MOTOR TRUCK REPAIR MANUAL

33rd Edition

First Printing

Editor-in-Chief
Louis C. Forier, SAE

Executive Editor
Larry Solnik, SAE

Managing Editor
Michael J. Kromida, SAE

Associate Editors
Dan Irizarry, SAE • Warren Schildknecht, SAE

Assistant-to-the-Editor
Katherine Keen

Editorial Assistants
**William Lilieholm, SAE • Keith D. Rasmussen
Patricia S. Lubetkin**

Published by
MOTOR

224 West 57th St., New York, N.Y. 10019

The Automotive Business Magazine

Printed in the U.S.A. © Copyright 1980 by The Hearst Corporation
Library of Congress Catalog Number: 75-643228

ISBN 0-87851-522-4

DECIMAL & MILLIMETER EQUIVALENTS

INCH	INCH	MM
1/64	.015625	.397
1/32	.03125	.794
3/64	.046875	1.191
1/16	.0625	1.587
5/64	.078125	1.984
3/32	.09375	2.381
7/64	.109375	2.778
1/8	.125	3.175
9/64	.140625	3.572
5/32	.15625	3.969
11/64	.171875	4.366
3/16	.1875	4.762
13/64	.203125	5.159
7/32	.21875	5.556
15/64	.234375	5.953
1/4	.25	6.350
17/64	.265625	6.747
9/32	.28125	7.144
19/64	.296875	7.541
5/16	.3125	7.937
21/64	.328125	8.334
11/32	.34375	8.731

INCH	INCH	MM
23/64	.359375	9.128
3/8	.375	9.525
25/64	.390625	9.922
13/32	.40625	10.319
27/64	.421875	10.716
7/16	.4375	11.113
29/64	.453125	11.509
15/32	.46875	11.906
31/64	.484375	12.303
1/2	.5	12.700
33/64	.515625	13.097
17/32	.53125	13.494
35/64	.546875	13.890
9/16	.5625	14.287
37/64	.578125	14.684
19/32	.59375	15.081
39/64	.609375	15.478
5/8	.625	15.875
41/64	.640625	16.272
21/32	.65625	16.669
43/64	.671875	17.065

INCH	INCH	MM
11/16	.6875	17.462
45/64	.703125	17.859
23/32	.71875	18.265
47/64	.734375	18.653
3/4	.75	19.050
49/64	.765625	19.447
25/32	.78125	19.884
51/64	.796875	20.240
13/16	.8125	20.637
53/64	.828125	21.034
27/32	.84375	21.431
55/64	.859375	21.828
7/8	.875	22.225
57/64	.890625	22.622
29/32	.90625	23.019
59/64	.921875	23.415
15/16	.9375	23.812
61/64	.953125	24.209
31/32	.96875	24.606
63/64	.984375	25.003
1		25.400

Special Service Tools

Throughout this manual references are made and illustrations may depict the use of special tools required to perform certain jobs. These special tools can generally be ordered through the dealers of the make vehicle being serviced. It is also suggested that you check with local automotive supply firms as they also supply tools manufactured by other firms that will assist in the performance of these jobs. The vehicle manufacturers special tools are supplied by:

American Motors & General Motors . . . . Service Tool Division
Kent-Moore Corporation
1501 South Jackson Street
Jackson, Michigan 49203

Chrysler Corp. . . . . Miller Special Tools
A Division of Utica Tool Co.
32615 Park Lane
Garden City, Michigan 48135

Ford Motor Co. . . . . Owatonna Tool Company
Owatonna, Minnesota 55060

INDEX

This Edition Covers Mechanical Specifications and Service Procedures on 1970–80 Models

TRUCK SECTION

Autocar 800	Dodge 937	Kenworth 1298
Brockway 803	Ford 1025	Mack 1302
Chevrolet 808	GMC 1141	Plymouth 937
Diamond Reo 924	International 1205	White 1333
	Jeep 1252	

GENERAL SERVICE SECTION

AXLES, DRIVING
- Eaton Axle Service 204
- Spicer Axle Service 239
- Timken Axle Service 241
- Locking Differentials 192
- Front Wheel Locking Hubs .. 505

BRAKES
- Adjustments 590
- Air Brake Service 620
- Anti-Skid Brakes 551
- Bendix Twinplex Brake 608
- Brake Booster Service 639
- Disc Brakes 661
- Hydraulic System Service .. 632
- Parking Brake Service 612
- Stopmaster Brake Service .. 599

CLUTCHES
- Air-Hydraulic Control 468
- Clutch Service 429

COOLING SYSTEM
- Variable Speed Fans 10

ELECTRICAL
- Alternator Service 52
- Dash Gauge Service 179
- Distributors, Standard 141
- Electronic Ignition 152
- Generator Service 11
- Ignition Coils and Resistors ... 7
- Starting Motor Service 29
- Starter Switch Service 21
- Tune Up Service 2

FUEL & EXHAUST
- Blue Ox Compression Brake . 677
- Crankcase Ventilation 748
- Emission Controls 750
- Fuel Pump Service 183
- Jacobs Engine Brake 678
- L.P.G. Carburetion 190
- Turbochargers 187

STEERING
- Manual Steering Gears 680
- Power Steering Gears 686

TRANSFER CASES 469

TRANSMISSIONS, Automatic
- Allison AT-540, 543 510
- Allison MT-640, 643, 644, 650, 653 & 654 CR 512
- Allison HT-740, 750 514
- Allison 6 Speed 518
- Powerglide (Aluminum Case) 522
- GMC Pow-R-Flo 522
- Chrysler Corp. Loadflite & A-345 534
- Ford 3 Speed (Cast Iron Case) 528
- Ford C6 531
- Ford C4 525
- Turbo Hydra-Matic 200 541
- Turbo Hydra-Matic 250 544
- Turbo Hydra-Matic 350 544
- Turbo Hydra-Matic 400 538
- Turbo Hydra-Matic 425 548
- Turbo Hydra-Matic 475 538

TRANSMISSIONS, Manual Shift
- Clark Transmissions 275
- Fuller Transmissions 289
- New Process Transmissions 329
- Spicer Transmissions 347
- Warner Transmissions 406

STOCK & FARM TRACTOR ENGINE SPECIFICATIONS

Allis-Chalmers 1361	Hercules 1356	Minneapolis-Moline .. 1379
Continental 1352	International Harvester .. 1371	Oliver 1382
Ford Tractor 1368	J. I. Case 1362	Waukesha 1358
Hall-Scott 1354	John Deere 1365	White 1384
	Massey-Ferguson ... 1376	

"The data reported herein has been compiled from authoritative sources. While every effort is made by the editors to attain accuracy, manufacturing changes as well as typographical errors and omissions may occur. The publisher then cannot be responsible nor does it assume responsibility for such omissions, errors or changes."

TUNE UP SERVICE

Engine tune-up has become increasingly important to the modern automotive engine with its vastly improved power and performance. With the emission control systems, improved electrical systems and other advances in design, engines have become more sensitive to usage and operating conditions, all of which have a decided effect on power and performance. Therefore, it is important that this service be performed on the engine at the recommended interval, or more often if conditions warrant.

In addition to the servicing of spark plugs, ignition points and condenser, a proper tune up includes a number of tests to check the condition of the engine and its related systems and uncover sources of future problems.

TUNE UP PROCEDURE

Since a quality tune up is dependent upon the proper operation of a number of systems, we have listed here in a logical sequence, the steps to be followed.
1. Diagnosis. This to consist of a compression test, cylinder balance test, oscilloscope check, manifold vacuum test, charging circuit and cranking voltage test.
2. Service spark plugs.
3. Service ignition system, secondary wiring, distributor and coil.
4. Check and service battery and charging system.
5. Service manifold heat valve, if used.
6. Service carburetor, linkage, fuel and air filters.
7. Check operation of various emission control devices.

Once these mechanical checks have been performed the tune up can be finalized. The final steps are:
1. Setting the dwell.
2. Setting slow idle, idle fuel mixture, choke and ignition timing.
3. Adjusting the fast idle.

4. Checking ignition output and secondary resistance.
5. Road test.

DIAGNOSIS & TESTING

Before a satisfactory tune up can be performed, the existing condition of the engine and its related systems must be determined. A tune up should not be attempted if tests indicate internal engine problems such as burnt valves, worn rings, blown head gasket, etc., until such conditions have been corrected.

Oscilloscope Test

Although oscilloscopes differ in many ways, they all display a light or "trace" on a screen which measures the voltage present at a given point and time. As the ignition system operates, its voltage creates a pattern on the screen. This pattern, when read in accordance with the manufacturers instructions for the particular unit, indicates the condition of the entire ignition system.

Compression Test

CAUTION: Should it become necessary to turn on the ignition switch to crank the engine under the hood for a compression test or for any other reason, it is highly recommended that the high tension cable be removed from the coil tower or from the distributor cap. This is necessary because on many vehicles the ignition and starter circuits are such that the ignition switch and/or starter solenoid may be damaged if this precaution is not taken. Another reason for removing the cable is to prevent the engine from starting accidentally.

The engine cannot be tuned to develop maximum power and smooth performance unless reasonably high and uniform compression pressure is obtained in each cylinder. The compression in each cylinder should, therefore, be tested before any other tune-up operations are performed.
1. Remove any foreign matter from around spark plugs by blowing out plug area with compressed air. Then loosen all plugs one turn.
2. Start engine and accelerate to a fast idle to blow out loosened carbon. Stop engine and remove spark plugs. *Cleaning out carbon in this manner is important in preventing false compression readings due to particles of carbon lodged under the valves.*
3. Remove air cleaner and block throttle and choke in wide open position.
4. Insert compression gauge firmly in spark plug opening and crank engine through at least four or five compression strokes to obtain highest possible reading.
5. Test and record compression of each cylinder and compare the maximum and minimum readings obtained. Refer to the tune-up charts in the truck chapters and determine if the minimum reading is within limits as indicated by the percentages in the chart in Fig. 1.
6. If one or more cylinders read low, inject about a tablespoon of engine oil on top of pistons in the low reading cylinders. Crank engine several times and recheck compression.
7. If compression comes up but does not reach normal it indicates worn piston rings. If compression does not improve, valves are sticking or seating poorly. If two adjacent cylinders indicate low compression and injecting oil does not improve the condition, the cause may be a head gasket leak between the cylinders.

Manifold Vacuum Test

Manifold vacuum is affected by carburetor adjustment, valve timing, ignition timing, condition of valves, cylinder compression, condition of positive crankcase ventilation system, and leakage of manifold, carburetor, carburetor spacer or cylinder head gaskets.

Because abnormal gauge readings may in-

MAXIMUM PSI	MINIMUM PSI		MAXIMUM PSI	MINIMUM PSI		MAXIMUM PSI	MINIMUM PSI	
	75%	80%		75%	80%		75%	80%
134	101	107	174	131	139	214	160	171
136	102	109	176	132	141	216	162	173
138	104	110	178	133	142	218	163	174
140	105	112	180	135	144	220	165	176
142	107	114	182	136	146	222	166	178
144	108	115	184	138	147	224	168	179
146	110	117	186	140	149	226	169	181
148	111	118	188	141	150	228	171	182
150	113	120	190	142	152	230	172	184
152	114	122	192	144	154	232	174	186
154	115	123	194	145	155	234	175	187
156	117	125	196	147	157	236	177	189
158	118	126	198	148	158	238	178	190
160	120	128	200	150	160	240	180	192
162	121	130	202	151	162	242	181	194
164	123	131	204	153	163	244	183	195
166	124	133	206	154	165	246	184	197
168	126	134	208	156	166	248	186	198
170	127	136	210	157	168	250	187	200
172	129	138	212	158	170			

Fig. 1 Compression pressure limit chart

TUNE UP SERVICE

dicate that more than one of the above factors are at fault, use care in analyzing an abnormal reading. For example, if the vacuum is low, the correction of one item may increase the vacuum enough so as to indicate that the trouble has been corrected. It is important, therefore, that each cause of an abnormal reading be investigated and further tests conducted, where necessary, in order to arrive at the correct diagnosis of the trouble. To check manifold vacuum, proceed as follows:

1. Operate engine for 30 minutes minimum at a fast idle speed to be sure engine is at normal operating temperature.
2. Connect an accurate vacuum gauge to the intake manifold vacuum fitting.
3. Operate engine at recommended idle speed with transmission selector lever in neutral.
4. Check vacuum reading on gauge.

Test Conclusions

NORMAL READING: 18 inches or more. Allowance should be made for the effect of altitude on the gauge reading. Engine vacuum will decrease with an increase in altitude.

LOW & STEADY: Loss of power in all cylinders possibly caused by late ignition or valve timing, or loss of compression due to leakage around piston rings.

VERY LOW: Intake manifold, carburetor, carburetor spacer or cylinder head gasket leak.

NEEDLE FLUCTUATES STEADILY AS SPEED INCREASES: A partial or complete loss of power in one or more cylinders caused by a leaking valve, cylinder head or intake manifold gasket, a defect in ignition system, or a weak valve spring.

GRADUAL DROP IN READING AT IDLE SPEED: Excessive back pressure in exhaust system.

INTERMITTENT FLUCTUATION: An occasional loss of power possibly caused by a defect in ignition system or a sticking valve.

SLOW FLUCTUATION OR DRIFTING OF NEEDLE: Improper idle mixture adjustment or carburetor, carburetor spacer or intake manifold gasket leak or crankcase ventilation system restricted.

Cylinder Balance Test

CAUTION: When performing engine diagnosis on vehicles equipped with catalytic converters, a "Cylinder Balance Test", Fig. 2, is not to be performed as damage to the catalytic converter will result. The alternate method of shorting out one cylinder at a time and noting the rpm drop of each individual cylinder can be used, but test should be performed as rapidly as possible.

It is sometimes difficult to locate a weak cylinder especially in an eight cylinder engine. A compression test, for example, will not locate a leaky intake manifold, a valve not opening properly due to a worn camshaft, or a defective spark plug.

With the cylinder balance test, the power output of one cylinder may be checked against another, using a set of grounding leads, Fig. 2. When the power of each cylinder is not equal, the engine will lose power and run roughly. The cylinder balance test is as follows:

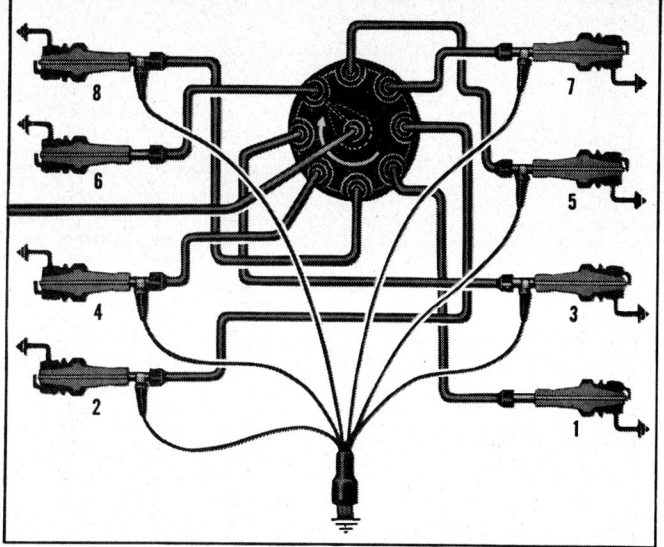

Fig. 2 Cylinder balance test connections. The firing order in this example is 1-8-4-3-6-5-7-2. Therefore, the cylinders to be tested together are 1-6, 8-5, 4-7, 3-2, using the grounding leads as shown.

1. Connect a tachometer and vacuum gauge.
2. Start engine and run it at fast idle.
3. Ground large clip of grounding leads and connect individual leads to all spark plugs *except the pair being tested* (see Fig. 1).
4. Divide the firing order in half and write down the first half over the second half. The cylinders to be tested together appear one over the other:

Firing Order	Pairs Tested
1-8-4-3-6-5-7-2	1-6, 8-5, 4-7, 3-2
1-2-7-8-4-5-6-3	1-4, 2-5, 7-6, 8-3
1-5-4-8-6-3-7-2	1-6, 5-3, 4-7, 8-2
1-5-4-2-6-3-7-8	1-6, 5-3, 4-7, 2-8
1-8-7-3-6-5-4-2	1-6, 8-5, 7-4, 3-2
1-6-5-4-3-2	1-4, 6-3, 5-2
1-5-3-6-2-4	1-6, 5-2, 3-4
1-4-5-2-3-6	1-2, 4-3, 5-6
1-3-4-2	1-4, 3-2

5. Operate engine on each pair of cylinders in turn and note engine rpm and manifold vacuum for each pair. A variation of more than one inch of vacuum or 40 rpm between pairs of cylinders being tested indicates that the cylinders are off balance.
6. To isolate one weak cylinder, short out one bank of cylinders at a time. The bank giving the lower readings will include the weak cylinder.

Spark Plugs

1. Examine firing ends of plugs for evidence of oil fouling, gas fouling, burned or overheated condition. *Oil fouling is usually identified by wet, sludgy deposits caused by excessive oil consumption. Gas fouling is identified by dry, black, fluffy deposits caused by incomplete combustion. Burned or overheated spark plugs are identified by white, burned or blistered insulator nose and badly burned electrodes. Improper fuel, insufficient cooling or improper ignition timing normally are the cause. Normal conditions are usually identified by white powdery deposits or rusty-brown to grayish-tan powdery deposits.*
2. Clean plugs with a suitable sand blast cleaner following the manufacturers instructions.
3. Remove carbon and other deposits from threads with a stiff wire brush.
4. Dress electrodes with a small file to secure flat, parallel surfaces on both center and side electrodes, Fig. 3.
5. Use a round wire gauge to check the gap, Fig. 4, and adjust by bending the side (never center) electrode to the proper specifications as shown in the *Tune Up Charts* in the vehicle chapters.
6. If gaskets are used, place new ones on plugs and torque them.

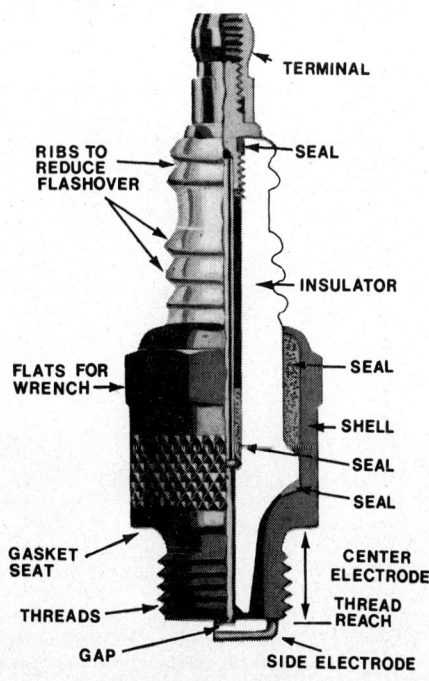

Fig. 3 Spark plug details

TUNE UP SERVICE

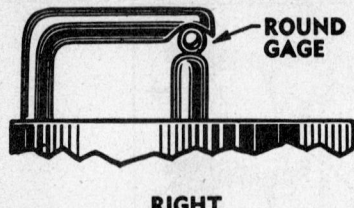
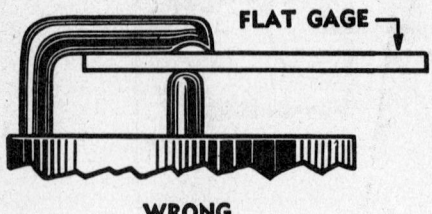

Fig. 4 Correct and incorrect spark plug gauges

CAUTION: Improper installation of spark plugs is one of the greatest single causes of unsatisfactory spark plug performance. Improper installation is the result of one or more of the following practices: 1) Installation of plugs with insufficient torque to fully seat the gasket; 2) excessive torque which changes gap settings; 3) installation of plugs on dirty gasket seal; 4) installation of plugs to corroded spark plug hole threads.

Failure to install plugs properly will cause them to operate at excessively high temperatures and result in reduced operating life under mild operation or complete destruction under severe operation where the intense heat cannot be dissipated rapidly enough.

Always remove carbon deposits in hole threads before installing plugs. When corrosion is present in threads, normal torque is not sufficient to compress the plug gasket (if used) and early failure from overheating will result.

Always use a new gasket (if required) and wipe seats in head clean. The gasket must be fully compressed on clean seats to complete heat transfer and provide a gas tight seal in the cylinder. For this reason as well as the necessity of maintaining correct plug gap, the use of correct torque is extremely important during installation.

Ignition System Service

1. Replace brittle or damaged spark plug wires. Install all wires to proper spark plug. The *Tune Up Charts* in the car chapters give firing orders should wires become mixed.
2. Tighten all ignition system connections.
3. Replace or repair any wires that are frayed, loose or damaged, Fig. 5.
4. Remove distributor cap, clean and inspect for cracks, carbon tracks and burned or corroded terminals. Replace cap if necessary.
5. Clean rotor and inspect for damage or deterioration. Replace rotor if necessary.
6. Check distributor centrifugal advance mechanism (if used) by turning distributor rotor in direction of running rotation as far as possible, then release rotor to see if springs return it to its retarded position. If rotor does not return readily, the distributor must be disassembled and cause of trouble corrected.
7. Check to see that the vacuum spark control operates freely by turning the movable breaker plate (if used) or distributor housing in a direction opposite to that of running rotation to see if the spring returns it to the retarded position. Any stiffness in the operation of the spark control will affect ignition timing. Correct any interference or binding condition noted.
8. Examine distributor points and clean or replace if necessary. Points with an overall gray color and only slight roughness or pitting need not be replaced.
9. Dirty points should be cleaned with a clean point file. Use only a few strokes of the file. The file should not be used on other metals and should not be allowed to become dirty or greasy. *Never use emergy cloth or sandpaper to clean points since particles will embed and cause arcing and rapid burning of points.* Do not attempt to remove all roughness nor dress the point surface down smooth. Merely remove scale or dirt.
10. Replace points that are badly burned or pitted. Where burned or badly pitted points are encountered, the ignition system and engine should be checked to determine the cause of the trouble so it can be eliminated. Unless the condition causing point burning is corrected, new points will provide no better service than the old points. See *Standard Distributor* chapter for an analysis of point burning or pitting, and for proper installation of points.

Battery & Cables

Inspect for signs of corrosion on battery, cables and surrounding area, loose or broken carriers, cracked or bulged cases, dirt and acid, electrolyte leakage and low electrolyte level. Fill cells to proper level with colorless, odorless drinking water.

The top of the battery should be clean and the battery hold-down bolts properly tightened.

For best results when cleaning batteries, wash first with a dilute ammonia or soda solution to neutralize any acid present and then flush off with clean water. Care must be taken to keep vent plugs tight so that the neutralizing solution does not enter the battery. The holddown bolts should be kept tight enough to prevent the battery from shaking around in its holder, but not so tight that the battery case will be placed under a severe strain.

To insure good contact, the battery cables should be tight on the battery posts. Oil battery terminal felt washer. If the battery posts or cable terminals are corroded, the cables should be cleaned separately with a soda solution and a wire brush. After cleaning and before installing the clamps, apply a thin coating of vaseline to the posts and cable clamps to help retard corrosion.

If the battery has remained undercharged, check for a loose generator belt, defective generator, high resistance in charging circuit, oxidized voltage regulator contact points, or a low voltage setting.

If the battery has been using too much water, the voltage regulator setting is too high.

Fan Belt & Generator

1. Inspect fan belt condition and check adjustment.
2. Inspect generator commutator and brushes for cleanliness or wear. The commutator should be cleaned if dirty and brushes should be replaced if worn down to less than half their original length. *The commutator may be cleaned by holding a strip of No. 00 sandpaper or a cleaning stone against it while the generator is operating.*
3. Replace or repair frayed or broken generator wires and tighten all wire connections.

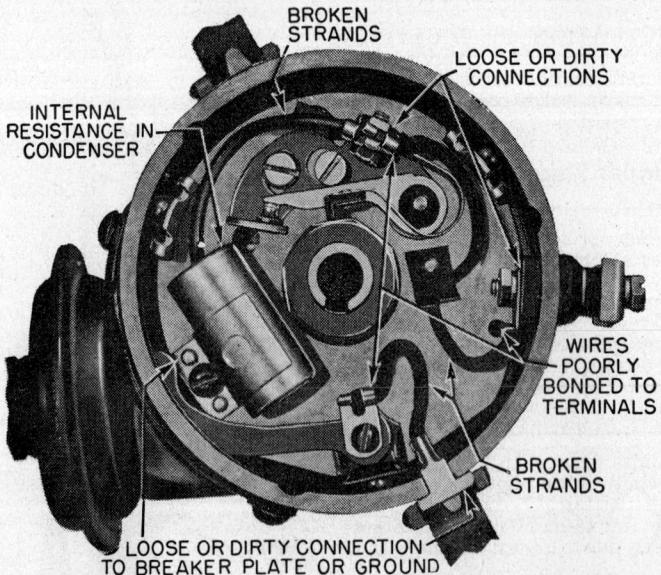

Fig. 5 What to look for when checking for high resistance in the primary circuit of the distributor. In addition to the points indicated, look for external circuit high resistance at ignition switch terminals, ammeter terminals, coil terminals and broken or poorly insulated wires in this circuit.

TUNE UP SERVICE

4. Lubricate generator by filling hinge cap oilers with light engine oil.

Ignition Timing

The use of a timing light, Fig. 6, is recommended for checking and setting ignition timing. This setting is critical especially on units equipped with emission control systems.

Some engines have a provision for monolithic method of ignition timing utilizing a timing receptacle designed to accept an electronic probe. The receptacle is usually mounted at the front of the engine and the electronic probe is connected to electronic equipment which reads out the engine timing. These engines can also be timed using a timing light.

NOTE: When setting timing, be sure idle speed is set lower than speed at which centrifugal advance begins. See *Distributor Specifications Chart* in truck chapters.

NOTE: The timing light should be connected to the proper spark plug lead by the use of an adapter. The boots around the connections should not be pierced to connect the light as this can cause spark arcing and misfiring.

Lacking a timing light, the timing can be set with the engine stopped by using a jumper light. Be sure to use a light bulb that corresponds with the vehicle voltage, Fig. 7.
1. Rotate engine until No. 1 cylinder is positioned at the specified timing mark.
2. Connect jumper light between distributor ignition terminal and ground.
3. Turn on ignition switch.
4. Loosen distributor and turn it in the direction of normal rotation until the points just close (light out). Then slowly turn the distributor in the opposite direction just to the exact point that the light goes on. Tighten distributor in this position.

CARBURETION

Since carburetion is dependent in several ways on both compression and ignition, it should always be checked last when tuning an engine. See the car chapter for adjustments for the unit you are interested in.

Before adjusting the carburetor, consider the factors outlined below and which definitely affect engine performance.

Performance Complaints

Flooding, stumble on acceleration or other performance complaints are in many instances caused by the presence of dirt, water or other foreign matter in the carburetor. To aid in diagnosing the cause of the complaint, the carburetor should be carefully removed from the engine without draining the fuel from the bowl. The contents of the fuel bowl may then be examined for contamination as the carburetor is disassembled.

Check the fuel in the bowl for contamination by dirt, water, gum or other foreign matter. A magnet moved through the fuel in the bowl will pick up and identify any iron oxide dust that may have caused intake needle and seat leakage.

Inspect gasketed surfaces between body and air horn. Small nicks or burrs should be smoothed down to eliminate air or fuel leakage. On carburetors having a vacuum piston, be especially particular when inspecting the top surface of the inner wall of the bowl around the vacuum piston passage. A poor seal at this location may contribute to a "cutting out" on turns complaint.

Fill the carburetor bowl with clean fuel before installing on manifold. This will help prevent dirt trapped in the fuel system from being dislodged by the free flow of fuel as the carburetor is primed. The operation of the floats and intake needle and seats may be checked under pressure if a fuel pump is used at the bench to fill the carburetor bowl. Operate the throttle several times and visually check the discharge from pump jets.

Poor Mileage and Engine Loading Complaints

Cases of poor mileage and engine loading may be due in many instances to sluggish choke valve opening during cold driveaway, caused by insufficient vacuum in choke housing, a plugged or restricted heat pipe or inlet in choke cover. To check for this condition, have engine warm and running at slow idle. Remove choke heat pipe and hold a finger over the heat inlet hole (hole is on choke housing on some carburetors). If there is little or no vacuum pull on the finger, check the choke housing for gasket leaks or plugged vacuum passages. If these are OK, check choke vacuum passages in carburetor between choke housing and manifold.

Dirty or Rusty Choke Housing

In cases where it is found that the interior of the choke housing is dirty, gummed or rusty while the carburetor itself is comparatively clean, look for a puncture or eroded manifold heat tube (if one is used).

Manifold Heat Control Valve

An engine equipped with a manifold heat control valve can operate with the valve stuck in either the open or closed position, Fig. 8. Because of this, an inoperative valve is frequently overlooked at vehicle lubrication or tune-up.

A valve stuck in the "heat-off" position can result in slow warm up, deposits in combustion chamber, carburetor icing, flat spots during acceleration, low gas mileage and spark plug fouling.

A valve stuck in the "heat-on" position can result in power loss, engine knocking, sticking or burned valves and spark plug burning.

To prevent the possibility of a stuck valve, check and lubricate the valve each time the vehicle is lubricated or tuned-up. Check the operation of the valve manually. To lubricate the valve, place a few drops of penetrating oil on the valve shaft where it passes through the manifold. Then move the valve up and down a few times to work the oil in. *Do not use engine oil to lubricate the valve as it will leave a residue which hampers valve operation.*

Idle Speed & Mixture Adjustments

Less Emission Controls

Start the engine and run it until it reaches normal operating temperature, at which time the choke valve should be wide open with the idle speed screw resting on lowest step of fast idle cam. Slowly turn the idle mixture screw a little at a time until the engine shows a tendency to hesitate and stall. Then turn it to the left until the engine runs smoothly. Continue turning the screw to the left until the fuel mixture is rich and the engine starts to "lope" or "gallop". Finally turn the screw to the right until the engine runs evenly.

On two-barrel carburetors, there is an idle mixture screw for each barrel. On four-barrel carburetors there are also two idle mixture screws on the primary side of the carburetor. When idle ports are provided on the secondary side, they are non-adjustable or they are rendered non-functional by being blocked with gaskets.

When adjusting the idle mixture on two and four-barrel carburetors, adjust one screw at a time until the engine runs smoothly as directed above. Then adjust the other screw in like manner.

After the idle mixture has been adjusted, it is recommended that a tachometer (engine speed indicator) be used to set the slow idle speed to the rpm indicated in the *Tune Up* table in the truck chapter.

With Emission Controls
1. With engine at operating temperature, set parking brake and block drive wheels.
2. Make sure choke valve is wide open.
3. On C.C.S. equipped vehicles, see that the air cleaner thermostatic valve is open.
4. On carburetors so equipped, hold hot idle compensator hole closed with eraser on pencil.
5. Turn air conditioner off or on according to directions given in *Tune Up Charts* in truck chapters.
6. Set idle mixture screw(s) for maximum idle rpm.
7. Adjust speed screw (or idle stop solenoid screw on C.C.S.) to obtain the specified

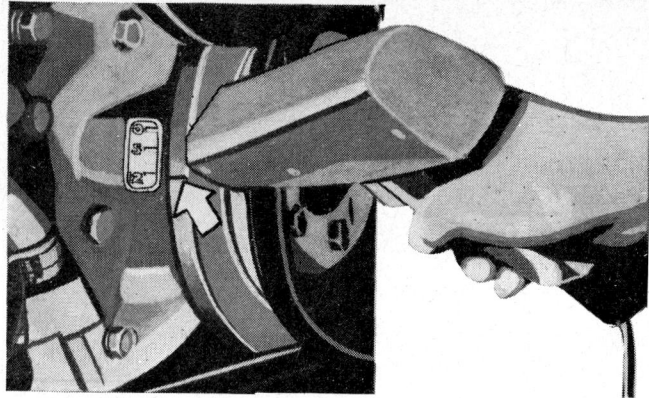

Fig. 6 Checking ignition timing with timing light

TUNE UP SERVICE

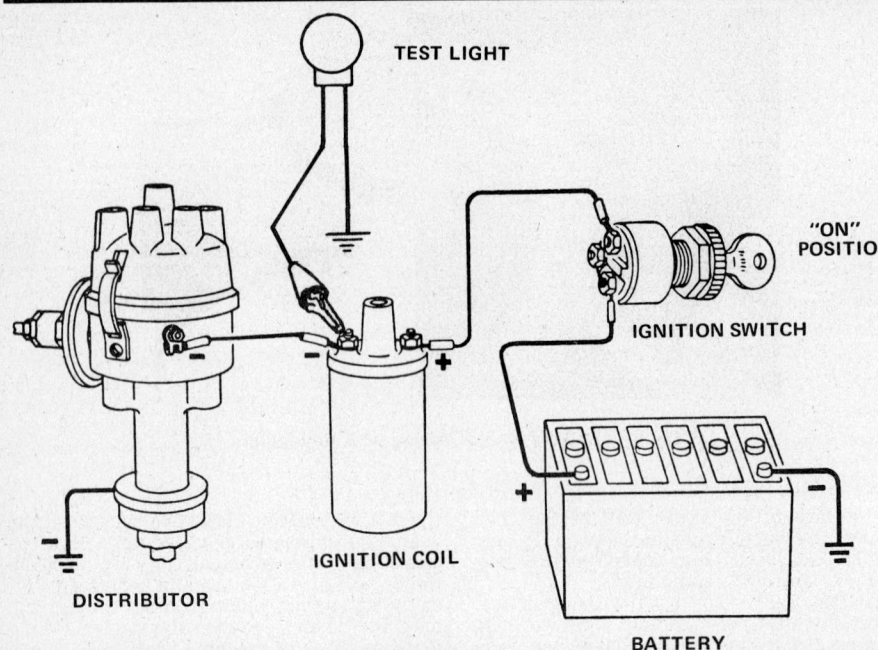

Fig. 7 Jumper light circuit for static ignition timing

rpm in Drive or Neutral as specified.
8. Set ignition timing according to specifications with vacuum advance line disconnected and hole in manifold plugged.
9. Adjust mixture screw IN to obtain a 20 rpm drop (lean roll).
10. Adjust mixture screw OUT 1/4 turn.
11. Repeat Steps 9 and 10 for second mixture screw (2 and 4 barrel carbs).
12. Readjust speed screw (or solenoid screw) if necessary to obtain specified rpm.
13. On C.C.S. with idle solenoid stop on carburetor, electrically disconnect solenoid and adjust carburetor idle speed screw to obtain 400 rpm in neutral, then reconnect wire to solenoid.

NOTE: Exact instructions for each C.C.S. equipped engine transmission combination is given for this Lean Roll (low idle) speed method on a decal permanently affixed to the vicinity of the radiator support.

Carburetor Flange

Check the flange for looseness on the manifold. If one of the flange nuts is loose as little as one-half turn, a sufficient amount of air will enter the intake manifold below the throttle plate to destroy engine idle and all engine performance.

If a tight fit cannot be obtained by tightening the nuts, install a new gasket but be sure that all the old gasket material has been removed.

Throttle Linkage

If the throttle linkage is adjusted so that the accelerator pedal will strike the floor board before the throttle plate is wide open, it will result in low top speed.

Fuel Lines

A restriction of the fuel line will result in an apparent vapor lock action or a definite cut-off of gasoline. This can generally be corrected by blowing out the line with compressed air. In some cases, it may be necessary to replace the line.

Fuel Pump

The pump should be tested to make sure that it will draw an adequate supply of fuel from the tank and deliver it to the carburetor under all conditions of operation. If the pump functions inefficiently, proper adjustment and operation of the carburetor is impossible because the fuel will not be maintained at the prescribed level in the idle passages and main discharge jet (or jets) of the carburetor under all operating conditions.

Fuel Tank

The fuel tank should not be overlooked as a possible source of trouble with carburetion. A shortage of fuel at the fuel pump or carburetor may be caused by material obstructing the mouth of the feed pipe in the tank, or by a restriction of the air vents in the filler cap and neck.

An unusual amount of dirt, water or gum in the fuel filter indicates that the tank is contaminated with these substances, which should be cleaned out to prevent future failure of the pump or carburetor.

Intake Manifold Leaks

Leakage of air into the intake manifold at any point will affect carburetion and general engine performance. Air may leak into the manifold through the joints at the carburetor or cylinder head, cracks in the manifold, cracks or poor connections in the windshield wiper or windshield washer hose lines, or the connections of any accessories which may be connected to the manifold. All such joints should be tested for leaks.

To test the intake manifold for leaks, apply oil from an oil can along the gasket joints with the engine idling. An air leak is indicated when oil is drawn past the gaskets by the suction of the engine. Tighten the nuts or cap screws holding the manifold to the engine and retest for leaks. If tightening fails to stop the leaks, replace the manifold gaskets. If the new gaskets fail to stop the leaks, carefully inspect the manifold for cracks and test any suspicious area with oil.

Air Cleaner

An air cleaner with a dirty element, or with oil that is dirty, too heavy, or too high in the sump, will restrict the air flow through the carburetor and cause a rich mixture at high speeds. In such a condition the air cleaner likewise will not properly remove dirt from the air, and the dirt entering the engine will cause rapid formation of carbon, sticking valves, and wear of piston rings and cylinder bores.

Automatic Choke

The choke mechanism must be inspected and cleaned to make sure it is operating freely. Sluggish action or sticking of the choke will cause excessive fuel consumption, poor performance during warm-up, and possibly hard starting.

The choke thermostat should be set in accordance with the average air temperature as well as the volatility of the fuel being used. It is desirable to have the thermostat set as lean as operating conditions permit in order to avoid an overrich mixture during engine warm-up.

Choke Thermostat

If necessary to adjust the choke more than two marks from the specified setting, either rich or lean, it indicates that the thermostat spring may be bent or has lost its tension.

PERFORMANCE TEST

After an engine has been tuned up, the car

Fig. 8 Operation of a typical manifold heat control valve

CLOSED HEAT ON   PARTLY OPEN HEAT MEDIUM   OPEN HEAT OFF

6

TUNE UP SERVICE

should be given a thorough and systematic road test to make certain that engine power and performance are up to standard under all operating conditions. The gasoline used in making the test must be of good quality and proper octane rating in order to obtain the performance described in the following tests.

Engine Warm Up

On vehicles with automatic chokes, a cold engine should operate on fast idle for two to five minutes, depending upon air temperature.

At 32 deg. F. the fast idle cam should move to the slow idle position in approximately 1/2 to 3/4 mile of driving. At higher temperatures, it should move to the slow idle position in a correspondingly shorter distance.

If the engine loads excessively or runs rich on warm up due to a rich choke setting, excessive fuel consumption, carbon formation, and spark plug fouling will result.

An engine which is adjusted for smooth idling in cold outside temperature will not idle smoothly for any length of time in a warm building, since the required carburetor adjustment will cause richness of mixture in the warmer atmosphere.

Gradual Acceleration Test

Starting at idling speed in high gear, gradually open the throttle to increase smoothly the speed of the car through the entire range. Note any roughness, flat spots, or surging in engine performance during acceleration, and the speed at which the unusual condition occurs.

Roughness or poor performance at speeds below 20 m.p.h. indicates improper carburetor idle adjustment, restriction in idle passages in carburetor, tight valve lash or sticking valves or faulty ignition.

Faulty ignition usually causes a more pronounced roughness than imperfect compression or carburetion.

Roughness or poor performance at speeds above 20 m.p.h. indicates restriction or improper settings in the high speed circuit of the carburetor, or faulty ignition.

Wide Open Throttle Acceleration Test

With the car running at idling speed in high gear, quickly press the accelerator pedal to the floor and hold it there, meanwhile noting the performance of the engine as the car is accelerated. Repeat the acceleration test, starting at different constant speeds throughout speed range of car. The car should accelerate smoothly without hesitation, spitting, or leading of the engine.

A hesitation, spitting, or a flat spot indicates that the accelerating pump is not discharging sufficient gasoline into the engine. Sluggishness or loading indicates that the accelerating pump is adjusted too rich.

Constant Speed Test

Hold the truck speed constant at various points through the speed range and note engine performance. The engine should operate smoothly without hesitation or surging under load at all constant speeds.

At some point between 15 and 22 m.p.h. with the car rolling along on a level road or slight upgrade, a slight leanness, surging or missing may be detected. Depressing or releasing the accelerator pedal slightly will eliminate this condition and no attempt should be made to correct it by altering carburetion or ignition. This condition seldom appears in the normal operation of the vehicle.

Spark Knock

Light detonation or spark knock will occur when operating with part throttle on a hard pull, even through the ignition is properly timed and high octane fuel is used. Light detonation also will occur when accelerating with fully opened throttle on a hard pull. These operating conditions are normal and no attempt should be made to eliminate light detonation by retarding the ignition timing.

If regular or low octane fuel is used, detonation will probably be excessive with the standard ignition timing, and it may be necessary to retard the timing, which will reduce fuel economy and over-all performance.

Extreme heavy detonation is injurious to any automobile engine. A car driven continuously under conditions and fuels which produce heavy detonation will overheat and lose power, with the possibility of damage to pistons and bearings.

IGNITION COILS & RESISTORS

IGNITION COILS

If poor ignition performance is obtained and the coil is suspected, it may be tested and the car or it may be removed for the test.

Ignition coils are often condemned when the trouble is actually in the ignition switch. A completely defective ignition switch will produce an open primary circuit, giving the same indications as if the coil were completely dead. A partly defective ignition switch will cause a weak spark. Both of these conditions are often blamed on the coil.

By cutting the ignition switch out of the circuit, it can easily be determined whether or not the coil is defective or whether fault lies with ignition switch.

In the absence of any testing equipment a simple check of an ignition coil can be made as follows: Turn on ignition switch with breaker points closed. Remove the high tension cable from the center socket of the distributor cap and hold it 1/4" to 3/8" away from a clean spot on the engine. If the coil and other units connected to it are in good condition a spark should jump from the wire to the engine. If not, use a jumper wire from the distributor terminal to the engine; if the primary is in good condition a spark will occur.

All ignition coils with metal containers can be tested for grounded windings by placing one test clip on a clean part of the metal container and touching the other clip to the primary and high tension terminals. If the lamp lights or tiny sparks appear at the points of contact, the windings are grounded and the coil should be replaced.

Coil Polarity

Most coils are marked positive and negative at the primary terminals. When installing or connecting a coil be sure to make the connections as shown in Figs. 1 and 2. A reversal of this polarity may affect the performance of the engine (or the radio).

If perchance the coil is not marked as to its polarity, it can be checked by holding any high tension wire about 1/4" away from its spark plug terminal with the engine running. Insert the point of wooden lead pencil between the spark plug and the wire, Fig. 3. If the spark flares and has a slight orange tinge on

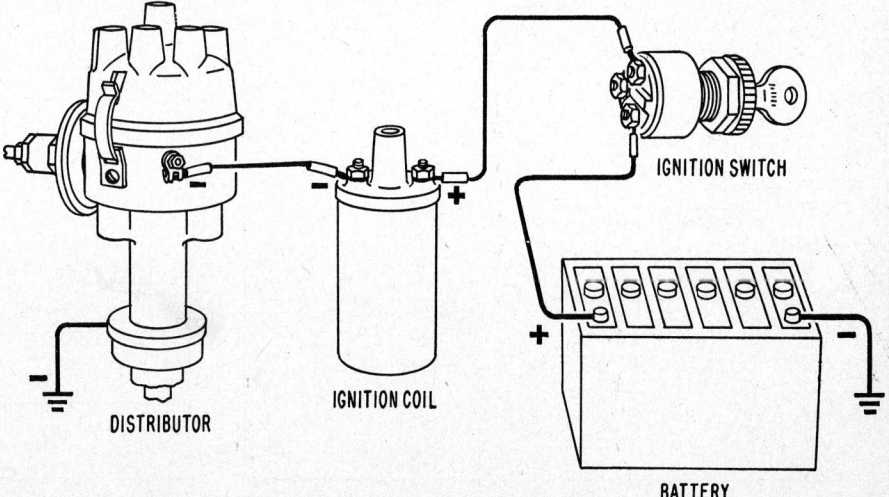

Fig. 1 Wiring connections for coil with negative grounded system

IGNITION COILS & RESISTORS

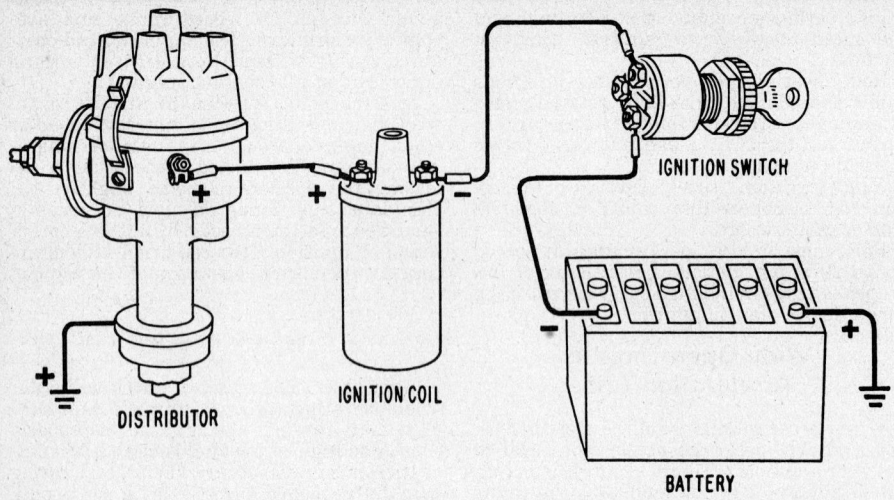

Fig. 2 Wiring connections for coil with positive grounded system

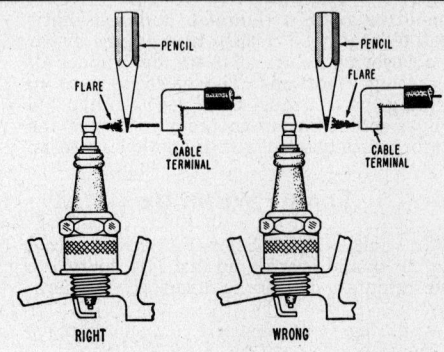

Fig. 3 Checking coil polarity

the spark plug side of the pencil, polarity is correct. If the spark flares on the cable side, coil connections should be reversed.

IGNITION RESISTORS

The purpose of the resistor is to prolong the service life of the distributor breaker points.

Block Type Ballast Resistors

Its basic purpose is to allow full battery voltage to the ignition coil during engine starting, and to reduce battery voltage to the coil when the engine is running. The higher voltage during starts means easier starts. But sustained high voltage to the breaker points can cause point failure. The reduced voltage during engine operation increases breaker point life.

These resistors are normally very dependable, But if one fails it can be one of the most difficult of all ignition system malfunctions to check out and diagnose. This type of resistor can fail in several ways. The resistance wire can separate, with a result similar to that caused by an open switch. An open resistor means that no current reaches the coil and the engine cannot operate. It is possible for the resistance wire to warp or bend enough to touch the side of the case and when this happens the engine may continue to run, but the overall performance would be poor.

Resistors can change value. Any creeping change in resistance value of a ballast resistor is invariably an increase in resistance. This means that coil output to the spark plugs is reduced proportionately. If a ballast resistor is slowly increasing in value the engine could gradually deliver less and less horsepower, particularly under high load conditions. An unsuspecting mechanic could unsuccessfully try to get the engine back to where it will deliver acceptable power output by changing spark plugs, adjusting timing, etc. Replacement of the faulty resistor is the only cure in this case.

To check a ballast resistor, replace it with one of known good quality. Then road-test the vehicle for improved performance.

It is important to remember that new spark plugs can temporarily mask the need for resistor replacement because new plugs require less voltage to fire. This is why a new-plug tune-up may prove satisfactory for a time. But if the ballast resistor is faulty, eventually the engine will misfire under load.

In Auto-Lite, Prestolite and Chrysler systems the resistor consists of an ordinary resistance wire that is sensitive to temperature, Fig. 4. The wire has a lower resistance value when cold than when hot. When the ignition is first turned on, more current will flow through the primary windings of the coil for a very short time until the resistor heats up.

In Delco-Remy and Ford systems, Figs. 5 and 6, the resistor is of the constant temperature type; that is, it is not affected by temperature and its resistance is approximately the same when cold as when hot. However, a feature is employed which shorts out the resistor while the engine is being cranked by the starter and automatically puts the resistance back in the coil circuit as soon as the starter switch is released. This is accomplished by bypassing the resistor through the starter solenoid. The solenoid has an additional terminal from which a wire runs directly to the coil.

On Delco-Remy systems, the resistor is bypassed by means of a "finger" inside the solenoid switch housing which is attached to the

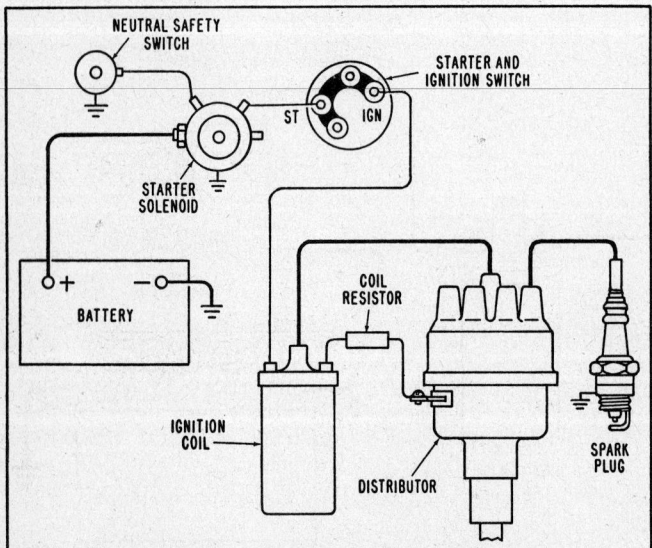

Fig. 4 Auto-Lite and Chrysler ignition circuit diagram with a temperature sensitive block-type resistor

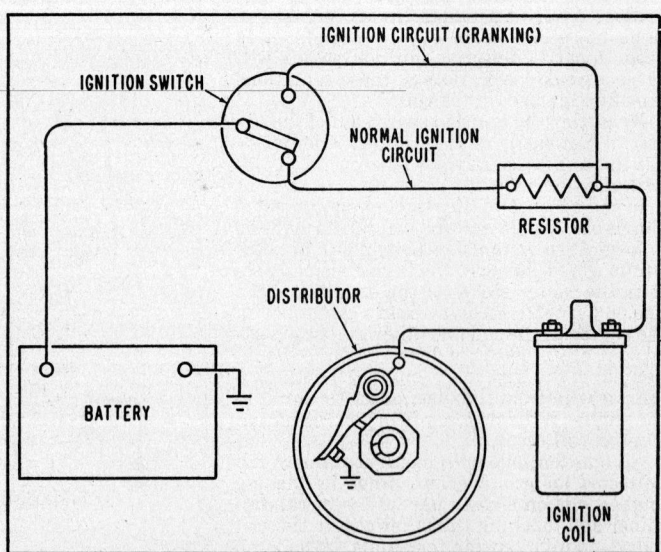

Fig. 5 Delco-Remy ignition circuit diagram with a constant temperature block-type resistor

IGNITION COILS & RESISTORS

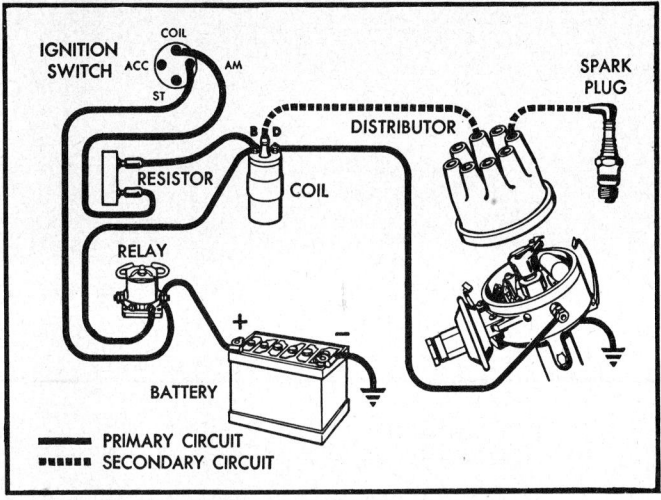

Fig. 6 Ford ignition circuit diagram with a constant temperature block-type resistor

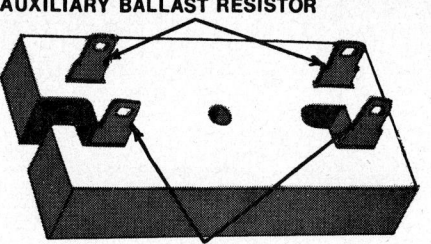

Fig. 7 Dual ballast resistor. Chrysler Corp. electronic ignition system

additional switch terminal.

On Ford systems, Fig. 6, the resistor is by-passed through a terminal on the starter relay which is connected directly to the positive terminal of the coil.

NOTE: If the engine fires when the ignition switch is turned on but quits when the switch is released to its running position, it indicates that the resistor is defective and must be replaced.

A dual ballast resistor, Fig. 7, is used on Chrysler Corp. vehicles equipped with electronic ignition. The normal side of the resistor is a compensating resistance in the primary circuit. At low engine speeds, current is maintained for a longer period of time in this side of the resistor, causing the unit to heat up, in turn increasing resistance. This increased resistance reduces the primary circuit voltage, protecting the ignition coil from high voltage at low engine speeds.

As engine speed increases, the period of time in which current is maintained in the normal side of the resistor is shorter, causing the unit to cool, in turn decreasing resistance. This decreased resistance permits the primary circuit voltage to increase for high speed operation.

During engine start, the normal side of the ballast resistor is by-passed, allowing full bat-

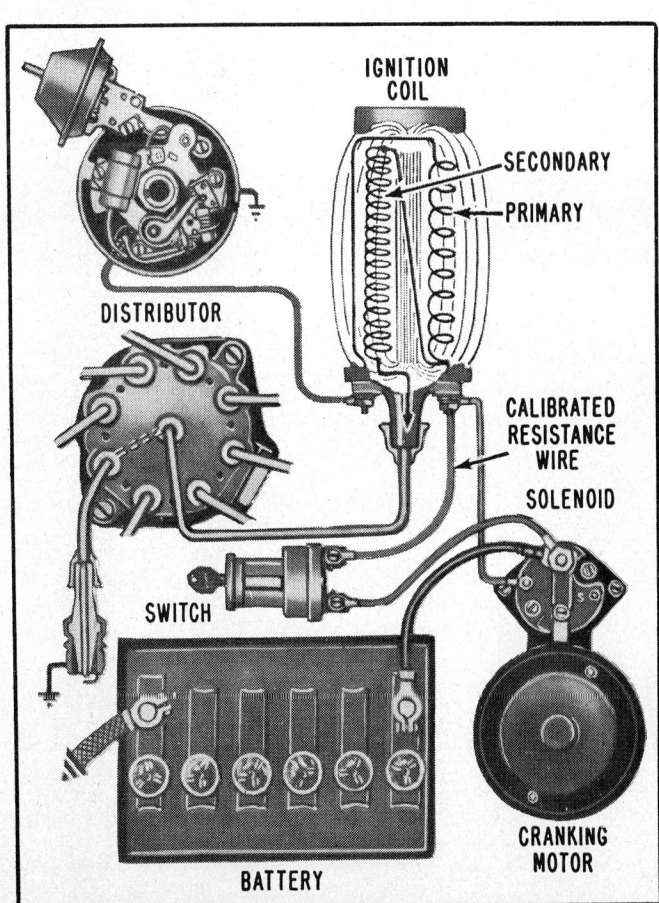

Fig. 8 Delco-Remy ignition circuit diagram with a resistance wire connected to a two-terminal ignition switch

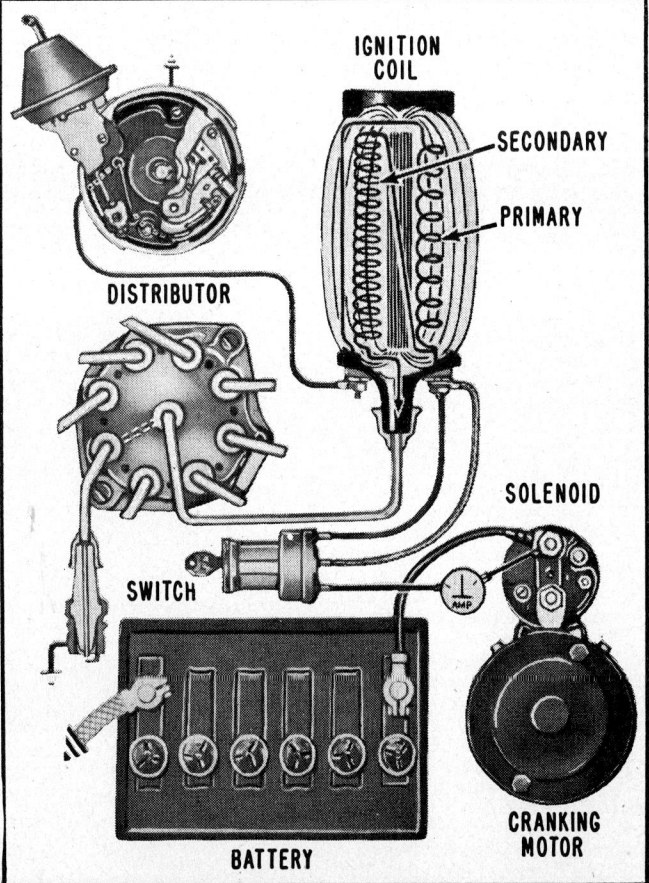

Fig. 9 Delco-Remy ignition circuit diagram with a resistance wire connected to a three-terminal ignition switch

IGNITION COILS & RESISTORS

tery voltage to be applied to the primary circuit.

The auxiliary side of the ballast resistor limits voltage to the control unit, thereby protecting the unit.

Wire Type Resistors

The special resistance wires used with 12-volt systems are five to six feet long and contained in the regular wiring harness. The wire is made of stainless steel or special alloy, plastic-coated and covered with a glass braid. There is relatively small temperature rise and the resistance wire is switched out of the circuit for starting and back in again for running.

With the Delco-Remy circuit shown in Fig. 8, the resistance wire is by-passed by means of a "finger" inside the starter solenoid housing which is attached to the additional switch terminal.

The Delco-Remy and Ford circuit diagrams shown in Figs. 9 and 10 have the resistance wire connected to a separate terminal on the ignition switch. When the ignition switch is released to its running position after the engine fires, the resistance wire is put back into the circuit.

NOTE: If the engine fires when the ignition switch is turned on but quits when the switch is released to its running position, it indicates that the resistance wire has lost its continuity or there is a bad connection at the resistor terminals. If the wire is defective, it must be replaced. To do this, first identify the terminal to which it is attached to the ignition switch (corresponding to the position of the ignition key when the engine is running). Then note the color code of the wire and disconnect it at both ends. Connect the new wire to the terminals and tape it to the main wiring harness. Finally, cut off the exposed sections of the defective wire.

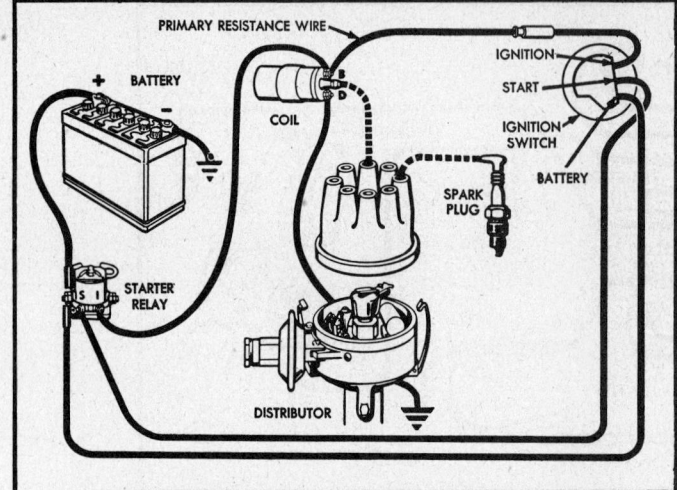

Fig. 10 Ford ignition circuit diagram with a resistance wire connected to a three-terminal ignition switch

CAUTION: Do not attempt to operate the engine for an extended length of time with the resistor shorted out by means of a jumper wire as the breaker points will burn up in short order.

VARIABLE SPEED FANS

DESCRIPTION

The fan drive clutch, Fig. 1, is a fluid coupling containing silicone oil. Fan speed is regulated by the torque-carrying capacity of the silicone oil. The more silicone oil in the coupling the greater the fan speed, and the less silicone oil the slower the fan speed.

Two types of fan drive clutches are in use. On one, Fig. 2, a bi-metallic strip and control piston on the front of the fluid coupling regulates the amount of silicone oil entering the coupling. The bi-metallic strip bows outward with a decrease in surrounding temperature and allows a piston to move outward. The piston opens a valve regulating the flow of silicone oil into the coupling from a reserve chamber. The silicone oil is returned to the reserve chamber through a bleed hole when the valve is closed.

On the other type of fan drive clutch, Fig. 3, a heat-sensitive, bi-metal spring connected to an opening plate brings about a similar result. Both units cause the fan speed to increase with a rise in temperature and to decrease as the temperature goes down.

In some cases a Flex-Fan is used instead of a Fan Drive Clutch. Flexible blades vary the volume of air being drawn through the radiator, automatically increasing the pitch at low engine speeds.

Fig. 1 Typical variable-speed fan installed

FAN DRIVE CLUTCH TEST

Run the engine at a fast idle speed (1000 rpm) until normal operating temperature is reached. This process can be speeded up by blocking off the front of the radiator with cardboard. Regardless of temperatures, the unit must be operated for at least five minutes immediately before being tested.

Stop the engine and, using a glove or a cloth to protect the hand, immediately check the effort required to turn the fan. If considerable effort is required, it can be assumed that the coupling is operating satisfactorily. If very little effort is required to turn the fan, it is an indication that the coupling is not operating properly and should be replaced.

SERVICE PROCEDURE

The removal procedure for either type of fan clutch assembly is generally the same for all trucks. Merely unfasten the unit from the water pump and remove the assembly from the truck.

CAUTION: To prevent silicone fluid from draining into fan drive bearing, do not place drive unit on bench with rear of shaft pointing downward.

The type of unit shown in Fig. 2 may be partially disassembled for inspection and cleaning. Take off the capscrews that hold the assembly together and separate the fan from

VARIABLE SPEED FANS

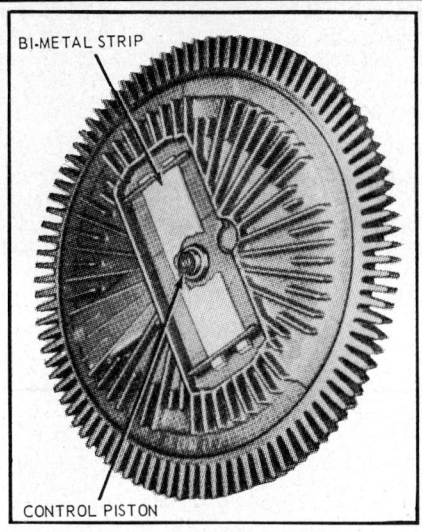

Fig. 2 Variable-speed fan with flat bi-metal thermostatic spring

the drive clutch. Next remove the metal strip on the front by pushing one end of it toward the fan clutch body so it clears the retaining bracket. Then push the strip to the side so that its opposite end will spring out of place. Now remove the small control piston underneath it.

Check the piston for free movement of the coupling device. If the piston sticks, clean it with emery cloth. If the bi-metal strip is damaged, replace the entire unit. These strips are not interchangeable.

When reassembling, install the control piston so that the projection on the end of it will contact the metal strip. Then install the metal strip with any identification numerals or letters facing the clutch. After reassembly, clean the clutch drive with a cloth soaked in solvent. Avoid dipping the clutch assembly in any type of liquid. Install the assembly in the reverse order of removal.

The coil spring type of fan clutch cannot be disassembled, serviced or repaired. If it does not function properly it must be replaced with a new unit.

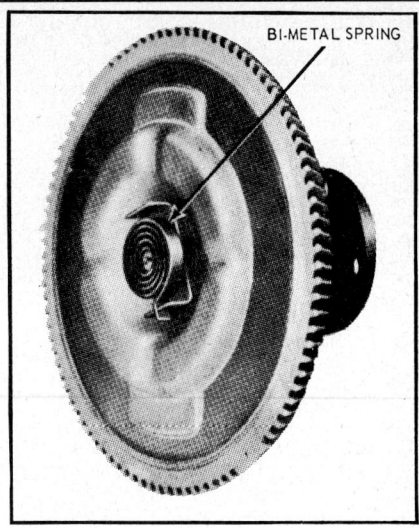

Fig. 3 Variable-speed fan with coiled bi-metal thermostatic spring

GENERATORS & REGULATORS

INDEX

Page No.

GENERATOR SERVICE

Generator Not Charging	12
Removing Generator	11
Replacing Brushes	12
Replacing With New Generator	13
Polarizing Generator	14
Motoring Generator	14

REGULATOR SERVICE

Replacing Regulator	14
Electrical Test Service Notes	15
Auto-Lite Electrical Tests	16
Delco-Remy Electrical Tests	17
Ford and Bosch Electrical Tests	16
Auto-Lite Mechanical Adjustments	19
Delco-Remy Mechanical Adjustments	20
Ford and Bosch Mechanical Adjustments	21

GENERATOR SERVICE

Removing Generator

Figs. 1 and 2 illustrate a typical generator. The following contains tips on servicing and replacing the generator. To replace the brushes, it is assumed that the generator is to be removed from the engine.

1. Remove the leads from the generator terminals, Fig. 3. Identify each lead in order that it can be replaced to the proper terminal. Note that the condenser (for radio suppression) is always attached to the "A" terminal and never to the "F" terminal.
2. The fan belt must be removed from the generator pulley. On some cars it is neces-

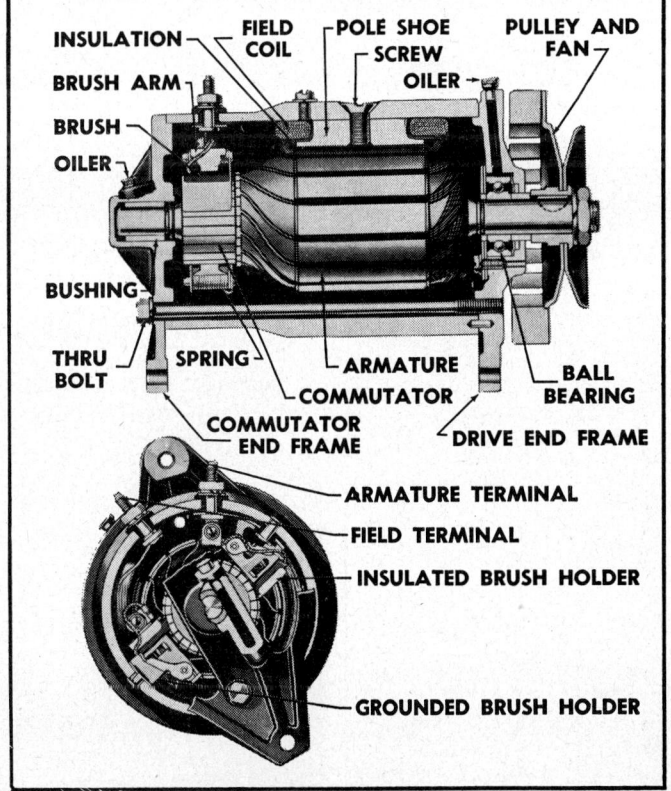

Fig. 1 End and sectional views of a typical magnetic switch

sary to remove the nut holding the belt tension idler pulley in place. With tension loosened, the belt can be removed.

3. Remove the generator by removing the bolts holding the generator lugs to the engine mounting bracket, Fig. 4. On some

GENERATORS & REGULATORS

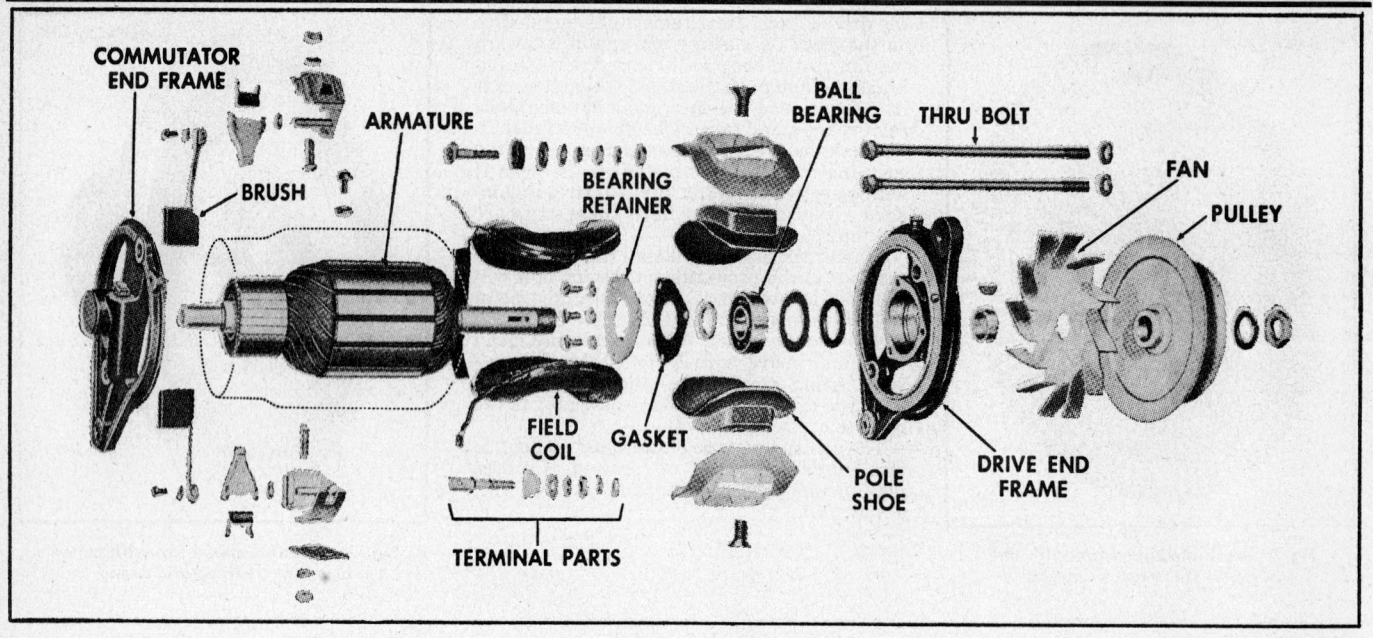

Fig. 2 Exploded view of generator

cars, it is necessary to remove the stud holding the adjusting bracket to generator end frame, Fig. 5. Loosen the nuts holding the generator to the engine mounting bracket. Move generator toward the engine to release the belt from the pulley. Remove mounting bolts and lift generator from bracket.

4. Some applications have a power steering pump driven by an extended generator shaft, Fig. 6. To remove this type generator, the pump must first be removed from the generator by loosening the two mounting screws. The pump can then be pulled off and the generator removed from the engine as previously described.

Replacing Brushes

1. Remove commutator end frame by first removing the through bolts. Some types of through bolts have hex heads whereas others have slotted screw heads. After bolts are removed, it may be necessary to lightly tap the end frame to remove it from the field frame, Fig. 7.

2. Remove drive end frame and armature assembly from field frame, Fig. 8.
3. With a cloth, clean inside of field frame assembly. *Do not dip field coils in any cleaning solvent or puncture field coil insulation during the cleaning process.*

GENERATOR NOT CHARGING

1. To check out the trouble, first make sure all connections at the generator and the regulator are clean and tight. Then run the engine at a fast idle speed. If the generator still fails to show a charge, proceed with step 2. But if a charge is indicated on the ammeter or if the indicator light goes out, there was a poor connection in the circuit.
2. If the generator field is internally grounded, connect a jumper wire from the regulator armature terminal to the field terminal. If the generator field is grounded externally through the regulator, ground the field terminal to the regulator base. In both cases, the regulator has been taken out of the circuit. Again run the engine, and if the generator now shows a charge the regulator is at fault.

CAUTION: *The foregoing procedure should not be used with double contact voltage regulators. With external ground systems (Delco-Remy), disconnect the field lead and ground it to the regulator base. With internal ground systems, disconnect the field lead and hold it against the armature terminal of the regulator. If this is not done, the lower set of contacts will burn, thereby making the regulator inoperative.*

3. If there is still no charge after the foregoing test, short out the circuit breaker and current regulator by connecting a jumper wire from the regulator armature termi-

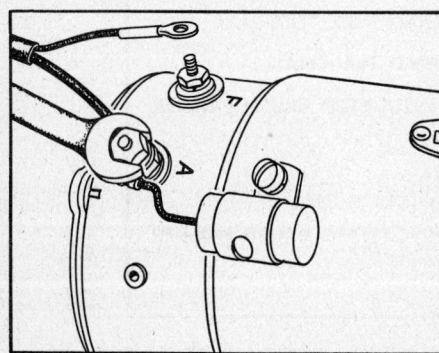

Fig. 3 Note that condenser is attached to the "A" terminal. If connected to the "F" terminal it would make the voltage regulator ineffective and the generator would overcharge.

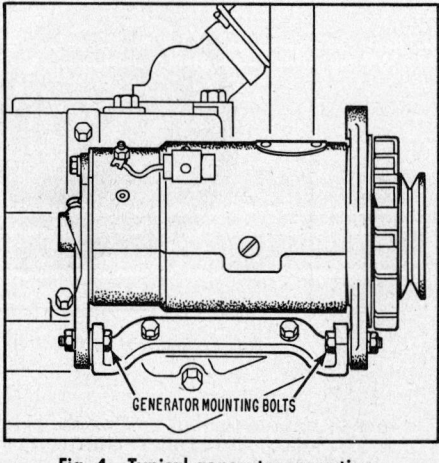

Fig. 4 Typical generator mounting

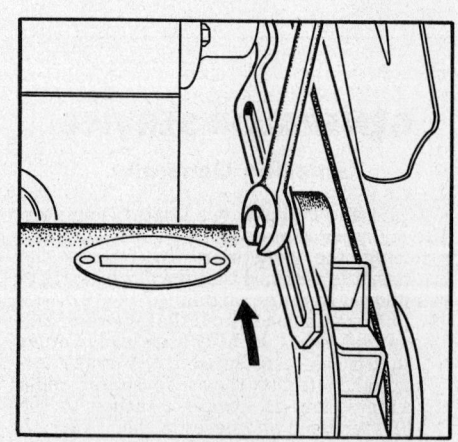

Fig. 5 Removing stud holding adjusting bracket to generator end frame

GENERATORS & REGULATORS

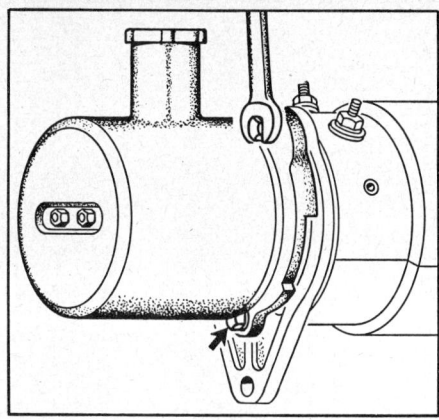

Fig. 6 Removing power steering pump from generator

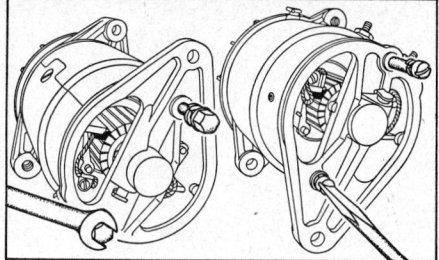

Fig. 7 Removing generator end frame from field frame

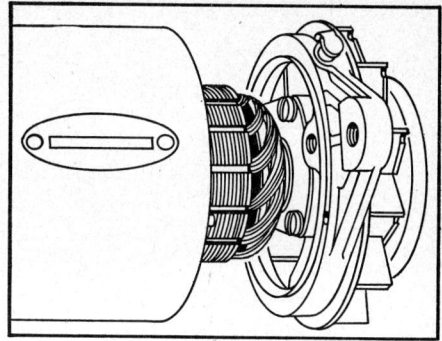

Fig. 8 Removing drive end frame and armature assembly

nal to the battery terminal. Again run the engine, and if the generator now shows a charge, the regulator is at fault. However, if there is still no charge, the trouble is probably in the generator itself, although it may be elsewhere in the charging circuit.

4. Clean commutator end frame, using a cloth dampened in solvent. Place a drop or two of oil in the bushing type bearing to facilitate reassembly.
5. Clean the armature and drive end assembly with an air hose. A clean dry rag may be used to wipe off dirt if an air hose is not available. *Do not use solvent of any kind on the armature.*
6. Examine commutator for high bars, high mica, pitted bars, or excessive wear. If any of these conditions are found, the commutator should be turned down on a lathe and the mica undercut, Figs. 9, 10, 11. Burned bars may indicate a defective armature which should be tested and replaced if necessary, Figs. 12, 13, 14.
7. If commutator appears to be in good condition except for dirt or minor corrosion, it may be cleaned with a fine grade of sandpaper. After cleaning, blow out abrasive particles left between commutator bars. *Never use emery cloth for this purpose as particles of emery may become embedded in the commutator bars and cause a short.*
8. Remove brushes from field frame. Wipe off brush holders with a rag dampened in solvent. Any corrosion on the brush bearing surface of the brush holders should be removed to permit freedom of brush movement.
9. If brush holders are mounted on the commutator end frame, remove necessary screws allowing complete removal of brushes.
10. Generators with cover bands need not be disassembled, unless so desired, for brush replacement. First remove the cover band and then remove the screws that attach the flexible brush leads to the brush holders. Then lift up on the brush spring arm and pull out the old brush. A new brush is then pushed down into position in the brush holder. The flexible leads of the brush are then re-fastened to the brush holder. If a field coil lead is present, it also must be fastened to the proper brush holder at this same time.
11. To insert new brushes into the brush holders attached to the field frame, push brush into holder from the bottom and shove it up all the way. This will allow the brush arm to lock the brush up into a position for installation over the commutator. Refasten flexible leads to commutator.
12. When brushes are installed, make sure the pre-formed angle on the brush matches the commutator contour.
13. Generators with brush holders mounted to the commutator end frame of the type shown in Fig. 15, should have their brushes inserted and flexible leads securely fastened in place before reassembling the end frame onto the field frame.
14. On some generators the brushes may be seated as shown in Fig. 16, using No. 00 sandpaper cut as wide as the commutator finished surface. Excessive use of sandpaper should be avoided since it will shorten the brush and decrease its life. Blow off abrasive dust and carbon after completing the seating process.
15. Another method of seating brushes after the generator is reassembled is to spread some brush seating compound on the commutator and then turn the armature by hand for 20 or 30 revolutions. Then blow out the carbon and dust residue left from the brush seating operation.
16. Before reassembling the generator, it may be desirable to check out the field coils and terminals. If so refer to Figs. 17 to 20.
17. When reassembling generators, make sure brushes are out of the way when brush assembly is slipped over commutator. In the event brushes are held up by the brush arm, make sure they are seated down on commutator before installing generator on engine.

Replacing With New Generator

1. When exchanging the existing generator with a new or replacement generator, it is necessary to remove the pulley and fan assembly from the old generator for use on the new generator. After the generator has been removed from the engine, it may be possible to remove the pulley nut by holding the pulley armature shaft by a belt, Fig. 21.
2. In the event that the pulley nut cannot be loosened by the belt method, it is necessary to disassemble old generator to remove the pulley, armature and drive end frame assembly. This assembly can then be placed in a vise and the pulley nut removed.
3. A pulley puller is then used to remove the pulley from the armature shaft, Fig. 22.

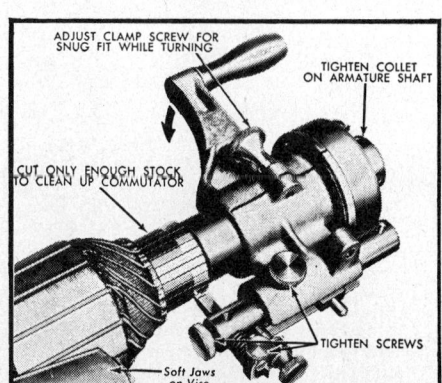

Fig. 9 Turning down commutator with a lathe

Fig. 10 Undercutting mica insulation. Depth of cut should be 1/32"

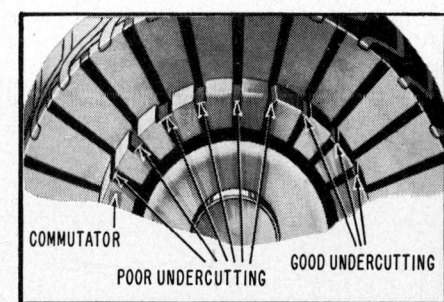

Fig. 11 Examples of proper and improper undercutting

GENERATORS & REGULATORS

Fig. 12 Testing armature for short circuit. As armature is rotated by hand, steel strip (hacksaw blade) will vibrate if short circuit exists.

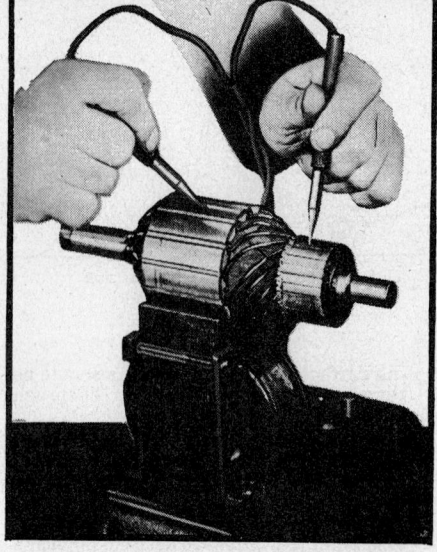

Fig. 13 Armature test for ground. Using test lamp, place test lead on armature core and the other lead on each commutator bar. If lamp lights armature is grounded and must be replaced.

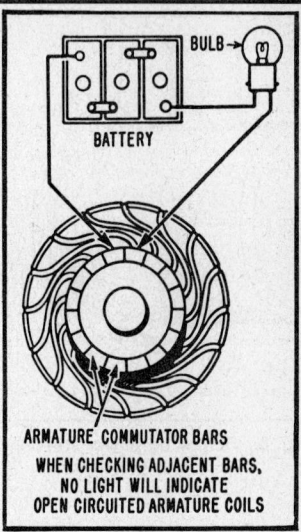

Fig. 14 Armature test for open circuit

4. Care should be exercised not to bend or distort either the pulley or fan blades during the removal process.
4. The fan and pulley assembly is then placed over the new generator shaft with the keyway in position over the key. Then lightly tap the pulley and fan assembly down on the shaft until the pulley nut can be started on the threaded end of the shaft.
5. After the generator is assembled and brushes properly seated the generator should be run as a motor, the procedure for which is given below. Mount the generator on the engine and tighten the pulley nut to force the pulley into position against the armature shaft shoulder. Use the vehicle belt as a holding device on the pulley.
6. Apply 8 to 10 drops of light engine oil to the oil cups if present on the generator. Sealed bearings do not require lubrication.

POLARIZING GENERATOR

After the generator is installed on the engine and all leads are connected, the generator must be polarized before starting the engine. The polarizing procedure depends upon whether the field is grounded externally or internally. This data is included in the *Generator and Regulator Specifications* charts in the vehicle chapters. Having determined which system is used, proceed as follows:

If the generator field is externally grounded, Fig. 23, momentarily connect a jumper wire from the "BAT" to the "GEN" or "ARM" terminals of the voltage regulator. Just a touch of the jumper of both terminals is all that is required:

If the generator field is internally grounded, Fig. 24, disconnect the field wire from the regulator and momentarily touch this wire to the regulator "BAT" terminal.

MOTORING GENERATOR

Run the generator as a motor by connecting the ground side of a battery to the generator housing. Connect the ungrounded side of the battery to the generator armature terminal.

On generators with externally grounded fields, connect a jumper wire from the generator field terminal to the generator frame. For internally grounded units connect a jumper wire from the armature terminal to the field terminal.

While motoring, the armature should rotate slowly. If it does not, it may be due to improper bearing fit or alignment, mechanical interference between armature and field coil pole shoes or improper end play. If end play appears excessive, check the tightness of the pulley nut. Make sure that the pole shoe screws are securely tightened. Two or three sharp raps on the generator frame with a rawhide or plastic hammer will often help to free the armature.

VOLTAGE REGULATORS, REPLACE

1. When working on voltage regulators, it is good practice first to remove the battery ground strap or cable from the battery post. This prevents any short circuits or accidental grounds from occurring.
2. To aid in correctly re-wiring to the replacement regulator, identify the wires in some manner that will aid in proper

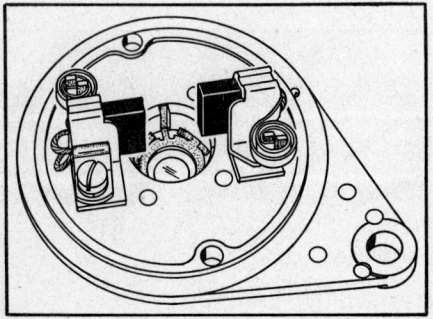

Fig. 15 Brushes mounted to commutator end frame

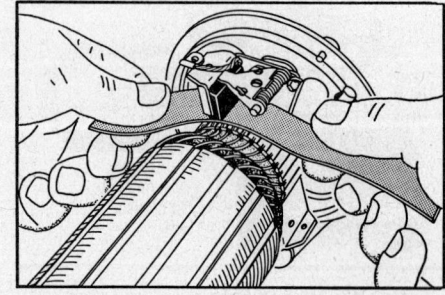

Fig. 16 Seating brushes with sandpaper

Fig. 17 Field coil test for open circuit. Using test lamp, place one test lead on field terminal and the other on the field coil lead to armature terminal. If lamp does not light, field coils are open and must be replaced (unless a loose soldered connection is found at field terminal).

GENERATORS & REGULATORS

Fig. 18 Field coil test for ground. Using a test lamp, place one test lead on generator frame (ground) and the other on field terminal. Be sure free end of field wire is not touching ground and field terminal insulation is not broken. If lamp lights, field coils are grounded. If ground cannot be located or repaired, field coils must be replaced.

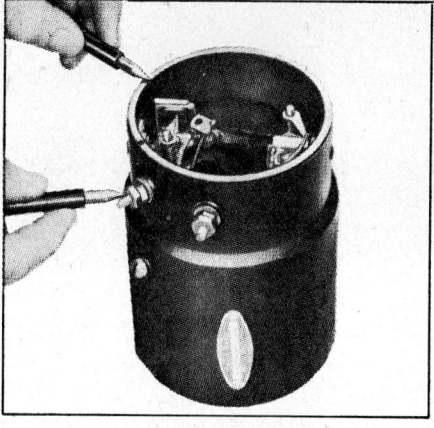

Fig. 19 Armature terminal test for ground. Using a test lamp, place one test lead on armature terminal and the other on generator frame. Be sure loose end of terminal lead is not touching ground. If lamp lights, armature terminal insulation through generator frame is broken down and must be replaced.

Fig. 20 Insulated brush holder test for ground. Using a test lamp, place one test lead on insulated brush holder and the other on ground. If lamp lights, brush holder is grounded due to defective insulation on frame.

installation.

3. Remove lead or leads connected to the battery terminal of the regulator.
4. Remove lead or leads connected to the armature terminal of the regulator. This terminal is marked "GEN" on Delco-Remy units, and "A" or "ARM" on Autolite, Ford and Bosch units. *If a condenser is present, note that it must be connected to the armature terminal only.*
5. Some regulators have a fuse connected to the regulator battery terminal. This fuse should be removed for use with the replacement regulator. Before installing the fuse, however, it should be tested for continuity with a test lamp. This is to make sure the fuse is not defective or "blown" which would result in an open circuit.
6. After the new regulator has been installed in position, scrape all lead connections or terminals clean to provide a good metal-to-metal contact when re-connected to the regulator terminals.
7. After all leads are connected and before the engine is started, the generator must be polarized as outlined previously.

ELECTRICAL TESTS ON REGULATORS

Service Notes

1. Do not attempt to adjust regulators unless its operation is thoroughly understood and accurate meters are available. Even a slight error in the setting of the unit may cause improper functioning, resulting in a rundown or overcharged battery, or damage to the generator or regulator.
2. When electrical tests are made at the regulator terminals, there is great danger of short circuiting the regulator and burning the contact reeds on Autolite units. Whenever possible it is better to connect test apparatus where there is no danger of damaging the regulator. For example:
3. When checking generator output on single contact voltage regulators, ground the field terminal at the generator rather

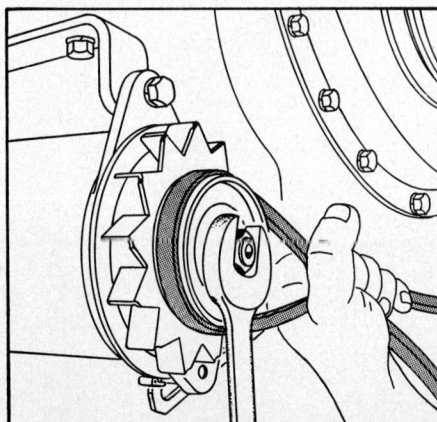

Fig. 21 Holding pulley tight with fan belt while loosening or tightening pulley nut.

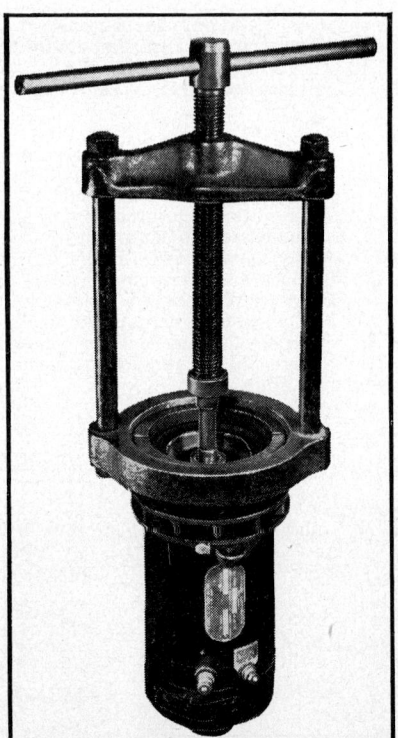

Fig. 22 Using puller to remove pulley

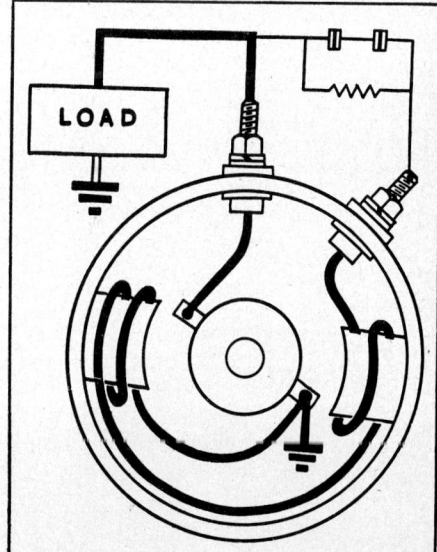

Fig. 23 Wiring diagram of a generator having the field grounded externally through the voltage regulator. This can readily be identified by the fact that the grounded brush has only its own lead connected to it.

GENERATORS & REGULATORS

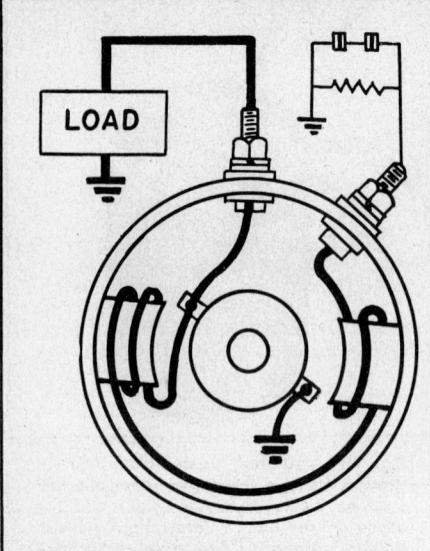

Fig. 24 Wiring diagram of a generator having the field grounded internally through the grounded brush. This can readily be identified by the fact that the grounded brush has both its own lead and the field lead connected to it.

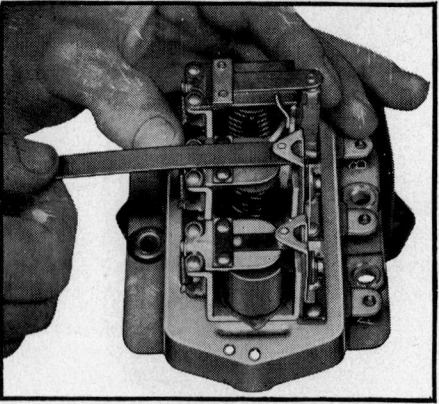

Fig. 25 Auto-Lite, Ford and Bosch regulator contacts should be filed parallel with length of armature.

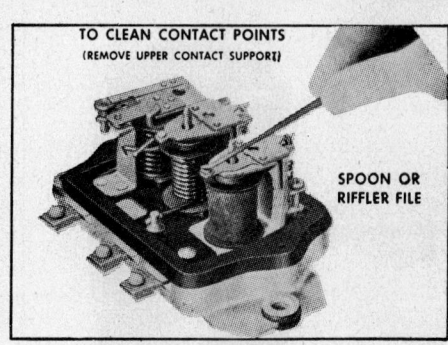

Fig. 26 Cleaning Delco-Remy regulator contact points

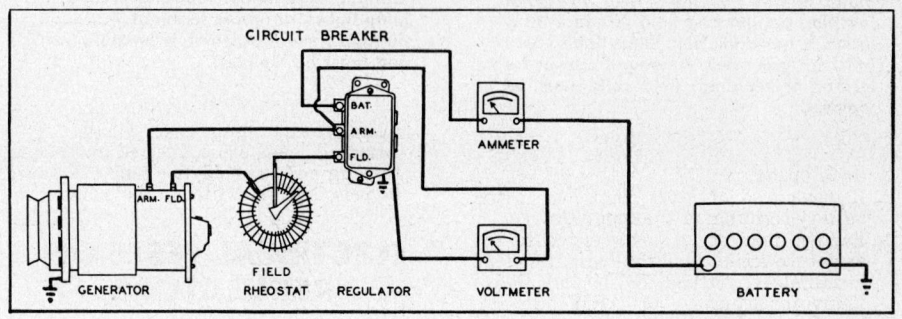

Fig. 27 Circuit breaker test for Auto-Lite, Ford and Bosch regulators

than at the regulator to avoid the possibility of grounding the regulator battery terminal with a screwdriver.

CAUTION: *When making this test on double contact voltage regulators, disconnect the field lead from the generator and ground this lead to the generator frame.*

4. Timing or trouble lights should be connected at the starter solenoid terminal rather than at the regulator battery terminal. This will avoid danger of the clip connector slipping off and simultaneously touching the battery and field terminal of the regulator.
5. Before testing or adjusting the regulator, be sure all connections in the charging circuit are clean and tight, and that the battery is fully charged. Check the generator output and be sure the regulator is the correct unit for use with the particular generator. Be sure regulator is properly grounded.
6. Always make the voltage regulator test before making the current regulator test.

When removing or installing the regulator cover, do not allow the cover to touch regulator parts, as this might cause a short circuit and damage the unit.

7. Before starting the tests make sure the contacts are clean and not rough or pitted. If this is not done, subsequent tests will only produce erratic meter indications. When cleaning Autolite, Ford and Bosch contacts, they should be filed parallel to the armature as shown in Fig. 25, using a No. 6 American Swiss cut equaling file. Do not file crosswise as grooves may form which would tend to cause sticking and erratic operation. Delco-Remy recommends the use of a spoon or riffler file, Fig. 26. After filing, use a strip of linen tape dampened with lighter fluid to clean the contacts; then run a strip of dry tape across the points to remove any residue left from filing.

AUTO-LITE, FORD & BOSCH ELECTRICAL TESTS

Circuit Breaker

1. With an ammeter connected as shown in Fig. 27, and a voltmeter connected from regulator armature terminal to regulator base, disconnect field lead from regulator field terminal and insert a variable resistance between field lead and its terminal.
2. Run engine at about 800 rpm. Turn variable resistance to the "all in" position. Then slowly reduce the resistance, noting the voltage reading just as the circuit breaker closes. The voltmeter will give a sharp fluctuation at that point and usu-

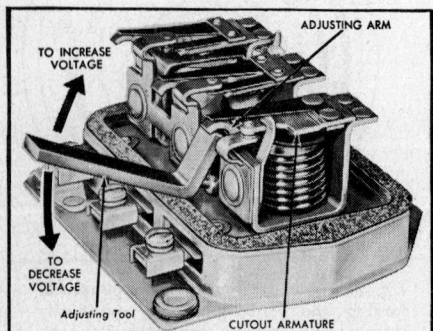

Fig. 28 Adjusting circuit breaker closing voltage on Ford and Bosch regulators

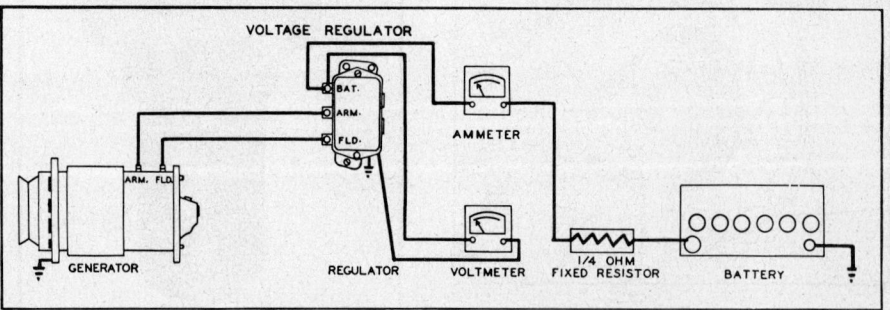

Fig. 29 Voltage regulator test on Auto-Lite, Ford and Bosch single contact voltage regulators

GENERATORS & REGULATORS

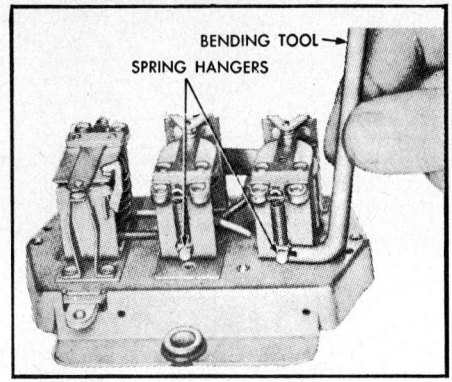

Fig. 29A Adjusting armature spring tension for Auto-Lite voltage and current settings.

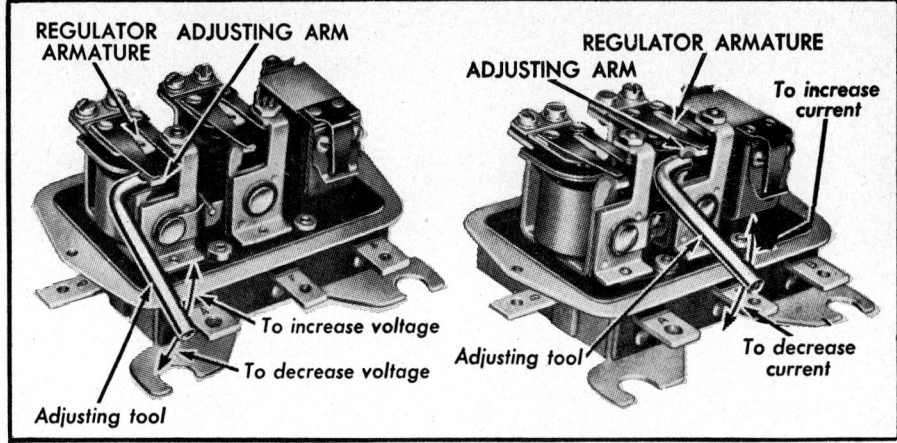

Fig. 30 Adjusting voltage regulator (left) and current regulator (right) on Ford and Bosch regulators

ally a slight click can be heard as the contacts close.

3. On Autolite units, if the closing voltage is not within specifications, remove the regulator cover and change the armature spring tension by bending the lower spring hanger. Bending the spring hanger down increases spring tension and raises the voltage, and vice versa.
4. If closing voltage is not within specifications on Ford and Bosch units, bend the adjusting arm upward to increase voltage, and vice versa, Fig. 28.

Single Contact Voltage Regulator

1. Leave the ammeter connected as shown and move the voltmeter clip from the regulator armature terminal to the regulator battery terminal, Fig. 29.
2. Disconnect the variable resistance from the regulator field terminal and reconnect the field lead. Then insert a ¼ ohm fixed resistor in series with the ammeter.
3. Increase engine speed to obtain about a 7 ampere charge and operate for about 15 minutes with regulator cover in place.
4. Stop and restart the engine to cycle the generator; then note voltage reading. If not within specifications, adjust as follows:
5. On Autolite units, adjust by bending lower spring hanger, Fig. 29A. Bending the hanger down increases spring tension

and raises voltage and vice versa.

6. On Ford and Bosch units, increase spring tension by bending adjusting arm upward to raise voltage and vice versa, Fig. 30.
7. Be sure to stop and restart ending and replace cover after each setting before taking voltage readings.

Ford & Bosch Double Contact Voltage Regulator

If proper voltage cannot be obtained by bending the spring hanger as directed for single contact voltage regulators, further adjustments are required as follows:

1. Disconnect ground terminal from battery.
2. Remove regulator from vehicle and take off cover.
3. Turn upper contact screw in or out to obtain a .040″ gap between armature core and armature, Fig. 31.
4. Turn lower contact screw in or out to obtain a .037″ gap between armature core and armature. While making adjustments, hold contact points together by pressing downward on screwdriver.

Current Regulator

1. Meters are connected as for the voltage regulator test except that the fixed resistor is removed and a carbon pile rheostat is connected across the battery as shown in Fig. 32 to allow full output. An alternate method for allowing the current regulator to operate is to operate the

starting motor for 15 to 20 seconds cranking the engine and turning on lights and accessories.

2. Operate engine at about 1800 rpm. Using the carbon pile, increase the load to lower the regulated system voltage approximately one volt and allow the current regulator to operate.

DELCO-REMY ELECTRICAL TESTS

Figs. 33 and 34 show the generator circuit using single contact voltage regulator and double contact voltage regulator, respectively. In making the following tests, the regulator must be at operating temperatures before taking meter readings. Operating temperature may be assumed to exist after not less than 15 minutes continuous operation with a charging rate of about 10 amperes and regulator cover in place.

CAUTION: *With charging circuits having the double contact voltage regulator, Fig. 34, it is extremely important never to ground the field terminal of the generator or regulator when these units are connected or operating together. To do so will burn up the upper set of voltage regulator contacts.*

For best results, the electrical tests must be made in the order given below.

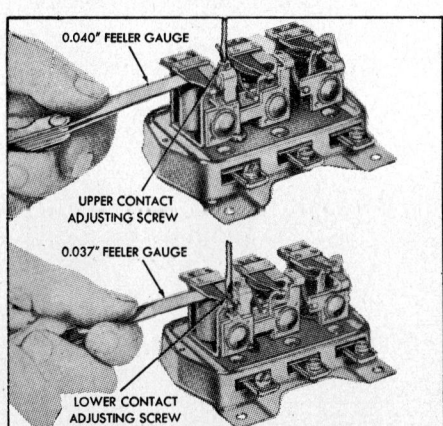

Fig. 31 Adjusting Ford and Bosch double contact voltage regulator

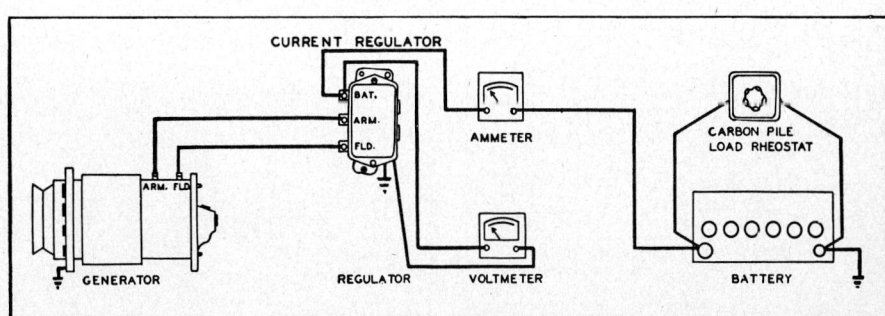

Fig. 32 Current regulator test on Auto-Lite, Ford and Bosch regulators

GENERATORS & REGULATORS

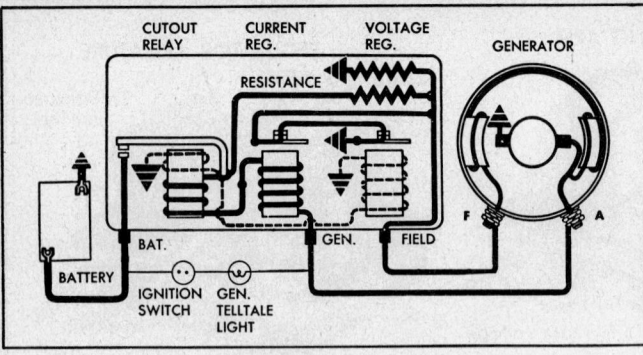

Fig. 33 Delco-Remy charging circuit with single contact voltage regulator

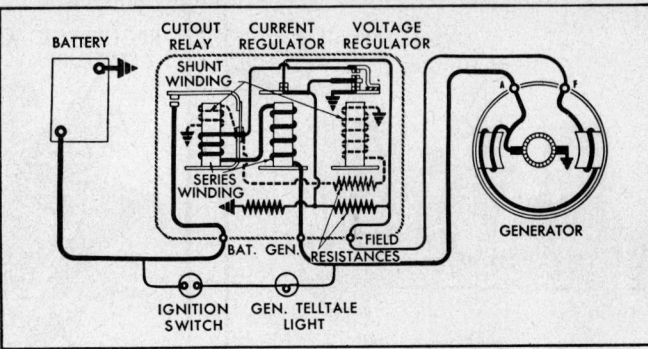

Fig. 34 Delco-Remy charging circuit with double contact voltage regulator

Single Contact Voltage Regulator

1. Make meter connections as shown in Fig. 35 (upper view), and operate the engine at about 1600 rpm for 15 minutes with the 1/4 ohm resistor in the circuit and cover in place to bring the regulator to operating temperature.
2. Cycle the generator by stopping the engine, then restarting and bringing generator speed back to 1600 engine rpm.
3. Note voltmeter reading and ambient temperature (temperature of air surrounding regulator 1/4" from cover). The voltage reading represents setting at ambient temperature. As shown in Fig. 36, setting will be different at other ambient temperatures. *If method of measuring ambient temperature is not available it may be assumed to be 40 degrees above room temperature.*
4. To adjust voltage setting, remove regulator cover and turn voltage regulator adjusting screw, Fig. 37. Turn screw clockwise to increase spring tension and raise voltage, and vice versa. *Final adjustment should always be made by turning screw clockwise to assure contact between screw head and spring support, Fig. 38.*
5. After each adjustment and before taking meter reading, replace cover and recycle generator, as in Step 2.

Double Contact Voltage Regulator

1. Make meter connections as shown in Fig. 35 (lower view).
2. With variable resistance turned out (minimum resistance), operate generator at a speed so that the voltage regulator is operating on the upper set of contacts. Continue to operate for 15 minutes to establish operating temperature. Regulator cover must be in place.
3. Cycle generator by turning variable resistance to the "open" position momentarily, then slowly decrease (turn out all) resistance. Regulator should again be operating on the upper set of contacts.
4. Note voltmeter reading and ambient temperature, and see Fig. 39 for correction factors.
5. Increase (turn in) resistance slowly until voltage regulator begins to operate on the lower set of contacts. The lower set should operate at a lower voltage than the upper set of contacts.
6. To adjust voltage setting on upper set of contacts, do so in the same manner as directed for single contact voltage regulators above.
7. For the lower set of contacts, the difference in voltage between the upper set and lower set is increased by *slightly* increasing the air gap between the armature and center of core and decreased by *slightly* decreasing the air gap, Fig. 40. This adjustment is made while the regulator is operating. If necessary to make this adjustment, recheck the voltage setting of both sets of contacts.

REGULATOR AMBIENT TEMPERATURE	VOLTAGE LOW	VOLTAGE HIGH
165°F	13.1	13.9
145°F	13.5	14.3
125°F	13.8	14.7
105°F	14.0	14.9
85°F	14.2	15.2
65°F	14.4	15.4
45°F	14.5	15.6

NORMAL SPECIFICATION RANGE
■ INDICATES PUBLISHED SPECIFICATIONS

Fig. 36 Delco-Remy single contact regulator temperature and voltage factors

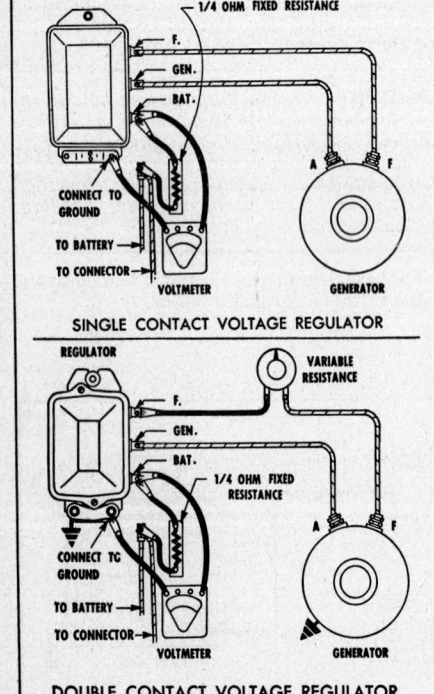

Fig. 35 Checking Delco-Remy voltage regulator setting

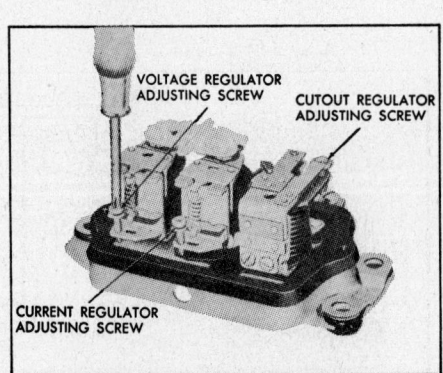

Fig. 37 Delco-Remy regulator adjusting screws

Fig. 38 Proper contact between regulator spring support and adjusting screw on Delco-Remy regulators.

GENERATORS & REGULATORS

REGULATOR AMBIENT TEMPERATURE	VOLTAGE LOW		HIGH
205°F	13.3	—	14.1
185°F	13.4	—	14.2
165°F	13.5	—	14.4
145°F	13.7	—	14.5
125°F	13.8	—	14.6
105°F	14.0	—	14.8
85°F	14.1	—	14.9
	NORMAL SPECIFICATION RANGE		

Fig. 39 Delco-Remy double contact regulator temperature and voltage factors.

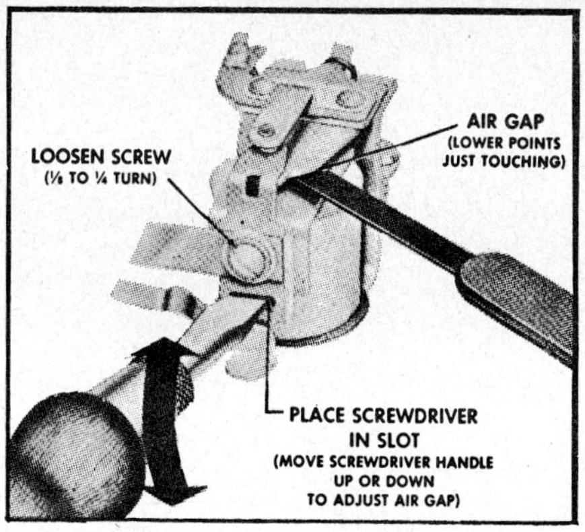

Fig. 40 Adjusting lower set of contacts on Delco-Remy double contact voltage regulator.

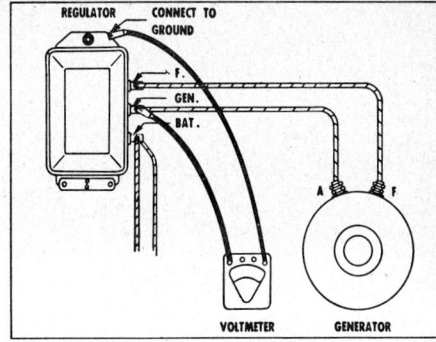

Fig. 41 Delco-Remy circuit breaker test

Circuit Breaker Closing Voltage

1. Connect as shown in Fig. 41.
2. Check closing voltage by slowly increasing generator speed and noting voltage at which points close. Decrease generator speed and make sure points open.
3. If not as specified, adjust voltage by turning adjusting screw clockwise to increase voltage and vice versa.

Current Regulator

1. Before making connections shown in Fig. 42, disconnect battery ground lead. After completing the hook-up, reconnect battery lead.
2. Turn on all lights and accessories and connect an additional load across the battery, such as a carbon pile or bank of lights, so as to drop the system voltage to 12.5–13.0 volts.
3. Operate generator at 1600 engine rpm for at least 15 minutes with cover in place to establish operating temperature.
4. Cycle the generator as previously directed and note current regulator setting.
5. Adjustment is made in the same manner as outlined for single contact voltage regulators (see Fig. 37).

Check For Oxidized Contacts

1. Oxidized contacts may be the cause of low generator output or a discharged battery.

To check for this condition, connect an ammeter into the circuit as shown in Fig. 43, and turn on headlights.
2. Operate generator at a speed that will produce a charge rate of 5 amperes.
3. Ground the "F" terminal of regulator as shown.

CAUTION: *On double contact regulators, remove lead from "F" terminal and*

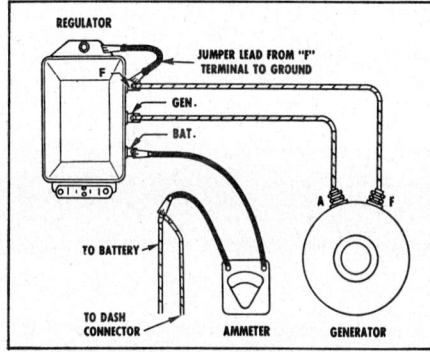

Fig. 43 Checking for oxidized regulator contact points. On double contact regulators do not use jumper wire as shown; instead remove lead from "F" terminal and ground this lead

ground this lead.

4. If generator output increases more than 2 amperes, oxidized contact points are indicated. Remove regulator from vehicle and clean points.

AUTO-LITE MECHANICAL ADJUSTMENTS

Current & Voltage Regulator Air Gaps

1. Use a pin type gauge which measures .048–.052". Insert gauge on point side of air gap and next to armature stop pin with contact points just separating, Fig. 44.
2. If an adjustment is necessary, loosen bracket screws and raise or lower contact point brackets until the foregoing clearance is obtained. Tighten screws securely after adjustment.
3. With armature held down so that stop rivet rests on magnet core, the point gap should be .015" when checked with a feeler gauge.

Circuit Breaker Air Gap

1. As shown in Fig. 45, use a flat gauge which measures from .031–.034". Insert gauge between armature and magnet core. Place gauge as near to hinge as possible.
2. To adjust, bend armature stop, Fig. 46, so

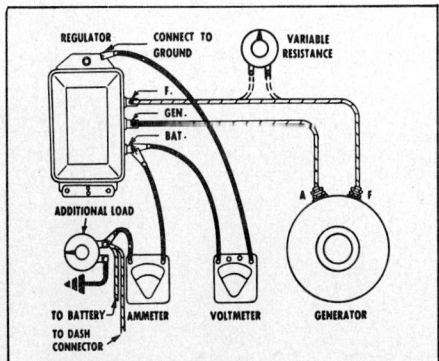

Fig. 42 Delco-Remy current regulator test

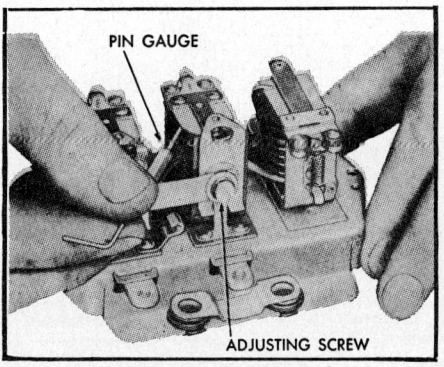

Fig. 44 Checking air gaps on Auto-Lite regulators

Fig. 45 Checking air gap on Auto-Lite circuit breaker

GENERATORS & REGULATORS

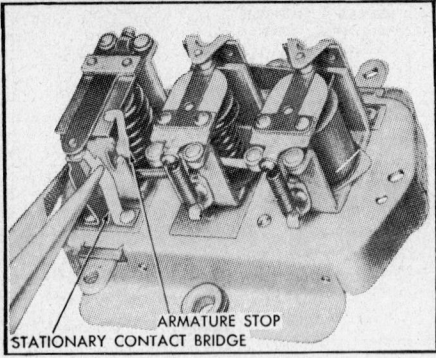

Fig. 46 Adjusting air gap on Auto-Lite circuit breaker

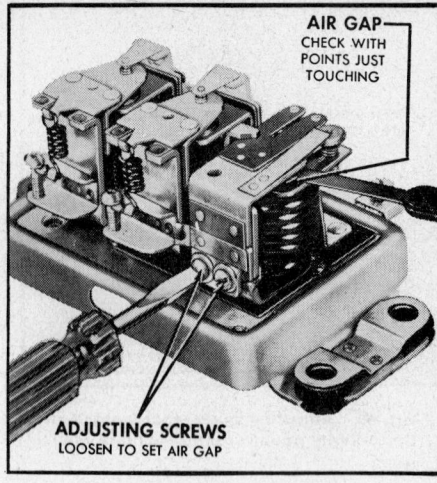

Fig. 47 Adjusting air gap on Delco-Remy circuit breaker

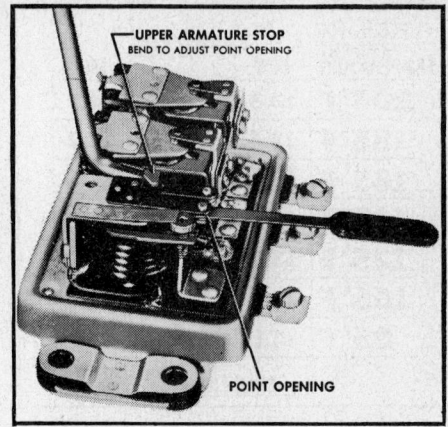

Fig. 48 Adjusting point opening on Delco-Remy circuit breaker

that space between core and armature is within the foregoing limits. The stop must not interfere with armature movement.
3. Adjust the contact gap to .015" by expanding or contracting the stationary contact bridge, Fig. 46. When making this adjustment, keep the contact points in alignment.

DELCO-REMY MECHANICAL ADJUSTMENTS

Circuit Breaker Air Gap & Point Opening

1. Place fingers on armature directly above core and move armature down until points *just* close. Then measure air gap between armature and center core, Fig. 47. Gap should be .020".
2. Check to see that both points close simultaneously. If not, bend spring finger so that they do.
3. To adjust air gap, loosen two screws at back of circuit breaker and raise or lower armature as required. Tighten screws after adjustment.
4. Check point opening with feeler gauge as shown in Fig. 48 and adjust to .020" by bending upper armature stop.
5. After both adjustments have been made, recheck closing voltage and make any necessary adjustments.

Voltage Regulator Air Gap On Single Contact Units

1. Referring to Fig. 49, push armature down to core and release it until contact points *just* touch. Then measure air gap with pin gauge between armature and center of core. Air gap should be .075".
2. On late units, adjust gap by turning nylon nut on top of regulator as shown. On earlier units, adjust as shown in Fig. 50.
3. After making adjustment, recheck voltage setting and make necessary adjustments.

Voltage Regulator Air Gap & Point Opening On Double Contact Units

Point Opening
1. With lower contacts touching, measure point opening between upper set of contacts. Opening should be .016".
2. On early units, adjust as shown in Fig. 51. On late units, adjust as shown in Fig. 52.

Air Gap
1. On late units, Fig. 53, with lower contacts touching, measure air gap and adjust as shown.
2. On early units, first make sure adjusting screw on top of armature is turned all the

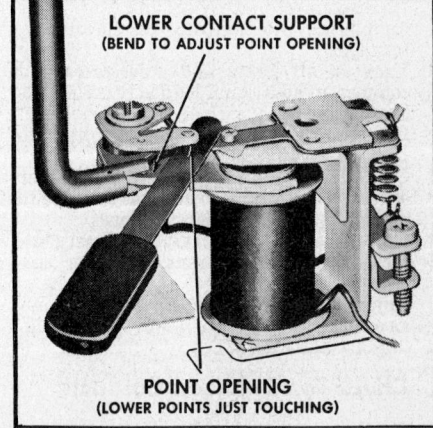

Fig. 51 Adjusting point opening on early type Delco-Remy double contact voltage regulator.

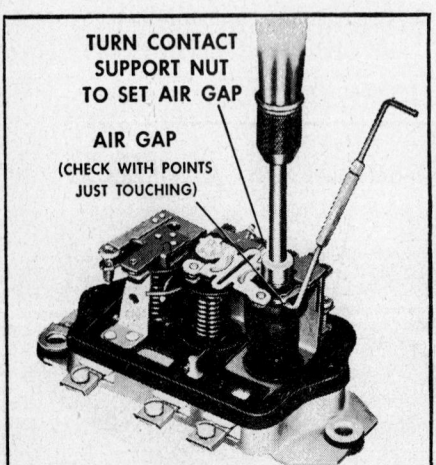

Fig. 49 Adjusting air gap on late type Delco-Remy single contact voltage regulator.

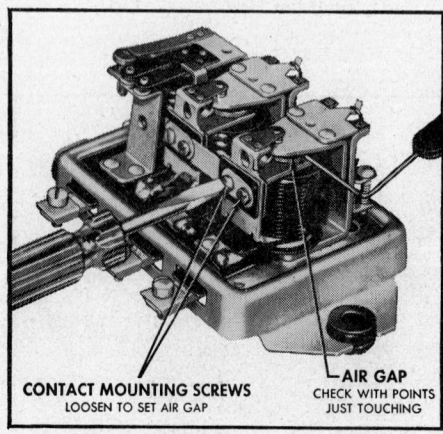

Fig. 50 Adjusting air gap on early type Delco-Remy single contact voltage regulator.

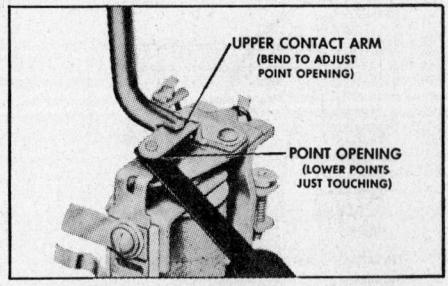

Fig. 52 Adjusting point opening on late type Delco-Remy double contact voltage regulator.

GENERATORS & REGULATORS

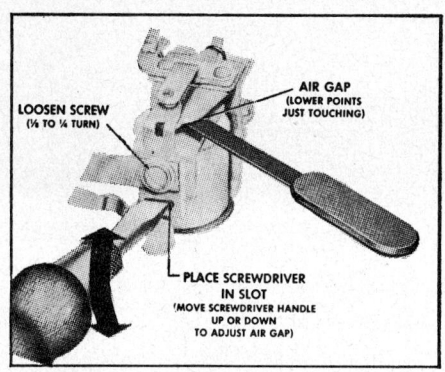

Fig. 53 Adjusting air gap on late type Delco-Remy double contact voltage regulator.

way in a clockwise direction. Then check and adjust the gap as shown in Fig. 54.

Current Regulator Air Gap

Check and adjust current regulator air gap in exactly the same manner as the single contact voltage regulator. Air gap should be .075". After making the adjustment, recheck current setting and adjust as required.

FORD & BOSCH MECHANICAL ADJUSTMENTS

No mechanical adjustments are provided on these regulators as they are of riveted construction. However, on double contact regulators, the upper and lower voltage regulator contact sets are provided with an adjustment. See text in connection with Fig. 31.

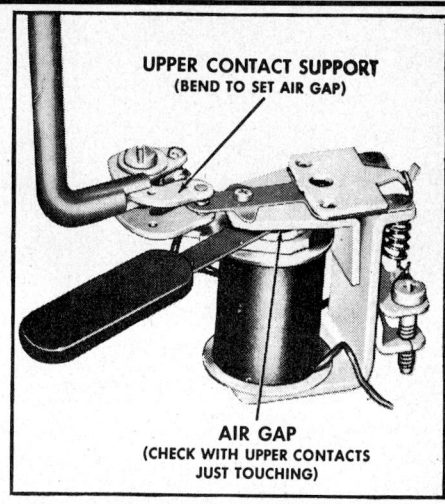

Fig. 54 Adjusting air gap on early type Delco-Remy double contact voltage regulator.

STARTING SWITCHES

Magnetic and solenoid switches are designed to perform mechanical jobs electromagnetically such as closing a heavy circuit or shifting the starter drive pinion with the engine flywheel ring gear for cranking. Switches of this type consist basically of contacts and a winding (or windings) around a hollow cylinder containing a movable core or plunger. When the winding (or windings) is energized by the battery through an external control circuit the plunger is pulled inward, producing the necessary mechanical movement.

MAGNETIC SWITCHES

Figs. 1 and 2 illustrate two typical Delco-Remy switches. The switch shown in Fig. 1 is not designed for disassembly and must be replaced if defective.

In the switch shown in Fig. 2 the terminals are assembled into a molded terminal ring which is held in place on the switch case by the cover and screws. Gaskets on both sides of the ring seal contact the compartment as a protection against moisture and dirt. The winding assembly is not removable from the case on this unit although the contact disk, plunger and plunger return spring can be removed after the cover is taken off.

Fig. 3 is a heavy duty magnetic switch. It is completely serviceable and easy to disassemble and assemble. To disassemble, remove the four terminal plate nuts and washers and take off the terminal plate assembly. The contact disk may be removed by taking off the castellated nut. It is necessary to remove the spring and washers on the plunger rod only when the rod needs to be disassembled. To remove the plunger, unscrew the large metal cover, take out the cotter pin in the plunger

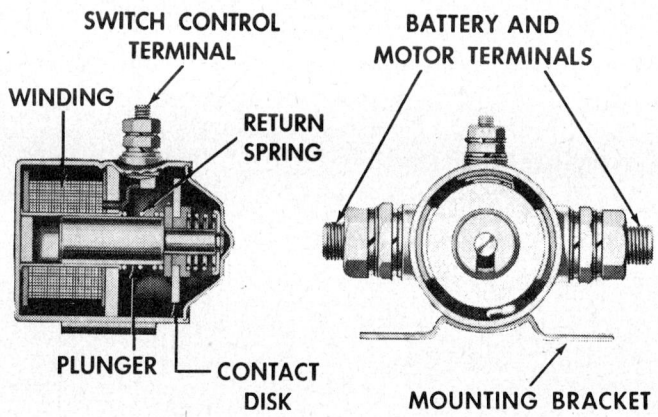

Fig. 1 End and sectional views of a typical magnetic switch

shaft, remove the spring retainer washer and spring, and withdraw the plunger. The winding and switch case is an integral assembly. The only parts that can be removed are the switch terminals. Before removing the switch terminals, the winding leads must be unsoldered from the terminal studs. Whenever the switch is disassembled, upon reassembly, locate the contact disk properly by turning the castellated nut in or out as required to obtain the dimension shown in Fig. 3 between the contact disk and edge of housing.

NOTE: On vehicles with overrunning clutch starting motors, a magnetic switch is normally used to shift the drive pinion into mesh and to close the starter circuit. There are two variations of three-terminal switches and also one type with four terminals. Any of these switches may be manufactured with either a grounded or insulated base. When installing a switch that is not marked "grounded base" or "insulated base", it must be checked out as follows, using a battery and test lamp connected in series.

THREE TERMINAL SWITCHES
1. If the switch has a grounded base the test lamp will light when connected between the starter ("S") terminal or ignition ("I") terminal and switch mounting bracket.
2. If the switch has an insulated base the test lamp will light when connected between the "S" and "I" terminals and either one of the 5/16" threaded studs.

STARTING SWITCHES

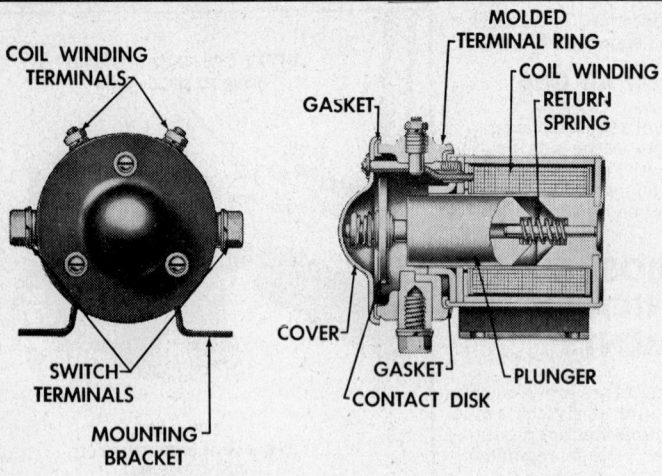

Fig. 2 End and sectional views of a sealed type magnetic switch which uses gaskets to seal the contact compartment.

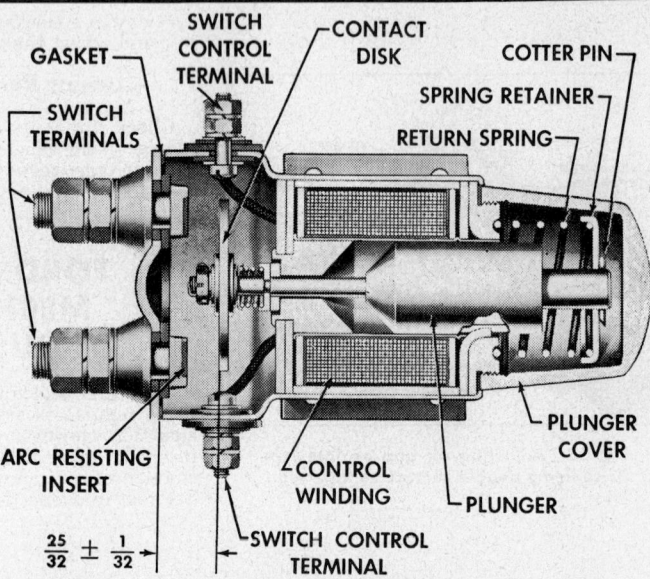

Fig. 3 Sectional view of heavy duty sealed type magnetic switch. To adjust the position of the contact disk, turn the nut on the disk in or out as required to obtained the dimension shown.

3. If the test lamp fails to light when connected between the "S" and "I" terminals and any external part of the switch, disassemble the switch to determine whether the base is grounded or insulated.

FOUR TERMINAL SWITCHES
1. If the switch has a grounded base the test lamp will light when connected between the "S" terminal and switch mounting bracket.
2. If the switch has an insulated base the test lamp will light when connected between the "S" and "I" terminals.
3. If the test lamp fails to light when connected between the "S" terminal and any other external part of the switch, disassemble the switch to determine whether it has an insulated or grounded base.

SOLENOID SWITCHES

The solenoid switch on a cranking motor not only closes the circuit between the battery and the cranking motor but also shifts the drive pinion into mesh with the engine flywheel ring gear. This is done by means of a linkage between the solenoid switch plunger and the shaft lever on the cranking motor. Some linkages are adjustable whole others are not. The linkage is not adjustable on the type shown in Fig. 4 but adjustment of the entire assembly is made by moving the switch on the motor frame.

Fig. 4 shows two views of a solenoid switch used on vehicles with 12-volt systems. Like other solenoid switches, this type is energized by the battery through a separate starting switch. Note, however, that the switch includes an additional small terminal and contact finger. This terminal has no functional duty in relation to the switch, but is used to complete a special ignition circuit during the cranking cycle only. When the solenoid is in cranking position, the finger touches the contact disk and provides a direct circuit between the battery and ignition coil.

Fig. 5 is an exploded view of the 12-volt solenoid switch shown in Fig. 4. When reassembling the switch the contact finger should be adjusted to touch the contact disk before the disk makes contact with the main switch terminals. There should be 1/16" to 3/32" clearance between the contact disk and the main terminals when the finger touches.

Fig. 6 is a wiring circuit of a typical solenoid switch. There are two windings in the solenoid: a pull-in winding (shown as dashes) and a hold-in winding (shown dotted). Both windings are energized when the external control switch is closed. They produce a magnetic field which pulls the plunger in so that the drive pinion is shifted into mesh, and the main contacts in the solenoid switch are closed to connect the battery directly to the cranking motor. Closing the main switch contacts shorts out the pull-in winding since this winding is connected across the main contacts. The magnetism produced by the hold-in winding is sufficient to hold the plunger in, and shorting out the pull-in winding reduces drain on the battery. When the control switch is open, it disconnects the hold-in winding from the battery. When the hold-in winding is disconnected from the battery, the shift lever spring withdraws the plunger from the solenoid, opening the solenoid switch contacts and at the same time withdrawing the drive pinion from mesh. Proper operation of the switch depends on maintaining a definite balance between the magnetic strength of the pull-in and hold-in windings.

This balance is established in the design by the size of the wire and the number of turns specified. *An open circuit in the hold-in winding or attempts to crank with a discharged battery will cause the switch to chatter.*

To disassemble the solenoid, remove nuts, washers and insulators from the switch terminal and battery terminal. Remove cover and take out the contact disk assembly.

When the solenoid has been removed from the starter motor for repair or replacement, the linkage must be adjusted to provide the correct pinion clearance or pinion travel when the solenoid is remounted on the motor. Some solenoids equipped with relays have an adjustable plunger stud but others must be moved on the motor frame to adjust pinion travel. When it is not feasible to tabulate the adjustment specifications for all starters like-

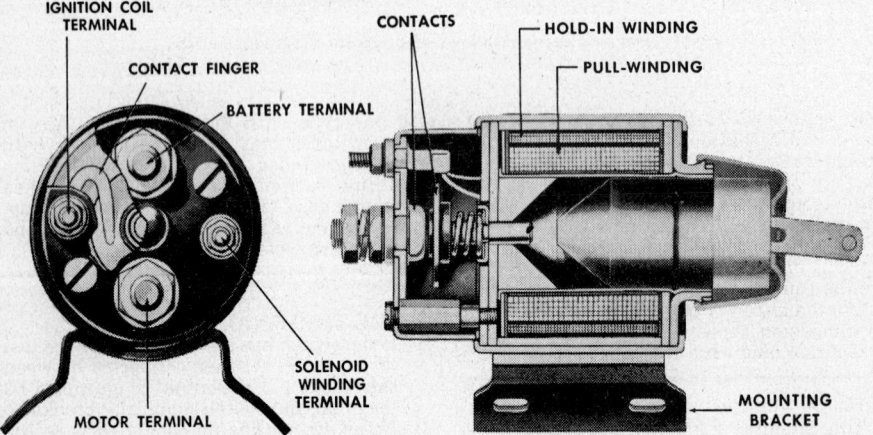

Fig. 4 End and sectional views of solenoid switch. The additional terminal and contact finger are used on 12-volt passenger car applications

STARTING SWITCHES

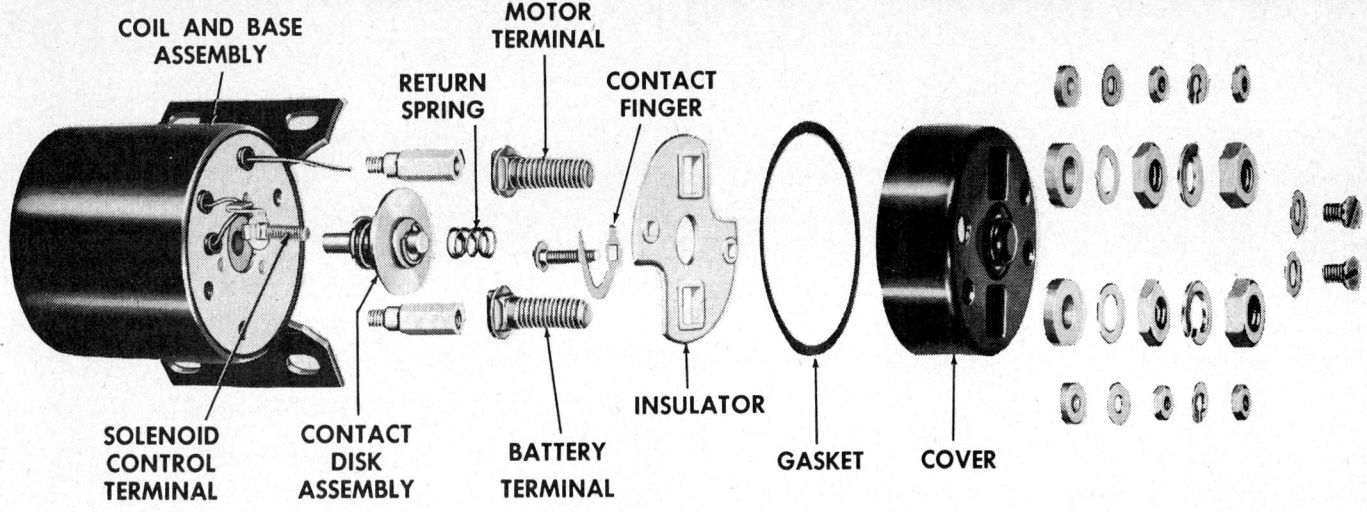

Fig. 5 Exploded view of solenoid switch shown in Fig. 4

ly to be found on trucks, the object of the adjustment is to prevent the drive from slamming against the drive housing.

Solenoid on Dyer Drive Starting Motor

Fig. 7 is an exploded view of this type of solenoid switch. Disassembly of the switch is made by removing the screws or nuts attaching the terminal plate assembly. The contact disk can be detached from the plunger and rod assembly by removing the castellated nut. The contact disk may sometimes require removal so that its face can be wire-brushed to remove corrosion.

On reassembly, the castellated nut should be tightened down so that the face of the disk is $1^{1}/_{32}''$ below the edge of the housing with the plunger in the retracted position. After assembly is completed, fill the bushing in the terminal plate through which the lead passes (where present) with sealing material to prevent entrance of dirt.

DELCO-REMY SERIES-PARALLEL SWITCHES

On Diesel and similar heavy-duty engines, cranking requirements are high and consequently it is desirable to use higher voltage cranking motors so that adequate cranking performance will be obtained. The series-parallel switch makes it possible to use two 12-volt batteries which are connected in parallel for normal operating conditions after the engine is started, but which are connected in series by means of the series-parallel switch to provide 24 volts for the cranking motor. Likewise, two 6-volt batteries can be connected either in parallel or in series to provide a 6-12 volt system.

Fig. 8 shows the construction of a solenoid-operated series-parallel switch. Mechanically-operated series-parallel switches are also used. In both types, however, the switch incorporates a heavy copper contact disk and heavy tungsten-faced main terminals which resist the effects of the arcs that occur when the circuits are broken. The main cranking current is carried through these contacts and terminals. In addition there are contacts to the ter-

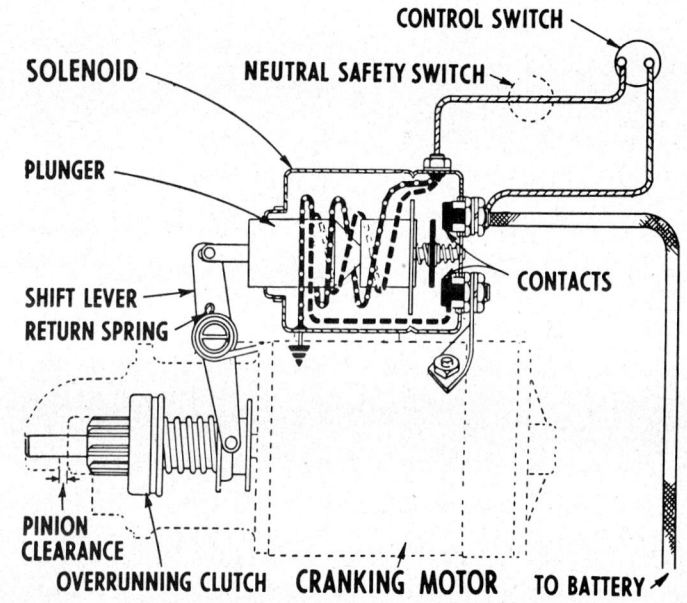

Fig. 6 Wiring circuit of typical solenoid switch

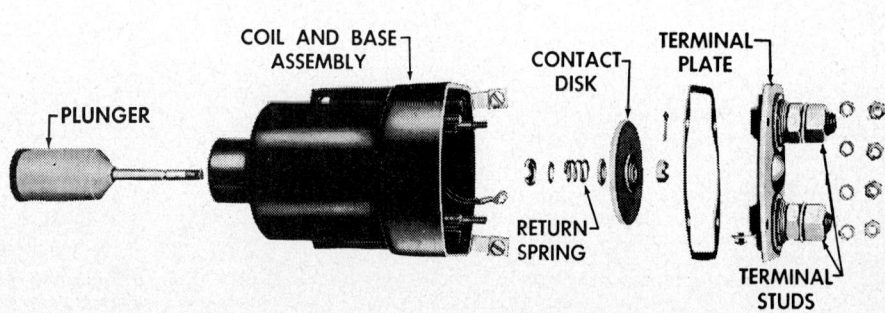

Fig. 7 Exploded view of heavy duty type solenoid used with Dyer cranking motor

STARTING SWITCHES

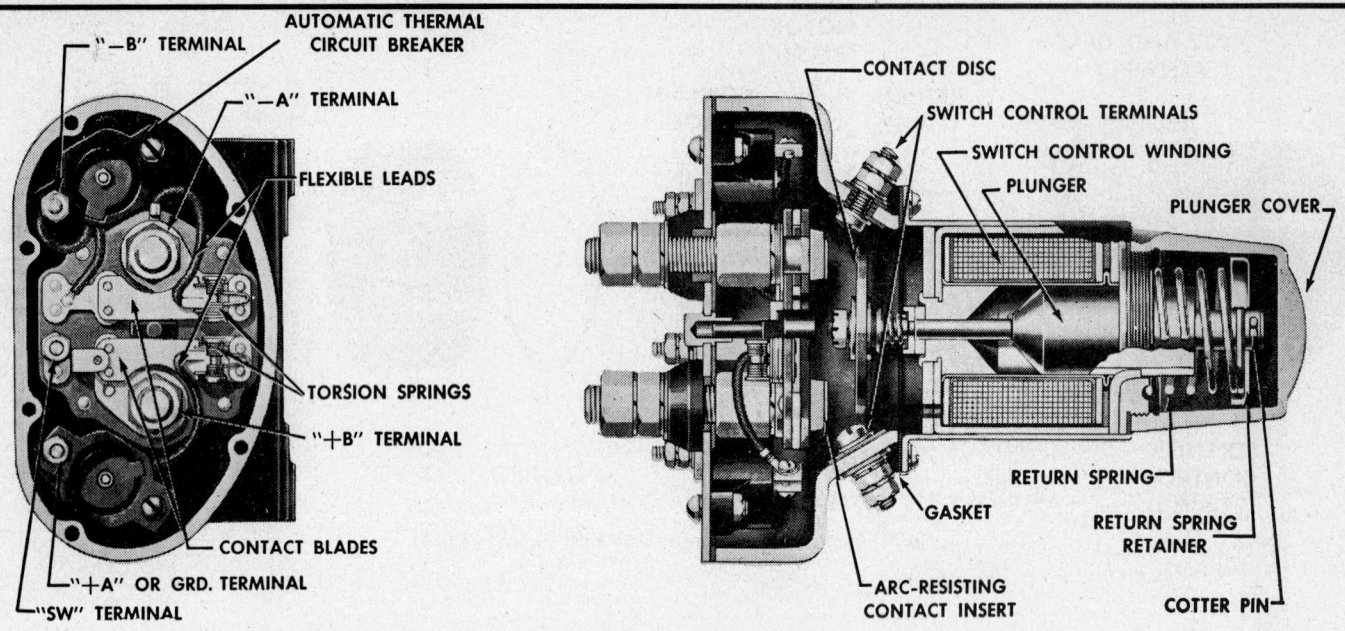

Fig. 8 End and sectional views of a Delco-Remy solenoid-operated series-parallel switch. In the end view the cover has been removed so the terminal plate assembly can be seen

minal plate which completes the parallel connections between the batteries for normal operation and also complete the connections that energize the cranking motor solenoid in the cranking position.

Fig. 9 is the wiring circuit of a (mechanically-operated) series-parallel system during normal operation of the vehicle. The main charging circuit is shown as a solid line. The current from the generator splits at the −A terminal, half of it going to the left-hand battery (dashed lines) and the other half going to the right-hand battery (dotted lines). Note that there are two circuit breakers or fuses in the right-hand battery circuit. Note also that an optional ammeter, as indicated, may be located in either of the two positions. The position in the −B to cranking motor circuit is preferable, however, since this circuit carries only the charging current while the other circuit (+A to "ground") must also carry the solenoid energizing current.

An ammeter sufficiently heavy to carry the solenoid current is generally unsatisfactory for reading small charging currents. In either position, the ammeter will indicate how much current is entering the right-hand battery, and if this is subtracted from the total shown in the main ammeter, the difference will be that which is entering the left-hand battery.

Fig. 10 illustrates the circuits during the cranking action when the series-parallel switch main contacts are closed (note that this diagram shows a solenoid-operated series-parallel switch). The series connections between the two batteries and the cranking motor are shown as a solid line, while the cranking motor solenoid circuit is shown as a dashed line.

As the switch is operated the solenoid plunger (or push rod in a mechanically-operated switch) strikes a small plunger in the contact plate assembly, causing the small contacts to be actuated so that the parallel connections between the two batteries are broken. Then the main contact disk connects the two main switch terminals (−A and +B); and as the small plunger completes its travel it connects the cranking solenoid through ground through the SW terminal (this circuit

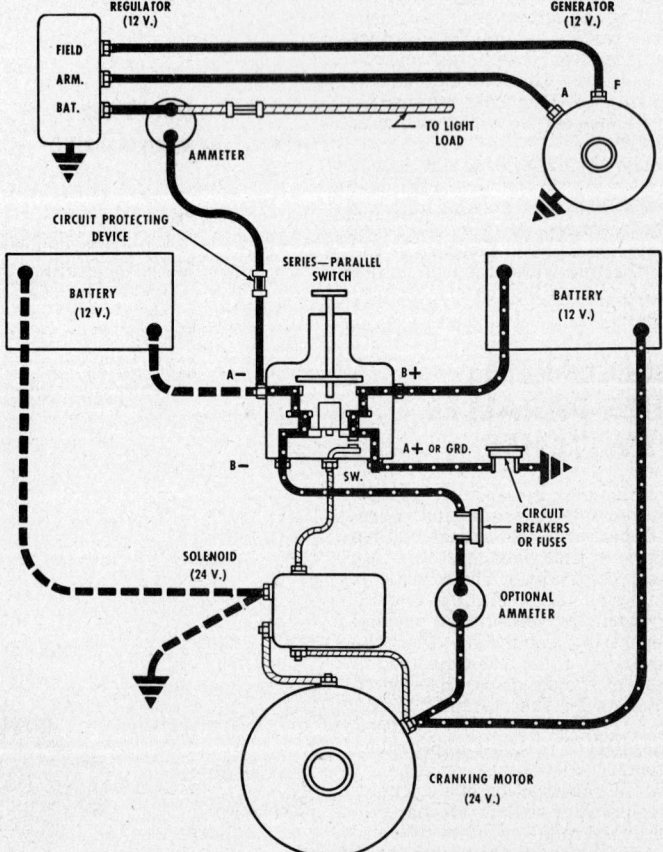

Fig. 9 Wiring diagram of a mechanically-operated series-parallel switch and cranking motor solenoid. This diagram shows the series-parallel switch completing the parallel connections between the batteries for normal operation of the vehicle's electrical equipment on 12 volts.

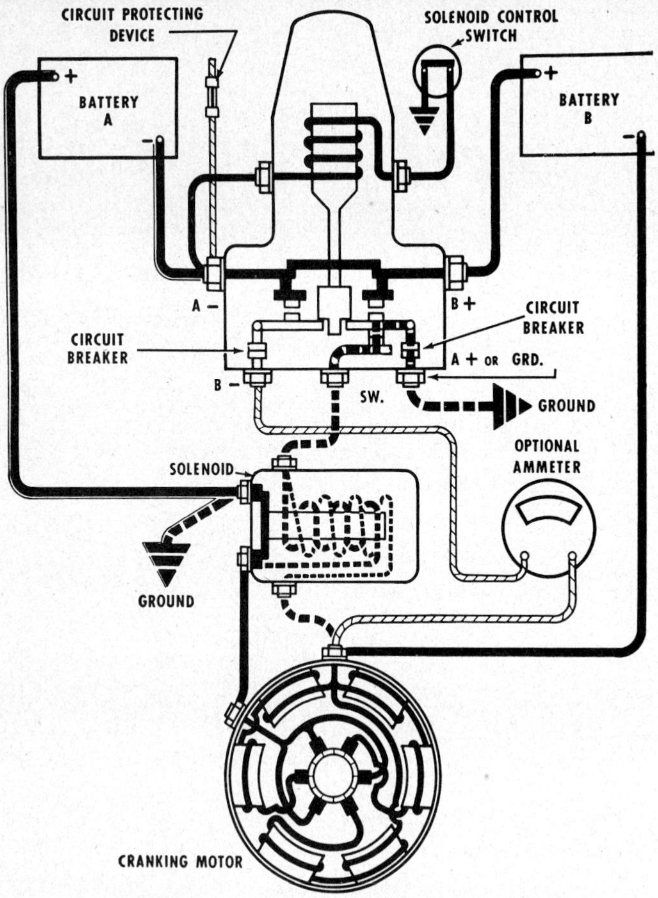

STARTING SWITCHES

Fig. 10 This diagram shows a (solenoid-operated) series-parallel switch completing the series connections between batteries so 24 volts are imposed on cranking motor.

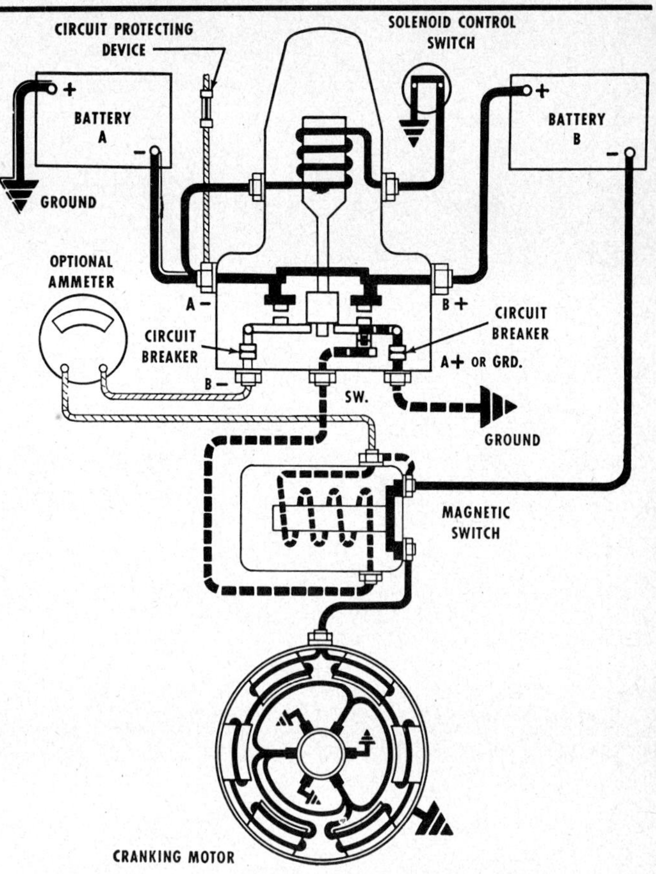

Fig. 11 Same as Fig. 10 except with magnetic type starter switch

is shown as a dashed line). Now the cranking motor solenoid operates and closes its contacts to complete the series connections through the cranking motor so that the motor operates.

After cranking has been accomplished and the series-parallel switch is released, the two batteries again become connected in parallel to provide 12-volt operation of the equipment.

a quick-break mechanism, consisting of a pair of triggers and a cam, causes the contact disk to be snapped away from the stationary contacts very quickly so that there is a very small amount of arcing.

Fig. 11 illustrates a solenoid-operated series-parallel switch used in conjunction with a cranking motor magnetic type switch. Figs. 12 and 13 are exploded views of the mechanical switch, while Fig. 14 is an exploded view of the solenoid-operated switch. These pictures can be used as guides whenever disassembly is required.

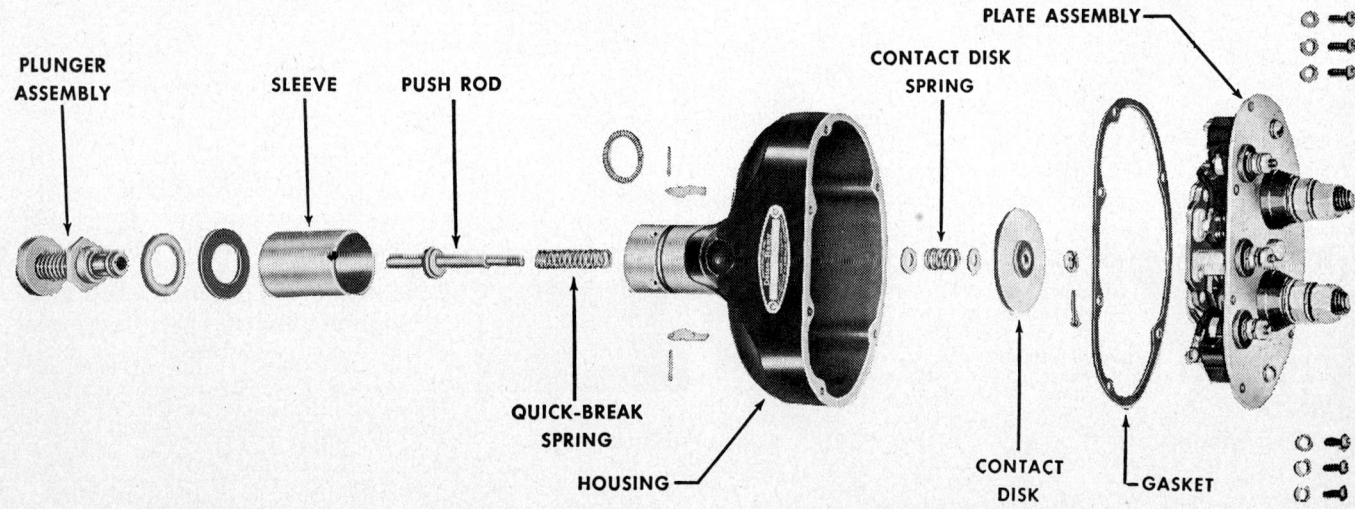

Fig. 12 Disassembled view of mechanically-operated series-parallel switch

STARTING SWITCHES

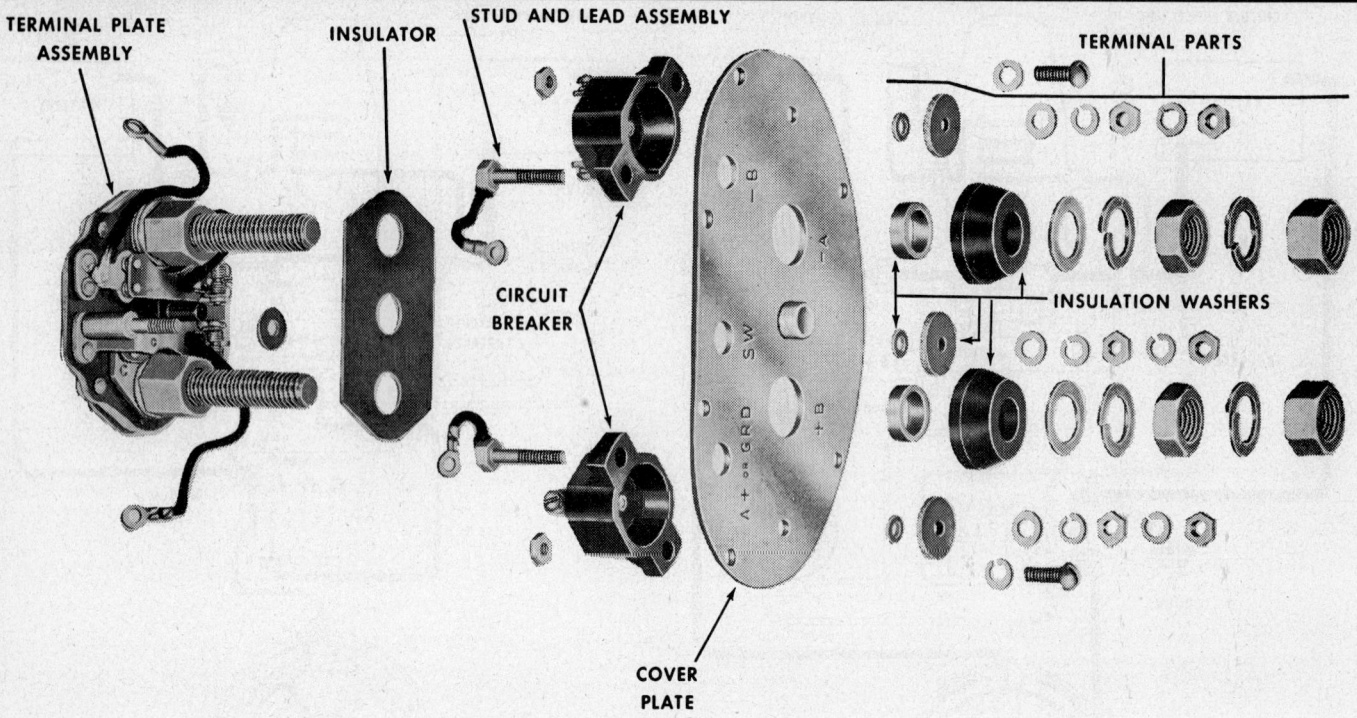

Fig. 13 Disassembled view of terminal plate assembly of switch shown in Fig. 12

DELCO-REMY SPLASHPROOF SERIES-PARALLEL & COMBINED SERIES-PARALLEL & MAGNETIC SWITCHES

Fig. 15 illustrates a low weight series-parallel switch and Fig. 16 pictures the combined series-parallel and magnetic switch of the same type construction. The switch shown in Fig. 15 can be used with either a solenoid or separate magnetic switch controlled starting motor. The switch shown in Fig. 16 is only used with a magnetic switch controlled starting motor and incorporates the magnetic switch with the series-parallel switch into the same splashproof container.

Series-Parallel Switch Used With Solenoid Operated Motor

Fig. 17 is a schematic wiring circuit of the series-parallel system in connection with the solenoid operated motor during the cranking operation. The sequence that takes place as the switch closes is as follows:

As the starting switch is closed, the solenoid coil within the series-parallel switch is energized, creating sufficient magnetic force to attract the series-parallel switch plunger. Movement of the plunger then closes the two main switch terminals and connects the two batteries in series with the motor. At the same time, the starter solenoid coil circuit is completed by a set of points mechanically closed by the series-parallel switch plunger. This completes the battery-to-starting motor circuit and allows cranking to take place.

After cranking has been accomplished and the starting switch is released, the two batteries again become connected in parallel with the series-parallel switch in its "at rest" position. This allows operation of the rest of the vehicle's electrical equipment at a system voltage of 12 volts. Note that there are two circuit breakers or fuses in the circuit of the "B" battery. These should be used in the location shown. The fuse capacity should be 50% of the generator rated output.

Series-Parallel Switch Used With Magnetic Switch Operated Motor

Fig. 18 is the schematic wiring circuit of this system. The position of the switch is that found in normal operation of the vehicle. The current from the generator divides at the terminal of the series-parallel switch, half of it going to the "A" battery, with the other half of the current going to the "B" battery through the series-parallel switch. Note that an optional ammeter, as indicated, may be located

Fig. 15 End and sectional view of Delco-Remy splashproof solenoid operated series-parallel switch

STARTING SWITCHES

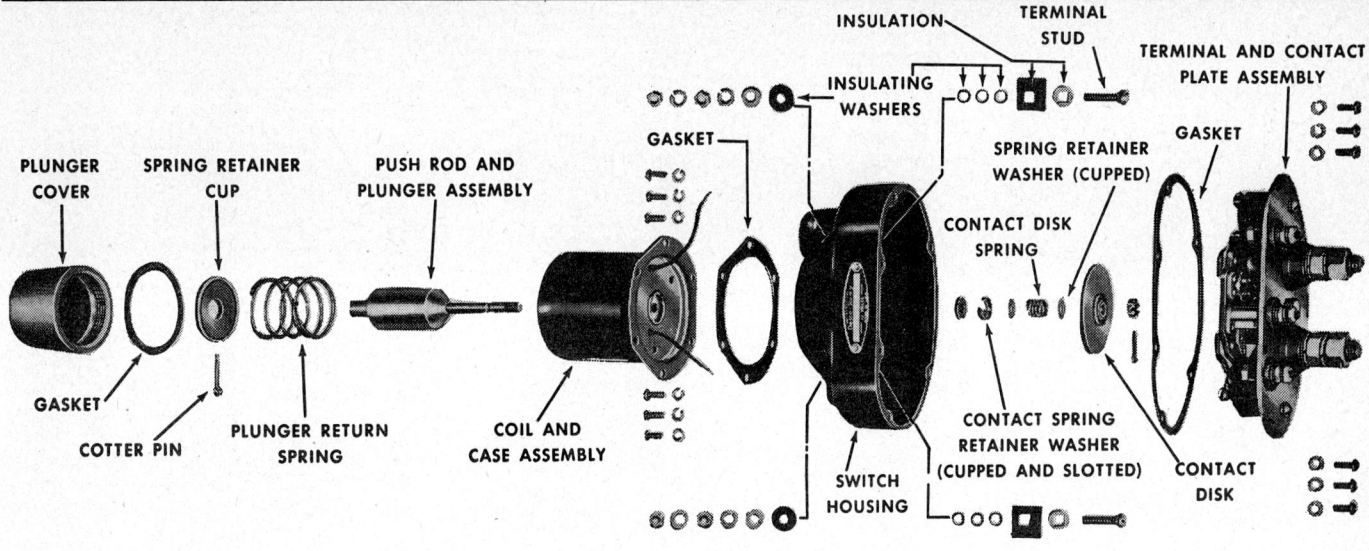

Fig. 14 Disassembled view of solenoid-operated series-parallel switch

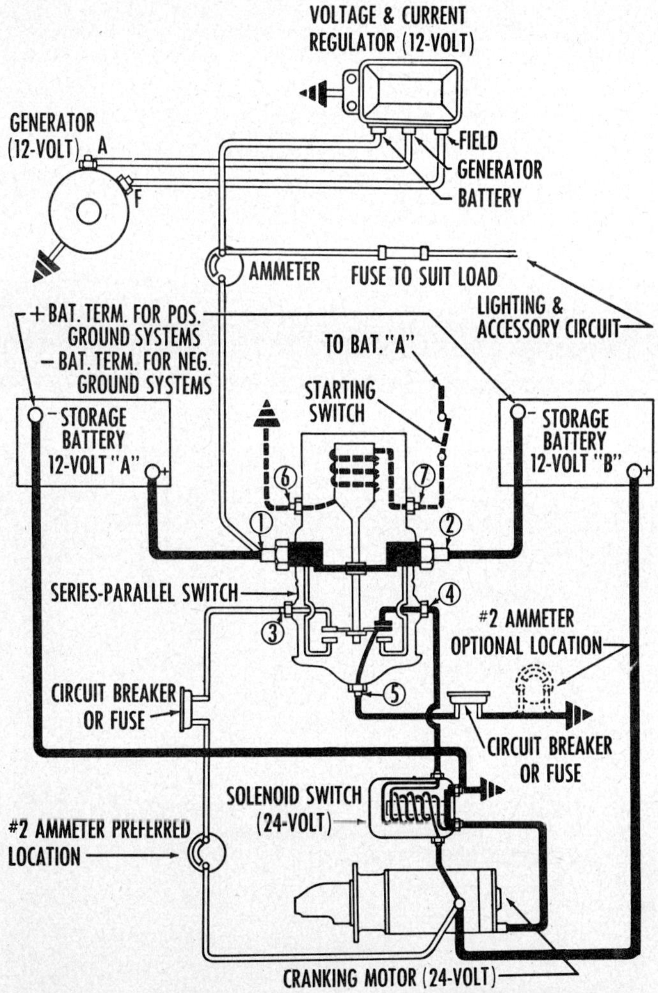

Fig. 17 Circuit diagram of series-parallel system with switch completing series connections between batteries for 24-volt starting motor operation. The motor is operated and controlled by a solenoid.

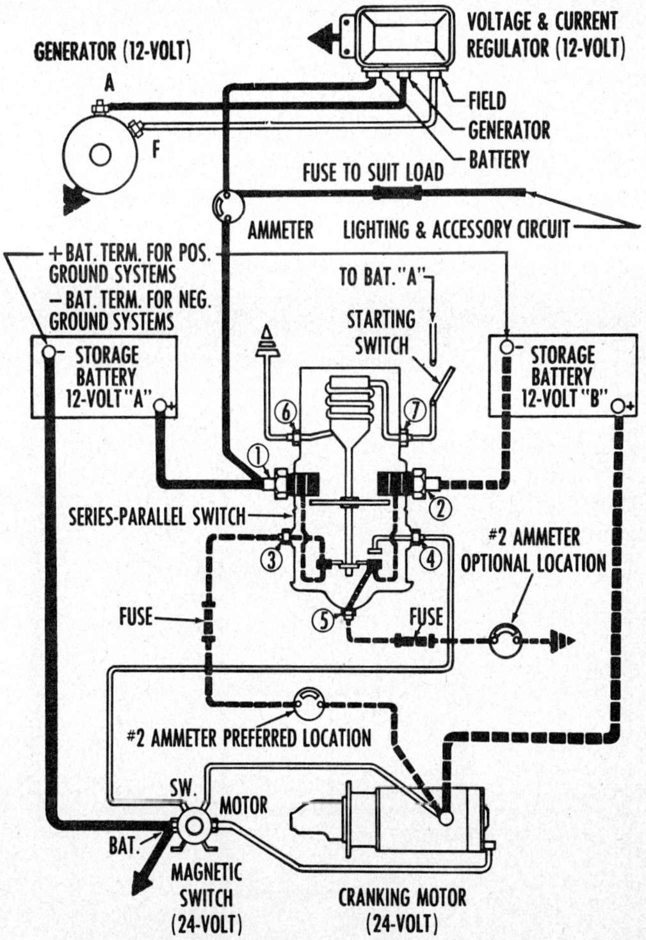

Fig. 18 Circuit diagram of series-parallel system with switch completing parallel connections between batteries for normal operation of vehicle electrical equipment at 12 volts. The starting motor is operated and controlled by a separately mounted magnetic switch.

STARTING SWITCHES

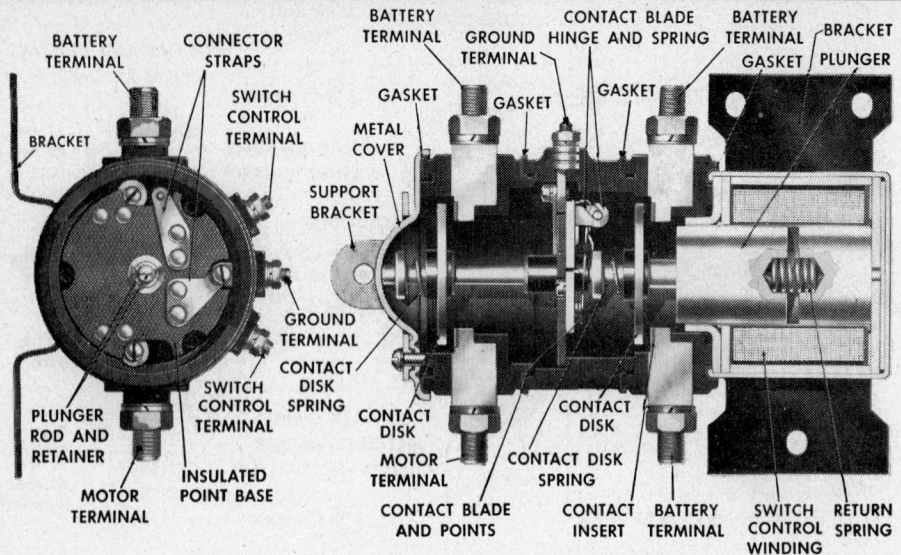

Fig. 16 End and sectional view of Delco-Remy splashproof solenoid operated combined series-parallel and magnetic switch

indicate how much current is entering the battery to the right, and if this is subtracted from the total shown on the main ammeter, the difference will be that which is entering the battery to the left.

Combination Series-Parallel Magnetic Switch Used With Bendix Drive Motor

Fig. 19 is a schematic wiring circuit of this system. As the starting switch is closed, the solenoid coil within the series-parallel switch is energized, creating sufficient magnetic force to attract the series-parallel switch plunger. The movement of the plunger then joins the two sets of large terminals. This connects both batteries in series with the cranking motor in order that 24 volts can be supplied for starting motor operation.

Fig. 20 shows the same switch after the starting switch is released and the series-parallel switch is in its "at rest" or charging position.

in either of two positions. The preferred location is shown since this circuit carries only the charging current while the other circuit must also carry the magnetic switch energizing current. An ammeter sufficiently heavy to carry the magnetic switch current is generally unsatisfactory for reading small charging currents. In either position, the ammeter will

WIRING INSTALLATION FOR SERIES-PARALLEL SWITCHES

Due to the high voltage of the starting circuit and the great amount of power available from the two batteries, it is essential that every precaution be taken to avoid short cir-

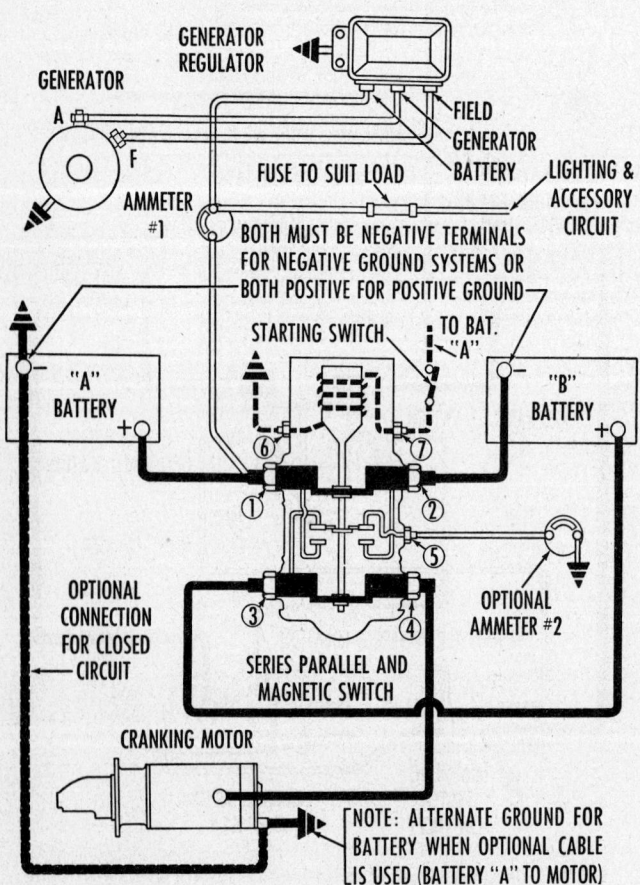

Fig. 19 Circuit diagram of combination series-parallel and magnetic switch completing series connections between batteries for 24-volt starting motor operation

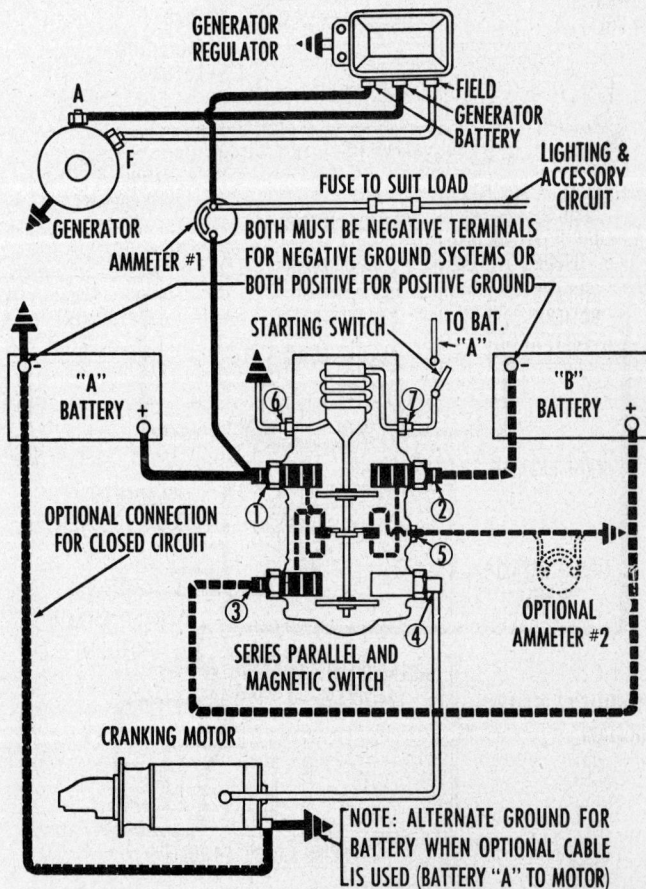

Fig. 20 Circuit diagram of combination series-parallel and magnetic switch completing parallel connections between batteries for normal operation of vehicle electrical equipment at 12 volts.

STARTING SWITCHES

cuits or grounds. All wires should be of sufficient size to carry the electrical load to which they are subjected without overheating. Stranded wire and cable should be used throughout to reduce the possibility of breakage due to vibration. All connections should be clean and tight and all terminal clips should be soldered to wires or cables.

Only resin flux should be used to solder electrical connections. Acid flux should never be used. All wires should be adequately insulated and supported at enough points to prevent movement and consequent chafing through the insulation. It is desirable that all terminals and clips, which are ordinarily left exposed, be protected by insulation. Thus, rubber boots, rubber tape or friction tape and shellac should be applied to cover all exposed terminals and clips. This will prevent accidental grounding of an exposed terminal which could cause serious damage to the system.

BATTERY CARE

For the best performance of the electrical system in which the series-parallel type switch is used, it is recommended that the "A" and "B" batteries be of the same capacity, size, age and manufacturer. This will assure both batteries of receiving approximately equal charging rates and the danger of overcharging one battery and undercharging the other will be reduced.

Since the electrical loads on most vehicles are tapped off of one battery, it is recommended that periodically the two batteries should be switched in position. This will lessen the possibility of one battery becoming cycled with resultant positive plate shed which can cause unequal battery capacities.

USE OF GLOW PLUGS FOR STARTING

On some applications, glow plus are used to provide some initial heating so that starting can be facilitated. The heater coil and glow plug circuit should be connected to the +B terminal and a quick-break push button switch installed between the SW terminal of the series-parallel switch and the SW terminal of the cranking motor solenoid. Closing the series-parallel switch supplies current to the heater coil and glow plugs. After the proper heating interval, cranking is then accomplished by closing the quick-break push button switch in the cranking motor-solenoid circuit.

STARTING MOTORS

INDEX

	Page No.
Starting Trouble Check-Out	29
Starting Motor Service	30
Chrysler Direct Drive Starter	31
Chrysler Reduction Gear Starter	32
Delco-Remy Standard Duty Enclosed Shift Lever Type Starter	35
Delco-Remy Heavy Duty Enclosed Shift Lever Type Starter	38
Ford Starter With Integral Positive Engagement Drive	42
Ford Solenoid Actuated Starter	44
Prestolite Starter With Positork Drive	45
Prestolite Starter With Inertia Drive	47
Starter Drive Service	47
Air Starting Motor	49

STARTING TROUBLE CHECK-OUT

When trouble develops in the starting motor circuit, and the starter cranks the engine slowly or not at all, several preliminary checks can be made to determine whether the trouble lies in the battery, in the starter, in the wiring between them, or elsewhere. Many conditions besides defects in the starter itself can result in poor cranking performance.

To make a quick check of the starter system, turn on the headlights. They should burn with normal brilliance. If they do not, the battery may be run down and it should be checked with a hydrometer.

If the battery is in a charged condition so that the lights burn brightly, operate the starting motor. Any one of three things will happen to the lights: (1) They will go out, (2) dim considerably or (3) stay bright without any cranking action taking place.

If Lights Go Out

If the lights go out as the starter switch is closed, it indicates that there is a poor connection between the battery and starting motor. This poor connection will most often be found at the battery terminals. Correction is made by removing the cable clamps from the terminals, cleaning the terminals and clamps, replacing the clamps and tightening them securely. A coating or corrosion inhibitor (vaseline will do) may be applied to the clamps and terminals to retard the formation of corrosion.

If Lights Dim

If the lights dim considerably as the starter switch is closed and the starter operates slowly or not at all, the battery may be run down, or there may be some mechanical condition in the engine or starting motor that is throwing a heavy burden on the starting motor. This imposes a high discharge rate on the battery which causes noticeable dimming of the lights.

Check the battery with a hydrometer. If it is charged, the trouble probably lies in either the engine or starting motor itself. In the engine, tight bearings or pistons or heavy oil place an added burden on the starting motor.

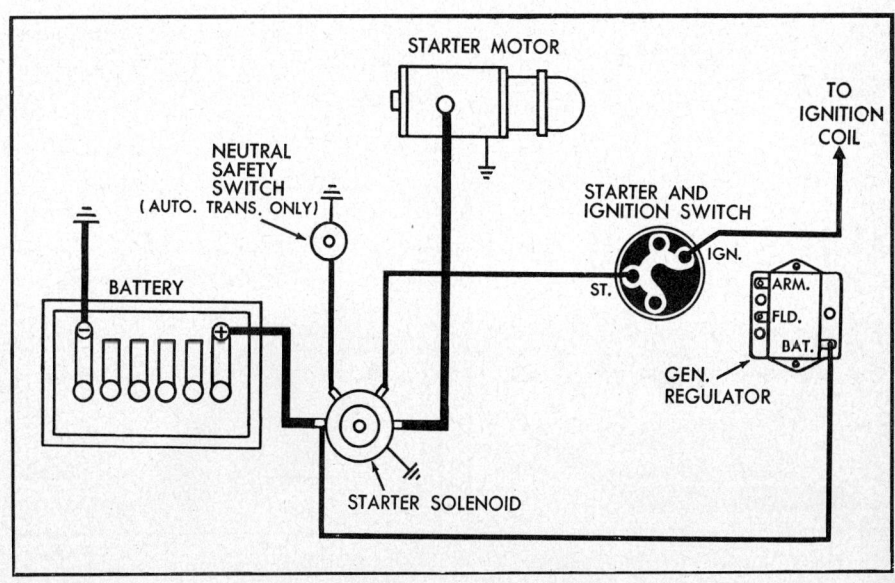

Fig. 1 Wiring diagram of a typical starter circuit

STARTING MOTORS

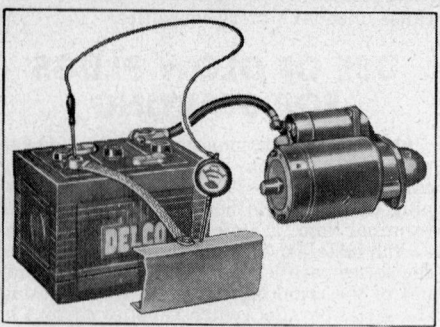

Fig. 2 Checking voltage drop between vehicle frame and grounded battery terminal post

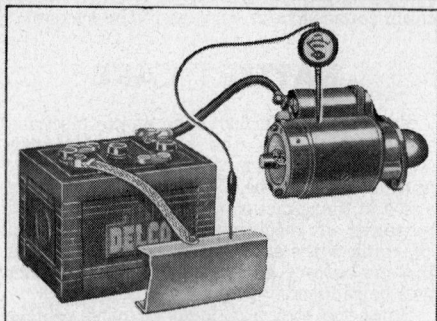

Fig. 3 Checking voltage drop between vehicle frame and starter field frame

Fig. 4 Checking voltage drop between ungrounded battery terminal post and battery terminal on solenoid

Low temperatures also hamper starting motor performance since it thickens engine oil and make the engine considerably harder to crank and start. Also, a battery is less efficient at low temperatures.

In the starting motor, a bent armature, loose pole shoe screws or worn bearings, any of which may allow the armature to drag, will reduce cranking performance and increase current draw.

In addition, more serious internal damage is sometimes found. Thrown armature windings or commutator bars, which sometimes occur on over-running clutch drive starting motors, are usually caused by excessive over-running after starting. This is the result of such conditions as the driver keeping the starting switch closed too long after the engine has started, the driver opening the throttle too wide in starting, or improper carburetor fast idle adjustment. Any of these subject the overunning clutch to extra strain so it tends to seize, spinning the armature at high speed with resulting armature damage.

Another cause of failure may be engine backfire during cranking which may result, among other things, from ignition timing being too far advanced.

To avoid such failures, the driver should pause a few seconds after a false start to make sure the engine has come completely to rest before another start is attempted. In addition, the ignition timing should be reset if engine backfiring has caused the trouble.

Lights Stay Bright, No Cranking Action

This condition indicates an open circuit at some point, in the starter itself, the starter switch or control circuit. The solenoid control circuit can be eliminated momentarily by placing a heavy jumper lead across the solenoid main terminals to see if the starter will operate. This connects the starter directly to the battery and, if it operates, it indicates that the control circuit is not functioning normally. The wiring and control units must be checked to locate the trouble, Fig. 1.

If the starter does not operate with the jumper attached, it will probably have to be removed from the engine so it can be examined in detail.

Checking Circuit With Voltmeter

Excessive resistance in the circuit between the battery and starter will reduce cranking performance. The resistance can be checked by using a voltmeter to measure voltage drop in the circuits while the starter is operated. There are three checks to be made:

1. Voltage drop between car frame and grounded battery terminal post (not cable clamp), Fig. 2.
2. Voltage drop between car frame and starting motor field frame, Fig. 3.
3. Voltage drop between insulated battery terminal post and starting motor terminal stud (or the battery terminal stud or the battery terminal stud of the solenoid), Fig. 4.

Each of these checks should show no more than one-tenth (0.1) volt drop when the starting motor is cranking for more than 30 seconds at a time to avoid overheating.

If excessive voltage drop is found in any of these circuits, make correction by disconnecting the cables, cleaning the connections carefully, and then reconnecting the cables firmly in place. A coating of vaseline on the battery cables and terminal clamps will retard corrosion.

NOTE: On some vehicles, extra long battery cables may be required due to the location of the battery and starter. This may result in somewhat higher voltage drop than the above recommended 0.1 volt. The only means of determining the normal voltage drop in such cases is to check several of these vehicles. Then when the voltage drop is well above the normal figure for all cars checked, abnormal resistance will be indicated and correction can be made as already explained.

STARTING MOTOR SERVICE

To obtain full performance data on a starting motor or to determine the cause of abnormal operation, the starting motor should be submitted to a no-load test and torque test. These tests are best performed on a starter bench tester with the starter mounted on it.

From a practical standpoint, however, a simple torque test may be made quickly with the starter in the car. Make sure the battery is

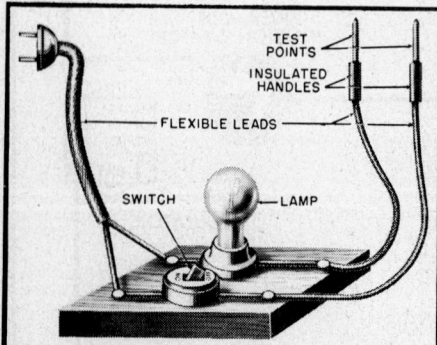

Fig. 5 A simple tester for making continuity and ground tests on armature and field windings

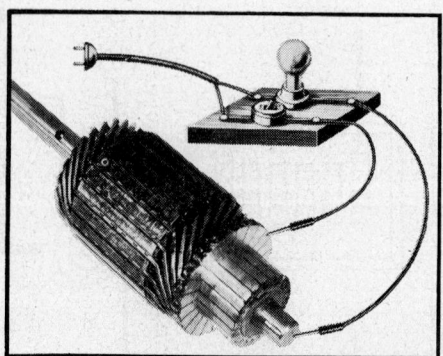

Fig. 6 Checking armature for grounds. If lamp lights armature is grounded and should be replaced

Fig. 7 Measuring commutator runout with a dial indicator. Mount shaft in V blocks and rotate commutator. If runout exceeds .003", commutator should be turned in a lathe to make it concentric.

STARTING MOTORS

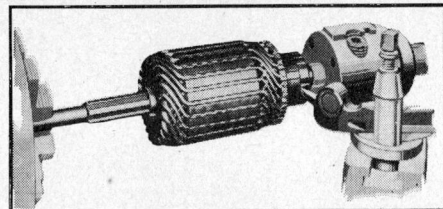

Fig. 8 Turning commutator in a lathe. Take light cuts until worn or bad spots are removed. Then remove burrs with No. 00 sandpaper.

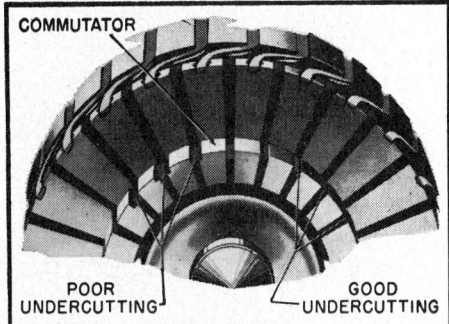

Fig. 9 Good undercutting should be .002" wider than mica insulation, 1/64" deep and exactly centered so that there are no burrs on the mica.

fully charged and that the starter circuit wires and terminals are in good condition. Then operate the starter to see if the engine turns over normally. If it does not, the torque developed is below standard and the starter should be removed for further checking.

Remove starter from engine and disassemble as outlined in the following text and make the tests as suggested in Figs. 6 through 11.

Fig. 10 Checking armature for short circuit. As armature is rotated by hand, steel strip (hacksaw blade) will vibrate if short circuit exists.

CHRYSLER DIRECT DRIVE STARTER

This Chrysler built starting motor, Fig. 12, is a four coil assembly with an over-running clutch type drive and a solenoid shift-type switch mounted on the motor. The brush holders are riveted to a separate brush plate and are not serviced individually. Brush replacement can be made by removing the commutator bearing end head.

Disassembly

1. Remove through bolts and tap commutator end head from field frame.
2. Remove thrust washers from armature shaft.

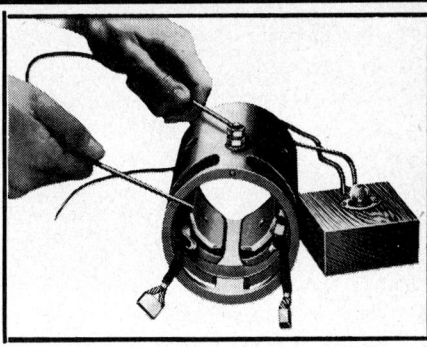

Fig. 11 Testing field coils for grounds. Lamp will light if a ground is present

3. Lift brush holder springs and remove brushes from holders.
4. Remove brush plate.
5. Disconnect field leads at solenoid connector.
6. Unfasten and remove solenoid and boot assembly.
7. Drive out over-running clutch shift fork pivot pin.
8. Remove drive end pinion housing and spacer washer.
9. Note position of shifter fork on starter and remove fork.
10. Slide over-running clutch pinion gear toward commutator end of armature. Drive stop retainer toward clutch pinion gear to expose snap ring and remove snap ring.
11. Slide clutch drive from armature shaft.
12. If it is necessary to replace the field coils, remove screw that holds ground brushes and raise brushes with the terminal and shunt wire up and away from field frame. Remove pole shoe screws and take out field coils.

Reassembly

1. Lubricate armature shaft and splines

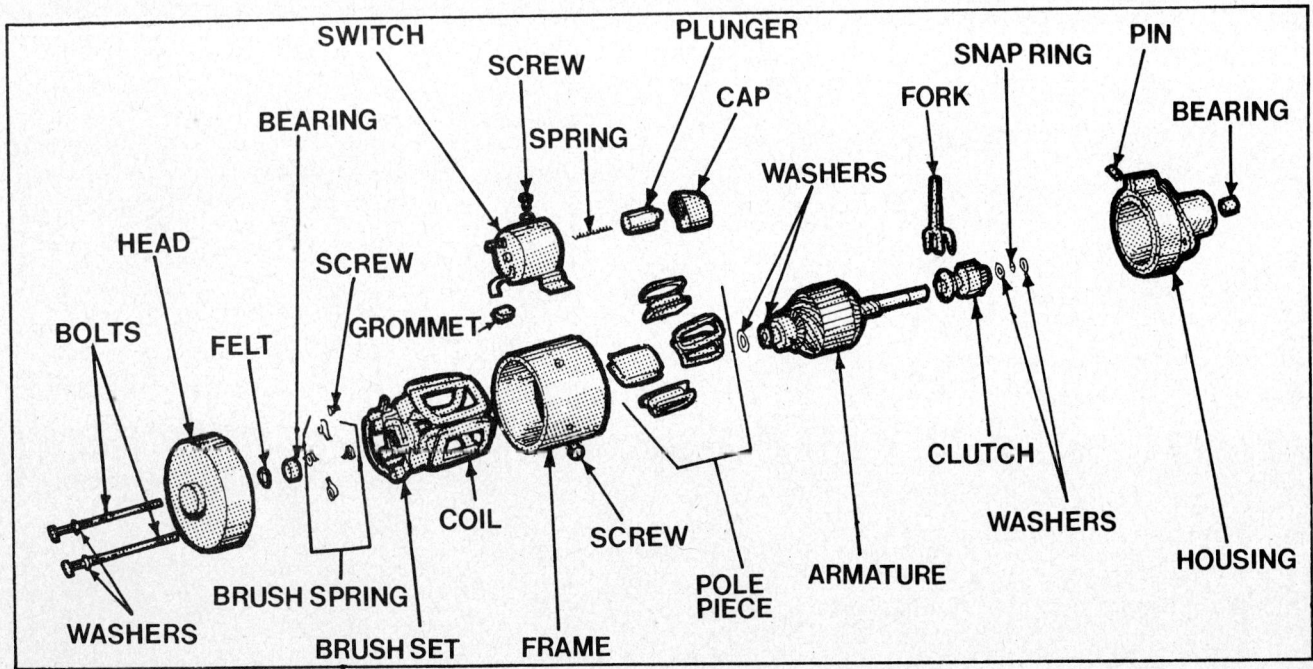

Fig. 12 Chrysler built direct drive starter

STARTING MOTORS

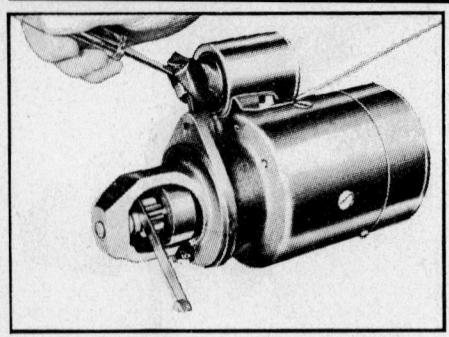

Fig. 13 Clearance between end of pinion and pin stop should be 1/8" with plunger seated and pinion pushed toward commutator.

nector.
10. Install brush holder ring, indexing tang of ring in hole of field frame.
11. Position brushes in brush holders. *Be sure field coil lead wires are properly enclosed behind brush holder ring and that they do not interfere with brush operation.*
12. Install thrust washer on commutator end of armature shaft to obtain .010" minimum end play.
13. Install commutator end head.
14. Install through bolts and tighten securely.

Adjusting Pinion Clearance

1. Place starter in vise with soft jaws and tighten vise enough to hold starter. *Place a wedge or screwdriver between bottom of solenoid and starter frame to eliminate all deflection in solenoid when making pinion clearance check.*
2. Push in on solenoid plunger link, Fig. 13 (not fork lever) until plunger bottoms.
3. Measure clearance between end of pinion and pin stop with plunger seated and pinion pushed toward commutator end. Clearance should be 1/8". Adjust by loosening solenoid attaching screws and move solenoid fore and aft as required.
4. Test starter operation for free running and install on engine.

CHRYSLER REDUCTION GEAR STARTER

This reduction gear starting motor, Fig. 14, has an armature-to-engine crankshaft ratio of 45 to 1; a 2 to 1 or 3½ to 1 reduction gear set is built into the motor assembly. The starter utilizes a solenoid shift. The housing of the solenoid is integral with the starter drive end housing.

Fig. 15 Terminal screw replacement, 1970-73 units

Fig. 16 Terminal screw replacement, 1974-79 units

Disassembly

1. Place gear housing of starter in a vise with soft jaws. *Use vise as a support fixture only; do not clamp.*

with SAE 10W or 30W rust preventive oil.
2. Install starter drive, stop collar (retainer), lock ring and spacer washer.
3. Install shifter fork over starter drive spring retainer washer with narrow leg of fork toward commutator. *If fork is not positioned properly, starter gear travel will be restricted, causing a lockup in the clutch mechanism.*
4. Install drive end (pinion) housing on armature shaft, indexing the shift fork with slot in drive end of housing.
5. Install shift fork pivot pin.
6. Install armature with clutch drive, shifter fork and pinion housing. Slide armature into field frame until pinion housing indexes with slot in field frame.
7. Install solenoid and boot assembly and tighten bolts securely.
8. Install ground brushes.
9. Connect field coil leads at solenoid con-

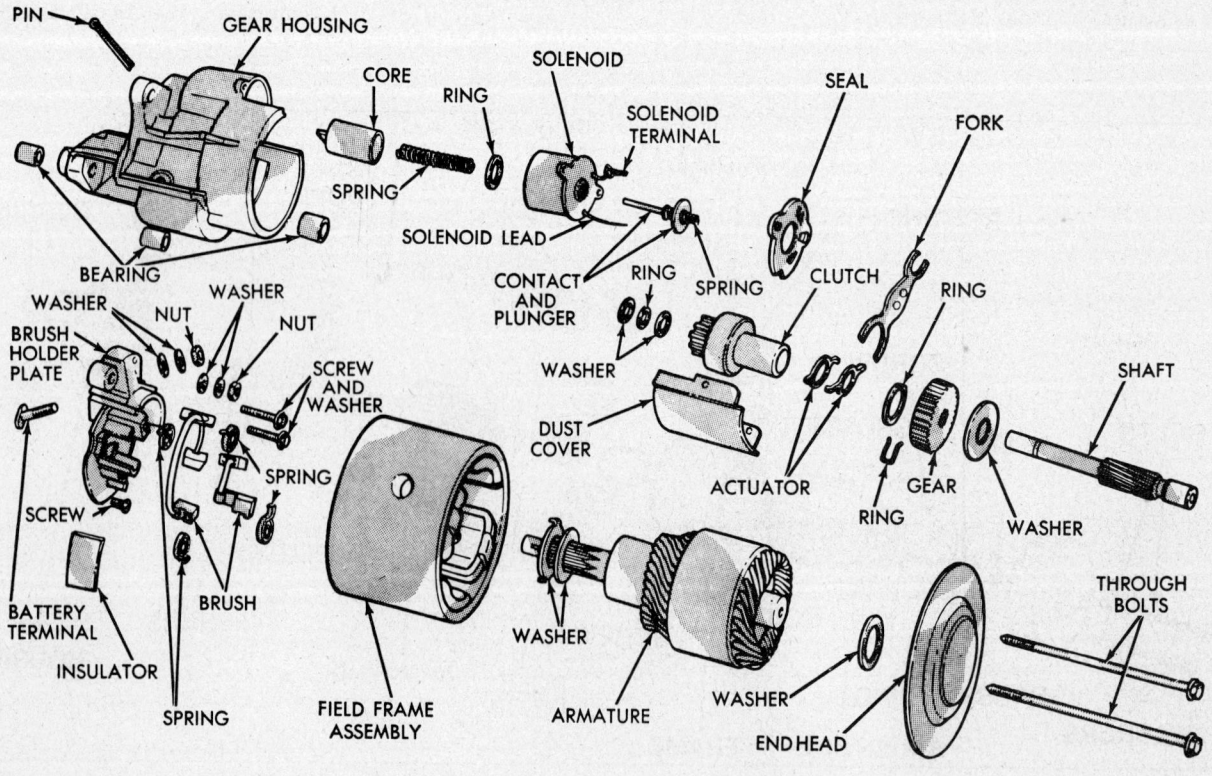

Fig. 14 Chrysler built reduction gear starter

STARTING MOTORS

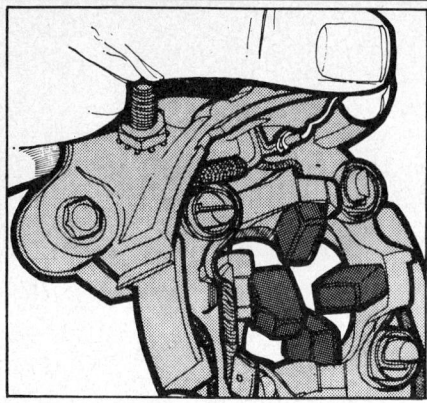

Fig. 17 Unwinding solenoid lead wire, all units (Typical)

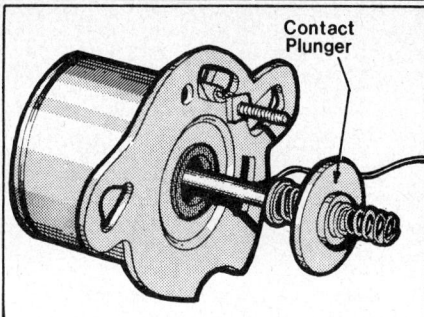

Fig. 18 Solenoid contact & plunger, all units (Typical)

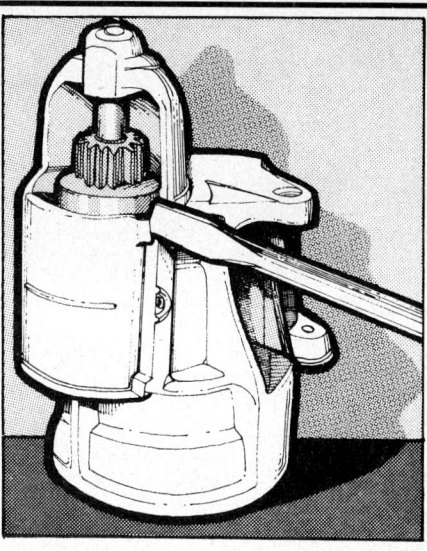

Fig. 19 Dust cover removal, all units (Typical)

2. Remove through bolts and starter end head assembly.
3. On 1970–73 units, carefully pull armature up and out of gear housing, and starter frame and field assembly. Remove steel and fiber thrust washer. *The wire of the shunt field coil is soldered to the brush terminal. One pair of brushes are connected to this terminal. The other pair of brushes is attached to the series field coils by means of a terminal screw. Carefully pull the frame and field assembly up just enough to expose the terminal screw and the solder connection of the shunt field at the brush terminal. Place two wood blocks between starter frame and gear housing, Fig. 15, to facilitate removal of terminal screw and unsoldering of shunt field wire at brush terminal.*
4. On 1974–80 units, carefully remove armature, then pull field frame assembly from gear housing to expose terminal screw.
5. On all units, support terminal screw with a finger, then remove terminal screw, Figs. 15 and 16.
6. On 1970–73 units:
   a. Unwrap shunt field coil lead from starter brush terminal.

   NOTE: The starter brush holder plate with the starter brush terminal, contact and brushes is serviced as an assembly.

   b. Unwrap solenoid lead wire and unwind wire from starter brush terminal, Fig. 17.
7. On 1974–80 units:
   a. Remove field frame assembly.
   b. Remove nuts attaching solenoid and brush holder plate assembly to gear housing, then the solenoid and brush plate assembly.
8. On all units, remove nut, steel washer and insulating washer from solenoid terminal.
9. On 1970–73 units, straighten solenoid wire and remove brush holder plate with brushes and solenoid as an assembly. Remove solenoid from gear housing well.
10. On 1974–80 units, unwind solenoid lead wire from brush terminal, Fig. 17, and remove screws securing solenoid to brush plate, then the solenoid from brush plate.
11. On all units, remove nut from battery terminal on brush plate, then the battery terminal.

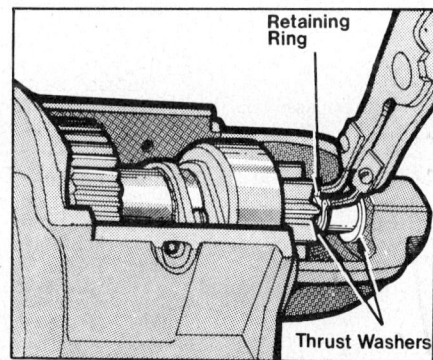

Fig. 21 Pinion shaft retaining ring replacement, 1970–73 units

12. Remove solenoid contact and plunger assembly from solenoid, Fig. 18, then the return spring from the solenoid moving core.
13. Remove dust cover from gear housing, Fig. 19.
14. Release retainer clip positioning driven gear on pinion shaft, Fig. 20.

NOTE: The retainer clip is under tension. Therefore, it is recommended that a cloth be placed over the retainer clip when released, preventing it from springing away.

15. On 1970–73 units, release retainer ring at front of pinion shaft, Fig. 21. On 1974–80 units, remove pinion shaft "C" clip, Fig. 22.

NOTE: On 1970–73 units, do not spread retainer ring greater than the outside diameter of the pinion shaft since lock ring damage may result.

16. On all units, push pinion shaft toward rear of housing, Fig. 23 and remove retainer ring and thrust washers, clutch and pinion assembly, with the two shift fork nylon actuators as an assembly, Fig. 24.
17. Remove driven gear and thrust washer.
18. Pull shifting fork forward and remove solenoid moving core, Fig. 25.
19. Remove shifting fork retainer pin, Fig. 26, and remove clutch shifting fork assembly.

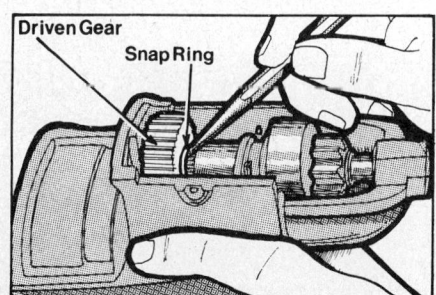

Fig. 20 Driven gear snap ring replacement, all units (Typical)

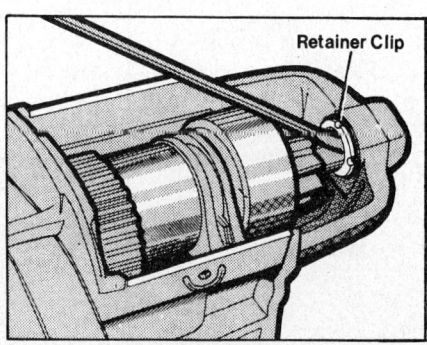

Fig. 22 Pinion shaft "C" clip replacement, 1974–79 units

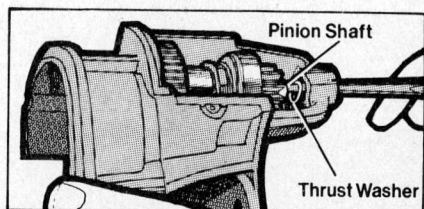

Fig. 23 Removing pinion shaft

STARTING MOTORS

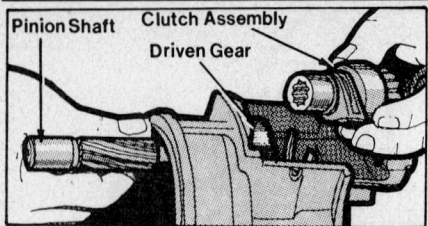

Fig. 24 Clutch assembly replacement, all units (Typical)

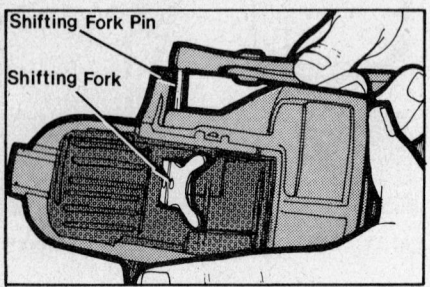

Fig. 26 Shifter fork pin replacement, all units (Typical)

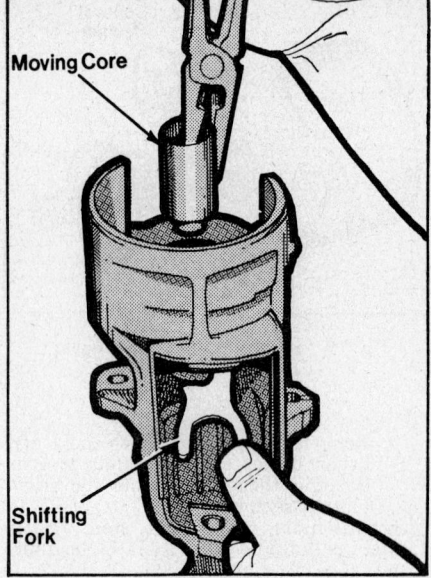

Fig. 25 Solenoid core replacement, all units (Typical)

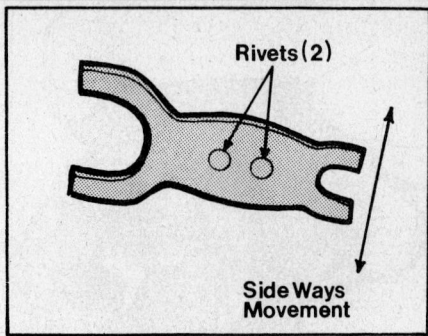

Fig. 27 Shifter fork assembly, all units (Typical)

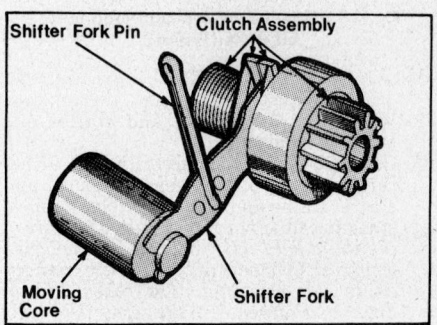

Fig. 28 Shifter fork & clutch assembly, all units (Typical)

Reassembly

NOTE: *The shifter fork consists of two spring steel plates assembled with two rivets, Fig. 27. There should be about 1/16" side movement to insure proper pinion gear engagement. Lubricate between plates sparingly with SAE 10 engine oil.*

1. Position shift fork in drive housing and install fork retaining pin, Fig. 26. One tip of pin should be straight, the other tip should be bent at a 15 degree angle away from housing. Fork and pin should operate freely after bending tip of pin.
2. Install solenoid moving core and engage shifting fork, Fig. 25.
3. Enter pinion shaft in drive housing and install friction washer and driven gear.
4. Install clutch and pinion assembly, Fig. 24, thrust washer, retaining ring, and thrust washer.
5. Complete installation of pinion shaft, engaging fork with clutch actuators, Fig. 28. *Friction washer must be positioned on shoulder of splines of pinion shaft before driven gear is positioned.*
6. Install driven gear snap ring, Fig. 20, then the pinion shaft retaining ring or "C" clip, Figs. 21 and 22.
7. Install starter solenoid return spring into movable core bore.

NOTE: Inspect starter solenoid switch contacting washer. If top of washer is burned, disassemble contact switch plunger assembly and reverse the washer.

8. Install solenoid contact plunger assembly into solenoid, Fig. 18. On 1970–73 units, reform the double wire to permit proper entry of terminal stud into brush holder with the double wires curved around the contactor. The contactor must not touch the double wires when the solenoid is energized after assembly. On 1974–80 units, ensure contact spring is properly positioned on shaft of solenoid contact plunger assembly.
9. On all units, install battery terminal stud in brush holder.

NOTE: Inspect contacts in brush holder. If contacts are badly burned, replace brush holder with brushes and contacts as an assembly.

10. Position seal on brush holder plate.
11. Install solenoid lead wire through hole in brush holder, Fig. 29 then the solenoid stud, insulating washer, flat washer and nut.

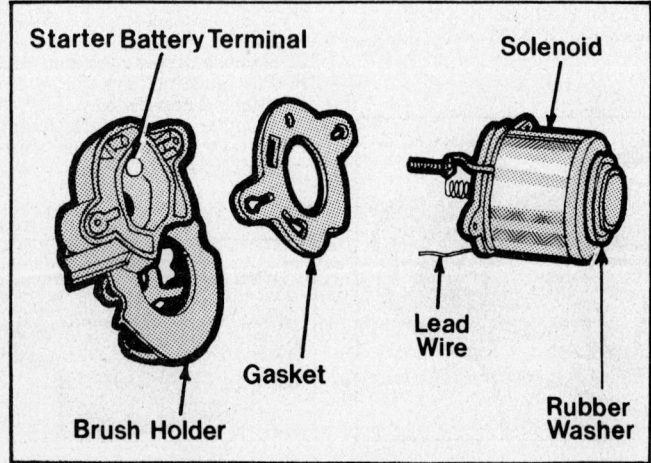

Fig. 29 Solenoid to brush holder plate assembly, all units (Typical)

Fig. 30 Solenoid & brush installation, all units (Typical)

STARTING MOTORS

Fig. 31 Installation of brushes & armature thrust washer, all units (Typical)

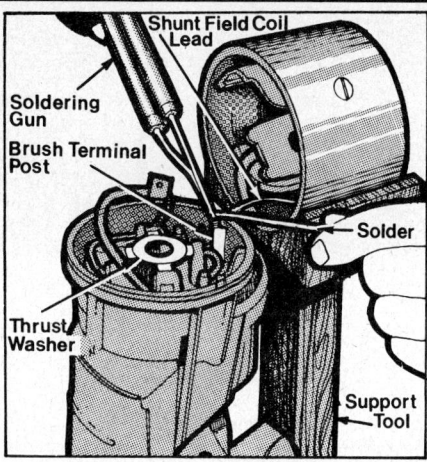

Fig. 32 Soldering shunt coil lead wire, 1970–73 units

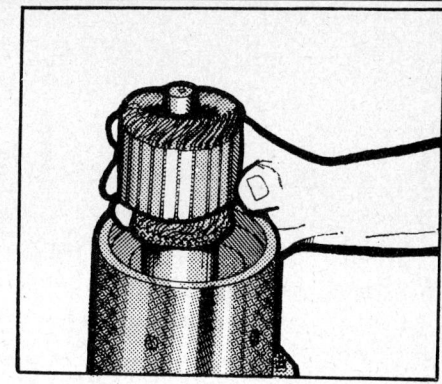

Fig. 33 Armature installation, all units (Typical)

12. Wrap solenoid lead wire around brush terminal post, Fig. 17, and solder with a high temperature resin core solder and resin flux.
13. Install brush holder attaching screws.
14. Install solenoid coil and brush plate assembly into gear housing bore and position brush plate assembly into starter gear housing, Fig. 30. Then install and tighten housing attaching nuts.
15. Install brushes with armature thrust washer, Fig. 31. This holds brushes out and facilitates proper armature installation.
16. On 1970–73 units, solder shunt coil lead wire to starter brush terminal, Fig. 32.
17. On all units, install brush terminal screws, Figs. 15 and 16.
18. Position field frame on gear housing and install armature into field frame and starter gear housing, Fig. 33, carefully engaging splines of shaft with reduction gear by rotating armature slightly to engage splines.
19. Install thrust washer on armature shaft. On 1970–73 units, install steel washer on armature shaft.
20. On all units, install starter end head assembly, then the through bolts.

DELCO-REMY STANDARD DUTY ENCLOSED SHIFT LEVER TYPE MOTOR

Except 1978–80 V8-350 Diesel

This type of starting motor, Fig. 34, has the solenoid shift lever mechanism and the solenoid plunger enclosed in the drive housing, thus protecting them from exposure to road dirt, icing conditions and splash. They have an extruded field frame and an overrunning clutch type of drive. The overrunning clutch is operated by a solenoid switch mounted to a flange on the drive housing.

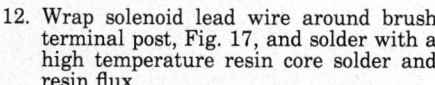

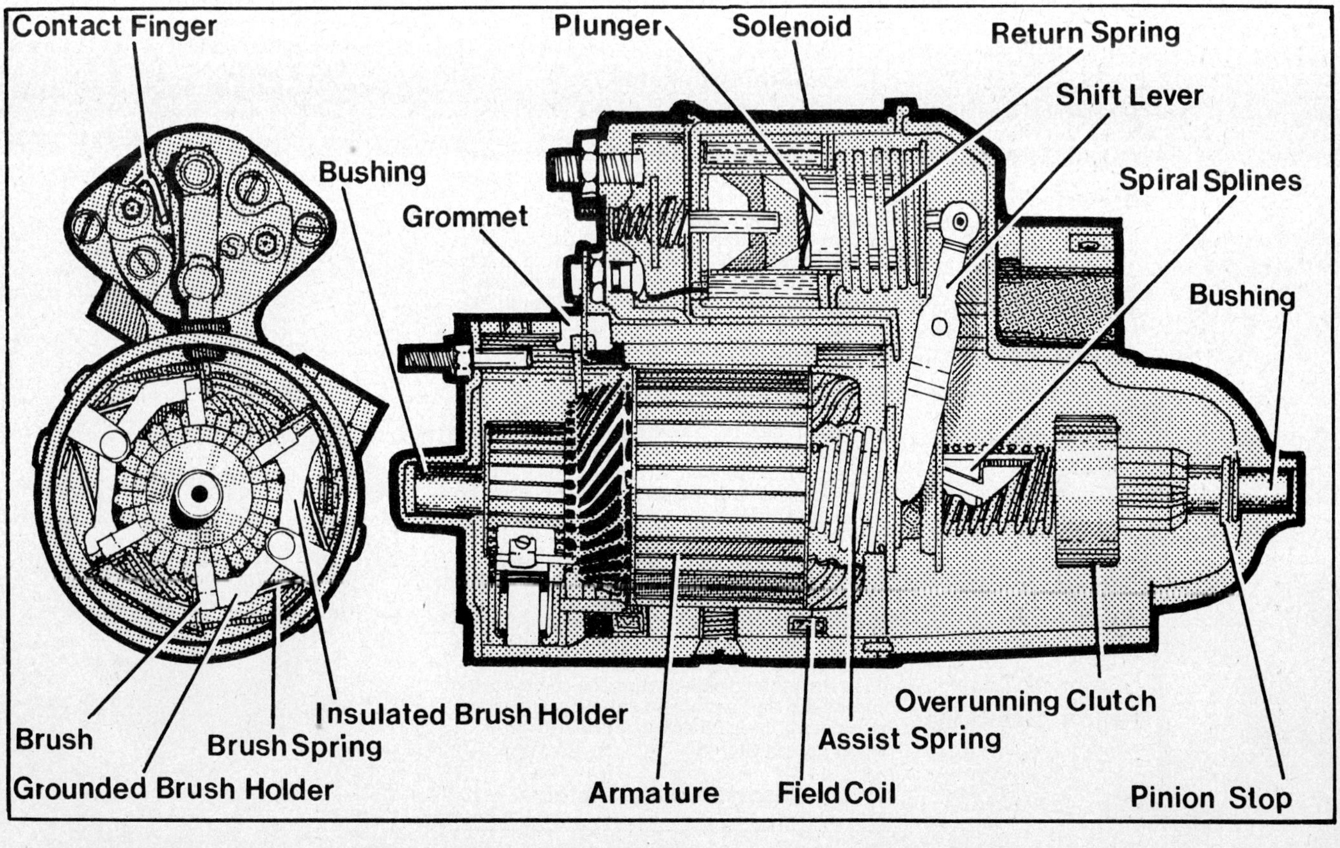

Fig. 34 Delco-Remy Standard Duty starter with enclosed shift lever (Typical)

STARTING MOTORS

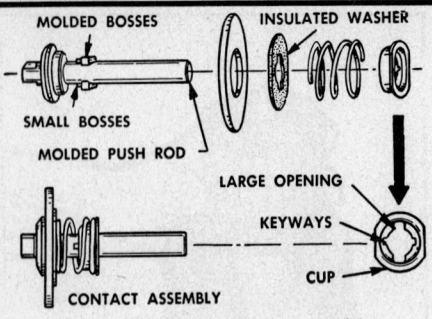

Fig. 35 Solenoid contact assembly

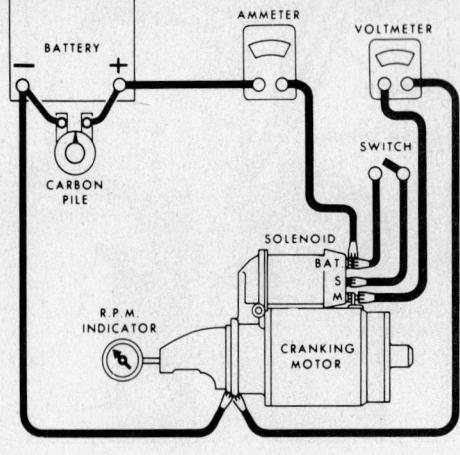

Fig. 36 Connections for checking free speed of motor

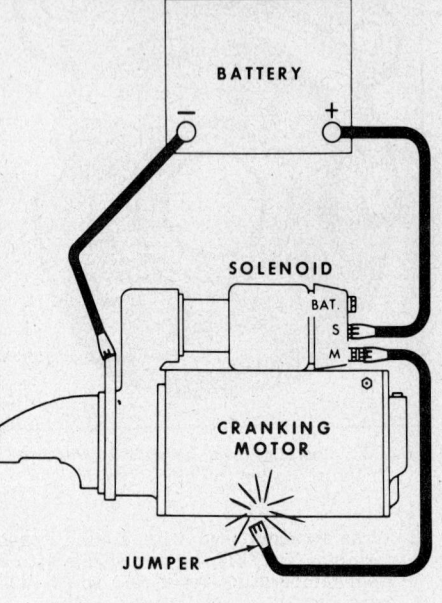

Fig. 37 Connections for checking pinion clearance

Solenoid

The solenoid is attached to the drive end housing by two screws. The angle of the nose of the plunger provides a greater bearing area between the plunger and core tube. A molded push rod, Fig. 35, is assembled in the contact assembly. A shoulder molded on the push rod and a cup that can easily be assembled to the rod and locked into position over two molded bosses holds the contact assembly in place.

To disassemble the cup from the push rod, push in on the metal cup and rotate 1/4 turn so the molded bosses on the rod are in line with openings in the cup, then slide the metal cup off the rod.

To assemble the metal cup on the rod, locate the parts on the rod as shown and align the large openings in the cup with the molded bosses on the rod): then push in on the cup and rotate it 1/4 turn so the small bosses on the rod fall into the keyways of the cup.

Solenoid Terminals

The terminals of the solenoid are assembled in a molded cover. Some solenoids have an additional small terminal which is identified with the letter "R". To this terminal is attached a small metal finger which makes contact with a disc inside the solenoid when it is energized. On the vehicle, this terminal is connected to the battery side of the ignition coil. The purpose of this is to short out the ignition resistor during cranking and thereby provide high ignition coil output for starting the engine.

Maintenance

Most motors of this type have graphite and oil impregnated bronze bearings which ordinarily require no added lubrication except at time of overhaul when a few drops of light engine oil should be placed on each bearing before reassembly.

Motors provided with hinge cap oilers should have 8–10 drops of light engine oil every 5000 miles, or every 300 hours of operation. Since the motor and brushes cannot be inspected without disassembling the unit, there is no service that can be performed with the unit assembled on the vehicle.

Starting Motor Test

Free Speed Check—With the circuit connected as shown in Fig. 36, use a tachometer to measure armature revolutions per minute. Failure of the motor to perform to specifications may be due to tight or dry bearings, or high resistance connections.

Pinion Clearance—There is no provision for adjusting pinion clearance on this type motor. When the shift lever mechanism is correctly assembled, the pinion clearance should fall within the limits of .010 to .140". When the clearance is not within these limits, it may indicate excessive wear of the solenoid linkage or shift lever yoke buttons.

Pinion clearance should be checked after the motor has been disassembled and reassembled. To check, disconnect motor field coil connector from solenoid terminal and insulate end. Connect one battery lead to solenoid switch terminal and the other lead to the solenoid frame, Fig. 37. Using a jumper lead connected to the solenoid motor terminal, momentarily flash the lead to the solenoid frame. This will shift the pinion into the cranking position until the battery is disconnected.

After energizing the solenoid with the clutch shifted toward the pinion stop retainer, push the pinion back toward the commutator end as far as possible to take up any slack movement; then check the clearance with feeler gauge, Fig. 38.

Disassembling Motor

NOTE: The 5 MT series starting motor will be used on some 1978–80 models, Fig. 39. On this type starting motor, the field coils and pole shoes are permanently bonded to the motor frame. The frame and field coils must be replaced as an assembly.

Normally the motor should be disassembled only so far as necessary to repair or replace defective parts.
1. Disconnect field coil connectors from solenoid "motor" terminal.
2. Remove thru bolts.
3. Remove commutator end frame and field frame assembly.
4. Remove armature assembly from drive housing. On some models it may be necessary to remove solenoid and shift lever assembly from the drive housing before removing the armature assembly.

IMPORTANT: *When solenoid is installed, apply sealing compound between field frame and solenoid flange (Fig. 40).*

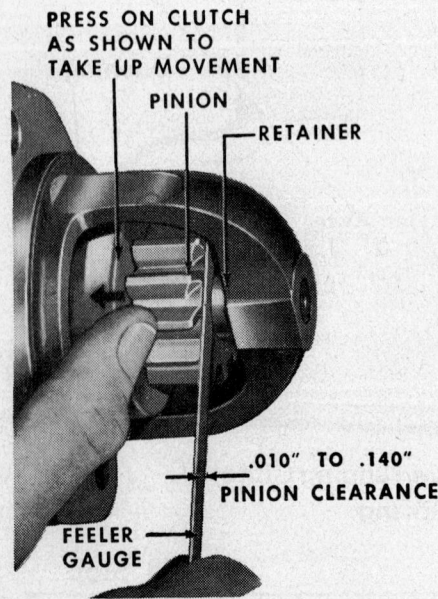

Fig. 38 Checking pinion clearance

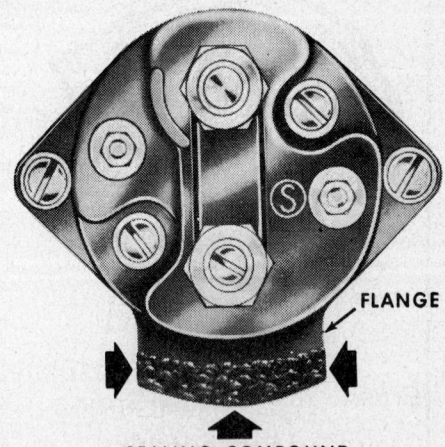

Fig. 40 Sealing solenoid housing to frame

STARTING MOTORS

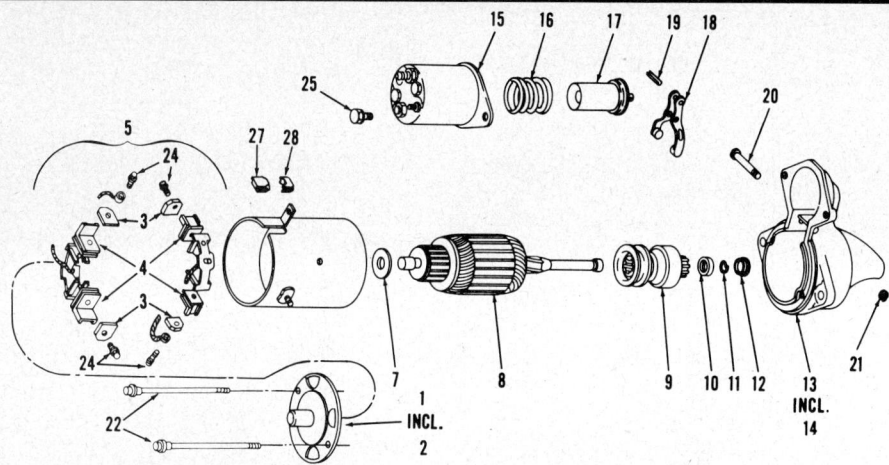

4. Slide retainer onto shaft with cupped surface facing end of shaft.
5. Stand armature on end on wood surface with commutator down. Position snap ring on upper end of shaft and hold in place with a block of wood. Hit wood block with a hammer forcing snap ring over end of shaft, Fig. 43. Slide snap ring into groove, squeezing it to ensure a good fit in groove.
6. Assemble thrust collar on shaft with shoulder next to snap ring.
7. Position retainer and thrust collar next to snap ring. With clutch pressed against assist spring, for clearance next to retainer, use two pairs of pliers at the same time (one pair on either side of shaft) to grip retainer and thrust collar. Then squeeze until snap ring is forced into retainer, Fig. 44.
8. Place 4 or 5 drops of SAE 10 oil in drive housing bushing. Make sure thrust collar is in place against snap ring and retainer; then slide armature and clutch assembly into place in drive housing.
9. Attach solenoid and shift lever assembly to drive housing. Be sure lever buttons are located between sides of clutch collar.
10. Position field frame over armature, *applying sealing compound between frame and solenoid flange, Fig. 40.* Position frame against drive housing, using care to prevent damage to brushes.
11. Place 4 or 5 drops of SAE 10 oil in bushing in commutator end frame. Make sure leather brake washer is on armature

1. FRAME—COMMUTATOR END
2. BRUSH AND HOLDER PKG.
3. BRUSH
4. BRUSH HOLDER
5. HOUSING—DRIVE END
6. FRAME AND FIELD ASM.
7. SOLENOID SWITCH
8. ARMATURE
9. DRIVE ASM.
10. PLUNGER
11. SHIFT LEVER
12. PLUNGER RETURN SPRINGER
13. SHIFT LEVER SHAFT
14. LOCK WASHER
15. SCREW—BRUSH ATTACHING
16. SCREW—FIELD LEAD TO SWITCH
17. SCREW—SWITCH ATTACHING
18. WASHER—BRAKE
19. THRU BOLT
20. BUSHING—COMMUTATOR END
21. BUSHING—DRIVE END
22. PINION STOP COLLAR
23. THRUST COLLAR
24. GROMMET
25. GROMMET
26. PLUNGER PIN
27. PINION STOP RETAINER RING
28. LEVER SHAFT RETAINING RING

Fig. 39 Disassembled view of Delco-Remy 5MT series starting motor

5. Remove overrunning clutch from armature shaft as follows:
   a. Slide thrust collar off end of armature shaft, Fig. 41.
   b. Slide a standard ½" pipe coupling or other metal cylinder of suitable size onto shaft so end of coupling or cylinder butts against edge of retainer. Tap end of coupling with hammer, driving retainer toward armature and off snap ring, Fig. 42.
   c. Remove snap ring from groove in shaft. If snap ring is too badly distorted during removal, use a new one when reassembling the clutch.
   d. Slide retainer, clutch and assist spring from armature shaft.

Reassembling Motor, Figs. 39 & 45

1. Lubricate drive end and splines of armature shaft with SAE 10 oil. *If heavier oil is used it may cause failure to mesh at low temperatures.*
2. Place "assist" spring on drive end of shaft next to armature, with small end against lamination stack.
3. Slide clutch assembly onto armature shaft with pinion outward.

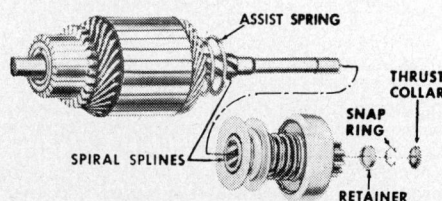

Fig. 41 View of armature and overrunning clutch

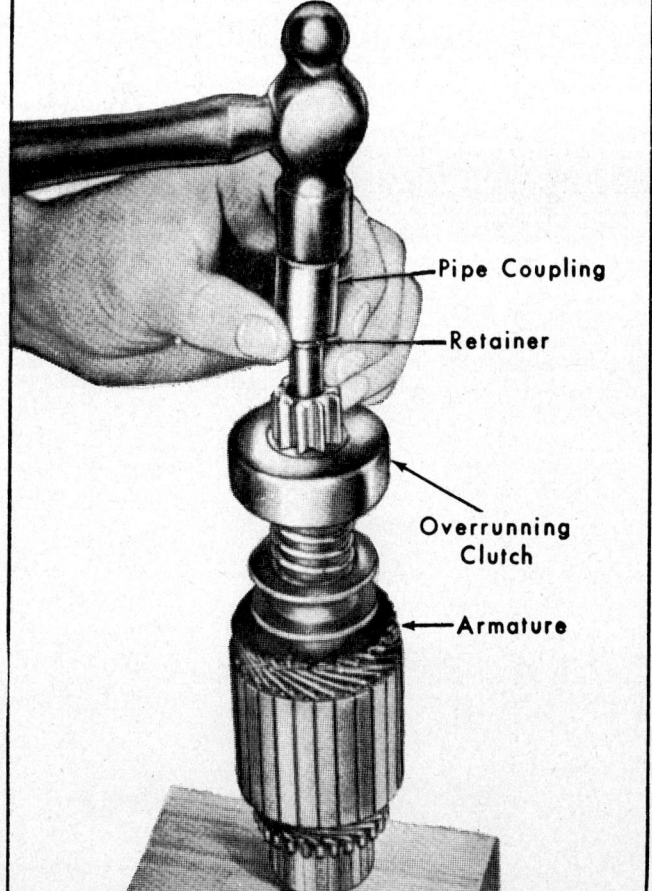

Fig. 42 Removing over-running clutch snap ring retainer

STARTING MOTORS

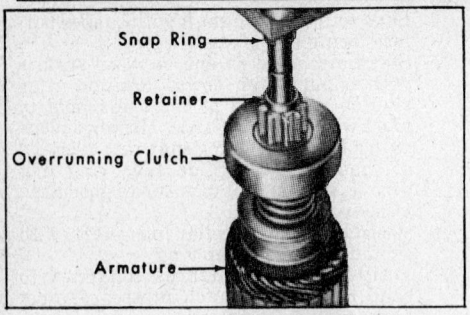

Fig. 43 Installing snap ring onto armature shaft

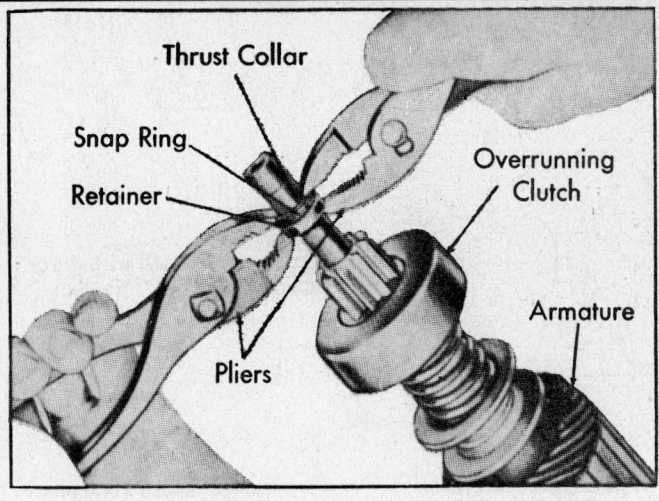

Fig. 44 Installing snap ring into retainer

shaft; then slide commutator end frame onto shaft.
12. Install thru bolts and tighten securely.
13. Reconnect field coil connectors to solenoid "motor" terminal.

Cleaning

The overrunning clutch, armature and fields should not be cleaned in any degreasing tank, or with grease dissolving solvents, since these would dissolve the lubricant in the clutch mechanism and would damage the insulation in the armature and field coils. It is suggested that all parts, except the clutch, be cleaned with oleum spirits and a brush. The clutch can be wiped with a clean cloth.

If the commutator is dirty it may be cleaned with No. 00 sandpaper; *never use emery cloth for this purpose.*

1978–80 V8-350 Diesel

Disassemble

1. Remove screw from field coil connector and solenoid mounting screws, then rotate solenoid 90° and remove solenoid with plunger return spring, Fig. 49.
2. Remove two through bolts, then commutator end frame with washer.
3. Remove end frame assembly from drive gear housing.
4. Remove shift lever pivot bolt.
5. Remove center bearing screws, then remove drive gear housing from armature shaft. Shift lever and plunger assembly, should fall from starter clutch.
6. Remove thrust washer or collar from armature shaft.
7. Position a 5/8 in. deep socket over shaft against retainer, then tap socket to move retainer off snap ring.
8. Remove snap ring from groove in shaft, then remove retainer, clutch assembly, fiber washer and center bearing from armature shaft.
9. Remove roll pin and separate shift lever and plunger.
10. Remove brush pivot pin and brush spring, then replace brushes as necessary.

Assemble

1. Lubricate drive end of armature with lubricant 1960954 or equivalent.
2. Install center bearing with bearing facing toward armature winding, then install fiber washer on armature shaft, Fig. 49.
3. Position clutch assembly on armature shaft with pinion facing away from armature.
4. Position retainer on armature shaft with cupped side facing end of shaft.
5. Install snap ring into groove on armature shaft, then install thrust washer.
6. Using two pliers, grip retainer and thrust washer or collar and squeeze until snap ring is forced into retainer and is held securely in groove on armature shaft.
7. Lubricate drive end housing bushing with lubricant 1960954 or equivalent.
8. Engage shift lever yoke with clutch and slide complete assembly into drive gear housing.
9. Install center bearing attaching screws and shift lever pivot bolt.
10. Install solenoid on drive gear housing.
11. Apply sealer No. 1050026 or equivalent to solenoid flange where field frame contacts solenoid.
12. Position field frame against drive gear housing on alignment pin, using care to prevent damage to brushes.
13. Lubricate commutator end frame bushing with lubricant 1960954 or equivalent.
14. Install washer on armature shaft and slide end frame onto shaft, then install and tighten through bolts.
15. Connect field coil connector to solenoid terminal, then check pinion clearance.

Pinion Clearance Check

1. Disconnect field coil connector from solenoid terminal and insulate carefully.
2. Connect one 12 volt battery lead to solenoid switch terminal and other lead to starter motor frame.
3. Flash a jumper lead momentarily from solenoid motor terminal to starter motor frame. This will shift pinion into cranking position until battery is disconnected.
4. Push pinion back as far as possible to take up any movement, then check pinion clearance using a feeler gauge. Pinion clearance should be .010–.140 in. If clearance is not within limits, check for improper installation or worn parts and replace as necessary.

DELCO-REMY HEAVY DUTY ENCLOSED SHIFT LEVER TYPE STARTER

In this type motor, Figs. 47, 48 and 49, the nose housing can be rotated to obtain a number of different solenoid positions with respect to the mounting flange, which is a feature that makes these motors adaptable to a wide variety of mounting applications.

Positive lubrication is provided to the bronze bushing located in the commutator end frame, in the lever housing, and in the nose housing by an oil saturated wick that projects through each bushing and contacts the arma-

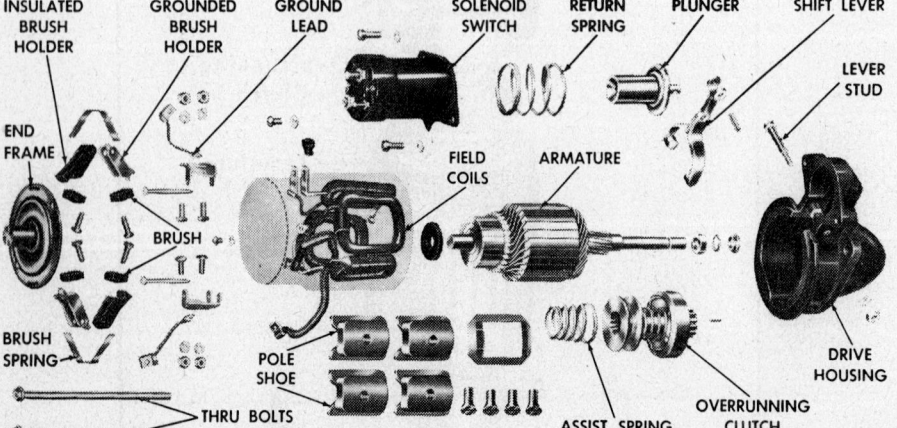

Fig. 45 Disassembled view of 10MT series starting motor (Typical)

STARTING MOTORS

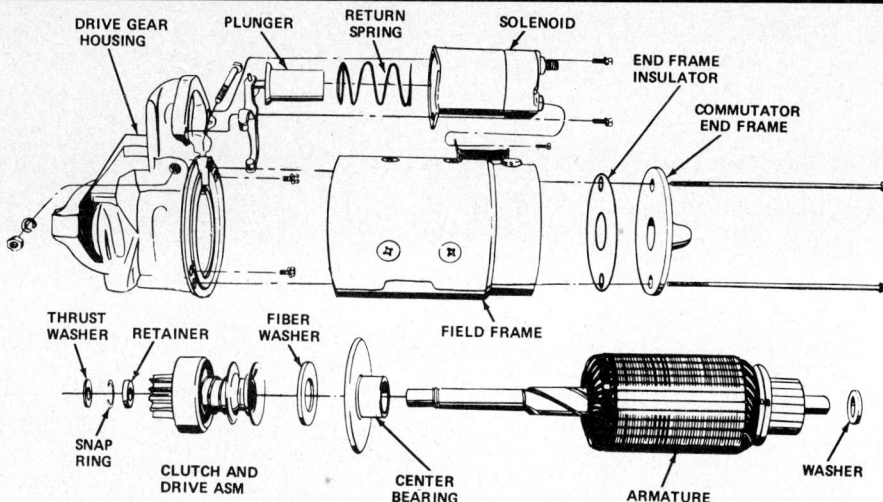

Fig. 46 Disassembled view of Delco-Remy 25MT series starting motor

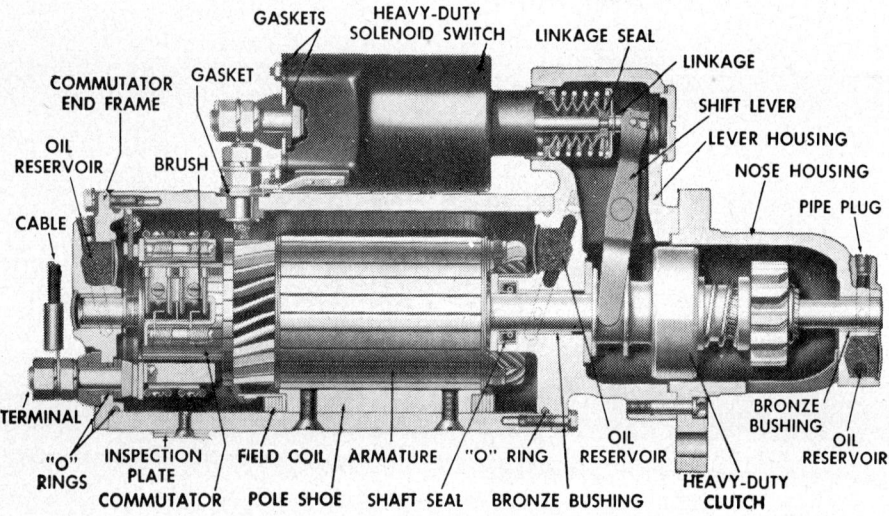

Fig. 47 Delco-Remy heavy duty enclosed shift lever type motor

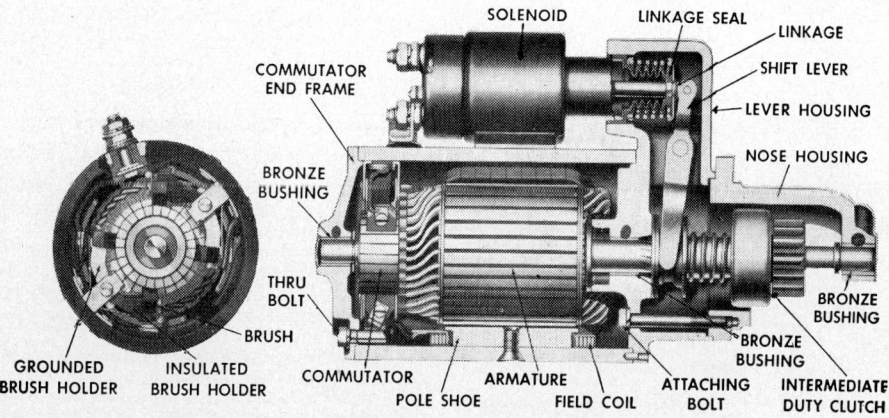

Fig. 48 Delco-Remy intermediate duty enclosed shift lever type motor (with through bolts)

ture shaft. Oil can be added to each wick by removing a pipe plug which is accessible on the outside of the motor.

Available as an optional feature is a waste-filled oil reservoir for each wick which makes available a larger supply of oil thereby extending the time required between lubrication periods. Another optional feature is "O" rings which can be added to resist entry of dirt and moisture into the entire motor assembly.

Many models feature a seal between the shaft and lever housing, and all models have a rubber boot or linkage seal over the solenoid plunger. The seal and the boot, when used together, prevent entry of transmission oil into the motor main frame and solenoid case, allowing the motor to be used on wet clutch applications.

Overrunning Clutches

As shown in Figs. 47, 48 and 49, two kinds of clutches, heavy duty or intermediate duty overrunning type, may be used with these motors. The clutches may be either the sprag type or the four-roll type. Both types are moved into mesh with the ring gear by the action of the solenoid. Once engaged, the clutch will not disengage during intermittent engine firing, which prevents damage to pinion and ring gear teeth. The pinion remains engaged until starting is assured and the solenoid circuit is interrupted.

Maintenance

Under normal operating conditions, no maintenance will be required between engine overhaul periods. At time of engine overhaul, motors without oil reservoirs and "O" rings, and "long life" motors incorporating "O" rings and oil reservoirs should be disassembled, inspected, cleaned and tested.

Adjustable Nose Housing

Two methods are employed to attach the nose housing to the lever housing. As shown in Fig. 47, one method attaches the nose housing to the lever housing by six bolts located around the outside of the housing. To relocate the housing, it is only necessary to remove the bolts, rotate the housing to the desired position, reinstall the bolts and torque them to 13-17 ft. lb. during reassembly.

In the second method, Fig. 48, the lever housing and commutator end frame are held to the field frame by thru bolts extending from the commutator end frame to threaded holes in the lever housing. The nose housing is held to the lever housing by internal attaching bolts. With this arrangement, it is necessary to partially disassemble the motor to provide access to the attaching bolts when relocating the nose housing.

To accomplish this, remove the electrical connector and the screws attaching the solenoid assembly to the field frame and then remove the thru bolts from the commutator end frame. Separate the field frame from the remaining assembly, and pull the armature away from the lever housing until the pinion stop rests against the clutch pinion. This will clear the nose housing attaching bolts so they can be removed, permitting relocation of the nose housing. During reassembly, torque the nose housing attaching bolts to 11-15 ft. lb

Starting Motor Tests

On intermediate duty motors with through bolts, make test connections as shown in Fig. 39. On intermediate motors without through

STARTING MOTORS

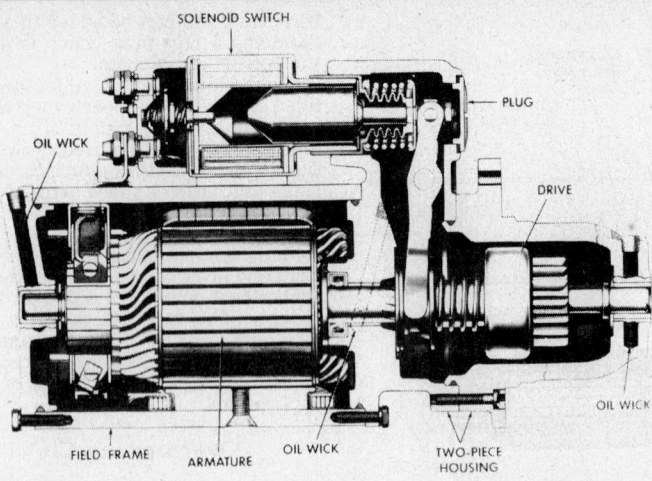

Fig. 49 Delco-Remy intermediate duty enclosed shift lever type motor (without through bolts)

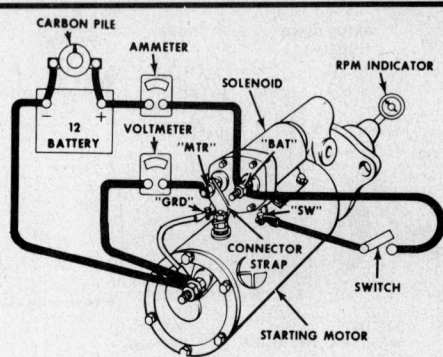

Fig. 50 Connections for checking free speed of motor

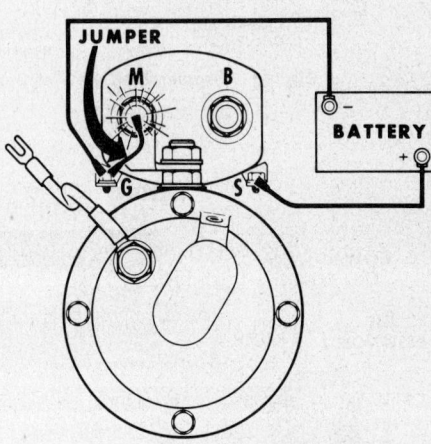

Fig. 51 Connections for checking pinion clearance

bolts and heavy duty motors, make test connections shown in Fig. 50.

Free Speed Test—Failure of the motor to perform to specifications may be due to tight or dry bearings, or high resistance connections.

Pinion Clearance: There are no provisions for adjusting pinion clearance on motors using the intermediate duty clutch. However, this should be checked after reassembly of motor to make sure the clearance is within specifications. On intermediate duty motors with through bolts, make test connections as shown in Fig. 37. On intermediate duty motors without through bolts, make test connections shown in Fig. 51. After energizing the solenoid with the clutch shifted toward the pinion stop retainer, push the pinion back toward the commutator end as far as possible to take up any slack movement, then check the clearance between pinion and pinion stop retainer with a feeler gauge, Fig. 52. If clearance is not within specified limits, check the solenoid linkage and shift lever yoke buttons for excessive wear.

The pinion clearance for motors using the heavy duty clutch is checked in the same manner as for intermediate duty clutches. The clearance for these motors, however, is measured as indicated in Fig. 53. The clearance is adjustable and is accomplished by removing the plug on the lever housing and turning the nut on the plunger rod inside the housing. Turn the nut clockwise to decrease clearance, and vice versa.

Disassembling Motor

Note the relative position of the solenoid, lever housing and nose housing so the motor can be reassembled in the same manner.

INTERMEDIATE DUTY MOTOR WITH THROUGH BOLTS

1979-80 Units
1. Remove through bolts, then remove end frame.
2. Remove spacer from commutator end of armature shaft, then separate field frame from lever housing assembly. Use care not to damage solenoid boot.
3. Disconnect field coil connector from solenoid motor terminal, then remove solenoid to end frame attaching screws and remove solenoid.
4. Remove nose housing attaching bolts, then separate nose housing from lever housing.
5. To remove drive assembly from lever housing, proceed as follows:
   a. Using a metal cylinder and a hammer, drive collar away from retainer ring, then remove retainer ring from armature shaft.
   b. Remove armature shaft from lever housing and separate driver assembly from shift lever fingers.
6. Remove solenoid plunger from lever housing:
   a. Remove expansion plugs from housing by piercing the plugs and prying out, Fig. 54.
   b. Using needle nose pliers, remove lever pin retainer clip, then remove pin and solenoid plunger from housing.
7. Disassemble shift lever from housing by piercing one of the small expansion plugs in lever housing. Drive shift lever pin out of housing, then remove shift lever from housing.
8. Inspect brake washer in lever housing and replace as necessary.

1970-78 Units
1. Disconnect field coil connector from solenoid motor terminal, and remove solenoid

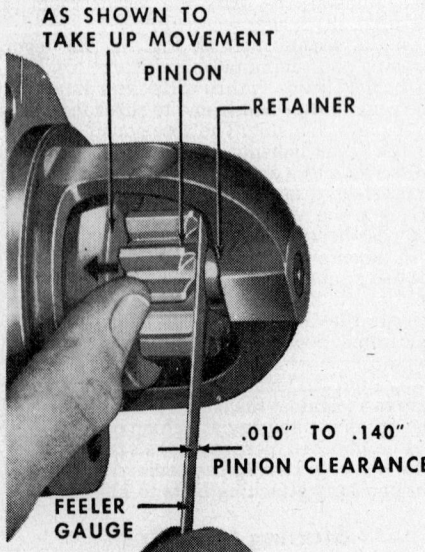

Fig. 52 Checking pinion clearance on intermediate duty motor

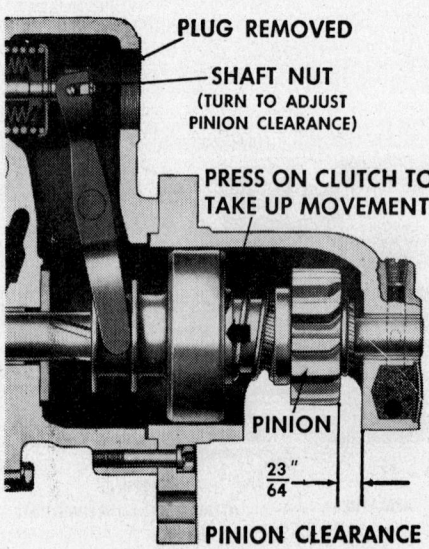

Fig. 53 Checking pinion clearance on heavy duty motor

STARTING MOTORS

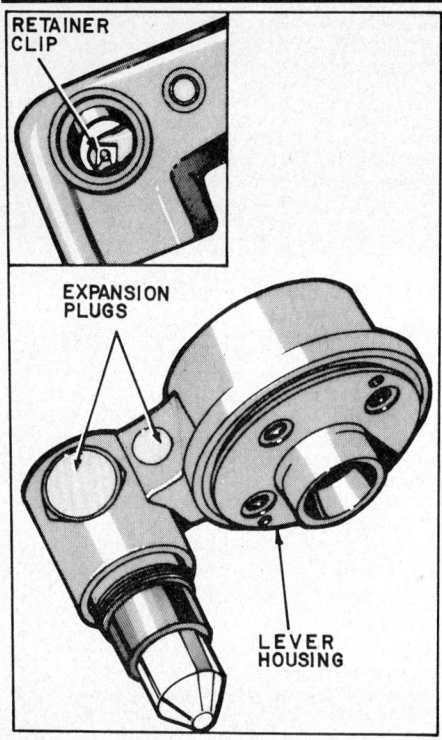

Fig. 54 Lever housing expansion plugs & shift lever retainer. Intermediate duty motor with through bolts

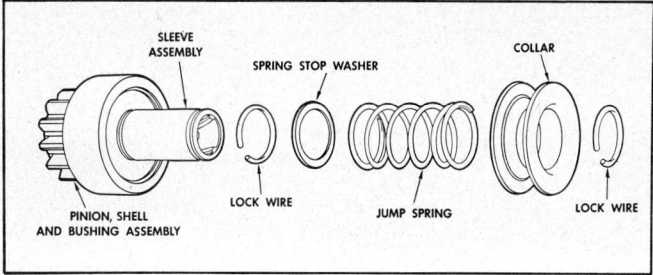

Fig. 55 Disassembled view of early type intermediate duty sprag clutch drive

mounting screws.
2. Remove thru bolts.
3. Remove commutator end frame from field frame and field frame from lever housing.
4. Remove nose housing attaching bolts and separate nose housing from lever housing.
5. Slide a 1/2" pipe coupling or other metal cylinder of suitable size onto shaft so end of coupling or cylinder butts against edge of retainer. Tap end of coupling with a hammer, driving retainer toward armature and off snap ring.
6. Remove snap ring from groove in shaft, using pliers or other suitable tool. If snap ring is too badly distorted during removal, use a new one when reassembling clutch.
7. Remove armature and clutch from lever housing.
8. Separate solenoid from lever housing.

INTERMEDIATE DUTY MOTORS WITHOUT THROUGH BOLTS

1. Remove screws attaching to nose housing to lever housing, then separate nose housing from motor.
2. Remove solenoid access plug from lever housing.
3. Remove bolts attaching lever housing to field frame.
4. Disconnect field coil lead from solenoid motor terminal.
5. Remove solenoid to frame attaching bolts.
6. Remove end frame and spacer from armature shaft.
7. Separate lever housing assembly from field frame.
8. Remove solenoid from lever housing. Use care not to damage solenoid boot.
9. Remove adjustment nut from solenoid plunger shaft.

10. Remove armature and drive assembly as follows:
   a. Using a metal cylinder and a hammer, drive stop collar away from retainer ring, then remove retainer ring from armature shaft.
   b. Remove armature shaft from lever housing and separate drive assembly from shift lever fingers.
11. Remove snap ring from shift lever retainer pin, then drive retainer pin from housing and remove shift lever.
12. Inspect brake washer in lever housing and replace as necessary.

HEAVY DUTY MOTORS

1. Disconnect field coil connector from solenoid motor terminal and lead from solenoid ground terminal.
2. On motors having brush inspection plates, remove plates and then brush lead screws. This will disconnect the field leads from the brush holders.
3. Remove attaching bolts and separate commutator end frame from field frame.
4. Separate nose housing and field frame from lever housing by removing attaching bolts.
5. Remove armature and clutch assembly from lever housing.
6. Separate solenoid from lever housing by pulling apart.

Intermediate Duty Sprag Clutch

1. Remove lock wire and collar from sleeve, Fig. 55 and 56.
2. Remove jump spring, spring stop washer and second lock wire.
3. Remove retainer ring and large washers. Do not remove sleeve or sprags from shell.
4. Lubricate sprags, Fig. 57, and saturate the felt washer with SAE 5W-20 oil. *Heavier oil must not be used.*
5. Reassemble washers and retaining ring.
6. Assemble lock wire in groove next to sprag; then assemble stop washer.
7. Assemble jump spring, collar and other lock wire.

8. Lubricate armature shaft with a few drops of SAE 10 oil before sprag clutch is reinstalled.

Heavy Duty Sprag Clutch

1. Remove cupped pinion stop and split washer, Figs. 58, 59 and 60. In removing cupped pinion stop, it will probably be damaged to the extent that a new one will be required on reassembly.
2. Remove pinion, spring and retainer cups.
3. Remove retainer ring and washers. *Do not remove collar sleeve and shell, or sprags from shell.*
4. Lubricate sprags and saturate felt washer with SAE 5W-20 oil—no heavier.
5. Reassemble washers and retainer ring.
6. Lubricate spiral spline on collar sleeve and shell with SAE 10 oil.
7. Assemble retainer cups and spring.
8. Assemble pinion with collar side toward spring, Figs. 58, 59 and 60.
9. Install new cupped pinion stop and split washer as shown. Stake cupped pinion stop in about 10 places with a round-nosed tool.

Cleaning

Follow cleaning instructions outlined for standard duty motors.

Reassembling Motor

The reassembly procedure for each type of motor is the reverse of disassembly. On motors using a snap ring and retainer on the shaft as a pinion stop, the ring and retainer can be assembled as follows:

With the retainer placed over the shaft with the cupped surface facing the end of the shaft, force the ring over the shaft with a light hammer blow and then slide the ring down into the groove. To force the retainer over the snap ring, place a suitable washer over the shaft and squeeze with pliers. Remove the washer, Fig. 61.

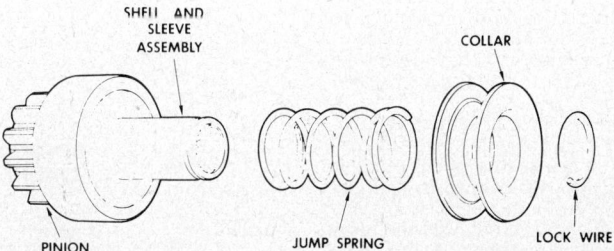

Fig. 56 Disassembled view of late type intermediate duty sprag clutch drive

STARTING MOTORS

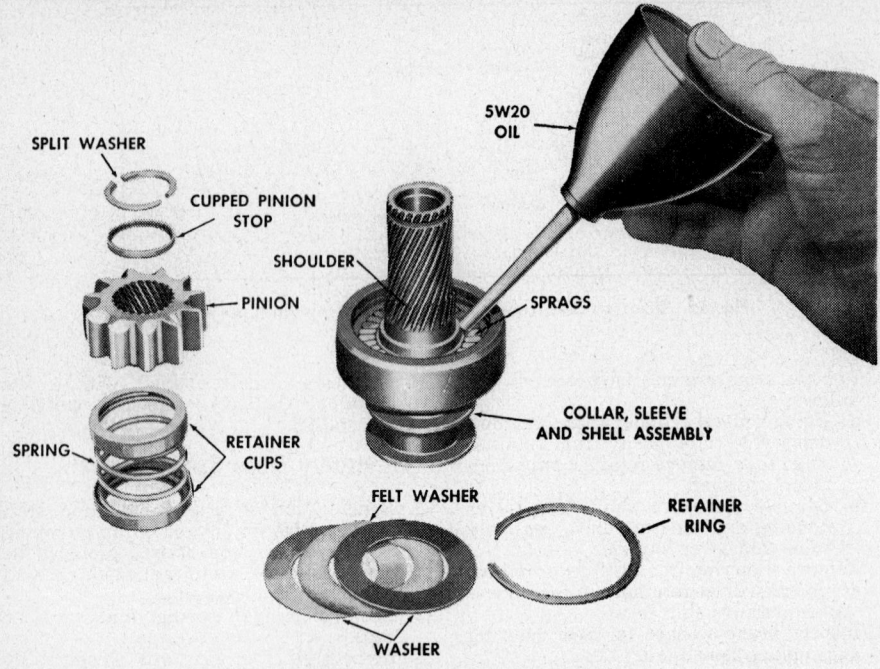

Fig. 57 Lubricating clutch sprags

To reassemble the end frame having eight brushes onto the field frame, pull the armature out of the field frame just far enough to permit the brushes to be placed over the commutator, Fig. 62. Then push the commutator end frame and the armature back against the field frame.

Lubrication

All wicks and reservoirs should be saturated with SAE 10 oil, and the splines underneath the clutch should be lubricated with a light coat of SAE 10 oil. *Heavier oil may cause failure to mesh at low temperatures.*

FORD STARTER WITH INTEGRAL POSITIVE ENGAGEMENT DRIVE

This type starting motor, Figs. 63 and 64 is a four pole, series parallel unit with a positive engagement drive built into the starter. The drive mechanism is engaged with the flywheel by lever action before the motor is energized.

When the ignition switch is turned on to the start position, the starter relay is energized and supplies current to the motor. The current flows through one field coil and a set of contact points to ground. The magnetic field given off by the field coil pulls the movable pole, which is part of the lever, downward to its seat. When the pole is pulled down, the lever moves the drive assembly into the engine flywheel, Fig. 65.

When the movable pole is seated, it functions as a normal field pole and opens the contact points. With the points open, current flows through the starter field coils, energizing the starter. At the same time, current also flows through a holding coil to hold the movable pole in its seated position.

When the ignition switch is released from the start position, the starter relay opens the circuit to the starting motor. This allows the return spring to force the lever back, disengaging the drive from the flywheel and returning the movable pole to its normal position, Fig. 66.

1970–77 Units

Disassembly

It may not be necessary to disassemble the starter completely to accomplish repair or replacement of certain parts. Thus, before disassembling the motor, remove the cover band and starter drive actuating lever cover. Examine brushes to make sure they are free in their holders. Replace brushes if defective or worn beyond their useful limit. Check the tension of each brush spring with a pull scale. Spring tension should not be less than 45 ounces. If disassembly is necessary, proceed as follows:

1. Remove cover band and starter drive actuating lever cover.
2. Remove through bolts, starter drive gear housing, drive gear retaining clip cup and starter drive actuating lever return spring. Some units incorporate needle bearings at the drive end. If needle bearings need not be replaced, insert a dummy shaft into the housing while removing the armature. This will prevent loss of bearings.
3. Remove pivot pin retaining starter gear actuating lever and remove lever and

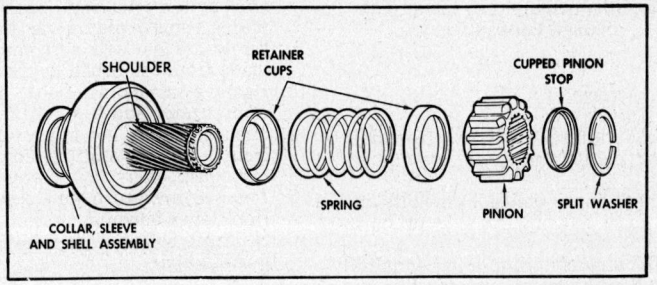

Fig. 58 Disassembled view of early type heavy duty sprag clutch drive

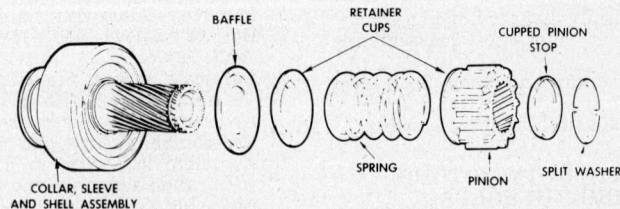

Fig. 59 Disassembled view of late type heavy duty sprag clutch drive

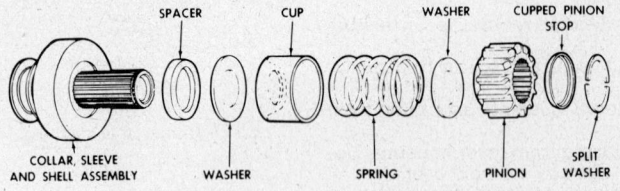

Fig. 60 Disassembled view of DR-250 clutch drive

STARTING MOTORS

armature.
4. Remove and discard spring clip retaining starter drive gear to end of armature shaft, and remove drive gear.
5. Remove commutator brushes from holders and remove brush end plate.
6. Remove two screws retaining ground brushes to frame, Fig. 67.
7. On the field coil that operates the drive actuating lever, bend tab up on field retainer and remove retainer.
8. Remove field coil retainer screws, Fig. 68. Unsolder field coil leads from terminal screw, and remove pole shoes and coils from frame.
9. Remove starter terminal nut and related parts. Remove any excess solder from terminal slot.

Reassembly
1. Install starter terminal, insulator, washers and retaining nut in frame, Fig. 67. Be sure to position slot in screw perpendicular to frame end surface.
2. Install field coils and pole pieces. As pole shoe screws are tightened, strike frame several sharp blows with a soft-faced hammer to seat and align pole shoes, then stake the screws.
3. Install solenoid coil retainer and bend tabs to retain tabs to frame.
4. Solder field coils and solenoid wire to starter terminal, using rosin core solder.
5. Check for continuity and grounds in the assembled coils.
6. Position solenoid coil ground terminal over ground screw hole nearest starter terminal.
7. Position ground brushes to starter frame and install retaining screws, Fig. 67.
8. Position starter brush end plate to frame with end plate boss in frame slot.
9. Install drive gear to armature shaft and install a new retaining spring clip.
10. Position fiber thrust washer on commutator end of armature shaft and install armature in frame.
11. Install starter drive actuating lever to frame and starter drive, and install pivot pin.
12. Position actuating lever return spring and drive gear housing to frame and install through bolts. Do not pinch brush leads between brush plate and frame.
13. Install brushes in holders, being sure to

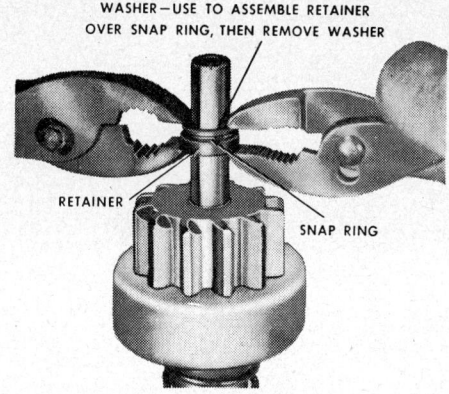

Fig. 61 Forcing retainer over snap ring

center brush springs on brushes.
14. Position drive gear actuating lever cover on starter and install brush cover band.
15. Check starter for free running and install on engine.

1978–80 Units

Disassemble Fig. 64
1. Remove cover screw, cover, through bolts, starter drive end housing and starter drive plunger lever return spring.
2. Remove plunger lever retaining pin, then remove lever and armature.
3. Remove stop ring retainer from armature shaft, then remove stop ring and starter drive gear assembly.
4. Remove brush end plate and insulator assembly.
5. Remove brushes from brush holder, then remove brush holder. Note position of brush holder to end terminal.
6. Remove two screws retaining ground brushes to frame.
7. Bend up edges of sleeve inserted in frame, then remove sleeve and retainer.
8. Detach field coil ground wire from copper

Fig. 62 Assembling end frame with eight brushes to field frame

tab on frame.
9. Using tool No. 10044-A, remove three coil retaining screws, Fig. 68. Cut field coil connection at switch post lead and pole shoes and coils from frame.
10. Cut positive brush leads from field coils, as close to field connection as possible.

Assemble Fig. 64
1. Position pole pieces and coils in frame, then install retaining screws using tool No. 10044-A, Fig. 68. As pole shoes are tightened, strike frame several times with a soft faced mallet to seat and align pole shoes, then stake screws.
2. Install plunger coil sleeve and retainer, then bend tabs to retain coils to frame.
3. Position grommet on end terminal, then insert terminal and grommet into notch on frame.
4. Solder field coil to starter terminal post strap.

NOTE: Use 300 watt soldering iron and rosin core solder.

5. Check coils for continuity and grounds.
6. Position brushes to starter frame and install retaining screws.
7. Apply a thin coat of Lubriplate 777 or equivalent to armature shaft splines.
8. Install drive gear assembly on armature shaft, then install stop ring and stop ring retainer.
9. Install armature into starter frame.
10. Position starter drive gear plunger to frame and starter drive assembly then install pivot assembly. Fill end housing bearing bore approximately 1/4 full with grease, then position drive end housing to frame.
11. Install brush holder, then insert brushes into holder and install brush springs.

NOTE: Ensure positive brush leads are properly positioned in slots on brush holder.

12. Install brush end plate. Ensure brush end plate insulator is properly positioned.
13. Install through bolts, then install starter drive plunger lever cover and tighten retaining screw.

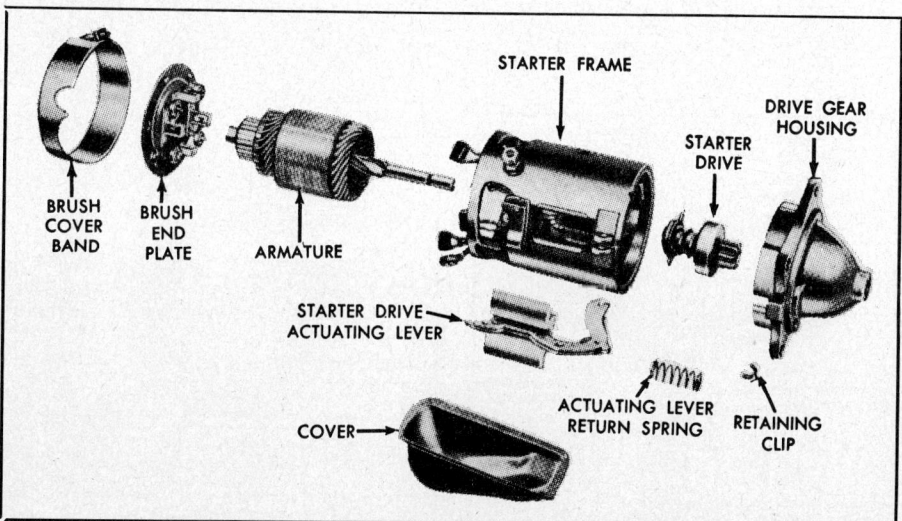

Fig. 63 Ford starter with an integral positive engagement drive 1970–77

43

STARTING MOTORS

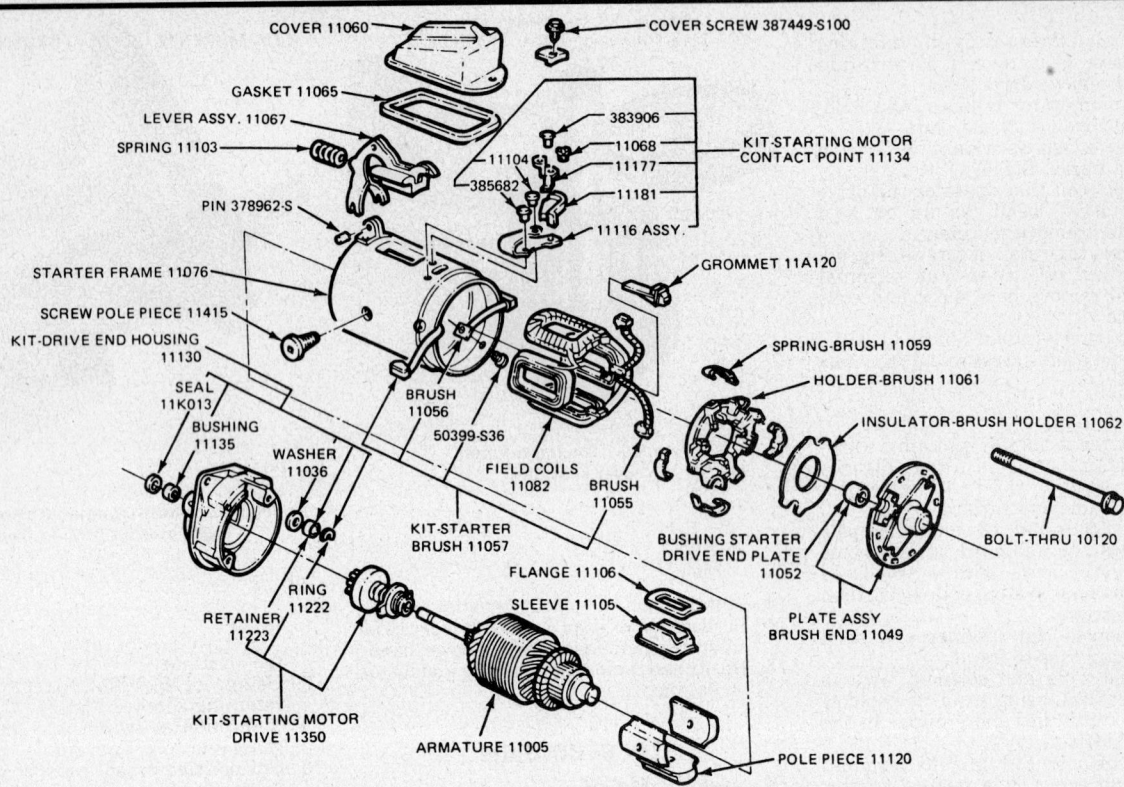

Fig. 64 Ford Motorcraft positive engagement starting motor. 1978–80

FORD MOTORCRAFT SOLENOID ACTUATED STARTER

Description

The solenoid assembly, in this unit, Fig. 69, is mounted to a flange on the starter drive housing which encloses the entire shift lever and solenoid plunger mechanism. The solenoid incorporated a pull-in winding and a hold-in winding.

Operation

As the solenoid is energized, it shifts the starting motor pinion into mesh with the engine flywheel ring gear.

At the same time, the solenoid contacts are closed and battery current flows to the motor, turning it and the engine.

After the engine starts, the starter drive is disengaged when the ignition switch is returned from the start position to the run position and the solenoid spring pushes the shift lever back, disengaging the starter drive from the flywheel ring gear.

The starting motor is protected by an overrunning clutch built into the starter drive.

Disassembly, Fig. 69

1. Disconnect the copper strap from the starter terminal of the solenoid, remove the retaining screws and remove solenoid.
2. Loosen retaining screw and slide brush cover band back on frame.
3. Remove commutator brushes from holders. Hold each spring away from the brush with a hook while sliding brush from holder.
4. Remove through bolts and separate end plates and frame.
5. Remove solenoid plunger and shift fork assembly.
6. Remove armature and drive assembly from frame. Remove drive stop ring and slide drive assembly from shaft. Remove fiber thrust washer from commutator end of shaft.
7. Remove drive stop ring retainer from shaft.

Reassembly, Fig. 69

1. Install drive assembly on shaft and in-

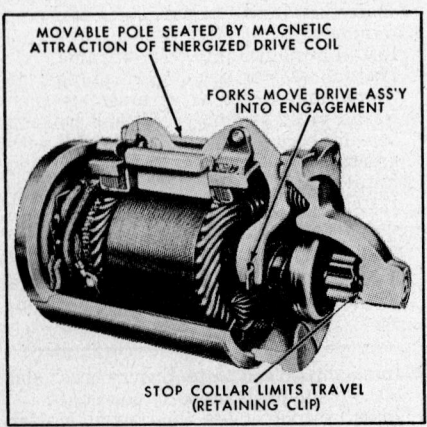

Fig. 65 Starter drive engaged

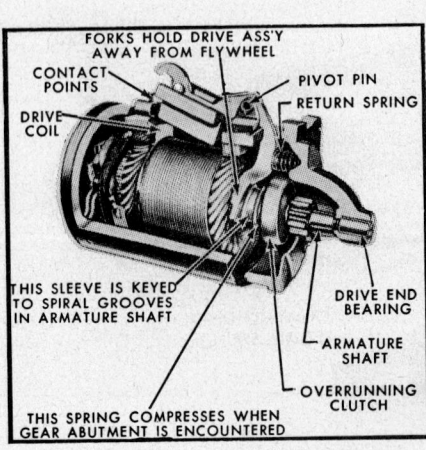

Fig. 66 Starter drive disengaged

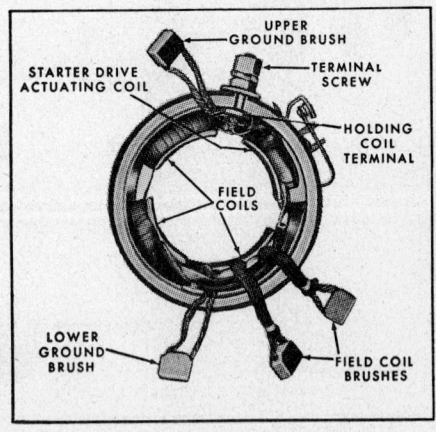

Fig. 67 Field coil assembly

STARTING MOTORS

stall new stop ring.
2. Install solenoid plunger and shift fork.
3. Place new retainer in drive housing and install armature and drive in housing. Be sure shift lever tangs properly engage drive assembly.
4. Install fiber washer on commutator end of shaft and position frame to drive housing, being sure to index frame and drive housing correctly.
5. Install brush plate assembly being sure to index it properly, install through bolts and tighten to 55-75 in. lbs.
6. Install brushes by pulling each spring away from holder with a hook to allow entry of the brush. Center the brush springs on the brushes. Press insulated brush leads away from all other components to prevent possible shorts.
7. Install rubber gasket and solenoid.
8. Connect copper strap to starter terminal of solenoid.
9. Position cover band and tighten retaining screw.
10. Connect starter to battery and check operation.

PRESTOLITE STARTER W/POSITORK DRIVE

This heavy duty starter is solenoid actuated and has an armature shaft center bearing. The indexing type Positork drive assures complete drive pinion engagement before the motor begins to rotate, thereby minimizing flywheel ring gear and drive pinion wear and also protects the starter from over-speeding.

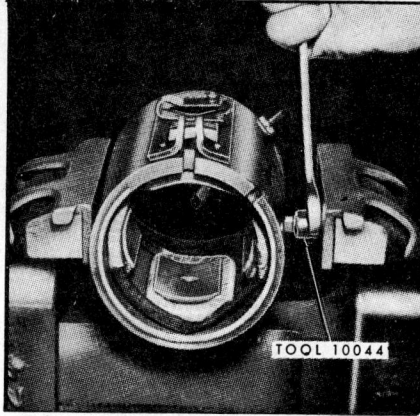

Fig. 68 Removing field coil pole shoe screws

Disassembly, Fig. 70

1. Remove plug and gasket from intermediate housing, then remove the nut from the end of the moving core shaft.

NOTE: To ease removal of adjusting nut, an adapter should be fabricated, Fig. 71. Drill a 3/16 inch hole through a piece of 3/8 inch square and 1 1/2 inches long stock. Install a 3/8 drive 1/2 inch socket onto nut, then install adapter onto socket. Insert a 3/32 inch allen wrench through adapter to hold the moving core shaft. While holding allen wrench, turn adapter with a 1/2 inch wrench.

2. Disconnect solenoid lead from the front motor terminal, then remove the nut and lockwasher from the motor terminal stud. Remove the four solenoid retaining screws and remove the solenoid.
3. Remove the nut, lockwasher and washers from the commutator end head, then remove the attaching bolts or screws and remove the commutator.
4. Remove the intermediate housing to frame and field assembly bolts then remove the frame and field assembly.
5. Remove the pipe plugs to expose the shift lever pin, then using a small drift or punch, drive the shift lever pin out of the intermediate housing.
6. Scribe or punch aligning marks on intermediate housing and pinion housing, then remove the attaching bolts and separate the two housings. Slide the intermediate housing and drive assembly off the armature.

Assembly

To assemble starter, reverse disassembly procedure while observing the following precautions:
1. When installing new bearings, always use the proper arbor to obtain correct fit. Remove felt oil wick from pinion housing reservoir before installing bearing. After bearings are installed, saturate felt wick with SAE 20 oil, then install felt wick and fill reservoir with SAE 20 oil.

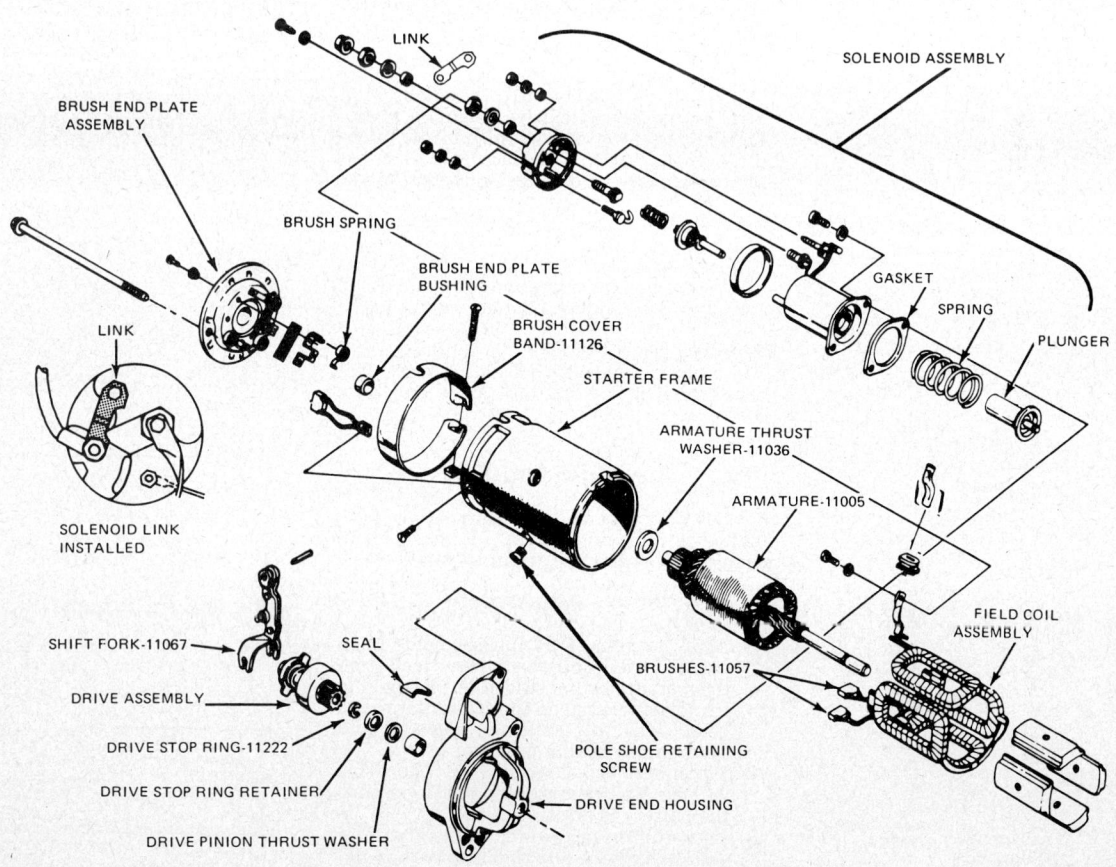

Fig. 69 Ford Motorcraft solenoid actuated starting motor

STARTING MOTORS

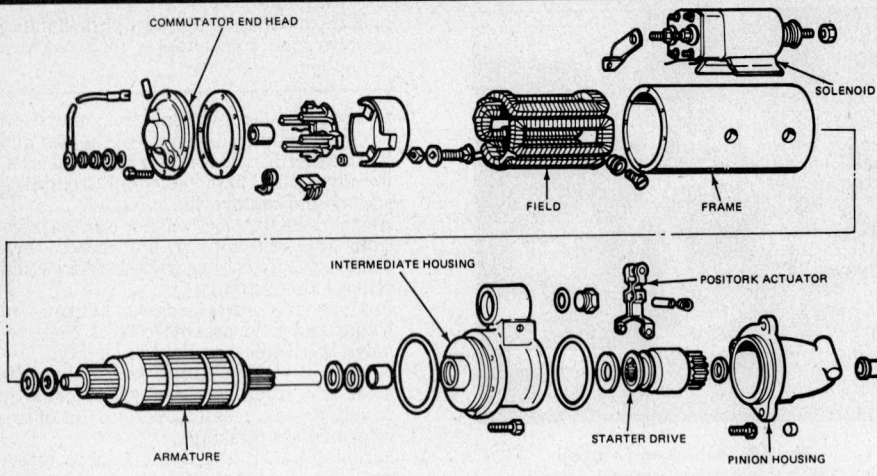

Fig. 70 Prestolite starter with Positork drive

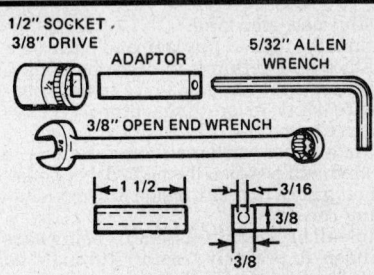

Fig. 71 Fabrication dimensions for adapter tool

2. Apply a light coat of grease to all O-ring seals prior to installation to prevent damaging seals during motor assembly.
3. Any sealing components that are worn or were damaged during removal, should be replaced.
4. Lubricate bearing surfaces of armature with SAE 10 oil. Lubricate shaft splines under drive assembly with low temperature EP grease.
5. When assembling intermediate and pinion housings, torque allen head retaining bolts to 8 ft. lbs.
6. After assembly, coat the insulation of the two terminal studs with sealing compound.

NOTE: Make sure to keep sealer off contact surfaces of terminal studs and nuts.

Inspection & Testing

Armature
1. Check armature for excessive wear, indications of excessive arcing, rough bearing surfaces on the shaft or damaged shaft splines.
2. If commutator is rough, it should be turned down. If commutator was originally undercut, undercut mica to a depth of 1/32 inch below commutator segments.
3. Check armature for shorts or grounds as described previously.

Field Coils
Check field coils for grounds as described previously. Assure that brushes or coil terminals are not grounded while checking field coils.

Brush Holder
Check brush holder assembly for grounds by touching one probe of test light to the holder and the other probe to each brush. If test light goes on, replace brush holder assembly.

Positork Drive
Clean drive assembly with solvent and wipe drive. Do not immerse drive assembly in solvent as this will wash away the internal lubrication which cannot be replaced. Check drive splines for wear or damage. Check to make sure that drive moves freely on armature shaft splines.

Pinion Housing
Inspect housing for cracks. Clean any paint or rust off the mounting flange.

Intermediate Housing
Inspect oil seal and bearing for wear. Replace seal if it is worn, or is hard and brittle.

Armature End Play
Adjust to obtain .005-.030 inch end play, by adding or removing thrust washers on the commutator end of the armature shaft.

Pinion Adjustment
1. Apply 12 volts to 24 volt solenoids, then momentarily connect a jumper lead from the motor terminal stud of the solenoid to the terminal stud on the commutator end head. This will shift the solenoid and drive into cranking position.
2. Disconnect the jumper wire. The drive will remain in the cranking position until the battery is disconnected.
3. Push the drive toward the commutator end to eliminate any backlash in the linkage and measure the clearance between the outside edge of the pinion and nose housing, Fig. 72. If the clearance is not within .020-.050 inch, adjust by turning the adjusting nut in or out as required.
4. Fabricate interference block, Fig. 73.

CAUTION: Due to the high amount of current passing through the series windings, the following tests should be made as quickly as possible.

5. Place the 63/64 inch side of the interference block against the drive gear, Fig. 74, then connect a 12 volt battery with a test light in series to 12 volt solenoids, or a 24-volt battery and test light in series to 24 volt solenoids.
6. If the test light goes on, the solenoid has been assembled incorrectly. Remove the solenoid cover and check the contact component assembly.
7. If the test light does not go on, connect a carbon pile and ohmeter to the circuit.
8. Place the 1/2 inch side of the interference block against the drive gear, Fig. 74, and adjust the voltage with the carbon pile. The test light must go on before 16 volts on 24 volt solenoids or 8 volts on 12 volt solenoids are reached. If the light does not go on as specified, turn the adjusting nut out until the light goes on as specified.
9. After adjusting, replace the plug and washer in the shift linkage cover.
10. Check all starters for 80 ampere draw at 11 volts. If current draw is excessive, check end play and bearing alignment. Normally several taps with a rawhide mallet will correct bearing misalignment.

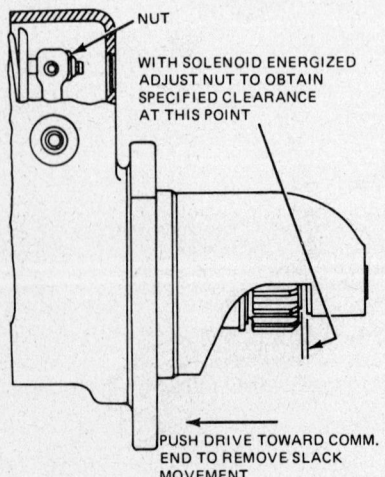

Fig. 72 Starter drive adjustment

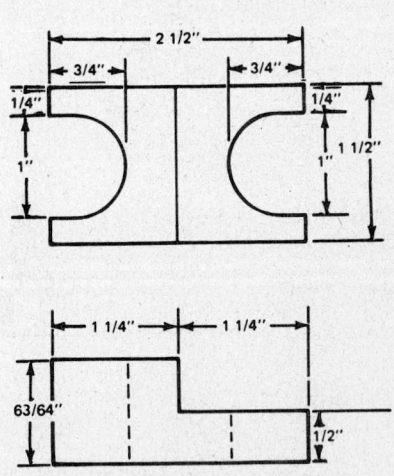

Fig. 73 Fabrication dimensions for interference block

STARTING MOTORS

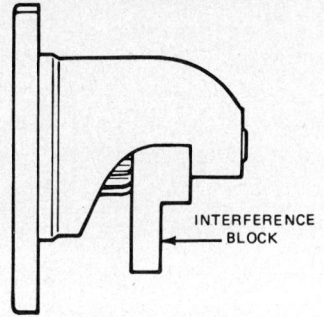

Fig. 74 Interference block installed

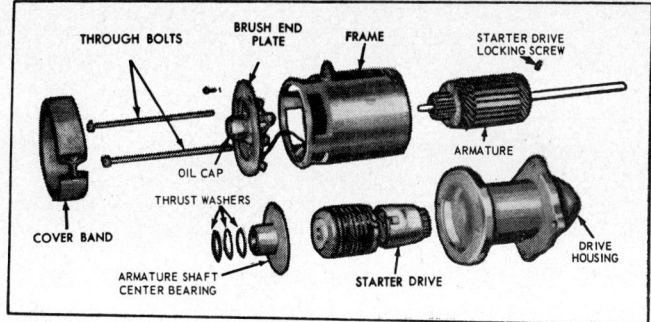

Fig. 75 Prestolite starter with inertia drive

PRESTOLITE STARTER W/INERTIA DRIVE

This heavy duty starter has an armature shaft center bearing and an inertia drive with an overrunning clutch protecting starter from overspeed.

Disassembly, Fig. 75

1. Remove cover band and brushes.
2. Remove through bolts then the end plate retaining screws.
3. Pull out armature, brush end plate and drive housing from frame.
4. Remove terminal from frame.
5. Remove field pole retaining screws and slide field poles out of frame.
6. If field brushes are to be replaced, unsolder the field brushes and solder the new brushes onto the field coil. If ground brushes are to be replaced, remove the rivets and rivet the new brushes onto the end plate.
7. To remove the starter drive, compress the drive spring slightly, then remove the locking screw and slide the drive off the shaft.

Assembly, Fig. 75

1. Position thrust washers, center bearing and starter drive on the shaft and install the locking screw.
2. Install armature assembly into drive housing so that slot center bearing support plate engages pin in drive housing and bearing is firmly seated in housing.
3. Install field coils, pole shoes and retaining screws. As the retaining screws are being tightened, tap the frame several times with a soft-face hammer to align and seat the pole shoes.
4. Install terminal, brush end plate and the six retaining screws.
5. Slide armature and drive housing into frame with frame dowel engaging the hole in the drive housing and install the through bolts.
6. Install the brushes making sure that springs are centered on the brushes and that insulated brushes are not grounded.
7. Install cover band, oil felt and oil cap. Add several drops of oil into oil cap opening.

STARTER DRIVE SERVICE

Starter drives fall into one or the other of two basic groups, the type that uses the principle of the over-running clutch, Figs. 76 and 77, and the Bendix, which uses the spinning nut principle, Figs. 78 and 79.

Starter drive troubles are easy to diagnose and they usually cannot be confused with ordinary starter difficulties. If the starter does not turn over at all or if it drags, look for trouble in the starter or electrical supply system. Concentrate on the starter drive or ring gear if the starter is noisy, if it turns but does not engage the engine, or if the starter won't disengage after the engine is started. After the starter is removed, the trouble can usually be located with a quick inspection.

Worn or chipped ring gear or starter pinion are the usual causes of noisy operation. Before replacing either or both of these parts, try to find out what caused the damage. With the Bendix type drive incomplete engagement of the pinion with the ring gear is a common cause of tooth damage. The wrong pinion clearance on starter drives of the overrunning clutch type leads to poor meshing of the pinion and ring gear and too rapid tooth wear.

A less common cause of noise with either type of drive is a bent starter armature shaft. When this shaft is bent, the pinion gear alternately binds and then only partly meshes with the ring gear. Most manufacturers specify a maximum of .003" radial run-out on the armature shaft.

When Clutch Drive Fails

The over-running clutch type drive seldom becomes worn that they fail to engage since they are directly activated by a fork and lever, Fig. 76. The only thing that is likely to happen is that, once engaged, it will not turn the engine because the clutch itself is worn out. A much more frequent difficulty and one that rapidly wears ring gear and teeth is partial engagement. Proper meshing of the pinion is controlled by the end clearance between the pinion gear and the starter housing or the pinion stop, if one is used.

The clearance is set with the starter off the vehicle and with the drive in the engaged position. While it is not feasible to list the clearances for all starters used on all trucks, the idea is to have enough clearance so that the drive does not slam against the end of the drive housing or pinion stop when it is engaged.

To check the clearance, supply current to the starter solenoid with the electrical connection between starter and solenoid removed. Supplying current to the solenoid but not the starter will prevent the starter from rotating during the test. Take out all slack by pushing lightly on the starter drive clutch housing while inserting the proper thickness feeler gauge between pinion and housing or pinion

Fig. 76 Overrunning clutch drive. When assembling make sure curved sides of yoke shoes are toward gear end of clutch. Reversed yoke shoes can cause improper meshing of pinion.

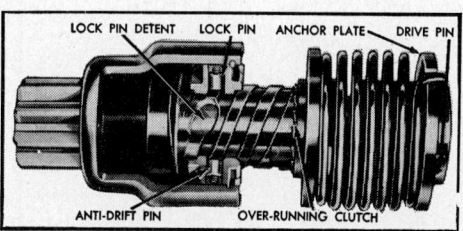

Fig. 77 Folo-Thru starter drive with Bendix spring

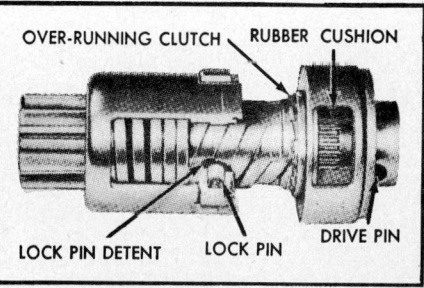

Fig. 78 Folo-Thru starter drive without Bendix spring

47

STARTING MOTORS

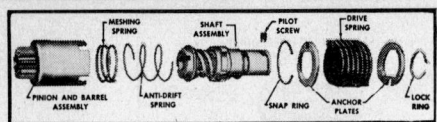

Fig. 79 Barrel type Bendix drive

stop, Fig. 80.

On a number of starters, the solenoids are completely enclosed in the starter housing and the pinion clearance is not adjustable. If the clearance is not correct, the starter must be disassembled and checked for excessive wear of solenoid linkage, shift lever mechanism, or improper assembly of parts.

On starters where the solenoid is exposed, the clearance can be adjusted either by loosening the screws holding the solenoid to the starter and moving the solenoid forward and backward, Fig. 81, or by screwing or unscrewing the link attached to the solenoid plunger, Fig. 82.

Failure of the over-running clutch drive to disengage is usually caused by binding between the armature shaft and the drive. If the drive, particularly the clutch, shows signs of overheating, it indicates that it is not disengaging immediately after the engine starts. If the clutch is forced to overrun too long, it overheats and turns a bluish color. For the cause of the binding, look for rust or gum between the armature shaft and the drive, or for burred splines. Excess oil on the drive will lead to gumming, and inadequate air circulation in the flywheel housing will cause rust.

Over-running clutch drives cannot be overhauled in the field so they must be replaced. In cleaning, never soak them in a solvent because the solvent may enter the clutch and dissolve the sealed-in lubricant. Wipe them off lightly with kerosene and lubricate them sparingly with SAE 10 or 10W oil.

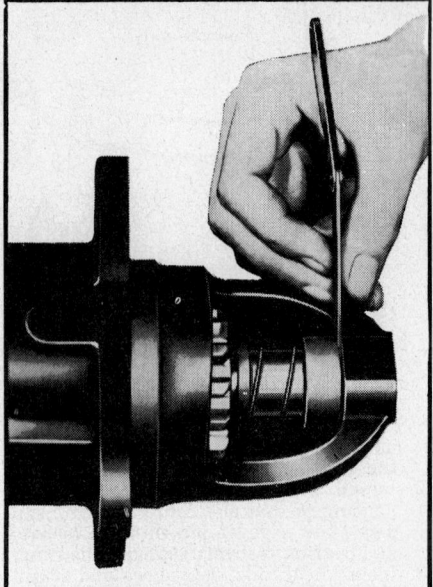

Fig. 80 Measuring overrunning clutch drive stop clearance. Do not compress anti-drift spring as this will give an incorrect clearance. If clearance is not present there is danger of the drive housing being broken as gear or collar slams back against it.

When Bendix Drive Fails

When a Bendix drive doesn't engage the cause usually is one of three things: either the drive spring is broken, one of the drive spring bolts has sheared off, or the screwshaft threads won't allow the pinion to travel to-

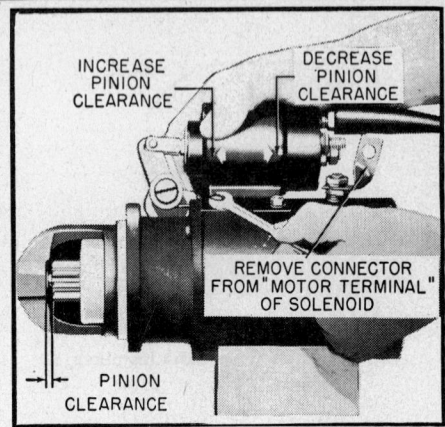

Fig. 81 Adjusting pinion clearance on overrunning clutch motor with an exposed solenoid having a non-adjustable plunger stud

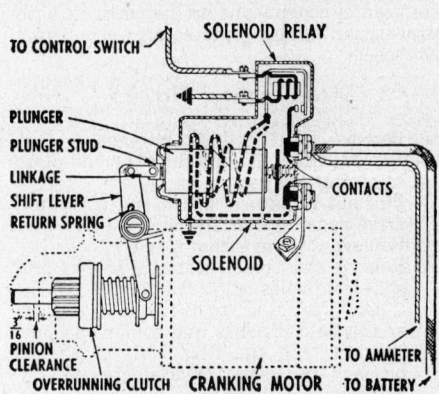

Fig. 82 Overrunning clutch motor equipped with adjustable plunger stud for adjusting pinion clearance

ward the flywheel. In the first two cases, remove the drive by unscrewing the set screw under the last coil of the drive spring and replace the broken parts. Gummed or rusty screwshaft threads are fairly common causes of Bendix drive failure and are easily cleaned with a little kerosene or steel wool, depending on the trouble. Here again, as in the cause of overrunning clutch drives, use light oil sparingly, and be sure the flywheel housing has adequate ventilation. There is usually a breather hole in the bottom of the flywheel housing which should be kept open.

The failure of a Bendix drive to disengage or to mesh properly is most often caused by gummed or rusty screwshaft threads. When this is not true, look for mechanical failure within the drive itself.

Bendix Folo-Thru Drive

This type of drive, Figs. 77, 78, is in wide use on late model starters. It incorporates a device that keeps the pinion engaged to the flywheel until the engine reaches a specified rpm. When replacing one of these drives, be sure that you have the correct drive for the vehicle. The drives are rated differently and the correct one must be used for the vehicle being serviced. The Folo-Thru, incidentally, is not supposed to be repaired in the field because of the danger of incorrectly assembling the carefully calibrated springs in the pinion head.

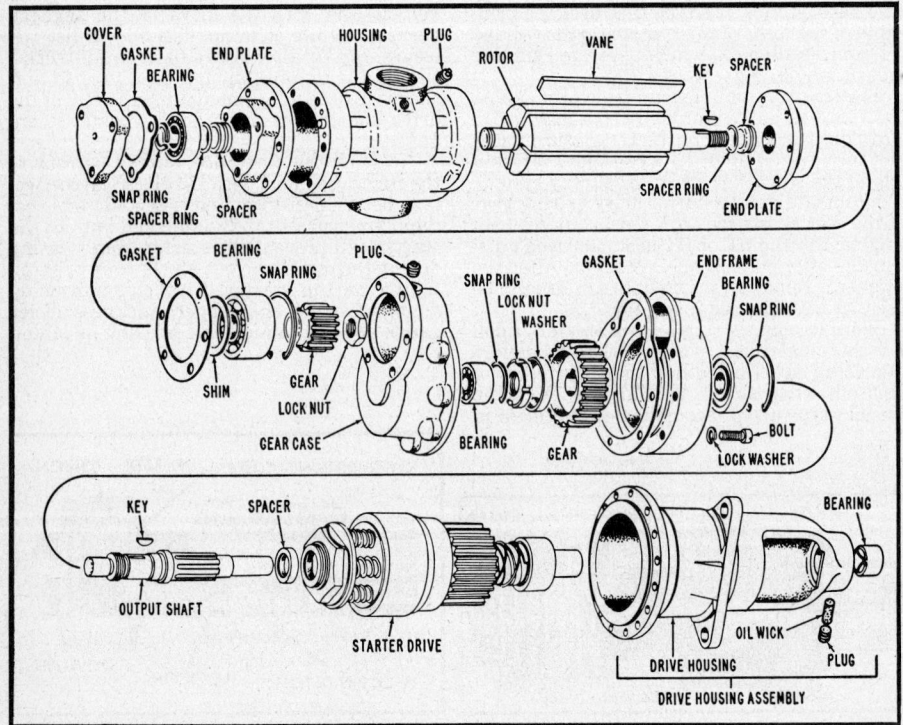

Fig. 83 "Startaire" air cranking motor

STARTING MOTORS

AIR STARTING MOTOR

The principle components of the "Startaire" assembly are a multi-vane type air rotor, a reduction gear assembly, and a friction clutch type drive. Compressed air in the correct volume and pressure range is used to provide the necessary cranking power. Fig. 83 shows an exploded view of an air cranking motor.

The motors are available in two sizes. Model 17 delivers approximately 17 horsepower at 100 psi air pressure with a pinion rpm of 2300. In general, model 17 cranks all engines up to approximately 1100 cubic inch displacement. Model 30 delivers approximately 30 horsepower at 100 psi air pressure with a pinion rpm of 2000. It is normally used on engines of 1100 cubic inch displacement or more.

Fig. 84 shows the various devices used in a "Startaire" installation. A pressure protection valve is used in the air supply line to protect the basic air system on the vehicle against complete loss of air during starting operation. A rubber seated single check valve permits maintenance of the Startaire system as a self-contained system in which leakage can be minimized. A control valve and air pressure gauge registering air pressures in the starting system are installed close to the driver's position. An air starting valve which opens or closes the air line between the starter reservoir and motor, as controlled by the control valve, is mounted on or close to the motor as possible. The motor is installed on the engine in the usual location provided for starting motors. One or two reservoirs are installed in the system to provide a sufficient volume of compressed air to the system. A tire valve, tire chuck and hose coupling are provided to replenish the system from an outside source should it be required.

Operation

For operation, 100 psi or more should register on the air starter system air gauge. Before starting the engine, be sure that all engine adjustments and prior starting procedures are carried out. Depress the knob on the control valve. This action allows air to turn the motor and engage the flywheel. The control valve knob should be kept fully depressed until the engine fires. Release the control valve immediately when the engine fires to allow the drive gear to disengage the flywheel.

Preventive Maintenance

1. Daily or as often as necessary, drain the reservoir to be sure clean dry air is delivered to the motor.
2. Monthly or about every 5000 miles of service, remove pipe plug or grease fitting at air inlet port or air inlet fitting at the motor and inject ½ pint of kerosene into the rotor assembly before operating the motor.

CAUTION: *Do not over-lubricate. Over-lubrication or use of lubricants of heavy consistency can cause improper operation. Do not perform the above flushing operation indoors as the kerosene will be discharged at the exhaust outlet with the first start. Also be certain that there is no open flame in the vicinity to ignite the exhaust*

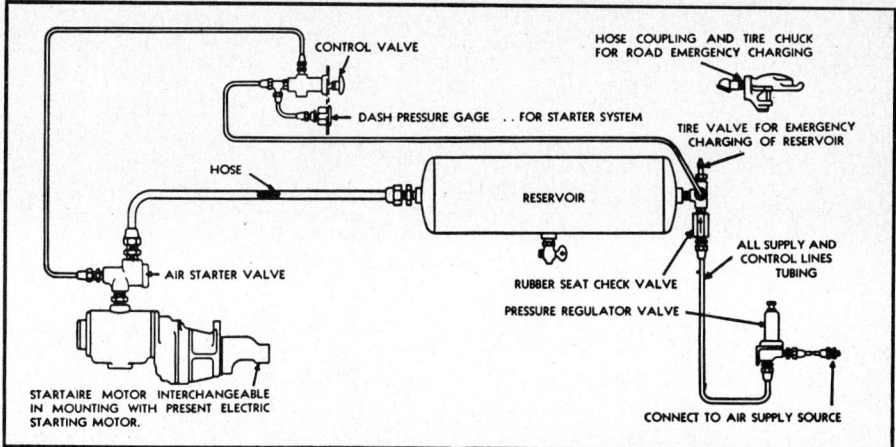

Fig. 84 Typical air starter installation

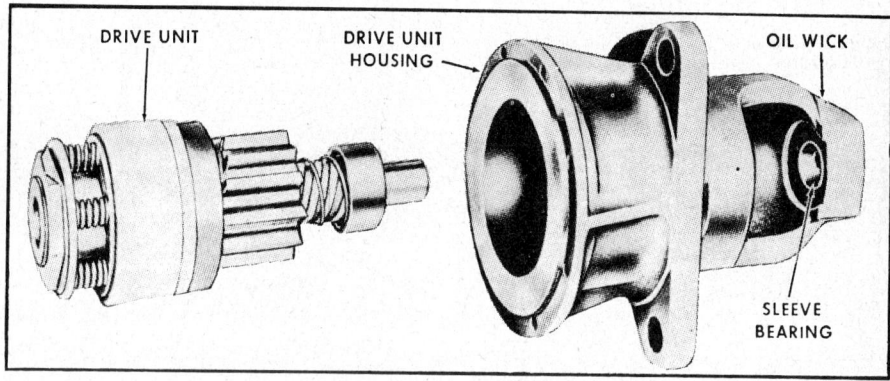

Fig. 85 Drive end and housing. Model 17

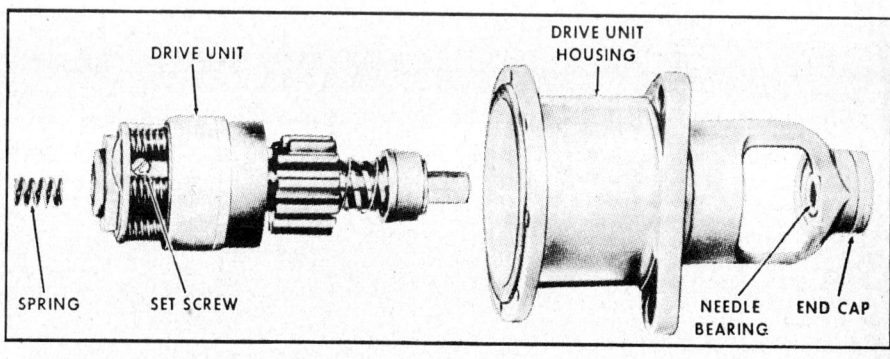

Fig. 86 Drive end and housing. Model 30

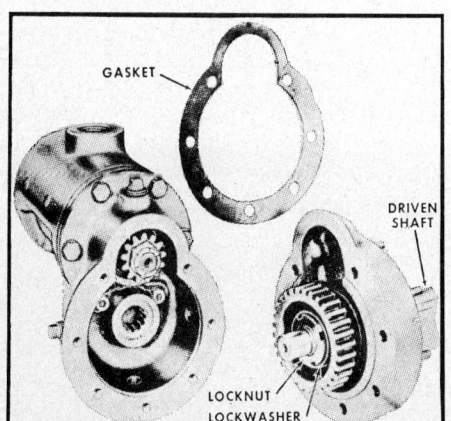

Fig. 87 Cover, shaft and gear. Model 17

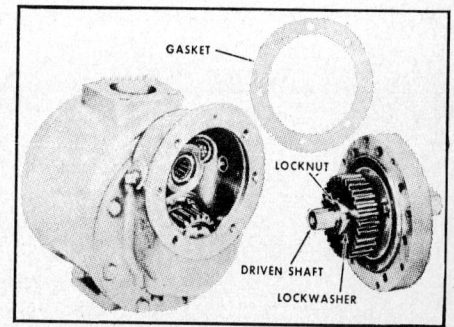

Fig. 88 Cover, shaft and gear. Model 30

STARTING MOTORS

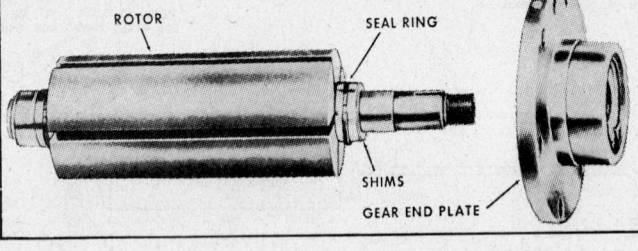

Fig. 89 Rotor and gear end plate. Model 17

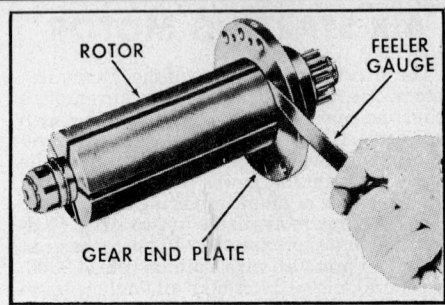

Fig. 90 Checking clearance between rotor and end plate. Model 17

kerosene.

3. Check to see that the motor mounting is secure to the flywheel housing. Check all air lines and valves in the system for leakage.
4. Test the operation of the motor. The unit should turn over the engine quickly and at high revolutions per minute. Be sure that air pressure and volume are correct for motor requirements in making this test.
5. To make a leakage test, first see that the system is fully charged and the control valve is in fully released position. Then check to be sure there is no measurable leakage at the exhaust port of motor, at control valve knob, at tire valve, or at other possible leakage points in the system.
6. Periodically check all other devices, fittings and air lines to be sure they are tight.

Remove & Install Motor

1. Disconnect air line at control valve on Model 17 or air line at motor on Model 30.
2. On Model 17, remove motor control valve.
3. Unfasten motor housing from flywheel housing and lift out motor.
4. Reverse removal procedure to install.

Disassemble Motor

1. After covering inlet and exhaust ports, clean the exterior of the motor.
2. The original position of the mating parts should be marked. *This is important because if the rotor housing is turned end for end when reassembled, the motor will rotate in the opposite direction, the pinion will not engage and the motor could rotate at dangerous speeds.*
3. Remove drive unit housing.
4. Remove drive unit by pulling off splines of driven shaft, Fig. 85. If necessary to replace sleeve bearing in drive housing, remove oil wick and press out bearing.
5. When disassembling Model 30, remove set screw in clutch to permit removal of drive unit from driven shaft, Fig. 86. This unit contains a spring at the end of the driven shaft. In Model 30, if it is necessary to replace the needle bearing in drive housing, drive off end cap and press out bearing.
6. Remove spacer from driven shaft on Model 17.
7. Remove capscrews from cover and remove cover, driven shaft and gear, Figs. 87 and 88.
8. Release lockwasher on driven gear and remove lock nut. Use puller to remove gear from driven shaft.
9. For Model 17, remove key and press driven shaft out of bearing. Remove snap ring and press bearing from gear case cover.
10. For Model 30, remove capscrews from bearing retainer plate and press bearing and shaft from cover after which press bearing from driven shaft.
11. Remove capscrews securing gear case to main housing, including the two capscrews inside the case.
12. Before removing gear case on Model 17, remove lock wire inside case. Then remove gear.
13. Remove snap ring from roller bearing and press out bearing which is a sliding fit in case.

Removing Model 17 Rotor

1. Remove gear end plate and rotor from housing. Dowels in main case position end plate correctly.
2. When removing rotor from main housing, inner race of roller bearing remains on rotor shaft. Do not remove it unless bearing is to be replaced.
3. Remove rotor vanes to protect them from damage.
4. Remove lock nut and take off drive gear from rotor shaft with the aid of a gear puller.
5. Remove key from rotor shaft and press

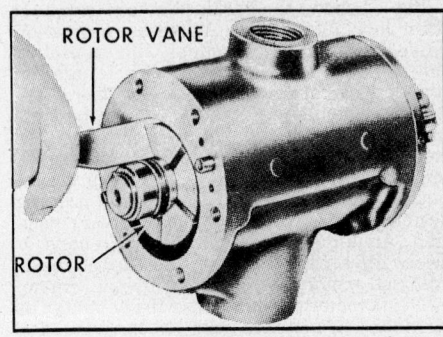

Fig. 91 Installing vanes. Model 17

rotor from bearing and gear end plate, using an arbor press.
6. Rotor and shaft are serviced as a unit. *A spacer is pressed on each rotor shaft. Do not remove spacer unless replacement is required. If rotor is to be reassembled using the same parts, the shims located between the spacer on the gear end of the rotor shaft and bearing inner race can be reused if not damaged.* Remove snap ring in gear end plate. Bearing is a light press fit in plate.
7. Remove plain end plate cover.
8. Remove plain end plate from housing and press out bearing.

Removing Model 30 Rotor

1. After removing drive gear from rotor shaft with a gear puller, remove gear end plate and bearing from rotor shaft. There are dowels on end plate for positioning

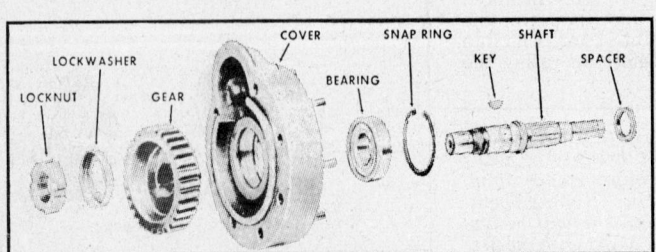

Fig. 92 Cover, driven shaft and gear parts. Model 17

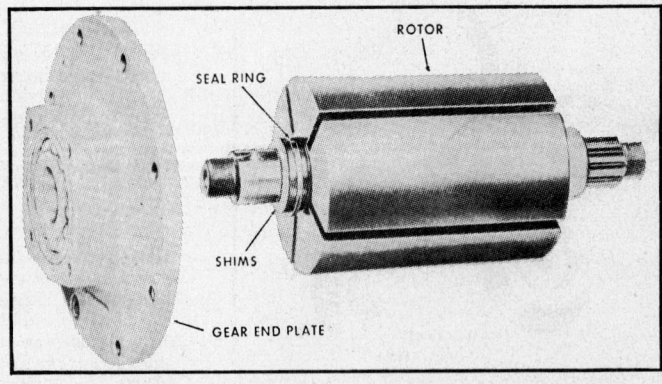

Fig. 93 Rotor and gear end plate. Model 30

STARTING MOTORS

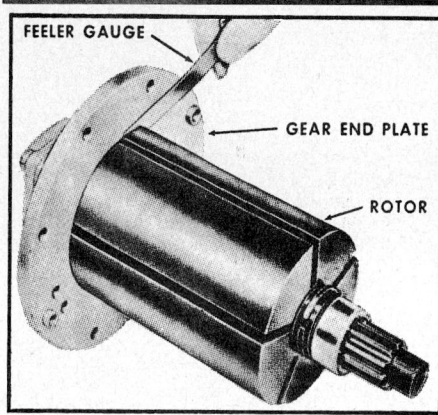

Fig. 94 Checking clearance between rotor and end plate. Model 30

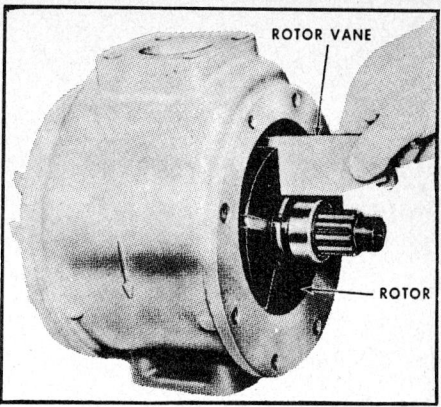

Fig. 95 Installing vanes. Model 30

plate correctly.
2. Remove snap ring holding roller bearing in gear end plate. Bearing is a light press fit in plate and can easily be removed.
3. Bearing inner race normally remains on shaft. Do not remove it unless a new bearing is required.
4. Remove plain end plate cover.
5. Remove end plate from main housing and lift end plate and rotor as a unit out of case.
6. Remove rotor vanes to protect them from damage. Release lockwasher and remove lock nut. Carefully press rotor from end plate or use a gear puller to remove end plate from rotor. Bearing is a light press fit in end plate. *Do not misplace or damage shims between rotor shaft shoulder and bearing inner race because the same shims can be used again for reassembly if the same parts are to be reused. The rotor and shaft are serviced as a unit only.*

Inspection of Parts

1. Clean and inspect all parts. Any broken or excessively worn parts must be replaced with new ones.
2. Inspect rotor, housing and end plates for cracks, abrasions, wear spots or build-up of foreign material. Cracked castings must be replaced. Rough or worn spots can sometimes be smoothed out with fine emery cloth. Deposits of gum, carbon, or other foreign material must be removed. Wash and dry all parts.
3. Rotor vanes should be inspected for cracks and wear and should normally be replaced.
4. Gears should be replaced if excessively worn or if teeth are broken.
5. For Model 30 the gear splines should be a light press fit on shaft splines. If fit is loose, replace parts.
6. Broken seal rings must be replaced.
7. Seal ring bores in end plates should be checked for excessive wear or roughness.
8. Seal ring grooves should be checked for visible wear.
9. Bearings should be checked for visible wear and replaced if necessary.
10. New gaskets should be used when reassembling.

Reassemble Model 17 Rotor

1. Install spacers and seal rings on rotor shaft. Press roller bearing on rotor shaft and install snap ring. Press bearing into gear end plate and replace bearing lock wire.
2. Place shims on gear end of rotor shaft. If same parts are being reused, use same shims if undamaged, as originally removed. If new parts are being used, use .015" of shims for initial installation, subject to adjustment as given below.
3. Press bearing and gear end plate on rotor shaft, Fig. 89. Install key, drive gear and locknut on rotor shaft.
4. Check clearance between rotor and gear end plate. Clearance should be .002 to .003", Fig. 90. Shims of .002, .003 and .005" are available for adjustment.
5. After obtaining proper clearance, install rotor and gear end plate in main housing.
6. Install valves in rotor through open end of housing, Fig. 91. Install bearing in plain end plate and apply end plate to main housing, using care to avoid breaking seal ring.
7. Install capscrews and, using a new gasket, fill cover half full of ball and roller bearing grease and install cover.
8. Install bearing and snap ring in gear case. Use a new gasket and install gear case. After installing capscrews, insert lock wire.
9. Press bearing on driven shaft with its seal facing spline end of shaft. Install key, driven gear, lockwasher and lock nut.
10. Install driven shaft, bearing and gear assembly in cover and install snap ring, Fig. 92. Before assembling cover to gear case, place about 6 ounces of general purpose grease in gear case. Use a new gasket and install cover, shaft and gear in case.
11. Install spacer over driven shaft and install drive unit on shaft.
12. If the sleeve bearing in end of drive unit has been removed, press new bearing into housing flush with end face and finish inside diameter to .751-.752" concentric with drive housing pilot diameter. If finishing tools are not available and bearing is worn, replace drive housing assembly.
13. Install oil wick after soaking it in SAE No. 10 engine oil. Install drive unit to gear case cover.

Reassemble Model 30 Rotor

1. Install bearing in plain end plate, and seal rings on rotor shaft.
2. Install bearing on rotor shaft.
3. Install spacer shims on plain end rotor shaft, Fig. 93. If new parts are being used, start with about .009" shim thickness for initial installation subject to adjustment as given below.
4. Press bearing and plain end plate over rotor shaft, using care to avoid breaking seal ring. Install lockwasher and lock nut. Do not flatten lockwasher until .003" end clearance between rotor and plain end plate is obtained.
5. Install new gasket between small cover and end plate and install cover temporarily. Check clearance as shown in Fig. 94. Adjust as necessary to obtain .003" clearance between rotor shaft shoulder and bearing inner race. Shims of .002, .003 and .005" thicknesses are available for adjustment.
6. After clearance is obtained, remove small cover and fill it half full with bearing grease and reinstall cover.
7. Install rotor and plain end plate on main housing. Install rotor vanes through open gear end of housing, Fig. 95. Press bearing into gear end plate and install snap ring.
8. Install gear end plate to main housing, using care to avoid breaking seal ring.
9. Install gear on rotor shaft. Install new lockwasher and pull gear into position and install lock nut.
10. Press roller bearing in gear, install washer and snap ring, Fig. 96.
11. Using new gasket between end plate and gear case, install gear case.
12. Press bearing on driven shaft with its seal facing drive unit. Install bearing and shaft in cover, and bearing retainer plate, Fig. 96.
13. Press driven gear over splined end of shaft and install lockwasher and lock nut.
14. Place about 8 ounces of general purpose grease in gear case and install case. Using a new gasket, install cover and gear sub-assembly to gear case.
15. Install two keys and drive unit on driven shaft after installing spring between end of driven shaft and drive unit. Install and tighten set screw in drive unit. Install needle bearing in housing flush with drive face. Fill end cap half full with bearing grease before pressing into place.

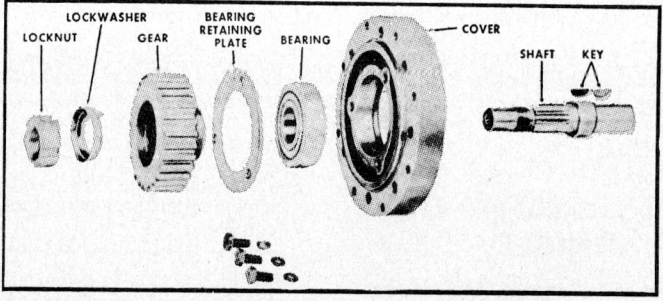

Fig. 96 Cover, driven shaft and gear parts. Model 30

ALTERNATORS

INDEX

	Page No.
Introduction	52
Service Precautions	52
Chrysler System	52
Delco-Remy Systems	64
Ford Systems	104
Leece-Neville Systems	127
Motorola Systems	119
Prestolite System	124

INTRODUCTION

Alternators under discussion here are of the modern type with built-in silicon diode rectifiers. Under normal operating conditions, these alternators have a rating of 30 to 150 amperes, depending upon the requirements of the vehicle, and usually deliver 5 to 10 amperes at curb idle speed.

Alternators are composed of the same functional parts as the conventional D.C. generator but they operate differently. The field is called a rotor and is the turning portion of the unit. A generating part, called a stator, is the stationary member, comparable to the armature in a D.C. generator. The regulator, similar to those used in a D.C. system, regulates the output of the alternator-rectifier system.

The power source of the system is the alternator. Current is transmitted from the field terminal of the regulator through a slip ring to the field coil and back to the ground through another slip ring. The strength of the field regulates the output of the alternating current. This alternating current is then transmitted from the alternator to the rectifier where it is converted to direct current.

These alternators employ a three-phase stator winding in which the phase windings are electrically 120 degrees apart. The rotor consists of a field coil encased between interleaved sections producing a magnetic field with alternate north and south poles. By rotating the rotor inside the stator, the alternating current is induced in the stator windings. This alternating current is rectified (changed to D.C.) by silicon diode rectifiers and brought out to the output terminal of the alternator.

Diode Rectifiers

Six silicon diode rectifiers are used and act as electrical one-way valves. Three of the diodes have ground polarity and are pressed or screwed into a heat sink which is grounded. The other three diodes (ungrounded) are pressed or screwed into and insulated from the end head; these diodes are connected to the alternator output terminal.

Since the diodes have a high resistance to the flow of current in one direction and a low resistance in the opposite direction, they may be connected in a manner that allows current to flow from the alternator to the battery in the low resistance direction. The high resistance in the opposite direction prevents the flow of current from the battery to the alternator. Because of this feature no circuit breaker is required between alternator and battery.

SERVICE PRECAUTIONS

1. Be certain that the battery polarity of the system is known so that the battery is connected to the proper ground. *Reversed battery polarity will damage rectifiers and regulator.*
2. If a booster battery is used for starting the vehicle, it must be connected to the vehicle battery properly to prevent damage to rectifiers and regulator. Negative cable from booster battery to negative terminal on vehicle battery, and positive booster cable to positive terminal.
3. When a fast charger is used to charge a vehicle battery, the vehicle battery cables should be disconnected *unless the charger is equipped with a special Alternator Protector,* in which case the vehicle battery cables need not be disconnected. Also the fast charger should never be used to start an engine as damage to rectifiers will result.
4. Lead connections to grounded rectifiers on Auto-Lite and Chrysler units should never be soldered as the excessive heat may damage the rectifiers.
5. Unless the system includes a load relay or field relay, grounding the alternator output terminal will damage the alternator and/or circuits. This is true even when the dystem is not in operation since no circuit breaker is used and the battery is applied to the alternator output terminal at all times. The field or load relay acts as a circuit breaker in that it is controlled by the ignition switch.
6. When adjusting the voltage regulator, do not short the adjusting tool to the regulator base as the regulator may be damaged. The tool should be insulated by taping or by installing a plastic sleeve.
7. Before making any "on vehicle" tests of alternator or regulator, the battery should be checked and the circuit inspected for faulty wiring or insulation, loose or corroded connections and poor ground circuits.
8. Check alternator belt tension to be sure belt is tight enough to prevent slipping under load.
9. The ignition switch should be off and the battery ground cable disconnected before making any test connections to prevent damage to the system.
10. The vehicle battery must be fully charged or a fully charged battery may be installed for test purposes.

Chrysler Alternators

Two types of alternators are used on Chrysler Corp. trucks, one has an external capacitor and is used with an electro-mechanical voltage regulator only, Figs. C2 and C3, and the isolated field unit using an electro-mechanical or electronic voltage regulator, Figs. C4 through C10.

The main components of the alternator are the rotor, stator, diodes, end shield and drive pulley. Direct current is available at the output "BAT" terminal. The function of the voltage regulator is to limit output voltage. This is accomplished by controlling the current flow in the rotor field coil, in turn controlling the strength of the rotor magnetic field. The electronic voltage regulator is a sealed, non-adjustable unit.

TESTING SYSTEM ON VEHICLE

W/Electro-Mechanical Regulator

FIELD CIRCUIT RESISTANCE TEST
1. Referring to Fig. C11, disconnect ignition wire at coil side of ballast resistor and connect a test ammeter and voltmeter in the circuit as shown. All lights and accessories should be turned off.
2. Turn ignition switch on and turn voltmeter selector switch to the low voltage scale and read the meter. The voltage should not exceed .55 volt. A reading in excess of .55 volt indicates high resistance in field circuit between battery and voltage regulator field terminal.
3. If high resistance is indicated, move negative voltmeter lead to each connection along the circuit to the battery. A sudden drop in voltage indicates a loose or corroded connection between that point and the last point tested. To test the terminals for tightness, attempt to move the terminal while observing the voltmeter. Any movement of the meter pointer indicates looseness.

NOTE: *Excessive resistance in the regulator wiring circuit will cause fluctuation in the ammeter.*

4. Turn ignition switch off, disconnect test instrument and reconnect ignition primary wire at the coil side of the ballast resistor.

CHARGING CIRCUIT RESISTANCE TEST

With battery in good condition and fully charged, first disconnect the battery ground cable to avoid accidental shorting of the charging or field circuit when making the test connections shown in Fig. C12.
1. With the test instruments connected as shown and with battery ground cable reconnected, start and operate engine at a speed to obtain 10 amperes flowing in the circuit.
2. The voltmeter should not exceed .3 volt. If a higher voltage drop is indicated, inspect, clean and tighten all connections in the charging circuit. A voltage drop test may be performed at each connection to locate the connection with excessive resistance.
3. Turn ignition switch off. Disconnect ground cable at battery to avoid acciden-

CHRYSLER ALTERNATORS

tal shorting of the charging or field circuit when disconnecting the test instruments. Connect battery lead to alternator "BAT" terminal and tighten securely. Connect ignition lead to regulator ignition terminal and reconnect ground cable at battery.

CURRENT OUTPUT TEST
1. With test instruments connected in circuit as shown in Fig. C13, connect an engine tachometer.
2. Start and operate engine at 1250 rpm.
3. Adjust carbon pile rheostat to obtain a reading of 15 volts on the test voltmeter.
4. Observe reading on test ammeter.
5. If the output is slightly less (5 to 7 amperes) than the rated output of the alternator, it may be an indication of an open-circuited diode or other internal alternator problem.
6. If the output is considerably lower than the rated output of the alternator, it may be an indication of a short-circuited diode or other internal alternator problem. In either case the alternator should be removed and tested.

NOTE: *Turn off the carbon pile rheostat immediately after observing reading on test ammeter.*

7. If the alternator current output tested satisfactorily, turn off the ignition switch and remove the jumper lead from the alternator field terminal and output terminal.

VOLTAGE REGULATOR TEST
Upper Contact Test
1. With engine at normal operating temperature and test instruments connected as shown in Fig. C14, start and operate the engine at 1250 rpm. Adjust carbon pile to obtain a 15 ampere output as indicated on the test ammeter.

NOTE: *No current reading on the ammeter would indicate either a low regulator setting or a blown fuse wire inside the voltage regulator between upper stationary contact and "IGN" terminal. Correct the cause and replace the fusible wire.*

2. Operate engine at 1250 rpm and a 15

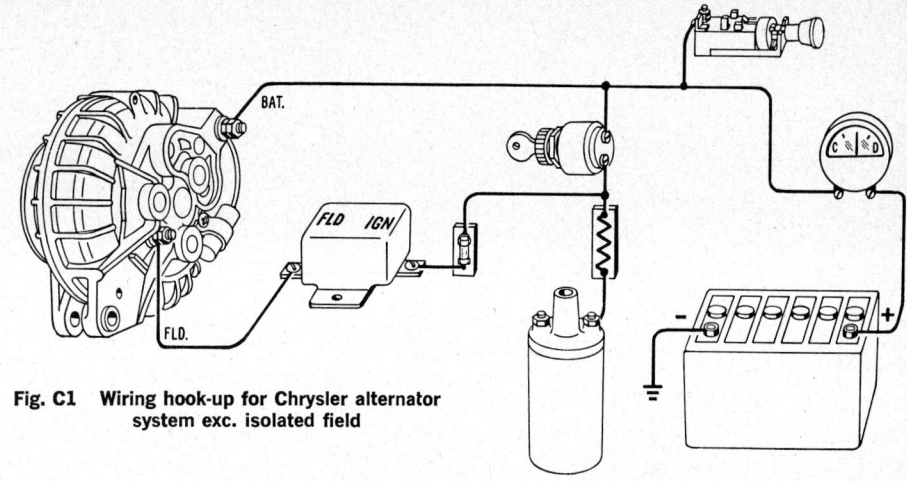

Fig. C1 Wiring hook-up for Chrysler alternator system exc. isolated field

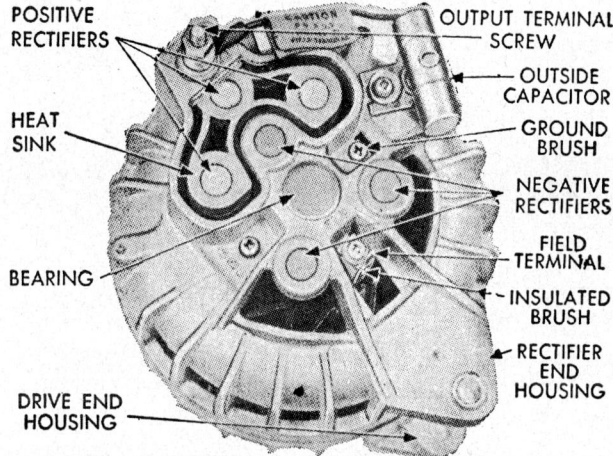

Fig. C2 Chrysler alternator with external capacitor

ampere load for 15 minutes to make sure entire regulator system is stabilized.

3. Measure temperature at regulator by holding a reliable thermometer ¼ inch from regulator cover.
4. Read test ammeter. With fully charged battery and 15 amperes flowing in circuit, voltmeter readings should be within specifications.
5. If regulator operates within specifications, proceed to the lower contact voltage test. If not, remove cover and adjust voltage setting as outlined under "Regulator Adjustments".

Lower Contact Voltage Test
1. Increase engine speed to 2200 rpm. Vary

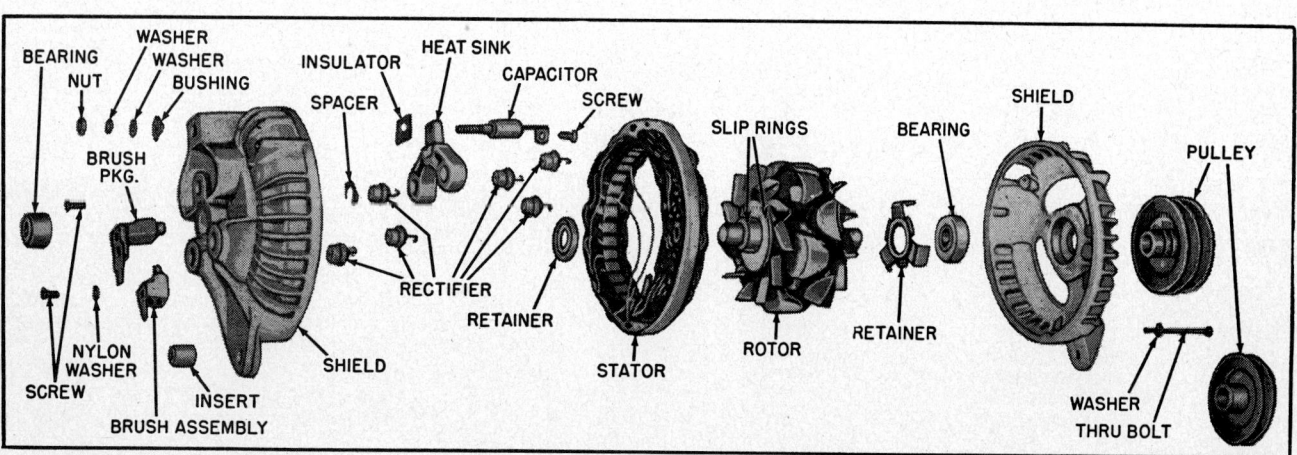

Fig. C4 Isolated field alternator disassembled. 1970–71

CHRYSLER ALTERNATORS

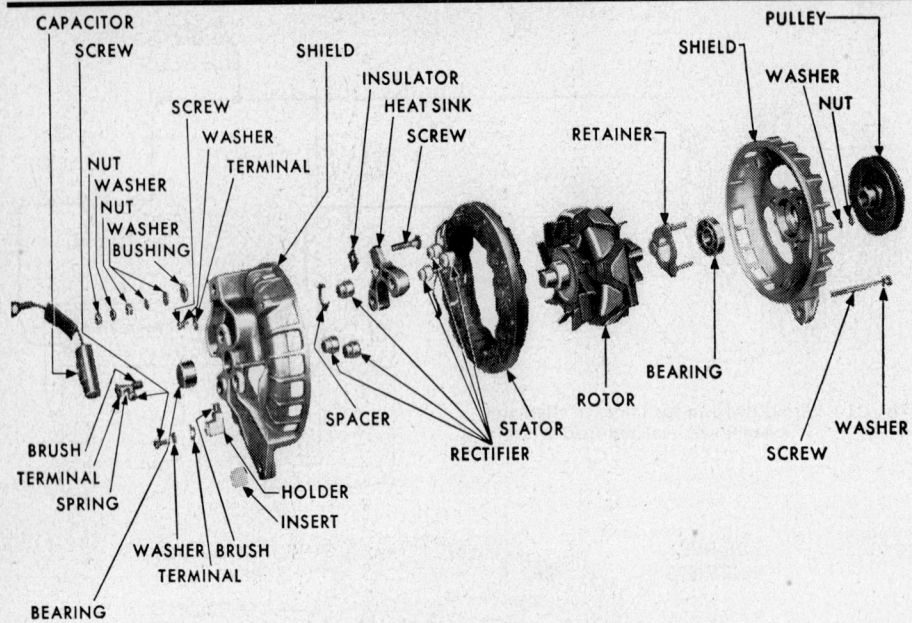

Fig. C3 Disassembled view of alternator with external capacitor

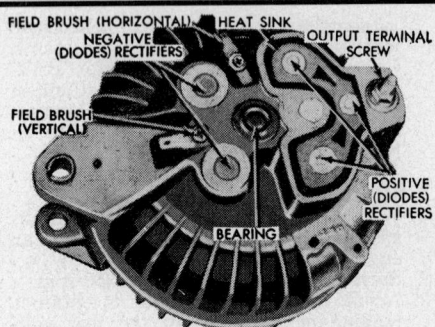

Fig. C5 Isolated field alternator. 1970-71

carbon pile to decrease current load to 7 amperes output as registered on test ammeter. The voltage should *increase* and amperage should *decrease*.

NOTE: *There will be a slightly higher voltage at higher engine speeds above 2200 rpm. However, this increased voltage must not exceed the voltage specified by more than .7 volt at any temperature range.*

2. If the regulator setting is outside the specified limits, the regulator must be removed to remove the cover.
3. To adjust the voltage setting, bend the regulator lower spring hanger *down to increase voltage*, or *up to decrease* voltage setting, Fig. C15. The regulator must be installed, correctly connected, and re-tested after each adjustment of the lower spring hanger.

NOTE: *If repeated readjustment is required, it is permissible to use a jumper wire to ground the regulator base to the fender splash shield for testing instead of reinstalling the regulator each time. However, it is important that the cover be reinstalled, the regulator connections correctly connected, and the regulator insulated to prevent grounding the regulator terminals or resistances. When testing, the regulator must be at the same attitude (or angle) as when installed on the vehicle.*

4. If the alternator and regulator tested satisfactorily, turn the ignition switch off. Disconnect battery ground cable, then the test instruments. Connect the leads to alternator and regulator. Finally reconnect battery ground cable.

REGULATOR ADJUSTMENTS

If the regulator cannot be adjusted for voltage control, or if the regulator performance is erratic or malfunctions, it may be necessary to adjust the air gap and contact point gap.

1. Remove regulator from vehicle and take off cover.
2. Insert a .048" wire gauge between regulator armature and core, next to stop pin on spring hanger side, Fig. C16.
3. Press down on armature (not contact spring) until it contacts wire gauge. Upper contacts should just open.

NOTE: *A battery and test light connected in series to the "IGN" and "FLD" terminals may be used to determine accurately the contact opening. When the contacts open, the test light will go dim.*

4. Insert a .052" wire gauge between armature and core, next to stop pin on spring hanger side.
5. Press down on armature until it contacts wire gauge. The contacts should remain closed and test light should remain bright.
6. If adjustment is required, adjust air gap by loosening the screw and moving the stationary contact bracket. Make sure air gap is measured with attaching screw fully tightened. Remeasure the gap as directed above.
7. Remove wire gauge. Measure lower contact gap with feeler gauge, which should be .012 to .016". Adjust lower contact gap by bending lower stationary contact bracket.
8. Install regulator cover and then the regulator. Finally, make electrical adjustments as outlined above.

W/Electronic Voltage Regulator

CHARGING CIRCUIT RESISTANCE TEST
1. Disconnect battery ground cable. Disconnect "Batt" lead at the alternator.
2. Complete test connections as per Fig. C17.
3. Connect battery ground cable, start engine and operate at idle.
4. Adjust engine speed and carbon pile to obtain 20 amps in the circuit and check voltmeter reading. Reading should not exceed .7 volts. If a voltage drop is indicated, inspect, clean and tighten all connections in the circuit. A voltage drop test at each connection can be performed to isolate the trouble.

CURRENT OUTPUT TEST
1. Disconnect battery ground cable, complete test connections as per Fig. C18 and start engine and operate at idle. *Immediately after starting, reduce engine speed to*

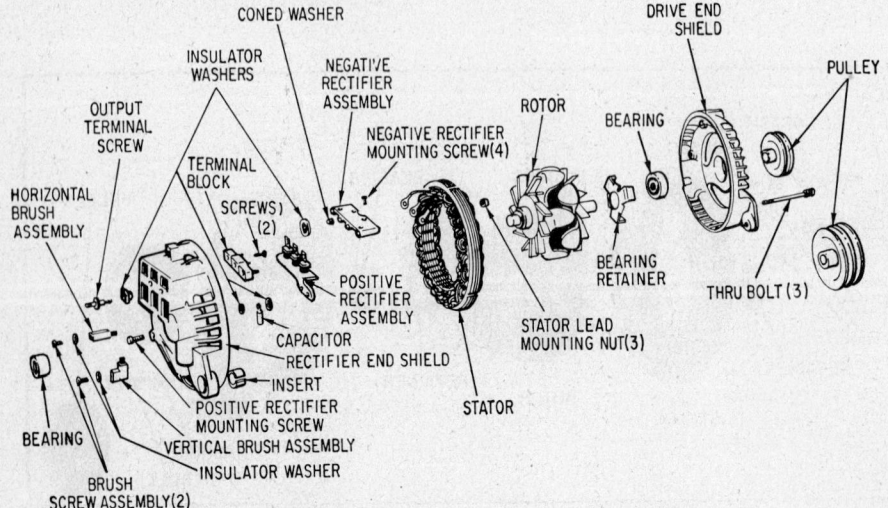

Fig. C6 Isolated field alternator disassembled. 1972-77 (Typical)

CHRYSLER ALTERNATORS

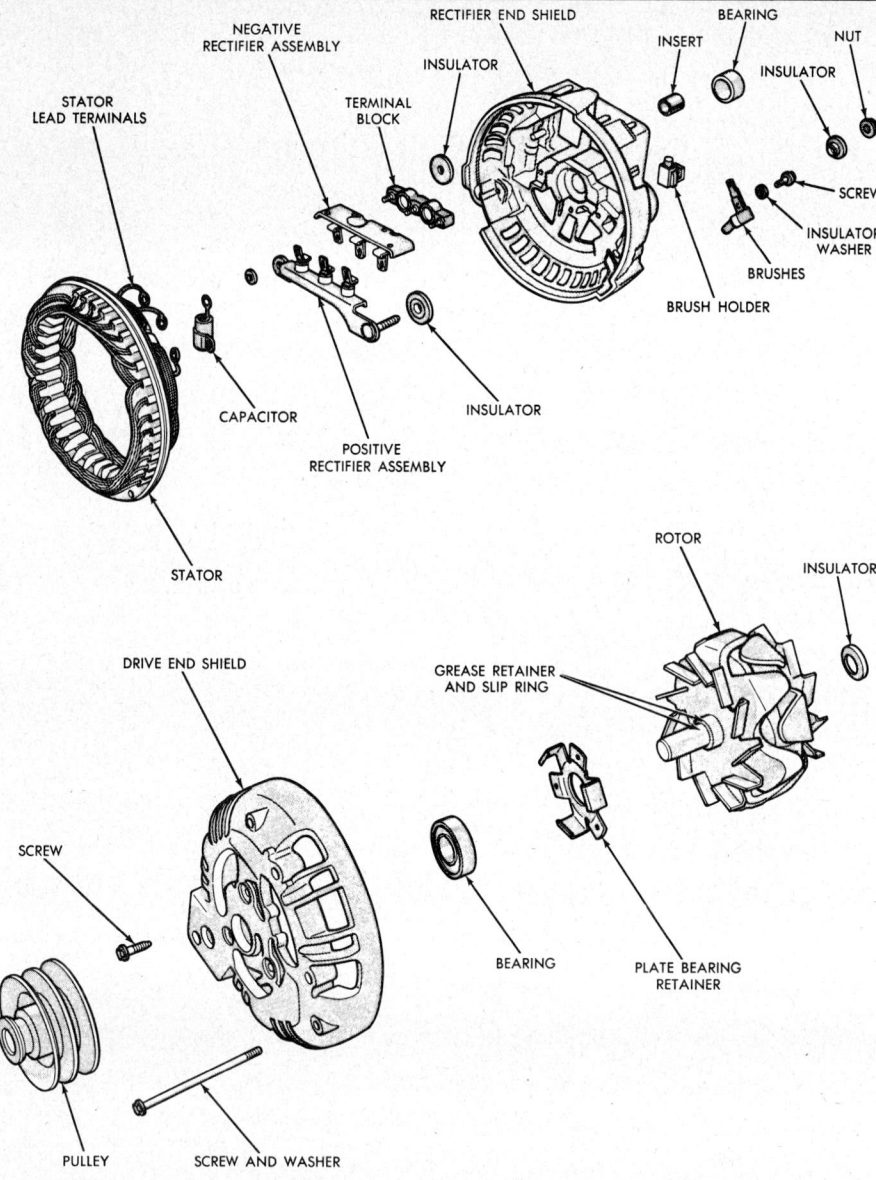

Fig. C7 Isolated field alternator disassembled. 1978–80

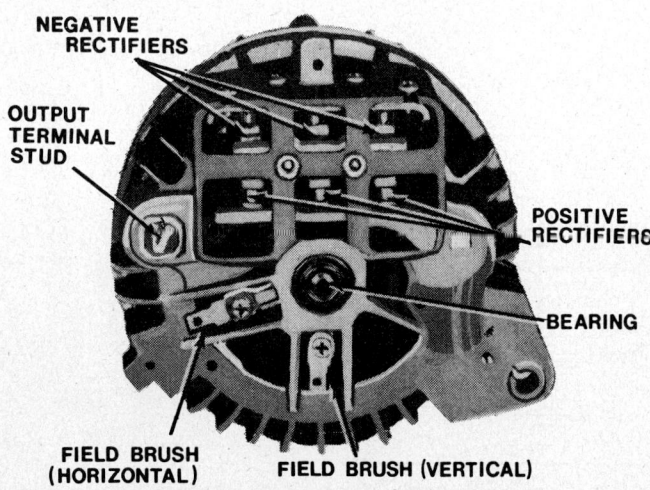

Fig. C8 Isolated field alternator. 1972–80

idle.

2. Adjust the carbon pile and engine speed in increments until a speed of 1250 rpm and 15 volts on all except 100 and 117 amp units. On 100 and 117 amp units, adjust carbon pile and engine speed in increments until a speed 900 rpm and 13 volts is obtained.

CAUTION: While increasing speed, do not allow voltage to exceed 16 volts.

3. Check ammeter reading. Output current should be within specifications.

VOLTAGE REGULATOR TEST

NOTE: Battery must be fully charged for test to be accurate.

1. Complete test connections as per Fig. C19.
2. Start and operate engine at 1250 rpm with all lights and accessories turned off. Voltage should be 13.9–14.6 if temperature at the regulator is 80 degrees F. and 13.3–14.0 at 140 degrees F.
3. It is normal for the car ammeter to show an immediate charge then gradually return to normal position.
4. If voltage is below limits, check for good voltage regulator ground, and voltage drop between regulator cover and body on low voltage scale of voltmeter.
5. Turn off ignition switch and disconnect regulator connector.
6. Turn on ignition switch but do not start engine. Check for battery voltage at the wiring harness terminal connected to the blue and green leads.

NOTE: Disconnect wiring harness from regulator when checking the leads.

7. Turn off ignition switch. If voltage is not present at either lead, the problem is in the vehicle wiring or alternator field circuit. *Use care to avoid bending the terminals with voltmeter probe.*
8. If Steps 4–7 tested satisfactorily, change voltage regulator and repeat Step 2. If voltage is slightly above limits, or is fluctuating, proceed as follows:
9. Check voltage regulator ground, check ground between vehicle body and engine.
10. Check ignition switch circuit between battery terminal of ignition switch and voltage regulator. If voltage is more than $\frac{1}{2}$ volt above limits, replace the regulator.

BENCH TESTS

If the alternator performance does not meet current output specification limits, it will have to be removed and disassembled for further tests and servicing.

To remove the alternator, disconnect the battery ground cable and the leads at the alternator. Then unfasten and remove the alternator from the vehicle.

Field Coil Draw

Exc. Isolated Field Alternator
1. Connect a test ammeter positive lead to the battery positive terminal of a fully charged battery.
2. Connect ammeter negative lead to the field terminal of the alternator.

CHRYSLER ALTERNATORS

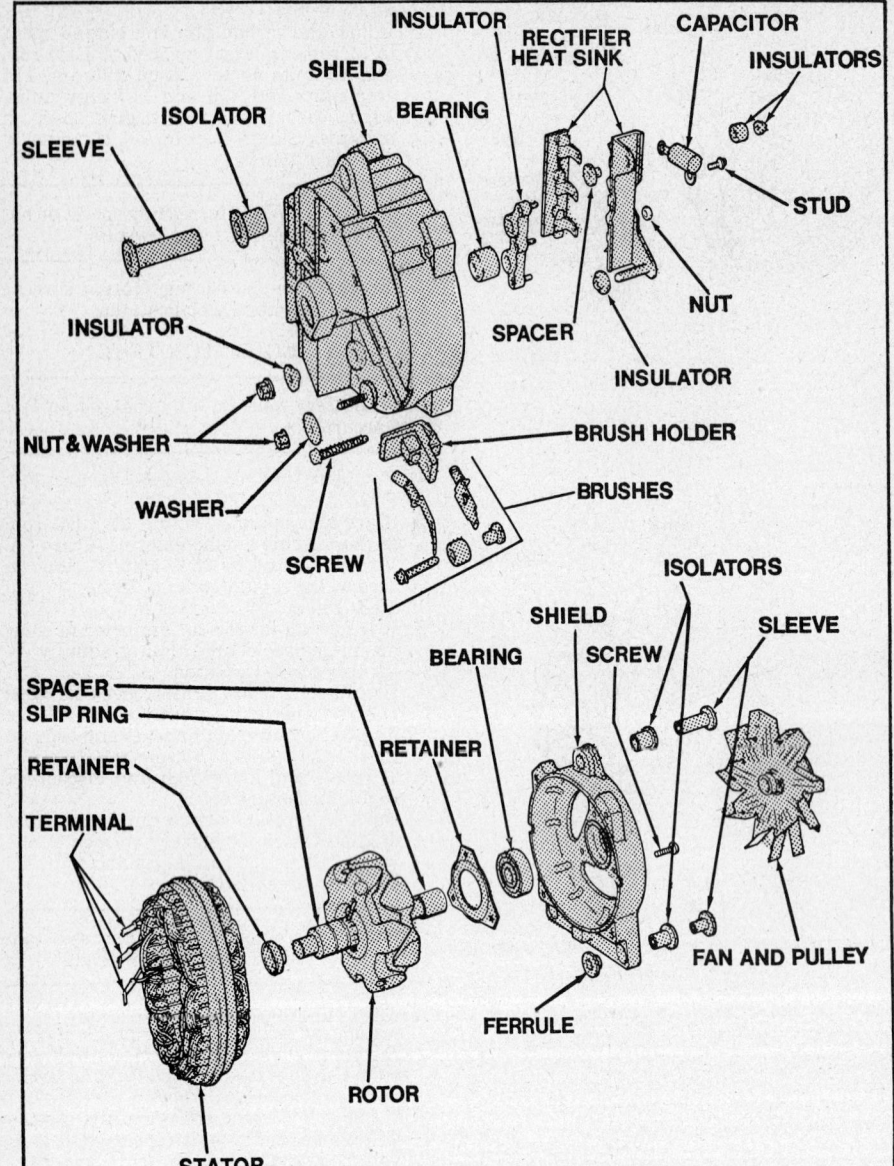

Fig. C9 100 & 117 amp alternator disassembled

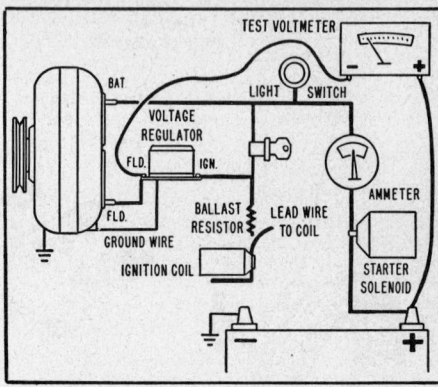

Fig. C11 Field circuit resistance test. With electro-mechanical regulator

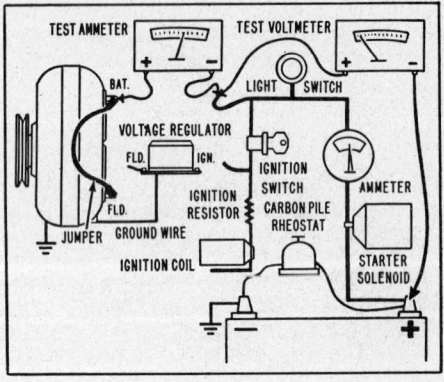

Fig. C12 Charging circuit resistance test. With electro-mechanical regulator

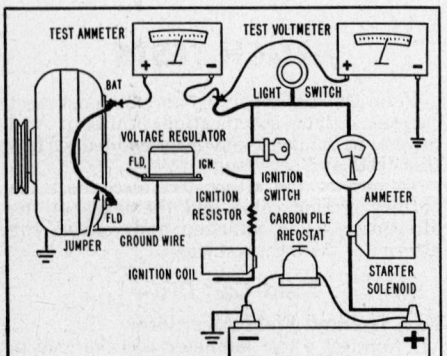

Fig. C13 Current output test. With electro-mechanical regulator

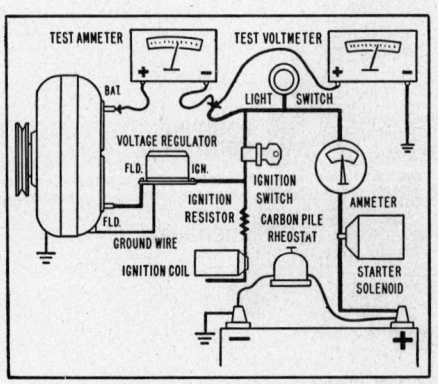

Fig. C14 Voltage regulator test. With electro-mechanical regulator

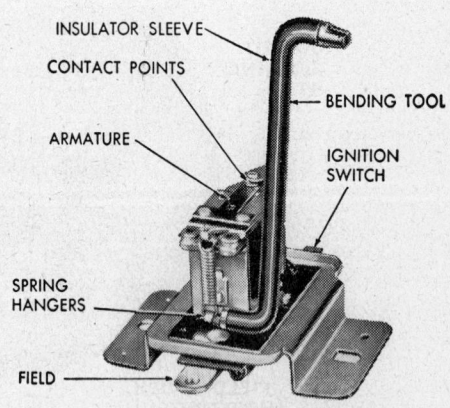

Fig. C15 Adjusting spring tension to obtain correct voltage

CHRYSLER ALTERNATORS

3. Connect a jumper wire to negative terminal of battery, and ground it to the alternator end shield.
4. Slowly rotate alternator rotor by hand. Observe ammeter reading. The field coil draw should be 2.3 to 2.7 amperes at 12 volts.

NOTE: *A low rotor coil draw is an indication of a high resistance in the field coil circuit (brushes, slip rings or rotor coil). A higher rotor coil draw indicates a possible shorted rotor coil or a grounded rotor.*

Isolated Field Alternator
1. Connect jumper wire between one alternator field terminal and the positive terminal of a fully charged battery.
2. Connect test ammeter positive lead to the other alternator field terminal and the ammeter negative lead to the negative battery terminal.
3. Slowly rotate alternator by hand. Field current draw at 12 volts should be 2.3–2.7 amps on 1970–71 units, 2.5–3.1 amps 1972–73 units, 2.5–3.7 amps on 1974–75 units and 4.5–6.5 amps on 1976–80 units.
4. A low rotor coil draw is an indication of high resistance in the field coil circuit, (brushes, slip rings or rotor coil). A high rotor coil draw indicates shorted rotor coil or grounded rotor.

Testing Alternator Internal Field Circuit

Exc. Isolated Field Alternator
1. To test the internal field circuit for a

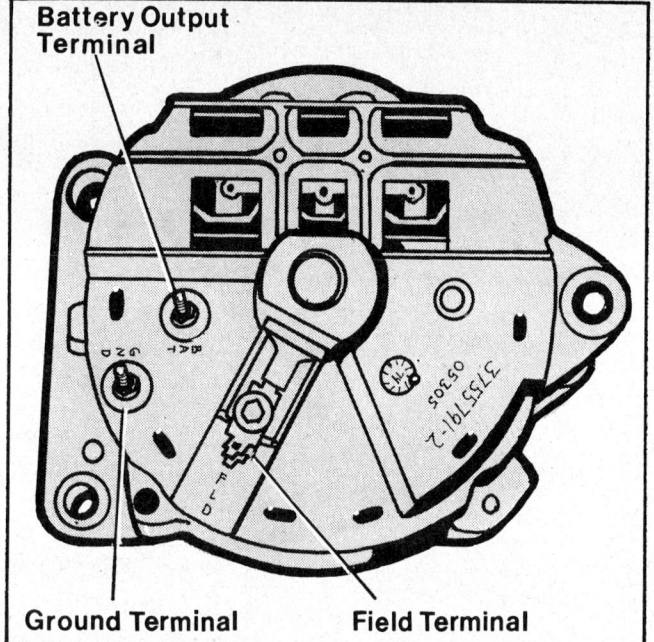

Fig. C10   100 & 117 amp alternator assembly

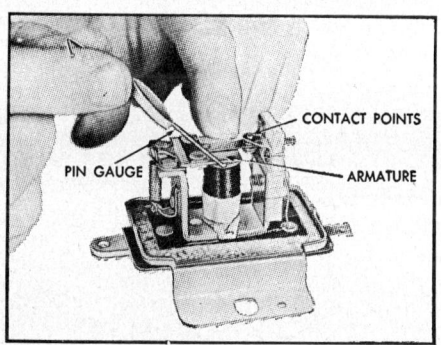

Fig. C16   Measuring armature air gap, electro-mechanical regulator

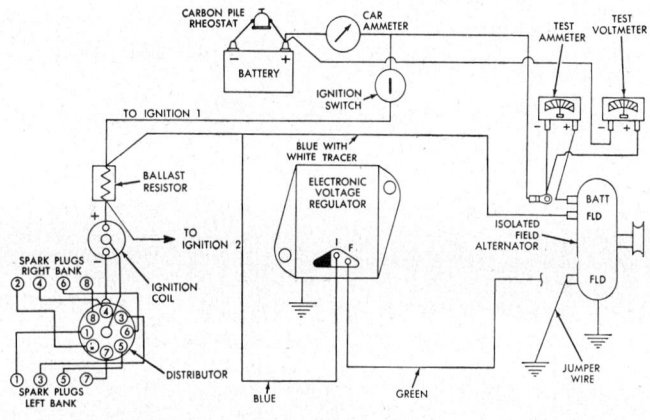

Fig. C17   Charging circuit resistance test with electronic regulator (Typical)

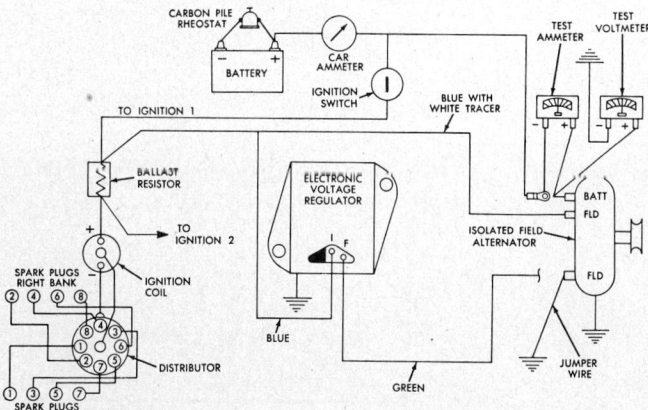

Fig. C18   Current output test with electronic regulator (Typical)

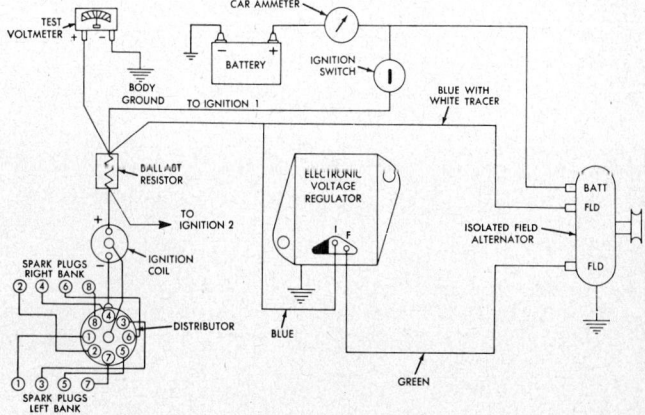

Fig. C19   Electronic voltage regulator test (Typical)

CHRYSLER ALTERNATORS

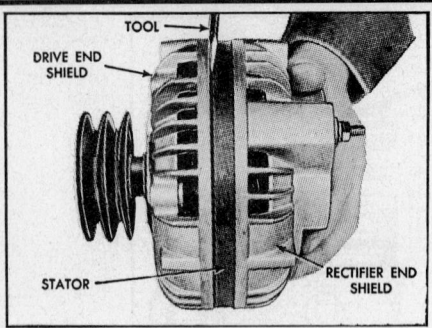

Fig. C20 Separating drive end shield from stator

ground, remove the ground brush. Touch one test prod from a 110 volt test lamp to the alternator insulated brush terminal and the remaining test prod to the end shield. If the rotor or insulated brush is not grounded, the lamp will not light.
2. If the lamp lights, remove insulated brush (noting how parts are assembled) and separate end shields by removing the three through bolts.
3. Again test by placing one of the test prods to the slip ring and the remaining test prod to the end shield. If the lamp lights, the rotor is grounded and requires replacement. If the lamp does not light after removing the insulated brush and separating the end shields, the insulated brush is grounded.
4. Examine the plastic insulator and screw. *The screw is a special size and must not be replaced by another size.*
5. Install insulated brush holder, terminal, insulated washer, shake proof washer and screw. *If the parts were not assembled in this order or if the wrong screw was used this could be the cause of the ground condition.*

Isolated Field Alternator, 1970-71
1. Touch one probe of a 110 volt test lamp to one of the alternator field brush terminals and the other to the end shield. If lamp lights, rotor assembly or a field brush is grounded.

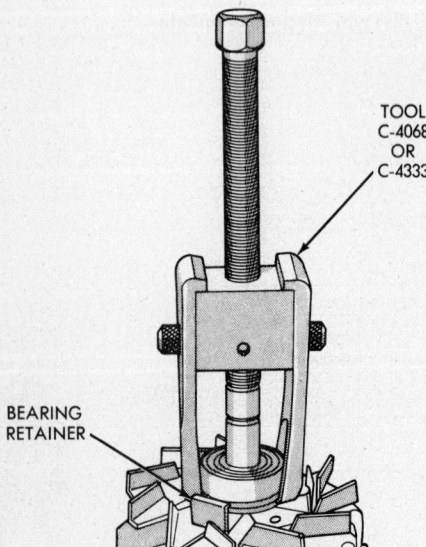

Fig. C23 Removing bearing from rotor shaft

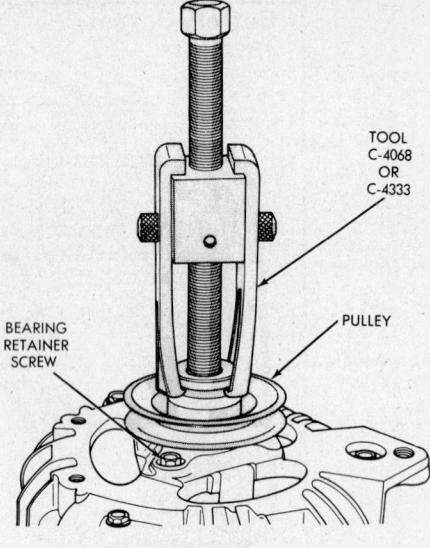

Fig. C21 Removing pulley

2. If lamp lights, remove field brush assemblies, remove through bolts and separate end shields.
3. Touch one test probe to a slip ring and the remaining probe to the end frame. If the lamp lights, rotor is grounded and must be replaced. If lamp does not light, cause is a grounded brush.

ALTERNATOR REPAIRS EXCEPT 100 & 117 AMP UNITS

Disassembly

To prevent possible damage to the brush assemblies, they should be removed before disassembling the alternator. The insulated (field) brush is mounted in a plastic holder which positions the brush against one of the slip rings. In this isolated field type alternator, both brushes are insulated and mounted in plastic holders. Disassembled views of all four types are shown in Figs. C3, C4, C6 and C7.
1. On 1970-71 units, remove retaining screw lockwasher, insulated washer and field terminal. Carefully lift plastic holder containing the spring and brush from the end housing.
2. On isolated field units, remove both brush screws, insulating nylon washers

Fig. C24 Removing or installing heat sink insulator

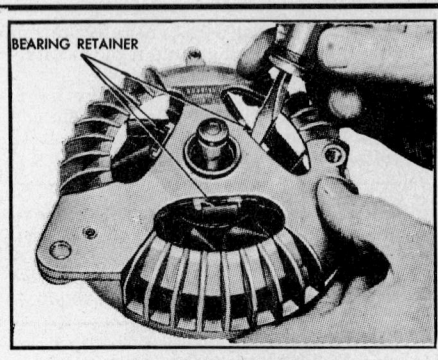

Fig. C22 Disengaging bearing retainer from end shield

and brush assemblies. On electromechanical units, remove ground brush retaining screw and lift the clip, spring and brush from end shield.

NOTE: *The stator is laminated; do not burr it or the end shield.*

3. Remove through bolts and pry between stator and drive end shield with a screwdriver. Carefully separate drive end shield, pulley and rotor from stator and diode rectifier shield, Fig. C20.
4. The pulley is an interference fit on the rotor shaft; therefore, a suitable puller must be used to remove it, Fig. C21.
5. Pry drive end bearing spring retainer from end shield with a screwdriver, Fig. C22.
6. Support end shield and tap rotor shaft with a plastic hammer to separate rotor from end shield.
7. The drive end ball bearing is an interference fit with the rotor shaft; therefore, a suitable puller must be used to remove it, Fig. C23.
8. On 1970-71 units, remove D.C. output terminal nuts and washers, terminal screw and capacitor, if used. Then remove heat sink and heat sink insulator, Fig. C24.
9. On 1972-80 units to remove rectifiers and heat sinks, loosen screws securing negative rectifier and heat sink assembly to end shield, remove the two outer screws and lift assembly from end shield.

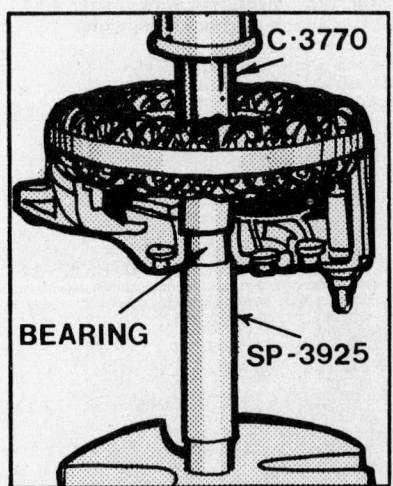

Fig. C25 Removing diode end shield bearing

CHRYSLER ALTERNATORS

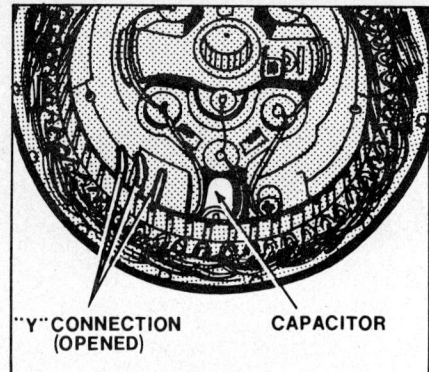

Fig. C26 Separating the three stator leads. 1970–71 units

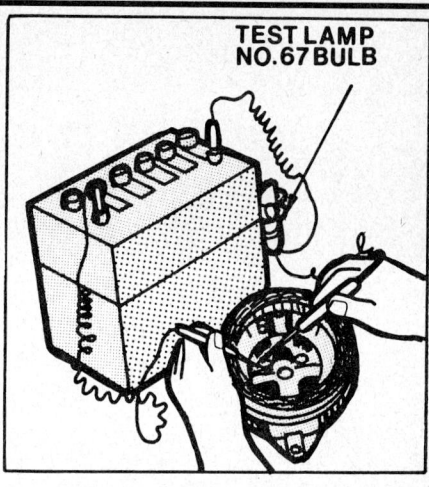

Fig. C27 Testing diodes with a test lamp

Remove nuts securing positive rectifier and heat sink assembly to insulated terminals in end shield. Then, remove capacitor ground screw and lift insulated washer, capacitor and positive rectifier and heat sink assembly from end shield.

10. The needle roller bearing in the rectifier end shield is a press fit. If it is necessary to remove the rectifier end frame needle bearing, protect the end shield by supporting the shield when pressing out the bearing as shown in Fig. C25.

Testing Diode Rectifiers

A special Rectifier Tester Tool C-3829 provides a quick, simple and accurate method to test the rectifiers without the necessity of disconnecting the soldered rectifier leads. This instrument is commercially available and full instructions for its use is provided. Lacking this tool, the rectifiers may be tested with a 12 volt battery and a test lamp having a No. 67 bulb. The procedure is as follows:

1. On 1970–71 units, separate the three stator leads at the "Y" connection, Fig. C26. Cut the stator connections as close to the connector as possible because they will have to be soldered together again. If they are cut too short it may be difficult to get them together again for soldering.
2. On 1972–80 units, remove nuts securing stator windings, positive and negative rectifier straps to terminal block. Remove stator winding terminals and pry stator from end shield.
3. On all units, connect one side of test lamp to positive battery post and the other side of the test lamp to a test probe. Connect another test probe to the negative battery post, Fig. C27.
4. On 1970–71 units, contact outer case of rectifier with one probe and other probe to rectifier center wire. On 1972–80 units, contact heat sink with one probe and strap on top of rectifier with the other probe.
5. On all units, reverse position of probes. If test lamp lights in one direction only, the rectifier is satisfactory. If test lamp lights in both directions, the rectifier is shorted. If test lamp lights in neither direction, the rectifier is open.

NOTE: *Possible cause of an open or a blown rectifier is a faulty capacitor or a battery that has been installed on reverse polarity. If the battery is installed properly and the rectifiers are open, test the capacitor capacity, which should be .50 microfarad plus or minus 20%.*

Testing Stator

1. On 1970–71 units, unsolder rectifiers from stator leads. On 1972–80 units, separate stator from end shields.
2. On 1970–71 units, insulate stator from rectifier shield with wood slats and using a 110 volt test lamp, Fig. C28, test stator for grounds by contacting one test probe to stator pole frame and the other to each stator lead. If test lamp lights, stator is grounded.
3. On 1972–80 units, using a 12 volt test lamp, Fig. C29, test stator for grounds. Contact one test probe to any pin on stator frame and the other to each stator lead. If lamp lights, stator is grounded.

NOTE: Remove varnish from stator frame pin to ensure proper electrical connection.

4. On all units, use a 12 volt test lamp to test stator for continuity. On 1970–71 units, connect one probe to all three stator leads at the "Y" connection and contact each of the three stator leads (disconnect from diodes), Fig. C30. On 1972–80 units, contact one stator lead with one probe and the remaining two leads with the other

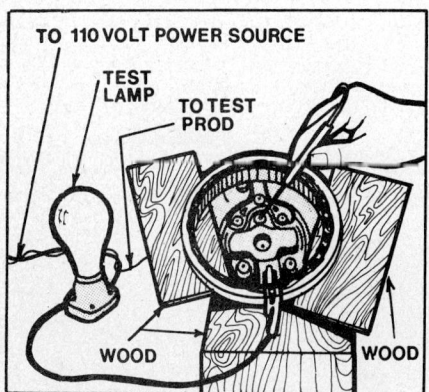

Fig. C28 Testing stator for grounds. 1970–71 units

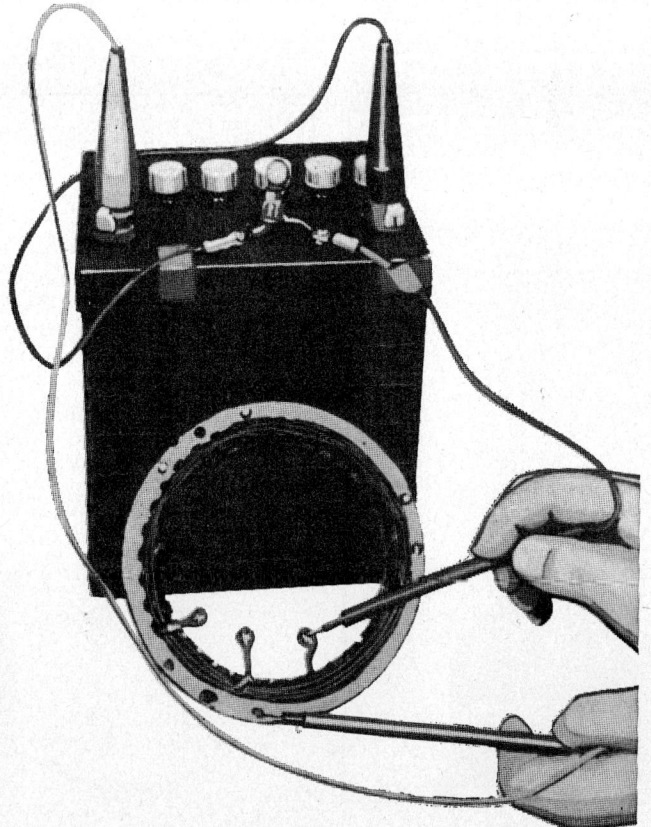

Fig. C29 Testing stator for grounds. 1972–80 units

CHRYSLER ALTERNATORS

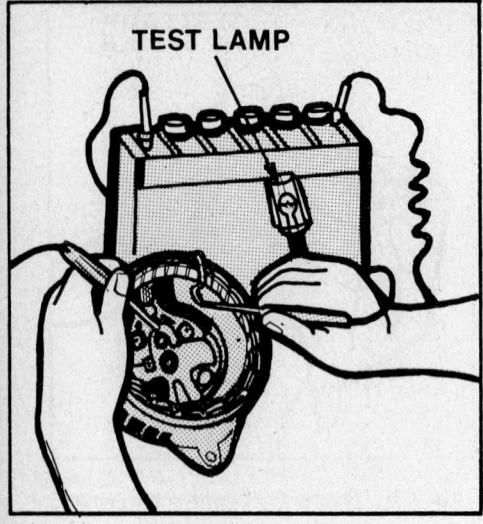

Fig. C30 Testing stator windings for continuity

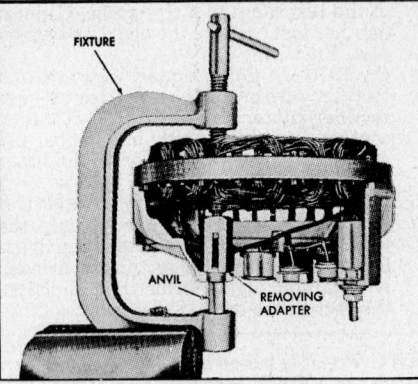

Fig. C31 Removing a diode

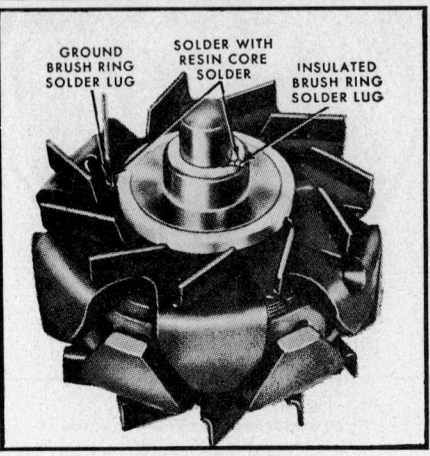

Fig. C32 Soldering points with slip ring installed

probe. On all units, if test lamp does not light, the stator has an open circuit.
5. Install new stator if one tested is defective.

Testing Rotor

1972-80

The rotor may be tested electrically for grounded, open or shorted field coils as follows:

Grounded Field Coil Test: Connect an ohmmeter between each slip ring and the rotor shaft. The ohmmeter should indicate infinite resistance. If reading is zero or higher, rotor is grounded.

Open or shorted Field Coil Test: Connect an ohmmeter between the slip rings. A resistance of 3 to 4 ohms on 1972-75 units and 1.5 to 2 ohms on 1976-80 units at room temperature indicates rotor is satisfactory. A reading of 4 to 6 ohms on 1972-75 units and 2.5 to 3 ohms on 1976-80 units, indicates the alternator was operated at a high underhood temperature, however, rotor is still satisfactory. Resistance below 3 ohms on 1972-75 units, below 1.5 ohms on 1976-80 units, indicates a shorted field coil. Resistances above 6.5 ohms on 1972-75 units, 3.5 ohms on 1976-80 units, indicates a high resistance in the field coils and further testing or rotor replacement is required.

Removing Rectifiers

1970-71
1. Three diodes are pressed into the heat sink and three in the end shield. When removing the diodes, it is necessary to support the end shield and/or heat sink to prevent damage to these castings.
2. Install the tools shown in Fig. C31, making sure bore of tool completely surrounds diode.
3. Carefully apply pressure to remove diode from end shield.

Replacing Slip Rings

NOTE: On 1975-80 units, slip rings and rotor are serviced as an assembly.

1. On 1970-74 units, remove rotor plastic grease retainer.
2. Unsolder field coil leads at solder lugs, Fig. C32.
3. Cut through copper of both slip rings at opposite points with a chisel, Fig. C33.
4. Break insulator and remove old ring.
5. Clean away dirt and particles of old slip ring from rotor.
6. Scrape ends of field coil lead wires clean for good electrical contact.
7. Position field coil wires aside and place new slip ring on rotor shaft so slip ring lugs are properly positioned for field coil wire connections, Fig. C34.
8. Place installing tool over rotor shaft and with a suitable press, press slip ring onto shaft, Fig. C35.

NOTE: With slip ring bottomed against fan, the field lead wire should clear the access hole, fan and pole piece.

9. Tin field coil lead wires, then coil each lead wire around slip ring lug with first wrap against lug shoulder and winding outward. Solder leads with resin core solder.
10. Test slip rings for ground with a 110 volt test lamp by touching one test lead prod to rotor pole shoe and remaining prod to slip rings. The lamp should not light. If lamp lights, slip rings are shorted to ground, possibly due to a grounded insulated field lead when installing slip ring.
11. If rotor is not grounded, lightly clean slip ring surfaces with No. 00 sandpaper and

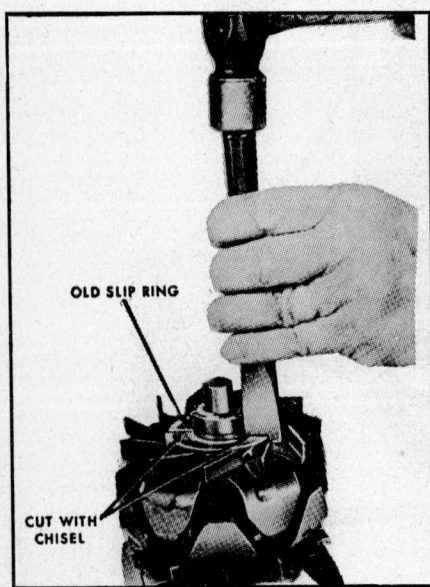

Fig. C33 Cutting old slip rings for removal

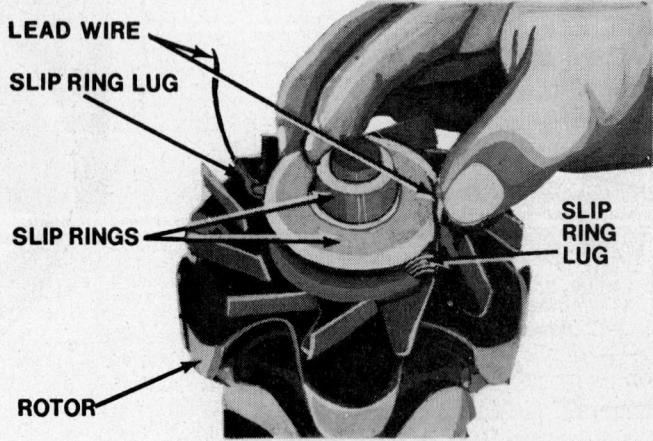

Fig. C34 Aligning slip ring with field lead wires

CHRYSLER ALTERNATORS

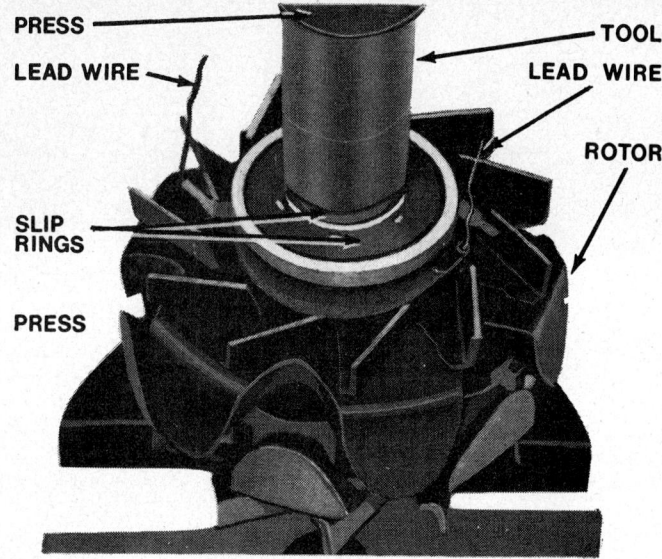

Fig. C35 Installing slip ring

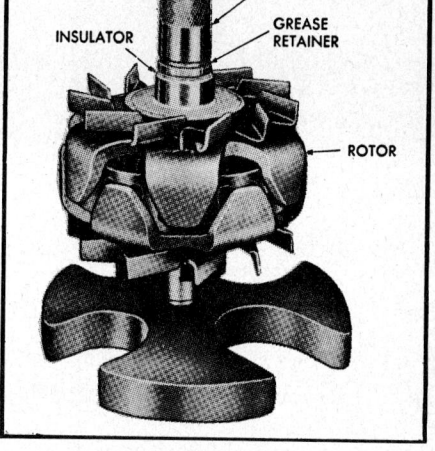

Fig. C36 Installing bearing grease retainer

assemble to alternator.
12. Position grease retainer gasket and retainer on rotor shaft and press retainer on shaft, Fig. C36. Retainer is properly positioned when inner bore of installer tool bottoms on rotor shaft.

Alternator, Assemble

1. On 1970-71 units:
   a. Install diodes, Fig. C37.

   NOTE: Do not hammer diode in any manner since this will fracture the thin silicon wafer in the diode, causing complete diode failure.

   b. Clean leads and mate stator lead with diode wire loop, then bend loop snugly around stator lead to provide a good electrical and mechanical connection. Solder wires with resin core solder, holding diode lead wire with pliers just below joint, Fig. C38. Pliers will act as a heat sink and protect diode.

   NOTE: After soldering, quickly cool soldered connection by touching a damp cloth against it. Also, this will aid in forming a solid joint.

   c. Push stator leads into slots in end shield and cement them to protect leads against possible interference with rotor fan (Cement is Mopar part No. 2299314). Test each diode to ensure proper installation.
2. On all units, install diode end shield bearing, Fig. C39.
3. Install drive end bearing in end shield with bearing retainer plate to hold bearing in position. Place assembly on rotor shaft and press into position, Fig. C40.
4. Press pulley onto rotor shaft until it contacts inner race of bearing.

   NOTE: Do not exceed 6800 lbs.

5. On 1970-71 units:
   a. Ensure heat sink insulator is properly positioned, then install capacitor stud through heat sink and end shield.
   b. Install insulating washers, lockwashers and lock nuts.
   c. Ensure heat sink and insulator are properly positioned, then tighten lock nut.
6. On 1972-80 units:
   a. Install output terminal stud and insulator through end shield. Then place positive heat sink assembly over studs, guiding rectifier straps over studs.
   b. Place capacitor terminal over capacitor end stud and install capacitor shoulder insulator. Ground the capacitor bracket to end shield with a metal screw. Install and tighten positive heat sink lockwashers and nuts.
   c. Slide negative rectifier and heat sink assembly into place, position straps on terminal block studs, then install and tighten attaching screws.
7. Position stator on diode end shield.
8. Position rotor end shield on stator and diode end shield.
9. Align through bolt holes in stator, diode end shield and drive end shield.
10. Compress stator and both end shields by hand and install through bolts, washers and nuts.
11. Install field brushes into vertical and horizontal holders. Place an insulating washer on each field brush terminal and install lockwashers and attaching screws.

   NOTE: Ensure that brushes are not grounded.

12. Rotate pulley slowly by hand to be sure rotor fans do not touch diodes, capacitor lead and stator connections.
13. Install alternator and adjust drive belt.

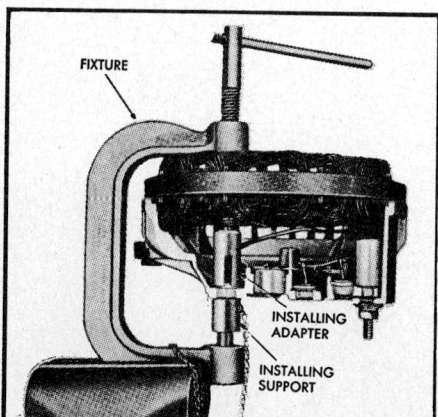

Fig. C37 Installing a diode. 1970-71 units

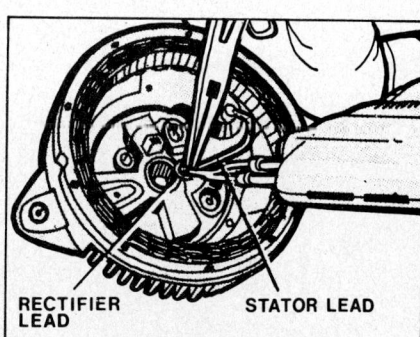

Fig. C38 Soldering diode & stator leads

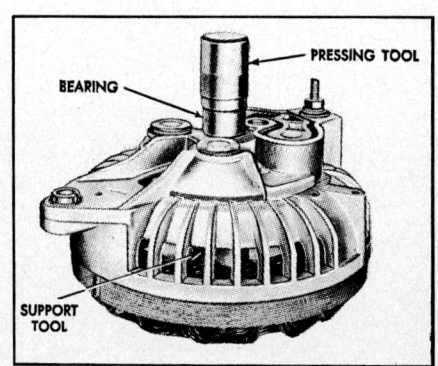

Fig. C39 Installing diode end shield bearing

CHRYSLER ALTERNATORS

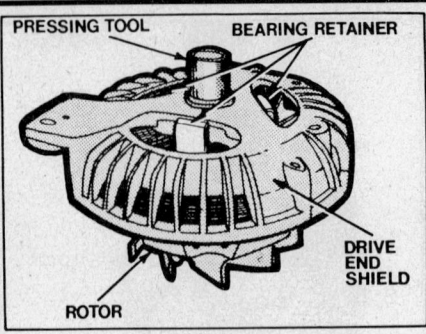

Fig. C40 Installing drive end shield & bearing

14. Connect leads to alternator.
15. Connect battery ground cable.
16. Start and operate engine and observe alternator operation.
17. If necessary, test current output and regulator voltage setting.

100 & 117 AMP ALTERNATOR REPAIRS

Disassembly & Testing

Separating End Shields
1. Remove brush holder screw and insulat-

Fig. C41 Separating end shields. 100 & 117 amp units

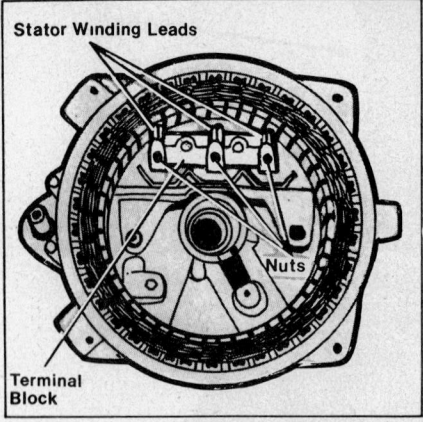

Fig. C42 Removing stator winding leads. 100 & 117 amp units

ing washer, then lift brush holder from end shield.
2. Remove the through bolts, then using a screwdriver, pry between the stator and end shield in the slot provided to separate end shields, Fig. C41.

Rectifier Testing
1. Remove stator winding leads to terminal block stud nuts, Fig. C42.
2. Lift stator winding leads and pry stator from end shield.
3. Using a 12 volt battery and a test lamp equipped with a #67 bulb, test rectifiers as follows:
   A. Connect one test probe to rectifier heat sink and the other test probe to the metal strap on top of rectifier, Fig. C43. Reverse the probes.
   B. If test lamp lights in one direction and does not light in the other, rectifier is satisfactory. If test lamp lights in both directions, rectifier is shorted. If test lamp does not light in either direction, rectifier is open.

Rectifier & Heat Sink Assembly Removal
1. Remove nut and insulator securing positive heat sink assembly to end shield stud.
2. Remove capacitor attaching screw.
3. Remove nut and insulator securing positive heat sink assembly stud to end shield, then remove positive heat sink assembly, Fig. C44, noting location of the insulators.
4. Remove screws securing negative heat sink assembly to end shield, then the negative heat sink assembly, Fig. C45.
5. Remove terminal block, then the capacitor and insulator.

Stator Testing
1. Contact one test lamp probe to outer diameter of stator frame and the other probe to each of the stator lead terminals, one at a time, Fig. C46.
2. If test lamp lights, the stator lead is grounded, requiring replacement.

NOTE: The stator windings are Delta Wound, therefore the windings cannot be tested for opens or shorts using a test lamp. If the stator is not grounded, and all other electrical circuits and alternator components test satisfactory, the stator may be open or shorted.

Pulley & Bearing Removal
1. Remove pulley with a suitable puller, Fig. C47.

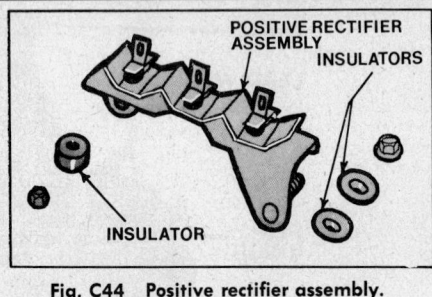

Fig. C44 Positive rectifier assembly. 100 & 117 amp units

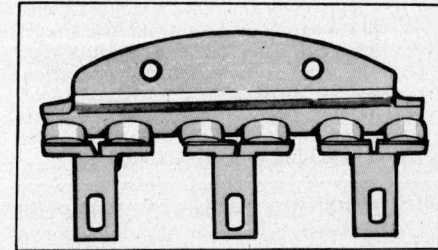

Fig. C45 Negative rectifier assembly. 100 & 117 amp units

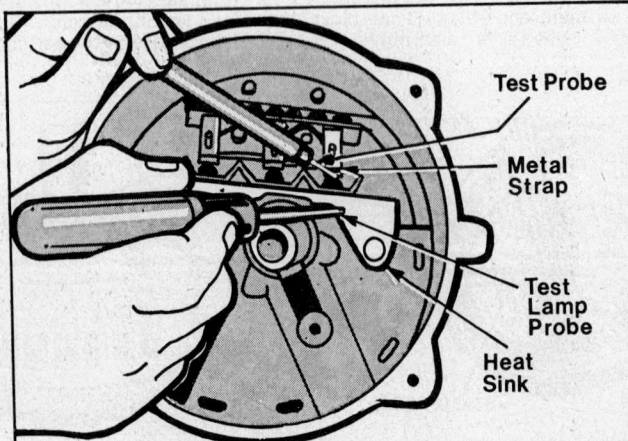

Fig. C43 Testing rectifiers with a test lamp. 100 & 117 amp units

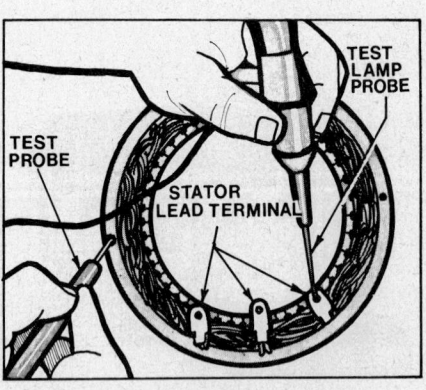

Fig. C46 Testing stator winding. 100 & 117 amp units

CHRYSLER ALTERNATORS

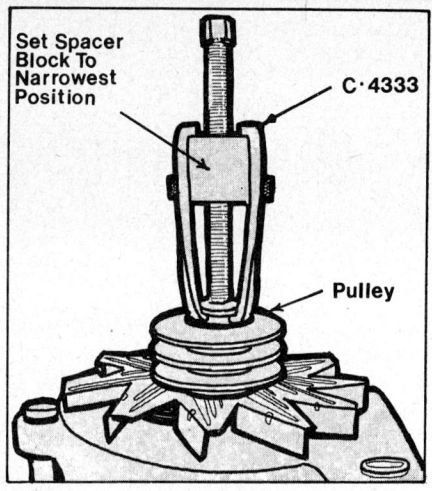

Fig. C47 Removing pulley. 100 & 117 amp units

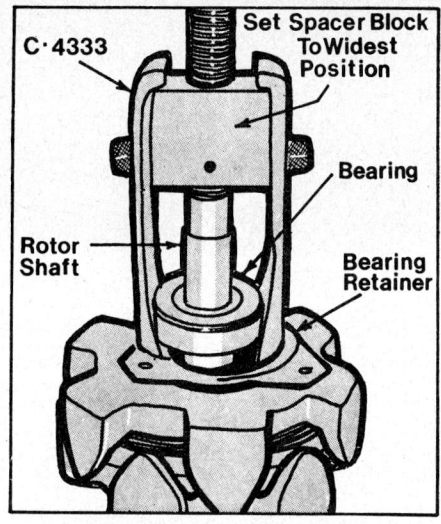

Fig. C48 Removing bearing from rotor shaft. 100 & 117 amp units

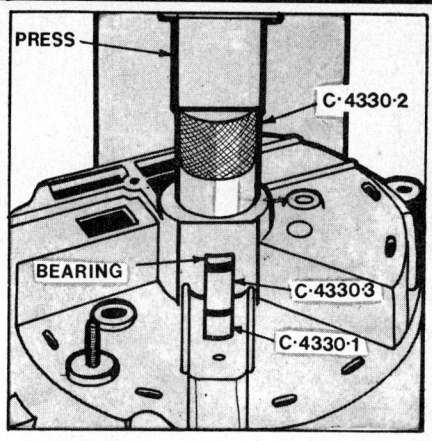

Fig. C49 Removing rectifier end shield bearing. 100 & 117 amp units

2. Remove bearing retainer to drive end shield attaching screws.
3. Support end shield and using a mallet, tap rotor from end shield.
4. Remove bearing with a suitable puller, Fig. C48.
5. If necessary to remove needle roller bearing in rectifier end shield, use tool C-4330, Fig. C49.

Rotor Testing

Grounded Field Coil Test: Connect a test lamp between each slip ring and the rotor shaft, Fig. C50. If test lamp lights, the rotor is grounded, requiring replacement.

Open Field Coil Test: Connect a test lamp between the slip rings, Fig. C51. If test lamp does not light, the rotor is open, requiring replacement.

Shorted Field Coil Test: Connect an ohmmeter between the slip rings, Fig. C39. If reading is below 1.7 ohms, the rotor is shorted.

High Resistance Test: with an ohmmeter connected across the slip rings, reading should be between 1.7 and 2.1 ohms at 80° F. If not, replace rotor.

Assembly

1. Press grease retainer onto rotor shaft, Fig. C49 (Omit tool C-4330-3).
2. Place rectifier end shield bearing on base of tool C-4330-1, Fig. C49 (Omit tool C-4330-3), then place rectifier end shield on top of bearing. Using tool C-4330-2, press end shield onto bearing until end shield contacts press base.
3. Install drive end bearing and retainer in drive end shield.
4. Position bearing and drive end shield on rotor and while supporting base of rotor shaft, press end shield onto shaft. Ensure rotor spacer is in place before pressing bearing and end shield on shaft.
5. Press pulley onto rotor shaft until it contacts inner race of bearing.

NOTE: Do not exceed 6800 lbs.

6. Place insulator and capacitor on positive heat sink mounting stud, then install capacitor mounting screw.
7. Place terminal block into position in rectifier end shield and install mounting screws.
8. Place negative heat sink into position, ensuring metal straps are properly located over studs on terminal block, then install negative heat sink mounting screws.
9. Place insulator over positive heat sink stud and install positive heat sink assembly into position in end shield, ensuring metal straps are properly located over terminal block studs. From inside end shield, place insulator on positive heat sink mounting stud, then install mounting nut. From outside end shield, place insulator on positive heat sink stud, then install mounting nut.
10. Place stator over rectifier end shield and install terminals on terminal block. Then, press stator pins into end shield and install terminal nuts.

NOTE: Route leads to avoid contact with rotor or sharp edge of negative heat sink.

11. Place rotor and drive end shield assembly over stator and rectifier end shield assembly, aligning bolt holes. Compress stator and both end shields, then install and torque through bolts to 40–60 inch lbs.
12. Install field brushes into brush holder with long terminal on bottom and the short terminal on top, Fig. C52. Then, install insulators and mounting screw.
13. Place brush holder on end shield, ensure it is properly seated and tighten mounting screw.
14. Slowly rotate pulley to ensure rotor poles do not contact stator winding leads.

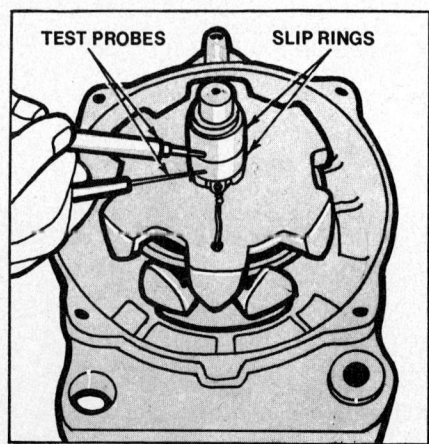

Fig. C50 Testing rotor for open or short circuits. 100 & 117 amp units

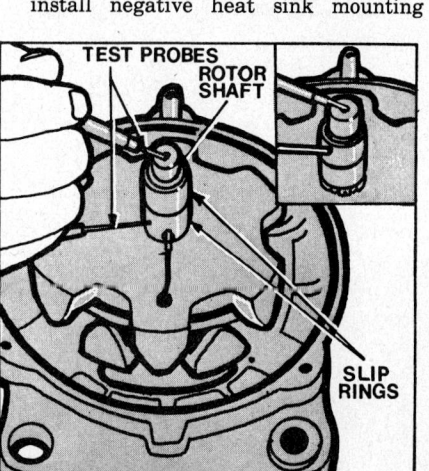

Fig. C51 Testing rotor for grounds. 100 & 117 amp units

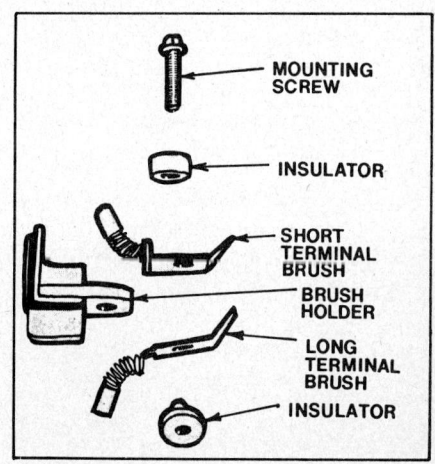

Fig. C52 Assembling field brushes. 100 & 117 amp units

Delco-Remy "Delcotron"

DESCRIPTION

Figs. 1 through 4 illustrate the four types of Delcotron alternators used on automotive truck applications. All models have the rotor mounted on ball or roller bearings, and each bearing has a supply of lubrication to provide long periods of service. Current to the coil winding mounted on the rotor is supplied through brushes riding on smooth slip rings.

All models develop three-phase A.C. voltage which is then rectified to a single D.C. voltage available at the output terminals of the alternator. All models are also designed to provide an output at engine idle, the amount depending on the application. They all are "self-limiting" in their maximum output, which occurs as the magnetic field produced by the current in the stator windings opposes in polarity and approaches in value the magnetic field provided by the rotor as the output increases. This causes the alternator to limit its own output to a maximum value.

OUTPUT TEST ON VEHICLE

Systems with Two-Unit or Transistorized Regulator

If evidence of an undercharged battery exists, test alternator output to determine if alternator is capable of producing its normal rated output.
1. Disconnect negative cable from battery.
2. Remove wire from "BAT" terminal on alternator and connect an ammeter between wire and "BAT" terminal on alternator, Fig. 5.
3. Install voltmeter between "BAT" terminal and "GRD" terminal on alternator.
4. Pull latch on regulator upward to disengage latch from connector lug, then pull wiring harness connector from regulator.

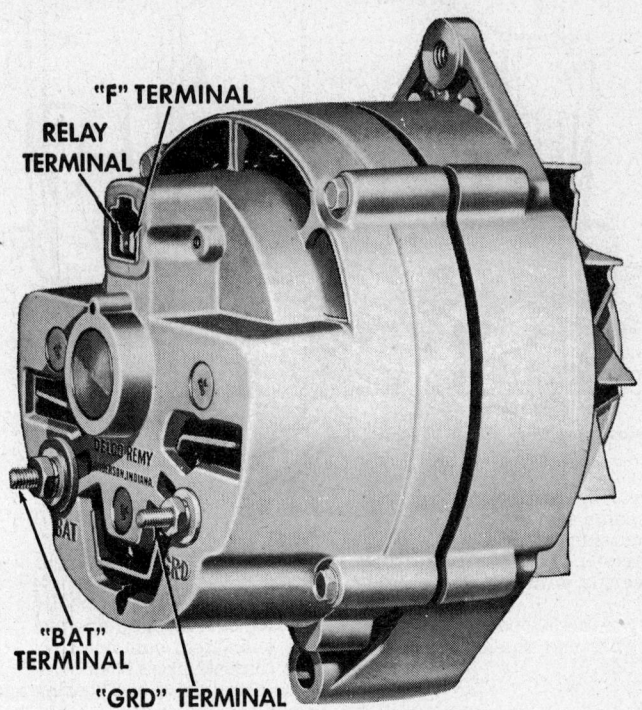

Fig. 1 Delcotron 5.5" 1D Series

With jumper lead, make connection between "F" terminal socket and #3 or "V" socket, Fig. 6.

CAUTION: With wiring connected as shown in Fig. 7, the voltage regulator is taken out of the circuit and causes the field to be energized by full battery voltage. Do not permit voltage to exceed setting specified for regulator. Refer to "Voltage" chart later on in this section.

NOTE: Instead of using a carbon pile, the headlights and heater switch can be turned on.

5. Connect tachometer to engine; connect battery cable, then start engine. Adjust engine speed and carbon pile (if used) or with accessories to provide rated voltage. Ratings for each generator are given in the Truck Chapters. If alternator does not produce current within its rated capacity, it can be considered defective and in need of repair.
6. Remove instruments and jumper lead, then make connections at alternator and regulator.
7. If no defects are discovered by the foregoing tests, yet the battery remains undercharged, the cause is probably a low voltage regulator setting.

Systems with Full Transistor Regulator

Two methods may be used for checking alternator output on these systems: Method using a special adapter (J-21600) installed in harness connector at voltage regulator or method not requiring use of an adapter.

Using Special Adapter (J-21600)
1. Connect voltmeter to adapter as shown in View A, Fig. 8.
2. Turn on ignition switch.
3. Operate alternator at specified speed and check for rated output. Load battery with

Fig. 2 Delcotron 6.2" 2D Series

DELCO-REMY "DELCOTRON"

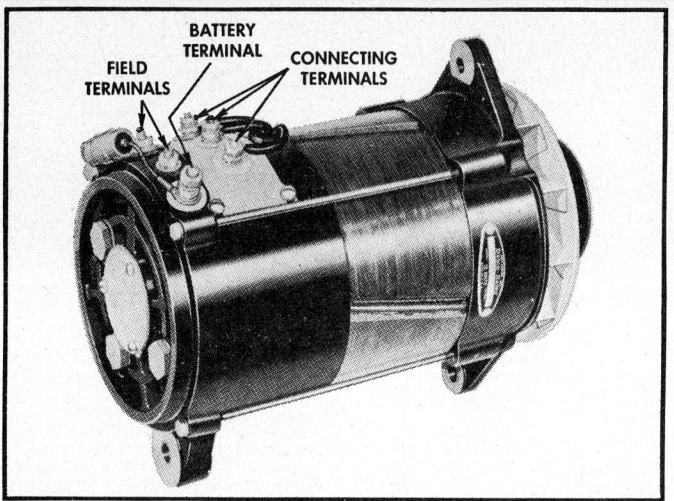

Fig. 3 Delcotron Series 3D

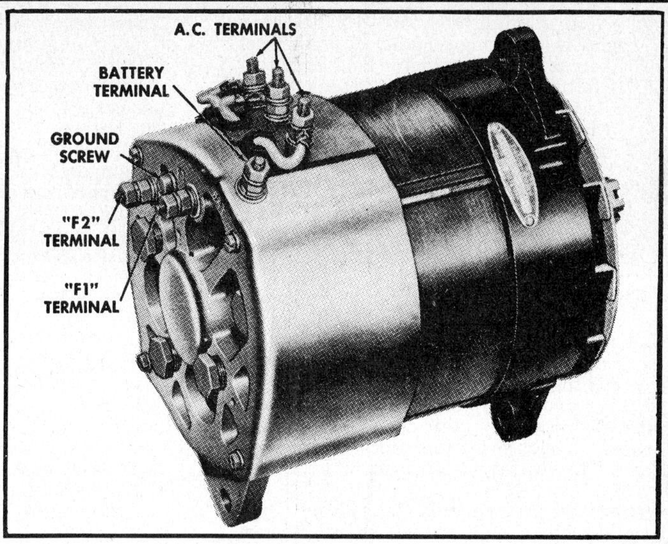

Fig. 4 Delcotron Series 4D

carbon pile or with accessories if needed to obtain rated output. If alternator does not provide rated output, replace or repair alternator.

Without Using Adapter
1. Separate harness connector at regulator.
2. Install voltmeter between alternator "BAT" terminal and base of alternator (to ground).
3. Connect a jumper lead between alternator "F" or "F2" terminal.
4. Load battery with carbon pile or accessories (headlight and heater switch on).
5. Start engine and operate at specified speed and check for rated output.
6. If rated output is not obtained, replace or repair alternator.

REGULATOR UNIT FIELD RELAY TEST ON VEHICLE

Systems with Two-Unit or Transistorized Regulator

If charge indicator shows no charge, the regulator field relay or possibly the alternator is at fault. To determine which, proceed as follows:
1. Make connections to regulator and connector terminals as shown in Fig. 9.
2. Start engine and operate at idle speed. Observe voltmeter reading. If reading is 5 volts or over, and indicator shows no charge, the field relay is defective and must be checked.
3. If voltmeter reading is below 5 volts, trouble is in the alternator.
4. The field relay closing voltage can be checked on the vehicle as follows (refer to Fig. 10 which shows hookup of test equipment):
   a. Connect a 100-150 ohm variable resistor and a voltmeter to adapter as shown. If a 0–50 ohms variable resistor unit is used, it will be necessary to add a 15 and a 115 ohm resistor in same series to provide required resistance.
   b. Turn resistor to the open or "full resistance" position. Leave ignition switch off.
   c. Slowly decrease resistance and note closing voltage. Voltage should be 1.5 to 2.7 for a two-unit regulator, or 2.3 to 3.5 volts for a transistorized regulator. If necessary, adjust as directed under applicable regulator section explained later.

FIELD RELAY CIRCUIT TEST

Separate Unit Type

Using Special Adapter J-21600
1. Connect voltmeter to adapter as shown in View A, Fig. 8.
2. Make sure ignition switch is off.
3. If voltmeter indicates battery voltage, the field relay contacts are stuck closed (replace relay). If reading is zero, proceed as follows:
4. Turn ignition switch on.
5. If voltmeter indicates battery voltage, relay is operating properly. Trouble is most likely in alternator field circuit.
6. If voltmeter indicates zero, check for excessive resistance or an open in wiring or in the ignition switch. If wiring and switch are satisfactory, replace relay.

Without Use of Special Adapter
1. Connect a voltmeter to No. 1 terminal of field relay and to ground.
2. Make sure ignition switch is off.
3. If voltmeter indicates battery voltage the relay points are stuck closed (replace relay).
4. If voltmeter indicates zero, turn ignition switch on.

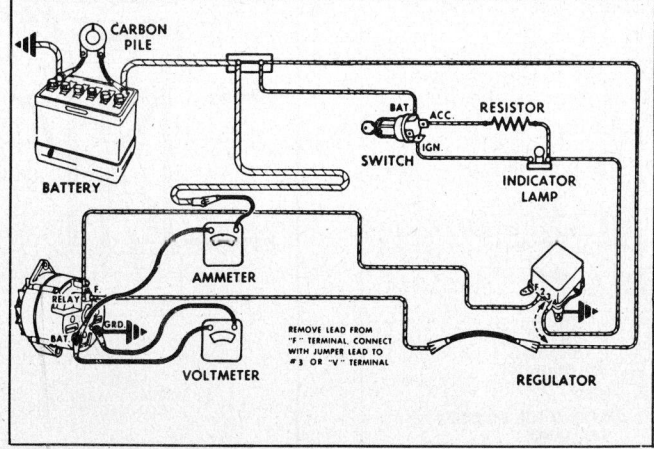

Fig. 5 Connections for testing alternator output with two-unit or transistorized regulator

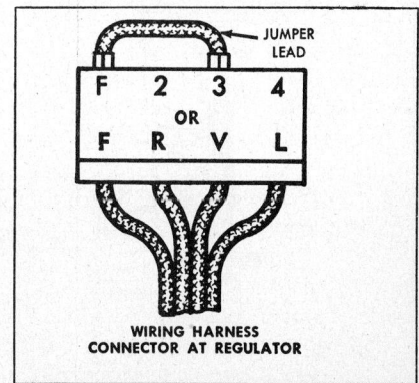

Fig. 6 Alternator output test on systems with two-unit or transistorized regulator. Jumper leads connected at regulator

DELCO-REMY "DELCOTRON"

5. If voltmeter indicates battery voltage, the relay is operating properly. Trouble most likely is in the alternator field circuit.
6. If voltmeter indicates zero, check for excessive resistance or an open in wiring or in ignition switch. If wiring and switch are satisfactory, replace field relay.

REGULATOR VOLTAGE TEST ON VEHICLE

The voltage at which the regulator operates varies with changes in ambient temperature. The ambient temperature is the temperature of air at a distance of 1/4" from the regulator. The full transistor regulator as used with 85 to 130 ampere systems is not noticeably affected by temperature changes. To check and adjust voltage setting, proceed as follows. *Do not remove regulator cover.*

Systems With Two-Unit Regulator
1. Refer to Fig. 11 which shows all test equipment connected into system. Fig. 12 shows use of special adapter and jumper lead at regulator.
2. Connect an ammeter and a 1/4 ohm resistor with a rating of 25 watts or more in series in the circuit at the "BAT" terminal on the alternator, Fig. 11. In the event the battery is discharged, the 1/4 ohm resistor will limit the alternator output to 10 amperes or less which is required when checking and adjusting the voltage setting.
3. Install special adapter as shown in Fig. 11. Use a 25 ohm 25 watt variable resistor in series with the alternator field windings at the regulator "F" terminal, and connect a jumper lead from the #3 adapter lead to the alternator "BAT" terminal as shown. Connect a voltmeter from #3 adapter lead to ground as shown. Turn the resistor to the closed or "no resistance" position.
4. Secure a thermometer close to regulator to establish operating temperature. With all accessories and lights off, start and operate engine for 15 minutes at 1500 engine rpm.
5. After warm-up, cycle alternator as follows:

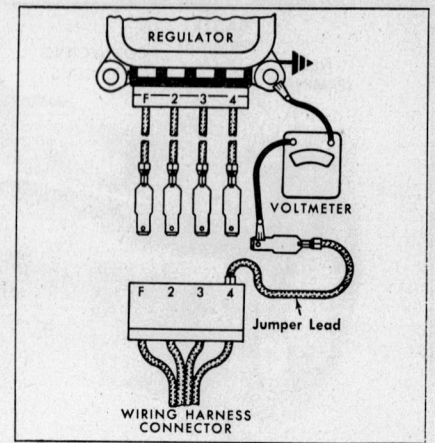

Fig. 7 Testing resistance wire on 1D Series

a. Turn variable resistor to "off" or "full resistance" position.
b. Disconnect lead at #4 terminal of harness connector momentarily, then reconnect lead.
c. Return variable resistor to the closed or "no resistance" position.
d. Bring engine speed up to approximately 2500 rpm and note voltage setting. Refer to voltage chart, Fig. 15, and specifications in Truck Chapters.

NOTE: The regulator unit should be operating on the upper or shorting contacts. If it will not operate on the upper contacts, the battery is in extreme state of discharge, and must be at least partially charged before proceeding with test.

6. To prevent accidental grounding and consequent damage to internal regulator parts when removing or installing regulator cover, perform the following steps in order listed.
a. Disconnect #4 lead at harness connector.
b. Disconnect jumper lead at alternator "BAT" terminal.

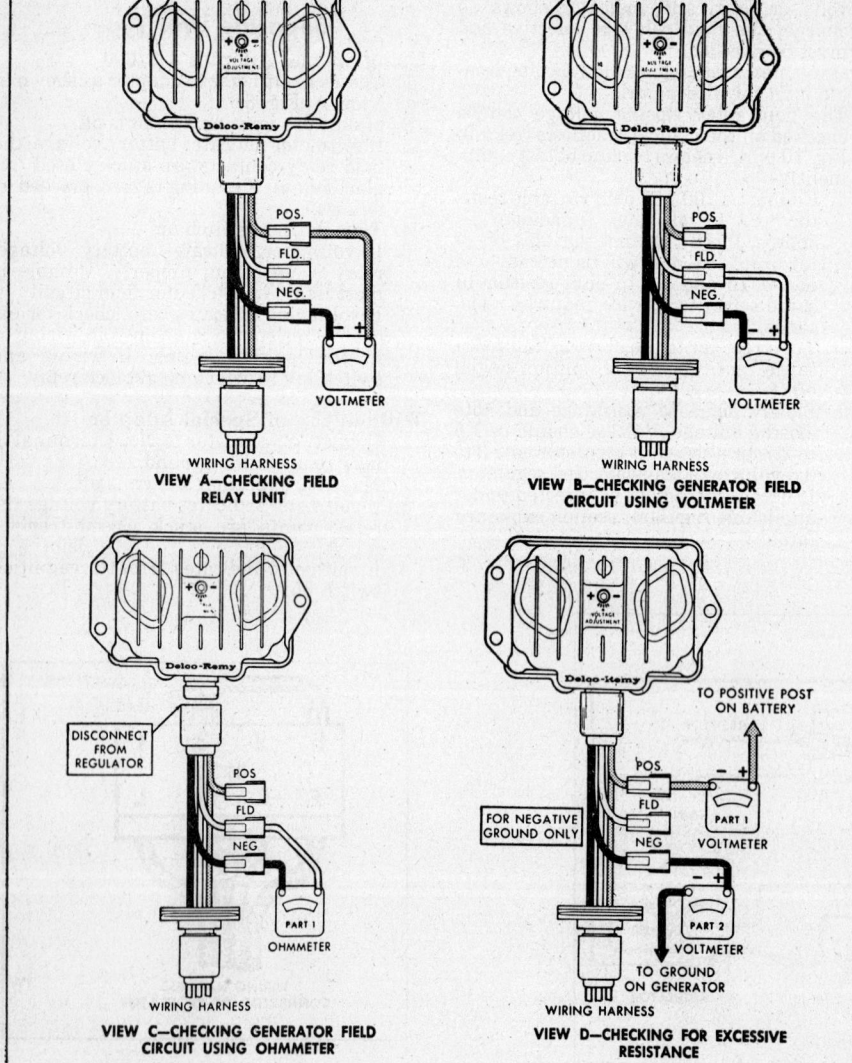

Fig. 8 Using adapter (J-21600) to check alternator output on Series 3D

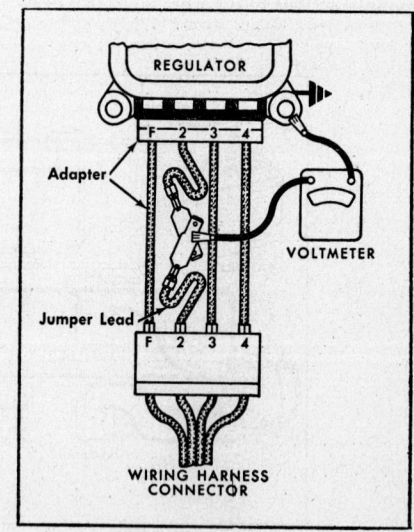

Fig. 9 Testing regulator field relay on two-unit or transistorized regulator

DELCO-REMY "DELCOTRON"

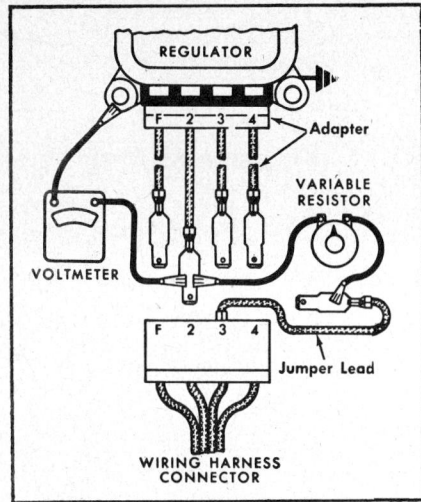

Fig. 10 Testing field relay closing voltage on two-unit or transistorized regulator

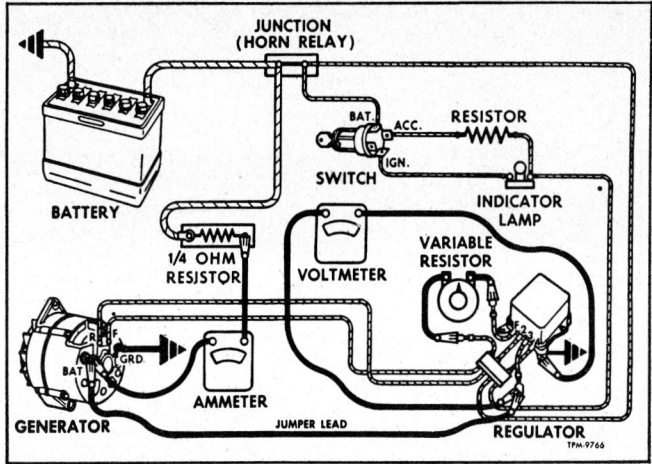

Fig. 11 Connections for testing closing voltage on two-unit regulators

c. Remove regulator cover.
d. Reconnect jumper lead to alternator "BAT" terminal.
e. Connect #4 lead to harness connector.
7. To adjust voltage setting, turn adjusting screw as shown in Fig. 13.

CAUTION: Always turn screw clockwise to make final setting to insure spring holder being against head of adjusting screw. If necessary, pry holder up against screw head before turning screw clockwise.

8. After making setting, cycle alternator again as outlined previously in step 5.
9. Operate engine at approximately 2500 rpm and note voltage setting. Readjust if necessary.
10. Check voltage setting while operating on lower set of contacts as follows:
    a. Slowly increase resistance of variable resistor with engine operating at 2500 rpm until regulator begins to operate on lower sets of contacts. Then note change in voltage reading. The upper set voltage should be 0.1 to 0.3 volts higher.

NOTE: The most desirable method for determining that the regulator is operating on the lower set of contacts when the cover is installed is to use earphones (if available) connected across the regulator "F" terminal to ground. As the variable resistor is turned, and operation changes from the upper set of contacts to the lower set, the earphone sound will fade away and stop completely and then return when the lower set of contacts begin to operate. The alternate method is visual observation, but this is less desirable because the cover must be removed which affects temperature stabilization.

b. If turning the variable resistor does not cause the regulator to operate on the lower set of contacts, return the variable resistor to the "no resistance" position. Turn the carbon pile to slightly load the battery, and then adjust the variable resistor to cause the regulator to operate on the lower set of contacts. Usually, turning on the vehicle headlights can substitute for the carbon pile.
c. The difference in voltage between the operation of the upper set of contacts and the lower set is increased by slightly increasing the air gap between the armature and center of core, and decreased by slightly decreasing the air gap, using the Nylon adjusting nut. This adjustment can be made while the regulator is operating. If necessary to make this air gap adjustment, recheck the voltage setting of both sets of contacts.

11. Always make final voltage test after regulator cover is installed, referring to step 6 for precautions when removing and installing cover.

Systems with Transistorized Regulator
1. Refer to chart, Fig. 15. Then make connections as shown in Fig. 14.
2. With switch on, operate engine at 1275 rpm for 15 minutes. *Leave cover on regulator.*
3. After the warm-up, cycle the alternator by turning off the ignition switch, stopping the alternator and temporarily disconnecting the jumper lead from the alternator. Then reconnect the jumper lead, re-run engine at 1275 rpm and note voltage reading.
4. To adjust setting, remove cover and turn adjusting screw shown in Fig. 16.

CAUTION: To avoid grounds, turn off switch and disconnect jumper lead when replacing cover. Always make final setting by turning screw clockwise. After turning screw, pry holder up against screw head, then turn clockwise to make setting.

5. Recycle alternator as explained in step 3, then turn on switch, operate engine at 1275 rpm and note voltage setting. Readjust if necessary.
6. Always recycle alternator before reading final voltage setting on voltmeter.

NOTE: When decreasing voltage, the alternator output may decrease to below the 3 amperes minimum allowable, or even to no output. If this happens, load battery with carbon pile rheostat connected across its posts, or turn on electrical accessories in order to obtain 3 to 30 amperes output required when adjusting the voltage setting. The transistor and diodes can be checked as explained later under "Transistorized Voltage Regulator."

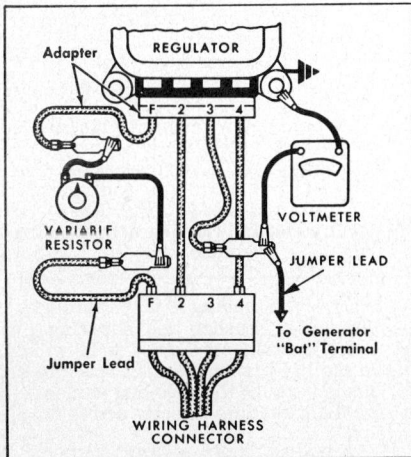

Fig. 12 Testing voltage setting on two-unit regulator

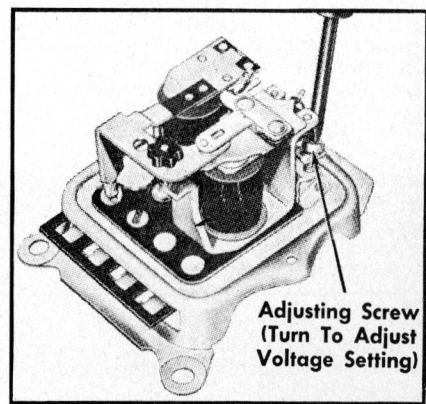

Fig. 13 Adjusting voltage setting on two-unit regulator

67

DELCO-REMY "DELCOTRON"

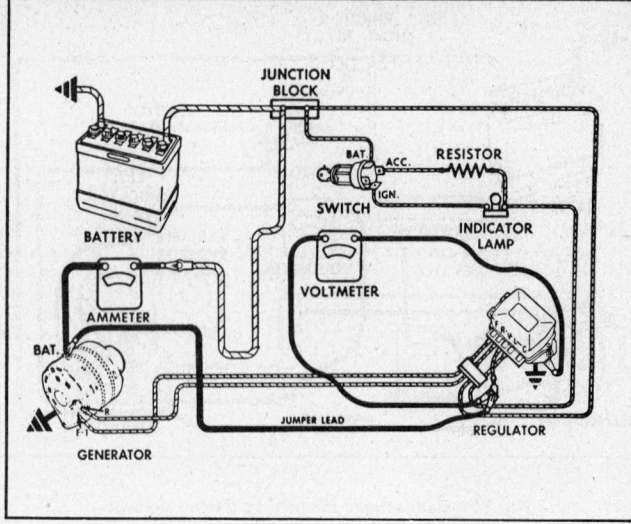

Fig. 14 Connections for testing voltage setting on transistorized regulator

Fig. 15 Voltage chart for various type regulators

VOLTAGE REGULATOR SPECIFICATIONS VS. AMBIENT TEMPERATURE

Regulator Ambient Temperature	Voltage High	Voltage Low
TWO-UNIT REGULATOR		
65°F.	15.0	13.9
85°F.	14.8	13.8
105°F.	14.6	13.7
125°F.	14.4	13.5
145°F.	14.2	13.4
165°F.	14.0	13.2
185°F.	13.9	13.1
TRANSISTORIZED REGULATOR		
65°F.	14.5	13.6
85°F.	14.5	13.4
105°F.	14.3	13.3
125°F.	14.2	13.2
145°F.	14	13
165°F.	13.8	12.8
FULL TRANSISTOR REGULATOR		
65°F.	14.9	14.1
85°F.	14.7	13.9
105°F.	14.5	13.7
125°F.	14.3	13.5
145°F.	14.2	13.4

Series 2D Systems with Full Transistor Regulator

1. Make connections as shown in View B, Part 1, Fig. 17, and record voltage drop.

   CAUTION: Do not leave jumper lead connected longer than five minutes.

2. Make connections as shown in View B, Part 2, Fig. 17, and record voltage drop.
3. Add voltage in step 3A to voltage in step 3B. If total voltage is above 2.5 volts, check system wiring for high resistance.
4. If total voltage in step 3C is below .25 volt, make connections as shown in View C, Fig. 17. Then with switch on, operate engine at 1275 rpm for 15 minutes. *Leave cover on regulator.* Place a thermometer 1/4" from regulator cover and compare voltage given in chart, Fig. 15. If voltage is not within specified range, replace regulator. If voltage is within specified range, remove plug and turn slotted adjusting button inside regulator, Fig. 18.
5. For an undercharged battery, raise voltage setting by turning one notch (clockwise). Then check for an improved battery condition after a service period of reasonable length. After two notches in each direction there is a positive stop.
6. For overcharged battery, lower voltage setting by turning one notch (counterclockwise). Then check for an improved battery condition after a service period of reasonable length.
7. If the regulator cannot be adjusted to a value within the specified range, replace the regulator.

NOTE: If repeated regulator failures are experienced on the vehicle, but no defects are found, a shorted, grounded or open alternator field winding, or grounded leads of an intermittent nature should be suspected.

85 to 130 Amp. Systems
1. Connect voltmeter to adapter as shown in View B, Fig. 8.
2. Turn all accessories off.
3. Operate alternator at approximately 3000 rpm (1200 engine rpm).
4. The alternator output should be at least 10 amperes below the rated output for this check. For example, if rated output is 85 amps the voltage setting output should be 75 amps or less.
5. To adjust voltage setting, see Fig. 18. If regulator cannot be adjusted to a value within the specified range, replace or repair the regulator.

NOTE: If repeated regulator failures are experienced on the vehicle, but no defects are found, a shorted, grounded or open alternator field winding, or grounded leads of an intermittent nature should be suspected.

TAILORING VOLTAGE SETTING

On Vehicle

Proper setting is obtained when the battery remains fully charged with a minimum use of water. If no circuit defects are found, yet the battery remains undercharged, raise the setting by 0.3 volt, then check the battery over a period of time to see if improvements were achieved. Reset regulator if necessary. If the system is overcharging, lower the setting by 0.3 volt, then check the battery over a period of time.

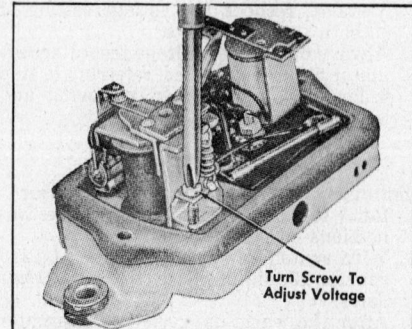

Fig. 16 Adjusting voltage setting on transistorized regulator

ALTERNATOR FIELD CIRCUIT CHECK

Series 3D & 4D Systems

1. Connect a voltmeter to adapter as shown in View B, Fig. 8.
2. Turn on ignition switch.
3. If voltmeter indicates 1 or 2 volts less than battery voltage, proceed to check alternator output explained previously.
4. If voltmeter indicates zero volts, the regulator is defective and must be replaced.

CAUTION: The regulator defect may have been caused by a defective alternator field. Check the field as follows before installing the new regulator.

5. Turn off ignition switch and disconnect battery ground strap.
6. Disconnect adapter from regulator.
7. Connect an ohmmeter to the adapter as shown in View C, Fig. 8.
8. If the ohmmeter indicates high, there is an open or excessive resistance in the field winding or in wiring between regulator positive terminal and alternator "F1" terminal (Lead E, Fig. 19).
9. If ohmmeter indicates low the winding is shorted or grounded.

NOTE: Since the reading is taken through the adapter, leads, brushes and slip rings, the ohmmeter reading on a good field winding will be slightly higher than the specified value. This is because the specified values is for an ohmmeter reading directly across the slip rings.

10. Disconnect ohmmeter and reconnect battery ground strap.

DELCO-REMY "DELCOTRON"

EXCESSIVE RESISTANCE TEST
Series 3D & 4D Systems

Excessive resistance in the sensing circuit, consisting of the wiring and voltage regulator, can cause an overcharged battery. If the trouble is not battery overcharge, proceed with the "Regulator Voltage Test" explained previously. Otherwise, proceed as follows:

1. Connect a voltmeter as shown in Part 1 and Part 2 in view D, Fig. 8.
2. Turn on ignition switch but do not start engine.
3. If the two voltmeter readings total more than 0.3 volt, check for excessive resistance in leads B, C and D, Fig. 19, which can cause an overcharged battery. If these leads are satisfactory, the field relay contacts may have excessive resistance. In this event, replace field relay unit.

VOLTAGE REGULATOR ADJUSTMENTS

CAUTION: Before removing a voltage regula-

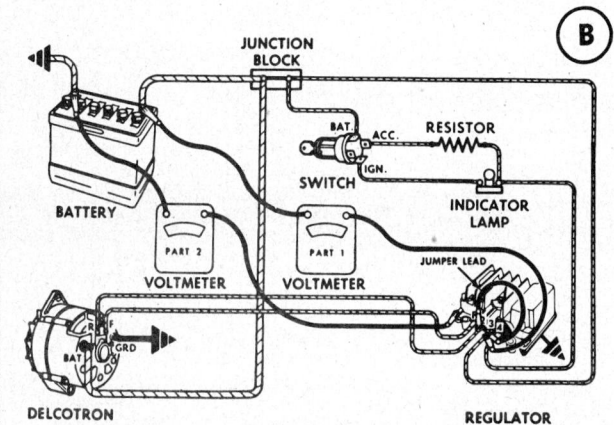
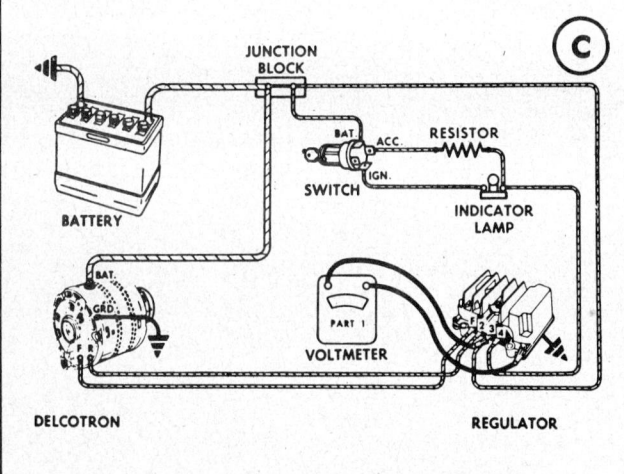
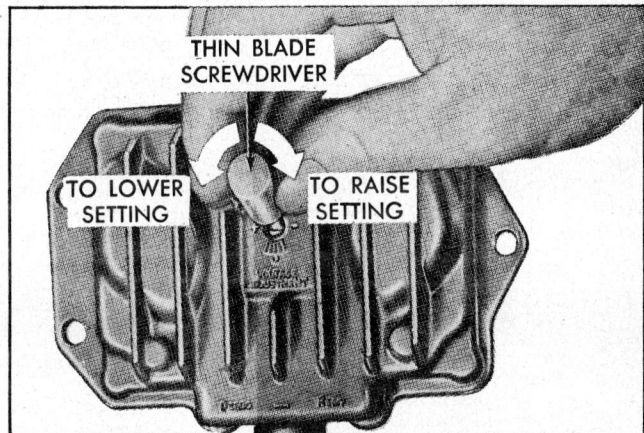

Fig. 18 Adjusting voltage setting on full transistor regulator

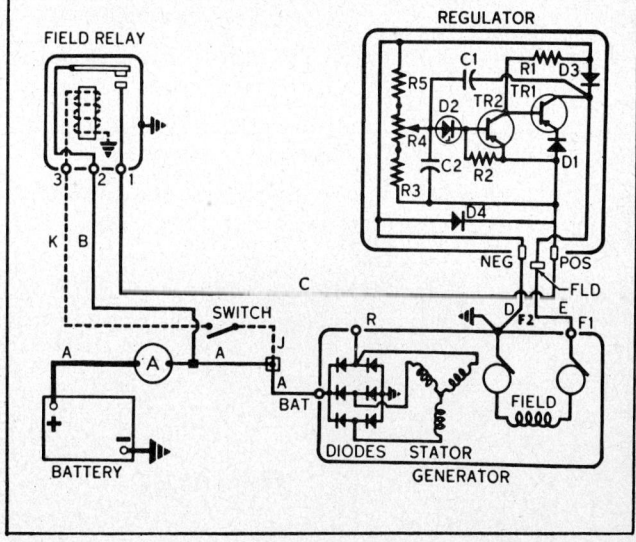

Fig. 17 Connections for testing regulator voltage setting on vehicle with full transistor regulator

11. If the voltmeter indicates battery voltage, the regulator is shorted and must be replaced, or the alternator field winding is open or grounded. Check the field winding as outlined above.

12. To check the regulator, connect a voltmeter as shown in View A, Fig. 8, and operate engine at moderate speed. If the voltage is uncontrolled and increases with speed to values above the specified setting range, replace or repair the regulator.

Fig. 19 Schematic diagram (typical) of Series 3D & 4D

69

DELCO-REMY "DELCOTRON"

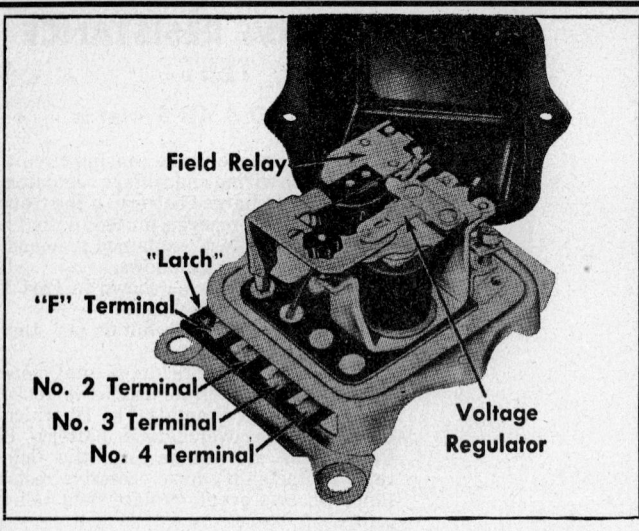

Fig. 20 Two-unit voltage regulator

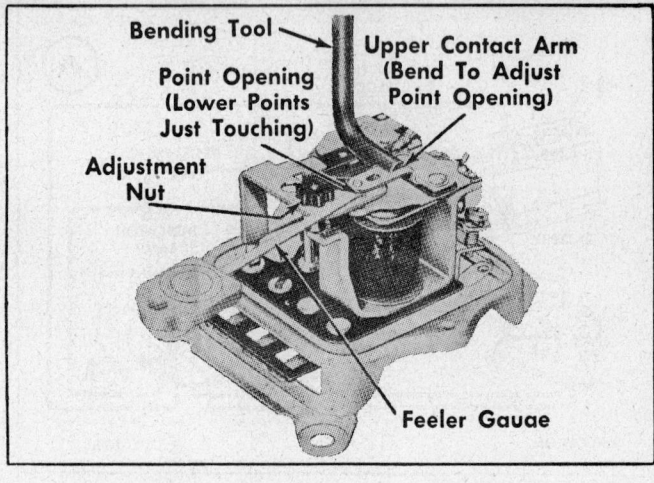

Fig. 21 Adjusting contact point opening

tor from a vehicle, be sure to disconnect one battery cable and leave it disconnected until after the unit is installed on the vehicle.

NOTE: In making the following adjustments, refer to the "Alternator Specifications" charts in the vehicle chapters for the proper feeler gauges to use to obtain the specified settings.

Two-Unit Regulators

Cleaning Contact Points, Fig. 20

If the points are dirty or oxidized, they must be cleaned before any adjustments are made since the cleaning may change the mechanical settings. The upper contacts may develop slight cavities. These surfaces should be cleaned to the bare metal, using #400 silicone carbide paper (or equivalent) folded over, then pulled back and forth between contacts.

It is not necessary to remove the cavities entirely. The lower contacts are of softer material; use a piece of cloth with solvent to remove any discoloration. *Do not use abrasive on these points.* After contacts have been cleaned, they should be washed with a solvent (non-toxic type) to remove any foreign material.

Adjusting Contact Point Opening

With the lower contacts touching, measure the opening between the upper contacts as shown in Fig. 21. Point opening should be as specified in the "Alternator Specifications" chart in the vehicle chapters. Adjust by bending the upper contact arm as shown, being careful not to bend the hinge.

Adjusting Air Gap

Measure the air gap between armature and core when the lower contacts are just touching as shown in Fig. 22. If the clearance is not as specified in the "Alternator Specifications" chart in vehicle chapters, turn the adjusting nut located on the contact support as required.

NOTE: Only an approximate air gap setting should be made by the feeler gauge method. The final setting must be whatever is required to obtain the specified difference in voltage between the upper and lower contacts. Instructions for making the final setting are explained previously under "Regulator Voltage Test On Vehicle."

Field Relay Unit

Cleaning Contact Points

If points appear to be pitted or burned, clean them with a thin cut file. Remove only enough material to clean points. Never use emergy cloth or sandpaper for this operation.

Adjusting Air Gap

Referring to Fig. 23, measure clearance between armature and core and exert just enough pressure on the armature to allow it to touch the feeler gauge. The gauge should be the thickness of the specified clearance in "Alternator Specifications" chart in the vehicle chapters. The contact points should just close at this time. Adjust by bending the flat contact support spring.

Adjusting Contact Point Gap

Referring to Fig. 24, measure gap between the contact points with the armature in its normal at rest position. If the gap is not according to the clearance listed in the "Alternator Specifications" chart in the vehicle chapter, adjust be bending the relay heel iron.

Adjusting Closing Voltage

To adjust the closing voltage, connect a 100–150-ohm variable resistor with an "OFF" position between the positive post of a 12-volt battery and the No. 2 terminal of the regulator.

Connect a jumper lead from the regulator base to the battery negative cable as a ground. Connect a voltmeter between the regulator No. 2 terminal and regulator base. Slowly decrease the resistance, noting the voltage at which the relay closes. Adjust the voltage to specifications by bending the armature heel

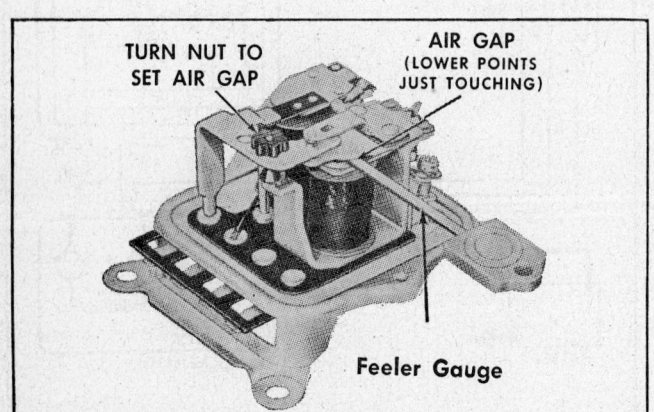

Fig. 22 Adjusting regulator air gap

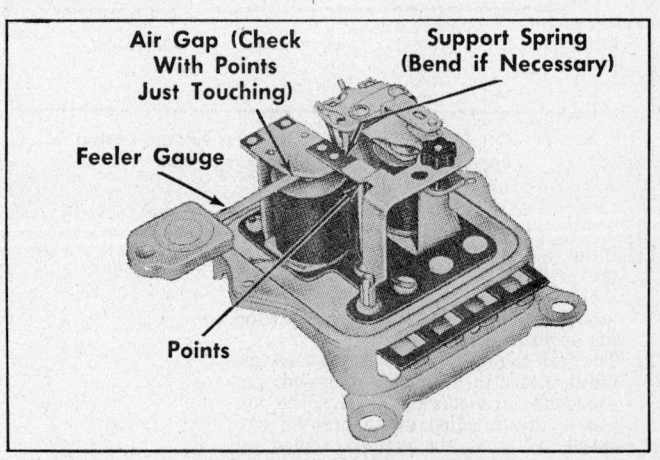

Fig. 23 Adjusting field relay air gap

DELCO-REMY "DELCOTRON"

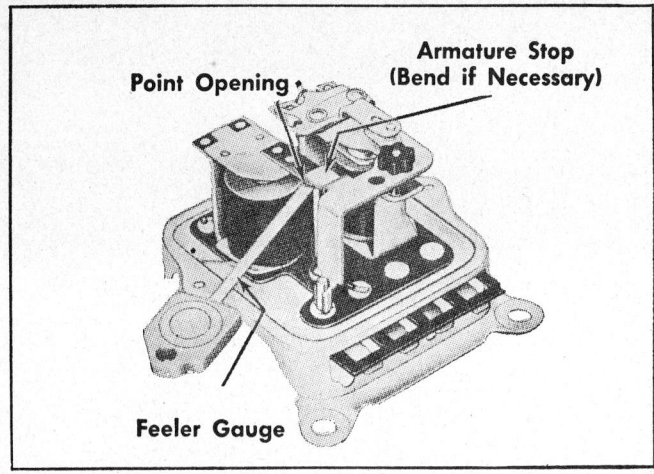

Fig. 24 Adjusting field relay contact points

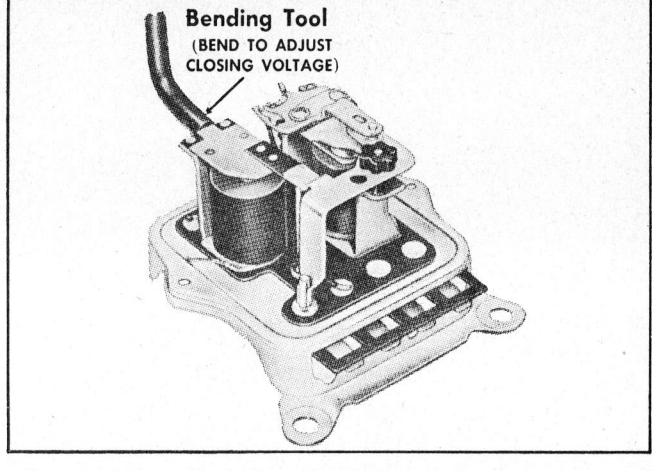

Fig. 25 Adjusting field relay closing voltage

iron shown in Fig. 25 (see "Alternator Specifications" in vehicle chapters).

Transistorized Regulator

When removing or installing the regulator, be sure to have one of the battery cables disconnected. After removing the regulator, remove the cover and inspect the various components, connections, and contact points for signs of damage, Fig. 26. When making adjustments, see the "Alternator Specifications" charts in the vehicle chapters.

Cleaning Contact Points

If the points are dirty or oxidized, they must be cleaned before any adjustments are made since the cleaning may change the mechanical settings. The contact surfaces may oxidize and develop a slight cavity. These surfaces should be cleaned to the bare metal, using a riffle file as shown in Fig. 27. It may be necessary to remove the point support as shown to provide file clearance. Do not file points excessively.

Adjusting Air Gap

Measure the gap between the armature and core, Fig. 28. Push down on the armature (not the flat spring that contains the movable point). The points should just touch when the armature bottoms on the proper feeler gauge. If the air gap is not as specified, loosen the contact bracket mounting screws and adjust the bracket, up or down as required. Make sure points are squarely aligned, then tighten screws and recheck air gap.

The regulator limiting voltage is adjusted after the unit is installed on the vehicle. See instructions for making final setting under "Voltage Regulator Check."

Field Relay

Adjusting Air Gap

Measure the clearance with a feeler gauge of the specified thickness between armature and core. Press down on the armature; the contact points should just touch when the armature bottoms. If the clearance is not as specified, adjust by carefully bending the flat contact support spring, Fig. 29.

Adjusting Point Opening

The point opening is measured in the open or at rest position. The opening should be as

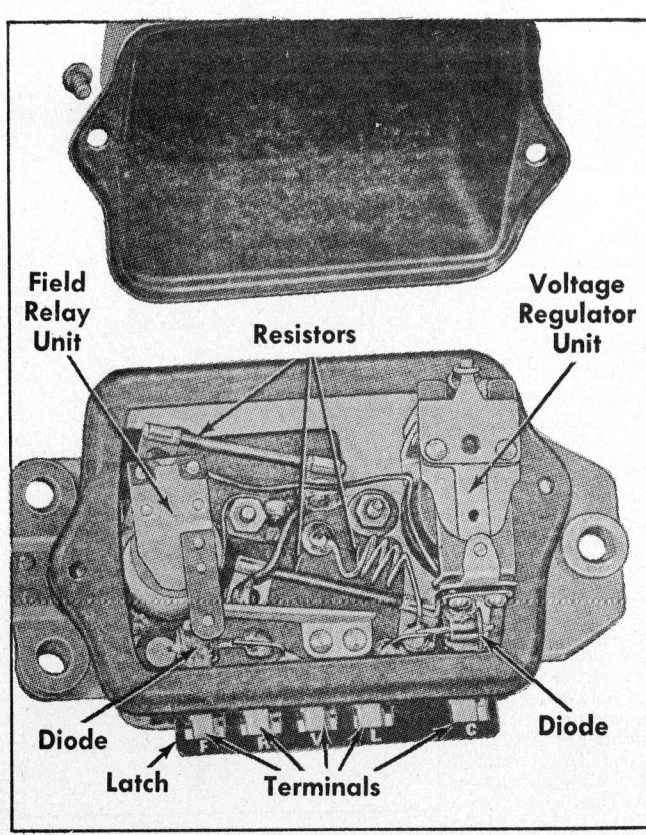

Fig. 26 Transistorized voltage regulator with cover removed

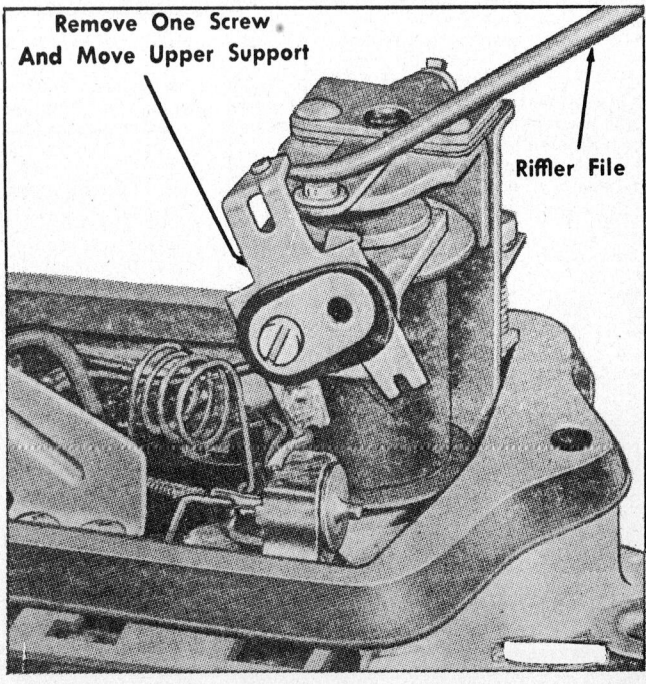

Fig. 27 Cleaning regulator contact points

DELCO-REMY "DELCOTRON"

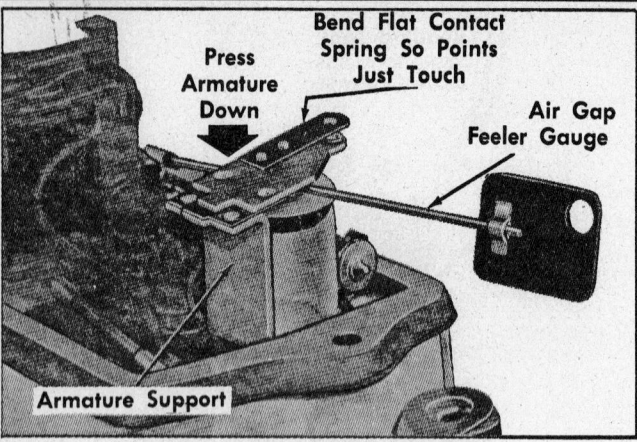

Fig. 28 Adjusting regulator air gap

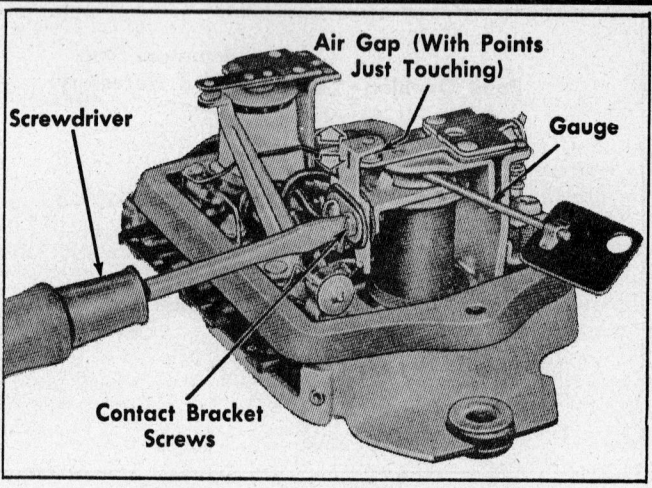

Fig. 29 Checking field relay air gap

specified and may be adjusted by bending the heel iron in the same manner as when adjusting the closing voltage, Fig. 30. This setting is in general a reference point and is not critical. If the air gap and closing voltage are correct, the relay will operate satisfactorily even though the point opening may not be exactly according to specifications.

Adjusting Closing Voltage

Connect a 100–150 ohm variable resistor with an "OFF" position between the positive post of a 12-volt battery and the "R" terminal of the regulator. Connect a jumper lead from the regulator base to the battery negative post as a ground. Connect a voltmeter to the "R" terminal and the regulator base, then slowly decrease the resistance, noting the voltage at which the relay closes. Adjust to the specified voltage by bending the heel iron, Fig. 30.

Transistor and Diode Check

Referring to Fig. 31, the transistor can be checked by connecting a jumper lead between the regulator "V" terminal and the positive post of a 12-volt battery. Use another jumper lead to ground the regulator frame to the negative battery post.

Connect a voltmeter between the "F" terminal and ground, manually close the field relay, and check the meter reading. Meter should indicate 8 or more volts. A reading under 8 volts indicates an open transistor that must be replaced.

With the field relay still held closed, manually open the voltage regulator and note the voltage. If the voltage is more than 2 volts, the transistor is shorted and must be replaced.

Disconnect the test leads.

If the transistor is open or shorted, replace the unit by removing the two retaining nuts and screws, then unsolder the connections (upper view, Fig. 31). When installing the new transistor, use rosin core solder (60% tin, 40% lead). Limit the soldering time to avoid damage to the transistor.

If the voltage setting was found to be high or low during the diagnosis, or a failed transistor was found, check the two regulator diodes, Fig. 32. It is necessary to unsolder the diode leads before testing. Using the test lamp as shown, check the current flow through the field diode, then reverse test lamp leads. Test lamp should light in one direction only. If lamp lights in both directions, the diode is defective and must be replaced. Check the suppression diode in the same manner.

To replace a diode, melt the solder from around its mounting and at lead connection. When installing the new diode, limit soldering time to a minimum as excessive heat may damage the diode.

NOTE: After performing the foregoing operations, install the unit in the vehicle and adjust the voltage setting as outlined previously under "Voltage Regulator Check."

Full Transistor Regulator

Four-Terminal Type, Fig. 33

This type regulator is composed of transistors, diodes, capacitors, and resistors. These components form a completely static electrical unit containing no moving parts. A combination field and light relay is also part of the entire assembly.

The function of the regulator in the charging circuit is to limit alternator voltage to a pre-set value by controlling the alternator field current.

Regulator Repairs

With the regulator removed from the vehicle, remove the cover and inspect the various components, connections, and field relay contact points for signs of damage.

If the field relay contact points are dirty or oxidized, they should be cleaned. The contact surfaces may oxidize and develop a slight cavity. These surfaces should be cleaned to the bare metal, using a riffler file. Do not file excessively.

If the voltage regulator cannot be adjusted to specifications listed in the "Alternator Specifications" charts in the vehicle chapters, replace the regulator assembly.

Three-Terminal Plug Type, Fig. 34

Like the four-terminal type, the regulator is an assembly composed principally of transistors, diodes, capacitors, and resistors. These components form a completely static electrical unit containing no moving parts.

A separate field relay is included in the control system to disconnect the regulator feed (positive) terminal from the battery circuit

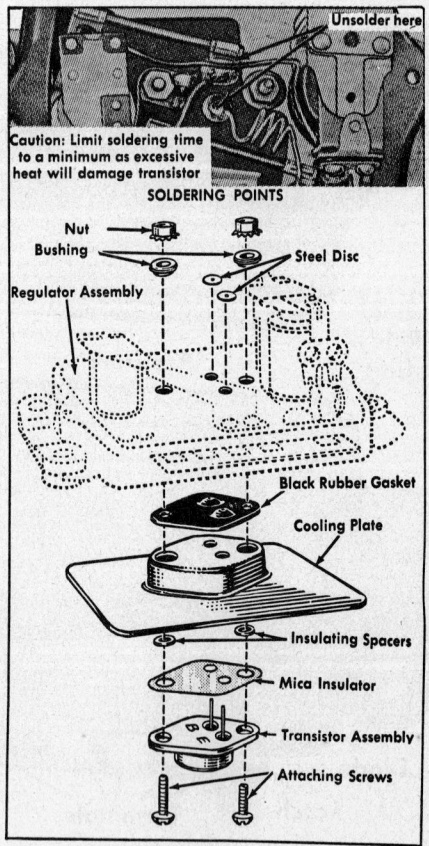

Fig. 31 Transistorized regulator installation views

Fig. 30 Adjusting field relay closing voltage

DELCO-REMY "DELCOTRON"

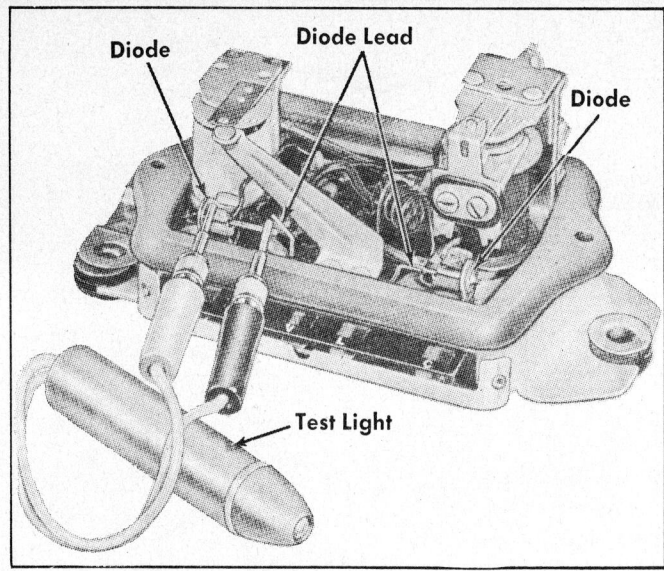

Fig. 32 Checking diodes with test lamp

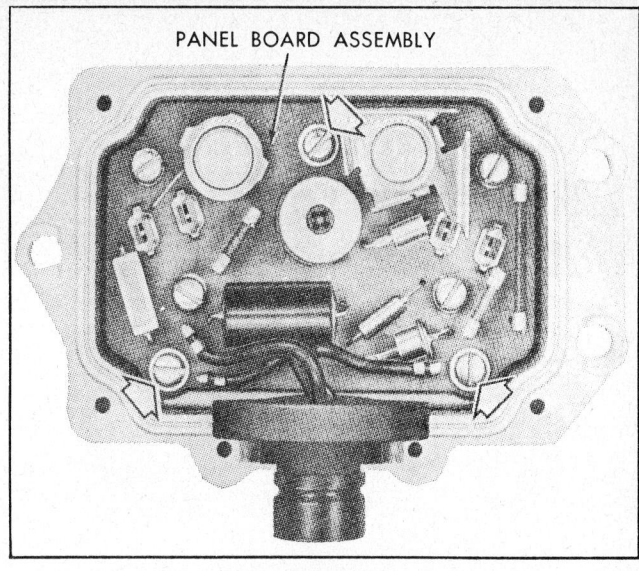

Fig. 35 Regulator with bottom plate removed

when the ignition switch is in the "OFF" position. Supression of radio interference is accomplished by a capacitor on the alternator.

CAUTION: The field wire terminal must not be grounded or flashed when the regulator is connected into the circuit as instant damage to the transistors will occur.

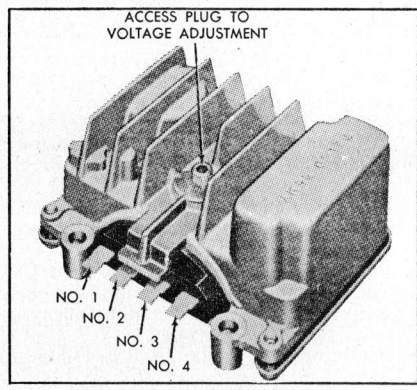

Fig. 33 Full transistor type voltage regulator with four terminals

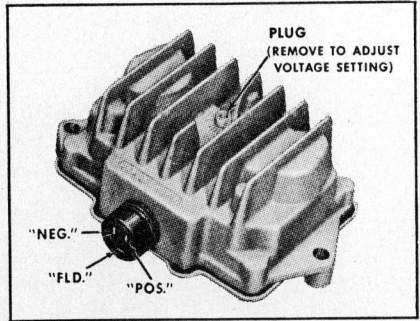

Fig. 34 Full transistor type voltage regulator with three-terminal plug

Analyzing System Troubles

If the trouble is located in the alternator during test procedures outlined previously, refer to the applicable alternator section for corrective procedures.

When analyzing the system, make sure all the connections between the battery, junction block, and alternator are clean and tight. Then remove the wiring harness connector from the regulator and connect adapter (J-21600) between wiring harness connector and the regulator.

Regulator Repairs

1. Remove bottom plate from regulator. Remove three panel board attaching screws identified by arrows, Fig. 35, and lift assembly from housing.
2. To aid in reassembly, note or make any identifying marks on the two transistors and their respective locations on the panel board and heat sink assembly, Fig. 36.
3. Note the insulators between the transistors and the heat sink, and the insulators separating the heat sink from the panel board, Fig. 36.
4. Remove the transistor attaching screws, and separate transistors and heat sink from panel board.

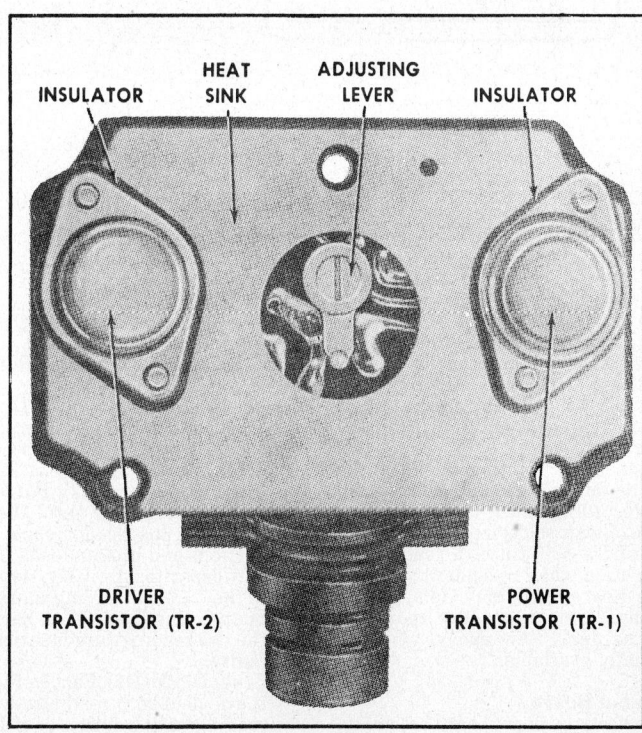

Fig. 36 Top side of regulator panel board

73

DELCO-REMY "DELCOTRON"

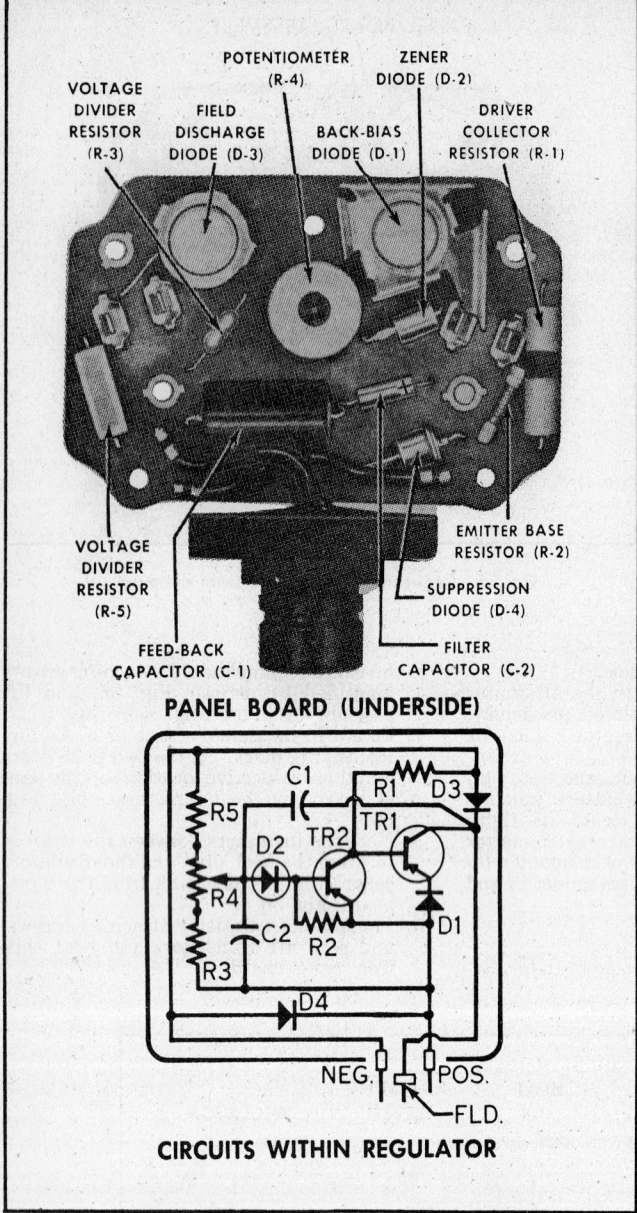

Fig. 37 Underside of regulator panel board

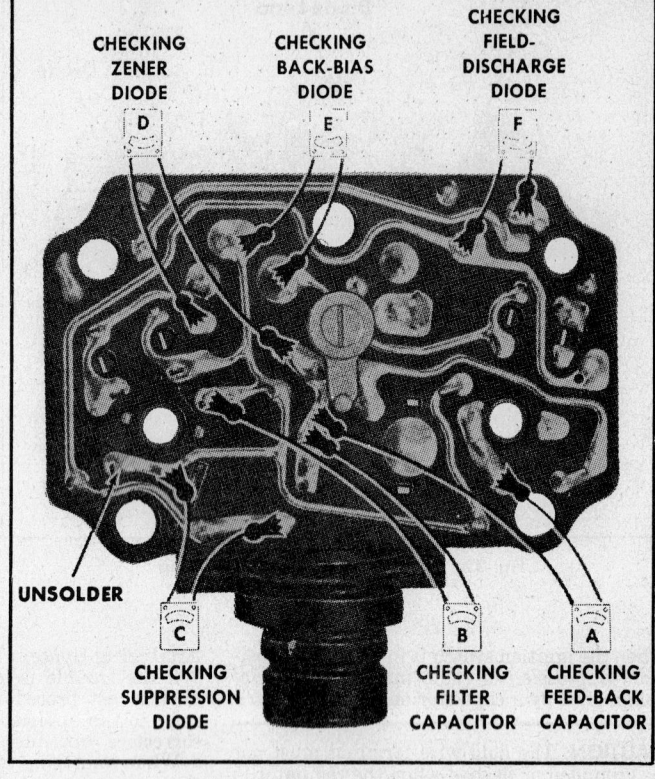

Fig. 38 Checking regulator circuits

5. With the transistors separated from the assembly, an ohmmeter may be used to check the transistors and components on the panel board for defects. An ohmmeter having a 1½ volt cell is recommended. The low range scale on the ohmmeter should be read.
6. If a component part on the panel board is found to be faulty, it should be replaced before proceeding with the remaining checks. A 25-watt soldering gun is recommended, and a 60% tin 40% lead solder should be used when re-soldering. Avoid excessive heat which may damage the panel board. Chip away any epoxy involved, and apply new epoxy, which is commercially available.

Checking Panel Board

In order to check the panel board assembly, it is necessary to unsolder the emitter-base resistor at the location shown in Fig. 38. In all the following checks, connect the ohmmeter as shown and then reverse the ohmmeter leads to obtain two readings. Refer to Figs. 36, 37, 38.

1. Feed-Back Capacitor (C1), Part A, Fig. 38: If both readings are zero, the capacitor is defective. Visually inspect for open soldered connections and broken leads.
2. Filter Capacitor (C2), Part B, Fig. 38: If both readings are zero, the capacitor is defective. Inspect for open soldered connections and broken leads. To assemble a new capacitor properly, note the location of the "+" identifying mark in Fig. 37.
3. Suppression Diode (C4), Part C, Fig. 38: If the two readings are identical the diode is faulty.
4. Zener Diode (D2), Part D, Fig. 38: Replace the diode if both readings are zero, if both readings are infinite, or if both readings are identical.
5. Back-Bias Diode (D1) Part E, Fig. 38: Replace diode if both readings are zero, if both readings are infinite or if both readings are identical.
6. Field Discharge Diode (D3), Part F, Fig. 38: Replace the diode if both readings are zero, if both readings are infinite, or if both readings are identical.
7. Driver-Collector Resistor, Part A, Fig. 39: If both readings are infinite the resistor is open.
8. Voltage-Divider Resistor (R3), Part B, Fig. 39: If one reading is infinite or nearly so, or if both readings are infinite or nearly so the resistor is open.
9. Voltage-Divider Resistor (R5), Part C, Fig. 39: If one reading is infinite or nearly so, or if both readings are infinite or nearly so, the resistor is open.
10. Potentiometer, Parts D and E, Fig. 39: If

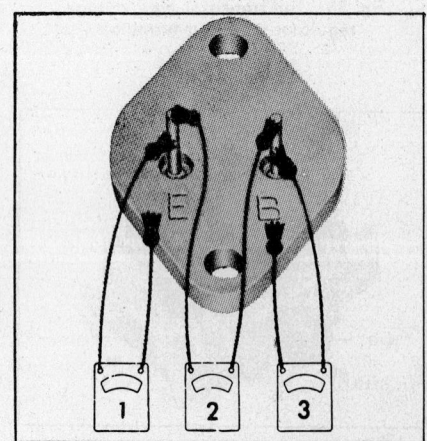

Fig. 40 Checking transistor for shorts

DELCO-REMY "DELCOTRON"

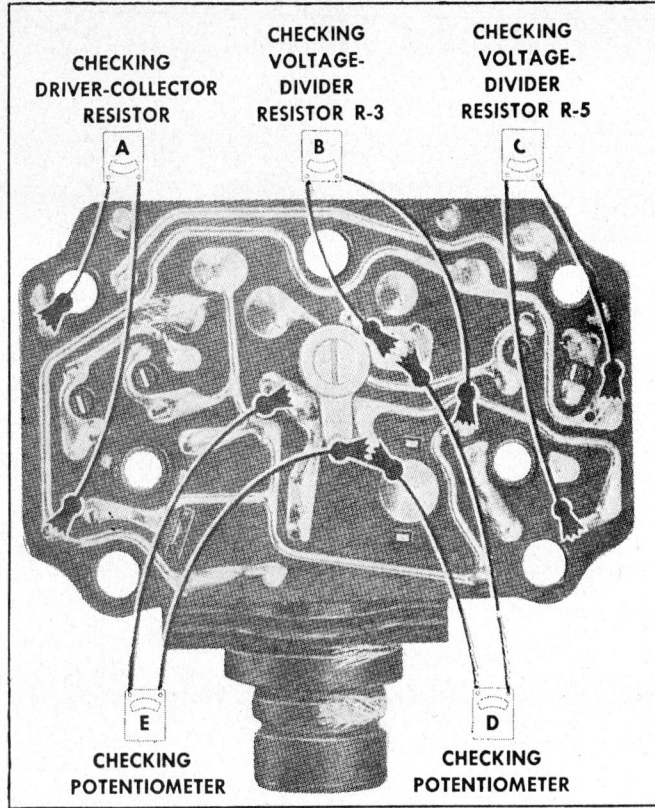

Fig. 39 Checking regulator circuits

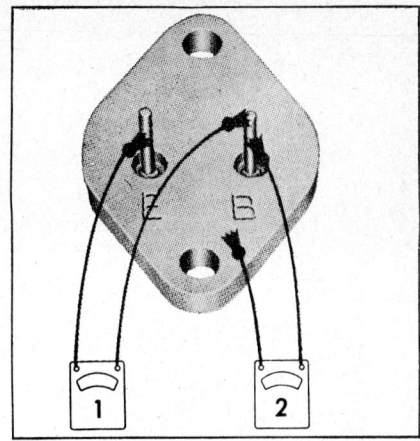

Fig. 41 Checking transistor for open

Relay Adjustments
Remove cover from relay, Fig. 42. Before attempting adjustment of the relay, make sure points are clean. Clean contacts with a thin, fine-cut contact file if pitted or burned.

Air Gap, Fig. 42
Disconnect wire from No. 2 terminal on relay. With contact points just touching, measure air gap (.010" minimum) between armature and center of coil. If necessary, adjust air gap by bending the lower point support.

Point Opening, Fig. 42
Measure point opening with armature up against stop. Correct dimension is .015 to .025". If necessary, adjust by bending armature stop.

Closing Voltage, Fig. 43
Connect an accurate reading voltmeter parallel with the relay operating circuit (No. 3 terminal to ground). Connect a variable resistance unit in series with the operating circuit (at No. 3 terminal). Turn ignition switch on. Adjust variable resistance until relay points close and note voltmeter reading. Points should close between 7 and 9 volts. Adjustment is made by bending armature spring post to increase or decrease spring tension on armature, Fig. 42.

one reading is infinite or nearly so in Part D, the potentiometer is open. If both readings are infinite in Part E, the potentiometer is open.

NOTE: When installing a new potentiometer, locate the adjusting lever in a vertical position, Fig. 36. Turn the potentiometer resistance adjustment to the middle position, then use a soldering iron to melt the adjusting lever into the potentiometer.

11. Emitter-Base Resistor: Since this resistor has been unsoldered from the panel board at one end, merely connect an ohmmeter across the resistor; an infinite reading indicates an open, in which case replace the resistor.
12. Driver and Power Transistors, Fig. 40: If both readings in Step 1 are zero or if both readings are very low or indentical, the transistor is shorted. Similarly, if both readings in Step 2 or in Step 3 are zero or very low and identical, the transistor is shorted.
13. Driver and Power Transistors (TR1 and 2), Fig. 41: If both readings in Step 1 are infinite or if both readings are very high and identical, the transistor is open. Similarly, if both readings in Step 2 are infinite or very high and identical, the transistor is open.

Reassembly and Final Check
During assembly, coat with silicone grease both sides of the flat insulators used between the transistors and heat sink, and also the heat sink on the side on which the transistors are mounted. The silicone grease increases heat condition.

Field Relay Unit
When used, the separate field relay unit completes the battery circuit to the voltage regulator, which in turn energizes the alternator field windings when the ignition switch is on. The procedure for checking the field relay on the vehicle is explained previously under "Field Relay Unit Test."

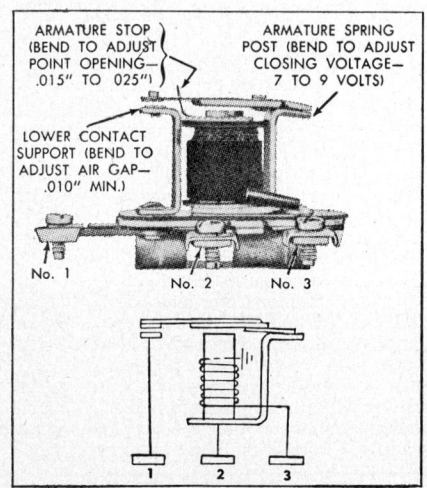

Fig. 42 Separate field relay unit

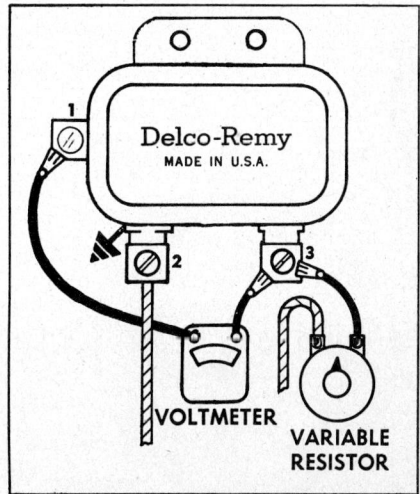

Fig. 43 Checking relay operation

DELCO-REMY "DELCOTRON"

Delcotron Series 1D

DISASSEMBLY

The alternator may be disassembled into major components shown in Fig. 1. After bench tests have been made, the slip ring end frame components may be disassembled if necessary to replace defective parts, Fig. 2.
1. Remove drive pulley and fan, Fig. 3.
2. Remove four thru-bolts that hold end frames together. Scribe a mark on end frames and stator frame to aid in locating parts when reassembling. Pry between stator frame and drive end frame to separate drive end frame and rotor from stator.

NOTE: Separation must be made between drive end frame and stator frame due to stator windings being attached to slip ring end frame assembly. Seal opening at end frame bearing with pressure-sensitive tape to prevent entry of dirt and other foreign material. Also tape bearing contact surface on end of rotor shaft to protect shaft from accidental damage. Do not use friction tape which could leave a gummy deposit on shaft.

3. If any lubricant from front end of rotor shaft has come in contact with brushes, wipe brushes clean. A nontoxic solvent may be used.
4. Remove three stator leads from terminals, Fig. 4. Remove stator from slip ring and end frame assembly.
5. Remove drive end frame and bearing assembly from rotor shaft. Note location of spacers at either end of bearing. There is one long spacer and one short spacer.

ELECTRICAL TESTS

Rotor Checks, Fig. 5

Checking for Ground with Test Lamp
Touch one test lamp lead to one of the slip rings and other lead to rotor pole or shaft. If lamp lights, windings are grounded and rotor assembly must be replaced.

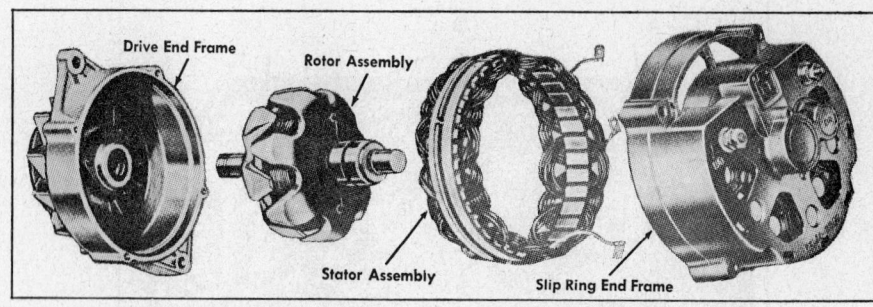

Fig. 1 Delcotron Series 1D alternator major components disassembled

Checking for Ground with Ohmmeter
Make test in same manner as with test lamp and observe reading. If reading is low indicating low resistance, the winding is grounded and rotor assembly must be replaced.

Checking for Open Circuit
Touch leads from lamp or ohmmeter to each of the slip rings. If lamp fails to light or if ohmmeter reading is high (infinite), the winding is open.

Checking for Shorted Rotor Winding
Either of two methods may be used to check rotor winding for shorts, 1) ammeter and battery method and 2) ohmmeter method.
1. Connect a 12-volt battery and ammeter in series with the two slip rings. Note ammeter reading. If reading is over 2.6 amperes, there is a short circuit in winding.
2. Connect ohmmeter leads to the two slip rings and note resistance reading. If resistance is less than 4.6 ohms, there is a short circuit in rotor winding.

NOTE: If an ohmmeter is not available, the resistance can be calculated by dividing the voltage by the current (amperes), using values from step 1 above.

If there are no defects found in the rotor assembly and alternator does not produce rated output when checked as outlined in "Alternator Output Test," trouble is in either the stator assembly or in the rectifying diodes.

Stator Checks, Fig. 6

1. Connect one test lamp lead or ohmmeter to any one of the three stator leads, and touch the other lead to the stator frame. If lamp lights or if ohmmeter reading is low, stator windings are grounded.
2. Connect test lamp leads or ohmmeter leads successively between pairs of stator winding leads. If lamp fails to light or if ohmmeter reading is high, an open circuit in stator windings is indicated.

NOTE: A short circuit in stator windings is difficult to locate without laboratory test equipment due to low resistance of the windings. However, if alternator output is below specified rating and none of the other tests show defects in other units, shorted stator windings are indicated. When defective stator windings are found, the complete stator assembly must be replaced.

Diode Checks, Fig. 7

Each of the six diodes may be checked electrically for a shorted or open condition, using either of the methods described below. Stator leads must be disconnected and lead from diode being tested must not be in contact with lead from other diode.

Checking Diodes with Ohmmeter
Use lowest range scale and a 1½ volt cell in ohmmeter. Connect one lead from ohmmeter to diode lead and other lead to diode case and note reading on ohmmeter. Reverse ohmmeter lead connections and note reading. If both readings are very low or if both readings are very high, the diode is defective. A good diode will show one low reading and one high reading. Check each diode in same manner.

NOTE: All diodes, if in good condition, will show one low reading and one high reading. But the respective reading at diodes in the heat sink will be opposite from those in the end frame assembly.

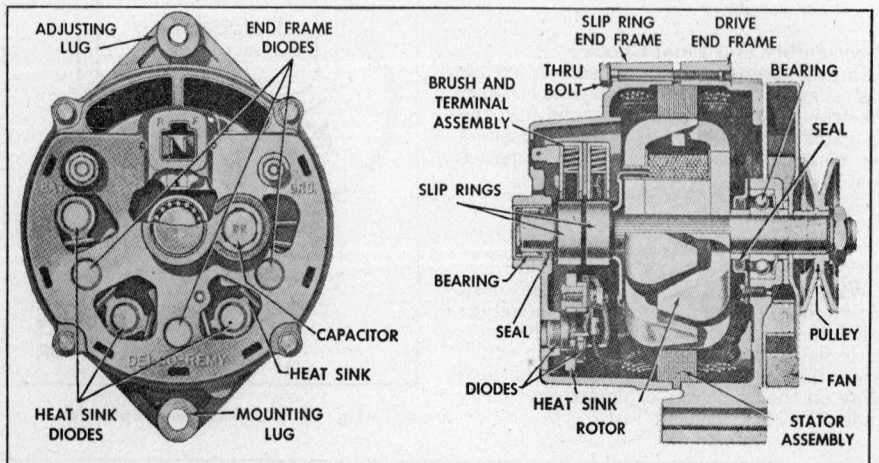

Fig. 2 Delcotron Series 1D alternator

76

DELCO-REMY "DELCOTRON"

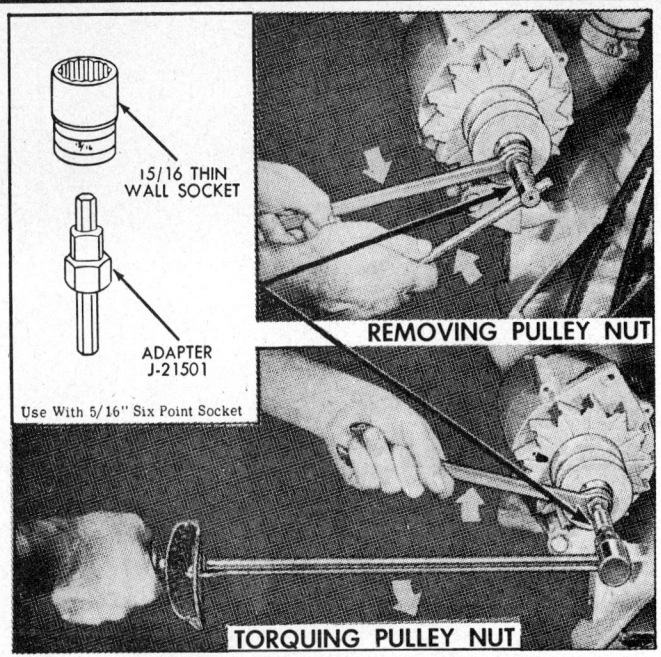

Fig. 3 Replacing pulley nut

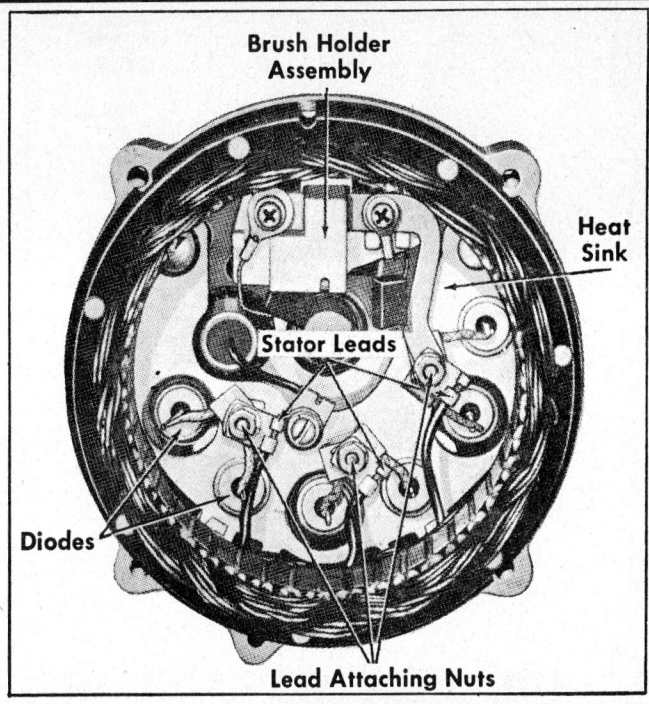

Fig. 4 Stator leads at junction studs

Checking Diodes with Test Lamp

An alternate method of checking diodes is to use a test lamp of not more than 12 volts in place of an ohmmeter. *Do not use 110-volt test lamp to check diodes.*

With stator leads disconnected, connect test lamp leads across each diode in same manner as given for the ohmmeter method. First check for current flow in one direction, then in reverse direction. If the test lamp lights in both checks, or fails to light in both checks, the diode is defective. When checking a good diode, the test lamp will light only when connected in one direction.

Special Testers

Special testers are available which operate without disconnecting stator. When using this type of equipment, follow manufacturer's instructions.

Capacitor Check, Fig. 7

The capacitor is pressed into retainer in the alternator end frame and capacitor lead is connected to the heat sink.

Since the capacitor rating is only 0.5 microfarads, it is impractical to test the capacitance with conventional equipment. However, when the alternator is disassembled for overhaul, a check should be made to be sure the insulation between elements is not permitting a current leak to ground.

Check can be made with a 12-volt test lamp or a 1½ volt ohmmeter. Connect one test lead to capacitor lead and other lead to condenser case. Wiggle the "pig tail" lead while observing ohmmeter or test lamp. If capacitor is good, the ohmmeter will show infinite (high) resistance or a test lamp will not glow during test.

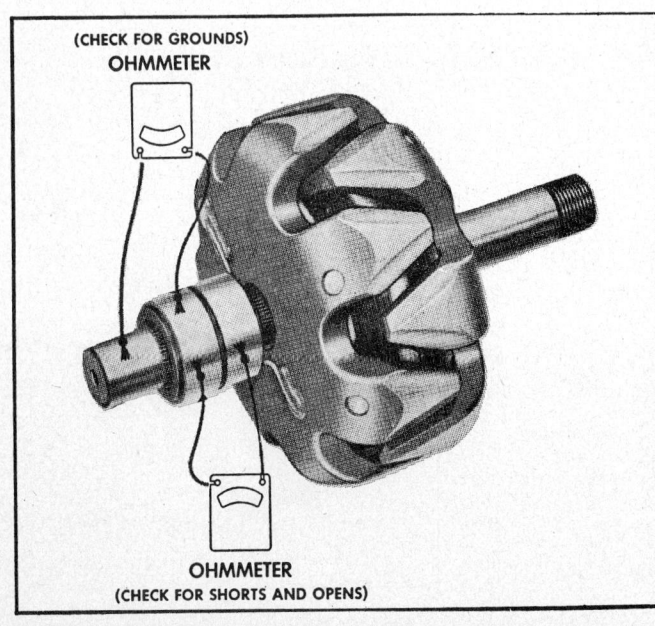

Fig. 5 Checking for grounded, shorted or open circuit in rotor

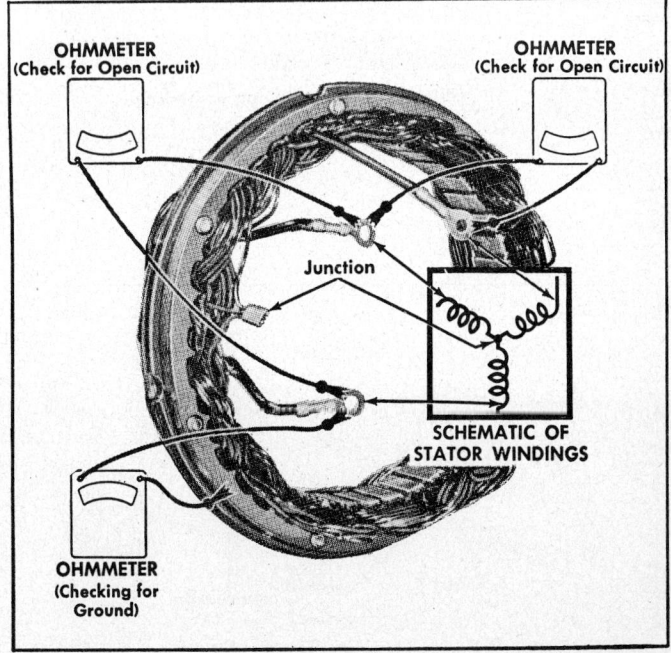

Fig. 6 Checking for grounded or open circuit in stator or windings

DELCO-REMY "DELCOTRON"

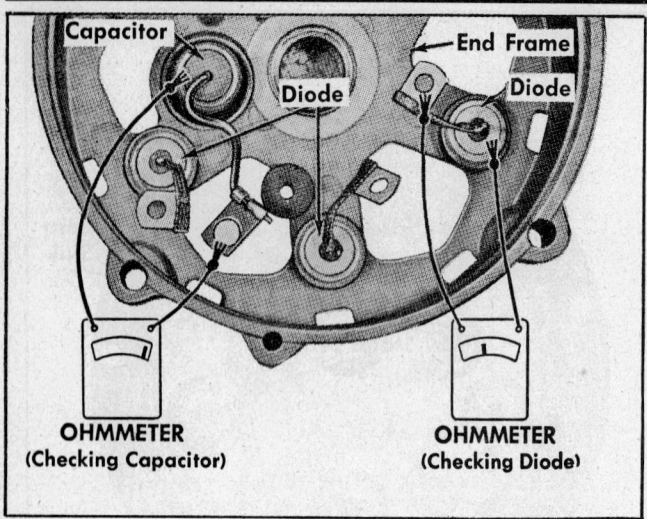

Fig. 7 Testing diode and capacitor

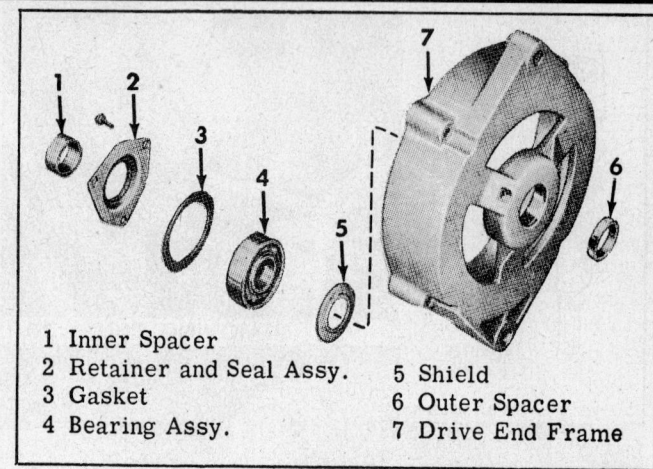

1 Inner Spacer
2 Retainer and Seal Assy.
3 Gasket
4 Bearing Assy.
5 Shield
6 Outer Spacer
7 Drive End Frame

Fig. 8 Drive end frame and bearing components

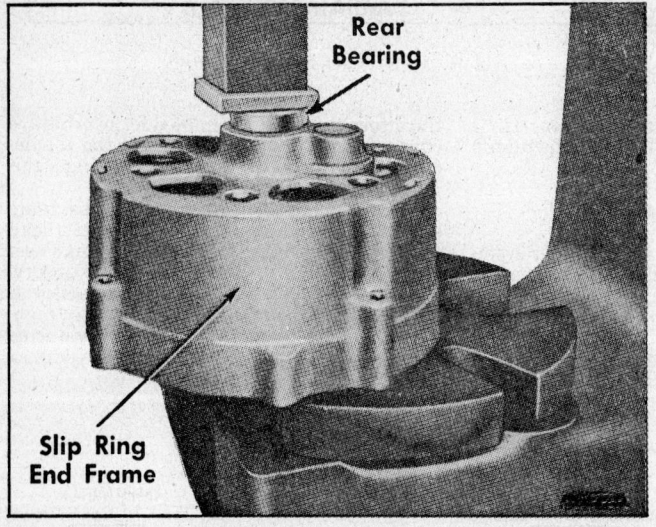

Fig. 9 Installing bearing in slip ring end frame

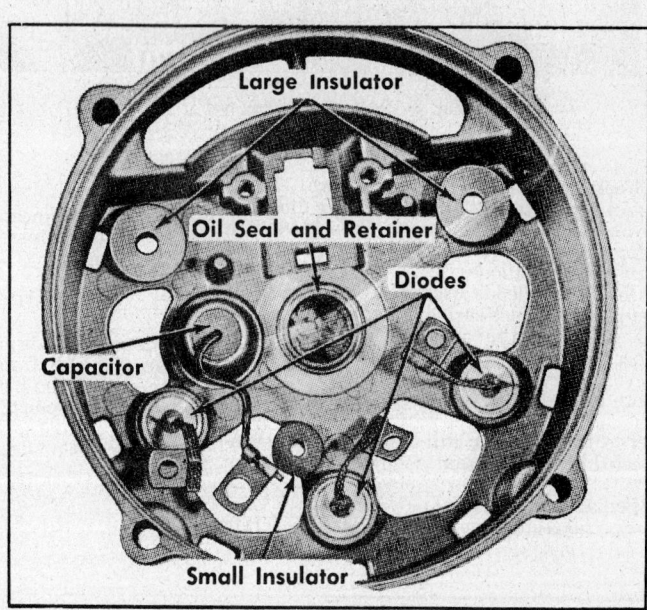

Fig. 11 Slip ring end frame with heat sink removed

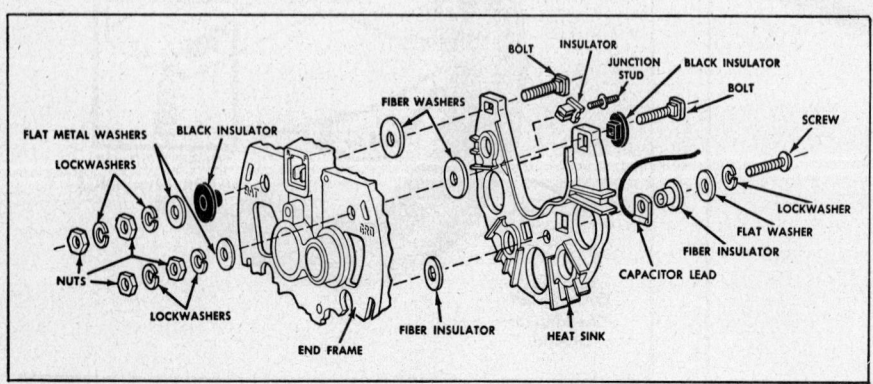

Fig. 10 Heat sink and associated parts disassembled

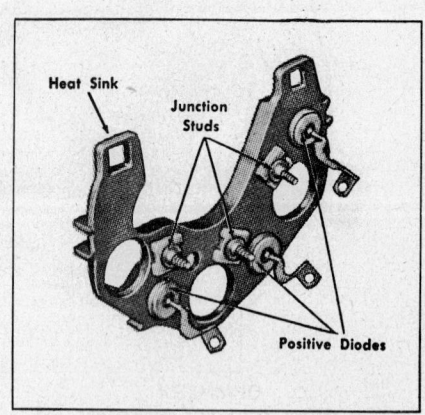

Fig. 12 Heat sink with positive diodes and junction studs installed

DELCO-REMY "DELCOTRON"

Any capacitor that allows current leakage as indicated by low ohmmeter reading must be replaced.

INSPECTION & REPAIRS

Inspection

1. Check drive end frame and bearing assembly for condition of bearing, felt seal, and retainer. Examine end frame for cracks and for damaged threads.
2. Rotor assembly should be inspected for scoring at slip rings and at surfaces contacted by shaft bearings. If shaft is damaged, a new rotor assembly should be installed.
3. Inspect brushes, brush springs and brush holder attached to slip ring end frame assembly. If brushes are worn to half of their original length or are damaged they must be replaced. Visually inspect brush springs; if distorted, worn or broken, replace with new springs.
4. Inspect rotor shaft bearing in slip ring end frame. If there is evidence that bearing has been run without lubricant, or if bearing is not in good condition, it must be replaced.

Repairs

Drive End Frame Bearing, Fig. 8
1. Remove retainer and seal from end frame (3 screws), then press bearing out of frame. Remove bearing shield from bearing recess in frame.
2. Place shield in recess and press bearing into place. Lubricant cavity in bearing and recess must not be packed solid, but should be only 1/4 filled.
3. Install bearing retainer and seal.

Slip Ring End Frame Bearing, Fig. 9
1. To remove bearing, use arbor press and a tube or shaft that just fits inside bore without interference. Support end frame and press from outer side to inner side of end frame.
2. Use a flat plate to press new bearing into end frame. Press from outer side of frame while supporting end frame. Use extreme care to avoid cocking bearing or placing undue strain on bearing. Outer (rear) end of bearing must be pressed in flush with outer surface of end frame.
3. Saturate felt seal with SAE 20 engine oil and install seal and steel retainer at inner end of bearing.

Heat Sink, Fig. 10
Heat sink and positive diodes can be replaced as an assembly after alternator is separated into major components. The following procedure covers replacing heat sink assembly on slip ring end frame:
1. If brush holder has not been removed from end frame, loosen screw that holds strap at brush holder so lower end of strap can be disengaged from junction terminal without bending strap. Also disengage negative diode leads from the three junction terminals if not previously done.
2. Remove "BAT" and "GRD" terminals with respective washers and insulators from end frame and heat sink.
3. Remove heat sink from end frame and the three insulating washers shown in Fig. 11.
4. With diodes and junction terminals installed in heat sink, place insulating washers in slip ring end frame, Fig. 11, then locate heat sink on washers in end frame. Be sure leads on diodes in end frame protrude through holes in heat sink. Assemble "BAT" and "GRD" termi-

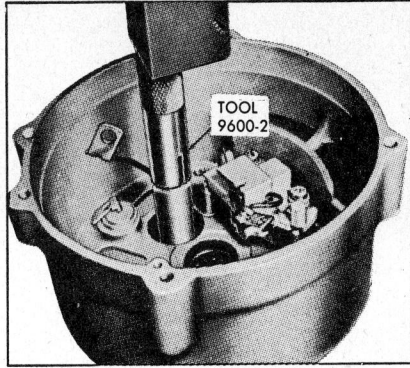

Fig. 13 Installing capacitor in end frame

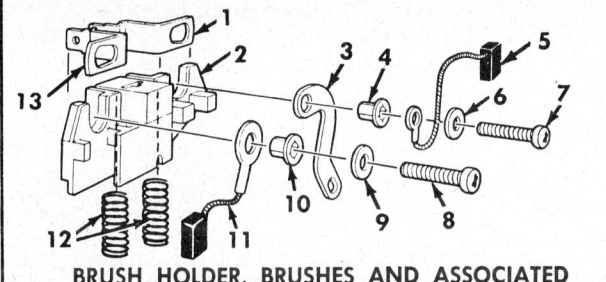

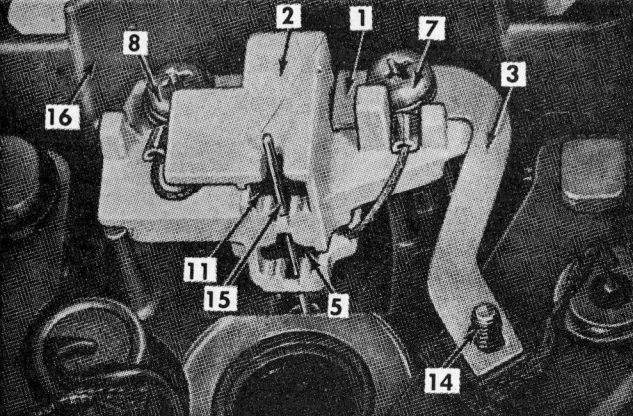

BRUSH HOLDER AND BRUSHES INSTALLED

1 Relay Terminal	10 Brush Insulator
2 Brush Holder	11 Field Current Brush
3 Strap	12 Brush Springs
4 Strap Insulator	13 Field Terminal
5 Ground Brush	14 Diode Junction Stud
6 Washer	15 Brush Retaining Pin
7 Ground Screw	(For Assembling Only)
8 Brush Holder Screw	
9 Washer	16 End Frame

Fig. 14 Brush and brush holder installation

 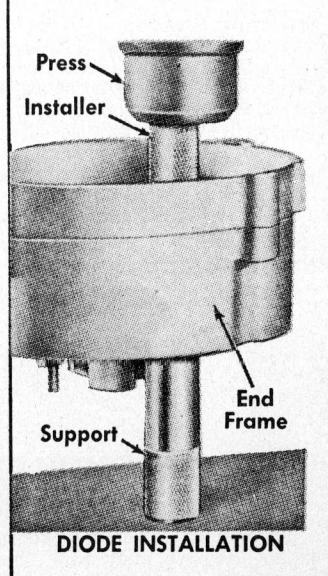

Fig. 15 Replacing diodes in end frame

DELCO-REMY "DELCOTRON"

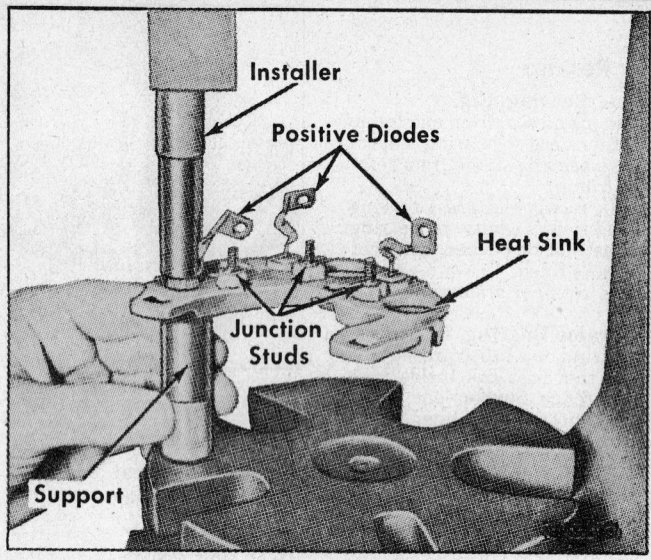

Fig. 16 Installing diodes in heat sink

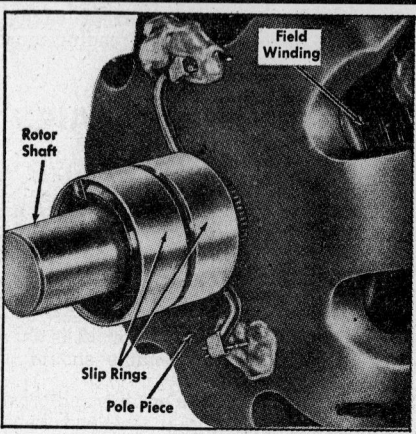

Fig. 17 Rotor and slip ring assembly

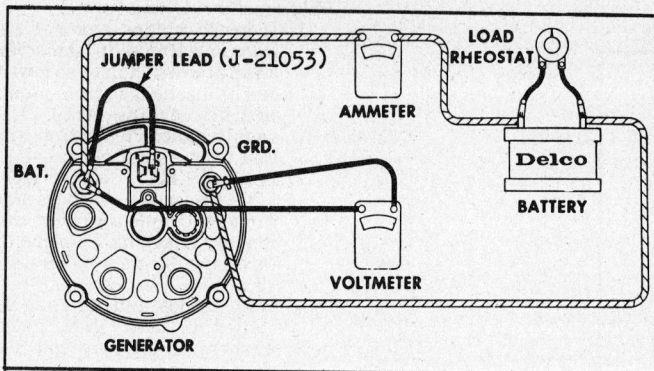

Fig. 18 Connections for bench-testing alternator

nal bolts, insulators and washers in the order shown in Fig. 10. Place lower end of strap on junction stud and tighten screw at brush holder.
5. Attach capacitor lead with screw, insulator, flat washer and lock washer, making sure insulating washer between heat sink and end frame is in place. Place diode leads in pairs on the three junction studs. *Do not install nuts on studs until stator is being assembled to slip ring end frame.*

Diode Junction Stud and Insulators

Diode junction studs and insulators are available for service replacement. Stud and insulator are shown in Figs. 10 and 12. To remove studs, support heat sink at flat side and press studs out of insulators. With pliers, remove insulators that are retained in heat sink by lugs.

Rotor Slip Ring Recondition, Fig. 17

Slip rings on rotor shaft may be cleaned with 400 grit or finer polishing cloth. Spin rotor in lathe to clean and polish slip rings.
Slip rings that are rough or out-of-round should be trued in a lathe to .002" total indicator reading. *Slip ring end of rotor shaft must not be gripped in lathe jaws.* Chuck rotor shaft only at pulley end.
Remove only enough material to make slip rings smooth and round. After lathe operation, finish slip ring surface with 400 grit or finer polishing cloth and blow away all dust.

ASSEMBLY

1. Place inner spacer on end of rotor shaft. Place drive end frame and bearing assembly on rotor shaft, then install outer spacer.
2. Place fan on rotor shaft, then install pulley, washer and nut, Fig. 3. Hold nut with wrench while turning shaft with torque wrench and hex driver in socket in shaft. Torque nut to 40-50 ft-lbs.
3. Assemble stator to slip ring end frame with stator leads engaging junction studs on heat sink. Be sure two diode leads and one stator lead are connected to each junction stud. Install lock washer and nut on each stud. Tighten "BAT" terminal stud to 20-25 inch-lbs torque. Tighten "GRD" terminal stud to 15-20 inch-lbs torque.
4. With slip ring brushes in respective holders and retained with pin or wire as shown in Fig. 14, place slip ring end frame assembly over rotor assembly. Refer to marks made at disassembly, align marks, then install through-bolts.
5. Pull out brush retaining wire or pin to allow brushes to contact with slip rings.

Bench Test After Assembly

Fig. 18 shows wiring connections for making alternator output test on bench. Refer to charts in Truck Chapters for specifications.

Delcotron Series 2D

DISASSEMBLE

1. Referring to Figs. 1 and 2, remove two nuts and washers from sockets and terminals. Remove relay wire, then remove socket and terminals.
2. Remove two capacitor and brush holder mounting screws and separate capacitor from brush holder. Lift brush holder and brushes out of cavity in end frame.

NOTE: Capacitor lead is attached to heat sink inside end frame. Avoid unnecessary strain on capacitor lead and relay lead. If brush springs remain inside alternator, remove them and place with brushes.

3. Remove nut from field relay terminal on brush holder to remove insulated brush.
4. Remove three slip ring end frame bolts and washers that secure end frame to stator shell. Remove three special nuts from

DELCO-REMY "DELCOTRON"

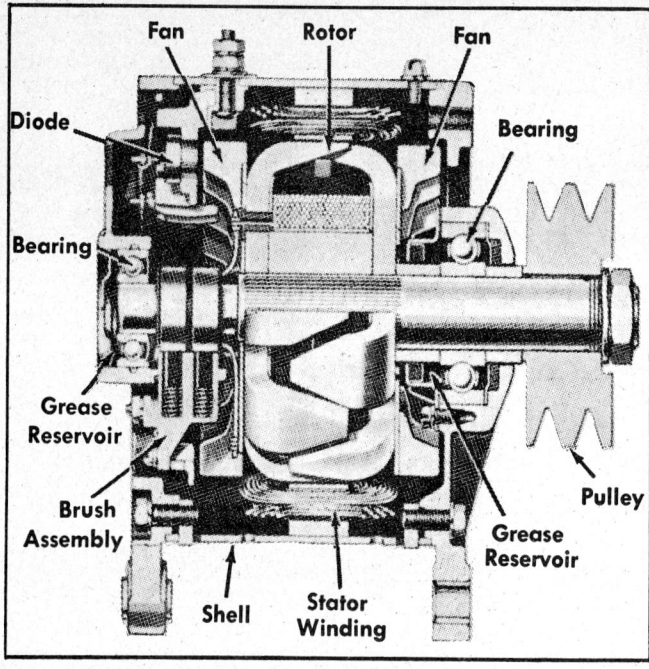

Fig. 1 Delcotron Series 2D

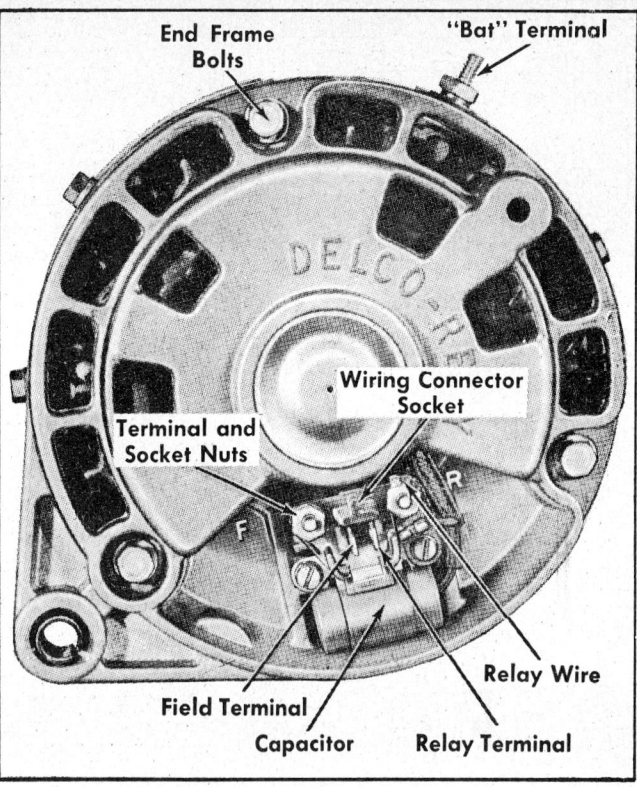

Fig. 2 Rear view of series 2D alternator

slots in stator shell.
5. Pry between stator shell and slip ring end frame to force end frame off rotor shaft rear bearing. Do not cock frame excessively as it is pried off. Fig. 9 shows slip ring end frame removed from alternator. Note that capacitor and relay leads must pass through opening in end frame as end frame is removed and must remain with stator assembly.
6. Remove three bolts, washers and special nuts that attach drive end frame to stator shell. Separate stator and shell from drive end frame and rotor.
7. Remove pulley and Woodruff key and slide end frame and two spacers off shaft. Further disassembly is not required unless inspection and tests indicate necessity for parts replacement.

ELECTRICAL TESTS

Rotor Checks, Fig. 3

Checking for Ground

When using a test lamp, touch one test lamp lead to one slip ring and other lead to rotor pole or shaft. If lamp lights, winding is grounded and rotor must be replaced.

When using an ohmmeter, make test in same manner as with test lamp and observe reading. If reading is low, indicating low resistance, the winding is grounded and rotor must be replaced.

Checking for Open Circuit

Touch leads from test lamp or ohmmeter to each of the slip rings. If lamp fails to light, or ohmmeter reading is high (infinite) the winding is open.

Checking for Shorted Winding

Either of two methods may be used to check rotor winding for shorts.
1. Ammeter and battery method: Connect 12-volt battery and ammeter in series with the two slip rings and note ammeter reading. If reading is over 4.4 amperes, these is a short circuit in winding.
2. Ohmmeter Method: Connect ohmmeter leads to the two slip rings and note the resistance reading. If the resistance is less than 2.7 ohms, there is a short circuit in rotor winding.

NOTE: If an ohmmeter is not available the resistance can be calculated by dividing the voltage by the current (amperes), using values from Step 1 above.

If there are no defects found in the rotor assembly and the alternator does not produce its rated output when checked as outlined in "Alternator Output Test," the trouble is either in the stator assembly or in the rectifying diodes.

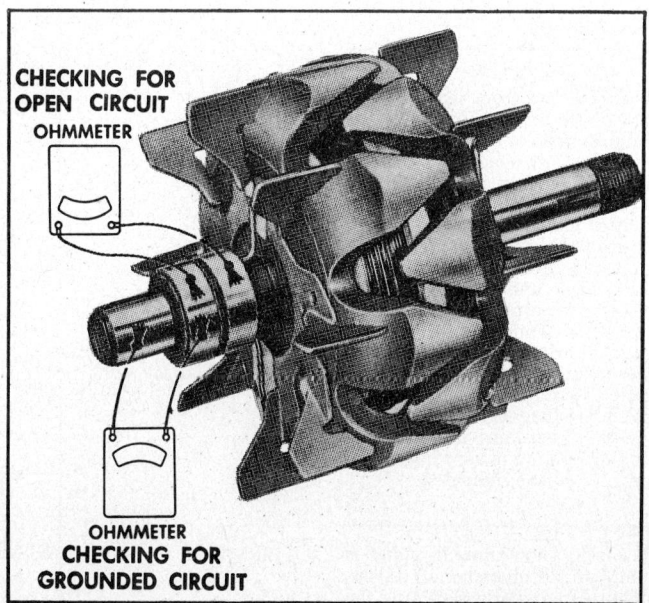

Fig. 3 Checking rotor for grounded, shorted or open circuit

DELCO-REMY "DELCOTRON"

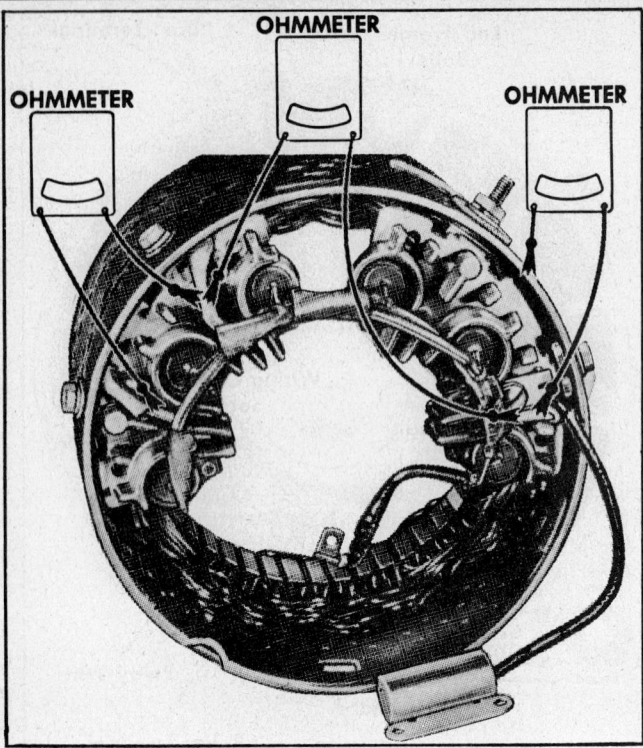

Fig. 4 Checking for grounded or open circuit in stator

Stator Checks, Fig. 4

CAUTION: Do not use test lamps of more than 12 volts. Higher voltage, such as 110-volt test lamp, will immediately destroy a diode if prods should accidentally contact a diode lead when checking the stator.

Due to the low resistance of the stator winding, it is not practical to check stator windings for short circuit without laboratory equipment. However, if all other electrical checks show units to be in good condition, but alternator fails to supply rated output, shorted stator windings are indicated.

1. Scrape epoxy coating from lead connections. Unsolder stator leads, using a minimum amount of heat to avoid damage to diodes to which stator leads are connected. An alternate method is to cut stator leads between coil and diodes. Leads must be spliced after making checks.
2. Check for grounded stator windings by attaching one lead from ohmmeter or test lamp to stator shell, and other lead to any one of the stator winding leads. If the test lamp glows or if ohmmeter shows very low reading, the windings are grounded.
3. To check for open circuits in stator windings, connect ohmmeter leads or test lamp leads successively between the pairs of stator leads. If test lamp fails to light, or if ohmmeter reading is very high (infinite) an open circuit is indicated.

NOTE: If these checks show that the stator is defective, a complete stator and shell assembly must be installed when reassembling the alternator.

Diode Checks, Fig. 5

Each diode in the two heat sinks should be checked individually for shorted or open condition when overhauling alternator. Diodes can be checked using either a 12-volt test lamp or an ohmmeter.

1. Disassemble alternator leaving only the shell, stator and heat sinks with diodes assembled.
2. Cut stator leads as shown, Fig. 5.
3. Using either a test lamp or ohmmeter, check No. 1 positive diode, starting with one test probe to "BAT" terminal and the other test probe to the light relay wire, then reverse this connection. If test lamp lights in both checks, diode is defective. When checking a good diode, test lamp will light only when connected in one direction.
4. If using an ohmmeter, and both readings are very low or if both readings are very high, the diode is defective. A good diode will indicate one low reading and one high reading.
5. To check No. 1 negative diode, place one of the probes on the light relay wire and

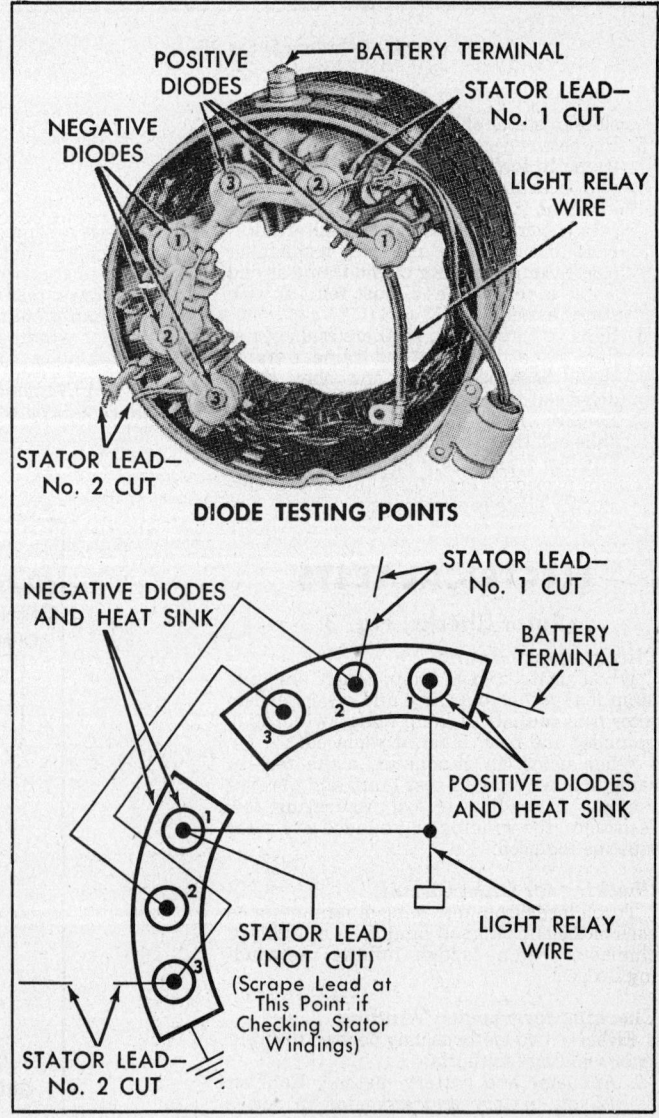

Fig. 5 Testing diodes

DELCO-REMY "DELCOTRON"

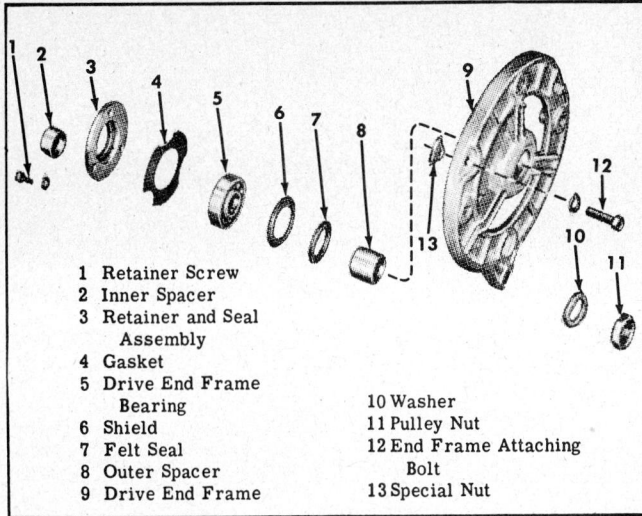

Fig. 6 Drive end frame and bearing components

1 Retainer Screw
2 Inner Spacer
3 Retainer and Seal Assembly
4 Gasket
5 Drive End Frame Bearing
6 Shield
7 Felt Seal
8 Outer Spacer
9 Drive End Frame
10 Washer
11 Pulley Nut
12 End Frame Attaching Bolt
13 Special Nut

Fig. 8 Diode replacement

the other probe on the negative heat sink. Reverse this connection to check this diode.

6. To check No. 2 positive diode, touch one probe to the No. 1 cut stator lead which comes from the diode (not lead that goes to stator) and the other probe to ground on stator shell. Reverse this connection to determine state of this diode.
7. To check No. 2 negative diode, place one probe to the No. 1 cut stator lead and ground the other probe on the negative heat sink. Then reverse connections to determine state of this diode.
8. To check No. 3 positive diode, place one probe on No. 2 cut stator lead (diode end) and ground other probe on positive heat sink. Then reverse connection to determine state of this diode.
9. To check No. 3 negative diode, place a probe on the No. 2 stator lead (diode end) and other probe on negative heat sink. Reverse these connections to determine state of this diode.

NOTE: If all six diodes check as being good, then the stator should be checked. In order to check the stator the third lead from the stator must also be cut. This will make it unnecessary to disturb the epoxy and solder at the No. 1 negative diode. Proceed to check the stator as outlined above.

If one or more diodes were found to be defective, replace diodes as directed under "Repairs."

Special Testers

Special testers are available which operate without disconnecting the stator. When using this type of equipment, follow the manufacturer's instructions.

Capacitor Check, Fig. 2

The capacitor is mounted to the alternator end frame and capacitor lead is connected to insulated heat sink.

Since the capacitor rating is only 0.5 microfarads, it is impractical to test the capacitance with conventional equipment. However, when the alternator is disassembled for overhaul a check should be made to be sure the insulation between elements is not permitting a current leak to ground.

Check can be made with a 12-volt test lamp or a 1½ volt ohmmeter. Connect one test lead to capacitance lead and other lead to capacitor case, Fig. 7. Wiggle "pig tail" lead while observing ohmmeter or test lamp. If capacitor is good, the ohmmeter will show infinite (high) resistance or a test lamp will not glow during test. Capacitor should be replaced if it does not measure up to this test.

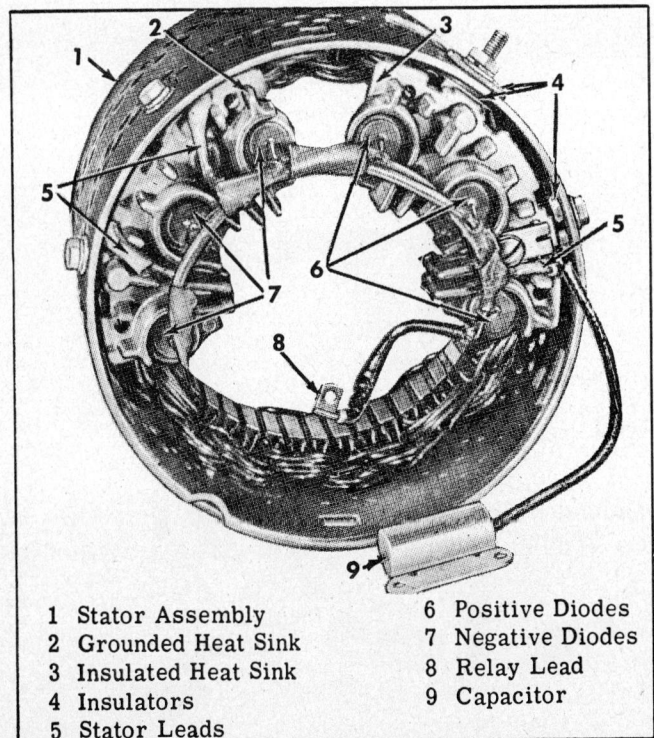

1 Stator Assembly
2 Grounded Heat Sink
3 Insulated Heat Sink
4 Insulators
5 Stator Leads
6 Positive Diodes
7 Negative Diodes
8 Relay Lead
9 Capacitor

Fig. 7 Heat sinks installed in rotor shell

DELCO-REMY "DELCOTRON"

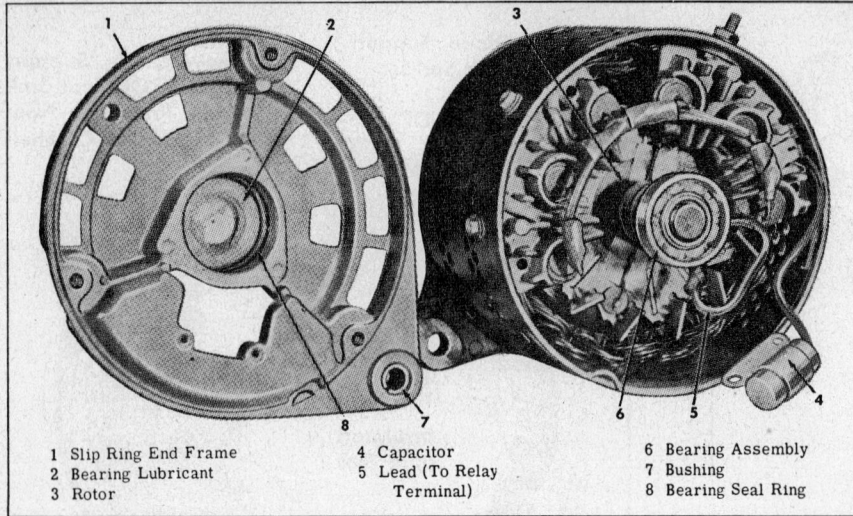

1. Slip Ring End Frame
2. Bearing Lubricant
3. Rotor
4. Capacitor
5. Lead (To Relay Terminal)
6. Bearing Assembly
7. Bushing
8. Bearing Seal Ring

Fig. 9 Slip ring end frame prepared for installation

INSPECTION & REPAIRS

Inspection

Clean all parts except bearings which must not be washed as they are packed with special lubricant.
1. Check drive end frame and bearing assembly for condition of bearing, felt seal and retainer, Fig. 6. Examine end frame for cracks and for other damage.
2. Inspect rotor shaft rear bearing. If there is evidence that the bearing has been run without lubricant, or if bearing is not in good condition, it must be replaced.
3. Rotor assembly should be inspected for scoring at slip rings, Fig. 3. If shaft is damaged a new rotor assembly should be installed at assembly.
4. Inspect brushes, brush springs and brush holder. If brushes are worn to half their original length or are damaged they must be replaced. Visually inspect brush springs; if distorted, worn or broken, replace with new springs.

Repairs

Drive End Frame Bearing, Fig. 6
1. Remove retainer and gasket from end frame, then press out bearing. Remove bearing shield and felt seal from bearing recess.
2. Place shield and seal in recess and press bearing into place. Lubricant cavity in bearing and recess must not be packed solid with lubricant but should be only one-half filled, otherwise bearing will overheat.
3. Install bearing retainer, seal and gasket.

Slip Ring Reconditioning

If slip rings on rotor shaft are scored or dirty, they may be cleaned with 400 grit or finer polishing cloth. Spin rotor in lathe to clean and polish slip rings.

Slip rings that are rough or out-of-round should be trued in a lathe to .002" total indicator reading. Remove only enough material to make slip rings smooth and round. After lathe operation, finish slip ring surface as directed above and blow away all dust.

CAUTION: Brush noise due to flat spots on slip rings may be present if slip rings are cleaned by hand without spinning rotor assembly.

Rotor Shaft Rear Bearing
1. Use a suitable puller or arbor press to remove bearing.
2. With shielded side of bearing toward slip rings, press bearing squarely onto rotor shaft until rear end of shaft protrudes .08 to .10 inch through bearing inner race.

Heat Sink Replacement

The two heat sinks, Fig. 7, are available with diodes for service replacement. The following operations are performed after alternator is disassembled into major components.

Negative (Grounded) Heat Sink
1. Cut or unsolder stator leads and diode connecting wires attached to three diodes in negative heat sink.
2. Unfasten heat sink from stator shell (2 bolts) and remove heat sink and diode assembly.
3. Attach heat sink and diode assembly to stator shell with two bolts, lock washers and special bushings. Two stator leads must fit in notches as shown in Fig. 7. Tighten bolts firmly while holding nuts with wrench.
4. Solder diode connecting wires and stator leads to diode stems, using rosin core (60% tin, 40% lead) solder, then coat diode leads with epoxy.

CAUTION: Do not use excessive heat in soldering leads to diode stems as excessively high temperature may damage the diode. Also avoid bending diode stems, as internal damage to diode may occur, resulting in diode failure.

5. Tape leads and connecting wires as shown in Fig. 7 to prevent wire movement which could eventually wear away insulation.

Positive (Insulated) Heat Sink
1. Detach capacitor from heat sink.
2. Cut or unsolder one stator lead, relay lead and three diode connecting wires which are soldered to diodes.
3. Remove nuts and washers from battery terminal at outer side of stator shell. Remove bolt, lock washer and special bushing which retains heat sink.
4. Remove heat sink and diode assembly and two insulators that are used to prevent contact between heat sink and stator shell.
5. To install, locate battery terminal insulator at inner side of stator shell with projecting flange piloted in terminal hole in shell. Set heat sink mounting bolt insula-

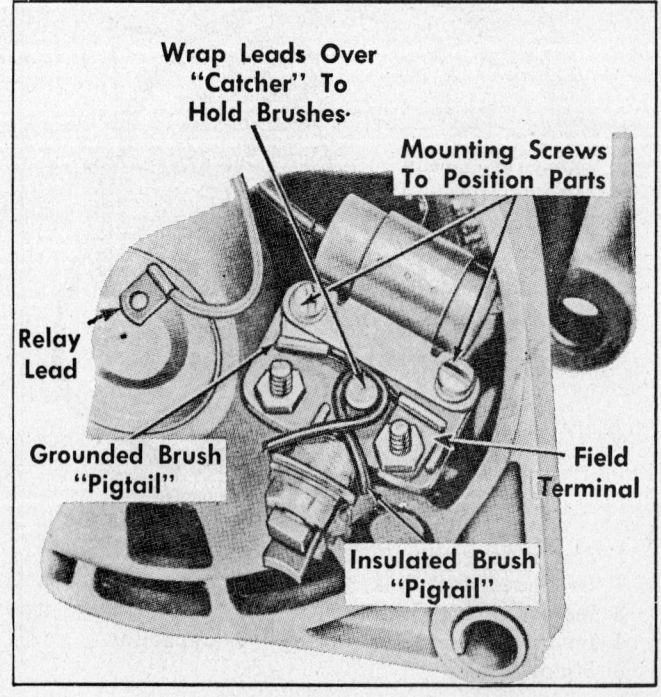

Fig. 10 Brushes and brush holder installation

DELCO-REMY "DELCOTRON"

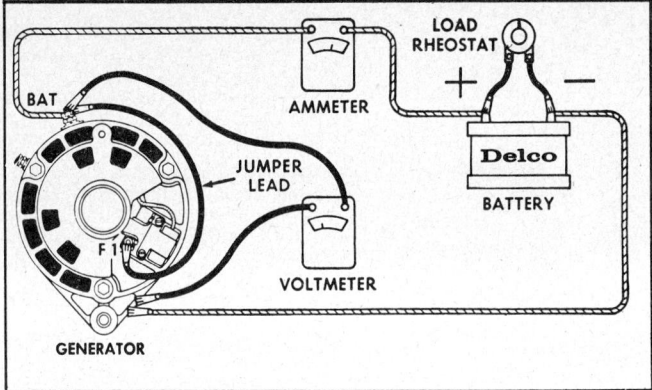

Fig. 11 Equipment and wiring connections for testing alternator on bench

tor in notch in heat sink, then position heat sink in stator shell.
6. Install mounitng bolt with lock washer and special bushing through stator shell and insulator and place nut on inner end of bolt at insulator.
7. Insert battery terminal (bolt) from inside stator shell, through heat sink and insulating washer.
8. Assemble flat fiber washer, steel washer, lock washer and nut on outer end of terminal. Tighten nuts firmly.
9. Referring to Fig. 7, solder diode connecting wires, one stator lead and relay lead to diode stems. Observe the caution previously mentioned to prevent diode damage due to heat or bending diode stems.
10. Tape leads and connecting wires to prevent wire movement, and attach capacitor lead to heat sink.

Diode Replacement, Fig. 8
With proper tools, any of the diodes may be replaced with heat sinks either removed or installed.

NOTE: Negative diodes have black markings on the case and positive diodes have red markings on the case. Note that the heat sink connected to the alternator output terminal is insulated from the shell and contains the positive diodes. The other heat sink is grounded to the shell and contains the negative diodes.

To replace a defective diode, scrape away epoxy coating, then cut only the the leads connected to that particular diode stem. Use diagonal cutters to clip the leads as close to the diode stem as possible. Then remove and install diodes as directed in Fig. 8. After diode is installed, resolder leads to diode stem. Limit soldering time to a minimum so excessive heat will not damage diode.

ASSEMBLE

Follow steps in sequence to assemble the alternator major components, referring to Fig. 1 for identification of various parts except as otherwise indicated.
1. Place inner (short) spacer on pulley end of rotor shaft, then install drive end frame and bearing assembly on rotor shaft with bearing inner race in contact with spacer.
2. Place outer (long) spacer on rotor shaft, then install pulley key and pulley. Retain pulley with spring washer and self-locking nut. Tighten pulley nut to 60 ft-lbs torque.
3. Place stator and shell assembly over rotor and into place at drive end frame. Dimples in stator shell serve to properly locate end frames on stator shell. While holding T-shaped nut in opening in stator shell, install drive end frame bolt and lock washer. Before tightening bolt, install remaining two bolts, lock washers and special nuts, then tighten the three bolts evenly and solidly.
4. Place rear bearing seal ring in groove in slip ring end frame and add recommended lubricant to cavity in bearing. Do not fill reservoir more than half full. Overfilling will cause bearing seal to be pushed out of place or bearing to become overheated.
5. Move slip ring end frame into position with recess in frame aligned with dimple in stator shell. Guide capacitor and relay lead out through brush holder opening in end frame. With slip ring end frame positioned on stator shell, assemble bolts, lock washers and special nuts to secure end frame to stator shell. Tighten bolts evenly and solidly.
6. Referring to Fig. 10, attach insulated alternator brush lead to brush holder with terminal bolt, nut and lock washer. Compress brush spring into brush slot, insert brush against spring and wrap brush spring over "catcher" as shown.
7. Insert two brush holder mounting screws and lock washers through holes in capacitor bracket, and place grounded brush lead on one screw as shown.
8. Insert mounting screws in holes in brush holder, then assemble brush spring and grounded brush in slot in brush holder and wrap lead around "catcher" to hold brush in place until brush holder is installed.
9. Move brush holder and capacitor into place and screw the two mounting screws into threads in end frame.
10. Disengage brush leads from "catcher" to permit brushes to move into contact with slip rings. Install wire connector socket and blade type terminals over terminal screws, attach relay lead on terminal screw as shown in Fig. 2, and install retaining nuts.

Test After Assembly

Fig. 11 shows wiring connections for making alternator output test on bench. Refer to chart in truck chapter for specifications.

CAUTION: When making battery connections, always connect negative terminal to alternator "GRD" terminal. Reversing battery connections will damage alternator.

Delcotron Series 3D

DISASSEMBLY

1. Separate terminal plate from terminals, then remove terminal plate and insulators.
2. Remove two large screws that attach brush holders onto slip ring end frame through window in frame side after removing plates.
3. Disconnect two lead clips that connect the two field terminals to brush holders.
4. Remove four thru-bolts.
5. Tap slip ring end frame lightly to achieve initial separation, then pry it from stator with two screwdrivers located between frames at opposite points.
6. Separate drive end frame from stator in same manner.
7. Referring to Fig. 2, remove shaft nut and washer, then remove pulley.
8. Use an arbor press to force rotor shaft from drive end frame.
9. To remove drive end bearing, detach bearing retainer plate and force bearing from housing.
10. Use a puller to remove slip ring end bearing and collar from shaft.

ELECTRICAL TESTS
Rotor Checks
Checking for Ground
Touch one lead of a 110-volt test lamp to one of the slip rings and the other lead to rotor shaft or laminations. If lamp lights, field windings are grounded.

Checking for Open Circuit
Touch leads from a 110-volt test lamp to each of the slip rings. If lamp fails to light, the windings are open.

Checking for Shorted Windings
Connect a 12-volt battery and ammeter in series with the two slip rings. If ammeter reading is over 6.6 amperes, there is a short circuit in windings.

NOTE: If there are no defects found in the

85

DELCO-REMY "DELCOTRON"

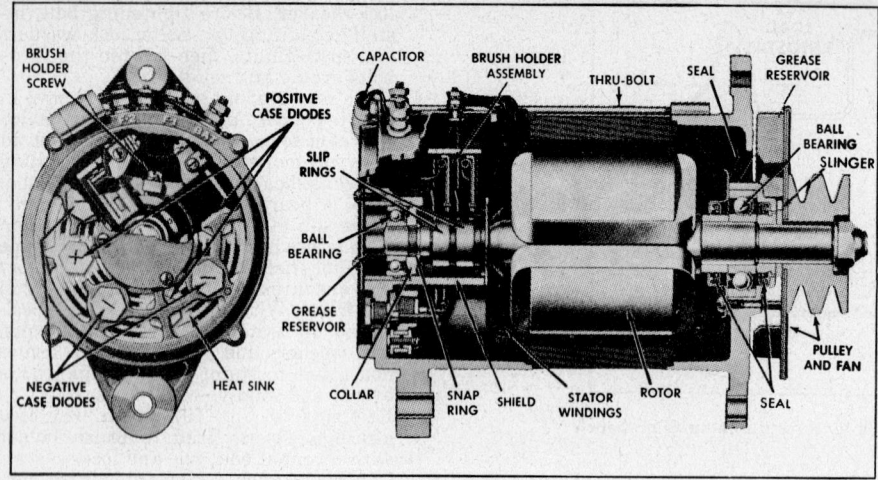

Fig. 1 Delcotron Series 3D

rotor and alternator does not produce its rated output when checked as outlined under "Alternator Output Test", the trouble is in either the stator or in the rectifying diodes.

Stator Checks

1. If a 110-volt test lamp lights when connected from any terminal in the stator windings to the stator frame, the windings are grounded. If the lamp fails to light when successively connected between each pair of stator leads, the windings are open.
2. A short circuit in the stator windings is difficult to locate without laboratory test equipment due to the low resistance of the windings. However, if all other electrical checks are normal and the alternator fails to supply its rated output, shorted stator windings are indicated.

Diode Checks

As shown in Fig. 1, six threaded-type diodes are mounted in the slip ring end frame. Three positive diodes are mounted in the slip ring end frame, and three negative diodes are mounted into a bracket or heat sink located in the frame. The heat sink is attached to but insulated from the slip ring end frame and is attached to the "BAT" terminal on the alternator. Note in Fig. 1 that all diodes are marked either with a + or − on the hexagonal head to identify the polarity of the case.

Diodes can be checked with an ohmmeter as shown in Fig. 3. The ohmmeter leads may be touched to each diode as shown without disconnecting the diodes or removing them from either the end frame or heat sink. Use an ohmmeter with a 1½ volt cell and a scale on which a 300-ohm value is at or near mid-scale. To determine the cell voltage of the ohmmeter, select the scale on the ohmmeter that is to be used, then connect the ohmmeter leads of a voltmeter. The voltmeter will indicate the ohmmeter cell voltage. *Do not use high voltage to test diodes, such as 110-volt test lamp.*

To check each diode, connect ohmmeter one lead to the diode case, and the other ohmmeter lead to the diode lead. Note ohmmeter reading. Then reverse ohmmeter lead connections and note the reading. Ohmmeter readings may vary considerably when checking different diodes. However, if both readings are 300 ohms or less, the diode is defective. Also if both readings are greater than 300 ohms the diode is defective. A good diode will give one very low and one very high reading. When checking each diode, push and then pull on the diode lead slightly to determine if there are loose connections within the diode.

INSPECTION & REPAIRS

Inspection

1. Clean all parts except the bearings, which should not be washed as they are packed with special lubricant.
2. Check drive end frame and bearing for condition of bearing and retainer. Examine end frame for cracks or other damage.
3. Inspect rotor shaft rear bearing. If there is evidence bearing has been run without lubricant, or if bearing is not in good condition, it must be replaced.
4. Rotor should be inspected for scoring at slip rings. If shaft is damaged, a new rotor should be installed at assembly.

Repairs

Drive End Frame Bearing
1. Remove four screws attaching retainer and seal to end frame.
2. Remove retainer and gasket, then press bearing out of end frame. Remove lip-type seal from bearing recess in end frame and discard.
3. Install seal in recess in end frame with lip toward reservoir.
4. Press bearing into recess. Lubricant cavity in bearing should not be packed solid with lubricant, but should be only one-half full.
5. Install bearing retainer and seal assembly and gasket.

CAUTION: Make sure shielded side of bearing is on side away from lubricant reservoir. Satisfactory bearing life will be obtained only if recommended lubrication procedures are followed.

Slip Ring Reconditioning
Slip rings that are rough or out-of-round should be trued in a lathe to .002" maximum indicator reading. Remove only enough material to make the rings smooth and round. Finish with 400 grit polishing cloth and blow away all dust.

Slip rings that must be replaced can be removed from the shaft with a gear puller after the leads have been unsoldered and the bearing, collar and snap ring have been removed. The new assembly should be pressed on with a sleeve that just fits over the shaft. This will apply all the pressure to the inner slip ring collar and prevent damage to the outer slip ring. Only pure tin solder should be used when reconnecting the field leads. Make sure the soldered connections are secure. New slip rings must be turned in a lathe to a smooth finish with .002" maximum indicator reading. Finish with 400 grit or finer polishing cloth.

Diode Replacement
Negative diodes have right-hand threads, and positive diodes have left-hand threads.
1. To replace any diode mounted in the end frame, disconnect diode lead from terminal, then remove the defective diode. For ease in removing the defective diode it is recommended that both the diode and end frame be heated in an oven to 150°F, or briefly immersed in hot water at a temperature just below the boiling point.
2. Before installing the new diode, lightly coat the threads with silicone grease or light engine oil. With the diode and end frame at room temperature, install the diode and torque to 160–190 inch-pounds. Since diodes use pipe threads, the depth of penetration may vary from one diode to another. Reconnect the diode lead to the terminal.

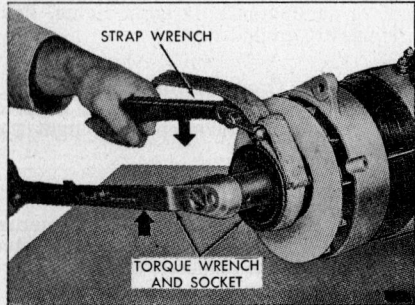

Fig. 2 Replacing alternator pulley nut

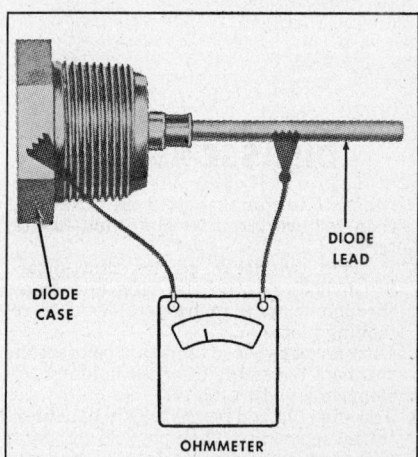

Fig. 3 Checking diodes with ohmmeter

DELCO-REMY "DELCOTRON"

3. To replace any diode mounted in the heat sink, first disconnect all three heat sink diode leads from the three terminals. Then remove the heat sink from the end frame and follow the procedure outlined for removing and installing a new one.

ASSEMBLY

1. Improvise a collar-type tool that just fits over the shaft to press the slip ring end frame bearing and collar with snap ring over shaft. Install collar so shoulder is against bearing inner race.
2. Install drive end frame bearing as outlined previously under "Repairs".
3. Place stator over rotor and into drive end frame. Notches in stator shell serve to properly locate end frame on stator shell.
4. Move slip ring end frame into position on stator shell and install four thru-bolts. Tighten bolts evenly and solidly.
5. Through opening in end frame, install brush and holder assembly and attach to slip ring end frame with two screws.
6. Tighten terminal plate over terminals, then assemble terminal plate and insulators to slip ring end frame.
7. Install terminal nuts and washers on three terminals located in terminal plate.

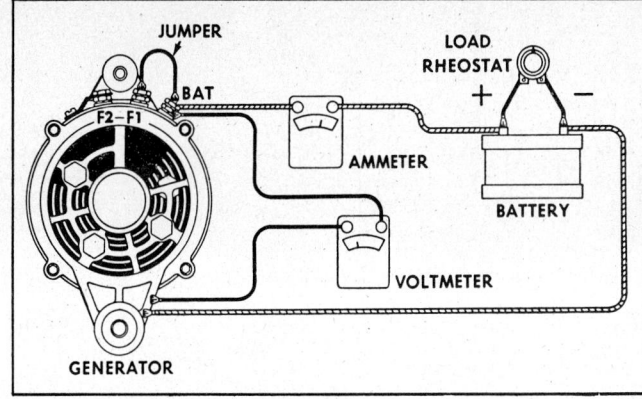

Fig. 4 Wiring connections for checking alternator output on bench

Bench Testing Alternator

Fig. 4 shows the wiring connections for making alternator output test on bench. Connect the jumper lead to the "BAT" and "F1" terminals as shown, operate at specified speed and check for rated output as listed in the "Alternator Specifications" chart in Truck Chapters.

When making battery connections, always connect negative terminal to alternator "GRD" terminal. Reversing battery connections will damage alternator.

Delcotron Series 4D

DISASSEMBLY

1. Referring to Fig. 1, remove four thru-bolts that attach slip ring end frame to drive end frame. Insert a thru-bolt into slip ring end frame and lift brushes off slip rings.
2. Remove drive end frame and rotor assembly. Remove nut and washer from rotor shaft, then use a suitable pulley to remove pulley and fan assembly.
3. When removing slip ring end frame bearing, care should be taken to press the shaft out against the inner bearing race. Because of the small space between the slip ring and the bearing, it may be necessary to secure the outer race of the bearing on this end of the rotor in order to remove it from the shaft. If this is necessary, the bearing may be ruined during removal, in which case a new bearing must be installed. When installing the bearing over the shaft, be sure to press against the inner race only.
4. Disconnect leads from three A.C. terminals, then separate slip ring end frame from stator assembly.

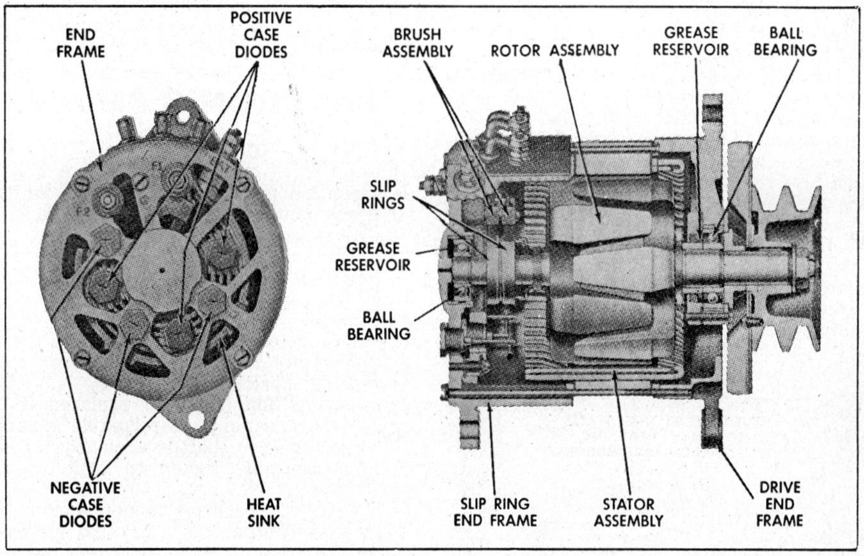

ELECTRICAL CHECKS

Rotor Checks

Checking for Grounds
Touch one lead of a 110-volt test lamp to one of the slip rings and the other lead to the rotor shaft or laminations. If the lamp lights, the field windings are grounded.

Checking for Open Circuit
Touch the leads from a 110-volt test lamp to each slip ring. If the lamp fails to light, the windings are open.

Checking for Shorted Windings
Connect a 12-volt battery and ammeter in series with the two slip rings. If ammeter reading is above 2.4 amperes, there is a short circuit in the winding.

Stator Checks

The stator windings may be checked for grounded or open windings with a 110-volt test lamp. Due to the low resistance of the stator windings, it is not practical to check stator windings for short circuits without laboratory test equipment. However, if all other electrical checks show units to be in good condition, but alternator fails to supply rated output,

Fig. 1 Delcotron Series 4D

shorted stator windings are indicated.

1. Check for grounded stator windings by attaching one lead from test lamp to stator frame and the other lead to any one of the stator winding leads. If test lamp lights, the windings are grounded.
2. Check for open circuits in stator windings by connecting test lamp leads successively between each pair of stator terminals. If lamp fails to light, the windings are open.

Diode Checks

With the drive end frame and rotor re-

DELCO-REMY "DELCOTRON"

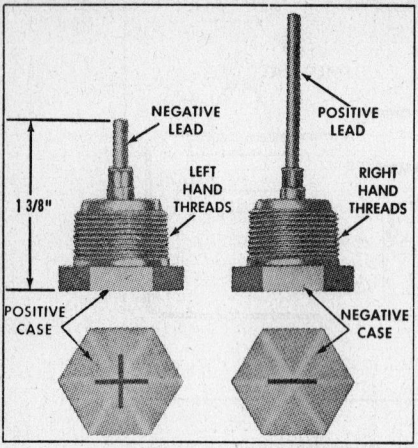

Fig. 2 Diode polarity markings

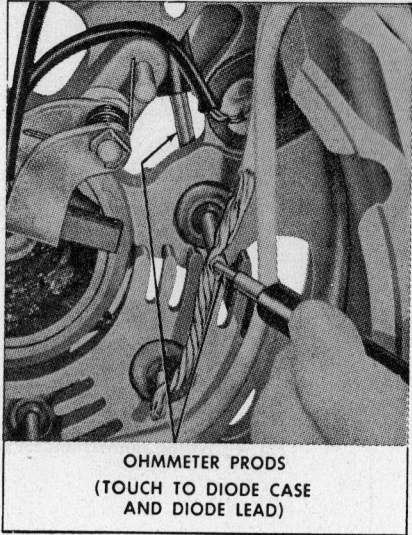

Fig. 3 Checking diodes

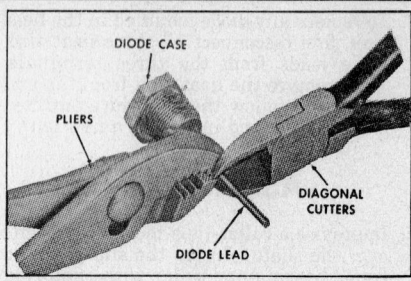

Fig. 4 Cutting diode leads

moved, the slip ring end frame can readily be separated from the stator by disconnecting the leads from the three terminals at top of alternator.

As shown in Fig. 2, there are six diodes mounted in the slip ring end frame. Three positive diodes are mounted in the slip ring end frame, and three negative diodes are mounted into a heat sink which is attached to but insulated from the slip ring end frame. The "BAT" terminal on the alternator is attached to the insulated heat sink.

All diodes are marked either with a + or − on the diode head to identify the polarity of the case. Diodes with a negative case have positive polarity leads whereas positive case diodes have negative polarity leads as shown in Fig. 2.

Diodes can be checked for defects with an ohmmeter as shown in Fig. 3. To check each diode, connect one of the ohmmeter leads to the diode case, and the other ohmmeter lead to the diode lead. Note the ohmmeter reading. Then reverse the ohmmeter connections and note the reading. Ohmmeter readings may vary considerably when checking diodes, but if both readings are 300 ohms or less, the diode is defective. Also, if both readings are greater than 300 ohms, the diode is defective. A good diode will give one low and one high reading.

When checking each diode, push and then pull diode lead slightly on the the diode lead to check for loose connections. Use an ohmmeter with a 1½ volt cell and a scale on which the 300 ohm value can be accurately read. To determine the cell voltage of the ohmmeter, select the scale on the ohmmeter which is to be used, then connect the ohmmeter leads to the leads of the voltmeter. The voltmeter will indicate the ohmmeter cell voltage. *Do not use high voltage to test diodes, such as a 110-volt test lamp.*

INSPECTION & REPAIRS

Inspection
1. Clean all parts except bearings which should not be washed as they are packed with special lubricant.
2. Check drive end frame and bearing for condition of bearing, felt seal and retainer. Examine end frame for cracks or other damage.
3. Inspect rotor shaft rear bearing. If there is evidence that bearing has been run without lubricant or if bearing is not in good condition, it must be replaced.
4. The rotor should be inspected for scoring at slip rings. If shaft is damaged, a new rotor assembly should be installed at assembly.
5. Inspect brushes, brush holders and brush springs. If brushes are worn to one-half their original length, they must be replaced.

Repairs
Slip Ring Reconditioning
1. Slip rings that are rough or out-of-round should be trued in a lathe to .002″ maximum indicator reading. Remove only enough material to make the rings smooth and round. Finish with 400 grain or finer polishing cloth and blow away all dust.
2. Slip rings that must be replaced can be removed from the shaft with a gear puller after the leads have been unsoldered and the shaft bearing has been removed. The new assembly should be pressed on with a sleeve that just fits over the shaft. This will apply all the pressure to the inner slip ring collar and prevent damage to the outer slip ring. Only pure tin solder should be used when reconnecting the field leads. Make sure the soldered connections are secure. New slip rings must be turned in a lathe to a smooth finish with .002″ maximum indicator reading. Finish with 400 grain or finer polishing cloth.

Diode Replacement
Negative diodes have right-hand threads and positive diodes have left-hand threads.

The diode in the service package has a long diode lead. If the diode is to be assembled into the heat sink, it is necessary to cut off the diode lead to an overall length of 1⅜″, Fig. 2. To cut off the diode lead, hold the diode lead with ordinary pliers or vise-grip pliers, and use diagonal cutters, Fig. 4, or a hacksaw.

CAUTION: Do not grip diode case when cutting the lead as this will place stress between the diode case and the diode lead, and will damage the diode internally.

1. To replace a diode that is mounted in the outside frame, use diagonal cutters to clip the flexible leads on each side of the diode lead. Clip the flexible leads as close to the diode lead as possible, Fig. 5. For ease in removing the defective diode, it is recommended that the diode and outside frame be heated in an oven to 150°F. or briefly immersed in hot water just below the boiling point.

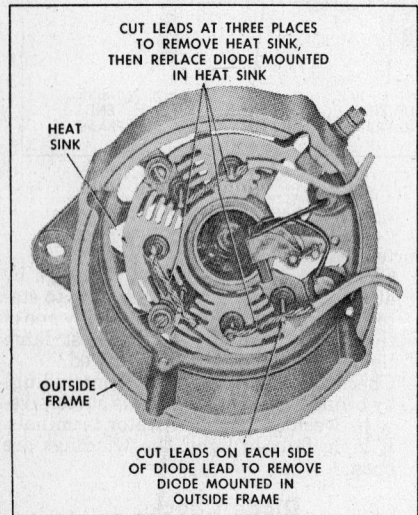

Fig. 5 Replacing diodes

Fig. 6 Checking brush spring tension

DELCO-REMY "DELCOTRON"

2. Before installing the new diode, lightly coat the threads with silicone grease or light engine oil. With the diode and outside frame at room temperature, install the diode and torque to 160-190 inch-pounds. Since diodes use pipe threads, the depth of penetration may vary from one diode to another.
3. Place the single diode lead clip furnished in service package over the diode lead, and place the ends of the flexible leads into the clip. (The two identical clips are not used when installing a diode in the outside frame.) Crimp the clip tightly over the flexible leads, and liberally solder leads to the clip, and the clip to the diode lead.

CAUTION: Use only 60% tin, 40% lead solder, or other solder with melting point of 360°F., or above. Do not hold the soldering iron on the leads any longer than necessary as excessive heat may damage the diode.

4. To replace a diode mounted in the heat sink, it is necessary to remove the heat sink from the end frame. This is accomplished by clipping with diagonal cutters the flexible lead as close to the diode lead as possible. Also clip the flexible leads midway between the other two pairs of diodes, Fig. 5. Then remove the "BAT" terminal and heat sink attaching screws, and the long leads from the nylon connector.
5. Complete the operation as given for the diodes in the outside frame.

Brush Replacement

The extent of brush wear can be determined by comparison with a new brush. If brushes are worn over half-way, they should be replaced. Replacement is accomplished by installing a new holder, brushes, leads, and terminal assembly. Note that there are both right- and left-hand holders and springs. Brush holders should be toward the right of their pivot pin as viewed from the outside of the rectifier end frame.

Brush spring tension should be checked as shown in Fig. 6. The spring tension scale should be hooked under the brush. The reading should be taken with the brush in the same position encountered when riding on the slip ring. A ten-ounce pull should register on the scale. Excessive tension will cause rapid wear, whereas low tension results in erratic alternator output and burning of slip rings. Defective springs cannot be adjusted, and therefore must be replaced.

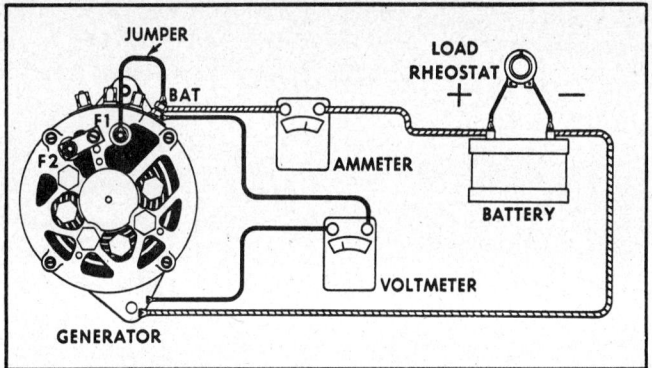

Fig. 7 Wiring connections for checking alternator output on bench

ASSEMBLY

1. Half-fill each reservoir with recommended lubricant.
2. Place inner spacer on pulley end of rotor shaft, then install drive end frame and bearing assembly on rotor shaft with bearing inner race in contact with spacer.
3. Place outer spacer on rotor shaft, then install pulley key and pulley. Retain pulley with self-locking nut and torque nut to 60 ft-lbs.
4. Place stator over rotor and into drive end frame.
5. Fill slip ring end frame bearing cavity half-full of approved lubricant.
6. Insert a thru-bolt through slip ring end frame to hold brushes off slip rings while moving slip ring end frame into position with stator shell. With slip ring end frame positioned on stator shell, install and tighten the four thru-bolts.
7. Connect leads to the three A.C. terminals.

Bench Test

Fig. 7 shows wiring connections for making alternator output test on bench. Refer to "Alternator Specifications" chart in Truck Chapters for specifications. While operating alternator at specified speed, adjust load rheostat to specified voltage. Ammeter will show alternator output which must be within range specified.

When making battery connections, connect negative terminal to alternator "GRD" terminal. Reversing battery connections will damage alternator.

Delcotron 10 & 27 SI (Type 100) Integral Charging Systems

DESCRIPTION

These units, Figs. 1, 2 and 3, feature a solid state regulator mounted inside the alternator slip ring end frame, Fig. 4, along with the brush holder assembly. All regulator components are enclosed in a solid mold with no need or provision for adjustment of the regulator. A rectifier bridge, containing six diodes and connected to the stator windings, changes A.C. voltage to D.C. voltage which is available at the output terminal. Generator field current is supplied through a diode trio which is also connected to the stator windings. The diodes and rectifiers are protected by a capacitor which is also mounted in the end frame.

NOTE: Some 1975-80 units incorporate a resistor in the warning indicator circuit. Fig. 5.

No maintenance or adjustments of any kind are required on this unit.

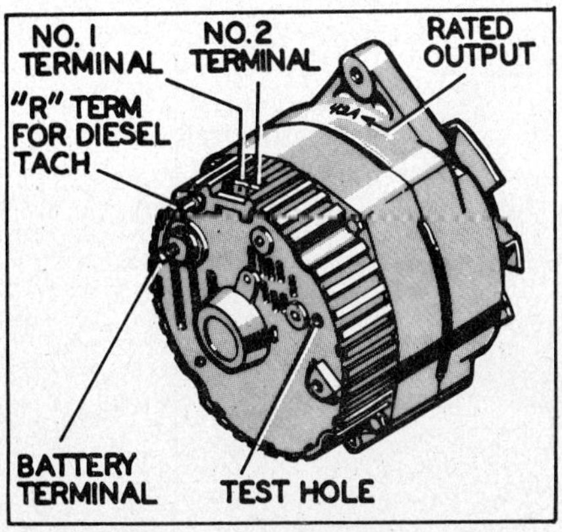

Fig. 1 Delcotron type 10 SI alternator (Typical)

TROUBLE SHOOTING

Undercharged Battery

1. Disconnect battery ground cable.
2. Disconnect wire at "BAT" terminal of alternator, connect ammeter, positive lead to "BAT" terminal and negative lead to wire.
3. Connect battery ground cable.
4. Turn on all accessories, then connect a carbon pile regulator across battery.
5. Operate engine at moderate speed, adjust carbon pile regulator to obtain maximum current output.
6. If ammeter reading is within 10 amps of rated output, alternator is not at fault.

NOTE: Alternator rated output is

89

DELCO-REMY "DELCOTRON"

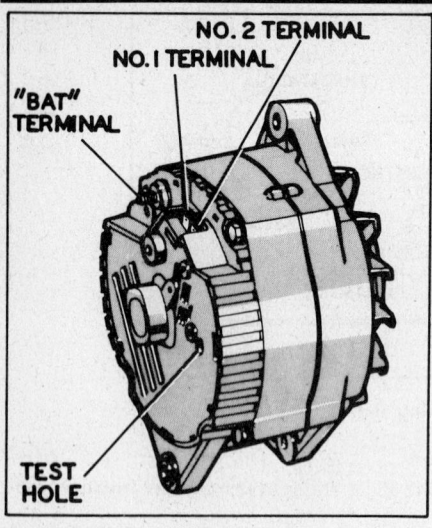

Fig. 2 Delcotron type 27 SI alternator

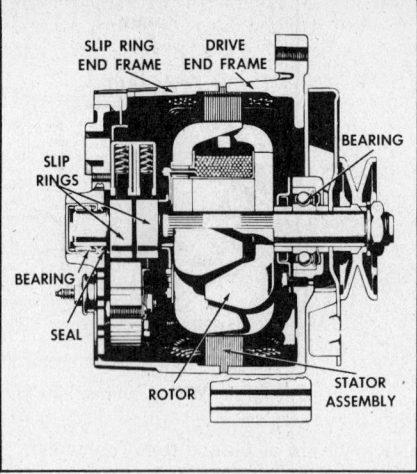

Fig. 3 Sectional view of Delcotron type SI alternator (Typical)

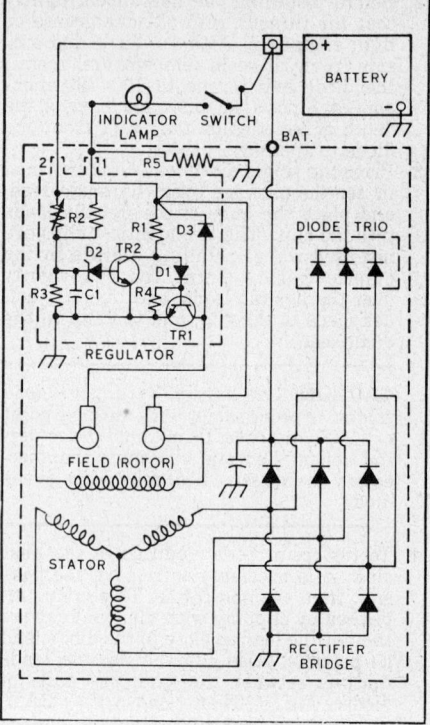

Fig. 5 Wiring diagram of charging circuit

stamped on alternator frame.

7. If ammeter reading is not within 10 amps of rated output, ground field winding by inserting screw driver in end frame hole, contacting tab. Fig. 6.

NOTE: Do not insert screw driver deeper than one inch, tab is usually located within 3/4 inch of casing surface.

8. If reading is within 10 amps of rated output, regulator must be replaced. If reading is not within limits, check field winding, diode trio, rectifier bridge and stator.
9. Turn off all accessories and disconnect ammeter and carbon pile regulator.

Overcharging Battery

1. Remove alternator from vehicle and separate end frames as outlined under "Alternator Disassembly."
2. Check field winding, if shorted replace rotor and regulator.
3. Connect ohmmeter from brush clip to end frame, set meter on low scale and note reading. Fig. 7.
4. Reverse leads, if both readings are zero remove screw from brush clip and inspect sleeve and insulator.
5. If sleeve and insulator are in good condition, then regulator is at fault and must be replaced.

ALTERNATOR DISASSEMBLY

NOTE: When pressing bearings or seals from end frames, support frames from inside.

1. Scribe mark across end frames and stator ring so parts can be installed in same position.
2. Remove four through bolts, then using screw driver in stator slot pry end frames apart, Fig. 8.

NOTE: Brushes may fall from holders and become contaminated with bearing grease, if so they must be cleaned prior to assembly.

3. Place tape over slip ring end frame bearing and shaft at slip ring end.
4. Remove nut, washer, pulley, fan and collar from rotor shaft, then slide drive end frame from shaft.
5. Remove bearing, retainer and seal from drive end frame.
6. Remove attaching bolts, then pry stator from slip ring end frame.
7. Remove capacitor, diode trio, rectifier bridge and battery terminal stud.
8. Remove resistor (if equipped), brush holder and regulator.
9. Remove bearing and seal from slip ring end-frame.

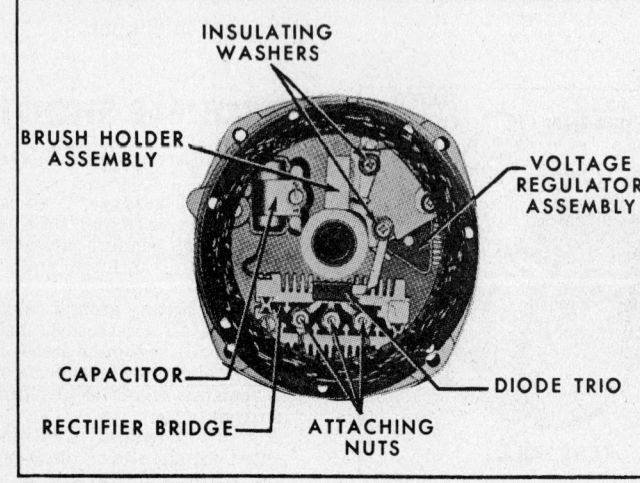

Fig. 4 Slip ring end frame. 10 & 27 SI (Type 100) Delcotron

Fig. 6 Grounding field winding

DELCO-REMY "DELCOTRON"

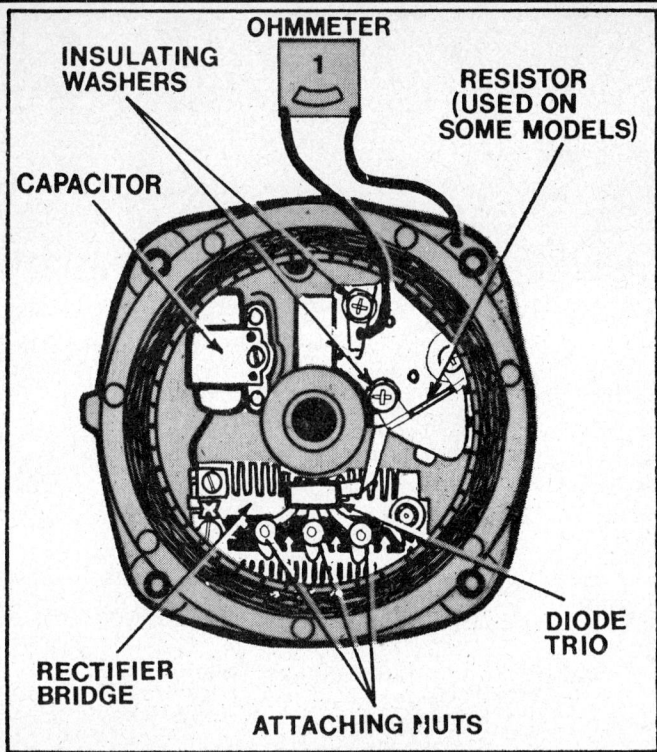

Fig. 7 Testing brush clip

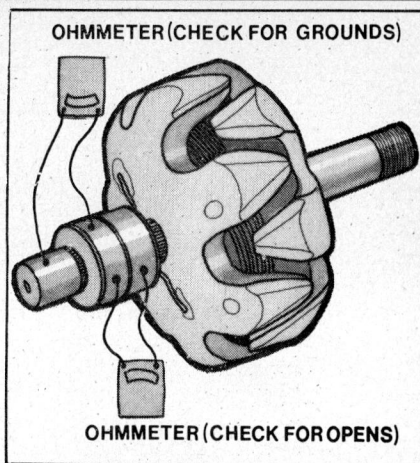

Fig. 9 Testing rotor and slip rings

5. If a reading above 3 ohms is obtained excessive resistance exists in windings.
6. Connect one ohmmeter lead to rotor shaft and touch slip rings with other lead, if any reading is obtained there is a ground in the circuit. Fig. 9.

NOTE: If any of the above problems are present the rotor assembly must be replaced.

BENCH TESTS

Rotor & Slip Ring Test

NOTE: Ohmmeter must be at low scale setting during this test.

1. Inspect rotor for wear or damage.
2. Touch ohmmeter leads to slip rings. Fig. 9.
3. If reading is high an open circuit exists in windings.
4. If reading below 2.5 ohms is obtained winding is shorted.

Stator Winding Test

1. Inspect stator for discolored windings, loose connections and damage.

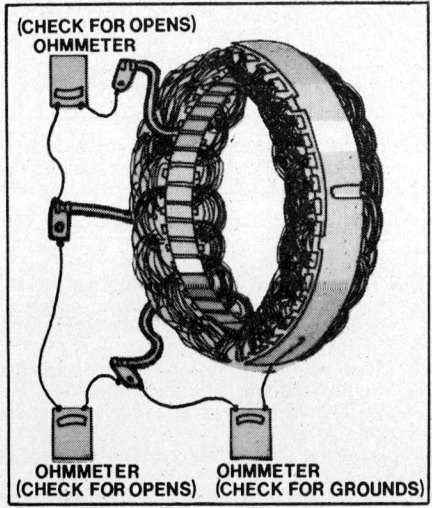

Fig. 10 Testing stator winding

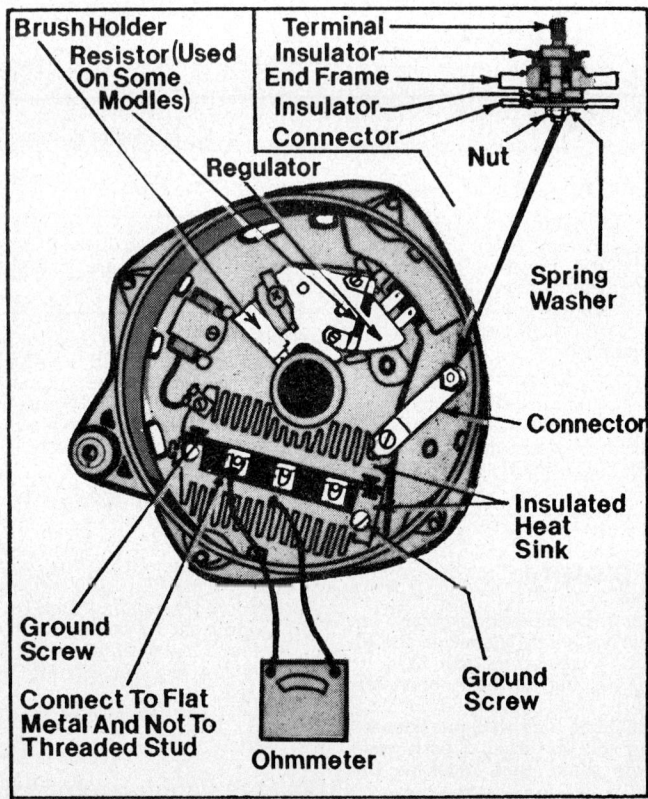

Fig. 12 Testing rectifier bridge diodes

DELCO-REMY "DELCOTRON"

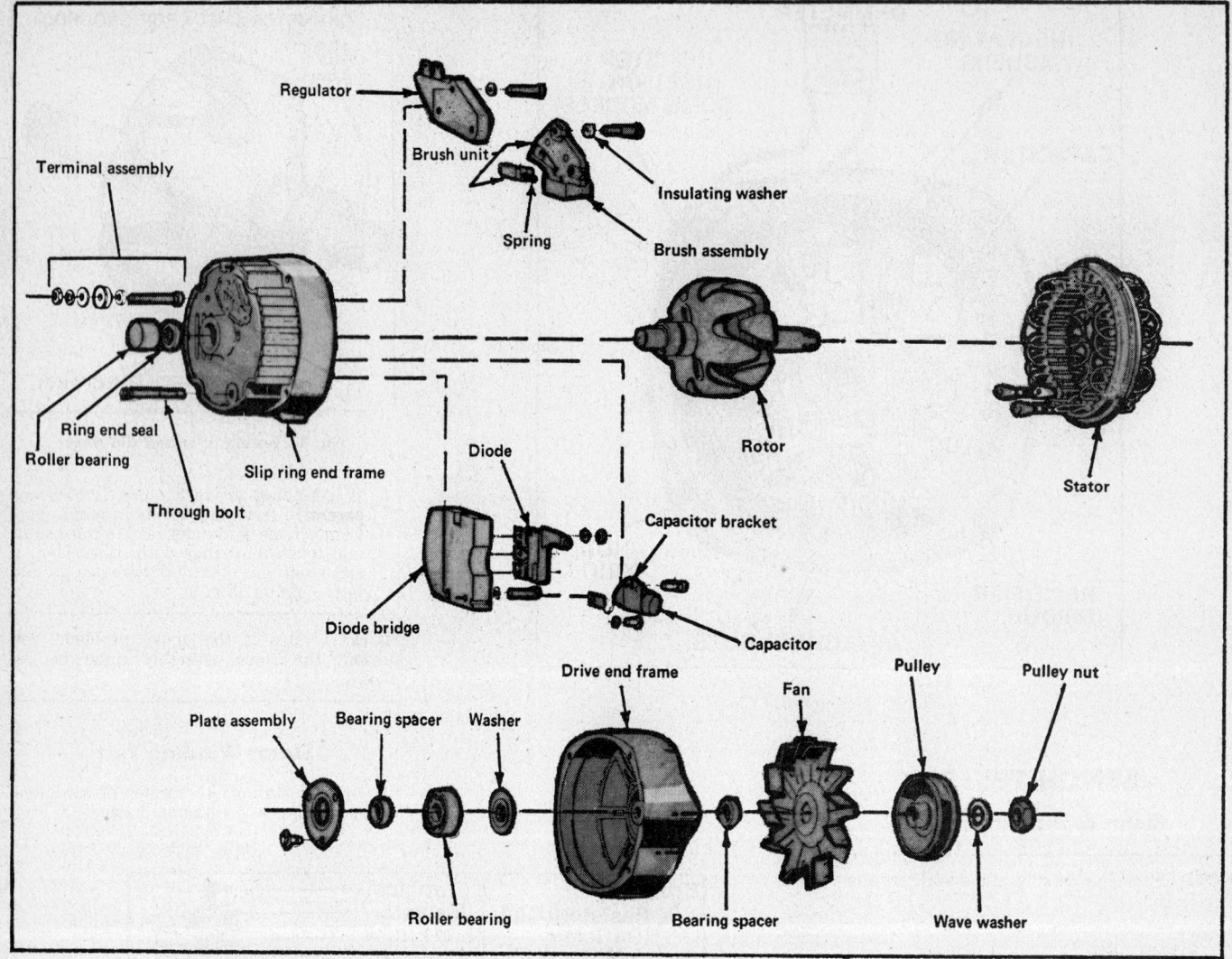

Fig. 8 Alternator disassembled

2. Connect an ohmmeter from stator lead to frame, if any reading is obtained windings are grounded. Fig. 10.
3. Connect ohmmeter between stator leads, if reading is high when connected between each pair of leads, an open circuit exists in windings.

NOTE: Shorted windings are difficult to locate without special equipment. If other tests indicate normal, but rated alternator output cannot be obtained, the windings are probably shorted.

Diode Trio

1. With diode unit removed, connect an ohmmeter to the single connector and to one of the three connectors, Fig. 11.
2. Observe the reading. Reverse ohmmeter leads.
3. Reading should be high with one connection and low with the other. If both readings are the same, unit must be replaced.
4. Repeat between the single connector and each of the three connectors.

NOTE: There are two diode units differeing in appearance. These are completely interchangeable.

The diode unit can be checked for a grounded brush lead while still installed in the end frame by connecting an ohmmeter from the brush lead clip to the end frame as in Steps 1 and 2 above. If both readings are zero, check for a grounded brush or brush lead.

Rectifier Bridge Test

1. Connect ohmmeter to the grounded heat sink and one of the three terminals, Fig. 12.
2. Observe the reading then reverse leads.
3. Reading should be high with one connection and low with the other. If both readings are the same, unit must be replaced.
4. Repeat test for each of the other terminals.

Voltage Regulator/Brush Lead Test

Connect an ohmmeter from the brush lead clip to the end frame, note reading, then reverse connections. If both readings are zero, either the brush lead clip is grounded or the regulator is defective.

ALTERNATOR ASSEMBLY

NOTE: When pressing bearings or seals, end frames must be supported from inside.

1. Lightly lubricate seal and position on slip ring end frame with lip facing toward rotor. Fig. 8.
2. Press seal part way into housing.
3. Position bearing and end plug on slip ring end frame, press bearing and plug in until flush with end frame.
4. Place regulator in end frame, install brushes and springs in brush holder, use pin to hold brushes in compressed position.
5. Install rectifier bridge and battery terminal stud.
6. Install diode trio, ensure current only flows one way through single connector.
7. Install capacitor.

DELCO-REMY "DELCOTRON"

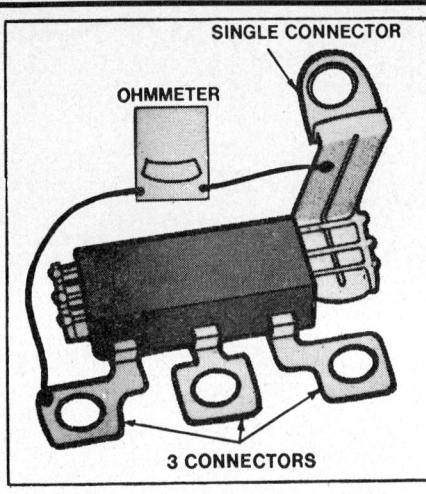

Fig. 11 Testing diode trio

8. Install stator, check the three leads for continuity, ensure stator is not grounded against case or holder.
9. Position slinger on drive end frame, then press ball bearing into end frame. Fig. 13.
10. Fill seal cavity ¼ full with special alternator lubricant, then install retainer.
11. Install rotor in drive end frame, then install collar, fan, pulley, washer and nut.
12. Align scribe marks on end frames and stator plate, install through bolts and remove brush retaining pins.

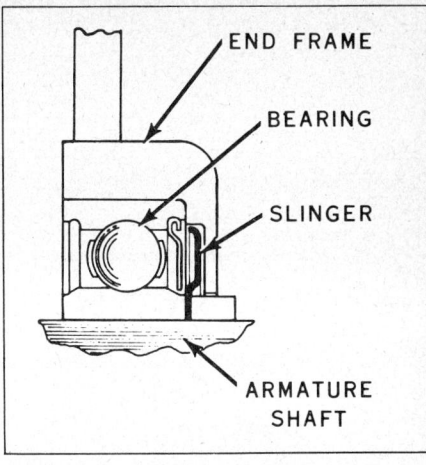

Fig. 13 Drive end frame bearing and slinger installed

Delcotron 25 SI Integral Charging System

DESCRIPTION

This unit, Fig. 1, features a solid state regulator mounted inside the alternator slip ring end frame, along with the brush holder assembly. All regulator components are enclosed in a solid mold with a provision for adjustment of the regulator. A rectifier bridge, containing six diodes and connected to the stator windings, changes A.C. voltage to D.C. voltage which is available at the output terminal. Generator field current is supplied through a diode trio which is also connected to the stator windings. The diodes and rectifiers are protected by a capacitor.

ALTERNATOR OUTPUT TEST

1. Install test equipment, Fig. 2.
2. With the carbon pile turned "Off", run engine at moderate speed and note voltage reading. Voltage should be 13 to 15 volts.
3. If voltage reading is above 15 volts, check regulator lead for proper connection. If satisfactory, check field coil for shorts. If field coil is shorted, replace field coil and regulator.
4. If voltage reading in step 2 is less than 13 volts increase engine speed and adjust carbon pile to obtain maximum current output. If maximum current is within 10 per cent of specified rating, the voltage

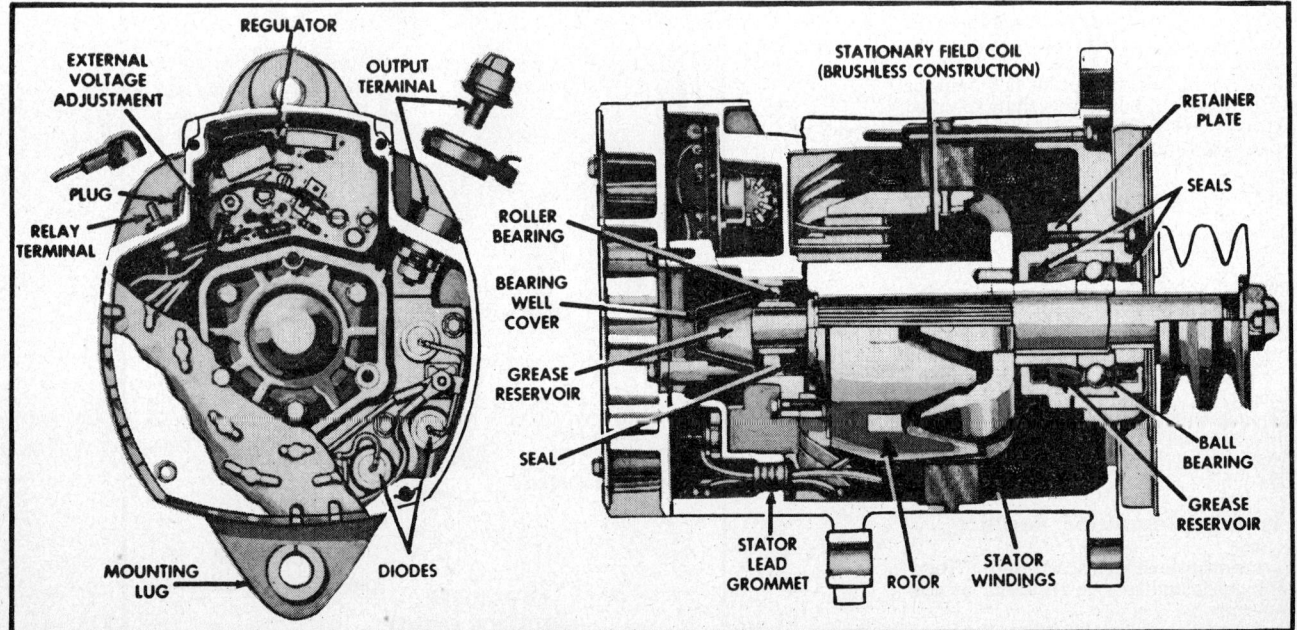

Fig. 1 Delcotron 25 SI Integral Charging System

DELCO-REMY "DELCOTRON"

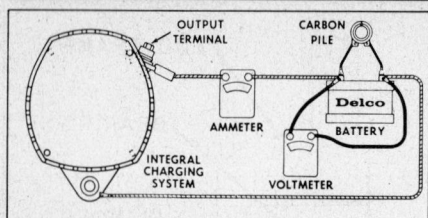

Fig. 2 Alternator output test connections

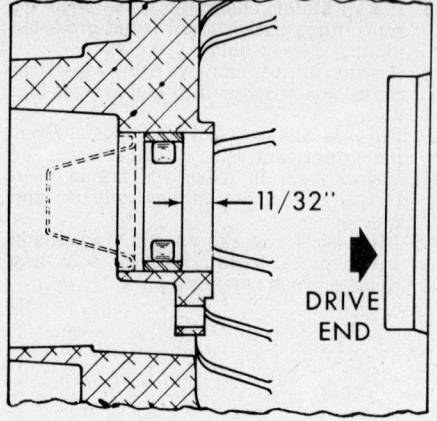

Fig. 4 Bearing location

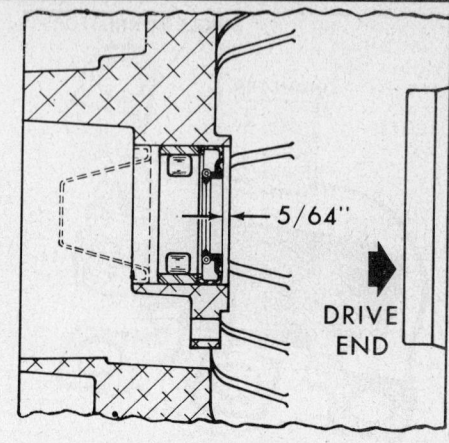

Fig. 5 Seal location

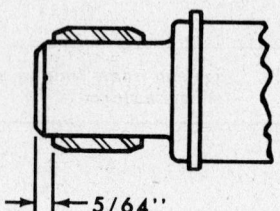

Fig. 3 Bearing inner race location

Diode, Replace

1. Disconnect regulator lead from heat sink, remove heat sink mounting screws and alternator output terminal, then the heat sink.

NOTE: Round insulators are located under the heat sink mounting screws and a flat insulator is located behind the heat sink.

regulator setting may be changed as follows.
  a. Remove pipe plug from alternator.
  b. Rotate adjusting screw one or two notches clockwise to raise voltage setting.

NOTE: For an overcharged battery condition, rotate adjusting screw counterclockwise to lower the voltage setting.

  c. Install pipe plug.
5. If maximum current output in step 4 is not within 10 per cent of specified rating and is less than 5 amps, check field coil and if open, replace only the field coil. If field coil is grounded or shorted, replace both the field coil and the regulator. If field coil tests satisfactory, replace regulator.
6. If maximum current output is 5 amps or more in step 4, but is less than specified rating, check field coil, stator and diodes as outlined under "Bench Tests".

ALTERNATOR DISASSEMBLY

1. Remove cover plate from slip ring end frame.
2. Remove shaft nut while holding shaft with a hex wrench inserted in hex hole in shaft end. Remove pulley, fan and slinger.
3. Remove four through bolts and separate slip ring end frame and stator assembly from drive end frame and rotor assembly.

Voltage Regulator, Replace

1. Disconnect three identically colored regulator leads and remove regulator attaching screws.
2. Disconnect regulator lead from heat sink and remove regulator.
3. Reverse procedure to install.

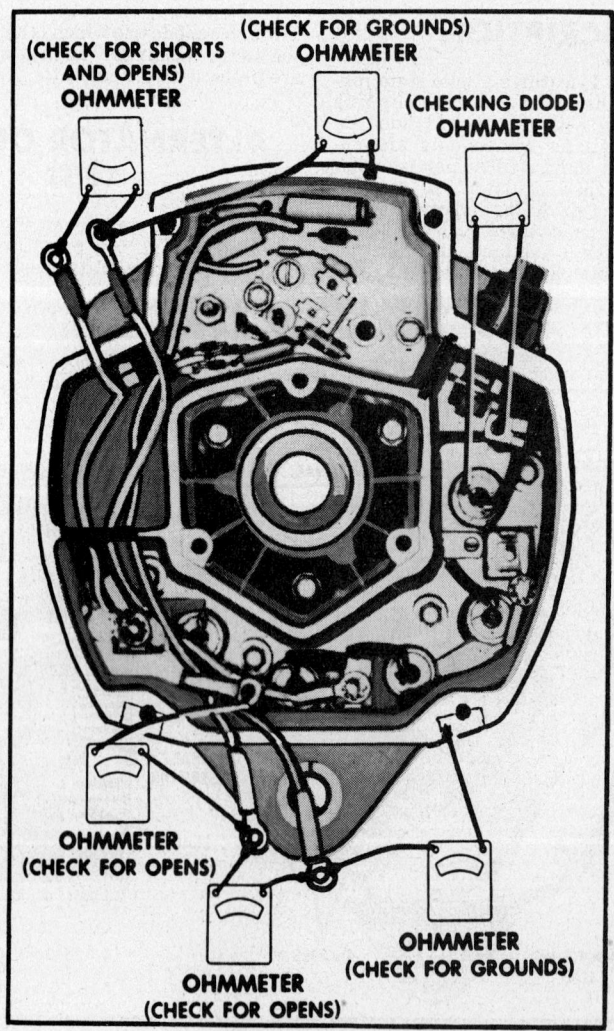

Fig. 6 Bench test connections

DELCO-REMY "DELCOTRON"

2. Support heat sink with tool J-9717-2 or a suitable equivalent, press diode from heat sink with tool J-9717-1 just enough to install tool J-23097 and slide hammer, tool J-6125. Pull diode from heat sink.
3. Press new diode into heat sink with tool J-9600-2.
4. Install heat sink, insulators and mounting screws. Note that silicone grease is applied to both sides of the flat insulator to provide the necessary heat transfer between the heat sink and end frame. Reapply the silicone grease as necessary.

Drive End Bearing, Replace

1. Remove shaft nut, pulley, fan and slinger.
2. Press rotor from end frame.
3. Remove retainer plate screws, retainer plate assembly, gasket and collar.
4. Press bearing from end frame.
5. Remove retainer plate and replace felt washer. Then, install retainer plate.
6. Press new bearing into end frame with the sealed side facing away from grease reservoir.
7. Fill grease reservoir approximately 1/2 full with a suitable lubricant, P/N 1948791 or equivalent.
8. Install gasket and new retainer plate assembly in end frame, then with collar on shaft, press rotor into end frame.
9. Install collar, slinger, fan, pulley and shaft nut.

Rectifier End Bearing, Replace

1. Pull inner race from shaft and press new inner race onto shaft to specified dimension, Fig. 3.
2. Remove old seal and bearing from housing.
3. To aid bearing installation, heat bearing in an oven to 200-300°F. Then, press against bearing outer race to install in proper location, Fig. 4.
4. Fill bearing well cover approximately 3/4 full with lubricant, P/N 1948791. A portion of the lubricant should contact bearing after assembly. Press bearing well cover into housing.
5. Lubricate seal lip and fill cavity between rubber lip and steel case of seal with lubricant. Then, install seal with lip facing toward bearing to specified dimension, Fig. 5.

BENCH TESTS

Field Coil Tests

1. Disconnect field coil leads from regulator.
2. To check for grounds, connect an ohmmeter between one field coil lead and the end frame, Fig. 6. If a low reading is noted, the field coil is grounded.
3. To check for shorts or opens, connect an ohmmeter between the two field coil leads, Fig. 6. If resistance reading is below 2.65-2.85 ohms, the field coil is shorted. If an infinite reading is noted, the field coil is open.

Diode & Stator Tests

1. Remove three stud nuts, three regulator leads, three stator leads, six diode leads and R terminal lead from stud. With ohmmeter set at low scale range, connect one lead to diode lead and other lead to alternator case, Fig. 6, and note reading. Reverse leads, one reading should be high and the other low. If both readings are the same the diode must be replaced.
2. To check for grounded stator windings, connect an ohmmeter from any stator lead to alternator case, Fig. 6, if a low reading is obtained stator windings are grounded. To check stator windings for an open circuit, connect an ohmmeter between each pair of stator leads, Fig. 6, if reading is high the windings are opened. To check stator windings for a short circuit special equipment must be used. If all other checks are normal but alternator fails to supply rated output stator windings may be shorted.
3. After tests are completed, install leads on each stud in the following order; two diode leads, stator lead, R terminal lead (on one stud only), regulator lead and nut.

ASSEMBLY

1. Align case components and install through bolts.
2. With oil slinger properly positioned over end frame boss, install fan, pulley, washer and shaft nut on shaft.

Delcotron 27 or 51 SI (Type 200) Integral Charging Systems

DESCRIPTION

This unit, Fig. 1, features a solid state regulator mounted inside the alternator slip ring end frame, along with the brush holder assembly. All regulator components are enclosed in a solid mold with a provision for adjustment of the regulator. A rectifier bridge, containing six diodes and connected to the stator windings, changes A.C. voltage to D.C. voltage which is available at the output terminal. Generator field current is supplied through a diode trio which is also connected to the stator windings. The diodes and rectifiers are protected by a capacitor which is also mounted in the end frame.

TROUBLE SHOOTING

Undercharged Battery

1. Check alternator drive belt tension and adjust if necessary. Also, check charging system for proper electrical connections.
2. Ensure battery is fully charged at this time.
3. Connect a voltmeter between the alternator "Bat" terminal and the ground, voltmeter check No. 1, Fig. 2. No voltage reading indicates an open circuit between the voltmeter connection and battery.
4. If battery voltage is obtained in step 3, disconnect battery ground cable. Connect voltmeter between battery terminals, voltmeter check No. 2, Fig. 2. Also, connect an ammeter between the battery terminals.
5. Connect battery ground cable.
6. Turn on all accessories, then connect a carbon pile regulator across battery.
7. Operate engine at moderate speed, adjust carbon pile regulator to obtain maximum current output.
8. If ammeter reading is within 10 amps of rated output, alternator is not at fault.

NOTE: Alternator rated output is stamped on alternator frame.

9. If ammeter reading is not within 10 amps of rated output, ground field winding by inserting screw driver in end frame hole, contacting tab. Fig. 3.

NOTE: Do not insert screw driver deeper than one inch, tab is usually located within 3/4 inch of casing surface.

10. If reading is within 10 amps of rated output, regulator must be replaced. If reading is not within limits, check field winding, diode trio, rectifier bridge and stator.
11. Turn off all accessories and disconnect ammeter and carbon pile regulator.

The voltage setting of this alternator may be adjusted to correct the undercharged condition. Remove voltage adjusting cap from alternator and raise the setting by rotating the cap in 90° increments. Note that in Fig. 4 the cap is set for medium high voltage. With position 2 aligned with the arrow, the setting is medium low. The "Lo" position is the lowest regulator setting and position "Hi" is the highest regulator setting. After adjusting the regulator setting, check for improved battery condition after a reasonable length of time in service.

Overcharged Battery

1. Ensure battery is fully charged and connect a voltmeter between the alternator "Bat" terminal and the ground, voltmeter check No. 1, Fig. 2.
2. Start engine and with all accessories turned on, increase engine speed to obtain maximum voltage reading.
3. If maximum voltage is above 15 volts, the alternator is defective.

95

DELCO-REMY "DELCOTRON"

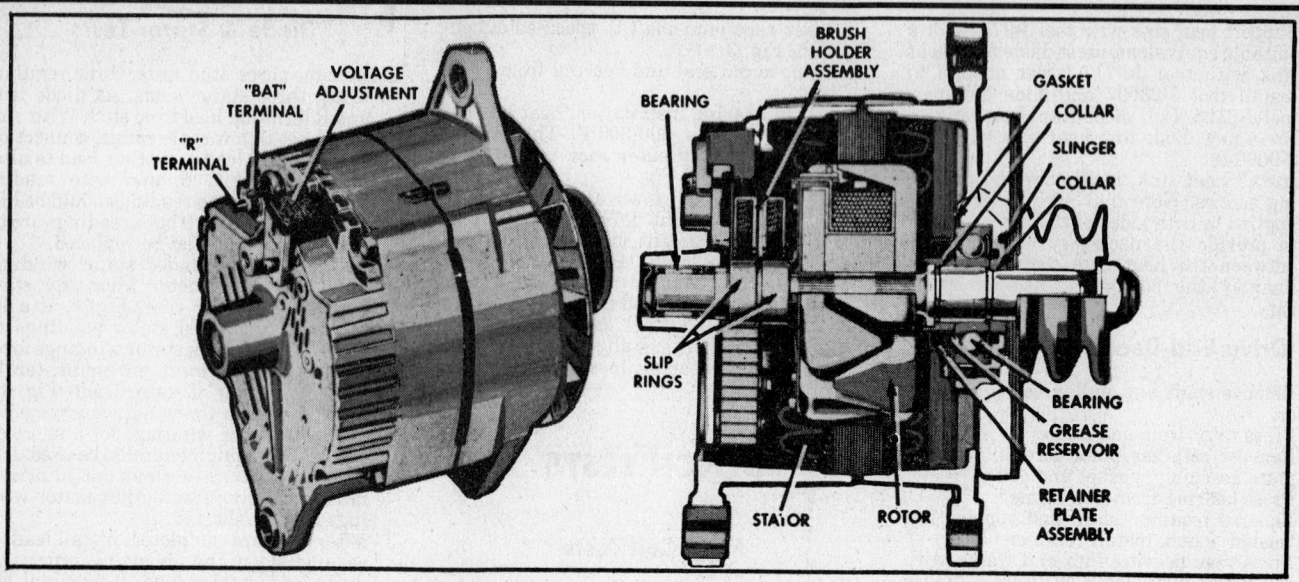

Fig. 1 Delcotron 27 & 51 SI (Type 200) Integral Charging System

ALTERNATOR DISASSEMBLY

1. Remove through bolts from drive end frame.
2. Separate slip ring end frame and stator assembly from drive end frame and rotor assembly.
3. Remove stator lead attaching nuts and separate stator from end frame.
4. Place a piece of pressure sensitive tape over bearing and shaft.
5. Inspect all leads for burned connections or opens. Check brushes for excessive wear and springs for distortion or discoloration.
6. During servicing and reassembly, hold brushes and springs in holder using a pin or toothpick inserted through end frame.

Drive End Bearing, Replace

1. Remove shaft nut, pulley, fan and slinger.
2. Press rotor from end frame.
3. Remove retainer plate screws, retainer plate assembly, gasket and collar.
4. Press bearing from end frame.
5. Remove retainer plate and replace felt washer. Then, install retainer plate.
6. Press new bearing into end frame with the sealed side facing away from grease reservoir.
7. Fill grease reservoir approximately ½ full with a suitable lubricant, P/N 1948791 or equivalent.
8. Install gasket and new retainer plate assembly in end frame, then with collar on shaft, press rotor into end frame.
9. Install collar, slinger, fan, pulley and shaft nut. Torque shaft nut to 70-80 ft. lbs.

Slip Ring Service

If the slip rings are dirty they may be cleaned with No. 400 silicon carbide paper and finish polished with crocus cloth. Spin the rotor in a lathe, or otherwise spin the rotor, and hold the polishing cloth against the slip rings until they are clean.

CAUTION: The rotor must be rotated in order that the slip rings will be cleaned evenly. Cleaning the slip rings by hand without spinning the rotor may result in flat spots on the slip rings, causing brush noise.

Slip rings that are rough or out-of-round should be trued in a lathe to .002" maximum runout as indicated on a dial gauge. Remove only enough material to make the rings smooth and round. Finish polish with crocus cloth and blow away all dust.

BENCH TESTS
Rotor & Slip Ring Test

NOTE: Ohmmeter must be at low scale setting during this test.

1. Inspect rotor for wear or damage.
2. Touch ohmmeter leads to slip rings. Fig.

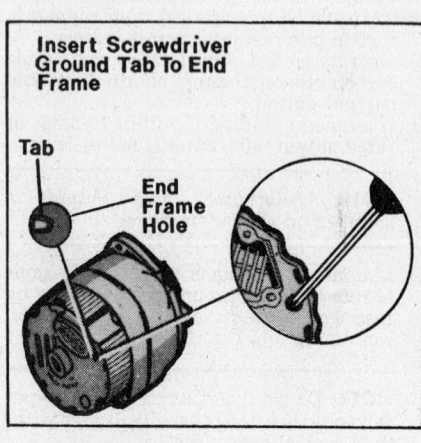

Fig. 2 System test connections

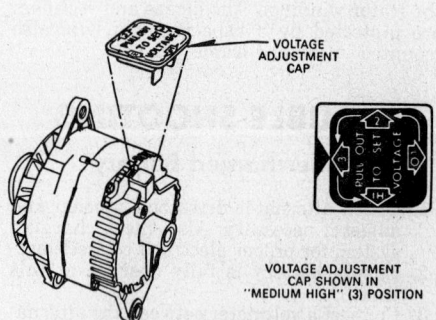

Fig. 3 Grounding field windings

Fig. 4 Voltage adjusting cap

DELCO-REMY "DELCOTRON"

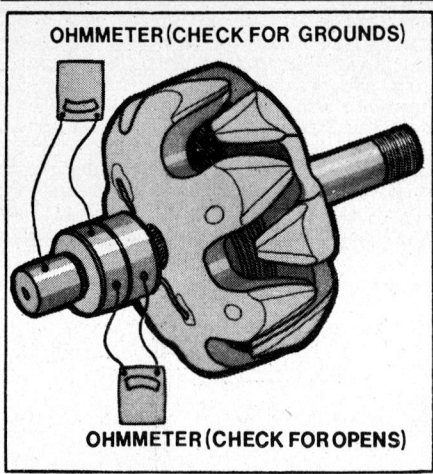

Fig. 5 Testing rotor & slip rings

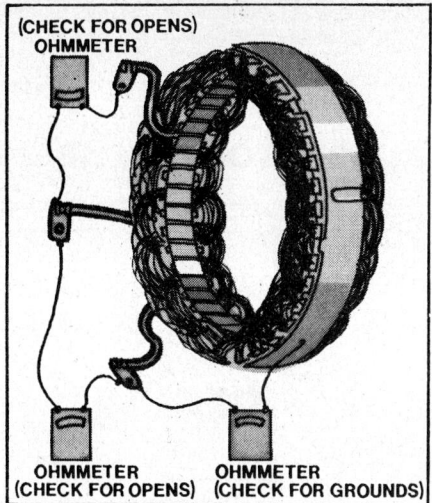

Fig. 6 Testing stator windings

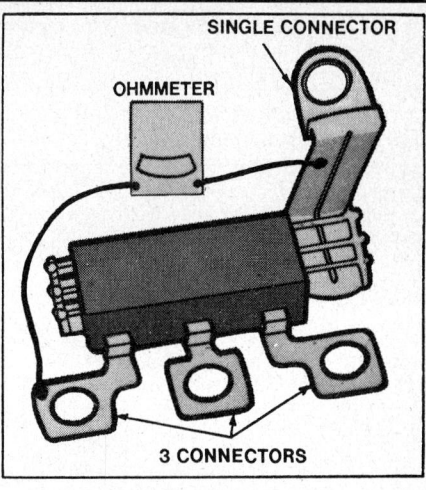

Fig. 7 Testing diode trio

5.
3. If no reading is obtained an open circuit exist in windings.
4. If reading below 3 ohms is obtained winding is shorted.
5. If a reading above 3 ohms is obtained excessive resistance exists in windings.
6. Connect one ohmmeter lead to rotor shaft and touch slip rings with other lead, if any reading is obtained there is a ground in the circuit. Fig. 5.

NOTE: If any of the above problems are present the rotor assembly must be replaced.

Stator Winding Test

1. Inspect stator for discolored windings, loose connections and damage.
2. Connect an ohmmeter from stator lead to frame, if any reading is obtained windings are grounded. Fig. 6.
3. Connect ohmmeter between stator leads, if reading is high when connected between each pair of leads, an open circuit exists in windings.

NOTE: Shorted windings are difficult to locate without special equipment. If other test indicate normal, but rated alternator output cannot be obtained the windings are probably shorted.

Diode Trio

1. With diode unit removed, connect an ohmmeter to the single connector and to one of the three connectors. Fig. 7.
2. Observe the reading. Reverse ohmmeter leads.
3. Reading should be high with one connection and low with the other. If both readings are the same, unit must be replaced.
4. Repeat between the single connector and each of the three connectors.

NOTE: There are two diode units differing in appearance. These are completely interchangeable.

The diode unit can be checked for a grounded brush lead while still installed in the end frame by connecting an ohmmeter from the brush lead clip to the end frame as in Steps 1 and 2 above. If both readings are zero, check for a grounded brush or brush lead.

Rectifier Bridge Test

1. Connect ohmmeter to the grounded heat sink and one of the three terminals. Fig. 8.
2. Observe the reading then reverse leads.
3. Reading should be high with one connection and low with the other. If both readings are the same, unit must be replaced.
4. Repeat test for each of the other terminals.

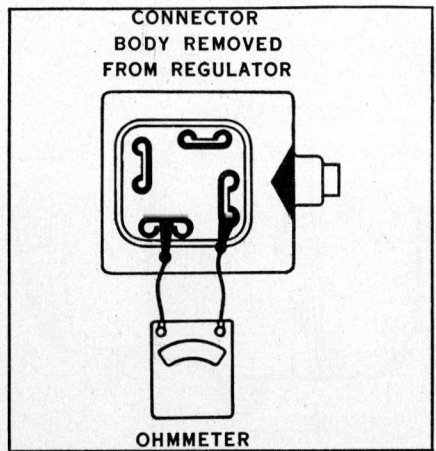

Fig. 9 Testing connector body

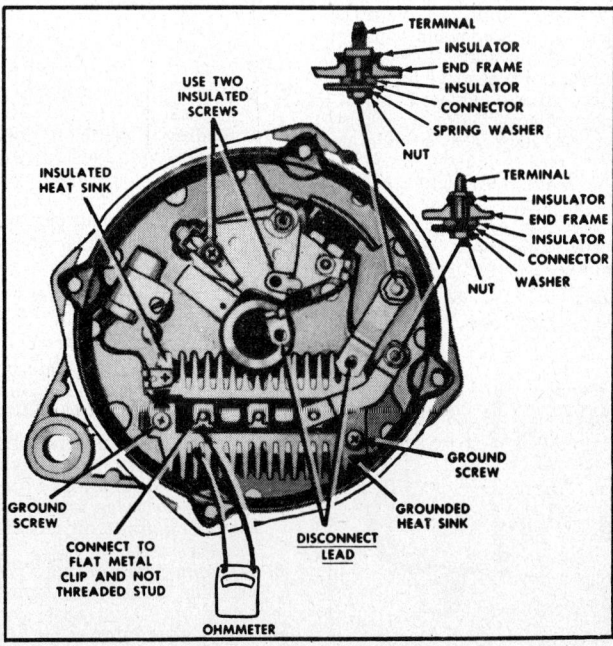

Fig. 8 Testing rectifier bridge

97

DELCO-REMY "DELCOTRON"

Regulator Test

NOTE: This test need only be performed if an overcharged condition was present.

1. Remove connector body from regulator.
2. Connect an ohmmeter, using middle range scale, to each adjacent pair of terminals, Fig. 9. If any reading is infinite, replace connector body.

ALTERNATOR ASSEMBLY

The alternator assembly procedure is the reverse of the disassembly procedure. However when installing the slip ring end frame assembly, remove tape from bearing and shaft, ensuring shaft is free from foreign material. With the brushes held in place with a pin, install shaft into end frame, using caution not to damage seal. After tightening the through bolts, remove brush retaining pin, allowing brushes to fall into place on the slip rings.

Delcotron 30 SI & 30 SI/TR Integral Charging System

DESCRIPTION

These units, Figs. 1 and 2 feature a solid state regulator mounted inside the rectifier end frame housing, Figs. 3, 4 and 5. Regulator voltage setting can be adjusted externally by repositioning a voltage adjustment cap. The 30 SI/TR unit is a standard 30 SI with a transformer-rectifier (TR unit) mounted on the end frame, Fig. 5. The TR unit provides a separate voltage to charge a cranking battery, which eliminates the need for a series-parallel switch.

TROUBLE SHOOTING

Undercharged Battery

30 SI

1. Check alternator drive belt tension and adjust if necessary. Also check charging system for proper electrical connections.
2. Ensure battery is fully charged at this time.
3. Connect a voltmeter between alternator "Batt" terminal and ground. No voltage reading indicates an open circuit between voltmeter connection and battery.
4. If battery voltage is obtained in step 3, disconnect battery ground cable. Connect an ammeter between "Batt" terminal of alternator and battery positive post, then connect battery ground cable.
5. Install a carbon pile regulator across battery, then operate engine at a moderate speed.
6. Turn on all accessories and adjust carbon pile regulator to obtain maximum current output.
7. If reading is within 10 amps of rated output, adjust voltage adjustment cap as outlined under "Voltage Setting".
8. If reading is not within 10 amps of rated output, the alternator must be disassembled and checked as outlined under "Alternator Disassembly".

30 SI/TR

NOTE: Do not allow leads or terminals to touch ground.

1. Remove TR unit attaching screws, then pull unit away from alternator to expose lead connections.
2. Disconnect three transformer leads from mounting studs on rectifier bridge then reinstall nuts.
3. Disconnect remaining TR unit lead from rectifier bridge heat sink, then reinstall screw.
4. Check alternator as outlined under 30 SI procedure.
5. If no defect is found, check TR unit rectifier bridge as follows:
   a. Connect one lead of ohmmeter to heat sink and other lead to terminal or flat metal connector, if equipped, Fig. 6.

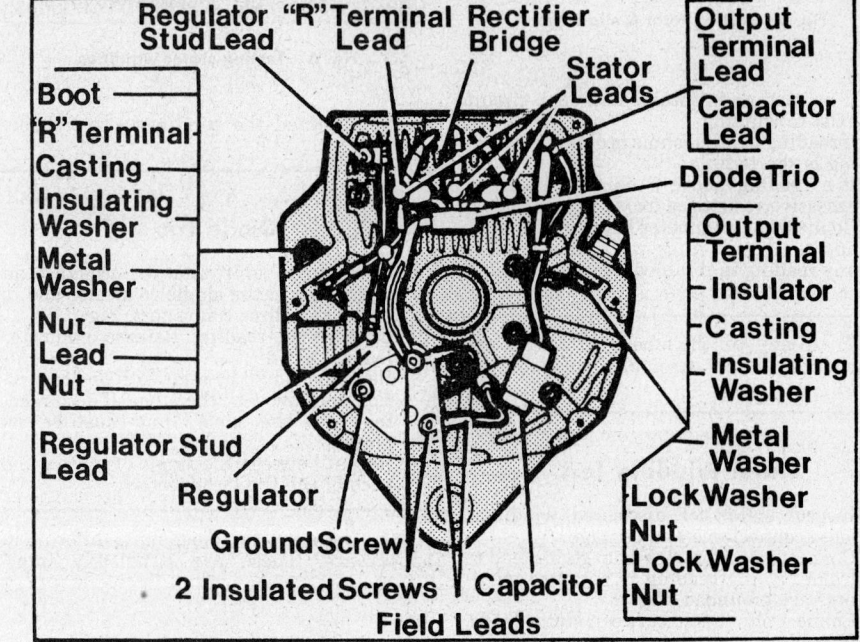

Fig. 3 Delcotron 30 SI negative ground unit

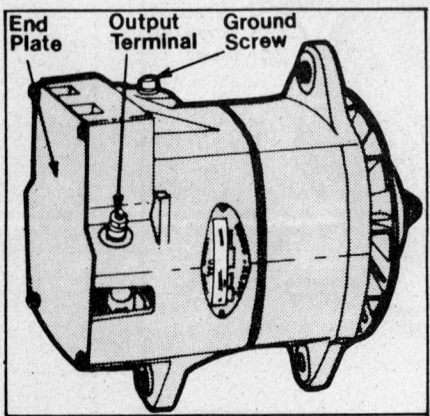

Fig. 1 Delcotron 30 SI alternator

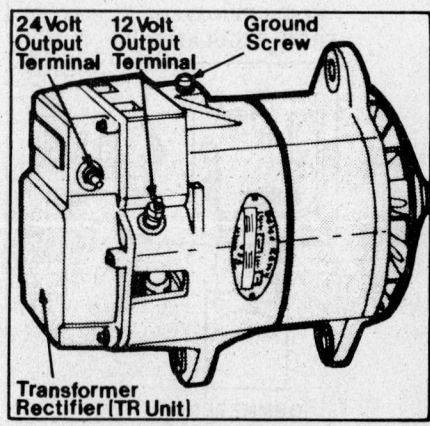

Fig. 2 Delcotron 30 SI/TR alternator

DELCO-REMY "DELCOTRON"

b. Note reading, then reverse leads using the same heat sink and terminal or metal connector.
c. One reading should be high and the other low.
d. If both readings are the same, replace rectifier bridge.
e. Repeat test on remaining two terminal or metal connectors using the same heat sink, then between other heat sink and each of the three terminals.
6. If no defects are found, install TR unit on alternator.
7. Disconnect lead from TR unit output terminal, then connect ammeter between terminal and lead.

NOTE: Do not allow terminal to touch ground.

8. Operate engine at moderate speed to obtain maximum output.
9. If specific gravity of cranking battery is 1.200 or below, charging rate of alternator should be 5 amps or higher. If charging rate is below 5 amps, replace TR unit transformer.

Overcharged Battery

NOTE: The TR unit on 30 SI/TR alternators does not require testing for this condition.

1. Operate engine at moderate speed to obtain maximum voltage output, ensure all accessories are turned off.
2. If voltage exceeds 15 volts on a 12 volt system, 30 volts on 24 volt system or 39

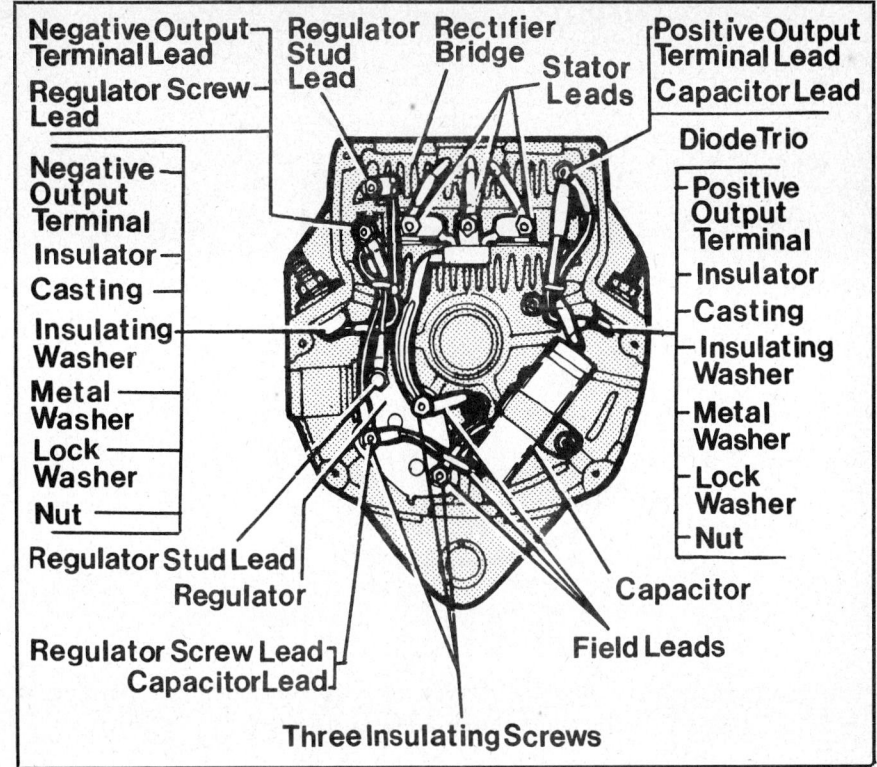

Fig. 4   Delcotron 30 SI insulated unit

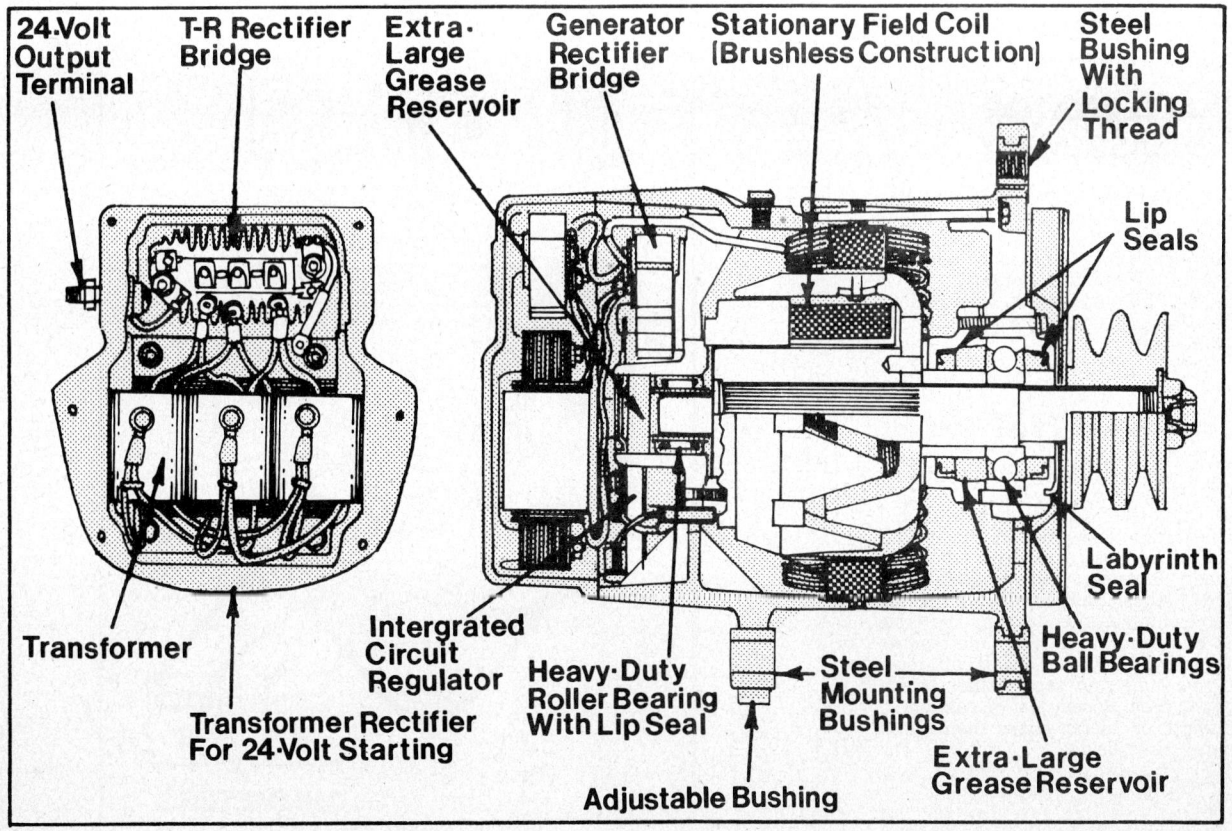

Fig. 5   Cross sectional view. Delcotron 30 SI/TR

DELCO-REMY "DELCOTRON"

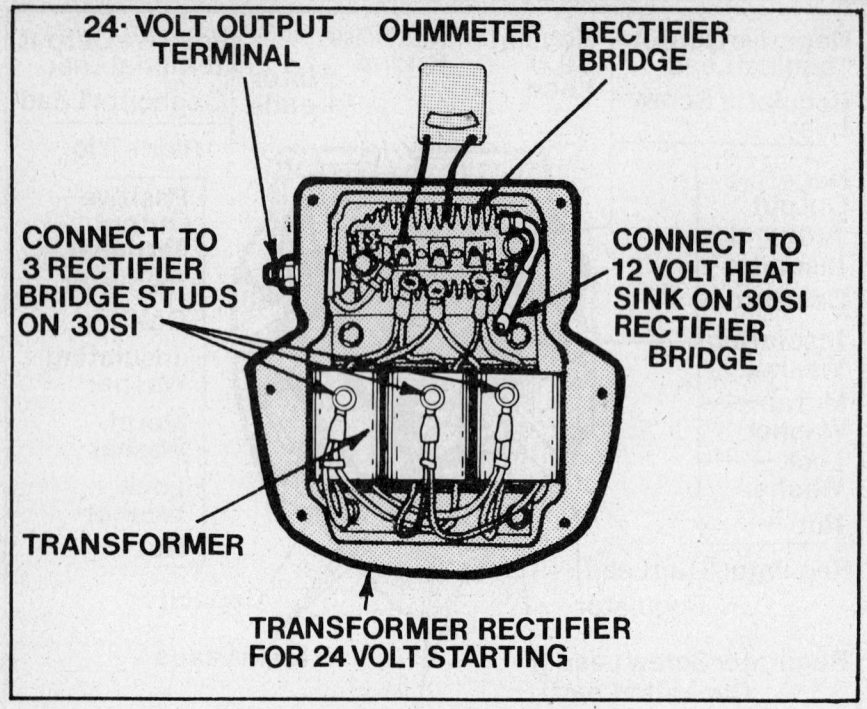

Fig. 6 Testing TR unit rectifier bridge diodes

volts on a 32 volt system, the alternator must be removed and disassembled and tested as outlined under "Alternator Disassembly".
3. If voltage does not exceed the above values, adjust voltage adjustment cap as outlined under "Voltage Setting".

ALTERNATOR DISASSEMBLY

1. Remove attaching screws and end plate.
2. Remove fan and pully, then remove four through bolts.
3. Separate drive end frame and rotor from rectifier end frame and stator.
4. Press rotor from end frame, then remove inner collar from end frame and outer collar from shaft.

BENCH TEST

Rectifier Bridge Check

Connect ohmmeter between heat sink and one of three terminals or clips, step 1 Fig. 7. If rectifier bridge is constructed with flat metal clips, connect ohmmeter leads to metal clips not threaded studs. Note ohmmeter reading then reverse ohmmeter leads using the same heat sink and terminal or clip. One reading should be high and the other low. If both readings are the same and the rectifier bridge should be replaced. Repeat test on remaining two terminals or metal clips, then check remaining rectifier bridge.

Field Coil Checks

Connect one ohmmeter to field coil lead and other lead to end frame, step 2 Fig. 7. If ohmmeter reading is low, field coil is grounded. Connect ohmmeter between field coil leads, step 3 Fig. 7. If ohmmeter is high (infinite), field coil is open.

Connect battery and ammeter in series with field coil. Note ammeter reading and refer to Alternator and Regulator Specification in truck chapter. An ammeter reading above specified value indicates shorted windings.

Diode Trio Check

Using an ohmmeter having a 1½ volt cell and set at low reading scale, connect one lead to the single connector and other lead to one of three connectors, Fig. 8. Note reading then reverse leads using the same two connectors. If both readings are the same, replace diode trio. One reading should be high and the other low. Use single connector and repeat test on remaining two connectors.

Stator Check

To check for grounded stator winding, connect one ohmmeter lead to any stator lead and other lead to metal frame, step 4 Fig. 7. Reading should be infinite, if not replace stator. Stator windings cannot be checked for opens or short circuits unless special test equipment is used. If regulator checks good, but alternator fails to supply rated output and stator windings are badly discolored, replace stator.

Regulator Check

The regulator cannot be checked with an ohmmeter. A special regulator tester must be used.

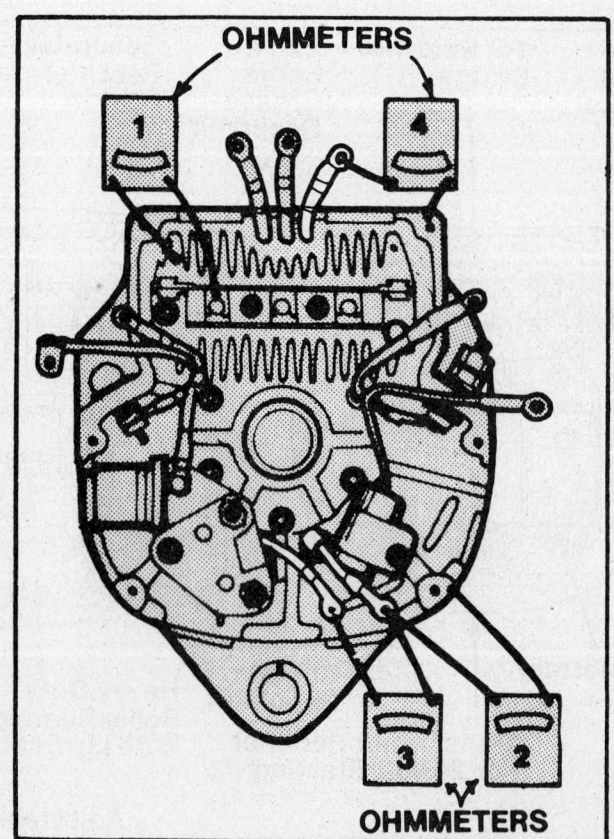

Fig. 7 Bench test connections

DELCO-REMY "DELCOTRON"

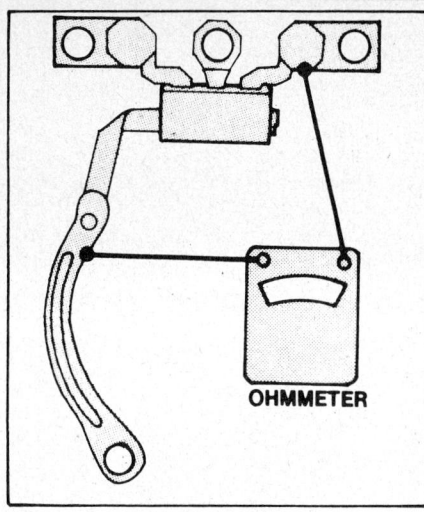

Fig. 8 Testing diode trio

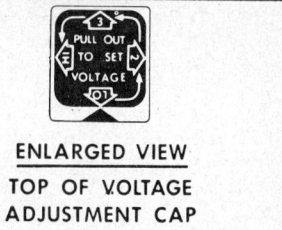

Fig. 9 Voltage adjusting cap

four retainer plate attaching screws, retainer plate and gasket. Push on inner race to remove bearing, then remove seals from end frame and retainer. Press new seals in with lip facing toward bearing. Press bearing in against outer race, then fill cavity half full with lubricant No. 1948791 or equivalent. Install retainer and four attaching bolts.

To replace rectifier end frame bearing, pull inner race from shaft and bearing from end frame. Install inner race on shaft and bearing in end frame with seal facing away from grease reservoir. Fill reservoir half full with lubricant No. 1948791 or equivalent.

ALTERNATOR ASSEMBLE

1. Install inner collar on shaft and outer collar on end frame under seal next to bearing.
2. While supporting outer collar, press rotor into drive end frame.
3. Assemble drive end frame and rotor to rectifier end frame and stator, then install four through bolts.
4. Install fan and pulley on rotor shaft.
5. Install end plate and attaching screws.

REPAIRS

Bearings, Replace

To replace drive end frame bearing, remove

VOLTAGE SETTING

Remove adjusting cap and rotate it ¼ turn in the desired direction, then reinstall cap, Fig. 9. There are four settings, LO-lowest voltage setting, 2-medium low voltage, 3-medium high voltage and HI-highest voltage setting. Alternator voltage should be 13 to 15 volts on a 12 volt system, 26 to 30 volts on a 24 volt system and 33 to 39 volts on a 32 volt system.

Delcotron 40 SI Integral Charging System

DESCRIPTION

This unit features a solid state regulator mounted inside the alternator slip ring end frame, Fig. 1, along with brush holder assembly. The voltage setting can be adjusted by repositioning the adjustment cap. The 100 amp model incorporates two rectifier bridges, each containing 6 diodes and connected to the stator winding, changes A.C. voltage to D.C. voltage which is available at the output terminal. The 145 amp model incorporates three rectifier bridges, each containing 6 diodes. Some models incorporate three A.C. terminals located on top of alternator. Alternator field current is supplied through a diode trio which is also connected to the stator windings. The diodes and rectifiers are protected by a capacitor which is also mounted in the end frame.

TROUBLE SHOOTING

Undercharged Battery

1. Disconnect battery ground cable.
2. Connect an ammeter between BAT terminal of alternator and battery positive post and reconnect battery ground cable.
3. Install a carbon pile regulator across battery, then operate engine at a moderate speed.
4. Turn on all accessories and adjust carbon pile regulator to obtain maximum current output.
5. If reading is within 10 amps of rated output, adjust voltage adjustment cap as described under "Voltage Setting".

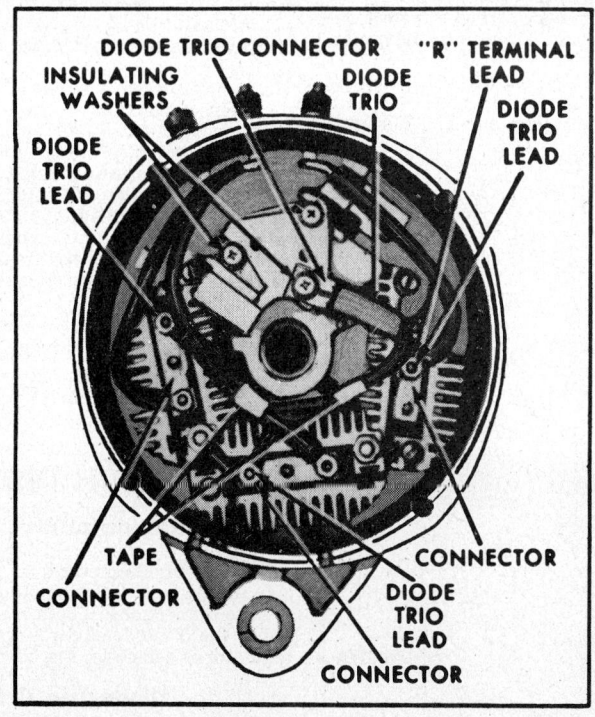

Fig. 1 Slip ring end frame components

DELCO-REMY "DELCOTRON"

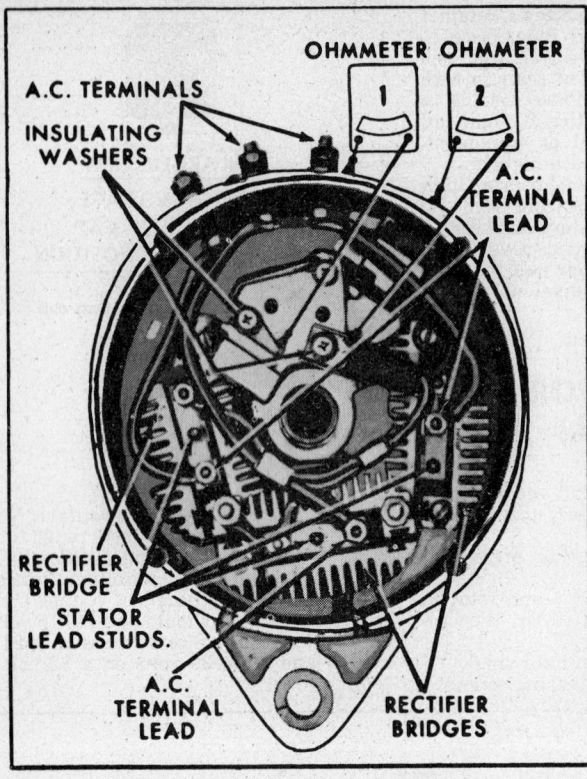

Fig. 2 Voltage regulator and brush lead test

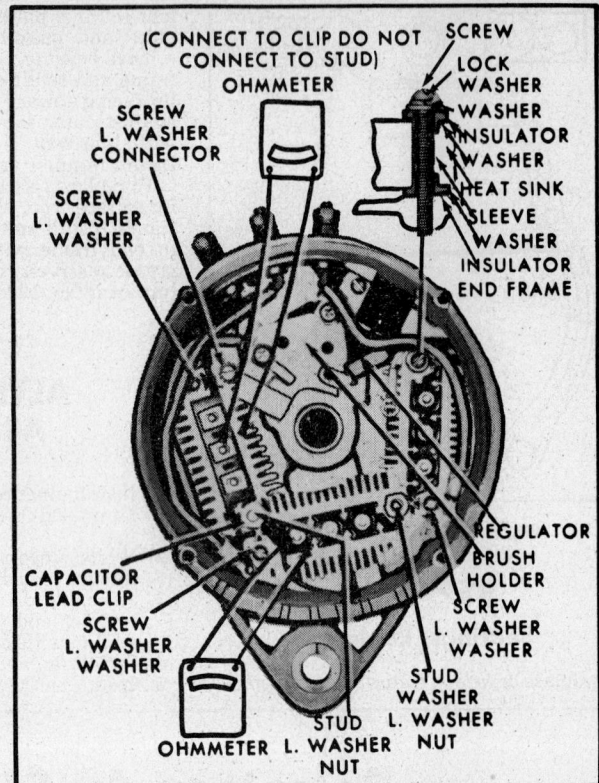

Fig. 5 Checking rectifier bridge

6. If reading is not within 10 amps of rated output, the alternator must be disassembled and checked, as described under "Alternator Disassembly".

Overcharged Battery

1. Connect a voltmeter between alternator BAT terminal and ground.
2. With all accessories turned off, start engine and increase speed until maximum voltage reading is obtained.
3. If voltage reading exceeds 15 volts, the alternator must be disassembled and checked, as described under "Alternator Disassembly".
4. If voltage reading does not exceed 15 volts, adjust voltage adjusting cap as described under "Voltage Setting".

ALTERNATOR DISASSEMBLY

1. With alternator secured in a vise, remove cover plate from slip ring end frame.
2. Using an allen wrench to hold rotor shaft in place remove pulley nut, pulley, fan, slinger and collar.
3. Remove four through bolts, then using a screw driver in stator slot separate slip ring end frame and stator assembly from drive end frame and rotor assembly.
4. Remove three stator lead to rectifier bridge attaching nuts, then separate stator from slip ring end frame.
5. Place tape over slip ring end frame bearing and shaft.

NOTE: Brushes may fall from holders and become contaminated with bearing grease, if so they must be cleaned prior to assembly.

BENCH TESTS

Voltage Regulator/Brush Lead Test

Connect an ohmmeter from the brush lead clip to the end frame, note reading, then reverse connections. If both readings are zero, either the brush lead clip is grounded or the regulator is defective, Fig. 2.

Diode Trio Test

Using an ohmmeter having 1½ volt cell and set at low reading scale, connect one lead to the single connector and the other lead to one of three connectors, Figs. 3 & 4. Note reading, then reverse leads using the same two connectors. If both readings are the same replace the diode trio. One reading should be high and the other low. Using single connector repeat test on the other two connectors.

Rectifier Bridge Test

Connect one lead of ohmmeter to grounded heat sink and other lead to terminal or flat metal connector, if equipped, Fig. 5. Note reading then reverse leads of the same heat sink and terminal or metal connector. One reading should be high and the other low. If both readings are the same the rectifier bridge must be replaced. Repeat test on the remaining two terminals or metal connectors, then check remaining rectifier bridges.

Rotor Field Winding Test

To check if winding is open, connect one ohmmeter to each slip ring, Fig. 6. If reading

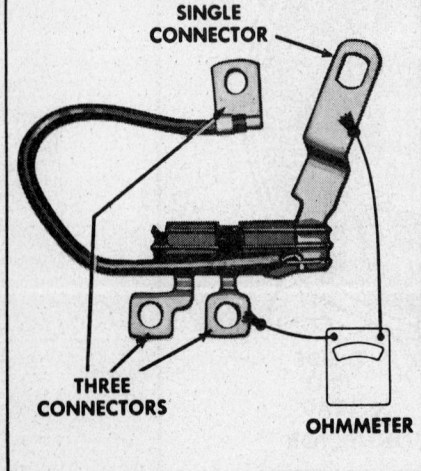

Fig. 3 Checking diode trio. 100 amp units

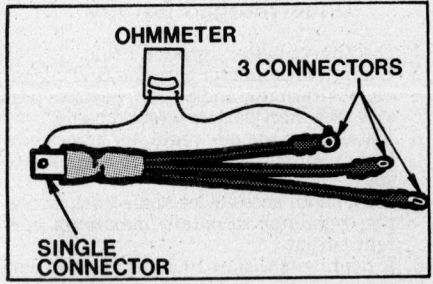

Fig. 4 Checking diode trio. 145 amp units

DELCO-REMY "DELCOTRON"

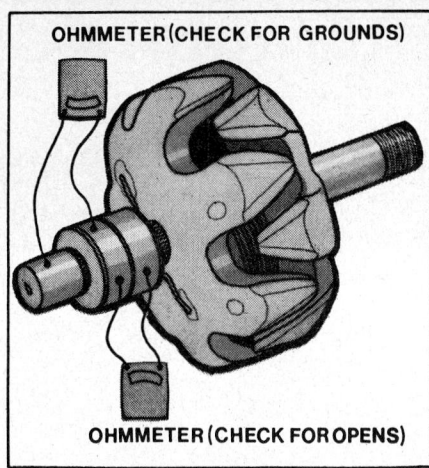

Fig. 6 Checking rotor

is high then the winding is open.

To check for a short circuit or excessive resistance connect an ammeter and battery in series with edges of two slip rings. The ammeter reading should be 4.0 to 4.5 amps at 80° F. If reading is above 4.5 amps the winding is shorted and the rotor and regulator must be replaced.

Rotor may also be checked for shorts by connecting an one ohmmeter lead to each slip ring. Ohmmeter reading should be 2.75 to 3.0 ohms. If reading is below 2.75 ohms the rotor is shorted.

Stator Test

To check for grounded stator winding, connect one ohmmeter lead to any stator lead and the other lead to metal frame, Fig. 7. If ohmmeter reading is low the stator windings are grounded. Stator windings can not be checked for opens or short circuits unless special test equiment is used. If alternator fails to supply rated output, but will supply at least 10 amperes, the stator windings may be shorted.

Regulator Test

If all other checks fail to show any defects

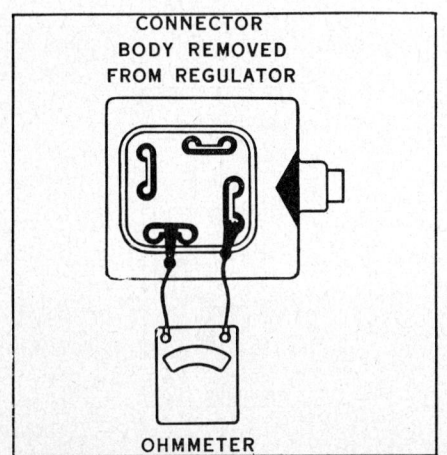

Fig. 8 Checking regulator connector body

and an overcharging condition exists, remove connector body from regulator and check as follows. With ohmmeter set to middle scale range, connect leads to each adjacent pair of terminals until four readings are obtained Fig. 8. If any reading is excessively high replace the connector body. If all previous checks are satisfactory but maximum current output is less than 10 amps or maximum voltage is over 15 volts, replace the regulator.

VOLTAGE SETTING

Remove adjusting cap and rotate it 1/4 turn in the desired direction, then reinstall cap, Fig. 9. There are four settings, LO—lowest voltage setting, 2—medium low voltage, 3—medium high voltage and HI—highest voltage setting. Alternator voltage should be 13 to 15 volts.

REPAIRS

Bearing Replace

The drive end frame bearing is sealed on both sides and cannot be lubricated. To replace bearing, press rotor from end frame, remove retainer plate and press bearing from end frame. Use a socket that just fits over outer race to press new bearing into end frame.

The slip ring end frame bearing cannot be relubricated, the bearing must be replaced. Using a suitable socket press bearing from end frame. Position new bearing on outside of end frame, then using a suitable socket press bearing in to specified dimension, Fig. 10. Fill plug with lubricant No. 1948791 or equivalent, ensure grease reservoir will be half full when plug is pressed into end frame and that lubricant will contact bearing when plug is installed. Press plug in until flush with end frame. Lubricate seal lip, then position seal on end frame with lip facing toward bearing, press seal in to specified dimension, Fig. 10.

Slip Ring Service

If the slip rings are dirty they may be cleaned with No. 400 silicon carbide paper and finish polished with crocus cloth. Spin the rotor in lathe, or otherwise spin the rotor, and until they are clean.

CAUTION: The rotor must be rotated in order that the slip rings will be cleaned evenly.

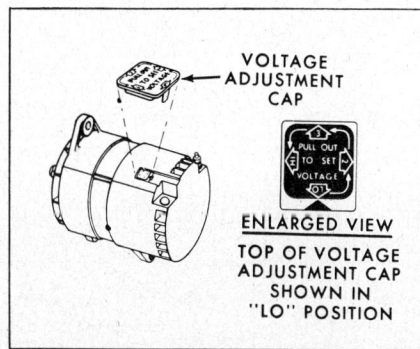

Fig. 9 Adjusting voltage setting

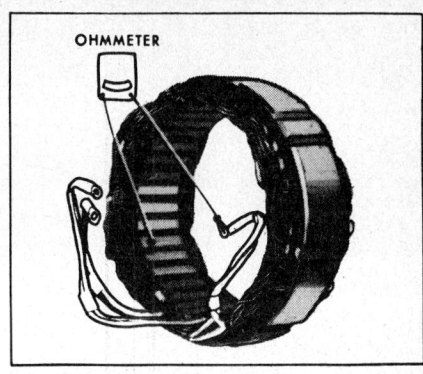

Fig. 7 Checking stator winding

Hold the polishing cloth against the slip rings. Cleaning the slip rings by hand without spinning the rotor may result in flat spots on the slip rings, causing brush noise.

Slip rings that are rough or out-of-round should be trued in a lathe to .002" maximum runout as indicated on a dial gauge. Remove only enough material to make the rings smooth and round. Finish polish with crocus cloth and blow away all dust.

ALTERNATOR ASSEMBLY

1. Remove tape from slip ring end frame bearing and shaft.
2. Use pin to hold brushes in compressed position.
3. Install three stator leads on rectifier bridges.
4. Install drive end frame and rotor assembly onto stator and slip ring end frame, use care when installing shaft into slip ring end frame to avoid damaging seal.
5. Install four through bolts.
6. Install collar, slinger, fan, pulley and pulley nut onto rotor shaft, torque pulley nut to 75 ft. lbs.
7. Remove pin holding brushes, then install cover plate onto slip ring and frame.

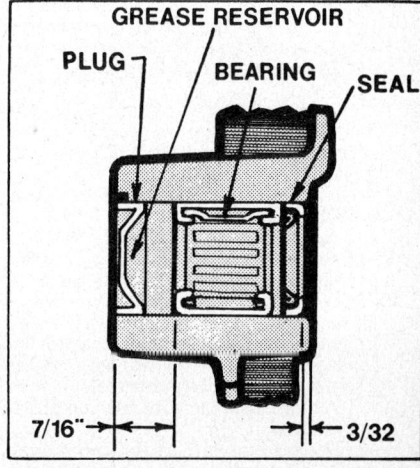

Fig. 10 Installing slip ring end frame bearing assembly

Ford Autolite/Motorcraft Alternators

DESCRIPTION

A charge indicator lamp or ammeter can be used in charging system.

If a charge indicator lamp is used in the charging system, Fig. F1, the system operation is as follows: when the ignition switch is turned ON, a small electrical current flows through the lamp filament (turning the lamp on) and through the alternator regulator to the alternator field. When the engine is started, the alternator field rotates and produces a voltage in the stator winding. When the voltage at the alternator stator terminal reaches about 3 volts, the regulator field relay closes. This puts the same voltage potential on both sides of the charge indicator lamp causing it to go out. When the field relay has closed, current passes through the regulator A terminal and is metered to the alternator field.

If an ammeter is used in the charging system, Fig. F2, the regulator I terminal and the alternator stator terminal are not used. When the ignition switch is turned ON, the field relay closes and electrical current passes through the regulator A terminal and is metered to the alternator field. When the engine is started, the alternator field rotates causing the alternator to operate.

NOTE: The ammeter indicates current flow into (charge) or out of (discharge) the vehicle battery.

Some 1978 and all 1979–80 Ford vehicles are equipped with new electronic voltage regulators, Figs. F3 and F4. These solid state regulators are used in conjunction with other new components in the charging system such as an alternator with a higher field current requirement, a warning indicator lamp shunt resistor (500 ohms) and a new wiring harness with a new regulator connector. When replacing system components, note the following precautions:

1. Always use the proper alternator in the system. If the new 1978–80 alternator is installed on previous model systems, it will destroy the electro-mechanical regulator. If the older model alternator is used on the new system, it will have a reduced output.
2. Do not use an electro-mechanical regulator in the new system since the wiring harness connector will not index properly with this type of regulator.
3. The new electronic regulators are color coded for proper installation. The black color coded unit is installed in systems equipped with a warning indicator lamp. The blue color coded regulator is installed in systems equipped with an ammeter.
4. The new systems use a 500 ohm resistor on the rear of the instrument cluster on vehicles equipped with a warning indicator lamp. Do not replace this resistor with the 15 ohm resistance wire used on previous systems.

On the new systems with an indicator lamp, closing the ignition switch energizes the warning lamp and turns on the regulator output stage. The alternator receives maximum field current and is ready to generate an output voltage. As the alternator rotor speed increases, the output and stator terminal voltages increase from zero to the system regulation level determined by the regulator setting.

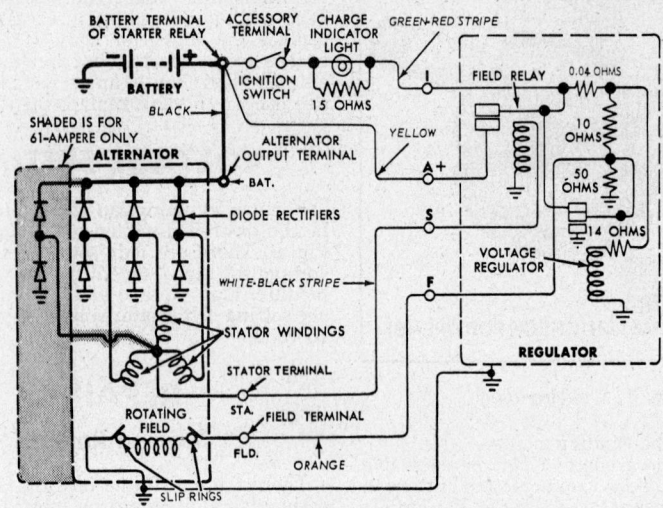

Fig. F1 Indicator light rear terminal alternator charging system (Typical)

When the ignition switch is turned off, the solid state relay circuit turns the output stage off, interrupting current flow through the regulator so there is not a current drain on the battery.

On vehicles equipped with an ammeter, the operating principle is similar.

NOTE: The ammeter indicates current flow into (charge) or out of (discharge) the vehicle battery.

SYSTEM TESTING
In-Vehicle Tests
1970–72 Units

ALTERNATOR OUTPUT TEST

When the alternator output test is conducted off the truck, a test bench must be used. Follow the procedure given by the test bench equipment manufacturer.

NOTE: When the alternator is removed from the vehicle for this purpose, always disconnect the battery ground cable as the alternator output connector is connected to the battery at all times.

1. Make the connections and tester knob adjustments, F5 and F6 (Output Test). Be sure that the field rheostat knob is at the OFF position at the start of this test.
2. Close the battery adapter switch. Start the engine, then open the battery adapter switch.
3. Increase the engine speed to approximately 2000 rpm (use a tachometer following the manufacturers instructions). Turn off all lights and electrical accesso-

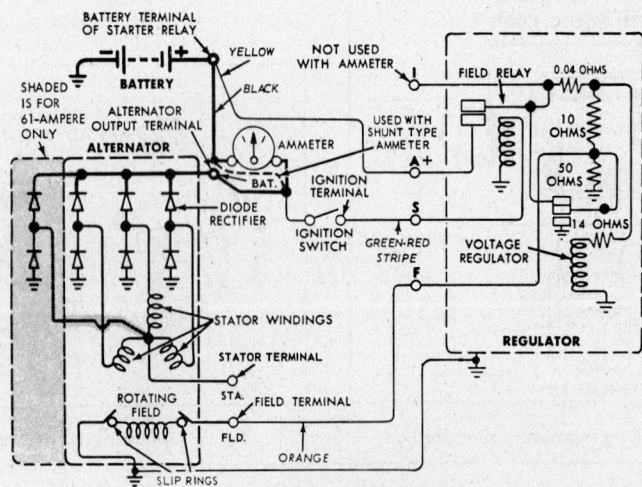

Fig. F2 Ammeter rear terminal alternator charging system (Typical)

Ford Autolite/Motorcraft Alternators

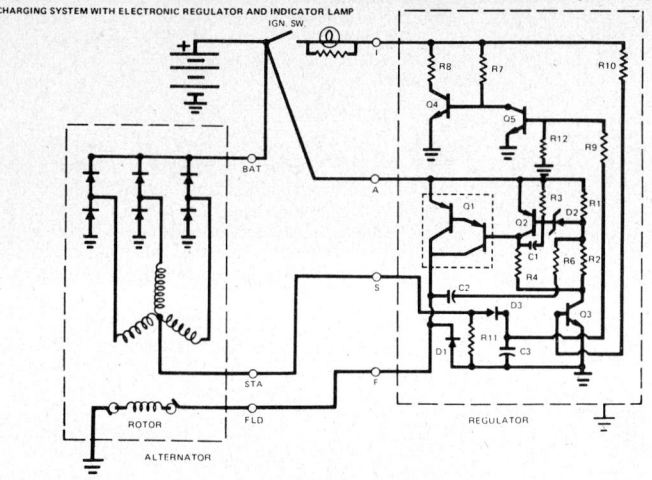

Fig. F3 Indicator light charging system with electronic voltage regulator

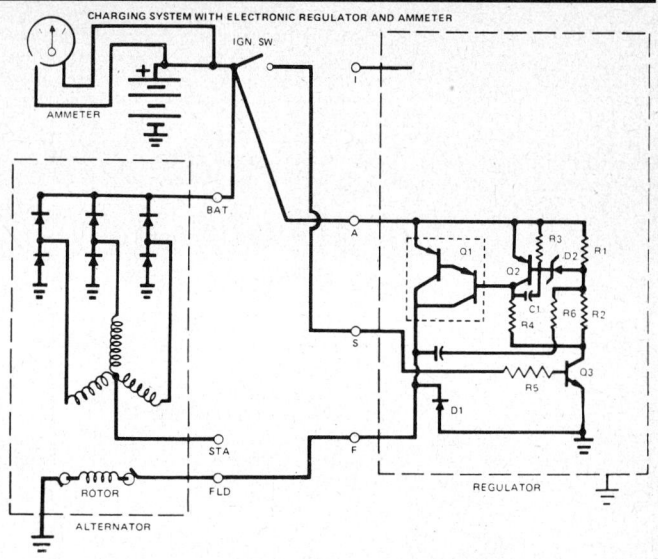

Fig. F4 Ammeter charging system with electronic voltage regulator

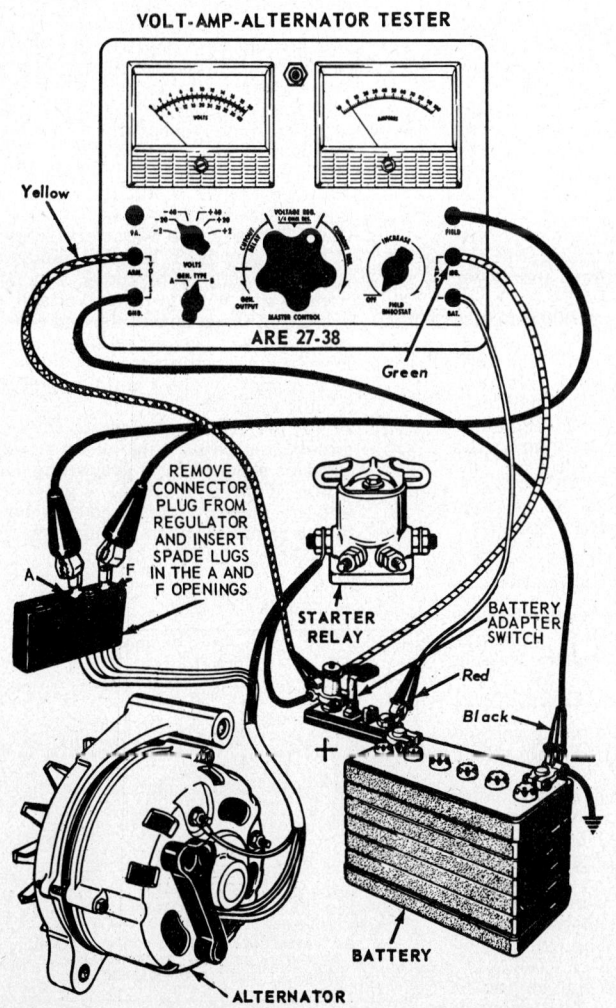

Fig. F5 Alternator output test

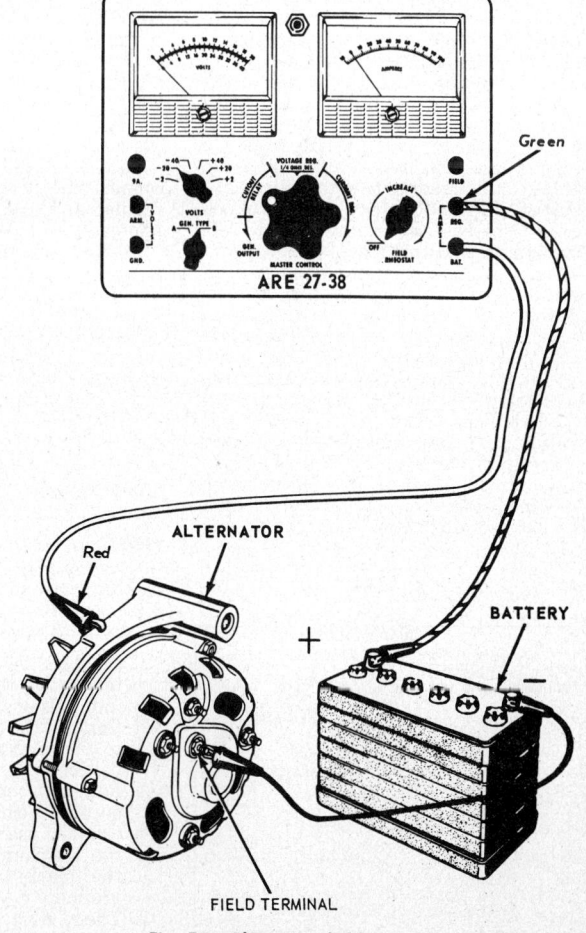

Fig. F6 Alternator field open or short circuit test

105

FORD AUTOLITE/MOTORCRAFT ALTERNATORS

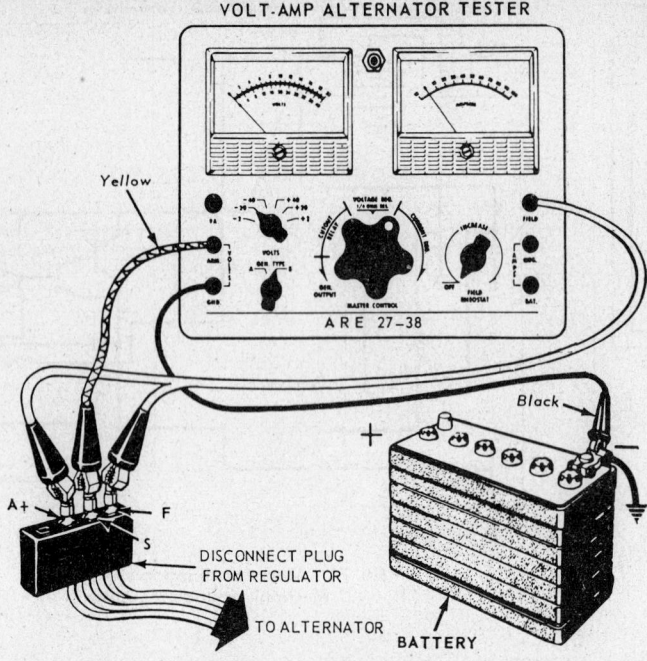

Fig. F7 Typical stator neutral voltage test

ries.

4. Turn the field rheostat clockwise until 15 volts is indicated on the voltmeter upper scale. Turn the master control clockwise until the voltmeter indicates between 11 and 12 volts. Holding the master control in this position, turn the field rheostat clockwise to its maximum rotation. Turn the master control counter clockwise until the voltmeter indicates 15 volts. Observe the ammeter reading. Add 2 amperes to this reading to obtain alternator output. If rated output cannot be obtained, increase the engine speed to 2900 rpm and repeat this step.
5. Return the field rheostat knob to OFF, release the master control knob, and stop the engine. Disconnect the test equipment, if no further tests are to be made.

If the alternator output is not O.K., it will be necessary to remove the alternator from the vehicle and perform the necessary bench tests to locate the defect.

An output of approximately 2 to 5 amperes below specification usually indicates an open alternator diode. An output of approximately 10 amperes below specification usually indicates a shorted alternator diode. An alternator with a shorted diode will usually whine, which will be most noticeable at idle speeds.

STATOR NEUTRAL VOLTAGE TEST

The alternator STA terminal is connected to the stator coil neutral or center point of the alternator windings, Figs. F1 and F2. The voltage generated at this point is used to close the field relay in the charge indicator light system.

To test for the stator neutral voltage, disconnect the regulator connector plug from the regulator. Make the connections and tester knob adjustments, Fig. F7.

Start the engine and run it at 1000 rpm (use a tachometer). Turn off all lights and accessories. Rotate the field rheostat clockwise until at least 6 volts is indicated on the voltmeter upper scale. If 6 volts or more is not obtained, remove the alternator and perform the diode and stator tests to determine which part of the alternator is damaged.

1973–80 Units

VOLTMETER TEST

NOTE: *All lights and electrical systems in the off position, parking brake applied, transmission in neutral and a charged battery (at least 1.200 specific gravity).*

1. Connect the negative lead of the voltmeter to the negative battery cable clamp (not bolt or nut).
2. Connect the positive lead of the voltmeter to the positive battery cable clamp (not bolt or nut).
3. Record the battery voltage reading shown on the voltmeter scale.
4. Connect the red lead of a tachometer to the distributor terminal of the coil and the black tachometer lead to a good ground.
5. Then, start and operate the engine at approximately 1500 rpm. With no other electrical load (foot off brake pedal and car doors closed), the voltmeter reading should increase but not exceed (2 volts) above the first recorded battery voltage reading. The reading should be taken when the voltmeter needles stops moving.
6. With the engine running, turn on the heater and/or air conditioner blower motor to high speed and headlights to high beam.
7. Increase the engine speed to 2000 rpm. The voltmeter should indicate a minimum reading of 0.5 volts above the battery voltage, Fig. F8.

NOTE: *If the above tests indicate proper voltage readings, the charging system is operating normally. Proceed to "Test Results" if a problem still exists.*

TEST RESULTS

1. If voltmeter reading indicates 2 volts over battery voltage (over voltage), proceed as follows:
   a. Stop the engine and check the ground connections between the regulator and alternator and/or regulator to engine. Clean and tighten connections securely and repeat the *Voltmeter Test Procedures*.
   b. If *over voltage* condition still exists, disconnect the regulator wiring plug from the regulator and repeat the *Voltmeter Test Procedures*.
   c. If *over voltage* still exists with the regulator wiring plug disconnected, repair the short in the wiring harness between the alternator and regulator. Then, replace the regulator and connect the regulator wiring plug to the regulator and repeat the *Voltmeter Test Procedures*.
2. On 1975–77 units, if voltmeter does not indicate more than $\frac{1}{2}$ volt above battery voltage, proceed as follows:
   a. Check for presence of battery voltage at alternator BAT terminal and the regulator plug A terminal, Fig. 10. Repair the wiring if no voltage is present at these terminals, and repeat the *Voltmeter Test Procedures*.
   b. If voltmeter reading does not increase $\frac{1}{2}$ volt above battery voltage, proceed to next step.
   c. Before performing other tests, the field circuit (regulator plug to alternator) must be checked for a grounding condition. If the field circuit is grounded and the jumper wire is used as a check at the regulator wiring plug from the

Fig. F8 Voltmeter test scale

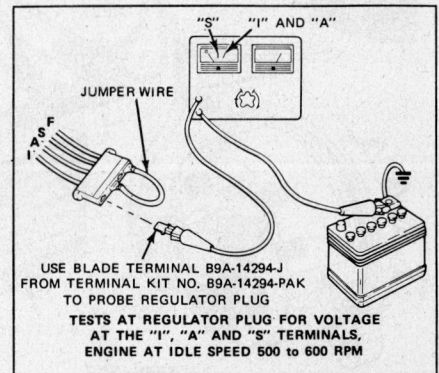

Fig. F9 Regulator plug voltage test

Ford Autolite/Motorcraft Alternators

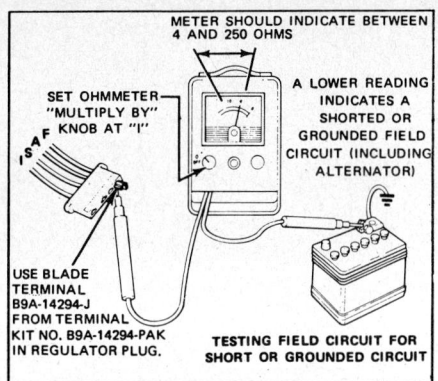

Fig. F10 Testing field circuit with Ohmmeter

A to F terminals, Fig. F9, excessive current will cause heat damage to the regulator wiring plug terminals and may burn the jumper wire, Fig. F9. Also, if the field circuit was grounded, the connector wire inside the regulator will be burned open and an under voltage condition will result.

d. The field circuit should be checked with the regulator wiring plug disconnected and an ohmmeter connected from the *F* terminal of the regulator wiring plug to the battery ground. The ohmmeter should indicate between 4 and 250 ohms, Fig. F10.

e. A check for the regulator burned-open wire is made by connecting an ohmmeter from the *I* to *F* terminals of the regulator, Fig. F11. The reading should indicate *O* (no resistance). If the reading indicates approximately *10 ohms*, the connector wire inside the regulator is burned open. *The field circuit grounded condition must be found and repaired before installing a new regulator.*

3. On 1978–80 units, if voltmeter does not indicate more than ½ volt above battery voltage, proceed as follows:
   a. Disconnect voltage regulator wire connector and connect an ohmmeter between wire connector F terminal and ground. Ohmmeter reading should indicate more than 3 ohms. If reading is less than 3 ohms, repair grounded field circuit and repeat Voltmeter Test procedure.
   b. If ohmmeter reading is more than 3 ohms, connect a jumper wire between voltage regulator wire connector terminals A and F, Fig. F12, then repeat Voltmeter Test procedure. If voltmeter reading is now more than ½ volt above battery voltage, the voltage regulator or wiring is defective, refer Regulator Test.
   c. If voltmeter still indicates less than ½ volt, disconnect jumper wire from voltage regulator wire connected and leave connector disconnected from regulator. Connect a jumper wire between alternator FLD and BAT terminals, Figs. F13 and F14, then repeat Voltmeter Test procedures.
   d. If voltmeter reading now indicates ½ volt or more above battery voltage, repair alternator to regulator wiring harness.
   e. If voltmeter still indicates less than ½ volt above battery voltage, stop engine and move voltmeter positive lead to alternator BAT terminal.
   f. If voltmeter now indicates battery voltage, the alternator should be removed, inspected and repaired. If zero volts is indicated, repair BAT terminal wiring.

FIELD CIRCUIT & ALTERNATOR TESTS

1. If the field circuit is satisfactory, disconnect the regulator wiring plug at the regulator and connect the jumper wire from *A* to the *F* terminals on the regulator wiring plug, Fig. F12.
2. Repeat the *Voltmeter Test Procedures*.
3. If the *Voltmeter Test Procedures* still indicate a problem of under voltage, remove the jumper wire at the regulator plug and leave the plug disconnected from the regulator, Figs. F13 and F14. Connect a jumper wire to the *FLD* and *BAT* terminals on the alternator, Figs. F13 and F14.
4. Repeat the *Voltmeter Test Procedures*.
5. If the *Voltmeter Test* are now satisfactory, repair the wiring harness from the alternator to the regulator. Then, remove the jumper wire at the alternator and connect the regulator wiring plug to the regulator.
6. Repeat the *Voltmeter Test Procedures*, to be sure the charging system is operating normally.
7. If the *Voltmeter Test* results still indicate under voltage, repair or replace the alternator. With the jumper wire removed, connect the wiring to the alternator and regulator.
8. Repeat the *Voltmeter Test Procedures*.

REGULATOR TESTS

S Circuit Test—With Ammeter
1. Connect the positive lead to the voltmeter to the S terminal of the regulator wiring plug Fig. F9. Turn the ignition switch to the ON position. *Do not start the engine.*
2. The voltmeter reading should indicate battery voltage.
3. If there is no voltage reading, disconnect the positive voltmeter lead from the positive battery clamp and repair the S wire lead from the ignition switch to the regulator wiring plug.
4. Connect the positive voltmeter lead to the positive battery cable terminal and repeat the *Voltmeter Test Procedures*.

S & I Circuit Test—With Indictor Light
1. With the engine idling, connect the positive lead of the voltmeter to the S terminal and then to the *I* terminal of the regulator wiring plug, Fig. F9. The voltage of the S circuit should read approximately

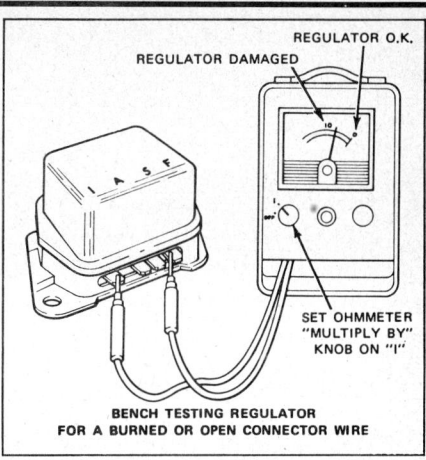

Fig. F11 Testing regulator for a burned or open connector wire

½ of the circuit.
2. If no voltage is present, repair the alternator or the wiring circuit at fault. Reconnect the positive voltmeter lead to the positive battery cable terminal and repeat the *Voltmeter Test Procedures*.
3. If the above tests are satisfactory, install a new regulator.
4. Then, remove the jumper wire from the regulator wiring plug and connect the wiring plug to the regulator. Repeat the *Voltmeter Test Procedures*.

Bench Tests

REAR TERMINAL ALTERNATOR

Field Open Or Short Circuit Test

The first part of this test will determine if the alternator portion of the field coil system, consisting of the field coil, the field coil slip rings and the field coil brush assembly is satisfactory. The second part of the test will indicate (in case of a field coil system malfunction), which of the above items is causing the malfunction.

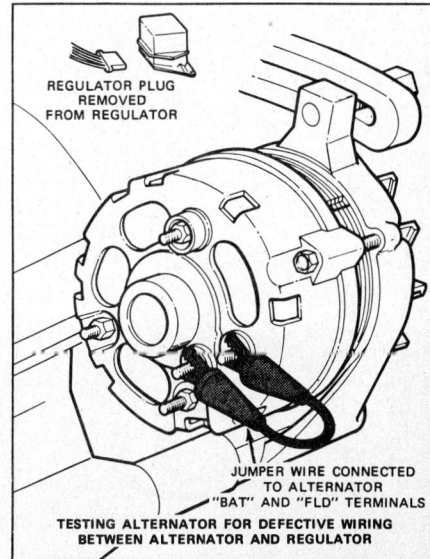

Fig. F13 Rear terminal alternator. Jumper wire connection

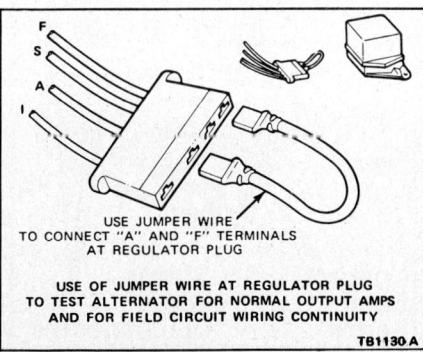

Fig. F12 Regulator plug. Jumper wire connection

FORD AUTOLITE/MOTORCRAFT ALTERNATORS

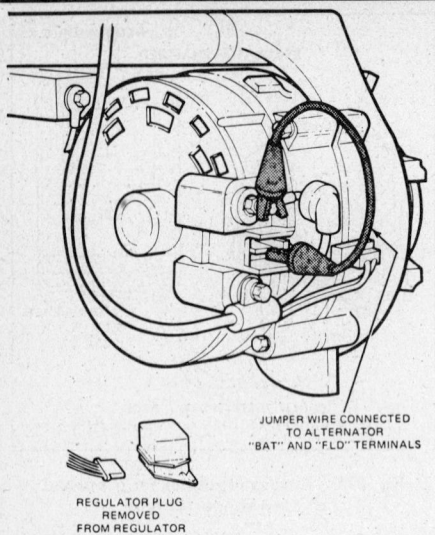

Fig. F14 Side terminal alternator. Jumper wire connection

Test Procedure

Make the connection, Fig. F6. The current draw, as indicated by the ammeter, should be to specification as listed in truck chapters. If there is little or no current flow, the field or brushes current flow considerably higher than that specified above indicates shorted or grounded field turns or brush leads touching. If the test shows that the field is shorted or open, determine if the field brush assembly or slip rings are at fault.

Disassemble unit front housing and rotor from the rear housing and stator, check the resistance of the rotor with ohmmeter. Set the ohmmeter multiply-by knob at 1 and calibrate the ohmmeter as indicated inside the ohmmeter cover.

Contact each ohmmeter probe to a slip ring. The resistance should be 3.5 to 5 ohms. A higher reading indicates a damaged slip ring soldered connection or a broken wire. A lower reading indicates a shorted wire or slip ring assembly.

Contact one ohmmeter probe to a slip ring and the other probe to the rotor shaft. The resistance should be infinite. Any reading other than infinite indicates a short to ground. Inspect the slip ring soldered terminals to make certain that they are not bent and touching the shaft or the excess solder is not grounding the rotor coil.

If the rotor checks indicate that it is in proper operating condition but the overall test, Fig. F6 indicates trouble, the brushes or brush assembly are the cause.

Diode Tests

Disassemble the alternator. Disconnect the rectifier assembly from the stator and connect leads, Fig. F15 or F16. To test one set of diodes, contact one probe to the diode plate and contact each of the three stator lead terminals with the other probe. Reverse the probes and repeat the test. Test the other set of diodes in the same way. On 61-ampere alternators, test the two additional diodes, Fig. F17.

All 6 tests (8 tests on 61-ampere alternator) should show a low reading of approximately 60 ohms in one direction and an infinite reading (no needle movement) with the probes reversed.

Open Or Grounded Stator Coil Tests

These tests are made to determine if the stator coil is operating properly. Disassemble the stator from the alternator and rectifier assembly.

Open Stator Test

Set ohmmeter multiple-by knob at 1. Connect the ohmmeter probes between each pair of stator leads. If the ohmmeter does not show equal readings between each pair of stator leads, the stator is open and must be replaced.

Grounded Stator Test

Connect the ohmmeter probes to one of the stator leads and to the stator laminated core. Be sure that the probe makes a good electrical connection with the stator core. The metal should show an infinite reading (no meter movement). If the meter does not indicate an infinite reading (needle moves), the stator winding is shorted to the core and must be replaced. Repeat this test for each of the stator leads.

SIDE TERMINAL ALTERNATOR

Rectifier Short or Grounded and Stator Grounded Test

Set ohmmeter Multiply By knob at 10, and calibrate meter.

Contact one ohmmeter probe to the alternator BAT terminal, Fig. F18, the other probe to the STA terminal (rear blade terminal). Then, reverse the ohmmeter probes and repeat the test. A reading of about 60 ohms should be obtained in one direction and no needle movement with the probes reversed. A reading in both directions indicates a bad positive diode, a grounded positive diode plate or a grounded BAT terminal.

Perform the same test using the STA and GND (ground) terminals of the alternator. A reading in both directions indicates either a bad negative diode, a grounded stator wind-

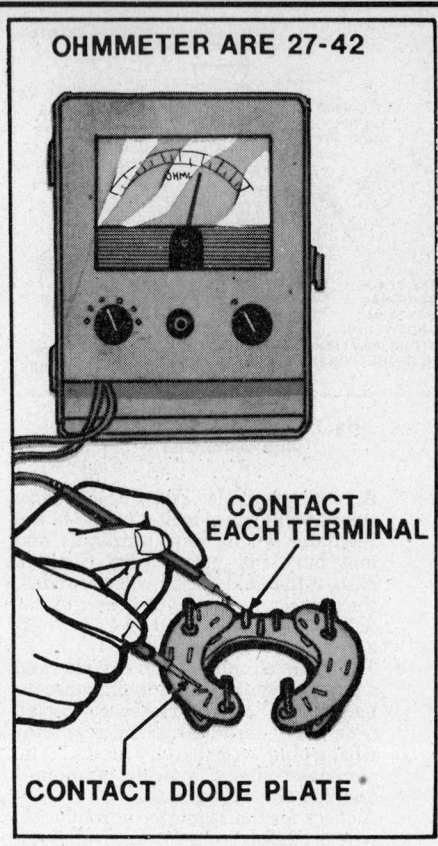

Fig. F15 Diode test. 38, 42 & 35 amp alternators

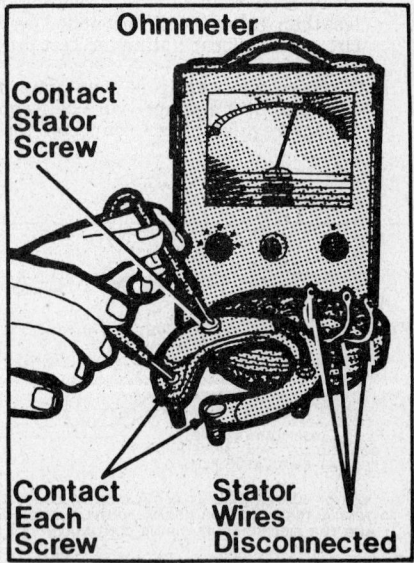

Fig. F17 Booster plate diode test 61-amp alternator

Fig. F16 Diode test. 65-amp rear terminal alternator

Ford Autolite/Motorcraft Alternators

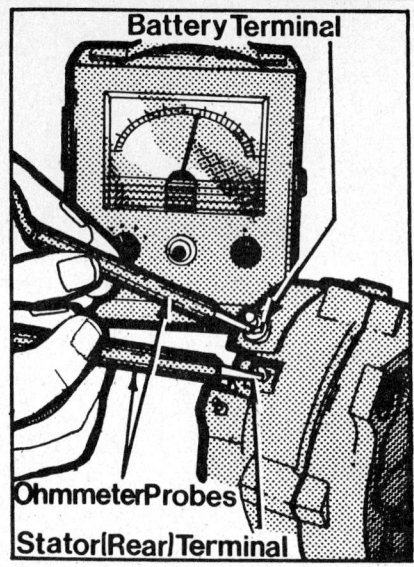

Fig. F18 Rectifier short or grounded and stator grounded test

Set ohmmeter Multiply By knob at 1000. Connect the ohmmeter probes to one of the stator leads and to the stator laminated core. Be sure that the probe makes a good electrical connection with the stator core. The meter should show an infinite reading (no meter movement). If the meter does not indicate an infinite reading (needle moves), the stator winding is shorted to the core and must be replaced. Repeat this test for each stator lead.

Rotor Open or Short Circuit Test

Disassemble the front housing and rotor from the rear housing and stator. Set the ohmmeter. Multiply By knob at 1 and calibrate meter.

Contact each ohmmeter probe to a rotor slip ring. The meter reading should be 3 to 5½ ohms. A higher reading indicates a damaged slip ring solder connection or a broken wire. A lower reading indicates a shorted wire or slip ring.

Contact one ohmmeter probe to a slip ring and the other probe to the rotor shaft. The meter reading should be infinite (no deflection). A reading other than infinite indicates the rotor is shorted to the shaft. Inspect the slip ring soldered terminals to be sure they are not bent and touching the rotor shaft, or that excess solder is grounding the rotor coil connections to the shaft. Replace the rotor if it is shorted and cannot be repaired.

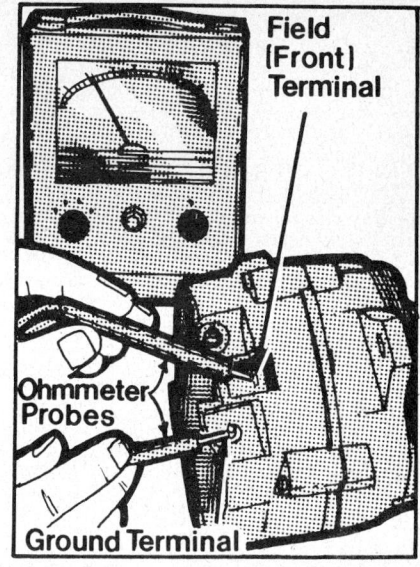

Fig. F19 Field open or short circuit test

ing, a grounded stator terminal, a grounded positive diode plate, or a grounded BAT terminal.

Infinite readings (no needle movement) in all four probe positions in the preceeding tests indicates an open STA terminal lead connection inside the alternator.

Field Open or Short Circuit Test

Set the ohmmeter Multiply By knob at 1 and calibrate meter.

Contact the alternator field terminal with one probe and the ground terminal with the other probe, Fig. F19. Then, spin the alternator pulley. The ohmmeter reading should be between 4 and 200 ohms, and should fluctuate while the pulley is turning. An infinite reading (no meter movement) indicates an open brush lead, worn or stuck brushes, or a bad rotor assembly. An ohmmeter reading less than 4 ohms indicates a grounded brush assembly, a grounded field terminal or a bad rotor.

Diode Test

Remove the rectifier assembly from the alternator. Set the ohmmeter Multiply By knob at 10 and calibrate meter.

To test one set of diodes contact one probe to the terminal bolt, Fig. F20 and contact each of the three stator lead terminals with the other probe. Reverse the probes and repeat the test. All diodes should show a low reading of about 60 ohms in one direction, and an infinite reading (no needle movement) with the probes reversed. Repeat the preceding tests for the other set of diodes except that the other terminal screw is used.

If the meter readings are not as specified, replace the rectifier assembly.

Stator Coil Open or Grounded Test

Disassemble the stator from the alternator.

Set ohmmeter Multiply By knob at 1, and calibrate meter. Connect the ohmmeter probes between each pair of stator leads (3 different ways). The ohmmeter must show equal readings for each pair of stator leads. Replace the stator if the readings are not the same.

REGULATOR TESTS
1970–71 UNITS
Voltage Limiter Test

Voltage limiter calibration tests must be

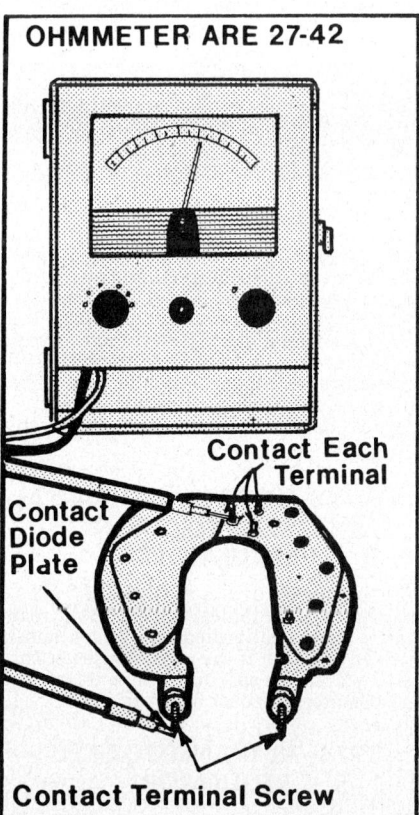

Fig. F20 Side terminal alternator diode test

made with the regulator cover in place and the regulator at normal operating temperature (equivalent to the temperature after 20 minutes of operation on the vehicle with the hood down).

For accurate voltage limiter testing, the battery specific gravity must be at least 1.230. If the battery is low in charge, either charge it to 1.230 specific gravity or substitute a fully charged battery, before making a voltage limiter test.

To test the voltage regulator on the vehicle, make the test connections to the battery, Fig. F21. Turn all accessories off, including door operated dome lights. Close the battery adapter switch, start the engine, then open the adapter switch. Attach a voltage regulator thermometer to the regulator cover. Operate the engine at approximately 2000 rpm for an additional 5 minutes. (Use a tachometer.)

When the battery is charged, and the voltage regulator has been temperature stabilized, the ammeter should indicate less than 10 amperes with the master control set at the ¼—OHM position.

Cycle the regulator as follows (mechanical regulators only): turn the ignition key to OFF to stop the engine, close the adapter switch, start the engine, and open the adapter switch. Increase the engine speed to 2000 rpm. Allow the battery to normalize for about one minute, then read the voltmeter. Read the thermometer and compare the voltmeter reading with the voltage, Fig. F22, for the ambient temperature indicated on the thermometer.

If the regulator voltage is not within specifications replace voltage regulator.

Field Relay Test Electro-Mechanical Regulator

Remove the regulator from the truck, and remove the regulator cover. Make the connections Fig. F23. Slowly rotate the field rheostat controls clockwise from the maximum counterclockwise position until the field relay contacts close. Observe the voltmeter reading at the moment that the relay contacts close. This is the relay closing voltage. If the relay closes immediately, even with the field rheostat close to the maximum counterclockwise position, push the red button between the two meters, and repeat the test. Relay unit must be replaced.

Ford Autolite/Motorcraft Alternators

Field Relay Test-Transistor Regulator

Disconnect the relay connector plug. Make the connections, Fig. F23. Slowly rotate the field rheostat control clockwise from the maximum counterclockwise position until the test light comes on. Observe the voltmeter reading at the moment that the light comes on. This is the relay closing voltage. If the relay closes immediately, even with the field rheostat close to the maximum counterclockwise position, push the red button between the two meters, and repeat the test. If the closing voltage is not to specification as listed in truck chapters, replace the relay.

1972–80 UNITS

The alternator must be adjusted within specification, and the charging system electrical connections must be clean and tight before testing the regulator.

1973–80 Regulator Test

For test procedures, refer to In Vehicle Tests, 1973–80 units, Regular Tests.

Calibration Test Procedure 1972–78 Electro-Mechanical Regulator

Connect the voltmeter positive lead to the battery positive terminal, and the negative lead to the battery negative terminal. Turn off all electrical loads. Then, check and record the voltmeter reading. Connect the red lead of a tachometer to the distributor terminal of the coil and the block tachometer lead to a good ground.

Place the transmission shift lever in the neutral or park position and start the engine. Increase the engine speed to 1800–2200 rpm for 2 or 3 minutes. Check and record the voltmeter reading, it should be 1 to 2 volts higher than the first reading. If the reading is less than 1 volt or greater than 2½ volts, replace the voltage regulator. If the reading is between 1 and 2 volts, turn on the headlights and heater blower. The voltage should not decrease more than ½ volt. Replace the regulator if the voltage drop is greater than ½ volt.

1970–73 TRANSISTORIZED REGULATOR ADJUSTMENTS

Regulator Voltage Limiter Adjustments

The only adjustment on the transistorized

Ambient Air Temperature °F	Voltage Limiter Setting (Volts)
50	14.1–15.1
75	13.9–14.9
100	13.7–14.7
125	13.6–14.6

Fig. F22 Voltage limiter setting vs ambient air temperature. Mechanical or transistor regulator

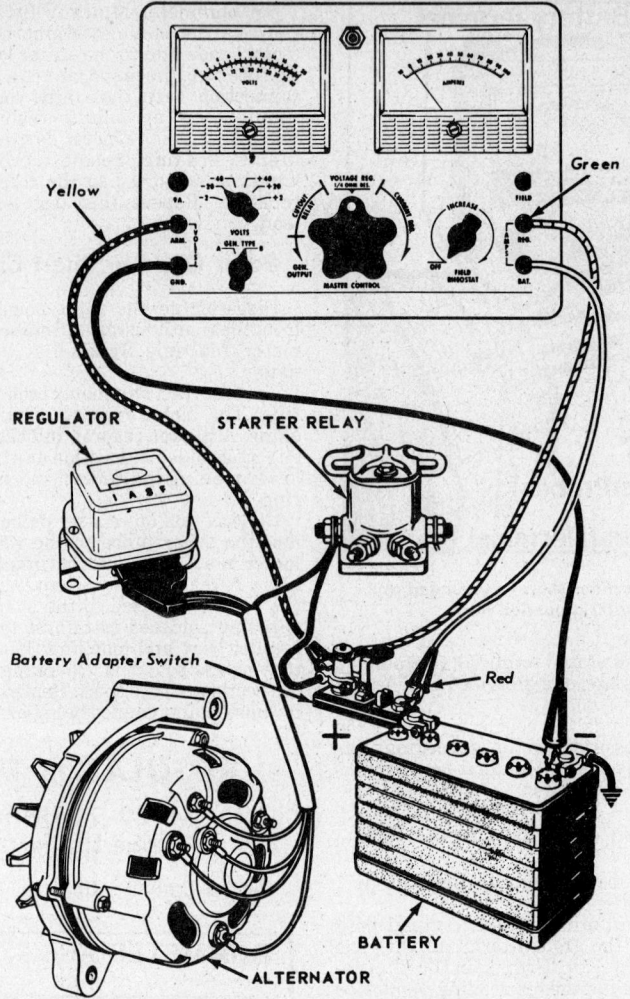

Fig. F21 Typical voltage limited tests

alternator regulator is the voltage limiter adjustment.

Adjustment of the transistor voltage limiter must be made with the regulator at normal operating temperature. Remove the regulator mounting screws and remove the bottom cover from the regulator. The voltage setting may be moved up or down by adjusting the 40-ohm adjustable resistor, Fig. F24. Use a fiber rod as a screw driver for this adjustment.

Follow "Regulator Tests" when making this adjustment.

1970–78 ELECTRO-MECHANICAL & 1978–80 ELECTRONIC REGULATORS

The electro-mechanical and electronic regulator is factory calibrated and sealed and is not to be adjusted. If the regulator is not calibrated within the specified limits as listed in truck chapters, it must be replaced.

1974–78 TRANSISTORIZED REGULATOR

The only adjustment of this regulator is the voltage limiter adjustment Fig. F25. This adjustment is made with regulator at normal operating temperature. Remove the regulator cover and using a fiber rod turn voltage adjusting screw clockwise to raise voltage setting or counter-clockwise to lower voltage setting. Refer to the "Alternator & Regulator Specifications" as listed in the individual truck chapters for proper voltage setting.

ALTERNATOR REPAIRS
Rear Terminal Alternator Exc. 65, 70, 85 & 90 Ampere Units

NOTE: Use a 100 watt soldering iron.

Disassembly

1. Mark both end housings and the stator with a scribe mark for assembly, Fig. F26.
2. Remove the three housing through bolts.
3. Separate the front housing and rotor from the stator and rear housing.
4. Remove all the nuts and insulators from

Ford Autolite/Motorcraft Alternators

the rear housing and remove the rear housing from the stator and rectifier assembly.
5. Remove the brush holder mounting screws and remove the holder, brushes, brush springs, insultor and terminal.
6. If replacement is necessary, press the bearing from the rear housing, supporting the housing on the inner boss.
7. If the rectifier assembly is being replaced, unsolder the stator leads from the printed-circuit board terminals, and separate the stator from the rectifier assembly.
8. Original production alternators will have one of three types of rectifier assembly circuit boards, Figs. F27 and F28; one has the circuit board spaced away from the diode plates with the diodes exposed. Another type is a single circuit board with built-in diodes. The third type circuit board has built-in diodes with an additional booster diode plate containing two diodes. This circuit board is used only in the 61-ampere alternator.

If the alternator rectifier has an exposed diode circuit board, remove the screws from the rectifier by rotating the bolt heads $1/4$ turn clockwise to unlock them and then remove the screws, Fig. F27. Push the stator terminal screw straight out on a rectifier with the diodes built into the circuit board, Fig. F28. Avoid turning the screw while removing to make certain that the straight knurl will engage the insulators when installing. Do not remove the grounded screw, Fig. F29.

On 61-ampere alternator rectifier, press the stator terminal screw from the circuit board, Fig. F30. When the terminal screw has moved about $1/4$ inch, remove the nut from the end of the screw and lift the screw from the circuit board.

NOTE: Do not twist the screw in the circuit board.

9. Remove the drive pulley nut, Fig. F31. Then, pull the lockwasher, pulley, fan, fan spacer, front housing and rotor stop from the rotor shaft.
10. Remove the three screws that hold the front end bearing retainer, and remove the retainer. If the bearing is damaged or has lost its lubricant, support the housing close to the bearing boss and press out the old bearing from the housing.
11. Perform a diode test and a field open or short circuit test.

Cleaning and Inspection

1. The rotor, stator, diodes and bearings are not to be cleaned with solvents. These parts are to be wiped off with a clean cloth. Cleaning solvent may cause damage to electrical parts or contaminate the bearing internal lubricant. Wash all other parts with solvent and dry them.
2. Rotate front bearing on drive shaft. Check for any scraping noise, looseness or roughness that would indicate that the bearing is excessively worn. As the bearing is being rotated, look for any lubricant leakage. If any of these conditions exist, replace the bearing.
3. Place the rear end bearing on the slip ring end of the shaft and rotate the bearing on the shaft. Make the same check for wear or damage as for the front bearing.
4. Check the housings for cracks. Check the front housing for stripped threads in the mounting holes. Replace defective housings.
5. Pulleys that have been removed and installed several times may have to be replaced because of the increase bore diameter. A pulley is not suitable for reuse if more than $1/4$ of the shaft length will enter the pulley bore with light pressure. Replace any pulley that is bent out

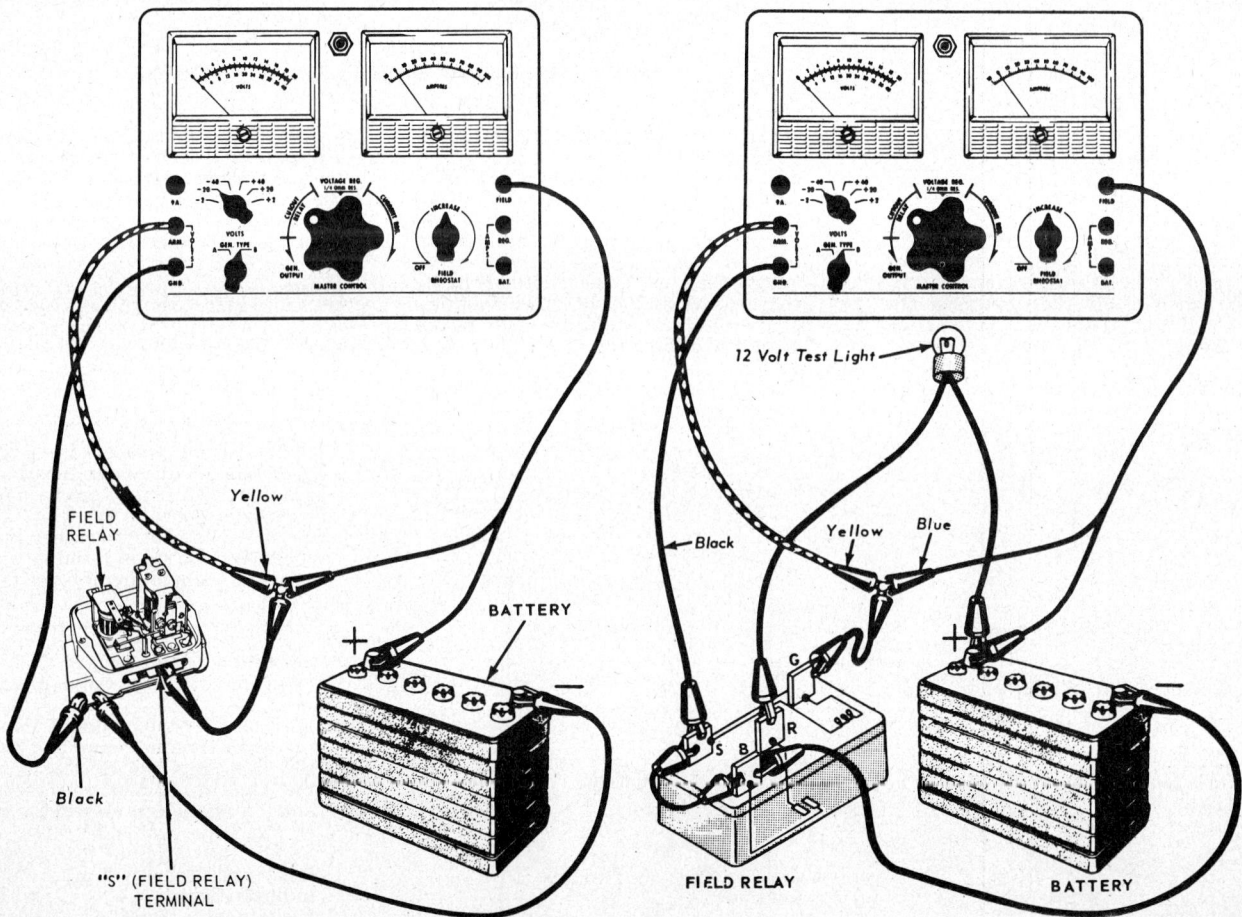

MECHANICAL REGULATOR TRANSISTOR REGULATOR

Fig. F23 Autolite regulators field relay test

Ford Autolite/Motorcraft Alternators

of shape. After installing the pulley, check for clearance between the fins and the alternator drive end housing.
6. Check all the wire leads on both stator and rotor for loose soldered connections and for burned insulation. Resolder poor connections and replace parts that show burned insulation.
7. Check slip rings for damaged insulation. Check the slip rings for runout as shown in Fig. F32. If the slip rings are more than .0005″ out of round, take a light cut (minimum diameter limit 1.22″) from the face of the rings to true them up. If the slip rings are badly damaged, the entire rotor will have to be replaced as they are serviced only as a complete assembly.
8. Replace the terminal spacer block assembly if the neutral terminal is loose. Replace any parts that are burned or cracked. Replace brushes that are worn to less than 5/16″ in length. Replace the brush spring if it has less than 7 to 12 ounces tension.

Assembly

1. The rotor, stator and bearings must not be cleaned with solvent. Wipe these parts off with a soft cloth.
2. Press the front bearing in the front housing bearing boss (put pressure on the outer race only), and install the bearing retainer, Fig. F26.
3. If the stop-ring on the rotor drive shaft was damaged, install a new stop-ring. Push the new ring on the shaft and into the groove.

NOTE: Do not open the ring with snap ring pliers as permanent damage will result.

4. Position the rotor stop on the drive shaft with the recessed side against the stop-ring.
5. Position the front housing, fan spacer, fan, pulley and lock washer on the drive shaft and install the retaining nut. Torque the retaining nut, Fig. F31, to 60–100 ft lbs.
6. If the rear housing bearing was removed, support the housing on the inner boss and press in a new bearing flush with the outer end surface.
7. Place the brush springs, brushes, brush terminal and terminal insulator in the brush holder and hold the brushes in position by inserting a piece of stiff wire in the brush holder, Fig. F33.
8. Position the brush holder assembly in the rear housing and install the mounting screws. Position the brush leads in the brush holder, Fig. F34.
9. 1970–80 Units—Wrap the three stator winding leads around the circuit board terminals and solder them. Position the stator neutral lead eyelet on the stator terminal screw and install the screw in the rectifier assembly, Fig. F35.
10. For a rectifier with the diodes exposed insert the special screws through the wire lug, dished washers and circuit board, Fig. F27. Turn them 1/4 turn counter-clockwise to lock them. For single circuit boards with built in diodes, insert the screws, straight through the wire lug, insulating washer and rectifier into the insulator, Fig. F29.

NOTE: The dished washers are to be used only on the circuit board with exposed diodes, Fig. F27. If they are used on the single circuit board, a short circuit will occur. A flat insulating washer is to be used between the stator terminal and the board when a single circuit board is used, Fig. F29.

11. For a rectifier with a booster diode plate (61 Ampere Alternator only), proceed as follows:
    a. Position the stator wire terminal on the stator terminal screw and position the screw into the rectifier. Position the square insulator over the screw and into the square hole in the rectifier, Fig. F36.
    b. Rotate the terminal screw until it locks in position. Then, press the screw in finger tight.
    c. Position the stator wire, Fig. F37. Press the terminal screw into the rectifier and insulator, Fig. F38.
12. Position the radio noise suppression capacitor on the rectifier terminals. On the circuit board with exposed diodes, install the STA and BAT terminal insulators,

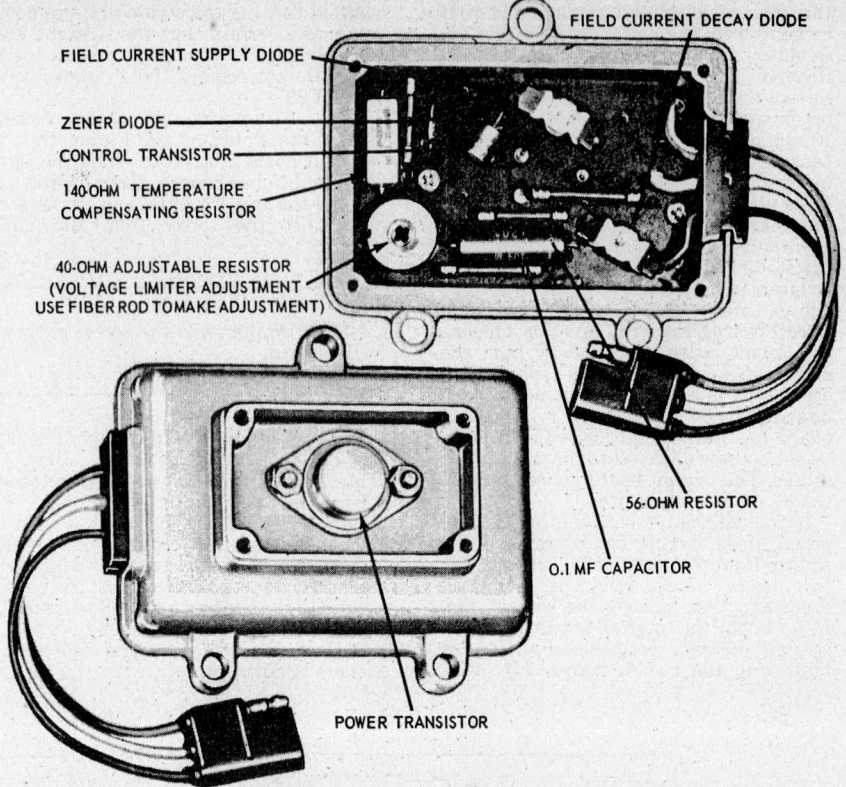

Fig. F24 Transistorized voltage regulator. 1970–73 units

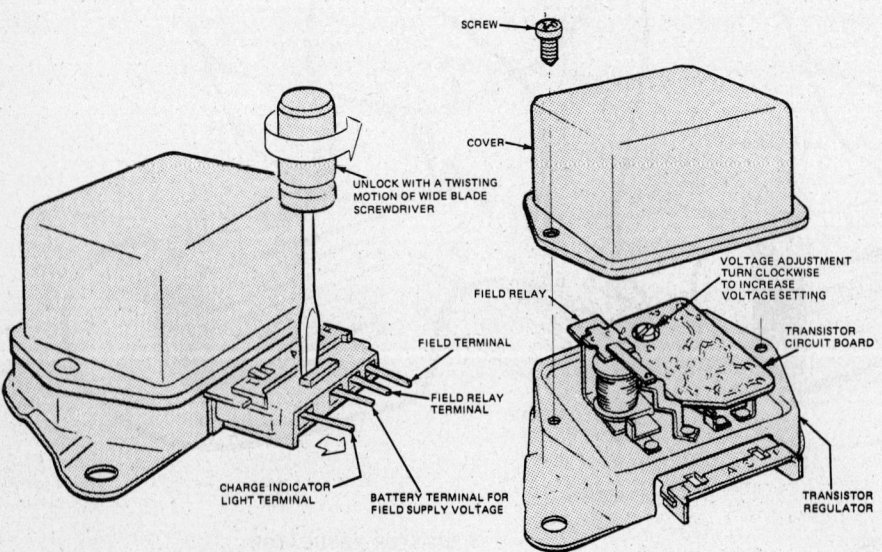

Fig. F25 Transistorized voltage regulator. 1974–78 units

Ford Autolite/Motorcraft Alternators

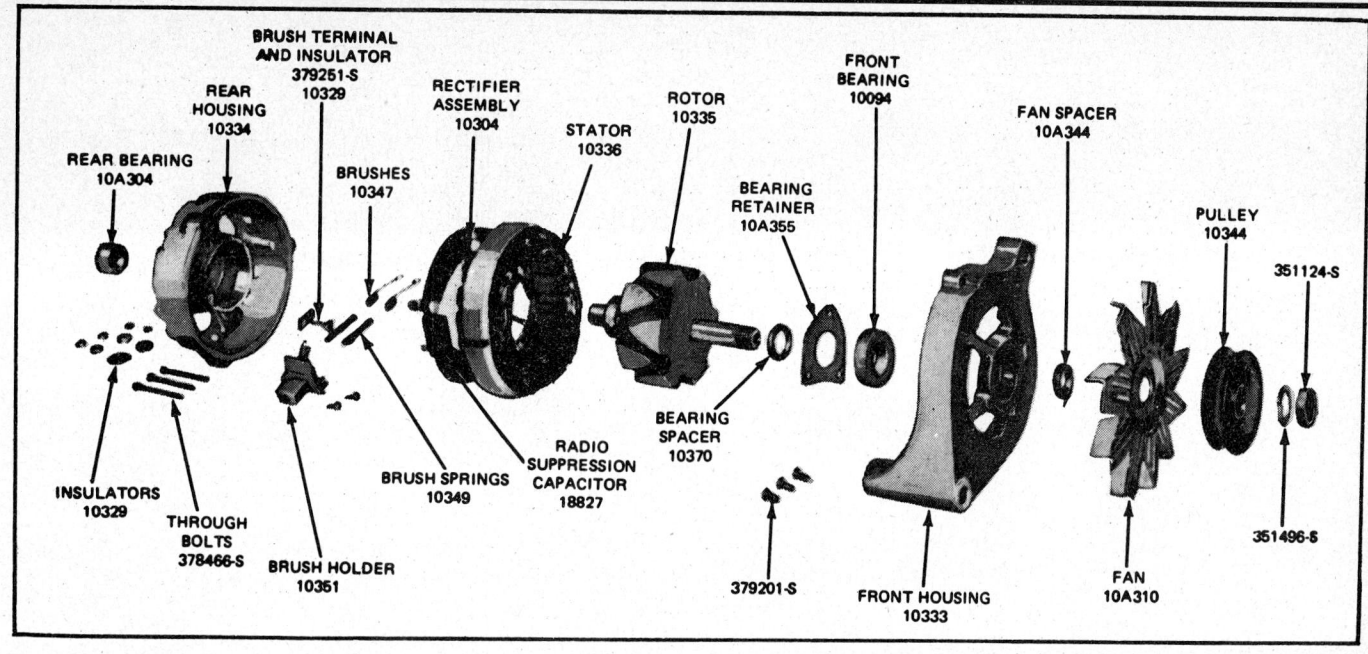

Fig. F26 Disassembled rear terminal alternator (Typical)

Fig. F35. On the single circuit board, position the square stator-terminal insulator in the square hole in the rectifier assembly, Fig. F29. Position the BAT terminal insulator, Fig. F39.

Position the stator and rectifier assembly in the rear housing. Make certain that all terminal insulators are seated properly in the recesses, Fig. F35. Position the STA (black), BAT (red) and FLD (orange) insulators on the terminal bolts, and install the retaining nuts, Fig. F40.

13. Wipe the rear end bearing surface of the rotor shaft with a clean lint-free rag.
14. Position the rear housing and stator assembly over the rotor and align the scribe marks made during disassembly. Seat the machined portion of the stator core into the step in both end housings. Install the housing through bolts. Remove the brush retracting wire, and put a daub of waterproof cement over the hole to seal it.

Rear Terminal 65, 70, 85 & 90-Ampere Alternator

NOTE: Use a 200 watt soldering iron.

Disassembly

1. Remove the brush holder and cover assembly from the rear end housing. Fig. F41.
2. Mark both end housings and the stator with a scribe mark for assembly.
3. Remove the three housing through bolts.
4. Separate the front housing and rotor from the stator and rear housing.
5. Remove the drive pulley nut, lock-washer, flat washer, pulley, fan, fan spacer and rotor from the front housing, Fig. F31.
6. Remove the three screws that hold the front bearing retainer, and remove the retainer. If the bearing is damaged or has lost its lubricant, support the housing close to the bearing boss and press out the bearing from the housing.
7. Remove all the nut and washer assemblies and insulators from the rear housing and remove the rear housing from the stator and rectifier assembly.
8. If replacement is necessary, press the bearing from the rear housing, supporting the housing on the inner boss.
9. Unsolder the three stator leads from the rectifier assembly, and separate the stator from the assembly.
10. Perform a diode test and an open and grounded stator coil test.

Assembly

NOTE: "Cleaning and Inspection" procedures,

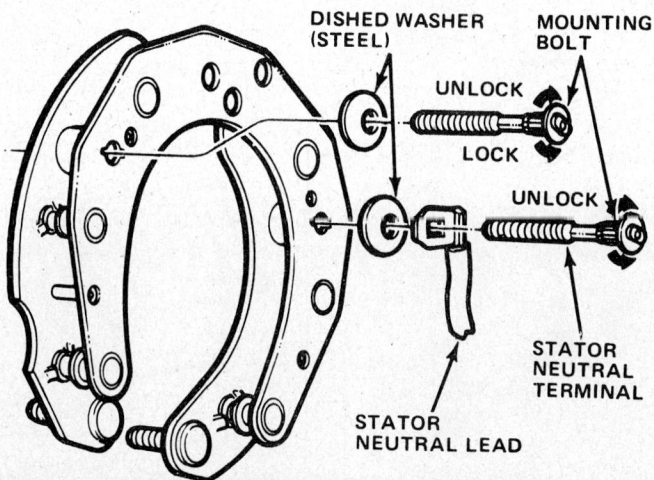

Fig. F27 Rectifier assembly with exposed diodes

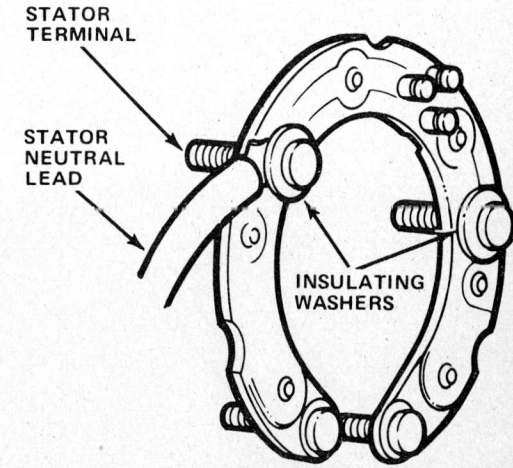

Fig. F28 Rectifier assembly with built-in diodes

Ford Autolite/Motorcraft Alternators

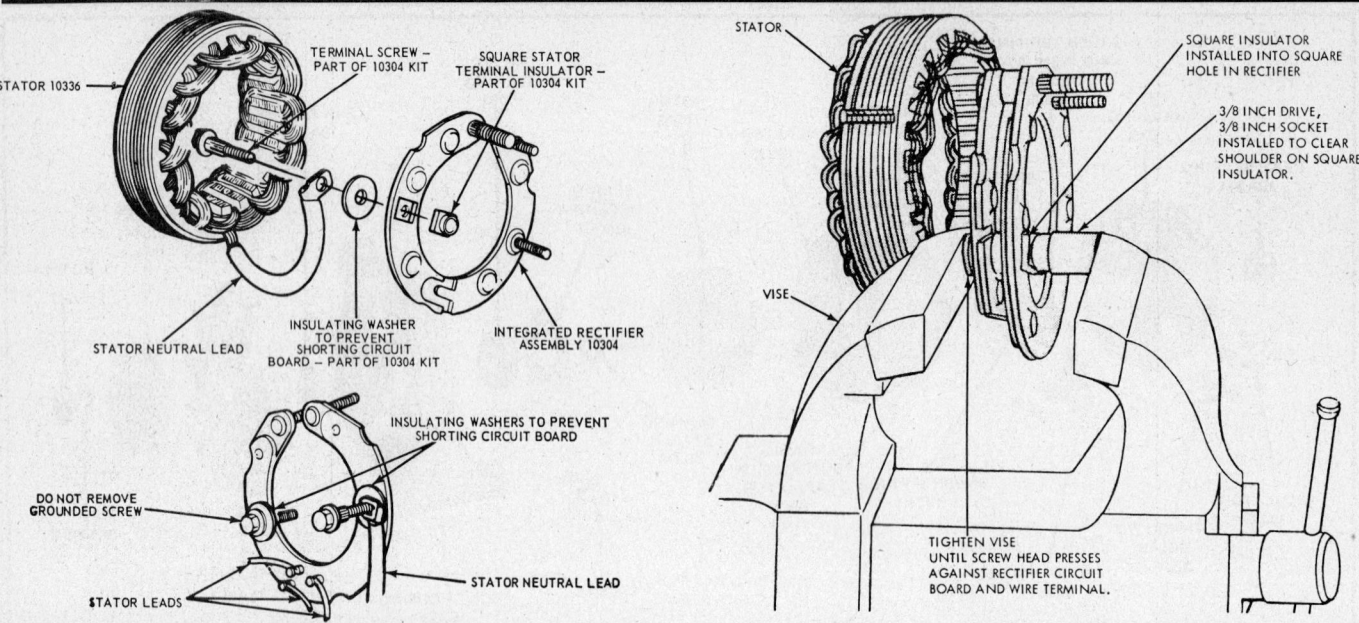

Fig. F29 Stator terminal installation. Integral rectifier circuit board

Fig. F30 Stator terminal screw removal. 61-amp alternator

are same as procedures used previously in this chapter.

1. If the front bearing is being replaced, press the new bearing in the bearing boss putting pressure on the outer race only. Then, install the bearing retainer, and tighten the retainer screws until the tips of the retainer touch the housing.
2. Position the rectifier assembly to the stator, wrap the three stator leads around the diode plate terminals and solder them, Fig. F42.
3. If the rear housing bearing was removed, press in a new bearing from the inside of the housing until the bearing is flush with the outer end surface. Put pressure on the bearing outer race only.
4. Install the BAT-GRD insulator, Fig. F42, and position the stator and rectifier assembly in the rear housing.
5. Install the STA (purple) and BAT (red) terminal insulators in the terminal bolts and install the nut and washer assemblies.

NOTE: Make certain that the shoulders on all insulators both inside and outside of the housing are seated properly before tightening the nuts.

6. Position the front housing over the rotor and install the fan spacer, fan, pulley, flat and lock washers and nut on the rotor shaft, Fig. F31.
7. Wipe the rear bearing surface of the rotor shaft with a clean lint free rag.
8. Position the rotor with the front housing into the stator and rear housing assembly, and align the scribe marks made during disassembly. Seat the machined portion of the stator core into the step in both housing, and install the through bolts.
9. Hold the brushes in position by inserting a stiff wire in the brush holder, Figs. F43 and F47.
10. Position the brush holder assembly into the rear housing and install the three mounting screws. Remove the brush retracting wire and put a daub of waterproof cement over the hole to seal hole.

Brush Replacement

1. Remove the brush holder and cover assembly from the rear housing.
2. Remove the terminal bolts from the brush holder and cover assembly, and remove the brush assemblies.
3. Position the new brush terminals on the terminal bolts and assemble the terminals, bolts, brush holder washers and nuts, Figs. F43 and F47. The insulating washer mounts under the FLD terminal nut. The entire brush and cover assembly is also available for service.
4. Depress the brush springs in the brush holder cavities and insert the brushes on top of the springs. Hold the brushes in position by inserting a stiff wire in the brush holder as shown in Figs. F43 and F47. Position the brush leads, Figs. F43 and F47.
5. Install the brush holder and cover assem-

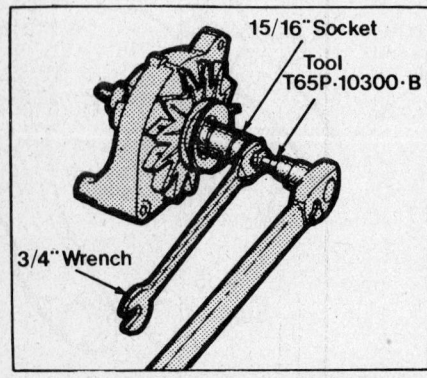

Fig. F31 Typical pulley removal

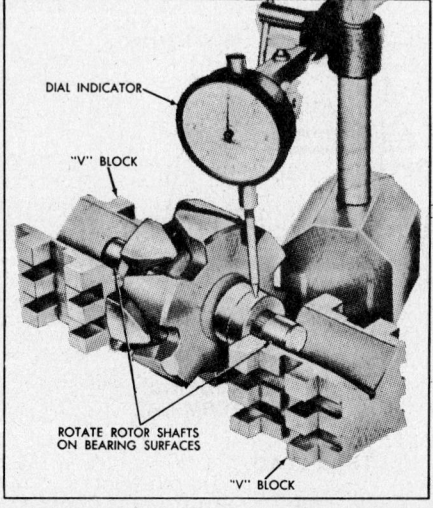

Fig. F32 Slip ring runout check

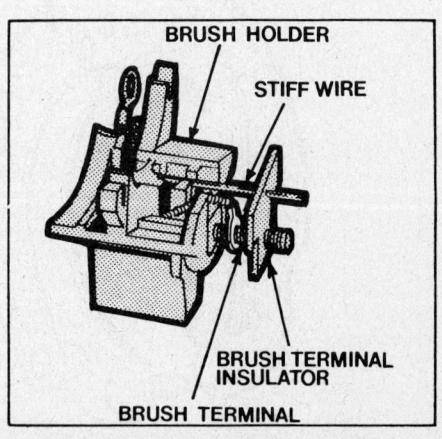

Fig. F33 Brush holder assembly

Ford Autolite/Motorcraft Alternators

Fig. F34 Typical brush lead positions

bly to the rear housing. Remove the brush retracting wire and put a daub of waterproof cement over the hole to seal it.

SIDE TERMINAL ALTERNATOR

Disassembly

NOTE: Use a 200 watt soldering iron.

1. Mark both end housings and the stator with a scribe mark for use during assembly, Fig. F44.
2. Remove the four housing through bolts, and separate the front housing and rotor from the rear housing and stator. Slots are provided in the front housing to aid in disassembly. *Do not seaprate the rear housing from the stator at this time.*
3. Remove the drive pulley nut, Fig. F31. Remove the lockwasher, pulley, fan and fan spacer from the rotor shaft.
4. Pull the rotor and shaft from the front housing, and remove the spacer from the rotor shaft, Fig. F44.
5. Remove three screws retaining the bear-

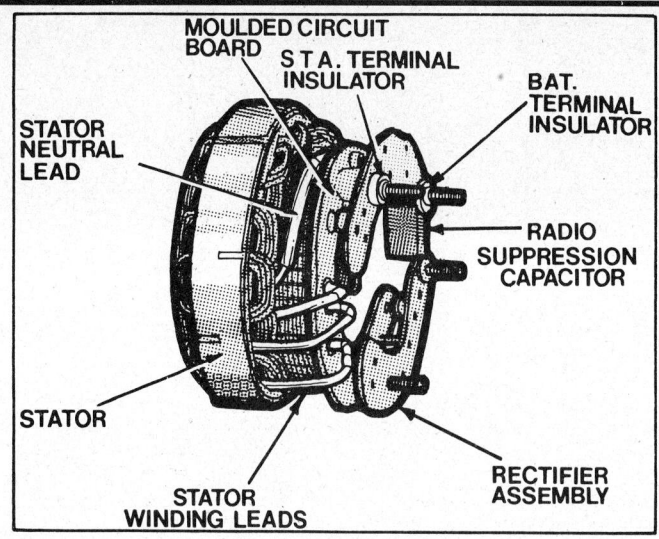

Fig. F35 Stator lead connections. Except 61-amp alternator

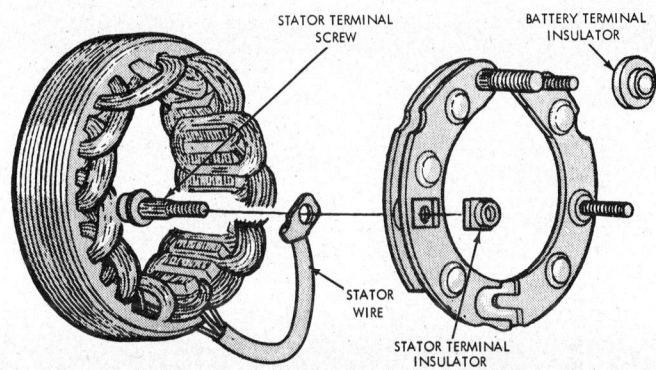

Fig. F36 Stator and rectifier assembly. 61-amp alternator

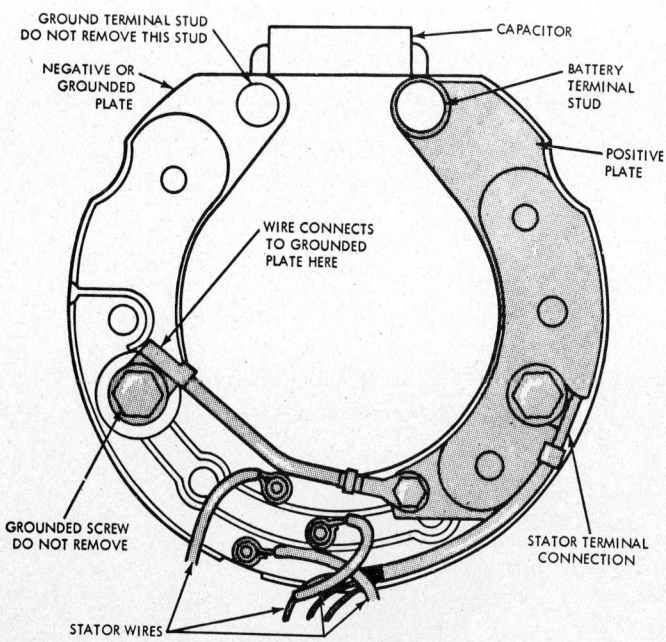

Fig. F37 Rectifier terminal locations. 61-amp alternator

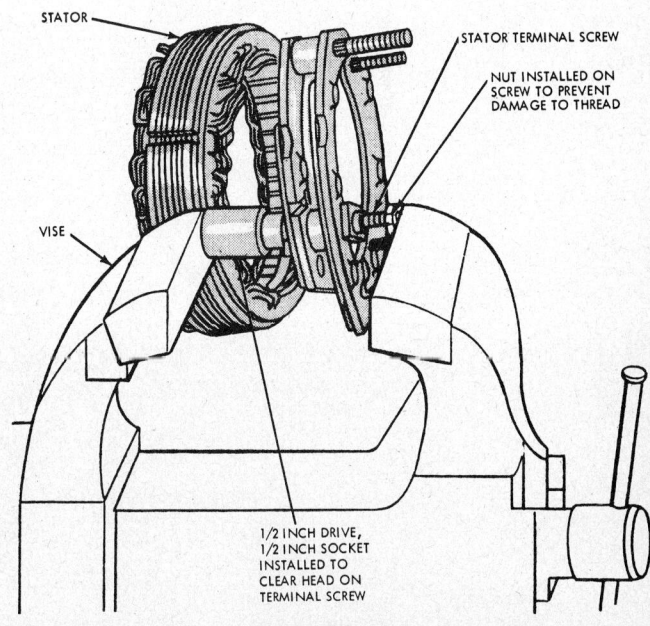

Fig. F38 Stator terminal screw installation. 61-amp alternator

115

Ford Autolite/Motorcraft Alternators

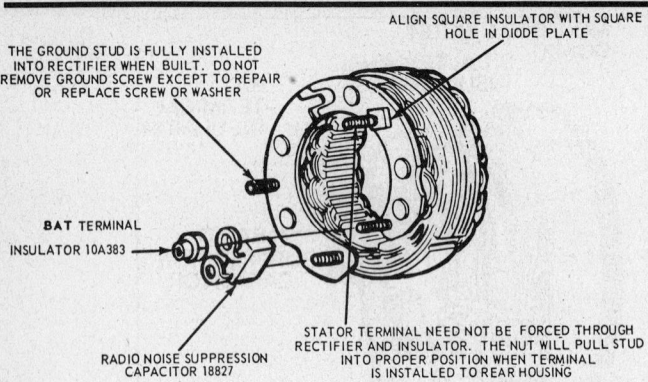

Fig. F39 Fiber-glass circuit board terminal insulators

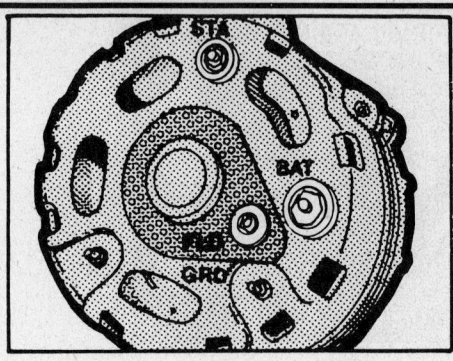

Fig. F40 Alternator terminal locations

ing to the front housing. If the bearing is damaged or has lost its lubricant, remove the bearing from the housing. To remove the bearing, support the housing close to the bearing boss and press the bearing from the housing.

6. Unsolder and disengage the three stator leads from the rectifier, Fig. F45.
7. Lift the stator from the rear housing.
8. Unsolder and disengage the brush holder lead from the rectifier.
9. Remove the screw attaching the capacitor lead to the rectifier.
10. Remove four screws attaching the rectifier to the rear housing, Fig. F45.
11. Remove the two terminal nuts and insulator from outside the housing, and remove the rectifier from the housing.
12. Remove two screws attaching the brush holder to the housing and remove the brushes and holder.
13. Remove sealing compound from rear housing and brush holder.
14. Remove one screw attaching the capacitor to the rear housing and remove the capacitor.
15. If bearing replacement is necessary, sup-

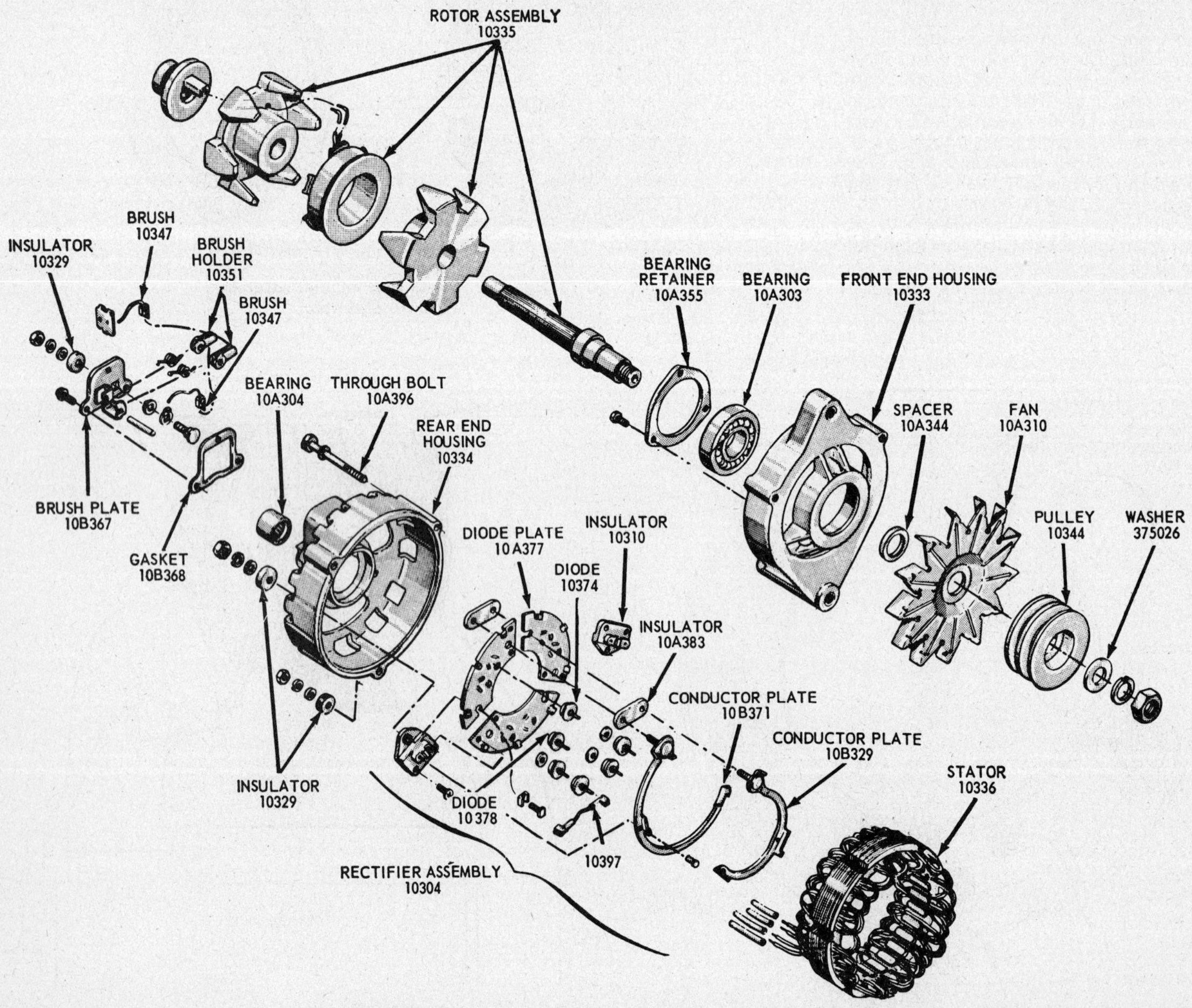

Fig. F41 Disassembled 65-amp rear terminal alternator (Typical)

Ford Autolite/Motorcraft Alternators

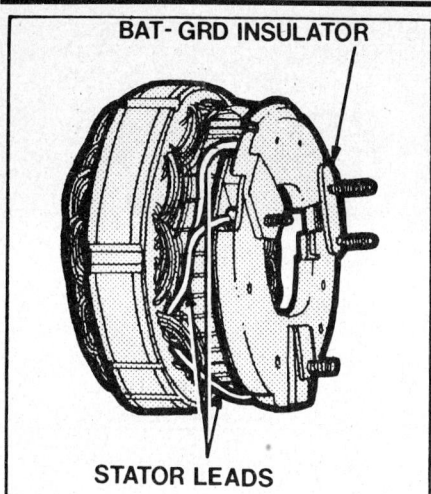

Fig. F42 Stator lead connections

port the rear housing close to the bearing boss and press the bearing out of the housing from the inside.

Assembly

NOTE: Refer to "Cleaning and Inspection" procedures before reassembly.

1. If the front housing bearing is being replaced, press the new bearing in the housing.

NOTE: *Put pressure on the bearing outer race only.* Then, install the bearing retaining screws.

2. Place the inner spacer on the rotor shaft and insert the rotor shaft into the front housing and bearing.
3. Install the fan spacer, fan, pulley, lockwasher and nut on the rotor shaft, Fig. F31. Torque nut to 60–100 ft. lbs.
4. If the rear bearing is being replaced, press a new bearing in from inside the housing until it is flush with the boss outer surface.
5. Position the brush terminal on the brush holder, Fig. F47. Install the springs and brushes in the brush holder, and insert a piece of stiff wire to hold the brushes in place, Fig. F47.
6. Position the brush holder in the rear housing and install the attaching screws. Push the brush holder toward the rotor shaft opening and tighten the brush holder attaching screws.
7. Position the capacitor to the rear housing and install the attaching screw.
8. Place the two cup shaped (rectifier) insulators on the bosses inside the housing, Fig. F46.
9. Place the insulator on the BAT (large) terminal of the rectifier, and position the rectifier in the rear housing. Place the outside insulator on the BAT terminal, and install the nuts on the BAT and GRD terminals *finger tight*.
10. Install but do not tighten the four rectifier attaching screws.
11. Tighten the BAT and GRD terminal nuts on the outside of the rear housing. Then, tighten the four rectifier attaching screws.
12. Position the capacitor lead to the rectifier and install the attaching screw.
13. Press the brush holder lead on the rectifier and solder securely, Fig. F45.
14. Position the stator in the rear housing and align the scribe marks. Press the three stator leads on the rectifier pins and solder securely, Fig. F45.
15. Position the rotor and front housing into the stator and rear housing, Align the scribe marks and install the four through bolts. Tighten two opposing bolts and then the two remaining bolts.
16. Spin the fan and pulley to be sure nothing is binding within the alternator.
17. Remove the wire retracting the brushes, and place a daub of waterproof cement over the hole to seal it.

Brush Replacement

Removal

1. Mark both end housings and the stator

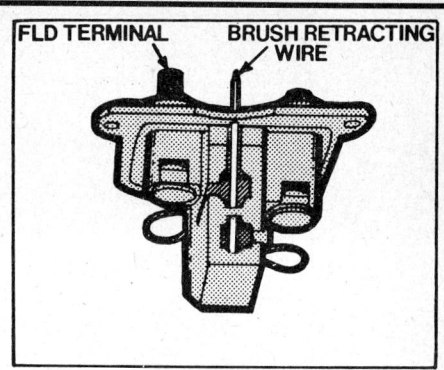

Fig. F43 Field brush assembly 65-amp alternator. 1970–73

with a scribe mark for use during assembly.

2. Remove the four housing through bolts, and separate the front housing and rotor from the rear housing and stator. Slots are provided in the front housing to aid in disassembly.

NOTE: *Do not separate the rear housing and stator.*

3. Unsolder and disengage the brush holder lead from the rectifier.
4. Remove the two brush holder attaching screws and lift the brush holder from the rear housing.
5. Remove the brushes from the brush holder.

Installation

1. Insert the brushes into the brush holder and position the terminal on the brush holder.
2. Depress the brushes and insert a 1½ inch piece of stiff wire, Fig. F47, to hold the brushes in the retracted position.
3. Position the brush holder to the rear housing, inserting the wire used to retract the brushes through the hole in the rear housing.

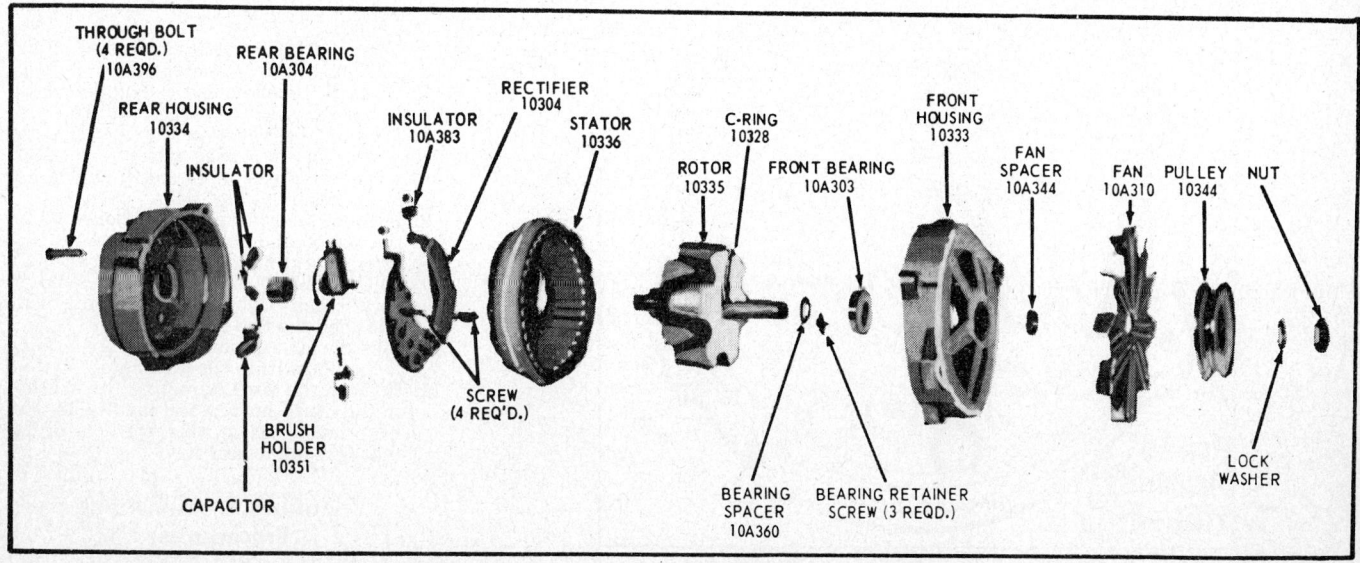

Fig. F44 Side terminal alternator disassembled (typical)

FORD AUTOLITE/MOTORCRAFT ALTERNATORS

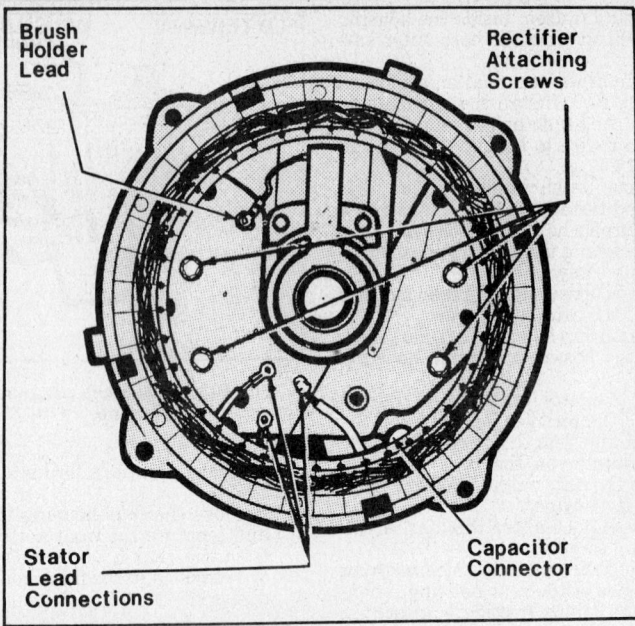

Fig. F45 Stator lead connections

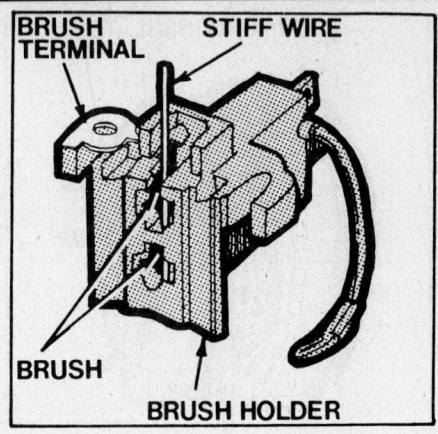

Fig. F47 Brush holder assembly

and stator at this time.

3. Unsolder and disengage the three stator leads from the rectifier, Fig. F45.
4. Unsolder and disengage the brush holder lead from the rectifier.
5. Remove the screw attaching the capacitor lead to the rectifier.
6. Remove four screws attaching the rectifier to the rear housing, Fig. F45.
7. Remove the terminal nuts and insulator from outside the housing, and remove the rectifier from the housing.

Installation

1. Insert a piece of wire through the hole in the rear housing to hold the brushes in the retracted position.
2. Place the two cup shaped (rectifier) insulators on the bosses inside the housing, Fig. F46.
3. Place the insulator on the BAT (large terminal) of the rectifier, and position the rectifier in the rear housing. Place the outside insulator on the BAT terminal, and install the nuts on the BAT and GRD terminals finger tight.
4. Install but do not tighten the four rectifier attaching screws.
5. Tighten the BAT and GRD terminal nuts on the outside of the rear housing. Then, tighten the four rectifier attaching screws.
6. Position the capacitor lead to the rectifier and install the attaching screw.
7. Press the brush holder lead on the rectifier pin and solder securely, Fig. F45.
8. Position the stator in the rear housing and align the scribe marks. Press the three stator leads on the rectifier pins and solder securely, Fig. F45.
9. Position the rotor and front housing into the stator and rear housing. Align the scribe marks and install the four through bolts. Partially tighten all four through bolts. Then, tighten two opposing bolts and then the two remaining bolts.
10. Spin the fan and pulley to be sure nothing is binding within the alternator.
11. Remove the wire retracting the brushes in the brush holder, and place a daub of waterproof cement over the hole in the rear housing to seal it.

Cleaning & Inspection Procedures

1. The rotor, stator, and bearings must not

4. Install the brush holder attaching screws. Push the brush holder toward the rotor shaft opening and tighten the attaching screws.
5. Press the brush holder lead on the rectifier pin and solder securely.
6. Position the rotor and front housing into the stator and rear housing. Align the scribe marks and install the four through bolts. Tighten two opposing bolts and then the two remaining bolts.
7. Spin the fan and pulley to be sure nothing is binding within the alternator.
8. Remove the wire retracting the brushes, and place a daub of waterproof cement over the hole to seal it.

Rectifier Replacement

Removal

1. Mark both end housings and the stator with a scribe mark for use during assembly, Fig. F44.
2. Remove the four housing through bolts, and separate the front housing and rotor from the rear housing and stator. Slots are provided in the front housing to aid in disassembly.

NOTE: *Do not separate the rear housing*

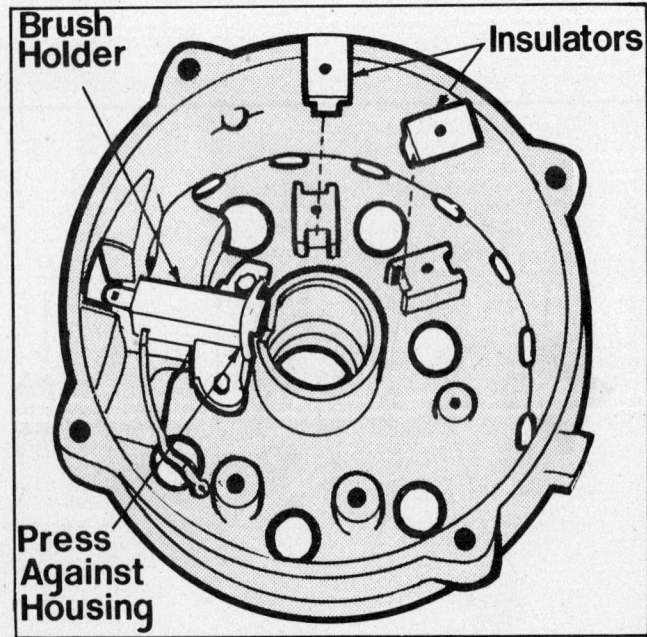

Fig. F46 Brush holder and rectifier insulators installed

FORD AUTOLITE/MOTORCRAFT ALTERNATORS

be cleaned with solvent. Wipe these parts off with a clean cloth.
2. Rotate the front bearing on the drive end of the rotor drive shaft. Check for any scraping noise, looseness or roughness that will indicate that the bearing is excessively worn. Look for excessive lubricant leakage. If any of these conditions exist, replace the bearing.
3. Inspect the rotor shaft at the rear bearing surface for roughness or severe chatter marks. Replace the rotor assembly if the shaft is not smooth.
4. Place the rear end bearing on the slip-ring end of the shaft and rotate the bearing on the shaft. Make the same check for noise, looseness or roughness as was made for the front bearing. Inspect the rollers and cage for damage. Replace the bearing if these conditions exist, or if the lubricant is lost or contaminated.
5. Check the pulley and fan for excessive looseness on the rotor shaft. Replace any pulley or fan that is loose or bent out of shape. Check the rotor shaft for stripped or damaged threads. Inspect the hex hole in the end of the shaft for damage.
6. Check both the front and rear housing for cracks. Check the front housings for stripped threads in the mounting gear. Replace defective housings.
7. Check all wire leads on both the stator and rotor assemblies for loose soldered connections, and for burned insulation. Resolder poor connections. Replace parts that show burned insulation.
8. Check the slip rings for nicks and surface roughness. If the slip rings are badly damaged, the entire rotor will have to be replaced, as it is serviced as a complete assembly.
9. Replace any parts that are burned or cracked. Replace brushes and brush springs that are not to specification.

Motorola Alternators

DESCRIPTION

1970

The electrical circuit of the alternator, Fig. M1, uses 6 silicon diodes in a full wave rectifier circuit. Since the diodes will pass current from the alternator to the battery or load but not in the reverse direction, the alternator does not use a circuit breaker.

The entire DC output of the system passes through the "Isolation Diode". This diode is mounted in a separate aluminum heat sink and is replaced as an assembly. The isolation diode is not essential for rectification. It is used to:
1. Provide an automatic solid state switch for illuminating the charge-discharge indicator light.
2. Automatically connect the voltage regulator to the alternator and battery when the alternator is operating.
3. Eliminate electrical leakage over the alternator insulators so that maximum leakage is less than one milliampere when the car is not in use.

1971-75

The electrical circuit, Fig. M2, of these units differs from previous units in that a field diode assembly is used. Also, on alternators used in 1973-75 Jeep vehicles equipped with a four barrel carburetor, an extra terminal is used on the rear housing which provides about seven volts of alternating current to the heating element of the electric assisted choke.

The field diode (diode trio) assembly incorporates three diodes mounted on a circuit board or on some 1974 & 1975 units, a potted type diode trio is used, Fig. M3. The input lead are connected to the stator windings in parallel with the positive diodes. The diode output leads are connected to a metal grommet in the circuit board and is secured to the insulated regulator terminal.

A portion of the alternating current and voltage developed in the stator windings is rectified by the field diode assembly. This voltage is sensed by the voltage regulator to provide current to the field windings. Fig. M4 shows the charging circuit.

Voltage Regulator

The voltage regulator is an electrical switching device sealed at the factory, requiring no adjustments. It senses the voltage appearing at the regulator terminal of the alternator and supplies the necessary field

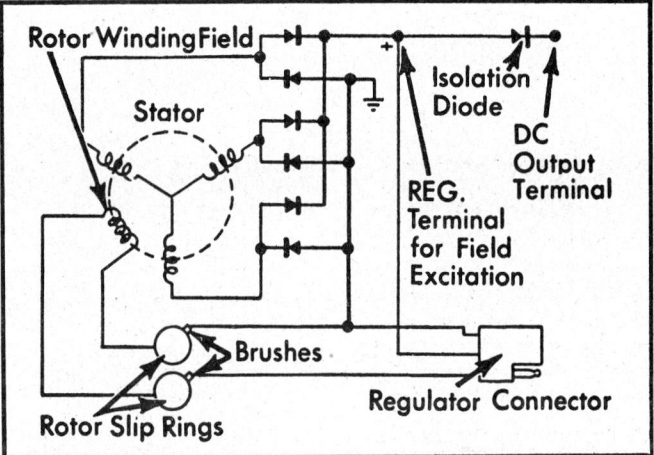

Fig. M1 Motorola alternator circuit diagram 1970 35 amp.

current for maintaining the system voltage at the output terminal.

TESTING SYSTEM IN VEHICLE

Alternator Output Test 1974-75

1. Connect a voltmeter to the battery, start engine and turn on headlamps.
2. Run engine for two minutes at 1000 RPM and observe voltmeter. If voltage remains above 13 volts, alternator and regulator are satisfactory.

1970-73

1. Connect test leads as shown in Fig. M5.
2. Turn ground polarity switch to Negative and voltage selector to 16 volt position. Place load control knob in Direct position.
3. Close battery post adapter switch, Fig. M6 and start engine. Run engine at 2000 RPM and allow to warm up.
4. Turn load control knob until highest reading is noted on ammeter. This reading should be within 10 amps of the alternator rated output. If not, further proceed with this test as outlined below.
5. Disconnect field and ground wire connector at alternator.
6. Connect a jumper wire (J-21053) to field terminal and connect one test lead to jumper and the other to output terminal, Fig. M7.
7. Close battery post adapter switch and start engine. Open adapter switch and run engine at 2000 RPM.
8. Slowly rotate field control knob clockwise and note highest ammeter reading. Do not allow voltage to exceed 16 volts.
9. Stop engine and install a jumper wire between ignition coil negative terminal and ground.

NOTE: Stator winding of 62 amp alternator is the same as the 51 & 55 amp.

10. Turn ground polarity switch to Positive and ignition switch ON. Note ammeter reading, which should not exceed 5 amps, and add this reading to reading taken in Step 8. Total reading should be approximately the same as alternator rated output. If not, alternator must be repaired.

Isolation Diode Test 1970

If a commercial diode tester is used, follow the Test Equipment Manufacturer's instructions. If a commercial tester is not

MOTOROLA ALTERNATORS

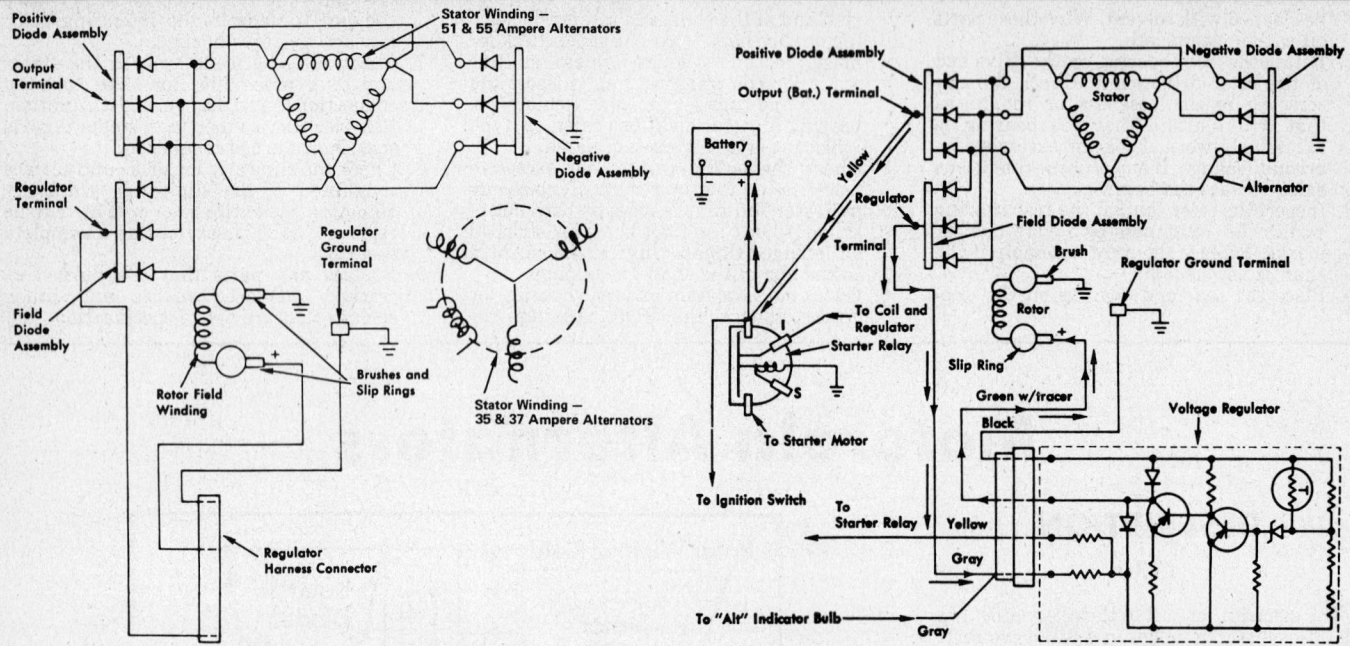

Fig. M2 Alternator circuit, 1971–75, 35, 37, 51, 55 & 62 amp.

Fig. M4 Charging circuit diagram, 1971–75 (typical)

available, use a DC Test Lamp.

CAUTION: *Do not use a 120 volt test lamp as diodes will be damaged.*

1. Connect test lamp to output terminal and regulator terminal of isolation diode.
2. Reverse test probes.
3. The test lamp should light in one direction but should not light in the other direction.
4. If the test lamp lights in both directions the isolation diode is shorted.
5. If the test lamp does not light in either direction, isolation diode is open.

Rectifier Diode Tests

Any commercial in-circuit diode tester will suffice to make the test. Follow Test Equipment Manufacturer's instructions.

Check diodes individually after the diodes have been disconnected from the stator. A shorted stator coil or shorted insulating washers or sleeves on positive diodes would make diodes appear to be shorted.

A test lamp will not indicate an open condition unless all three diodes of either assembly are open. However, a shorted diode can be detected. The test is not 100% effective but can be used if so desired when an in-circuit diode tester is not available.

The test lamp should light in one direction but not in the other direction. If the test lamp lights in both directions, one or more of the diodes of the assembly being tested is shorted. If the test lamp does not light in either direc-

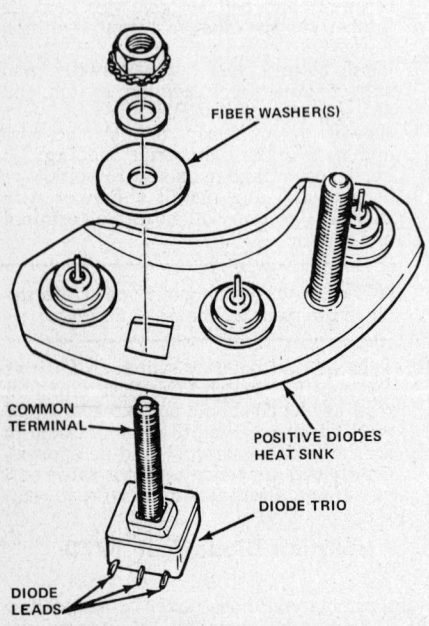

Fig. M3 Potted type diode trio. 1974–75

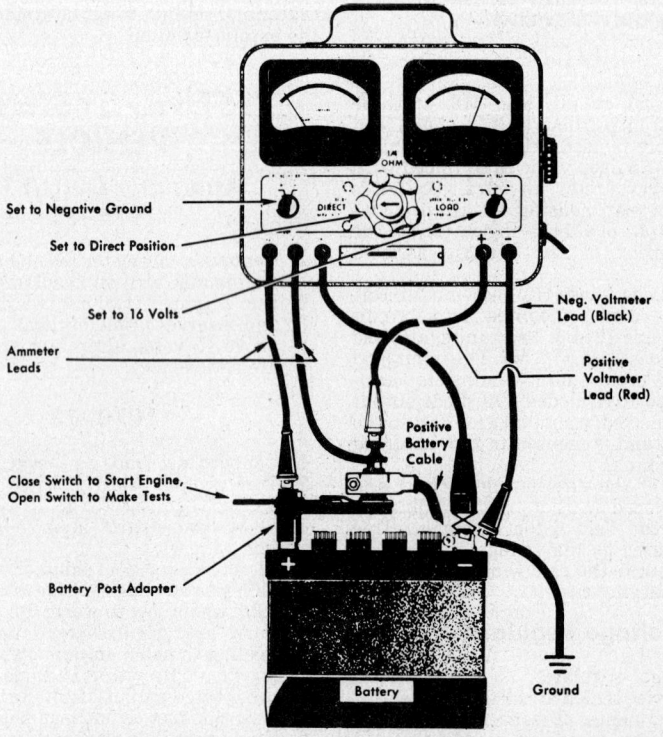

Fig. M5 Alternator test connections

MOTOROLA ALTERNATORS

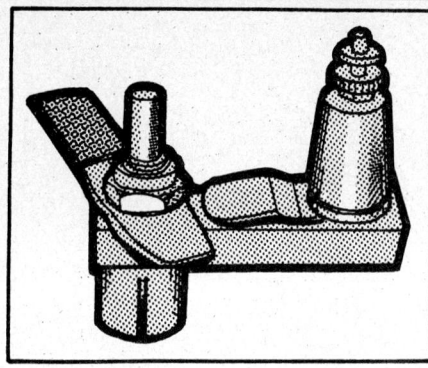

Fig. M6 Battery post adapter tool which provides a convenient method for connecting ammeter leads of volt-ammeter tester to charging system

1970-73

1. With test equipment connected, Fig. M4, run engine at 2000 RPM and open battery post adapter switch.
2. Place load control knob in the 1/4 ohm position. Voltmeter reading should be 14.0 to 14.8 volts for 1970 units or 13.8 to 14.2 for 1971-73 units. The reading is taken when the unit is at 80° F. If voltage is not within above limits, replace voltage regulator.

ALTERNATOR REPAIRS

Disassembly, Figs. M8 & M9

Brush Assembly

The brush assembly can be removed in most cases with the alternator on the vehicle. The spring clip is bent back so that the field terminal plug can be removed. Remove the two self-tapping screws, field plug retainer spring and cover. Pull brush assembly straight out far enough to clear locating pins, then lift brush assembly out. The complete brush assembly is available for replacement.

Isolation Diode, 1970

Remove the 2 lock nuts securing the isolation diode to the rear housing and slide it off the studs. The diode is replaced as an assembly.

Rear Housing

Remove the 4 through bolts and nuts. Carefully separate the rear housing and stator from the front housing by using 2 small screwdrivers and prying the stator from the front housing at 2 opposing slots where the "through bolts" are removed. Do not burr the stator core which would make assembly difficult.

CAUTION: *Do not insert screwdriver blade deeper than 1/16" to avoid damaging stator winding.*

Stator and Diode Assembly

Do not unsolder stator-to-diode wire junction. Remove stator and diode as an assembly. Avoid bending stator wire at junction holding positive and negative diode assembly from housing.

Remove 4 lock nuts and insulating washers. The insulating washers and nylon sleeves are used to insulate the positive plate studs from the housing. With the 4 nuts removed, the stator can be separated from the rear housing by hand.

Diode Replacement

To replace field diode assembly, remove nylon sleeve, insulating washer and hold-down nut from regulator stud. Unsolder field diode wires from positive diodes. *When replacing positive or negative diodes, make note of diode assembly to stator connections, and make sure replacement diode assembly connections are the same. The positive diode assembly has red markings, the negative black markings.*

In soldering and unsoldering leads from diodes, grasp the diode lead with pliers between the diode and stator lead to be removed. This will give better heat dissipation and protect the diode. Do not exert excessive stress on diode lead.

Rotor

The rotor should only require removal from the front housing if there is a defect in the field coil itself or in the front bearing. Front and rear bearings are permanently sealed, self-lubricating type. If the front housing must be removed from the rotor, use a two-jaw puller to remove the pulley. The split spring

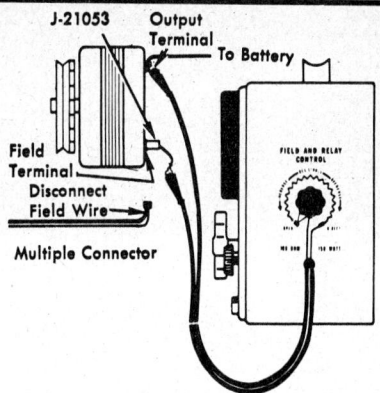

Fig. M7 Alternator output test with external field control

tion, *all three diodes in the assembly are open.* Check diodes individually after disassembly to ascertain findings.

NOTE: *A shorted stator coil would appear as a shorted negative diode. Also check stator for shorts after disassembly.*

Field Diode Test

1. Using a voltmeter, connect positive lead to alternator output terminal and negative lead to regulator terminal.
2. Start and run engine at idle speed. The voltmeter should then read .6 volt or less. If reading is over .6 volt, replace field diode assembly.

Voltage-Regulator Test 1974-75

1. Connect a voltmeter to the battery, start engine and turn on headlamps.
2. Run engine at 1000 RPM for several minutes to establish voltage regulator operating temperature.
3. Voltage should be within 13.1 to 14.3 volts when regulator temperature is between 100°F and 150°F.

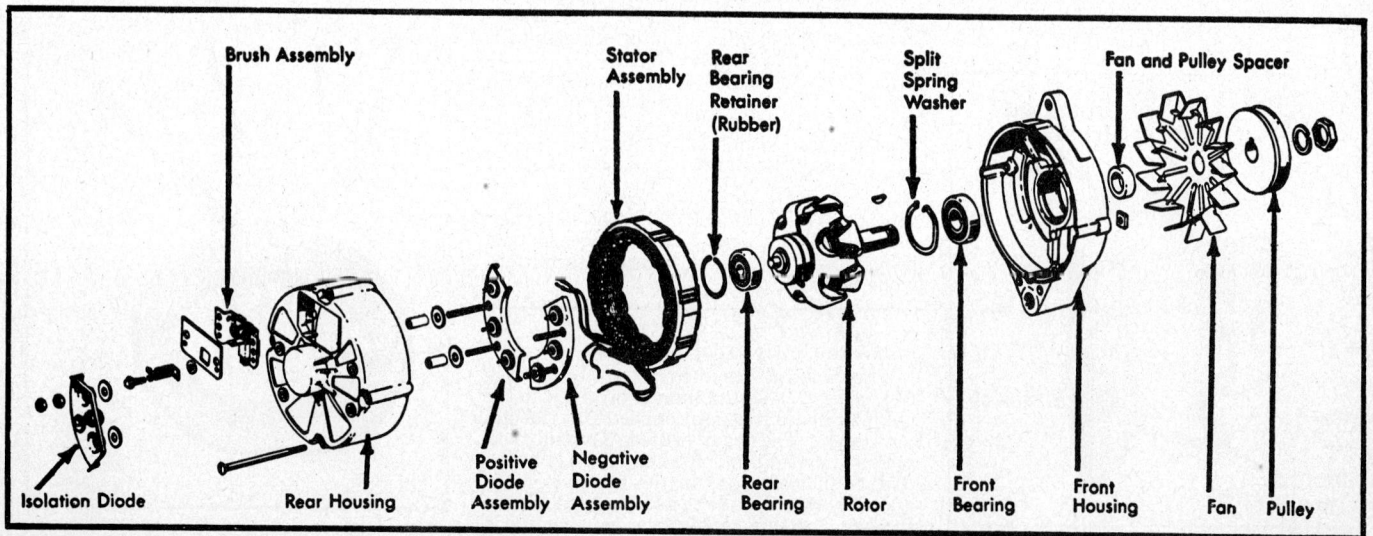

Fig. M8 Motorola alternator disassembled. 1970 (typical)

121

MOTOROLA ALTERNATORS

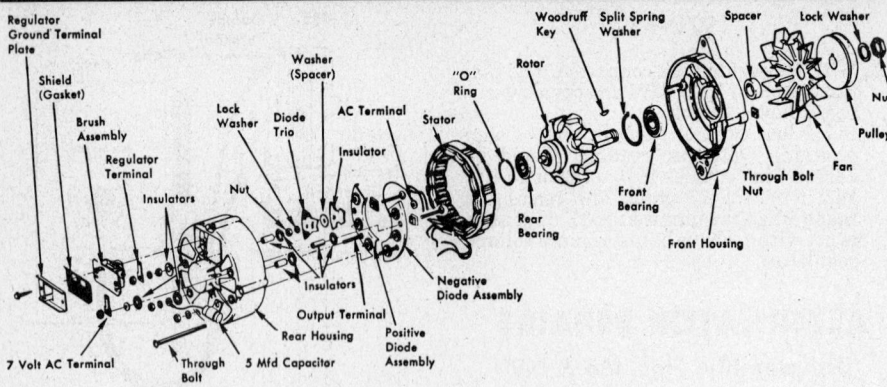

Fig. M9 Alternator disassembled. 1971–75 NOTE: Model shown has AC terminal for 1973–75 electric choke

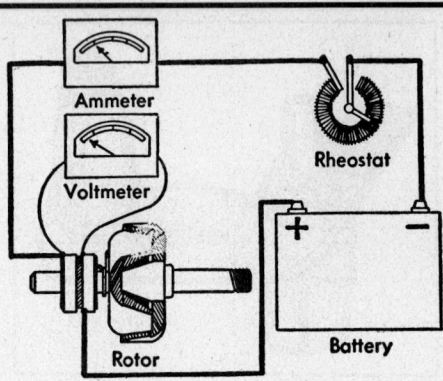

Fig. M10 Field coil test

washer must be loosened with snap ring pliers through the opening in the front housing. Remove the washer only after the housing is removed. The rotor and front bearing can be removed from the front housing by tapping the rotor shaft slightly.

NOTE: *Make certain that the split spring washer has been removed from its groove before attempting to remove the front housing from the bearing.*

Alternator Bench Tests

Field Coil Test

The rotor should be tested for grounds and for shorted turns in the winding. The ground test is made with test probes connected in series with a 110 volt test lamp. Place one test probe on the slip ring and the other probe on the rotor core. If the bulb lights the rotor is grounded.

To test for shorted turns, check rotor field current drawn as shown in Fig. M10. Slowly reduce resistance of rheostat to zero. With full battery voltage applied to the field coil, the field current should be as listed in Alternator Specifications tables in front of Truck chapters. Excessive current draw indicates shorted turn in field winding.

Brush Insulation Test

Connect an ohmmeter or a test lamp to the field terminal and bracket. Resistance should be high (infinite) or test lamp should not light. If resistance is low or if test lamp lights, brush assembly is shorted and must be replaced.

Brush Continuity Test

Connect an ohmmeter to field terminal and brush. Use an alligator clip to assure good contact to brush, test points "A" and "C" in Fig. M11.

CAUTION: *Do not chip brush.*

Resistance reading should be zero. Move brush and brush lead wire to make certain that brush lead wire connections are not intermittent. Resistance reading should not vary when brush and lead wire are being moved around. Connect ohmmeter to bracket and grounded brush, test points "E" and "D", Fig. M11. Resistance reading should be zero.

1974-75 Diode Tests

Diode Trio: Unsolder diode trio leads and using a 12 volt meter which draws a one amp maximum load, connect test leads providing current path, Fig. M12. Hold this connection for at least two minutes, then reverse test leads immediately. Test each diode in this manner. If current flows in both directions, neither direction or flows intermittently, the diode trio must be replaced.

Rectifier Diodes: The same method of testing is used for the rectifier diodes as for the diode trio, Fig. M13. However, a 15 amp load is used when testing the rectifier diodes.

NOTE: A diode can be tested for opens or shorts using an ohmmeter. Reason for applying an electrical load to the diodes, in turn generating heat, is to detect intermittent diode failures.

Stator in-Circuit Test

When making the in-circuit stator leakage test, some consideration must be given to the rectifier diodes that are connected to the stator winding. The negative diode assembly will conduct in one direction when properly polarized. A shorted diode in the negative diode assembly would make the stator appear to be shorted. For this reason, the rectifier plate assembly and stator must be checked individually after alternator has been disassembled if the problem is localized to the stator.

CAUTION: *Use a special diode continuity light or a DC test lamp. Do not use a 120 volt test lamp as diodes will be damaged.*

1. Connect the test lamp to a diode terminal of the negative assembly and ground terminal.
2. Reverse test probes. The lamp should light in one direction but not in the other.
3. If the test lamp does not light in either direction, this indicates that all three rectifiers in the negative diode assembly are open.
4. If the test lamp lights in both directions, the stator winding is shorted to stator or one of the negative diodes is shorted.
5. Check stator again when it is disassembled from diode assemblies.
6. With alternator disassembled, connect an ohmmeter or test lamp probes to one of the diode terminals and to stator.

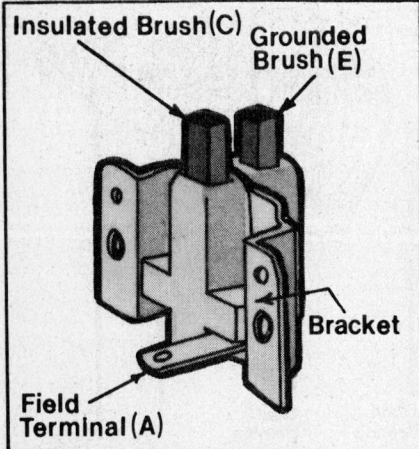

Fig. M11 Brush assembly test

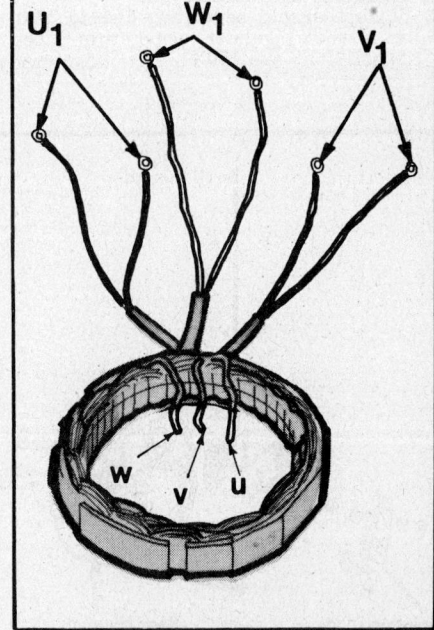

Fig. M14 Stator coil shorts and continuity tests

MOTOROLA ALTERNATORS

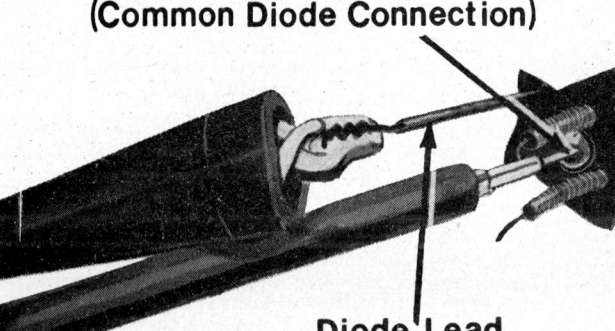

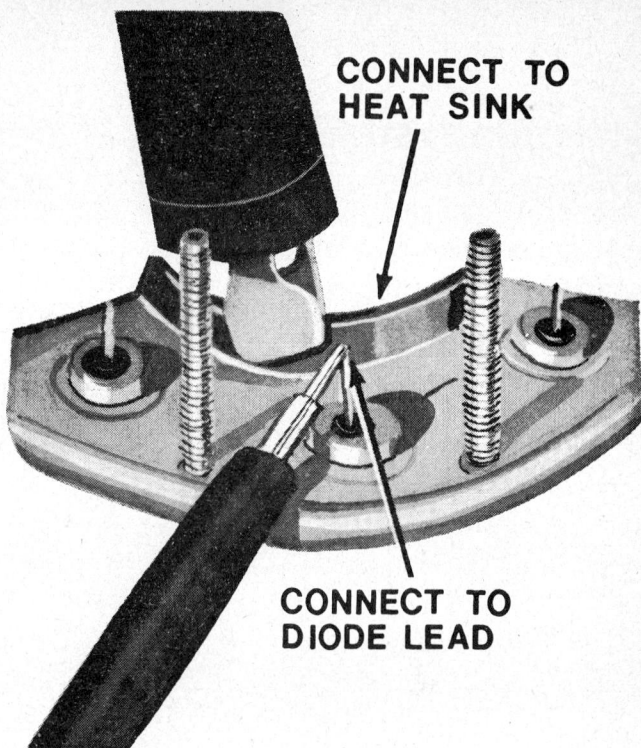

Fig. M13 Rectifier diodes bench test. 1974-75 alternators

Fig. M12 Diode trio bench test. 1974-75 alternators

7. Resistance reading should be infinite or test lamp should not light.
8. If resistance reading is not infinite or test lamp lights, high leakage or a short exists between stator winding and stator. In either case, stator should be replaced.

Stator Coil Shorts Test
1. This test checks for shorts between stator coil windings. The winding junctions must be separated as shown in Fig. M13. An ohmmeter or test lamp may be used.
2. Connect one of the test probes to test point "U" and the other to test point "V" and then to test point "W". Resistance should be infinite or test lamp should not light.
3. Connect test probes to test V and W. Resistance should be infinite or test lamp should not light. In either test, if the resistance reading is not infinite or the test lamp lights, high leakage or a short exists between stator windings. Stator should be replaced.

Stator Continuity Test
1. Measure resistance of each winding in stator between test points U and U1, V and V1, W and W1, Fig. M14. Resistance should be a fraction of an ohm (approximately .1 Ohm). An extremely accurate instrument would be necessary to ascertain short turns. Only an open condition can be detected with a commercial type ohmmeter.
2. If the alternator has been disassembled because of an electrical malfunction, replace stator only after all other components have been checked and found to be satisfactory.

Assemble Alternator
1. Clean bearing and inside of bearing hub of front housing. Support front housing and, using a suitable driver, apply sufficient pressure to outside race of bearing to seat bearing.
2. Insert split spring washer hub of front housing, seating washer into groove of hub.

NOTE: *Do not use a screwdriver or any small object to compress washer that can slip off and damage bearing seal. Make certain that split spring washer has been installed prior to assembling front housing and rotor.*

3. Use sufficient pressure to seat front bearing against shoulder on rotor shaft. The bearing drive tool must fit the inner race of bearing.
4. Install fan and pulley.
5. Use a 7/16" socket to fit inside race of near bearing and apply sufficient pressure to drive bearing against shoulder of rotor shaft.
6. Assemble front and rear housings.
7. Make certain that rear bearing is properly seated in rear housing hub and that diode wires are properly dressed so that rotor will not contact diode wires.
8. Align stator slots with rear housing through bolt holes, then align front housing through bolt holes with respect to rear housing.

NOTE: *The position of the brush assembly and belt adjusting screw boss must be in the same relative position to each other.*

9. Spin rotor to make certain that rotor is not contacting diode wires. Install through bolts.
10. Before mounting isolation diode, make certain that positive rectifier diode plate has been properly insulated from housing.
11. Install brush assembly, cover and field plug retainer spring.

123

Prestolite Alternators

TESTING SYSTEM IN VEHICLE

Charging Circuit Resistance Test

1. Make connections as shown in Fig. P1.
2. Adjust engine speed and electrical load to obtain amperes in the charging circuit. The voltage drop in this circuit should not exceed .2 volt. If more, locate and correct cause of high resistance before proceeding with tests.
3. With the same operating conditions as in Step 2, connect voltmeter leads from ground battery terminal to alternator frame, and from alternator to regular base. In neither case should the voltage reading exceed .04 volt. If more, locate and correct cause of high resistance ground connections.

Alternator Output Test

1. Make test connections as shown in Fig. P2. *Be sure rheostat is "Off" before connecting leads.*
2. Connect a tachometer, start engine and adjusts its speed to 1750 rpm. Adjust rheostat to obtain 14.2 volts and observe ammeter reading. It should be as specified for the alternator being serviced.
3. If the alternator fails to reach rated output, it should be removed from the vehicle for repairs. A slightly low ammeter reading may indicate an open rectifier while a considerably lower reading may indicate a shorted rectifier.
4. If the output is only slightly low, a temperature check may be made to determine whether a rectifier is open. With the alternator operating as for the output test, place a bulbtype thermometer (250° scale) on the base of each rectifier heat sink for the rectifier bank being checked.
5. The rectifier temperature will normally be several degrees higher than the heat sink temperature. If the rectifier is open its temperature will be the same as that of the heat sink in which it is located.

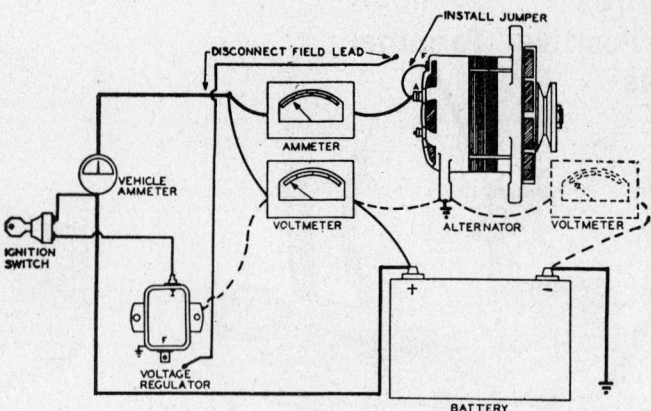

Fig. P1 Meter connections for testing voltage drop in charging circuit

6. If the rectifier is shorted the temperature of the entire heat sink in which it is located will be abnormally high.

Voltage Regulator Test

The first part of this test checks the operating voltage of the regulator when operating on the upper contract. Make test connections as shown in Fig. P3. *Be sure the ignition switch is off when connecting the field lead. Grounding of the field circuit while the ignition switch is on will damage the regulator.*

1. To test voltage regulator setting, start engine and adjust its speed to 750 rpm. Turn on lights and accessories to obtain a 10-ampere charge rate. Operate the system at this speed and load for 15 minutes to normalize the temperature. (This regulator is temperature compensated.)
2. Cycle the system by stopping and restarting the engine; then note the voltmeter reading. If seriously out of adjustment a rough setting may be made. The final setting is not made until the "spread" between operation on the upper contact and operation on the lower contact is established. This value is determined in the next part of the test which checks voltage when the regulator is operating on the lower contact.
3. Test connections remain as for the previous part of the test. Increase engine speed to 1500 rpm and turn off all lights and accessories. Voltage should increase and amperage should decrease. The "spread" in voltage between this reading and the reading noted in the first part of the test should be from .1 to .3 volt.
4. If the "spread" is greater or less than specified, remove the regulator cover and adjust by loosening the stationary contact support screw and moving the support up or down. Raising the support will increase voltage "spread", and vice-versa.
5. Replace the cover and reduce engine speed to 750 rpm and repeat the first part of the test with the regulator operating on the upper contact. If the voltage setting is not within specifications, remove the cover and adjust by bending the lower spring hanger. Replace the cover and cycle after each trial adjustment to obtain accurate readings.

Indicator Light Relay Test

1. Make meter connections as shown in Fig.

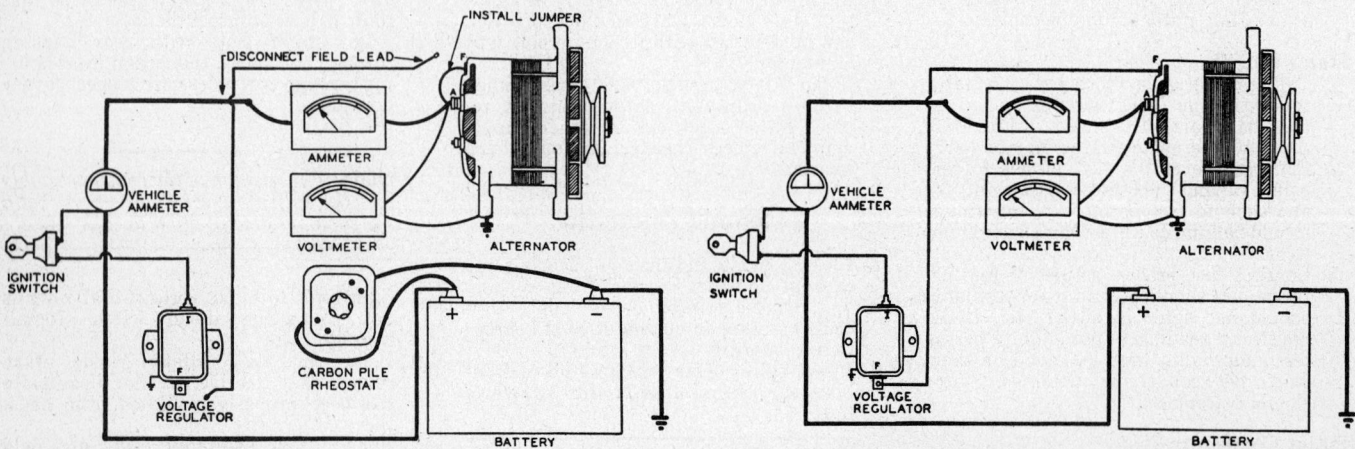

Fig. P2 Meter connections for testing alternator output

Fig. P3 Meter connections for testing voltage regulator

PRESTOLITE ALTERNATORS

P4. If the vehicle indicator light cannot be seen while making this test, connect a 12-volt test lamp, using a No. 57 bulb between the "L" and "B" terminals of the regulator.

2. Turn the rheostat to the "resistance in" position and operate the engine at approximately 800 rpm. Slowly cut out resistance and observe the ammeter reading when the vehicle indicator or test light goes out. It should be 4 to 7 amperes.
3. To adjust relay contact opening amperage, remove the cover and bend the lower armature spring hanger up or down. Increasing the spring tension raises the setting, and vice versa. Replace the cover and recheck.

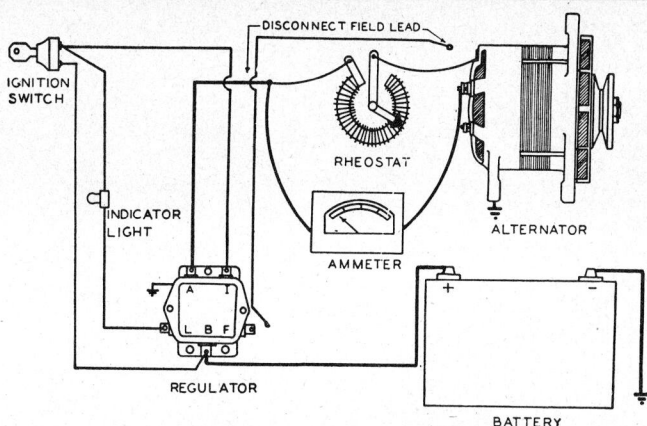

Fig. P4 Meter connections for testing indicator light relay operation

BENCH TESTS

If the voltage regulator is unstable or cannot be adjusted to specifications in the above test, remove and regulator from the vehicle for further tests and adjustments.

Voltage Regulator Contact Gap

Contact gap is checked by placing a .010" gauge between the lower movable contact and the lower stationary contact. Adjust by bending the upper stationary contact up or down. Be sure that proper contact alignment is maintained.

Voltage Regulator Air Gap

To check the voltage regulator armature air gap, connect a No. 57 bulb in series with a 12-volt battery between the regulator field terminal and base.

Place a .034" round wire gauge between the armature and core on the side of the brass stop rivet nearest the center of the core head.

The lower movable contact should barely touch the lower stationary contact when the armature is pressed down against the gauge and the lamp should light. With a .038" gauge between the armature and core the light should go out.

To adjust to the above specifications, loosen the stationary bracket attaching screw and move the bracket up or down. *This is a preliminary adjustment only as the air gap may be changed when voltage "spread" is established as outlined previously.*

Servicing Regulator Contacts

If the contacts are rough or oxidized, they may be cleaned with an American Swiss No. 6 equalling cut file. After filing, the contacts should be cleaned with a strip of linen tape saturated with a few drops of lighter fluid and drawn between the contacts. Then repeat with a dry strip of tape to remove fluid.

ALTERNATOR REPAIRS

When repairing an alternator, Fig. P5, complete disassembly may not be required. In some cases it will be necessary only to perform those operations that are required to repair or replace the defective part. However, the following material covers the complete overhaul procedure.

Disassambly

1. Remove through bolts and tap lightly on end heads to separate them from stator.
2. Remove drive end head and rotor.
3. Remove nuts, etc., from rectifier bracket studs. Separate slip ring end from stator.
4. Both brushes are located in slip ring end housing and should be replaced if worn to 5/16" or less. Remove brushes, being careful that the brush springs are not lost when brushes are removed from holders.
5. Remove pulley and fan.
6. Remove drive end head and bearing, Fig. P6.
7. Remove three scews from retainer plate and press bearing out of drive end head, using tool shown in Fig. P13.
8. Remove roller bearing from slip ring end head, Fig. P7.
9. If rectifiers must be removed, cut rectifier wire as near to crimpled sleeve as possible. Then remove rectifiers, Fig. P8.

Inspection

1. When disassembled, all parts should be wiped clean and inspected for wear, distortion or signs of overheating or mechanical interference.
2. Stator windings and leads should be examined for insulation failures or defects. A shorted phase winding or rectifier will normally be evidenced by discoloration.
3. The stator can be checked for shorted windings with an internal-external growler. The test is made with the stator leads disconnected from rectifiers.
4. The stator can be checked for grounded windings with a 110-volt test lamp and test probes. *Do not make this test with rectifiers connected to stator leads.*
5. Test rectifiers as described below.

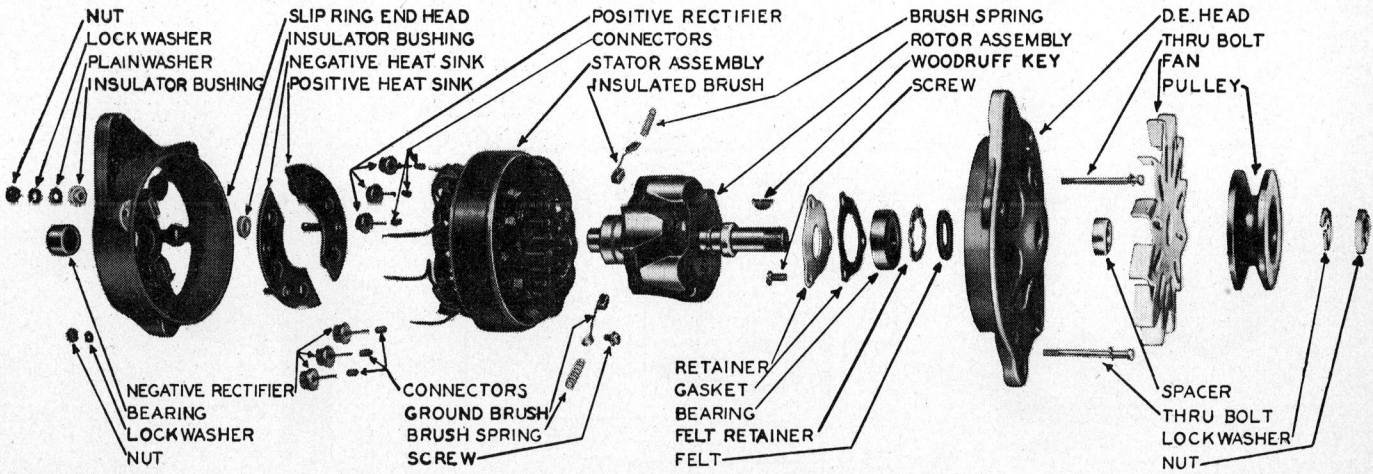

Fig. P5 Exploded view of a Prestolite alternator

125

PRESTOLITE ALTERNATORS

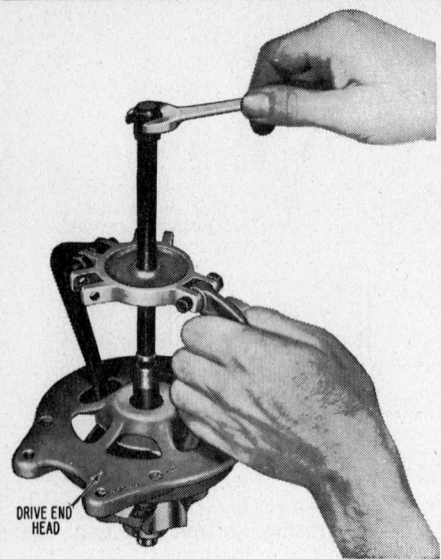

Fig. P6 Removing drive end head and bearing

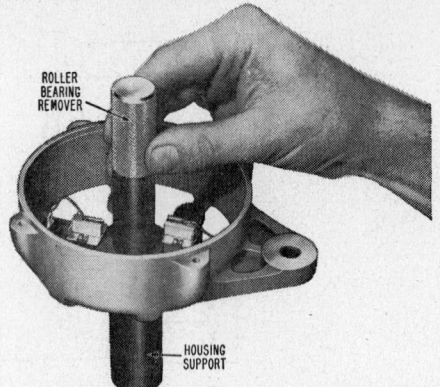

Fig. P7 Removing roller bearing from slip ring end head

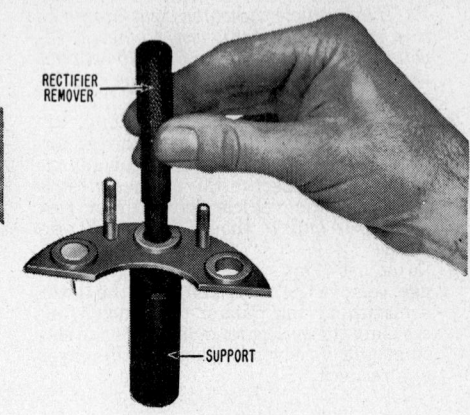

Fig. P8 Removing rectifiers from heat sink

6. The rotor should be tested for grounds and for shorted turns in the winding. The ground test is made with the test probes connected in series with a 110-volt test lamp as shown in Fig. P9. If bulb lights, rotor winding is grounded. To test for shorted turns, check rotor field current draw as shown in Fig. P10. Using the rheostat, adjust voltage to 10 volts and read field current draw on ammeter. Reading should be 2.34 to 2.42 amps at room temperature (70°F). Excessive current draw indicates shorted turns in field winding.

Assembly

1. Press rectifiers in heat sink, Fig. P11. *Rectifiers are identified by red markings on positive and black markings on negative.* Strip the insulation back about 1/4" on stator leads and reconnect them to rectifiers. The connector sleeves should be crimped on rectifier leads. *Do not solder these connections as the excessive heat may damage rectifiers.*
2. Install roller bearing, Fig. P12. Enclosed end of bearing should be flush with outer surface of end frame when installed.
3. Install felt retainer and crinkle washer and press bearing into drive end frame. Use a flat block 2" square so that pressure is exerted on outer race. Replace retainer plate and gasket on end frame. Make sure snap ring and retainer are in place on rotor shaft and press end frame on, Fig. P13. Press bearing down against snap ring retainer.
4. Replace spacer on shaft and install Woodruff key, fan and pulley.
5. Install brush springs and brushes. Eyelet on ground brush lead is fastened to end frame with a screw. The blade terminal on the insulated brush lead is pushed into the slot in field terminal insulator bushing. A tab on blade terminal snaps into insulator bushing. If damaged, this bushing may be replaced.
6. To spread brushes so they will clear slip rings when end head is installed, a wire slip can be made and used as shown in Fig. P14. This clip can be fashioned from a coat hanger or 1/8" welding rod cut and bent to the dimensions shown. File a "V" groove in ends of wire clip so that it will contact brush leads when inserted through holes in end head.
7. Install negative rectifier heat sink in slip ring end head and install lockwashers and nuts. Install insulator bushings on positive heat sink studs and install heat sink in end head. Install outer insulator bushings, washers and nuts.
8. Manually press stator in position on slip ring end head and install assembled drive end head and install assembled drive end head and rotor. Make sure that through bolt holes line up on the two end heads. Install and tighten through bolts.
9. Remove brush spreader clip and make sure brush leads do not drag on rotor and that rotor turns freely when rotated by hand. Test alternator when assembled.

TESTING RECTIFIERS

There are two methods of testing diode rectifiers. One method requires the use of Tool C-3829. The other is to make the tests with a No. 57 bulb test lamp. The advantage of the former over the latter is that it is not necessary to perform the time consuming job of separating the soldered leads. (The instrument is available through the Miller Mfg. Co., Alliance, Ohio.)

If the current output test indicates that the alternator is not operating within specifications, remove the alternator from the vehicle and proceed as follows:
1. Perform a field coil draw test to provide an indication of the alternator field.
2. Open the alternator by first removing the brushes and then the alternator through bolts. Separate the drive end housing from rectifier end housing.
3. Inspect alternator components, paying special attention to the condition of the slip rings for indications of oil and for being burnt or worn. Check the brushes for evidences of sticking in the holder or housing.
4. Inspect the bearing surfaces of the rotor shaft at the rectifier end and the bearing.

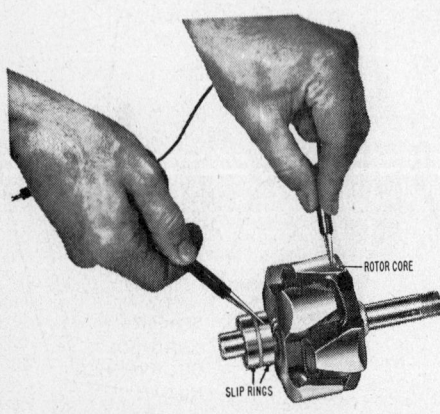

Fig. P9 Testing rotor for grounds

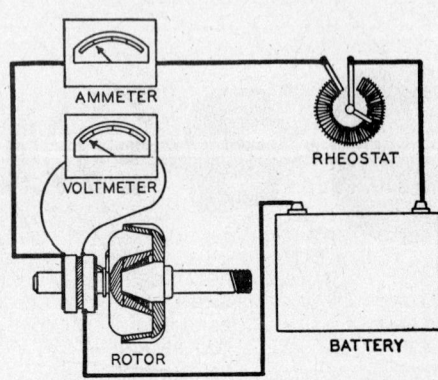

Fig. P10 Meter connections for testing rotor field current draw

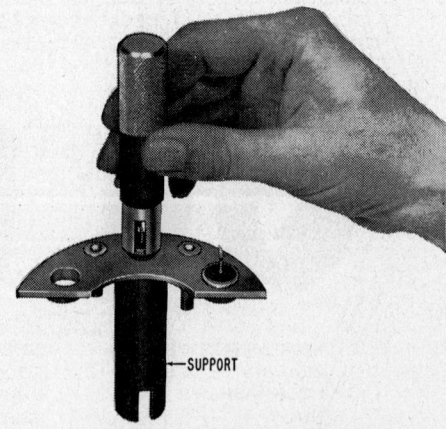

Fig. P11 Installing rectifiers in heat sink

PRESTOLITE ALTERNATORS

Fig. P12 Installing roller bearing

Fig. P13 Installing drive end head and bearing

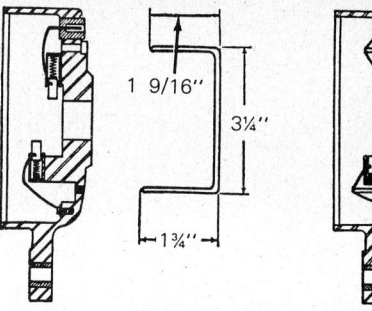

Fig. P14 Brush spreader clip. Right view shows clip installed

Make sure rectifier leads are in good condition, especially at the connections. The insulation should not be worn or broken.

Testing Rectifiers With Test Lamp

1. With alternator disassembled and rectifier leads disconnected, proceed as follows:
2. With a No. 57 test lamp, connect one side of the lamp to the positive battery post and the other side of the lamp to a test probe. Connect another test probe to the negative battery post.
3. Touch the outer case of the rectifier with one probe and the other probe to the wire in the center of the rectifier.
4. Reverse the probes.
5. If the test lamp lights in one direction the rectifier is good. If the lamp lights in both directions the rectifier is shorted. If the lamp does not light in either direction the rectifier is open.

Leece-Neville Alternators

SERIES 6000, 6200

These alternators, Fig. L1, are the 40 and 50 ampere, three-phase type. The slip rings and brushes, which carry field current to the rotor coil, are enclosed for protection from abrasive dust yet are readily accessible for inspection and servicing. One brush is grounded to simplify the circuit.

The rectifier cells, or diodes, are mounted in the slip ring end housing and are internally connected to the stator windings. One end of each of the three stator windings, or phases, is connected to a positive and a negative diode. The other ends of the stator windings are connected together forming a "Y" type connection. The three negative and the three positive diodes are pressed (in sets) into two plates called "heat sinks". These multiple-purpose heat sinks serve as mountings for the diodes, as radiation plates for heat dissipation, and also as current conductors.

The two-element regulator used with these alternators consists of a voltage regulator and a load relay which is connected to the auxiliary terminal on the ignition switch, Fig. L2. The load relay, controlled by the ignition switch, functions as a reverse current relay. When the ignition switch is turned on, the relay contacts close to energize the field coil in the alternator.

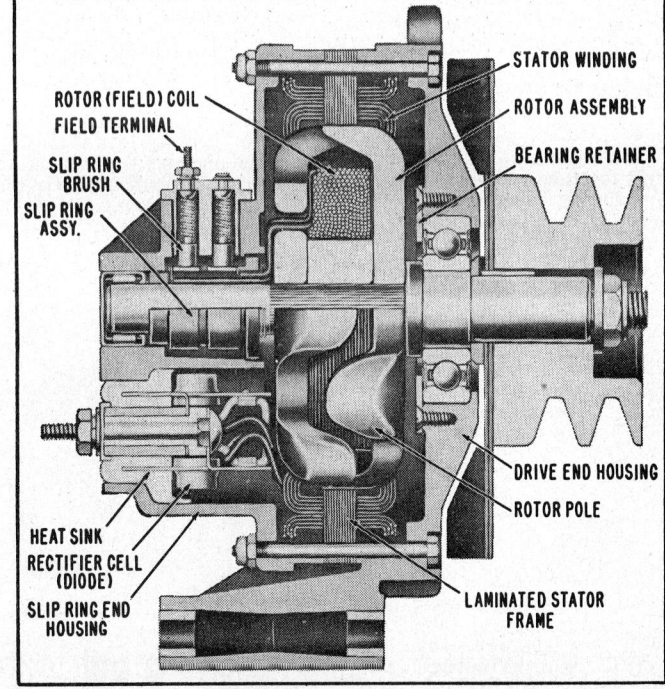

Fig. L1 Sectional view of Leece-Neville 6000 Series alternator

Testing System In Vehicle

Low or No Output

The field circuit must be closed in order to energize the rotor coil before the alternator can generate current.

A quick check of the field circuit can be made (with engine shut off) by turning on ignition switch and disconnecting the field terminal lead at the voltage regulator and then momentarily striking the FLD terminal with it.

If a medium spark is obtained, field circuit is closed. If spark is very light, a poor brush contact at the slip rings, or a poor connection, is indicated. If no spark is obtained, short or broken brushes, collapsed brush springs, poor or broken solder connections at the slip rings, or an open in the rotor coil, is indicated. A very heavy spark would indicate a short in the rotor coil. (Reconnect FLD terminal lead after

LEECE-NEVILLE ALTERNATORS

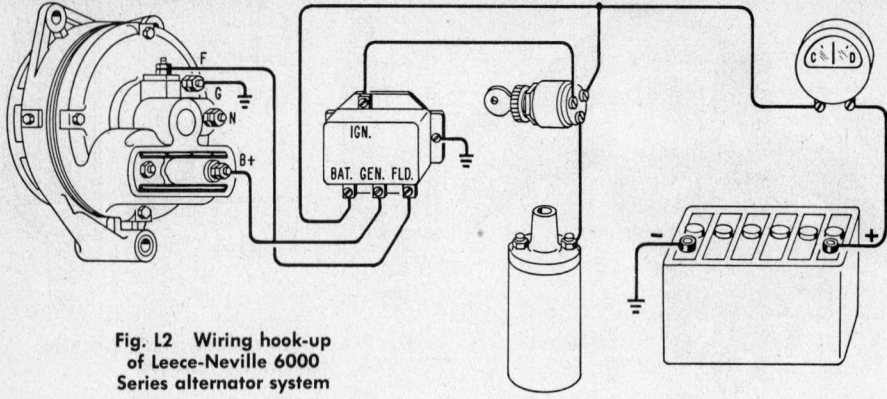

Fig. L2 Wiring hook-up of Leece-Neville 6000 Series alternator system

making this check.)

If field circuit is found to be closed, alternator can be checked for output as follows:

With the engine at idle speed, remove the "F" lead from the alternator and attach a jumper wire from the "F" terminal to the "B" terminal. This jumper connection will take the regulator out of the circuit and allow the alternator to operate at full field strength.

If the alternator shows a high rate of charge when running with full field strength, the alternator is functioning and the problem lies with the regulator, system wiring on battery.

If the alternator shows a very low or no rate of charge when running with full field strength, the alternator will have to be removed from the engine and checked as outlined below if the system wiring and battery are good.

Bench Test

1. Remove pulley, fan and spacer from shaft. Remove brushes. Remove through bolts holding unit together and remove drive end housing and rotor assembly.
2. To test the rotor without removing it from end housing, measure the resistance of the coil by placing the prods of an ohmmeter on the slip rings. If the meter reads from 3.8 to 4.2 ohms the rotor is good. If very little resistance is read, it would indicate a possible shorted coil circuit. Check for loose or broken wire at the slip rings. If no resistance is read, the coil is open. Should no loose or broken wires be detected at the slip rings, the short or open is within the rotor coils and the rotor is beyond repair.
3. Upon removal of the brushes it is found that the brush springs are collapsed, the rotor has a shorted coil and the rotor should be replaced.
4. Check the slip ring brushes or springs. If the brushes or springs are cracked, broken or burned, they should be replaced. Brushes worn to a length less than 3/16" are too short and must be replaced.
5. If the rotor checks good, the stator and rectifier sections should be tested. This can be accomplished without removing the stator and rectifier sections from the slip ring end housing.

Rectifier Tests On Units Having An "N" Terminal

Place the positive prod of an ohmmeter on the "N" terinal at the slip ring end housing and the negative prod on the "B" terminal. With the prods in this position, the meter will read approximately 4 to 5 ohms and indicate that this is the positive section rectifiers. With the prods reversed, the meter needle will read infinity (excessive resistance) which will indicate that the rectifiers are good. Color coding on the bottom of rectifiers is red.

Place the negative prod of the ohmmeter on the "N" terminal and the positive prod on the "GRD" terminal. The ohmmeter will read approximately 4 to 5 ohms and indicate that this is the negative ground secton. Reversing the position of the prods will make the meter read infinity. Color coding on bottom of rectifiers is black.

Rectifier Tests On Units Without "N" Terminal

Since there is no "N" (neutral) terminal, it will be necessary to make the tests at the rectifier sections.

Place the negative prod of an ohmmeter on any one of the three lead connections between the stator and rectifier cells. Place the positive prod on the heat sink of the insulated section of rectifier. The meter should read 4 to 5 ohms. Reverse the prod position and the meter should read infinity and indicate that this is the positive or grounded section of rectifiers.

Place the positive prod on any one of the lead connections between stator and rectifier cells and the negative prod on the opposite heat sink. The meter should read 4 to 5 ohms. Reverse the prod positions and the meter will read infinity indicating that this is the negative rectifier section.

NOTE: *When making the above tests, if the meter readings do not fall in the category mentioned above, one or more of the rectifiers in the section are not operating properly and the section should be replaced. When replacing rectifiers, be certain that the correct section is grounded.*

Alternate Rectifier Test

If an ohmmeter is not available a #57 bulb may be used to test the silicon rectifiers. This test is basically the same except that the bulb and battery replaces the ohmmeter.

If the bulb lights in one direction only the rectifiers are good.

If the bulb lights in both directions one or more of the cells in the section are shorted and the section found bad should be replaced.

If the bulb does not light in either direction one or more of the cells in the section are open and the section should be replaced.

Rectifier Section, Replace

To replace one or both rectifier sections, remove the nuts, etc. from the "B" terminal and the bolt holding the rectifier sections opposite the "B" terminal, and in the case of negative ground units, the "N" terminal. Remove stator and rectifier section from slip ring housing and unsolder the stator leads from the rectifier section or sections to be replaced.

When resoldering the rectifier sections to the stator leads, care must be exercised to

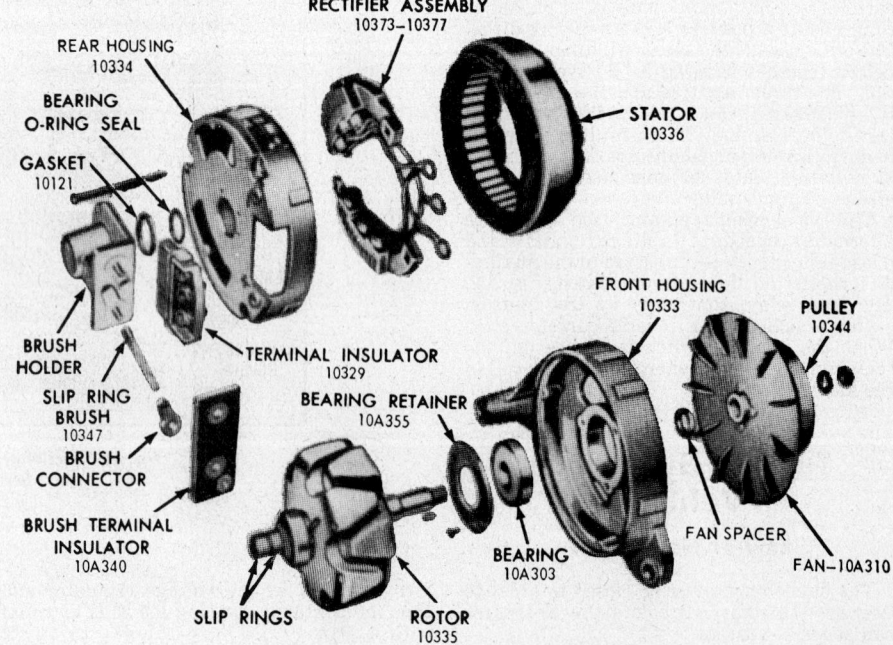

Fig. L3 1970–73 60, 65, 70 & 1973–80 70, 105 & 1979–80 130 amp. alternator disassembled (typical)

LEECE-NEVILLE ALTERNATORS

apply only enough heat to insure a good connection. Overheating may damage the rectifier cells.

Stator Ground Test

To ground test the stator it will be necessary to unsolder the AC stator leads from the rectifiers. Check each stator phase for grounds to the stator core. A 110 volt test lamp is used for this test. No circuit should be present.

Stator Winding Continuity Test

With the test lamp check the continuity of each of the three stator phases. Each phase should show a closed circuit.

Disassembly & Inspection

After the foregoing tests are completed and the part or parts found inoperative are replaced, the following inspection and cleaning of parts should be done.

Rotor

If the rotor has seen considerable service and the slip rings appear to be worn, they should be replaced. Check shaft threads. Press rotor from housing using an arbor press.
To disassemble rotor, unsolder both field coil leads from the slip rings and, using a small puller, carefully pull off the rings. In some cases it will be impossible to save the old slip rings due to the tight fit on the shaft.
To clean the rotor it may be washed with a brush dipped in a cleaning solvent or paint thinner. Rinse with another brush dipped in unleaded gasoline or kerosene and then wipe with a dry cloth or blow dry with compressed air. *Do not immerse complete rotor in the cleaning fluid.*

Stator

After visual inspection finds the stator free of broken or cracked insulation or other damage which would cause failure, the stator can be cleaned in the same manner described for the rotor.

Brushes, Bearings, Etc.

Replace worn or broken brushes, insulation washers, etc. and inspect all tapped holes for good threads. It is recommended that bearings be replaced at time of overhaul.
Remove bearing retainer screws and bearing retainer from drive end housing. Tap or press out bearing. With bearing removed, housing can be immersed in cleaning solvent or paint thinner for cleaning.
The slip ring end housing bearing needs no special tool for removal or replacement. It may be tapped or pressed out. However, a piece of fiber or similar material should be placed over the new bearing when installing to prevent damage.

Reassembly

The alternator should be assembled in the reverse order of disassembly. Care should be exercised not to damage the housing pilots and stator windings. When completely assembled, spin the rotor by hand for free rotation check.
Reinstall the alternator on the vehicle and run it "full field" as outlined under Alternator System Check.

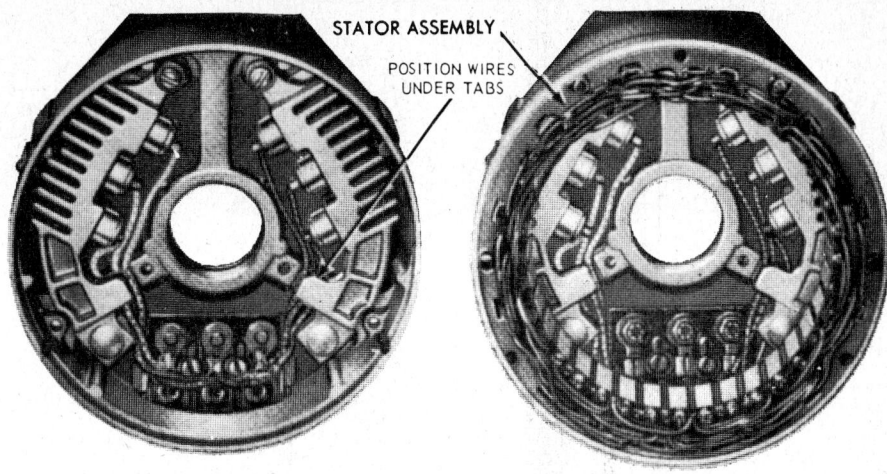

Fig. L4 Slip ring end housing, rectifier & stator assembly, 1970–73 60, 65, 70 & 1973–80 70, 105 & 1979–80 130 amp. alternator

Regulator, Adjust

Load Relay

To check the load relay, connect leads from a 12 volt battery to the ground and ignition terminals on the regulator, with a variable resistor in series with one lead. Connect a voltmeter across the "IGN" and "GRD" terminals.
Start with all the resistance cut in and then gradually decrease it to allow the voltmeter reading to rise. The load relay should close at 5.8 to 6.2 volts.
To raise closing voltage, increase spring tension by bending lower arm of the spring bracket. To lower closing voltage decrease spring tension.

Voltage Regulator

To check the voltage regulator remove the cover. Connect one voltmeter lead to the regulator "BAT" terminal and the other lead to the regulator or alternator ground. Then connect a pair of earphones of not less than 1,000 ohms resistance to the "FLD" and "GEN" regulator terminals to hear the operation of the regulator contacts. *After each of the three steps in the test, open the ignition switch to bring the alternator speed to zero.*

1. Raise alternator speed slowly and listen for the vibration indicating the start of regulation on the upper contacts. This should start within the range of 13.9 and 14.3 volts. To increase the voltage, bend the arm of the spring bracket down. To lower the voltage, bend the arm up.
2. Slowly increase alternator speed past the start of regulation until the vibration ceases. Continue until the voltage reaches its maximum value, just before the lower set of contacts starts to vibrate. The maximum should be 14.7 and is adjusted as outlined in Step 1.
3. Increase alternator speed slowly past maximum voltage until the regulator armature vibrates on the lower contacts. The operating voltage should be 13.9 to 14.3 volts. To increase the voltage, increase the armature core gap; reduce the core gap to lower the voltage. The gap is adjusted by loosening the locking screw on the contact block to raise or lower the block.

60, 65, 70, 1973–80 105 1979–80 130 AMP. ALTERNATORS

System Testing

Testing procedures for these alternators are same as the procedures outlined in the "Ford Alternator" section of this chapter.

Alternator Repairs

Disassembly

1. Remove pulley nut, pulley, fan, shaft key and spacer.
2. Remove brushes and terminal insulator, then brush holder assembly from housing, Fig. L3.
3. Remove through bolts and separate brush end housing and stator from alternator.
4. Remove AC terminal nuts and stator from end housing.
5. Remove rotor from drive end housing with a gear puller or a suitable press, then front bearing retainer and bearing from housing.
6. Unsolder field leads from slip rings and remove slip rings and bearing from rotor shaft.
7. Remove rectifier assembly bolts, terminals and insulators, then the rectifier assembly and stator terminal insulator.

Assembly

1. Press bearing onto slip ring end of rotor shaft, putting pressure on bearing inner race. Heat slip rings, then carefully press slip rings onto rotor shaft and solder field leads to slip rings.
2. Press bearing into drive end housing, putting pressure on bearing outer race.
3. Press drive end housing and bearing onto rotor shaft, putting pressure on bearing inner race.
4. Install stator insulator and rectifier insulators. Place rectifier assemblies into housing and install mounting screws and terminals, ensuring rectifiers are insulat-

LEECE-NEVILLE ALTERNATORS

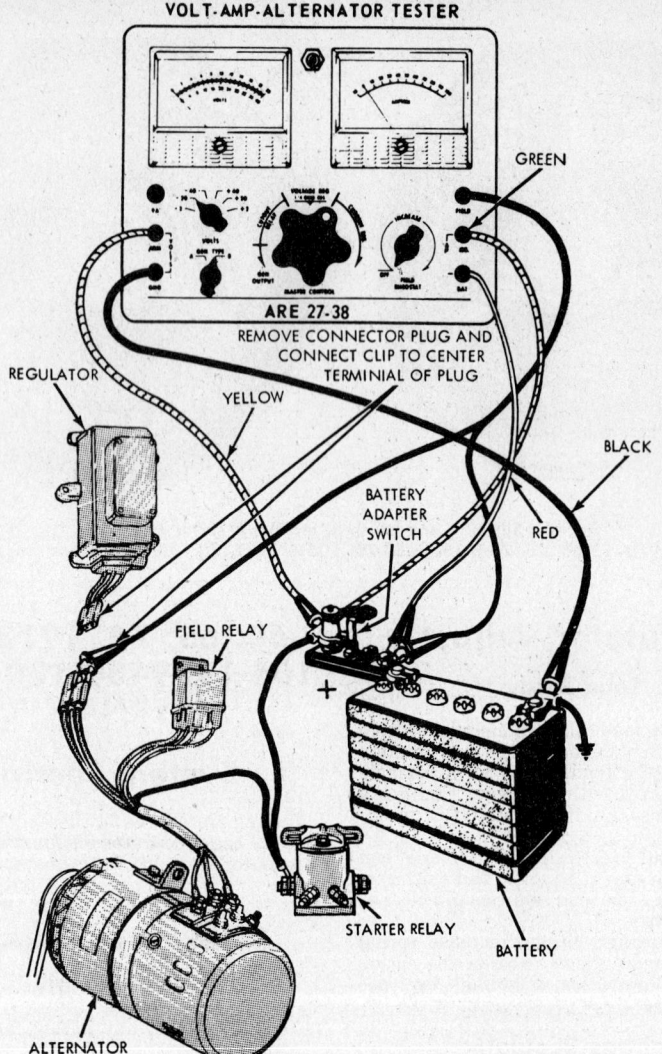

Fig. L5 Alternator output test, 1970-72 105 amp alternator

ed from end frame and wires are under tabs extending from heat sinks therefore preventing interference with rotor, Fig. L4.
5. Install stator and align through bolt holes with end housing. Place stator terminals over rectifier terminals and install nuts, Fig. L4.
6. Place brush end housing and stator assembly over rotor and install and tighten through bolts.
7. Install brush holder with "O" ring between holder and frame, place brushes and springs into holder with extruded portion of brush connectors against terminal screw shoulders. Hold brush connectors in position and install terminal insulator.
8. Install spacer, shaft key, fan, puller and nut.

1970-72 105 AMP. ALTERNATOR

In Vehicle Tests

Alternator Output Test

When the alternator output test is conducted off the car, a test bench must be used. Follow the procedure given by the test bench equipment manufacturer.

NOTE: When the alternator is removed from the vehicle for this purpose, always disconnect the battery ground cable as the alternator output connector is connected to the battery at all times.

Test Procedure

1. Make the connections and tester knob adjustments, Fig. L5. (Output test). Be sure that the field rheostat knob is at the OFF position at the start of this test.
2. Close the battery adapter switch. Start the engine, then open the battery adapter switch.
3. Increase the engine speed to approximately 2000 rpm (use a tachometer following the manufacturers instructions). Turn off all lights and electrical accessories.
4. Turn the field rheostat clockwise until 15 volts is indicated on the voltmeter upper scale. Turn the master control clockwise until the voltmeter indicates between 11 and 12 volts. Holding the master control in this position, turn the field rheostat clockwise to its maximum rotation. Turn the master control counter clockwise until the voltmeter indicates 15 volts. Observe the ammeter reading. Add 2 amperes to this reading to obtain alternator output. If rated output cannot be obtained, increase the engine speed to 2900 rpm and repeat this step.
5. Return the field rheostat knob to OFF, release the master control knob, and stop the engine. Disconnect the test equipment, if no further tests are to be made.

If the alternator output is not O.K., it will be necessary to remove the alternator from the vehicle and perform the necessary bench tests to locate the defect.

An output of approximately 2 to 5 amperes below specification usually indicates an open alternator diode. An output of approximately 10 to 14 amperes below specification usually indicates a shorted alternator diode. An alternator with a shorted diode will usually whine, which will be most noticeable at idle speeds.

Bench Tests

Field Open or Short Circuit Test

Make the connections, Fig. L6. The current draw, as indicated by the ammeter, should be to specification as listed in truck chapters. If there is little or no current flow, the field or brushes current flow considerably higher than that specified above indicates shorted or grounded field turns or brush leads touching. If the test shows that the field is shorted or open, determine if the field brush assembly or slip rings are at fault.

If the alternator has output at low rpm and no output at high rpm, centrifugal force may be causing the rotor windings to short to ground. Put the alternator on a test stand and repeat the preceding test. Run the alternator at high speed druing the test. If the test shows that the field is shorted or open and the field brush assembly or slip rings are not at fault, the entire rotor must be replaced.

Diode Test

Disassemble the alternator and disconnect the diode leads from the collector plates. With the ohmmeter multiply-by knob set at 10, connect one probe to the diode lead and the other probe to the diode body. Note reading and reverse the probes. All diodes should show a reading of approximately 60 ohms in one direction and an infinite reading in the other direction.

Open Or Grounded Stator Coil Tests

These tests are made to determine if the stator coil is operating properly. Disassemble the stator from the alternator and rectifier assembly.

Open Stator Test

Set ohmmeter multiply-by knob to 1. Connect the ohmmeter probes between each pair of stator leads. If the ohmmeter does not show equal readings between each pair of stator leads, the stator is open and must be replaced.

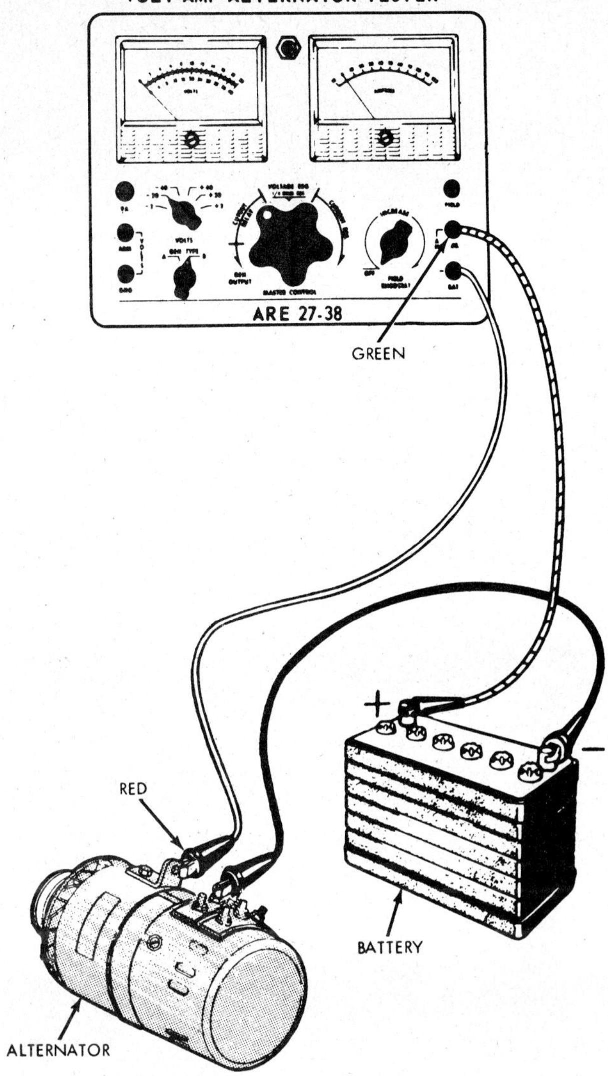

LEECE-NEVILLE ALTERNATORS

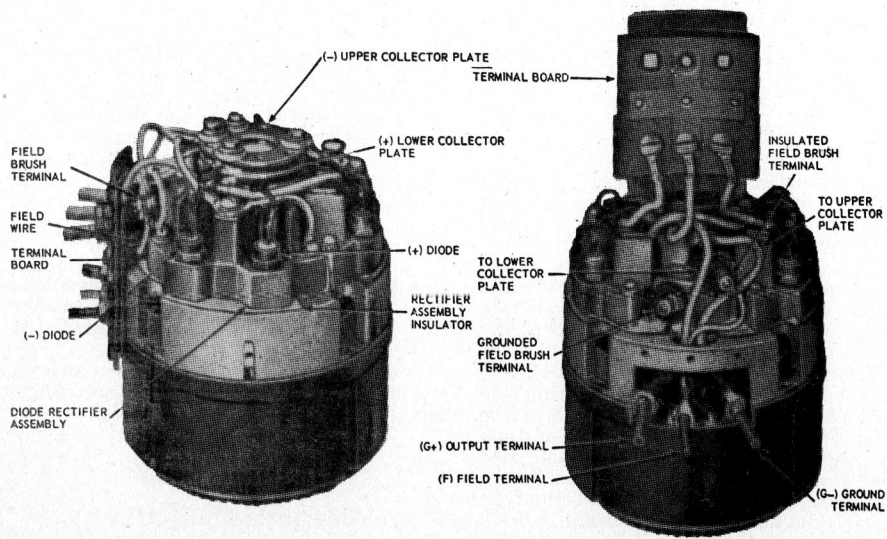

Fig. L6 Field open or short circuit test, 1970–72 105 amp. alternator

Fig. L8 Collector plates & lead assembly, 1970–72 105 amp. alternator

Grounded Stator Test

Connect the ohmmeter probes to one of the stator leads and to the stator laminated core. Be sure that the probe makes a good electrical connection with the stator core. The metal should show an infinite reading (no meter movement). If the meter does not indicate an infinite reading (needle moves), the stator winding is shorted to the core and must be replaced. Repeat this test for each of the stator leads.

Alternator Repairs

Disassembly

1. Remove alternator mounting brackets, pulley, fan, woodruff key and spacer from rotor shaft. Remove dust shields.
2. Remove screws securing stator and terminal board leads to rectifier assemblies, Fig. L7. Label leads for identification during assembly.
3. Remove screws securing terminal board to brush end housing, nut retaining field lead to brush holder, brush holders, springs and brushes from housing.
4. Remove through bolts and separate drive end housing and rotor from the stator and brush end housing, then remove stator.
5. Remove screws securing drive end bearing retainer to end housing, then rotor from drive end housing.
6. Press front bearing off rotor shaft and slide bearing retainer and spacer from shaft.
7. Unsolder field lead from rear slip ring and press slip ring off shaft. Repeat for forward slip ring.
8. Remove insulating washer and snap ring from rotor shaft and press rear bearing off shaft.
9. Remove screws, washers and insulators securing circular copper collector plates to brush end housing, then terminal board from brush end housing.

NOTE: Screws also secure diode leads and terminal board output leads. Label leads for identification during assembly.

10. Remove screws from each rectifier assembly, rectifiers, insulators and stator winding insulators from brush end housing.
11. Disassemble terminal board and wire assembly if damaged.

Assembly

1. If stator is replaced, transfer locating plate to new stator.
2. Assemble terminal board wires, if disassembled, and place stator winding insulators into brush end housing, then install insulators and rectifiers onto brush end housing.
3. Place terminal board and wiring, circular collector plates, insulators and washers on brush end housing and install retaining screws, Fig. L8.

NOTE: Screws also retain diode leads and terminal output leads. The "G" lead and positive diode leads connect to inner collector plate.

4. Press rear bearing onto rotor shaft, putting pressure on bearing inner race. Install snap ring, ensuring field leads are in the recess of rotor shaft.

131

Leece-Neville Alternators

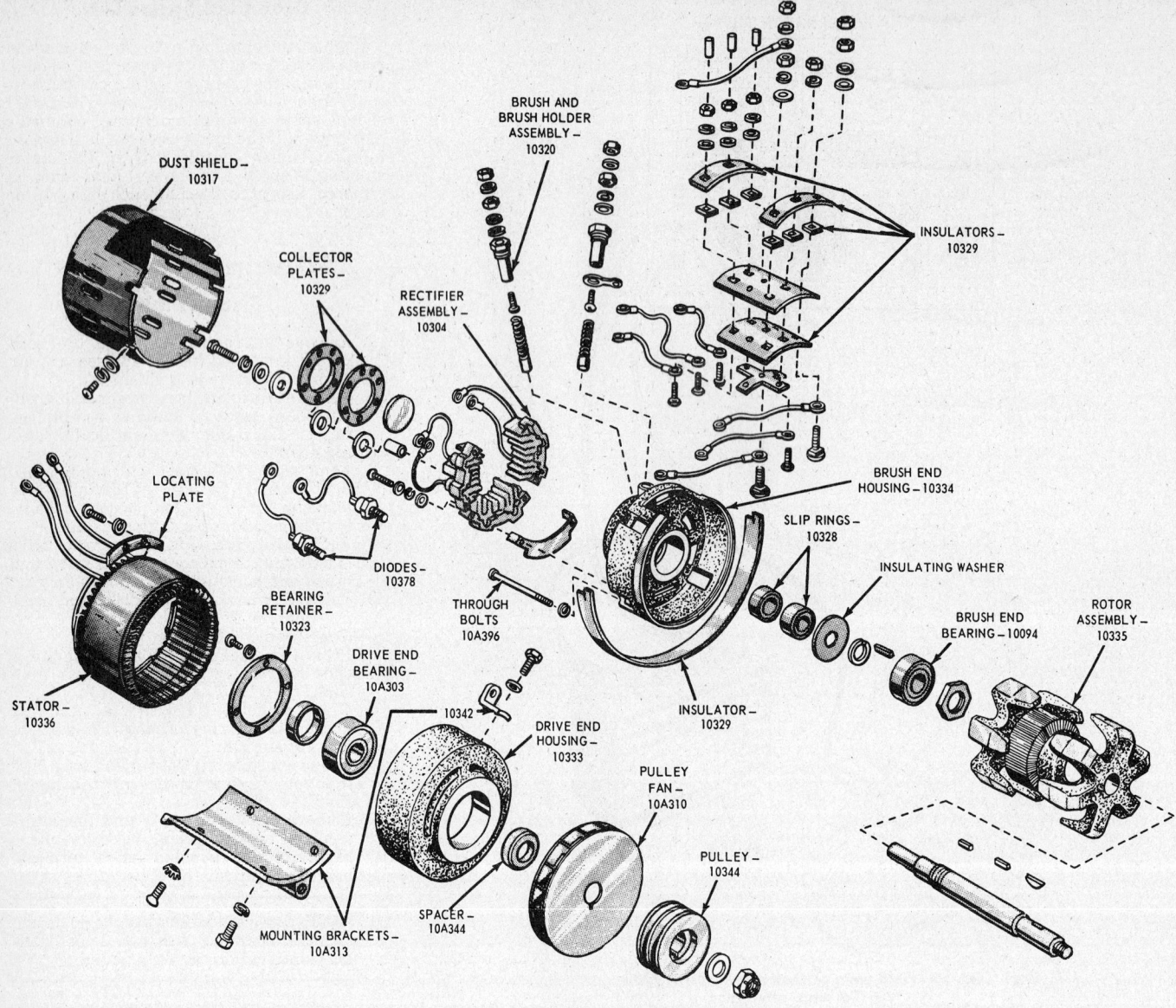

Fig. L7 1970-72 105 amp. alternator disassembled

5. Place insulating washer on rotor shaft and press forward slip ring onto shaft. Solder field lead to forward slip ring, then press rear slip ring onto shaft and solder field lead to rear slip ring.
6. Place bearing into drive end housing and install bearing retainer.
7. Place bearing spacer on the rotor shaft drive end. Press drive end housing and bearing onto rotor shaft drive end, applying pressure on bearing inner race.
8. Place stator on brush end housing, followed by the rotor and drive end housing on stator and brush end housing assembly. Install the through bolts.
9. Install brushes, springs and brush holder into brush end housing and connect field wire to brush holder terminal. Install terminal board to brush end housing screws, ensuring "GT", "F" and "G" terminal lugs are clear of stator windings and frame.
10. Position terminal board and stator leads to the respective rectifiers and install retaining screws.
11. Install dust shield, spacer, Woodruff key, fan, pulley, washer and nut.
12. Install alternator mounting brackets.

SERIES SI

The alternator shown in Fig. L9 is a self-rectifying system integral type unit, having a built-in solid state regulator and interconnecting wiring, Figs. L10, L11 and L12. The major parts consist of the rotor, stator, drive end and slip ring end housings, and the regulator assembly. The stator is composed of a large number of windings assembled on the inside of a laminated core attached to the alternator frame. As the rotor turns, two brushes mounted behind the slip ring end housings, and the regulator assembly. The stator is composed of a large number of windings assembled on the inside of a laminated core attached to the alternator frame. As the rotor turns, two brushes mounted behind the slip ring end housing, carry current through the slip rings to the field coil mounted on the rotor shaft and to the regulator. The alternating current produced is rectified by six silicon rectifier elements mounted on the slip ring end housing which is internally connected to the positive and negative terminal screws of the regulator. Six external terminals (G+, lamp, G− and three A.C. terminals), are provided for connections to the system of the vehicle.

The three A.C. terminals are internally connected to the rectifier heat sinks which in turn are connected to the stator winding transformers, mobile power units and load relay rectifiers. These terminals can also be used to test the silicon rectifiers when the alternator is installed on the vehicle.

One slip ring brush is internally connected to the "F" terminal on the stator and the terminal of the other brush is grounded.

Bench Test

Alternator Output Test

1. Strap unit in test stand and make connec-

LEECE-NEVILLE ALTERNATORS

Fig. L9 SI type Leece-Neville alternator

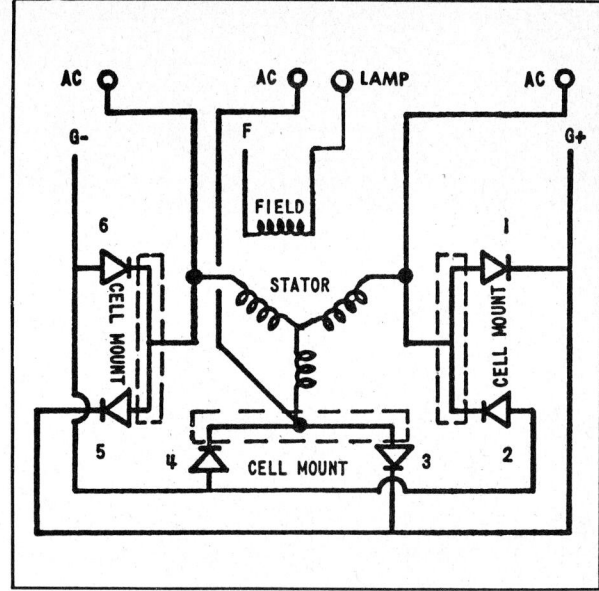

Fig. L10 Internal wiring diagram

tions as shown in Fig. L13.

NOTE: Leave carbon pile in "OFF" position or disconnected. Also use a fully charged battery.

2. Connect carbon pile and operate alternator to 2500 rpm. Adjust carbon pile to obtain maximum current output.
3. If ampere reading is within 10% of rated 105 amp system, the charging system is not defective.
4. If reading is not within 10% proceed as follows: Operate alternator at 2000 rpm and adjust carbon pile to place 10 amp load on system.
5. Adjust voltage regulator setting until voltmeter reads 13.9 to 14.1 volts.

NOTE: A hole is provided in the end cover to adjust the regulator. Turn clockwise to increase voltage or counterclockwise to decrease.

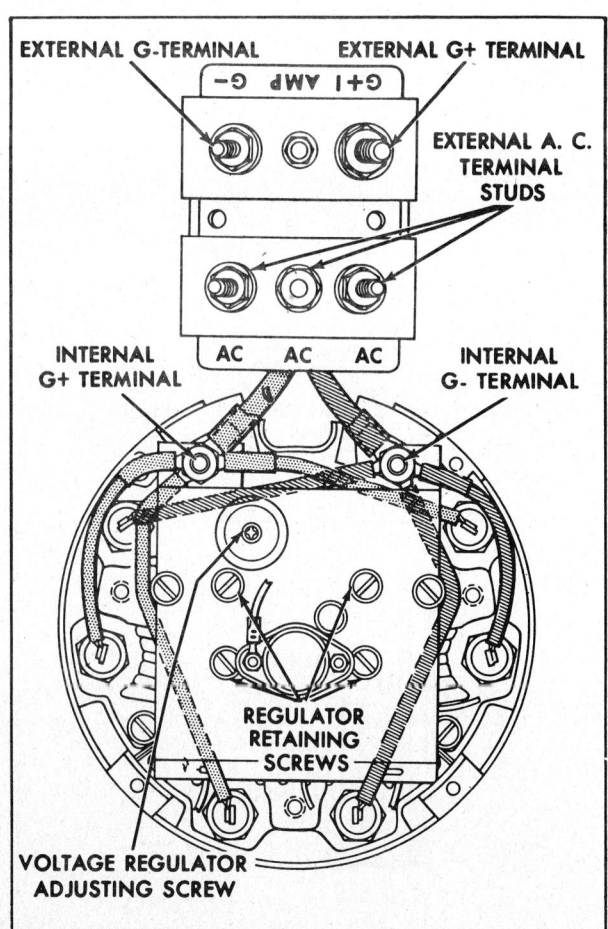

Fig. L11 Terminals & wiring connections

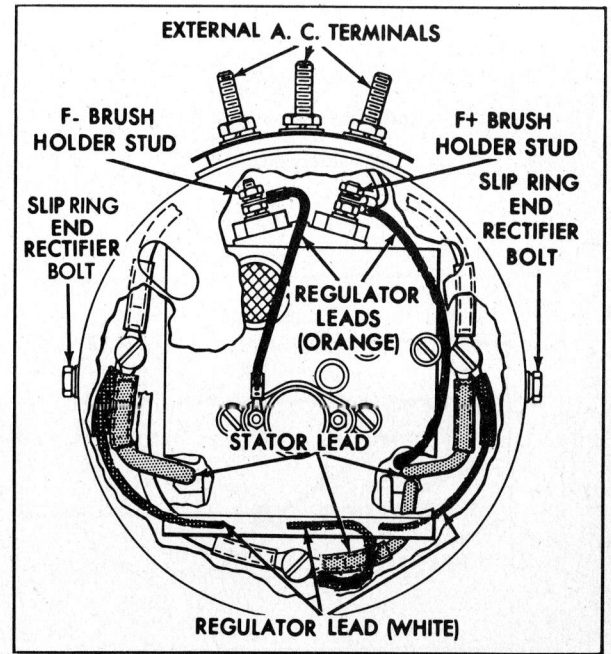

Fig. L12 Regulator terminals & wiring

133

LEECE-NEVILLE ALTERNATORS

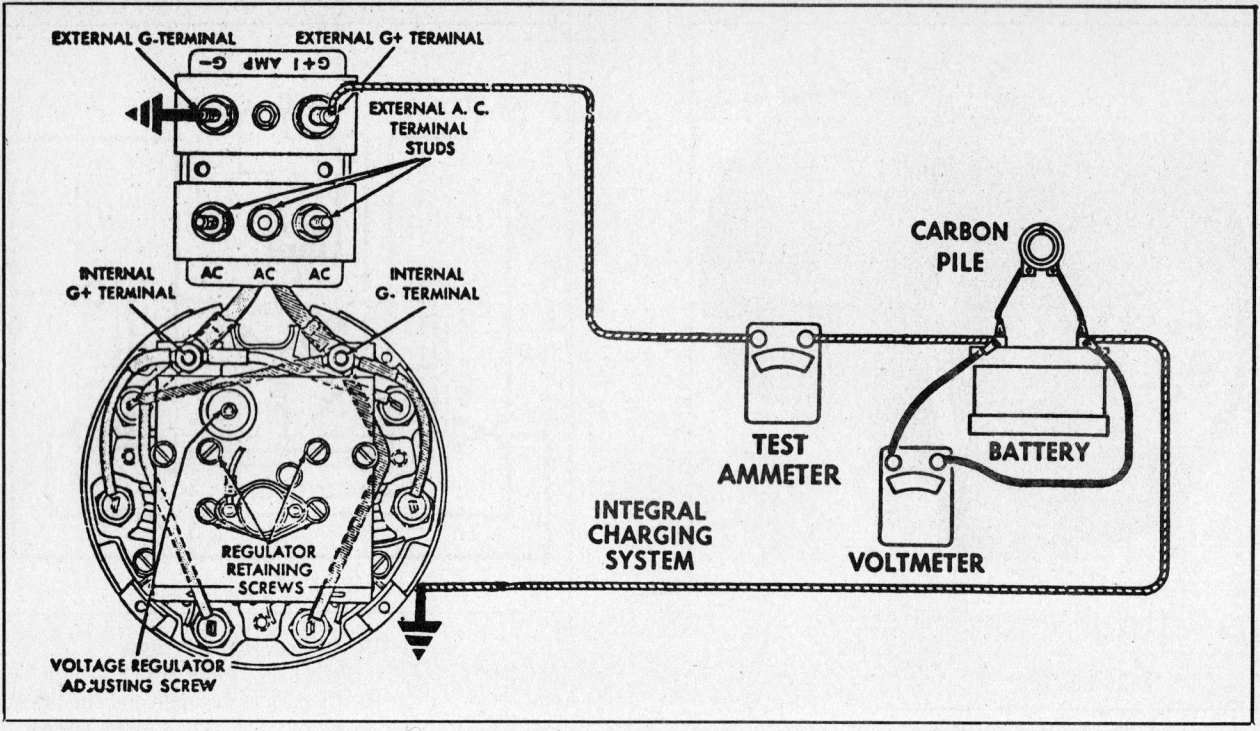

Fig. L13 Output test connections

6. Repeat steps 1 and 2 to check for normal operation. If unit remains abnormal, make Regulator Voltage Test, otherwise install unit in vehicle and make final adjustment.
7. Install voltmeter at battery. Run engine at 800 rpm. Voltmeter should read 13.5 to 14.1. Adjust regulator if necessary.

Regulator Voltage Test

This test can be made on or off the vehicle and will determine whether the alternator or regulator is at fault when there is low output.
1. Make connections as shown in Fig. L13.
2. Loosen bolts and remove slip ring end rectifier cover.
3. Disconnect field lead from (F−) brush holder stud.
4. Connect external ground jumper wire to (F−) brush holder stud.

NOTE: Unit is now full-fielded and will have no voltage control. Do not exceed 1700 alternator rpm or 500-600 engine rpm.

5. Install suitable ammeter in series at G+ external terminal and voltmeter across battery terminals.

NOTE: Remove all external load from battery by turning off carbon pile.

6. Connect battery and run at 1500 alternator rpm. If there is no positive ammeter reading and battery voltage does not show rise proceed to step 7.
7. Connect a jumper from G+ terminal to F+ brush holder after removing existing wires.

NOTE: Leave ground jumper connected.

8. Repeat steps 5 and 6. If voltage increases, replace regulator. If it does not increase, replace alternator.

Rectifier Test

Make note of wiring to each rectifier. With wiring disconnected at terminals, make individual rectifier test as shown in Fig. L14. The results are as follows.
1. If the bulb lights in only one direction, the rectifier is good.
2. If bulb lights in both directions, rectifier is shorted.

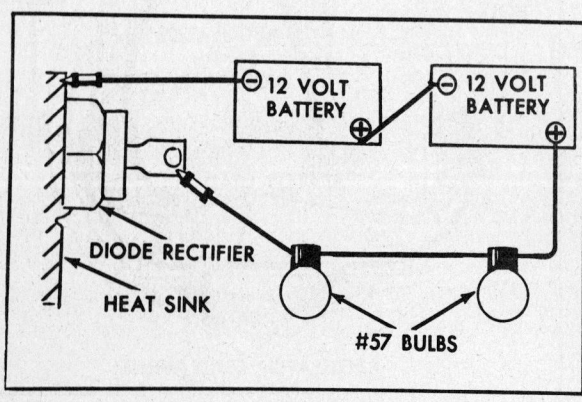

Fig. L14 Rectifier test

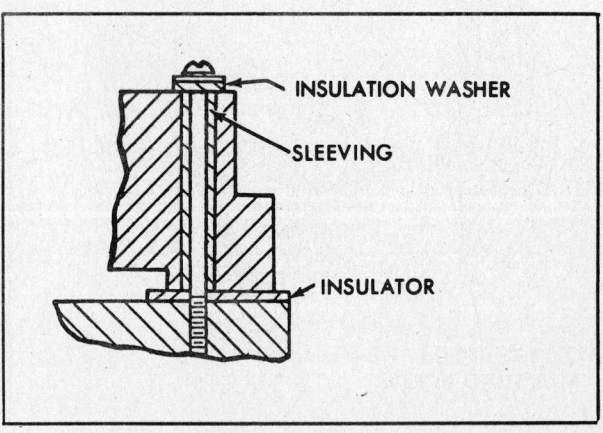

Fig. L15 Rectifier mount insulation

LEECE-NEVILLE ALTERNATORS

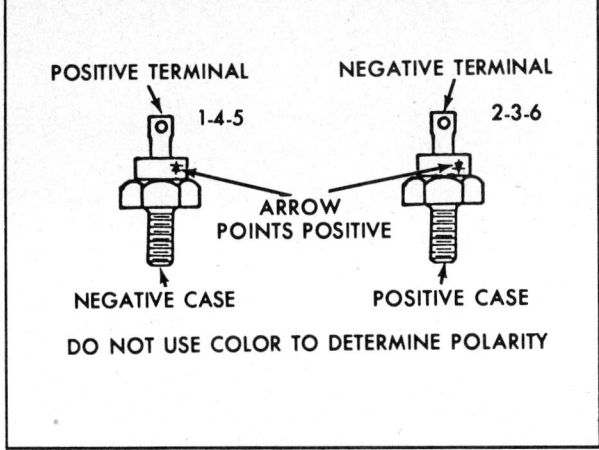

Fig. L16 Rectifier markings

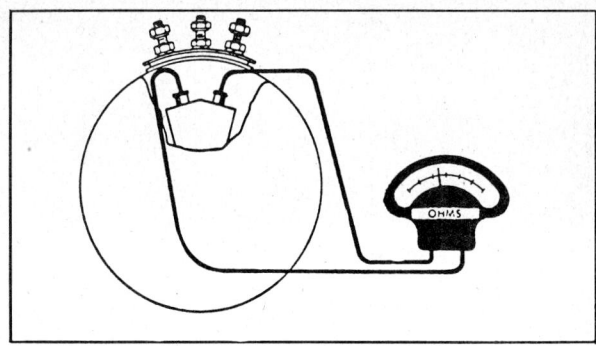

Fig. L18 Rotor coil resistance test

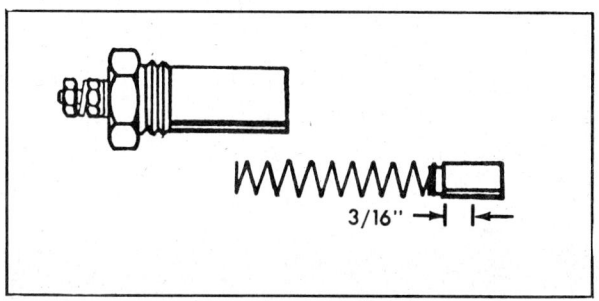

Fig. L19 Minimum serviceable brush length

3. If bulb does not light in either direction, rectifier is open.

Rectifier Mount Ground Test

1. With a 110 volt test lamp, check each of the three cell mounts for grounds to the alternator frame. If a ground is present between mount and frame check the insulator under the mount and the insulation of the attaching screws, Figs. L15 and L16.

Stator Ground Test

Remove external grounding jumper if used. Check each stator phase for grounds to the frame, Fig. L17. A 110 volt test lamp is used. There should be no circuit present.

Stator Winding Continuity Test

With an ohmmeter or test lamp, check the continuity of each of the three stator phases, Fig. L17. Each phase should show a closed circuit or indicate a low resistance, the test lamp should light.

Stator Phase Test

With the alternator on test block, connect a 12 volt battery to the field circuit and run the alternator at 800 rpm. Connect an AC voltmeter or test lamp of the same voltage as the system, across the three A.C. terminals in turn. Voltage or lamp brilliancy should be the same across phases 1-2, 2-3, 1-3. A pronounced difference indicates shorted or grounded stator windings.

Rotor Coil Test

1. Remove bolts attaching cover to slip ring end frame and remove cover.
2. Referring to Fig. L18, remove nuts, washers and leads from F+ and F− brush terminals. Remove brush holders and brushes with springs.
3. To check for ground, place one ohmmeter or test lamp prod on case and the other test lead through brush holder opening on slip ring. If ohmmeter reads high or test lamp lights, rotor coil is open.
4. To check for an open circuit, insert ohmmeter prods into brush holder openings and make direct contact with each of the two slip rings. If ohmmeter reading is very low or test lamp does not light, rotor coil circuit is open.
5. Test rotor coil for short by setting ohmmeter on direct scale and place prods on each slip ring. Ohmmeter reading should be from 4.9 to 5.3 ohms. If lower than 4.9 ohms, coil is shorted or has a loose or poor solder connection.

NOTE: If brush springs were collapsed, the rotor may have shorted turns within the coil.

Slip Ring Brushes

Check the brushes and springs. If cracked,

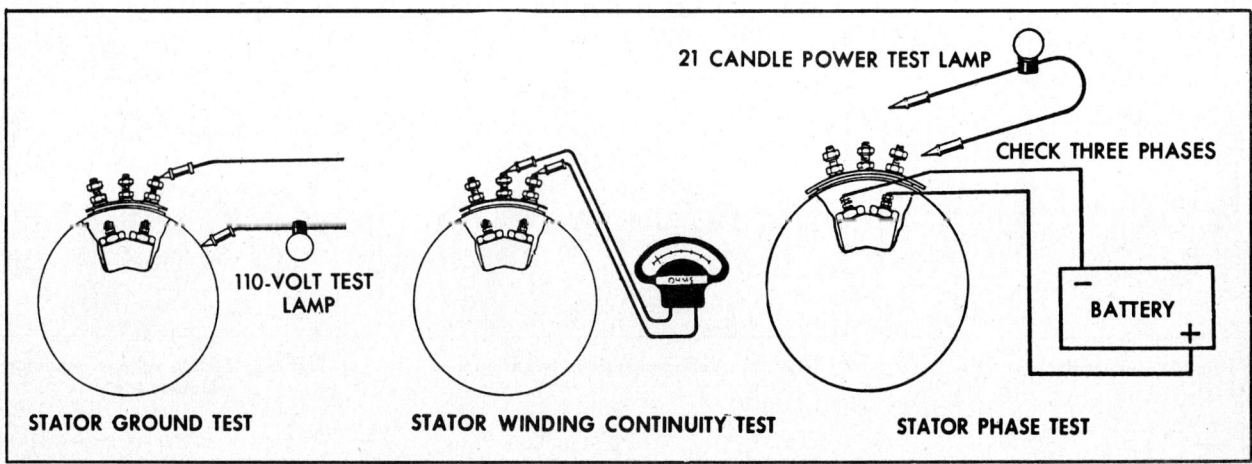

Fig. L17 Stator checks

135

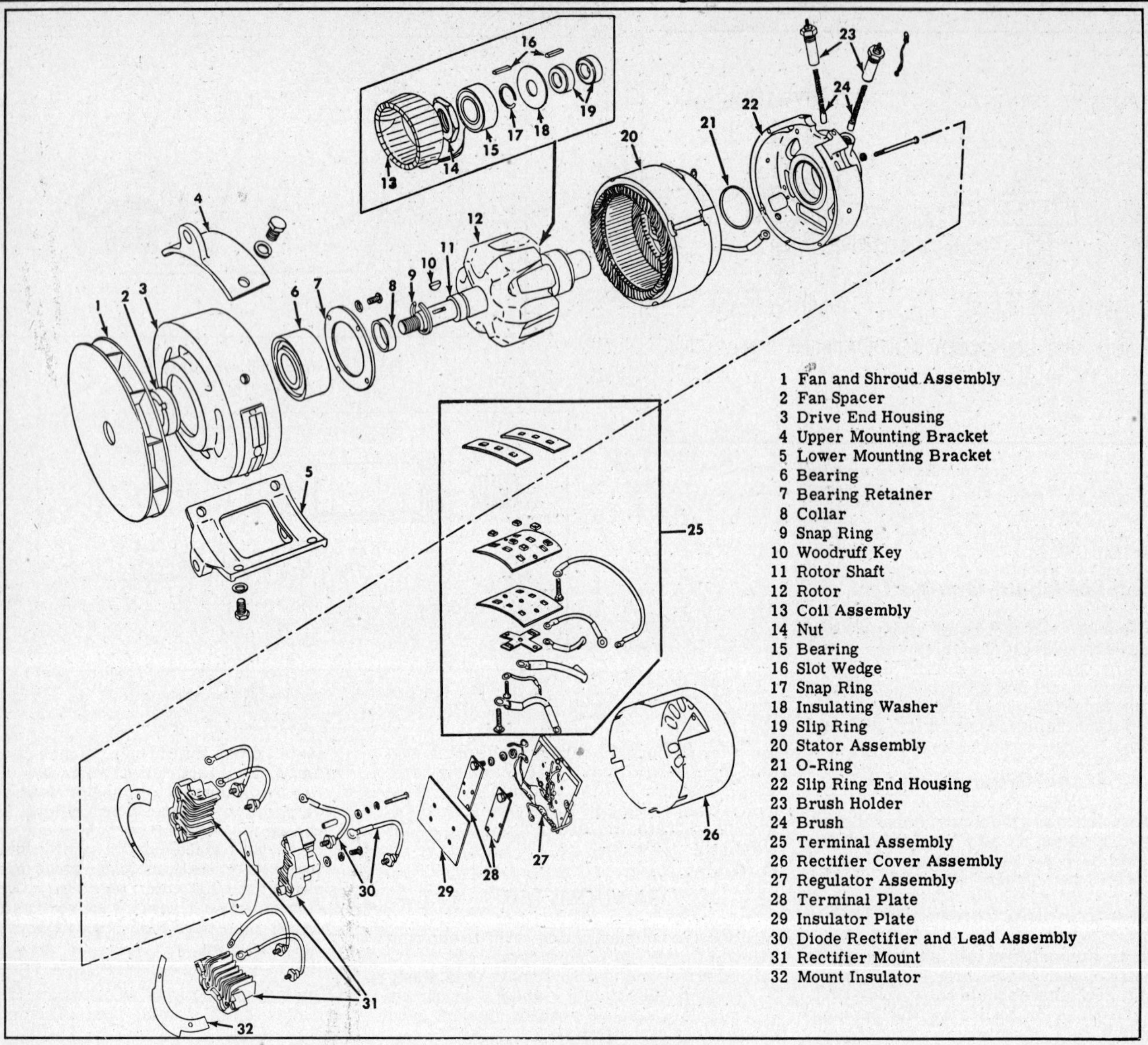

LEECE-NEVILLE ALTERNATORS

1 Fan and Shroud Assembly
2 Fan Spacer
3 Drive End Housing
4 Upper Mounting Bracket
5 Lower Mounting Bracket
6 Bearing
7 Bearing Retainer
8 Collar
9 Snap Ring
10 Woodruff Key
11 Rotor Shaft
12 Rotor
13 Coil Assembly
14 Nut
15 Bearing
16 Slot Wedge
17 Snap Ring
18 Insulating Washer
19 Slip Ring
20 Stator Assembly
21 O-Ring
22 Slip Ring End Housing
23 Brush Holder
24 Brush
25 Terminal Assembly
26 Rectifier Cover Assembly
27 Regulator Assembly
28 Terminal Plate
29 Insulator Plate
30 Diode Rectifier and Lead Assembly
31 Rectifier Mount
32 Mount Insulator

Fig. L20   Type SI alternator exploded

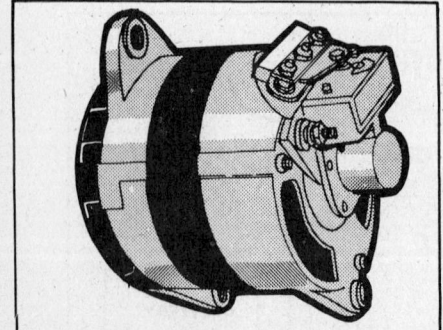

Fig. L21   Alternator assembly

Fig. L22   Voltage regulator adjustment

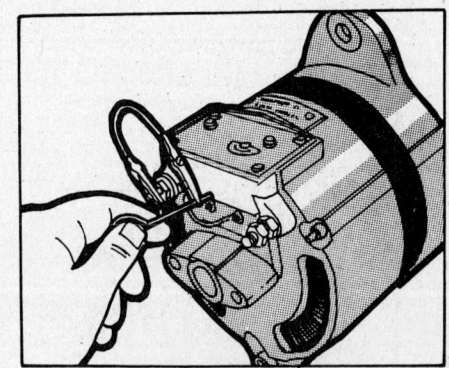

Fig. L23   Testing voltage regulator & diode trio

LEECE-NEVILLE ALTERNATORS

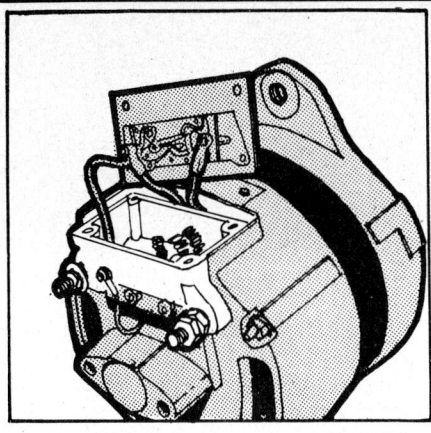

Fig. L24 Removing brush & spring assemblies

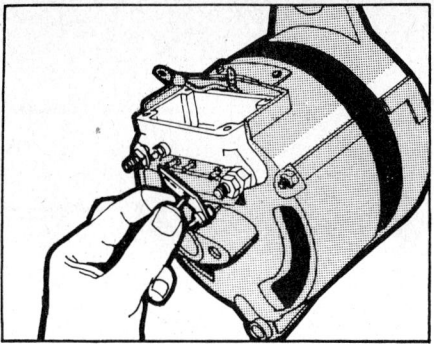

Fig. L25 Removing diode trio

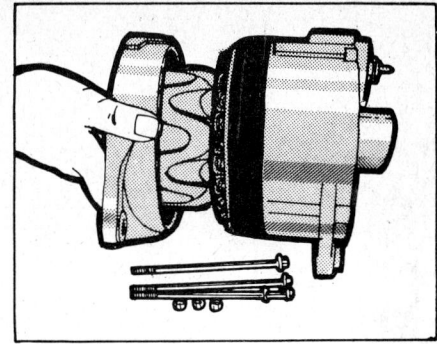

Fig. L26 Separating drive end housing from stator

broken or burned, they should be replaced. Brushes worn to less than 3/16" must be repaced, Fig. L19.

Alternator Disassembly

Refer to Fig. L20 for exploded view of alternator.
1. Remove mounting brackets.
2. Place a strap wrench or equivalent around alternator drive pulley and remove shaft nut. Using a puller, remove pulley from rotor shaft. Remove fan, shaft key and fan spacer.
3. Remove slip ring end cover. Remove screws in terminal block mounting plate. Raise terminal block to clear brush holders.
4. Make note of wiring on brush holders and remove brush holders and brushes.
5. Make note of wiring on heat sinks and disconnect A.C. leads.
6. With a socket, take out four screws holding housings and stator and pull off the slip ring end housing . If necessary tap around the housing with a rawhide mallet to free the pilot surfaces. Remove the composition dust shield under the circular bus bars by removing one screw and loosening the two remaining screws to reveal the rotor shaft.
7. Remove stator from drive end housing and rotor. It may be necessary to use a rawhide mallet.
8. Press drive end housing from shaft.
9. Remove bearing retainer screws and bearing retainer from drive end housing. Tap or press out drive end bearing.

NOTE: If the rotor bearings, slip rings and coil are in good condition, further disassembly is unnecessary.

Rotor Disassembly

1. Unsolder both field coil leads from slip rings and using a small puller, carefully pull off the rings.
2. Take of the insulation washer and snap ring in front of the bearing and pull bearing from shaft. Save wedge removed from the lead slot under bearing and remove nut.
3. Loosen field coil lead clip and free the coil lead.
4. Holding rotor in vise, tap off slip ring end rotor half. Remove square key.
5. Remove rotor coil.
6. Using a press push shaft out of hub and remaining rotor half.
7. Remove snap ring and square key.

NOTE: Keep the rotor halves together in marked pairs, to eliminate rebalancing of the assembled rotor.

SERIES 2300JB, 2500JB, 2600JB, 2601JB & 2700JB

These alternators are 14 volt self load limiting units incorporating a fully adjustable integral solid state voltage regulator Fig. L21. Six silicon diodes, mounted in heat sinks, convert alternating current from the delta wound stator into direct current. A capacitor, connected between the heat sinks, assists in supressing transient voltage spikes which may cause diode damage and failure. The brushes and voltage regulator, installed in a waterproof housing, may be replaced or inspected without disassembling the unit. An external relay terminal is provided for charge light relays or other accessories which may require current from such a source. These units incorporate ungrounded output terminals and may be utilized on either positive or negative ground systems.

Trouble Shooting

To determine if problem lies in alternator or regulator, connect a voltmeter across battery and note reading. Start engine, if voltmeter reading rises excessively, the charging system may be defective or require adjustment. With engine operating at approximately 1000 RPM, remove voltage regulator cap and attempt to bring voltage within the 13.6 to 14.2 volt range by turning the adjusting screw, Fig. L22. If voltage cannot be lowered in this manner, the regulator is probably defective and should be replaced.

If alternator voltage cannot be raised, either alternator, regulator or diode trio are defective. Connect one jumper wire lead to alternator negative output terminal and other lead to a piece of stiff wire approximately 1½ inches long Fig. L23. Insert stiff piece of wire into small hole in end of brush holder so it firmly contacts the outer brush holder so it firmly contacts the outer brush terminal. Operate engine at fast idle, if voltmeter reading now rises, the alternator is not at fault and diode trio should be checked as outlined under Bench Test. If diode trio checks out, the regulator should be replaced.

To check alternator output across each phase, construct a test light from a two filament sealed beam unit connected in such a manner that filaments are in parallel. If test lamp is noticeably dimmer on one or two

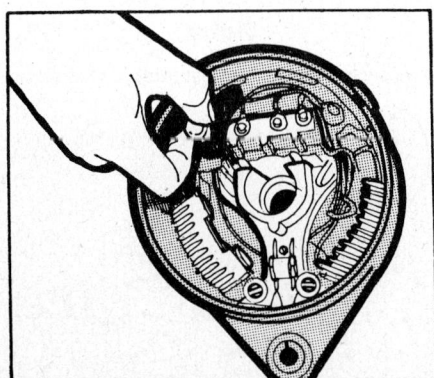

Fig. L27 Removing capacitor

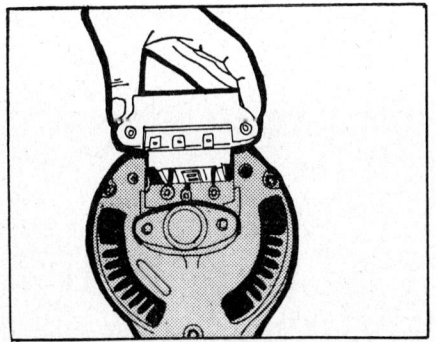

Fig. L28 Removing terminal stud insulating bushings

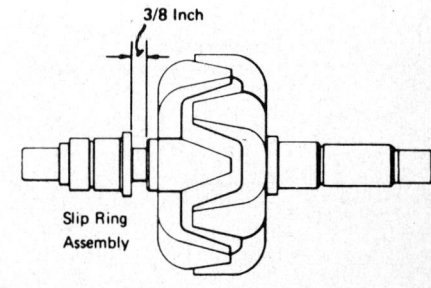

Fig. L29 Slip ring installation

LEECE-NEVILLE ALTERNATORS

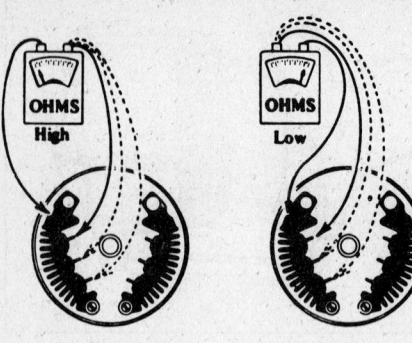

Fig. L30 Positive heat sink tests   Fig. L31 Negative heat sink tests

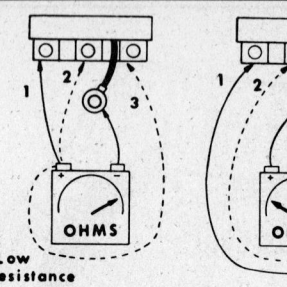

Fig. L32 Diode trio tests

phases, a defective diode trio, stator or power diode is indicated.

Alternator Disassembly

1. Remove nut, pulley and fan.

   NOTE: Use a suitable puller to remove pulley to avoid damaging shaft and threads.

2. Remove four regulator attaching screws, then lift regulator and disconnect red and black leads.
3. Disconnect lead from diode trio to terminal on regulator housing. Loosen inner nut, which will allow blue regulator lead to be withdrawn from under terminal screw, then remove regulator.
4. Remove brush and spring assemblies from housing, Fig. L24.
5. Remove three attaching nuts and lift diode trio from AC terminal studs, Fig. L25.
6. Remove three through bolts, then separate rotor and drive end housing from stator and slip ring end housing, Fig. L26.

   NOTE: Ensure stator remains attached to slip ring end housing when separating to avoid damaging stator leads.

7. Remove three nuts attaching stator leads to terminals and remove stator.
8. Remove positive and negative output terminals, note location of red and black regulator leads on heat sinks.
9. Remove hex head attaching screws, then remove capacitor connected between heat sinks, Fig. L27.
10. Remove regulator housing, note location of gasket which seals brush compartment.
11. Remove terminal stud insulating bushings from housing, Fig. L28.
12. Remove two screws, lock washers, guard washers and insulating washers which retain lower portion of heat sinks.
13. Remove heat sinks, note location of insulating washers and bushings.
14. Pry metal dust cover from housing.

Slip Ring, Replace

1. Unsolder slip ring leads and position them clear of rotor coil eyelets.
2. Using a suitable puller, remove slip ring assembly from rotor shaft.
3. Clean rotor shaft, then apply a small amount of "Loctite Grade A" on shaft in area where slip rings are to be installed.
4. Position slip rings on shaft so that leads are aligned with rotor coil eyelets.
5. Carefully press slip ring onto shaft until there is a clearance of ⅜ inch between rotor and inner edge of slip ring, Fig. L29

Bench Test

Heat Sink

To test positive heat sink, connect ohmmeter positive lead to heat sink and contact each of the three diode terminals with negative lead, Fig. L30. A high ohmmeter reading should be obtained, if any of the three diodes shows low resistance, the diode is shorted. Reverse ohmmeter leads and repeat test. A low ohmmeter reading should be obtained, if any of the three diodes show high resistance, the diode is open.

To test negative heat sink, connect ohmmeter negative lead to heat sink and contact each of the three diode terminals with positive lead, Fig. L31. If a resistance is obtained, the diode is shorted. Reverse ohmmeter leads and repeat test. If a high resistance is obtained, the diode is open.

NOTE: If a shorted or open diode is detected, the entire heat sink assembly should be replaced.

Diode Trio

Connect ohmmeter negative lead to diode trio output lead and positive lead to each of three copper terminal pads, Fig. L32. A low ohmmeter reading should be obtained. Reverse ohmmeter leads and repeat test. A high ohmmeter reading should be obtained. Any diode trio which does not conform to the above test should be replaced.

Capacitor

Connect ohmmeter between capacitor terminals. A low reading would indicate a shorted or leaking capacitor, Fig. L33.

Rotor

Connect one ohmmeter lead to rotor shaft and other lead to slip ring, Fig. L34. If ohmmeter reading is other than infinite, the rotor coil is grounded and the rotor should be replaced.

Connect ohmmeter between two slip rings and note reading, Fig. L35. Reading should be 4.4-4.8 ohms for 2300JB models manufactured prior to date code 7406, 2.5-2.8 ohms for 2300JB, 2601JB models and 1.9-2.3 ohms for 2700JB models. If resistance readings differ significantly from these figures, replace rotor.

NOTE: Before replacing rotor, ensure soldier joints at slip ring leads are in good condition.

Stator

Using a 115-220 volt test lamp, check stator

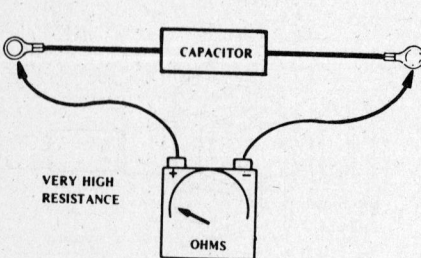

Fig. L33 Testing capacitor for short

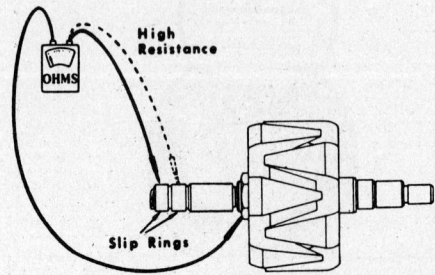

Fig. L34 Rotor coil ground test

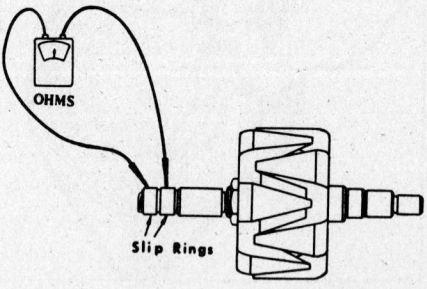

Fig. L35 Rotor coil resistance test

LEECE-NEVILLE ALTERNATORS

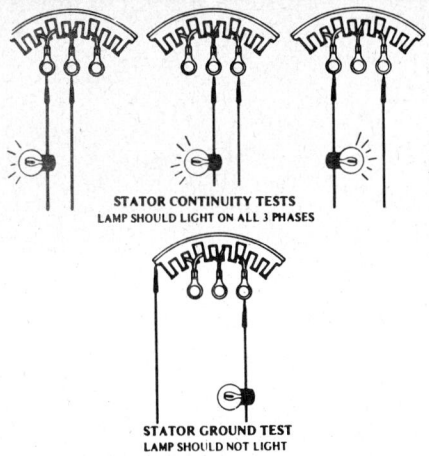

Fig. L36 Testing stator

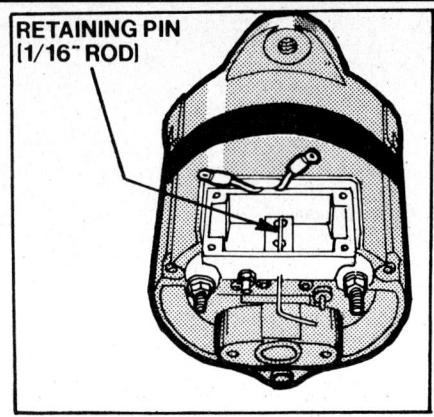

Fig. L37 Brush installation

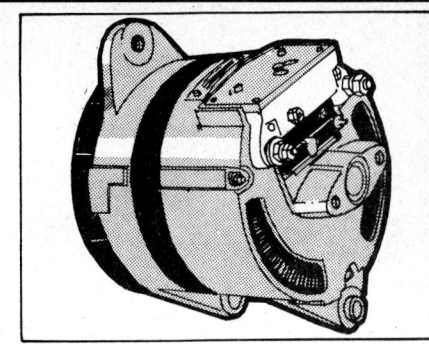

Fig. L38 Alternator assembly

for continuity between phases, Fig. L36. Test lamp should light on all three phases. To test stator for grounds, contact one stator lead against stator core and other lead to each of three stator leads, Fig. L36. Test lamp should not light. Stator that appear overheated or have charred insulation should be replaced regardless of test results.

Alternator Assemble

1. Install heat sinks on slip ring end housing, ensure upper and lower insulating washers are properly positioned. Install but do not tighten attaching screws, lock washers, guard washers and insulating washers.
2. Install terminal bolts and regulator lead wires.

NOTE: Red lead goes to positive heat sink and black lead to negative heat sink.

3. Install insulating bushings on each terminal bolt, then install regulator housing. Ensure red and black regulator leads are properly routed through cutaway section of end frame, then install and tighten terminal bolt nuts.
4. Tighten lower heat sink attaching screws, then install capacitor.

5. Install stator leads on terminals, then align stator on end frame and install two through bolts to hold stator position.
6. Press drive end housing and bearing onto rotor shaft.

NOTE: Use a sleeve around shaft and press on inner race to prevent damaging bearing.

7. Install rotor and drive end housing on stator and slip ring end housing, then install through bolts and torque to 50 to 60 in. lbs.
8. Apply a small amount of SRI 2 grease in housing, then carefully press metal dust cap into place.
9. Install diode trio.
10. Insert outer brush and spring assembly into housing, then compress brush spring. Insert a pin through rear of housing to hold brushes in compressed position, Fig. L37. Install remaining brush in same manner.
11. Connect red and black leads to regulator, then attach blue regulator lead to diode terminal. Position regulator on end frame housing and loosely install attaching screws, then remove brush retaining pins and tighten attaching screws.
12. Install diode trio lead and attaching nut.
13. Install spacer, key, fan, pulley and nut. Torque nut to 70-80 ft. lbs.

NOTE: The shaft end play designed into this unit will vary from .004-.012 inch.

Regulator Adjustment

With battery in fully charged condition and all accessories turned off, connect voltmeter across battery. Remove cap from adjusting screw, then start engine and operate at approximately 1000 RPM. Turn adjusting screw counter clockwise to lower charging voltage and clockwise to raise charging voltage, Fig. L22. The ideal voltage setting will be a value which maintains a fully charged without resulting in an excessive usuage of battery water. After adjusting replace adjusting screw cap.

NOTE: Do not force adjusting screw past its stop as damage may result.

Regulator, Replace

1. Remove four screws and carefully lift regulator from housing, Fig. L24.
2. Disconnect red and black lead from regulator noting their position to aid in assembly.
3. Remove lead from diode trio to regulator terminal. Loosen inner nut which will allow blue regulator lead to be withdrawn under head of terminal screw.
4. Remove regulator, then lift brush and spring assemblies from housing.

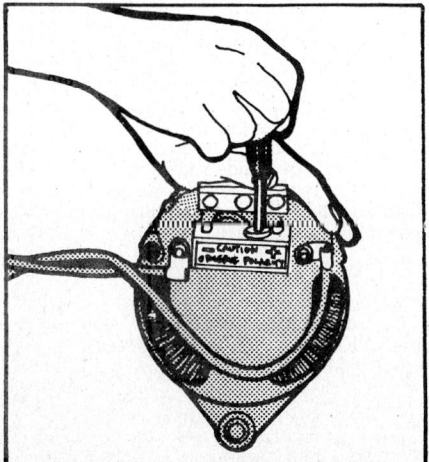

Fig. L39 Voltage regulator adjustment

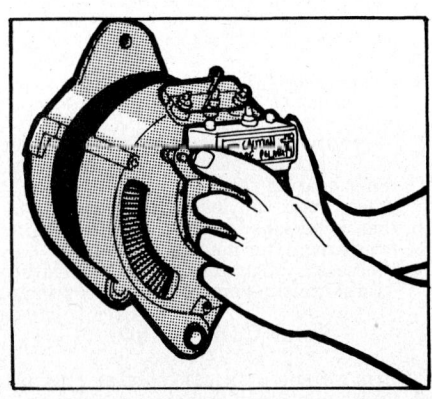

Fig. L40 Remove brush housing assembly

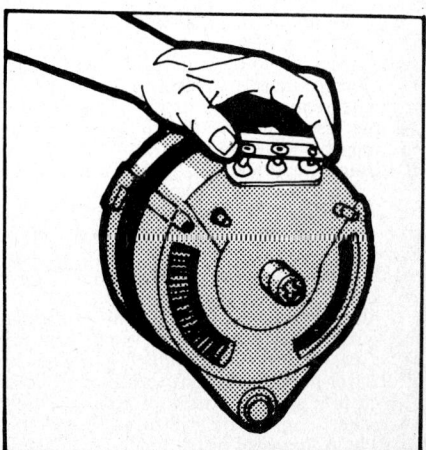

Fig. L41 Remove diode trio from AC terminal studs

LEECE-NEVILLE ALTERNATORS

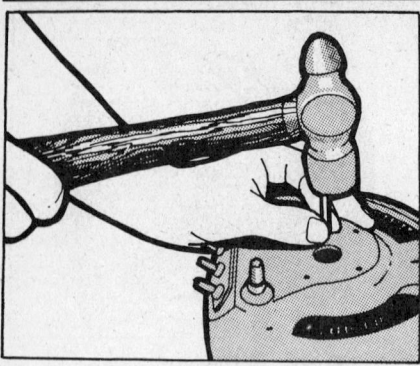

Fig. L42 Removing seal

5. Position brush and spring assembly in housing, then compress brush springs. Insert pin through rear of housing to hold brushes in compressed position. Fig. L37.
6. Connect red and black leads to regulator, then install blue regulator lead on diode terminal screw and tighten screw.
7. Position regulator on housing and loosely install attaching bolts.
8. Remove brush retaining pins, then tighten regulator attaching bolts.
9. Connect diode trio lead to regulator terminal, then install protective caps on terminal screws.

SERIES 3425JA, 4425JA & 4625JA

These alternators are self load limiting units incorporating a fully adjustable integral solid state voltage regulator, Fig. L38. Six silicon diodes, mounted in heat sinks, convert alternating current from delta would stator into direct current. A capacitor, connected between heat sinks, assist in suppressing transient voltage spikes which may cause diode damage and failure. The brushes and voltage regulator, installed in a waterproof housing, may be replaced or inspected without disassembling the unit. An external relay terminal is provided for chargelight relays on negative ground systems only. These units incorporate ungrounded output terminals and may be utilized on either positive or negative ground systems.

Trouble Shooting

To determine if problem lies in alternator or regulator, connect a voltmeter across battery and note reading. Start engine. If voltmeter reading rises excessively, the charging system may be defective or require adjustment. With engine operating at approximately 1000 RPM, remove voltage regulator cap and attempt to bring voltage within the 13.6 to 14.2 volt range by turning the adjusting screw, Fig. L39. If voltage cannot be lowered in this manner, the regulator is probably defective and should be replaced.

If alternator voltage cannot be raised, either alternator, regulator or diode trio are defective. Connect one jumper wire lead to alternator negative output terminal and other lead to a piece of stiff wire approximately 1½ inches long. Insert stiff piece of wire into small hole in end of brush holder so it firmly contacts the outer brush terminal. Operate engine at fast idle. If voltmeter reading now rises, the alternator is not at fault and diode trio should be checked as outlined under Bench Test. If diode trio checks out, the regulator should be replaced.

To check alternator output across each phase, construct a test light from a two filament sealed beam unit connected in such a manner that filaments are in parallel. If test lamp is noticeably dimmer on one or two phases, a defective diode trio, stator or power diode is indicated.

Alternator Disassembly

1. Remove nut, washer, pulley, fan, key and spacer.

NOTE: Use a suitable puller to remove pulley to prevent damage to shaft and threads.

2. Remove diode trio lead from top of regulator, then remove nuts from positive and negative output terminals.
3. Remove four regulator attaching screws, then carefully remove regulator and brush holder assembly, Fig. L40.
4. Remove three attaching nuts and lift diode trio from AC terminal studs, Fig. L41.
5. Remove through bolts, then separate rotor and drive end housing from stator and slip ring housing.

NOTE: Ensure stator remains attached to slip ring and housing when separating to avoid damaging stator leads.

6. Remove three nuts attaching stator leads to terminals, then remove stator.
7. Remove positive and negative output terminals.
8. Remove hex head attaching screws, then remove capacitor connected between heat sinks.
9. Remove two screws, lock washers, guard washers and bushings securing lower end of heat sinks, then remove heat sinks.
10. If slip ring end housing bearings are to be replaced, remove seal, Fig. L42, then using a suitable puller, remove bearing.
11. Press drive end housing bearings are to be replaced, remove four screws and bearing retainer, then press bearing and seal from housing.

Slip Ring Replace

1. Straighten slip ring tabs, then unsolder both connections.
2. Using a suitable puller, remove slip ring assembly.
3. Clean rotor shaft and apply a small amount of Loctite Grade A on shaft in area where slip rings are to be installed.
4. Position slip ring assembly on shaft aligning slot in slip ring with slot in shaft.
5. Carefully press slip ring assembly on shaft until the assembly is against the inner bearing race.
6. Solder rotor coil leads to slip ring tabs, then bend tabs to allow for clearance in brush-regulator housing.
7. If necessary, truse up slip rings in a lathe. Maximum slip ring run out is .002 inch.

Rotor Coil Replace

1. Remove slip ring assembly as outlined under Slip Rings Replace.
2. Remove nut and slot insulator from shaft.

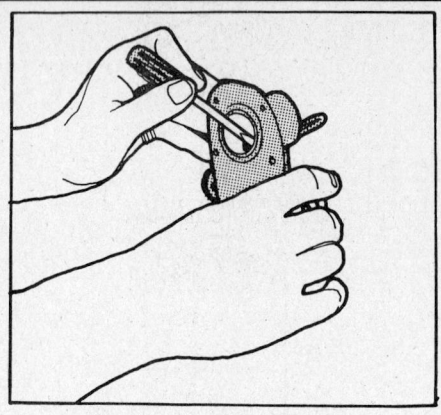

Fig. L43 Brush installation.

3. Using a suitable puller, remove inner bearing race.
4. Remove rotor halves, coil and hub from shaft and separate.
5. Install new rotor coil and dress leads.
6. Reverse procedure to install. When installing nut coat threads with "Loctite Grade A" and torque to 110 ft. lbs. Press on inner bearing race until a clearance of 9/64 inch is obtained between inner edge of race and nut threads.

BENCH TEST

To test positive heat sink, connect ohmmeter positive lead to heat sink and contact each of the three diode terminals with negative lead Fig. L30. A high ohmmeter reading should be obtained, if any of the three diodes shows low resistance, the diode is shorted. Reverse ohmmeter leads and repeat test. A low ohmmeter reading should be obtained, if any of the three diode shows high resistance, the diode is open.

To test negative heat sink, connect ohmmeter negative lead to heat sink and contact each of the three diode terminals with positive lead Fig. L31. If a low resistance is obtained, the diode is shorted. Reverse ohmmeter leads and repeat test. If a high resistance is obtained, the diode is open.

NOTE: If a shorted or open diode is detected, the entire heat sink assembly should be replaced.

Diode Trio

Connect ohmmeter negative lead to diode trio output lead and positive lead to each of three copper terminal pads Fig. L32. A low ohmmeter reading should be obtained. Reverse ohmmeter leads and repeat test. A high ohmmeter reading should be obtained. Any diode to which does not conform to the above test should be replaced.

Capacitor

Connect ohmmeter between capacitor terminals Fig. L33. A low reading would indicate a shorted or leaking capacitor.

Rotor

Connect one ohmmeter to rotor shaft and other lead to slip ring Fig. L34. If ohmmeter reading is other than infinite, the rotor coil is

LEECE-NEVILLE ALTERNATORS

grounded and should be replaced.

Connect ohmmeter between slip rings and note reading Fig. L35. Ohmmeter reading should be 3.0-3.3 ohms, if reading differs significantly, replace rotor coil.

NOTE: Before replacing rotor coil, ensure soldered joints at slip ring leads are good condition.

Stator

Using a 115-220 volt test lamp, check stator for continuity between phases, Fig. L36. Test lamp should light on all three phases. To test stator for grounds, contact one stator lead against stator core and other lead to each of three stator leads, Fig. L36. Test lamp should not light. Stator that appear overheated or have charred insulation should be replaced regardless of test results.

Alternator Assemble

1. Press drive end frame bearing into housing with seal facing outward, if removed.

NOTE: When pressing bearing in, apply force to outer race to avoid damaging bearing.

2. Press new bearing seal into bearing retainer, then fill cavity of seal with SRI-2 grease or equivalent.
3. Install retainer, seal and four attaching screws on drive housing, then lubricate bearing seal with grease.
4. Press housing and bearing assembly onto rotor shaft.

NOTE: Use a sleeve around shaft so that force will be exerted on inner race of bearing.

5. Install heat sinks, ensure upper and lower insulating washers and bushing are properly positioned.
6. Install capacitor between heat sinks.
7. Press in rear slip ring housing seal until flush with rear of housing, then fill seal cavity with SRI-2 grease or equivalent.
8. Pack new bearing with grease, then press into slip ring end housing.
9. Pack cavity with grease, then press seal into housing with metal lip facing inside of housing.
10. Position stator on slip ring end housing, then connect leads and install nuts.
11. Install protective cap over slip rings, then assemble drive end housing and rotor to stator and slip ring housing.
12. Ensure both housings are aligned, then install through bolts and torque nuts to 50-60 in. lbs.
13. Install diode trio on AC terminals.
14. Install regulator and brushes on housing, then connect positive and negative regulator leads.
15. Compress brushes, then install retaining pin through hole in housing to hold brushes in the compressed position, Fig. L43.
16. Apply a small amount of "Loctite Grade A" to regulator housing retaining screws then install and tighten screws.
17. Remove brush retaining pins, then install nuts on alternator output terminals.
18. Connect diode trio lead to regulator charge light terminal and output leads to alternator output terminals.

Regulator Adjustment

With battery in fully charged condition and all accessories turned off, connect voltmeter across battery. Remove cap from adjusting screw, then start engine and operate at approximately 1000 RPM. Turn adjusting screw counter clockwise to lower charging voltage and clockwise to raise charging voltage, Fig. L39. The ideal voltage setting will be a value which maintains a fully charged battery without resulting in an excessive usage of battery water. After adjusting replace adjusting screw cap.

NOTE: Do not force adjusting screw past its stop as damage may result.

Regulator Replace

1. Remove diode trio lead from regulator charge light terminal.
2. Remove nuts from positive and negative output terminals.
3. Remove four attaching screws and regulator and brush holder assembly.
4. Remove nuts securing regulator positive and negative leads.
5. Install regulator and brushes on housing, then connect positive and negative regulator leads.
6. Compress brushes, then install retaining pin through hole in housing to hold brushes in the compressed position, Fig. L43.
7. Apply a small amount of "Loctite Grade A" to regulator housing retaining screws then install and tighten screws.
8. Remove brush retaining pins, then install nuts on alternator output terminals.
9. Connect diode trio lead to regulator charge light terminal and output leads to alternator output terminals.
10. Momentarily flash field by connecting a jumper wire between charge light terminal and positive output terminal.

DISTRIBUTORS, STANDARD

The ignition system can be divided as follows, Fig. 1.
1. Battery to supply current.
2. Ignition wiring to carry current to the units in the system.
3. Ignition switch to control the circuit.
4. Ignition coil to increase the voltage delivered to the spark plugs.
5. A distributor to distribute current to each cylinder.
6. Spark plugs to ignite the fuel in each cylinder.

But inasmuch as the "Tune Up" chapter deals with such service as comes within the province of tuning up an engine—such as batteries, spark plugs, etc.—this chapter will discuss the functions and service requirements of the distributor itself, together with any additional data not included in the "Tune Up" chapter.

BREAKER CONTACT POINTS

Contact Analysis

The normal color of points should be a light gray. If the contact surfaces are black it is usually caused by oil vapor or grease from the cam. If they are blue, the cause is usually excessive heating due to improper alignment, high resistance or open condenser circuit.

If the contacts develop a crater or depression on one point and a high spot of metal on the other, the cause is an electrolytic action transferring metal from one contact to the other, Fig. 2. This can be the result of some unusual operation of the vehicle. A slow-speed driver in city traffic or door-to-door delivery vehicles will be one extreme, and high-speed, long distance driving would be the other extreme. It may also be due to an unbalanced ignition system, which can sometimes be improved by a slight change in condenser capacity. If the mound is on the positive point, Fig. 3, install a condenser of greater capacity; if on the negative point, Fig. 4, use a condenser of lesser capacity.

One of the most common causes of point failure is the presence of oil or grease on the contact surfaces, usually from over-lubrication of the wick at the top of the cam or too much grease on the rubbing block of the breaker arm.

Breaker Point Gap

Correct contact point opening is important, especially during starting and low speed operation. If points are set too close, arcing and burning will occur, causing hard starting and poor low speed performance. If points are set too wide, the cam angle or dwell will be too small to allow saturation of the coil at high engine speeds, resulting in weak spark.

Contact point opening has a direct bearing on cam angle or dwell which is the number of degrees that the breaker cam rotates from the time the points close until they open again, Fig. 5. The cam angle or dwell increases as point opening is decreased and vice versa. In view of the importance of point opening to low speed engine performance and cam dwell to high speed engine performance, the cam angle or dwell should be checked after adjusting and aligning points. This is done on a distributor testing machine, following the manufacturers instructions.

Breaker Arm Spring Tension

Breaker arm spring tension is important. If the tension is too great the arm will bounce,

141

DISTRIBUTORS, Standard

causing an interruption of the current in the coil and misfiring. If the spring tension is too little, the rubbing block will not follow the cam, causing a variation in cam dwell. The spring tension should always be set at the high limit as given in the *Distributor Specifications* chart in truck chapter, as it will be reduced as the rubbing block wears.

Hook a spring scale on the breaker arm and pull in a straight line as shown in Fig. 6. Take a reading as the points start to separate under the slow and steady pull of the scale. If the tension is not within specification, loosen the screw that holds the end of the point spring and slide the end of the spring in or out as necessary. Tighten the screw and recheck the spring tension.

Breaker Point Alignment

Check alignment of points with points closed, Fig. 7. Align new points where necessary but do not attempt to align used points. Instead, replace used points where serious misalignment is observed. After aligning points, adjust point gap.

Adjusting Breaker Gap

Specifications for breaker gap, *as measured with a wire gauge,* is listed in the *Tune Up Specifications* in truck chapters. However, if at all possible, this opening should be set on a distributor testing machine or with a dial indicator, Fig. 8. This not only eliminates the possibility of an incorrect gap setting but if the points are slightly rough but otherwise in alignment, there is the danger of obtaining an incorrect gap, as shown in Fig. 9.

The advantage of a distributor testing machine is that it not only measures cam angle or dwell but it also uncovers irregularities between cam lobes, point bounce, alignment of rubbing block with cam, alignment of contacts and breaker arm spring tension.

Auto-Lite & Chrysler Single Point Set Adjustment

Adjustment of breaker gap is accomplished by loosening the lock screw in the stationary point and moving the adjusting screw as required to obtain the correct breaker gap.

Delco-Remy Internal Adjustment Breaker Points

An opening in the point set assembly allows for easy dwell angle or breaker point adjustment, Fig. 10.

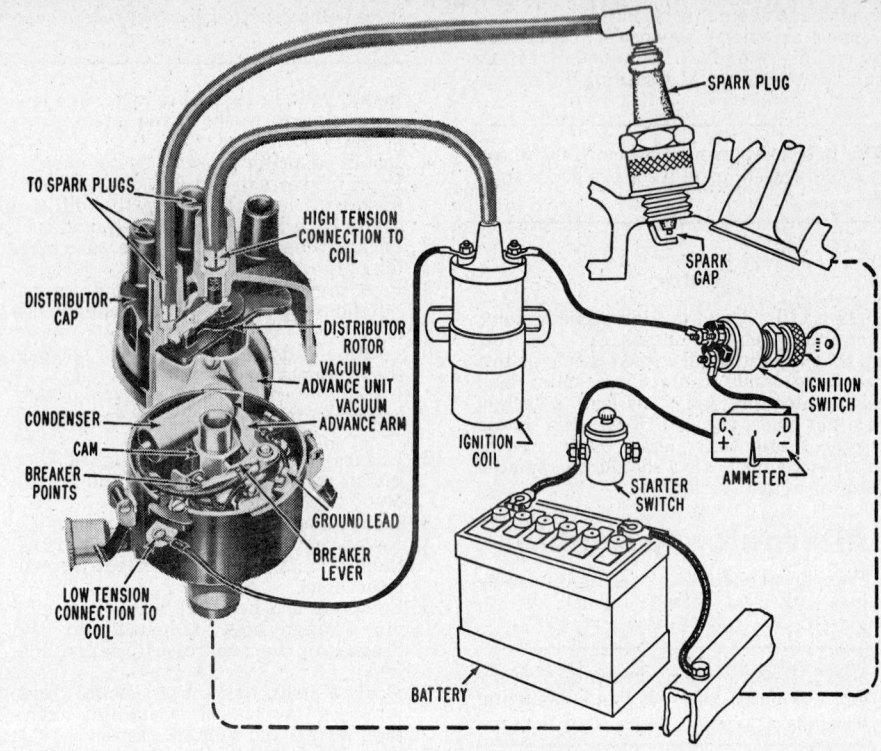

Fig. 1 Typical ignition system

Delco-Remy External Adjustment Breaker Points

With engine running at idle speed, the breaker gap is adjusted by first raising the window provided in the cap and inserting a "hex" wrench into the adjusting screw, Fig. 11. Turn the adjusting screw clockwise until the engine begins to misfire. Then give the wrench one-half turn in the opposite direction which will provide the proper breaker gap. If a dwell meter is to be used, turn the adjusting screw until the correct angle is obtained.

NOTE: Beginning with 1973, some General Motors V-8 trucks may be equipped with the new Uni-Set breaker points (one piece points and condenser). If the Uni-Set points and con-

denser is not available for service the following alternatives can be applied.
1. A conversion kit is available (Part No. 1876065) which contains a breaker plate, contact set, radio shields, condenser and wick.
2. If the existing breaker plate has tapped holes for the condenser clamp and radio shields, it need not be changed and the conversion kit is not necessary. You can install the previous two piece points and condenser but you must obtain and install the radio shields.

Holley Breaker Points

The breaker point set is attached to the

Fig. 2 Showing how metal from one contact transfer to the other

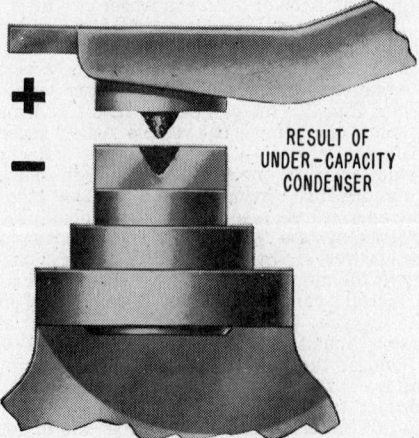

Fig. 3 Mound on positive point

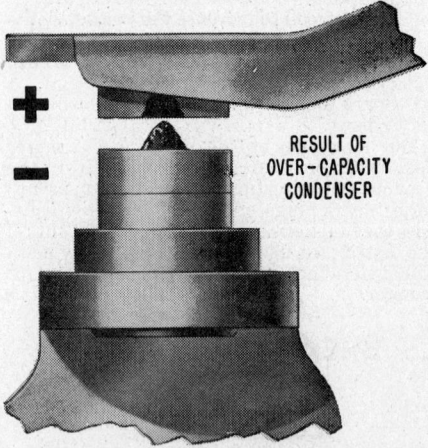

Fig. 4 Mound on negative point

142

DISTRIBUTORS, Standard

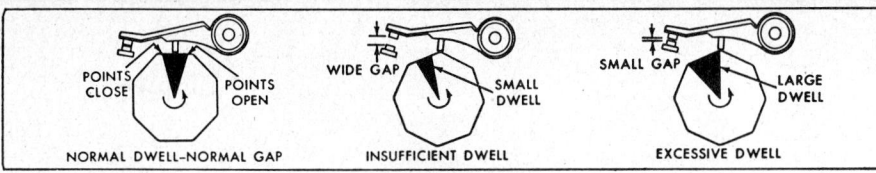

Fig. 5 Cam angle or dwell

movable breaker plate. A slot in the stationary point bracket allows for easy breaker point adjustment, Fig. 13.

CONDENSER

A condenser should not be condemned because the points are burned or oxidized. Oil vapor, or grease from the cam, or high resistance may be the cause of such a condition.

Condensers should be tested with a good condenser tester for leakage, breakdown, capacity, and resistance in series in the condenser circuit. Manufacturers of condenser testers furnish complete instructions as to their use.

CENTRIFUGAL ADVANCE

Except for Holley "full vacuum" distributors, all other distributors utilize an automatic advance mechanism which functions by virtue of centrifugal weights. Some distributors employ both centrifugal and vacuum advance mechanisms, while others make use of only the centrifugal mechanism.

When engine speed increases, the spark must be introduced in the cylinder earlier in the cycle in order that the fuel charge can be ignited and will have time to burn and deliver its power to the piston. To provide this spark advance based on engine speed, the centrifugal governor mechanism is used.

This mechanism, Fig. 14, consists of centrifugal advance weights which throw out against spring tension as the engine speed increases. This movement imparts, through a toggle arrangement, rotational motion to the breaker cam, causing it to rotate a number of degrees with respect to the distributor drive shaft. This causes the lobes on the cam to close and open the contact earlier in the cycle so that the spark is induced and is delivered to the cylinder earlier with respect to the position of the upward moving piston.

In servicing the distributor, all weights should be removed from the hinge pins, cleaned and checked for excessive wear, either in the weights or pins, or the plate which is slotted for the movement of the pins on top of the governor weights. Replacement should be made if there is any appreciable wear in the slots, as any wear at this point would change the characteristic of the spark advance.

If these parts are in good condition, the hinge pins should be lubricated before being reassembled, by greasing the hinge pins and filling the pockets in the governor weights with grease. Do not use vaseline for this purpose as its melting point is comparatively low.

When installing new centrifugal governor assemblies, it is important that the spacer washers between the housing and shaft be installed correctly. If incorrectly installed, the governor assembly will be too high, causing it to rub against the bottom of the breaker plate.

On some distributors, both springs are alike, while on others there is one heavy and one light spring, as in Fig. 14. Another combination that may be found is an additional flat spring on the outside of the outer spring posts, Fig. 15. As the governor speed is increased, the flat springs are first pulled against the

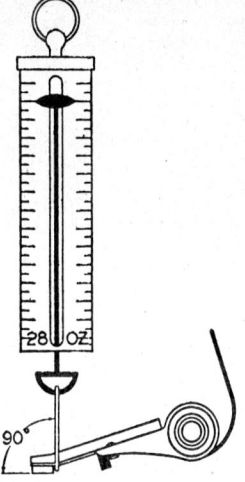

Fig. 6 Measuring breaker arm spring tension

posts by the eyes of the coil springs to provide a rapid spark advance of a few degrees before the coil springs pull against the spring posts.

VACUUM ADVANCE
Conventional Type

The two types of vacuum advance mechanisms used on Auto-Lite and Delco-Remy distributors are illustrated in Figs. 17 and 18. Both types make use of a spring-loaded diaphragm which is connected through linkage to the distributor. The spring loaded side of the diaphragm is air tight and is connected through a vacuum line to the carburetor above the throttle plate so that idling performance will not be affected.

When the throttle is open vacuum from the intake manifold is introduced into the vacuum advance mechanism and the diaphragm is pulled against the spring causing the distributor to advance.

In Fig. 16 the mechanism is attached to the distributor breaker plate so that the breaker plate rotates. In Fig. 17, the mechanism is connected to the distributor body so that the entire distributor moves. In both cases, the rotational movement carries the contact points around to an advanced position so that the breaker cam closes and opens the points earlier in the cycle.

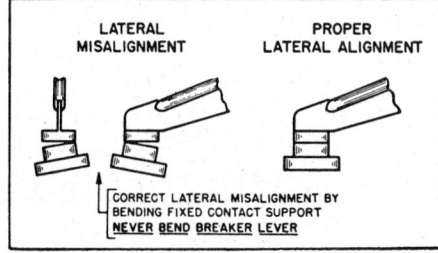

Fig. 7 Breaker point alignment

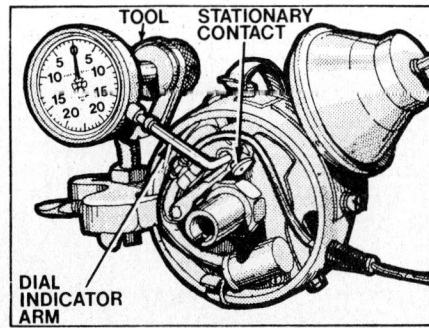

Fig. 8 Dial indicator for measuring breaker gap

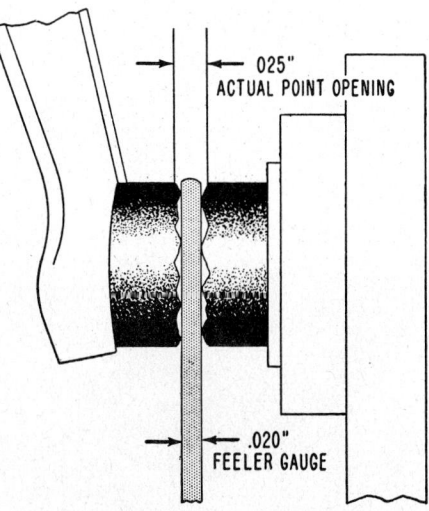

Fig. 9 Why flat feeler gauge will not provide accurate point spacing if points are rough

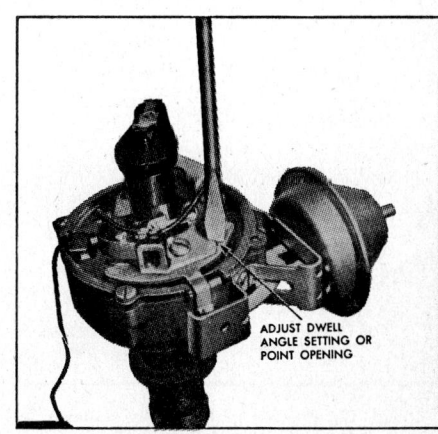

Fig. 10 Breaker point setting

DISTRIBUTORS, Standard

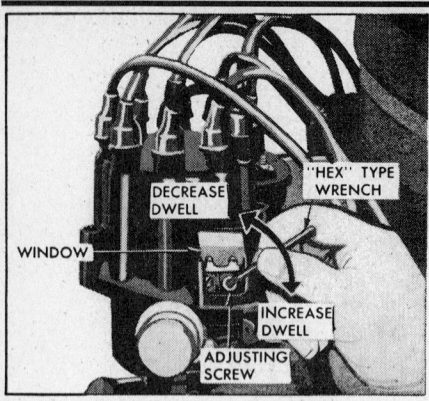

Fig. 11 Adjusting breaker point gap through window in distributor cap

See Holley Distributor Service for vacuum advance data for these units.

Emission Control Types

Chrysler C.A.P.
The Chrysler vacuum advance units incorporate a vacuum advance control valve in the advance vacuum circuit to provide the necessary retard during closed throttle operation.

Chrysler C.A.S.
Some Chrysler C.A.S. engines have a solenoid incorporated in the distributor vacuum advance mechanism to retard the ignition timing when the throttle is closed. At closed throttle, electrical contacts on the carburetor throttle stop, with idle adjusting screw in the closed position, cause the distributor solenoid to energize. This retards the ignition timing to provide reduced exhaust emissions under hot idle conditions. Cold or part throttle starting is not penalized because the distributor solenoid is not energized unless the hot idle adjusting screw is against the throttle stop contact. Timing must be set at closed throttle to give accurate setting.

Ford Dual-Diaphragm
This unit consists of two independent diaphragms. The outer diaphragm uses carburetor vacuum to advance timing. The inner diaphragm uses intake manifold vacuum to provide additional retard during closed throttle operation.

General Motors CCS
In this system, the advance is the ported type, that is the vacuum take-off is located above the throttle plate(s) so that during periods of closed throttle operation there is little or no vacuum reaching the advance unit and timing is retarded. As soon as the throttle is cracked, vacuum reaches the advance unit and timing is advanced.

NOTE: Some models of the Chevrolet V8-307 engine use the conventional type advance unit.

Prestolite IBP Distributors

Used on some Dodge trucks, this distributor uses a very different type vacuum spark advance. Unlike other systems which either rotate the breaker plate or the entire distributor when manifold vacuum is high, the IBP breaker plate is pivoted in such a way that the points swing in an arc about the cam when the vacuum advance unit is in operation. Thus, cam angle and breaker point gap change as high manifold vacuum advances the spark. For this reason cam angle should be checked with the vacuum line disconnected and the point gap checked or adjusted when the vacuum advance unit is in full retard position.

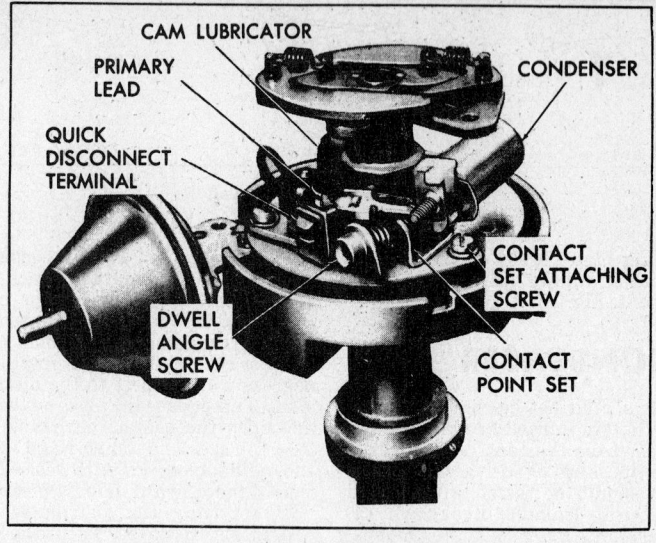

Fig. 12 Delco-Remy one piece breaker point & condenser (Uni-Set)

PRESTOLITE & CHRYSLER DISTRIBUTOR SERVICE

Shaft & Bushing Wear Test

1. Remove distributor from vehicle and clamp distributor in a vise. Use extreme caution not to damage distributor.
2. Install a dial indicator on housing so plunger rests against moveable contact arm when rubbing block is on the highest point of a cam.
3. Place a wire loop around distributor shaft and hook a spring scale on the other end of the loop. Apply a one pound pull in line with indicator plunger and read movement on indicator. Movement must not exceed .006 inch. If movement exceeds limit, replace either housing or shaft on Chrysler distributors or bushing or shaft on Prestolite distributors to bring move-

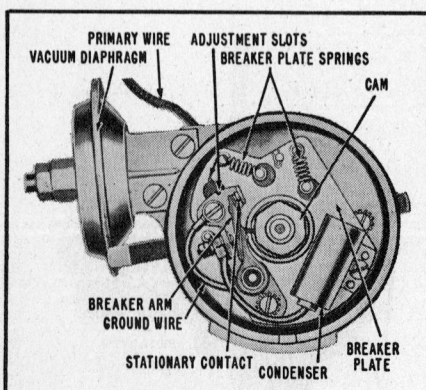

Fig. 13 Breaker plate details. Holley Loadamatic distributor. Note slot for adjusting breaker gap

Fig. 14 Top view of Delco-Remy distributor with breaker plate removed to show centrifugal advance mechanism

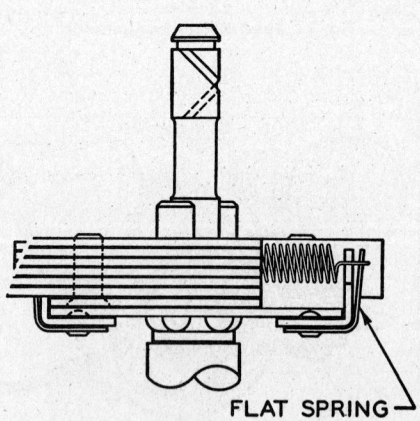

Fig. 15 Flat spring used on some governors to provide a rapid spark advance

DISTRIBUTORS, Standard

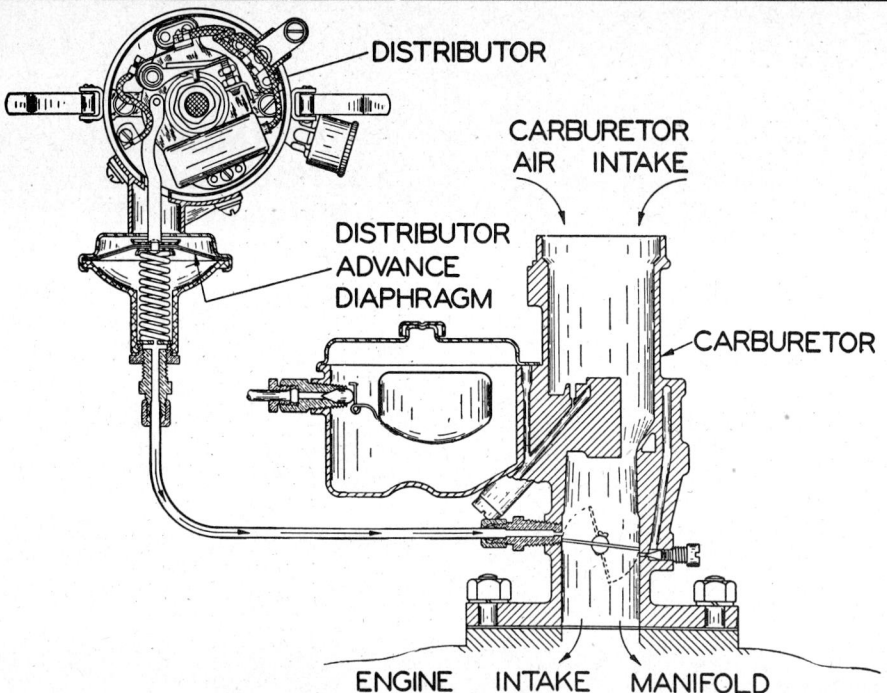

Fig. 16 Auto-Lite vacuum advance mechanism of type mounted of distributor. Breaker plate is supported on a ball bearing, and breaker plate alone rotates in the housing as vacuum conditions

ers.
11. Test breaker arm spring tension and adjust breaker gap.
12. Lubricate felt pad in top of distributor cam with 3 to 5 drops of light engine oil and install rotor.

DELCO-REMY DISTRIBUTOR SERVICE

External Adjustment Type

If the distributor has been disassembled, refer to Fig. 22 for guidance when reassembling.
1. Place gasket on shaft housing.
2. Place felt washer around bushing in housing.
3. Install vacuum advance unit.
4. Install breaker plate in housing and spring retainer on upper bushing.
5. Install condenser.
6. Install breaker point set.
7. Install cam and weight base assembly on shaft. If lubrication in grooves at top of shaft was removed during disassembly, replace with Plastilube #2 or its equivalent.
8. Install shaft and cam weight assembly in housing.
9. Using a pin, install driven gear to shaft.
10. Install advance weights and springs.
11. Install cam lubricator.
12. Install rotor.
13. Check breaker arm spring tension and adjust breaker gap.

Internal Adjustment Type

If the distributor has been disassembled, refer to Fig. 23. When assembling, Fig. 24 shows the details of the breaker plate and attaching parts.
1. Replace cam assembly to shaft. Lubricate top end of shaft with light engine oil prior to replacing.
2. Install weights on their pivot pins. Install weights, weight cover and stop plate.
3. Lubricate shaft and install in housing.

ment back within tolerance.
If the distributor has been disassembled, reassemble as follows, referring to Figs. 18 and 19 for guidance.
1. Check operation of centrifugal weights and weight springs for distortion. Lubricate governor weights.
2. Inspect all bearing surfaces and pivot pins for roughness, binding, or excessive looseness.
3. Install cam spacer (chamfered end down) on distributor shaft.
4. Slide cam and yoke on distributor shaft. Engage weight lugs with slots in yoke as shown in Fig. 20. Install cam retaining clip, being sure it is properly seated in distributor shaft groove.
5. Lubricate and install two concave washers for Prestolite distributors, or a single flat thrust washer for Chrysler distributors. Position washers on shaft and slide shaft into distributor body. On Chrysler six cylinder distributors, if drive gear is worn or damaged, replace as follows:
   a. Install thrust washer and old gear on shaft and install pin. Scribe a line centered between two gear teeth from center to edge of shaft and in line with center of rotor electrode.
   b. Remove pin and gear. Clean burrs from around pin hole and install new gear.
   c. Place a .007 inch feeler gauge between gear and thrust washer and drill a .124–.129 inch hole in gear and shaft about 90 degrees from old hole in shaft and with scribe line centered between gear teeth and in line with center of rotor electrode as shown in Fig. 21.

NOTE: If new pin hole location appears to interfere with shaft oil groove, rotate gear to centerline of next pair of gear teeth and align with scribe line on shaft.

d. Install pin.
6. Position lower thrust washer and drive collar on lower end of shaft and install retainer pin.
7. Install oiler wick and oiler.
8. Install breaker plate assembly, align condenser lead, breaker point spring, primary lead and install attaching screw.
9. Install felt wick in top of distributor cam.
10. Attach vacuum advance unit arm to breaker plate and install retainer. Install vacuum unit attaching screws and wash-

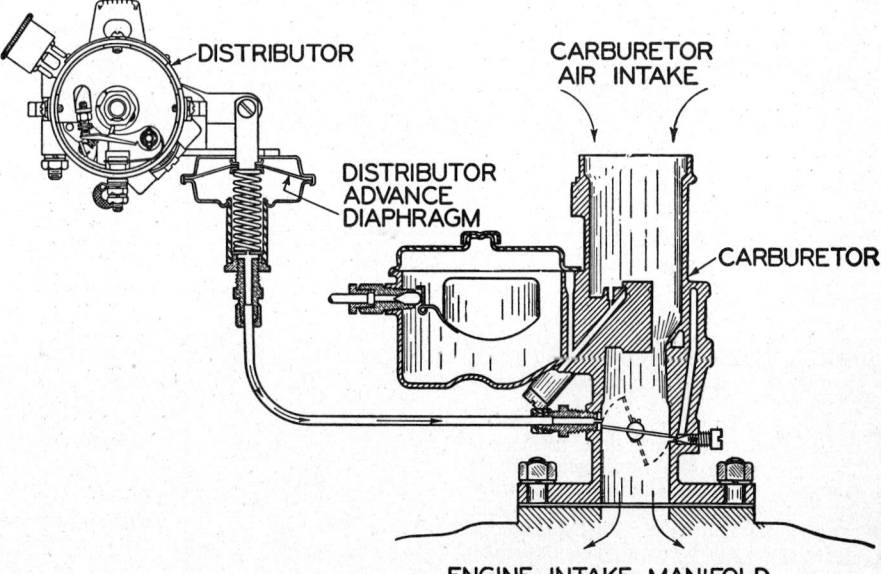

Fig. 17 Auto-Lite vacuum advance mechanism of type clamped around distributor so that entire distributor is rotated as vacuum conditions change

DISTRIBUTORS, Standard

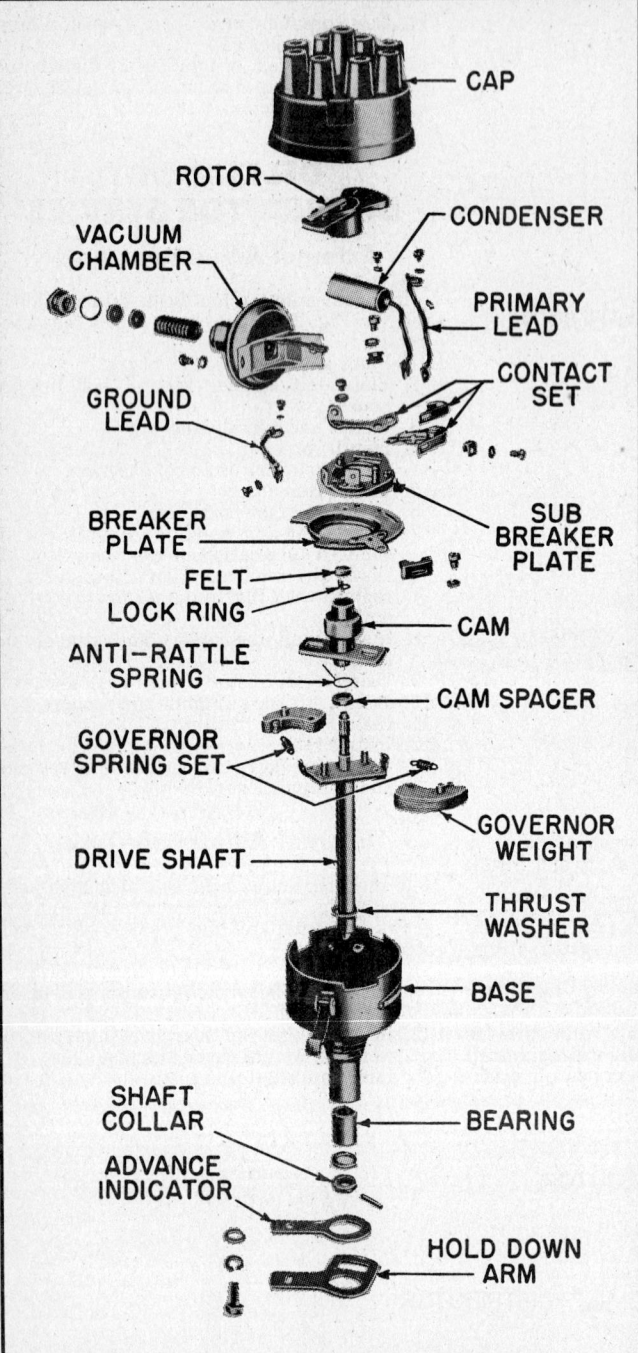

Fig. 18 Disassembled view of a typical Prestolite distributor

breaker gap.
9. Install rotor.

D-R EXTERNAL ADJUSTMENT TYPE DISTRIBUTOR WITH BUILT-IN SPEED GOVERNOR

Except for the built-in maximum speed governor, Fig. 25, this distributor is similar to the standard external adjustment type.

The governor mechanism, encased in a chamber in the distributor housing, is assembled on and revolves with the distributor shaft. Disassembly, assembly and adjustment of the governor mechanism is made through external openings in the casting that are cov-

4. Install thrust washers and driven gear to shaft and secure with roll pins. Check to see that shaft turns freely. Install driven gear with mark on hub in line with rotor segment.
5. Install breaker plate.
6. Attach condenser and breaker point set in proper location with appropriate attaching screws, Fig. 24. Connect primary and condenser leads to breaker point set quick disconnect terminal. *Contact point set pilot must engage matching hole in breaker plate.*
7. Attach vacuum control assembly to distributor housing, using upper mounting holes.
8. Adjust breaker arm spring tension and

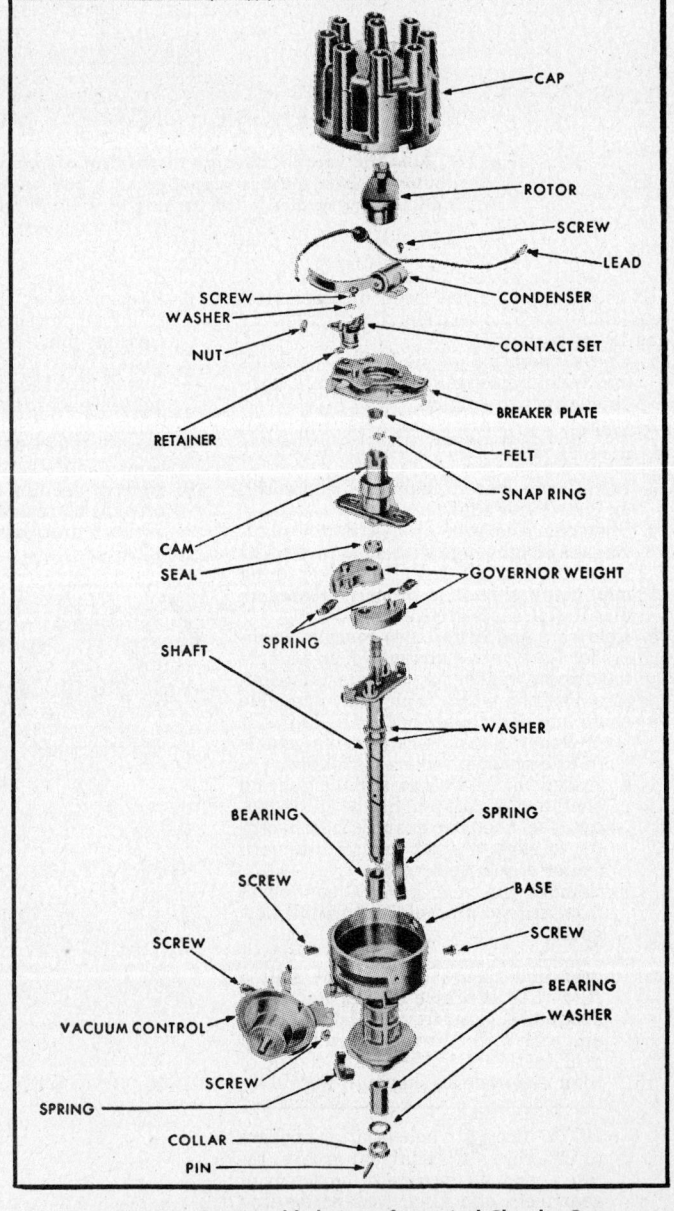

Fig. 19 Disassembled view of a typical Chrysler Corp. (V-8 distributor)

DISTRIBUTORS, Standard

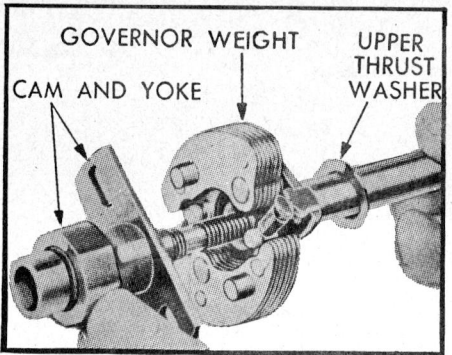

Fig. 20 Distributor shaft details

When the distributor shaft revolves, the centrifugal force of the weight pulls against the spring, causing the valve shaft to move transversely in the main shaft. The slots on the valve shaft move into the main shaft of the distributor, gradually restricting the flow of air. When this restriction occurs, vacuum is created in the carburetor actuator, causing it to move the butterfly valve in the carburetor, thereby governing the engine speed. When the valve shaft in the distributor does not restrict air flow, air is brought from the air cleaner through the distributor. An overriding feature on the carburetor butterfly valve allows the foot pedal to control the butterfly valve position except when the vacuum diaphragm pull is sufficient to overcome the opposing spring force.

Governor Adjustment

The distributor governor mechanism can be adjusted off the vehicle to an approximate setting by using an approved tester and the following procedure:

1. With the "spinner" valve (centrifugal valve) adjusted so that at least two threads on the valve are showing behind the nut, mount the distributor in the tester.
2. Screw vacuum adapter into lower vacuum opening on distributor housing.
3. With vacuum hose pinched or bent double to prevent leakage through the hose, adjust vacuum so that gauge reads 5.0" Hg. Release hose, then repeat adjustment until reading returns to 5.0" Hg each time the hose is pinched.
4. Attach vacuum hose to adapter on dis-

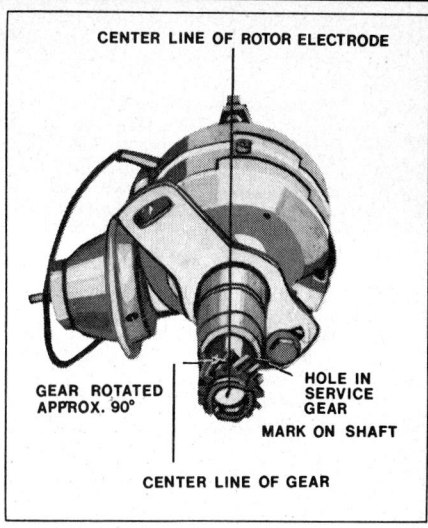

Fig. 21 Gear tooth alignment, Chrysler 6 cyl. distributor

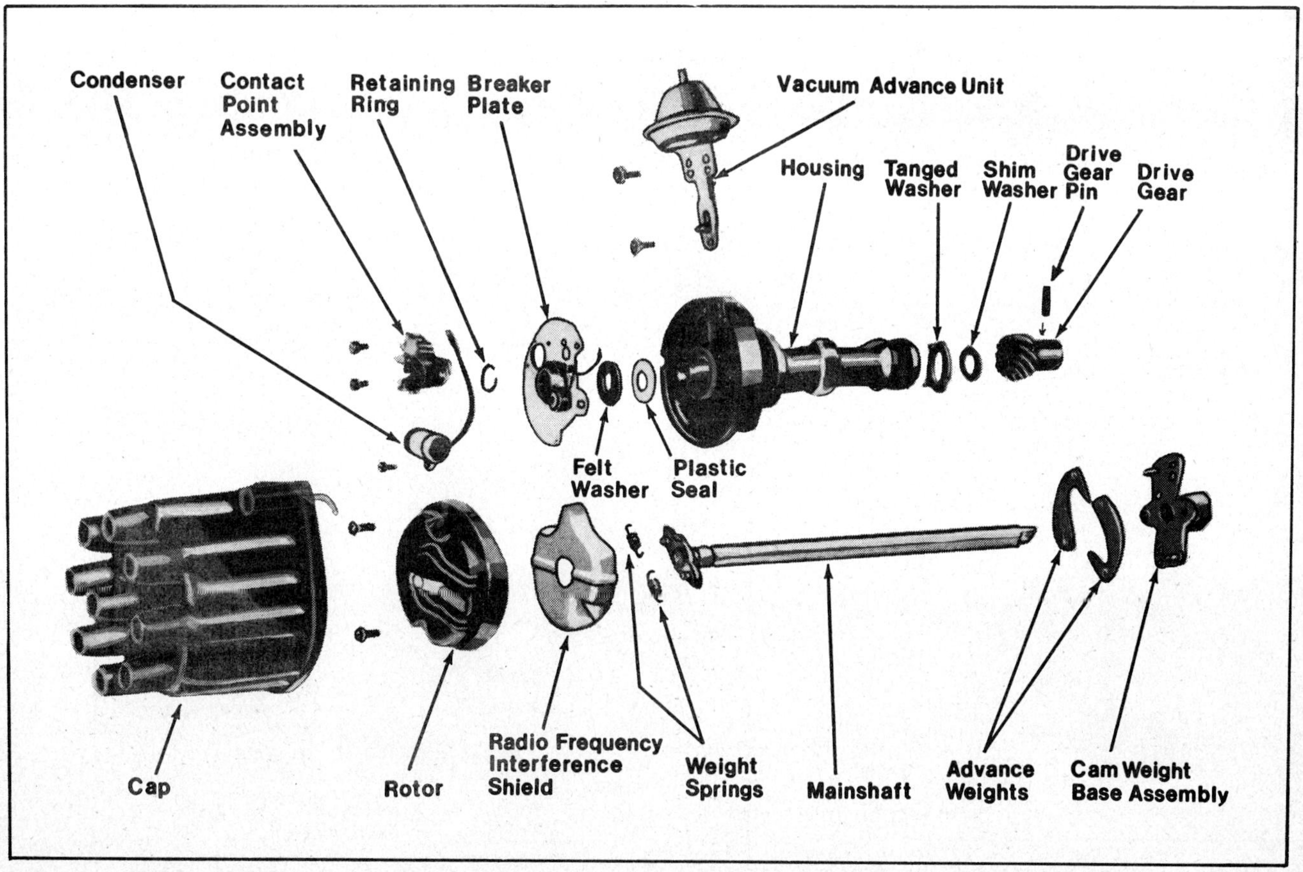

tributor and start tester. Increase speed until vacuum reading reaches a maximum value. This maximum value will vary, depending on the type "spinner" parts used, but will probably be above 3.8" Hg.
5. After this maximum reading has been reached, slowly decrease distributor speed until vacuum gauge pointer falls back .1" Hg. The speed at which this .1"

ered with a removable cover band.

The governor assembly consists of a valve shaft extending through the distributor main shaft. One end of the shaft has a slotted head, whereas the opposite end is threaded to take the adjusting nut. Assembled to the slotted head of the valve shaft is a plain washer, a ballast weight, and a rubber shock absorbing sleeve inside the weight. Assembled on the opposite end is a return spring and a self-locking adjusting nut.

Fig. 26 shows a simplified diagram of the air flow and vacuum connections between the carburetor and distributor. An air line connects the carburetor air cleaner to the governor chamber in the distributor housing. A vacuum line connects the lower opening in the distributor housing to the carburetor actuator.

Fig. 22 Delco-Remy external adjustment distributor

DISTRIBUTORS, Standard

Hg drop occurs will be the approximate no-lead governed speed. (Bear in mind that distributor rpm is half engine rpm when making this adjustment.)
6. Final adjustment must be made with the distributor on the vehicle. Road testing is necessary for accurate full-throttle governing; however, it can be assumed that full-throttle governed speed will be about 200 rpm below no-lead governed speed. Therefore, the governed speed can be checked by operating the engine at high speed in neutral.
7. To adjust distributor governing mechanism, stop the engine, remove the cover band from the distributor and turn the centrifugal valve adjusting nut, Fig. 26, holding opposite end of shaft with a screwdriver as adjusting nut is turned.
8. To increase speed limit setting, turn adjusting nut clockwise, and vice-versa.
9. When the cover band is replaced, be sure it covers the openings and is tight so as to prevent dirt from entering the chamber.

AUTOLITE/MOTORCRAFT DUAL ADVANCE DISTRIBUTOR

This distributor, Figs. 27 and 28, is similar to conventional design in that both a centrifugal advance mechanism is provided to regulate ignition timing according to speed and a vacuum advance unit to regulate ignition timing according to load. However, unlike other make distributors, the centrifugal advance mechanism can be adjusted through a slot in the breaker plate.

Adjust centrifugal advance before adjusting vacuum advance. If the correct advance is not indicated when tested on a distributor machine, bend one spring bracket with a screwdriver through the hole in the breaker plate, Fig. 29. Bend bracket away from distributor shaft to decrease advance and toward shaft to increase advance. Identify bracket after adjustment is made. After an adjustment has been made to one spring, check the minimum advance point again. Then operate distributor at the specified rpm to give an advance just below maximum. If this advance is not up to specifications, bend the other spring bracket

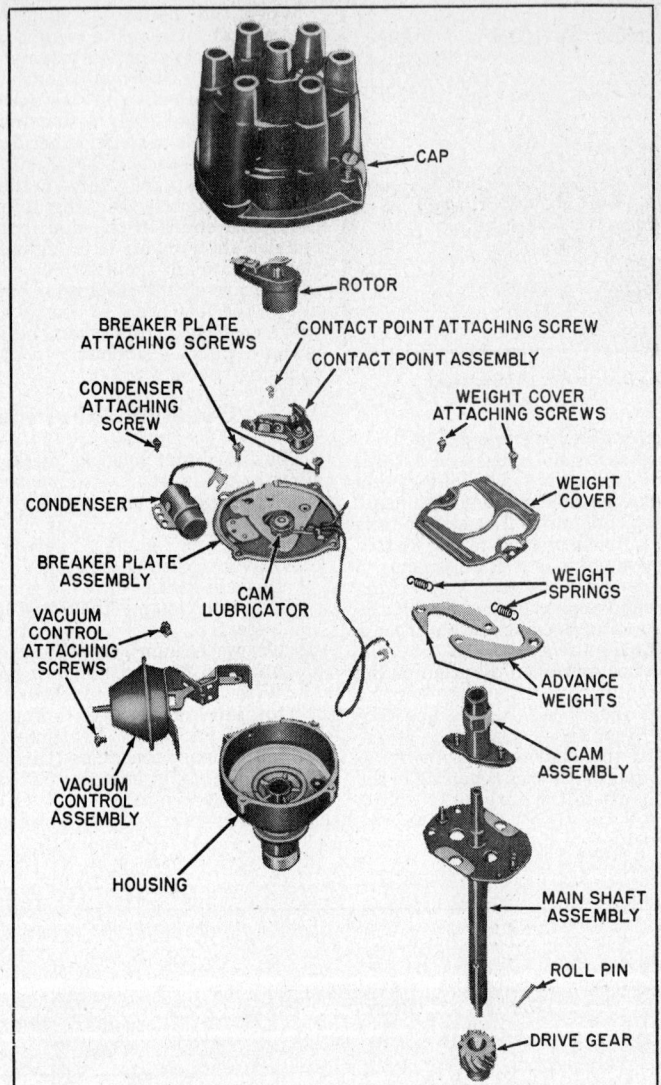

Fig. 23 Delco-Remy internal adjustment distributor

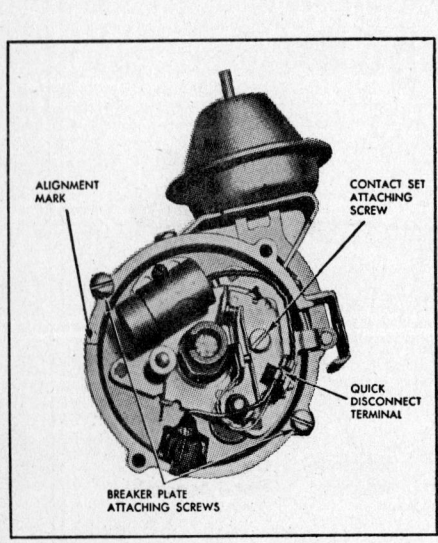

Fig. 24 Breaker plate installation. Delco-Remy internal adjustment distributor

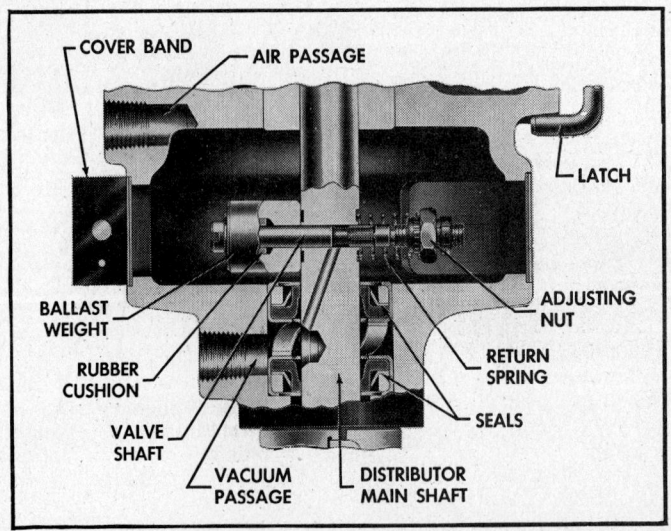

Fig. 25 Delco-Remy distributor speed governor mechanism

DISTRIBUTORS, Standard

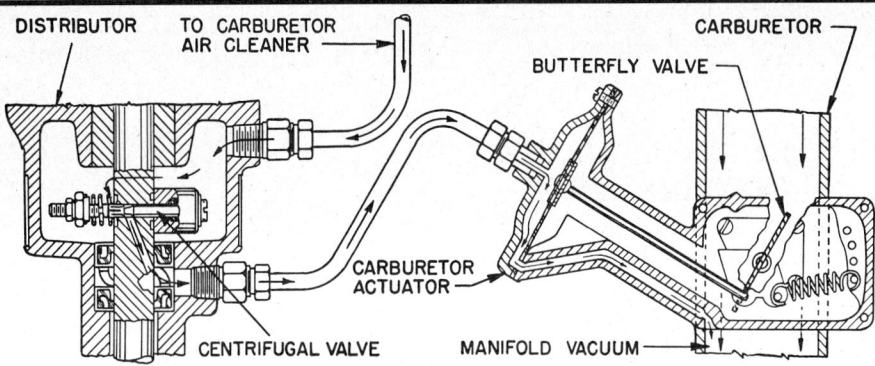

Fig. 26 Air flow and vacuum connections between carburetor and Delco-Remy governed distributor (typical)

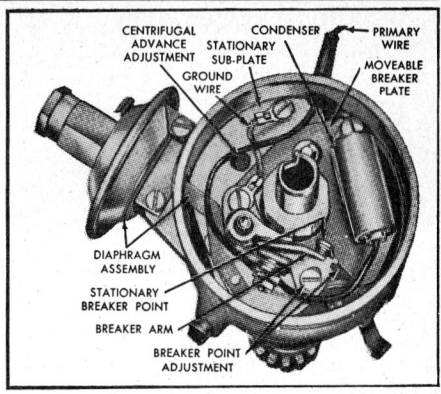

Fig. 27 Breaker plate installation. Autolite/Motorcraft dual advance distributor

to give the correct advance.

Vacuum advance on all 1970-71 distributors and 1972 units used on Super Duty engines can be adjusted by changing the calibrated washers between the vacuum chamber spring and nut, Fig. 30. The addition of one washer will decrease advance and the removal of a washer will increase advance.

Vacuum advance on 1972 distributors except with Super Duty engines and on all 1973-74 units can be adjusted by turning an allen head screw inside the vacuum unit, Fig. 31. Turning the screw clockwise increases advance and counter-clockwise decreases advance.

Distributor Service

If the distributor has been disassembled, refer to Fig. 28 for guidance upon reassembly.

1. Oil shaft and slide it into distributor body.
2. Place collar in position on shaft and align holes in collar and shaft, then install a new pin.
3. Install distributor cap clamps.
4. Check shaft end play with feeler gauge placed between collar and base of distributor. If shaft end play is not within .024–.035", replace shaft and gear.
5. Fill grooves in weight pivot pin with ball bearing grease.
6. Position weights in distributor.
7. Install weight springs, being sure proper weight, spring and adjustment bracket are assembled together.
8. Install upper thrust washer.
9. Fill grooves in upper portion of distributor shaft with ball bearing grease.
10. Install cam assembly, being sure that slots in cam engage pins in weights.
11. Install cam retainer. Apply a light film of cam lubricant to cam lobes. Saturate wick with 10W engine oil. Install wick in cam.
12. Position stationary sub plate in distributor. Install one end of ground wire under plate retaining screw close to diaphragm mounting flange.
13. Position movable breaker plate in distributor. Install spring washer on pivot pin. Place flat washer on spring washer. Be sure protruding edges of spring washer are facing upward. Install retainer.
14. Install new breaker point assembly. Install ground wire on breaker point attaching screw furthest from point adjustment slot.
15. Install condenser.
16. Working from inside to outside of distributor housing, pass primary wire through opening in distributor. Pull wire through opening until locating stop is flush with inside of distributor.
17. Connect condenser wire and primary wire to breaker points.
18. Position diaphragm and hook its link over pin on breaker plate. Install diaphragm attaching screws. Secure link with retainer. Install oil seal.

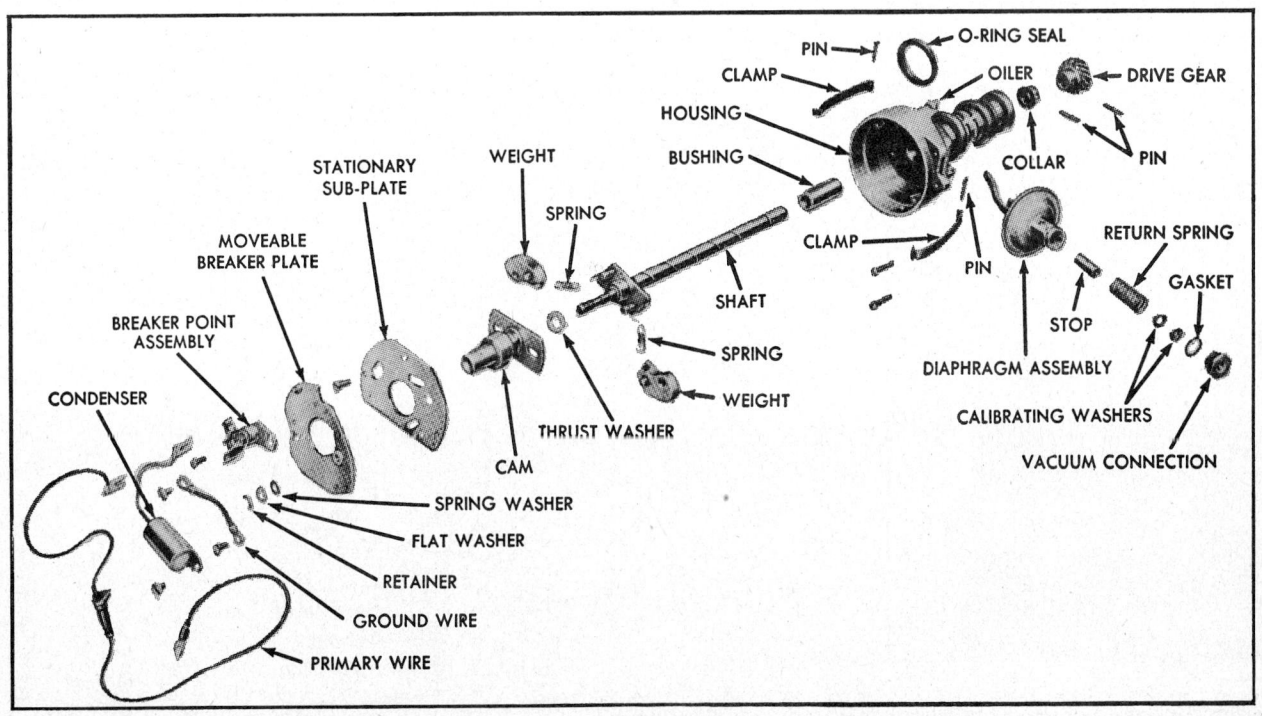

Fig. 28 Disassembled view of Autolite/Motorcraft dual advance distributor

DISTRIBUTORS, Standard

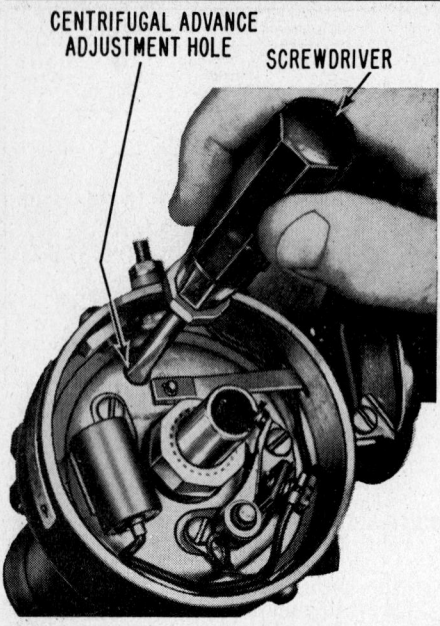

Fig. 29 Adjustment of centrifugal advance

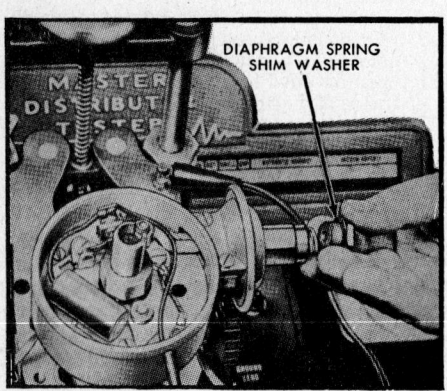

Fig. 30 Vacuum advance adjustment. Autolite/Motorcraft all 1970–71 & 1972 exc. Super Duty distributors

Fig. 31 Vacuum advance adjustment. Autolite/Motorcraft 1972 exc. Super Duty & all 1973–74 distributors

19. Adjust breaker arm spring tension, align and adjust breaker points and check and adjust cam dwell, centrifugal and vacuum advance.

HOLLEY "ROTO-VANCE" DISTRIBUTOR

This distributor, Fig. 32, functions as a standard ignition unit and in addition acts as a control unit for the engine speed governor valves located below the carburetor. Fig. 33.

The distributor-governor consists of an adjusting nut, a calibrating spring and governor weight. Below governing speed the weight cannot overcome the spring tension and the air inlet port is open. Thus air is permitted to flow through the distributor shaft, the governor air line and through the engine governor. This air is at atmospheric pressure.

With an increase of engine speed and distributor shaft rotational speed, centrifugal force is exerted on the weight and it moves out against spring tension. Continued increases of engine speed moves the weight far enough to close off the air inlet port. Closing the air inlet port permits vacuum pressure to be impressed on one side of the engine governor diaphragm. The opposite side of the diaphragm is vented to atmospheric pressure through a connecting line to the fresh air inlet line. The resulting pressure differential on the diaphragm causes the throttle valve to be moved towards a partially closed position against the throttle valve plate governor spring tension.

A decrease in engine speed allows the distributor governor valve weight spring to push the weight towards the distributor shaft, thus opening the inlet port and neutralizing the pressure differential on the diaphragm. The governor throttle plate is returned to its fully open position by the engine governor spring.

Automatic Advance Adjustment

Install distributor on a test bench and remove the adjusting hole cover plug. Check the operation of the automatic advance against specifications given in Truck Chapters. Adjust the weight springs by screwing in or out on the adjusting nuts, Fig. 34, turning both nuts the same amount. Turning in on the nuts will increase the tension and the rpm

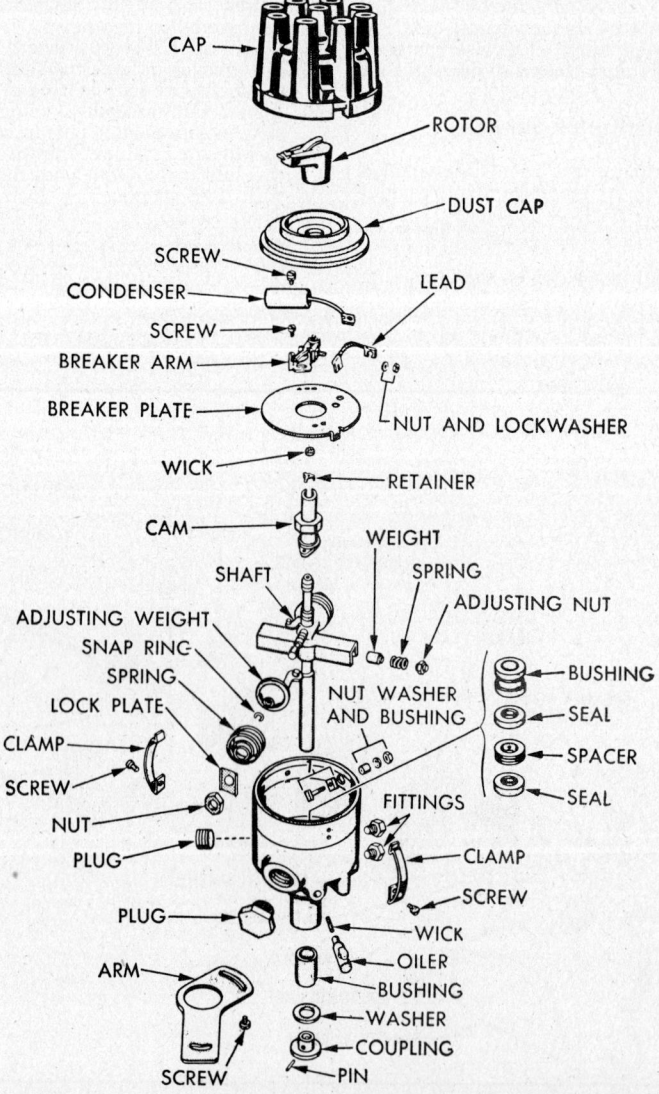

Fig. 32 Holley "Roto-Vance" (carburetor governor control) distributor

DISTRIBUTORS, Standard

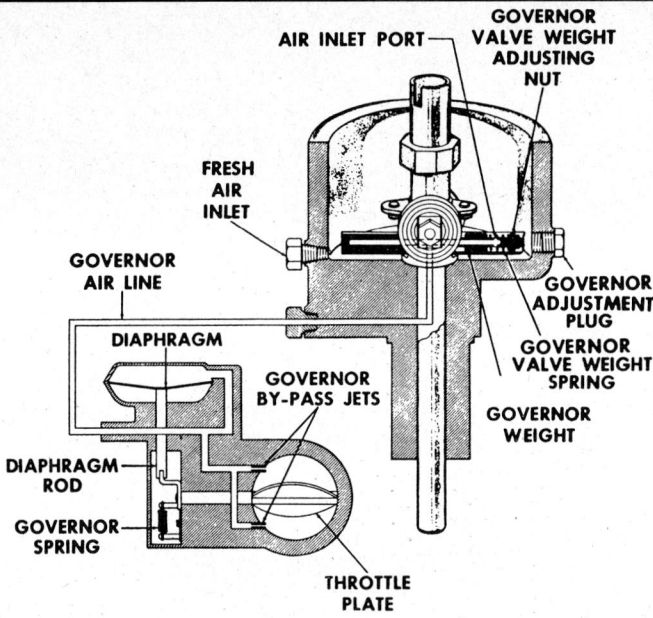

Fig. 33 Diagrammatic view of governor system. Holley "Roto-Vance" distributor

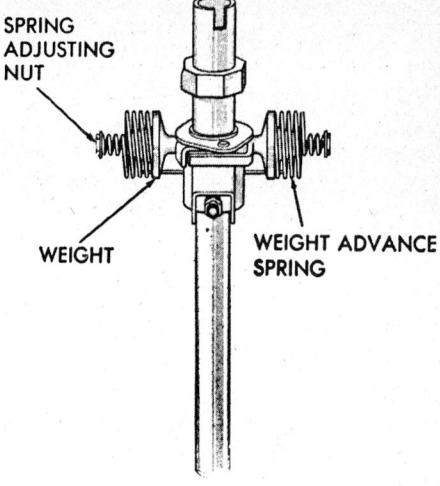

Fig. 34 Adjusting advance weight springs. Holley "Roto-Vance" distributor

required to move the weights and will give a retarded advance. Loosening the nuts will allow the weights to move at a slower rpm and will cause the timing to advance earlier. *Be sure nut flats index lock plate.* Where the initial setting is correct but the advance does not follow specifications it is an indication that the advance springs are faulty or the distributor cam is binding on the shaft.

CAUTION: Care should be taken when adjusting the advance mechanism to approximate the specified curve as closely as possible. The spark timing of the engine in operating range is determined directly by the accuracy of the distributor advance mechanism. *It is important to remember that a one-degree error in the distributor advance settings will produce a two-degree error in spark timing when operating in the engine.*

Testing Engine Speed Governor Valve In Test Stand

Operate the test stand vacuum pump. Pinch the end of the vacuum hose and record the highest vacuum reading obtained. Connect the vacuum line to the lowest fitting on the distributor. Make certain that no leaks are present.

Without rotating the distributor shaft, note the vacuum reading on the gauge. If the passages in the distributor are free of obstructions, a desirable very low reading should be obtained. An undesirable high reading will indicate that obstructions in the passages are present, caused by dirt or other causes. The distributor should then be thoroughly checked to determine cause and corrections made.

NOTE: Some test machines have a pipe cleaner type of restrictor. For these tests this restrictor should be removed or an inaccurate reading will be obtained. The vacuum line in the machine must be open.

Rotate the distributor shaft and gradually increase the speed while observing the vacuum gauge. When the distributor shaft speed reaches the rpm necessary to move the governor weight out on its shaft and close the air inlet port, the vacuum reading will "jump" to a high reading almost instantly. The vacuum reading at this rpm and at all higher speeds should be within one or two inches (Hg) of the reading recorded at the start of the test. If the vacuum reading is within the specified one to two inches of the previous reading, it is an indication that the weight valve is sealing the inlet port and that no noticeable leaks are apparent.

Decrease the distributor shaft speed gradually while observing the vacuum gauge. When the speed drops slightly below the governor closing speed, the air inlet port should open, causing a rapid drop in vacuum.

HOLLEY 1500 DISTRIBUTOR

This distributor is designed so that it is available with centrifugal advance, vacuum advance, a governor control valve and a tachometer drive, or with any combination of

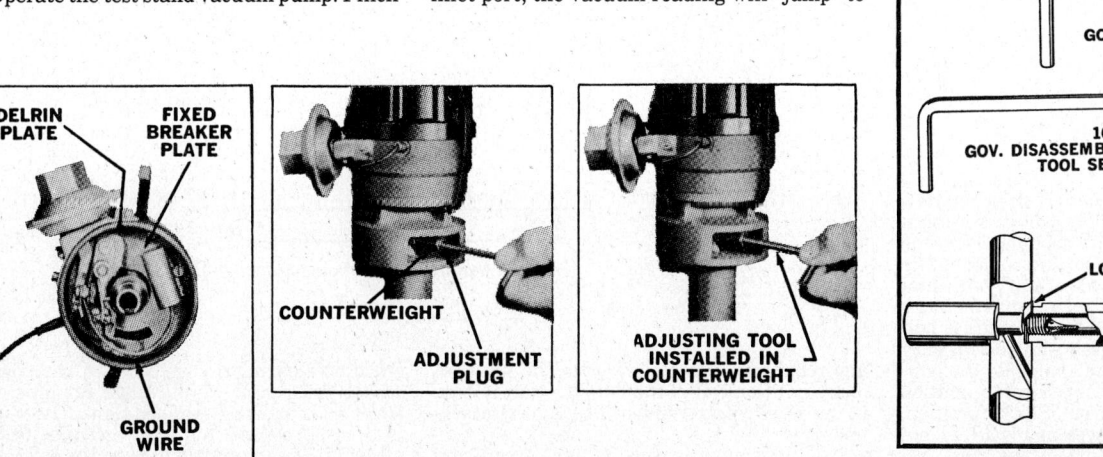

Fig. 35 Holley 1500 distributor

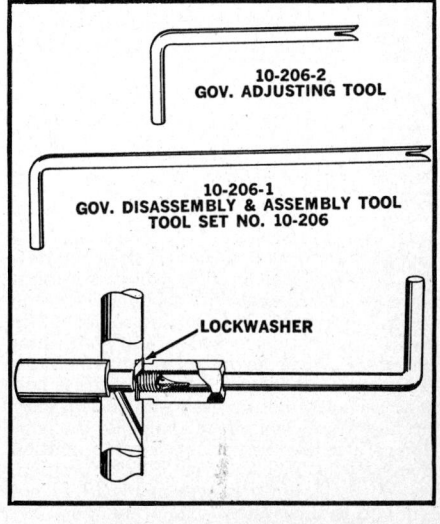

Fig. 36 Governor service tools for Holley 1500 distributor

DISTRIBUTORS, Standard

these features. The governor valve is identical in function to that used with the "Roto-Vance" distributor. The distributor also features a fixed breaker plate and a movable plate on which the breaker points are mounted, Fig. 35.

Distributor Service

The movable breaker plate can easily be removed as a unit with the old breaker points. New breaker points can then be installed and aligned with ease and reinstalled as an assembly in the distributor. Spring tension and breaker gap are tested and adjusted in the conventional manner.

Governor, Adjust

For adjustment on the engine, the shorter tool shown in Fig. 36 is used because other engine components are in the way. The longer tool is necessary for disassembly and assembly of the governor valve. These tools are available from any Holley distributor.
1. Remove governor service band and gasket assembly.
2. Remove hex head plug at adjusting end of valve, using a $1/8''$ Allen wrench.
3. Install slotted end of tool over spring adjusting nut.

NOTE: The spring type adjusting screw cannot be adjusted with a screwdriver or by any other means except by this special tool.

Disassemble Governor Valve

1. Remove service band and gasket.
2. Bend ears of lockwasher from governor counterweight.
3. Remove hex head plug.
4. Slip a $7/16''$ deep socket over the long disassembly tool and loosen counterweight.
5. Hold tool in fixed position and unscrew counterweight by rotating deep socket with the fingers.
6. When spring adjusting screw is completely out of governor counterweight, let the socket and counterweight slide up the shaft of the tool, and push the valve spring and adjusting nut out of the opening in the opposite side of the distributor.

ELECTRONIC IGNITION

INDEX

	Page No.
American Motors:	
BID	152
Solid-State	155
Chrysler	158
Delco-Remy:	
Capacitor Discharge	161
High Energy Ignition	164
Transistor Controlled	161
Ford:	
Breakerless	169
Duraspark	169
Holley	173
Prestolite	176

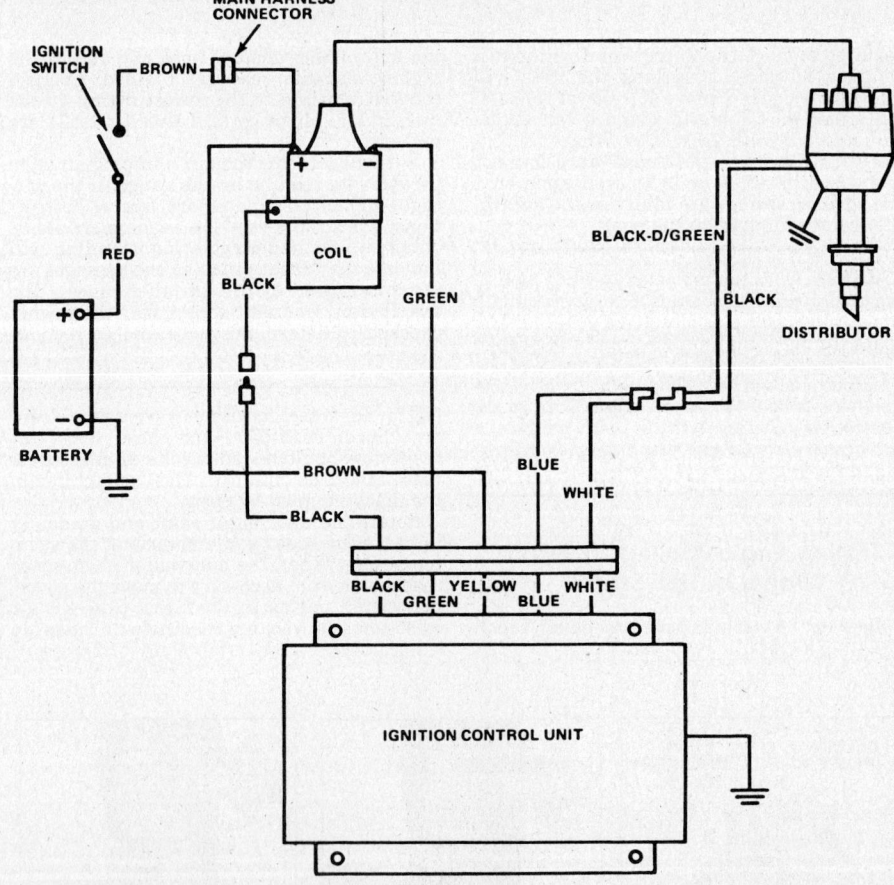

Fig. 1 American Motors BID ignition system wiring

AMERICAN MOTORS BREAKERLESS INDUCTIVE DISCHARGE (BID) IGNITION SYSTEM

Description

The BID ignition system incorporates four major units; an electronic control unit, ignition coil, distributor and high tension wires, Fig. 1. The electronic control unit is a solid-state, moisture resistant module with the components sealed in a potting compound to resist vibration and environmental conditions. Since the control unit has an internal current regulator, a resistance wire or ballast resistor is not necessary in the primary circuit. Battery voltage is applied to the ignition coil positive terminal when the ignition switch is in the "On" or "Start" position, therefore, an ignition system bypass is not required in this system. The primary coil circuit is electronically regulated by this unit.

The ignition coil is of standard construction and requires no special service. The function of the ignition coil in the BID ignition system is the same as for conventional ignition systems.

The distributor is conventional except the contact points, condenser and cam are replaced by a sensor and trigger wheel, and since no wearing occurs between the trigger wheel and sensor, dwell angle remains constant and requires no adjustment. The sensor is a small coil of fine wire and receives an alternating current signal from the electronic control unit. The sensor develops an electromagnetic field used to detect the presence of

Electronic Ignition

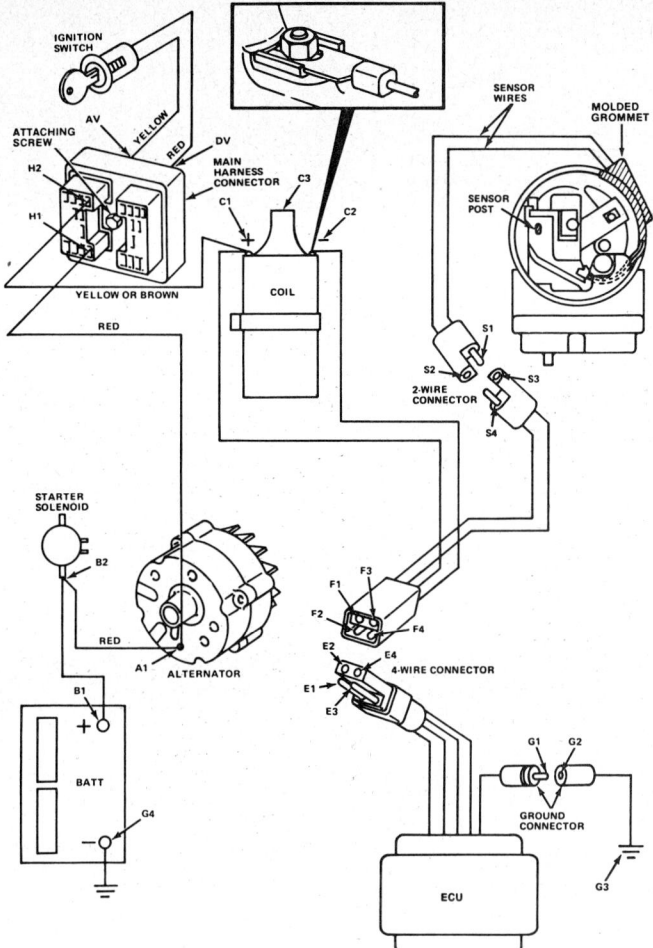

Fig. 2 BID ignition system checkpoints

metal which are the leading edges of the trigger wheel teeth.

Operation

When the ignition switch is placed in the "Start" or "Run" position, the control unit is activated. An oscillator within the control unit excites the sensor coil, in turn developing the electromagnetic field. When a leading edge of a trigger wheel tooth enters the electromagnetic field, the tooth reduces the sensor oscillation strength to a predetermined level, in turn activating the demodulator circuit. The demodulator circuit controls a power transistor located in series with the coil primary circuit. The power transistor switches the coil primary circuit off, thereby inducing a high voltage in the coil secondary winding. The high voltage is then delivered to the spark plugs through the distributor rotor, cap and high tension wires.

Troubleshooting, Fig. 2

1. Disconnect Electronic Control Unit (ECU) ground wire and the four wire connector. Using a small wire brush and solvent, clean the terminals. Leave connectors disconnected.
2. Disconnect battery cables, then momentarily move ignition switch to START and allow it to move to ON.
3. Measure resistance of entire ignition feed circuit by connecting an ohmmeter to battery positive B1 and F3 terminal in the 4-wire connector.
4. If resistance is less than 1 ohm, tighten main harness connector attaching screw to fully seat connector. If resistance is 1 ohm or more, isolate trouble area by connecting the ohmmeter and measuring the resistance of each portion of the ignition feed circuit between the following terminals: B1 and B2, B2 and A1, A1 and H1, F3 and C1, C1 and H2, H1 and H2, AV and DV. Clean, tighten or reposition connectors as needed.
5. Inspect coil primary connections for looseness and proper assembly. Wire terminals must be between channel washer and nut, channel washer tabs must be facing up. Reposition and tighten as needed.
6. Connect an ohmmeter between F3 and F4 terminals to measure coil primary circuit resistance. If resistance is 1-2 ohms, proceed to step 7. If resistance is less than 1 ohm, replace coil and proceed to step 8. If resistance is more than 2 ohms, isolate trouble and insure that the resistance between the following terminals is as follows: C1 and C2; 1-2 ohms, F3 and C1; 0 ohms, F4 and C2; 0 ohms. Replace coil or repair trouble area and proceed to step 7. If coil was replaced, proceed to step 8.
7. Measure coil secondary resistance by removing coil secondary wire from coil and connecting ohmmeter between C1 and C3.

NOTE: Set ohmmeter to the 1,000 ohm scale before testing secondary resistance.

If resistance is 9,000–15,000 ohms, reconnect coil secondary wire and proceed to step 8. If resistance is less than 9,000 ohms or more than 15,000 ohms, replace coil and reconnect coil secondary wire and proceed to Step 8.

8. Remove distributor cap, rotor and dust cover and check for 1.6–2.4 ohms resistance between F1 and F2 terminals.

NOTE: Pull and flex sensor wires, firmly squeeze molded sensor grommet at distributor, and apply firm side to side pressure on sensor post while checking resistance.

If resistance is as specified and steady, proceed to step 10. If resistance is too high or low, or if needle fluctuates or wavers, proceed to step 9.

9. Disconnect 2 wire connector and check for 1.6–2.4 ohms resistance between S1 and S2 terminals.

NOTE: Pull and flex sensor wires, firmly squeeze molded sensor wire grommet at distributor, and apply firm side to side pressure on sensor post.

If resistance is as specified and steady, proceed to step 10. If resistance is too high or two low, or if needle fluctuates or wavers, replace sensor and proceed to step 10.

10. Using a small wire brush and solvent, clean terminals S1, S2, S3 and S4.
11. Measure resistance of ECU ground circuit by connecting an ohmmeter between terminal G2 and battery negative cable G4. Resistance should be 0 ohms. Clean and tighten connections as needed.
12. Using pliers, squeeze terminals, E1, E2, E3, E4 and G1 until terminals have a distinct oval shape, thereby assuring a tight fit when terminals are connected.
13. Using petroleum jelly, coat the male terminals in the 4 wire connector and ground connectors and around the outer edge of the terminal end of the ECU 4 wire connector.
14. Connect the 4 wire and ground connectors.
15. Connect Pulse Simulator J-25331 to the S3 and S4 terminals and reconnect battery cables. Remove coil secondary wire from distributor and place end of wire ½ inch from ground, then with ignition switch ON, operate simulator and observe for spark across the ½ inch gap. If spark jumps gap, proceed to step 17. If spark does not jump gap, proceed to step 16.
16. Disconnect wire from coil negative terminal, then connect one pulse simulator clip to the coil negative terminal and connect the remaining clip to the ground. With ignition switch ON, operate pulse simulator and observe for spark across the ½ inch gap when button is released. If spark jumps the gap, replace ECU unit and proceed to step 17. If spark does not jump gap, replace coil before proceeding to step 17.

NOTE: If ECU unit is replaced, squeeze and lubricate the connectors as described

153

Electronic Ignition

in steps 12 and 13.

17. Disconnect pulse simulator. Before connecting 2-wire connector, squeeze and lubricate terminals as described in steps 12 and 13. Connect coil negative wire.
18. Inspect distributor cap for cracks and carbon tracks. Replace as necessary. Install dust cover, rotor, distributor cap and coil secondary wire.

NOTE: If the malfunction still exists after performing the above procedure, connect an engine oscilloscope and measure the ignition dwell. A scope must be used because a dwell meter will not accurately measure the dwell on this system. Start the engine and observe the dwell readings, then lower the hood being careful not to squeeze the oscilloscope leads between the fender and hood and allow the engine and wiring harness to warm up for 10 minutes. Prior to, during and after the engine warm up period, the dwell must be 23° on V8 engines and 32° for 6 cylinder engines and the dwell must not vary more than 3° at any time. If the dwell readings are as specified at all times, the malfunction may be caused by the fuel system. If the fuel system checks out OK and the malfunction still exists, replace the ECU unit and recheck the dwell. If the dwell readings are still not as specified above, replace the ignition wiring harness and recheck the dwell above. If the dwell is below specifications, disconnect the 4-wire connector and measure the sensor circuit resistance and integrity as described in step 8. If sensor circuit resistance and integrity are within specifications, replace ECU unit. If sensor circuit resistance is too high or too low, or if needle fluctuates, replace the sensor. Be sure to squeeze and lubricate the terminals as described in steps 12 and 13.

Component Replacement

1. Place distributor in a suitable holding fixture and remove cap, rotor and dust shield, Fig. 3.
2. Using a small gear puller, remove trigger wheel. Ensure puller jaws are gripping trigger wheel inner shoulder to prevent trigger wheel damage. Also, use a thick flat washer or nut as a spacer and do not press against small center shaft.
3. Loosen sensor locking screw approximately three turns, lift sensor lead grommet from distributor bowl and pull sensor leads from slot around sensor spring pivot pin. Release sensor spring, ensure spring clears sensor leads and slide sensor from bracket.

NOTE: The sensor locking screw utilizes a tamper proof head design and requires tool J-25097 for removal. However, if special tool is not available, use a small needlenose plier to remove screw. The service (replacement) sensor has a standard slotted head screw.

4. If vacuum control unit is to be replaced, remove retaining screw and vacuum unit.
5. Install new vacuum control unit and assemble sensor, sensor guide, flat washer and retaining screw.

NOTE: Install retaining screw far enough to hold assembly together and ensure it does not protrude past bottom of sensor.

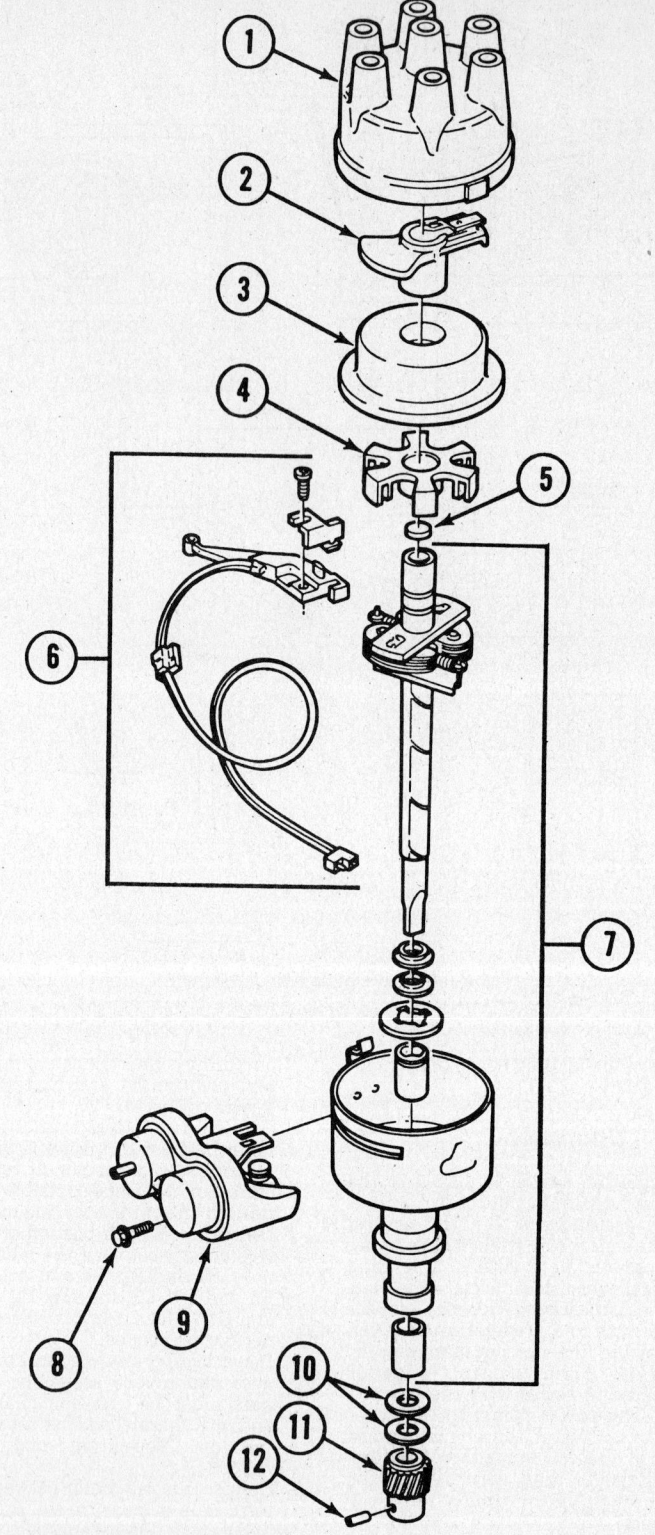

1. DISTRIBUTOR CAP
2. ROTOR
3. DUST SHIELD
4. TRIGGER WHEEL
5. FELT
6. SENSOR ASSEMBLY
7. HOUSING
8. VACUUM CONTROL SCREW
9. VACUUM CONTROL
10. SHIM
11. DRIVE GEAR
12. PIN

Fig. 3 Exploded view of BID distributor

ELECTRONIC IGNITION

6. If vacuum control has been replaced and original sensor is being used, replace special head screw with standard slotted head screw.
7. Install sensor assembly on vacuum chamber bracket, ensuring tip of sensor located properly in summing bar. Place sensor spring on sensor and route sensor leads around spring pivot pin, Fig. 4. Install sensor lead grommet and position leads away from trigger wheel.
8. Install sensor positioning gauge over yoke, ensure gauge is against flat of shaft, and move sensor sideways until gauge can be positioned. Snug retaining screw and check sensor position by removing and installing gauge, Fig. 5. When gauge can be removed and replaced without sensor side movement, sensor is positioned properly. Tighten retaining screw and check sensor position.
9. Place trigger wheel on yoke and check if sensor core is positioned approximately in center of trigger wheel legs. Bend a .050 inch gauge wire to dimension specified in Fig. 6, and place between trigger wheel legs and sensor base. Press trigger wheel onto yoke until legs contact gauge wire.
10. Apply 3 to 5 drops of light engine oil to felt wick in top of yoke, then install dust shield, rotor and cap.

AMERICAN MOTORS SOLID STATE IGNITION SYSTEM

This ignition system, Fig. 7, is used on 1978-80 vehicles. The solid state ignition system consists of the ignition switch, electronic ignition control unit, ignition coil, primary resistance wire and bypass, distributor and spark plugs.

The electronic ignition control unit is a solid state, moisture resistant module. The component parts are sealed in a potting material to resist vibration and environmental conditions. The control unit is incorporated with reverse polarity protection and transient voltage protection.

The distributor incorporates a sensor and trigger wheel. Current flowing through the ignition coil creates a magnetic field in the primary windings. When the circuit is opened, the magnetic field collapses and induces a high voltage in the coil secondary windings. This circuit is electronically controlled by the electronic ignition control unit. The distributor sensor and trigger wheel provide the signal to operate the control unit. The trigger wheel is mounted on the distributor shaft and has one tooth for each cylinder. The sensor, a coil of fine wire mounted to a permanent magnet, develops an electromagnetic force that is sensitive to the presence of ferrous metal. The sensor detects the trigger wheel teeth as the teeth pass the sensor. When a trigger wheel tooth approaches the pole piece of the sensor, it reduces the reluctance of the magnetic field, increasing field strength. Field strength decreases as the tooth moves away from the pole piece. This increase and decrease of field strength generates an alternating current which is interpreted by the electronic ignition control unit. The control unit then opens and closes the ignition coil primary circuit.

Since there are no contacting surfaces and no wear occurs, dwell angle requires no adjustment. The dwell angle is electronically controlled by the electronic ignition control unit. When the coil circuit is switched open, an electronic timer in the control unit keeps the circuit open only long enough for the spark to discharge. Then, it automatically closes the ignition coil primary circuit.

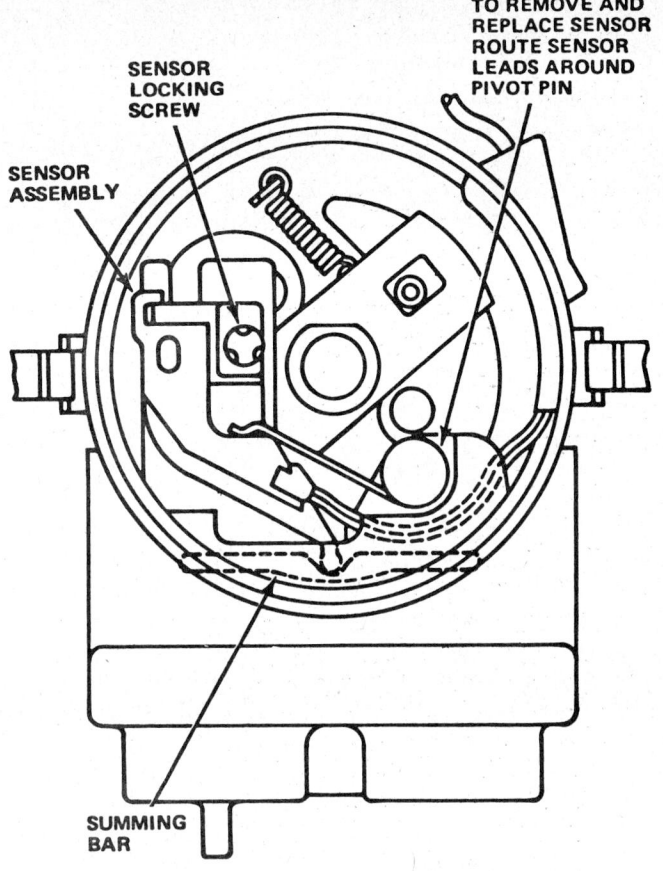

Fig. 4 Sensor installation

Trouble Shooting

Secondary Circuit Test
1. Disconnect coil wire from distributor cap and, using insulated pliers, hold wire approximately 1/2 inch from a good engine ground.
2. Crank engine and observe wire for spark. If no spark occurs, proceed to Step 5. If spark occurs, proceed to Step 3.
3. Reconnect coil wire to distributor cap. Remove wire from one spark plug.

CAUTION: Do not remove wires from spark plugs on cylinders 3 or 5 on six cylinder engines or cylinders 3 or 4 on V8 engines when performing this test since the sensor may be damaged.

4. Using insulated pliers, hold wire approximately 1/2 inch from a good engine ground. Crank engine and observe wire for spark. If spark occurs, check for fuel system problems or incorrect ignition timing. If no spark occurs, check for defective distributor cap, rotor or spark plug wires.
5. If no spark occurs at coil wire, measure coil wire resistance. If resistance is greater than 10,000 ohms, replace wire.
6. If malfunction still exists, proceed to the following tests or diagnosis procedures.

Intermittent Failure Diagnosis
Since intermittent failure may be caused by loose or corroded terminals, defective components, poor ground connections or defective wiring, it is necessary to check all wiring connections in the ignition system. Also, refer to Fig. 8 for further diagnosis.

Ignition Coil Primary Circuit Test
1. Turn ignition switch "On" and connect a voltmeter between ignition coil positive terminal and the ground. If voltage is 5.5-6.5 volts, proceed to Step 2. If battery voltage is noted, proceed to Step 4. If voltage is below 5.5 volts, disconnect condenser lead. If voltage is not 5.5-6.5 volts, replace condenser. If voltage is still not within specifications, proceed to Step 6.
2. Turn ignition switch to "Start" and measure voltage at coil positive terminal while cranking engine. If battery voltage is present while cranking engine, the ignition coil primary circuit is satisfactory. If voltage present is less than battery voltage, proceed to Step 3.
3. Check for shorted or open circuit in wire attached to starter "I" terminal. Check for defective starter solenoid. Repair as necessary.
4. Place ignition switch in "On" position, disconnect wire from starter solenoid "I" terminal and measure voltage at ignition coil positive terminal. If voltage drops to 5.5-6.5 volts, replace starter solenoid. If voltage remains constant at battery voltage, connect a jumper wire between ignition coil negative terminal and the ground. If voltage drops to 5.5-6.5 volts, proceed to Step 5. If not, repair defective resistance wire and repeat Step 2.
5. Check continuity between ignition coil

ELECTRONIC IGNITION

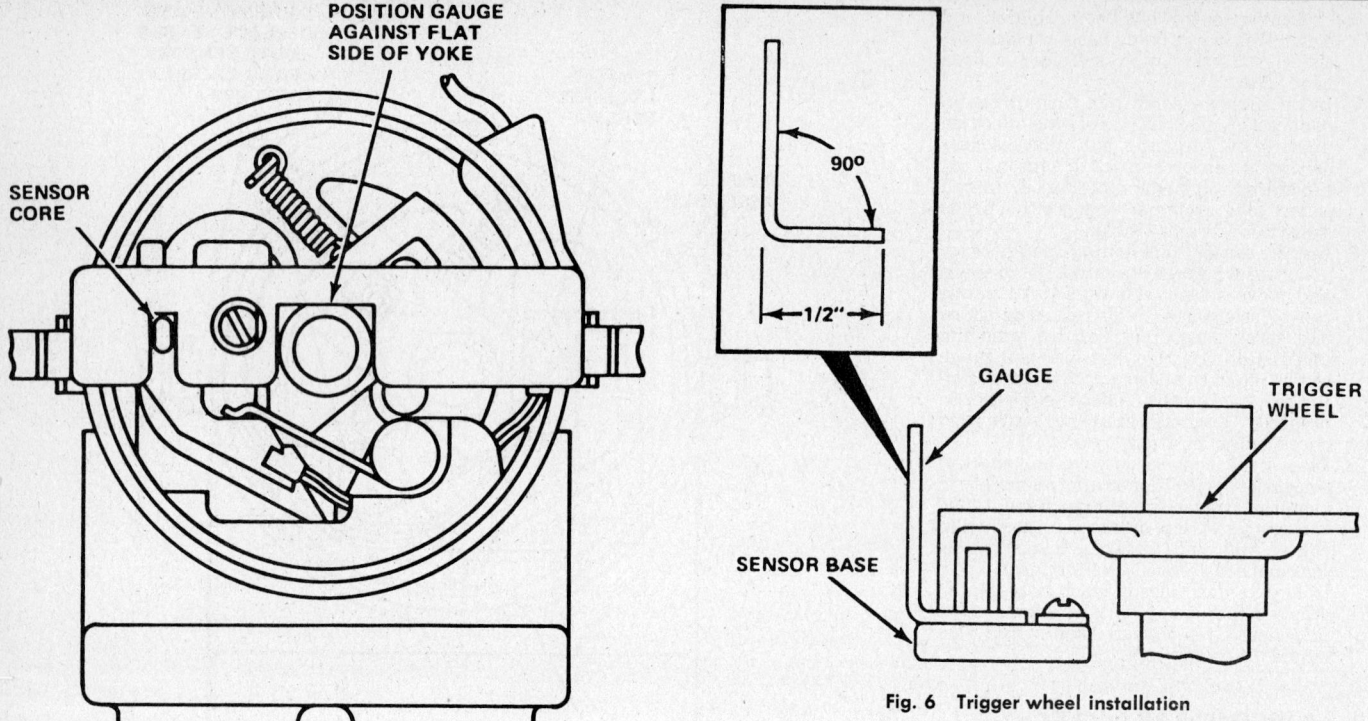

Fig. 5 Positioning sensor

Fig. 6 Trigger wheel installation

negative terminal and terminal "D4", Fig. 7. Also, check continuity between terminal "D1" and the ground. If continuity is present, replace electronic ignition control unit. If continuity is not present, locate and repair open circuit.
6. Turn ignition switch "Off" and measure resistance between ignition coil positive terminal and the dash connector "AV", Fig. 7. If resistance is greater than 1.40 ohms, repair or replace resistance wire. If resistance is 1.30–1.40 ohms, proceed to Step 7.
7. With ignition "Off", measure resistance between dash connector "AV" and ignition switch terminal "I1", Fig. 7. If resistance is greater than .1 ohm, check and repair terminal connections at dash connector or defective wiring.

Coil Test
1. Inspect ignition coil for oil leaks, exterior damage and carbon tracks. If satisfactory, proceed to Step 2. If not, replace ignition coil.
2. Disconnect ignition coil connector and connect ohmmeter between coil terminals. If resistance is 1.13–1.23 ohms at 75° F. or 1.5 ohms at 200° F., proceed to Step 3. If not, replace ignition coil.
3. Connect ohmmeter between ignition coil center tower and the plus or minus terminal. Resistance should be 7700–9300 ohms. If not replace ignition coil.

Sensor & Control Unit Test
1. Disconnect the four wire connector at the control unit, Fig. 7. Disconnect coil wire from center tower of distributor and hold wire approximately 1/2 inch from a good engine ground with insulated pliers, then turn ignition "On". If spark is observed at coil wire, proceed to next step. If not, proceed to Step 5.
2. Measure resistance between terminals "D2" and "D3" of the harness connector, Fig. 7. If resistance is 400–800 ohms, proceed to Step 6. If not, proceed to next step.

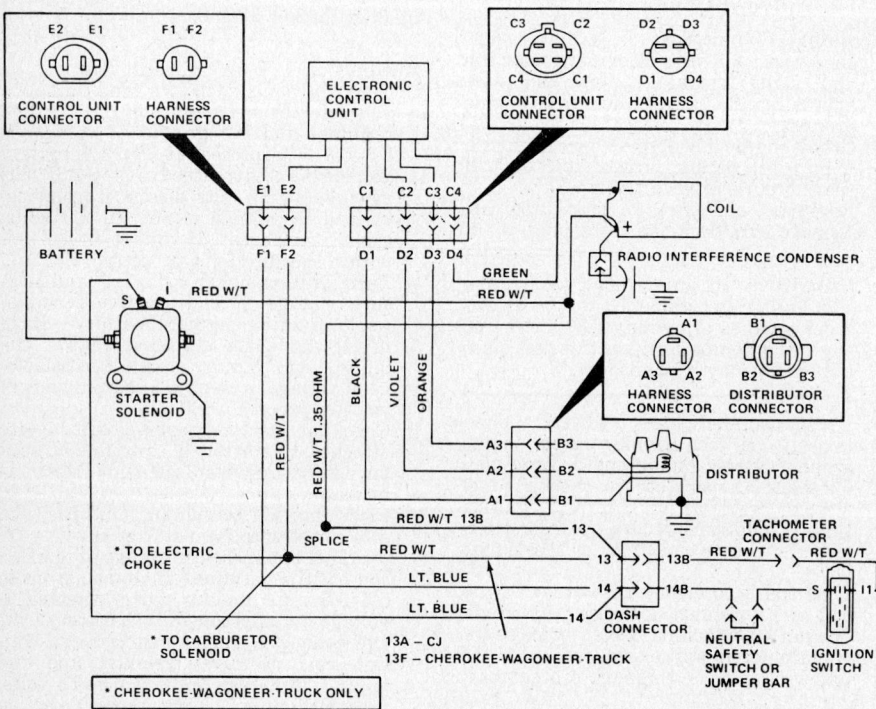

Fig. 7 American Motors solid state ignition system schematic

ELECTRONIC IGNITION

3. Disconnect and connect the three wire connector at distributor and measure resistance between terminals "D2" and "D3" of the harness connector, Fig. 7. If resistance is now between 400–800 ohms, proceed to Step 6. If not, disconnect three wire connector at distributor and proceed to next step.
4. Measure resistance between terminals "B2" and "B3" of the distributor connector, Fig. 7. If resistance is not 400–800 ohms, repair or replace harness between three wire and four wire connector.
5. Connect an ohmmeter between terminal "D1" of the harness connector, Fig. 7, and the battery negative terminal. If reading is below .002 ohm, repeat Step 2. If not, check for an improper ground. Check ground cable resistance, distributor to engine block resistance and distributor ground screw to terminal "D1" resistance, Fig. 7.
6. Using a voltmeter connected between terminals "D2" and "D3" of the harness connector, Fig. 7, observed reading while cranking engine. If voltmeter reading fluctuates, it indicates proper sensor and trigger wheel operation. If not, the trigger wheel is defective or the distributor is not rotating.

Ignition Feed To Control Unit Test

NOTE: Perform the "Ignition Coil Primary Circuit Test" before performing this test.

1. Disconnect two wire connector from control unit and connect a voltmeter between terminal "F2" and the ground, Fig. 7. Turn ignition "On". If voltmeter reading is within .2 volts of battery voltage, replace control unit and proceed to Step 3. If voltmeter reading is not within .2 volt of battery voltage, proceed to next step.
2. Locate and repair cause of voltage reduction as noted in Step 1. Check for a corroded dash connector or defective ignition switch. Then, check for spark at coil wire. If not, replace control unit.
3. Connect the two wire connector at control unit and disconnect the four wire connector from control unit. Connect an ammeter between terminal "C1" and the ground, Fig. 7. If ammeter reading is 1 ± .1 amp., the system is satisfactory. If ammeter reading is higher or lower, replace module.

Current Flow Test

1. Remove connector from coil.
2. Depress plastic barb and remove positive wire from connector. Remove negative wire in same manner.
3. Connect an ammeter between coil positive terminal and the disconnected positive wire.
4. Connect a jumper wire between coil negative terminal and the engine ground.
5. Turn ignition "On" and note ammeter reading. Reading should be approximately 7 amps. and not exceeding 7.6 amps. If reading exceeds 7.6 amps., replace ignition coil.
6. Remove jumper wire from coil negative

Condition	Possible Cause	Correction
ENGINE FAILS TO START (NO SPARK AT PLUGS)	1. No voltage to ignition system 2. Electronic Control Unit ground lead inside distributor open, loose or corroded. 3. Primary wiring connectors and fully engaged. 4. Coil open or shorted. 5. Electronic Control Unit defective. 6. Cracked distributor cap. 7. Defective rotor.	1. Check battery, ignition switch and wiring. Repair as required. 2. Clean, tighten or repair as required. 3. Clean and fully engage connectors. 4. Test coil. Replace if faulty. 5. Replace Electronic Control Unit. 6. Replace cap. 7. Replace rotor.
ENGINE BACKFIRES BUT FAILS TO START	1. Incorrect ignition timing. 2. Moisture in distributor. 3. Distributor cap faulty. 4. Ignition wire not in correct firing order.	1. Check timing. Adjust as required. 2. Dry cap and rotor. 3. Check cap for loose terminals, cracks and dirt. Clean or replace as required. 4. Install in correct order.
ENGINE RUNS ONLY WITH KEY IN START POSITION	1. Open in resistance wire or excessive resistance.	1. Repair resistance wire.
ENGINE CONTINUES TO RUN WITH KEY OFF	1. Defective starter solenoid. 2. Defective ignition switch.	1. Replace solenoid. 2. Replace switch.
ENGINE DOES NOT OPERATE SMOOTHLY AND/OR ENGINE MISFIRES AT HIGH SPEED	1. Spark plugs fouled or faulty. 2. Ignition cables faulty. 3. Spark advance system(s) faulty. 4. "I" terminal shorted to starter terminal in solenoid. 5. Trigger wheel pin missing. 6. Distributor wires installed in wrong firing order.	1. Clean and gap plugs. Replace as required. 2. Check cables. Replace as required. 3. Check operation. Repair as required. 4. Replace solenoid. 5. Install pin. 6. Install wires correctly.
EXCESSIVE FUEL CONSUMPTION	1. Incorrect ignition timing. 2. Spark advance system(s) faulty.	1. Check timing. Adjust as required. 2. Check operation. Repair as required.
ERRATIC TIMING ADVANCE	1. Faulty vacuum advance assembly. 2. Centrifugal weights sticking.	1. Check operation. Replace if required. 2. Remove dirt, corrosion.
TIMING NOT AFFECTED BY VACUUM	1. Defective vacuum advance unit. 2. Advance unit adjusting screw too far counterclockwise. 3. Sensor pivot corroded.	1. Replace vacuum advance unit. 2. Turn screw clockwise to bring advance curve within specifications. 3. Clean pivot.
INTERMITTENT OPERATION	1. Loose or corroded terminals. 2. Defective sensor. 3. Defective control unit. 4. Loose ground connector in distributor. 5. Wires to distributor shorted together or to ground.	1. Clean and tighten terminals. Apply electrical grease. 2. Perform sensor tests. 3. Perform control unit tests. 4. Clean and tighten connection. 5. Check for frayed, pinched or burned wires.

Fig. 8 American Motors solid state ignition system service diagnosis chart

Electronic Ignition

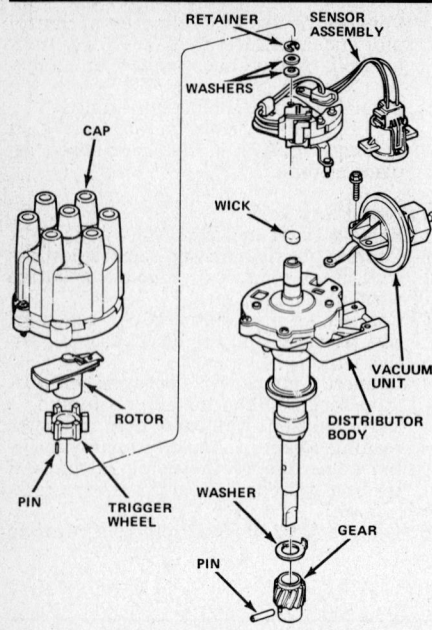

Fig. 9 American Motors distributor used with solid state ignition system (Typical)

terminal and connect the coil green wire to negative terminal. Ammeter reading should be approximately 4 amps. If reading is less than 3.5 amps., check for poor connections at the three wire and four wire connectors or a poor ground at distributor ground screw. If reading is greater than 5 amps., the control unit is defective, requiring replacement.

7. Start and run engine. Ammeter reading should be 2–2.4 amps. If not, replace control unit.

Distributor Service

Trigger Wheel & Sensor, Replace

1. Remove distributor cap and rotor, Fig. 9.
2. Remove trigger wheel with a suitable gear puller. Use a flat washer to prevent gear puller from contacting inner shaft. The trigger wheel may also be removed by using two screwdrivers to pry trigger wheel upward. Remove pin.
3. On six cylinder distributors, remove sensor retainer and washers from pivot pin on base plate.
4. On V8 distributors, remove sensor snap ring from shaft, then the retainer from vacuum unit to sensor drive pin and position vacuum unit lever aside.
5. On all distributors, remove ground screw from harness tab.
6. Remove sensor assembly from distributor housing.
7. Reverse procedure to assemble.

Vacuum Unit, Replace

1. Disconnect vacuum hose.
2. On six cylinder distributors, remove vacuum unit attaching screws and the vacuum unit, Fig. 9. It is necessary to tilt the vacuum unit to disengage the link from the sensor pin and also loosen the base plate screws for clearance.
3. On V8 distributors, remove distributor cap and the retainer from the sensor pin. Remove vacuum unit attaching screws and the vacuum unit, Fig. 9.
4. Reverse procedure to install. If a new vacuum unit is installed, it must be calibrated as follows:
   a. Insert an appropriate size allen wrench into vacuum hose tube of original vacuum unit. Rotate allen wrench clockwise and note the number of turns required to bottom the adjusting screw.
   b. Insert allen wrench into vacuum hose tube of replacement vacuum unit. Turn the allen wrench clockwise until the adjusting screw is bottomed, then rotate allen wrench counterclockwise the number of turns noted in the previous step.

CHRYSLER SYSTEM

This system, Fig. 10, is composed of a magnetic distributor, an electronic control unit, a wiring harness, a production coil and a dual ballast resistor.

The distributor is essentially the same as the conventional type except the contacts have been replaced by a pickup coil and the cam by a reluctor. With a conventional contact type system, the voltage necessary to fire the spark plugs is developed by interrupting the current flowing through the primary of the ignition coil by opening a set of contacts. With the Electronic System, the voltage is produced the same way except that the current is interrupted by a transistor in the electronic control unit. This happens each time the control unit receives a "timing" pulse from the distributor magnetic pickup.

Since the magnetic pickup, reluctor and the control unit, which replace the contact points and cam, do not normally change or wear out with service, engine timing and dwell does not require periodic adjusting. This minimizes regular ignition maintenance to cleaning and replacing the spark plugs.

Trouble Shooting

Engine Will Not Start—Fuel System OK
1. Dual ballast.
2. Faulty ignition coil.
3. Faulty pickup or improper pickup air gap.
4. Faulty wiring.
5. Faulty control unit.

Engine Surges Severly—Not Lean Carburetor
1. Wiring.
2. Faulty pickup leads.
3. Ignition coil.

Engine Misses—Carburetion Good
1. Spark plugs.
2. Secondary cables.
3. Ignition coil.
4. Wiring.
5. Control unit.

System Testing

NOTE: To completely test components and circuits of the electronic ignition system, special testers should be used. However, in event the testers are not available, the following procedures may be utilized. A voltmeter with a 20,000 volt/ohm rating and an ohmmeter using a 1.5 volt battery for power should be used for testing. Before performing any electrical tests, ensure all wiring is properly connected.

Harness Wiring Test

1. Check battery voltage and note reading.
2. Disconnect harness connector from control unit.

CAUTION: Before disconnecting or connecting harness connector, ensure ignition switch is in the "Off" position.

3. Turn ignition switch to "On" position.
4. Connect the voltmeter between harness connector cavity No. 1 and the ground. Voltage reading should be within 1 volt of battery voltage earlier noted. If not, check circuit between cavity No. 1 and the battery, Fig. 11.
5. Test harness connector cavities numbers 2 and 3 in same manner. If voltage is not within specifications, check circuits between cavities numbers 2 and 3 and the battery, Figs. 12 and 13.
6. Turn ignition switch to "Off" position.

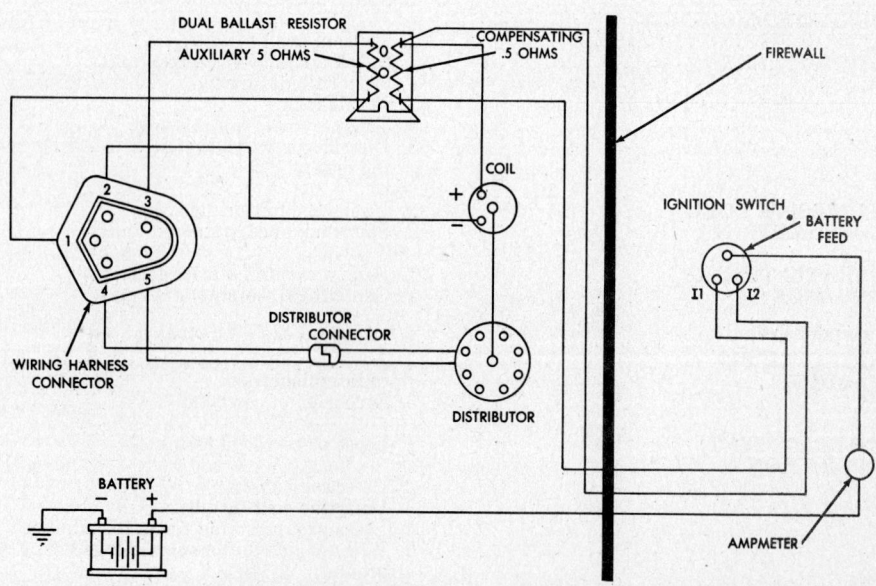

Fig. 10 Chrysler electronic ignition system wiring

158

Electronic Ignition

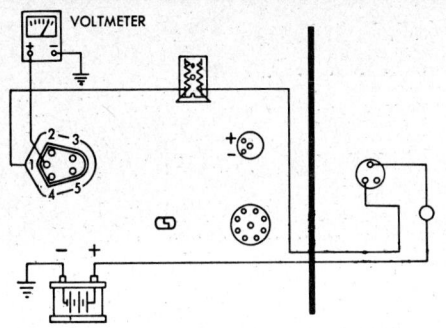

Fig. 11 Harness wiring test, No. 1 cavity

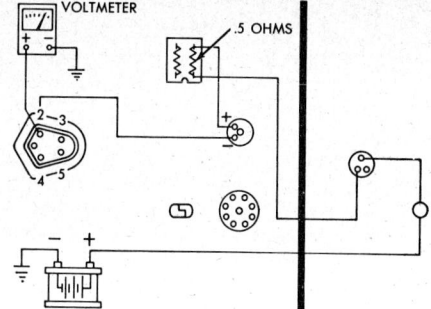

Fig. 12 Harness wiring test, No. 2 cavity

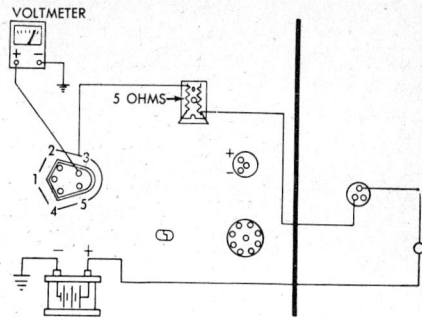

Fig. 13 Harness wiring test, No. 3 cavity

Distributor Pick-up Coil Test

1. Connect an ohmmeter between harness connector cavities numbers 4 and 5, Fig. 14. Resistance reading should be 150 to 900 ohms.
2. If reading is not as specified in above step, disconnect distributor dual lead connector and connect ohmmeter between the two leads on distributor side of connector, Fig. 15. If resistance is not between 150 and 900 ohms, replace pick-up coil.
3. Connect one ohmmeter lead to a good ground and the other lead to either connector of the distributor. If ohmmeter shows a reading, the pickup coil must be replaced.

Control Unit Ground Circuit Test

Connect an ohmmeter between control unit connector pin No. 5 and the ground, Fig. 16. If ohmmeter indicates infinite resistance, tighten bolts securing control unit to firewall and recheck resistance. If reading is still infinite, replace control unit.

Distributor Service

Distributor Shaft & Bushing Wear Test

1. Remove distributor from vehicle and clamp distributor in a vise. Use extreme caution not to damage distributor.
2. Attach a dial indicator to housing so plunger rests against reluctor sleeve.
3. Place a wire loop around reluctor sleeve and hook a spring scale on the other end of the loop. Apply a one pound pull in line with indicator plunger and read movement on indicator. Movement must not exceed .006 inch. If movement exceeds limit, replace either housing or shaft to bring movement back within tolerance.

Distributor Disassemble

1. Remove rotor and vacuum advance unit, Figs. 17 and 18.
2. Remove reluctor by prying up from bottom of reluctor using two screwdrivers with a maximum blade width of 7/16 in. Use care not to damage or distort reluctor teeth.
3. Remove two screws and lockwashers attaching lower plate to distributor housing, then lift out lower plate, upper plate and pick-up coil as an assembly. Do not remove distributor cap clamp springs.
4. On six cylinder units, if distributor housing, or shaft and governor assembly are to be replaced, proceed as follows:
   a. If gear is worn or damaged, scribe a line on end of shaft from center to edge, so that line is centered between two gear teeth, Fig. 19. Do not scribe line completely across shaft. Remove distributor drive gear retaining pin and slide gear off end of shaft.

   NOTE: Support hub of gear so that pin can be driven out without damaging shaft.

   b. If necessary use a file to clean burrs from around pin hole area on shaft, then remove lower thrust washer.
   c. Push shaft upward and remove from distributor body.
5. On eight cylinder units, if distributor housing, shaft, reluctor sleeve or governor weights are to be replaced, proceed as follows:
   a. Remove distributor shaft retaining pin and slide retainer off end of shaft.
   b. If necessary, use a file to clean burrs from around pin hole area on shaft, then remove lower thrust washer.
   c. Push shaft upward and remove from distributor housing.

Distributor Assemble

1. Lubricate and test operation of governor weights. Inspect weight springs for distortion and bearing surfaces and pins for damage.
2. Lubricate upper thrust washer and install onto shaft. Install shaft into housing, Figs. 17 and 18.
3. On 6 cylinder units, install lower thrust washer and distributor gear and roll pin. If a replacement distributor gear is to be installed, proceed as follows:
   a. Install thrust washer and replacement gear on rotor shaft. Position pin hole in replacement gear approximately 90 degrees from hole in distributor shaft, with scribed line made during disassembly between gear teeth, Fig. 19.

   NOTE: On replacement distributor gears, the roll pin hole is located higher than the original gear roll pin hole, so that distributor shaft will not be weakened when the shaft is rotated 90 degrees and drilled to accomodate the replacement gear.

   b. Before drilling through shaft and gear, place a .007 in. feeler gauge between gear and thrust washer and observe that centerline between two gear teeth is in line with centerline of rotor electrode, Fig. 20. Drill a .124 to .129 in. hole and install roll pin.

   NOTE: Support gear hub when installing roll pin so gear teeth will not be damaged.

4. On eight cylinder units, install distribu-

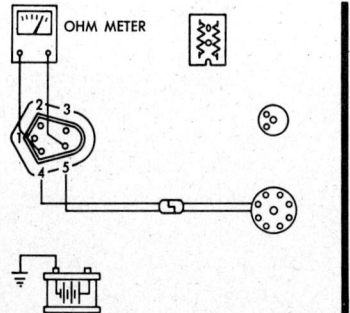

Fig. 14 Pick-up coil test, cavity Nos. 4 & 5

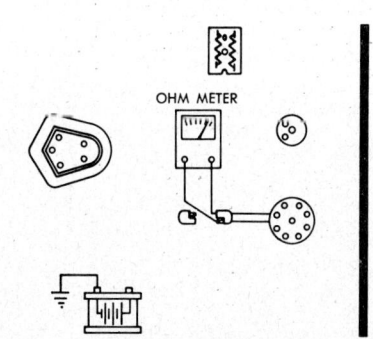

Fig. 15 Pick-up coil test, distributor lead connector

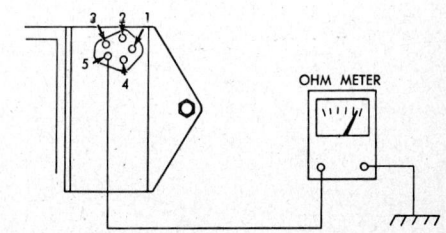

Fig. 16 Control unit ground circuit test

ELECTRONIC IGNITION

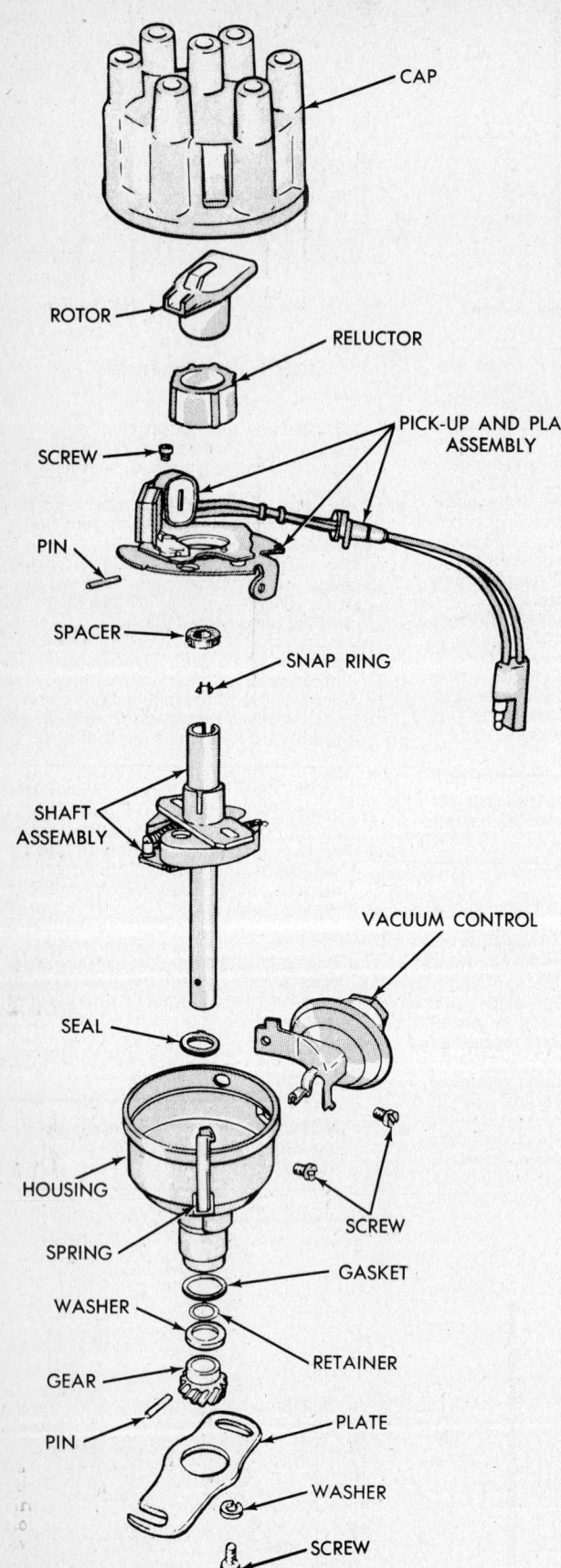

Fig. 17 Disassembled view of Chrysler electronic 6 cylinder distributor

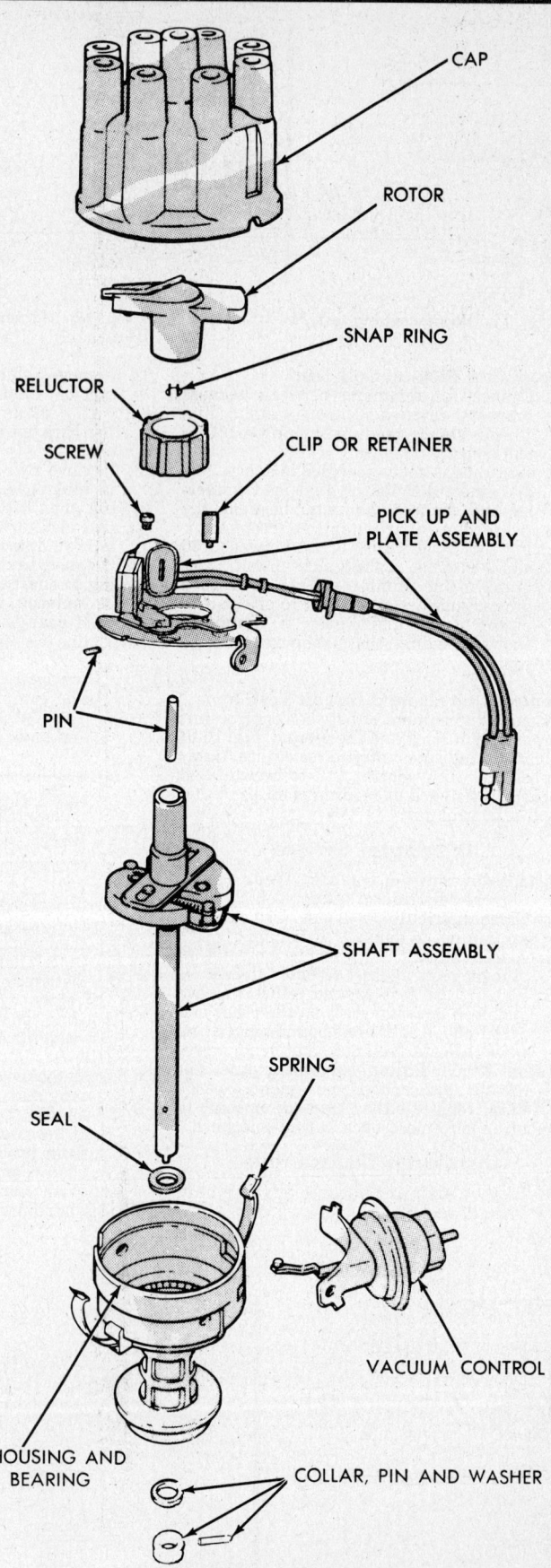

Fig. 18 Disassembled view of Chrysler electronic 8 cylinder distributor

Electronic Ignition

tor shaft retainer and pin. Fig. 18.
5. On all units, install lower plate, upper plate and pick-up coil assembly, Figs. 17 and 18.
6. Attach vacuum advance unit to pick-up plate, then install vacuum advance unit attaching screws and washers.
7. Position reluctor keeper pin into place on reluctor sleeve, then slide reluctor down reluctor sleeve and press firmly into position. Install keeper pin.
8. Lubricate felt pad located in top of reluctor sleeve with one drop of light engine oil, then install rotor.

Pick-up Replacement & Air Gap Adjustment

1. With distributor removed from vehicle, perform Steps 1 to 3 as outlined in Distributor Disassemble.
2. Remove pick-up coil and upper plate by depressing retainer clip and moving it away from mounting stud. Pick-up coil cannot be removed from upper plate.
3. Lightly lubricate upper plate pivot pin and lower plate support pins with distributor lubricant. Install upper plate pivot pin through smallest hole in lower plate and install retainer clip.

NOTE: The upper plate must ride on the support pins on the lower plate.

4. Install lower and upper plates and pick-up coil as an assembly and install distributor into vehicle.
5. To set air gap, align one reluctor tooth with pick-up pole and install a non-magnetic feeler gauge—.008 inch on except 1977-79 units or .006 inch on 1977-79 units, between reluctor tooth and pick-up pole, Fig. 21. Rotate pick-up coil until contact is made between reluctor tooth, feeler gauge and pick-up pole. Tighten pick-up coil hold down screw and remove feeler gauge. The feeler gauge should be removed without force. If not, readjust gap.
6. Perform a secondary gap check with a feeler gauge—.010 inch on except 1977-79 units or .008 inch on 1977-79 units. Do not force feeler gauge between reluctor tooth and pick-up pole since it is possible to do so. Apply vacuum to vacuum control unit. Pick-up should not contact reluctor tooth. Readjust air gap if contact occurs.

NOTE: If pick-up contacts reluctor teeth on one side of shaft only, the distributor shaft most likely is bent and shaft replacement is required.

DELCO-REMY SYSTEMS CAPACITOR DISCHARGE (CD) & TRANSISTOR CONTROLLED

Both systems employ an identical Magnetic Pulse Breakerless distributor. This unit, Fig. 22, resembles a conventional distributor. However, in the Magnetic Pulse distributor, an iron timer core replaces the conventional breaker cam, Fig. 23. The timer core has the same number of equally spaced projections as engine cylinders. The timer core rotates inside a magnetic pick-up assembly, which replaces the conventional breaker plate, contact

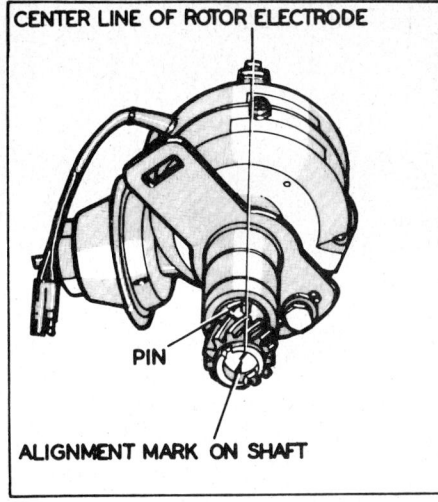

Fig. 19 Scribe line on distributor shaft. 6 cylinder units

point set and condenser assembly.

The magnetic pick-up assembly consists of a ceramic permanent magnet, a pole piece and pick-up coil. The pole piece is a metal plate having equally spaced internal teeth, one tooth for each cylinder in the engine. The magnetic pick-up assembly is mounted over the main bearing on the distributor housing and is actuated by the vacuum control unit to provide vacuum advance. The timer core is moved by conventional advance weights to provide centrifugal (mechanical) advance.

Ignition Pulse Amplifier

Transistor Controlled Type

This type amplifier, Fig. 24, consists primarily of transistors, resistors, diodes and condensers mounted on a printed circuit panel board. Since there are no moving parts, the control unit is a completely static assembly.

Fig. 25 shows a wiring diagram showing the complete circuit. Note that there are two separate ballast resistors used. The resistor connected directly to the switch is by-passed during cranking, whereas the other resistor is always in the circuit. The use of two resistors

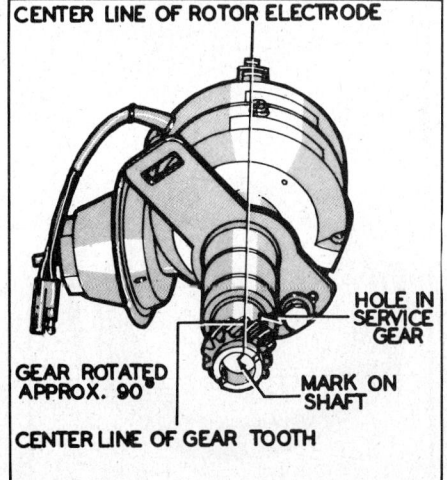

Fig. 20 Aligning gear teeth with center line of rotor electrode. 6 cylinder units

permits the required value of resistance to be by-passed during cranking.

In order to fire the spark plug, it is necessary to induce a high voltage in the ignition coil secondary winding by closing and opening the circuit to the coil primary winding. When the switch is closed (engine not running) current flows through part of the circuit. The current comes from the battery, through the switch and ballast resistor to the amplifier unit. Current then flows to two transistors and three resistors, thence to the coil primary winding and ballast resistor to ground, thus completing the circuit back to the battery.

Capacitor Discharge Amplifier

This type amplifier, Fig. 26, consists of transistors, diodes, resistors, a thyristor and a transformer. These components are mounted on a printed circuit panel board. Like the earlier amplifier, it is a solid state unit with no moving parts.

With a capacity of delivering 30,000 volts almost instantaneously, it can fire burned, fouled or even damp spark plugs. As a result, spark plug life is extended several times longer than normal in conventional systems. Because of the extremely high voltage it delivers (about one-third more than the conventional system) the CD system offers faster cold weather starting as well as improved ignition performance throughout the engine speed range.

In the CD system, the ignition coil primary is connected across a high voltage capacitor (condenser). The capacitor is charged to about 300 volts during the time the spark plugs are not firing. On impulse signal voltage from the distributor, the capacitor discharges this high voltage into the ignition coil primary.

Due to the transformer action in the coil, this high voltage primary is increased many times to produce the high voltage secondary to fire the spark plug. Fig. 27 shows a typical circuit diagram.

Voltage is supplied to the transformer which operates through a rectifying bridge circuit of four diodes to keep the capacitor charged. A zener diode limits this charge to 300 volts. This capacitor voltage is maintained at its maximum value during cranking even through battery voltage may be well below its normal 12 volts. This is due to the transformer which acts as a free-running oscillator during cranking. The adverse effect on ignition normally present in conventional ignition systems, especially during cold weather cranking, are therefore eliminated in the CD ignition system.

As the engine turns, the vanes on the rotating timer core in the distributor line up with the internal teeth on the pole piece. This establishes a magnetic path through the center of the pick-up coil. This voltage (after amplification) is applied at the gate of the Thyristor, causing it to turn on. The charged capacitor then discharges through the thyristor and primary winding of the special ignition coil, inducing the high voltage in the secondary winding to fire the spark plug. This special ignition coil acts as a step-up transformer to fire the spark plug when the primary current *increases*. This contrasts with the conventional ignition system in which the secondary voltage is induced when the distributor contacts open and the primary current *decreases*.

Periodic Service

Since the amplifier in both systems is completely static, and the distributor shaft and bushings have permanent-type lubrication, no periodic maintenance is required. The dis-

ELECTRONIC IGNITION

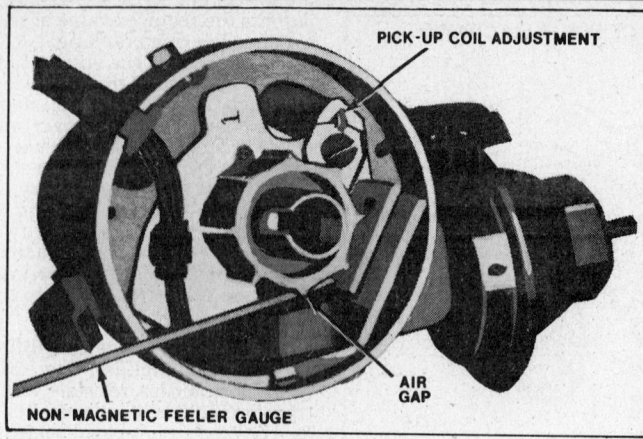

Fig. 21 Adjusting air gap

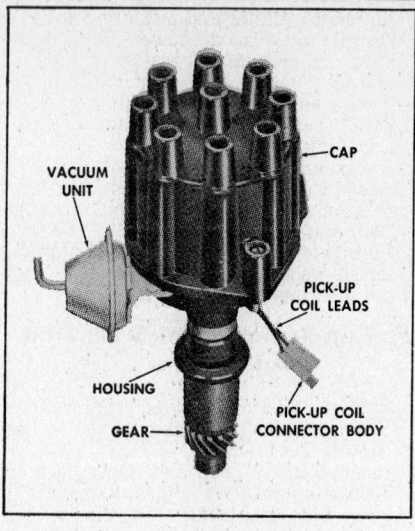

Fig. 22 Delco-Remy Magnetic Pulse distributor

tributor lower bushing is lubricated by engine oil through a splash hole in the distributor housing, and a housing cavity next to the upper bushing contains a supply of lubricant which will last between engine overhaul periods. At time of engine overhaul, the upper bushing may be lubricated by removing the plastic seal and then adding SAE 20 oil to the packing in the cavity. A new plastic seal will be required since the old one will be damaged during removal.

Trouble Shooting Procedure

Faulty engine performance usually will be evidenced by one of the following conditions: 1. Engine will not run at all. 2. Engine will start but not run. 3. Engine will miss or surge. *The special coil used in both systems cannot be tested on a conventional coil tester.*

Engine will not run at all

To determine if the ignition system is operating, hold one spark plug lead about 1/4 inch from the engine block and crank the engine. If sparking occurs, the trouble most likely is not ignition. If sparking does not occur, and the vehicle fuel system is satisfactory, check the ignition system. The spark plugs, wiring, distributor cap and rotor can be checked in the conventional manner. Only the coil requires a different procedure.

The special coil can be checked for primary and secondary winding continuity with an ohmmeter. With leads disconnected from coil, connect ohmmeter across primary terminals. If reading is infinite, winding is open. To check the secondary, connect ohmmeter to high voltage center tower and coil case. An infinite reading means coil secondary is open. *When checking secondary, use middle or high resistance range on ohmmeter.*

Checking Amplifier:
1. Temporarily connect a jumper lead from amplifier housing to a good ground.
2. If engine now will start and run, the amplifier is not properly grounded.
3. Detach positive and negative leads from coil. Note carefully the color code so wires can be reconnected in the same manner.
4. Connect a bulb between the two leads, Fig. 28.
5. Crank engine.
6. If bulb flickers on and off, amplifier is operating properly. In this case, recheck secondary system for the cause of "no run" condition.
7. If bulb does not flicker on and off, check distributor.

Distributor checks:
1. On CD system, be sure that the two distributor leads are connected to distributor connector body, Fig. 29.
2. With distributor connector disconnected from harness connector, connect an ohmmeter (1), Fig. 30, to the two terminals on distributor connector.
3. Connect a test stand vacuum source to the distributor and observe ohmmeter reading throughout vacuum range. (Distributor need not be removed from engine).
4. Any reading outside the 550–770 ohm range indicates a defective pick-up coil in distributor.
5. Remove one ohmmeter (2) lead, Fig. 30, from connector body and connect to ground.
6. Observe ohmmeter reading throughout vacuum range.
7. Any reading less than infinite indicates a defective pick-up coil.
8. Reconnect harness connector to distributor connector.

Continuity checks—CD System

Carefully inspect all wiring connections to

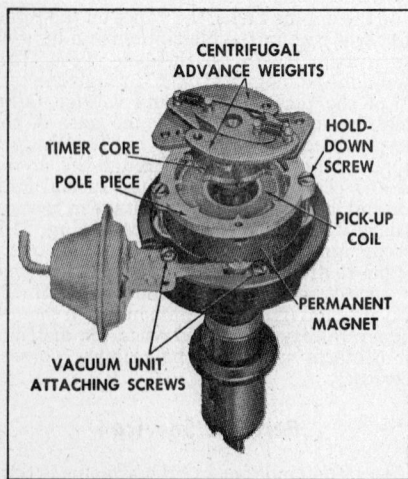

Fig. 23 Magnetic Pulse distributor components

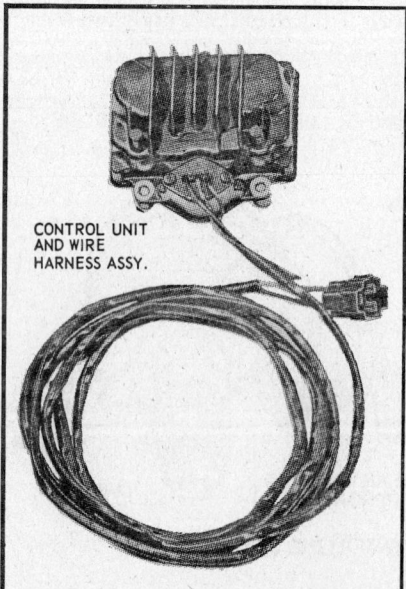

Fig. 24 Transistor controlled amplifier

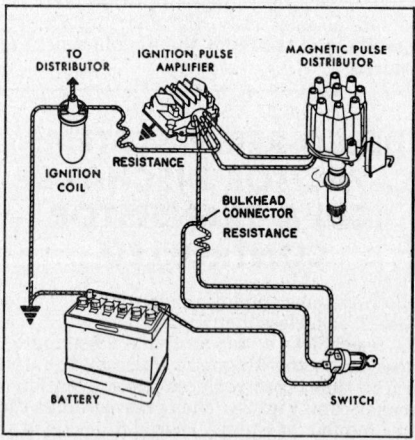

Fig. 25 Circuit diagram of transistor controlled system

ELECTRONIC IGNITION

Fig. 26 Capacitor Discharge (CD) amplifier unit

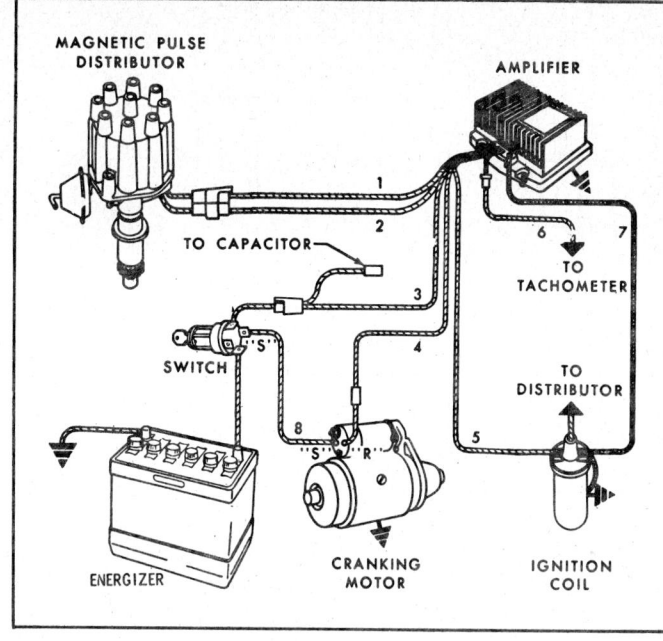

Fig. 27 CD ignition circuit (typical)

be sure that they are clean and tight. If satisfactory, disconnect amplifier No. 3 and No. 4 leads, Fig. 29, from the two connectors, then proceed as follows:

1. Connect voltmeter from ground to No. 4 connector lead.
2. Turn switch to "Start" position.
3. If reading is zero, circuit is open between connector body and battery.
4. If reading is obtained, connect voltmeter from ground to No. 3 connector lead.
5. Turn switch to the run position.
6. If reading is zero, circuit is open between connector body and switch.
7. If reading is obtained, replace amplifier.

Engine will start but not run—CD System

If engine starts but then stops when switch is returned to the run position, proceed as follows:

1. Be sure that leads are properly connected to No. 3 lead connector body.
2. If satisfactory, connect a voltmeter from ground to the terminal connector inside the connector.
3. Turn switch to run position.
4. If reading is zero, lead between connector and ignition switch is open.
5. If reading is obtained, replace amplifier.

Engine miss or surge:

The vehicle fuel system should be checked in the usual manner. If satisfactory, check the ignition system in the usual manner except the special coil which should be checked with an ohmmeter as described above.

A poorly ground amplifier can cause an engine miss or surge. If it is properly grounded and the plugs, wiring, cap and coil are satisfactory, the most likely cause for the miss or surge is a defective amplifier.

Distributor Service

Remove distributor in the usual manner, being sure to note position of rotor, then pull distributor up until rotor just stops turning and again note position of rotor. To insure correct timing of the distributor, it must be installed with the rotor correctly positioned as noted above.

If necessary to remove secondary wires from cap, mark position on cap tower for lead to No. 1 cylinder. This will aid in reinstallation of leads.

If the engine has been turned after the distributor was removed, it will be necessary to install a jumper wire and crank engine until the timing mark on vibration damper indexes with the proper mark on the engine front cover. If both valves of No. 1 cylinder are closed, the piston will be on top dead center of the firing stroke.

Fig. 31 shows an exploded view of the distributor.

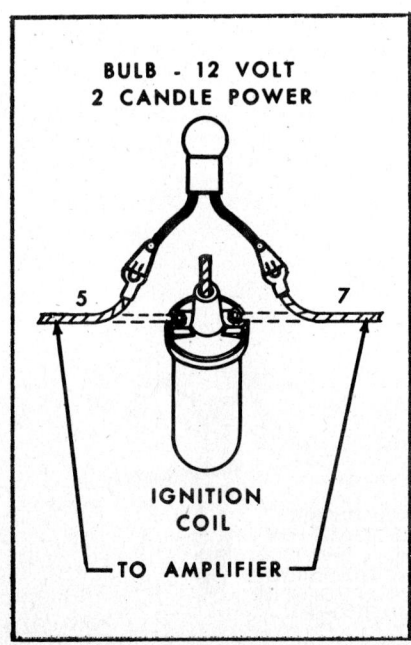

Fig. 28 Amplifier output test

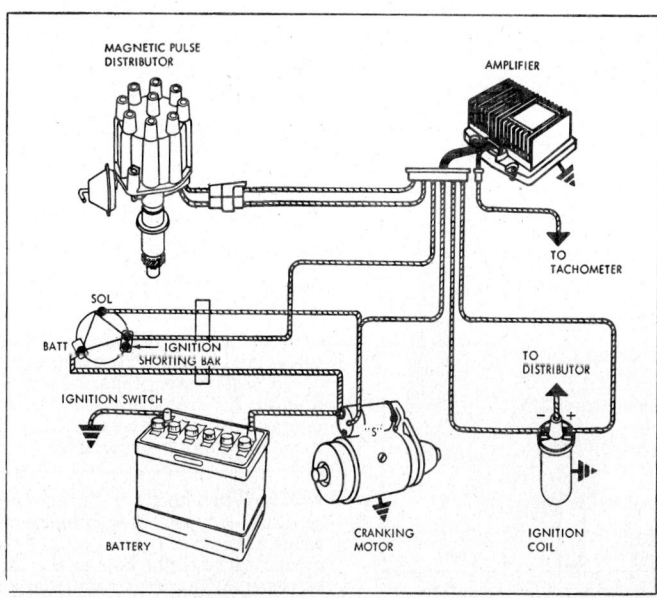

Fig. 29 Pictorial diagram of CD system

ELECTRONIC IGNITION

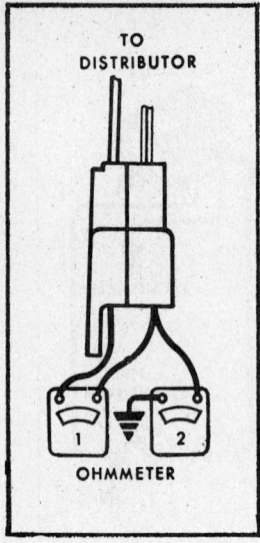

Fig. 30 Distributor test

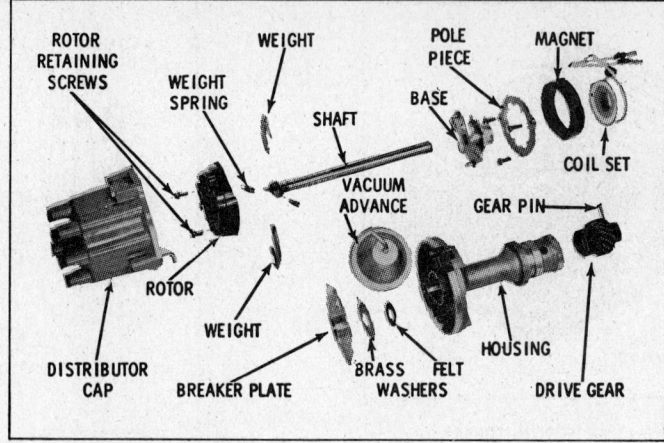

Fig. 31 Exploded view of Magnetic Pulse distributor

No adjustments can be made on either system and no periodic maintenance is required.

DELCO-REMY HIGH ENERGY IGNITION SYSTEM (H.E.I.)

The H.E.I. system utilizes an all electronic module, pickup coil and timer core in place of the conventional ignition points and condenser (the condenser is used for noise suppression only). Point pitting and rubbing block wear resulting in retarded ignition timing, is eliminated.

NOTE: H.E.I. components are not interchangeable with "Unit Distributor" Components.

Since the coil is part of the H.E.I. distributor there is no need for distributor-to-coil primary (breaker points to coil negative lead) or secondary lead (high voltage lead).

NOTE: On late 1975 and all 1976-79 coils, the primary and secondary windings have been separated and a secondary coil ground lead is incorporated into the assembly, Fig. 32.

The main features of H.E.I. system differentiating this system from the "Unit Ignition" system are shown in Figs. 33, 34 and 35.

The magnetic pickup consists of a rotating timer core attached to the distributor shaft, a stationary pole piece, permanent magnet and pickup coil.

When the distributor shaft rotates, the teeth of the timer core line up and pass the teeth of the pole piece inducing voltage in the pickup coil which signals the all-electronic module to open the ignition coil primary circuit. Maximum inductance occurs at the moment the timer core teeth are lined up with the teeth on the pole piece. At the instant the timer core teeth start to pass the pole teeth, the primary current decreases and a high voltage is induced in the ignition coil secondary winding and is directed through the rotor and high voltage leads to fire the spark plugs.

NOTE: Since this is a full 12 volt system it does not require a resistance wire.

The vacuum diaphragm is connected by linkage to the pole piece. When the diaphragm moves against spring pressure it rotates the pole piece allowing the poles to advance relative to the timer core. The timer core is rotated about the shaft by conventional advance weights, thus providing centrifugal advance.

CAUTION: Never connect to ground the "tach" terminals, Fig. 33, of the distributor connector as this will damage the electronic circuitry of the module.

A convenient tachometer connection is incorporated in the wiring connector on the side of the distributor, Figs. 33 and 35. However due to its transistorized design, the high energy ignition system will not trigger some models of engine tachometers.

NOTE: When using a timing light to adjust ignition timing, the connection should be made at the No. 1 spark plug. Forcing foreign objects through the boot at the No. 1 terminal of the distributor cap will damage the boot and could cause engine misfiring.

The spark plug boot has been designed to form a tight seal around the spark plug and should be twisted 1/2 turn before removal.

System Diagnosis

1976-79 UNITS WITH INTERNAL COIL

Refer to H.E.I. diagnosis charts, Figs. 36 and 37, for diagnosis procedures.

1974-75 ALL & 1976-77 UNITS WITH EXTERNAL COIL

With the wiring connector properly attached to connector at side of distributor cap and all the spark plug leads properly connected at plugs and at distributor terminals, proceed as follows:

Engine Will Not Start
1. Connect voltmeter between "Bat" terminal lead on distributor connector and ground and turn on ignition switch.
2. If voltage is zero, there is an open circuit between the distributor and the bulkhead connector; or between the bulkhead connector and the ignition switch; or between the ignition switch and the starter solenoid. Repair as required.
3. If reading is battery voltage, hold one spark plug lead with insulated pliers approximately 1/4 inch away from a dry

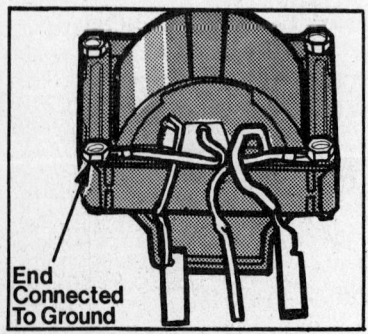

Fig. 32 H.E.I. coil, late 1975 & 1976-78 units

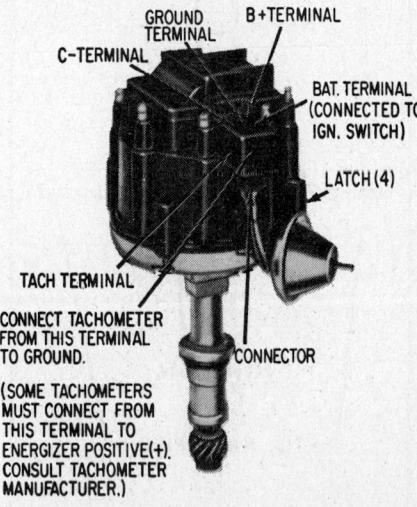

Fig. 33 H.E.I. distributor external components. Internal coil units

ELECTRONIC IGNITION

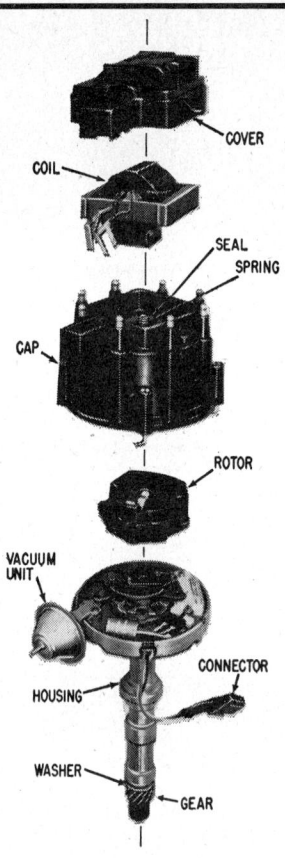

Fig. 34 H.E.I. distributor internal components. Internal coil units

area of engine block and crank engine. If a spark is visible, the distributor has been eliminated as source of trouble. Check spark plugs and fuel system.
4. If there is no visible spark, perform the "Component Checkout" and proceed as described further on.

Engine Starts But Runs Rough
1. Check for proper fuel delivery to carburetor.
2. Check all vacuum hoses for leakage.
3. Visually inspect and listen for sparks jumping to ground.
4. Check ignition timing
5. Check centrifugal advance mechanism for proper operation.
6. Remove spark plugs and check for unusual defects, such as very wide gap, abnormal fouling, cracked insulators (inside and out), etc.
7. If no defects are found, perform the "Component Checkout" procedure as described below.

Component Checkout
1. Remove cap and coil assembly.
2. Inspect cap, coil and rotor for spark arc-over.
3. On internal coil units:
   a. Connect ohmmeter, Fig. 38, step 1. If ohmmeter reading is other than zero or very near to zero, the ignition coil must be replaced.
   b. If no ohmmeter reading was observed in step 1, reconnect ohmmeter both ways, Fig. 38, step 2. If both ohmmeter readings are infinite on high scale, replace ignition coil.
4. On inline 4 and 1975-77 6 cylinder engines:
   a. Connect ohmmeter, Fig. 39, step 1. If reading is not infinite, replace coil.
   b. Connect ohmmeter, Fig. 39, step 2. If reading is not zero or near zero, replace coil.
   c. Connect ohmmeter, Fig. 39, step 3. If reading is infinite, replace coil.
5. Connect an external vacuum source to the vacuum advance unit. Replace vacuum unit if inoperative.
6. If vacuum unit is operating properly, connect ohmmeter, Fig. 40, step 1. If ohmmeter reading on middle scale in not infinite at all times, pick-up coil must be replaced.
7. With ohmmeter connected, Fig. 40, step 2, ohmmeter reading must be within 500 to 1500 ohms at all times. If not replace pick-up coil.

NOTE: Tester J-24624 is required to test the module. If this tester is not available, and malfunction still exists after performing the above checks, replace module.

Service Note

Some 1974-75 G. M. vehicles equipped with High Energy Ignition Systems (H.E.I.) may encounter a no-start condition or engine miss. These conditions may be caused by the battery ignition wire installed in such a way that the connector in distributor cap is bent and jammed on wrong side of blade in ignition wire connector, Fig. 41. To correct this condition proceed as follows:
1. Pry latch on black ignition wire connector and remove it from distributor, then unlock tang on blade and remove connector from blade.
2. Straighten blade, if bent. Bend tang on blade outboard to insure a positive lock when blade is reinstalled.
3. Slide connector over blade aligning tang with groove in connector until it bottoms, then pull lightly on wire to insure a positive lock.
4. Inspect blade in distributor cap connector. If bent, straighten and center.
5. Reinstall ignition wire connector by

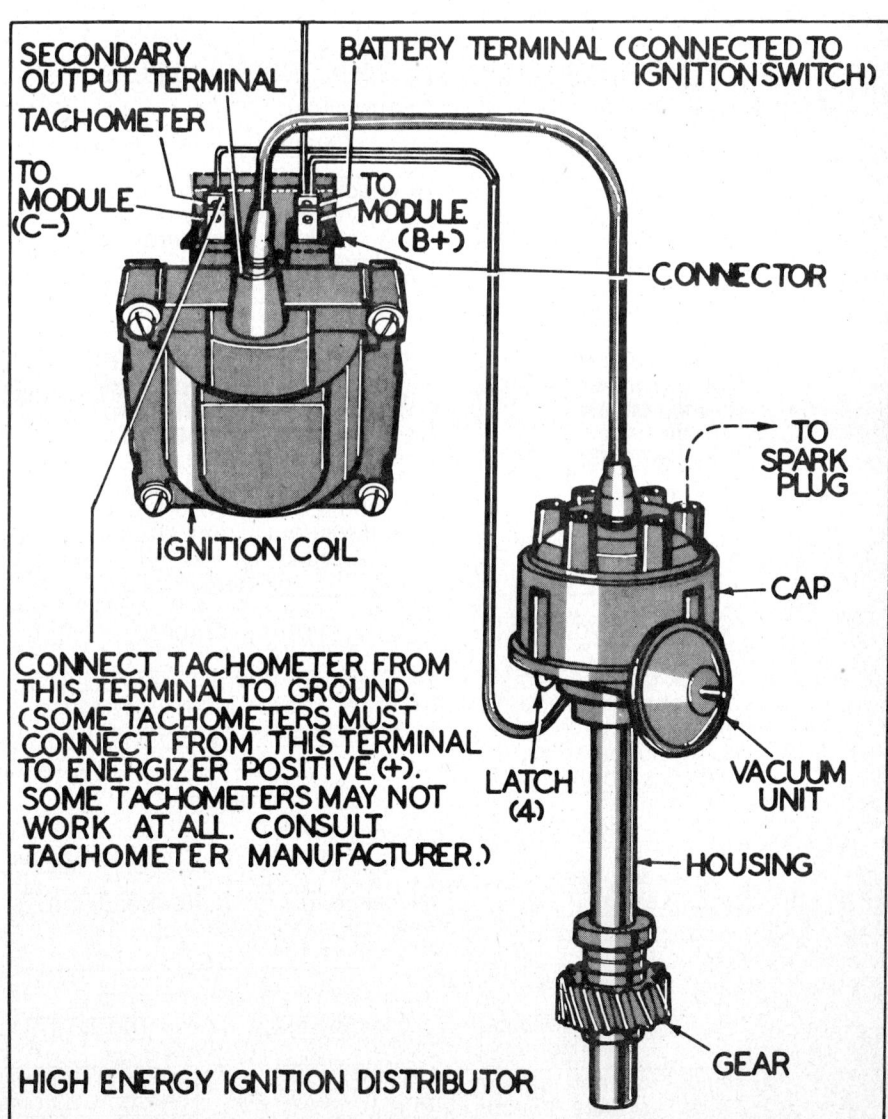

Fig. 35 HEI distributor components. External coil units

ELECTRONIC IGNITION

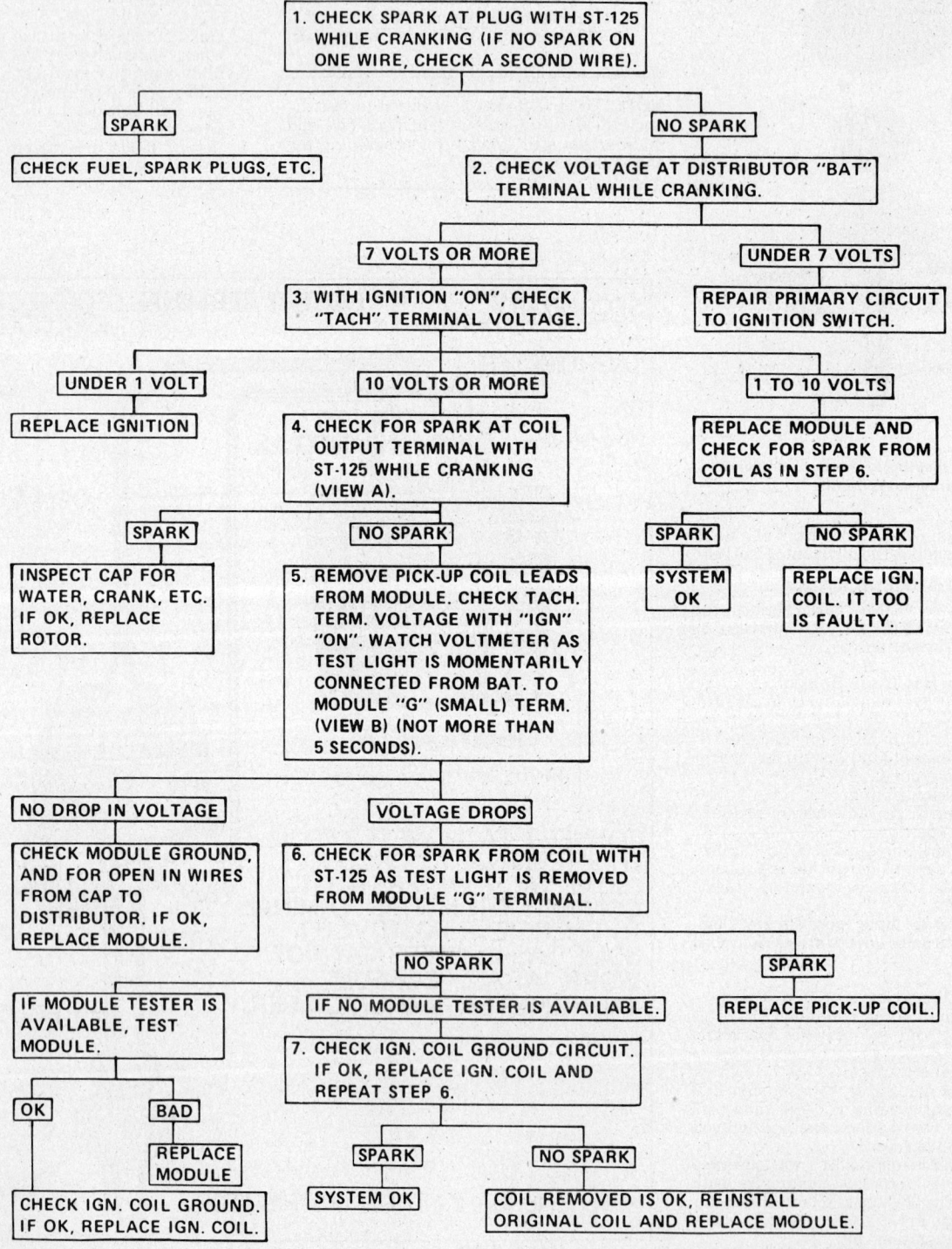

Fig. 36 H.E.I. diagnosis chart (part 1 of 2). 1976-80 units

ELECTRONIC IGNITION

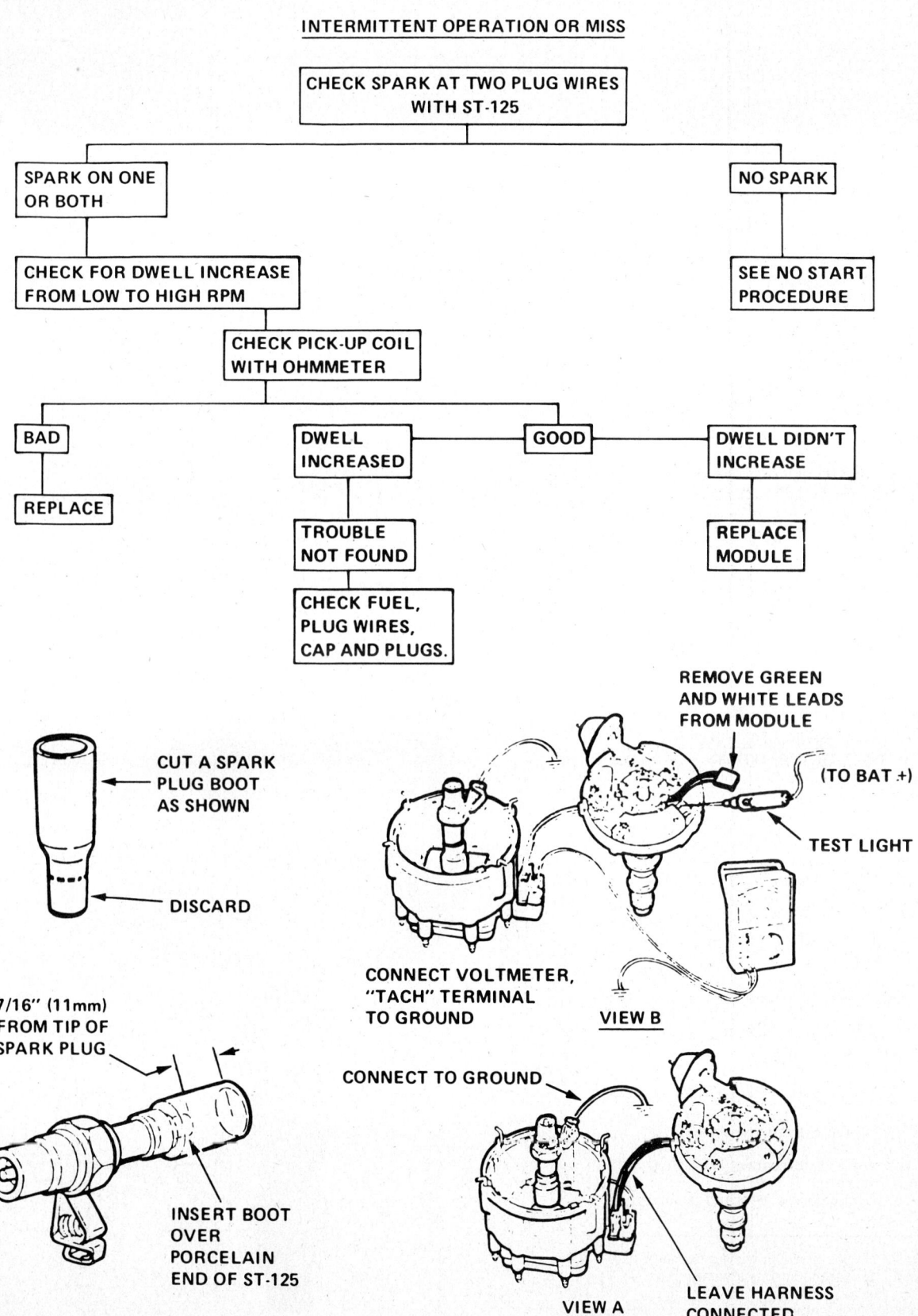

Fig. 37 H.E.I. diagnosis chart (part 2 of 2). 1976–80 units

ELECTRONIC IGNITION

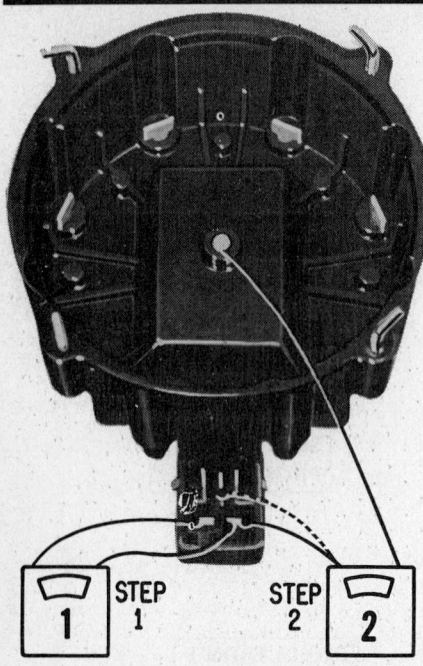

Fig. 38 H.E.I. distributor ignition coil ohmmeter tests. Internal coil units

CAUTION: At installation, coat bottom of new module with dielectric lubricant (furnished with new module) to aid in heat transfer into distributor housing. Failure to appy lubricant will cause excessive heat at module and premature module failure.

POLE PIECE, MAGNET OR PICK-UP COIL REPLACEMENT, FIG. 42

Removal
1. With distributor removed, disconnect wires at module terminals.
2. Remove roll pin from drive gear by driving out with 1/8 inch diameter drift punch.
3. Remove gear, shim and the tanged washer from distributor shaft. Remove any burrs that may have been caused by removal of pin.
4. Remove distributor shaft from housing.
5. Remove washer from upper end of distributor housing.

NOTE: Bushings in the housing are not serviceable.

6. Remove three screws securing pole piece to housing and remove pole piece, magnet and pick-up coil.

Installation
1. Install pick-up coil, magnet and pole piece and loosely install three screws holding pole piece.
2. With washer installed at top of housing, install distributor shaft and rotate to check for proper clearance between pole piece teeth and timer core teeth.
3. If necessary, realign pole piece to provide adequate clearance and secure properly.
4. Install tanged washer, shim and drive gear (teeth up) to bottom of shaft. Align drive gear and install new roll pin.
5. Connect all wires to module terminals.

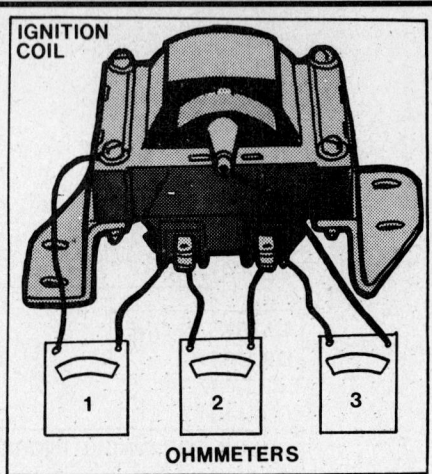

Fig. 39 HEI distributor ignition coil ohmmeter test. External coil units

pushing straight up until latch is locked. The blade on distributor connector should be toward lock tab on ignition wire connector. When correctly installed, the connector should move freely while in the locked position.
6. Start engine and move connector. If engine does not start or misses, recheck above procedure.

Components Replace

IGNITION COIL REPLACEMENT, INTERNAL COIL UNITS, FIG. 34
1. Remove screws holding distributor cover to distributor cap and remove distributor cover.
2. Remove four screws holding coil to cap.
3. Remove harness connector and battery wire from side of distributor cap.
4. Push coil leads out of position in cap and remove coil.
5. Reverse procedure to install.

EXTERNAL COIL UNITS, FIG. 35
1. Disconnect ignition switch to coil lead from coil.
2. Disconnect coil to distributor leads from coil.
3. Remove coil to engine retaining screws and remove coil.
4. Reverse procedure to install.

MODULE REPLACEMENT, FIG. 42
1. Disconnect wiring harness connector at side of distributor cap and remove distributor.
2. Remove rotor and disconnect wire from module terminals.
3. Remove two mounting screws and remove module.

NOTE: Two types of H.E.I. wiring harness are used. The second type is a wiring harness, connector and capacitor which is serviced as an assembly.

4. Reverse procedure to install.

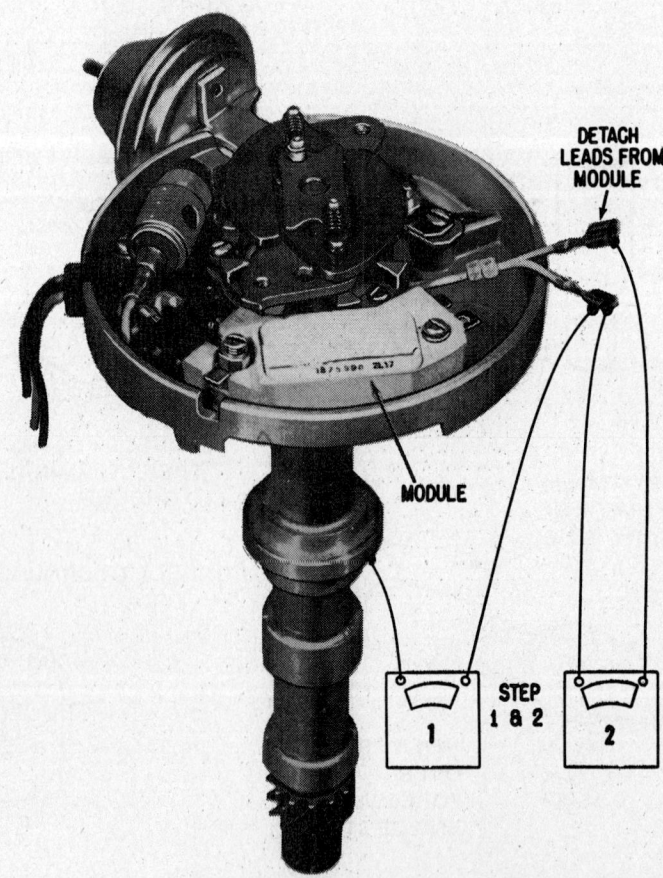

Fig. 40 H.E.I. distributor pickup coil ohmmeter test

ELECTRONIC IGNITION

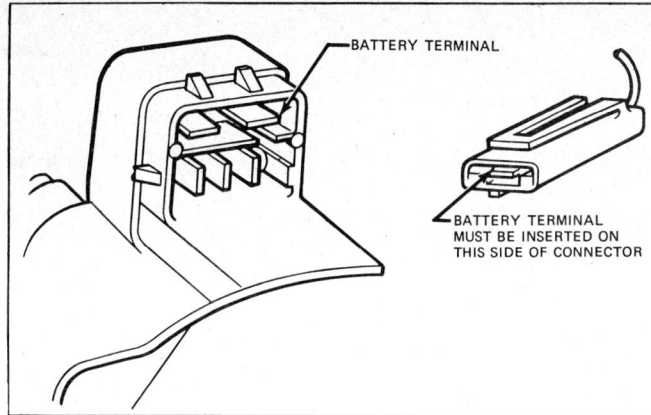

Fig. 41 H.E.I. distributor cap connector

Distributor Service

NOTE: If distributor has been disassembled, refer to Fig. 43 during reassembly.

1. Liberally apply silicone to bottom of module and install module and retaining screws.

   CAUTION: Failure to apply silicone lubricant will cause excessive heat build-up at module and premature module failure.

2. Install capacitor and harness making certain that ground lead is under capacitor and retaining screw.
3. Install vacuum advance unit and retaining screws.
4. Place felt wick under pick-up coil plate and lubricant with engine oil, then install pick-up coil and retain with waved C-washer.
5. Install distributor shaft into housing, then install drive gear onto shaft and install new roll pin.
6. On internal coil units, install arc seal, coil and coil cover.

FORD BREAKERLESS (B/L) & DURA SPARK SOLID STATE IGNITION SYSTEMS

The B/L and Dura Spark ignition systems do not use points and are controlled by an electronic module. The Dura Spark system uses higher spark plug voltages during the starting and running modes, permitting the use of wider spark plug gaps required to ignite the leaner air/fuel mixtures.

Two versions of the Dura Spark system are used. The Dura Spark I incorporates a new module ignition coil, distributor cap and adaptor, rotor and ignition wires. The module has a built-in current regulator which reduces overheating of the coil and module during operation. The ignition coil has revised primary and secondary windings necessary to supply the higher spark plug voltages. The Dura Spark II system, Fig. 44, uses a new distributor cap and adaptor, rotor and ignition wires. The higher spark plug voltage in this system is obtained by reducing the value of the ballast resistor in the primary side of the ignition system.

The electronic module, Figs. 44 and 45, is the brain of this system and is well protected from outside elements such as heat and shock. The heat sink containing all the electronic devices is sealed in a mixture of epoxy and sand. This module can not be disassembled and must be replaced if malfunctioning.

NOTE: On some high altitude models, a special Dura Spark II module plus a barometic pressure switch, allow base engine timing to be modified to suit altitude conditions. These units have three wire connectors, Fig. 46. All other elements and performance characteristics of this module are identical in both modes of operation to the basic Dura Spark II system.

New oil filled ignition coils are used, therefore conventional ignition coils are not to be used with these system. The proper B/L coil is easily identified as it is all blue and terminals are labeled differently from conventional ignition coils "BAT" (battery) and "DEC" (Distributor Electronic Control), Fig. 47.

The ignition switch energizes the module through the white wire while engine is cranking and through the red wire when engine is running.

The distributor shaft and armature rotation, Fig. 48, causes the armature poles to pass by the core of the magnetic pick-up assembly, in turn cutting the magnetic field and signaling the electronic module, Figs. 49 thru 53, through the orange and purple wires to break the primary ignition current, thus inducing secondary voltage in the coil to fire the spark plugs. The coil is then energized again by the primary circuit and ready for the next spark cycle. This primary circuit is controlled by a timing circuit in the module.

The ignition system is protected against electrical current produced during normal vehicle operation and against reverse polarity or high voltage accidentally applied if vehicle is jump started.

Total diagnosis of the system requires only a volt-ohmmeter tester.

CAUTION: The ignition system will be damaged if other than volt-ohm test procedures are used to check alternator output. This alternator test procedure is outlined in the "Ford Autolite/Motorcraft Alternator" section, under "Voltmeter Test."

Do not use the volt-amp test procedure or any other test that utilizes a knife switch on the battery terminal.

Since the interval between the time that the module activates the primary ignition circuit and the time the distributor signal turns it off varies with engine speed, a dwell measurement is insignificant.

System Diagnosis

If the ignition system is suspected of a malfunction inspect for loose connections and perform the "Secondary Ignition Checkout" procedure in the Trouble Shooting Chapter elsewhere in this manual. Since the secondary circuit is identical to that of a conventional ignition system.

If no spark is observed during the above test, check the ignition coil high tension wire, replace if damaged. If no damage is observed at the coil wire, disconnect the three-way and four-way connectors at the electronic module and make tests at the harness connectors.

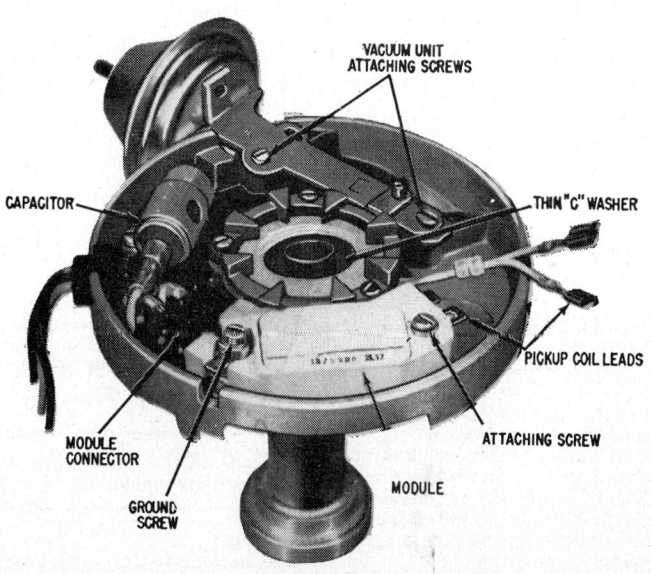

Fig. 42 H.E.I. distributor component replacement

Electronic Ignition

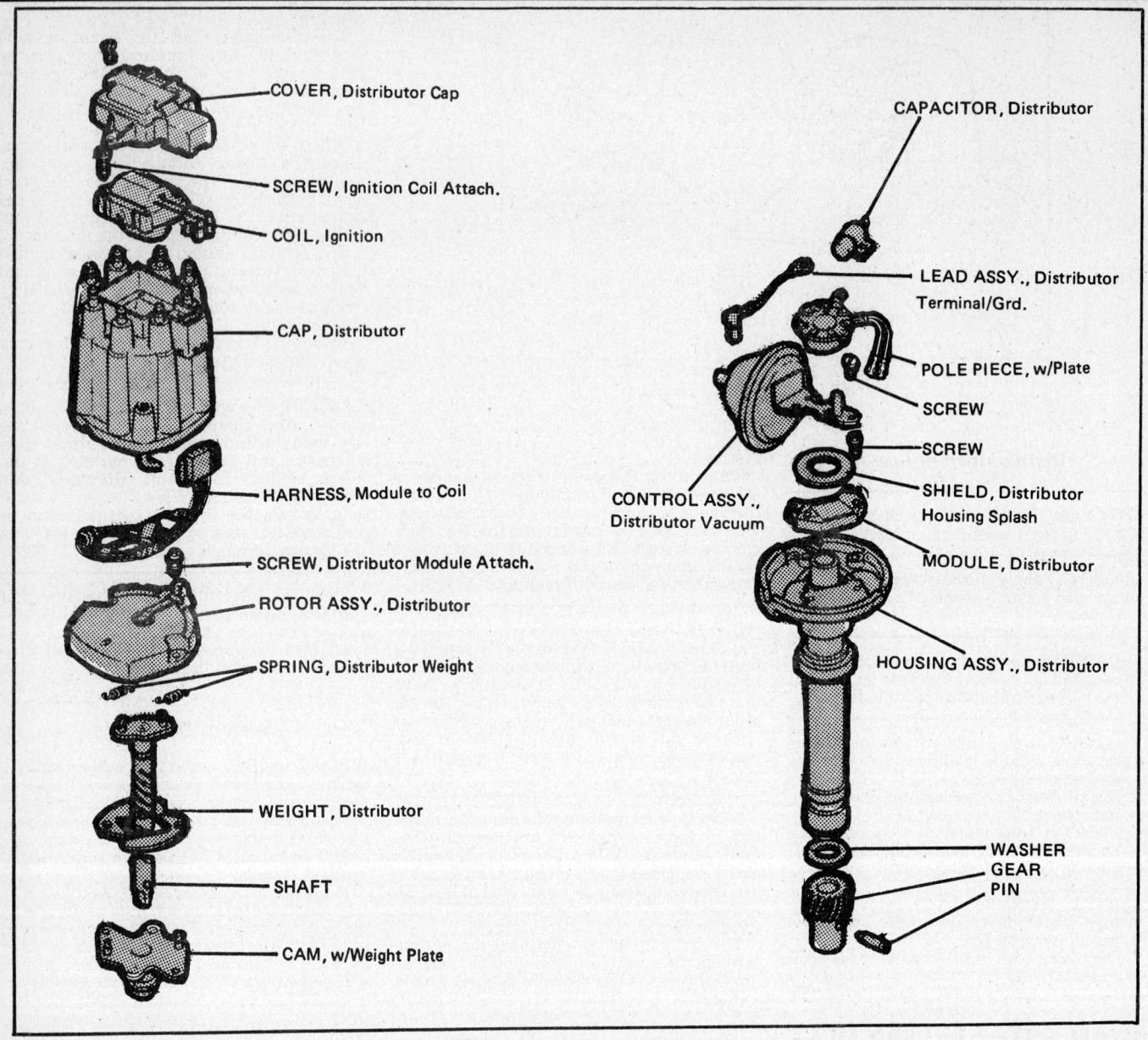

Fig. 43 Exploded view of HEI distributor (typical)

NOTE: Do not make test at the module terminals.

SERVICE NOTE

If a no start condition exists during wet weather/high humidity conditions, the cause may be high voltage leakage to ground at the coil to distributor wire boots due to excessive moisture and contamination (such as salt). To correct this condition proceed as follows:
1. Clean all moisture and dirt accumulation from exposed surfaces on the distributor cap and coil tower without removing wires from the cap or coil tower. If there is evidence of wire damage replace as necessary. Attempt to start the engine.
2. If the engine still does not start, remove the distributor to coil high tension wire and clean the coil tower, the center tower of the distributor cap and the distributor to coil wire. Apply Dow 4X or GE G-624 Silicone grease to the outer surfaces of the coil tower and the center tower of the cap and re-install the coil wire insuring that both ends are fully seated.
3. If condition persists, replace the coil to distributor high tension wire to provide new sealing qualities at the boots seals.

Voltage Test At Harness Connectors, Figs. 54 Thru 57

NOTE: If all the following tests comply with specifications replace the module.

Key On
1. Check for battery voltage between pin #3 for 1974 & 1977-79 or #4 for 1975-76 and engine ground. If voltage is less than specified, the voltage feed wire to the module is damaged and must be repaired.
2. Check for battery voltage between pin #5 for 1974 & 1977-79 or #1 for 1975-76 and engine ground. If voltage is less than specified proceed as follows:
   a. Without disconnecting the coil, connect voltmeter between coil "BAT" terminal and engine ground.
   b. Connect a jumper wire between the coil "DEC" terminal and engine ground.
   c. With all lights and accessories off, turn on the ignition switch.
   d. A satisfactory primary circuit will register between 4.9 to 7.9 volts for Breakerless and Dura Spark II systems, or 11 to 14 volts for Dura Spark I systems
   e. If less than specified volts register on voltmeter, check for worn primary circuit insulation, broken wire strands or

Electronic Ignition

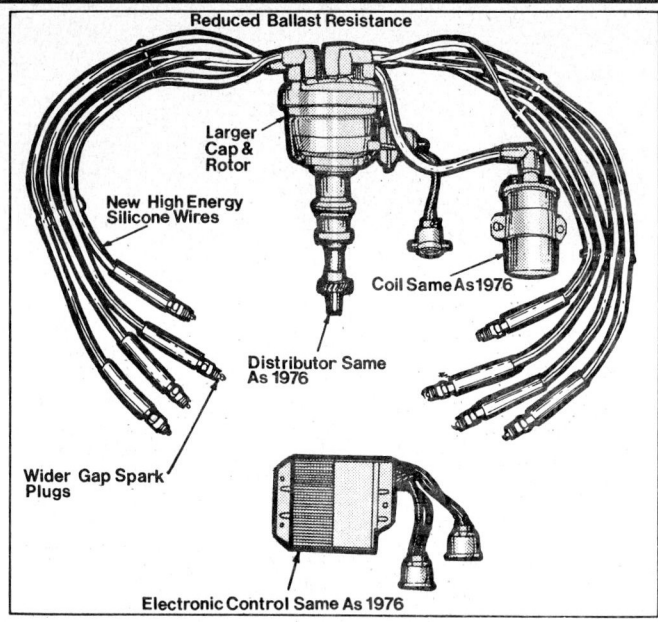

Fig. 44 1977-79 Ford Dura Spark ignition system exc. California (Typical)

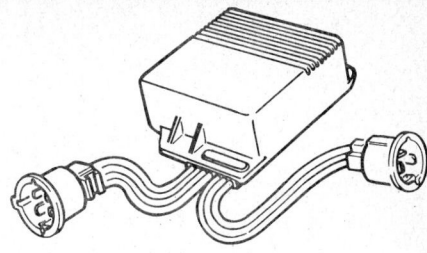

Fig. 45 Ford breakerless electronic module

loose-corroded terminals.

f. On Breakerless and Dura Spark II systems, if voltage reading registered on voltmeter is greater than 7.9 volts, check and replace if necessary the resistance wire.

Cranking Engine
1. Check for 8 to 12 volts between pin #1 for 1974 & 1977-79 or pin #5 for 1975-76 and engine ground. On 1974-75, if voltage is not within specifications, the voltage feed wire to the module is damaged. On 1976-79, if reading is not more than 6 volts, the ignition by-pass circuit is open or grounded from either the starter solenoid or the ignition switch to pin #5 or primary connections at coil.
2. Check for 1/2 volt oscillation (using the 2.5 volt scale) between pin #7 and #8 for 1974 and 1977-79 pin #7 and #3 for 1975 or pin #3 and #8 for 1976. If the voltmeter does not register this oscillation, visually inspect distributor components.

Make sure that the toothed armature is not damaged, is tight on sleeve and secured properly with the alignment pin. Fig. 48. If armature is not damaged and is rotating properly when cranking the engine and voltmeter is not oscillating, replace the magnetic pickup (stator assembly).

Resistance Test At Harness Connectors, Figs. 54 Thru 57

Key Off
1. Connect an ohmmeter between pin #7 and #8 for 1974 and 1977-79, pin #7 and #3 for 1975 and pin #8 and #3 for 1976, resistance should be 400 to 800 ohms. Connect ohmmeter between pin #6 and 1974 and 1977-79, pin #8 for 1975 or pin #7 for 1976 and ground. Resistance should be zero ohms. Connect ohmmeter between pin #7 or #8 for 1974 and 1977-79, pin #7 or #3 for 1975 or pin #8 or #3 for 1976 and ground, resistance

should be more than 70,000 ohms. If any of the above checks do not comply with specifications, the magnetic pick-up assembly (stator assembly) is not functioning and must be replaced.
2. Check secondary coil resistance between pin #3 for 1974 and 1977-79 or pin #4 for 1975-76 and coil tower. Also check primary coil resistance between pin #5 for 1974 and 1977-79 or pin #1 for 1975-76 and pin #4 for 1974, pin #6 for 1975 or coil "Bat" terminal for 1976. If secondary coil resistance is not within 7,000 to 13,000 ohms, or primary coil resistance is not within 1 to 2 ohms for Breakerless and Dura Spark II, or .5 to 1.5 for Dura Spark 1, diagnose coil separately from rest of system. Follow procedures for testing standard ignition coils as outlined in the "TUNE UP SERVICE" chapter under "Ignition Coils & Resistors."
3. Check for a resistance of more than 4.0 ohms between pin #5 for 1974 or pin #1 for 1975-76 and engine ground. If resistance is less than specified, locate the short to ground either at the coil "DEC" terminal or in the green wire, Fig. 38.
4. If a resistance of 1.0 to 2.0 ohms is not obtained between pins #3 for 1974 and 1977-79 or pin #6 for 1975 and #4, replace the primary resistance wire.

Component Replacement

MAGNETIC PICKUP ASSEMBLY

Removal
1. Remove distributor cap and rotor, then disconnect distributor wiring harness plug, Fig. 48.
2. Using two screw drivers, pry armature from advance plate sleeve and remove roll pin.
3. Remove snap ring securing pickup assembly to base plate. On 6 cylinder models, remove washer and wave washer.
4. On all models, remove snap ring securing vacuum advance link to pickup assembly.
5. Remove pickup assembly ground screw and lift assembly from distributor.
6. Disconnect vacuum advance link from pickup assembly post.

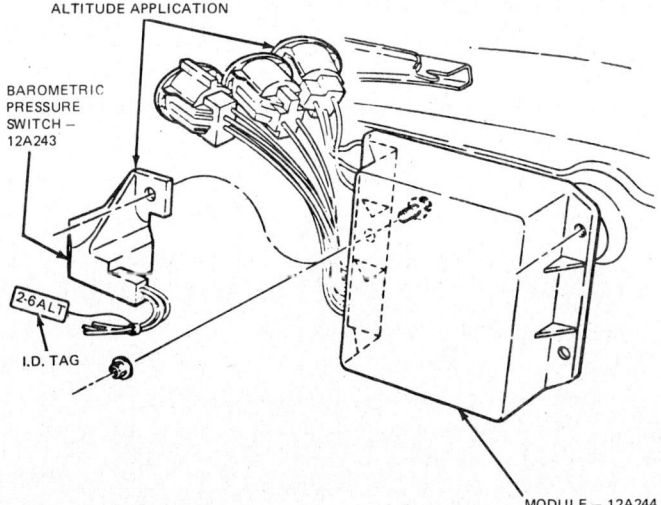

Fig. 46 Ford Dura Spark II electronic module. High altitude models with dual mode timing

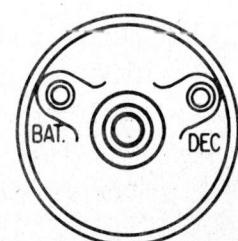

Fig. 47 Ford electronic ignition coil identification

171

ELECTRONIC IGNITION

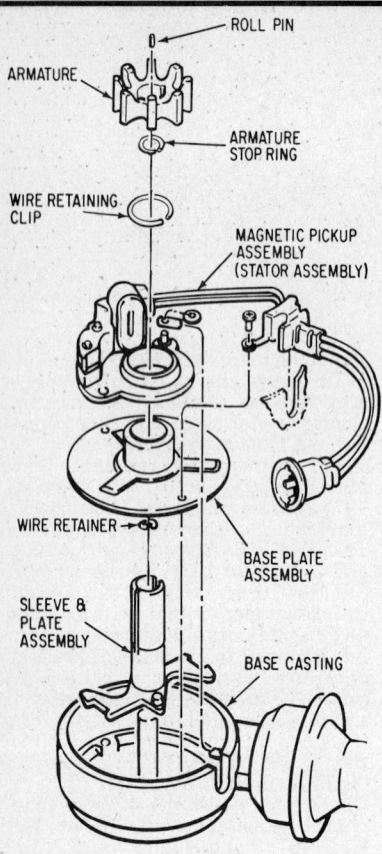

Fig. 48 Ford breakerless (B/L) distributor

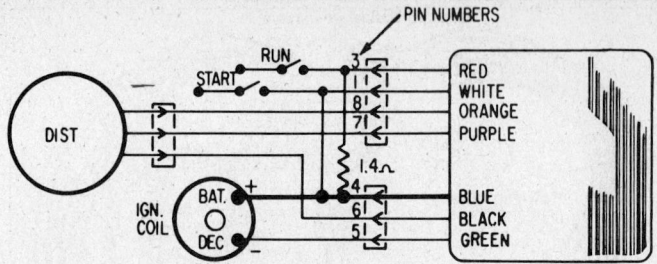

Fig. 49 1974 Ford breakerless primary circuit

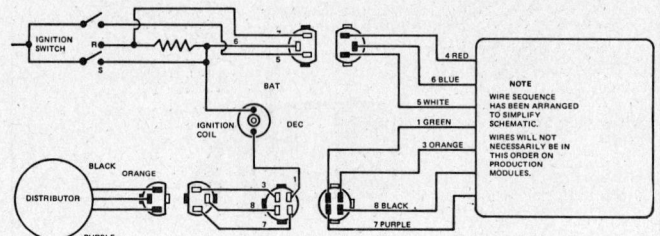

Fig. 50 1975 Ford breakerless ignition primary circuit

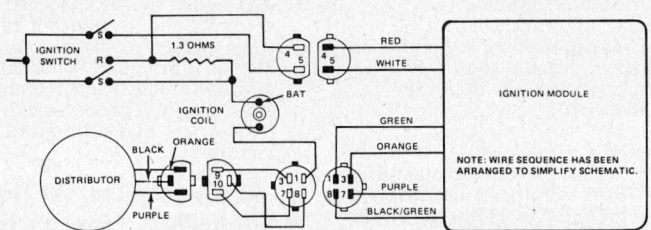

Fig. 51 1976 Ford breakerless ignition primary circuit

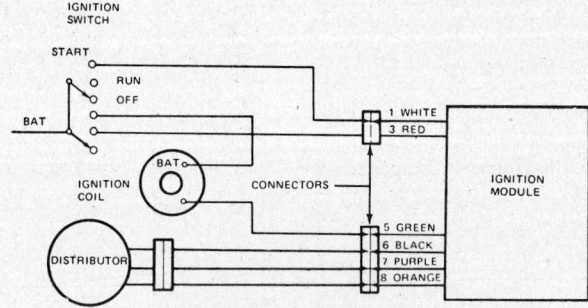

Fig. 52 Ford Dura Spark 1 ignition primary circuit

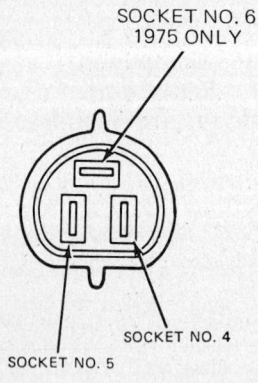

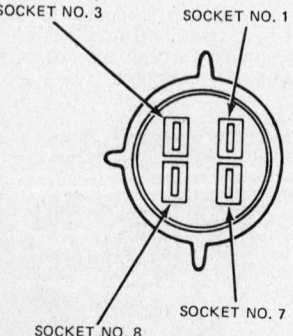

Fig. 55 1975-76 Ford breakerless ignition female harness connectors (System test points)

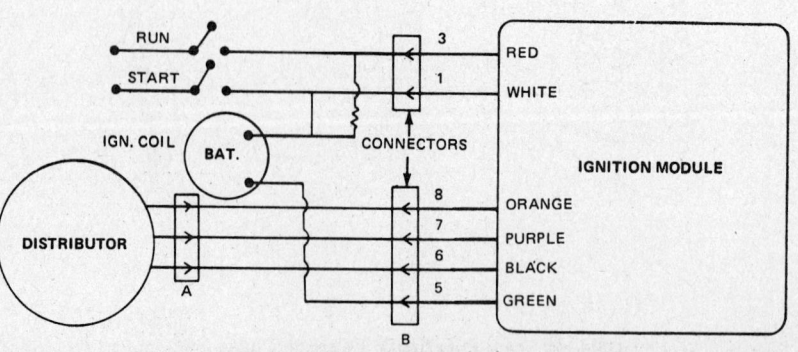

Fig. 53 Ford Dura Spark II ignition primary circuit

Electronic Ignition

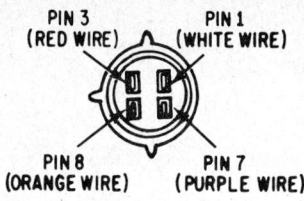

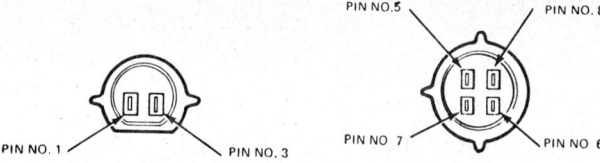

Fig. 56 Ford Dura Spark I ignition female harness connectors (system test points)

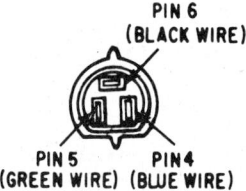

Fig. 54 1974 Ford breakerless ignition female harness connectors (System test points)

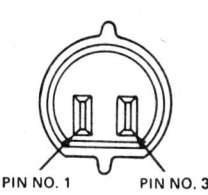

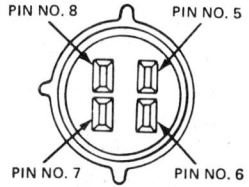

Fig. 57 Ford Dura Spark II ignition female harness connectors (system test points)

Installation
1. Position pickup assembly over base plate and slide wiring harness into slot on side of distributor housing, Fig. 48.
2. On 6 cylinder models, install washers. On all models, install snap ring securing pickup assembly to base plate.
3. Position vacuum advance link on pickup assembly post and install snap ring.
4. Insert ground screw through wiring harness tab and install on base plate.
5. Install armature on advance plate sleeve, ensure roll pin is engaged in slot.
6. Install distributor rotor and cap, then connect distributor wiring harness plug to vehicle wiring harness.

VACUUM ADVANCE UNIT, REPLACE
1. Remove distributor cap and rotor.
2. Disconnect vacuum lines, then remove snap ring that secures vacuum advance link to pickup assembly.
3. Remove vacuum advance attaching screws, then tilt unit downward to disconnect link.
4. Carefully remove unit from distributor.
5. Reverse procedure to install.

FIXED BASE PLATE, REPLACE
1. Remove distributor cap and rotor.
2. Remove vacuum advance unit and magnetic pickup assembly.
3. Remove attaching screws and lift base plate from distributor.
4. Reverse procedure to install.

HOLLEY (IH) BREAKERLESS IGNITION SYSTEM
(EXTERNAL ELECTRONIC CONTROL UNIT)

Description

This ignition system incorporates four major units; an electronic control unit, ignition coil, distributor and high tension wires, Fig. 58. The electronic control unit is a solid-state, moisture resistant module with the components sealed in a potting compound to resist vibration and environmental conditions. Since the control unit has an internal current regulator, a resistance wire or ballast resistor is not necessary in the primary circuit. Battery voltage is applied to the ignition coil positive terminal when the ignition switch is in the "On" or "Start" position, therefore, an ignition system bypass is not required in this system. The primary coil circuit is electronically regulated by this unit.

The ignition coil is of standard construction and requires no special service. The function of the ignition coil in this ignition system is the same as for conventional ignition systems.

The distributor is conventional except the contact points, condenser and cam are replaced by a sensor and trigger wheel, and since no wearing occurs between the trigger wheel and sensor, dwell angle remains constant and requires no adjustment. The sensor is a small coil of fine wire and receives an alternating current signal from the electronic control unit. The sensor develops an electromagnetic field used to detect the presence of metal which are the leading edges of the trigger wheel teeth.

Troubleshooting

Ensure all electrical connections are correct

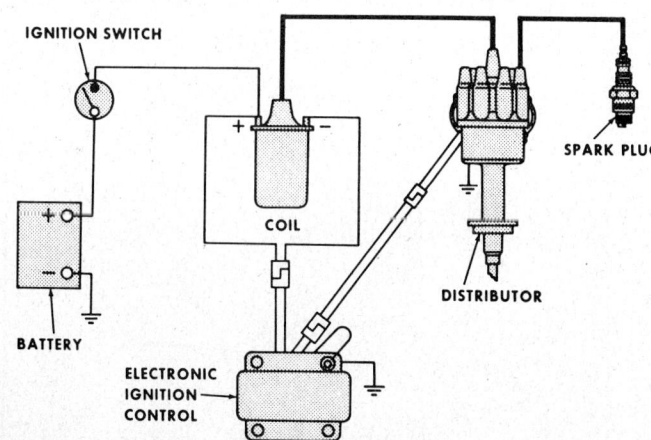

Fig. 58 Holley (International Harvester) breakerless ignition system (External electronic control unit type)

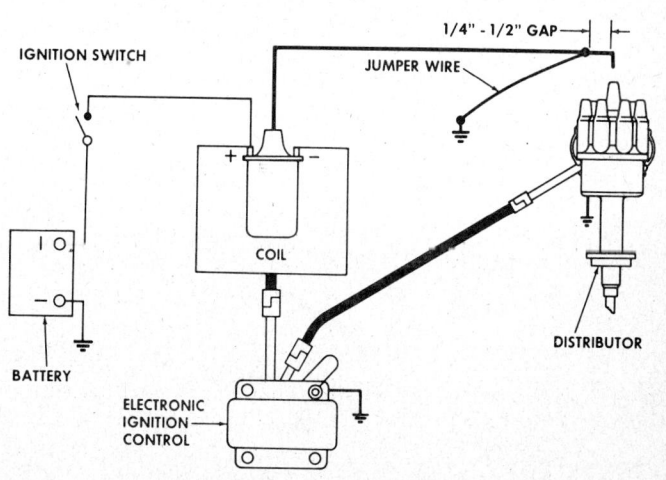

Fig. 59 Checking spark at coil wire

173

ELECTRONIC IGNITION

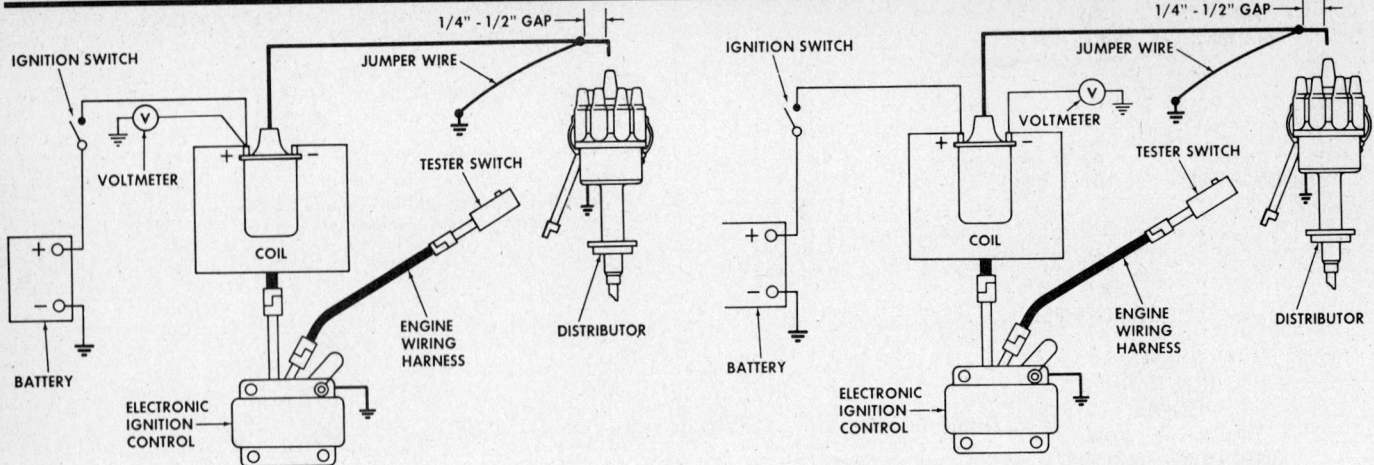

Fig. 60 Checking spark at coil wire with tester switch & jumper wire

Fig. 61 Checking voltage at ignition coil positive terminal

and battery is fully charged before proceeding with the following checks.

1. Disconnect a high tension cable from a spark plug, hold cable approximately 1/2 inch from a suitable ground and crank engine. If spark jumps between the cable and the ground, system is satisfactory.
2. If no spark occurs in step 1, disconnect coil wire from distributor cap and connect a jumper wire to the coil wire approximately 1/4–1/2 inch from distributor end and the ground, Fig. 59. Crank engine and observe for spark between the coil wire distributor end terminal and the jumper wire. If spark occurs, the distributor cap or rotor is faulty and must be replaced.
3. If no spark occurs in step 2, disconnect distributor primary wiring connector and connect tester switch SE-2503 into wiring harness, Fig. 60. Turn ignition switch "On" and press tab on tester switch. If spark occurs between coil wire distributor end and jumper wire, the distributor sensor unit is defective, requiring replacement.
4. If no spark occurs in step 3, connect a voltmeter between the coil positive terminal and the ground, Fig. 61, then turn ignition switch "On". If voltage indicated is less than battery voltage, a high resistance exists between the battery and the coil positive terminal. Check wiring and repair as necessary.
5. If indicated voltage was equal to battery voltage in step 4, connect a voltmeter between the coil negative terminal and the ground, Fig. 62, then turn ignition switch "On". A voltage under 5 volts or over 8 volts indicates a defective coil and must be replaced. If indicated voltage is between 5 and 8 volts, press tab on tester switch. Voltage should increase to battery voltage. Release tester switch tab and voltage should decrease to 5 to 8 volts. If voltage does not increase or decrease, the electronic ignition control unit is defective and must be replaced. If voltage increases and decreases, but no spark occurs between coil wire distributor end and jumper wire, the ignition coil is defective, requiring replacement.

Shaft & Bushing Wear Test

1. Clamp distributor in a soft jawed vise.
2. Remove distributor rotor.
3. Install a dial indicator so the plunger contacts trigger wheel.
4. Place one end of a wire loop around rotor shaft and hook a spring scale around the other end.
5. Apply 5 pounds of pull on spring scale and observe dial indicator reading. If reading exceeds .006 inch, replace distributor shaft bushings.

Distributor Disassemble

1. Remove rotor and dust cover.
2. Remove vacuum advance diaphragm rod "E" ring retainer, advance unit mounting screws, then the vacuum advance unit.
3. Pull sensor wiring seal/retainer from distributor housing slot, remove sensor plate mounting screws and lift plate assembly from housing, Fig. 63.
4. Remove epoxy sealer from sensor mounting screw, then remove mounting screw, disengage wiring clip from plate and remove sensor.
5. Remove retaining spring from underside of lower plate, Fig. 64, separate upper and lower plates, then remove three nylon "Buttons" from upper plate, Fig. 65.
6. Remove felt lubrication wick and trigger wheel retainer from shaft, Fig. 66, then slide trigger wheel from shaft and remove slider blocks, Fig. 67.
7. Remove advance weight springs, advance weights, bushings and thrust washers.
8. Measure distributor shaft end play which should be .035–.040 inch. If not, replace distributor shaft and gear.
9. Drive roll pin from gear and shaft and press gear from shaft.
10. Remove distributor shaft from housing.

Distributor Assemble

1. Install new bushings in advance weight

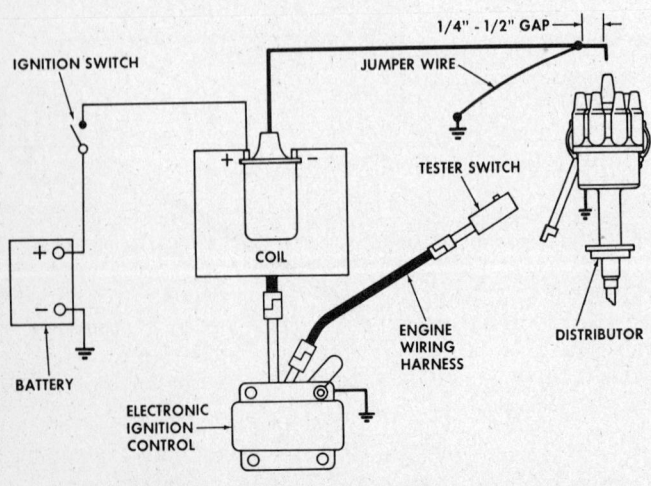

Fig. 62 Checking voltage at ignition coil negative terminal

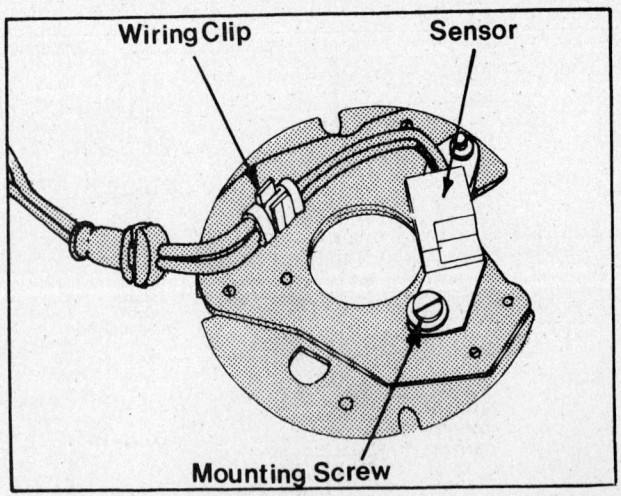

Fig. 63 Removing sensor

Electronic Ignition

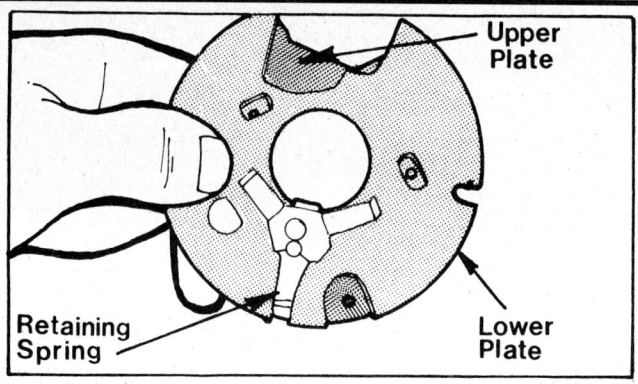

Fig. 64 Removing plate retaining spring

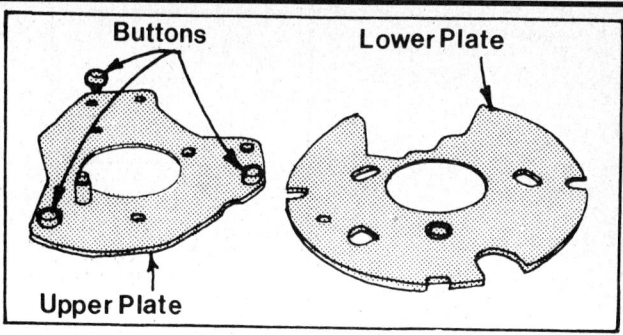

Fig. 65 Upper & Lower plates

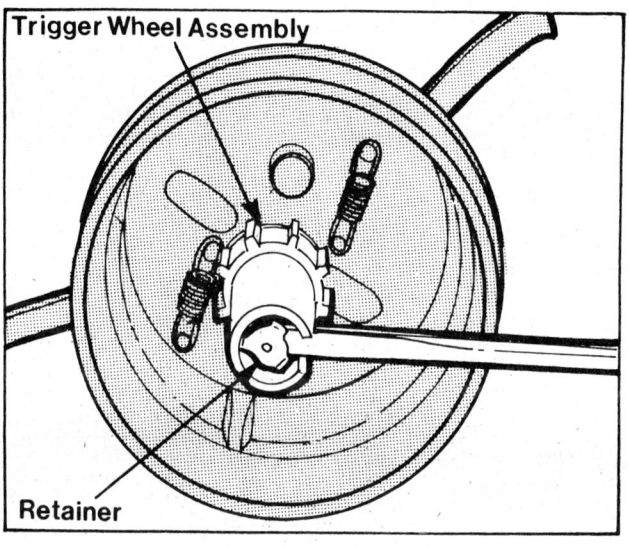

Fig. 66 Removing trigger wheel retainer

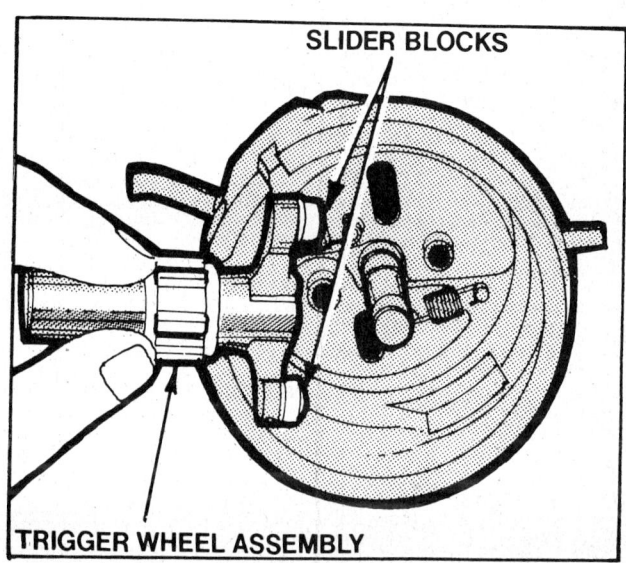

Fig. 67 Removing trigger wheel

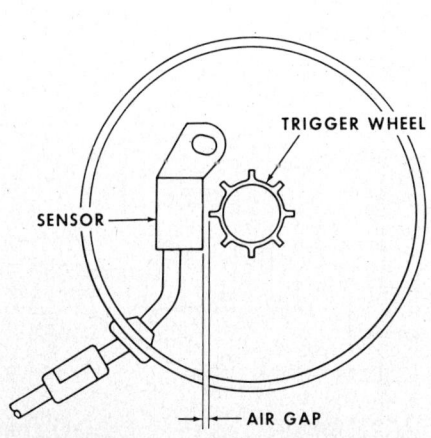

Fig. 68 Adjusting air gap

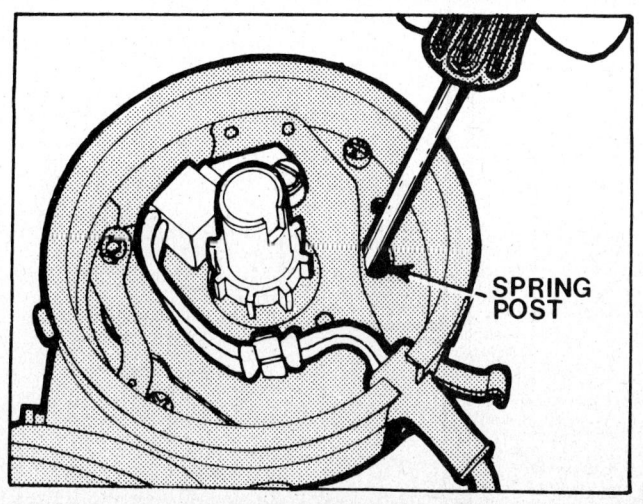

Fig. 69 Adjusting centrifugal advance

175

ELECTRONIC IGNITION

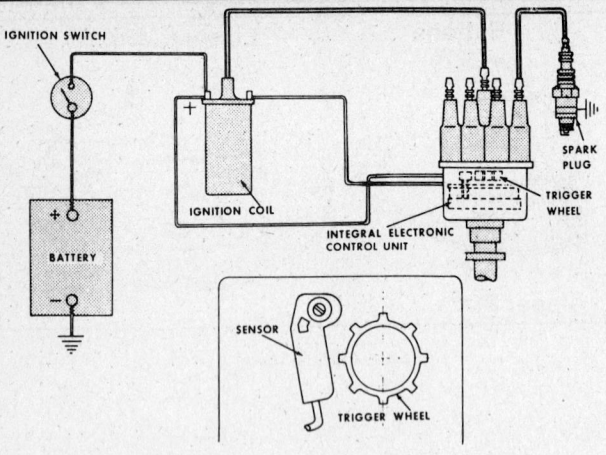

Fig. 70 Prestolite (International Harvester) breakerless ignition system (Internal electronic control unit type)

Fig. 71 Checking for spark at spark plug

bores, new thrust washers on advance weight pins, then place advance weights on pins and install new advance springs.
2. Lubricate trigger wheel pilot surface with distributor cam lubricant. Grooves in pilot diameter should be filled and lands between grooves should have a thin film of lubricant. The reservoir in the center should be filled to depth of lands with lubricant.
3. Install new slider blocks on trigger wheel, then place trigger wheel on shaft pilot surface with slider block flats aligned with slots in advance weights and push trigger wheel into position.
4. Install trigger wheel retainer and felt lubrication wick.
5. Lubricate distributor shaft with engine oil, then slide shaft into distributor housing.
6. Press gear onto distributor shaft, aligning roll pin hole in gear with hole in shaft. If a new distributor shaft is used, a new gear must be installed. Press new gear onto shaft until specified shaft end play is obtained. Using roll pin hole in the gear as a guide, drill roll pin hole in shaft. Install roll pin.
7. Install three nylon "Buttons" in upper plate and assemble upper plate to lower plate and install retaining spring.
8. Place sensor on upper plate and loosely install mounting screw. Install plate assembly into housing and tighten retaining screws, then place sensor wiring seal/retainer into housing slot.
9. Install vacuum advance unit on housing, connect diaphragm rod to sensor plate pin and install the "E" ring retainer and advance unit mounting screws.
10. To adjust trigger wheel to sensor air gap, rotate trigger wheel until one tooth is aligned with center of sensor and, using a suitable feeler gauge, adjust air gap to .008 inch, Fig. 68. Tighten sensor mounting screw and recheck air gap.
11. To adjust centrifugal advance, install distributor on distributor test stand. Check advance at each specified test speed. If advance is not within limits, adjust by bending spring posts, Fig. 69. To increase advance, bend post toward distributor shaft thereby decreasing spring tension. Decrease advance by bending post away from shaft thereby increasing spring tension.

PRESTOLITE (IH) BREAKERLESS IGNITION SYSTEM
(INTEGRAL ELECTRONIC CONTROL UNIT)
Description

This ignition system incorporates two major units: a distributor and an ignition coil, Fig. 70. The distributor is conventional except that a trigger wheel and an electronic control unit (Circuit board and sensor) replace the usual distributor cam, contact points and condenser.

The electronic control unit is associated with the primary side of the ignition system and electronically makes and breaks the primary circuit in response to rotation of the trigger wheel. The control unit circuit board is of solid state design and its components are sealed in a waterproof and vibration resistant compound. The sensor is a small coil, wound of fine wire, which is a metal detector. The metal that the sensor detects is the teeth of the trigger wheel.

The electronic circuit board and sensor are mounted on the distributor plate assembly. The sensor leads are soldered to the circuit board. The electronic control unit (Circuit board, sensor and plates) is serviced as an assembly.

Troubleshooting

Ensure all electrical connections are correct and the battery is fully charged before proceeding with the following checks.
1. Disconnect a high tension cable from a spark plug, hold cable approximately 1/2 inch from a suitable ground and crank engine, Fig. 71. If a spark jumps between the cable and the ground, the system is

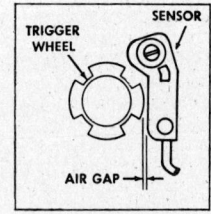
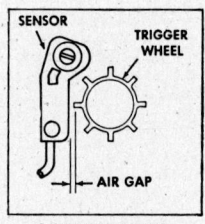

Fig. 73 Trigger wheel to sensor air gap

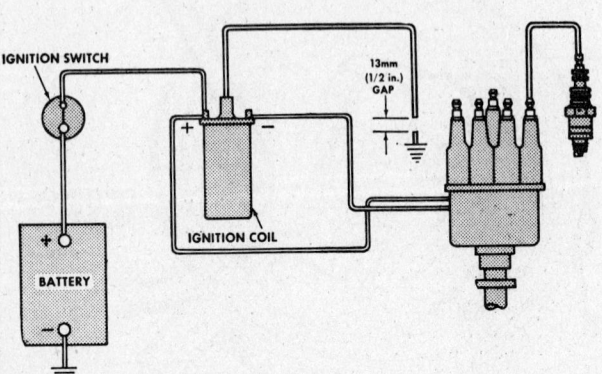

Fig. 72 Checking for spark at coil wire

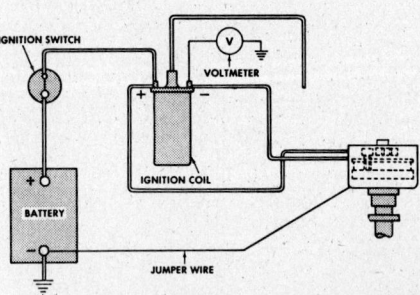

Fig. 74 Testing primary voltage

ELECTRONIC IGNITION

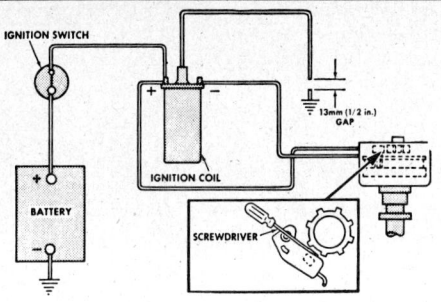

Fig. 75 Testing voltage at ignition coil negative terminal

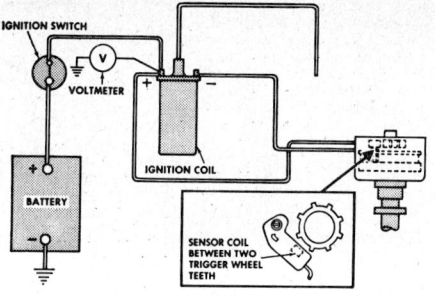

Fig. 77 Testing voltage at ignition coil negative terminal with brown wire disconnected

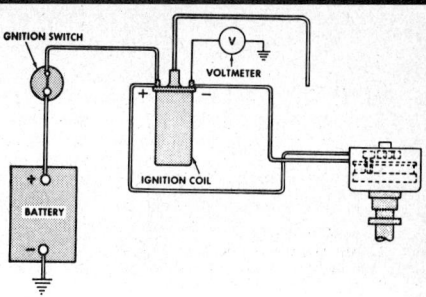

Fig. 78 Testing electronic control unit operation

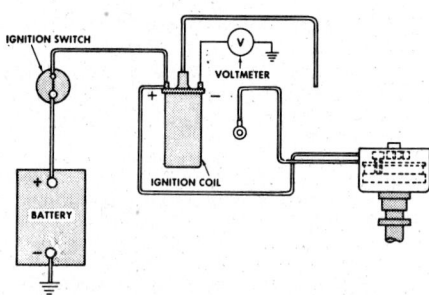

Fig. 76 Testing voltage at ignition coil negative terminal with jumper wire installed

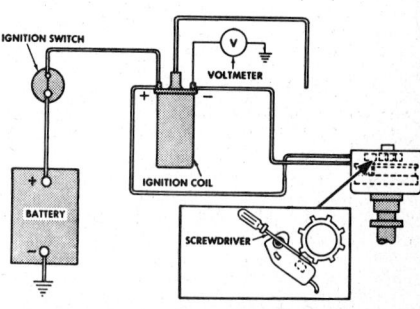

Fig. 79 Testing ignition coil operation

satisfactory.

2. If no spark occurs in Step 1, disconnect coil wire from distributor cap. Insert an extension adapter into boot and engage into cable terminal. Hold cable approximately ½ inch from a suitable ground and crank engine, Fig. 72. If spark occurs, the problem may be the distributor cap, rotor or high tension leads.
3. If no spark occurs in Step 2, check trigger wheel to sensor air gap. Remove distributor cap, rotor and shield. Crank engine to align one of the trigger wheel teeth with the sensor coil, Fig. 73. Check air gap between trigger wheel tooth and sensor. The air gap should be .008 inch. Adjust air gap, if necessary, and repeat Step 2. If no spark occurs, proceed to next step.
4. Crank engine to position sensor coil between two trigger wheel teeth. Connect a voltmeter between the ignition coil positive terminal and the ground, Fig. 74. Turn ignition switch "On" and note voltmeter reading. If voltage is lower than battery voltage, a high resistance exists between the battery and the ignition coil. If battery voltage is present, proceed to next step.
5. Connect voltmeter between the ignition coil negative terminal and the ground with the sensor coil position between two trigger wheel teeth, Fig. 75. Observe voltmeter reading with ignition "On". If reading is 5 to 8 volts, proceed to next step. If reading is 12 to 13 volts, connect a jumper wire between distributor housing and battery negative terminal and observe voltmeter, Fig. 76. If the voltage remains at 12–13 volts, the electronic control unit in the distributor is defective, requiring replacement. If the voltage changes to 5 to 8 volts with the jumper wire connected, a problem exists in the ground circuit between the distributor and the battery. If the voltage is 0 to 5 volts, disconnect the voltmeter, remove the brown wire from the ignition coil negative terminal and reconnect the voltmeter between the ignition coil negative terminal and the ground, Fig. 77. If voltage remains at 0 to 5 volts, the ignition coil is defective, requiring replacement. If voltage increases to 12 to 13 volts, the electronic control unit is faulty. Reconnect the brown wire to the ignition coil negative terminal.
6. Connect voltmeter between the ignition coil negative terminal and the ground, Fig. 78. With ignition "On", place a screwdriver blade against face of sensor, Fig. 78. Voltage should increase to 12 to 13 volts. Remove the screwdriver blade and voltage should drop to 5 to 8 volts. If so, proceed to next step. If not, replace electronic control unit.
7. Disconnect coil wire from distributor cap and insert an extension adapter into boot and engage into cable terminal. Hold cable approximately ½ inch from a suitable ground. With ignition "On", observe for spark each time a screwdriver blade is placed across the sensor face, Fig. 79. If no spark occurs, the sensor coil is defective, requiring replacement.
8. After replacing components, remove test equipment and repeat Step 1.
9. Connect a dwell meter to engine. Operate engine and observe dwell reading. It may be necessary to readjust the trigger wheel to sensor air gap to obtain specified dwell.

Primary Voltage Drop Test, Fig. 80
1. Remove distributor cap, rotor and shield.

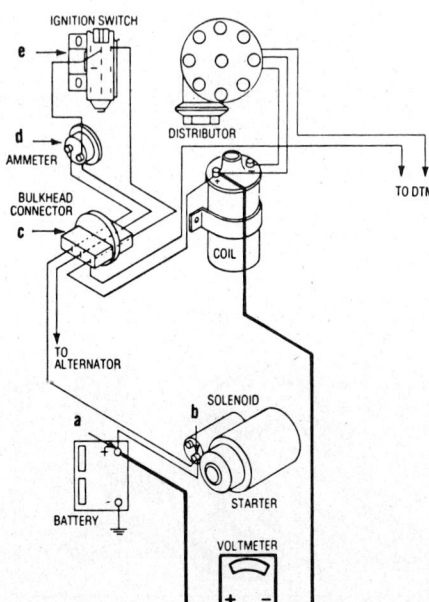

Fig. 80 Primary voltage drop test

Crank engine to position sensor coil between two trigger wheel teeth.
2. Connect voltmeter positive lead to battery positive terminal and the voltmeter negative lead to the ignition coil positive terminal.
3. Turn ignition "On" and observe voltmeter reading. A reading of less than 1 volt should be obtained.
4. Check circuit conditions by observing voltmeter while moving the connectors at the following locations: battery cables, starter solenoid battery terminal, dash panel bulkhead connector, ammeter terminals and ignition switch connections.
5. If a reading fluctuation or an upswing of the voltmeter needle is observed, a poor connection exists and must be corrected.

Shaft & Bushing Wear Test

1. Clamp distributor is a soft jawed vise.
2. Remove distributor rotor and shield.
3. Install a dial indicator so the pluger contacts the trigger wheel.
4. Place one end of a wire loop around the rotor shaft and hook a spring scale around the other end.
5. Apply ½ pound of pull on spring scale and observe dial indicator reading. Apply ½ pound of pull in opposite direction and observe dial indicator reading.
6. Peak to peak side play is the total of the two readings in Step 5. If the side play exceeds .006 inch, replace distributor shaft bushings.

Distributor Disassemble

1. Remove rotor and shield, Fig. 81.
2. Remove vacuum advance diaphragm rod "E" ring retainer, advance unit mounting screws and the vacuum advance unit, Fig. 82. Remove felt washer from diaphragm rod pin on sensor advance plate, Fig. 82.
3. Remove electronic control unit (Circuit board, sensor and plate assembly), Fig. 83, as follows:

177

ELECTRONIC IGNITION

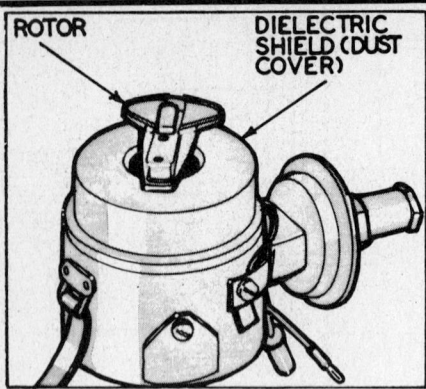

Fig. 81 Distributor rotor & shield

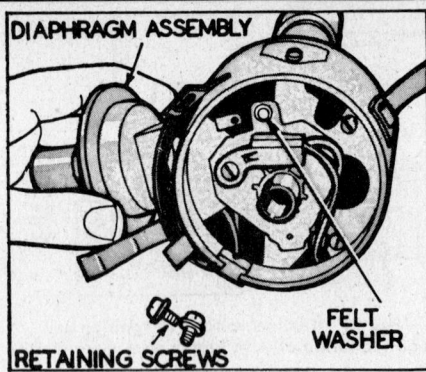

Fig. 82 Vacuum advance assembly

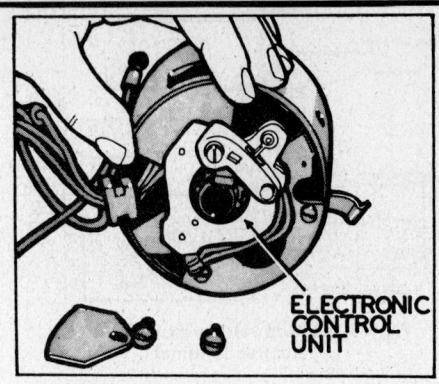

Fig. 83 Electronic control unit installation

a. Remove distributor plate (Control unit) mounting screws.
b. Pull wiring grommet from slot in distributor housing.
c. Lift control unit assembly from housing.
4. Measure distributor shaft end play between thrust washer and gear, Fig. 84, or thrust washer and thrust collar, Fig. 85. If end play exceeds .035–.040 inch on 4-196 and V8-345, 392 units, .004–.018 inch on V8-404, 446 units or .002–.010 inch on V8-537 units, replace upper and lower thrust washers.
5. Drive roll pin from gear and shaft. Press gear or thrust collar and lower thrust washers from shaft.
6. Remove distributor shaft from housing. Use care not to lose the upper thrust washers.

Distributor Assemble

NOTE: If a new distributor shaft is being installed, a new distributor driven gear or thrust collar and new thrust washers must be installed.

1. Install distributor shaft into housing as follows:
   a. Place new upper thrust washers on shaft. Units with a tachometer drive use one thrust washer, Fig. 86, while all others use two. On units using two thrust washers, Fig. 87, install the outer washer first with the lip facing toward lower end of shaft. Install the inner washer with lip facing toward lower end of shaft and seated on the lip of the outer washer.
   b. Lubricate distributor shaft with engine oil.
   c. Slide distributor shaft into housing carefully to avoid damaging lower oil seal, if installed.
2. Install new lower thrust washers on shaft. Units used on V8-537 engines use one thrust washer, Fig. 88, while all others use two. On units using two thrust washers, Fig. 89, install inner washer first with the lip facing toward the distributor housing. Install outer washer with the lip facing toward distributor housing and seated on the lip of the inner washer.
3. If original distributor driven gear or thrust collar is being installed, position gear or thrust collar on distributor shaft and align roll pin hole in gear or thrust collar with roll pin hole in shaft. Install driven gear or thrust collar roll pin.
4. If a new distributor driven gear or thrust collar is being installed, position gear or thrust collar on distributor shaft and align hole with roll pin hole in distributor shaft. Support distributor assembly and drill a hole through other side of gear or thrust collar. Install roll pin.

NOTE: A new gear or thrust collar has the roll pin hole drilled in one side only.

5. If a new distributor shaft and gear or thrust collar are being installed, position gear or thrust collar on distributor shaft and adjust distributor shaft end play. End play should be .035–.040 inch on 4-196 and V8-345, 392 units, .004–.018 inch on V8-404, 446 units and .002–.010 inch on V8-537 units. Then, support distributor assembly and, using the existing hole in gear or thrust collar as a guide, drill roll pin hole in distributor shaft and other side of gear or thrust collar. Install roll pin.
6. Install electronic control unit (Circuit board, sensor and plate assembly) as follows:
   a. Apply a small amount of grease under the three thrust buttons.
   b. Place control unit assembly and wiring grommet in distributor housing.
   c. Install distributor plate (Control unit) mounting screws.
7. Place vacuum advance diaphragm assembly on distributor housing and install mounting screws.
8. Install felt washer on diaphragm rod pin of sensor advance plate. Lubricate felt washer with engine oil.
9. Connect diaphragm rod to pin on sensor advance plate and install flat washer, if used, and rod retaining "E" clip.
10. Adjust trigger wheel to sensor air gap,

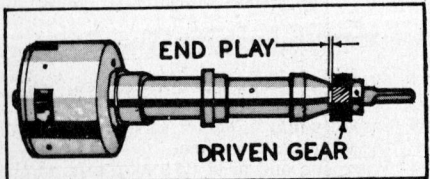

Fig. 84 Checking distributor shaft end play. Units with driven gear

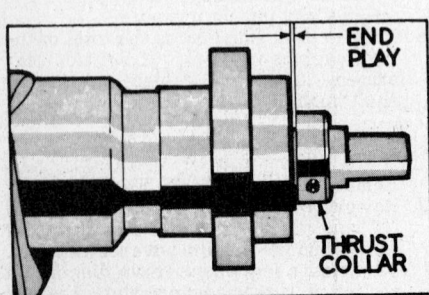

Fig. 85 Checking distributor shaft end play. Units with thrust collar

Fig. 86 Upper thrust washer installation. Units with tachometer drive

Fig. 87 Upper thrust washer installation. Units less tachometer drive

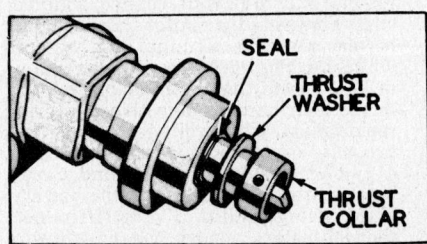

Fig. 88 Lower thrust washer installation. V8-537 units

ELECTRONIC IGNITION

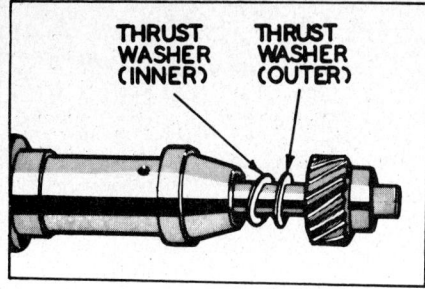

Fig. 89 Lower thrust washer installation. Exc. V8-537 units

Fig. 73, as follows:
  a. Rotate trigger wheel until one tooth is aligned with centerline of sensor.
  b. Using a feeler gauge, measure air gap between sensor and end of tooth. Air gap should be .008 inch. If not, move sensor to obtain proper air gap. Tighten sensor mounting screw and recheck air gap.
11. To adjust centrifugal advance, install distributor on distributor test stand. Check advance at each specified speed. If advance is not within limits, adjust by bending spring posts, Fig. 90. To increase advance, bend spring post toward distributor shaft thereby decreasing spring tension. To decrease advance, bend spring posts away from distributor shaft thereby increasing spring tension.
12. Install shield, rotor and distributor cap.

Fig. 90 Adjusting centrifugal advance

DASH GAUGES

TESTING

Gauge failures are often caused by defective wiring or grounds. Therefore, the first step in locating trouble should be a thorough inspection of all wiring and terminals. If wiring is secured by clamps, check to see whether the insulation has been severed thereby grounding the wire. In the case of a fuel gauge installation, rust may cause failure by corrosion at the ground connection of the tank unit.

CONSTANT VOLTAGE TYPE

Voltage Regulator Test

1. Turn on ignition switch.
2. Check voltage at gauge feed wire at one of the gauges.
3. Voltage should oscillate between zero and about 10 volts.
4. If it does not, voltage regulator is defective, or there is a short or ground between voltage regulator and gauges.

Dash Gauge Tests

1. Turn off ignition switch.
2. Connect the terminals of two series-connected flashlight batteries to the gauge terminals in question (fuel, oil or temperature).
3. The three volts of the batteries should cause the gauge to read approximately full scale.
4. If the gauge unit is inaccurate or does not indicate, replace it with a new unit.
5. If the gauge unit still is erratic in its operation, the sender unit or wire to the sender unit is defective.

Fuel Tank Gauge Test

1. Test the dash gauge as outlined above.
2. If dash gauge is satisfactory, remove flashlight batteries.
3. Then disconnect wire at tank unit and ground it momentarily to a clean, unpainted portion of the vehicle frame or body *with ignition switch on*.
4. If the dash gauge still does not indicate, the wire is defective. Repair or replace the wire.
5. If grounding the new or repaired wire causes the gauge to indicate, the tank unit is faulty and should be replaced.

Oil & Temperature Sending Unit Tests

1. Test dash gauge as outlined above.
2. If dash gauge is satisfactory, remove flashlight batteries.
3. Then start engine and allow it to run to warm up to normal temperature.
4. If no reading is indicated on the gauge, check the sending unit-to-gauge wire by removing the wire from the sending unit and momentarily ground this wire to a clean, unpainted portion of the engine.
5. If the gauge still does not indicate, the wire is defective. Repair or replace the wire.
6. If grounding the new or repaired wire causes the dash gauge to indicate, the sending unit is faulty.

VARIABLE VOLTAGE TYPE

The procedure given herewith applies to AC, Auto-Lite and Stewart-Warner systems. The following method quickly checks the gauge system to determine which component (sender or receiver) of a given system is defective.

Fuel Gauge Tank Unit Method

1. Use a spare fuel gauge tank unit known to be correct.
2. To test whether the dash gauge in question (fuel, oil or temperature) is functioning, disconnect the wire at the gauge which leads to the sending unit.
3. Attach a wire lead from the dash gauge terminal to the terminal of the "test" tank gauge, Fig. 1.
4. Ground the test tank unit to an unpainted portion of the dash panel and move the float arm.
5. If the gauge operates correctly, the sending unit is defective and should be replaced.
6. If the gauge does not operate during this test, the dash gauge is defective and should be replaced.

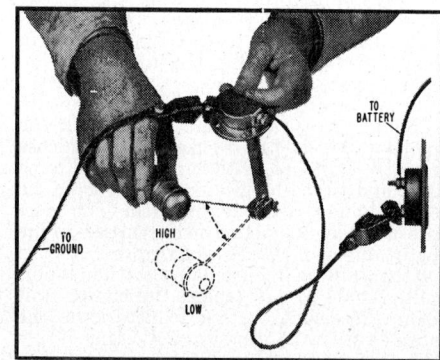

Fig. 1 Hook-up for testing dash gauge with a spare tank unit

AMMETERS

This instrument shows whether the battery is being charged by the generator or alternator or is being discharged by lights, radio, engine, etc. If a constant discharge is indicated on the ammeter, it is a signal that the battery is being run down. It is often a signal that the generator is out of order. Since both a charged battery and a working generator are very necessary—especially with vehicles equipped with many electricity-consuming devices such as heater, defroster, fog lights, radio, etc.—an inoperative ammeter should be given prompt attention.

The typical ammeter, Fig. 2, consists of a frame to which a permanent magnet is attached. The frame also supports an armature and pointer assembly.

When no current flows through the ammeter, the magnet holds the pointer armature so that the pointer stands at the center of the dial. When current passes in either direction through the ammeter, the resulting magnetic field attracts the armature away from the effect of the permanent magnet, thus giving a reading proportional to the strength of the current flowing.

179

DASH GAUGES

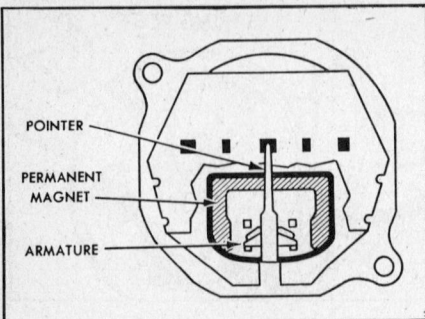

Fig. 2 Drawing of typical automobile ammeter

Trouble Shooting

When the ammeter apparently fails to register correctly, there may be trouble in the wiring which connects the ammeter to the generator and battery or in the generator or battery themselves.

To check the connections, first tighten the two terminal posts on the back of the ammeter. Then, following each wire from the ammeter, tighten all connections on the ignition switch, battery and generator. Chafed, burned or broken insulation can be found by following each ammeter wire from end to end.

All wires with chafed, burned or broken insulation should be repaired or replaced. After this is done, and all connections are tightened, connect the battery cable and turn on the ignition switch. The needle should point slightly to the discharge (−) side.

Start the engine and speed it up a little above idling speed. The needle should then move to the charge side (+), and its movement should be smooth.

If the pointer does not behave correctly, the ammeter itself is out of order and a new one should be installed.

GENERATOR INDICATOR LIGHT

A red generator or alternator "no charge" light is used on many cars in lieu of an ammeter. This light flashes on if the battery is discharging and the generator or alternator is not supplying current.

The light should glow when the ignition is turned on and before the engine is started. If the bulb does not light, either the bulb is burned out or the indicator light wiring has an open circuit. After the engine is started, the light should be out at all times with the alternator system. With the D.C. generator system, the light should also be out at all times with the engine running except in cases where the engine idling speed is set too low; however, when the engine is speeded up the light should go out.

If the light fails to go out when the engine is running, the drive belt may be loose or missing or the generator or alternator or voltage regulator may be defective.

Light Circuit With D.C. Generator

The light is usually connected between the armature terminal of the generator regulator and the necessary terminal on the ignition switch, Fig. 3. If the ignition switch is on and the cutout relay contacts are open, the light will glow, indicating that the generator is not electrically connected to the battery. As soon as the generator is speeded up, the cutout relay contacts close. This by passes the indicator light and thus indicates that the battery is electrically connected to the generator.

Light Circuit With Alternator

A double contact voltage regulator together with a field relay is used on Delco-Remy and Ford alternators when used with the indicator light. The circuit is as follows:

With the ignition switch turned on (engine not running), current flow is through the ignition switch through the indicator light on the dash panel. From there it goes to a terminal of the regulator (marked "4" or "L" on Delco-Remy or "I" on Ford). The circuit continues through the lower contacts of the voltage regulator (held closed by a spring), out the "F" terminal of the regulator, in the "F" terminal of the alternator, through a brush and slip ring, through another brush and slip ring to ground.

After the engine is started, the voltage output of the alternator immediately closes the field relay. This causes battery voltage from the battery terminal of the regulator (marked "3" or "V" on Delco-Remy, "B" on Ford) to be present at the "4", "L" or "I" terminal. Since battery voltage is present on both sides of the indicator light, the light goes out.

If the generator light comes on with the engine running, the charging circuit should be tested as soon as possible to determine the cause of the trouble.

OIL PRESSURE INDICATOR LIGHT

Many trucks utilize a warning light on the instrument panel in place of the conventional dash indicating gauge to warn the driver when the oil pressure is dangerously low. The warning light is wired in series with the ignition switch and the engine unit—which is an oil pressure switch.

The oil pressure switch contains a diaphragm and a set of contacts. When the ignition switch is turned on, the warning light circuit is energized and the circuit is completed through the closed contacts in the pressure switch. When the engine is started, build-up of oil pressure compresses the diaphragm, opening the contacts, thereby breaking the circuit and putting out the light.

Trouble Shooting

The oil pressure warning light should go on when the ignition is turned on. If it does not light, disconnect the wire from the engine unit and ground the wire to the frame or cylinder block. Then if the warning light still does not go on with the ignition switch on, replace the bulb.

If the warning light goes on when the wire is grounded to the frame or cylinder block, the engine unit should be checked for being loose or poorly grounded. If the unit is found to be tight and properly grounded, it should be removed and a new one installed. (The presence of sealing compound on the threads of the engine unit will cause a poor ground).

If the warning light remains lit when it normally should be out, replace the engine unit before proceeding further to determine the cause for a low oil pressure indication.

The warning light sometimes will light up or will flicker when the engine is idling, even though the oil pressure is adequate. However,

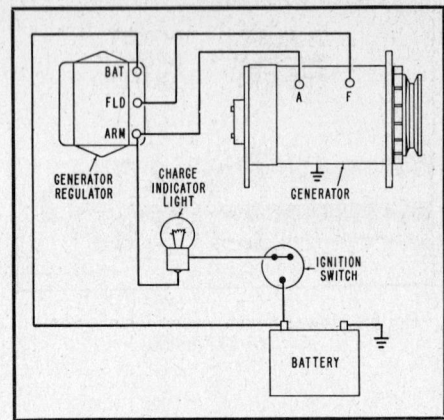

Fig. 3 Wiring diagram of a typical charge indicator light circuit

the light should go out when the engine is speeded up. There is no cause for alarm in such cases; it simply means that the pressure switch is not calibrated precisely correct.

TEMPERATURE INDICATOR LIGHTS

A temperature (bimetal) switch, located in cylinder head, controls the operation of a "Cold" temperature indicator light with a green lens and a "Hot" temperature indicator light with a red lens. When the cooling system water temperature is below approximately 110 degrees F., the temperature switch grounds the "Cold" indicator circuit and the green light goes on. When the green light goes out, the water temperature is high enough so that the heater can be turned on and be effective.

NOTE: *The car should never be subjected to full throttle accelerations or high speeds until after the green light has gone out.*

If the engine cooling system is not functioning properly and the water temperature should reach a point where the engine approaches an overheated condition, the red light will be turned on by the temperature switch.

NOTE: *As a test circuit to check whether the red bulb is functioning properly, a wire which is connected to the ground terminal of the ignition switch is tapped into its circuit. When the ignition is in the "Start" (engine cranking) position, the ground terminal is grounded inside the switch and the red bulb will be lit. When the engine is started and the ignition switch is in the "On" position, the test circuit is opened and the bulb is then controlled by the temperature switch.*

Trouble Shooting

If the red light is not lit when the engine is being cranked, check for a burned out bulb, an open in the light circuit, or a defective ignition switch.

If the red light is lit when the engine is running, check the wiring between light and switch for a ground, temperature switch defective, or overheated cooling system.

If the green light is not lit when ignition is

DASH GAUGES

on and engine cold, check for a burned out bulb, an open in the light circuit, or a defective temperature switch.

If the green light stays on after normal engine warm-up period, check for a ground between light and switch, defective temperature switch, or a defective cooling system thermostat.

PRESSURE EXPANSION TYPE OIL GAUGES

The pressure expansion type oil gauge, Fig. 4, consists of a metal case enclosing a dial, frame and mechanism. The dash unit is connected by a tube to the oil line leading from the oil pump. Oil pressure from the pump is carried by the tube to the dash unit where it causes a Bourdon tube to straighten out slightly. This straightening of the Bourdon tube causes the pointer movement.

The Bourdon tube is an oval tube, bent in a circular shape and closed except for a connection to the oil pump. When oil pressure is applied to the Bourdon tube, it tends to expand to make a circular cross section, and in so doing straightens out slightly.

The amount of expansion and straightening depends upon the amount of pressure applied to the tube. One end of the tube is fixed while the other is linked to the pointer. While no spring is necessary to return the pointer to zero, a spring is often used to keep a slight tension on the pointer and to take up any slack in the linkage, thus reducing vibration or fluctuation of the pointer.

Trouble Shooting

Pressure expansion type gauges are subject to two kinds of trouble: (1) The gauge shows a very low pressure at normal engine speed and temperature; (2) the pointer is jumpy, sticky or uneven in its movement.

If the pointer on the gauge is sticky, jumpy or uneven in its movement, it cannot be fixed. Install a new gauge of the same make as the one removed.

If the gauge is inoperative, disconnect the tube from the back of the gauge. Check for possible plugging of the tube by holding the disconnected end over a pan or other receptacle and starting the engine. The oil should flow from the tube at a steady rate. If it does not, check the tube for kinks, leaks and plugging. If none of these conditions is evident, the oil pump should be removed and checked for damage or wear.

If the foregoing inspection shows that oil pressure is reaching the gauge, remove the gauge from the instrument panel. Inspect to see if the small hole leading into the Bourdon tube is open and clean it out with a pin. Make sure there is no binding on the pointer or other parts. Connect the unit to the oil line and again check its operation. If it still will not operate, replace it with a new gauge of the same make as the one removed.

ELECTRICAL OIL PRESSURE GAUGES

This oil pressure indicating system incorporates an instrument voltage regulator, electrical oil pressure gauge and a sending unit which are connected in series. The sending unit consists of a diaphragm, contact and a variable resistor. As oil pressure increases or decreases, the diaphragm actuated the contact on the variable resistor, in turn controlling current flow to the gauge. When oil pressure is low, the resistance of the variable resistor is high, restricting current flow to the gauge, in turn indicating low oil pressure. As oil pressure increases, the resistance of the variable resistor is lowered, permitting an increased current flow to the gauge, resulting in an increased gauge reading.

Trouble Shooting

Disconnect the oil pressure gauge lead from the sending unit, connect a 12 volt test lamp between the gauge lead and the ground and turn ignition ON. If test lamp flashes, the instrument voltage regulator is functioning properly and the gauge circuit is not broken. If the test lamp remains lit, the instrument voltage regulator is defective and must be replaced. If the test lamp does not light, check the instrument voltage regulator for proper ground or an open circuit. Also, check for an open in the instrument voltage regulator to oil pressure gauge wire or in the gauge itself.

NOTE: If test lamp flashes and gauge is not accurate, the gauge may be out of calibration, requiring replacement.

VAPOR PRESSURE TYPE TEMPERATURE GAUGES

Made by both AC and Auto-Lite, this type gauge, Fig. 5, is a remotely controlled thermometer which tells the temperature of the engine coolant. The dash unit is the Bourdon tube type having a capillary tube and bulb attached to the unit. This tube and bulb are filled with a liquid and sealed. When the bulb is heated by the engine coolant, the confined liquid generates vapor pressure which is transmitted through the capillary tube to the Bourdon tube in the gauge. This Bourdon tube is similar to that described for the pressure expansion type oil pressure gauge and is linked to a pointer in the same manner. The complete gauge is calibrated to read directly in degrees.

Trouble Shooting

If the gauge does not give a reasonably accurate indication of the coolant temperature and it is certain that no other part of the cooling system is at fault, the complete unit must be removed and tested as follows:
1. Drain the water from the cooling system.
2. Loosen the plug which holds the vapor pressure bulb in the engine block.
3. Pry loose the adapter which seats on the bulb. Do not pull up on the tube until the adapter and bulb are free as this may damage the capillary tube and bulb. A light tap on the adapter with a screw driver blade will often free the bulb for easy removal.
4. Remove the vapor pressure bulb from the engine block.
5. Place the vapor pressure bulb in a pail of hot water, together with a thermometer which reads up to 200 degrees F. or higher, Fig. 6. The thermometer must be reasonably accurate in the hot water.
6. Leave the bulb and thermometer in the hot water long enough to allow the gauge to come to its indication. If the gauge is OK the pointer should register the same temperature as the thermometer.
7. If this test shows that the trouble is in the temperature gauge itself, install a new gauge of the correct make, as there is nothing to fix.

ELECTRICAL TEMPERATURE GAUGES

This temperature indicating system consists of a sending unit, located on the cylinder head, electrical temperature gauge and an instrument voltage regulator. As engine temperature increases or decreases, the resistance of the sending unit changes, in turn controlling current flow to the gauge. When engine temperature is low, the resistance of the sending unit is high, restricting current flow to the gauge, in turn indicating low engine temperature. As engine temperature increases, the resistance of the ending unit decreases, permitting an increased current flow to the gauge, resulting in an increased temperature reading.

Trouble Shooting

Trouble shooting for the electrical temperature indicating system is the same as for the electrical oil pressure indicating system previously described.

SPEEDOMETERS

The following material covers only that service on speedometers which is feasible to perform by the average service man. Repairs on the units themselves are not included as they require special tools and extreme care when making repairs and adjustments and only an experienced speedometer mechanic should attempt such servicing.

The speedometer has two main parts—the indicating head and the speedometer drive cable. When the speedometer fails to indicate speed or mileage, the cable or cable housing is probably broken.

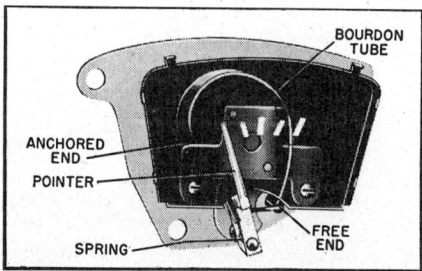

Fig. 4 Pressure expansion type oil gauge. The gauge is connected by a tube to the oil line and the oil pressure causes the Bourdon tube to straighten, which moves the pointer.

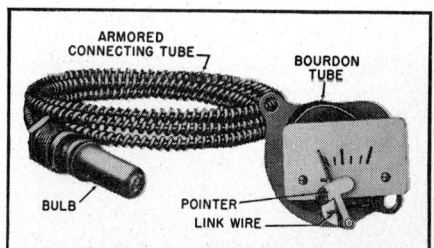

Fig. 5 Auto-Lite vapor pressure temperature gauge. This gauge is similar to the oil pressure expansion gauge

DASH GAUGES

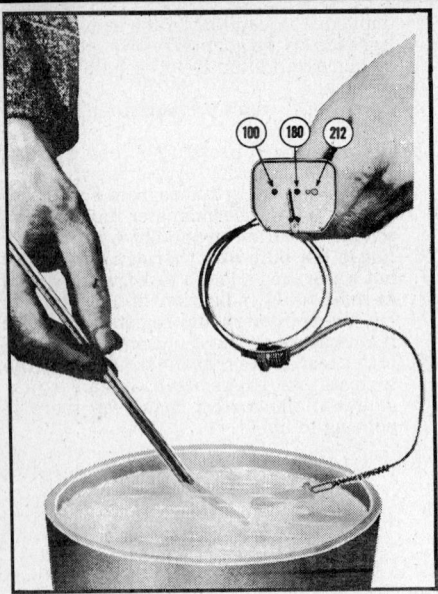

Fig. 6 Testing vapor pressure temperature gauge in hot water and a thermometer

Fig. 7 Typical vacuum gauge

except for the last six inches of cable. Too much lubricant at this point may cause the lubricant to work into the indicating head.

Installing Cable

During installation, if the cable sticks when inserted in the housing and will not go through, the housing is damaged inside or kinked. Be sure to check the housing from one end to the other. Straighten any sharp bends by relocating clamps or elbows. Replace housing if it is badly kinked or broken. Position the cable and housing so that they lead into the head as straight as possible.

Check the new cable for kinks before installing it. Use wide, sweeping, gradual curves where the cable comes out of the transmission and connects to the head so the cable will not be damaged during its installation.

Arrange the housing so it does not lean against the cylinder head because heat from the engine may dry out the lubricant.

If inspection indicates that the cable and housing are in good condition, yet pointer action is erratic, check the speedometer head for possible binding.

The speedometer drive pinion should also be checked. If the pinion is dry or its teeth are stripped, the speedometer may not register properly.

The transmission mainshaft nut must be tight or the speedometer drive gear may slip on the mainshaft and cause slow speed readings.

VACUUM GAUGE

This gauge, Fig. 7, measures intake manifold vacuum. The intake manifold vacuum varies with engine operating conditions, carburetor adjustments, valve timing, ignition timing and general engine condition.

Since the optimum fuel economy is directly proportional to a properly functioning engine, a high vacuum reading on the gauge relates to fuel economy. For this reason some manufacturers call the vacuum gauge a "Fuel Economy Indicator." Most gauges have colored sectors the green sector being the "Economy" range and red the "Power" range. Therefore, the vehicle should be operated with gauge registering in the green sector or a high numerical number, Fig. 7, for maximum economy.

Fuel Economy Warning System

This system actually monitors the engine vacuum just like the vacuum gauge, but all it registers is a low vacuum. The light on the instrument panel warns the vehicle operator when engine manifold vacuum drops below the economical limit. Switch operation is similar to that of the oil pressure indicating light, except that the switch opens when vacuum is applied, rather than oil pressure.

Trouble Shooting
Fuel Economy Warning Light

The fuel economy warning light should go on when the ignition is turned on. If it does not light, disconnect the wire from the fuel economy vacuum switch connector and ground the wire to the frame or cylinder block. Then if the warning light still does not go on, check for burned out indicating bulb or an open in the harness between the vacuum switch and instrument panel. If the warning light goes on, circuit is functioning and the vacuum switch should be checked for proper ground. Remove and clean the mounting bracket screws and also the mounting surfaces.

If system still does not operate perform the following:

With the electrical connector and vacuum tube disconnected from the switch, connect a self-powered test light to the switch electrical connector and to the vacuum gauge mounting bracket. Attach a vacuum pump to gauge (Rotunda Model No. ZRE-10662 hand operated). If the following conditions are not met the switch has to be replaced:
1. With vacuum applied test light should be "Off".
2. With no vacuum to the vacuum switch test light should be "On".

If the warning light remains lit when it normally should be out, check vacuum hose to vacuum switch for damage or plugged condition.

Speedometer Cable

Most cables are broken due to lack of lubrication, or a sharp bend or kink in the housing.

A cable might break because the speedometer head mechanism binds. If such is the case, the speedometer head should be repaired or replaced before a new cable or housing is installed.

A "jumpy" pointer condition, together with a sort of scraping noise, is due, in most instances, to a dry or kinked speedometer cable. The kinked cable rubs on the housing and winds up, slowing down the pointer. The cable then unwinds and the pointer "jumps."

To check for kinks, remove the cable, lay it on a flat surface and twist one end with the fingers. It if turns over smoothly the cable is not kinked. But if part of the cable flops over as it is twisted, the cable is kinked and should be replaced.

Lubrication

The speedometer cable should be lubricated with special cable lubricant every 10,000 miles. At the same time, put a few drops of the lubricant on the wick in the speedometer head.

Fill the ferrule on the upper end of the housing with the cable lubricant. Insert the cable in the housing, starting at the upper end. Turn the cable around carefully while feeding it into the housing. Repeat filling the ferrule

FUEL PUMPS

MECHANICAL FUEL PUMP

Fig. 1 illustrates a schematic drawing of a typical fuel system in which a combination fuel and vacuum pump is incorporated. Figs. 2 and 3 illustrate two typical diaphragm fuel pumps. Fig. 4 differs in that the pump has a vacuum booster section. The booster section has nothing to do with the fuel system except that it is operated by the pump arm.

Fuel Pump Operation

During the first or suction stroke, the rotation of the eccentric on the camshaft operates the pump operating arm which pulls the lever and diaphragm downward against the pressure of the diaphragm spring, producing a suction in the pump chamber. The suction holds the outlet valve closed and pulls the inlet valve open, making the fuel flow from the supply tank through the inlet up through the inlet valve into the pump chamber. During the return stroke, the diaphragm is forced up by the diaphragm spring, the inlet valve closes and the outlet valve is forced open, allowing the fuel to flow through the outlet to the carburetor.

Vacuum Section Operation

The vacuum section of combination pumps operates the windshield wipers at almost constant speed. The rotation of the camshaft eccentric in this type pump also operates the vacuum booster section by actuating the pump arm which pushes a link and bellows diaphragm downward, expelling air in the vacuum chamber through its exhaust valve out into the intake manifold of the engine. On the return stroke of the pump arm, the diaphragm is moved upward, producing a suction in the vacuum chamber. This suction operates the vacuum section and draws air through the inlet passage from the windshield wiper.

Fuel Pump Performance

It is essential that the fuel pump deliver sufficient fuel to supply the requirements of the engine under all operating conditions and that it maintain sufficient pressure in the line between the pump and carburetor to keep the fuel from boiling and to prevent vapor lock.

Excessive fuel pump pressure holds the carburetor float needle valve off its seat, causing high gasoline level in the float chamber which in turn increases gasoline consumption.

The pump usually delivers a minimum of ten gallons of gasoline per hour at top engine speeds, under an operating pressure of from 2 to 6 psi (depending on the installation). The highest operating pressure will be attained at idling speed and the lowest at top speed.

Fuel Pump Tests

The fuel pump can be tested on the car with a pressure gauge, a hose and a pint measuring can. With this equipment, it is possible to check the fuel pump to see if it is delivering the proper amount of gasoline at the correct pressure.

Pressure Test

To make the pressure test, disconnect the fuel pipe at the carburetor inlet and attach the pressure gauge and hose between the carburetor inlet and the disconnected fuel pipe, Fig. 5. Take the pressure reading with the engine running. The pressure should be within the limits permissible for the particular vehicle installation. The pressure should remain constant or return very slowly to zero when the engine is stopped.

Capacity Test

To make this test, connect the hose so the pump will deliver gasoline into the pint measure held at carburetor level. Run the engine at idle speed and note the time it takes to fill the measure. On the average it should take from 20 to 30 seconds, depending on the pump being tested.

When Pressure Is Low

Low pressure indicates extreme wear on one part, small wear on all parts, ruptured diaphragm, dirty valve or gummy valve seat.

Wear in the pump usually occurs at the rocker arm pivot pin and on the contacting surfaces of the rocker arm and links. Due to the leverage design, wear at these points is multiplied five times in the movement of the diaphragm. It is apparent, therefore, that very little wear will materially reduce the stroke of the diaphragm. The worn parts must

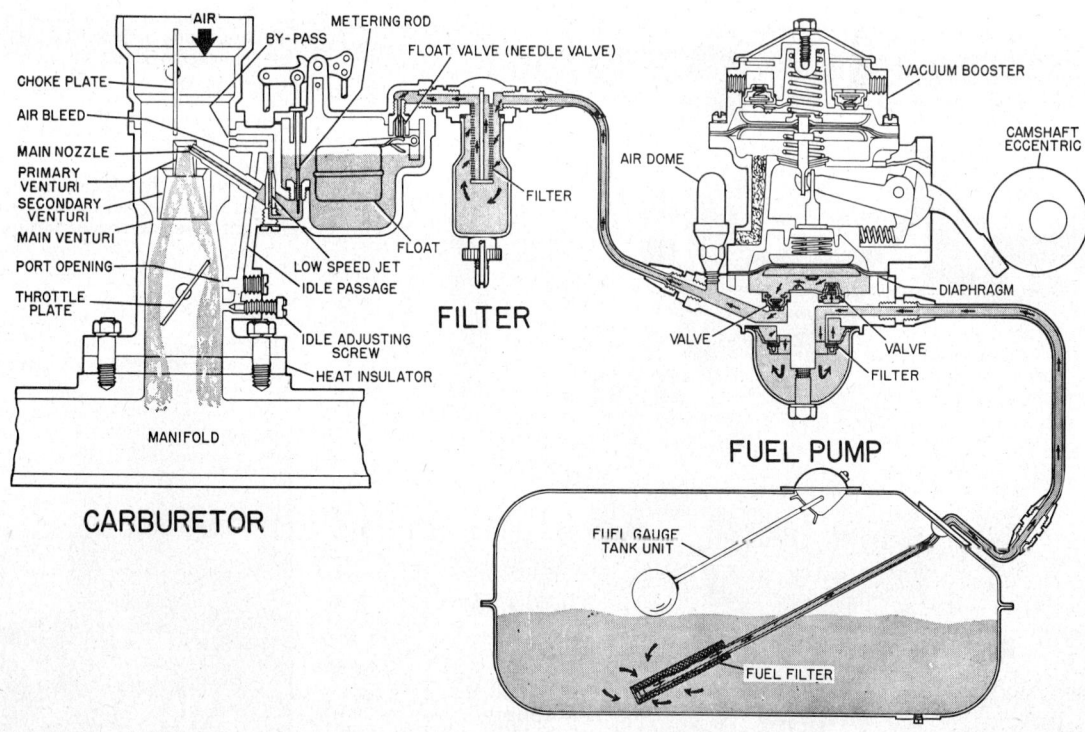

Fig. 1 Diagram of fuel system in operation

FUEL PUMPS

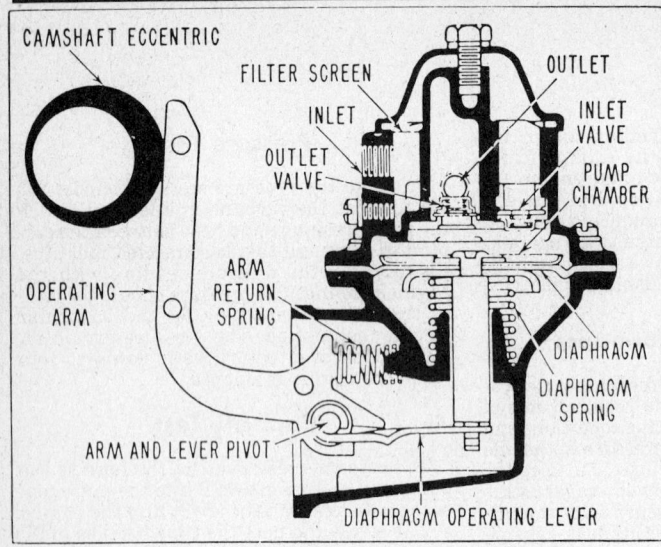

Fig. 2 Fuel pump with built-in fuel filter

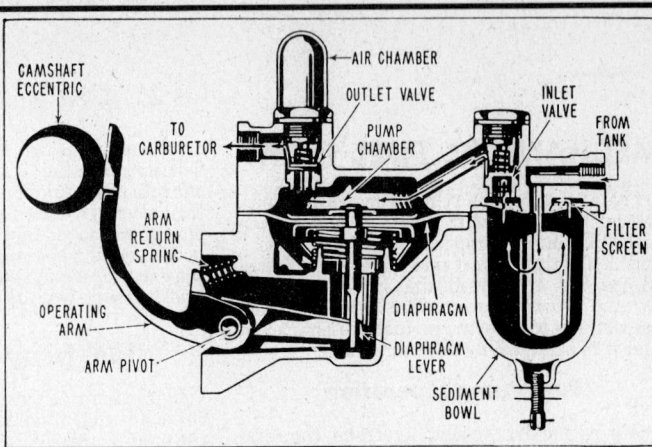

Fig. 3 Fuel pump with separate fuel filter

be replaced for a satisfactory correction.

The diaphragm pull rod has an oil seal around it which prevents the hot oil vapors from the crankcase coming in contact with the diaphragm. If this seal is damaged, the oil vapors have a tendency to shorten the life of the diaphragm.

The first three conditions—extreme wear on one part, small wear on all parts and ruptured diaphragm—are brought about by usage, while dirty and/or poor fuel is usually the cause of valve trouble.

When Pressure Is High

High pressure is caused by a tight diaphragm, fuel between diaphragm layers, diaphragm spring too strong, pump link frozen to rocker arm.

A tight diaphragm will stretch slightly on the down stroke. As the pump operates, the diaphragm will rebound on the up stroke beyond its normal position, much as a stretched rubber band when it is suddenly released. This rebound will cause a higher than normal pressure in the pump chamber.

A loose diaphragm retainer nut or poor riveting on the diaphragm assembly may allow fuel to seep between the diaphragm layers. This will cause a bulge in the diaphragm and have the same effect as a diaphragm that is too tight.

A diaphragm spring that is too strong also causes a high pressure, for the diaphragm will operate longer before pressure of the fuel on the diaphragm will overcome the diaphragm spring.

On a combination pump there are times when the operating parts may become badly corroded and the links freeze to the rocker arm. In this condition the pump operates continually, resulting in a very high pressure and a flooding carburetor.

The remedy for all these conditions is to remove the pump for replacement or repair, using a repair kit.

When Capacity Is Low

A pump is extra efficient and will never starve the engine when it supplies fuel equal to or above the capacity of the pump. The pressure, of course, must be within specifications.

Low capacity is usually caused by an air leak at the intake pipe at these points: fuel pipe fitting at pump, bowl flange or diaphragm flange, fuel bowl. (It is assumed that the conditions of too little fuel have already been checked and the fuel pump is the cause of the difficulty.)

An air leak at the fuel pipe fittings indicate either poor installation of pump or a defective fitting. The fitting should be tightened or replaced.

A leak at the diaphragm flange may be caused by a warped cover casting, loose diaphragm cover screws or foreign material be-

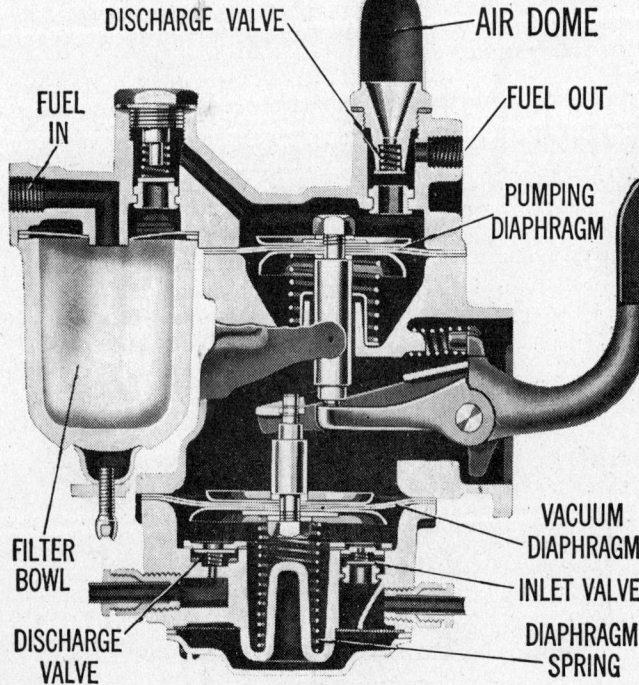

Fig. 4 Fuel pump with fuel filter and vacuum booster for windshield wiper operation

Fig. 5 Testing fuel pump pressure

FUEL PUMPS

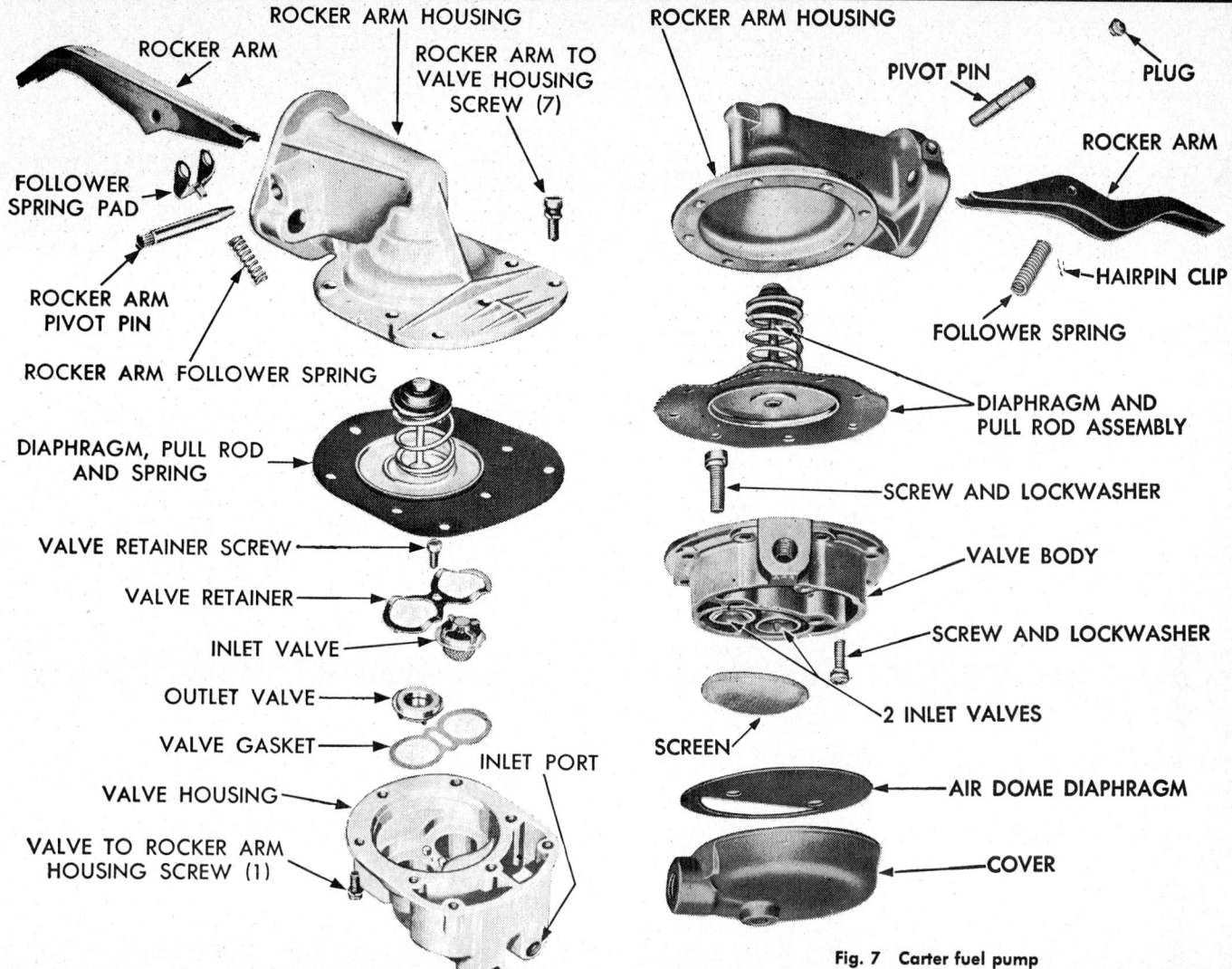

Fig. 6 Auto-Lite fuel pump

Fig. 7 Carter fuel pump

tween cover casting and diaphragm.

A leak at the bowl flange of the cover casting can usually be corrected by the installation of an extra gasket. A warped top cover indicates that the pump must be replaced.

A chipped glass or bent metal bowl may cause a leak at the bowl flange as may a defective gasket or foreign material between gasket and bowl or cover casting. A chipped glass bowl must be replaced while a dented metal bowl can be straightened.

Vacuum Pump Troubles

To assist the manifold vacuum to operate the windshield wiper at a uniform rate under any engine load is the only function of the vacuum pump. Of course, "uniform rate" infers a wet windshield and not one covered with snow or ice. Failure to do the above indicates difficulty in either the vacuum system of the pump, windshield wiper motor, or tubes and connections.

Symptoms of trouble in the vacuum section show up in four ways: oil consumption, slow windshield wiper action, poor idle, noise.

In some cases it has been found that an engine which has given very good oil mileage suddenly appears to be using oil. Upon investigation, it will often be found that the vacuum booster has a ruptured diaphragm and is drawing oil fumes from the crankcase into the intake manifold. This can be checked by removing the cover of the vacuum section.

When the windshield wiper slows down excessively under engine load, it usually is an indication of a ruptured vacuum diaphragm or defective valve action in the vacuum pump. This condition may not be discovered immediately as the windshield wipers may not be used for long intervals.

Oil will be evidenced in the cover casting recesses if the diaphragm is ruptured. The pump should be removed and the diaphragm replaced.

On some vehicles the engine will idle very poorly when the vacuum diaphragm is ruptured. This is true when the tube from the vacuum pump is connected to one end of the intake manifold. The air leak through the vacuum section will give those cylinders on the end a lean mixture which results in a miss or poor idle. In many cases, this leads one to believe the valves of the engine are sticking; but if they are ground, the miss or poor idle remains.

This condition can be checked by removing the vacuum pump tube at the manifold and plugging the hole. If the miss or rough idle disappears, the trouble is an air leak through the pump or tube connections. The pump should be removed and repaired or the connections tightened to eliminate this trouble.

Sometimes a combination pump will give off a peculiar grunting sound on idle. In some cases this can be remedied by stuffing curled horse hair into the pump breather.

Vacuum Pump Test

With a combination fuel and vacuum pump the windshield wiper should operate at 80 to 100 strokes per minute through all ranges of car speed and load. The windshield should be wet when the test is made, otherwise the action will be slow.

Checking With Vacuum Gauge

To check the vacuum section, disconnect both inlet and outlet tubes and attach a vacuum gauge to the inlet (side that goes to windshield wiper). It is assumed that the engine, windshield wiper motor and blade, and connecting tubing have been checked and are in satisfactory condition.

Read the gauge when the engine is running at 100 rpm (about 20 mph). It should read

185

FUEL PUMPS

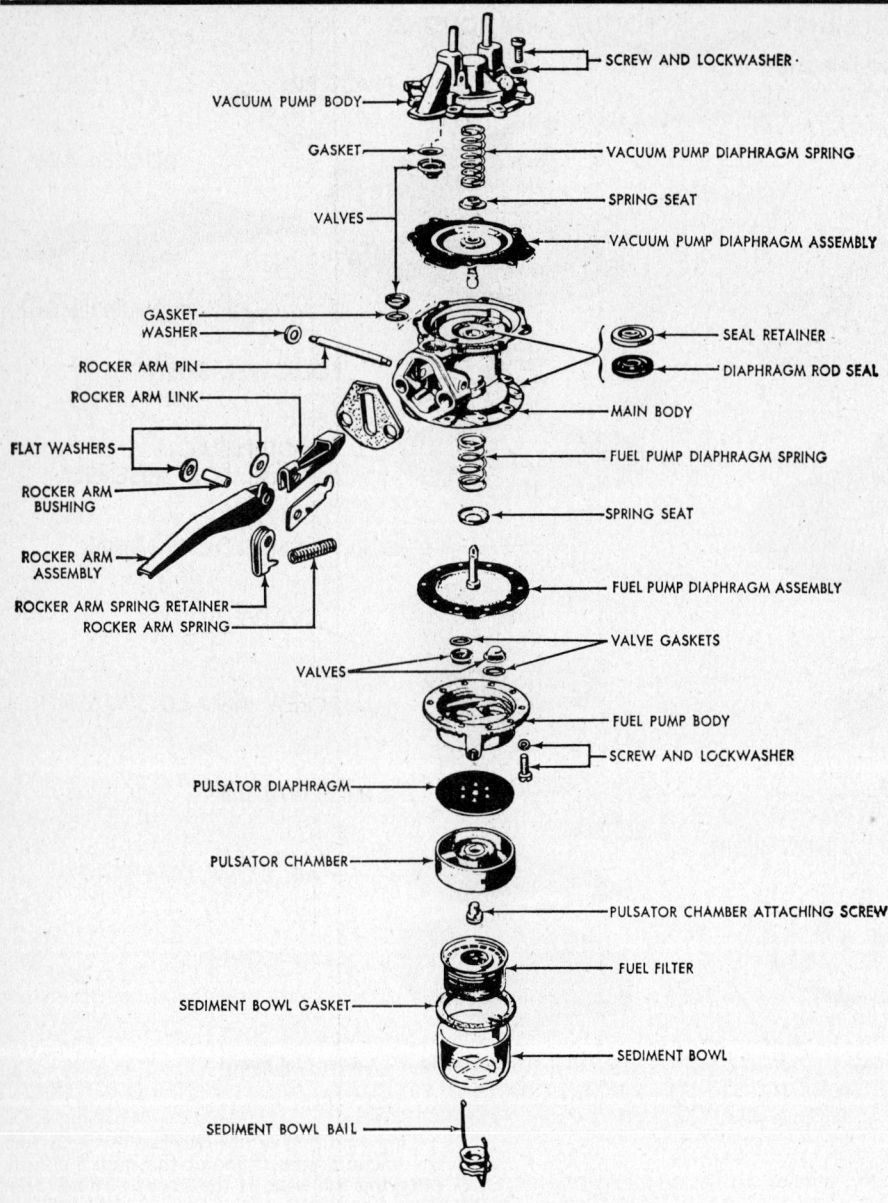

Fig. 8 A.C. combination pump with four vacuum valves and built-in fuel filter

from 7 to 12 inches of vacuum on a normal pump. If the reading is less than 7, the pump should be removed and repaired or replaced. When making this test, the tube to the manifold should be plugged and the pump outlet should always be open or damage may result to the mechanism.

Checking Without Gauge

Disconnect the outlet tube (to manifold) from the pump and plug the end. Then operate the engine from idle through slow acceleration to about 40 mph. If the wiper starts operating at about 15 mph and reaches full speed at about 40 mph, the vacuum section is okay. If it does not operate, it may be the windshield wiper motor. This can be checked by connecting the intake manifold directly to the windshield wiper tube. Then slowly accelerate the engine from idle to about 25 mph. The wiper should operate at full speed. If it does not it can be assumed that the wiper motor or tubing is defective.

Fuel Pump Service

NOTE: Most modern fuel pumps are sealed, non-serviceable units. These pumps cannot be repaired and must be replaced when defective.

Illustrated are representative fuel pumps among the many models that have been produced. Before disassembling any pump, scribe a mark across the housings in such a manner that they may be reassembled with inlet and outlet fitting holes in correct location.

When disassembled, clean all parts except diaphragms) in solvent and blow dry with compressed air. Examine the diaphragm for cracks, torn screw holes or ruptures. If deteriorated, install new diaphragm and pull rod assembly. Check the strainer screen and if found to be corroded or clogged, install a new screen. Check the rocker arm for wear or scoring on that portion which contacts the camshaft eccentric. If arm is scored or worn, install a new one. When reassembling a pump, do not use shellac or other adhesive on a diaphragm.

IN-TANK MOUNTED ELECTRIC FUEL PUMPS

Some trucks use an in-tank, positive displacement electric fuel pump. This pump has an enclosed, dry motor driving the impeller and in some applications, a magnetic coupling between the pump motor and impeller is incorporated to protect the motor in event of impeller seizure.

The pump is actuated by a primer switch on the dash panel before engine starting is attempted. This delivers a positive supply of fuel to the carburetor. Some units incorporate an oil pressure safety switch which de-activates the pump when the engine has stopped or in the event of excessively low oil pressure.

AUTO PULSE ELECTRIC FUEL PUMP

This bellows type pump, Fig. 10, has a magnetic activating coil in the base with a drive spring through the center of the coil. A pressure screw is incorporated to increase or reduce the drive spring pressure to control output pressures. The armature and contacts are located above the coil. The drive spring presses against a vertical shaft to which the upper contacts and one-piece metal bellows are attached. The bellows, in addition to performing the pumping action, acts as a seal between the pumping chamber and the electric mechanism. The pumping chamber is above the electric mechanism and consists of an inlet and outlet valve through which the fuel flows. A screen is located in the top, or dome, of the pump.

Operation

On the intake stroke the coil is energized, extending the bellows and compressing the drive spring. The bellows then returns to its normal position in the pressure stroke, pushing fuel through the outlet valve. The contacts are open during this interval. At the end of the pressure stroke, the contacts close, energizing the coil and drawing the armature and bellows downward on the intake stroke. Electrical contact is made for only a short time during the intake stroke. This cycle is repeated as long as fuel is required.

Trouble Shooting

Disconnect the fuel line at the carburetor and turn on the ignition switch. If ample fuel flows, the pump is okay. If the pump races but fuel does not flow in sufficient volume, the cause is an air leak in the suction portion of the fuel line. If fuel does not flow at all, inspect the fuel lines for restrictions or check the electrical connections for a shorted or open circuit. If all is in order and the pump still does not operate, remove the pump and replace or repair as necessary.

Disassembly

1. Take off the filter bowl and screen.
2. Remove two screws attaching filter base to pump base.
3. The electrical unit of the pump may be exposed by removing the lower cover.

FUEL PUMPS

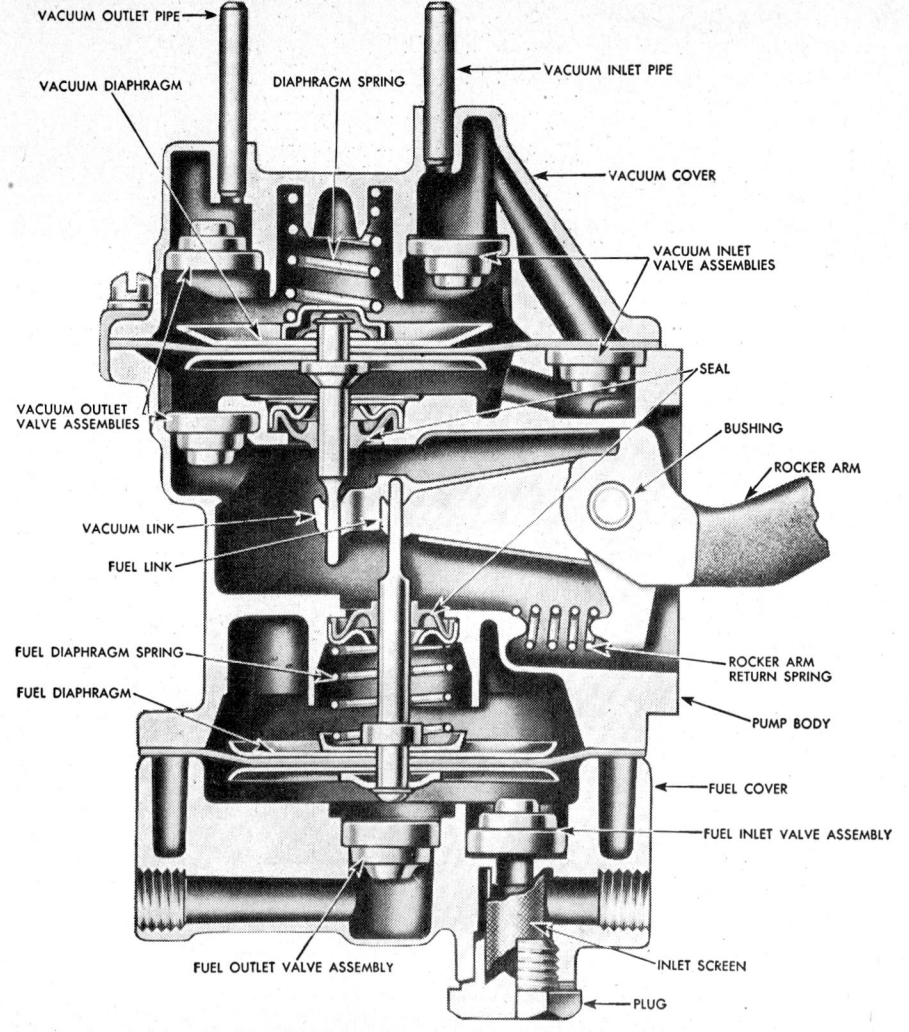

Fig. 9 A.C. combination pump with four vacuum valves

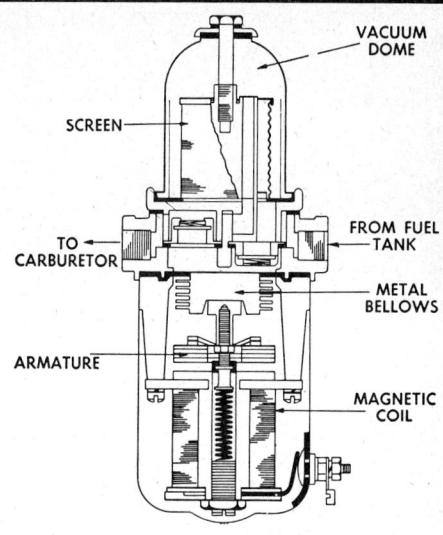

Fig. 10 Auto Pulse electric fuel pump

4. To separate the coil from the rest of pump, remove the pressure nut screw. Then use a 1/4" magneto wrench and loosen the drive screw nut below the bellows stud.
5. Insert a thin screwdriver into the coil hole and loosen the drive screw.
6. Remove the coil mounting screws.
7. Separate the coil from the armature by removing the armature mounting screws.
8. The bellows are removed by taking out the four bellows ring screws from the pump base.
9. Take out the bellows ring, bellows, gasket and air seal gasket.

Inspection

Wash the filter and bowl in solvent and blow dry with compressed air. The valves may be resurfaced with crocus cloth. Clean the faces of the pump base and bellows ring with a soft, dry cloth. Replace all defective electrical parts.

Assembly

Reverse the disassembly procedure to reassemble the pump, bearing in mind the following: Always use a new bellows when rebuilding this type pump. Make sure the inlet and outlet valves are not tight in their chambers. Use new gaskets throughout the assembly.

TURBOCHARGERS

A turbocharger is essentially an exhaust driven blower, the purpose of which is to increase engine power by supplying compressed air to the combustion chambers, permitting greater fuel consumption at an efficient air-fuel ratio. The turbocharger is not connected to the engine power train; therefore, it is not a horsepower parasite during operation. The unit automatically responds to engine load demands without any control connections between turbocharger and engine.

In outward appearance, turbochargers are made in various shapes but they are of two general types. In one type the unit consists basically of a compressor (main) housing and a turbine housing, Fig. 1. The other type consists primarily of a compressor housing, a turbine housing and a separate bearing housing. This design is shown mounted on a diesel engine in Fig. 2.

In both types the turbine housing encloses the turbine wheel and provides an exhaust outlet and inlet. The turbine housing also incorporates a nozzle ring which directs the exhaust gases to the turbine wheel. The nozzle ring is designed to increase the velocity of the exhaust gas before it enters the turbine wheel. The hot gases, expanding through the turbine housing, rotate the turbine wheel, thus producing power to drive the compressor.

The compressor housing in both types encloses the compressor wheel and provides an air inlet and outlet. Intake air from the engine air cleaner enters the compressor housing, is centrifugally compressed by the action of the wheel, and is supplied to the intake manifold of the engine.

The turbocharger shown in Figs. 1 and 3 is provided with a semi-floating sleeve bearing which is lubricated with oil from the engine lubrication system. A piston ring type oil seal prevents leakage at the turbine end of the shaft, while a mechanical-face type seal is usually used at the compressor end.

The turbocharger shown in Figs. 2 and 4 is lubricated by oil from the engine lubricating system also. Passages in the main housing direct oil under pressure to the bearings. The oil circulating through the bearing housing acts as a heat barrier between the hot turbine and compressor, and helps carry away heat generated in the bearings. From the bearing housing, the oil returns by gravity to the engine oil sump. Seal rings are used at each end of the shaft to prevent lubricating oil from entering the turbine or compressor.

TURBOCHARGERS

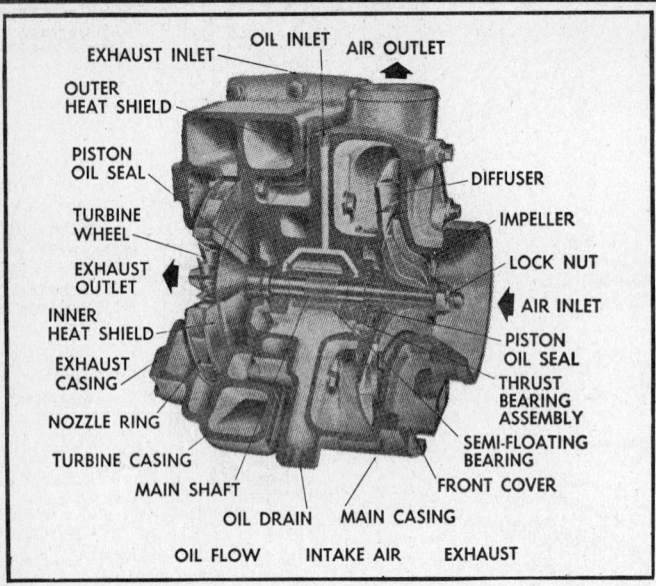

Fig. 1 Cutaway view of a Cummins turbocharger without a separate bearing housing

Fig. 2 Turbocharger with separate bearing housing mounted on a diesel engine

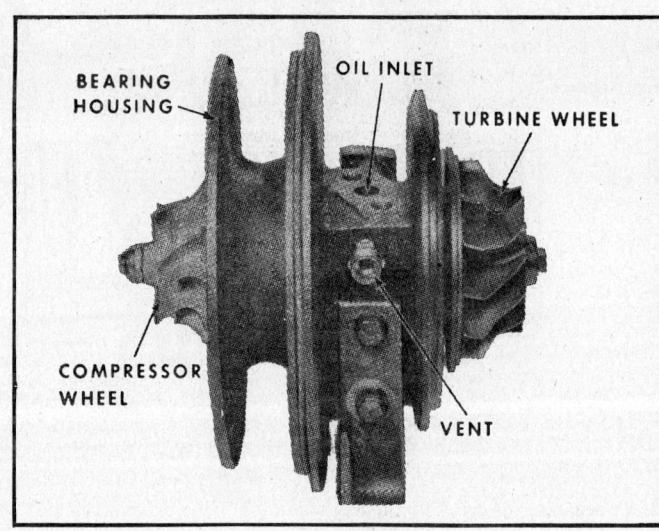

Fig. 4 Turbocharger with separate bearing housing

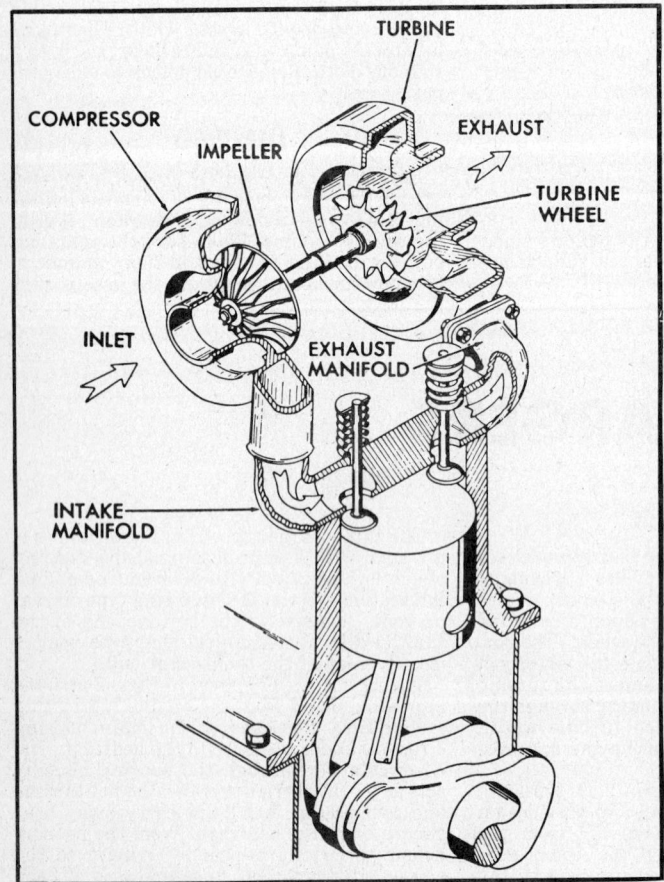

Fig. 3 Turbocharged gasoline engine

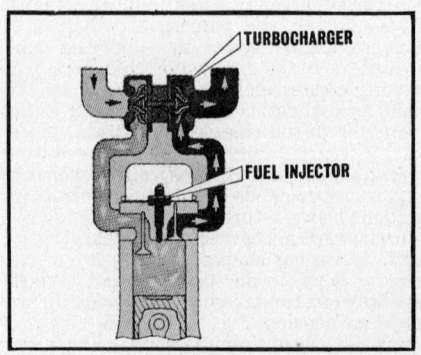

Fig. 5 Turbocharged diesel engine

TURBOCHARGERS

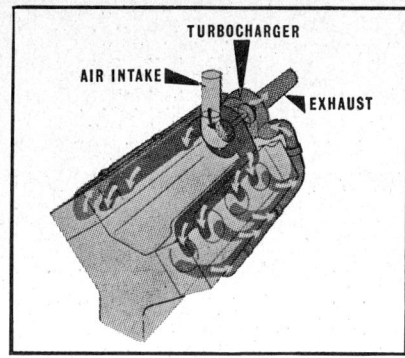

Fig. 6 Air and exhaust flow in turbocharged engine

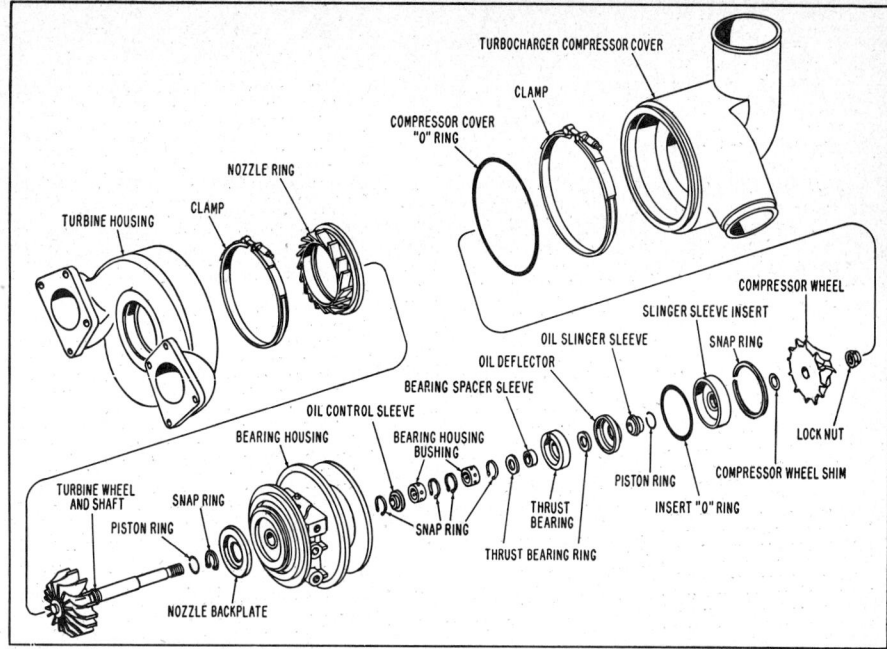

Fig. 7 Exploded view of a turbocharger with separate bearing housing

OPERATION

In a normal breathing engine (one that is neither turbocharged nor supercharged) air enters the engine at atmospheric pressure, mixes with a specified amount of fuel, and is burned in the combustion chamber, producing a certain amount of power.

On a turbocharged diesel engine, Fig. 5, the turbocharger supplies air under pressure to the intake manifold. Thus a greater amount of air enters the combustion chamber. The fuel injection system is calibrated to inject the correct amount of fuel for the increased volume of air. In a gasoline engine, Fig. 3, the principle is the same except that the carburetor is calibrated to provide the correct amount of fuel for the increased volume of air.

The turbocharger, in addition to exhaust volume and velocity, depends upon exhaust heat. Under loaded conditions, at maximum fuel delivery, the turbocharger becomes very efficient and supplies the increased air volume needed to support proper combustion.

Since the turbine speed is governed by the exhaust energy of the engine at any speed, the turbocharger delivers the correct volume of air at any throttle position. Also, less air resistance at higher elevations allows the turbocharger to spin faster and maintain correct air delivery, thereby avoiding the power loss and excessive smoking that occurs on a normal breathing engine and supercharged engines at high altitudes.

Summary: Engine exhaust is directed into the turbine housing. As the exhaust passes through the nozzle ring vanes, it gains velocity and strikes the turbine wheel vanes. This action spins the turbine wheel shaft to which the compressor wheel is attached. As the compressor wheel turns, it draws air from the air cleaner into the compressor housing, compresses it and forces it into the intake manifold. This provides a greater volume of air in the combustion chamber. Because a greater volume of air is delivered to the combustion chamber, a greater amount of fuel is required to obtain the correct air-fuel mixture. This increased consumption of fuel, at the correct air-fuel ratio, results in increased power output.

Service Precautions

NOTE: Regardless of their rugged appearance, turbochargers are to be handled with extreme care. The internal parts are manufactured to close tolerances and are sensitive to the accumulation of dirt, nicks and scratches. The turbine wheel, compressor impeller, shaft and related parts form a balanced assembly which rotates at very high speeds (65,000 rpm and higher in many applications). Bending of the turbine or compressor vanes or removal of any vane material during servicing could cause a serious out-of-balance condition which could quickly destroy the turbocharger. Therefore, *any major repairs to the unit should be performed by a specialty shop having the necessary special tools and equipment to do the work in accordance with the manufacturer's instructions and specifications.*

Because of the greater air flow requirements of a turbocharged engine, it is extremely important that the air intake system be kept clean. The air cleaner must be serviced at recommended intervals to avoid power loss due to air cleaner restriction and to prevent possible entry of dirt into the turbocharger and engine.

Turbocharging an engine is more than merely bolting on the turbocharger and driving away. The installation must be carefully engineered to provide the best performance and to avoid "over-charging" which would be destructive. Also, the engine must be designed to handle the greater air and fuel flow, higher pressures and temperatures, and increased torque and power output.

MAINTENANCE
General Handling

1. Prevent the entrance of foreign material by covering or plugging all openings into the turbocharger when the unit has been removed from the engine. Covers must remain in place until the unit is installed and all connections are secured.
2. All connections to the turbocharger (manifolds and piping) must be clean and free of foreign material, since serious damage to the turbocharger or engine could result. All connections must be air-tight.
3. Exhaust stacks of extra long length and other fixtures must not be rigidly attached to the turbocharger.
4. For initial running when installing a new or rebuilt turbocharger or after the engine has been shut down for 30 days or more or when engine oil filters have been changed, it is recommended that 4 or 5 ounces of oil (same type and grade as used in the engine) be injected into the oil inlet opening in the turbocharger. This will provide initial lubrication for the turbocharger bearings until normal engine lubrication is established.
5. If engine oil becomes contaminated by water, the turbocharger must be drained to prevent sludge formation. It is recommended that after an engine overhaul, an oil inlet filter be installed and used during the first 5 to 25 hours of operation and then removed, as this filter can clog with carbon that is normally suspended in the oil of a diesel engine.
6. It is imperative that the air cleaner be serviced at recommended intervals because of the oil carry-over and power losses that can be incurred with a restricted air cleaner.

NOTE: Air flow requirements for turbocharged diesel engines are considerably greater than for a non-turbocharged engine of the same size running at the same speed. Air inlet accessories must minimize the restriction of this higher air flow and maintain performance of the turbocharger unit.

7. The engine crankcase breather should be cleaned periodically to be sure there is no restriction.
8. During normal operation, the turbocharger should be free from vibration or unusual noises.
9. The exhaust stack should be covered to prevent water from entering and damaging the turbine during shutdown periods or when unit is being transported.
10. Periodic inspection of the compressor wheel should be made to check for soft carbon deposits, damaged blades, interference or excessive end play.

TURBOCHARGERS

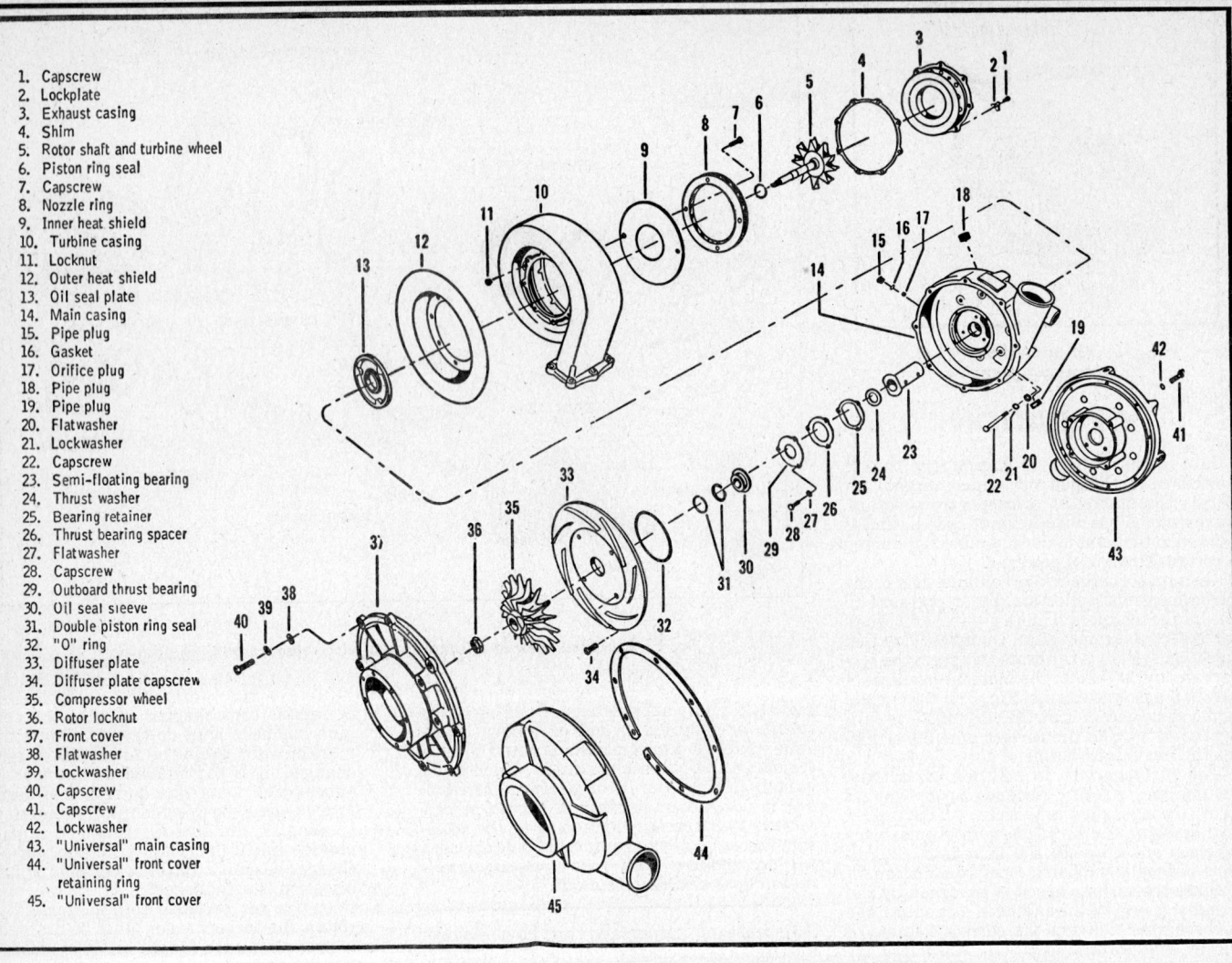

1. Capscrew
2. Lockplate
3. Exhaust casing
4. Shim
5. Rotor shaft and turbine wheel
6. Piston ring seal
7. Capscrew
8. Nozzle ring
9. Inner heat shield
10. Turbine casing
11. Locknut
12. Outer heat shield
13. Oil seal plate
14. Main casing
15. Pipe plug
16. Gasket
17. Orifice plug
18. Pipe plug
19. Pipe plug
20. Flatwasher
21. Lockwasher
22. Capscrew
23. Semi-floating bearing
24. Thrust washer
25. Bearing retainer
26. Thrust bearing spacer
27. Flatwasher
28. Capscrew
29. Outboard thrust bearing
30. Oil seal sleeve
31. Double piston ring seal
32. "O" ring
33. Diffuser plate
34. Diffuser plate capscrew
35. Compressor wheel
36. Rotor locknut
37. Front cover
38. Flatwasher
39. Lockwasher
40. Capscrew
41. Capscrew
42. Lockwasher
43. "Universal" main casing
44. "Universal" front cover retaining ring
45. "Universal" front cover

Fig. 8 Exploded view of a turbocharger without a separate bearing housing

LPG CARBURETION

INTRODUCTION

LPG (liquid petroleum gas) is an ideal engine fuel similar to gasoline. Both are a product of crude oil but they differ in that LPG is more volatile; that is it wants to boil or become a vapor at ordinary atmospheric temperatures. When used in an internal combustion engine, LPG is converted from a liquid in the fuel tank to a dry gas before reaching the combustion chamber. By good carburetion and perfect mixing of dry gas with air, uniform distribution throughout the manifold is achieved. With gasoline, or wet fuel, this uniform mixture and distribution is not attained.

With complete burning at a rate slower than gasoline, LPG makes for smoothness of operation because of prolonged power impulses on the power stroke and more uniform bearing pressures.

Being a dry gas, crankcase dilution is minimized and likewise all ill effects such as thinning of the lubricating oil and washing the lubricating oil from the cylinder walls with resultant cylinder wear are eliminated. Lubricating oil can be safely used much longer than on gasoline due to the elimination of carbon deposits, dirt, acid, and water content in the lubricating oil.

Harmful carbon within the engine is eliminated. There is no exhaust smoke or obnoxious odors. The time interval between engine shut-downs for overhaul is prolonged. Rings, valves, cylinders, and all moving parts lubricated from the crankcase last longer, resulting in a very substantial reduction in cost of keeping equipment in operation.

DESCRIPTION

Butane and propane gases, captured at the refinery and liquified by being put under pressure, are blended to a desired mixture and pumped as a liquid under pressure into specially constructed heavy steel tanks mounted on the truck. Tank pressures will vary from 20 to 175 psi (pounds per square inch) depending on the butane-propane mixture and atmospheric temperature. By reason of this tank pressure, no fuel pump is necessary. L. P. Gas tanks are never filled 100% full as 10% to 20% space must be allowed above the liquid for expansion.

Fig. 1 shows the flow diagram of the system.

Filtering

From the tank the liquid is piped to a liquid filter where scale from tank and fittings, and dirt or other solids are removed. From the filter, the L. P. Gas goes into the regulating unit. Final filtering is accomplished through a fine metal screen inserted in the fuel inlet connection of the regulator to further eliminate passage of undersirable foreign matter into the regulator.

Primary or High Pressure Regulation

Liquid butane is dropped from tank pres-

LPG CARBURETION

sure (20–175 psi) down to a regulated 1 to 10 psi. By use of the oil-controlled pressure regulator, the pressure is maintained at 1 psi with engine stopped and 10 psi when engine is running.

Vaporization

This function is performed by the vaporizer coils heated by hot water circulated by the engine. The high pressure valve would freeze up under the rapid expansion of gases were it not for the application of heat. This is accomplished by taking hot water from the water manifold, directing it first around the expansion valve, then around the heating coils to vaporize the expanded fuel, then returning it to the intake side of the water pump.

In starting a cold engine, there is sufficient differential in temperature between the extremely cold expanding butane and the parts surrounding the valve to provide latent heat for initial vaporization. However, it is desirable, especially in cold weather, to take vapor from the supply tank for starting and engine warm-up.

Final Pressure Regulation

The final regulator in the regulating unit further reduces the pressure of the completely vaporized butane from its 1 to 10 psi to slightly below atmospheric pressure. This final or "metering" regulator is actuated by engine vacuum or "suction" by the intake stroke which opens the final fuel regulator sufficiently to allow enough fuel to pass along to the carburetor to run the engine according to throttle opening. It actually regulates the supply of gas and shuts off the supply when the engine is stopped.

Idling System

The final regulator also contains the idling system. Even though most fuel used for idling enters the carburetor through the main gas orifice, additional and supplemental fuel for idling is taken from the final regulator and by-passed to a point in the carburetor directly above the throttle disc. The idle adjustment is in this line. This source of idling fuel is independent of the main gas supply to the carburetor and is controlled by an entirely different system. The two sources combine to produce the correct idling mixture.

Carburetion

From the regulating unit, the L. P. Gas is piped to the carburetor for final mixing and proportioning of the fuel with air. The carburetor is closely related to the final regulator of the regulating unit and with the two in correct coordination, air-fuel ratios are automatically controlled for greatest power, economy and flexibility.

The carburetor has an "easy-starting" feature wherein by pulling the choke entirely shut, a separate air-gas mixing device is put into operation to produce a pre-determined starting mixture. A separate adjustment is provided on the carburetor for adjusting the starting mixture. When the choke is released, the starting device is rendered inoperative and the main carburetor air-fuel orifices come into play. Therefore, the choke must be entirely *closed* for starting and entirely *open* for running.

A fuel economizer, actuated by manifold vacuum, is also utilized to reduce fuel consumption when operating at less than 80% full power.

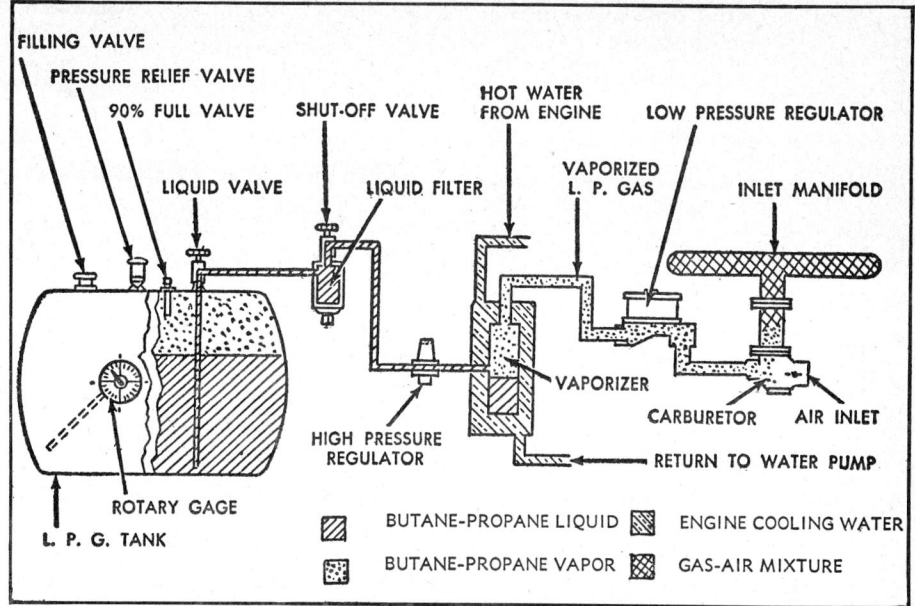

Fig. 1 Fuel diagram of LPG (liquid petroleum gas) fuel system

LPG SAFETY MEASURES

When Servicing Truck

1. To avoid accumulation of gas-air mixtures in and around a truck caused by undetected leaks, select a place where there is good air circulation.
2. Keep as far as possible from hot dip tanks, hot water cleaners, steam cleaners, welders or any device operating with an open flame or which may produce sparks such as cutting, welding, grinding, chiseling or any such similar operation.
3. If the truck is placed over a pit or near one, a fan should be put in the pit for ventilation as the gas is heavier than air and can easily accumulate in a pit with no air circulation. Nearby open stairways, or elevator shafts leading to basements should be provided with air circulation to keep gas out, or basements should be ventilated.
4. Absolutely no smoking.

Preparing Truck for Service

1. Before taking the truck into the shop for service, exhaust all fuel from the system by shutting off the main valves at the fuel tanks and allowing the engine to run until it stops. Then turn off the ignition.
2. Before towing a disabled vehicle into the shop, shut the valve at the tank and bleed the fuel system of all fuel and gas.
3. Never bring a vehicle into the shop without first checking the fuel system and fuel tanks for leaks.

Before Starting Repairs

1. Remember that the fuel system is pressurized.
2. Make certain the tank valves are tightly closed and all fuel exhausted from the lines before starting any repair work on the fuel system.
3. Make certain there are no leaks before doing any repair work on any part of the vehicle.
4. Place a fire extinguisher close by so it can be quickly put to use.

5. It is advisable to place Danger and No Smoking signs on each side of the vehicle as well as warn other people who might wander into the shop.

When LPG Gets on Fire

LPG should be allowed to burn until, if possible, the source of fuel is shut off. A fire extinguished before this is accomplished can and may result in dangerous accumulations of gas which might result in a more serious flash or explosion.

When Servicing Fuel System

1. Replace worn or defective fittings.
2. Treat all threaded connections with an insoluble lubricant such as Permatex or aviation gasket maker.
3. Check entire system for leaks after connecting it up.
4. LPG is treated with rather an offensive strong compound or odorant as a warning agent to indicate even small quantities of gas leakage.

Checking For Leaks

1. Detection of the peculiar odor indicates a possible leak. If detected, do not turn on or off any lights or electrical switches on any device or vehicle. Immediately tow vehicle outdoors until leak is located and danger eliminated.
2. Frosting of connections indicates leakage at that point.
3. Normally there should be a slight film of frost on the hex headed plug and boss just above the inlet fuel line connection to the regulator.
4. Never use open flame to check for leakage.
5. Brush a lather of soap on with a soft brush which will indicate the presence of leaks.
6. All rubber hose regardless of length used anywhere in the fuel line or piping system should be very carefully inspected for loose connections or any sign of checking, cracking, etc. At the least sign of injury or deterioration replace immediately.

191

LPG CARBURETION

When Serviced and Checked for Leaks

1. Do not start engine first.
2. Raise hood and allow air to circulate around engine to drive out any possible accumulation of gas.
3. Check fuel in tank with rotary gauge located on tank to make sure fuel supply is available.
4. To start engine open vapor valve *slowly*.
5. Turn on ignition and start engine with choke fully closed and throttle 1/4 open.
6. After engine starts open choke completely for normal operation.
7. Operate engine at fast idle until water temperature reaches 125°.
8. Turn *on* liquid valve.
9. Turn *off* vapor valve.

Precautions

1. LPG is not intended for any use other than to run the engine.
2. Do not use it as a substitute for solvents to clean parts, seats, cushions, trim, etc.
3. Do not use it in place of compressed air to inflate tires, blow out lines, or any other object or device which can be operated by air.
4. Do not perform any repair work on tanks. Have the necessary tank work performed by qualified firms who service such containers who are informed as to regulations, inspection and test after any repairs are made.
5. Never check fuel tanks without first shutting off engine.

CONVERTER TROUBLE SHOOTING

No Fuel At Converter Inlet

1. Check voltage at filter fuelock coil.
2. Defective filter fuelock coil.
3. Plugged filter.
4. LPG tank empty.
5. Crushed fuel line.

No Fuel To Carburetor With Primer Switch Actuated

1. Primary orifice in primary regulator plugged.
2. Missing primary spring in primary regulator.
3. Secondary regulator valve stuck in closed position.
4. Secondary regulator levers not adjusted properly.
5. Secondary regulator primary plunger not opening valve.
6. Defective primer switch.
7. Defective primer coil.
8. Check primer wiring for proper connections.

Fuel Leaking Through Primary Regulator

1. Dirty or defective valve seat.
2. Broken diaphragm.
3. Distorted valve lever.
4. Improperly installed spring or washers.

Fuel Leaking Through Secondary Regulator

1. Dirt on valve seat.
2. Missing spring.
3. Improperly adjusted levers.
4. Primer plunger too long.
5. Actuated primer.

Freezing

NOTE: Repeated freezing may loosen back cover screws or cause cover distortion.

1. Converter mounted too high.
2. Converter hose fittings too small or restricted by internal corrosion.
3. Internal fuel leak within converter.

LOCKING DIFFERENTIALS

The main purpose of these differentials is that they supply a greater percentage of torque to the wheel with better traction and still furnishes to the wheel with poorer traction as much torque as it is able to absorb under the circumstances.

In the conventional differential the wheel easiest to turn receives the power. Therefore, when traction conditions under the rear wheels are not the same, the driving force is limited by the wheel with the poorer traction (easiest to turn) even though one wheel is on good traction surface.

These locking differentials do not permit shock loads or full engine torque to be transmitted to one axle shaft. They provide power to both rear wheels and maintain the differential action that is necessary when the vehicle is turning a corner to permit the outer wheel to turn faster than the inner wheel.

NOTE: "On car" type wheel balancers are not recommended for use on rear wheels of cars equipped with a locking differential. The rear wheel will drive if in contact with the ground or with a block even though the opposite wheel is raised. *However, this type of wheel balancer may be used by removing the wheel opposite of the one being balanced with the complete assembly raised.*

SPICER POWR-LOK

Fig. 1 shows the cone clutch type whereas Fig. 2 illustrates the plate clutch type. Each assembly consists of two case halves, two cross

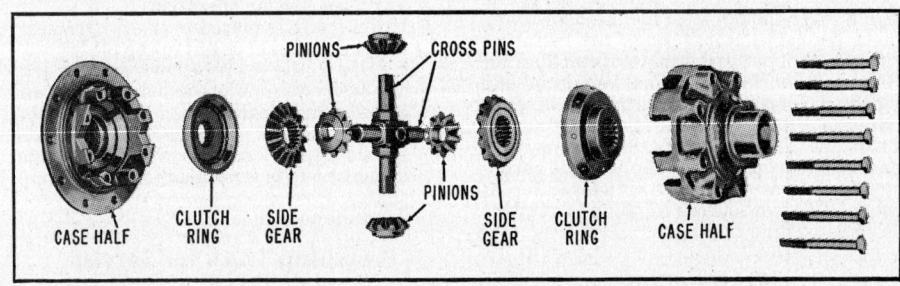

Fig. 1 Cone clutch type of POWR-LOK differential

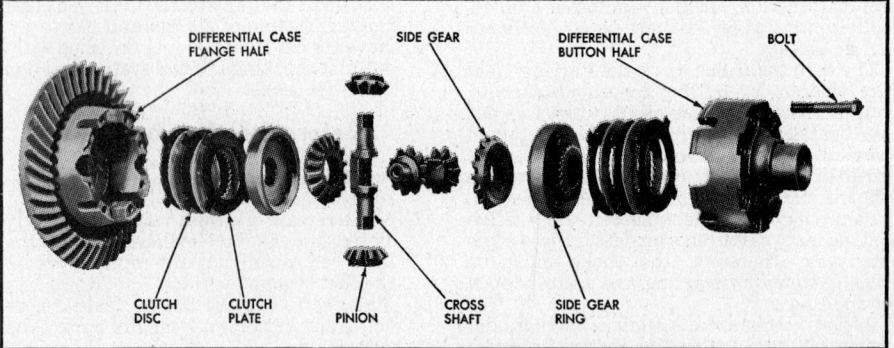

Fig. 2 Plate clutch type of POWR-LOK differential

LOCKING DIFFERENTIALS

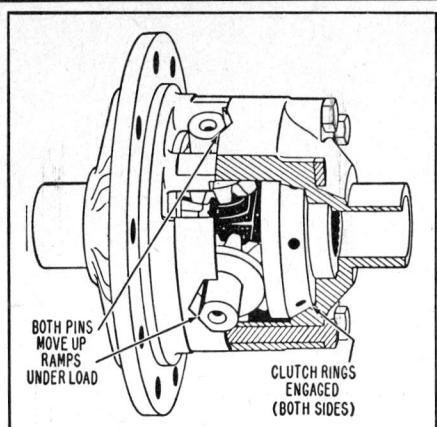

Fig 3. Differential action when moving straight ahead

CAUTION: Do not attempt to spin a wheel under power with a jack under only one side; both wheels must be clear of the ground. If one wheel remains in contact with the ground, there is a possibility that when spinning the other wheel, friction of the clutch rings or clutch disc may set the vehicle in motion.

Servicing Cone Clutch Type

This type differential, Fig. 1, must be replaced as a unit as individual parts are not available. It is furnished less ring gear and side bearings.

Servicing Plate Clutch Type

Before disassembling the differential, scribe a line across the differential case halves for alignment upon reassembly. Then, after removing the attaching bolts, separate the case halves and remove the differential parts.

Note the relative position of the friction plates, friction discs and Belleville spring plates (if used) so that they may be reassembled in the proper sequence, Figs. 5, 6 and 7.

Inspect all parts. See that there are no worn, cracked or distorted clutch plates. All parts must be free of nicks, burrs or any imperfections that will reduce the efficient operation of the unit.
1. Assemble differential as suggested in Figs. 5, 6 and 7.
2. Make sure the side gear retainer will

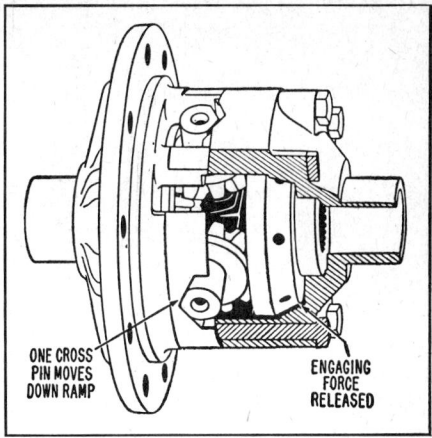

Fig. 4 Differential action when turning a corner

pins held together by a thrust block, differential pinions, side gears, and clutch rings (Fig. 1) or clutch plates (Fig. 2).

The cross pins are made with a movable joint at the center to permit each one to move independently while in continuous engagement. The pin ends are made in the form of a V, and a similar V is machined in each case half to provide a ramped cam surface.

In Fig. 1, the clutch ring is fitted over each bevel side gear and mates with a cone surface machined in each half of the differential case.

In Fig. 2, the clutch plates operate between the flat surface on the clutch retainer and the machined surface in each half of the differential case.

Operation

As the vehicle is put in motion, the driving force moves the cross pin up the ramp of the cam surface, applying a load to the clutches and restricts turning of the differential through the friction of the clutches on the mating surfaces in the differential case, Fig. 3. This provides a torque ratio between the axle shafts which is based on the amount of friction in the differential and the amount of load that is being applied to the differential.

When turning a corner this process is, in effect, partially reversed, Fig. 4. The differential gears become a planetary gear set, with the gear on the inside of the curve becoming the fixed gear of the planetary. The outer gear of the planetary overruns as the outside wheel on the curve has a further distance to travel. With the outer gear overrunning and the inner gear fixed, the differential pinions are caused to rotate, but since they are restricted by the fixed gear, they must first move the cross pins back down the cam surface, relieving the thrust load of the clutch on its mating surface in the differential case. Thus when turning a corner, the differential, for all practical purposes, is similar to a conventional differential and the wheels are free to rotate at different speeds.

With locking differentials, certain characteristics must be taken into consideration. Under average driving conditions, such as straight ahead, reverse, extreme right and left turns, the operation will be the same as with the conventional differential. However, a little more backlash may be noticed due to the lateral movement of the differential cross pins. In addition, a slight chatter may occur under surge torque with one wheel on a slippery surface. These conditions are considered normal.

rotate with a slight drag when in the case. Repeat for opposite side.
3. Install side gear on ring gear flange half.
4. With ring gear flange half in a vertical position, install one shaft and gears, making certain that notch in shaft is up.
5. Install side gear in other half of case.
6. Hold the remaining case half through the bearing trunnion and install it on the ring gear flange half, being sure scribed mark made previously is in alignment.
7. Insert axle shafts to align side gear ring

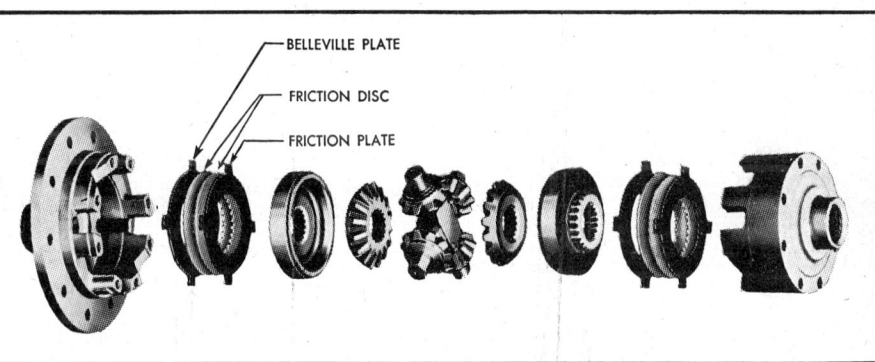

Fig. 5 Plate clutch type of POWR-LOK differential (4 stack unit) with Belleville spring plates at outside of stacks

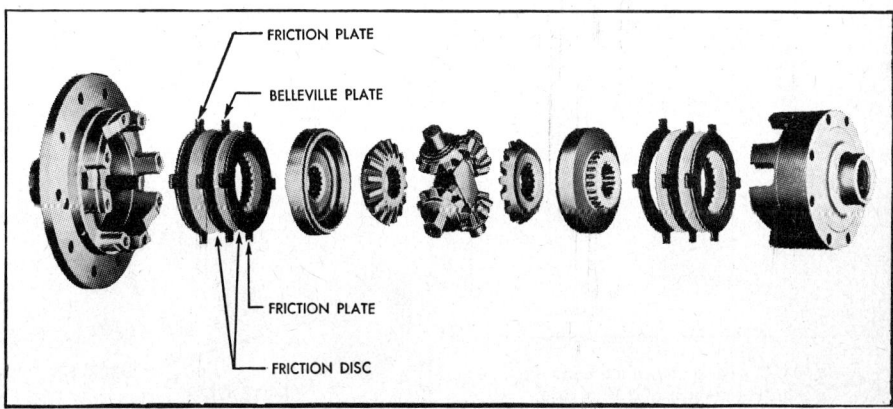

Fig. 6 Plate clutch type of POWR-LOK differential (5 stack unit) with Belleville spring plates in center of stacks

LOCKING DIFFERENTIALS

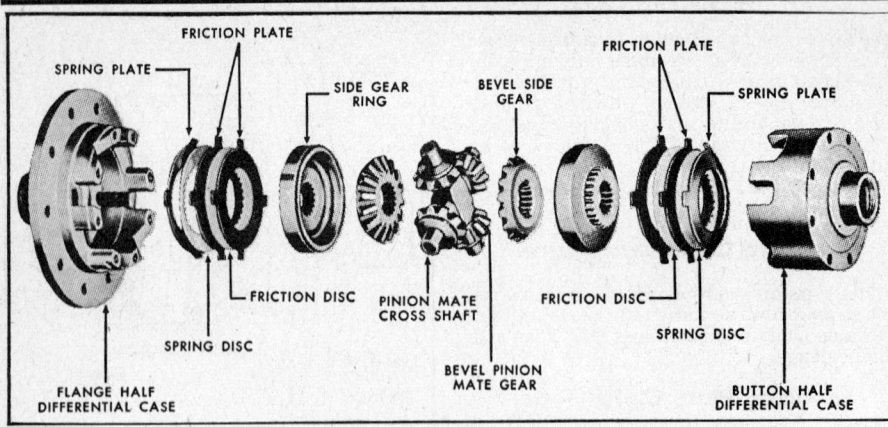

Fig. 7 Plate clutch type of POWR-LOK differential (5 stack unit) with Belleville spring plates at outside of stacks

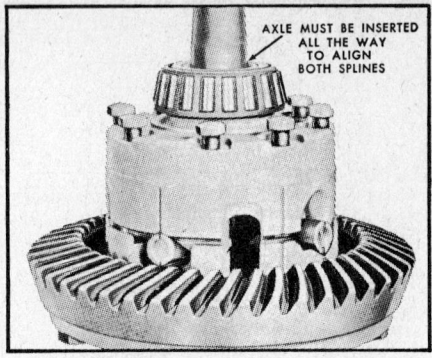

Fig. 8 Aligning splines of side gear and side gear ring before tightening attaching bolts

with bevel side gear, Fig. 8. If this is not done there may be some difficulty when installing axle shafts during final assembly. Tighten attaching bolts evenly to 35–45 ft-lb.

8. Check clearance between pinion mate shaft and the V of the case, Fig. 9. Do this by placing shim stock or feeler gauges on both ends of the same shaft and on opposite sides of the V. The clearance should be approximately .015″.

Installation Note

Make sure the spline end of the axle shaft does not interfere with the pinion mate shafts. This can be checked with a steel tape by measuring from the bottom of the axle shaft bearing bore to the pinion mate shafts. Then measure the axle shafts from the corresponding point of the bearing to the end of the spline. The minimum clearance required is 1/8″. Grind off the spline end of the axle shaft if it is too long. Check the other axle shaft in the same manner.

CAUTION: Use rear axle lubricant of the type specially recommended for locking differentials. Failure to use the proper lubricant will result in chattering or other serious malfunction.

FORD EXC. TRACTION-LOK

Disassembly

1. Referring to Fig. 10, mark one differential bearing cap and the mating support to help position the parts properly during assembly of the carrier.
2. Remove bearing adjusting nuts and lift differential assembly out of carrier.
3. Remove differential bearings.
4. Loosen *alternate* drive gear attaching bolts evenly to release the spring pressure between differential case and cover.
5. Remove differential case cover and then the drive gear.
6. Remove clutch plates.
7. Remove two Belleville springs.
8. Remove clutch hub, side gear and thrust washer.
9. Drive out differential pinion shaft lock pin.
10. Drive out differential pinion shaft. Then remove pinion gears and thrust washers.

Assembly

1. Lubricate all parts during assembly. Referring to Fig. 10, place side gear and thrust washer in differential case.
2. With soft-faced hammer, drive pinion shaft into case only far enough to retain a pinion thrust washer and pinion gear.
3. Place a second pinion and thrust washer in position, and drive pinion shaft into place. *Carefully line up pinion shaft retainer holes.*
4. Place second pinion and thrust washer in position. Drive pinion shaft into place. Install pinion shaft retainer. *The retainer must not extend beyond the machined surface of the case.*
5. Insert two 2″ × 7/16″ bolts through differential flange and thread them 3 or 4 turns into the drive gear as a guide in aligning drive gear bolt holes. Press or tap drive gear into position.
6. Clamp differential case in a vise. Install differential side gear on pinion gears. Place clutch hub on side gear and place thrust washer on hub.
7. Insert two 3/16 × 2″ dowel pins into differential case. Place a steel plate on differen-

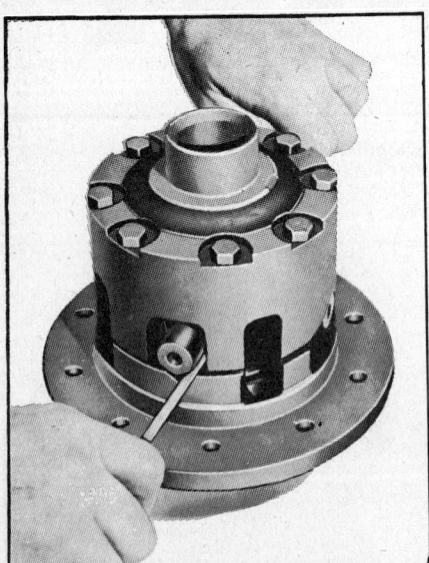

Fig. 9 Checking clearance between pinion mate shaft and V in case. Feeler gauges must be inserted on both ends of same shaft and on opposite sides of V

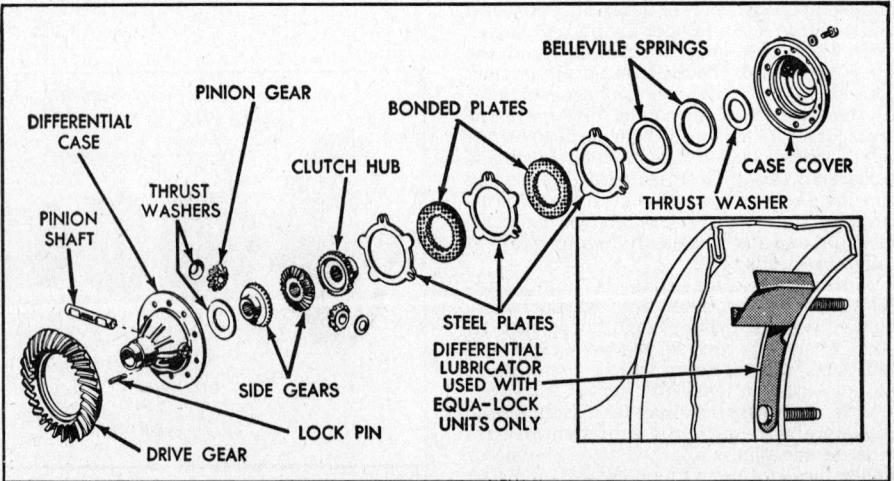

Fig. 10 Ford differential, exc. Traction-Lok

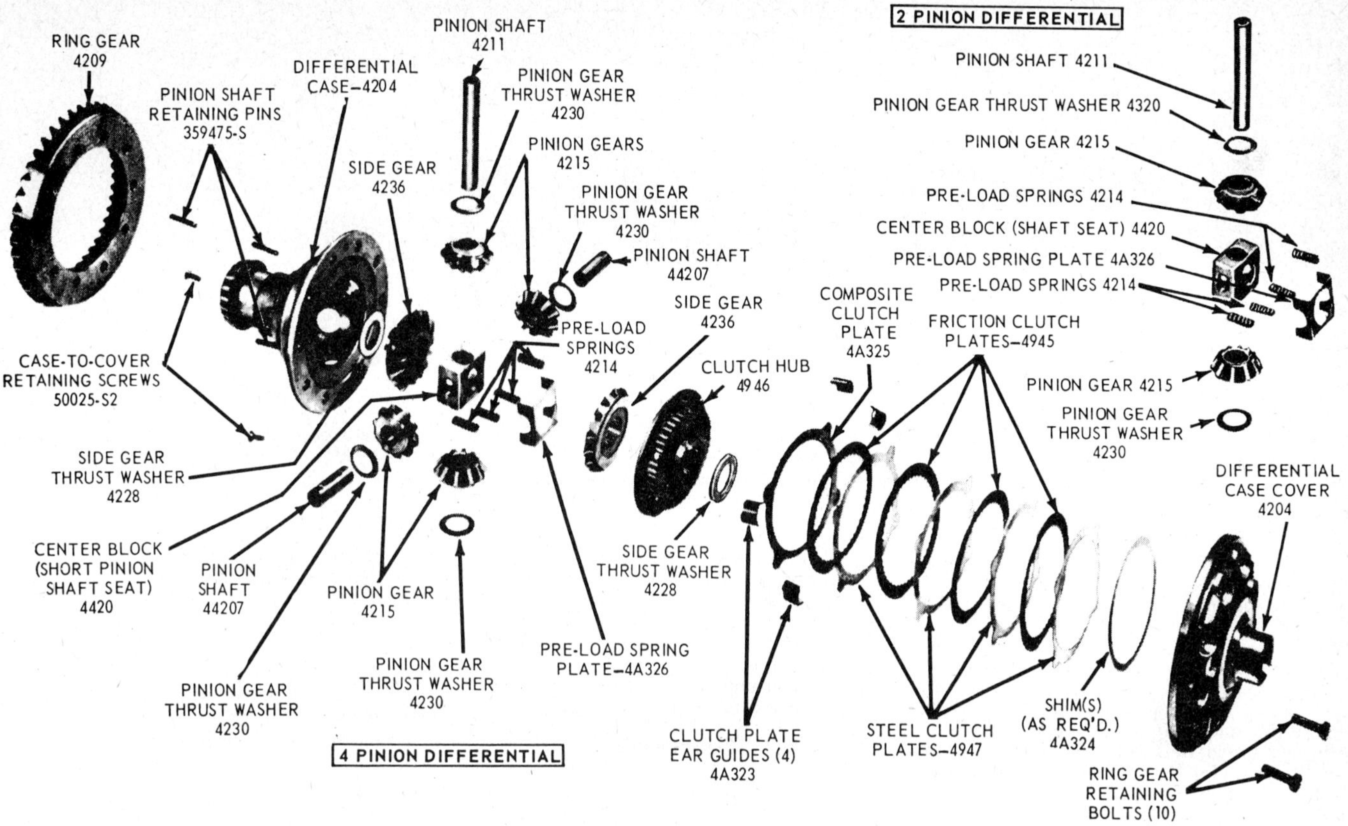

LOCKING DIFFERENTIALS

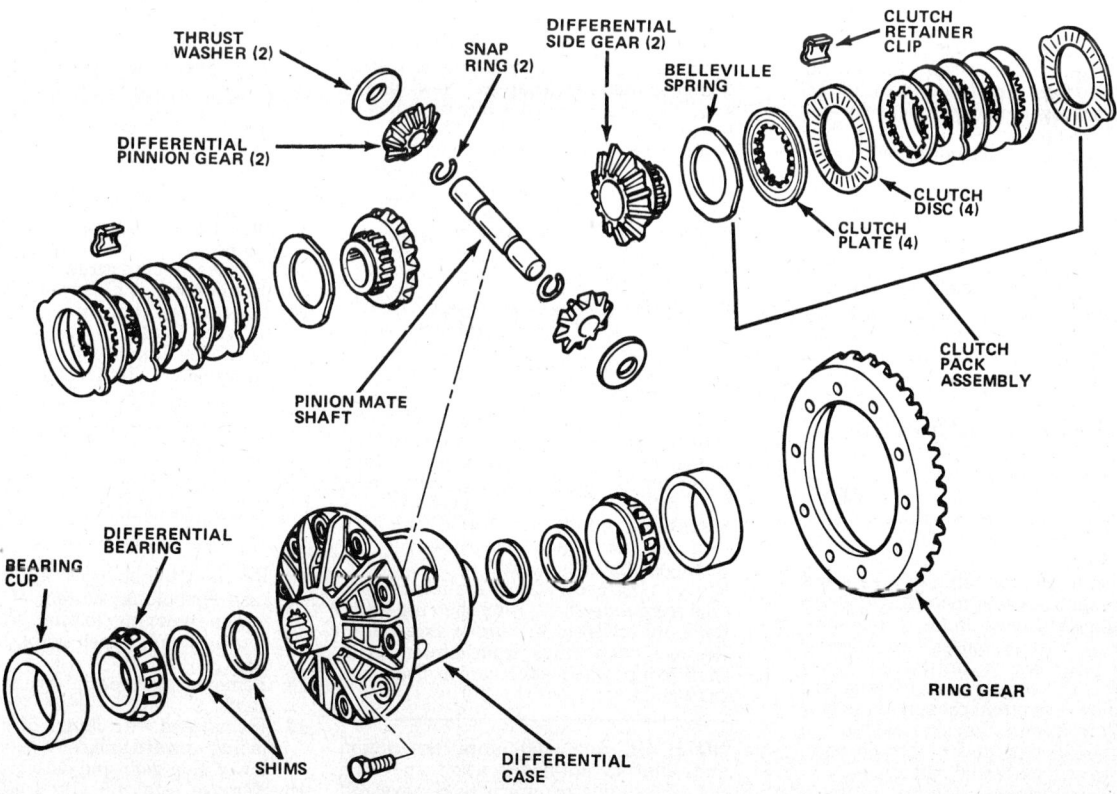

Fig. 11 Ford Traction-Lok differential

Fig. 12 Dana Trac-Lok locking differential, exc. Model 70 (Typical)

195

LOCKING DIFFERENTIALS

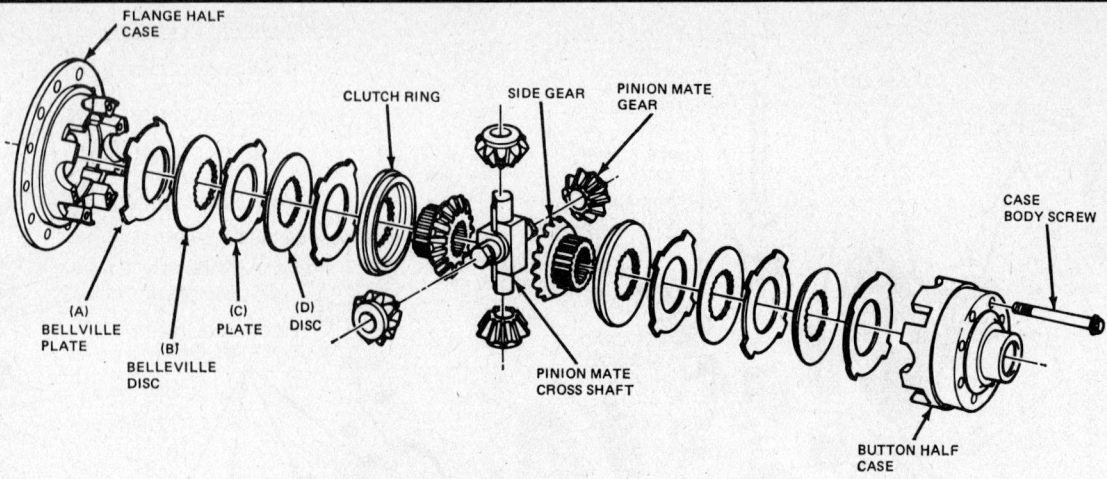

Fig. 15 Dana Trac-Lok locking differential, Model 70

tial case so that slots in dog ears straddle dowel pins. *Lubricate all differential parts so that an accurate torque check can be made.*
8. Place a bonded plate on steel plate. Make sure bonded plate inner spline teeth properly engage hub spline. Assemble remaining plates: a steel plate, a bonded plate and lastly a steel plate.
9. Place two Belleville springs on the top steel plate. Both springs are assembled with concave sides down.
10. Place differential case cover on case and start bolts.
11. Tighten bolts evenly and alternately across the diameter of drive gear. As the bolts are tightened the Belleville springs are compressed and the case and cover are pulled together.
12. Torque the bolts to 65–75 ft-lbs.
13. Check torque required to rotate one side gear while the other side gear is held. Ignore the torque required to start the side gear turning. The torque required to keep it moving steadily should be between 155 and 195 ft-lbs. If not within these limits, check for improper assembly.
14. Install differential in carrier.

CAUTION: Use rear axle lubricant of the type specially recommended for locking differentials. Failure to use proper lubricant will result in chattering or other serious malfunction.

FORD TRACTION-LOK

Disassembly

1. Referring to Fig. 11, remove ring gear-to-differential case bolts. Remove ring gear.
2. With case in press or using two bolts and nuts through ring gear mounting holes to compress case halves and overcome preload spring tension, loosen two Allen or Phillips head screws until only a few threads of the screws are still engaged then remove case from press and tap cover to spring it loose. Remove screws.
3. With cover facing down, remove case, preload spring plate and springs.
4. From cover, remove side gear, clutch guides, hub and clutch discs.
5. Drive pinion shaft lock pins from case.
6. With brass drift, drive long pinion shaft from case, driving from end opposite lock pin hole.
7. Remove two short pinion shafts by driving each shaft from center outward. Lift out center block, pinion gears, thrust washers and side gear.
8. Remove differential bearings.

Reassembly

1. With case mounted in a soft jawed vise, place a side gear in case.
2. Install pinion gears, center block and pinion shafts. Position center block so long shaft is driven through rough side and short shaft through machined side. Install lock pins.
3. Install pre-load springs and position pre-load plate over springs, straddling center block over narrower machined width.
4. Install selective shim in cover.
5. Starting with a composite plate, install clutch plates alternately. New plates should be soaked in gear lubricant before installation.
6. Install four guides and side gear.
7. Place two halves in press, compress springs and install two Allen or Phillips head screws and tighten evenly.
8. Install ring gear and tighten evenly to 65–80 ft-lbs.

DANA TRAC-LOK

Exc. Model 70

Disassembly, Fig. 12
1. Mount one axle shaft in a vise with the splined end facing upward. Do not allow end of shaft to extend more than 2 3/4 inch above top of vise. This prevents the shaft from fully entering the side gear.
2. Mount differential case on axle shaft with ring gear bolt heads facing upward.
3. Remove ring gear bolts.
4. Loosen ring gear with a mallet, remove case from axle shaft, then the ring gear.
5. Remount differential case on axle shaft.
6. Remove snap rings from pinion mate shaft using two screwdrivers to disengage snap rings.

NOTE: On model 60 units, the pinion mate shaft is retained by a roll pin. Use a 3/16 inch diameter punch to remove roll pin.

7. Remove pinion mate shaft with a suitable drift and hammer.

NOTE: The gear rotating tool J-23781 is required to perform the following steps. The tool consists of three parts: gear rotating tool, forcing screw and step plate.

8. Install step plate in lower differential side gear.
9. Position pawl end of gear rotating tool on step plate.
10. Insert forcing screw through top of case and thread into gear rotating tool.

NOTE: Apply a small amount of grease to centering hole in step plate and oil forcing screw threads before using forcing screw.

11. Center forcing screw in step plate and tighten screw to move differential side gears away from pinion gears.
12. Remove pinion gear thrust washers with a .030 feeler gauge or shim stock. Insert gauge or shim stock between washer and case and withdraw thrust washer and gauge.
13. Tighten forcing screw until movement of pinion gears is observed.
14. Insert pawl end of gear rotating tool between teeth of one differential side gear. Pull handle of tool to rotate side and pinion gears. Remove the pinion gears as gears appear in case opening.

NOTE: It may be necessary to adjust the tension applied on the belleville springs by the forcing screw before the gears can be rotated in the case.

15. Retain upper side gear and clutch pack in case by holding bottom of rotating tool while removing forcing screw. Remove rotating tool, upper side gear and clutch pack.
16. Remove differential case from axle shaft.
17. Invert case with flange or ring gear side facing upward and remove step plate tool, lower side gear and clutch pack.
18. Remove retainer clips from both clutch packs to permit separation of plates and discs.

LOCKING DIFFERENTIALS

Assembly, Fig. 12
1. Lubricate differential gear teeth, thrust faces, splines and the clutch discs and plates.
2. Assemble clutch packs placing discs and plates in original position. Then, install retainer clips.
3. Install clutch packs on differential side gears, then install one assembly in case.

NOTE: Ensure clutch packs remain assembled on side gear splines and the retainer clips are fully seated in case pockets.

4. Mount case assembly on axle shaft while clutch packs in place. Ensure that the side gear and axle shaft splines are properly aligned when mounting case on shaft. Also, ensure that the clutch packs are properly assembled in case.
5. Install step plate tool in side gear. Apply a small amount of grease to centering hole of step plate.
6. Install remaining clutch pack and side gear.

NOTE: Ensure clutch packs remain assembled on side gear splines and the retainer clips are fully seated in case pockets.

7. Position gear rotating tool in upper side gear.
8. Hold side gear and gear rotating tool in position and insert forcing screw through top of case and thread into gear rotating tool.
9. Install both differential pinion gears into case, ensuring that gear bores are aligned.
10. Tighten forcing screw to compress belleville springs and provide clearance between teeth of pinion and side gears.
11. Place pinion gears in case and insert rotating tool pawl between side gear teeth. Rotate side gears by pulling on tool handle and install pinion gears.

NOTE: If the side gears will not rotate, adjust belleville spring load. Loosen or tighten forcing screw to permit side gear rotating.

12. Rotate side gears until shaft bores are aligned with case bores.
13. Lubricate pinion gear thrust washers.
14. Tighten or loosen forcing screw to permit thrust washer installation. Install thrust washers using a small screwdriver to guide washers into position. Ensure that the shaft bores in the thrust washers and gears are properly aligned with case bores.
15. Remove forcing screw, gear rotating tool and step plate.
16. Lubricate pinion mate shaft and seat shaft in case using a hammer. Ensure that the snap ring grooves in shaft are exposed to permit snap ring installation.
17. Install pinion mate shaft snap rings.

NOTE: On models 60 units, align the shaft and shaft retaining pin bore and case pin bore. Drive the shaft into position and install retaining pin. If the case is mounted in a vise with the machined side of the ring gear flange facing upward, use a 5/16 inch diameter punch to install the retaining pin. Seat the pin until the punch bottoms in case bore. If the case is mounted in a vise with the machined side of the ring gear flange facing downward, place a piece of tape around a 3/16 inch diameter punch approximately 1 3/4 inch from end of punch. Install retaining pin until edge of tape is flush with pin bore.

18. Remove case from axle shaft.
19. Place ring gear on case and install ring gear bolts finger tight.
20. Remount case on axle shaft and tighten ring gear bolts.

Model 70
Disassembly, Fig. 13
1. Scribe a mark between the differential case halves to be used during assembly. Also, mark the pinion mate shafts and corresponding ramps for assembly in original locations.
2. Clamp differential assembly in a soft jawed vise.
3. Loosen but do not remove the case half retaining bolts.
4. Place assembly on bench with the ring gear half down and remove case half retaining screws.
5. Remove the cover half of the case.
6. Remove upper mate shaft, side gear, side gear ring and clutch pack. Retain parts with cover half of case so they can be installed in original position.
7. Remove lower mate shaft, side gear, side gear ring and clutch pack from drive gear case half.

Assembly, Fig. 13
1. Place side gear ring from ring gear half of

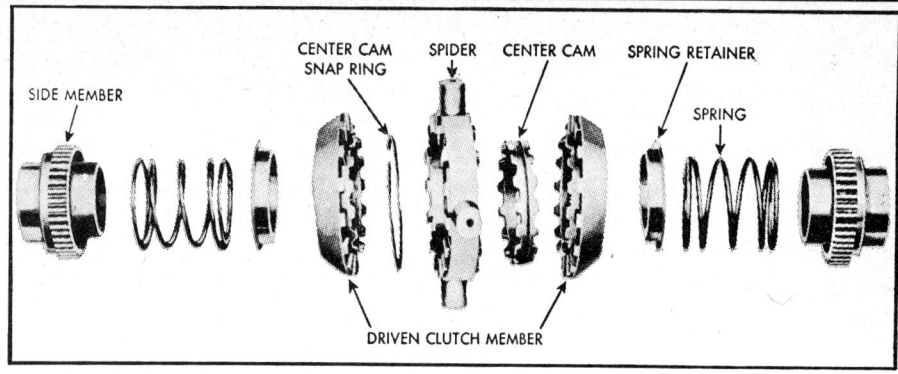

Fig. 14 NoSPIN locking differential

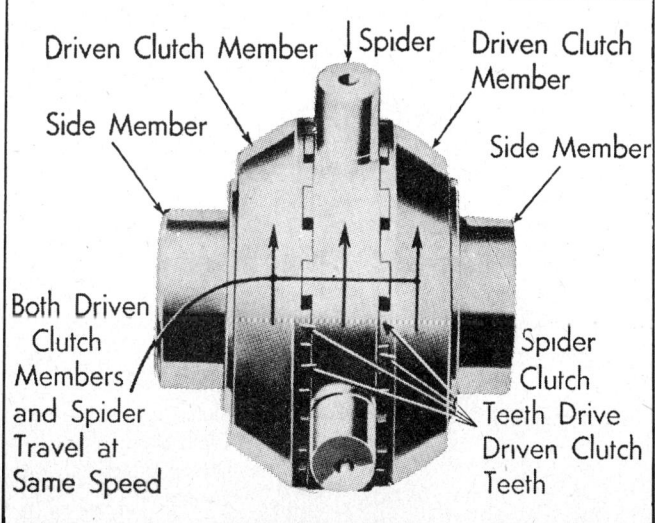

Fig. 15 NoSPIN differential action when moving straight ahead

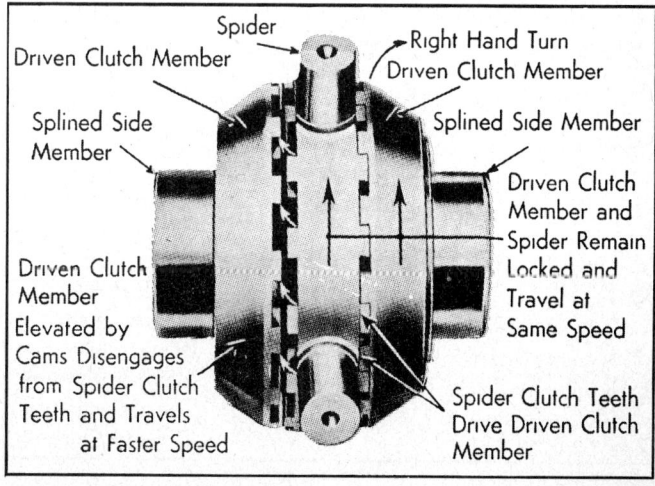

Fig. 16 NoSPIN differential action when making a forward right turn

LOCKING DIFFERENTIALS

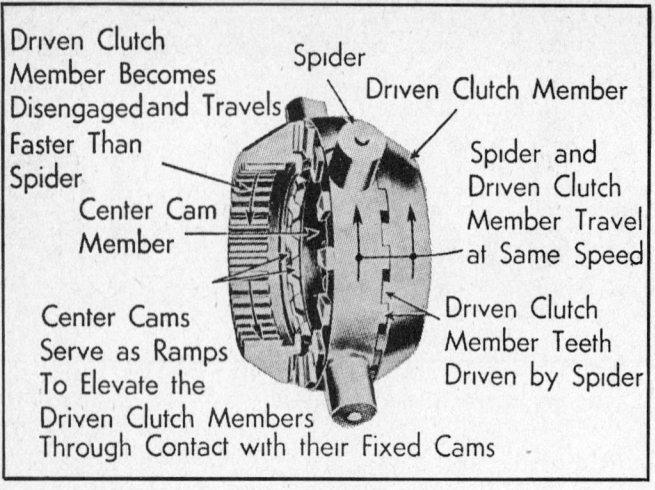

Fig. 17 Cross sectional view of NoSPIN differential when making a forward right turn

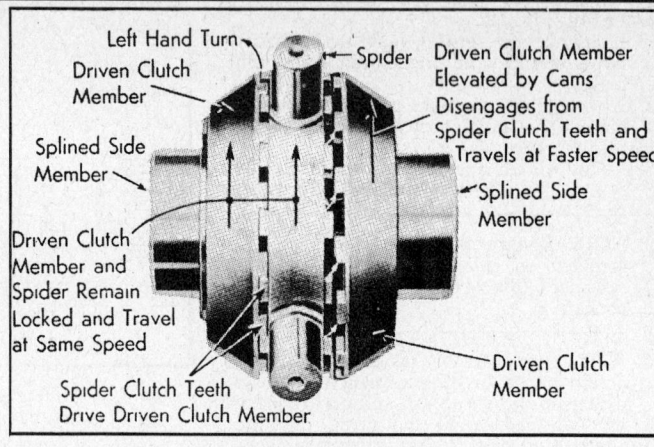

Fig. 18 NoSPIN differential action when making a forward left turn

case on a pinion flange or other suitable fixture so the case is approximately 4 inches above bench.
2. Lubricate clutch plates and assemble clutch pack on side gear ring.
3. Place ring gear side of case over clutch pack and side gear ring. Ensure that the clutch plate lugs enter the slots in the case and that the case bottoms on the clutch pack.
4. Invert the assembly. Hold assembly together while inverting.
5. Install the ring gear case half side gear in side gear ring.
6. Install axle shaft spacer in cross shaft.
7. Install the ring gear case half pinion mate shaft and pinions on the side gear ring.
8. Install the cover half pinion mate shaft and pinions.
9. Place side gear on pinions, then the side gear ring on side gear.
10. Assemble clutch pack on side gear ring, aligning clutch pack lugs.
11. Install cover half of case over assembly, aligning the marks made during disassembly.
12. Install the case half retaining bolts, turning the bolts to engage a few threads only.
13. Insert axle shafts into assembly and align the splines of the side gears and side gear rings. With the axle shafts in position, torque case half retaining bolts to 35-45 ft. lbs.
14. Remove axle shafts.
15. If the differential has been assembled properly, each pinion mate cross shaft should be tight on its ramp. However, if clearance is present, it should not exceed .010 inch and be equal at all four cross shaft ends.

NoSPIN DIFFERENTIAL

Fig. 14 illustrates the components of this unit while Figs. 15 through 20 show how it works.

NOTE: Before disassembling the differential case, insert a bolt through the center of the NoSPIN unit (axle shaft openings) with a flat washer on each end against the side members, Fig. 21. Thread a nut on the bolt against the flat washer finger tight. This will prevent possible injury caused by the unit flying apart due to the spring pressure within itself during disassembly of the differential case.

Disassembly

1. Remove nuts from differential case and lift out NoSPIN unit. Mount unit in a small press, Fig. 22.
2. Apply enough pressure on head of bolt to release spring pressure against nut.
3. Remove nut and flat washer by reaching underneath the press.
4. Slowly release press and allow unit to disassemble itself until spring pressure is fully released.
5. Remove unit from press and remove parts. The center cam may be removed

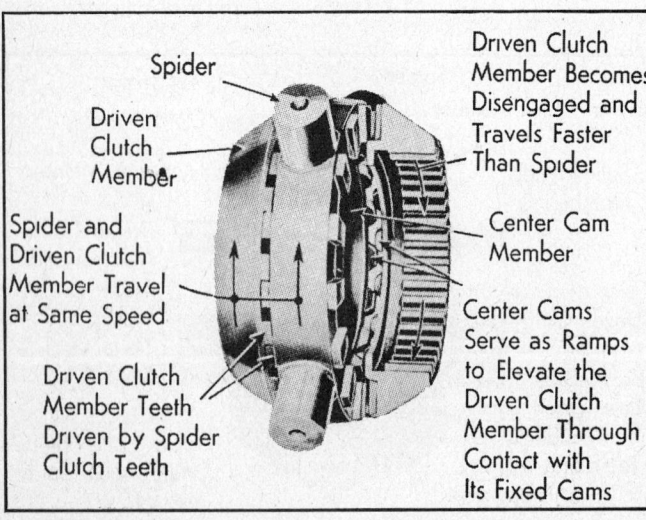

Fig. 19 Cross sectional view of NoSPIN differential when making a forward left turn

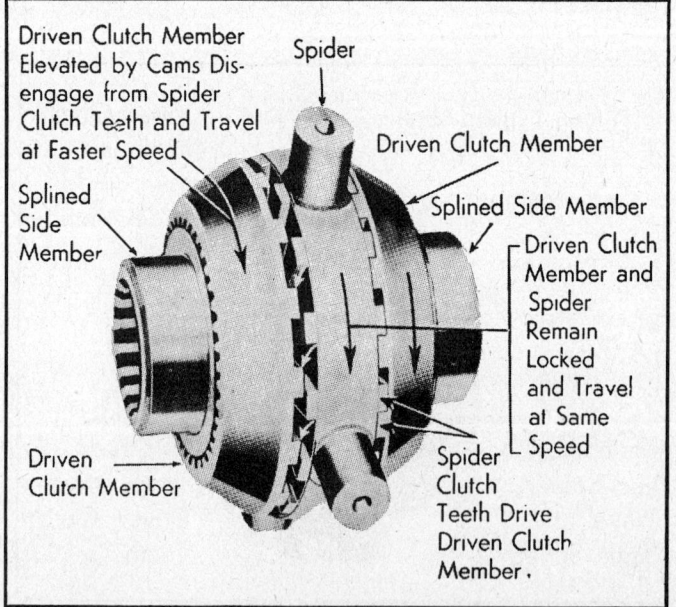

Fig. 20 NoSPIN differential when making a rearward right turn

LOCKING DIFFERENTIALS

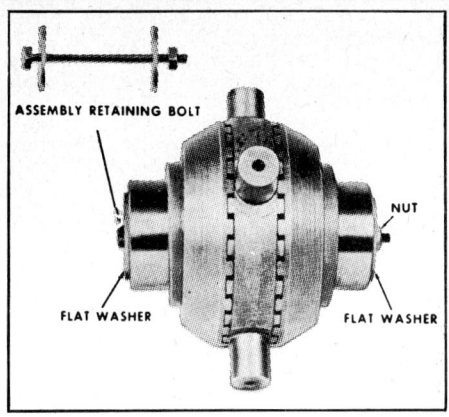

Fig. 21 Inserting assembly retaining bolt

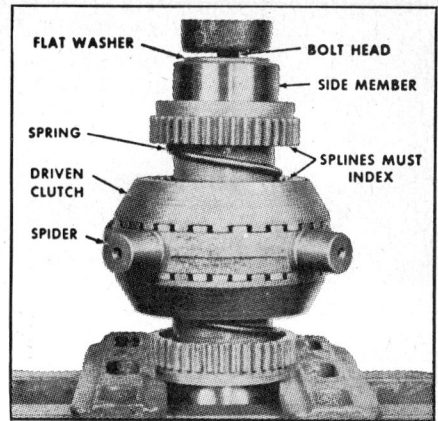

Fig. 22 Release of spring pressure

NoSPIN unit with a flat washer against the side member, and mount unit in press, Fig. 22.
7. Compress springs by pressing on head of bolt and index splines of side members with those of driven clutch members. *Keep entire unit aligned in press to prevent it from kicking out while springs are being compressed.*
8. Compress unit until side member splines are completely indexed and flush with driven clutch member.
9. Install flat washer on bolt against side member and thread nut on bolt finger tight so it has the appearance of Fig. 21 when removed from press.

from the spider by expanding the snap ring with small screwdrivers or wedges. However, it is not necessary to remove the center cam from the spider even if only one part is damaged since the center cam, snap ring and spider are not serviced separately—only as an assembly.
6. Wash all parts with cleaning solvent. Inspect all mating surfaces and teeth for possible wear or damage. Replace all worn or damaged parts upon reassembly. Lubricate all parts with SAE-30 oil during reassembly.

Reassembly

1. Place side member upright and install spring on same.
2. Place spring retainer on spring with flange end toward side member.
3. Install driven clutch member on spring retainer.
4. Place spider on driven clutch member, indexing teeth of same.
5. Install other driven clutch member, spring retainer, spring and side member on spider.
6. Insert a bolt through the center of the

TRACTION EQUALIZER
Cartridge Type

Fig. 23 is a cross-sectional view of this device. It consists of an internally splined cartridge, Fig. 24. One end mates with the externally splined differential case extension. The shell is loaded with a series of specially treated clutch plates which are splined alternately on the inside and outside diameters to match the internal splines of the cartridge and the external splines on the lengthened axle shaft splines. A series of Belleville spring washers maintain a constant pressure on the clutch plates. Oil scoops automatically pick up the standard axle lubricant.

Operation

During a straight forward drive, the drive torque is transmitted to the wheels in the same manner as with a conventional rear axle. Likewise, straight rearward driving employs the same principles as does the conventional rear axle.

When making a turn, differential action is required in order to permit the outside wheel to travel a greater distance, and faster, than the inside wheel. While differentiation takes place within the differential case, the outer wheel ground traction overpowers the clutch pack friction, thereby causing the clutch plates to rotate. This action takes place constantly in both units mounted on the axle shafts as the vehicle deviates minutely from a straight forward or straight rearward drive.

Differential Removal

1. Remove plug from bottom of axle housing and drain lubricant.
2. Back off and remove Traction Equalizer retaining set screws from housing, Fig. 25. *If only axle shafts are to be removed, do not disturb cartridge set screws.*
3. Remove axle shaft drive nuts and washers.
4. Hold a short drift firmly against center of axle shaft flange *between raised circular lugs* and strike drift a sharp blow to loosen tapered dowels. *Do not strike raised circular lugs with hammer as the lugs are liable to shatter and explode. Do not pry shaft loose. Pry bars, chisels and wedges will damage hub, shaft, flange and oil seals.*
5. Remove dowels and pull out axle shafts.
6. If cartridge remains on differential case splines when axle shaft is removed, insert long hooked rod through housing sleeve. Hook cartridge on inside, pull off differential case splines and leave in housing.
7. Disconnect universal joint at pinion shaft.
8. Disconnect power unit (if equipped).
9. Remove carrier-to-housing stud nuts and washers, leaving the two top nuts partial-

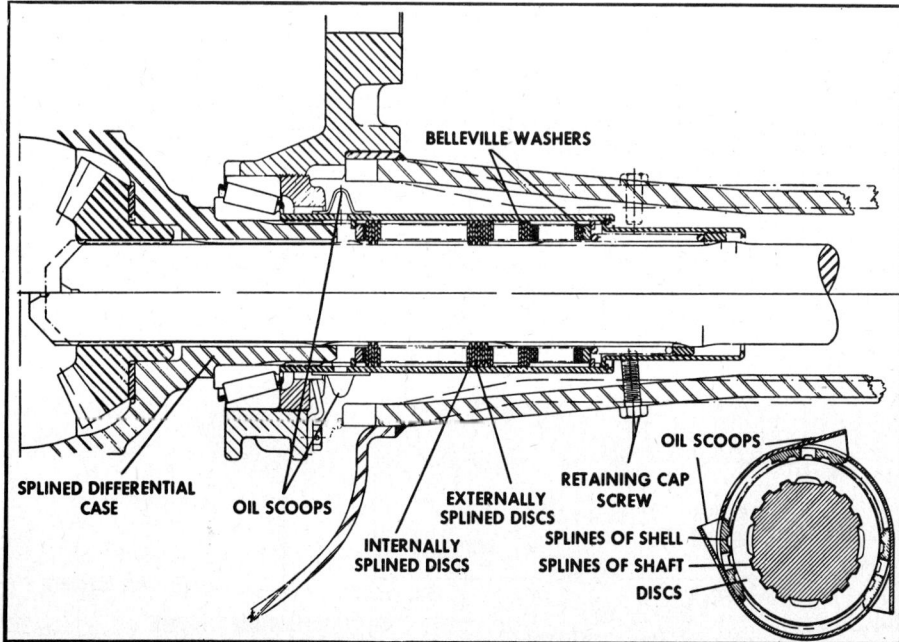

Fig. 23 Cross sectional view of Traction Equalizer differential

Fig. 24 Traction equalizer cartridge

LOCKING DIFFERENTIALS

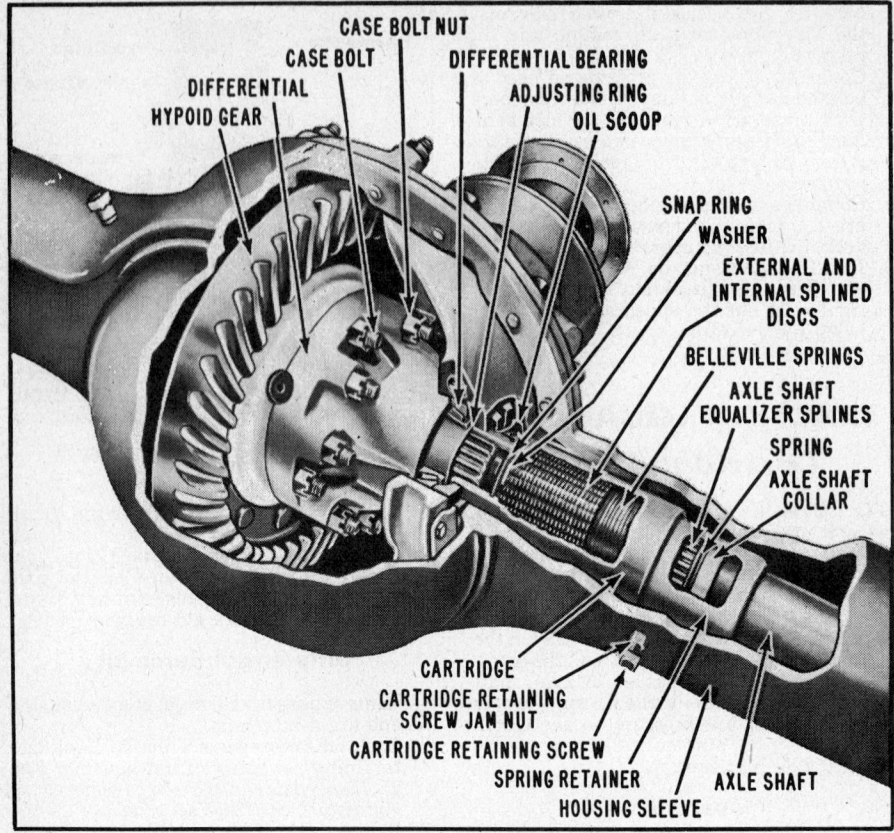

Fig. 25 Cutaway view of rear axle is showing Traction Equalizer unit

ly screwed on studs to prevent carrier from falling.
10. Break carrier loose from housing with a rawhide mallet (remove tapered dowels where used).
11. To remove carrier from a front mounted axle, place a roller jack under carrier, remove the two top nuts and work carrier free. To remove carrier from a top mounted axle, use a chain fall and puller screws in holes provided.

Disassembly

1. Place cartridge assembly under a press with oil scoop end down. A slight press pressure on the retainer assembly in the cartridge will compress the spring and permit removal of the outer snap ring.
2. Remove snap ring. Release press pressure and remove retainer, spring and axle collar.
3. Replace cartridge under press, oil scoop end down. Insert a mandrel with flange end up. Apply a slight pressure to compress Belleville springs and remove retaining snap ring.
4. Release press pressure and remove mandrel. Invert cartridge assembly and place over a post or bar to keep internal parts in order. Hold internal parts down with a sleeve (or equivalent tool) and lift off cartridge shell.
5. Clean and inspect shell and snap ring at oil scoop end.

Inspection & Repair

1. Wire internal parts together in original order and clean in kerosene or diesel fuel oil (not gasoline). Dry immediately after cleaning, using lintless, absorbent paper towels or wiping rags free of abrasive

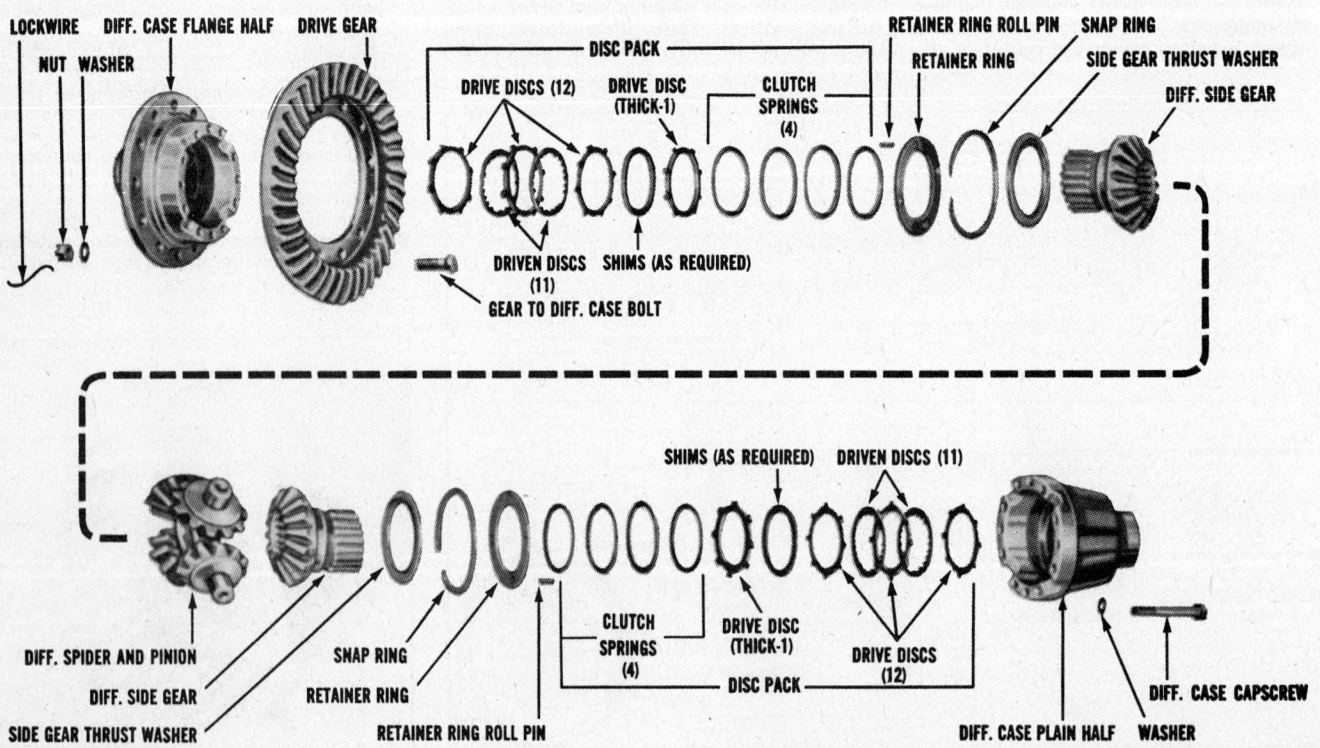

Fig. 26 Exploded view of self contained Traction Equalizer

LOCKING DIFFERENTIALS

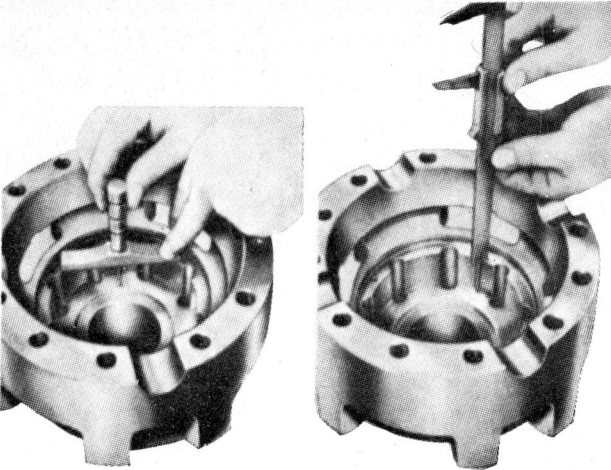

Fig. 27 Measuring depth of clutch bore in case half

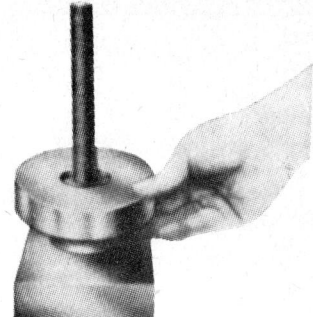

Fig. 28 Disc pack platform in place

material.
2. Replace dry internal parts on post and remove wire.
3. Remove any accumulation of grit, dirt or gum from housing bowl and sleeve. Clean housing with solvent and dry with compressed air.
4. Inspect housing for cracks, loose studs, nicks or burrs at machined surfaces. Remove nicks or burrs with a stone or file.
5. Make all necessary repairs or parts replacement before installing drive unit and cartridge in housing.

Reassembly

1. Install snap ring at oil scoop end (if removed).
2. Place cartridge shell with oil scoop end down over mandrel.
3. Starting with a thick washer and following with discs and Belleville springs, take internal parts from post, one at a time. Inspect and re-oil with axle shaft lubricant, install in shell and over mandrel. *Discs are to be installed alternately starting with an externally splined disc. Belleville springs are to be installed in alternating groups of four starting with concave side down toward last disc which is to be an externally splined disc. If discs bind in cartridge, tap into position with a screwdriver; do not force down as they will be cocked.*
4. Carefully remove mandrel, being careful not to misalign splines, and insert mandrel at top of cartridge with flange end up.
5. Place cartridge under press and apply a slight pressure to compress Belleville springs and install snap ring.
6. Release press pressure and mount a dial indicator so that its stem is against the top of the mandrel flange.
7. Apply a slight pressure and read dial indicator for movement required to compress discs and springs. Compression should be .120″ to .160″. If compression is more than desired, add one or more splined discs, being sure last disc is externally splined. (Discs are about .040″ thick.)
8. Release press pressure and remove mandrel. Install axle shaft collar, spring and retainer with chamfered edge of collar up.
9. Compress spring with slight pressure and install snap ring.
10. Insert axle shafts in housing and carefully mount cartridges on splined ends of shafts through housing bowl opening. Withdraw shafts and cartridges from housing just enough to allow clearance for carrier installation.
11. Install carrier in housing.
12. Complete assembly of one axle shaft in housing. Engage shaft with splines in side gear. Install taper dowels, lockwashers and nuts. Restrain pinion shaft and rotate hub or wheel until cartridge engages splines on differential case. Install other axle shaft in same manner.
13. Install housing drain plug and insert lubricant.
14. Insert cartridge retaining set screw and jam nut to prevent loss of lubricant.
15. Drive vehicle in a circle to permit second cartridge to engage splines on differential case.
16. Turn each cartridge set screw until it touches spring retainer, then back off screw 1½ to 2 turns and tighten jam nut to 30-35 ft. lbs.

Self Contained Type

When servicing this unit, Fig. 26, a clamping fixture must be used to permit the tension to be slowly released when the snap ring is removed. Both halves of the unit are serviced in the same manner.

Inspection

Parts having ground and polished surfaces such as gears, bearings, bearing journals and differential case halves, should be cleaned in a suitable solvent such as kerosene or diesel fuel oil. Do not use gasoline or any alkaline or hot tank solution.

Inspect all parts for pitted, scored or worn surfaces. Thrust washers must be replaced in sets. The use of a combination of old and new parts will result in premature failure.

Assembly

Preload Check
1. Using a depth micrometer, measure

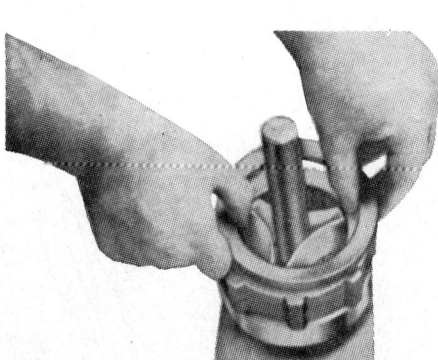

Fig. 29 Installing Belleville springs, concave side up

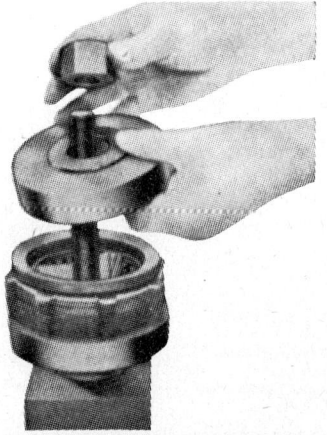

Fig. 30 Installing nut to compress pack

Fig. 31 Measuring height of pack

LOCKING DIFFERENTIALS

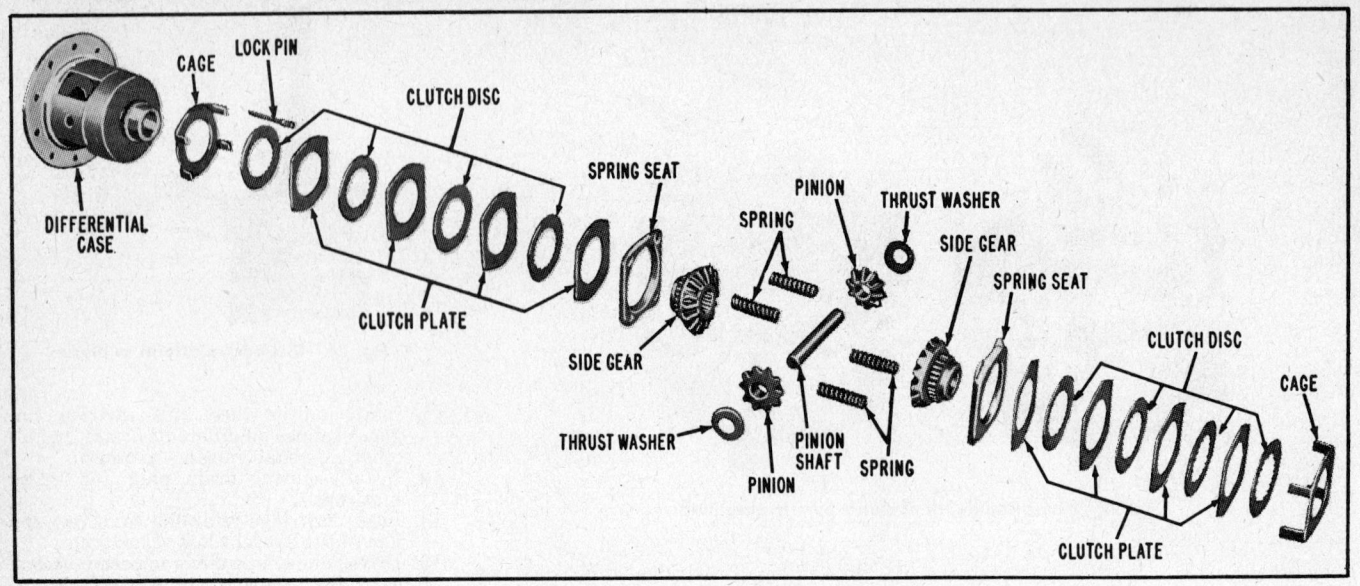

Fig. 32 Spring-loaded "Positraction" locking differential disassembled

depth of clutch bore in case half, Fig. 27, and record measurement.
2. Using a fixture as shown in Fig. 27, position the 1" thick spacer over the locating washer of fixture.
3. Place disc pack on platform. Omit shims at this time.
4. Place drive disc over disc pack.
5. Position four Belleville springs, concave side up, over thick disc, Fig. 28.
6. Place pressure plate, washer and nut over disc pack and tighten nut to 110–120 ft. lbs. to compress pack.
7. Using a Vernier gauge, measure height of pack, Fig. 30. Measure between top of disc pack platform (1" spacer) and bottom of pressure plate. Record measurement.
8. Subtract pack height obtained in step 7 from bore depth obtained in step 1. A shim pack of .004–.009" less than the difference of these two measurements should be used. If the desired shim pack exceeds .040", one of the old drive may be used as part of the shim pack.
9. Remove nut washer and pressure plate from fixture. Remove complete clutch pack and set aside for later use.
10. The unit is now ready for assembly.

DANA POSITRACTION

Disassembly, Fig. 32

1. Remove ring gear and install spring tool shown in Fig. 33, making sure spring jaws are securely indexed between spring coils.

2. Compress tool until spring is compressed enough to slide out of retainer seats. Repeat on remaining springs.
3. Remove differential pinions by rotating side gear with axle shaft until they move around to large opening in case. Pry clutch pack away from pinion until pinion drops out. Remove pinion thrust washers.
4. Remove clutch packs and side gears.

Inspection

1. Clean and inspect side gear thrust surfaces, pinion gear thrust surfaces and thrust washers for excessive wear and replace as required.
2. Inspect clutch pack for excessive wear or or overheating and, if necessary, replace as a unit.

Reassembly

1. Place clutch pack cages into case with side tabs up and flat sides parallel with flat sides in case.
2. Place aluminum spring seat plate over side gear.
3. Alternately place clutch plate and clutch disc on side gear until assembly of pack is complete. Make sure clutch discs index with teeth in side gear.

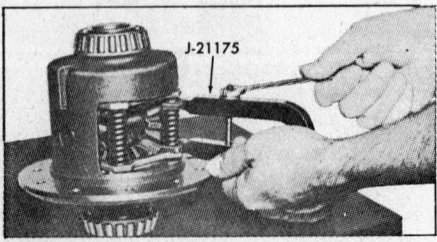

Fig. 33 Spring removal

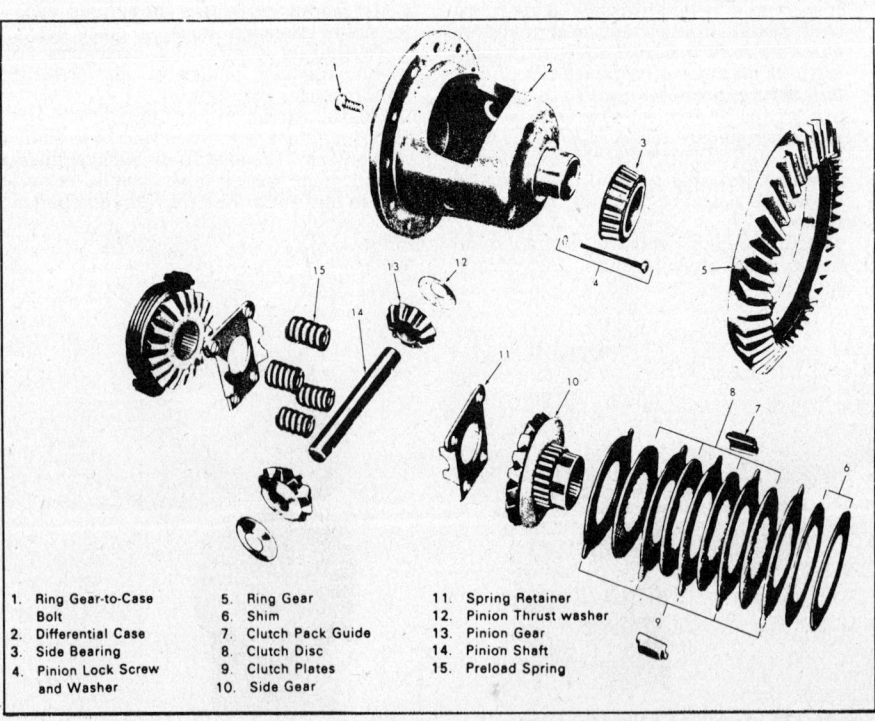

1. Ring Gear-to-Case Bolt
2. Differential Case
3. Side Bearing
4. Pinion Lock Screw and Washer
5. Ring Gear
6. Shim
7. Clutch Pack Guide
8. Clutch Disc
9. Clutch Plates
10. Side Gear
11. Spring Retainer
12. Pinion Thrust washer
13. Pinion Gear
14. Pinion Shaft
15. Preload Spring

Fig. 34 Eaton locking differential

LOCKING DIFFERENTIALS

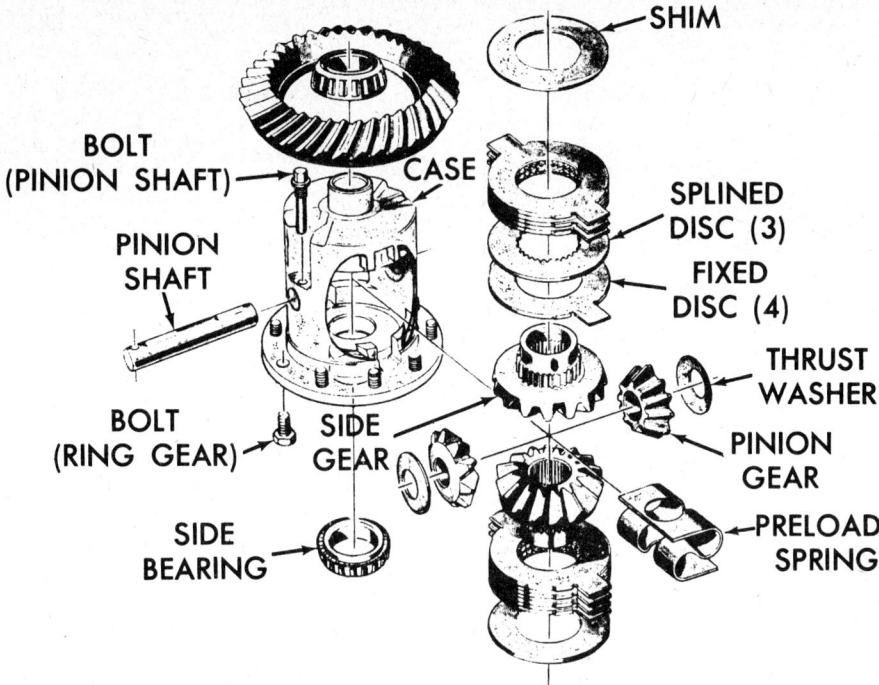

Fig. 35 GM Corp. locking differential disassembled

16. Insert thrust washers behind pinion gears.
17. Install pinion shaft and retain with lock bolt, tightening lock bolt to 15–25 ft-lbs.
18. Check side gear splined hole to be certain it is in line with hole in preload spring retainer. Spring retainer can be moved slightly to correct alignment.

GM CORP.

Disassembly, Fig. 35

1. Remove pinion shaft lock screw, then remove pinion shaft from case.
2. Using a brass drift drive preload spring from case.
3. Remove pinion gears and washers, followed by the side gears.
4. Remove clutch plate guides and separate shims and clutch plates from side gears. Keep clutch plates in their original location in clutch pack.
5. Clean and inspect all parts and replace as required.

Reassembly

1. Apply recommended lubricant to clutch plates and discs.
2. Alternately position clutch plates on side gear, starting and ending with a clutch plate having external lugs.
3. Place spacer against plate having external lugs then install shims. Make sure to install the same spacer and shims or an equal amount on the clutch pack for a starting point.
4. Repeat foregoing procedure on other clutch pack.
5. Install one side gear with clutch pack and shims in case.
6. Position two pinion gears and thrust washers on side gear and install pinion shaft.
7. Compress clutch pack by inserting a screwdriver between side gear and pinion shaft.
8. Install dial indicator with contact button against pinion gear.
9. Rotate pinion gear, clearance should be .001–.006 inch.
10. If clearance is more than .006 inch, add shims between clutch pack and case. If clearance is less than .001 inch, remove shims. A .002 inch shim will change clearance about .001 inch. Recheck clearance after adding or subtracting shims.
11. Remove side gear and repeat procedure with opposite clutch on opposite side of case.
12. Remove pinion shaft, pinions and thrust washers.
13. Install remaining side gear and clutch pack with correct shims in case.
14. Place pinion gears on side gears and rotate into correct position.
15. Install thrust washers behind pinion gears and align.
16. Insert pinion shaft into case through thrust washer and part way into pinion gear. This will keep pinion gears aligned while driving preload spring into place.
17. Position preload spring next to side gears and drive into place.
18. Push pinion shaft into position and align lock screw hole in shaft with hole in case. Install lock screw and torque to 15 ft. lbs.

---

4. Install clutch pack and side gear assemblies in case. Tilt case on its side to prevent side gears from falling out.
5. Place pinion gear between side gears through large opening in case. Rotate side gears and install second pinion directly opposite first. Install pinion thrust washers.
6. Place clutch spring in jaws of tool shown in Fig. 33. Compress spring to about 1.90" and carefully insert into spring seats. Release spring and remove tool. Repeat for remaining springs.
7. Install ring gear.
8. Place differential in carrier.
9. Test operation of differential as outlined at the beginning of this chapter.

EATON

1. Remove pinion shaft lock screw and pull pinion shaft from case, Fig. 34.
2. Remove preload spring retainer and springs.
3. Rotate side gears until pinions are in open area of case and pick out pinions and thrust washers.
4. Remove a side gear, clutch pack and shims, noting shim location in case to aid in reassembly. Remove side gear clutch pack and shims from opposite side. If side gear or clutch pack cannot be removed readily, drive it out with a brass drift.
5. Remove clutch plate guides and separate shims and clutch plates from side gears.

NOTE: Keep clutch plates in their original location in clutch pack.

Inspection

1. If pinion shaft, pinions or side gears are excessively scored, pitted or worn, replace parts affected.
2. Inspect clutch plates for scored, worn, cracked or distorted condition. If any of these conditions exist, new clutch plates must be installed.

Reassembly

1. Alternately position nine clutch plates on side gear, starting and ending with a plate with external lugs.
2. Install two clutch guides over clutch plate lugs.
3. Install same shims which were removed or an equal amount on clutch plate.
4. Repeat above steps on other clutch pack.
5. Install one side gear with clutch pack and shims in case.
6. Position two pinion gears and thrust washers on side gear and install pinion shaft.
7. Compress clutch pack by inserting a screwdriver or wedge between side gear and pinion shaft.
8. Install a suitable dial indicator with contact button against pinion gear.
9. Rotate pinion gear. Clearance should be .001" to .006".
10. If clearance is more than .006", add shims between clutch pack and case. If clearance is less than .001", remove shims. A .002" shim will change clearance about .001". Recheck clearance after adding or subtracting shims.
11. Remove side gear and repeat procedure with remaining clutch pack on opposite side of case.
12. Remove pinion shaft, pinions and thrust washers.
13. Install remaining side gear and clutch pack with correct shims in case.
14. Place pinion gears on side gears and rotate into correct position.
15. Compress preload springs and drive preload retainer and springs between side

EATON DRIVING AXLES

INDEX

	Page No.
Model Index and Lube Capacities	204
Torque Settings	204
Axle Adjustments (All Models)	205
Single Reduction Axle Service	209
Two-Speed Axle Service	212
Double Reduction Planetary Axle Service	214
"D" Series Tandem Drive Axle Service	215
"M" Series Tandem Drive Axle Service	222
Three-Speed Tandem Drive Axles	236

LUBRICANT CAPACITIES

Lubricant capacities are given as a guide only. The capacities of two similar axles in the same series may vary considerably due to design changes and the vehicle manufacturers' installation. The actual service capacity may be determined by carefully measuring the amount of lubricant necessary to fill the assembly to the correct level and measuring the lubricant again when it is drained. The vehicle should be on a level floor when this inspection is made.

Single Reduction Axles

Model	Capacity, Forged Housing	Pints, Fabricated Housing
1315	19	19
1614-5, 1618-9	24	25
1790A-1A	29	26
1792-3	29	26
1862-3, 1880-1	29	26
1890-1, 2, 3	29	26
1910-1	34	—
1918-9	34	—
2010-1	38	—
2018-9	38	—
17101, 121	31	—
17120	29	—
18101, 121	33½	—
18301	33	—
19121	35½	—
23121	34	—

Two Speed Axles

Model	Capacity, Forged Housing	Pints, Fabricated Housing
1350	19	19
13600-2	19	19
13800-2	19	19
15201	17	—
16220	20	—
16221	24	—
16244	22½	—
16500-1	24	25
16600-1	24	25
16802-3	24	25
17201, 221	31	—
17202, 222	22	—
17220	29	—
17500-1	29	26
17800-1	29	26
18201, 221	33½	—
18222	28½	—
18500-1, 2, 3	29	26
18800-1, 2, 3	29	26
19201	34	—
19202	29½	—

Two Speed Axles, continued

Model	Capacity, Forged Housing	Pints, Fabricated Housing
19221	36	—
19500-1, 2, 3	34	—
19800-1	34	—
20500-1, 2, 3	38	—
20800-1	38	—
22221	29	—
22500-1	35	—
23221	34	—

Planetary Double Reduction Axles

Model	Capacity, Forged Housing	Pints, Fabricated Housing
350	19	19
3800, 3802	19	19
6600-1	24	25
6802-3	24	25
7800-1	29	26
8802-3	29	26
9502-3	34	—
9800-1	34	—
0502-3	38	—
0800-1	38	—
2500-1	35	—
18302, 322	28½	—
45AR	38	—

Tandem Drive Axles

Model	Capacity, Forged Housing	Pints, Fabricated Housing
22MF, MR	12	—
22M (Power Divider)	9	—
28MF, MR	17	—
28M (Power Divider)	9	—
30DS, DT, DP	30	—
30DSC, DTC, DPC	28	—
30D-3	30	—
30RS, RT, RP	27	—
30R-3	27	—
32MF	29	—
32M (Power Divider)	3	—
32MR	32	—
34DS, DT, DP	29	—
34DSC	32½	—
34DSE	32	—
34 DTC, DTE	32	—
34DPC, DPE	32	—
34D-3, C	29	—
34D-3E	24	—
34RS, RT, RP	32	—
34R-3	32	—
36MF	24	—
36M (Power Divider)	3	—
36MR	24	—
38DPC	35½	—
38 DS, DT, DP	29	—
38DSC	34	—
38DSE	31	—
38DTC, DPE	31	—
38D-3	29	—
38D-3C, D	27	—
38RS, RT, RP	32	—
38R-3	32	—
42D-3	31	—
42DT, DP	31	—
42DPB, DPD	29	—
42RT, RP	29	—
44DSC, DTC	20	—
50DP	24	—
50MF (In Rear Filler Hole)	20	—
50MF (In Front Filler Hole)	2	—
50M (Power Divider)	6	—
50MR (In Rear Filler Hole)	20	—
50MR (In Front Filler Hole)	2	—
440DPC	20	—
DS380	29	—

TORQUE SETTINGS

Thread Size	Ft Lbs.
1/4–20	18–25
5/16–18	18–25
3/8–16	35–45
3/8–24	25–35
7/16–14	50–70 ①
7/16–14	35–50 ②
7/16–20	50–70
1/2–13	80–100
1/2–20	80–100
9/16–12	100–125
9/16–18	125–150 ③
9/16–18	95–125 ④
9/16–18	150–175 ⑤
5/8–11	150–175
5/8–18	135–160 ⑥
5/8–18	150–175 ⑦
5/8–18	160–185 ⑧
11/16–11	175–200
3/4–10	200–225
13/16–10	225–250
7/8–9	300–350
1–20	225–350
1 1/8–18	325–450 ⑪
1 1/8–18	500–700 ⑩
1 1/8–18	175–200 ⑨
1 1/4–12	400–600 ⑬
1 1/4–12	175–200 ⑫
1 1/4–18	400–600
1 1/2–18	175–200 ⑮
1 1/2–18	500–700 ⑭
1 3/4–12	600–800 ⑰
1 3/4–12	175–200 ⑯
2–12	700–900

①—Differential case.
②—Inspection cover to axle housing. Also oil collector drum to differential case on D Series forward axles.
③—Gear support case on two speed and planetary double reduction axles.
④—Ring gear to case on M Series axles.
⑤—Bolt locations other than specified in notes ③ and ④.
⑥—Ring gear to differential case on single reduction axles.
⑦—Herringbone gear to differential case on M Series forward axles, and gear case support on two-speed and planetary double reduction axles.
⑧—Differential case to axle housing on two-speed, planetary double reduction, D Series forward and rear axles, and M Series forward axles.
⑨—Drive pinion nut on two speed and planetary double reduction axles.
⑩—Input and output shaft nuts on M Series axles.
⑪—Bolt locations other than specified in notes ⑨ and ⑩.
⑫—Output shaft nut on D Series forward axles.
⑬—Bolt locations other than specified in note ⑫.
⑭—Drive pinion nut on D Series forward axle and M Series rearward axle.
⑮—Bolt locations other than specified in note ⑭.
⑯—Input shaft nut on M Series forward axle.
⑰—Bolt locations other than specified in note ⑯.

EATON DRIVING AXLES

Axle Adjustments

PROCEDURE

Measuring ring gear to drive pinion backlash and checking tooth contact pattern before disassembly, plus "punch marking" components for related position are recommended procedures for easier adjustment of axle after reassembly. If major axle parts are replaced, these identifying marks and reference measurements may not necessarily provide correct adjustment. However, usual return of parts to the identifying marks will serve as a reference to position parts as near as possible to correct adjustment.

The following is an outline of axle adjustment procedure and includes information on when adjustment should be performed and references to detailed instructions:

1. *Power Divider Input and Output Shaft Bearing Clearances.* These adjustments are made during reassembly of power divider. Refer to individual axle instructions.
2. *Drive Pinion Bearing Preload.* This adjustment is made before installing drive pinion (see below).
3. *Drive Pinion Position Adjustment.* Initial or preliminary adjustment is made during reassembly (see below).
4. *Differential Bearing Preload.* This adjustment is made in combination with ring gear and drive pinion adjustments (see below).
5. *Ring Gear and Drive Pinion Backlash.* Adjustments are given below.
6. *Ring Gear Tooth Contact.* Check ring gear tooth contact when adjusting ring gear and drive pinion (see below).
7. *Ring Gear Thrust Block Clearance.* This adjustment is made after drive pinion adjustments are completed and before differential carrier is installed in axle housing. Refer to individual axle instructions.
8. *Wheel Bearing Adjustments.* Procedure is given further on in this chapter.

DRIVE PINION BEARING PRELOAD

If the original pinion spacer can be used in reassembly, this should provide a close to correct adjustment of pinion bearing preload. If original spacer cannot be used start with spacer thickness recommended in Fig. 1.

Fig. 2 Checking drive pinion bearing preload with torque wrench (pinion in vise)

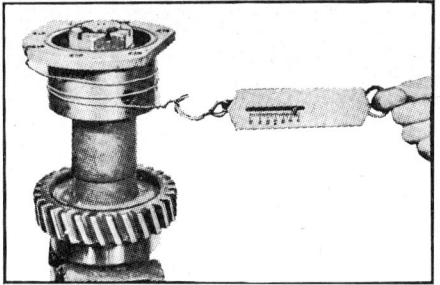

Fig. 3 Checking drive pinion bearing preload with spring scale for Tandem Drive Axles (pinion in vise)

With drive pinion, bearings, bearing cage and other related parts (oil seal and retainer removed) assembled and lubricated, measure and adjust pinion bearing preload.

Torque Wrench Method

1. Mount an adapter on pinion bearing cage, Fig. 2.
2. Hold drive pinion in a vise or arbor press. If an arbor press is used, apply approximately 5 tons pressure to bearings.
3. Rotate bearing cage by hand several revolutions to assure normal bearing contact. Then rotate bearing cage with a torque wrench and note torque reading as cage is rotated.
4. Correct bearing preload is indicated by a torque of 15 to 35 inch lbs. If incorrect, adjust by changing pinion bearing spacer. Use a thicker spacer to decrease preload or a thinner one to increase preload. *Do not use shim stock to increase thickness of spacer; always use correct size spacer.*

Spring Scale Method

1. Wrap a soft wire around bearing cage, Figs. 3 and 4.
2. Hold drive pinion in a vise or arbor press. If a press is used, apply approximately 5 tons pressure to bearings.
3. Pull scale on a line tangent to the cage outside diameter as shown with the scale attached to the wire and note scale reading.
4. To calculate torque from scale reading measure cage radius (see Fig. 1). Then multiply radius times scale reading. Example: With cage radius 2½" and scale pull 12 lbs., torque would be 12 × 2½ or 30 in. lbs.
5. Correct bearing preload is indicated by a torque of 15 to 35 inch lbs. If incorrect, use a thicker spacer to decrease preload and a thinner one to increase preload. *Do not use shim stock to increase thickness of spacer; always use correct size spacer.*

DRIVE PINION POSITION

Drive pinion position in relation to ring gear is adjusted by adding or removing shims between pinion bearing cage and differential carrier or power divider case.

To assist in adjustment of ring gear and pinion, pinion should be positioned as near as possible to the correct position during reassembly. This can be accomplished as follows:

If the original ring gear and pinion are used in reassembly, use same size and quantity of shims removed during disassembly. If a new ring gear and pinion are used in reassembly, use shim pack recommended in Fig. 1.

The drive pinion position may also be set with a depth gauge. Fig. 1 also shows the basic dimensions used for gauge setting.

RING GEAR & DRIVE PINION

Except Model 42M Tandem

1. With differential bearings lubricated and bearing cap screws tightened *finger tight,* adjust ring gear and pinion as follows, referring to Figs. 5 and 6 for tooth contact pattern identification. Also refer to Fig. 7 for tooth nomenclature.

NOTE: *Adjustment of bearing adjusters to change ring gear position is affected by the relative mounting positions of the ring gear and drive pinion. The following instructions are for axles with ring gear on left-hand side of drive pinion. Left and right-hand instructions in parentheses (left-hand) (right-hand) are for axles with ring gear on right-hand side of drive pinion.*

2. Tighten differential bearing adjusters to correctly seat bearing cups.
3. Loosen right-hand (or left-hand) bearing adjuster until it is very loose. Tighten left-hand (or right-hand) bearing adjuster until backlash is removed between ring gear and drive pinion. Tightening left-hand (or right-hand) adjuster moves ring gear toward drive pinion.
4. Tighten right-hand (or left-hand) bearing

Fig. 4 Checking drive pinion bearing preload with spring scale (pinion in press)

EATON DRIVING AXLES

adjuster until snug, then continue to tighten adjuster two additional notches. This will normally position ring gear within the specified .006 to .016" backlash. This adjustment will also preload differential bearings. Tightening right-hand (or left-hand) adjuster moves ring gear away from drive pinion.

5. Tighten differential bearing capscrews to correct torque, then measure ring gear movement with a dial indicator, Fig. 8, to determine specific backlash.
6. Paint ring gear teeth and check tooth contact pattern. Compare pattern with those illustrated in Figs. 5 and 6. If contact pattern similar to "A" is obtained, adjustment is correct.
7. If Pattern "B" is indicated, loosen left-hand (or right-hand) bearing adjuster and tighten right-hand (or left-hand) adjuster equal amounts. Recheck tooth contact pattern. If pattern is not corrected, continue to move bearing adjusters (the same number of notches) until proper lengthwise pattern is obtained.
8. If Pattern "C" is indicated, loosen right-hand (or left-hand) bearing adjuster and tighten left-hand (or right-hand) adjuster equal amounts. Recheck tooth pattern. If pattern is not corrected, continue to turn bearing adjusted equal amounts until proper lengthwise bearing pattern is obtained.
9. If Pattern "D" or "E" is indicated, adjustment of drive pinion position is necessary. Add or remove pinion bearing cage shims to move drive pinion as pattern indicates. When drive pinion position is changed, the adjustment may affect lengthwise bearing. If necessary, readjust backlash for proper lengthwise bearing. Recheck tooth contact pattern.
10. When correct tooth pattern "A" is obtained, install adjuster locks and cotter pins. Lock wire differential bearing capscrews.

Model 42M Tandem Axle

For easier adjustment, it is recommended that the differential assembly and power divider assembly be removed from the differential carrier. In the following instructions, it is assumed that only the countershaft assembly and bearings are installed in differential carrier. Refer to Fig. 5 for tooth contact pattern and Fig. 7 for tooth nomenclature.

1. To adjust countershaft bearings, turn left-hand bearing adjuster until two or three threads are engaged. Tighten right-hand bearing cage until end play is removed from countershaft bearings.
2. To preload countershaft bearings, continue to tighten right-hand bearing cage until resistance is felt when rotating countershaft. *This preload adjustment can be maintained during ring gear adjustment by turning bearing adjuster and cage equal amounts.* Preload should be 10 to 22 inch lbs.
3. Install power divider assembly.
4. To adjust ring gear backlash, loosen right-hand bearing cage and tighten left-hand bearing adjuster (the same number of turns) until .006 to .016" backlash is obtained. Measure backlash with dial indicator, Fig. 8.
5. Paint ring gear teeth and check tooth contact pattern. Compare pattern with those shown in Fig. 5.
6. If Pattern "B" is indicated, loosen left-hand bearing adjuster and tighten right-hand bearing cage equal amounts. Recheck tooth pattern. If pattern is not corrected, continue to move bearing cage and adjuster (the same number of notches) until proper lengthwise bearing pattern is obtained.
7. If Pattern "C" is indicated, loosen right-hand bearing cage and tighten left-hand bearing adjuster equal amounts. Recheck tooth pattern. If pattern is not corrected, continue to turn bearing cage and adjuster equal amounts until proper lengthwise bearing pattern is obtained.
8. If Pattern "D" or "E" is indicated, adjustment of drive pinion is necessary. Add or remove pinion bearing cage shims to move drive pinion as pattern indicates. When drive pinion position is changed, the adjustment may affect lengthwise bearing. If necessary, readjust backlash for proper lengthwise bearing. Recheck tooth contact pattern.
9. When Pattern "A" is obtained, install countershaft bearing covers, gaskets and capscrews. Install differential assembly.

WHEEL BEARING ADJUSTMENT

Wheel bearings should be adjusted to provide .001 to .010" end play.

1. Remove outer nut and lockwasher.
2. While turning wheel in both directions, tighten inner nut until a slight bind on nut is present.
3. Back off inner nut 1/3 turn to permit wheel to rotate freely.
4. Install lockwasher and outer nut, and lock both nuts in this position.

	AXLE MODELS	Dimensions for Drive Pinion Bearing Preload Adjustment		Dimensions for Drive Pinion Position Adjustment	
		PINION BEARING SPACER	PINION BEARING CAGE RADIUS	PINION BEARING CAGE SHIM PACK	PINION DEPTH GAUGE SETTING
SINGLE REDUCTION AXLES	1315	0.528	2⅛	0.046	3.28125
	1614	0.637	2½	0.043	3.5625
	1618	0.528	2⅛	0.030	4.125
	1790A, 1862	0.639	2½	0.030 + 0.125 Spacer	4.2187
	1792, 1892	0.190	2¹³⁄₁₆	0.040 + 0.125 Spacer	4.0625
	1910, 2010	0.185	3⅛	0.040	4.600
2-SPEED AXLES	1350, 13800	0.530	2⅛	0.040	3.6244
	13600	0.330	2²³⁄₃₂	0.045	4.28125
	13602	0.330	2²³⁄₃₂	0.165	4.28125
	13802	0.527	2⅛	0.040 + 0.250 Spacer *	3.6244
	16500	0.530	2⅛	0.040	4.125
	16600	0.331	3	0.056	4.8125
	16802	0.528	2⅛	0.043	4.125
	17500, 18500	For replacement, use 17800 or 18802 Gear Set plus 0.250 in. Bearing Cage Spacer			4.4062
	17800, 18802	0.638	2½	0.037	4.4062
	19502, 20502	0.188	2¹³⁄₁₆	0.040	4.7812
	22501	0.185	3⅛	0.040	5.4375
PLANETARY DOUBLE REDUCTION AXLES	45AR, 0502, 9502	0.188	2¹³⁄₁₆	0.040	4.7812
	2501	0.185	3⅛	0.040	5.4375
	3800	0.530	2⅛	0.040	3.6244
	3802	0.527	2⅛	0.040 + 0.250 Spacer †	3.6244
	6600	0.331	3	0.056	4.8125
	6802	0.528	2⅛	0.043	4.125
	7800, 8802	0.638	2½	0.037	4.4062
TANDEM DRIVE AXLES	22MF	0.530	2⅛	0.050	3.253
	22MR	0.530	2⅛	0.040	3.253
	28MF	0.530	2⅛	0.050	3.4725
	28MR	0.640	2⁷⁄₁₆	0.040	3.4725
	30DS, 30DT, 30DP	0.638	2½	0.040	4.125
	30RS	0.528	2⅛	0.030	4.125
	30RT, 30RP	0.528	2⅛	0.043	4.125
	32MF	0.637	2¹⁵⁄₃₂	0.050	4.2187
	32MR	0.639	2½	0.030	4.2187
	34DS, 34DT, 34DP	0.642	2¹³⁄₁₆	0.056	4.4062
	34RS	0.639	2½	0.030 + 0.125 Spacer	4.2187
	34RT, 34RP	0.638	2½	0.037	4.4062
	36MF	0.638	2¹⁵⁄₃₂	0.060	4.875
	36MR	0.177	3⅛	0.040	4.875
	38DS, 38DT, 38DP	0.642	2¹³⁄₁₆	0.056	4.4062
	38RS	0.639	2½	0.030 + 0.125 Spacer	4.2187
	38RP, 38RT	0.638	2½	0.037	4.4062
	42DT, 42DP	0.642	2¹³⁄₁₆	0.056	4.4062
	42RT, 42RP	0.638	2½	0.037	4.4062
	42MF	0.638	2¹⁵⁄₃₂	0.060	2.8125
	42MR	0.175	3⅜	0.060	2.8125

* spacer not used on all model 13802 axles.   † spacer not used on all model 3802 axles.

Fig. 1 Eaton axle drive pinion adjustment specifications

EATON DRIVING AXLES

The ring gear tooth contact patterns illustrated are approximate shapes. Actual contact may vary, however the same general shape should be obtained. When adjusting gear sets that have been in service, tooth contact may vary because of wear. To obtain best results, strive to obtain a pattern coinciding with original patterns.

Pattern "A"
CORRECT TOOTH CONTACT

Correct adjustment is obtained when pattern of tooth bearing *(both lengthwise and profile)* appear as shown.

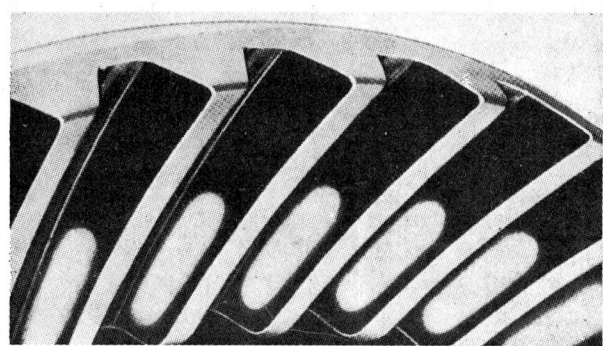

Pattern "A"

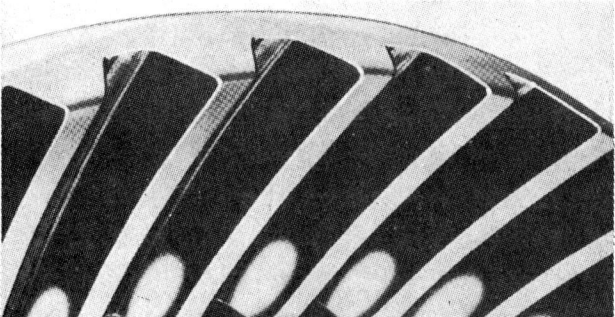

Pattern "B"
CONCENTRATED BEARING AT TOE

Not enough backlash . . . move ring gear *away* from drive pinion to increase lengthwise bearing. This may change the profile bearing to some extent and an adjustment of the pinion may be required.

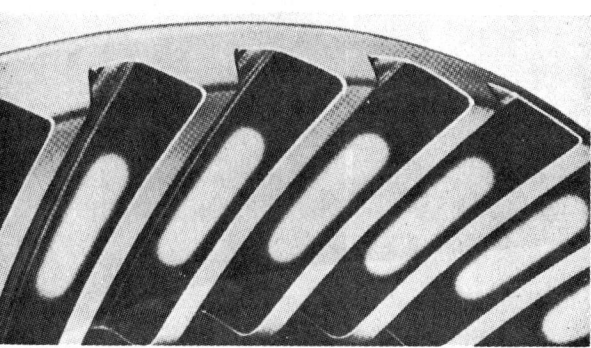

Pattern "C"
CONCENTRATED BEARING AT HEEL

Too much backlash . . . move ring gear *toward* drive pinion to obtain correct lengthwise bearing. This may change the profile bearing to some extent and an adjustment of the pinion may be required.

Pattern "D"
PROFILE BEARING HIGH

Pinion is out too far . . . remove shims to move drive pinion toward ring gear. Then move ring gear away from pinion to obtain correct lengthwise bearing.

Pattern "E"
PROFILE BEARING LOW

Pinion is in too far . . . add shims to move drive pinion away from ring gear. Then move ring gear toward pinion to obtain correct lengthwise bearing.

Fig. 5 Correct and incorrect tooth contact patterns for all models except 22M, 28M, 36M Tandem Axles

EATON DRIVING AXLES

The ring gear tooth contact patterns illustrated are approximate shapes. Actual contact may vary, however the same general shape should be obtained. When adjusting gear sets that have been in service, tooth contact may vary because of wear. To obtain best results, strive to obtain a pattern coinciding with original patterns.

Pattern "A"
CORRECT TOOTH CONTACT

Correct adjustment is obtained when pattern of tooth bearing *(both lengthwise and profile)* appear as shown.

Pattern "A"

Pattern "B"
CONCENTRATED BEARING AT TOE

Not enough backlash . . . move ring gear *away* from drive pinion to increase lengthwise bearing. This may change the profile bearing to some extent and an adjustment of the pinion may be required.

Pattern "C"
CONCENTRATED BEARING AT HEEL

Too much backlash . . . move ring gear *toward* drive pinion to obtain correct lengthwise bearing. This may change the profile bearing to some extent and an adjustment of the pinion may be required.

Pattern "D"
PROFILE BEARING HIGH

Pinion is out too far . . . remove shims to move drive pinion toward ring gear. Then move ring gear away from pinion to obtain correct lengthwise bearing.

Pattern "E"
PROFILE BEARING LOW

Pinion is in too far . . . add shims to move drive pinion away from ring gear. Then move ring gear toward pinion to obtain correct lengthwise bearing.

Fig. 6 Correct and incorrect tooth contact pattern for Tandem Axle Models 22MF, 22MR, 28MF, 28MR, 36MF, 36MR

EATON DRIVING AXLES

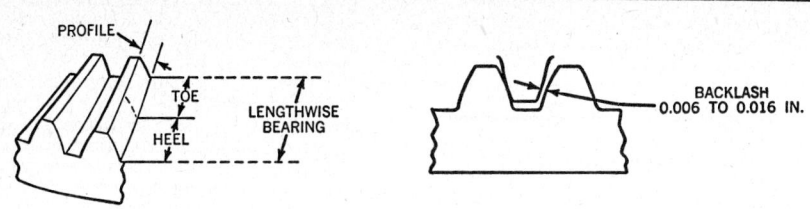

Ring Gear Tooth Nomenclature

check tooth contact pattern

Tooth contact pattern consists of the lengthwise bearing and profile bearing. The lengthwise bearing is the bearing along the tooth of the ring gear. The profile bearing is the bearing up and down the tooth (See fig. 206). In determining correct ring gear tooth contact, these two types of bearings must be considered separately to obtain proper results in combination.

With differential bearings adjusted correctly, paint at least ten ring gear teeth with red lead or prussian blue. Turn ring gear by hand a few revolutions in both directions to obtain impressions (or patterns) of tooth contact. Compare contact patterns with those shown in figure 208 or 209. If tooth contact patterns are not correct, move ring gear and/or drive pinion as necessary to adjust for correct pattern. Keep in mind that ring gear movement affects lengthwise bearing and that drive pinion movement affects the profile bearing.

Adjust to obtain correct tooth contact on drive side of teeth. Under this condition, the coast side tooth contact is usually satisfactory.

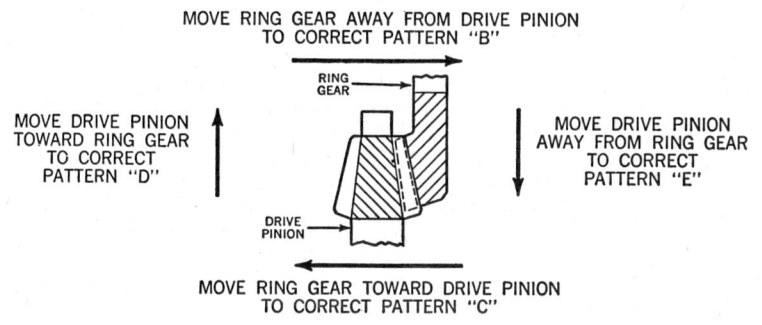

Fig. 7 Ring gear and drive pinion movement to obtain correct tooth contact pattern

Fig. 8 Measuring ring gear backlash with dial indicator

Eaton Single Reduction Axles

DISASSEMBLE

Differential Carrier, Fig. 9

1. Drain lubricant.
2. Disconnect propeller shaft and remove axle shafts.
3. Unfasten and remove differential carrier from axle housing and discard gasket.
4. Unscrew pipe plug, then remove spring and oil distributor (if used).
5. Remove ring gear thrust block from end of adjusting screw after removing locknut and screw (if used).
6. Punch mark differential bearing caps and carrier for correct location on reassembly. Also punch mark differential bearing adjusters for correct location of adjuster locks.
7. Remove differential bearing caps and adjusters. Tilt ring gear away from pinion and lift out differential assembly.
8. Remove pinion bearing cage-to-carrier capscrews. Drive pinion assembly out of carrier, being careful not to allow assembly to fall on flange. *Note size and quantity of shims under bearing cage flange for easier adjustment during reassembly.*

Drive Pinion

1. Hold companion flange in vise, then remove cotter pin, nut and flat washer.
2. Drive pinion out of flange.
3. Remove pinion bearings cage assembly. Remove oil seal retainer, flange flat washer (if used) and outer bearing cone from cage. Discard bearing cage cork seal.
4. If replacement is necessary, remove bearing cups from cage, using suitable puller. Remove oil seal and felt seal from seal retainer.
5. Remove bearing spacer washer (if used) and spacer from pinion.
6. Remove inner bearing cone and pilot bearing from pinion, using suitable pullers.

Differential

1. Punch mark differential cases for correct location in reassembly. Separate case halves and lift off plain half.
2. Lift out differential spider, pinions and thrust washers.
3. Remove bearing cones from differential cases with a split-type puller.
4. To remove ring gear from flanged differential, drill off the flat head of rivets (on ring gear side) and drive out rivets. Some ring gears are fastened with bolts and locknuts.

REASSEMBLE

Differential, Fig. 10

1. Rivet (cold) ring gear to flanged differential case, using a press. Compress rivets from 44 to 48 tons on Model 1315 and from 47–50 on all other models. If bolts and locknuts are used, tighten to correct torque. Lubricate internal parts of differential during reassembly.
2. Press bearing cones on differential cases.
3. Assemble spider, pinions and thrust washers in flanged differential case. Then tap plain differential case into place, aligning punch marks made during disassembly. Install capscrews, bolts and nuts. Tighten nuts and capscrews to correct torque and lockwire capscrews and nuts.

209

EATON DRIVING AXLES

Drive Pinion, Fig. 11

1. Press pilot bearing on drive pinion and stake in four places as shown in Fig. 12.
2. Press inner bearing cone on pinion. Place spacer and washer (if used) on pinion.
3. If removed, press bearing cups into pinion bearing cage. Install new felt seal and oil seal in oil seal retainer.
4. Lubricate drive pinion bearings, then place pinion bearing cage and outer bearing cone on drive pinion. *Do not install oil seal retainer until pinion bearing adjustment is completed.*
5. Temporarily assemble companion flange to pinion as follows: Place companion flange flat washer (if used) on drive pinion. Press flange on pinion. Install and tighten pinion nut to correct torque. Rotate pinion bearing cage while tightening nut. Check pinion bearing preload adjustment as outlined previously.
6. With pinion bearings correctly adjusted, remove companion flange. Install new cork seal in groove of pinion bearing cage. Install oil seal retainer, then reinstall companion flange, flat washer and pinion nut. Tighten nut to correct torque and install cotter pin.

Differential Carrier

1. Install same quantity and size shims that were removed in disassembly on pinion bearing cage, then install drive pinion assembly in carrier. Install and tighten capscrews to correct torque.
2. Thread thrust block adjusting screw (if used) far enough into carrier to mount thrust block. Lubricate and install thrust block on end of adjusting screw.
3. Place differential assembly in carrier and install differential bearing cups, adjusters and caps. Install and finger tighten differential bearing capscrews. Tighten adjusters to correctly seat differential bearings. Adjust ring gear and drive pinion as outlined previously.
4. With ring gear and pinion correctly adjusted, and differential bearing capscrews tightened to correct torque, install cotter pins to secure adjuster locks. Lock wire capscrews.
5. Install oil distributor (if used), spring and pipe plug.
6. Adjust thrust block clearance as follows: Tighten adjusting screw to position thrust block against ring gear. Loosen adjusting screw $1/8$–$1/4$ turn to obtain .010 to .015" clearance between thrust block and ring gear. Tighten locknut. Bend ear of lock against nut to secure adjustment.

Install Carrier In Housing

1. Using a new gasket, install carrier in axle housing. Install capscrews and tighten to correct torque.
2. Install axle shaft and connect propeller shaft. Fill housing with correct lubricant.

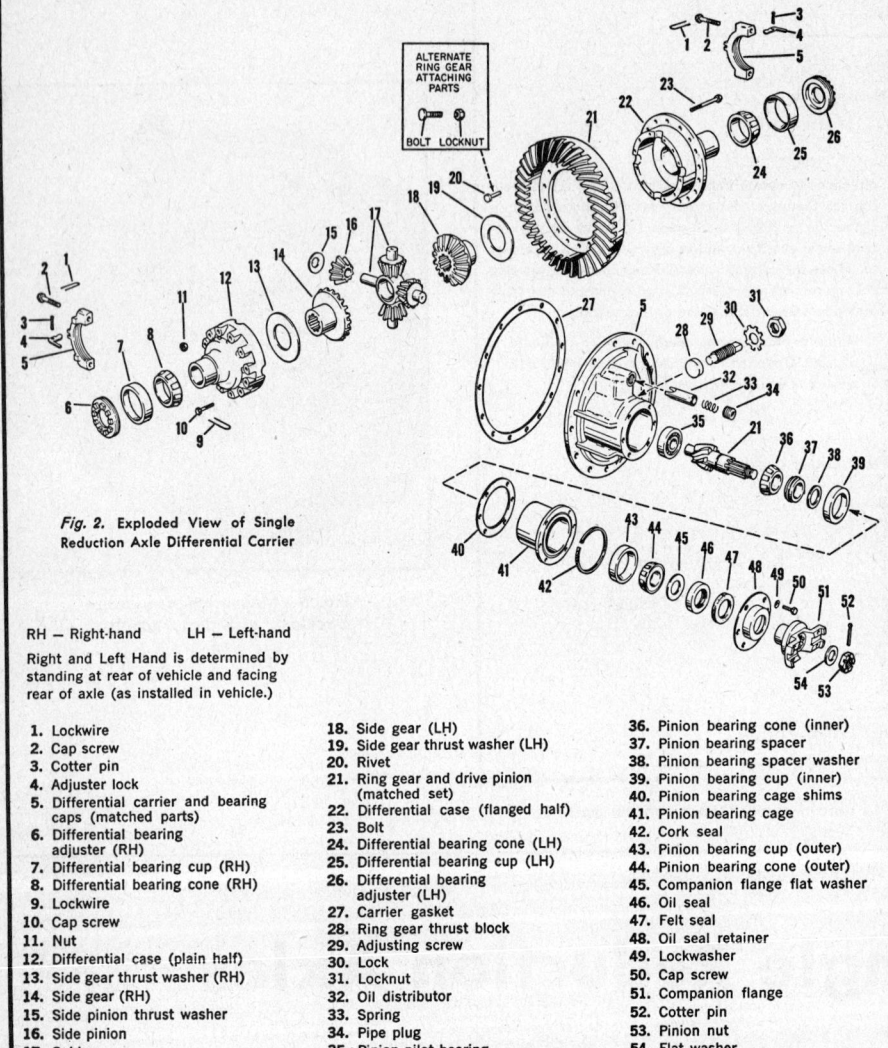

Fig. 2. Exploded View of Single Reduction Axle Differential Carrier

RH — Right-hand   LH — Left-hand

Right and Left Hand is determined by standing at rear of vehicle and facing rear of axle (as installed in vehicle.)

1. Lockwire
2. Cap screw
3. Cotter pin
4. Adjuster lock
5. Differential carrier and bearing caps (matched parts)
6. Differential bearing adjuster (RH)
7. Differential bearing cup (RH)
8. Differential bearing cone (RH)
9. Lockwire
10. Cap screw
11. Nut
12. Differential case (plain half)
13. Side gear thrust washer (RH)
14. Side gear (RH)
15. Side pinion thrust washer
16. Side pinion
17. Spider
18. Side gear (LH)
19. Side gear thrust washer (LH)
20. Rivet
21. Ring gear and drive pinion (matched set)
22. Differential case (flanged half)
23. Bolt
24. Differential bearing cone (LH)
25. Differential bearing cup (LH)
26. Differential bearing adjuster (LH)
27. Carrier gasket
28. Ring gear thrust block
29. Adjusting screw
30. Lock
31. Locknut
32. Oil distributor
33. Spring
34. Pipe plug
35. Pinion pilot bearing
36. Pinion bearing cone (inner)
37. Pinion bearing spacer
38. Pinion bearing spacer washer
39. Pinion bearing cup (inner)
40. Pinion bearing cage shims
41. Pinion bearing cage
42. Cork seal
43. Pinion bearing cup (outer)
44. Pinion bearing cone (outer)
45. Companion flange flat washer
46. Oil seal
47. Felt seal
48. Oil seal retainer
49. Lockwasher
50. Cap screw
51. Companion flange
52. Cotter pin
53. Pinion nut
54. Flat washer

Fig. 9 Disassembled view of Eaton Single Reduction Axle Differential Carrier

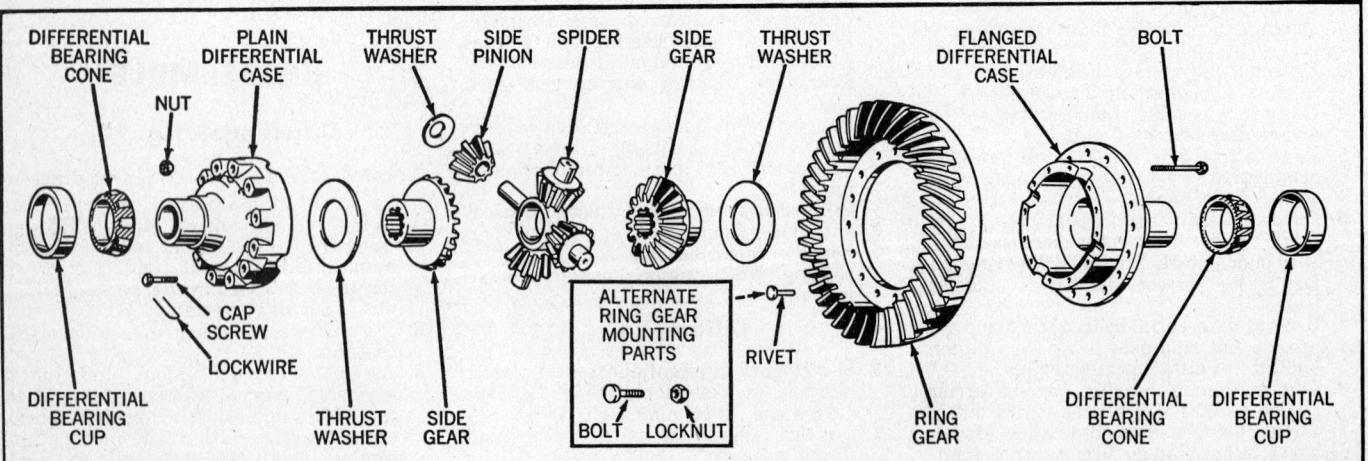

Fig. 10 Disassembled view of differential

EATON DRIVING AXLES

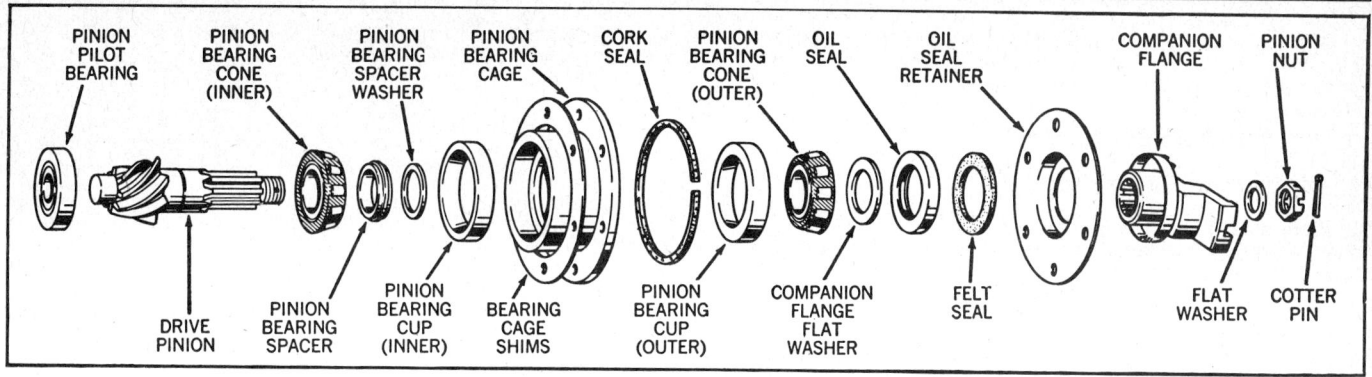

Fig. 11 Disassembled view of drive pinion. Companion flange flat washers and pinion bearing spacer washers are not used on all axles

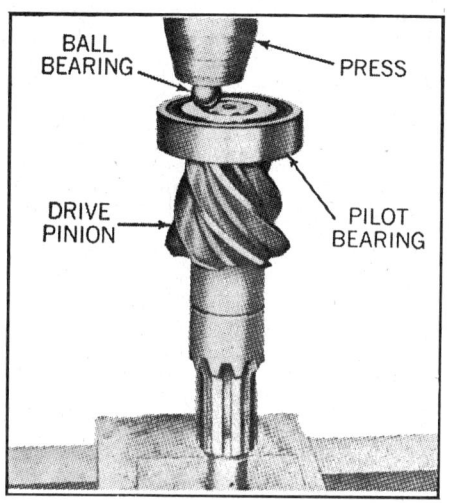

Fig. 12 Staking drive pinion pilot bearing (stake in four places)

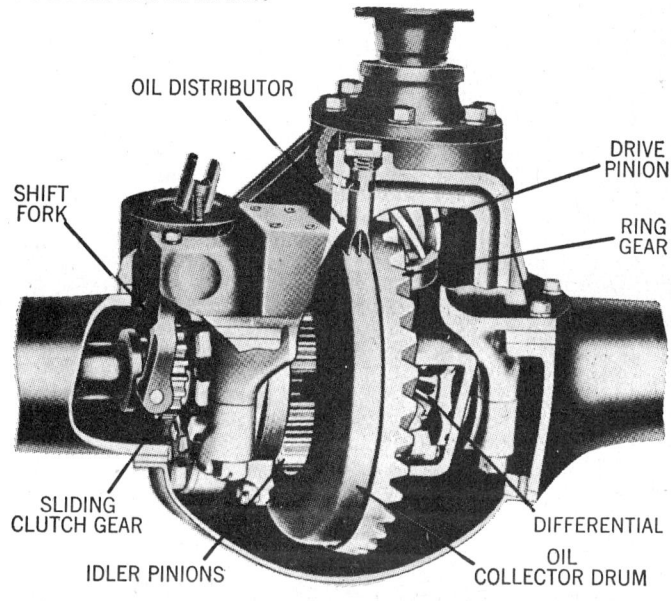

Fig. 13 Cutaway view of Eaton Two Speed Axle assembly

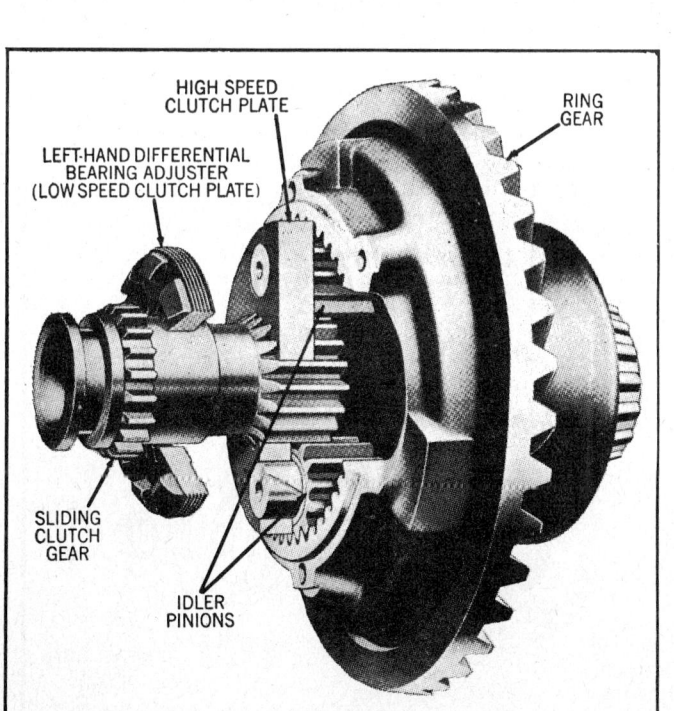

Fig. 14 Sliding clutch gear position for high axle ratio

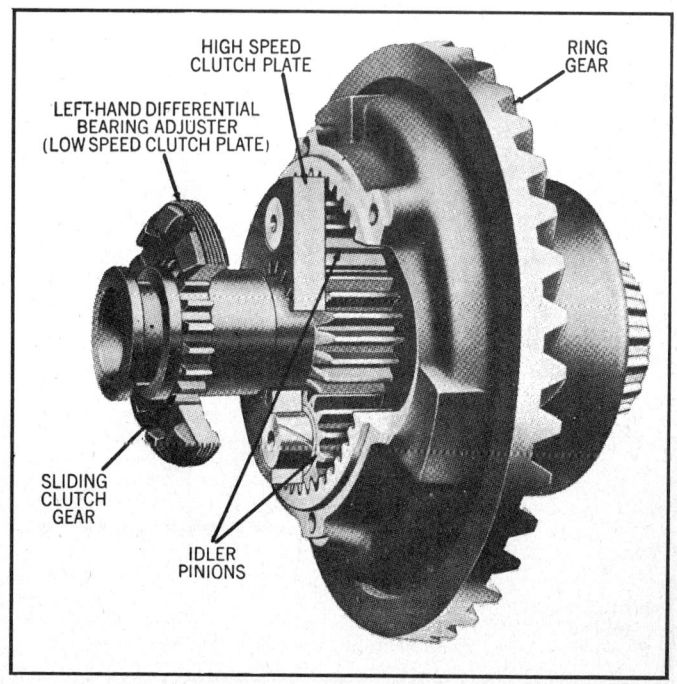

Fig. 15 Sliding clutch gear position for low axle ratio

211

EATON DRIVING AXLES

Eaton Two Speed Axles

DISASSEMBLE
Differential Carrier, Fig. 16

1. Place axle in low range. Remove shift unit nuts and washers. Disconnect electric wires, air tubing or vacuum tubing as necessary to remove shift unit.
2. Drain lubricant. Disconnect propeller shaft and remove axle shafts. Unfasten and lift differential carrier from axle housing. Discard carrier gasket.
3. Unscrew pipe plug and remove spring and oil distributor.
4. Remove seal and spring from shift fork. Remove expansion plugs and drive out shift fork shaft. Disengage and remove shift fork.
5. Remove sliding clutch gear. *If preliminary inspection reveals that ring gear and drive pinion are satisfactory, check backlash and tooth pattern for easier adjustment in reassembly.*
6. Punch mark right-hand differential bearing adjuster for location of lock in reassembly. Cut lockwire and remove differential bearing cap screws. Remove right-hand differential bearing cap, bearing adjuster and lock.
7. Cut lockwire and remove left-hand differential bearing cap, bearing adjuster and lock as an assembly to assure correct position of ring gear during reassembly.
8. Tilt up planetary end of differential, then lift out differential assembly.
9. Remove pinion bearing cage-to-differential carrier capscrews. Then drive pinion assembly out of carrier, being careful not to allow assembly to fall on flange. *Note size and quantity of shims on bearing cage flange* for easier adjustment in reassembly.

Drive Pinion

1. Hold companion flange in vise and, after removing cotter pin, nut and flat washer, drive pinion out of flange.
2. Remove pinion bearing cage assembly, oil seal retainer assembly (flanged or pressed-in type) flange flat washer (if used) and outer bearing cone from pinion bearing cage.
3. Discard pinion bearing cage cork seal (used only with flanged type oil seal retainer).
4. Remove oil seal and felt seal from oil seal retainer. If replacement is necessary, remove bearing cups from cage, using suitable puller.
5. Remove pinion bearing spacer washer (if used) and spacer from drive pinion.
6. Remove inner bearing cone and pilot bearing, using pullers.

Differential

1. Remove locknuts and bolts holding gear support cases together. Tap alternately on opposite sides of ring gear with a soft-faced hammer until ring gear is free of flange on support case.
2. Lift off left-hand support case, oil collector drum and thrust washer.
3. Lift off ring gear.
4. Pry off high-speed clutch plate, then remove idler pinions and pins.
5. Lift out differential assembly. Remove support case thrust washer.
6. Punch mark differential cases for correct location in reassembly. Cut lockwires and remove capscrews, then lift off right-hand differential case.
7. Lift out long-hub side gear and thrust washer.
8. Lift out spider, pinions and thrust washers. Remove short-hub side gear and thrust washer from left-hand differential case.
9. To remove differential bearing cones, place pilot punch in holes provided in gear case support. Tap on bearing cone inner race, alternately through each hole until cone is removed. Remove bearing cones from both support cases in the same manner.

REASSEMBLE
Differential, Fig. 17

1. Press bearing cones on gear support case.
2. Place thrust washer and short-hub side gear in left-hand differential case. Assemble side pinions and thrust washers to spider, then place this assembly in left-hand differential case.
3. Place long-hub side gear with thrust washer on side pinions. Place right-hand differential case over differential gears, aligning punch marks on both cases. Then install capscrews and tighten to correct torque. Lockwire capscrews.
4. Place right-hand support case thrust washer and differential assembly in right-hand support case. Install spider and pinions. Place high speed clutch plate on idler pinions. *Make certain that chamfered teeth of clutch plate are positioned toward idler pinions.*
5. Mount ring gear, oil collector drum, thrust washer and left-hand support case on right-hand support case. *During assembly of these parts, temporarily place two bolts in mounting holes. This procedure will assure bolt hole alignment as these parts are assembled into final position.* Secure assembly with bolts and locknuts. Temporarily install sliding clutch gear and rotate idler pinions to make sure parts are assembled correctly. Tighten locknuts to correct torque.

Drive Pinion, Fig. 18

1. Press pinion pilot bearing on drive

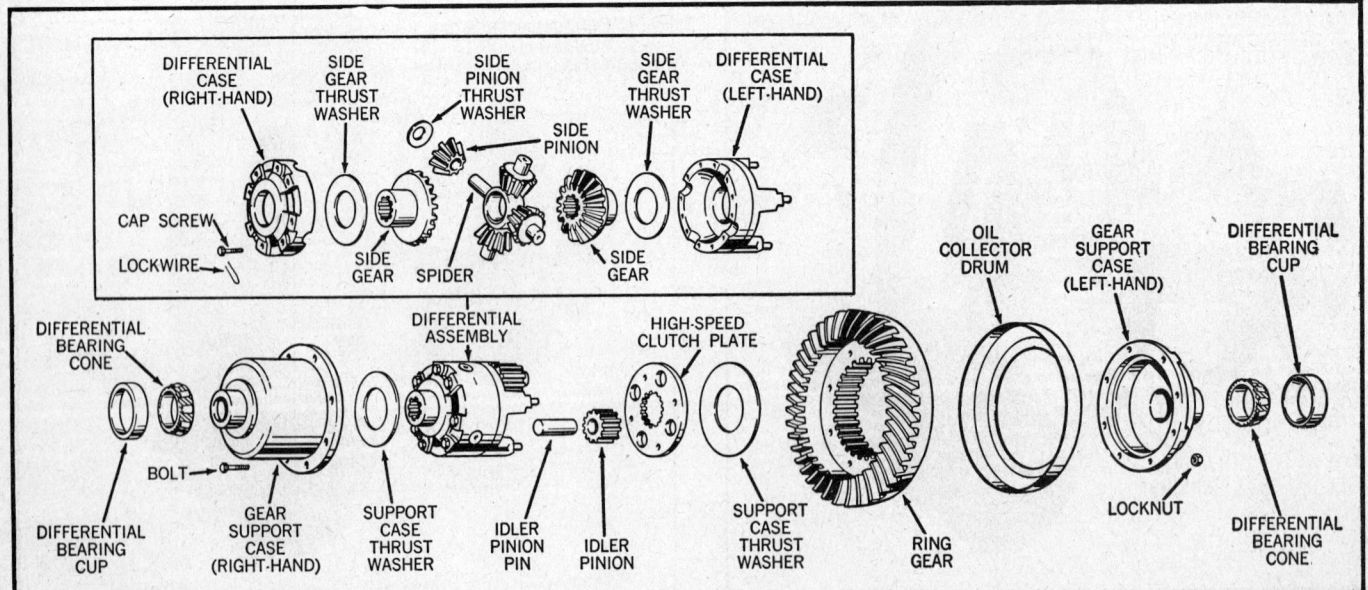

Fig. 17 Disassembled view of differential assembly

EATON DRIVING AXLES

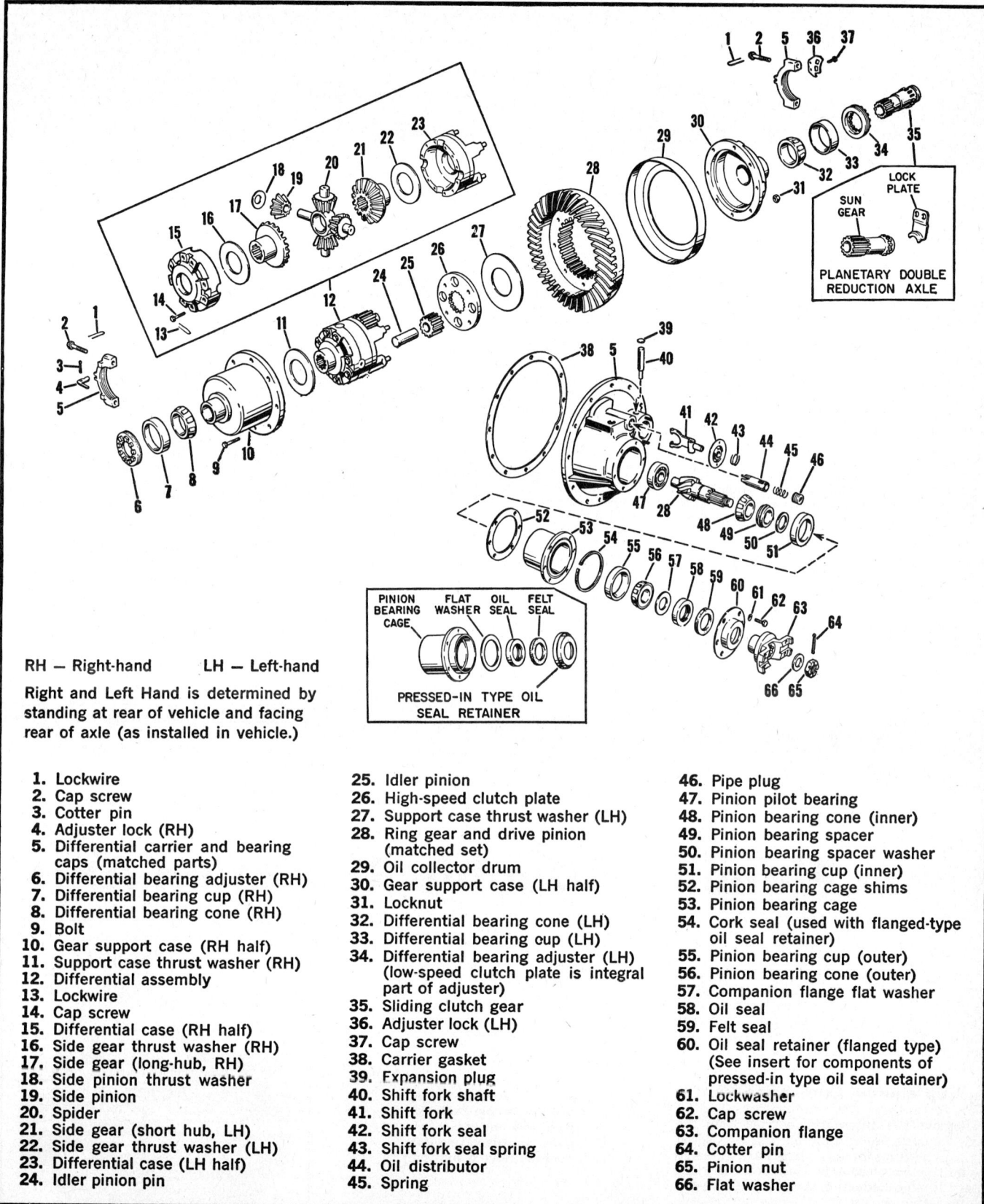

RH — Right-hand   LH — Left-hand

Right and Left Hand is determined by standing at rear of vehicle and facing rear of axle (as installed in vehicle.)

1. Lockwire
2. Cap screw
3. Cotter pin
4. Adjuster lock (RH)
5. Differential carrier and bearing caps (matched parts)
6. Differential bearing adjuster (RH)
7. Differential bearing cup (RH)
8. Differential bearing cone (RH)
9. Bolt
10. Gear support case (RH half)
11. Support case thrust washer (RH)
12. Differential assembly
13. Lockwire
14. Cap screw
15. Differential case (RH half)
16. Side gear thrust washer (RH)
17. Side gear (long-hub, RH)
18. Side pinion thrust washer
19. Side pinion
20. Spider
21. Side gear (short hub, LH)
22. Side gear thrust washer (LH)
23. Differential case (LH half)
24. Idler pinion pin
25. Idler pinion
26. High-speed clutch plate
27. Support case thrust washer (LH)
28. Ring gear and drive pinion (matched set)
29. Oil collector drum
30. Gear support case (LH half)
31. Locknut
32. Differential bearing cone (LH)
33. Differential bearing cup (LH)
34. Differential bearing adjuster (LH) (low-speed clutch plate is integral part of adjuster)
35. Sliding clutch gear
36. Adjuster lock (LH)
37. Cap screw
38. Carrier gasket
39. Expansion plug
40. Shift fork shaft
41. Shift fork
42. Shift fork seal
43. Shift fork seal spring
44. Oil distributor
45. Spring
46. Pipe plug
47. Pinion pilot bearing
48. Pinion bearing cone (inner)
49. Pinion bearing spacer
50. Pinion bearing spacer washer
51. Pinion bearing cup (inner)
52. Pinion bearing cage shims
53. Pinion bearing cage
54. Cork seal (used with flanged-type oil seal retainer)
55. Pinion bearing cup (outer)
56. Pinion bearing cone (outer)
57. Companion flange flat washer
58. Oil seal
59. Felt seal
60. Oil seal retainer (flanged type) (See insert for components of pressed-in type oil seal retainer)
61. Lockwasher
62. Cap screw
63. Companion flange
64. Cotter pin
65. Pinion nut
66. Flat washer

Fig. 16 Disassembled view of differential carrier for Two Speed Axle

213

EATON DRIVING AXLES

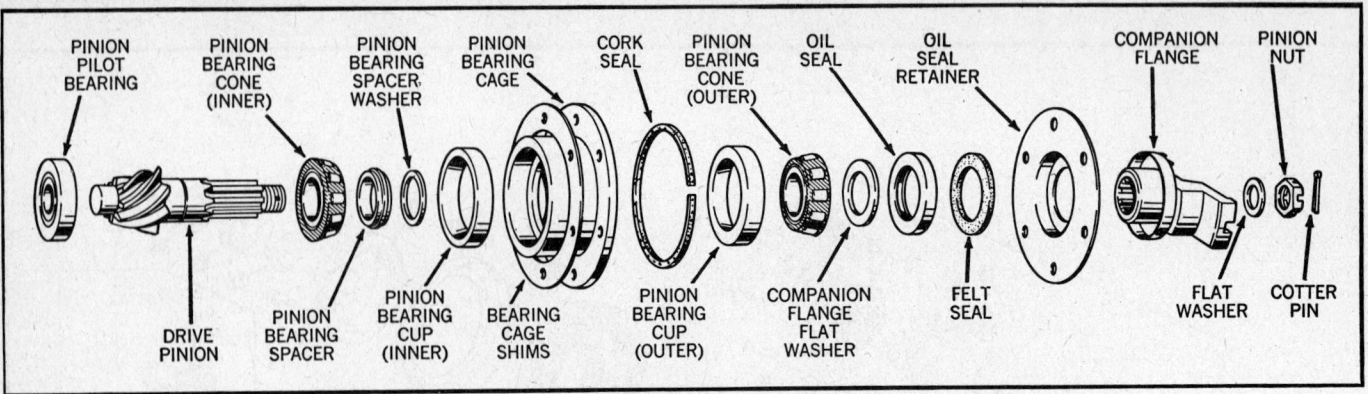

Fig. 18 Disassembled view of drive pinion. Companion flange flat washers and pinion bearing spacer washers are not used on all axles

pinion, then stake in place as shown in Fig. 12.
2. Press inner bearing cone on drive pinion.
3. If removed, press bearing cups in bearing cage.
4. Install new felt seal and oil seal in retainer.
5. Lubricate drive pinion bearings. Place pinion bearing spacer, spacer washer (if used), bearing cage and outer bearing cone on drive pinion. *Do not install oil seal retainer until pinion bearing adjustment is completed.*
6. Temporarily assemble companion flange as follows: Place flange flat washer (if used) on drive pinion. Press flange on pinion and install flat washer and pinion nut, tightening nut to correct torque. *Rotate bearing cage while tightening pinion nut.* Check pinion bearing preload adjustment as outlined previously.
7. To install oil seal retainer assembly (after drive pinion bearings are correctly adjusted) remove nut, flat washer and companion flange. Install oil seal retainer assembly (*pressed-in type mounts in recess of bearing cage with flat washer positioned between cage recess and oil seal retainer. Flanged-type is attached with same capscrews that fasten bearing cage*). Install companion flange, flat washer and nut, tightening nut to correct torque.

Differential Carrier

1. Using same quantity and size of shims that were removed during disassembly on pinion bearing cage flange, install drive pinion assembly in carrier. Install bearing cage capscrews and lockwashers, tightening capscrews to correct torque. Lubricate differential bearings during reassembly.
2. Place differential assembly in carrier and install differential bearing cups. Install assembled left-hand differential bearing cap, adjuster and lock. Install right-hand differential bearing cap and adjuster. Install and finger tighten differential bearing capscrews. Tighten right-hand bearing adjuster to seat differential bearings. Adjust ring gear and drive pinion as outlined previously.
3. With ring gear and drive pinion correctly adjusted, tighten differential bearing cap screws to correct torque. Then install cotter pins to secure locks and lockwire capscrews.
4. Install sliding clutch gear.
5. Install and engage shift fork with sliding clutch gear. Install shift fork shaft and expansion plugs.
6. Place seal on shift fork with bottom hole (stamped on seal) over lower stud. Install spring on seal.
7. Install oil distributor, spring and pipe plug in carrier.

Install Carrier In Housing

1. Using a new gasket, install differential carrier in axle housing. Install and tighten capscrews to correct torque. Install axle shafts and connect propeller shaft. Fill housing with correct lubricant.
2. Install electric shift unit or air-torsion spring unit on carrier, engaging swivel with slot in shift fork shaft. Install mounting nuts and washers. For electric shift, connect electric wires. For air-torsion spring shift, connect air line to unit.

Eaton Planetary Double Reduction Axles

This axle assembly, Fig. 19, is designed to provide a compact unit with heavy-duty load capacity. This is accomplished by incorporating a rugged ring gear and drive pinion set and a durable planetary unit in a single axle housing.

Differential Carrier Service

Remove the differential carrier from the axle housing as outlined for the two speed axle. Procedures for disassembly are the same as for the two speed axle. However, the Planetary Double Reduction Axle does not use a shift mechanism.

A sun gear is used in place of the sliding clutch gear. To remove the sun gear, remove the retainer which holds the sun gear in position, then remove sun gear.

Fig. 19 Power flow through Planetary Double Reduction Axle. This unit is similar to the two speed unit but it does not have a shift unit

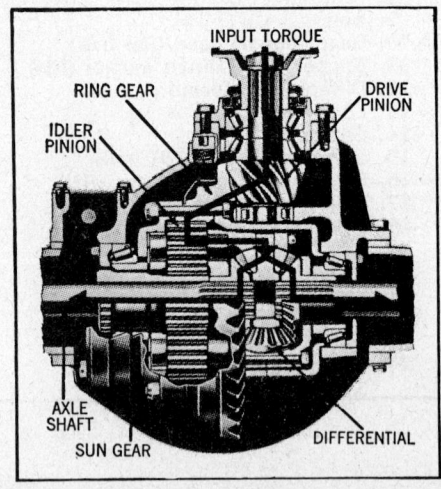

EATON DRIVING AXLES

Eaton "D" Series Tandem Drive Axles

The Series "D" driving unit consists of two axles coupled by a power divider. Three different combinations are available:
1. A single reduction forward axle with power divider, and a single reduction rearward axle.
2. A two-speed forward axle with power divider, and a two-speed rearward axle.
3. A planetary double reduction forward axle with power divider, and a planetary double reduction rearward axle.

Disassemble

It is recommended, but not necessary, that the axle housing cover be removed to replace the differential carrier and power divider assembly.
1. Drain lubricant, disconnect propeller shafts at companion flanges and remove axle shafts.
2. Remove companion flange from output shaft.
3. Remove axle housing cover and discard gasket.
4. To disassemble axle housing cover, remove oil seal from output shaft opening, using a suitable puller. Remove snap ring from output shaft opening, then press rear bearing from axle housing cover. *Rear bearing sleeve is mounted on output shaft.*
5. Disconnect lockout shift lever connections.
6. If axle is "Two-Speed", remove shift units, referring to "Two-Speed Axle" Section.
7. After removing stud nuts and lockwashers, lift and pull differential carrier and power divider out of axle housing.

Carrier & Power Divider, Figs. 20, 21, 22

1. If preliminary inspection reveals that ring gear and drive pinion are satisfactory, check backlash and tooth contact pattern for easier adjustment in reassembly.
2. Remove carrier cover from carrier.
3. Lift inter-axle differential off output shaft side gear.
4. Before disassembling inter-axle differential, punch mark cases for correct position during reassembly. Cut lockwire and remove nuts and bolts. Separate cases and remove thrust washers, side pinions, bushings and spider.

Output Shaft

1. Drive output shaft from differential carrier, driving at companion flange end of shaft.
2. To disassemble output shaft, remove snap ring, then lift off side gear assembly. Discard output shaft "O" rings. If replacement is necessary, remove bushing from bore of output shaft.
3. To remove output shaft front bearing from side gear, place side gear assembly in press with split-type puller plates under front bearing, then press side gear out of front bearing.

Input Shaft

1. Remove snap ring from input shaft, then lift off helical side gear, thrust washer and "D" washer. If replacement is necessary, press bushings from bore of side gear.
2. Remove companion flange from input shaft.
3. Remove input shaft bearing cover and shims. *Note size and quantity of shims for easier adjustment during reassembly.* Remove oil seal and felt seal from bearing cover.
4. Drive input shaft out of differential carrier cover.
5. To remove bearing from input shaft, place assembly in a press with threaded end of input shaft upward. Then press input shaft out of bearing.

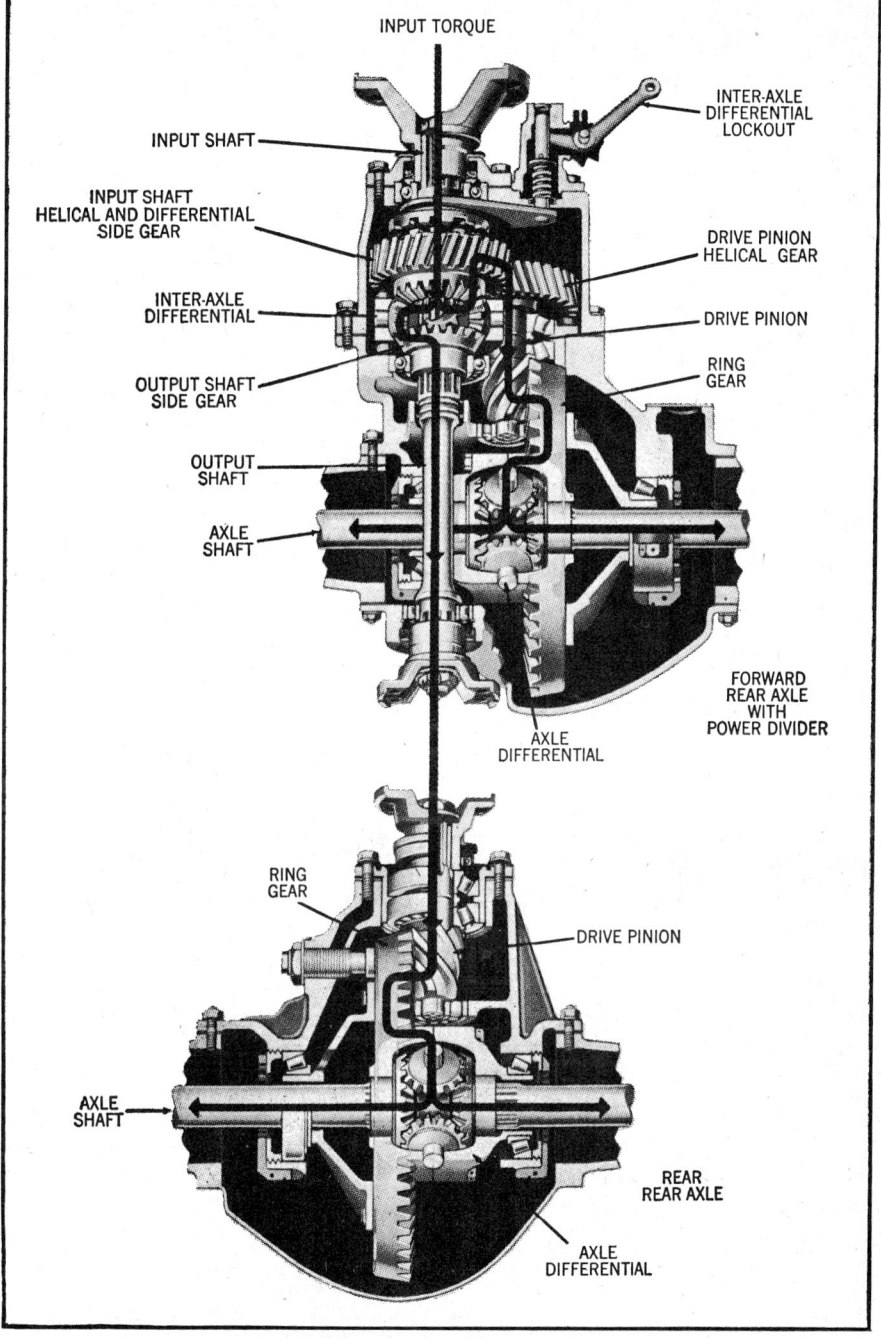

Fig. 20 Power flow through Single Reduction "D" Series Tandem Drive Axle

EATON DRIVING AXLES

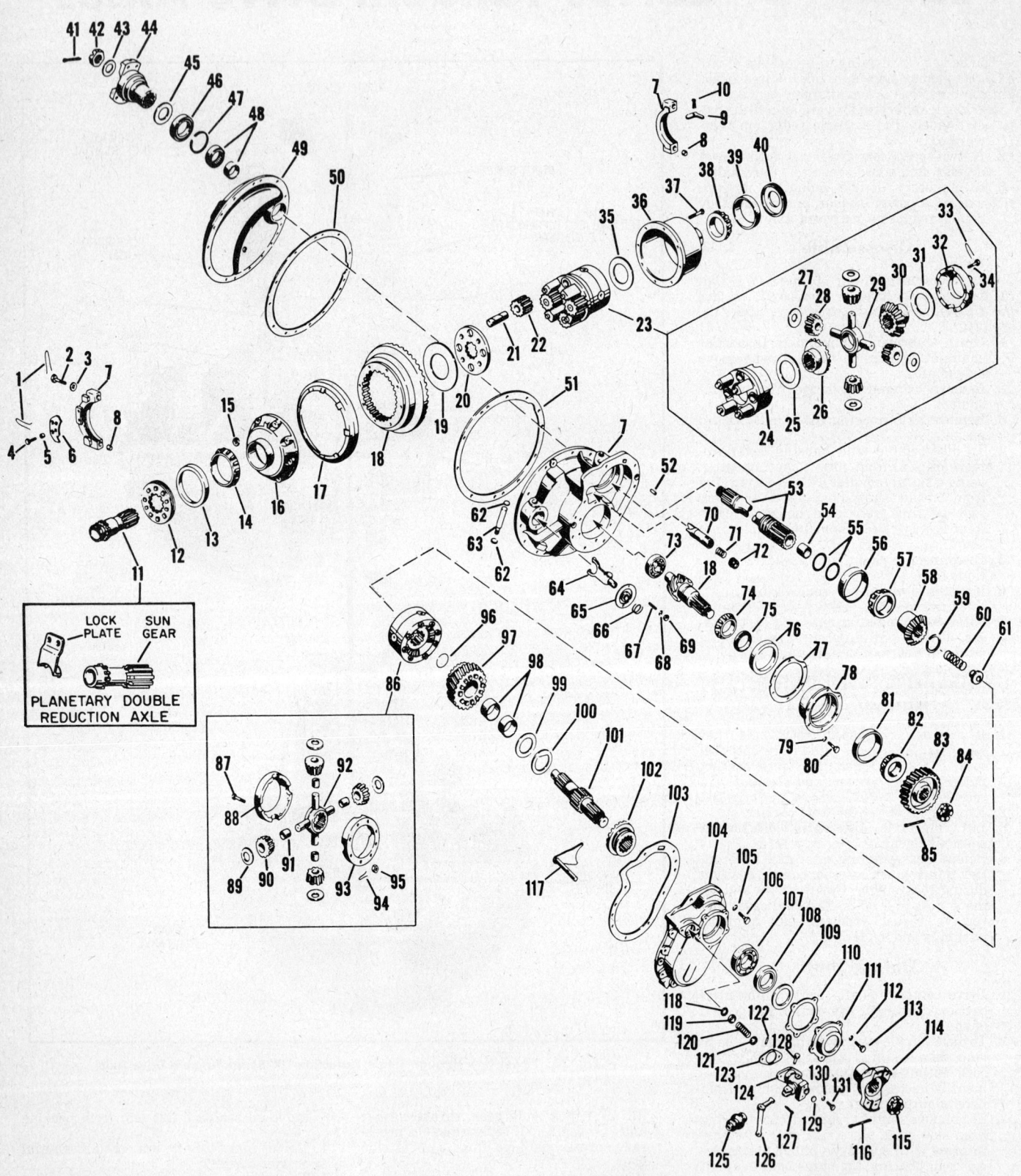

Fig. 21 Disassembled view of forward rear axle for Two-Speed and Planetary Double Reduction "D" Series Tandem Drive Axles

EATON DRIVING AXLES

Forward Rear Axle for 2-Speed and Planetary Double Reduction "D" Series Tandem Drive Axles

RH — Right-hand   LH — Left-hand

Right and Left Hand is determined by standing at rear of vehicle and facing rear of axle (as installed in vehicle)

1. Lockwire
2. Cap screw
3. Flat washer
4. Cap screw
5. Dowel bushing
6. Adjuster lock (RH)
7. Differential carrier and bearing caps (matched parts)
8. Dowel bushing
9. Adjuster lock (LH)
10. Cotter pin
11. Sliding clutch gear
12. Differential bearing adjuster (RH) (low speed clutch plate is integral part of adjuster)
13. Differential bearing cup (RH)
14. Differential bearing cone (RH)
15. Locknut
16. Gear support case (RH half)
17. Oil collector drum
18. Ring gear and drive pinion (matched set)
19. Support case thrust washer (RH)
20. High speed clutch plate
21. Idler pinion pins
22. Idler pinions
23. Differential asembly
24. Differential case (RH half)
25. Side gear thrust washer (RH)
26. Side gear (short hub, RH)
27. Side pinion thrust washer
28. Side pinion
29. Spider
30. Side gear (long hub, LH)
31. Side gear thrust washer (LH)
32. Differential case (LH half)
33. Lockwire
34. Cap screw
35. Support case thrust washer (LH)
36. Gear support case (LH half)
37. Bolt
38. Differential bearing cone (LH)
39. Differential bearing cup (LH)
40. Differential bearing adjuster (LH)
41. Cotter pin
42. Output shaft nut
43. Flat washer
44. Output companion flange
45. Rear bearing retainer washer
46. Oil seal
47. Rear bearing snap ring
48. Output shaft rear bearing and sleeve (matched parts)
49. Axle housing cover
50. Cover gasket
51. Carrier gasket
52. Dowel pins
53. Output shaft
54. Output shaft bushing
55. Output shaft "O" rings
56. Output shaft front bearing cup
57. Output shaft front bearing cone
58. Output shaft side gear
59. Output shaft snap ring
60. Output shaft holdout spring
61. Output shaft holdout thrust washer
62. Expansion plug
63. Shift fork shaft
64. Shift fork
65. Shift fork seal
66. Seal spring
67. Stud
68. Lockwasher
69. Stud nut
70. Oil distributor
71. Spring
72. Pipe plug
73. Pinion pilot bearing
74. Pinion bearing cone (inner)
75. Pinion bearing spacer
76. Pinion bearing cup (inner)
77. Pinion bearing cage shims
78. Pinion bearing cage
79. Lockwasher
80. Cap screw
81. Pinion bearing cup (outer)
82. Pinion bearing cone (outer)
83. Pinion helical gear
84. Pinion nut
85. Cotter pin
86. Inter-axle differential assembly
87. Bolt
88. Inter-axle differential case (female half)
89. Side pinion thrust washer
90. Side pinion
91. Side pinion bushing
92. Spider
93. Inter-axle differential case (male half)
94. Lockwire
95. Nut
96. Input shaft snap ring
97. Helical and differential side gear
98. Helical and differential side gear bushings
99. Helical and differential side gear thrust washer
100. Helical and differential side gear "D" washer
101. Input shaft
102. Input shaft sliding clutch
103. Differential carrier cover gasket
104. Differential carrier cover
105. Lockwasher
106. Cap screw
107. Input shaft bearing
108. Oil seal
109. Felt seal
110. Bearing cover shims
111. Bearing cover
112. Lockwasher
113. Cap screw
114. Input companion flange
115. Input shaft nut
116. Cotter pin
117. Shift fork and push rod
118. Felt seal
119. Seal retainer
120. Compression spring
121. Retainer washer
122. Retainer washer pin
123. Shift lever bracket gasket
124. Shift lever bracket
125. Shift lever boot
126. Shift lever
127. Cotter pin
128. Clevis pin
129. Expansion plug
130. Lockwasher
131. Cap screw

EATON DRIVING AXLES

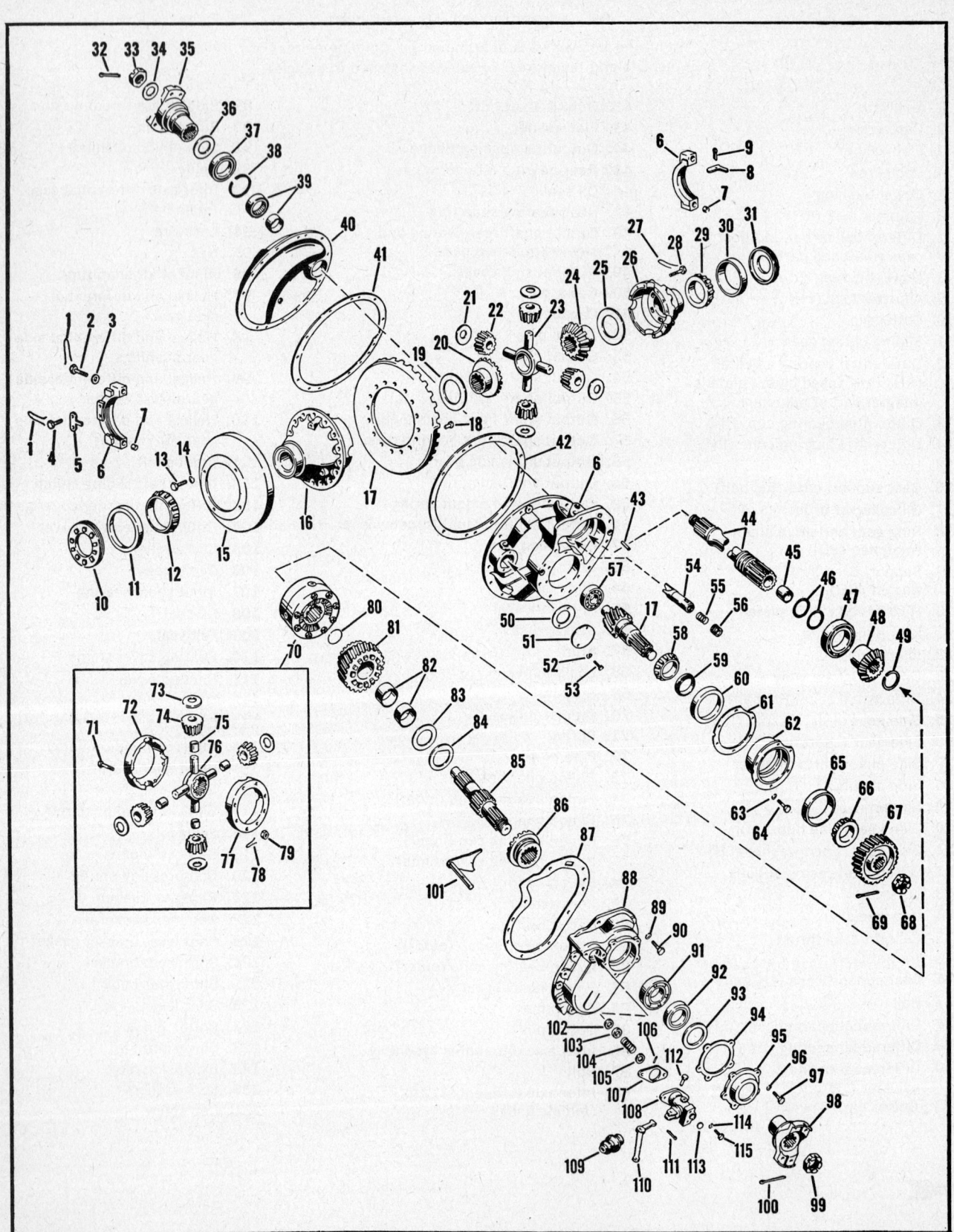

Fig. 22 Disassembled view of forward rear axle for Single Reduction "D" Series Tandem Drive Axle

EATON DRIVING AXLES

RH — Right-hand   LH — Left-hand
Right and Left Hand is determined by standing at rear of vehicle and facing rear of axle (as installed in vehicle)

1. Lockwire
2. Cap screw
3. Flat washer
4. Cap screw
5. Adjuster lock (RH)
6. Differential carrier and bearing caps (matched parts)
7. Dowel bushing
8. Adjuster lock (LH)
9. Cotter pin
10. Differential bearing adjuster
11. Differential bearing cup (RH)
12. Differential bearing cone (RH)
13. Cap screw
14. Lockwasher
15. Oil collector drum
16. Differential case (RH half)
17. Ring gear and drive pinion (matched set)
18. Rivet
19. Side gear thrust washer (RH)
20. Side gear (RH)
21. Side pinion thrust washer
22. Side pinion
23. Spider
24. Side gear (LH)
25. Side gear thrust washer (LH)
26. Differential case (LH half)
27. Lockwire
28. Cap screw
29. Differential bearing cone (LH)
30. Differential bearing cup (LH)
31. Differential bearing adjuster (LH)
32. Cotter pin
33. Output shaft nut
34. Flat washer
35. Output companion flange
36. Rear bearing retainer washer
37. Oil seal
38. Rear bearing snap ring
39. Output shaft rear bearing and sleeve (matched parts)
40. Axle housing cover
41. Cover gasket
42. Carrier gasket
43. Dowel pins
44. Output shaft
45. Output shaft bushing
46. Output shaft "O" rings
47. Output shaft front bearing
48. Output shaft side gear
49. Output shaft snap ring
50. Hole cover gasket
51. Hole cover
52. Lockwasher
53. Cap screw
54. Oil distributor
55. Spring
56. Pipe plug
57. Pinion pilot bearing
58. Pinion bearing cone (inner)
59. Pinion bearing spacer
60. Pinion bearing cup (inner)
61. Pinion bearing cage shims
62. Pinion bearing cage
63. Lockwasher
64. Cap screw
65. Pinion bearing cup (outer)
66. Pinion bearing cone (outer)
67. Pinion helical gear
68. Pinion nut
69. Cotter pin
70. Inter-axle differential assembly
71. Bolt
72. Inter-axle differential case (female half)
73. Side pinion thrust washer
74. Side pinion
75. Side pinion bushing
76. Spider
77. Inter-axle differential case (male half)
78. Lockwire
79. Nut
80. Input shaft snap ring
81. Helical and differential side gear
82. Helical and differential side gear bushings
83. Helical and differential side gear thrust washer
84. Helical and differential side gear "D" washer
85. Input shaft
86. Input shaft sliding clutch
87. Differential carrier cover gasket
88. Differential carrier cover
89. Lockwasher
90. Cap screw
91. Input shaft bearing
92. Oil seal
93. Felt seal
94. Bearing cover shims
95. Bearing cover
96. Lockwasher
97. Cap screw
98. Input companion flange
99. Input shaft nut
100. Cotter pin
101. Shift fork and push rod
102. Felt seal
103. Seal retainer
104. Compression spring
105. Retainer washer
106. Retainer washer pin
107. Shift lever bracket gasket
108. Shift lever bracket
109. Shift lever boot
110. Shift lever
111. Cotter pin
112. Clevis pin
113. Expansion plug
114. Lockwasher
115. Cap screw

EATON DRIVING AXLES

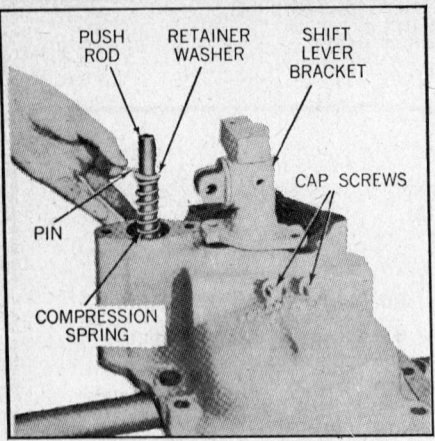

Fig. 23 Vacuum-operated lockout details

Lockout Mechanism (Vacuum Type)

Either vacuum-operated or air-operated lockout may be used on "D" Series Axles. The air-operated type is covered further on. The following instructions are for the vacuum-operated lockout.

1. Pull boot off lockout shift lever. Remove clevis pin and remove shift lever.
2. Referring to Fig. 23, remove shift lever bracket. Compress compression spring, then remove pin, retainer washer and compression spring from shift fork and push rod.
3. Lift input shaft sliding clutch and shift fork and push rod assembly from differential carrier cover.

Final Disassembly

1. Before removing differential assembly, remove cotter pin and loosen drive pinion helical gear nut.
2. Be sure to remove pipe plug, spring and oil distributor from differential carrier before attempting to remove differential assembly. *Refer to separate sections of this chapter for instructions covering the three types of axles used with the "D" Series combination.*
3. Removing and disassembling the drive pinion is covered in the separate sections of this chapter for the three axle types used, with the following variations:
   a. The drive pinions for the individual axles are equipped with companion flanges. For this type installation, the pinion bearing cage capscrews are accessible to permit removal of pinion with flange assembled.
   b. The drive pinion for "D" Series Tandem Axles are equipped with a helical gear, Fig. 24, which must be removed to gain access to pinion bearing cage capscrews. Therefore, to remove drive pinion, remove nut previously loosened before differential removal.
   c. Mount bearing puller on helical gear, gripping gear with puller legs and placing puller screw against pinion. Then pull gear off pinion. Remove capscrews from bearing cage and then remove drive pinion assembly.

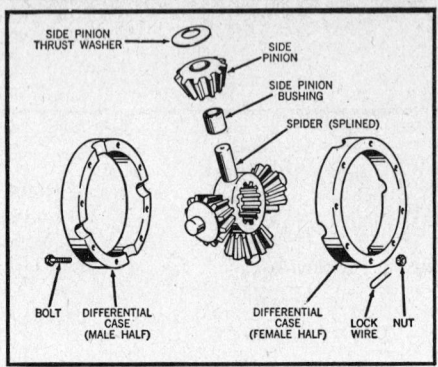

Fig. 26 Disassembled view of inter-axle differential

REASSEMBLE
Drive Pinion

Refer to separate sections of this chapter for instructions covering the three types of axles except for the following variation:

The drive pinions for the standard axle units are equipped with companion flanges. The pinion bearing cage capscrews are accessible to permit installation of pinion with companion flange installed.

The drive pinion for the "D" Series Tandem Axle units are equipped with a helical gear, Fig. 24, and the bearing cage capscrews cannot be installed with the helical gear attached to the drive pinion. Install the pinion in these

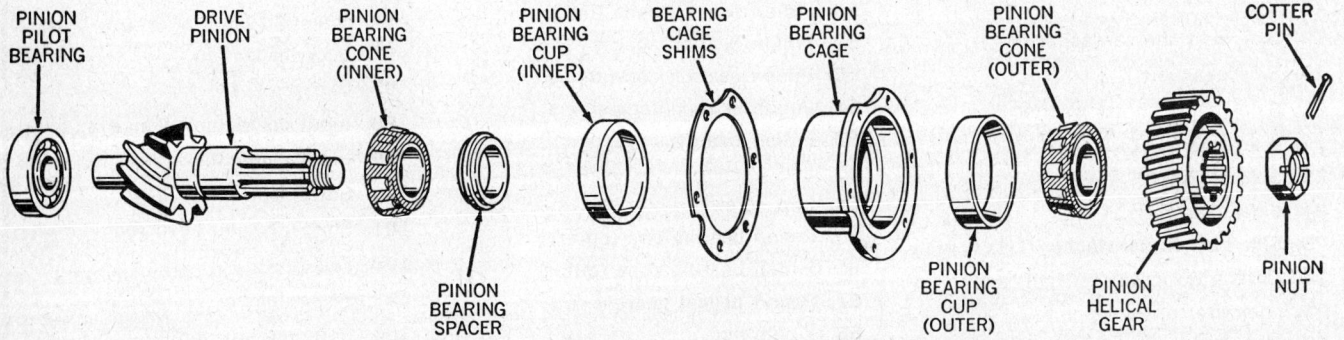

Fig. 24 Disassembled view of "D" Series drive pinion

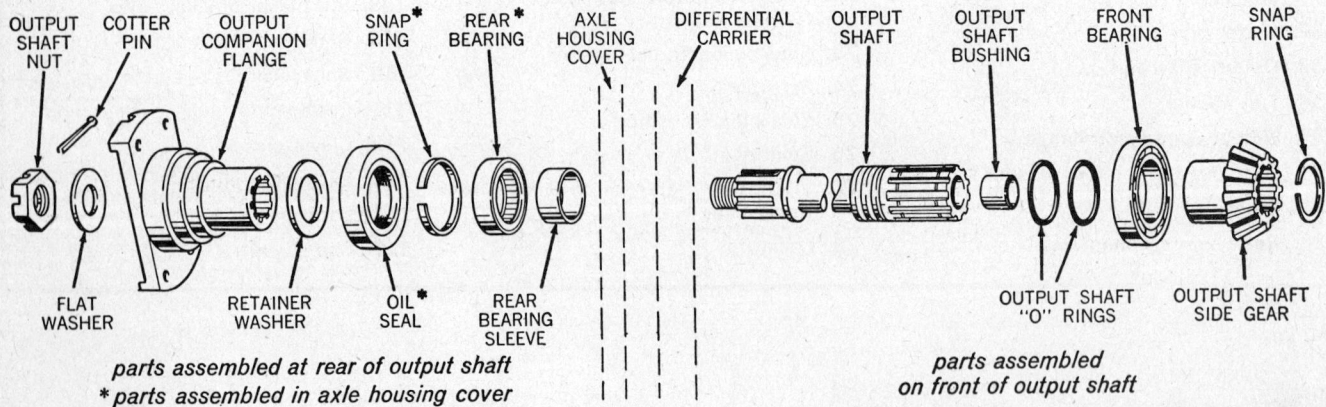

Fig. 25 Disassembled view of output shaft and axle housing cover parts

EATON DRIVING AXLES

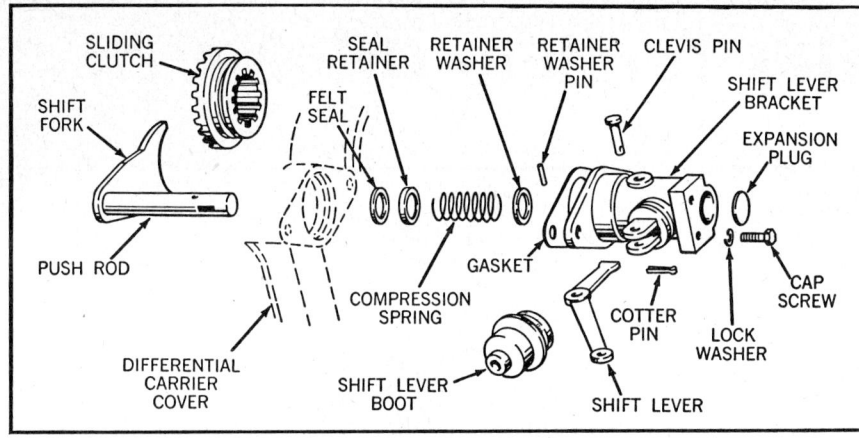

Fig. 27 Disassembled view of vacuum-operated lockout mechanism

axles with the helical gear removed. After pinion is installed, place helical gear on pinion. Install and tighten pinion nut to correct torque, then install cotter pin.

With drive pinion and differential assembled in differential carrier and correctly adjusted, install power divider components as follows:

Output Shaft

1. If removed, press bushing in bore of output shaft.
2. Press front bearing on output shaft side gear. Place side gear assembly on output shaft and install snap ring.
3. Install two "O" rings in grooves of output shaft.
4. Lubricate output shaft "O" rings, front bearing and bushing, then install output shaft assembly in differential carrier by tapping front bearing into bearing bore of carrier.

Inter-Axle Differential, Fig. 26

1. Install bushings, side pinions and thrust washers on journals of differential spider. Lubricate all parts during reassembly.
2. Place spider assembly in male differential case. Install female case, aligning punch marks made during disassembly, and secure with bolts and nuts. Tighten nuts to correct torque and install lockwire.
3. Place inter-axle differential on output shaft side gear. Position differential with nuts away from output shaft side gear.

Lockout Mechanism (Vacuum Type), Fig. 27

Instructions for the air-operated type lockout is covered further on.

1. Install felt seal and seal retainer in recess in carrier cover. Engage lockout shift fork with groove in input shaft sliding clutch. Place this assembly in differential carrier cover.
2. Place compression spring and retainer washer on push rod, depress spring and install retainer washer pin. Coat spring and retainer washer with grease.
3. Install new gasket and shift lever bracket on differential carrier cover and install capscrews and lockwashers. Tighten screws to correct torque. If removed, install grease fitting in bracket.
4. Place lockout shift lever in bracket, engaging slot in push rod. Install clevis pin and cotter pin.
5. Place boot over shift lever and secure boot to bracket.

Input Shaft, Fig. 28

1. Press bearing on threaded end of input shaft.
2. Place input shaft assembly in differential carrier cover, engaging sliding clutch.
3. Install felt seal and oil seal in input shaft bearing cover. Using same size and quantity of shims removed during disassembly, install shims and bearing cover on carrier cover. Install capscrews finger tight, with lockwashers. *To check bearing adjustment or determine thickness of shims required, install bearing cover on carrier cover without shims. Install and tighten capscrews finger tight. Then, using a feeler gauge, measure clearance between bearing cover and carrier cover. This clearance measurement plus .003" would equal the thickness of shims required for correct bearing clearance.*
4. Install input companion flange and nut on input shaft. Tighten nut to correct torque and install cotter pin. Tighten input shaft bearing cover capscrews to correct torque.
5. If removed, press two bushings in bore of helical side gear. Place "D" washer, thrust washer and helical side gear assembly on input shaft. Install snap ring on input shaft to secure these parts.

Differential Carrier Cover

1. Place new cover gasket on differential carrier.
2. Place carrier cover on differential carrier, aligning dowel pins with holes in cover. *During reassembly of cover to carrier, slowly rotate input shaft to engage its splines with splines in bore of inter-axle differential spider.*
3. Carefully install two cover capscrews, watching for possible binding between cover and carrier. If cover assembles to carrier without bind, install remaining capscrews and tighten to correct torque.
4. After cover is assembled to carrier, check operation of inter-axle differential. Hold output shaft stationary and rotate input shaft companion flange. If the assembly differentiates, the unit is correctly assembled.

Carrier & Power Divider

1. Place new gasket on carrier. Install carrier and power divider assembly into axle housing. Install and tighten stud nuts to correct torque.
2. Assemble axle housing cover, Fig. 25, as follows: Press output shaft rear bearing in cover. Install snap ring to secure bearing. Press oil seal in same opening in axle housing cover.
3. Place new gasket on axle housing and install axle housing cover, taking care not to damage oil seal. Install stud nuts and lockwashers and tighten nuts to correct torque.
4. Install rear bearing sleeve in output shaft. Install retainer washer, output companion flange, flat washer and nut. Tighten nut to correct torque and install cotter pin.
5. Install axle shafts and fill axle with correct lubricant. Connect propeller shafts. On Two-Speed Axles, install shift units. Make lockout shift lever connections.

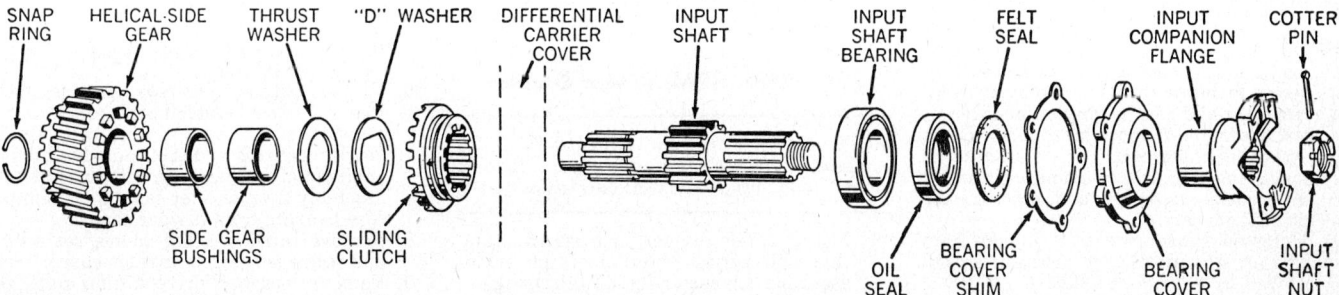

Fig. 28 Disassembled view of input shaft

EATON DRIVING AXLES

Eaton "M" Series Tandem Drive Axles

MODELS 22M, 28M, 32M, 36M

This series of axles consist of two axle units coupled by a single propeller shaft and a power divider unit. The forward rear axle on Models 22M, 28M, 32M and 36M are single reduction units combined with a power divider. The rearward rear axle is also a single reduction unit similar to the standard Eaton Single Reduction Axle, Fig. 29.

Model 42M consists of three units: Two knee-mounted double reduction axle units and a power divider. The power divider is mounted on the forward rear axle. An inter-axle propeller shaft connects the rearward rear axle to the power divider.

NOTE: *Inasmuch as the rearward rear axle is similar to the standard Eaton Single Reduction Axle, refer to that section of this chapter for service procedures. The following material covers the procedures on the forward rear axle.*

DISASSEMBLE
Carrier & Power Divider

1. Drain lubricant. Disconnect propeller shafts and remove axle shafts.
2. Disconnect lockout shift lever.
3. Unfasten and remove differential carrier and tower divider assembly from axle housing.
4. If preliminary inspection reveals that ring gear and drive pinion are satisfactory, check backlash with dial indicator and take a tooth contact pattern for reference and easier adjustment in reassembly.
5. Remove pinion bearing cage cover. Remove and discard cork seal. Hold input and output companion flanges and loosen (but do not remove) pinion nut.
6. Hold input companion flange and loosen (but do not remove) flange nut.
7. Hold output companion flange and loosen (but do not remove) flange nut.
8. Punch mark differential bearing caps and carrier for correct location in reassembly. Also punch mark differential bearing adjusters for correct location of adjuster locks, Fig. 30.
9. Cut lockwires and remove differential bearing cap screws, caps, adjusters, locks and bearing cups from both sides of differential.
10. On Models 22M, 28M and 36M, remove differential assembly from carrier.
11. On Model 32M, straighten ear of lock and loosen nut. Loosen thrust block adjusting screw to move thrust block away from ring gear and permit removal of differential assembly. Remove oil collector drum attaching capscrews. Tilt differential to move ring gear away from pinion and lift differential assembly and oil collector drum from carrier.
12. Unfasten and remove power divider from carrier. On Models 22M, 28M and 32M, the differential must be removed from the carrier before removing the power divider. On Model 36M, the power divider may be removed with the differential assembled in the carrier.

36M Power Divider

The 36M power divider is the same as Model 42M axle. Refer to 42M instructions given further on.

22M, 28M, 32M, Power Divider

NOTE: *Reference to "front" indicates the input companion flange side of power divider. "Rear" indicates differential carrier side.*

1. Mount power divider in a repair stand that will permit rotation of the entire assembly for easier handling during reassembly.
2. Remove input flange nut and flange.
3. Loosen (but do not remove) input shaft front bearing cover, Fig. 31.
4. Remove nuts securing power divider case cover to case. Then, using a suitable puller, grip front bearing cover with puller legs and position puller screw against input shaft. Pull bearing cover and case cover assembly from case.
5. Remove loosened output flange nut, flat washer and flange.
6. Remove output shaft rear bearing cover. Remove oil seal and felt seal from bearing cover.
7. Working at rear end of output shaft, drive shaft out of rear bearing. Lift output shaft assembly from divider case, then remove rear bearing from divider case.
8. Remove inner bearing sleeve set screw and lockwasher from divider case.
9. Remove loosened drive pinion nut and tongued washer. Drive pinion assembly out rear of divider case. Remove outer bearing cone from bearing cage.

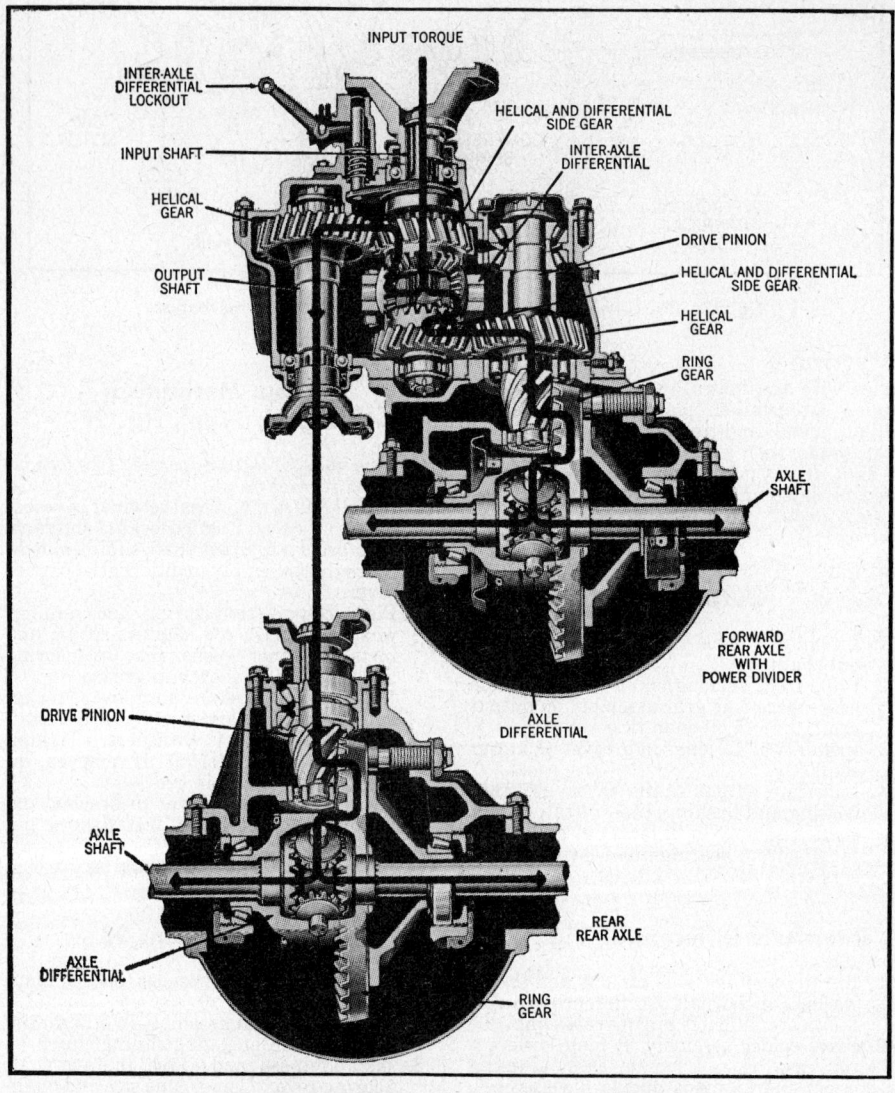

Fig. 29 Power flow through M Series Tandem Drive Axles

EATON DRIVING AXLES

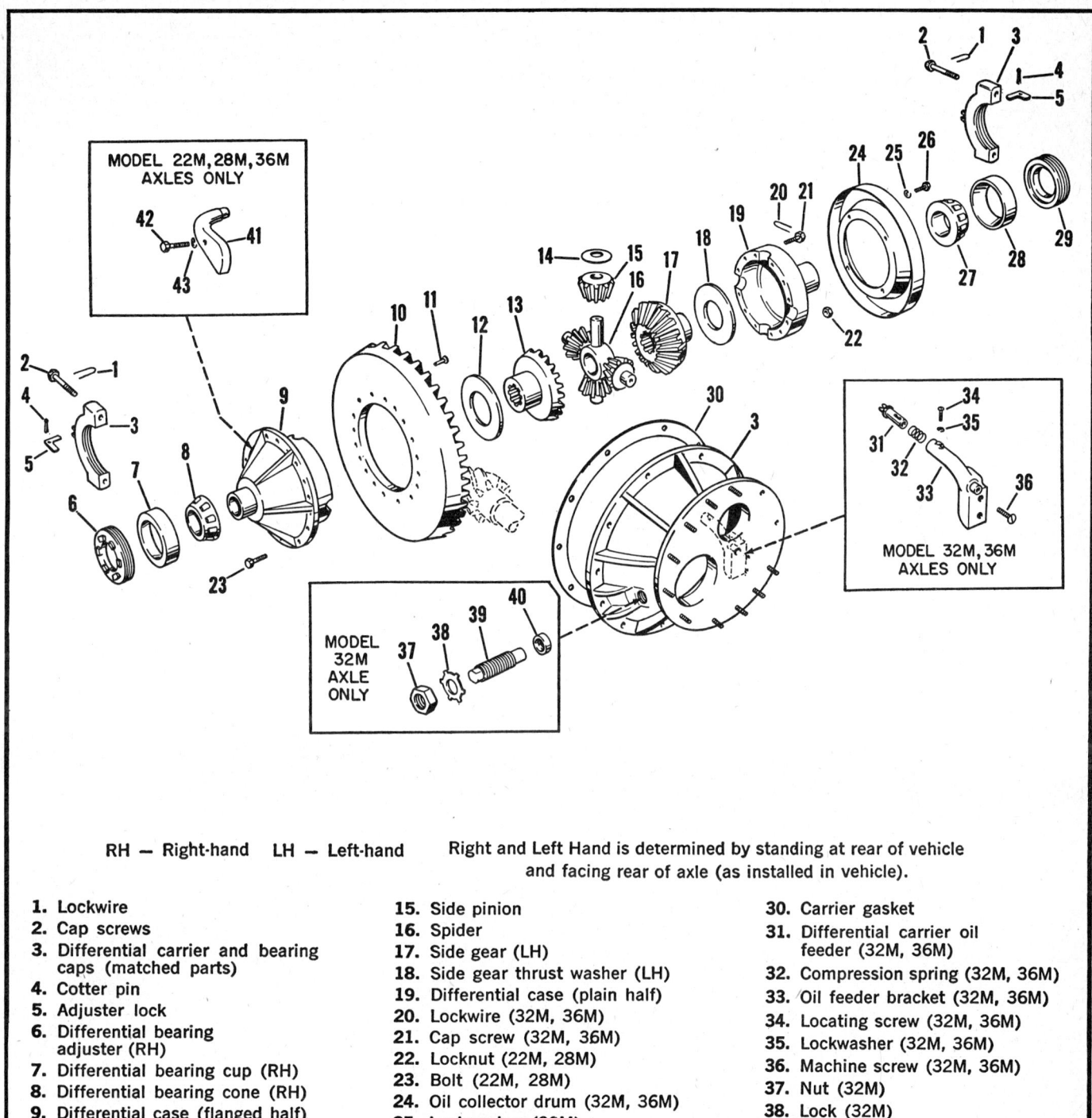

RH — Right-hand   LH — Left-hand   Right and Left Hand is determined by standing at rear of vehicle and facing rear of axle (as installed in vehicle).

1. Lockwire
2. Cap screws
3. Differential carrier and bearing caps (matched parts)
4. Cotter pin
5. Adjuster lock
6. Differential bearing adjuster (RH)
7. Differential bearing cup (RH)
8. Differential bearing cone (RH)
9. Differential case (flanged half)
10. Ring gear and drive pinion (matched set)
11. Ring gear rivet
12. Side gear thrust washer (RH)
13. Side gear (RH)
14. Side pinion thrust washer
15. Side pinion
16. Spider
17. Side gear (LH)
18. Side gear thrust washer (LH)
19. Differential case (plain half)
20. Lockwire (32M, 36M)
21. Cap screw (32M, 36M)
22. Locknut (22M, 28M)
23. Bolt (22M, 28M)
24. Oil collector drum (32M, 36M)
25. Lockwasher (32M)
26. Oil collector drum cap screw (32M)
27. Differential bearing cone (LH)
28. Differential bearing cup (LH)
29. Differential bearing adjuster (LH)
30. Carrier gasket
31. Differential carrier oil feeder (32M, 36M)
32. Compression spring (32M, 36M)
33. Oil feeder bracket (32M, 36M)
34. Locating screw (32M, 36M)
35. Lockwasher (32M, 36M)
36. Machine screw (32M, 36M)
37. Nut (32M)
38. Lock (32M)
39. Adjusting screw (32M)
40. Ring gear thrust block (32M)
41. Differential oil lubricator (22M, 28M, 36M)
42. Cap screw (22M, 28M, 36M)
43. Lockwasher (22M, 28M, 36M)

Fig. 30 Disassembled view of differential carrier for Models 22M, 28M, 36M

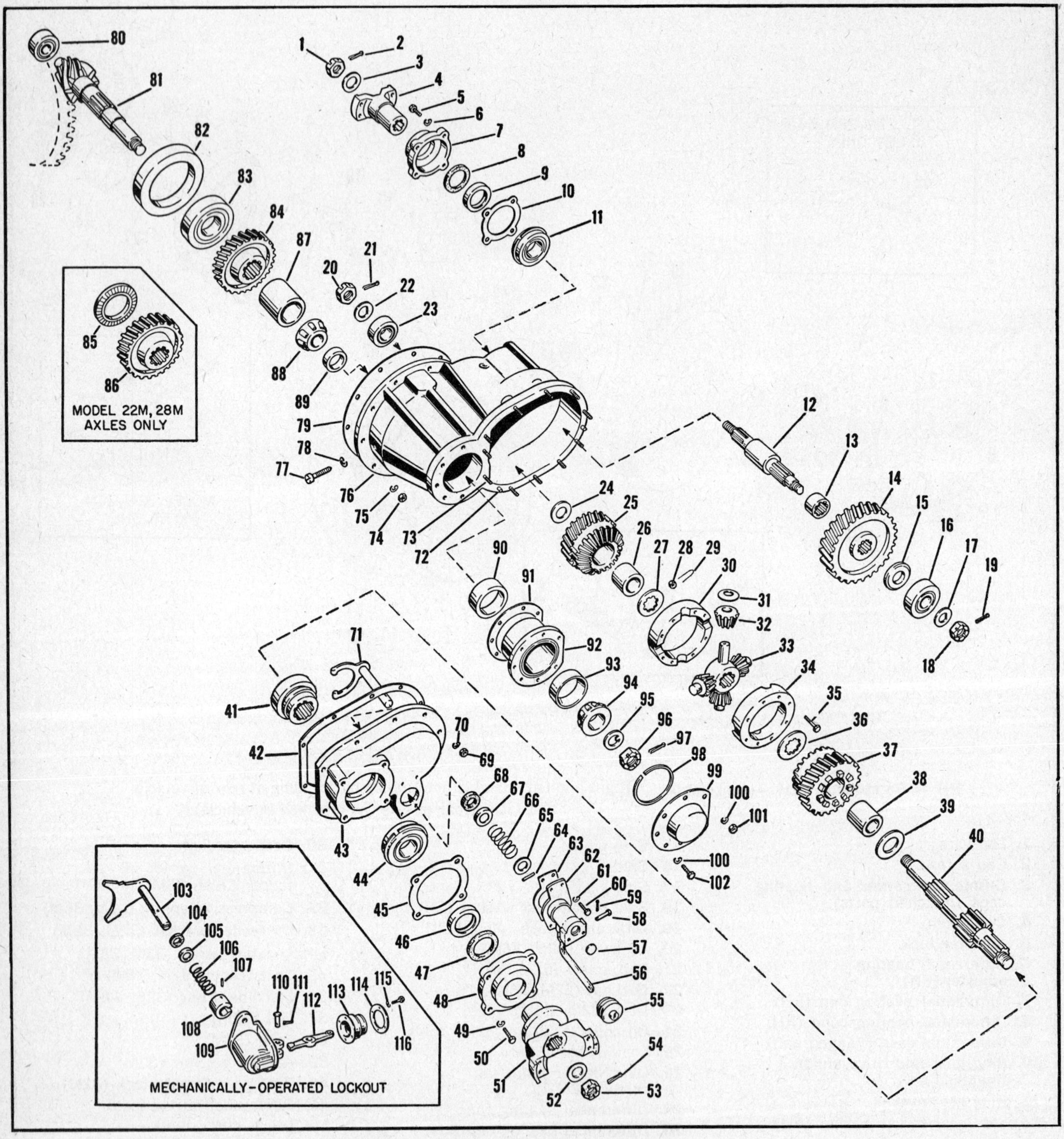

EATON DRIVING AXLES

Fig. 31 Disassembled view of power divider for Models 22M, 28M, 32M

224

EATON DRIVING AXLES

Reference to "FRONT" indicates the input companion flange side of power divider. "REAR" indicates the differential carrier side.

1. Flange nut
2. Cotter pin
3. Flat washer
4. Output companion flange
5. Cap screw
6. Lockwasher
7. Output shaft bearing cover (rear)
8. Felt seal
9. Oil seal
10. Bearing cover gasket
11. Output shaft bearing (rear)
12. Output shaft
13. Helical gear spacer
14. Output shaft helical gear
15. Front bearing spacer washer
16. Output shaft bearing (front)
17. "D" washer (32M)
18. Output shaft nut (front)
19. Cotter pin
20. Input shaft nut (inner)
21. Cotter pin
22. "D" washer
23. Input shaft bearing (rear)
24. Rear bearing spacer washer
25. Helical and differential side gear (rear)
26. Helical and differential side gear bushing (rear, short)
27. Differential spider splined washer (rear)
28. Nut
29. Lockwire
30. Inter-axle differential case (male half, rear)
31. Side pinion thrust washer
32. Side pinion
33. Spider
34. Inter-axle differential case (female half, front)
35. Bolt
36. Differential spider splined washer (front)
37. Helical and differential side gear (front)
38. Helical and differential side gear bushing (front, long)
39. Input shaft spacer washer
40. Input shaft
41. Sliding clutch
42. Power divider case cover gasket
43. Power divider case cover
44. Input shaft bearing (front)
45. Bearing cover gasket
46. Oil seal
47. Felt seal
48. Input shaft bearing cover (front)
49. Lockwasher
50. Cap screw
51. Input companion flange
52. Flat washer
53. Flange nut
54. Cotter pin
55. Shift lever boot
56. Shift lever
57. Expansion plug
58. Shift lever clevis pin
59. Cotter pin
60. Cap screw
61. Lockwasher
62. Shift lever bracket
63. Shift lever bracket gasket
64. Retainer washer pin
65. Retainer washer
66. Compression spring
67. Seal retainer
68. Felt seal
69. Stud nut
70. Lockwasher
71. Shift fork and push rod
72. Dowel pins
73. Stud
74. Stud nut
75. Lockwasher
76. Power divider case
77. Bearing sleeve set screw
78. Lockwasher
79. Power divider case gasket
80. Pinion pilot bearing
81. Drive pinion and ring gear (matched set)
82. Inner bearing sleeve
83. Pinion bearing (inner)
84. Helical gear (32M)
85. Helical gear seal (22M, 28M)
86. Helical gear (22M, 28M)
87. Pinion spacer (long)
88. Pinion bearing cone (inner)
89. Pinion bearing spacer
90. Pinion bearing cup (inner)
91. Shims
92. Pinion bearing cage
93. Pinion bearing cup (outer)
94. Pinion bearing cone (outer)
95. Tongued washer
96. Pinion nut
97. Cotter pin
98. Cork seal
99. Pinion bearing cage cover
100. Lockwasher
101. Stud nut
102. Cap screw

LEGEND FOR INSERT
(Mechanically-Operated Lockout)

103. Shift fork and push rod
104. Felt seal
105. Seal retainer
106. Compression spring
107. Rod bushing pin
108. Rod bushing
109. Shift lever bracket
110. Shift lever clevis pin
111. Cotter pin
112. Shift lever
113. Shift lever boot
114. Boot retainer
115. Lockwasher
116. Cap screw

EATON DRIVING AXLES

10. Remove pinion bearing cage and shims from divider case. *Note quantity and size of shims under cage flange for easier adjustment during reassembly.* If replacement is necessary, remove bearing cups from cage.
11. Remove cotter pin from input shaft inner nut. Temporarily place companion flange on input shaft. Hold flange and remove nut and "D" washer from input shaft.
12. Place divider case in press with front helical gear supported, then press on rear of input shaft until shaft end clears rear bearing. Remove input shaft assembly from divider case, and also rear bearing.
13. To disassemble input shaft, lift rear bearing spacer washer and rear helical side gear off input shaft. Place input shaft in press with splined end down and spacer washer resting on press plate. Then press input shaft out of component parts.
14. To disassemble inter-axle differential, punch mark differential cases for location on reassembly. Cut lockwire and remove nuts and bolts holding cases together. Separate cases, then remove spider, side pinions and thrust washers.
15. To disassemble drive pinion, remove sleeve from inner bearing. Place drive pinion in arbor press with teeth down and disassemble in two steps as follows: (a) Place press support plates under helical gear; then press pinion out of bearing spacer, inner bearing cone, long pinion spacer and helical gear. (b) Place bearing puller plates between pinion teeth and inner race of inner bearing and press pinion out of inner bearing. Remove pilot bearing from pinion, using press or suitable puller.
16. To disassemble output shaft, remove cotter pin from output shaft front nut. Temporarily install companion flange on rear end of output shaft. Hold flange and loosen output shaft front nut. Remove nut and "D" washer ("D" washer used on 32M only). Place output shaft in press with splined end down and helical gear resting on press plate. Press shaft through front bearing, spacer washer and helical gear. Remove helical gear spacer.

Power Divider Case Cover

NOTE: *Either vacuum-operated, air-operated or mechanically-operated lockout may be used on "M" Series axles. The air-operated lockout is covered further on. The following instructions are for vacuum-operated type. Mechanically-operated lockout varies slightly from the vacuum type (refer to insert in Fig. 31 for components).*

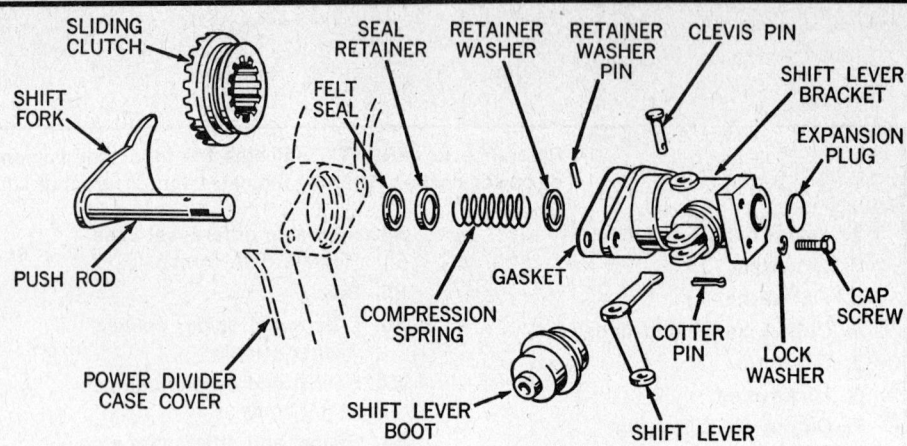

Fig. 32 Disassembled view of vacuum-operated lockout

1. Remove loosened capscrews, lockwashers and front bearing cover from divider case cover. Remove oil seal and felt seal from bearing cover.
2. Remove sliding clutch and input shaft front bearing from case cover.
3. Push back shift lever boot. Remove clevis pin and shift lever. Unfasten and remove shift lever bracket from case cover.
4. Depress compression spring. Then remove pin, retainer washer and compression spring from push rod.
5. Withdraw shift fork and push rod from case cover. Remove seal retainer and felt seal from case cover.

Axle Differential, Models 22M, 28M

1. Punch mark differential cases for correct location in reassembly. Remove locknuts and bolts and lift off plain differential case.
2. Remove differential components from ring gear side of case.
3. Remove capscrew, lockwasher and lubricator from flanged differential case.
4. Remove bearing cones from differential cases, using split-type bearing puller.
5. To remove ring gear from flanged differential case, drill off the flat head of rivets (on ring gear side) and drive out rivets.

32M Axle Differential

1. Punch mark differential cases for correct location in reassembly. Cut lockwire and remove differential case cap screws. Lift off plain differential case.
2. Remove differential components ring gear side of differential case.
3. Remove bearing cones from differential case, using split-type bearing puller. To remove ring gear from flanged differential case, drill off flat head of rivets (on ring gear side) and remove rivets.

36M Axle Differential

1. Punch mark differential cases for correct location in reassembly. Cut lockwire and remove differential case capscrews. Lift off oil collector drum and plain differential case.
2. Remove differential components from flanged differential case.
3. Remove capscrew, lockwasher and differential lubricator from flanged differential case.
4. Remove bearing cones from differential cases, using split-type bearing puller. To remove ring gear from flanged differential case, drill off flat head of rivets (on ring gear side) and remove rivets.

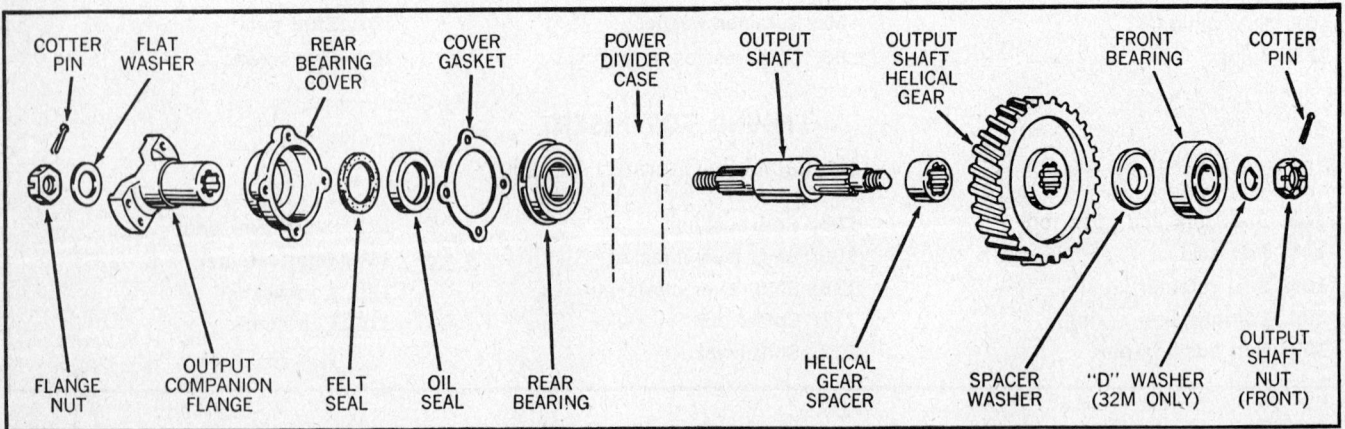

Fig. 33 Disassembled view of output shaft

EATON DRIVING AXLES

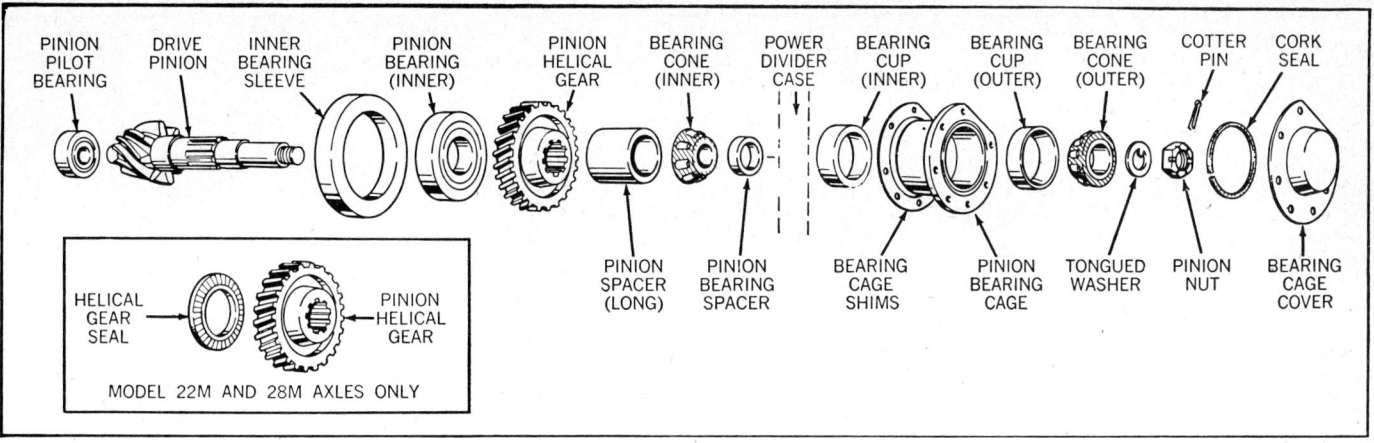

Fig. 34 Disassembled view of drive pinion

REASSEMBLE

36M Power Divider

NOTE: *The power divider assembly for Model 36M is the same as 42M. Refer to 42M instructions further on for procedures.*

22M, 28M, 32M, Power Divider

NOTE: *Partially reassemble shafts and case covers before reassembling power divider case.*

Power Divider Case Cover (Vacuum Type)

NOTE: *The following instructions are for the vacuum-type lockout. Mechanically operated lockout varies slightly from the vacuum type (refer to insert in Fig. 31). The air-operated type is covered further on. A disassembled view of the vacuum-type lockout is shown in Fig. 32.*

1. Install input shaft front bearing in divider case cover.
2. Place felt seal and seal retainer in recess in case cover. Insert push rod through case cover opening. Place compression spring and retainer washer on push rod, compress spring and install retainer washer pin. Coat spring and retainer washer with grease.
3. Install shift lever bracket and gasket over push rod and install capscrews and lockwashers.
4. Position shift lever on bracket, engaging end of lever with slot in push rod. Install clevis and cotter pins to connect lever to bracket.
5. Place boot on shift lever and bracket.
6. Depress shift lever and position sliding clutch in case cover engaging shift fork in clutch grooves.

Output Shaft, Fig. 33

1. Press helical gear spacer on front end of output shaft. Then press helical gear, spacer washer and front bearing on output shaft.

2. Temporarily place companion flange on rear end of output shaft. Place output shaft in vise with rear end down, gripping flange in vise jaws.
3. Install "D" washer (32M only) on output shaft. Install and tighten output shaft front nut to correct torque. Install cotter pin.

Drive Pinion, Fig. 34

1. Press pilot bearing on drive pinion and stake in four places (see Fig. 12).
2. Lubricate and press inner bearing on drive pinion, positioning bevel side of bearing toward pinion teeth.
3. On Models 22M and 28M, install oil seal in helical gear, positioning segment springs inside. Press helical gear on drive pinion, placing seal towards inner bearing. On Model 32M, press helical gear on pinion with short hub toward inner bearing.
4. Press long spacer on pinion. Press inner bearing cone on pinion.
5. If removed, press bearing cups in pinion bearing cage.
6. Lubricate pinion bearings. Temporarily place bearing cage, spacer, outer bearing cone, tongued washer and nut on pinion. Tighten nut to correct torque. Rotate pinion bearing cage while tightening nut. Check pinion bearing preload adjustment as already explained at the beginning of this chapter.
7. With pinion bearings correctly adjusted, remove temporarily installed nut, tongued washer, outer bearing cone and bearing cage from pinion.

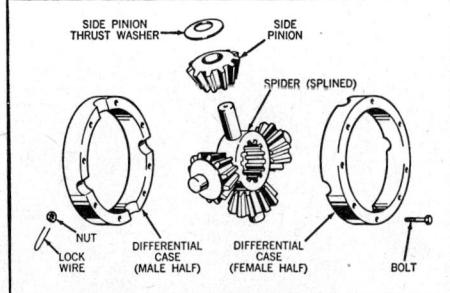

Fig. 35 Disassembled view of inter-axle differential

Inter-Axle Differential, Fig. 35

1. Lubricate parts during reassembly. Place side pinions and thrust washers on spider journals. Assemble spider assembly and case halves, aligning punch marks made during disassembly. Install bolts and nuts to secure case halves. Tighten nuts to correct torque and lockwire.

Input Shaft, Fig. 36

1. Temporarily install flange nut on front end of input shaft to protect threads during assembly. Place input in press, with shaft supported at nut and install parts on shaft as follows:
2. Place spacer washer on shaft.
3. Press fornt helical side gear bushing on shaft. Lubricate bushing, then install front helical side gear over bushing. *Bushing and gear must rest firmly against spacer washer.*
4. Place front spider splined washer on shaft. Place inter-axle differential on shaft, positioning bolt heads toward companion flange. Place rear spider splined washer on shaft, *making certain splines are engaged with input shaft splines.*
5. Press rear helical side gear bushing on shaft. Lubricate bushing, then install rear helical side gear over bushing. *Bushing and gear must rest firmly against splined washer.*
6. Place rear bearing spacer washer on shaft.
7. Temporarily place a "dummy sleeve" (1½" I.D. × 1" long), "D" washer and input shaft inner nut on shaft. Tighten nut to correct torque, then rotate shaft parts by hand. Gears and interaxle differential should rotate freely without bind. After testing, remove temporarily installed parts.

Power Divider

1. Temporarily install companion flange on input shaft. Place input shaft in vise, with front end down and gripping flange in vise jaws.
2. Place power divider case, front side down, over input shaft. With rear bearing spacer washer on input shaft, install rear bearing in divider case bore and on input shaft. Install "D" washer and inner nut on shaft. Tighten nut to correct torque and install cotter pin. Install output shaft rear bearing in divider case. Lubricate bearing. With new felt seal and oil seal

227

EATON DRIVING AXLES

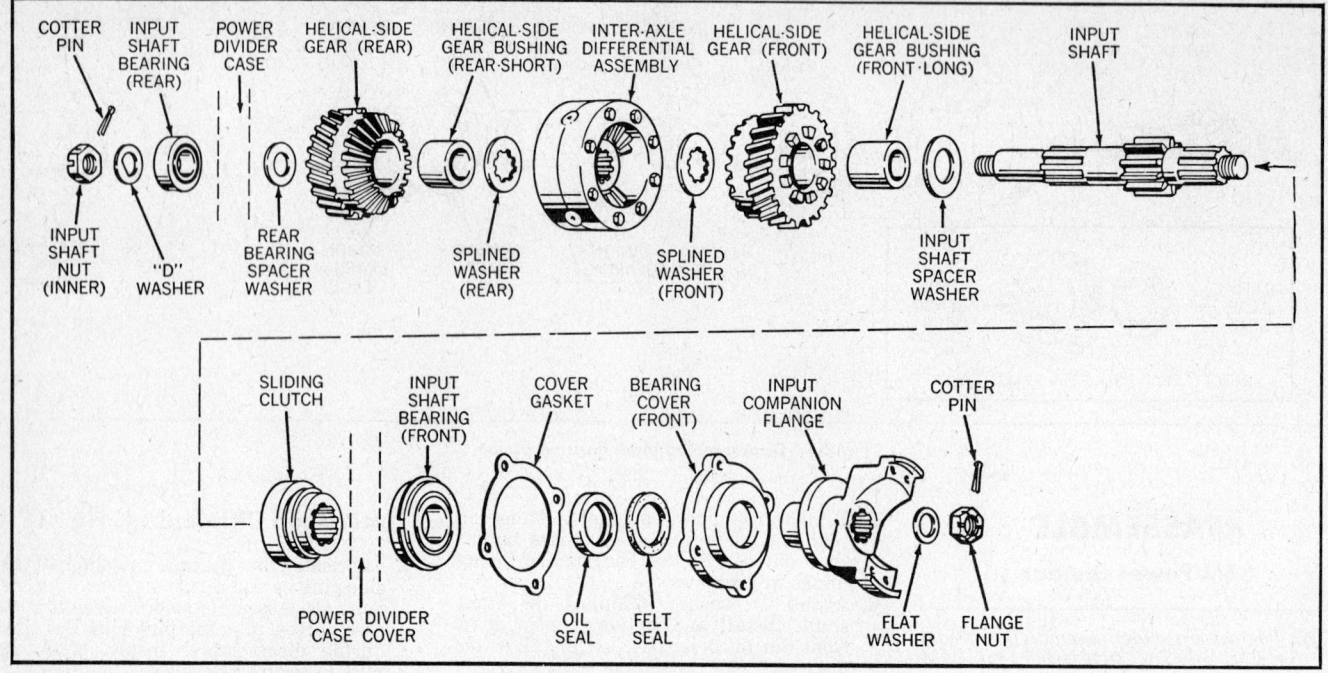

Fig. 36 Disassembled view of input shaft

installed in rear bearing cover, install gasket and bearing cover on divider case. Install cover capscrews and lockwashers.
3. Remove divider case and input shaft assembly from vise.
4. Position divider case with front side up. Place output shaft in case, taking care not to damage rear bearing oil seal.
5. Place gasket and case cover on divider case. Make certain sliding clutch engages splines of input shaft. Fasten cover to case and tighten stud nuts to correct torque.
6. Install felt seal and oil seal in input shaft front bearing cover. Place gasket and bearing cover on case cover. Install capscrews and lockwashers but do not tighten until companion flange is installed.
7. Install companion flange flat washer and nut. Tighten nut to correct torque and insert cotter pin. Now tighten front bearing cover capscrews to correct torque.

8. Install same quantity and size shims that were removed in disassembly on pinion bearing cage. Place shims and cage in divider case.
9. Insert drive pinion through opposite side of divider case until inner bearing cone is seated in inner bearing cup. Then place outer bearing cone, tongued washer and nut on drive pinion. Tighten nut to correct torque and insert cotter pin.
10. Install new cork seal in cage groove. Install cage cover and tighten nuts and capscrews to correct torque.
11. Insert bearing sleeve in divider case and over pinion inner bearing. Align sleeve hole with hole in case, then install set screw and lockwasher.
12. Loosen capscrews holding output shaft bearing cover. Install companion flange, flat washer and nut on output shaft. Tighten nut to correct torque and insert cotter pin. Tighten bearing cover capscrews to correct torque.

22M, 28M Axle Differential, Fig. 37

1. Rivet (cold) ring gear to flanged differential case, placing flat side head of rivets on ring gear side. Compress rivets to 34–38 tons on Model 22M or 40–42 tons on 28M.
2. Press bearing cones on differential cases. If removed, install oil lubricator in flanged differential case and secure with capscrew and lockwasher.
3. Lubricate parts during assembly. Place thrust washer and right-hand side gear in flanged differential case. Assemble side pinions and thrust washers to spider, then place this assembly on flanged differential case. Place left-hand side gear and thrust washer on side pinions.
4. Tap plain differential into place, aligning previously made punch marks. Draw case halves together with four bolts and lock

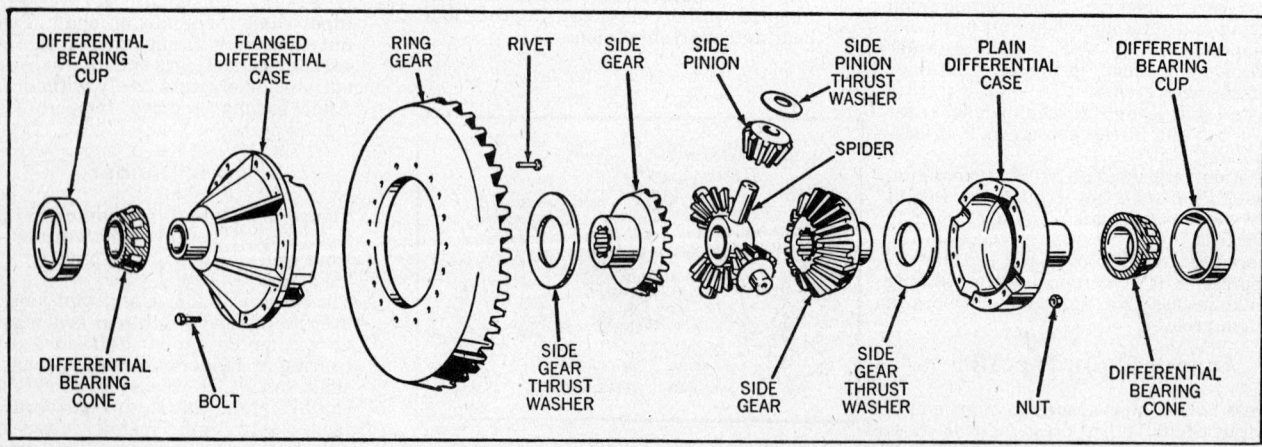

Fig. 37 Disassembled view of axle differential for Models 22M, 28M

EATON DRIVING AXLES

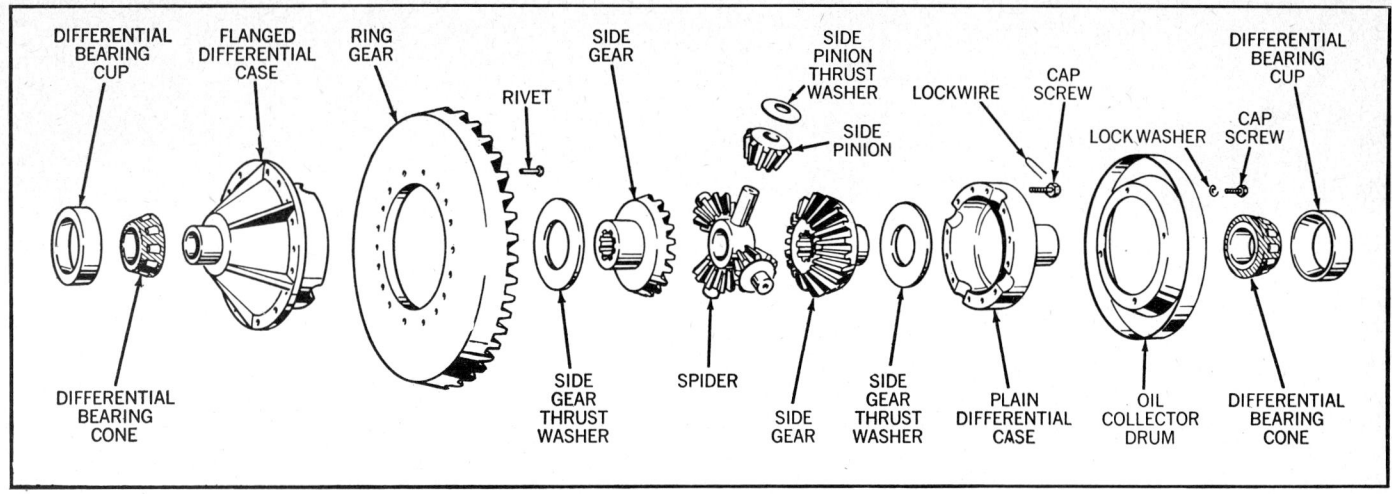

Fig. 38   Disassembled view of axle differential for Models 32M, 36M

nuts. Check assembly for free rotation. Install remaining bolts and locknuts and tighten all nuts to correct torque.

32M Axle Differential, Fig. 38

1. Rivet ring gear to flanged differential case, compressing rivets to 47–50 tons.
2. Press bearing cones on differential case. Lubricate parts during assembly.
3. Assemble differential parts in flanged differential case.
4. Tap plain differential case into place, aligning previously made punch marks. Do not install oil collector drum at this time, but assemble drum to case after differential is installed in carrier.
5. Install four large tapped head capscrews, equally spaced, to draw case halves together. Check assembly for free rotation. Install eight remaining capscrews and tighten all to correct torque. Lock with wire.

36M Axle Differential, Fig. 38

1. Rivet ring gear to flanged differential case, compressing to 39–41 tons.
2. Press bearing cones on differential cases. If removed, install oil lubricator in flanged differential case.
3. Assemble differential parts in flanged differential case. Then tap plain differential case half into place, aligning previously made punch marks.
4. Place oil collector drum on plain differential case. Install four capscrews to draw case halves together. Check assembly for free rotation. Install remaining capscrews and tighten all to correct torque.

Final Assembly

1. Using a new gasket, place power divider on differential carrier. Install and tighten stud nuts to correct torque.
2. On Models 22M, 28M and 36M, install differential in carrier as follows: Lubricate differential bearings. Place differential in carrier and install differential bearing cups, adjusters and caps, aligning punch marks previously made on caps. Install and finger-tighten bearing capscrews. Tighten adjusters to correctly seat bearings. Adjust ring gear and drive pinion as per instructions at the beginning of this chapter. When correctly adjusted, tighten bearing capscrews to correct torque. Install cotter pins to secure adjuster locks and lock capscrews with wire.
3. On Model 32M, install differential in carrier as follows:
   a. Lubricate differential bearings. Place oil collector drum on left-hand side of differential, but do not install capscrews. Place differential and drum in carrier and install bearing cups, adjusters and caps. Install and finger-tighten bearing cap screws.
   b. Secure oil collector drum to plain differential with four capscrews and lockwashers.
   c. Tighten bearing adjusters to seat bearings. Adjust ring gear and pinion as described at the beginning of this chapter.
   d. With ring gear and pinion correctly adjusted, tighten bearing capscrews to correct torque. Install cotter pins to secure adjuster locks and lockwire capscrews.
   e. Tighten thrust block adjusting screw to position thrust block against ring gear. Loosen adjusting screw (1/8 to 1/4 turn) to obtain .010–.015" clearance between thrust block and ring gear. Tighten nut and bend ear of lock to secure adjustment.

Install Assembly In Axle Housing

1. Using a new gasket, install differential and power divider assembly in axle housing. Install capscrews and stud nuts and lockwashers. Tighten screws or nuts to correct torque.
2. Connect lockout shift lever.
3. Install axle shafts and connect propeller shafts.
4. Fill axle with correct lubricant.

MODEL 42M

Rearward Rear Axle

Instructions for the rearward rear axle are essentially the same as the forward rear axle except for removal of the power divider and drive pinion.

The rearward rear axle is not equipped with a power divider. The drive pinion for the rearward rear axle is mounted in a bearing cage at the front side of the differential carrier. The drive pinion can be removed and installed as a complete assembly, consisting of pinion, bearings, cage and companion flange.

Disassembly and reassembly of the differential assembly and countershaft are the same as instructions for the forward rear axle which follows:

DISASSEMBLE FORWARD REAR AXLE

1. Drain lubricant. Disconnect propeller shafts and remove axle shafts.
2. Disconnect lockout shift lever.
3. Unfasten and remove carrier and power divider from axle housing. *If preliminary inspection reveals that ring gear and drive pinion are satisfactory, check backlash with dial indicator and take a tooth contact pattern for reference and easier adjustment during reassembly.*
4. Remove pinion cage cover. Remove and discard cork seal. Hold input and output companion flanges and loosen (but do not remove) pinion nut.
5. Hold input flange and loosen (but do not remove) flange nut.
6. Hold output flange and loosen (but do not remove) flange nut.
7. Unfasten and lift power divider from differential carrier.

Differential Carrier, Fig. 39

1. Punch mark differential bearing caps and carrier for correct location during reassembly.
2. Remove bearing caps and lift differential out of carrier. Remove outer bearing races from differential cases.
3. Unscrew oil distributor plug, spring and distributor.
4. Punch mark countershaft bearing covers and carrier for correct location during reassembly. Remove covers from both sides.
5. Punch mark countershaft bearing cage (right-hand), bearing adjuster (left-hand) and differential carrier for correct location on reassembly. Then remove bearing cage and adjuster from carrier. Remove cage seal.
6. Remove oil reservoir from carrier.
7. Position herringbone pinion halfway through right-hand bearing cage opening, then tilt countershaft to position ring gear at top and lift out countershaft.

EATON DRIVING AXLES

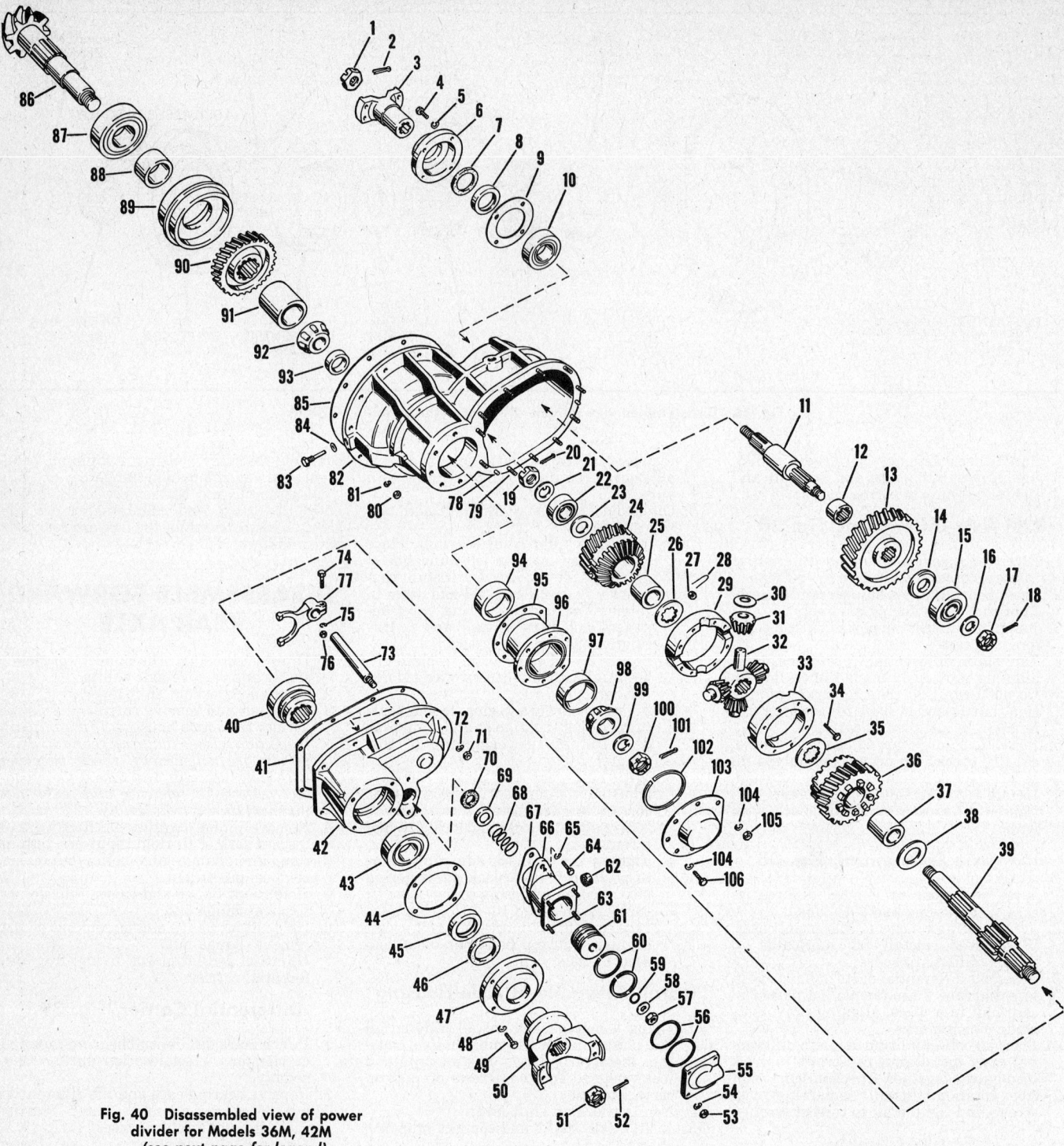

Fig. 40 Disassembled view of power divider for Models 36M, 42M (see next page for legend)

Differential

1. If match marks are not present, make marks to assure correct position of each case half in reassembly.
2. Unfasten and separate herringbone gear and case halves.
3. Lift herringbone gear and left-hand case off right-hand case and remove differential components.
4. Place side gear in vise and drive left-hand case from herringbone gear and case support.
5. Remove snap rings from case halves.
6. Remove bearing inner race from case halves using a split-type bearing puller.

Countershaft

1. Remove capscrews and oil collector disc.
2. If match marks are not present, make marks to assure correct position of ring gear on countershaft flange.
3. Remove ring gear from countershaft.
4. Remove bearing cones from countershaft using a split-type bearing puller.

Power Divider, Fig. 40

1. Remove input flange. Loosen (do not remove) capscrew on input shaft front bearing cover.
2. Remove divider cover to case stud nuts. Using suitable bearing puller, grip front bearing cover with puller legs and puller screw against input shaft. Pull bearing cover and case cover from case.
3. Remove output flange.
4. Working at rear end of output shaft, drive shaft end out of rear bearing. Lift output

EATON DRIVING AXLES

Reference to "FRONT" indicates the input companion flange side of power divider. "REAR" indicates the differential carrier side.

1. Flange nut
2. Cotter pin
3. Output companion flange
4. Cap screw
5. Lockwasher
6. Output shaft bearing cover (rear)
7. Felt seal
8. Oil seal
9. Bearing cover shim
10. Output shaft bearing (rear)
11. Output shaft
12. Helical gear spacer
13. Output shaft helical gear
14. Front bearing spacer washer
15. Output shaft bearing (front)
16. Tongued washer
17. Output shaft nut (front)
18. Cotter pin
19. Input shaft nut (inner)
20. Cotter pin
21. Tongued washer
22. Input shaft bearing (rear)
23. Rear bearing spacer washer
24. Helical and differential side gear (rear)
25. Helical and differential side gear bushing (rear, short)
26. Differential spider splined washer (rear)
27. Nut
28. Lockwire
29. Inter-axle differential case (male half, rear)
30. Side pinion thrust washer
31. Side pinion
32. Spider
33. Inter-axle differential case (female half, front)
34. Bolt
35. Differential spider splined washer (front)
36. Helical and differential side gear (front)
37. Helical and differential side gear bushing (front, long)
38. Input shaft spacer washer
39. Input shaft
40. Sliding clutch
41. Power divider case cover gasket
42. Power divider case cover
43. Input shaft bearing (front)
44. Bearing cover shim
45. Oil seal
46. Felt seal
47. Input shaft bearing cover (front)
48. Lockwasher
49. Cap screw
50. Input companion flange
51. Flange nut
52. Cotter pin
53. Stud nut
54. Lockwasher
55. Shift cylinder cover
56. Shift cylinder cover grommets
57. Push rod nut
58. Flat washer
59. Push rod grommet
60. Piston felt oilers
61. Shift cylinder piston
62. Shift cylinder body filter
63. Cover stud
64. Cap screw
65. Lockwasher
66. Shift cylinder body
67. Shift cylinder body gasket
68. Compression spring
69. Seal retainer
70. Felt seal
71. Stud nut
72. Lockwasher
73. Push rod
74. Bolt
75. Lockwasher
76. Nut
77. Shift fork
78. Dowel
79. Stud
80. Stud nut
81. Lockwasher
82. Power divider case
83. Bearing sleeve set screw
84. Lockwasher
85. Power divider case gasket
86. Drive pinion and ring gear (matched set)
87. Pinion bearing (inner)
88. Pinion inner bearing spacer (42M only)
89. Inner bearing sleeve
90. Helical gear
91. Pinion spacer (long)
92. Pinion bearing cone (inner)
93. Pinion bearing spacer
94. Pinion bearing cup (inner)
95. Shims
96. Pinion bearing cage
97. Pinion bearing cup (outer)
98. Pinion bearing cone (outer)
99. Tongued washer
100. Pinion nut
101. Cotter pin
102. Cork seal
103. Pinion bearing cage cover
104. Lockwasher
105. Stud nut
106. Cap screw

shaft from divider case, then remove bearing from case.
5. Remove inner bearing sleeve set screw from divider case.
6. Remove loosened pinion nut and tongued washer. Drive pinion out rear of divider case. Remove outer bearing cone from bearing cage.
7. Remove pinion bearing cage and shims from front side of divider case. *Note size and quantity of shims removed for easier adjustment in reassembly.* If replacement is necessary remove bearing cups from cage.
8. Remove input shaft assembly. This can easily be accomplished by temporarily installing companion flange and nut on end of shaft. Use flange to lift assembly from case.

Input Shaft & Inter-Axle Differential

1. Place input shaft in vise, gripping companion flange. Loosen and remove inner nut and tongued washer.
2. Place input shaft in press, with front helical side gear down and input shaft front spacer washer resting on press plates. Press shaft out of component parts.
3. Punch mark differential cases for correct location in reassembly. Cut lockwire and remove bolts holding cases together. Separate case halves and remove differential components.

Drive Pinion

1. On Model 36M, remove sleeve from inner

EATON DRIVING AXLES

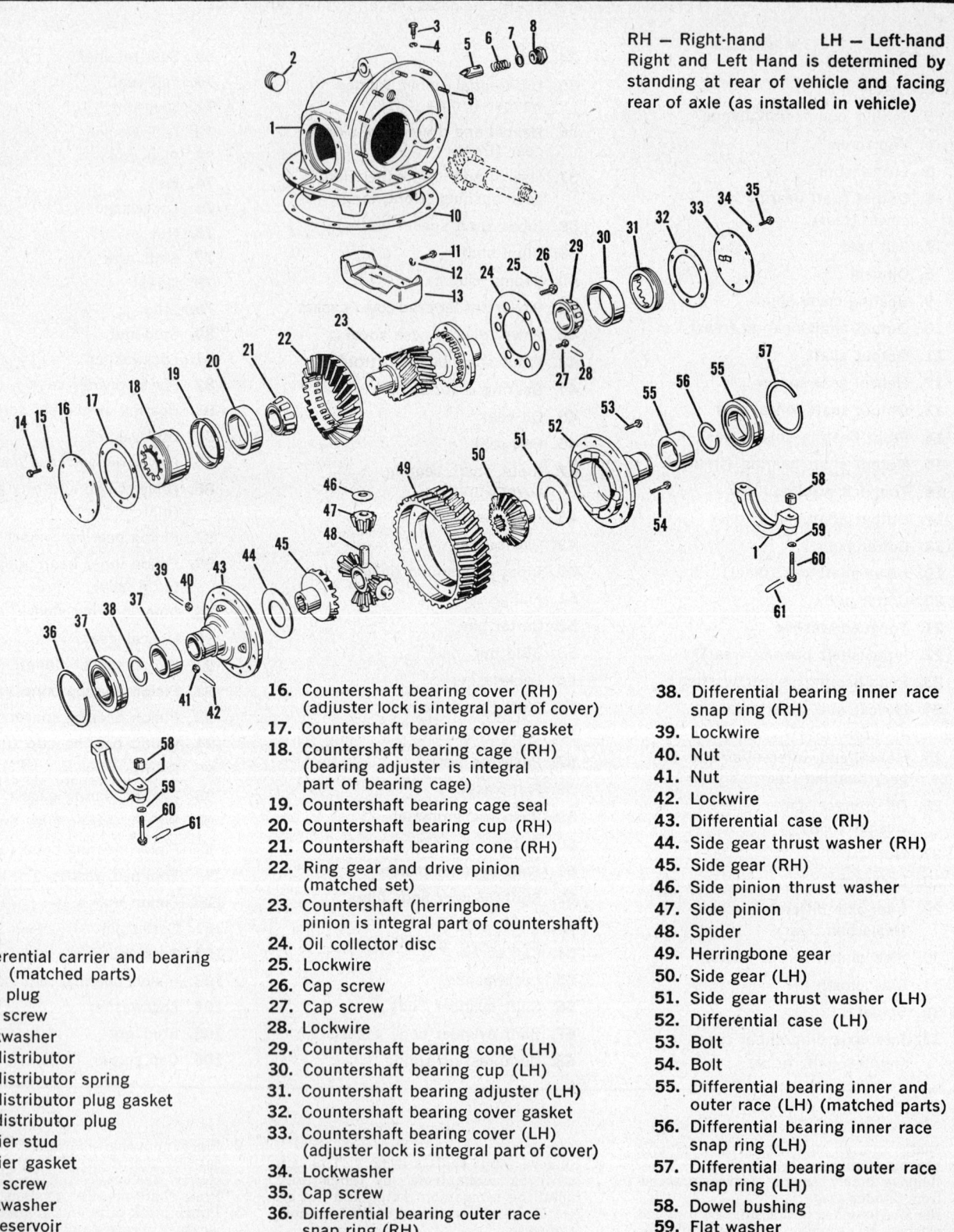

RH — Right-hand LH — Left-hand
Right and Left Hand is determined by standing at rear of vehicle and facing rear of axle (as installed in vehicle)

1. Differential carrier and bearing caps (matched parts)
2. Pipe plug
3. Cap screw
4. Lockwasher
5. Oil distributor
6. Oil distributor spring
7. Oil distributor plug gasket
8. Oil distributor plug
9. Carrier stud
10. Carrier gasket
11. Cap screw
12. Lockwasher
13. Oil reservoir
14. Cap screw
15. Lockwasher
16. Countershaft bearing cover (RH) (adjuster lock is integral part of cover)
17. Countershaft bearing cover gasket
18. Countershaft bearing cage (RH) (bearing adjuster is integral part of bearing cage)
19. Countershaft bearing cage seal
20. Countershaft bearing cup (RH)
21. Countershaft bearing cone (RH)
22. Ring gear and drive pinion (matched set)
23. Countershaft (herringbone pinion is integral part of countershaft)
24. Oil collector disc
25. Lockwire
26. Cap screw
27. Cap screw
28. Lockwire
29. Countershaft bearing cone (LH)
30. Countershaft bearing cup (LH)
31. Countershaft bearing adjuster (LH)
32. Countershaft bearing cover gasket
33. Countershaft bearing cover (LH) (adjuster lock is integral part of cover)
34. Lockwasher
35. Cap screw
36. Differential bearing outer race snap ring (RH)
37. Differential bearing inner and outer race (RH) (matched parts)
38. Differential bearing inner race snap ring (RH)
39. Lockwire
40. Nut
41. Nut
42. Lockwire
43. Differential case (RH)
44. Side gear thrust washer (RH)
45. Side gear (RH)
46. Side pinion thrust washer
47. Side pinion
48. Spider
49. Herringbone gear
50. Side gear (LH)
51. Side gear thrust washer (LH)
52. Differential case (LH)
53. Bolt
54. Bolt
55. Differential bearing inner and outer race (LH) (matched parts)
56. Differential bearing inner race snap ring (LH)
57. Differential bearing outer race snap ring (LH)
58. Dowel bushing
59. Flat washer
60. Cap screw
61. Lockwire

Fig. 39 Disassembled view of differential carrier for Model 42M

EATON DRIVING AXLES

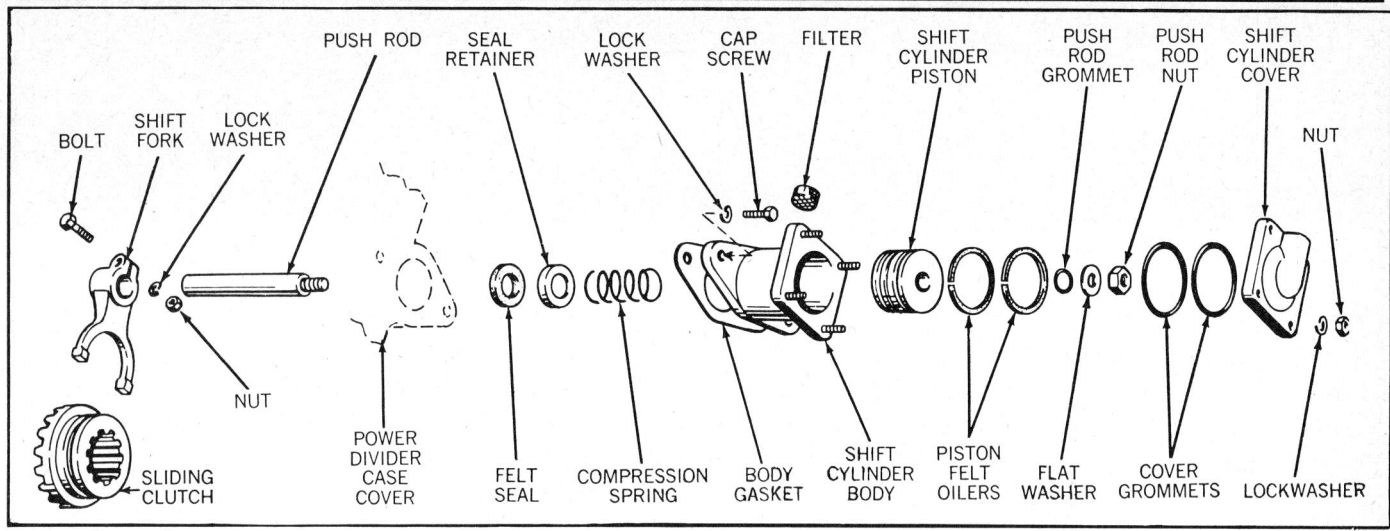

Fig. 41 Disassembled view of air-operated lockout mechanism

bearing. Place pinion in press with pinion teeth down. Then first press pinion out of bearing spacer, inner bearing cone, long spacer and helical gear. Then press pinion out of inner bearing.

2. On Model 42M, remove pinion bearing spacer. Then first press pinion out of inner bearing cone, long spacer, helical gear and inner bearing sleeve. Then press pinion out of inner bearing spacer and inner bearing.

Output Shaft

1. Remove cotter pin from output shaft front nut. Temporarily place companion flange on shaft. Then remove front nut, tongued washer and flange.
2. Place output shaft in press with rear end of shaft down and helical gear resting on press plates. Press shaft out of front bearing, spacer washer and helical gear. Remove helical gear spacer.

Divider Case Cover (Air-Operated Lockout)

Either air-operated or mechanically-operated lockout may be used on 36M and 42M axles. Refer to insert in Fig. 31 for components of mechanically-operated lockout. The following instructions are for air-operated lockout.

1. Remove cover from shift cylinder body. Discard grommets. Remove nut, flat washer and grommet from push rod.
2. Remove shift cylinder body from case cover.
3. Remove compression spring from push rod. Remove sliding clutch and shift fork from case cover.
4. Remove front bearing cover and shims. Note size and quantity of shims removed for easier adjustment during reassembly. Remove oil seal and felt seal from bearing cover. Remove input shaft bearing from case cover.

REASSEMBLE

Divider Case Cover (Air Operated), Fig. 41

1. Press front input shaft bearing in divider case cover.
2. Place felt seal and seal retainer in recess in case cover. Assemble push rod to shift fork and secure with nut, bolt and lockwasher.
3. Assemble shift fork and sliding clutch to case cover as follows: Partially insert push rod in case cover, engaging sliding clutch with shift fork, then push this assembly into correct mounting position in case cover.
4. Place compression spring, gasket and shift cylinder body over push rod and onto case cover. Secure body with capscrews and lockwashers. *Piston felt oilers should be soaked in SAE-30 oil for one hour prior to assembly.*
5. Install felt oilers on piston and insert piston assembly in body and on push rod. Place grommet on push rod, then install flat washer and nut.
6. Install grommets on cylinder cover, then install cover, nuts and lockwashers on shift cylinder body.

Output Shaft, Fig. 42

1. Press helical gear spacer on front end of shaft. Then press helical gear, bearing spacer washer and front bearing on shaft.
2. Temporarily place companion flange on rear end of shaft. Place shaft in vise with rear end down, gripping flange in vise jaws.
3. Install tongued washer on shaft. Install and tighten shaft front nut to correct torque. Install cotter pin.

Drive Pinion, Fig. 43

1. Lubricate and press inner bearing on pinion, positioning bevel side of bearing toward pinion teeth.
2. On Model 42M, press inner bearing spac-

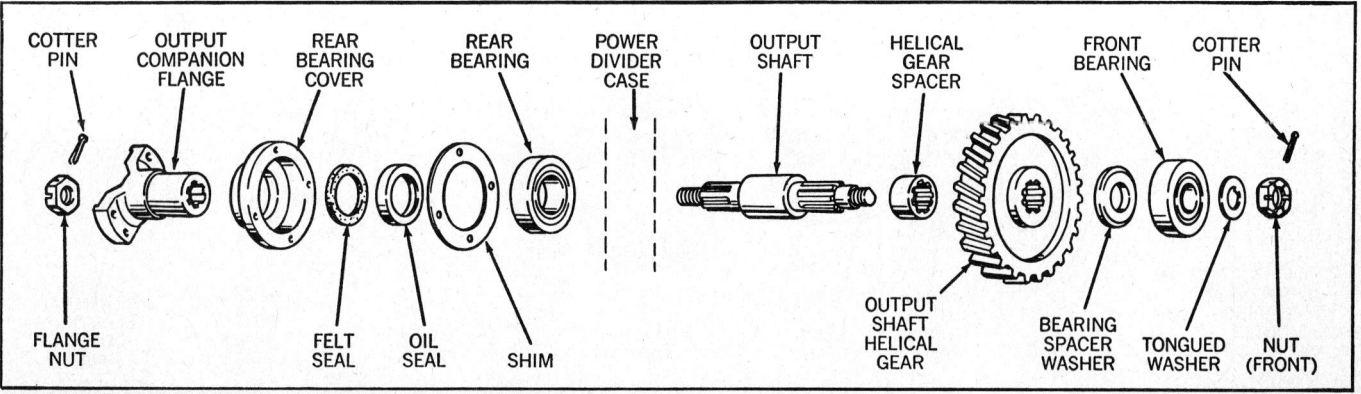

Fig. 42 Disassembled view of output shaft for Models 36M, 42M

EATON DRIVING AXLES

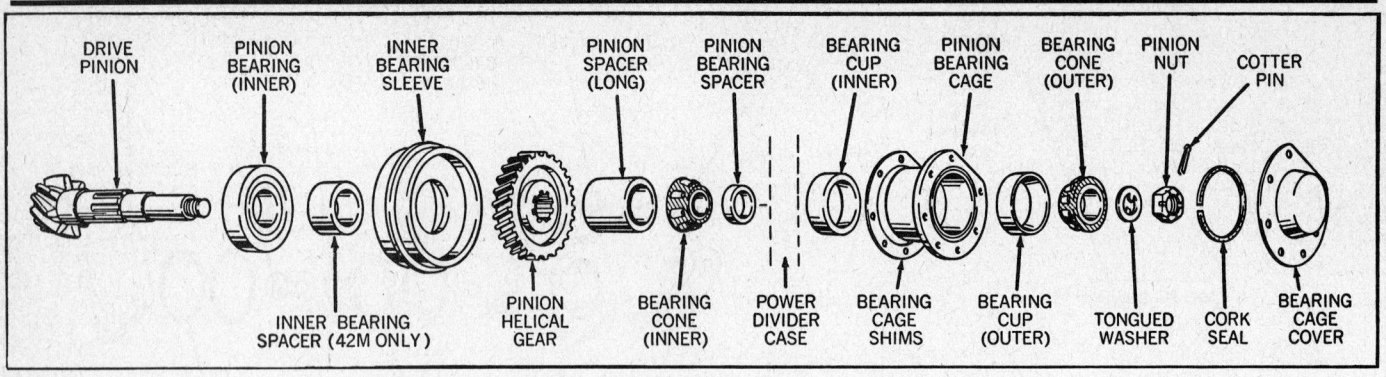

Fig. 43 Disassembled view of drive pinion for Models 36M, 42M

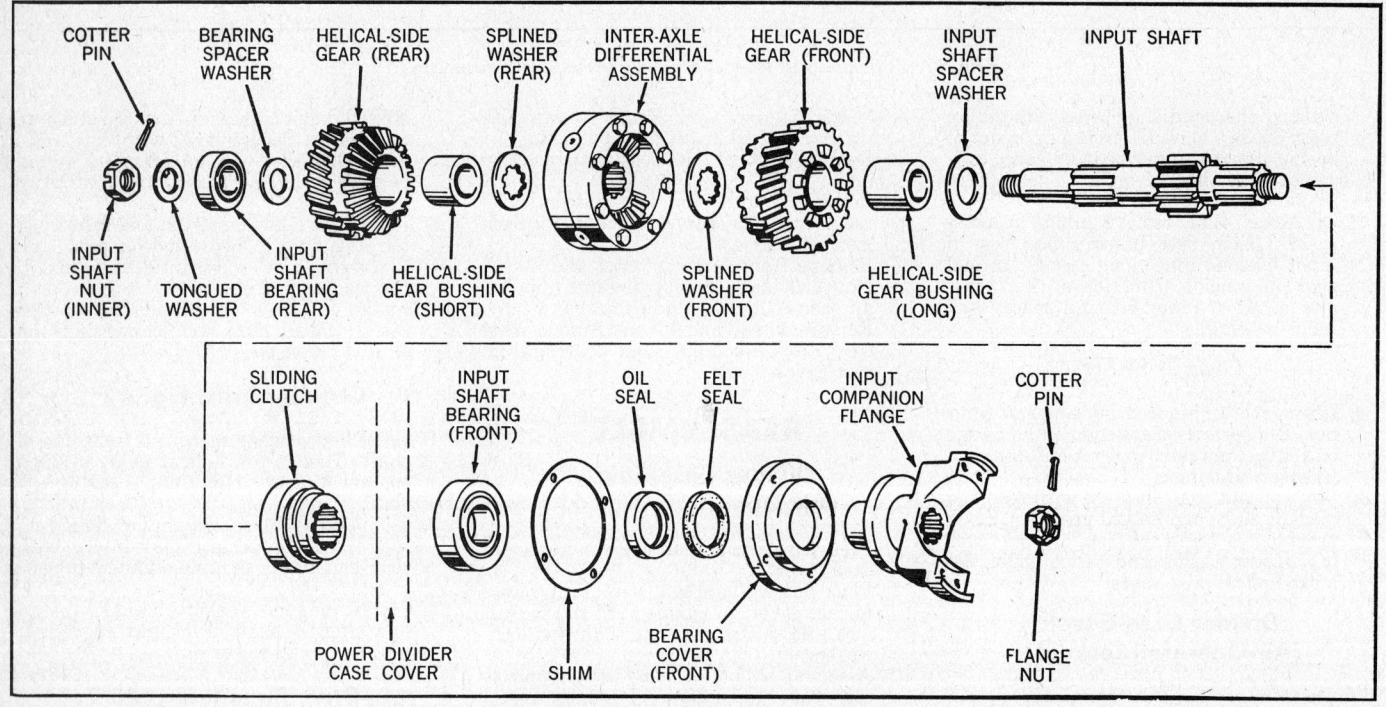

Fig. 45 Disassembled view of input shaft for Models 36M, 42M

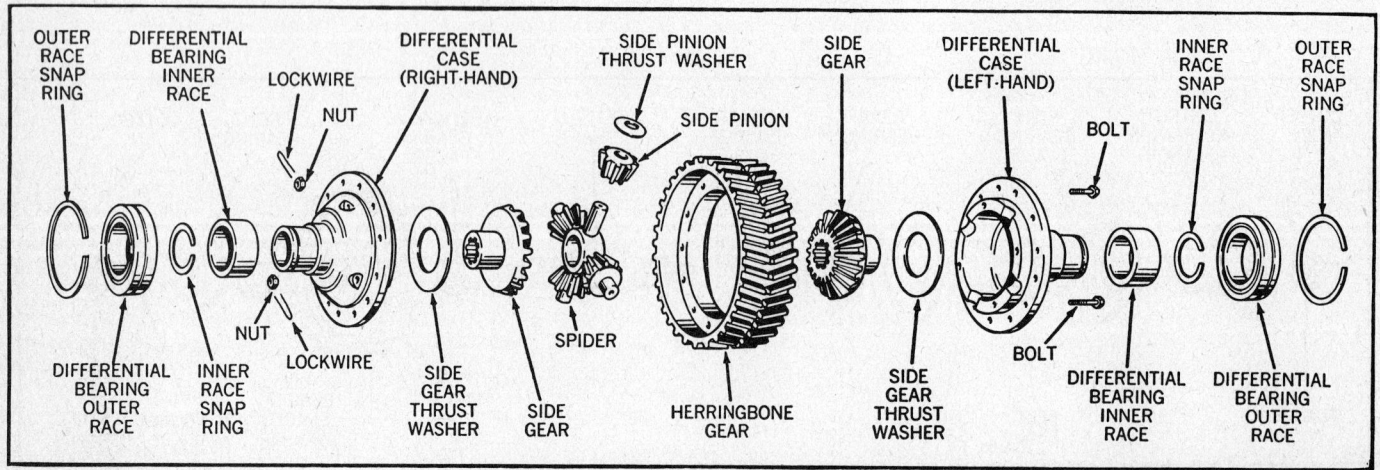

Fig. 46 Disassembled view of axle differential for Model 42M

EATON DRIVING AXLES

er and inner bearing sleeve on pinion. *On Model 36M, install inner bearing sleeve when pinion is assembled to power divider case (spacer is not used).*
3. Press helical gear in pinion splines, making certain long hub is against inner bearing spacer (42M). On Model 36M, long hub is against inner bearing.
4. Press long pinion spacer and inner bearing cone on pinion.
5. If removed, press pinion bearing cups n bearing cage.
6. Lubricate pinion bearings. Temporarily place bearing cage, bearing spacer, outer bearing cone, tongued washer and nut on pinion. Tighten nut to correct torque, rotating bearing cage while tightening nut. Check pinion bearing preload as instructed at the beginning of this chapter.
7. With pinion bearing preload correctly adjusted, remove temporarily installed parts from pinion.

Inter-Axle Differential, Fig. 44

Lubricate parts during reassembly. Place side pinions and thrust washers on spider journals. Assemble spider assembly and case halves, aligning previously made punch marks. Secure case halves with bolts and nuts, tightening nuts to correct torque. Lock nuts with wire.

Input Shaft, Fig. 45

1. Temporarily install flange nut on front end of shaft to protect threads during assembly. Place shaft in a press, with shaft supported at nut and install parts on shaft as follows:
2. Place spacer washer on shaft. Press long helical side gear bushing on shaft. Lubricate bushing, then install front helical side gear on bushing. *Bushing and gear must rest firmly against spacer washer.*
3. Place front spider splined washer on shaft. Place inter-axle differential on shaft, positioning bolt heads toward companion flange. Place rear spider splined washer on shaft. *Make certain washer splines are engaged with shaft splines.*
4. Press short helical side gear bushing on shaft. Lubricate bushing, then install rear helical side gear over bushing. *Bushing and gear must rest firmly against splined washer.*
5. Place rear bearing spacer washer on shaft. Temporarily place a dummy sleeve (1½" I.D. × 1" long), tongued washer and shaft inner nut on shaft. Tighten nut to

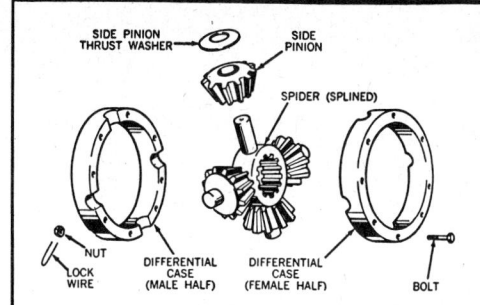

Fig. 44 Disassembled view of inter-axle differential for Models 36M, 42M

correct torque. Rotate shaft parts by hand; they should rotate freely without binding.
6. After testing assembly for free movement, remove temporarily installed parts. Then press rear bearing on shaft and install tongued washer and inner nut. Tighten nut to correct torque and install cotter pin.

Power Divider, Fig. 40

1. Position divider case with rear side up.
2. Lubricate and install output shaft rear bearing in divider case.
3. Install felt seal and oil seal in output shaft rear bearing cover. Using same size and quantity of shims removed at disassembly, install shims and bearing cover on divider case. Install (but do not tighten) cover capscrews and lockwashers until companion flange is installed.
4. *To check bearing clearance to determine thickness of shims required, install bearing cover on divider case without shims. Install and finger-tighten cover capscrews. Then, using a feeler gauge, measure clearance between bearing cover and divider case. This clearance measurement plus .003" would equal the thickness of shims required for correct bearing clearance.*
5. Rotate divider case to position front side up. Insert assembled input shaft, engaging rear bearing in bore of divider case.
6. Insert assembled output shaft in divider case, inserting end of shaft through rear bearing and taking care not to damage oil seal.
7. Using new case cover gasket, place divider case cover on divider case, engaging sliding clutch splines with input shaft splines. Install stud nuts and lockwash-

ers. Tighten stud nuts to correct torque.
8. Install felt seal and oil seal in input shaft front bearing cover.
9. Using same size and quantity of shims removed in disassembly, install shims and bearing cover on divider case cover. Install capscrews and lockwashers but do not tighten until companion flange is installed. Check bearing clearance as explained for output shaft bearings above.
10. With front bearing cover capscrews loose, install companion flange on input shaft and secure with flange nut. Tighten nut to correct torque and install cotter pin. Tighten front bearing cover capscrews to correct torque.
11. Install same size and quantity of shims removed as disassembly on pinion bearing cage, then install cage on divider case. Temporarily install capscrews to retain cage during pinion installation.
12. With divider case rear side up, and with output shaft rear bearing cover capscrews loose, install companion flange on output shaft, taking care not to damage oil seal. Install and tighten flange nut to correct torque and install cotter pin. Tighten rear bearing cover capscrews to correct torque.
13. Lubricate pinion bearings. Install partially assembled pinion in divider case.
14. On Model 42M, position inner bearing sleeve in case bore and end of pinion through inner bearing cup. Align sleeve with set screw hole in case and install set screw and lockwasher.
15. Install pinion bearing spacer, outer pinion bearing cone, tongued washer and pinion nut. Tighten nut to correct torque and install cotter pin.
16. Remove temporarily installed bearing cage capscrews. Install new cork seal in cage groove. Install cover and tighten nuts and capscrews to correct torque.
17. On Model 36M, place inner bearing sleeve on pinion inner bearing and in divider case. Align sleeve with set screw hole in case and install set screw and lockwasher.

Differential, Fig. 46

1. Press bearing inner races on differential case halves and install snap rings.
2. Lubricate parts during reassembly.
3. Place herringbone gear on left-hand differential case. Place thrust washer and side gear in left-hand case. Assemble side pinions and thrust washers to spider, then place this assembly in left-hand case. Place right-hand side gear on side pinions.

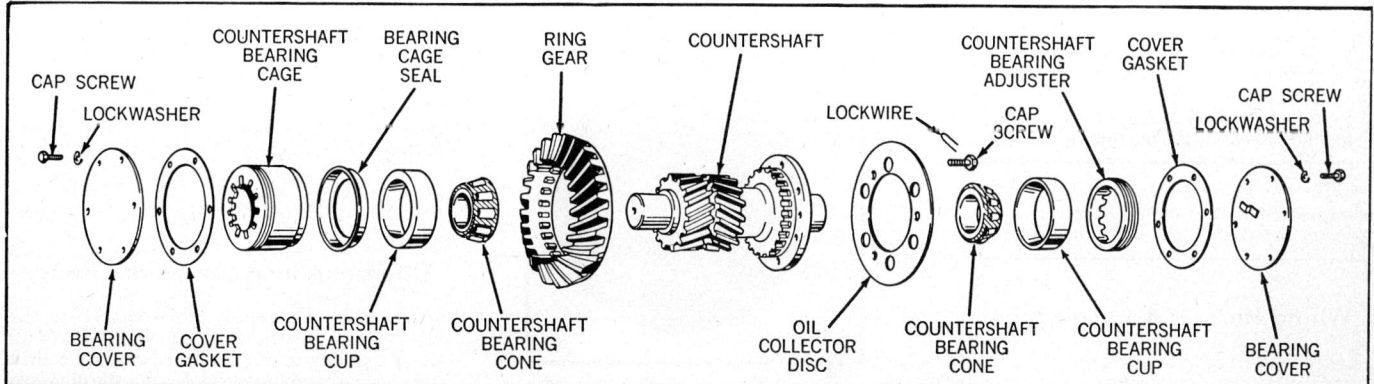

Fig. 47 Disassembled view of countershaft for Model 42M

EATON DRIVING AXLES

4. Place side gear thrust washer on right-hand side gear. Position right-hand case over left-hand case, aligning matching marks on each case and, using bolts as guides, drive right-hand case into herringbone gear.
5. Install bolts with heads positioned on left-hand side and tighten to correct torque. *The four oversize bolts are mounted midway between spider arms. Lock nuts with wire.*

Countershaft, Fig. 47

1. Place ring gear on countershaft, aligning punch marks.
2. Place oil collector disc on opposite side of countershaft flange.
3. Install and tighten capscrews to correct torque. Lock screws with wire.
4. Press bearing cones on end of countershaft.

Final Assembly

1. Place countershaft in differential carrier.
2. Lubricate bearings. Install bearing cups.
3. Install left-hand bearing adjuster in carrier, engaging only two or three threads.
4. Install right-hand bearing cage.
5. Tighten bearing cage to preload countershaft bearings as explained at the beginning of this chapter.
6. With new gasket in place on carrier, install power divider on carrier. Install and tighten lockwashers and nuts to correct torque.
7. Adjust ring gear and pinion for proper tooth contact (explained earlier).
8. After correct adjustment, install countershaft bearing cover gaskets, bearing covers, capscrews and lockwashers. Tighten screws to correct torque.
9. Place oil reservoir in carrier.
10. Lubricate bearing outer races. If removed, place snap rings on differential bearings. Place outer races on inner races, then install in carrier. Install bearing caps, making certain that snap rings rest in grooves in carrier and caps.
11. Install bearing capscrews and lockwashers and tighten to correct torque. Lock screws with wire.
12. Insert oil distributor in carrier and install capscrew and lockwasher. Install spring, gasket and plug.
13. Install differential carrier and power divider in axle housing.
14. Connect lockout shift lever.
15. Install axle shafts and connect propeller shafts.
16. Fill axle with correct lubricant.

Eaton Three-Speed Tandem Axles

DESCRIPTION

The Eaton Three-Speed Tandem Drive Axle consists of two planetary-type, two-speed axle units, coupled with a power divider and an inter-axle differential.

One control switch, mounted on the gear shift lever, effects the speed changes. This manually-operated switch controls operation of an Air-Torsion Spring Shift System which, in turn, shifts the axles from one ratio to next.

Service instructions on the shift system are given below. Axle instructions are covered in the Eaton Two-Speed Axle Section of this chapter.

Control Switch

The control switch, Fig. 48, is a three-position switch mounted on the gear shift lever and is manually operated by the vehicle driver. The switch controls current flow through the electrical system to operate the speedometer adapters and solenoid valves.

Speedometer Adapters

As shown in Fig. 49, two speedometer adapters are mounted in the system and compensate for drive shaft speed variations between low, intermediate and high axle range. In the low range the adapters are unexcited. In intermediate range one adapter is energized to 1:1 ratio while the other adapter is unexcited. In high range both adapters are energized to 1:1 ratio. The foregoing arrangement is accomplished by connecting each adapter in parallel to one of each of the two solenoid valves in the system.

NOTE: *For systems that use the front wheel drive speedometer, the speedometer adapters are not required in the electrical system.*

Wiring Harness & Circuit Breaker

Electric wiring in the system is a completely assembled unit including a circuit breaker. Individual wires in the harness are identified by various colors, Fig. 49. The circuit breaker is connected to the wire leading from the power source. If a short circuit occurs, the circuit breaker will open and cut off electrical current to the system.

Solenoid Valves

Two solenoid valves provide the link between the electrical control system and the air-torsion spring shift units. When the solenoids are energized, air is allowed to travel to the air shift units and thus shift the axles. When the solenoid valves are de-energized, by movement of control switch, air pressure supply is shut off allowing the air-torsion spring shift unit to bleed air through the solenoid valve exhaust port. In units with an electric lockout, an additional solenoid valve controls air pressure supply to operate the lockout unit mounted on the power divider.

Lockout With Low Pressure Switch

A low pressure switch is included in the shift system. This switch is mounted in the lockout valve and prevents the use of the inter-axle differential lockout except when the axles are in low ratio. When the lockout is engaged this switch immediately allows the axles to go to low ratio, no matter what range they were in previously. With lockout engaged, the axles cannot be shifted.

Fig. 48 Eaton three speed axle control switch

Lockout With Electric Switches

The electric type lockout consists of two electric switches and a solenoid valve, Fig. 49. One switch is located in the vehicle cab and the other is mounted on the forward rear axle shift unit. This type system permits lockout to engage in low range only. When the shift unit is in intermediate and high range position, the electric switch at the shift unit is open. This prevents completion of the electrical circuit to the lockout solenoid valve.

Air-Torsion Spring Shift Unit

This unit is mechanically connected to the axle shift fork and shifts the axle. The unit includes an air chamber and a torsion spring drive assembly. A diaphragm, operated by air pressure, moves a push rod. The end of the push rod connects to a spring winding lever. This lever is part of the torsion spring drive assembly, which acts to move the shift fork and change axle range as described under *System Operation*.

SYSTEM OPERATION

Operation In High Range

When control switch is moved to "HI" position, current to the two solenoid valves allows air to pass from its supply through the valves and be applied to the air shift diaphragm on both forward and rearward driving axles.

Diaphragm movement operates the push rod on each unit which, in turn, moves the spring winding levers. The spring winding levers increase the load placed on the torsion springs. When this occurs, the axles are ready to shift to high range. When torque on the gears is relieved by closing and opening the throttle, or declutching, the shift is completed.

Operation In Intermediate Range

When the control switch is moved to the "INT" position, the solenoid valve shuts off the air supply to the rearward rear axle shift unit, and the solenoid valve for the forward rear axle remains open, allowing the forward axle shift unit to retain its air. Thus, when

EATON DRIVING AXLES

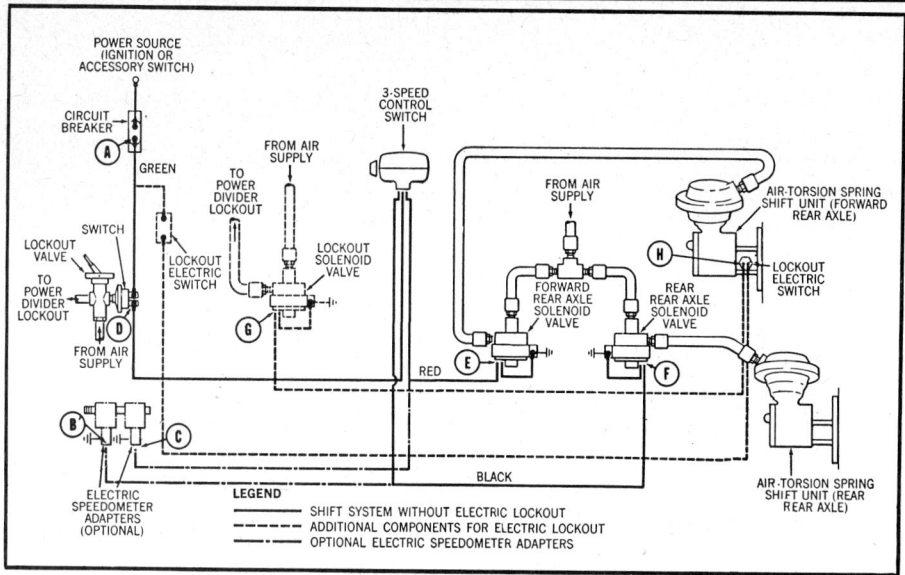

Fig. 49 Eaton air-torsion spring shift system diagram

torque on the gears is relieved by closing and opening the throttle, or declutching, the rearward rear axle is shifted to low range and the forward rear axle remains in high range. The shift is now completed to intermediate.

Operation In Low Range

When the control switch is moved to the "LO" position, both solenoid valves shut off the air supply. Air pressure in the air-torsion spring shift units bleeds back through the solenoid valves and air lines. Pressure on diaphragm is released. Push rod moves toward diaphragm and moves spring winding lever. Additional load is placed on torsion spring, providing a condition ready for axle to shift to low range. When torque on gears is relieved by closing and opening throttle, or declutching, the shift to low range is completed.

TROUBLE SHOOTING

If the axle will not shift, test system as follows, using a 12-volt test lamp at the terminal references indicated in Fig. 49.

Circuit Breaker Operation

Disconnect circuit breaker lead wire ("A"). Connect test lamp across terminal "A" and ground on vehicle frame. Turn on ignition (or diesel accessory switch) and observe test lamp operation:
If lamp lights and stays on continuously, circuit breaker and lead wire are satisfactory.
If lamp does not light, check for poor electrical connections or broken lead wire. If these are satisfactory, circuit breaker is faulty.
If lamp does not light immediately then starts to flash on and off, the circuit breaker is faulty.

Control Switch & Wiring Harness

1. Check harness for damage or worn insulation that may cause a ground connection, especially where harness passes through cab floor. Check for short circuits between wire terminals.
2. To determine condition of control switch, it is recommended that a new switch be temporarily installed. However, if a new switch is not available, check its operation with the test lamp as follows:

NOTE: *Under actual installation conditions, lead wires to speedometer adapters could be transposed without affecting operation. However, in the following tests it is assumed that the black and red wires are connected as shown in Fig. 49.*

3. Disconnect wires at speedometer adapter terminals "B" and "C" and at solenoid terminals "E" and "F". Turn ignition on and alternately connect test lamp leads to disconnected lead wires. Operate control switch and observe test lamp for following conditions:
4. When test lamp is connected to speedometer adapter lead wire "B", lamp should light when control switch is in "HI" position. Lamp should go out with control switch in "INT" or "LO" position.
5. When test lamp is connected to lead wire ("C"), lamp should light in "HI" or "INT" position. Lamp should go out in "LO" switch position.
6. When test lamp is connected to solenoid valve lead wire "E", lamp should light in "INT" and "HI" positions of control switch. Lamp should go out when switch is in "LO" position.
7. When test lamp is connected to solenoid lead wire "F", lamp should light in "HI" position, and should go out when control switch is in "INT" or "LO".
8. If test indications are correct in the foregoing tests, current supply is correct to speedometer adapters and solenoid valves.
9. If lamp does not light correctly, trouble may be a short circuit in wiring harness or control switch, or a wire in harness may be broken.

Solenoid Valve Operation

1. Disconnect solenoid lead wires at terminals "E", "F" and "G". Also disconnect air lines leading to respective shift unit.
2. Install an air pressure gauge in air line opening in solenoid valve.
3. Apply power supply (vehicle voltage) to solenoid terminal and observe pressure gauge reading. Operating pressure should approximate reservoir pressure.
4. If gauge indicates approximate reservoir pressure, solenoid operation is satisfactory. If gauge indicates low or no pressure, solenoid is faulty.

Air Torsion Spring Shift Unit Operation

If electrical system is satisfactory and axle does not shift correctly, trouble may be caused by a faulty spring shift unit which should be disassembled and repaired.

Speedometer Adapter Operation

Before condemning speedometer adapter operation, make certain that ground connection is satisfactory. If testing is required, proceed as follows:
1. Disconnect lead wire at terminal "B".
2. Connect test lamp to disconnected wire terminal and ground on vehicle frame.
3. Turn ignition switch on and observe test lamp. Test lamp should light in high range and should go out in intermediate and low ranges.
4. To test other speedometer adapter, disconnect wire at terminal "C".
5. Connect test lamp to disconnected wire and ground on vehicle frame.
6. Lamp should light in intermediate and high ranges, and should go out in low range.
7. If lamp indications are correct, current supply to adapters is correct.
8. If lamp indications are correct and axle shifts normally but speedometer does not operate properly, replace faulty adapter.
9. If test lamp indications are not correct, trouble is in wiring harness or control switch.

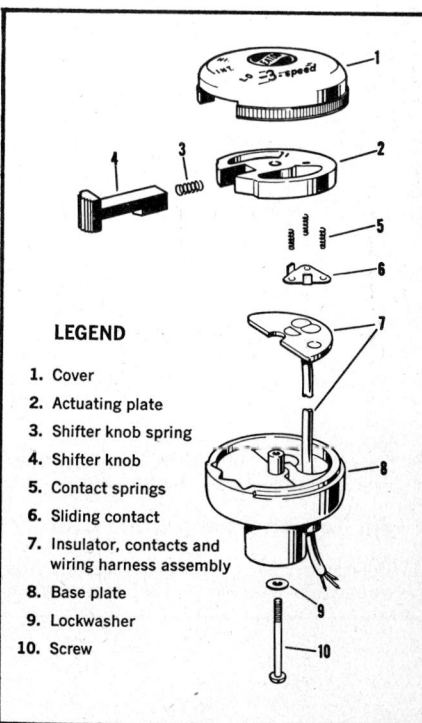

LEGEND
1. Cover
2. Actuating plate
3. Shifter knob spring
4. Shifter knob
5. Contact springs
6. Sliding contact
7. Insulator, contacts and wiring harness assembly
8. Base plate
9. Lockwasher
10. Screw

Fig. 50 Control switch disassembled

EATON DRIVING AXLES

Low Pressure Switch Operation

1. Place control switch in "HI".
2. Turn on ignition switch, then engage inter-axle differential lockout.
3. Air should bleed from shift system and axles should shift to low range.
4. If this does not occur, check low pressure switch circuit with test lamp as follows:
5. Disconnect wire at terminal "D".
6. Connect test lamp to terminal "D" and ground on vehicle frame.
7. Turn on ignition switch.
8. Place lockout valve in engaged and disengaged positions, and observe test lamp.
9. In disengaged position, lamp should light. If not, check for poor electrical connection or broken lead wire. If wire and connections are satisfactory, low pressure switch is faulty.
10. In the engaged position, lamp should not light. If it does, low pressure switch is faulty.

Electric Switch As Shift Unit

1. Disconnect wire at terminal "H".
2. Connect test lamp to terminal "H" and ground.
3. Close manual electrical lockout switch and operate control switch in all positions.
4. Test lamp should light in "LO" and should not light in "INT" and "HI".
5. Replace faulty switch.

UNIT REPAIRS

Control Switch

1. Referring to Fig. 50, disconnect wires at end of switch wiring harness, and unscrew switch from gear shift lever.
2. Remove screw from mounting side of switch and lift off over, actuating plate, shifter knob, knob spring, contact springs and contact.
3. Remove insulator, contacts and wiring harness from base plate.

REASSEMBLE

1. Pass wire harness through base plate, positioning insulator in recessed area in base plate.
2. Lightly coat contacts and pivot hub (at center of base plate) with non-melting silicone grease.
3. Hold actuating plate (top side down) in one hand and install three springs and sliding contact in correct mounting position. Place base plate over actuating plate with other hand.
4. Hold actuating and base plates together with one hand and install spring and shifter knob.
5. Continue to hold actuating plate in mounting position and install cover. Fasten cover to base plate with screw and lock washer.
6. Thread switch onto shift lever and connect wiring harness (see Fig. 49).

Air Torsion Spring Shift Unit

1. Referring to Fig. 51, disconnect air line connection from shift lever cover (when

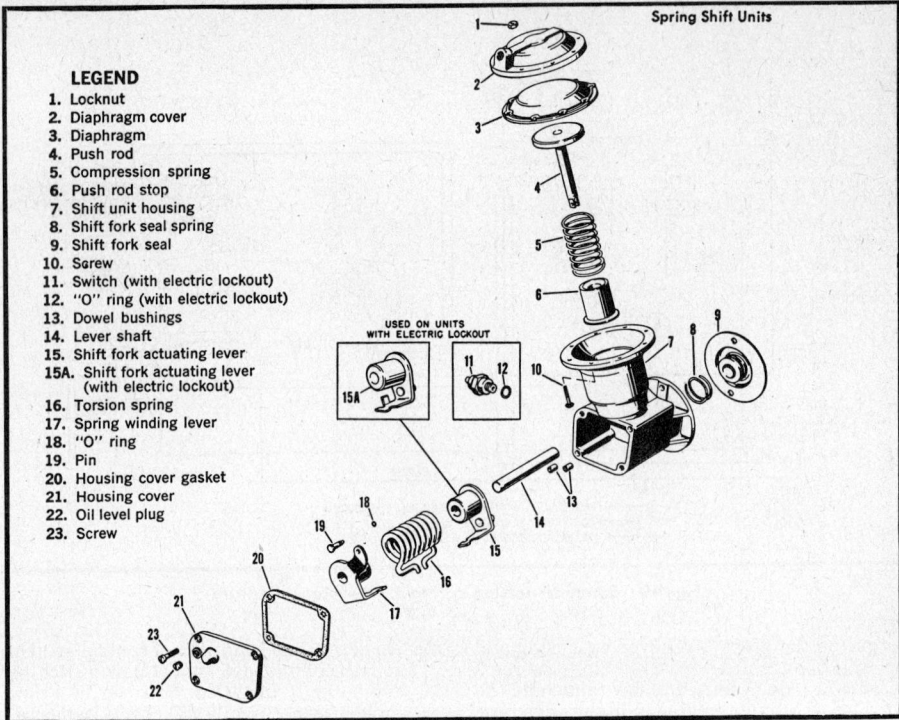

Fig. 51 Air torsion spring shift unit disassembled

LEGEND
1. Locknut
2. Diaphragm cover
3. Diaphragm
4. Push rod
5. Compression spring
6. Push rod stop
7. Shift unit housing
8. Shift fork seal spring
9. Shift fork seal
10. Screw
11. Switch (with electric lockout)
12. "O" ring (with electric lockout)
13. Dowel bushings
14. Lever shaft
15. Shift fork actuating lever
15A. Shift fork actuating lever (with electric lockout)
16. Torsion spring
17. Spring winding lever
18. "O" ring
19. Pin
20. Housing cover gasket
21. Housing cover
22. Oil level plug
23. Screw

equipped with electric locknut disconnect wires at switch).
2. Unfasten and lift shift unit off studs.
3. Remove shift fork seal and spring.

NOTE: Shift unit need not be completely disassembled to replace torsion spring drive assembly. Air pressure applied to opening in diaphragm cover will move push rod enough to remove or install pin which connects push rod to spring winding lever.

DISASSEMBLE

1. Remove housing cover and drain lubricant.
2. Remove diaphragm and cover from housing.
3. When equipped with electric lockout, unscrew switch and O-ring from housing.
4. Place housing in a vise and compress spring until pin which connects push rod and spring winding lever together, can be removed.
5. Remove pin and O-ring.
6. Carefully open vise until tension on compression spring is completely relieved.
7. Remove housing from vise and remove push rod, compression spring and push rod stop from housing.
8. Remove lever shaft and lift torsion spring drive from housing. Do not disassemble these parts unless replacement is necessary.

REASSEMBLE

1. Place torsion spring drive in housing. Insert lever shaft through torsion spring drive and into hole provided in housing.
2. Place push rod stop, compression spring and push rod in housing.
3. Place housing in vise. Close vise to compress spring until pin can be installed to connect push rod to spring winding lever.
4. Install O-ring on pin, then insert pin in openings provided in spring winding lever and push rod end.
5. Remove housing from vise.
6. Place shift fork seal on studs and differential carrier. Install spring on seal.
7. Place shift unit on mounting studs and make certain shift fork actuating lever engages slot in shift fork. Install stud nuts and lock washers.
8. Place diaphragm and cover on housing and secure with screws and lock nuts. Tighten lock nuts to 50-60 inch-lbs. After initial torquing, retighten until 50-60 inch-lbs is permanently maintained.
9. Install dowel bushings (if removed), gasket and housing cover. Secure cover and torque screws to 35-40 inch-lbs.
10. When equipped with electric lockout, install switch and O-ring in housing, and connect wiring to switch.
11. Connect air line to shift unit cover.

Lubrication

1. Use SAE 10 engine oil all year.
2. Each 10,000 miles or three months, remove level plug in cover and check oil level. Level should be even with bottom of filler hole.
3. At least twice a year remove housing cover and drain oil. Wash parts thoroughly and air dry. Reinstall cover and remove level plug. Fill through oil hole to bottom of filler hole.

SPICER DRIVING AXLES

Spicer axles are of the integral carrier, hypoid gear type and are available in two and four pinion models, Figs. 1 and 2. Pinion and differential bearing preload and ring gear and pinion backlash adjustments are made through use of shim packs. Axle assembly and axle shaft replace procedures are covered in the applicable truck chapters. The following service procedures apply to both front and rear axle carriers.

Differential Carrier, Disassemble

1. Remove axle shafts as outlined in applicable truck chapter. Axle shafts may be pulled out far enough to clear differential side gears.
2. Drain lubricant and rear cover.
3. Make sure differential side bearing caps and axle housing are marked, then remove the side bearing caps.
4. Pry differential from housing, Fig. 3.
5. Remove side bearing cups.
6. Pull off side bearing and adjusting shims, tagging the shims for identification on reassembly.
7. Unfasten ring gear from case.
8. Drive out differential pinion shaft pin and pull out the shaft, pinions and side gears.
9. Hold companion flange from turning and remove flange nut.
10. Pull flange from pinion shaft.
11. Remove pinion from carrier by tapping on front end with soft hammer.
12. Remove pinion shaft bearing oil seal and bearings from carrier, keeping separate the shim pack at each bearing.

Pinion & Bearings, Replace

If the original ring gear and pinion are being used in the original carrier, use the original shim packs at each bearing, Fig. 4. If a new pinion or differential carrier is installed, note the markings on the end of the pinion gear and on the differential carrier to obtain the correct thickness of shimming to be used with these parts from your supplier. The shims behind the rear bearing establishes the correct pinion depth.

1. Press the rear pinion bearing cup in the housing with the proper thickness of shims. Press the rear pinion bearing on the shaft.
2. Install the front bearing cup and shims, and front bearing.
3. Install the companion flange and, while holding the flange from turning, tighten the nut to a torque load of 200–220 ft. lbs.

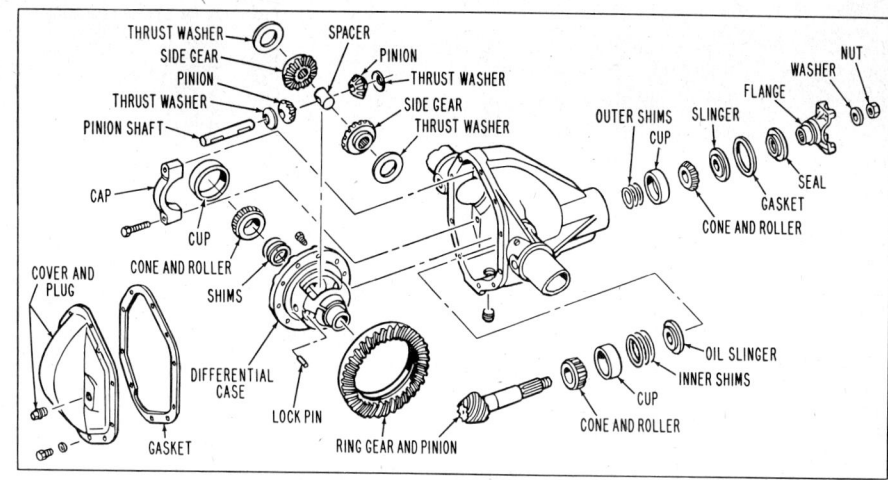

Fig. 1 Spicer 2 pinion driving axle

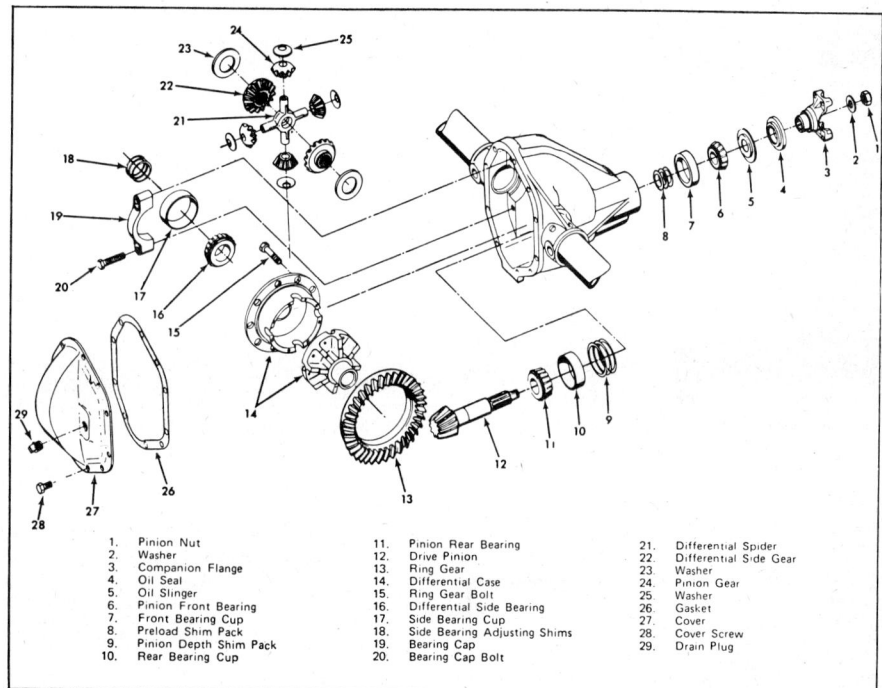

Fig. 2 Spicer 4 pinion driving axle

SPICER DRIVING AXLE SPECIFICATIONS

Model	Ring Gear & Pinion Backlash		Pinion Bearing Preload			Differential Bearing Preload		
	Method	Adjustment	Method	New Bearings Inch-Lbs.	Used Bearings Inch-Lbs.	Method	New Bearings Inch	Used Bearings Inch
27	Shims	.005–.010	Shims	10–25	—	Shims	.015	.015
30	Shims	.005–.009	Shims	15–35	10–20	Shims	.015	.015
44	Shims	.005–.010	Shims	20–40	10–20	Shims	.015	.015
53	Shims	.005–.010	Shims	10–25	—	Shims	.015	.015
60, 61	Shims	.005–.009	Shims	20–40	10–20	Shims	.015	.015
70	Shims	.005–.010	Shims	20–40	10–20	Shims	.015	.015

SPICER DRIVING AXLES

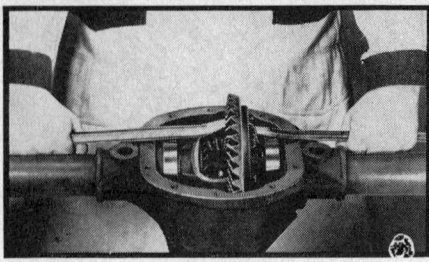

Fig. 3 Prying differential from housing

4. Check pinion bearing preload with an inch-pound torque wrench. Measure amount of torque required to turn pinion. If preload is not within specifications, add or remove shims from behind front bearing to obtain correct preload.
5. Remove the companion flange and install a new oil seal (well soaked). Reinstall the companion flange and tighten the nut to a torque load of 200–220 lb. ft.

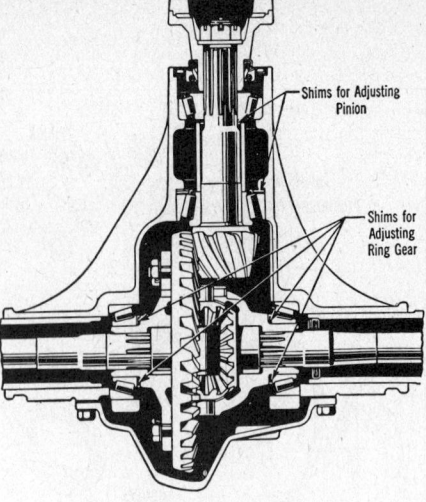

Fig. 4 Differential and pinion bearing adjustments

Fig. 6 Installing differential in housing

Ring Gear, Replace

1. Install guide pins in every other hole in the ring gear. These pins can be made from 1½" long capscrews with heads cut off the ends slotted.
2. Make sure back face of ring gear and face of case are free of dirt and burrs and slip gear over pilot diameter of case.
3. Install every other ring gear bolt. Draw them up evenly and snugly so ring gear face is flush with face of case.
4. Remove guide pins and install remaining bolts.

Differential Carrier, Assemble

The differential bearings are adjusted by shims, Fig. 4. These shims also establish the ring gear position with the pinion. Therefore, backlash must be checked whenever a bearing adjustment is made.

The correct bearing adjustment is one which will provide a .015–.020" pinch fit when the differential unit is assembled into the carrier. To make the adjustment, install the bearing cones without shims and place the assembly in the housing with the bearing cups. Force the unit to one side and check the clearance between the bearing cup and differential case with a feeler gauge, Fig. 5. When the clearance is determined, select shims of this amount plus .015–.020" extra to establish the proper pre-load.

Remove the differential bearings again and divide the shims into two packs of equal thickness and install on each side and replace the

Fig. 5 Checking clearance between bearing cup and differential case

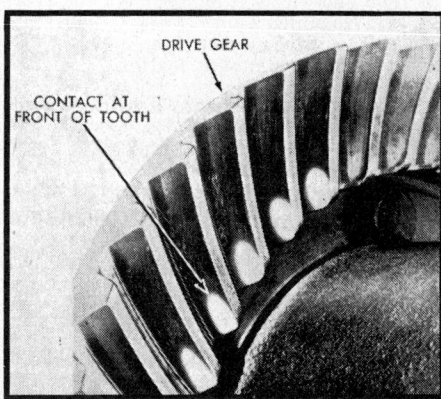

Fig. 9 Short toe contact. Move drive gear away from pinion

Fig. 7 Ring gear and pinion backlash adjustment

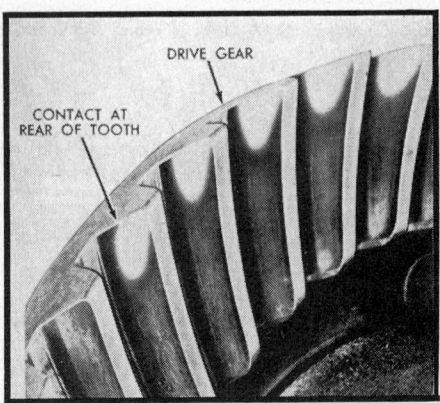

Fig. 8 Short heel contact. Move drive gear toward pinion

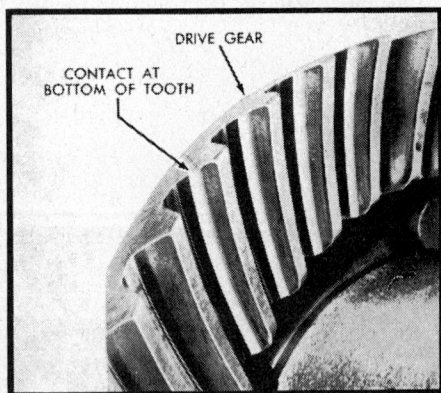

Fig. 10 Contact too low and narrow. Pinion should be moved away from center of axle

SPICER DRIVING AXLES

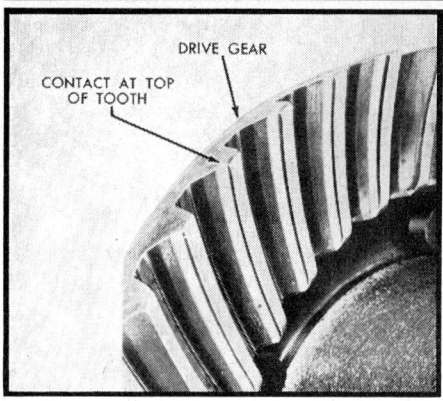

Fig. 11 Contact too high and narrow. Pinion should be moved toward center of axle

Fig. 12 Correct tooth contact

sure the ring gear teeth mesh with the pinion teeth before tapping the bearings in place. After the bearing cups are firmly in place, install the bearing caps. The bearing caps and gasket surface of the housing are marked with a horizontal numeral and on the other side by a vertical numeral. The position of the numerals should correspond when reinstalling the bearing caps.

Ring Gear & Pinion Backlash, Adjust

Mount a backlash gauge indicator on the carrier and start checking for the correct backlash between the ring gear and pinion. If the backlash is not within specifications, it will be necessary to change the arrangement of the shims back of the bearings. Make corrections in backlash according to Fig. 7, bearing in mind that shims removed from one side must be installed on the opposite side so that the total shim thickness of the right and left side will remain unchanged and the bearing adjustment undisturbed.

Gear Tooth Contact Pattern

Allowable variations in the carrier or drive

bearings. Reinstall the unit in the carrier. This operation is made easier by cocking the bearing cups slightly when the differential is placed in the housing and then tapping them lightly with a mallet, Fig. 6. However, when installing the differential in the housing, be

pinion may cause the pinion to be too far in or out even when shimmed properly. Thus, the tooth contact must be tested and corrected as necessary or the gears may be noisy.

Paint the ring gear teeth with a light coating of red lead, white lead or prussian blue. Revolve the gears and observe the contact, referring to Figs. 8 to 12.

TIMKEN (Rockwell) DRIVING AXLES

LUBRICANT CAPACITIES

Lubricant capacities are given as a guide only. The capacities of two similar axles of the same series may vary considerably due to design changes and the vehicle manufacturer's installation. The actual service capacity may be determined by carefully measuring the amount of lubricant necessary to fill the assembly to the correct level and measuring the lubricant again when it is drained. The vehicle should be on a level floor when this inspection is made.

Single Axles

Model	Oil, Pints
A-150	5½
B-100	10
B-140	12
B-150	3½
C-100	12½
D-100	12½
D-140	13
E-100	15
E-105	12½
E-150	9
E-300	13①
E-350, 370	22①
F 30	6
F-35	7
F-37	7
F-38	10
F-46	10
F-50	10
F-53	12
F-54	11
F-56	14
F-58	15
F-75	9
F-77	10
F-100	13
F-106	13½
F-140	14
F-141	18
F-147	14
F-200	12
F-223	16
F-233, 234, 235	23
F-300	16
F-337	24
F-340	16①
F-400	16
F-409	28
F-501	10
F-544	10
F-551, 552	11
F-580, 583	15
F-2090	12
F-3100	16
F-3110	26
F-3200	22
F-4700	40
F-4710	32
F-7900	40
F-7910	32
FS-4711	32
FDS-75	13
FDS-750	7
FDS-1600	23
FDS-1800	35
G-161	21
G-340	24①
G-341	22①
G-361	21①
H-100	20
H-140	21
H-141	18
H-150	11
H-162	20
H-170	26½
H-171	27
H-200	28①
H-240	22①
H-262	23
H-300	26①
H-340	22①
H-350, 360, 370	24①
H-362	26
L-100	23
L-140	24
L-162	24
L-200	31①
L-240	22①
L-300	29①
L-340	22①
L-345	33
L-350	24①
L-362	26
L-370	32①
LT-200	31①
LT-300	29①
QT-140	24
QT-200	31①
QT-230	44③
QT-240	34①
QT-300	29①
QT-330	44③
QT-340	32①
Q-100	31
Q-200	34①
Q-245	34①
Q-246A	36
Q-300	32①
Q-345	32①
Q-346A	34
Q-350	34①
Q-370	34①
Q-380	36①
Q-390	36①
RT-240	32①
RT-340	32①
RT-341A	34
R-100	30
R-140, 160	28
R-163	34
R-170	43
R-171B	44½
R-200	36①
R-230	36①

TIMKEN (Rockwell) DRIVING AXLES

Model	Oil, Pints	Model	Oil, Pints	Model	Oil, Pints
R-230 ③	45 ①	SRHR	36	SQW	40 ③
R-300	34 ①	SSHD	32 ②	3010, SD	19
R-330	35 ①	SSHR	28	3010, SW	14
R-330 ③	44 ①	SRT-235	45 ①	3013, SW	23
R-390	60 ①	SRT-335	44 ①	3020, SD	31
R-2090	10	SLD	28	3020, SFD	31
R-3100	20	SLDD	28 ②	3020, SFDD	31 ③
S-200	38 ①	SQD	22	3020, SW	28
S-300	39 ①	SQDD	22 ②	3022, SW	27
U-200	38 ①	SRD	22	472, SD	28
U-300	39 ①	SRDD	22 ②	473, SD	28
		STD	28	700, SBD	7
		STDD	30	760, SBD	5
		STDDA	30	1000, SBD	8
		SUDD	46	1055, SBD	19
Tandem Axles		SUDDA	46	1500, SBD	12
Model	Oil, Pints	4600, SFD	28	1555, SBD	26
SDHD	16 ②	4600, SFDD	28 ②	3000, SD	19
SDHR	16	4700, SFD	28	3000, SW	19
SFDD	28	4700, SFDD	28 ②	3002, SW	17
SFHD	17 ②	75, SFD	16	3456, SW	24
SFHR	16½	157, SFD	9	3458, SW	33
SHHD	26 ②	353, SD	24		
SHHR	26	375, SFD	23		
SLHD	32½ ②	450, SFD	36		
SLHR	32	454, SD	26		
SQHD	34 ②	456, SW	28		
SQHP	40 ②	457, SW	28		
SQHR	31	460, SW	28		
SQTT-335	44 ①	460, SFD	29		
SRHD	37 ②	SQW	33		

①—Add one pint of lubricant to pinion cage when new or reconditioned drive unit is installed.
②—Add two pints of lubricant to inter-axle differential housing when new or reconditioned drive unit is installed in addition to specified amount of lubricant in housing.
③—Housing cover 6½" deep overall.

Single Reduction Axles

INDEX

	Page No.
Model Index and Lube Capacities	241
Single Reduction Axles	242
Double Reduction Axles	246
Two Speed Double Reduction Axles	253
Single Reduction Thru-Drive Tandem Axles	258
Double Reduction Thru-Drive Tandem Axles	262
Worm Drive Axles	269
Electric Shift for Two Speed Axles	272

DISASSEMBLE

Remove Carrier From Housing

1. Remove plug from bottom of housing and drain lubricant.
2. Remove axle shaft drive stud nuts and lockwashers.
3. Rap axle shafts sharply in center of flange to free dowels. Remove taper dowels and pull out axle shafts. *Prying shafts loose will damage hubs and oil seals.*
4. Disconnect universal at pinion shaft.
5. Remove carrier-to-housing stud nuts and washers. Loosen two top nuts and leave on studs to prevent carrier from falling.
6. Break carrier loose from axle housing with rawhide mallet.
7. Remove top nuts and washers and work carrier free, using puller screws in holes provided. A small pinch bar may be used to straighten carrier in housing bore. However, the end must be rounded to prevent indenting carrier flange. A roller jack may be used to facilitate removal of carrier.

Disassemble Carrier, Fig. 1

1. To remove differential and gear assembly, cut lock wire. Remove capscrews and adjusting nut locks.
2. Center punch one differential carrier leg and bearing cap to identify for proper reassembly.
3. Remove bearing cap stud nuts or capscrews, bearing caps and adjusting nuts.
4. Loosen jam nut and back off thrust block

Fig. 2 Measuring pinion bearing preload

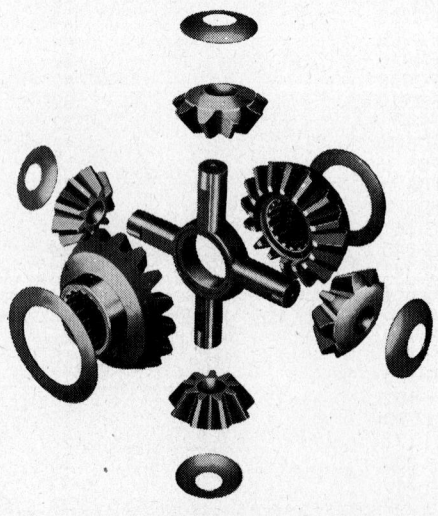

Fig. 3 Differential pinion and side gear assembly

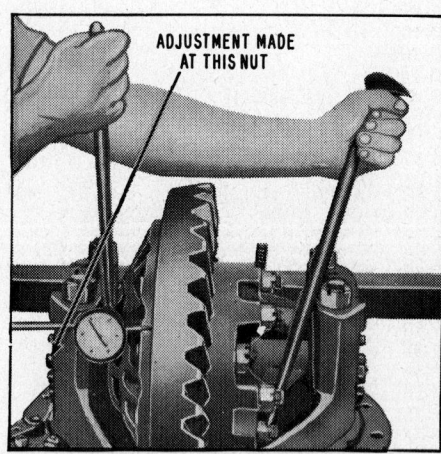

Fig. 4 Adjusting differential bearing preload

TIMKEN (Rockwell) DRIVING AXLES

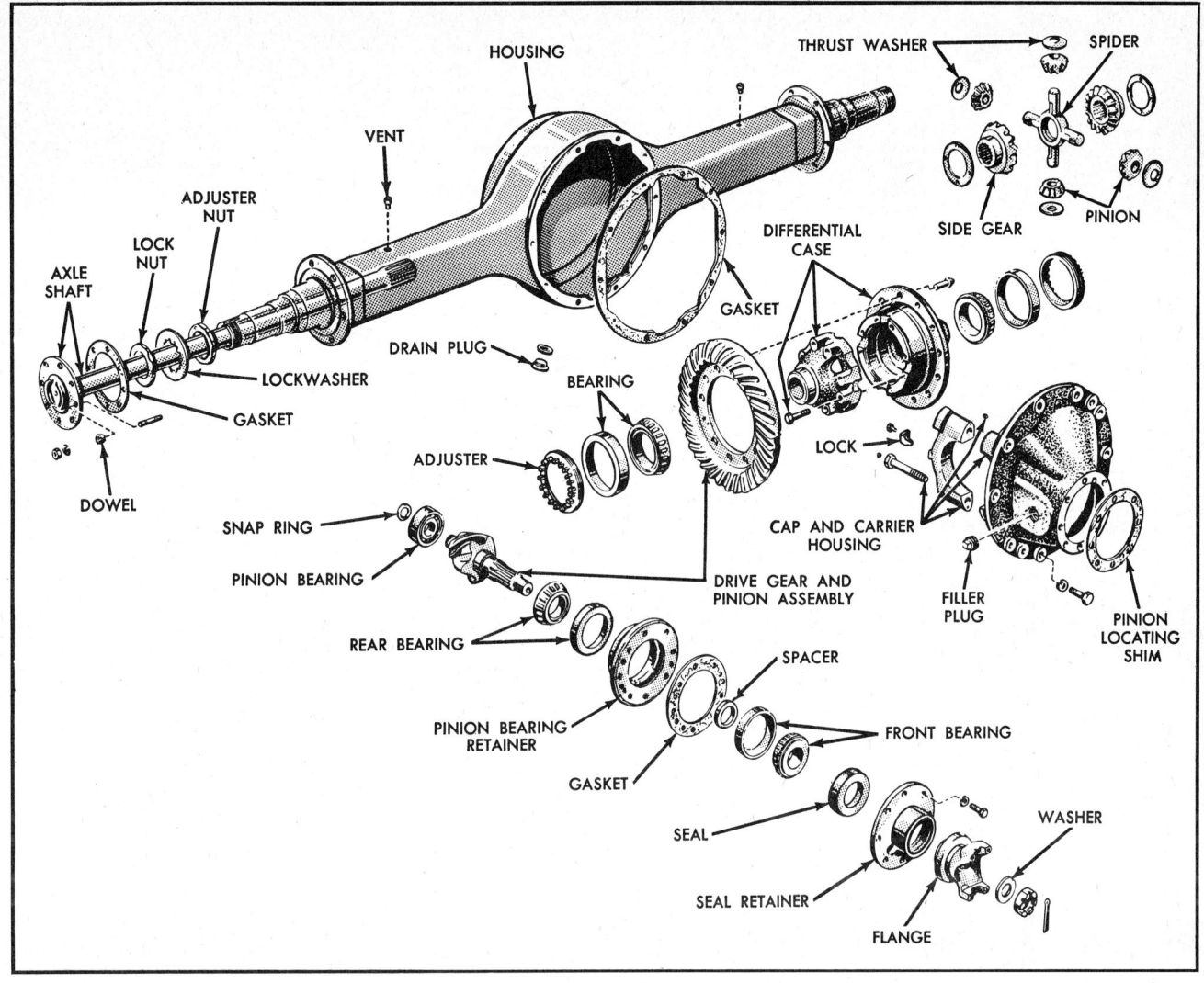

Fig. 1 Timken (Rockwell) single reduction axle (typical)

adjusting screw.
5. Lift out differential and gear assembly.
6. Remove thrust block from inside of carrier housing.

Disassemble Differential & Gear

1. If original identification marks are not clear, mark differential case halves with a punch or chisel for correct alignment upon reassembly.
2. Cut lock wire, remove bolts and separate case halves.
3. Remove spider, pinions, side gears and thrust washers.
4. To remove ring gear rivets, carefully center punch rivets in center of head. Use a drill 1/32" smaller than body of rivet to drill through head. Then press out rivets.
5. If necessary to remove differential bearings, remove with a suitable puller.

Removing Pinion & Cage

1. Hold flange or yoke with suitable tool and remove pinion shaft nut and washer.
2. Remove flange or yoke with a suitable puller. *Driving flange off will cause runout.*

3. Remove pinion cage stud nuts or capscrews.
4. Remove bearing cover and oil seal assembly.
5. Remove bearing cage, using puller screws in holes provided. *The use of a pinch bar will damage shims. Driving pinion from inner end with a drift will damage bearing lock ring groove.*
6. Wire shim pack together to facilitate adjustment on reassembly.

Disassemble Pinion & Cage

Both splined and tapered pinion shafts are used in single reduction carriers. Where the tapered shaft is used, the thrust bearings are adjusted by means of adjusting and lock nuts. On the splined shaft, this adjustment is secured with a selective spacer or spacer combination.

Splined Shaft
1. Tap shaft out of cage with a soft mallet and press shaft from cage.
2. Remove outer bearing from cage.
3. Remove spacer or spacer combination from pinion shaft.
4. If necessary to replace rear thrust bearing or radial bearing, remove with suitable puller.
5. Remove oil seal from bearing cover.

Tapered Shaft
1. Straighten lock washer, and remove lock nut, washer, adjusting nut and thrust washer.
2. Tap pinion out of cage with a soft mallet or press shaft from cage.
3. Remove bearing from cage.
4. Remove bearings from shaft with suitable puller if necessary.
5. Remove oil seal from bearing cover.

REPAIRS

1. Replace all worn or damaged parts. Hex nuts with rounded corners, all lock washers, oil seals and gaskets should be replaced.
2. Remove nicks, mars or burrs from machined or ground surfaces. Threads must be clean and free to obtain accurate adjustment and correct torque. A fine mill file or India stone is suitable for this purpose. Studs must be tight prior to reassembling of parts.
3. All bronze bushed differential pinions should be ball burnished after bushing

243

TIMKEN (Rockwell) DRIVING AXLES

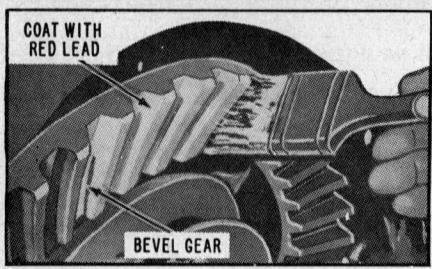

Fig. 5 Painting ring gear teeth for obtaining tooth contact impressions

installation. Install bushing with a small stepped drift. The small O.D. should be .010" smaller than the bushing burnished I.D. and 1½ times bushing length. Always install bushings so end is even with I.D. chamfer or about 1/16" below the spherical surface.
4. When assembling components, use a press where possible.
5. Tighten all nuts to the specified torque (see torque limits following service instructions). Use soft iron locking wire to prevent possibility of wire breakage.
6. The burrs, caused by lockwashers, at the spot face of stud holes of cages and covers should be removed to assure easy reassembly of these parts.

REASSEMBLY OF CARRIER

Pinion & Cage

Splined Shaft
1. Press rear thrust and radial bearings firmly against pinion shoulders with a suitable sleeve that will bear only on bearing inner race.
2. Install radial bearing lock ring and squeeze ring into pinion shaft groove with pliers.
3. If new cups are to be installed, press firmly against pinion bearing cage shoulders.
4. Lubricate bearings and cups with light machine oil.
5. Insert pinion and bearing assembly in pinion cage and position spacer or spacer combination over pinion shaft.
6. Press front bearing firmly against spacer.
7. Rotate cage several revolutions to assure normal bearing contact.
8. While in press under pressure, check bearing preload torque. Wrap soft wire around cage and pull on a horizontal line with a spring scale, Fig. 2. If a press is not available, the pinion nut may be tightened to the correct torque and preload checked.
9. The correct pressures and torque for checking pinion bearing preload are as follows:

Thread Size	Pressure	Torque, Ft. Lbs.
1" x 20	6 tons	300–400
1¼" x 18	11 tons	800–1100
1½" x 12	14 tons	800–1100
1½" x 18	14 tons	800–1100
1⅓" x 12	14 tons	800–1100

10. Use rotating torque, not starting torque. If rotating torque is not within 5 to 15 pound inches, use thinner spacer to increase or thicker spacer to decrease preload. Assuming pinion cage diameter to be 6", the radius would be 3" and with 5 pounds pull would equal 15 pound inches of preload torque.
11. Press flange or yoke against forward bearing and install washer and pinion shaft nut.
12. Place pinion and cage over carrier studs, hold flange and tighten pinion shaft nut to correct torque. Flange must be held with a suitable tool or fixture to tighten nut.
13. Recheck pinion bearing preload torque. If rotating torque is not within 5 to 15 pound inches, repeat the foregoing procedure.
14. Hold flange and remove pinion shaft nut and flange.
15. Lubricate pinion shaft oil seal and cover outer edge of seal body with a non-hardening sealing compound. Press seal against cover shoulder with a seal driver.
16. Install new gasket and bearing cover.
17. Press flange against forward bearing and install washer and pinion shaft nut.
18. Tighten to correct torque and install cotter key. *Do not back off nut to align cotter key holes.*

Tapered Shaft
1. Press rear thrust and radial bearings firmly against pinion shaft shoulder.
2. Install radial bearing lock ring and squeeze ring into pinion shaft groove with pliers.
3. If new cups are to be installed, press firm-

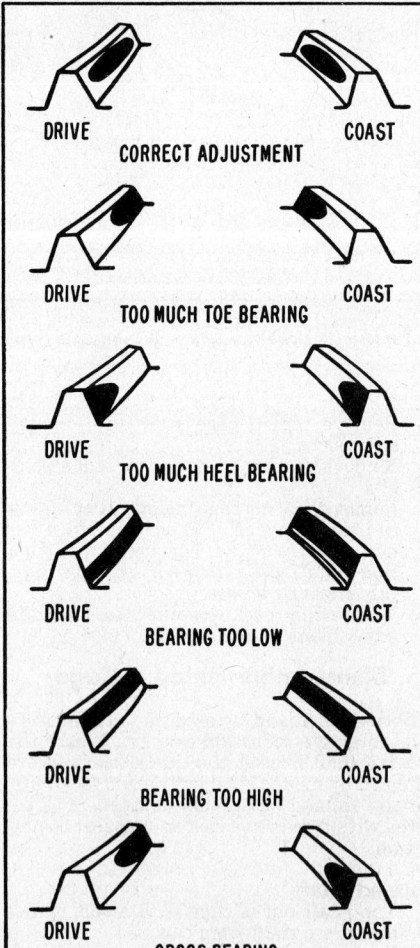

Fig. 6 Location, size and shape of tooth contacts

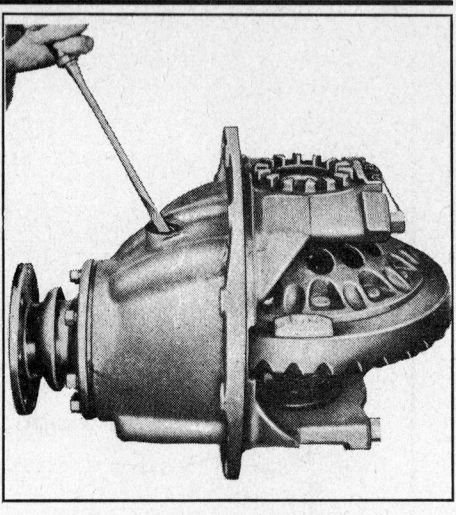

Fig. 7 Showing thrust block placed on back face of ring gear

ly against pinion cage shoulders.
4. Lubricate bearings and cups with light machine oil.
5. Install forward bearing, thrust washer and adjusting nut.
6. Install new lockwasher and lock nut.
7. Adjust pinion bearing preload to 5 to 15 pound inches with lock nut tightened securely against washer. *Lock nut must be tight to secure correct preload.*
8. Bend lock washer when correct preload has been obtained.
9. Lubricate pinion shaft oil seal and cover outer edge of seal body with a non-hardening sealing compound. Press seal against cover shoulder with a seal driver.
10. Install new gasket and bearing cover. Cover should be carefully installed to prevent cutting seal on keyway.
11. Install key, press flange on taper and install washer and pinion shaft nut.
12. Tighten to correct torque and install cotter key. *Do not back off nut to align cotter key holes.*

Install Pinion & Cage
1. Install correct shim pack. Locate thin shims on both sides for maximum sealing ability.
2. Position pinion and cage assembly over studs and tap into position with soft mallet.
3. Install lock washers and stud nuts or capscrews. Tighten to correct torque.

Assemble Differential & Gear
1. Rivet ring gear to case half with new rivets. Rivets should not be heated, but always upset cold. When the correct rivet is used, the head being formed will be at least 1/8" larger in diameter than the rivet hole. The head will then be approximately the same height as the preformed head. Excessive pressure will cause distortion of the case holes and result in gear eccentricity. Bolts are available for service replacement of rivets.
2. Lubricate differential case inner walls and all component parts with axle lubricant.
3. Position thrust washer and side gear in ring gear and case half, Fig. 3.
4. Place spider with pinions and thrust washers in position.

TIMKEN (Rockwell) DRIVING AXLES

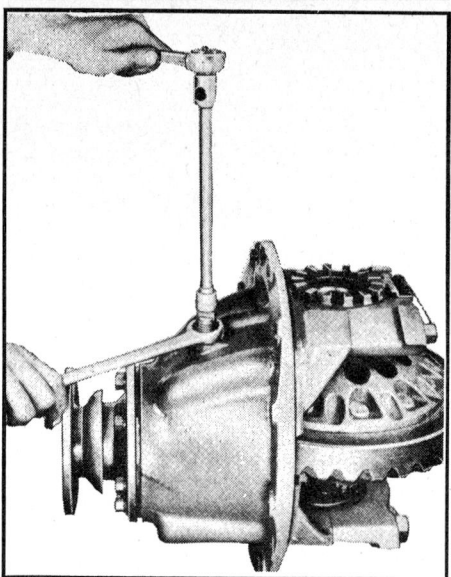

Fig. 8 Adjusting clearance between thrust block and back face of ring gear

Adjusting Differential Bearing Preload

1. Using dial indicator at back face of ring gear, Fig. 4, loosen bearing adjusting nut *on side opposite gear only* enough to notice end play on dial indicator.
2. Tighten same adjusting nut only enough to obtain zero end play.
3. Check gear for runout. If runout exceeds .008", remove differential and check for cause.
4. Tighten adjusting nuts *one notch each* from zero end play to preload differential bearings.

Check Ring Gear Backlash

If original gears are reused the backlash should be the same as before disassembly. For new gears the new backlash should be from .006" to .012". Adjust backlash by moving ring gear only. This is done by backing off one adjusting ring and advancing the opposite ring the same amount.

Check Gear Tooth Contact

Temporarily bolt up the pinion and cage to the differential carrier and coat the ring gear teeth with oiled red lead, Fig. 5. When the pinion is rotated, the red lead is squeezed away by the contact of the teeth, leaving bare areas the exact size, shape and location of the contacts. If these contacts are not acceptable, shims must be added to or removed from the shim pack located between the pinion cage flange and differential carrier housing. It may be necessary to make several attempts at the

5. Install component side gear and thrust washer.
6. Align mating marks and position component case half. Draw assembly together with four bolts or capscrews equally spaced.
7. Check assembly for free rotation of differential gears and correct if necessary.
8. Install remaining bolts and capscrews. Tighten to correct torque and lock with wire.
9. If bearings are to be replaced, press squarely and firmly on differential case halves.

Install Bearing Cups In Carrier Leg Bores

1. Temporarily install bearing cups or threaded adjusting rings and bearing caps. Tighten capscrews to proper torque.
2. The bearing cups must be a hand push fit in the bores, otherwise the bores must be re-worked with a scraper or some emery cloth until a hand push fit is obtained. Use a blued bearing cup as a gauge and check the fits as work progresses.

Install Differential & Gear

1. After checking related parts, coat differential bearing cones and cups with rear axle lubricant.
2. Place cups over assembled bearing cones and position differential assembly in carrier.
3. Insert bearing adjusting nuts and turn hand-tight against bearing cups.
4. Install bearing caps in correct location as marked and tap lightly in position. *If bearing caps do not position properly, adjusting nuts may be cross-threaded. Remove caps and reposition the adjusting nuts. Forcing caps into position will result in irreparable damage to carrier housing or bearing caps.*
5. Install flat washers where used and stud nuts or capscrews. Tighten to correct torque.

CAP SCREWS AND STUD NUTS

LOCATION	DIAMETER	NO. THREADS	TORQUE — LB. FT. MIN.	TORQUE — LB. FT. MAX.
Pinion cage	3/8"	16	27	35
	1/2"	13	81	104
	9/16"	12	116	149
	5/8"	11	160	205
Carrier to housing	7/16"	14	53	67
	1/2"	20	92	118
	5/8"	18	185	235
	3/4"	16	320	415
Differential case bolt	1/2"	20	92	118
	9/16"	18	130	167
	5/8"	18	185	235
	3/4"	16	320	415
Pinion shaft	7/8"	20	175	250
	1"	20	300	400
	1 1/4"	18	700	900
	1 1/2"	18	800	1100
	1 1/2"	12	800	1100
	1 3/4"	12	800	1100
Differential bearing adjusting nut lock	5/16"	18	16	20
	1/2"	13	81	104

DIFFERENTIAL BEARING CAP CAP SCREWS OR STUD NUTS
(Earlier Axle Models Without Hardened Washers)

CAP SCREW OR STUD NUT DIAMETER	CAP SCREW OR COARSE STUD THREAD	STUD NUT OR FINE THREAD	TORQUE — LB. FT. MIN.	TORQUE — LB. FT. MAX.
5/8"	11	18	130	170
3/4"	10	16	230	300
7/8"	9	14	345	440
7/8"	14	14	380	485
1"	14	14	380	485

DIFFERENTIAL BEARING CAP CAP SCREWS OR STUD NUTS
(Later Axle Models Employing Hardened Washers)

CAP SCREW OR STUD NUT DIAMETER	CAP SCREW OR COARSE STUD THREAD	STUD NUT OR FINE THREAD	TORQUE — LB. FT. MIN.	TORQUE — LB. FT. MAX.
5/8"	11	18	160	205
3/4"	10	16	290	370
7/8"	9	14	470	595
7/8"	14	14	510	655
1"	14	14	580	745

Fig. 9 Torque settings for Timken (Rockwell) single reduction axles. Specifications apply to parts coated with machine oil. For dry (or "as received") parts, increase torque 10%. For parts coated with multi-purpose gear oil, decrease torque 10%. Nuts on studs to use same torque as for driving the stud

TIMKEN (Rockwell) DRIVING AXLES

right selection of shims to obtain the correct tooth contact, Fig. 6.

Sharper tooth contact impressions may be obtained by applying a small amount of resistance to the gear with a flat steel bar and using a wrench to rotate the pinion. When making adjustments, check the drive side of the ring gear teeth. Coast side contact should be automatically correct when drive side contact is correct. As a rule coating about 12 teeth is sufficient for checking purposes.

Install Thrust Block

1. Remove thrust block adjusting screw and lock nut.
2. Place thrust block on rear face of ring gear, Fig. 7, and rotate gear until hole in thrust block is aligned with adjusting screw hole.
3. Install adjusting screw and lock nut and tighten screw enough to locate thrust block firmly against back face of ring gear.
4. To secure correct adjustment of .010" to .015" clearance Fig. 8, loosen adjusting nut 1/4 turn and lock securely with nut.
5. Recheck to assure minimum clearance of .010" during full rotation of ring gear.

Install Carrier In Housing

1. Install new gasket over housing studs.
2. Roll carrier into position on roller jack. Start carrier into housing with four flat washers and nuts equally spaced. *Do not drive carrier into housing with a hammer at the carrier stud flange. The flange may easily be distorted and cause severe oil leakage.*
3. Install lock washers and stud nuts on any studs under carrier housing offsets. *It is impossible to start these nuts after carrier is drawn into housing.*
4. Tighten the four nuts over flat washers alternately to draw carrier squarely into axle housing.
5. Remove nuts and flat washers. Install taper dowels, lock washers and stud nuts. Tighten to correct torque.
6. Connect universal at pinion shaft and install axle shafts.

Lubrication

1. Fill axle housing to correct level with specified lubricant.
2. Lubricate universal joint.
3. Jack up both rear wheels and operate vehicle in high transmission gear at approximately 25 mph for five minutes to assure satisfactory lubrication of all parts. *Do not operate with one wheel jacked up. Operation in this manner will result in over-heating the differential spider with resultant galling or shearing of spider pins.*

Double Reduction Axle

DISASSEMBLE

Remove Carrier From Housing

Front Mounted Carrier

The procedures for removing the differential carrier from the axle housing and removing the differential and drive gear from the carrier is the same as outlined for the single reduction axle. During the procedure which follows, refer to Figs. 1 and 2.

Top Mounted Carrier
1. Drain lubricant from housing.
2. Remove axle shaft stud nuts, lock washers and tapered dowels.

NOTE: To loosen the dowels, use a brass drift and hammer driving against the center of the axle shaft head, inside the circular driving lugs. Do not strike the circular driving lugs since the lugs may splinter or shatter.

3. Remove axle shafts and the front and rear propeller shafts.
4. Remove carrier to housing stud nuts and washers.
5. Loosen carrier from housing with a mallet and remove tapered dowels.
6. Pull carrier from housing with suitable lifting equipment.

Differential Case & Drive Gear

1. If original identification marks are not clear, center punch case halves for correct alignment on reassembly.
2. Cut lock wire, remove long bolts and separate case halves.
3. Remove spider, pinions, side gears and thrust washers.
4. Remove short bolts and separate gear from case half.
5. Remove differential bearings with suitable puller if necessary.
6. Remove drive gear rivets as directed for the Single Reduction Axle.

Pinion & Cage Assembly

1. Remove cage stud nuts or capscrews and lockwashers. Lift out cage assembly. *If cage is not free, tap it loose, using a soft drift on inner face of pinion or use puller screws in holes provided.*
2. Wire shim pack together to facilitate adjustment on reassembly.
3. Place pinion cage over carrier studs or secure with three capscrews. Hold flange and remove pinion shaft nut.
4. Press pinion shaft out of flange or yoke and cage.
5. Remove adjusting spacers or shims.
6. If necessary to renew the pinion or rear bearing, remove bearing with suitable puller.
7. Press front bearing and pinion shaft oil seal from cage. On assemblies where bearing cover is used, remove seal assembly from cover.

Cross Shaft Assembly

1. Remove stud nuts or capscrews and lockwashers from cross shaft bearing cage (side opposite drive gear).
2. Force off bearing cage with small pinch bar between back of gear and carrier housing (puller screw holes are also provided).
3. Wire shim pack together to facilitate adjustment on reassembly.
4. Remove cross shaft assembly.
5. Cut lock wire, remove capscrews and bearing retainer plate from gear end of shaft.
6. Press shaft from gear and bearing.
7. If necessary to replace bearing, remove bearing from opposite end of cross shaft with a suitable puller.
8. If necessary to replace bearing cups, remove cross shaft bearing cover or cage (drive gear side). Wire shim pack together to facilitate adjustment on reassembly.

REPAIRS

Precautions when making repairs on this axle are the same as outlined for the Single Reduction axle.

REASSEMBLY

Cross Shaft

1. Insert key and start shaft into drive gear in line with keyway or splines.
2. Press shaft squarely into drive gear. Gear must be firmly against cross shaft shoulder. *To facilitate installation, drive gear may be heated in oil from 200 to 250 degrees F.* Install capscrews where used.
3. Press bearing firmly against cross shaft shoulder on spur gear end.
4. Install bearing retainer plate and capscrews on drive gear end. Tighten to

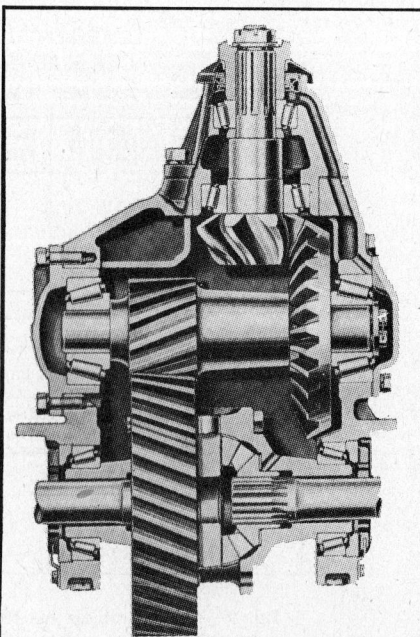

Fig. 1 Cutaway view of Timken (Rockwell) Double Reduction Axle (typical)

TIMKEN (Rockwell) DRIVING AXLES

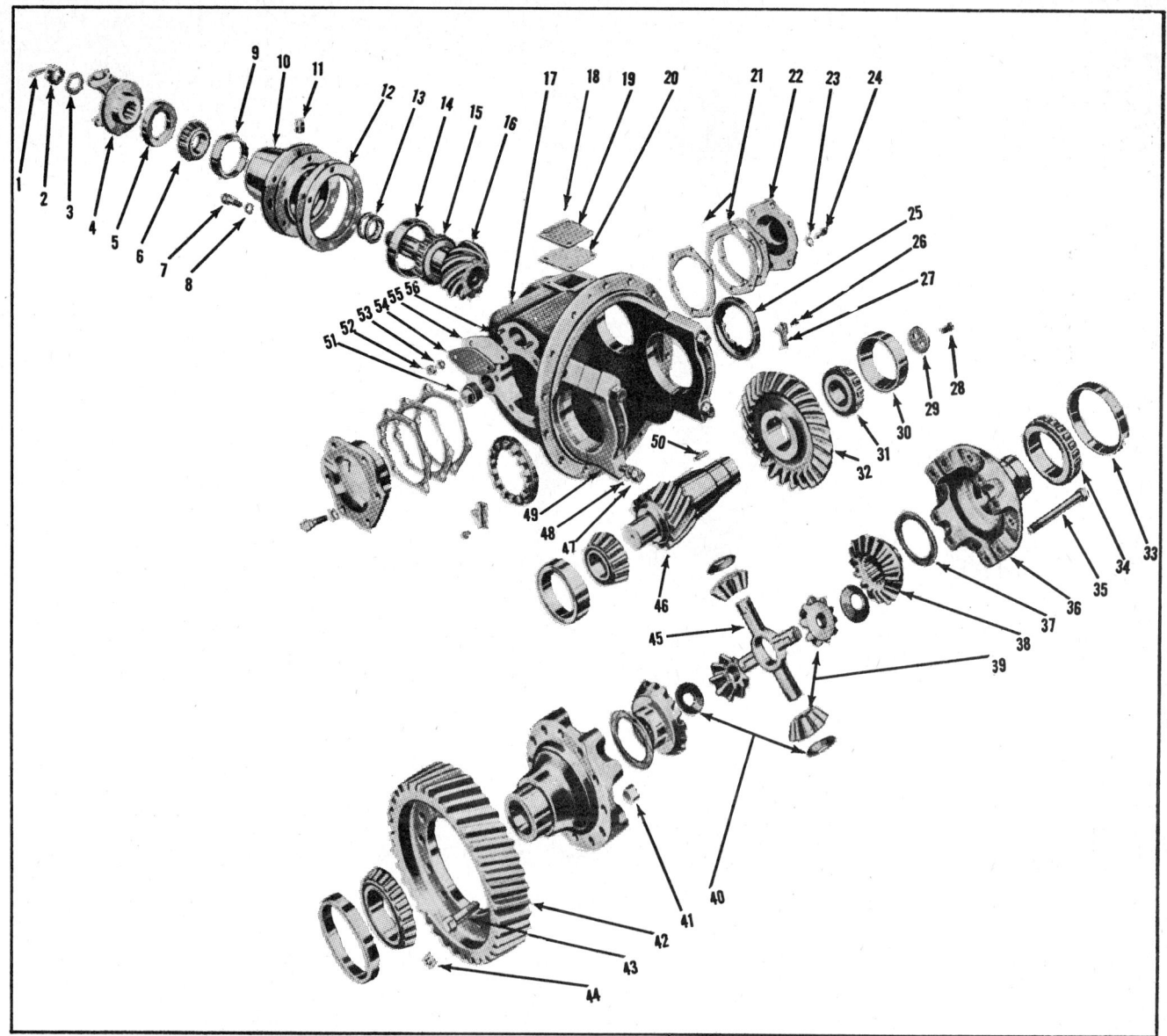

1. Cotter key
2. Yoke nut
3. Washer
4. Yoke and slinger assembly
5. Oil seal
6. Drive pinion outer bearing
7. Cap screw
8. Lock washer
9. Drive pinion outer bearing cup
10. Drive pinion bearing cage
11. Oil fill plug
12. Drive pinion shims
13. Drive pinion bearing spacer
14. Drive pinion inner bearing cup
15. Drive pinion inner bearing
16. Drive pinion
17. Differential carrier housing
18. Cap screw
19. Inspection hole cover
20. Gasket
21. Cross shaft cover shims
22. Cross shaft cover
23. Lock washer
24. Cap screw
25. Differential bearing adjusting nut
26. Cap screw
27. Differential bearing adjusting nut lock
28. Cap screw
29. Cross shaft bearing retainer
30. Cross shaft bearing cup
31. Cross shaft bearing
32. Drive gear
33. Differential bearing cup
34. Differential bearing
35. Differential case bolt
36. Differential case
37. Differential side gear thrust washer
38. Differential side gear
39. Differential pinion
40. Differential pinion thrust washer
41. Gear to case bolt nut
42. Helical spur gear
43. Gear to case bolt
44. Differential case bolt nut
45. Differential spider
46. Cross shaft (integral with spur pinion)
47. Differential bearing cap cap screw
48. Washer
49. Differential bearing cap
50. Square key
51. Oil level and fill plug
52. Stud nut
53. Lock washer
54. Shift shaft hole cover
55. Gasket
56. Stud

Fig. 2 Disassembled view of front mounted Timken (Rockwell) Double Reduction Axle

TIMKEN (Rockwell) DRIVING AXLES

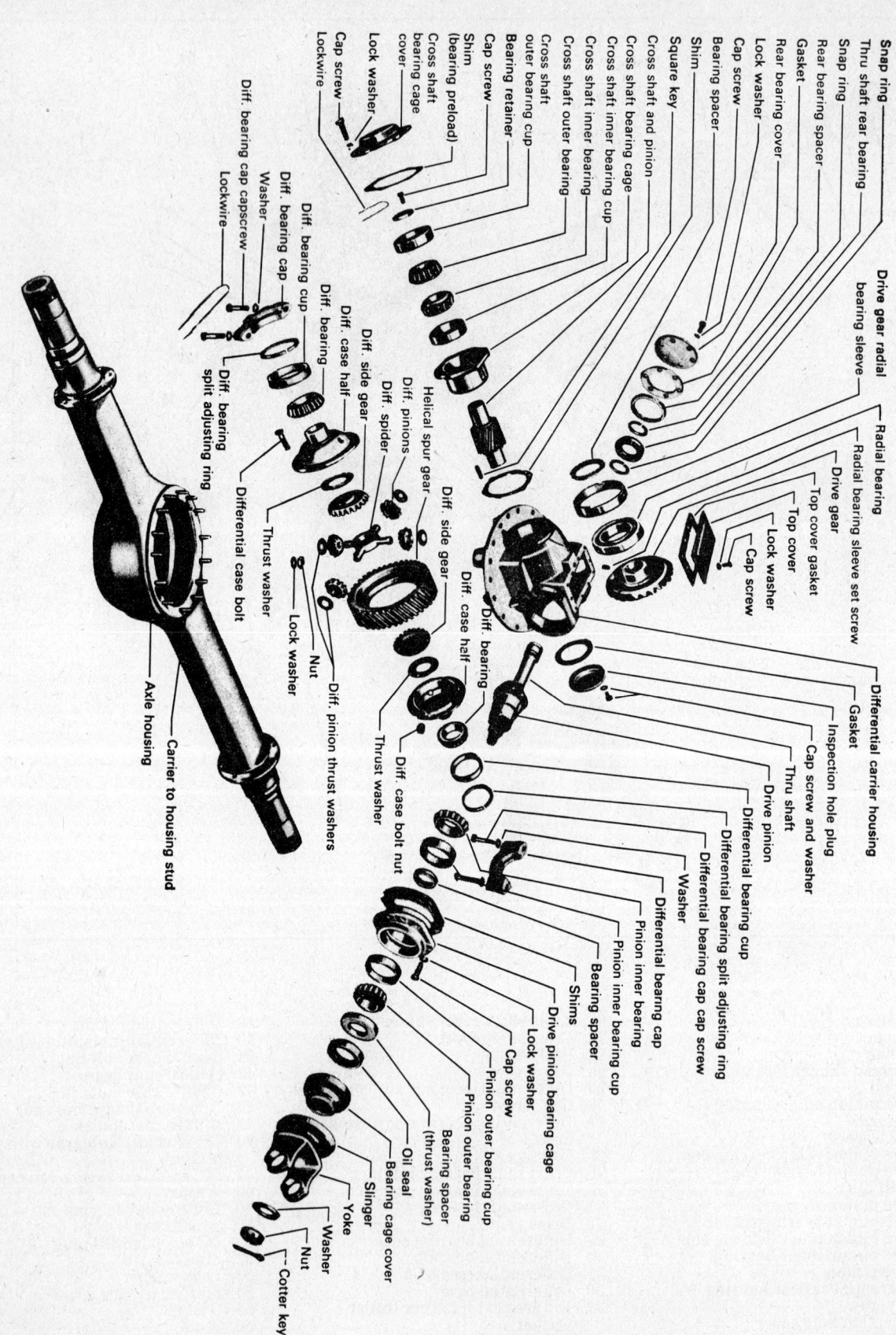

Fig. 3 Disassembled view of top mounted Timken (Rockwell) Double Reduction Axle, Series STD & STDD

TIMKEN (Rockwell) DRIVING AXLES

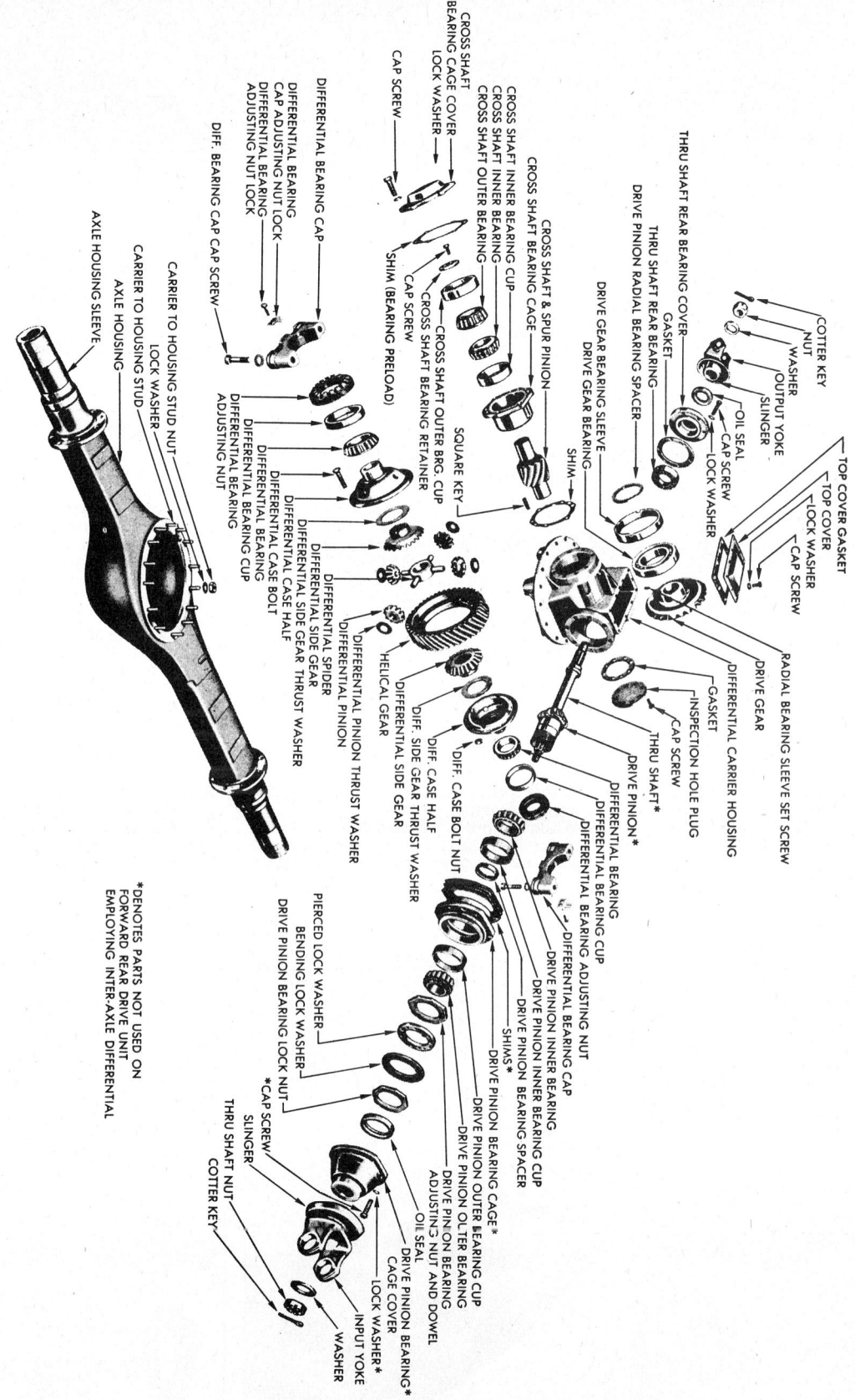

Fig. 3A Disassembled view of top mounted Timken (Rockwell) Double Reduction Axle, Series SRDD, SFDD, SUD & SUDD

TIMKEN (Rockwell) DRIVING AXLES

Fig. 4 Checking preload torque on cross shaft bearing

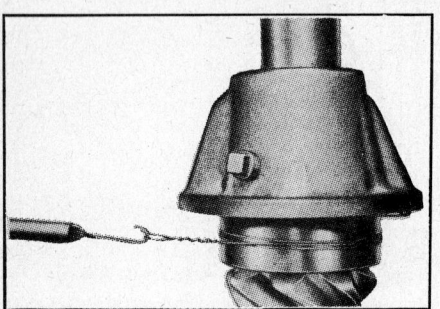

Fig. 4A Checking preload torque on pinion bearing

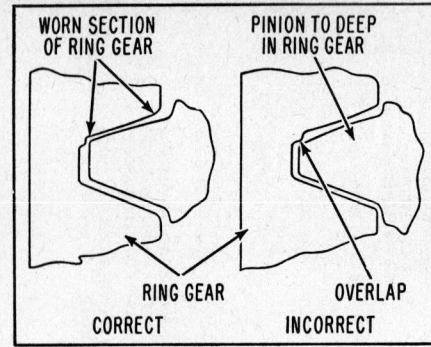

Fig. 5 Adjusting drive gear lash

Fig. 6 Checking drive gear lash with dial indicator

correct torque and lock with soft wire.
5. Lubricate cross shaft bearings and cups with light machine oil.
6. If bearing cover or cage on drive gear side has been removed, replace using the correct shim pack. Tighten stud nuts or capscrews to correct torque. If cover has not been removed, retighten stud nuts or capscrews to correct torque.
7. Ease cross shaft assembly past differential bearing supports and position in bearing cup.
8. Press bearing firmly against drive gear, using a suitable sleeve.
9. Install correct shim pack and start cross shaft bearing cage into carrier housing.
10. Tap bearing cage into position with soft mallet. Install lockwashers and stud nuts or capscrews and tighten to correct torque.
11. Rotate assembly several revolutions before checking bearing preload to assure full bearing contact.
12. Check cross shaft bearing preload torque. Wrap soft wire around pinion and pull on a horizontal line with a spring scale, Fig.

4. Assuming spur gear diameter to be 4", the radius would equal 2". Thus, five pounds pull on the scale would equal 10 pound-inches bearing preload torque. Use rotating, not starting torque.
13. To obtain correct preload torque of 5 to 15 pound-inches, add or remove shims from pack under bearing cage on side opposite bevel gear.

Assemble Pinion & Cage

1. Press rear bearing squarely and firmly against pinion gear shoulder.
2. Press bearing cups squarely and firmly against pinion cage shoulder.
3. Lubricate bearing and cups with light machine oil.
4. Insert pinion and bearing assembly in pinion cage.
5. Install selective spacer over pinion shaft with bevel side toward pinion shaft shoulder.
6. Press front bearing squarely and firmly against selective spacer with a suitable sleeve.
7. Rotate cage several revolutions to assure normal bearing contact.
8. While in press under pressure, check pinion bearing preload torque. Wrap soft wire around pinion cage and pull on a horizontal line with a spring scale, Fig. 4A. If a press is not available, the preload may be checked with the flange or yoke installed and the nut tightened to the correct torque. The correct pressures or torques for checking pinion bearing preload are as follows:

Thread Size	Pressure	Torque, Lb. Ft.
1" × 20	6 tons	300–400
1¼" × 18	11 tons	700–900
1½" × 12	14 tons	800–1100
1½" × 18	14 tons	800–1100
1⅓" × 12	14 tons	800–1100

9. Assuming pinion cage diameter to be 6" the radius would be 3". Four pounds pull on the scale would equal 12 pound-inches bearing preload torque. Use rotating, not starting torque. If rotating torque is not within 5 to 15 pound-inches, use a thinner spacer to increase or a thicker spacer to decrease bearing preload.
10. Press flange or yoke firmly against pinion forward bearing.
11. Place pinion and cage assembly over carrier studs or secure with capscrews. Hold flange and tighten pinion shaft nut to correct torque. If rotating torque is not within 5 to 15 pound-inches, repeat foregoing procedure.
12. Hold flange and remove pinion shaft nut and yoke or flange.
13. Lubricate pinion shaft oil seal. Coat outer edge of seal body with a non-hardening sealing compound and press seal firmly against cage or cover shoulder. Install bearing cover where used with capscrews.
14. Reinstate flange or yoke. Tighten pinion shaft nut to correct torque.

Install Pinion & Cage

1. The oil passage holes in carrier housing, gasket, shim pack and pinion bearing cage must be aligned.
2. Install cross shaft assembly as outlined previously.
3. Install correct shim pack.
4. Install pinion cage assembly, lockwashers and stud nuts or capscrews. Tighten to correct torque.

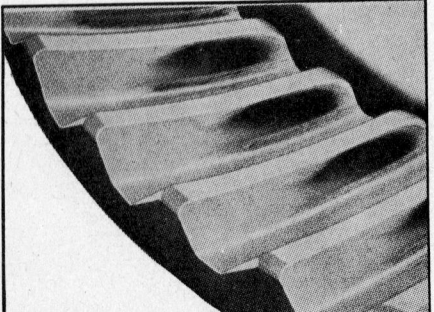

Fig. 7 Satisfactory tooth contact (gears unloaded)

Fig. 8 Satisfactory tooth contact (gears loaded)

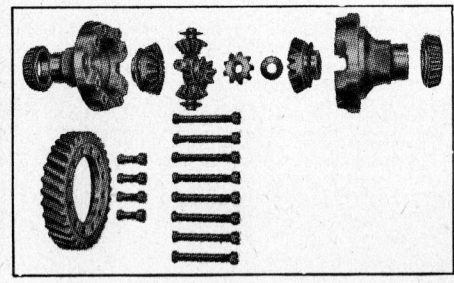

Fig. 9 Differential and gear assembly

TIMKEN (Rockwell) DRIVING AXLES

WRENCH TORQUE FOR PINION SHAFT NUTS

DIAMETER OR SIZE	THREADS PER INCH	TORQUE—LB. FT. MIN.	TORQUE—LB. FT. MAX.
7/8"	20	175	250
1"	20	300	400
1 1/4"	18	700	900
1 1/2"	12	800	1100
1 1/2"	18	800	1100
1 3/4"	12	800	1100

DIFFERENTIAL BEARING CAP
CAP SCREWS OR STUD NUTS
(Earlier Axle Models Without Hardened Washers)

CAP SCREW OR STUD NUT DIAMETER	CAP SCREW OR COARSE STUD THREAD	STUD NUT OR FINE THREAD	TORQUE—LB. FT. MIN.	TORQUE—LB. FT. MAX.
5/8"	11	18	126	140
3/4"	10	16	225	250
7/8"	9	14	330	370
7/8"	14	14	375	415
1"	14	14	375	415

DIFFERENTIAL BEARING CAP
CAP SCREWS OR STUD NUTS
(Later Axle Models Employing Hardened Washers)

CAP SCREW OR STUD NUT DIAMETER	CAP SCREW OR COARSE STUD THREAD	STUD NUT OR FINE THREAD	TORQUE—LB. FT. MIN.	TORQUE—LB. FT. MAX.
5/8"	11	18	160	180
3/4"	10	16	290	320
7/8"	9	14	470	520
7/8"	14	14	510	570
1"	14	14	570	630

Fig. 10 Torque specifications for Timken Double Reduction Axles

Checking Drive Gear Lash

Generally, if original gears are being installed, red leading of teeth will not indicate the same contact as new gears and can be misleading. Gears that have been in service for long periods form running contacts due to wear of teeth. Therefore, the thickness of the original shim pack plus approximately .015" additional shim stock should be maintained to check gear lash. In the event that gear lash is in excess of maximum tolerance, as stated under gear adjustment, reduce gear lash only in the amount that will avoid overlap of the worn tooth section, Fig. 5. Bevel gear lash can only be reduced to a point of maintaining smooth rotation of bevel gears.

Smoothness or roughness can be noted by rotating the bevel gear. If a slight overlap, Fig. 5, takes place at the worn tooth section, rotation will be rough. Generally with the original gears, tone should be satisfactory. Fig. 6 shows how a dial indicator is used to check bevel gear lash.

Drive Gear Adjustment for Correct Tooth Contact

Checking tooth contact is accomplished by means of oiled red lead applied lightly to the drive gear teeth. When the pinion is rotated, the red lead is squeezed away by the contact of the teeth, leaving bare areas the exact size, shape and location of the contacts.

With adjustments properly made (pinion at correct depth and backlash set at .010") the contacts shown in Figs. 7 and 8 will be procured. The area of contact favors the toe and is centered between the top and bottom of the tooth.

The hand-rolled pattern shown in Fig. 7, will result in a pattern centered in the length of the tooth when the gears are under load, shown in Fig. 8. The loaded pattern will be almost full length and the top of the pattern will approach the top of the gear tooth.

After the correct contacts shown have been established with a backlash of .010", open the backlash to measure .020 to .026".

Recheck Cross Shaft Bearing Preload

1. Remove pinion and cage, keeping shim pack intact.
2. Tighten cross shaft bearing cage and cover stud nuts or capscrews to the correct torque.
3. Recheck cross shaft bearing preload torque.
4. Add or remove shims from pack under cross shaft bearing cage on the side opposite drive gear only as necessary to obtain correct bearing preload torque.
5. Replace pinion cage and install lockwashers, nuts or capscrews.
6. Tighten bearing cage stud nuts to correct torque.
7. Reinstall pinion and cage over shim pack determined by correct gear adjustment.
8. Install lockwashers and stud nuts and tighten to correct torque.

Drive Gear Backlash Adjustment

1. Adjust gear backlash to .020 to .026" (regardless of what markings might be etched on the gear set) by transposing cross shaft bearing cage or cover shims.
2. To move gear away from pinion, remove shims from pack under cross shaft bearing cage on opposite side of gear and add shims of equal thickness to pack under cross shaft bearing cover or cage on gear side. Shims should be transposed in this manner to maintain established preload.
3. To move gear toward pinion, remove shims from pack from under cross shaft bearing cover or cage on the gear side and add shims of equal thickness to pack under cross shaft bearing cage on the opposite side.

Assemble Differential & Spur Gear

When new spur gears or a new differential case is installed, the differential case holes must be line-reamed with the gear in order to assemble, using correct size bolts or rivets.

Type Using Long and Short Bolts, Fig. 9
1. Join spur gear to either differential case half with short bolts.
2. Lubricate differential case inner walls and all components parts with axle lubricant.
3. Install thrust washer and side gear in one of the case halves. Place spider with pinions and thrust washers in position. Install other side gear and thrust washer.
4. Check assembly for free rotation and correct if necessary.
5. Install remaining bolts and tighten to correct torque.
6. Install lock wire.
7. Press differential bearings squarely and firmly on differential case halves.

Type Using Rivets or Short Bolts
1. Lubricate differential case inner walls and all component parts with axle lubricant.
2. Install thrust washer and side gear in one of the differential case halves.
3. Position spur gear on case half.

Location	Diameter	Threads Per Inch	Torque Lb. Ft. Min.-Max.
Carrier to Housing	7/16"	14	52-58
	7/16"	20	52-58
	1/2"	13	82-91
	1/2"	20	82-91
	5/8"	11	160-180
	5/8"	18	160-180
Pinion Cage	3/8"	16	33-37
	7/16"	14	52-58
	7/16"	20	52-58
	1/2"	13	82-91
	1/2"	20	82-91
	9/16"	12	116-129
	9/16"	18	116-129
	5/8"	11	160-180
Cross Shaft Bearing Cage and Cover	1/2"	13	82-91
	1/2"	20	82-91
	9/16"	12	116-129
	9/16"	18	116-129
	5/8"	11	160-180
Cross Shaft Bearing Lock	7/16"	14	42-45
	9/16"	12	92-101
Differential Bolts	3/8"	16	33-37
	7/16"	14	52-58
	1/2"	20	92-102
	9/16"	18	130-145
	5/8"	18	185-205
	3/4"	16	320-360
Adjusting Nut Lock	5/16"	18	15-17
Inspection Cover	3/8"	16	26-29
Shift Unit (Mounting)	3/8"	16	26-29
Shift Unit Lock Nut, Set Screw and Clamp Screw	3/8"	24	30-33
	7/16"	20	30-33
Shift Unit Travel Limiting Screws	1/2"	13	55-60
	5/8"	11	30-35

Fig. 11 Torque specifications for capscrews or stud nuts on front-mounted Timken (Rockwell) Double Reduction Axles. Torques given apply to parts coated with machine oil. For dry (or "as received") parts, increase torque 10%. For parts coated with multi-purpose gear oil, decrease torque 10%. Nuts on studs to use same torque as for driving the stud

TIMKEN (Rockwell) DRIVING AXLES

LOCATION	DIAMETER	NO. THREADS	TORQUE LB. FT. MIN.	TORQUE LB. FT. MAX.
INTER-AXLE DIFFERENTIAL GROUP				
Case (Input) Shaft Nut	1-3/4 1-3/4	12 20	300	400
Cover Capscrews	7/16	14	60	77
Housing to Carrier Capscrews	1/2	13	93	120
Case Bolts and Nuts	1/2	20	105	135
Shift Yoke Adjusting Screw Jam Nut	3/8	24	43	56
Shift Yoke Bolt and Nut	3/8	24	43	56
SHIFT UNIT AND HOUSING GROUP				
Housing Capscrews and Studs	3/8	16	27	35
Shift Shaft Stopscrew Nut	1/2	20	75	96
DRIVE PINION GROUP				
Bearing Adjusting Nut	3-3/8	12	800	1000
Bearing Jam Nut	3-3/8	12	1000	1200
THROUGH SHAFT GROUP				
Rear Bearing Cage Capscrews	3/8	16	38	49
Rear Bearing Cage Cover Capscrews	3/8	16	38	49
Rear (Output) Nut	1-1/2 1-3/4	18 12	300	400
CROSS SHAFT GROUP				
Cover (L.H.) Capscrews	3/8	16	27	35
Bearing Cage Cover (R.H.) Capscrews	1/2 9/16	13 12	66 130	85 170
Bearing Retainer (Washer) Capscrews	7/16 9/16	14 12	60 130	77 170
MAIN DIFFERENTIAL AND CARRIER GROUP				
Bearing Adjusting Nut Lock Capscrews	5/16	18	16	20
Bearing Cap Capscrews	3/4 7/8	10 9	290 480	320 520
Case and Gear to Case Bolts and Nuts	9/16	18	148	190
Top Cover Capscrews	3/8	16	38	49

Fig. 12 Torque specifications for capscrews or stud nuts on top mounted Timken (Rockwell) Double Reduction Axles

NOTE: Torques given apply to parts coated with machine oil. For dry (or "as received") parts, increase torque 10%. For parts coated with multi-purpose gear oil, decrease torque 10%. Nuts on studs to use same torque as for driving the stud

4. Place spider with pinions and thrust washers in position and install other side gear and thrust washer.
5. Align mating marks and position other case half.
6. Draw either bolted or riveted assembly together with four bolts equally spaced and check for free rotation of differential gears.
7. Install remaining bolts or rivets together as required. Install rivets as directed for the Single Reduction Axle.

Final Assembly & Installation

The installation of bearing cups in carrier leg bores, of differential assembly in carrier and of carrier in axle housing is the same as outlined for the Single Reduction Axle.

TIMKEN (Rockwell) DRIVING AXLES
Two Speed Double Reduction Axles

Fig. 1 shows the various types of Timken (Rockwell) two speed double reduction drive axles. The first reduction is through a hypoid pinion and gear. The hypoid pinion and gear set operates in conjunction with either of two sets of helical gears and pinions of different ratios. This second reduction is selective between high and low ratio.

The hypoid pinion is mounted on two tapered roller bearings in a pinion cage. The hypoid gear is locked on the cross shaft by a press fit and key. The cross shaft is mounted on tapered roller bearings and carries two free-rolling helical pinions. Both helical pinions engage helical gears attached to the differential, which is mounted on tapered roller bearings.

To establish and maintain differential bearing preload, these axles may incorporate any one of the three types of carrier leg and cap machining shown in Figs. 2, 3 and 4.

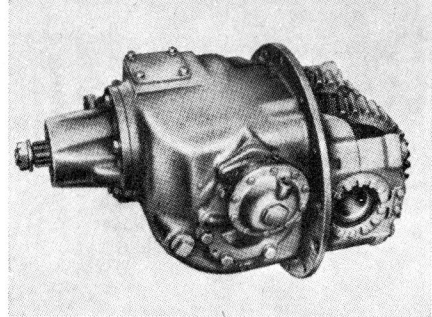
FRONT MOUNTED DRIVE UNIT

TOP MOUNTED DRIVE UNIT

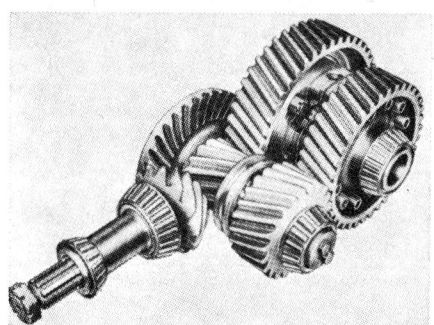
FRONT MOUNTED GEAR TRAIN

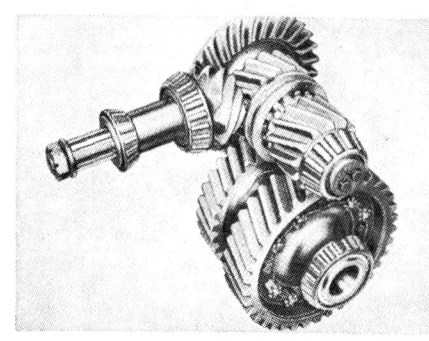
TOP MOUNTED GEAR TRAIN

Fig. 1 Timken (Rockwell) two-speed double reduction axles

REMOVING CARRIER FROM AXLE HOUSING

Front Mounted Type

1. Drain lubricant from housing.
2. Remove axle shafts.
3. Disconnect U-joint at pinion shaft.
4. Disconnect power shift unit.
5. Remove carrier-to-housing stud nuts, leaving two top nuts partially screwed on studs to prevent carrier from falling.
6. Break carrier loose from axle housing with a soft mallet. Remove tapered dowels if present.
7. Place a roller jack under carrier, remove two top nuts and work carrier free, using puller screws in holes provided. A small pinch bar may be used to straighten carrier in housing bore. However, be sure the end is rounded to prevent indenting carrier flange circle.

Top Mounted Type

1. Perform Steps 1 through 5 as outlined above.
2. Then break carrier loose from housing with soft mallet and remove tapered dowels. If necessary, back out studs.
3. Pull carrier straight out of housing with chain falls, boom, "A" frame or puller screws. A small pinch bar may be used to straighten carrier in housing bore. However, be sure end of punch is rounded to prevent indenting carrier flange circle.

DISASSEMBLE, FIG. 5

1. Center punch one carrier leg and bearing cap to identify for proper reassembly.
2. Remove capscrews and adjusting ring locks (where used).
3. Remove bearing cap, screws, bearing cups and adjusters.
4. Lift out differential and gear.
5. If original identification marks are not clear, center punch differential case halves for correct alignment upon reassembly.
6. Separate case halves and remove differential components.
7. Remove short bolts or rivets and separate

Fig. 2 Type with threaded adjusting rings on both sides. This type positions differential as well as preloading bearings by moving threaded rings in or out

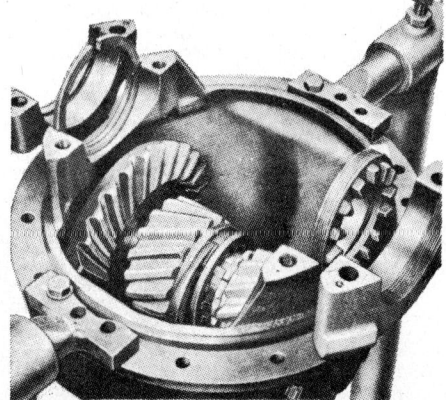
Fig. 3 Type with threaded ring on one side and split ring on opposite side. Split ring and groove locates differential whereas threaded ring is moved in or out to preload bearings

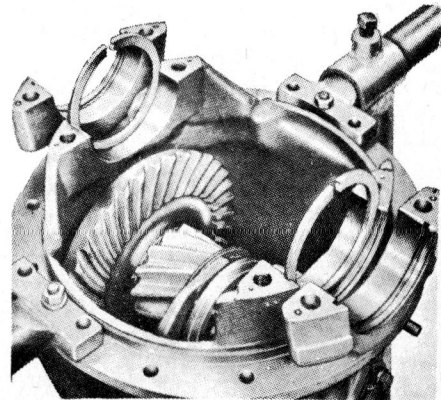
Fig. 4 Type with split rings on both sides. Bearing preload is established by using various thickness split rings. Differential positioning is automatic

TIMKEN (Rockwell) DRIVING AXLES

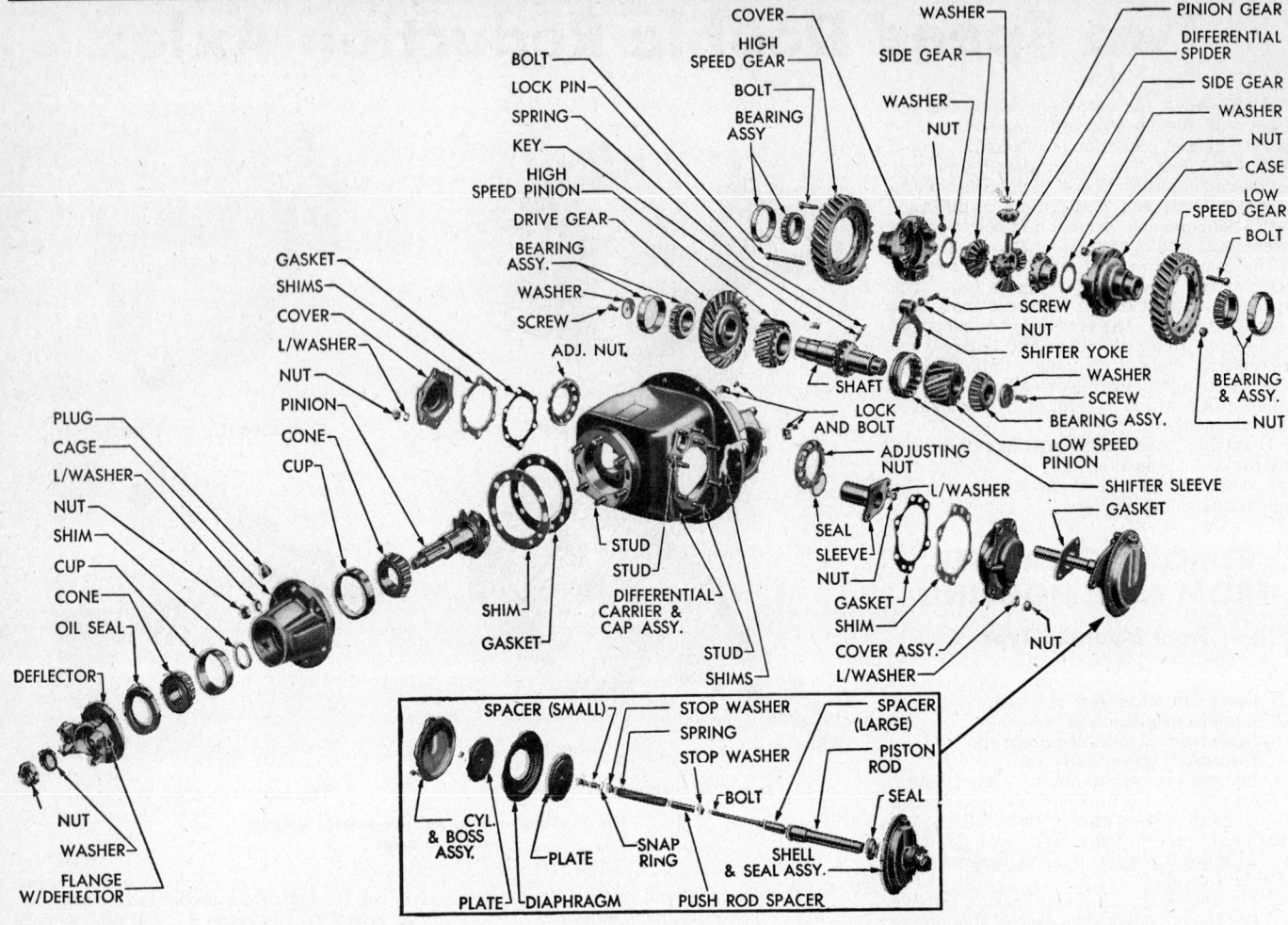

Fig. 5 Exploded view of Timken (Rockwell) two speed double reduction axle of the front mounted type with vacuum shift unit

gears from case when gear or case is to be replaced. Remove differential bearings with suitable puller when desired.
8. Hold flange and remove pinion shaft nut. Remove attaching capscrews and lift out pinion cage. If cage is not free, tap loose with a soft drift on inner face of pinion or use puller screws in holes provided.
9. Wire pinion cage shims together to facilitate adjustment on reassembly.
10. Press pinion shaft out of flange and cage. Remove adjusting spacers.
11. If necessary to replace pinion or rear bearing, remove bearing with suitable puller.
12. Press front bearing and pinion shaft oil seal from cage.

Remove Side Mounted Shift Unit

1. Remove lockwire at fork locking screw.
2. Loosen lock nut on shift fork lock screw and remove screw and nut.
3. Remove two shift unit stud nuts and washers.
4. Remove shift unit and shaft assembly and lift out shift fork.
5. Tap sleeve from carrier with a soft mallet.
6. Wire shim pack to keep intact for proper adjustment on reassembly.

Remove Front Mounted Shift Unit

1. Remove four shift unit adapter screws and washers.
2. Remove shift unit and adapter assembly from carrier.

Remove Cross Shaft

1. Remove capscrews from cross shaft bearing cage (side opposite hypoid gear).
2. Force out bearing cage with small pinch bar between back of hypoid gear and carrier housing (puller screw holes also provided).
3. Wire shim pack together to facilitate adjustment on reassembly.
4. On models with front mounted shift units, remove lockwire and set screw holding shift fork on shift shaft. Slide shaft out and remove fork from inside housing.
5. Thread out cross shaft assembly. Some wide ratio carriers will require removal of high speed pinion and bearing from cross shaft before removing cross shaft from carrier. On these units, proceed as follows:
6. Raise cross shaft through cage bore. Remove bearing retaining plate. Use puller to remove bearing. Remove high speed helical pinion from cross shaft. Thread out cross shaft. *Some wide range carriers will permit using cross shaft to that high speed pinion and bearing can be pulled off together.*

Disassemble Cross Shaft

1. Remove capscrews and retaining plates.
2. Press cross shaft from hypoid gear and bearing. Lift off helical pinion and remove shift collar, poppets and springs.
3. Replace shift collar and press shaft through remaining helical pinion and bearing.
4. If necessary to replace cross shaft bearing cups, remove cross shaft bearing cover (hypoid gear side). Wire shim pack together to facilitate adjustment on reassembly.
5. Remove cups from cages with suitable puller. Cup in cover side of carrier can be removed by tapping.

Service Notes

1. Replace all worn or damaged parts. Hex nuts with rounded corners, all lock washers, oil seals and gaskets should be replaced.
2. Remove nicks, mars or burrs from machined or ground surfaces. Threads must be clean and free to obtain accurate adjustment and correct torque. A fine mill file or India stone is suitable for this purpose. Studs must be tight prior to reassembling parts.
3. All bronze bushed differential pinions should be ball burnished after bushing

TIMKEN (Rockwell) DRIVING AXLES

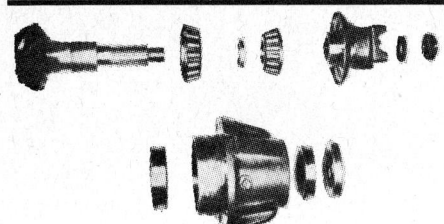

Fig. 6 Hypoid pinion and cage assembly

installation. Install bushing with small stepped drift. The small O.D. should be .010″ smaller than the bushing burnished I.D. and 1½ times bushing length. Always install bushings so end is even with the I.D. chamfer or about 1/16″ below the spherical surface.

4. Burrs, caused by lock washers at the spot face of stud holes of cages and covers should be removed to assure easy reassembly of these parts.

REASSEMBLE CARRIER
Hypoid Pinion & Cage

1. Refer to Fig. 6. Press rear bearing squarely and firmly against pinion shaft shoulder.
2. Press bearing cups squarely and firmly against pinion cage shoulder.
3. Lubricate bearing and cups with light machine oil.
4. Insert pinion and bearing in cage.
5. Install selective single or combination spacers over pinion shaft.
6. Install single spacer with O.D. bevel toward outer bearing cone. Install two combination spacers with I.D. bevels opposite each other and large flat faces together. *Spacers must be installed in this manner to prevent interference with outer bearing cone roller cage.*
7. Press front bearing squarely and firmly against selective spacer with suitable sleeve.
8. Rotate cage several revolutions to assure normal bearing contact.
9. While in press under pressure, check pinion bearing preload torque. Wrap strong cord around pinion cage and pull on a horizontal line with a spring scale, Fig. 7.
10. If a press is not available, pinion nut may be tightened to the correct torque and preload checked as follows:

Pinion Shaft Thread Size	Nut Torque Ft. Lbs.	Equivalent Pressure In Tons
1″ × 20	300–400	6
1¼″ × 18	700–900	11
1½″ × 12	800–1100	14
1½″ × 18	800–1100	14
1¾″ × 12	800–1100	14
2″ × 16	800–1100	14
2⅛″ × 12	800–1100	14

Example: Assuming pinion cage diameter to be 6″, the radius would be 3″, and with 4 pounds pull on scale would equal 12 inch pounds bearing preload torque.

11. Read rotating pounds pull on scale (not starting pounds pull). If rotating torque is not within 5 to 15 inch pounds, use a thinner spacer to increase or a thicker spacer to decrease preload torque.
12. Press flange or yoke firmly against forward pinion bearing.
13. Use carrier as a convenient holding fixture for pinion and cage assembly. Hold flange and tighten shaft nut to correct torque.
14. Recheck pinion bearing preload torque. If rotating torque is not within 5 to 15 inch pounds repeat foregoing procedure.
15. Hold flange and remove pinion shaft nut and yoke or flange.
16. Lubricate pinion shaft oil seal. With suitable sleeve, press seal firmly against bearing cage shoulder.
17. Reinstall yoke or flange and tighten nut to correct torque.
18. Remove pinion and cage assembly from carrier.

Cross Shaft Assembly

1. Refer to Figs. 8 and 9. Lubricate inner bearing surfaces on helical pinions with axle lubricant.
2. Position high or low speed helical pinion (depending on type of carrier) on cross shaft with splined row of teeth toward cross shaft teeth.
3. Install key and start cross shaft and pinion in hypoid gear in line with keyway.
4. Press shaft squarely into hypoid gear. *Cross shaft of all wide range ratio carriers*

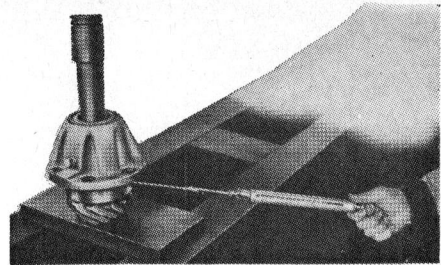

Fig. 7 Checking pinion bearing preload

and a number of conventional ratio carriers employ no hypoid gear shoulder. Extreme care must be exercised to assure pinion end play of .010″ minimum.

5. Check helical pinion end play with feeler gauge, Fig. 10. End play must be .010″ minimum to .026″ maximum. *On conventional ratio carriers where definite gear stop is provided by cross shaft shoulder, it is still necessary to have this end play. To facilitate installation, hypoid gear may be heated in oil to 200–250°.*
6. Press bearing firmly against hypoid gear using suitable sleeve. Install bearing retaining plate and capscrews.
7. Install poppets and springs and coat with axle lubricant.
8. Align all three tapered shift collar splines with poppets and position with shift collar marked "low side" toward low speed helical pinion. Due to tooth spacing, some shift collars can be assembled in one position only. *Some wide range ratio carriers will require installing cross shaft in carrier before assembly of high speed helical pinion and bearing on cross shaft. On these units skip Steps 9 to 12.*
9. Install opposite helical pinion (high or low speed depending on carrier) with splined teeth toward cross shaft teeth.
10. Press cross shaft bearing squarely and firmly against cross shaft shoulder using suitable sleeve.
11. Check low speed pinion end play which must be a minimum of .010″. Less than .010″ may result in seizure.
12. Install bearing retaining plates and capscrews.

Install Cross Shaft In Carrier

Gaskets at the pinion cage, cross shaft covers

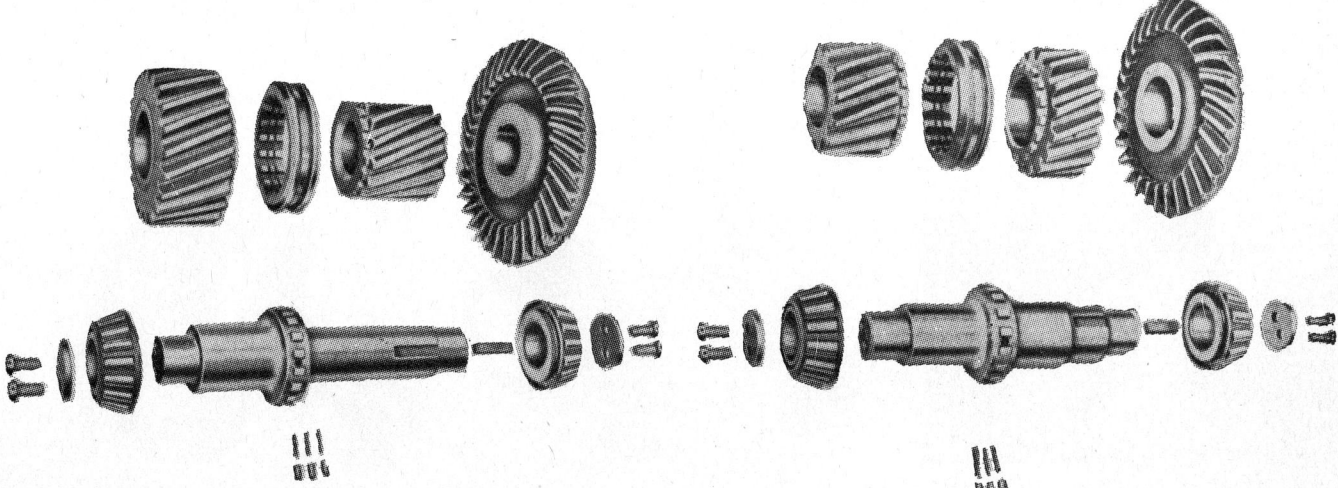

Fig. 8 Wide range ratio and some conventional ratio cross shaft assembly

Fig. 9 Most conventional ratio cross shaft assemblies

TIMKEN (Rockwell) DRIVING AXLES

Fig. 10 Checking helical pinion end play with feeler gauge

Fig. 11 Checking cross shaft bearing preload

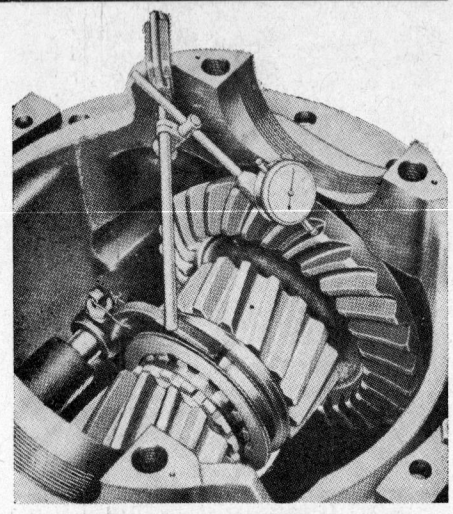

Fig. 12 Using dial indicator to determine gear lash

and cages have not been used in units produced for several years. Therefore, when assembling a drive unit formerly using gaskets, add approximately .015" shim stock to original shim pack to maintain correct bearing preload and gear adjustment. Thin shims should be located on both sides of pack to obtain maximum sealing ability.

Wide Range Ratio Carriers

On wide range ratio carriers requiring assembly of high speed helical pinion and bearings after cross shaft is in the carrier, proceed as follows:

1. Lubricate cross shaft bearings and cups with light machine oil.
2. Install cross shaft assembly (minus high speed helical pinion) into carrier with cage or cover of hypoid side removed.
3. Install high speed pinion and set up in a press so that bearing retaining plate at hypoid side of cross shaft may be rested on a support at cover or cage opening.
4. Press bearing opposite hypoid gear onto shaft. Install bearing retaining plate and capscrews.
5. Install bearing cage or cover with shim pack on hypoid side of carrier. Replace capscrews and lock washers, then tighten to proper torque. *Should a press not be available, cross shaft bearing opposite gear side may be installed with a suitable driver placed against the inner race of bearing providing gear side of shaft is blocked up against bearing retainer. Do not drive or press bearings onto cross shaft with opposite bearing resting on cage or in cup. To do so will cause brinelling of the cup and roller surfaces.*

All Other Carriers

On carriers permitting complete assembly of cross shaft before threading into carrier housing, proceed as follows:

1. Lubricate bearings and cups with light machine oil.
2. If bearing cover or cage on hypoid gear side has been removed, replace it using correct shim pack.
3. Thread cross shaft past differential bearing supports and position in bearing cup.
4. On carriers with front mounted shift units, position shift fork and install shift shaft. Align lock nut hole in fork with shaft indent and tighten lock screw and nut. Wire lock screw to fork.
5. Start bearing cage (side opposite hypoid gear) into carrier housing.
6. Tap bearing cage into position with soft mallet. Install capscrews.

Check Cross Shaft Bearing Preload

1. In checking cross shaft bearing preload torque, always rotate cross shaft and gear assembly several revolutions before checking preload to assure normal bearing contacts.
2. Lock low speed pinion and cross shaft with shift collar. Wrap a strong cord around pinion and pull on a horizontal line with a pound spring scale, Fig. 11. Assuming the pinion diameter to be 4",

the radius would be 2", and with a pull of 7 pounds on the scale, the bearing preload would be 14 inch pounds of preload torque.

3. Read rotating pull (not starting pull). If preload torque is not within 5 to 15 inch pounds, add shims under cage (opposite hypoid gear) to decrease or remove shims to increase preload torque.

Install Pinion & Cage

1. Install pinion cage with original shim pack. Install capscrews and tighten.
2. Adjust hypoid gear backlash to .014–.020" (regardless of what markings might be etched on gear set) by transposing cross shaft bearing cage or cover shims, Fig. 12.
3. To move bevel gear away from pinion, remove shims from pack under cross shaft bearing cage on side opposite bevel gear and add shims of equal thickness to pack under cross shaft bearing cover or cage on bevel gear side. *Shims should be transposed in this manner to maintain established preload.*
4. To move bevel gear toward pinion, remove shims from pack under cross shaft bearing cover or cage on bevel gear side and add shims of equal thickness to pack under cross shaft bearing cage on side opposite bevel gear. *The actual backlash*

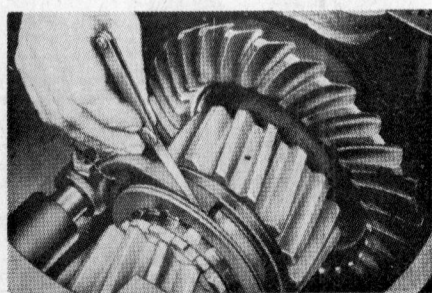

Fig. 13 Checking clearance of shift fork pads in shift collar with feeler gauge

Fig. 14 Differential pinion and side gear assembly

Fig. 15 Checking differential bearing preload

TIMKEN (Rockwell) DRIVING AXLES

changes approximately .008" for each .010" movement of the gear.

5. Check gear tooth contact for correct adjustment as outlined in the *Single Reduction Axle* section.

Install Shift Units

Power Actuated Side Mounted Type

1. Tap shift unit sleeve into carrier housing over original shim pack. Install lock washers and stud nuts.
2. Install new flange gasket. Hold shift fork in position. Align lock screw holes in shift shaft and slide shift unit and shaft into position.
3. Tighten fork screw and lock nut to 30–35 ft. lbs.
4. Install shift unit lock washers and stud nuts.
5. Check clearance of shift fork pads in shift collar with gauge, Fig. 13. Clearance should not be less than .010" on each side of fork in both high and low speed positions. *When checking clearance, shift collar must be flush with end face of spur pinion in both high and low speed positions.* Add or remove shims from pack under sleeve to obtain correct adjustment.
6. Check operation of shift unit. Ten pounds of air may be used to check vacuum type unit by applying air to opposite side of diaphragm, using vent opening on the single line shift unit.

Power Actuated, Front Mounted Type

1. Check bellcrank buttons and remove any scores at operating faces.
2. Place shift fork, collar and shift unit in high speed position. They must be in the same position to install shift unit.
3. Install new gasket and position shift unit with bellcrank in slot of shift shaft. Install lockwashers and capscrews. Do not disturb Allen set screw or travel positioning screw unless shift fork adjustments are needed. If adjustments are required, proceed as follows:
4. With fork and collar shifted to engage helical pinion next to hypoid gear, adjust Allen screw and lock nut in top of carrier so that fork is centered in collar groove within .005".
5. With fork and collar shifted to engage helical pinion away from hypoid gear, adjust hex head screw and lock nut in cross shaft cage so that fork is centered in collar groove within .005". When checking clearance, shift collar must be flush with end face of spur pinion in both high and low speed positions.
6. Check operation of shift unit in same manner as outlined for side mounted shift unit.

Assemble Differential

1. Join high and low speed spur gears to their respective case halves with bolts or rivets as desired. *When new spur gears or differential cases are installed, the case holes may require line reaming with the gear in order to assemble correct size bolts or rivets. When rivets are used they should be upset cold (not heated).*
2. Lubricate differential case inner walls and all parts with axle lubricant, Fig. 14.
3. Install thrust washer and side gear in one case half. Place spider with pinions and thrust washers in position. Install component side gear and thrust washer.
4. Align mating marks, position component case half and draw assembly together with four long bolts or capscrews equally spaced.
5. Check assembly for free rotation of differential gears and correct if necessary.
6. Install and tighten remaining bolts and secure with lock wire.
7. Press differential bearings squarely and firmly on case halves.

Install Bearing Cups In Carrier Leg Bores

1. Temporarily install bearing cups, threaded adjusting rings (where used) and bearing caps and tighten capscrews.
2. Bearing cups must be a hand push fit in bores otherwise bores must be re-worked with a scraper or emery cloth until a hand push fit is obtained. Use a blued bearing cup as a gauge and check fits as work progresses. This applies to all three types of carrier leg bores.
3. On carriers employing adjuster rings, if the rings cannot be turned by hand or with a maximum force of 10 lbs. applied at one end of a 2-ft. wrench (20 ft. lbs. torque) the O.D. should be slightly reduced with a fine mill file or use others that turn more freely. Be sure adjusting rings and threads are free from burrs or nicks.

Install Differential

1. After checking related parts, coat bearings with axle lubricant.

WRENCH TORQUE FOR PINION SHAFT NUTS

DIAMETER OR SIZE	THREADS PER INCH	TORQUE—LB. FT.	
		MIN.	MAX.
7/8"	20	175	250
1"	20	300	400
1 1/4"	18	700	900
1 1/2"	12	800	1100
1 1/2"	18	800	1100
1 3/4"	12	800	1100

DIFFERENTIAL BEARING CAP CAP SCREWS OR STUD NUTS
(Earlier Axle Models Without Hardened Washers)

CAP SCREW OR STUD NUT DIAMETER	CAP SCREW OR COARSE STUD THREAD	STUD NUT OR FINE THREAD	TORQUE—LB. FT.	
			MIN.	MAX.
5/8"	11	18	130	170
3/4"	10	16	230	300
7/8"	9	14	345	440
7/8"	14	14	380	485
1"	14	14	380	485

DIFFERENTIAL BEARING CAP CAP SCREWS OR STUD NUTS
(Later Axle Models Employing Hardened Washers)

CAP SCREW OR STUD NUT DIAMETER	CAP SCREW OR COARSE STUD THREAD	STUD NUT OR FINE THREAD	TORQUE—LB. FT.	
			MIN.	MAX.
5/8"	11	18	160	205
3/4"	10	16	290	370
7/8"	9	14	470	595
7/8"	14	14	510	655
1"	14	14	580	745

Fig. 16 Torque specifications for capscrews or stud nuts for Timken (Rockwell) Two Speed Double Reduction Axles

NOTE: Torques given apply to parts coated with machine oil. For dry (or "as received") parts, increase torque 10%. For parts coated with multi-purpose gear oil, decrease torque 10%. Nuts on studs to use same torque as for driving the stud.

TIMKEN (Rockwell) DRIVING AXLES

2. Place bearing cups over assembled bearing cones and position differential in carrier.
3. On the threaded adjusting ring type (see Fig. 2) insert rings and turn them hand tight against bearing cups. Position bearing caps in place.
4. On type with one threaded adjusting ring and one split ring (see Fig. 3) position split ring in groove of carrier leg and insert threaded adjusting ring on opposite side. Turn threaded ring hand tight against bearing cup. Install bearing caps.
5. With the split ring type (see Fig. 4) insert one ring in carrier leg groove. Move differential over so that face of bearing cup is held tightly against inserted ring. Install opposite split ring by tapping it into groove with a blunt end drift, tapping on lower I.D. of ring. Install bearing caps.
6. Install and tighten carrier leg screws.

Adjusting Differential Bearing Preload

Type With One or Two Threaded Rings
1. On units employing two threaded rings center helical gears in relation to helical pinions by means of the threaded rings.
2. Using a dial indicator as shown in Fig. 15 and starting with a definite amount of end play adjust differential bearings to zero end play. A pair of pinch bars may be used as shown. Rotate assembly several revolutions each time adjusting rings are moved before checking end play to assure normal bearing contact.
3. Tighten adjusting rings 1 3/4 to 2 1/2 notches (total of both rings) to correctly preload bearings.
4. Install ring locks and capscrews (where used) and install lock wire.

Type Employing Two Split Rings
1. Temporarily install differential in carrier and center between carrier leg grooves.
2. Insert thin split rings making certain that there is clearance between bearing cup faces and rings (do not install bearing caps).
3. Measure end play as shown in Fig. 15.
4. Remove and measure thickness of thin rings. To the total thickness of the two thin rings add the end play figure plus another .017 to .022" to obtain total thickness of the two thicker rings required to obtain proper bearing preload. Hardened split rings are ground in increments of .005".
5. When proper bearing preload has been established complete the assembly of the differential. Install unit in axle housing in reverse order of removal.

Location	Diameter	Threads Per Inch	Torque Lb. Ft. Min.-Max.
Carrier to Housing	7/16"	14	53-67
	7/16"	20	53-67
	1/2"	13	81-104
	1/2"	20	81-104
	5/8"	11	160-205
	5/8"	18	160-205
Pinion Cage	3/8"	16	33-43
	7/16"	14	53-67
	7/16"	20	53-67
	1/2"	13	81-104
	1/2"	20	81-104
	9/16"	12	116-149
	9/16"	18	116-149
	5/8"	11	160-205
Cross Shaft Bearing Cage and Cover	1/2"	13	81-104
	1/2"	20	81-104
	9/16"	12	116-149
	9/16"	18	116-149
	5/8"	11	160-205
Cross Shaft Bearing Lock	7/16"	14	42-54
	9/16"	12	94-120
Differential Bolts	3/8"	16	33-43
	7/16"	14	53-67
	1/2"	20	92-118
	9/16"	18	130-167
	5/8"	18	185-235
	3/4"	16	320-415
Adjusting Nut Lock	5/16"	18	16-20
Inspection Cover	3/8"	16	27-35
Shift Unit (Mounting)	3/8"	16	27-35
Shift Unit Lock Nut, Set Screw and Clamp Screw	3/8"	24	31-39
	7/16"	20	31-39
Shift Unit Travel Limiting Screws	1/2"	13	55-60
	5/8"	11	30-35

Fig. 17 Torque specifications for capscrews or stud nuts for Timken (Rockwell) Two Speed Double Reduction Axles

NOTE: Torques given apply to parts coated with machine oil. For dry (or "as received") parts, increase torque 10%. For parts coated with multi-purpose gear oil, decrease torque 10%. Nuts on studs to use same torque as for driving the stud.

Single Reduction Thru-Drive Tandem Axles

DESCRIPTION

This type drive, Fig. 1, utilizes a modified conventional single reduction axle for the forward rear axle and a conventional single reduction axle for the rearward axle. A power divider or inter-axle differential is mounted integrally with the forward axle. This type of drive permits a tandem hook-up with a minimum of angles in the drive line.

The pinion bearing preload is adjusted and maintained by a hardened precision spacer between the inner and outer tapered bearings. The differential bearing preload is adjusted and maintained by threaded adjusting rings located in the carrier legs and caps.

The inter-axle differential may be engaged or disengaged by a power actuated shift unit which moves a sliding collar on the through shaft splines. The shift unit is controlled by a selector switch or lever within the cab of the vehicle and may be engaged or disengaged under any normal operating conditions.

The inter-axle differential when engaged (unlocked) divides the engine torque between the forward and rearward axles; when disengaged (locked) it converts the two axles to a through drive type tandem.

DISASSEMBLE

Remove Unit From Housing

1. Disconnect forward and rear propeller shafts.
2. Drain lubricant from axle housing and inter-axle differential.
3. Remove axle shafts as outlined for standard single reduction axles.
4. Remove shift shaft housing assembly.
5. Disassemble and remove shift lever attaching nut, button, lever, cup and spring. The body fit bolt should not be removed.
6. Remove thru-shaft, cage and yoke, Fig. 4. To free cage from case bore it may be necessary to tap yoke with a soft mallet. While thru-shaft assembly is being threaded out, the sliding clutch must be eased along the shaft at the shift lever opening. When thru-shaft clears opening, the clutch may be lifted out.

TIMKEN (Rockwell) DRIVING AXLES

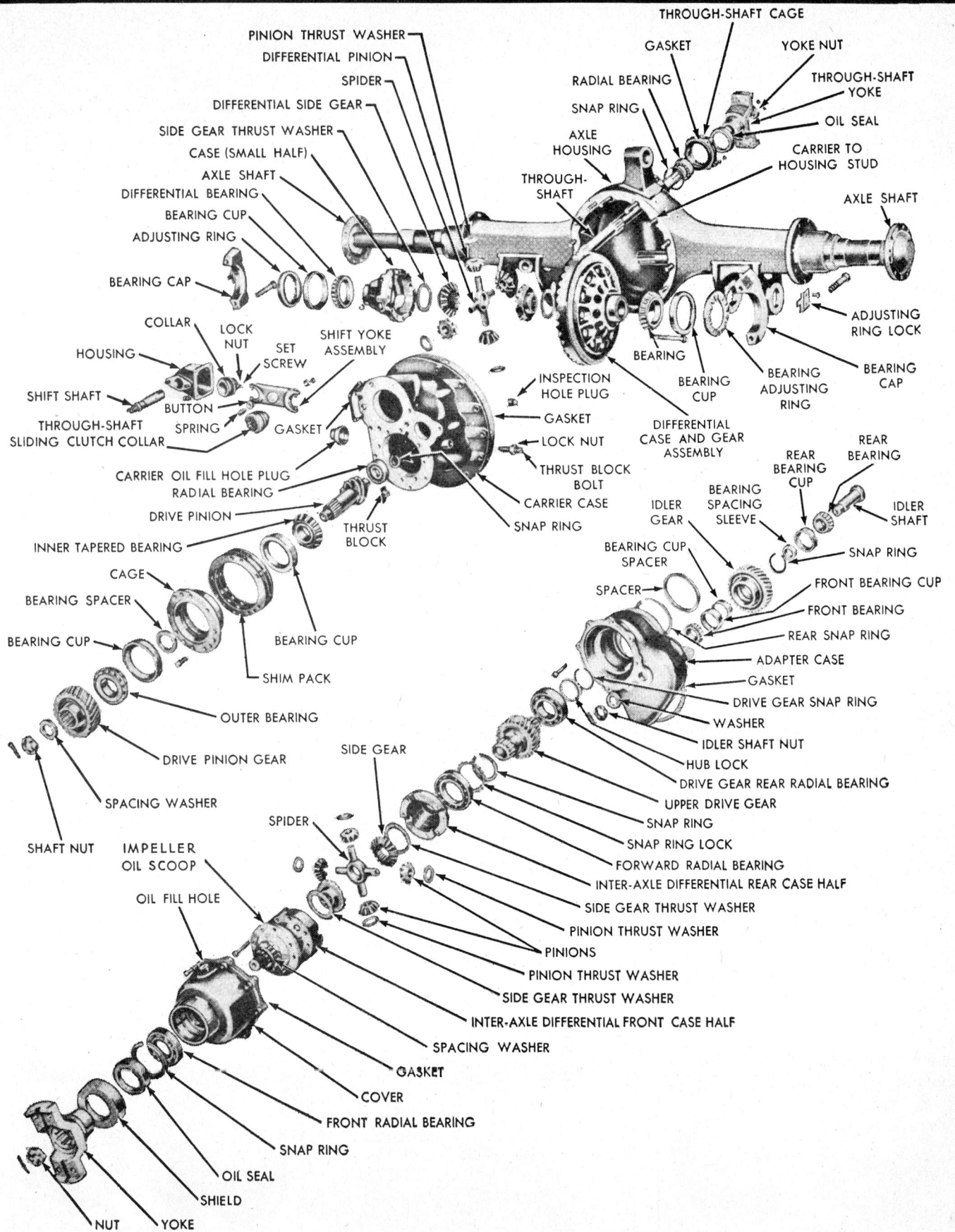

Fig. 1 Type 3 single reduction tandem drive forward axle. This unit differs from Type 2 in that it employs splines instead of dog teeth on the inter-axle differential, as shown in Figs. 2 and 3. Type 1 is similar to Type 2 except that the impeller (oil scoop), oil baffles, etc. used in Type 2 are not employed in Type 1.

TIMKEN (Rockwell) DRIVING AXLES

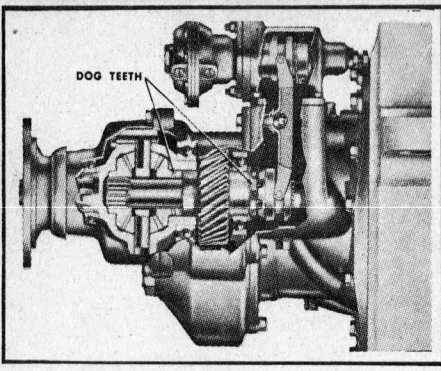

Fig. 2 Types 1 and 2 inter-axle differential shift mechanism

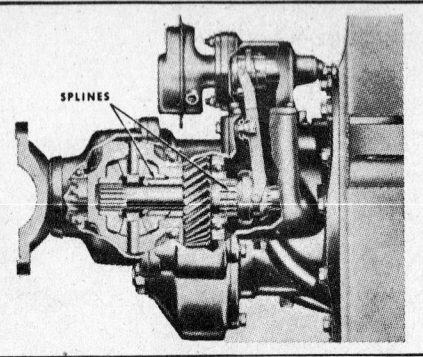

Fig. 3 Type 3 inter-axle differential shifting mechanism

Fig. 4 Removing thru-shaft and cage

7. Remove carrier from axle housing in same manner outlined for the standard single reduction axle.

Disassemble Thru-Shaft

1. After removing nut, use puller to remove yoke.
2. Press thru-shaft from cage, using a suitable sleeve against bearing inner race.
3. Remove cage snap ring, Fig. 5. Then tap radial bearing out of bore from seal end. If seal is damaged or worn, press out with suitable sleeve. If seal is in good condition, do not disturb.

Disassemble Inter-Axle Differential

1. Separate inter-axle differential and adapter case from carrier case, Fig. 6.
2. Unfasten and lift inter-axle differential from adapter case, Fig. 7.
3. Remove input shaft flange or yoke nut.
4. Press inter-axle differential from cover.
5. If original identification marks are not clear, mark differential case halves with a punch for correct alignment on reassembly.
6. Disassemble case halves and remove differential components.
7. On Types 1 and 2, remove radial bearings from differential case halves with a suitable puller, pulling against inner race of bearing. On Type 3, do not remove radial bearing from case unless replacement is necessary.
8. To disassemble adapter case, tap upper drive gear back until gear touches case. Remove spacer and snap ring from bearing outer race. Tap drive gear out of adapter case, Fig. 9. Do not remove radial bearing from gear hub unless replacement is necessary. If necessary, fold back tab locks and remove hub snap ring. Then remove bearing with suitable puller.
9. To disassemble idler gear, remove nut and spacing washer. Remove shaft and slide out gear and bearing. Remove tapered bearings and tap out cups and related parts, Fig. 10.

Main Differential Case, Ring Gear & Drive Pinion

Service procedures on these components are the same as outlined for the standard single reduction axle.

REASSEMBLE

Main Differential Case, Ring Gear & Drive Pinion

Assembly procedure, adjusting pinion bearing and differential bearing preloads, checking ring gear and pinion backlash are the same as described for the standard single reduction axles. Complete the assembly and adjustment of these parts, then proceed with the adapter case and inter-axle as follows:

Assemble Adapter Case

1. Install snap ring and press idler gear inner bearing cup squarely against snap ring.
2. Insert idler gear cup spacing sleeve against opposite side of snap ring.
3. Press idler gear outer bearing cup squarely against spacing sleeve.
4. Position idler gear inner and outer bearings into cups with hardened bearing spacer (or combination of two spacers) between them. *Some of the Type 1 drive units do not incorporate the idler bearing spacer or the idler shaft "O" ring. These parts should be added to any of the units that do not have them.*
5. Slide complete assembly through adapter case drive pinion opening. *On Types 1 and 2, position assembly so that bearings are aligned with adapter case shaft hole. On Type 3, temporarily push the assembly to the far side of the pocket and proceed to install upper drive gear assembly.*
6. On Types 1 and 2, tap idler shaft through idler gear so that inner bearing is squarely against idler shaft shoulder.

Idler Shaft Bearing Adjustment

On Types 1 and 2, this adjustment is made before assembling the upper drive gear. On Type 3, first assemble the upper drive gear, then make the adjustment as follows:

1. Hold adapter case and idler gear securely in a vise with jaws clamped on flattened end of idler shaft.
2. Install washer and nut and torque nut from 350 to 400 ft. lbs.
3. Measure idler shaft bearing end play with a dial indicator mounted to adapter case proper with stem set against idler gear face. End play should be .001"–.005".
4. If not within these limits, use a thinner or thicker spacer or combination of two spacers as required.
5. After proper end play has been established, remove washer and nut. Insert "O" ring and reinstall washer and nut. Tighten nut from 350 to 400 ft. lbs. and install cotter key.

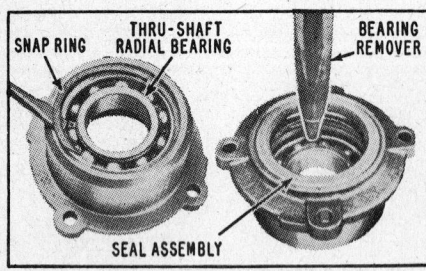

Fig. 5 Removing thru-shaft radial bearing

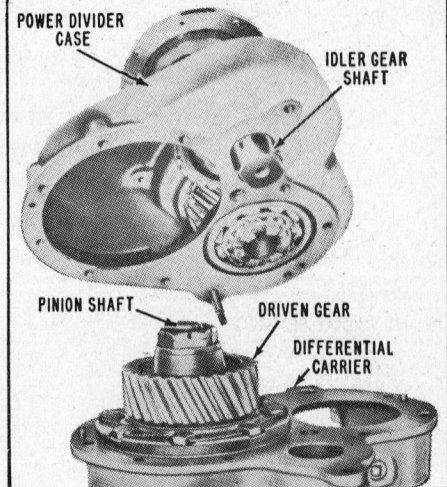

Fig. 6 Lifting power divider from differential carrier

Fig. 7 Separating power divider cover from case

TIMKEN (Rockwell) DRIVING AXLES

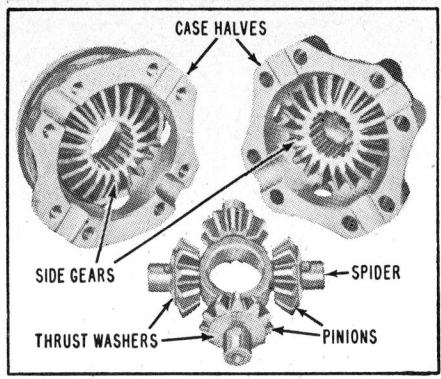

Fig. 8 Inter-axle differential parts

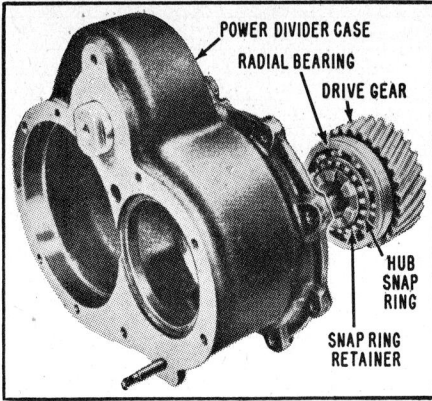

Fig. 9 Drive gear and bearing removed from case

Fig. 10 Idler gear components

Assemble Upper Drive Gear

On Type 3, this gear is assembled before adjusting idler shaft bearing, the procedure for all types being as follows:
1. If rear bearing has been removed for replacement, press new bearing on hub using a suitable sleeve against bearing inner race.
2. Install tabbed lock ring and hub snap ring.
3. With radial bearing outer race snap ring removed, position drive gear in case. Tap assembly through bore until gear touches wall of case.
4. Install radial bearing outer race snap ring in the groove. Tap gear back so that snap ring seats in recess in case.
5. On Types 1 and 2, install spacer over outer race of bearing against snap ring.
6. On Type 3, position spacer over bearing with flat toward pinion cage bore. Position idler assembly so that bearings are lined up with idler shaft hole. Tap idler shaft through gear so that inner bearing is squarely against idler shaft shoulder.

Assemble Inter-Axle Differential

1. Lubricate differential case walls and all components parts with axle lubricant.
2. Position thrust washer and rear side gear into rear case half.
3. Place spider with pinions and thrust washers into position.
4. Install forward side gear and thrust washer.
5. Align mating marks, position forward case half and draw together with case capscrews. Types 2 and 3 employ an impeller over forward case half.
6. Tighten case capscrews to correct torque.
7. Check for free rotation of gears and correct if necessary.
8. On Types 1 and 2, install forward radial bearing spacer and press on forward and rear radial bearings.

Install Inter-Axle Differential

Types 1 and 2
1. If snap ring was removed, reinstall in nose of cover.
2. Install cover-to-case gasket. Position cover over inter-axle differential and tap down with a sleeve until forward radial bearing seats against snap ring.
3. Position cover and differential over upper drive gear hub and tap down until rear radial bearing snap ring seats in adapter case recess. It may be necessary to rotate the assembly slightly to line up the dog teeth.
4. Install capscrews and lockwashers and draw cover and adapter case together. Tighten capscrews to specified torque.
5. Install cover oil seal with suitable driver.

Type 3
1. If cover was disassembled, install forward radial bearing and snap ring.
2. Install spacer on input shaft.
3. Position cover over input shaft and tap down until radial bearing seats against spacer.
4. Install gasket and position cover and differential over upper drive gear hub. Tap assembly into position. It will be necessary to line up the splines of the drive gear with those of the side gear.
5. Install capscrews and lockwashers and torque to specifications.
6. Install cover oil seal with suitable driver.

Assemble Adapter Case & Inter-Axle Differential to Carrier

1. Mount carrier in stand in upright position. Install gasket and place adapter case over carrier. The idler shaft flat must be lined up with corresponding flat in carrier.
2. Install lockwashers and capscrews and torque to specifications.

Final Assembly

1. Install carrier in axle housing in a manner outlined for standard single reduction axles.
2. Install thru-shaft rear radial bearing into cage and lock in place with snap ring.
3. Press bearing and cage on splined end of thru-shaft with suitable sleeve.
4. Install thru-shaft cage oil seal with suitable driver.
5. Enter thru-shaft and cage with new cage gasket into cage bore at rear of axle housing until forward end of shaft is even with shift lever opening.
6. Install sliding clutch collar over forward

CAP SCREWS OR STUD NUTS

LOCATION ON UNIT	DIA. INCH	THDS. NO.	TORQUE MIN.	TORQUE MAX.	LOCATION ON UNIT	DIA. INCH	THDS. NO.	TORQUE MIN.	TORQUE MAX.
Shift Unit	3/8"	24	38	49	Pinion Shaft Nut	1 3/4"	12	800	1100
Carrier to Housing	1/2"	20	81	104	Diff. Bearing Adj. Lock	5/16"	18	15	17
	5/8"	18	160	205					
	3/4"	16	325	420	Through-Shaft Rear Cage	3/8"	24	38	49
						7/16"	14	60	77
Shift Shaft Adjusting Screw Lock Nut	1/2"	20	66	85	Inter-Axle Diff. Case Bolt	7/16"	14	60	77
						1/2"	20	93	120
Input Shaft Yoke or Flange Nut	1 3/4"	12	300	400	Input Cage	7/61"	14	60	77
Pinion Cage Cap Screw	1/2"	13	82	91	Pinion Cover	3/8"	24	38	49

REPLACEMENT—DIFFERENTIAL GEAR TO CASE BOLTS

DIFFERENTIAL CARRIER	SERVICE BOLT	NUT	LOCKWIRE	ORIGINAL RIVET	SPOTFACE DIAMETER	TORQUE LBS. FT. MIN.	TORQUE LBS. FT. MAX.
Q—gearing	15X-786	N-210-1	LW-1610	RV-71014	1 3/8"	186	205
R—gearing	15X-659	N-210-1	LW-1610	RV-71016	1 3/8"	186	205

Fig. 11 Torque specifications for Timken (Rockwell) Single Reduction Thru-Drive Tandem Axles, Two Gear Units

NOTE: Torques given apply to parts coated with machine oil. For dry (or "as received") parts, increase torque 10%. For parts coated with multi-purpose gear oil, decrease torque 10%. Nuts on studs to use same torque as for driving the stud.

TIMKEN (Rockwell) DRIVING AXLES

end of shaft through shift housing opening. Ease shaft into forward side gear of inter-axle differential, while at the same time passing clutch collar onto collar splines.

7. Install thru-shaft cage capscrews and washers and torque to specifications.
8. Install over shift lever bolt the shift lever spring, cup and lever. Lever inner yoke must be properly located in collar groove at this time. Install shift lever button and nut. Tighten nut securely and install cotter key.
9. Position gasket and shift housing against drive unit, making sure that shift lever yoke is properly located in shift collar groove.
10. Install shift housing capscrews and torque to specifications.

Adjusting Shift Shaft

1. Adjust positioning screw at rear of shift housing as follows: With shift shaft moved back its full travel, locking the inter-axle differential, turn adjusting screw in until end of screw touches end of shift shaft.
2. From this point proceed 1 to 1¼ turn more and lock adjusting screw with jam nut. This will allow approximately .012" clearance between the yoke and groove of collar and thus eliminate yoke and collar wear. The shift collar provides a definite stop against housing wall when shifted in the opposite direction.

Install Thru-Shaft Yoke

1. Install yoke on splines with suitable sleeve. Install washer and nut.
2. By using a holder on yoke, tighten yoke nut to proper torque and install cotter key.

BOLT AND STUD NUTS					CAP SCREWS				
LOCATION ON UNIT	DIA. INCH	THDS. NO.	TORQUE — LB. FT. MIN.	MAX.	LOCATION ON UNIT	DIA. INCH	THDS. NO.	TORQUE — LB. FT. MIN.	MAX.
Shift Unit	⅜"	24	27	35	Through-Shaft Cage	⅜"	16	27	35
Carrier to Housing	½"	20	81	104	Carrier to Adapter Case	7/16"	14	60	77
	⅝"	18	160	205	Pinion Cage	½"	13	93	120
Shift Shaft Adjusting Screw Lock Nut	½"	20	45	50	Inter-Axle Cover	7/16"	14	42	54
Through-Shaft Yoke and Input Shaft Yoke Nuts	1"	20	300	400	Inter-Axle Differential Case	7/16"	14	53	67
	1¼"	18	300	400		½"	13	93	120
	1½"	18	300	400	Shift Housing	⅜"	16	27	35
Differential Case Cap Screws	½"	13	93	120					
	⅝"	18	210	270	Shift Collar Set Screw	⅜"	24	12	16
Bearing Cap Cap Screws	⅝"	11	130	170					
	¾"	10	230	300					

REPLACEMENT—DIFFERENTIAL GEAR TO CASE BOLTS

TANDEM MODEL CARRIER	SERVICE BOLT	NUT	LOCK WIRE	ORIGINAL RIVET	SPOTFACE DIAMETER	TORQUE — LB. FT. MIN.	MAX.
DHD —	15X-775	N-28-1	LW-1610	RV-7812	1⅛"	105	135
FHD —	15X-775	N-28-1	LW-1610	RV-7812	1⅛"	105	135
†LHD —	15X-666	N-29-1	LW-1610	RV-7913	1⅜"	130	170
†QHD —	15X-666	N-29-1	LW-1610	RV-7913	1⅜"	130	170
‡LHD —	15X-786	N-210-1	LW-1610	RV-71014	1⅜"	185	235
‡QHD —	15X-786	N-210-1	LW-1610	RV-71014	1⅜"	185	235

† Original production had 9/16" rivets and require 9/16" bolts and nuts for service.
‡ Current production has ⅝" rivets and require ⅝" bolts and nuts for service.

Fig. 12 Torque specifications for Timken (Rockwell) Single Reduction Thru-Drive Tandem Axles, Three Gear Units

NOTE: Torques given apply to parts coated with machine oil. For dry (or "as received") parts, increase torque 10%. For parts coated with multi-purpose gear oil, decrease torque 10%. Nuts on studs to use same torque as for driving the stud.

Double Reduction Thru-Drive Tandem Axles

In these units, Fig. 1, tapered roller bearings support the forward and rear ends of the thru-shaft and pinion assembly of spiral bevel gear units. Bearing preload is adjusted and maintained by shim packs between carrier machined surfaces and bearing covers. Yokes or flanges, held in place by thru-shaft nuts, press against the bearing cones or spiral bevel pinion splined to thru-shaft.

The thru-shafts of hypoid gear drive units are supported at the forward end by tapered roller bearings in a cage and at the rear end by a straight roller bearing. Pinion bearing preload is adjusted and maintained by a hardened precision spacer between inner and outer tapered bearings which are held in place on the thru-shaft by separate thru-shaft nuts.

Hypoid gear top-mounted forward drive units may be equipped with an inter-axle differential of the planetary type which divides engine torque between the forward and rear axles. The differential is equipped with a lock-up device which converts the tandem assembly to a thru-drive tandem. The lock-up is actuated by an air chamber and is controlled in the vehicle cab. It can be engaged and disengaged under all normal operating conditions. Fig. 2 illustrates the early

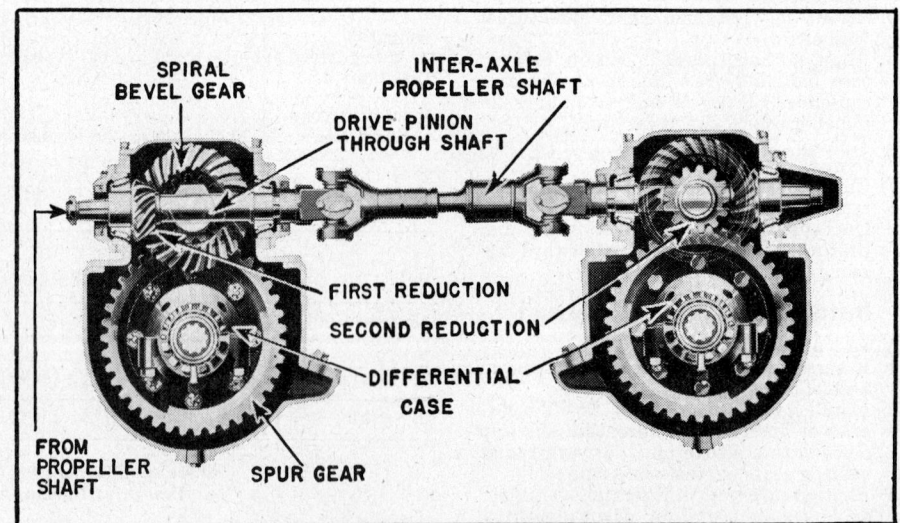

Fig. 1 Timken (Rockwell) double reduction, top-mounted thru-drive axles. Both hypoid and spiral bevel gears are used in the first reduction. Either straight spur or helical gears are used in the second reduction.

TIMKEN (Rockwell) DRIVING AXLES

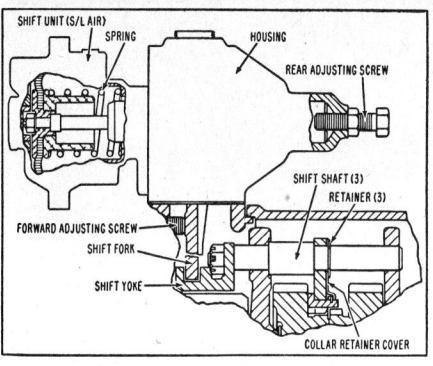

Fig. 2 Shift unit assembly (early models)

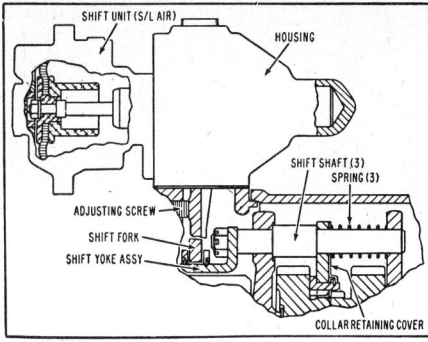

Fig. 3 Shift unit assembly (later models)

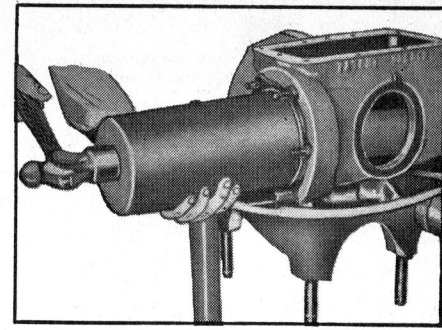

Fig. 4 Installing pinion, bearing and thru-shaft assembly with sleeve shown

design shift unit, while Fig. 3 is the current design.

DISASSEMBLE

During the disassembly process, be sure to keep any shims found with parts intact and identified so that when reassembling, adjustment of unit involved will be facilitated.

1. Drain axle and inter-axle differential housing.
2. Remove axle shafts and carrier from housing.
3. Match mark one differential carrier leg and bearing cap for identification on reassembly.
4. Lift out differential. Before dismantling differential, match mark case halves for proper alignment on reassembly.
5. Remove pinion and thru-shaft on models not equipped with inter-axle differential.
6. If inter-axle differential is used, remove shift unit.
7. Remove inter-axle differential bearing and cover assembly. Hoist inter-axle differential out with a chain fall.
8. Disassemble thru shaft.
9. Disassemble inter-axle differential.
10. Disassemble cross shaft.

REASSEMBLY

Service Note

The thru-shaft, pinion and bearing assembly of the spiral bevel type drive units must be installed in the carrier before the cross shaft assembly is installed. This permits determining the thickness of shim packs that control pinion bearing preload without interference of the cross shaft assembly. The thru-shaft assembly is then removed and the cross shaft assembly installed. Cross shaft bearing preload must be established at this time before final installation of the thru-shaft assembly with previously determined shim packs.

The cross shaft assembly of hypoid gear units must be installed in the carrier first so cross shaft bearing preload can be established without interference of the thru-shaft and pinion assembly. The thru-shaft, pinion, bearing and cage may be assembled at the bench and then installed in the carrier.

Assemble Spiral Bevel Pinion & Thru-Shaft

1. Press tapered bearing on pinion.
2. Coat pinion and thru-shaft splines with heavy grease and press parts together. *Press parts together about 1/4" to 3/8", then relieve press pressure to permit them to realign themselves to prevent distortion and damage. Continue the pressing operation until parts are correctly assembled.*
3. Install pinion, bearing and thru-shaft in drive unit. Install pinion bearing cup with suitable sleeve, Fig. 4.
4. Install spacer (if used) over splined end of thru-shaft and tighten nut on spacer end of thru-shaft.
5. Coat seal with non-hardening sealing compound and install in bearing covers. Lubricate sealing element of seal.
6. Install bearing cover and seal assembly (where used) and original shim pack over splined end of thru-shaft. Tighten cover nuts.
7. Install bearing opposite pinion firmly against shaft shoulder.
8. Install bearing cup in drive unit, rotating shaft to position all bearing rollers.
9. Install bearing cover and seal over original shim pack and tighten stud nuts.

Measuring Thru-Shaft Bearing Preload

1. As shown in Fig. 5, wrap strong cord around thru-shaft and pull on a horizontal line with a pound scale.
2. The preload specification for tapered roller bearings at opposite ends of thru-shaft is zero thru-shaft end play to 5 inch pounds torque.
3. Alter shim pack under bearing cover at end opposite pinion so there is no thru-shaft end play when measured with a dial indicator and so bearing preload torque does not exceed 5 inch pounds.
4. For example, assuming thru-shaft, diameter is 1½", the radius is 3/4" and with 4 pounds pull on scale, preload torque is 3 inch pounds.
5. Read rotating pounds pull (not starting pull). If preload torque is not within specified limits, add shims under bearing cover at end opposite pinion to decrease torque or remove shims at same location to increase preload torque.
6. Complete bearing adjustments before installing flanges or yokes.
7. Remove thru-shaft. Keep both shim pack with their respective covers to maintain established bearing preload.

Assemble Cross Shafts

Check I.D. of sleeve and O.D. of radial bearing and replace either or both of these parts if there is more than .006" clearance between them. When new, these parts have a clearance

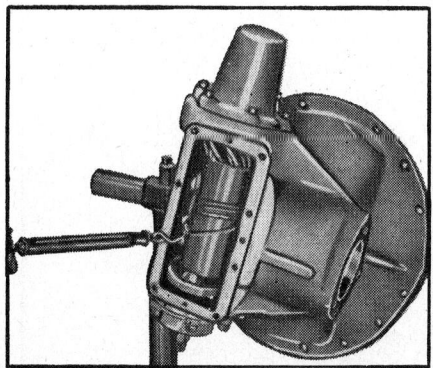

Fig. 5 Measuring thru-shaft bearing preload

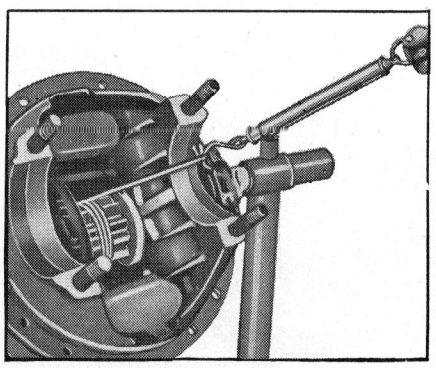

Fig. 6 Measuring Type 1 cross shaft bearing preload

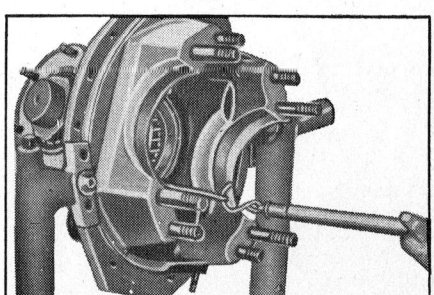

Fig. 7 Measuring Type 2 cross shaft bearing preload

TIMKEN (Rockwell) DRIVING AXLES

Fig. 8 Install inner bearing on Type 3 cross shaft, using wood block as shown

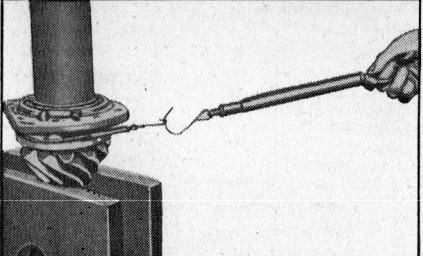

Fig. 9 Measuring pinion bearing preload on hypoid gear unit

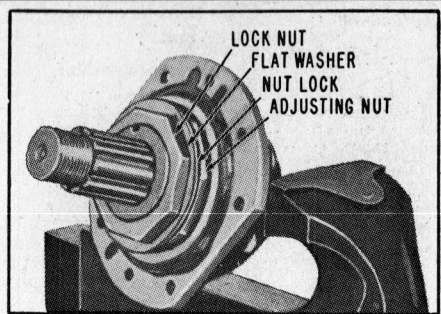

Fig. 10 Position of pinion locking components on hypoid gear units

of .0024" to .004". The radial bearing must be free to float in the sleeve.

Check the I.D. of the bearing bore on older drive units that do not have replaceable sleeves. If the I.D. is more than .006" larger than the bearing O.D., replace carrier and cap assembly with the newer type carrier and cap that incorporates replaceable sleeves.

If sleeve is to be replaced, press new sleeve firmly against housing shoulder. Drill hole for lock screw and remove burrs from sleeve. Install and tighten lock securely or install pin and stake in place.

Assemble Type 1 Cross Shaft
Gear Journal Fit to Cross Shaft

1. Install 6 studs at cross shaft flange. Assemble radial bearing on gear hub with large radius of bearing inner race toward back of gear.
2. Install bearing washer on gear hub against bearing with chamfer of spacer away from bearing. Install spacers with I.D. chamfer so chamfer is next to radius at root of pinion teeth. *A large flat washer is used at this location when O.D. of pinion teeth is smaller than I.D. of bearing.*
3. Coat I.D. of gear with heavy grease. Install gear, bearing and spacer assembly in drive unit sleeve and block up to hold in place.
4. Inspect entering end of cross shaft and remove any nicks or burrs. Coat O.D. of shaft and I.D. of gear with heavy grease.
5. Position housing in press with thru-shaft chamber down and gear supported on suitable sleeve.
6. Align key in cross shaft with key-way in gear hub and press shaft firmly against gear, bearing and spacer. *Continue pressing to exert 10 to 20 tons pressure in excess of that required for secure assembly.*
7. Install tapered bearing cage original shim pack (which controls gear position) over cross shaft cage studs.
8. Apply graphite lubricant to cross shaft tapered bearing journal and assemble inner and outer bearings, using suitable sleeves.
9. Install cage and bearing assembly in drive unit, pressing against outer bearing cone with suitable sleeve. Be sure oil holes in cage are aligned with oil holes in drive unit.
10. Assemble bearing retainer plate with two capscrews and secure with lock wire.
11. Install bearing cage cover over original shim pack (which control tapered bearing preload) over studs next to cage flange.
12. Assemble bearing cage cover, lock washers and stud nuts.
13. Wrap a strong cord around spur pinion, Fig. 6, and pull on a horizontal line on pound scale to measure cross shaft bearing preload torque. Proper preload torque is 5 to 15 inch pounds, which is equivalent to 2½ to 7½ pounds pull on scale.
14. Read rotating pull (not starting pull). If torque is not within limits, add shims between cover and cage to decrease, or remove shims to increase torque.
15. Install thru-shaft and pinion.
16. Adjust pinion and gear to secure correct gear tooth contact and backlash.

Assemble Type 2 Cross Shaft
Gear Splined to Hub, Hub Keyed to Cross Shaft

1. Apply graphite to cross shaft tapered bearing journal. Press inner bearing firmly against shaft shoulder with suitable sleeve.
2. Assemble gear to hub, aligning 6 gear-to-hub capscrew holes. Tighten screws securely.
3. Position drive unit on press bed with thru-shaft chamber up, and install radial bearing in drive unit sleeve. Large radius of bearing inner race must be toward bevel gear.
4. Support inner race of radial bearing with sleeve and press gear and hub assembly into bearing.
5. Turn drive unit over in press with thru-shaft chamber down, and support gear, hub and bearing assembly on sleeve with notches in end that fit over capscrew heads.
6. Inspect entering end of cross shaft and remove any nicks or burrs. Coat O.D. of shaft with heavy grease.
7. Align keyway in hub with key in cross shaft and press shaft and inner tapered bearing assembly firmly against hub.
8. Remove drive unit from press and install 6 cross shaft cage studs.
9. If tapered bearing cup has been removed from cross shaft cage, reassemble in press using sleeve to install cup firmly against cage shoulder.
10. Install original shim pack (which controls gear backlash) over studs, and cross shaft cage over shim pack, *aligning oil holes in cage with oil holes in drive unit.*
11. Install outer tapered bearing using suitable sleeve.

Fig. 11 Assemble rear gear against insert with locking teeth up

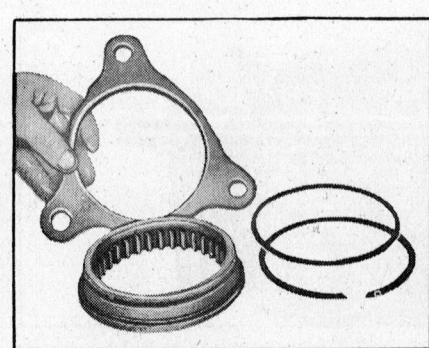

Fig. 12 Assemble yoke to shift collar

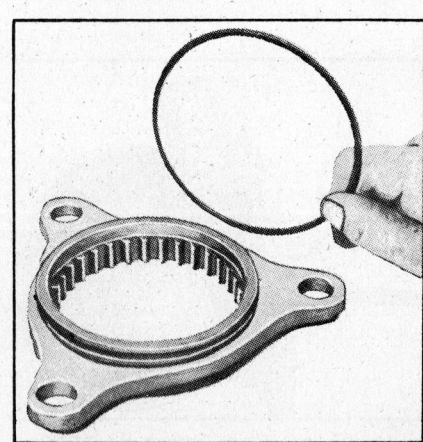

Fig. 13 Assemble spacer over collar yoke

TIMKEN (Rockwell) DRIVING AXLES

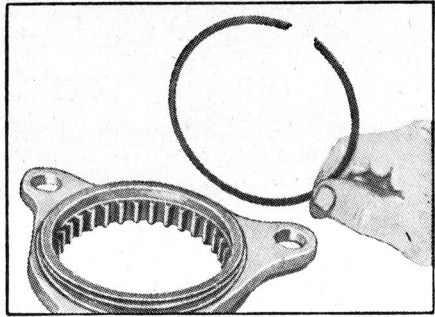

Fig. 14 Install retainer in shift collar groove

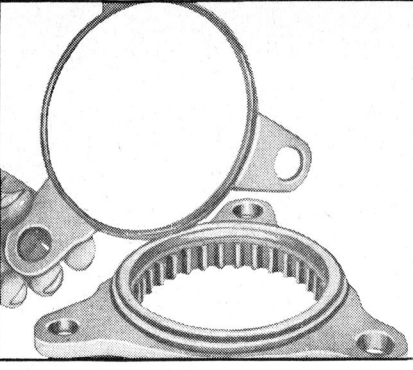

Fig. 15 Position stamped collar retainer cover over retainer

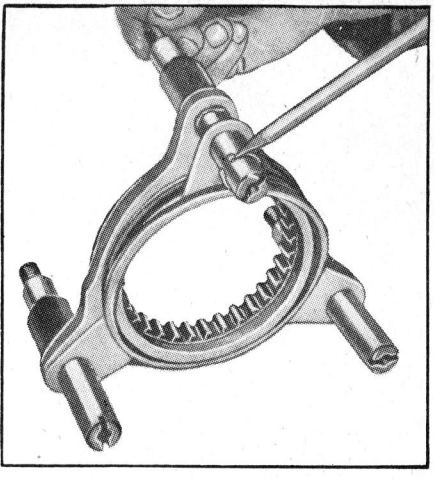

Fig. 16 Assemble shift shafts in collar and yoke and install snap rings in grooves as indicated

12. Install cross shaft bearing adjusting nut. Tighten nut as cross shaft is revolved to position all bearing rollers.
13. Measure cross shaft bearing preload torque by wrapping strong cord around spur pinion, Fig. 7, and pull on a horizontal line with pound scale. Preload torque should be 5 to 15 inch pounds which is equivalent to 2½ to 7½ pounds pull on scale.
14. Read rotating pull (not starting pull). If torque is not within limits, tighten bearing adjusting nut to increase, or loosen nut to decrease torque. Back off adjusting nut ¼ to ⅓ turn. Then install nut lock, flat washer and jam nut. Tighten jam nut to 500 ft. lbs. Recheck bearing preload. When correct, bend flat washer over jam nut.
15. Install thru-shaft and pinion.
16. Adjust pinion and gear to secure correct gear tooth contact and backlash.
17. Remove stud nuts and flat washers. Install bearing cage cover gasket, cover, stud nuts and lock washers.

Assemble Type 3 Cross Shaft

Gear Splined to Cross Shaft

1. Install radial bearing in drive unit with large radius of bearing inner race toward bevel gear.
2. Position drive unit in press with thru-shaft chamber up. Coat O.D. of shaft with heavy grease and press parts together about ¼" to ⅜". Then release press pressure to permit parts to align themselves to prevent distortion and damage. Continue pressing operation until parts are properly assembled.
3. Align gear and cross shaft capscrew holes and assemble gear to shaft. Torque capscrews to 65-85 ft. lbs.
4. Block up gear as shown in Fig. 8. Apply graphite lubricant to cross shaft tapered bearing journal. Install inner bearing firmly against shaft shoulder with suitable sleeve.
5. If tapered bearing cup has been removed, press cup firmly against shaft shoulder.
6. Install original shim pack (which controls gear backlash) over cross shaft cage studs, and cage over shim pack, aligning oil holes in cage with oil holes in drive unit. Install 4 evenly spaced nuts over thick flat washers to hold assembly in place. Tighten nuts securely.
7. Install outer tapered cross shaft bearing with suitable sleeve.
8. Install bearing adjusting nut. Tighten nut as cross shaft is being revolved to correctly position all bearing rollers.
9. Measure cross shaft bearing preload.

Wrap strong cord around spur pinion, Fig. 7, and pull on horizontal line with pound scale. Perload torque is 5 to 15 inch pounds which is equivalent to 2½ to 7½ pounds pull on scale. If preload is not within limits, tighten bearing adjusting nut to increase, or loosen nut to decrease preload torque.

10. Back off adjusting nut ¼ to ⅓ turn. Install nut lock, flat washer and jam nut. Tighten jam nut to 500 ft. lbs. Recheck bearing preload. When correct, bend flat washer over jam nut.
11. Install gear cover spacers, cover and 3 capscrews. Install pinion and thru-shaft. Adjust pinion and gear for correct gear

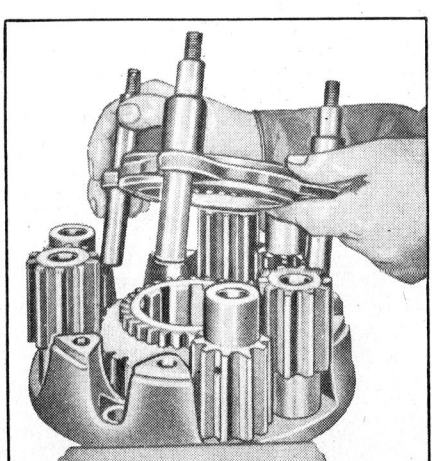

Fig. 17 Install pinions and shift yoke, collar and shaft assemblies, mating internal teeth of collar with teeth of rear side gear

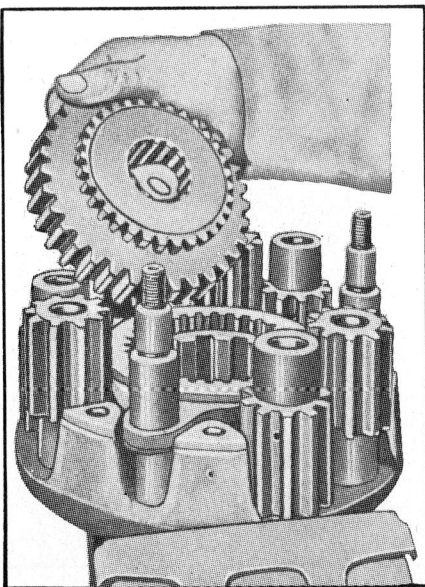

Fig. 18 Install forward differential gear. Turn gears to be sure all parts are correctly assembled and free-moving. Install forward thrust washer

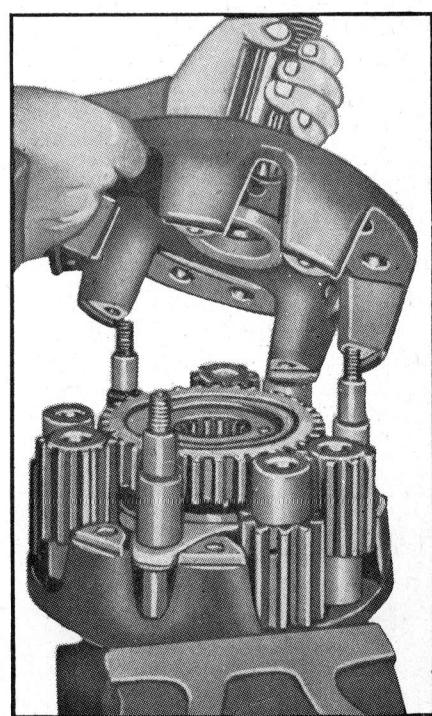

Fig. 19 Install forward case half, being sure to align match marks on case halves

TIMKEN (Rockwell) DRIVING AXLES

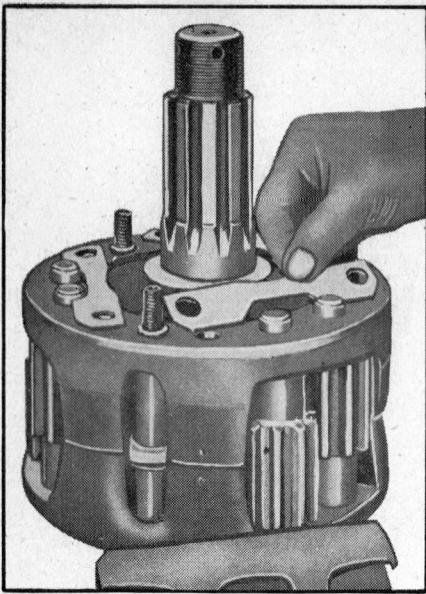

Fig. 20 Install pinion shaft locks

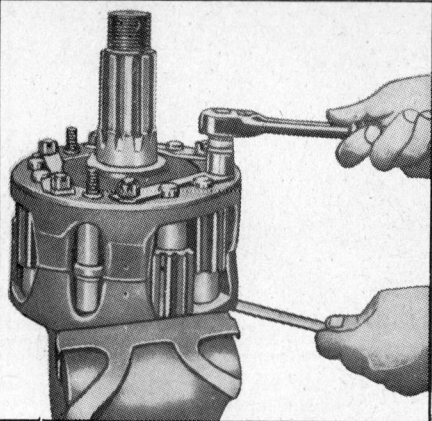

Fig. 21 Fasten case halves together. Check assembly for free movement by rotating pinions

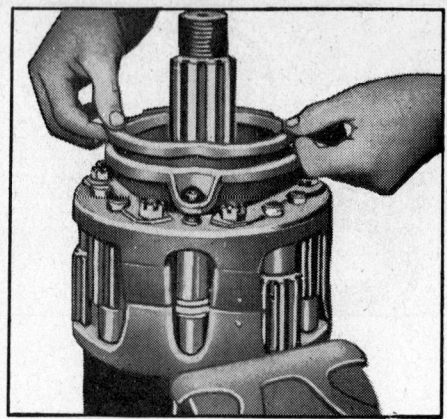

Fig. 22 Install shift collar. Tighten nuts to 65–85 ft. lbs. Be sure shift collar and shafts work up and down freely. If necessary rap assembly at several points on case to free up parts

backlash and tooth contact.
12. Remove stud nuts and flat washers. Install cage cover gasket, cover, nuts and lockwashers.

Install Hypoid Pinion & Thru-Shaft

1. Press pinion bearing cups in cage firmly against shoulder.
2. Coat thru-shaft O.D. and rear bearing inner race I.D. with heavy grease. *Press rear bearing inner race against rear shoulder of thru-shaft of forward carriers and rear carriers that have double splined end shafts. On rear carriers with short single end thru-shafts, install rear bearing inner race retainer, then press race in place and install outer retainer.*
3. Coat pinion and thru-shaft splines with heavy grease. Begin assembly operation in a press and press parts together 1/4" to 3/8". Then relieve press pressure to permit parts to realign themselves to prevent distortion and damage. Continue pressing operation until all parts are correctly assembled.
4. Lubricate all bearing journals with a few drops of engine oil and press inner pinion bearing firmly in place.
5. Position original bearing spacer next to bearing, being sure O.D. chamfer is toward outer bearing.
6. Install cage and cup and outer bearing. Press bearing firmly against selective spacer with suitable sleeve, rotating cage to assure normal bearing contact.
7. Measure pinion bearing preload torque while in press under 9 tons pressure. Wrap strong cord around cage pilot, Fig. 9, and pull on a horizontal line with a pound scale. The preload torque should be 5 to 15 inch lbs. which is equivalent to 2 1/2 to 7 1/2 pounds pull on scale. Use a thinner spacer to increase or a thicker spacer to decrease preload.
8. Remove assembly from press and install and tighten inner nut. Assemble as shown in Fig. 10. When properly tightened, bend lock washer over nut flat.
9. Install thru-shaft rear bearing with suitable sleeve. Check position in forward carrier with cover and seal assembly. In rear carriers with long thru-shaft (both ends splined) check position with cast end cover. In rear carriers with short thru-shaft, use large bearing spacer as a gauge.
10. Loosely install two guide studs in cage capscrew holes to aid reassembly. Position original shim pack over studs so oil holes are aligned. Carefully tap pinion, cage and thru-shaft in place.
11. Install and tighten 4 capscrews over flat washers to hold pinion cage firmly in place while checking hypoid tooth contact. Alter shim packs under cross shaft bearing cage to secure correct tooth contact.
12. Coat pinion oil seal with non-hardening sealing compound and install in cover. Lubricate sealing element.
13. Remove 4 capscrews and guide studs. Coat outer machined surface of cage and inside of cover with gasket cement. Install new gasket on cage flange.
14. Install cover and seal. Apply gasket cement to all covers and mating surfaces and install covers.
15. On rear drive units with thru-shafts splined at both ends, assemble parts as follows: Narrow spacer next to rear bearing inner race. Wide spacer next to narrow spacer. Nut washer, then rear nut.
16. Install forward yokes or flanges. Install narrow spacer at rear end of forward carrier thru-shaft, then yoke or flange.

Assemble Inter-Axle Differential

Assemble inter-axle differential as shown in Figs. 11 to 25. Then proceed with the

Fig. 23 Install ball bearing in housing cover

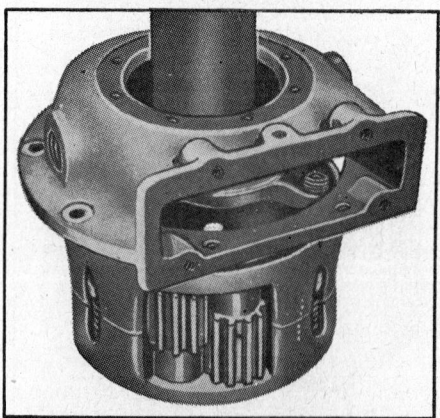

Fig. 24 Assemble cover and bearing assembly to differential. Use a small sleeve over input shaft against bearing inner race. Rotate cover to be sure it clears differential

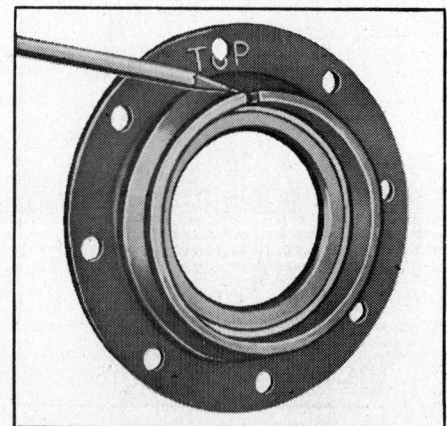

Fig. 25 Install retainer with slot indicated up, aligned with oil hole in cover

TIMKEN (Rockwell) DRIVING AXLES

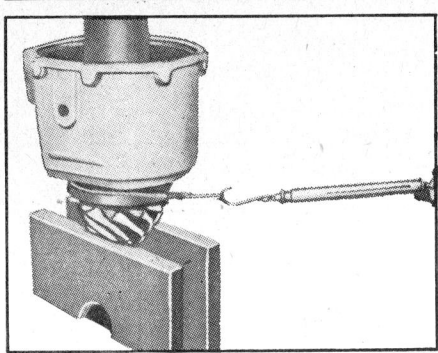

Fig. 26 Measuring pinion bearing preload

assembly as follows:
1. Position new gasket on cover and install bearing and seal retainer.
2. Carefully inspect completed assembly to be sure capscrew ends do not interfere with shift yoke or shift rings.
3. Install yoke or flange, washer and nut.

Assemble Hypoid Pinion & Quill

1. Press pinion bearing cups against housing shoulder. Assemble rear bearing inner race inner retainer. Coat quill O.D. and race I.D. with heavy grease and press race in place. Install outer retainer.
2. Lubricate all bearing journals with a few drops of engine oil and press inner bearing on pinion and quill assembly.
3. Install original spacer on inner bearing with O.D. chamfer of spacer toward outer (forward) bearing.
4. Position housing and cup assembly on pinion. Press bearing firmly against selective spacer with suitable sleeve, rotating housing to assure normal bearing contact.
5. Measure pinion bearing preload while in press under 9 tons pressure. Wrap strong cord around housing pilot, Fig. 26, and pull on a horizontal line with a pound scale. Preload should be 5 to 15 inch pounds which is equivalent to $2\frac{1}{2}$ to $7\frac{1}{2}$ pounds pull on scale.
6. Use a thinner spacer to increase or a thicker spacer to decrease preload. Tighten adjusting nut and recheck preload.
7. Install pinion quill rear bearing in carrier with suitable sleeve. Check location with thru-shaft ball bearing retainer.
8. Loosely install 2 guide studs in carrier if capscrews are used to hold housing in place. Position original shim pack over studs so oil holes are aligned. Carefully tap pinion, housing and gear assembly in place.
9. Install 4 equally spaced capscrews or stud nuts to hold assembly in place while checking hypoid gear tooth contact. Alter shim pack under cross shaft bearing cage and inter-axle differential housing to secure correct tooth contact.
10. Install remaining capscrews or stud nuts and secure with lock wire.

Install Inter-Axle Differential

1. Turn carrier so pinion and quill assembly is in vertical position and loosely install 3 guide studs in differential housing. Position gasket in place and install differential and cover. Revolve differential back and forth to engage splines of pinion with rear gear. Install capscrews.
2. Revolve differential to be sure it is free turning. If not, remove it and inspect parts.
3. Check position of oil scoop for interference at helix baffle at left inside housing of early models.
4. Install and tighten 2 capscrews at shift lever housing. Secure with lock wire.

Install Shift Unit Housing

1. Hold shift unit in vise and install push rod in housing and fork, Fig. 27. Be sure round button of fork faces front. Assemble push rod in place with sleeve.
2. Place copper gasket over end of push rod and install diaphragm assembly. Hold push rod with screwdriver while starting nut over lock washer. Be sure flats of push rod fit in slot of diaphragm insert as nut is tightened. Tighten nut to 4-6 ft. lbs. Install shift unit cover plug.
3. Attach assembly to cover with 2 capscrews over lock washers. Install 2 tapered dowels, special lock washers and stud nuts.

Adjust Shift Fork (Late Models)

This adjustment is for later models without shift shaft springs that have both forward and rear adjusting screws. Always check shift fork location with feeler gauge, Fig. 28, to be sure there is .010" clearance (minimum) at guide rings or groove.

Lockout Disengaged, Forward Adjusting Screw
1. Back off adjusting screw lock nut so screw is free turning.
2. Shift assembly to disengaged position with power chamber.
3. Turn in adjusting screw until it is finger-tight against fork.
4. Turn in screw $\frac{1}{2}$ revolution more to center fork in groove.
5. Tighten lock nut.

Lockout Engaged, Rear Adjusting Screw
1. Back off adjusting screw lock nut so screw is free turning.
2. Shift assembly to engaged position with power chamber. Be sure shift collar is fully engaged with rear gear.
3. Turn in screw until it is finger-tight against push rod.
4. Turn in screw $\frac{1}{2}$ revolution more to center fork in groove. Tighten lock nut.

Adjust Shift Fork (Early Models)

This adjustment is for early models that have shift shaft springs and only a forward adjusting screw. With lockout disengaged, adjust as follows:
1. Back off adjusting screw lock nut.

Fig. 28 Adjusting shift fork, using feeler gauge

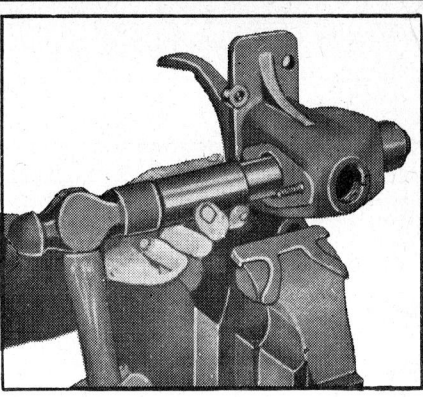

Fig. 27 Installing shift unit push rod

2. Turn screw in finger-tight against fork. This forces fork against inner guide ring.
3. Back off screw $\frac{1}{2}$ revolution to center fork between guide rings.
4. Tighten lock nut.

Install Thru-Shaft

1. Coat seal body and seat with non-hardening sealing compound and install in cover with suitable sleeve. Lubricate sealing element.
2. Install thru-shaft ball bearing firmly against shaft shoulder and assemble shaft and bearing in retainer.
3. Position new gasket over studs and install shaft assembly. Be sure thru-shaft splines mesh with forward gear of inter-axle differential. Do not force in place.
4. Install cover and seal with new gasket. Alternately tighten 4 evenly spaced stud nuts to draw assembly in place and correctly position pinion quill rear bearing. Install and tighten stud nuts.
5. Install thru-shaft yoke or flange.

Tooth Contact & Gear Backlash

Tooth contact may be checked as outlined in the *Single Reduction Axle* section. Spiral bevel gear first reduction units have shim packs between the forward and rear thru-shaft tapered bearing covers and the carrier to control pinion position. Hypoid gear first reduction units have a single shim pack between the pinion cage and carrier or inter-axle differential housing and carrier to control pinion position. A shim pack between the cross shaft bearing cage flange and carrier controls the

Fig. 29 Installing split ring

TIMKEN (Rockwell) DRIVING AXLES

BOLT AND STUD NUTS

LOCATION	DIAMETER	NO. THREADS	NUT THICKNESS	TORQUE—LB. FT. MIN.	TORQUE—LB. FT. MAX.
Push Rod Nut	5/16"	18		4	6
Shift Unit	3/8"	24		39	42
Pinion, Thru-Shaft and Cross Shaft Bearing Cages and Covers and Inter-Axle Differential Housings	3/8"	24	3/8"	39	42
	7/16"	20		61	66
	1/2"	20		73	80
	1/2"	20	7/16"	94	102
	1/2"	20		94	102
	9/16"	18		132	145
	5/8"	18		186	205
Carrier to Housing	1/2"	20		94	102
	5/8"	18		186	205
	3/4"	16		325	360
Axle Differential Case Bolt	1/2"	20		94	102
	9/16"	18		132	145
	5/8"	18		186	205
	3/4"	16		325	360
Inter-Axle Differential Shift Shaft Nut	1/2"	20		65	85
Inter-Axle Differential Case Bolt Nut	1/2"	20		94	102
Inter-Axle Differential Shift Housing	7/16"	20		61	66
Shift Fork Adjusting Screw Lock Nut	1/2"	20	6/16"	40	55
Shift Fork Set Screw Lock Nut	3/8"	24		30	33
Pinion Shaft, Thru-Shaft and Inter-Axle Differential Case Shaft	1"	20		300	400
	1 1/4"	18		700	900
	1 1/2"	18		800	1100
	1 1/2"	12		800	1100
	1 3/4"	12		800	1100
Pinion Bearing Adjusting and Lock Nut	3 3/8"	12		1000	1200

CAP SCREWS

LOCATION	DIAMETER	NO. THREADS	TORQUE—LB. FT. MIN.	TORQUE—LB. FT. MAX.
Differential Bearing Adjusting Nut Lock	5/16"	18	15	17
	1/2"	13	85	91
Cross Shaft Bearing Lock	7/16"	14	42	45
	1/2"	20	73	80
	9/16"	12	92	101
Inter-Axle Differential Shift Unit Housing	7/16"	14	54	58
Pinion, Thru-Shaft and Cross Shaft Bearing Cages and Covers and Inter-Axle Differential Housings	3/8"	16	26	29
	1/2"	13	85	91
	9/16"	12	120	129
	5/8"	11	168	180
Inter-Axle Differential Housing Cover and Bearing Retainer	3/8"	24	30	33
	7/16"	14	54	58
Differential Carrier Top, Rear and Side Covers	3/8"	16	26	29
Inter-Axle Differential Shift Fork Set Screw	3/8"	24	30	33

AXLE DIFFERENTIAL BEARING-CAP CAP SCREWS OR STUD NUTS

CAP SCREW OR STUD NUT DIAMETER	CAP SCREW OR COARSE STUD THREAD	STUD NUT OR FINE THREAD	TORQUE—LB. FT. MIN.	TORQUE—LB. FT. MAX.
5/8"	11	18	127	140
3/4"	10	16	230	250
7/8"	9	14	345	370
7/8"	14	14	375	415
1"	14	14	570	630

Fig. 30 Torque specifications for double reduction thru-drive tandem axles. Torques given apply to parts coated with machine oil. For dry (or "as received") parts increase torques 10%. For parts coated with multipurpose gear oil decrease torques 10%. Nuts on studs use same torque as driving the stud

position of the first reduction spiral bevel or hypoid gear in all top-mounted double reduction drive units.

Set backlash to the amount specified on gear O.D. When backlash is not specified on gear set to .006–.012".

Be sure all bearing preloads are within specified limits before checking tooth contacts. Transpose equal amounts of shims between front and rear pinion bearing covers of spiral bevel drive units to maintain correct bearing preload while adjusting tooth contact. Add or remove shims between pinion cage or inter-axle differential housing of hypoid drive gear units to alter pinion location. Change the location of spiral bevel or hypoid gear by altering the thickness of the shim pack between the cross shaft bearing cage flange and carrier.

In hypoid gearing the actual backlash changes .008" for each .010" movement of the gear. In spiral bevel gearing, the actual backlash changes .007" for each .010" movement of the gear.

Install Axle Differential

1. Press differential bearings firmly against case shoulders. Coat inside of case and all differential parts with rear axle lubricant.
2. Assemble differential case half and gear. Install side gear thrust washers, side gears and pinion gears, thrust washers and spider.
3. Note case alignment marks and assemble opposite case half. Hold assembly together with 4 bolts and nuts and check for free rotation of parts.
4. Install remaining case bolts so heads are locked by machined relief in case half. Be sure case halves are assembled to gear so there is adequate nut clearance. Check clearance in carrier before completing assembly.

NOTE: Apply Loctite grade 277 to the case bolts. Allow Loctite to cure for 4 hours before adding oil and 24 hours before subjecting axle to heavy duty use.

5. When a new gear or differential case is installed, the case holes must be line-reamed with the gear in order to assemble the parts, using the correct size rivets or bolts. Align case halves and hold together with 4 bolts. Line ream the holes and clean parts before assembly.

Install Differential Bearing Cups

1. Temporarily install bearing cups, threaded adjusting rings (when used) securely.
2. Bearing cups must be a hand push fit in bores, otherwise bores must be re-worked with a scraper or emery cloth until a hand push fit is obtained. Use a blued bearing cup as a gauge and check fit as work progresses.

Bearings With Two Threaded Adjusting Nuts

1. Apply rear axle lubricant to bearing cups and cones. Position cups over cones and install in carrier.
2. Insert differential bearing adjusting nuts and turn hand tight against bearing cups.
3. Install bearing caps. Install and tighten stud nuts or capscrews.
4. Alternately loosen one adjusting nut and tighten the other while turning the differential to assure normal bearing contact and to keep bearing cups straight in the bores.
5. With a dial gauge, establish zero end play. Then tighten adjusting nuts 1 3/4 to 2 1/2 notches (total for both nuts) tight to correctly preload bearings.

TIMKEN (Rockwell) DRIVING AXLES

6. Install adjusting nut locks and capscrews.

Type With Two Split Rings
1. With differential and bearings installed, insert thin split rings, making certain that there is clearance between bearing cup faces and rings (do not install bearing caps).
2. With a dial indicator, measure end play of differential by shifting assembly back and forth between rings with a pair of small pinch bars placed between carrier legs and spur gears.
3. Remove and measure thickness of rings. To the total thickness of the 2 thin rings add the end play figure plus another .017" to .022" to obtain the total thickness of the 2 thicker rings required to obtain proper bearing preload. Split rings are available in increments of .005".
4. Insert one split ring in carrier leg groove. Move differential over so that face of bearing cup is held tightly against inserted ring. Rings should be positioned in carrier leg grooves so that split portion will locate in center of cap.
5. Install opposite split ring by tapping it into the carrier leg, Fig. 29, tapping on I.D. of ring opposite split portion.
6. Install differential bearing caps and install capscrews.

Timken Worm Drive Axle

This type axle, Fig. 1, incorporates a forged, ground and polished worm of alloy steel and a worm wheel compounded of special phosphor-bronze. Worm drive units are usually incorporated in tandem drive vehicles where high engine horsepower is required to move heavy loads and where chassis design may be a factor limiting drive unit size.

Remove Drive Unit from Housing
1. Disconnect U-joints at ends of worm shafts. Remove plug at bottom of housing and drain lubricant.
2. Remove axle shafts.
3. Remove attaching stud nuts and break drive unit loose from axle housing with soft mallet and remove tapered dowels. Dowels must be removed before drive unit can be lifted from housing. Back out housing studs if necessary.

DISASSEMBLE DRIVE UNIT
1. Remove flange nuts and stud nuts or capscrews from tapered cage cover. Hold forward yoke or flange or rear drive unit while loosening tapered bearing jam nut.
2. Pull yokes or flanges from worm shaft with suitable puller. Remove key (if used) from worm shaft.
3. Match mark one differential bearing cap and carrier leg to identify at reassembly.
4. Remove all locking wire and worm wheel baffle (if used). Remove differential bearing caps, bearing cups, adjusting nuts and differential assembly.

Disassemble Differential Unit

Two types of differential assemblies are used. One uses bolts and nuts to hold differential case halves to worm wheel; the other uses rivets.
1. To disassemble the bolt-on type, match mark differential case halves and worm wheel so parts can be correctly identified if they are to be reused. Drive bolts from assembly with brass drift and pull assembly apart.
2. To disassemble the riveted-on type, match mark differential case halves and worm wheel for identification on reassembly if parts are to be re-used. Drill out rivets. Tap differential case half free and remove side gear and thrust washer. Turn worm wheel over and repeat operation.
3. Match mark two halves of differential driving ring at matching lugs for reassembly. Some driving rings have a dowel and hole in respective halves to insure correct assembly.
4. Drive or press driving ring, spider, pinion and thrust washer assembly from worm wheel. Then separate halves of driving ring to disassemble spider and pinions.

Remove Worm Shaft
1. Remove worm shaft and tapered bearing

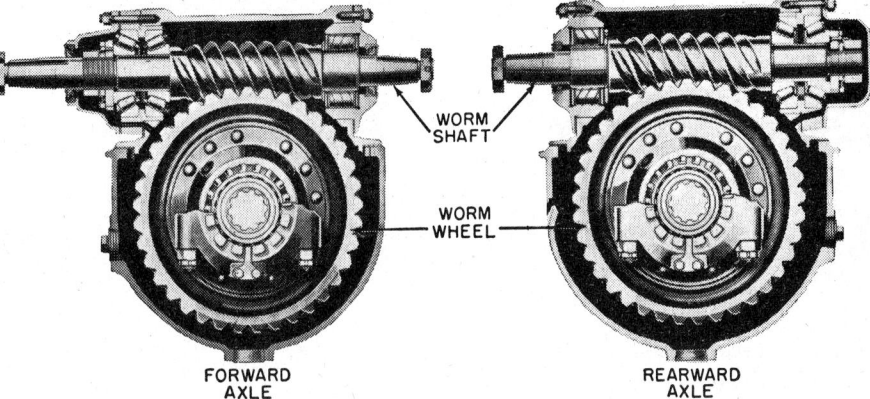

Fig. 1 Timken worm drive tandem axle units. Some units have the tapered bearing cage at the rear of both drive units. The tapered bearings shown are maintained by adjusting nuts. Units of more recent design have selective spacers to establish and maintain tapered bearing adjustment

Fig. 2 Removing straight roller bearing outer race lock screw

Fig. 3 Removing oil baffle (when used)

Fig. 4 Installing selective bearing spacers

TIMKEN (Rockwell) DRIVING AXLES

Fig. 5 Measuring worm shaft tapered bearing preload

Fig. 6 Installing worm shaft assembly

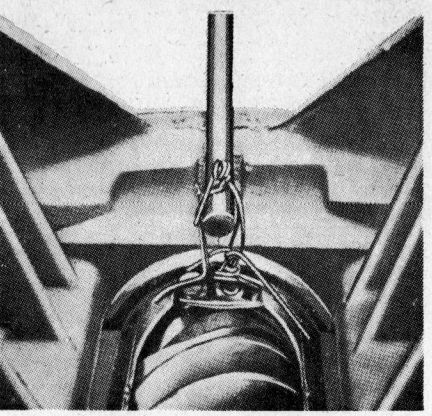

Fig. 7 Wire threaded through oil baffle holes to contract baffle

cage from drive unit by tapping on end opposite tapered bearing cage.
2. Remove roller bearing or self-aligning bearing end of drive unit. Remove bearing cage or straight roller bearing cover and seal assembly. Remove roller bearing spacer (if used), roller bearing, and outer race lock screws. Fig. 2.
3. Carefully tap race from drive unit with brass drift. Remove roller bearing from cage and seal as required.
4. Remove worm shaft oil baffle (if used), Fig. 3. Identify location of one end of baffle to aid in reassembly.

Disassemble Worm Shaft & Tapered Bearing Cage

1. Remove attaching nut and related parts and press shaft out of bearing cage. Do not lose selective spacers that are between bearings.
2. Tap hardened steel spacer from roller bearing end of worm shaft.
3. Remove bearing cups from cage with suitable puller.
4. Remove seals or felts from front and rear covers or cages.

REASSEMBLY

Replace worm wheels that have worn or broken teeth and worm shafts where there is evidence of checked or damaged case hardening.

Inspect differential for pitted, scored or worn thrust surfaces of differential case halves, thrust washers, spider trunnions and differential gears. *Thrust washers must be replaced in sets. The use of a combination of old and new thrust washers will result in premature failure.* Check for wear or damage to differential gear teeth. Inspect spider trunnions for looseness in differential case or driving ring bores.

Worm & Tapered Bearing Cage

1. Press inner and outer tapered bearing cups in cage with suitable sleeve.
2. Position outer tapered bearing on suitable sleeve in press. Place cage and cup on outer bearing.
3. Position original selective spacers in cage on outer bearing, Fig. 4.
4. Press worm shaft into cage and bearing as cage is rotated to assure normal bearing contact. *Begin the assembly operation in the press making sure the parts are properly aligned. Press the parts together about 1/4" to 3/8", then relieve the press pressure to permit them to realign themselves to prevent distortion or damage.* Continue the pressing operation until the parts are correctly assembled.
5. Install and tighten adjusting nut.

Tapered Bearing Preload

As shown in Fig. 5, wrap strong cord around tapered bearing cage three or four times and attach a pound scale to cord end. Pull scale on horizontal line and read pounds pull. Use rotating pounds pull (not starting pull). Tapered bearing preload may be measured while the assembly is in the press under pressure. The following table gives equivalent nut torques and press pressures:

Worm Shaft Thread Size	Specified Nut Torque Ft. Lbs.	Equivalent Press Pressure In Tons
1" x 20	300-400	6
1 1/4" x 18	700-900	11
1 1/2" x 12	800-1100	14
1 1/2" x 18	800-1100	14
1 3/4" x 12	800-1100	14
2" x 16	800-1100	14
2 1/8" x 12	800-1100	14

Compute bearing preload torque by multiplying radius of bearing cage pilot by the number of pounds pull. For example, assume diameter of cage pilot is 6", the radius is 3". If the scale reading is one pound rotating pull, the bearing preload is 3 inch pounds. Tapered bearing preload should be zero worm shaft end play to 5 inch pounds maximum torque. If in excess of 5 inch pounds when nut is correctly tightened, remove nut and outer bearing cone and substitute a thicker spacer. If less than zero worm shaft end play, remove spacer and add one thinner than the one removed. Continue this procedure until correct bearing preload is obtained.

Adjust splined worm shaft tapered bearing preload in the same manner, omitting the seal and cover assembly (where used) until correct preload is obtained.

Position nut lock and washer (where used) over adjusting nut and tighten jam nut. Check tapered bearing preload and readjust if necessary. Carefully tap steel washer on opposite end of worm shaft.

Assemble Worm Shaft In Drive Unit

1. Coat oil seals with non-hardening sealing compound and assemble in cover or cage

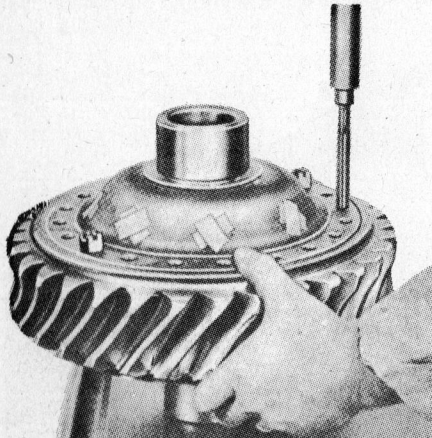

Fig. 8 Differential case holes covered with masking tape to prevent chips from falling into gear assembly when line-reaming case-to-worm wheel holes for bolt or rivet installation

Fig. 9 Differential components used with riveted case

TIMKEN (Rockwell) DRIVING AXLES

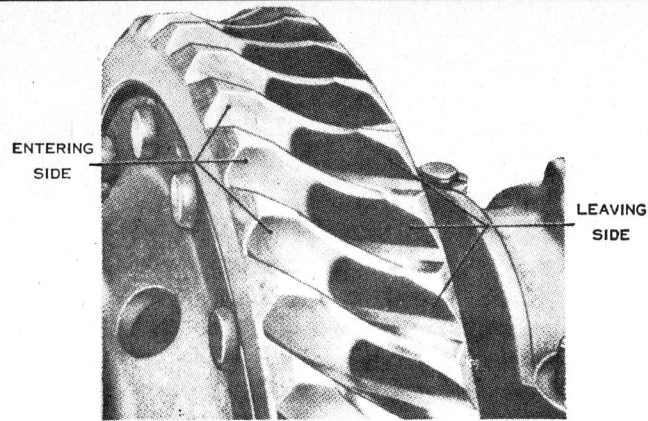

Fig. 10 Satisfactory tooth contact. Starting at leaving side 30 to 60% full tooth length

with suitable sleeve.
2. Install roller bearing outer race (where used) in drive unit with suitable sleeve. Be sure lock screw holes are properly aligned. Install and tighten bearing lock screw.
3. Note identifying location marks previously made on worm shaft oil baffle (new baffles have stenciled installation directions).
4. Install baffle so its tangs engage notches in drive unit. Position new gasket over tapered bearing cage studs.
5. Install worm shaft and bearing cage assembly in drive unit, Fig. 6.
6. Thread two or three strands of wire through oil baffle holes and twist wire to contract baffle, Fig. 7.
7. Tap worm shaft assembly into drive unit so baffle will fit against I.D. of tapered bearing cage. *Cut and remove wire, being sure no small bits of wire drop into drive unit.*
8. Install new gasket over tapered bearing cage flange and install cage cover or cover and seal assembly. Tighten stud nuts over lock washers.
9. Install roller bearing in opposite end of drive unit, or install self-aligning bearing and cage with new gasket. Install roller bearing outer washer and dowel assembly (if used).
10. Position new gasket over cover or cage and install assembly. Tighten stud nuts or capscrews.
11. When aluminum cover and seal assemblies are used, large flat steel washers are located beneath stud nut or capscrew lock washers.

Assemble Worm Wheel & Differential

Bolt-On Type
1. Assemble worm wheel to differential case half, carefully noting case matching marks. A suitable drift can be used in aligning case half and worm wheel holes.
2. Turn assembly over and install side gear thrust washer and side gear in case half.
3. Assemble differential pinions and thrust washers on spider. Install spider and pinion assembly in case half.
4. Install opposite side gear and thrust washer. Install opposite case half, carefully noting case matching marks.
5. Install two 7/16" × 4½" bolts in assembly and tighten nuts. Check assembly for free rotation of gears.
6. *When a anew worm wheel or differential case is installed, the case holes must be line-reamed with the worm wheel holes to properly reassemble, using correct size bolts. Use care to prevent ream chips from falling into assembly. Case holes may be covered with masking tape, Fig. 8, or plugged with stoppers.*
7. Remove two bolts used to hold assembly together.
8. Install differential assembly bolts so heads are locked by case half flange shoulder and safety wire holes in bolts are roughly parallel to worm wheel O.D. Install and tighten nuts. The two case halves are usually identical except for width of bolt circle flange shoulder. Install bolts so that bolt heads will fit snugly against locking shoulder of one case half.
9. Lock bolts in groups of four with soft iron wire. Install differential bearings with suitable sleeve. Lubricate assembly.

Riveted Type
1. Assemble pinion and thrust washers on spider. Assemble spider assembly in half of differential driving ring.
2. Place assembly in worm wheel driving ring slots and assemble other half of driving ring, Fig. 9. Note previously made matching marks (or dowel and its hole) in matching driving ring lugs.
3. Support worm wheel on steel blocks and assemble driving ring and spider assembly to wheel by driving it in wheel slots with a soft hammer. Continue procedure until driving ring assembly is flush with machined face of worm wheel.
4. Install side gear and thrust washer. Assemble differential case half to worm wheel and driving ring assembly, noting differential case matching marks. A suitable drift can be used to aid in aligning case half-to-worm wheel holes.
5. Turn assembly over and install opposite side gear and thrust washer and case half. Note matching marks on case half.
6. Hold assembly together with two 7/16" × 4½" bolts. Check for free rotation of gears.
7. *When a new worm wheel or differential case is installed, the case holes must be line-reamed with worm wheel holes to properly reassemble, using the correct size rivets. Use care to prevent rivet chips from falling into assembly. Case holes may be covered with masking tape, Fig. 8.*
8. Install rivets cold. When correct, rivet head being formed will be at least 1/8" larger in diameter than rivet hole. The formed head should not be more than 1/16" lower than preformed head as excessive pressure may distort assembly and result in unsatisfactory tooth contact.
9. Install differential bearings with suitable sleeve. Lubricate assembly.

Install Differential

1. Note identifying marks on bearing caps and install bearing cups, nuts and caps. Tighten nuts or capscrews. Then remove caps, cups and nuts. Lubricate parts and reassemble again, tightening nuts or capscrews securely.
2. Alternately loosen one adjusting nut and tighten the opposite nut while turning assembly to straighten bearing cups in bores and assure normal bearing contact.
3. Mount dial indicator to contact machine face of worm wheel and check end play. Established a .000" end play (no preload condition in bearings).
4. Tighten adjusting nuts 1¾ to 2½ notches tight (total for both nuts) to correctly preload bearings.

Worm Tooth Patterns

The worm wheel teeth have an entering side (where the worm shaft teeth enter) and a leaving side (where the worm shaft teeth leave). The entering sides of the teeth have the flattest angle while the leaving sides are

Fig. 11 Not enough leaving side contact. Move worm wheel to leaving side

Fig. 12 Contact at entering side. Move worm wheel to entering side

TIMKEN (Rockwell) DRIVING AXLES

almost straight or vertical.

The proper tooth contact during operation under load is approximately 80% of the tooth length, starting at the leaving side of the tooth, progressing toward the entering side of the tooth. *Do not have worm tooth patterns to have contact at the entering side.*

The correct tooth contact, when turned by hand before operation under load, should be 30 to 60% of worm wheel tooth length, starting at the leaving side of the tooth. To establish correct tooth contact, proceed as follows:

1. Apply a thin coating of Prussian blue to 6 or 8 worm wheel teeth.
2. Set the worm to its maximum amount of backlash, using a dial indicator.
3. Rotate worm shaft to wipe blue from worm wheel, indicating tooth contact.
4. Move worm wheel to one side or the other until contact, starting at the leaving side is 30 to 60% of full tooth length, Fig. 10.
5. Always use drive side of teeth when making adjustments as coast side will automatically show a satisfactory pattern when drive side contact is correct. If tooth pattern shows as illustrated in Figs. 11 and 12, adjust as indicated. As a rule it is necessary to move the worm wheel only a few thousandths of an inch to alter tooth contact.
6. To adjust, move differential bearing adjusting nuts about 1/4 turn at a time until proper tooth contact is obtained. Maintain differential bearing preload during adjustment by first loosening the adjusting nut on the side toward which the differential is to be moved and tightening the opposite adjusting nut the same amount. *Make normal wear adjustments at the left hand bearing only. This will maintain correct worm and wheel alignment.*

Final Assembly

1. Tighten differential bearing cap nuts or capscrews. Install nut locks and lock screws and secure with lock wire.
2. Install and tighten yoke and flange nuts.
3. With new gasket, install drive unit in housing. First install lock washer and stud nuts under any drive unit and housing offset. It is impossible to start these nuts after drive unit is tight in housing.
4. Install tapered dowels (where used). Alternately tighten nuts.
5. Connect U-joints at worm shaft. Install axle shafts and connect brake lines.

BOLTS AND STUD NUTS				
LOCATION	DIA.	NO. THDS.	TORQUE—LB. FT. MIN.	MAX.
Oil Baffle	5/16"	24	16	18
Carrier to Housing	1/2"	20	92	102
	5/8"	18	185	205
	3/4"	16	320	360
Worm Shaft Covers and Cages	7/16"	20	59	66
	1/2"	20	92	102
	9/16"	18	130	145
Differential Assembly and Worm Wheel Bolt	1/2"	20	92	102
Worm Shaft Yoke or Flange Nut	1"	20	300	400
	1 1/4"	18	700	900
	1 1/2"	12	800	1100
	1 1/2"	18	800	1100
	1 3/4"	12	800	1100
Worm Shaft Bearing Locknut	1 1/2"	12	800	1100
	2"	16	800	1100
	2 1/8"	12	800	1100
CAP SCREWS				
Adjusting Nut Lock	5/16"	18	15	17
	5/16"	24	16	18
Oil Baffle	3/8"	16	26	29
Carrier to Housing	1/2"	13	82	91
Roller Bearing Race Lock	1/2"	13	82	91
Worm Shaft Covers and Cages	7/16"	14	52	58
	1/2"	13	82	91
	9/16"	12	116	129

DIFFERENTIAL BEARING CAP CAP SCREWS OR STUD NUTS (Earlier Axle Models Without Hardened Washers)				
CAP SCREW OR STUD NUT DIAMETER	CAP SCREW OR COARSE STUD THREAD	STUD NUT OR FINE THREAD	TORQUE—LB. FT. MIN.	MAX.
5/8"	11	18	126	140
3/4"	10	16	225	250
7/8"	9	14	330	370
7/8"	14	14	375	415
1"	14	14	375	415

DIFFERENTIAL BEARING CAP CAP SCREWS OR STUD NUTS (Later Axle Models Employing Hardened Washers)				
CAP SCREW OR STUD NUT DIAMETER	CAP SCREW OR COARSE STUD THREAD	STUD NUT OR FINE THREAD	TORQUE—LB. FT. MIN.	MAX.
5/8"	11	18	160	180
3/4"	10	16	290	320
7/8"	9	14	470	520
7/8"	14	14	510	570
1"	14	14	570	630

Fig. 13 Torque specifications for Timken worm drive axles

Electric Shift Unit For Two-Speed Axles

DESCRIPTION

Basically, the shift unit, Fig. 1, consists of an electric motor, a worm shaft and wheel, an eccentric and a connecting rod. The electric motor drives the worm shaft and wheel; the eccentric is attached to the worm wheel and drives the connecting rod which operates the shift shaft.

The actual shifting is done by a double acting compressing spring contained in the push rod. This spring is mounted on the shift shaft which is attached to the connecting rod. As the connecting rod pushes (or pulls) the shift shaft, the spring cocks and, in turn, pushes or pulls on the push rod and shift collar. When the driving torque is relieved (by releasing the accelerator or clutch) the spring pressure will complete the shift.

SIDE MOUNTED TYPE

Removal

1. Disconnect electric harness at terminals at shift unit cover.
2. Remove attaching screws and filler plug from cover.
3. Screw a threaded tool into the filler plug hole and pull the cover from the housing. The tool is made from a 1/8 × 27 pipe plug welded to the end of a T handle. *Do not pry cover from housing.*
4. Drive roll pin from shift shaft, using tool having a 5/8" body and a 5/32" nose section. *If the roll pin is in line with the worm shaft, it will be necessary to change the position of the shift shaft before the pin can be driven out.*
5. To change the position of the shift shaft, turn on the vehicle ignition switch. Shift the unit to the desired position by touch-

TIMKEN (Rockwell) DRIVING AXLES

21. Electric Switch and Shift Cover Nut
22. Electric Switch and Shift Cover Washer
23. Electric Switch and Shift Cover Bushing
24. Electric Switch and Shift Cover Insulator
25. Electric Switch Assembly
26. Electric Switch Nut
27. Worm Wheel Cap Screw and Lock Washer—Short
28. Ball Bearing
29. Adjusting Screw Jam Nut
30. Adjusting Screw
31. Oil Seal Assembly
32. Snap Ring
33. Roll Pin
34. Shift Shaft Assembly
35. Push Rod
36. Shift Housing to Sleeve Gasket
37. Push Rod Sleeve
38. Push Rod Sleeve Shim
39. "O" Ring

1. Shift Motor Assembly
2. Shift Motor Lock Nut
3. Worm Shaft Spring Thrust Washer
4. Worm Shaft Spring
5. Worm Shaft Spring Washer
6. Worm Shaft
7. Worm
8. Worm Shaft Spring Retainer
9. Shift Motor Gasket
10. Shift Housing
11. Shift Housing Cover Gasket
12. Worm Wheel Cap Screw and Lock Washer—Long
13. Worm Wheel
14. Eccentric
15. Eccentric Connecting Rod
16. Eccentric Cover
17. Eccentric Shaft
18. Shift Cover
19. Shift Cover Attaching Screws
20. Shift Cover Filler Plug

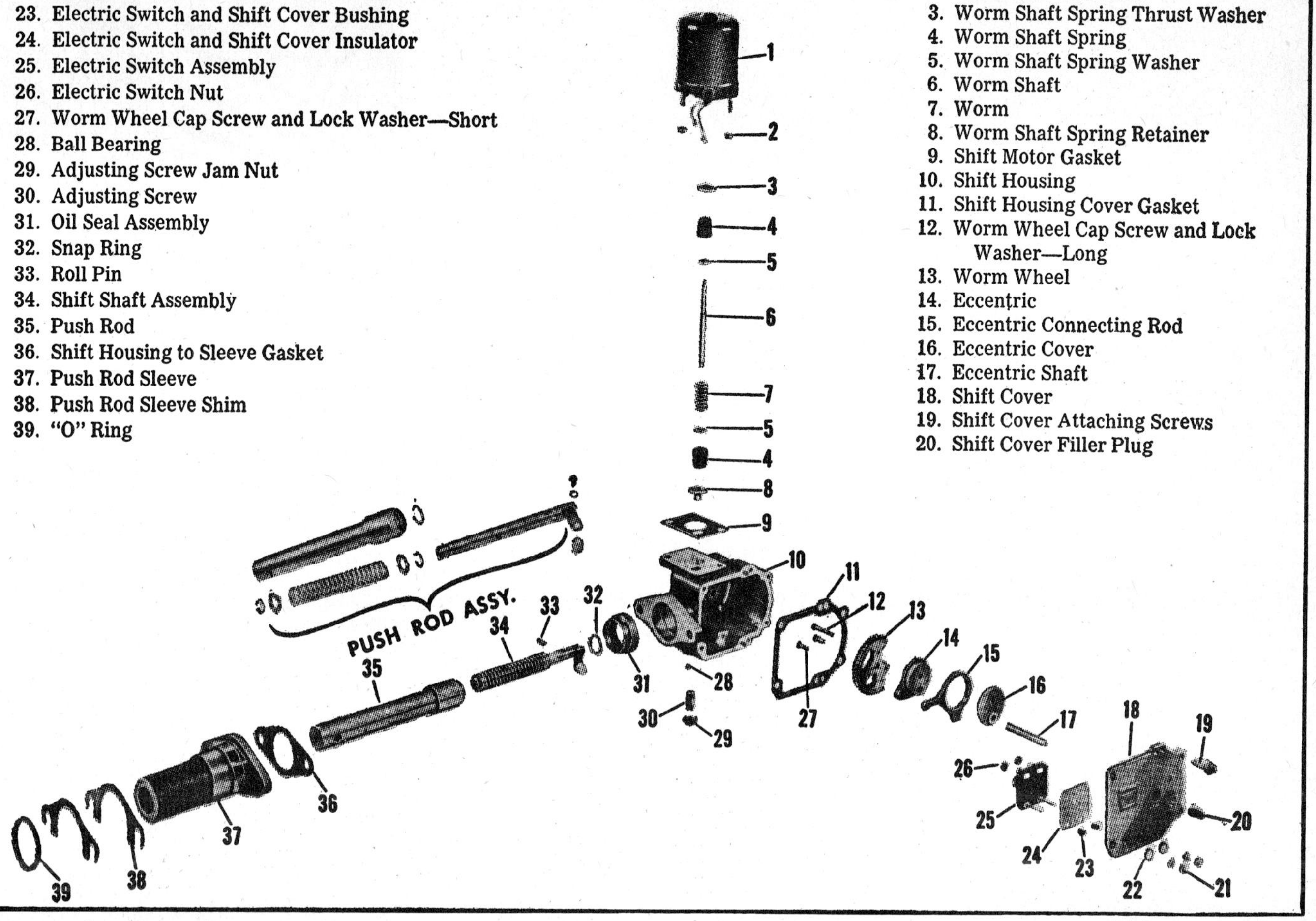

Fig. 1 Electric shift for two speed axles

ing the hot lead of the wiring harness to the left-hand terminal on the shift unit cover. It is not necessary to attach the cover to the housing. *If the shift motor is not operating, disconnect the wires at the inner face of the cover and remove the motor as outlined under Disassembly. Then install a new motor and shift the unit to the desired position. In case a new motor is not available, use a slotted tool that fits over the tang of the worm shaft and turn it until the shift shaft changes position.*

6. Unfasten and remove shift unit. Do not damage oil seal located in flange section.

Disassembly

1. Disconnect wires from terminals on inside face of cover.
2. Remove two stud nuts and star washers that hold motor to housing.
3. Carefully break loose motor and remove it and gasket from housing.
4. Loosen jam nut and remove adjusting screw. *Do not lose ball bearing that rides in recess of adjusting screw.*
5. Remove worm shaft assembly and disassemble it if necessary. *The spring retainer at bottom of worm shaft is pressed on and cannot be removed by hand. However, it can be removed by holding it in a vise and driving the shaft out.*
6. Remove worm wheel and eccentric assembly. To disassemble, hold assembly in vise and remove three capscrews and lockwashers. Drive eccentric shaft out of assembly.

Reassembly

1. Reassemble worm shaft and position it in shift housing.

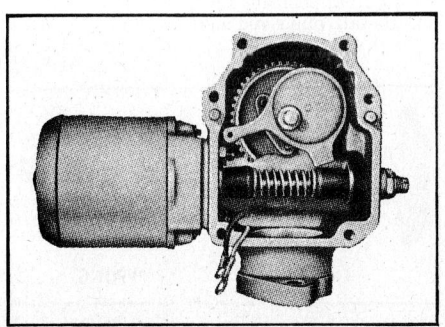

Fig. 2 Worm wheel and eccentric installed

Fig. 3 Shift unit in neutral position

Fig. 4 Location of gears on cross shaft with conventional ratio

TIMKEN (Rockwell) DRIVING AXLES

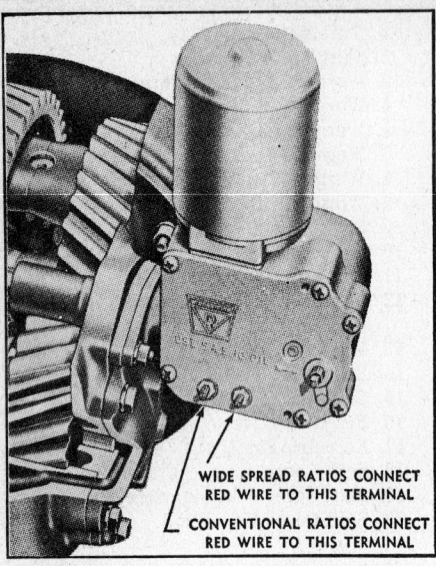

Fig. 5 Electric shift wiring hook-up

6. Remove cover from housing, using a tool made from a $1/8 \times 27$ pipe plug welded to the end of a T handle and screwed into filler plug hole. Do not pry cover.
7. Move shift unit to neutral position as shown in Fig. 3.
8. Move cross shaft shift collar to neutral (central) position.
9. Install new shift housing to sleeve gasket.
10. Position shift unit over mounting studs. Do not damage oil seal installed in flange section of shift housing.
11. Move connecting rod into slot in end of shift shaft.
12. Install lockwashers and mounting stud nuts. Tighten nuts to 26–29 ft. lbs. torque.
13. Line up hole in connecting rod with hole in end of shift shaft.
14. When holes are lined up, drive roll pin into place with a suitable driver.
15. Install gasket and cover. *To install cover, shift unit and axle assembly must be in neutral position to avoid damaging the switches.*
16. Fill unit to bottom of filler hole with SAE 10 motor oil. Install filler plug.

Connect Electric System

If a vacuum or air shift unit is being replaced by the electric type, it will be necessary to install an electric hook-up from the cab of the vehicle to the electric shift unit.

If the spur pinions on the cross shaft are located in the conventional manner, with the HI speed (larger) pinion next to the drive gear, Fig. 4, connect the red wire to the terminal indicated in Fig. 5, with the black wire connected to the other terminal.

If the spur pinions are located in the wide range manner, with the LO (smaller) pinion next to the drive gear, Fig. 6, connect the red wire to the terminal indicated in Fig. 5, with the black wire connected to the other terminal.

Check Operation of Shift Unit

1. Turn on ignition switch.
2. Flip switch button in cab to operate shift unit. One man can operate switch while another observes movement of shift collar on cross shaft through pinion cage bore.
3. Check to make sure shift collar completes shift into both HI range and LO range. The engaging teeth on shift collar must completely engage corresponding teeth of spur pinions. Incomplete shifts can cause serious axle failures.

Adjustments

1. Shift collar travel can be equalized by altering the shim pack installed behind flange of push rod sleeve.
2. Check clearance of shift fork pads in shift collar with feeler gauge, Fig. 7. Clearance should not be less than .010″ on each side of fork in both HI and LO speed positions. *When checking shift fork clearance, shift collar must be flush with end face of engaged spur pinion.*
3. Add or remove shims from pack under sleeve to obtain correct adjustment.

Final Assembly

1. If above adjustments are satisfactory, install shims, pinion and cage assembly, and capscrews.
2. Connect universal joint at pinion shaft.
3. Load vehicle and test operation of shift unit under actual operating conditions.

Fig. 6 Location of gears on cross shaft with wide range ratio

FRONT MOUNTED TYPE

Removal

1. Disconnect wires from terminals on shift cover.
2. Unfasten and remove shift unit from carrier. *The push rod must be drawn in toward shift housing before it can be removed from carrier, otherwise it will not clear bore in carrier.*
3. To move push rod to correct position, first turn on ignition switch. Then shift the unit by touching the hot lead of the wiring harness to the right-hand terminal. If shift motor is not working, see procedure under *Change Position of Shift Shaft* in the Side Mounted Type procedure. Do not attempt to force or pry shift unit from carrier.

Disassembly

1. Remove cover attaching screws and filler plug.
2. Screw a threaded tool into filler plug hole and pull off cover. Tool can be made from a $1/8 \times 27$ pipe plug welded to the end of a T handle. Do not pry off cover.
3. Drive roll pin from shift shaft. *If roll pin is in line with worm shaft, it will be necessary to change position of shift shaft by turning the worm.*
4. Remove two stud nuts and separate shift unit from push rod and bracket assembly.
5. Proceed with disassembly as outlined for the Side Mounted Type.

Reassembly

1. Install worm shaft assembly, shift motor, adjusting screw, and worm wheel and eccentric assembly as outlined for the Side Mounted Type.
2. Place worm shaft and worm wheel in the neutral position (see Fig. 3).
3. Install push rod and bracket assembly.

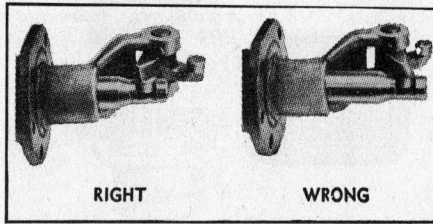

Fig. 8 Positioning push rod to permit entry in carrier bore

2. Install shift motor with gasket to housing. Slot in motor shaft fits over tang of worm shaft.
3. Install and tighten two locking stud nuts that secure motor.
4. Place ball bearing in recess of adjusting screw.
5. Turn adjusting screw in until the ball bearing is snug against bottom of worm shaft. Then back off screw $1/8$ turn for proper adjustment. Hold adjusting screw in place and tighten lock nut. Check to see that worm shaft turns freely by hand.
6. Reassemble worm wheel and eccentric. *The eccentric shaft should protrude an equal distance at top and bottom of the assembly.* Install assembly in position shown in Fig. 2.
7. Connect electric leads on inside face of shift cover. Attach red wire to terminal closet to flange of shift unit.

Installation

1. Position shift fork in cross shaft shift collar groove.
2. Slide push rod into shift fork. Line up set screw hole in fork with recess in push rod.
3. Install shift fork set screw and tighten jam nut to 30–33 ft. lbs. torque. Be sure set screw enters recess in push rod.
4. Lock set screw to fork with wire.
5. Remove screws from shift unit cover.

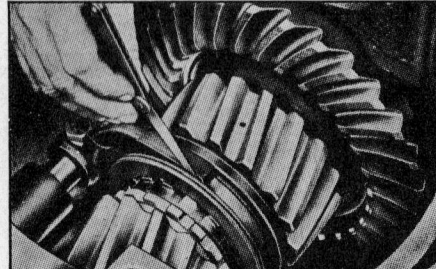

Fig. 7 Checking clearance of shift fork pads in shift collar with feeler gauge

TIMKEN (Rockwell) DRIVING AXLES

Tighten nuts to 26–29 ft. lbs. torque.
4. Slide connecting rod into slot at end of shift shaft.
5. Line up hole in connecting rod with hole in shift shaft and install roll pin with suitable driver.
6. Connect wire leads at inside face of shift cover. Attach red wire closest to flange of shift unit.
7. Install cover with new gasket. The shift unit must be in neutral position when cover is installed to avoid damage to switches.

Installation

1. Move cross shaft shift collar to engage spur pinion opposite drive gear.
2. Shift the unit to the corresponding position (with push rod drawn in toward shift unit housing, Fig. 8). Push rod must be in "right" position, otherwise it will not fit in carrier bore. *To shift the unit, use a battery and two leads; ground one lead and touch the other to the right-hand terminal on the cover.*
3. Install new gasket and slide shift unit into carrier bore.
4. Remove inspection cover from top of carrier and look inside to guide push rod bell-crank into slot in shift shaft.
5. Install and tighten attaching capscrews to 26–29 ft. lbs. torque.
6. Fill unit with SAE 10 motor oil to filler plug hole. Install filler plug.

Fig. 9 Shift collar travel adjustment. Front mounted type

Connect Electric System & Check Operation

Connect wires as outlined for the Side Mounted Type. Check the operation of the shift unit as outlined for the Side Mounted Type, observing the movement of the shift collar through the inspection hole at top of carrier.

Adjustments

Shift collar travel can be adjusted by the stop screws installed in the carrier assembly, Fig. 9. One stop screw is installed in cross shaft bearing cage, opposite the drive gear, and the other is installed in top of the carrier. *Do not disturb settings of stop screws unless shift fork adjustments are required.*

1. If necessary to adjust, first be sure fork and collar are shifted to engage the helical pinion next to the drive gear. Then adjust the stop screw and lock nut in the top of the carrier so that the fork is centered in the collar groove within .005".
2. With fork and collar shifted to engage pinion away from drive gear, adjust stop screw and lock nut in the cross shaft bearing cage so that the fork is centered in the collar groove with .005".
3. When checking shift fork clearance in collar groove, collar must be flush with end face of spur pinion in both the HI and LO speed positions.

CLARK TRANSMISSIONS

SERVICE INDEX

	Page No.
250 Series	275
260 Series	276
280 Series	284
300 Series	276
320 Series	284
380 Series	284
390 Series	279
400 Series	281
2600 Series	276

LUBE CAPACITY

MODEL	OIL, PINTS	MODEL	OIL, PINTS
250V, 250VO, 251VO	9	320	—
261F	12	325V	—
262-1V	11½	327V	—
264V, 264VO	11½	380	13
265V, 265VO	11½	390	8
267V, 267VO	12	401V, 406V	20
268V, 268VO	6	407V, 408V	20
269V	12	2621V, 2622V	12
280VO, 282V, 285V	12	2651V	11½
300V, 301V	12	2653V	12
305V, 307V, 308V, 308VO	15	2681V	11½

250 SERIES

Five Speed Synchronized Units, Figs. 1 and 2

When assembling the transmission, use new snap rings, cotter pins, gaskets and oil seals. Lubricate each moving part as it is being assembled, and coat all bushings with a light film of petroleum before installation.

Assembling Mainshaft

1. Clamp mainshaft in vise with front end up and install 3rd gear with internal teeth down and slip on thrust washer.
2. Place lock pin in 4th gear bushing (5th on O.D. units) and position bushing on shaft with lock pin toward upper end. Install gear on bushing with hub upward. Install thrust washer and snap ring.
3. Check end play of 4th gear. If not between .008–.012" replace thrust washer with one of a size that will provide correct end play. Thrust washers are available in four thicknesses ranging from .111" to .125".
4. Remove assembly from vise and install 2nd gear with internal teeth toward front. Install low-reverse gear with fork slot toward front.

Assemble Transmission

1. Install countershaft front bearing snap ring in case, then install new expansion plug in countershaft bore in case. Be sure to expand plug enough to prevent oil leakage.
2. Install countershaft front bearing in case. Install thrust washer on front end of shaft. Tip rear end of countershaft down and lower into case. Push shaft forward and insert it in front bearing.
3. Place rear bearing snap ring on bearing. Position bearing on countershaft with snap ring toward rear and install bearing on shaft.
4. Install reverse idler gear assembly in case with smaller gear toward rear of case. Drive reverse idler shaft into case until slot in shaft is flush with case. Install retainer in slot and secure with lock washer and bolt.
5. Tilt rear of mainshaft downward, inserting end of shaft through rear bore in case. Then lower front end of shaft until it is in line with pilot bearing opening and move assembly forward into position.
6. Place synchronizer on shaft with longer hub forward.
7. Install rear bearing on mainshaft with snap ring groove toward rear. Install snap ring on bearing and tap bearing onto mainshaft until snap ring is seated against case. Install speedometer drive gear spacer and gear on rear of shaft and pilot bearing on front end.
8. Install main drive gear and bearing in case. Tap front end of shaft with soft hammer until snap ring in bearing is seated against case. Position new gasket

CLARK TRANSMISSIONS

of proper thickness on case and install bearing retainer. Be sure that oil holes in retainer and gasket are aligned with hole in case.

9. Place countershaft rear bearing cap and gasket on case and install lock washers and bolts.
10. Install mainshaft rear bearing retainer with new seal and gasket.
11. Install 1st-reverse shift fork in case with fork engaged in sliding gear groove. Insert shift rail through hole in rear of case and through fork. Drive rail into case until edge of lock slot is flush with case. Install rail lock plate and secure with capscrew.
12. Place 1st-reverse rocker arm in case and install pivot bolt and nut.
13. Place new gasket on top of case and with gears in neutral, install gearshift housing, being sure shift forks engage slots in gears.
14. Install emergency brake and U-joint flange. Shift transmission into gear and tighten flange nut. If cotter pin holes do not line up, always tighten nut (not loosen) until cotter pin can be inserted.

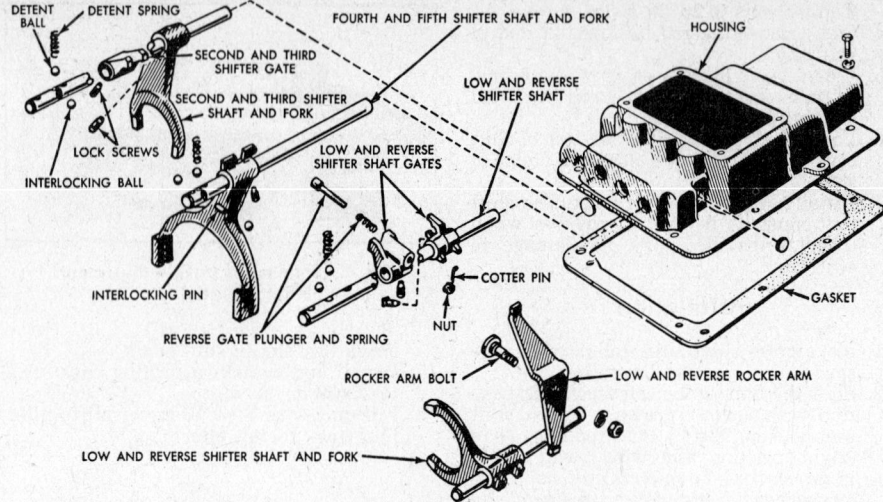

Fig. 1 Clark 250 Series gearshift housing

260, 2600 & 300 SERIES

4 and 5 Speed Synchronized Units, Figs. 3 and 4

When assembling the transmission, use new snap rings, cotter pins, gaskets and oil seals. Lubricate each moving part as it is being assembled, and coat all bushings with a light film of petrolatum before installation.

Assembling Mainshaft

1. Clamp mainshaft in vise with soft jaws with front end up.
2. Position 2nd speed gear on mainshaft with internal teeth facing up.
3. Place 2nd gear retainer washer in position of shaft.
4. Install 2nd gear retaining ring in groove of shaft over locating ring.

Four Speed Models

1. Place 2nd speed synchronizer on mainshaft with counterbore in shift hub down.
2. Position synchronizer support over shaft above synchronizer and install locating washer.
3. With lock pin in place in fluted bushing, install fluted bushing on shaft with lock pin toward upper end. Tap bushing into place.
4. Position 3rd speed gear on mainshaft with toothed hub up.
5. Install 3rd speed gear retaining washer on mainshaft, rotating gear so external teeth on washer mesh with internal teeth of gear.
6. Install snap ring on mainshaft, making sure it is securely locked in place.
7. Check end play on 3rd gear, which must be .004″ to .012″. Retaining washers of various thicknesses are available to obtain required end play.
8. Remove mainshaft from vise and install 3rd and 4th synchronizer assembly with lip on shift hub toward front.
9. Install 1st and reverse gear on shaft with fork slot toward front.

Five Speed Models

1. Referring to Figs. 3 and 5, place 2nd and 3rd speed synchronizer on mainshaft with counterbore in shift hub down.
2. Position 3rd speed gear on shaft with toothed hub down.
3. Install 3rd speed gear locating washer on shaft over 3rd speed gear.
4. With lock pin in place in fluted bushing, install fluted bushing on mainshaft with lock pin toward upper end. Tap bushing into position.
5. Position 4th speed gear on mainshaft with toothed hub up.
6. Install 4th speed gear retaining washer on splines of mainshaft, rotating gear to align external teeth of washer with internal teeth of gear so washer will drop into place.
7. Install snap ring on shaft so it is securely locked in groove. Check end play on 4th gear, which should be .005″ to .012″. Retaining washers are available in various thicknesses to obtain required end play.
8. Remove assembly from vise and install 4th and 5th speed synchronizer with lip on shift hub toward the front.
9. Install 1st and reverse speed gear with fork slot toward front.

Assemble Transmission

NOTE: If countershaft front bearing was previously removed and not reinstalled, install bearing as follows, using care not to damage the bearing during installation:

1. Using a suitable sleeve and an arbor press or hammer, press bearing in transmission case from clutch housing end of case. Open end of bearing goes toward rear of case.
2. Press bearing .007″ below front face of case.
3. Tap rear end of countershaft down and lower into transmission case, running rear of countershaft through opening for bearing in rear of case far enough so front countershaft can be lowered into position. Push countershaft forward into position in front bearing.
4. Install countershaft rear bearing, being sure snap ring is in groove in outer race of bearing. Press bearing into place on shaft with snap ring toward rear. Press bearing into case until snap ring contacts case.
5. Install snap ring in groove in countershaft to retain bearing, being sure it is well seated in groove.
6. Insert one reverse idler bearing in reverse idler gear; then install bearing spacer and the second bearing in gear.
7. Install reverse idler gear in case with bevel on gear toward rear of case.
8. Insert reverse idler shaft through opening in rear of case and into idler gear. Make sure groove for retainer lock in rear of shaft is at bottom of shaft. Drive shaft in until inner edge of groove is flush with transmission case. Install retainer lock and lock screw.
9. Install mainshaft assembly in case by tilting rear end down and lowering into and through opening in rear of case, which is provided for rear bearing. Lower front end in line with pilot bearing opening. Move mainshaft forward into position, lifting assembly so 2nd gear will clear countershaft oil slinger.
10. Position mainshaft rear bearing over end of shaft with snap ring in outer race of bearing facing the rear.
11. Using a suitable sleeve and hammer, drive bearing on mainshaft and into case until snap ring on bearing contacts case.
12. Slide pilot bearing on front end of mainshaft.
13. Position main drive gear and bearing into opening in front of case so that drive gear engages and meshes with countershaft gear and snap ring on bearing contacts case. It may be necessary to use a suitable sleeve and hammer to drive gear and bearing into position.
14. Install a new gasket on main drive gear bearing cap. Install bearing cap on case and tighten screws securely. *Oil return hole in bearing cap must line up with oil hole in transmission case.*
15. Install countershaft rear bearing cap and new gasket.
16. Install spacer washer and speedometer drive gear on mainshaft.
17. Install mainshaft rear bearing cap and oil seal and new gasket.
18. Install 2nd speed gear oil scraper to transmission case.
19. Install brake drum and flange.
20. Lock transmission in two speeds at once and install companion flange nut, torquing it to 250 ft. lbs. Then advance nut to nearest cotter pin hole and install cotter

CLARK TRANSMISSIONS

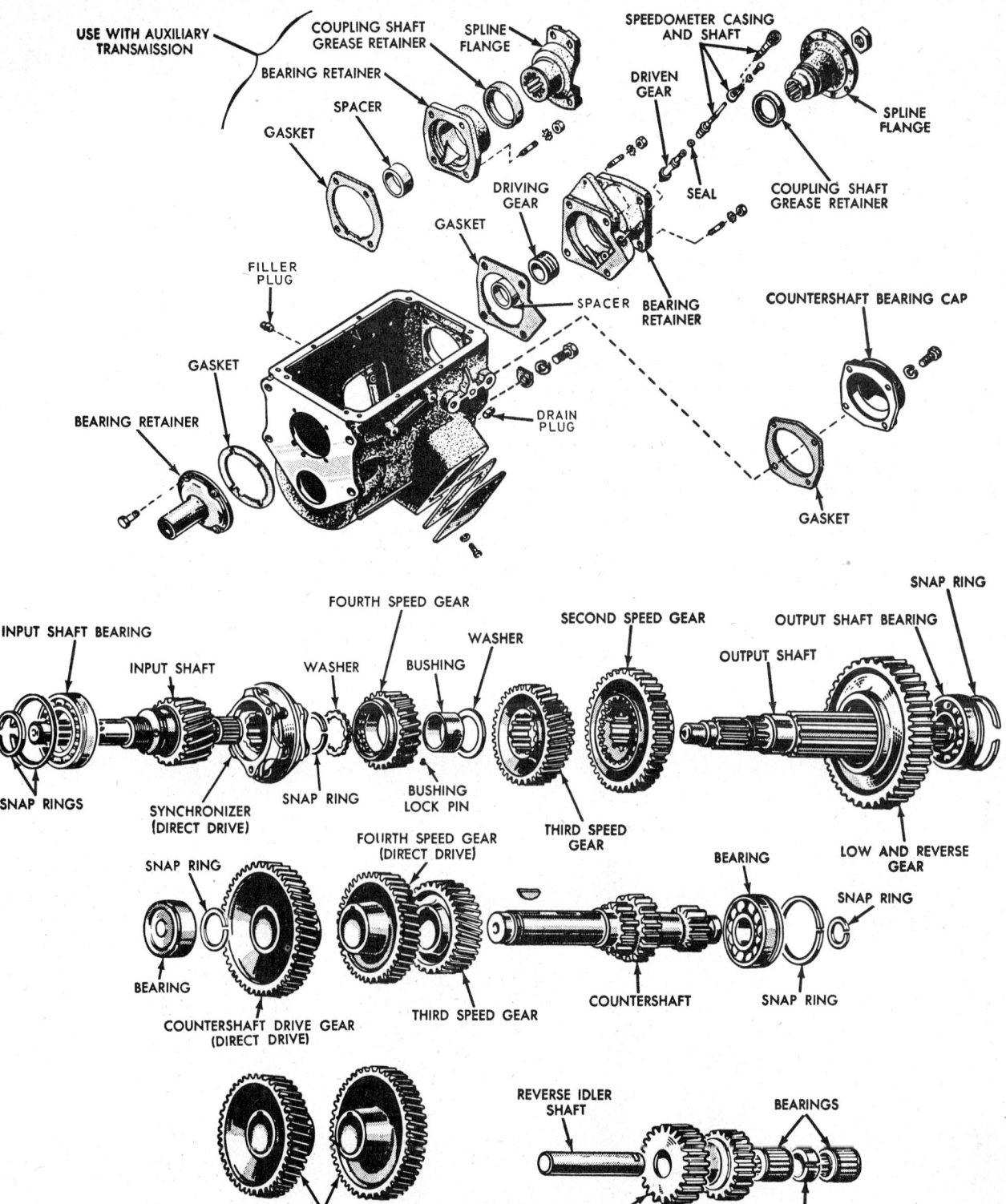

Fig. 2 Clark 250 Series five speed synchronized transmissions

CLARK TRANSMISSIONS

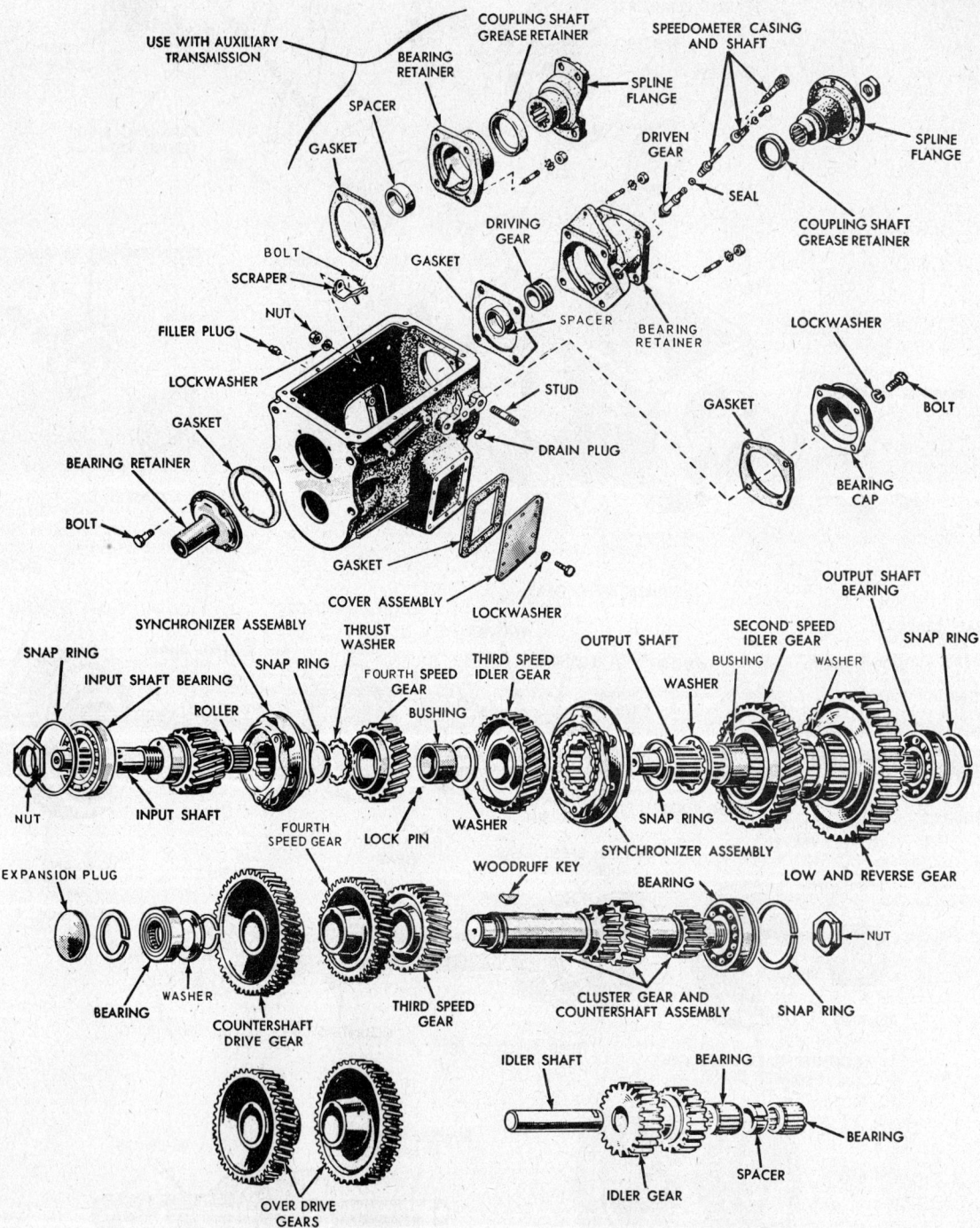

Fig. 3 Clark 260 and 300 Series four and five speed synchronized transmissions

CLARK TRANSMISSIONS

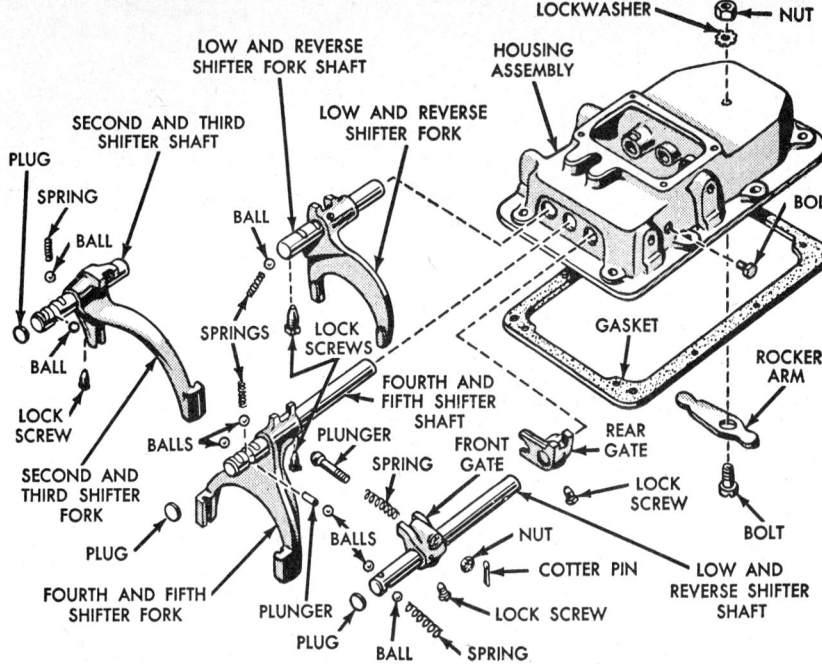

Fig. 4 Clark 260 and 300 Series gearshift housing

   pin.
21. Install shift bar housing with new gasket, being sure forks engage slots and rings in gears.
22. Install control cover and new gasket on shift bar housing.
23. Make sure transmission is in neutral by holding brake drum and turning main drive gear.
24. Install speedometer driven gear and adapter, hand brake parts, P.T.O. covers, and clutch housing.

390 SERIES

Transmission Disassemble, Fig. 5A

1. Remove remote control or shift tower from shifter housing, then remove shifter housing and back-up light switch.
2. Remove U-joint assembly and drive shaft from parking brake drum.
3. Remove parking brake actuating lever from linkage.
4. Remove spline flange, then remove bolts retaining carrier plate to transmission housing and slide plate with brake shoes and retaining springs off transmission.
5. Lock transmission in two gears, then remove retaining nut and drum from output shaft.
6. Remove output shaft rear bearing retainer and speedometer drive gear.
7. Remove countershaft rear bearing retainer and snap ring.
8. Remove input shaft bearing retainer and pull input shaft out of case.

NOTE: Use care to avoid dropping output shaft pilot bearing rollers into transmission case.

9. Push output shaft rearward until rear bearing is exposed, then using a puller, remove rear bearing.
10. Remove output shaft from case.
11. Remove reverse idler shaft and lift idler gear, bearing and thrust washers from case.
12. Push countershaft rearward until rear bearing is exposed, then using a puller, remove bearing and oil slinger.
13. Lift countershaft from case, then if countershaft front bearing or pilot bearing is to be replaced, remove clutch housing.
14. If pilot bearing is to be replaced, press bearing from case.

NOTE: Do not hammer or drive out bearing, as damage or distortion to the bearing bore will result.

Output Shaft Assemble

1. Place output shaft with forward end up in a soft jawed vise.
2. Place third gear on output shaft with clutching teeth down, then install the locking washer and snap ring.
3. Turn outer shaft over and install third gear synchronizer ring and second and third synchronizer assembly.
4. With clutching teeth of second gear down, coat inside diameter of gear with high quality heavy grease to retain needle rollers, then install first row of needle rollers.
5. Install bearing spacer, then install the second row of needle rollers and outer bearing spacer.
6. Install second gear, being careful not to catch needle rollers on edge of spline or snap ring groove.
7. Install second gear split washer locating ball and split washer on output shaft, then install retainer ring over split washer.
8. Coat inside of reverse gear with grease and install bearing spacers and bearings.
9. Install reverse gear on output shaft, then position shaft hub sleeve and shift hub and install shift hub sleeve snap ring.
10. Install spacers and bearings in first gear and install first gear on output shaft.
11. Install first gear retaining washer and output shaft bearing.

NOTE: Make certain that bearing is tight against washer.

12. Turn output shaft over and install fourth gear with clutching teeth facing upward.
13. Place fourth gear synchronizer ring on clutching teeth of fourth gear, then install fourth and fifth shift hub sleeve on output shaft.
14. Install fourth and fifth synchronizer and fifth speed synchronizer ring on output shaft.
15. Install thrust bearing and race.

Countershaft Assemble

1. Install fourth speed gear key in slot on shaft, then place fourth speed gear on shaft with long hub facing toward front.
2. Install countershaft main drive gear key in keyway in shaft.
3. Install countershaft drive gear on shaft with long hub facing toward rear.
4. Install snap ring on countershaft.

Input Shaft Assemble

1. Press bearing on input shaft.
2. Install needle bearings, washer and snap ring.

Gear Shifter Housing

1. Place first and reverse rocker arm on pivot pin, then install reverse latch plunger, spring and retaining plug.
2. Install the four poppet springs and poppet balls, noting the first and reverse shift fork rail poppet ball in pocket.
3. Align one tapered interlock cross pin with the hole in the first and reverse shaft rail, then position rail on poppet ball with rail in neutral position, noting position of the

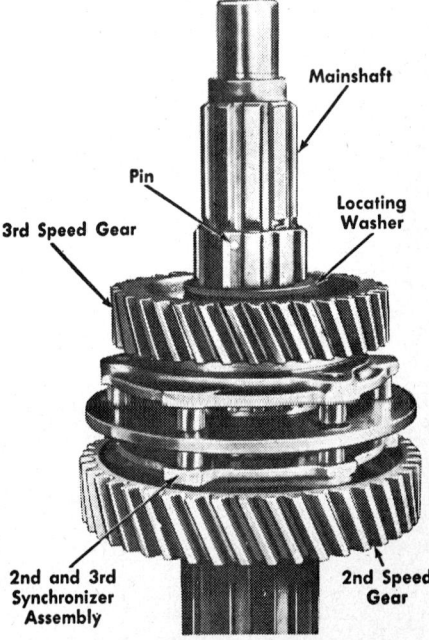

Fig. 5 Clark 260 and 300 Series five speed mainshaft assembly with fourth speed gear removed

279

CLARK TRANSMISSIONS

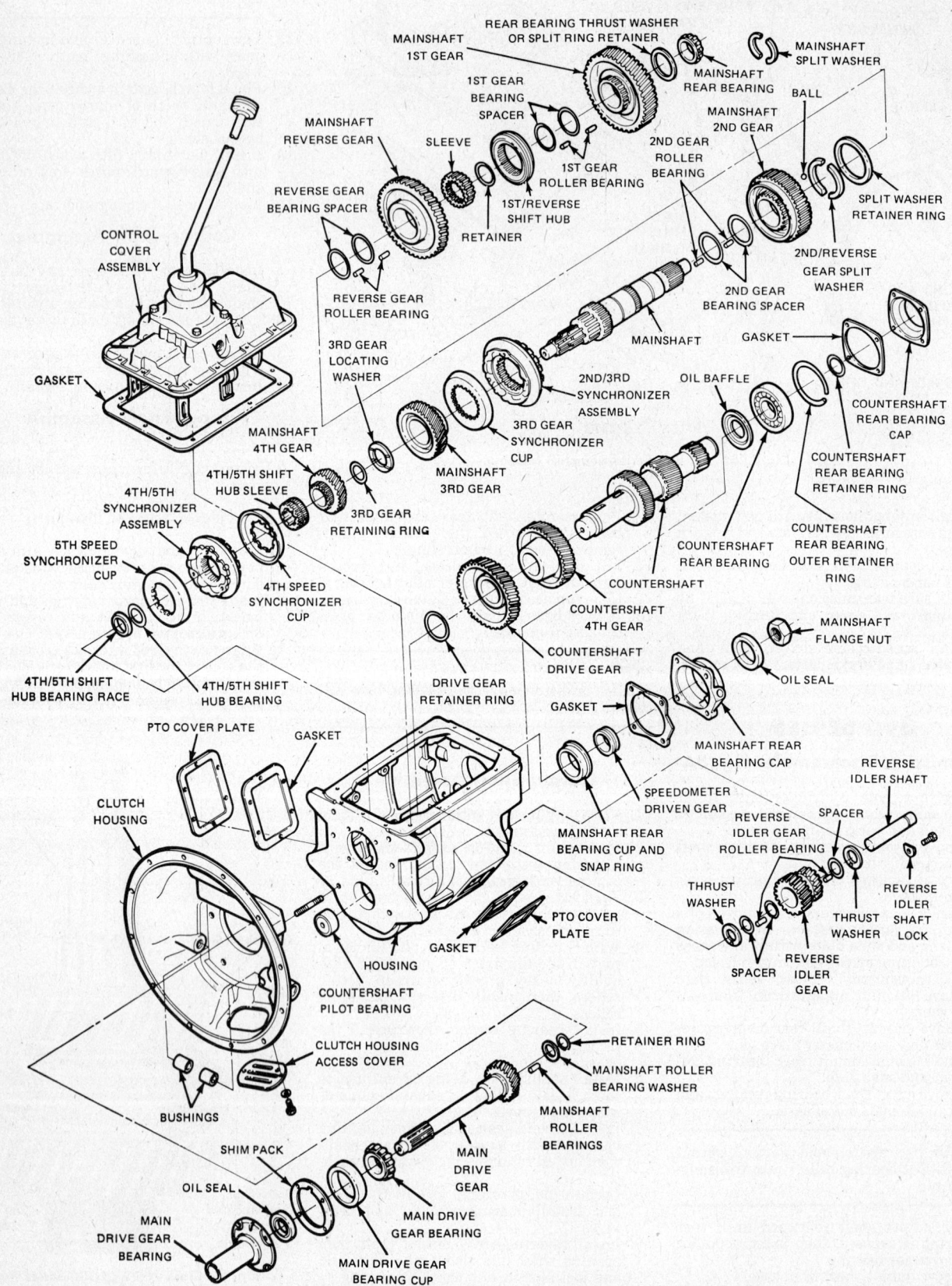

Fig. 5A Clark 390 Series five speed synchronized transmissions

CLARK TRANSMISSIONS

tapered interlock cross pin in relation to rail.
4. Install interlock cross pin in second and third shift rail, then position rail on poppet ball in neutral position with interlock pin aligned with first interlock tapered pin. Install second interlock tapered pin aligned with interlock cross pin hole.
5. Position fourth and fifth shift fork and rail assembly on poppet ball in neutral position, then raise rear of rail slightly to align second interlock tapered pin with cross hole in rail. Note positions of tapered interlock pins and shift rails.
6. Install first and reverse shift fork and rail assembly on poppet ball in neutral position. Align first and reverse rocker arm in notch at rear of rail.
7. Position rear rail support, then install washers and screws and tighten screws slightly.
8. Install interlock tapered supports, then tap fourth and fifth shift fork rearward to fourth speed position.
9. Position front rail support and install washers and screws. Torque screw to 20–25 ft. lbs.
10. Tap fourth and fifth shift fork rail assembly forward to neutral position.

Transmission Assemble

1. Coat front countershaft needle bearings with grease and install them into front countershaft bore.
2. Tip rear of countershaft down and lower it into case, then push countershaft forward and insert shaft into front bearing.
3. Position countershaft rear bearing oil slinger and bearing on shaft, then drive bearing into bore and install rear bearing retainer.

NOTE: Support countershaft drive gear while driving shaft to prevent damage to front bearing.

4. Coat reverse idler thrust washers with grease and place them into case.
5. Insert bearings in reverse idler gear bore and place gear assembly into transmission case with small gear toward rear of case.
6. Insert reverse idler shaft through hole in case, then through reverse idler gear, and into forward support boss.
7. Drive reverse idler shaft into case until slot in shaft aligns with lock bolt hole, then install retainer and lock bolt and tighten lock bolt securely.
8. Tilt rear of output shaft assembly down and insert end of shaft through output shaft bore in case. Lower front end of output shaft until it is aligned with pilot bearing opening and move assembly forward into position.
9. Insert pilot bearing in input shaft bore.
10. Position input shaft and bearings into forward end of transmission case, then tap front end of shaft until snap ring is seated against case.

NOTE: Make sure that clutching teeth of input shaft gear mesh with fifth speed synchronizer without binding.

11. Position new gasket on input shaft bearing retainer making sure that oil return holes in retainer and gasket are properly aligned with oil return hole in case. Position retainer on case, then install bolts and torque to 15–20 ft. lbs.
12. Place output shaft rear bearing on shaft and drive bearing into bore until snap ring is seated against case.
13. Place countershaft rear bearing cap and gasket on case, then install washers and bolts and torque bolts to 20–25 ft. lbs.
14. Install speedometer drive gear on output shaft and install a new seal on output shaft bearing retainer making sure that seal is correctly installed.
15. Place a new gasket and bearing retainer on case, then install washers and bolts and torque bolts to 60 ft. lbs.
16. Install parking brake flange and torque yoke retaining nut to 400–450 ft. lbs.
17. With transmission in neutral, position gear shifter housing over gears, aligning shift forks with gear shift hubs.

NOTE: If gear shifter housing is in neutral and transmission is in neutral, the transmission drive gear should turn without brake drum or output shaft turning.

18. Install shifter housing bolts and torque to 20–25 ft. lbs. Install remote control or shift tower and torque bolts to 20–25 ft. lbs.

400 SERIES

Five Speed Synchronized Units

Because of the increasingly higher engine speeds and extended periods of high gear operation, positive lubrication of the mainshaft is provided in this transmission in the form of a mainshaft pump that supplies mainshaft gear bushings and bearings with adequate oil at all times.

The pump is composed of a rotor which surrounds and is driven by the input shaft, a single free-floating vane confined in the rotor, and a stationary housing provided by the input shaft bearing cap which forms an eccentric bore for the single vane to contact.

Assemble Sub-Assemblies

When assembling the transmission, use new snap rings, cotter pins, gaskets and oil seals. Lubricate each moving part as it is being installed. Coat all bushings with a light coat of petrolatum before installation. Refer to Fig. 6.

Assemble Mainshaft

1. Clamp mainshaft in a soft-jawed vise with front end up.
2. Install mainshaft 2nd gear bushing sleeve and lock pin. Pin must be installed toward pilot end of mainshaft with oil hole in sleeve lined up with oil hole in shaft, Fig. 7.
3. To insure a proper tight stack-up between the 2nd gear bushing sleeve, selective retaining washer and snap ring, proceed as follows:
   a. Before 2nd gear is installed on bushing sleeve, place retaining washer on shaft and hold down securely on bushing sleeve.
   b. While holding snap ring parallel to retaining washer, slip snap ring into ring groove in mainshaft. Select variable thickness retaining washers until one is selected that will allow snap ring to fit securely in groove, Fig. 8.
   c. Remove selected washer and install 2nd gear and bushing over bushing sleeve.
   d. Place selected washer in position; then install snap ring into shaft groove. End play on 2nd gear must be .004" to .010".
4. Place 2nd and 3rd synchronizer with large end of hub toward rear on splines of mainshaft and drop into position. Install 3rd speed gear locating thrust washer on shaft.
5. Position 3rd gear and bushing over mainshaft with toothed hub down and drop into place.
6. Position 4th gear locating washer on shaft.
7. With lock pin in place in 4th gear bushing sleeve, install bushing sleeve on shaft with lock pin toward pilot or front end of shaft. It may be necessary to use a suitable sleeve and hammer to properly install sleeve. *Oil hole in sleeve must line up with oil hole in mainshaft.*
8. To insure proper stack-up between 4th gear locating washer, bushing sleeve, selective retainer washer and snap ring, follow the same procedure outlined for the 2nd gear parts.
9. Install 4th and 5th speed synchronizer with large end of hub toward rear.

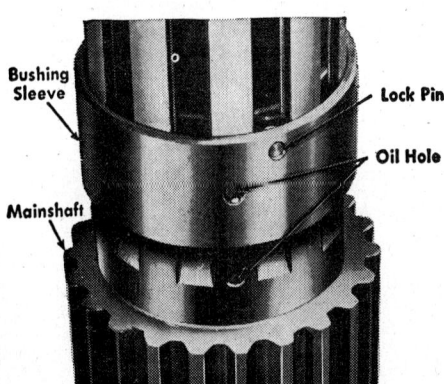

Fig. 7 Clark 400 Series. Installing mainshaft second gear bushing sleeve

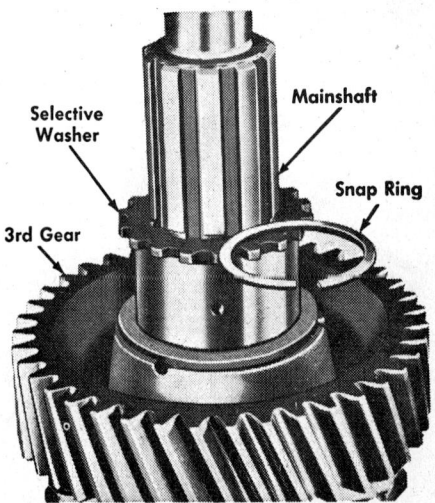

Fig. 8 Clark 400 Series. Selecting fourth gear variable thickness retaining washer

CLARK TRANSMISSIONS

Fig. 6 Clark 400 Series pressure lubricated five speed synchronized transmissions

CLARK TRANSMISSIONS

10. Press pilot bearing on front end of mainshaft. Remove assembly from press and cover it with clean cloth until ready for installation.

Assemble Transmission

1. Install countershaft from bearing in bore of case, applying pressure on outer race of bearing only.
2. Place countershaft front bearing spacer in position on front end of countershaft.
3. Tip rear of countershaft down and lower assembly into transmission case, running rear end of countershaft through rear bearing opening in case far enough to permit front of countershaft to be lowered into place. Push countershaft forward into proper position.
4. Using hammer and suitable installer sleeve, install countershaft rear bearing. Install rear bearing retainer nut loosely.
5. Insert two roller bearings, separated by spacer, into hub of reverse idler gear.
6. Lower reverse idler gear into position in case. Gear with chamfered teeth goes toward rear of case.
7. Insert reverse idler shaft through rear of case, through reverse idler gear and into forward support boss. The shaft should be driven in until forward face of slot in shaft is flush with rear face of case and slot lined up to permit installation of locking plate.
8. Install reverse idler shaft lock on idler shaft, engaging lock with slot in shaft. Secure lock to shaft with cap screw.
9. Position mainshaft 1st gear and bushing and reverse gear in case.
10. Install mainshaft in case by tilting rear end of assembly down and lowering into and through reverse gear, 1st gear, and opening in rear of case. Lower front end of shaft in line with pilot bearing opening in case and move assembly forward in proper position.
11. Install pressure rotor backing plate on main drive gear.
12. Position pressure rotor drive pin on drive gear.
13. Install pressure rotor on drive gear, with side of rotor marked "Front" toward front of transmission away from backing plate. With rotor drive pin at top and vane slot of rotor at bottom, see that oil inlet hole in rotor is on left side of rotor vane slot, Fig. 9.
14. Position new O-ring seal in groove in pressure rotor backing plate.
15. Install bearing cap on main drive gear, aligning oil inlet and outlet holes between rotor backing plate and drive gear bearing cap. Align word "Top" on cap with "Top" on backing plate.
16. Position main drive gear, bearing cap, pressure rotor, and new gasket into case so the main drive gear engages and meshes with countershaft drive gear. *Oil inlet and outlet holes must line up with oil holes in transmission case and word "Top" on bearing cap toward top of case.* Install four cap screws and tighten securely.
17. Install mainshaft 1st gear thrust washer; then, using a suitable installer sleeve and hammer, install mainshaft rear bearing.
18. Lock transmission gears in two speeds at same time and tighten countershaft rear bearing nut. Draw nut up tight and stake in position.
19. Position speedometer gear on mainshaft.
20. If previously removed, install new mainshaft rear bearing cap oil seal, using a suitable sleeve and hammer. Lip of seal goes toward front of bearing cap.
21. Install mainshaft and countershaft rear bearing caps and new gaskets.
22. With transmission still "locked up", install hand brake companion flange and retainer nut.
23. Install speedometer driven gear and adapter, P.T.O. covers and drain plugs.
24. Install pressure rotor oil gallery magnetic plug in case.
25. Install clutch housing, shift bar housing, control top oil baffle and control top assembly, Fig. 10.
26. Make sure transmission is in neutral by holding brake drum and turning main drive gear.
27. Install hand brake parts.

---

1 Clutch Housing	29 Lock Washer	55 Mainshaft 2nd Gear Bushing Sleeve
2 P.T.O. Cover	30 Countershaft Front Bearing	56 Mainshaft 2nd Gear and Bushing Assy.
3 Gasket	31 Front Bearing Spacer	57 2nd Gear Retainer Washer - Selective
4 Cap Screw	32 Countershaft Drive Gear Retainer Ring	58 2nd Gear Retainer Snap Ring
5 Filler Plug	33 Countershaft Drive Gear	59 2nd and 3rd Synchronizer Assy.
6 Transmission Case	34 Drive Gear Spacer	60 Mainshaft 3rd Gear Thrust Washer
7 Countershaft Rear Bearing	35 Countershaft 4th Gear	61 Mainshaft 3rd Gear and Bushing Assy.
8 Rear Bearing Retainer Nut	36 Countershaft 3rd Gear	62 Mainshaft 4th Gear Locating Washer
9 Rear Bearing Cap	37 Countershaft Gear Keys	63 Mainshaft 4th Gear Bushing Sleeve
10 Speedometer Drive Gear	38 Countershaft	64 Mainshaft 4th Gear and Bushing Assy.
11 Rear Bearing Cap	39 Reverse Idler Shaft Lock	65 4th Gear Retainer Washer - Selective
12 Rear Bearing Cap Oil Seal	40 Lock Screw	66 4th Gear Retainer Snap Ring
13 Hand Brake Companion Flange	41 Reverse Idler Shaft	67 4th and 5th Synchronizer Assy.
14 Companion Flange Nut	42 Reverse Idler Gear Bearing	68 Mainshaft Pilot Bearing
15 Driven Gear Adapter	43 Bearing Spacer	69 Main Drive Gear O-Ring
16 Speedometer Driven Gear	44 Reverse Idler Gear	70 Rotor Vane
17 Gasket	45 Reverse Idler Gear Bearing	71 Rotor Drive Pin
18 Gasket	46 Main Drive Gear Bearing Cap	72 Bushing Sleeve Pin
19 Mainshaft Rear Bearing	47 Pressure Rotor	
20 Mainshaft 1st Gear Thrust Washer	48 Rotor Backing Plate	
21 Drain Plug	49 Bearing Retainer Nut	
22 Clutch Housing Stud Nut	50 Main Drive Gear Bearing	
23 Lock Washer	51 Main Drive Gear	
24 Oil Gallery Magnetic Plug	52 Mainshaft	
25 Clutch Housing Cover	53 Mainshaft Reverse Gear	
26 Lock Washer	54 Mainshaft 1st Gear and Bushing Assy.	
27 Cover Screw		
28 Bearing Cap Attaching Screw		

← Fig. 6

CLARK TRANSMISSIONS

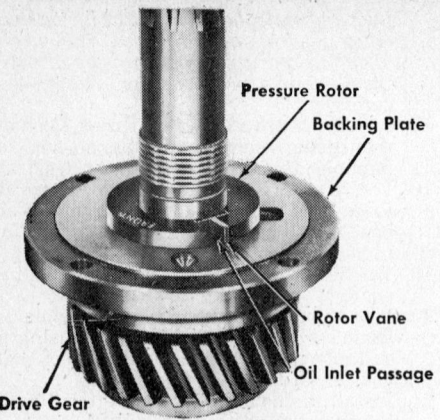

Fig. 9 Clark 400 Series. Oil pressure rotor installed

280 SERIES

Transmission Disassemble, Fig. 11

1. Remove shifter housing.
2. Remove parking brake and drum.
3. Remove mainshaft rear bearing cap and speedometer drive gear.
4. Remove countershaft rear bearing cap and snap ring.
5. Remove main drive gear.
6. Pry mainshaft rearward to expose rear bearing. Remove snap ring and pull off rear bearing.
7. Raise front end of mainshaft and lift assembly out of case.
8. Remove reverse idler lock.
9. Use puller to remove reverse idler gear shaft.
10. Remove reverse idler gear, bearings and two spacers.
11. Pry countershaft rearward to expose rear bearing, then remove snap ring from bearing.
12. Use puller to remove countershaft rear bearing and oil slinger.
13. Raise front end of countershaft and lift assembly out of case.
14. Disassemble mainshaft and countershaft as required.

Mainshaft Assemble, Fig. 12

1. Install 2nd speed gear retainer ring, locating washer and 2nd speed gear on mainshaft with clutch teeth up. Install 2nd gear retainer ring.
2. Install 2-3 shift hub sleeve and sleeve retainer ring.
3. Install 2-3 synchronizer assembly.
4. Install 3rd speed gear with clutch teeth down, then install locating washer.
5. Install 3rd gear retainer ring.
6. Install 4th speed gear with clutch teeth up. Note chamfer on 4-5 shift hub sleeve. Chamber must go down. Install bottom cup of 4-5 synchronizer on 4th gear clutch teeth before installing 4-5 shift hub sleeve. Install sleeve retainer ring.
7. Install 4-5 synchronizer on shift hub sleeve.
8. Turn mainshaft over and install 1st-reverse sliding gear with shift fork slot down.

Transmission Assemble

1. Coat countershaft pilot needle bearings with heavy grease to hold them in place until countershaft is installed.

2. Tip rear of countershaft down and into transmission case. Feed rear of countershaft through rear countershaft bearing bore. Move countershaft forward and into pilot bearing.
3. Position oil slinger and start rear bearing. Drive rear bearing on countershaft and into rear bearing bore.

NOTE: Countershaft drive gear must be supported on each side with a 1/4" flat bar to prevent damage to countershaft pilot bearing. Install bearing retainer ring.

4. Use heavy grease on reverse idler thrust washers to hold them in place.
5. Insert two reverse idler gear bearings in idler gear.
6. Install reverse idler gear, then insert idler shaft through case and idler gear.

NOTE: Idler shaft lock groove must line up with lock bolt hole. Drive shaft into position. Install shaft lock and bolt. Torque bolt to 20-25 ft-lbs.

7. Install mainshaft assembly in case.
8. Assemble pilot bearing in main drive gear as follows: If a new pilot bearing is to be used it comes from the factory with a plastic sleeve. Stand drive gear on end. Set bearing and sleeve over bearing pocket in drive gear. Slide bearing rollers and cage from plastic sleeve into bearing pocket. If old pilot bearing is being used, set rollers in bearing cage and hold in place with a rubber band. Slide bearing rollers and cage from rubber band into bearing pocket.
9. Install main drive gear assembly in case. Clutch teeth must enter 5th speed synchronizer cup without binding.
10. Press oil seal into drive gear bearing cap with lip of seal up. Shellac a new gasket to bearing cap, using care so as not to cover oil return groove in bearing cap. Install bearing cap with oil grooves lined up with oil holes in case. Torque to 20-25 ft-lbs.
11. Install parking brake and drum.
12. With transmission gears in neutral, install shift control assembly. Torque bolts to 20-25 ft-lbs.

320 & 380 SERIES

Transmission Disassemble, Fig. 13

1. Remove shifter housing.
2. Remove parking brake (if used).
3. Pull companion flange from rear end of mainshaft.
4. Remove speedometer driven gear and adapter (if used) from mainshaft rear bearing cap.

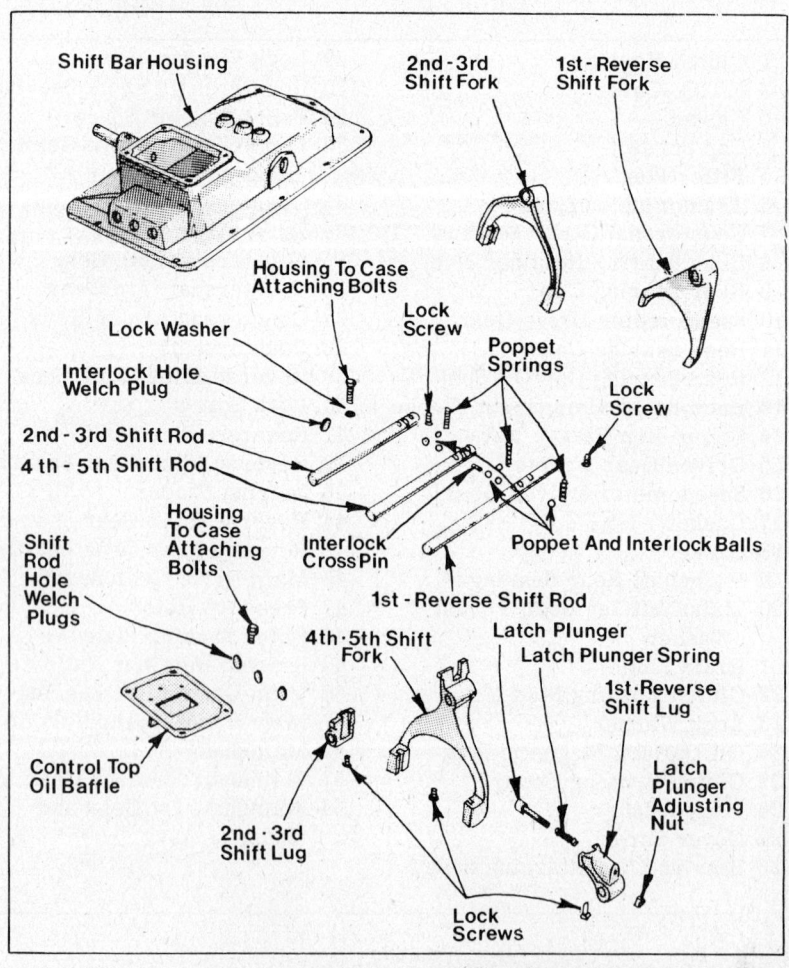

Fig. 10 Clark 400 Series gearshift housing

CLARK TRANSMISSIONS

5. Remove mainshaft and countershaft rear bearing caps.
6. Remove countershaft rear bearing nut.
7. Remove clutch release bearing and support from main drive gear.
8. Remove clutch release yoke.
9. Remove main drive gear bearing cap.
10. Remove main drive gear and bearing from front of transmission case.
11. Remove speedometer drive gear and spacer (if used).
12. Push mainshaft toward rear of case far enough to expose rear bearing, then pull bearing from mainshaft.
13. Tilt front end of mainshaft and lift out through top of case.
14. Remove reverse idler gear and related parts.
15. Push countershaft toward rear far enough to remove snap ring from rear bearing, then pull off bearing.
16. Raise front end of countershaft and lift assembly through top of case.
17. Disassemble mainshaft and countershaft as required.

Main Drive Gear Assemble, Fig. 14

1. Lubricate main drive gear bearing and shaft. Start bearing straight on shaft of drive gear with bearing snap ring toward pilot end of gear. Support front inner race of bearing and press gear into bearing tight against front face of gear.
2. Install bearing retainer nut or snap ring.
3. If a new pilot bearing is to be used it comes from the factory with a plastic sleeve. Stand drive gear on end. Set bearing and sleeve over bearing pocket in drive gear. Slide bearing rollers and cage from plastic sleeve into bearing pocket. When new bearing is used always install new pilot bearing race on mainshaft. If old pilot bearing is used, set rollers in bearing cage and hold in place with a rubber band. Slide bearing rollers and cage from rubber band into bearing pocket.

Countershaft Assemble, Fig. 14

1. Install Woodruff keys in 3rd and 4th gear slots. Lubricate countershaft and bore of each gear before installing gears on countershaft.
2. Press 3rd speed gear straight on countershaft with long hub of gear toward rear. Align keyway in gear with key and press gear tight against shoulder on shaft.
3. Press 4th speed gear on countershaft in same manner used for 3rd speed gear. Long hub of gear goes toward rear.
4. Install drive gear spacer and key.
5. Press drive gear onto countershaft with long hub toward rear.
6. Install snap ring in countershaft groove.

Mainshaft Assemble, Fig. 14

1. Clamp mainshaft in a vise with front end up.
2. Drop 2nd speed gear locating washer into position over mainshaft.
3. With lock pin in place in 2nd gear bushing sleeve, install bushing sleeve on mainshaft with lock pin toward upper end of mainshaft.
4. To insure proper tight stack-up between 2nd gear locating washer and bushing sleeve, 2nd gear retaining washer and snap ring, the following procedure should be used:
   a. Before 2nd gear is installed on bushing sleeve, place retaining washer on

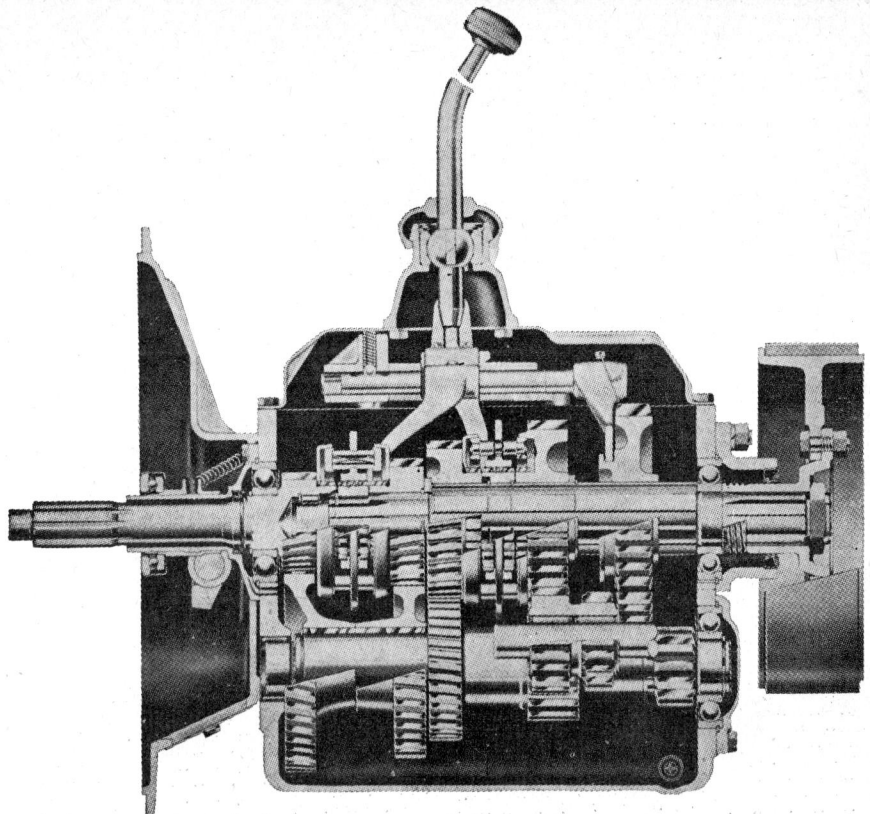

Fig. 11 Sectional view of Clark 280 Series five-speed transmission

mainshaft and hold down securely against bushing sleeve.
   b. Holding snap ring parallel to retaining washer, slip snap ring into its groove in mainshaft.
   c. Select variable thickness 2nd gear retaining washers until a washer is selected that will assure a tight stack-up through the assembly.
   d. Remove selected washer and install 2nd gear over bushing sleeve.
   e. Place selected washer in position on shaft and install snap ring so it is locked securely in groove. End play of 2nd gear must be a minimum of .006".
5. Place 2-3 speed synchronizer with long end of hub toward rear on splines of mainshaft and drop into position. Install 3rd speed gear locating thrust washer on mainshaft.
6. Position 3rd gear and bushing assembly over mainshaft with toothed hub down and drop into place. Position 4th gear locating washer on mainshaft.

NOTE: When assembling 4th gear bushing sleeve and lock pin assembly, make certain sleeve lock pin is centered in a spline of mainshaft before pressing sleeve into place. Failure to do this may shear head of lock pin and cause bushing seizure, Fig. 15.

7. With lock pin in place in 4th gear bushing sleeve, install bushing sleeve on mainshaft with lock pin toward pilot or front end of mainshaft. It may be necessary to use a suitable sleeve and hammer to install sleeve properly.
8. To insure a tight stack-up between 4th gear locating washer, bushing sleeve, gear selective retaining washer and snap ring, the following procedure must be used:
   a. Before 4th gear is installed on bushing sleeve, place retaining washer on mainshaft and hold down against bushing sleeve.
   b. While holding snap ring parallel to retaining washer, slip snap ring into its groove in mainshaft. Select variable thickness retaining washers until a washer is selected that will assure a tight stack-up through the assembly, Fig. 16.
   c. Remove selected washer and install 4th speed gear and bushing assembly over bushing sleeve.
   d. Place selected washer into position, then install snap ring into groove in mainshaft. End play of 4th speed gear must be a minimum of .006".
9. Remove assembly from vise and install 4-5 speed synchronizer on mainshaft with long end of hub toward rear.
10. Install 1st-reverse gear on mainshaft with shift fork slot toward front.

Transmission Assemble
Countershaft Installation

1. Install countershaft front bearing in case. Apply pressure on outer race of bearing only.
2. Place countershaft front bearing spacer on forward end of countershaft.
3. Tip rear end of countershaft assembly down and lower into case, running rear of countershaft through opening for rear bearing in rear of case far enough so front of countershaft can be lowered into position. Push countershaft forward into position in front bearing.

Clark Transmissions

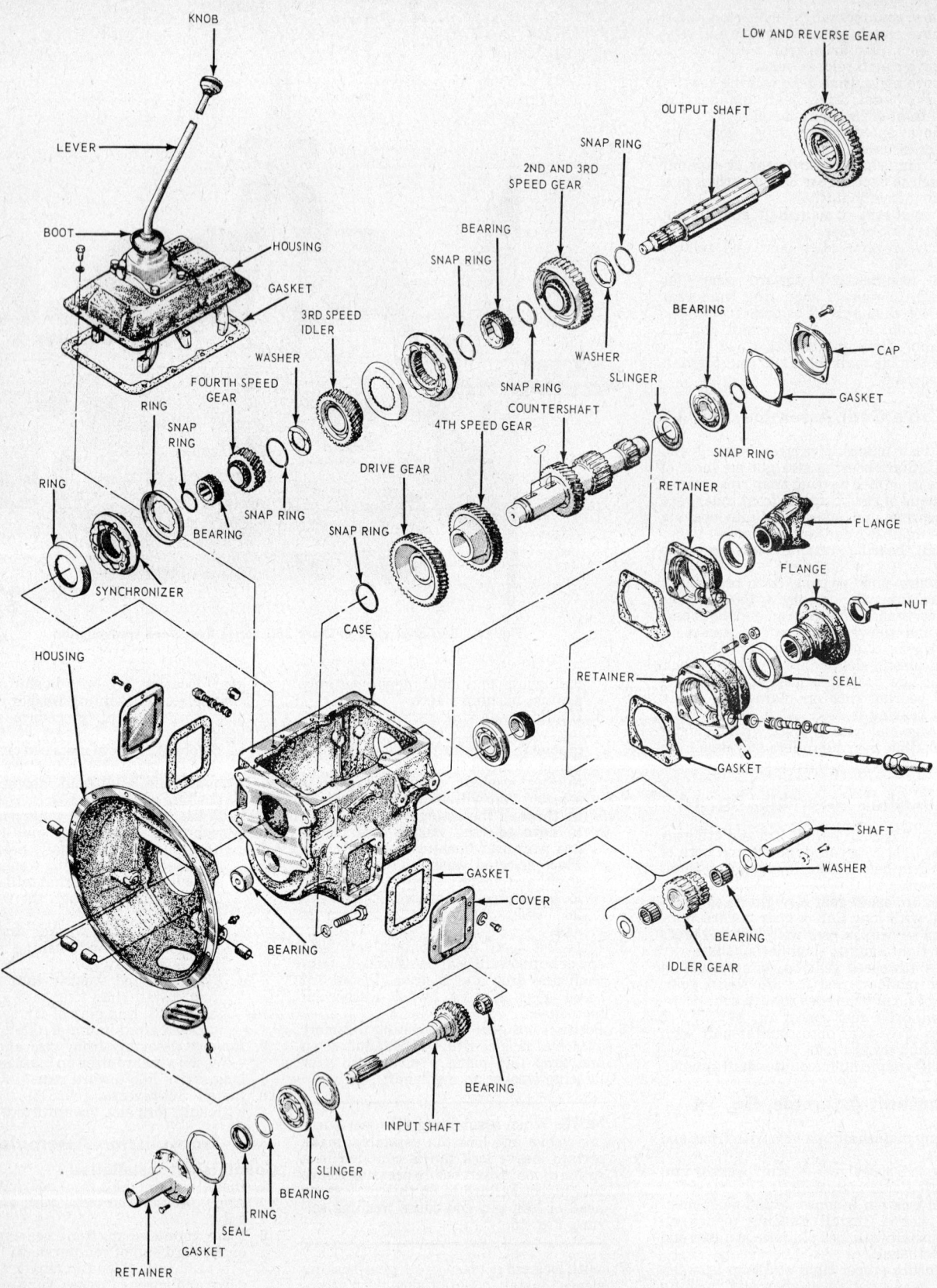

Fig. 12 Exploded view of Clark 280 Series transmission

CLARK TRANSMISSIONS

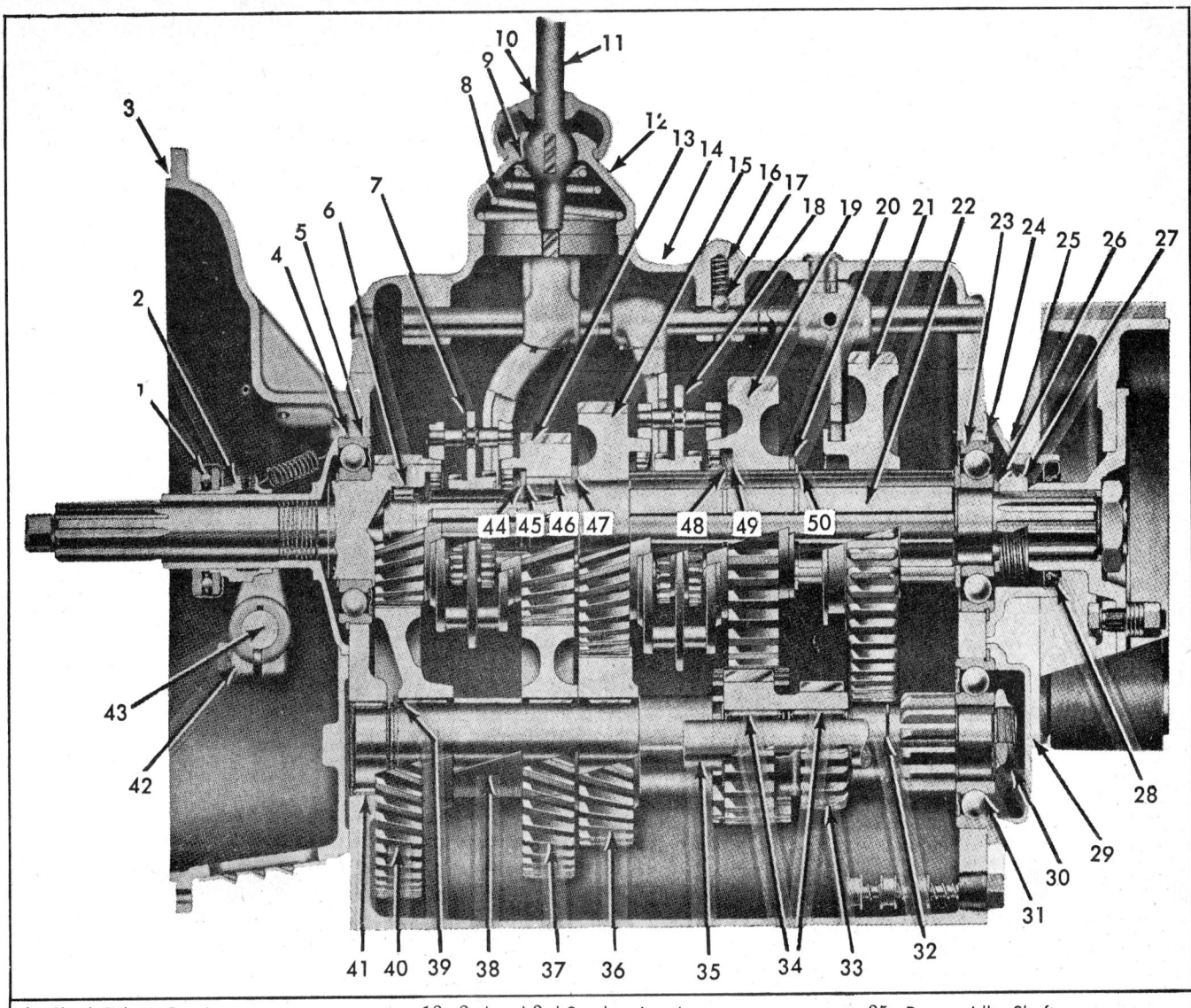

1. Clutch Release Bearing
2. Release Bearing Support
3. Clutch Housing
4. Drive Gear Bearing Retainer Ring
5. Drive Gear Bearing
6. Mainshaft Pilot Bearing
7. 4th and 5th Synchronizer Assy.
8. Gearshift Lever Spring
9. Spring Seat Washer
10. Dust Cover
11. Gearshift Lever
12. Control Tower
13. Mainshaft 4th Speed Gear
14. Shift Bar Housing
15. Mainshaft 3rd Speed Gear
16. Poppet Spring
17. Poppet Ball
18. 2nd and 3rd Synchronizer Assy.
19. Mainshaft 2nd Speed Gear
20. 2nd Gear Locating Washer
21. Mainshaft 1st and Reverse Gear
22. Mainshaft
23. Mainshaft Rear Bearing
24. Mainshaft Rear Bearing Snap Ring
25. Mainshaft Rear Bearing Cap
26. Speedometer Drive Gear Spacer
27. Speedometer Drive Gear
28. Rear Bearing Cap Oil Seal
29. Countershaft Rear Bearing Cap
30. Countershaft Rear Bearing Retainer Nut
31. Countershaft Rear Bearing
32. Countershaft
33. Reverse Idler Gear
34. Reverse Idler Gear Bearings
35. Reverse Idler Shaft
36. Countershaft 3rd Speed Gear
37. Countershaft 4th Speed Gear
38. Countershaft Drive Gear Spacer
39. Snap Ring
40. Countershaft Drive Gear
41. Countershaft Front Bearing
42. Clutch Release Yoke
43. Release Yoke Cross Shaft
44. Snap Ring
45. 4th Speed Gear Retainer Washer
46. 4th Speed Gear Bushing Sleeve
47. 4th Speed Gear Locating Washer
48. Snap Ring
49. 2nd Speed Gear Retainer Washer
50. 2nd Speed Gear Snap Ring

Fig. 13 Sectional view of Clark 320 & 380 Series five-speed transmission. Typical

CLARK TRANSMISSIONS

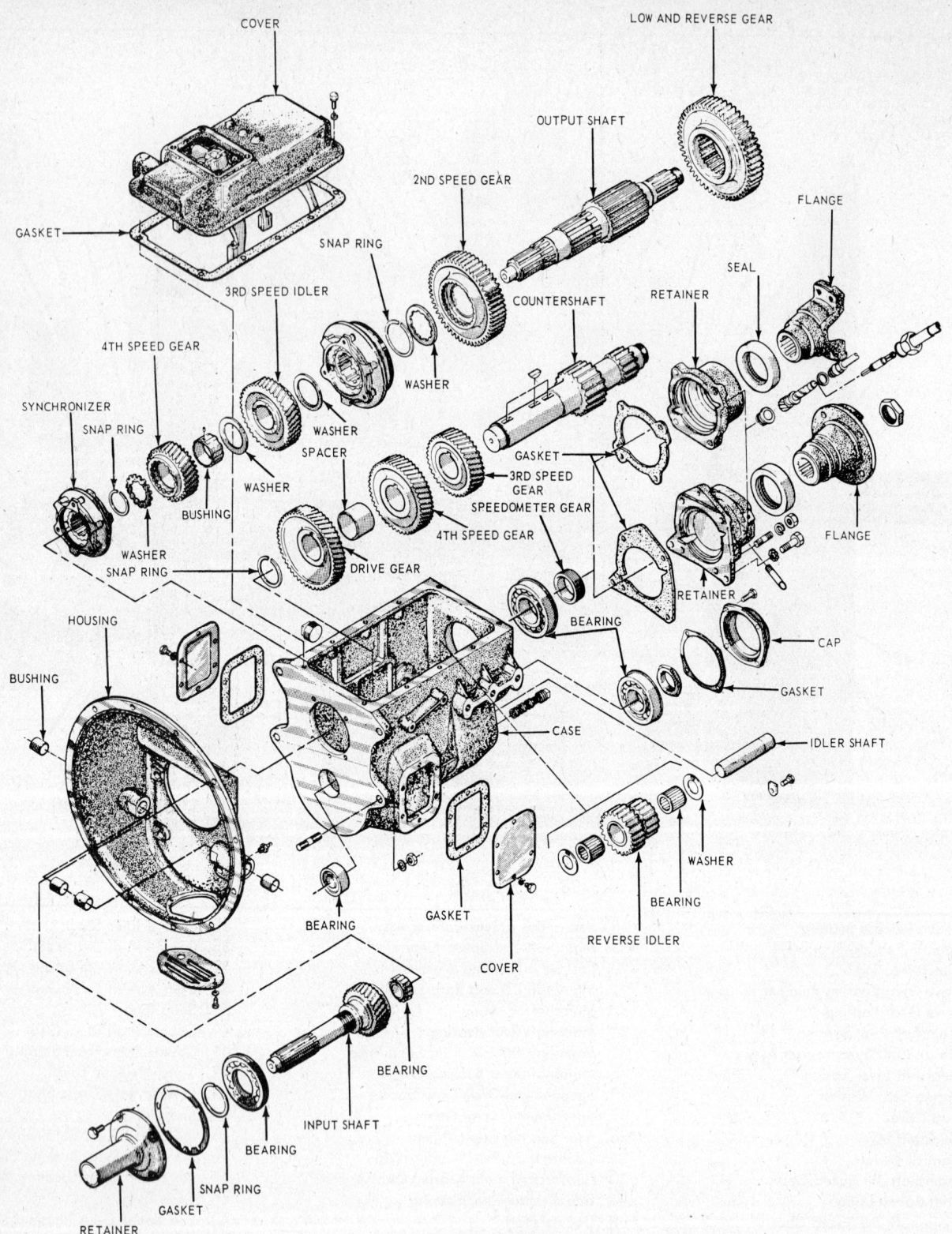

Fig. 14 Exploded view of Clark 320 & 380 Series transmission. Typical

CLARK TRANSMISSIONS

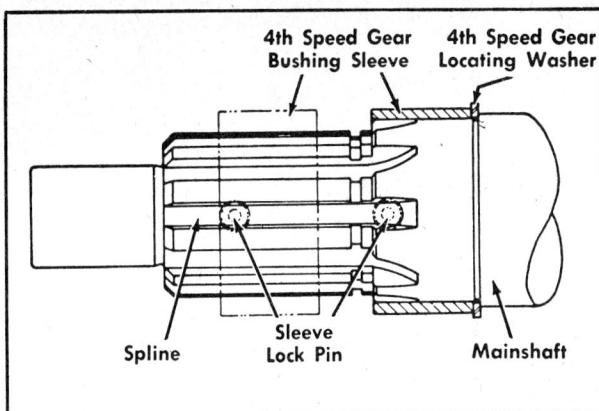

Fig. 15 Sleeve lock properly installed. Clark 320 & 380 Series. Typical

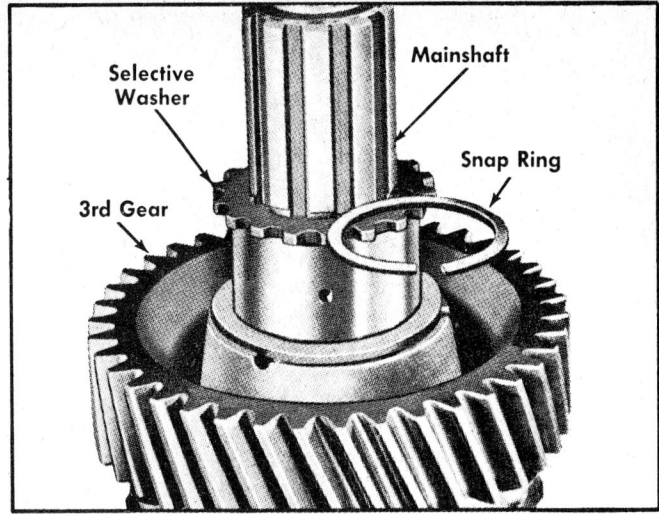

Fig. 16 Selecting 4th speed gear variable thickness retainer washer. Clark 320 & 380 Series. Typical

4. Install countershaft rear bearing. Be sure snap ring is in position in groove of outer race of bearing. Press bearing into place on countershaft with snap ring toward rear. Press bearing into case until snap ring contacts case.
5. Install countershaft rear bearing nut loosely.

Reverse Idler Gear Installation
1. Insert one reverse idler gear bearing in idler gear, then install bearing spacer and second bearing in bore of idler gear.
2. Install reverse idler gear assembly in case with chamfered teeth on gear toward rear of case.
3. Insert reverse idler gear shaft through opening in rear of case, into idler gear and into forward support boss. Make sure groove for retainer lock in rear of idler shaft is at bottom of shaft. Drive shaft in until inner edge of groove is flush with transmission case. Install retainer lock with bolt and lock washer.

Mainshaft Installation
1. Install mainshaft assembly into case by tilting rear end down and lowering into and through opening in rear of case. Lower front end in line with pilot bearing opening. Move mainshaft forward into position.
2. Position rear bearing over end of mainshaft with snap ring in outer race of bearing, facing the rear.
3. Drive mainshaft rear bearing on mainshaft and into case until snap ring on bearing contacts case.
4. Position main drive gear and bearing assembly into front of case so that drive gear engages and meshes with countershaft drive gear and snap ring on bearing contacts case. It may be necessary to use a sleeve and hammer to drive gear and bearing into case.
5. Install main drive gear bearing cap with new gasket on transmission case. Oil return hole in bearing cap must line up with oil hole in case.
6. Install clutch release bearing return spring clip under head of bolt when installing bearing cap.
7. Lock transmission in two gears at the same time to lock it up. Tighten countershaft rear bearing nut. After nut is driven up tight, stake it in position with punch and hammer.
8. Install countershaft rear bearing cap with new gasket.
9. Install speedometer drive gear spacer and drive gear (if used) on mainshaft.
10. Install mainshaft rear bearing cap with new gasket.
11. Install parking brake drum (if used) and companion flange on rear end of mainshaft.
12. With transmission still locked in two speeds, install and torque flange nut to 250 ft-lbs.
13. Place transmission gears in neutral and install shifter housing.

FULLER TRANSMISSIONS

Model	Speeds	Oil, Pts.	Page
3-65 Series	3 Aux.	13	325
5A-33, 330	5	11	322
5B-33, 330	5	11	322
5F-33	5	11	322
5A-43, 130	5	16	322
5A-62, 620	5	18	322
5A-65, 650	5	24	322
5C-65, 650	5	24	322
5C-67, 720	5	24	322
5CA-720	5	24	322
5H-74, 5HA-74	5	12	324
5W-74	5	24	322
5WA-74	5	24	322
4C-75	4 Aux.		327
R46	8	19	309
R96, R960	10	33	316
RT610	10	12	295
RT613	13	16	290

Model	Speeds	Oil, Pints	Page
RT906	6	26	290
RT910, RTF910	10	26	290
RT12510, RTF12510	10	25	290
RTO910, RTOF910	10	26	290
RTO-913	13	24	290
RT-915, RTO-915	15	28	290
RT-9513	13	27	302
RT-12513	13	27	302
RTF-9513	13	27	302
RTO-9513	13	27	302
RTOF-9513	13	27	302
RTOO-9513	13	27	302
RTOOF-9513	13	27	302
RTQ9513	13	27	290
T-905, TO-905	5	22	290

FULLER TRANSMISSIONS

RT, RTF, RTO, RTQ, T, TO Models With Twin Countershafts

DESCRIPTION

Series T transmission is shown in Fig. 1. As shown it is a five speed unit and is similar to the main transmission of the RT Series, Figs. 2, 3, 4. The "O" in RTO and TO units indicate that the transmissions include an overdrive ratio. The "F" in RTF models are of the same construction except for the forward position of the gearshift lever.

The twin countershaft design splits torque equally between the two shafts providing a high torque capacity-to-weight ratio. Because of torque splitting, each gear set carries the load, greatly reducing the face width of each gear.

Another unique design feature is the floating gear principle. The mainshaft gears, when not engaged, "float" between the countershaft gears, eliminating the need for gear sleeves and bushings. All gears are in constant mesh and have spur type teeth.

The 910 models have ten forward speeds and two reverse speeds, consisting of a five-speed front section and a two-speed auxiliary or range section. First through fifth speeds are obtained by using the five gear ratios in the front section through the low-speed gear of the auxiliary section. Sixth through tenth speeds are obtained by using the five gear ratios in the front section through the high speed (direct drive) auxiliary section.

The 913 and 9513 models have 13 progressive forward ratios and two reverse, consisting of a five-speed front section, a synchronized two-speed range section, and an overdrive splitter gear. One ratio in the front section is used only in low range as a low-low or starting gear. The remaining ratios (four) in the front section are used once through the reduction (low) gear in the range section and once through direct (high) in the range section. While in high range the four ratios can be split by the overdrive splitter to give eight speeds in high range.

The 915 models have 15 speeds forward and three reverse speeds, consisting of the five-speed front section which is identical to the 910 front section, and a three-speed auxiliary or range section. Both sections are contained in one case, the rear plate being extended to accommodate the auxiliary gears. The 15 speeds are obtained by using the five speeds in the front section through direct drive (high range) through the low speed range gear, and through the hole gear of the auxiliary section for deeper reduction provides the 15 forward speeds.

The range shift between high and low is made automatically by air upon preselection by the driver. The hole gear in the 915 models is engaged by air when selected by the driver.

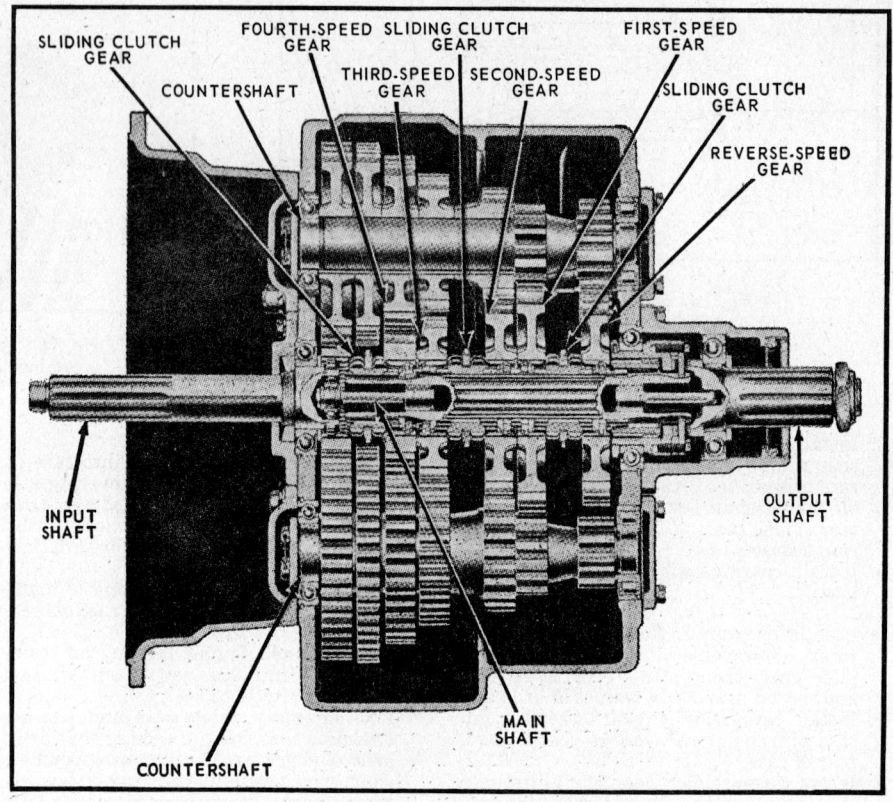

Fig. 1 Sectional view of Fuller T Series twin countershaft transmission

DISASSEMBLE TRANSMISSION

Preparation, Series T

1. Remove bolts that attach shifting bar housing to transmission case. Tap housing with soft hammer to free it from case, then lift from transmission.
2. Lock mainshaft by engaging two gears at one time, then remove companion flange nut and remove flange.
3. Remove attaching screws and pry off rear bearing cover, Fig. 5.
4. Remove speedometer drive gear or spacer and bearing washer from output shaft or from cover.
5. Remove rear bearing from output shaft, Fig. 6. In some instances this bearing will remain in rear cover, in which case; it should be removed from cover.
6. Remove lock wire and the two flat key attaching bolts, Fig. 7. Lift keys from output shaft.
7. Remove outshaft shaft, Fig. 8.
8. Remove clutch release mechanism from flywheel housing. Unfasten and lift flywheel housing from transmission case.

NOTE: At this point the balance of the procedure for disassembling the transmission is the same as given for the compound RT units.

Separation of Main & Auxiliary Units (All Models)

1. Disconnect air hoses at air valve.
2. Remove air filter and air regulator valve assemblies.
3. Remove air valve from adapter plate.
4. Remove alignment sleeve, spring and actuating pin from air valve adapter plate, then remove plate from transmission.
5. With transmission in neutral, remove gearshift housing cover.
6. Lock transmission in two gears and remove U-joint flange.
7. Unfasten auxiliary section from main transmission. Install three puller screws in tapped holes of rear plate and tighten them alternately and evenly to move auxiliary section to rear just enough to break gasket seal.
8. Attach chain hoist to auxiliary section and continue to move it to the rear until free of transmission, Fig. 9.
9. Unfasten and remove clutch housing from transmission.

ALL EXC. 610, 9513 & 12513 SERIES

Main. Trans. Disassemble

NOTE: All references to any part of the auxiliary sections do not apply, of course, to the five-speed (T Series).

1. Remove snap ring from the inside of the

FULLER TRANSMISSIONS

auxiliary drive gear.
2. Remove mainshaft rear quill support plate from bore of auxiliary drive gear and remove coupling. Remove coupling snap ring.
3. Cut lock wire and remove bolts that attach bearing retainer ring to case. Insert three puller screws in tapped holes of retainer ring and tighten bolts evenly and alternately to pull assembly from case, Fig. 11.
4. Secure auxiliary drive gear in a vise and remove bearing nut (left-hand thread). Then press on drive gear bearing retainer ring and bearing from gear.
5. Move mainshaft reverse gear to rear as far as possible and remove reverse gear snap ring. Then move reverse gear forward and against low-speed gear and into engagement with sliding clutch gear. Remove snap ring and reverse gear splined spacer from mainshaft.
6. Working from inside of case, remove left reverse idler shaft nut and washer.
7. Remove plug, Fig. 12, from reverse idler shaft bore. Using an impact puller, remove reverse idler gear shaft. Remove thrust washer and gear.
8. If necessary, remove bearing inner race from reverse idler shaft, and bearing from reverse idler shaft.
9. Move mainshaft to rear as far as possible to separate mainshaft gears from countershaft gears. Tilt front of mainshaft and lift from case.
10. Cut lock wire and remove bolts that attach bearing retainer to front of countershaft. Remove snap ring from rear of countershaft.
11. Using a mallet and soft drift, drive countershaft to rear as far as it will go. This will partially unseat front bearing from shaft and rear bearing from case bore.
12. Use a puller to remove countershaft rear bearing from shaft and case bore.
13. Move countershaft forward until front bearing is clear of case, then pull bearing from shaft. Remove left countershaft bearings in like manner.
14. Remove input shaft bearing retainer bolts and, working from inside of case, tap input shaft forward and remove bearing retainer. Remove snap ring from input shaft bearing.
15. Move input shaft to rear and lift from case.
16. Move front of right countershaft toward center of case and, at the same time, lift it from case. Remove left countershaft in like manner.
17. Working from inside case, remove right reverse idler shaft and nut, then remove component parts in same manner as left-hand assembly.
18. Disassemble shifter housing, mainshaft and countershaft as required.

Main Sub-Assemblies, Assemble
Countershaft Assemble, Fig. 13 and 13A

NOTE: Except for the number of teeth on the PTO gears, the countershafts are identical and are assembled in the same manner.

1. Install front washer over rear of countershaft and position keys in keyways.
2. Press countershaft gears on shaft one at a time, starting with the drive gear. The drive, PTO, 3rd and 1st speed gears are

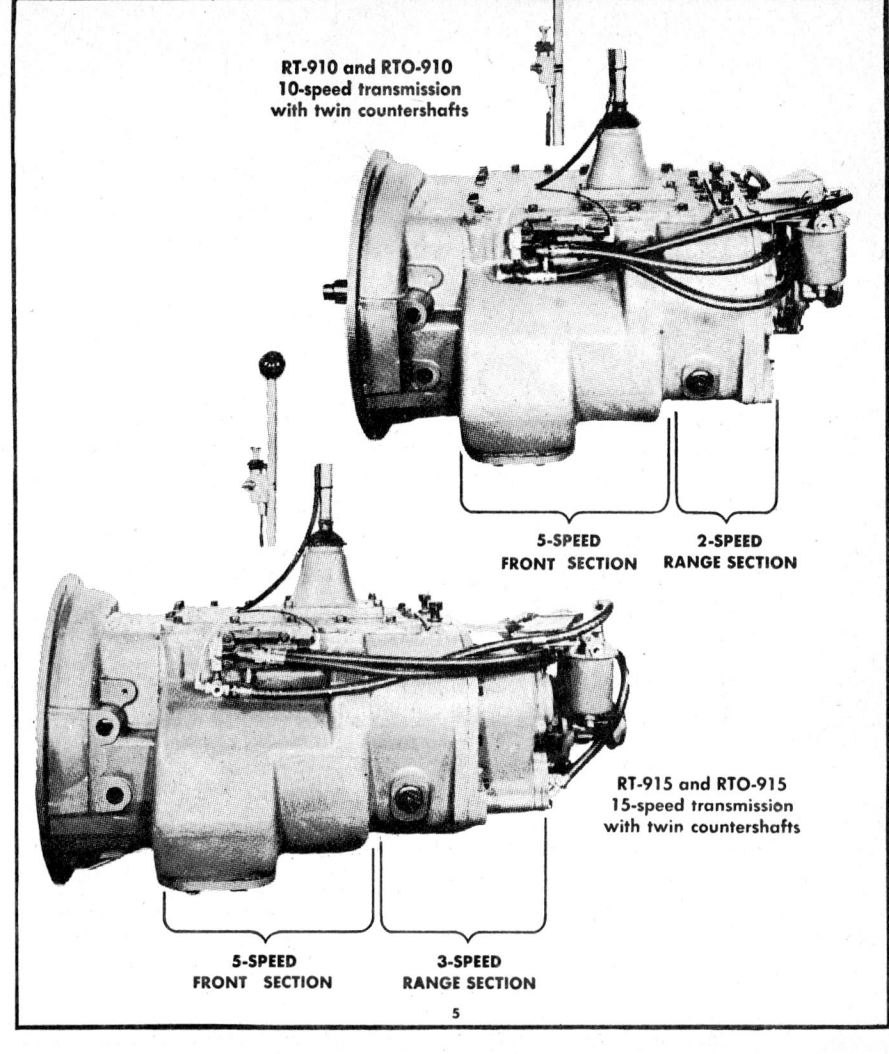

Fig. 2 Exterior view of Fuller RT twin countershaft compound transmissions. The 9513 & 12513 Series is similar to RT-915 and RTO-915 Series

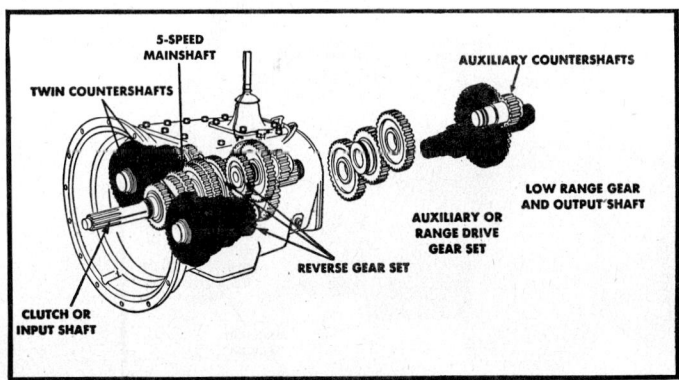

Fig. 3 Expanded view of RT-910 transmission

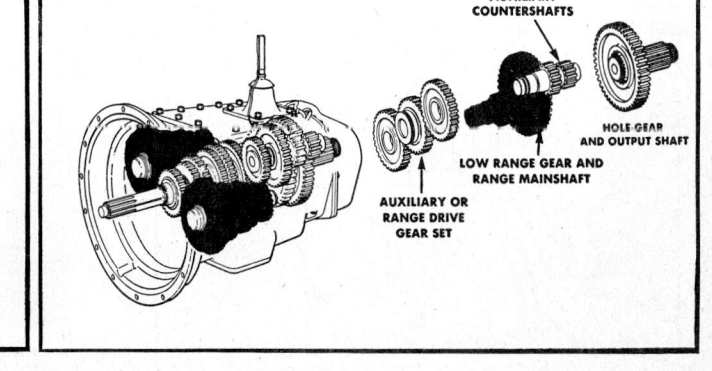

Fig. 4 Expanded view of RT-915 transmission

FULLER TRANSMISSIONS

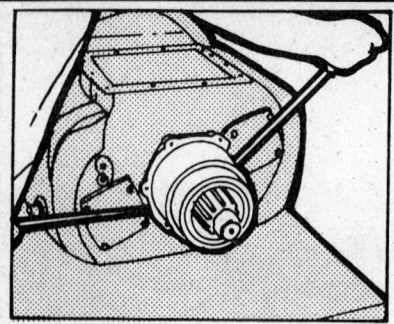

Fig. 5 Removing rear bearing cover. T Series

Fig. 6 Removing rear bearing from output shaft. Series T

Fig. 7 Removing output shaft screws. Series T

installed with long hubs to the rear; the 4th, 2nd and reverse gears are installed with long hubs to the front. The left countershaft has a 47 tooth PTO gear; the right side a 45 tooth gear. After installing the PTO gear, mark the assembly either left or right to correspond with the installed PTO gear.
3. Install snap ring on rear of countershaft.

Input Shaft, Assemble, Fig. 14
1. Install snap ring in drive gear if it was removed.
2. Install drive gear on shaft with snap ring toward front.
3. Install drive gear spacer.
4. Press drive gear bearing on shaft with snap ring toward front.
5. Install and tighten bearing attaching nut (left-hand thread). Peen nut in slots milled in shaft.

Mainshaft Assemble, Fig. 15
1. Except for the reverse gear, install snap ring in each gear if it was removed.
2. Place mainshaft in a vise with front end up.
3. Install reverse gear washer (flat side down) in fifth groove from top of mainshaft.
4. From bottom, install long key in keyway in shaft so that forward end is moved through slot of reverse gear washer. Keep snap ring groove in key to the rear and to the outside. Move key upward to engage washer as it is placed on mainshaft.
5. Install 1st-reverse sliding clutch gear on shaft, making sure that keyway is lined up with key in shaft.
6. Install 1st speed gear on shaft with snap ring up. Engage splines of gear with splines of spacer.
7. With snap ring down, install 2nd speed gear on shaft and against 1st gear.
8. Install 2nd gear spacer and washer on shaft (flat sides down). Move key upward through slot in 2nd gear washer until it reaches second groove from top of mainshaft.
9. Align keyway in 2-3 speed sliding clutch with key, and position clutch on mainshaft.
10. Install 3rd gear washer (flat side up) in second groove from top of mainshaft, then move key upward to engage washer.
11. Install 3rd gear spacer with flat side against washer.
12. Install 3rd gear (snap ring up) on shaft and onto splines of spacer.
13. With snap ring down, install 4th speed gear on shaft against 3rd speed gear.
14. With flat side up, install 4th speed gear spacer into 4th gear hub.
15. Install 4th speed gear washer (flat side down) on shaft and move key upward to engage washer.
16. Install 4-5 speed sliding clutch gear, aligning large slot in clutch gear with keyway in shaft.
17. Install front quill bearing if it was removed. When installing the bearing, be sure to use a suitable tool so that the quill is not pushed into the mainshaft. Install front quill snap ring.
18. Remove mainshaft from vise and align snap ring groove in key with snap ring groove in mainshaft.
19. Install reverse gear on mainshaft and move it as far forward as possible into engagement with sliding clutch gear. *Do not install reverse gear spacer and snap ring until mainshaft assembly is installed in transmission.*
20. Install front mainshaft coupling snap ring on shaft and key, securing key to mainshaft.

Gearshift Housing Assemble, Fig. 16
1. Install shifter shaft through rear bores of housing with neutral and detent notches to rear. Keep shafts in neutral position when installed.
2. Place housing in a vise with plunger side up.
3. Install 1st-reverse shifter shaft in bottom bore and through shift fork. Install set screw and secure with lock wire.
4. Install actuating plunger in front opening of housing, and a ¾" interlock ball in rear opening.
5. Position 2-3 speed shift shaft through shift block and fork. *Be sure to install interlock pin in bore at neutral notch.* Install set screws and secure with lock wire. *Keep shift shaft so that interlock pin remains in vertical position during remainder of assembly. Rotating the shaft*

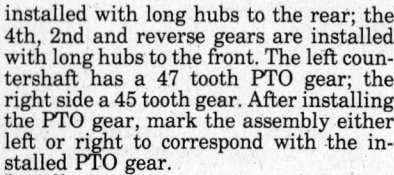

Fig. 8 Removing output shaft. Series T

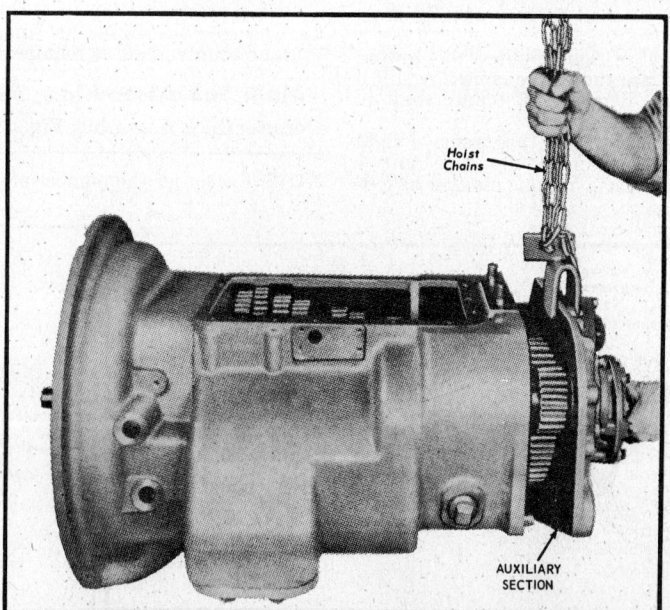

Fig. 9 Separation of auxiliary section. RT-910 shown

FULLER TRANSMISSIONS

Fig. 10 Removing auxiliary section shift cylinder housing and fork

will cause interlock pin to jam into tension spring bores.

6. Install 3/4" ball in rear opening in housing.
7. Position 4-5 speed shift shaft in upper bore and through shift block and fork. Install set screws and secure with lock wire.
8. Remove shift housing from vise and place on work bench. Install three detent balls and springs into top of housing.

Auxiliary Section

Disassemble

1. Remove shift cylinder cover.
2. Remove nut from end of shifter shaft. Using puller screws, remove piston from shift cylinder.
3. Remove bolts attaching shift cylinder housing to rear plate.
4. Cut lock wires and remove set screws from shifting fork. If necessary, rotate shift cylinder housing to expose set screws.
5. Push shifter shaft to inside, through fork hub, and out of cylinder housing. Remove shift fork and shift cylinder housing from plate.
6. To remove countershaft gear, remove snap ring and press gear from each shaft.

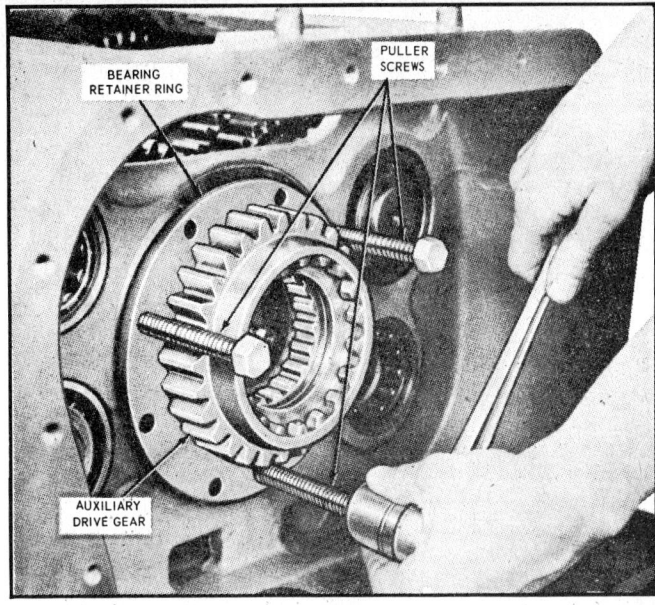

Fig. 11 Removing auxiliary drive gear

7. Place synchronizer assembly on work bench. Remove direct (high range) cone synchronizer ring from pins of low-speed synchronizer ring. *Place a cloth over ring during removal to catch the three springs installed in bores of direct cone synchronizer.*
8. Remove sliding clutch gear from pins of low-speed synchronizer.
9. Remove inner bearing spacer from output shaft, Fig. 17.
10. Using front face of low-speed gear as a base, press shaft through gear, washer and bearing. Remove splined and stepped washers from shaft.

Assemble Sub-Assemblies

1. Set output shaft on work bench with threaded end up. Install stepped and splined washers on shaft, Fig. 17. Be sure small diameters are toward threaded end of shaft.
2. Install low-speed gear on shaft (flat side up). Then install cone-shaped washer with flat side against gear.
3. Install bearing on shaft with taper toward threaded end.
4. Install inner bearing spacer on shaft and against bearing.
5. Place low-speed synchronizer ring on work bench with pins up. Then install clutch sliding gear on pins.
6. Install three springs into bores of direct synchronizer ring, Fig. 18, and install direct synchronizer over pins of low-speed synchronizer ring.
7. Apply pressure to direct synchronizer ring to compress springs and fully seat

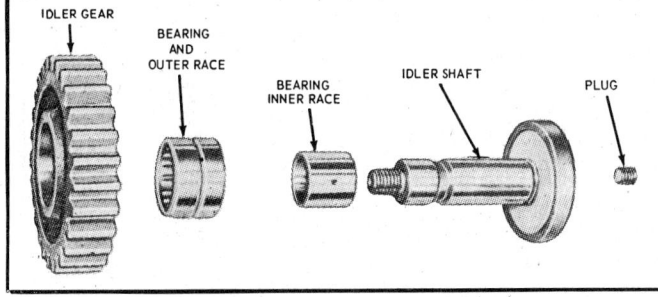

Fig. 12 Reverse idler shaft components, except 9513 & 12513

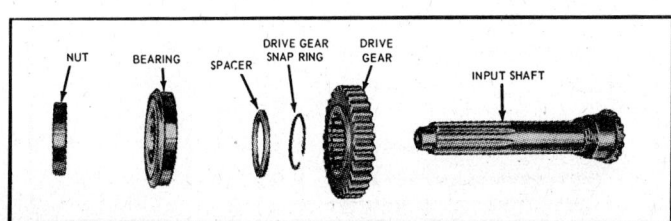

Fig. 14 Main transmission input shaft disassembled

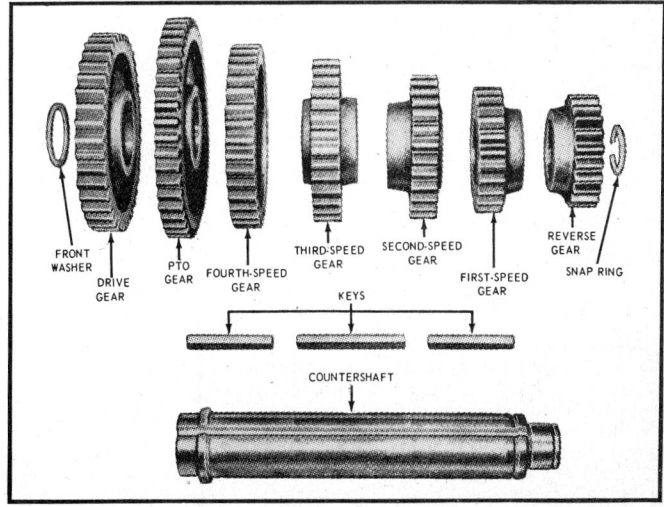

Fig. 13 Main transmission countershaft disassembled, all except 613, 913, 9513 & 12513 Series

FULLER TRANSMISSIONS

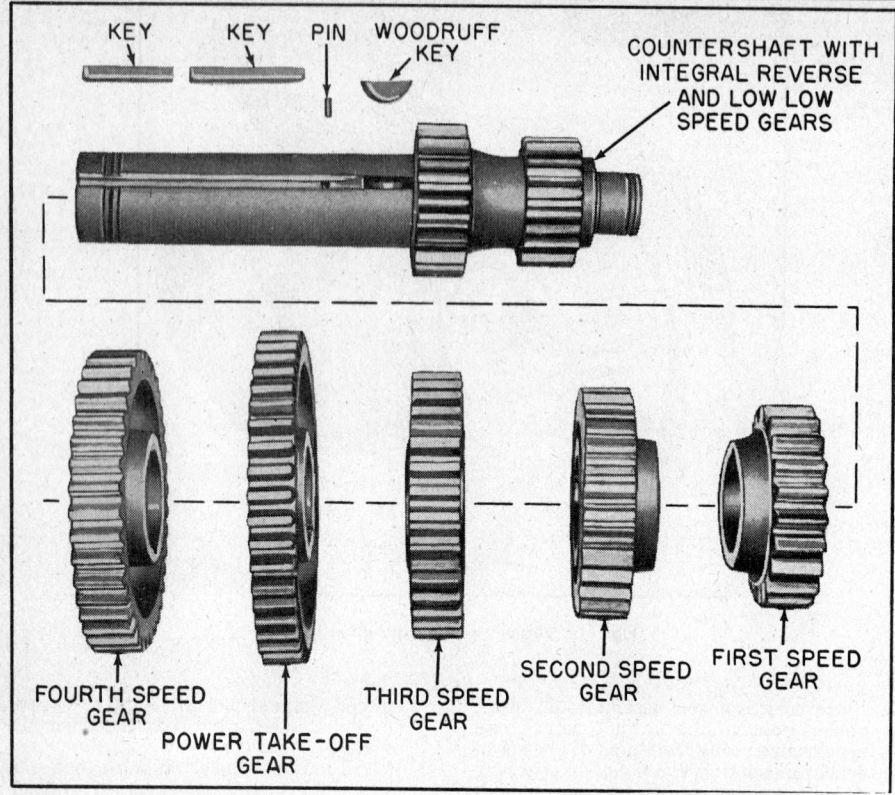

Fig. 13A Main transmission countershaft disassembled. 613, 913, 9513 & 12513 Series

direct synchronizer on pins of low-speed synchronizer.
8. Install Woodruff key on each countershaft and press countershaft into each drive gear. Install snap ring on front end of each shaft.

Assemble Auxiliary Section

1. With rear plate on work bench, place front cup (taper to inside) of rear bearing into rear bore of plate.
2. Place bearing outer spacer on front cup. Place rear cup on spacer and tap the two cups and spacer into rear plate bore.
3. Place rear plate over output shaft. Be sure that the bearing on shaft is seated on rear plate front bearing cup.
4. Install rear bearing on output shaft. Install new seal in rear bearing cover (if it was removed). Position cover to rear plate and install attaching bolts.
5. Install synchronizer assembly on output shaft with low-speed synchronizer ring toward low-speed gear.
6. To install and time auxiliary countershafts, mark gear tooth which is stamped "O" on small diameter low-range gear of each countershaft. This tooth will be aligned with the keyway in the countershaft drive gear. These two teeth, one on each countershaft, must both mesh at the same time with the output shaft low-speed gear and be in directly opposite positions.
7. Mark any two adjacent teeth on the output shaft low-speed gear. Then mark the two adjacent teeth which are directly opposite the first set marked. There should be the same number of teeth between the markings on each side of the gear.
8. Place rear plate assembly on blocking with threaded end of output shaft up. Make sure blocking is also placed under the synchronizer assembly to prevent it from dropping from the output shaft.
9. Place each countershaft into position and place blocking under each shaft. For correct timing, place marked teeth of countershafts into mesh with the low-speed gear. Install rear bearing on each countershaft. Recheck gears to be sure they are correctly timed.
10. Position rear bearing retainer plate on each countershaft and secure them with bolts and lock wire. Install rear bearing covers.
11. Install new O-ring in shift cylinder bore if it was removed.
12. Position shift fork in sliding clutch gear and install shift cylinder into bore of rear plate.
13. Insert threaded end of shift shaft through front of shift cylinder, through shift fork hub and into cylinder bore. Install set screws and secure with lock wire.
14. Install new O-rings on shift cylinder piston if they were removed.
15. Position piston in shift cylinder bore and secure with elastic stop nut.
16. Position cover on shift cylinder (air port to upper left) and secure with bolts.

Main Trans. Assemble

1. Install plug in right reverse idler shaft. Install needle bearings in bore of reverse idler gear if they were removed. Install bearing inner race on reverse idler shaft if it was previously removed.
2. Insert threaded end of idler shaft through right wall of case. As shaft is moved forward, install reverse idler gear and thrust washer. *Be sure needle bearings in gear are seated evenly on shaft inner race before moving shaft forward.* The thrust washer should be positioned between gear and boss, with slot toward gear.
3. Position washer over threaded end of shaft and secure with elastic stop nut.
4. To install and time countershaft assemblies, mark drive gear tooth that aligns with keyway of each countershaft. This tooth will be stamped with an "O." Position left and right countershaft assemblies in case. *Make sure that left countershaft has larger 47-tooth PTO gear.*
5. Mark any two adjacent gear teeth on the input shaft drive gear. Then mark two adjacent teeth which are directly opposite the first set marked.
6. Install input shaft through front bore from inside of case. Move shaft as far forward as possible and install snap ring on input shaft bearing.
7. Using a wood block, center front end of left countershaft in case bore. Then mesh the marked tooth on left countershaft drive gear with the two teeth marked on the input shaft main drive gear.

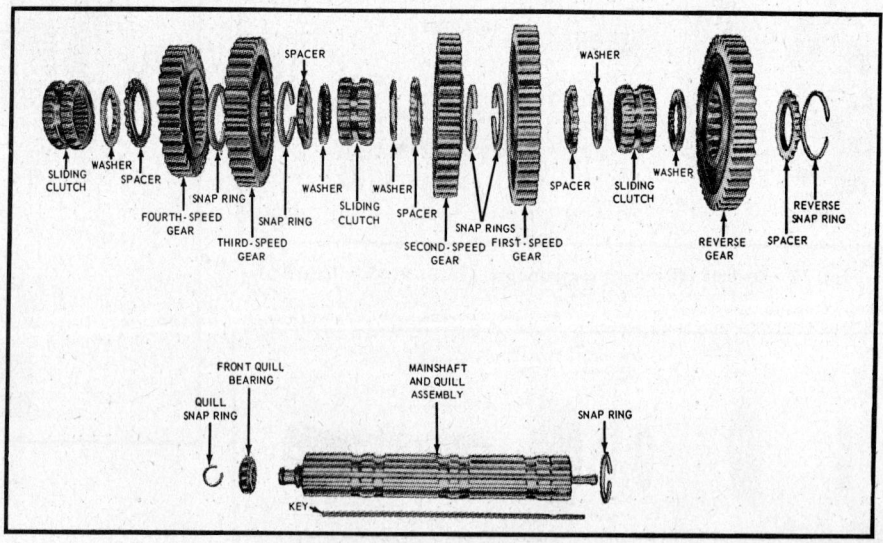

Fig. 15 Main transmission mainshaft disassembled. All except 9513 & 12513

FULLER TRANSMISSIONS

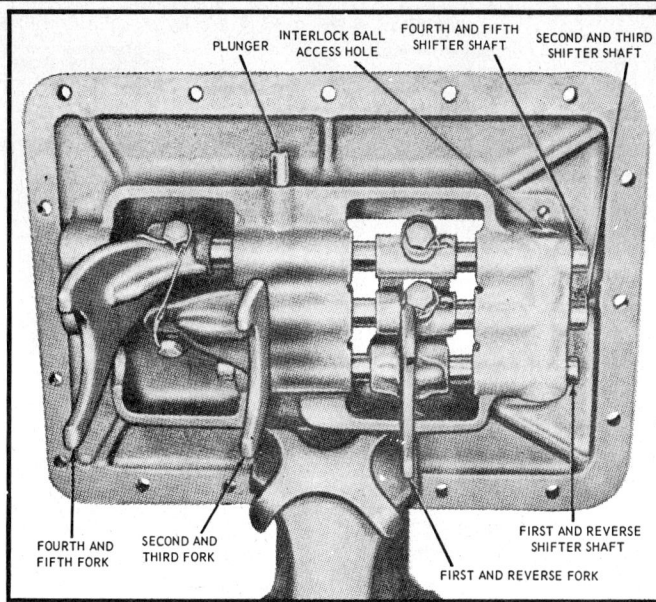

Fig. 16 Gearshift housing assembled

4. Position inner bearing outer race in adapter, then apply sealer to adapter gasket. Make sure adapter oil return hole is aligned, then install gasket and adapter.
5. Install inner bearing cone. Position spacer and install outer bearing cone. Position outer bearing outer race. Install bearing lock plate and secure bolts with lock wire.
6. Apply sealer to adapter cap gasket and install gasket and cap.
7. After tilting case back to its normal position, install idler gear and shaft. Be sure flat on shaft will align with lock plate. Install lock plate.
8. Position output shaft sliding gears in case, then position output shaft in case. Check for proper gear engagement.
9. Install rear bearing.
10. Position input shaft bearing snap ring in case bore. Position input shaft assembly and install bearing retainer gasket and retainer, using sealer on gasket.
11. Install clutch housing and speedometer drive gear.
12. After installing a new seal in rear bearing retainer, install gasket and retainer, using sealer on gasket.
13. Install parking brake shoe and connect brake linkage.
14. With transmission locked in two gears, install brake drum and flange.
15. Adjust parking brake. Install gearshift housing, using sealer on gasket.

Joining Main & Auxiliary Sections

1. Install clutch housing to transmission case. Using a chain hoist, install auxiliary section to transmission. It may be necessary to rotate drive gear to properly mesh gears. Install and securely tighten attaching bolts.
2. With transmission locked in two gears, install speedometer drive gear and U-joint flange on mainshaft. *If speedometer drive gear is not used, be sure to install replacement spacer of the same width.*
3. Install gearshift housing cover to transmission. Install air valve plate and housing. Install air valve and air regulator valve assemblies, and connect air hoses at air valve.

RT610

Separation of Main & Auxiliary Units

1. Disconnect nylon air lines from air valve and remove gear shift lever housing, lever and control valve as an assembly. Then disconnect air line and clamp between air valve and regulator.
2. Remove air regulator and filter assembly, then remove air lines between air valve and air cylinder in auxiliary section.
3. Remove air valve and actuating spring and pin from valve bore, then remove gear shift lever housing or control housing from shift bar housing.
4. Remove shifting bar housing from transmission, then lock transmission by engaging two gears with mainshift sliding clutch gears and remove output shaft nut flange.
5. Remove auxiliary section attaching screws, then install puller screws in tapped holes of auxiliary section and tighten screws evenly until housing can be removed, Fig. 9.
6. Remove clutch release mechanism and

---

8. With countershaft as far to rear as possible, install rear bearing on shaft and into case bore.
9. Remove wood block and install front bearing on countershaft and into case bore. Install snap ring on rear of countershaft.
10. Position bearing retainer plate on front of countershaft and secure with attaching bolts and lock wire.
11. After installing left countershaft assembly in case, install right countershaft in like manner.
12. Position input shaft bearing retainer to case and secure with attaching bolts.
13. Lower mainshaft assembly in case. Place bar across top of case and install support wire under forward sliding clutch gear, Fig. 19.
14. Align mainshaft assembly, making sure mainshaft gears and mating countershaft gears are properly engaged, and that quill bearing is seated in pocket of main drive gear. Remove support wire and bar. *Keep mainshaft in forward position during installation of left reverse idler gear so that gears will not slip out of mesh.*
15. Install plug in left reverse idler shaft. Install needle bearings in bore of reverse idler gear if they were removed. Install bearing inner race on reverse idler shaft if it was previously removed.
16. Insert threaded end of reverse idler shaft through left wall of case. As shaft is moved forward, install reverse idler gear and thrust washer. *Be sure needle bearings in gear are seated evenly on shaft inner race before moving shaft forward.* The thrust washer should be positioned between gear and boss with slot toward gear. Install washer over threaded end of shaft and install elastic stop nut.
17. Move mainshaft reverse gear to the rear so that it engages reverse idler gears. Then install reverse gear spacer (flat side inward) into hub of reverse gear. Install reverse gear snap ring.
18. If auxiliary drive gear was disassembled, place bearing retainer on gear and press bearing into place. Apply Loctite to threads of drive gear and nut and install nut (left-hand thread).
19. Position auxiliary drive gear assembly in rear case bore and install attaching bolts. Wire bolts in groups of three.
20. Pull mainshaft as far to rear as possible and install mainshaft coupling snap ring. Place coupling gear and rear quill support plate in bore of auxiliary drive gear and install snap ring.
21. Install auxiliary countershaft front bearings into reverse idler shaft bores.

Series T Final Assembly

1. Install countershaft front bearing in case bore. Position front bearing spacer and gasket and install retainer.
2. Position countershaft assembly in case, then tilt case so that rear face is up.
3. Position two wood blocks of equal thickness between drive gear and case.

Fig. 17 Auxiliary section output shaft. All except 9513 & 12513

FULLER TRANSMISSIONS

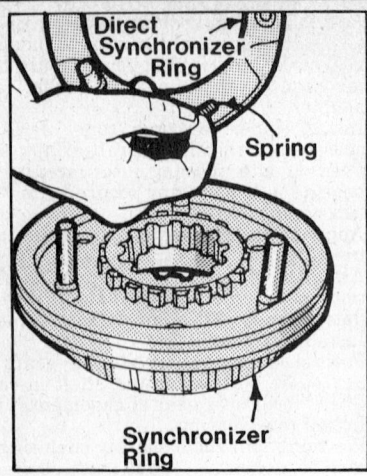

Fig. 18 Installing synchronizer springs

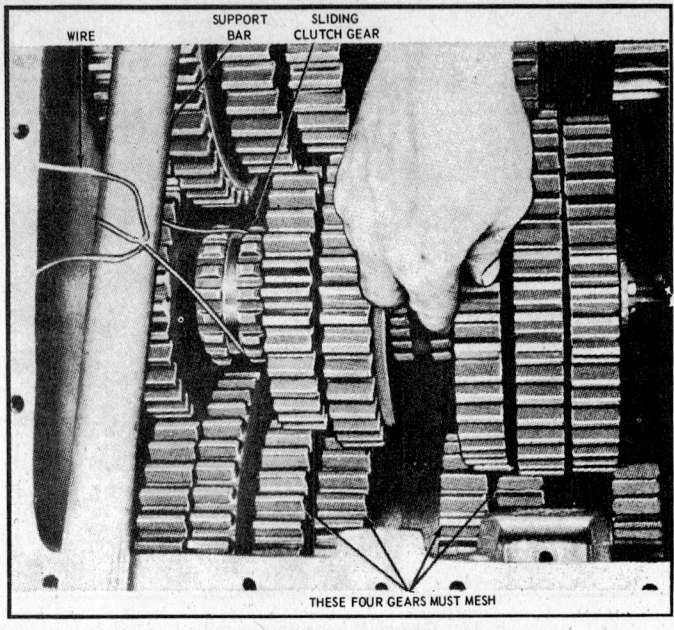

Fig. 19 Aligning mainshaft countershaft gears

clutch housing and remove front gear cover.

Main Trans. Disassemble

1. Remove right countershaft snap ring from rear bearing bore of case, Fig. 20, then using a soft bar and hammer, drive against rear of countershaft, moving assembly forward as far as possible to expose front bearing snap ring groove.

   NOTE: If front bearing cannot be exposed, use punch between hub of countershaft drive gear and inner race of bearing to move gear forward on shaft.

2. Install snap ring removed from rear bearing bore into exposed bearing snap ring groove, then loosen capscrews at bearing retaining rings of auxiliary drive gear. This will allow movement to rear of countershaft and mainshaft assemblies.
3. Using soft bar and hammer, drive against front of countershaft and move countershaft assembly rearward as far as possible, thereby moving front bearing forward on shaft. Then, again using soft bar and hammer, drive against countershaft and move countershaft forward as far as possible to unseat bearing from case bore. Using puller, remove bearing.
4. Using a soft curved bar and hammer from inside case, drive rear countershaft bearing rearward far enough to expose snap ring groove in rear bearing. Install snap ring into groove in rear bearing and using puller, remove countershaft rear bearing.
5. Move drive gear and shaft forward as far as possible, then remove bearing retaining snap ring from groove in shaft.
6. Hold shaft in position and tap drive gear forward to unseat bearing from case, then using puller, remove bearing.
7. Remove drive gear washer, and remove snap ring from inside diameter of drive gear, then pull shaft forward and from splines of drive gear.
8. Remove bushing from pocket in clutch shaft, if necessary.
9. Position drive gear rearward and against 4th speed gear, engaging teeth of sliding clutch gear, then remove capscrews and the two bearing retainer rings from case.
10. Remove coupling snap ring from groove in mainshaft located in bore of auxiliary drive gear, then tap against front of mainshaft to move auxiliary drive gear bearing rearward, exposing bearing snap ring.
11. Using pry bars, remove auxiliary drive gear assembly from case bore and from splines of mainshaft, then remove snap ring from groove in auxiliary gear and press or drive bearing from auxiliary drive gear.
12. Using pry bar, remove bearing from idler bore in case, then remove rear idler washer and holder from bore. If necessary bend holder lugs and remove washer from holder.
13. Remove idler gear from case and remove idler bearing from reverse idler gear.
14. Remove front idler washer from case, then block right countershaft to the right as far as possible and lift mainshaft assembly from case.
15. Remove drive gear and 4th-5th sliding clutch from mainshaft, then from inside hub of 4th speed gear, remove snap ring from groove in mainshaft, Fig. 21.
16. Remove 4th and 3rd speed gears and washers, remove 2nd-3rd speed sliding clutch, remove long key from mainshaft slot, remove 2nd and 1st speed gears and washers, remove 1st-reverse sliding clutch and remove reverse gear and washer.
17. Lift right countershaft assembly from case, then remove bearings from left countershaft in same manner in which bearings were removed from right countershaft.

   NOTE: Both left and right countershaft assemblies are disassembled in the same manner as their construction is identical.

18. Remove snap ring from front of countershaft, Fig. 22, and press the drive gear then the 4th speed gear from shaft.
19. Using the rear face of PTO gear as a base in press, press the 3rd speed gear, the PTO gear and 2nd speed gear cluster from shaft. If necessary, remove Woodruff key, long key and roll pin from shaft.
20. Using curved pry bar, remove reverse idler gear bearing from idler bore in case, then remove rear idler washer and holder from bore. If necessary, bend holder lugs and remove washer from holder.
21. Remove reverse idler gear from case, then remove idler bearing from reverse idler gear and remove front idler washer from case.

Main Trans. Assemble

1. Install small, flat, right reverse idler gear front washer on pin in lower right of case, then set reverse gear in position next to washer, with long hub to the rear.
2. Install needle bearing through rear bore and into hub of reverse gear, then place rear washer in holder with oil slots down and bend lugs to secure washer.
3. Place washer and holder into reverse gear case bore, with oil slots toward gear and holder flange to the rear.
4. Install auxiliary countershaft front bearing into reverse gear case bore to hold reverse idler gear assembly in position.

NOTE: The front portion of the auxil-

Fig. 20 Removing right countershaft snap ring. RT610

FULLER TRANSMISSIONS

iary countershaft is used as a journal for the reverse idler gear. Countershafts are identical and assembled in the same manner.

5. If removed, install roll pin, long key and Woodruff key in countershaft slots.
6. Press PTO and 2nd speed gear cluster on countershaft with PTO gear to the front, then press 3rd speed gear on shaft with long hub to the rear, 4th speed gear with long hub to the front and drive gear with long hub to the rear.
7. Install snap ring into groove at front of shaft, Fig. 23.
8. On each countershaft drive gear, mark the gear tooth aligned with the keyway in shaft and is stamped with an "O", Fig. 24.
9. First place left countershaft and then right countershaft into place in case. Do not install bearings.
10. Place mainshaft in vise with pilot end down and keeping keyway free for insertion of long key.

NOTE: Each mainshaft gear is held in place by locking the gear splined washer to the mainshaft with key. There is one splined washer for each gear. Splined washers for the reverse, 1st, 2nd and 3rd speed gears are identical. The 4th speed gear splined washer is of smaller diameter.

11. Install 2nd speed gear washer at 2nd speed gear location and insert key from bottom to lock washer in place, then install 2nd speed gear on splined washer with clutching teeth down.
12. Install 1st speed gear on shaft and against 2nd speed gear with clutching teeth up, then insert splined washer in hub of 1st speed gear. Align washer with mainshaft splines and move key up to lock washer in position.
13. Install 1st-reverse gear splined washer, aligning slot in clutch with key, then install reverse gear splined washer, align keyway and lock with key.
14. Reposition assembly in vise with pilot end up.
15. Install 2nd-3rd speed sliding cluth, aligning keyway in sliding clutch with key in shaft.
16. Install 3rd speed gear splined washer and lift key to install washer under pin in key to lock in position.
17. Install 3rd speed gear on mainshaft and slign gear splines with those of washer, Fig. 25.
18. Install 4th speed gear on mainshaft with clutching teeth up and against 3rd speed gear, then install 4th speed gear splined washer on mainshaft and in hub of 4th speed gear.
19. Install snap ring into mainshaft groove which will hold 4th speed gear in position, then install 4th-5th speed sliding clutch on mainshaft and engage it with 4th speed gear.
20. Mark two adjacent teeth of drive gear (5th speed gear) and mark the two adjacent teeth which are directly opposite the set marked. There should be the same number of teeth between markings on each side of the gear.
21. Install drive gear in mainshaft and against 4th speed gear with snap ring in drive gear to the front.
22. Remove assembly from vise and install reverse gear on rear of mainshaft, engaging splines of gear with those of splined washer on mainshaft.
23. Move both countershafts toward case wall as far as possible and position mainshaft assembly in case. Block under front of mainshaft to center it in front of case bore.
24. Press bearing on auxiliary drive gear with snap ring towards gear, then install bearing retaining snap ring in auxiliary drive gear shoulder groove.
25. Center mainshaft in rear bore of case and install auxiliary drive gear on splines of mainshaft, then seat auxiliary drive gear bearing in rear bore of case.
26. Install coupling snap ring in mainshaft groove in hub of auxiliary drive gear, then install the two bearing retainer plates on the case and attach both upper and lower plates using a double locking lug for each plate. Tighten screws and secure by bending locking lugs.
27. If removed, install bushing in pocket of clutch shaft. Install flush with shaft making certain that oil hole in shaft is not plugged.
28. Install clutch shaft in splines of drive gear, moving gear forward against wall of case, then install ring in groove in inside diameter of drive gear.
29. Install the drive gear spacer on shaft and drive gear bearing on shaft and into case bore, then install bearing retaining snap ring in groove in clutch with taper towards the outside.
30. Place left countershaft into mesh mainshaft gears, aligning the marked timing tooth on countershaft drive gear with the two marked timing teeth on main drive gear.
31. Hold left countershaft in position and install front and rear bearings, then center rear of left countershaft in rear bore of case with wood block. Partially install front and rear countershaft bearings, then using a flanged bearing driver, complete seating both front and rear bearings.
32. Install snap ring in groove in rear bore of case, then place right countershaft into mesh with mainshaft gears, aligning the

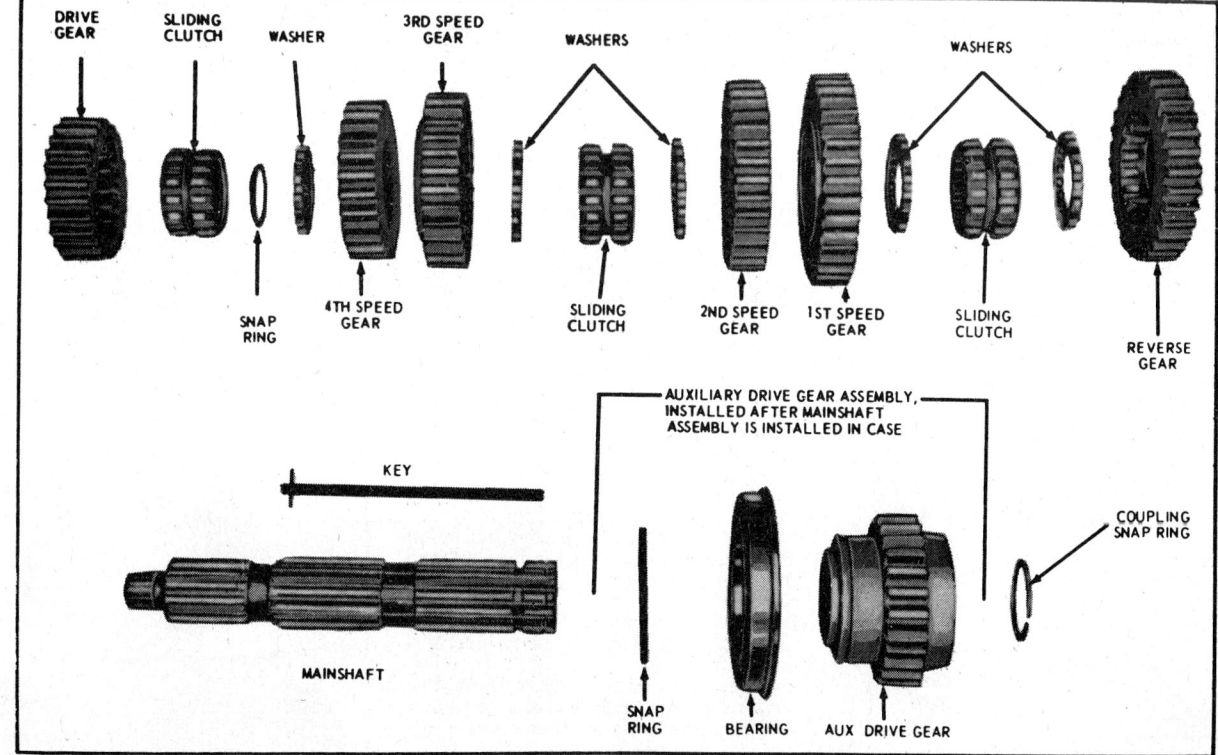

Fig. 21 Mainshaft and auxiliary drive gear. RT610

FULLER TRANSMISSIONS

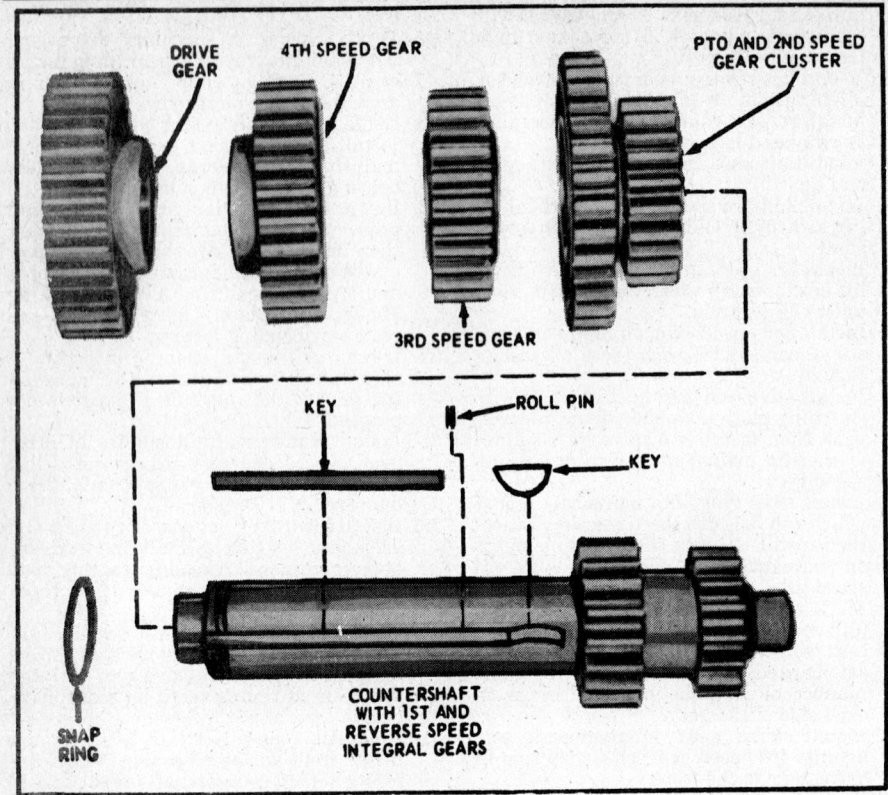

Fig. 22 Front section countershaft. RT610

Fig. 23 Installing front countershaft snap ring. RT610

complete assembly.
9. Remove shaft and yoke from synchronizer assembly, then cut lock wire, remove lock screws and remove yoke from shaft.
10. Place larger low range synchronizer ring on bench, then turn and pull upward to remove high range synchronizer from pins.

NOTE: The three springs located in high range synchronizer housing will be released as high range synchronizer is removed from pins.

11. Remove sliding clutch from low range synchronizer pins.
12. Remove dust seal, air port extension and air cylinder from housing, then remove O-ring from small bore in cylinder, if necessary.
13. Drive or press against rear of tailshaft to move low speed gear and tailshaft assembly forward and from rear bearing, Fig. 30.
14. Remove rear washer and low speed gear from rear of shaft and remove spline washer from hub of low speed gear.
15. Move mainshaft rear bearing rearward and out of housing, then using bearing driver, remove rear countershaft bearings from housing.

Auxiliary Section, Assemble

1. Make certain that magnetic cleaner is installed in recess of auxiliary case.
2. For timing purposes, mark any two adja-

marked tooth on countershaft drive gear with the two marked timing teeth on main drive gear, Fig. 26.
33. Hold right countershaft in position and install front and rear bearings in same manner as installed on left countershaft.
34. Install snap ring in groove in rear bore of case and install left-reverse idler gear front washer on pin in upper left of case, then install needle bearing in hub of reverse idler gear and position reverse idler gear with long hub facing rearward.
35. If removed, place rear washer in holder with oil slot down, and bend lugs to secure washer, then place washer and holder into reverse gear case bore, with oil slots toward gear and holder flange to the rear.
36. Install the auxiliary countershaft front bearing into the reverse idler case bore to hold the reverse idler gear assembly in position.

NOTE: The front portion of the auxiliary countershaft is used as a journal for the reverse idler gear.

Auxiliary Section, Disassemble

1. Using puller, remove output shaft bearing, then remove rear bearing cover and if necessary, remove seal from cover.
2. Remove speedometer gear or replacement spacer from output shaft and remove speedometer gear washer.
3. Using a long punch from inside housing, move outer races of countershaft rear bearings rearward approximately 1/2 inch, Fig. 27.
4. Pull countershafts forward and out of housing, then remove bearing inner race from rear of countershaft, Fig. 28.
5. Remove snap ring from groove in front of shaft and press drive gear forward and from shaft. If necessary, remove key from countershaft.
6. Remove air cylinder cover and remove nut and lock washer from air cylinder piston shaft.
7. Using compressed air, remove piston, Fig. 29. If necessary, remove O-ring from outside diameter of piston, then remove copper seal from shaft.
8. Remove synchronizer assembly, shift yoke and piston shaft out of housing as

Fig. 24 Marking countershaft drive gear for timing purposes. RT610

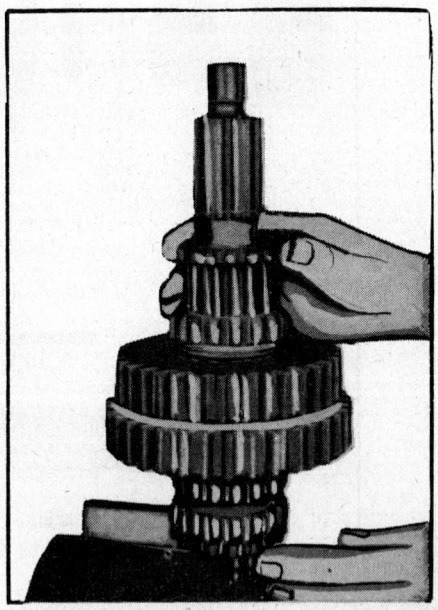

Fig. 25 Assembling mainshaft. RT610

FULLER TRANSMISSIONS

Fig. 26 Meshing countershaft and low speed gear for proper timing. RT610

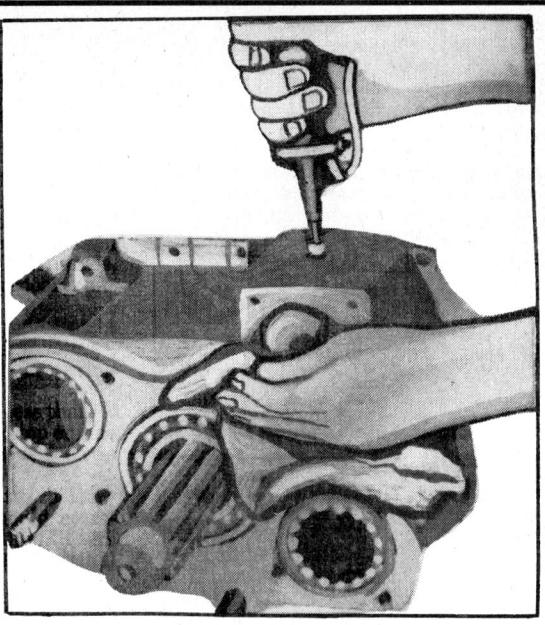

Fig. 29 Removing piston from auxiliary section. RT610

Fig. 27 Moving outer countershaft races rearward. RT610

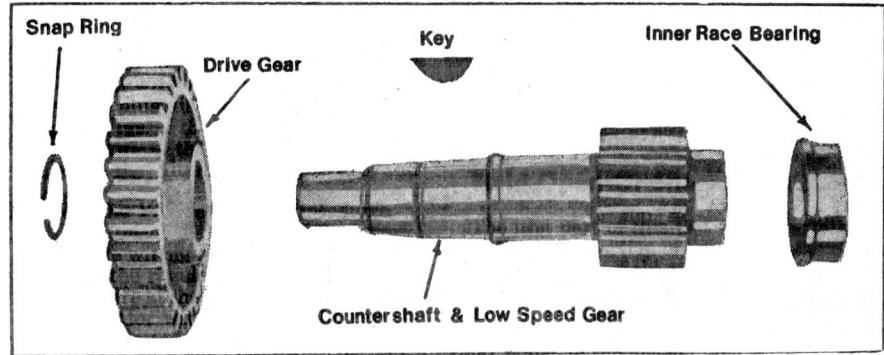

Fig. 28 Auxiliary section countershaft. RT610

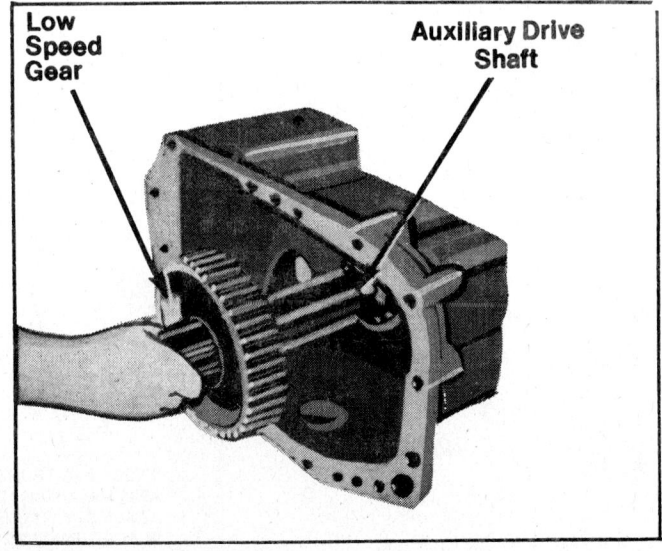

Fig. 30 Removing low speed gear and tailshaft. RT610

Fig. 31 Marking timing tooth on low speed gear for timing purposes. RT610

299

FULLER TRANSMISSIONS

cent gear teeth on low speed gear, then mark the two adjacent teeth which are directly opposite the first set marked. There should be the same number of teeth between the markings on each side of the gear.

3. Place splined spacer in hub of low speed gear with shoulder facing rearward, then install low speed gear and spacer over rear of shaft and against shoulder with clutching teeth to the front.
4. Install low speed gear washer on shaft and against gear with chamfer facing rearward.
5. Position tailshaft with forward end down and place auxiliary housing over rear of shaft so that shaft extends through rear bore.
6. Seat mainshaft rear bearing securely on shaft and in bore, then install O-ring into slot of small bore of range shift air cylinder.
7. Install cylinder in housing with small bore in cylinder aligned with air port in top of auxiliary section, then install dust cover and air port extension through housing and into bore of air cylinder.
8. Place shifting yoke on piston shaft with fork facing threaded end, then align slots in shaft with bores in yoke hub and install the two lock screws. Secure with safety wire.
9. Place yoke in slot of sliding clutch with threaded end of piston shaft towards the larger low range synchronizer, then place entire assembly into auxiliary housing and thread splined sliding clutch onto tailshaft and insert piston shaft into cylinder bore.
10. Install copper seal on threaded end of piston shaft and install O-ring on outside diameter of piston.
11. Install lock washer and nut on shaft to secure piston, then install gasket and cylinder cover and torque retaining bolts to 35–45 ft. lbs.
12. With larger low range synchronizer ring facing down with pins up, place sliding clutch with recessed side up on pins of low range synchronizer.
13. Install the three springs into bores in high range synchronizer ring as shown in Fig. 18.
14. Place high range synchronizer ring over pins of low speed synchronizer, seating springs against pins.
15. Apply pressure to high range synchro-

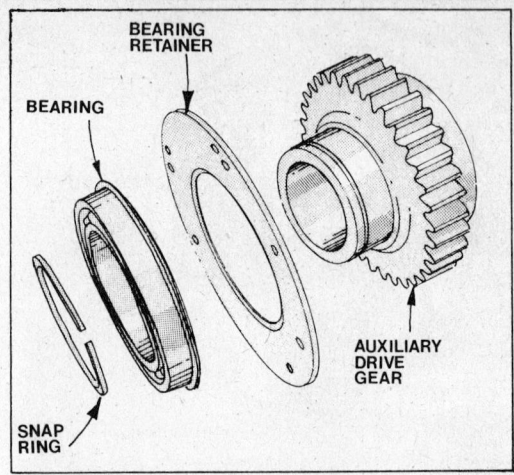

Fig. 32 Auxiliary gear assembly. 9513 & 12513 Series

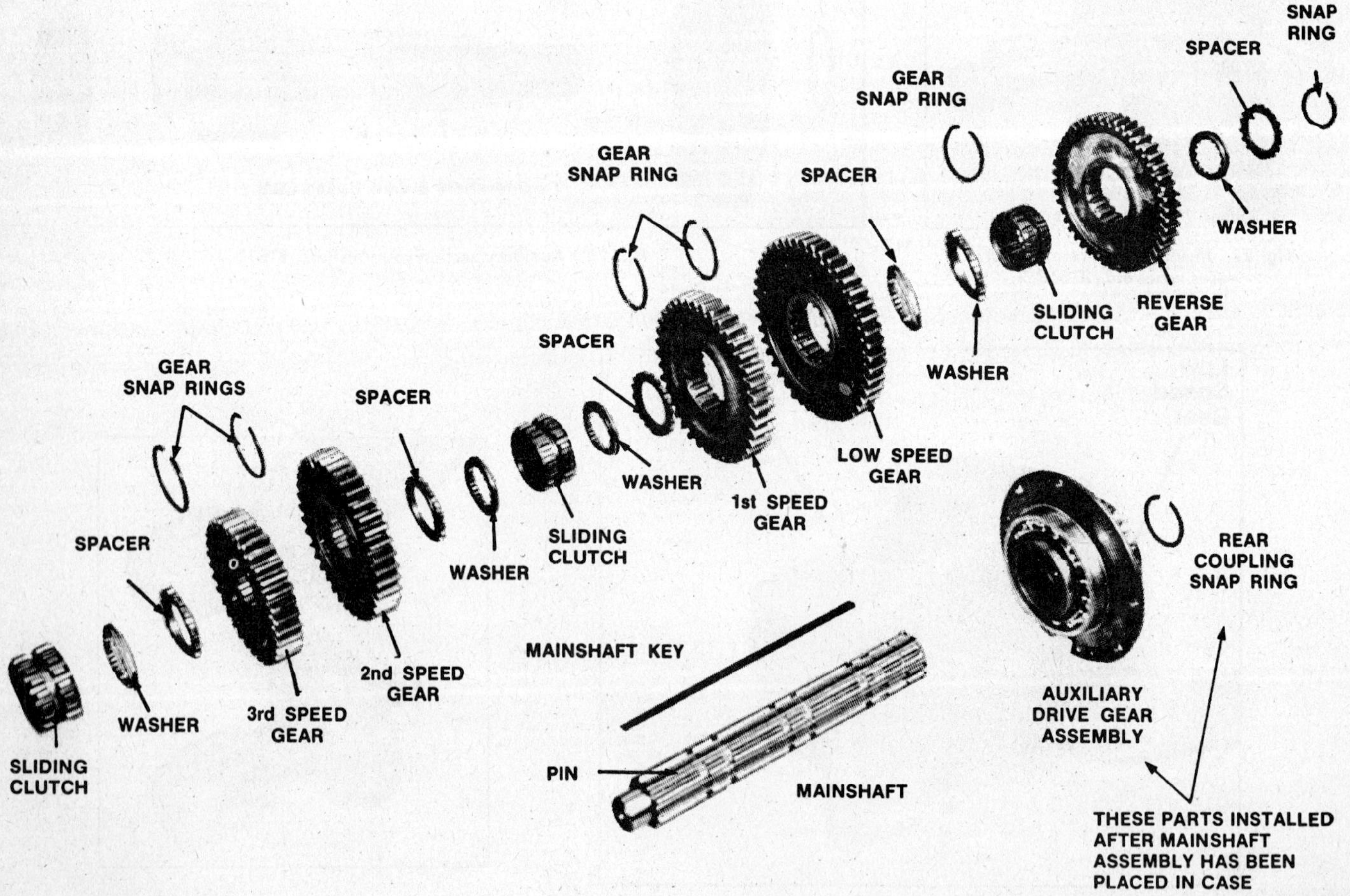

Fig. 33 Mainshaft assembly. 9513 & 12513 Series

FULLER TRANSMISSIONS

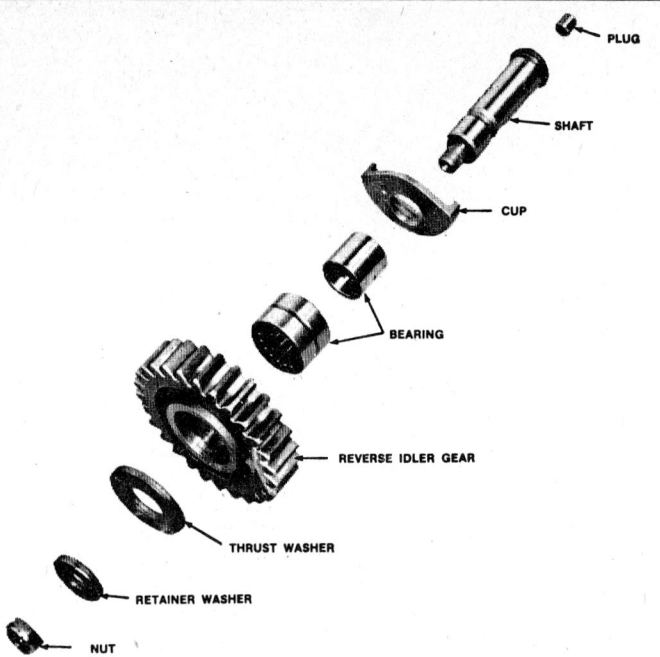

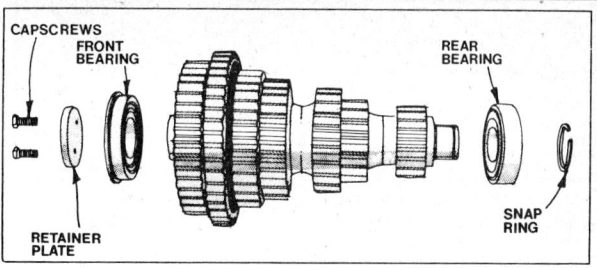

Fig. 35 Countershaft bearing assembly. 9513 & 12513 Series

Fig. 34 Reverse idler gear assembly. 9513 & 12513 Series

nizer ring to compress springs and seat pins of low range synchronizer fully into bores of high range synchronizer ring.
16. If removed, install keys into countershaft keyways, then press drive gear onto each countershaft with long hub facing rearward and install snap ring in front of each countershaft.
17. Install bearing inner race on rear of each countershaft.
18. For timing purposes, mark tooth on countershaft low speed gear that is aligned with the drive gear keyway and is stamped with an "O", Fig. 31.
19. Partially seat outer races of countershaft rear bearings and place countershafts into position in auxiliary housing, then as the countershafts are installed, mesh marked low speed gear tooth on each countershaft between each set of marked gear teeth of low speed gear.
20. With countershafts positioned, complete installation of countershaft rear bearings on shaft and into case bore.
21. Install speedometer gear rear washer on tailshaft and against bearing with chamfered inside diameter towards bearing and install speedometer gear or replacement spacer on shaft and against washer. If removed, install oil seal into rear bearing cover with lip of seal facing rearward.
22. Install rear bearing cover with speedometer bore up and to the left, then torque retaining bolts to 35-45 ft. lbs. and install front output shaft bearing.

Joining Main & Auxiliary Sections

1. Referring to Figs. 9, 27 & 28, install drive gear bearing cover and clutch housing, and torque stud nuts to 170-180 ft. lbs.
2. If equipped, install the clutch release mechanism.

NOTE: The two reverse gears and washers must be in perfect alignment with center of case bores as the front of the auxiliary countershafts must be inserted through these parts during auxiliary section installation. A heavy grease will help hold washers in place. Also check rear of front section to make certain that all snap rings have been installed.

3. Install auxiliary section of front section, aligning auxiliary section on dowel pins and the extended portion of auxiliary countershafts with reverse idler gears. The clutch shaft may be rotated to facilitate installation.

NOTE: The auxiliary section can also be installed with front section in a vertical position, by placing clutch housing on blocks and using a chain hoist to lower auxiliary section into position.

4. Install auxiliary section attaching screws, then lock transmission by engaging two gears with mainshaft sliding clutches.
5. Make certain that speedometer gear washer and speedometer gear or replacement spacer are installed on tailshaft, then install companion flange and torque retaining nut to 380-470 ft. lbs.
6. With shift bars and sliding clutches on mainshaft in neutral position, install shifting bar housing on transmission, fitting yokes into yoke slots of corresponding clutch gears. Torque attaching capscrews to 35-45 ft. lbs.
7. Making certain that shifting notches on bars in shifting bar housing are aligned in neutral position, install gear shift lever housing on shifting bar housing, fitting lower end of lever into notches in shifting block and yokes. Install all except rear left attaching screws and torque to 35-45 ft. lbs.
8. If removed, install fittings on air valve and install actuating pin and spring in transmission bore.
9. Make certain that alignment sleeve is installed in air valve.

NOTE: Before installing alignment sleeve, check bore in air valve to make sure the piston is either in a forward or rearward position. Piston can be moved with pencil or compressed air.

10. Install air valve on transmission and torque screws to 15-20 ft. lbs. Actuating plunger in case will fit into alignment sleeve in air valve.
11. Install fittings, air lines, regulator and

Fig. 36 Countershaft gears timing marks

FULLER TRANSMISSIONS

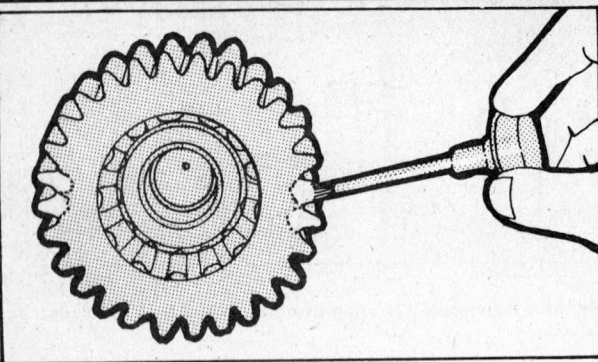

Fig. 37 Drive gear timing marks

Fig. 38 Left countershaft gear and dirve gear correctly meshed

filter assembly, gear shift lever housing, lever and control valve. Tighten all attaching nuts and bolts securely.

9513 & 12513 SERIES

Main Trans., Disassemble

1. Remove mainshaft rear coupling snap ring and bearing retainer screws. Remove bearing retainer using three puller screws, Fig. 11, then remove snap ring and press retainer ring and bearing from drive gear, Fig. 32.
2. Remove snap ring from reverse gear, Fig. 33. Move reverse gear into engagement with sliding clutch and remove auxiliary countershaft front bearings from left reverse idler gear bore using an inside jawed puller.
3. Remove nut, washer and plug from idler shaft, pull idler shaft from gear and idler boss, then remove reverse idler gear and thrust washer, Fig. 34.

NOTE: To remove mainshaft assembly, it is necessary to remove right countershaft bearings.

4. Remove snap ring from rear of right countershaft, Fig. 35, and use a soft bar from inside case to move the rear bearing to the rear and off the shaft.
5. Remove the front right bearing retainer plate, Fig. 35. Using a soft bar and mallet, drive the countershaft about a 1/2 inch to the rear then drive the countershaft as far forward as possible to expose the front bearing snap ring then remove the front bearing using a puller.
6. Place a rubber band around mainshaft to retain key and remove mainshaft.
7. Remove 3rd-4th speed sliding clutch, front coupling snap ring, mainshaft key, reverse gear spacer and washer from mainshaft, Fig. 33.
8. Remove reverse gear and 1st-reverse sliding clutch from mainshaft then remove remaining parts and align gear washers with splines. If necessary remove snap rings from gears.
9. Remove snap ring and retainer plate from left countershaft, then remove front and rear bearings in the same manner as they were removed from the right countershaft.
10. Remove drive gear front bearing cover then tap drive gear outward and remove snap ring, then remove drive gear from inside case.
11. Remove drive gear nut where peened into shaft and remove nut, Fig. 14.
12. Press shaft from drive gear and bearing. If necessary, remove snap ring from drive gear, Fig. 14. Inspect bushing in pocket of input shaft and replace if necessary.

NOTE: Countershaft assemblies are identical except for the number of teeth on PTO gears and are disassembled in the same manner.

13. Remove right and left countershaft assemblies from case, Fig. 13A.
14. Press the 4th, PTO, 3rd and second speed gears off the countershaft.

NOTE: This will require a press of at least a 25 ton capacity. Do not use PTO gear as a base for pressing as its large diameter makes it susceptible to damage.

15. Press 1st speed gear and remove the keys from the countershaft, Fig. 13A.
16. Remove right reverse idler gear bearing and assembly in the same manner as the left reverse idler gear assembly was removed, Fig. 34.

Front Section, Assemble

1. Install plug and cup on reverse idler shaft then install bearing inner race on shaft against cup, Fig. 34. Press needle bearing into reverse idler gear.
2. Place reverse idler gear and thrust washer into case and install shaft into

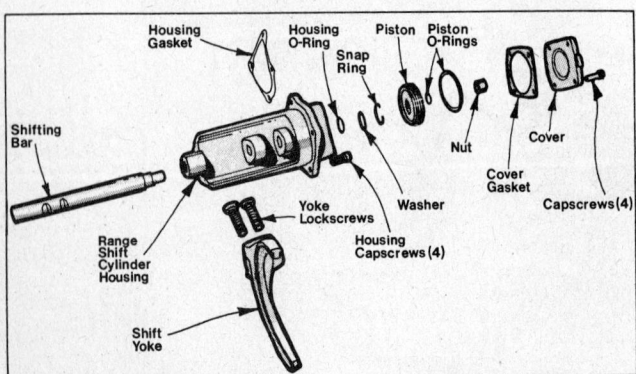

Fig. 39 Range shift cylinder assembly

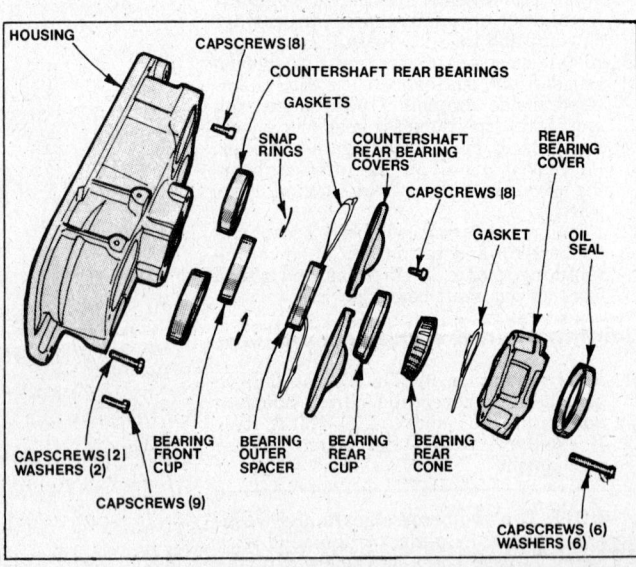

Fig. 40 Auxiliary section bearing assembly

FULLER TRANSMISSIONS

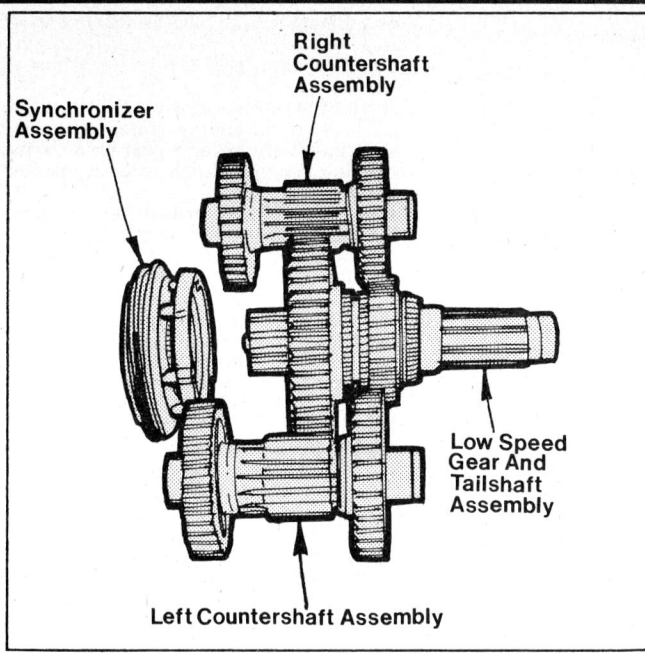

Fig. 41 Auxiliary section gear assembly

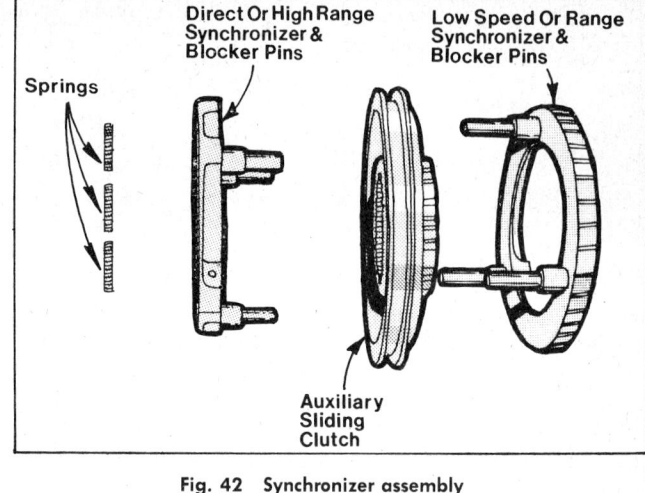

Fig. 42 Synchronizer assembly

bore.

NOTE: Make certain needle bearing in gear seats on inner race evenly before completing installation of shaft.

3. Install stop nut and retainer washer on shaft then install auxiliary countershaft front bearing outer race into reverse idler bore, Fig. 34.
4. Install pin and keys in countershaft then press first speed gear on countershaft with long hub of gear facing front of shaft, Fig. 13A.
5. Press second speed gear with long hub of gear facing rear of shaft followed by the third speed gear with long hub of gear facing front of shaft, Fig. 13A.
6. Press the PTO gear with tapered edge of teeth facing rear of shaft followed by the fourth speed gear with the long hub of gear facing rear of shaft, Fig. 13A.
7. Mark the timing tooth that is aligned with keyway on each countershaft and is stamped with an "O", Fig. 36.
8. Place the left countershaft assembly (47 tooth PTO gear) and the right countershaft assembly (45 tooth PTO gear) into the case. Do not install bearings.
9. Install snap ring into drive gear and install drive gear on input shaft with snap ring facing forward, Fig. 14.
10. Install spacer and press drive gear bearing onto shaft, Fig. 14.
11. Apply Loctite grade AVV to threads of gear nut then install nut and torque to 250–300 ft. lbs., Fig. 14.

NOTE: All threads must be dry and free of dirt and grease.

12. Peen nut into slots of shaft, then for timing purposes mark any two adjacent teeth on drive gear plus the two adjacent teeth directly opposite, Fig. 37.

NOTE: Check to make certain input shaft

bushing is in good condition. If replacement is necessary, press bushing flush into shaft. If the three oil holes are restricted by bushing, drill out with a 5/32 inch drill. Radial clearance between bushing and pilot should be .040–.045 inch.

13. Install input shaft from inside of case and install bearing snap ring.
14. Place blocking tool or wooden block in the case bore, to center rear of left countershaft then mesh marked tooth on left countershaft with marked teeth on drive gear, Fig. 38.
15. Install front countershaft bearing, remove blocking and install rear countershaft bearing.
16. Install front bearing retainer plate and safety wire and install snap ring in groove at rear of shaft.

Mainshaft, Assemble

1. Install snap ring in all mainshaft gears except the reverse speed gear and make sure that roll pin is in place in mainshaft near pilot end, Fig. 33.

NOTE: Axial end play is .005–.038 inch for the reverse speed gear and .005–.012 inch for the forward speed gears. Washers are used to obtain the correct limits and are available in six thicknesses as follows:

Axial Clearance (End Play) Washer Table

Part No.	Limits	Color
14274	.248–.250	White
14275	.253–.255	Green
14276	.258–.260	Orange
14277	.263–.265	Purple
14278	.268–.270	Yellow
14279	.273–.275	Black

Always use the low limit washer (14274) in the reverse, 1st and 3rd speed gear positions.

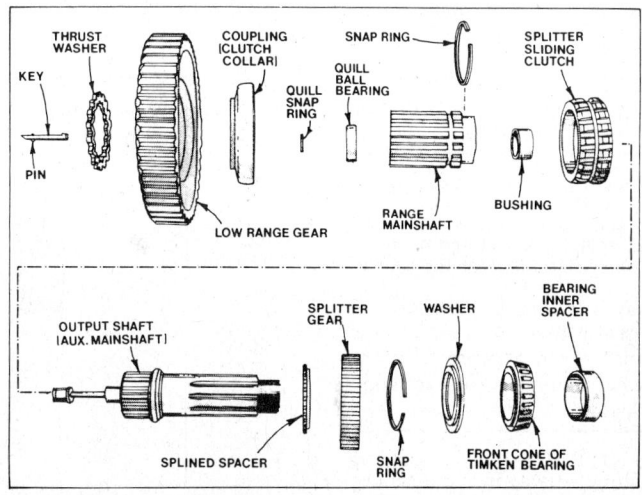

Fig. 43 Tailshaft and low range gear assembly

303

FULLER TRANSMISSIONS

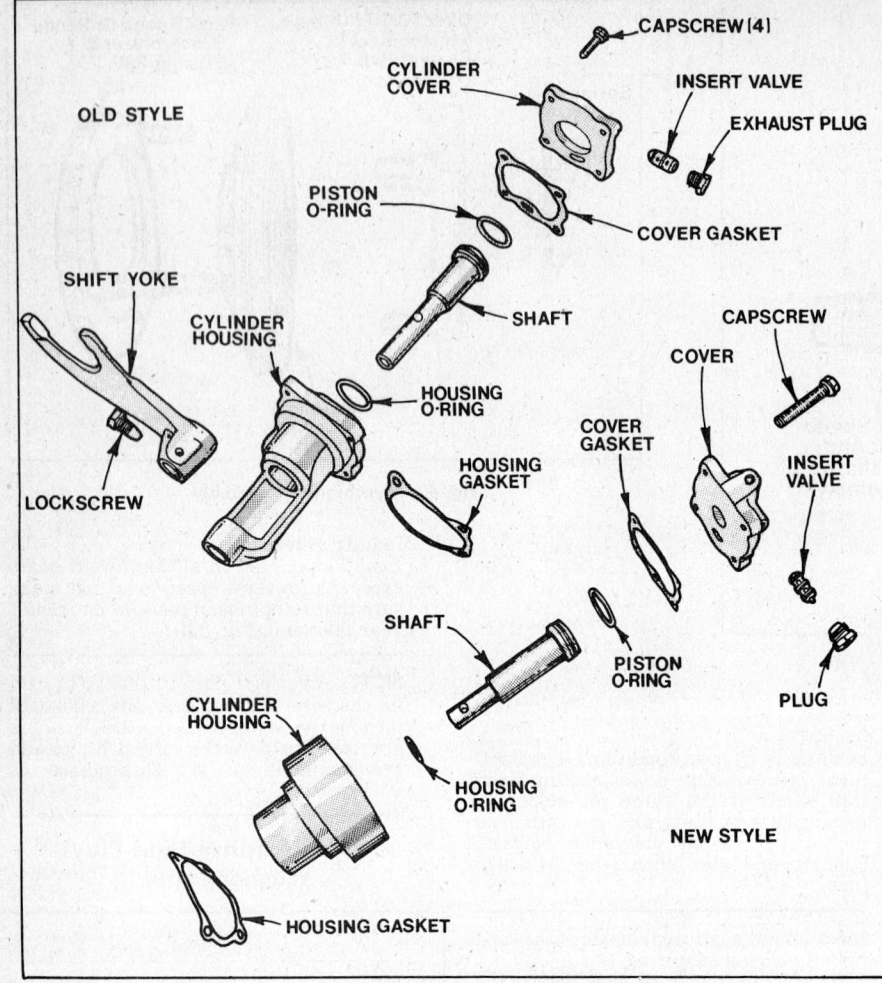

Fig. 44 Splitter shift cylinder assembly

For reference purposes, the gear washers are internally splined and the spacers are externally splined and there is one washer and one spacer for each gear.

2. With mainshaft in a vise, place 3rd speed gear washer (14274) over rear of shaft and down to lowest groove in shaft with flat side up, then turn washer to align internal splines with mainshaft splines and temporarily install key in spline to keep washer aligned.

NOTE: Do not use square cut spline inside washer for locking purposes.

3. Install 3rd speed gear spacer (flat side facing down) followed by 3rd speed gear (clutching teeth facing down).
4. Install 2nd speed gear (clutching teeth facing up) then install spacer into hub of gear.
5. Remove key and install washer, align with splines of mainshaft.

NOTE: Use correct limit washer to obtain specified end play.

6. Install key and the 1st-2nd speed sliding clutch, aligning keyway in sliding clutch with key.
7. Remove key and install 1st speed washer (14274) with flat side up then align splines and reinstall key.
8. Install the 1st speed gear spacer (flat side facing down), 1st speed gear (clutching teeth facing down) and low speed gear (clutching teeth facing up).
9. Install low speed gear spacer in hub of gear (flat side facing up) then remove key and install correct low speed gear washer with flat side facing down to obtain specified clearance, align splines and reinstall key.
10. Install low-reverse sliding clutch, aligning keyway in sliding clutch with key, then install the reverse gear onto sliding clutch, engaging clutch in both low and reverse gear.
11. Remove key and install reverse gear washer (14274) then align splines, reinstall key and install reverse spacer (flat side facing down).
12. Install snap ring in second groove from top with gap of snap ring placed at key location then temporarily place a rubber band on mainshaft to hold key in place.
13. Remove assembly from vise and install 3rd-4th speed sliding clutch.
14. Install assembly into case with rear of mainshaft through rear bearing bore and lower into position, then move mainshaft forward to seat pilot end of shaft in bushing of input shaft and remove rubber band.
15. To time and install the right countershaft assembly, mesh timing tooth on right countershaft with timing teeth of drive gear and mesh countershaft gears with mainshaft gears.
16. Using blocking tool, center rear of countershaft in bore and center rear of mainshaft in bore.

NOTE: Accurate centering of mainshaft is important.

17. Install front and rear countershaft bearings, then install front bearing retainer plate and safety wire. Install rear bearing snap ring.
18. Install plug, cup and bearing inner sleeve on reverse idler shaft then press bearing in bore of reverse idler gear, Fig. 34.
19. With thrust washer and reverse idler gear in position, insert shaft through gear and seat into bore making sure needle bearing is aligned with bearing sleeve then install washer and nut.
20. Seat outer race of auxiliary countershaft front bearing in reverse idler bore, then mesh mainshaft reverse gear with reverse idler gears and install snap ring into mainshaft reverse gear.
21. To reassemble and install auxiliary drive gear, place retainer on auxiliary drive gear, press on bearing and install snap ring in gear shoulder groove, Fig. 32.
22. Seat bearing in bore fitting drive gear

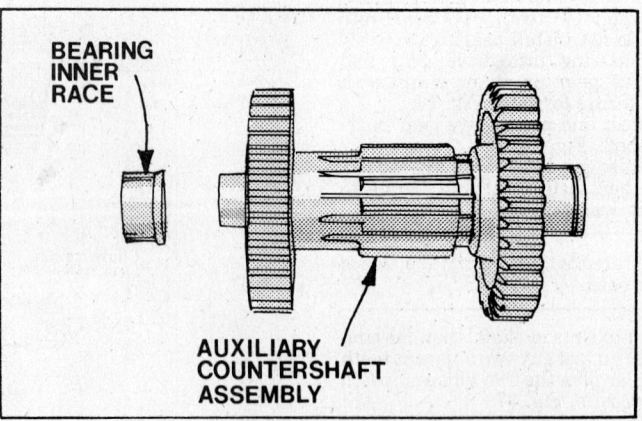

Fig. 45 Auxiliary countershaft assembly

FULLER TRANSMISSIONS

Fig. 46 "O" stamped tooth on overdrive gear marked for proper timing

Fig. 47 Left countershaft gear and splitter gear correctly meshed

with splines of mainshaft, install screws, safety wire, then install rear coupling snap ring.
23. Install front bearing cover and gasket then install clutch housing and torque the four bolts to 70–75 ft. lbs. and the six nuts to 170–185 ft. lbs.
24. Using a chain hoist attach the auxiliary section to the front section.
25. Install speedometer drive gear on flange and install flange on output shaft.

NOTE: If speedometer gear is not used, install a spacer of same width.

26. Lock transmission in two gears and tighten flange nut to 450–500 ft. lbs.

NOTE: Failure to torque and pull flange tightly into place will result in damage to the rear bearing.

Auxiliary Section
Disassemble
1. Remove shift cylinder cover and shift bar stop nut, Fig. 39 then apply a small amount of compressed air through the supply port to remove piston.
2. Remove cylinder retaining screws and remove shift yoke screws.

NOTE: The cylinder may be rotated to expose the screws, Fig. 39.

3. Remove the shift bar from the cylinder, then the cylinder from the housing and the shift yoke from the sliding clutch gear followed by the snap ring, washer and O-ring, Fig. 39.
4. Remove the two countershaft rear bearing covers and the two snaprings, Fig. 40.
5. Drive countershafts forward about 1/2 inch then rearward to expose snap rings and remove countershaft bearings, Fig. 40.
6. Separate front ends of countershafts and remove synchronizer assembly. Pull direct synchronizer from blocker pins of low speed synchronizer and remove sliding gear from low speed synchronizer, Figs. 41 and 42.

NOTE: Place a cloth over ring before removal as springs in direct ring will be released, Fig. 42.

7. Remove key from splines of range mainshaft, Fig. 43, then align splines of low speed gear washer with splines of shafts.
8. Remove the low speed gear, washer and clutching collar from shaft, Fig. 43 and then the right countershaft from housing.
9. Remove shift lock screw and splitter gear shift cylinder cover. If necessary remove insert valve cover and valve, Fig. 44.
10. Remove shift shaft, shift yoke, cylinder housing, Fig. 44 and left countershaft assembly, Fig. 47.
11. Drive output shaft assembly out of rear bearing and remove bearing inner spacer from shaft.
12. Press output shaft from splitter gear and bearing front cone and remove snap ring from output shaft quill, Fig. 43.
13. Pull range mainshaft from quill using the sliding clutch as a puller base and remove ball bearing, bushing and snap ring from mainshaft, Fig. 43.
14. Remove rear bearing cover, oil seal, bearing rear cone, cups and outer spacer from housing.
15. Pull bearing inner race from the front of each countershaft, Fig. 45.

NOTE: It may be necessary to start inner race with a pry bar between shoulder of shaft and bearing race.

NOTE: The auxiliary countershaft, drive gear and overdrive gear are one piece and cannot be disassembled.

Reassembly
1. For timing purposes, mark the tooth on each overdrive gear which is stamped with an "O", Fig. 46.
2. Heat countershaft bearing inner race and install it on shaft, seated against shaft shoulder, Fig. 45.
3. Place splitter gear sliding clutch on output shaft with internal splines toward threaded end, Fig. 43.
4. Press range mainshaft bushing into bore so that it is about 1/16 inch below face of shaft, Fig. 36, and install snap ring in splines of range mainshaft, Fig. 43.
5. Install range mainshaft on quill of output shaft, Fig. 43.

NOTE: Radial clearance between quill and bushing is .025–.030 inch.

6. Install quill ball bearing and snap ring into output shaft quill, Fig. 43.

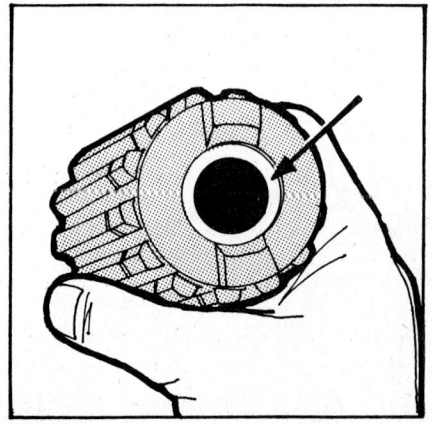

Fig. 48 Bushing pressed in about 1/16 inch below face of mainshaft

Fig. 49 Splitter gear timing marks

FULLER TRANSMISSIONS

Fig. 50 Right countershaft gear and splitter gear correctly meshed

7. Install snap ring into splitter gear, Fig. 43. For timing purposes mark any two adjacent teeth on the splitter gear, then mark the two adjacent teeth directly opposite, Fig. 49.
8. Place output shaft assembly in a vise with threaded end facing up. Install splined washer with shoulder facing up, splitter gear with clutching teeth facing down and rear washer with flat side facing up, Fig. 43.
9. Heat front cone of Timken bearing and install on shaft against washer, followed by the inner spacer, Fig. 43.

CAUTION: Do not heat bearing over 275° F.

10. Start front cup of bearing (taper facing inside) into rear bore of housing, place outer spacer on front cup and place rear cup onto spacer, then tap lightly and evenly to seat it in the bore, Fig. 40.
11. Place auxiliary housing over output shaft, seating front cup on front cone of bearing then heat rear cone of bearing and install on shaft and into rear cup, Fig. 40.
12. Install oil seal flush into rear bearing cover, Fig. 40, then install cover onto case making sure that output shaft is rearward as far as possible.

NOTE: Use star washer at speed bore location to prevent oil leakage.

13. Position left countershaft in place, meshing marked tooth on countershaft gear between marked teeth on splitter gear, Fig. 47.
14. Install O-ring in splitter cylinder bore then install yoke onto slot of sliding clutch gear. Insert splitter cylinder into housing and place hub of yoke into cylinder, Fig. 44.
15. Install O-ring on piston and shift shaft into cylinder through yoke hub. Install lockscrew and secure with safety wire, Fig. 44.
16. Install splitter insert valve and exhaust screw into cover, Fig. 44, then install cover with exhaust screw facing down and supply port to the right.
17. Position right countershaft in place, meshing marked tooth on countershaft gear between marked teeth on splitter gear, Fig. 50, then install clutching collar on range mainshaft against snap ring with clutching teeth facing the rear, Fig. 43.
18. Install low range gear on mainshaft against clutching collar, Fig. 43 and install splines into hub or low range gear aligning washer splines with shaft splines. Lock low range gear in place by inserting key between splines of shaft and washer, Fig. 51.
19. Place sliding clutch gear on pins of low speed synchronizer and install the three springs in direct synchronizer, Figs. 18 and 42.
20. Place direct synchronizer over pins of low speed blocker pins and compress springs to fully seat direct synchronizer on pins of low speed synchronizer, then install the synchronizer assembly on output shaft.

NOTE: Make certain that marked timing teeth on countershaft gears are aligned with the marked timing teeth on splitter gear.

21. Block against housing or mount housing in a vise and install rear bearings on countershafts and into case bores making certain that bearings are fully against shoulders so that snap ring groove is fully exposed.
22. Install snap ring on each countershaft and install bearing covers, Fig. 40.
23. Install O-ring, washer and snap ring in bore of shift cylinder, Fig. 39.
24. Install the range shift yoke into slot of sliding clutch then install shift cylinder into housing and place hub of shift yoke in place in cylinder.

NOTE: With newer type range cylinders, make certain that long hub of shift yoke is facing the rear plate.

25. Install the shift bar and the two yoke lockscrews, Fig. 39, and safety wire, then install cylinder housing screws with air port facing up.
26. Install O-rings on piston and install piston in cylinder with flat side out, then install nut on shifting bar and cover onto shift cylinder with air port towards upper left side.

Gearshift Housing, Fig. 52

Disassembly
1. After removing springs from housing, remove housing from transmission, invert housing and remove steel balls.
2. Place housing in vise, remove yoke lockscrews, 3rd-4th speed shift bar, 1st-2nd speed shift bar and interlock pin.
3. Remove actuating plunger, low-reverse speed shift bar and interlock balls.

Assembly
1. Install low-reverse shifting bar and yoke then torque lockscrew to 45-55 ft. lbs. and safety wire.
2. Install the actuating plunger and the 3/4 inch interlock ball in the rear boss.
3. Install 1st-2nd speed shifting bar, yoke and block, inserting interlock pin in bore of neutral notch of bar then install lockscrews and safety wire. On "F" models, use short lockscrew in shift block.

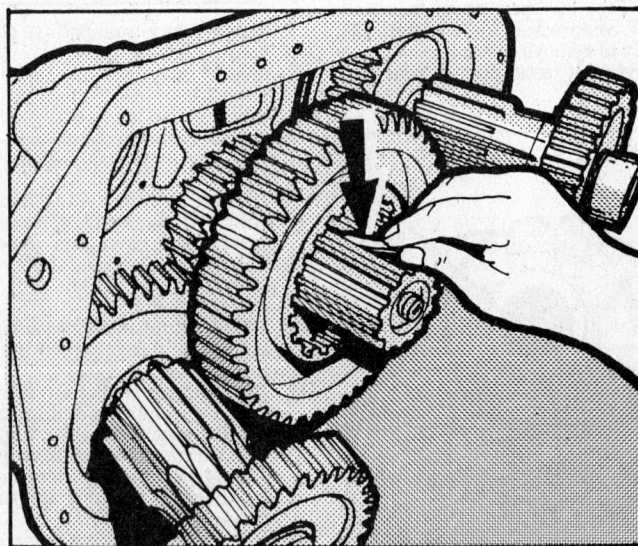

Fig. 51 Low range gear locked in place with key inserted between splines of shaft and washer

FULLER TRANSMISSIONS

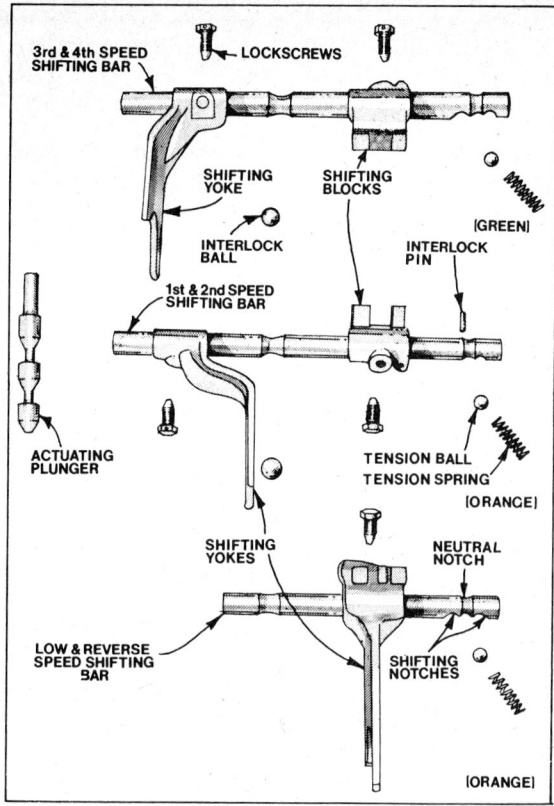

Fig. 52 Shifting bar assembly

Air Leaks
1. With gear shift lever in neutral, coat all air lines and fittings with soapy water and check for leaks, moving control button to both positions.
2. If there is a steady leak out control valve exhaust or bottom port, an O-ring is defective in the control valve.
3. If there is a steady leak out breather on air valve, an O-ring is defective in the air valve. This may also indicate a leak in the shift cylinder.

Air Regulator
1. With gear shift lever in neutral, check exhaust port on bottom of air regulator. If there is a steady leak it indicates a ruptured diaphragm, or dirt and rust have clogged the regulator piston in the input port of the seal. Inspect and replace diaphragm if necessary. Clean regulator.
2. Cut off air pressure and install an air gauge in air line at output port of regulator. Bring vehicle air pressure to normal, which should be a steady pressure of 58 to 62 psi. Move range control button up and down; the pressure should drop during each shift and then return quickly to the original reading. If gauge readings do not conform to the above, proceed as follows:
3. If gauge shows full line pressure the diaphragm is ruptured and should be replaced.
4. A pulsating gauge indicates loose lock ring which attaches two sections of regulator.
5. Regulated pressure can be changed by the addition or removal of shims. Add shims to raise air pressure; remove shims to lower the pressure. One shim is equal to

4. Install the next 3/4 inch interlock ball.
5. Install 3rd-4th speed shifting bar, yoke, block and lockscrews and safety wire.
6. Install the three tension balls in bores in proper bar locations.
7. Install shifting bar housing on transmission and fit yoke forks into sliding clutch gears and install screws.
8. Install tension springs in bores at bar locations.

NOTE: Install green spring in 3rd-4th speed bar location.

RANGE SHIFT AIR SYSTEM

System Check-Out

The following checks are to be made with normal vehicle air pressure of approximately 60 psi but with the engine off. Refer to Fig. 53, for check points.

Incorrect Hook-Up
1. With gear shift lever in neutral, move control button up and down.
2. If lines are crossed between control valve and air valve the control button will not stay in an up position and transmission will not stay in high range.
3. If lines are crossed between air valve and shift cylinder, transmission range gearing will not correspond with button position. This will have to be tested by starting vehicle and, with control button down, engaging low speed gear.

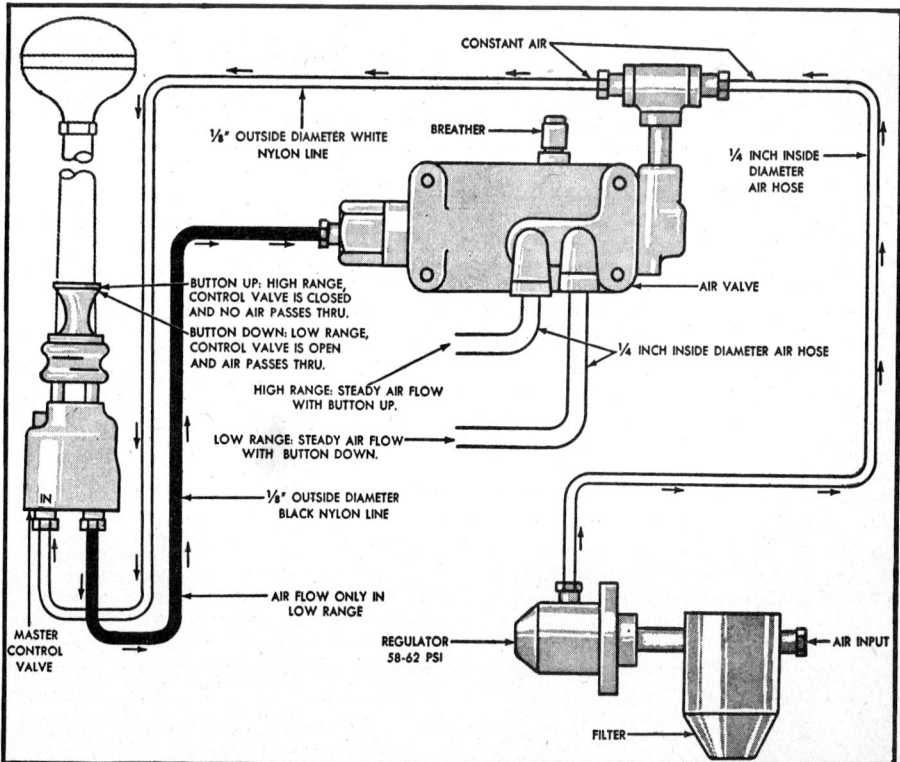

Fig. 53 Transmission air system. RT-910. On RT-915 models the hole gear is engaged by air for deeper reduction

FULLER TRANSMISSIONS

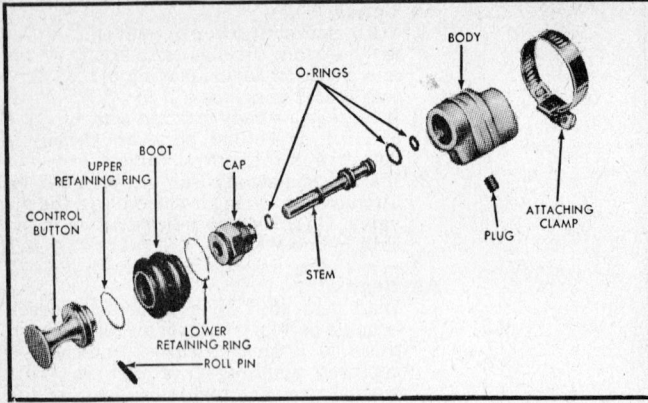

Fig. 54 Range shift control valve disassembled

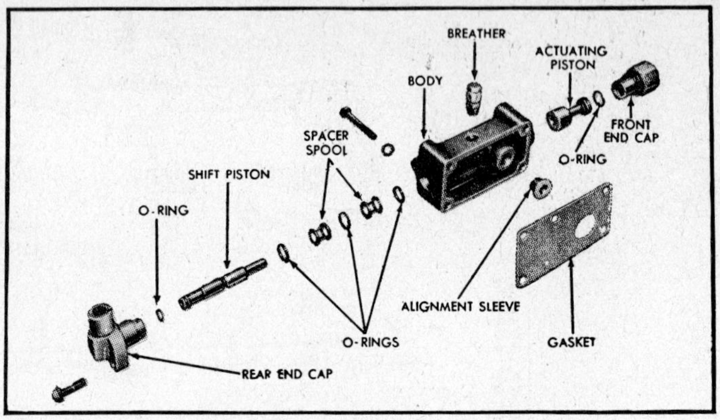

Fig. 55 Air valve disassembled

approximately 2 psi pressure change.
6. Only as a last resort should an adjustment be made with the screw in end cap of regulator. This adjustment has been set for correct operating limits. Any deviation from these limits will in most cases be caused by dirt or worn parts. Adjustment of screw will give only a temporary remedy. Turning screw clockwise raises air pressure; turning screw out lowers air pressure.

Control Valve
1. With gear shift lever in neutral, pull control button up to high range and disconnect 1/8" black nylon air line at air valve.
2. When control button is pushed down, a steady blast of air should flow from the disconnected line. Air will shut off when button is pulled up. This indicates that control valve is operating correctly. Reconnect air line if control valve does not operate correctly, check for leaks, restrictions and defective O-rings.

High Range Check
1. With gear shift lever in neutral, push control button down and disconnect high range air line from shift cylinder cover.
2. Pull control button up. There should be a steady flow of air from high range air line. Push button down to shut off air. If air escapes from high range port in cover with button down, this indicates a defective O-ring on piston in shift cylinder.
3. Make sure vehicle engine is shut off and move gear shift lever to a gear position. Pull control button up; there should be no air at the high range line. Move shift lever to neutral; there should now be a steady flow of air from high range line. Push button down to shut off air and reconnect line.
4. If air system operated incorrectly, it indicates that air valve is defective or that actuating parts in shifting bar housing are jammed or defective.

Low Range Check
1. With gear shift lever in neutral, pull control button up and disconnect low range air line at shift cylinder.
2. Repeat procedure under "High Range Check", reversing the position of control button in order to check low range operation.

Range Shift Cylinder
1. If any of the seals in the range shift cylinder are defective the range shift will be affected. The degree of lost air, or course, will govern the degree of failure, from slow shift to complete failure to shift.
2. Failure to shift into either low or high range indicates a steady leak out breather in air valve in both ranges.
3. Failure to shift into low range is due to pressurizing of transmission. Make sure cylinder bore is clean to prevent damage to piston seal. Use only a very light amount of shellac or Permatex on cover gasket to prevent clogging cylinder. Tighten capscrews securely.

Hole-Gear Air System 915 Units
Air Input Check
1. With gear shift lever in neutral and normal vehicle air pressure, loosen connection at air input (end port) of deep reduction valve (in cab) until it can be determined that there is a constant flow of air at this point. Reconnect line.
2. If there is no air at this point, there is a restriction in the line between deep reduction valve and air valve. Also check to make sure this line is connected to constant supply.

Deep Reduction Valve (In Cab)
1. With deep reduction valve lever to "IN", remove line from deep reduction valve at port in hole-gear shift cylinder; there should be no air at this point.
2. Move deep reduction valve lever to "OUT". There should now be a constant air flow from the line. Move lever to "IN" to shut off air. If the above conditions do not exist, deep reduction valve is faulty or there is a restriction in air line.

Hole-Gear Shift Cylinder
If any of the seals in the hole-gear shift cylinder are defective, the hole-gear shift will be affected. The degree of lost air, of course, will govern the degree of failure, from slow shift to complete failure to shift.

AIR SYSTEM SERVICE
Shift Control Valve, Fig. 54
1. Disconnect two nylon air lines at air valve on transmission. If desired, gear shift lever housing can now be removed from transmission without disconnecting remainder of control valve air lines and without removing control valve from shift lever.
2. Disconnect two nylon air lines at control valve on shift lever.
3. Remove ball grip from shift lever.
4. Loosen mounting clamp and remove control valve and clamp from shift lever.
5. Remove nylon air lines, sheathing and O-ring clamp from shift lever.

Air Regulator & Filter
1. Disconnect and remove air line between air valve and air regulator, including hose clamp.
2. On RT-915 models, remove air line between air regulator and hole gear shift cylinder.
3. Turn out capscrews and remove air regulator and filter assembly from transmission or from vehicle frame if so mounted.
4. Turn large hex nut from threads of air regulator.
5. Turn air regulator from nipple.
6. Remove bracket and nipple from air filter.

Air Valve, Fig. 55
1. Disconnect air lines between air valve and shift cylinder in rear plate of transmission.
2. If necessary, remove fittings from shift cylinder.
3. Turn out four capscrews and remove air valve from adapter plate.
4. Remove alignment sleeve from air valve or from bore in adapter plate.
5. Remove spring and actuator pin from bore in adapter plate.
6. Turn out capscrews and two Allen head screws and remove adapter plate.
7. If necessary, remove fittings from air valve.

FULLER TRANSMISSIONS

Fuller Roadranger R-46 Eight-Speed Transmission

DESCRIPTION

The Fuller R-46 Roadranger 8-speed transmission, Fig. 1, combines a four-speed front (or main) section with a two-speed auxiliary (or rear) section to provide a total of eight forward and two reverse speeds.

The transmission should always be filled through the auxiliary filler plug opening. Openings between the front and rear sections allow the lubricant to seek its proper level in both cases. Fill to the level of the filler opening in the auxiliary case. Overfilling will slow the action of the auxiliary synchronizing clutches, and the extra drag caused may result in damage to the synchronizer discs.

The power flow of the transmission is controlled by manipulation of the gearshift lever and the air-powered range shift control, Fig. 2. The air-powered range shift control system consists of a master valve mounted on the gearshift lever and a slave valve mounted on the shift bar housing on the transmission that are connected by nylon air hose. The air system provides for smooth operation. Each gear shift should be double-clutched.

TROUBLE SHOOTING

NOTE: Before removing the transmission from the truck for inspection, always check for possible trouble in the clutch, drive shaft, universal joints or rear axle.

Noisy Transmission

Excessive noise may be caused by misalignment due to loose mounting bolts, paint on the clutch housing or transmission faces, flywheel housing misalignment, loose parts, dirt or metal chips in the lubricant, or insufficient lubricant.

Transmission noise may also be caused by worn or damaged parts, which requires the removal of the transmission to replace worn parts.

Transmission Shifts Hard

Check the clutch pedal free travel adjustment and clutch parts. Inspect the transmission linkage for binding caused by bent or worn parts. Hard shifting may also be caused by improper lubricant in the transmission.

Transmission Jumps Out of Gear

Improper shifting may cause the transmission to jump out of gear. Be sure the gears are completely engaged before releasing the clutch pedal.

Check the transmission linkage adjustment and make necessary corrections. Check for excessive end play caused by wear in the shift forks, sliding gear fork grooves, thrust washers, output shaft or countershaft bearings, or clutch pilot bearing or bushing.

Inspect the detent springs in the gear shift housing and replace any that are broken or damaged. Check clutch housing alignment with the engine.

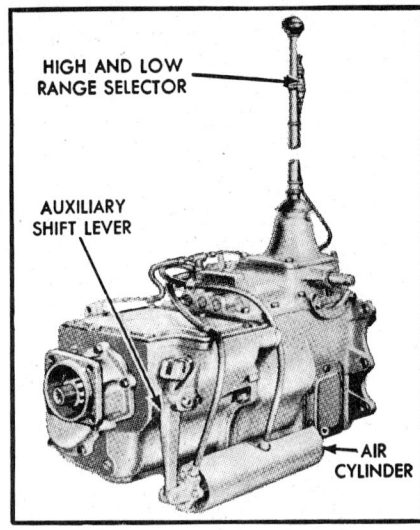

Fig. 1 Roadranger R-46 transmission

Oil Leakage

Oil leaks may be caused by overfilling the transmission or by using a lubricant that expands and foams while the truck is in operation.

Loose gear shift housing cover screws may allow the lubricant to escape between the housing and transmission case. Check the condition of the bearing retainers and gaskets. See that the transmission vent is open.

Bind in Air Cylinder or Connecting Linkage

With the auxiliary section in high range, relieve the pressure in the air system and disconnect the piston rod of the air cylinder. Slowly move the piston several times through

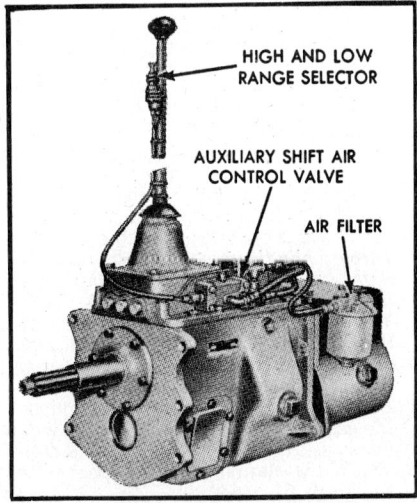

Fig. 2 Roadranger R-46 transmission

the complete stroke cycle. If either bind or drag is evident, disassemble the cylinder to find the cause. When connecting the piston, check the entire linkage for bind resulting from misalignment.

Leak in Air Lines

Raise the air pressure in the lines to normal and coat all connections in the system with soapy water to locate leaks. Disassemble the leaky connections, coat them with sealing compound and reassemble. Replace worn, leaky air hose, and repair or replace connectors, lines and hoses which continue to leak.

Leak in Air Cylinder

With the air system at normal line pressure and shift lever in neutral, disconnect the hose at the air cylinder which is not under pressure. Check the open port in the cylinder for a leak past the piston leathers. If no leak is found, connect the hose.

Move the shift lever to neutral and move the range selector handle to its opposite position. At the air cylinder, disconnect the air hose which is *not* now under pressure. Check the open port for a leak past the piston leathers; if no leak is found, connect the hose.

Check for a leak at the seal in the cylinder cap where the piston rod enters the cylinder.

If the above procedures disclose a leak, disassemble the cylinder and check the leathers, barrel, seal and piston rod. Replace any defective parts.

Defective Air Valve

Disconnect air hoses at the cylinder and cap each hose securely. After raising the air pressure to normal, move the shift lever to neutral and raise and lower the range selector handle. With each movement of the handle a short, fast blast of air should be heard at the breather valve. If the air exhaust is not as described, the valve is defective and the "O" rings should be replaced.

With the gear shift lever in neutral and selector handle in low-range position, check the breather valve for an escape of air past the pressure (outside) "O" ring. Move the selector handle to the opposite position and recheck the breather valve for a leak past the pressure "O" ring.

With the engine not running and with normal line pressure, move the shift lever in a geared position and then move the range selector handle to its opposite position. With movement of the selector handle a short, fast blast of air should be heard at the breather valve. After the initial exhaust, check the breather valve for continued escape of air past the pre-exhaust (inside) "O" ring.

Move the shaft lever to neutral to allow the air valve to complete the shift. Again move the shift lever to a geared position and move the selector handle to its opposite position. After the initial exhaust, check the breather valve for continued escape of air past the pre-exhaust "O" ring.

If a leak is found at the breather valve after either a complete range shift or pre-exhaust of the air valve, replace both "O" rings.

FULLER TRANSMISSIONS

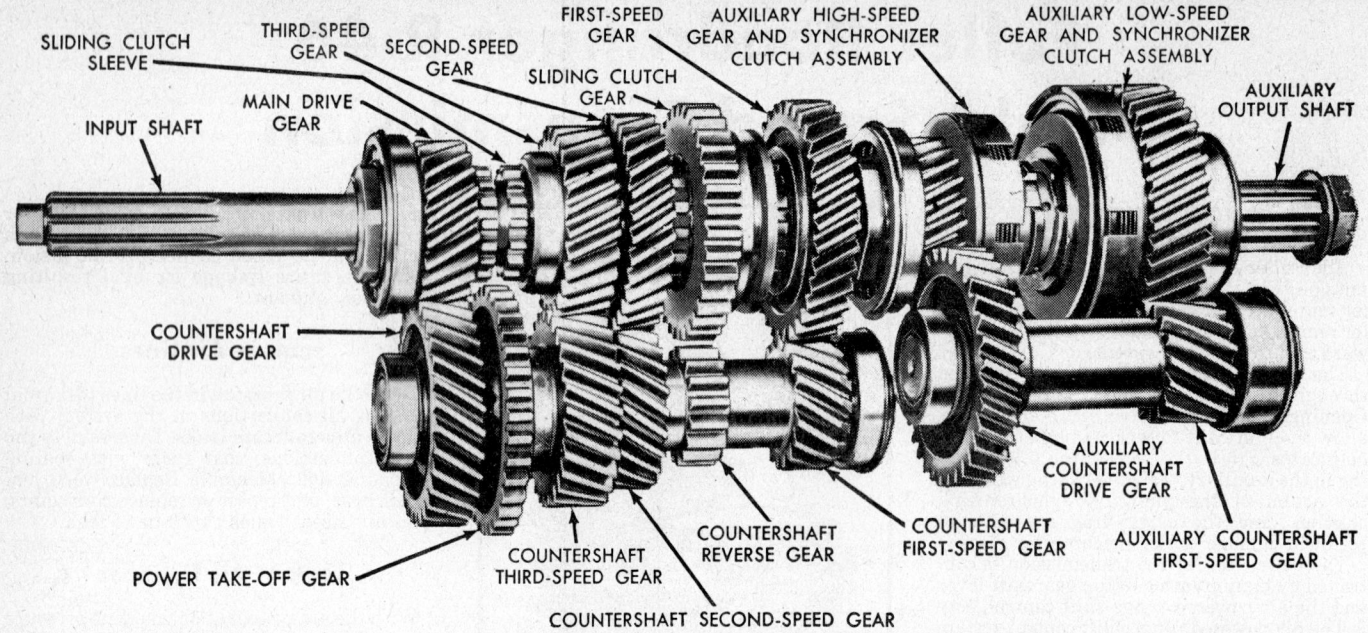

Fig. 3 Roadranger R-46 eight speed transmission

Block in Air System

Raise the air pressure to normal and move the shift lever to neutral. At the air cylinder, disconnect the hose which is not under pressure and move the range selector handle to its opposite position. If no air block exists, a loud, continuous air blast will escape from the disconnected hose. Move the range selector handle to its opposite position and reconnect the loose hose to the cylinder.

Move the range selector handle to its opposite position and proceed as above with the other hose. If this check reveals an air block, it can be located by inspection of the air valve and/or by inspection of the air lines.

TRANSMISSION REMOVAL

The procedure for removing the transmission varies somewhat depending upon the truck in which it is used. In general, however, it is accomplished as follows:
1. Bleed air reservoirs.
2. Drain transmission.
3. Disconnect drive shaft.
4. Set parking brake and remove companion flange nut.
5. Remove parking brake assembly.
6. Disconnect speedometer cable at transmission.
7. Remove parking brake lever.
8. Move selector control cable to high range position and remove cable retaining clamps.
9. Disconnect cable at connector joint and remove cable and cable tube.
10. Remove gear shift lever housing.
11. Disconnect air line from air filter.
12. Disconnnect air lines from air cylinder and remove cylinder from transmission.
13. Remove four lower transmission mounting bolts and install guide studs in the two lower holes.
14. Raise front axle on blocks and position jack under transmission.
15. Install safety chain.
16. Remove transmission support.
17. Remove two upper attaching bolts and remove transmission from truck.

TRANSMISSION INSTALL

Installation of the transmission is the reverse of the removal procedure. However, observe the following:
1. Torque the transmission-to-clutch housing bolts to 120–130 ft. lbs.
2. Torque the brake shoe support bolts to 180–220 ft. lbs.
3. Torque the companion flange nut to 275–350 ft. lbs.
4. Torque the gearshift housing attaching bolts to 35–40 ft. lbs.
5. During installation of the selector cable, eliminate unnecessary bends, and do not bend the cable on a radius of less than 4 inches.
6. On tilt-cab models, route the connector end of the cable along the frame before attempting to adjust the cable. Position the frame clamps on the cable but do not attach the clamps to the frame.
7. Push the selector handle all the way down to the cable ring and shift the air valve into high range position.
8. Partially fill the cable tube with Lubriplate and slide it over the end of the long cable.
9. Attach the connector ends of the two cables and move the cable rearward into its bore in the valve housing.
10. Push the cable casing into the connector tube until it contacts the cable joint. *The selector handle must be held up in the high range position during this operation.*
11. With the cable casing in position against the joint, install the cable clamp and spacer on the adapter. *Tighten the bolts finger-tight.*
12. Position the control cable and clamps on the gear shift lever and tighten the clamp bolts securely. On tilt-cab models do not attach the clamps to the frame at this time.
13. Loosen bolts that attach cable clamp and spacer to adapter.
14. Push selector handle down until there is 1/8″ clearance between bottom of selector handle and cable ring, Fig. 5. *This clearance should not exceed 1/8″.*
15. Tighten cable clamp bolts to adapter 10–15 ft. lbs., being careful not to pinch cable casing.
16. Check operation of control cable, making certain that air valve shifts freely into both high and low range positions.
17. On tilt-cab models, install frame clamps.
18. Install transmission cover plate and close air reservoir valves.
19. Fill transmission with lubricant, start engine and check for air leaks.

AIR VALVE SERVICE

Removal

1. Remove floor mat and plate.
2. Move selector control cable to high range position and remove cable clamp and spacer from adapter.
3. Disconnect long and short shift cables at connector joint, Fig. 6.
4. Disconnect 3 hoses at air valve and remove valve housing mounting bolts.
5. Remove air valve and plate, Fig. 7.
6. Remove Allen screw which holds adapter to gearshift housing and remove adapter.
7. Remove lockout spring and pin from bore in gearshift housing.

Disassembly

1. Remove 3 air line fittings from valve housing.
2. Remove breather valve, Fig. 8.
3. Remove Allen head pipe plug from center opening in side of valve housing.
4. Remove short control cable only for replacement. Remove Allen set screw from end of lower swivel and pull cable from swivel through opening in front end of valve housing, Fig. 8.
5. Remove upper and lower swivels and

FULLER TRANSMISSIONS

spring by prying outward at lower swivel. Spring tension will free both swivels as lower swivel clears side of housing.
6. Lift out slide bar, spacer and shift fork.
7. Remove welch plug from front end of housing by carefully forcing plug outward with small punch. *Inserts in housing must not be moved or damaged as plug is removed.*
8. Remove valve through welch plug opening by pushing with small screwdriver at shift fork slot.
9. Remove "O" rings from valve.

Inspection

1. Clean and inspect all parts, replacing as necessary.
2. Check tension of actuator and swivel springs, and examine the upper and lower swivels for wear or damage.
3. Check the slide bar, spacer and shift fork for wear or rust, and replace the 4 "O" rings if one or more show wear or damage.
4. Coat the slide bar, spacer, shift fork, lower swivel and contact points with Automatic Transmission Fluid.

Assemble

1. Install "O" rings on valve.
2. Position valve in housing with shift fork slot toward front of housing, and install welch plug.
3. Position slide bar, spacer and shift fork in housing. *Shift fork must engage groove in valve and spacer must be positioned between slide bar and shift fork, Fig. 8.*
4. It short cable was removed from lower swivel, pass new cable completely through swivel. Stake cable securely through set screw hole in swivel. Install set screw.
5. Push connector end of cable through its opening in front of valve housing.
6. Position upper swivel and spring guide and bracket in ends of spring, and position lower swivel in yoke of spring guide.
7. Compress spring until upper swivel enters its depression in slide bar and lower swivel rides on lower track in housing.
8. To provide maximum projection of cable, move slide bar to rear of housing.
9. Install Allen head pipe plug in center opening in side of housing.
10. Install breather valve and 3 air hose fittings.

Installation

1. Install lockout spring and pin in gearshift housing bore.
2. Position adapter and install retaining screw.
3. Position valve plate and air valve, install 4 mounting bolts and connect 3 hoses. Torque bolts to 10–15 ft. lbs.
4. Connect long and short shift cables and pull cable tube toward rear until it bottoms in valve housing.
5. Install cable retaining clamp and spacer on adapter and adjust cable as outlined under *Transmission, Install.*

AUXILIARY SECTION SERVICE

Separation of Main and Auxiliary Transmissions

1. Disconnect 3 air hoses at air control valve and remove the 2 valves-to-cylinder hoses from transmission.
2. Remove air filter and air hose.
3. Remove air valve and plate from air valve adapter. *Do not lose small horseshoe spacer in air valve.*
4. With assembly shifted into neutral, remove main transmission gear shift housing assembly and auxiliary cover.
5. Remove auxiliary rear bearing cover and speedometer drive gear.
6. With a small punch, relieve the auxiliary countershaft rear bearing nut where it is staked to shaft. Shift main transmission into two gears and remove countershaft rear bearing nut. *This nut has a right-hand thread.*
7. Shift main transmission into neutral and auxiliary unit into low range. Remove lock wire from groove at front end of auxiliary high speed synchronizer clutch housing. Remove 3 set screws (in lock wire groove) which secure high speed synchronizer clutch housing to auxiliary drive gear, Fig. 9. Move clutch housing to rear against auxiliary shifting yoke.
8. Remove upper front nuts from two studs inside auxiliary case.
9. Remove 6 nuts retaining auxiliary case to main case.
10. Remove auxiliary case from main case by tapping with a soft mallet.

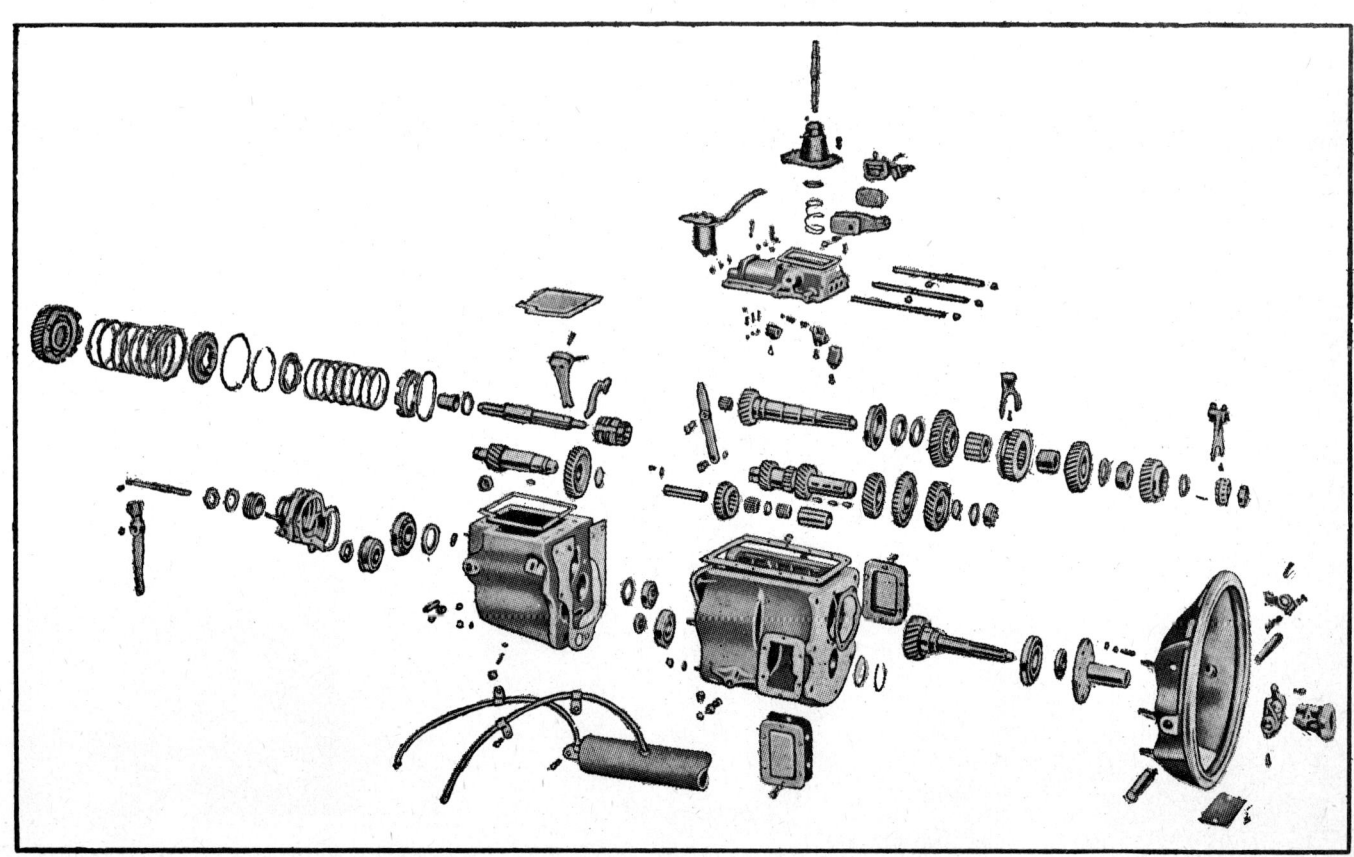

Fig. 4 Roadranger R-46 eight-speed transmission disassembled

FULLER TRANSMISSIONS

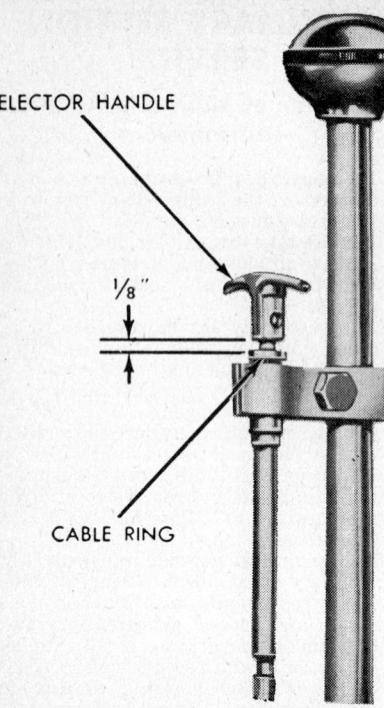

Fig. 5 Selector handle adjustment

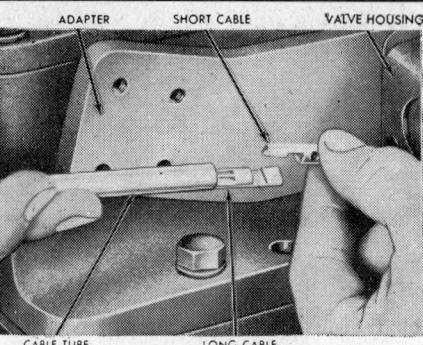

Fig. 6 Long and short shift cable connection

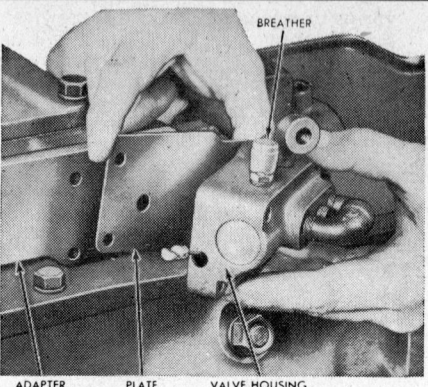

Fig. 7 Air valve and plate

Disassemble

1. Remove auxiliary detent spring cap from boss under shift fork shaft, and remove spring and ball.
2. Remove shift lever fulcrum pin lock plate and withdraw pin, using a slide hammer.
3. Remove shift lever.
4. Remove swivel pin from shift shaft.
5. To remove shift fork, cut lock wire and remove shift fork lock screws. Withdraw shift shaft and remove fork and fork shoe.
6. Remove oil seal from shift shaft bore in rear of case.
7. Remove auxiliary output shaft pilot bearing.
8. Using a soft mallet, tap auxiliary output shaft forward out of rear bearing. Remove shaft by forcing it forward out of case through front bearing bore.
9. Remove low speed gear, high speed synchronizer clutch and low speed thrust washer from case.
10. Remove output shaft rear bearing from case by lightly tapping bearing outer race with soft drift.
11. To remove countershaft, tap shaft to rear until rear bearing is out of case. Remove rear bearing from shaft, using a suitable puller.
12. Tilt countershaft and remove it from top of case.
13. Remove front countershaft bearing by tapping lightly on outer race with a soft mallet. If countershaft drive gear is to be replaced, press it off the shaft.
14. To dismantle the output shaft assembly, Fig. 10, first remove the sliding clutch gear.
15. Press the output shaft 5/8" through low speed gear front thrust washer and bushing. *Pressing the shaft more than 5/8" will damage the small Woodruff key and thrust washer.* Move thrust washer forward against shoulder of shaft and press shaft through bushing until key is completely exposed. Remove key and press washer and bushing off shaft.
16. Disassembly of the two clutches is the same. At the rim of the clutch, remove the wire stop for the pressure plate retaining snap ring. Remove snap ring, pressure plate and discs from housing.

Inspection

Check the surfaces of all thrust washers. Washers scored and/or reduced in thickness should be replaced. Synchronizer discs scored, burned or warped should be replaced. Bearing covers grooved or showing wear from thrust of adjacent bearings should be replaced. Check oil return threads in bearing covers. If the sealing action of the threads has been destroyed by contact from the input and output shafts, replace the covers.

Assemble

1. Both synchronizer clutches are assembled the same way. Start with an inner disc (projections at inside diameter) and alternately place one inner and one outer disc in housing, until 8 discs have been installed, Fig. 11.
2. Install pressure plate and snap ring. *Lock wire hole in rim of gear must be between open ends of snap ring.*
3. Install lock wire in housing rim and bend wire up internally and down externally. *Internal end must not extend above housing.*
4. Press countershaft drive gear on shaft, Fig. 12.

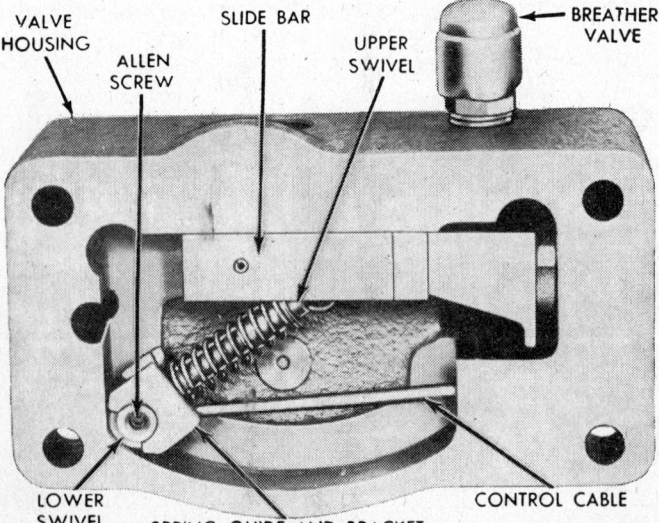

Fig. 8 Air valve

Fig. 9 Removal of one screw from high-speed synchronizer clutch housing

FULLER TRANSMISSIONS

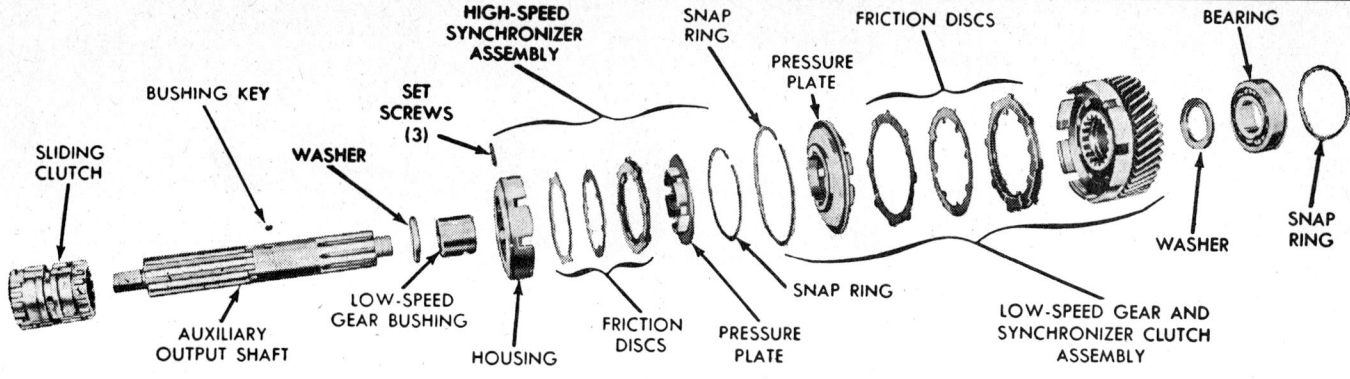

Fig. 10 Auxiliary section output shaft

5. To assemble output shaft, refer to Fig. 10 and proceed as follows:
6. Install low speed gear front thrust washer on rear of shaft *with beveled edge toward front of shaft.*
7. Install Woodruff key and press low speed gear bushing onto shaft until thrust washer is firmly seated against spline shoulder.
8. Install new oil seal in shift shaft bore.
9. Position snap ring on countershaft front bearing and install bearing in case. Tap lightly with soft mallet if necessary.
10. Position countershaft front bearing thrust washer on countershaft and install it in case.
11. Position snap ring on countershaft rear bearing and install bearing, using a suitable bearing driver.
12. Place low speed gear and high speed clutch in case, making sure low gear teeth engage those of low countershaft gear.
13. Install output shaft through front of case, threading it through high speed clutch and low gear until low gear is fully seated on sleeve.
14. Position low gear rear thrust washer on output shaft *with beveled edge toward low gear.*
15. Install snap ring on output shaft rear bearing.
16. Block front of output shaft and install bearing in case, using suitable bearing driver.
17. Install sliding clutch on output shaft through front bearing bore with word "front" toward front end of shaft. Thread sliding clutch through both synchronizer clutches until it engages pocket in low gear. *Interference can be eliminated during installation of sliding clutch by turning synchronizer clutches until lugs on inside diameters line up with grooves in sliding clutch.*
18. Install shoe in shift fork. *Countersunk holes in fork must be up and rib in shoe must face the rear.*
19. Install shoe and fork in sliding clutch.
20. Insert shift shaft in case through fork. End of shaft with milled flats should be to rear. Make sure notches in shaft line up with holes in fork but do not install lock screws.
21. Shift sliding clutch into low speed position and install auxiliary detent spring, ball and cap. Torque cap to 25-35 ft. lbs.
22. Install swivel pin on outer end of shift shaft.
23. Position shift lever on swivel pin. Insert fulcrum pin in case and through shift lever, lining up milled slot in pin with lock screw hole. Drive fulcrum pin into case until slot is flush with case.
24. Install fulcrum pin lock, capscrew and lockwasher, and torque to 20-25 ft. lbs.
25. Install shift fork lock screws and torque to 50-60 ft. lbs.
26. Install safety wires in shift fork screws.

Joining Main and Auxiliary Transmissions

1. Shift auxiliary section into low range. Move high speed clutch to rear against auxiliary shift fork.
2. Install auxiliary output shaft pilot bearing in bore of auxiliary drive gear.
3. Install new gasket between two transmission cases.
4. Attach main and auxiliary cases by fitting auxiliary section over gear which projects from end of mainshaft of main transmission. At the same time, fit auxiliary case over studs which project from rear of main case. The mainshaft rear bearing must be seated in shallow bore in rear of main case before two sections are joined.
5. Install retaining nuts holding two cases together and torque to 65-70 lbs. ft. *Do not overlook the nuts on the two upper studs on the inside of the auxiliary case.*
6. Shift main transmission into two gears and torque auxiliary countershaft rear bearing nut to 250-300 ft. lbs. *This nut has a right-hand thread.* Stake nut at milled slots, and shift transmission into neutral.
7. Move high speed synchronizer clutch forward against auxiliary drive gear.
8. Line up three holes in outside diameter of high speed synchronizer housing with holes in projections on drive gear.
9. Fit high speed clutch on projections of drive gear and move it forward until flush against shoulder of gear, at the same time keeping holes in line.
10. Install three set screws which retain clutch to drive gear. Tighten screws securely and then back them off until the slots are parallel with lock wire grooves in synchronizer housing.
11. Install lock wire in groove at front end of synchronizer housing and through slotted heads of set screws.
12. Install speedometer drive gear.
13. Install auxiliary rear bearing cover with new gasket and torque bolts to 25-35 ft. lbs.
14. Install auxiliary transmission cover and

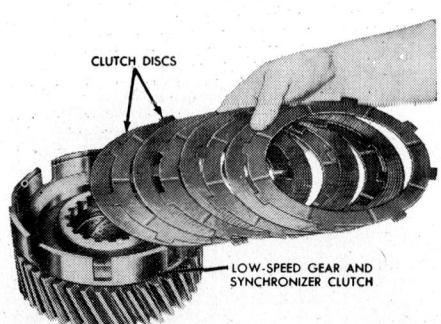

Fig. 11 Positioning synchronizer discs

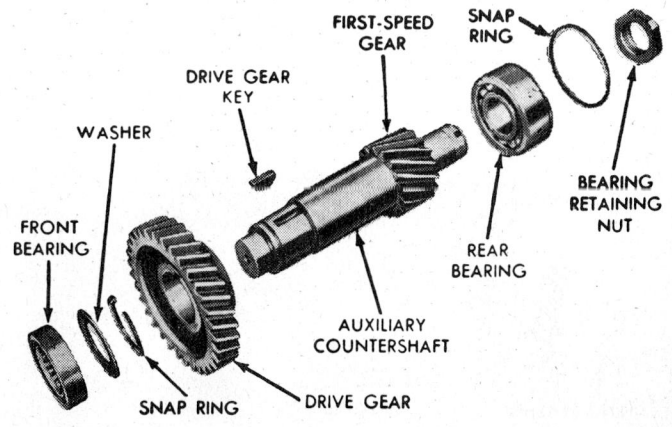

Fig. 12 Auxiliary section countershaft and related parts

FULLER TRANSMISSIONS

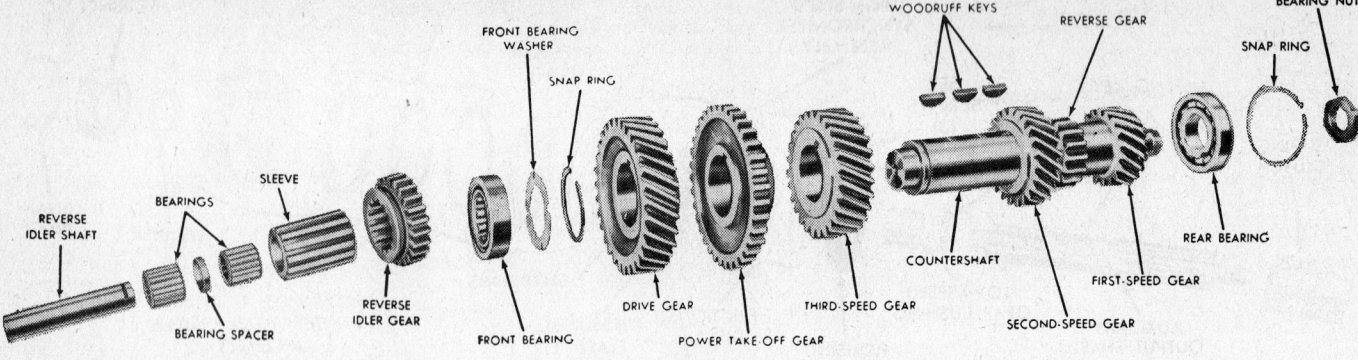

Fig. 13 Reverse idler shaft and related parts

Fig. 14 Countershaft and related parts

gasket and torque bolts to 35–40 ft. lbs.
15. Shift gear shift housing in neutral and install with new gasket. Shift forks must enter grooves in mainshaft sliding gears and reverse shift lever must engage reverse shift gate. Torque gear shift housing bolts to 35–40 ft. lbs.
16. Install air filter.
17. Install air valve and plate on air valve adapter. Torque bolts to 10–15 ft. lbs. Make sure small horseshoe spacer is installed between slide bar and shift fork.
18. Connect air hose to front of air filter and top fitting of air valve.
19. Install two air cylinder hoses and clamps on transmission and connect hoses to air control valve.

4 SPEED MAIN SECTION

NOTE: Separate the main and auxiliary transmission as outlined previously. Then disassemble the main section as follows:

Disassemble

1. Using a small punch, unstake countershaft rear bearing nut. Shift transmission into two gears and remove nut *which has a right-hand thread.*
2. Remove input shaft bearing retainer and pull shaft and bearing out of front of case as an assembly.
3. If input shaft bearing is to be removed, unstake retaining nut and remove the nut, *which has a left-hand thread.* Shift transmission into neutral.
4. To remove mainshaft, shift reverse gear into mesh with countershaft, and shift sliding gear forward into second speed position. Then lift mainshaft from case.
5. Remove nut from reverse shift lever pivot pin on left side of transmission case. Force pin out of case and remove lever and pin.
6. Remove reverse idler shaft retainer through opening in rear of case.
7. Remove shaft by threading a capscrew into the shaft and use a slide hammer to pull shaft from case.
8. Remove splined reverse sleeve with reverse gear, bearings and spacer.
9. Remove reverse idler gear from sleeve.
10. Remove caged bearings and spacer from sleeve, Fig. 13.
11. To remove countershaft, pry it to rear until rear bearing is out of case.
12. Using a suitable bearing puller, remove bearing from countershaft.
13. Lift countershaft out of case.
14. To remove countershaft front bearing, rap front of case sharply with a mallet to jar bearing backward, and remove it from case.
15. To disassemble input shaft, remove bearing nut and press bearing from shaft.
16. If countershaft gears are to be removed, remove snap ring and press gears off shaft one at a time, Fig. 14. Remove Woodruff keys from shaft.

Mainshaft, Disassemble

1. Secure mainshaft assembly in a soft-jawed vise.
2. Remove pilot bearing.
3. Tap sliding clutch off shaft.
4. At pilot end of shaft and between the splines, pry out third speed gear washer locking key. Remove washer and gear, Fig. 15.
5. Position mainshaft in a press, using sliding clutch gear as a base and press mainshaft $1/8''$ through third speed gear bushing and thrust washer. If a press is not available, pry bushing upward. *Travel of*

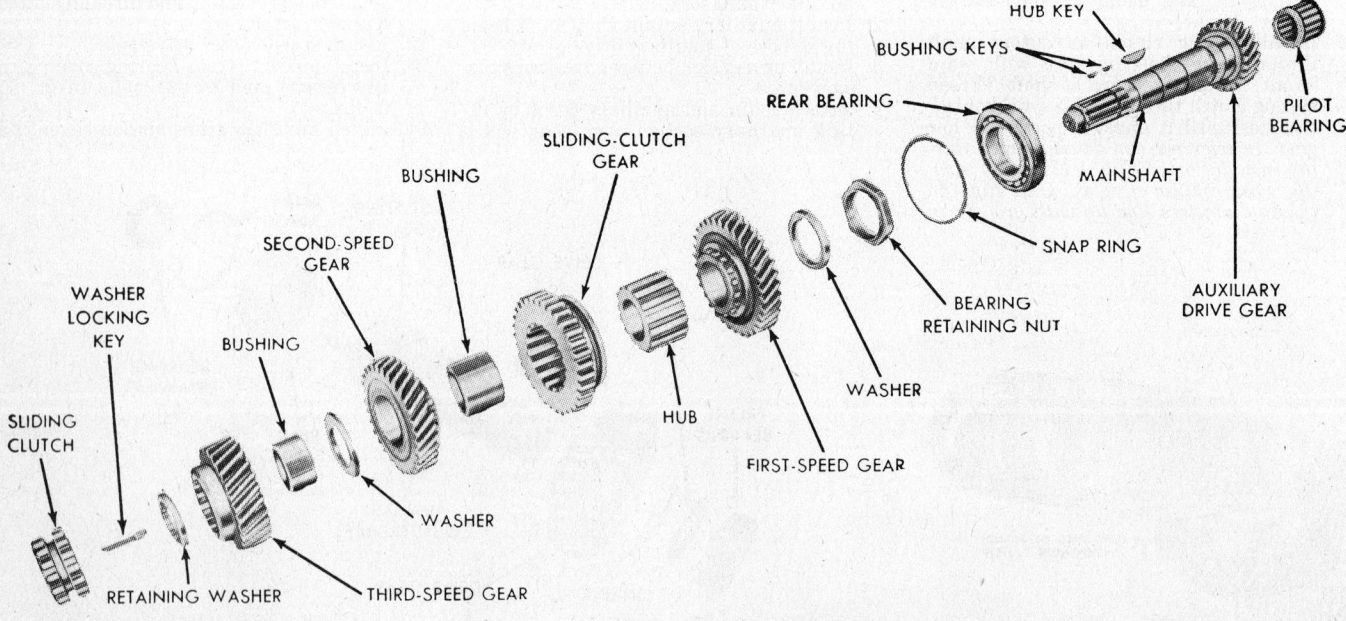

Fig. 15 Transmission mainshaft related parts

FULLER TRANSMISSIONS

mainshaft as limited to 1/8" by the small Woodruff key installed under the sleeve. Pressing the shaft more than 1/8" will shear the key and damage the washer.

6. Pry third gear bushing upward on shaft to expose Woodruff key, Fig. 16, and remove key.
7. Using weight of sliding clutch gear, jar second speed gear, third gear bushing and thrust washer off shaft.
8. Remove sliding gear.
9. Position mainshaft in press. Then press shaft out of first speed gear, sliding gear hub and second gear bushing.
10. Remove Woodruff keys from shaft and remove first gear thrust washer.
11. Unstake and remove mainshaft rear bearing nut, which has a left-hand thread.
12. Press rear bearing from mainshaft.

Mainshaft, Assemble

1. Press mainshaft rear bearing on shaft with snap ring groove toward front and install snap ring.
2. Install gear bearing retaining nut and torque to 300–350 lbs. ft. Stake nut at slots milled into shaft.
3. Install first gear rear thrust washer with beveled edge on the I.D. toward rear of shaft.
4. Install first gear with clutching teeth toward front of shaft, Fig. 15.
5. Install large Woodruff key which prevents movement of sliding clutch gear hub.
6. Position sliding clutch gear hub on shaft with beveled edge of the I.D. toward rear of shaft. Line up keyway with key and press shaft through hub until hub is tight against shoulder of shaft. *When pressing shaft through hub hold first gear against its rear thrust washer.*
7. Install sliding clutch gear on its hub with fork slot to rear.
8. Install small Woodruff key which prevents movement of second gear bushing.
9. Position second gear bushing on shaft, making sure keyway is lined up with Woodruff key.
10. Press or tap bushing into position making sure it fits tightly against hub.
11. Install second gear with clutching teeth toward rear.
12. Install third gear rear thrust washer with beveled edge at the I.D. to rear.
13. Install Woodruff key which prevents movement of third gear sleeve.
14. Line up keyway in third gear bushing with the key, and press or tap bushing into position. Bushing must fit tightly against rear thrust washer.
15. Install third speed gear with internal clutching teeth toward front of shaft.
16. Install third gear retaining washer with beveled edge of lugs at the I.D. to rear.

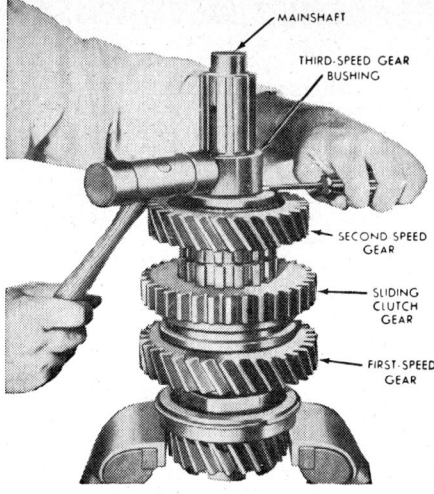

Fig. 16 Gaining access to third speed gear washer locking key

Turn washer in its groove until lugs are under splines on shaft. The thick end of this key must enter slot in washer. Check end clearance between third gear and its thrust washer, which must be .006" to .012". Adjust to specified clearance by selecting a third gear retaining washer of the proper thickness. These washers are available in thicknesses of .253–.255", .258–.260" and .263–.265".

17. Install sliding clutch with word "front" toward front of shaft.
18. Install mainshaft pilot bearing on mainshaft with roller retaining snap ring to rear of shaft.

Main Transmission, Assemble

1. Install countershaft front bearing in its bore.
2. Lower countershaft into case and position front of shaft into front bearing.
3. Install countershaft rear bearing, using a suitable bearing driver.
4. Install countershaft rear bearing retaining nut finger-tight. This nut has a right-hand thread.
5. Install bearings and spacer in splined reverse gear sleeve, Fig. 13.
6. Install reverse gear in splined sleeve. Position gear and sleeve in case *with shift fork groove in gear toward front of transmission.*
7. Insert reverse idler shaft in case and through bearings and spacer. Line up slot in shaft with lock screw hole in case.
8. Drive shaft into case until front edge of milled slot in shaft is flush with case wall.
9. Install reverse idler shaft retainer and torque capscrew to 20–25 lbs. ft.
10. Install reverse shifting lug in bottom or gear end of reverse lever. Insert lug in lever from side opposite bosses. Install snap ring on grooved end of lug.
11. Position reverse shifting lever in case, and guide lug into groove in reverse sliding gear.

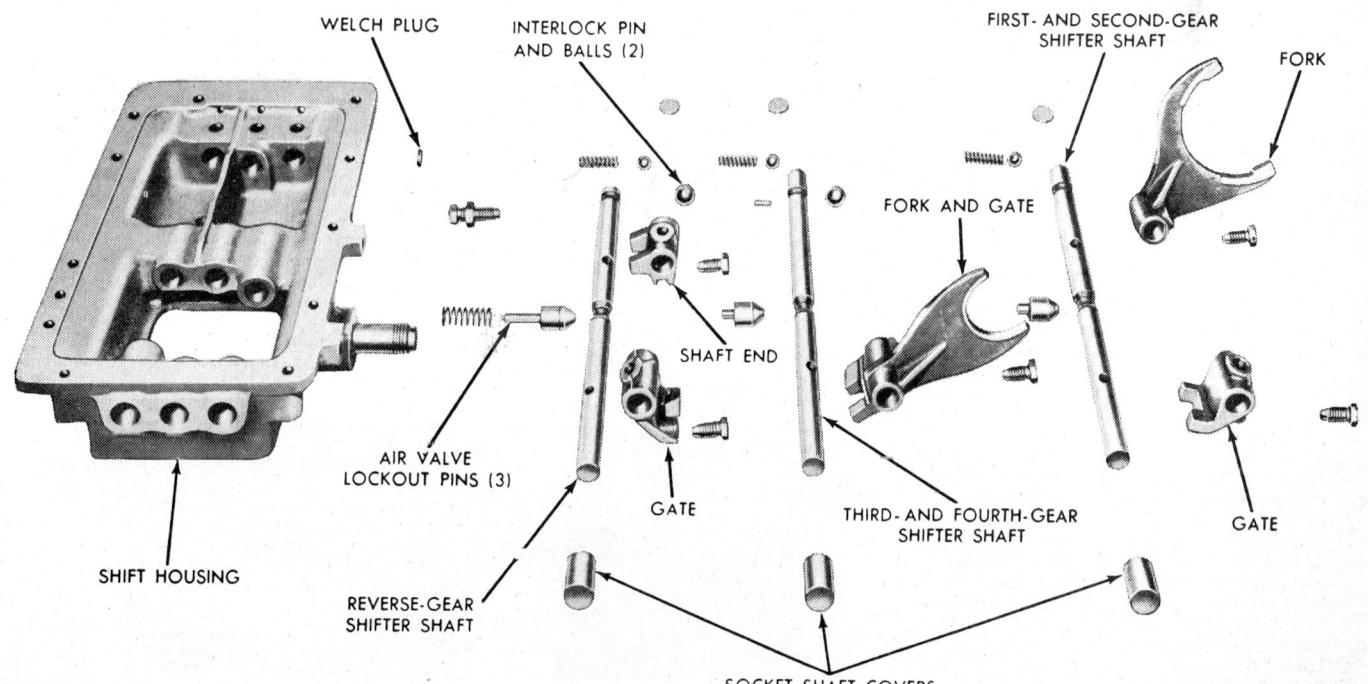

Fig. 17 R-46 gearshift mechanism

FULLER TRANSMISSIONS

12. Line up hole in lever with hole in case and install pivot pin through lever and case. Install washer and nut on pivot pin and torque nut to 100–115 ft. lbs.
13. Shift reverse idler shaft into mesh with countershaft and move mainshaft sliding gear into mesh with second speed gear clutching teeth.
14. Lower mainshaft assembly into case, making sure all mainshaft and countershaft gears properly engage, and that the rear bearing is seated in its shallow bore in rear face of case.
15. Install input shaft, making sure mainshaft pilot bearing enters bore in input shaft. Block against rear of mainshaft as input shaft is installed.
16. Shift transmission into two gears and torque countershaft rear bearing nut to 225–275 ft. lbs. Stake nut in place.
17. If input shaft bearing was removed, install retaining nut and torque to 250–300 ft. lbs. Stake nut in place.
18. Shift transmission into neutral. Install input shaft bearing cover and gasket, making sure oil return hole in cover lines up with hole in case. Torque bolts to 25–35 ft. lbs.

GEARSHIFT MECHANISM

Disassemble, Fig. 17

1. Remove the air valve adapter plate and lock pin and spring from the bore in the air valve mounting surface.
2. Remove the welch plug from the interlock bore on the left side of the shift housing and, with air valve mounting face down, mount housing in a soft-jawed vise.
3. Make sure all shifter shafts are in neutral. Then remove lock wires and lock screws from shifting forks and gates, Fig. 17.
4. Remove welch plugs from rear of shift housing.
5. Remove shifter shafts, top one first, by driving them out front of housing. The detent springs and balls, interlock pin and balls, and intermediate air valve lockout pins must not be lost as shafts are removed. A detent spring and steel ball are depressed by each shaft and will be released from the bore as the shaft clears the hole in the rear hub.

Inspection

Shift forks and gates should be checked for wear. Check forks for alignment. Check lock screws in forks and gates. Replace parts showing wear or misalignment. Retighten and rewire lock screws. Check neutral notches in shafts for wear from interlock balls. Shafts indented at points adjacent to neutral notches should be replaced. Check spring tension on shift lever. Replace tension spring and washer if lever moves too freely. Check shift lever pivot pin and slot in lever for wear. Check auxiliary shift fork and shoe for wear. Replace if necessary.

Assemble

Reverse the order of disassembly to assemble the shift housing. Be sure the interlock pin is in the shaft. Torque shift gate and fork lock screws to 50–60 ft. lbs.

Fuller R-96 & R-960 Roadranger Ten-Speed Transmission

Description

These transmissions, Figs. 1 and 2, consist of a five-speed main (front) section and a two-speed auxiliary (rear) section which provides ten forward and two reverse speeds shifted with one lever. The ten forward speeds are obtained by using the ratios of the five-speed section twice; the first time with the auxiliary section in low gear so that the ratios in the five-speed section are compounded by the auxiliary low gear; the second time with the auxiliary section in high gear. The two reverse speeds are obtained by using reverse in the five-speed section through either high or low gear of the auxiliary section.

Separating Sections

1. Disconnect three air hoses at air control valve. Remove clamps and remove hoses with air cylinder.
2. Remove air filter and air regulator valve (with bracket and hose).
3. Remove air valve housing and its plate from adapter.
4. With transmission in neutral, remove gearshift housing and auxiliary cover.
5. Drain transmission and remove oil filter.
6. Remove brake drum, lock transmission in two gears and remove U-joint flange.
7. Remove parking brake shoe assembly.
8. Shift auxiliary unit in low range.
9. To hold mainshaft of front unit in position during removal of auxiliary section, block large sliding gear forward, Fig. 3. Use a block of wood about two inches wide, and be sure the sliding gear is engaged with the adjacent gear.
10. Secure auxiliary section on a hoist.
11. Remove nuts holding the two sections together. Do not overlook the two upper front nuts that are inside the auxiliary section, Fig. 4.
12. In the right and left sides of the flange at the rear of the main section, locate the two 1/2" tapped holes. In each of these, start a hardened bolt about 2 1/2" long, Fig. 5. *Do not try to separate the sections at this time.*
13. Line up one of the two depressions in the O.D. of the clutch disc carrier with the auxiliary countershaft drive gear, Fig. 6, so that there will be clearance when transmission cases are separated.
14. Now separate cases by evenly tightening the bolts started in Step 12. Then remove the bolts.

Fig. 1 Fuller Roadranger R-96 ten-speed transmission

FULLER TRANSMISSIONS

Disassemble Main Trans.

1. Remove wood block (Fig. 3) and, while keeping sliding gear engaged, move mainshaft rearward until it clears input shaft. Remove mainshaft.
2. Remove input shaft bearing retainer bolts. Then, working inside of case, force out input shaft, including bearing, nut and bearing retainer.
3. Remove retainer from input shaft and bearing snap ring from case.
4. Remove reverse idler gear shaft, gear and bearing from case, then remove bearing from gear.
5. Remove bearing retainer washer from rear end of countershaft.
6. Remove countershaft front bearing retainer and bearing spacer.
7. After driving countershaft far enough rearward to expose rear bearing, pull the bearing.
8. After removing the countershaft, remove outer race of countershaft front bearing from case.

Disassemble Sub-Assemblies

Front Unit Mainshaft

1. After removing wire stop from clutch disc carrier, remove pressure plate snap ring from carrier, Fig. 7.
2. Remove pressure plate and friction discs, *keeping discs in order of original assembly*.
3. Remove mainshaft pilot bearing.
4. After removing washer locking key, Fig. 8, turn washer so that it aligns with shaft spline grooves. Remove 4th speed gear and washer (3rd on R-960).
5. Using rear face of 3rd speed gear (2nd on R-960) as a base, press shaft through bushing and gear, Fig. 9. *Do not let shaft drop.* Remove clutch sleeve.
6. Using rear face of 2nd speed gear (1st on R-960) as a base, press shaft through two bushings and gear, Fig. 10.
7. Remove large and small Woodruff keys from shaft.
8. On R-96 only: Using rear face of 1st speed gear as a base, press shaft through bushing, washer and gear until front end of bushing meets lower end of large keyway, Fig. 11. *Pressing the shaft further will damage washer.* Then move gear and washer back to the rear and pry bushing off shaft. Remove Woodruff key now exposed, Fig. 12, then remove washer and two sliding gears.
   a. On R-960 only: Using rear face of sliding gear as a base, press shaft through bushing, washer and gears until front end of bushing meets lower end of large keyway. *Pressing shaft further will damage washer.* Then move gear and washer back to rear with gear

Fig. 2 Fuller Roadranger R-960 ten-speed transmission

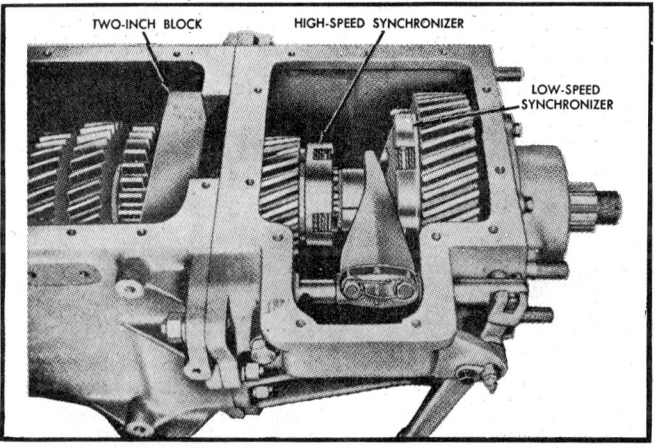

Fig. 3 Preparation for separation of cases

Fig. 4 Auxiliary upper front stud nuts

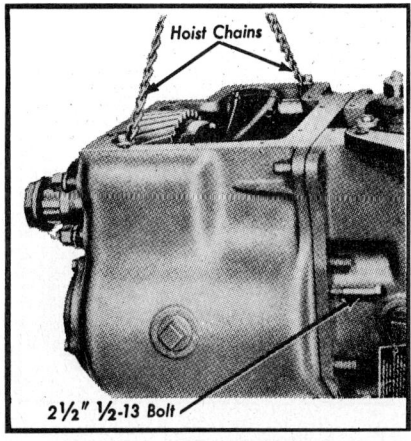

Fig. 5 Separation of cases

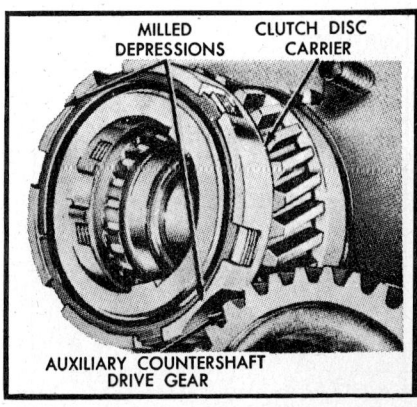

Fig. 6 Clutch disc carrier clearance

FULLER TRANSMISSIONS

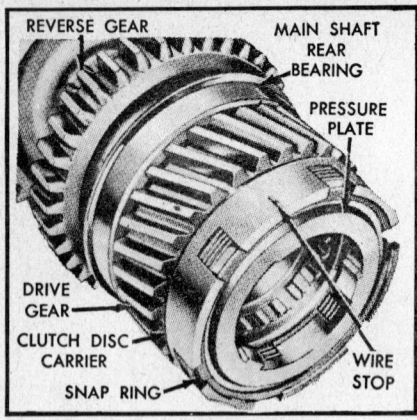

Fig. 7 Rear end of mainshaft

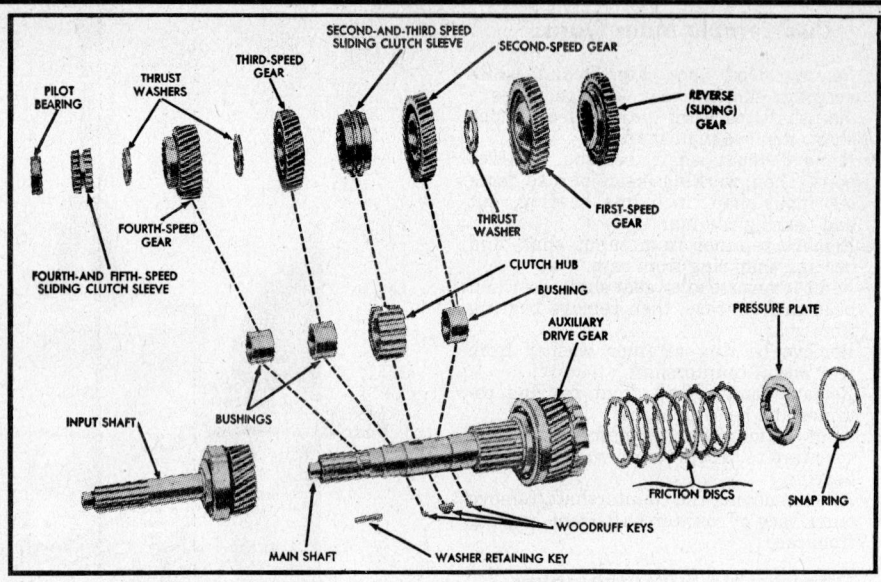

Fig. 8 Mainshaft disassembled

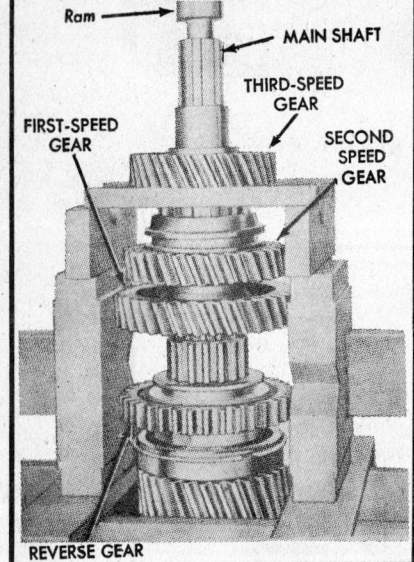

Fig. 9 Removing 4th speed gear bushing

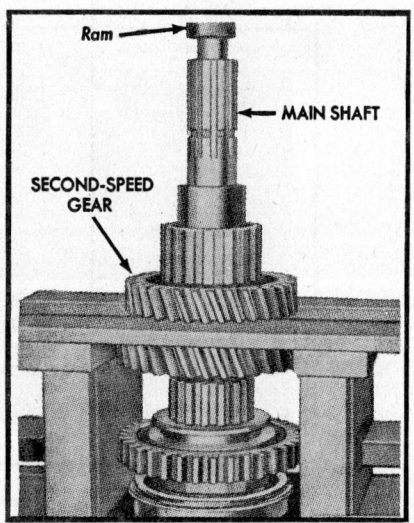

Fig. 10 Removing 3rd speed gear bushing and hub

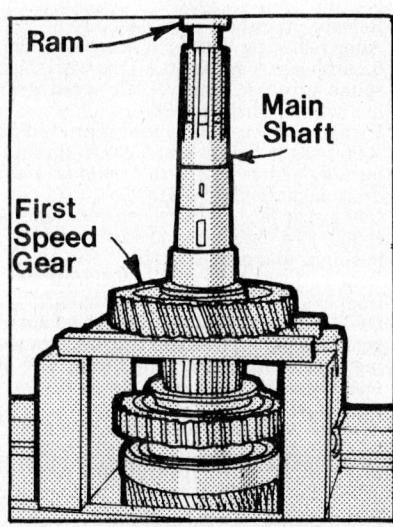

Fig. 11 Removing 2nd speed gear bushing

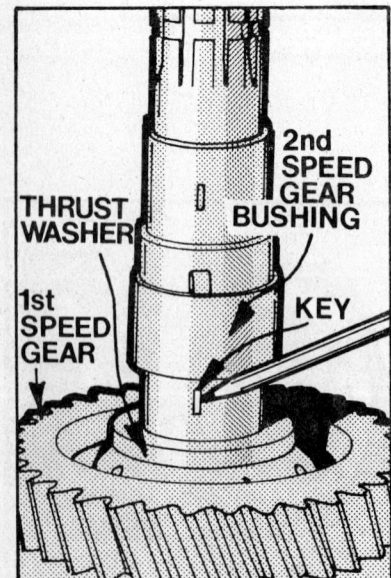

Fig. 12 Second speed gear bushing key

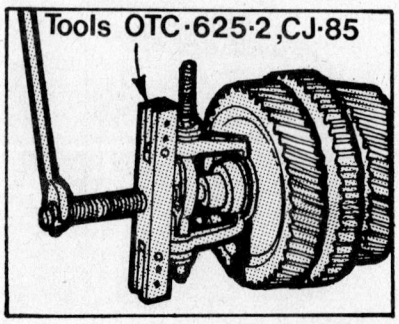

Fig. 13 Removing main countershaft front bearing inner race

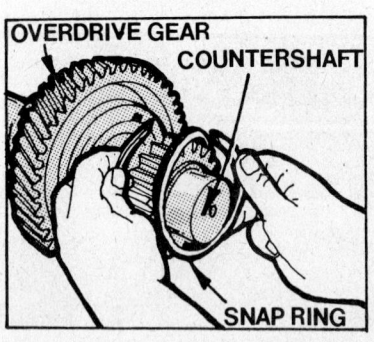

Fig. 14 Spiral snap ring (R-960 only)

FULLER TRANSMISSIONS

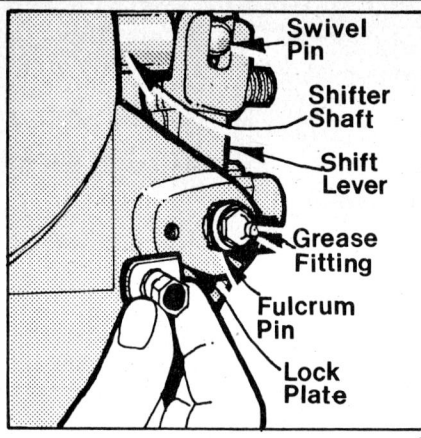

Fig. 15 Fulcrum pin lock plate

against shoulder of shaft. Press shaft through bushing and remove Woodruff key, washer and gears.
9. Mount shaft in soft-jawed vise, relieve peening on bearing nut and remove nut *which has a left-hand thread*.
10. Jar shaft on a block of wood to remove bearing.

Front Unit Input Shaft
Mount shaft in a soft-jawed vise. Relieve peening on bearing nut and remove nut *which has a left-hand thread*. Press or jar bearing front shaft.

Front Unit Countershaft
1. After removing snap ring at front end of shaft, use a puller to remove bearing inner race, Fig. 13.
2. Press off gears *one at a time,* beginning with the drive gear. On R-960, remove spiral type snap ring at rear of overdrive gear before pressing off this gear, Fig. 14. Remove Woodruff keys.

Auxiliary Section
1. Remove shift lever lock plate and grease fitting, Fig. 15.
2. Remove shift lever fulcrum pin, then remove lever and swivel pin.
3. Remove cap, spring and detent ball, Fig. 16.
4. To remove shift fork, cut lock wire and remove fork lock screws. Withdraw shifter shaft and remove fork.
5. Remove bearing retainer and countershaft retaining washer.
6. Using a soft drift, drive output shaft forward through front bearing bore. Remove low-speed gear and rear thrust washer from case, Fig. 17.
7. Remove output shaft rear bearing from case.
8. To remove countershaft, tap shaft rearward until rear bearing is outside its bore. Use a puller to remove bearing, Fig. 18.
9. Remove countershaft assembly from case, and front bearing from its bore.
10. If countershaft or gear is to be replaced, remove snap ring at front of shaft, then press shaft through gear. Remove Woodruff key.
11. To dismantle auxiliary output shaft, position it in a soft-jawed vise and use a puller to remove pilot bearing, Fig. 19.
12. After removing sliding clutch, position shaft in a press. Use low-speed gear thrust washer as a base and press the shaft 1 3/8" through bushing and washer, Fig. 20. *If shaft is pressed further, washer will be damaged.*
13. Move washer against shoulder of shaft and, using front end of bushing as a base, press shaft through bushing, Fig. 21. Remove Woodruff key and thrust washer.
14. To disassemble low-speed gear assembly, first remove wire stop from low-speed clutch disc carrier, then remove pressure plate snap ring.
15. Remove pressure plate and friction discs, *keeping discs in order of original assembly.*

Disassemble Gearshift Housing
1. Carefully remove detent spring retainer, springs and balls from upper side of housing. Remove plug from bore on air valve side of housing.

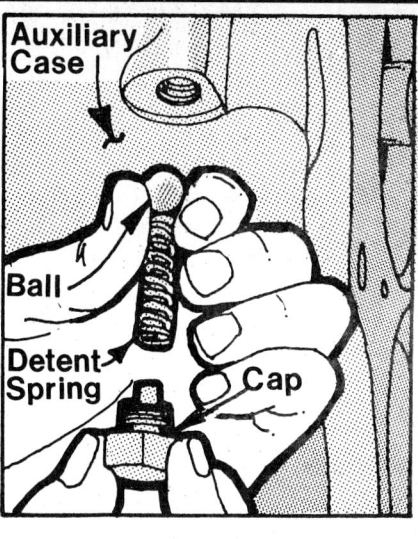

Fig. 16 Auxiliary detent spring, cap and ball

2. Mount air valve side of housing in a vise and, *with all shafts in neutral,* remove set screws from all forks and gates.
3. Remove adapter, Fig. 20, and interlock spring and plunger, Fig. 23.
4. After removing welch plugs from shifter shaft bores, remove shafts, *being sure not to lose interlock plungers and balls as the last shaft is removed,* Fig. 22.

Assemble Gearshift Housing
1. Shifter shafts should be positioned through front of housing with notches to the front. Mount housing in vise with air valve face upward.
2. Position 1st-reverse (overdrive-reverse on R-960) shifter shaft in bottom of bore, through gate and through fork, Fig. 23. Install and safety-wire set screws.
3. Install 3/4" interlock ball in front opening (air valve side) and air valve intermediate lockout plunger in rear opening, Fig. 24. Move shaft to neutral.
4. Position 2nd-3rd (1st-2nd on R-960) shifter shaft in center bore and through shift fork. *Don't forget the lockout pin that must be inserted in its hole at neutral notch.* Install and safety-wire screws.
5. Repeat Step 3 and move shaft to neutral.
6. Position 4th-5th (3rd-4th on R-960) shifter shaft in upper bore and through shift fork. Install and safety-wire retaining screws.

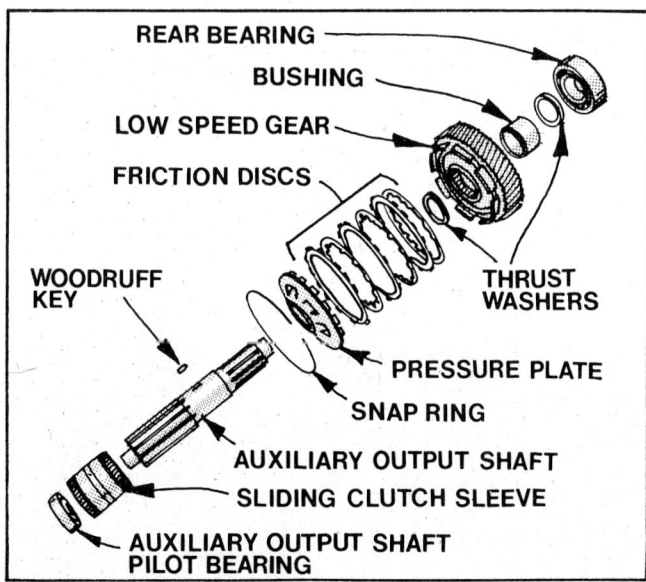

Fig. 17 Auxiliary output shaft (R-960 only)

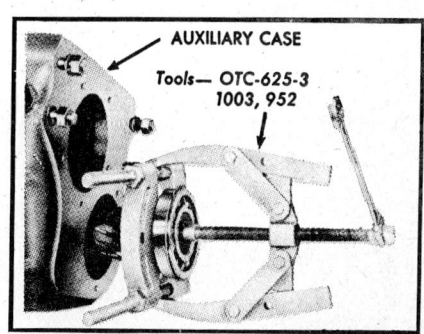

Fig. 18 Removing auxiliary countershaft rear bearing

FULLER TRANSMISSIONS

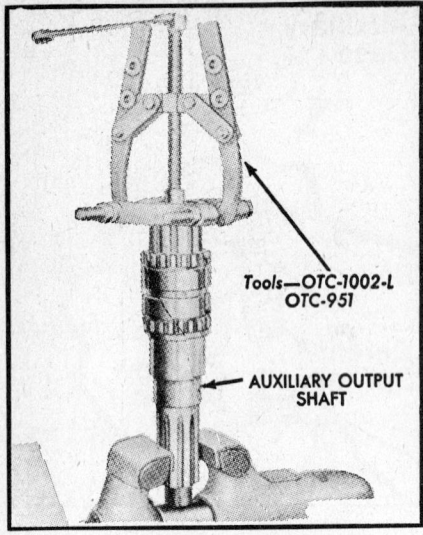

Fig. 19 Removing auxiliary output shaft pilot bearing

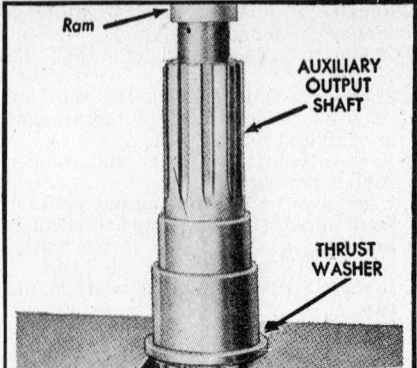

Fig. 20 Removing auxiliary shaft bushing

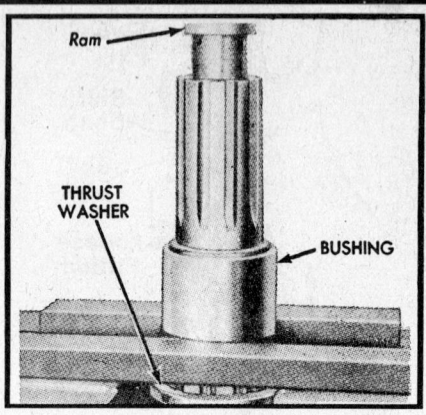

Fig. 21 Pressing auxiliary output shaft through bushing

7. After positioning detent balls and spring in top of housing, install detent spring retainer.
8. Apply sealer to welch plugs and install them in housing. Install plug in bore of air valve side of housing.
9. Install third interlock plunger and its spring, then install adapter.

Auxiliary Section, Assemble

1. Position friction discs in low-speed gear. Start with an inner disc (projections at inside diameter) and alternately one inner and one outer disc in housing until six discs have been positioned, Fig. 25. The last inner disc to be installed will have four bent lugs that should be positioned toward pressure plate.
2. Install pressure plate and snap ring. The lock wire hole in rim of gear must be between open ends of snap ring.
3. Cut a new stop wire and install it in housing rim between open ends of snap ring. Bend wire up internally and down externally. The internal end must not extend above the housing.
4. To assemble output shaft, install low-speed gear front thrust washer with *beveled face to front*, Fig. 26.
5. Position Woodruff key and low-speed gear bushing, and press bushing onto shaft.
6. Position sliding clutch on shaft and install pilot bearing.
7. To install countershaft drive gear, position the key and press gear on shaft. Install snap ring on shaft, Fig. 27.
8. Position countershaft in case, then turn case up on its front surface.
9. Install countershaft rear bearing on shaft and in case bore.
10. Position case in its normally upright position and install inner race of countershaft front bearing. Install outer race.
11. Install rear bearing retainer washer, install and safety-wire bolts.
12. Position output shaft low-speed gear in case, meshing teeth with those on countershaft.
13. Position output shaft through front bearing bore. Move sliding clutch gear through synchronizer assembly into engagement with low-speed gear. Install rear thrust washer with polished face next to gear.
14. Install output shaft rear bearing.
15. Install speedometer drive gear spacer and gear, and bearing retainer.
16. Position auxiliary shift fork and its shaft in case. Install lock screws and wire them securely.
17. With transmission shifted in low, install detent ball, spring and cap.
18. Position swivel pin in end of shifter shaft, then install shift lever and fulcrum pin.
19. Line up fulcrum pin slot with lock screw hole and drive pin into case until inner edge of slot is flush with boss. Install lock plate and grease fitting for the pin.

Assemble Main Trans. Sub-Assemblies

Countershaft, Fig. 28
1. Install Woodruff keys and press gears on, one at a time, over front end of shaft.
2. Install inner race of front bearing on shaft. Install gear retaining snap ring.
3. On R-960, press on overdrive gear (long hub to rear). Install spiral type snap ring.

Input Shaft
1. Press on input shaft bearing with shield toward front of shaft.
2. Install bearing nut (left-hand thread). Tighten nut and peen it into the milled slots.

Mainshaft, Fig. 8
1. Press on rear bearing with snap ring toward front. Install retaining nut (left-hand thread) and peen nut in four places

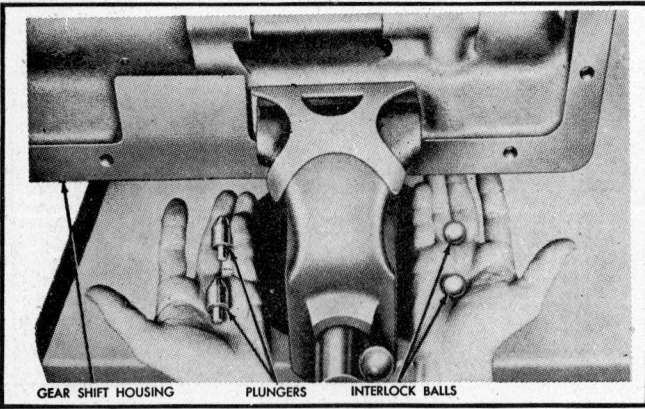

Fig. 22 Interlock plungers and balls

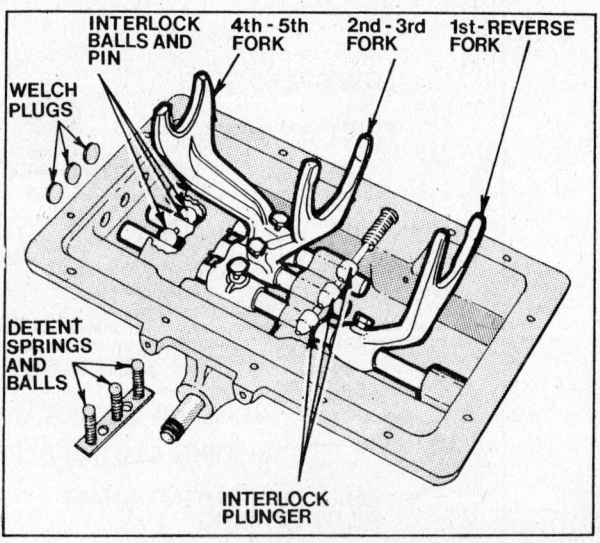

Fig. 23 Shift mechanism

FULLER TRANSMISSIONS

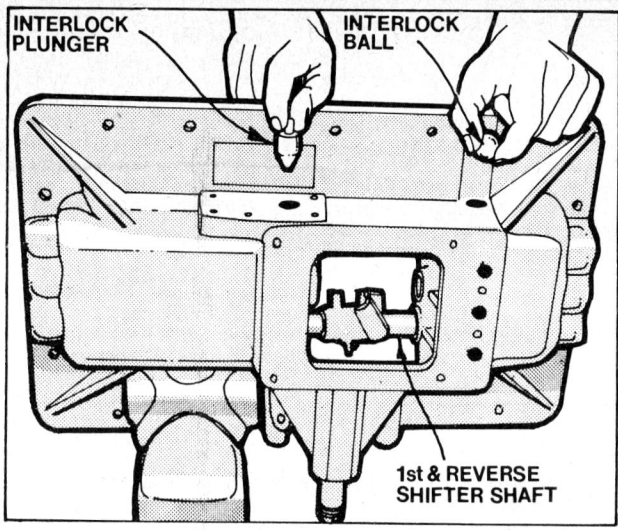

Fig. 24 Interlock ball and plunger installation

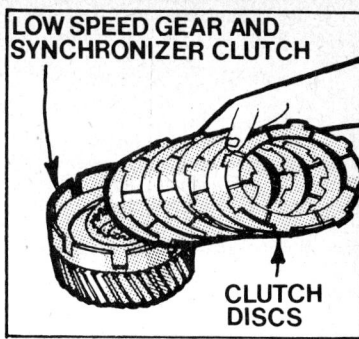

Fig. 25 Positioning synchronizer discs

90° apart.
2. Install sliding gear with fork groove to front.
3. Install 1st speed gear (overdrive gear on R-960) *with clutching teeth to rear*.
4. Install 2nd speed gear washer (1st speed on R-960).
5. Install 2nd speed gear bushing (1st speed on R-960). Bushing must be tight against washer.
6. Install 2nd speed gear (1st speed on R-960) *with clutching teeth to front*.
7. With large Woodruff key installed, press on clutch hub. Hub must be tight against gear.
8. After installing shift collar, the small Woodruff key and its bushing, install 3rd speed gear (2nd speed on R-960) *with clutching teeth to rear*.
9. Install 4th speed gear (3rd speed on R-960) washer, *with ID chamfered edge to rear*.
10. Install 4th speed gear (3rd speed on R-960) bushing and its gear, *with internal clutching teeth to front*.

11. After positioning the internally splined front washer, *with chamfered end of splines to rear,* turn washer in its groove until lugs on its ID are under projecting mainshaft splines.
12. Install washer locking key, making sure that lower end engages washer.
13. Install sliding clutch gear with the word "Front" toward pilot end of shaft. Install pilot bearing with snap ring groove to rear.
14. The high- and low-speed synchronizers are assembled in the same manner. Position high-speed synchronizer discs in their original order in the synchronizer housing. Install pressure plate, retaining snap ring and wire stop.

Assemble Main Trans.

1. Install outer race of countershaft front bearing and spacer.
2. Install countershaft in case and install rear bearing.
4. Install rear bearing retainer.

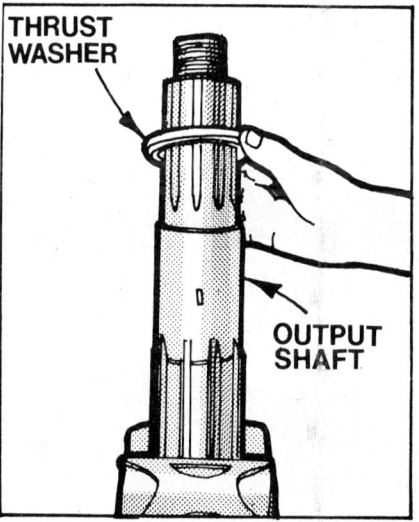

Fig. 26 Thrust washer installation

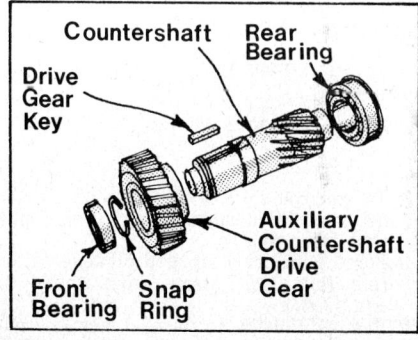

Fig. 27 Auxiliary countershaft

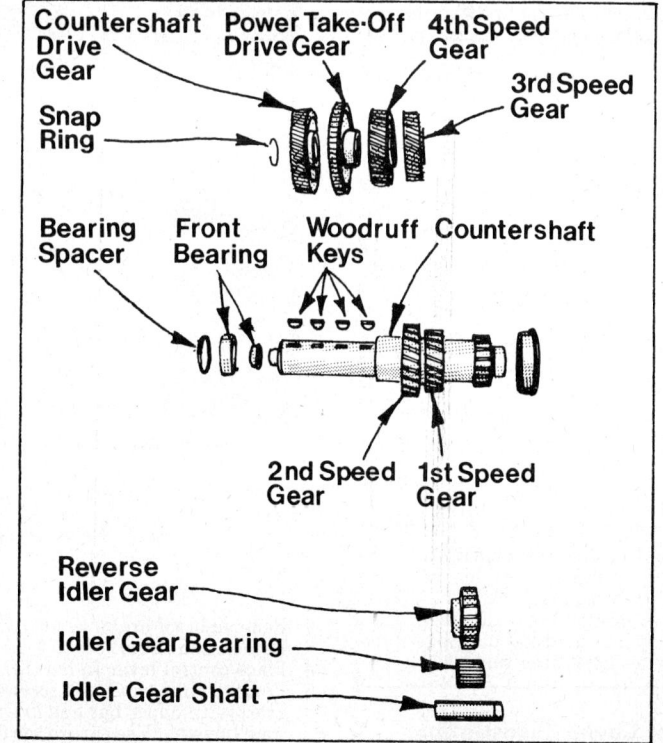

Fig. 28 Main countershaft

321

FULLER TRANSMISSIONS

5. After positioning bearing in reverse gear, install gear in case *with long hub to front*.
6. Using a soft drift, drive reverse gear shaft into place until front edge of shoulder is flush with rear face of case.
7. To install mainshaft, engage sliding gear with adjacent gear and lower shaft assembly into case. Be sure that corresponding countershaft gears and that rear bearing seats in its bore.
8. Install input shaft bearing retaining ring in its case bore.
9. Block rear end of mainshaft and install input shaft assembly. Install input shaft bearing retainer, making sure oil drain groove in retainer lines up with drain hole in case.

Joining Front & Rear Sections

1. With auxiliary section in low gear and new gasket in place, move auxiliary section into place. Before moving auxiliary all the way forward, be sure that one of the two depressions in the OD of the clutch disc carrier is lined up to provide clearance at the countershaft drive gear. Also line up the ID lugs of the pressure plate with the corresponding grooves in the OD of the auxiliary sliding clutch gear.
2. With case faces flush, install lockwashers and nuts on attaching studs, including the two upper studs on the inside of the auxiliary, Fig. 4.
3. Install auxiliary section cover.
4. After making sure that speedometer gear washer and gear are installed, install parking brake assembly.
5. Install U-joint flange and brake drum.
6. Install air valve plate and housing.
7. Install air filter and air regulator valve assemblies, and connect the three air hoses at the air control valve.
8. Install oil filter and lubricant.

Air Valve Service

For air valve service and trouble shooting data, follow instructions given in the Fuller R-46 transmission section.

Fuller Five-Speed Conventional Transmissions
5-33, 5-43, 5-62, 5-65, 5-72, 5W-74

Disassemble Transmission

Before dismantling a transmission, carefully clean the outside of the case to avoid the possibility of introducing dirt or other foreign material into the unit. This is important because dirt, being an abrasive, is highly detrimental to highly polished parts such as bearings, sleeves and bushings. These, as well as other parts, should be cleaned as removed and protectively wrapped until ready for use.

In removing the control cover, do not force it off the transmission. Forcing may spring the yokes out of alignment and cause partial engagement or gear interference. Follow the directions relative to shifting and the cover can easily be removed. If binding occurs, a slight manipulation or movement to one side or the other will free it.

When disassembling the control cover, all parts should be laid on a clean bench in the same sequence as removed. This procedure will not only simplify reassembling the yokes and bars in their proper places but will also reduce the possibility of omitting the small yoke bar interlock parts. If these parts are left out, the unit will shift into two speeds at the same time.

Unless absolutely necessary, the clutch housing should not be detached from the case. If it is detached, extreme care should be taken when reassembling the housing to maintain the alignment between its machined face and the mainshaft bores in the case; also the concentricity of the mainshaft bores and the flange pilot.

NOTE: The disassembly procedure which follows is based on the assumption that the transmission has been taken from the chassis and that all supplementary equipment such as universal joint companion flanges and brake assemblies have been removed.

Control Cover, Disassemble

1. Shift transmission into 1st speed.

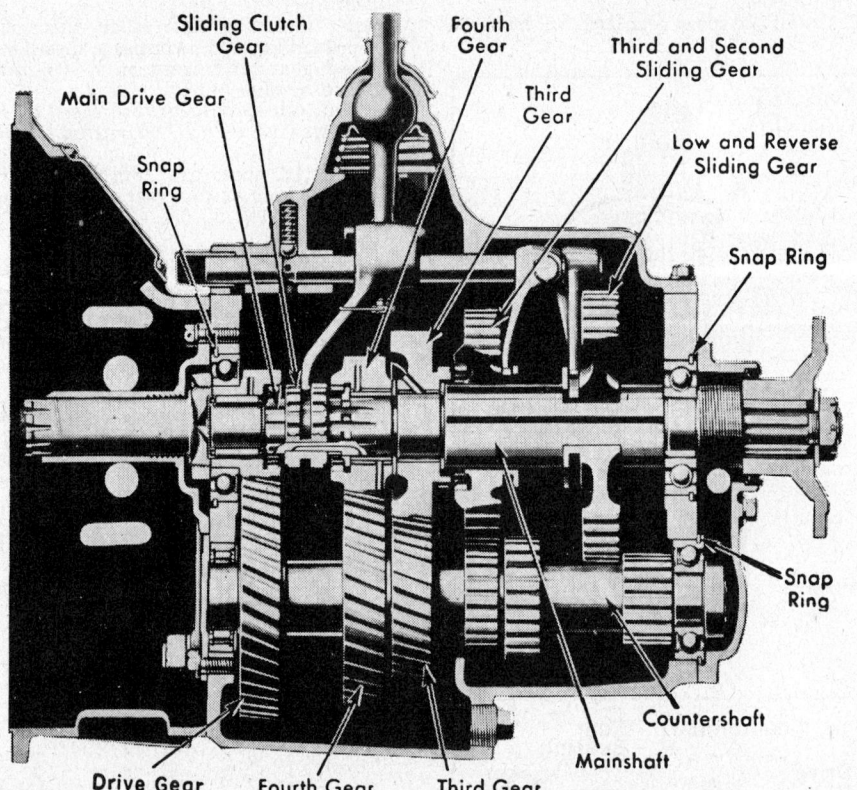

Fig. 1 Fuller five speed transmission. Series 5-33, 330, 5-43, 430

2. Remove hand brake lever.
3. Detach and lift off cover.
4. Place control lever in neutral.
5. Remove shift yoke lock screws.
6. Start with upper bar and drive shift bars from housing. Use care to see that none of the small yoke bar locking parts are lost as bars are removed.
7. To remove shift lever, take off rubber grip, and latch spoon if lever is equipped with latch rod.
8. Force dust cover up and off lever after removing lock screw from those so equipped.
9. Remove tension spring and washer from inside lever housing, and withdraw shift lever.

FULLER TRANSMISSIONS

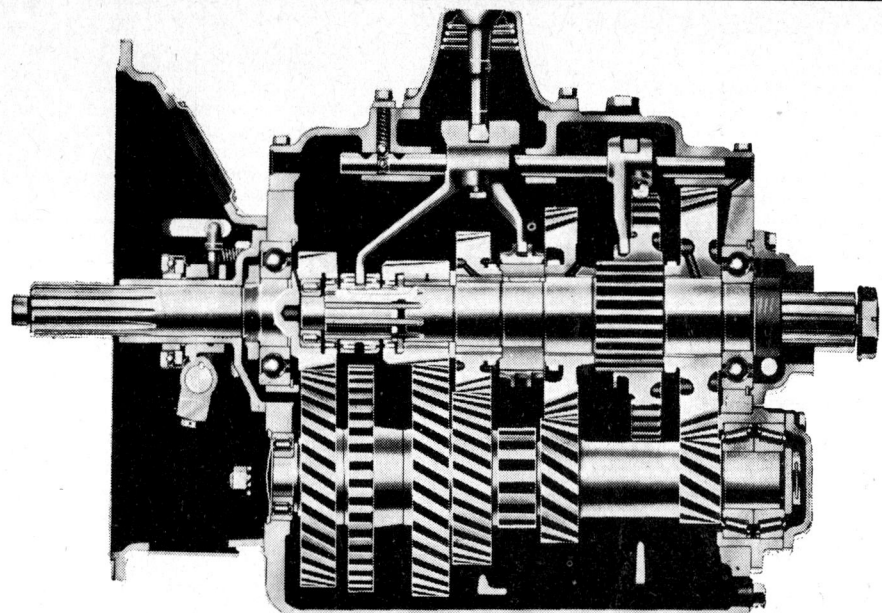

Fig. 2 Fuller five speed transmission. Series 5-72, 720, 5W-74

3. Replace bushings in gears having excessive radial clearance.

Assembling Bushed Gears

When assembling either new or rebushed gears on the mainshaft or countershaft, be sure that they move freely after having been assembled in their proper places. Clean all mounting parts and coat with clean oil before replacing gears.

Installing Bushings in Mainshaft Helical Gears

1. Remove old bushing.
2. Clean bore of gear carefully and remove all burrs.
3. Lubricate outside diameter of bushing and inside diameter of gear.
4. Carefully press bushing fully into gear.
5. Face off any projecting end of bushing.
6. Drill oil holes in bushing through holes in gear, making sure all holes are open.
7. Remove all burrs resulting from drilling and break all sharp edges on ends of bushing.

Installing Bushings in Reverse & Countershaft Gears

1. Remove old bushing, clean bore of gear and remove all burrs.
2. Press bushing fully into gear.
3. Spin over the projecting ends of the bushing.
4. Open the ends of the oil grooves with a file.
5. Drill oil holes in bushing through holes in gear, making sure all holes are open.
6. Remove all ridges and burrs resulting from drilling and spinning operations.

Mainshaft, Disassemble

1. Remove rear bearing covers from mainshaft and countershaft.
2. Lock gears and remove bearing lock nut from end of countershaft.
3. Pull mainshaft and countershaft assemblies to the rear.
4. Remove mainshaft rear bearing.
5. Tilt mainshaft and remove through top of case, leaving sliding gears inside case.
6. Remove loose sliding gears from case.
7. To remove gears and sleeve from mainshaft, remove pilot bearing and sliding clutch, using the latter to free bearing.
8. Remove mainshaft gear retaining washer key.
9. Rotate mainshaft gear retaining washer until its inside lugs line up with grooves in shaft.
10. Remove mainshaft bushed gears, sleeve and washers, using the rear bushed gear to start the sleeves.

Main Drive Gear, Disassemble

1. Remove clutch release mechanism.
2. Remove drive gear bearing cover.
3. Withdraw gear.

Reverse Gears, Disassemble

1. Remove high speed reverse shifting bar and yoke from inside the case (Models 62, 620, 65, 650, 72, 720).
2. Withdraw shaft or shafts and remove gear or gears from case.

Countershaft, Disassemble

1. Remove countershaft rear bearing.
2. Tilt countershaft and remove through top of case.
3. To disassemble countershaft, remove gear retaining snap ring.
4. Press gears from shaft one at a time.

Reassembly Instructions

With the exception of a few specific points, the general instructions for reassembly are merely the reversal of those for disassembly. The exceptions are as follows and should be given careful attention.

Clearances

1. On mainshaft helical bushed gears, replace worn washers to assist in maintaining original fit.
2. Hold end play of both gears to a minimum of .006″. Check with dial indicator or feeler gauge.

Fig. 3 Fuller five speed transmission. Series 5-62, 620, 5-65, 650

FULLER TRANSMISSIONS

U-Joint Flange

The mainshaft is held in its proper place by the universal joint companion flange. The omission of parts between the flange and bearing, or failure to pull the flange tightly into place will allow the mainshaft to move endwise with resultant damage to the pilot bearing, mainshaft and main drive gear.

Sliding Clutches

All sliding clutches should be assembled to the shaft with the counterbore toward the bushed gears. An exception is the sliding clutches in 43 and 430 series, which have no counterbore. They are marked, however on one end with the word "front," and must be assembled with the marked end toward the front of the transmission.

Power Take-Off

When attaching a power take-off, be sure sufficient filler blocks and gaskets are used to prevent the gears from meshing too deeply. If the gears bottom, they will damage not only themselves but also the transmission case.

Fuller Series 5H Five-Speed Transmissions

Disassemble Transmission

1. With transmission in neutral, remove gearshift housing.
2. With transmission locked up in two gears, remove output shaft flange nut.
3. Remove flange and brake drum as a unit, and disconnect parking brake linkage as required so that brake shoe assembly can be removed.
4. Remove output shaft rear bearing retainer and speedometer drive gear. Remove oil seal from retainer.
5. After removing clutch release mechanism, remove six stud nuts (inside clutch housing) and then remove clutch housing.
6. Remove input shaft bearing retainer, then pull out input shaft and bearing assembly. If necessary, use a soft drift from inside of case. Remove bearing retainer snap ring from case bore.
7. Mount input shaft in a vise and relieve bearing nut peening. Remove nut which has a left-hand thread. If bearing is to be replaced, press or jar it from shaft.
8. Remove countershaft rear bearing adapter cap. Remove retainer plate from rear end of countershaft.
9. Remove countershaft rear bearing adapter, using puller screws in holes provided in adapter.
10. Drive output shaft forward until it stops solidly, then drive it to the rear until rear bearing snap ring is exposed. Remove bearing. If bearing is to be replaced, remove the snap ring, Fig. 1.
11. Remove output shaft and gears, except sliding gears. Lift sliding gears out of case.
12. Remove countershaft rear bearings and spacer from retainer.
13. After removing reverse idler shaft retainer, remove shaft, then idler gears and bearings.
14. Move countershaft rearward to clear front bearing, then remove shaft and gears from case.
15. Remove countershaft front bearing retainer, gasket, bearing and spacer.
16. Disassemble output shaft and countershaft as required.

Gearshift Housing, Assemble

1. Referring to Fig. 2, position housing (left-hand side up) in a vise and install rocker arm and pivot.
2. Insert rocker arm shift shaft through webs and gates and install set screws.
3. Insert 2-3 shaft into housing and through its fork. Install set screw.

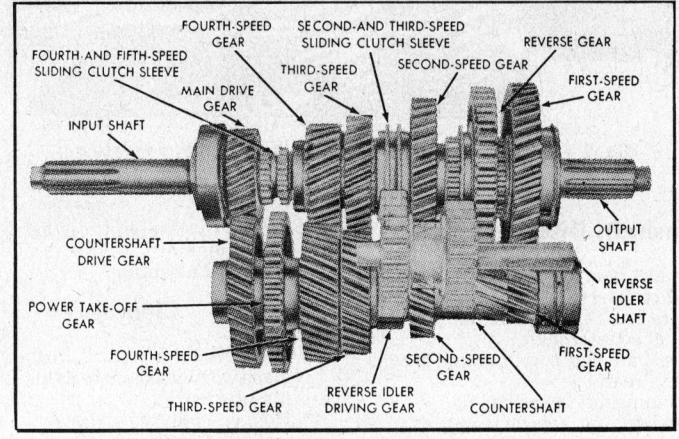

Fig. 1 Gear train of Series 5-74 five-speed transmission

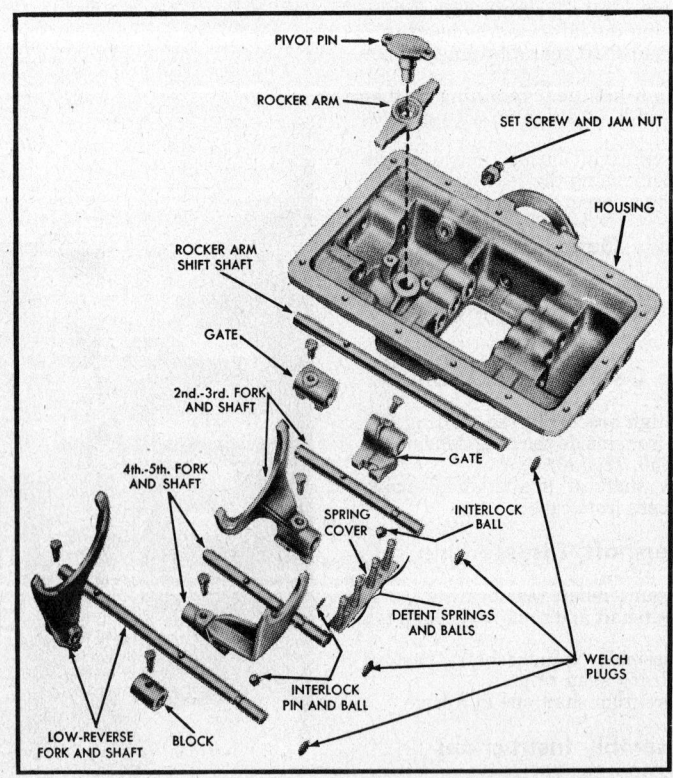

Fig. 2 Gearshift housing disassembled. Series 5-H-74, 740

FULLER TRANSMISSIONS

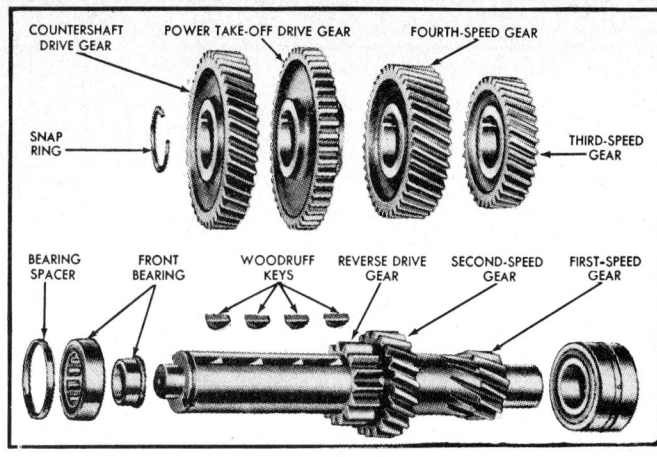

Fig. 3 Countershaft disassembled. Series 5-H-74, 740

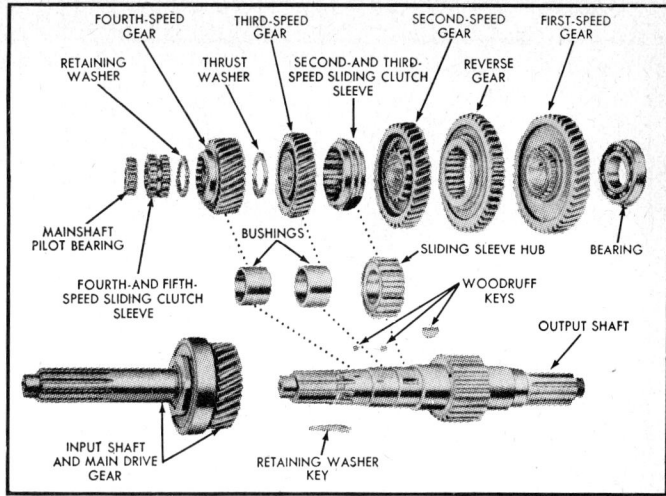

Fig. 4 Main drive line disassembled. Series 5-H-74, 740

4. Position a ¾" interlock ball in housing opening between 2-3 and 4-5 shafts.
5. Insert 4-5 shaft into housing and through its fork. Insert interlock pin into shaft as neutral notch enters web. Install lock screw.
6. Install remaining ¾" interlock ball.
7. Insert low-reverse shaft through housing, block and fork. Install set screws.
8. Safety wire all set screws and pivot pin retaining bolts.
9. Install four ½" steel balls and detent springs. Be sure all shafts are in neutral position so that balls will fit in their slots.
10. Install detent spring cover and new gasket.
11. Install plugs in shift shaft openings of housing.
12. Start set screw and jam nut and tighten screw until it bottoms. Back off ½ turn and tighten jam nut.

Countershaft Assemble, Fig. 3

1. Install Woodruff keys and press gears on one at a time.
2. Press on front bearing inner race and install drive gear snap ring.

Output Shaft Assemble, Fig. 4

1. Install Woodruff keys for sleeve hub and 3rd speed gear bushing.
2. Position 2nd gear (clutching teeth front) on shaft, then press sleeve hub (recessed end to front) tightly against gear.
3. Press 3rd gear bushing on shaft and against sleeve hub. Position clutch sleeve on its hub.
4. Position 3rd gear (clutching teeth to rear) on its bushing.
5. Install thrust washer (chamfer to rear) and install remaining key.
6. Press 4th gear bushing on shaft and position 4th gear (hub forward) on bushing.
7. Install retaining washer and measure clearance between 4th gear and its thrust washer. If clearance is not within the limits of .006 to .012", select the required retaining washer to result in the specified end play.
8. Install retaining washer key and clutch sleeve (recessed end to rear).
9. Install pilot bearing in input shaft gear pocket.
10. If input shaft bearing was removed, install new bearing with shielded side toward front.

Assemble Transmission

1. Install countershaft front bearing in case bore.
2. Position front bearing spacer and gasket and install retainer.
3. Position countershaft in case, then tilt case so that its rear face is up.
4. Position two wood or fiber blocks of equal thickness between drive gear and case.
5. Position inner bearing outer race in adapter, then apply sealer to adapter gasket. Make sure adapter oil return hole is aligned, then install gasket and adapter.
6. Install inner bearing cone.
7. Position spacer and install outer bearing cone. Position outer bearing outer race.
8. Install bearing lock plate and safety wire bolts.
9. Apply sealer to adapter cap gasket and install gasket and cap.
10. After tilting case back to its normal position, install idler gear and shaft. Be sure flat on shaft will align with lock plate. Install lock plate.
11. Position output shaft sliding gears in case, then install output shaft in case. Check for proper gear engagement with countergears.
12. Install output shaft rear bearing.
13. Install input shaft bearing snap ring in case bore.
14. Position input shaft, then install gasket and bearing retainer, using sealer on gasket.
15. Install clutch housing and speedometer drive gear.
16. After installing new seal in rear bearing retainer, install gasket and retainer, using sealer on gasket.
17. Install parking brake shoe assembly and connect brake linkage.
18. With transmission locked in two gears, install brake drum and flange.
19. Adjust parking brake and install gearshift housing, using a new gasket.

Fuller Separate Auxiliary Transmissions

3-65 SERIES

Disassemble Transmission

1. Referring to Fig. 1, remove shifter mechanism.
2. Remove rear cover, speedometer drive gear and washer from output shaft.
3. From inside of case, drive output shaft to the rear, forcing rear bearing out of its seat in case bore.
4. Use puller to remove rear bearing.
5. Remove low-speed clutch gear through output shaft rear bearing bore.
6. Lift output shaft through top of case.
7. Drive countershaft rearward until rear bearing cap has been forced from case.
8. Move countershaft rearward as far as it will go.
9. Remove retaining nuts from input shaft from bearing cover.
10. Drive input shaft backward into case and lift assembly out through top of case.
11. Remove input shaft front bearing cover.
12. Remove front bearing spacer.
13. Place bearing cover in a vise.
14. Drive bearing forward against oil seal, forcing both out through front of case.
15. Disassemble output shaft and counter-

FULLER TRANSMISSIONS

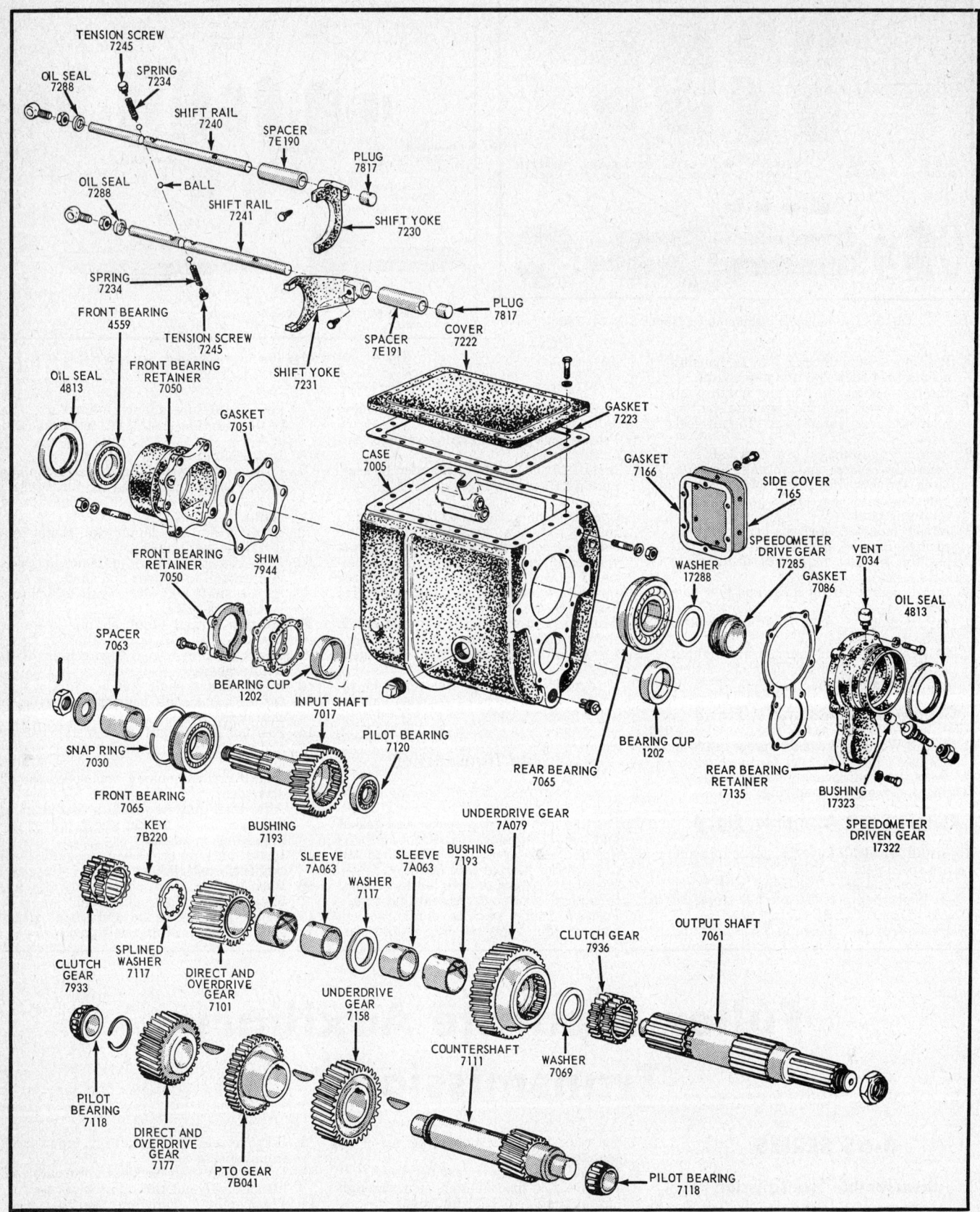

Fig. 1 Exploded view of 3-65 Series three-speed auxiliary transmission

FULLER TRANSMISSIONS

shaft as required.

Countershaft Assemble, Fig. 1

1. Insert Woodruff keys in shaft.
2. Press overdrive, PTO and direct drive gears on shaft one at a time. Shaft must center gear bore on chamfered side of gear.
3. Install snap ring on front end of countershaft.
4. Install pilot bearings on each end of countershaft.

Output Shaft Assemble, Fig. 1

1. Place output shaft in vise with front end up.
2. Install underdrive gear rear washer with waffle side facing up.
3. Install underdrive gear bushing.
4. Install underdrive gear on shaft with internal clutching teeth facing down.
5. Position underdrive gear rear thrust washer on shaft.
6. Install overdrive gear.
7. Install overdrive gear splined washer with thrust surface toward gear. Turn washer in its groove until lugs on inside diameter line up with splines on output shaft.
8. Install washer key in keyway between splines of output shaft.
9. Install direct and overdrive clutch gear with counterbore to rear.
10. Install output shaft pilot bearing.

Assemble Transmission

1. Install countershaft in case with rear bearing protruding through rear bore.
2. Remove snap ring from input shaft main bearing.
3. Press input shaft main bearing on shaft, leaving approximately $1/2$" space between bearing and drive gear.
4. Install input shaft from inside of case, driving shaft forward until main bearing snap ring groove is clear of case.
5. Install snap ring on main bearing.
6. Block rear of input shaft and, using a sleeve-type bearing installer, drive bearing backward until it seats against drive gear shoulder.
7. Install countershaft front bearing cup in case bore.
8. Move countershaft forward until front bearing seats in bearing cup.
9. Install countershaft rear bearing cup in case bore.
10. Install countershaft rear bearing cover and tighten capscrews.
11. Install countershaft front bearing cover and tighten securely. Then remove bearing cover and measure distance bearing cup protrudes from case. This distance should be .003–.005". Add or subtract shims as required.
12. Remove rear bearing cover.
13. Lower output shaft assembly into case, engaging helical gears of output shaft with those of countershaft.
14. Insert pilot bearing into drive gear bore.
15. Slide underdrive clutch gear onto shaft with chamfered end of clutch facing underdrive gear.
16. Drive output shaft rear bearing into place in case bore.
17. Install speedometer gear washer with chamfered side in, then install speedometer gear.
18. Install output shaft rear bearing cover. Install oil seal in cover.
19. Install input shaft front bearing cover but do not tighten retaining nuts at this time.
20. Install input shaft spacer and outer bearing in cover bore.
21. Tighten input shaft bearing cover nuts.
22. Install oil seal in front bearing cover.
23. Insert direct and overdrive shift bar into lower set of shift bar holes in case. This bar must pass direct and overdrive yoke and spacer. Spacer must be installed to rear of yoke.
24. Install yoke lock screw and wire securely.
25. Insert one $1/2$" steel ball in poppet spring hole located between the two shift bars.
26. Be sure direct-overdrive shift bar is in neutral. Insert underdrive shift bar through spacer and shift yoke. Spacer should locate in front of shift yoke. Install shift bar in upper set of holes in case.
27. Install yoke lock screw and wire securely.
28. Shift the bars into neutral. Install poppet balls, springs and plugs in both upper and lower poppet holes.
29. Install top cover and tighten screws securely.

4-C-75 FOUR SPEED

Disassemble Transmission

1. Referring to Fig. 2, remove shifter mechanism.
2. Lock mainshaft in two gears at once. Then remove nuts and take off universal joint companion flanges from input and output shafts.
3. Place transmission gears in neutral.
4. Remove capscrews from rear cover.
5. Move sliding 1st and 2nd speed gears forward on output shaft into engagement with 2nd speed gear on countershaft.
6. Drive output shaft rearward until rear bearing cover is forced approximately $1/4$" from case.
7. Place a wood block between rear of case and 1st speed gear.
8. Pry rear bearing cover from case.
9. Remove oil seal from cover.
10. Remove speedometer gear and washer from rear of output shaft.
11. Remove wood block and move output shaft to rear, forcing rear bearing from its seat in case bore.
12. Use a puller to remove output shaft rear bearing.
13. Lift output shaft out through top of case, then remove sliding gear from case.
14. Remove countershaft rear bearing plate.
15. Remove countershaft front bearing cover.
16. From outside of case, drive countershaft rearward until front and rear bearings are forced out of their seats in case bores and 1st speed gear is completely exposed outside the case.
17. Force input shaft rearward until shaft is unseated from bearings.
18. Lift input shaft out of case.
19. Remove front bearing cover.
20. Remove input shaft gear bearing spacer from inside of bearing cover.
21. Remove input shaft front bearing and oil seal from inside of bearing cover.
22. Force input shaft main bearing out through front of case bore.
23. Remove countershaft rear bearing with a puller.
24. Lift countershaft out top of case.
25. Disassemble output shaft and countershaft as required.

Countershaft Assemble, Fig. 2

1. Install Woodruff keys in countershaft keyways.
2. Press overdrive gear on shaft with long shoulder toward rear.
3. Press on PTO gear with long shoulder to the rear.
4. Press drive gear on shaft with long shoulder to the rear.
5. Install snap ring in its groove at front end of shaft.
6. Install front bearing on shaft. Bearing must be flush with end of shaft with stamped face forward.

Output Shaft Assemble, Fig. 2

1. Mount output shaft in a vise with front end up.
2. Install 2nd speed gear on shaft with clutching teeth down.
3. Install overdrive gear rear washer with waffle side down.
4. Install overdrive gear bushing on shaft, fitting bushing tight against washer.
5. Install overdrive gear on bushing, clutching teeth up.
6. Install splined washer in its groove, flat side down.
7. Turn splined washer in its groove until lugs on inside diameter line up with splines of output shaft.
8. Install washer key in its keyway between lugs of splined washer.
9. Install sliding clutch gear on shaft with counterbore toward rear.
10. Install pilot bearing on front of shaft, chamfered inner diameter down.
11. Remove assembly from vise and install sliding gear over rear of shaft with yoke slot facing forward.

Transmission, Assemble

1. Place countershaft assembly in bottom of case, inserting rear of shaft through rear bore of case until 1st gear is completely exposed.
2. Remove snap ring from input shaft main bearing.
3. Press input shaft main bearing on shaft, leaving approximately 1" space between bearing and gear.
4. Install input shaft from inside of case. Be sure front bearing is not cocked in case bore.
5. Move input shaft and bearing forward until bearing snap ring groove is exposed, then install snap ring.
6. Using a sleeve-type bearing installer, force main bearing against shoulder of gear.
7. Install input shaft front bearing cover. Install lockwashers and nuts but do not tighten at this time. Install spacer in bearing cover.
8. Install front bearing on input shaft with shielded side out.
9. Tighten bearing cover nuts securely. Install oil seal in cover.
10. Work countershaft forward and insert front bearing into case bore. At the same time, mesh countershaft drive gear with input shaft drive gear.
11. Install rear bearing in countershaft and into case bore. Bearing must seat against shoulder of shaft.
12. Install rear bearing retainer plate. Tighten capscrews evenly and install lockwire.
13. Install front bearing cover.
14. Move output shaft sliding gear into engagement with 2nd speed gear.

FULLER TRANSMISSIONS

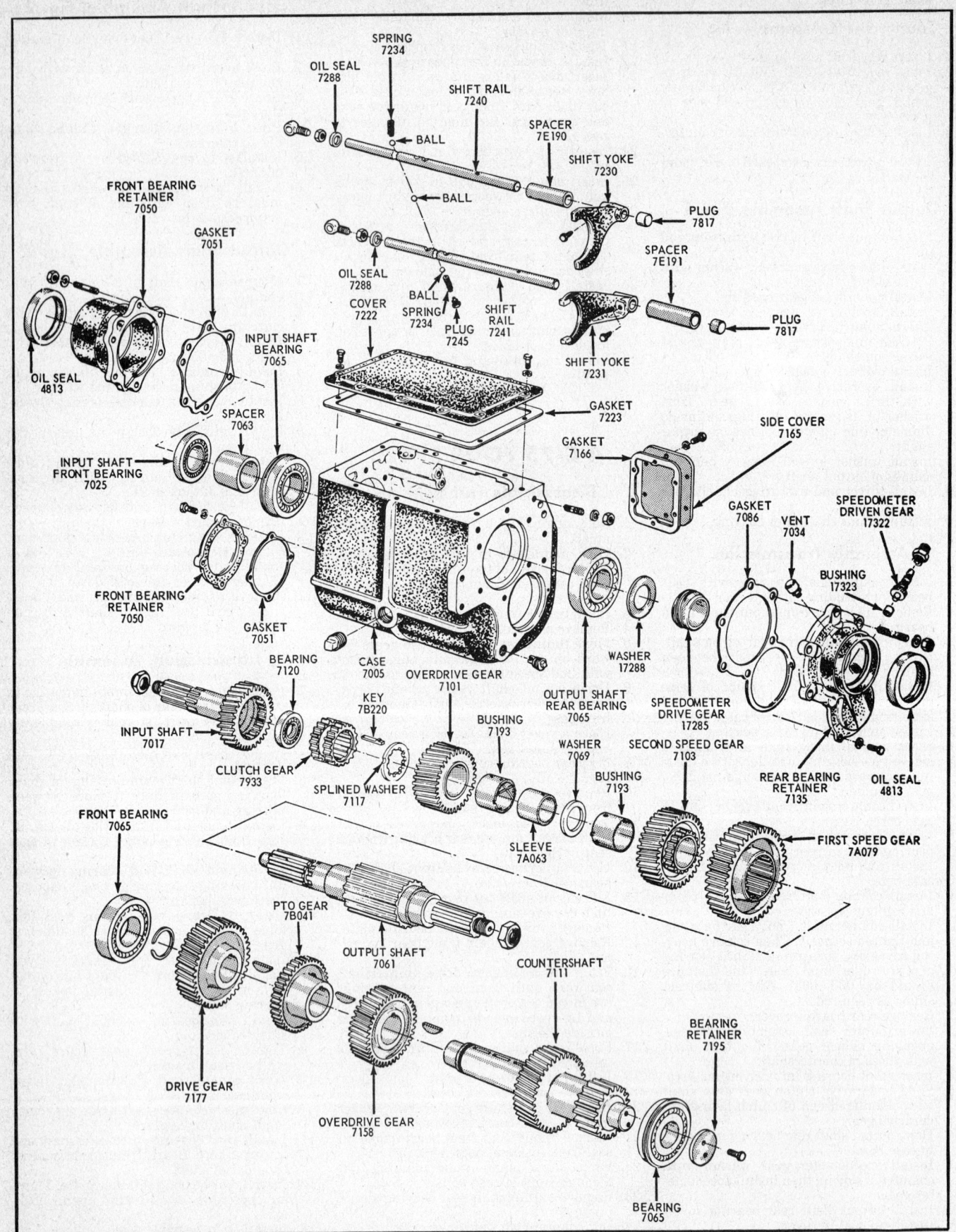

Fig. 2 Exploded view of 4-C-75 four speed auxiliary transmission

FULLER TRANSMISSIONS

15. Lower output shaft into case, engaging output shaft gears with mating gears on countershaft. At the same time, fit output shaft pilot bearing into drive gear bore.
16. Block front face of 2nd speed gear to prevent output shaft movement. Install output shaft rear bearing in case bore. Bearing should seat against shoulder of shaft with stamped numbers forward.
17. Remove block and install speedometer gear washer and drive gear on rear of shaft.
18. Install rear bearing cover.
19. Install oil seal in rear cover.
20. Install vent in rear bearing cover.
21. Lock output shaft by engaging two gears. Install companion flange on shaft, being sure flange is tight against speedometer gear.
22. Install companion flange to input shaft.
23. Move gears to neutral position.
24. Install direct-overdrive shift bar through shift yoke and long spacer and into lower set of shift bar bores. At the same time, insert shift yoke into yoke slot on clutch gear. Install lock screw and wire securely.
25. Place shift bar in neutral and install steel interlock ball in angled boss at top of case.
26. Install 1st, 2nd shift bar into upper shift bar bore, through short spacer and shift yoke. Keep lower shift bar in neutral to prevent interlock ball from jamming upper shaft bar during installation. Install lock screw and wire securely.
27. With both shift bars in neutral, install lower tension ball, spring and plug on side of case.
28. Install top tension ball and spring in top face of case. Install top cover.

NEW PROCESS TRANSMISSIONS

INDEX & LUBE CAPACITY

Model	Speeds	Oil, Pts.	Page
245, 275	5	12	329
420	4	5½	329
433, 434, 435	4	7	331
445	4	7	337
540, 541, 542	5	10	335
745	3	3¾	339
875, 895	5	8	342
5401, 2, 3, 4	5	10	335
7550, 7590	5	22	343

SERIES 245, 275

Disassemble, Figs. 1, 2

1. Remove nut from output shaft.
2. Remove parking brake, universal joint spline flange and parking brake drum.
3. Remove gearshift housing.
4. Remove power take-off covers and gaskets.
5. Remove speedometer driven gear and bearing from output shaft bearing retainer.
6. Remove output shaft bearing retainer and slide speedometer drive gear and spacer from output shaft.
7. Remove input shaft bearing retainer and pull shaft and bearing out through front of case.
8. Slide synchronizer assembly off output shaft and lift shaft out of case.
9. Pull reverse idler gear shaft out of case and lift out gear.
10. Remove countershaft front bearing retainer, unfasten retainer washer and remove washer.
11. Remove bolts from countershaft rear bearing cap. Tap countershaft toward rear until bearing cap and bearing is forced out of case.
12. Lift out countershaft front bearing.

Disassemble Sub-Assemblies

Input Shaft—Remove lock nut from end of shaft and remove bearing. Remove snap ring from shaft bore and remove output shaft pilot bearings. Remove snap ring from output shaft bearing.

Output Shaft—Slide low and reverse gear and 2nd speed gear from shaft. Remove snap ring and remove 4th and 5th gear synchronizer hub. Slide 4th speed gear (5th gear on overdrive units) and thrust washer from shaft. Remove bushing from gear and pin from bushing.

Slide off 3rd speed gear and thrust washer and remove bearing rollers from gear. Separate synchronizer parts and inspect for wear or damage. Reassemble with new parts as necessary.

Countershaft—Remove thrust washer from front end of countershaft. Press gear cluster off shaft and drive key from shaft slot.

Reverse Idler Gear—Remove thrust washer from bore of gear and remove bearing rollers and spacer.

Assemble Sub-Assemblies

Reverse Idler Gear—Install spacer in gear. Coat bearing rollers with grease and install 31 rollers in each end of gear. Install washer at each end of gear next to rollers.

Countershaft—Install spacer on shaft and key in slot. Press gear cluster on shaft until gear is seated against spacer. Position thrust washer on forward end of shaft.

Output Shaft—Coat 3rd speed gear rollers with lubricant and install rollers in bore of gear. Place thrust washer on shaft and slide gear on shaft with spur gear teeth toward rear.

Install lock pin in 4th speed gear bushing (5th speed gear on overdrive units). Place thrust washer on shaft and install bushing. Install gear on bushing with shorter teeth toward front.

Position clutch gear on shaft and install snap ring in shaft groove. Check 3rd speed gear end play. If not within .006–.008″, replace snap ring with one of the proper thickness to give correct end play.

Position 2nd speed gear on shaft with shift fork groove toward rear. Install low and reverse gear on shaft with shift fork groove toward front of shaft. Assemble synchronizer as shown in Fig. 1.

Input Shaft—Install bearing on shaft. Install lock nut and tighten until bearing is firmly seated against gear shoulder. Install snap ring in shaft bearing groove.

Coat pilot bearing rollers with grease, and install in bore of input shaft. Secure bearings with snap ring.

Installation in Case

1. Install snap ring on countershaft front bearing and tap bearing into case.
2. Position countershaft in case and insert forward end in front bearing.
3. Tap countershaft rear bearing and cap into case and onto countershaft. Install bolts and lockwashers.
4. Install countershaft front bearing retaining washer and retainer.
5. Position reverse idler gear in case and tap idler shaft into case until notch in shaft is flush with rear face of case. Install shaft retainer.
6. Place output shaft in case and slip on synchronizer.
7. Install input shaft through front of case. Tap assembly into case until bearing snap ring is seated in recess in case. Install and tighten bearing retainer.
8. Position output shaft into pilot bearing, then install shims on rear of output shaft. Install snap ring on output shaft bearing and tap bearing into case bore until snap ring is seated against rear face of case. Install spacer and speedometer drive gear on output shaft.
9. Install output shaft bearing retainer and tighten securely.
10. Check end play of synchronizer. If not within .040–.060″, change shims at rear of output shaft until correct end play is obtained.
11. Install speedometer driven gear and bearing, and power take-off covers.
12. Place gears in neutral and install gearshift housing, tightening bolts to 30–40 ft. lbs. torque.
13. Slide parking brake drum onto output shaft and place band and lever on drum. Install bolts to case and torque them to 30–40 ft. lbs.
14. Install parking brake band anchor spring and adjusting screw, then adjust brake.

SERIES 420

Disassemble, Fig. 3

1. Remove nut from companion yoke.
2. Remove hand brake linkage and band.
3. Pull off brake drum and companion yoke.
4. Remove transmission cover.
5. Remove rear bearing retainer and seal assembly, and speedometer drive gear.
6. Remove main drive gear bearing retainer, gear and bearing.
7. Remove snap ring and pull rear bearing from case. Remove shim pack and tie shims together for reassembly.
8. Remove synchronizer snap ring and slide synchronizer gear forward. Then slide

329

NEW PROCESS TRANSMISSIONS

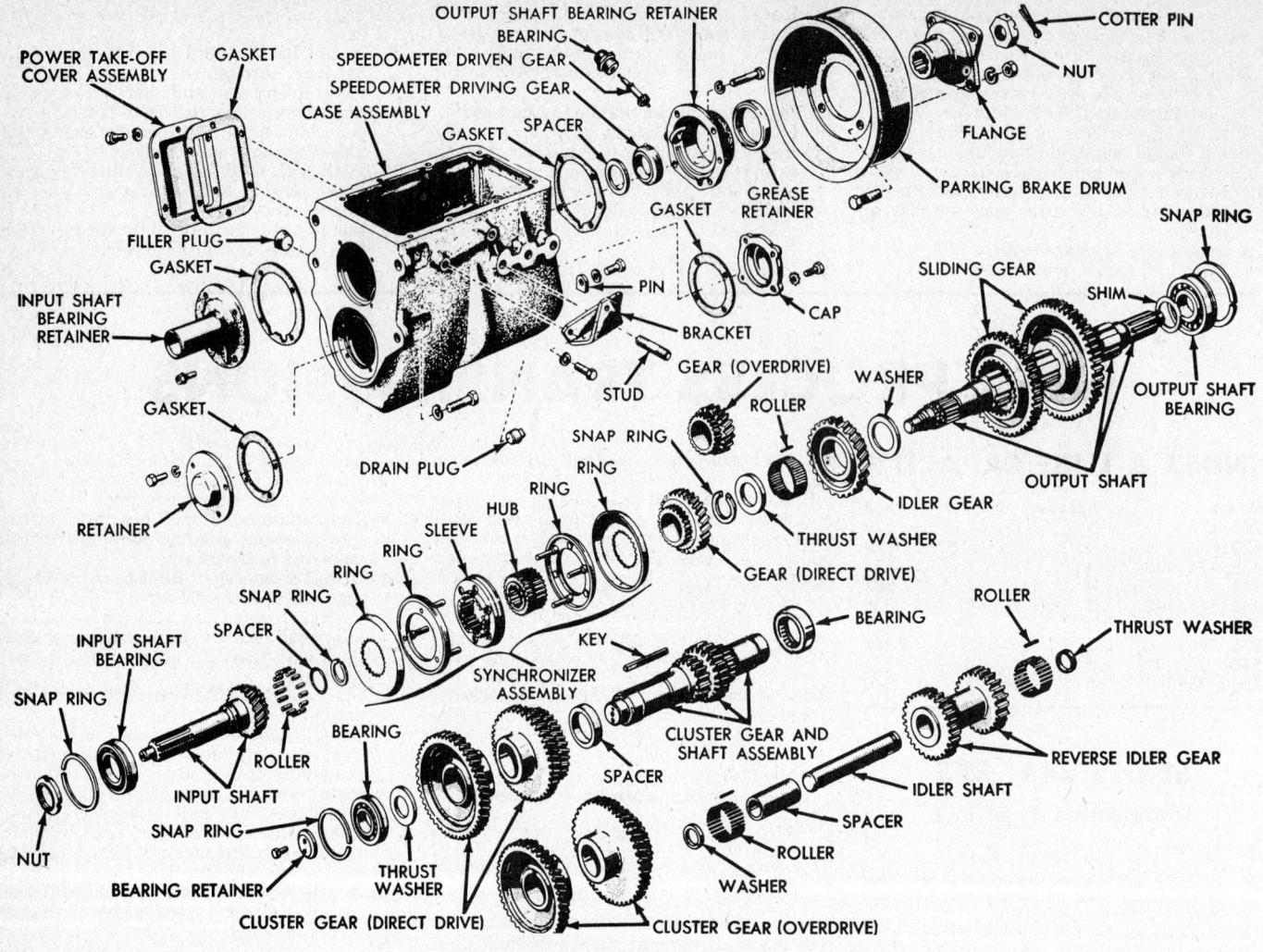

Fig. 1 New Process five speed transmission. Series 245, 275

synchronizer from mainshaft.
9. Lift mainshaft assembly out of case through sliding gears. Then remove sliding gears from case.
10. Remove reverse idler shaft lock plate, pull out shaft and lift gear from case.
11. Remove rear countershaft bearing retainer and bearing. Then remove front countershaft retainer, cap screws and lock plate, and remove bearing.
12. Lift countershaft assembly from case.

Reassembly

Reverse Idler Gear—Install spacer in gear. Coat roller bearings with grease and install a complete set of 31 rollers in each end of the gear. Install a thrust washer in each end of the gear.

Countershaft—Install spacer and drive key in shaft keyway. Remove all burrs from key and shaft and press gear cluster onto shaft until gears bottom on spacer. Then install thrust washer on forward end of shaft.

Mainshaft—Coat third speed gear roller bearings with grease and place in third speed gear. Install thrust washer on mainshaft. Position third speed gear with spur teeth toward rear of shaft and slide gear on shaft.
Install lock pin in fourth speed gear (fifth on overdrive units). Place thrust washer on shaft and install bushing on shaft. Position fourth (or fifth) speed gear with shortest teeth toward front end of shaft. Install gear on bushing.

Install mainshaft synchronizer gear on mainshaft and secure with snap ring in shaft groove. Check snap ring for proper thickness by testing third speed gear end play. Snap rings are available in .002″ steps each to obtain desired end play of .006 to .008″.

Position second speed gear with shift fork groove toward rear of shaft and slide gear on shaft.

Main Drive Gear—Install bearing on shaft. Install lock nut and tighten securely to seat bearing against gear shoulder. Install snap ring in bearing groove. Lubricate mainshaft pilot bearing and place it in main drive gear bore.

Installation in Case

Countershaft—Install snap ring on countershaft front bearing and tap bearing into case. Lower countershaft in case and insert shaft into front bearing. Install new gasket on rear bearing retainer and tap rear bearing and retainer assembly into case and on countershaft. Install retainer cap screws and lock washers and tighten securely. Install countershaft front bearing lock plate and secure screws with lock wire. Install front bearing retainer, using a new gasket, and tighten securely.

Reverse Idler Gear—Place gear in position and tap shaft through case and gear until notch in shaft is flush with rear face of transmission case. Install shaft lock plate.

Mainshaft & Main Drive Gear—Place low and reverse gear in case. Lower mainshaft into case, passing it through low and reverse gear. Then insert shaft through rear of case far enough to install synchronizer parts one at a time on front end of shaft.

Insert main drive gear in case, tapping it with a soft hammer until the bearing snap ring is seated against case. Install main drive gear bearing retainer, using a new gasket, and tighten securely.

Place synchronizer outer stop ring on main drive gear and position front end of mainshaft into pilot bearing. Then install shim pack (as removed) on rear end of mainshaft.

Install snap ring on mainshaft rear bearing. Tap bearing into case until retainer seats against case. Install speedometer gear on mainshaft. Install mainshaft rear bearing retainer, using new gaskets, and tighten securely.

Install companion yoke and nut, tightening nut from 95–135 ft. lbs. torque. Check gears in neutral and in all speeds for free rotation.

NEW PROCESS TRANSMISSIONS

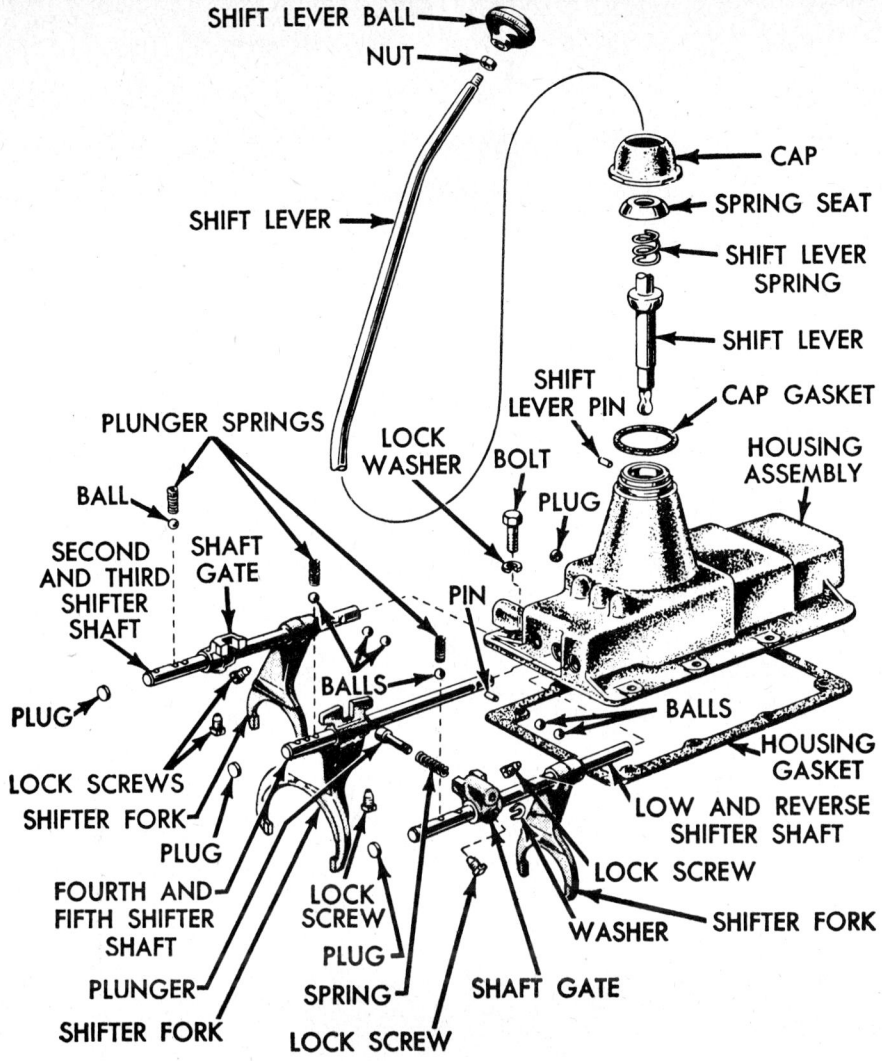

Fig. 2 New Process 245 and 275 gearshift housing

Check synchronizer end play by placing feeler gauges diametrically opposite each other. End play should be .040 to .060"; if not within these limits, adjust by removing or adding shims at the rear of the case to obtain the desired result.

With gears in neutral, install a new gasket and install the transmission cover. Tighten cover screws to 30–40 ft. lbs. torque.

Install hand brake and fill transmission with correct amount of lubricant.

SERIES 433, 434, 435

Transmission Disassemble, Fig. 3A

1. With transmission in neutral, remove gearshift housing.
2. Lock transmission in two gears and remove output flange nut, yoke and brake drum.
3. Remove speedometer drive pinion and mainshaft rear bearing retainer.
4. Remove drive pinion bearing retainer.
5. Rotate drive pinion gear to align space in pinion gear teeth with countershaft drive gear teeth and remove drive pinion gear and tapered roller bearing from transmission.
6. Remove snap ring, washer and pilot roller bearing from recess in drive pinion gear.
7. Using a brass drift placed in front center of mainshaft, drive mainshaft to rear, then when mainshaft rear bearing clears case, remove rear bearing and speedometer gear (with spacer) using a puller.
8. Move mainshaft assembly rearward and tilt front of mainshaft up.
9. Remove roller thrust bearing, synchronizer and stop rings, and mainshaft.
10. Remove reverse idler lock screw and lockplate.
11. Using a brass drift, drive idler gear rearward, then pull shaft and lift reverse idler gear from case.
12. Remove gearing retainer at rear end of countershaft.
13. Tilt cluster gear assembly and work it out of case.
14. Using a suitable driver, remove front bearings from case.

Disassemble Sub-Assemblies

Mainshaft

1. Remove clutch gear snap ring, then remove clutch gear, synchronizer outer stop ring to third speed gear shim(s) and third gear.
2. Using two screwdrivers, remove split lock ring, then remove second speed gear and synchronizer.
3. Remove first and reverse sliding gear.

Reverse Idler Gear

Do not disassemble idler gear. If satisfactory operation is doubtful, replace entire assembly complete with bearings.

Drive Pinion & Bearing Retainer

1. Using a suitable tool, remove roller bearing from pinion shaft.
2. Remove snap ring, washer and pilot rollers from gear bore.
3. Using a puller, remove bearing race from front bearing retainer.
4. Remove pinion shaft seal.

Shifter Housing

1. Remove roll pins from first and second speed shift fork and gate.
2. Push shift rail out through front to force expansion plug out of cover and remove rail, fork and gate.

NOTE: Cover detent ball access hole in cover to prevent ball and spring from flying out as rail clears hole.

NEW PROCESS TRANSMISSIONS

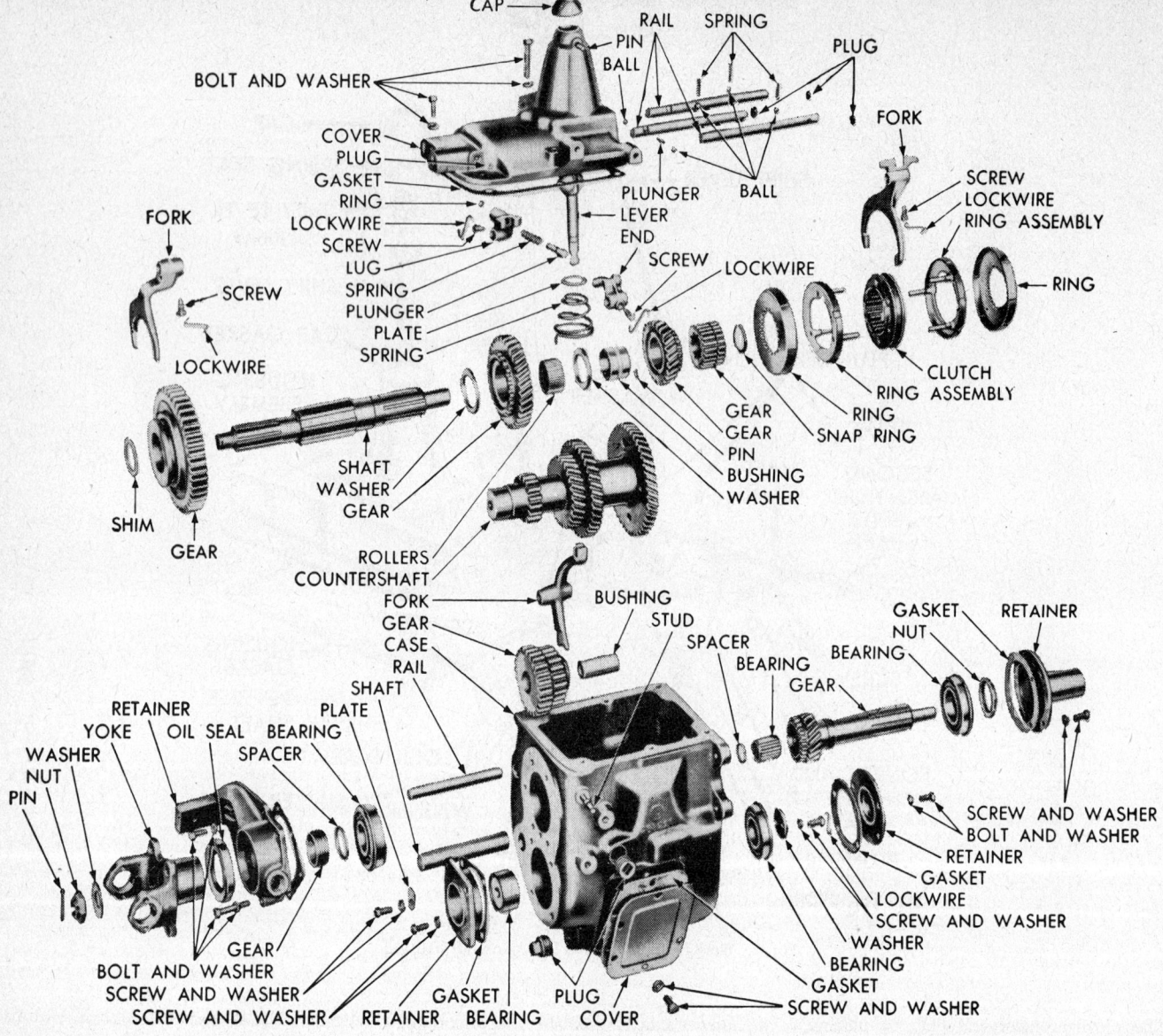

Fig. 3 New Process 420 Series four speed transmissions

3. Remove third and fourth speed rails, then remove reverse rail.
4. Compress reverse gear plunger, then remove retaining clip, plunger and spring from gate.

Assemble Sub-Assemblies

When assembling sub-assemblies, use new expansion plugs, gaskets and seals. Lubricate all parts with clean transmission lubricant. Where grease is recommended, use oil soluble grease. Make certain that oil return passages are not obstructed with grease.

Mainshaft
1. Place mainshaft in soft jawed vise with rear end up and install first and reverse gear making sure that two spline springs (if used) are inside of gear.
2. Reverse mainshaft in vise with forward end up.
3. Assemble second speed synchronizer spring and synchronizer brake to second speed gear, then install snap ring making sure that snap ring tangs are facing away from gear.
4. Slide second speed gear onto front of output shaft making sure that synchronizer brake is toward rear, then install the two piece lock ring and install third speed gear.
5. Install shim(s) between third speed gear and third and fourth speed synchronizer stop ring. Check end play. If end play is not within .050–.070 inch, add or remove shims as necessary to bring end play to specifications.

Drive Pinion & Bearing Retainer
1. Using an arbor press and a wooden block placed on pinion gear, press gear into bearing until it contacts bearing inner race.
2. Coat roller bearings with a light coat of grease to hold rollers in place and insert into pocket of drive pinion.
3. Install washer and snap ring.
4. Press seal into bearing retainer making sure that lip of seal is toward mounting plate.
5. Press bearing race into retainer.

Shifter Housing, Fig. 3B
1. Install spring on reverse gear plunger, then compress spring into reverse shift gate and install retaining clip.
2. Install reverse shift rail into cover and place detent spring and ball in position, then depress ball and slide rail over it.
3. Install gate and fork on rail, then install a new roll pin in gate and fork.
4. With reverse fork in neutral position, install the two interlock plungers in their bores.
5. Install interlock pin in third and fourth speed shift rail, then install rail in same manner as reverse shift rail.
6. Install first and second speed shift rail in same manner as reverse shift rail, making certain that interlock plunger is in

NEW PROCESS TRANSMISSIONS

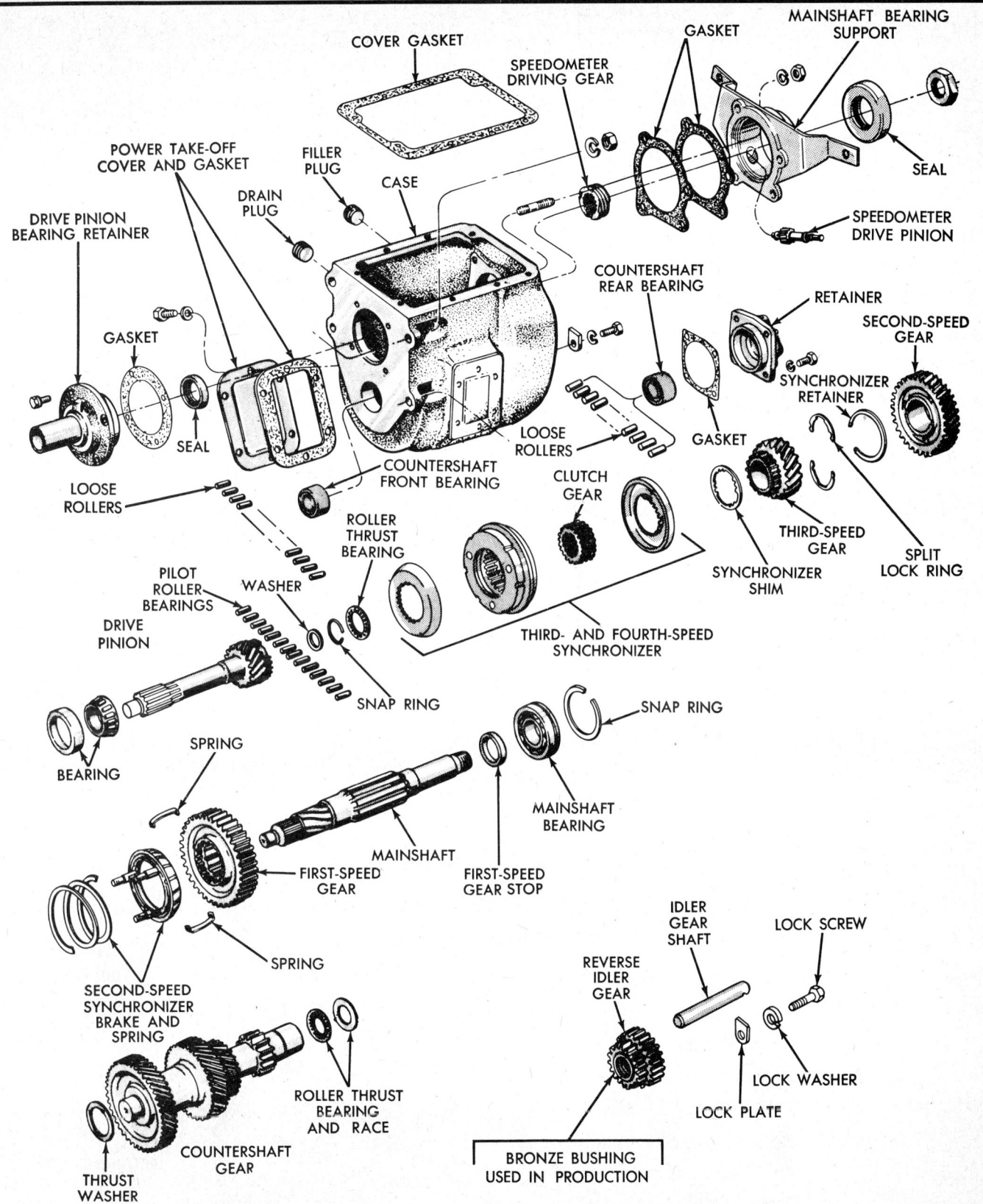

Fig. 3A New Process four speed transmission. Series 433, 434, 435

NEW PROCESS TRANSMISSIONS

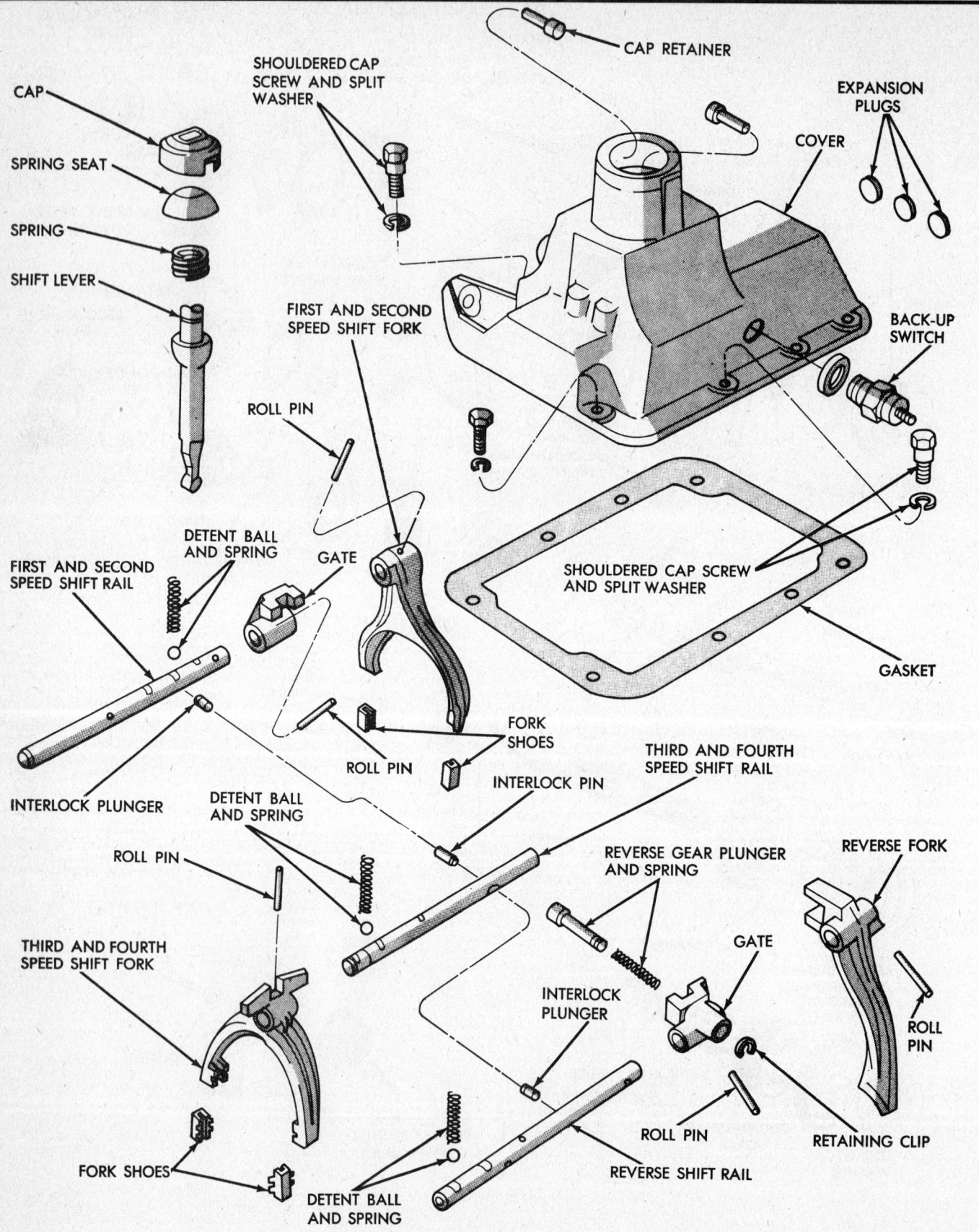

Fig. 3B Shifter housing disassembled. Series 433, 434, 435

NEW PROCESS TRANSMISSIONS

place.

NOTE: Check interlocks by shifting reverse shift rail into reverse position. It should be impossible to shift all other rails when this rail is shifted.

7. If installing shift lever, lubricate spherical ball seat and place cap in position.
8. Install back-up light switch, if used.
9. Install new expansion plugs in bores of rail holes and install interlock hole plug.

Transmission Assemble

1. Press front roller bearing into case until cage is flush with front of case and lubricate bearings with a light coat of grease.
2. Position transmission with front of case facing down. If uncaged roller bearings are being re-used, hold rollers in place with a light coat of grease.
3. Lower countershaft assembly into case, placing thrust washer tangs in slots in case and inserting front end of shaft into bearing.
4. Place countershaft rear roller thrust bearing on countershaft and hold in place with a light coat of grease.
5. Align countershaft assembly and install retainer gasket, retainer and bearing, then install and tighten screws.
6. Place reverse idler gear and bearing assembly in case.
7. Align reverse idler shaft so lock plate groove in shaft is properly aligned to install lock plate.
8. Tap reverse idler shaft far enough into case to start reverse gear, then while holding gear in position, tap shaft through case and gear.
9. Install lock plate, washer and screw. Make certain that gear turns freely on shaft.
10. Lower rear end of mainshaft into case, then while holding first speed gear on shaft, maneuver shaft through rear bearing opening.

NOTE: With shaft assembly moved to rear of case, make sure that third and fourth speed synchronizer and preselected shims remain in place.

11. Install roller thrust bearing.
12. Place a wood block between front of case and front of mainshaft.
13. Using a suitable size sleeve against inner race of bearing, install rear bearing onto shaft and into case until snap ring is flush against case.
14. Install drive pinion shaft and bearing assembly making sure pilot rollers remain in place.
15. Install spacer, speedometer gear, gasket and bearing retainer.
16. Place drive pinion bearing retainer over pinion shaft without gasket, then while holding retainer tight against bearing, measure clearance between retainer and case using a feeler gauge. Install a gasket shim pack .010–.015 inch greater than clearance measured between retainer and case to obtain the required .007–.017 inch pinion shaft end play. After retainer bolts are tightened, recheck end play.
17. Check for .050–.070 inch synchronizer end play after all mainshaft components are in place and properly tightened, using two sets of equal size feeler gauges Fig.

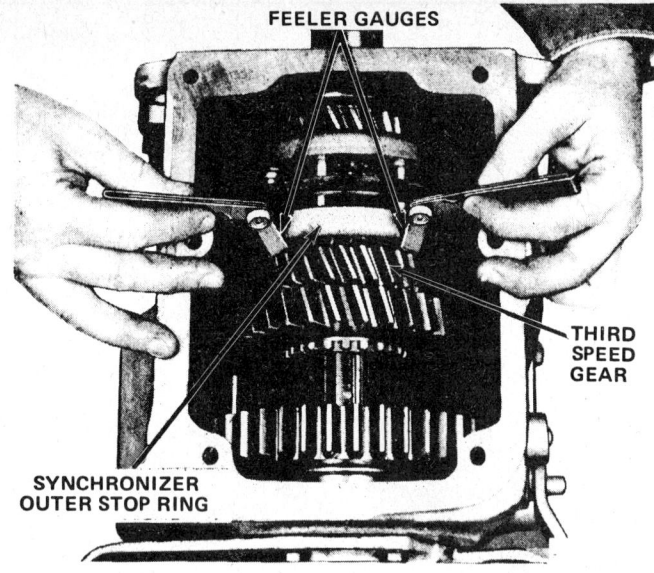

Fig. 3C Checking synchronizer end play. Series 433, 434, 435

3C. If necessary, disassemble mainshaft and change shims to retain end play within specifications.
18. Install speedometer drive pinion, yoke flange, drum and brake assembly and output flange nut.
19. Shift gears into all speed positions and check for freedom of operation.

NOTE: Before installing shifter housing, fill transmission with lubricant, then oil all exposed transmission parts to avoid damage to transmission at start up.

20. Move gears into neutral position, then lower cover and new gasket over transmission, engaging forks into proper gears.
21. Install one shouldered alignment screw in each of the holes on each side of cover located next to the front hole. Check gears for freedom by shifting gears with a long screwdriver inserted in cover tower.
22. Install remaining cover screws.

SERIES 540, 541, 542, 5400

Disassemble, Fig. 4

1. Remove nut from output shaft.
2. Remove parking brake, universal joint spline flange and parking brake drum.
3. Remove gearshift housing.
4. Remove power take-off covers and gaskets.
5. Remove speedometer driven gear and bearing from output shaft bearing retainer.
6. Remove output shaft bearing retainer and slide speedometer drive gear and spacer from output shaft.
7. Remove input shaft bearing retainer and pull shaft and bearing out through front of case.
8. Slide synchronizer assembly off output shaft and lift shaft out of case.
9. Pull reverse idler shaft out of case and lift out gear.
10. Remove countershaft front bearing retainer, unfasten retainer washer and remove washer.
11. Remove bolts from countershaft rear bearing cap. Tap countershaft toward rear of case until bearing cap and bearing is force out of case.

Disassemble Sub-Assemblies

Clutch Shaft—Remove lock nut from end of shaft and remove bearing. Remove snap ring from shaft bore and remove output shaft pilot bearings. Remove snap ring from output shaft bearing.

Mainshaft—Slide low and reverse gear and 2nd speed gear from shaft. Remove snap ring and remove 4th and 5th gear synchronizer hub. Slide 5th speed gear and thrust washer from shaft. Remove bushing from gear and lock pin from bushing.

Slide off 3rd speed gear and thrust washer and remove bearing rollers from gear. Separate synchronizer parts and inspect for wear or damage. Reassemble with new parts as necessary.

Countershaft—Remove thrust washer from front end of countershaft. Press gear cluster off shaft and drive key from shaft slot.

Reverse Idler Gear—Some models of these transmissions are equipped with a bushing type reverse idler gear, whereas others have roller bearing type gear. Remove thrust washers from bore of gear and remove bearing rollers and spacer (if equipped).

Assemble Sub-Assemblies

Reverse Idler Gear—If roller bearings are used, install spacer in gear. Coat bearing rollers with grease and install 31 rollers in each end of gear. Install washer at each end of gear next to rollers.

Countershaft—Install spacer on shaft and key in slot. Press gear cluster on shaft until gear is seated against spacer. Position thrust washer on forward end of shaft.

Mainshaft—Coat 3rd speed gear rollers with lubricant and install rollers in bore of gear. Place thrust washer on shaft and slide gear on shaft with spur gear teeth toward rear.

335

NEW PROCESS TRANSMISSIONS

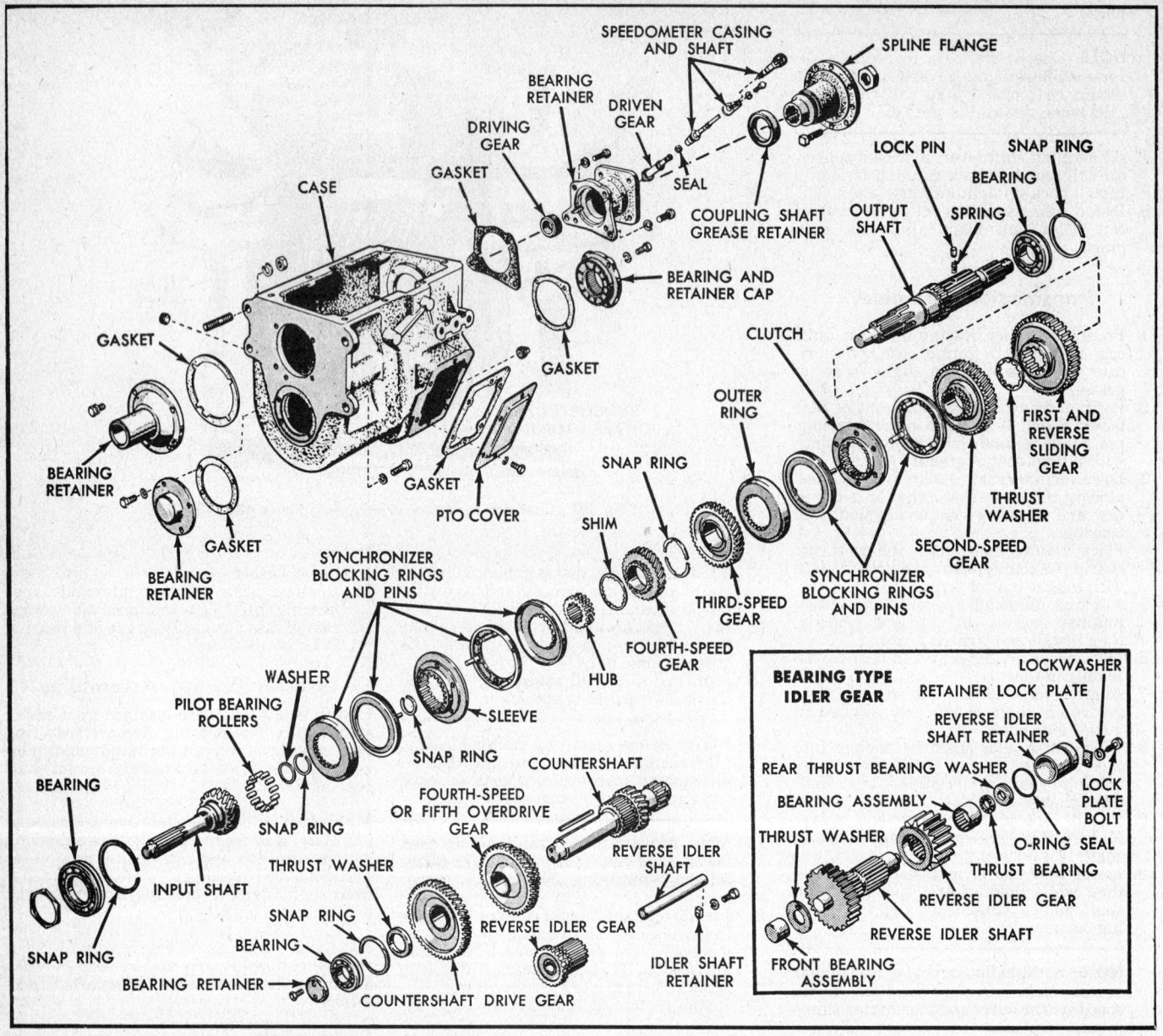

Fig. 4 New Process 540 and 5400 Series five speed transmission

Install lock pin in 5th speed gear bushing. Place thrust washer on shaft and install bushing. Install gear on bushing with shorter teeth toward front.

Position clutch gear on shaft and install snap ring in shaft groove. Check 3rd speed gear end play. If not within .006–.008", replace snap ring with one of the proper thickness to give correct end play.

Position 2nd speed gear on shaft with shift fork groove toward rear. Install low and reverse gear on shaft with shift fork groove toward front of shaft. Assemble synchronizer as shown in Fig. 4.

Input Shaft—Install bearing on shaft. Install lock nut and tighten until bearing is firmly seated against gear shoulder. Install snap ring in shaft bearing groove.

Coat pilot bearing rollers with grease and install in bore of input shaft. Secure bearings with snap ring.

Installation in Case

1. Install snap ring on countershaft front bearing and tap bearing into case.
2. Position countershaft in case and insert forward end in front bearing.
3. Tap countershaft rear bearing and cap into case and onto countershaft. Install bolts and lockwashers.
4. Install countershaft front bearing retaining washer and retainer.
5. Position reverse idler gear in case and tap idler shaft into case until notch in shaft is flush with rear face of case. Install shaft retainer.
6. Place output shaft in case and slip on synchronizer.
7. Insert input shaft through front of case. Tap assembly into case until bearing snap ring is seated in recess in case. Install and tighten bearing retainer.
8. Position output shaft into pilot bearing, then install shims on rear of output shaft. Install snap ring on output shaft bearing and tap bearing into case bore until snap ring is seated against rear face of case. Install spacer and speedometer drive gear on output shaft.
9. Install output shaft bearing retainer and tighten securely.
10. Check end play of synchronizer. If not within .040–.060", change shims at rear of output shaft until correct end play is obtained.

NOTE: The clearance on new synchronizer assemblies should be .070–.095 inch.

11. Install speedometer driven gear and bearing. Install power take-off covers.
12. Place gears in neutral and install gearshift housing, tightening bolts to 30–40 lb. ft. torque.
13. Slide parking brake drum onto output

NEW PROCESS TRANSMISSIONS

shaft and place band and lever on drum. Install bolts to case and torque them to 30–40 ft. lb.

14. Install parking brake band anchor spring and adjusting screw, then adjust brake.

MODEL 445

Disassemble, Fig. 5

1. Drain lubricant from transmission and remove gearshift cover.

NOTE: The two bolts opposite the tower are shouldered to properly position cover and are provided with lockwashers. Make certain that these alignment bolts are correctly located and tightened before installing cover.

2. Lock transmission in two gears and remove mainshaft nut and yoke.
3. Remove mainshaft rear extension housing and speedometer drive gear.
4. Remove pinion front bearing retainer and gasket, then rotate drive pinion gear to align pinion gear with countershaft drive gear teeth and remove drive pinion gear and tapered roller bearing from transmission, Fig. 6.
5. Remove thrust bearing, then push mainshaft assembly rearward of transmission and tilt front of mainshaft up, Fig. 7, and remove mainshaft from case.
6. Remove reverse idler lock plate, then using tool C-603, pull idler shaft from case and lift out reverse idler gear.

NOTE: If tool C-603 is not available, the reverse idler shaft may be driven out the rear of the case with a hammer and brass drift. DO NOT ATTEMPT TO DRIVE IDLER SHAFT FORWARD, as it is a shouldered shaft and a broken case will result.

7. Remove countershaft rear bearing retainer, then slide countershaft rearward, up and out of case, Fig. 8.
8. Drive countershaft from bearing assembly forward and out of transmission case.

SUB ASSEMBLIES, DISASSEMBLE

1. Place mainshaft vertically in soft jawed vise with front end up, then lift 3rd-4th synchronizer and high speed clutch gear off mainshaft and remove third speed gear.
2. Remove 2nd speed gear snap ring with snap ring pliers and lift off thrust washer, Fig. 9.

NOTE: The thrust washer must be positioned with ground surface toward 2nd speed gear when the mainshaft is reassembled.

3. Remove 2nd speed gear and lift off low speed synchronizer and clutch gear from mainshaft.
4. Using a gear puller, remove tapered bearing from rear of mainshaft, then remove 1st speed gear snap ring and thrust washer and lift off 1st speed gear.

COVER AND SHIFT FORK ASSEMBLY, FIG. 10

NOTE: The shift cover should be disassembled only if it is necessary to replace a shift fork, a shaft or the cover.

1. Using a square type or spiral wound "easy out" mounted in a tap handle, remove roll pin from 1st-2nd speed shift fork and roll pin from shift gate.
2. Push 1st-2nd speed shift rail out of rear of cover, driving out expansion plug and remove shift fork and gate. Be sure to cover detent hole to prevent loss of detent ball and spring.
3. Remove 3rd-4th speed shift rail in same manner as in steps 1 and 2.
4. Compress reverse gear plunger and remove retaining clip. Remove plunger and spring from gate.

CLEANING & INSPECTION

Wash all bearings in clean solvent and check all rollers and races for wear, pitting and spalled areas. Replace parts as necessary.

Check operating gear teeth for wear or pitting on tooth faces. Gears which have been

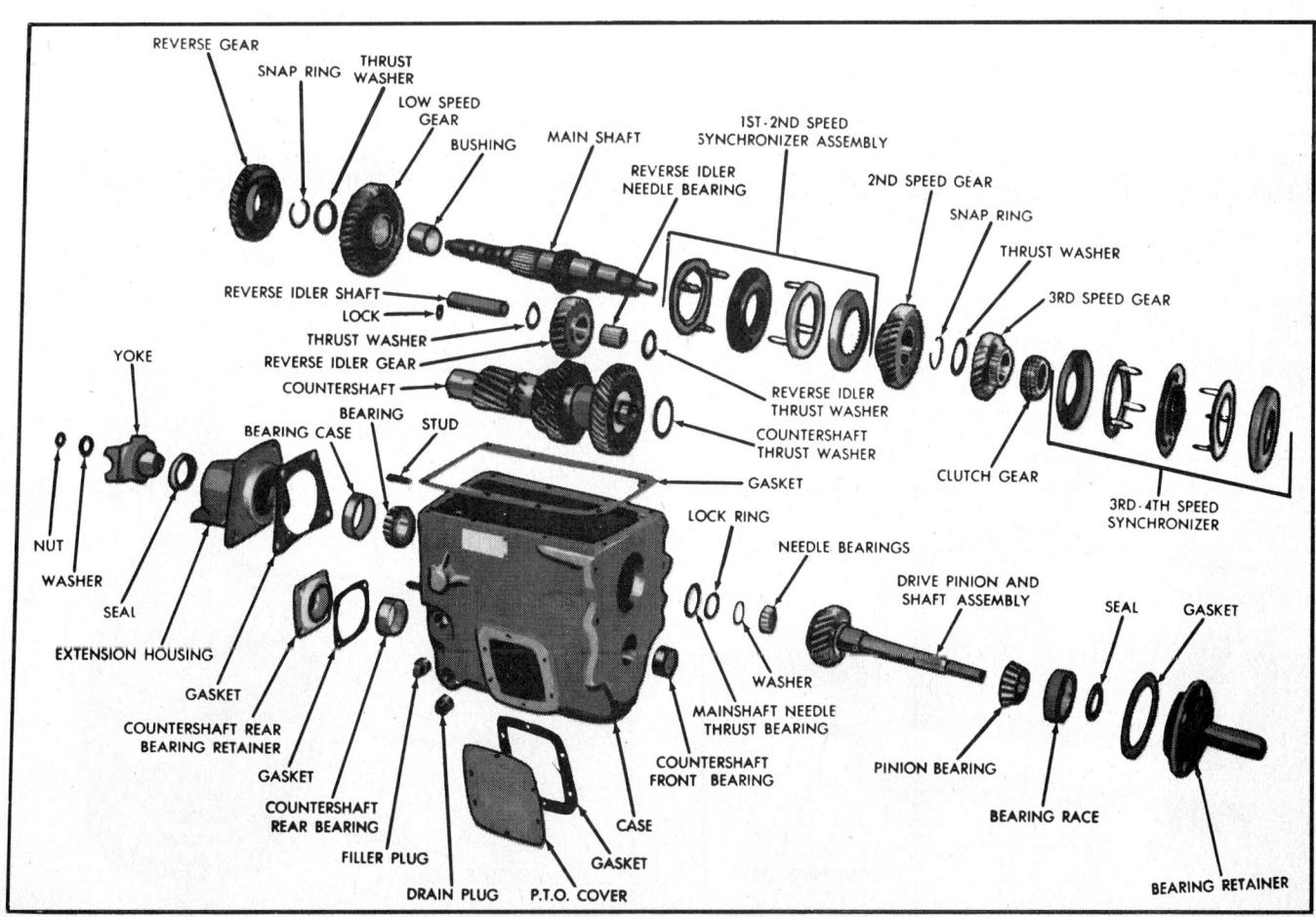

Fig. 5 New Process Model 445 four speed transmission

NEW PROCESS TRANSMISSIONS

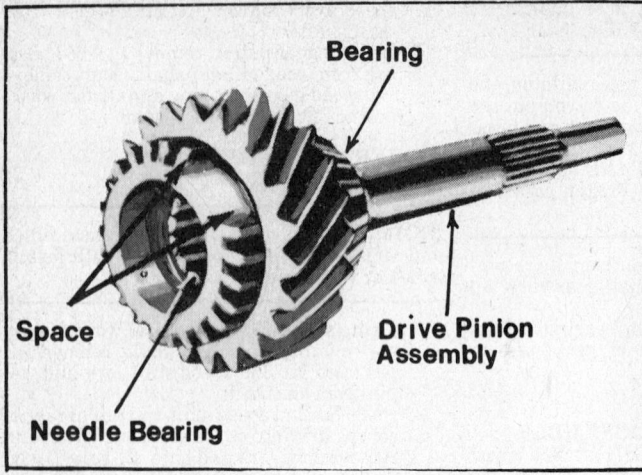

Fig. 6 Drive gear. Model 445

shortened or tapered from clashing during gear shifts should be replaced. If excessive axial gear clearance is found, check snap rings, washers, spacers and gear hubs for excessive wear. Proper axial clearance must be maintained on all mainshaft gears. Replace parts as necessary.

Check splines on mainshaft for excessive wear. If sliding gears, clutch hubs or flanges have been worn into the sides of the splines, the shaft should be replaced.

Check reverse idler gear shaft and rollers for wear and replace as necessary.

Check synchronizer for burrs and uneven or excessive wear at contact surfaces. Check blocker pins for excessive wear or looseness. Check synchronizer contact surfaces on all affected gears for excessive wear.

Check shift bar housing forks and gates for wear at pad and lever slot, check all forks for alignment, check roll pin fit in forks and gates and check neutral notches of shift shafts for wear from interlock balls. Shafts which are indented at points adjacent to neutral notches should be replaced. Replace all worn or damaged parts.

Check all other parts for cracks and fractures. Replace or repair as necessary. Cracked castings may be welded or brazed as long as cracks do not extend into bearing bores or bolting surfaces.

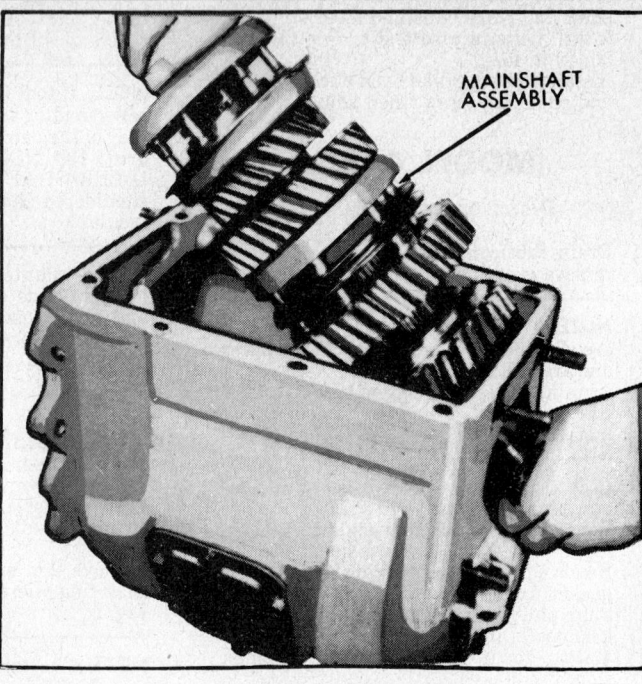

Fig. 7 Removing mainshaft. Model 445

Transmission, Assemble
MAINSHAFT

NOTE: Prior to assembly, lubricate all parts with clean transmission lubricant and replace all expansion plugs, gaskets and seals.

1. Place mainshaft in vertical position with rear end up and lubricate with transmission oil.
2. Slide 1st speed gear over mainshaft with clutch facing down and install thrust washer and snap ring.
3. Install reverse gear over end of mainshaft with fork groove down, then install mainshaft rear bearing and using appropriate size sleeve and tool C-4040, press bearing on inner race.
4. Reverse mainshaft in vise.
5. Install low speed synchronizer and slide 2nd speed gear over mainshaft, then install keyed thrust washer over mainshaft, with ground side facing 2nd gear. Secure with snap ring.
6. Install 3rd speed gear and one shim on mainshaft, then install 3rd-4th synchronizer over mainshaft, making certain that slotted end of clutch gear is positioned toward 3rd speed gear.

GEAR SHIFT COVER, ASSEMBLE, FIG. 10

1. Grease interlock slugs and slide into

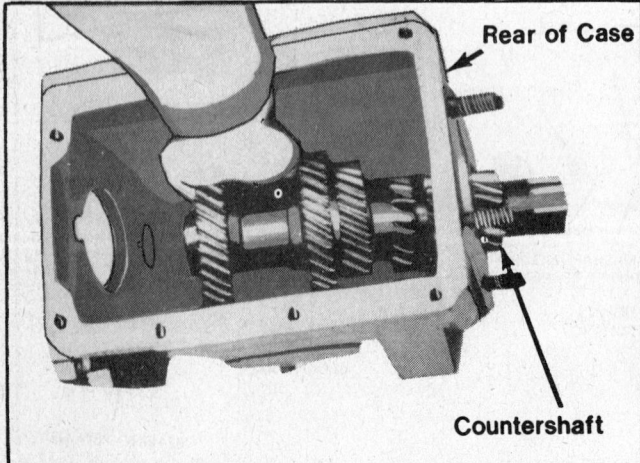

Fig. 8 Removing countershaft. Model 445

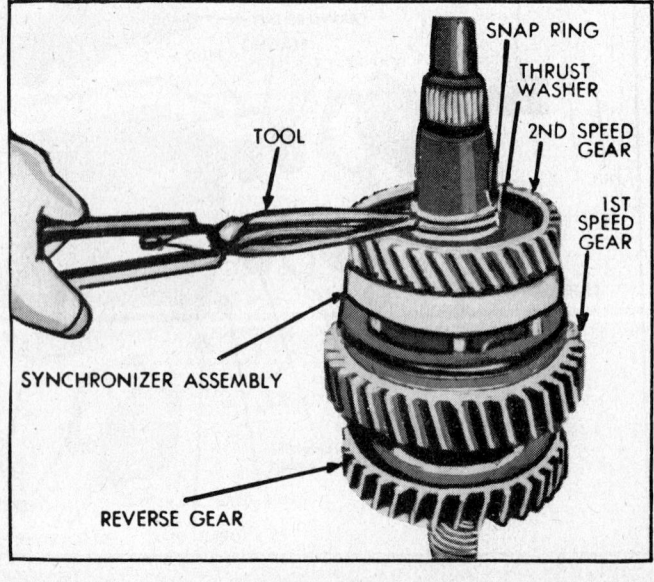

Fig. 9 Removing 2nd-speed gear snap ring. Model 445

NEW PROCESS TRANSMISSIONS

openings in shift rail supports.
2. Insert and slide reverse shift rail through reverse shift plate and shift fork.
3. Secure reverse shift plate and shift fork with roll pin, then install interlock pin into 3rd-4th shift rail and secure with grease.
4. Slide 3rd-4th shift rail into rail support from rear of cover, through 3rd-4th speed shift fork and over poppet ball and spring, then secure 3rd-4th speed shift fork to rail with roll pin.
5. Making sure interlock slug is in place, slide 1st-2nd speed shift rail into case through shift fork and shift gate. Hold poppet ball and spring down until shift rail passes and secure 1st-2nd speed shift fork and shift gate with roll pins.

SUB-ASSEMBLY, INSTALLATION
1. Using a 1 3/8 inch socket as driver, install countershaft front bearing in case. Grease needle bearings prior to installation. Hold bearings in place in bearing retainer with socket of appropriate diameter while seating retainer. Drive retainer until flush with front of case.
2. Install tanged thrust washer on countershaft with tangs facing out and install countershaft into case.
3. Install countershaft rear bearing retainer over countershaft rear bearing and using new washer, position retainer with curved segment toward bottom of case.
4. Install reverse idler gear with chamfer toward rear of case, then while holding thrust washers and needle bearings in position, slide reverse idler shaft into case through idler gear. Make certain that shaft lock notch is down and at rear of shaft and install shaft lock and bolt.
5. Place mainshaft vertically in a soft jawed vise with front end up.
6. Mount drive gear on top of mainshaft, then measure clearance between high speed synchronizer and drive gear with two feeler gauges. If clearance is geater than .043–.053 inch, install synchronizer shims between third speed gear and synchronizer brake drum of the thickness required to bring clearance within specifications. After required shim thickness has been determined, remove drive gear from mainshaft.
7. Insert assembled mainshaft into case and place thrust washer over pilot end of mainshaft.
8. Position drive gear so that the cutaway portion of gear is facing down, then slide drive gear into front of case engaging mainshaft pilot in pocket of drive gear.
9. Slide drive gear front bearing retainer over shaft with no gasket or bolts, then install mainshaft rear bearing retainer and tighten retainer bolts.
10. Hold retainer against front of transmission case and measure clearance between front bearing retainer and front of case with feeler gauge. Remove front bearing retainer.
11. Install a gasket pack on front bearing retainer which is .010–.015 inch thicker than the clearance measured in above step. Install front bearing retainer and tighten bolts. This will insure the required .007–.017 inch gear end play.
12. The front synchronizer end play float must be checked before installation of transmission cover. Measure end play float by inserting two feeler gauges diametrically opposite one another between 3rd speed gear and synchronizer stop ring. Accurate measurement can be made only after all mainshaft components are

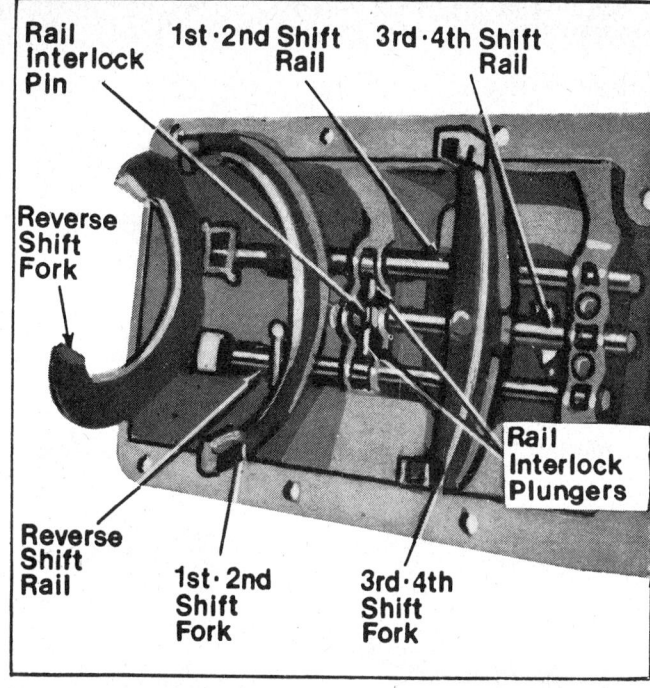

Fig. 10 Cover and shift fork assembly. Model 445

in place and tightened securely. If front synchronizer end play is not within .050–.070 inch, shims should be added or removed as required between 3rd speed gear and synchronizer stop ring.
13. Install yoke and retaining nut on mainshaft, then lock transmission in two gears and torque yoke nut to 125 ft. lbs.
14. Shift transmission into neutral and install cover gasket, then shift transmission and cover into 2nd and carefully lower cover into position. It may be necessary to position reverse gear to permit shift fork to engage groove.
15. Install and tighten cover aligning screws, then install remaining cover screws and tighten all screws evenly and securely.

SERIES 745

Disassemble, Fig. 11
1. Remove parking brake drum and flange.
2. Remove speedometer pinion.
3. Remove speedometer drive gear.
4. Remove parking brake.
5. Remove rear bearing seal.
6. Remove transmission cover.
7. Remove drive pinion bearing retainer.
8. When removing drive pinion and bearing from case, slide synchronizer front inner stop ring from clutch teeth on pinion as assembly is being removed from case.
9. Remove snap ring which locks drive pinion bearing on shaft.
10. Press bearing off shaft and remove oil slinger.
11. Remove mainshaft pilot bearing snap ring and remove 15 rollers.
12. Remove seal from retainer.

DISASSEMBLE MAINSHAFT
1. Remove mainshaft rear bearing snap ring.
2. Slide mainshaft and rear bearing to the rear until bearing is out of case.
3. Remove synchronizer from mainshaft.
4. Remove 2–3 shift fork.
5. Remove synchronizer clutch gear snap ring.
6. Remove synchronizer clutch gear 2nd gear and low-reverse gear from mainshaft.

NOTE: *If synchronizer clutch gear cannot be removed easily from the mainshaft, position the low-reverse fork and sliding gear to the rear of case. Then, using a plastic hammer, tap mainshaft back out of synchronizer cluth gear.*

7. Remove mainshaft and bearing out through rear of case, while stripping mainshaft of gears.

COUNTERSHAFT
1. Using a countershaft bearing arbor, drive countershaft toward rear of case until small key can be removed from countershaft.
2. Drive countershaft the remaining way out of the case (toward the rear) keeping arbor tight against end of countershaft to prevent loss of roller bearings.
3. Remove cluster gear and thrust washers.
4. Remove rollers (88), washers (4) and center spacer from cluster gear.

REVERSE IDLER GEAR
1. Using a blunt drift, drive reverse idler shaft toward rear of case far enough to remove key from shaft.
2. Drive shaft all the way out and remove idler gear and bearing assembly.
3. Remove thrust washers and needle bearings (22).

GEARSHIFT MECHANISM
1. Using a small punch, remove low-reverse gear lever shaft tapered lock pin by driving it toward the top of the transmission case.

NEW PROCESS TRANSMISSIONS

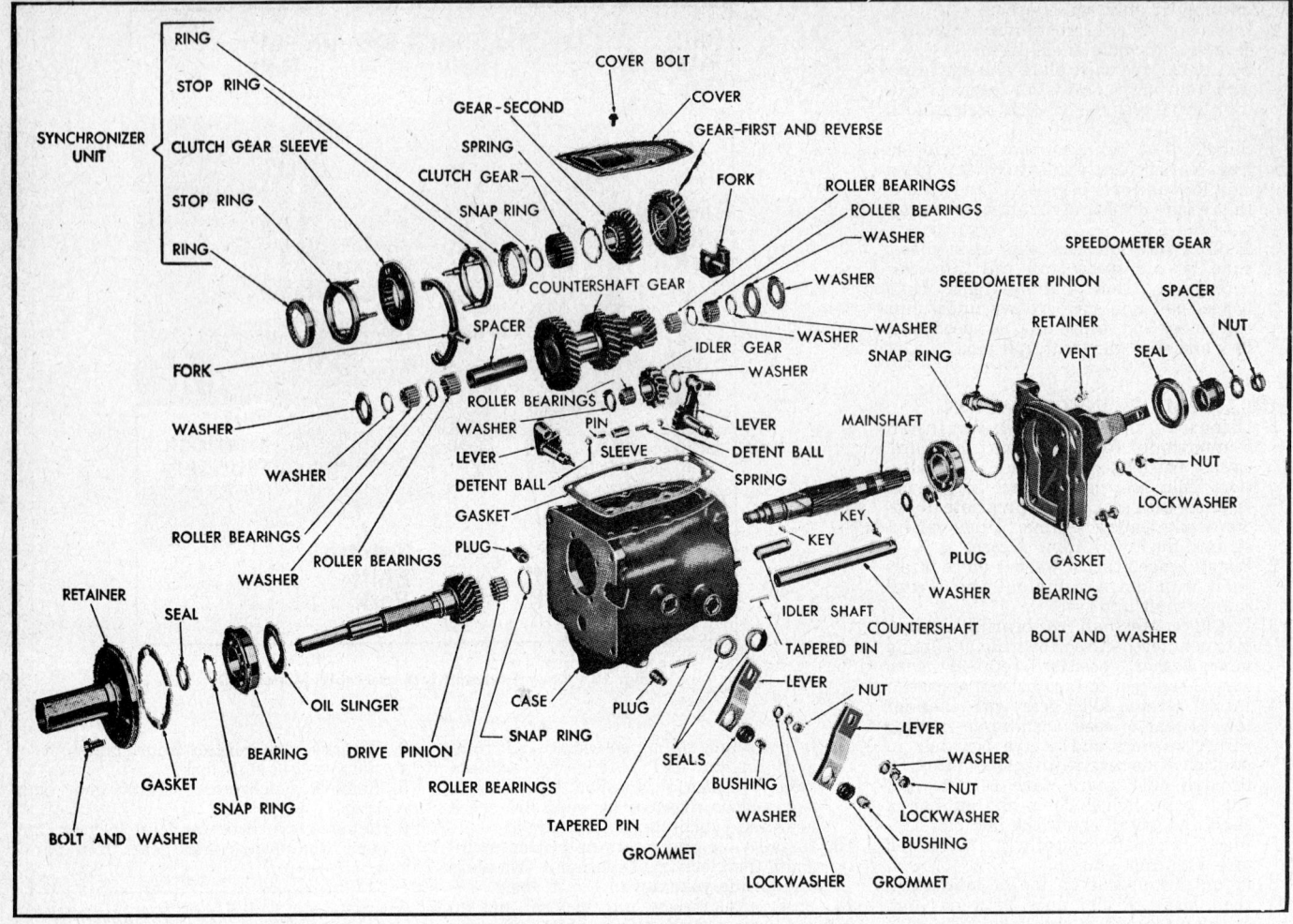

Fig. 11 New Process 745 three speed transmission

2. Remove 2-3 lever pin in same manner.
3. Remove lever shafts from case, taking care not to lose spring-loaded detent balls.
4. Remove interlock sleeve, spring, pin and balls.

Assemble

DRIVE PINION & BEARING
1. Place oil slinger on drive pinion.
2. Place bearing on pinion shaft with outer snap ring away from gear.
3. Press bearing into position so it is seated firmly against oil slinger and pinion gear.
4. Install bearing snap ring on shaft.
5. Coat 15 roller bearings with heavy grease and install them in cavity at rear of drive pinion. Install roller bearing snap ring.

COUNTERSHAFT
1. Place bearing spacer in center of cluster gear bore and use an arbor to assist in assembling roller bearings. Use heavy grease to hold bearings in place and install a row of 22 rollers next to one end of spacer.
2. Place a spacer ring next to rollers and install another row of 22 rollers next to spacer ring.
3. Install another spacer ring at outside end of second row of rollers.
4. At opposite end of cluster gear bore, install two more rows of rollers in same manner.
5. With a small amount of heavy grease to hold it in place, install front thrust washer on arbor at front end of cluster gear, with tabs outward.
6. Install tabbed rear thrust washer on arbor against rear of cluster gear with tabs positioned in grooves provided in cluster gear.
7. Install remaining rear thrust plate on rear thrust washer.
8. Align tabs of front thrust washer vertically to index with notches in transmission case. Position cluster gear and arbor assembly in case. Make sure thrust washers are not dislodged from arbor, and engage thrust washer tabs in case grooves, while sliding assembly into place.
9. Using countershaft, drive arbor forward out of cluster gear and through bore in front of case. Before driving countershaft all the way into case with soft hammer, insert shaft key and continue to drive countershaft forward until it is 1/64" below rear face of case.

REVERSE IDLER
1. Position arbor in reverse idler gear and, using heavy grease, install 22 roller bearings in gear around an arbor.
2. Place front and rear thrust washers at each end of gear and position assembly in case with chamfered end of gear teeth toward front.
3. Insert reverse idler shaft into bore at rear of case, pushing arbor toward front of transmission.
4. With shaft keyway aligned with recess in case, drive shaft forward, inserting key before keyway is obscured. Continue driving shaft forward until 1/64" below rear face.

GEARSHIFT MECHANISM
1. Install two lever shaft seals in case.
2. Install low-reverse gear lever shaft in case bore.
3. Install low-reverse gear lever shaft lock pin at top of hole and driving it in firmly to prevent leakage or loss of pin.
4. Place interlock parts in position in case in order: sleeve, ball, spring, pin and ball.
5. Place 2-3 lever shaft in case and, using a suitable tool to depress detent ball against spring tension push lever shaft firmly into position so it prevents ball from escaping.
6. Install 2-3 lever shaft lock pin.
7. Place low-reverse fork in lever shaft with offset toward rear of transmission.

NEW PROCESS TRANSMISSIONS

MAINSHAFT

1. While holding low-reverse sliding gear in position in fork, with hub extension to rear, insert mainshaft with rear bearing through rear of case and into sliding gear.
2. Place synchronizer energizer spring and then the inner stop ring on clutch teeth of 2nd speed gear. Install 2nd speed gear on mainshaft.
3. Install synchronizer clutch gear on mainshaft with shoulder to front.
4. Select thickest synchronizer clutch gear snap ring that can be used and install it in mainshaft groove. Make sure ring is bottomed all the way around in groove.
5. Check clearance between clutch gear and 2nd gear. Clearance should be .002″ to .016″.

NOTE: *End play in excess of .016″ may cause 2nd speed gear "jump out".*

6. Hold synchronizer clutch gear sleeve front inner and two outer rings together with pins properly entered in holes in synchronizer gear sleeve and with gear sleeve engaged in groove of 2–3 shift fork, position fork on gear fork shaft.
7. While holding synchronizer parts and fork in position, slide mainshaft forward, placing synchronizer clutch gear into clutch sleeve and at the same time guiding mainshaft rear bearing into case bore.
8. While continuing to hold synchronizer parts in position, tap mainshaft forward until rear bearing bottoms in case bore.
9. Install mainshaft rear bearing snap ring in groove in case bore.

DRIVE PINION

1. Install new seal in retainer until it bottoms on seat of counterbore.
2. Place synchronizer front inner ring in position in front outer ring and guide drive pinion through case bore.
3. Engage splines on rear of pinion with inner stop ring, and tap drive pinion into case until outer snap ring on pinion bearing is against transmission case.
4. Place drive pinion bearing retainer, without gasket, over pinion shaft and against case. While holding retainer with hand pressure against case, measure clearance between retainer and case with a feeler gauge.
5. Select a gasket .003″ to .005″ thicker than the clearance found. This eliminates end play of front bearing in case and also insures sealing.
6. Install and tighten front bearing retainer bolts to 200 inch-lbs.
7. Install plug or back-up light switch (if equipped) with gasket and tighten securely.

REAR BEARING RETAINER

1. Install new seal in rear bearing retainer.
2. Install rear bearing retainer with new gasket and torque bolts to 50 ft-lbs.
3. Install parking brake assembly.
4. Place speedometer drive gear on main shaft and install parking brake drum and flange assembly. Install washer and nut and torque to 175 ft-lbs.
5. Install speedometer pinion and gear-shift operating levers, tightening nuts to 180 inch-lbs.

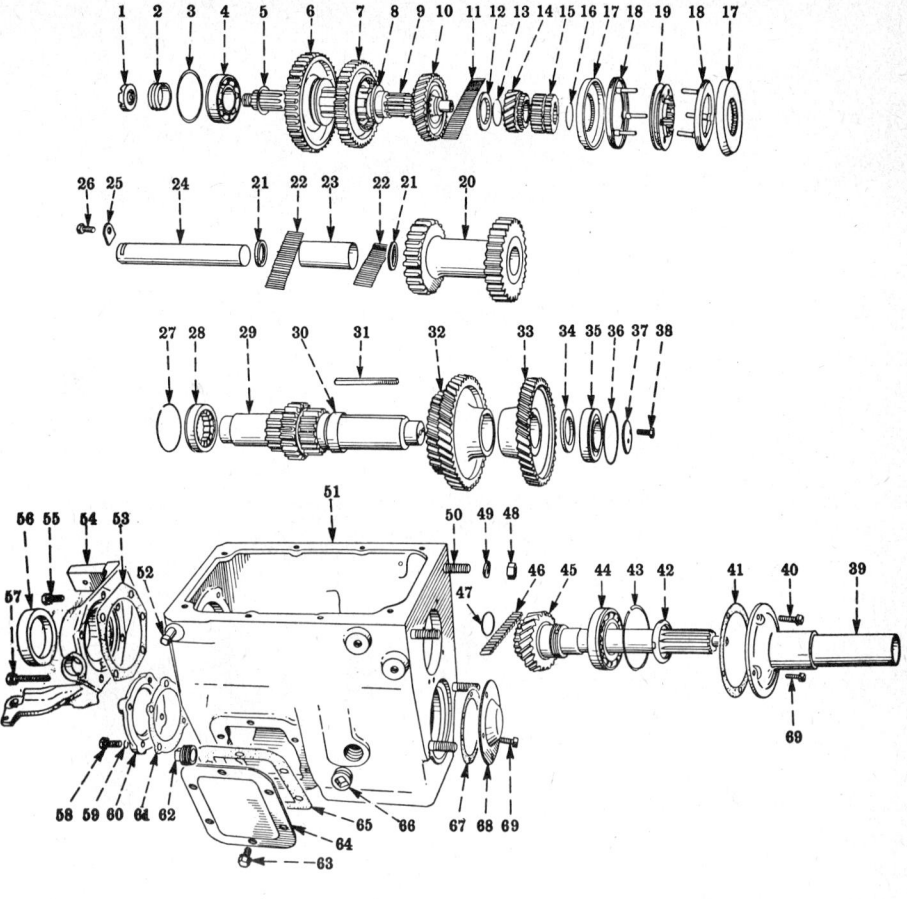

1. Mainshaft nut
2. Speedometer drive gear
3. Snap ring
4. Bearing
5. Shim
6. Low and reverse gear
7. Second and third gear
8. Thrust washer
9. Mainshaft
10. Third speed gear
11. Bearing
12. Thrust washer
13. Snap ring
14. Overdrive gear
15. Synchronizer clutch gear
16. Snap ring
17. Synchronizer ring
18. Synchronizer ring
19. Synchronizer clutch
20. Reverse idler gear
21. Spacer
22. Bearing
23. Spacer
24. Reverse idler shaft
25. Lock
27. Snap ring
28. Bearing
29. Countershaft
30. Spacer
31. Key
32. Third and fourth gear
33. Drive gear
34. Thrust washer
35. Bearing
36. Snap ring
37. Plate
39. Retainer
41. Gasket
43. Snap ring
44. Bearing
45. Main drive gear
46. Bearing
47. Spacer
51. Case
53. Gasket
54. Retainer
56. Seal
60. Bearing cover
61. Gasket
62. Drain plug
64. Cover
65. Gasket
66. Plug
67. Gasket
68. Cover

Fig. 12 New Process five speed transmissions. Models 875, 895

NEW PROCESS TRANSMISSIONS

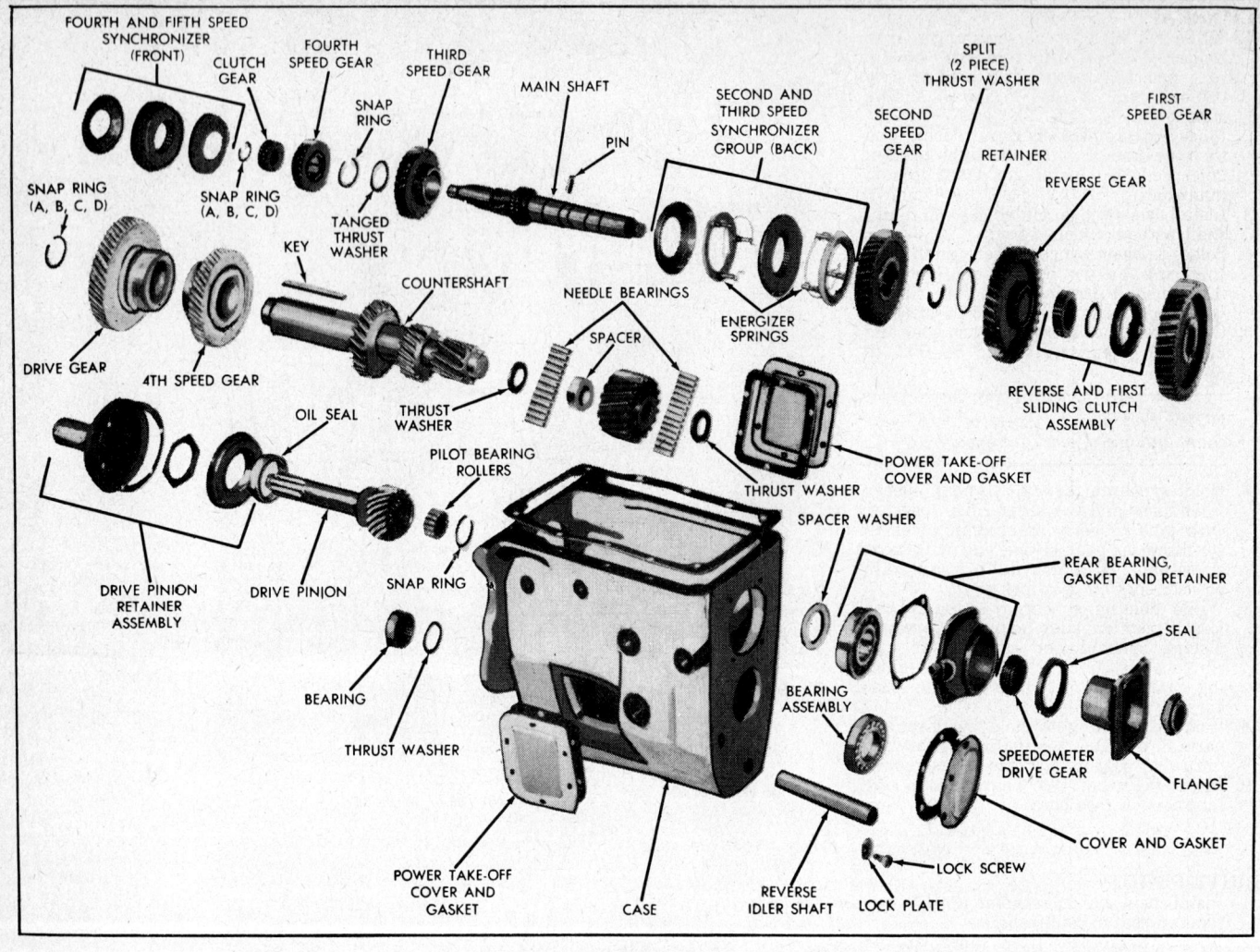

Fig. 13 New Process 7500 Series five speed transmission

SERIES 875, 895

Disassemble, Fig. 12

1. Drain transmission.
2. Remove hand brake band and drum.
3. Remove transmission control housing.
4. Remove mainshaft rear bearing retainer, noting the number of gaskets present.
5. Remove oil seal and speedometer drive gear.
6. Remove main drive gear bearing retainer, noting the number of gaskets used.
7. Remove main drive gear.
8. Tap mainshaft to rear until rear bearing is free of case.
9. Remove synchronizer.
10. Use puller to remove bearing from rear of mainshaft. Remove shims and note number used as they control floating clearance of synchronizer.
11. Lift mainshaft assembly from case.
12. Remove reverse idler gear shaft from rear of case and lift out reverse idler gear.
13. Remove front and rear countershaft bearing covers, and bearing retainer plate from end of countershaft.
14. Tap front end of countershaft toward rear of case until rear bearing is free of case. Then lift countershaft and gear assembly out of case.

Reassembly

1. Install reverse idler gear assembly in case before installing countershaft gear assembly. This will permit clearance for removal of pilot shaft used to assemble bearings in idler gear.
2. A wood pilot shaft or a discarded idler gear shaft cut to a length of five inches may be used to facilitate assembling bearings in reverse idler gear. Diameter of wood pilot shaft should be 1 1/16".
3. A bench assembly of the reverse idler gear and bearings should be made before installing in case. Position pilot shaft and long spacer in idler gear. Insert 31 needle bearings and short spacer between pilot shaft and idler gear. Insert 31 needle bearings and short spacer in same manner at opposite end of idler gear. Position gear and bearing assembly in case. Push shaft flush against pilot shaft, permitting pilot to be removed from case. Remove pilot shaft from inside of case.
4. The mainshaft third speed gear bearing consists of 50 individual needle bearings. To assemble bearings, position thrust washer and third speed gear on mainshaft. Insert each needle bearing between gear and mainshaft.
5. Select a snap ring of correct thickness that will provide proper running clearance of mainshaft third speed gear. Snap rings are available in three thicknesses (.090", .093", .096") for this purpose.
6. Select a snap ring for securing the clutch gear that will hold the gear tight against the shoulder on mainshaft. Four thicknesses (.087", .090", .093", .096") are available for this purpose. To check for the thickness required temporarily install the synchronizer clutch gear on the mainshaft before installing the overdrive gear and third speed gear. Insert snap ring in groove on mainshaft and check the gear for tightness.
7. The main drive gear bearing lock nut should be tightened sufficiently to seat bearing against gear shoulder.
8. Like parts of the synchronizer assembly are interchangeable. Preassembling of this unit before installing on the mainshaft is not required since parts may be installed individually.
9. Check and replace all thrust washers showing signs of excessive wear.
10. The mainshaft front and rear bearing retainers fit or end play for their respective bearing is controlled by gaskets. Install bearing retainers and cap screw, check clearance between each retainer and case with a feeler gauge. Then select a gasket or gaskets about .005" thicker than the clearance between retainer and

NEW PROCESS TRANSMISSIONS

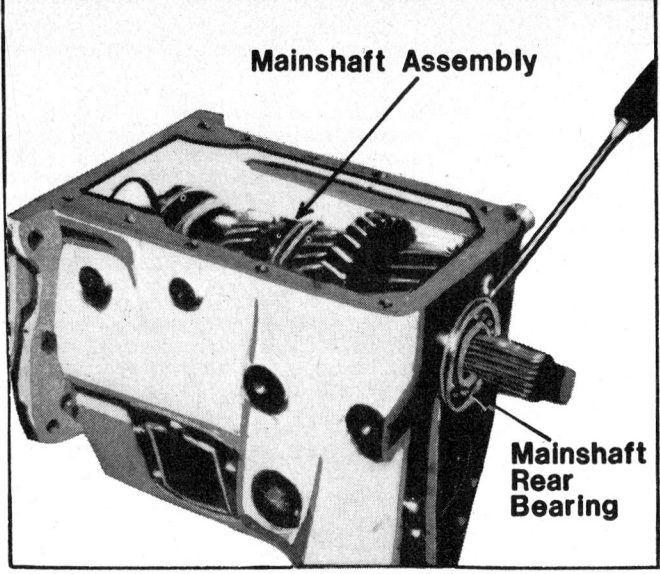

Fig. 13A Removing rear bearing from mainshaft. 7500 Series

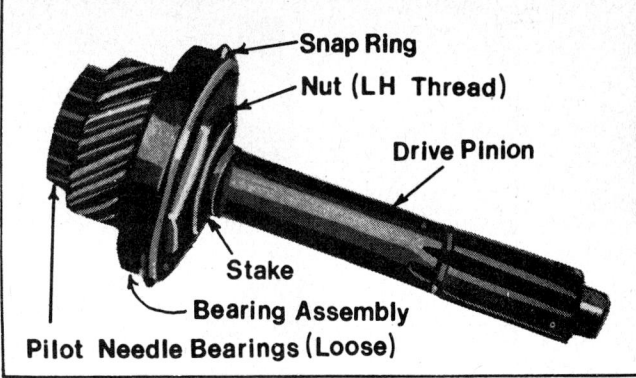

Fig. 14 Drive pinion shaft assembly. 7500 Series

case. Remove retainer, install selected gasket or gaskets and retainer. This will give a satisfactory condition as to bearing end play and sealing of transmission.

SERIES 7500

Disassemble

SHIFT COVER & PARKING BRAKE

1. Remove parking brake assembly (if used), then shift transmission into neutral and remove shift cover retaining bolts and shift cover.

   NOTE: Second screw from front on each side is shouldered to properly align shift cover.

2. Lock transmission in two gears and remove output shaft flange nut, then remove brake drum (if used) and yoke assembly by lightly tapping with a soft hammer.

   NOTE: The yoke and drum are balanced as a unit, and unless replacement of parts is required, the yoke and drum should be removed as an assembly.

3. Remove brake band assembly bracket (if used), support bolts and lock-washers and remove brake band assembly as a complete unit.

CHECKING FRONT SYNCHRONIZER END PLAY FLOAT

Before removal and disassembly of drive pinion and mainshaft, measure end-play between synchronizer outer stop ring and 4th speed gear. Record reading for reference during assembly. Note deviation from desired .070–.090 inch allowable end play so that correction shims can be installed during assembly. Thick or thin shims are available as required.

DRIVE PINION, BEARING RETAINER & MAINSHAFT

1. Remove drive pinion bearing retainer, Fig. 13.
2. Remove drive pinion gear and ball bearing from transmission. Pull on pinion shaft or rap on face of case with brass hammer.
3. Remove speedometer drive pinion and mainshaft rear bearing retainer, then place a brass drift in front center of mainshaft and drive rearward.
4. Using a puller or two large screwdrivers, Fig. 13A, remove rear bearing from mainshaft, then when mainshaft rear bearing clears case, remove rear bearing and speedometer gear using a puller.
5. Move mainshaft assembly rearward and tilt front of mainshaft up, then while holding 1st-reverse gear and 4th-5th speed synchronizer, lift assembly out of case.

REVERSE IDLER SHAFT & COUNTERSHAFT, FIG. 13

1. Remove reverse idler lock screw and lock plate, then using a brass drift held at an angle, drive idler shaft rearward and pull out.
2. Remove reverse idler gear and thrust washer from case.

   NOTE: Loose needle bearings should be replaced with all new needle bearings. Never mix old with new.

   NOTE: If excessive side and end play are not found and teeth are not badly worn or chipped, countershaft gears may not require replacement. However, if continued use seems questionable, the countershaft should be removed.

3. Remove countershaft rear bearing retainer, gasket and bearing, then tip countershaft upward and remove from case. Remove thrust washers from front end of countershaft.
4. Using a suitable driver from inside of

Fig. 14A Installing mainshaft rear bearing. 7500 Series

NEW PROCESS TRANSMISSIONS

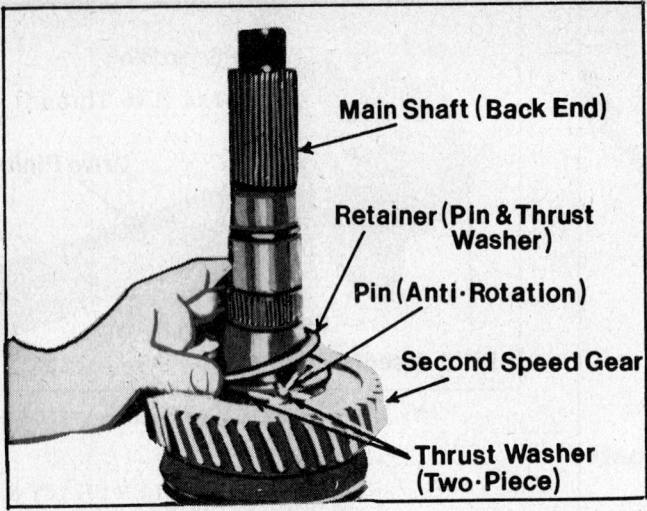

Fig. 15 Installing or removing 2nd-speed gear. 7500 Series

MAINSHAFT, FIG. 15
1. Remove spacer washer and first speed gear from mainshaft, then remove retaining ring and 1st-reverse clutch and clutch gear assembly and reverse gear.
2. Remove 2nd speed gear (retaining) thrust washer assembly. This two piece thrust washer consists of two halves held in position on the mainshaft and prevented from turning by a pin in mainshaft together with a retainer ring.
3. Remove 2nd speed gear, then remove back (2nd-3rd speed) synchronizer assembly. The 2nd-3rd speed clutch is integral with mainshaft.
4. Remove snap ring, then remove front (4th-5th speed) synchronizer assembly, clutch gear and 4th speed gear.
5. Remove retaining snap ring, tanged thrust washer and 3rd speed gear.

SHIFT COVER & FORKS, FIG. 16

NOTE: Shift cover and forks should be disassembled only if rails, poppets or interlock plungers are worn or springs broken allowing end play or simultaneous movement of rails, and if shift forks or cover itself needs replacing.

1. Mark each fork and rail for location during assembly and place shift forks and rails in neutral. Mount cover in a soft jawed vise or bench fixture and remove spiral pins from shift forks and shift lugs. Spiral pins may be removed using an "easyout" installed in a tap handle.
2. Drive short, 1st-reverse shift rail rearward and out of transmission cover and remove fork.
3. Remove first-reverse shift rail pivot bolt and nut and remove crossover lever.

case, remove countershaft front needle bearing by tapping on bearing cage.

NOTE: It is not usually necessary to disassemble countershaft, unless if after inspection, damage or malfunction warrants disassembly.

5. Remove snap ring, then place countershaft assembly in a suitable press with blocks supporting drive gear and carefully press shaft.
6. Repeat above procedure supporting 4th speed gear and remove key.

DRIVE PINION, FIG. 14
1. Remove snap ring and washer holding pilot needle bearings in place and remove bearings.
2. Relieve staked area, then remove drive pinion ball bearing retainer nut and remove ball bearing.

NOTE: Retainer nut has left hand thread.

3. Remove snap ring from drive pinion ball bearing and seal from drive pinion bearing retainer.

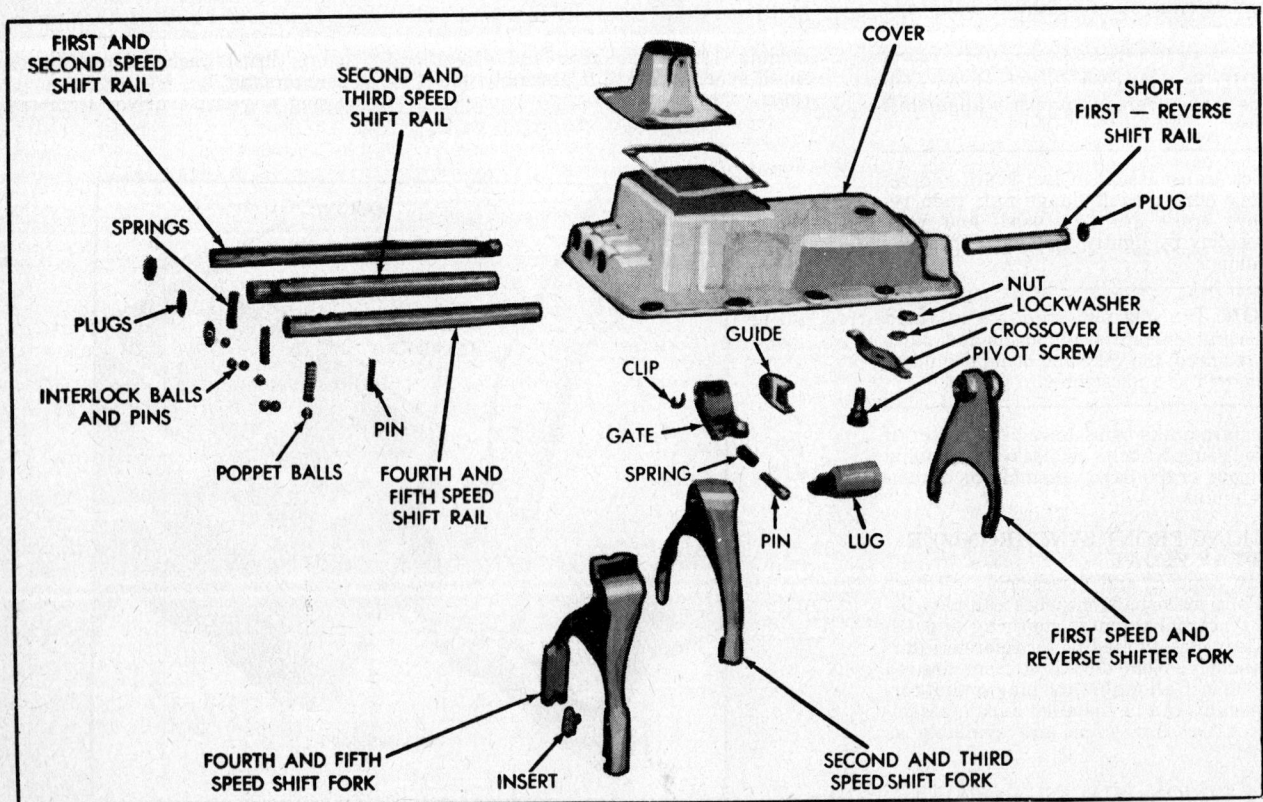

Fig. 16 Shift cover and fork assembly. 7500 Series

NEW PROCESS TRANSMISSIONS

4. Drive 4th–5th and 2nd–3rd speed shift rails forward and out of transmission cover, then remove 1st-reverse shift rail in same manner.

   NOTE: Place a towel over shift rails while driving shift rails out, to prevent loss of poppet balls and springs.

5. Remove the four interlock balls and pin from cover.

   NOTE: Make certain that pin and balls are out by shaking or jarring cover sharply on a block of wood.

Sub-Assembly, Assemble

NOTE: During assembly, use new expansion plugs, gaskets and seals and lubricate all parts with transmission fluid. Where grease is specified, use an oil soluble grease such as Multi-Purpose Grease NLGI Grade 2 or equivalent. Make certain that all oil returns are free of grease or obstructions. Clean and inspect all parts and replace as necessary. Clean and inspect transmission case and wipe all bores and bearing surfaces before reassembly.

Check synchronizers for burrs, uneven or excessive wear at threads and check blocker pins for excessive wear or looseness. Check synchronizer contact surfaces on gears for excessive wear. If replacement is required, replace front (4th–5th speed) synchronizer along with outer stop rings. Replace back (2nd–3rd speed) synchronizer parts as required.

MAINSHAFT FIGS. 13 & 15
1. Place mainshaft with forward end up in a soft jawed vise, then place third speed gear on shaft with clutching teeth facing down and install tanged thrust washer and snap ring.
2. Place 4th speed gear on shaft with clutching teeth up.

   NOTE: Referring to dimension recorded during disassembly, select shims which will provide .070–.090 inch end play between 4th speed gear and front synchronizer, Fig. 15. Thick and thin shims are available.

3. Place 4th speed synchronizer clutch gear (with oil slots down) on mainshaft. Select a snap ring of greatest thickness (available in four sizes, marked A, B, C or D) to eliminate all clutch gear end play.
4. Remove mainshaft from vise and install 2nd–3rd synchronizer group.

   NOTE: Synchronizer sleeve is marked "FRONT" for proper installation.

5. Place second speed gear on shaft and thrust washer retaining pin in hole in mainshaft, then position the two thrust washer halves on mainshaft and install the thrust washer retaining ring with large diameter making contact with 2nd speed gear, Fig. 15.
6. Install reverse gear, then position reverse and 1st speed clutch gear on mainshaft and install retaining snap ring. Select a snap ring of greatest thickness (available in four sizes marked A, B, C or D) to eliminate all clutch gear end play.
7. Position sliding clutch on clutch gear, then install 1st speed gear and spacer on mainshaft.

CHECKING BACK SYNCHRONIZER END-PLAY FLOAT, FIG. 17
Checking end float (.070–.090") at back synchronizer (2nd–3rd speeds) should be performed during assembly of the mainshaft assembly. This can be done by using two equal sized feeler gauges diametrically opposite each other between 3rd speed gear outer stop ring and third speed gear itself.

NOTE: Extreme care should be used to make sure that all synchronizer parts are assembled correctly and parallel and that the feeler gauges are inserted close to the mainshaft and up on the shoulder of 3rd speed gear, otherwise an erroneous reading will result.

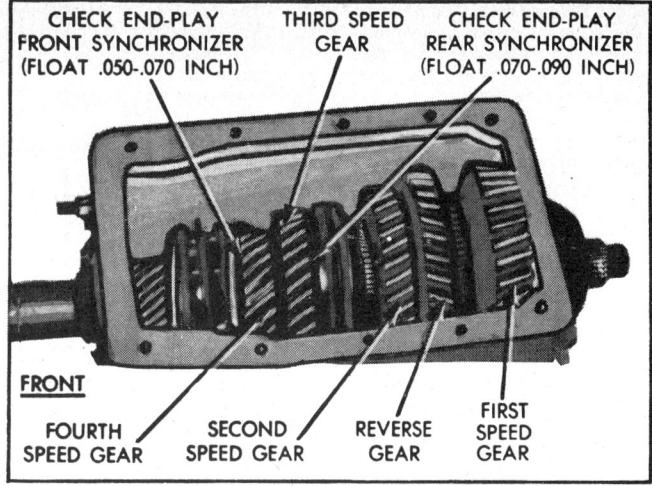

Fig. 17 Checking end-play. 7500 Series

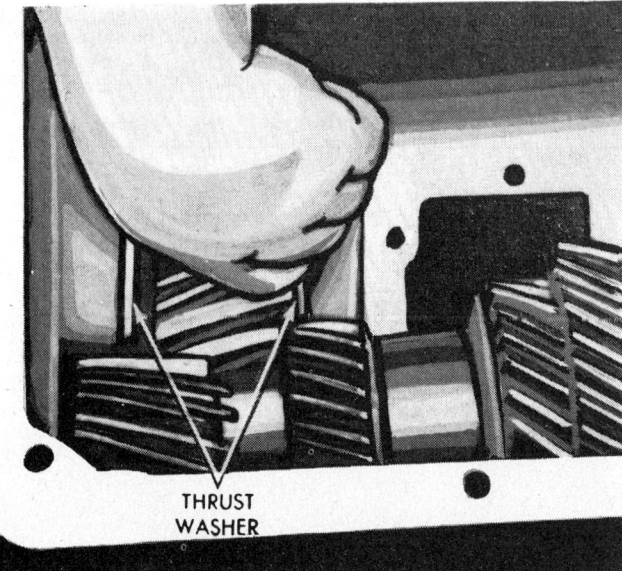

Fig. 18 Reverse idler installation. 7500 Series

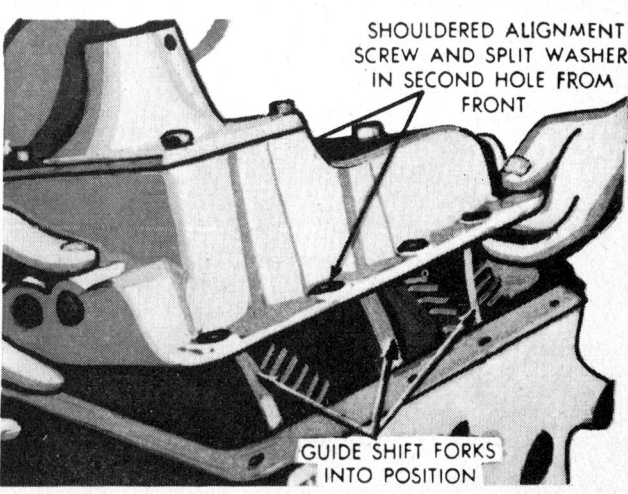

Fig. 19 Shift cover and fork installation. 7500 Series

345

NEW PROCESS TRANSMISSIONS

If the end play float is less than .070 inch or more than .090 inch, install new component parts for the synchronizer assembly. This may require new gears if thrust faces are worn, as shims cannot be used at this point.

COUNTERSHAFT, FIG. 13
1. With keys positioned on countershaft, press on gears until properly seated.

NOTE: Make certain that key does not climb out of position as gear is being pressed on.

2. Install snap ring on countershaft. Select a snap ring of greatest thickness (available in four sizes, marked A, B, C or D) to eliminate possible end play.
3. Install washer on countershaft drive gear.

DRIVE PINION, FIG. 14
1. Grease needle bearings and install into pocket drive gear and install washer and snap ring.
2. Press large bearing onto pinion shaft making sure bearing is properly seated, then install bearing retainer nut and tighten securely. Stake in place.

NOTE: Nut has left hand thread.

3. Install snap ring on large bearing, making certain it is properly seated.

SHIFT COVER & FORKS, FIG. 17
1. Push 1st-reverse shift rail into cover bore far enough to permit installation gates, poppet ball springs and roll pins. Move shift rail into neutral position.
2. Coat the four interlock balls and pin with grease, then place two balls in interlock bore, moving both balls toward shift rail and seating ball in neutral notch.
3. Place interlock pin in hole located in 2nd-3rd speed shift rail. Install 2nd-3rd speed shift rail, gate and fork as in step one and move rail into neutral position.
4. Install the two remaining balls into interlock bore, then push 4th-5th speed shift rail into cover bore and install shift fork and move shift rail into neutral position.
5. Position crossover lever in such a manner that the short 1st-reverse shift rail, fork and roll pin can be installed.
6. Position crossover lever and align notches in both long and short 1st-reverse shift rails.
7. Install pivot bolt through crossover lever and transmission cover and install and tighten nut.
8. Install new welch plugs.

Transmission Reassembly
COUNTERSHAFT
1. If removed, install front bearing assembly into countershaft bearing bore.
2. Grease thrust washer and position it into transmission case, then install countershaft front bearing journal into front bearing, seated against thrust washer. Make sure to keep centerline of countershaft aligned with rear bearing bore during installation to prevent damage to countershaft front bearing.
3. Install countershaft rear roller bearing assembly, gasket and cover and tighten screws securely.

NOTE: Check countershaft for .008–.020 inch end play clearance. Clearance can be adjusted by changing countershaft rear bearing cover gasket.

REVERSE IDLER, FIG. 18
1. With new needle bearing held in place on each side of spacer with grease, place reverse idler gear and thrust washers into position in case.
2. Drive shaft through case and gear using a hammer and brass drift. Be sure needles stay in place and lock strap slit in shaft will line up so that lock strap, cap and screw can be installed.
3. Install lock strap on shaft and tighten screw securely.

MAINSHAFT & DRIVE PINION, FIG. 14
1. Carefully lower rear end of mainshaft into case while holding 1st speed gear and spacer washer from slipping off shaft.
2. Using a wooden block at front of mainshaft, drive mainshaft bearing onto shaft and into case, Fig. 14A.
3. Install drive pinion by carefully driving on bearing outer race and forcing it into case while guiding front end of mainshaft into pilot bearing pocket. Make certain bearing is fully seated.
4. Press oil seal into retainer until it is seated. Do not press beyond this point.
5. Install bearing retainer and gasket and tighten retainer screws securely.

MAINSHAFT FLANGE
1. Install speedometer gear on output shaft, then install oil seal into retainer until seal makes contact with its seat. Do not press beyond this point.
2. Install retainer and gasket and tighten retainer screws securely.
3. Position universal joint flange and brake drum (if used) on output shaft.
4. Lock transmission in two gears and install and torque output shaft nut to 125–175 ft. lbs.

CHECKING FRONT SYNCHRONIZER END-PLAY FLOAT
End-play float of .050–.070 inch should be checked just before transmission cover is installed. Follow the same procedure used for initial back synchronizer end play check, except place feeler gauges between 4th speed gear and outer stop pins.

NOTE: If end play float is not within .050–.070 inch, shims should be removed or added between 4th speed gear and outer stop ring of synchronizer.

NOTE: Correct readings can only be obtained after all mainshaft components are properly assembled and tightened.

NOTE: If end-play float is not within .050–.070 inch, shims should be removed or added between 4th speed gear and outer stop ring of synchronizer. Add shims as necessary and recheck clearance.

TRANSMISSION SHIFT COVER, FIG. 19

NOTE: After completing assembly of main case and just before installing cover assembly, recheck rear synchronizer end-play float of .070–.090 inch. If it is not within these limits, install new parts as necessary to correct end-play float.

1. With transmission gears and cover placed in neutral, carefully lower cover into place while guiding shift forks into position.
2. Install shouldered aligning screws and split lockwashers in second hole from front and finger tighten.
3. Install remaining screws and tighten all screws securely after cover is properly seated.
4. Before installing shifter, make certain that transmission shifts through all gears.

SPICER TRANSMISSIONS

SERVICE INDEX

SERIES	SPEEDS	PAGE
3000	5	347
5000	5	347
6000	5	348
7000	5	352
8000	4	353
8000	5	354
8125	12	361
8500	4	353
8500	5	354
8700	4	353
8700	5	354

SST Split Torque Units

1007-2A, B	7	370

SERIES	SPEEDS	PAGE
1007-2C, D	7	370
1007-3A, B	7	370
1010-2A	10	373
1062-A, B	6	370
1211-3A	11	370
1262-A	6	370
1263-T	6	370

Compound Units

7016 (4 x 4)	16	381
7216 (4 x 4)	16	381
8016 (4 x 4)	16	391
8216 (4 x 4)	16	391
8512 (4 x 3)	12	398

SERIES	SPEEDS	PAGE
8516 (4 x 4)	16	398
8716 (4 x 4)	16	398

Auxiliary Units

1241	4	355
5831	3	349
6041	4	358
7041	4	350
7231	3	349
8031	3	361
8035	3	361
8341	4	350
8345	4	350
9441	4	403

LUBRICANT CAPACITY BY MODELS

MODEL	PINTS
3152, 3153	10
5052, 5252	17
5652	13
5662	17
5752, 5753, 5756	13
5852, 5853	13
6052	18
6253	17
6352, 6354	17
6452, 6453, 6454	17
6455, 6456	17
6553	18
6852, 6853, 6854, 6855	17
7016, 7216 (4 x 4)	28
7352	18
7452, 7453	18
8012, 8212 (4 x 3)	36
8016, 8216 (4 x 4)	36
8041, 8045	16

MODEL	PINTS
8051, 8055	24
8052, 8054	24
8125, 8125-U	28
8241, 8245	16
8251, 8255	24
8312, 8612	28
8440, 8445	18
8516	36
8552	24
8716	36
1006-2A	③
1007-2A	③
1007-2B, C, D	①
1007-3A, B	①
1010-2A	41
1062-A, B, C	②
1211-3A	28
1214-2A	①
1252-A	28

MODEL	PINTS
1262-A	②
1263-A	②

Auxiliary Units

1241	14
5831	4
6041	8
6231	8
7041	11
7231	8
8031, 8035	12
8341, 8345	12
9341	18
9441	12

①—front case 41 pints, rear case 10 pints
②—fill until oil runs out of fill hole
③—front case 38 pints, rear case 10 pints

3000 & 5000 SERIES

Five Speed Synchronized Type, Figs. 1 and 2

1. To disassemble remove gearshift housing.
2. Remove brake drum, spline flange, brake shoe, mainshaft rear bearing retainer, speedometer drive gear and spacer.
3. Remove countershaft rear bearing retainer and nut.
4. Remove left side power take-off cover.
5. Use puller to remove reverse idler shaft.
6. With hard wood block against front side of second speed gear, drive mainshaft toward rear until rear bearing is free of case. Remove snap ring and bearing.
7. Slide first speed gear off as mainshaft is removed from case.
8. Remove input shaft from case.
9. Remove countershaft rear bearing.
10. Work countershaft toward rear until it clears front bearing and lift assembly out of case.
11. Remove countershaft front bearing retainer and tap bearing out of case.
12. Remove reverse idler gear.

Assemble Mainshaft

1. Place 2nd speed gear on output shaft with clutch teeth toward front.
2. Install two Woodruff keys in mainshaft. Then press 2nd-3rd synchronizer clutch gear on mainshaft.
3. Place 2nd-3rd speed synchronizer, 3rd gear and 3rd gear sleeve on mainshaft. Press sleeve onto shaft until it bottoms on synchronizer clutch gear. *Third speed gear slots must line up with Woodruff keys in mainshaft.*
4. Install snap ring at front of 3rd gear sleeve.
5. Install 4th gear, thrust washer and snap ring on mainshaft.
6. Install 4th-5th synchronizer.

Assemble Transmission

1. Tap countershaft front bearing into case. Install bearing retainer with new gasket. Line up oil holes in retainer, gasket and case.
2. Place assembled countershaft in case and start shaft into front bearing. Drive rear bearing onto shaft and into case.
3. Install reverse idler and power takeoff cover.
4. Tap input shaft and bearing into case and install mainshaft pilot roller.
5. Install input shaft retainer without gasket and tighten bolts to bottom retainer on bearing snap ring. Check clearance between retainer gasket surface and case. Use gaskets that will prevent oil leakage and any end play. Install retainer with oil hole in line with gasket and case holes.
6. Install low-reverse gear on mainshaft and position assembly in case. Drive mainshaft bearing into position.
7. Install and tighten countershaft nut to 350–450 ft. lbs. on 1966–72 models and 500–550 ft. lbs. on 1966–73 models. Install bearing retainer and torque bolts to 60–80 ft. lbs.
8. Install new seal in mainshaft rear bearing retainer, tightening bolts to 60–80 ft. lbs.
9. Install brake shoe, spline flange and

SPICER TRANSMISSIONS

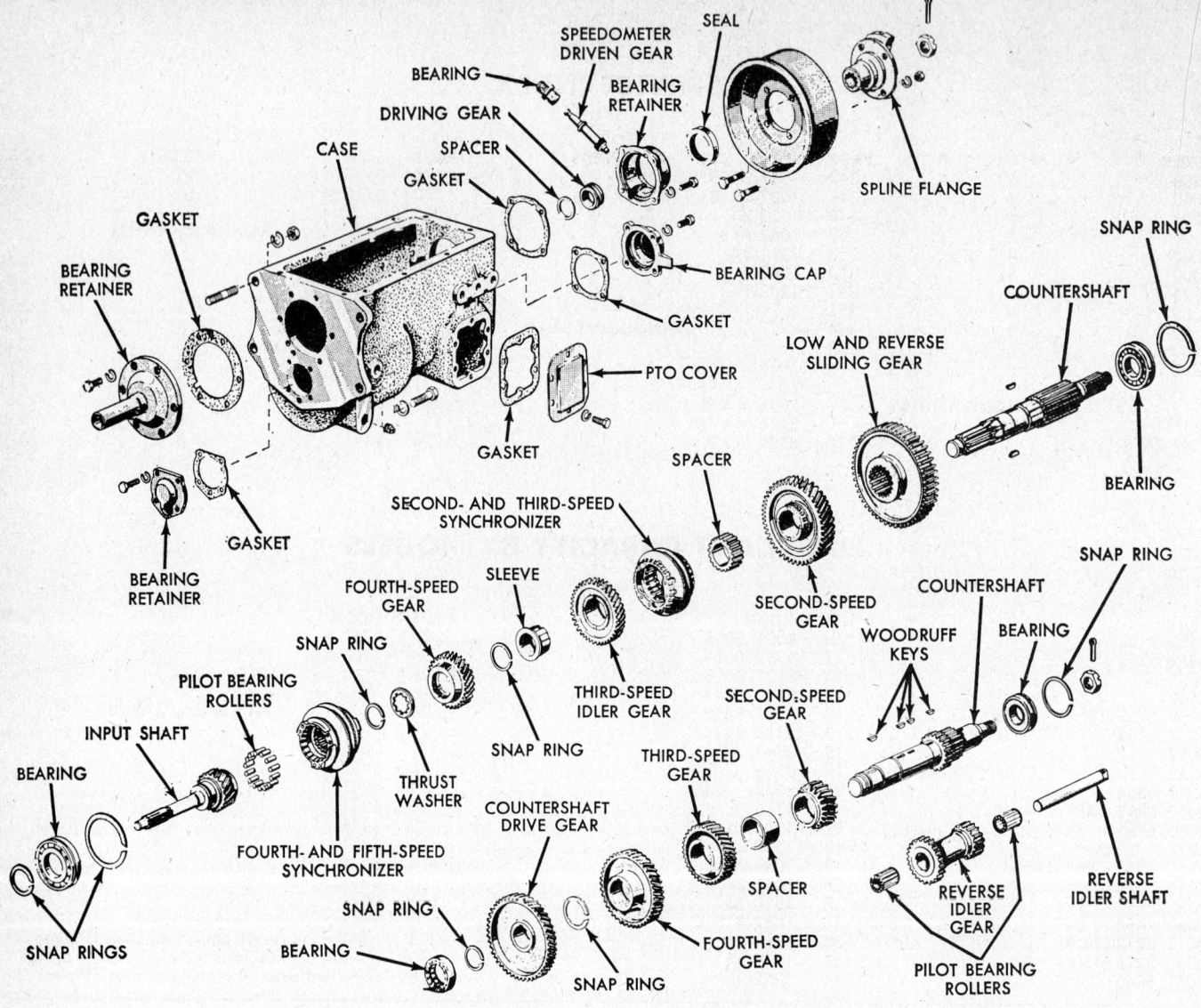

Fig. 1 Spicer 3000 and 5000 Series five speed synchronized transmissions

nut.
10. Shift gears into neutral and install gearshift housing.

6000 SERIES

Five Speed Synchronized Type, Figs. 3 and 4

1. To disassemble, remove gearshift housing.
2. Remove brake drum, spline flange and brake shoe.
3. Remove rear bearing retainers from mainshaft and countershaft. Then remove speedometer drive gear and spacer from mainshaft.
4. Remove countershaft rear nut.
5. Remove reverse idler gear shaft.
6. Using a hard wood block against front side of 2nd speed gear, drive mainshaft toward rear until rear bearing clears case. Remove snap ring and bearing from shaft.
7. Slide low-reverse gear from shaft as mainshaft is removed from case. Remove pilot rollers from input shaft.
8. Remove input shaft from case.
9. Remove snap ring and bearing from rear of countershaft. Slide countershaft toward rear of case until shaft clears front bearing and lift assembly out of case.
10. Remove countershaft front bearing retainer and tap bearing out of case.

Assemble Mainshaft

1. Slide 2nd speed gear and synchronizer clutch gear onto shaft. Install clutch gear retaining snap ring.
2. Slide 2nd-3rd synchronizer onto shaft, and press on 3rd speed gear.
3. Install 4th speed gear sleeve and 4th gear. Position thrust washer and install snap ring. Slide 4th-5th speed synchronizer onto shaft. Then slip low-reverse sliding gear on shaft.

Assemble Transmission

1. Tap countershaft front bearing into case. Install retainer with new gasket, lining up oil holes in retainer, gasket and case.
2. Start assembled countershaft into front bearing. Drive rear bearing onto shaft and into case.
3. With bearings in reverse idler gear, install gear in case, lining up flat surface on rear end of idler shaft with position of lock tang on countershaft rear bearing retainer. Drive shaft into position.
4. Position mainshaft assembly in case. With wood block at front end of shaft, drive rear bearing into place.
5. Insert pilot rollers into input shaft, holding rollers with Lubriplate. Last roller must be inserted endwise.
6. Install input shaft and bearing.
7. Lock transmission in two gears and install and tighten countershaft rear bearing nut to 350-450 ft. lbs. on 1966-72 models and 500-550 ft. lbs. on 1973-76 models.
8. Install countershaft rear bearing retainer.
9. Install new oil seal in mainshaft bearing retainer. Place speedometer gear and spacer on mainshaft. Install bearing re-

SPICER TRANSMISSIONS

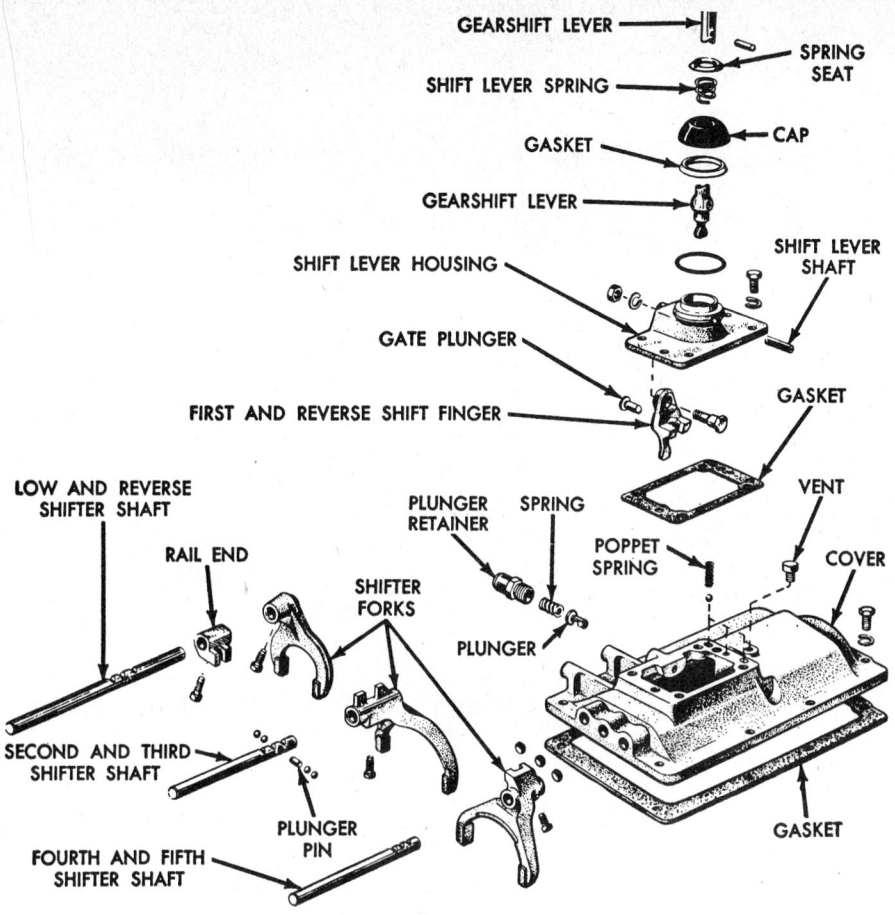

Fig. 2 Spicer 3000 and 5000 gearshift housing

Assembly Notes

After countershaft is assembled, measure clearance between rear bearing cap and case. Then select a shim or shims that will provide .001–.003" end play. When adjustment is satisfactory torque bolts to 45–55 ft. lbs.

When assembling the output shaft, position direct and overdrive hub with face of hub stamped "X" toward front end of shaft. Install underdrive hub with face stamped "X" toward rear of shaft.

Assemble Transmission

1. With gears in neutral and new gasket on case, place gearshift housing on gasket with outer ends of shift rods toward front of transmission and each shift fork engaged in its proper groove, Fig. 6. Torque housing bolts to 45–50 ft. lbs.
2. Install transmission trunnion, making certain it does not bind on bearing retainer.
3. Install U-joint flange and yoke on input shaft and torque nut to 275–350 ft. lbs.
4. Install transmission mounting bracket and torque bolts to 40–45 ft. lbs.
5. Install brake shoe assembly and rear U-joint flange (and drum) and torque nut to 275–350 ft. lbs.

7231 SERIES

Three Speed Auxiliary Type, Figs. 7, 8, 9 & 10

1. Remove gearshift housing.
2. Remove input shaft yoke.
3. Remove trunnion from front bearing retainer.
4. Remove output shaft flange and brake drum, brake shoe and output shaft bearing retainer.
5. Remove countershaft rear bearing cap and shims. Tie shims together for use at reassembly.
6. Remove input shaft assembly.
7. Tap underdrive gear toward rear until bearing clears case. Pull bearing off shaft.
8. Remove underdrive sleeve and hub through rear bearing bore and remove output shaft.
9. Drive countershaft toward rear until rear bearing cup clears case. Slide countershaft toward rear and lift out assembly. Remove countershaft front bearing cup.

Assemble Transmission

1. Install countershaft front bearing cup. Lower gear end of shaft into rear bearing bore and position shaft in case. Install rear bearing cup.
2. Position countershaft rear bearing cap without shims. Measure clearance between cap and case. Select shims that will provide .001–.003" end play, and tighten bolts.
3. Position output shaft in case and slide hub and underdrive sleeve onto shaft. With rear end of output shaft extended beyond rear of case, drive rear bearing onto shaft. Drive bearing on shaft until it firmly seats in bore.
4. Install new oil seal in output shaft bearing retainer. Install speedometer gear on shaft and install bearing retainer, tightening bolts to 45–50 ft. lbs.
5. Install input shaft and bearing retainer as a unit.
6. Install parking brake shoe and tighten

---

tainer.
10. Install input shaft retainer without gasket and tighten bolts to bottom retainer on bearing snap ring. Check clearance between retainer gasket surface and case, which should be .010–.015". Select gasket pack that will seal oil and also prevent end play at bearing snap ring.
11. Install input shaft retainer with oil hole in line with gasket and case holes.
12. Install brake shoe assembly.
13. Install U-joint flange and parking brake drum.
14. With transmission in neutral, install gearshift housing.

Oil Pump

The oil pump (when used) is bolted to the inner side of the clutch housing. The pump is fitted with a non-adjustable pressure relief valve consisting of a ball and spring held in place by a pipe plug in the side of the oil pump housing.

When assembling the pump, press the drive gear on the shaft so that the distance from the front end of the shaft to the front side of the gear measures 17/32". This dimension should be maintained to prevent excessive wear on the side of the gear.

Assemble the oil pump driving gear and shaft in the housing. Press the driven gear shaft in the housing and then on the shaft. Assemble the relief valve and spring and install the pipe plug. Position the housing gasket, being sure the oil holes in the case are not covered by the gasket. Fill the oil pump with gear oil and fasten the assembly in place, being sure the oil holes line up.

5831 SERIES

Three Speed Auxiliary Type, Figs. 5 and 6

1. To disassemble, remove gearshift housing.
2. Remove input shaft U-joint yoke.
3. Remove flange and brake drum from output shaft.
4. Remove brake shoe assembly.
5. Remove rear mounting bracket.
6. Remove output shaft rear bearing retainer and remove speedometer gear from shaft.
7. Remove input shaft bearing retainer and bearing spacer.
8. Remove countershaft rear bearing cap and shims. Tie shims together for use at reassembly.
9. Tap underdrive gear toward rear until bearing clears case. Remove bearing from shaft. Remove underdrive sleeve and hub through rear bearing bore.
10. Tilt front of output shaft upward and slide it out of case.
11. Remove pilot rollers from input shaft. Remove snap ring and tap input shaft and bearing into case.
12. Drive countershaft toward rear until rear bearing cup is out of case. Remove countershaft front bearing cup from case.

349

SPICER TRANSMISSIONS

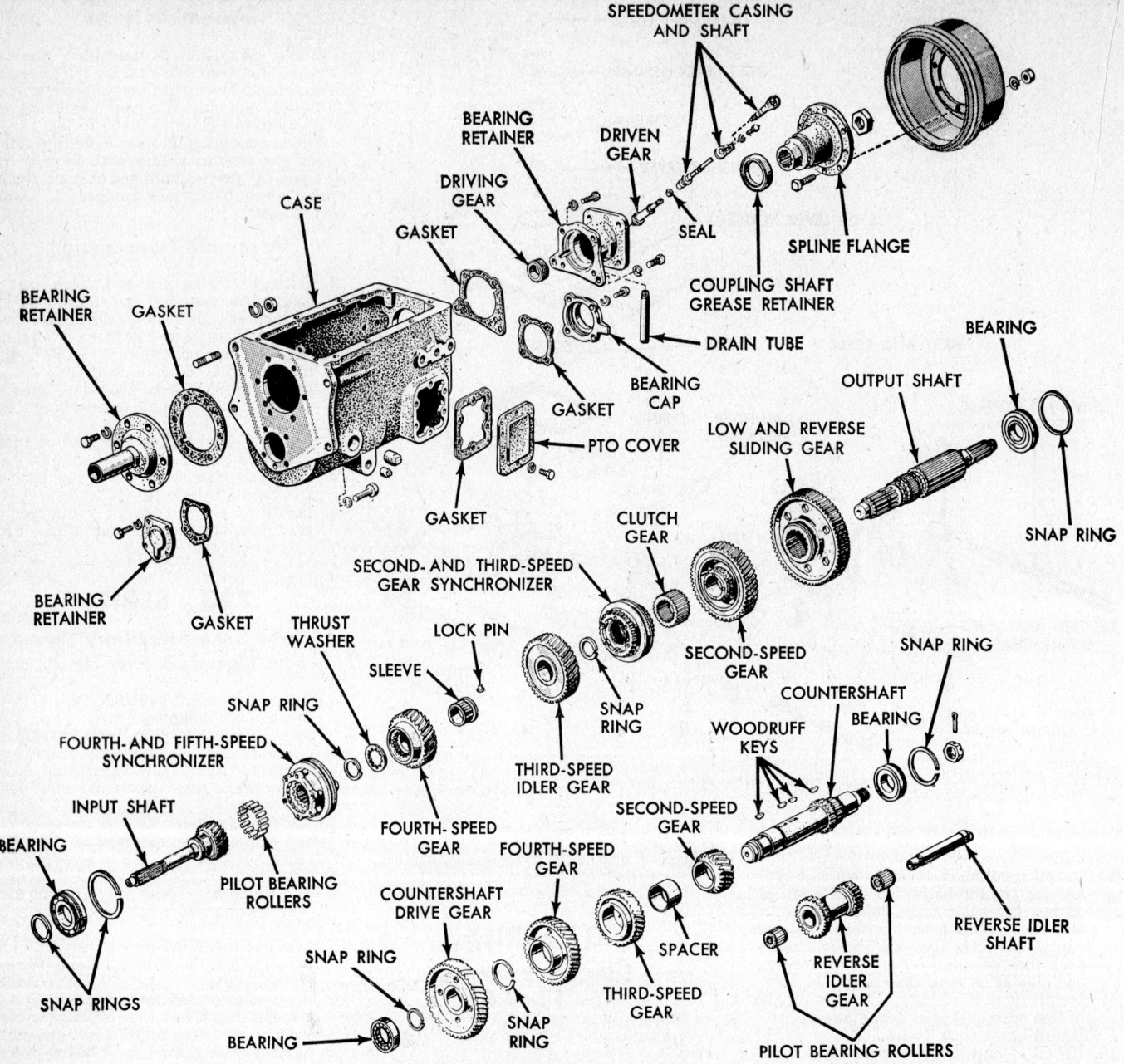

Fig. 3 Spicer 6000 Series five speed synchronized transmission

bolts to 180–220 ft. lbs.
7. Install output shaft flange and tighten nut to 275–350 ft. lbs. If brake drum was removed, install it and tighten nuts to 70–75 ft. lbs.
8. Install trunnion but do not tighten bolt. Position input shaft yoke on shaft, install nut and torque to 275–350 ft. lbs.
9. Install gearshift housing.

7041, 8341, 8345
Four Speed Auxiliary Type, Figs. 11 to 14

1. Remove gearshift housing.
2. Remove flange (and drum) from output shaft.
3. Remove input shaft U-joint flange and dust deflector.
4. Remove trunnion and front bearing retainer cap.
5. Remove lockwashers from retainer cap bolts and reinstall cap. Then after removing bolts from retainer, use puller to remove retainer and front bearing. Remove cap and tap bearing out of retainer.
6. Remove brake shoe, output shaft bearing retainer, speedometer drive gear and 1st gear spacer washer.
7. After sliding input shaft as far forward as possible, tap output shaft forward to start shaft out of its bearing. Then slide output shaft and bearing rearward until there is clearance for a standard bearing puller. Pull bearing from shaft and remove 1st gear thrust washer.
8. Place two 1" thick wood blocks between input shaft and 3rd-4th clutch gear. Press output shaft forward until clutch gear lock ring is exposed. Remove two machined halves and wood blocks.
9. Pull output shaft out through rear of case, noting that there are double rows of bearing rollers in 1st, 2nd and 4th speed gears.
10. Remove input shaft through top of case and pilot bearing from shaft. Remove sleeve and inner bearing race from shaft.
11. Remove countershaft front bearing retainer washer, bearing cap and gasket. Press countershaft toward rear until shaft is freed from front bearing and rear bearing is out of case. Remove bearing

Spicer Transmissions

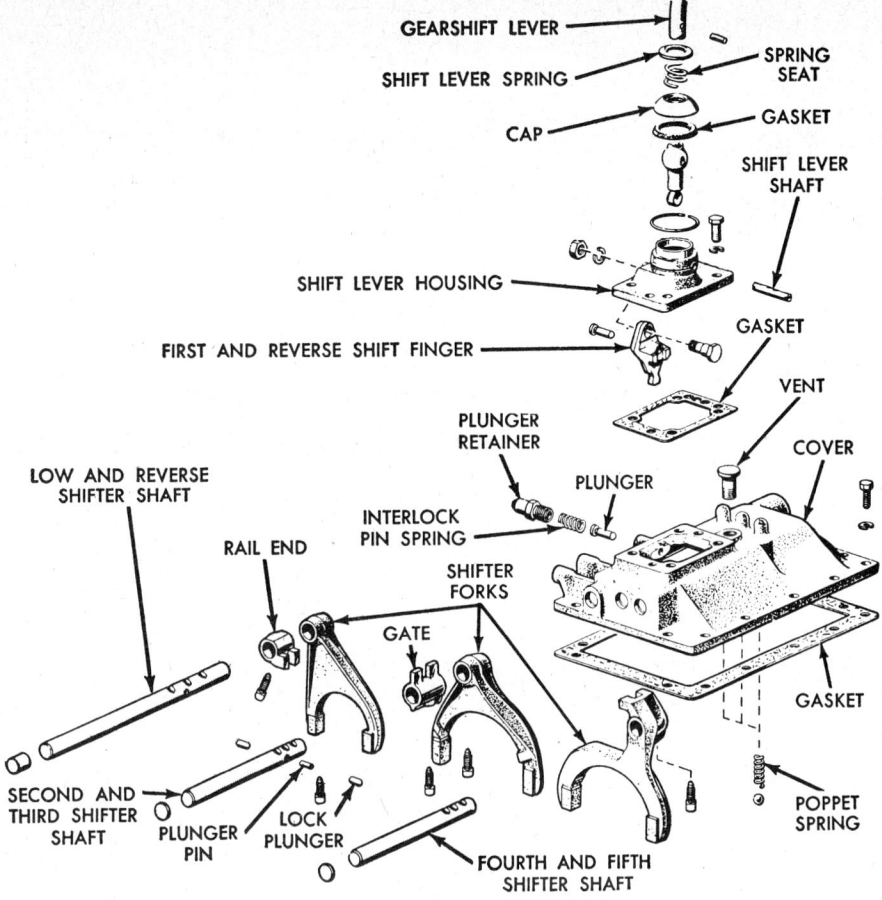

Fig. 4 Spicer 6000 Series gearshift housing

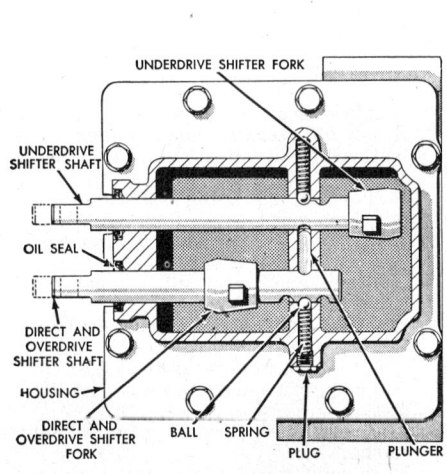

Fig. 6 Spicer 5831 Series gearshift housing

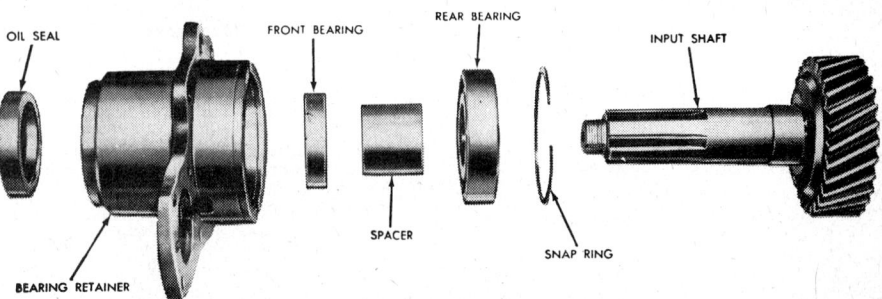

Fig. 7 Series 7231 input shaft parts

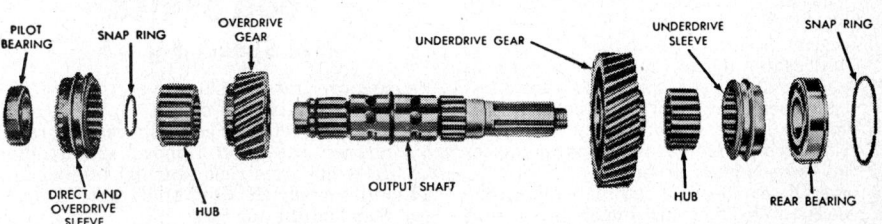

Fig. 8 Series 7231 output shaft parts

351

SPICER TRANSMISSIONS

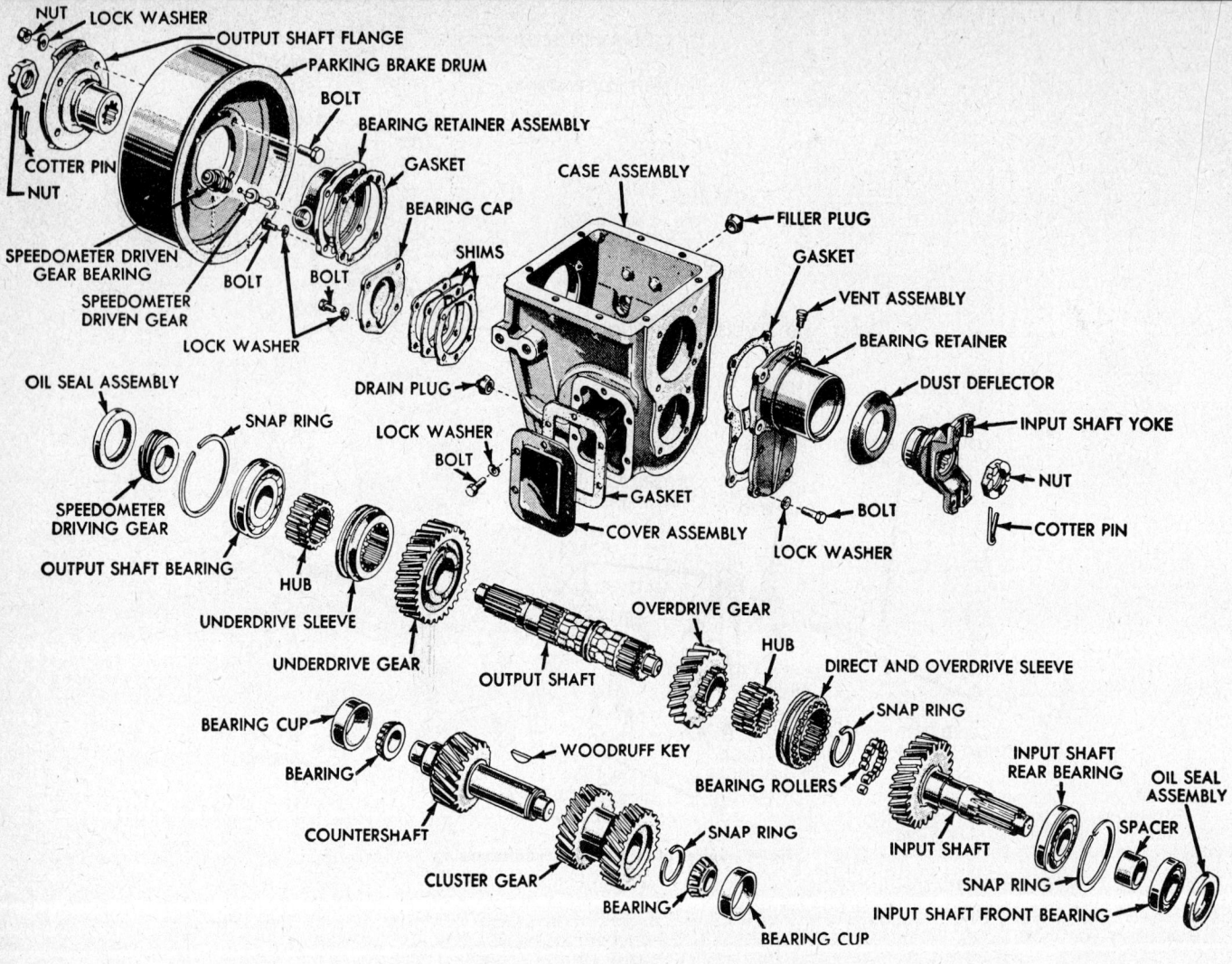

Fig. 5 Spicer 5831 Series three speed auxiliary transmission

from shaft and front bearing from case.
12. Remove countershaft from case, front end first.

Assemble Transmission

1. Assemble and install countershaft in case, being sure oil drain hole in rear bearing cap is at bottom and torque bolts to 45-50 ft. lbs.
2. Assemble and install input shaft in case.
3. Assemble and install output shaft components in case. Then with two 1" thick wood blocks between input shaft and 3rd-4th clutch gear, press output shaft forward until shaft lock ring groove is beyond 3rd-4th clutch gear. Remove wood blocks. Slide 3rd-4th clutch gear forward and make sure that both parts of lock ring will center inside counterbore of clutch gear. Pull output shaft rearward until components are drawn into position.
4. Install output shaft bearing with snap ring groove to rear. Install spacer washer and speedometer drive gear.
5. Install rear bearing retainer and torque bolts to 65-75 ft. lbs. Install brake shoe assembly, output shaft flange and drum and torque nut to 275-350 ft. lbs.
6. Install input shaft bearing retainer and gasket, tightening large bolts to 75-100 ft. lbs. and small ones 25-30 ft. lbs. Install front bearing in retainer. Install bearing cap and gasket. Torque bolts to 40-50 ft. lbs.
7. Install trunnion with finished surface toward front and torque bolt to 50-55 ft. lbs.
8. After positioning dust reflector, install input shaft flange, tightening nut to 275-350 ft. lbs.
9. After aligning shaft forks with clutch sleeves, install shift cover and gasket and torque nuts and bolts to 45-50 ft. lbs.

7000 SERIES

Five Speed, Fig. 15

1. Remove transmission cover.
2. Remove universal flange.
3. Unfasten retainer cap from rear of transmission case and remove speedometer drive gear and rear bearing retainer.
4. Pull overdrive shift shaft out through rear and lift out fork.
5. Remove overdrive housing countershaft cover and unscrew lock bolts that retain overdrive gears to countershaft.
6. Reach into overdrive housing and remove bolts which fasten this housing to main case.
7. Pull overdrive housing and gears to rear and force rear bearing from mainshaft.
8. Push mainshaft to rear until intermediate bearing is free of case.
9. Tilt mainshaft and lift assembly out through top.
10. Remove bell housing and main drive gear bearing cap.
11. Unscrew nut from main drive gear shaft and push drive gear into case and lift it out.
12. Remove snap ring from front end of countershaft.
13. Push countershaft to rear until bearing is free of case, then lift countershaft out through top.
14. Push out reverse idler shaft and lift out gear.
15. To disassemble the mainshaft, slip off sliding gear and clutch sleeve. Unscrew clutch gear retaining nut and strip mainshaft, being careful not to lose any of the bearing rollers.
16. Reverse the above procedure to assemble the transmission.

SPICER TRANSMISSIONS

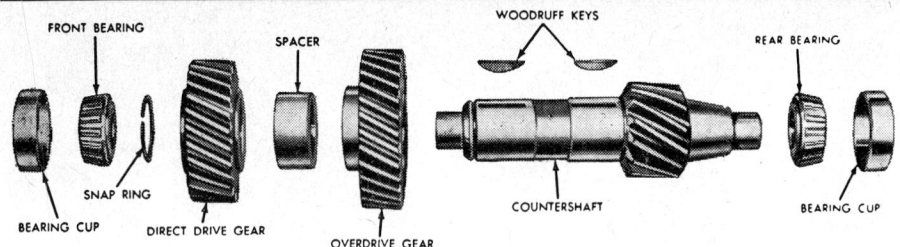

Fig. 9 Series 7231 countershaft parts

8000, 8500, 8700 SERIES, 4 SPEED

Disassemble, Fig. 16

1. Shift transmission into reverse gear, remove cover screws and lift off shift cover.
2. Remove nut and pull off companion flange.
3. Remove mainshaft rear bearing cap and take off speedometer drive gear, spacer and thrust washer.
4. Slide mainshaft to rear far enough to free rear bearing from case and use a suitable puller to remove bearing.
5. Remove clutch release yoke and shafts.
6. Remove cap screws from main drive gear bearing cap and, using a suitable puller, remove bearing cap and main drive gear.
7. Remove mainshaft pilot bearing from drive gear pocket.
8. Lift mainshaft assembly out of case by its front end.
9. Remove countershaft rear bearing cap and the bearing retainer washer from rear end of countershaft.
10. Pull reverse idler gear shaft out with a puller.
11. Remove reverse idler gear, sleeve and bearing assembly.
12. Move countershaft to rear far enough to free rear bearing from case. Then use puller to remove bearing.
13. Slide countershaft to rear until front bearing is out of case and lift out assembly.

Main Drive Gear, Disassemble

1. Remove snap ring from inside of bearing cap.
2. Place bearing cap in arbor press and push bearing and main drive gear out of bearing cap.
3. Remove nut and press bearing off main drive gear.

Mainshaft, Disassemble

1. Remove 3rd and 4th speed clutch collar.
2. Remove low speed gear, being careful not to lose any of the needle bearings.
3. Remove low and 2nd speed clutch gear.
4. Remove 3rd and 4th speed clutch gear snap ring.
5. Place mainshaft assembly in arbor press with rear end down and press mainshaft through gears. Use care to see that none of the needle bearings and 3rd speed gear lock balls are lost as they fall out.

Countershaft, Disassemble

1. Use puller to remove front bearing.
2. Remove countershaft drive gear snap ring.
3. Place assembly in arbor press and press countershaft through gears.

Mainshaft, Assemble

1. Coat inside bore of low speed gear with heavy grease. Then place two rows of needle bearings (72 per row) on inside of low speed gear with spacer between rows.
2. Assemble needle bearings in 2nd and 3rd speed gears in same manner.
3. Place mainshaft in vise with rear end down.
4. Place 2nd speed gear on mainshaft with clutch teeth to rear.
5. Place 3rd speed gear sleeve on mainshaft with flanged end of sleeve toward rear. Line up two notches on inside of sleeve with mainshaft splines. Place two sleeve lock balls in notches of sleeve and press sleeve on mainshaft.
6. Place 3rd speed gear on mainshaft with clutch teeth to front.
7. Place 3rd and 4th speed clutch gear on mainshaft with hub of gear toward front and press in place. Then lock assembly with a new snap ring.
8. Place 3rd and 4th speed clutch collar on clutch gear with longer hub to rear.
9. Take mainshaft from vise and place low and 2nd speed clutch gear with shift fork collar to rear.
10. Place low speed gear on mainshaft with clutch teeth to front.
11. Grease one side of low speed gear thrust washer and place its greased side against low speed gear.

Transmission, Assemble

Reassembly of the transmission is largely

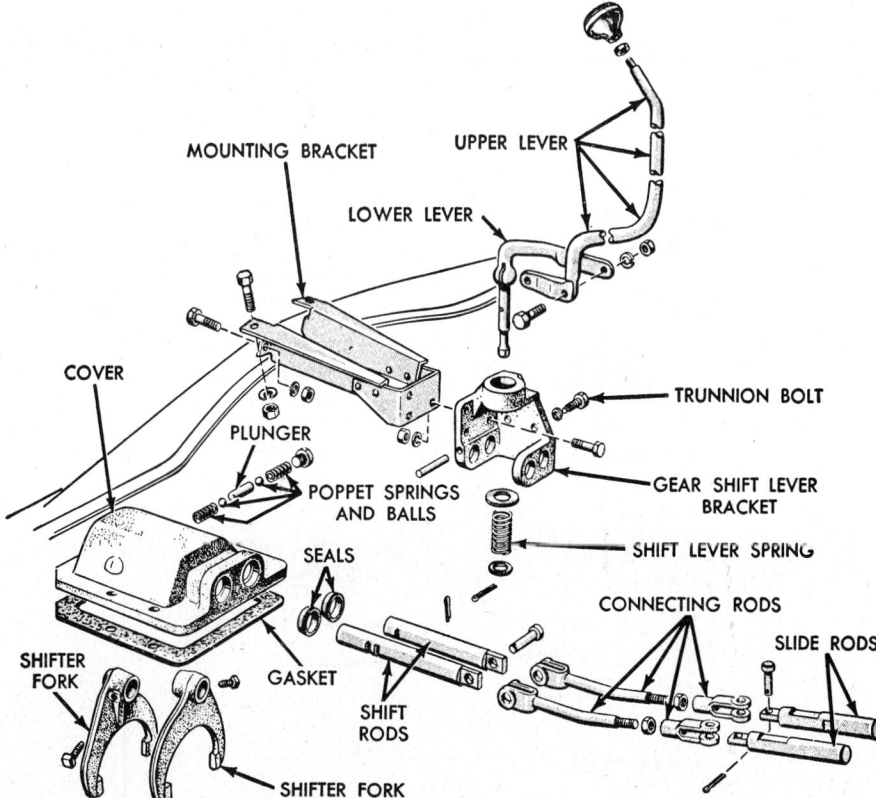

Fig. 10 Spicer 7231 Series gearshift housing

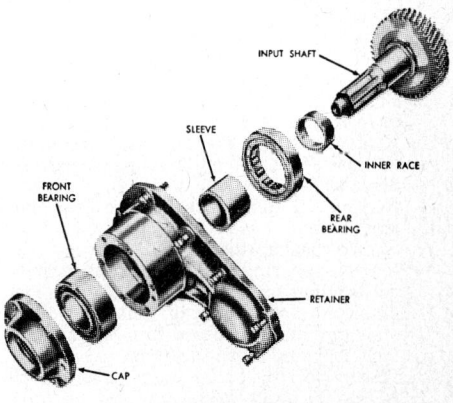

Fig. 11 Spicer 8341 Series input shaft parts

353

SPICER TRANSMISSIONS

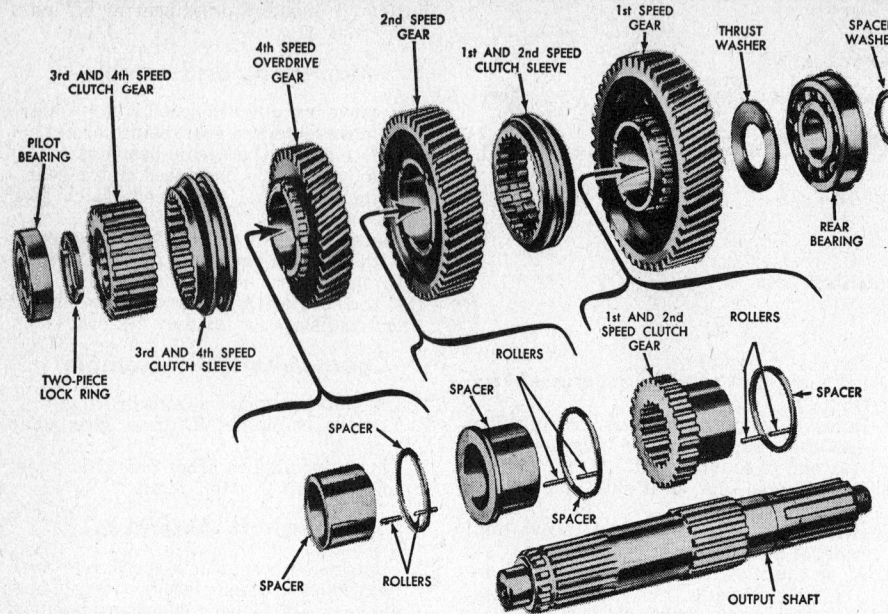

Fig. 12 Spicer 8341 Series output shaft parts

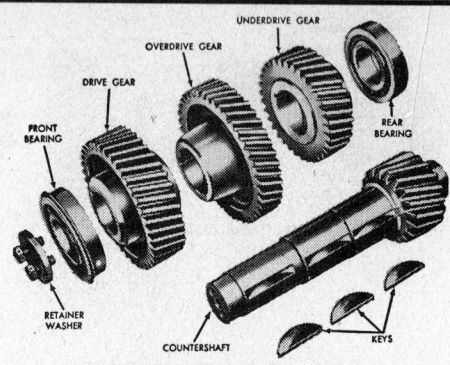

Fig. 13 Spicer 8341 Series countershaft parts

the reverse of the disassembly procedure. However, the following should be noted:
1. Place reverse idler gear and sleeve in case with shift fork collar to rear of case.
2. Make sure flat on rear end of reverse idler shaft is lined up so countershaft rear bearing cap will lock shaft in place.
3. Main drive gear bearing cap is marked "Top" and should be so installed.
4. Be sure mainshaft rear bearing cap and gasket are installed with oil drain holes lined up.

8000, 8500, 8700 SERIES, 5 SPEED

Disassemble, Fig. 17

1. Shift transmission into reverse.
2. After removing cap screws, lift cover and shift forks off transmission.
3. Remove nut and pull off companion flange.
4. Remove mainshaft rear bearing cap.
5. Remove speedometer drive gear or spacer from mainshaft.
6. Slide mainshaft to rear until rear bearing is free of case. Then use a suitable puller to remove bearing.
7. Remove overdrive gear lower shift fork guide shaft and remove shift fork.
8. Remove transmission rear end cover.
9. Remove overdrive gear and bearing spacer from mainshaft.
10. Remove nut from rear end of countershaft and use a suitable puller to remove overdrive sleeve.
11. Remove countershaft overdrive gear and shift collar.
12. Slide mainshaft toward rear to bring center roller bearing out of case far enough to get a puller or "C" clamp on the outside diameter of the bearing. Then tap rear end of mainshaft toward front which will move bearing off shaft.
13. Loosen bearing puller or "C" clamp and slide mainshaft back and get another hold on center mainshaft roller bearing and again tap mainshaft forward as far as possible.
14. Repeat this procedure until center roller bearing is out of case and off mainshaft.
15. Remove clutch release yoke and shafts.
16. Remove cap screws from main drive gear bearing cap and with a suitable puller remove cap and main drive gear out of case, using the two puller screw holes provided.
17. Remove main drive gear pilot bearing from mainshaft.
18. Tilt front end of mainshaft upward and lift assembly out of case.
19. Remove cap screws and take off countershaft rear bearing retainer and thrust washer.
20. Place a suitable puller in threaded hole in reverse idler gear shaft and pull out shaft.
21. Remove reverse idler gear and sleeve and bearing assembly.
22. Move countershaft to the rear until rear bearing is out of case. Then use a puller to remove rear bearing.
23. Slide countershaft toward rear until front end is out of case. Then lift assembly out by its front end.

Main Drive Gear, Disassemble

1. Remove snap ring on inside of bearing cap.
2. Place bearing cap in press and push bearing and main drive gear out of cap.
3. Remove bearing nut and press bearing from main drive gear.

Mainshaft, Disassemble

1. Remove 3rd and 4th speed clutch collar.
2. Remove low speed gear and needle roller bearings, being careful not to lose any of the rollers.
3. Remove low and 2nd speed clutch gear.
4. Remove snap ring from front end of mainshaft and press gears off shaft. Use care to see that needle bearings and 3rd speed gear sleeve lock balls are not lost during the pressing operation.

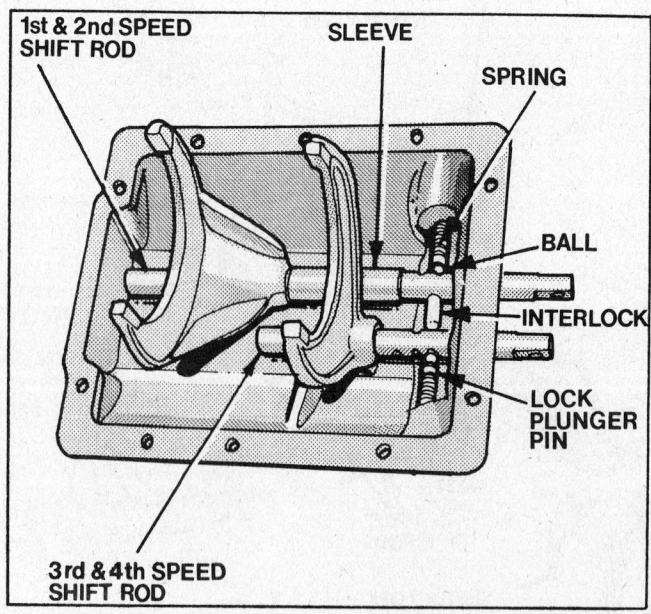

Fig. 14 Spicer 8341 Series gearshift housing

Spicer Transmissions

Countershaft, Disassemble

1. Use puller to remove front bearing.
2. Remove countershaft drive gear snap ring.
3. Press off countershaft gears one at a time by placing gears on bed of press and pushing countershaft out of gears.

Mainshaft, Assemble

1. Coat inside bore of low speed gear with heavy grease.
2. Place two rows of needle bearings (71 per row) on inside of low speed gear with spacer between rows.
3. Assemble needle bearings in 2nd and 3rd speed gears in same manner.
4. Place mainshaft in vise with rear end down.
5. Place 2nd speed gear on mainshaft with clutch teeth to rear of shaft.
6. Place 3rd speed gear sleeve on shaft with flanged end toward rear. Line up the two notches on inside of sleeve with mainshaft spline and place two sleeve lock balls in notches of sleeve. Then press sleeve on mainshaft.
7. Place 3rd speed gear on mainshaft sleeve with clutch teeth to front.
8. Press 3rd and 4th speed clutch gear on mainshaft with its hub to front. Then install snap ring in front of clutch gear.
9. Place 3rd and 4th speed clutch collar on clutch gear with longer hub to rear.
10. Remove mainshaft from vise and place low and 2nd speed clutch gear on mainshaft with shift fork collar to rear.
11. Place low speed gear on rear of mainshaft with clutch teeth to front.
12. Grease one side of mainshaft low speed gear thrust washer and place on mainshaft with greased side against low gear.

Transmission, Assemble

Reassembly of the transmission is largely a matter of reversing the disassembly procedure. However, the following should be noted:
1. Shift fork collar of reverse idler gear should be to rear of case.
2. When installing reverse idler gear shaft, make sure flat on rear of shaft is lined up so countershaft rear bearing retainer will lock reverse idler shaft in place.
3. Mainshaft pilot bearing must be assembled on shaft with snap ring in outer race to rear.
4. Main drive gear bearing cap is marked "Top" and it should be so installed.
5. Make sure countershaft overdrive gear clutch collar is installed with hub of collar toward gear. Make sure collar is a free slide fit on spline hub of gear.
6. When installing overdrive shift fork and shaft, place shift fork guide shaft in hole provided in rear of case. Tap it through case and line up shift fork and tap shaft on through hole in center support in main case.

1241 SERIES

4 Speed Auxiliary Unit, Disassemble, Figs. 18 & 19

1. Remove shifter housing, then lock transmission in two gears, remove yoke nuts, using a suitable puller remove companion flanges or yokes.

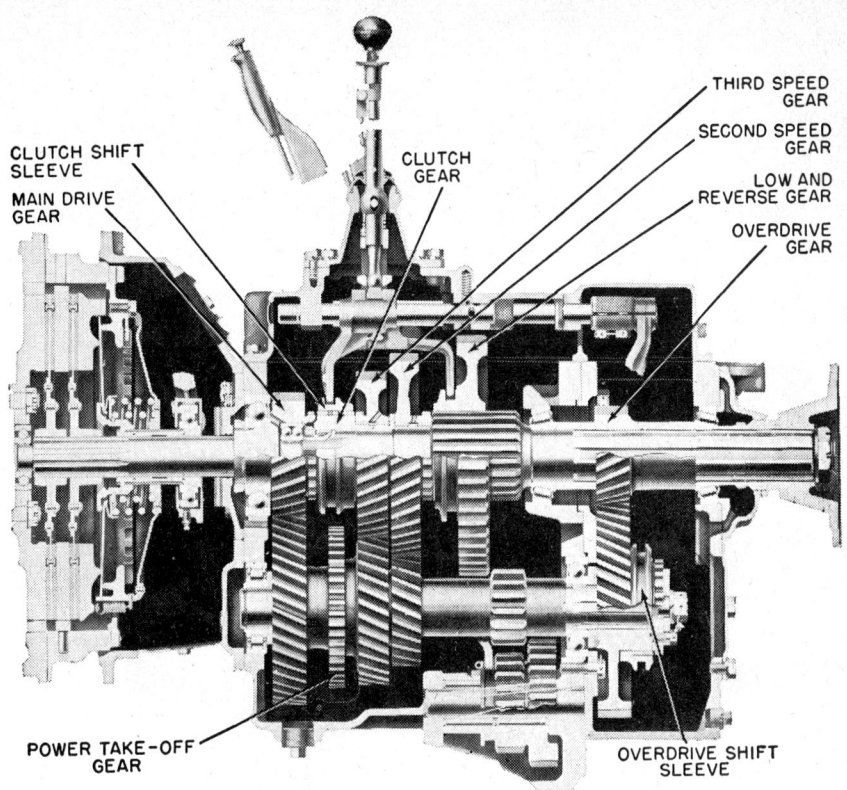

Fig. 15 Spicer Series 7751, 7851 five speed transmissions

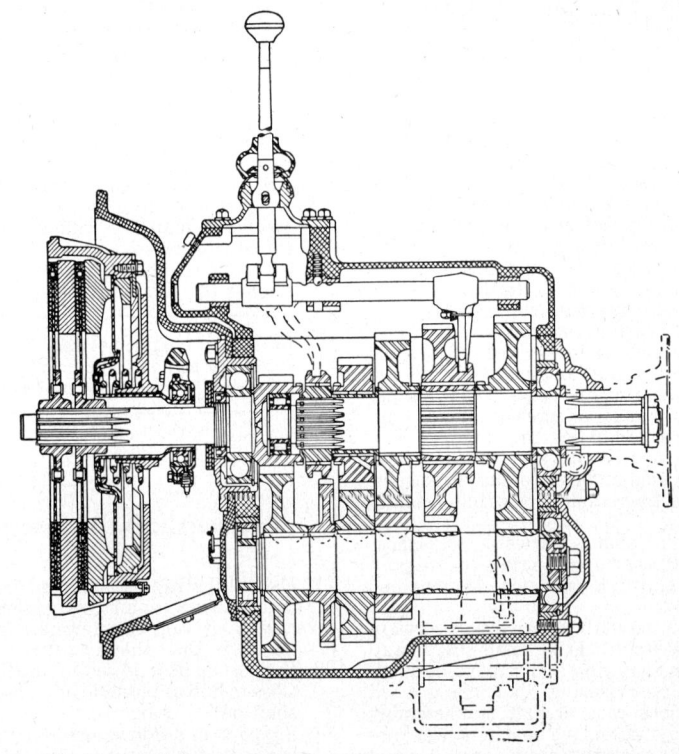

Fig. 16 Spicer 8000, 8500, 8700 Series four speed transmissions

SPICER TRANSMISSIONS

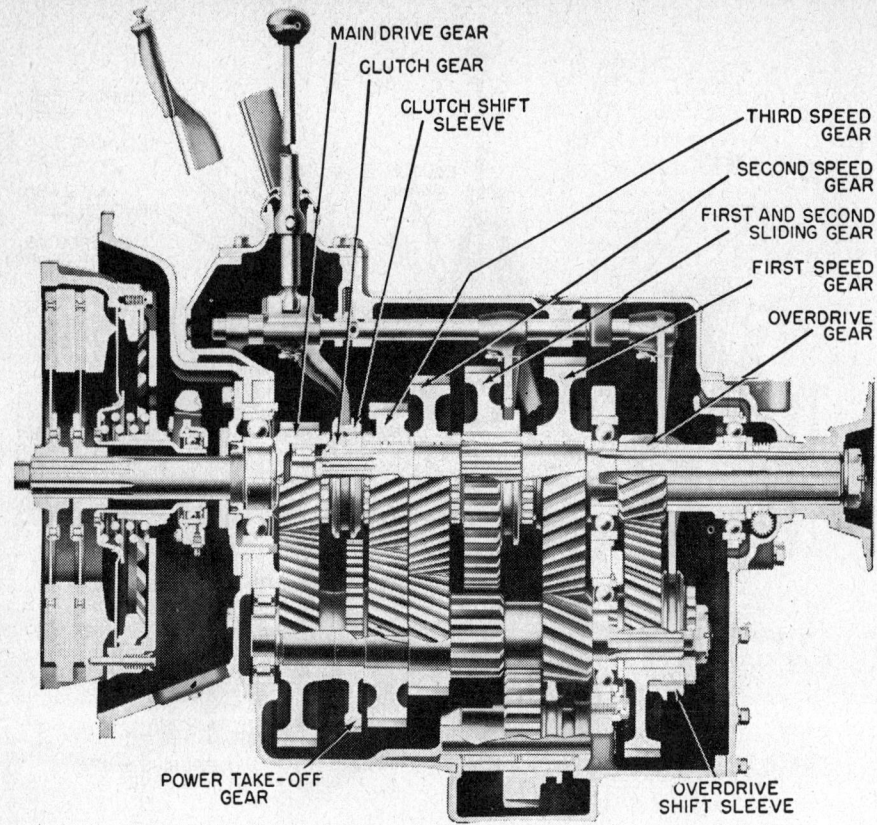

Fig. 17 Spicer 8000, 8500, 8700 Series five speed. Some models have double row ball bearing at rear of mainshaft

NOTE: Do not hammer on these parts as this could cause dimensional distortion and failure of these and other related parts.

2. Remove front transmission hanger (if used) then remove front bearing cap from bearing retainer. Remove front bearing seal only if it requires replacement.
3. Remove drive gear bearing retainer screws. Using a soft hammer, tap trunnion bearing face of drive gear bearing retainer until two pry bars can be inserted between case and retainer. Pry evenly with both bars until bearing retainer and drive gear can be removed.
4. Support bearing retainer on its flange and press drive gear free of bearing retainer, bearings and spacer.
5. Remove bearing and spacer from retainer then using a large screwdriver, pry out drive gear pocket bearing.
6. Remove mainshaft rear bearing caps, both the front and rear countershaft bearing caps then remove bearing retainer plate.
7. Force mainshaft rearward to expose mainshaft bearing snap ring, install puller on snap ring and remove bearing and spacer.
8. Force countershaft sub-assembly forward to expose front bearing snap ring install puller on snap ring and remove bearing.
9. Remove rear bearing, then using a lift strap, move countershaft sub-assembly rearward and remove bearing outer race and roller assembly from inner bearing race and shaft.

NOTE: Do not remove inner race from shaft unless bearing must be replaced.

10. With bearings removed from either or both countershafts, move the countershaft to side of case, then using a lift strap around clutch collar, lift the mainshaft sub-assembly up and out of the case.
11. Remove Lo-Lo gear, thrust washers, snap rings and clutch collar from mainshaft.
12. Remove snap ring located under bore of overdrive gear and slide overdrive gear, thrust washers, snap ring and underdrive gear and its parts off mainshaft then remove the remaining snap ring.

NOTE: All snap rings and thrust washers should be removed from the gear bores at this time for cleaning and inspection.

Countershaft, Disassemble

1. Using lift strap behind head end gear, lift right countershaft sub-assembly from case. Left side countershaft may be removed in the same manner.
2. Support head end with parallel bars as close to hub as possible and press countershaft out of gear.
3. Support underdrive gear with parallel bars as close to hub as possible and press countershaft out of gears.

Countershaft, Reassemble

NOTE: Coat the bores of gears with oil before pressing them onto the countershaft. Install the keys for each gear one at a time as the countershaft is pressed into each gear.

1. Press key closest to countershaft gear into place. Support underdrive gear with long hub facing up and press shaft key into gear.
2. Press second key into place. Support overdrive gear with long hub facing down and press shaft and key until gear seats firmly against face of underdrive gear.
3. Press third key into place. Support direct drive gear with long hub facing up and press shaft and key until gear seats firmly against face of overdrive gear.

NOTE: Tooth timing mark "V" must align with the center of gear keyway and the third key must be slightly under the face of the direct drive shaft.

Mainshaft, Reassemble

NOTE: Prior to assembly, inspect all thrust washers in gear bores for heavy face galling or gear tooth indentations. Replace as necessary.

1. Lubricate thrust washers with #30 engine oil.
2. Install clutch collar over rear end of mainshaft ahead of first snap ring groove at rear of shaft and install snap ring into last groove on shaft.
3. Install Lo-Lo gear with snap ring and thrust washers on rear of shaft and locate internally splined thrust washer against snap ring then install spacer with flanged portion toward face of Lo-Lo gear and shoulder of mainshaft.
4. From the front of the mainshaft install the second snap ring in the groove and install underdrive gear sub-assembly along with snap ring and thrust washers.

NOTE: Internally splined thrust washer should rest against shaft snap ring.

5. Install overdrive gear sub-assembly with snap ring and thrust washers, the gear internal snap ring should face toward the underdrive gear.
6. Place snap ring on last groove on mainshaft, install second clutch collar on front of mainshaft then place assembly in the bore and in mesh with overdrive gear.

Drive Gear Components, Reassembly

1. Press drive gear into the first bearing until race of bearing bottoms against front face of drive gear.
2. Press the pocket bearing firmly against pocket shoulder into the drive gear with the pocket bearing part number visible when pressed in bore.
3. Install spacer followed by the bearing retainer onto the drive gear bearing, then

SPICER TRANSMISSIONS

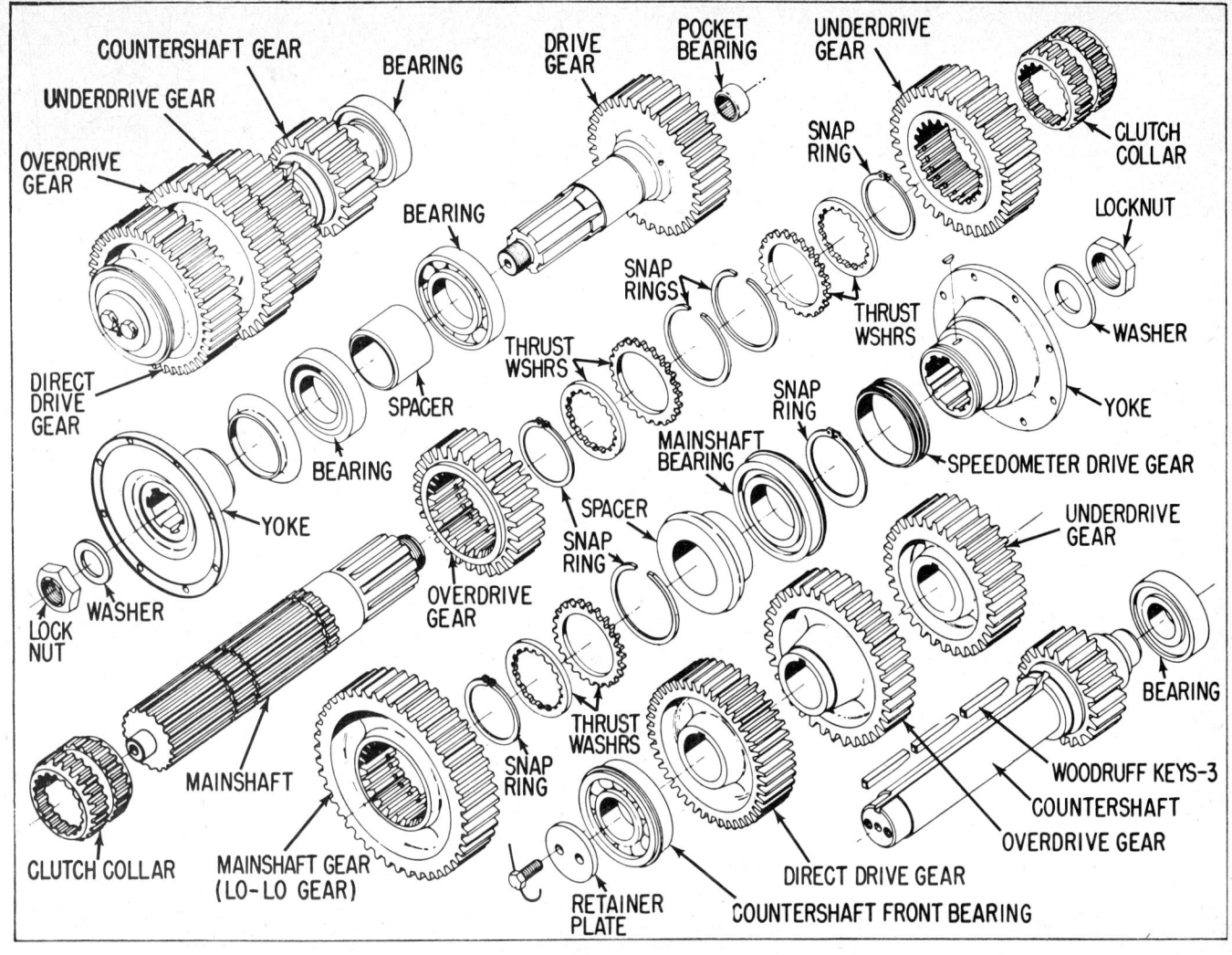

Fig. 18 Gear assembly. Spicer 1241 four speed auxiliary transmission

install the second bearing retainer and bearing and press until it seats firmly against face of spacer and shoulder of bore in the retainer.

4. Assemble front bearing cap and gasket onto bearing retainer and torque screws to 40–50 ft. lbs.

Countershafts, Installation

1. Place either of countershaft sub-assemblies into the left side of case (as viewed from rear of case) with timing mark of head end gear toward center of case.

   NOTE: This mark must be aligned with the drive gear timing mark later during reassembly.

2. Place remaining countershaft sub-assembly into the right side of the case with the timing mark on the head end gear facing toward center of case.

   NOTE: Do not install front or rear countershaft bearings until the mainshaft sub-assembly is installed in the case.

Mainshaft Sub-Assembly, Installation

1. Using a chain hoist and sling around Lo-Lo underdrive shift collar, lower mainshaft assembly into the approximate center of case rear bore then block mainshaft front stem with a piece of wood or brass plate.
2. Install mainshaft rear bearing on rear of shaft and drive bearing onto shaft and into bore of case then install the bearing snap ring.
3. Install speedometer drive gear (if removed) and rear bearing caps and gaskets then dip screws in sealer and torque to 60–80 ft. lbs.
4. Install front drive gear and bearing cap assembly then dip capscrews in sealer and torque to 60–80 ft. lbs.

   NOTE: With all timing gears painted, bring timing teeth of countershaft head end gears, pointing toward center of the case and the two timing teeth aligning with the timing teeth of the countershaft gears.

5. Remove sling from mainshaft clutch collar and disengage shift collar from under overdrive gear and move clutch collar to neutral position on the mainshaft.

Final Assembly

1. Assemble rear bearing inner race onto the countershaft then locate the sling behind the head end gear. Centralize countershaft to case front bore and align timing teeth with the drive gear timing tooth. Install countershaft bearing onto shaft and into case bore, seat bearing snap ring into case bore.
2. Install retaining plate and leave screws loose then lock transmission in two gears by placing clutch collar into Lo-Lo gear bore and direct drive gear bore.
3. Install outer race and roller assembly of countershaft rear bearing onto shaft and into bore of case against shaft shoulder.
4. Install countershaft rear bearing cap and gasket and torque screws to 40–50 ft. lbs., torque retaining plate screws to 60–80 ft. lbs., then install countershaft front bearing cap and gasket and torque screws to 40–50 ft. lbs.
5. Move clutch collars into their neutral positions on the mainshaft, align timing marks on right side countershaft with drive gear timing marks which are parallel to bottom of case, if they were moved out of mesh.

SPICER TRANSMISSIONS

6. Assemble rear bearing inner race to countershaft and using a sling on right countershaft in same manner as before, mesh head and gear timing teeth into drive gear timing tooth.
7. With timing teeth in place, install countershaft bearing onto the front of the right shaft and into bore of case, then install snap ring against face of case and install shaft retaining plate.
8. Install outer race and roller assembly onto shaft and into bore of case and against shoulder of shaft.
9. Install countershaft rear bearing cap and torque screws to 40-50 ft. lbs. then install countershaft front capscrews and torque to 60-80 ft. lbs. and install front bearing cap and torque screws to 40-50 ft. lbs.
10. Move clutch collars back into bore of gears and lock transmission in two gears then place front transmission hanger over front bearing cap.
11. Install end yokes or flanges onto drive gear stem and mainshaft splines, then install washers and locknuts, torque lock nuts to 550-600 ft. lbs.
12. Move clutch collar out of bore of gear and leave it engaged with drive gear, then turn drive gear end yoke or flange turning transmission. If timing teeth have been set correctly, the entire gear train will turn freely. If the unit locks up after several turns, the timing teeth have not been aligned correctly.
13. If transmission locks up, disengage shift collar from drive gear and turn drive gear in reverse rotation until timing marks or paint marks come into view showing alignment or misalignment. If misalignment has occurred it will be necessary to retime the shafts.
14. If timing is correct, move clutch collar to its neutral position on the mainshaft and install shifter housing.

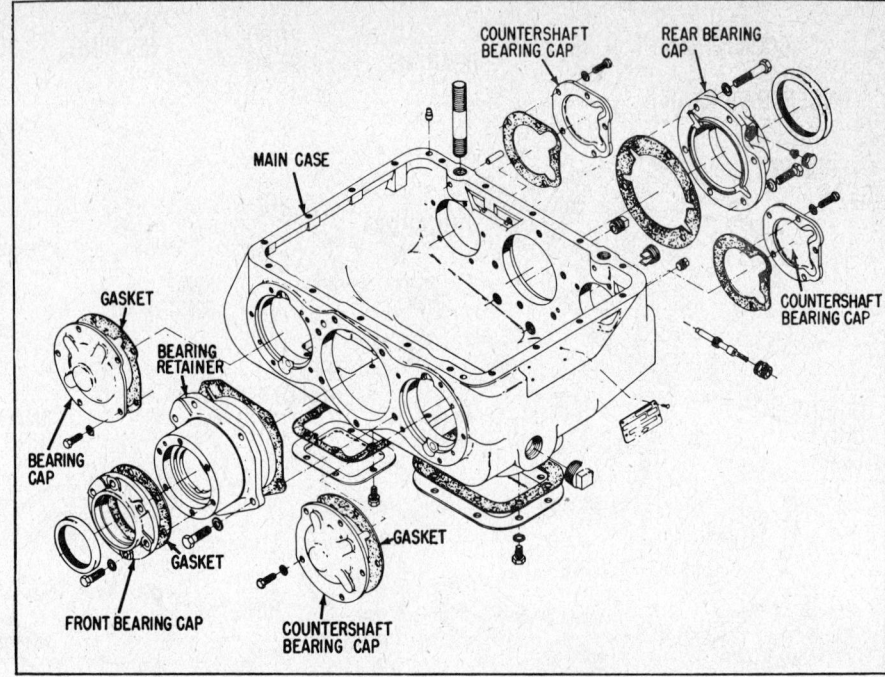

Fig. 19 Case assembly. Spicer 1241 four speed auxiliary transmission

6041 SERIES

4 Speed Auxiliary
Disassemble, Fig. 20

1. Remove transmission cover.
2. Remove both propeller shaft flanges.
3. Remove support from main drive gear bearing cap.
4. Remove countershaft rear bearing cap, noting number of shims under cap.
5. Remove mainshaft rear bearing cap, oil seal, and speedometer driven gear in cap. Then remove oil seal and driven gear from cap and sleeve.
6. Remove main drive gear bearing cap with bearings, gear, seal and seal cap.
7. Remove speedometer drive gear.
8. With suitable puller, press mainshaft with front pilot bearing, overdrive gear snap ring, overdrive and direct clutch gear, collar and overdrive gear out through front of case, leaving first speed gear, first and second clutch gear and collar, and second speed gear and sleeve in case. Remove these items from case after removing mainshaft.
9. Remove mainshaft rear bearing.
10. Drive countershaft toward rear far enough to force rear bearing cap out of case. Using snap ring pliers, remove countershaft second speed gear snap ring from groove, slide second gear forward, then lift countershaft assembly out of case.
11. Remove countershaft front bearing cup from case.
12. Remove power take-off covers, and drain and filler plugs from case.
13. Disassemble sub-assemblies as required. If countershaft is to be disassembled, gears should be marked so that correct position will be known when installing.

Countershaft, Assemble

1. Drive gear keys in countershaft slots. Then using arbor press and suitable driver, press countershaft overdrive gear and drive gear into place.
2. Install new snap ring in groove at forward end of drive gear.
3. Press cone on front end of countershaft, making sure that cone seats firmly against countershaft.
4. Install second speed gear front snap ring over end of countershaft and position snap ring in groove in countershaft.
5. Install second gear on countershaft, then position rear snap ring in groove.
6. Press bearing cone on rear end of countershaft, making sure cone seats firmly against countershaft.

Mainshaft, Assemble

1. Place mainshaft in vise with front end up. Then apply heavy gear oil on bearing surfaces.
2. Install overdrive gear and overdrive and direct clutch gear with shoulder toward overdrive gear.
3. Install snap ring in groove at front end of mainshaft.
4. Install overdrive and direct clutch gear collar with external teeth toward front end of mainshaft.
5. Install mainshaft pilot bearing, using suitable bearing replacer.

Main Drive Gear Assemble

1. Apply transmission lubricant to bearings before installing.
2. Press bearing cups into cap and install inner bearing on drive gear. Then install bearing spacer on drive gear.
3. Place drive gear and bearing in arbor press with bearing spacer in place.
4. Apply pressure on front bearing inner race, using a piece of 2" diameter tubing about 4" long over end of shaft. Bearing cup should turn readily but not spin on shaft with pressure applied. If bearing adjustment is too loose or too tight, select correct spacer (available in several sizes). After correct spacer has been installed, remove assembly from press.
5. If seal has been removed from seal cap, press new seal in cap.
6. Place washer in position against bearing cone. Then install seal cap with new gasket. Install cap bolts and tighten securely.

Transmission, Assemble

1. Install countershaft front bearing cup in transmission case bore.
2. Lower countershaft assembly in case with rear end of shaft out through rear bearing bore. Then move assembly forward so that front bearing enters cup.
3. Install drive gear bearing cap temporarily with new gasket. Tighten cap screws evenly and firmly. Then slide countershaft second speed gear on shaft and install snap ring in groove ahead of second speed gear.
4. Install rear bearing cup. Using same thickness of shims as was removed at disassembly, install rear bearing cap temporarily. Tighten cap bolts, meanwhile turning countershaft by hand. If any binding of countershaft bearings is noted before cap bolts are fully tightened, remove cap and add shims. If cap bolts are tightened with a shim pack which is too thin, bearings will be damaged. Three sizes of shims (.003", .010" and .030") are available for use in adjusting countershaft bearings. Bearing adjustment is

SPICER TRANSMISSIONS

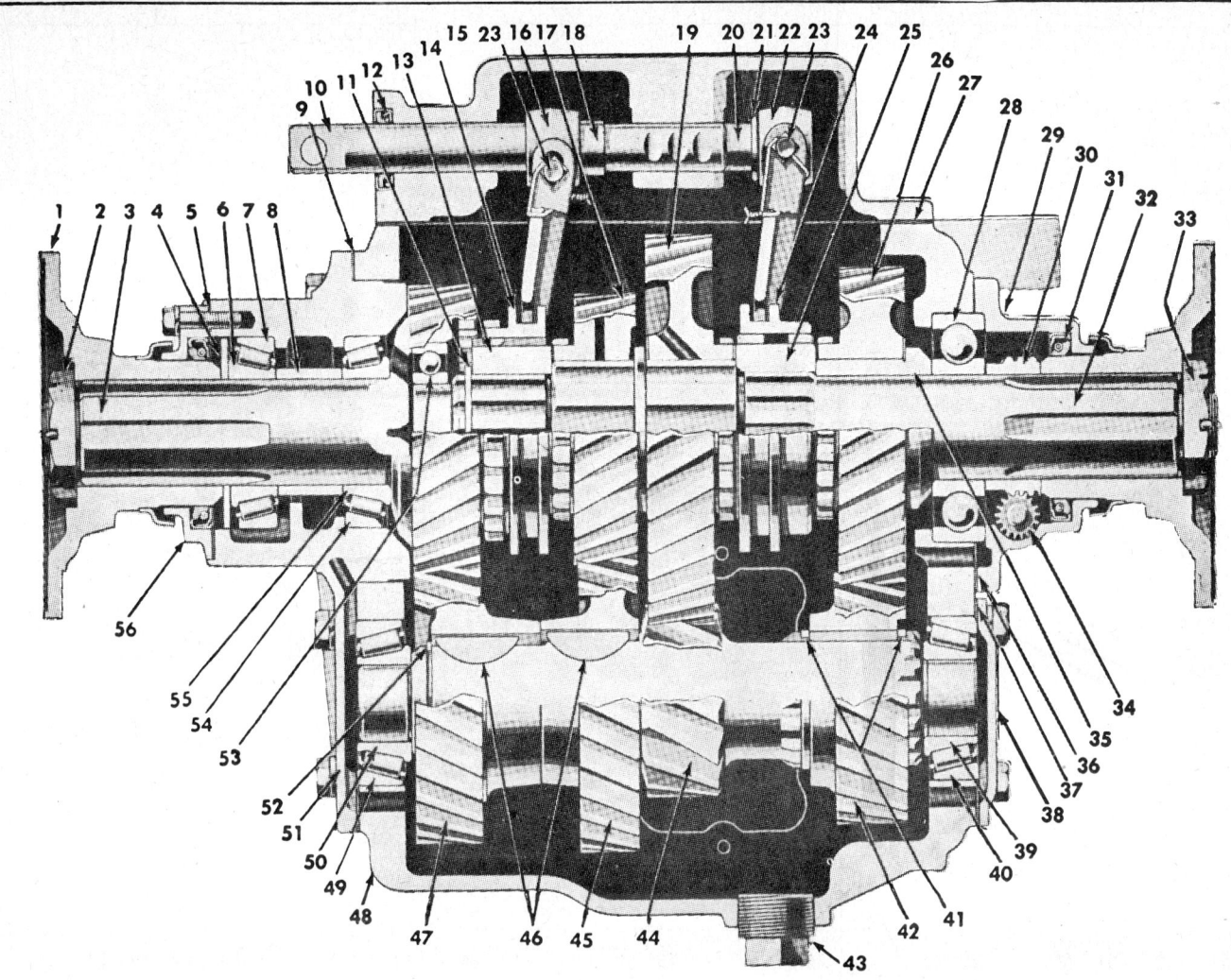

1. Propeller Shaft Flange
2. Main Drive Gear Nut
3. Main Drive Gear
4. Companion Flange Washer
5. Seal Gasket
6. Outer Bearing Cone
7. Outer Bearing Cup
8. Drive Gear Bearing Spacer
9. Bearing Cap Gasket
10. Direct and Overdrive Shift Rod
11. Mainshaft Overdrive Gear Snap Ring
12. Shift Rod Oil Seal
13. Overdrive and Direct Clutch Gear
14. Overdrive and Direct Clutch Collar
15. Shifter Housing (Cover)
16. Direct and Overdrive Shift Fork
17. Mainshaft Overdrive Gear
18. Shift Rod Spacer
19. Mainshaft 1st Speed Gear
20. 1st and 2nd Shift Rod
21. Shift Rod Spacer
22. 1st and 2nd Shift Fork
23. Shift Fork Screw
24. 1st and 2nd Speed Clutch Gear Collar
25. 1st and 2nd Speed Clutch Gear
26. Mainshaft 2nd Speed Gear
27. Shifter Housing Gasket
28. Mainshaft Rear Bearing Assembly
29. Mainshaft Rear Retainer Cap Assembly
30. Speedometer Drive Gear
31. Oil Seal
32. Mainshaft
33. Mainshaft Nut
34. Speedometer Driven Gear
35. Mainshaft 2nd Speed Gear Sleeve
36. Retainer Cap Gasket
37. Rear Bearing Cap Adjusting Shims (0.003, 0.010 and 0.030)
38. Countershaft Rear Bearing Cap
39. Countershaft Rear Bearing Cone
40. Countershaft Rear Bearing Cup
41. Countershaft 2nd Speed Gear Snap Rings
42. Countershaft 2nd Speed Gear
43. Drain Plug
44. Countershaft 1st Speed Gear
45. Countershaft Overdrive Gear
46. Countershaft Keys
47. Countershaft Drive Gear
48. Transmission Case
49. Countershaft Front Bearing Cup
50. Countershaft Front Bearing Cone
51. Main Drive Gear Bearing Cap
52. Countershaft Drive Gear Snap Ring
53. Mainshaft Front Bearing
54. Bearing Cup
55. Bearing Cone
56. Seal Cap

Fig. 20 Spicer Series 6041 four speed auxiliary

SPICER TRANSMISSIONS

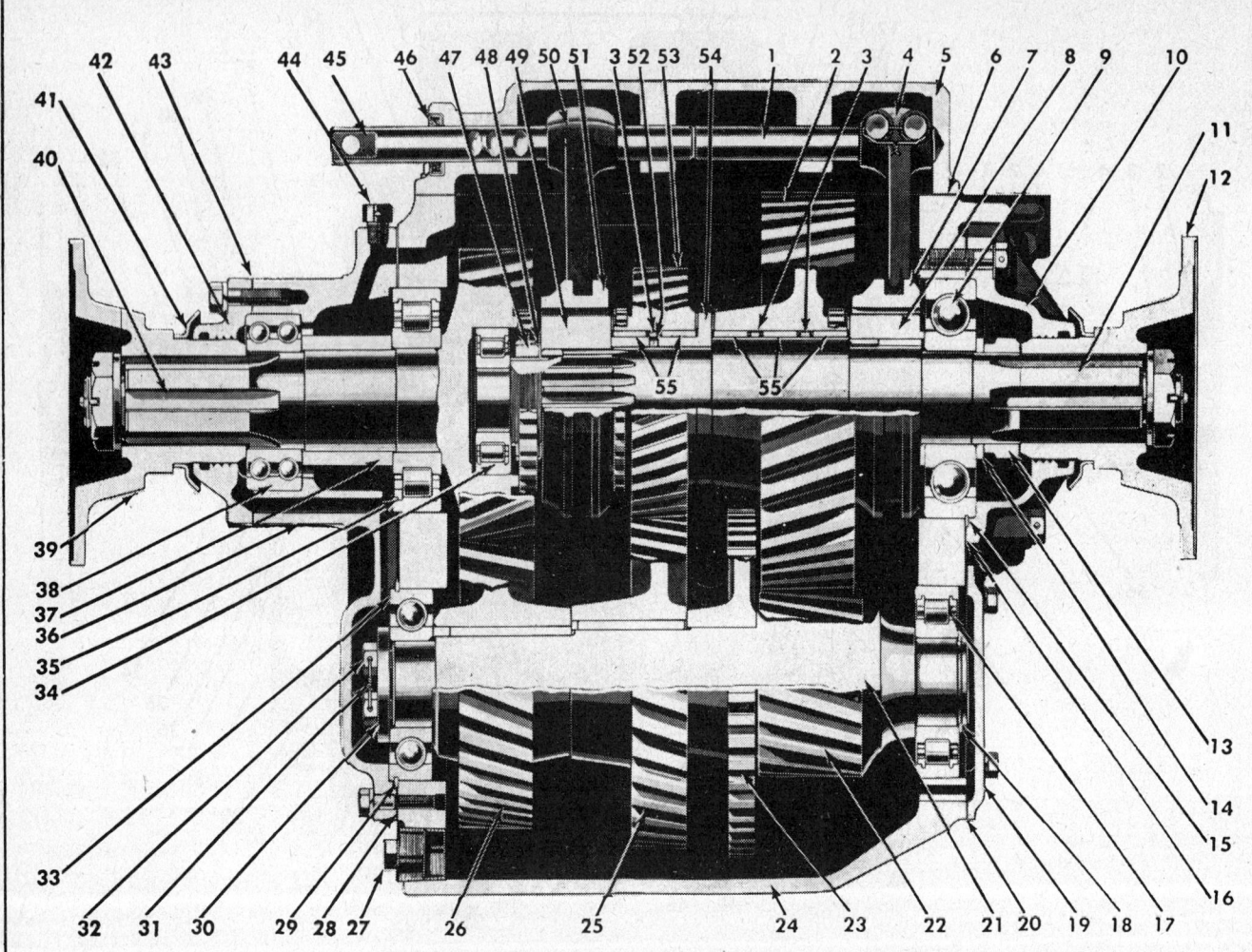

1. Low (1st) Shift Rod
2. Low (1st) Speed Gear
3. Bearing Spacer
4. Low (1st) Speed Shift Fork
5. Cover
6. Cover Gasket
7. Low (1st) Speed Shift Collar
8. Low (1st) Speed Clutch Gear
9. Mainshaft Rear Bearing
10. Mainshaft Rear Bearing Cap
11. Mainshaft
12. Flange
13. Speedometer Drive Gear
14. Spacer Washer
15. Snap Ring
16. Gasket
17. Countershaft Rear Bearing
18. Bearing Snap Ring
19. Countershaft Rear Bearing Cap
20. Cap Gasket
21. Countershaft
22. Low (1st) Speed Gear Teeth (8031-C)
    Low (1st) Speed Gear (8031-G, 8035-G)
23. Power Take-Off Drive Gear
24. Case
25. Countershaft Overdrive Gear
26. Countershaft Drive Gear
27. Drain Plug
28. Bearing Cap Gasket
29. Bearing Snap Ring
30. Bearing Retainer Washer
31. Lock Wire
32. Washer Cap Screw
33. Countershaft Front Bearing
34. Drive Gear Pocket Bearing
35. Drive Gear Rear Bearing
36. Drive Gear Bearing Cap
37. Bearing Spacer
38. Drive Gear Front Bearing
39. Propeller Shaft Flange
40. Main Drive Gear
41. Guard
42. Front Bearing Cap
43. Gasket
44. Vent
45. Direct and Overdrive Shift Rod
46. Shift Rod Oil Seal
47. Clutch Gear Lock Nut
48. Lock Washer
49. Clutch Gear
50. Direct and Overdrive Shift Fork
51. Shift Collar
52. Locating Pin
53. Mainshaft Overdrive Gear
54. Sleeve
55. Needle Bearings

Fig. 21 Spicer Series 8031, 8035 three speed auxiliary transmissions

SPICER TRANSMISSIONS

correct when countershaft can be turned without evidence of binding and without perceptible end play.

5. Remove main drive gear bearing cap. Lower mainshaft first speed gear, first and second clutch gear and collar, and second speed gear into case. Then guide mainshaft assembly through front of case and through gears. Slide second speed gear sleeve into hub of second gear through rear of case.
6. Using new gasket, install main drive gear bearing cap with main drive gear and bearings on front of case, guiding mainshaft pilot bearing into pocket of main drive gear. Tighten cap bolts securely.
7. Press mainshaft rear bearing onto mainshaft and into case, then place speedometer drive gear on shaft with shoulder toward front of transmission.
8. Install mainshaft rear bearing cap and gasket and tighten capscrews securely.
9. Install propeller shaft flange on mainshaft and tighten nut to a torque of 350–400 ft. lbs.
10. Place transmission front support bracket on trunnion at bearing cap, install front flange and tighten nut to a torque of 350–400 ft. lbs.
11. Install cover, being sure that shift forks enter grooves in shift collars.
12. Install breather in cover, and drain plugs.

8031, 8035 SERIES

3 Speed Auxiliaries
Disassemble, Fig. 21

1. Remove transmission cover.
2. Lock mainshaft by placing gears in two speeds at same time, remove nuts and pull off both flanges.
3. Remove front bearing cap and bearing as a unit.
4. Remove washer from front end of countershaft.
5. Remove mainshaft rear bearing cap and pull speedometer drive gear and washer off mainshaft.
6. Move main drive gear forward as far as possible and force mainshaft and gears rearward, thereby forcing mainshaft rear bearing out of case.
7. Use a suitable puller to remove bearing from mainshaft.
8. Slide low speed shift collar off mainshaft and remove through rear of case.
9. Raise front end of mainshaft and lift from case, passing low speed gear teeth through power take-off gear teeth.
10. Move main drive gear rearward, forcing bearing out of bore. Then lift assembly out through top of case.
11. Remove countershaft rear bearing cap. Then push countershaft forward until front bearing is free of case, after which use puller to remove bearing.
12. Move countershaft rearward until rear bearing is out of case. Then remove snap ring and bearing from countershaft. The assembly may then be lifted out of the case by its front end.

Mainshaft, Disassemble

1. Support mainshaft assembly with front side of low speed gear on bed plate of arbor press.
2. Apply pressure on rear of mainshaft to force low speed clutch gear off mainshaft. Use care to prevent loss of needle bearings as mainshaft is pressed out of gear.
3. Grip mainshaft in vise with front end up. Then remove mainshaft pilot bearing from shaft, and remove clutch gear lock nut.
4. Set mainshaft in arbor press with flange on sleeve resting on bed plate. Press on front end of mainshaft to force sleeve with mainshaft overdrive gear and bearings and clutch gear off mainshaft.
5. Slide gear off sleeve, being careful not to lose bearings.

Mainshaft, Assemble

1. Place locating pin in hole in sleeve. Apply heavy grease on surface of sleeve to hold bearings in place. Then stand sleeve on end with flange down and arrange needle bearings and spacer around sleeve. Use 63 bearings in each row. Carefully lower overdrive gear over sleeve and spur teeth toward front of mainshaft.
2. Hold mainshaft in vise with front end up. Then lower overdrive gear and sleeve assembly over front end of mainshaft, carefully guiding head of locating pin into milled slot of mainshaft. Press sleeve flange tightly against mainshaft shoulder.
3. Press direct drive clutch gear on mainshaft up against sleeve. Then install lock washer and nut. Tighten nut securely and bend lock washer against flats on nut.
4. Grip mainshaft in vise with rear end up. Apply heavy transmission grease on mainshaft surface contacted by low speed gear rollers. Then arrange two rows of needle bearings separated by a spacer around mainshaft. Use 63 rollers in each row.
5. Set low speed gear over bearings with spur teeth upward. Drop other spacer over rearward end of mainshaft and insert remaining 63 rollers at gear hub.
6. Install clutch gear on splines at rear of gear with flat side of gear toward front.
7. Install pilot bearing on forward end of mainshaft and install shift collar.

Transmission, Assemble

Reassembly procedure is largely the reverse of disassembly procedure. However, the following should be noted:

1. When installing main drive gear and mainshaft, place main drive gear in place from inside of case, moving the assembly forward as far as possible. Lower mainshaft and gears into case with rear end extending through rear bearing bore. Install low gear shift collar on clutch gear, inserting collar through bearing bore in case.
2. Move mainshaft forward so that mainshaft pilot bearing enters pocket of main drive gear. Then install rear mainshaft bearing, spacer washer and speedometer drive gear.
3. Be sure to install front bearing cap gasket so oil passage is not obstructed.
4. Companion flange nuts should be torque tightened to 240–310 ft. lbs.

Spicer 8125 & 8125-U 12 Speed Units

INDEX

	Page No.
Sub-assemblies, Disassemble	365
Sub-assemblies, Assemble	366
Transmission, Assemble	367
Transmission, Disassemble	363
Transmission, Install	363
Transmission, Remove	362

This transmission, Figs. 1 and 2, is made semi-automatic to obtain twelve speeds forward and six reverse with only three shift lever positions. To accomplish the preselected but automatic shifts, air actuated power cylinders built into each end of the shifter housing are used to make the input gear splits and hi-lo range shifts. Air pressure that makes these shifts is admitted and exhausted from opposite ends of the double acting cylinders through a control valve operated by cables attached to the gear shift lever.

Service Bulletin

In an effort to minimize parts mix-up and misapplication, the following information is presented for guidance of parts for both models 8125 and 8125-U transmissions.

In effect there are three types of 12-speed transmissions in use: (1) the fully synchronized model 8125, (2) the desynchronized hand shift model sometimes called "dehorned" model 8125, and (3) the unsynchronized (hand shifts only) model 8125-U. This could be a factory built or a field conversion, using Spicer changeover kits 311329X for No. 1 or 311582X for No. 2 clutch housings.

As noted above the major difference between 8125 and 8125-U is the omission of the hand-shifted synchronizers.

The most critical items involved in parts mix-ups are the high range countershafts with their matching collars and gears, Fig. A. Although these two countershafts look alike and their overall lengths are the same, the splined section for the sliding clutch gear (80-466-18) has been lengthened and the "hopping-guard" is moved rearward on the 8125-U, Fig. B. This change means that clutch gear (80-466-18) and 1-2/7-8 speed gear (80-196-14) *must* be used with (80-30-8) countershaft.

In the high range countershaft synchronizer 310950X or the clutch gear from a cut-up synchronizer and a 1-2/7-8 speed gear 310949X were used with (80-30-8) countershaft, a "walking out" of 3-4/9-10 gear posi-

361

SPICER TRANSMISSIONS

tion would probably occur. Also, clutch gear (80-196-14) *cannot* be used with 8125 countershaft (80-30-1).

The 3-4/9-10 speed gear (80-196-8) from a model 8125 can be used with either countershaft if necessary. The tooth pointing is slightly different from the 3-4/9-10 gear (80-195-15) but not enough to prevent its use in an emergency.

In model 8215-U unsynchronized units using the Spicer pull-type clutch, a clutch brake is usually provided. To make room for the clutch brake, the clutch housing and drive gear are made 3/8" longer. The bearing cap is also changed to provide a full face instead of four pads for the brake. When the clutch brake is used it *must* be 311299X. The 8000 Series three-piece clutch brake (125C21 washer and 200C4 disc) is too small on the outside diameter to give effective braking surface on the bearing cap of an 8125-U, Fig. C.

Mainshaft drive gears 310769X and 311300X, Fig. D, differ primarily because of a steel synchronizer cone on one end and the type of tooth pointing on the clutch teeth. If necessary the 8125 gear (310769X) could be used with the 5-6/11-12 clutch gear (80-466-19) in an 8125-U.

The blocker pins in the 5-6/11-12 synchronizer (310706X) may be cut to salvage the sliding clutch gear, Fig. E. This gear, as well as 80-466-19, is symmetrical and may be reversed for longer parts life with either the B or C type units mentioned at the beginning of this bulletin.

TRANSMISSION, REMOVE

1. Disconnect linkage and remove forward and reverse shift lever.
2. Drain air reservoir tanks to bleed all air from transmission air system.
3. Disconnect air control valve cable controls by removing capscrew, end plate and sleeves from rear of valve body, Fig. 3.
4. If necessary, push range "T" handle down and rotate splitter control handle clockwise to move both plungers to their rear position. Remove locknuts and rubber rings from end plungers.
5. Loosen upper and lower cable locknuts from front of valve body. Do not remove cable adapter plugs.
6. Grasp cables and pull cable castings and inner wires free of valve body and plungers. Plungers need not be removed from valve body.
7. Place rubber rings inside locknuts and tighten finger tight on plungers. Install sleeves, end plate and capscrew to prevent loss.
8. Remove shift tower connector block and upper shift tower.
9. Disconnect clutch release linkage and remove release shaft.
10. Drain lubricant.
11. Disconnect upper and lower oil filter lines at oil pump and drain. Remove can and cartridge, Fig. 4.
12. Disconnect electrical lead to oil temperature sending unit and remove sending unit to prevent breakage during removal.
13. Remove propeller shaft and parking brake linkage. Disconnect speedometer cable.
14. Disconnect forward and reverse shift lever bracket and linkage at shift rod attaching stud (if equipped).
15. Position suitable jack under transmission and pick up its weight.
16. Remove rear transmission support.
17. Remove all capscrews from bell housing and pull transmission back free of engine. Slide transmission back until pinion shaft clears clutch release bearing housing. Then lower transmission.

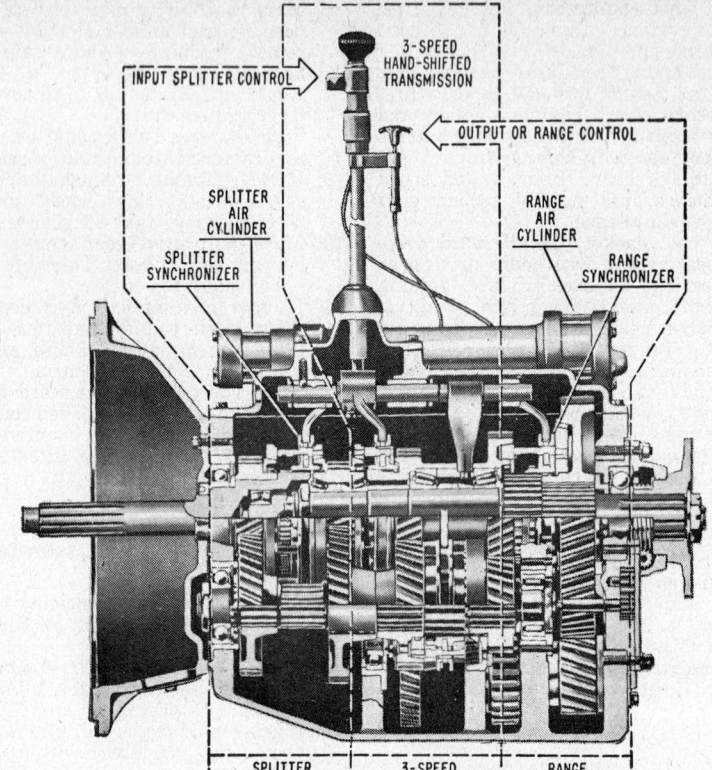

Fig. 1 Spicer 8125 transmission

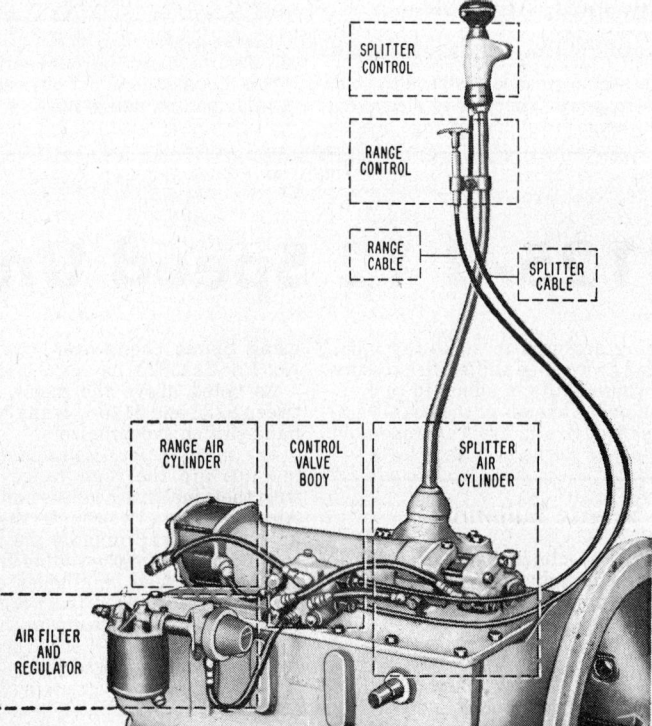

Fig. 2 Spicer 8125 transmission shift control

SPICER TRANSMISSIONS

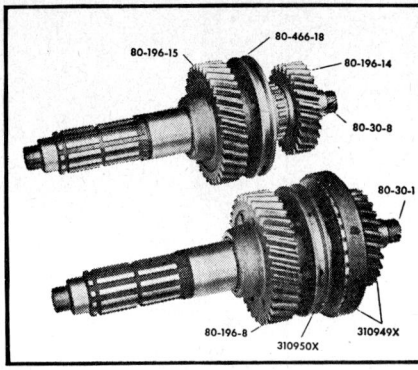

Fig. A   Countershafts

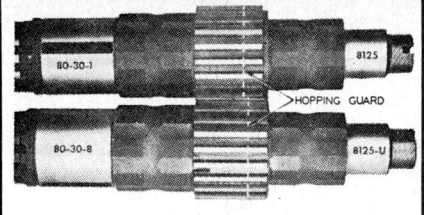

Fig. B   Sliding clutch gears

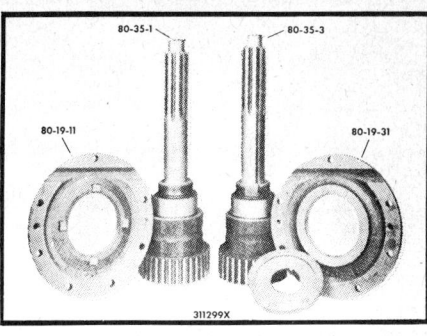

Fig. C   Clutch brakes

Fig. D   Main drive gears

Fig. E   Synchronizer sleeves

TRANSMISSION, INSTALL

1. Use an old pinion shaft or aligning tool to check alignment of clutch discs. Shift transmission into one of the manual gear shift positions. Apply a light coat of lubriplate to splines and entire surface of pinion shaft.
2. Place transmission on a suitable jack and position under truck. Adjust to align transmission with engine.
3. Start pinion gear shaft into clutch release bearing. Enter transmission slowly while checking proper positioning of clutch release bearing housing in clutch release yoke. It may be necessary to rotate end yoke or flange slowly to align splines of pinion shaft with hubs of clutch discs.
4. Enter pilot on bell housing into clutch housing and align capscrews. Start all capscrews and tighten evenly around bell housing. Install rear transmission support.
5. Connect speedometer cable to adapter or driven gear.
6. Install parking brake linkage. Install bracket and connect forward and reverse control cable.
7. Connect propeller shaft.
8. Connect air line to transmission air filter. Close drain cocks on air tanks.
9. Install new filter cartridge. Connect oil lines from filter to pump as shown in Fig. 4. Install temperature sending unit (if removed) and connect lead wire.
10. Install specified type and quantity of transmission oil.
11. Connect clutch release linkage and mount clutch release cylinder (if equipped). Set release bearing clearance to $1/8''$.
12. Remove capscrew, end plate and sleeves. Pull both plungers to rear and remove locknuts with rubber rings, Fig. 3.
13. Loosen locknuts at front of valve body and insert splitter cable inner wire through lower cable adapter, passing inner wire through plunger.
14. Bottom outer casing of splitter cable in adapter and tighten locknut (190 inch-lbs) to clamp casing. Insert range cable inner wire through upper cable adapter, passing inner wire through plunger. Bottom outer casing in adapter and tighten locknut to 190 inch-lbs.
15. Set range "T" handle so that a $1/4''$ gap exists between "T" handle and body, Fig. 5. Remove knob, spacer and splitter lever from shift lever stud.

CAUTION: *Take care not to lose small ball bearing in pocket inside splitter lever.*

16. Position inner sleeve so that $1/8''$ gap exists between bottom of sleeve and shoulder, Fig. 6.
17. At valve body, slide rubber rings over inner wires of splitter and range cables, seating rings against plungers. Assemble locknuts over wires and tighten securely (30 inch-lbs.) to plungers.
18. Assemble splitter control by setting lever over sleeve, noting that inner guide ball registers in spiral groove of sleeve. Install spacer and shift knob. Check operation of splitter control by rotating lever clockwise and counterclockwise. Lever should move easily through a 90 degree arc. Check range control by pulling up and pushing down on "T" handle. Handle should move freely through $1/2$ its travel and should not bottom against body in down position, Fig. 5.
19. Install forward and reverse lever and connect linkage.

DISASSEMBLE TRANS.

1. Disconnect filter-to-cylinder air line at cylinder and remove air filter and bracket.
2. Remove remaining shift housing bolts and use a sling to remove housing. *The*

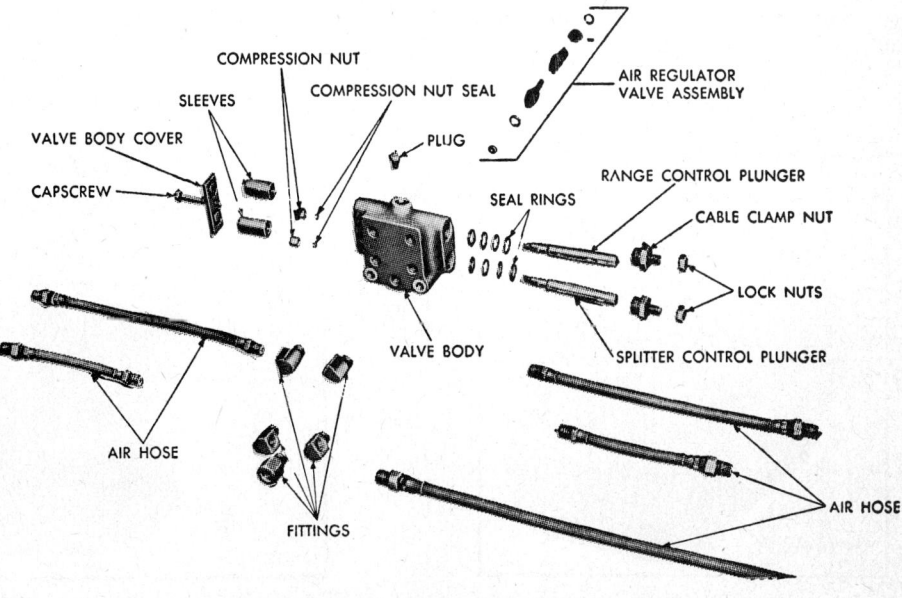

Fig. 3   Air control valve body disassembled

363

SPICER TRANSMISSIONS

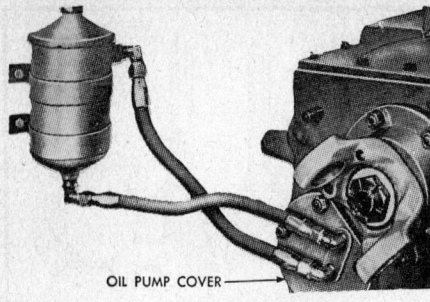

Fig. 4 Transmission oil filter

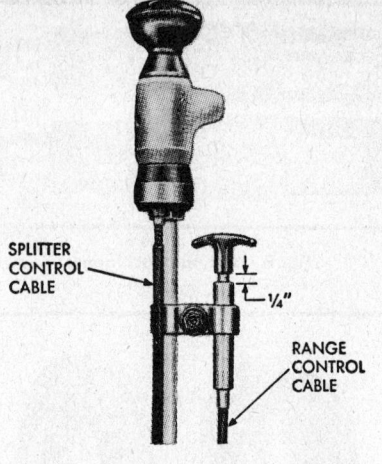

Fig. 5 Range control cable setting

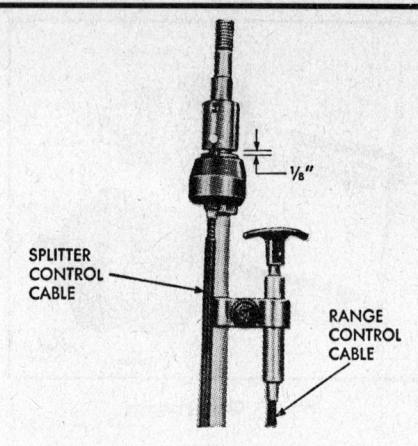

Fig. 6 Splitter control cable setting

transmission must be in Lo-Range and left edge of shifter housing must swing up and to the right, Fig. 7.
3. Remove shift fork shoes and housing gasket.
4. Remove clutch housing (8 nuts) and release mechanism.
5. Back off parking brake adjustment and lock transmission in two gears.
6. Remove output flange and brake drum.
7. Disconnect parking brake linkage, remove brake shoe assembly, speedometer drive and driven gear, and oil seal.
8. Remove transmission rear support.
9. Remove output shaft rear bearing retainer cap and gasket.
10. Remove Lo-Range countershaft rear bearing cap and gasket.
11. Remove oil pump cover plate and gasket, Fig. 8.
12. Install bolts shown in Fig. 9 into threaded holes in oil pump body and run bolts down evenly until body and gasket are removed from case.
13. Relieve staking on Lo-Range countershaft rear bearing lock nut and remove nut and washer.
14. Relieve staking on input shaft and Hi-Range front countershaft nut.
15. Remove input shaft nut (left-hand thread) and remove Hi-Range countershaft front nut and washer.
16. Remove input shaft bearing cap nuts.
17. Use a floor crane with lifting sling, support output shaft and cluster gear.
18. Install the two bolts shown in Fig. 10 into the blind holes in input shaft bearing retainer and remove retainer. *Keep input shaft in place against output shaft by tapping with a mallet while pulling retainer.* Remove bearing from retainer.
19. Remove input shaft, thrust washer and front drive gear from shaft, Fig. 11,

through front bearing bore and, remove input shaft from case.
20. Remove clutch housing gasket.
21. Remove output shaft rear bearing retainer and gasket, using two 7/16-14 puller bolts.
22. Remove output shaft rear bearing spacer from shaft or retainer. *Use a suitable puller as required but do not pull on seal ring. Remove seal rings from spacer.*
23. Remove Lo-Range interlock pin from its boss.
24. Remove output shaft from case. Rock shaft to get Lo-Range gear to clear case.
25. Remove Lo-Range gear and range synchronizer from output shaft.
26. Position output shaft horizontally in a vise (holding shaft splines) with cluster gear resting on bench.
27. Cut lock wire and remove Hi-Range countershaft shift fork set screw.
28. Remove welch plug from rear of case by tapping Hi-Range shift rod rearward through hole in case. Remove shift fork as shaft is removed from case.
29. Remove Hi-Range countershaft rear bearing nut.
30. Disengage Hi-Range countershaft front driven gear rear snap ring from its groove and slide front driven gear back against Hi-Range rear driven gear, Fig. 12.
31. Drive Hi-Range countershaft forward un-

til front bearing and retainer are exposed for a suitable puller.
32. Remove Hi-Range countershaft front bearing and retainer, Fig. 13; then remove shaft assembly from case. Remove bearing from retainer.
33. Remove Lo-Range shift rod detent plunger, spring and retainer from outside of case, Fig. 14.
34. After removing shift fork set screw, move Lo-Range shift rod forward out of case and remove fork. Pry shift rod seal from case.
35. Drive Lo-Range countershaft rearward until rear bearing and retainer are exposed. Pull rear bearing, retainer and gasket from shaft. Tap bearing out of retainer.
36. Remove spacer and drive gear from shaft through rear bearing bore.
37. Lift Lo-Range countershaft from case.
38. Remove reverse idler shaft lock plate and remove shaft, using a drift.
39. Lift reverse idler gear assembly and thrust washers from case and separate the parts, Fig. 15.
40. Remove Hi-Range countershaft rear bearing retainer screws, Fig. 12. Then use two 7/16-14 puller screws to remove retainer from case. Tap bearing out of retainer.
41. Remove Lo-Range countershaft front

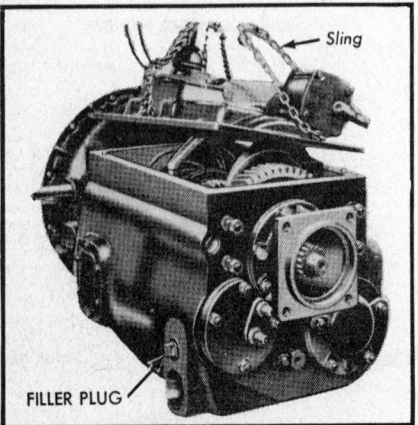

Fig. 7 Removing shift housing

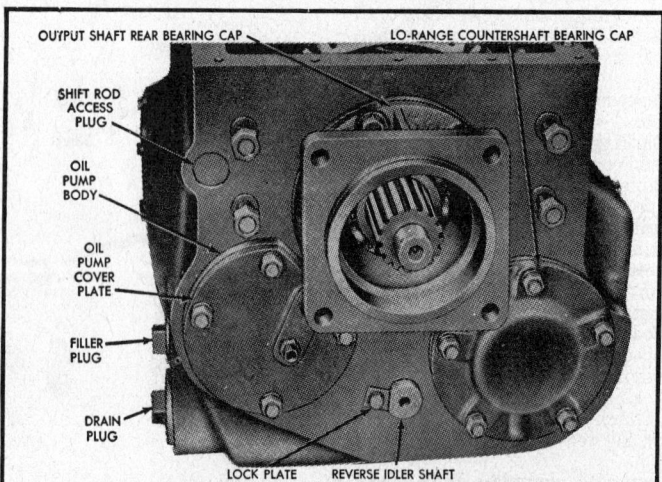

Fig. 8 Transmission rear face

SPICER TRANSMISSIONS

Fig. 9 Removing oil pump body

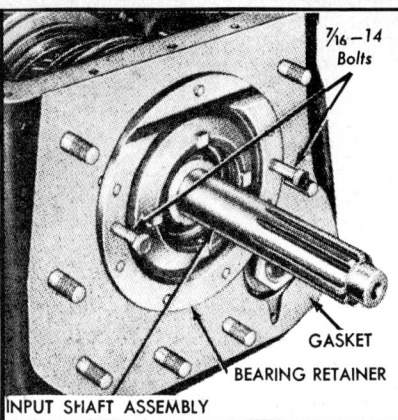

Fig. 10 Removing input shaft bearing retainer

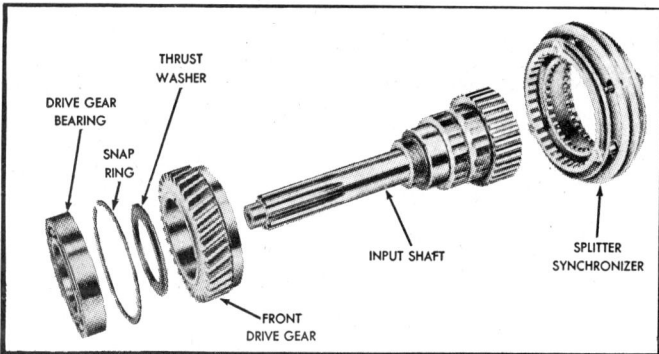

Fig. 11 Input shaft assembly

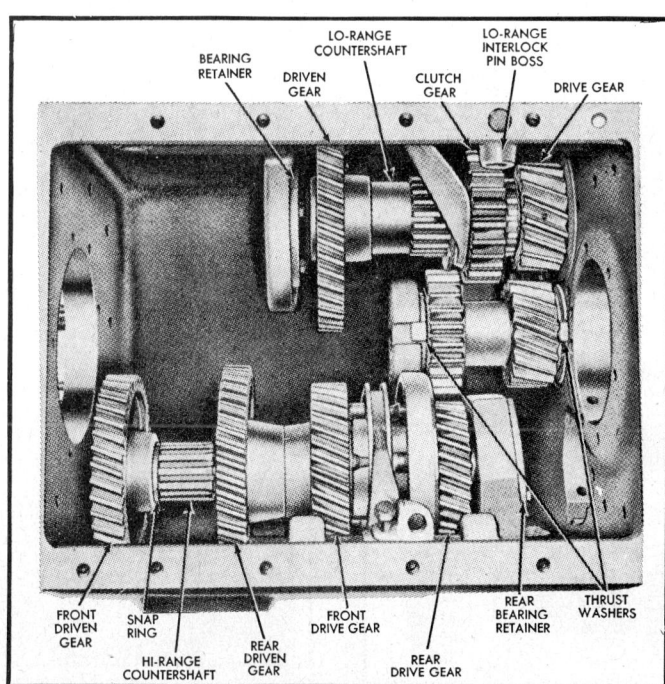

Fig. 12 Transmission with output shaft removed

bearing retainer, Fig. 12, using two 7/16-14 puller screws. Remove retainer from case. Tap bearing out of retainer.
42. If necessary, pry out welch plug above Lo-Range detent mechanism, Fig. 14.
43. Shift case to let interlock pin drop out of case.

DISASSEMBLE SUB-ASSEMBLIES

Oil Pump

1. Drive pin from shaft and remove gears from pump body.
2. Press drive gear from shaft and remove Woodruff key.
3. Drive driven gear shaft from body.
4. Drive driven gear bushing from gear.
5. Press drive shaft bushing from body.

Output Shaft

1. Tap pilot bearing from shaft.
2. Remove drive gear bearing lock nut.
3. Tap splitter synchronizer forward and remove front bearing cone and rear drive gear. Remove bearing spacers and shim pack. Wire shim pack together.
4. Remove splitter synchronizer from shaft. *Parts for this synchronizer are not serviced.*
5. Remove shaft from vise and position in a press, using rear face of cluster gear as a base. Press output shaft down through rear drive gear bearing cone, spacer and cluster gear, Fig. 16.
6. Remove cluster gear bearing spacers and shim pack from output shaft. Wire shim pack together.
7. Remove cluster gear rear bearing cone Fig. 17.
8. Remove cluster gear bearing snap ring from cluster gear, Fig. 16.
9. Position cluster gear in press with rear face of gear down. Press cluster gear bearing cups and spacers free of cluster gear, Fig. 18.
10. Place range synchronizer on bench with Hi-Range cone up. Lift up to remove Hi-Range cone from clutch gear. *Watch for three poppets and springs, Fig. 19.*
11. With synchronizer on bench (resting on Lo-Range cone) use a small screwdriver to compress poppets back into clutch gear, Fig. 20, and remove gear from Lo-Range cone.
12. Remove oil metering plug from front end of output shaft.

Hi-Range Countershaft

1. Lift off front bearing inner race, thrust washer, rear drive gear and synchronizer assembly. *Parts for synchronizer are not serviced.*
2. Remove snap ring from front end of shaft and remove front driven gear, Fig. 21.
3. Lift off previously disengaged snap ring from countershaft and remove rear driven gear snap ring.
4. Using rear driven gear as a base, press gear from shaft.
5. Remove drive gear Woodruff key from countershaft and slide front drive gear from shaft.

Lo-Range Countershaft

1. Remove sliding clutch gear from rear end of shaft, Fig. 22.
2. Remove driven gear snap ring.
3. Press off driven gear and remove Wood-

365

SPICER TRANSMISSIONS

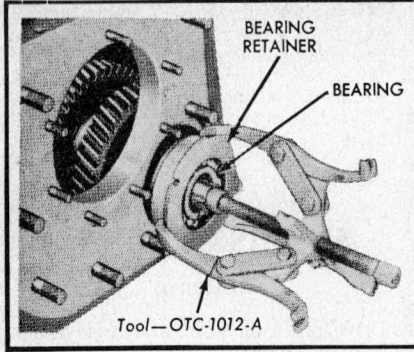

Fig. 13 Removing countershaft front bearing and retainer

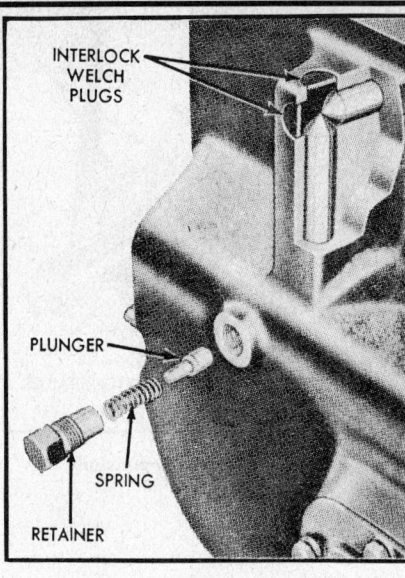

Fig. 14 Lo-Range countershaft detent mechanism

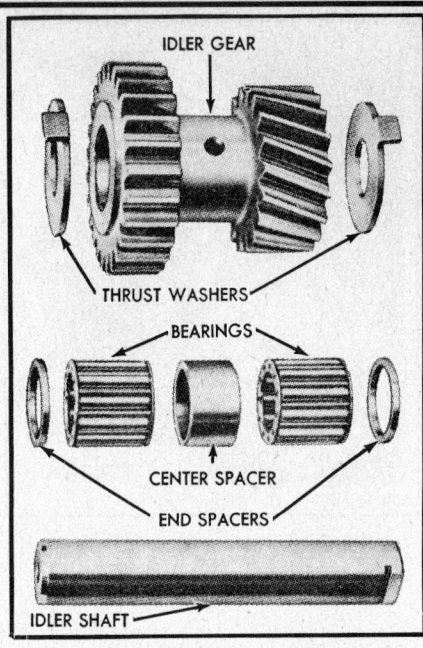

Fig. 15 Idler shaft assembly

ruff key.
4. Press off countershaft front bearing inner race, Fig. 23.

ASSEMBLE SUB-ASSEMBLIES

Lo-Range Countershaft, Fig. 22

1. Install Woodruff key and press driven gear on shaft.
2. Install driven gear snap ring.
3. Press on front bearing inner race.
4. Position sliding clutch gear as shown. Apply Lubriplate to bore of drive gear.

Hi-Range Countershaft, Fig. 21

1. After coating bore of front drive gear with Lubriplate, position gear on shaft.
2. Install Woodruff key and press rear driven gear on shaft.
3. Install rear driven gear snap ring.
4. Position front driven gear rear snap ring over shaft and slide it back against snap ring.
5. Install front driven gear and its snap ring.
6. Apply Lubriplate to front drive gear clutch teeth, the splines of Hi-Range countershaft, the clutch teeth of the synchronizer, the rear drive gear and the fluted bearing surface of shaft.
7. Install synchronizer and rear drive gear.
8. Position thrust washer *with flat side against rear driven gear* on shaft.
9. Tap rear bearing inner race on shaft.

Output Shaft, Fig. 16

1. Install oil metering plug in shaft bore.
2. Position Lo-Range cone on bench with pins up and with poppets and springs in gear. With three spacer tools, position gear on cone. Remove tools, Figs. 19 and 20.
3. Position remaining three poppets and springs in clutch gear. Compress poppets and install Hi-Range cone. Check action of assembled synchronizer.
4. Position cluster gear on press with larger face up, Fig. 24. Position front bearing cone in gear.
5. Position front bearing cup, outer spacer and rear bearing cup. Then press these parts into cluster gear, Fig. 24.

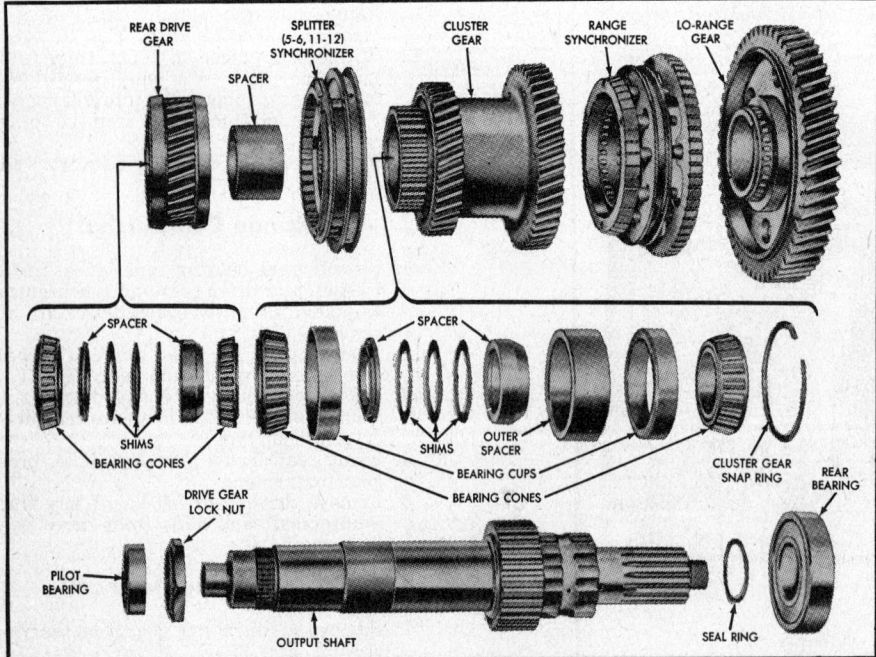

Fig. 16 Output shaft assembly

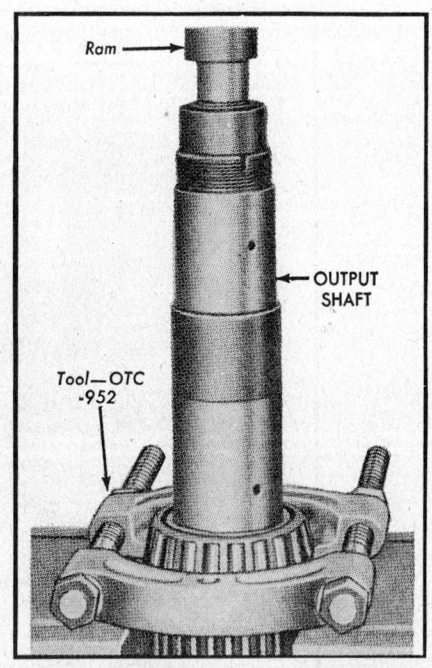

Fig. 17 Removing output shaft cluster gear rear bearing cone

SPICER TRANSMISSIONS

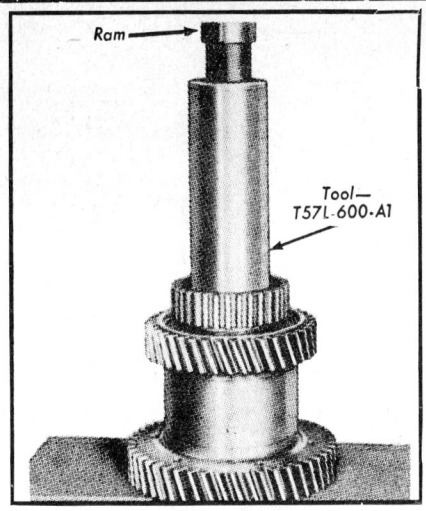

Fig. 18 Removing cluster gear bearings and related parts

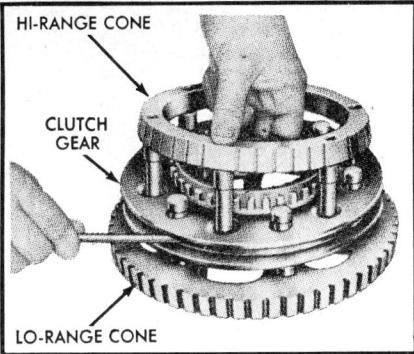

Fig. 19 Removing range synchronizer Hi-Range cone

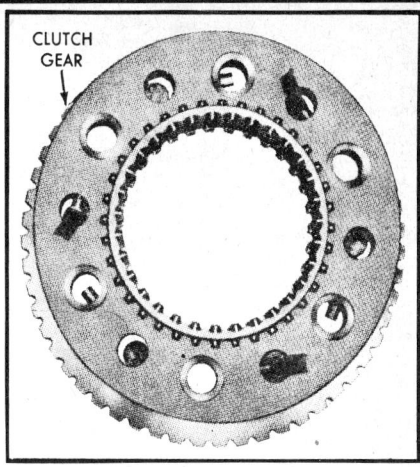

Fig. 20 Range synchronizer cone installation

6. Install cluster gear snap ring (tapered side up) in groove inside of cluster gear. Be sure that ring is fully seated.
7. Press cluster gear rear bearing cone on output shaft, Fig. 25.
8. Install remaining cluster gear spacers and shim pack on output shaft.
9. Press cluster gear assembly on output shaft, Fig. 26. Press on front bearing cone to position gear on shaft. *It is essential that end play of the output shaft cluster gear and output shaft drive gear be held to .002–.004" loose.*
10. Install a 5½" length of 3" ID diameter tubing on output shaft, Fig. 27. Install output shaft lock nut.
11. Seat cluster gear bearings by pressing down on cluster gear and rotating it back and forth through about 90 degrees.
12. Mount a dial indicator to check end play, Fig. 27. Make a reference mark where indicator point touches cluster gear and set dial indicator to zero. Pull up on gear and rotate it back and forth through approximately 90 degrees to seat the other roller bearings.
13. Rotate the cluster gear to line up reference mark with indicator and read indicator while pulling up on cluster gear, Fig. 27. If necessary, remove cluster gear and adjust shim pack to obtain .002–.004" end play.
14. After securing correct end play adjustment, remove nut and tubing spacer.
15. Install splitter synchronizer on output shaft and position long spacer inside cluster gear.
16. Install rear drive gear rear bearing cone on shaft, Fig. 16. Then position rear drive gear internal spacers and shim pack.
17. Position rear drive gear and install front bearing cone.
18. Install rear drive gear lock nut.
19. Mount a dial indicator and check end play, Fig. 28. Determine end play of output shaft rear drive gear by following a similar procedure to that outlined in Steps 11, 12 and 13. End play should be .002–.004".
20. Stake drive gear bearing lock nut after final assembly of drive gear, then remove output shaft from vise.
21. Set output shaft sub-assembly on bench with rear end of shaft overhanging edge of bench. Apply Lubriplate to splines and fluted bearing surface of output shaft as well as clutch teeth of synchronizer and gear.
22. Position range synchronizer on shaft with Hi-Range cone toward cluster.
23. Apply Lubriplate to rear clutch teeth of range synchronizer as well as to clutch teeth and pilot of Lo-Range gear.

Oil Pump

1. Press a new drive shaft bushing into oil pump body, allowing 1/16" clearance between end of bushing and edge of gear pocket.
2. Press new bushing into driven gear.
3. Burnish drive shaft bushing and idler gear bushing with a .5070–.5065" steel ball.
4. Press a new driven gear shaft into pump body until flush with body.
5. Position driven gear on shaft and check rotational freedom.
6. Tap Woodruff key into drive shaft, then press shaft into gear flush with gear face.
7. Assemble drive shaft and gear assembly into pump body and check rotation of pump gears for freedom. Pump must rotate freely.
8. Press pin through hole in end of drive shaft and equalize pin projection on each side of shaft.
9. If pump rotates freely, lubricate gears with heavy engine oil as a means of priming the pump.

ASSEMBLE TRANSMISSION

1. Drop Lo-Range countershaft vertical interlock pin into case. Install welch plug, Fig. 14.
2. Install Lo-Range countershaft shift rod

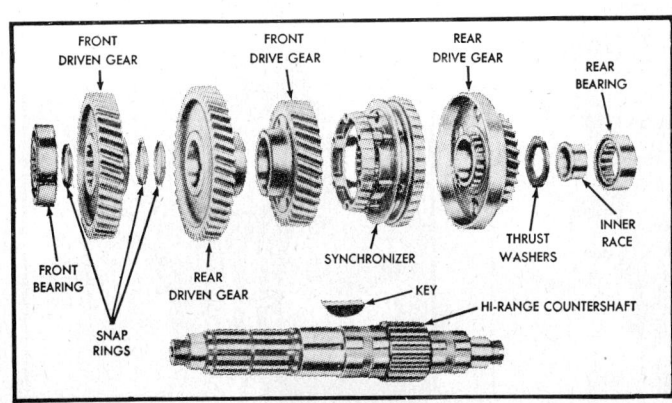

Fig. 21 Hi-Range countershaft assembly

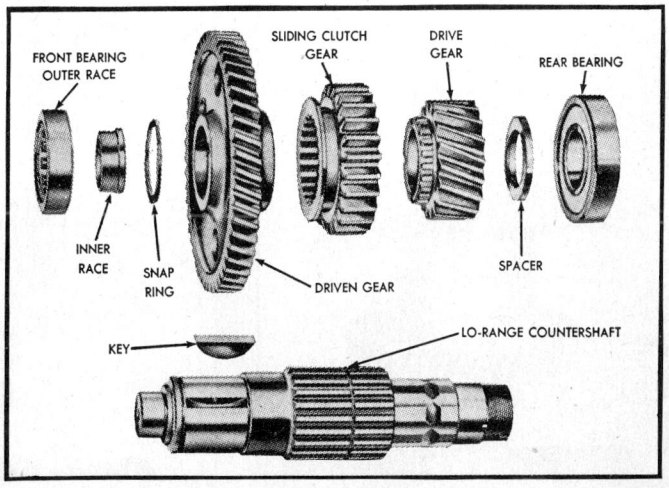

Fig. 22 Lo-Range countershaft assembly

367

SPICER TRANSMISSIONS

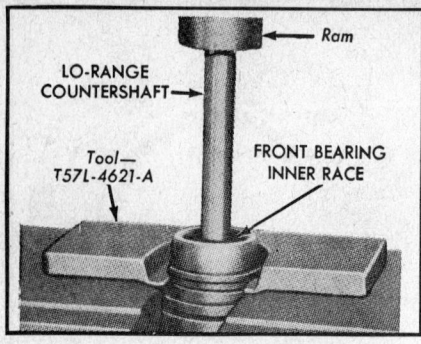

Fig. 23 Removing Lo-Range countershaft front bearing inner race

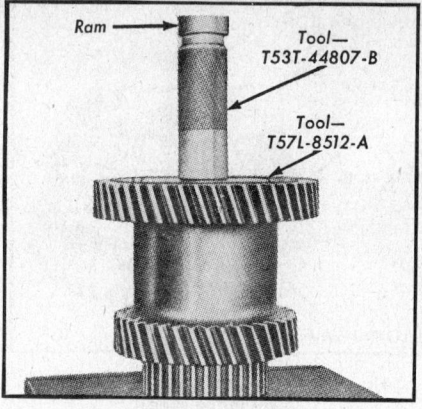

Fig. 24 Assembly of cluster gear

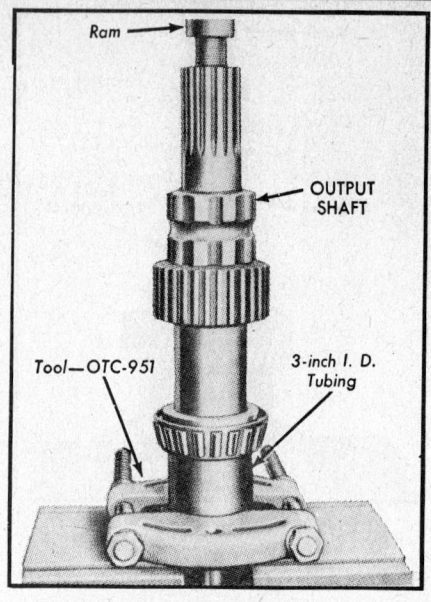

Fig. 25 Cluster gear rear bearing cone installation

oil seal in case. Coat bushing and seal with Lubriplate.
3. Coat idler shaft bearings and three spacers with Lubriplate and assemble these parts in reverse idler gear, Fig. 15.
4. Position Lo-Range countershaft front bearing outer race in its retainer.
5. Install two pilot studs (7/16-14) in case to align Lo-Range countershaft front bearing retainer and tap retainer into position. Remove pilot studs.
6. Install bearing retainer bolts and secure with lock wire.
7. Position Hi-Range countershaft rear bearing in its retainer.
8. Install two 7/16-14 pilot studs in case to align Hi-Range countershaft rear bearing retainer and tap retainer into position. Remove pilot studs.
9. Install bearing retainer bolts and secure with lock wire.
10. Apply Lubriplate to reverse idler gear thrust washers and position them in case, Fig. 12.
11. Install reverse idler gear assembly, Fig. 15, aligning flat at rear of shaft to mate with lock plate. Install lock plate.
12. With Lo-Range countershaft in case, slide drive gear onto shaft.
13. Position gear spacer and apply sealing compound to rear bearing retainer gasket. Position gasket over studs.
14. Tap bearing retainer onto shaft and into case bore. Install bearing.
15. Install flat washer and rear bearing lock nut; *hand-tighten nut.*
16. Start Lo-Range countershaft shift rod from the front through seal and bushing assembly. As rod enters case, tighten shift fork on sliding clutch gear and slide shift rod through fork. Lift interlock pin and push rod into final position.
17. Install set screw and secure with lock wire.
18. Install Lo-Range shift rod detent plunger, spring and retainer, Fig. 14.
19. Position Hi-Range countershaft in case and position front bearing and retainer. Line up the alignment notch with the lock pin and drive front bearing and retainer into case.
20. Install flat washer and nut on front of shaft and *hand-tighten nut.*
21. Tap Hi-Range countershaft front driven gear forward and lock in place with snap ring. Make sure snap ring seats in groove.
22. Position High-Range countershaft shift fork in synchronizer and install shift fork in synchronizer and shift fork rod through rear rod boss, shift fork and front boss.
23. Install fork screw and secure with lock wire.
24. Apply sealing compound to a welch plug and install in shift rod access hole at rear of transmission case.
25. Position output shaft Lo-Range gear (clutch teeth to front) in transmission case. Lower output shaft into transmission case and guide splined end of shaft through Lo-Range gear and rear bearing bore. Align Lo-Range gear with range synchronizer and move output shaft to rear as far as possible.
26. Install output shaft pilot bearing, then align all gears to mesh properly.
27. Install Lo-Range interlock pin in case, Fig. 14.
28. Coat splines and fluted bearing surface of input shaft with Lubriplate and position on output shaft. If input shaft does not enter freely, tap end of shaft lightly. *Do not force assembly because self-aligning bearing may be tipped.*
29. Coat clutching surface of front drive gear with Lubriplate and install gear on output shaft.

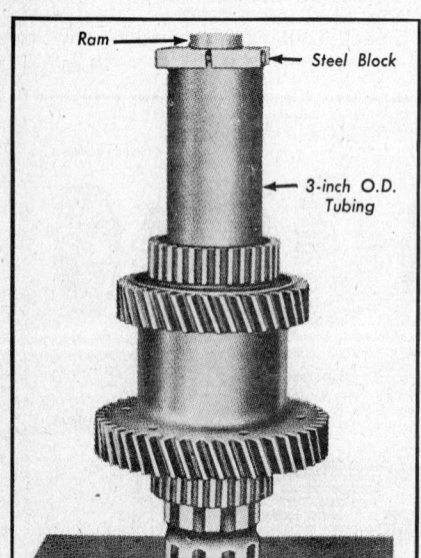

Fig. 26 Installing cluster gear assembly

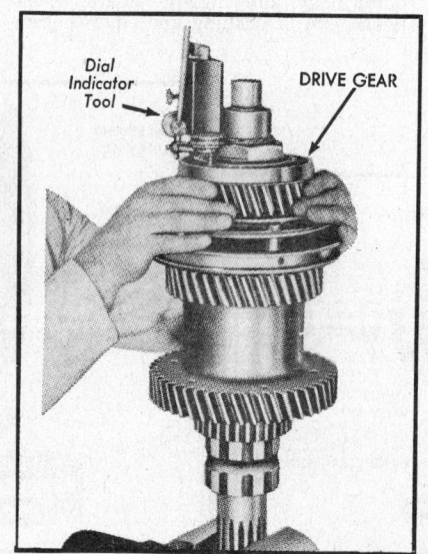

Fig. 27 Checking cluster gear end play

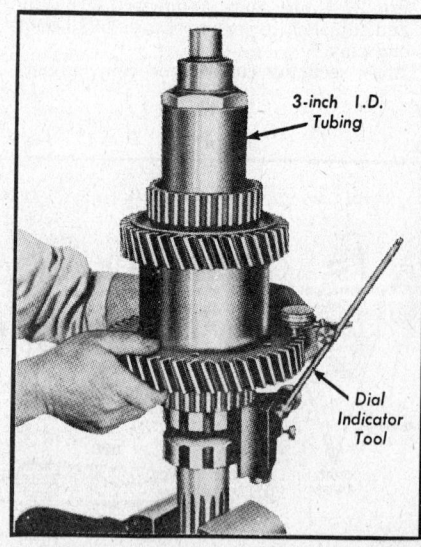

Fig. 28 Checking drive gear end play

SPICER TRANSMISSIONS

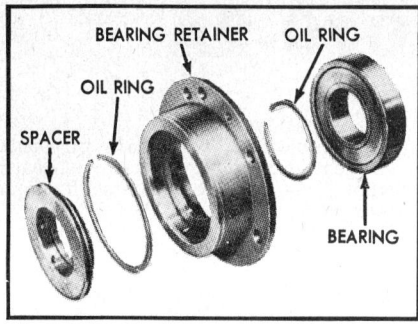

Fig. 29 Output shaft bearing retainer assembly

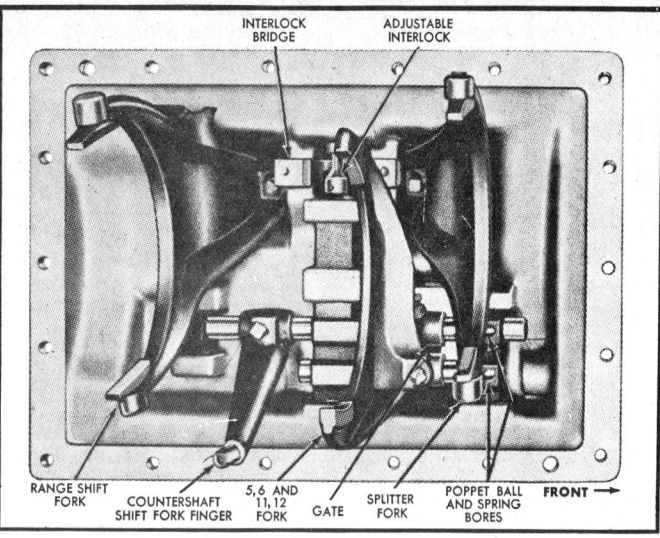

Fig. 31 Assembled gearshift housing

30. Install thrust washer on input shaft with flat against front drive gear, Fig. 11.
31. Apply sealing compound on clutch housing gasket and place gasket on front studs.
32. Tap input shaft bearing and retainer into position. It may be necessary to lift input shaft for alignment of bearing retainer stud holes with studs.
33. Install bearing retainer stud nuts.
34. Install input shaft bearing nut *handtight*. Lock transmission in two gears and tighten the following: input shaft nut, Hi-Range countershaft front nut, and Lo-Range countershaft rear nut. Stake these nuts in one place. *Do not use a prick-punch in grooves or threads.*
35. Apply sealing compound to output shaft rear bearing retainer gasket and place gasket on studs. Be sure to align oil return hole in gasket with oil return hole in case.
36. Assemble output shaft bearing retainer components, Fig. 29.
37. Position output shaft rear bearing retainer over case studs.
38. Block front of output shaft Lo-Range gear to prevent any forward movement of gear.
39. Install seal ring on output shaft and against spacer.
40. Drive output shaft bearing into retainer. After bearing bottoms against output shaft, remove block from case. Use a pry bar between Lo-Range gear and back of transmission case to pull bearing retainer into case.
41. Apply sealing compound to rear bearing retainer cap gasket, align drain hole and install gasket on studs. Install cap and tighten nuts.
42. Apply sealing compound to Lo-Range countershaft rear bearing cap gasket, align drain hole and install gasket. Install cap and tighten nuts.
43. Apply sealing compound to oil pump body gasket and position on studs.
44. Install oil pump, making sure that drive pin mates with Hi-Range countershaft.
45. Apply sealing compound to oil pump cover gasket and install gasket and cover.
46. Install transmission rear support, speedometer gears and oil seal.
47. Install brake shoe assembly on rear retainer cap. Connect parking brake linkage.
48. Lock transmission in two gears and install output shaft flange, brake drum and nut. Shift transmission to neutral and adjust parking brake.
49. Install oil pick-up screen and cap with gasket.
50. Install clutch housing and release mechanism. Apply sealing compound to clutch housing gasket and place gasket on case. Fill transmission (through top opening) with proper amount of lubricant.
51. If disassembled, assemble shift housing as suggested in Figs. 30 and 31. Then position shift housing above transmission. Stick shift fork shoes to forks with grease. Lower shift housing and align all shoes and forks.
52. Install air filter assembly.
53. Install and tighten shift housing bolts.
54. Connect air filter air line to cylinder and install transmission.

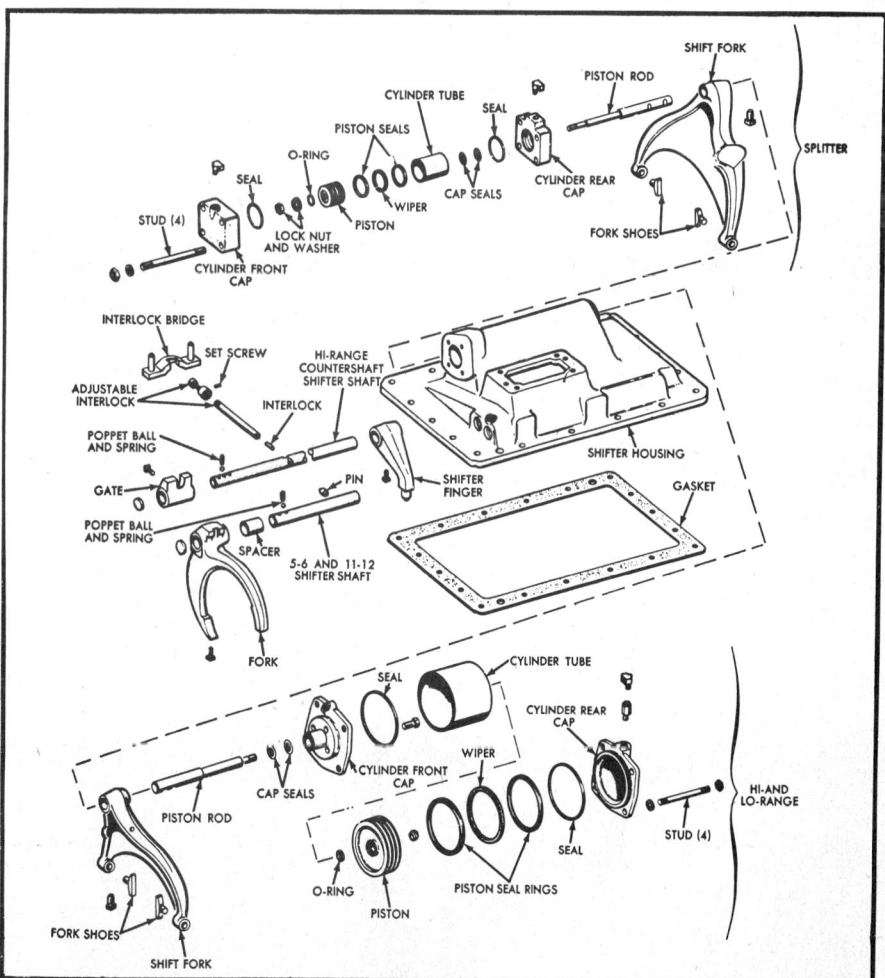

Fig. 30 Gearshift housing disassembled

SPICER TRANSMISSIONS
Spicer SST Series Exc. 1010-2A

REAR CASE & GEARS
Partial Disassembly

1. Remove capscrews and lockwashers from rear section piston body and remove assembly from case face and off piston and "O" ring. Remove piston body gasket.
2. Remove shift piston locknut from shaft and remove piston, Fig. 1.
3. Lift and place complete transmission unit vertically resting on two 4" × 4" wooden blocks under clutch bell pilot face.
4. Remove 16 capscrews and washers from rear cover.
5. Using a chain hoist, with rope sling slipped through end yoke bores, lift complete rear cover assembly off dowel pins.
6. Remove gasket from either rear case housing or the case cover, Fig. 2.
7. Remove fork rod, fork and stop spacer with shift collar from mainshaft gear.
8. Before removing either countershaft gears with front cones from mating mainshaft gear, pay particular attention to the timing marks or paint marks on web face of gears. Turn head end gear until timing marks align to each other.
9. Pull countershaft gears with front cone straight back to separate from front cup.
10. If it is necessary to remove the mainshaft head end gear, unstake tang of lockwasher from groove of locknut to remove locknut.
11. Use puller to remove pocket bearing from shaft.
12. Slide gear with thrust washer off splines of shaft.
13. Inspect lip of oil seal for damage or wear.

Disassembly for Overhaul of Rear Unit

1. Remove locknut from end of output shaft and remove end yoke or companion flange.
2. Remove output shaft bearing cap and gasket. Inspect lip of oil seal and replace seal if lip wear or damage is found.
3. Pull back on output shaft to expose snap ring on shaft bearing. Use puller on snap ring and pull bearing off shaft. Remove thrust spacer.
4. Remove piston body and gasket from case face and off piston.
5. Remove shift piston locknut and piston from shaft.
6. Remove rear cover from dowel pins by lifting straight up. Remove cover gasket and inspect "O" ring in piston rod hole of cover. Do not remove shift rod welch plug unless necessary.
7. Remove rear cover countershaft bearing caps with shims. Tie shims together and lay aside.
8. Remove cups from countershaft bores of cover. Inspect cups for wear, pitting or abnormal contamination wear.
9. Remove output shaft and gear as an assembly from rear case.
10. Remove piston shift rod with fork and stop spacer as an assembly. Clutch collar will pull away with fork.
11. Before removing countershafts, turn head end gear until timing marks align to each other. Then remove countershafts from rear case.
12. If countershaft bearing cones require replacement, use splitter puller tool to remove cones from countershaft ends.
13. Unstake lockwasher from groove of locknut and remove locknut and washer from end of mainshaft.
14. Use puller and remove pocket bearing from shaft.
15. Slide mainshaft gear and thrust washer from end of shaft.
16. Unfasten and remove rear case and gasket from front unit.
17. Inspect lip of oil seal in rear case centerbore. Also inspect cups in countershaft bores. Replace seal and cups if badly worn or mutilated.
18. Remove air vent and wash with cleaning solution. Replace vent on rear case being careful not to overtighten as this can cause collapse of vent body.
19. Reassembly is done in reverse order of disassembly.

MAIN CASE & GEARS
Disassemble
Figs. 3 and 4

1. To disassemble, remove gearshift housing.
2. Remove clutch housing from main case.

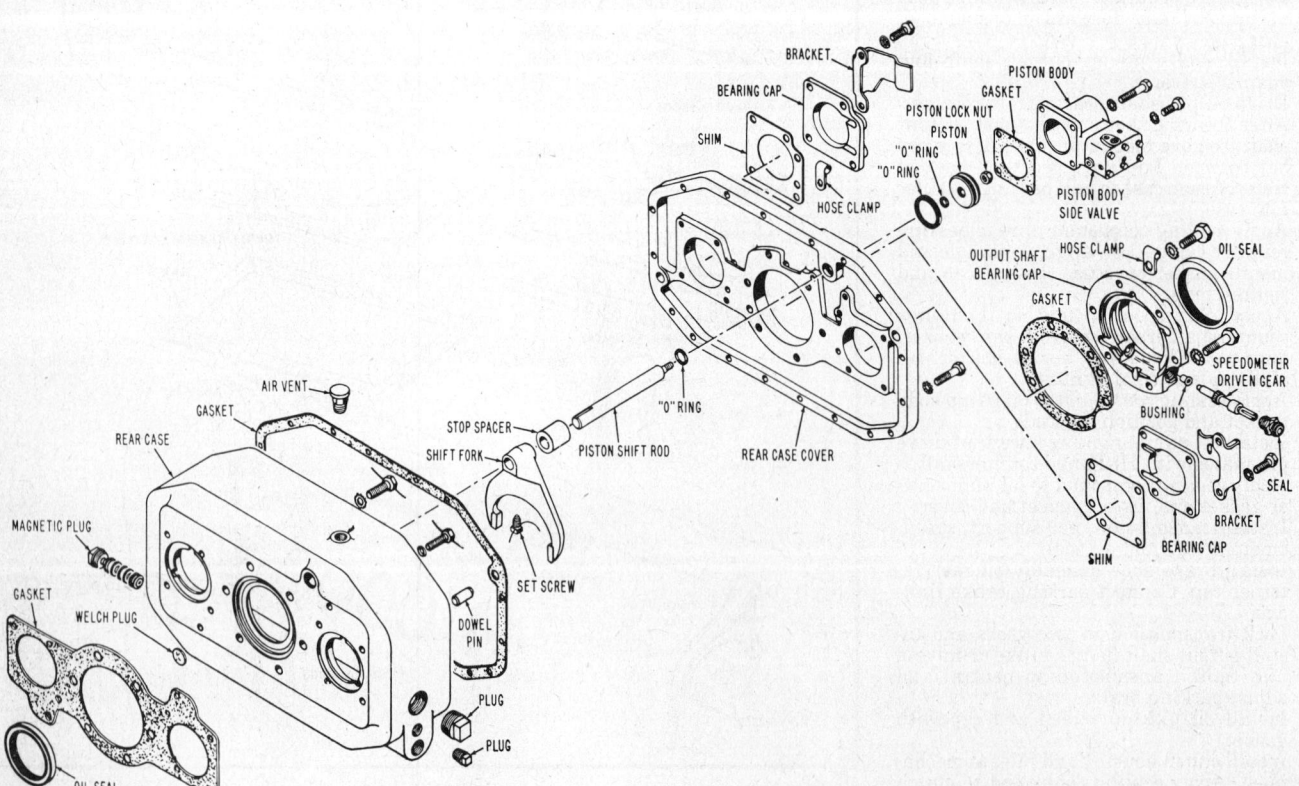

Fig. 1 Rear case cover components

Spicer Transmissions

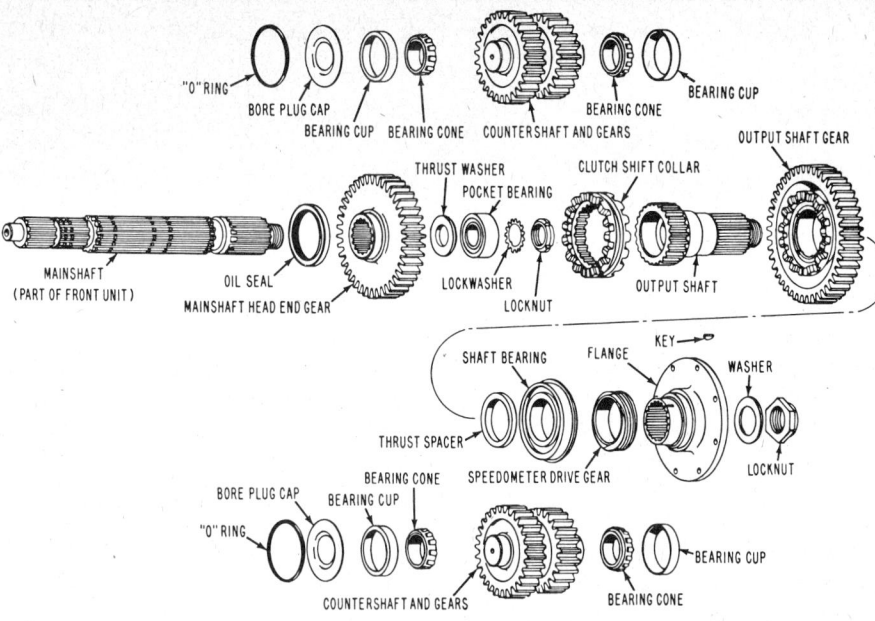

Fig. 2 Rear case gears

ball from case. Leave idler gear in place for later removal after mainshaft is removed.
15. Place a sling or wire around 2nd-3rd shift collar to support mainshaft. Using chain hoist on sling, lift out mainshaft.
16. Remove upper idler gear.
17. Remove right then left side countershafts.
18. Remove lower idler gear.
19. Countershaft, Fig. 5, and mainshaft, Fig. 6, sub-assemblies can now be disassembled.

Assemble Mainshaft, Fig. 6

1. Position mainshaft vertically in vise with output end resting on bed and soft jaws clamping splined area.
2. Install thrust washer on mainshaft to shoulder near output splines.
3. Install snap ring and seat securely in bottom groove of mainshaft.
4. Assemble 1st-reverse clutch collar on shaft and rest collar on snap ring.
5. Install second snap ring in groove closest to 1st-reverse clutch collar.
6. Install thrust washer on shaft.
7. With thrust washer and snap ring assembled into 1st speed gear, assemble gear sub-assembly on shaft with 35° chamfer in gear bore toward clutch collar.
8. Assemble second set of thrust washers and snap ring into second speed gear. Assemble gear sub-assembly on shaft with 35° chamfer up.

Rotate main drive gear until timing marks on back face of drive gear and countershaft drive gears match. Lock transmission into 1st and 6th gears and remove both countershaft front locknuts and mainshaft rear locknut.
3. Using a suitable puller, remove flange and washer.
4. Remove mainshaft rear bearing cap, speedometer gear, bushing and seal.
5. Engage collar into 5th speed gear and use a pry bar against the front face of the collar to force the mainshaft rearward to expose rear bearing snap ring. Install a puller on snap ring and pull bearing from shaft.
6. Remove thrust washer and split rings from shaft.
7. Remove snap ring located in reverse gear bore.
8. Engage 1st-reverse shift collar under reverse gear. Slide reverse gear and collar forward, butting gear against 1st speed gear. Wire or tie both gears together.

NOTE: The countershaft gears will support the mainshaft sub-assembly with mainshaft rear bearing and drive gear sub-assembly removed from the main case.

9. Remove cap screws and lock washers from countershaft rear bearing cap. Separate cap from case.
10. Remove drive gear bearing cap retaining screws and separate cap from case.
11. Remove drive gear sub-assembly from the case bore by pulling forward on the drive gear splined stem.
12. Using a 1¾" dia. × 6" long soft metal bar, drive backward on the front ends of both countershafts. Force shaft backward to allow bearings to creep forward to expose bearing snap ring. Install suitable puller to bearing snap ring and remove bearings.
13. Move countershaft to expose rear bearing so a bearing split tool can be installed on the front side of the bearing. Remove snap ring from countershaft end. Install puller arms on split tool and remove bearing.
14. Remove upper idler gear shaft and lock

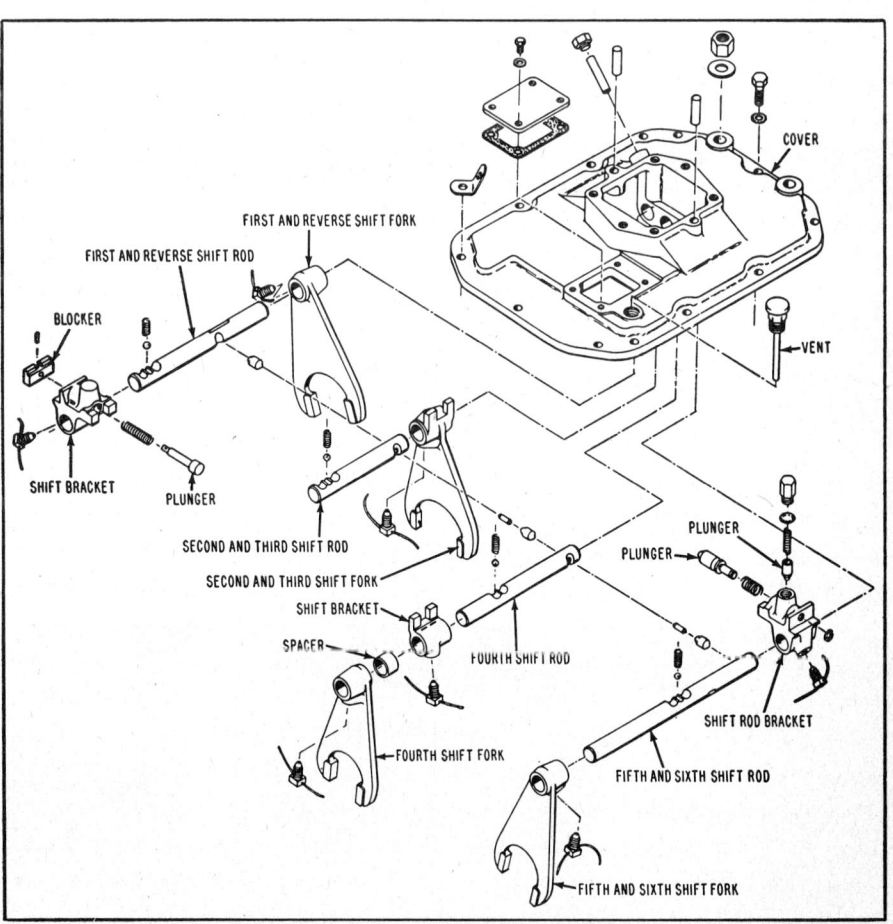

Fig. 3 Spicer SST gearshift housing

SPICER TRANSMISSIONS

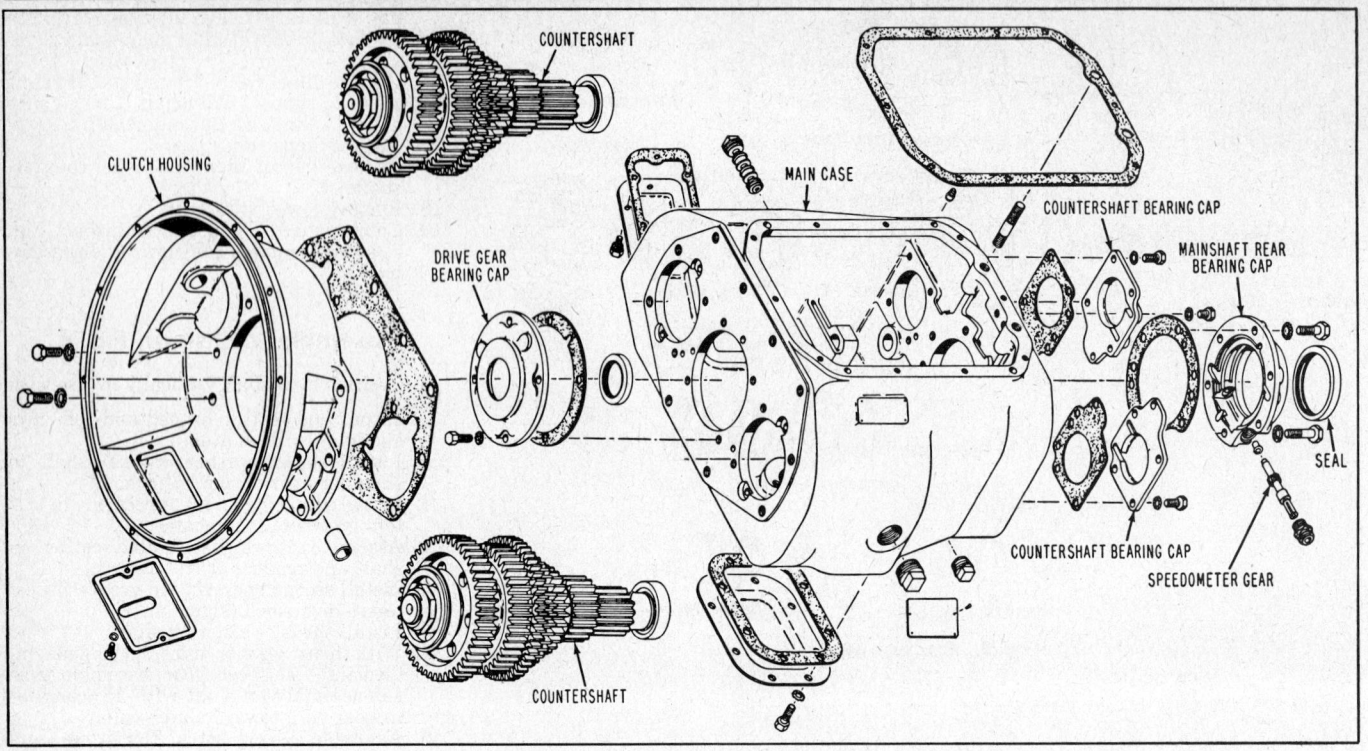

Fig. 4 Spicer SST gear case components

9. Install snap ring.
10. Install 2nd-3rd clutch collar and fourth snap ring. Install thrust washers.
11. Assemble snap ring into 3rd speed gear. Install gear with chamfer down toward clutch collar.
12. Assemble washers and snap ring into 4th speed gear and install gear with chamfer up. Install snap ring.
13. Assemble 4th speed clutch collar on shaft. Install snap ring.
14. Assemble snap rings and thrust washers into 5th speed gear and install gear onto shaft with chamfer up. Install snap ring.
15. Install 5th-6th speed clutch collar on shaft.
16. Remove assembly from vise and place on work bench.
17. Slide 1st-reverse shift collar into bore of 1st gear. Slide thrust washer on end of shaft against snap ring. *Do not install thrust washer or snap ring into bore of reverse gear at this time.*
18. Assemble reverse gear on the rear of the shaft. Slide it forward onto clutch collar. Match gear teeth, butt both gears together and wire the two gears together.
19. The remaining mainshaft parts are assembled after the mainshaft has been placed in the case.

Assemble Transmission

1. Install one of the countershaft sub-assemblies in the case on the left side with timing mark of head and gear toward the center of the case.
2. Assemble two idler shaft bearings and spacer into bore of reverse idler gear.
3. Place one of the reverse idler gears into mesh with countershaft. Do not install idler shaft at this time.
4. Install remaining countershaft into right side of case with head end timing mark toward center of case. Install other idler gear, idler gear shaft and lock ball.

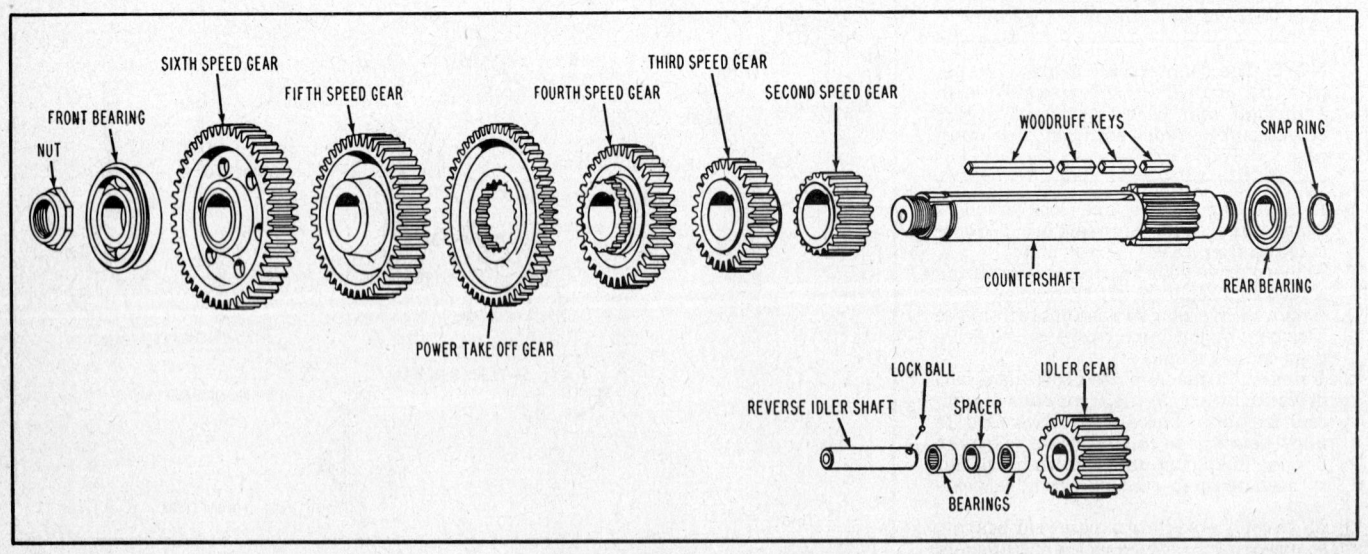

Fig. 5 Spicer SST mainshaft. Exploded

Spicer Transmissions

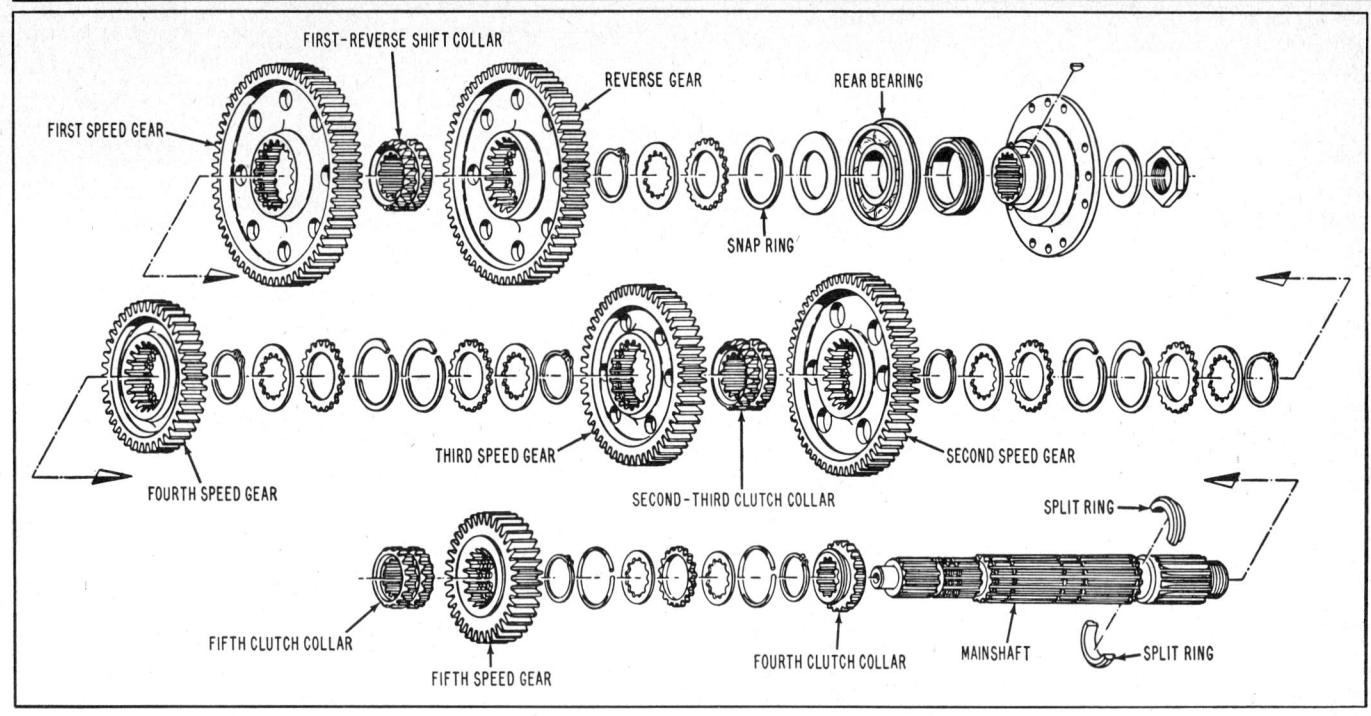

Fig. 6 Spicer SST countershaft. Exploded

Tap shaft flush with case. Do not install countershaft bearings at this time.
5. Using chain hoist, install mainshaft.
6. Install thrust washers on output end of mainshaft and cut tie wire from 1st-reverse gears.
7. Install split rings with flanges toward gears.
8. Install remaining thrust washers and snap rings on mainshaft.
9. Install drive gear and bearing cap.

NOTE: Mainshaft and both countershafts must be correctly timed. Be sure timing teeth of countershaft head end gears align with timing teeth (two) on mainshaft before completing assembly.

10. Install mainshaft rear bearing and remove chain hoist.
11. Install reverse idler shaft into upper reverse idler gear. Install lock ball in shaft and tap shaft end flush with case.
12. During final assembly and tie-up of countershafts, both countershafts must be supported to maintain proper gear timing. Using care not to disturb timing, install countershaft bearings and lock nuts.
13. After all shafts are installed, recheck gear timing and if timing is correct, complete assembly of transmission.

Spicer SST 1010-2A Unit

DISASSEMBLY

1. Using a 15/16 inch socket remove six clutch housing-to-gear case external cap screws and lock washers, Fig. 1. Remove four internal cap screws and lockwashers from inside the clutch housing with a 3/4 inch socket.
2. Using a soft head hammer, tap the clutch housing off the gear case and the OD pilot of the drive gear front bearing cap, Fig. 1. Remove the clutch housing gasket if torn or damaged.
3. Rotate the main drive gear until the timing marks on the outside diameter of the curvic ring of the splitter drive gear align with the timing marks on the back face of the two countershaft head-end drive gears, Fig. 2. Lock the splitter shift clutch collar into the curvic ring of the splitter drive gear.
4. On the mainshaft, shift the clutch collar into the 1st-2nd gear to lock the transmission in two gears, Fig. 2.
5. Remove both countershaft front lock nuts and the yoke lock nut on the mainshaft, Fig. 2.
6. Remove the yoke from the mainshaft, Fig. 2, with a suitable puller. The washer will come off with the yoke.
7. Remove the capscrews and lock washers from the mainshift rear bearing cap with a 3/4 inch socket, Fig. 1. Separate bearing cap from the gear case and gasket. Remove speedometer drive gear and bushing, if used. Remove the seal, if damaged.
8. At the mainshaft, position a pry bar between the splitter shift clutch collar and the 9th-10th gear curvic tooth ring, Fig. 2. Force the mainshaft subassembly rearward to expose the snap ring on the mainshaft rear bearing. Install a suitable puller on the snap ring and pull the bearing off the shaft.
9. Remove thrust washer from the mainshaft, then the split rings, Fig. 2. Remove snap ring located in the bore of the reverse gear. Use a long thin-lipped screw driver to work the snap ring from groove in the gear bore and rearward to remove snap ring from the gear and mainshaft.
10. Pull upper reverse idler gear shaft from gear case, Fig. 3. Recover the idler shaft lock ball. Leave the idler gear in place and force to side of case where it should remain until after the mainshaft subassembly has been removed.
11. On the mainshaft, engage 1st-Reverse clutch collar with reverse gear then slide the reverse gear and collar forward until reverse gear butts against the 1st-2nd speed gear, Fig. 2. Wire or tie both gears together.
12. Remove capscrews and lock washers from both countershaft rear bearing caps and separate the caps from gear case and gaskets, Fig. 1. The air filter and regulator mounting brackets will come off with the bearing caps. Do not remove the connecting nylon line between the air filter and regulator unless damaged. Position the two assemblies with connecting line aside.
13. Remove the capscrews and lockwashers from the drive gear front bearing cap and separate the cap from the gear case and gasket, Fig. 1.
14. Disengage drive gear front bearing snap ring from drive gear and pull the bearing and snap ring forward on drive gear

373

SPICER TRANSMISSIONS

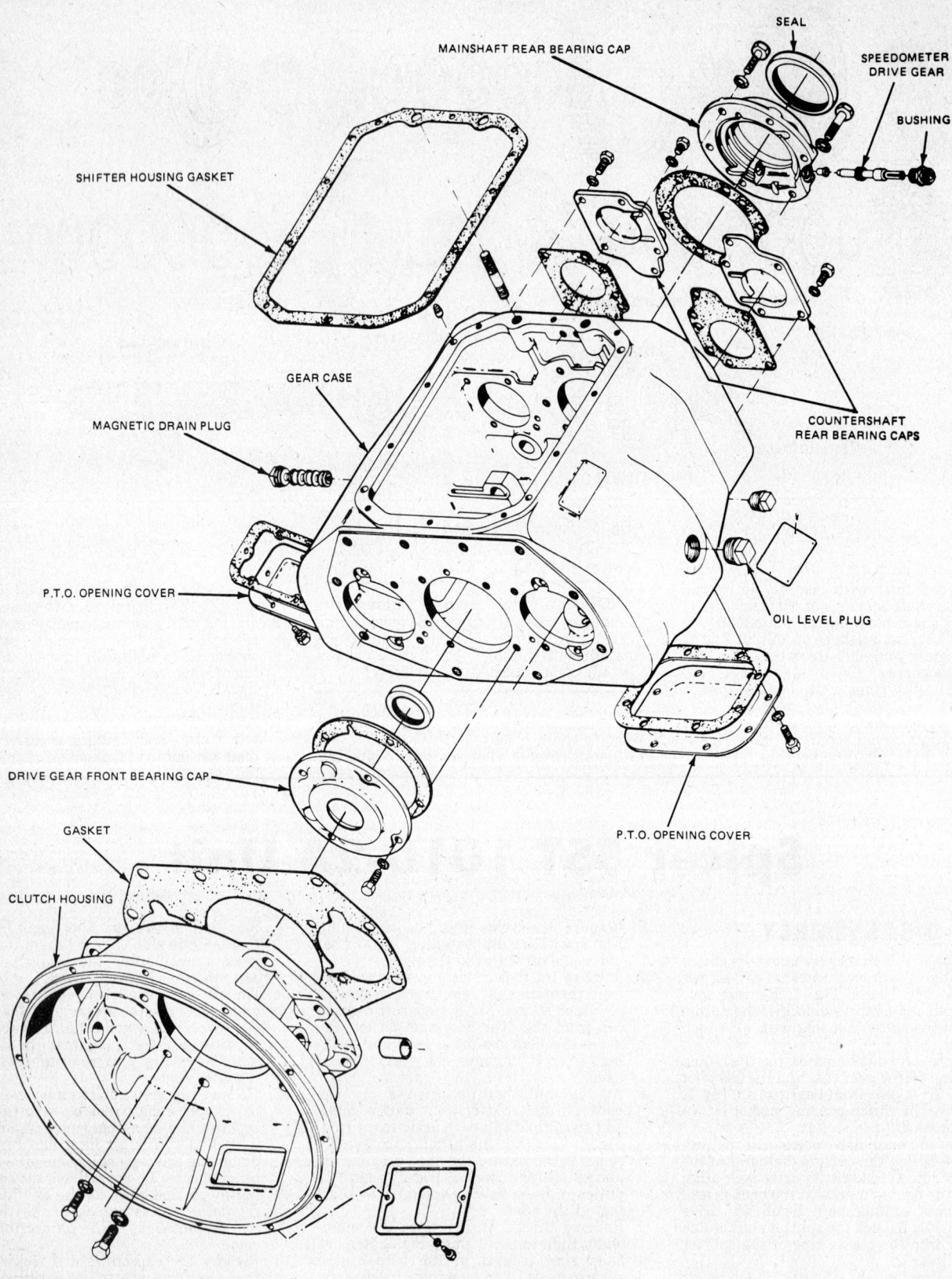

Fig. 1 Gear case & clutch housing

SPICER TRANSMISSIONS

spline stem as far as possible, Fig. 2. This will make the snap ring accessible slightly forward of the gear case face. Using a suitable puller on the bearing snap ring, remove the front bearing from drive gear.
15. Force the two countershafts rearward so front bearings can creep forward to expose the bearing snap rings, Fig. 4. Install puller tool arms on bearing snap ring and remove bearings from shafts.
16. At each countershaft, maneuver the assembly rearward to expose the rear bearing so a bearing split tool can be installed on the front side of the bearing, Fig. 4. Remove the rear bearing snap ring, install puller tool arms on the split tool, and pull the bearing from the rear end of the countershaft.
17. To obtain clearance for removing the mainshaft assembly, force the two countershaft sub-assemblies and the drive gear assembly forward as far as possible. Also, keep the mainshaft as far back as possible.
18. Place a sling rope around 3rd-4th/5th-6th clutch collar, Fig. 2, to support the mainshaft assembly. Using suitable lifting equipment, lift the mainshaft sub-assembly from the gear case.
19. Remove the upper idler gear subassembly, Fig. 3.
20. Remove the drive gear sub-assembly from the case, Fig. 2.
21. Remove the right side (looking from rear of case) countershaft sub-assembly from the case, Fig. 2.
22. Remove the left side countershaft sub-assembly from the case, Fig. 2.
23. Pull the lower reverse idler gear shaft out of the gear case, Fig. 3. Remove idler gear sub-assembly from the case.

SUB-ASSEMBLY SERVICE

Shifter Housing

Disassembly

1. Remove four retaining screws and lock washers and the splitter piston housing from shifter housing, Fig. 5.
2. Clamp splitter control in a soft jawed vise with the splitter piston rod shift bracket facing upward. Cut lock wire and remove set screw from the shift bracket.
3. Remove splitter piston housing cover.
4. Remove the actuating piston and rod from the shift bracket and out of the piston housing by pulling on rod lock nut.

NOTE: If the piston O-rings are damaged by cuts or have flat spots on air sealing surfaces, replace as necessary.

5. Remove the splitter air control valve body from the piston housing.
6. Remove the two valve plungers from valve body. Inspect the O-rings on both plungers for cuts or flat-spot wear on sealing surfaces, replace as necessary.
7. Install required new O-rings on the plungers and lubricate with silicon grease.
8. Reassemble plungers into the valve body, install the valve body on the piston housing with the six retaining screws and lock washers.
9. Place the piston on the actuation piston rod and secure to rod with the lock nut hand tight.
10. Install the piston and rod into the cylindrical housing, Fig. 5. When the rod end protrudes through the front boss, install the shift bracket on the rod with the extended hub of the bracket toward the welch plug.
11. Locate the shift bracket in the proper position on the piston rod, install the set screw, and secure with a lock wire.

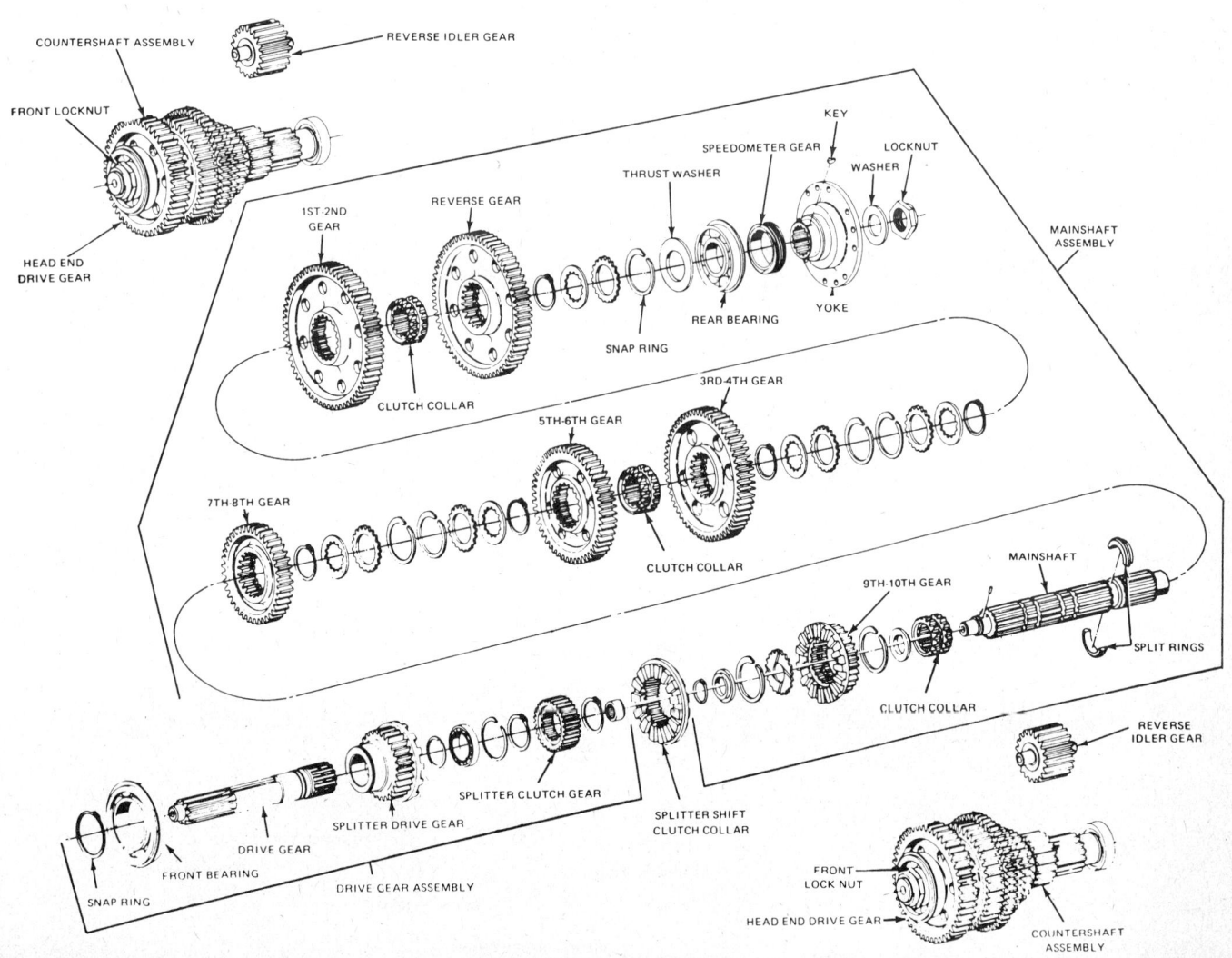

Fig. 2 Sub-assembly installation in transmission case

SPICER TRANSMISSIONS

12. Tighten the piston rod lock nut.
13. Install splitter piston housing cover and gasket, lock washers and retaining screws.
14. Position the air valve sub-assembly aside for later installation on the shifter housing.
15. Remove shoes from the splitter shift fork.
16. Place the edge of the shifter housing in a vise with rods and forks exposed and the front of the housing to the right, or lay the shifter housing on a work bench with forks up and the front of the housing to the left.
17. Cut and remove all wires, then loosen and remove all set screws from shift forks.
18. Turn the splitter shift rod 90 degrees in either direction to preload the poppet detent pin into the recess hole of the center boss on the shifter housing.
19. With a soft drift and hammer, tap the splitter shift rod to the left. As the rod clears housing center boss, remove the detent pin and the poppet spring from the recess hole in the boss. As the rod clears the splitter fork, remove the fork from the rod and the rod from the housing front boss.
20. Tap the 7th-8th/9th-10th shift rod to the left. Remove the bracket as it clears the rod. Remove the poppet ball and spring as the rod clears the front boss. Remove the shift fork as it clears the rod. Then, remove the rod from the front boss.
21. Tap the 3rd-4th/5th-6th shift rod to the left. Remove the poppet ball and spring from the housing boss. Remove the shift rod interlock pin if it should dislodge from the rod during rod movement. Remove the shift fork as it clears the rod, then the rod from the front boss.
22. Remove the (housing boss) interlock pin located internally in the rear boss between the two shift rod (3rd-4th/5th-6th, and 7th-8th/9th-10th) bores.
23. Tap the 1st-2nd/Reverse shift rod to the left and remove the shift fork as it clears the rod. Remove the poppet ball and spring from the housing boss. Remove the bracket sub-assembly as it clears the rod and the rod from the front boss.
24. Remove the second interlock pin located

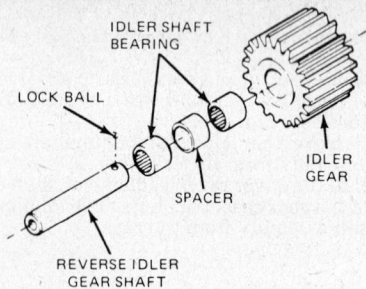

Fig. 3 Idler gear, disassembled

internally in the boss between the two shift rod (3rd-4th/5th-6th and 1st-2nd/Reverse) bores.

25. To disassemble the 1st-2nd/Reverse shift bracket, clamp the trunion ends in a vise. Shear the block retainer pin using a flat-head punch against the small diameter end of the plunger. Strike the plunger end with a sharp blow to shear the pin. Check the block and plunger for excessive wear, and check the spring for broken coils or weak tension.
26. Remove vent from the top surface of the shifter housing.
27. Remove old gaskets and sealing material from the machined surfaces of the shifter housing and top of the gear case.
28. Examine the shift fork shoes for excessive wear. Sharp corners of the shoes should be chamfered slightly with a hand grinder to allow entry of oil between the shoes and shift collar, thereby reducing wear on these surfaces.
29. Check the 1st/reverse blocker pins which are located on the internal side of the shifter housing, Fig. 5. If either pin shows excessive wear or galling, drive it out with a flat head punch. Press a new pin into its hole in the shifter housing flush with the top surface of the housing. This will allow proper length extension to the internal location of the shifter housing.

Assembly

1. If 1st-2nd/reverse shift bracket was disassembled, clamp the trunion ends of the bracket in a vise and insert the plunger and spring into the plunger hole of the bracket, Fig. 5. Pre-load the plunger with a C clamp.
2. Assemble the block to the bracket so the end of the plunger enters the hole in the block. The step on the block must face inward against the block, Fig. 5. Assembling the block outward will cause 1st-2nd/reverse gear block-out.

   Align the plunger pin hole with the block pin hole, and install the lock pin with a .084 inch flat head punch. Tap the C clamp from the plunger and move the plunger in and out to be sure plunger moves freely.
3. Place the shifter housing on a bench with the inside of the housing facing up and the front of the housing to the left.
4. Check all four shift rods to ensure free movement in the boss bores without excessive radial movement. Remove the rods and lightly coat both the rods and the bores in the shifter housing with grease. Install the rods in the bores.
5. Coat interlock pin with heavy grease and insert into the 1st-2nd/reverse shift rod bore through the hole in rear boss.
6. Install and pre-load the poppet spring and ball in the poppet detent bore of 1st-2nd/reverse rod location.
7. To install the 1st-2nd/reverse shift rod and bracket: start the end of the rod, farthest from set screw countersunk holes, through the rear boss of the housing. Assemble bracket on the rod with top boss of the bracket down and the shift gate towards the lower opening. Tap rod sharply to remove the poppet loading tool and slide the rod into the front boss. Assemble the shift fork on the rod with the extended hub of fork to the right. Position the fork and bracket properly on the rod, install the set screws and install the lock wires. Move the shift rod until the poppet ball registers in the neutral detent of the rod.
8. Install and preload the poppet spring and ball in the poppet detent bore of 3rd-4th/5th-6th shift rod location of the boss.
9. To install the 3rd-4th/5th-6th shift rod and fork: coat the small interlock pin, Fig. 5, with heavy grease and insert into the

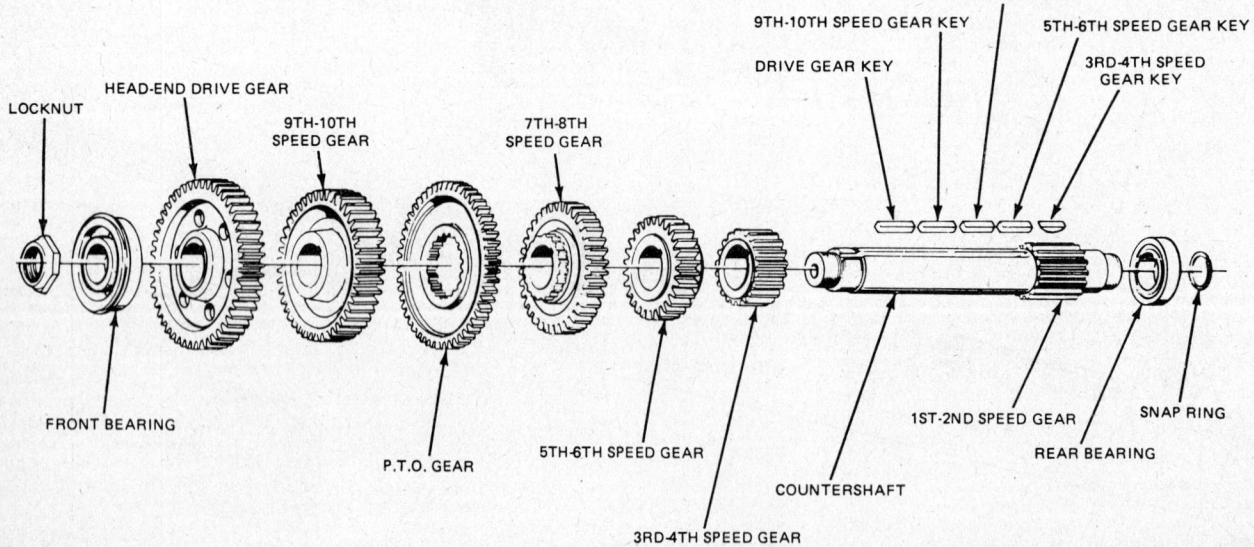

Fig. 4 Countershaft, disassembled

SPICER TRANSMISSIONS

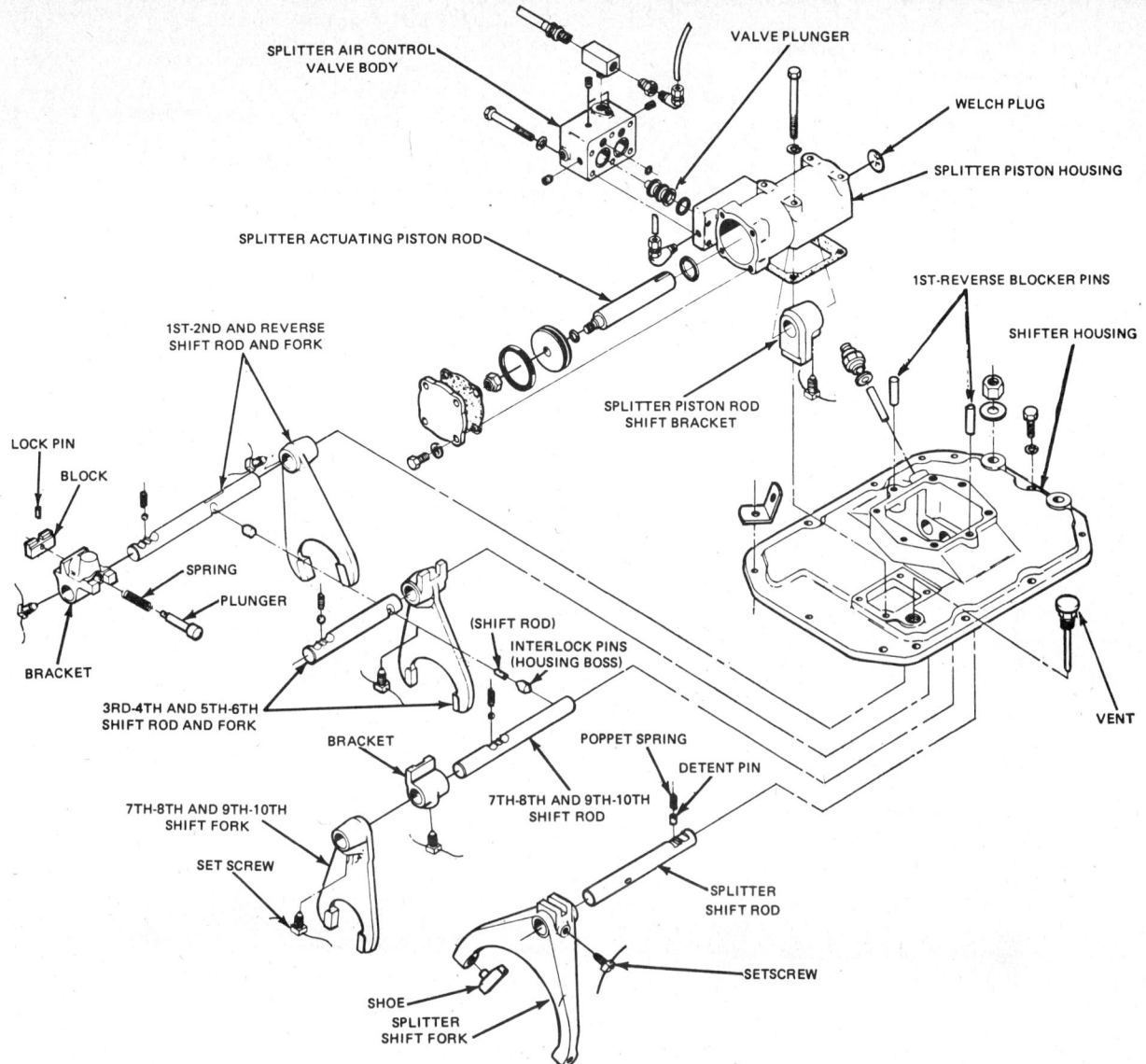

Fig. 5 Shifter housing, disassembled

hole of the shift rod. Enter the rod with interlock pin to the right through the rear boss. Assemble the fork to the rod with fork hub to the left. As the rod enters the front boss, tap it sharply to remove the poppet loading tool. Properly position the shift fork on the rod, install the set screw and secure with the lock wire. Move the rod until the poppet registers in the neutral detent of the rod.

10. Coat the interlock pin with heavy grease and insert into 7th-8th/9th-10th shift rod bore through the hole in the rear boss. Install the poppet spring and ball in the poppet detent bore of 7th-8th/9th-10th shift rod location of the boss.
11. To install the 7th-8th/9th-10th shift rod, bracket and fork: enter the rod end (farthest from interlock detent) into the rear boss. Assemble the bracket on the rod with the shift gate downward. Tap the rod sharply to remove the poppet loading tool in the front boss. Assemble the fork to the rod with fork hub to the left. Properly position the bracket and fork on the rod, install the set screws, and install the lock wires. Move the rod until the poppet registers in the neutral detent of the rod.
12. Install and pre-load the poppet spring and ball in the poppet detent bore of the splitter shift rod location of the boss.
13. To install the splitter shift rod and fork: enter the rod (detent end) into the front boss with detent facing up. Assemble the fork to the shaft with fork extended hub to the right and hub shift gate down. Tap the rod sharply to remove the poppet loading tool. Turn the rod 180 degrees so the poppet pin locates in the rod detent. Properly position the fork on the rod, install the set screw and secure with the lock wire. Move the rod until the poppet registers in the left detent of the rod. This locates the splitter fork in the LO position of splitter-to-transmission gear.
14. Shift 1st-2nd/reverse speed shift fork into gear position and try to shift the other two shift rods (3rd-4th/5th-6th and 7th-8th/9th-10th). If all interlocks are functioning, the rods should be locked in neutral position.
15. Return the 1st-2nd/reverse shift fork to neutral positions and check the movement of each of the other shift rods to the rods move readily and completely into each gear position.
16. Turn the shifter housing assembly over (top up). Install vent in the tapped hole in the top surface of the housing using sealer on the threads, Fig. 5. Tighten vent securely, but be careful not to collapse the body of the vent by over-tightening.
17. Assemble the splitter piston housing and splitter control valve body sub-assembly to the shifter housing with gasket, Fig. 5. As the assembly is mounted to the housing engage the pad on the splitter piston rod shift bracket into the splitter shift fork. Secure the assembly to the housing with four capscrews and lock washers.
18. Coat the trunions of the splitter fork shoes with heavy grease and insert the shoes in the splitter fork.
19. Position complete shifter housing aside for later assembly to gear case.

SPICER TRANSMISSIONS

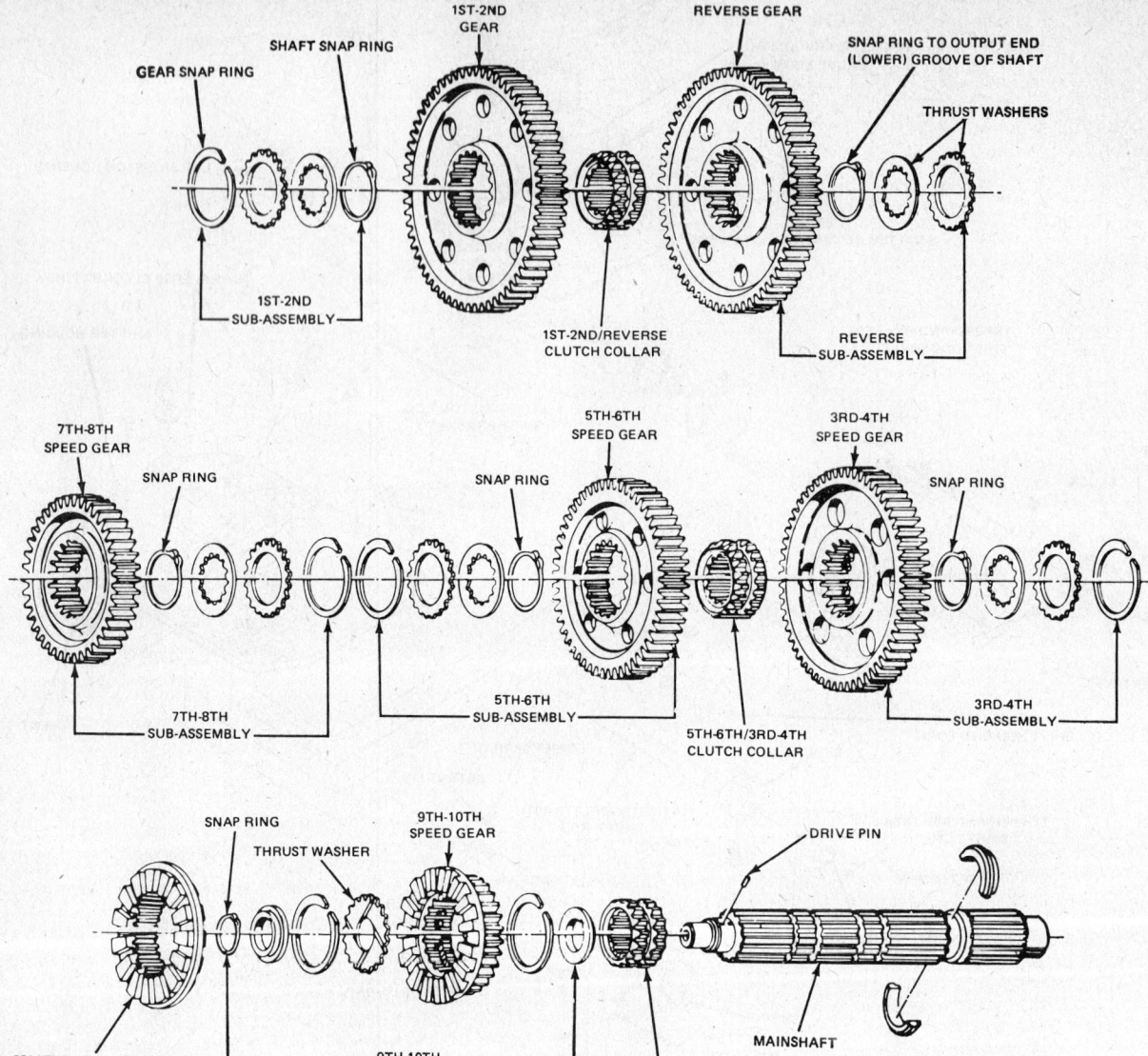

Fig. 6 Mainshaft, disassembled

Mainshaft

Disassembly
1. Remove snap ring from front of mainshaft, and slide the 9th-10th gear sub-assembly off the shaft drive pins, Fig. 6.
2. Remove 7th-8th/9th-10th clutch collar from shaft.
3. Remove the snap ring from the shaft groove, then the 7th-8th speed gear sub-assembly.
4. Remove 5th-6th gear sub-assembly and the snap ring from the shaft groove.
5. Remove 5th-6th/3rd-4th clutch collar from shaft.
6. Remove snap ring from the 3rd-4th speed gear bore, and the 3rd-4th speed gear sub-assembly.
7. Remove the wire used to fasten the 1st-2nd speed gear to the reverse gear when the mainshaft was removed from the gear case.
8. Remove 1st-2nd gear sub-assembly from the shaft and the snap ring from the shaft groove.
9. Remove 1st-2nd/reverse shift collar from shaft.
10. Remove reverse gear sub-assembly from the (rear) output end of the shaft.

Assembly
Before assembly inspect all thrust washers. If heavy face galling or tooth wear is indicated, the thrust washers should be replaced. Lubricate thrust washers with 30 weight engine oil on the thrust faces.
1. Clamp the mainshaft vertically in a vise with the output end splines of the shaft resting on the bed and the soft jaws clamping on the splined area.
2. Install internal tooth thrust washer on the mainshaft and let it rest on the shoulder near the output splines. The external tooth thrust washer is installed after the mainshaft sub-assembly has been installed in the gear case.
3. Install the snap ring in the lower groove of the shaft, Fig. 6. Make sure the ring is seated securely in the groove.
4. Assemble 1st-2nd/reverse clutch collar with either end of collar down. Rest the collar against the snap ring.

NOTE: Clutch collars are identical parts. They can be installed in any of the gear positions. Either end can be installed on the shaft at time of assembly.

5. Install 1st-2nd sub-assembly snap ring in the shaft groove closest to the 1st-2nd/reverse clutch collar, Fig. 6.
6. Install the internal tooth snap ring on the shaft to snap ring rests on the snap ring.
7. With both thrust washers and the large snap ring assembled into the 1st-2nd speed gear, install the 1st-2nd sub-assembly on the shaft so the chamfer in the bore of the gear extends down toward the clutch collar.
8. Assemble second set of thrust washers and large snap ring into the 3rd-4th speed gear and install the 3rd-4th sub-assembly on the shaft, chamfer up. Rest 3rd-4th speed gear against the face of the 1st-2nd speed gear. Install third (shaft) snap ring in shaft groove under the bore of the 3rd-4th speed gear.
9. Assemble 3rd-4th/5th-6th clutch collar so clutch collar rests in the bore of 3rd-4th

SPICER TRANSMISSIONS

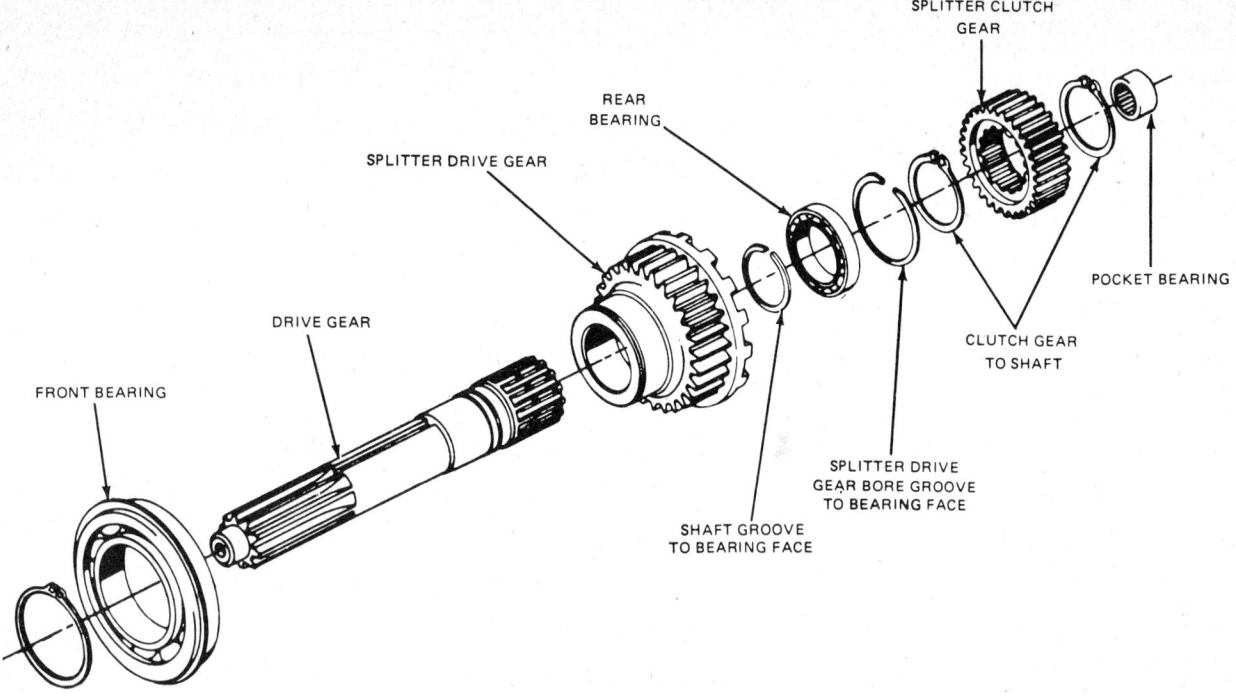

Fig. 7 Drive gear, disassembled

speed gear.
10. Install the fourth (shaft) snap ring in the shaft groove closest to 3rd-4th/5th-6th clutch collar.
11. Install two thrust washers, one internal and one external, on the shaft, resting on the snap ring.
12. Assemble the large snap ring into the 5th-6th speed gear and assemble the gear chamfer in bore down toward the clutch collar.
13. Assemble the fourth set of washers and the large snap ring into the 7th-8th speed gear. Assemble the 7th-8th gear sub-assembly chamfer up and resting against the face of the 5th-6th gear. Install the fifth snap ring in the shaft groove under the bore of the 7th-8th speed gear.
14. Assemble the 7th-8th/9th-10th speed clutch collar on the shaft.
15. If 9th-10th speed gear was disassembled, reassemble one large snap ring in the gear bore groove, install the thrust washer and lock the parts together with the second large snap ring, Fig. 6.
16. If replacement of drive pins on the front of the mainshaft is not necessary, install the 9th-10th sub-assembly on the mainshaft.
17. Lock up all the 9th-10th gear parts on the shaft by installing the small ring in the shaft groove. Install curvic shift collar on the 9th-10th gear curvic ring.
18. Remove the complete assembly from the vise and place it on a work bench.
19. Slide 1st-2nd/reverse clutch collar into the bore of the 1st-2nd speed gear. Also, slide the internal tooth thrust washer on the rear end of the shaft against the snap ring.
20. Do not install the external tooth thrust washer or large snap ring into the bore of the reverse gear at this time. Assemble only the reverse gear on the rear end of the mainshaft. Assemble the reverse gear with the chamfer of clutch teeth toward

the clutch collar. Match the O.D. teeth of the clutch collar to the 1st-2nd speed gear internal teeth. Butt both gears together and tie with wire.

The remaining parts, Fig. 2, relative to the reverse gear and rear end of the mainshaft will be assembled to their respective places after the mainshaft sub-assembly has been placed in the gear case.

Countershaft

Use an arbor press with parallel bars to remove all the gears except 9th and 10th speed gear.

Disassembly
1. Support the head end drive gear, Fig. 4, with parallel bars as close to the hub as possible and press the countershaft from gear.
2. Remove 9th-10th speed gear from the countershaft with a suitable puller tool engaged in the lightener holes in the web of the gear.
3. Lift the P.T.O. gear off the splined teeth of the 7th-8th speed gear, Fig. 4.
4. Support the 7th-8th speed gear with parallel bars under the gear teeth, and press the shaft from gear.
5. Support the 3rd-4th speed gear with parallel bars under and as close to the hub as possible. Then press the countershaft out of both 5th-6th and 3rd-4th speed gears.

Assembly
Coat bores of all gears with oil before pressing the gears on the countershaft. The key to each gear should be installed in the shaft keyway one at a time. If the keys become mutilated or burred, use a mill file to align the sides and remove burrs.
1. Press 3rd-4th speed key into place on the countershaft, Fig. 4. Support the 3rd-4th speed gear and set the countershaft and key into position under the arbor. Align the key with the gear keyway and press the shaft and key into the gear. Seat the gear firmly against the face of the 1st-2nd speed gear. If the key crept out from 3rd-4th speed gear face, tap the key back flush with the gear face or slightly under the gear face.
2. Press the $1^{9}/_{16}$ inch, 5th-6th speed gear key into place on the countershaft. Support the 5th-6th speed gear on the bars with the long hub up. Set the shaft into the gear under the press. Align the key with the gear keyway and press the shaft and key into the gear. Set the gear firmly against the face of the 3rd-4th speed gear. If the key crept out of position, tap it back flush with the face of the gear or slightly under the gear face.
3. Press the $2^{3}/_{8}$ inch, 7th-8th speed gear key into place on the countershaft. Support the 7th-8th speed gear on the bars with the splined teeth on the hub down. Set the shaft into the gear under the arbor press. Align the gear keyway with the key and press the shaft and key into the gear. Seat the gear face firmly against the face of the 5th-6th speed gear. Ensure the key is flush with or under the face of the gear.
4. Slide the P.T.O. gear onto the splined teeth of the 7th-8th speed gear with the long hub of the P.T.O. gear against the face of 7th-8th speed gear.
5. Press the $2^{7}/_{16}$ inch, 9th-10th speed gear key into the keyway on the countershaft. Support the 9th-10th speed gears on the bars with the long hub end down. Set the shaft into the gear holding the P.T.O. gear in mesh with its mating gear, Fig. 4. Align the gear keyway with the key and press the shaft and key into the gear. Seat the gear firmly against the face of the 7th-8th speed gear. Ensure the key is flush with or slightly under the face of the gear.
6. Press the head end drive gear key into the keyway on the countershaft. Support the

SPICER TRANSMISSIONS

head end (splitter) drive gear on the bars with the long hub facing upward.

NOTE: Be sure that the timing mark on the tooth web of the gear is in alignment with the center of the gear keyway.

Set the shaft into the gear, align the gear keyway with the key, and press the shaft and key into the gear. Seat the gear face firmly against the face of the 9th-10th speed gear. Ensure the key face is flush with or slightly under the face of the gear.

NOTE: The front and rear bearings will be installed after the countershaft is installed in the gear case.

Drive Gear

Disassembly
1. If the pocket bearing replacement is necessary, use a small puller tool to dislodge it from the pocket of the drive gear, Fig. 7.
2. Remove the clutch gear-to-shaft outer snap ring and the splitter clutch gear from the drive gear splines. Remove the clutch gear-to-shaft outer snap ring.
3. Remove large snap ring from the bore of the splitter drive gear, and force the splitter drive gear from the rear bearing.
4. Remove the shaft groove-to-bearing face snap ring from the drive gear and shaft assembly, Fig. 7. Support the rear bearing on a press bed and press the drive gear and shaft assembly out of the bearing.

Assembly
1. Support rear bearing in an arbor press (inner race of bearing) and press the drive gear shaft assembly into the bearing. Seat the shaft groove-to-bearing face snap ring into its groove, Fig. 7.
2. Assemble shaft and bearing assembly into the bearing bore of the splitter drive gear. Seat the bearing to the bore face of the splitter drive gear and assemble the gear bore groove-to-bearing face snap ring.
3. Install clutch gear-to-shaft inner snap ring in the groove near the bore of the splitter drive gear. Assemble the splitter clutch gear on the shaft and install the second (outer) snap ring on the shaft to secure the clutch gear to the shaft, Fig. 7.
4. Support the drive gear sub-assembly in an arbor press resting the front face of the splitter drive gear on the press bed. Press the pocket bearing into the pocket or small inner bore of the drive gear and shaft assembly. The pocket bearing part number must be visible when pressed into the bore. The opposite end of the bearing is made of softer metal. Press the bearing so bearing is recessed 1/16 inch under the gear face.
5. Do not install the front bearing and snap ring at this time. The drive gear assembly must be installed in the gear case bore from the internal side after the countershaft assemblies have been placed into position on the bottom of the case. The front bearing and snap ring is then installed on the drive gear assembly and into the case bore from the outside. Set the drive gear assembly aside for later installation into the gear case.

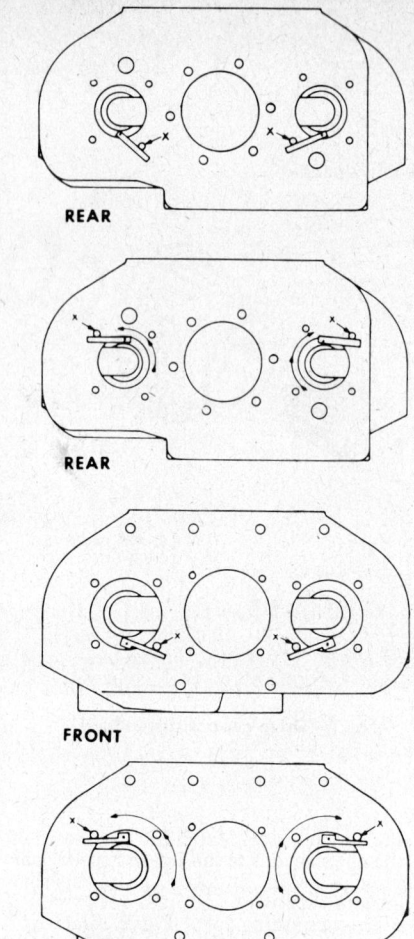

REAR

REAR

FRONT

FRONT

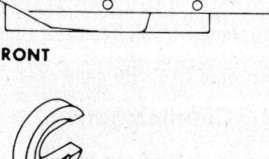

3/8"-16 NC-2 CAP SCREW

Fig. 8 Positioning pilot tools in countershaft bearing bores

ASSEMBLY

The timing teeth on the head end of the countershafts and on the splitter drive gear, Fig. 2, are designated by a timing mark (letter V). The back face of these three gear teeth should be painted with a bright color before installing any of the sub-assemblies.

The sub-assemblies should be installed in the gear case by performing the following procedures in the specified order.

Countershafts, Reverse Idler Gears, & Drive Gear Assembly Installation

1. Place either of the countershaft sub-assemblies inside the gear case on the left side with the head-end gear towards the front bore of the case, Fig. 2. Rotate the head-end gear until the timing mark points inward toward the center of the case and the tooth itself is parallel with the bottom of the case.
2. Assemble the two idler shaft bearings with a spacer between the bore of each reverse idler gear, Fig. 3.
3. Position either of the reverse idler gears in the upper bore of the case in mesh with the teeth on the rear end of the countershaft.

NOTE: Do not install the upper idler gear shaft until after the mainshaft is installed.

4. Check if the magnetic drain plug is in place on the right side of the gear case, Fig. 1. If the plug is in the case, remove it so plug will not be damaged during later installation of the lower reverse idler gear.
5. Place the remaining countershaft assembly inside of the gear case on the right side with the head end gear toward the front bore of the case, Fig. 2. Rotate the head end gear until the timing mark points inward toward the center of the case and the timing tooth itself is parallel with the bottom of the case.
6. Position the remaining idler gear to the lower boss location in the gear case. Roll the idler gear on the mating teeth of the countershaft to align the gear bearing bore with the hole in the case. Install the idler shaft into the gear bore, Fig. 3. Install the lock ball into hole in the shaft just before the ball comes into the recess of the gear case. Tap the end of the shaft until it is flush with the face of the case.
7. Do not install the countershaft front and rear bearings at this time. Allow the countershafts to lay free in the bottom of the case.
8. Install the drive gear assembly, Fig. 2, into the gear case center bore from the inside of the case.

Mainshaft Installation

1. Place a sling rope around 3rd-4th/5th-6th clutch collar, Fig. 2, to support the mainshaft assembly. (Using suitable lifting equipment,) lift the mainshaft assembly from the work bench and lower it into the gear case in partial mesh with the countershaft gears. Support the mainshaft in proper position until all bearings and the upper reverse idler shaft have been assembled in the case.
2. Install the external-tooth thrust washer over the output (rear) end of the mainshaft and slide it forward against the internal-tooth thrust washer previously installed during mainshaft assembly, Fig. 2. Force both washers forward against the snap ring already installed on the mainshaft.
3. Unfasten the 1st-2nd speed gear from the reverse gear. Slide the reverse gear rearward into approximate location on the reverse gear bore thrust washers internal and external teeth.
4. Install the large snap ring into the location groove of the bore on the reverse gear, Fig. 2. Use a long thin-lipped screwdriver to work the snap ring into the gear groove.
5. Coat the two split rings, Fig. 2, with heavy grease and install the rings into the recess on the rear of the mainshaft with ring flanges facing the gears.
6. Coat the thick thrust washer with heavy grease and install it on the mainshaft against the flange face of the split rings,

SPICER TRANSMISSIONS

Fig. 2.

7. Install the pilot tool for the mainshaft rear bearing bore. The tool will help align the mainshaft and gears with the drive gear assembly that is already installed in the front center bore of the case.
8. Support the front end of each countershaft with a countershaft front bearing bore tool, Fig. 8.
9. Turn the countershaft head end gears around until the V timing marks point inward toward each other and the timing teeth are parallel with the bottom of the case. Position the two timing marks on the splitter drive gear (curvic ring) where they will match and mate with the timing teeth on the countershaft gears, Fig. 2.
10. Install the snap ring on the drive gear front bearing, and seat the bearing with the snap ring against the face of the gear case, Fig. 2.
11. Install the drive gear front bearing cap with gasket, Fig. 1. Align the oil port holes of the case to the oil return holes on the bearing cap.
12. Dip the cap screws in sealer and attach the bearing cap to the case with cap screws and washers.
13. Remove bearing bore pilot tool from the case center rear bore and mainshaft. Slide the three clutch collars into their neutral positions on the mainshaft, Fig. 2.
14. Start the inner race of the mainshaft rear bearing, Fig. 2, on the mainshaft with the mainshaft rear bearing pilot tool against the bearing face. Use the drive tubing of the tool to drive against the pilot tool and force the bearing onto the shaft and into the bore of the case. Seat the bearing snap ring against the face of the case.
15. Relieve the hoist tension on the sling rope and remove the rope from the mainshaft.
16. Install the shaft into the upper reverse idler gear bore, Fig. 3. Install the shaft lock ball in its hole in the shaft just before the ball enters the recess in the case. Tap the end of the idler shaft flush with the case face.

Final Assembly

1. Support the rear end of each countershaft with a countershaft rear bearing bore pilot tool, Fig. 8. As the pilot tools are inserted into the bores keep the timing teeth in correct mesh with each other.
2. As each front piloting tool is removed and the front bearing installed, both countershafts must be held in proper position relative to the timing teeth mesh and the timing marks must be held in place.
3. Remove the pilot tool from the left countershaft front bore. Install the left countershaft front bearing, Fig. 4. Use the face of the pilot tool on the front end of the bearing to drive the bearing on the shaft and into the case bore. Seat the bearing snap ring to the face of the case.
4. Install the left countershaft front locknut on the shaft and tighten against the bearing face hand tight.
5. Remove the pilot tool from the right countershaft front bore and install the right countershaft front bearing in the same manner as the left countershaft described in Step 3.
6. Remove tools and chain hoist from the countershafts.
7. Install the right countershaft front lock nut on the shaft and tighten against the bearing face hand tight.
8. Lock the transmission in two gears by engaging the splitter shift clutch collar to the curvic ring of the splitter drive gear and by shifting the 1st-2nd; reverse clutch collar into the 1st-2nd speed gear, Fig. 2. Tighten both countershaft front bearing lock nuts.
9. Remove the pilot tool from the left countershaft rear bore and install the countershaft rear bearing.

NOTE: The bearing must be assembled with the snap ring toward the outside of the transmission case. Do not assemble the bearing with the snap ring toward the inside of the transmission.

10. Use the pilot tool tubing to drive the bearing on the shaft and into the bore of the case. Install the snap ring on the shaft.
11. Remove pilot tool from the right countershaft rear bore and install the right countershaft rear bearing in the same manner as for the left countershaft described in Steps 9 and 10.
12. If the speedometer gear was removed, install it into the mainshaft rear bearing cap. Install rear bearing cap with the oil return holes of the bearing cap aligning the oil port holes in the case.
13. Dip the bearing cap retaining screws in sealer, install the screws with washers.
14. Assemble both countershaft rear bearing caps with gaskets to the face of the gear case. Secure the caps with retaining screws and washers.
15. Install the end yoke with washer on the mainshaft output splines, Fig. 2.
16. Install the mainshaft locknut, Fig. 2.

17. Move the 1st-2nd/reverse clutch collar into its neutral position, Fig. 2. Leave the splitter shift clutch collar engaged in the splitter drive gear.
18. Roll the gear train by turning the drive gear stem. If tooth timing marks are in their correct positions, the entire gear train will roll freely. If the timing teeth have been set incorrectly or have moved from proper position, the gear train will roll lock up after several turns of the drive gear.
19. If the unit locks up, disengage the shift collar from the splitter drive gear. Turn the drive gear in reverse rotation until the timing marks or painted teeth come into alignment or close mis-match. If mismatch appears, the timing was set incorrectly at the time of assembly or the timing teeth escaped positioning during final tie-up. If this is the case, the shafts must be re-timed.
20. If timing is correct, shift all clutch collars, except the splitter shift collar, into their neutral positions for later installation of the shifter housing assembly, Fig. 2. Move the splitter shift clutch collar into mesh with the 9th-10th speed gear so that it will be in proper position for later assembly with the splitter shift fork, Fig. 5.

Now proceed with installation of the clutch housing and related parts.

Clutch Housing Installation

1. Using the drive gear front bearing cap as a pilot, position the clutch housing gasket to the front face of the gear case, Fig. 1.
2. Set the clutch housing in place using the drive gear bearing cap as a guide.
3. Dip the capscrews in sealer, attach the clutch housing to the gear case with capscrews (six external and eight internal) and washers, Fig. 1.
4. Install clutch release yoke and short shaft to the clutch housing. Assemble the long shaft to the yoke. Align the keyway with the slots in the yoke and assemble the key, lockwashers and capscrews.
5. Replace the P.T.O. opening covers and gaskets if removed.
6. Install magnetic drain plug on right side of gear case and the oil level plug on the left side, Fig. 1.
7. Install shifter housing gasket on the gear case, Fig. 1.
8. Check the shifter housing assembly to see all shift forks are in neutral position, Fig. 5. Install the shifter housing to the gear case so all shift forks engage their pertinent clutch collars.

Spicer 7016 & 7216—16-Speed Unit

DESCRIPTION

These transmissions consist of a four-speed main unit and a four-speed auxiliary unit joined together in one compact assembly, Fig. 1. The mainshaft in each unit is supported by a single-row roller bearing at the front and a single-row ball bearing at the rear of the shaft. The countershaft in the front unit is supported by a single-row roller bearing at the front; a single-row ball bearing supports the shaft at the rear. The reverse idler gear is supported by two roller-type bearings that are recessed inside the idler gear and revolve on the idler shaft. The countershaft in the rear unit is supported by one single-row tapered roller bearing at each end of the shaft. All gears are helical-mesh type, except the reverse idler and main unit PTO, which are spur type.

Controls for shifting the transmission may be of several types, depending on truck model applications: The one-piece gearshift lever type, the remote prop shaft type, and remote rod and lever type.

The transmission should be overhauled in the sequence outlined unless only one unit is to be worked on or a specific problem has been correctly diagnosed, then complete overhaul is not required. Remove drain plugs from both units and drain before attempting disassembly.

SEPARATING UNITS

1. Remove shifter housing assembly, Figs. 2, 3 and 4.
2. From inside near top of rear case, cut lock wire and remove four capscrews and lockwashers.

SPICER TRANSMISSIONS

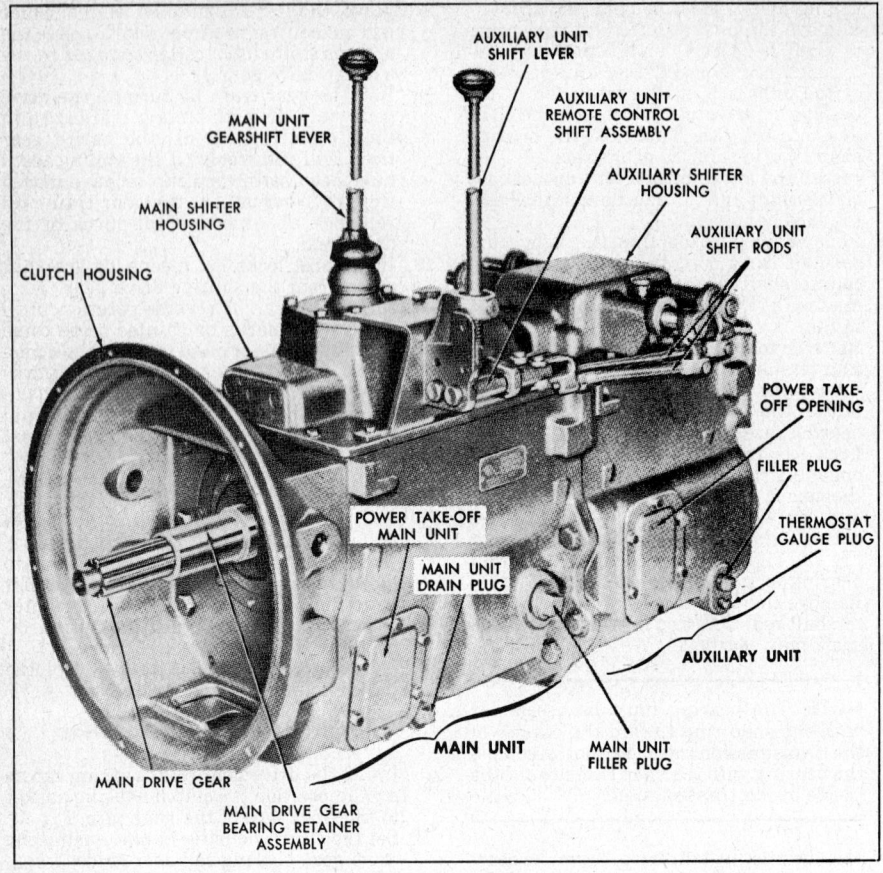

Fig. 1 Exterior view of transmission

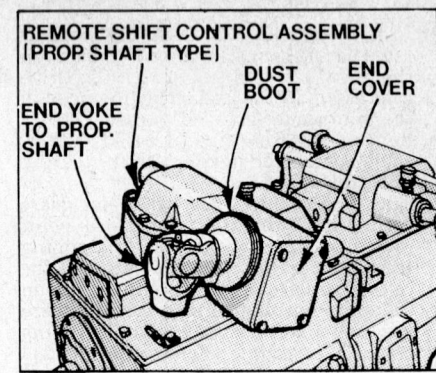

Fig. 2 Prop shaft type remote control

remove countershaft rear bearing nut.

NOTE: The procedure and ease of disassembly for this series transmission varies with the internal gearing and gear ratios provided. If gear ratios are such that the main drive gear is smaller than the case bearing bore, remove drive gear and bearing. If the drive gear is larger than the case bore, it is necessary to remove the mainshaft assembly before the drive gear can be removed from the case.

2. Remove capscrews from main drive gear bearing cap and then use two $7/16''$ puller screws to remove bearing cap and main drive gear assembly as shown in Fig. 8.

NOTE: Fourteen loose rollers are used for a pilot bearing between drive gear and mainshaft. Remove rollers from drive gear pocket or from bottom of case if they fell out when gear was removed.

3. Support rear unit with a bridge chain as shown in Fig. 5, across top of two internal capscrew holes while performing the next step.
4. From outside of case, remove eight remaining capscrews, three of which are located on filler plug side of main unit and five on the opposite side of the rear unit.
5. Using a pry bar, separate the two units, leveling the rear unit with a chain fall as shown in Fig. 6.

DISASSEMBLE FRONT UNIT

Main Drive Gear, Fig. 7

1. Lock transmission in two gears, then

Mainshaft & Gears, Fig. 9

1. Remove auxiliary unit mainshaft front bearing from auxiliary drive gear.
2. Cut lock wire and remove two washer bolts and retainer washer.

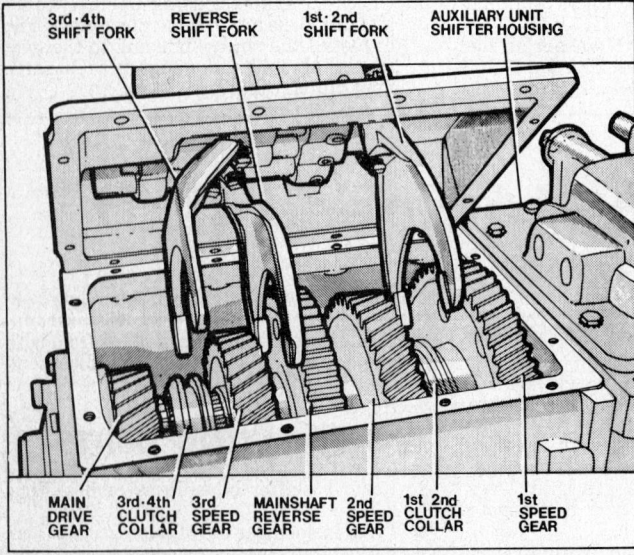

Fig. 3 Removal of front unit shifter housing

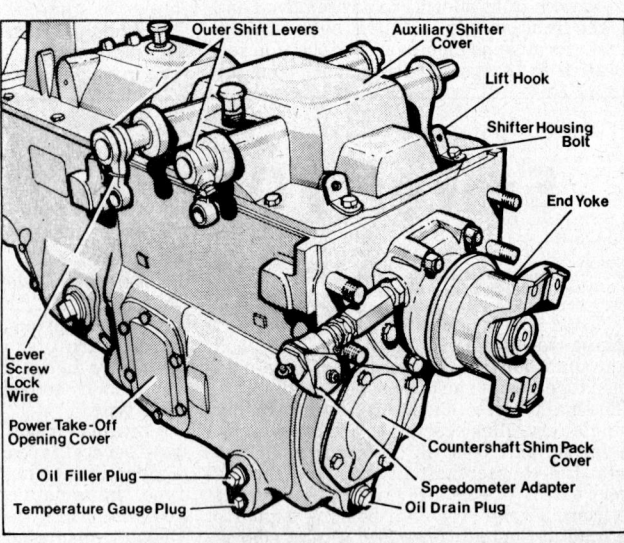

Fig. 4 Rear side view of transmission

SPICER TRANSMISSIONS

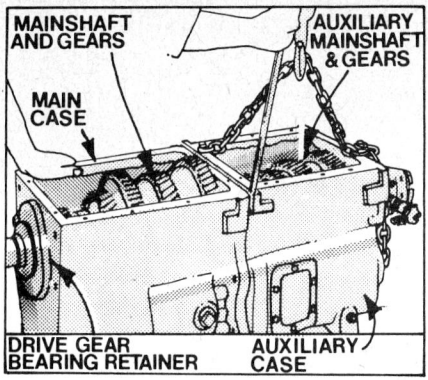

Fig. 5 Separating front and rear units

DISASSEMBLE REAR UNIT

Mainshaft, Fig. 14

1. Lock transmission in two gears and remove yoke nut. Then use a suitable puller to remove end yoke from mainshaft.
2. Referring to Fig. 15, remove capscrews from mainshaft and countershaft rear bearing caps. Separate bearing caps from gaskets and case, remove shim pack and tie together; then set aside for installation later.
3. Press rear bearing oil seal from cap. Remove speedometer bushing if it needs to be replaced at this time.
4. Remove speedometer drive gear and mainshaft rear bearing thrust washer if loose.
5. Use a soft hammer and tap forward on rear of mainshaft to start bearing off shaft.
6. Slide mainshaft and gears to rear of case as far as possible. Remove rear bearing with suitable puller, clamping on bearing snap ring.
7. Remove mainshaft rear bearing washer.
8. Remove mainshaft direct and overdrive clutch collar from its clutch gear by sliding forward off gear. Remove mainshaft in manner shown in Fig. 11.

Countershaft, Fig. 16

1. Remove snap ring from front of shaft and use a soft drift and hammer to tap countershaft forward, dislodging front bearing cup from case.
2. Remove countershaft rear and front snap rings from grooves, move rings forward on shaft as far as possible, then slide low speed gear forward as far as possible.
3. Use a soft drift to tap countershaft rearward to remove rear bearing cup from case. Lift countershaft up and out of case. The 1st speed gear need not be removed unless damaged.

3. Remove four bolts from drive gear bearing retainer.
4. Use a suitable puller to remove shaft and gear assembly, Fig. 10. First speed gear may be left in case for easier removal of shaft and gears as shown in Fig. 11.

Reverse Idler Gear, Fig. 12

1. Remove capscrew along with reverse idler gear shaft lock plate. Use a long through-bolt with a 1¾" × 6" tube and flat washer to pull reverse idler gear shaft from rear of case.
2. A slide hammer may be used as an option when removing shaft. Remove reverse idler gear sub-assembly as idler shaft pulls free. Remove thrust washers.

Countershaft, Fig. 13

1. Move countershaft assembly toward rear of case until rear bearing is free of case bore. Use a suitable puller to remove bearing from countershaft.
2. With countershaft free of front bearing, lift front end first and remove countershaft assembly from case. Inspect inside of case for lost rollers or reverse idler thrust washers.

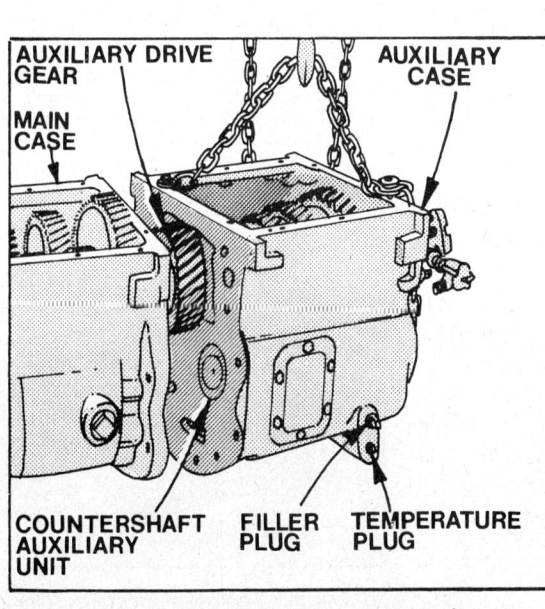

Fig. 6 Front and rear units separated

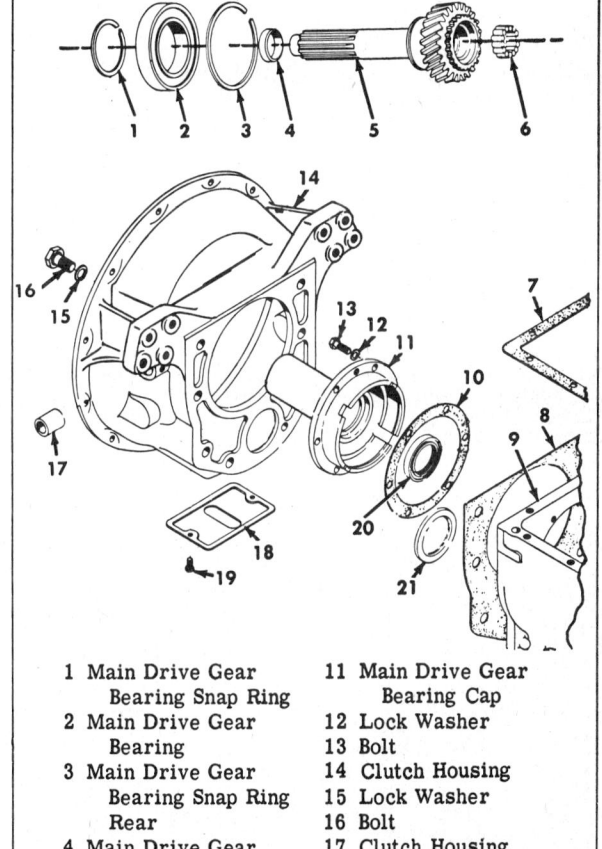

1. Main Drive Gear Bearing Snap Ring
2. Main Drive Gear Bearing
3. Main Drive Gear Bearing Snap Ring Rear
4. Main Drive Gear Wear Sleeve
5. Main Drive Gear
6. Mainshaft Front Bearing Rollers
7. Shifter Housing Gasket
8. Clutch Housing Gasket
9. Main Case
10. Main Drive Gear Bearing Cap Gasket
11. Main Drive Gear Bearing Cap
12. Lock Washer
13. Bolt
14. Clutch Housing
15. Lock Washer
16. Bolt
17. Clutch Housing Bushing
18. Clutch Housing Hand Hole Cover
19. Bolt
20. Main Drive Gear Bearing Cap Oil Seal
21. Countershaft Front Bearing Retainer

Fig. 7 Main drive gear and clutch housing components

SPICER TRANSMISSIONS

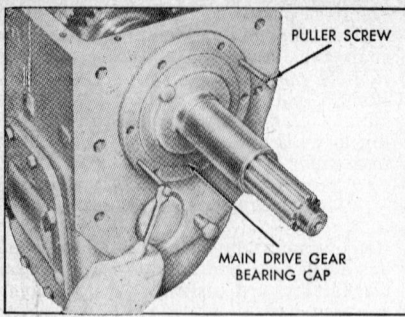

Fig. 8 Removal of main drive gear bearing cap

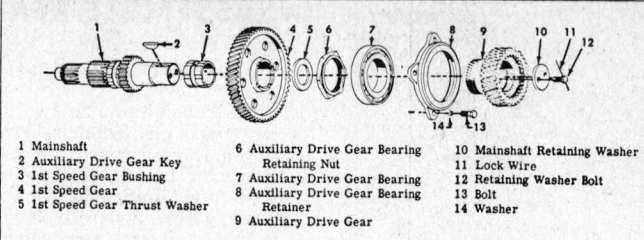

1. Mainshaft
2. Auxiliary Drive Gear Key
3. 1st Speed Gear Bushing
4. 1st Speed Gear
5. 1st Speed Gear Thrust Washer
6. Auxiliary Drive Gear Bearing Retaining Nut
7. Auxiliary Drive Gear Bearing
8. Auxiliary Drive Gear Bearing Retainer
9. Auxiliary Drive Gear
10. Mainshaft Retaining Washer
11. Lock Wire
12. Retaining Washer Bolt
13. Bolt
14. Washer

Fig. 9 Front unit mainshaft and gears

DISASSEMBLE SUB-ASSEMBLIES

Gearshift Housings

Refer to Figs. 17 through 25 and, if necessary, disassemble shifter housing as suggested by the illustrations.

Front Unit Mainshaft, Fig. 26

1. With assembly on bench, remove 3-4 clutch collar by sliding it off clutch gear.
2. Remove snap ring holding 3-4 clutch gear on shaft and remove gear.
3. Remove 1-2 clutch collar and 1st speed gear if not left in case.
4. Remove 1st speed gear bushing from shaft along with keys.
5. Remove 3rd speed gear from its sleeve, also reverse gear.
6. The 3rd speed gear sleeve and reverse clutch gear can be removed by placing shaft and 2nd speed gear in an arbor press. Support gear close to hub to prevent damage, then press shaft from sleeve and clutch gear.
7. Inspect 3rd speed gear sleeve pin for wear and replace if necessary.
8. Unstake drive gear bearing retainer nut (left-hand thread) and remove nut.
9. Place mainshaft drive gear and bearing assembly vertically in an arbor press with front threaded end up; use two 1/4" thick plates to support under bearing retainer. Press drive gear free from bearing and retainer.
10. Press retainer free from bearing.

Front Unit Countershaft, Fig. 13

1. From inside case remove countershaft front bearing from case bore.
2. Remove drive gear snap ring, 3rd gear snap ring, and 2nd gear snap ring.
3. Press gears off countershaft one at a time by supporting under gear as close to hub as possible. Remove keys one at a time as each gear is pressed from shaft.
4. If inner race of bearing remained on shaft at time of removal from case, remove it at this time. Use puller or drive off with drift tool.

Front Unit Reverse Idler, Fig. 13

1. Remove two sets of idler gear bearings and spacers from bore of idler gear.
2. If spacers are not with gear assembly, retrieve them from bottom of case.
3. Although bearings are identical, it is advisable to install in same location otherwise a different wear pattern will result.
4. Reverse idler gear shaft is larger on outer end; it must be installed in same position.

Rear Unit Mainshaft, Fig. 14

1. Slide 1st speed gear and 1-2 clutch collar off rear of shaft.
2. Remove 1st speed gear bushing if sleeve was not removed with gear.
3. Remove clutch gear snap ring.
4. Using a support under rear of 2nd speed gear, press mainshaft free of direct and overdrive clutch gear and from overdrive gear and sleeve.
5. Remove overdrive gear lock pin from inside overdrive sleeve.

Rear Unit Countershaft, Fig. 16

1. Use a puller to remove front and rear bearing cones.
2. Remove drive gear snap ring and support drive gear underneath with parallel bars as close to hub as possible. Press shaft free of gear.
3. Remove overdrive gear snap ring and support overdrive gear with bar stock on underside, then press countershaft free of gear.
4. Support 2nd speed gear in similar manner and press shaft free of gear.

ASSEMBLE SUB-ASSEMBLIES

Gearshift Housings

Refer to Figs. 17 through 25 and, if disassembled, assemble shifter housing as suggested by the illustration.

Front Unit Countershaft, Fig. 13

IMPORTANT: All countershaft gears should fit tight on the shaft. Since a shrink fit of .0015" to .003" is built into new parts, it presents a field assembly problem. If heat is needed to expand gear bores, boiling water, hot oil, steam or heat lamps are satisfactory. Do not exceed 250°F.

CAUTION: Do not use hot plates, acetylene torches or other methods that will turn the steel blue or straw color, and damage the heat-treated gears. If heat is not used, it is advisable to coat the gear bores with white lead to prevent galling or seizing of parts.

1. Assemble keys to shaft securely.
2. Using a suitable arbor press, support 2nd speed gear on its hub with chamfer and long end of hub up. Usually two pieces of 5/8" bar stock will serve this purpose well. Place countershaft in bore of gear. Align key and keyway and press shaft into gear until firmly seated against shoulder. Install 2nd speed gear snap ring.
3. Install 3rd speed gear snap ring on shaft. Using suitable bar stock, support 3rd speed gear as close to center of hub as possible to prevent damage to gear while pressing on shaft. Long end of gear hub should face down with chamfer up. Place shaft in bore and align key with keyway of gear. Press shaft into gear until firmly seated against snap ring face.
4. Support PTO gear in like manner on the short hub end, with chamfer and long end of hub up. Place shaft in chamfered bore, align key with gear keyway and press shaft into gear until seated firmly against 3rd speed gear.

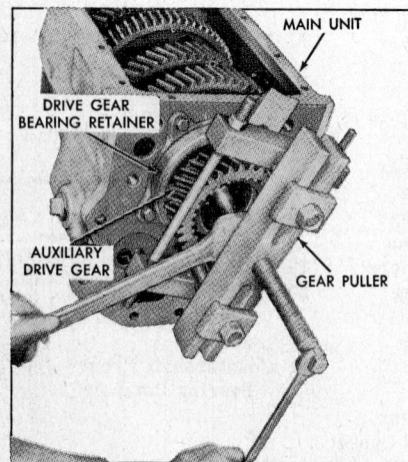

Fig. 10 Removal of auxiliary drive gear

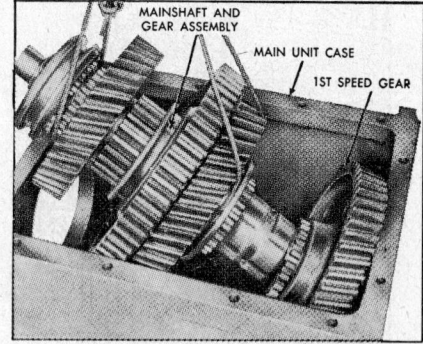

Fig. 11 Removal of mainshaft from main case

SPICER TRANSMISSIONS

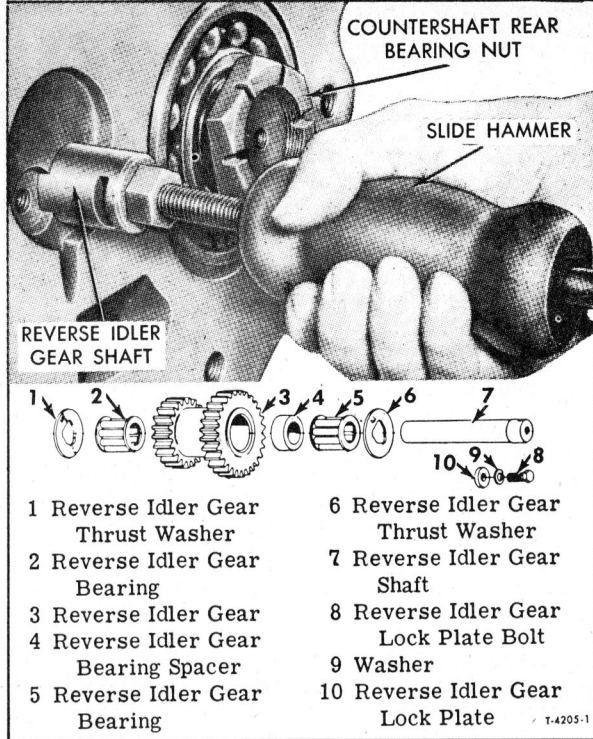

Fig. 12 Removal of reverse idler gear shaft

1. Reverse Idler Gear Thrust Washer
2. Reverse Idler Gear Bearing
3. Reverse Idler Gear
4. Reverse Idler Gear Bearing Spacer
5. Reverse Idler Gear Bearing
6. Reverse Idler Gear Thrust Washer
7. Reverse Idler Gear Shaft
8. Reverse Idler Gear Lock Plate Bolt
9. Washer
10. Reverse Idler Gear Lock Plate

5. Support drive gear on short end of hub with long hub and chamfer up. Place shaft in bore, align key with keyway, and press shaft into gear until firmly seated against PTO gear. Install drive gear snap ring on shaft to lock drive gear to shaft.
6. Press inner race of front roller bearing (flange toward gears) onto shaft until firmly seated against shoulder.

Front Unit Reverse Idler, Fig. 13

1. Hand-pack roller bearings with grease and install inside reverse idler gear at each end with spacer between the two bearings. Place the two thrust washers with assembly for installation with idler gear later.

Front Unit Main Drive Gear, Fig. 26

1. Place drive gear bearing on arbor press, supported underneath with bar stock at shoulder of inner race and with shield of bearing facing up. Press drive gear into inner bearing race until seated firmly against shoulder of drive gear.
2. Install snap ring in groove of drive gear, being sure it is properly seated.
3. Replace wear sleeve at this time if it was removed during disassembly.
4. To install a new bearing cap oil seal, press seal out of cap. Clean cap seal opening. Coat outside diameter of seal with gasket cement and press seal into cap. Lip of seal should face toward bearing. Coat lip of seal with caster oil or equivalent.
5. Place drive gear bearing cap over bearing and press cap into position. Install snap ring in groove provided on inside at rear of cap.
6. Assemble 14 pocket bearing rollers in drive gear. Coat bore of pocket with thick coat of chassis grease to set rollers in place. It is necessary to slide last roller in position endways because of the wedge effect of the other rollers.

Front Unit Mainshaft, Fig. 26

1. Fasten mainshaft vertically in a vise, using soft jaws to clamp on keyway end of shaft.
2. Install 2nd speed gear on shaft with clutch teeth down.
3. Install reverse clutch gear to shaft spline.
4. Install reverse gear to reverse clutch gear spline with fork groove up.
5. Install 3rd speed gear sleeve pin in sleeve. Slide sleeve on shaft, with flange of sleeve down, and head of sleeve pin in proper location in spline of shaft.
6. Install 3rd speed gear on shaft with teeth up and over sleeve.
7. Slide 3-4 clutch gear on shaft.
8. Install 3-4 clutch gear snap ring in groove to secure gear on shaft.
9. Remove mainshaft assembly from vise.
10. Assemble 1-2 clutch collar with long collar toward 2nd gear.
11. Install 1st gear bushing. Assemble 1st gear over bushing with clutch teeth of gear toward (or facing) 2nd gear. Install thrust washer against hub face of gear.
12. Assemble keys to shaft grooves.

NOTE: A rope or wire sling should be attached to the middle section of the mainshaft for easier lifting and positioning, Fig. 11.

13. Press bearing into main drive gear bearing retainer cap. Use a suitable tool to press on outer edge of bearing race.
14. Turn bearing and its retainer over on opposite side on press bed. Support inner race of bearing as close to center as possible to avoid damage to bearing. Press auxiliary drive gear into bearing bore until it seats against inner race of bearing.
15. Remove assembly from press. Install bearing retainer nut on drive gear. Hold gear in suitable manner in a vise and torque nut to 550–600 ft-lbs. Stake nut in three equally spaced places in grooves on drive gear provided for this purpose.

Rear Unit Countershaft, Fig. 16

CAUTION: All countershaft gears should fit tight on the shaft. As a shrink fit of .0015" to .003" is built into new parts, it presents a field assembly problem. If heat is used to expand gear bores, boiling water, hot oil or steam are usually satisfactory. Do not exceed 250°F.
Do not use hot plates, acetylene torches or other methods that would turn steel blue or straw color and damage the heat-treated gears. If heat is not used, it is advisable to coat

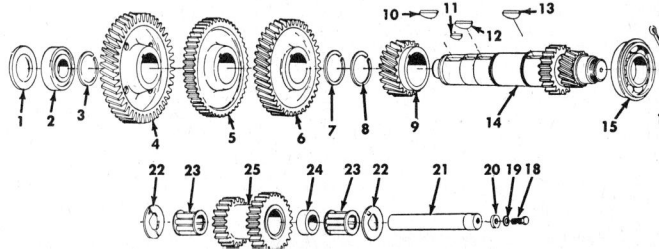

1. Countershaft Front Bearing Retainer
2. Countershaft Front Bearing
3. Countershaft Drive Gear Snap Ring
4. Countershaft Drive Gear
5. Countershaft PTO Gear
6. Countershaft 3rd Speed Gear
7. Countershaft 3rd Speed Gear Snap Ring
8. Countershaft 2nd Speed Gear Snap Ring
9. Countershaft 2nd Speed Gear
10. Countershaft Gear Key
11. Countershaft Gear Key
12. Countershaft Gear Key
13. Countershaft Gear Key
14. Countershaft
15. Countershaft Rear Bearing
16. Countershaft Rear Bearing Nut Cotter Pin
17. Countershaft Rear Bearing Nut
18. Reverse Idler Shaft Lock Bolt
19. Reverse Idler Shaft Lock Washer
20. Reverse Idler Shaft Lock Plate
21. Reverse Idler Gear Shaft
22. Reverse Idler Gear Thrust Washer
23. Reverse Idler Gear Bearing
24. Reverse Idler Gear Bearing Spacer
25. Reverse Idler Gear

Fig. 13 Front unit countershaft and reverse idler gears

SPICER TRANSMISSIONS

the gear bores heavily with white lead to prevent galling or seizing of parts.

1. Install keys to shaft, seating them firmly.
2. Support 2nd speed gear in arbor press with long hub down and chamfer up. Set countershaft into position. Align keys with keyways and press shaft into gear until seated firmly against gear hub.
3. Support hub of overdrive gear with long hub down and chamfer up. Set countershaft into position. Align key with keyway and press shaft into gear. Seat shoulder firmly against shoulder of 2nd speed gear.
4. Assemble overdrive gear snap ring to lock 2nd and overdrive gear on shaft.
5. Support drive gear in press with long hub and chamfer up. Set countershaft in position, align key with keyway and press shaft into gear until seated firmly against shoulder.
6. Install drive gear snap ring.
7. Support countershaft in press. Use tubing to press and seat cones of front and rear tapered roller bearings against countershaft shoulders.

Rear Unit Mainshaft, Fig. 14

1. Lubricate all mainshaft free-running gear bearing bores with a light film of grease as gears are assembled to shaft. *Do not plug oil holes with grease.*
2. Position mainshaft vertically in a vise, using soft jaws to clamp on output splines.
3. Install 2nd gear to shaft with clutching teeth down. Insert new lock pin inside fluted overdrive sleeve. Do not press or drive against ground thrust face or flange of sleeve.
4. With flanged end of overdrive sleeve down, align lock pin with mainshaft spline. Push or tap fluted sleeve onto shaft against shoulder on shaft.
5. Install overdrive gear on shaft with clutch teeth up.
6. Install 3-4 clutch gear to shaft. Secure with snap ring. Assemble drive gear pocket bearing to front of shaft. Since bearing fits tight on surface of shaft, it will be necessary to use tubing to drive bearing on. To avoid damage, drive against inner race of bearing. Assemble 3-4 speed clutch collar on clutch gear. *Assemble roller bearing with snap ring in outer race so that snap ring is toward mainshaft.*
7. Turn mainshaft end for end in vise and clamp on 3-4 speed clutch gear.
8. Assemble 1-2 speed clutch collar with long hub down and toward 2nd speed gear.
9. Slide 1st speed gear bushing on shaft and coat fluted area with light grease.
10. Assemble 1st speed gear to shaft sleeve with clutching teeth toward front of mainshaft.

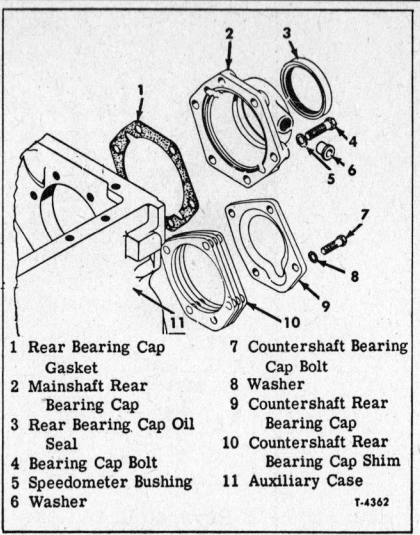

1 Rear Bearing Cap Gasket
2 Mainshaft Rear Bearing Cap
3 Rear Bearing Cap Oil Seal
4 Bearing Cap Bolt
5 Speedometer Bushing
6 Washer
7 Countershaft Bearing Cap Bolt
8 Washer
9 Countershaft Rear Bearing Cap
10 Countershaft Rear Bearing Cap Shim
11 Auxiliary Case

Fig. 15 Auxiliary unit rear bearing caps

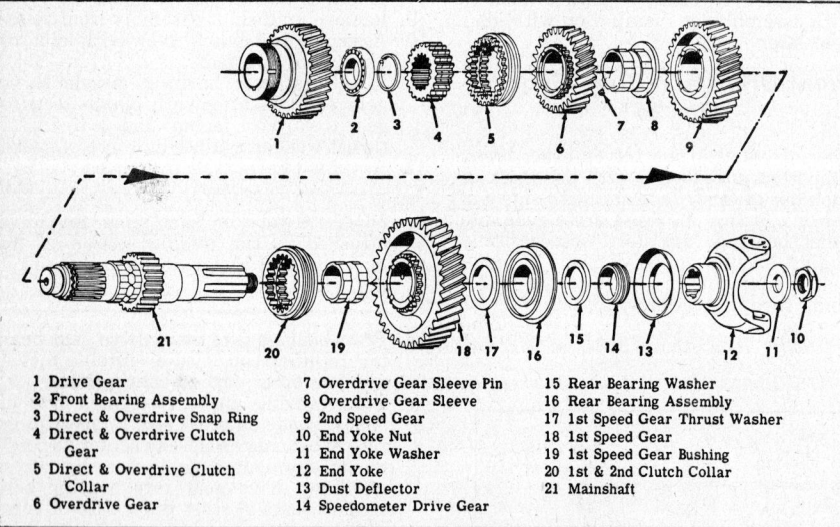

1 Drive Gear
2 Front Bearing Assembly
3 Direct & Overdrive Snap Ring
4 Direct & Overdrive Clutch Gear
5 Direct & Overdrive Clutch Collar
6 Overdrive Gear
7 Overdrive Gear Sleeve Pin
8 Overdrive Gear Sleeve
9 2nd Speed Gear
10 End Yoke Nut
11 End Yoke Washer
12 End Yoke
13 Dust Deflector
14 Speedometer Drive Gear
15 Rear Bearing Washer
16 Rear Bearing Assembly
17 1st Speed Gear Thrust Washer
18 1st Speed Gear
19 1st Speed Gear Bushing
20 1st & 2nd Clutch Collar
21 Mainshaft

Fig. 14 Auxiliary unit mainshaft and gears

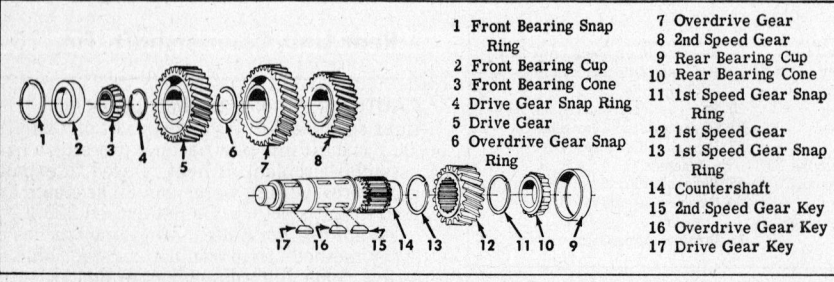

1 Front Bearing Snap Ring
2 Front Bearing Cup
3 Front Bearing Cone
4 Drive Gear Snap Ring
5 Drive Gear
6 Overdrive Gear Snap Ring
7 Overdrive Gear
8 2nd Speed Gear
9 Rear Bearing Cup
10 Rear Bearing Cone
11 1st Speed Gear Snap Ring
12 1st Speed Gear
13 1st Speed Gear Snap Ring
14 Countershaft
15 2nd Speed Gear Key
16 Overdrive Gear Key
17 Drive Gear Key

Fig. 16 Auxiliary unit countershaft components

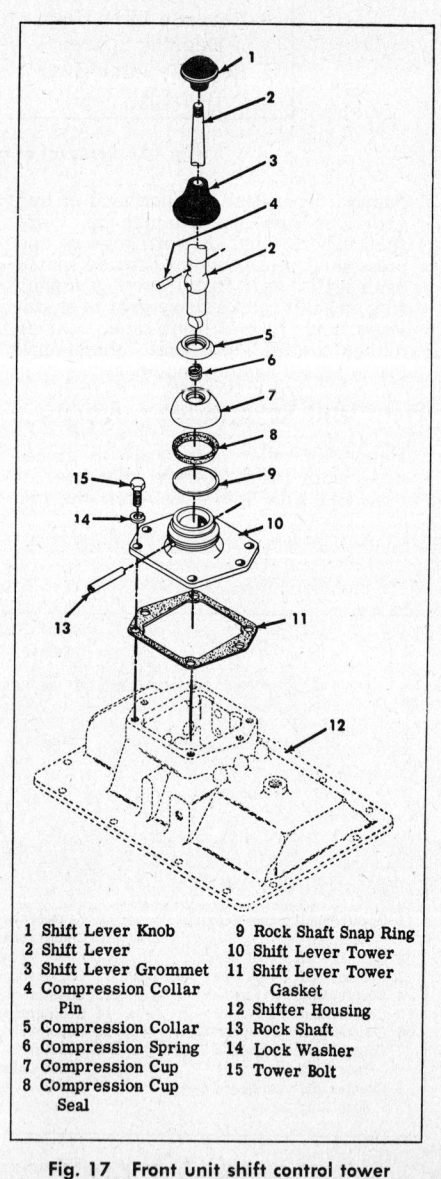

1 Shift Lever Knob
2 Shift Lever
3 Shift Lever Grommet
4 Compression Collar Pin
5 Compression Collar
6 Compression Spring
7 Compression Cup
8 Compression Cup Seal
9 Rock Shaft Snap Ring
10 Shift Lever Tower
11 Shift Lever Tower Gasket
12 Shifter Housing
13 Rock Shaft
14 Lock Washer
15 Tower Bolt

Fig. 17 Front unit shift control tower

SPICER TRANSMISSIONS

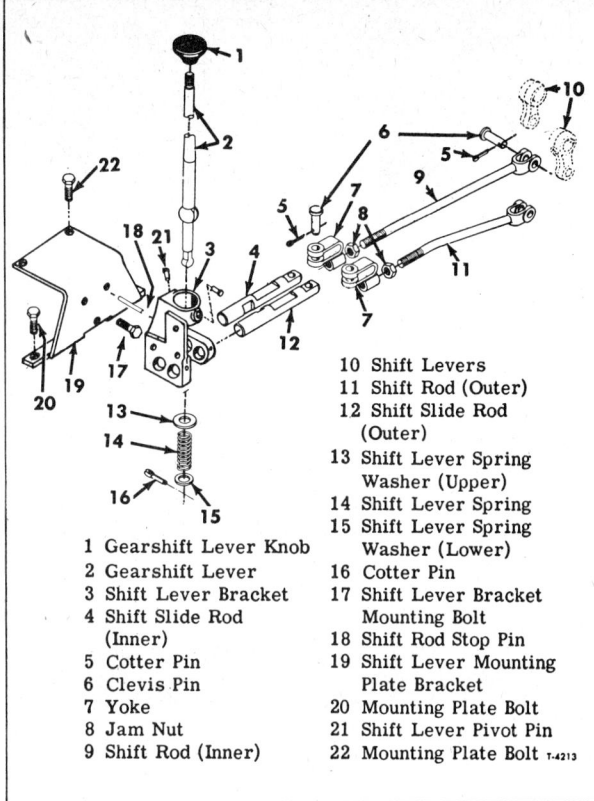

Fig. 18 Auxiliary unit shift control and bracket

1 Gearshift Lever Knob
2 Gearshift Lever
3 Shift Lever Bracket
4 Shift Slide Rod (Inner)
5 Cotter Pin
6 Clevis Pin
7 Yoke
8 Jam Nut
9 Shift Rod (Inner)
10 Shift Levers
11 Shift Rod (Outer)
12 Shift Slide Rod (Outer)
13 Shift Lever Spring Washer (Upper)
14 Shift Lever Spring
15 Shift Lever Spring Washer (Lower)
16 Cotter Pin
17 Shift Lever Bracket Mounting Bolt
18 Shift Rod Stop Pin
19 Shift Lever Mounting Plate Bracket
20 Mounting Plate Bolt
21 Shift Lever Pivot Pin
22 Mounting Plate Bolt

Mainshaft

1. Lift shaft and gear assembly into case by means of overhead hoist and wire and chain sling, Fig. 11. Position gears so they mesh with countershaft gears.
2. Lubricate two keys and mainshaft diameter with grease or white lead for easier assembly of bearing retainer and drive gear, and assemble to shaft.

NOTE: Two methods can be used to press the auxiliary drive gear and bearing retainer assembly on mainshaft and keys. The first method requires the use of a hydraulic press with a minimum press power of 50 tons. If not available, the second method using puller arrangement will be necessary.

3. If a hydraulic press is available, a case bore pilot and spacer block is required. The block diameter should be $6^{1}/_{2}''$ with a thickness of $1^{3}/_{4}''$.
   a. With mainshaft and gears assembled in case, move entire case to hydraulic press. Before placing unit on press bed, insert spacer block tool into front bore of case. Place case with front end down on press and opening to gears facing press operator.
   b. Place auxiliary drive gear and bearing retainer on end of mainshaft and in line with keys. With a light press, start drive gear and retainer on shaft and keys. Visually align bearing outer race diameter with case bore as assembly is pressed on shaft. Just before bearing retainer flange has bottomed itself against the case surface, adjust retainer flange holes to case holes. Press drive gear and bearing retainer on shaft until flange is flush against face of case.
   c. Relieve press pressure and remove unit from press. Install lock plate to rear of mainshaft and secure with bolts. Torque bolts to 40-45 ft-lbs. Then tie with lock wire, Fig. 27.
   d. With bearing retainer flange holes aligned with holes in case, install and torque bolts to 40-50 ft-lbs.

ASSEMBLE FRONT UNIT

Countershaft

1. Before installation of countershaft and gears in case, check case front bearing retainer. It must be installed in front bearing bore securely. Install outer cup of front bearing into case bore.
2. Lower countershaft assembly into case with rear end through opening. Align front end of shaft with front bearing. Tap into partial position.

NOTE: To prevent damage to front bearing as rear bearing is being driven on countershaft, place two strips of $3/8''$ flat stock between countershaft drive gear and front wall of case.

3. Position bearing on rear end of countershaft with shield and snap ring of bearing facing toward rear. Align shaft and bearing with case bore. Use tubing to drive bearing until seated against shoulder of shaft.
4. Remove $3/8''$ strips of flat stock. Tap shaft the rest of the way or until snap ring of rear bearing rests against recessed shoulder of rear bearing bore.
5. Start and turn bearing nut against bearing finger-tight. Nut will be tightened after mainshaft and main drive gear have been assembled in case.

Reverse Idler Gear

1. Position idler gear in case with large gear toward rear. Place thrust washers one at each end of gear. Mesh with countershaft gear teeth and align bore of bearings with bore in case.
2. Insert idler gear shaft (long end first) through opening in rear of case and into idler gear bearings. Align slot on rear of shaft for lock plate and tap into final position.
3. Install lock plate into case and secure with capscrew and lockwasher.

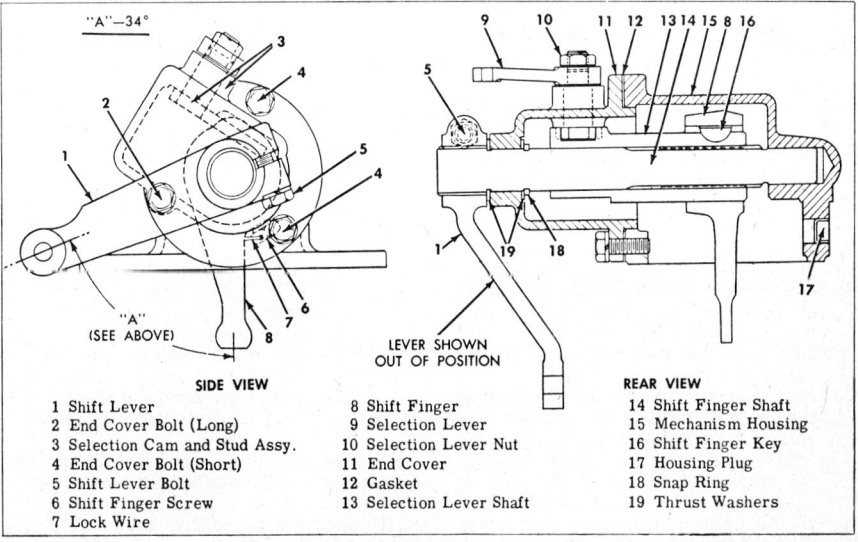

1 Shift Lever
2 End Cover Bolt (Long)
3 Selection Cam and Stud Assy.
4 End Cover Bolt (Short)
5 Shift Finger Screw
6 Shift Finger Screw
7 Lock Wire
8 Shift Finger
9 Selection Lever
10 Selection Lever Nut
11 End Cover
12 Gasket
13 Selection Lever Shaft
14 Shift Finger Shaft
15 Mechanism Housing
16 Shift Finger Key
17 Housing Plug
18 Snap Ring
19 Thrust Washers

Fig. 19 Lever type remote control

387

SPICER TRANSMISSIONS

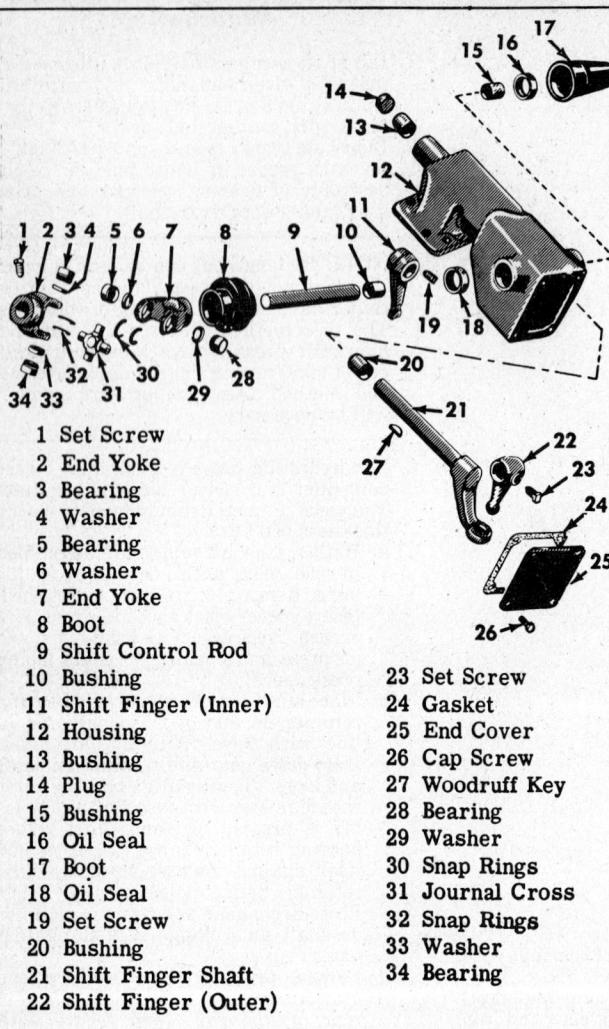

1 Set Screw
2 End Yoke
3 Bearing
4 Washer
5 Bearing
6 Washer
7 End Yoke
8 Boot
9 Shift Control Rod
10 Bushing
11 Shift Finger (Inner)
12 Housing
13 Bushing
14 Plug
15 Bushing
16 Oil Seal
17 Boot
18 Oil Seal
19 Set Screw
20 Bushing
21 Shift Finger Shaft
22 Shift Finger (Outer)
23 Set Screw
24 Gasket
25 End Cover
26 Cap Screw
27 Woodruff Key
28 Bearing
29 Washer
30 Snap Rings
31 Journal Cross
32 Snap Rings
33 Washer
34 Bearing

Fig. 20 Prop shaft type remote control

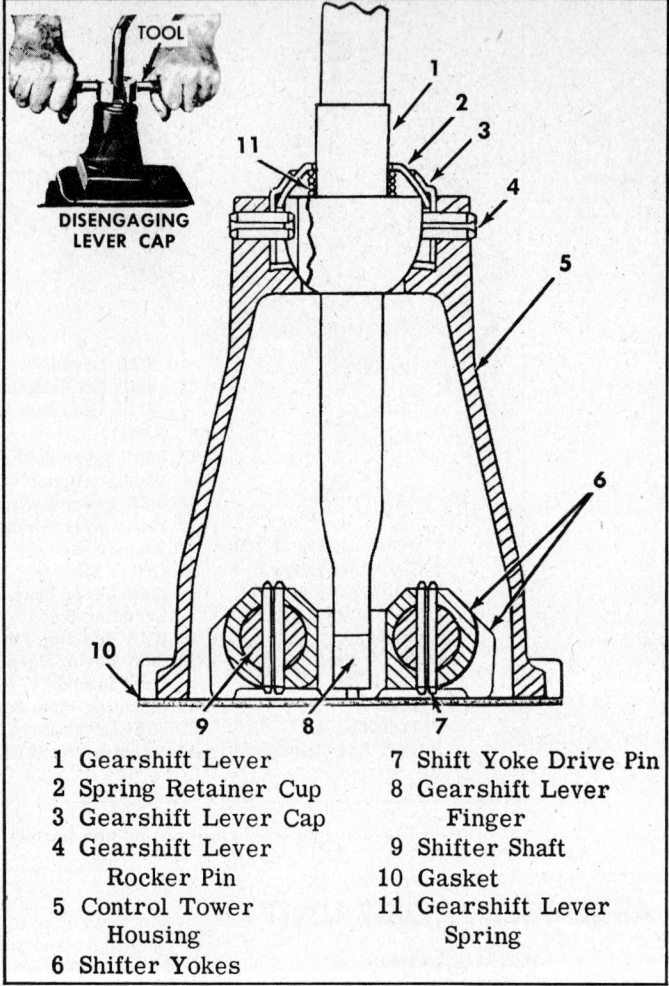

1 Gearshift Lever
2 Spring Retainer Cup
3 Gearshift Lever Cap
4 Gearshift Lever Rocker Pin
5 Control Tower Housing
6 Shifter Yokes
7 Shift Yoke Drive Pin
8 Gearshift Lever Finger
9 Shifter Shaft
10 Gasket
11 Gearshift Lever Spring

Fig. 21 Auxiliary unit type shift tower

4. If the puller arrangement method is to be used it will be necessary to make a push spacer to the following dimensions:
   a. Use round steel stock $2^{11/16}$" in diameter and cut to $2^{3/8}$" long. Drill two $9/16$" holes $5/8$" from center of spacer for each hole. Drill holes completely through stock from one end to the other. These holes must be drilled accurately enough to line up with holes in mainshaft.
   b. Secure two hardened bolts ($1/2$-20 and $4^{7/8}$" in length) plus two thrust washers to fit bolt diameter, and several flat washers of same hole diameter size. Install spacer washers on bolts and position washer against underside of bolt head. Place each bolt into holes of spacer push tool and through bolt holes in auxiliary drive gear. Start bolts into threaded bolt holes in back end of mainshaft.
   c. Progressively tighten each bolt, using the spare washers under bolt heads to obtain full movement of drive gear onto mainshaft and keys. Before bearing retainer bottoms against face of case, align flange holes to case holes. Finish tightening bolts until bearing retainer is flush against case.
   d. Remove special bolts and push spacer from shaft. Secure bearing retainer to case and torque bolts to 40-50 ft-lbs. Install lock plate and torque bolts to 40-50 ft-lbs. Install lock wire as shown in Fig. 27.
5. Assemble 3-4 clutch gear collar on clutch gear before assembling main drive gear and bearng cap sub-assembly to transmission.

Main Drive Gear

1. Check drive gear pocket to make sure that all 14 rollers are properly positioned inside pocket.
2. Apply gasket cement to drive gear bearing cap gasket and stick gasket on cap. Apply cement to opposite side of gasket.
3. Install drive gear and bearing cap to front of case. Use a soft head hammer to tap into position and check on pocket rollers to make sure they are still intact.
4. Secure bearing cap to case and torque bolts to 60-80 ft-lbs.
5. Secure case firmly and lock gears, then tighten countershaft rear bearing nut to 400-450 ft-lbs.
6. Place gears in neutral and rotate drive gear to check for free rotation of all gears and shafts.

ASSEMBLE REAR UNIT

Countershaft

1. Lower rear end of countershaft assembly into auxiliary case. Slide end of shaft and 1st speed gear out through rear of case. Lower front of shaft into its approximate position and maintain alignment with a cable, or support underneath by blocking up at countershaft drive gear.
2. Use a soft hammer to tap front and rear roller bearing cups into case and over bearing cones on countershaft. Install snap ring to front bore of case.
3. Assemble rear bearing cap and shim pack to case. Torque capscrews to 35-40 ft-lbs. Check bearing end play. Add or remove shims as required to obtain .001" to .003" play. Individual shims are available in various thicknesses.
4. After correct adjustment is made, remove rear bearing cap and coat both sides of shim pack with gasket cement. Install bearing cap and torque capscrews to 35-40 ft-lbs.

Mainshaft

1. Lower rear of shaft assembly, Fig. 11, into case and out through rear bearing bore.

SPICER TRANSMISSIONS

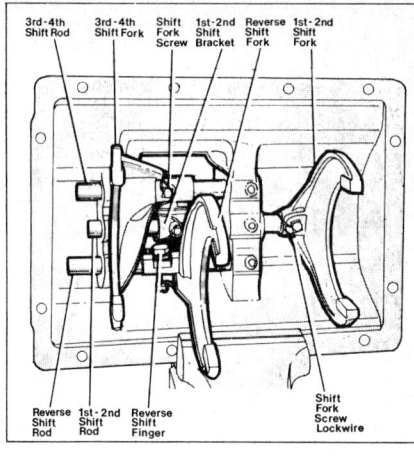

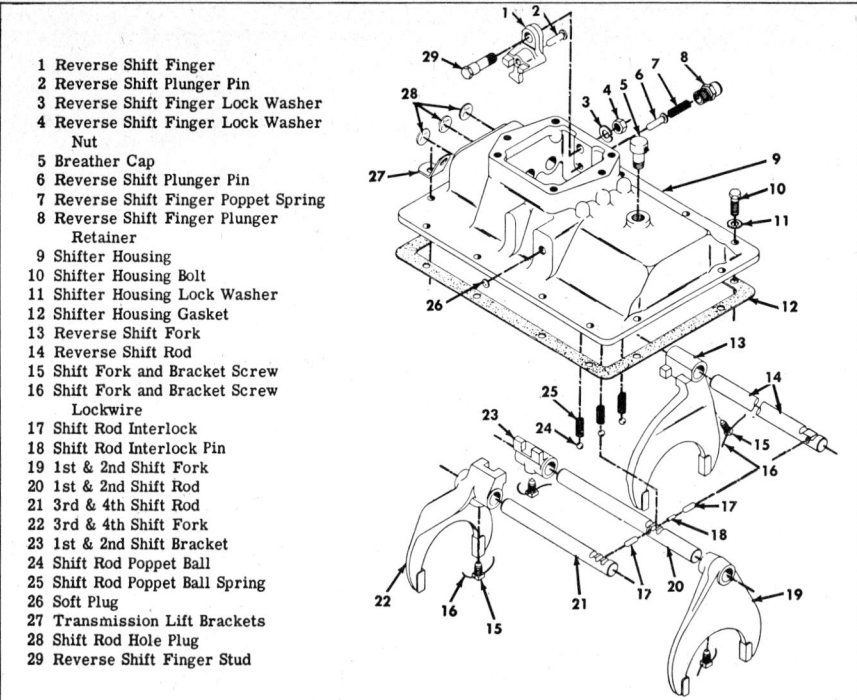

1. Reverse Shift Finger
2. Reverse Shift Plunger Pin
3. Reverse Shift Finger Lock Washer
4. Reverse Shift Finger Lock Washer Nut
5. Breather Cap
6. Reverse Shift Plunger Pin
7. Reverse Shift Finger Poppet Spring
8. Reverse Shift Finger Plunger Retainer
9. Shifter Housing
10. Shifter Housing Bolt
11. Shifter Housing Lock Washer
12. Shifter Housing Gasket
13. Reverse Shift Fork
14. Reverse Shift Rod
15. Shift Fork and Bracket Screw
16. Shift Fork and Bracket Screw Lockwire
17. Shift Rod Interlock
18. Shift Rod Interlock Pin
19. 1st & 2nd Shift Fork
20. 1st & 2nd Shift Rod
21. 3rd & 4th Shift Rod
22. 3rd & 4th Shift Fork
23. 1st & 2nd Shift Bracket
24. Shift Rod Poppet Ball
25. Shift Rod Poppet Ball Spring
26. Soft Plug
27. Transmission Lift Brackets
28. Shift Rod Hole Plug
29. Reverse Shift Finger Stud

Fig. 22 Main unit shifter housing

Fig. 23 Front shifter housing

Lower front of shaft into position and mesh all gears with countershaft gears.
2. Coat thrust face of 1st speed gear washer with light grease and assemble on rear of mainshaft, with flat face toward 1st speed gear.
3. Use a 3/4" piece of stock to block mainshaft across drive gear bearing cap opening at front of case. Position mainshaft rear bearing on shaft with snap ring to rear. Use care to align outer race of bearing with case bore. Drive bearing on shaft with suitable piece of tubing against inner race of bearing until bearing is seated against washer. Remove 3/4" stock and tap bearing into case bore until snap ring seats against case.
4. If necessary, replace speedometer drive gear bushing in rear bearing cap.
5. Apply a light coat of gasket cement to O.D. of rear bearing cap oil seal. Press into cap.
6. Apply gasket cement to rear bearing cap gasket and place gasket on cap. Align oil passages as necessary.
7. Apply cement to other side of gasket. Assemble bearing cap and gasket to rear of case. Dip threads of bolts in gasket cement and install in case with washers. Torque bolts to 60–80 ft-lbs.
8. Assemble end yoke to mainshaft. Install flat washer and nut and torque nut to 400–450 ft-lbs.

ASSEMBLE FRONT & REAR UNITS

1. Install clutch housing to front unit, tightening retaining bolts to 90–95 ft-lbs. Install clutch release parts to clutch housing if previously removed.
2. Position front unit up vertically on clutch housing.
3. Secure rear unit direct and overdrive clutch gear collar to overdrive gear, or insert collar into rear of auxiliary drive gear. Note that clutch teeth of clutch collar point toward auxiliary drive gear.
4. Assemble gasket on front unit rear case surface. Install mainshaft front bearing in auxiliary drive gear bore.
5. Lift rear unit with chain fall safely attached to output yoke and suspend unit vertically over front unit.
6. Carefully lower rear unit into place. Use caution to align rear unit mainshaft with front bearing in rear of auxiliary drive gear of front unit with teeth of countershaft drive gear of auxiliary unit.
7. Bolt two units together, using the four drilled head bolts and lock-washers on upper inside holes of rear unit case.
8. Install remaining bolts, then progressively tighten and pull cases together. Torque all bolts to 120–150 ft-lbs. Secure four inside bolts with lock wire. Tie two side bolts together.
9. Use chain fall to lift entire assembly and lower to a horizontal position.
10. Install shifter housing.

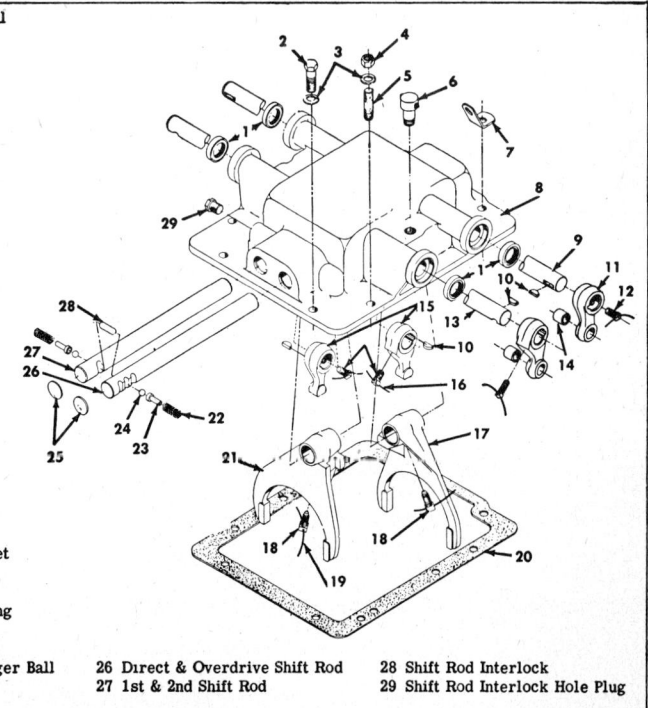

1. Outer Shift Lever Seal
2. Shifter Housing Cap Screw
3. Shifter Housing Cap Screw Lock Washer
4. Housing Stud Nut
5. Shifter Cover Stud
6. Breather
7. Lift Bracket
8. Auxiliary Shifter Housing
9. Cross Shaft Rod
10. Cross Shaft Woodruff Key
11. Outer Shift Lever
12. Outer Shift Lever Set Screw
13. Cross Shaft Rod
14. Outer Shift Lever Bushing
15. Inner Shift Finger
16. Inner Finger Screw Lockwire
17. 1st & 2nd Shift Fork
18. Inner Finger Lock Screw
19. Inner Finger Lock Screw Lockwire
20. Shifter Housing Gasket
21. Direct & Overdrive Shift Fork
22. Shift Rod Poppet Spring
23. Shift Rod Poppet Plunger
24. Shift Rod Poppet Plunger Ball
25. Shift Rod Hole Plug
26. Direct & Overdrive Shift Rod
27. 1st & 2nd Shift Rod
28. Shift Rod Interlock
29. Shift Rod Interlock Hole Plug

Fig. 24 Auxiliary unit shifter housing

SPICER TRANSMISSIONS

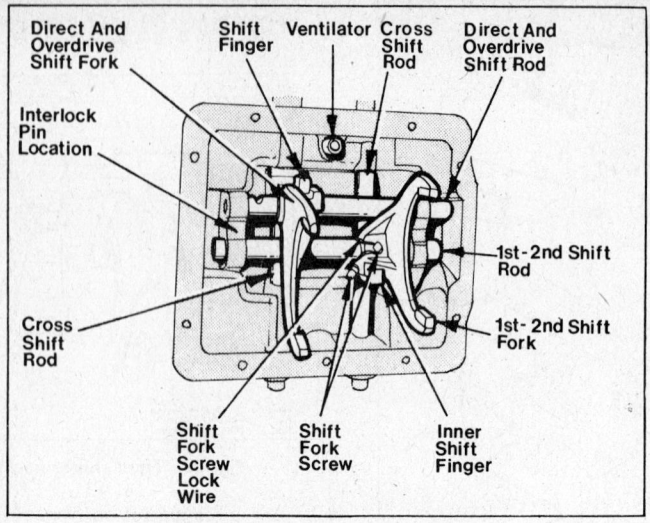

Fig. 25 Auxiliary shifter housing

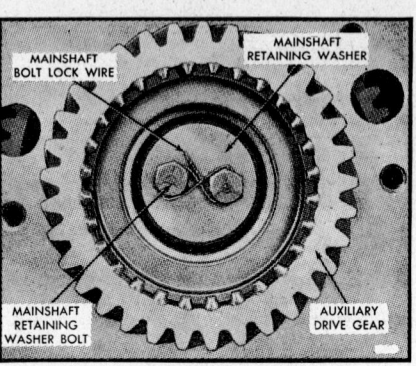

Fig. 27 Auxiliary drive gear and lock plate installed

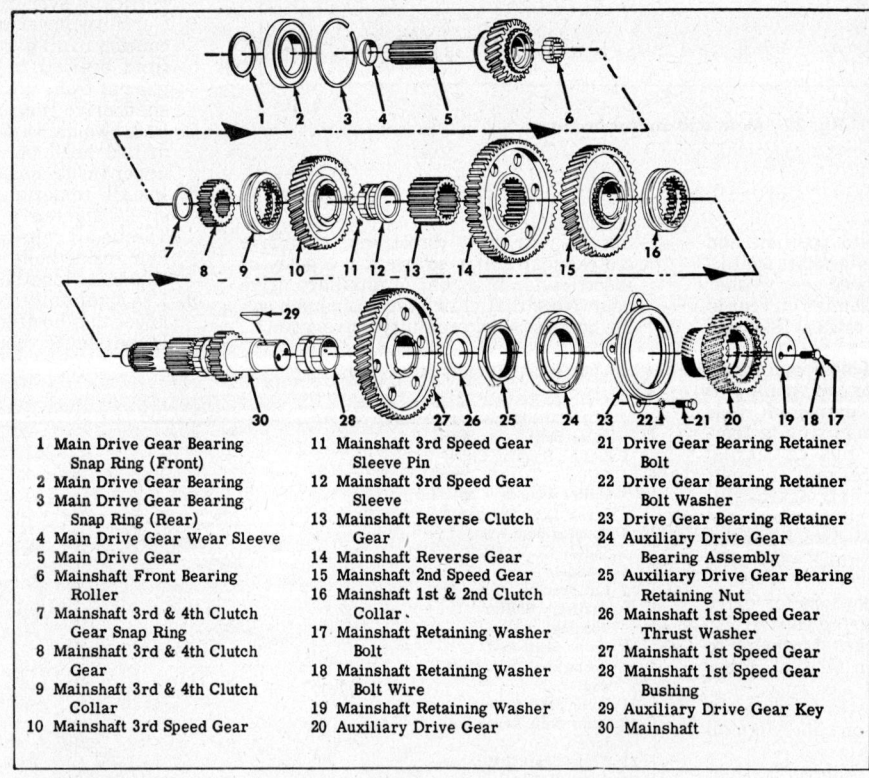

1. Main Drive Gear Bearing Snap Ring (Front)
2. Main Drive Gear Bearing
3. Main Drive Gear Bearing Snap Ring (Rear)
4. Main Drive Gear Wear Sleeve
5. Main Drive Gear
6. Mainshaft Front Bearing Roller
7. Mainshaft 3rd & 4th Clutch Gear Snap Ring
8. Mainshaft 3rd & 4th Clutch Gear
9. Mainshaft 3rd & 4th Clutch Collar
10. Mainshaft 3rd Speed Gear
11. Mainshaft 3rd Speed Gear Sleeve Pin
12. Mainshaft 3rd Speed Gear Sleeve
13. Mainshaft Reverse Clutch Gear
14. Mainshaft Reverse Gear
15. Mainshaft 2nd Speed Gear
16. Mainshaft 1st & 2nd Clutch Collar
17. Mainshaft Retaining Washer Bolt
18. Mainshaft Retaining Washer Bolt Wire
19. Mainshaft Retaining Washer
20. Auxiliary Drive Gear
21. Drive Gear Bearing Retainer Bolt
22. Drive Gear Bearing Retainer Bolt Washer
23. Drive Gear Bearing Retainer
24. Auxiliary Drive Gear Bearing Assembly
25. Auxiliary Drive Gear Bearing Retaining Nut
26. Mainshaft 1st Speed Gear Thrust Washer
27. Mainshaft 1st Speed Gear
28. Mainshaft 1st Speed Gear Bushing
29. Auxiliary Drive Gear Key
30. Mainshaft

Fig. 26 Main unit mainshaft and gears

Spicer Transmissions
Spicer 8016 & 8216—16 Speed Unit

DESCRIPTION

This unit consists of two 4-speed transmissions joined together with a separate shift lever for each unit. The shift lever for the rear unit is mounted on a bracket bolted to the front unit. The rear unit is operated by means of shift rods from the shift control assembly.

When used on a Tilt Cab model, it is equipped with a remote control cab unit and transmission slave unit, with the rear unit being shifted by means of control cables attached to a shift control assembly in the cab, similar to the controls used with auxiliary transmissions.

Figs. 1 through 5 are exploded views of the various shift control assemblies. The following material covers the disassembly and reassembly of the front and rear gear boxes.

SEPARATING UNITS

1. From inside of rear case, cut lock wire and remove two capscrews.
2. Use a bridge chain across the two internal capscrew holes to support rear unit.
3. Remove six remaining capscrews joining front and rear units from outside case.
4. Using a pry bar, separate the two units, leveling rear unit with a chain fall.

NOTE: As the two units are separated, the mainshaft drive gear bearing retainer, Fig. 6, will pull free of rear case. This allows the integral mainshaft rear drive pinion to pass through the front bearing bore of the rear case and remain with the front unit.

The pocket bearing is the separable type. It may remain intact on the rear mainshaft, stay in the drive pinion pocket or the bearing may separate as the cases are parted.

DISASSEMBLE FRONT UNIT—FIG. 6

Drive Pinion & Clutch, Disassemble

1. Lock transmission in two gears by engaging 3-4 speed clutch collar with drive gear and reverse sliding gear with 2nd speed gear.
2. Remove countershaft rear bearing retaining lockscrew. Remove washer from retaining pin.
3. Remove capscrew attaching *long* clutch release shaft to clutch release yoke. Remove key. Tap release shaft free of yoke and remove through side of clutch housing. Slide yoke and *short* shaft toward inside of housing and remove as a unit.
4. Remove four capscrews from drive pinion bearing cap. Use two 7/16" puller screws to free bearing cap and drive pinion assembly from case bore. Remove as an assembly.
5. Remove snap ring from drive pinion bearing cap and press cap free of bearing.
6. Remove nut from drive pinion.
7. Support outer race of bearing and press drive pinion free of bearing.
8. Remove mainshaft pocket bearing.

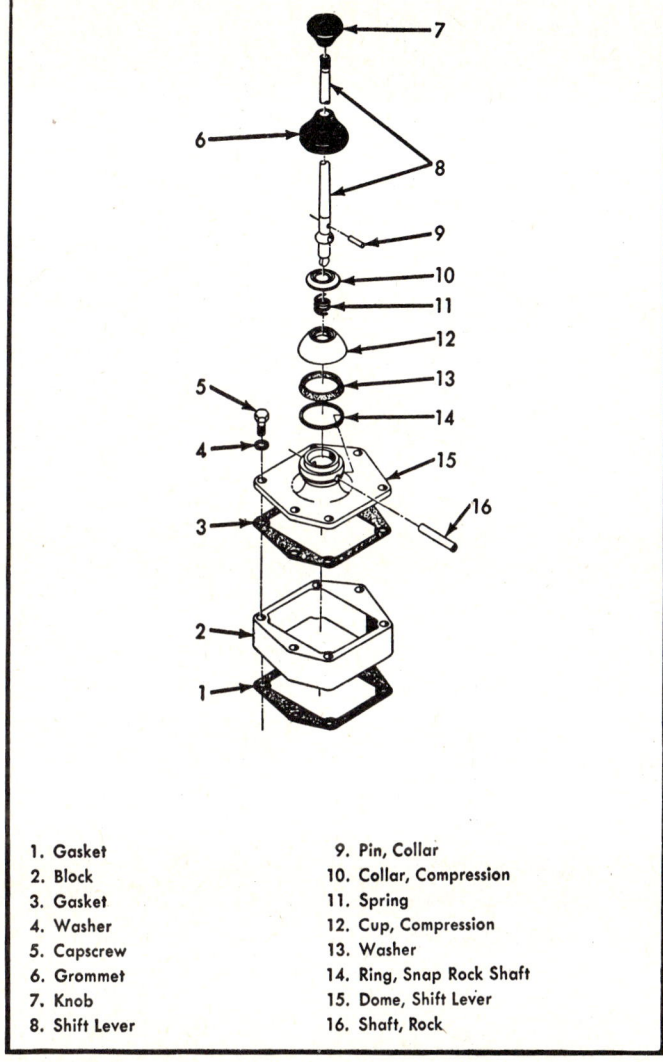

1. Gasket
2. Block
3. Gasket
4. Washer
5. Capscrew
6. Grommet
7. Knob
8. Shift Lever
9. Pin, Collar
10. Collar, Compression
11. Spring
12. Cup, Compression
13. Washer
14. Ring, Snap Rock Shaft
15. Dome, Shift Lever
16. Shaft, Rock

Fig. 1 Front unit overhead control

Mainshaft, Disassemble

1. Remove front pocket bearing or parts if any remained on mainshaft.
2. Remove rear pocket bearing or parts if any remained while separating the units.
3. Unstake mainshaft 3-4 clutch gear locknut. Using a spanner wrench, remove locknut *which has a left-hand thread*.
4. Slide 3-4 clutch collar from clutch gear.

NOTE: It is impossible to remove the mainshaft from internal gears without dropping any or all of the 154 roller bearings used in the bore of the 1st speed gear. Use caution to prevent loss of bearings as mainshaft is removed from gear.

5. Using a long drift, remove mainshaft by tapping rearward through gears and sleeves, removing each sub-assembly as mainshaft is being tapped through in the following order: (a) 3-4 clutch gear, (b) 3rd gear with sleeve, roller bearings and spacer, (c) 2nd gear with sleeve, bearings and spacer, (d) reverse sliding gear with clutch gear, (e) 1st speed gear with spacer and remaining needle bearings.
6. Remove 1st speed gear thrust washer.
7. Unstake bearing locknut and remove with wrench or hammer and drift. *Nut has a left-hand thread.*
8. Place mainshaft and bearing sub-assembly vertically in arbor press with front end up and press shaft free of bearing.
9. Press bearing retainer free of bearing. Discard two retainer seals.

Reverse Idler Gear, Disassemble

1. Remove reverse idler shaft lock plate.
2. Using a puller bolt and a piece of suitable tubing, remove idler gear shaft.
3. Remove idler gear, two sets of bearings

391

SPICER TRANSMISSIONS

and sleeve as an assembly.
4. Remove two sets of bearings and gear from sleeve. Remove key.

Countershaft, Disassemble

1. Remove rear bearing retainer capscrew, lockwasher and retainer wahser.
2. Move countershaft sub-assembly toward rear of case until rear bearing is free of case bore. Use a suitable puller to remove bearing from countershaft.
3. Remove countershaft from case by lifting front end up first.
4. Use a suitable puller to remove countershaft front bearing from case bore.
5. Remove countershaft drive gear snap ring.
6. Press gears off countershaft one at a time by supporting behind gears as close to hub as possible.
7. Remove woodruff keys.

Clutch Housing, Remove

NOTE: It is not necessary to remove clutch housing unless it is damaged or if gasket is allowing oil leak.

1. If removal is required, it will be necessary to remove main drive pinion bearing cap if not done previously during disassembly.
2. Remove capscrews from inside clutch housing. *One capscrew is located outside of housing at lower left corner of front case.* Tap housing free of case and remove gasket.

REASSEMBLE FRONT UNIT, FIG. 6

Countershaft, Assemble

NOTE: If woodruff keys or keyways were burred during disassembly, dress with a file before assembly to prevent metal chips from lodging between gear hub faces.

1. Install and seat keys in countershaft.
2. Using a suitable arbor press, support 2nd speed gear on hub with chamfer up. Place countershaft in bore, align key and keyway and press shaft into gear until seated firmly against shoulder.
3. Support 3rd speed gear with chamfer up. Press countershaft in bore, align key and keyway, and press shaft into gear until firmly seated against 2nd speed gear.
4. Support P.T.O. drive on long hub with chamfer up. Place countershaft in bore, align key and keyway, and press shaft into gear until seated firmly against P.T.O. gear.
5. Support countershaft drive gear on short hub and chamfer up. Place countershaft in bore, align key and keyway, and press shaft into gear until seated firmly against P.T.O. gear.
6. Install snap ring on countershaft to lock drive gear in place.
7. Press front roller bearing on countershaft until inner race seats firmly against shoulder on shaft.

Countershaft Installation

1. Lower countershaft assembly into case with rear end through rear bearing bore.

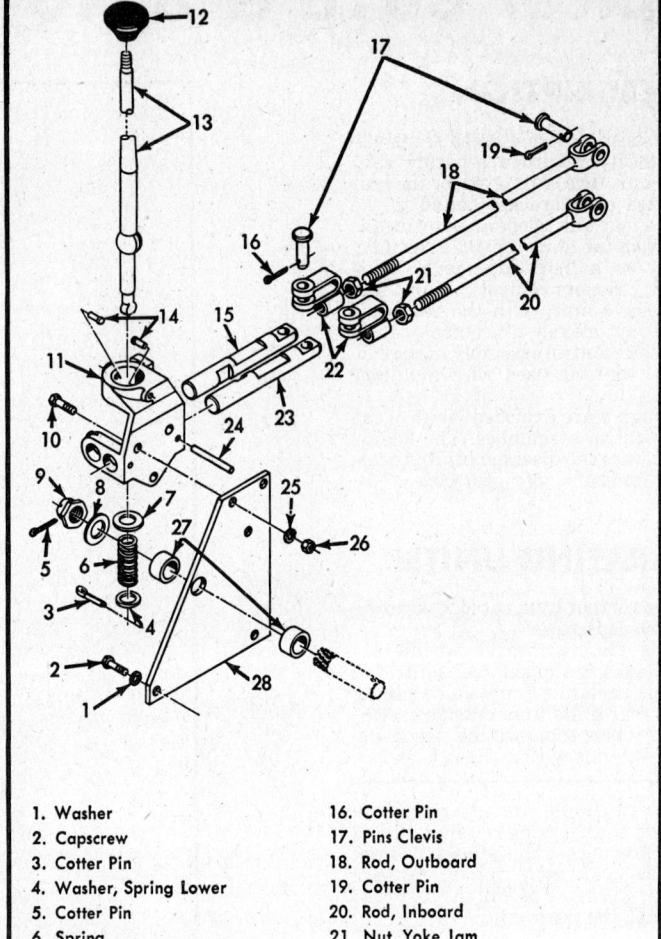

1. Washer
2. Capscrew
3. Cotter Pin
4. Washer, Spring Lower
5. Cotter Pin
6. Spring
7. Washer, Upper
8. Washer, Stud Mounting Plate
9. Nut, Mounting Plate Stud
10. Capscrew
11. Bracket, Shift Lever
12. Knob
13. Lever
14. Pin, Shift Lever Pivot
15. Slide, Outboard
16. Cotter Pin
17. Pins Clevis
18. Rod, Outboard
19. Cotter Pin
20. Rod, Inboard
21. Nut, Yoke Jam
22. Yoke, Offset Clevis
23. Slide, Inboard
24. Pin, Stop
25. Washer
26. Nut, Lever Bracket and Plate Screw
27. Sleeve, Bracket Mounting Plate Stud
28. Plate, Shift Lever Bracket

Fig. 2 Rear unit stick control

Align front end of countershaft with front bearing bore and tap into partial position.

NOTE: To prevent damage to front bearing as rear bearing is being driven on countershaft, place two strips of 3/8" flat stock between countershaft drive gear and front wall of case.

2. Position rear bearing on countershaft with shield inward and external snap ring toward rear. Align shaft and bearing with case bore and, using tubing, drive against inner race until bearing is seated on shoulder.
3. Remove steel strips and tap countershaft assembly the remaining way in, or until external snap ring seats against case.
4. Install rear bearing retainer.

Assemble & Install Reverse Idler

1. Install key in sleeve.
2. Install gear in sleeve.

NOTE: The sleeve has been ground to accommodate a hopping guard to prevent "walking" out of reverse. The gear must be assembled on the sleeve with shift fork collar toward rear. Make sure gear slides freely on key.

3. Grease two sets of bearings and install in sleeve bore.
4. Install assembly in case.
5. Insert reverse idler gear shaft (plain end first) through hole in rear of case and through idler gear assembly. Align "flat" on rear of shaft for lock plate and tap into position. Install lock plate.

Assemble Drive Pinion

NOTE: The drive pinion and bearing cap assembly should be installed temporarily to

Spicer Transmissions

facilitate assembly of mainshaft through the gears stacked inside the case. After mainshaft installation, the drive pinion and bearing cap must be removed to install mainshaft locknut, pocket bearing and gasket.

1. Position drive pinion under arbor press with shield up. Support inner race of bearing and press drive pinion into bearing.
2. Using a vise with soft jaws, clamp on teeth of drive pinion and install bearing locknut. This is a left-hand thread. Tighten locknut 300–350 ft-lbs. and stake in two places.
3. Place bearing cap over drive pinion bearing and press cap into position.
4. Seat snap ring in groove provided inside rear of cap to lock bearing in place.

Install Clutch Housing & Drive Pinion

1. If clutch housing has been removed it must be installed at this time. Using a light coating of gasket cement install gasket on case.
2. Position clutch housing case studs or retain with capscrews and lockwashers. *Do not tighten at this time.*
3. Install drive pinion and bearing cap assembly in bore of clutch housing and transmission case. Bearing cap will align clutch housing bore with transmission case bore. Tighten front bearing cap.
4. Tighten clutch housing capscrews or locknuts, whichever are provided. With cast iron case, tighten capscrews or studs to 90–95 ft-lbs; with aluminum case 70–75 ft-lbs.

Assemble & Install Mainshaft

NOTE: Due to the one-piece design of the front unit mainshaft and rear drive gear, the shaft must be assembled through the rear bearing retainer bore. Mainshaft installation is accomplished with the front case, front drive pinion and clutch housing set up vertically on two 4 × 4 wooden blocks.

The temporary installation of drive pinion and front bearing cap assembly holds the vertical stack-up of mainshaft gears and sleeves in their approximate position and alignment inside case during installation of mainshaft.

1. Place 3rd speed gear sleeve on flange end and coat lower one inch and flange with grease. Install one row of 71 needle bearings to sleeve.
2. Install spacer on sleeve and coat upper end of sleeve with grease. Then install second row of needle bearings on sleeve.
3. Install 3rd speed gear on needle and sleeve assembly with clutch teeth up.
4. Install 3-4 clutch gear collar on clutch gear and set in position on 3rd speed gear and sleeve assembly.
5. Engage clutch collar with 3rd speed gear. Grasp sub-assembly securely, turn over and set in position on drive pinion inside case. Allow clutch collar to drop down and engage clutch teeth on drive pinion to hold alignment.
6. Place 2nd speed gear sleeve on a suitable flat plate and coat lower one inch with grease. Install one row of 77 needle bearings on sleeve. Install spacer. Coat upper end with grease. Install second row of 77 needle bearings.
7. With clutch teeth down, install 2nd speed gear over sleeve and needles. Apply an extra heavy coat of grease along ends of needle bearings and face of 2nd speed gear to seal needles in place. Using the plate, turn assembly over quickly and stack in position on 3rd speed gear and sleeve in case.
8. Install 1-2 and reverse clutch gear in 1-2 and reverse sliding gear and stack in position in case on 2nd speed sleeve.

NOTE: Shift collar of sliding gear should be up. Line up assembly by allowng gear to drop down and engage clutch teeth of 2nd speed gear.

9. Place 1st speed gear with clutch teeth facing down into position on gear stack. *Do not install needle bearings at this time.*
10. Position mainshaft drive gear bearing retainer under arbor and press mainshaft drive gear bearing into retainer. Use a suitable tool to permit pressing on outer race of bearing.
11. Turn bearing and retainer assembly over on arbor. Support inner race of bearing and press mainshaft drive gear through bearing until bearing seats against shoulder of mainshaft.
12. Remove mainshaft and bearing sub-assembly from arbor press and install locknut, (left-hand thread). Tighten to 500–550 ft-lbs and stake nut in groove provided.
13. Install two retainer and bearing seals in grooves provided in bearing retainer.
14. Using a mainshaft installing tool, Fig. 10, with a hoist, suspend mainshaft and bearing assembly vertically over rear bearing bore in case.

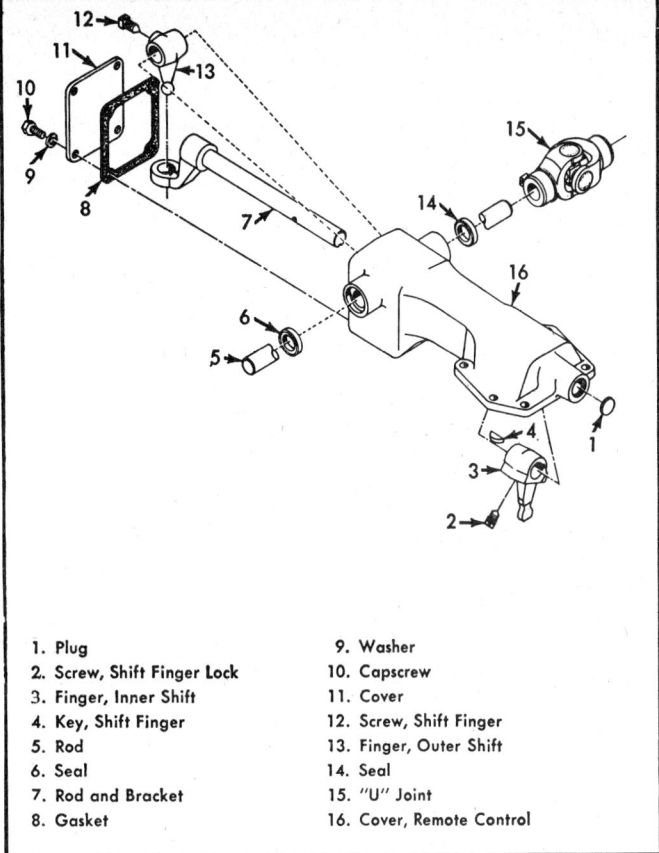

1. Plug
2. Screw, Shift Finger Lock
3. Finger, Inner Shift
4. Key, Shift Finger
5. Rod
6. Seal
7. Rod and Bracket
8. Gasket
9. Washer
10. Capscrew
11. Cover
12. Screw, Shift Finger
13. Finger, Outer Shift
14. Seal
15. "U" Joint
16. Cover, Remote Control

Fig. 3 Front unit remote control

15. Lower mainshaft slowly into bore of sleeves and clutch gear. Carefully align shaft with splines of 3-4 clutch gear and 1-2 reverse clutch gear by slowly rotating shaft and tapping lightly. When shaft bottoms into position, *mark drive gear position on case*, so mainshaft can be reassembled without difficulty.
16. Use a 2" spacer to hold reverse idler in position to allow mainshaft to rotate.
17. Use caution to hold gear stack in alignment and remove mainshaft out of rear bearing bore.

Install Mainshaft in Gear Stack

1. Stand mainshaft rear drive gear sub-assembly on bench with small end up.
2. Apply a coat of grease to 1st speed gear thrust washer and install on mainshaft, seating it securely on shoulder ahead of locknut.
3. Apply a coat of grease approximately one inch wide to ground diameter of mainshaft above thrust washer. Install one row of 77 needle bearings on mainshaft. Install spacer and seat against end of needle bearings. Apply a coat of grease to the upper shaft area and install the second row of 77 needle bearings on mainshaft. Apply a liberal coat of grease to hold bearing on shaft during assembly.
4. Using a light coat of grease, install gasket on transmission cae.
5. Carefully turn and suspend mainshaft sub-assembly (with bearings intact) vertically with hoist.
6. Position sub-assembly over case and gear stack, and rotate shaft to align reference marks on transmission case and drive

393

SPICER TRANSMISSIONS

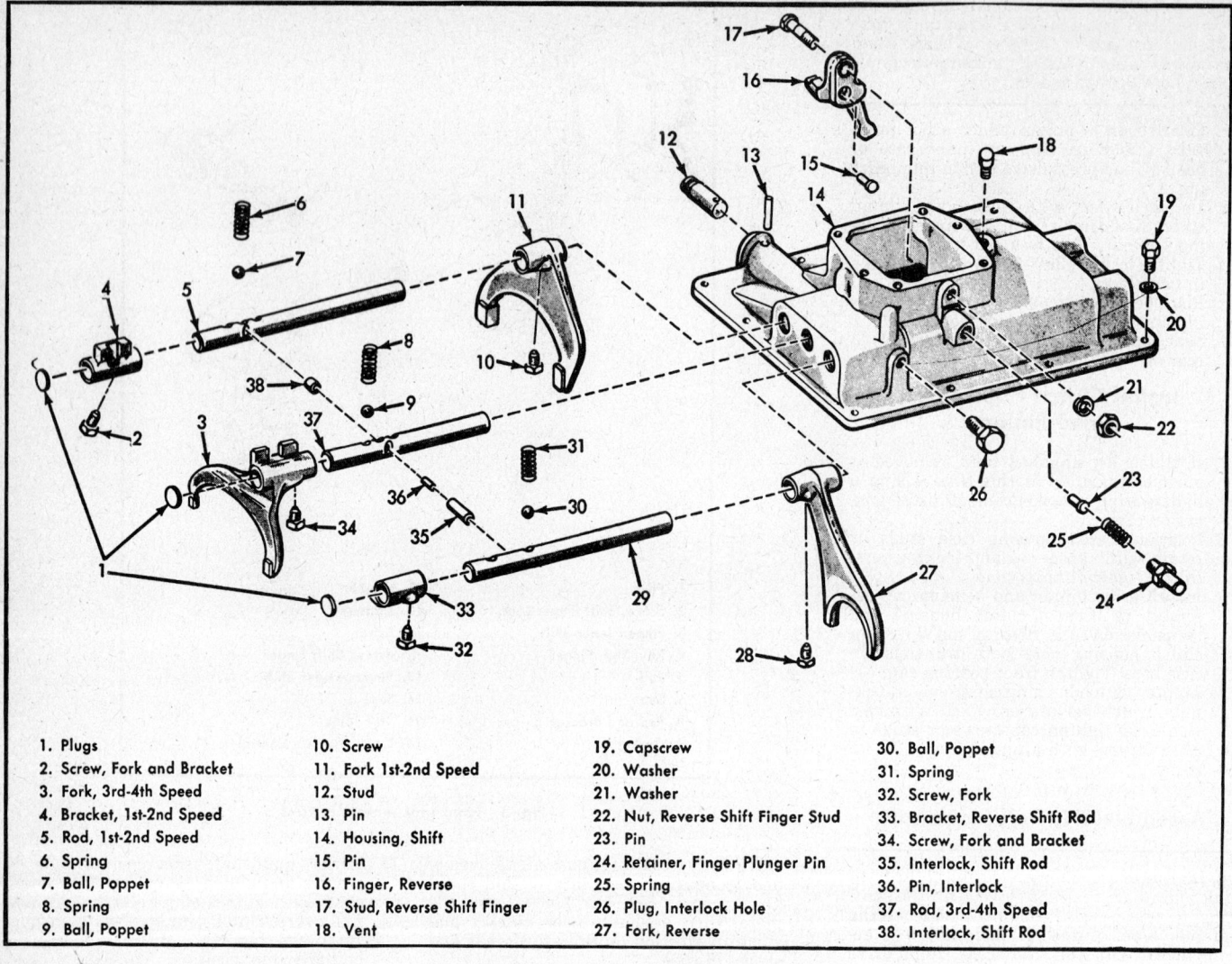

1. Plugs
2. Screw, Fork and Bracket
3. Fork, 3rd-4th Speed
4. Bracket, 1st-2nd Speed
5. Rod, 1st-2nd Speed
6. Spring
7. Ball, Poppet
8. Spring
9. Ball, Poppet
10. Screw
11. Fork 1st-2nd Speed
12. Stud
13. Pin
14. Housing, Shift
15. Pin
16. Finger, Reverse
17. Stud, Reverse Shift Finger
18. Vent
19. Capscrew
20. Washer
21. Washer
22. Nut, Reverse Shift Finger Stud
23. Pin
24. Retainer, Finger Plunger Pin
25. Spring
26. Plug, Interlock Hole
27. Fork, Reverse
28.
29.
30. Ball, Poppet
31. Spring
32. Screw, Fork
33. Bracket, Reverse Shift Rod
34. Screw, Fork and Bracket
35. Interlock, Shift Rod
36. Pin, Interlock
37. Rod, 3rd-4th Speed
38. Interlock, Shift Rod

Fig. 4 Front unit shift housing

gear.

7. Lower mainshaft into position, using caution to align shaft with sleeves and clutch gear splines. The last 1½" are usually the most difficult of the assembly since mainshaft splines must index and align with the splines of 3-4 speed clutch gear and spline of 1-2 and reverse clutch gear. Relax chain support and tap lightly while rotating back and forth slowly to complete spline assembly.
8. Line up dowel pin, Fig. 9, with notch in mainshaft and drive bearing retainer in case bore.
9. If removed, insert assembled pocket bearing in drive gear end of mainshaft.

DISASSEMBLE REAR UNIT—FIG. 7

Remove & Disassemble Mainshaft

1. Remove pocket bearing from front end of mainshaft. Use a suitable puller if necessary to remove inner race.
2. Lock unit in two gears at once to prevent mainshaft from turning.
3. Remove mainshaft rear flange or end yoke locknut and flat washer.
4. Use a suitable puller to remove flange or yoke.
5. Remove both mainshaft and countershaft rear bearing caps.
6. Press out rear bearing cap seal from mainshaft cap. Remove speedometer bushing if replacement is necessary.
7. Remove speedometer drive gear or spacer and mainshaft rear bearing thrust washer if loose.
8. Use two pieces of hardwood to block 3-4 speed clutch gear against inside of case. Using a brass drift, drive mainshaft forward to expose 3-4 speed clutch gear split lock ring.
9. Remove blocks, split lock ring, 3-4 speed clutch collar and clutch gear.
10. Using a brass drift, drive mainshaft rearward.

NOTE: As mainshaft moves, rear bearing and thrust washer will be forced out of rear case bore. Needle bearings used with 1st speed gear may begin to fall out. Use care to prevent their loss.

11. Continue to drive mainshaft rearward and strip off all loose parts.
12. Using a suitable arbor press, support remaining assembly on thrust washer and press shaft out of rear bearing and 1st speed gear thrust washer. If speedometer gear and rear bearing washer could not be removed previously, they will press off with bearing.

Remove & Disassemble Countershaft

1. Remove retainer from front of countershaft.
2. Using a brass drift, drive countershaft rearward to clear front bearing. Rear bearing will be driven out of case.
3. Using a suitable puller, remove rear bearing from countershaft.
4. Lift countershaft assembly from case.
5. Remove front bearing by tapping with soft hammer from inside case.
6. Using an arbor press, remove counter shaft drive gear, 4th and 2nd gears. Care should be used to support each gear as close to hub as possible.

394

SPICER TRANSMISSIONS

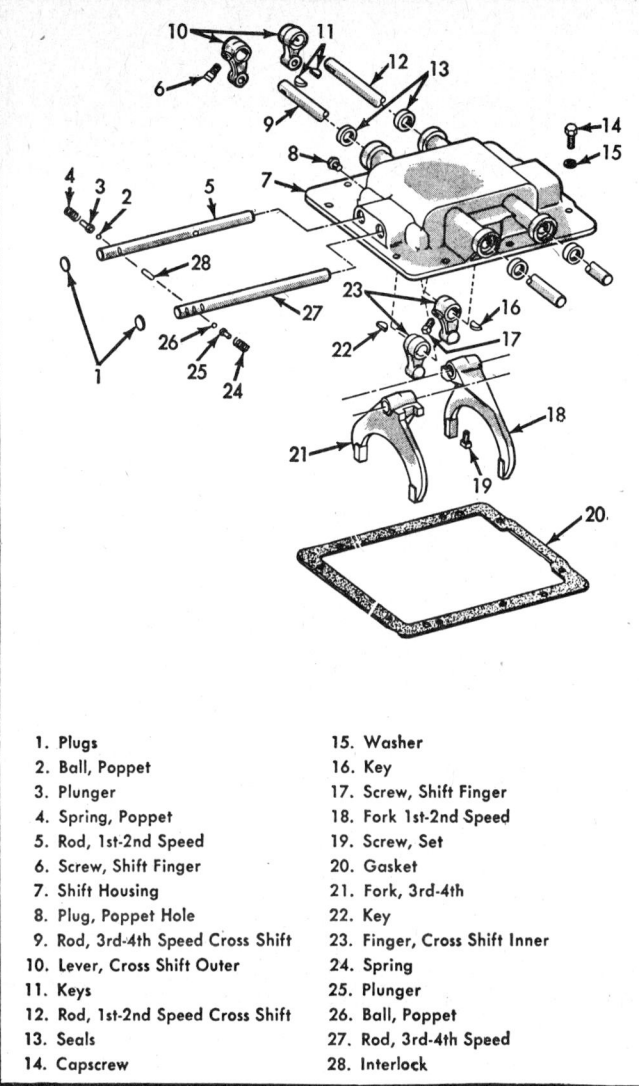

1. Plugs
2. Ball, Poppet
3. Plunger
4. Spring, Poppet
5. Rod, 1st-2nd Speed
6. Screw, Shift Finger
7. Shift Housing
8. Plug, Poppet Hole
9. Rod, 3rd-4th Speed Cross Shift
10. Lever, Cross Shift Outer
11. Keys
12. Rod, 1st-2nd Speed Cross Shift
13. Seals
14. Capscrew
15. Washer
16. Key
17. Screw, Shift Finger
18. Fork 1st-2nd Speed
19. Screw, Set
20. Gasket
21. Fork, 3rd-4th
22. Key
23. Finger, Cross Shift Inner
24. Spring
25. Plunger
26. Ball, Poppet
27. Rod, 3rd-4th Speed
28. Interlock

Fig. 5 Rear unit shift housing

ASSEMBLE REAR UNIT, FIG. 7

Assemble Countershaft

NOTE: All countershaft gears should fit tight on the shaft. As a shrink fit of .0015" to .003" is built into new parts, it presents a service problem. If heat is used to expand gear bores, boiling water, hot oil or steam are usually satisfactory. Do not exceed 250 deg. F. Do not use flame.

If heat is not used, it is advisable to coat the gear bores heavily with white lead to prevent seizing or galling of parts. If keys or keyways are burred, dress up with a file before assembly.

1. Install keys in countershaft.
2. Support hub of 2nd speed gear in an arbor press with long hub and chamfer up. Place countershaft in position, align key with keyway and press shaft into gear until shoulder seats firmly against gear.
3. Support hub of 4th speed gear in arbor press with long hub down and chamfer up. Place countershaft in position, align key with keyway and press shaft into gear until seated firmly blocking up drive gear.
4. Support hub of countershaft drive gear in arbor with long hub and chamfer up. Press countershaft into gear until seated firmly against 4th speed gear.

NOTE: A two-piece or separable roller bearing is now being used in production transmissions. It is recommended that this two-piece bearing be used as a replacement part.

5. Press inner race of rear bearing on rear of countershaft with lip or flange seated firmly against shoulder of 1st speed gear.

Install Countershaft

1. Lower rear end of countershaft into case with end of shaft and 1st speed gear through rear bearing bore. Lower front of countershaft into its approximate position and maintain alignment with a cable

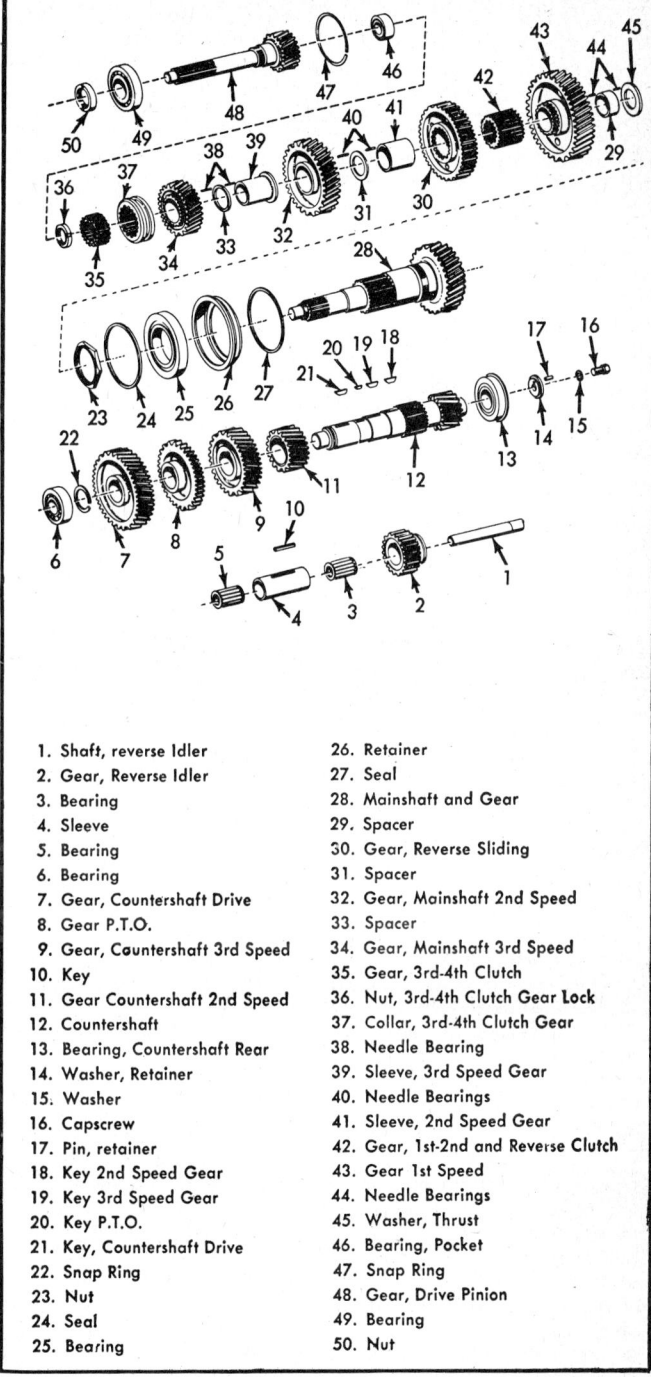

1. Shaft, reverse Idler
2. Gear, Reverse Idler
3. Bearing
4. Sleeve
5. Bearing
6. Bearing
7. Gear, Countershaft Drive
8. Gear P.T.O.
9. Gear, Countershaft 3rd Speed
10. Key
11. Gear Countershaft 2nd Speed
12. Countershaft
13. Bearing, Countershaft Rear
14. Washer, Retainer
15. Washer
16. Capscrew
17. Pin, retainer
18. Key 2nd Speed Gear
19. Key 3rd Speed Gear
20. Key P.T.O.
21. Key, Countershaft Drive
22. Snap Ring
23. Nut
24. Seal
25. Bearing
26. Retainer
27. Seal
28. Mainshaft and Gear
29. Spacer
30. Gear, Reverse Sliding
31. Spacer
32. Gear, Mainshaft 2nd Speed
33. Spacer
34. Gear, Mainshaft 3rd Speed
35. Gear, 3rd-4th Clutch
36. Nut, 3rd-4th Clutch Gear Lock
37. Collar, 3rd-4th Clutch Gear
38. Needle Bearing
39. Sleeve, 3rd Speed Gear
40. Needle Bearings
41. Sleeve, 2nd Speed Gear
42. Gear, 1st-2nd and Reverse Clutch
43. Gear 1st Speed
44. Needle Bearings
45. Washer, Thrust
46. Bearing, Pocket
47. Snap Ring
48. Gear, Drive Pinion
49. Bearing
50. Nut

Fig. 6 Front unit gears and related parts

395

SPICER TRANSMISSIONS

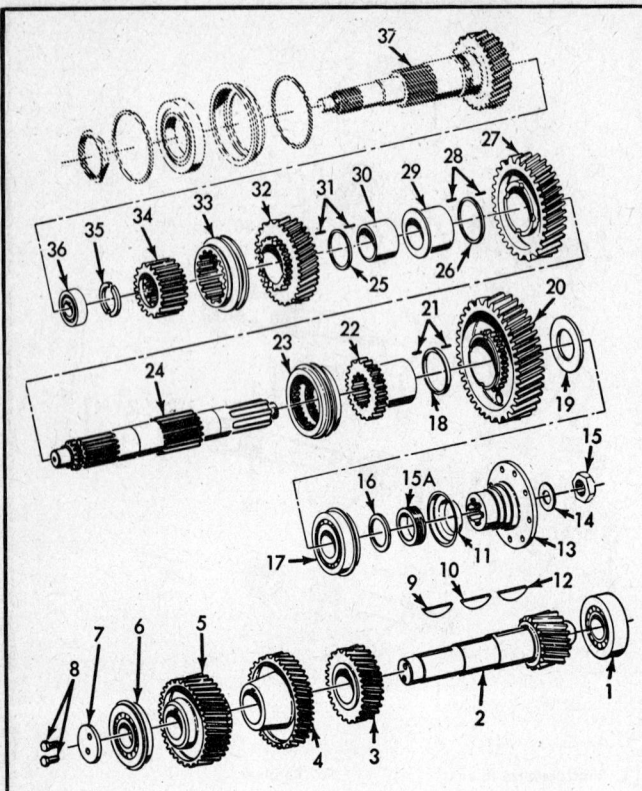

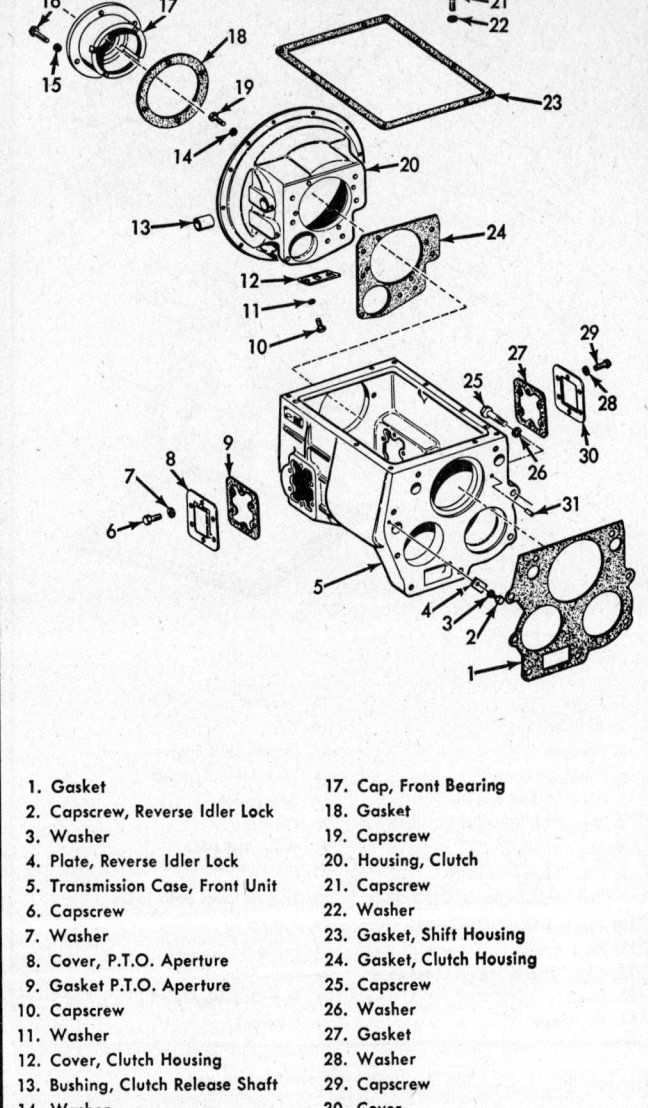

1. Bearing, Countershaft Rear
2. Countershaft
3. Gear, Countershaft 2nd Speed Underdrive
4. Gear, Countershaft 4th Speed Overdrive
5. Gear, Countershaft Drive
6. Bearing, Countershaft Front
7. Washer, retainer
8. Capscrews, Retainer
9. Key, Countershaft Drive Gear
10. Key, Countershaft 4th Speed Gear
11. Finger
12. Key, Countershaft 2nd Speed Gear
13. Flange
14. Washer, Flange Nut
15. Flange Nut
16. Washer
17. Bearing, Mainshaft Rear
18. Spacer
19. Washer, thrust
20. Gear, 1st speed Mainshaft Underdrive
21. Needle Bearings
22. Gear, Mainshaft 1st-2nd Speed Clutch
23. Collar, Mainshaft 1st-2nd Speed Clutch Gear
24. Auxiliary Mainshaft
25. Spacer
26. Spacer
27. Gear, Mainshaft 2nd Speed Underdrive
28. Needle Bearings
29. Sleeve, Mainshaft 2nd Speed Gear
30. Sleeve, Mainshaft 4th Speed Gear
31. Needle Bearings
32. Gear, Mainshaft 4th Speed Overdrive
33. Collar, Mainshaft 3rd-4th Speed Clutch Gear
34. Gear, Mainshaft 3rd-4th Speed Clutch
35. Lock Ring 3rd-4th Speed Clutch Gear
36. Bearing, Drive Pinion Pocket
37. Gear, Drive Pinion

Fig. 7 Rear unit gears and related parts

1. Gasket
2. Capscrew, Reverse Idler Lock
3. Washer
4. Plate, Reverse Idler Lock
5. Transmission Case, Front Unit
6. Capscrew
7. Washer
8. Cover, P.T.O. Aperture
9. Gasket P.T.O. Aperture
10. Capscrew
11. Washer
12. Cover, Clutch Housing
13. Bushing, Clutch Release Shaft
14. Washer
15. Washer
16. Capscrew
17. Cap, Front Bearing
18. Gasket
19. Capscrew
20. Housing, Clutch
21. Capscrew
22. Washer
23. Gasket, Shift Housing
24. Gasket, Clutch Housing
25. Capscrew
26. Washer
27. Gasket
28. Washer
29. Capscrew
30. Cover
31. Dowel Pin

Fig. 8 Front unit transmission case

Assemble Mainshaft

1. Place 1-2 speed clutch gear on bench with flange down. Apply a light coat of grease approximately one inch wide to ground area above flange. Install one row of 72 needle bearings on clutch gear. Install spacer. Apply a light coat of grease above spacer and install the second row of 72 needle bearings. *Do not plug holes in gears with grease.*
2. With clutch teeth down, install 1st speed gear on clutch gear and over needles and spacer. Set this assembly aside.
3. Coat 2nd speed gear sleeve on thrust face and ground surface with grease and install two rows of 72 needle bearings with spacer in between.
4. Install 2nd speed gear on sleeve and bearings with clutch teeth on gear away from flange. Set this assembly aside.
5. Place 4th speed gear sleeve on a plate and

support or by blocking up drive gear.
2. Align outer race of rear bearing (two-piece) with inner race and rear bore and tap flush with case.
3. Using a light coating of gasket cement on gasket, install countershaft rear bearing cap. Secure capscrews dipped in gasket cement. Tighten to 35–40 ft-lbs in cast iron case or 20–25 ft-lbs with aluminum case.
4. Position front bearing on countershaft with external snap ring away from case. Use a 4×4 hard wood block to wedge between rear case wall and 2nd speed gear. Drive against inner race of bearing until seated against hub of drive gear.
5. Secure bearing with retainer washer and capscrews. Tighten capscrews to 45–50 ft-lbs. Secure with lockwire.

SPICER TRANSMISSIONS

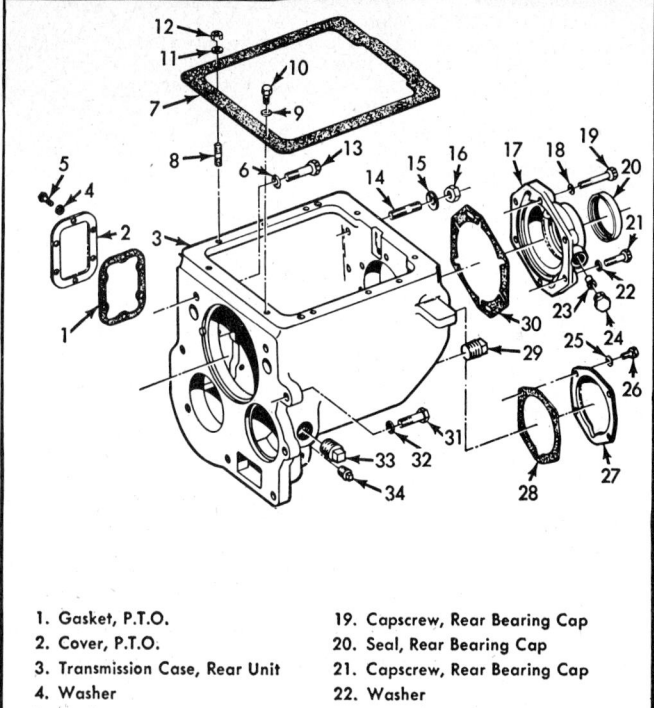

1. Gasket, P.T.O.
2. Cover, P.T.O.
3. Transmission Case, Rear Unit
4. Washer
5. Capscrew
6. Washer
7. Gasket, Shift Housing
8. Stud
9. Washer
10. Capscrew
11. Washer
12. Nut
13. Capscrew
14. Stud
15. Washer
16. Nut
17. Cap, Mainshaft Rear Bearing
18. Washer
19. Capscrew, Rear Bearing Cap
20. Seal, Rear Bearing Cap
21. Capscrew, Rear Bearing Cap
22. Washer
23. Bushing, Speedometer
24. Plug
25. Washer
26. Capscrew
27. Cap, Countershaft Rear Bearing
28. Gasket
29. Plug, Oil Drain
30. Gasket, Mainshaft Rear Bearing Cap
31. Capscrew
32. Washer
33. Plug, Oil Filler
34. Plug, Temperature Indicator

Fig. 9 Rear unit transmission case

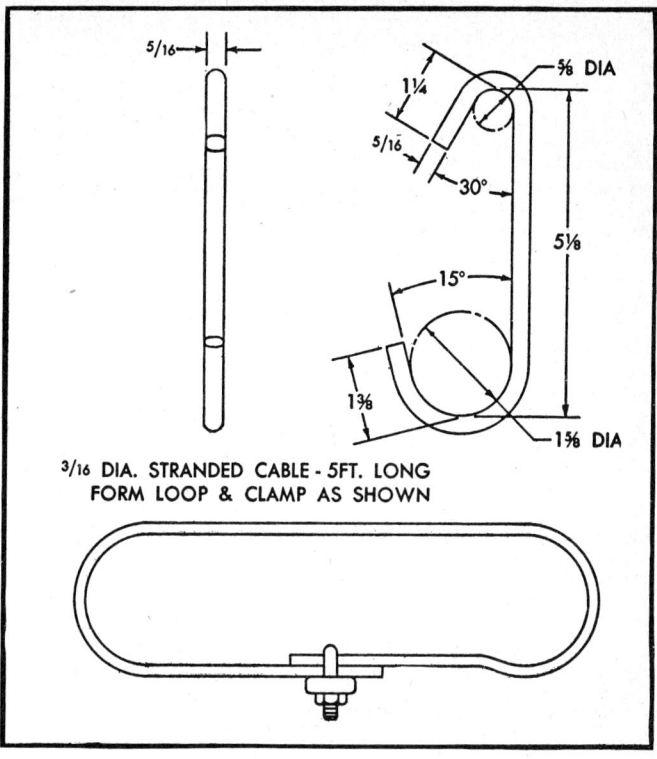

Fig. 10 Dimensions for lifting sling and hook for installing mainshaft

coat lower one inch with grease. Install one row of 62 needle bearings.
6. Install 4th speed gear on sleeve and bearings with clutch teeth of gear up. Set this assembly aside.

Install Mainshaft Sub-Assemblies

1. Position 1st speed gear and sleeve assembly in rear of case with clutch teeth toward front. Mesh with countershaft gear. Install 1-2 clutch collar on 1st speed gear with extended hub toward gear.
2. Place 2nd speed gear sleeve assembly in case with clutching teeth of gear toward 1st speed gear, and mesh with countershaft 2nd speed gear. Move clutch collar to neutral to hold assemblies in relationship.
3. Coat thrust faces and splines of mainshaft with light grease. Enter pilot bearing and through rear bearing bore until mainshaft has passed through 2nd gear sleeve approximately one inch.
4. Place 4th speed gear and sleeve assembly in case with clutch teeth away from 2nd speed gear. Slide mainshaft forward through bore of sleeve.
5. Install 3-4 speed clutch collar on clutch gear. Extended hub of collar goes toward front as does lock ring counterbore in end of gear. Position gear and collar in case and install on mainshaft spline.
6. Block 3-4 clutch gear and tap mainshaft through until locking groove in shaft is beyond clutch gear.
7. Coat two clutch gear lock rings with heavy grease and place them in groove provided.
8. Tap mainshaft rearward and make sure lock rings center inside of counterbore of 3-4 clutch gear.
9. Install 1st speed gear thrust washer on rear of mainshaft next to 1st speed gear.
10. Position mainshaft rear bearing onto mainshaft with external snap ring away from case. Use a 3/4" thick strip of flat stock to block front of mainshaft against inside of case. Use a pinch bar to roll mainshaft into position to align outer race of bearing with case bore. Using a suitable piece of tubing, drive on inner race until bearing is seated against 1st speed gear thrust washer.
11. Remove 3/4" block and continue to tap bearing into case bore until snap ring is seated against case.
12. Install rear bearing washer and speedometer gear or spacer on mainshaft.
13. Apply a light coat of gasket cement on OD of rear bearing cap oil seal and press into cap.
14. Using a light coat of gasket cement on cap and gasket, install rear bearing cap. Be sure to align oil passages. Secure with capscrews. Tighten to 45–50 ft-lbs in cast iron case or 25–30 ft-lbs in aluminum case.
15. Install end yoke or flange on mainshaft with pusher tool. *Do not drive flange or yoke on shaft without provisions to keep shaft from moving forward.*
16. Install flat washer and locknut. Lock transmission in two gears and tighten to 350–450 ft-lbs. Install cotter pin.
17. Shift clutch collars back into neutral and make sure all shafts turn freely.
18. The drive pinion pocket bearing is a separable part. Due to the vertical method of joining the front and rear units, the inner race may be pressed on the front end of the rear mainshaft or the outer race may be placed in the "pocket" of the front unit drive gear. *Flanged end of inner race goes toward 3rd speed clutch gear.*

Joining Front & Rear Units

1. Tie 3-4 clutch gear collar to 3rd speed gear, Fig. 6.
2. Pick up rear unit with a chain hoist attached to the output end yoke or flange.
3. Lower rear unit into place, using care to align rear mainshaft with pocket bearing and mainshaft drive gear teeth with countershaft drive gear as the units meet.
4. Bolt cases together using the two drilled head capscrews with star washers on top inside holes in rear case. Install lockwire. Using remaining capscrews on stud nuts with lockwashers to secure cases, tighten

397

SPICER TRANSMISSIONS

to 95–100 ft-lbs with cast iron case or 70–75 ft-lbs with aluminum case.
5. Use a chain hoist to lift complete assembly and lower to a horizontal position.
6. Remove capscrews and washer from front drive pinion bearing cap. Use two 7/16" puller screws and remove front pinion and bearing cap from case.
7. Install clutch gear locknut (left-hand thread) to front of mainshaft. Lock transmission in two gears and tighten locknut 300–350 ft-lbs.
8. Unlock transmission gears and make sure mainshaft rotates freely before staking locknut to groove provided in mainshaft.
9. Install pocket bearing on end of mainshaft.
10. Using a light coat of gasket cement on bearing cap and gasket, prepare to install drive pinion and bearing cap on transmission.
11. Use a large screwdriver to roll mainshaft up into proper position to aid alignment of pocket bearing with bearing bore of drive pinion.
12. Secure drive pinion bearing cap to case. Tighten to 25–28 ft-lbs. Rotate front drive pinion to make sure all gears and shafts turn freely.

Spicer 8512, 8516 & 8716–12 & 16 Speed Units

These transmissions, Figs. 1 and 2, consist of an 8500 four-speed main transmission coupled with a three-speed auxiliary unit on 8512 and a four-speed auxiliary unit on 8516 and 8716. Inasmuch as the main unit is covered elsewhere in this section, the following material will be confined to the auxiliary units only.

Separating Front & Rear Units

1. Unfasten and lift off shifter housing from rear case.
2. From inside of rear case (near the top), cut lockwire and remove two attaching capscrews.
3. Use a bridge chain across the same two internal capscrew holes to support rear unit as next step is performed.
4. Remove 11 remaining attaching capscrews and bolts from outside of case.
5. Using a pry bar to wedge between front and rear case, separate the two units, leveling the rear unit with a chain fall.

NOTE: As the two cases are separated, the mainshaft drive gear bearing retainer will pull free of the rear case. This allows the integral mainshaft rear drive gear to pass through the front bearing bore of the rear case and remain with the front unit. The pocket bearing is the separable type. It may remain intact on the rear mainshaft, stay in the drive gear pocket or the bearing may separate as the two cases are parted.

Three Speed Rear Unit

Mainshaft Disassemble
1. If necessary, use a suitable puller to remove inner race of pocket bearing from front of mainshaft.
2. Unstake clutch gear lockwasher from locknut at front of mainshaft. If used, pull

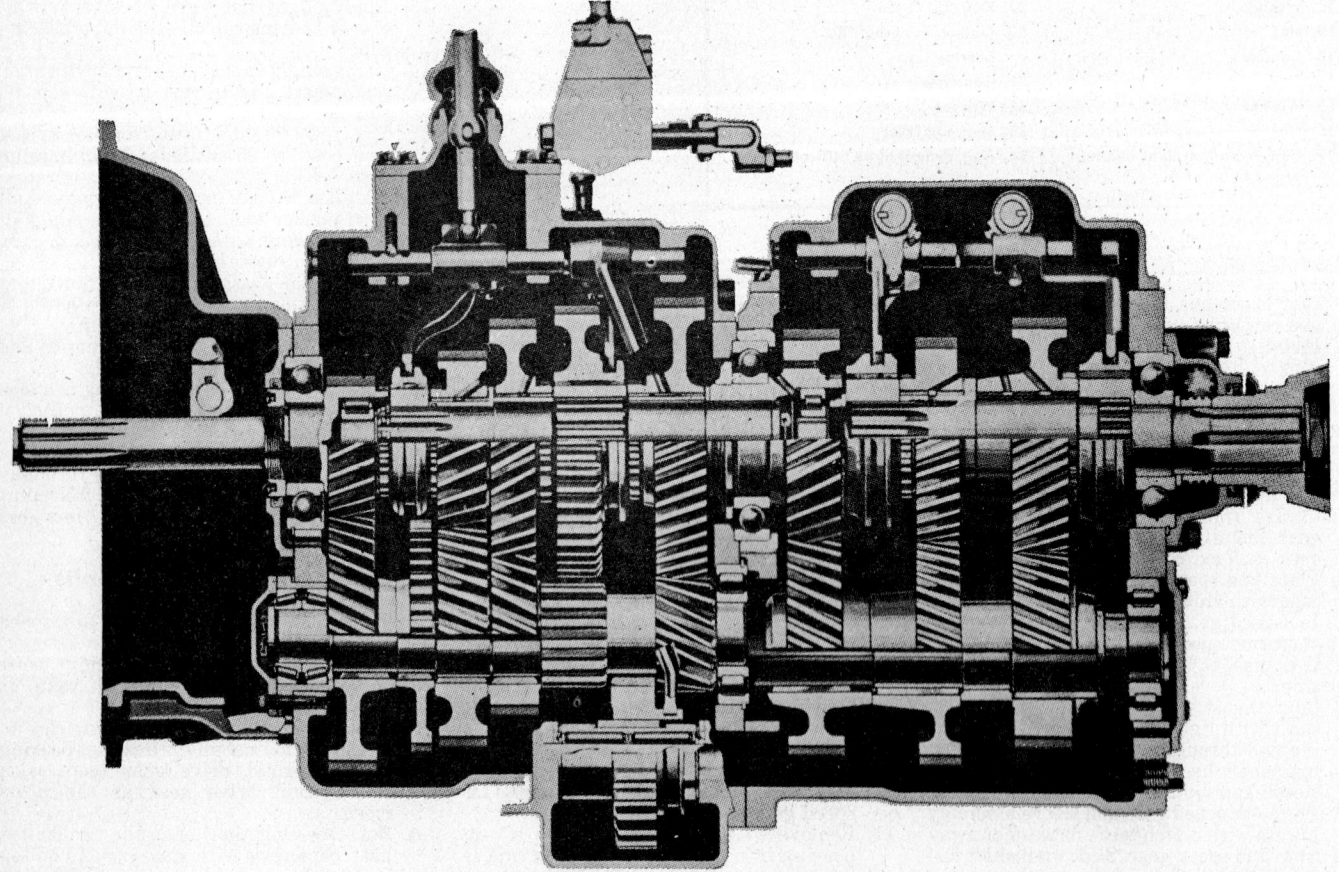

Fig. 1 Spicer Model 8512 12-speed transmission. Assembly consists of a Series 8500 four-speed front unit and a three-speed auxiliary unit

SPICER TRANSMISSIONS

Fig. 2 Spicer Models 8516 and 8716 16-speed transmission. Assembly consists of a Series 8500 four-speed front unit and a four-speed auxiliary unit

cotter pin from rear flange or end yoke locknut.
3. Lock rear unit in two gears by engaging the 2-3 clutch collar with 3rd gear and 1st speed clutch collar with 1st speed gear.
4. Use a piloted tool and impact wrench (or hammer and drift) to loosen locknut. *Locknut has a left-hand thread. Do not remove from shaft at this time.*
5. Remove rear output flange (or end yoke) locknut.
6. Remove flange (or end yoke).
7. Remove mainshaft and countershaft rear bearing caps and gaskets.
8. Remove speedometer drive gear (or spacer) and mainshaft rear bearing thrust washer.
9. Tap or slide mainshaft and gear assembly out rear bearing bore until stopped by 1st speed gear.
10. Remove loosened 2-3 speed clutch gear locknut from front of mainshaft.
11. Remove 2-3 speed clutch gear collar and clutch gear (if slip fit) from front of shaft.
12. Use suitable puller on snap ring to remove ball bearing from rear of mainshaft.
13. Lift remaining assembly, front end first, out top of case.

CAUTION: Do not allow parts to slip off rear of shaft as assembly is removed. Three rows of 62 needle bearing and two spacers contained between 1st speed gear and shaft are loose and can be easily lost.

14. Disassemble mainshaft.

Countershaft Disassembly, Fig. 3
1. Cut lockwire and remove front bearing retaining washer.
2. With brass drift, drive countershaft rearward to clear front bearing, which will remain in case bore. Rear bearing will be driven out of case.
3. Remove snap ring from rear end of shaft and use a suitable puller to remove rear bearing.
4. Lift countershaft assembly out top of case.
5. Remove front bearing by tapping with soft hammer from inside of case.
6. Press countershaft out of gears one at a time by supporting each gear with parallel bars as close to hub as possible.
7. Remove exposed Woodruff keys.
8. Support 1st speed gear and press countershaft out of P.T.O. drive gear spacer at the same time. Remove remaining Woodruff key.

Countershaft, Reassemble, Fig. 3
All countershaft gears should fit tight on the countershaft. As a shrink or interference fit of .0015" to .003" is built into new parts, it presents a field assembly problem.
If heat is used to expand gear bores, boiling water, hot oil or steam are usually satisfactory. Do not exceed 250°F. Do not use hot plates or acetylene torches or any method that will turn the steel blue or straw color and damage the heat treated gears.
If heat is not used, it is advisable to coat the gear bores with white lead to reduce galling or seizing of parts.
When in doubt about which end of the hub to assemble on the shaft first, look for the chamfered end of the bore.
If Woodruff keys or keyways are mutilated or burred during disassembly, clean up with a file before reassembling. This will help prevent metal chips from getting between gear hub faces.

1. Assemble rearmost Woodruff key to countershaft.
2. In a suitable arbor press, support 1st speed gear on hub, with long hub and chamfer up. Place countershaft into position, align key with keyway and press into gear until shoulder on countershaft seats firmly against gear.
3. Assemble P.T.O. drive gear spacer to shaft and seat against gear. Assemble remaining two Woodruff keys to countershaft, seating keys securely.
4. Again, in arbor press, support under hub of 3rd speed gear with long hub down and chamfer up, place countershaft into position, align key with keyway and press into gear until seated against spacer.
5. In a similar manner, support countershaft drive gear with long hub and chamfer up. Press countershaft subassembly into gear until seated against 3rd speed gear.

NOTE: Either one piece or separable bearings will be found as the rear countershaft bearing.

SPICER TRANSMISSIONS

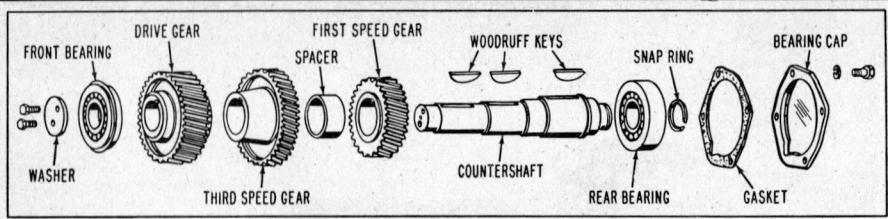

Fig. 3 Countershaft components of the 8512 three-speed rear unit

If a separable bearing is used, press on the inner race with flange seated against shoulder of countershaft. Assemble snap ring to retain bearing.

Installation of Countershaft

1. Lower countershaft sub-assembly into case with rear end of shaft and hub of 1st speed gear out rear bearing bore. Lower front of countershaft into its approximate position. Maintain alignment with a cable support or by blocking under countershaft drive gear.

   NOTE: If a one-piece bearing is used, assemble countershaft at this time. This bearing is a tight fit. Block the front end of the countershaft with a 1/2" thick piece of flat steel stock about 8 to 10" long and use tubing to drive on the inner race of rear bearing. Seat bearing firmly on shaft and secure with snap ring.

2. Remove steel plate and move countershaft and rear bearing assembly forward at the same time, tapping outer race of rear bearing into case bore.
3. Use a light coating of gasket cement and assemble countershaft rear bearing cap gasket to bearing cap. Apply gasket cement to case side of gasket and apply to case.
4. Dip capscrews in gasket cement and assemble to case with lockwashers and torque capscrews to 25–32 ft-lbs.
5. Position front bearing on countershaft with snap ring away from face of case. Use a 2 × 4 hard block to wedge between rear case wall and 1st speed gear. Use tubing to drive against inner race of bearing until snap ring seats against front face of case.
6. Lock front bearing to countershaft with retainer washer and capscrews. Torque capscrews to 40–50 ft-lbs and secure with lockwire.

Assemble and Install Mainshaft, Fig. 4

1. Using a suitable arbor press, support extended hub of 1st speed clutch gear and insert mainshaft into spline of clutch gear. Press shoulder of mainshaft flush against clutch gear.
2. Place mainshaft vertically in a vise with soft jaws gripping spline of output end.
3. Coat thrust face of 1st speed clutch gear and about 3/4" of the mainshaft bearing diameter with grease. Assemble one row of 62 rollers to mainshaft. Assemble spacer to mainshaft and slide down into position against end of needle bearings.

   NOTE: Due to variations in tolerances and to provide better bearing lubrication, the manufacturer recommends that needle bearings should NOT completely encircle the shaft. Space for approximately one needle bearing should be left unfilled on all Spicer needle bearing applications. This will aid in preventing seizures by allowing easier oil entry and free movement of needle bearings.

   If it is more convenient to assemble needle bearings to inside of gears rather than on shaft and sleeve, the method is applicable.

4. Apply a light coat of grease to middle mainshaft bearing area and assemble second row of 62 needle bearings to shaft. In a similar manner, assemble second spacer and third row of 62 needle bearings. Use grease to hold bearings in place.
5. Assemble 1st speed gear over bearings and spacers with clutch teeth down toward clutch gear.
6. Insert new lockpin in sleeve and assemble sleeve on shaft so that pin registers with the one extended spline. If necessary to drive sleeve on shaft, use a tube against end of sleeve only. Seat flange against shoulder of shaft and 1st speed gear.
7. Coat thrust face and about one inch of third speed sleeve with light grease. Assemble one row of 62 needle bearings to sleeve. Assemble spacer over sleeve and down against needle bearings. Apply grease to upper end of sleeve and assemble second row of 62 needle bearings to sleeve.
8. With clutch teeth up, assemble 3rd speed gear over sleeve bearings and spacer.
9. Assemble 3rd speed clutch gear to mainshaft splines with ground end down or toward 3rd speed gear.
10. Assemble 3rd speed gear flat washer, lock washer and lock nut to end of mainshaft. Torque left-hand thread lock nut to 550–600 ft-lbs. Bend tangs of lock washer into slots of nut.
11. Remove mainshaft sub-assembly from vise and install in case with output end of mainshaft through rear bearing bore. Lower front of mainshaft into position and mesh all gears.
12. Maintain approximate alignment of mainshaft by supporting with cable and chain hoist. Assemble 1st speed clutch gear collar to clutch gear, with extended hub toward 1st speed gear.
13. Position rear bearing on mainshaft with snap ring to rear. Use a 3/4" thick flat steel strip to block front of mainshaft against inside of case. With tubing, drive on inner race until bearing seats against 1st speed clutch gear. Use caution to align outer race of bearing with case bore.
14. Assemble rear bearing washer and speedometer gear (or spacer washer) to mainshaft and seat against washer.
15. If necessary, replace speedometer gear bushing in rear bearing cap.
16. Apply a light coat of gasket cement to O.D. of rear bearing cap oil seal and press into cap.
17. Apply gasket cement to mainshaft rear bearing cap gasket and position on cap. Align oil passages.
18. Apply gasket cement to other side of gasket and assemble bearing cap and gasket to rear of case. Dip capscrews in gasket cement and assemble to case with copper washers. Torque capscrews to 60–80 ft-lbs. Secure with lock wire.
19. Assemble end yoke or flange to mainshaft with pusher tool. Do not drive onto mainshaft without provisions to stop shaft from moving forward (see Step 13).
20. Assemble 3rd speed clutch gear collar to clutch gear.
21. Assemble flat washer and lock nut. Lock transmission in two gears and torque flange nut to 400–450 ft-lbs.
22. Shift clutch collars back into neutral and make sure all shafts turn freely.
23. Use pressure type oil can to force lubricant in oil holes and end slots of all floating gears on mainshaft to flush out grease and insure initial lubrication of over-running gears and bearings.
24. Drive gear pocket bearing is a separable part. Due to the vertical method of assembling the rear unit to the front unit, the

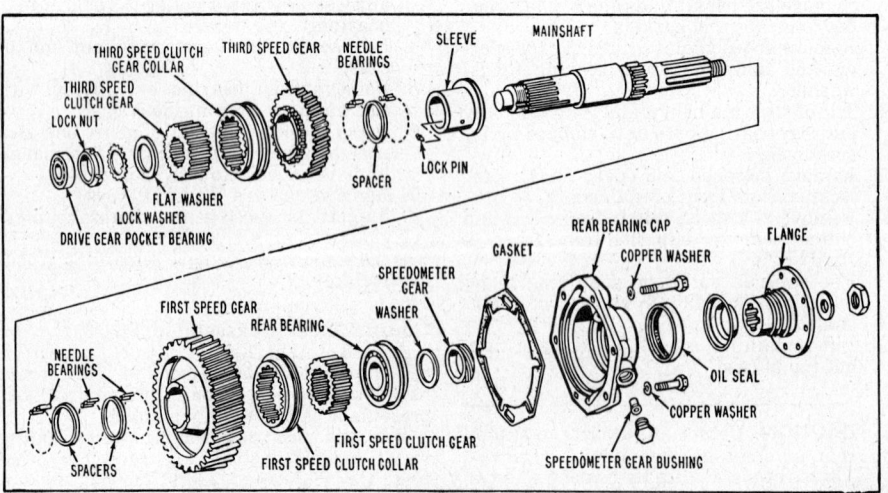

Fig. 4 Mainshaft components of the 8512 three-speed rear unit

SPICER TRANSMISSIONS

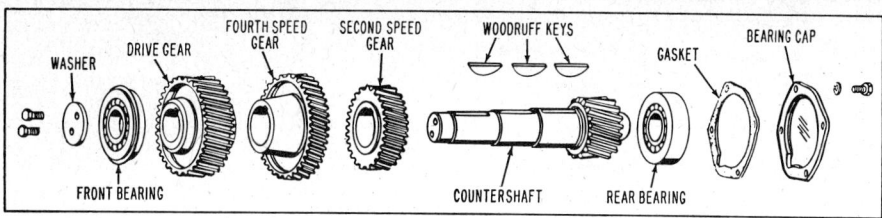

Fig. 5 "A" ratio countershaft components of the 8500 four-speed auxiliary unit

inner race must be pressed on the front end of the rear mainshaft or placed intact in the pocket of the drive gear. Flanged end of inner race assembles toward 3rd speed clutch gear. Use tubing to drive against inner race until seated against shoulder on shaft.

Joining Front and Rear Units

1. Tie the 3-4 clutch gear collar to 3rd speed gear or assemble collar to rear of mainshaft. Long snout of clutch collar points toward mainshaft.
2. Pick up rear unit with a chain hoist attached to output end yoke or companion flange and suspend vertically over front unit.
3. Lower rear unit into place, using caution to align rear mainshaft with pocket bearing of front mainshaft and drive gear teeth with countershaft drive gear.
4. Bolt cases together using two drilled head capscrews and star washers on top inside holes of rear case.
5. Assemble five capscrews with new star washers through flange on righthand side of front case into rear case. Three capscrews and washers assembled from rear into right-hand side of front case.
6. The longest through bolt assembles front to rear in bottom center hole of cases. Two shorter bolts assemble to left of bottom center. Use washer and nuts on all bolts.
7. After starting all capscrews and bolts, progressively tighten and pull cases together. Torque capscrews and nuts to 120-150 ft-lbs. Secure internal capscrews with lockwire.
8. Lower complete assembly in a horizontal position with a chain hoist.

Four Speed Rear Unit

NOTE: The 4 × 4 rear unit is produced with "A" or "B" ratio. This designation will always be found on the name plate as the letter following the model number. For example: 8516-3A or 8716-5B. All "A" models are *deep* Lo-Lo units and all "B" models are *splitter* Lo-Lo units. Only the procedure for removal and installation of the countershafts differ with the "A" and "B" units. Removal and installation of mainshaft is the same for both units.

Mainshaft, Remove and Disassemble

1. Remove shifter housing.
2. Separate rear unit from front unit.
3. Remove pocket bearing from front end of mainshaft. Use suitable puller if necessary to remove inner race.
4. Lock unit in two gears at once and remove mainshaft rear flange or end yoke lock nut. If countershaft is to be removed unstake countershaft lock nut and remove while the gears are locked.
5. Use puller to remove end yoke or flange.
6. Unfasten and remove mainshaft and countershaft rear bearing caps.
7. Press out rear bearing cap oil seal and check for damage. Remove speedometer bushing if it is to be replaced.
8. Remove speedometer drive gear or spacer and mainshaft rear thrust washer if loose.
9. Use two pieces of hard wood to block the 3-4 speed clutch gear against inside of case. With a brass drift, drive mainshaft forward to expose the 3-4 speed clutch gear split lock ring.
10. Remove hard wood blocks and split ring. Remove 3-4 speed clutch collar and clutch gear if it is a slip fit.
11. With brass drift, begin to drive mainshaft rearward.

NOTE: As mainshaft moves, rear bearing and thrust washer will be forced out of rear case bore. Needle bearings used with 1st speed gear may begin to fall out. Use care to prevent their loss.

12. Continue to drive mainshaft rearward. As shaft clears bores, strip the mainshaft of parts.
13. Using a suitable arbor press, support remaining assembly on thrust washer and press shaft out of rear bearing and 1st speed thrust washer. If speedometer gear and rear bearing washer could not be removed previously, they will press off with bearing.

"A" Ratio Countershaft, Disassemble

1. Remove front bearing washer.
2. With brass drift, drive countershaft rearward to clear front bearing which will remain in case bore. Rear bearing will be driven out of case. Use a puller to remove rear bearing from countershaft.
3. Lift countershaft out of case.
4. Remove front bearings by tapping out with soft hammer from inside of case.
5. Press countershaft out of gears one at a time by supporting each gear with parallel bars as close to hub as possible. Woodruff keys need not be removed unless worn or hoose. First speed gear is integral with shaft and cannot be separated.

"B" Ratio Countershaft, Disassemble

1. Remove lock nut and washer.
2. Move countershaft forward to expose snap ring on front bearing. Use suitable puller to remove bearing from countershaft.
3. Block drive gear against moving and tap countershaft rearward until split spacer between drive gear and 4th speed gear can be removed.

NOTE: Early production models had a one-piece bearing assembly. Later production models use a separable bearing which greatly simplifies assembly and disassembly.

4. If a one-piece bearing is used remove roller retaining snap ring from inner race of rear bearing. Remove snap ring from outer race of bearing if present.
5. If snap rings are not exposed, tap countershaft forward to move drive gear back on countershaft splines (where split spacer was removed). Inner race of rear bearing will move forward out of roller cage and outer race will remain in case bore.

NOTE: If old style bearing could not be separated by snap ring removal, use a large chisel as a wedge between face of 1st speed gear and outer race of bearing to start inner race off countershaft. Use drift and hammer to complete removal.

6. With rear of countershaft free of bearing, lift rear end first and remove remaining assembly out through top of case.
7. Slide drive gear forward off countershaft.
8. Press countershaft out of gears one at a time by supporting each gear with parallel bars as close to hub as possible. Woodruff keys need not be removed unless worn or loose. The 1st speed gear is integral with the shaft and cannot be separated.

"A" Ratio Countershaft Assemble, Fig. 5

1. With Woodruff keys in place and seated securely, support hub of 2nd speed gear in an arbor press with long hub and chamfer up. Place countershaft into position and press shaft into gear until shoulder on countershaft seats firmly against gear.
2. Support hub of 4th speed gear with long hub down and chamfer up. Press shaft into 4th speed gear until it is seated firmly against 2nd speed gear.
3. Support hub of drive gear with long hub and chamfer up. Press countershaft into gear until it is seated firmly against 4th speed gear.
4. Press inner race of rear bearing on rear of shaft with lip or flange seated against shoulder of 1st speed gear.

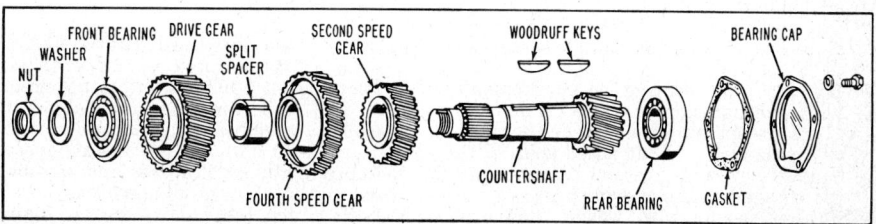

Fig. 6 "B" ratio countershaft components of the 8500 four-speed auxiliary unit

401

SPICER TRANSMISSIONS

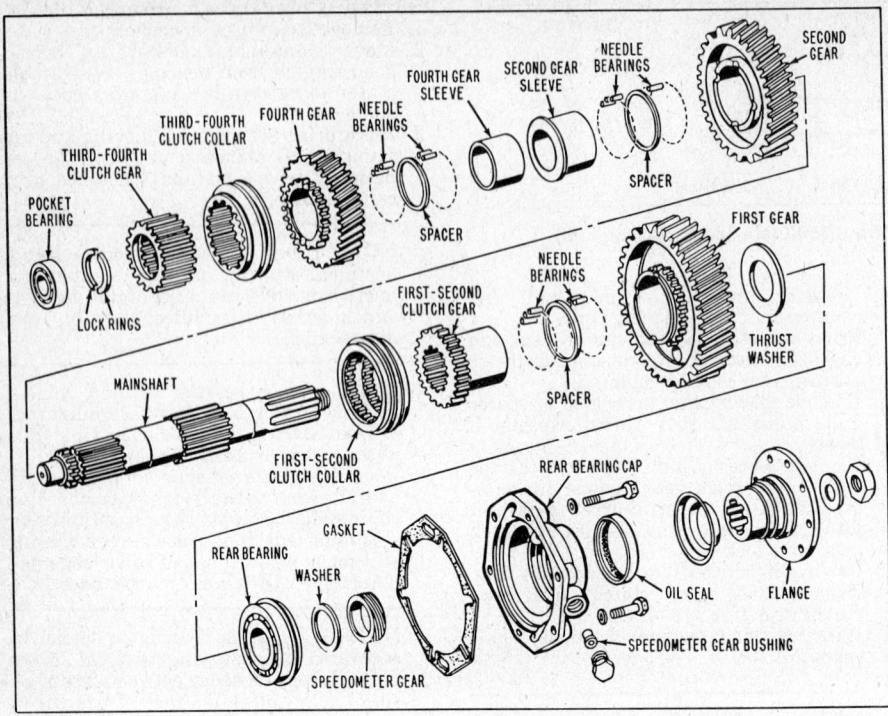

Fig. 7 Mainshaft components of the 8516 and 8716 four-speed auxiliary unit

"B" Ratio Countershaft Assemble, Fig. 6
1. With Woodruff keys in place and seated securely, support hub of 2nd speed gear in an arbor press with long hub and chamfer up. Press countershaft into gear until shoulder on countershaft seats firmly against gear.
2. Support hub of 4th speed gear with long hub down and chamfer up. Press shaft into 4th speed gear until seated firmly against 2nd speed gear.
3. Press inner race of rear bearing on rear of shaft with lip or flange seated against shoulder of 1st speed gear.
4. Assemble drive gear to front of countershaft and gear sub-assembly with long hub of drive gear toward front of countershaft. Slide gear to rear until it butts against 4th speed gear.

"A" Ratio Countershaft Installation
1. Lower rear end of countershaft assembly into case with end of shaft and 1st speed gear through rear bearing bore. Lower front of countershaft into its approximate position and maintain alignment with a cable support or by blocking up drive gear.
2. Align outer race of rear bearing with inner race and rear bore and tap flush with case.
3. Use light coat of gasket cement and assemble gasket to rear bearing cap. Apply cement to other side of gasket and assemble cap and gasket to case.
4. Dip capscrews in gasket cement and install with lockwashers. Torque capscrews to 25–32 ft-lbs.
5. Position front bearing on countershaft with external snap ring away from case. Use a 4 × 4 hard block to wedge between rear case wall and 2nd speed gear. With tubing, drive inner race of bearing until seated against hub of drive gear.
6. Secure bearing with washer and capscrews. Torque to 40–50 ft-lbs and secure with lock wire.

"B" Ratio Countershaft Installation
1. Assemble rear bearing to case and tap outer race in flush with face of case.
2. Use light coat of gasket cement to both sides of gasket and install bearing cap. Dip capscrews in gasket cement, install and torque to 25–32 ft-lbs.
3. Lower front of countershaft into case with end through front case bore. Lower rear end of countershaft into its approximate position and move toward rear until inner race on shaft is inserted in rollers of rear bearing.
4. Use a cable and chain hoist to support countershaft in its correct position. Block countershaft from moving while tapping drive gear forward on splines until stopped by front of case.
5. Assemble split spacer to shaft. Move drive gear back and make sure both halves are seated in counterbores of drive gear and 4th speed gear.
6. Position front bearing on countershaft with external snap ring away from case. Use a 2 × 4 hard block to wedge between rear case and 1st speed gear. Use tubing to drive against inner race of bearing until seated firmly against face of drive gear.
7. Remove block and tap bearing back until snap ring seats against case.
8. Place flat washer against bearing and run lock nut up finger tight. Nut will be tightened after the mainshaft is installed.

Mainshaft Assemble (both ratios) Fig. 7
1. Place 1–2 speed clutch gear on bench with flange down. Apply a light coat of grease about 1" wide to ground area above the flange. Assemble one row of 72 needle bearings to clutch gear. Install spacer. Apply light coat of grease and assemble second row of 72 needle bearings.
2. With clutch teeth down toward flange assemble 1st speed gear to clutch gear and over needle bearings and spacer. Place gear and sleeve assembly to one side.
3. In a similar manner, coat 2nd speed gear sleeve on thrust face and ground surface with grease and apply two rows of 72 needle bearings with spacer between.
4. Assemble 2nd speed gear to sleeve and bearings with clutch teeth of gear away from flange. Place gear and sleeve assembly aside.
5. Place 4th speed gear sleeve on flat plate and coat lower 1" with light grease. Assemble one row of 62 needle bearings to sleeve, add spacer and in like manner, assemble second row of 62 needle bearings.
6. Assemble 4th speed gear to sleeve and bearings with clutch teeth of gear up. Place this assembly aside.

Mainshaft Final Assembly
1. Position 1st speed gear and sleeve in rear of case with clutch teeth toward front of case. Mesh with countershaft gear. Assemble 1–2 speed clutch collar to 1st speed gear with extended hub toward gear.
2. Place 2nd speed gear and sleeve assembly in case with clutching teeth of gear toward 1st speed gear and mesh with countershaft gear. Move clutch collar to neutral to hold assemblies in relationship.
3. Coat thrust faces and splines of mainshaft with light grease. Enter pilot bearing end through rear bearing bore until mainshaft has passed through 2nd gear sleeve about 1".
4. Place 4th speed gear and sleeve in case with clutch teeth forward or away from 2nd speed gear. Slide mainshaft forward through bore of sleeve.
5. Assemble 3–4 speed clutch collar to clutch gear. Extended hub of collar assembles toward front as does lock ring counterbore in end of gear. Position gear and collar in case and assemble to mainshaft spline.
6. Block 3–4 clutch gear and tap mainshaft through until locking groove in mainshaft is beyond clutch gear.
7. Coat the two clutch gear lock rings with heavy grease and place in groove provided in mainshaft.
8. Tap mainshaft rearward and make sure lock rings center inside of counterbore of 3–4 clutch gear.
9. Assemble 1st speed gear thrust washer on rear of mainshaft next to 1st speed gear.
10. Position mainshaft rear bearing onto mainshaft with external snap ring away from case. Use a ¾" thick steel strip of flat stock to block front of mainshaft against inside of case. Use a pinch bar to roll mainshaft into position to align outer race of bearing with case bore. With tubing, drive on inner race until bearing is seated against 1st speed gear thrust washer.
11. Remove ¾" blocking and continue to tap bearing into case bore until snap ring is seated against case.
12. Assemble rear bearing washer and speedometer gear or spacer to mainshaft and seat against rear bearing.
13. If necessary, replace speedometer gear bushing in rear bearing cap.
14. Apply a light coat of gasket cement to O.D. of rear bearing cap oil seal and press into cap.
15. Apply gasket cement to gasket and fasten onto bearing cap. Align oil passages.
16. Apply cement to other side of gasket and assemble bearing cap and gasket to rear

SPICER TRANSMISSIONS

of case. Dip capscrews in gasket cement and install with copper washers. Torque capscrews to 60–80 ft-lbs and secure with lock wire.
17. Assemble end yoke or flange to mainshaft with pusher tool. Do not drive on either piece without provision to stop shaft from moving forward.
18. Assemble flat washer and lock nut. Lock transmission in two gears and torque lock nut to 400–450 ft-lbs.
19. Torque countershaft front lock nut to 550–600 ft-lbs and stake nut in slot in shaft.
20. Shift clutch collars back into neutral and make sure all shafts turn free.
21. Use pressure type oil can to force lubricant down oil holes and end slots of all floating gears on mainshaft to flush out grease and to insure initial lubrication of overrunning gears and bearings.
22. Drive gear pocket bearing is a separable part. Due to the vertical method of reassembling the rear unit to the front unit, the inner race may be pressed on the front end of the rear mainshaft or, with the outer race, be placed in the drive gear pocket. Note that flanged end of inner race assembles toward 3rd speed clutch gear. If necessary, use tubing to drive against inner race until it seats against spline shoulder.
23. Assemble rear unit to front unit in reverse order of disassembly and install shifter housing.

Spicer 9441 Four-Speed Auxiliary Unit

This transmission, Fig. 1, is designed to utilize splash and pump feed lubrication for all internal bearings, bushings, shafts and gears.

Mainshaft, Disassemble, Fig. 2

1. Remove shifter housing.
2. Lock transmission in two gears.
3. Remove drive gear and mainshaft companion flange (or end yoke) nuts.
4. Use a puller to remove drive gear and mainshaft companion flange or end yokes.
5. Remove front transmission hanger (if used) from drive gear rear bearing cap.
6. Disconnect oil line from front bearing fitting. Disconnect oil lines from fittings on front pump. If it is not necessary to remove the oil lines connected to the case bottom oil screen and filter, leave these oil lines intact.
7. Disconnect oil line from mainshaft rear bearing cap and countershaft rear bearing cap fitting.
8. Separate drive gear front bearing cap from drive gear rear bearing cap.
9. Unfasten drive gear rear bearing cap. Use a soft hammer and tap on trunnion bearing face of drive gear rear bearing cap until it is separated from case far enough to use two pry bars between case and cap.
10. Pry evenly with both bars until bearing cap and front drive gear bearing are free of drive gear. Remove bearing spacer from drive gear.
11. Tap front bearing free of bearing cap.
12. Unfasten and separate mainshaft rear bearing cap from case. Check and remove speedometer bushing if it is to be replaced.
13. Remove speedometer drive gear (or spacer) and bearing thrust washer from rear of mainshaft, using puller tool.
14. Remove bearing retainer with tapered roller bearing, cups and gasket from case.
15. Use two pry bars to slide mainshaft and gear assembly toward rear of case as far as possible.

NOTE: Some of the needle bearings used with the Lo-Lo gear may fall as the mainshaft moves rearward. Use care not to lose these needles if they are to be used again.

16. Place a 1/2" thick aluminum or brass block

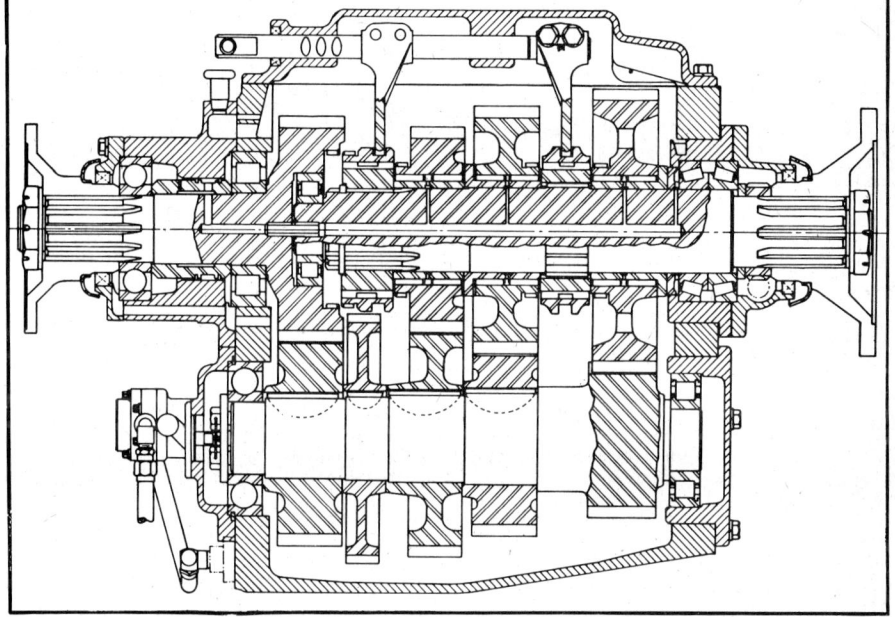

Fig. 1 Sectional view of Spicer Model 9441 four-speed auxiliary transmission

between main drive gear and mainshaft direct and overdrive clutch gear.
17. Tap forward on rear of mainshaft until lock rings are exposed from direct and overdrive clutch gear.
18. Remove 1/2" block and remove lock rings.
19. Pull mainshaft out through rear bearing bore, lifting loose parts out through top of case as mainshaft is being withdrawn.

NOTE: If transmission is to be rebuilt using old drive gear and mainshaft, be sure to clean out the shaft center oil reservoir orifices.

20. Before attempting to remove drive gear, countershaft must be removed from front and rear bores by sliding assembly to the rear. This allows drive gear to pass by front face of countershaft power take-off gear.
21. Slide drive gear and inner race off its bearing rearward and lift out through top of case. Remove inner race of bearing. If necessary, remove oil tube from pocket of drive gear.
22. Tap outer race of drive gear roller bearing out of front bearing bore of case. Remove pocket bearing from drive gear.

Countershaft, Disassemble, Fig. 3

1. Remove front bearing cap.
2. Remove rear bearing cap and bearing.
3. Push countershaft rearward and out of front bearing.
4. Lift front end of countershaft up and out of case.
5. Support P.T.O. gear with parallel bars under and as close to hub as possible and press countershaft free from drive gear and P.T.O. gear.
6. Support 2nd speed gear and press countershaft free from 4th and 2nd speed gears. Remove exposed Woodruff keys.

Countershaft, Resasssemble, Fig. 3

CAUTION: All gears should fit tight on countershaft. As a shrink (or interference) fit of

403

SPICER TRANSMISSIONS

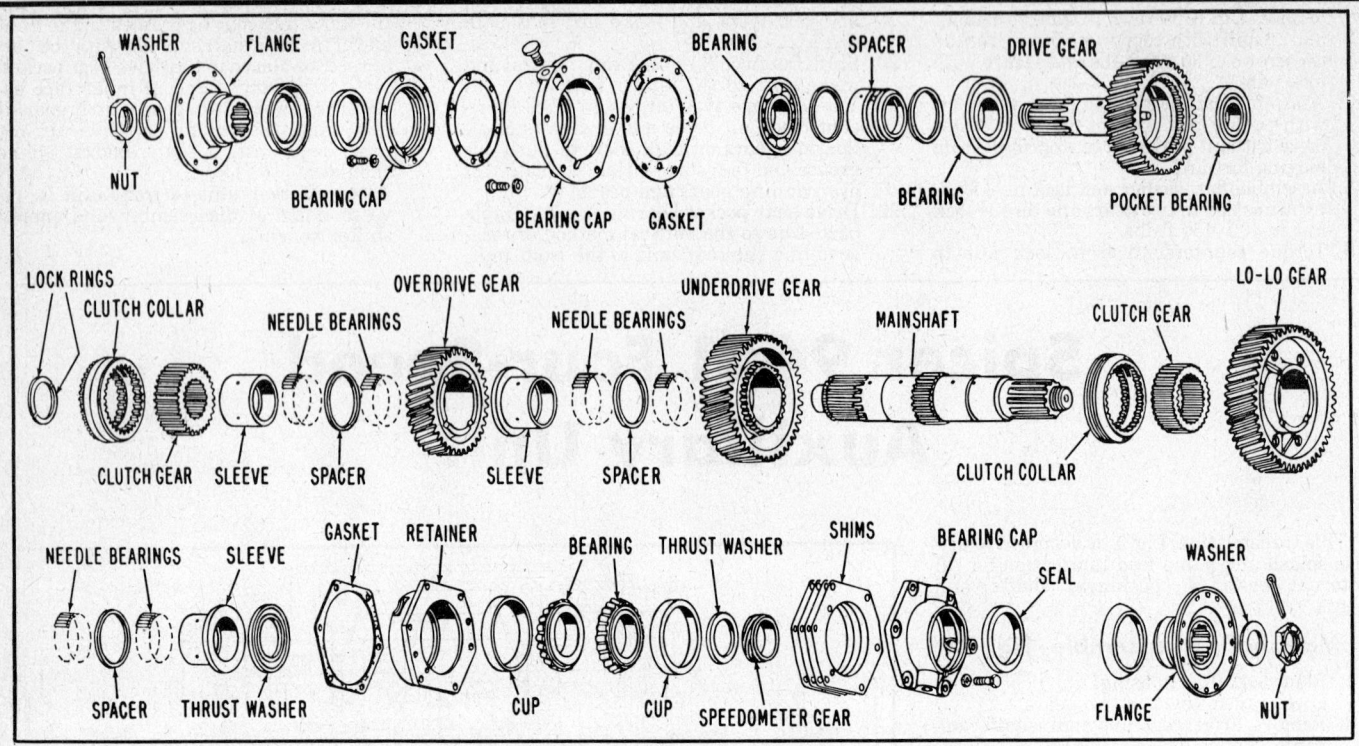

Fig. 2 Mainshaft components. Spicer 9441

.0015" to .003" is built into new parts, it presents a field assembly problem.

If heat is used to expand gear bores, boiling water, hot oil or steam are usually satisfactory. Do not exceed 250°F. Do not use hot plates, acetylene torch or other methods that will turn the steel blue or straw color and damage the heat treated gears.

If heat is not used, it is advisable to coat the gear bores heavily with white lead to prevent galling or seizing of parts.

When in doubt as to which end of the hub to assemble on the shaft first, look for the chamfered end in the bore.

1. Assemble all Woodruff keys in countershaft keyways.
2. Support 2nd speed gear on arbor press with chamfer up. Set countershaft into position. Align keys with keyway and press shaft into gear. Seat shoulder firmly against low gear.
3. Support 4th speed gear with long hub down and chamfer up. Align keys with keyway and press shaft into gear firmly against shoulder of 2nd gear.
4. Support P.T.O. gear with long hub up and chamfer up. Align keys with keyway and press shaft into gear firmly against shoulder of 4th speed gear.
5. Support drive gear with long hub down and chamfer up. Align key with keyway and press shaft into gear firmly against shoulder of P.T.O. gear.

Countershaft, Install

1. Assemble bearing to rear of countershaft.
2. Using a rope or wire sling placed in center of countershaft assembly, use hoist to lower assembly in case. Lower rear end of shaft into case and slide small end of shaft out rear bearing bore.
3. Place gasket to rear bearing cap using gasket cement.
4. Slide bearing cap and gasket onto shaft and secure cap to case. Hand tighten capscrews at this time.
5. With front end of countershaft in its approximate position, assemble front bearing onto shaft and seat snap ring against case.
6. Assemble lock plate to end of shaft and torque capscrews to 35-40 ft-lbs. Secure screws with lock wire.
7. Be sure bearing cap is in proper position on rear face of case. Torque capscrews to 35-40 ft-lbs.

CAUTION: Make certain pump coupling is on pump drive shaft, as pump is driven by coupling through slot in countershaft end.

8. Install front bearing cap with pump and gasket to case. Line up oil passages in gasket and bearing cap with main case. Torque capscrews to 35-40 ft-lbs.

Main Drive Gear, Assemble

1. Press inner race of bearing with flanged end toward teeth of drive gear. Seat flange of inner race securely against shoulder.
2. Lower front end of drive gear, with inner race of bearing, through top opening and slide it forward through bore of case. Tap outer race of bearing through front of case, using a soft hammer. Position drive gear in outer race of bearing.
3. Install spacer with sealing rings on drive gear shaft.
4. Install drive gear bearing cap with gasket over sealing rings with spacer on case. Line up oil passages in gasket and bearing cap. Secure with lockwashers and capscrews. Install breather cap if removed.
5. Press bearing into bearing cap.
6. Press oil seal in bore of front bearing cap.
7. Assemble front bearing cap and oil seal with gasket to bearing cap. Line up oil passage in gasket and bearing cap. Torque capscrews to 35-40 ft-lbs.
8. Install outer race of bearing into bore of drive gear. Install oil tube into bore of drive gear. This tube must be concentric with bore within .002" total indicator reading.

Mainshaft, Assemble & Install

1. Position case, with gears assembled, in a vertical position with front end down. Lubricate all mainshaft bearing bores with light grease as gears are assembled. Do not plug oil holes with grease.
2. Install collar on clutch gear and set these into clutch teeth of main drive gear. Using heavy grease in 3rd speed (or overdrive) gear, assemble one row of 56 needle bearings in bore. Place spacer in bore and assemble second row of 56 needle bearings in bore of gear.
3. Slide sleeve into needle bearing bore of gear. Place gear assembly with clutch teeth down on top of clutch gear. Use care not to drop or lose any needle bearings.
4. Use heavy grease in bore of 2nd speed gear. Assemble one row of 56 needle bearings in bore. Place spacer in bore and assemble second row of 56 needle bearings.
5. Place a 1/2" thick collar or spacers between overdrive gear and front face of underdrive gear. Slide sleeve into needle bearing bore of gear with flanged end of sleeve away from clutch teeth. Place gear as-

SPICER TRANSMISSIONS

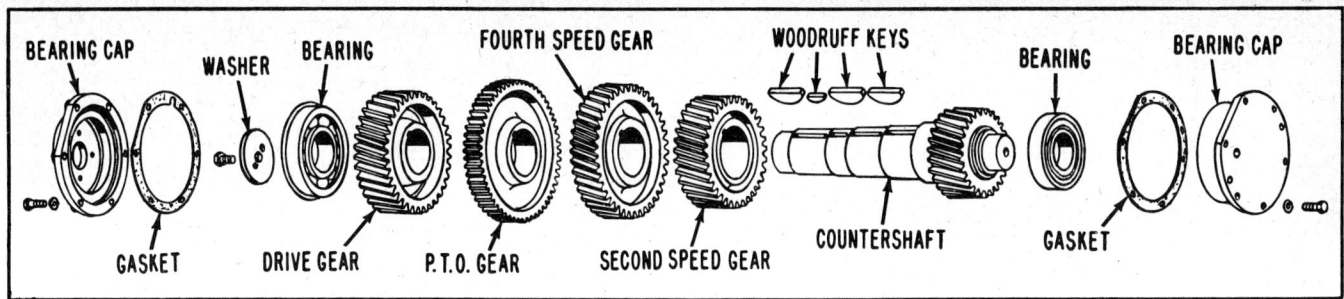

Fig. 3 Countershaft components. Spicer 9441

sembly with clutch teeth up on top of 3rd speed or overdrive gear.
6. Assemble clutch collar to clutch gear and place on top of 2nd speed gear.
7. Use heavy grease in bore of 1st speed gear. Assemble 56 needle bearings in one end of bore. Place spacer in bore and assemble 56 needle bearings on other end of bore.
8. Place 1st speed gear assembly with clutch teeth down on top of clutch gear.
9. Slide mainshaft through all gears. Allow inner race of bearing on front of shaft to seat in rollers of outer race of bearing in drive gear.

CAUTION: Before placing mainshaft into gears, notice drill point mark in back of input spline tooth for alignment teeth of clutch gears. Assemble inner race of bearing on end of mainshaft to be lowered into drive gear pocket bearing outer race.

10. Assemble 1st speed sleeve, with flange up, into 1st speed gear needle bearing bore. Install thrust washer with flat side against flange face of sleeve.
11. Apply gasket cement to gasket and install on bearing retainer. Assemble bearing retainer to case. Note word "Top" for proper location and line up oil passages.
12. Install front tapered bearing cup in retainer. Use tubing to press bearing cone on mainshaft. Leave rear cone and cup out of bearing retainer at this time as they will be assembled during a later step.
13. Lower entire case assembly to horizontal position. Pull 1/2" collar or spacers from between overdrive gear and underdrive gear.
14. Use pry bars on front face of clutch gear and move gears to rear as far as possible. Tap rear end of mainshaft with a soft hammer until lock ring groove is fully exposed. Use heavy grease to coat faces of lock rings and install in shaft groove.
15. To secure lock rings in place, use a pry bar on rear face of 1st speed gear and force gears forward. This will secure lock rings under clutch gear.
16. Assemble 2nd tapered roller bearing cone on shaft, and 2nd tapered cup into retainer. Assemble spacer and speedometer drive gear (if used) on shaft.
17. If oil seal was removed from rear bearing cap, use gasket cement on O.D. of seal and press into bearing cap. Press in new speedometer bushing (if removed).
18. Assemble rear bearing cap and shim pack to case.

CAUTION: Line up of oil hole on shims with oil hole in retainer is required. Blocking of retainer oil hole by improper shim placement will deprive tapered bearings of lubrication.

19. Secure bearing cap and shim pack and torque capscrews to 35-40 ft-lbs.
20. Assemble end yoke or companion flange and flat washer to rear of shaft. Tighten nut firmly but do not torque at this time.
21. Check end play of mainshaft taper roller bearings. Fasten dial indicator to back face of case with dial indicator shaft on end face of mainshaft. Set dial indicator on "zero".
22. Using body weight and hands, rotate flange or yoke back and forth about 30° while pushing forward. Read indicator until it ceases to change. Leaving indicator as it reads, pull back and twist flange or yoke until reading again ceases to change. Total end play should be .003 to .005". Add or remove shims as required to obtain the desired result.
23. After adjustment is made, remove nut, flange or yoke and rear bearing cap. Coat I.D. and O.D. of shim pack with gasket cement to obtain a good seal. Secure rear cap and torque capscrews to 35-40 ft-lbs.

Final Assembly

1. Lock transmission in two gears.
2. If proper tools are not available, block front or rear face of gears with 3/4" stock. Use tubing to install flange or yoke. Tighten drive gear and mainshaft flange or yoke nuts to 400-450 ft-lbs.
3. Shift clutch collars back into neutral and make sure all shafts turn free.
4. Use a pressure type oil can to force lubricant down the oil holes and end slots of all floating gears on mainshaft to flush out grease and insure initial lubrication of overrunning gears and bearings.

WARNER TRANSMISSIONS

Index & Lube Capacity

Model	Speeds	Oil, Pts.	Page
T9, T9A	4	6	406
T10	4	①	416
T14A	3	2½	419
T15A	3	2¾	419
T16	3	①	411
T18	4	①	411
T19	4	6½	420
T85	3	①	406
T86	3	①	407
T87D	3	6	408
T87E	3	5½	408
T89B	3	3	408
T89C	3	3½	408
T90	3	①	407
T96	3	①	408
T97	4	7	406
T98, T98A	4	8	411
T150	3	2¾	422
T176	4	3½	426

①—Capacities vary. Fill to bottom of filler hole.

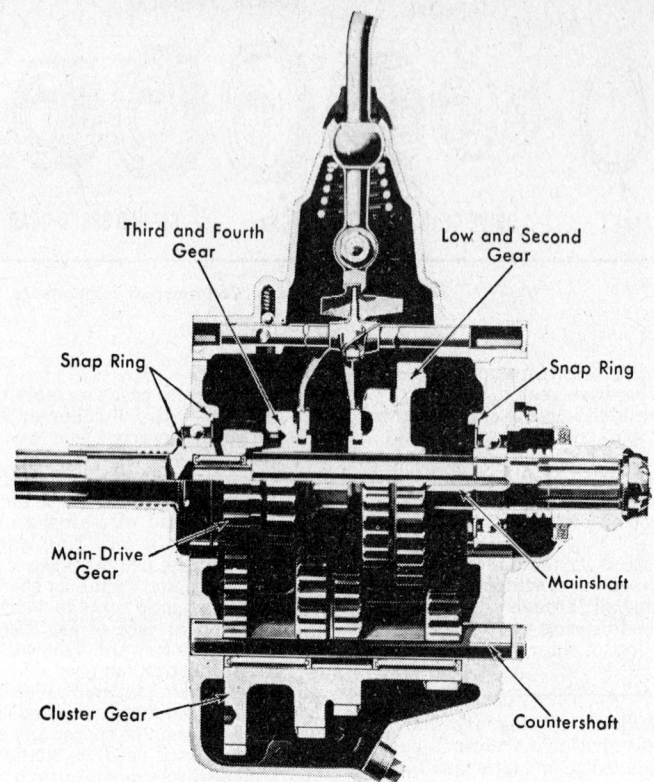

Fig. 1 Warner T9, T97 Series four speed transmission

T9, T97 SERIES

Disassemble, Fig. 1

1. Take off the transmission cover.
2. Unscrew the nut from the universal flange.
3. Remove the hand brake mechanism.
4. Remove universal flange.
5. Remove main drive gear bearing retainer and pull drive gear out through front.
6. Take off mainshaft rear bearing retainer oil seal and speedometer drive gear.
7. Before removing the mainshaft, chalk-mark the relationship of the mainshaft splines with the mating splines in the sliding gears so that these parts may be assembled in the original position, as the gears are a selective fit on the mainshaft splines.
8. Grasp the mainshaft gears and pull the mainshaft and rear bearing out through the rear. Then lift out the loose gears.
9. Remove the counter shaft lock plate, push the shaft through the rear and lift out the cluster gear.
10. Drive out the reverse shift rail and lift out the fork.
11. Push the reverse idler shaft out through the rear and lift out the gear.

Reassembly

Reverse the order of the above procedure to assemble the unit. And when installing the mainshaft, be sure to match the marked gear splines with the mainshaft splines.

T85 SERIES

Three Speed, Fig. 2

1. To disassemble, remove gearshift housing.
2. Remove mainshaft nut and parking brake.
3. Remove U-joint flange, speedometer gear and spacer.
4. Remove mainshaft and rear bearing retainer rearward out of case as a unit.
5. Remove mainshaft pilot bearing.
6. Remove main drive gear bearing retainer. After removing large snap ring, tap drive gear and bearing back into case, removing it through rear of case.
7. Drive countershaft backward out of case and remove cluster gear assembly.
8. Remove reverse idler gear.
9. To disassemble mainshaft, remove snap ring from its front end. Mark relationship of synchronizer hub and sleeve and slide synchronizer and gears off shaft.

Assemble Transmission

1. Install reverse idler gear and shaft with chamfered teeth ends toward front.
2. Install cluster gear assembly in bottom of case. Tang on front washer fits into slot in case thrust face. Tab on rear steel washer must be up.
3. Install main drive gear bearing and snap ring from front until snap ring bottoms on case.
4. Install drive gear retainer without gasket and finger tighten retainer bolts.
5. Install oil slinger on drive gear shaft with grease and with dished side away from bearing.
6. Install drive gear shaft with oil slinger in case and shaft into bearing.
7. Remove drive gear retainer and install spacer washer and thickest snap ring that will fit. Snap rings are available in thicknesses of .086″ to .103″.
8. Tape drive gear shaft forward out of case as far as gear will allow. Then install mainshaft pilot in bore of drive gear, using grease to hold rollers in place.
9. Install synchronizer stop ring on rear end of drive gear shaft, coating inside of stop ring with grease.

Assemble Mainshaft

1. Press rear bearing on mainshaft. Install rear snap ring into rear bearing retainer housing and tap mainshaft with bearing into retainer. Install thickest snap ring that will fit in front of rear bearing. Snap rings are available in thicknesses of .088″ to .100″.
2. Assemble gears and synchronizer on mainshaft. Grease synchronizer stop ring before assembling, and make sure stop rings are free.
3. Install mainshaft, being sure that one of the pilot bearings is not forced off position and block oil hole in mainshaft.
4. Tap main drive gear to rear until snap ring seats on case.

Final Assembly

1. Turn transmission to help align cluster gear to install countershaft.
2. When countershaft is close to end of case, install key and drive it into case.
3. Turn rear bearing retainer into position and torque retainer bolts to 65–75 ft. lbs.
4. Install new gasket on main drive gear bearing retainer, install retainer and torque bolts 25–30 ft. lbs. Select gasket or gaskets that will seal lubricant and prevent end play between snap ring and retainer. Gaskets are available in thicknesses of .10″ to .025″.
5. Install spacer, speedometer drive gear and flange.

WARNER TRANSMISSIONS

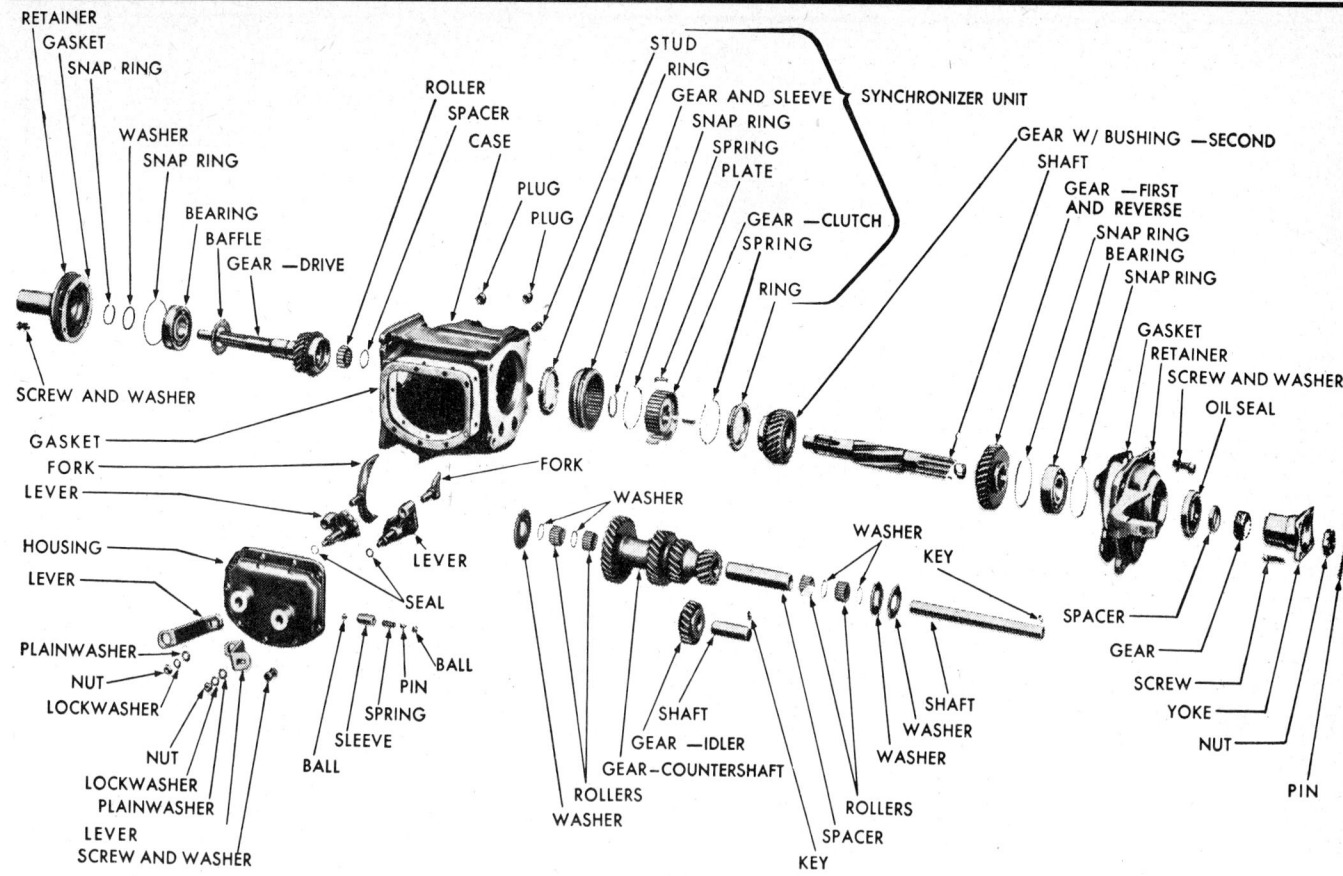

Fig. 2 Warner T85 Series three speed transmission

6. Install parking brake.
7. Shift transmission into neutral. Place 2nd-3rd fork on clutch gear sleeve and place gearshift housing with new gasket on case.

Gearshift Linkage

For any adjustment to bring shift lever to horizontal plane with lever in neutral position, adjust length of 2nd-3rd control rod at its swivel.

The crossover movement of lever should be made without binding or interference. If slots in lever are not aligned, the gearshift tube pin strikes corner of slot. To bring slots in line, adjust low-reverse rod.

T86, T90 SERIES

Three Speed, Fig. 2A

1. Remove shift housing or cover from top of case. On floor shift models, remove shift rails and forks from shift housing.
2. Remove front main drive gear bearing retainer and two socket head screws supporting oil collector inside case, if equipped.
3. Tap front end of countershaft to loosen lock plate, then remove lock plate.
4. With a brass drift, drive countershaft through rear of case and countershaft gear set will drop to bottom of case.
5. Remove mainshaft rear bearing adapter, then mainshaft and gears from case through rear bearing adapter opening.
6. If equipped with oil collector, drive main drive gear into case far enough to remove the collector.
7. Remove main drive gear and on column shift models, remove shift forks.
8. Remove countershaft gear set and thrust washers from bottom of case, then washers, needle bearings and spacer from gear set.
9. With a brass drift, drive reverse idler gear shaft into case, then remove reverse idler gear and shaft.

Assemble Transmission

Reverse above procedure to assemble transmission, observing the following:

1. When replacing either transmission case or transfer case, if used, ensure drilled oil holes on case mating surfaces match and correct gasket is used.
2. Place reverse idler gear and shaft into case, ensuring slot at shaft end is aligned properly to allow lock plate installation.
3. Install spacer, washers and countershaft needle bearings into countershaft gear hub. Place a washer and a set of roller bearings at each end of spacer. Add a set of roller bearings and a washer at each end, completing the assembly. Place countershaft gear set into case, however, do not install countershaft in final position until mainshaft and main drive gear have been installed.
4. Install low and reverse sliding gear on main shaft with shift shoe groove facing front of transmission.
5. To assemble synchronizer unit: Install the two springs in high and intermediate clutch hub with spring tension opposing each other. Install three synchronizer shifting plates into three slots in hub with smooth side of plates facing outward. Hold plates in position then slip second and direct speed clutch sleeve over hub with the long beveled edge toward long part of clutch hub. Install one blocking ring on each side of hub. Place assembly on mainshaft with beveled edge of clutch sleeve toward front end of shaft.
6. Install main drive gear bearing onto main drive gear shaft with tool KF-128A.
7. When installing main shaft, ensure main drive gear needle bearing rollers are correctly positioned.
8. Install front and rear bearing retainers on mainshaft and rotate transmission mainshaft, allowing gears to mesh and permitting alignment and installation of countershaft.
9. To install countershaft gear set: Install large bronze thrust washer at front of case with lip entered in slot of case. Install steel thrust washer at rear of case and partially insert the countershaft into case to hold washer in position. Align slot in countershaft with slot in reverse idler gear shaft, permitting installation of lock plate. Ensure thrust washers are positioned properly, then place bronze thrust washer against rear end of gear and place gear in its running position. Drive countershaft through countershaft gear set and case. When installed, the countershaft gear set should have .012 to .018 inch end play. End play is obtained by the selective thickness of rear steel thrust washers available in thicknesses of .0555 and .0625 inch.

WARNER TRANSMISSIONS

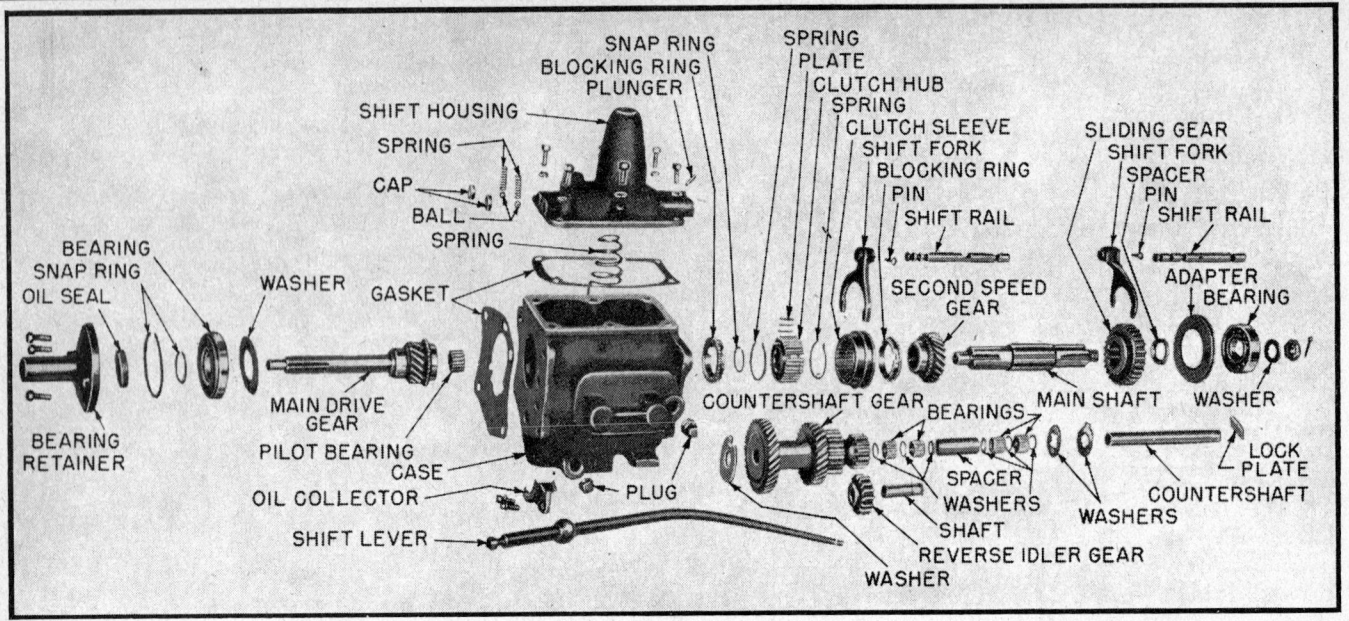

Fig. 2A Warner T86, T90 Series three speed transmission with floor shift

T87 SERIES

Three Speed, Figs. 3 and 4

1. Remove gearshift housing.
2. Remove parking brake.
3. Remove mainshaft bearing retainer.
4. Drive countershaft out through rear of case.
5. Use puller to remove mainshaft bearing.
6. Remove input shaft retainer and tap shaft and bearing as far forward as possible.
7. Remove mainshaft assembly.
8. Remove input shaft. If bearing is to be replaced, assemble with thickest snap ring that will fit.
9. Use puller to remove reverse idler shaft.
10. Remove reverse idler gear and countershaft gear cluster.

Assemble Transmission

1. Install reverse idler gear and shaft.
2. Install cluster gear assembly with front thrust washer tip hooked into groove on inside of case. Check end play (.006–.020"). Change thrust washers as required.
3. Install assembled mainshaft. Place a short 2 × 4 block between input shaft and mainshaft. Slide mainshaft bearing baffle and bearing onto shaft. Baffle must be installed so it does not rub bearing outer race. Drive bearing onto shaft.
4. Install mainshaft pilot rollers in input shaft, holding them with grease.
5. Place front blocking ring on synchronizer and start input shaft bearing in case.
6. Drive mainshaft bearing into case.
7. Tap input shaft and bearing into place. Install retainer without gasket and tighten bolts to bottom retainer on snap ring. With feeler gauge, check clearance between gasket surface and case. Select a gasket or gaskets that will seal oil and eliminate all clearance.
8. Raise cluster gear and insert countershaft. Then install retainer in notches in countershaft and reverse idler shaft. Drive both shafts toward front so that retainer is tight against gasket and torque bolts to 25-37 ft. lbs.
9. Install speedometer gear and spacer, mainshaft bearing retainer and gasket, and parking brake. Tighten output shaft nut to 90-125 ft. lbs.
10. Install gearshift housing.

T89 SERIES

Three Speed, Figs. 5 and 6

1. Remove gearshift housing.
2. Remove parking brake.
3. Tap main drive gear forward as far as possible.
4. Push countershaft out of rear of case.
5. Remove mainshaft assembly.
6. Remove main drive gear; then bearing.
7. Drive reverse idler gear shaft out of rear of case.
8. Lift out countershaft gear cluster.
9. Disassemble mainshaft.

Assemble Transmission

1. Place assembled countershaft gear cluster in case. Tang on front thrust washer fits into slot in case surface. Tab on rear steel washer must be up.
2. Install countershaft. Check end play (.006–.020"). Change thrust washers as required.
3. Install reverse idler gear shaft with chamfered teeth ends to front. Drive shaft in nearly flush with case and insert Woodruff key.
4. Tap input shaft bearing in case until snap ring bottoms in case. Install bearing retainer without gasket and barely tighten retainer capscrews. Lightly coat baffle with grease to hold it in place and install it on input shaft at rear of bearing with dished side away from bearing. Drive shaft into bearing with hard wood block.
5. Remove input shaft bearing retainer and install spacer washer and snap ring on input shaft. Install thickest snap ring that will fit. Then tap input shaft as far forward as possible and install pilot bearing rollers, holding them with grease.
6. Install mainshaft and bearing in bearing retainer casting, using the thickest snap ring that will fit.
7. Assemble mainshaft and secure with snap ring at front of shaft.
8. With new gasket, install mainshaft rear bearing retainer.
9. Tap input shaft bearing toward rear until outer snap ring bottoms on case.
10. Install countershaft gear cluster and insert Woodruff key in countershaft.
11. Torque mainshaft rear bearing retainer bolts to 65-75 ft. lbs.
12. Install and tighten input shaft bearing retainer to 25-30 ft. lbs., using a gasket or gaskets that will seal lubricant and prevent end play between snap ring and retainer.
13. Install parking brake.
14. Install shift housing cover with new gasket.

T96 SERIES

Three Speed, Fig. 6A

1. Remove transmission cover and shift levers.
2. Remove front retainer and gasket and front bearing snap rings.
3. Align notch in clutch shaft with 3rd speed gear and use suitable puller to remove clutch shaft using care not to lose rollers.
4. Remove front bearing with puller.
5. Remove extension case and remove snap rings that retain speedometer drive gear.
6. Remove speedometer gear using care not to lose drive ball.
7. Remove gear bearing snap rings and remove rear bearing with a puller.
8. Move mainshaft to side and remove shift forks.
9. Place front synchronizer in 2nd speed position and remove mainshaft by tilting front of shaft up and lifting through top of

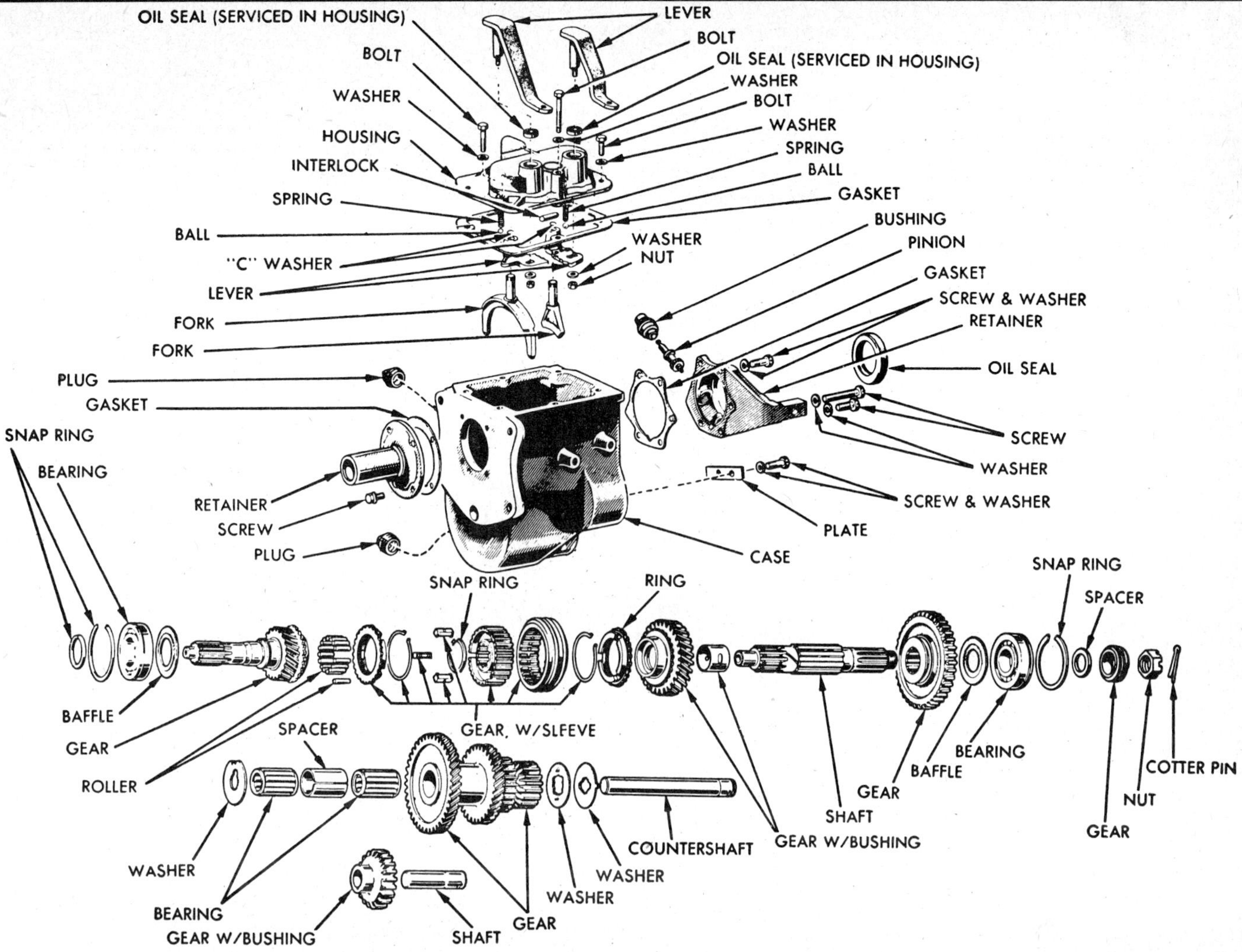

WARNER TRANSMISSIONS

Fig. 3 Warner T87 Series three speed transmission

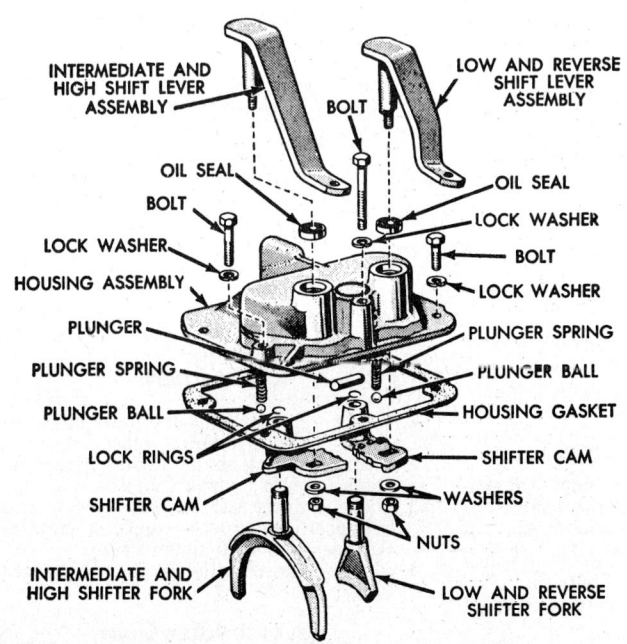

Fig. 4 Warner T87 Series gearshift housing

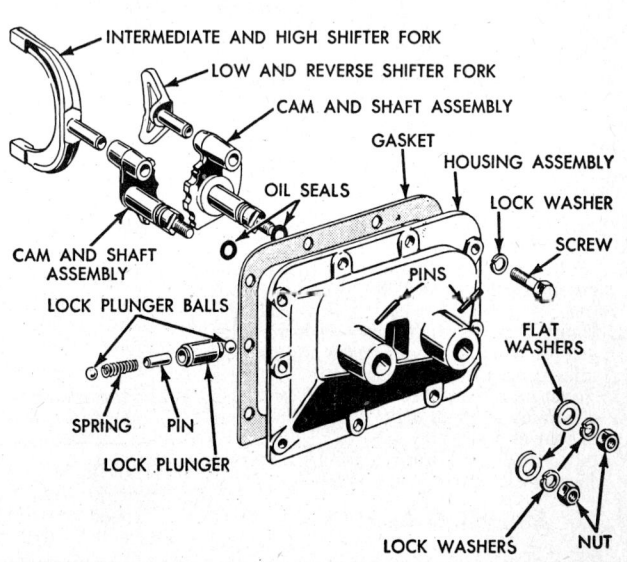

Fig. 6 Warner T89 Series gearshift housing

WARNER TRANSMISSIONS

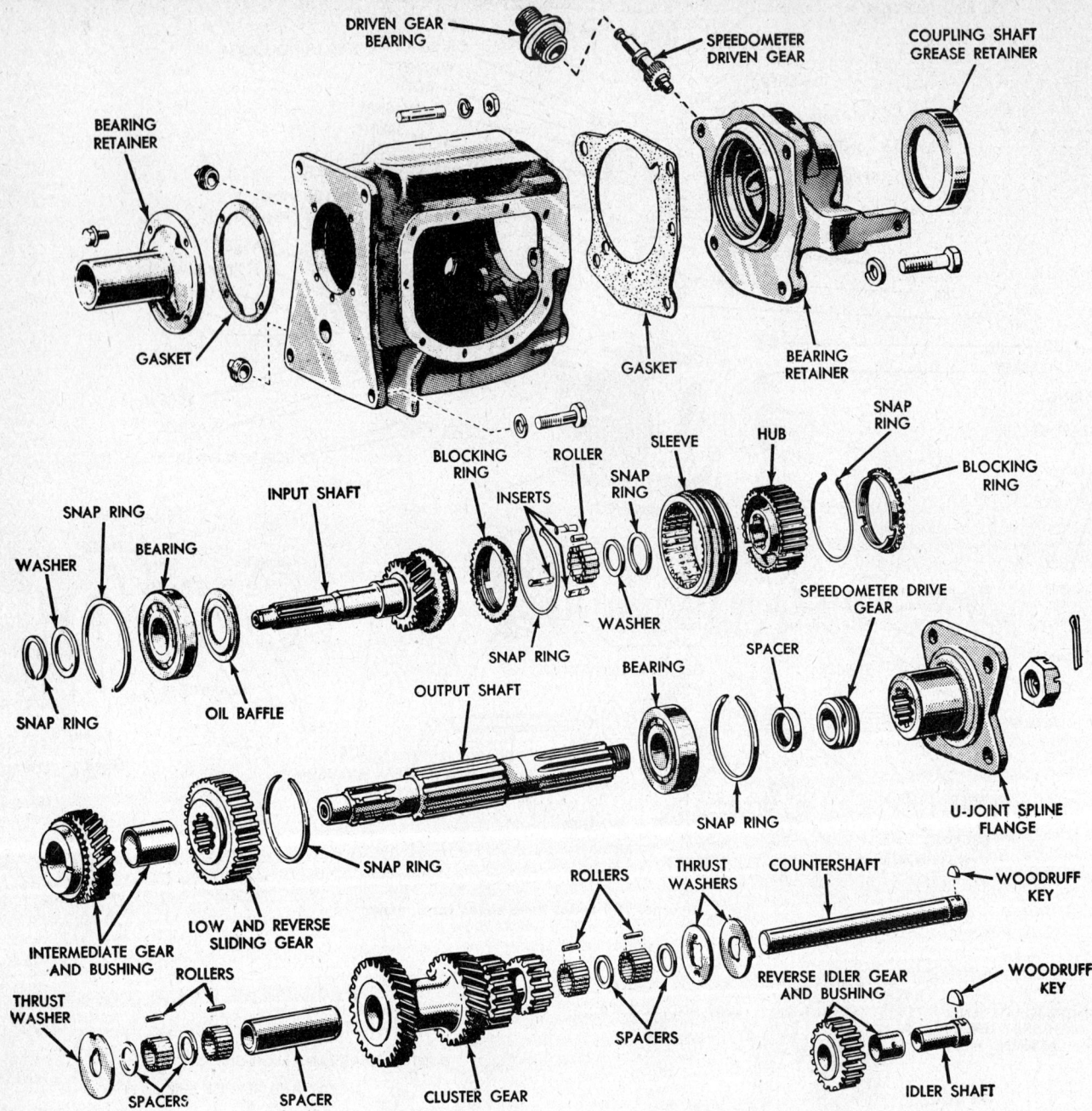

Fig. 5 Warner T89 Series three speed transmission

case.

10. Use a punch to remove roll pins from shift shafts and push shafts into case. Detent assembly may now be removed from case.

11. Using a brass drift drive reverse idler gear shaft out of gear of case and remove idler gear. Do not lose rollers.

12. To retain rollers in countershaft gear, use a dummy shaft to drive countershaft out of rear of case.

13. After disassembling mainshaft carefully inspect all bearings and gear.

Mainshaft Assemble

1. Place low speed and rear synchronizer on mainshaft and install rear synchronizer snap ring.

NOTE: Snap rings are available in select thicknesses. Clearance between first gear and collar on mainshaft must be .003–.012".

2. Place 2nd speed gear and 2nd & 3rd synchronizer on shaft and install snap ring.

NOTE: Snap rings are available in select thicknesses. Clearance between 2nd speed gear and color on mainshaft must be .003–.010".

3. Slide reverse speed gear on mainshaft and set assembly aside to be installed later.

Countergear

1. Coat bore at each end of counter gear with grease to hold rollers in place.
2. Install dummy shaft in countergear and install spacer, washers and rollers.
3. Place countergear in transmission case and position thrust washers at each end so tabs align with slots in case.
4. Use a plastic mallet to install countershaft.

Reverse Idler Gear

1. Coat bore of idler gear with grease to

WARNER TRANSMISSIONS

retain rollers.
2. Install idler gear in case and position thrust washers.
3. Use plastic mallet to install idler gear shaft.

Shifter Shafts

1. Partially install shifter shafts in transmission case.
2. Align detent assembly with shifter shafts and case stud.
3. Push shift detent assembly and shift shafts into place and install roll pins.

Mainshaft Installation

1. Place front synchronizer in 2nd speed position and place mainshaft in case.
2. Move mainshaft to side and install shift forks by pulling detent lever up and placing forks in the shifting assembly.
3. Position mainshaft assemble in center of case and place rear bearing on mainshaft, drive bearing into position and install snap ring.
4. Install speedometer gear and snap ring.

Final Assembly

1. Install rollers in clutch shaft using grease to retain them.
2. Slide clutch shaft into position through front of case.
3. Install front bearing, snap rings, gasket and retainer.
4. Replace seal if necessary and install extension housing, shift levers and case cover.
5. Fill transmission with lubricant and check operation.

T18, T98 SERIES

Four Speed, Figs. 7 thru 8B

NOTE: Case assembly shown is used on Ford trucks. Jeep vehicles have power take-off located on left side of case.

1. Remove parking brake.
2. Remove mainshaft bearing retainer.
3. Remove countershaft-reverse idler shaft lock.
4. Remove gearshift housing.
5. Remove mainshaft bearing.
6. Remove input shaft bearing.
7. Drive out countershaft.
8. Remove input shaft through front end of case.
9. Pull out reverse idler shaft.
10. Remove reverse gear shifter arm from case.
11. Remove mainshaft assembly through top of case.
12. Remove power take-off cover and roll cluster gear toward top of case until small end of assembly can be pushed through mainshaft bearing bore in case.

Assemble Transmission

1. Position case with power take-off opening downward.
2. Hold thrust washer at front end of inner thrust plate at rear end of cluster gear to prevent rollers from falling out of gear. Position gear in bottom of case and install outer thrust plate.
3. Install reverse idler gear and shaft with slot in end of shaft down at rear face of case.

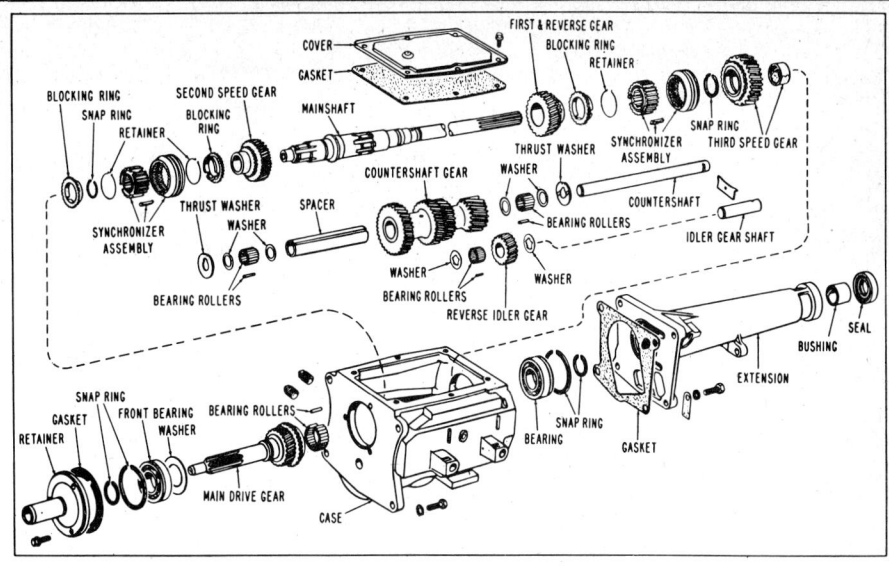

Fig. 6A Warner T96 Series three speed transmission

4. Install countershaft through cluster gear with slot in end of shaft facing downward. Cluster gear end play should be .006–.020". Change thrust washers as required.
5. Install pilot rollers in input shaft. Place baffle on shaft so it does not rub bearing race. Position input shaft in bore of case, working from inside of case. Install high speed synchronizer blocking ring on input shaft gear.
6. Install mainshaft assembly, inserting forward end in input shaft. Use a stop yoke tool over synchronizer rings to prevent jamming rings.
7. Install input shaft bearing and install thickest snap ring that will fit.
8. Install input shaft and bearing in case and install snap rings on both bearings.
9. Install input shaft retainer without gasket. Tighten bolts enough to bottom retainer on snap ring. Measure clearance between retainer gasket surface and case and select a gasket or gaskets that will seal oil and eliminate clearance. Tighten bolts to 25–30 ft. lbs.
10. Slide second speed synchronizer to rear and install reverse gear shifter arm.
11. Install reverse idler shaft-countershaft retainer and gasket. Torque retainer bolts to 25–37 ft. lbs.
12. Install speedometer gear and spacer, mainshaft bearing retainer and gasket. Make sure longest retainer bolt is in proper hole. Torque bolts to 25–35 ft. lbs.
13. Install gearshift housing and torque bolts to 30–35 ft. lbs.
14. Install U-joint flange and parking brake drum. Torque mainshaft nut to 90–125 ft. lbs.

T16 SERIES

Disassemble, Fig. 9

1. Remove side cover and shift forks.
2. Unfasten attaching screws and rotate extension housing clockwise to expose reverse idler gear shaft.
3. Drive reverse idler shaft and its woodruff key out through rear of case, Fig. 10.
4. Rotate extension housing counter-clockwise to expose countershaft and use a brass drift at front of shaft to drive shaft and its woodruff key out rear of case, Fig. 11.
5. With countergear dropped to bottom of case remove entire mainshaft and extension assembly through rear of case, Fig. 12. Remove mainshaft pilot roller bearings from clutch gear.
6. Expand snap ring in extension and remove extension from rear bearing and mainshaft by tapping on end of mainshaft, Fig. 13.
7. Remove clutch gear bearing retainer, bearing snap ring and washer from mainshaft, Fig. 14.
8. Drive clutch gear through its bearing into case, Fig. 15, and remove bearing by tapping out from inside of case.
9. Remove countergear assembly from case.

Mainshaft Disassembly

1. Remove snap ring and strip front of mainshaft, Fig. 16.
2. Remove rear bearing snap ring, Fig. 17.
3. Support reverse gear with press plates and press on rear of mainshaft to remove reverse gear, rear bearing, special washer, snap ring and speedometer drive gear from rear of mainshaft.

CAUTION: When pressing rear bearing be sure special washer is clear of snap ring groove. Also, be careful to center gear, bearing, washer and snap ring on mainshaft before attempting to press off speedometer drive gear.

4. Remove low-reverse sliding clutch hub snap ring from mainshaft, Fig. 18, and remove clutch assembly, blocker ring and low gear from mainshaft.

Synchronizer Clutch Keys & Springs

NOTE: The clutch hubs and sliding sleeves are a selected assembly and should be kept together as originally assembled. However, the two keys and springs may be replaced if worn

411

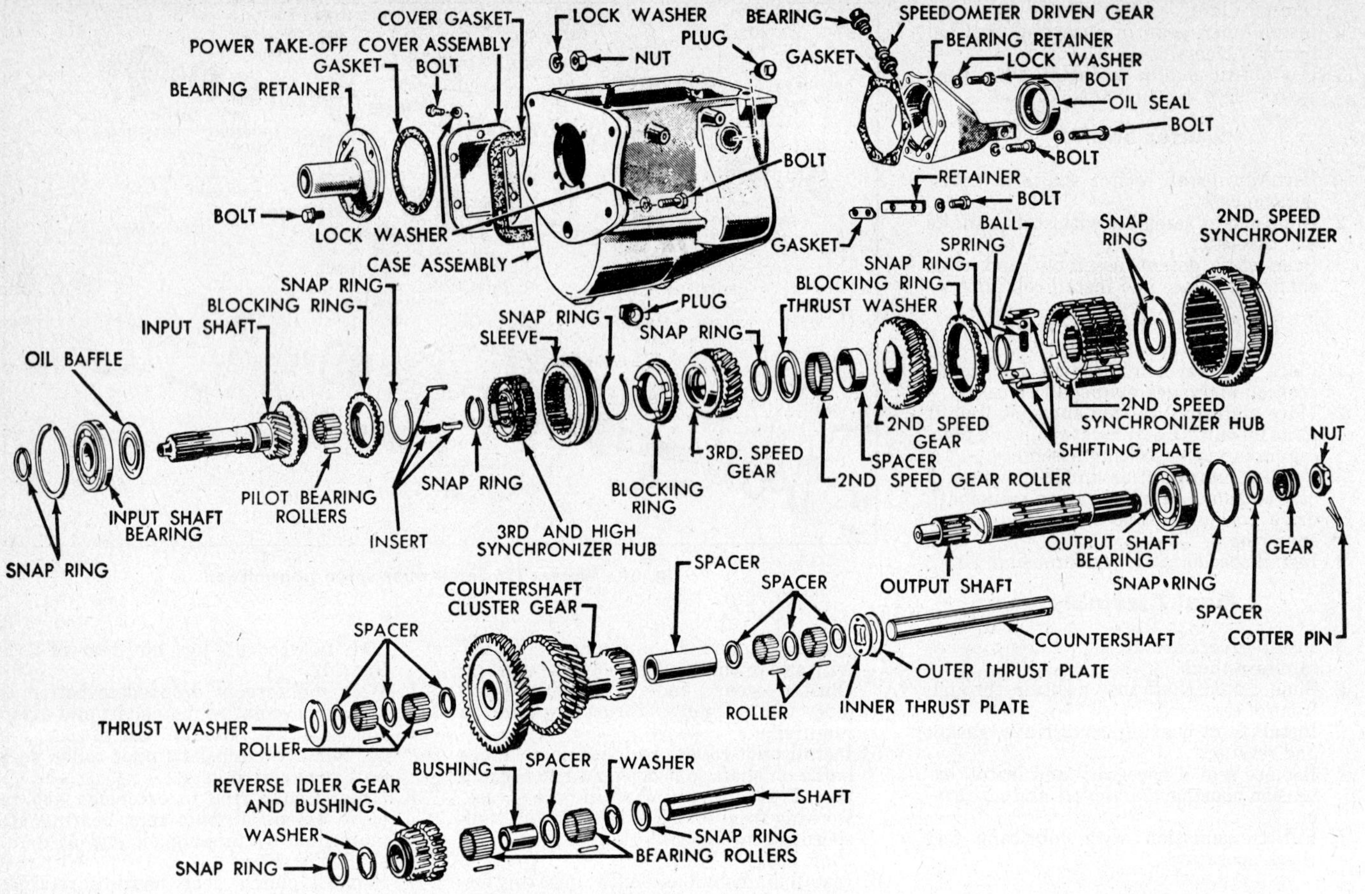

WARNER TRANSMISSIONS

Fig. 7 Warner T98 Series four speed transmission

or broken.

1. If relation of hub and sleeve are not already marked, mark for assembly purposes.
2. Push hub from sliding sleeve. Keys will fall free and springs may easily be removed.
3. Place two springs in position (one on each side of hub) so all three keys are engaged by both springs, Fig. 19. Place keys in position and, holding them in place, slide sleeve onto hub, aligning marks made previously.

Mainshaft Reassemble

1. Referring to Fig. 20, install 1st gear on rear of mainshaft with gear clutching teeth to rear.
2. Install 1st gear blocking ring over 1st gear tapered cone end area with clutch key notches toward rear.
3. Install 1st-reverse sliding clutch assembly over rear of mainshaft, being careful to engage three keys with notches of blocker ring. Properly installed, straightest side of clutch hub and taper of sliding sleeve should both be toward rear of mainshaft (see Fig. 9).
4. Install snap ring in front of 1st-reverse clutch hub, Fig. 18.

NOTE: Snap ring is available in three thicknesses. Use thickest snap ring that will assemble with all parts stacked tight

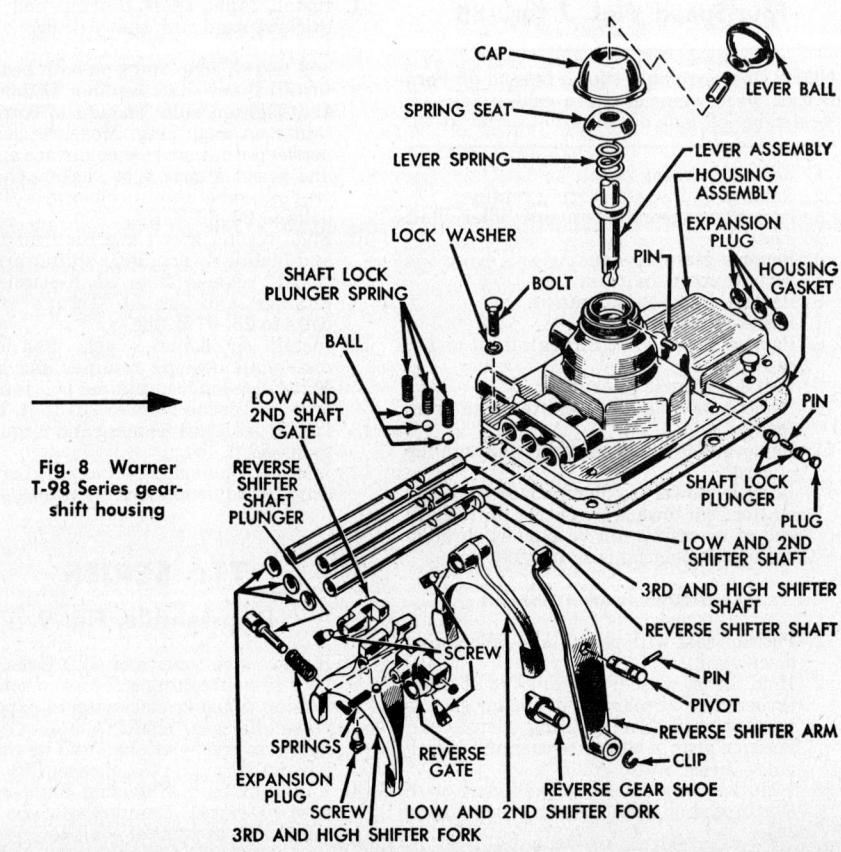

Fig. 8 Warner T-98 Series gearshift housing

WARNER TRANSMISSIONS

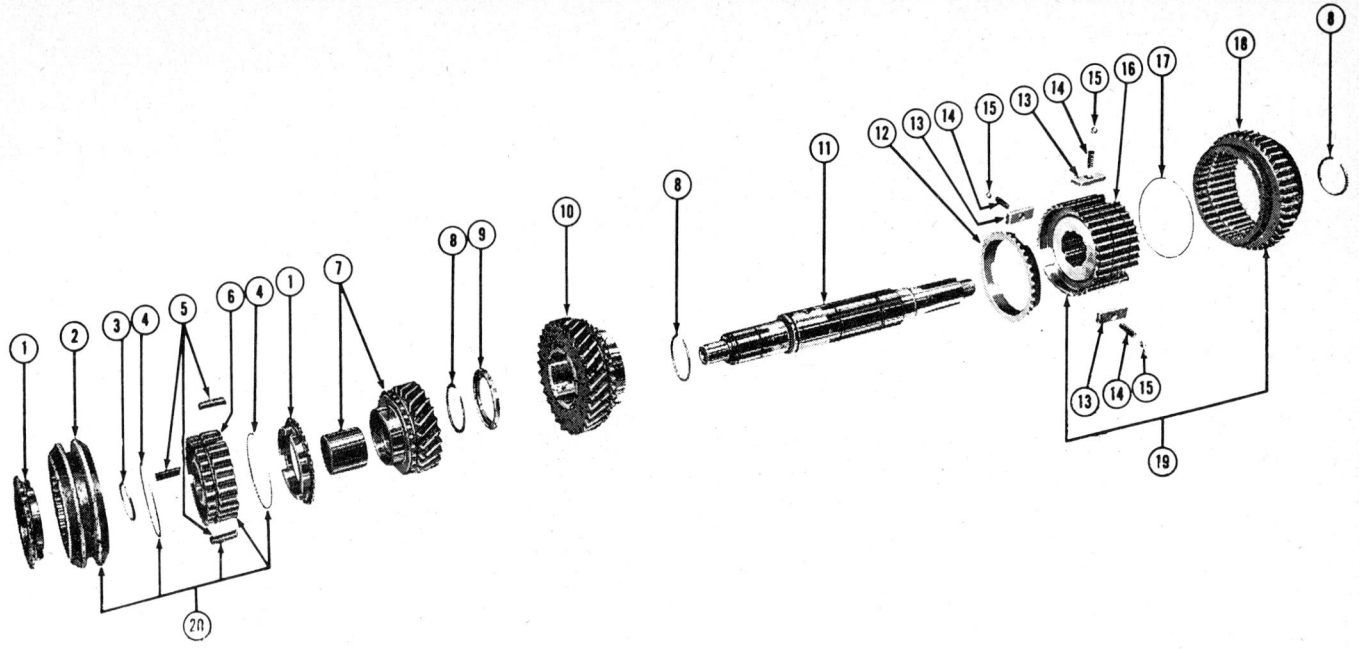

1—Blocking Ring
2—Direct and Third Clutch Sleeve
3—Snap Ring
4—Spring
5—Shifting Plate
6—Direct and Third Clutch Hub
7—Third Speed Gear Assembly
8—Snap Ring
9—Thrust Washer
10—Second Speed Gear
11—Mainshaft
12—Blocking Ring
13—Shifting Plate
14—Poppet Spring
15—Ball
16—Low and Second Clutch Hub
17—Retaining Ring
18—Low and Second Speed Gear
19—Second Speed Synchronizer Assembly
20—Direct and Third Synchronizer Assembly

Fig. 8A T18 Series mainshaft disassembled

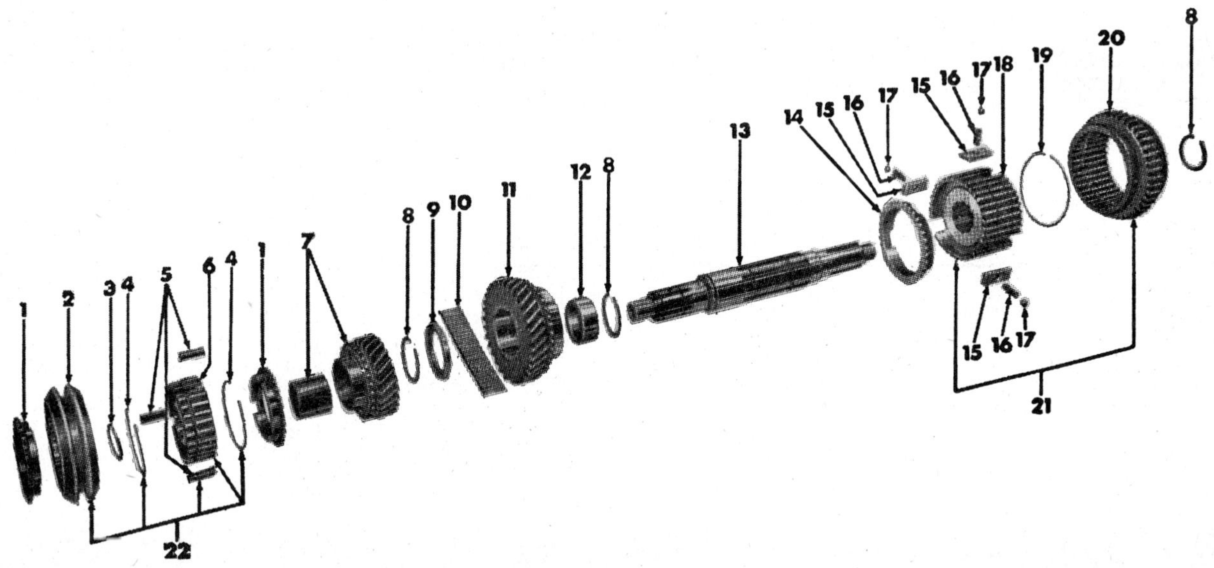

1—Blocking Ring
2—Direct-and-Third Clutch Sleeve
3—Snap Ring
4—Lock Ring
5—Shifting Plate
6—Direct-and-Third Clutch Hub
7—Third-Speed Gear Assembly
8—Snap Ring
9—Thrust Washer
10—Bearing Rollers
11—Second-Speed Gear
12—Spacer
13—Mainshaft
14—Blocking Ring
15—Shifting Plate
16—Poppet Spring
17—Ball
18—Low-and-Second Clutch Hub
19—Retaining Ring
20—Low-and-Second Speed Gear
21—Second-Speed Synchronizer Assembly
22—Direct-and-Third Synchronizer Assembly

Fig. 8B T98 Series mainshaft disassembled

413

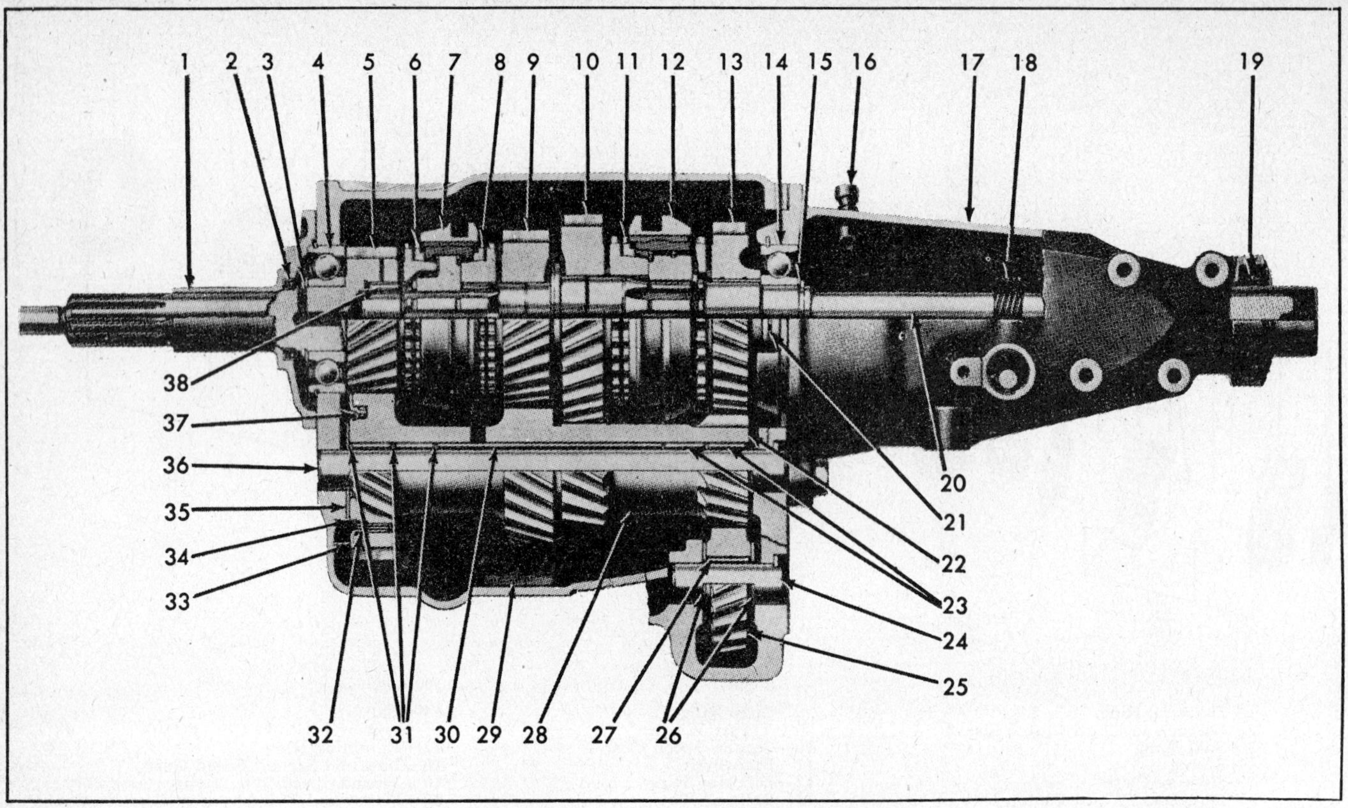

WARNER TRANSMISSIONS

Fig. 9 Warner T16 Series three speed fully synchronized transmission

1. Bearing Retainer
2. Lip Oil Seal
3. Snap Ring and Special Washer
4. Clutch Gear Bearing
5. Clutch Gear
6. 3rd Speed Blocker Ring
7. 2-3 Sliding Clutch Sleeve
8. 2nd Speed Blocker Ring
9. Second Speed Gear
10. First Speed Gear
11. 1st Speed Blocker Ring
12. 1st and Reverse Sliding Clutch Sleeve
13. Reverse Gear
14. Mainshaft Rear Bearing
15. Snap Ring and Special Washer
16. Vent
17. Extension
18. Speedo Drive Gear
19. Extension Oil Seal
20. Mainshaft
21. Extension to Bearing Retainer Ring
22. Countergear Thrust Washer
23. Roller Bearings
24. Reverse Idler Shaft
25. Reverse Idler Gear
26. Thrust Washer
27. Roller Bearings
28. Countergear
29. Magnet
30. Tube Spacer
31. Washers
32. Roll Pin
33. Dampener Plate
34. Spiral-Lox Retainer
35. Countergear Thrust Washer
36. Countergear Shaft
37. Dampener Spring
38. Mainshaft Pilot Bearings

endwise.

5. Install reverse gear over mainshaft with gear clutch teeth toward front.
6. Press rear bearing on mainshaft with its outer race snap ring groove closest to reverse gear.
7. Install rear bearing special washer and snap ring to mainshaft, Fig. 17.

NOTE: This snap ring is available in six thicknesses. Use thickest snap ring that will assemble with all parts stacked tight endwise.

8. Press speedometer drive gear on rear of mainshaft until centered on shaft boss.
9. Install 2nd speed gear over front of mainshaft with gear clutch teeth toward front.
10. Install blocker ring over 2nd gear tapered cone end with clutch key notches toward front.
11. Install 2-3 sliding clutch assembly over front of mainshaft, engaging clutch keys with notches of 2nd gear blocker ring.

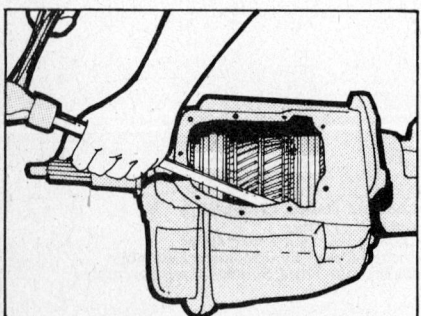

Fig. 10 Removing reverse idler shaft

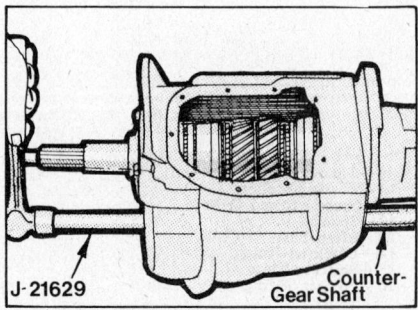

Fig. 11 Removing countershaft

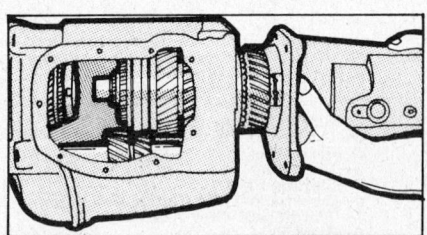

Fig. 12 Removing mainshaft and extension from case

WARNER TRANSMISSIONS

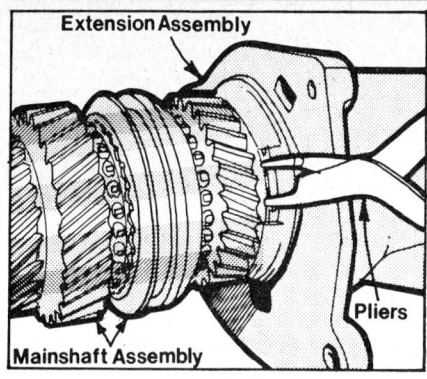

Fig. 13 Extension-to-rear bearing snap ring

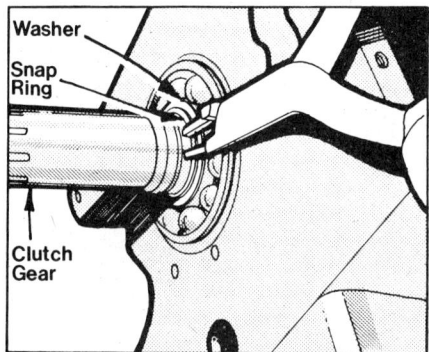

Fig. 14 Clutch gear bearing-to-gear snap ring

Properly installed, the straightest side of clutch hub should be toward rear and clutch sliding sleeve taper should be toward front of mainshaft (see Fig. 9).

12. Install 2-3 clutch hub snap ring to mainshaft, Fig. 16.

NOTE: This snap ring is available in four

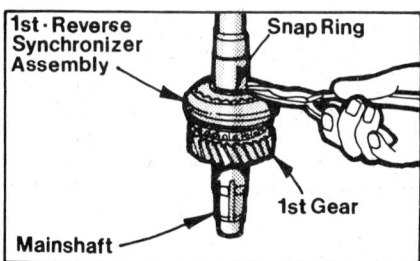

Fig. 18 First-reverse clutch hub snap ring

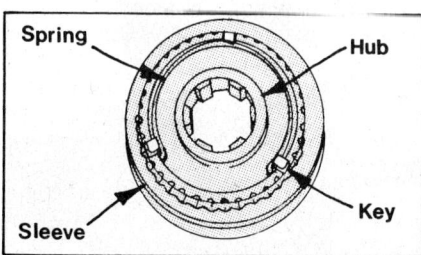

Fig. 19 2nd-3rd synchronizer clutch

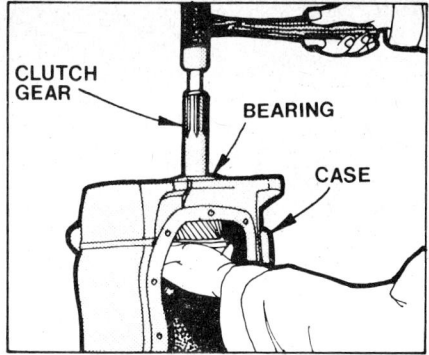

Fig. 15 Removing clutch gear from bearing and case

thicknesses. Use thickest snap ring that will assemble with all parts stacked tight endwise.

Assemble Transmission

1. Insert tube spacer and a double row of roller bearings and bearing retainer washers at each end of countergear, using grease to hold them in place, Fig. 22.
2. Place countergear assembly through case rear opening along with a tanged thrust washer (tang away from gear) at each end (large washer at front). Install countershaft and woodruff key from rear of case, Fig. 23.

CAUTION: Be sure countershaft picks up both thrust washers and that washer tangs are aligned with their notches in case.

3. Attach a dial indicator as shown in Fig. 24 and check end play of countergear. If end play is greater than .025" new thrust washers must be installed.

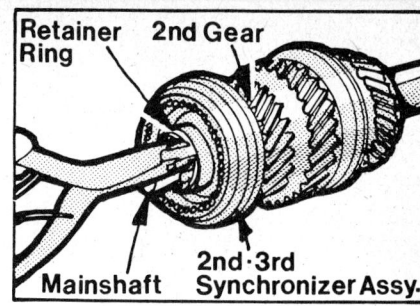

Fig. 16 2nd-3rd clutch hub snap ring

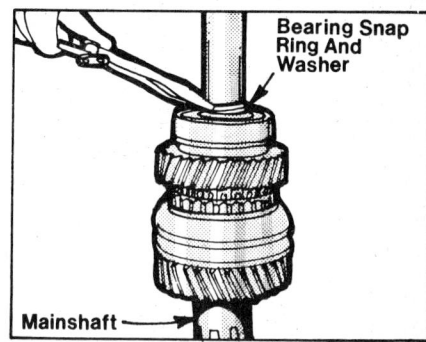

Fig. 17 Rear bearing-to-mainshaft snap ring

4. Use grease to hold 25 reverse idler gear roller bearings in position and place gear and bearings along with a thrust washer on each end into position inside case so that bevelled edge of gear teeth face toward front of case.
5. Load pilot bearing rollers and spacer into clutch gear with grease to hold them in place and position gear in case. *Do not install clutch gear bearing at this time.*
6. Stand case on end with clutch gear shaft through hole in bench or stand, and place 3rd gear blocker ring over clutch gear.
7. Install mainshaft assembly through rear

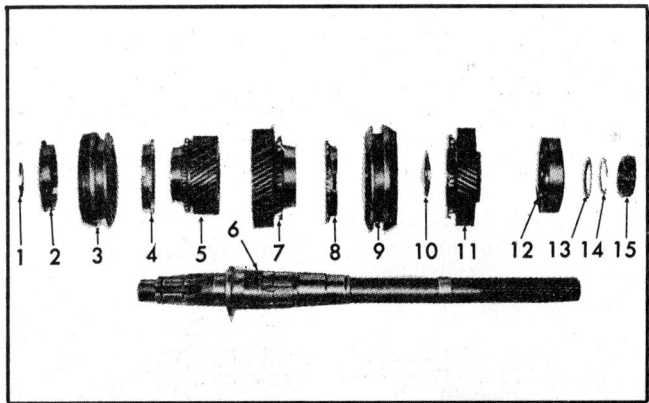

1. Snap Ring
2. 3rd Speed Blocker Ring
3. 2-3 Clutch Assembly
4. 2nd Speed Blocker Ring
5. 2nd Speed Gear
6. Mainshaft
7. 1st Speed Gear
8. 1st Speed Blocker Ring
9. 1st Reverse Clutch Assembly
10. Snap Ring
11. Reverse Gear
12. Rear Bearing
13. Special Washer
14. Snap Ring
15. Speedo Drive Gear

Fig. 20 Mainshaft disassembled

415

WARNER TRANSMISSIONS

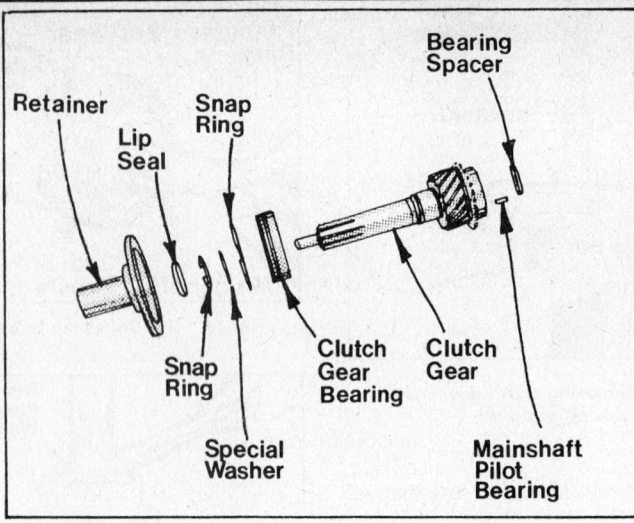

Fig. 21 Clutch gear components

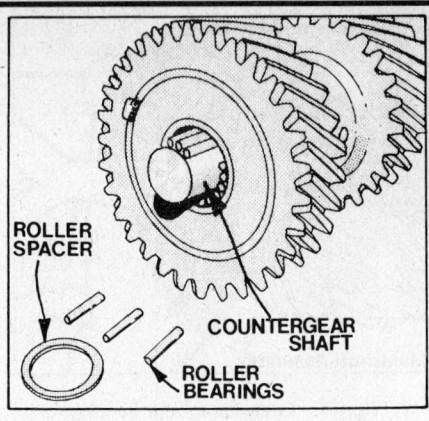

Fig. 22 Loading countershaft bearings

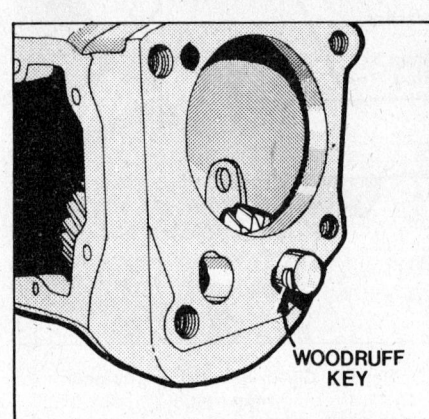

Fig. 23 Installing countershaft

of case, picking up spacer, pilot bearings and 3rd gear blocker rings, Fig. 25.
8. Install reverse idler gear shaft and woodruff key. *Be sure shaft picks up both thrust washers during installation.*
9. Install extension gasket on rear of case and, using snap ring pliers, expand snap ring, Fig. 13, and install extension over mainshaft and rear bearing. Be sure snap ring has started over bearing, then install and tighten extension case bolts. *Use graphite sealer on the two lower bolts.*
10. Tap on front of clutch gear shaft to force rear bearing snap ring to seat in its groove.

NOTE: This snap ring is available in five thicknesses. Use thickest snap ring that will assemble with all parts stacked tight endwise.

11. Install snap ring in outer race of clutch gear bearing. If snap ring groove is partially inside case opening, tap on inside bearing outer race with a long drift used through side cover opening.

NOTE: If mainshaft does not turn freely, check clutch sliding sleeves for neutral positions and that blocker rings are free on their gear cone surfaces.

12. Install gaskets and clutch gear bearing retainer and lip seal with oil drain passages at bottom and tighten. *Use graphite sealer on threads of retainer bolts.*

NOTE: Install two retainer-to-case gaskets (one .010″ and .015″) to replace the one .025″ production gasket removed.

13. Install shift forks to clutch sleeve grooves with 1st-reverse fork "hump" toward bottom of case, Fig. 26.
14. Install side cover and gasket. *The two rear side cover-to-case bolts have special oil sealing splines and must be used at these two "through" hole locations.*

T10 SERIES

Disassemble, Fig. 27

1. Shift transmission into 2nd gear and remove side cover.
2. Remove front bearing (clutch gear bearing) retainer and gasket.
3. Remove backup lamp switch and plunger from transmission. Drive lock pin from reverse shifter lever boss, Fig. 28 and pull shifter partially out of case to disengage the reverse shifter fork from reverse gear.
4. Remove rear extension retaining bolts. Tap extension with a soft hammer in a rearward direction to start removal. Remove extension and gasket. Remove the rearward portion of reverse idler gear from case.
5. Shift transmission into 3rd gear to prevent mainshaft from turning and remove snap ring from rear splines of mainshaft.

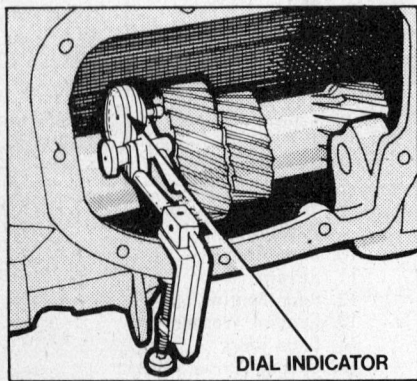

Fig. 24 Checking countergear end play

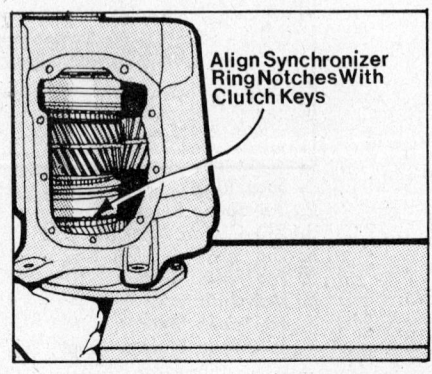

Fig. 25 Installing mainshaft assembly

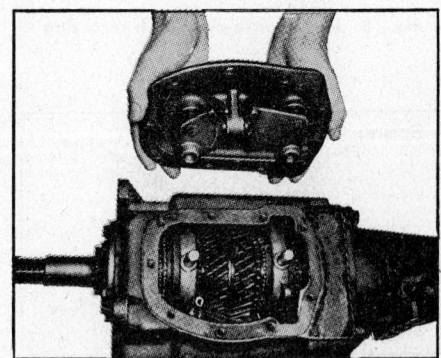

Fig. 26 Installing side cover assembly

WARNER TRANSMISSIONS

Using puller, remove speedometer gear, Fig. 29. Remove reverse gear from mainshaft.

6. Remove the self-locking bolt attaching the rear bearing retainer to the transmission case. Remove case to retainer alignment pin with pair of channel locks or vise-grips.
7. Rotate rear bearing retainer until countergear shaft lines up with reverse idler shaft hole in retainer. Using a dummy shaft, drive counter gear shaft out rear of case, Fig. 30, letting countergear drop to bottom of case.

NOTE: Leave dummy shaft inside countergear to retain needle bearings.

8. Slide 3rd-4th gear clutch sleeve forward on hub. Remove mainshaft and rear bearing retainer assembly from case. If 4th gear synchronizer ring has fallen off during removal, remove it from case. The clutch gear roller bearings may also fall into the case. Remove all loose roller bearings from case as well as any rollers retained in clutch gear.
9. Remove front reverse idler gear and thrust washer from case.
10. Remove clutch gear shaft snap ring (do not remove snap ring on outer bearing race). Press clutch gear out of front bearing into case, Fig. 31.
11. Front inside case, tap out front main bearing and snap ring.
12. Remove countergear and its tanged thrust washer from case.
13. Remove mainshaft front snap ring, Fig. 32. Slide 3rd and 4th speed clutch assembly, 3rd speed gear, and synchronizing ring from mainshaft.
14. Spread rear bearing retainer snap ring and slide retainer from mainshaft.
15. Remove mainshaft rear snap ring and spacer. Support 1st speed gear using press plates and press rear bearing and 1st gear from mainshaft, Fig. 33.
16. Remove 1st and 2nd speed clutch assembly snap ring. Slide clutch assembly and 2nd speed gear from mainshaft.

Cleaning & Inspection

1. Wash transmission case inside and out with cleaning solvent and inspect for cracks. Inspect front face of case for burrs and, if present, dress them off with a fine cut mill file.
2. Wash front and rear bearings in cleaning solvent. Blow out bearings with compressed air. *Do not allow bearings to spin; turn them slowly by hand. Spinning bearings will damage race and balls.*
3. Make sure bearings are clean, then lubricate them with light engine oil and check them for roughness. Roughness may be determined by turning outer race by hand.
4. All main drive gear and countergear bearing rollers should be inspected closely and replaced if they show wear. Inspect countershaft and replace if necessary.

Replace all worn spacers.

5. Inspect all gears and first speed gear bushing (or sleeve) and, if necessary, replace all that are worn or damaged.

Synchronizers
Clutch hubs and sliding sleeves are a select-

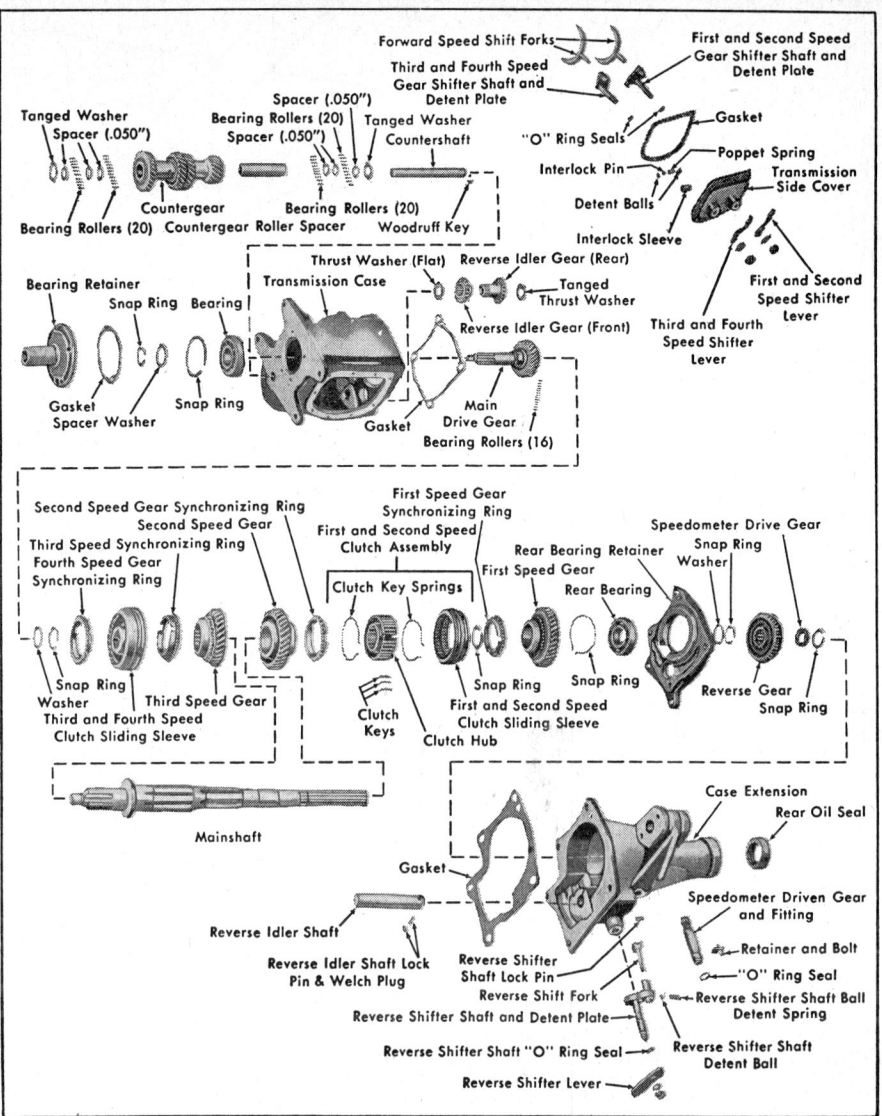

Fig. 27 Exploded view of Warner four speed transmission

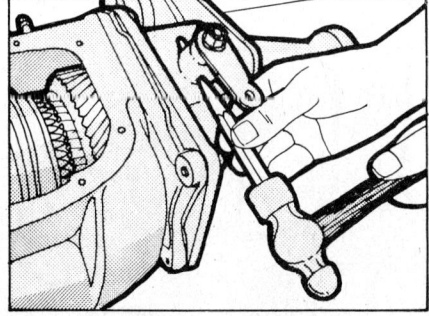

Fig. 28 Removing reverse shifter shaft lock pin

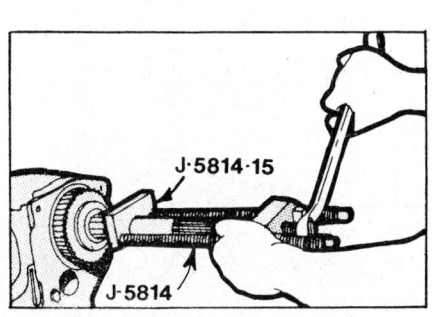

Fig. 29 Removing speedometer gear

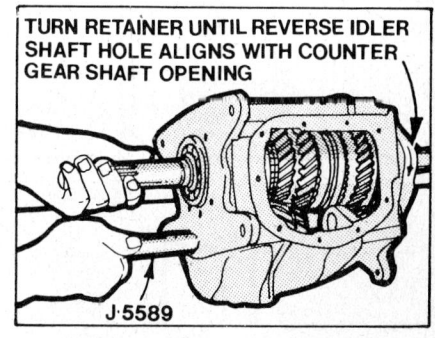

Fig. 30 Removing countergear shaft

417

WARNER TRANSMISSIONS

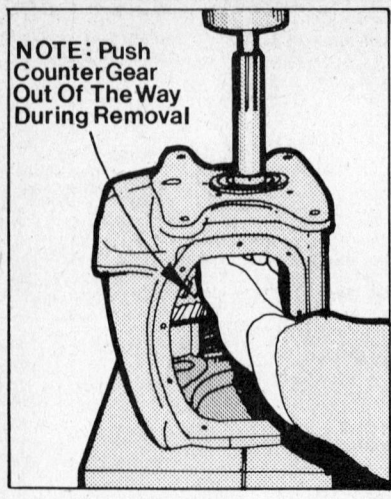

Fig. 31 Removing clutch gear

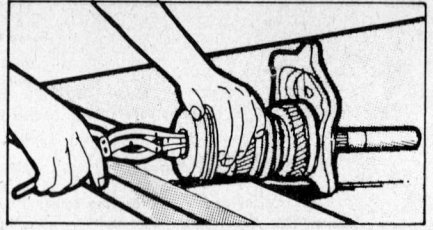

Fig. 32 Removing mainshaft front snap ring

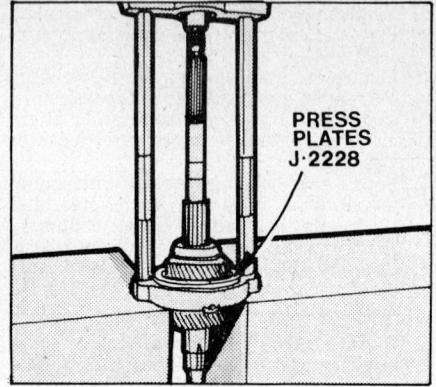

Fig. 33 Removing mainshaft rear bearing

ed assembly and should be kept together as originally assembled, but the three keys and two springs may be replaced if worn or broken.

Push hub from sliding sleeve. Keys will fall free and springs may be easily removed. To assemble, place the two springs in position (one on each side of hub) so tanged end of each spring falls into same keyway in hub. Place keys in position and, holding them in place, slide hub into sleeve.

Assemble Mainshaft

1. From rear of mainshaft, assemble the 2nd speed gear (with hub of gear toward rear of shaft).
2. Install 1st-2nd synchronizer clutch assembly to mainshaft (sliding clutch sleeve taper toward the rear, hub to front) together with a synchronizer ring on both sides of the clutch assemblies so the keyways line up with the clutch keys.
3. Install new select fit snap ring (thickest that will assemble) in groove on mainshaft at rear of clutch assembly.
4. Install 1st speed gear (with hub toward front) and supporting inner race, press the rear bearing onto the mainshaft with the snap ring groove toward the front of the transmission, Fig. 34.
5. Install spacer and new select fit snap ring (thickest that will assemble) on mainshaft behind rear bearing.
6. Install the third speed gear (hub to front of transmission) and the 3rd speed gear synchronizer ring (notches to front of transmission).
7. Install the 3rd and 4th speed gear clutch assembly (hub and sliding sleeve) with taper toward the front making sure that the keys in the hub correspond to the notches in the 3rd speed gear synchronizing ring.
8. Install new selective fit snap ring (thickest that will install) in the groove in the mainshaft in front of the 3rd and 4th speed clutch assembly.
9. Install the rear bearing retainer over end of mainshaft. Spread the snap ring in the plate allowing the snap ring to drop around the rear bearing. Release snap ring when it aligns with groove in rear bearing.
10. Install the reverse gear (shift collar to rear).
11. Press speedometer drive gear onto the mainshaft using a suitable press plate. Position the speedometer gear to get a measurement of 4½" from the center of the gear to the flat surface of the rear bearing retainer, Fig. 35.

Assemble Countergear

1. Install roller spacer in countergear.
2. Using heavy grease to retain rollers, install 20 rollers in either end of countergear, two spacers, 20 more rollers, then one spacer.
3. Assemble rollers and spacers in the same manner in other end of countergear. Then insert dummy shaft in countergear to retain rollers.

Assemble Transmission

1. Rest case on its side with side cover opening toward you. Place countergear tanged thrust washers in place, retaining them with heavy grease, making sure that tangs are resting in notches in case.
2. Place countergear assembly in bottom of case, making sure that tanged thrust washers are not knocked out of place.
3. Press bearing onto main drive gear with snap ring groove to front.
4. Install spacer washer and selective fit snap ring in groove on gear stem.
5. Install main drive gear assembly through side cover opening and into position in transmission front bore. Tap lightly into place with a soft hammer, if necessary. Place snap ring in groove in front bearing.
6. With transmission resting on its front face, move countergear into mesh with main drive gear, making sure thrust washers remain in place. Install key in end of countershaft and, from front of case, tap or press shaft until end of shaft is flush with rear of case and dummy shaft is displaced.
7. Attach dial indicator as shown in Fig. 36 and check end play of countergear. End play must not be more than .025".

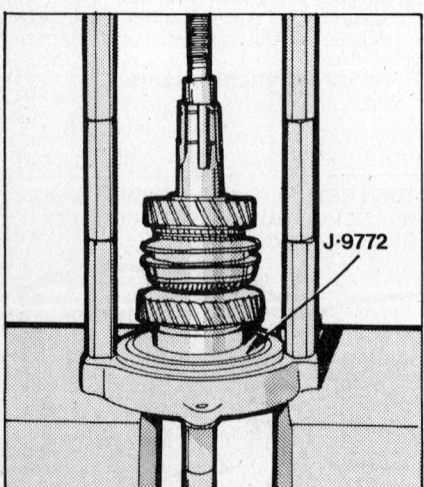

Fig. 34 Installing mainshaft rear bearing

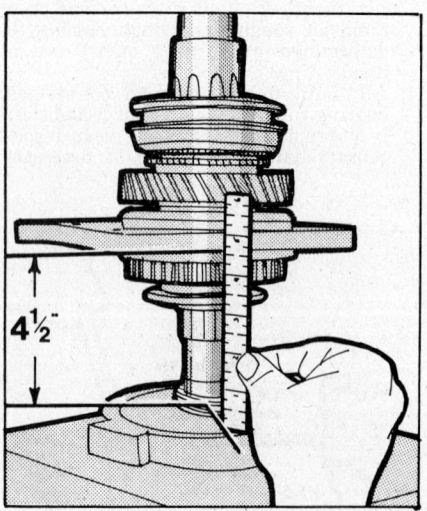

Fig. 35 Installing speedometer gear

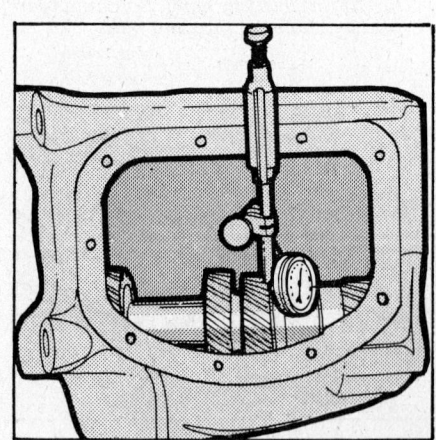

Fig. 36 Checking countergear end play

WARNER TRANSMISSIONS

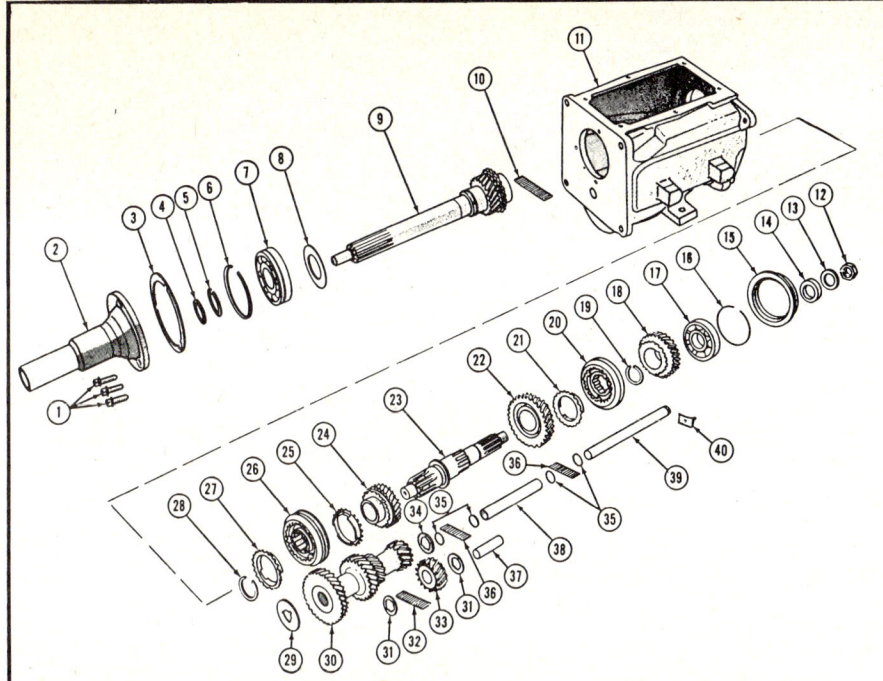

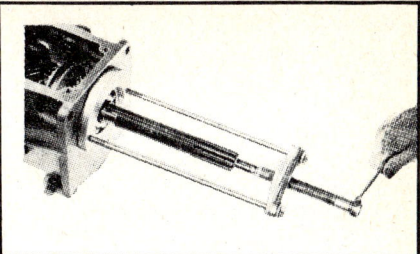

Fig. 38 Removing main drive gear bearing

Fig. 39 Removing mainshaft

1. Screws
2. Retainer
3. Gasket
4. Seal
5. Snap ring
6. Snap ring
7. Main drive bearing
8. Oil slinger
9. Main drive gear
10. Rollers
11. Case
12. Nut
13. Flatwasher
14. Spacer
15. Bearing adapter
16. Snap ring
17. Mainshaft bearing
18. Reverse gear
19. Snap ring
20. Low synchronizer assembly
21. Blocking ring
22. Low gear
23. Mainshaft
24. Second gear
25. Blocking ring
26. 2-3 synchronizer assembly
27. Blocking ring
28. Snap ring
29. Thrust washer
30. Countergear
31. Washer
32. Rollers
33. Reverse idler gear
34. Thrust washer
35. Spacer washer
36. Rollers
37. Reverse idler shaft
38. Spacer
39. Countershaft
40. Lockplate

Fig. 37 T14A, T15A three speed transmission

8. Install 14 rollers into main drive gear, using heavy grease to hold them in place. Place gasket in position on front face of rear bearing retainer, using heavy grease to hold it in position.
9. Install 4th gear synchronizing ring on main drive gear with clutch key notches toward rear of case.
10. Position reverse idler gear thrust washer (untanged) on machined face of ear cast in case for reverse idler shaft. Position front reverse idler gear on top of thrust washer, with hub facing toward rear of case.
11. Lower mainshaft assembly into case, making certain that notches on 4th gear synchronizing ring correspond to keys in synchronizer.
12. Install self-locking bolt attaching rear bearing retainer to case.
13. From rear of case, insert rear reverse idler gear, engaging splines with portion of gear within case.
14. Using heavy grease, place gasket into position on rear face of rear bearing retainer.
15. Install remaining tanged thrust washer into place on reverse idler shaft, being sure tang on washer is in notch in idler thrust face of extension.
16. Place two synchronizers in neutral position. *If locking-up of gears is encountered, a small amount of petrolatum may be applied to the 1st speed gear synchroniz-*

ing ring, enabling it to turn freely on 1st speed gear hub.
17. Pull reverse shifter shaft to left side of extension and rotate shaft to bring reverse shift fork to extreme forward position in extension. Line up front and rear reverse idler gears, making sure front thrust washer is in place.
18. Start extension into case by carefully inserting reverse idler shaft through reverse idler gears. Slowly push it on shifter shaft until shift fork engages reverse gear shift collar. When fork engages, rotate shifter shaft to move reverse gear rearward, permitting extension to slide onto transmission case.
19. Install extension and retainer to case attaching bolts, and extension to retainer attaching bolts. Use suitable sealer on the lower right attaching bolt.
20. Adjust reverse shifter shaft so that groove in shaft lines up with hole in boss and drive in lock pin from top of boss.
21. Install main drive gear bearing retainer and gasket, being sure oil well lines up with oil outlet hole.
22. Install shift fork in each synchronizer sleeve. With both synchronizers in neutral, install side cover with gasket. Use suitable sealer when installing lower right cover bolt.
23. Install shifter levers, lock washers and nuts.

T14A & T15A SERIES

Disassemble, Fig. 37

1. Remove housing cover and gasket from top of transmission case.
2. Remove nut and flat washer securing transfer case drive gear on the mainshaft. Remove transfer case drive gear, adapter and spacer.
3. Remove main drive gear bearing retainer and gasket.
4. Remove main drive gear and mainshaft bearing snap rings.
5. Using suitable puller, remove main drive gear and mainshaft bearings, Fig. 38.
6. Remove main drive gear from case.

NOTE: T15A unit must be shifted into second gear to permit removal of the mainshaft and gear assembly.

7. Remove mainshaft and gears as assembly through the case cover opening, Fig. 39.
8. On remote shift units, remove the shifter forks by removing the roll pins from the shift lever shafts and housing. From inside the transmission case, slide the shift levers and interlock assembly toward the outside of the case and remove shifter forks and lever assemblies.
9. Remove lockplate by tapping lightly on the front end of the countershaft and reverse idler shaft. Remove lockplate from the slots in the shafts.
10. Using a suitable drift, drive countershaft rearward out of case. Remove countergear assembly, thrust washers and bearings.
11. Drive reverse idler shaft rearward out of

419

WARNER TRANSMISSIONS

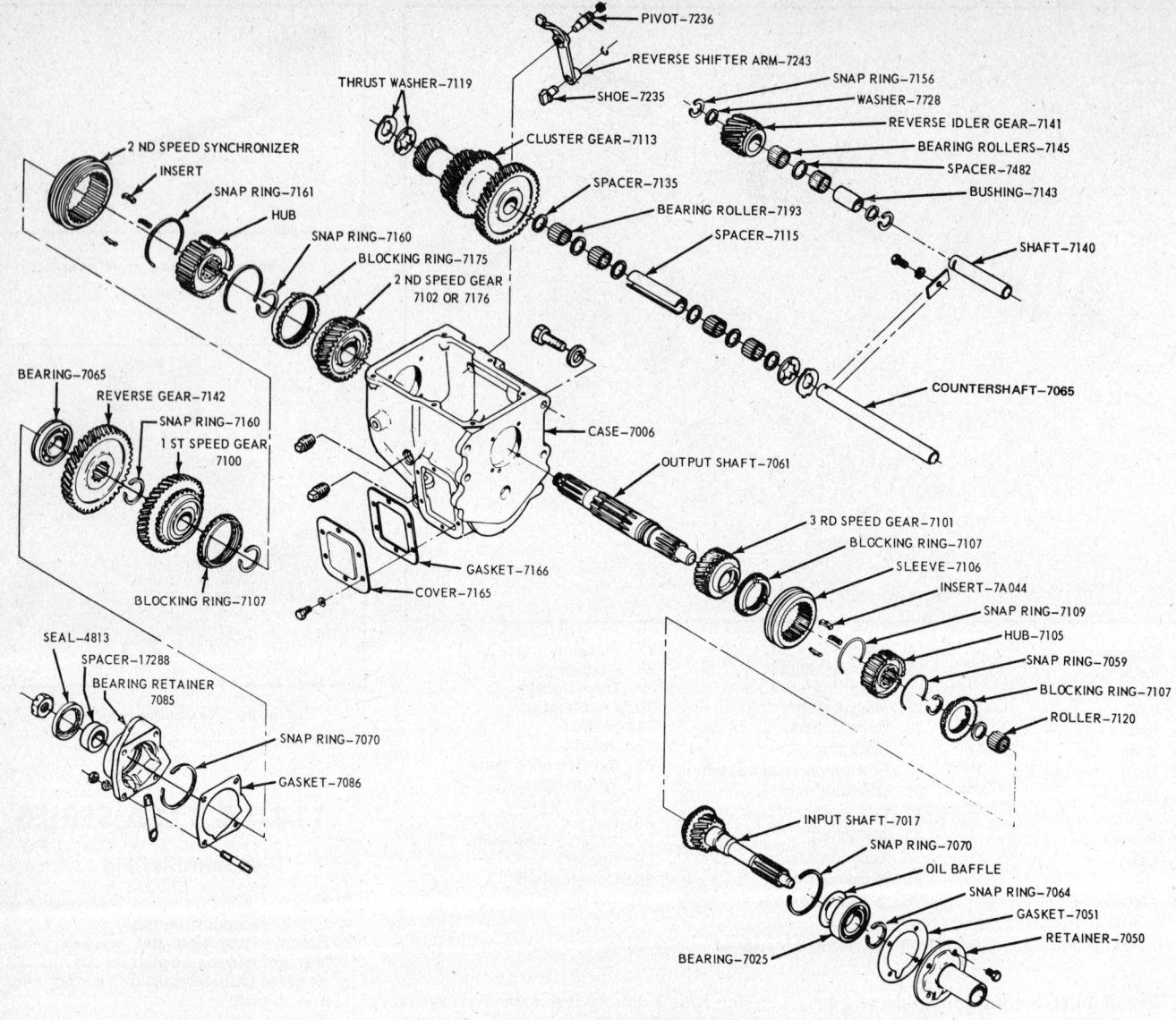

Fig. 40 Exploded view of Warner T19 four speed transmission

case. Remove idler gear.

Mainshaft, Disassemble

1. Remove clutch hub snap ring and 2-3 synchronizer assembly from the mainshaft.
2. Remove 2nd speed gear.
3. Remove reverse gear from mainshaft.
4. Remove clutch hub, snap ring, and low synchronizer assembly from the mainshaft.
5. Remove first speed gear from mainshaft.

Transmission, Reassemble

1. Install reverse idler gear assembly, making sure that the slot end of the idler shaft is aligned to receive the lockplate.
2. Assemble countershaft center spacer, bearing spacers and rollers in the countergear. Using a suitable dummy shaft to retain rollers, install gear in case and with thrust washers in place, install countershaft through rear of case with the lockplate slot toward the rear and aligned to receive lockplate.
3. Locate the lockplate in the two shafts and tapping alternately, drive shafts in until lockplate is tight against case.
4. Install mainshaft and gear assembly as a unit through the top cover opening of the transmission case.

NOTE: On remote shift units, the shifter forks and levers must be installed at this time. T15A transmission interlock levers are stamped and must be installed in the respective locations. T14A levers are interchangeable.

5. Using a screwdriver, depress interlock lever while installing shift fork into shifter lever and synchronizer clutch sleeve. Be sure poppet spring is properly installed. Install tapered pins securing lever shafts in case.
6. Install main drive gear and oil retainer into case with the cutaway part of the gear downward. Guide main drive gear onto mainshaft using care not to drop the rollers.
7. Install main bearings and snap rings.
8. Install main drive gear bearing retainer. Make sure oil drain holes are aligned.
9. Install transmission cover.

T19 SERIES

Disassemble, Fig. 40

1. Remove gear shift housing, Fig. 41, then the parking brake drum, with the transmission locked in two gears remove U-joint flange and oil seal.
2. Remove speedometer driven gear and bearing assembly.
3. Remove output shaft bearing retainer and speedometer drive gear and spacer, then remove output bearing retainer studs from case, Fig. 40.
4. Remove output shaft bearing snap ring, then using suitable tool remove bearing.
5. Remove countershaft and idler shaft retainer and power take-off cover.
6. Remove input shaft bearing snap ring and bearing.
7. Remove oil baffle.

WARNER TRANSMISSIONS

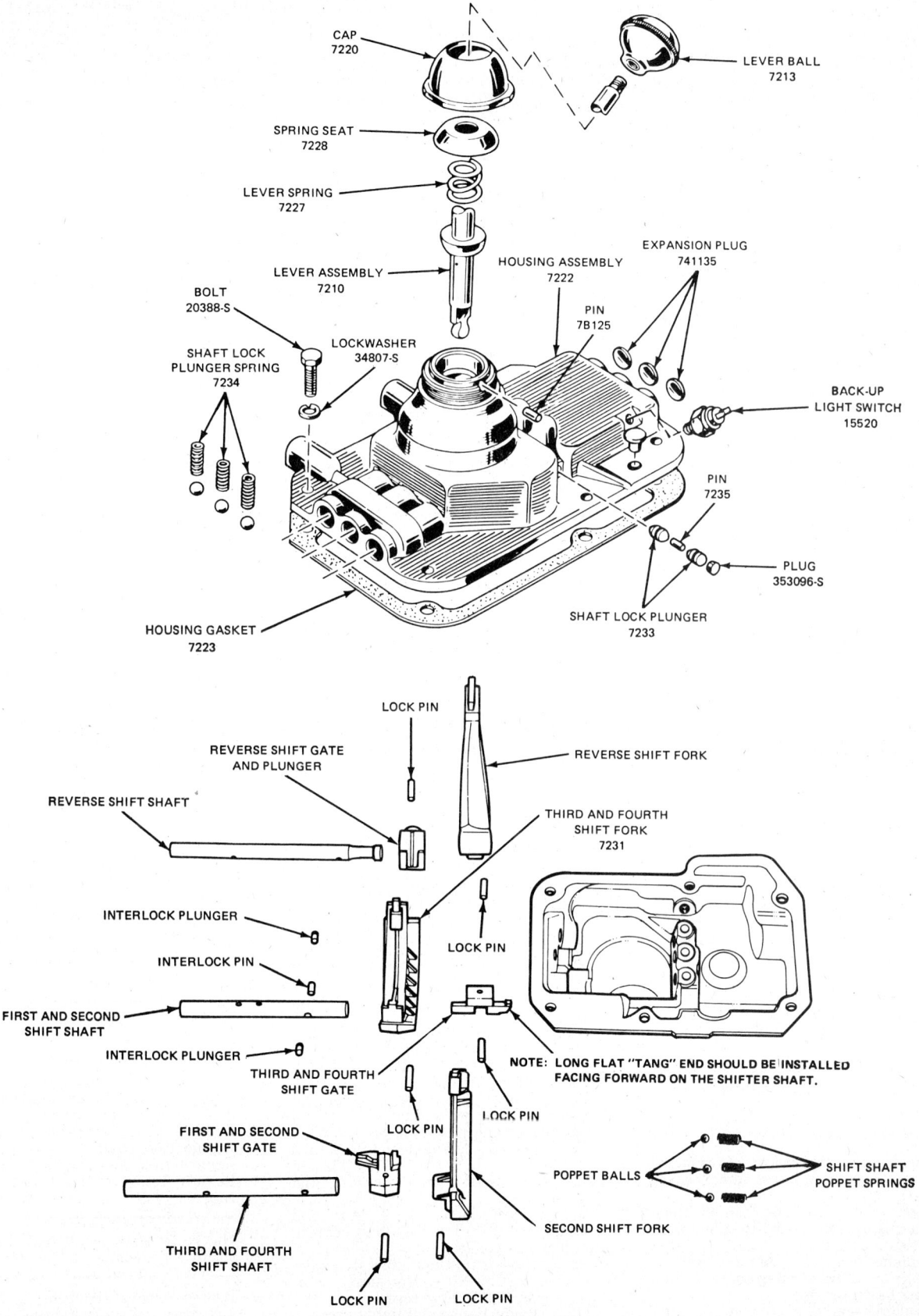

Fig. 41 Gear shift housing. Warner T19

WARNER TRANSMISSIONS

8. Remove roll pin from reverse gear shifter arm shaft, then remove shaft from shifter and lift shifter from case.
9. Remove output shaft and gear assembly from case.
10. Using a dummy shaft, drive countershaft out from front of transmission.

NOTE: Keep dummy shaft in contact with countershaft to avoid dropping rollers.

11. Remove input shaft and synchronizer blocking ring, then using a suitable puller remove idler shaft.
12. Remove idler gear and countershaft gear, use care not to lose rollers.

Output Shaft

Disassembly
1. Remove 3rd-4th speed synchronizer hub snap ring from output shaft, then slide synchronizer assembly and 3rd gear from shaft.
2. Press reverse gear from output shaft.
3. Remove 1st speed gear snap ring, then slide gear from shaft.
4. Remove 1st-2nd speed synchronizer snap ring, then slide synchronizer from shaft.
5. Remove snap ring from rear of 2nd speed gear, then remove gear and thrust washer.

Assemble
1. Install 2nd speed gear thrust washer and snap ring on shaft, then hold shaft in vertical position and install 2nd speed gear.
2. Install snap ring at rear of 2nd speed gear, then position blocking ring on gear.
3. Press 1st-2nd speed synchronizer onto shaft and install snap ring.
4. Install 1st speed gear and snap ring on shaft.
5. Press reverse gear onto shaft, then remove shaft from press and install 3rd speed gear and synchronizer blocking ring.
6. Install snap ring with openings staggered at both ends 3rd-4th speed synchronizer hub.
7. Place inserts into synchronizer sleeve and position sleeve on hub.
8. Slide synchronizer assembly onto output shaft and install snap ring at front of synchronizer assembly.

NOTE: Slots in blocking ring must be aligned with synchronizer inserts.

Countershaft Gear

Disassemble
Remove dummy shaft, pilot bearing rollers, bearing spacers and center spacer from countershaft gear.

Assemble
1. Position long bearing spacer into countershaft gear bore, then insert dummy shaft in spacer.
2. Position gear in vertical position, then install spacer and place 22 pilot roller bearings in gear bore.
3. Position bearing spacer on top of rollers, then install 2 more roller bearings and another bearing spacer.
4. Place a large washer against end of countershaft gear to prevent rollers from dropping out then turn assembly over.
5. Install rollers and spacers in other end of countershaft gear.

Reverse Idler Gear

Disassemble
Remove snap ring from end of gear, then remove bearing rollers thrust washers, bearing spacer and bushing.

Assembly
1. Install snap ring in one end of idler gear, then set gear on end with snap ring facing bottom.
2. Position thrust washer and bushing in gear bore, then install 37 bearing rollers between bushing and gear bore.
3. Install spacer on top of rollers then install 37 more bearing rollers.
4. Place remaining thrust washer on rollers and install snap ring.

Assemble Transmission

1. Lubricate all parts with transmission oil, then position countershaft gear assembly in case.
2. Position idler gear assembly in case, then install idler shaft and shifter arm.

NOTE: Position idler shaft so that slot at rear will engage retainer.

3. Drive countershaft in through rear of case forcing dummy shaft out through front.

NOTE: Position countershaft so that slot at rear will engage retainer.

4. Install thrust washers as necessary to obtain countershaft end play of .006 to .020 inch.
5. Install countershaft and idler shaft retainer.
6. Position oil baffle and input shaft pilot rollers so that baffle will not rub on bearing race, then position input shaft in case and install blocking ring.
7. Install output shaft assembly in case.
8. Using a suitable tool drive input shaft bearing onto shaft then install thickest select fit snap ring that will fit on bearing. Snap ring is available in thicknesses of, .117-.119, .120-.122, .123-.125 and .127-.129 inch. Install input shaft snap ring.
9. Install output shaft bearing.
10. Install input shaft bearing retainer without gasket and tighten bolts only enough to bottom retainer on bearing snap ring. Measure distance between retainer and case and select a gasket that will seal and also prevent end play retainer and snap ring. Gaskets are available in thicknesses of .008-.011, .0135-.0165, .018-.022 and .0225-.0275 inch. Install gasket and tighten bolts.
11. Position speedometer drive gear and spacer, then install output shaft bearing retainer and gasket.
12. Install brake drum then lubricate extension housing bushing, seal and U joint flange with ball joint grease.
13. Install U joint flange and tighten bolt.

MODEL T-150

Disassembly, Fig. 42

1. Remove transfer case to transmission attaching bolts, then separate transfer case from transmission.
2. Remove shift control housing, Fig. 43.
3. Move 2-3 synchronizer sleeve forward and the 1st.-reverse sleeve rearward to lock the mainshaft.
4. Remove transfer case gear lock nut, flat washer and drive gear.
5. Move both synchronizers back to the Neutral position.
6. Remove fill plug.
7. Remove countershaft roll pin with a 3/16 inch punch. The roll pin is accessible through fill plug opening.
8. Remove countershaft and access plug using tool J-25232. Remove countershaft from rear of case. Permit countershaft gear to remain at bottom of case after countershaft removal.
9. Punch alignment marks in front bearing cap and transmission case for assembly reference.
10. Remove front bearing cap and gasket.
11. Remove large lock ring from front bearing.
12. Remove clutch shaft and front bearing assembly with tool J-6654-01.
13. Remove 2-3 synchronizer blocking ring from clutch shaft or synchronizer hub.
14. Remove rear bearing and adapter using a suitable drift and hammer.
15. Remove mainshaft and geartrain assembly. Tilt splined end of shaft downward and lift the forward end of the shaft up and out from case.
16. Remove countershaft gear and tool as an assembly.
17. Remove countershaft gear thrust washers, countershaft roll pin and any mainshaft pilot roller bearings which may have fallen into the case during clutch shaft removal.
18. Remove reverse idler gear shaft. Insert a brass drift through clutch shaft bore in front of case and tap shaft until end of shaft with roll pin clears countershaft bore in rear of case, then remove shaft.
19. Remove reverse idler gear and thrust washers.

SUB-ASSEMBLY DISASSEMBLY

Mainshaft
1. Remove retaining snap ring from front of mainshaft.
2. Remove 2-3 synchronizer assembly and the second gear. Mark hub and sleeve for assembly reference.

NOTE: Observe position of insert springs and inserts for assembly reference.

3. Remove insert springs from 2-3 synchronizer. Remove the three inserts and separate sleeve from synchronizer hub.
4. Remove snap ring and tabbed thrust washer from shaft.
5. Remove first gear and blocking ring.
6. Remove 1st.-reverse hub retaining snap ring.

NOTE: Observe position of inserts and spring for assembly reference.

7. Remove sleeve and gear, insert spring and three inserts from hub.
8. Remove oil slinger and spacer from rear

WARNER TRANSMISSIONS

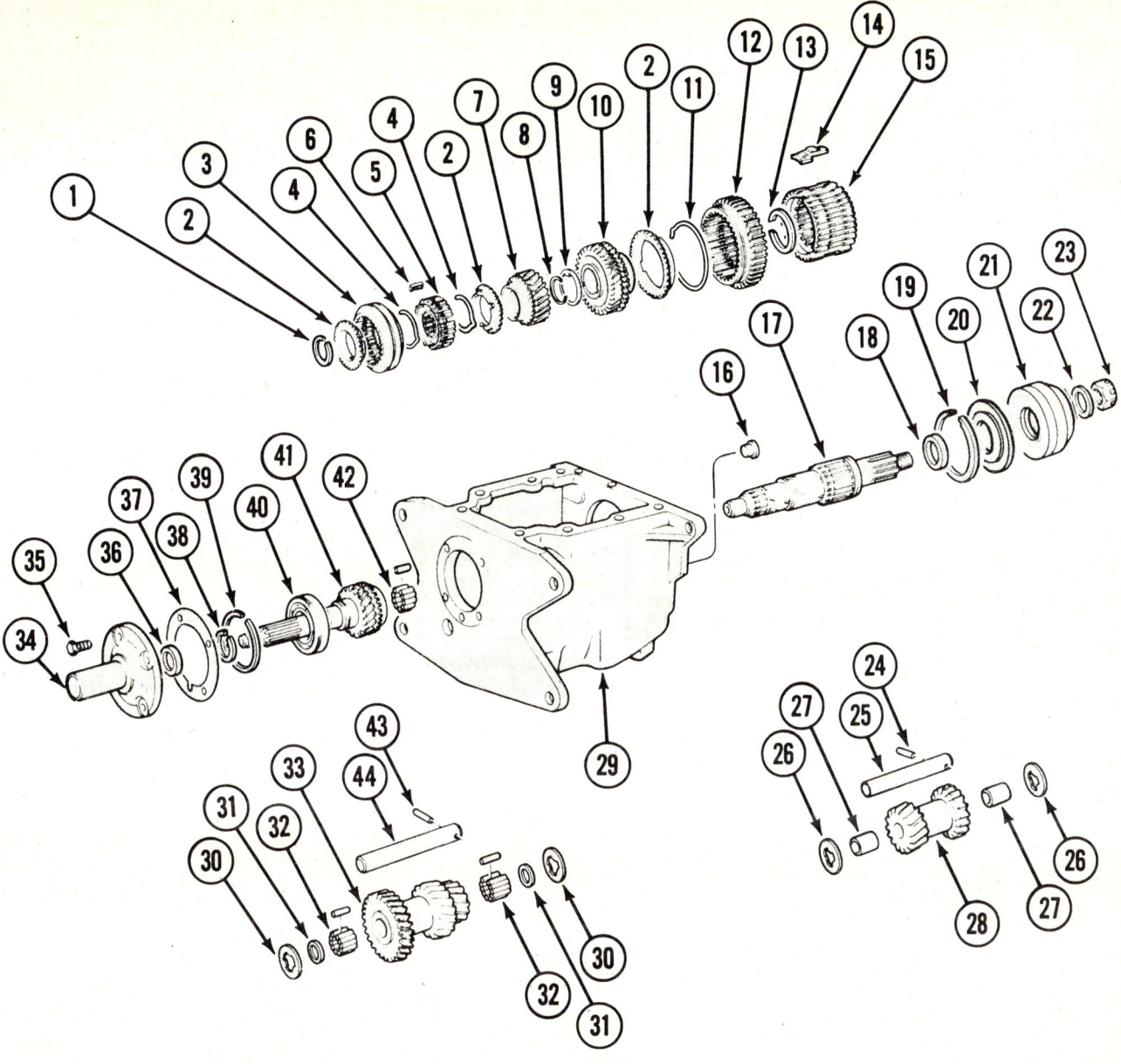

1. MAINSHAFT RETAINING SNAP RING
2. SYNCHRONIZER BLOCKING RINGS (3)
3. SECOND-THIRD SYNCHRONIZER SLEEVE
4. SECOND-THIRD SYNCHRONIZER INSERT SPRING (2)
5. SECOND-THIRD HUB
6. SECOND-THIRD SYNCHRONIZER INSERT (3)
7. SECOND GEAR
8. FIRST GEAR RETAINING SNAP RING
9. FIRST GEAR TABBED THRUST WASHER
10. FIRST GEAR
11. FIRST-REVERSE SYNCHRONIZER INSERT SPRING
12. FIRST-REVERSE SLEEVE AND GEAR
13. FIRST-REVERSE HUB RETAINING SNAP RING
14. FIRST-REVERSE SYNCHRONIZER INSERT (3)
15. FIRST-REVERSE HUB
16. COUNTERSHAFT ACCESS PLUG
17. MAINSHAFT
18. MAINSHAFT SPACER
19. REAR BEARING ADAPTER LOCK RING
20. OIL SLINGER/SPACER
21. REAR BEARING AND ADAPTER ASSEMBLY
22. WASHER
23. LOCKNUT
24. ROLL PIN
25. REVERSE IDLER GEAR SHAFT
26. THRUST WASHER
27. BUSHING (PART OF IDLER GEAR)
28. REVERSE IDLER GEAR
29. TRANSMISSION CASE
30. THRUST WASHER (2)
31. BEARING RETAINER (2)
32. COUNTERSHAFT NEEDLE BEARINGS (50)
33. COUNTERSHAFT GEAR
34. FRONT BEARING CAP
35. BOLT (4)
36. FRONT BEARING CAP OIL SEAL
37. GASKET
38. FRONT BEARING RETAINER SNAP RING
39. FRONT BEARING LOCKRING
40. FRONT BEARING
41. CLUTCH SHAFT
42. MAINSHAFT PILOT ROLLER BEARINGS
43. ROLL PIN
44. COUNTERSHAFT

Fig. 42 Model T150 3 speed transmission, disassembled

WARNER TRANSMISSIONS

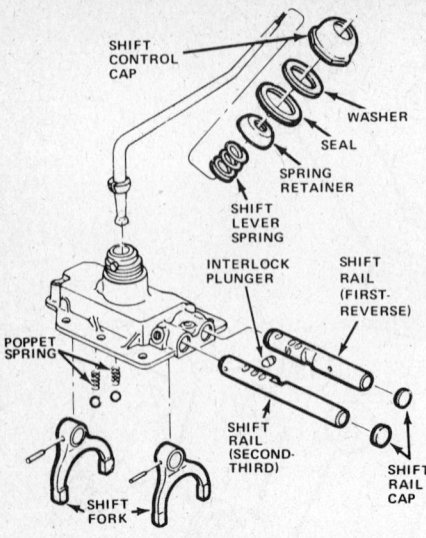

Fig. 43 Shift control housing, disassembled. Model T150

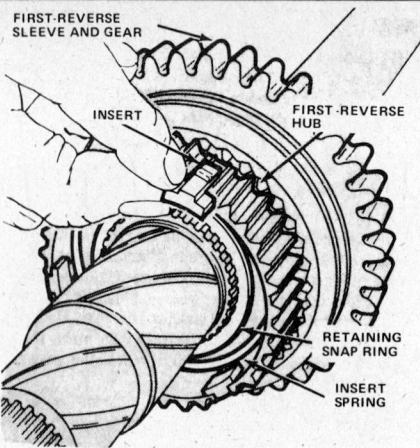

Fig. 44 1st-reverse hub insert installation

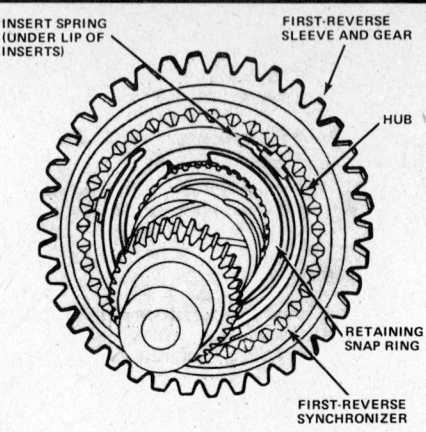

Fig. 45 Snap ring & insert spring positioning in 1st-reverse hub

of mainshaft.
9. Remove hub from output shaft using a suitable press.

NOTE: Do not attempt to hammer the press-fit hub from the shaft since damage to the hub and shaft will occur.

Clutch Shaft
1. Remove front bearing retaining snap ring and any remaining roller bearings.
2. Press front bearing from shaft.

NOTE: Do not attempt to hammer the bearing from the shaft since damage to the shaft and bearing will occur.

Rear Bearing & Adapter
1. Clamp rear bearing adapter in a soft-jawed vise.
2. Remove rear bearing retaining snap ring.
3. Remove bearing adapter from vise.
4. Press bearing from adapter with a suitable press.
5. Remove bearing adapter lock ring.

Assembly, Fig. 42

1. Lubricate reverse idler gear shaft bore and bushings with transmission lubricant.
2. Coat transmission case reverse idler gear thrust washer surfaces with petroleum jelly, then install thrust washers into case.

NOTE: Ensure that the locating tabs on the thrust washers are engaged into case slots.

3. Install reverse idler gear. Align gear bore, thrust washers and case bores, then install reverse idler gear shaft from rear of case. Align and seat roll pin in shaft in counterbore in rear of case.
4. Measure reverse idler gear end play by inserting a feeler gauge between thrust washer and gear. End play should be .004–.018 inch. If not, replace thrust washers.
5. Coat needle bearings and bearing bores in countershaft gear with petroleum jelly. Insert tool J-25232 in bore of gear and install 25 needle bearings and one retainer in each end of gear.
6. Coat countershaft gear thrust washer surfaces with petroleum and place thrust washers in the case.

NOTE: Ensure that the locating tabs on the thrust washers are engaged into case slots.

7. Insert countershaft into rear case bore far enough to secure the rear thrust washer in position. This prevents the thrust washer from being displaced when countershaft gear is installed.
8. Install countershaft gear but do not install roll pin. Align gear bore, thrust washers and case bores, then install countershaft.

NOTE: Do not remove tool J-25232 completely.

9. Measure countershaft gear end play by inserting a feeler gauge between thrust washer and the countershaft gear. End play should be .004–.018 inch. If not, replace thrust washers. After proper end play is obtained, install arbor tool fully in countershaft gear. Permit gear to remain at bottom of case. Leave countershaft in rear case bore to secure thrust washer in position.

NOTE: The countershaft gear must remain at bottom of case to provide clearance for installation of the mainshaft and clutch shaft assemblies.

10. Coat all mainshaft splines and machined surfaces with transmission lubricant.
11. Start 1st-reverse synchronizer hub onto output shaft splines by hand. The end of

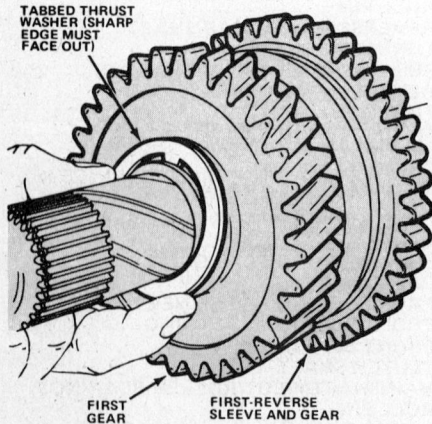

Fig. 46 First gear thrust washer installation

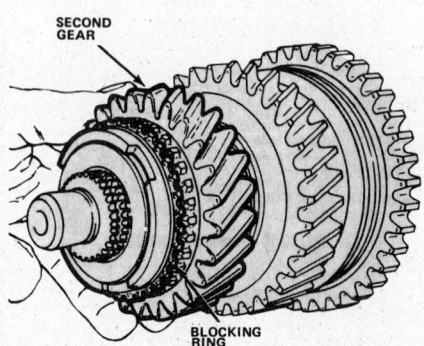

Fig. 47 Second gear installation

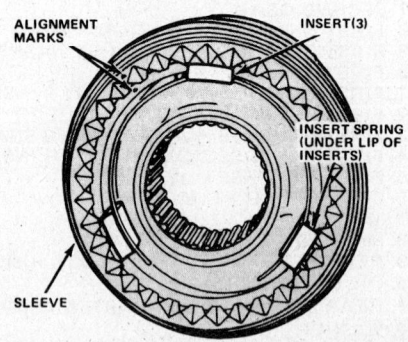

Fig. 48 2nd-3rd synchronizer assembly

WARNER TRANSMISSIONS

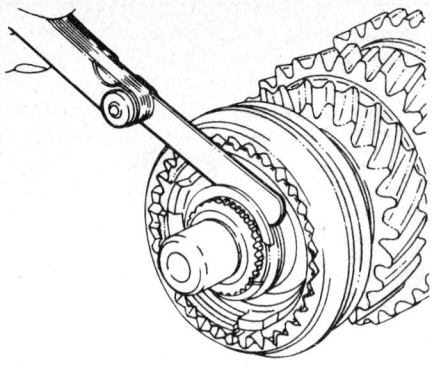

Fig. 49 Measuring mainshaft end play

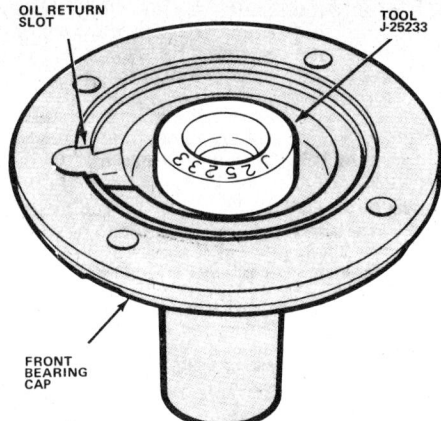

Fig. 50 Front bearing cap oil seal installation

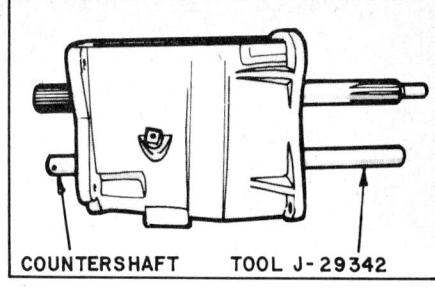

Fig. 51 Countershaft replacement

the hub with the slots should face toward front of shaft. Use a suitable press to complete installation of the hub, then install retaining snap ring in the most rearward groove in shaft, Fig. 44.

NOTE: Do not attempt to hammer the hub onto shaft since damage to shaft and hub will occur.

12. Coat 1st-reverse hub splines with transmission lubricant.
13. Install 1st-reverse sleeve and gear halfway onto hub. The gear end of the sleeve must face toward rear of shaft. Align sleeve and hub using alignment marks made during disassembly.
14. Install insert springs into 1st-reverse hub. Ensure the spring is bottomed in hub and covers all three insert slots. Position the three "T" shaped inserts into hub with small ends in hub slots, Fig. 44. Push the inserts fully into hub so the inserts seat on the insert spring, then slide 1-reverse sleeve and gear over inserts until inserts engage in sleeve, Fig. 45.
15. Coat bore and blocking ring surface of first gear with transmission lubricant and place first gear blocking ring on tapered surface of gear.
16. Install first gear on mainshaft. Rotate gear until notches in blocking ring engage inserts in 1st-reverse hub, then install tabbed thrust washer, with sharp edge facing outward, and retaining snap on mainshaft, Fig. 46.

17. Coat bore and blocking ring surface of second gear with transmission lubricant and place second gear blocking ring on tapered surface of gear.
18. Install second gear on mainshaft with tapered surface of gear facing toward front of shaft, Fig. 47.
19. Install one insert spring into 2-3 hub. Ensure that the spring covers all three insert slots in hub. Align 2-3 sleeve to hub using alignment marks made during disassembly, and start sleeve onto hub.
20. Place three inserts into hub slots and on top of insert spring, then push sleeve fully onto hub to engage inserts in sleeve, Fig. 48. Install remaining insert spring in the exact same position as the first spring. The ends of both springs must cover same slots in hub and not be staggered.

NOTE: The inserts have a small lip on each end. When properly installed, this lip will fit over the insert spring.

21. Install 2-3 synchronizer assembly on mainshaft. Rotate second gear until notches in blocking ring engages inserts in 2-3 synchronizer assembly.
22. Install retaining snap ring on mainshaft and measure end play between snap ring and 2-3 synchronizer hub with a feeler gauge, Fig. 49. End play should be .004–.014 inch. If not, replace thrust washer and all snap rings on output shaft assembly.

23. Install spacer and oil slinger on rear of mainshaft.
24. Install mainshaft assembly into case. Ensure 1st.-reverse sleeve and gear is in Neutral (centered) position on hub so gear end of sleeve will clear top of case when output shaft assembly is installed.
25. Press rear bearing into rear bearing adapter using a suitable press.
26. Install rear bearing retaining ring and bearing adapter lock ring in adapter.
27. Support mainshaft assembly and install rear bearing and adapter assembly into case. Use a mallet to seat adapter into case.
28. Press front bearing onto clutch shaft. Install bearing retaining snap ring on clutch shaft and lock ring in front bearing groove.

NOTE: When properly installed, the snap ring groove in the front bearing will be nearest to the front of the clutch shaft.

29. Coat bearing bore of clutch shaft with petroleum jelly.
30. Install 15 roller bearings in clutch shaft bore.
31. Coat blocking ring surface of clutch shaft with transmission lubricant and place blocking ring on shaft.
32. Support mainshaft assembly and install clutch shaft through front bearing bore in case. Seat mainshaft pilot in clutch shaft roller bearings and tap front bearing into place with a mallet.
33. Apply a thin film of sealer to front bearing cap gasket and place gasket on case. Ensure that the gasket notch is aligned with the oil return hole in case.
34. Replace front bearing cap oil seal. Remove old seal with a screwdriver and drive new seal into bearing cap with tool J-25233, Fig. 50.

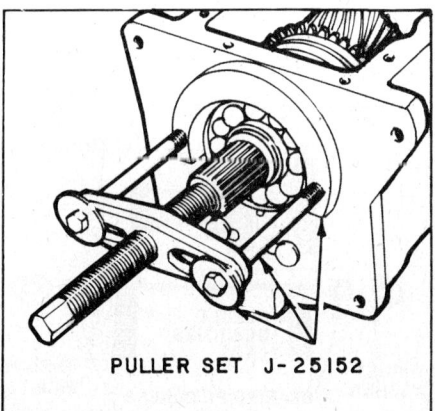

Fig. 52 Rear bearing removal

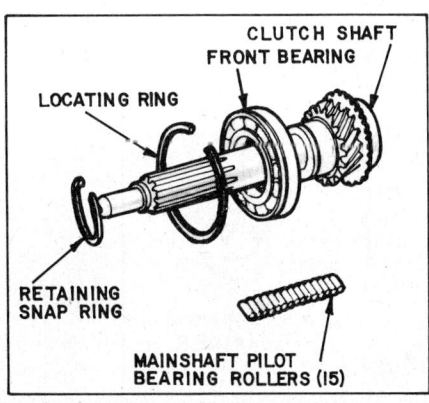

Fig. 53 Clutch shaft & front bearing assembly

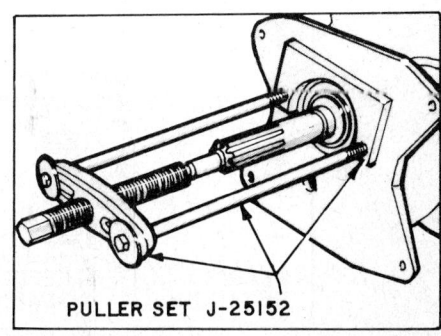

Fig. 54 Clutch shaft & front bearing removal

WARNER TRANSMISSIONS

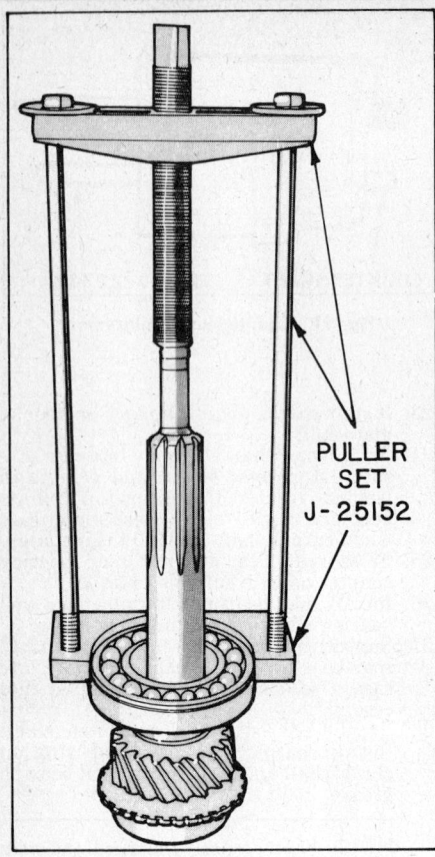

Fig. 55 Removing front bearing from clutch shaft

35. Install front bearing cap and torque attaching bolts to 33 ft. lbs.

NOTE: When installing the front bearing cap, align the cap and case index marks. Also, ensure that the cap oil return slot and case oil return hole are aligned.

36. Fabricate a wire loop approximately 18 to 20 inches long. Pass the wire loop under the countershaft gear assembly, then raise countershaft gear with loop. Align countershaft gear bore with front thrust washer and countershaft and start countershaft into gear. Align roll pin hole in countershaft and roll pin holes in case, then complete countershaft installation.
37. Install countershaft access plug in rear of case, seating plug with a mallet.
38. Install countershaft roll pin in case. Use a magnet or pair of needlenose pliers to insert pin in case. Use a 1/2 inch diameter punch to seat pin. Install fill plug.
39. Shift synchronizer sleeves into all gear positions to check for proper operation. If clutch shaft and mainshaft binds in Neutral position, check for sticking blocking rings on the first or second speed gear tapers.
40. Shift both synchronizers into gear to prevent gear rotation.
41. Install transfer case drive gear. Install and torque retaining nut to 150 ft. lbs.
42. Shift synchronizers into Neutral position.
43. Attach transmission to transfer case. Torque attaching bolts to 30 ft. lbs.

MODEL T-176

Disassembly

1. Remove transfer case from transmission. Drain lubricant from transmission.
2. Remove shift control housing.

NOTE: Two of the housing attaching bolts are of the dowel pin type. Note location of the bolts during disassembly.

3. Using arbor tool J-29342, tap countershaft from rear of case, Fig. 51.
4. Remove rear bearing locating ring and snap ring. Using a suitable puller, remove rear bearing from case, Fig. 52.
5. Scribe alignment marks on front bearing cap and transmission case, then remove front bearing cap and gasket and oil seal from cap.

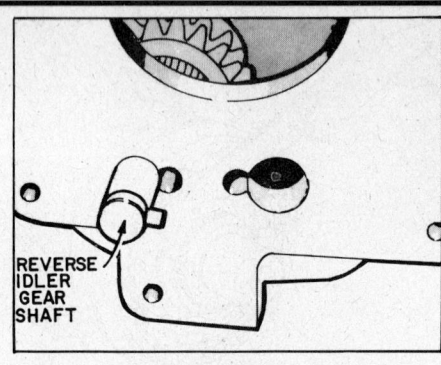

Fig. 56 Reverse idler gear shaft replacement

6. Remove locating ring and retaining snap ring from front bearing, Fig. 53.
7. Using suitable puller, remove clutch shaft and front bearing from case, Fig. 54.
8. Remove 3rd-4th gear blocking ring from clutch shaft or synchronizer hub.
9. Press front bearing from clutch shaft, Fig. 55.
10. Remove mainshaft pilot bearing rollers from clutch shaft, Fig. 53.
11. Move 3rd-4th gear synchronizer sleeve rearward to 3rd gear position. Tilt rear end of mainshaft downward and lift front upward and remove mainshaft and geartrain assembly.
12. Remove countershaft gear and arbor tool as an assembly.
13. Remove countershaft gear thrust washers and any fallen mainshaft pilot bearing rollers from the case.
14. Remove reverse gear idler shaft from rear of case. Remove gear assembly and thrust washers, Fig. 56.
15. Remove needle bearings and retainers from gear assembly, Fig. 57. Note position of sliding gear and remove from reverse idler gear.
16. Remove arbor shaft tool from countershaft gear and remove needle bearing and retainers, Fig. 58.

Mainshaft, Disassemble
1. Remove 3rd-4th synchronizer snap ring from front of mainshaft, Fig. 59.
2. Remove 3rd-4th assembly from shaft, then slide hub from sleeve. Remove insert springs and three inserts and blocking ring. Note position of insert springs for reassembly.
3. Remove 3rd gear from shaft.
4. Remove 2nd gear snap ring, gear, block-

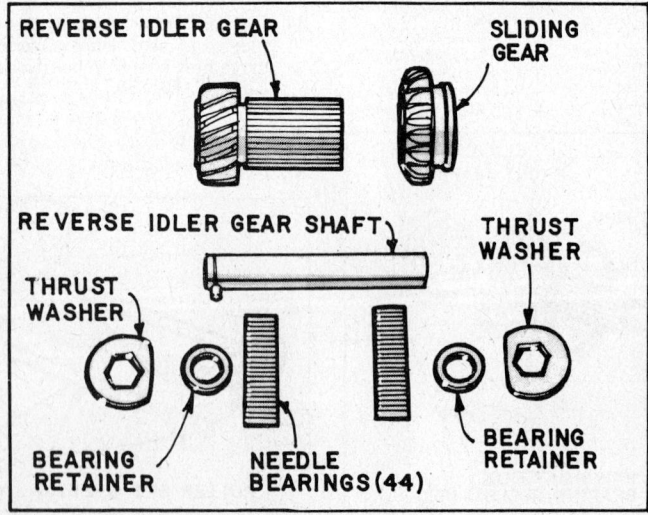

Fig. 57 Reverse idler gear assembly

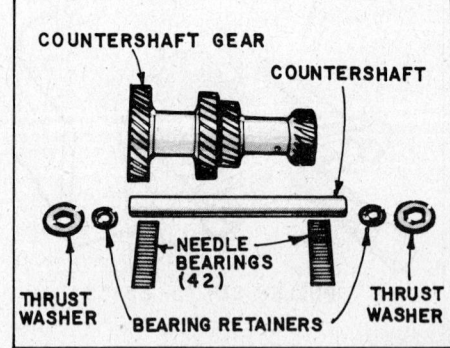

Fig. 58 Countershaft gear assembly

WARNER TRANSMISSIONS

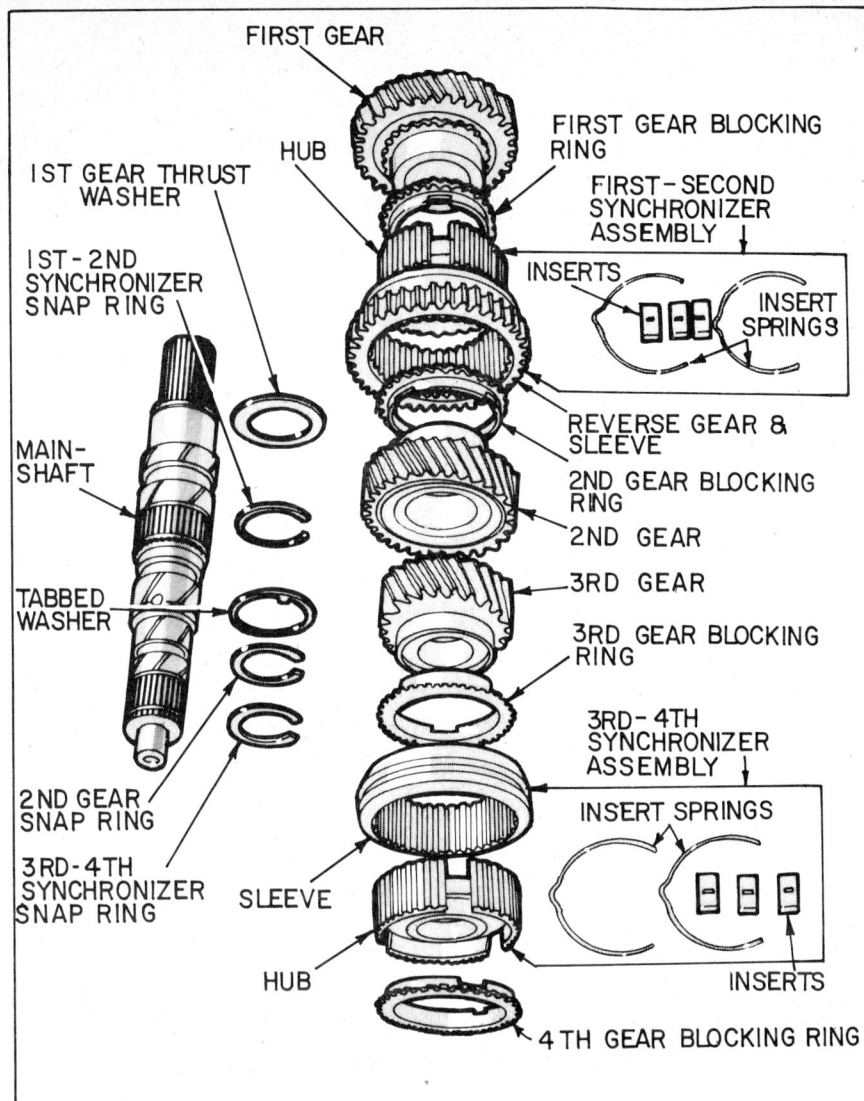

Fig. 59 Mainshaft assembly, Model T176

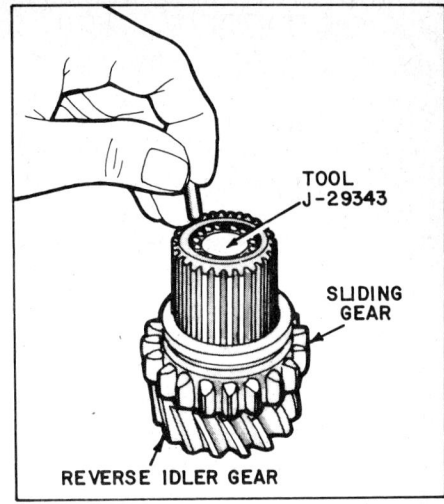

Fig. 60 Reverse idler gear needle bearing installation

ing ring and tabbed washer from shaft, Fig. 59.

5. Remove snap ring from 1st-2nd gear synchronizer hub. Remove hub, reverse gear and sleeve as an assembly. Mark hub and sleeve for assembly reference. Remove insert springs, inserts, sleeve and gear from hub.
6. Remove first gear thrust washer, then the first gear and blocking ring from shaft.

Assembly

1. Lubricate and assemble reverse idler gear and sliding gear, Fig. 57.
2. Install arbor tool J-29343 in reverse idler gear. Install 22 needle bearings and one retainer at each end of gear, Fig. 60.
3. Lubricate reverse idler gear thrust washers with petroleum jelly and install in case.

NOTE: Install thrust washers with flats facing the mainshaft and engage the washer locating tabs into slots of case.

4. Install reverse idler gear assembly into case, Fig. 61. Install reverse idler shaft from rear of case, Fig. 56. Ensure that roll pin seats in case recess.
5. Measure reverse idler gear end play by inserting a feeler gauge between thrust washer and gear. End play should be 0.004 to 0.018 inch. If not, replace thrust washers.

6. Lubricate countershaft gear bore, needle bearings and bearing bores in gear with petroleum jelly. Install arbor tool in bore of gear and install 21 needle bearings and one retainer in each end of gear.
7. Lubricate countershaft gear thrust washers with petroleum jelly and position in case.

NOTE: Install thrust washers with the locating tabs in slots of case.

8. Insert countershaft into rear case bore just enough to hold rear thrust washer in position. This will prevent thrust washer from being displaced during countershaft gear installation.
9. Install countershaft gear. Align gear bore, thrust washers, bores in case and install countershaft partially into case. Ensure arbor tool enters shaft bore at front of case.

NOTE: Do not remove countershaft arbor tool completely.

10. Measure countershaft gear end play with a feeler gauge inserted between gear and thrust washer. End play should be 0.004 to 0.018 inch. If not, replace the thrust washers. After correct end play has been

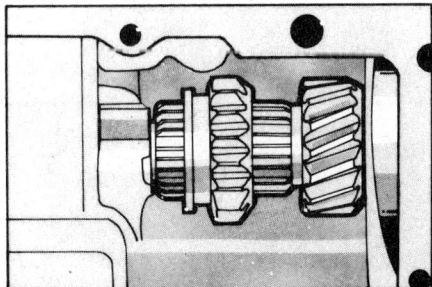

Fig. 61 Reverse idler gear installation

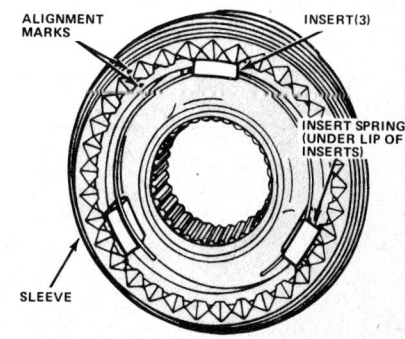

Fig. 62 Synchronizer insert spring installation

WARNER TRANSMISSIONS

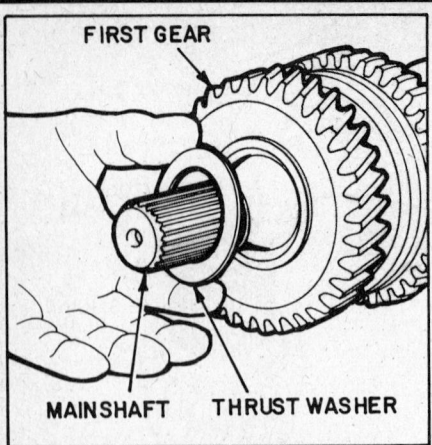

Fig. 63 First gear & thrust washer installation

obtained, reinstall arbor tool in counter shaft gear and allow gear to remain at bottom of case. Leave countershaft in rear case bore to retain thrust washer in position.

NOTE: Countershaft gear must remain at bottom of case to allow clearance for mainshaft and clutch shaft installation.

11. Lubricate mainshaft, synchronizer assemblies and gear bores with transmission lubricant.
12. Assemble 1st-2nd synchronizer hub and reverse gear and sleeve, Fig. 59:
    a. Install gear and sleeve on hub and place assembly flat on bench.
    b. Install the inserts into the hub slots.
    c. Install the insert spring. Position loop-end of spring in one insert, compress spring ends and insert the spring ends under lips of remaining two inserts, Fig. 62.
    d. Turn assembly over and install remaining insert spring as described in previous step. However, install this spring so open end is 180° opposite first spring.
13. Install assembled 1st-2nd synchronizer hub and reverse gear and sleeve on mainshaft, Fig. 59.
14. Install 1st-2nd synchronizer snap ring on mainshaft.
15. Install 1st gear and blocking ring on rear of mainshaft and the first gear thrust washer, Fig. 63.
16. Install new tabbed washer on mainshaft. Ensure that washer tab is seated in mainshaft tab bore, Fig. 64.
17. Install 2nd gear and blocking ring on mainshaft, then a new 2nd gear snap ring.
18. Install 3rd gear and blocking ring on mainshaft.
19. Assemble 3rd-4th synchronizer, Fig. 59:
    a. Install sleeve on synchronizer hub. Align parts using reference marks.
    b. Place assembled hub and sleeve flat on bench.
    c. Install the inserts into the hub slots.
    d. Install insert spring. Position loop-end of spring in one insert, compress spring ends and insert under lips of remaining two inserts, Fig. 62.
    e. Turn assembly over and install remaining insert spring as described in previous step. However, position this spring so open end faces 180° opposite first spring.
20. Install 3rd-4th synchronizer assembly on mainshaft.
21. Install new 3rd-4th synchronizer retaining snap ring on mainshaft and measure end play between hub and snap ring, Fig. 49. End play should be 0.004 to 0.014 inch. If not, replace snap rings and thrust washers.
22. Install mainshaft assembly into case. The synchronizers must be in neutral position so sleeves will clear top of case.
23. Install locating snap ring on front bearing, then install the front bearing partially onto clutch shaft.

NOTE: Do not install bearing completely since the shaft will not clear the countershaft gear during installation.

24. Lubricate bearing bore in clutch shaft and mainshaft roller bearings with petroleum jelly. Install 15 roller bearings in clutch shaft bearing bore.

CAUTION: Do not use chassis grease or other heavy grease in the clutch shaft bore since improper lubrication of the roller bearings may result.

25. Lubricate blocking ring surface of clutch shaft with transmission lubricant and position blocking ring on shaft.
26. Support mainshaft assembly and insert clutch shaft through front bearing bore in case. Seat mainshaft pilot hub in clutch shaft roller bearings and tap front bearing and clutch shaft into case using suitable mallet.
27. Install front bearing cap and tighten bolts finger tight.
28. Position rear bearing on mainshaft. Do not install bearing locating snap ring at this time. Start bearing onto shaft and into case bore using tool J-29345. Remove tool and finish bearing installation using suitable mallet. Install retaining snap ring when bearing is fully seated.

NOTE: To seat bearing on mainshaft, the bearing must be driven into case deeper than the locating snap ring would allow. Therefore, do not install the locating snap ring until after the bearing is fully seated on the shaft and the retaining snap ring is installed.

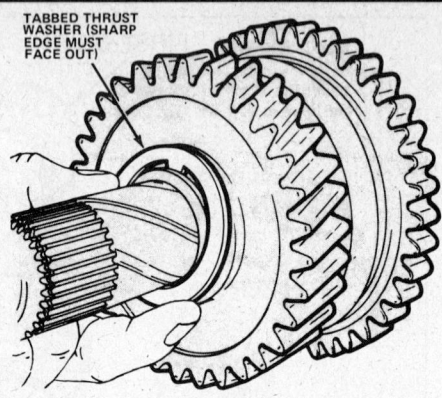

Fig. 64 Tabbed thrust washer installation

29. Remove front bearing cap, seat front bearing fully on clutch shaft and install bearing retaining snap ring.
30. Apply a thin film of sealer to front bearing cap gasket and position on case. Ensure that notch in gasket and oil return hole in case are aligned.
31. Remove front bearing cap oil seal using suitable tool. Install new seal using tool J-25233, Fig. 50.
32. Install front bearing cap and torque cap bolts to 12 ft. lbs.
33. Install locating ring on rear bearing. Reseat bearing in case if necessary.
34. Install countershaft as follows:
    a. Turn transmission case on end. Position case at edge of workbench with clutchshaft facing downward. Ensure that countershaft bore in front of case is accessible.
    b. Have an assistant hold case in position.
    c. Align countershaft gear bores with thrust washers and case bores and tap shaft into place.

NOTE: The arbor tool will be driven through opposite end of case.

CAUTION: Do not damage thrust washers during installation of countershaft. Ensure that the washers, case bores and gear bores are aligned when installing countershaft.

35. Check operation of synchronizer sleeves in all gear positions. If clutch shaft or mainshaft appear to bind in neutral position, check for blocking rings sticking on gears. Use a screwdriver to free any sticking rings.
36. Fill transmission with 3.5 pints of SAE 85W-90 gear lubricant.
37. Install shift control housing with new gasket. Torque housing bolts to 12 ft. lbs.
38. Install transmission on transfer case.

HEAVY DUTY CLUTCHES
Lipe DP Clutch

As shown in Figs. 1 and 2, DP type clutches are single and two plate direct pressure units. The nameplate attached to the flywheel ring (cover) identifies the cover plate as to the serial number and model number. Driven discs are stamped with an assembly number.

This type clutch can be serviced easily without the use of special tools. It is of the dry disc, push type construction, with no internal clutch adjustment to compensate for wear. The only adjustment is made by adjusting the clutch pedal free travel, which should be maintained at $1\frac{1}{2}''$.

Servicing the Clutch

After the clutch is disassembled, clean all parts thoroughly. Inspect all parts as indicated below.

Pressure Plate

The pressure plate must be replaced if:
1. Friction surface is severely heat checked.
2. It is warped in excess of .015″.
3. Driving slots are worn.
4. Pin holes are elongated.

The pressure plate may be salvaged if the friction surface cleans up by regrinding any amount up to a maximum of $\frac{1}{32}''$ from "Dimension C", Fig. 3, and chart, Fig. 4. *Using a heat checked or warped pressure plate will cause the facings to disintegrate quickly.*

Intermediate Plate

The intermediate plate in the two plate clutches may not be used if the driving slots are worn or deep cracks are present on either friction surface. If the clearance between the contact face of the driving pins in the flywheel is over .012″, it is recommended that the intermediate plate and driving pins be replaced. If the driving slots or pins are not worn and the plate is not warped over .015″, it may be reground. However, it is recommended that the grinding be kept to a minimum with not over .015″ being removed from either side for a total of .030″ (see chart, Fig. 4 for thickness specifications).

Pressure Springs

It is of vital importance that the pressure springs have proper tension. They should be checked for compression weight in accordance with the weight given in the chart, Fig. 4.

CAUTION: Underweight springs will reduce clutch capacity and possibly cause clutch slippage; therefore, to insure best clutch performance, it is recommended that new springs be installed.

Eyebolts, Release Levers and Links

It is extremely important that the pin be a tight press fit in the eyebolt. If looseness is detected, replace with a new eyebolt assembly. If the pin is worn, replace with a new eyebolt assembly. The eyebolt and adjusting nut threads must be free fitting, but not excessively loose.

If the release lever pin holes are worn or elongated, replace levers. If release lever buttons are worn, replace with new buttons.

If link holes are worn or elongated, replace links.

Disc Assembly

The disc should be replaced if the hub splines are worn, disc is distorted, disc is cracked or broken. If the disc is acceptable for relining, use a Lipe Facing Kit to obtain correct rivets and the proper facing material of original specifications, Fig. 4.

Fig. 6 illustrates the correct riveting for types of facings to be used. The left view shows the correct method of riveting fabric facings, using a star set anvil, resulting in the split end of the rivet conforming to the tapered counterbore of the facing. The roll set type rivet should be used for installing metallic facings, Fig. 6, right view.

Lubrication

Place a small amount of high melting point grease on the driving lugs of the flywheel ring (cover) and mating slots in the pressure plate, as well as the pins.

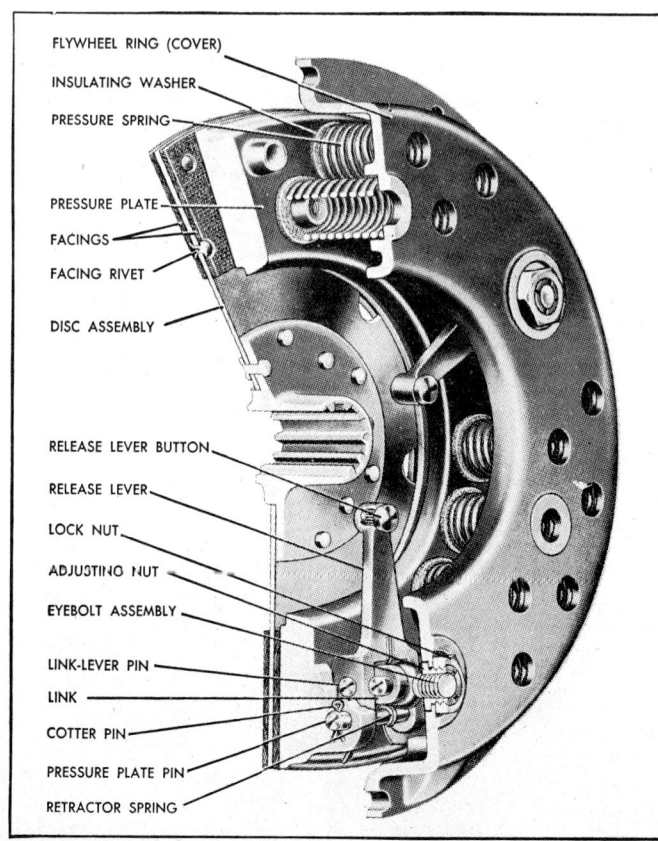

Fig. 1 Lipe DP single plate clutch

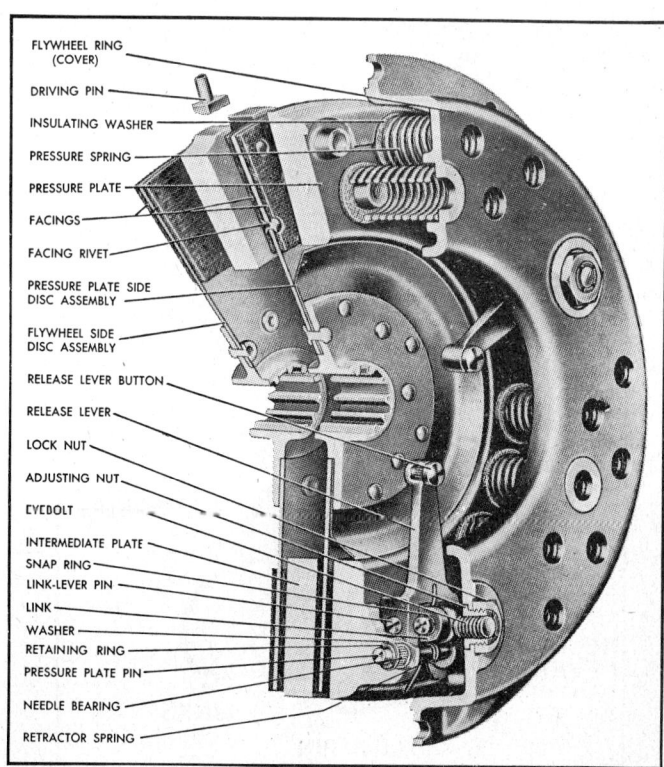

Fig. 2 Lipe DP two plate clutch

HEAVY DUTY CLUTCHES

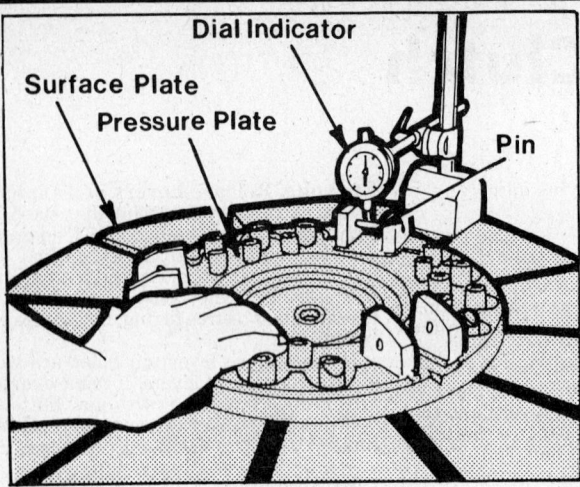

Fig. 3 Checking Dimension "C" on DP clutch

Fig. 5 Aligning drive pins in two plate clutch cover

Flywheel Ring (Cover)

The flywheel ring must be replaced if any cracks are present, driving lugs are worn, or if it is distorted.

The 14" and 15" single plate units and 15" two plate clutches have milled lugs in the flywheel which engage with machined surfaces of the release lever bosses on the pressure plates.

The 14" two plate unit has replaceable driving pins while in the 13" single plate the pressure plate engages the cover through slots machined in the cover. A check of the clearance or wear of the driving surfaces in either cover can be made by using a new pressure plate as a gauge. There should not be less than .004" or more than .014" movement possible between the two mating parts. A tight fit may hamper smooth engagement and release while too loose a fit may cause noise.

In replacing the driving pins in the 14" two plate cover, extreme care must be taken to assure accurate alignment. A straight edge and a square placed as indicated in Fig. 5 will serve to properly align the driving pins. It is recommended that a .0015" feeler gauge be used as an aid. Pins may be turned with a 1½" open end wrench and must be held securely while tightening the lock nuts. The driving pins must be a drive fit into the flywheel ring.

Nuts should be torqued to 30 ft-lbs.

CAUTION: Burred edges on flange surface should be filed so as to assure flange being drawn tight to rim of engine flywheel at time of clutch installation. Replace retractor springs with new springs.

Clutch Assembly

1. Place pressure plate on arbor press with friction surface down.
2. Assemble adjusting nut to eyebolt assembly so that 3 or 4 threads are showing on inside of adjusting nut (use new links only).
3. Assemble the two links to eyebolt, install same to release lever assembly, using link lever pin, Fig. 7.
4. At this point, install retractor spring with the hook end seated in groove of lever, running under eyebolt assembly to groove in pressure plate.
5. Then assemble to pressure plate, inserting pressure pin through coiled loop of retractor spring. Make sure cotter pin hole of pressure plate pin is parallel to pressure plate and install cotter pin, Fig. 8.

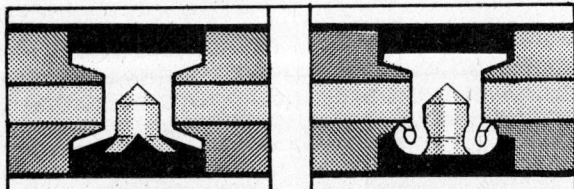

Fig. 6 Left view shows correct riveting for fabric or non-metallic facings; right view shows proper riveting for metallic facings

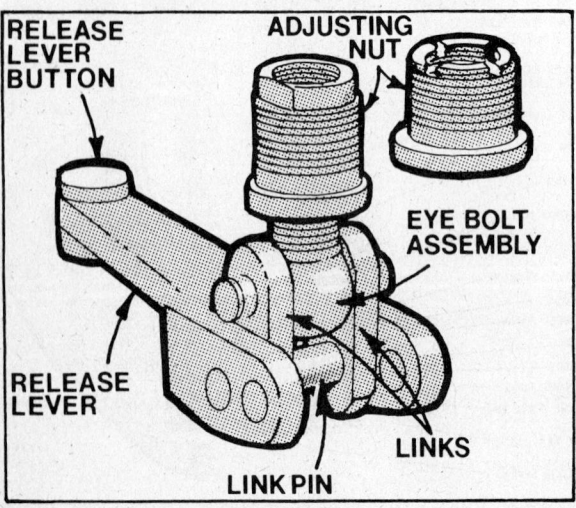

Fig. 7 Assemble eyebolt and related components as shown

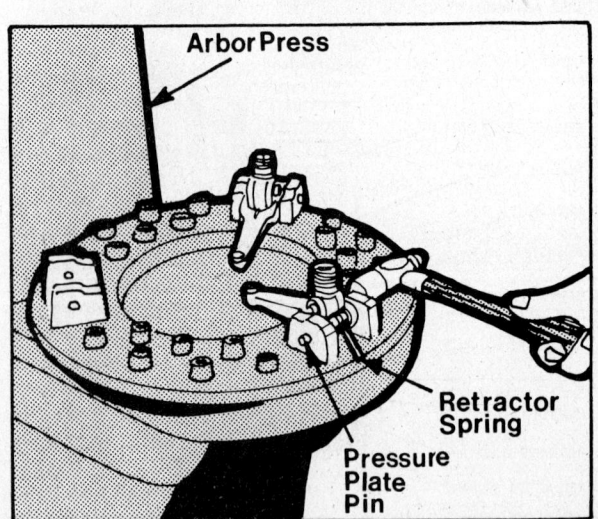

Fig. 8 Assembling release levers to pressure plate

HEAVY DUTY CLUTCHES

Model Number	Dimension "A"	Flywheel Depth + .005" − .005"	Facing Thickness	PRESSURE SPRING DATA			PRESSURE PLATE DATA
				Quantity	Color	Minimum Weight✦	Dimension "C" New
140-51-374	1"	1.187"	3/16"	21	Dark Maroon	130 lbs. @ 1 27/32"	1.687"
140-51-490	1"	1.187"	3/16"	21	Bronze	250 lbs. @ 1 31/32"	1.687"
140-51-496	1"	1.187"	3/16"	21	Dark Maroon	130 lbs. @ 1 27/32"	1.687"
140-51-501	1"	1.187"	3/16"	21	Aluminum	225 lbs. @ 1 31/32"	1.687"
140-51-505	1"	1.187"	3/16"	21	Aluminum	225 lbs. @ 1 31/32"	1.687"
150-51-506	1 1/8"	1.750"	3/16"	27	Purple	170 lbs. @ 2 1/16"	1.875"
140-51-519	1"	1.187"	7/32"	21	Dark Maroon	130 lbs. @ 1 27/32" ✦	1.687"
140-51-520	1"	1.187"	3/16"	21	Dark Maroon	130 lbs. @ 1 27/32"	1.687"
140-51-521	1"	1.594"	3/16"	21	Pink	120 lbs. @ 2 3/32"	1.968"
140-51-526	1"	1.187"	3/16"	21	Pink	120 lbs. @ 2 3/32"	1.687"
150-51-529	1 1/8"	1.750"	3/16"	21	Purple	170 lbs. @ 2 1/16"	1.875"
140-52-531†	1"	1.406"	5/32"	21	Dark Maroon	130 lbs. @ 1 27/32"	1.687"
130-51-532	31/32"	Flat	5/32"	20	Dark Maroon	130 lbs. @ 1 27/32"	1.406"
150-51-534	1 1/8"	1.750"	3/16"	21	Purple	170 lbs. @ 2 1/16"	1.875"
140-51-535	1"	1.187"	3/16"	21	Light Green	150 lbs. @ 1 27/32"	1.687"
140-51-536	1"	1.187"	3/16"	21	Light Green	150 lbs. @ 1 27/32"	1.687"
140-51-537	1"	1.187"	3/16"	21	Light Green	150 lbs. @ 1 27/32"	1.687"
140-51-538	1"	1.187"	3/16"	21	Dark Maroon	130 lbs. @ 1 27/32"	1.687"
140-51-539	1"	1.187"	3/16"	21	Dark Maroon	130 lbs. @ 1 27/32"	1.687"
150-51-544**	5/16"	1.750"	3/16"	27	Purple	170 lbs. @ 2 1/16"	1.875"
130-51-547	31/32"	Flat	5/32"	20	Dark Maroon	130 lbs. @ 1 27/32"	1.406"
140-51-549	1"	1.594"	3/16"	21	Pink	120 lbs. @ 2 3/32"	1.968"
150-51-551	15/16"	1.593"	3/16"	21	Purple	170 lbs. @ 2 1/16"	1.875"
130-51-552	31/32"	Flat	5/32"	12	Dark Maroon	130 lbs. @ 1 27/32"	1.406"
140-51-556	15/16"	1.187"	7/32"	18	Dark Maroon	130 lbs. @ 1 27/32" ✦	1.687"
150-52-557††	1 1/8"	2.937"	5/32"	24	Purple	170 lbs. @ 2 1/16"	1.875"
150-51-558**	1 1/8"	1.750"	3/16"	27	Purple	170 lbs. @ 2 1/16"	1.875"
150-51-562**	5/16"	1.750"	3/16"	21	Purple	170 lbs. @ 2 1/16"	1.875"
150-51-564**	1 1/8"	1.750"	3/16"	21	Purple	170 lbs. @ 2 1/16"	1.875"
150-51-565**	1 1/8"	1.750"	3/16"	21	Purple	170 lbs. @ 2 1/16"	1.875"
150-51-570**	1 1/8"	1.750"	3/16"	18	Purple	170 lbs. @ 2 1/16"	1.875"
140-51-575	1"	1.187"	3/16"	18	Dark Maroon	130 lbs. @ 1 27/32"	1.687"
150-51-579**	1 1/8"	1.750"	3/16"	27	Bronze	250 lbs. @ 1 31/32"	1.875"
150-51-580	1 1/8"	1.750"	3/16"	21	Purple	170 lbs. @ 2 1/16"	1.875"
140-52-581†	1"	1.406"	5/32"	15	Dark Maroon	130 lbs. @ 1 27/32"	1.687"
140-51-583	1"	1.594"	3/16"	21	Blue	150 lbs. @ 2 3/32"	1.968"
150-51-586**	1 1/8"	1.750"	3/16"	18	Purple	170 lbs. @ 2 1/16"	1.875"
150-52-587††	1 1/8"	2.937"	5/32"	18	Purple	170 lbs. @ 2 1/16"	1.875"
130-51-588	31/32"	Flat	5/32"	16	Dark Maroon	130 lbs. @ 1 27/32"	1.406"
140-52-589†	1"	1.406"	5/32"	12	Dark Maroon	130 lbs. @ 1 27/32"	1.687"
150-51-595	1 3/8"	1.312"	7/32"	24	Purple	170 lbs. @ 2 1/16"	1.875"
140-51-599	1"	1.187"	3/16"	21	Light Green	150 lbs. @ 1 27/32"	1.687"
150-51-608	1"	1.594"	3/16"	24	Purple	170 lbs. @ 2 1/16"	1.875"
150-51-634**	1 1/8"	1.750"	3/16"	21	Purple	170 lbs. @ 2 1/16"	1.875"
150-51-654**	5/16"®	1.750"	3/16"	27	Purple	170 lbs. @ 2 1/16"	1.875"
150-51-655	15/16"	1.594"	3/16"	21	Purple	170 lbs. @ 2 1/16"	1.875"
150-51-656	15/16"	1.594"	3/16"	24	Purple	170 lbs. @ 2 1/16"	1.875"
150-51-657**	5/16"®	1.750"	3/16"	21	Purple	170 lbs. @ 2 1/16"	1.875"
150-51-658**	1 1/8"	1.750"	3/16"	27	Purple	170 lbs. @ 2 1/16"	1.875"
150-51-659	1 1/8"	1.750"	3/16"	21	Purple	170 lbs. @ 2 1/16"	1.875"
150-51-660**	1 1/8"	1.750"	3/16"	18	Purple	170 lbs. @ 2 1/16"	1.875"
150-51-661**	1 1/8"	1.750"	3/16"	24	Purple	170 lbs. @ 2 1/16"	1.875"
150-51-662**	5/16"®	1.750"	3/16"	18	Purple	170 lbs. @ 2 1/16"	1.875"
150-51-672	1 3/8"	1.312"	7/32"	24	Purple	170 lbs. @ 2 1/16"	1.875"
150-51-685**	5/16"®	1.750"	3/16"	24	Purple	170 lbs. @ 2 1/16"	1.875"
150-52-696	25/32"	2.796"	5/32"	18	Purple	170 lbs. @ 2 1/16" ✦	1.875"
150-51-714	1 1/8"	1.750"	3/16"	24	Purple	170 lbs. @ 2 1/16"	1.875"
155-51-728	1 3/8"	1.312"	7/32"	18	Purple	170 lbs. @ 2 1/16"	1.875"
150-52-739	1 1/8"	2.937"	5/32"	24	Purple	170 lbs. @ 2 1/16"	1.875"
150-52-745	1 1/8"	2.937"	5/32"	24	Purple	170 lbs. @ 2 1/16"	1.875"
150-52-747	25/32"	2.796"	5/32"	21	Purple	170 lbs. @ 2 1/16" ✦	1.875"
150-52-748	25/32"	2.796"	5/32"	24	Purple	170 lbs. @ 2 3/32" ✦	1.875"
155-51-766	1 3/8"	1.312"	7/32"	21	Purple	170 lbs. @ 2 1/16"	1.875"
155-51-767	1 3/8"	1.312"	7/32"	24	Purple	170 lbs. @ 2 1/16"	1.875"
155-51-768	1 3/8"	1.312"	7/32"	27	Purple	170 lbs. @ 2 1/16"	1.875"
150-51-771	1 1/8"	1.750"	3/16"	18	Light Green	150 lbs. @ 1 27/32"	1.875"
150-51-775	1 1/8"	1.750"	3/16"	15	Purple	170 lbs. @ 2 1/16"	1.875"
140-51-814	1 3/16"	1.594"	3/16"	21	Blue	150 lbs. @ 1 27/32"	1.986"

**Also Applicable to engine flywheel depth of 1.812" with 7/32" facing thickness.

†Intermediate Plate Thickness .754 + .000 − .003

††Intermediate Plate Thickness .832 + .000 − .003

✦Height listed is not necessarily the working height when assembled.

Fig. 4 Lipe DP clutch chart

HEAVY DUTY CLUTCHES

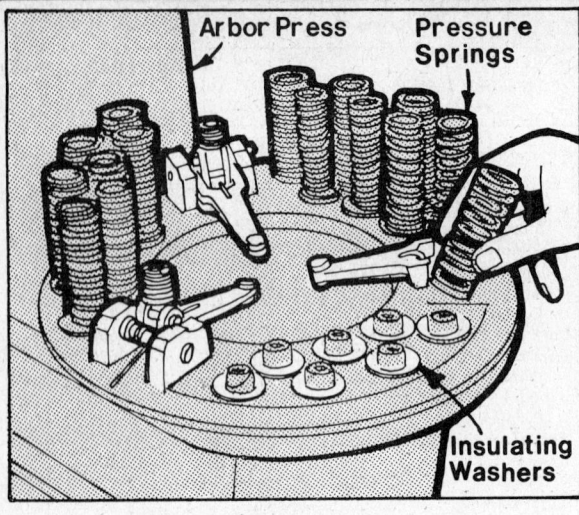

Fig. 9 Installing insulating washers and pressure springs

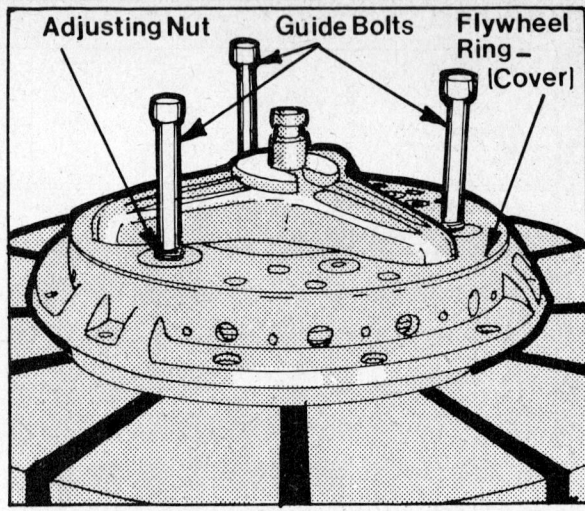

Fig. 10 Installing flywheel ring (cover) and guide bolts

6. Place insulating washers over bosses on pressure plate and install pressure springs, Fig. 9.
7. Place flywheel ring (cover) over assembly. If original parts are used, line up driving lugs marked "O" with driving slot marked "O".
8. To facilitate assembly, install guide bolts into adjusting nut until contact is made with end of eyebolt, Fig. 10.
9. Compress flywheel ring (cover) gradually, making sure that the three driving lugs enter properly into the driving slots in the pressure plate, and the pressure springs are properly seated on the pressure plate and in the seats provided in the flywheel ring (cover). Pull adjusting nut through holes in cover with guide bolts previously installed.
10. Remove guide bolts and assemble adjusting screw locknuts, making sure they are drawn tight to cover, Fig. 11.
11. Install hold-down bolts with standard washers in holes provided in flywheel ring (cover) and tapped holes in pressure plate (3 required), Fig. 11.

NOTE: An alternate procedure is to use a 7/16" wood block between release lever and underside of cover.

12. The press can now be released and the clutch cover assembly removed.

Clutch Installation

Inspect Engine Flywheel
1. Check flywheel for correct depth, Fig. 4.
2. Make sure release bearing and flywheel pilot bearing are in useable condition. Pilot bearing should be a finger press fit in flywheel and on transmission drive shaft.
3. Friction face of flywheel should be smooth and clean.

CAUTION: Friction face of flywheel must be free of heat cracks, score marks and foreign matter, as the presence of any one of these conditions will cause the clutch facings to quickly disintegrate.

Installing Single Plate Clutch
1. Try cover in flywheel before inserting driven disc to make sure it is a free fit in flywheel.
2. Install driven disc in flywheel, making sure long end of hub faces cover.
3. To facilitate assembly of transmission to engine, the use of a spare splined pilot shaft to align the driven disc while bolting the clutch in place is essential.

NOTE: The side of the driven disc that faces the clutch pressure plate has a chamfer on the end of the splined hub to facilitate the insertion of the transmission drive shaft.

4. Bolt the clutch to the flywheel and screw in each bolt until it contacts cover plate. Then gradually tighten opposite bolts until assembly is drawn up tight and completely into flywheel.
5. Remove the three hold-down bolts previously installed.

NOTE: It is very important that the correct capscrews be used when attaching the 13" cover to flywheel. The shank of the attaching capscrews are a close fit to the holes in this cover and the shank extends into the counterbore in the flywheel. If the flywheel has been excessively remachined, this counterbore may become too shallow, which will necessitate replacing the flywheel.

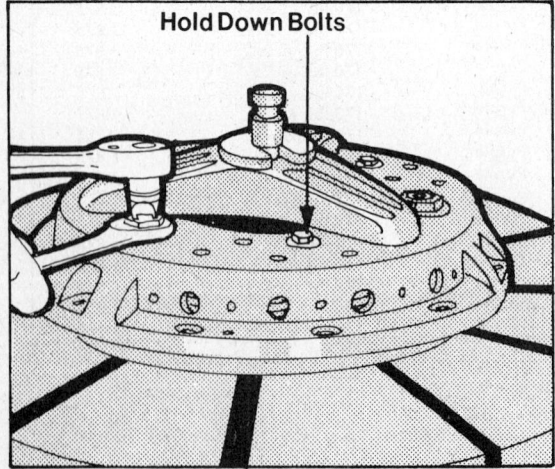

Fig. 11 Installing adjusting screw lock nuts and hold-down bolts

Clutch Size & Type	Release Bearing Clearance	Normal Release Bearing Travel	Total Bearing Travel Required
13" Single Plate	1/8"	7/16"	9/16"
14" Single Plate	1/8"	7/16"	9/16"
15" Single Plate	1/8"	7/16"	9/16"
13" Two Plate	1/8"	1/2"	5/8"
14" Two Plate	1/8"	1/2"	5/8"
15" Two Plate	1/8"	1/2"	5/8"

Fig. 12 DP clutch release travel chart

HEAVY DUTY CLUTCHES

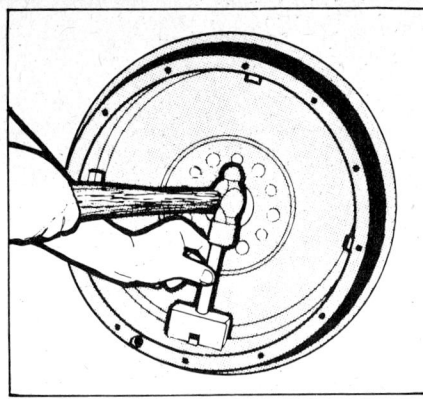

Fig. 12 Aligning drive pins in flywheel, using Lipe tool T-10670

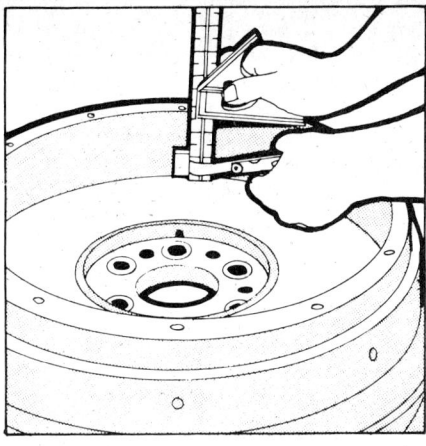

Fig. 14 Aligning drive pins in flywheel, using machinist square and feeler gauge

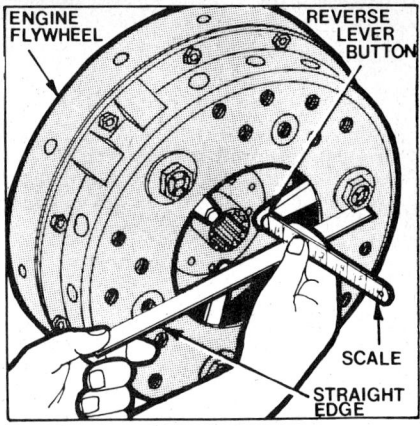

Fig. 15 Checking Dimension "A" on clutches with cast cover

Installing Two Plate Clutch

1. The four intermediate plate driving pins must be removed if the flywheel is to be machined. Pins with worn contact faces must be replaced.
2. The driving pins must be installed with the contact face square to the friction face of the flywheel.

NOTE: To insure perfect alignment, it is recommended that a tool, Fig. 13, be used. If this tool is not available, place a machinist square firmly on the flywheel rim and make sure the contact face of the driving pins have even contact with the square, Fig. 14.

3. The 14" two plate clutch driving pins are held in place by locknuts on the threaded end projecting through the flywheel which must be securely tightened. The 15" two plate driving pins may be locked in place by cup point Allen screws located in the bottom of the tapped holes used for attaching the cover to the flywheel.
4. After the driving pins are properly aligned and secured, and a new pilot bearing installed, the clutch is ready to be installed into the flywheel. It is essential that a splined shaft of the correct size for the pilot bearing and driven discs be used to align the driven discs before the cover is installed to the flywheel.
5. Install one disc in the flywheel and then place the intermediate plate on the driving pins and check for lash or free play at the driving slots. The intermediate plate should fit over the driving pins with not less than .007" clearance at the contact faces, which will permit free movement of the intermediate plate. If the clearance exceeds .012", the intermediate plate may cause some noise when the clutch is disengaged.
6. With the splined alignment shaft holding the driven discs in position, the cover assembly can now be attached to the flywheel. Attaching capscrews should be evenly tightened until cover is drawn tight to the flywheel.

NOTE: New cover assemblies have wooden blocks positioned between release levers and cover which facilitate assembly of cover to flywheel. Make sure these blocks are removed after clutch installation.

7. If the cover has been repaired or rebuilt, the lever heights should be checked after installation to flywheel. Use a straightedge and 6" scale as an "A" dimension gauge as indicated in Fig. 15. Refer to Fig. 4 for correct lever setting.
8. Always start with the levers low and keeping some tension on the lock nuts at all times, turn both the lock nut and adjusting nuts in a clockwise direction to raise the levers to the desired setting. When the correct height has been obtained, hold the adjusting nut firmly while tightening the lock nut.

Adjusting to Dimension "A"

Satisfactory operation of the clutch is absolutely dependent upon the accuracy of the release lever adjustment since the pressure plate must operate parallel with the engine flywheel.

Set the release levers to the proper Dimension "A" by turning the adjusting nuts and measuring with a straightedge and scale. The release lever buttons should be the same distance from the ground surface of the bosses on the flywheel ring (cover). After Dimension "A" has been set, tighten lock nuts securely, at the same time holding the adjusting nut from turning. Use the tool shown in Fig. 16 for holding slotted adjusting nut.

On the stamped DP cover, Dimension "A" is obtained in the same manner as described for the cast cover above. Use the straightedge and scale as shown in Fig. 17 with the straightedge in the grooves adjacent to the adjusting nuts. The straightedge must also be at right angles to and over the end of the release lever. The release lever buttons must be the same distance from the grooves in the flywheel ring (cover).

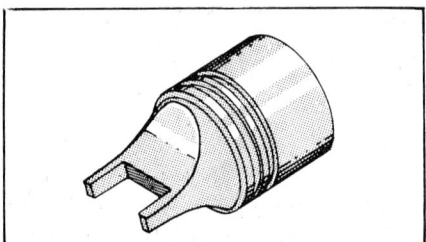

Fig. 16 Lipe tool for holding slotted adjusting nut

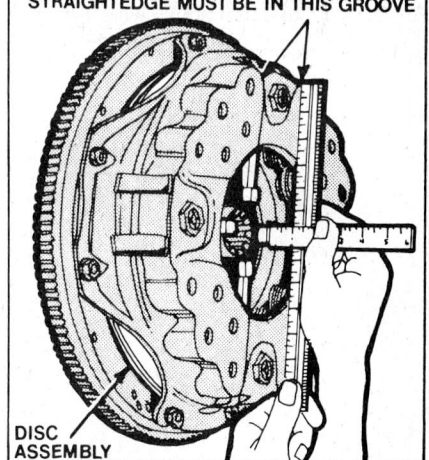

Fig. 17 Checking Dimension "A" on clutches with stamped cover

HEAVY DUTY CLUTCHES

Lipe DLB Clutch

The Lipe DLB clutch is a direct pressure, dry disc design, incorporating a push type release bearing, Fig. 1 and 2. The DLB units are available in a 13 inch, two plate design and a 14 inch, single plate design.

Clutch Pedal Adjustment

Proper clutch pedal free play is approximately $1\frac{1}{2}''$. If inspection indicates that the free play is less than $\frac{1}{2}''$, immediate adjustment of the clutch pedal linkage should be made to restore $1\frac{1}{2}''$. This $1\frac{1}{2}''$ free play normally results in $\frac{1}{8}''$ clearance between clutch release levers and release bearing.

Servicing the Clutch

After the clutch is disassembled, clean all parts thoroughly. Inspect all parts as indicated in the following procedure. If in doubt about any part, replace with a new one.

Pressure Plate
The pressure plate must be replaced if friction surface is severely heat checked, it is warped in excess of .015", driving surfaces are worn, or pin holes are elongated.

It is recommended that not over $\frac{1}{32}''$ be removed from friction face by regrinding. See Fig. 3 and refer to Fig. 4 for thickness of new pressure plates, "Dimension C".

Install new bearings by pressing on the end of the bearing on which part numbers are stamped. This prevents damage to bearing case.

Intermediate Plate
The intermediate plate in two plate clutches should not be re-used if there is over .012" clearance between the driving lugs and the mating slots in the flywheel. It is recommended that grinding of the intermediate plate be kept to a minimum with not over .015" being removed from either side for a total of .030". See Fig. 4 for thickness specifications.

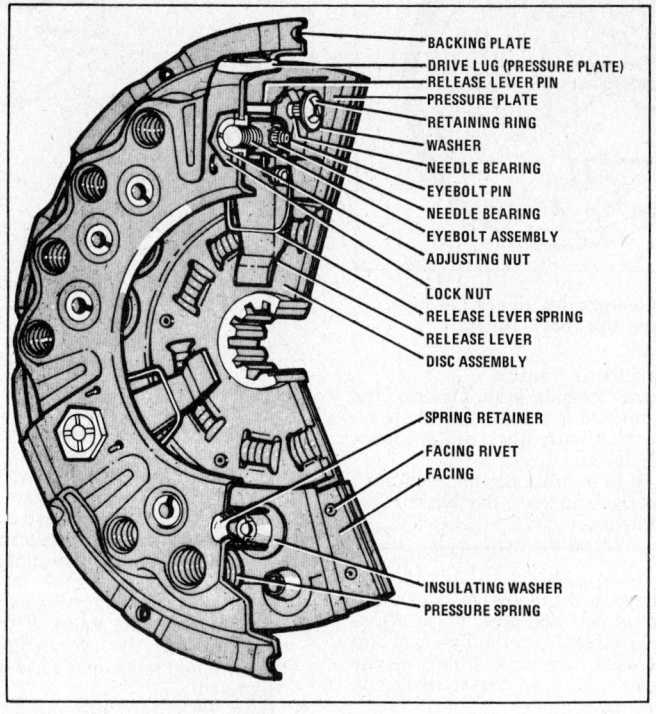

Fig. 1 Lipe DLB single plate clutch

Flywheel Ring (Cover)
Inspect flywheel ring (cover) for distortion or cracks. Bolting flanges should be flat to within .015" when checked on a surface plate.

Pressure Springs, Fig. 5
It is of vital importance that the pressure springs be checked for compression weight in accordance with the weight listed in the chart, Fig. 4. Under-weight springs will reduce clutch capacity and possibly cause clutch slippage. Therefore, to insure best clutch performance, new springs should be installed.

Eyebolt and Adjusting Nut
When installing new bearings, use a suitable tool and press on the end of the bearing having numbers stamped thereon. This will prevent damage to bearing cage.

In cover assemblies not incorporating needle bearings, the eyebolt pin hole is elongated

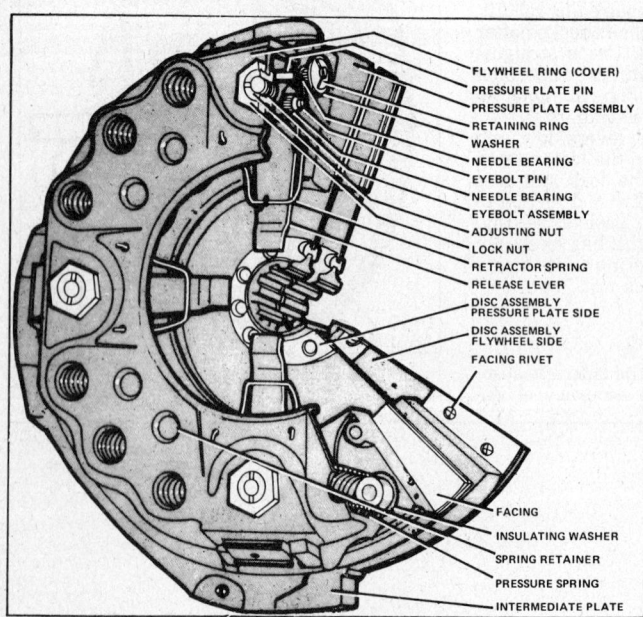

Fig. 2 Lipe DLB two plate clutch

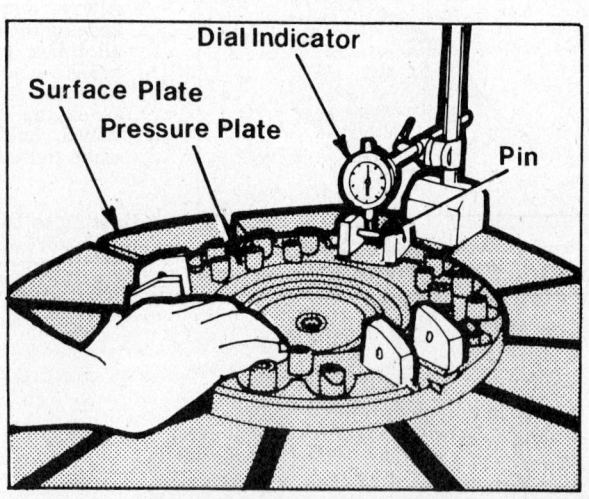

Fig. 3 Checking Dimension "C" on DLB clutches

HEAVY DUTY CLUTCHES

Model	Dimension "A"	Flywheel Depth +.005" −.005"	Facing Thickness	Pressure Spring Data			Pressure Plate Data
				Quantity	Color	Minimum Weight Lbs. @ Inch	Dimension "C" New
130-62-702	1 1/16	1.062	5/32	16	Dk. Maroon Stripe	133 @ 1 27/32	1.531
130-62-987	1 1/16	1.062	5/32	12	Dk. Maroon Stripe	133 @ 1 27/32	1.531
130-302-1140 ①	1 1/16	1.062	5/32	12	Lt. Green Stripe	153 @ 1 27/32	1.531
130-302-1508	1 1/16	1.062	5/32	16	Dk. Maroon Stripe	133 @ 1 27/32	1.531
130-302-1544	1 1/16	1.062	5/32	12	Dk. Maroon Stripe	133 @ 1 27/32	1.531
140-301-1086	2 9/32	Flat	3/16	18	Dk. Maroon Stripe	133 @ 1 27/32	1.687
140-301-1107	2 9/32	Flat	11/64	21	Lt. Green Stripe	153 @ 1 27/32	1.687

①—Some pressure plate assemblies were manufactured with 16 pressure springs and can be identified by a blue dot on the pressure plate cover. If a 12 spring unit is being reworked and 16 springs are desired, a blue dot should be added to the cover. The 16 springs used are 8 light green stripe (Tension—153 lbs. @ 1 27/32 inch) and 8 dark maroon stripe (Tension—133 lbs. @ 1 27/32 inch) positioned as shown in Fig. 5.

Fig. 4 Lipe DLB clutch chart

to allow the pin to move as the clutch is disengaged. If this hole indicates wear the eyebolt should be replaced. Eyebolt and adjusting nut threads must be free fitting but not excessively loose.

Release Lever Assembly

The release levers must be replaced if the holes for the eyebolt and pressure plate pins are worn, or if worn severely by the release bearing.

Release levers used in needle bearing clutches have elongated holes for eyebolt pins, whereas levers for standard pin clutches have round holes for both the pressure plate and eyebolt pins.

Driven Disc Assembly

The disc should be replaced if the hub splines are worn, disc is distorted, cracked or broken. If the disc is acceptable for lining, use Lipe Facing Kit to obtain correct rivets and facing material.

Make sure proper riveting method is used. See Fig. 6 in the DP clutch section for riveting method with fabric and metallic facings.

NOTE: Field relining of dampener or cushioned type disc assemblies is not recommended. Facing Kits, including original equipment facings with proper rivets are only available for non-cushioned clutches. Other component parts, such as marcels (cushioned segments) or coil springs are not available for service replacement. The rigid type disc without cushioned facings may be relined if the steel disc is not distorted or cracked and the hub splines are not worn over .010".

Clutch Assembly

1. Apply a small amount of NGLI #2 multi-purpose, lithium grease on all pins. Also, on two plate clutches, apply grease on driving lugs of flywheel ring and mating slots in pressure plate.

NOTE: Do not over lubricate.

2. Support pressure plate in an arbor press with suitable blocks so the flywheel ring (cover) can be pressed over the pressure plate without contacting base of press.
3. Assemble adjusting nuts to eyebolts, then to the release levers using new pins.
4. Assemble levers to pressure plate and install release lever pins.

NOTE: Clutches with needle bearings require flat washers installed on both ends of the pins.

5. Position insulating washers over spring bosses on pressure plate, then install pressure springs on bosses. Refer to Fig. 5 if two types (Color coded) springs are used.

NOTE: If the base of the spring boss is equipped with webs, do not use the insulating washers.

6. Assemble release lever springs on flywheel ring (cover) and position flywheel ring over pressure springs, ensuring each spring is properly positioned in the ring.

NOTE: Be sure to align the "O" marks on the pressure plate and flywheel ring.

7. Press flywheel ring (cover) into position ensuring the pressure plate driving lugs are engaged in the flywheel ring slots.
8. Pull adjusting nuts through flywheel ring

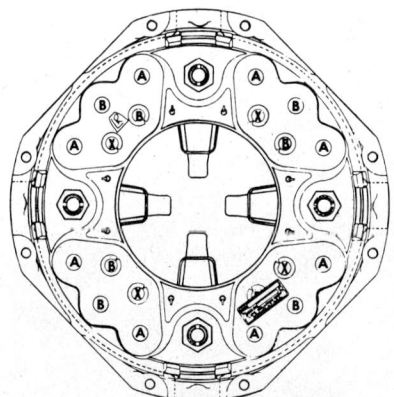

Ⓐ LOCATION OF PRESSURE SPRING w/DARK MAROON STRIPE
Ⓑ LOCATION OF PRESSURE SPRING w/LIGHT GREEN STRIPE
Ⓧ DO NOT ASSEMBLE SPRINGS ON THESE LOCATORS

Fig. 5 Pressure spring location

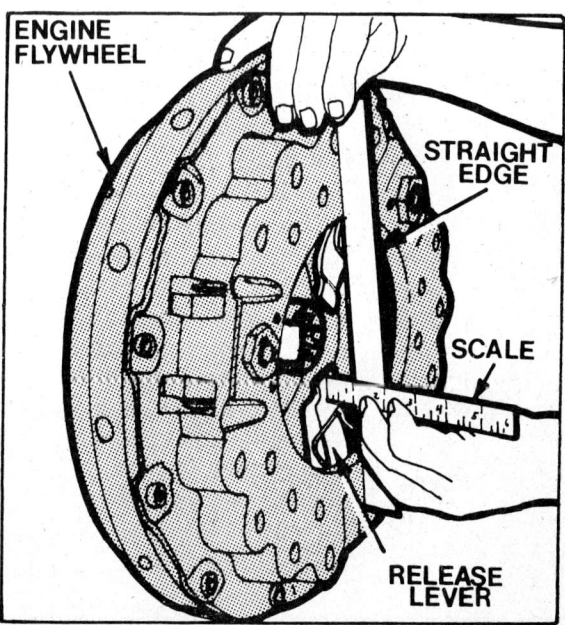

Fig. 6 Checking Dimension "A" on DLB clutches

HEAVY DUTY CLUTCHES

(cover) and install lock nuts.
9. Before releasing press, install four 1/4" 20 × 2 1/4" bolts on 13 inch units or three 1/4" 20 × 2 1/4" bolts on 14 inch units through flywheel ring (cover) into the tapped holes in the pressure plate.
10. The release levers must be adjusted to the proper height and lock nuts tightened as follows:
    a. Dimension "A" is the distance from the top of the flywheel ring (cover) to ends of release levers. (Applies only to field repaired or rebuilt clutches.)
    b. See chart, Fig. 4, for correct "A" dimension for unit being serviced. Satisfactory operation of the clutch depends greatly upon the accuracy of the lever setting as this controls the parallel movement of the pressure plate.
    c. A straightedge and scale will provide a means of checking the "A" dimension. Fig. 6 shows the special tools available for slotted adjusting nuts.
    d. Adjusting the lever height is facilitated by starting with the levers low and with lock nut just snug. Turn adjusting nut and lock nut as a unit clockwise until the lever is raised the desired height. Then hold slotted nut firmly and tighten lock nut.
11. Check recessed type flywheels for proper depth as listed in chart, Fig. 4.

Lipe DPB Clutch

The Lipe DPB clutch is a direct pressure unit. The clutch requires no maintenance other than maintaining release bearing clearance which is accomplished by normal linkage adjustment, Figs. 1 and 2.

Identifying Models

The name plate attached to the flywheel ring (cover) identifies the cover plate as to the serial number and model number. For example, model number 120-61-615 is interpreted as follows: 120 indicates that it is a 12" clutch. The '61' between the dashes indicates the clutch to be a single plate type DPB unit, and 615 is the parts list number. A '61' indicates that the assembly is equipped with needle bearings; a '62' indicates a two plate assembly with needle bearings.

There are four types of disc assemblies available with the numbering system set up to identify each type. An assembly number is stamped on the disc.

Clutch Pedal Adjustment

Proper clutch pedal free play is approximately 1 1/2". If inspection indicates that the free play is less than 1/2", immediate adjustment of the clutch pedal linkage should be made to restore to 1 1/2". This 1 1/2" free play normally results in 1/8" clearance between clutch release levers and release bearing.

Some two plate DPB assemblies are equipped with intermediate plate separator springs and adjusting screws. These units may require periodic adjustment to maintain the .020" clearance recommended clearance between the end of the adjusting screws and the intermediate plate.

The adjustment must be made with the clutch in the engaged position. The adjusting screws should be turned clockwise until they just contact the intermediate plate. At this point a 1/2 turn (counterclockwise) of the screws will produce a .020" clearance. Lock the adjusting screws in position by tightening the lock nuts.

NOTE: When replacing or repairing the clutch assembly, it is recommended that the separator springs and adjusting screws be removed from the assembly before installation.

Servicing the Clutch

After the clutch is disassembled, clean all parts thoroughly. Inspect all parts as indicated in the following procedure. If in doubt about any part, replace with a new one.

Pressure Plate

The pressure plate must be replaced if friction surface is severely heat checked, it is warped in excess of .015", driving surfaces are worn, or pin holes are elongated.

It is recommended that not over 1/32" be removed from friction face by regrinding. See

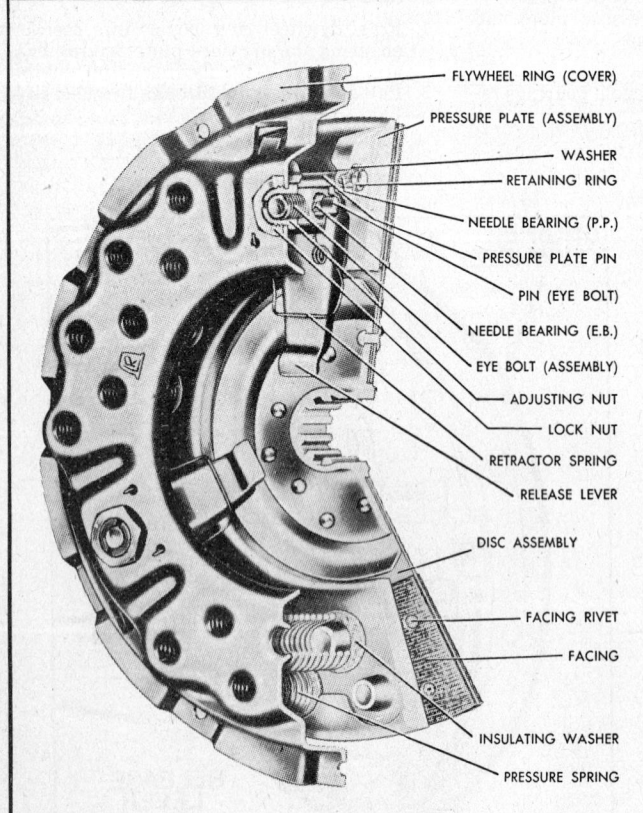

Fig. 1 Lipe DPB single plate clutch

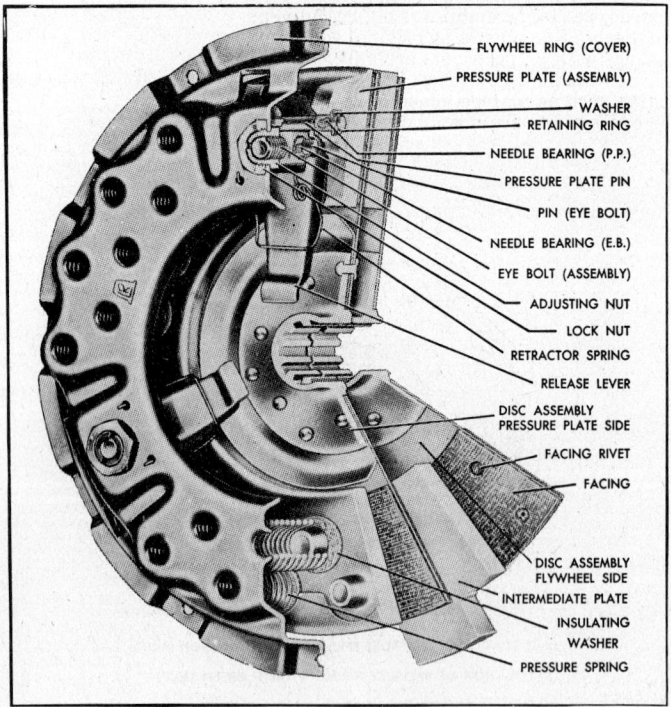

Fig. 2 Lipe DPB two plate clutch

HEAVY DUTY CLUTCHES

Model Number	Dimension "A"	Flywheel Depth +.005" −.005"	Facing†† Thickness	PRESSURE SPRING DATA			PRESSURE PLATE DATA
				Quantity	Color	Minimum Weight in lbs.§	Dimension "C" New
120-61-615	1 3/16"	Flat	5/32"	12	No Color	170 @ 1 27/32"	1.468
130-61-619	1 1/16"	Flat	5/32"	16	Dark Maroon	130 @ 1 27/32"	1.531
140-61-623	29/32"	Flat	3/16"	21	Light Green	150 @ 1 27/32"	1.687
130-62-625**	1 1/16"	1.062	5/32"	20	Dark Maroon	130 @ 1 27/32"	1.531
120-61-627	1 3/16"	Flat	5/32"	12	Light Green	150 @ 1 27/32"	1.468
120-61-628	1 1/16"	Flat	5/32"	12	Red Stripe	170 @ 1 27/32"	1.468
120-62-629*	1 3/16"	1.062"	5/32"	12	Light Green	150 @ 1 27/32"	1.468
120-61-631	1 3/16"	Flat	5/32"	12	Light Green	150 @ 1 27/32"	1.468
120-61-633	1 3/16"	Flat	5/32"	12	Light Green	150 @ 1 27/32"	1.468
140-61-635	29/32"	Flat	3/16"	21	Dark Maroon	150 @ 1 27/32"	1.687
130-61-642	1 1/16"	Flat	5/32"	20	Dark Maroon	130 @ 1 27/32"	1.531
130-61-647	1 1/16"	Flat	5/32"	20	Dark Maroon	130 @ 1 27/32"	1.531
140-61-648	29/32"	1.187	3/16"	21	Light Green	150 @ 1 27/32"	1.687
140-62-650†	29/32"	1.093	5/32"	15	Dark Maroon	130 @ 1 27/32"	1.687
140-61-651	29/32"	1.187	3/16"	21	Light Green	150 @ 1 27/32"	1.687
140-61-652	29/32"	Flat	3/16"	21	Dark Maroon	130 @ 1 27/32"	1.687
140-61-653	29/32"	1.187	3/16"	21	Dark Maroon	130 @ 1 27/32"	1.687
140-62-665†	29/32"	1.093	5/32"	18	Dark Maroon	130 @ 1 27/32"	1.687
140-61-666	29/32"	1.187	3/16"	18	Dark Maroon	130 @ 1 27/32"	1.687
120-61-667	1 3/16"	Flat	5/32"	12	Red Stripe	180 @ 1 27/32"	1.468
130-61-669	1 3/16"	Flat	5/32"	16	Dark Maroon	130 @ 1 27/32"	1.531
130-61-670	1 3/16"	Flat	5/32"	20	Dark Maroon	130 @ 1 27/32"	1.531
120-62-675*	1 3/16"	1.062	5/32"	09	Light Green	150 @ 1 27/32"	1.468
140-61-684	27/32"	1.187	7/32"	18	Dark Maroon	130 @ 1 27/32"§	1.687
140-61-689	29/32"	Flat	3/16"	18	Dark Maroon	130 @ 1 27/32"	1.687
140-61-695	29/32"	Flat	3/16"	21	Dark Maroon	130 @ 1 27/32"	1.687
150-61-697	1"	1.750	3/16"	24	Purple	170 @ 2 1/16"	1.937
130-62-699**	1 1/16"	1.062	5/32"	20	Dark Maroon	130 @ 1 27/32"	1.531
130-62-700**	1 1/16"	1.062	5/32"	16	Dark Maroon	130 @ 1 27/32"	1.531
140-62-701	29/32"	1.093	5/32"	18	Dark Maroon	130 @ 1 27/32"	1.687
130-62-702**	1 1/16"	1.062	5/32"	16	Dark Maroon	130 @ 1 27/32"	1.531
140-61-703	29/32"	1.187	7/32"	21	Dark Maroon	130 @ 1 27/32"§	1.687
140-62-704†	29/32"	1.093	5/32"	21	Dark Maroon	130 @ 1 27/32"	1.687
140-61-706	29/32"	Flat	3/16"	21	Light Green	150 @ 1 27/32"	1.687
140-61-707	29/32"	1.187	3/16"	21	Dark Maroon	130 @ 1 27/32"	1.687
150-62-708	1"	1.093	5/32"	24	Purple	170 @ 2 1/16"	1.937
140-61-711	29/32"	1.187	3/16"	18	Dark Maroon	130 @ 1 27/32"	1.687
140-61-712	29/32"	1.187	3/16"	18	Dark Maroon	130 @ 1 27/32"	1.687
140-61-713	29/32"	Flat	3/16"	18	Dark Maroon	130 @ 1 27/32"	1.687
140-61-718	29/32"	1.187	3/16"	18	Dark Maroon	130 @ 1 27/32"	1.687
150-62-719	1"	1.093	5/32"	18	Purple	170 @ 2 1/16"	1.937
140-61-720	29/32"	1.187	3/16"	14	Dark Maroon	130 @ 1 27/32"	1.687
140-61-721	29/32"	Flat	3/16"	15	Dark Maroon	130 @ 1 27/32"	1.687
140-61-723	29/32"	1.187	3/16"	12	Light Green	150 @ 1 27/32"	1.687
130-61-724	1 1/16"	Flat	5/32"	12	Dark Maroon	130 @ 1 27/32"	1.531
130-61-725‡	7/8"	Flat	5/32"	20	Dark Maroon	130 @ 1 27/32"	1.531
120-61-726	1 1/16"	Flat	5/32"	12	No Color	170 @ 1 27/32"	1.468
140-62-727	29/32"	1.093	5/32"	15	Dark Maroon	130 @ 1 27/32"	1.687
150-61-731	1"	1.750	3/16"	18	Purple	170 @ 2 1/16"	1.937
130-61-734	1 1/8"	Flat	5/32"	20	Dark Maroon	130 @ 1 27/32"	1.531
140-62-735†	29/32"	1.093	5/32"	21	Light Green	150 @ 1 27/32"	1.687
130-62-736	29/32"	1.477	5/32"	12	Light Green	150 @ 1 27/32"	1.750
150-61-738	1"	1.750	3/16"	21	Purple	170 @ 2 1/16"	1.937
150-62-743	1"	1.093	5/32"	21	Purple	170 @ 2 1/16"	1.937
140-61-761	29/32"	1.187	3/16"	21	Dark Maroon	130 @ 1 27/32"	1.687
140-61-773	29/32"	1.187	3/16"	21	Dark Maroon	130 @ 1 27/32"	1.687
150-61-776	1"	1.750	3/16"	15	Purple	170 @ 2 1/16"	1.937
140-62-778	29/32"	1.093	5/32"	21	Dark Maroon	130 @ 1 27/32"	1.687
140-62-779	29/32"	1.093	5/32"	18	Dark Maroon	130 @ 1 27/32"	1.687
140-62-780	29/32"	1.093	5/32"	15	Dark Maroon	130 @ 1 27/32"	1.687
140-62-781	29/32"	1.093	5/32"	21	Light Green	150 @ 1 27/32"	1.687
140-61-785	29/32"	Flat	3/16"	15	Dark Maroon	130 @ 1 27/32"	1.687

Fig. 3 Lipe DPB clutch chart (Part 1 of 2)

Continued

HEAVY DUTY CLUTCHES

Model Number	Dimension "A"	Flywheel Depth +.005" −.005"	Facing†† Thickness	PRESSURE SPRING DATA			PRESSURE PLATE DATA
				Quantity	Color	Minimum Weight in lbs.§	Dimension "C" New
170-62-789	1 7/32"	1.562	5/32"	32	Orange	355 @ 2 17/32"	1.875
120-62-791	1 3/16"	1.062	3/32"	9	Light Green	150 @ 1 23/32"	1.468
150-62-794	1"	1.093	5/32"	15	Purple	170 @ 2 1/16"	1.937
130-62-798	2 9/32"	1.477	5/32"	12	Light Green	150 @ 1 27/32"	1.750
130-61-802	1 3/16"	Flat	3/32"	16	Dark Maroon	130 @ 1 27/32"	1.531
140-61-805	2 3/32"	.976	3/32"	18	Dark Maroon	130 @ 1 27/32"	1.687
120-61-806	1 3/16"	Flat	5/32"	12	Dark Maroon	130 @ 1 27/32"	1.468
130-61-807	1 3/16"	Flat	5/32"	12	Dark Green Stripe	90 @ 1 27/32"	1.531
				4	Dark Maroon	130 @ 1 27/32"	
130-61-808	1 3/16"	Flat	5/32"	20	Dark Green Stripe	90 @ 1 27/32"	1.531
130-61-809	1 3/16"	Flat	5/32"	16	Dark Maroon	130 @ 1 27/32"	1.531
140-61-810	2 9/32"	1.187	3/16"	15	Dark Green Stripe	90 @ 1 27/32"	1.687
				3	Light Green	150 @ 1 27/32"	
140-61-811	2 9/32"	1.187	3/16"	6	Dark Maroon	130 @ 1 27/32"	1.687
				15	Dark Green Stripe	90 @ 1 27/32"	
120-61-812	1 3/16"	Flat	5/32"	6	Light Green	150 @ 1 27/32"	1.468
				6	Dark Green Stripe	90 @ 1 27/32"	
120-61-813	1 3/16"	Flat	5/32"	9	Dark Maroon	130 @ 1 27/32"	1.468
				3	No Color	170 @ 1 27/32"	
130-61-817	1 1/16"	Flat	5/32"	16	Dark Maroon	130 @ 1 27/32"	1.531
140-61-818	2 9/32"	Flat	3/16"	21	Light Green	150 @ 1 27/32"	1.687
140-61-819	2 9/32"	Flat	3/16"	18	Dark Maroon	130 @ 1 27/32"	1.687
170-61-821	1 7/32"	.396	3/32"	24	Orange	355 @ 2 17/32"	1.875

INTERMEDIATE PLATE THICKNESS   * 12" − .676 − .000   ** 13" − .676 − .000   † 14" − .754 − .000
                                                    + .003   + .003   + .003

†† Facings on 12" and 13" cushioned driven discs are 3/64" thick.
‡ "A" Dimension was 1 1/16".   § Height listed not necessarily working height when assembled.

Fig. 3   Lipe DPB clutch chart (Part 2 of 2)

Fig. 4 and refer to Fig. 3 for thickness of new pressure plates.

Install new bearings by pressing on the end of the bearing on which part numbers are stamped. This prevents damage to bearing case.

Intermediate Plate

The intermediate plate in two plate clutches should not be re-used if there is over .012" clearance between the driving lugs and the mating slots in the flywheel. It is recommended that grinding of the intermediate plate be kept to a minimum with not over .015" being removed from either side for a total of .030". See Fig. 3 for thickness specifications.

Flywheel Ring (Cover)
1. Inspect flywheel ring (cover) for distortion or cracks. Bolting flanges should be flat to within .015" when checked on a surface plate.
2. All DPB flywheel rings or covers are of stamped construction. The only wear points are the slots which engage the driving lugs of the pressure plate. If these driving surfaces are worn to the extent that, with a new pressure plate installed and an excess of .012" clearance is present, replace the cover assembly.
3. A clearance of at least .004" is required between driving surfaces of the flywheel ring (cover) and pressure plate. An excessive amount of clearance may cause noise or allow the pressure plate to shift off center and create an unbalanced condition.
4. Some DPB cover assemblies are piloted to the flywheel by an accurately machined O.D. of the flywheel ring (cover) which fits into a recess or rim on the flywheel. In other DPB units the assembly is piloted by body fitted capscrews which hold the assembly onto the flywheel. In this case the tapped holes in the flywheel will have a reamed recess to receive the special attaching screws. It is important that the correct capscrews be used where the cover is piloted by this method.

Pressure Springs

It is of vital importance that the pressure springs be checked for compression weight in accordance with the weight listed in the chart, Fig. 3. Under-weight springs will reduce clutch capacity and possibly cause clutch slippage. Therefore, to insure best clutch performance, new springs should be installed.

Eyebolt and Adjusting Nut

When installing new bearings, use a suitable tool and press on the end of the bearing having numbers stamped thereon. This will prevent damage to bearing cage.

In cover assemblies not incorporating needle bearings, the eyebolt pin hole is elongated to allow the pin to move as the clutch is disengaged. If this hole indicates wear the eyebolt should be replaced. Eyebolt and adjusting nut threads must be free fitting but not excessively loose.

Release Lever Assembly

The release levers must be replaced if the holes for the eyebolt and pressure plate pins

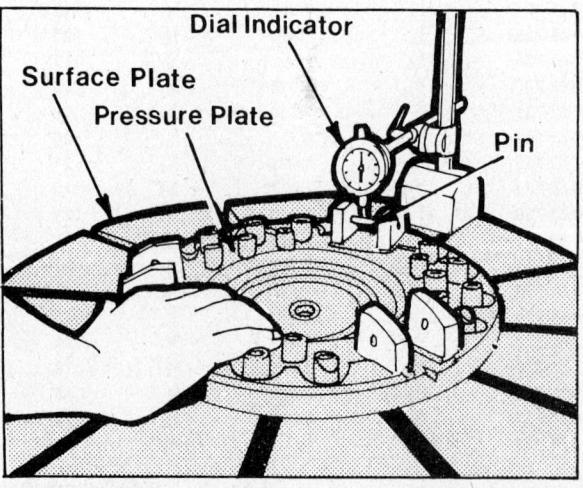

Fig. 4   Checking Dimension "C" on DPB clutches

HEAVY DUTY CLUTCHES

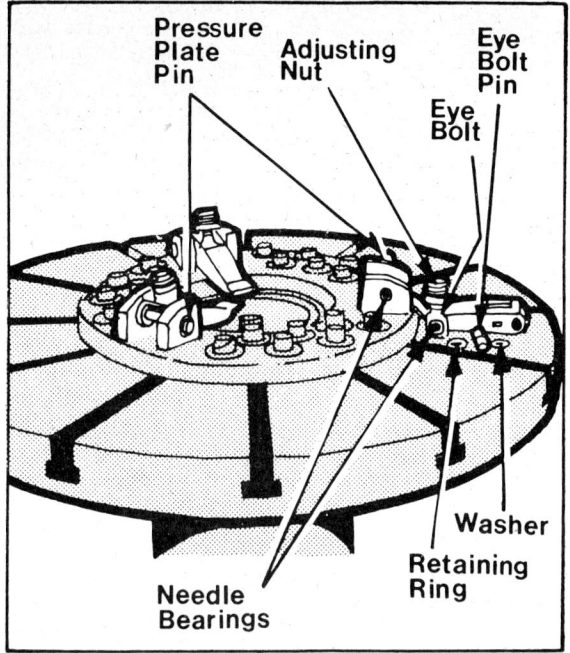

Fig. 5 Assembly of eyebolts and release levers

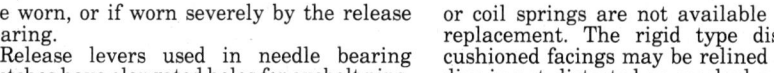

Fig. 6 Installation of release levers

are worn, or if worn severely by the release bearing.

Release levers used in needle bearing clutches have elongated holes for eyebolt pins, whereas levers for standard pin clutches have round holes for both the pressure plate and eyebolt pins.

Driven Disc Assembly

The disc should be replaced if the hub splines are worn, disc is distorted, cracked or broken. If the disc is acceptable for lining, use Lipe Facing Kit to obtain correct rivets and facing material.

Make sure proper riveting method is used. See Fig. 6 in the DP clutch section for riveting method with fabric and metallic facings.

NOTE: Field relining of dampener or cushioned type disc assemblies is not recommended. Facing Kits, including original equipment facings with proper rivets are only available for non-cushioned clutches. Other component parts, such as marcels (cushioned segments) or coil springs are not available for service replacement. The rigid type disc without cushioned facings may be relined if the steel disc is not distorted or cracked and the hub splines are not worn over .010".

Clutch Assembly

1. Place pressure plate on arbor press with friction face down.
2. Assemble adjusting nuts to eyebolts, then assemble to release lever, using new pins, Fig. 5.
3. Assemble levers to pressure plate and install retaining rings on pressure plate pins, Fig. 6.
4. Place insulating washers over spring bosses on pressure plate and install pressure springs, Fig. 6.
5. Install new retractor springs to flywheel ring (cover), Fig. 7.
6. Place cover over pressure srpings, making sure each spring is properly positioned. If original pressure plate and cover are being used, line up the "O" marks on pressure plate and cover.
7. The cover can now be pressed into position, using care to engage driving lugs into slots of cover to avoid distortion.
8. After cover has been pressed into position, the adjusting nuts may be pulled up through the holes in the cover and lock nuts installed, Fig. 8.
9. The 12" cover should have three $1/4$" $\times$ 20 $\times$ $2 1/4$" capscrews and the 14" cover should have three $3/8$" $\times$ 16 $\times$ $2 1/4$" capscrews installed through cover into tapped holes in pressure plate to hold it under compression when assembling to flywheel. All other DPB covers can be held in compression by placing $7/16$" wooden blocks between release lever and cover.
10. The press can now be released and cover assembly removed for attachment to flywheel where levers must be adjusted to proper height, and lock nuts tightened securely. See Dimension "A" on chart, Fig. 3.

Clutch Installation

Check Engine Flywheel
1. Check recessed type flywheels for proper

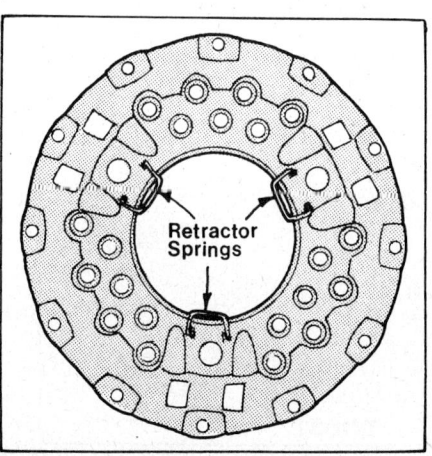

Fig. 7 Installation of retractor springs

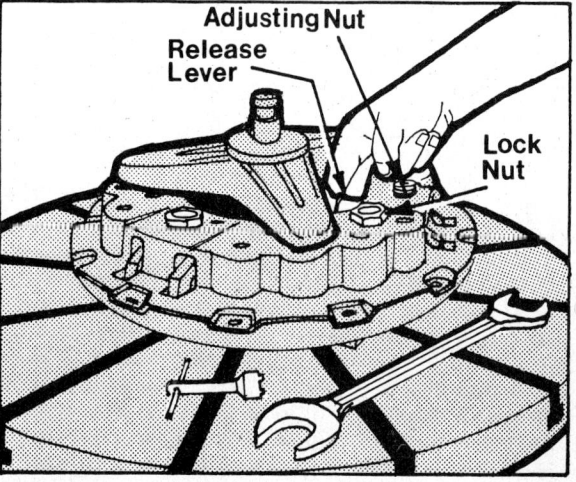

Fig. 8 Installation of lock nuts

439

HEAVY DUTY CLUTCHES

Clutch Size & Type	Release Bearing Clearance	Normal Release Bearing Travel	Total Bearing Travel Required
12" Single Plate	1/8"	11/32"	15/32"
13" Single Plate	1/8"	7/16"	9/16"
14" Single Plate	1/8"	7/16"	9/16"
15" Single Plate	1/8"	7/16"	9/16"
17" Single Plate	1/8"	7/16"	9/16"
12" Two Plate	1/8"	1/2"	5/8"
13" Two Plate	1/8"	1/2"	5/8"
14" Two Plate	1/8"	1/2"	5/8"
15" Two Plate	1/8"	1/2"	5/8"
17" Two Plate	1/8"	1/2"	5/8"

Fig. 9 DPB clutch release travel chart

depth as listed in chart, Fig. 3.
2. Replace release bearing and carrier, and flywheel pilot bearing. Pilot bearing should be a hand press fit in the flywheel recess and transmission drive gear. The release yoke or fork should contact the release bearing carrier pads evenly to prevent a bind on the front bearing cap extension.
3. The friction face of the flywheel must be free from heat cracks, score marks or taper. The presence of any of these conditions will have an adverse effect on clutch function and life.

Installing Single Plate Clutch
1. Check cover assembly on flywheel without the disc for proper fit.
2. Install driven disc, making sure that it is properly positioned and insert an aligning shaft.

CAUTION: Normally the long end of the driven disc hub extends toward the transmission, but in a few instances the long end may face toward the engine. Make sure that the disc hub does not come within 5/32" of the pilot bearing.

3. Bolt cover to flywheel, tightening each capscrew gradually until cover is drawn up tight. Remove wooden blocks or hold-down capscrews before removing aligning shaft.
4. See Fig. 9 for release travel specifications.

NOTE: Some cover assemblies are piloted to the flywheel by capscrews with a machined shank which fits the reamed holes in the cover. The machined shank extends through the cover into a recessed or counterbored hole in the flywheel. If the flywheel has been remachined several times to remove heat cracks or scores, the counterbored holes may not be deep enough to allow complete tightening of the capscrews. This will necessitate replacing the flywheel.

Installing Two Plate Clutch
1. The DPB two plate units have an intermediate plate with driving lugs which fit into mating slots of the flywheel.
2. Before installing one of these units, the intermediate plate should be set into the driving slots and clearances checked. A minimum of .006" is recommended to allow for free movement of the intermediate plate.
3. In some vehicles, the two plate assemblies are equipped with separator springs and adjusting screws. When necessary for such an assembly to be removed for repairs or replacement, the separator springs should be removed from the flywheel and the adjusting screws from the replacement unit before the installation is made.
4. The two driven discs will be marked either flywheel side or pressure plate side and must be so installed. In no instances shall the hubs be allowed to approach the pilot bearing or come together within 5/32".
5. When installing two plate clutches, it is essential that a splined shaft or an aligning shaft be used with a key to properly align the two driven discs. Otherwise the instructions for installing these clutches are the same as for single plate clutches.

NOTE: To obtain complete disengagement of DPB clutches, the release levers must be actuated a specified distance from the engaged position. Assuming the release bearing clearance is 1/8" (between levers and bearing) when clutch is in the engaged position, the release bearing must move forward 1/8" to take up this clearance before it contacts the release levers and then move the normal amount of travel required to disengage the clutch as shown in the chart, Fig. 9.

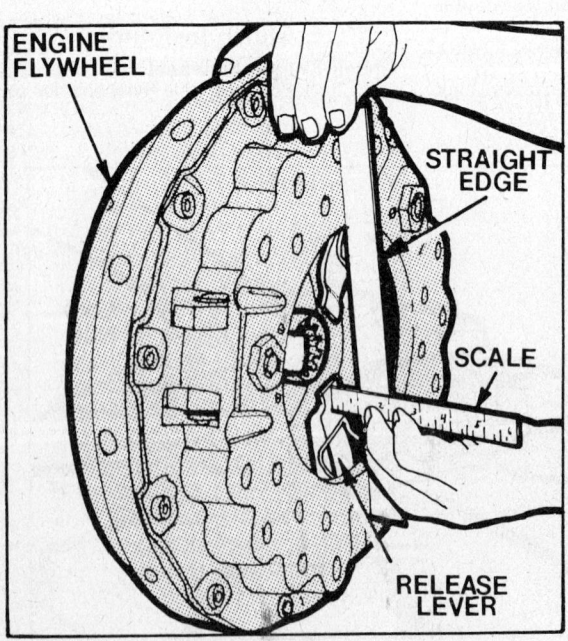

Fig. 10 Checking Dimension "A"

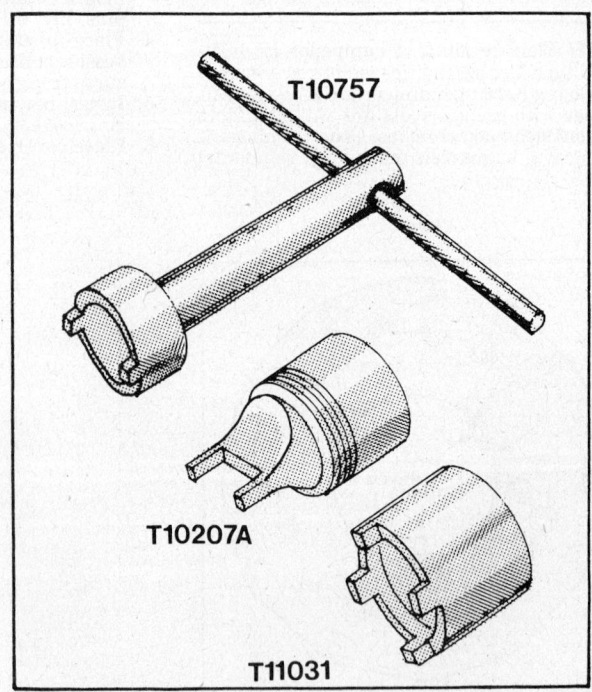

Fig. 11 Lipe tools for slotted adjusting nuts

HEAVY DUTY CLUTCHES

Adjusting Lever Heights

Dimension "A"
1. This dimension is the distance from the top of the flywheel ring (cover) to ends of release levers, Fig. 10. (Applies only to field repaired or rebuilt clutches.)
2. See chart, Fig. 3, for correct "A" dimension for unit being serviced. Satisfactory operation of the clutch depends greatly upon the accuracy of the lever setting as this controls the parallel movement of the pressure plate.
3. A straightedge and scale will provide a means of checking the "A" dimension. Fig. 11 shows the special tools available for slotted adjusting nuts.
4. Adjusting the lever height is facilitated by starting with the levers low and with lock nut just snug. Turn adjusting nut and lock nut as a unit clockwise until the lever is raised the desired height. Then hold slotted nut firmly and tighten lock nut.

Lipe ML Clutch

The Lipe ML clutch is a multiple lever unit of the adjustable, dry disc, push type construction, Figs. 1 and 2. Maintenance can be accomplished easily without the use of special tools. Adjustment, to compensate for facing wear, is accomplished by removing shims. This operation also restores the original spring pressure and does not disturb the running balance of the clutch.

Identifying Models

The model and serial numbers of the clutch cover plate are stamped on the machined surface of the cover or on the name plate. Driven disc assemblies are stamped with a model number.

Periodic Inspection

It is recommended that the clutch be kept in proper adjustment by periodic inspection of the Dimension "A", which is referred to in Fig. 3 and in the clutch adjustment chart.

Clutch Adjustment

Checking Dimension "A"
1. With clutch in engaged position, place Gauge T-2187 between face of clutch release sleeve and release bearing, Fig. 4.
2. Turn thumb screw of gauge to just contact ground surface of clutch cover.
3. As shown in Fig. 3, Dimension "A" is the distance from underside of gauge to end of thumb screw.
4. Block clutch pedal in released position. This prevents bending of adjusting straps and facilitates loosening of adjusting nuts.
5. Loosen adjusting nuts five full turns.
6. Remove clutch pedal block or jack to allow the adjusting plate to move back for easy removal of shims.
7. Use sharp nose pliers or cotter pin puller to remove shims, Fig. 5. Removing one shim from each stud reduces Dimension "A" by approximately $3/32"$. Likewise, adding one shim increases Dimension "A" by $3/32"$. *Make sure that an equal quantity of shims remains on each stud before proceeding.*
8. Again block clutch pedal to disengage clutch. This prevents bending of adjusting straps and facilitates tightening of adjusting nuts.
9. Tighten adjusting nuts, remove pedal block or jack and recheck Dimension "A"

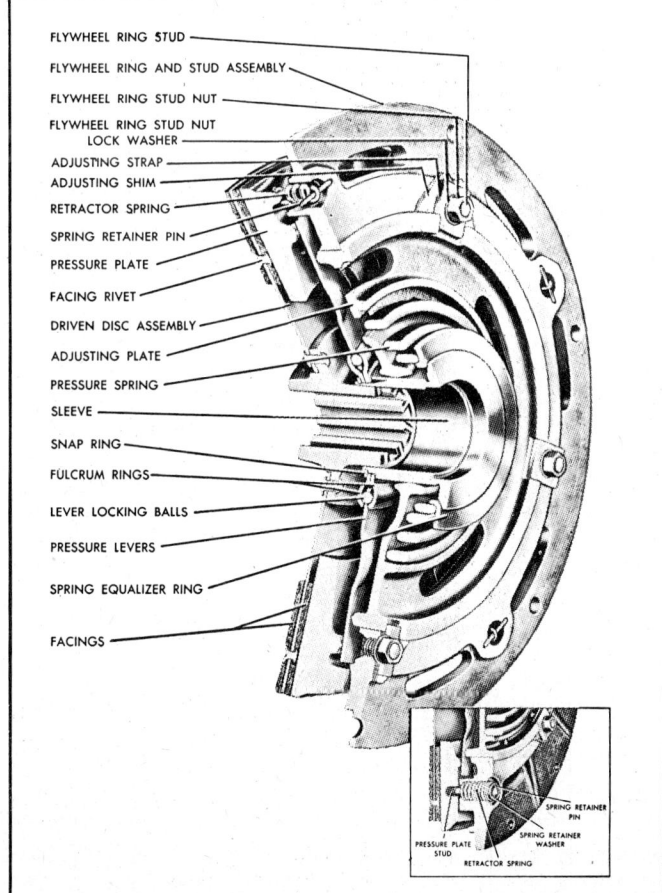

Fig. 1 Lipe ML 12", 13", 14" single plate clutch. Inset shows type of pressure plate retractor spring on 15" single plate and 14" and 15" two plate clutches

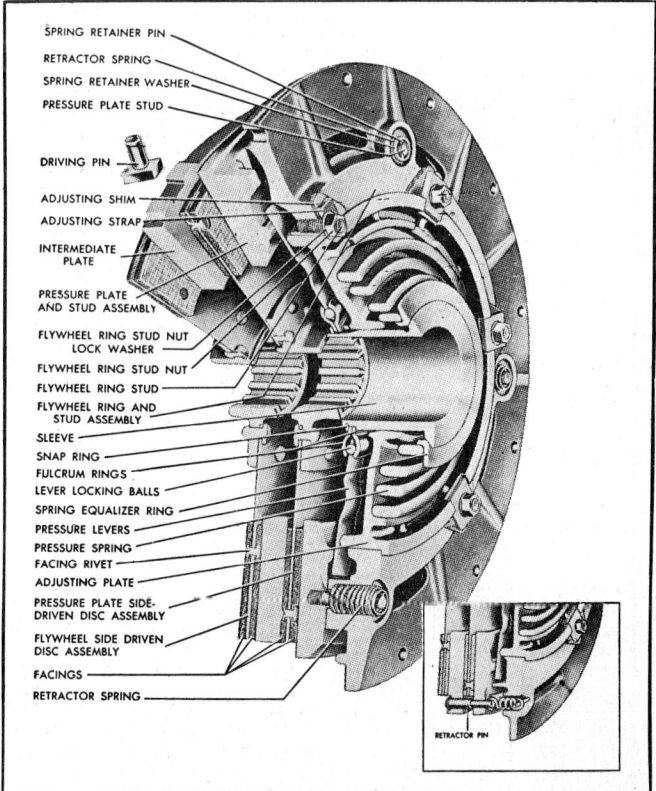

Fig. 2 Lipe ML 14" and 15" two plate clutch. Inset shows type of pressure plate retractor spring and pin on 13" two plate clutch

441

HEAVY DUTY CLUTCHES

Number Model	Inch Size	Dimension "A" +1/16"−0"	Quantity of Shims	Flywheel Depth	Facing Thickness	Pressure Sprg. Reference No.	Pressure Plate Reference
120-1-018	12	1"	6	1.920"	5/32"	9	A
130-1-021	13	1 1/16"	8	1.500"	5/32"	2	B
140-1-022	14	1 3/16"	8	1.312"	5/32"	10	D
140-1-023	14	1 3/16"	8	1.312"	5/32"	10	D
130-1-025	13	1"	6	1.843"	9/64"	2	F
140-1-026	14	1 1/4"	6	1.812"	9/64"	4	D
140-1-027	14	1 1/4"	7	1.812"	9/64"	10	D
150-1-028	15	1 3/8"	6	1.812"	5/32"	4	E
130-1-029	13	2 1/8"	6	1.843"	9/64"	3	F
120-1-030	12	1 1/16"	4	1.875"	1/8"	9	A
130-1-033	13	1"	6	1.843"	9/64"	10	F
140-1-038	14	1 1/16"	7	1.812"	9/64"	2	D
120-1-039	12	1 1/16"	4	1.875"	1/8"	10	A
140-1-041	14	1 1/4"	6	1.812"	9/64"	6	D
130-1-043	13	1"	6	1.843"	9/64"	2	B
120-1-044	12	1"	6	1.920"	5/32"	10	A
130-1-045	13	1 1/16"	7	1.500"	5/32"	10	B
130-2-054	13-2	1 15/16"	8	2.937"	1/8"	6	G
130-1-063	13	1"	6	1.812"	9/64"	10	F
140-1-086	14	1 1/16"	7	1.812"	9/64"	10	D
130-1-087	13	1"	6	1.843"	9/64"	2	B
140-1-089	14	1 1/4"	8	1.312"	5/32"	6	D
130-1-092	13	1"	6	1.843"	9/64"	10	F
130-2-096	13-2	1 15/16"	8	2.937"	1/8"	4	C
140-1-102	14	1 1/16"	7	1.812"	9/64"	10	D
130-1-103	13	1"	6	1.843"	9/64"	9	F
120-1-112	12	1"	6	1.920"	5/32"	10	H
140-1-114	14	1 1/4"	6	1.812"	9/64"	4	D
140-1-116	14	1 3/16"	8	1.312"	5/32"	10	I
130-1-117	13	1 1/16"	8	1.500"	5/32"	10	F
140-1-126	14	1 1/16"	7	1.812"	9/64"	10	K
140-1-127	14	1 1/4"	6	1.812"	9/64"	4	K
130-1-128	13	1"	6	1.843"	9/64"	2	F
130-2-132	13-2	1 1/4"	8	2.937"	1/8"	6	C
140-1-138	14	1 1/4"	6	1.812"	9/64"	15	D
150-1-145	15	1 1/8"	8	1.812"	5/32"	6	E
150-1-146	15	1 1/8"	7	1.812"	5/32"	4	E
150-1-147	15	1 1/8"	7	1.812"	5/32"	6	E
150-1-148	15	1 1/8"	8	1.812"	5/32"	4	E
150-1-149	15	1 1/8"	8	1.812"	5/32"	8	E
150-1-150	15	1 1/8"	8	1.812"	5/32"	13	E
150-1-151	15	1 1/8"	7	1.812"	5/32"	15	E
150-1-152	15	1 1/8"	7	1.812"	5/32"	8	E
150-2-162	15-2	1 1/8"	7	2.937"	5/32"	4	E
150-2-163	15-2	1 1/8"	7	2.937"	5/32"	8	E
150-1-171	15	1 1/8"	7	1.812"	5/32"	6	E
140-1-175	14	1 1/16"	7	1.812"	9/64"	10	K
130-1-176	13	2 1/8"	6	1.843"	9/64"	3	F
150-2-177	15-2	1 1/8"	7	2.937"	5/32"	4	E
150-2-178	15-2	1 1/8"	12	2.937"	5/32"	8	E
150-2-179	15-2	1 1/8"	12	2.937"	5/32"	6	E
140-2-181	14-2	1 1/16"	8	2.937"	9/64"	4	J
140-2-182	14-2	1 1/4"	7	2.937"	9/64"	8	J
150-1-187	15	1 1/8"	7	1.812"	5/32"	4	E
150-1-191	15	1 3/8"	14	1.812"	5/32"	8	E
150-1-192	15	1 3/8"	14	1.812"	5/32"	23	E
150-1-193	15	1 3/8"	14	1.812"	5/32"	8	E
140-1-195	14	1 1/16"	6	1.812"	9/64"	2	D
150-1-199	15	1 1/8"	7	1.812"	5/32"	4	E
150-1-200	15	1 1/8"	8	1.812"	5/32"	8	E
120-1-226	12	1 1/16"	8	1.875"	1/8"	2	A
130-1-227	13	1"	8	1.843"	9/64"	10	F
130-1-232	13	1"	8	1.843"	9/64"	10	F
140-1-234	14	1 3/16"	8	1.312"	5/32"	4	I
150-1-241	15	1 1/8"	7	1.812"	5/32"	4	E
150-1-247	15	1 1/8"	8	1.812"	5/32"	13	E
150-2-261	15-2	1 1/8"	12	2.937"	5/32"	8	E
140-1-266	14	1 3/16"	9	1.187"	9/64"	4	M
120-1-287	12	1 1/8"	8	1.875"	5/32"	10	A
140-1-293	14	1 1/8"	8	1.812"	9/64"	10	D
150-1-295	15	1 3/16"	7	1.812"	5/32"	4	E
120-1-300	12	1 1/8"	8	1.875"	1/8"	9	A
150-1-301	15	1 1/8"	8	1.812"	5/32"	8	E
120-1-302	12	1 1/8"	8	1.875"	1/8"	2	A
130-1-307	13	1 1/16"	6	1.812"	9/64"	10	F
140-1-308	14	1 3/8"	6	1.812"	9/64"	4	D
150-1-310	15	1 3/16"	8	1.812"	5/32"	6	E
140-1-311	14	1 1/8"	8	1.812"	9/64"	2	D
140-1-312	14	1 3/8"	9	1.812"	9/64"	6	D
120-1-314	12	1 1/16"	6	1.920"	5/32"	10	H
140-1-315	14	1 1/4"	11	1.187"	9/64"	4	M
150-1-316	15	1 3/16"	7	1.812"	5/32"	4	E
150-1-317	15	1 3/16"	7	1.812"	5/32"	13	E
130-1-318	13	1 1/16"	6	1.843"	9/64"	9	F
130-1-319	13	1 1/16"	6	1.843"	9/64"	2	F
130-1-320	13	1 1/16"	6	1.843"	9/64"	10	F
150-2-321	15-2	1 3/16"	12	2.937"	5/32"	6	E
150-2-322	15-2	1 3/16"	12	2.937"	5/32"	4	E
150-2-323	15-2	1 3/16"	12	2.937"	5/32"	8	E
150-1-326	15	1 3/16"	7	1.812"	5/32"	13	E
140-2-327	14-2	1 1/8"	8	2.937"	9/64"	4	J
140-2-328	14-2	1 1/8"	7	2.937"	9/64"	8	J
150-2-329	15-2	1 3/16"	12	2.937"	5/32"	8	E
130-2-334	13-2	1 3/8"	8	2.937"	1/8"	4	C
120-1-331	12	1 1/8"	6	1.920"	5/32"	9	A
140-1-332	14	1 3/8"	7	1.812"	9/64"	10	I
130-1-333	13	1 1/16"	6	1.843"	9/64"	10	F
130-1-334	13	1 1/16"	6	1.843"	9/64"	2	B
140-1-335	14	1 3/8"	8	1.812"	9/64"	10	K
140-1-336	14	1 3/8"	9	1.812"	9/64"	4	K
150-1-337	15	1 3/16"	7	1.812"	5/32"	8	E
150-1-338	15	1 3/16"	7	1.812"	5/32"	6	E
150-1-339	15	1 3/16"	7	1.812"	5/32"	4	E
120-1-340	12	1 1/8"	8	1.875"	1/8"	10	A
120-1-341	12	1 1/8"	8	1.875"	5/32"	9	A
120-1-342	12	1 1/8"	8	1.875"	5/32"	2	A
150-1-343	15	1 3/8"	14	1.812"	5/32"	23	L
150-1-344	15	1 3/8"	14	1.812"	5/32"	8	L
130-2-347	13-2	1 3/8"	8	2.937"	1/8"	6	C
120-1-359	12	1 1/8"	8	1.875"	5/32"	9	N
120-1-360	12	1 1/8"	8	1.875"	5/32"	2	N
120-1-361	12	1 1/8"	8	1.875"	5/32"	10	N
130-1-362	13	1 1/16"	7	1.843"	5/32"	10	B
150-2-371	15-2	1 3/16"	12	2.937"	5/32"	6	L
150-2-372	15-2	1 3/16"	12	2.937"	5/32"	4	L
150-2-373	15-2	1 3/16"	12	2.937"	5/32"	8	L
140-2-378	14-2	1 1/16"	8	2.937"	9/64"	6	J
150-1-387	15	1 3/16"	11	1.750"	5/32"	8	E
130-41-397	13	1 1/16"	8	1.500"	5/32"	74	F
140-31-400	14	1 1/4"	8	1.312"	5/32"	73	I
130-1-407	13	1 1/16"	8	1.843"	5/32"	10	F
150-2-411	15-2	1 3/16"	12	2.937"	5/32"	8	L
150-41-420	15	1 1/8"	8	1.812"	5/32"	73	E
140-1-425	14	1 1/8"	8	1.812"	9/64"	10	I
150-1-465	15	1 3/16"	8	1.812"	5/32"	8	E
150-1-466	15	1 3/16"	8	1.812"	5/32"	13	E
150-1-467	15	1 3/16"	8	1.812"	5/32"	13	E
150-1-468	15	1 3/16"	7	1.812"	5/32"	8	L
150-2-469	15-2	1 3/16"	12	2.937"	5/32"	8	L
150-2-470	15-2	1 3/16"	12	2.937"	5/32"	8	L

Continued

HEAVY DUTY CLUTCHES

Model Number	Inch Size	Dimension "A" +1/16"−0"	Quantity of Shims	Flywheel Depth	Facing Thickness	Pressure Sprg. Reference No.	Pressure Plate Reference No.
140-2-471	14-2	1 1/8"	7	2.937"	9/64"	8	J
140-1-474	14	1 3/8"	9	1.812"	5/32"	8	D
140-41-475	14	1 1/4"	9	1.812"	5/32"	73	I
140-41-483	14	1 1/4"	8	1.312"	5/32"	73	I
150-41-486	15	1 1/8"	8	1.812"	5/32"	73	E
130-41-487	13	1 1/8"	8	1.500"	5/32"	74	F
140-41-495	14	1 1/4"	9	1.812"	5/32"	73	I
140-1-504	14	1 3/8"	9	1.812"	5/32"	4	I
140-1-508	14	1 1/4"	11	1.187"	9/64"	4	M
140-1-509	14	1 3/8"	9	1.812"	9/64"	4	I
140-1-510	14	1 3/8"	6	1.812"	9/64"	4	D
150-2-514	15-2	1 3/8"	12	2.937"	5/32"	4	L
130-2-515	13-2	1 3/8"	8	2.937"	1/8"	4	C
150-1-516	15	1 3/8"	8	1.812"	5/32"	4	E
140-2-517	14-2	1 1/8"	7	2.937"	9/64"	4	J
150-1-518	15	1 3/16"	11	1.750"	5/32"	13	E
150-1-528	15	1 3/16"	8	1.812"	5/32"	8	E
130-1-540	13	1 7/16"	9	1.843"	5/32"	4	F
150-2-546	15-2	1 3/8"	12	2.937"	5/32"	8	L
140-1-555	14	1 5/16"	11	1.187"	5/32"	4	M
140-1-611	14	1 1/8"	8	1.812"	5/32"	10	I
130-1-621	13	2 3/16"	9	1.843"	5/32"	3	F
150-1-693	15	1 3/8"	8	1.812"	5/32"	13	L
140-2-765	14-2	1 1/8"	8	2.937"	5/32"	8	J
140-1-822	14	1 3/8"	9	1.812"	5/32"	4	P

MODEL NO.—Is the number stamped on machined surface of the cover, on which adjusting shims are supported, or on the name plate.

INCH SIZE—Refers to the approximate diameter of the driven disc assembly or pressure plate, which determines the clutch size.

DIMENSION "A"—Is the dimension indicated as "A" on the assembly drawing (Fig. 7) and (Fig. 2), and has a limit from plus 1/16" to minus 0".

QUANTITY OF SHIMS—Is the approximate number of adjusting shims required on each stud, to give correct DIMENSION "A". This applies only when the clutch is new in a flywheel of the correct depth and when correct facings are used on the driven disc assembly. This quantity may vary one shim. Fewer shims are required in a used or worn clutch. OBTAIN DIMENSION "A" REGARDLESS OF NUMBER OF SHIMS REQUIRED.

FLYWHEEL DEPTH—Is the correct dimension from the flywheel friction face to the face of the rim. This dimension must not vary more than plus or minus .005"

FACING THICKNESS—Is the correct dimension of each facing on the disc assembly.

PRESSURE SPRING REFERENCE NO.—Is the reference number listed in the chart below to correspond with the LIPE part number.

Reference Number	Lipe Pressure Spring Number	Spring Color	Pounds Minimum Weight
2	C5-2	Yellow	360 Lbs. at 1 1/4"
3	C5-3	———	360 Lbs. at 2 1/4"
4	C5-4	Black	480 Lbs. at 1 1/4"
6	C5-6	Green	440 Lbs. at 1 1/4"
8	C5-8	Orange & White	575 Lbs. at 1 1/4"
9	C5-9	Blue	330 Lbs. at 1 1/4"
10	C5-10	Red	415 Lbs. at 1 1/4"
13	C5-13	Orange & Blue	630 Lbs. at 1 1/4"
15	C5-15	Red & Green	400 Lbs. at 1 1/4"
23	C5-23	Green & White	375 Lbs. at 1 1/4"
73	C5-73	Brown (Rd. Wire)	650 Lbs. at 1 1/8"
74	C5-74	Orange (Rd. Wire)	490 Lbs. at 1 1/8"

PRESSURE PLATE REFERENCE NO.—Is the reference number listed in the chart below to correspond with the LIPE part number.

Reference Number	Lipe Pressure Plate Number	Distance From Top of Fulcrum Edge to Friction Surface (New)
A	C1-2	.914"
B	C1-3	1.000"
C	C1-6	1.088"
D	C1-7	.975"
E	AC1-9	.977"
F	C1-16	1.013"
G	C1-19	1.026"
H	C1-23	.926"
I	C1-24	.980"
J	AC1-25	1.046"
K	C1-27	.975"
L	AC1-42	.977"
M	C1-61	.918"
N	C1-76	.916"
O	C1-118	.980"
P	C1-140	.980"

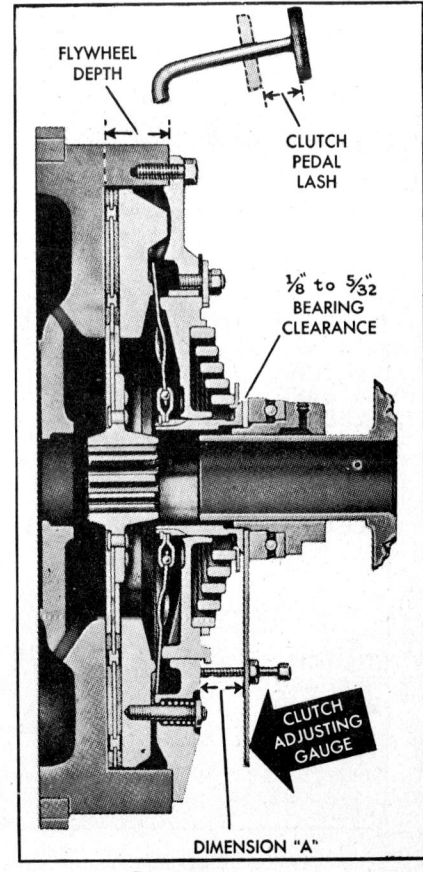

Fig. 3 Clutch specifications and adjustments for chart identification

HEAVY DUTY CLUTCHES

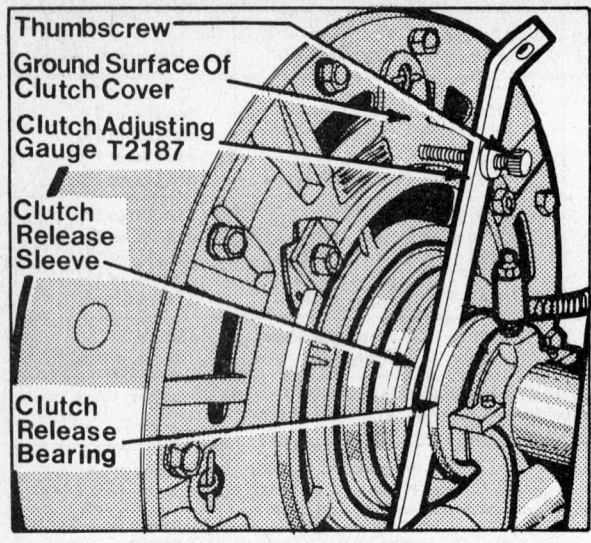

Fig. 4 Installation of clutch adjusting gauge

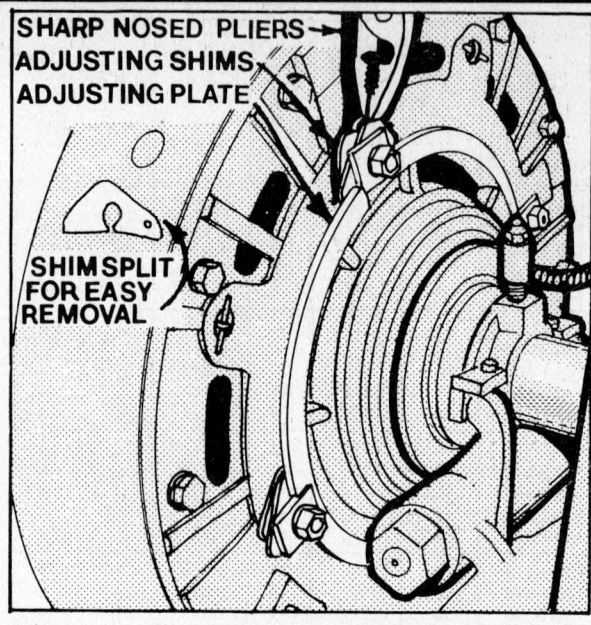

Fig. 5 Removing adjusting shims

before proceeding.
10. Check clearance between clutch release sleeve and release bearing, Fig. 6. If clearance is not 1/8", adjust vehicle clutch pedal linkage to obtain this 1/8" clearance. This 1/8" clearance normally results in 1 1/2" of clutch pedal free travel.

Clutch Service

1. Place clutch cover assembly on table of press with assembly resting on pressure plate, Fig. 7.
2. Compress pressure spring.
3. Remove four retractor spring retaining pins, being careful not to over-stretch springs.
4. Place assembly on table of press with assembly resting on face of release sleeve, Fig. 8.
5. Using metal yoke as shown (or suitable blocks of wood) compress assembly and lock press in position.
6. Remove snap ring from groove of sleeve. The fulcrum rings, pressure levers and lever locking balls can now be removed.
7. Slowly release press to allow pressure spring, sleeve and remaining parts to be removed.

Inspection & Repair

After clutch is disassembled, clean all parts thoroughly. Inspect all parts as indicated below and replace any part that appears doubtful.

Pressure Plate
1. Inspect fulcrum edge for excessive wear. Compare fulcrum edge with cross section view of a new fulcrum edge, Fig. 9. If fulcrum edge "land" exceeds 1/16" in width, replace with a new pressure plate. *Any amount worn from fulcrum edge directly reduces total available clutch wear.*
2. Inspect friction surface of pressure plate for burning, heat cracking and distortion. If friction surface is badly scored, heat checked, warped, or dished in excess of .015", install a new pressure plate. *A scored or distorted pressure plate will cause the facings to disintegrate quickly.*

Flywheel Ring
1. Inspect flywheel ring for cracks; if present, replace with new one.
2. Inspect slots for indentation caused by pressure plate lugs. If indented, replace with a new flywheel ring.
3. Inspect flanged surface for burred edges. Burred edges on flange surface should be filed to assure flange being drawn tight to rim of engine flywheel when clutch is being installed.

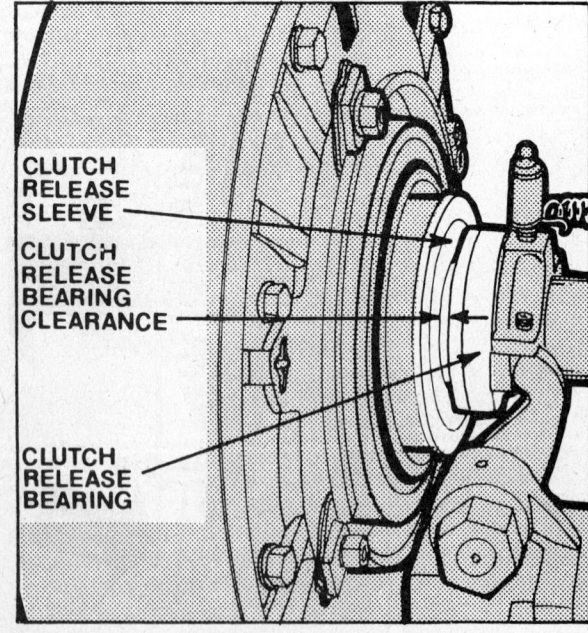

Fig. 6 Checking clearance between clutch release sleeve and release bearing

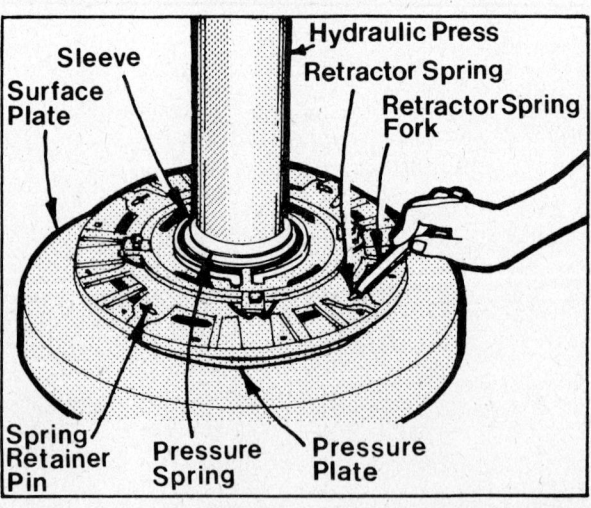

Fig. 7 Clutch cover mounted on press

HEAVY DUTY CLUTCHES

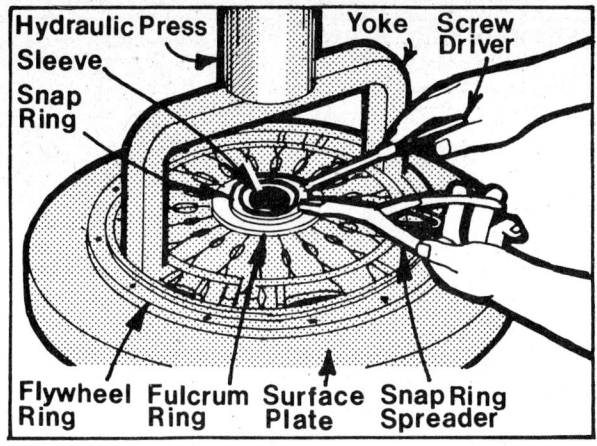

Fig. 8 Removing snap ring from sleeve groove

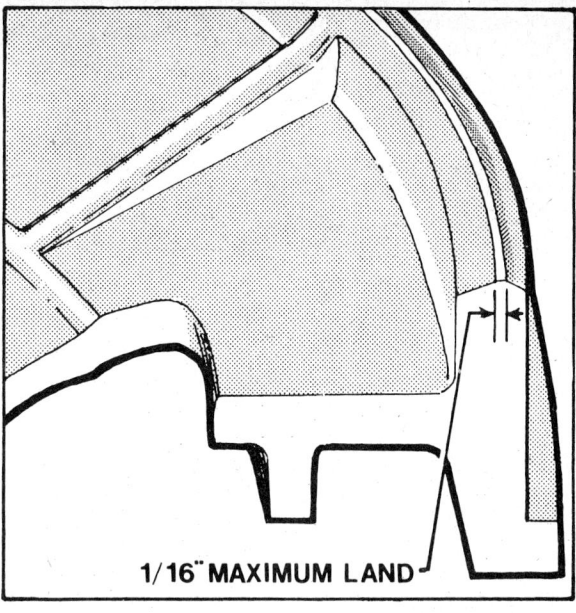

Fig. 9 Cross section view of a new fulcrum edge

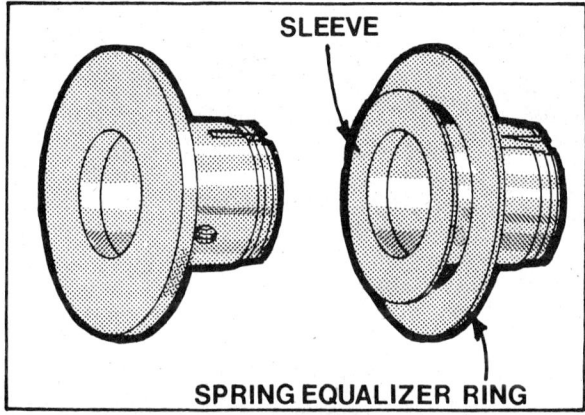

Fig. 10 Construction of release sleeves

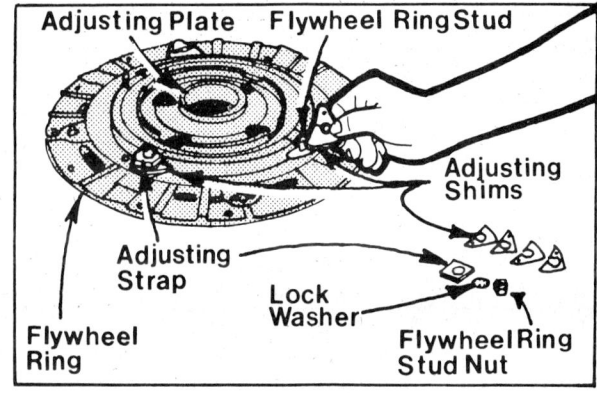

Fig. 11 Installing adjusting plate and shims

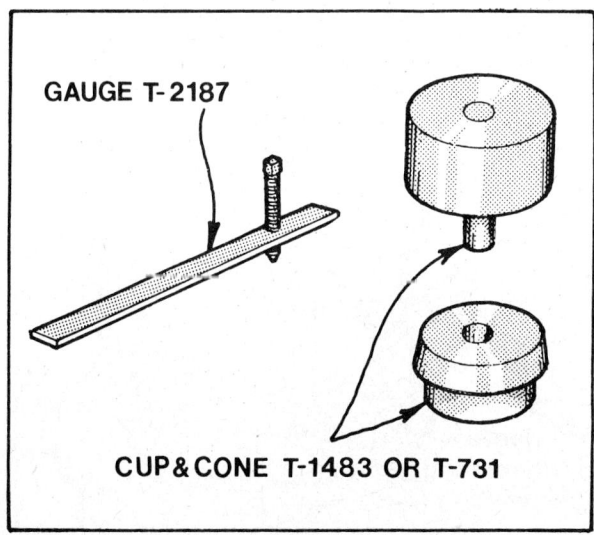

Fig. 12 Clutch overhaul tools

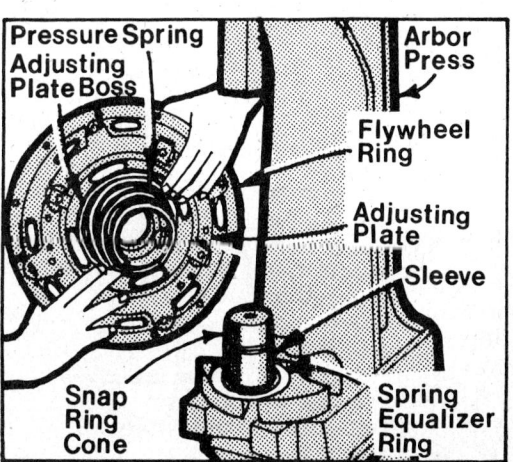

Fig. 13 Installing pressure spring in adjusting plate and assembling to sleeve

HEAVY DUTY CLUTCHES

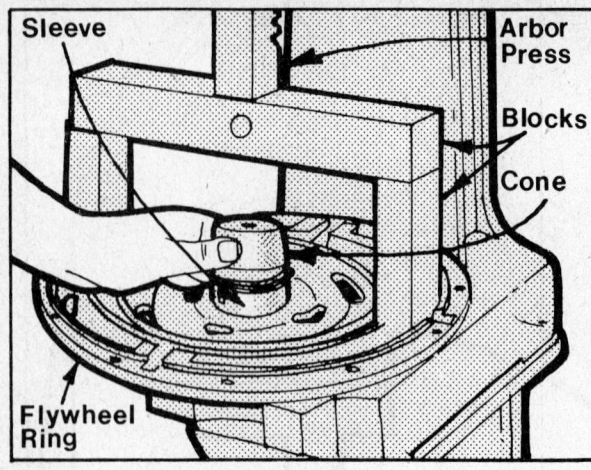

Fig. 14 Compressing the assembly

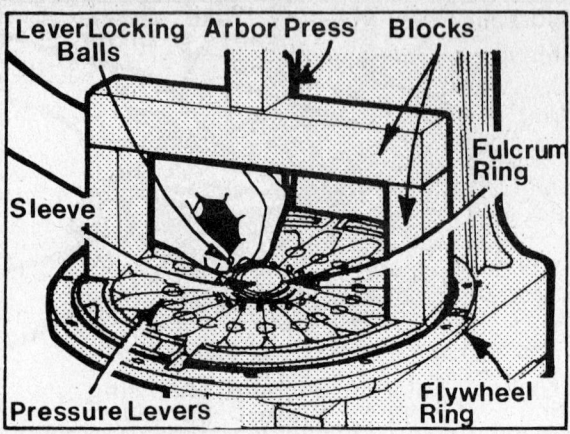

Fig. 15 Installing clutch lever locking balls

Adjusting Straps and Plate
1. Inspect straps for wear and bent condition. Worn or bent straps will prevent proper clamping of adjusting plate to flywheel ring.
2. Inspect fulcrum edge for excessive wear as shown in Fig. 9.
3. Inspect bore of adjusting plate for excessive wear. Release sleeve must be a free sliding fit in bore.
4. Inspect bottom of adjusting strap slots for excessive wear. Worn slots will prevent proper clamping of adjusting plate to flywheel ring.

Sleeve and Pressure Spring
1. Inspect sleeve for excessive wear or indentations of flange. If wear is indicated, replace with a new sleeve.
2. Inspect snap ring groove for wear, nicks or burrs. Any of these conditions will prevent proper seating of snap ring.
3. It is recommended that all one-piece type sleeves be replaced with the improved equalizer type sleeve and mating spring equalizer ring, Fig. 10.
4. Pressure springs should be checked for compression weight in accordance with the weights given in the *ML Clutch Chart*. Under-weight springs will cause excessive clutch slippage.

Fulcrum Rings and Pressure Levers
1. If fulcrum rings are worn or warped, install new rings.
2. Inspect pressure levers to see that they are not bent or excessively worn from contact with fulcrum edges of adjusting plate, pressure plate and fulcrum rings. If these conditions are present, install new levers.

Intermediate Plate and Driving Pins
1. On two plate clutches, inspect friction surfaces of intermediate plate for heat cracks, scoring or distortion. If any of these conditions exist, replace with a new plate.
2. Inspect driving slots of intermediate plate for wear; also driving pins. If either is worn, replace with new parts.

Driven Disc Assembly
Inspect disc assembly for cracks, worn splines, and warped or dished condition. If any of these conditions exist, install a new disc assembly.

Clutch Assembly
1. Assemble adjusting plate to flywheel ring. Install adjusting shims, Fig. 11, using the number of shims required on each stud to obtain the proper Dimension "A" (See ML Clutch Chart).
2. Place sleeve on arbor press with face down. Set equalizer ring over sleeve on to beveled edge of sleeve flange with flat side of ring down. Insert cone portion of snap ring assembling tool, Fig. 12, in end of sleeve.
3. Place pressure spring on adjusting plate with end of large coil abutting the small

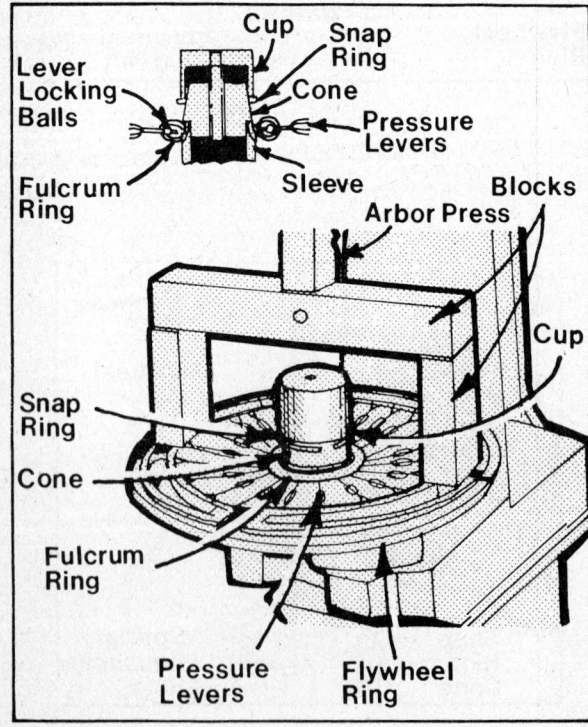

Fig. 16 Installing clutch snap ring

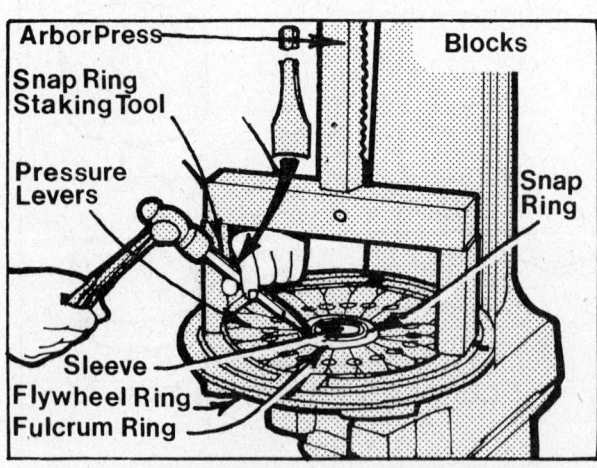

Fig. 17 Locking clutch snap ring

HEAVY DUTY CLUTCHES

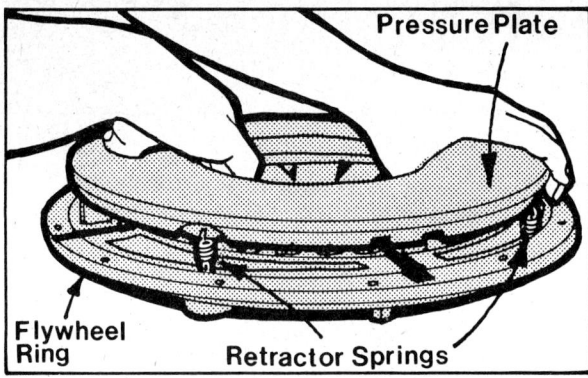

Fig. 18 Installing retractor springs

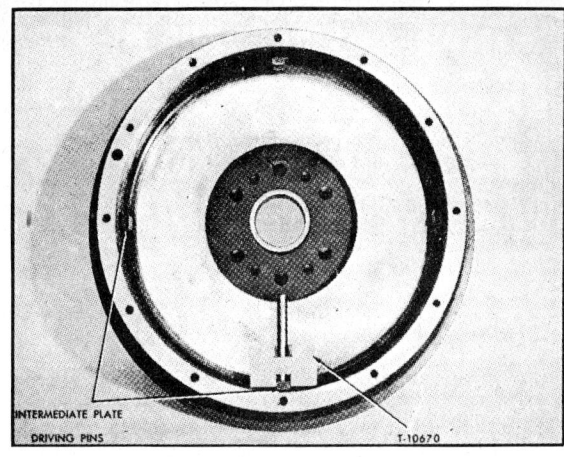

Fig. 19 Driving pin alignment gauge for two plate clutches

boss in the adjusting plate, Fig. 13.
4. Place flywheel ring, adjusting plate and pressure spring over the sleeve, seating small coil of spring on spring equalizer ring.
5. Using block system shown in Fig. 14, slowly compress assembly to allow sleeve to slip through bore of adjusting plate. *Be sure equalizer ring is seated properly on top coil of pressure spring.*
6. Place one fulcrum ring, cupped side up, over sleeve until it is seated firmly.
7. Arrange twenty pressure levers around sleeve. If ribbed levers are used, the raised side of lever must face pressure plate.
8. Using lever locking balls of proper size, insert one in hole at end of each lever, Fig. 15.
9. Install other fulcrum ring, cupped side down, over sleeve, making sure levers do not overlap.
10. Reinsert coned tool into sleeve and set a new snap ring over coned tool with open ends of snap ring at right angles to keyways of sleeve. Place cupped tool on snap ring and tap until snap ring is seated into sleeve groove, Fig. 16.
11. Remove cup and cone from sleeve and, with snap ring staking tool, Fig. 17, starting opposite open ends of snap ring, work each way until snap ring is seated well into groove of sleeve.

CAUTION: Test each of the twenty levers to see that they are locked securely by a ball and that they do not overlap. Release press and remove blocks.

12. Hook four retractor springs in pressure plate, Fig. 18. Place pressure plate and springs in position on the assembly, with driving lugs of pressure plate fitting into driving slots of flywheel ring.

NOTE: The driving lugs should fit free in the slots of flywheel ring with a clearance of .004" to .006". If original pressure plate is used, reassemble with driving lug marked "O" in driving slot marked "O". Turn assembly over and compress to facilitate installing retainer pins in retractor springs. This will prevent spring from becoming over-stretched.

Clutch Installation

Single Plate Clutch
1. Try cover plate assembly in flywheel before inserting driven disc to make sure it is a free fit in flywheel.
2. After installing driven disc, bolt clutch to flywheel and screw in each bolt until it contacts cover plate. Then gradually tighten opposite bolts until assembly is drawn tight to flywheel.
3. Check for Dimension "A" as outlined previously.
4. To facilitate the assembly of transmission to engine, the use of a spare splined pilot shaft to align the driven disc while bolting the clutch in place is essential. The pressure plate end of the driven disc hub has been chamfered to facilitate the insertion of the drive shaft, whereas the flywheel end of the hub is left plain.

Two Plate Clutch
1. Inspect the four intermediate driving pins to make certain that shank of pins are press fitted into flywheel rim, and that heads are squarely aligned with friction face. Use tool shown in Fig. 19 to facilitate the alignment of the driving pins.
2. Make sure that there is clearance between heads of driving pins and driving slots in intermediate plate by placing intermediate plate over pins.

NOTE: The intermediate plate should fit over the driving pins with perceptible circumferential lash before clutch is assembled to flywheel. A clearance of .007" to .011" is required.

3. The 13" two plate clutch incorporates retractor spring pins to retract intermediate plate when clutch is released. This necessitates the driven disc next to the pressure plate being in place before the intermediate plate is assembled to the cover plate.
4. The two discs for the two plate clutch may or may not be identical or interchangeable. In most cases they will not be interchangeable and will be marked either flywheel side or pressure plate side. They must be positioned according to the mark next to or adjacent to the respective part. In no instance shall the hubs be allowed to approach pilot bearing or come together within 5/32".
5. Bolt cover to flywheel. Screw in each bolt until it contacts cover plate. Then gradually tighten opposite bolts until assembly is drawn tight to flywheel.
6. Check for proper Dimension "A" as listed in the *ML Clutch Chart*.
7. Use an aligning shaft when installing transmission to prevent damage to driven discs which will cause clutch drag.

NOTE: To obtain complete disengagement of ML clutches, the sleeve must be moved a specified distance from the engaged position. Assuming the release bearing clearance (distance between sleeve and bearing) to be 1/8" when clutch is in the engaged position, the release bearing must move forward 1/8" to take up this clearance before it contacts the sleeve and then move the normal amount of travel to disengage the clutch as shown in Fig. 20.

Clutch Size & Type	Release Bearing Clearance	Normal Sleeve Travel	Total Bearing Travel Required
12" ML Single Plate	1/8"	3/8"	1/2"
13" ML Single Plate	1/8"	7/16"	9/16"
14" ML Single Plate	1/8"	7/16"	9/16"
14" RML Single Plate	1/8"	5/16"	7/16"
15" ML Single Plate	1/8"	1/2"	5/8"
15" RML Single Plate	1/8"	1/2"	5/8"
13" ML Two Plate	1/8"	1/2"	5/8"
14" ML Two Plate	1/8"	1/2"	5/8"
15" ML Two Plate	1/8"	1/2"	5/8"

Fig. 20 Lipe ML clutch release travel chart

HEAVY DUTY CLUTCHES

Lipe PT Clutch

The Lipe PT clutch is a pull-type, dry disc, non-adjustable design, incorporating an adjustable sleeve connecting the release levers to the release bearing. Adjustment of this sleeve compensates for facing wear, maintains pedal lash and provides operating clearance for the clutch brake. Anti-friction bearings are provided in the release lever system resulting in low release load on the pedal.

Identifying Models

The name plate attached to the flywheel ring (cover) identifies the cover plate as to the serial number and part number. Driven disc assemblies are stamped with an assembly number. See Chart, Fig. 2 for clutch data.

Clutch Pedal Adjustment

The proper clutch pedal "free travel" is approximately 1½". If inspection indicates the free travel of the clutch pedal is less than ½", immediate adjustment of the release sleeve should be made to restore the proper 1½" free travel, Fig. 3. This 1½" free travel normally results in ⅛" clearance between the release yoke and the bearing carrier wear pads or at the cross shaft adjustment, Fig. 4.

Linkage Adjustment

1. Be sure release bearing sleeve is properly adjusted and locked before attempting to adjust the external linkage to set the pedal lash.
2. If vehicle is equipped with a hydraulic release, refer to the vehicle chapter in this manual or to the vehicle manufacturer's maintenance manual for specifications relating to master and slave cylinder adjustments.
3. Master cylinder operating lever must be adjusted so that the piston can retract fully and uncover the compensating port.
4. The cross shaft lever should travel the same distance on each side of the vertical centerline of the cross shaft, Fig. 4.

Transmission Removal

When removing the transmission from the vehicle, disconnect the external linkage as it will be necessary to allow the release yoke to turn up and over the release bearing housing as the transmission is being moved away from the engine. Clutch may now be removed for inspection.

Flywheel Inspection

1. Remove worn intermediate plate drive pins.

   NOTE: Most flywheels have socket head set screws holding these pins in place which must be loosened before the driving pins can be removed. If the engine flywheel has no provision for set screws, it is recommended that four holes be drilled, tapped and set screws installed. Use 5/16" drill and 3/8" × 16 tap.

2. Flywheel friction surface must be free of heat checks, scoring and taper. For proper depth, see *PT Clutch Chart*, Fig. 2.
3. Replace flywheel pilot bearing. If pilot bearing bore is worn, re-bore and sleeve to obtain proper bearing fit.
4. If flywheel is being replaced on engine crankshaft, it should be dial indicated for engine manufacturer's specifications for acceptable runout.

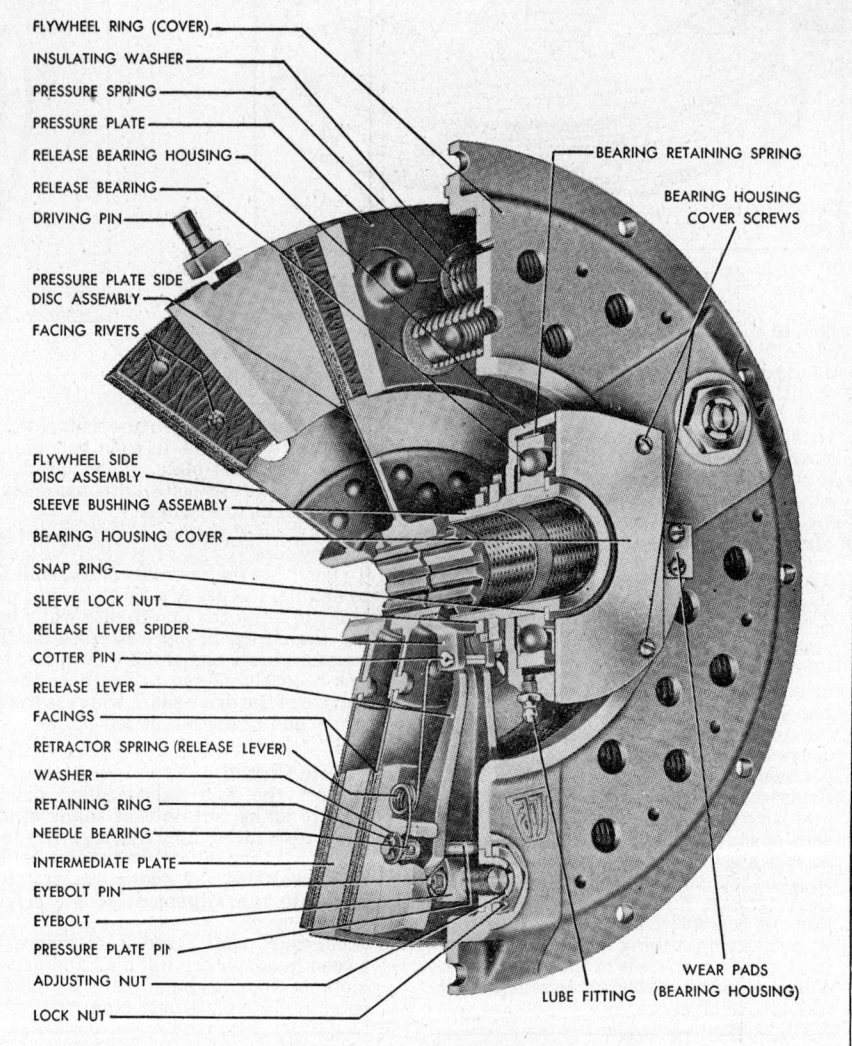

Fig. 1 Type PT two plate clutch

Clutch Service

Disassemble
1. Remove bearing housing and sleeve from spider.
2. Remove cotter pins from lever spider. Lower lever spider assembly and turn it sufficiently to clear levers and remove.
3. Place cover assembly on arbor press with pressure plate down.
4. Compress assembly to relieve spring tension and remove lock nuts.
5. Release press slowly; then remove flywheel ring (cover), pressure springs and insulating washers.
6. Remove retaining rings from pressure plate pins and remove pins to disassemble release levers and eyebolts.

Release Sleeve and Bearing
1. To disassemble, remove housing cover.
2. Remove snap ring, then press sleeve and bushing from bearing.
3. Remove wear pads from bearing housing.

Inspection

After cover is disassembled, clean all parts thoroughly. Inspect all parts as indicated below and replace any that appear doubtful.

Pressure Plate

The pressure plate must be replaced if the friction surface is severely heat checked, it is warped in excess of .015, or if there is excessive wear at the driving slots.

The pressure plate may be salvaged if the friction surface cleans up by regrinding, not to exceed 1/32" maximum from Dimension "C",

HEAVY DUTY CLUTCHES

Model Number	Dimension "A"	Flywheel Depth +.005" -.005"	Facing Thickness	PRESSURE SPRING DATA			PRESSURE PLATE DATA
				Quantity	Color	Minimum Wt. in Lbs.	Dimension "C" New
140-72-760	1 9/32"	2.937	3/16"	21	Dk. Maroon	130 @ 1-27/32"	1.875
140-72-786	1 9/32"	2.937	3/16"	18	Dk. Maroon	130 @ 1-27/32"	1.875
140-72-787	1 9/32"	2.937	3/16"	15	Dk. Maroon	130 @ 1-27/32"	1.875
140-72-788	1 9/32"	2.937	3/16"	21	Lt. Green	150 @ 1-27/32"	1.875
140-72-816	1 9/32"	2.937	3/16"	12	Dk. Maroon	130 @ 1-27/32"	1.875
*140-72-901	1 9/32"	2.937	3/16"	21	Dk. Maroon	130 @ 1-27/32"	1.875
†140-72-917	1 9/32"	2.937	3/16"	18	Dk. Maroon	130 @ 1-27/32"	1.875
‡140-72-919	1 9/32"	2.937	3/16"	21	Lt. Green	150 @ 1-27/32"	1.875
‡140-72-920	1 9/32"	2.937	3/16"	21	Dk. Maroon	130 @ 1-27/32"	1.875

Intermediate Plate Thickness .630 +.000" -.005"
*(1) C25-53 intermediate plate, (4) C26-32 drive pins only included, can use 140-72-760 2-760
†(1) C25-53 intermediate plate, (4) C26-32 drive pins only included, can use 140-72-786 2-786
‡ Equipped for 2"-10C spline.

Fig. 2 Type PT clutch chart

Fig. 6, (see *PT Clutch Chart* for specification).

Always replace needle bearings by pressing on that end of the bearing on which part numbers are stamped. This prevents damage to bearing case.

All Other Parts

Inspect and repair all other parts as outlined for the DP two plate clutch section of this chapter.

Clutch Assembly

1. Place pressure plate on arbor press face down, Fig. 7.
2. Assemble adjusting nuts to eyebolts, then use new pins to assemble to release lever.
3. Install release levers, using new pins and retaining rings. Check proper positions of retractor springs, Fig. 7.
4. Place insulating washers over spring bosses and install pressure springs.
5. Press flywheel ring (cover) into position, using care to engage driving lugs into mating slots of pressure plate as springs are being compressed.
6. Pull adjusting nuts up through holes in cover and install lock nuts, Fig. 8.
7. Install three 3/8" x 16 x 2 1/4" hold-down capscrews through cover into tapped holes in pressure plate. This holds pressure springs in a compressed state to facilitate assembly to engine flywheel.
8. Release press and remove clutch.

Release Bearing and Housing

1. To assemble, place release bearing housing over sleeve and bushing assembly and press bearing onto sleeve and install snap ring. Be sure bearing is tight to snap ring (see Fig. 5).
2. Install bearing retaining spring in housing opposite grease fitting hole.
3. Hand pack bearing and housing with high temperature lubricant such as Esso "Alert" 275 or equivalent. *Chassis or all purpose lubricants are not satisfactory for clutch release bearings.*

Clutch Installation

1. Be sure flywheel and intermediate plates are in good condition. Also check for free fit of cover on flywheel.
2. Be sure that intermediate drive pins are a free fit in holes in flywheel rim and that heads are perfectly square to friction surface. Lipe Tool shown in Fig. 9 will assist in installing new pins and assure that they are properly aligned. If tool mentioned is not available, a machinist's square and feeler gauge may be used to check for squareness.
3. After pins are installed, try intermediate

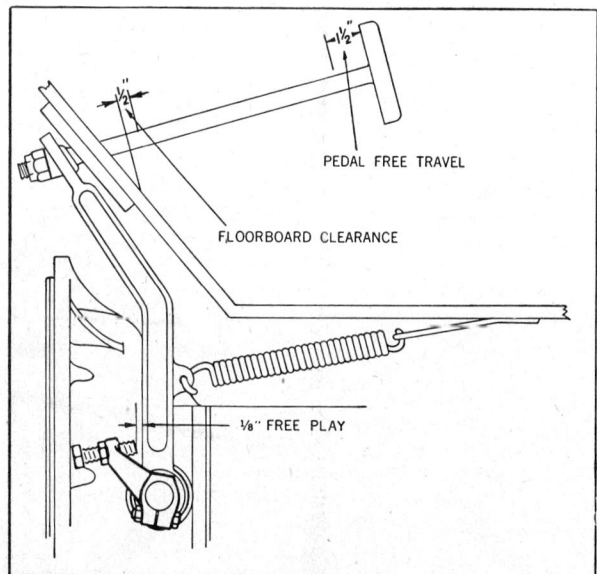

Fig. 3 Adjusting clutch pedal linkage

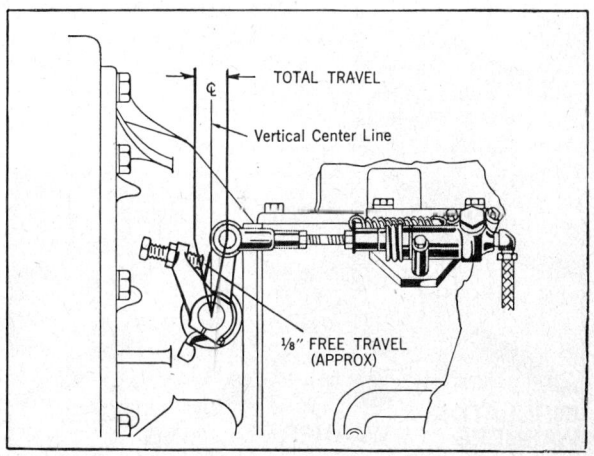

Fig. 4 Hydraulic release linkage (typical)

HEAVY DUTY CLUTCHES

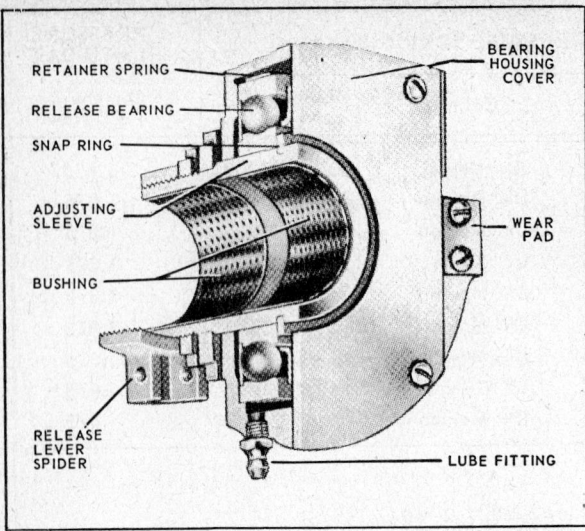

Fig. 5 Release sleeve and bearing assembly

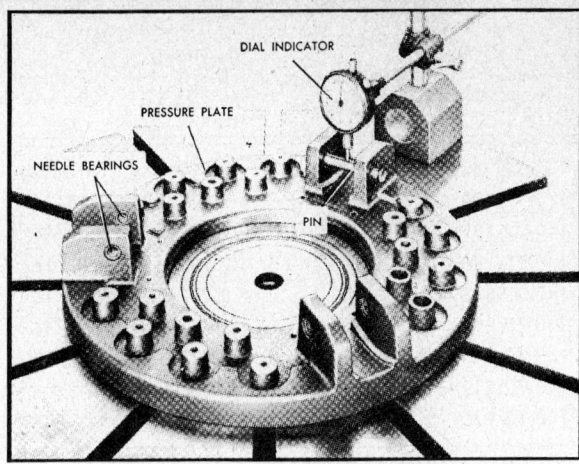

Fig. 6 Checking Dimension "C"

plate for fit over pins. With new pins and new intermediate plate, there should be .006" to .014" clearance. Try plate in different positions and select the one that provides the greatest freedom of movement. Mark the plate for location to the flywheel and then lock the drive pins in place with the socket head or Allen set screws.

4. Driven discs are marked "Pressure Plate Side" and "Flywheel Side" to indicate their proper positions.
5. The cover assembly may now be installed on the flywheel, but before tightening capscrews, install an aligning shaft through the two hubs and into the pilot bearing.
6. Cover capscrews may now be tightened progressively around the flywheel to 35 to 40 ft-lbs torque.
7. Remove the three hold-down bolts from cover before removing the aligning shaft or disc assemblies may fall out of position.

Clutch Adjustment

1. If cover assembly is new or a genuine Lipe exchange unit, the levers will not require adjustment.
2. If cover assembly has been repaired or rebuilt locally, the lever heights must now be adjusted to the correct "A" dimension as listed in the chart, Fig. 2. A hook type rule, Fig. 10, will facilitate taking the "A" dimension measurement. The tool shown in Fig. 11 is available for turning the slotted adjusting nut.
3. The best method of adjusting PT release levers is to make an initial adjustment so that the levers are all high or with an "A" dimension of about 1". Then with the lock nut just tight enough to prevent lost motion, the lock nut and adjusting nut may be turned clockwise as a unit until the exact "A" dimension is obtained. Then hold the adjusting nut still and tighten lock nut to 60 ft-lbs torque.
4. Install release sleeve and bearing assembly into spider. Be sure to include sleeve lock nut and thread sleeve well into spider.

Transmission Installation

1. Place the two brake friction discs on the transmission clutch shaft with the keyed steel disc between the friction discs. *These parts are not used with a synchronized transmission.*
2. Raise transmission and enter spline shaft into release sleeve assembly.
3. Square up transmission and move it forward to enter driven disc hubs, at the same time allow the release yoke to pass over the top of the release bearing housing and fall into its normal operating position on the bearing housing wear pads.

NOTE: An alternate method of installing the transmission to the engine is as follows: Instead of installing the release bearing and sleeve assembly into the release lever spider, the release sleeve and bearing is placed on the transmission with the release yoke in its operating position. Then after the transmission has been raised into position and started forward, the adjusting sleeve must be threaded into the release lever spider. If this method is used, care must be taken that the transmission is not moved up to the engine faster than the sleeve and spider are threaded together or cotter pins may be damaged.

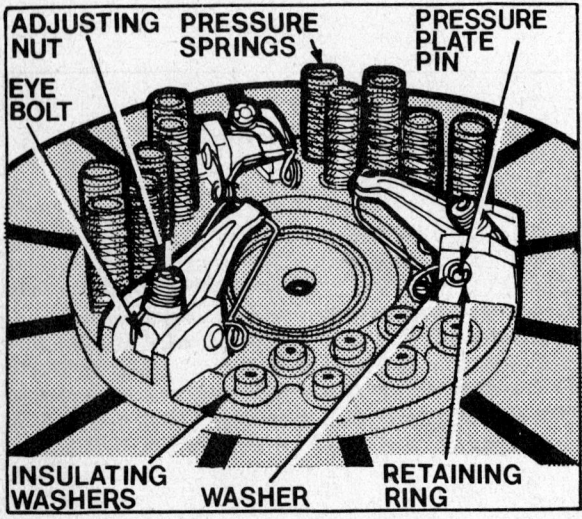

Fig. 7 Pressure plate assembly

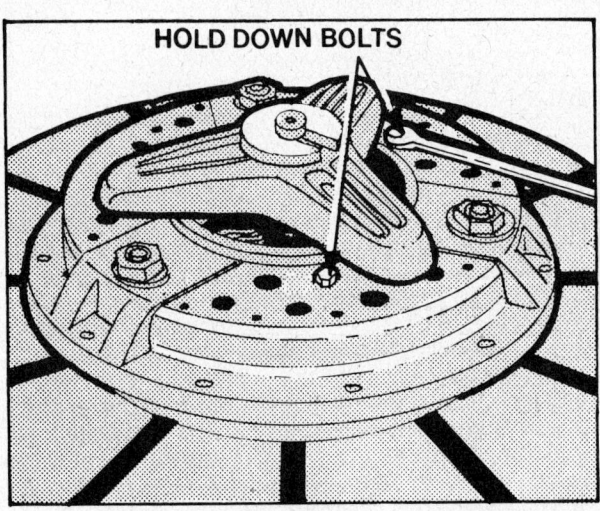

Fig. 8 Installation of hold-down bolts and lock nuts

HEAVY DUTY CLUTCHES

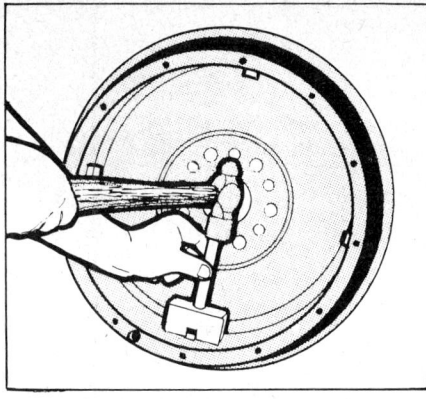

Fig. 9 Driving pin alignment gauge (T-10670)

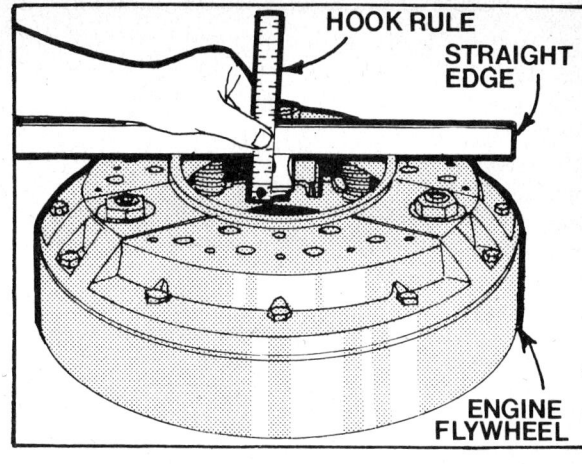

Fig. 10 Checking Dimension "A"

Release Bearing Adjustment

1. After the transmission has been securely attached to the engine, the release sleeve must be adjusted until there is 3/8" to 7/16" between the contact surface of the release bearing housing and the front brake disc.

   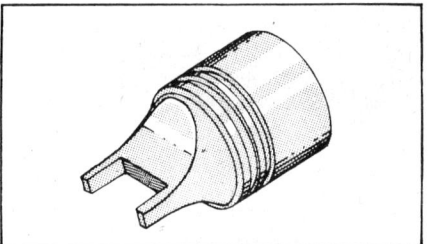

   Fig. 11 Lipe Tool T-10207A for slotted adjusting nut

   CAUTION: Keep tension on release yoke while turning adjusting nut. Do not attempt to secure the sleeve lock nut to the release lever spider until the pedal linkage has been connected and adjusted for "free travel".

2. Following the preliminary adjustment of the pedal linkage, check the release bearing travel by pressing down on the clutch pedal. The release bearing housing should contact the clutch brake disc just before the clutch pedal makes contact with the floor board. Depress the pedal a few times and recheck the 3/8" to 7/16" distance between the release bearing housing and brake disc.

3. Hold or block the clutch pedal down while the lock nut is turned up to release lever spider and securely tightened.

   CAUTION: Always disengage the clutch while the lock nut is being locked or unlocked but have the clutch engaged while turning the release sleeve to obtain the 3/8" to 7/16" distance which must be rechecked and adjusted as facing wear occurs.

Lipe TC Clutch

The Lipe TC "Constant Capacity" clutch is of the non-adjustable, dry disc type which automatically compensates for facing wear, Figs. 1 and 2. As facings of the disc assembly wear through normal use, the toggle lever angle, which is formed by the release lever and toggle link, increases in efficiency as it straightens out and induces an increased pressure against the facings. Thus a "Constant" clutch torque capacity is maintained throughout the life of the clutch facings.

NOTE: If inspection indicates that clutch pedal free travel is less than 1/2", immediate adjustment of the clutch linkage should be made to restore the proper 1 1/2" free travel of the pedal.

Clutch Removal

1. Install two 3/8" × 16 × 3" hold-down bolts as shown in Fig. 3, through holes in spring retainer, and thread these bolts into the tapped holes in the pressure plate provided for this purpose. Tighten sufficiently to compress the springs and free the levers.
2. Remove capscrews holding clutch to flywheel and remove clutch.

Clutch Disassembly

1. Unfasten and lift off flywheel ring (cover).
2. Place clutch on table of an arbor or drill press. Place block across the spring retainer and hold springs in a compressed position so the hold-down bolts can be removed; then slowly release the spring tension.
3. Release lever and link sub-assemblies can now be removed from pressure plate by removing cotter pins at ends of pressure plate pins.
4. To remove toggle link from release lever, drive out locking pin.
5. The needle bearings in the release levers can be removed by the use of a suitable driver and arbor press; the same applies to the removal of the fulcrum guide buttons.

Inspection & Repairs

Pressure Plate

It is recommended that not more than 1/32" be machined from the pressure plate friction surface. If not more than this amount or any portion thereof is removed, the clutch should be reassembled, using hole "A" of toggle link (see Fig. 10).

IMPORTANT: When machining amounts in excess of 1/32", it is essential that resurfaced dimension "B" (shown in chart) be obtained and clutch reassembled using hole "B" of toggle link. Dimension "B" is measured from the top of the pin to the friction surface of the pressure plate. It is important that these instructions be followed, otherwise short clutch life or incomplete clutch release (drag) will result.

Flywheel Ring (Cover)

Inspect cover for wear of driving lugs and cover pin holes. Cover should fit freely in slots of pressure plate with approximately .006" clearance between lugs and mating slots in pressure plate. Cover should be checked for distortion by placing it flange face down on surface plate. If cover incorporates driving pins, make certain pins are tight and squarely aligned.

Lever and Link Assembly

Referring to Fig. 4, inspect lever for condition of toggle link hole; if elongated or worn, replace lever. Check milled slot in underside of lever; if excessively worn by fulcrum studs, replace lever. Latest design release lever incorporates a removable fulcrum guide button, as shown in Fig. 4, that can easily be

HEAVY DUTY CLUTCHES

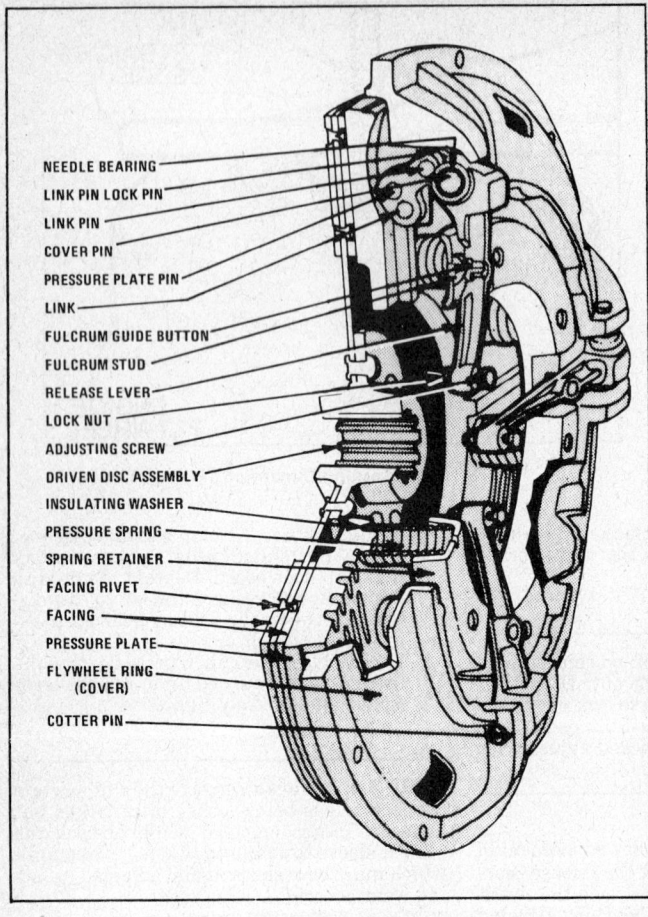

Fig. 1 Lipe TC single plate clutch

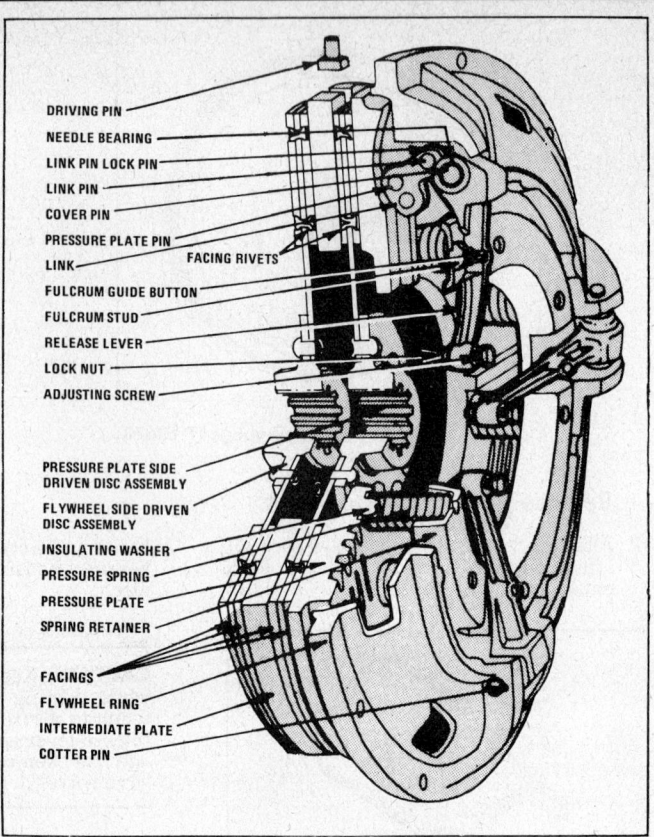

Fig. 2 Lipe TC two plate clutch

replaced if worn. If needle bearings do not rotate freely, replace.

When installing new needle bearings, press them in flush with lever. Make certain they are installed in lever with part number (stamped on end of bearing cage) facing outward, as pressing on other end of bearing cage will damage bearing. Pack needle bearing with a small amount of high melting point grease. Use correct grease and do not over-lubricate.

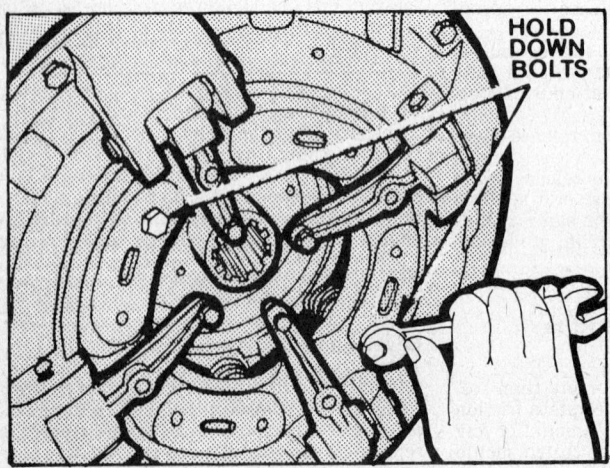

Fig. 3 Installing hold-down bolts

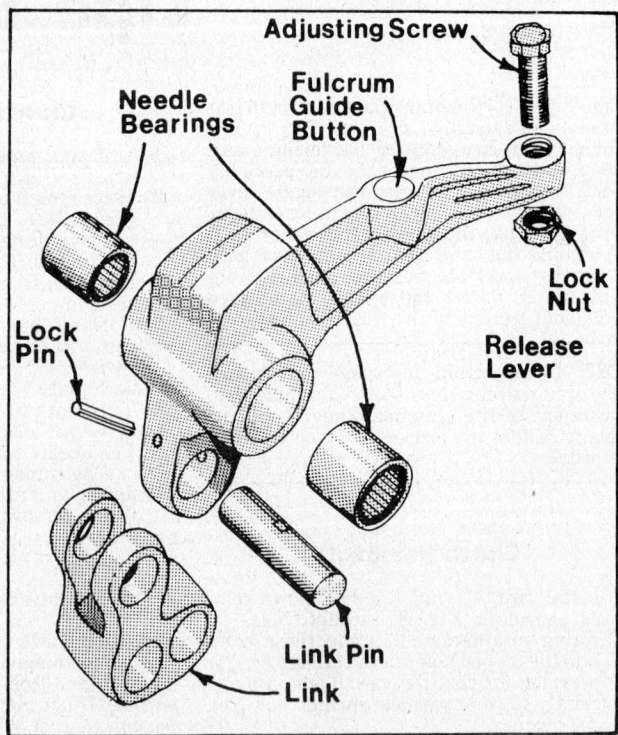

Fig. 4 Lever link and associated parts

HEAVY DUTY CLUTCHES

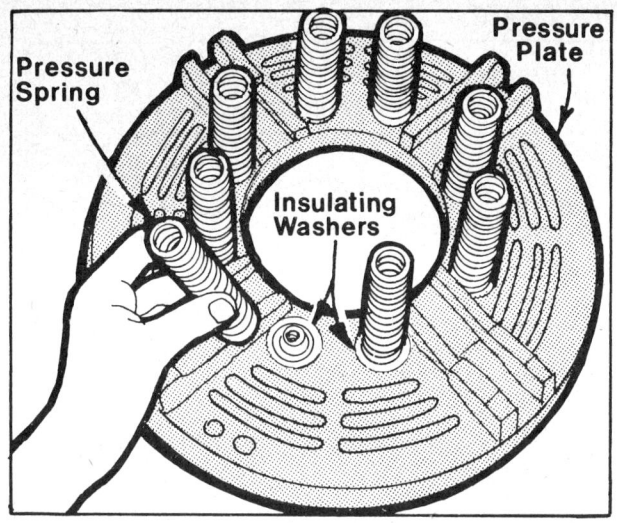

Fig. 5 Placing springs over insulating washers

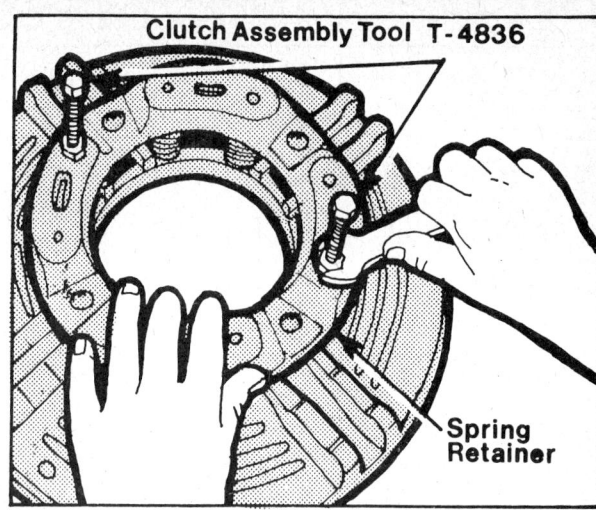

Fig. 6 Compressing pressure springs

Notice condition of lever adjusting screws. If they are worn where contacted by release bearing, install new screws in levers. Inspect fulcrum studs in spring retainer for wear. Replace if wear is indicated.

Driven Discs

Inspect and reface driven discs as outlined for other model clutches, being sure to use the proper riveting method for fabric and metallic facings.

Clutch Assembly

1. Place a small amount of high melting point grease on driving lugs of cover and mating slots in pressure plate, as well as pins and fulcrum studs. Do not over-lubricate as grease on facings will cause clutch to grab or slip.
2. Place insulating washers over spring locating bosses on pressure plate, Fig. 5. Use two washers under each spring if refaced pressure plate is installed to compensate for material ground off. Do not use two washers unless pressure plate has been refaced to dimension shown in chart under column "B Dimension Refaced".
3. Place springs over insulating washers on pressure plate, Fig. 5.
4. As shown in Fig. 6, install spring retainer over pressure springs and compress springs with the hold-down bolts used when clutch was removed. Draw nuts down against top of spring retainer to compress springs to an overall height of approximately 2″.

   NOTE: An alternate method is to use an arbor or drill press to compress the springs. Place a block across the spring retainer. Install the hold-down bolts to hold the springs fully compressed. The hold-down bolts or the Lipe tool, Fig. 7, must remain in place until clutch has been bolted to flywheel.

5. As shown in Fig. 8, assemble toggle link to release lever, placing lever in slot of toggle link and insert link pin. Align milled notch of link pin with lock pin hole in lever with use of suitable tool before driving in lock pin. Lock pin should be driven in flush with lever surface.

   THREE HOLE LINK: The proper link hole to use will depend on whether or not the pressure plate has been refaced. Toggle link hole "A", Fig. 10, is assembled to the pressure plate if a NEW pressure plate is used. Hole "B" is assembled only if the pressure plate has been refaced. See Chart indicating correct new and refaced pressure plate dimensions with respect to each clutch model.

6. Assemble sub-assembly, Fig. 9.

7. Place flywheel ring (cover) into position, aligning lugs in underside of cover with mating slots in pressure plate. If original pressure plate is used, be sure that cover registers with aligning "O" mark stamped on O.D. of both cover and pressure plate.
8. Referring to Fig. 11, start longest cover pins through cover, at the same time lifting or placing small blocks of proper thickness between top of work bench and underside of cover flange so as to align two opposite levers, and drive cover pins through needle bearings in levers into place.

Clutch Installation

1. Be sure hold-down bolts are used to hold springs compressed and free from release levers before clutch is assembled to flywheel.
2. Make sure flywheel is the correct depth and friction face is smooth and clean (see Chart for flywheel depth specifications).
3. Try cover plate assembly in flywheel before inserting driven disc to make certain clutch pilot diameter is a free fit in flywheel.
4. Install driven disc with pressure plate end of hub that has chamfered or pointed ends on splines to assist in the insertion of transmission drive shaft toward you.
5. Install spare splined shaft or clutch aligning arbor through disc hub into flywheel

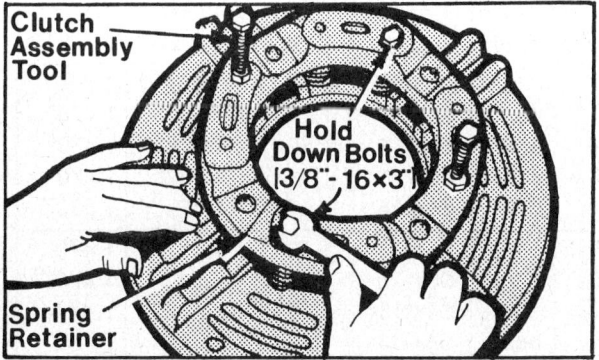

Fig. 7 Clutch assembly tool and hold-down bolts

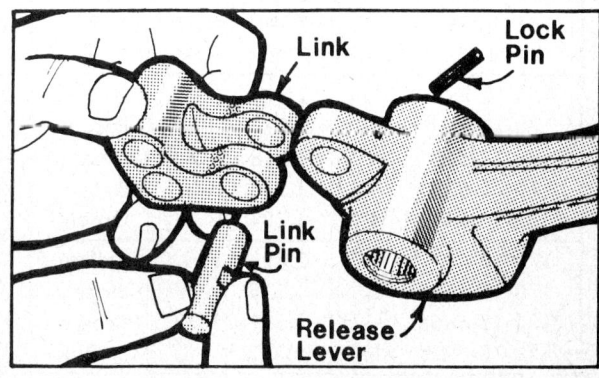

Fig. 8 Installing link to lever

HEAVY DUTY CLUTCHES

LIPE TC CLUTCH DATA CHART

Model Number†	Dimension "A"	Flywheel Depth +.007"/−.000"	Facing Thickness	PRESSURE SPRING DATA		DIMENSION "B" (New)		PRESSURE PLATE REFACING DATA (Dimension "B" Refaced)		
				Color	Minimum Weight	New ±.002"	Assemble Using Hole "A" of Link	Reassemble Using Hole "A" of Link C64-20	Reassemble Using Hole "B" of Link C64-20 or C64-16	Reassemble Using Hole "B" of Link C64-13
170-11-239	11/32"	1.218"	3/16"	White	125 @ 2¼"	1.656"	C64-16	1.594"	1.532"	1.470"
155-11-244	15/32"	1.781"	5/32"	White	125 @ 2¼"	1.718"	C64-16	1.656"	1.594"	1.532"
170-12-248*	11/32"	2.321"	5/32"	Green	240 @ 2¼"	1.656"	C64-13	1.594"	1.532"	1.470"
170-11-264	11/32"	1.218"	3/16"	Yellow	170 @ 2¼"	1.656"	C64-16	1.594"	1.532"	1.470"
170-12-277*	11/32"	2.321"	5/32"	White	125 @ 2¼"	1.656"	C64-13	1.594"	1.532"	1.470"
170-12-278*	11/32"	2.321"	5/32"	Brown	115 @ 2¼"	1.656"	C64-13	1.594"	1.532"	1.470"
170-11-279	11/32"	1.218"	3/16"	Green	240 @ 2¼"	1.656"	C64-16	1.594"	1.532"	1.470"
170-11-281	3/8"	Flat	3/16"	Red	100 @ 2⅜"	1.656"	C64-16	1.594"	1.532"	1.470"
155-11-282	15/32"	1.625"	5/32"	Red	100 @ 2⅜"	1.500"	C64-16	1.438"	1.376"	1.314"
155-11-284	15/32"	1.625"	5/32"	Red	100 @ 2⅜"	1.500"	C64-16	1.438"	1.376"	1.314"
155-11-285	15/32"	1.781"	5/32"	Red	100 @ 2⅜"	1.718"	C64-16	1.656"	1.594"	1.532"
155-11-289	15/32"	1.625"	5/32"	Red	100 @ 2⅜"	1.500"	C64-16	1.438"	1.376"	1.314"
170-11-349	11/32"	1.218"	3/16"	White	125 @ 2¼"	1.656"	C64-16	1.594"	1.532"	1.470"
155-11-350	15/32"	1.781"	5/32"	White	125 @ 2¼"	1.718"	C64-16	1.656"	1.594"	1.532"
170-12-351*	11/32"	2.321"	5/32"	Brown	115 @ 2¼"	1.656"	C64-13	1.594"	1.532"	1.470"
170-12-352*	11/32"	2.321"	5/32"	White	125 @ 2¼"	1.656"	C64-13	1.594"	1.532"	1.470"
170-12-353*	11/32"	2.321"	5/32"	Yellow	170 @ 2¼"	1.656"	C64-13	1.594"	1.532"	1.470"
155-11-354	15/32"	1.781"	5/32"	Red	100 @ 2⅜"	1.718"	C64-16	1.656"	1.594"	1.532"
170-11-355	11/32"	1.218"	3/16"	Yellow	170 @ 2¼"	1.656"	C64-16	1.594"	1.532"	1.470"
170-11-367	11/32"	1.218"	3/16"	Red	100 @ 2⅜"	1.656"	C64-16	1.594"	1.532"	1.470"
170-12-368*	11/32"	2.321"	5/32"	Brown	115 @ 2¼"	1.656"	C64-13	1.594"	1.532"	1.470"
170-12-369*	11/32"	2.321"	5/32"	White	125 @ 2¼"	1.656"	C64-13	1.594"	1.532"	1.470"
170-12-370*	11/32"	2.321"	5/32"	Yellow	170 @ 2¼"	1.656"	C64-13	1.594"	1.532"	1.470"
155-11-377	15/32"	1.781"	5/32"	Yellow	170 @ 2¼"	1.718"	C64-16	1.656"	1.594"	1.532"
155-11-379	15/32"	1.781"	5/32"	Lt. Blue	150 @ 2¼"	1.718"	C64-16	1.656"	1.594"	1.532"
170-11-383	11/32"	1.156"	3/16"	Gray	280 @ 2⅝"	1.656"	C64-16	1.594"	1.532"	1.470"
170-12-388*	11/32"	2.321"	5/32"	Green	240 @ 2¼"	1.656"	C64-13	1.594"	1.532"	1.470"
170-11-389	11/32"	1.218"	3/16"	White	125 @ 2¼"	1.656"	C64-16	1.594"	1.532"	1.470"
170-11-452	11/32"	1.218"	3/16"	Lt. Blue	150 @ 2¼"	1.656"	C64-16	1.594"	1.532"	1.470"
155-11-457	15/32"	1.781"	5/32"	Black	200 @ 2¼"	1.718"	C64-16	1.656"	1.594"	1.532"
170-11-458	11/32"	1.218"	3/16"	Black	200 @ 2¼"	1.656"	C64-16	1.594"	1.532"	1.470"
170-11-460	11/32"	1.218"	3/16"	Yellow	170 @ 2¼"	1.656"	C64-16	1.594"	1.532"	1.470"
170-12-477*	3/4"	2.321"	5/32"	Green	240 @ 2¼"	1.656"	C64-13	1.594"	1.532"	1.470"
170-12-479*	11/32"	2.321"	5/32"	Lt. Blue	150 @ 2¼"	1.656"	C64-13	1.594"	1.532"	1.470"
170-12-481*	11/32"	2.321"	5/32"	Black	200 @ 2¼"	1.656"	C64-13	1.594"	1.532"	1.470"
170-12-482*	11/32"	2.321	5/32"	Green	240 @ 2¼"	1.656"	C64-13	1.594"	1.532"	1.470"
170-12-522*	11/32"	2.321	5/32"	Brown	115 @ 2¼"	1.656"	C64-13	1.594"	1.532"	1.470"
170-11-523	3/4"	1.218	3/16"	Gray	280 @ 2⅝"	1.656"	C64-16	1.594"	1.532"	1.470"
170-11-527	11/32"	1.218	3/16"	Gray	280 @ 2⅝"	1.656"	C64-16	1.594"	1.532"	1.470"
155-11-613	15/32"	1.781	5/32"	Green	240 @ 2¼"	1.718"	C64-16	1.656"	1.594"	1.532"
170-12-640*	11/32"	2.321	5/32"	Yellow	170 @ 2¼"	1.656"	C64-13	1.594"	1.532"	1.470"
170-11-664	11/32"	1.218	3/16"	Black	200 @ 2¼"	1.656"	C64-16	1.594"	1.532"	1.470"
170-12-686*	11/32"	2.321	5/32"	Brown	115 @ 2¼"	1.656"	C64-13	1.594"	1.532"	1.470"
170-12-690*	11/32"	2.312	5/32"	Lt. Blue	150 @ 2¼"	1.656"	C64-13	1.594"	1.532"	1.470"

Continued

HEAVY DUTY CLUTCHES

LIPE TC CLUTCH DATA CHART—Continued

Model Number†	Dimension "A"	Flywheel Depth +.007"/-.000"	Facing Thickness	PRESSURE SPRING DATA		DIMENSION "B" (New)		PRESSURE PLATE REFACING DATA (Dimension "B" Refaced)		
				Color	Minimum Weight	New ±.002"	Assemble Using Hole "A" of Link	Reassemble Using Hole "A" of Link C64-20	Reassemble Using Hole "B" of Link C64-20 or C64-16	Reassemble Using Hole "B" of Link C64-13
170-12-709*	11/32"	2.312"	5/32"	White	125 @ 2¼"	1.656"	C64-13	1.594"	1.532"	1.470"
170-12-710*	¾"	2.312"	5/32"	Black	200 @ 2¼"	1.656"	C64-13	1.594"	1.532"	1.470"
170-12-715*	¾"	2.312"	5/32"	Lt. Blue	150 @ 2¼"	1.656"	C64-13	1.594"	1.532"	1.470"
170-12-722*	11/32"	2.321"	5/32"	Gray	280 @ 2⅝"	1.656"	C64-13	1.594"	1.532"	1.470"
170-12-733*	¾"	2.321"	5/32"	Yellow	170 @ 2¼"	1.656"	C64-13	1.594"	1.532"	1.470"
170-12-737*	11/32"	2.321"	5/32"	Black	200 @ 2¼"	1.656"	C64-13	1.594"	1.532"	1.470"
170-12-741*	11/32"	2.321"	5/32"	Lt. Blue	150 @ 2¼"	1.656"	C64-13	1.594"	1.532"	1.470"
170-12-744*	¾"	2.321"	5/32"	Black	200 @ 2¼"	1.656"	C64-13	1.594"	1.532"	1.470"
170-12-746*	11/32"	2.321"	5/32"	Green	240 @ 2¼"	1.656"	C64-13	1.594"	1.532"	1.470"
170-12-777*	¾"	2.321"	5/32"	Gray	280 @ 2⅝"	1.656"	C64-13	1.594"	1.532"	1.470"
170-12-799	¾"	2.321"	5/32"	Gray	280 @ 2⅝"	1.656"	C64-13	1.594"	1.532"	1.470"

* If the intermediate plate also requires refacing, remove the difference between dimension new and the dimension refaced as a total amount of material to be removed from the intermediate plate and pressure plate friction surfaces. Thickness of new intermediate plate is .749". Reassemble as indicated.

† Model number is the number stamped on the name plate attached to cover.
Dimension "A" refers to proper setting of release lever adjusting screw.
Dimension "B" is the distance from top of pin to ground surface of pressure plate.

pilot bearing to center disc assembly.
6. Install cover plate assembly to flywheel.

NOTE: Push inner ends of release levers in toward flywheel before starting to tighten the opposite capscrews attaching clutch to flywheel. Screw in each capscrew until it contacts clutch cover. Then gradually tighten the opposite capscrew until clutch is drawn tight to flywheel. Do not force clutch into flywheel with attaching capscrews as the clutch may be damaged. Remove hold-down bolts from clutch.

Adjusting Release Levers

Using a straight-edge and scale, set adjusting screws in ends of release levers to the proper Dimension "A" (see chart). Dimension "A" is the distance from ground surface of raised lever bosses of flywheel ring (cover) to heads of lever adjusting screws when clutch is bolted to flywheel and in the engaged position. The contact points of these adjusting screws should be set a uniform distance from underside of straight-edge. The adjusting screws must be in the same plane within 1/32". To change the position of the adjusting screws, loosen lock nuts and turn screw as required to obtain "Dimension A".

Vehicle Clutch Linkage

Check vehicle clutch linkage for excessive wear and resulting lost motion that can cause incomplete release of clutch (clutch drag) and improper release bearing clearance, which causes clutch slippage. Replace worn parts.

IMPORTANT: Set the vehicle clutch release linkage so as to provide 1/8" release bearing clearance between contact face of bearing and ends of clutch release lever adjusting screws. This usually results in 1½" of clutch pedal free travel.

Two Plate Clutches

1. Check driving pins and intermediate

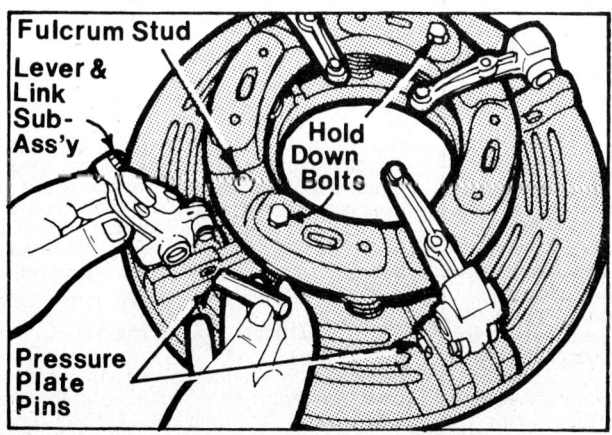

Fig. 9 Installing link to lever sub-assembly

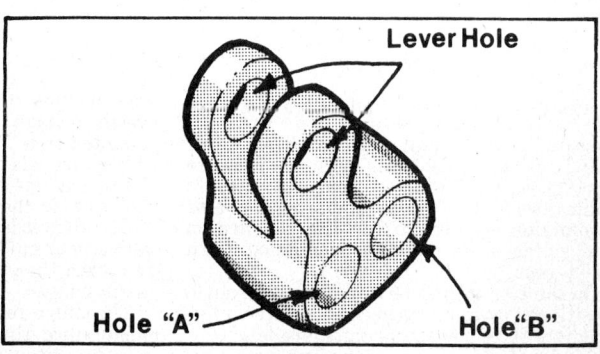

Fig. 10 Toggle link

HEAVY DUTY CLUTCHES

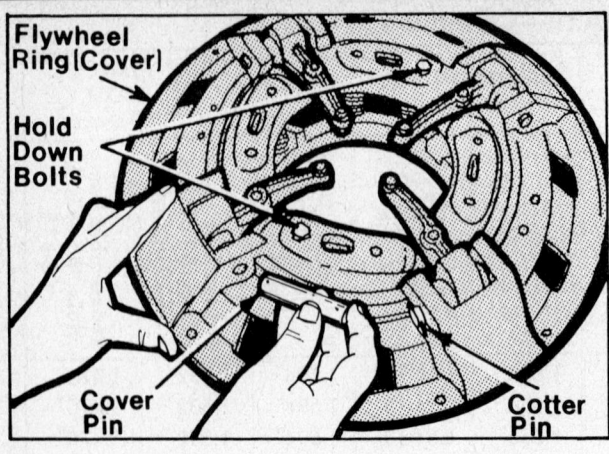

Fig. 11 Installing cover pins

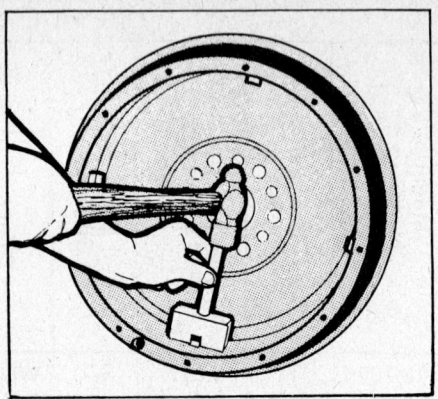

Fig. 12 Aligning drive pin in flywheel using Lipe tool T-10670

plate for wear.

2. Driving pins should be installed in flywheel with a press fit and squarely aligned with friction face of flywheel. It is recommended that the tool shown in Fig. 12 be used. If this tool is not available, place a machinist's square firmly against the rim of the flywheel and make certain the contact face of the driving pins have even contact with the square, Fig. 13.
3. Check clearance between heads of driving pins and driving slots in mating intermediate plate over the pins, making certain the plate fits freely before clutch is assembled to engine. If excessive clearance exists, new parts should be installed.
4. Try clutch in flywheel before installing driven discs and intermediate plate to be sure clutch pilot diameter is a free fit in flywheel bore.
5. When installing intermediate plate, be sure its rotation will be in the direction of the arrows appearing on one side of the plate near the bore.
6. When installing the driven discs, note that the one marked "Flywheel Side" should be installed with this mark next to the friction face of the flywheel. The disc marked "Pressure Plate Side" is installed with this mark next to the friction face of the pressure plate. This is important to prevent hub interference.
7. Use a spare spline shaft to align driven discs so as to make the installation of the transmission easier.

Release Lever Travel

To obtain complete disengagement of TC clutches, the release levers must be actuated a specified distance from the engaged position. Assuming the release bearing clearance to be $1/8''$ when the clutch is in the engaged position, the release bearing must move forward $1/8''$ to take up this clearance before it contacts the release levers, and then move the normal amount of travel required to disengage the clutch as shown in the chart, Fig. 14.

Fig. 13 Aligning drive pin in flywheel using machinist's square and feeler gauge

Clutch Size and Type	Release Bearing Clearance	Normal Release Bearing Travel	Total Bearing Travel Required
15½ TC Single Plate	$1/8''$	$7/16''$	$9/16''$
17 TC Single Plate	$1/8''$	$7/16''$	$9/16''$
17-2 TC Two Plate	$1/8''$	$1/2''$	$5/8''$

Fig. 14 TC clutch release travel chart

Spicer Clutches

Description

These clutches, Figs. 1 and 2 are of the dry disc, adjustable, pull type, multiple lever units utilizing centrally located pressure springs entirely isolated from the pressure plate itself. They are available with one or two plates, with the driven disc mounted on the spline shaft of the transmission main drive gear.

In the 13", 14" and 14" two-plate with angle positioned pressure springs models, the intermediate drive plate is mounted inside a "cup" type flywheel and carried on four drive pins (six pins for the 14" two-plate with angle positioned pressure springs) mounted in the flywheel. However, in the 15½" models, the intermediate drive plate has external lugs which engage slots in the flywheel ring mounted on a "flat" type flywheel, Fig. 3.

In all models the pressure plate is driven by four drive lugs or drive pins which mate with four slots in the clutch flywheel ring.

On all models, the pressure plate also carries four pull-back springs and anchor pins to retract the pressure plate when the clutch is disengaged.

The clutch release bearing rotates continuously since the inner race turns with the release sleeve and flywheel. However, the clutch release bearing carries a thrust load only when the clutch is released. Bronze, graphite-impregnated bushings are used to reduce friction when the flywheel and main drive gear are turning at different speeds.

The spring plates of all clutches are ventilated and incorporate air scoops to circulate cooling air through the clutch whenever the engine is running.

Clutch Adjustments

The need for an internal adjustment is indicated by a reduction in clutch pedal free travel. In general the clutch should be adjusted for approximately $1½''$ of free pedal travel. When the free pedal travel diminishes to $½''$, the

HEAVY DUTY CLUTCHES

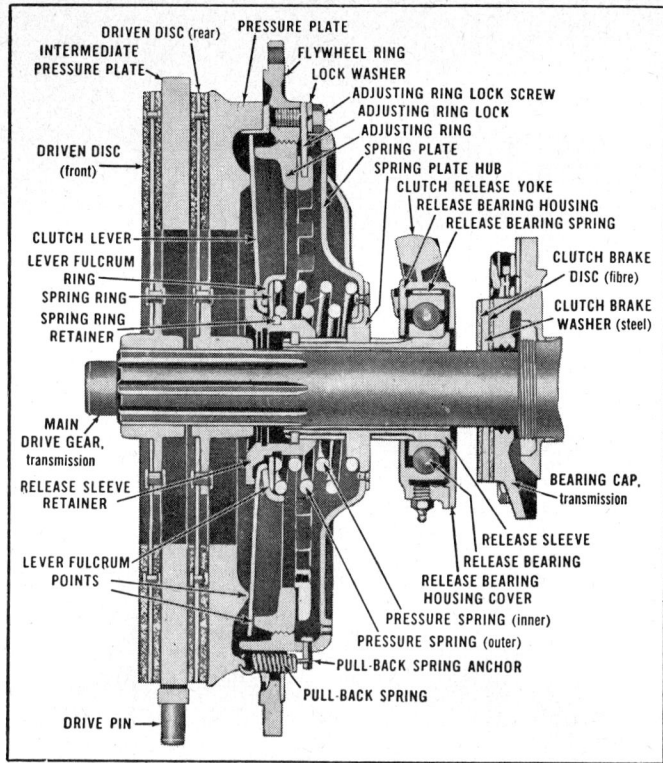

Fig. 1 Sectional view of Spicer 13" and 14" clutches

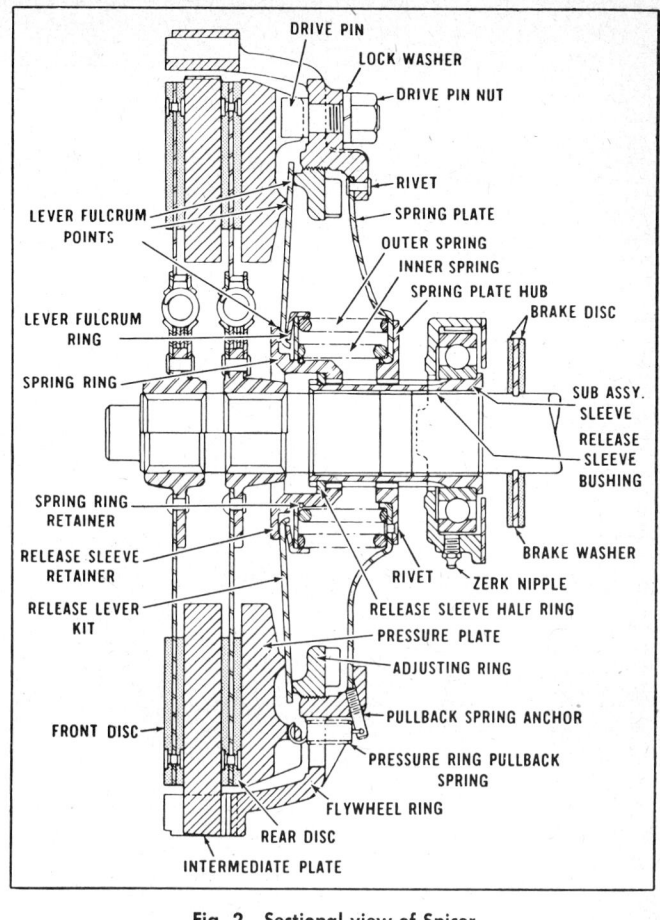

Fig. 2 Sectional view of Spicer 15½" clutch (less angle positioned springs)

internal adjustment must be made.

NOTE: Adjusting the external clutch linkage to restore the original free pedal travel will not compensate for an improperly adjusted clutch. Make the internal adjustment first and then check and reset the external linkage, if required.

Adjustment with Clutch Brake

If the clutch installation is used with a clutch brake or a non-synchronized transmission, the internal clutch adjustment should be checked by measuring the clearance (gap) between the clutch release bearing housing cover and the clutch brake, Fig. 4. The average adjustment with clutch brake is given below with a tolerance of plus or minus 1/32":

13" two plate	1/2"
14" single plate	7/16"
14" two plate	1/2"
15½" single plate	9/16"
15½" two plate	1/2"

On clutch brake applications the release bearing housing cover should contact the clutch brake washer when the clutch pedal is at least one inch from the floor. Idle the engine and make sure the clutch releases fully before the clutch brake comes into action. Gears should be shifted freely without noticeable drag of clutch plates when clutch is released. If the clutch does not release before the clutch brake comes into action, make an internal clutch adjustment.

Adjustment without Clutch Brake

If the clutch installation is used with a synchronized transmission or without the clutch brake, the internal adjustment should be checked between the clutch release bearing housing and the clutch spring hub, Fig. 4. The average adjustment is given below with an allowable tolerance of plus or minus 1/32":

13" two plate	23/32"
14" single plate	3/8"
14" two plate	19/32"
15½" single plate	17/32"
15½" two plate	19/32"

With Hydraulic Release

If the vehicle is equipped with a hydraulic clutch release cylinder the truck manufacturer's instructions should be followed. However, points that should be kept in mind when setting the clutch release mechanism are:

1. That there be 1/8" free travel somewhere in the linkage.
2. That the hydraulic clutch release lever travels equally on each side of the vertical centerline.
3. That the slave cylinder travel is sufficient to give a clean clutch release.

On some applications the external clutch lever is twice as long as the clutch release yoke. This gives a two to one ratio, or the slave cylinder piston must travel one inch to give 1/2" clutch release travel. In any case, an average of 1/2" clutch release bearing travel should be provided for proper release of all Spicer heavy duty clutches.

Internal Clutch Adjustments

1. Remove inspection cover at bottom of clutch housing.
2. Measure clearance between release bearing housing and clutch brake or spring plate hub, according to the installation. If the clearance is more or less than that listed above, readjust clutch as follows:
3. Rotate engine flywheel until adjusting ring lock is exposed, then remove lock.
4. Release clutch by blocking clutch pedal down towards floor.
5. Use a pry bar to turn adjusting ring. Turn counterclockwise to move release bearing housing toward the flywheel: turn clockwise to move housing away from flywheel. Rotation or movement of one lug position will move release bearing approximately .020".
6. Unblock clutch pedal to engage clutch.
7. Recheck clearances as in Step 2.
8. After clutch has been properly adjusted, install locking device in notch provided in adjusting ring.
9. Check clearance between release yoke fingers and release bearing housing pads, or clearance between clutch release lever adjusting arm and linkage if an external arm is used. This clearance should be 1/8". It is important that this clearance be provided to allow for facing wear and clutch pedal free travel. When clutch is properly adjusted, the free pedal travel should be approximately 1½".

Remove & Disassemble

All Except Units with Angle Positioned Pressure Springs

A suitable sling or transmission jack should be used to properly support and maintain the engine-transmission alignment when removing or installing a transmission on the engine. Do not allow the front end of the transmission to drop and hang unsupported in the splined hubs of the clutch discs to avoid bending or

457

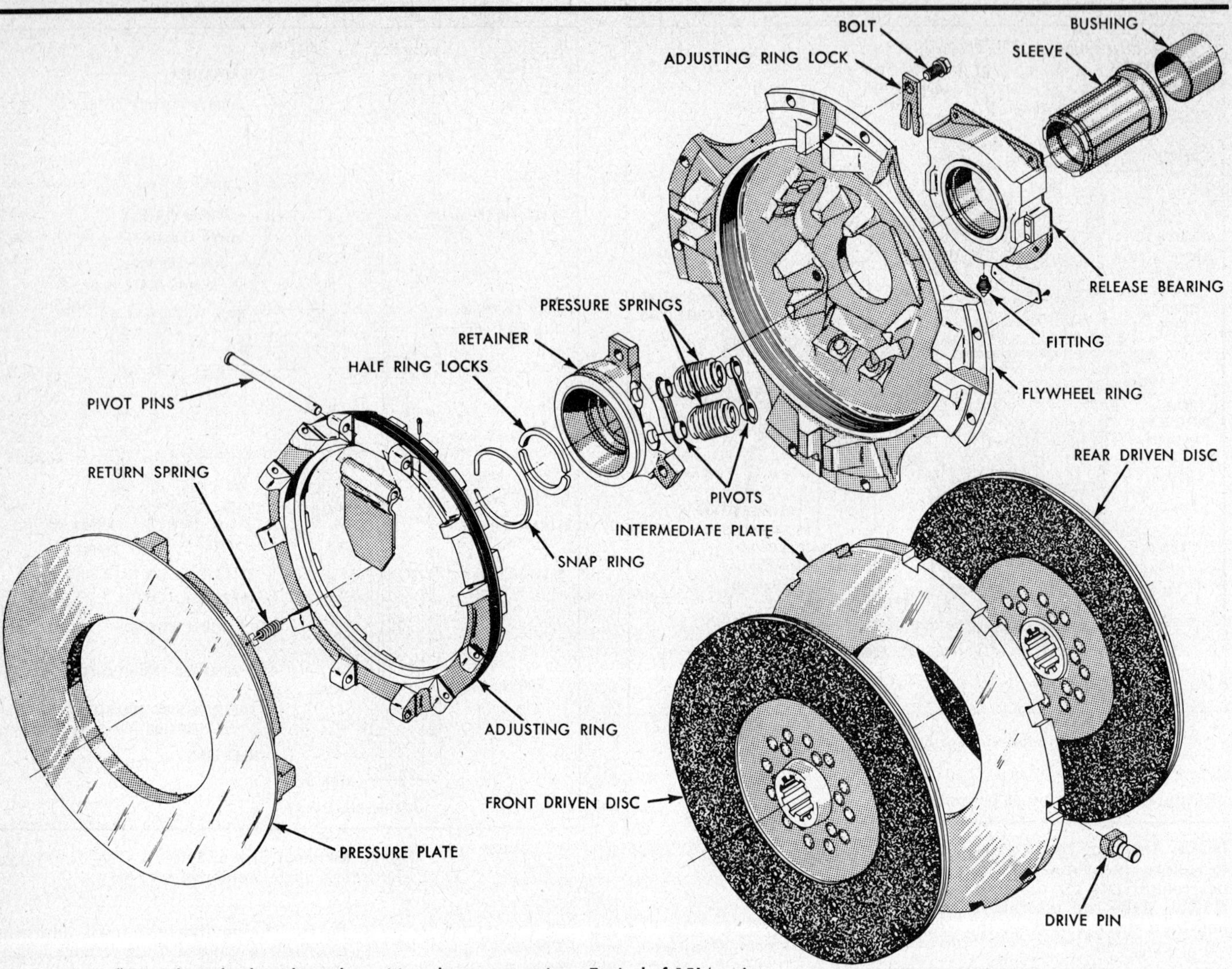

HEAVY DUTY CLUTCHES

Fig. 3 14" two plate clutch with angle positioned pressure springs. Typical of 15½" units, except that the 15½" units have external lugs on intermediate plate

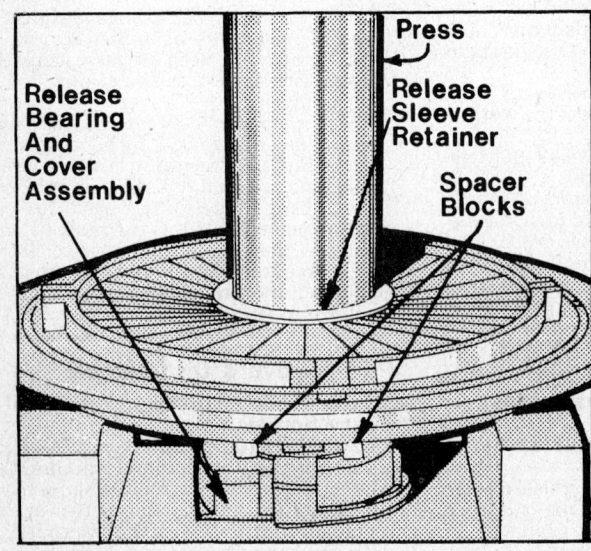

Fig. 5 Position or spacer blocks

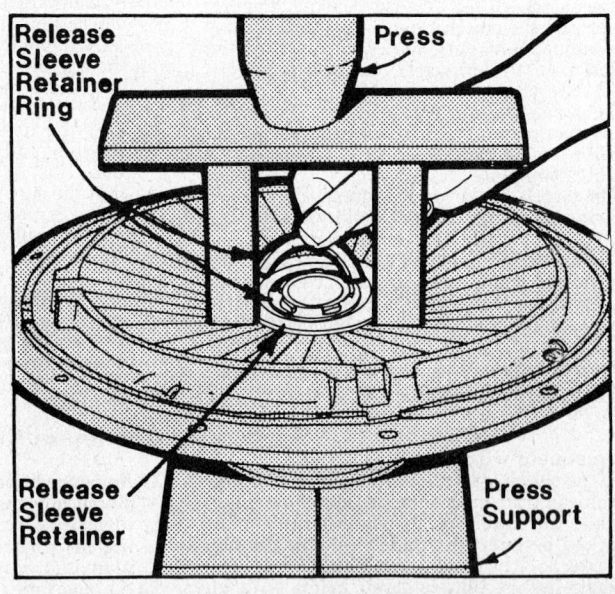

Fig. 6 Release sleeve retainer split ring

HEAVY DUTY CLUTCHES

distorting the driven discs. Disconnect the external linkage from the clutch release arm to permit the clutch release yoke to turn up and pull free of the release bearing thrust pads.

1. Prior to actual clutch removal, assemble a clutch disc aligning tool to the driven disc and release bearing assembly. Also remove two clutch-flywheel mounting capscrews from the upper part of the flywheel and insert two guide studs (5" long) in these holes.
2. After the transmission has been removed, insert two ¾" spacer blocks of wood between the clutch release bearing and spring plate hub, Fig. 5. This facilitates removal of clutch-to-flywheel capscrews and protects pullback springs from excessive tension.
3. Remove clutch retaining capscrews and remove pressure plate and flywheel ring assembly.
4. Remove driven disc or discs and intermediate plate.
5. Remove drive pins from flywheel. If Allen head set screws are used to retain drive pins, they must be removed to free drive pins.
6. To disassemble pressure plate, flywheel ring and lever assembly, first unhook the pull-back springs and remove pressure plate.
7. Press down on two places on outside of flywheel ring and remove spacer blocks.
8. Place assembly under arbor press with release bearing down. Use a spacer so pressure is exerted on release sleeve.
9. Press down on release sleeve retainer, Fig. 6, and remove split lock rings.
10. Remove spring ring retainer, Fig. 7.
11. Lift off spring ring and clutch levers, Fig. 8.
12. Clean and inspect all parts and discard any part that appears doubtful.

Units with Angle Positioned Pressure Springs

1. With transmission removed, install a clutch disc aligning tool into the driven disc and release bearing. Install two ¾ inch wood blocks between clutch release bearing housing and clutch flywheel rings, Fig. 9, as the clutch retaining bolts are loosened. These blocks will relieve the heavy spring load.
2. Remove all bolts and slide clutch assembly back with caution keeping aligning tool in place thus retaining disc and intermediate plate.
3. Carefully remove aligning tool, rear disc,

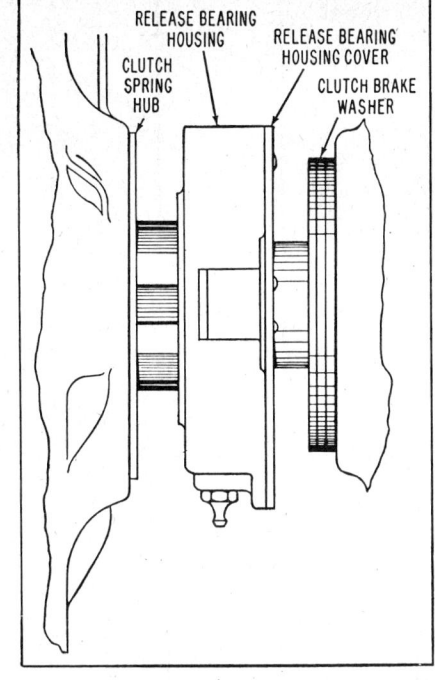

Fig. 4 Clutch adjusting points

intermediate plate and front disc.

4. Remove ring lock bolt, then using a screwdriver pry out ring lock.
5. With driven discs and intermediate plate removed, place clutch assembly upside down on flat surface then remove the four return springs, Fig. 25 and lift off the pressure plate.
6. Turn adjusting ring and lever assembly counterclockwise until free of flywheel, Fig. 10.
7. Remove snap ring from release sleeve retainer and install three ⅜" × 5" threaded rods through clearance holes in release sleeve retainer and into holes in flywheel ring, Fig. 11.

NOTE: Threaded rods must be flush with back of flywheel ring to prevent interference with bearing cover.

8. Install nuts onto rods. Place assembly on an arbor press with a short piece of tubing 2½ inch to 2¾ inch outside diameter used to support the release sleeve. Compress retainer until drive lugs bottom against flywheel ring and tighten nuts against retainer, Fig. 12.

NOTE: Do not support against clutch release bearing cover rivet heads.

9. Raise arbor, tilt assembly and remove wood blocks.
10. Support release sleeve as in step 8 and remove half ring locks, Fig. 13. Remove release sleeve and bearing assembly through rear of clutch.
11. Compress retainer to relieve load on nuts, then back off nuts and relieve load from springs. Remove springs and pivots, Fig. 14.
12. Remove cotter pins from pivot pins then the pins and levers.

Assemble

13" & 14" Units Without Angle Positioned Springs, Fig. 15

1. Place two flat springs in top side of bearing housing, one on top of the other. Use only one spring on the 14" single plate clutch.
2. Place release bearing in bearing housing, compressing springs.
3. Place bearing cover on housing and secure with two short rivets. The two hardened thrust plates as well as the bearing cover are assembled with four long rivets. Secure assembly with bolts, lock washers and nuts.
4. Install grease nipple if open bearings are used. Omit grease nipple and plug this opening if double-sealed bearings are used.
5. Press clutch release sleeve assembly in bearing housing, using an arbor press, Fig. 16.
6. Assemble four pull-back spring anchors in flywheel ring. Hook pull-back springs in anchors and clinch with pliers so an-

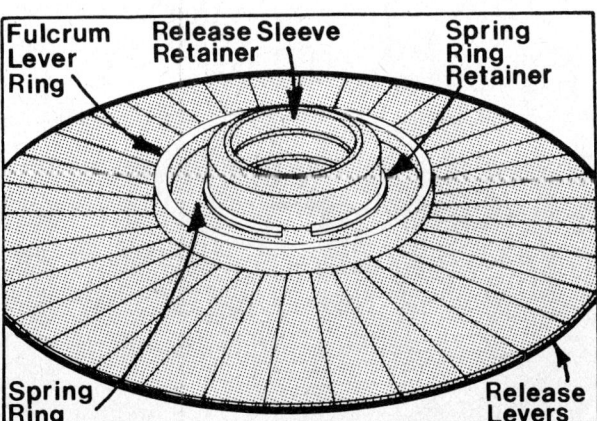

Fig. 7 Release sleeve retainer and lever assembly

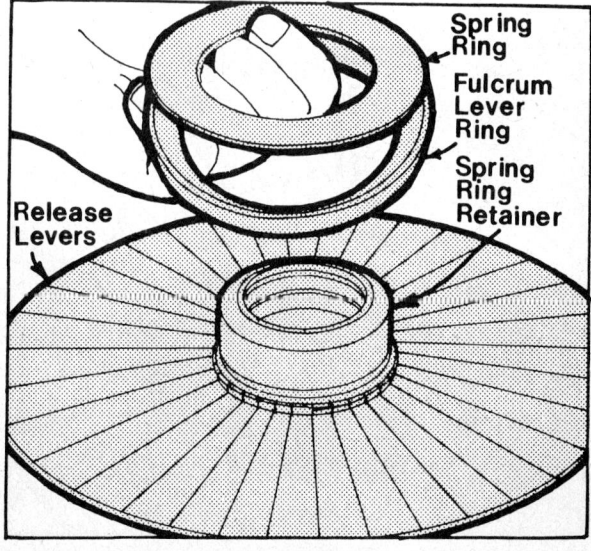

Fig. 8 Spring ring and fulcrum lever ring

459

HEAVY DUTY CLUTCHES

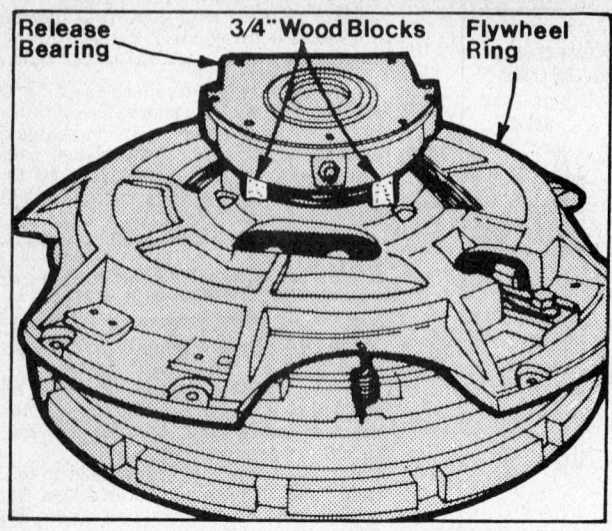

Fig. 9 Wood blocks positioned between release bearing and flywheel ring

Fig. 10 Removing adjusting ring

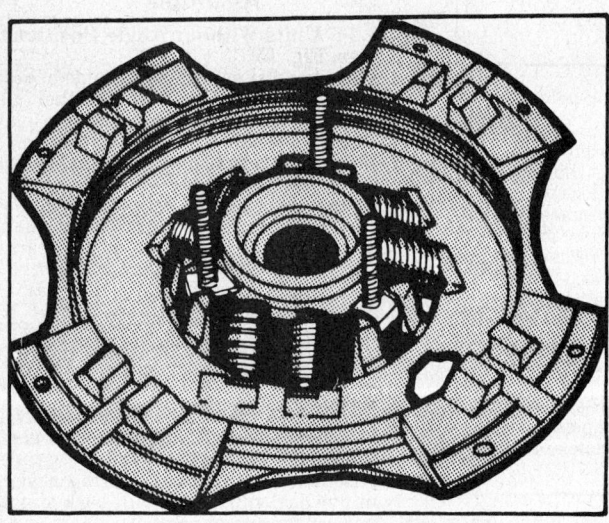

Fig. 11 Flywheel ring with threaded rods installed

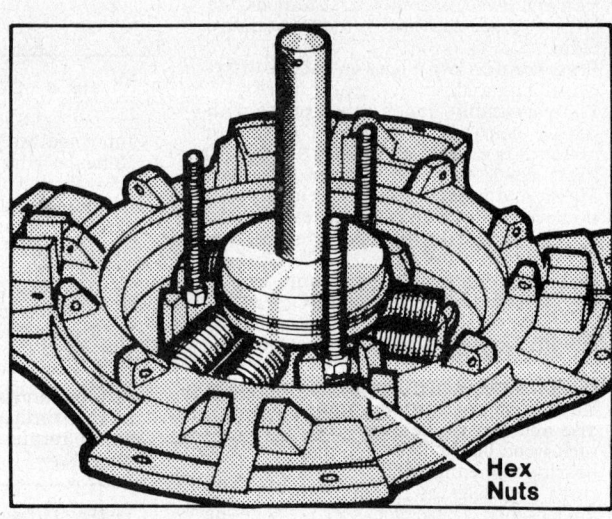

Fig. 12 Retainer ring in compressed position

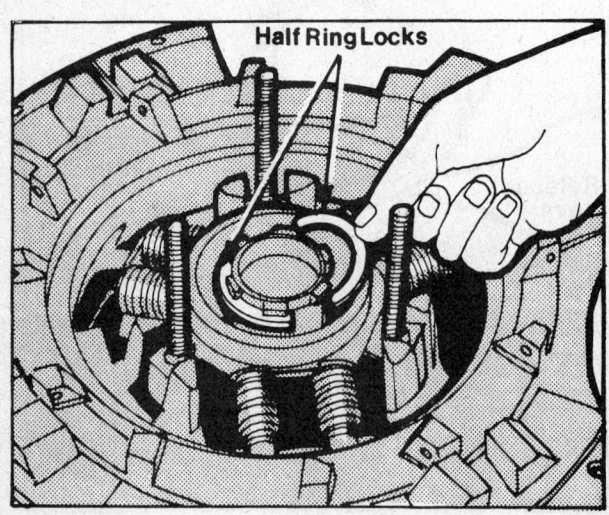

Fig. 13 Removing of installing half ring locks

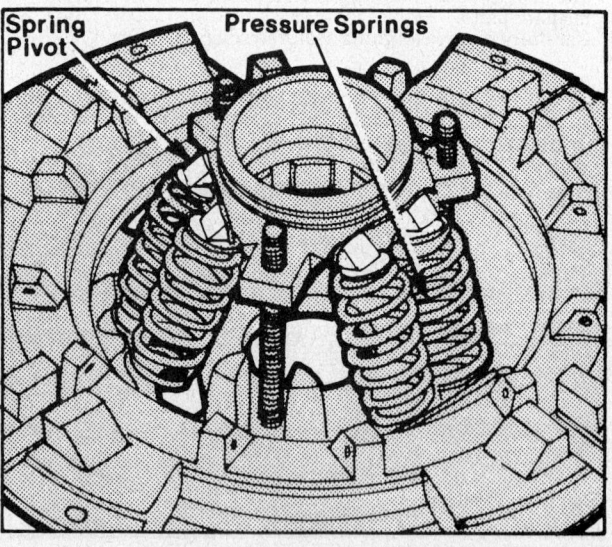

Fig. 14 Removing or installing pressure springs

HEAVY DUTY CLUTCHES

chors and springs do not fall out.
7. Screw adjusting ring into flywheel ring with adjusting notches down. Be sure adjusting ring turns freely. Powdered graphite mixed with oil and applied to threads will insure easy adjustment after clutch has been in service. Set adjusting ring to the dimension shown in Fig. 17 from fulcrum of ring to face of flywheel ring. Secure adjusting ring with lock, lockwasher and lock screw.
8. Continue with assembly by referring to Figs. 18 through 25.

15½" Units Without Angle Positioned Springs

NOTE: Inasmuch as an exploded view of these units and suitable detailed illustrations are not currently available, refer to Fig. 2 and earlier 15½" clutch pictures for identification of parts referred to below.

Release Sleeve Retainer & Lever
1. Place release sleeve retainer on bench with flanged end down and assemble 35 levers and hooked end up around retainer. *This clutch is so designed that sufficient space for one more lever may be available; however, do not use more than 35 levers.*
2. Install release lever fulcrum ring and spring ring down over hooked end of levers.
3. Install spring ring retainer to hold sub-assembly intact during assembly.

Flywheel Ring & Spring Plate
1. Coat threads of adjusting ring with powdered graphite mixed with oil. Assemble adjusting ring to flywheel ring with "notches" down. Preset adjusting ring 2⅞" below face of flywheel ring. Be sure adjusting ring turns freely in flywheel ring. Turn flywheel ring over and lock adjusting ring in position.
2. Set pressure plate on wooden bridge on bed of arbor press. Position four drive pins in slots and wedge with .004" to .008" shim stock.
3. Place flywheel ring and plate sub-assembly down over pressure plate and drive pins, aligning threaded end of drive pins with bosses of flywheel ring. Tap ring to start all drive pins securely. Use a short piece of tubing and, moving progressively, press each drive pin into place a little at a time. Avoid bending or forcing pins into position with one pass of the press.
4. Clamp clutch sub-assembly to bed of press with block of wood on spring plate hub. Use a long bolt through a flywheel mounting bolt hole to prevent the assembly from turning. Assemble lock nuts and lock washers to drive pins. Torque all lock nuts to 145 ft-lbs.
5. Remove assembly from press and set up-side down on bench. *Use care when removing clutch ring from press to prevent pressure plate from dropping free and causing personal injury or damage to pressure plate.*
6. Pry pressure plate free of driving pins (if necessary) and remove shim stock wedges. Check and make sure pressure plate slides freely on end of drive lugs. Realign drive pins if necessary to free up pressure plate.

Release Bearing & Sleeve
1. Assemble two flat springs inside and across top of release bearing housing with ends of springs inside cast relief sections.

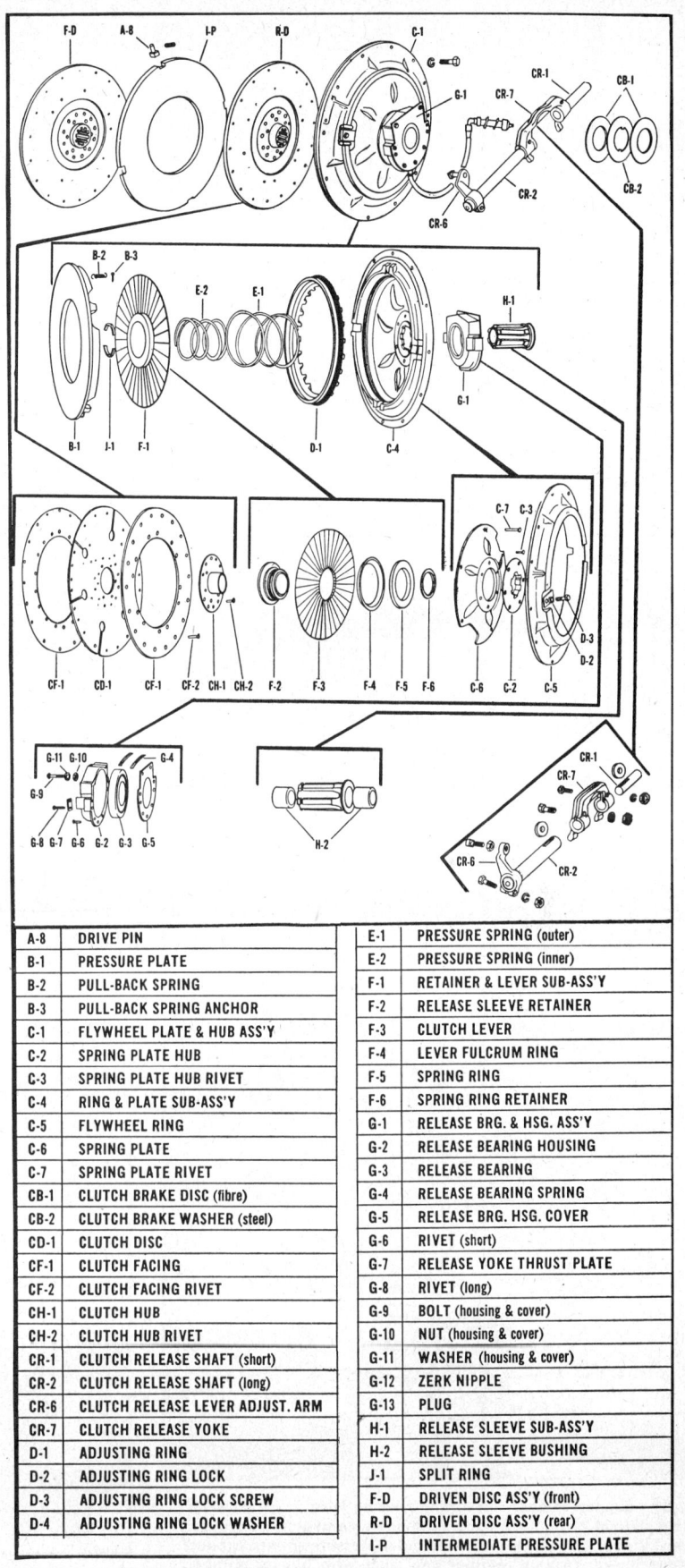

A-8	DRIVE PIN	E-1	PRESSURE SPRING (outer)
B-1	PRESSURE PLATE	E-2	PRESSURE SPRING (inner)
B-2	PULL-BACK SPRING	F-1	RETAINER & LEVER SUB-ASS'Y
B-3	PULL-BACK SPRING ANCHOR	F-2	RELEASE SLEEVE RETAINER
C-1	FLYWHEEL PLATE & HUB ASS'Y	F-3	CLUTCH LEVER
C-2	SPRING PLATE HUB	F-4	LEVER FULCRUM RING
C-3	SPRING PLATE HUB RIVET	F-5	SPRING RING
C-4	RING & PLATE SUB-ASS'Y	F-6	SPRING RING RETAINER
C-5	FLYWHEEL RING	G-1	RELEASE BRG. & HSG. ASS'Y
C-6	SPRING PLATE	G-2	RELEASE BEARING HOUSING
C-7	SPRING PLATE RIVET	G-3	RELEASE BEARING
CB-1	CLUTCH BRAKE DISC (fibre)	G-4	RELEASE BEARING SPRING
CB-2	CLUTCH BRAKE WASHER (steel)	G-5	RELEASE BRG. HSG. COVER
CD-1	CLUTCH DISC	G-6	RIVET (short)
CF-1	CLUTCH FACING	G-7	RELEASE YOKE THRUST PLATE
CF-2	CLUTCH FACING RIVET	G-8	RIVET (long)
CH-1	CLUTCH HUB	G-9	BOLT (housing & cover)
CH-2	CLUTCH HUB RIVET	G-10	NUT (housing & cover)
CR-1	CLUTCH RELEASE SHAFT (short)	G-11	WASHER (housing & cover)
CR-2	CLUTCH RELEASE SHAFT (long)	G-12	ZERK NIPPLE
CR-6	CLUTCH RELEASE LEVER ADJUST. ARM	G-13	PLUG
CR-7	CLUTCH RELEASE YOKE	H-1	RELEASE SLEEVE SUB-ASS'Y
D-1	ADJUSTING RING	H-2	RELEASE SLEEVE BUSHING
D-2	ADJUSTING RING LOCK	J-1	SPLIT RING
D-3	ADJUSTING RING LOCK SCREW	F-D	DRIVEN DISC ASS'Y (front)
D-4	ADJUSTING RING LOCK WASHER	R-D	DRIVEN DISC ASS'Y (rear)
		I-P	INTERMEDIATE PRESSURE PLATE

Fig. 15 Exploded view of 13" and 14" clutches

HEAVY DUTY CLUTCHES

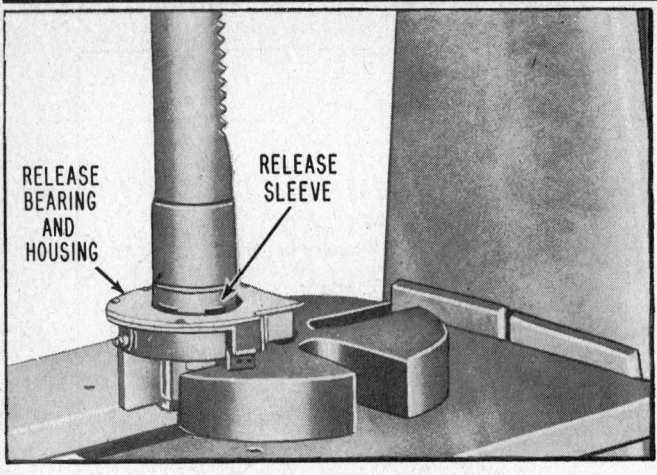

Fig. 16 Pressure clutch release sleeve into bearing housing

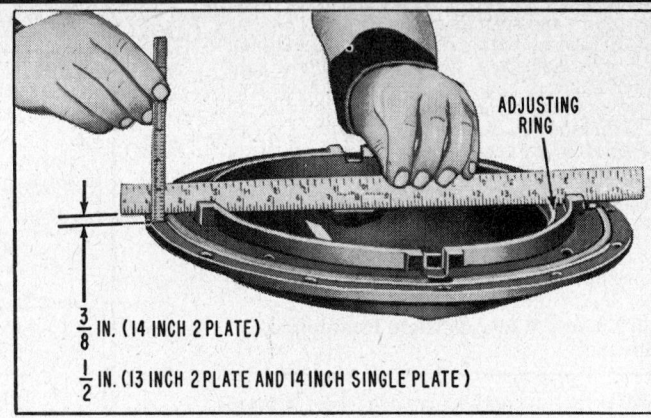

Fig. 17 Adjusting ring settings, measured from fulcrum of ring to face of flywheel ring

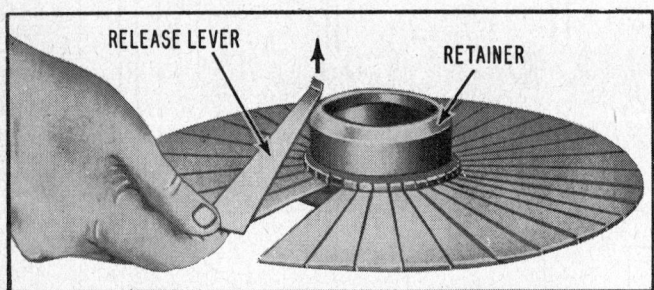

Fig. 18 Place retainer on bench with flange down and assemble levers with hook up around retainer

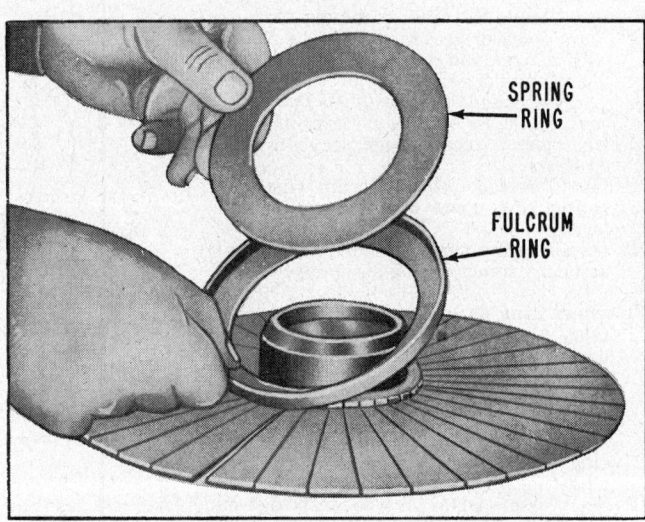

Fig. 19 Install fulcrum ring and spring ring

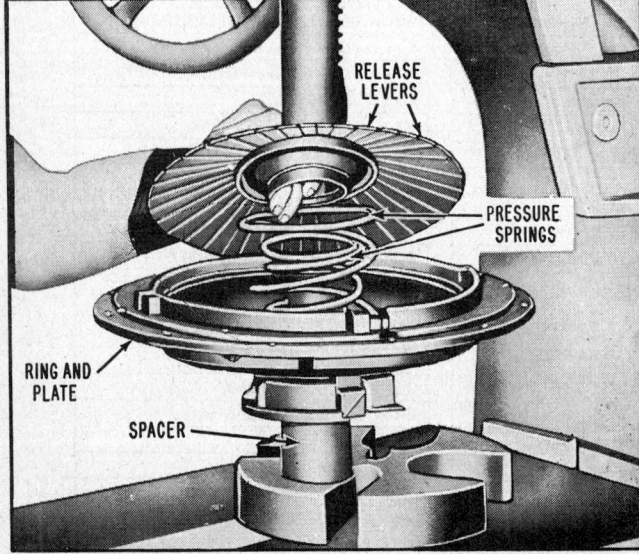

Fig. 21 Support release sleeve and bearing (sleeve up) on press with a piece of 2" tubing, 3" long. Position ring and plate down over release sleeve. Assemble inner and outer pressure springs around release sleeve. Position retainer and lever with hub of retainer down and inside springs

Fig. 20 Install snap ring

HEAVY DUTY CLUTCHES

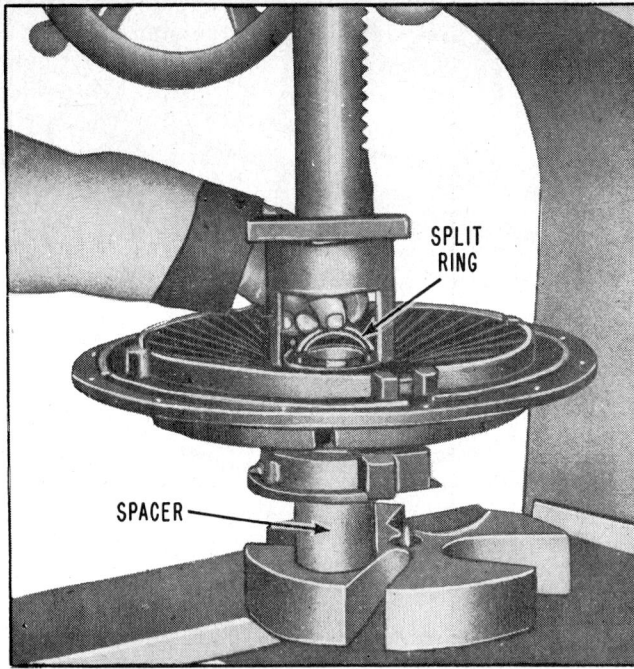

Fig. 22 Use two 3/4" × 6" long blocks of wood to compress springs. Lock lever retainer to release sleeve by installing split ring in groove of sleeve

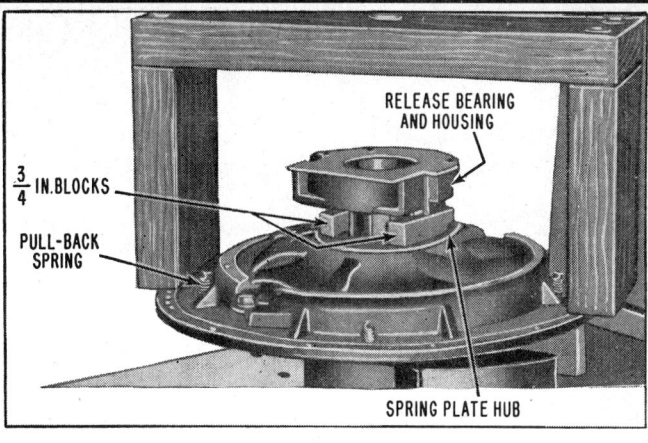

Fig. 23 Turn assembly over and rend end of sleeve on piece of 2" tubing. Use pieces of 2 × 4 placed as shown to compress clutch springs, and install two 3/4" blocks as shown

Hand pack bearing with proper lubricant and assemble bearing to housing, compressing flat springs. Seat bearing against machined flats inside housing.

2. Coat edge of release housing with a suitable sealer and assemble cover to housing with five short rivets. Assemble new hardened thrust plates to housing with long rivets. Rivet heads must be set tight to maintain grease-tight seat between bearing housing and cover. Assemble grease fitting to housing and fill cavity with proper grease.

Assemble 1¾" 10 Spline Unit

Place release bearing and cover on press with cover up. Press release sleeve sub-assembly into release bearing, making sure shoulder of sleeve is seated against inner race of bearing.

Assemble 2" 10 Spline Unit

Set release sleeve sub-assembly vertically on bed of press, splined end down. Position release bearing assembly on sleeve, with cover up. Use a 2⅜" thin wall tubing and press inner race of bearing onto ground diameter of sleeve. *Do not press on rivet heads or cover during this assembly.* Assemble snap ring to end of sleeve. Make sure inner race of bearing is seated firmly against snap ring.

Completing Assembly

1. Support release sleeve with bearing assembly on the press bed with a piece of 2½" × 2¾" tubing about 3" long. *Do not support this assembly on the release bearing cover as this will result in distortion and excessive end loading on the ball bearing.*

2. Position flywheel ring and spring plate assembly, with adjusting ring and pressure plate drive pins in place over release sleeve.
3. Assemble inner and outer pressure springs to release sleeve and resting on spring plate.
4. Assemble release sleeve retainer and lever sub-assembly, with splined hub end of retainer down and inside of pressure springs.
5. Use a small wooden bridge to compress pressure springs and permit assembly of half-ring locks.
6. Seat half-ring locks securely in groove of release sleeve and make sure retainer is not cocked or stuck, but slides back freely into its proper position when the press load is released.
7. Turn clutch over on press and rest end of release sleeve on piece of 2½" tubing. Use the 2 × 4 bridge to compress the pressure springs and install two 3/4" blocks of wood between release bearing housing and spring plate hub.
8. Set pressure plate on the 2 × 4 bridge with pull-back springs crimped to pressure plate. Stand springs up and set flywheel ring down over pressure plate, using care to align pull-back springs with cast slots provided in flywheel ring.
9. Check to make sure pull-back spring anchor pins are screwed completely into cover. Use long-nose pliers and hook

Fig. 24 Remove from press. Place clutch on bench with release bearing down. Install pressure plate to flywheel ring. Check clearance between driving lugs on pressure plate and drive slots in flywheel ring. Clearance should be .004" to .008"

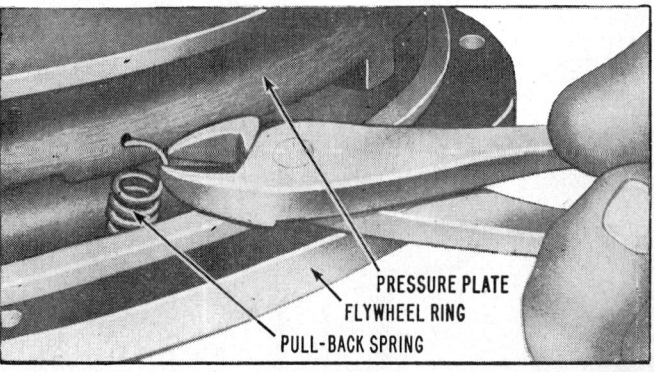

Fig. 25 Hook four pull-back springs in holes in pressure plate

HEAVY DUTY CLUTCHES

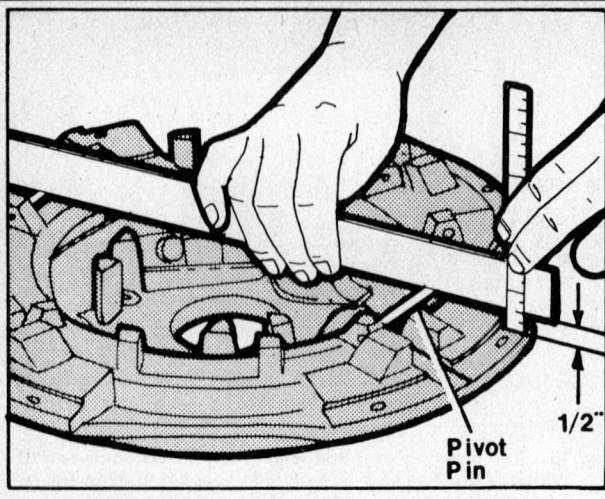

Fig. 26 Pre-setting adjusting ring. Except 15½" units

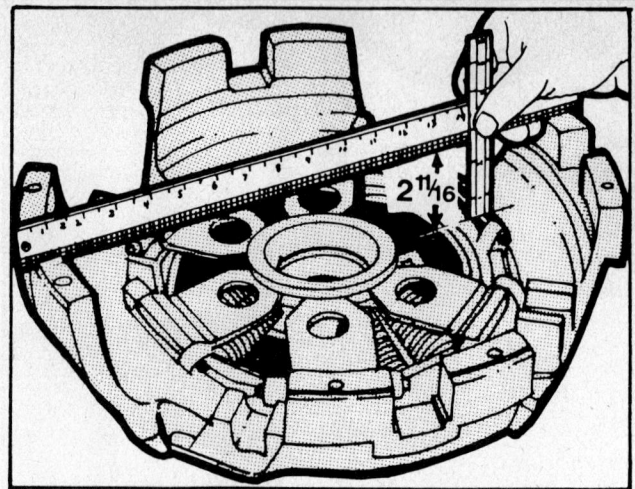

Fig. 27 Pre-setting adjusting ring. 15½" units

springs to anchor pins.
10. Using the rear disc as a spacer, assemble intermediate plate to clutch flywheel ring. Use a feeler gauge to check driving lug clearance in slots. Slot clearance should be .006" to .011".

Units with Angle Positioned Pressure Springs
1. Coat all threads of adjusting ring and flywheel ring with molykote or equivalent.
2. Assemble adjusting ring to flywheel ring with notches down. Pre-set adjusting ring by placing two pivot pins in adjusting ring bosses directly opposite each other. Using two straight edges, measure dimension from flywheel ring mounting surface to straight edge, this distance should be about ½ inch for 14 inch clutches, Fig. 26, or 2 11/16 for 15½ inch clutches, Fig. 27.
3. Install three threaded rods into flywheel ring and install hex nut on opposite side of ring and place spring pivots into flywheel ring and retainer. Place release sleeve retainer in position guided by rod, and install pressure springs, Fig. 14.
4. Place hex nuts on the three threaded rods and draw down enough to hold release sleeve retainer in place.
5. Place flywheel ring and release sleeve retainer assembly on arbor press. Depress retainer against flywheel ring then turn nuts on threaded rods tightly against flywheel ring, Fig. 12.

NOTE: Make certain that springs are seated in pivots.

6. Remove assembly from press then install release sleeve and bearing assembly through flywheel ring and release sleeve retainer. Install half ring locks, Fig. 13.
7. Place the ¾ inch wood blocks between flywheel ring and release bearing housing and place assembly on arbor press supporting sleeve on tubing previously used. Compress retainer to relieve load and remove threaded rods and wood blocks, Fig. 28.
8. Install snap ring above half ring locks and place levers between adjusting ring bosses, with the narrow end in groove of release sleeve retainer. Move adjusting ring as necessary to insert pivot pins and return adjusting ring to previous position.

NOTE: Raised area of lever fulcrum must be facing pressure plate. Each pivot pin has a flat surface on the head, this pivot pin surface must be mated with milled surface on adjusting ring boss.

9. Install cotter pins in pivot pin holes from outside in, flatten cotter pin head to insure clearance between flywheel ring lugs and adjusting ring.
10. Place pressure plate in drive slots or flywheel ring. Check clearance between driving lugs on pressure plate and drive slots in flywheel ring. This clearance should be .004–.008 inch, Fig. 24.
11. Install the four return springs, Fig. 25 and the adjusting ring lock and bolt.
12. Install drive pins in flywheel making sure that shanks of drive pins are press fit in the flywheel rim and the heads are square with friction face, Fig. 29.

Clutch Installation

13", 14" and 14" Two-Plate with Angle Positioned Pressure Springs
1. On all except the 14" Two-Plate with angle positioned pressure springs, install four pins in flywheel, making sure shanks of pins are press fit in flywheel

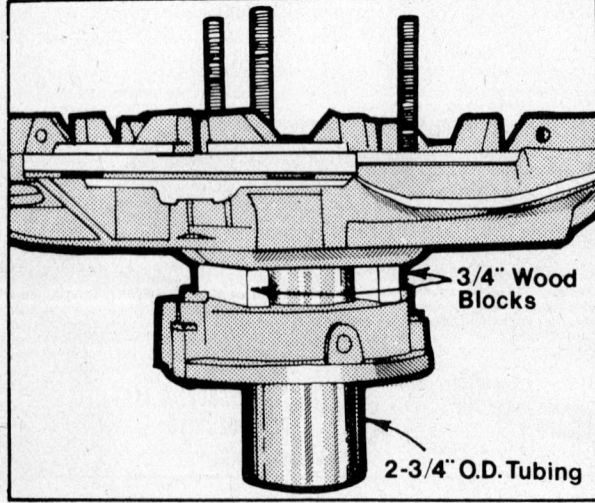

Fig. 28 Supporting sleeve with tube and wood blocks.

Fig. 29 Installing and checking drive pins for squareness

HEAVY DUTY CLUTCHES

rim and heads are square with friction face.
2. Check clearance of slots in intermediate plate by positioning plate on drive pins. Measure clearance between drive pins and slots, which should be .006″ to .010″, and measured on same side of pins. If alignment and clearance are satisfactory, remove intermediate plate and lock drive pins in place with Allen head screws if provided in design.
3. Place front driven disc in flywheel with hub of flange towards transmission. On 14″ single plate clutch, install long hub of clutch disc towards transmission.
4. Install intermediate plate in flywheel, locating drive slots on drive pins.
5. Install rear driven disc with long hub of clutch disc towards transmission.
6. Position pressure plate and flywheel ring on flywheel and start capscrews to hold in place. Insert an aligning arbor or spare transmission main drive gear through clutch and align both discs. Tool should be inserted into pilot bearing to insure central location of discs.
7. Tighten clutch to flywheel capscrews evenly, progressing around the flywheel to prevent cocking and binding of flywheel ring pilot. Tighten capscrews to 35–40 ft-lbs torque.
8. Remove wooden blocks from between release bearing housing and flywheel ring. Then remove spline aligning tool.

Installing 15½″ Units
1. Insert spline aligning tool through clutch to align clutch discs and keep parts in place during assembly of flywheel.
2. Position assembly on flywheel, making sure that pilot end of aligning tool has entered pilot bearing.
3. Tighten capscrews gradually and evenly around flywheel. Final tightening to be 35–40 ft-lbs torque.
4. Remove wooden blocks from between clutch release bearing housing and flywheel housing. Then remove aligning tool and install transmission.

Installing Transmission
1. If clutch brake is used, place two fiber discs with a steel washer between them on main drive gear.
2. Rotate clutch release yoke so that top is back towards transmission.
3. Shift transmission into gear.
4. Position clutch release bearing housing so that flat section is at top.
5. Install transmission. Turn companion flange to align splines of drive gear with clutch driven discs. As transmission is entering clutch and flywheel, turn fingers of clutch release yoke down over clutch release bearing housing into their proper position.
6. After transmission is secured to engine, check internal clutch adjustment as outlined at the beginning of this discussion. After setting the internal adjustment, adjust external clutch linkage to provide 1½″ free pedal travel.

Long CF Clutches

DESCRIPTION

Long CF clutches are of the single-plate, dry-disc type consisting of two basic assemblies, the driven disc and the clutch cover assembly, Fig. 1. The driven disc is splined to the transmission main drive gear. The cover assembly is bolted to the engine flywheel. The pressure plate is driven by the cover through the release lever mounting lugs which extend through openings in the cover. Coil type pressure springs between the cover and pressure plate force the pressure plate against the driven member when the clutch is engaged.

No adjustment for wear is provided in the clutch itself. An individual adjustment is provided for locating each lever. In manufacturing the adjusting nuts are locked in place and should never be disturbed unless the clutch is dismantled for replacement of parts.

The clutch release bearing and support assembly slides on the transmission main drive gear bearing retainer. The release bearing on vehicles having a release fork instead of a lever is equipped with a lubrication fitting which is accessible after removing the clutch underpan. The pilot bearing, pressed into a recess in the flywheel, carries the forward end of the transmission main drive gear. This bearing requires lubrication only at time of overhaul.

The release fork (if used) is ball stud mounted in the clutch housing, with inner end of fork engaging a groove in the release bearing collar for actuating the release levers. The clutch is disengaged by a foot pedal and, in some cases, hydraulically connected to the release fork or lever.

Disassembly
1. Mark pressure plate and clutch cover so they may be reassembled in correct position to maintain the original balance.
2. Place cover and pressure plate assembly on arbor press bed with pressure plate resting on spacers ⅜″ thick, Fig. 2. Place a bar across the cover as shown, clearing all thrust plate bolts and yoke adjusting nuts. Turn arbor press screw down against bar and force cover down against press bed, compressing the pressure springs.
3. Remove two capscrews attaching each thrust plate to clutch cover. Remove adjusting nut from each release lever yoke. Remove thrust plates.
4. Slowly release arbor press until pressure of springs is relieved. Remove clutch cover from pressure plate. Remove pressure springs, then remove pressure plate and release lever assembly from arbor press bed and place on bench.
5. It is not necessary to remove yokes from levers or to remove levers from pressure plate unless necessary to replace parts.

Inspection & Repairs

Prior to inspection, wash all parts in cleaning solvent except the driven disc assembly. Wipe off the driven disc assembly. Inspect all clutch components and also flywheel and pilot bearing.

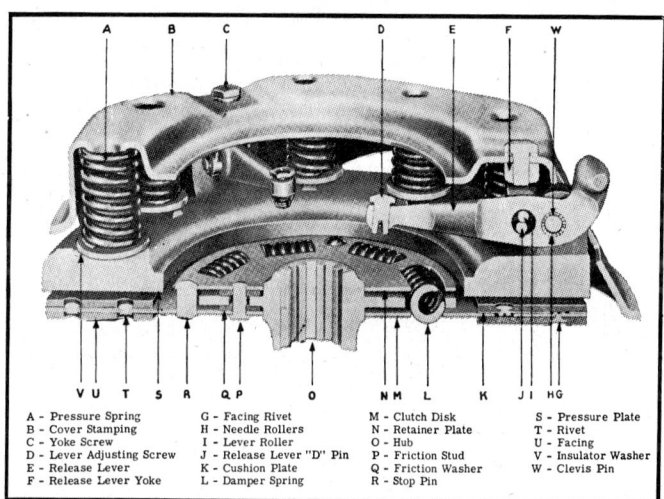

Fig. 1 Cutaway view of a typical long CF clutch

A - Pressure Spring
B - Cover Stamping
C - Yoke Screw
D - Lever Adjusting Screw
E - Release Lever
F - Release Lever Yoke
G - Facing Rivet
H - Needle Rollers
I - Lever Roller
J - Release Lever "D" Pin
K - Cushion Plate
L - Damper Spring
M - Clutch Disk
N - Retainer Plate
O - Hub
P - Friction Stud
Q - Friction Washer
R - Stop Pin
S - Pressure Plate
T - Rivet
U - Facing
V - Insulator Washer
W - Clevis Pin

Pressure Plate
The pressure plate must be replaced if the friction surface is severely heat checked or scored; if it is warped in excess of .015″ or if the driving lug slots are worn or the pin holes elongated.

The pressure plate may be salvaged if the friction surface cleans up by removing a maximum of 1/16″ of metal by machining.

Clutch Cover
Inspect clutch cover for distortion or cracks. Clutch cover flange should be flat within .015″ when checked on a surface plate.

Place cover over pressure plate and check clearance between driving lugs on pressure plate and edge of slots in cover, Fig. 3. Clearance should be not less than .008″ or more than .015″.

Release Levers
1. Check ends of release levers that contact release bearing support for wear. If excessive wear is evident, or if necessary to

HEAVY DUTY CLUTCHES

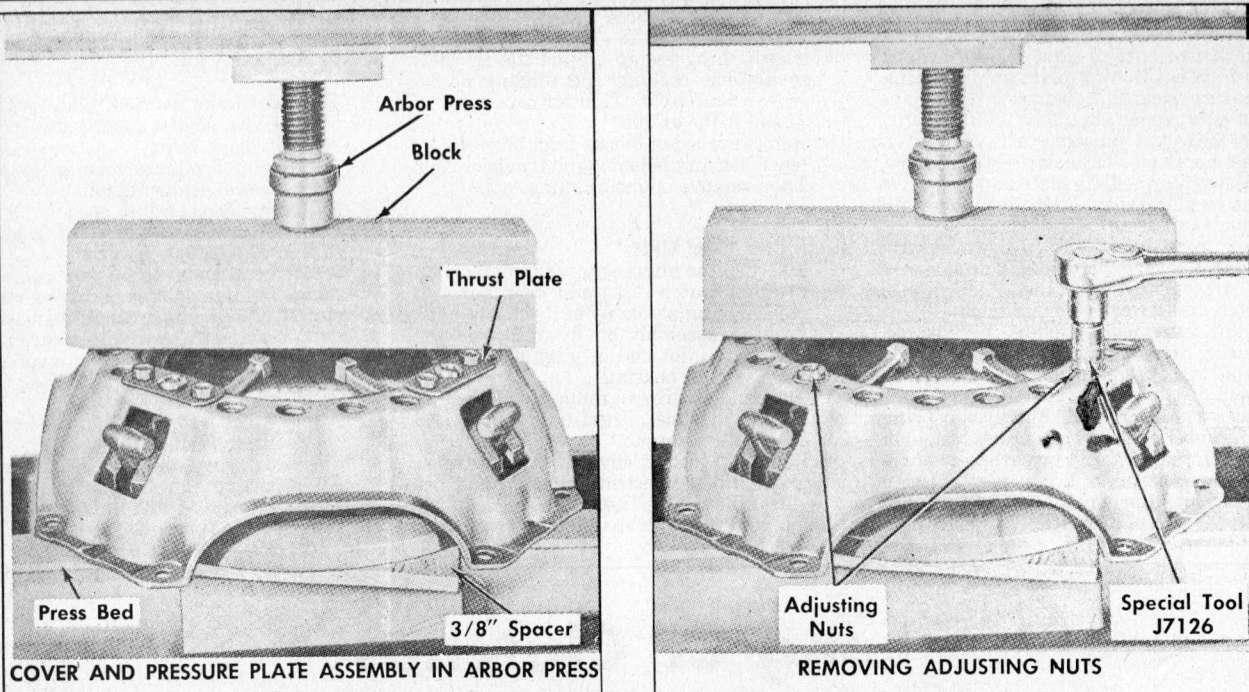

Fig. 2 Disassembling cover and pressure plate

remove levers and yokes, remove as follows:

2. Grind off swaged end of pins securing release levers in pressure plate lugs and remove pins. Remove release levers and needle bearing rollers from pressure plate. Remove pins securing yokes on release levers in same manner.
3. Inspect needle bearing bores in release levers for wear or damage. Replace levers or bearing rollers if damage is evident.
4. A pilot pin is required for installing release levers and yokes. Chamfer both ends of pin. Lay one release lever on its side on bench and place pilot pin in release yoke hole. Coat needle bearings with Lubriplate 320 or equivalent, then insert rollers around pilot pin, Fig. 4. Position release lever yoke over release lever, then insert new pin through yoke and bearings in lever, pushing out pilot pin. Use a chisel to spread end of pin to secure in place. Do not spread pin far enough to bend or distort yoke.
5. Install release lever in lugs on pressure plate, using pilot pin in same manner. Assemble and install the other release levers and yokes in same manner.

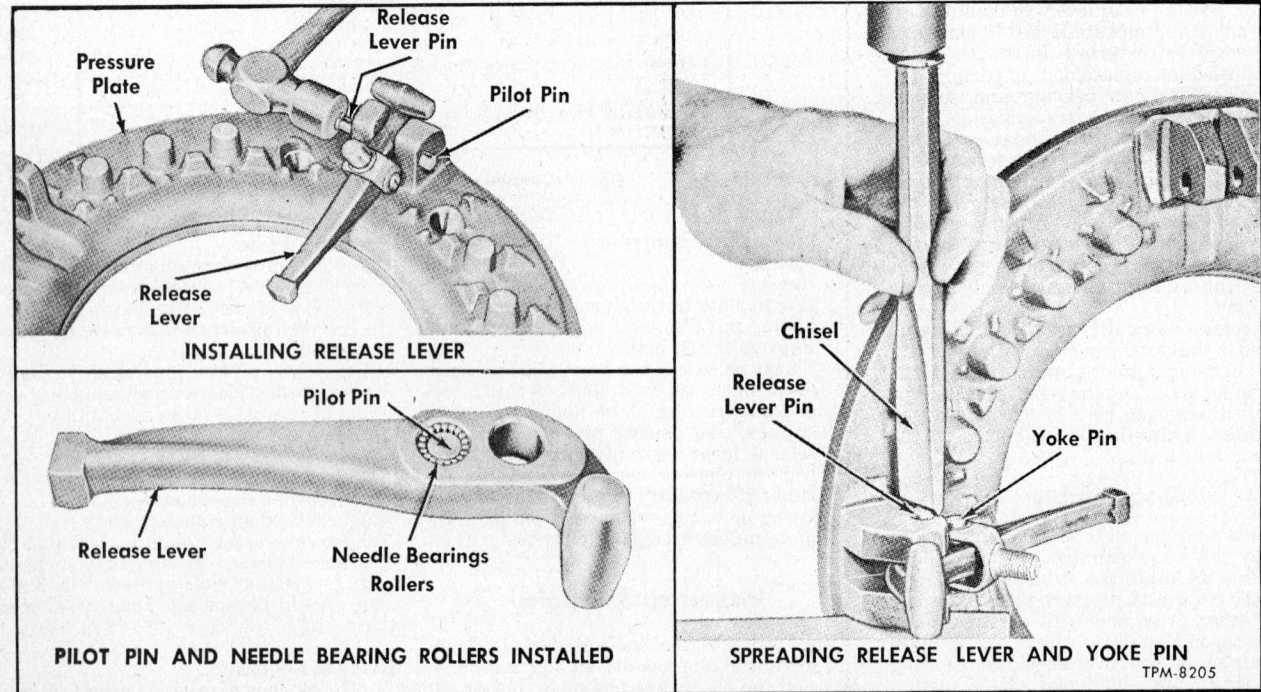

Fig. 4 Assembling and installing release lever

HEAVY DUTY CLUTCHES

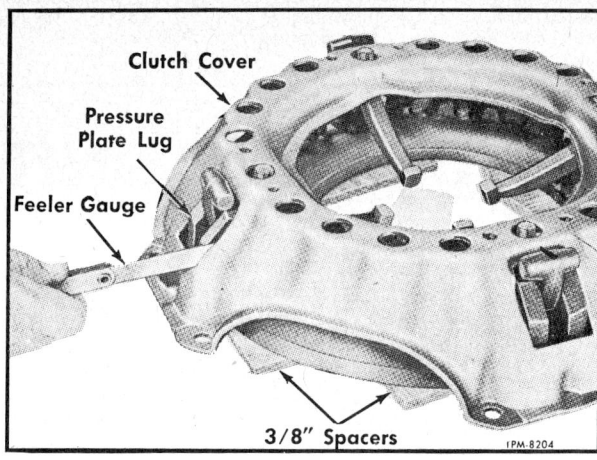

Fig. 3 Checking lug-to-cover clearance

Assembly

1. Place pressure plate face down on arbor press bed on 3/8" thick spacers, (see Fig. 2).

NOTE: If face of pressure plate was machined, shims of a thickness equal to the amount of metal removed must be installed over each spring post on pressure plate. Shims can be made locally.

2. Place a pressure spring on each spring post on pressure plate, Fig. 5.
3. Place clutch cover over springs, with release lever counterweights and yokes extending through holes in cover, and with marks made prior to disassembly aligned. If a new unmarked pressure plate or cover is used, the cover and pressure plate should be balanced after completely assembled.
4. Place bar across cover, clearing all thrust plate capscrew holes and release lever yokes.
5. Turn arbor press screw down against bar and force cover down against press bed, compressing springs. Install adjusting nut on each release lever yoke until yoke end is flush with end of nut.
6. Place thrust plate over each release lever adjusting nut and attach with two capscrews, but do not tighten. Remove assembly from press.

Release Levers, Adjust

Satisfactory operation of the clutch is dependent upon the accuracy of the lever adjustment, since the pressure plate must be parallel with the flywheel. The method of checking the position of the levers depends upon the equipment available. Regardless of how the levers are adjusted, they must be in the same plane within .005".

To make the adjustment, remove the flywheel from the engine of the vehicle being worked on. Use a new driven disc or a gauge plate of the exact same thickness as the driven disc to be used in the clutch being serviced. Adjust the levers by screwing the adjusting nut on each lever until all levers are in the same plane within .005".

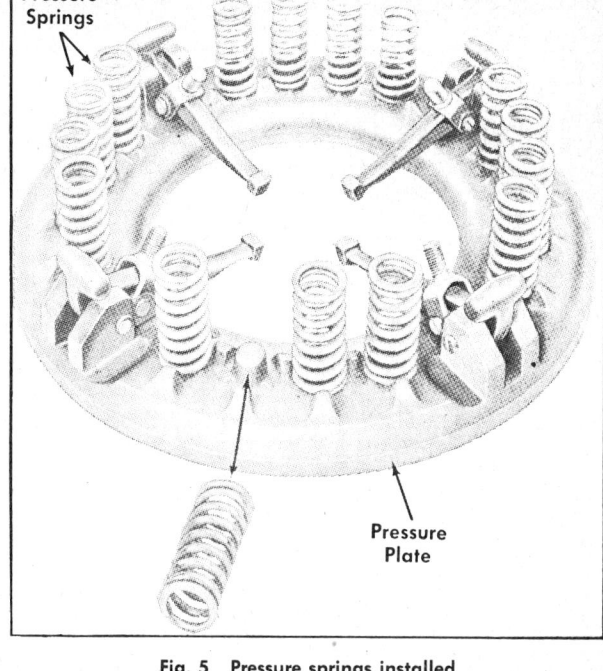

Fig. 5 Pressure springs installed

The foregoing remarks may be used if the specifications for the specific clutch being worked on are not available. For example, Fig. 6 illustrates the method of adjusting a 13" clutch. The adjustment to be made on this specific clutch model calls for a scale dimension of 1 1/32" from edge of straightedge to crown of lever tip.

Final Assembly

After completing adjustments, tighten thrust plate capscrews. Install wood blocks between release levers and cover plate to keep plate retracted until clutch is installed. Remove clutch from flywheel.

NOTE: If a new pressure plate or cover was installed, the complete assembly must be balanced within one-ounce-inch by attaching balance weights as required to side of cover with capscrews. Balance weights are available in three sizes—light, medium and heavy.

Installation

1. Place driven disc against engine flywheel, being sure portion of hub that goes to the front is placed to the front. While holding driven disc in place, move clutch cover assembly into position against driven disc. Insert an aligning tool or an old transmission main drive gear through the driven disc hub and into pilot bearing.
2. Install cover-to-flywheel bolts and lock washers. Tighten bolts alternately one turn at a time to compress clutch pressure springs evenly and to prevent possible distortion of cover flange. Remove aligning tool and wood blocks (if used) between levers and cover.
3. If release fork is used, install fork and fork ball stud by pushing it on until ball snaps into recess in fork.
4. Coat outside and inside grooves of release

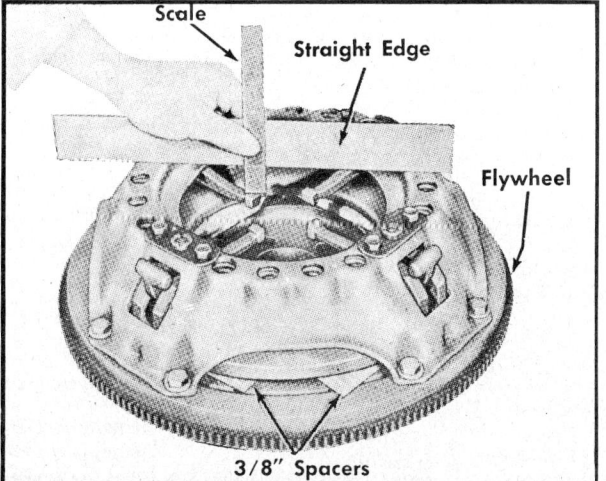

Fig. 6 Adjusting release levers

HEAVY DUTY CLUTCHES

bearing support with a small quantity of high temperature grease.

5. Before installing transmission on vehicles using release fork instead of a release yoke, release bearing and support assembly must be placed in fingers of release fork. Install transmission assembly.

MINI-PAK CLUTCH AIR-HYDRAULIC UNIT

This unit, Fig. 1, is a clutch assistor consisting of a combined compressed air and hydraulic assembly used to supply power for clutch operation on vehicles equipped with a hydraulic clutch cylinder. Clutch actuation is obtained with low clutch pedal effort while retaining "drive feel" during clutch engagement. In the event of power failure, clutch actuation is made in the usual manner except that increased pedal effort is required by the driver. The assembly consists of the following basic components:
1. A compressed air cylinder containing an air pressure operated piston and push rod.
2. A hydraulic cylinder and piston.
3. An air pressure control valve containing a hydraulic pressure operated piston, an air pressure poppet, an atmospheric pressure poppet valve and an air pressure control diaphragm.

Operation

To disengage the clutch, the clutch pedal is depressed which forces fluid out of the clutch hydraulic cylinder under pressure into the clutch assistor hydraulic cylinder and control valve piston chamber, Fig. 2. When fluid pressure acting upon the control hydraulic piston reaches a predetermined value, the valve poppet closes the atmospheric port and opens the air pressure port. This action admits compressed air to the air pressure side of the air cylinder, Fig. 3. The force from the air pressure applied to the air piston is transmitted through the push rod to the hydraulic piston of the clutch assistor and through the clutch push rod to the clutch release lever to disengage the clutch.

To engage the clutch, the driver gradually releases the foot pressure on the clutch pedal.

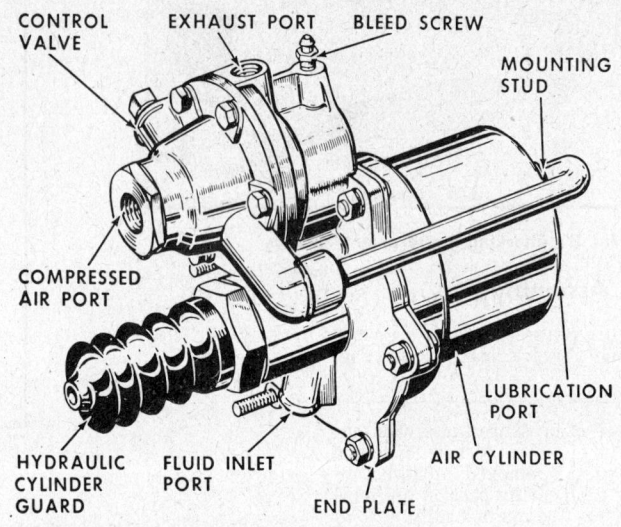

Fig. 1 Clutch air-over-hydraulic power unit

As pressure is reduced in the clutch assistor hydraulic cylinder, pressure will also be reduced in the clutch assistor hydraulic cylinder and control valve chamber. The air pressure applied to the air pressure piston will also be reduced. Fluid is then returned from the clutch assistor hydraulic cylinder in accordance with release of air pressure. When foot pressure on the clutch pedal is released sufficiently to allow the control valve to close the air pressure port and reopen the atmospheric port of the clutch assistor, the clutch is fully engaged.

Adjustment

The free pedal travel will be slight (approximately 1/4") and can be compared to the free travel that is acceptable for the pedal of hydraulic brake systems. The clutch assistor should be adjusted to provide complete engaging and disengaging of the clutch when the pedal is depressed and released. An average of 1/2" clutch release bearing travel should be provided for proper release of the clutch. The stroke of the clutch assistor hydraulic cylinder should be approximately 1 13/16".

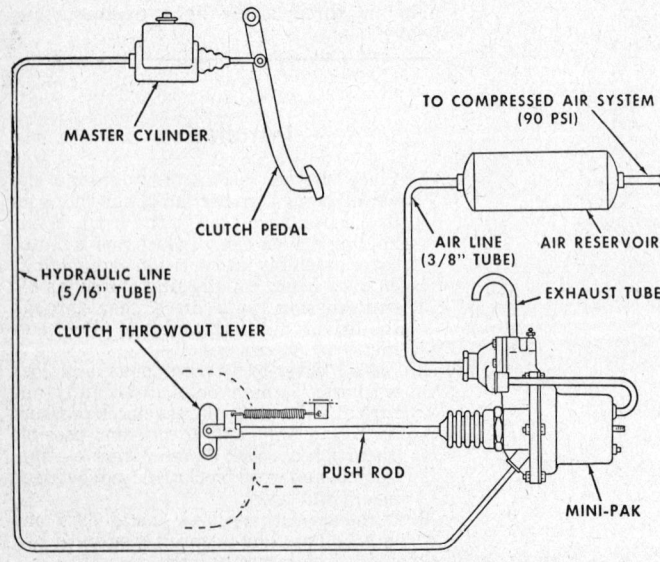

Fig. 2 Schematic diagram of typical air-hydraulic power unit

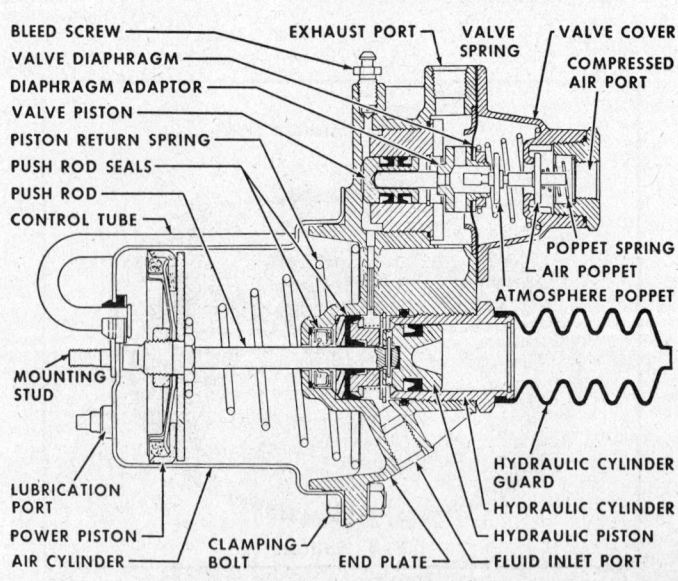

Fig. 3 Sectional view of air-hydraulic power unit

MINI-PAK AIR HYDRAULIC UNIT

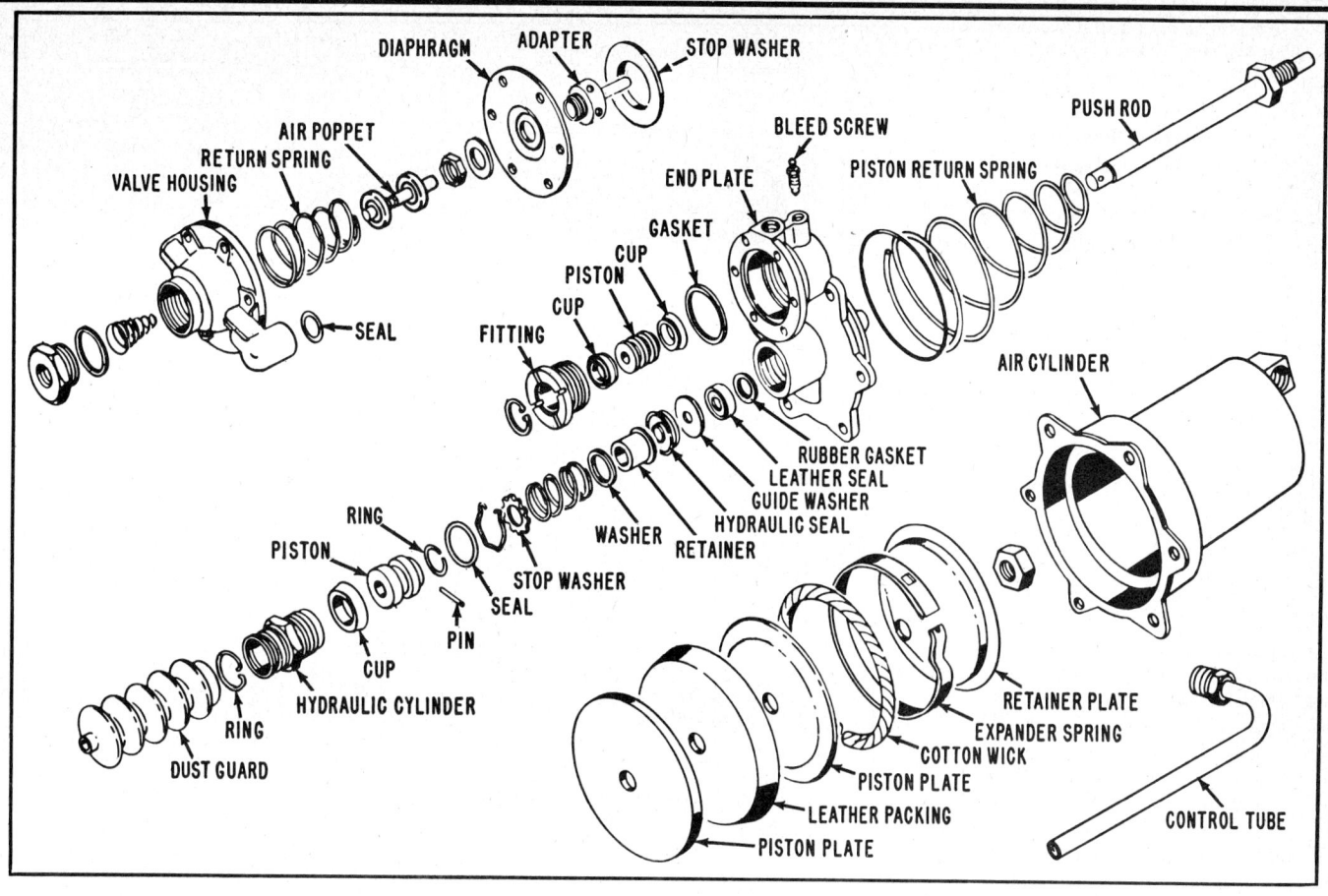

Fig. 4 Exploded view of air-hydralic power unit

Repairs

When overhauling the clutch assistor, refer to Fig. 4 as a guide. Be very careful when handling hydraulic system parts to prevent their coming in contact with mineral oils or grease. *Do not handle hydraulic piston cups or seals with greasy hands.* When overhauling the clutch assistor, always use a repair kit and install all the parts contained in the kit regardless of the condition of the old parts. If replacement of the air cylinder leather piston packing is necessary, use a piston packing kit in addition to the repair kit.

Lubrication

Do not lubricate the clutch assistor until it has been permanently installed on the vehicle. This is a safeguard. The clutch assistor should be lubricated every 10,000 miles or every six months, whichever occurs first, with vacuum cylinder oil.

To lubricate, remove the 1/8" pipe plug located in the end of the air cylinder shell and inject vacuum cylinder oil through this port until oil begins to run out, then replace pipe plug. *During lubrication, the engine should be shut off and the clutch assistor should be in the released position.*

TRANSFER CASES

DESCRIPTION

A transfer case is a gear box located between the main transmission and the rear axle. Its purpose is to transfer power from the transmission to the front driving axle as well as the rear driving axle. It also provides an extra gear reduction (LO) in the power train of the vehicle.

Most units are available with a Power Take Off and a parking brake. Every unit incorporates a Front Axle Declutch which is used to drive the front axle whenever the vehicle encounters steep grades or rough terrain. These accessories are actuated by separate shift levers located in the cab of the vehicle.

Fig. 1 shows a typical hook-up of a three-shaft transfer case, while Figs. 2 and 3 illustrate a typical hook-up of a four-shaft transfer case used with a 4 × 4 and a 6 × 6 vehicle, respectively.

TIMKEN/ROCKWELL THREE SHAFT UNIT

Disassembly

1. Referring to Figs. 4 and 5, remove drain plug and drain lubricant.
2. Remove power take-off unit and wire shims together for reassembly.
3. Remove front axle declutch unit.
4. Remove input and output shaft yokes or companion flanges.
5. Remove range shift shaft and fork.
6. Remove shift cover. Cover is spring-loaded and should be held down during removal to prevent injury. Take out detent ball, plunger and spring.
7. Loosen shift fork nut and screw shift shaft out of fork and slide it out of case.
8. Loosen set screw in mainshaft driving clutch and remove clutch and oil dam.
9. Drive tapered pins from cover and remove cover.
10. Lift mainshaft assembly from case.
11. Lift out axle drive shaft assembly and then remove idler assembly.

Disassemble Power Take-Off

1. Remove yoke from power take-off shaft.
2. Remove oil filler plug from cage. Then remove detent capscrew, spring and ball.
3. Remove oil seal cage, shims and gasket.
4. Through oil filler plug hole, loosen shift fork set screw. Disconnect shift lever and pull shift shaft from housing.

469

TRANSFER CASES

5. Use a bronze drift and drive power take-off shaft from housing. Remove shift fork and sliding clutch. *Do not disassemble further unless bearings need replacing.*

Disassemble Front Axle Declutch Unit

1. With suitable puller, remove declutch shaft yoke.
2. Remove bearing cage from housing.
3. Remove detent parts from housing.
4. Unscrew filler plug and loosen shift fork set screw.
5. Slide shift shaft out of housing. If necessary, remove shift and shaft oil seal.
6. Remove sliding clutch and shift fork.
7. If necessary, press apart bearing cage assembly. Remove outer bearing cup and oil seal.

Disassemble Shaft Assemblies

1. To disassemble mainshaft, press off front bearing and remove sliding gear. Press drive gear, bearing spacer and rear tapered bearing from shaft. Remove ball bearings and spacer from drive gear.
2. To disassemble axle drive shaft, remove set screw and pull off driving clutch. Press rear bearing and gear from shaft. Press off front bearing. Remove pilot bushing from shaft with a suitable puller if necessary.
3. To disassemble idler shaft, remove snap ring at low gear end. Slide off speedometer drive gear and remove Woodruff key. Remove front bearing snap ring. Press off low gear and remove spacer. Invert assembly and remove bearing retainer. Press off high gear and bearing.

Disassemble Case & Cover

1. Remove mainshaft front seal cage and idler shaft front bearing cap from transfer case housing.
2. Remove idler shaft bearing cover.
3. Pull axle drive shaft rear bearing cage, using puller screws. Wire shims together for reassembly. If necessary, press mainshaft rear bearing cup from cover.

Assemble Axle Drive Shaft

1. Referring to Fig. 6, press pilot bushing into bore at front of shaft.
2. Press front bearing into place.
3. Press driven gear and rear bearing into place, using a suitable sleeve that bears against inner race.
4. Slide driving clutch onto shaft and install set screw. Screw must enter recess in shaft.

Assemble Idle Shaft

1. Referring to Fig. 7, press low gear and tapered bearing into place on shaft. *Use a sleeve that will clear bearing journal.*
2. Install bearing snap ring, and Woodruff key in keyway.
3. Place speedometer drive gear on shaft and install outer snap ring.
4. Invert assembly and install spacer and high gear. Place bearing on shaft and press into position. Install bearing retainer, capscrews and lock wire.

Assemble Mainshaft

1. Referring to Fig. 8, tap rear ball bearing into gear with suitable sleeve against outer race.
2. Position bearing spacer in gear and tap front ball bearing into gear.
3. Press gear assembly onto shaft until it seats against shoulder on shaft.
4. Position spacer and press rear tapered bearing onto shaft.
5. Install sliding gear and front bearing. *Do not install oil dam and power take-off driving clutch until after transfer case cover has been attached.*

Assemble Front Axle Declutch Unit

1. Referring to Fig. 9, hold shift fork in place inside declutch housing and install sliding clutch. Position fork in groove.
2. Slide shift shaft through housing bore and into shift fork. Install and tighten set screw. Install oil filler plug.
3. Install detent ball, spring, lockwasher and lock screw in housing. Tighten lock screw.
4. Install inner and outer bearing cups in declutch bearing cage.
5. Press inner bearing on shaft with suitable sleeve.
6. Position bearing spacer on shaft and then install bearing cage.
7. Press outer bearing onto shaft. *Do not install oil seal at this time.*
8. Mount cage in vise and install yoke or flange and tighten nut to specified torque.
9. Check bearing adjustment by using a dial indicator at the end of the shaft as shown in Fig. 10. *Since the specified bearing adjustment is zero end play and zero preload, there should be no reading on the dial gauge.*
10. If there is no end play in the assembly, turn the shaft by hand to check for bearing preload. There should be no more than a slight drag on the shaft.
11. If there is end play in the assembly, use a thinner spacer between the bearings; if there is preload, use a thicker spacer.

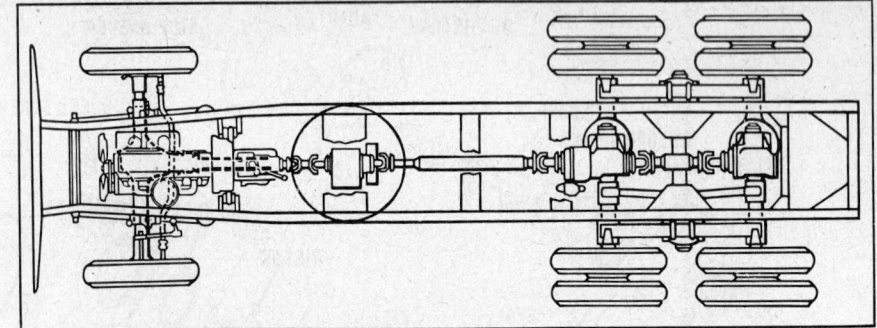

Fig. 1 Typical hook-up of a three shaft transfer case on a 6 × 6 vehicle

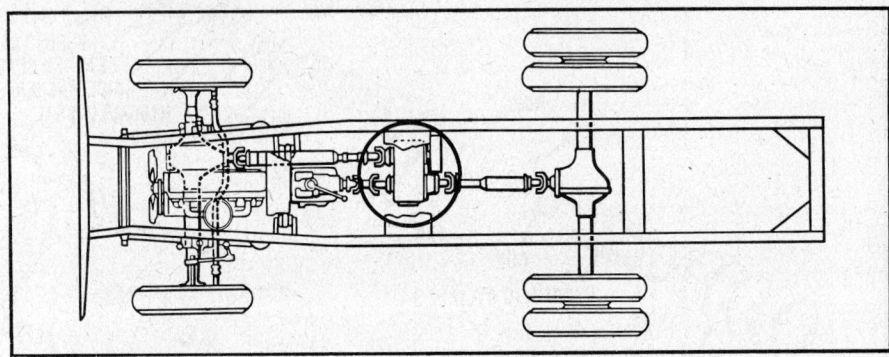

Fig. 2 Typical hook-up of a four shaft transfer case on a 4 × 4 vehicle

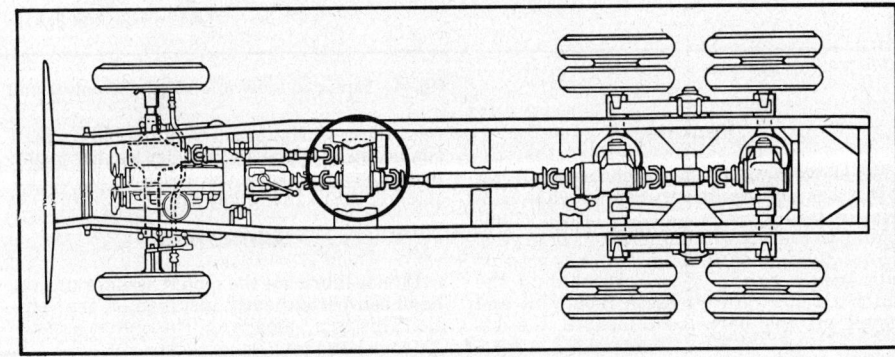

Fig. 3 Typical hook-up of a four shaft transfer case on a 6 × 6 vehicle

Transfer Cases

Fig. 12 Checking end play of power take-off unit

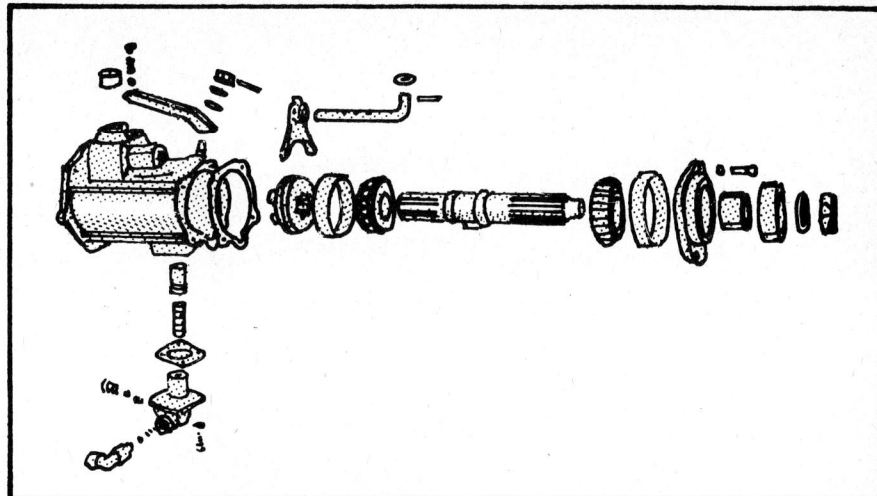

Fig. 13 Pump type P.T.O. Pump is actuated by an eccentric located on the P.T.O. shaft to assure proper lubrication during "stationary" operation of the P.T.O.

very slight bit of end play should be felt.

Final Assembly

1. Position shift fork in transfer case so that it fits in groove of mainshaft sliding gear.
2. Slide shift shaft into case and screw it into shaft fork.
3. Tighten bolt in shift fork and secure with lockwashers and nut.
4. Install detent ball in transfer case. Position plunger in detent spring and install in case.
5. Place shift fork cover gasket, breather plate and cover on case. Press cover down to compress detent plunger spring. Hold down cover and install lockwashers and capscrews.
6. Install yoke or flange on mainshaft and tighten nut to specified torque.
7. Install companion flange at rear of axle drive shaft. Tighten nut to specified torque.

Lubrication

Install and tighten drain plug. Turn transfer case upright and pour 1/2 pint of recommended lubricant through filler plug opening. Add some oil to P.T.O. and front axle declutch unit. Do not fill unit to specified level until it is installed in the vehicle. Test operation of transfer case in all ranges.

TIMKEN/ROCKWELL T-233 FOUR SHAFT UNITS

Disassemble

1. Referring to Fig. 15, remove all yokes or flanges.
2. Remove P.T.O. assembly or rear cover if P.T.O. is not used.
3. Remove transfer case cover.
4. Remove detent balls and springs.
5. Pull both shift shafts out through front of case if possible. Otherwise, use a soft metal drift and drive shafts and expansion plugs out through rear of case.
6. Remove oil seals from front of case if necessary.
7. Lift out range and declutch forks.
8. Pull front output shaft and declutch collar from case.
9. Slide a bar through front output shaft gear and tap out small and large expansion plugs located in brake section.
10. Remove brake drum, brake hub retaining ring and hub with a suitable puller. Remove brake shoes and lever, and brake backing plate.
11. Remove idler shaft front and rear bearing caps. Wire forward cap shims together for reassembly.
12. Remove bearing retainer plate from front end of idler shaft and press shaft out through rear of case. Lift out low gear, spacer and front bearing.
13. Remove high gear. Tap front bearing cup from case. Remove snap ring and press rear bearing from idler shaft.
14. Remove front output gear rear bearing cap and gasket.
15. Take off bearing snap ring and tap front output gear into case. Reach through cover opening and lift out gear and bearing. Press off radial bearing.
16. Take off rear output shaft front and rear bearing caps. Wire shims together for reassembly.
17. Remove input shaft front bearing cover. Wire shim pack together for reassembly.
18. Using a block of wood between sliding gear and case, press out input shaft and front bearing. Do not pound on shaft if gear becomes bound. Lift out sliding gear, drive gear and spacer. Remove front bearing from shaft.

Assemble P.T.O. Unit

1. If this unit was disassembled, refer to Fig. 16 and proceed as follows:
2. Install ball bearings on P.T.O. shaft.
3. Position wiper against inner bearing. Install snap ring in groove of outer bearing.
4. Slide shaft into housing and install sliding clutch on inner end.
5. Position new gasket and install oil seal cage.
6. Place shift fork in groove of sliding clutch. Slide shift shaft into bore of fork.
7. Line up recess in shaft with set screw and tighten screw. Lock wire set screw to fork.
8. Install expansion plug in shift shaft hole.
9. If necessary, replace shift shaft oil seal in front of housing.

BOLT AND STUD NUTS

LOCATION ON UNIT	DIA. INCH	NO. THDS.	TORQUE—LB FT. MIN.	MAX.
Case and Cover	3/8"	16	38	42
Main Shaft and Rear Bearing Cap	7/16"	14	60	66
P.T.O. to Cover	7/16"	14	60	66
Drive Shaft Rear Bearing Cap	7/16"	14	60	66
Declutch to Case	7/16"	14	60	66
Declutch Housing Cap	3/8"	16	38	42
Main Shaft Yoke Nut	1 1/4"	18	300	400
Declutch Shaft Yoke Nut	1 1/4"	18	300	400
Drive Shaft Yoke Nut	1 1/4"	18	300	400
P.T.O. Shaft Yoke Nut	1"	20	300	400

CAP SCREWS

LOCATION ON UNIT	DIA. INCH	NO. THDS.	TORQUE—LB FT. MIN.	MAX.
Shift Cover	3/8"	16	38	42
Idler Shaft Front and Rear Bearing Caps	7/16"	14	60	66
Main Shaft Front Bearing Cap	7/16"	14	60	66
Idler Shaft Bearing Retainer	7/16"	14	60	66
P.T.O. Housing Cap	5/16"	18	22	24

Fig. 14 Torque specifications for three shaft transfer case. Torques given are for parts coated with machine oil. For dry (or "as received") parts, increase torque 10%. For parts coated with multipurpose gear oil, decrease torque 10%. Nuts on studs use same torque as for driving the stud

TRANSFER CASES

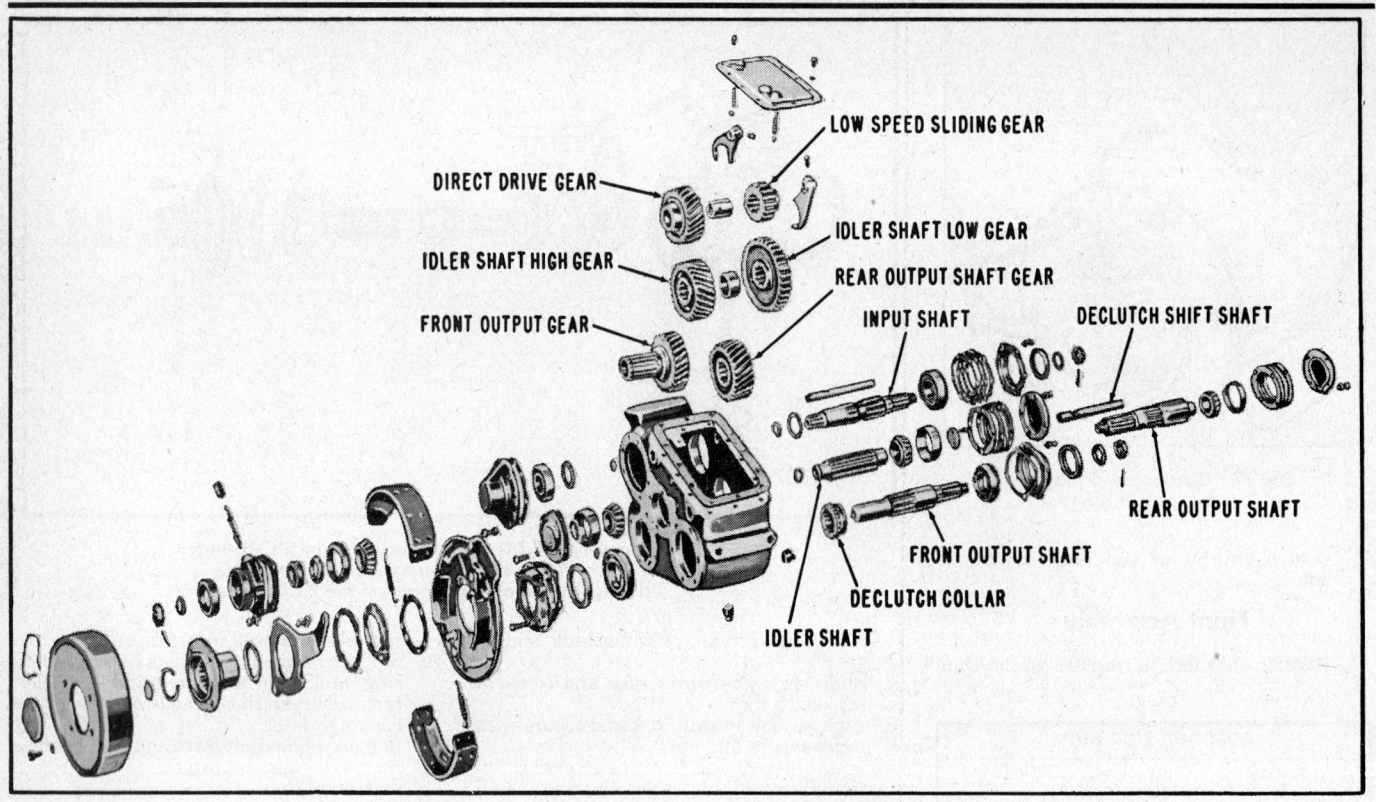

Fig. 15 Timken/Rockwell T-233 "clover leaf" four shaft transfer case

Assemble Input Shaft

1. Referring to Fig. 17, install front bearing on shaft with shielded side against shoulder.
2. Start shaft into case. Mount sliding gear, spacer and drive gear (with bushing) on shaft.
3. Tap shaft into position using a suitable sleeve against inner race of front bearing.
4. Position original shim pack plus .010" more to make sure there is end play in the assembly. Install front cover and tighten capscrews.
5. Place thrust washer on shaft and install rear bearing with shielded side toward inside.
6. Position new gasket and attach the P.T.O. or cover to rear side of case.
7. Mount a dial indicator on the unit. Set the stem against the front end of the input shaft and check the amount of end play in the assembly. Remove enough shims from under the bearing cap to arrive at an adjustment of .003–.005" end play.
8. Reposition bearing cap, insert capscrews and torque to specifications. Remove P.T.O. for convenience in handling transfer case.

Install Rear Output Shaft

1. Referring to Fig. 18, press front bearing onto shaft with suitable sleeve.
2. Hold rear output gear in position inside case and slide shaft through it.
3. Install front bearing cup and original shim pack plus .010". Install bearing cover with lockwashers and tighten capscrews.
4. Press rear bearing on shaft with a suitable sleeve. Then tap bearing cup into position.
5. Install spacer and speedometer drive gear over shaft.
6. Position new gasket, bearing cap and oil seal over shaft. Install lockwashers and capscrews and tighten to specified torque.
7. Rotate shaft to seat bearings. Mount a dial indicator against rear end of shaft to check the amount of end play in the assembly. Remove enough shims from under the front bearing cap to obtain an adjustment of zero end play and zero preload.

Install Front Output Gear

The front output gear must be installed in the case before the idler assembly is installed.

1. Install ball bearing on hub of gear.
2. Position gear and bearing in case and install snap ring on bearing.
3. Install rear bearing cap over new gasket. Insert capscrews and lockwashers and tighten to specified torque.

Fig. 16 Power take-off for Timken/Rockwell T-233 four shaft transfer case

TRANSFER CASES

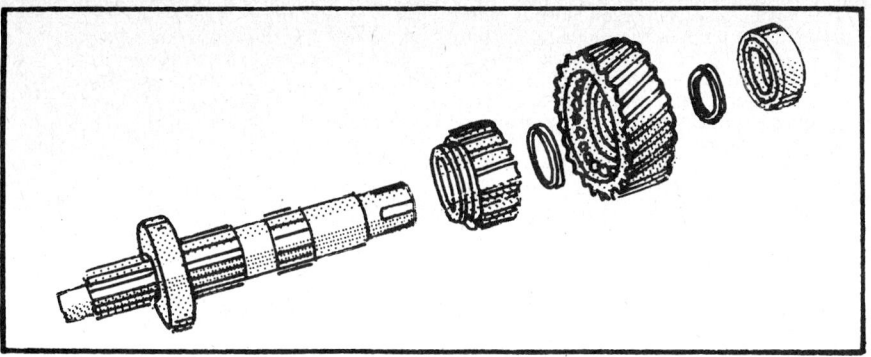

Fig. 17 Input shaft components. Timken/Rockwell T-233 four shaft case

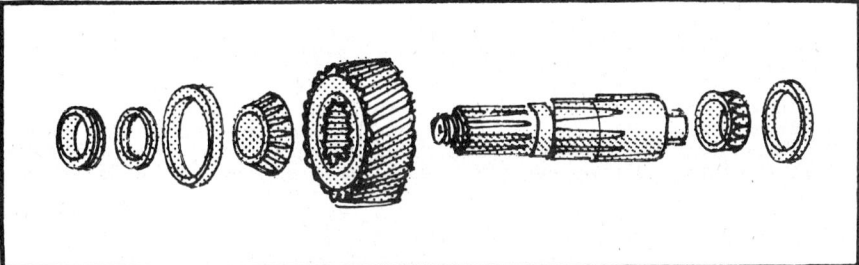

Fig. 18 Rear output shaft components. Timken/Rockwell T-233 four shaft case

Fig. 19 Idler gear components. Timken/Rockwell T-233 four shaft case

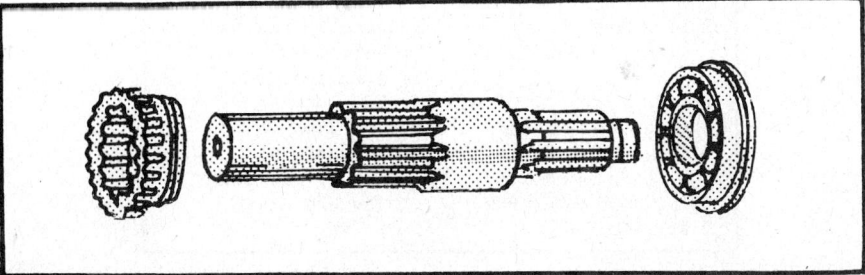

Fig. 20 Front output shaft components. Timken/Rockwell four shaft case

Install Idler Gear

1. Referring to Fig. 19, press rear bearing on idler shaft. Install snap ring.
2. Hold high gear in position inside case and tap idler shaft through it with a soft hammer. Short hub side of gear goes to the outside (rear).
3. Install rear spacer on shaft and then install low gear with long hub toward outside (front) of case.
4. With shaft in position, install rear bearing cup in case. Use a new gasket and install rear bearing cap, lockwashers and capscrews. Tighten to specified torque.
5. Drive front bearing onto idler shaft. Hold shaft rigid to avoid damaging rear bearing and cup. Install bearing retainer plate. Lock wire capscrews.
6. Tap front bearing cup into place.
7. Install enough shims to set up end play in the idler assembly. Install front bearing cap and secure with lockwashers and capscrews.
8. Mount a dial indicator on the case with the stem set against the inside face of the low gear. Check the amount of end play by working the assembly back and forth with two pry bars. Remove enough shims to obtain .003–.005″ end play.

Install Front Output Shaft

1. Referring to Fig. 20, install bearing on shaft with bearing snap ring toward outside.
2. Install sliding collar on shaft and slide shaft into case.
3. With shaft in position, install new gasket, bearing cap and oil seal, lockwashers and capscrews. Tighten to specified torque.

Install Parking Brake

1. Position new gasket and mount backing plate, deflector and stamped washer. Insert capscrews and star washers and tighten to specified torque.
2. Position brake lever on backing plate.
3. Position brake shoes on backing plate with actuating pawl in web slot.
4. Hook up brake shoe return springs.
5. Slide brake hub over splines of front output gear. Install retaining ring.
6. Install brake drum. Tighten capscrews to specified torque and lock with wire.
7. Install expansion plugs. The smaller plug goes in the bore of the front output gear and the larger in the brake drum.

Install Shift Shafts

1. If necessary, install new shift shaft oil seals in case.
2. Position declutch fork in collar.
3. Grease declutch shift shaft and slide it into case and through fork.
4. With shift shaft in position, insert and tighten set screw and lock with wire.
5. Position range shift fork in sliding gear.
6. Slide range shift shaft through fork. Install and tighten set screw and lock with wire.
7. Install expansion plugs at rear of case.
8. Place detent balls and springs in case.
9. Install cover with new gasket and tighten capscrews to specified torque.
10. Install P.T.O. with new gasket.
11. Install yokes or flanges and nuts and torque to specifications.

Lubrication

Install drain plug. Turn transfer case up-

TRANSFER CASES

LOCATION ON UNIT	DIAMETER	NO. THREADS	TORQUE—LB. FT	
			Min.	Max.
Top cover	3/8"	16	38	42
Bearing caps (all)	3/8"	16	38	42
Brake drum	7/16"	14	60	66
Brake mounting	7/16"	14	60	66
P.T.O. to case	3/8"	16	38	42
P.T.O. bearing cap to housing	3/8"	16	38	42
P.T.O. top cover	3/8"	16	38	42
YOKE OR FLANGE NUTS				
Input shaft	1"	20	300	400
Front output shaft	1"	20	300	400
Rear output shaft	1"	20	300	400
P.T.O shaft	1"	20	300	400

Fig. 21 Torque specifications for four shaft transfer case. Torques given apply to parts coated with machine oil. For dry (or "as received") parts, increase torque 10%. For parts coated with multipurpose gear oil, decrease torque 10%. Nuts on studs use same torque as for driving the stud

right and pour 1/2 pint of recommended gear lubricant through filler plug opening. Add some oil to P.T.O. Do not fill unit to specified level until it is installed in the vehicle.

COLEMAN MODELS 22 & 42

Model 22 declutcher type transfer case transmits power to the front axle only when required. It does not provide differential action between front and rear axles. The transfer case must be disengaged except when needed for traction.

Model 42 transfer case transmits power to the front axle at all times with full differential action between front and rear output shafts. The differential may be locked out for positive drive front and rear. The differential should always be unlocked under conditions of good traction.

Both models are two speed units (direct and low) and are shifted by two shift levers through the cab floor.

Disassembly

1. Position unit on bench with front housing down. Remove parking brake parts.
2. Turn assembly over and remove front output shaft end yoke.
3. Remove input shaft end yoke.
4. Remove external parts from case.
5. Remove snap ring and use a suitable puller to remove output shaft, Fig. 22.
6. Remove front output shaft sliding lock gear from front housing.
7. Remove center shaft front bearing cap and shim set from front housing. *Tag shim set for reassembly.*
8. Remove input shaft front bearing cap and shim set from front housing. *Tag shim set for reassembly.*
9. Turn case over and remove output shaft bearing case and shim set. *Tag shim set for reassembly.*

NOTE: On Model 42, rear output shaft, ball bearing assembly and speedometer drive gear will come out with bearing cap. After removing bearing cap and shaft, remove differential assembly from rear of case.

On Model 22, pull rear output shaft assembly out of case rear housing. Output shaft consists of shaft, outer bearing, speedometer drive gear, bearing spacer, rear output shaft gear, inner bearing assembly, pilot bushing, and two output shaft gear keys.

10. Remove center shaft bearing cap from rear housing.
11. Remove P.T.O. cover.
12. Using a spanner wrench, remove first input shaft high gear rear bearing nut. Then remove second shaft high gear rear bearing nut.
13. Remove input shaft high gear rear bearing from shaft.
14. Remove P.T.O. adapter from rear housing.
15. Separate front and rear housings.
16. Remove declutcher or differential shift bar and fork from rear housing. Remove high-low shift bar and fork.
17. Remove input shaft from high speed gear, and high speed gear from rear housing.
18. Remove center shaft assembly.
19. Remove shift bars from forks.
20. Using a plastic hammer, tap rear output shaft inner bearing cup from rear housing. Tap center shaft rear bearing cup out of rear housing.
21. Tap center shaft front bearing cup and input shaft front bearing cup out of front housing.

Reassembly

After disassembling sub-assemblies as required to install new parts, reassemble the transfer case in the reverse order of disassembly, observing the following:

1. Use all new gaskets and oil seals.
2. When installing shims and bearing caps, be sure oil drain-back holes and passages are not covered.
3. Great care should be taken in setting tapered roller bearings so they are neither too tight nor too loose. As a general guide, the front output shaft bearing should be set from .003" to .005" loose.
4. The input shaft high gear rear bearing should be set from .000" to .002" clearance.
5. Both center shaft bearings should be set from .003" to .005" loose.
6. The lower rear output shaft bearing should be set from .003" to .005" loose.
7. To adjust bearings, tighten bearings caps to a snug fit. Then measure the gap between inside of bearing cap and housing with a feeler gauge. Add the foregoing dimensions to the measured gap for total shim thickness. Shims are available in .005", .0075" and .020" thicknesses.

DANA MODEL 21

This manually-shifted transfer case controls the power from the engine and transmission to the front driving axle. There are two positions for the transfer case: front axle drive engaged and front axle drive disengaged.

As shown in Fig. 25, when the transfer case front shaft clutch collar is in neutral, power from the main transmission drives the transfer case input shaft gear. The shaft gear drives the idler shaft and the gear that free

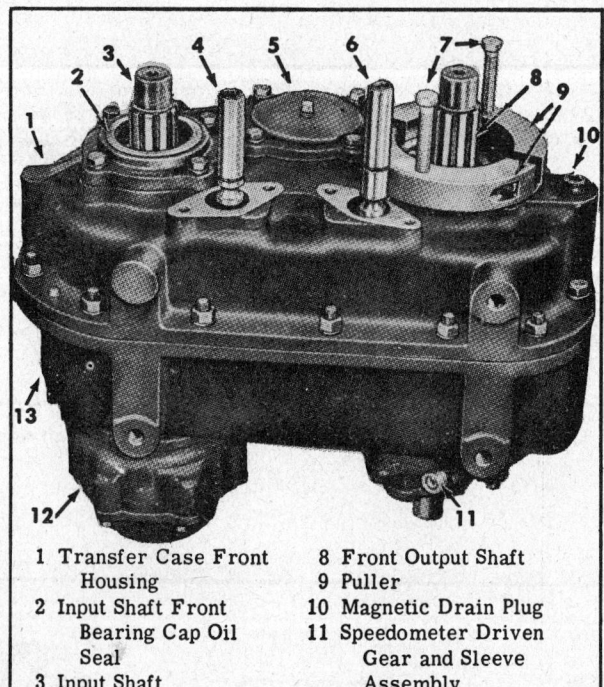

1 Transfer Case Front Housing
2 Input Shaft Front Bearing Cap Oil Seal
3 Input Shaft
4 High-Low Shift Bar
5 Center Shaft Front Bearing Cap
6 Declutcher Shift Bar
7 Puller Screws
8 Front Output Shaft
9 Puller
10 Magnetic Drain Plug
11 Speedometer Driven Gear and Sleeve Assembly
12 Power Take-off Adapter
13 Transfer Case Rear Housing

Fig. 22 Removing front output shaft assembly. Coleman units

TRANSFER CASES

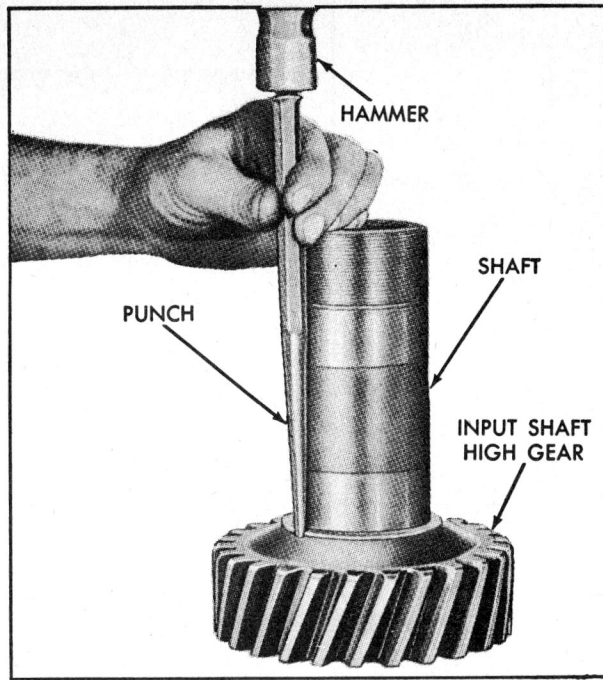

Fig. 23 Removing input shaft high gear bearing cup. Coleman units

runs on the front output shaft.

There is only power delivered to the rear axle because of the direct hook-up of the main transmission to the rear wheel output shaft.

When the transfer case shift lever is shifted into the 4-wheel drive position, it pulls the front output shaft collar forward into engagement with the clutch teeth of the main drive gears. This locks the front output shaft to the idler shaft gear.

The power from the main transmission flows from the drive gear in two directions: Direct drive to the rear axle flows through the rear output shaft. Direct drive to the front axle flows through the idler shaft drive gear through the front output shaft gear direct to the front axle.

Disassembly

1. Remove case cover, Fig. 26.
2. Remove set screw securing shift fork to rail. Tap shift rail rearward, then remove shift rail cap from rear of case.
3. Remove shift rail and fork.
4. Remove detent spring and ball that engages front drive shift rail.
5. Remove front and rear flanges.
6. Remove rear bearing retainer and output shaft as an assembly.
7. Remove front and rear idler shaft covers.
8. Drive idler shaft and rear idler bearing rearward and out of case. Then lift front bearing and idler gear from case.
9. Remove front output shaft bearing retainer and gasket. Remove retainer seal if worn or damaged.
10. Remove front output shaft rear cover and shims. Tie shims together for reassembly.
11. Tap end of front output shaft toward front of case to remove front bearing cup. Remove rear bearing cup by tapping front output shaft rearward.
12. Wedge front output shaft front bearing away from main drive gear to allow removal of snap ring from its groove in shaft. Then drive output shaft and rear bearing out of case.
13. Lift sliding gear, main drive gear, front bearing, thrust washer and snap ring from case.
14. Remove shift rail seal from case bore if it is worn or damaged.

Reassembly

After disassembling sub-assemblies as required to install new parts, Figs. 27, 28, 29, reassemble transfer case as follows:

1. While holding drive gear, sliding gear and thrust washer in case, install front output shaft through gears and washer

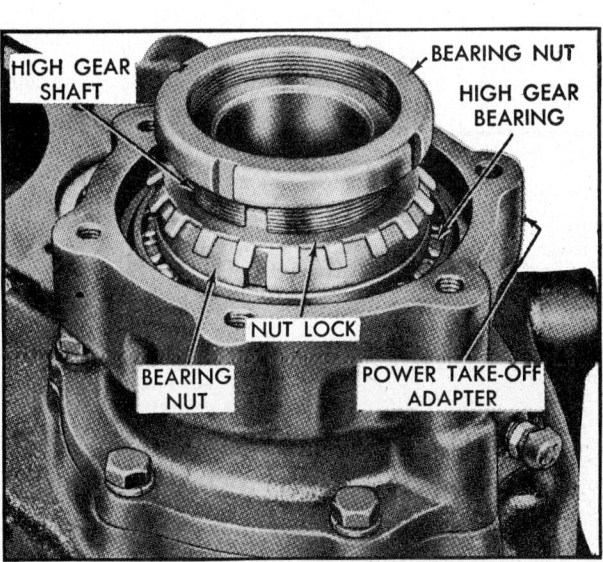

Fig. 24 Installing input shaft high gear bearing nuts. Coleman units

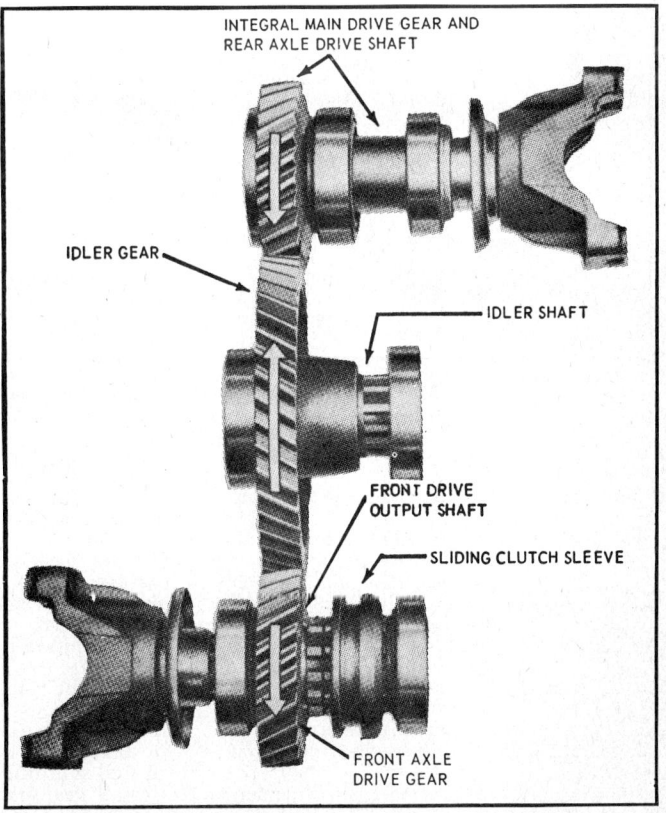

Fig. 25 Ford single speed transfer case gear train

TRANSFER CASES

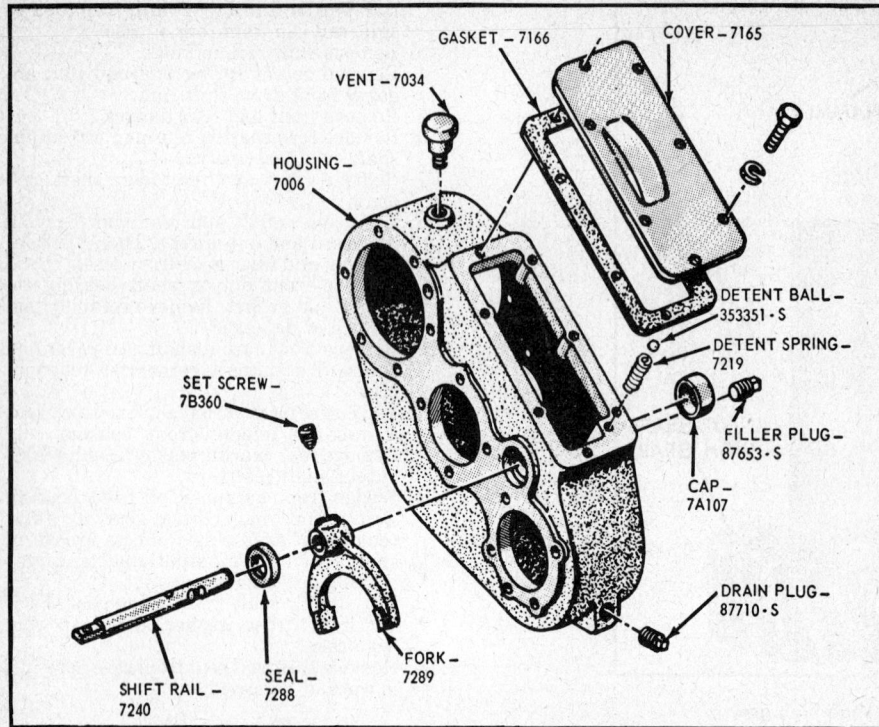

Fig. 26 Dana model 21 transfer case housing and related parts

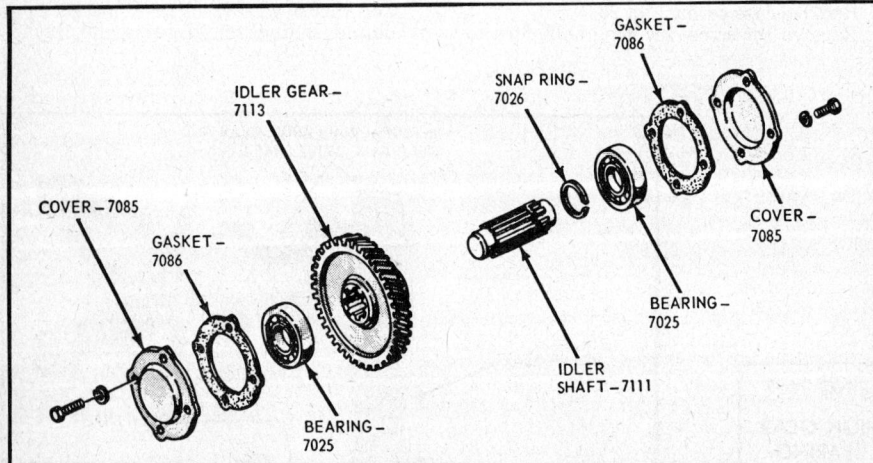

Fig. 27 Dana model 21 transfer case idler shaft assembly

from rear of case, Fig. 29. Install snap ring.
2. Install front output shaft rear bearing cup.
3. Install front output shaft rear bearing cover and shims to case. Apply gasket sealer to attaching bolts and tighten bolts. With cover installed, apply gasket sealer to outer edges of adjusting shims.
4. Install front output shaft front bearing on shaft. Install front bearing cup.
5. If front bearing retainer oil seal was removed, install a new seal. Install bearing retainer and gasket to case.
6. Install flange, O-ring, washer and nut on front output shaft.
7. Install dial indicator on front drive output shaft and check end play. End play should be .003" to .005". If necessary,

increase or decrease shim pack thickness at front output shaft rear cover.
8. Install idler gear in case and install idler shaft through gear. Install front bearing on shaft.
9. Install front and rear idler covers and gaskets to case.
10. Install a new shaft rail seal in case if it was removed.
11. Install shift rail detent ball and spring in top of case.
12. Slide shift rail into case, and position shift fork on rail as rail enters case. Depressing ball and spring will allow rail to pass. Secure fork to rail with set screw. Install shift rail cap.
13. Install rear output shaft and bearing retainer to case.
14. Install flange, O-ring, washer and nut on

rear output shaft.

NEW PROCESS EXC. MODELS, 203 & 205
Disassembly

Rear Output Shaft
1. Loosen rear output shaft yoke nut, Fig. 30.
2. Remove front bearing retainer.
3. Remove front output shaft rear bearing retainer bolts and tap output shaft to remove shaft, gear and rear bearing retainer. Remove sliding clutch front output gear and bearing which will have remained in case, Fig. 31.
4. Remove gear retaining ring and discard, Fig. 32. Remove thrust washer and pin from shaft.
5. Remove gear, needle bearings and spacer. If necessary to replace front output shaft rear bearing, replace bearing and retainer as a unit.

Shift Rail & Fork Assemblies
1. Remove two poppet nuts, springs and, using a magnet, remove the balls.
2. Using a punch, remove cup plugs on top of case.
3. With both shift rails in neutral, remove shift fork pins, Fig. 33.
4. Remove clevis pins and shift rail link.
5. Remove shift rails, upper (range) rail first, Fig. 34.
6. Remove shift forks and sliding clutch from case.
7. Remove front output high gear, washer and bearing. Remove shift rail cup plugs.
8. Remove snap ring in front of bearing. Tap shaft out rear of case. Tap bearing out of case.
9. Tap case on P.T.O. and remove two interlock pins from inside of case.

Idler Gear
1. Remove idler gear shaft nut.
2. Remove idler shaft rear cover.
3. Tap idler shaft out of case, Fig. 35.
4. Remove idler gear from case.

Assembly, Fig. 36

The procedure for reassembling the transfer case is largely the reverse of the disassembly. However, observe the following:
1. Torque idler shaft lock nut to 100-200 ft.-lbs.
2. Install idler shaft cover with flat located adjacent to front output shaft rear cover.
3. Tip case on P.T.O. opening when installing range rail lock pin.
4. When installing front output shaft snap ring, position the snap ring so the opening is opposite the pin.
5. Torque yoke lock nut to 100-200 ft.-lbs.

DANA MODEL 20 & NEW PROCESS 205
Disassembly

1. Remove cover from bottom of case.
2. Remove poppet hole retainer cap screws from the outside of the front bearing retainer.
3. Remove intermediate gear shaft lock plate at rear side of transfer case.

TRANSFER CASES

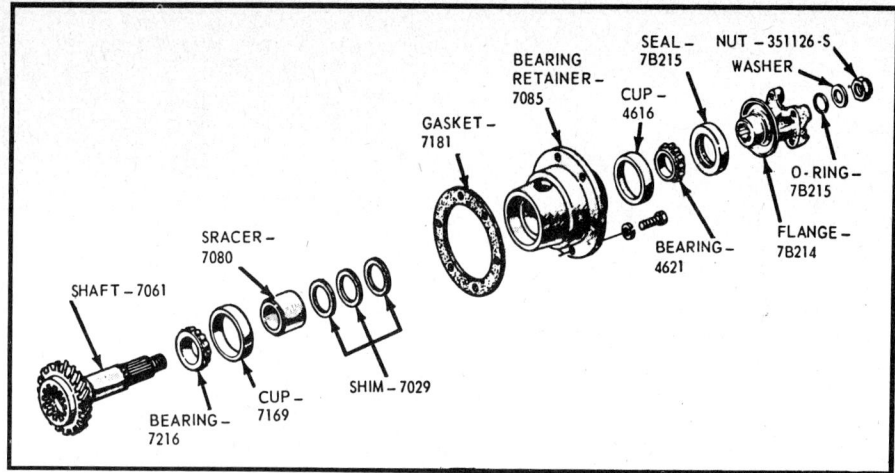

Fig. 28 Dana model 21 transfer case rear drive output shaft assembly

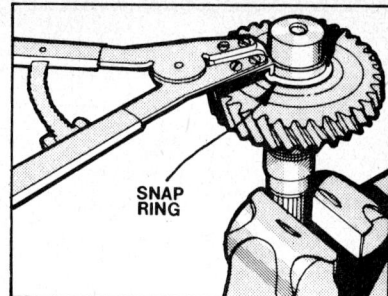

Fig. 32 Removing gear retaining ring. New Process

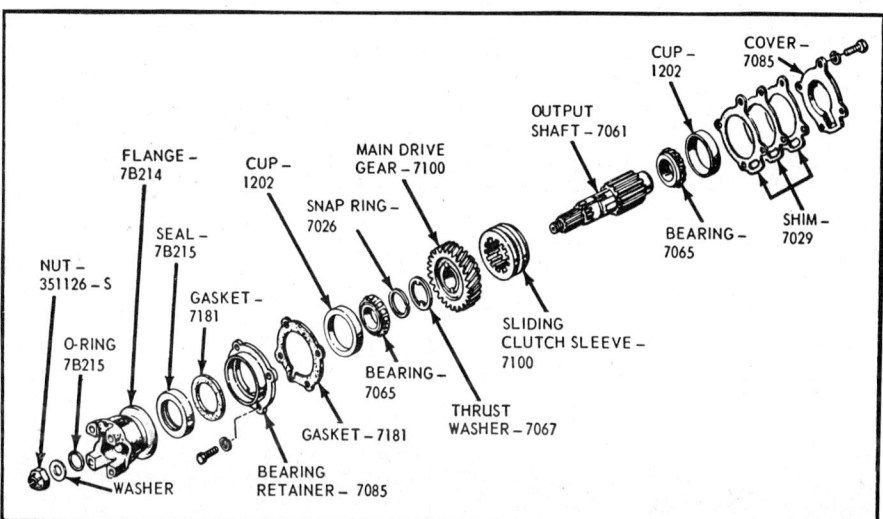

Fig. 29 Dana model 21 transfer case front output shaft assembly

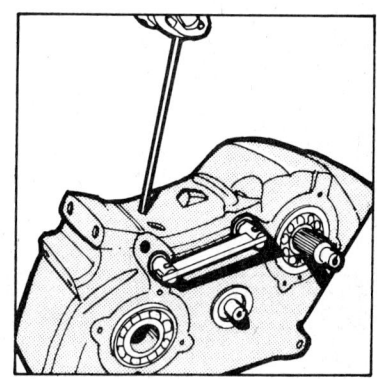

Fig. 33 Removing shift fork pins. New Process

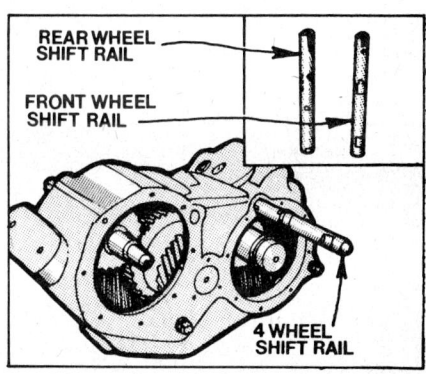

Fig. 34 Shift rail removed. New Process

4. Using dummy shaft, drive intermediate shaft out of rear of case, Fig. 37. Remove intermediate gear and thrust washers from case.
5. Remove complete rear output shaft sub assembly, Fig. 38.
6. Remove front output shaft yoke.
7. Loosen dog set screw from 2-wheel drive shaft fork. Rotate shift rail to pre-load poppet ball and pull rail out of the housing. Remove shift fork and clutch gear from case. Remove poppet ball and spring from retainer.
8. Remove front output shaft rear cover and shims.
9. Remove front output shaft bearing retainer and gasket.
10. Tap on front end of front output shaft removing shaft from rear of case, Fig. 39.

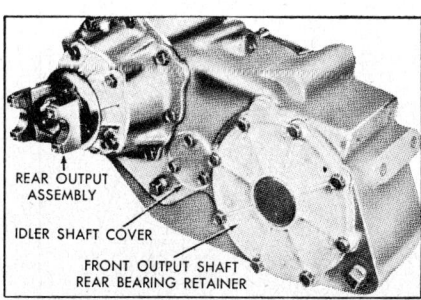

Fig. 30 Rear view of transfer case. New Process

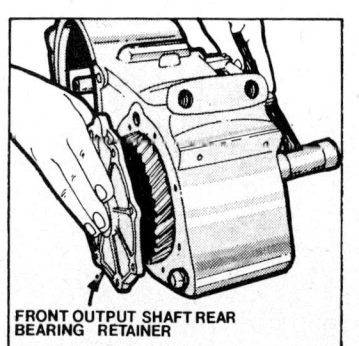

Fig. 31 Removing front output shaft rear bearing retainer. New Process

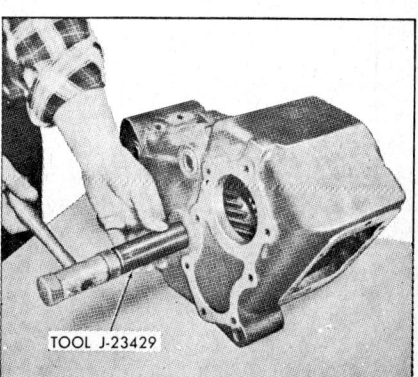

Fig. 35 Removing idler gear shaft. New Process

479

1
2
3
4
5
6
7
8
9
10
11
12
13
14
15
16
17
18
19
20
21
22
23
24
25
26
27
28
29
30
31
32
33
34
35
36
37
38
39
40
41
42
43
44
45
46
47
48
49
50
51
52
53
54
55
56

1
2
3
4
5
6
7
8
9
10
11
12
13
14
15
16
17
18
19
20
21
22
23
24
25
26
27
28
29
30
31
32
33
34
35
36
37
38
39
40
41
42
43
44
45
46
47
48
49
50
51
52
53
54
55
56
57
58
59
60
61
62
63
64
65
66
67
68
69
70
71
72

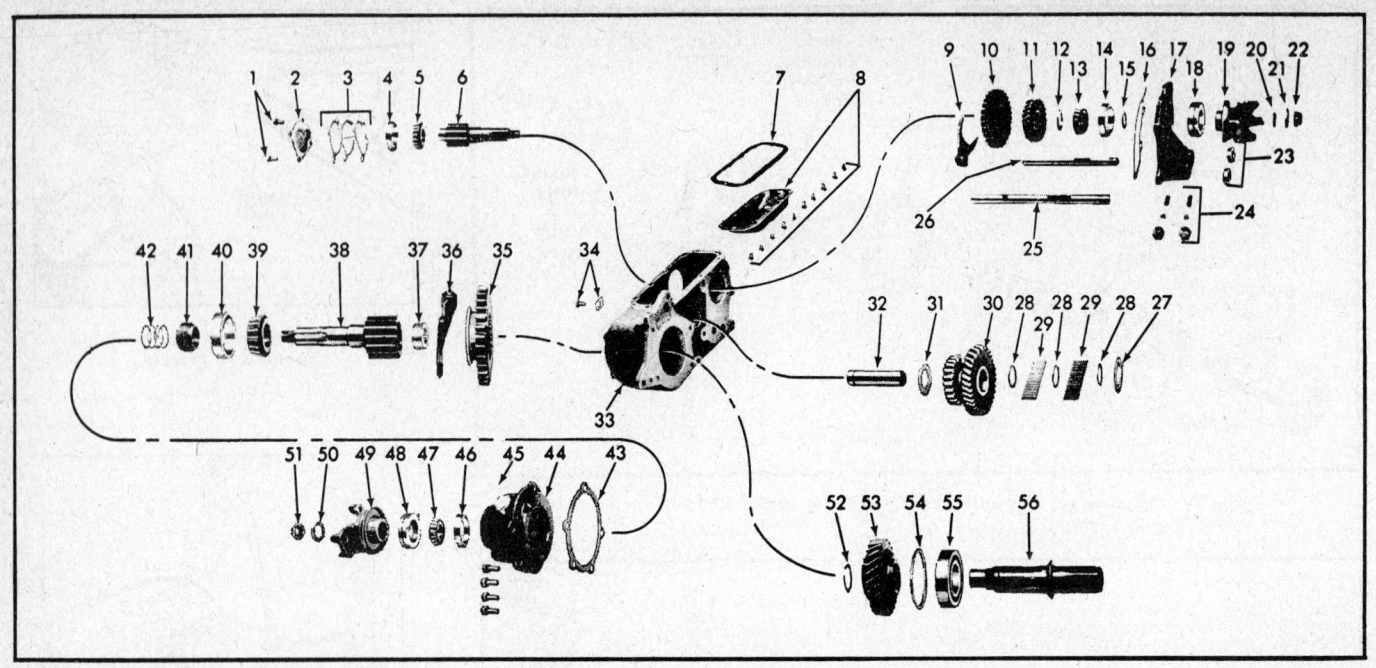

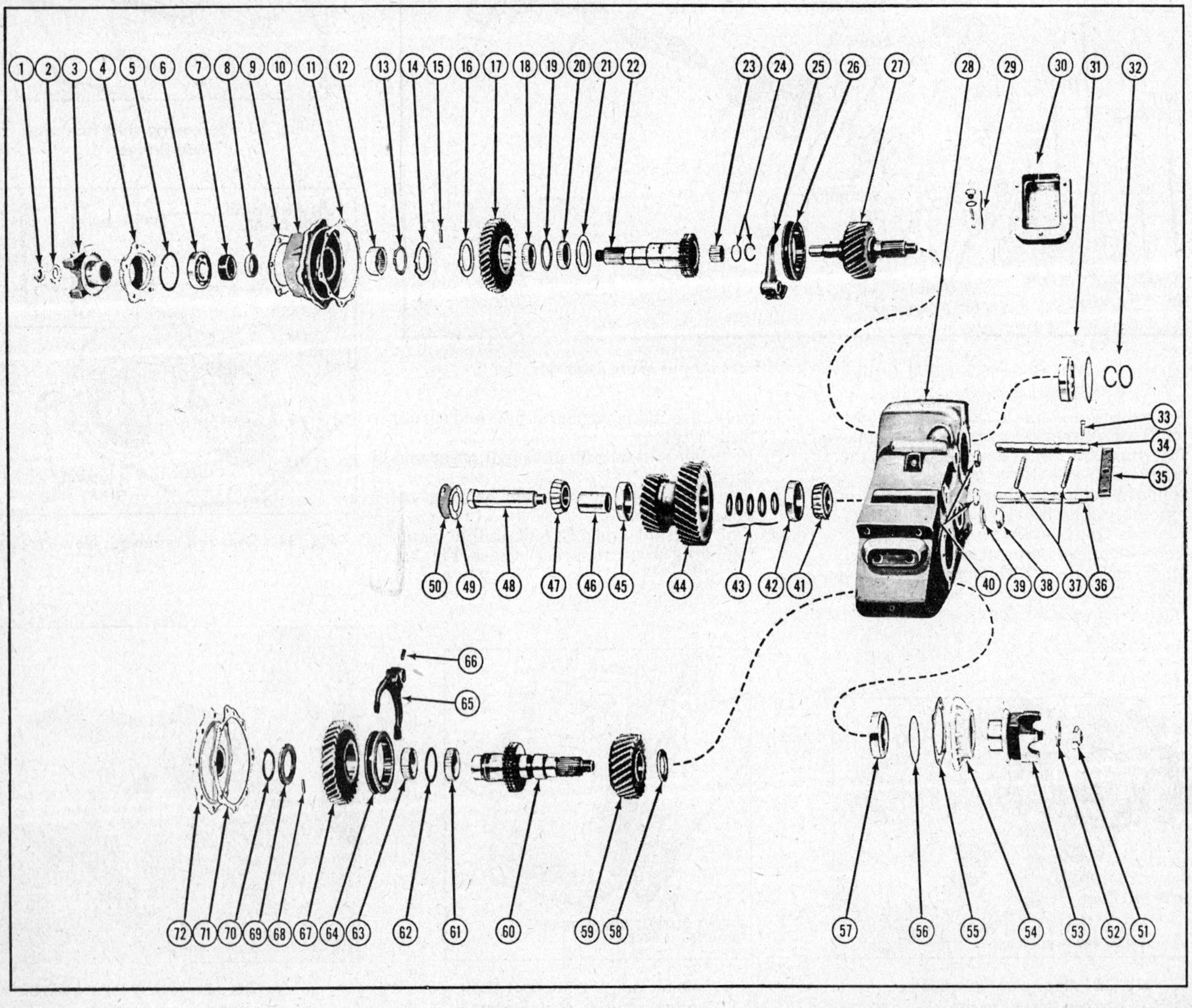

TRANSFER CASES

1. Cover Bolts (4)
2. Front Output Shaft Rear Cover
3. Front Output Rear Cover Shims
4. Front Output Rear Bearing Cup
5. Front Output Rear Bearing
6. Front Output Shaft
7. Bottom Cover Gasket
8. Bottom Cover and Bolts
9. Front Wheel Drive Shift Fork
10. Front Output Sliding Gear
11. Front Output Gear
12. Thrust Washer
13. Front Output Bearing
14. Front Output Bearing Cup
15. Spacer
16. Front Output Bearing Retainer Gasket
17. Front Output Bearing Retainer
18. Seal
19. Output Yoke Assembly
20. "O" Ring
21. Washer
22. Locknut
23. Shifter Rail Seals
24. Poppet Ball, Spring and Cap Screw
25. Rear Wheel Drive Shift Rail
26. Front Wheel Drive Shift Rail
27. Tanged Thrust Washer
28. Spacer
29. Needle Bearings
30. Intermediate Gears
31. Tanged Thrust Washer
32. Intermediate Shaft
33. Transfer Case
34. Intermediate Shift Lockplate and Bolt
35. Rear Wheel Sliding Gear
36. Rear Wheel Drive Shift Fork
37. Pilot Bearing
38. Rear Output Shaft
39. Rear Output Front Bearing
40. Rear Output Front Bearing Cup
41. Speedometer Drive Gear
42. Rear Output Shaft Shims
43. Rear Retainer Gasket
44. Rear Output Bearing Retainer
45. Rear Retainer Bolts (10)
46. Rear Output Rear Bearing Cup
47. Rear Output Rear Bearing
48. Rear Output Retainer Seal
49. Rear Output Yoke Assembly
50. Spacer
51. Locknut
52. Snap Ring (Input Shaft)
53. Direct Drive Gear
54. Snap Ring (Part of Adapter Assembly)
55. Bearing (Part of Adapter Assembly)
56. Input Shaft

Fig. 36 New Process exc. 203 & 205 transfer case. Exploded

1. Rear Output Shaft Locknut
2. Washer
3. Yoke
4. Bearing Retainer and Seal Assembly
5. Snap Ring
6. Bearing
7. Speedometer Gear
8. Spacer
9. Gasket
10. Housing
11. Gasket
12. Bearing
13. Snap Ring
14. Thrust Washer
15. Thrust Washer Lock Pin
16. Thrust Washer (Tanged)
17. Low Speed Gear
18. Needle Bearings
19. Spacer
20. Needle Bearings
21. Tanged Washer
22. Rear Output Shaft
23. Needle Bearings
24. Washer and Retainer
25. Shift Fork
26. Sliding Clutch
27. Input Shaft
28. Transfer Case
29. Poppet Plug, Spring and Ball
30. P.T.O. Gasket and Cover
31. Input Shaft Bearing and Snap Ring
32. Snap Ring and Rubber 'O' Ring
33. Shift Link Clevis Pin
34. Range Shift Rail
35. Shift Rail Connector Link
36. Front Wheel Drive Shift Rail
37. Interlock Pins
38. Rear Idler Lock Nut
39. Washer
40. Shift Rail Seals
41. Idler Shaft Bearing
42. Bearing Cup
43. Shims
44. Idler Gear
45. Bearing Cup
46. Spacer
47. Idler Shaft Bearing
48. Idler Shaft
49. Cover Gasket
50. Rear Cover
51. Front Output Shaft Locknut
52. Washer
53. Yoke
54. Bearing Retainer and Seal
55. Gasket
56. Snap Ring
57. Front Bearing
58. Thrust Washer
59. Front Wheel High Gear
60. Front Output Shaft
61. Needle Bearings
62. Spacer
63. Needle Bearing
64. Sliding Clutch Gear
65. Shift Fork
66. Roll Pin
67. Front Output Low Gear
68. Thrust Washer Lock Pin
69. Thrust Washer
70. Snap Ring
71. Rear Cover Gasket
72. Rear Cover and Bearing

Fig. 41 Dana Model 20 & New Process 205 transfer case. Exploded

TRANSFER CASES

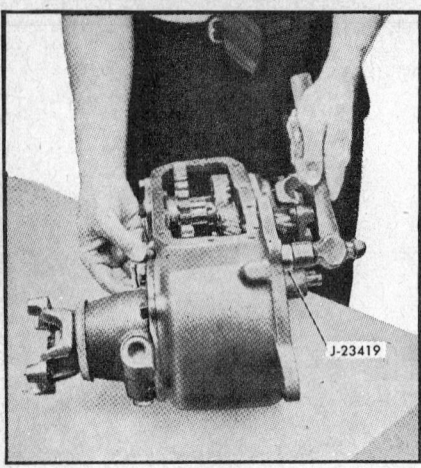

Fig. 37 Removing intermediate gear shaft. Dana Model 20

Remove gears and washers as they clear shaft. Remove rear bearing cup. Remove front bearing cap as required, using suitable puller.
11. Press rear bearing from shaft, Fig. 40.
12. Loosen dog set screw from the 4-wheel drive shift fork. Swing fork and gear toward cover opening and lift out gear. Rotate shift rail to pre-load poppet ball and pull rail out of retainer. Remove fork as it clears shift rail and remove poppet ball and spring from retainer.
13. Remove shift rail seals with a suitable puller.
14. Remove front and rear drive bearing retainer seals.

Assembly, Fig. 41

The procedure for reassembly is largely the reverse of the disassembly. However, observe the following:
1. When installing front wheel drive shift fork, set screw boss should face front of case.
2. Rear wheel drive clutch gear shift collar should face rear of case.
3. When installing shift rail poppet balls and springs, use long (yellow) spring on rear wheel drive shift rail and short (red) spring on front wheel shift rail.
4. Torque front output shaft yoke lock nut to 200–250 ft.-lbs.

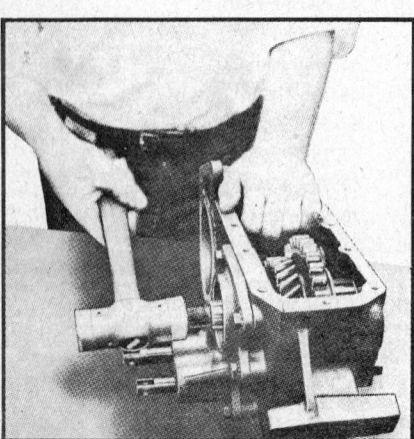

Fig. 39 Removing front output shaft. Dana Model 20

5. Intermediate shaft is a press fit into case front bore. Align lock plate slot in shaft with bolt hole before installing shaft in front bore.
6. Torque rear output shaft yoke lock nut to 200–250 ft.-lbs.

SPICER MODEL 18

Disassembly, Fig. 42

1. Remove propeller shaft flange, brake assembly and linkage.
2. Remove lower cover, Fig. 42.
3. Remove lock plate.
4. Drive intermediate shaft to rear of case, being careful not to lose thrust washers.
5. Remove intermediate gear, thrust washers and roller bearings through bottom of case.
6. Shift front wheel drive to engaged position (shaft forward) and remove poppet plugs, springs and balls on both sides of output bearing cap.
7. Remove output bearing cap together with the universal joint end yoke, clutch shaft, bearing, clutch gear, fork and shift rod. Use care not to lose the interlock.
8. Remove output shaft snap ring and thrust washer.
9. Use a rawhide mallet to drive against the front end of the mainshaft to start the rear bearing from the case. As the shaft is removed, the gears will remain in the case and can be taken out through the bottom, also the snap ring and thrust washer.
10. Remove set screw in sliding gear shift fork and take out the shift rod.
11. Disassemble the front and rear bearing caps as required.

Reassembly Notes

Reverse the order of the above procedure to assemble the transfer case. But when rear bearing cap assembly is installed, check the end movement of the mainshaft which determines the adjustment of the tapered roller bearings. For correct bearing adjustment, the shaft should have from .004″ to .008″ end play. Adjustment is made by selective shim installation between the cap and case. Shims .003″, .010″ and .031″ thicknesses are available for this adjustment. Do not install the rear cap oil seal until the bearings are properly adjusted.

SPICER MODELS 20 & 21

Disassembly, Figs. 43 & 44

1. Remove rear bearing cap bolts and rear bearing cap assembly.
2. Remove bottom cover and lock plate.
3. Install a dummy shaft, tool W-280 and drive intermediate shaft out from rear of case, then remove intermediate gear through bottom of case.

NOTE: Tool W-280 should be centered in intermediate gear assembly to prevent interference with thrust washers.

4. Remove front output shaft nut, washer and yoke, Fig. 45. Remove oil seal with a suitable puller.
5. Remove rear cover and with a mallet, tap front output shaft rearward to drive rear bearing cup from case.
6. On Model 20, cut safety wire and remove

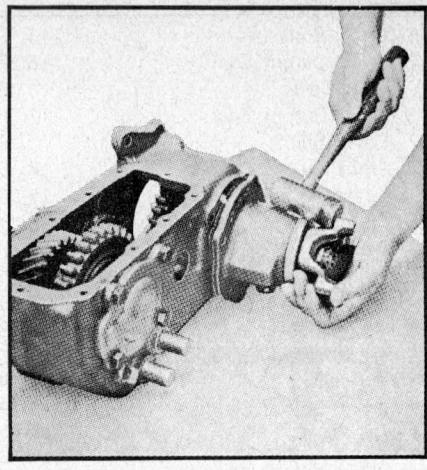

Fig. 38 Removing rear output shaft sub-assembly. Dana Model 20

inner shift fork bolt. Tap inner shift rod to the rear and remove shift rod cap, then drive inner shift rod out from front of case. Remove main gear and inner shift fork.
7. On all models remove shift rod housing from case.
8. Remove front bearing cone from front output shaft using a wedge forcing it between bearing and front output shaft gear. Remove snap ring, then the output shaft through rear of case. Remove output shaft gear, thrust washer and bearing roller assembly through bottom of case.
9. On Model 20, remove output shaft sliding gear from outer shift fork. On Model 21, remove output sliding clutch gear from front wheel drive shift fork. On all models, remove fork.

NOTE: Model 21 has a shift fork stop between the shift fork and rear of case.

Reassembly

1. Place outer or front wheel drive shift rod partially into case and install outer or front wheel drive shift fork on rod, aligning shift rod fork bolt hole with countersunk hole in rod. Install and torque shift

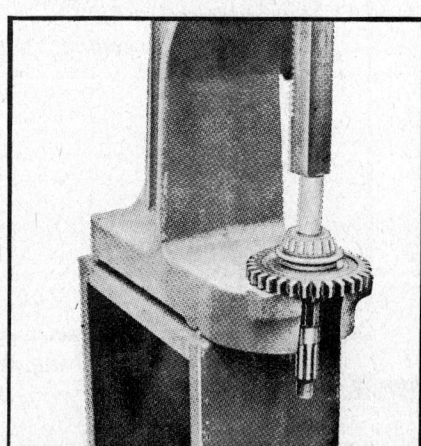

Fig. 40 Removing front output shaft rear bearing. Dana Model 20

TRANSFER CASES

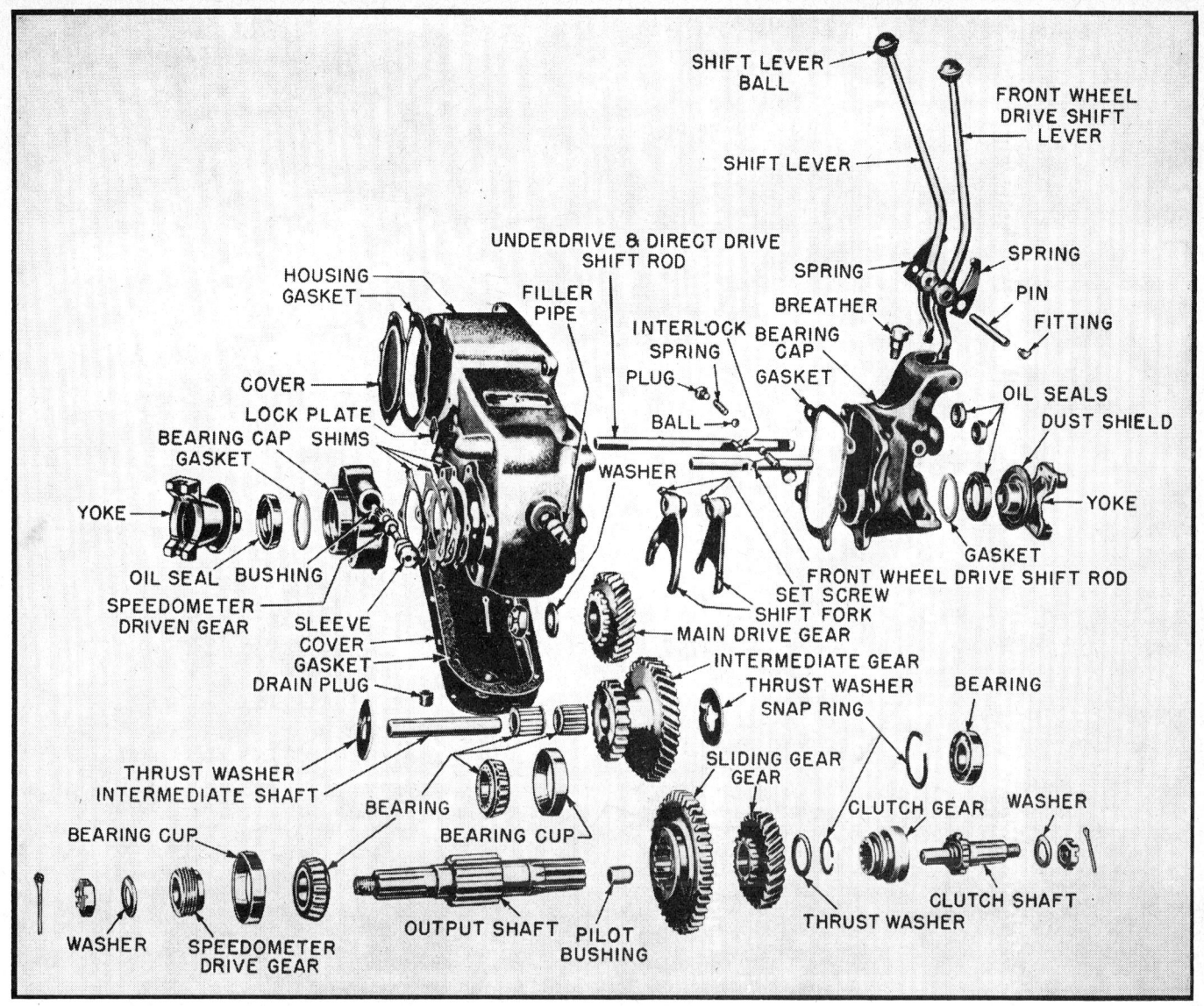

Fig. 42 Spicer single range Model 18 transfer case. Exploded view

fork bolt to 12 to 15 ft. lbs. and safety wire bolt.
2. On Model 20, place front output shaft sliding gear in shift fork with gear facing front of case. On Model 21, install sliding clutch gear with bevel facing front of case.
3. Install rear cone and roller onto front output shaft, position output shaft gear in case and install output shaft. Install front cone, roller and front and rear bearing cups.
4. Install shift rod housing and on Model 21, hold shift rod interlock ball down when housing is placed over shift rod.
5. Install rear cover shim set and cover. Check output shaft bearing adjustment using a dial indicator. Bearing adjustment should be .002–.005 inch. If not, change rear cover shims to obtain specified clearance. Shims are available in thicknesses of .003", .010" and .031".
6. On Model 20, position outer shift rod to allow shift rod interlocks to enter detents in rod when inner shift rod is installed in shift rod housing. Start inner shift rod into housing and install inner shift fork into case.
7. On all models, install mainshaft gear on fork with gear facing front of case and push shift rod into case and through fork, aligning countersunk hole in rod with shift fork bolt hole. Install and torque shift rod bolt to 12-15 ft. lbs. and safety wire bolt.
8. Install rear thrust washer and hold in place by starting intermediate shaft into case. Install front thrust washer and hold in place with grease. Align tang on thrust washers with grooves in case.
9. Install intermediate gear into case and drive intermediate shaft into gear, inturn forcing dummy shaft out of case. Install intermediate shaft lock plate and torque bolt to 12-15 ft. lbs.
10. Install rear bearing cap assembly and torque bolts to 28-32 ft. lbs.
11. Install shift rod cups approximately 3/8 inch into case.
12. Install lower cover gasket and cover, torque bolts to 12-15 ft. lbs.
13. Install front and rear yoke oil seals, oil seal gaskets and felt oil seals.
14. Install front and rear propeller shaft yokes and torque nuts to 225-250 ft. lbs.

WARNER QUADRA-TRAC

Case Disassembly

1. Remove front and rear output shaft yokes.
2. If unit is not equipped with reduction unit, remove power take-off cover and the sealing ring from transfer case rear cover, Fig. 46.
3. Remove cover from transfer case. Position cover with drive chain downward and place a 2 × 4 × 6 inch block of wood under sprocket.
4. If not equipped with reduction unit, expand snap ring securing drive hub and sleeve to drive sprocket rear splines and remove hub and sleeve.
5. If equipped with reduction unit, remove pinion cage from drive sprocket rear splines.
6. Remove cover from drive sprocket and

TRANSFER CASES

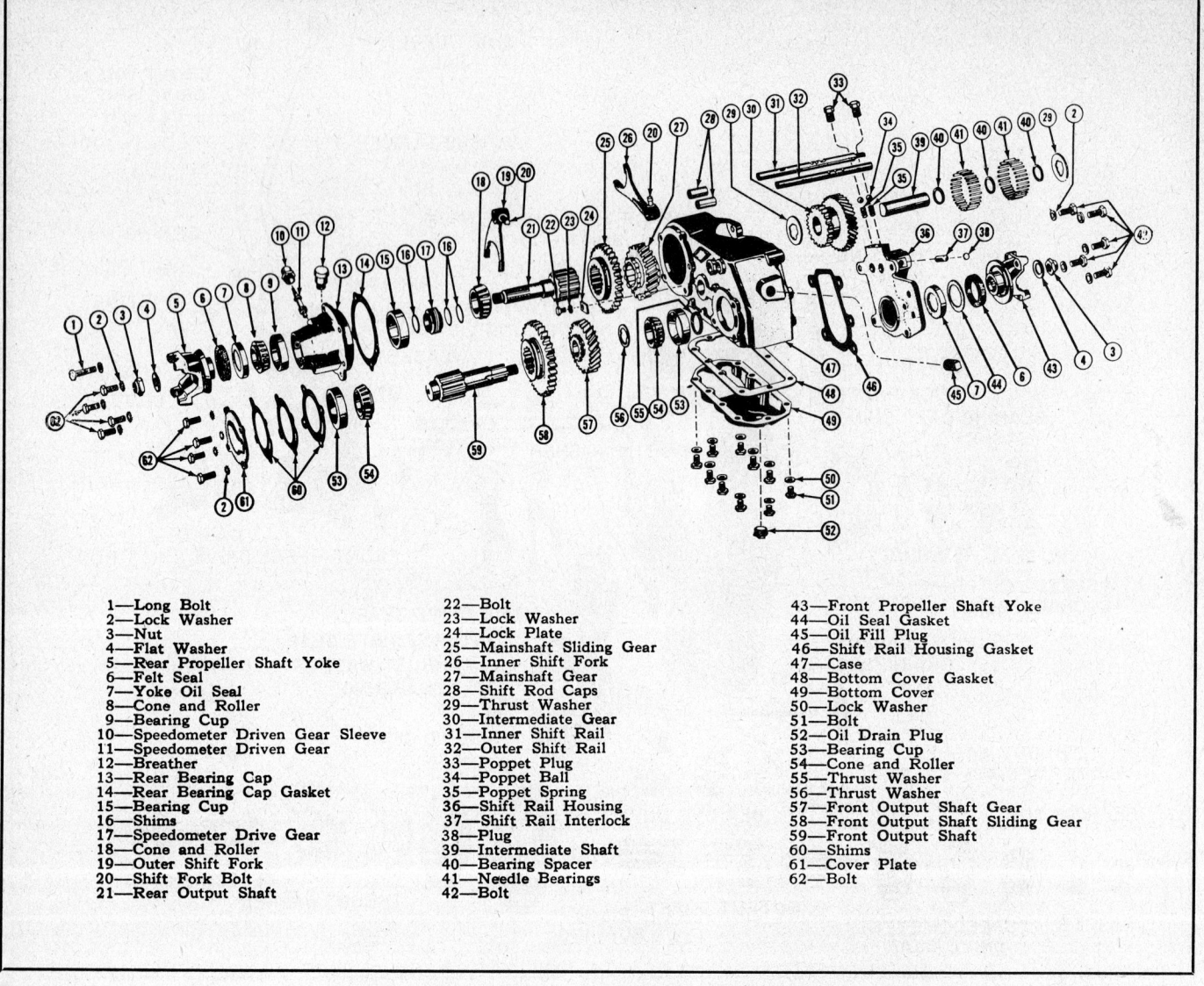

Fig. 43 Spicer dual range Model 20 transfer case. Exploded view

1—Long Bolt
2—Lock Washer
3—Nut
4—Flat Washer
5—Rear Propeller Shaft Yoke
6—Felt Seal
7—Yoke Oil Seal
8—Cone and Roller
9—Bearing Cup
10—Speedometer Driven Gear Sleeve
11—Speedometer Driven Gear
12—Breather
13—Rear Bearing Cap
14—Rear Bearing Cap Gasket
15—Bearing Cup
16—Shims
17—Speedometer Drive Gear
18—Cone and Roller
19—Outer Shift Fork
20—Shift Fork Bolt
21—Rear Output Shaft
22—Bolt
23—Lock Washer
24—Lock Plate
25—Mainshaft Sliding Gear
26—Inner Shift Fork
27—Mainshaft Gear
28—Shift Rod Caps
29—Thrust Washer
30—Intermediate Gear
31—Inner Shift Rail
32—Outer Shift Rail
33—Poppet Plug
34—Poppet Ball
35—Poppet Spring
36—Shift Rail Housing
37—Shift Rail Interlock
38—Plug
39—Intermediate Shaft
40—Bearing Spacer
41—Needle Bearings
42—Bolt
43—Front Propeller Shaft Yoke
44—Oil Seal Gasket
45—Oil Fill Plug
46—Shift Rail Housing Gasket
47—Case
48—Bottom Cover Gasket
49—Bottom Cover
50—Lock Washer
51—Bolt
52—Oil Drain Plug
53—Bearing Cup
54—Cone and Roller
55—Thrust Washer
56—Thrust Washer
57—Front Output Shaft Gear
58—Front Output Shaft Sliding Gear
59—Front Output Shaft
60—Shims
61—Cover Plate
62—Bolt

differential, slide drive sprocket toward differential and remove chain.

Sub-Assembly Service

Differential Disassembly

1. Apply identification markings on case sprocket and end caps to ensure proper assembly.
2. Remove screws attaching front end cap to case sprocket, then remove end cap, thrust washers, preload springs, brake cone and side gear from case sprocket. Repeat for rear end cap, Fig. 46.
3. Remove pinion shaft lock pin and drive out the pinion shaft from case sprocket with a suitable drift.

Inspection

Clutch, thrust surfaces and shaft bores may be polished. Small smooth score marks and machine marks are acceptable. Case sprocket teeth will show a polished wear pattern, whereas pinion and side gears will have a "rough machined" appearance. The pinion shaft should be straight and fit snugly into case sprocket. The thrust washers should be flat and preload springs should be dished approximately 3/32 inch. Clean all parts of differential before assembly.

Differential Reassembly

During reassembly, bearing and thrust surfaces must be coated with lubricant, Jeep P/N 8123004.

1. Install pinion shaft sprocket approximately 3 inches into case and place pinion thrust washers and gears on shaft in proper sequence. Fully drive shaft into sprocket, aligning lock pin holes in shaft and case.
2. Slide pinion gears apart and mesh either front or rear side gear with pinion gears. Install brake cone over side gear followed by large thrust washer, preload springs, small thrust washer and end cap, Fig. 46.
3. Install pinion shaft lock pin and mesh remaining side gear with pinion gears. Install brake cone over side gear followed by large thrust washer, preload springs, small thrust washer and end cap.
4. Install front and rear output shafts into differential and rotate shafts so both shafts are aligned having entered the brake cone splines and tighten end cap screws.

Bearing Replacement

Refer to Figs. 47 thru 50 when replacing differential or drive sprocket needle bearings. Install drive sprocket rear needle bearings with removal tools, Fig. 50, with tool #W361-1 installed into the case bore.

Front and rear output shaft annular bearings are retained by selected thickness snap rings. The outer snap ring is available in the following thickness ranges: .060"–.063", .064"–.066", .067"–.069" and .070"–.072". The inner snap ring is available only in a thickness of .060–.063 inch. These bearings can be removed by hand or with a brass drift, if necessary. When removing the rear output shaft bearing, remove speedometer gear, then the outer snap ring and bearing. When installing outer snap ring, install proper snap ring to provide .001–.003 inch bearing end play.

Diaphragm Control, Shift Fork & Lock-Up Hub Disassembly

1. Remove vent cover and sealing ring.

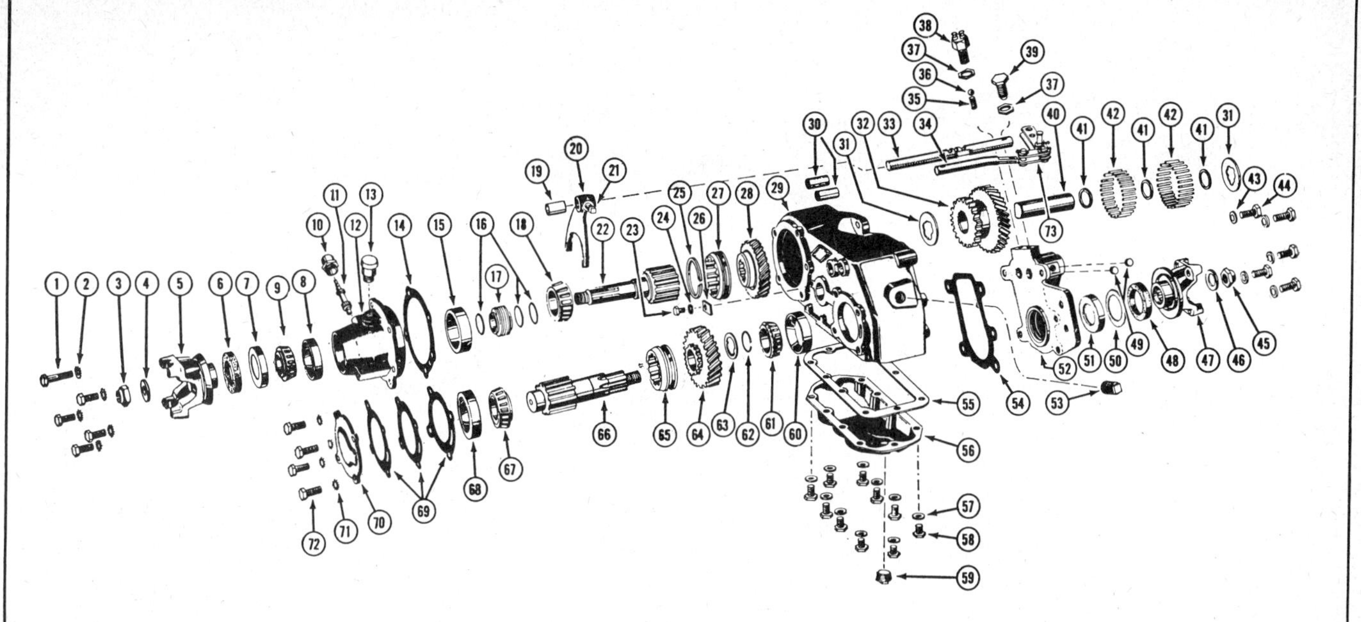

TRANSFER CASES

Fig. 44 Spicer single range Model 21 transfer case. Exploded view

1—Bolt
2—Lockwasher
3—Nut
4—Flat Washer
5—Rear Propeller Shaft Yoke
6—Felt Seal
7—Yoke Oil Seal
8—Bearing Cup
9—Cone and Roller
10—Speedometer Driven Gear Sleeve
11—Speedometer Driven Gear
12—Rear Bearing Cap
13—Breather
14—Rear Bearing Cap Gasket
15—Bearing Cup
16—Shims
17—Speedometer Drive Gear
18—Cone and Roller
19—Shift Rod Stop
20—Front-Wheel-Drive Shift Fork
21—Shift Rod Bolt
22—Rear Output Shaft
23—Bolt
24—Lockwasher
25—Snap Ring
26—Lock Plate
27—Stationary Clutch Gear
28—Mainshaft Gear
29—Case
30—Shift Rod Caps
31—Intermediate Gear
32—Intermediate Gear
33—Front-Wheel-Drive Shift Rod
34—Dummy Shift Rod
35—Spring
36—Shift Rod Interlock Ball
37—Lock Nut
38—Indicator Light Switch
39—Bolt
40—Intermediate Shaft
41—Bearing Spacer
42—Needle Bearings
43—Lockwasher
44—Bolt
45—Nut
46—Flat Washer
47—Front Propeller Shaft Yoke
48—Felt Seal
49—Plug
50—Oil Seal Gasket
51—Yoke Oil Seal
52—Front Bearing Cap
53—Oil Fill Plug
54—Shift Housing Gasket
55—Bottom Cover Gasket
56—Bottom Cover
57—Lockwasher
58—Bolt
59—Oil Drain Plug
60—Bearing Cup
61—Snap Ring
62—Snap Ring
63—Thrust Washer
64—Front Output Shaft Gear
65—Sliding Clutch Gear
66—Front Output Shaft
67—Cone and Roller
68—Bearing Cup
69—Shims
70—Cover Plate
71—Lockwasher
72—Bolt
73—Shift Linkage

2. Remove shift fork retaining rings from diaphragm control rod.
3. Remove dowel pin and insert a small magnet into dowel pin hole, Fig. 51. Remove diaphragm control from case cover, detent ball and spring.

NOTE: The diaphragm control is held by the detent ball and spring.

4. Remove shift fork, shifting shoes and lock-up hub.

Diaphragm Control, Shift Fork & Lock-Up Hub Reassembly

1. Lubricate and install shifting shoes and lock-up hub into shift fork.
2. Install fork and hub assembly into case cover with care not to separate lock-up hub from fork, Fig. 52.
3. Slide diaphragm control into case cover, past the fork but not further than the detent ball hole. Insert detent spring and ball into hole, using a 1/4 inch punch, depress detent ball and slide diaphragm control rod past ball.
4. Install shift fork retaining rings and diaphragm control retaining dowel pin.
5. Install sealing ring and vent cover.

Case Reassembly

1. Place drive sprocket on a 2×4×6 inch block of wood with differential assembly about 2 inches from sprocket with front end down. Place drive chain around sprocket and differential, ensure chain is engaged with sprocket and differential teeth. Remove slack from chain, Fig. 53.
2. Install rear output shaft into differential and shift lock-up hub to rear of case cover.
3. With grease holding drive sprocket thrust washer in position on cover. Align and position cover on drive sprocket and differential. Rotate output shaft to align with lock-up nub.
4. Assemble drive hub, drive sleeve and snap ring. If not equipped with reduction unit, install drive hub and sleeve assembly on drive sprocket, ensuring snap ring seats properly.
5. If equipped with reduction unit, ensure oil baffle is positioned properly and install pinion cage and snap ring.
6. Install front output shaft, thrust washer and front case gasket onto case.
7. Insert oil tube into case bore located at front output shaft bearing boss, then insert a 5/16 × 6 inch rod into oil tube.
8. Position case onto drive sprocket and differential assembly. Using the 5/16 × 6 inch rod to align oil tube with case cover. Install and torque case to cover screws to 15-25 foot lbs.

NOTE: Rotate drive sleeve to ensure drive sprocket thrust washer is correctly positioned. Sleeve should turn without binding.

9. Install power take-off sealing ring and cover.
10. Install speedometer gear onto rear output shaft and the front and rear output shaft oil seals into case bores.
11. Install front yoke and torque nut to 90-150 ft. lbs.

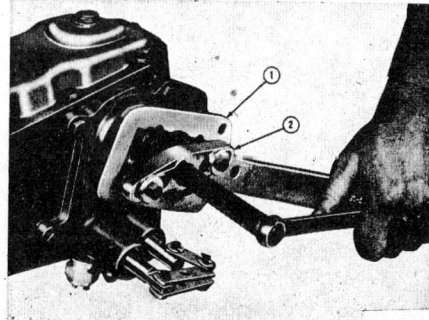

①Tool C-3281. ②Tool W-172.

Fig. 45 Removing universal joint flange. Spicer Models 20 & 21 transfer cases

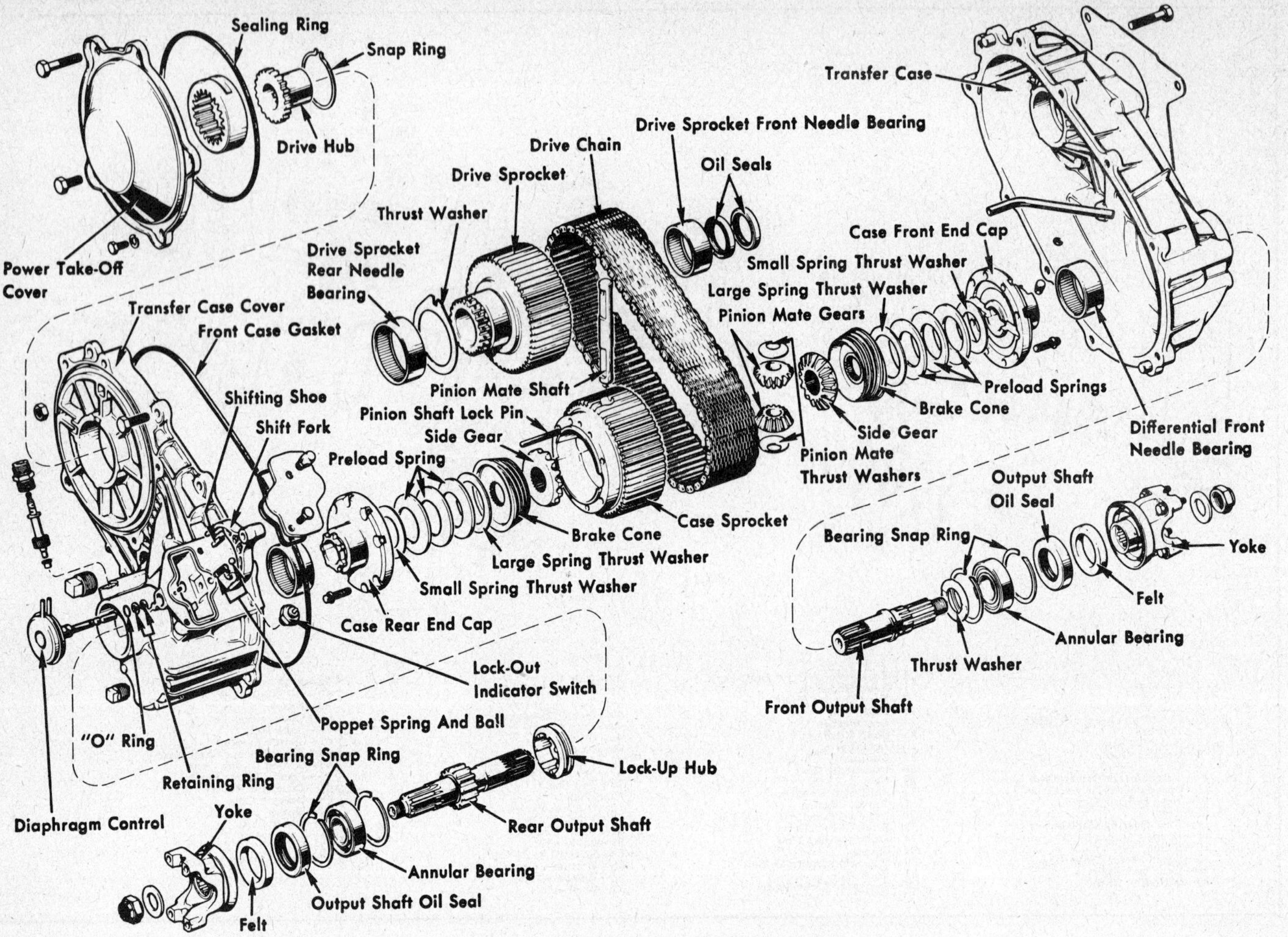

TRANSFER CASES

Fig. 46 Warner Quadra-Trac transfer case. Disassembled

WARNER QUADRA-TRAC REDUCTION UNIT

Disassembly

1. Remove power take-off cover and gasket.
2. Remove reduction mainshaft snap ring and spacer, pull reduction mainshaft and sun gear assembly forward out of housing. Remove mainshaft needle bearings, Fig. 54.
3. Remove ring gear, reduction collar plate, pinion cage lock plate, shift collar hub and the reduction collar hub assembly from housing.
4. Using a mallet, tap shift collar hub from pinion cage lock plate. Remove pinion cage lock plate and needle bearing, ring gear, reduction collar plate and shift collar hub.
5. Remove reduction collar hub and needle bearings from shift collar hub.
6. Remove snap rings retaining reduction collar plate hub and ring gear to reduction collar plate.
7. Remove needle bearing and direct drive

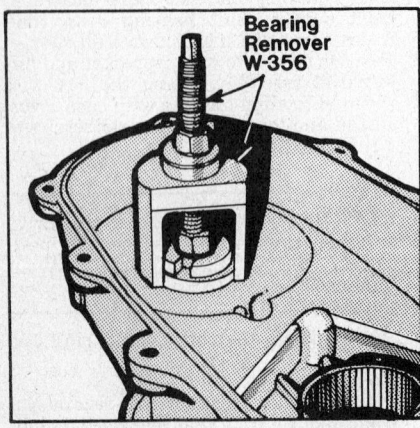

Fig. 47 Warner Quadra-Trac differential drive sprocket needle bearngs removal (typical)

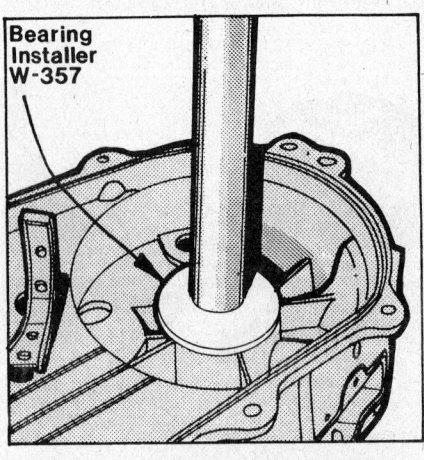

Fig. 48 Warner Quadra-Trac differential needle bearings installation (typical)

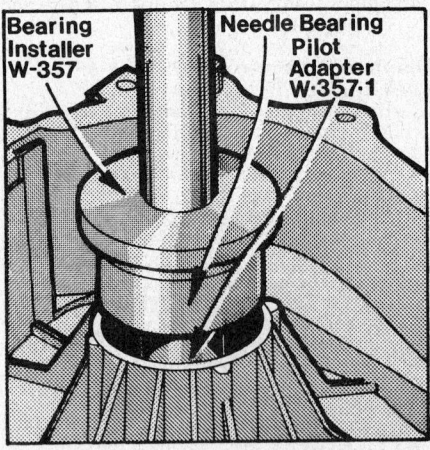

Fig. 49 Warner Quadra-Trac drive sprocket front needle bearing installation

TRANSFER CASES

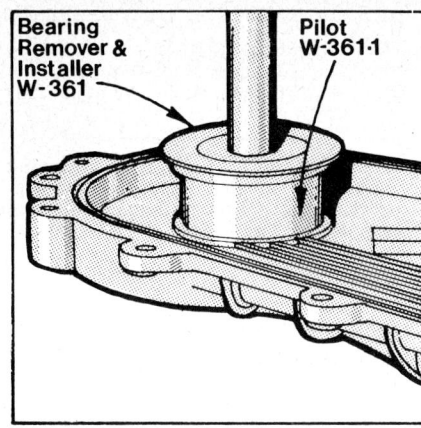

Fig. 50 Warner Quadra-Trac drive sprocket rear needle bearing removal

Fig. 51 Warner Quadra-Trac diaphragm control removal

Fig. 53 Warner Quadra-Trac drive chain installation

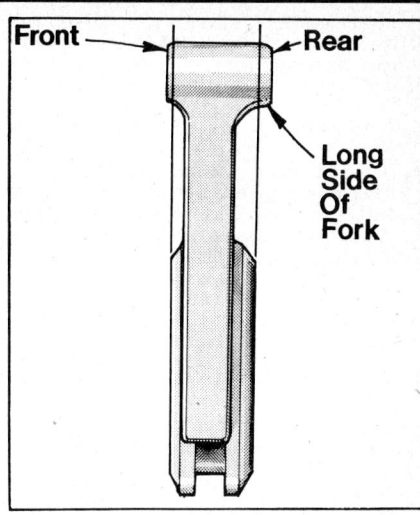

Fig. 52 Warner Quadra-Trac lock-up hub & shift fork assembly

sleeve from reduction shift collar.
8. With the control lever move reduction shift collar to center detent, move collar away from shift fork and disengage fork. Move fork rearward to direct drive detent and collar toward fork, align outer teeth on collar and inner teeth on reduction holding plate. Move fork and collar forward to reduction detent and remove reduction shift collar.
9. Remove rear snap ring and annular bearing.
10. Remove shift fork locating spring pin, large expansion plug and shift rail taper plugs.
11. Remove control lever from shift lever.
12. Drive spring pin out from shift fork and rail with a 3/16 inch punch, slide rail out of fork and remove fork.
13. Remove shift rail poppet ball, drive poppet taper plug into rail bore and remove plug and poppet spring.
14. Remove shift lever retaining pin and lever assembly.
15. Remove snap ring and reduction holding plate.

Reassembly

1. Install reduction holding plate with locating pin indexed in reduction housing shift fork locating spring pin holes in plate aligned with holes in the housing, Fig. 55. Install holding plate snap ring with tabs forward.
2. Install shift lever assembly into housing with lever and rearward. Place "O" ring in groove on shift lever shaft and move shift lever assembly inward to a position allowing installation of shift lever locating taper pin.
3. Install shift rail with grooved end first into rail rear bore and rotate rail so flat side is adjacent to poppet spring. Slide rail so shift fork is meshed with shift

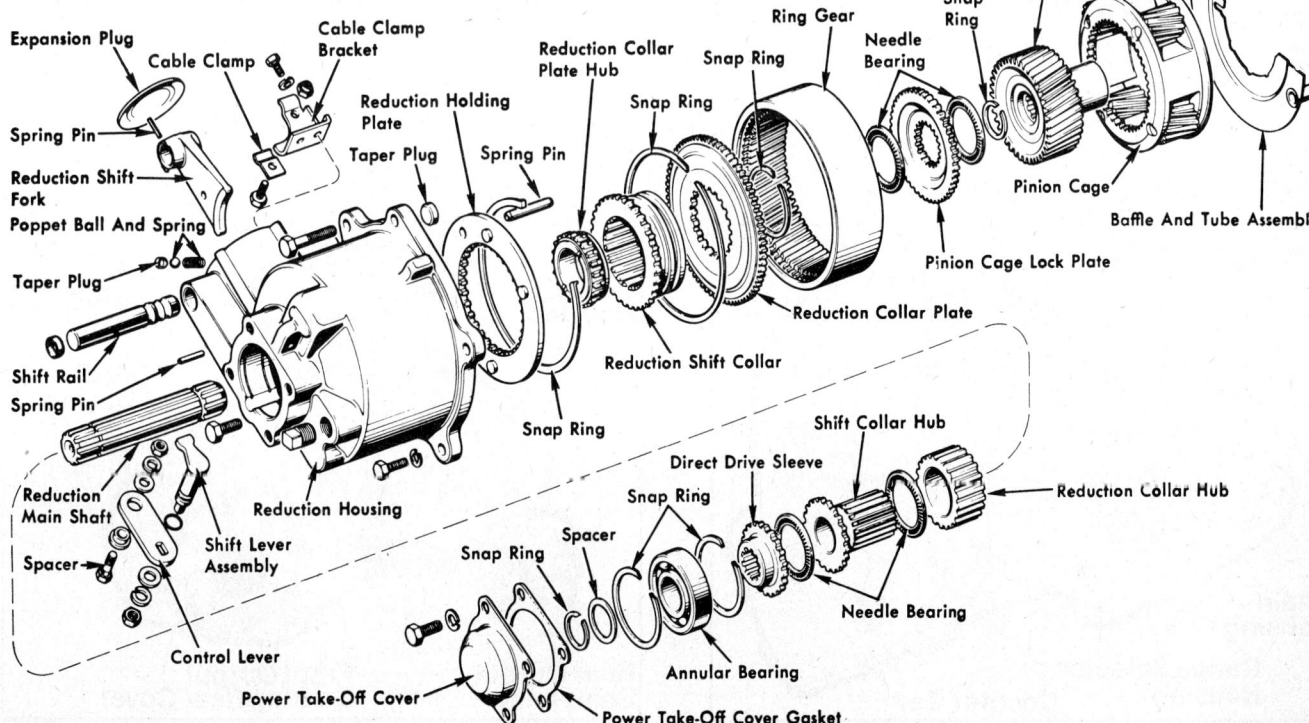

Fig. 54 Warner Quadra-Trac reduction unit. Disassembled

487

TRANSFER CASES

lever assembly and rail, move rail through fork so end of rail is even with edge of poppet bore.

4. Place poppet ball on end of spring and with a spring pin, depress ball and slide shift rail over ball as far as possible. Remove pin, slide rail to first detent position and rotate rail flat side facing shift lever assembly and spring bore aligning with spring pin bore in shift fork. Align spring pin holes in shift rail and fork, install spring pin flush with fork.
5. Install shift rail taper plugs, poppet bore taper plug and rail cover expansion plug.
6. Install shift fork locating spring pin and control lever.
7. Place shift fork in center detent. Mesh reduction shift collar outer teeth with reduction holding plate inner teeth. Move fork to rear detent and shift collar away from fork, aligning groove in collar with shift fork. Move collar toward fork, engaging collar groove with fork.
8. Install direct drive sleeve into reduction shift collar with needle bearing surface and pointed ends of outer teeth forward. Adequately lubricate needle bearing and install against direct drive sleeve.
9. Install needle bearing and reduction collar hub onto shift collar hub. Install ring gear, reduction collar plate and hub assembly onto shift collar hub.

NOTE: A needle bearing is not used between reduction collar plate hub and reduction collar hub.

10. Install needle bearing onto shift collar hub and between reduction collar plate hub. Install pinion cage lock plate on shift collar hub so lock plate is snug against needle bearing. Install assembly into housing, rotating ring gear or pinion cage lock plate to align splines. Place needle bearing on shift collar hub and pinion cage lock plate.
11. Install reduction mainshaft and sun gear assembly into shift collar hub through the direct drive sleeve and annular bearing, rotating assembly to align splines. Use a drift to tap mainshaft fully rearward.

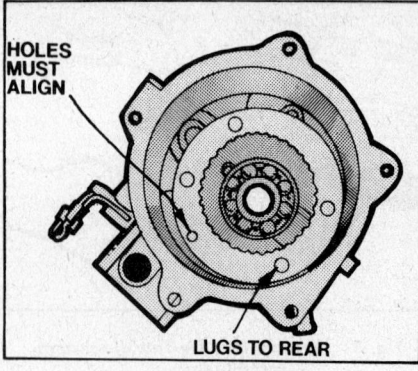

Fig. 55 Warner Quadra-Trac reaction unit holding plate installation

12. Install rear spacer and snap ring. Snap rings are available in various thickness ranges of .089″–.091″, .092″–.094″, .095″–.097″, .099″–.101″ and .103″–.105″. Install appropriate snap ring to provide .004–.009 inch spacer clearance.
13. Install power take-off gasket and cover and torque cover screws to 15–25 ft. lbs.

NEW PROCESS MODEL 203

Case Disassembly

1. Remove front output rear cover located on side of range selecter and drain lubricant, Figs. 56 and 57.
2. Remove rear output shaft retaining nut, washer and flange, Fig. 58.

NOTE: Tap dust cover shield rearward on shaft to gain clearance to remove bolts and install tool.

3. Remove front bearing retainer, Fig. 59, then using a hoist, position assembly on blocks in an upright position.
4. Remove rear output shaft retaining bolts then disengage assembly from transfer case and slide carrier unit from shaft.

NOTE: Install a suitable size band type hose clamp on input shaft to prevent losing bearings when removing input shaft assembly.

5. Raise shift rail, drive out pin retaining shift fork to rail and remove shift rail poppet ball plug, gasket spring and ball from case, Figs. 57 and 59.

NOTE: Use a small magnet to remove ball from case.

6. Push shift rail down, lift up on lockout clutch and remove shift fork from clutch assembly.
7. Remove front output shaft rear bearing retainer bolts and tap on front of shaft or carefully pry retainer from shaft and discard gasket. Recover any roller bearings which may fall from rear cover.

NOTE: If replacing bearing, press bearing out. Press new bearing in until it is flush with output bearing rear cover.

8. Pry out output shaft front bearing then disengage front output shaft from chain and remove shaft from transfer case, Fig. 59.
9. Remove intermediate chain housing bolts and remove intermediate housing from range box.
10. Remove chain from intermediate housing, then remove lockout clutch, drive gear and input shaft from range box.

NOTE: Install a suitable size band type hose clamp on end of input shaft to prevent losing roller bearings which may fall out if clutch assembly is pulled off input shaft.

11. Pull up on shift rail and disconnect rail from link then remove input shaft assembly from range box.

Inspection

With the transfer case totally disassembled into sub-assemblies. These sub-assemblies

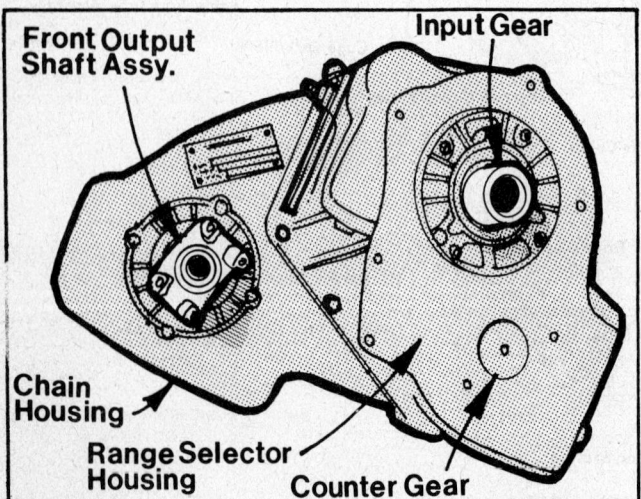

Fig. 56 New Process 203 transfer case. Front view

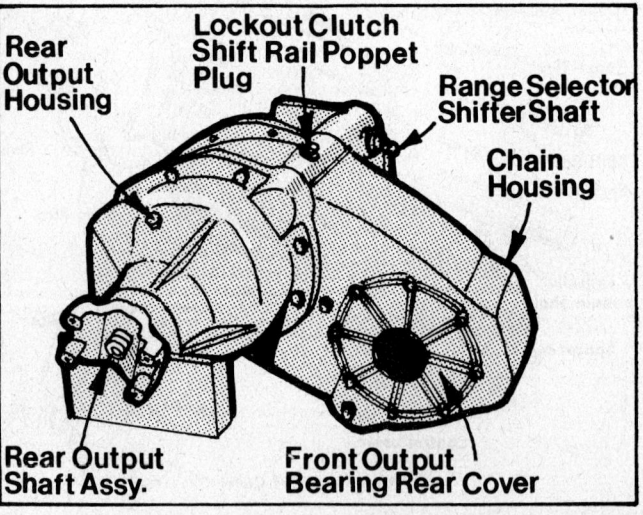

Fig. 57 New Process 203 transfer case. Rear view

TRANSFER CASES

should be further disassembled for cleaning and inspection.

Place all bearings, rollers, shafts and gears in cleaning solution and allow to remain long enough to loosen all accumulated lubricant. Bearings should be moved up and down and turned slowly in solvent. Dry all parts with compressed air. When drying bearings direct air so as to avoid spinning the bearings. When cleaning transfer case, cover or housing, make certain that all traces of gasket are removed from surfaces.

Inspect all bearings and rollers for evidence of chipping, cracking, or worn spots that would render bearing unfit for further use. Bearings are non-adjustable and if worn or damaged, must be replaced. Inspect shaft splines, drive chain and gears.

Sub-Assembly Service

Differential Carrier Disassemble, Fig. 59
1. Remove carrier assembly bolts and separate carrier sections, then lift pinion gear and spider assembly from carrier.

NOTE: Make certain that undercut side of pinion gear spider faces toward front side gear.

2. Remove pinion thrust washers, pinion roller washers, pinion gears and roller bearings from spider unit.
3. Clean, inspect and replace parts as necessary.

Differential Carrier Reassembly
1. Using petroleum jelly, insert roller bearings into pinion gears.

NOTE: A total of 132 bearings are required with 33 bearings in each pinion.

2. Install pinion roller washer, pinion gear, roller washer and thrust washer on each leg of spider.
3. Install spider assembly in front half of carrier with undercut surface of spider thrust spacer facing toward gear teeth.
4. Align marks on carrier sections and position carrier halves together then install retaining bolts and torque to 45 ft. lbs.

Lockout Clutch Disassembly, Fig. 59
1. Remove front side gear from input shaft assembly and remove thrust washer, roller bearings (123 total) and spacers from front side gear bore. Note position of spacers to facilitate reassembly.
2. Remove the snap ring retaining the drive sprocket to the clutch assembly, then slide the drive sprocket out from the front side gear and remove the lower snap ring.
3. Remove sliding gear, spring and spring cup washer from front side gear.
4. Clean, inspect and replace parts as necessary.

Lockout Clutch Reassembly
1. Install spring cup washer, spring and sliding clutch gear on front side gear.
2. Install snap ring retaining sliding clutch to front side gear.
3. Using petroleum jelly, load (123) roller bearings and spacers in front side gear.
4. Install thrust washer in gear end of the front side gear, then slide sprocket onto clutch splines and install retaining ring.

Input Shaft Disassembly, Fig. 59
1. Slide thrust washer and spacer from shaft, then remove snap ring retaining

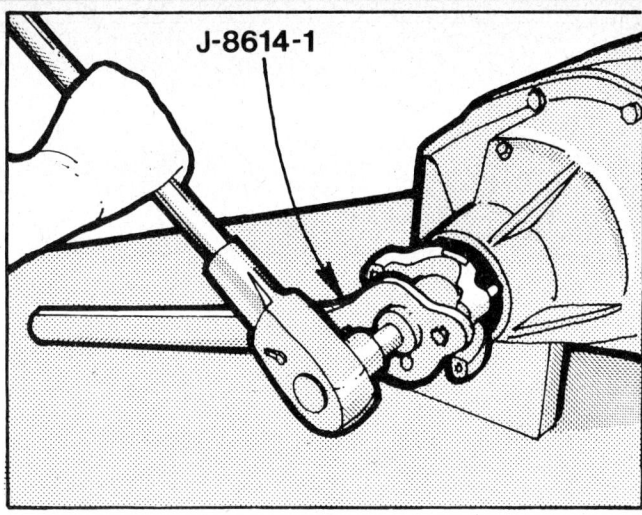

Fig. 58 Removing rear output flange. New Process 203 transfer case

input bearing retainer assembly to shaft. Remove bearing retainer assembly from shaft.
2. Support low speed gear and tap shaft out from the gear and thrust washer.

NOTE: Observe thrust washer pin locations in shaft.

3. Remove snap ring retaining input bearing in bearing retainer, then tap bearing out from the retainer.
4. Remove pilot roller bearings (15 total) and O-ring from input shaft.
5. Clean, inspect and replace parts as necessary.

Input Shaft Reassembly
1. Press bearing into retainer with ball loading slots toward concave side of retainer.
2. Install large snap ring retaining bearing in the retainer.

NOTE: Use size A, B, C or D snap ring to provide tightest fit.

3. Install low speed gear on shaft with clutch end facing toward gear end of shaft and position thrust washers onto shaft, aligning slot in washer with pin in shaft. Slide or tap washer into place.
4. Position input bearing retainer onto shaft and install snap ring, holding bearing in position on shaft.

NOTE: Use size A, B, C, or D snap ring to provide tightest fit.

5. Slide spacer and thrust washer onto shaft and align spacer with locator pin.
6. Using heavy grease, install (15) roller bearings and O-ring on end of shaft.

Removing Shifter Assembly, Fig. 59
1. Remove poppet plate spring, plug and gasket, then disengage sliding clutch gear from input gear. Remove clutch fork and sliding gear from case.
2. Remove shift lever retaining nut, upper shift lever, shift lever snap ring and lower lever.
3. Push shifter shaft assembly down and remove lockout clutch connector link.

NOTE: Long end of connector link engages poppet plate.

4. Remove shifter shaft assembly and separate the inner and outer shifter shafts. Remove and discard O-rings.
5. Inspect poppet plate for damage. If necessary drive pivot shaft from case and remove poppet plate and spring from case.

Removing Input Gear Assembly, Fig. 59
1. Remove input gear bearing and remove large snap ring from bearing.
2. Tap input gear and bearing out from the case then remove snap ring retaining input shaft bearing with the shaft and remove bearing from input gear.

Removing Countergear Assembly, Fig. 59
1. Using tool J-24745, remove countershaft from cluster gear and remove cluster gear assembly.

NOTE: Recover roller bearings (72 total) from gear case and shaft.

2. Remove countergear thrust washers.
3. Clean, inspect and replace parts as necessary.

Installing Countergear Assembly
1. Using tool J-24745 and heavy grease, install (72) roller bearings and spacers in countergear bore.
2. Using heavy grease, position countershaft thrust washers in case. Engage tab on washers with slot in case thrust surface.
3. Position countergear assembly in case and install countershaft through front face of range box and into gear assembly. Flat on countershaft face should face forward and must be aligned with case gasket.

Installing Input Gear Assembly
1. Install bearing (without large snap ring) on input gear shaft positioning snap ring groove outward and install new retaining ring on shaft. Position input gear and bearing in housing.

TRANSFER CASES

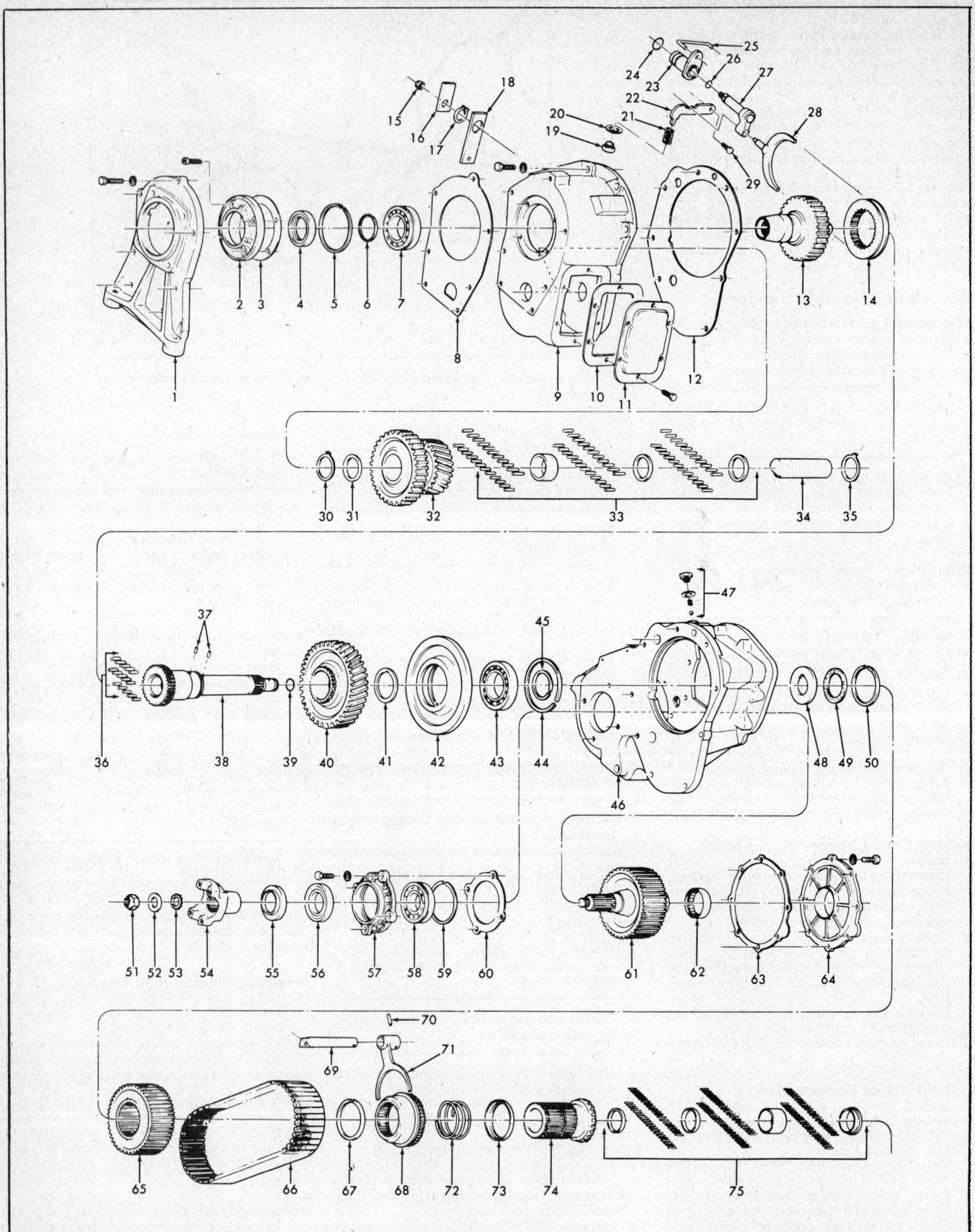

TRANSFER CASES

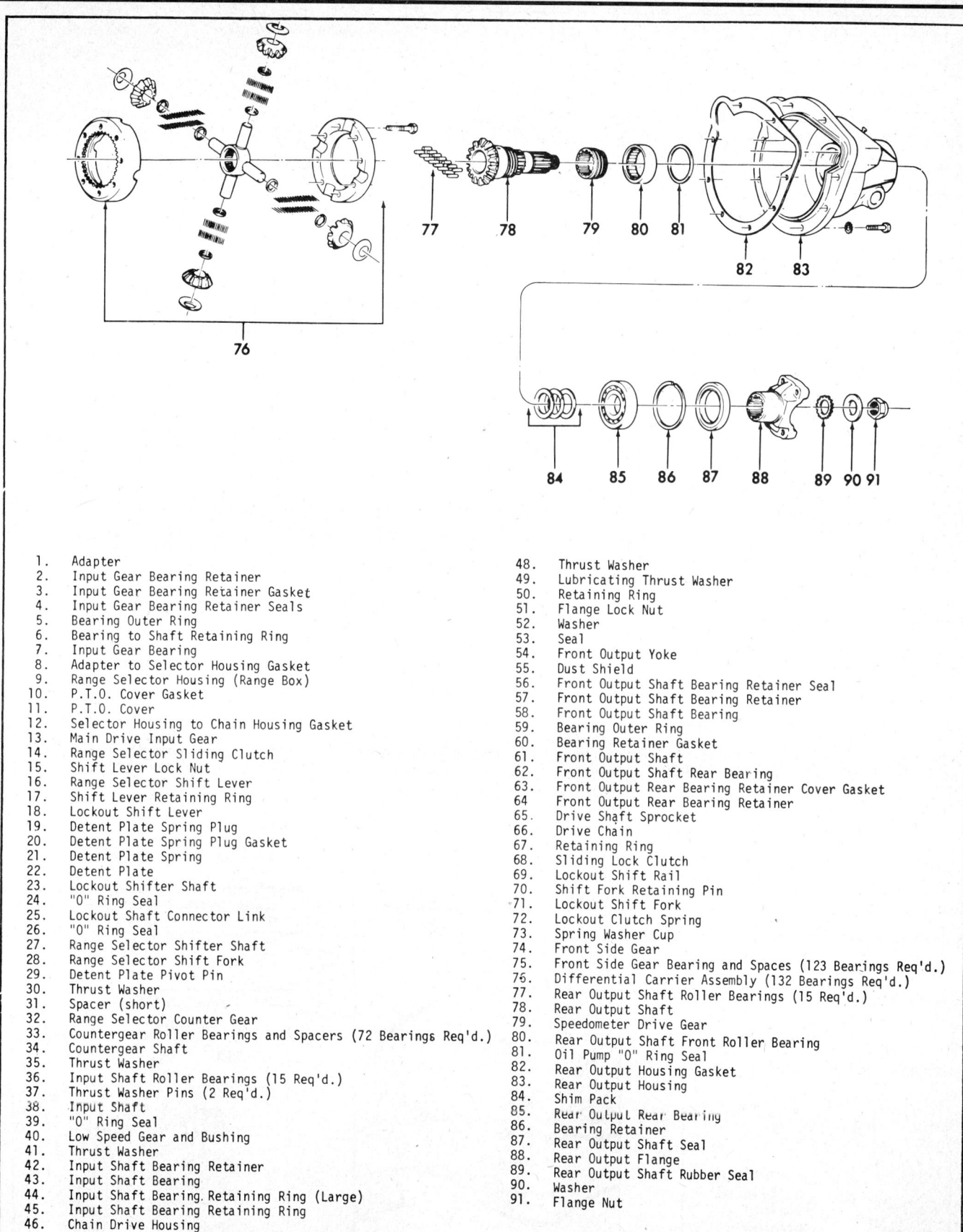

1. Adapter
2. Input Gear Bearing Retainer
3. Input Gear Bearing Retainer Gasket
4. Input Gear Bearing Retainer Seals
5. Bearing Outer Ring
6. Bearing to Shaft Retaining Ring
7. Input Gear Bearing
8. Adapter to Selector Housing Gasket
9. Range Selector Housing (Range Box)
10. P.T.O. Cover Gasket
11. P.T.O. Cover
12. Selector Housing to Chain Housing Gasket
13. Main Drive Input Gear
14. Range Selector Sliding Clutch
15. Shift Lever Lock Nut
16. Range Selector Shift Lever
17. Shift Lever Retaining Ring
18. Lockout Shift Lever
19. Detent Plate Spring Plug
20. Detent Plate Spring Plug Gasket
21. Detent Plate Spring
22. Detent Plate
23. Lockout Shifter Shaft
24. "O" Ring Seal
25. Lockout Shaft Connector Link
26. "O" Ring Seal
27. Range Selector Shifter Shaft
28. Range Selector Shift Fork
29. Detent Plate Pivot Pin
30. Thrust Washer
31. Spacer (short)
32. Range Selector Counter Gear
33. Countergear Roller Bearings and Spacers (72 Bearings Req'd.)
34. Countergear Shaft
35. Thrust Washer
36. Input Shaft Roller Bearings (15 Req'd.)
37. Thrust Washer Pins (2 Req'd.)
38. Input Shaft
39. "O" Ring Seal
40. Low Speed Gear and Bushing
41. Thrust Washer
42. Input Shaft Bearing Retainer
43. Input Shaft Bearing
44. Input Shaft Bearing Retaining Ring (Large)
45. Input Shaft Bearing Retaining Ring
46. Chain Drive Housing
47. Lockout Shift Rail Poppet Plug, Gasket, Spring and Ball.
48. Thrust Washer
49. Lubricating Thrust Washer
50. Retaining Ring
51. Flange Lock Nut
52. Washer
53. Seal
54. Front Output Yoke
55. Dust Shield
56. Front Output Shaft Bearing Retainer Seal
57. Front Output Shaft Bearing Retainer
58. Front Output Shaft Bearing
59. Bearing Outer Ring
60. Bearing Retainer Gasket
61. Front Output Shaft
62. Front Output Shaft Rear Bearing
63. Front Output Rear Bearing Retainer Cover Gasket
64. Front Output Rear Bearing Retainer
65. Drive Shaft Sprocket
66. Drive Chain
67. Retaining Ring
68. Sliding Lock Clutch
69. Lockout Shift Rail
70. Shift Fork Retaining Pin
71. Lockout Shift Fork
72. Lockout Clutch Spring
73. Spring Washer Cup
74. Front Side Gear
75. Front Side Gear Bearing and Spaces (123 Bearings Req'd.)
76. Differential Carrier Assembly (132 Bearings Req'd.)
77. Rear Output Shaft Roller Bearings (15 Req'd.)
78. Rear Output Shaft
79. Speedometer Drive Gear
80. Rear Output Shaft Front Roller Bearing
81. Oil Pump "O" Ring Seal
82. Rear Output Housing Gasket
83. Rear Output Housing
84. Shim Pack
85. Rear Output Rear Bearing
86. Bearing Retainer
87. Rear Output Shaft Seal
88. Rear Output Flange
89. Rear Output Shaft Rubber Seal
90. Washer
91. Flange Nut

Fig. 59 New process 203 transfer case legend & exploded view of differential carrier assembly & rear output housing (first design)

TRANSFER CASES

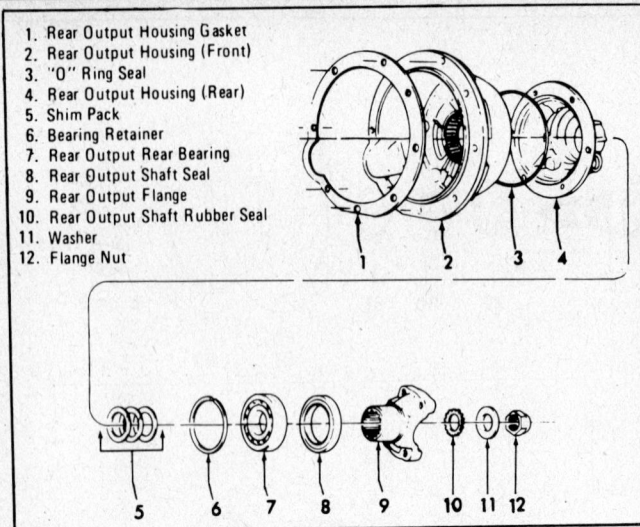

Fig. 59A New Process 203 transfer case rear output housing (second design) exploded view

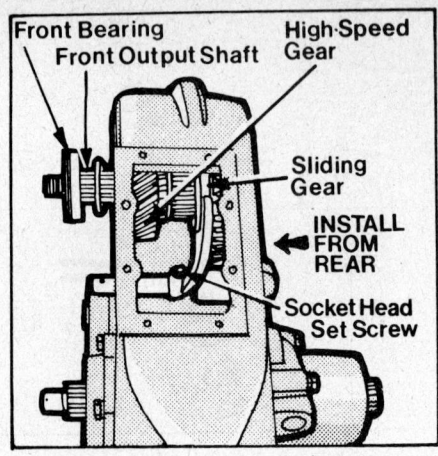

Fig. 60 Replacing front output shaft

NOTE: Use size A, B, C or D snap ring to provide tightest fit.

2. Install snap ring onto bearing.
3. Align oil slot in retainer with drain hole in case and install input gear bearing retainer, gasket and bolts. Torque bolts to 30 ft. lbs.

Installing Shifter Shaft Assembly

1. Install poppet plate and pivot pin assembly into housing. Use sealant on pin.
2. Install new O-rings on inner and outer shifter shafts then lubricate O-rings and assemble inner shaft into the outer shaft.
3. Push shifter shafts into housing, engaging long end of locknut clutch connector link to the outer shifter shaft before the shaft assembly bottoms out in housing.
4. Install lower shift lever, retaining ring, upper shift lever and shifter shaft retaining nut.
5. Install shift fork and sliding clutch gear. Push fork up into shifter shaft assembly to engage poppet plate, sliding gear forward onto the input shaft gear.
6. Install poppet plate spring, gasket and plug into top of housing. Check spring engagement with poppet plate.

Input Gear Bearing Replacement, Fig. 59

1. Remove bearing retainer and gasket.
2. Remove snap ring retaining bearing on the shaft. Pry bearing from case and remove it from shaft.

NOTE: Inspect input gear for burrs, scoring, heat discoloration etc. and inspect seal in retainer. Replace as necessary.

3. Install bearing and snap ring onto input gear shaft. Position bearing to case and tap into place using a small hammer.

NOTE: Use size A, B, C or D snap ring to provide tightest fit.

4. Install new snap ring on shaft and position new gasket and bearing retainer to housing. Install bolts and torque to 30 ft. lbs.

Input Gear Bearing Retainer Seal Replacement

1. Remove bearing retainer bolts, retainer and gasket.
2. Pry seal out of retainer.
3. Install seal using tool J-21359.
4. Install bearing retainer and gasket and torque bolts to 30 ft. lbs.

Rear Output Shaft Housing Disassembly, Fig. 59

1. Remove speedometer driven gear from housing and if not already removed, remove flange nut, washer and flange from shaft.
2. Using a soft hammer, tap on flange end of pinion and remove pinion from carrier. If speedometer drive gear is not on the pinion shaft, reach into carrier and remove it from housing.
3. Using a screwdriver, pry seal out and pry behind open ends of snap ring retaining rear bearing in housing and remove snap ring.
4. Tap rear bearing out, then using a long drift inserted through rear opening drive the front bearing out of housing.

Rear Output Shaft Housing Reassembly

1. Using grease, position seal in bore and press roller bearing into place until it bottoms in housing.

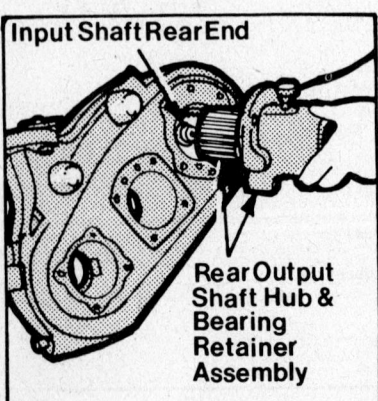

Fig. 61 Replacing rear output shaft & bearing

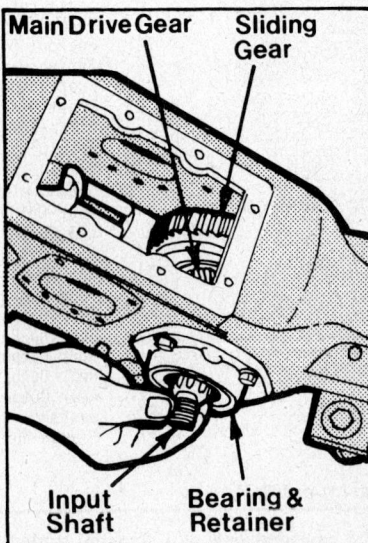

Fig. 62 Replacing input shaft

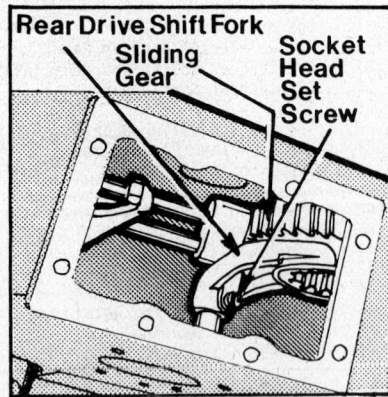

Fig. 63 Rear drive shift fork & sliding gear installation

TRANSFER CASES

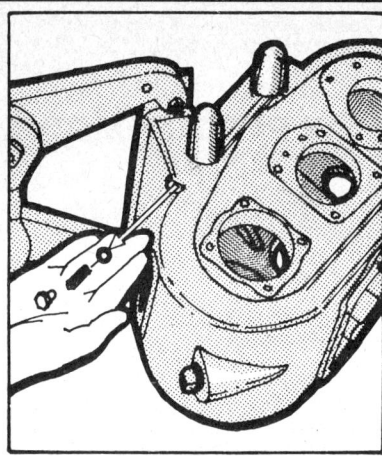

Fig. 64 Front drive shift rail detent ball, spring & plug installation

2. Tap rear bearing into place and install snap ring retaining bearing in case.

NOTE: Use size A, B, C or D snap ring to provide tightest fit.

Torque Specifications

Intermediate Case to Range Box Bolts	30 ft. lbs.
Front Output Bearing Retainer Bolts	30 ft. lbs.
Output Shaft Yoke Nuts	150 ft. lbs.
Front Output Rear Bearing Retainer Bolts	30 ft. lbs.
Differential Assembly Screws	45 ft. lbs.
Rear Output Shaft Housing	30 ft. lbs.
Poppet Ball Retainer Nut	15 ft. lbs.
Power Take Off Cover Bolts	15 ft. lbs.
Front Input Bearing Retainer Bolts	20 ft. lbs.
Filler Plug	25 ft. lbs.

3. Using tool J-22388, drive rear seal into

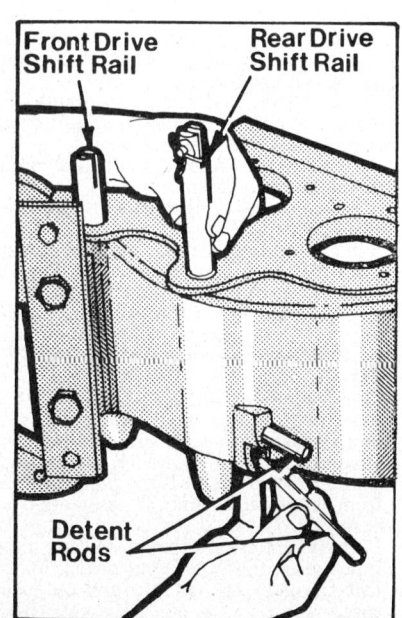

Fig. 66 Shaft rail & detent plugs installation

housing until it is about 1/8–3/8 inch below housing face.
4. Install speedometer drive gear and shims (approximately .050 inch thick), install shaft into carrier through front opening.
5. Install flange, washer and nut. Leave nut loose until shim requirements are determined (approximately .060 inch thick).
6. Install speedometer driven gear into housing.

Front Output Shaft Bearing Retainer Seal, Replacement
1. Pry out seal from retainer.
2. Clean and inspect retainer.
3. Apply sealer to outer diameter of seal and install using tool J-22836 into retainer.

Front Output Shaft Rear Bearing, Replacement
1. Remove rear cover and gasket from transfer case.
2. Press out old bearing and press in new bearing until it is flush with opening. Use a block of wood over bearing.
3. Install cover and gasket and torque bolts to 30 ft. lbs.

Transfer Case Reassembly, Fig. 59
1. Place range box on blocks with input gear side facing down and position range box to transfer case gasket on input housing.
2. Install lockout clutch and drive sprocket assembly on input shaft assembly.

NOTE: Install a 2 inch band type clamp on end of shaft to prevent losing bearings from clutch assembly.

3. Install input shaft, lockout clutch and drive sprocket assembly into range box, aligning tab on bearing retainer with notch in gasket.
4. Connect lockout clutch shift rail to the connector link and position rail in housing bore. Rotate the shifter shaft while lowering shift rail into the housing, to prevent the link and rail from being disconnected.
5. Install chain into housing, positioning chain around outer wall of housing then install chain housing onto range box, engaging the shift rail channel of the housing to the shift rail. Position chain onto input drive sprocket.
6. Install front output sprocket into case engaging drive chain with sprocket. Rotate drive gear to aid in positioning chain onto drive sprocket.
7. Install shift fork onto clutch assembly and shift rail, then push clutch assembly into drive sprocket. Install roll pin retaining shift fork to shift rail.
8. Install front output shaft bearing, retainer, gasket and bolts.
9. Install front output shaft flange, gasket, seal, washer and nut. Install bolts in flange and tap dust shield into place.
10. Install front output shaft rear bearing retainer, gasket and bolts.

NOTE: If rear bearing was removed, place new bearing on outside face of cover and press into cover until bearing is flush with opening.

11. Install front output shaft flange, gasket, seal, washer and retaining nut. Tap dust shield back into place after installing flange bolts.
12. Install front output shaft rear bearing

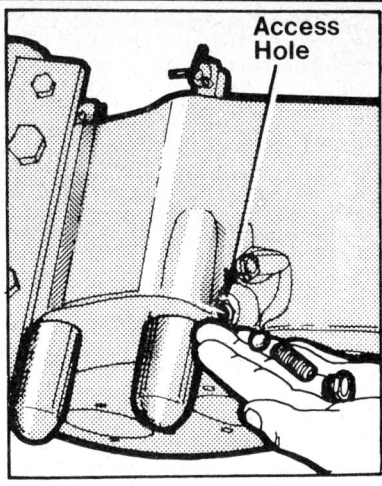

Fig. 65 Rear drive shift rail detent ball spring & plug installation

retainer, gasket and retaining bolts.
13. Install differential carrier assembly on input shaft with bolt heads facing rear of shaft.
14. Install rear output housing, gasket and bolts. Load bearings in pinion shaft.
15. Install speedometer gear and shims (about .050 inch) onto the output shaft.
16. Position the rear output of the rear assembly onto the rear output housing of the front assembly. Make sure that O-ring is properly positioned on the front section of the output housing.

NOTE: Make sure that vent is in the upward position.

17. Install flange, washer and retaining nut. Leave nut loose until shim requirements are determined.
18. Check shim requirements as follows:
    a. Make sure that output shaft retaining nut is loose about .060 inch.
    b. Install a dial indicator in such a manner as to contact the end of the output shaft.
    c. Push in rear output shaft to its full travel while rotating front output yoke and holding rear output yoke stationary. Set dial indicator to zero on the

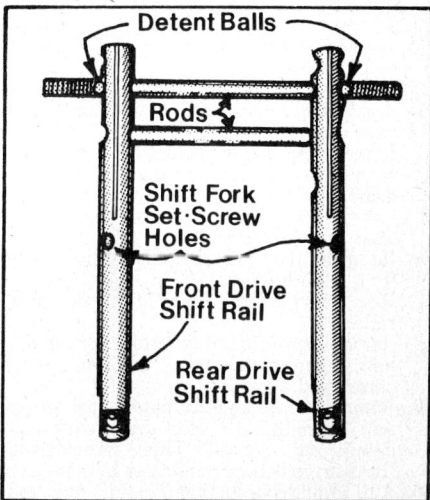

Fig. 67 Shift mechanism

TRANSFER CASES

highest reading obtained.
d. Pry out rear output shaft yoke until the maximum reading is obtained on the dial indicator. The allowable end play is .001–.010 inch. Add or remove shims as required to obtain the allowable end play.
e. Check to make sure that end play is not too tight after the nut has been tightened, by holding the rear yoke stationary and rotating the front yoke. If the yoke can be rotated by hand and the "bumps" are felt, the end play is acceptable.
19. Install the speedometer driven gear into the housing.
20. Install lockout clutch shift rail poppet ball, spring and plug.
21. Install poppet plate spring, gasket and plug, if not installed previously.
22. Install shift levers on shifter shafts.
23. Torque all bolts, lock nuts and plugs to specifications listed above.

DANA MODEL 24

Disassembly

1. Remove power take-off cover plate, then the idler shaft bearing retainers.
2. With a mallet, tap idler shaft and bearing rearward until rear bearing can be removed from case.
3. Remove idler shaft, two gears and spacer.
4. Remove idler shaft front bearing from case.
5. Remove flange retaining nuts from front output shaft, rear output shaft and input shaft. Then, remove the flanges and washers.
6. Remove the front and rear bearing retainers from the front output shaft.
7. Tap front output shaft and the rear bearing through the gears and case, Fig. 60, then remove high speed gear from case.
8. Remove the front output shaft front bearing and washer from case.
9. Remove set screw retaining front drive shaft fork to shift rail, then the front output shaft sliding gear from case.
10. If input shaft oil seal replacement is necessary, remove seal with a suitable puller.
11. Remove the rear output shaft bearing retainer, then the speedometer drive assembly from the retainer.
12. With a mallet, tap on the front of the input shaft to loosen the rear output shaft assembly from case, then remove the rear output shaft and bearing retainer assembly, Fig. 61.
13. Tap the input shaft through front bearing, main drive gear, sliding gear and from case, Fig. 62.
14. Remove main drive gear from case, then with a mallet, drive the input shaft front bearing from case.
15. Remove set screw retaining rear drive shift fork to shift rail, Fig. 63.
16. Remove rear output shaft sliding gear from case, Fig. 63.
17. Remove shift rail link from the two shift rails.
18. Remove retaining plug, detent spring and ball engaging the front drive shift rail detent rod, Fig. 64.
19. Remove retaining plug, detent spring and ball engaging the rear drive shift rail detent rod, Fig. 65. Then, remove the front drive detent rod access hole plug.
20. Pull front drive shaft rail to fully outward position.
21. Pull rear drive shift rail outward to permit the two detent rods to slide from case, Fig. 66.
22. Remove front and rear drive shift rails and forks from case.
23. Remove shift rail seals from case with a suitable puller.

Assembly

1. Press new oil seals into place in the case or bearing retainers.
2. If necessary, replace bearings on input shaft and the front and rear output shafts with a suitable press.
3. Slide front drive shift rail into case and position shift fork on rail.

NOTE: When installing the shift rails, the detents should be positioned as shown in Fig. 67.

4. Insert the two detent rods into case, Fig. 66, then install the rear drive shift fork, and hold the detent rods and shift fork in position as the rear drive shift rail is inserted as far as possible.
5. Pull the front drive shift rail out to the next detent and push the rear drive shift rail fully into position. Then, push the front drive shift rail back into position.
6. Install rear drive shift rail detent ball, spring and retaining plug, then the access hole plug, Fig. 65.
7. Install front drive shift rail detent ball, spring and retaining plug, Fig. 64.
8. Install shift rail link in the two shift rails.
9. Place the rear output shaft sliding gear in the shift fork and secure with set screw to rear drive shift rail, Fig. 63.
10. Install input shaft front bearing and retainer assembly. Coat retainer and attaching bolts with a suitable sealer.
11. Install main drive gear into case and slide input shaft through rear of case, main drive gear and the front bearing and retainer, Fig. 62.
12. Install roller bearing into splined hub of rear output shaft. Then, install the shaft and bearing retainer assembly, ensuring the output shaft is aligned with the input shaft, Fig. 61. Coat the case, bearing retainer and bolts with suitable sealer.
13. Place front output shaft sliding gear in the shift fork and secure with set screw to the front drive shift rail.
14. Hold sliding gear and high speed gear in position, install the front output shaft and rear bearing assembly through the two gear from the rear of case.
15. Install front output shaft rear bearing retainer and gasket. Coat retainer and bolts with a suitable sealer.
16. Install washer and front bearing, front bearing retainer and gasket. Coat retainer and bolts with a suitable sealer.
17. Install flange, washer, flange retaining nuts and cotter key on the input shaft, front output shaft and the rear output shaft.
18. Install the idler shaft gears into case, then the idler shaft and rear bearing assembly from the rear of case. Install rear bearing retainer plate, applying sealer to plate and bolts.
19. Place spacer on front of idler shaft, then the front bearing. Tap bearing into place with a mallet.
20. Install washer, retaining nut and cotter key on front of idler shaft.
21. Install idler shaft front bearing retainer plate. Apply sealer to the plate and bolts.
22. Install power take-off cover plate. Apply sealer to plate and bolts.

NEW PROCESS MODEL 208

Disassembly, Fig 68

1. Remove fill and drain plugs. Drain lubricant from transfer case.
2. Remove front and rear yokes. Discard the yoke seal washers and yoke nuts.
3. Rotate transfer case and position on wood blocks with the front case resting on the wood. If necessary cut "V" notches in the blocks so the front case rests squarely on the blocks.
4. Remove lock mode indicator switch and washer.
5. Remove detent bolt, spring and ball.
6. Mark relationship between rear retainer and case for alignment at reassembly.
7. Remove rear retainer attaching bolts, then the rear retainer attaching bolts, then the rear retainer and pump housing as an assembly. Do not pry retainer from case. If necessary, use a plastic mallet to tape retainer.
8. Remove pump housing from retainer then the pump seal from housing. Discard the seal.
9. Remove speedometer drive gear from mainshaft.
10. Remove oil pump from mainshaft noting position of pump for reassembly. The side of the pump facing toward inside of case is recessed.
11. Remove rear case to front case retaining bolts, then the rear case from front case.

NOTE: To remove rear case, insert a suitable screwdriver into th slots in the case ends and gently pry upward. Do not attempt to wedge the case halves apart at any point on the mating surfaces.

12. Remove front output shaft rear thrust bearing assembly. Note position of bearing and races for reassembly.
13. Remove driven sprocket retaining snap ring.
14. Remove drive sprocket retaining snap ring, then the thrust washer and spacer washer, if equipped.
15. Remove drive and driven sprockets and the drive chain as an assembly. Lift evenly on both sprockets to remove.
16. Remove front output shaft and front thrust bearing assembly.
17. Remove sprocket carrier stop ring and clutch spring, Fig. 69.
18. Remove sliding clutch, mode fork and mode fork spring as an assembly, Fig. 70. Then remove shift rail.
19. Remove sprocket carrier, needle bearing upper retainer, thrust washer and mainshaft needle bearings as an assembly, Fig. 71.
20. Remove mainshaft.
21. Remove annulus gear retaining ring and thrust washer, then the annulus gear and range fork as an assembly. Rotate fork counter-clockwise to disengage fork lug from range sector and lift assembly from case, Fig. 72.
23. Remove mainshaft thrust bearing from input gear, then the input gear, Fig. 74. Lift the gear straight up and out from case.
24. Remove input gear thrust bearing and race, Fig. 75. Note position of bearing and

TRANSFER CASES

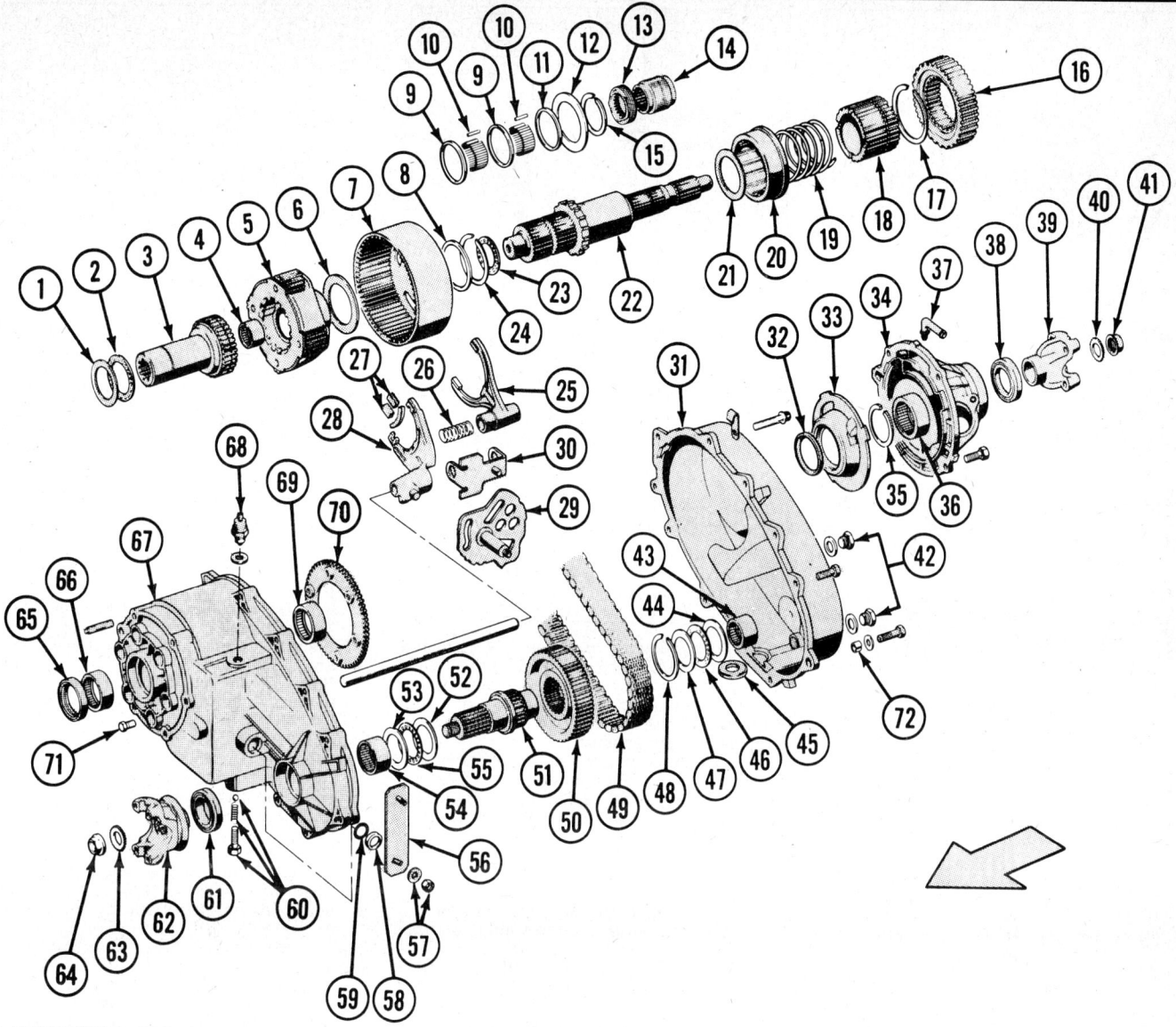

1. INPUT GEAR THRUST WASHER
2. INPUT GEAR THRUST BEARING
3. INPUT GEAR
4. MAINSHAFT PILOT BEARING
5. PLANETARY ASSEMBLY
6. PLANETARY THRUST WASHER
7. ANNULUS GEAR
8. ANNULUS GEAR THRUST WASHER
9. NEEDLE BEARING SPACERS
10. MAINSHAFT NEEDLE BEARINGS (120)
11. NEEDLE BEARING SPACER
12. THRUST WASHER
13. OIL PUMP
14. SPEEDOMETER GEAR
15. DRIVE SPROCKET RETAINING RING
16. DRIVE SPROCKET
17. SPROCKET CARRIER STOP RING
18. SPROCKET CARRIER
19. CLUTCH SPRING
20. SLIDING CLUTCH
21. THRUST WASHER
22. MAINSHAFT
23. MAINSHAFT THRUST BEARING
24. ANNULUS GEAR RETAINING RING
25. MODE FORK
26. MODE FORK SPRING
27. RANGE FORK INSERTS
28. RANGE FORK
29. RANGE SECTOR
30. MODE FORK BRACKET
31. REAR CASE
32. SEAL
33. PUMP HOUSING
34. REAR RETAINER
35. REAR OUTPUT BEARING
36. BEARING SNAP RING
37. VENT TUBE
38. REAR SEAL
39. REAR YOKE
40. YOKE SEAL WASHER
41. YOKE NUT
42. DRAIN AND FILL PLUGS
43. FRONT OUTPUT SHAFT REAR BEARING
44. FRONT OUTPUT SHAFT REAR THRUST BEARING RACE (THICK)
45. CASE MAGNET
46. FRONT OUTPUT SHAFT REAR THRUST BEARING
47. FRONT OUTPUT SHAFT REAR THRUST BEARING RACE (THIN)
48. DRIVEN SPROCKET RETAINING RING
49. DRIVE CHAIN
50. DRIVEN SPROCKET
51. FRONT OUTPUT SHAFT
52. FRONT OUTPUT SHAFT FRONT THRUST BEARING RACE (THIN)
53. FRONT OUTPUT SHAFT FRONT THRUST BEARING RACE (THICK)
54. FRONT OUTPUT SHAFT FRONT BEARING
55. FRONT OUTPUT SHAFT FRONT THRUST BEARING
56. OPERATING LEVER
57. WASHER AND LOCKNUT
58. RANGE SECTOR SHAFT SEAL RETAINER
59. RANGE SECTOR SHAFT SEAL
60. DETENT BALL, SPRING AND RETAINER BOLT
61. FRONT SEAL
62. FRONT YOKE
63. YOKE SEAL WASHER
64. YOKE NUT
65. INPUT GEAR OIL SEAL
66. INPUT GEAR FRONT BEARING
67. FRONT CASE
68. LOCK MODE INDICATOR SWITCH AND WASHER
69. INPUT GEAR REAR BEARING
70. LOCKPLATE
71. LOCKPLATE BOLTS
72. CASE ALIGNMENT DOWELS

Fig. 68 New Process model 208 transfer case, disassembled

TRANSFER CASES

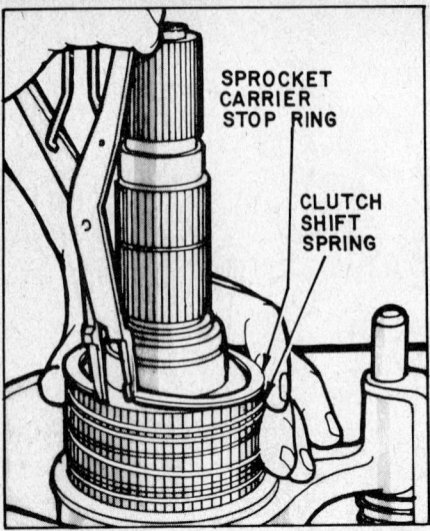

Fig. 69 Sprocket carrier stop ring & clutch spring replacement

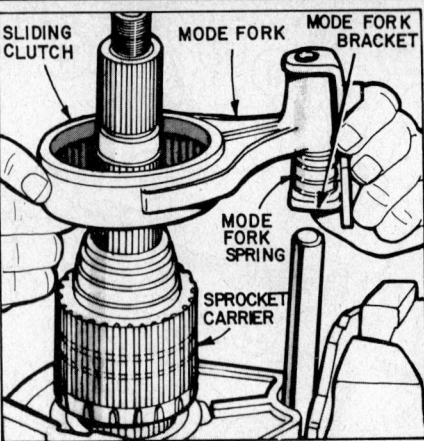

Fig. 70 Mode fork, spring, bracket & sliding clutch replacement

Fig. 71 Sprocket carriers, bearing retainers, thrust washer & needle bearing replacement

race for reassembly.
25. Remove range sector operating lever attaching nut and washer, then the lever. Remove sector shaft seal and seal retainer.
26. Remove range sector.
27. Inspect lock plate. If lock plate is loose, worn or damaged, remove lock plate.
28. Remove output shaft seals from front and rear case seal bores.

Sub-Assembly Service

Lock Plate, Replace
1. Remove and discard lock plate attaching bolts.
2. Remove lock plate from case, Fig. 68.
3. Coat the case and lock plate surfaces around the bolt holes with Loctite 515 sealer or equivalent.
4. Position new lock plate in the case and align bolt holes in lock plate and case.
5. Coat new lock plate attaching bolts with Loctite 271 sealer or equivalent.
6. Install and torque lock plate attaching bolts to 30 ft. lbs.

BEARING, BUSHING & SEAL REPLACEMENT

NOTE: The following bearings, bushings and seals are replaced using special service tools. However, they may also be replaced using suitable equivalent tooling and when using these tools, care should be taken as not to damage any components.

Also, all the bearings used must be correctly positioned to prevent covering the bearing oil feed holes. After replacing any bearing, check position of bearing to ensure that the oil feed hole is not obstructed or blocked by the bearing.

Rear Output Bearing & Seal, Replace
1. Remove bearing retaining snap ring and tap bearing from retainer with a mallet.
2. Remove rear seal using a suitable screwdriver or drift.
3. Install new bearing using tool J-7818. Ensure that shielded side of bearing faces toward inside of case.
4. Install bearing retaining snap ring.
5. Install new rear seal using tools J-8092 and J-29162.

Front Output Shaft Front Bearing, Replace
1. Remove bearing using tools J-8092 and J-29168.
2. Install new bearing using tools J-8092 and J-29167.
3. Remove tools and check bearing position to ensure that oil feed hole is clear.

Front Output Shaft Rear Bearing, Replace
1. Remove bearing using tools J-26941 and slide hammer J-2619-01.
2. Install new bearing using tools J-8092 and J-29163.
3. Remove tools and ensure that oil feed hole is clear and that the bearing is seated flush with edge of case bore to permit space for the thrust bearing assembly.

Input Gear Front & Rear Bearing, Replace
1. Remove both bearings simultaneously with tools J-8092 and J-29170.
2. Install new bearings one at a time. Install the rear bearing first, then the front bearing. Use tools J-8092 and J-29169.
3. Remove tools and check position of bearing to ensure that the oil feed hole is clear

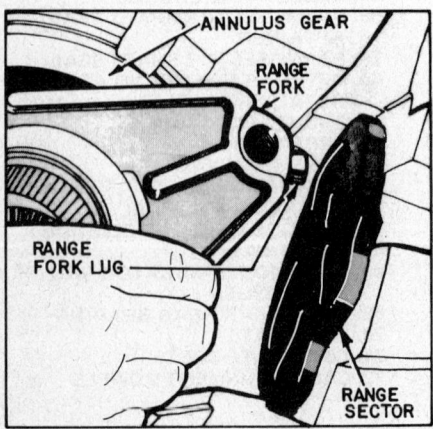

Fig. 72 Annulus gear & range fork replacement

Fig. 73 Planetary thrust washer & planetary assembly replacement

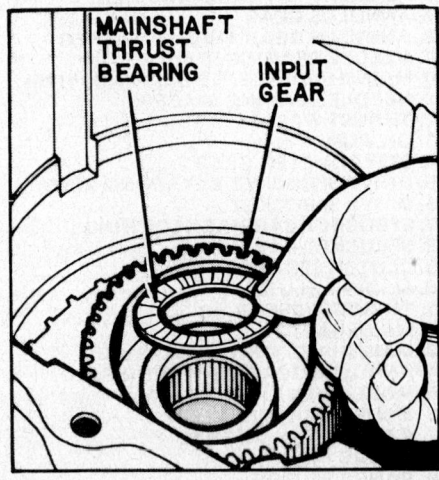

Fig. 74 Mainshaft thrust bearing & input gear replacement

TRANSFER CASES

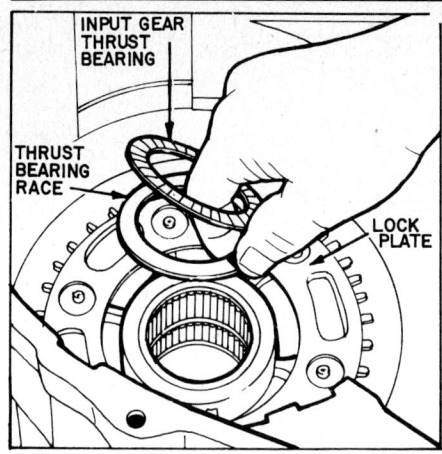

Fig. 75 Input gear thrust bearing & race replacement

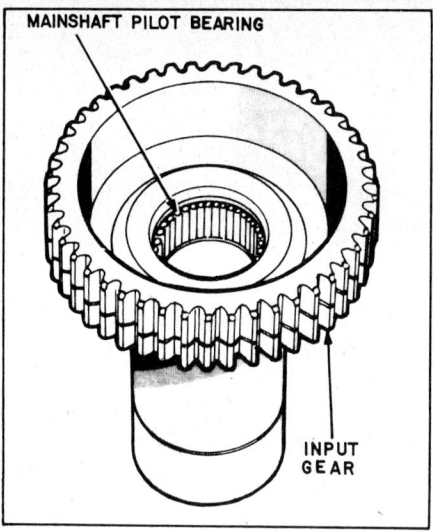

Fig. 76 Mainshaft pilot bearing installation

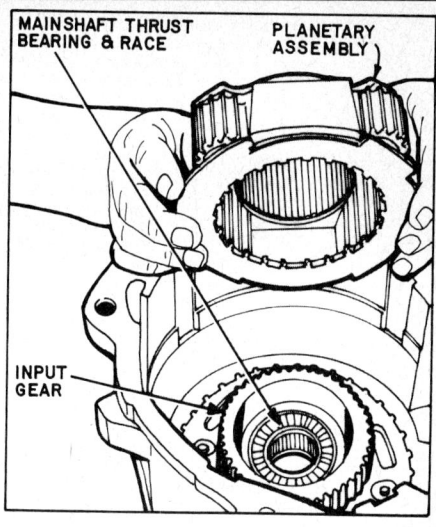

Fig. 77 Input gear, mainshaft thrust bearing & planetary installation

and that the bearings are flush with the case bore surfaces.

Mainshaft Pilot Bearing, Replace
1. If bearing cannot be removed by hand, remove by using slide hammer J-2619-01 and J-29369-1. A similar internal type blind hole bearing puller may also be used.
2. Install new bearing using tools J-8092 and J-29174.
3. Remove tools and check position of bearing to ensure that the oil feed hole is clear and that the bearing is seated flush with edge of bearing bore, Fig. 76.

Annulus Gear Bushing, Replace
1. Remove bushing with tools J-8092 and J-29185.
2. Install new bushing with tools J-8092 and J-29185-2.
3. Remove any metal chips made by bushing replacement.

Assembly, Fig. 68

NOTE: During assembly, lubricate all components with 10W-30 engine oil or petroleum jelly where indicated only. Do not use any other types of lubricant.

1. Install input gear race and thrust bearing into front case, then the input gear, Fig. 77.
2. Install mainshaft thrust bearing in input gear, Fig. 77.
3. Install range sector shaft seal and seal retainer, then the range sector.
4. Install operating lever on range sector shaft. Install and torque shaft washer and lock nut to 18 ft. lbs.
5. Install planetary assembly over input gear and ensure that the assembly is fully seated and meshed with the gear.
6. Install planetary thrust washer on planetary hub.
7. Install inserts into range fork, if removed.
8. Engage range fork into annulus gear and install annulus gear over planetary assembly. Ensure that the range fork lug is inserted fully into range sector slot.
9. Install annulus gear thrust washer and retaining snap ring.
10. Align shift rail bores in the case and range fork and install shift rail.

NOTE: The shift rail bore in the case must be dry and not contain any oil. A small amount of oil may prevent the shift rail from seating completely and also may prevent front case installation.

11. Install mainshaft. Ensure that the mainshaft thrust bearing is seated properly in the input gear before installing mainshaft.
12. Thickly coat sprocket carrier bore with petroleum jelly and position bearing retainer at center of carrier bore.
13. Coat mainshaft needle bearings with petroleum jelly and install 60 needle bearings in each end of sprocket carrier bore. 120 needle bearings are used.
14. Install bearing retainer in each end of sprocket carrier bore and position the thrust washer on the bottom of the carrier, Fig. 78.

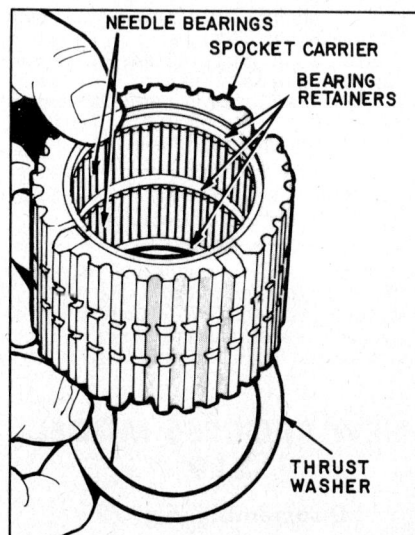

Fig. 78 Sprocket carrier components assembly

15. Align the assembled carrier and needle bearings with the mainshaft and install the assembly on the mainshaft. Use caution as not to dislodge the needle bearings.
16. Assemble the mode fork, fork spring and bracket. Engage the fork in the sliding clutch and install the assembly onto the shift rail and mainshaft.
17. Install clutch spring and stop ring on sprocket carrier.

NOTE: If the sprocket carrier has two ring grooves, install the stop ring in the upper groove only.

18. Install front output shaft front thrust bearing assembly in front case. The proper installation sequence is: thick race, thrust bearing, then thin race.
19. Install front output shaft.
20. Install sprockets and drive chain as an assembly. Position the sprockets in the chain, aligning the sprockets with the shafts and install the assembly.

NOTE: Ensure that the drive sprocket is installed with the recessed side of the sprocket facing toward the inside of the case.

21. Install spacer and thrust washer on drive sprocket, then the sprocket retaining snap ring.
22. Install driven sprocket retaining snap ring.
23. Install front output shaft rear thrust bearing assembly on front output shaft. The proper installation sequence is: thin race, thrust bearing, then thick race.
24. Install oil pump on mainshaft. Ensure that the recessed side of the pump faces toward inside of case.
25. Install speedometer drive gear on mainshaft.
26. Install magnet in front case, if removed.
27. Apply Loctite 515 sealer or equivalent to mating surface of front case. Then, install rear case onto front case.

NOTE: Ensure that the front output shaft

TRANSFER CASES

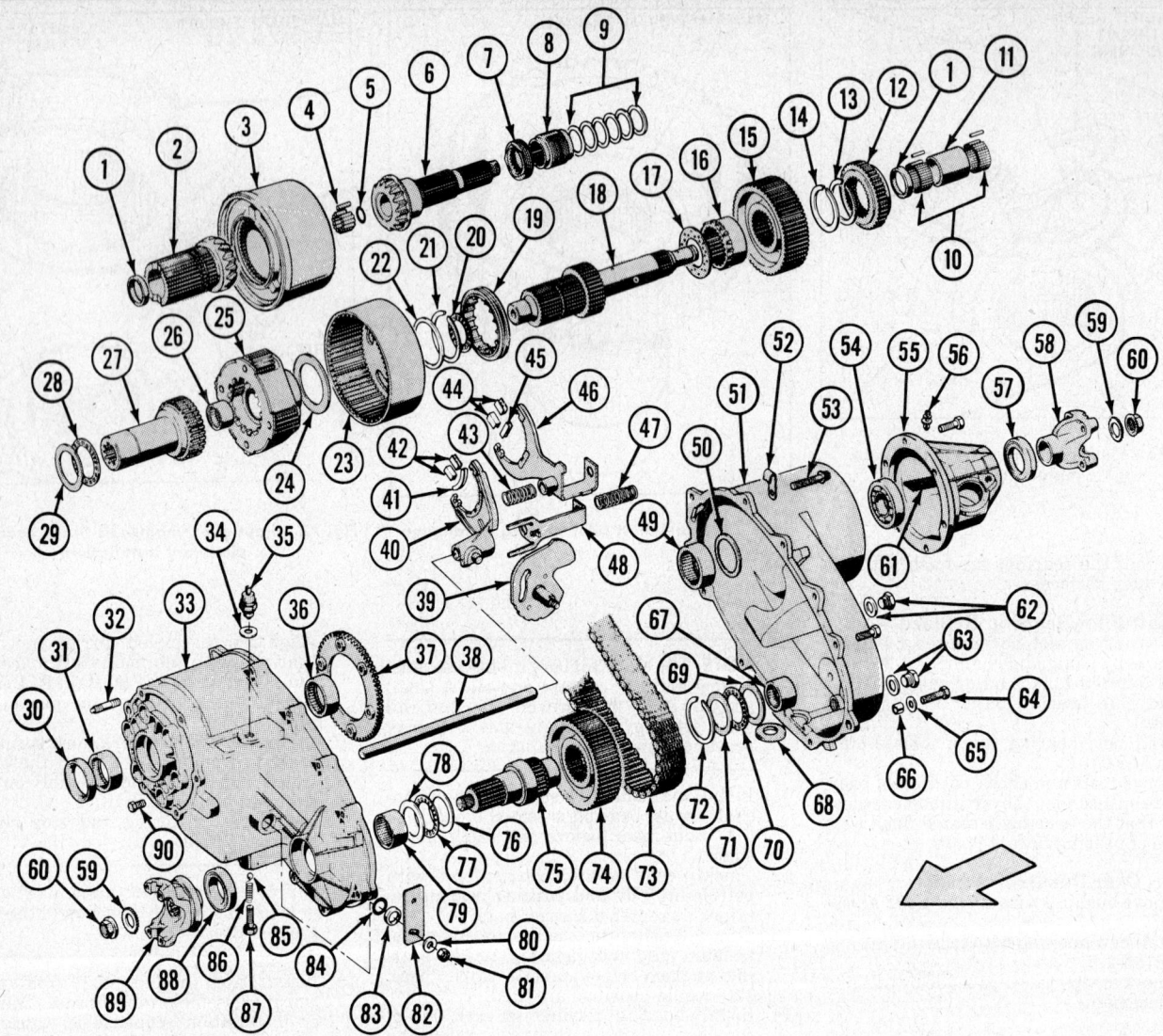

rear thrust bearing assembly is properly seated in the rear case.

28. Align case bolt holes and alignment dowels and install retaining bolts. Alternately torque bolts to 23 ft. lbs.

NOTE: Flat washers are installed on the two bolts at opposite ends of the case.

29. Install rear output bearing in rear retainer, then install retaining snap ring.
30. Install seal into pump housing. Apply petroleum jelly to pump housing tabs. Install housing into rear retainer.
31. Apply Locktite 515 sealer or equivalent to mating surface of rear retainer. Align rear retainer and case alignment marks made during disassembly and install retainer.
32. Install and torque retainer bolts to 23 ft. lbs.
33. Install oil seal into rear retainer bore. Coat the seal lip with petroleum jelly prior to installation.
34. Install washer and indicator switch. Torque switch to 18 ft. lbs.
35. Lightly apply Locktite 515 sealer or equivalent to detent retainer bolt, then install detent ball, spring and bolt. Torque bolt to 23 ft. lbs.
36. Install drain plug and gasket. Torque drain plug to 18 ft. lbs.
37. Install oil seal in front case output shaft bore.
38. Install front and rear yokes.

NOTE: The yoke with the collar is installed on the front output shaft.

39. Install yoke seal washer and yoke nuts. Torque yoke nuts to 120 ft. lbs.
40. Install 6 pints of 10W-30 engine oil into transfer case through fill plug.
41. Install and torque fill plug to 18 ft. lbs.

NEW PROCESS MODEL 219

Disassembly, Fig. 79

1. Remove fill and drain plugs. Drain lubricant from transfer case.
2. Remove front and rear output shaft yokes. Discard yoke seal washers and yoke nuts.
3. Mark relationship between rear retainer and rear case for alignment at reassembly.
4. Remove rear retainer attaching bolts, then the rear retainer. If necessary use a mallet to loosen retainer. Do not pry from case.
5. Remove differential shim and speedometer drive gear from rear output shaft, Fig. 80. Tag the shim or shims for assembly reference.

NOTE: The speedometer drive gear is installed with the long end facing toward the case. Note the gear position for assembly.

6. Remove rear output bearing snap ring, then the bearing from retainer with a mallet.

NOTE: The rear output bearing has one shielded side. Note position for assembly.

TRANSFER CASES

1. MAINSHAFT REAR BEARING SPACER – SHORT (2)
2. SIDE GEAR
3. VISCOUS COUPLING AND DIFFERENTIAL ASSEMBLY
4. MAINSHAFT REAR PILOT ROLLER BEARINGS (15)
5. MAINSHAFT O-RING
6. REAR OUTPUT SHAFT
7. OIL PUMP
8. SPEEDOMETER GEAR
9. DIFFERENTIAL END PLAY SHIMS (SELECTIVE)
10. MAINSHAFT NEEDLE BEARINGS (82)
11. MAINSHAFT REAR BEARING SPACER
12. CLUTCH GEAR
13. CLUTCH GEAR LOCATING RING
14. DRIVE SPROCKET LOCATING RING
15. DRIVE SPROCKET
16. SIDE GEAR CLUTCH
17. MAINSHAFT THRUST WASHER
18. MAINSHAFT
19. CLUTCH SLEEVE
20. MAINSHAFT THRUST BEARING
21. ANNULUS GEAR RETAINING RING
22. ANNULUS GEAR THRUST WASHER
23. ANNULUS GEAR
24. PLANETARY THRUST WASHER
25. PLANETARY ASSEMBLY
26. MAINSHAFT FRONT PILOT BEARING
27. INPUT GEAR
28. INPUT GEAR THRUST BEARING
29. INPUT GEAR THRUST BEARING RACE
30. INPUT GEAR OIL SEAL
31. INPUT GEAR FRONT BEARING
32. FRONT CASE MOUNTING STUD (6)
33. FRONT CASE
34. LOCK MODE INDICATOR SWITCH GASKET
35. LOCK MODE INDICATOR SWITCH
36. INPUT GEAR REAR BEARING
37. LOW RANGE LOCKPLATE
38. SHIFT RAIL
39. RANGE SECTOR
40. RANGE FORK
41. RANGE FORK INSERT
42. RANGE FORK PADS
43. MODE FORK SPRING
44. MODE FORK PADS
45. MODE FORK INSERT
46. MODE FORK
47. SHIFT RAIL SPRING
48. MODE FORK BRACKET
49. REAR OUTPUT SHAFT BEARING
50. REAR OUTPUT SHAFT BEARING SEAL
51. REAR CASE
52. WIRING CLIP
53. SPLINE BOLT
54. REAR OUTPUT BEARING
55. REAR RETAINER
56. VENT
57. OUTPUT SHAFT OIL SEAL
58. REAR YOKE
59. YOKE SEAL WASHER
60. YOKE LOCKNUT
61. VENT CHAMBER SEAL
62. FILL PLUG AND GASKET
63. DRAIN PLUG AND GASKET
64. REAR CASE BOLT
65. WASHER (2)
66. CASE ALIGNMENT DOWEL
67. FRONT OUTPUT SHAFT REAR BEARING
68. MAGNET
69. FRONT OUTPUT SHAFT REAR THRUST BEARING RACE (THICK)
70. FRONT OUTPUT SHAFT REAR THRUST BEARING
71. FRONT OUTPUT SHAFT REAR THRUST BEARING RACE (THIN)
72. DRIVEN SPROCKET RETAINING SNAP RING
73. DRIVE CHAIN
74. DRIVEN SPROCKET
75. FRONT OUTPUT SHAFT
76. FRONT OUTPUT SHAFT FRONT THRUST BEARING RACE (THIN)
77. FRONT OUTPUT SHAFT FRONT THRUST BEARING
78. FRONT OUTPUT SHAFT FRONT THRUST BEARING RACE (THICK)
79. FRONT OUTPUT SHAFT FRONT BEARING
80. WASHER
81. LOCKNUT
82. OPERATING LEVER
83. RANGE SECTOR SHAFT SEAL RETAINER
84. RANGE SECTOR SHAFT SEAL
85. DETENT BALL
86. DETENT SPRING
87. DETENT RETAINING BOLT
88. FRONT OUTPUT SHAFT SEAL
89. FRONT YOKE
90. LOCKPLATE BOLTS

Fig. 79 New Process model 219 transfer case, disassembled

7. Remove rear output shaft seal from rear retainer using a suitable screwdriver or a punch.
8. Position transfer case on wood blocks with the front case resting on the wood. If necessary, cut "V" notches in the blocks so the front case rests squarely on the blocks.
9. Remove rear case to front case attaching bolts, then the rear case from front case. To remove, insert suitable screwdrivers into notches at case ends to pry rear case from front case.

NOTE: The two case end bolts have flat washers and alignment dowels. Note bolt, dowel and washer locations for assembly.

10. Remove rear output shaft and viscous coupling as an assembly, Fig. 81. If necessary, tap shaft with a plastic mallet to remove.
11. Remove "O" ring seal and pilot roller bearings from mainshaft.
12. Remove rear output shaft from viscous coupling.
13. Remove shift rail spring from rail.
14. Remove plastic oil pump from shaft bore in rear case. Note pump position for reassembly. The side of the pump with the recess must face toward shaft bore when installed.
15. Remove rear output shaft bearing seal from case using a suitable screwdriver to pry seal from seal bore.
16. Remove front output shaft thrust bearing assembly, Fig. 82. Tag the assembly for installation reference.
17. Remove driven sprocket retaining snap ring.
18. Remove drive sprocket, drive chain, driven sprocket, side gear clutch and clutch gear as an assembly, Fig. 83. Place assembly on bench and mark components for reassembly reference.
19. Remove needle bearings and bearing spacers from mainshaft or side gear bore. A total of 82 needle bearings and three spacers are used.
20. Remove side gear/clutch gear assembly from drive sprocket, Fig. 83. Remove two snap rings, then the clutch gear from the side gear, Fig. 84. Note position of snap rings and gears for reassembly.
21. Remove side gear clutch, mainshaft thrust washer and the remaining (short) mainshaft needle bearing spacer.
22. Remove front output shaft and shaft thrust bearing assembly, Fig. 85. Note installation sequence of thrust bearing assembly. The proper sequence is: thin race, bearing, then thick race.
23. Remove front output shaft seal from front case using a suitable screwdriver or punch.
24. Remove shaft rail spring from shaft rail if not previously removed.
25. Remove clutch sleeve, mode fork and mode fork spring as an assembly, Fig. 86.
26. Remove mainshaft thrust washer, then the mainshaft. Pull mainshaft straight up to remove.
27. Move range operating lever downward to the last detent position, then disengage range fork lug from range sector slot.
28. Remove annulus gear retaining snap ring and thrust washer, then the annulus gear and range fork as an assembly, Fig. 87.
29. Remove planetary thrust washer from planetary assembly hub, then the planetary assembly, Fig. 88.
30. Remove mainshaft thrust bearing from input gear, then the input gear, thrust bearing and race.
31. Remove range sector detent ball and spring retaining bolt, then the ball and

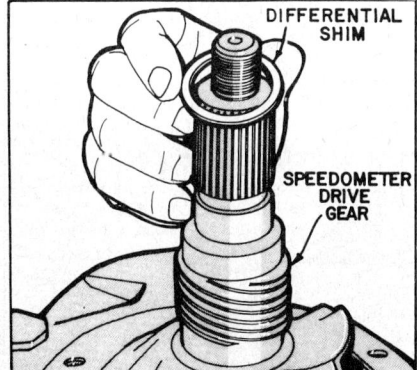

Fig. 80 Differential shim & speedometer drive gear replacement

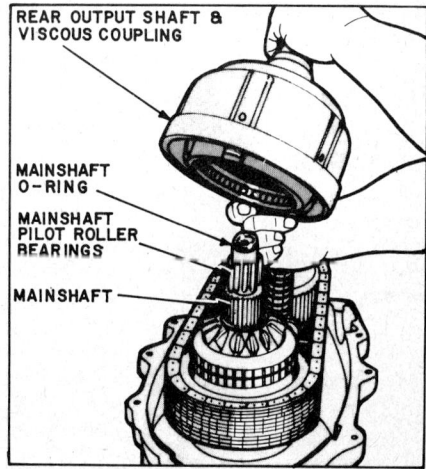

Fig. 81 Rear output shaft & viscous coupling replacement

TRANSFER CASES

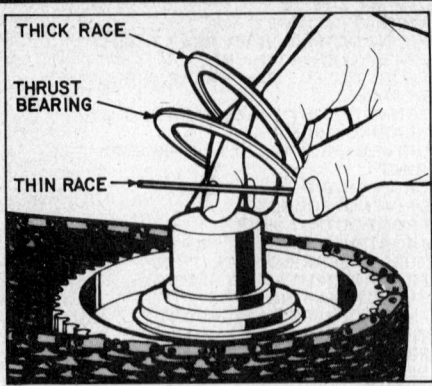

Fig. 82 Front output shaft rear thrust bearing assembly replacement

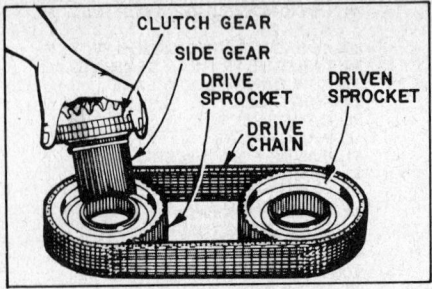

Fig. 83 Side gear, clutch gear, sprockets & chain assembly

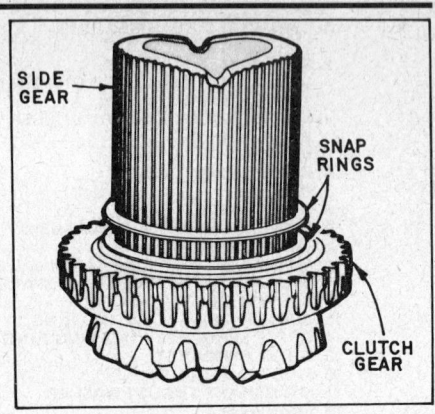

Fig. 84 Side gear components

spring.
32. Remove range sector and operating lever attaching nut and lock washer, then the lever.
33. Remove sector, then the range sector shaft "O" ring and retainer.
34. Remove input gear oil seal from front case using a suitable screwdriver or punch.

Sub-Assembly Service

Lock Plate, Replace
1. Remove and discard lock plate attaching bolts.
2. Remove lock plate from case.
3. Coat case and lock plate surfaces around bolt holes with Loctite 515 sealer or equivalent.
4. Place new lock plate in case and align bolt holes in lock plate and case.
5. Coat new lock plate attaching bolts with Loctite 271 sealer or equivalent.
6. Install and torque lock plate attaching bolts to 30 ft. lbs.

BEARING & BUSHING REPLACEMENT

NOTE: The following bearings and bushings are replaced using special service tools. However, they may also be replaced using suitable equivalent tooling and when using these tools, care should be taken as not to damage any components.

Also, all the bearings used must be correctly positioned to prevent covering the bearing oil feed holes. After replacing any bearing, check position of bearing to ensure that the oil feed hole is not obstructed or blocked by the bearing.

Rear Output Shaft Bearing, Replace
1. Remove bearing using tools J-8092 and J-29165.
2. Install new bearing with tools J-8092 and J-29166.
3. Remove tools and check position of bearing to ensure that the oil feed hole is clear.

Front Output Shaft Front Bearing, Replace
1. Remove bearing with tools J-8082 and J-29168.
2. Install new bearing with tools J-8092 and J-29167.
3. Remove tools and check position of bearing to ensure that the oil feed hole is clear.

Front Output Shaft Rear Bearing, Replace
1. Remove bearing with tools J-26941 and J-2619-01.
2. Install new bearing with tools J-8092 and J-29163.
3. Remove tools and check position of bearing to ensure that oil feed hole is clear and that the bearing is seated flush with the edge of the bore in the case to permit clearance for thrust bearing assembly.

Input Gear Front & Rear Bearings, Replace
1. Remove both bearings simultaneously with tools J-8092 and J-29170.
2. Install new bearing one at a time. First, install the rear bearing, then the front bearing. Bearings are installed with tools J-8092 and J-29169.
3. Remove tools and check position of bearings to ensure that the oil feed holes are clear and that the bearings are flush with the case bore surfaces.

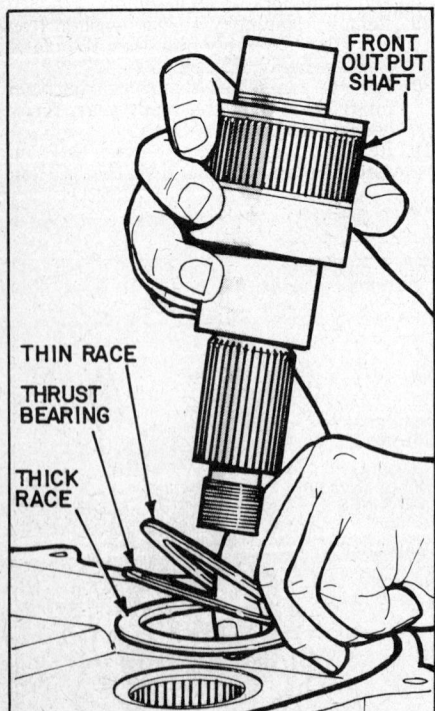

Fig. 85 Front output shaft & shaft front thrust bearing replacement

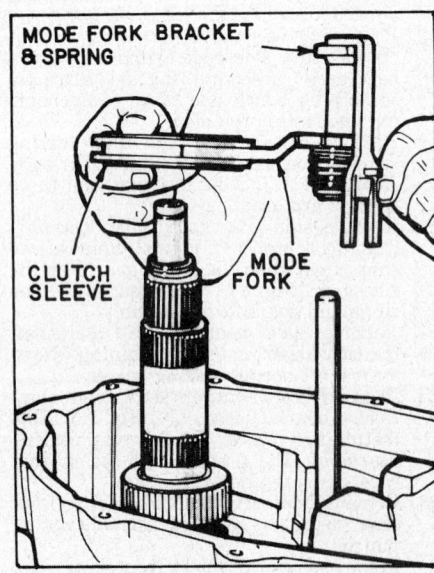

Fig. 86 Clutch sleeve & mode fork replacement

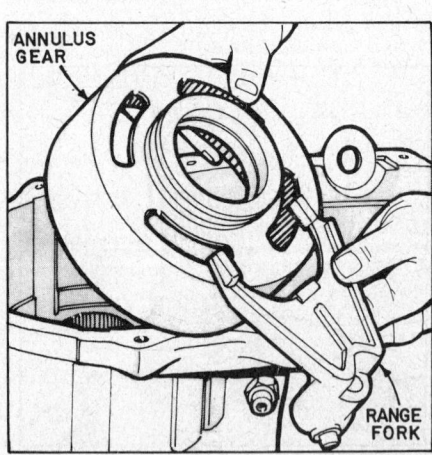

Fig. 87 Annulus gear & range fork replacement

TRANSFER CASES

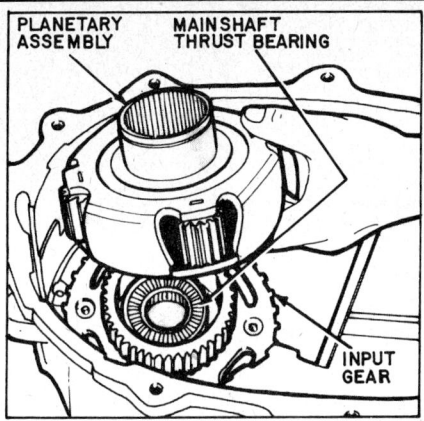

Fig. 88 Planetary assembly replacement

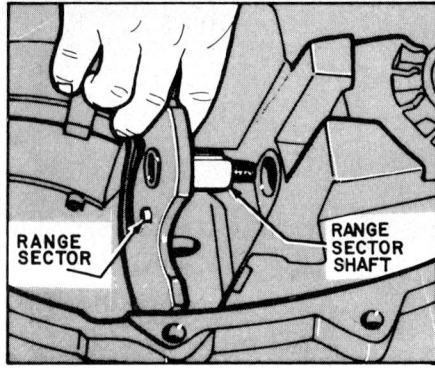

Fig. 89 Range sector installation

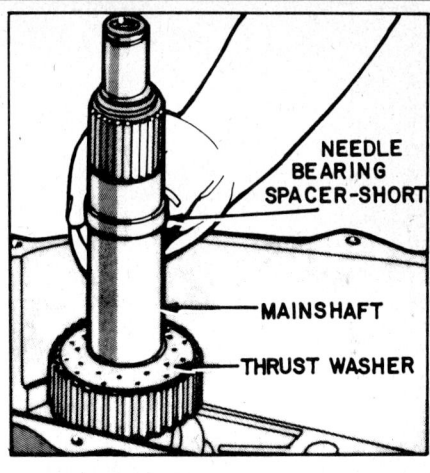

Fig. 90 Mainshaft installation

Mainshaft Front Pilot Bearing, Replace
1. If bearing cannot be removed by hand, use tools J-2619-01 and J-29369. A similar internal type blind hole bearing puller may also be used.
2. If necessary, install new bearing with tools J-8092 and J-29174.
3. Remove tools and check position of bearing to ensure that the oil feed hole is clear and that the bearing is seated flush with edge of bearing bore.

Rear Output Bearing, Replace
1. Remove snap ring, then the bearing using a mallet or brass punch.
2. Install new bearing with tools J-8092 and J-7818.

NOTE: Ensure that the shielded side of the bearing faces toward the inside of the transfer case after installation.

3. Install bearing snap ring.

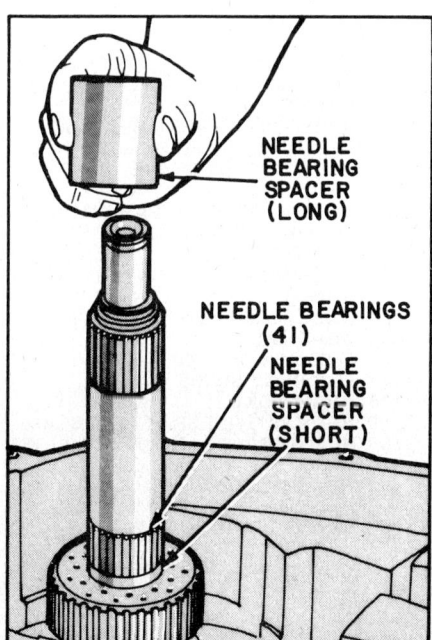

Fig. 91 Mainshaft needle bearings & spacer installation

4. Install new seal with tool J-29162.

Annulus Gear Bushing, Replace
1. Remove bushing with tools J-8092 and J-29185.
2. Install new bushing using the same tools.
3. Remove any metal chips caused by bushing replacement.

Assembly, Fig. 79

NOTE: During assembly, lubricate all components with 10W-30 engine oil or petroleum jelly where indicated only. Do not use any other types of lubricant.

1. Install new input gear and rear output shaft bearing oil seals. Seat the seals flush with the edge of seal bore or in seal groove in the case. Coat seal lips with petroleum jelly after installation.
2. Install input gear thrust bearing race in the case counterbore.
3. Install input thrust bearing on input gear, then install the gear and bearing assembly into case.
4. Install mainshaft thrust bearing into bearing recess in input gear.
5. Install planetary assembly on input gear. Ensure that the planetary pinion teeth mesh fully with the input gear.
6. Install planetary thrust washer on planetary hub.
7. Install new sector shaft "O" ring and retainer in shaft bore in the case.
8. Install range sector in front case, Fig. 89. Install operating lever on sector shaft, then the lever attaching washer and lock nut on shaft. Torque lock nut to 17 ft.

Fig. 92 Mode fork, spring & bracket assembly

lbs.
9. Install detent ball, spring and retaining bolt into front case detent bore. Torque retaining bolt to 22 ft. lbs.
10. Move range sector to last detent position.
11. Assemble annulus gear and range fork. Install the assembly on and over planetary assembly. Ensure that the annulus gear is meshed fully with planetary pinions.
12. Insert range fork lug in range sector detent slot.
13. Install annulus thrust washer and annulus retaining ring on annulus gear hub.
14. Align mainshaft thrust washer in input gear, if necessary.
15. Install mainshaft and ensure that the shaft is seated fully in the input gear, Fig. 90.
16. Install mainshaft thrust washer on mainshaft.
17. Install short mainshaft needle bearing spacer on the shaft, Fig. 91.
18. Liberally coat mainshaft needle bearing surface with petroleum jelly and to all 82 needle bearings. Install 41 needle bearings on the shaft, Fig. 91. Ensure that bearings are in the vertical position and seated on the short spacer.
19. Install the long mainshaft needle bearing spacer on the shaft, Fig. 91. Lower the spacer onto previously installed needle bearings. Avoid displacing bearings.
20. Align shift rail bore in the case with bore

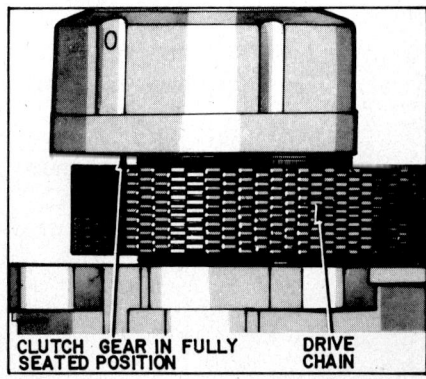

Fig. 93 Seating viscous coupling on clutch gear

TRANSFER CASES

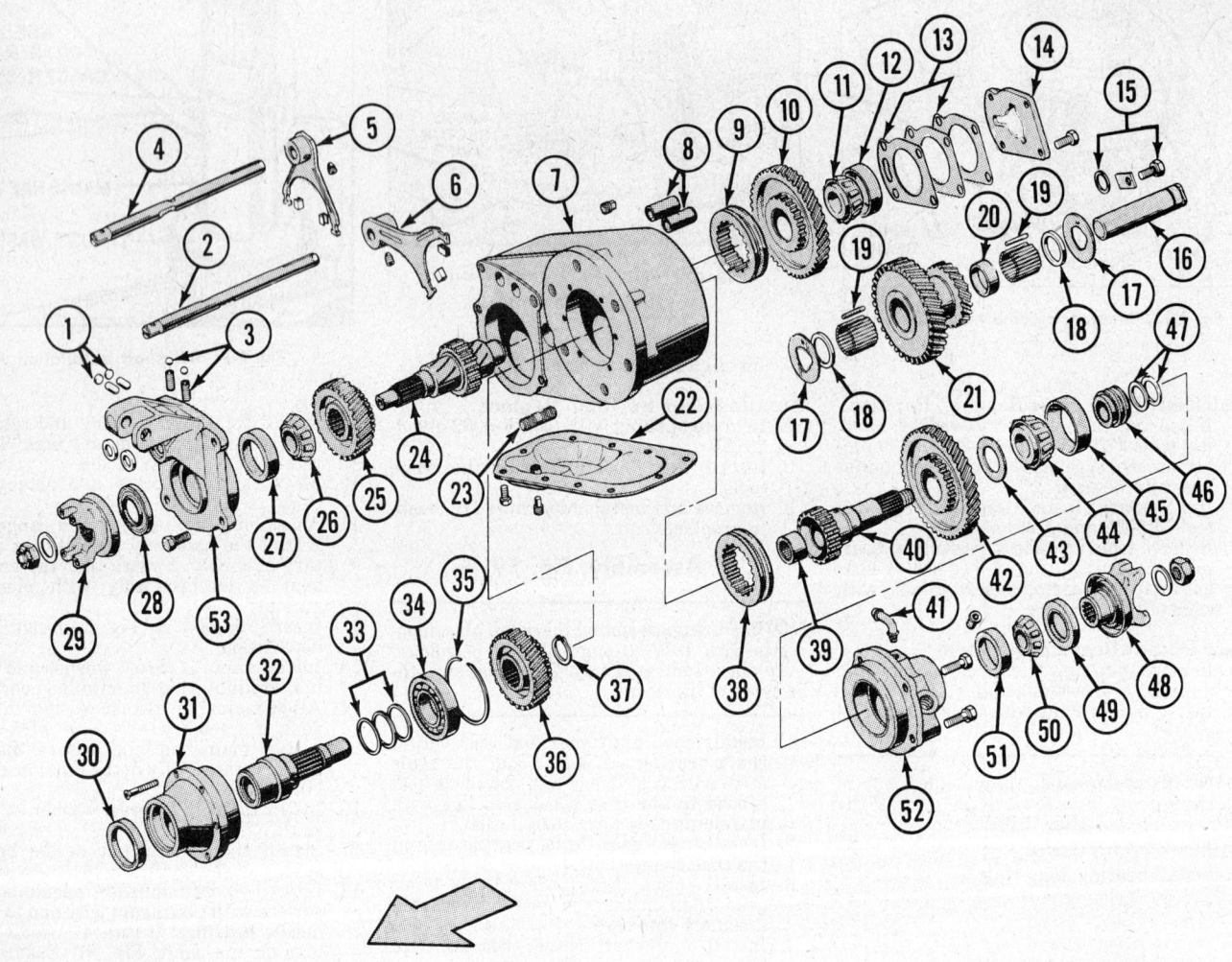

1. INTERLOCK PLUGS AND INTERLOCKS
2. SHIFT ROD – REAR OUTPUT SHAFT FORK
3. POPPET BALLS AND SPRINGS
4. SHIFT ROD – FRONT OUTPUT SHAFT FORK
5. FRONT OUTPUT SHAFT SHIFT FORK
6. REAR OUTPUT SHAFT SHIFT FORK
7. TRANSFER CASE
8. THIMBLE COVERS
9. CLUTCH SLEEVE – FRONT OUTPUT SHAFT
10. CLUTCH GEAR – FRONT OUTPUT SHAFT
11. BEARING – FRONT OUTPUT SHAFT REAR
12. RACE – FRONT OUTPUT SHAFT BEARING
13. END PLAY SHIMS – FRONT OUTPUT SHAFT
14. COVER PLATE
15. LOCK PLATE, BOLT AND WASHER
16. INTERMEDIATE GEAR SHAFT
17. THRUST WASHER
18. BEARING SPACER (THIN)
19. INTERMEDIATE GEAR SHAFT NEEDLE BEARINGS
20. BEARING SPACER (THICK)
21. INTERMEDIATE GEAR
22. BOTTOM COVER
23. STUD (CASE-TO-TRANS.)
24. FRONT OUTPUT SHAFT
25. FRONT OUTPUT SHAFT GEAR
26. FRONT OUTPUT SHAFT BEARING (FRONT)
27. FRONT OUTPUT SHAFT BEARING RACE
28. OIL SEAL
29. FRONT YOKE
30. SEAL
31. SUPPORT – INPUT SHAFT
32. INPUT SHAFT
33. SHIMS
34. INPUT SHAFT BEARING
35. INPUT SHAFT BEARING SNAP RING
36. REAR OUTPUT SHAFT GEAR
37. SNAP RING
38. CLUTCH SLEEVE – REAR OUTPUT SHAFT
39. INPUT SHAFT REAR BEARING (NEEDLE) (OR PILOT BEARING)
40. REAR OUTPUT SHAFT
41. VENT
42. CLUTCH GEAR – REAR OUTPUT SHAFT
43. THRUST WASHER
44. BEARING – REAR OUTPUT SHAFT FRONT
45. RACE – REAR OUTPUT SHAFT BEARING
46. SPEEDOMETER DRIVE GEAR
47. END PLAY SHIMS
48. REAR YOKE
49. REAR OUTPUT SHAFT OIL SEAL
50. BEARING – REAR OUTPUT SHAFT REAR
51. BEARING RACE
52. REAR BEARING CAP
53. FRONT BEARING CAP

Fig. 95 Dana model 300 transfer case, disassembled

TRANSFER CASES

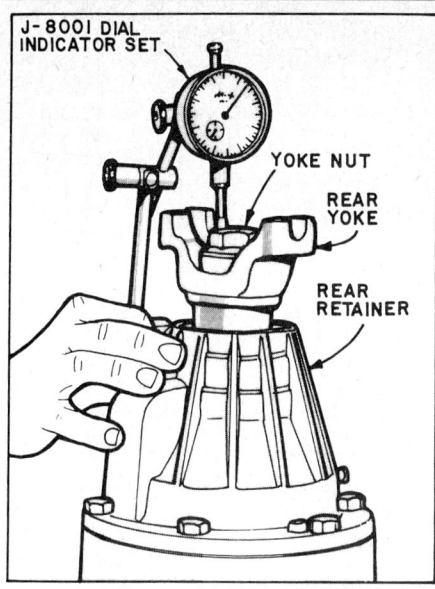

Fig. 94 Checking differential end play

in range fork and install shift rail.

NOTE: The shift rail bore in the case must be dry and not contain any oil. A small amount of oil may prevent the shift rail from seating completely and also may prevent rear case installation.

21. Assemble mode fork, mode fork spring and mode fork bracket, Fig. 92.
22. Install clutch sleeve in mode fork. Ensure that the sleeve is positioned so the I.D. numbers on the sleeve face upward after the sleeve is installed.
23. Align clutch sleeve and mode fork assembly with shift rail and install assembly onto shift rail and mainshaft. Ensure that the clutch sleeve is meshed with the mainshaft gear.
24. Lubricate the remaining 41 mainshaft needle bearings and place bearings on shaft.
25. Install side gear clutch on mainshaft with clutch gear teeth facing downward. Ensure that the gear teeth mesh with the clutch sleeve.
26. Install the remaining short mainshaft needle bearing spacer. Avoid displacing the bearings.
27. Install front output shaft front thrust bearing assembly into front case. The correct assembly sequence is: thick race, thrust bearing, then thin race.
28. Install front output shaft into front case.
29. Install clutch gear on side gear. The tapered side of the clutch gear teeth must face toward side gear teeth.
30. Install clutch gear and drive sprocket locating snap rings on side gear. Install the snap rings so the rings face each other.
31. Position drive and driven sprockets in drive chain and install the assembled side and clutch gears in the drive sprocket.
32. Install assembled drive chain, sprockets and side gear on mainshaft and front output shaft. Align sprockets with shafts, then, keeping the assembly level, lower the assembly onto both shafts simultaneously. Avoid displacing mainshaft needle bearings during chain and sprockets installation.
33. Install driven sprocket retaining snap ring.
34. Install front output shaft rear thrust bearing assembly onto front output shaft. The proper installation sequence is: thin race, thrust bearing, then thick race.
35. Install shift rail spring on shift rail.
36. Install new "O" ring on mainshaft pilot bearing hub.
37. Thickly coat mainshaft pilot roller bearing hub and pilot roller bearings with petroleum jelly. Install rollers onto shaft.
38. Install rear output shaft in viscous coupling. Ensure that the shaft is seated fully.
39. Install assembled viscous coupling and rear output shaft on mainshaft. Align mainshaft pilot hub with pilot bearing bore in rear output shaft and lower assembly onto mainshaft. Avoid displacing pilot roller bearings during installation.
40. Align clutch gear teeth with viscous coupling teeth and seat the coupling fully onto the clutch gear, Fig. 93.

NOTE: When properly installed, the clutch gear teeth will not be visible or extend past the coupling.

41. Install magnet into front case, if removed.
42. Thoroughly clean mating surfaces of front and rear cases. Apply Loctite 515 sealer or equivalent to mating surface of front case and to all case attaching bolts.
43. Install rear case onto front case. Align case dowels and install case attaching bolts. Torque attaching bolts to 22 ft. lbs.

NOTE: The two case end bolts require flat washers.

44. Install oil pump on rear output shaft and seat into case. Install the pump so the recessed side faces toward inside of case.
45. Install speedometer drive gear and differential shim on output shaft.
46. Install vent chamber seal in rear retainer, if removed.
47. Align and install rear retainer on rear case. Install retainer bolts finger tight only.
48. Install yoke onto rear output shaft. Install yoke nut finger tight only.
49. Install a dial indicator onto retainer with the plunger contacting the top of the yoke nut, Fig. 94.
50. Install yoke on front output shaft and rotate the front shaft 10 complete revolutions.
51. Rotate front output shaft again and note end play reading on dial indicator. End play should be .002 to .010 inch. If end play is not within specifications, remove rear retainer and add or remove differential shims as required. Recheck end play.
52. Remove both output shaft yokes.

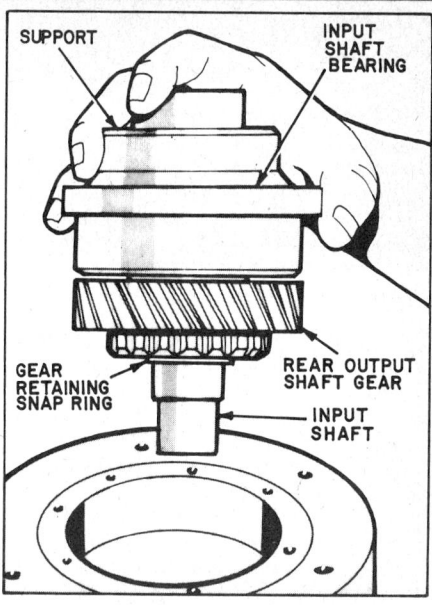

Fig. 96 Front support, input shaft & rear output shaft gear replacement

Fig. 97 Shift fork setscrew replacement

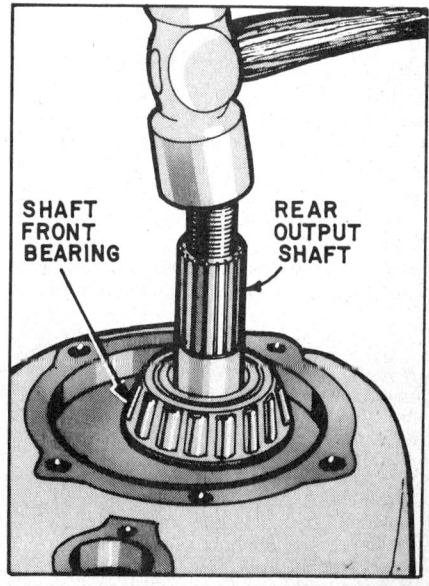

Fig. 98 Rear output shaft front bearing removal

TRANSFER CASES

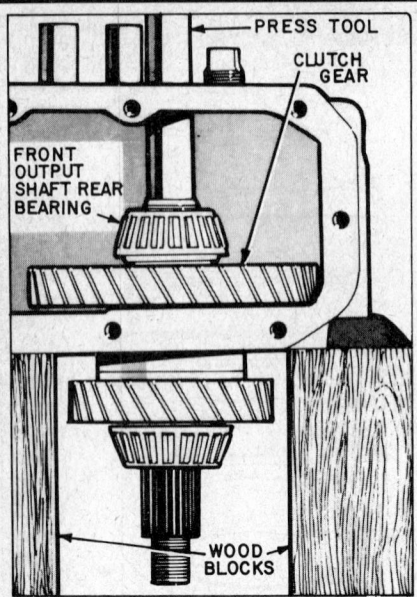

Fig. 99 Front output shaft front bearing removal

from case using a suitable mallet and punch.
13. Remove and discard intermediate shaft "O" ring.
14. Remove intermediate gear assembly and thrust washers.

NOTE: The thrust washers have locating tabs which must fit into notches in the case at reassembly.

15. Remove needle bearings and bearing spacers from intermediate gear.

NOTE: There are 48 needle bearings and 3 bearing spacers in the intermediate gear.

16. Remove rear bearing cap attaching bolts, then the cap. Tap on the output shaft to aid cap removal. The rear bearing cap is coated with a sealant. Use a putty knife to break the seal, then work knife around edge to loosen and remove cap.
17. Remove end play shims and speedometer drive gear from rear output shaft.
18. Remove and discard rear output shaft oil seal. Remove bearings and races from rear bearing cap.
19. Remove setscrews, retaining front and rear output shaft shift forks on shift rods, Fig. 97.
20. Remove shift rods. Insert a punch through clevis pin holes in rods and rotate rods while pulling out from case.

NOTE: When the shift rods are free of the front cap, avoid losing the shift rod poppet balls and springs.

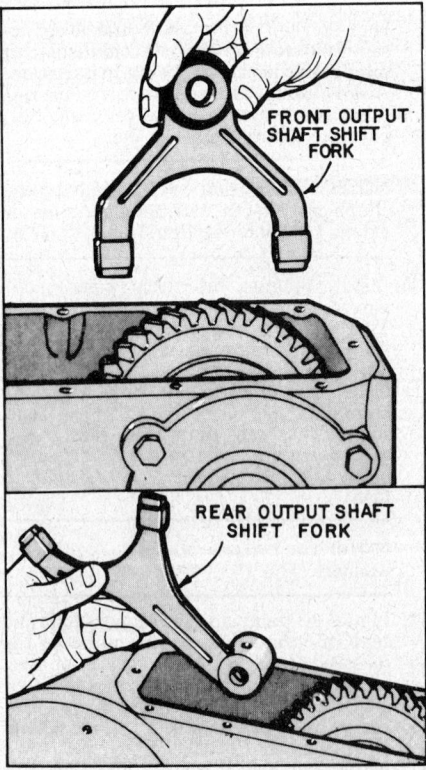

Fig. 101 Shift fork installation

Fig. 100 Front output shaft rear bearing installation

21. Remove shift forks from case.
22. Remove bolts attaching front cap to case, then the cap. The front cap is coated with a sealant. Use a putty knife to break the seal, then work knife around edge to loosen and remove cap.
23. Remove front output shaft and shift rod oil seals from front cap.
24. Remove front bearing race from front bearing cap with tool J-29168.
25. Remove cover plate bolts, then the plate and end play shims from case.
26. Move front output shaft toward front of case.
27. Remove front output shaft rear bearing race from case.
28. Remove rear output shaft front bearing, Fig. 98. Position case on wood blocks. Seat clutch gear on case interior surface and tap shaft from bearing with a suitable mallet.

NOTE: If bearing is difficult to remove, use a suitable press.

29. Remove rear output shaft front bearing, thrust washer, clutch gear and output shaft from case.
30. Remove front output shaft rear bearing using a suitable press, Fig. 99.

NOTE: Support the case with wood blocks located at either side of case core to prevent damage to case.

31. Remove transfer case from press.
32. Remove front output shaft, clutch gear and sleeve, and the shaft rear bearing from case.
33. Remove front output shaft front bearing with tool J-22192-01 and a suitable press.
34. Remove front output shaft gear from shaft.
35. Remove input shaft rear needle bearing from rear output shaft with tool J-29369-1. Support output shaft in a vise during bearing removal.
36. Remove shift rod thimbles.

Assembly, Fig. 95

1. Apply Loctite 220 sealer or equivalent to shift rod thimbles, then install the thimbles.
2. Install front output shaft gear onto front

53. Install new front and rear yoke seals if not previously installed.
54. Install rear retainer bolts and apply Loctite 515 sealer or equivalent to mating surface of retainer and to the bolts. Install and torque retainer bolts to 22 ft. lbs.
55. Install new yoke seal washers on output shafts, then the yokes. Install and torque new yoke nuts to 110 ft. lbs.
56. Install and torque drain plug to 18 ft. lbs.
57. Install 4 pints of 10W-30 engine oil into transfer case through fill plug.
58. Install and torque fill plug to 18 ft. lbs.

DANA MODEL 300

Disassembly, Fig. 95

1. Remove shift lever assembly.
2. Remove bottom cover. The bottom cover is coated with a sealant. Use a putty knife to break the seal, then work the knife around the edge to loosen and remove cover.
3. Remove front and rear yokes. Discard yoke nuts.
4. Remove socket head screws attaching the input shaft support to the case, then the support, rear output shaft gear and input shaft as an assembly, Fig. 96. The support is coated with a sealant. Use a putty knife to break the seal, then work knife around the edge to loosen and remove support.
5. Remove rear output shaft clutch sleeve from case.
6. Remove and discard snap ring retaining the rear output shaft gear on input shaft. Remove the gear.
7. Remove and discard input shaft bearing snap ring.
8. Remove input shaft and bearing from support. Tap end of input shaft with a mallet to aid removal.
9. Remove input shaft bearing and end play shims from shaft using a suitable press.
10. Remove input shaft oil seal from support. Discard the seal.
11. Remove intermediate shaft lock plate bolt and lock plate.
12. Remove intermediate shaft. Tap shaft

TRANSFER CASES

output shaft. Ensure that the clutch teeth on the gear face face toward shaft gear teeth.
3. Install front bearing on front output shaft using a suitable press. Ensure that the bearing is seated against the gear.
4. Install front output shaft into case, then the clutch sleeve and clutch gear on shaft.
5. Install front output shaft rear bearing with a suitable press, Fig. 100.

NOTE: Install an old yoke nut on the shaft to prevent thread damage.

6. Install input shaft rear beedle bearing in rear output shaft with tool J-19179.
7. Place rear output shaft clutch gear in case and insert rear output shaft into gear.
8. Install thrust washer and front bearing on rear output shaft using a suitable press.
9. Install shims and bearing on input shaft using a suitable press.
10. Install new input shaft oil seal into input shaft support using tool J-19184.
11. Install input shaft and bearing in support. Install new bearing snap ring.
12. Install rear output shaft gear on input gear. Install new gear retaining snap ring.
13. Using a feeler gauge, measure clearance between input gear and the gear retaining snap ring. Clearance should not exceed .003 inch. If clearance exceeds specification, disassemble input shaft and add shims between input shaft and shaft bearing.
14. Install clutch sleeve on rear output shaft.
15. Apply Loctite 515 sealer or equivalent to mating surface of input shaft support and install assembled support, shaft and gear into case. Use two support bolts to align the support on case and tap support into position with a mallet.
16. Install and torque socket head screws in support to 10 ft. lbs.
17. Install rear bearing cap front bearing race using tool J-9276-3.
18. Install rear bearing cap rear bearing using tool J-29182.
19. Position rear output shaft rear bearing in rear bearing cap.
20. Install rear output shaft yoke oil seal with tool J-25160.
21. Install speedometer gear and end play shims on rear output shaft.
22. Apply Loctite 515 sealer or equivalent to mating surface of rear bearing cap, then install the cap. Use two cap bolts to align bolt holes and tap rear cap into place with a suitable mallet. Install and torque cap bolts to 35 ft. lbs.
23. Install rear output shaft yoke. Torque new lock nut to 120 ft. lbs.
24. Check rear output shaft end play as follows:
   a. Install a dial indicator onto bearing cap and position indicator so the plunger contacts end of shaft.
   b. Move output shaft back and forth to check end play. End play should be .001-.005 inch.
   c. If end play is not within specifications, remove or add shims between speedometer drive gear and output shaft rear bearing.
25. Install front output shaft rear bearing race.
26. Install front output shaft end play shims and cover plate. Install and torque cover plate bolts to 35 ft. lbs.

NOTE: Apply Loctite 220 sealer or equivalent to bolt threads prior to installation.

27. Install front output shaft front bearing race using tools J-8092 and J-29181.
28. Install front output shaft yoke oil seal using tool J-25160.
29. Install shift rod oil seals using tool J-25167.
30. Apply Loctite 515 sealer or equivalent to mating surface of front bearing cap, then install the cap. Use two bolts to align cap and case bolt holes and tap cap into position with a mallet. Torque cap bolts to 35 ft. lbs.
31. Check front output shaft end play as follows:
   a. Seat rear bearing cup against cover plate by tapping end of front output shaft with a mallet.
   b. Install a dial indicator on front bearing cap so the plunger contacts end of output shaft.
   c. Move output shaft back and forth to check end play. End play should be .001-.005 inch.
   d. If end play is not within specifications, remove or add shims between cover plate and case. If shims are added, seat rear bearing cup as outlined previously before rechecking end play.
32. Install front output shaft yoke. Install and torque new lock nut to 120 ft. lbs.
33. Insert front and rear output shaft shift forks into case, Fig. 101.
34. Install front output shaft shift rod poppet ball and spring into front bearing cap.
35. Compress poppet ball and spring and install front output shaft shift rod partially into case. Insert front output shaft shift rod through shift fork. Align setscrew hole in shift fork, then install and torque setscrew to 14 ft. lbs.
36. Install rear output shaft shift rod poppet ball and spring into front bearing cap.
37. Compress poppet ball and spring and install rear output shaft shift rail partially into case.

NOTE: Before installing shift rail, ensure that the front output shaft shift rod is in the neutral position and that the interlocks are seated in the front bearing cap bore.

38. Insert rear output shaft shift rod through shift fork. Align setscrew holes in fork and rod. Install and torque setscrew to 14 ft. lbs.
39. Insert tool J-25142 in intermediate gear and install needle bearings and spacers into gear.
40. Install intermediate gear thrust washers into case. Ensure that the washer tangs are aligned with grooves in case. Secure thrust washers in position with petroleum jelly.
41. Install new "O" ring seal on intermediate shaft.
42. Position intermediate gear into case.
43. Install intermediate shaft in case core. Tap shaft into gear until shaft forces tool J-25142 from case.
44. Install intermediate shaft lock plate and bolt. Torque bolt to 23 ft. lbs.
45. Install bottom cover. Apply Loctite 515 sealer or equivalent to mating surface of cover. Install and torque cover bolts to 15 ft. lbs.

FRONT WHEEL LOCKING HUBS
Used With Front Driving Axles

SPICER EXTERNAL TYPE HUB-LOK

Description

As shown in Figs. 1 and 1A, the splines on the inside diameter of the inner clutch ring assembly mesh with the axle shaft splines, and the assembly is held to the axle shaft by a snap ring. The splines on the outside diameter of the outer clutch and cam assembly mesh with the wheel hub splines. Therefore, when the outer clutch assembly is pushed in so that its teeth engage the teeth of the inner clutch assembly, the wheel hub is locked to the axle shaft.

The outer clutch and cam assembly, the retaining plate, and the actuating knob come as one assembly which is retained to the wheel hub with a snap ring. Turning the actuating knob engages the clutch teeth.

Operation

"L" POSITION

When the transfer case is shifted into the position for driving the front axle, turn the actuating knob so that it is aligned with the letter L. If the clutch teeth do not engage with the knob turned to this position, the clutch teeth are butted and a slight movement of the wheel in either direction complete the lock.

The front axle will now drive the wheel.

"F" POSITION

When the transfer case is to be shifted into the position for driving the rear axle only, turn the actuating knob so that it is aligned with the letter F. This will disengage the clutch teeth and thus unlock the wheel hub from the axle shaft. The wheel will now turn free on the axle.

CAUTION: *Be certain that the transfer case is shifted into two-wheel drive position before disengaging the Hub-Lok.*

FRONT WHEEL LOCKING HUBS

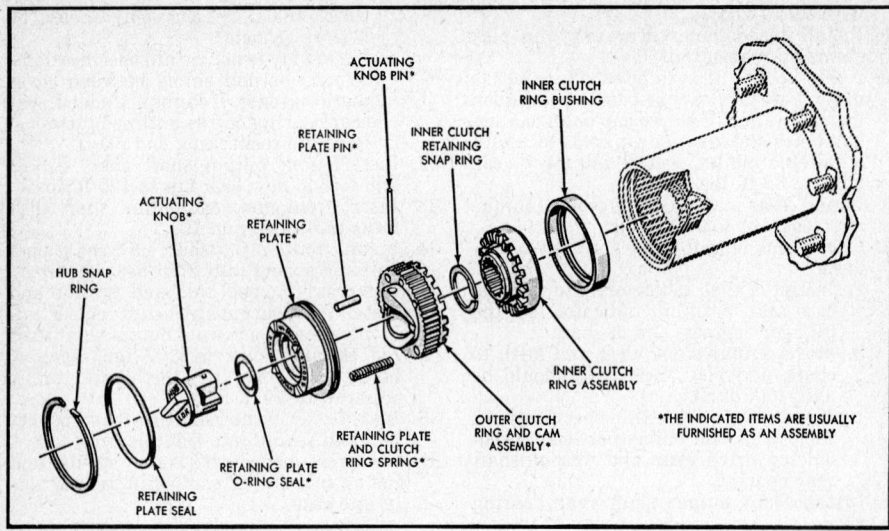

Fig. 1 Spicer external type Hub-Lok disassembled, 1970-71

1970-71

Removal

1. Remove Hub-Lok retaining snap ring from I.D. of wheel hub, Fig. 1.
2. Remove actuating knob, retaining plate and outer clutch ring as a unit, then remove O-ring seal from outer clutch ring.
3. Remove inner clutch retaining snap ring from axle shaft.
4. Remove inner clutch ring from axle shaft.
5. Remove inner clutch ring bushing from wheel hub.

Installation

1. Place inner clutch ring bushing into wheel hub with flange outward. Be sure bushing bottoms on offset in wheel hub.
2. Slide inner clutch ring onto axle shaft splines with clutch teeth facing outward. Push clutch ring inward until it seats in inner bushing. Lock inner clutch ring to axle shaft with a new snap ring.
3. Install O-ring seal in groove of outer clutch ring. Start outer clutch ring assembly into wheel hub with splines matching those in hub. Push clutch ring into hub far enough to install hub snap ring.
4. Install hub snap ring. Make sure that it is well seated in groove in I.D. of hub.

1972-79

Removal

1. Remove hub screws and washers, then slide gear hub housing away from hub.
2. Remove inner metal gasket, gear hub housing and the outer gasket.
3. With actuator knob in "Lock" position, remove clutch gear snap ring, clutch gear and pressure spring.
4. With actuator knob in the "Free" position, drive cam lock pin from assembly with a suitable punch.
5. Remove actuating cam from knob, then the knob retaining snap ring and the knob from knob retainer.
6. Remove axle shaft snap ring, inner clutch gear and bushing.

Installation

1. Lubricate bushing and splines of inner clutch gear then assemble the inner clutch gear to bushing and install assembly onto axle shaft. Ensure inner clutch gear splines are aligned with axle shaft splines.
2. Install axle shaft snap ring.
3. Lubricate "O" ring groove in actuator knob with "O" ring lubricant and install "O" ring onto actuator knob.
4. Install actuating knob into retainer with knob in "Free" position, then the retaining snap ring.
5. Install actuating cam onto knob, aligning the cam ears with retainer slots.
6. Install cam lock pin through cam groove and actuating knob holes. Ensure pin ends are flush with outside diameter of cam.
7. Turn actuator cam to "Lock" position and lubricate cam grooves.
8. Install pressure spring, outer clutch gear and snap ring. Ensure snap ring is properly seated in the cam groove.
9. Turn actuator knob to "Free" position and lubricate outer spline and teeth of outer clutch gear.
10. Install outer retainer gasket, gear hub housing and inner metal masket, then install two retaining screws to position the assembly.
11. Install hub assembly to axle and tighten retainer screws. Turn actuator knob to "Lock" position.
12. Install remaining retainer screws and torque all screws to 30-35 ft. lbs.

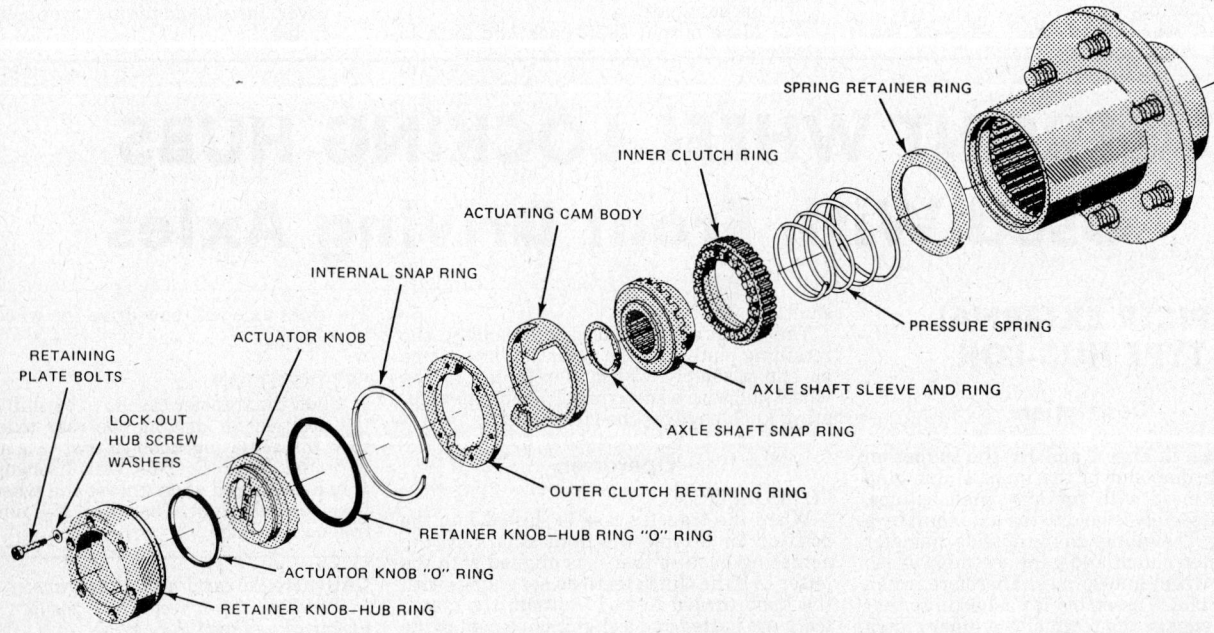

Fig. 1A Spicer external type Hub-Lok disassembled, 1972-79

FRONT WHEEL LOCKING HUBS

SPICER INTERNAL TYPE HUB-LOK

Referring to Fig. 1B, the parts shown can be replaced individually. However, the actuator knob, actuator cam body, axle shaft sleeve and ring and the inner clutch ring are exposed to wear when the Hub-Lok is engaged. These parts should be checked carefully during inspection.

If the actuator knob is worn or damaged but the actuating cam ring is in good condition, then replace only the knob. Replace both parts only if both show evidence of wear or damage.

The same attention should be given to the axle shaft sleeve and ring and the inner clutch ring. If wear or damage is evident on the axle shaft sleeve and ring but the inner clutch shows none, then replace only the axle shaft sleeve and ring. Replace both parts only if they both show signs of wear or damage.

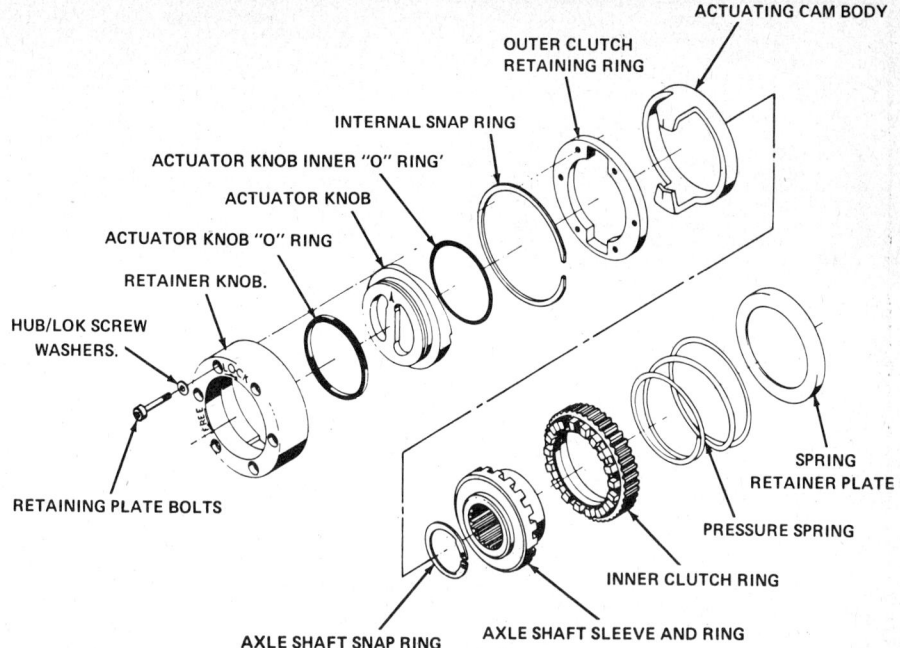

Fig. 1B Spicer internal type Hub-Lock disassembled

Removal

1. Remove hub screws and washers, then the hub ring and knob.
2. Remove internal snap ring from hub groove.
3. Remove cam body ring and clutch retainer assembly from hub and disassemble components.
4. Remove axle shaft snap ring.
5. Remove drive gear and clutch gear.
6. Remove coil spring and spring retainer ring.

Installation

1. Lubricate hub inner splines with suitable grease.
2. Install spring retainer ring with recessed undercut side facing inboard. Ensure the ring seats against bearing.
3. Install coil spring with large end positioned against retainer ring.
4. Lubricate and install axle shaft sleeve and ring and the inner clutch ring. Ensure the teeth are meshed for ease of assembly. Also, it may be necessary to rock the hub to align the splines.
5. Install axle shaft snap ring. Ensure snap ring is fully seated in the shaft groove.
6. Install actuating cam body ring into outer clutch retaining ring, then install assembly into hub.
7. Install internal snap ring. Ensure snap ring is fully seated in the hub groove.
8. Lubricate cam ears with Lubriplate and apply a small amount of "O" ring lubricant in groove of actuating knob. Install outer "O" ring.
9. Install knob in hub ring, then the assembly on axle with the knob in locked position. Install retaining screws and ensure retaining ring is positioned properly in the hub.
10. Torque lock-out hub screws to 35-40 inch lbs.

CUTLAS SELECTIVE DRIVE HUB

The outstanding operational advantage of this type hub, Fig. 2, is its "preset" feature. Turning the control knob from two-wheel drive to four-wheel drive "presets" the hub to automatically engage the axle shaft when the transfer case is shifted into four-wheel drive. The axle shaft is not engaged until the shift into four-wheel drive is made.

Knurling on the control knob provides a firm gripping surface. An O-ring seal under the control knob keeps out all foreign matter. The control knob makes only a quarter turn, and snaps in place for positive positioning.

WARN LOCKING HUB

As shown in Fig. 3, turning the clutch controls to the "L" or lock position connects the wheel hubs to the axle shafts. Therefore, when the transfer case is driving the front axle and the controls are in the "L" position, the wheels are driven by the axle shafts. When the transfer case is not driving the front axle, the clutch controls are turned to the "F" or free position to disconnect the wheel hubs from the axle shafts. The wheels now rotate freely but the axle shafts remain stationary.

Description

The locking hub consists of two major assemblies, the coupling assembly and the clutch body which are retained to each other by eight Allen screws, Fig. 4.

The inner coupling rides on the needle bearings in the inside diameter of the outer coupling. The two couplings are held together by the coupling snap ring. When the coupling assembly is installed, the inside diameter of the inner coupling splines to the axle shaft and the outside diameter of the outer coupling splines to the wheel hub. The engine assembly is retained to the axle shaft by a snap ring at the inner coupling.

The clutch body consists of the clutch control and actuator assembly, the drive pins and the clutch ring.

Operation

"L" POSITION

When the control is rotated clockwise to the "L" position, the worm drive of the actuator threads into the clutch ring forcing it to move inward and engage the lands and grooves of the inner coupling. The clutch ring cannot rotate with the actuator because the clutch ring is dowelled to the clutch body and coupling by the drive pins going through the slots in the O.D. of the clutch ring.

Power is now transferred from the meshed axle shaft and inner coupling to the clutch ring through the engaged lands and grooves. From the clutch ring the power passes through the drive pins to the clutch body and to the outer coupling which is splined to the

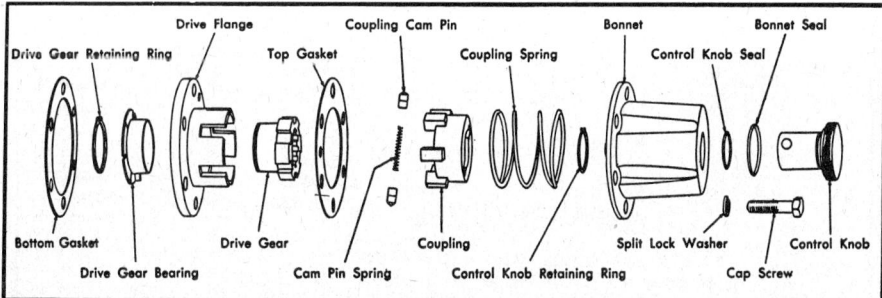

Fig. 2 Cutlas Selective Drive hub disassembled

FRONT WHEEL LOCKING HUBS

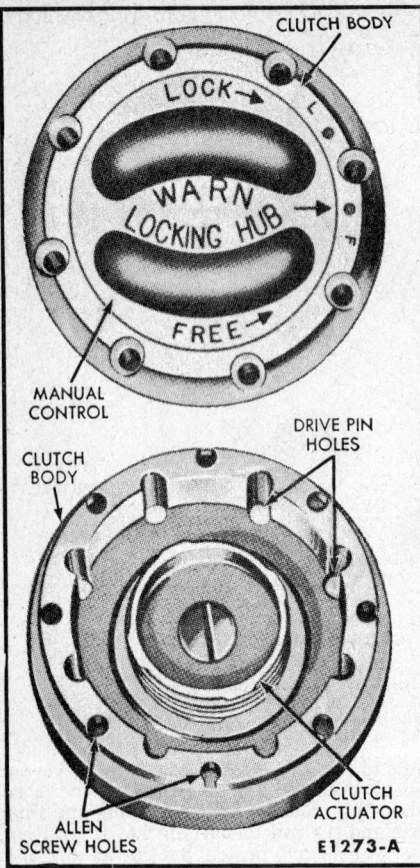

Fig. 3 Warn Locking Hub

wheel hub.

"F" POSITION

When the control is rotated counterclockwise to the "F" position, the worm drive of the actuator pulls the clutch ring outward to disengage it from the lands and grooves of the inner coupling. The clutch ring, clutch body, outer coupling and wheel now are all free to rotate independently of the axle shaft. The inner coupling becomes stationary with the axle shaft to which it is splined. The outer coupling, to which the wheel is splined, rotates around the inner coupling through the needle bearing assembly in the I.D. of the outer coupling.

Removal

1. Remove the eight retaining screws and clutch body from the coupling assembly, Fig. 4.
2. Remove coupling-to-axle shaft snap ring.
3. Remove coupling assembly from wheel hub and axle shaft.

Disassembly

1. Referring to Fig. 4, remove outer drive pins and O-ring seal from clutch body.
2. Remove clutch ring from actuator worm drive by rotating ring clockwise.
3. Remove coupling snap ring and separate inner coupling from outer coupling.
4. Remove bronze thrust washer.
5. Remove needle bearing assembly from outer coupling with a suitable puller. *This step is not necessary for cleaning purposes.*

Assembly

1. Press needle bearing assembly into outer coupling. To avoid damage, press against name surface of bearing.
2. Install bronze thrust washer on inner coupling, then install inner coupling into outer coupling.
3. Secure two couplings together by installing snap ring.
4. Install clutch ring onto actuator by turning ring counterclockwise on worm drive.
5. Rotate control knob to "F" position and turn clutch body in until it bottoms on clutch body. Turn clutch ring further until drive pin slots on ring are aligned with drive pin holes in clutch body. Proper alignment is necessary to insure complete disengagement of clutch ring from inner coupling when unit is in "F" position.
6. Install O-ring on clutch body, and drive pins in their holes in body.

Installation

1. Install coupling assembly to axle shaft and wheel hub and secure to axle shaft with snap ring.
2. Install clutch body assembly to coupling assembly, being sure that all drive pins are in place.
3. Install and tighten clutch body retaining screws.

I. H. LOCKING HUBS

Manual Type—Fig. 5

When the hub is engaged, full power is transmitted to both front wheels. Disengagement, with front axle not driving, allows the front wheels to "Free Wheel" and the axle shafts and differential gears to remain idle, saving unnecessary wear.

Lock-o-matic Type—Fig. 6

This type hub, when set in the "Free" position, automatically locks the front wheel and axle shaft together the moment torque is applied to the front axle. The hub controls, therefore, do not have to be changed regardless of whether the vehicle is being operated in two- or four-wheel drive. It is necessary to set the control in the "Lock" position only when engine braking is required (down steep hills, on ice, etc.).

Operation

To engage the locking hubs, turn brass controls (one on each hub) clockwise to "Lock" position. Arrow in center of controls must point directly at dot located on rim of hub. You can feel the brass control "seat" itself when it is properly positioned. If the arrow does not point directly at the dot, the control will not seat itself. Thus, the gears will not completely engage and the pressure may force off the end of the hub.

To disengage the hubs, turn brass controls counter-clockwise to "Free" position. Here again, the arrow must point directly at the dot on the rim, otherwise the gears may rake against each other.

When the controls are properly positioned, the gears are completely engaged or disengaged and units will not be damaged.

Precautions

1. Use fingers only to turn controls. If controls do not move freely with finger effort, move vehicle slightly in either direction in two-wheel drive, standard gear range. If hubs do not now turn freely, look for external damage or dirt around controls. *Do not force controls with tools.*
2. Do not drive vehicle unless controls on both hubs are properly positioned and both are set the same.
3. To avoid excessive torque loads on the rear axle, do not drive vehicle equipped with *manual locking hubs* in the low range of transfer case with hubs set in "Free" position. This does not apply to the Lock-O-Matic hub because it automatically locks the wheel with the axle shaft when torque is applied. Therefore, no increased load is placed on the rear axle.
4. During vehicle operation, arrow in center of control must always point directly to one of the dots on the rim of the hub. Also, both hubs must be set the same.

Removal

1. Remove bolts holding clutch body to hub body.

CAUTION: *Use only a thin wall socket to remove these bolts. Heavier sockets may force in recessed wall.*

2. Lift off clutch body, holding it erect so as not to let the drive pins slide out of body.

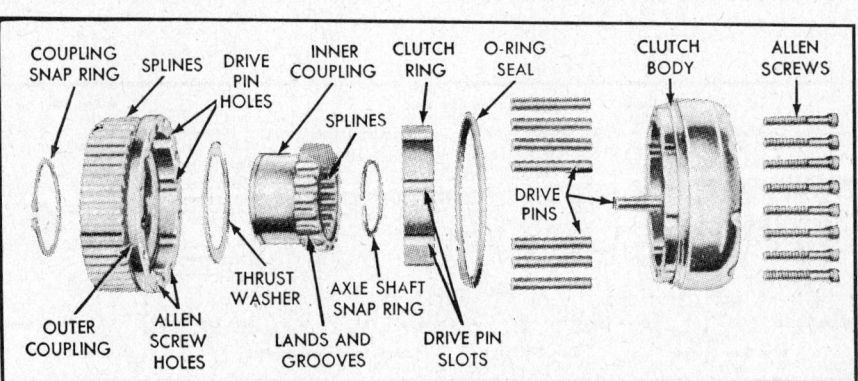

Fig. 4 Warn Locking Hub disassembled

FRONT WHEEL LOCKING HUBS

Fig. 5 I.H. (International Harvester) Locking Hub (manual type)

3. Remove lock ring holding hub body to axle shaft and pull off hub body.
4. If necessary to remove drag shoe from axle spindle, loosen hex-head set screw and unscrew drag shoe from spindle.

Manual Type, Disassemble, Fig. 7

1. Remove snap ring and pull axle shaft hub out of hub body, noting from which side of hub body the axle shaft hub is extracted. If necessary needle bearing assembly may be removed from hub body.
2. Using a small chisel, remove staked-over metal retaining clutch hex-head screw, being careful not to damage screw.
3. Remove hex-head screw with Allen wrench. Lift out clutch screw and clutch ring. Clutch ring may be separated from clutch screw by unscrewing it.
4. Turn clutch body face down to remove the twelve drive pins.
5. Remove disc from bottom center of clutch body.
6. Place thumb inside clutch body on center of control assembly and push outward.
7. Remove O-ring seal and outer oil seal from control dial. Dowel pin may be lifted out of control dial.

NOTE: *The poppet ball and spring located in the control dial cannot be serviced; therefore, if damaged, the control assembly must be replaced.*

Manual Type, Assemble, Fig. 7

1. Place axle shaft hub into hub body and secure with snap ring in groove in end of axle shaft hub.
2. Apply a small amount of chassis lube on bearing side and in grooves of control assembly.
3. Install new O-ring seals on control assembly.
4. Place disc on inside (clutch side) of clutch body.
5. Assemble clutch screw into clutch ring from back side. Be certain clutch screw works freely. If it is sticky in any position, tap lightly on back side.
6. Drop in clutch ring and screw assembly.

NOTE: *Clutch screw must be flush with back edge of clutch ring.*

7. Insert twelve drive pins. *Try clutch ring for free siding fit on drive pins. If it does not move freely from top to bottom, lift out clutch ring and screw assembly and turn it to another position. If it still does not move freely, it should be removed and the clutch ring, body and drive pins examined for damage.*
8. Apply a light grade of chassis lube to inside face of clutch body and disc (from front side of clutch body). Hold hand over drive pins to prevent their falling out.
9. Position control assembly with dowel pin into face of clutch body so the arrow stops on the dot marked "Free". Install and tighten the 1/4" flat-head screw into the control assembly.
10. To check clutch screw setting, turn control from "Lock" to "Free" position and back several times. Control should snap into both positions. In "Free" position, clutch ring should just clear bottom of clutch body.

NOTE: *If clutch ring is set too far above bottom of clutch body when set in the "Free" position, axle shaft hub will rub face of clutch ring.*

11. Stake dowel pin and flat-head screw.
12. Turn control to "Free" position and apply a thin coating of light grade chassis lube around clutch screw and drive pins.

Lock-O-Matic Type, Disassemble

1. Referring to Fig. 8, remove lock ring retaining axle shaft hub into hub body. Pull axle shaft hub and roller cage assembly out of hub body, noting side of hub from which gear teeth extend.
2. Remove ten rollers from roller cage. Take

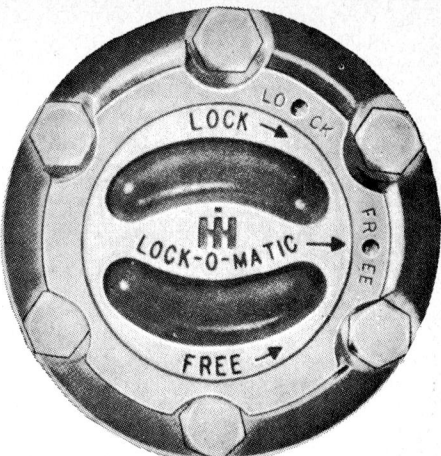

Fig. 6 I.H. (International Harvester) (Lock-O-Matic)

out centering spring.
3. Remove lock ring located in second groove on axle shaft hub. This permits axle shaft hub to be separated from roller cage.
4. Pull axle shaft hub out of roller cage.

NOTE: *The corner points of axle shaft hub must be aligned with grooves in friction shoes to permit removal of hub.*

5. Remove locking ring located in roller cage in end opposite friction shoes.
6. Remove friction shoe spring and lift out friction shoes from roller cage.

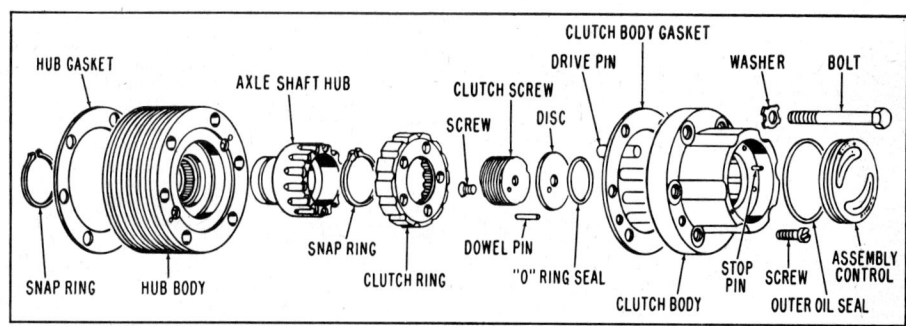

Fig. 7 I.H. (International Harvester) manual type locking hub disassembled

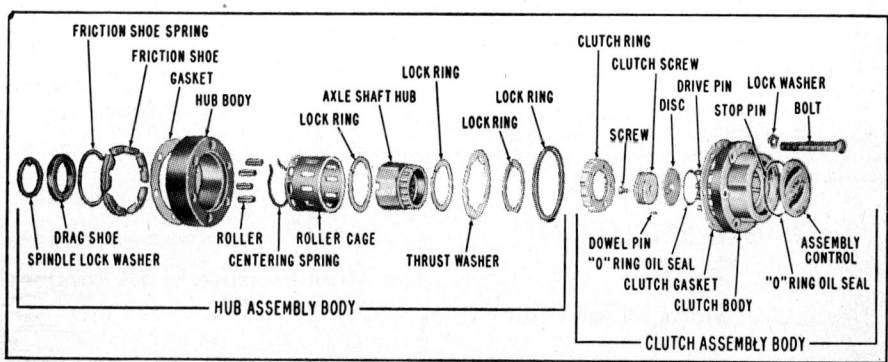

Fig. 8 I.H. (International Harvester) Lock-O-Matic disassembled

509

FRONT WHEEL LOCKING HUBS

7. Remove lock ring and thrust washer from hub body.
8. Disassembly of the Lock-O-Matic clutch body is identical to that of the manual type.

Lock-O-Matic Type, Assemble

1. Referring to Fig. 8, install thrust washer in hub body. Place lock ring in its groove in hub body to hold thrust washer in position.
2. Position friction shoes into roller cage. Install spring.
3. Install lock ring into end opposite friction shoes of roller cage.
4. Insert axle shaft hub into roller cage against lock ring.

NOTE: *Points on axle shaft hub must be aligned with grooves in friction shoes to permit entry.*

5. Install lock ring into second groove on axle shaft hub.
6. Slip centering spring into back side of axle shaft hub.

NOTE: *The two ends of spring go into the slot in cage which is longer than the rest.*

7. Place a small amount of light grade chassis lube into all slots of cage and into bore of hub body.
8. Hold hub and cage assembly with clutch end up and insert ten rollers into cage slots.
9. Slip axle shaft hub and cage assembly into hub body from back side. Install lock ring into remaining groove in axle shaft hub.

NOTE: *To hold axle shaft hub while lock ring is being installed, place it on a piece of 2 1/4" diameter bar stock.*

10. Assemble clutch body in the same manner described for the manual type clutch body.

AUTOMATIC TRANSMISSIONS

INDEX

	Page No.
CHRYSLER UNITS	
Chrysler Corp. Loadflite	534
Chrysler Corp. A-345	534
FORD UNITS	
Ford C4	525
Ford FMX (Cast Iron Case)	528
Ford C6	531

	Page No.
GENERAL MOTORS UNITS	
Allison AT-540, 543	510
Allison HT-740, 750	514
Allison MT-640, 643, 644, 650, 653, 653CR	512
Allison (Powermatic, Reomatic, Torqmatic, Transmatic)	518

	Page No.
Chevrolet Powerglide	522
GMC Pow-R-Flo	522
Turbo Hydra-Matic 200	541
Turbo Hydra-Matic 250	544
Turbo Hydra-Matic 350	544
Turbo Hydra-Matic 400	538
Turbo Hydra-Matic 425	548
Turbo Hydra-Matic 475	538

Allison AT-540 & 543

DESCRIPTION

This transmission, Fig. 1, has four forward speeds and reverse. Shifting within the four ranges selected by the operator is fully automatic. A simple 3 element torque converter transmits power from the engine to the transmission gearing. The torque converter serves as both a fluid coupling and a torque multiplier. Ratios for the four forward speeds and reverse are established by planetary gearing which is controlled by hydraulic clutches. All gearing is in constant mesh.

TROUBLE SHOOTING GUIDE

Automatic Shifts at Too High Speed

1. Governor valve stuck.
2. Vacuum modulator hose to engine kinked or leaking (light throttle shifting delayed).
3. Vacuum modulator failed.
4. Mechanical actuator cable kinked, broken or improperly adjusted.
5. Mechanical actuator malfunctioning.

Automatic Shifts at Too Low Speed at Full Throttle

1. Governor valve stuck.
2. Governor spring weak.
3. Mechanical actuator cable kinked, broken or improperly adjusted.
4. Mechanical actuator malfunctioning.

Low Main Pressure in All Ranges

1. Low oil level.
2. Oil filter element clogged.
3. Seal ring on oil pickup tube leaking or missing.
4. Main pressure regulator valve spring weak.
5. Control valve body leakage.
6. Valves sticking.
7. Oil pump worn or damaged.

Low Main Pressure in First Gear, Normal Pressure in Other Ranges

1. First gear circuit of control valve body leakage.
2. Excessive leakage at first-and-reverse piston seals.

Buzzing Noise Occurring Intermittently

1. Low oil level.
2. Air leak at oil intake pipe.
3. Clogged filter.
4. Aerated oil.

AUTOMATIC TRANSMISSIONS

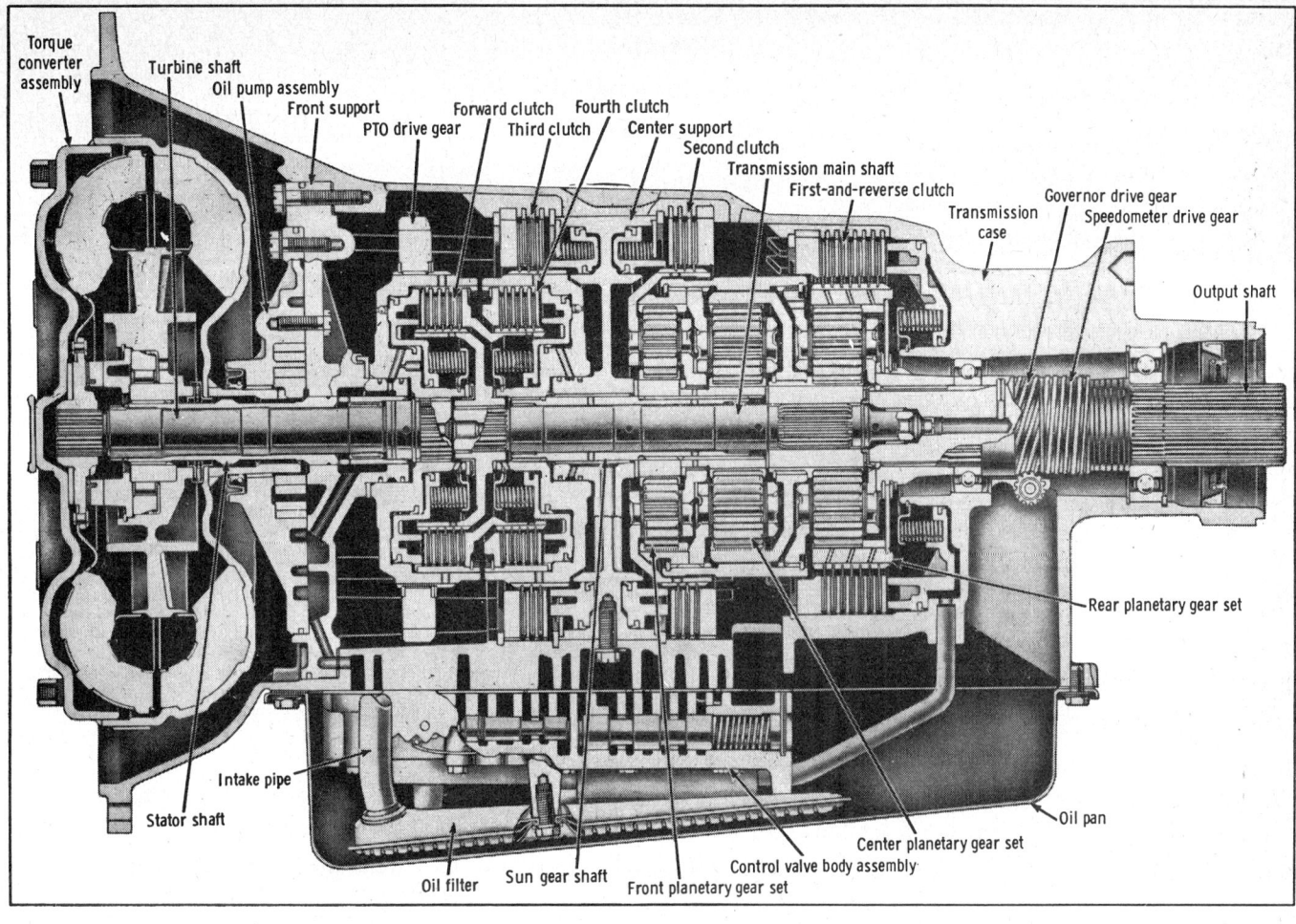

Fig. 1 Sectional view of AT 540 & 543 four speed automatic transmission

Excessive Creep in First and Reverse Gears

1. Engine idle speed too high.

Low Lubrication Pressure

1. Oil level low.
2. Excessive internal oil leakage.
3. Cooler lines restricted or leaking.

Oil Leaking into Converter Housing

1. Engine crankshaft rear oil seal leakage.
2. Charging oil pump, lip type seal at converter leaking.
3. Seal ring around O.D. of oil pump leaking.
4. Cracked weld in converter assembly, leaking.

Transmission Heating Up in All Ranges

1. Oil level low.
2. Oil level high.
3. Engine cooling system restricted.
4. Oil cooler lines restricted.
5. Broken parts in converter.

No Response to Movement of Shift Lever

1. Range selector linkage unhooked.
2. Range selector linkage defective or broken.
3. Main pressure low.
4. Range selector not engaged at control valve.

High Stall Speed

1. Oil level low.
2. Clutch pressure low.
3. Forward clutch slipping (forward).
4. First-and-reverse clutch slipping.

Low Stall Speed

1. Engine not performing efficiently (may be due to high altitude).
2. Broken converter parts.

Rough Shifting

1. Manual selector linkage out of adjustment.
2. Control valves sticking.
3. Vacuum modulator valve sticking.
4. Vacuum modulator hose kinked or leaking.
5. Engine idle speed too fast.
6. Governor valve malfunctioning.
7. Mechanical actuator cable kinked, broken or improperly adjusted.
8. Mechanical actuator malfunctioning.

Engine Overspeeds on Full Throttle Upshift

1. Piston seals leaking or clutch plates slipping in range involved.
2. Forward clutch piston seals or clutch plates slipping (all upshifts).
3. Broken seal rings on front support hub.
4. Sticking governor valve.

Excessive Slippage or Chatter in One Range

1. Clutch slippage in that range clutch.
2. Excessive oil leakage in range piston seals.
3. Oil leakage in valve components for that range.

Dirty Oil

1. Failure to change oil at specified intervals.
2. Excessive heat.
3. Clutch failure.
4. Damaged oil filter.

Oil Leak at Output Shaft

1. Faulty or missing seal at output flange.

AUTOMATIC TRANSMISSIONS

Slippage in All Forward Gears

1. Oil level low.
2. Clutch pressure low.
3. Forward clutch slipping.

Slippage in Fourth and Reverse Gear Only

1. Fourth clutch slipping.
2. Broken seal rings on support assembly hub.

Slippage in Reverse and First Gear; Proper Function in Other Forward Gears

1. First-and-reverse clutch slipping.

Vehicle Moves Forward in Neutral

1. Range selector linkage out of adjustment.
2. Forward clutch failed and dragging.

Vehicle Moves Backward in Neutral

1. Range selector linkage out of adjustment.
2. Fourth clutch failed and dragging.

Throws Oil Out of Transmission Filler Tube

1. Dipstick loose.
2. Oil level too high.
3. Breather stopped up.

MAINTENANCE

Oil Level

The transmission oil level should be checked every 1000 miles. Oil should be added only when the level is below the ADD mark. The safe operating level is from the ADD mark to the FULL mark. One quart of oil changes the level about 1/2" on the dipstick. In order to check the oil level, the transmission must be at operating temperature (160° to 220°F). Shift the transmission through all ranges to fill all cavities and passages. Vehicle must be level and transmission in Neutral when checking oil.

Changing Oil

The oil and oil filter should be changed every 25,000 miles or 12 months, whichever occurs first. The transmission should be at operating temperature when oil is drained. This will insure quicker and better drainage.

Remove the oil fill tube from the oil pan and allow oil to drain. Unfasten the oil pan and replace the internal oil filter. Replace the pan gasket with a new one when installing the pan. Only Dexron fluid is recommended for use in this transmission.

NOTE: Governor oil filter screen should be cleaned or replaced at each oil change.

Allison MT-640, 643, 644, 650, 653 & 654CR

DESCRIPTION

The MT-640, 643 and 644, 653 & 654CR Fig. 1, has four forward speeds and one reverse. The MT-650, 643 and 644, 653 and 654CR Fig. 2, has five forward speeds and one reverse. Shifting within any of the forward ranges selected by the operator is fully automatic.

A simple three element torque converter transmits power to the transmission gearing. The torque converter which serves as both a fluid coupling and a torque multiplier, has a stall ratio of 2.3:1.

A lockup clutch automatically locks the turbine to the flywheel. When the vehicle reaches a certain speed, hydraulic pressure automatically applies the clutch. When the lockup clutch is applied, the engine output is directed to the transmission gearing at a ratio of 1:1. A decrease in speed automatically releases the lockup clutch.

The planetary gear sets are controlled by six hydraulic-applied clutches. All gearing is in constant mesh.

TROUBLE SHOOTING GUIDE

Automatic shifts at Too High Speed

1. Governor valve stuck.
2. Vacuum signal valve spring adjustment too tight.
3. Valves sticking.

Automatic Shifts at Too Low Speed

1. Governor valve stuck.
2. Governor spring weak.
3. Vacuum signal valve spring adjustment.
4. Stuck modulator valve.
5. Modulator valve spring adjustment too loose.

Low Main Pressure in All Ranges

1. Low oil level.
2. Oil filter clogged.
3. Intake pipe seal leaking or missing.
4. Main pressure regulator valve spring weak.
5. Control valve body leakage.
6. Trimmer valves, relay valves or main pressure regulator valves stuck.
7. Worn or damaged oil pump.

Low Main Pressure in One Operating Range, Normal in Other Ranges

1. Leakage in clutch apply circuit for specific range.
2. Excessive leakage at clutch seals for specific range.

Excessive Creep in First and Reverse

1. Idle setting too high.

Low Lubrication Pressure

1. Oil level too low.
2. Excessive internal leakage.
3. Cooler lines restricted or leaking.
4. Lubrication valve spring weak.

Oil Leaking Into Converter Housing

1. Worn converter pump hub seal.
2. Converter pump hub worn at seal area.
3. Worn rear engine seal.

Transmission Overheating in All Ranges

1. Oil level too low.
2. Oil level too high.
3. Restricted oil cooler.

No Response To Shift Lever Movement

1. Shift selector linkage disconnected.
2. Shift selector linkage broken or defective.
3. Low main pressure.
4. Shift selector not engaged at control valve.

Rough Shifting

1. Shift selector linkage incorrectly adjusted.
2. Control valves sticking.
3. Sticking modulator valve or spring incorrectly adjusted.
4. Modulator actuator cable kinked or incorrectly adjusted.

Dirty Oil

1. Oil not changed at proper intervals.
2. Overheating.
3. Clutch failure.
4. Damaged oil filter.

Oil Leakage At Output Shaft

1. Worn or damaged output shaft seal.
2. Flange worn at seal area.

High Stall Speed

1. Low oil level.

AUTOMATIC TRANSMISSIONS

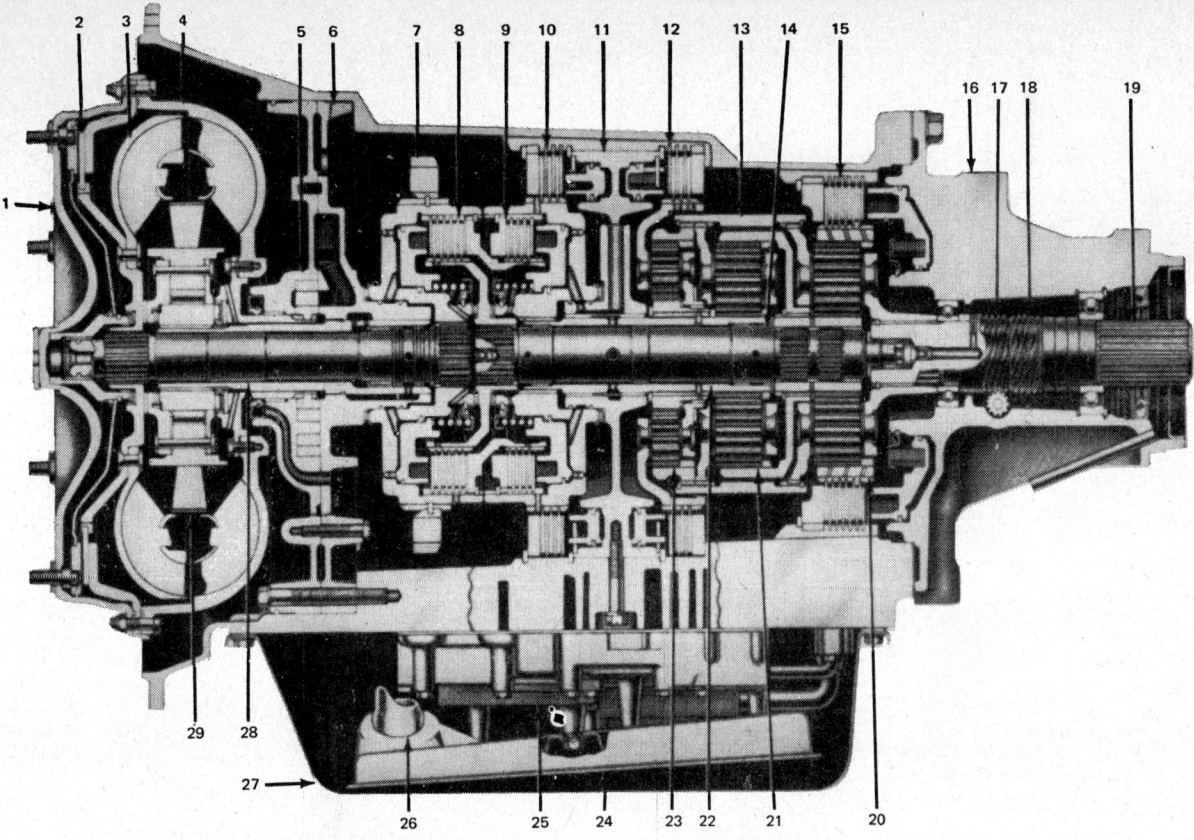

1 - Converter cover
2 - Lockup clutch
3 - Converter turbine
4 - Converter pump
5 - Oil pump
6 - Front support and valve assembly
7 - Power takeoff gear
8 - Forward clutch
9 - Fourth clutch
10 - Third clutch
11 - Center support
12 - Second clutch
13 - Planetary connecting drum
14 - Transmission main shaft
15 - First clutch
16 - Transmission rear cover
17 - Governor drive gear
18 - Speedometer drive gear
19 - Output shaft
20 - Rear planetary gear set
21 - Center planetary gear set
22 - Center sun gear shaft
23 - Front planetary gear set
24 - Oil filter
25 - Control valve assembly
26 - Intake pipe
27 - Oil pan
28 - Turbine shaft
29 - Converter stator

Fig. 1 Sectional view of MT-640, 643, 644 four speed automatic transmission

2. Low clutch pressure.
3. Forward clutch slipping.
4. First clutch slipping.

Low Stall Speed

1. Inefficient engine operation (may be due to high altitude).
2. Broken converter parts.

Clutch Slippage in All Forward Gears

1. Low oil level.
2. Clutch (main) pressure low.
3. Forward clutch slipping.
4. Front support hub seals worn or broken.

Clutch Slippage in First and Reverse

1. First clutch slipping.

Clutch Slippage in Second or Third (MT 640); or Third or Fourth (MT 650) Only

1. Clutch for specific range slipping.

Clutch Slippage in Fourth and Reverse Only

1. Fourth clutch slipping.
2. Center support hub seal worn or broken.

Clutch Slippage in First Only (MT 650)

1. Low clutch slipping.

Vehicle Moves in Neutral

1. Shift selector linkage out of adjustment.

Oil Overflowing From Filler Tube

1. Loose dipstick.
2. Oil level too high.
3. Clogged breather.
4. Worn dipstick gasket.

MAINTENANCE

Oil Level

The transmission oil level should be checked every 6000 miles. Oil level should be at the "Full" mark or slightly below, but never above the "Full" mark when engine and transmission are at normal operating temperatures.

In order to check oil level, the transmission must be at operating temperature (160°-220°F) and the vehicle in a level position. Apply parking brake and momentarily select each gear, then place selector lever in Neutral and check oil level.

Oil & Filter Change

Oil and filter should be changed every 25,000 miles or 12 months, which ever occurs first. The transmission should be at opearting temperature when oil is changed. This will ensure quicker and better drainage.

Remove oil pan drain plug and gasket from pan and allow oil to drain thoroughly. Remove oil pan attaching bolts and pan and gasket. Replace internal oil filter, then install oil pan, new gasket and drain plug. Only Dexron fluid is recommended for use in this transmission.

NOTE: Both governor oil filter screens should be cleaned or replaced at each oil change.

AUTOMATIC TRANSMISSIONS

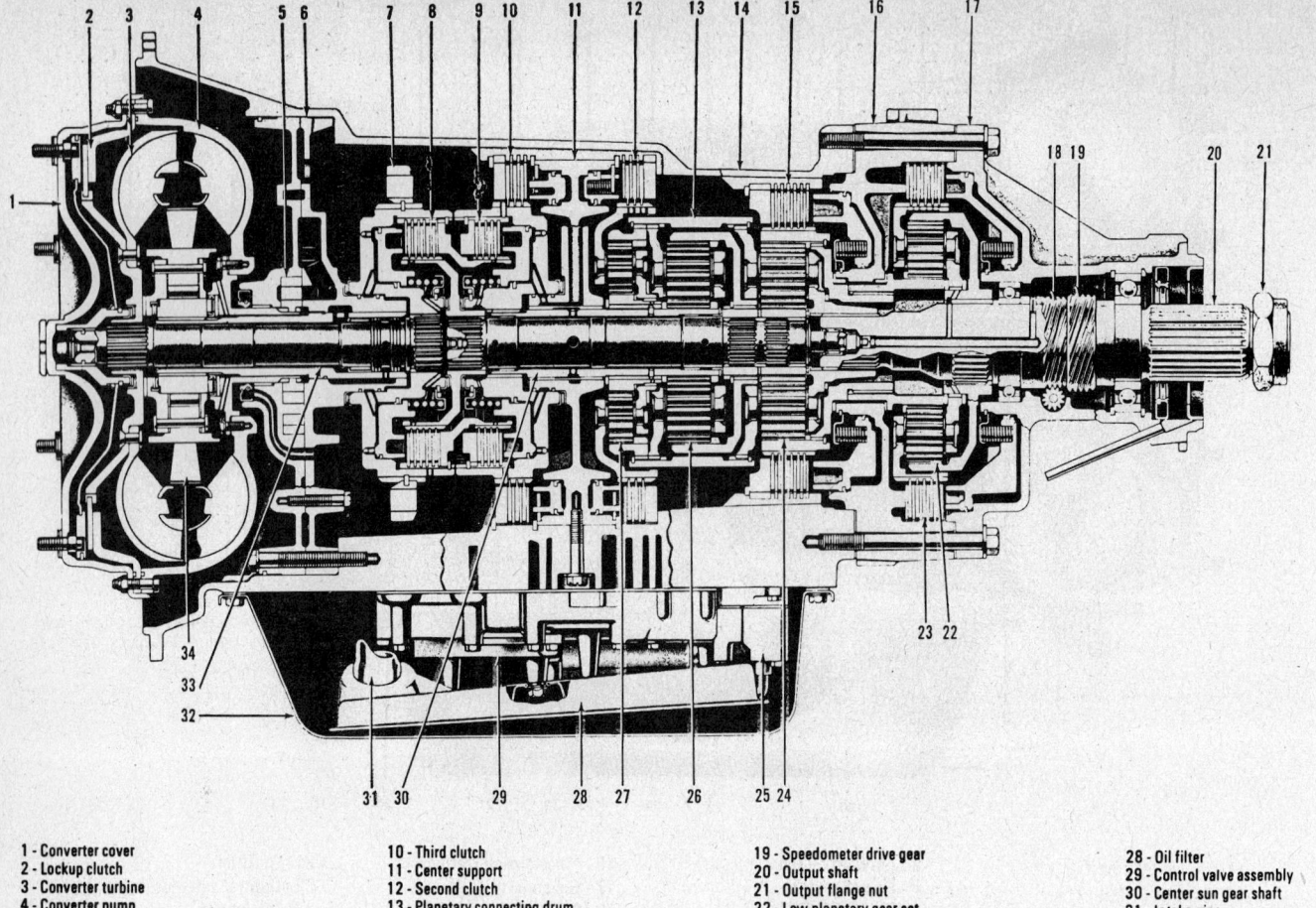

1 - Converter cover
2 - Lockup clutch
3 - Converter turbine
4 - Converter pump
5 - Oil pump
6 - Front support and valve assembly
7 - Power takeoff gear
8 - Forward clutch
9 - Fourth clutch
10 - Third clutch
11 - Center support
12 - Second clutch
13 - Planetary connecting drum
14 - Transmission housing
15 - First clutch
16 - Adapter housing
17 - Rear cover
18 - Governor drive
19 - Speedometer drive gear
20 - Output shaft
21 - Output flange nut
22 - Low planetary gear set
23 - Low clutch
24 - Rear planetary gear set
25 - Low shift valve
26 - Center planetary gear set
27 - Front planetary gear set
28 - Oil filter
29 - Control valve assembly
30 - Center sun gear shaft
31 - Intake pipe
32 - Oil pan
33 - Turbine shaft
34 - Converter stator

Fig. 2 Sectional view of MT-640, 653, 654CR five speed automatic transmission

Allison HT-740, 750

DESCRIPTION

The 740 units consist of four forward speeds and the 750 units consist of five forward speeds. Shifting is fully automatic on the HT-740D, Fig. 1, 750CRD, Fig. 2, models, while the HT-750DRD, Fig. 3, models must be manually shifted out of first gear, but the remaining ranges are fully automatic.

A simple three element torque converter transmits power from the engine to the transmission gearing. The dual purpose torque converter is a torque multiplier and a fluid coupling. Depending on application, the three combinations of converters which are used provide a stall ratio of 2.8:1, 2.2:1 or 2.1:1.

The lockup clutch which locks the turbine element of the torque converter to the flywheel is automatically applied by hydraulic pressure when the vehicle attains sufficient speed. A decrease in speed automatically releases the clutch. When the lockup clutch is applied, the engine output is directed to the transmission gearing at a ratio of 1:1.

Some HT-700D units incorporate a built in hydraulic retarder which is primarily a vaned rotor attached to the torque converter turbine output shaft. When the annually operated control valve admits oil into the vaned chamber surrounding the rotor, the retarder assists in slowing the vehicle.

These transmissions are provided with provisions for mounting a power take-off unit either on the transmission housing or converter housing. The transmission mounted PTO units are converter driven, while the converter housing mounted PTO units are engine driven.

On HT-740 units, ratios for the forward speeds are established by three planetary gear sets and are controlled by five hydraulically applied clutches. On HT-750 units, ratios for the forward speeds are established by four planetary gear sets and are controlled by six hydraulically applied clutches. All gearing on both the HT-740, 750 are in constant mesh.

TROUBLE SHOOTING GUIDE

Automatic Shifts Occur at Too High Speed

1. Shift signal valve spring too tight.
2. Governor valve stuck.
3. Valves sticking.

Automatic Shifts Occur at Too Low Speed

1. Governor valve stuck.
2. Weak governor spring.
3. Shift signal valve spring adjustment too loose.
4. Stuck modulator valve.

AUTOMATIC TRANSMISSIONS

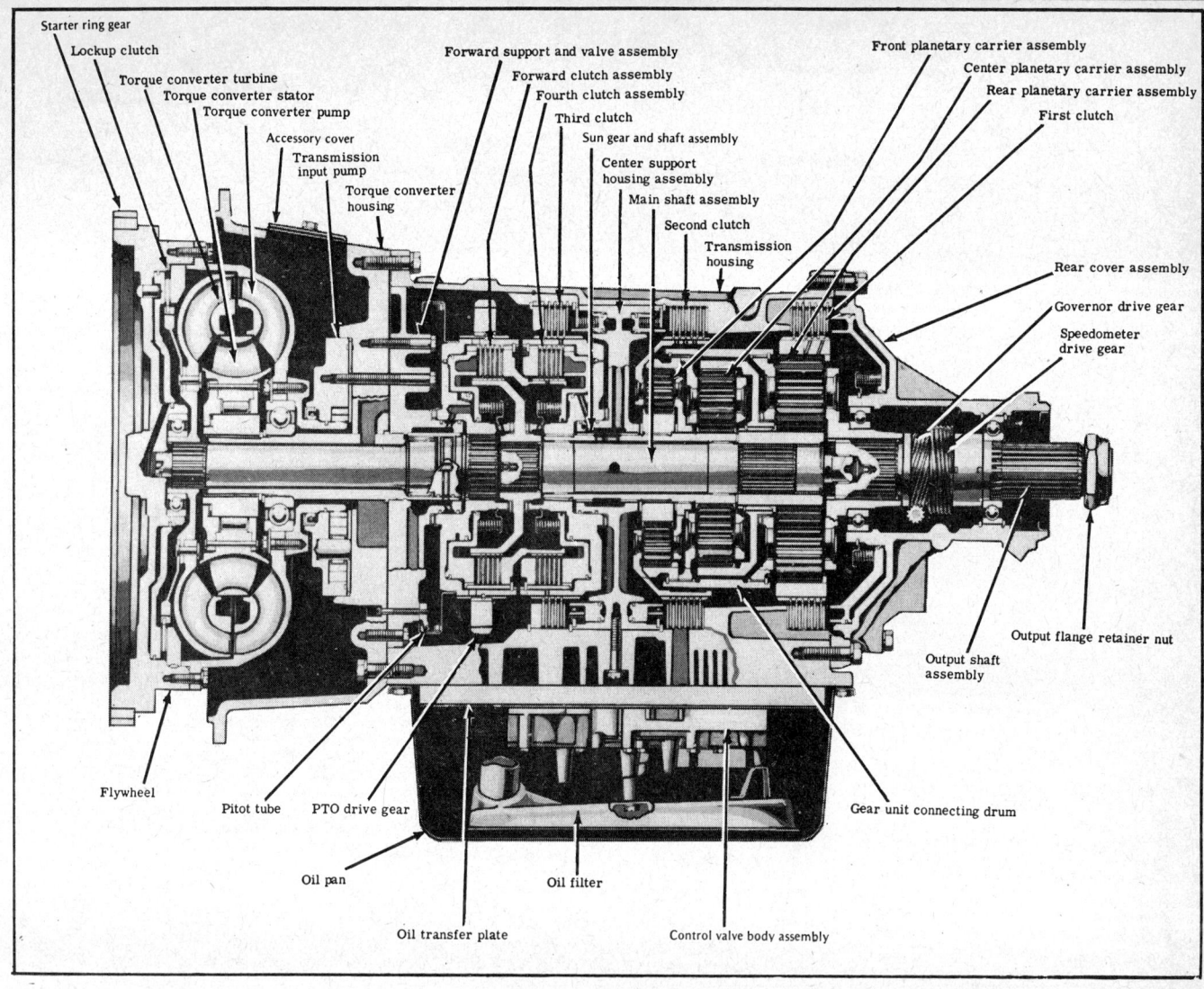

Fig. 1 HT-740 transmission

5. Modulator valve spring adjustment too loose.

Low Main Pressure In All Ranges

1. Low oil level.
2. Clogged oil filter element.
3. Seal at oil intake pipe (filter output) leaking or missing.
4. Weak main pressure regulator valve spring.
5. Control valve body leakage.
6. Trimmers, relays, and/or main pressure regulator valves stuck.
7. Worn or damaged oil pump.

Low Main Pressure In One Operating Range, Normal In All Other Ranges

1. Leakage in clutch apply circuits for specific range.
2. Excessive leakage at clutch piston seals for specific range.

Excessive Creep in First and Reverse Gears

1. Idle throttle setting too high.

Low Lubrication Pressure

1. Oil level too low.
2. Excessive internal oil leakage.
3. Restricted or leaking cooler lines.
4. Weak lubrication valve spring.

Oil Leaking Converter Housing

1. Converter hub seal worn.
2. Converter hub worn at seal area.
3. Engine rear seal worn.

Transmission Overheating In All Ranges

1. Low oil level.
2. High oil level.
3. Restricted cooler at oil or coolant side.

No Response to Shift Lever Movement

1. Range selector linkage disconnected.
2. Worn or defective range selector linkage.
3. Low Main Pressure.
4. Range selector disengaged at control valve.

Rough Shifting

1. Range selector linkage maladjusted.
2. Sticking control valves.
3. Sticking modulator valve or spring adjustment too tight.
4. Modulator actuator cable kinked or out of adjustment.

Contaminated Oil

1. Failure to change oil at proper intervals.
2. Overheating.
3. Damaged oil filter.
4. Clutch failure.

Oil Leaking At Output Shaft

1. Output flange seal worn or damaged.
2. Output flange worn at seal area.

High Stall Speed

1. Low oil level.
2. Low clutch pressure.
3. Slipping forward clutch (forward).
4. First clutch slipping.
5. Fourth clutch slipping (reverse).
6. Low clutch slipping (5 speed).

515

AUTOMATIC TRANSMISSIONS

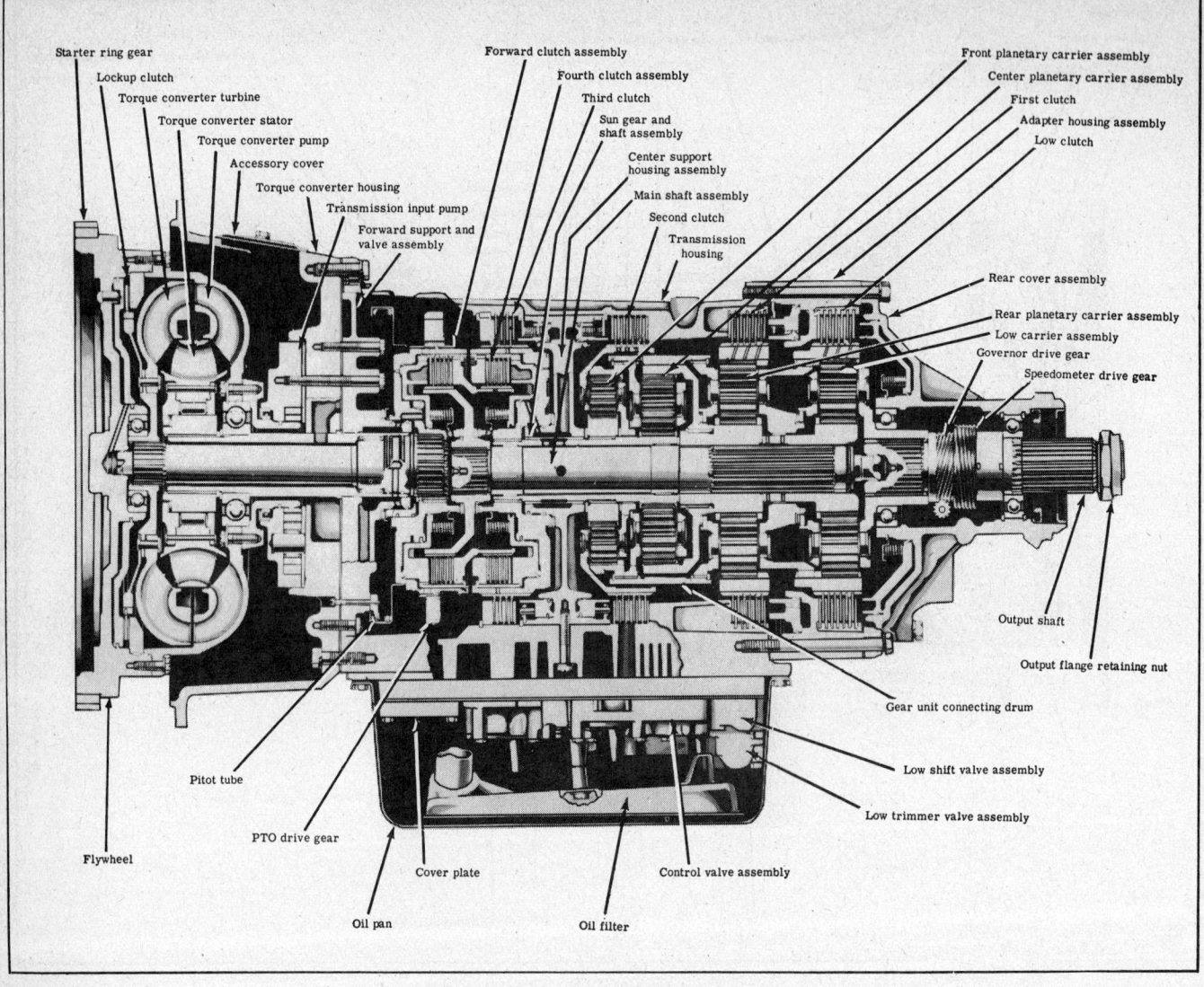

Fig. 2 HT-750 CRD transmission

Low Stall Speed

1. Engine not performing efficiently. (May be due to high altitude).
2. Damaged converter.

Clutch Slippage In All Forward Gears

1. Low oil level.
2. Low clutch (main) pressure.
3. Foward clutch slipping.
4. Seal rings on front support hub worn or broken.

Clutch Slippage In First and Reverse Only (740 D units)

1. First clutch slippage.

Clutch Slippage In All Forward Gears But No Slippage In Reverse

1. Forward clutch slipping.

Clutch Slippage In Fourth and Reverse Gears Only (740D units)

1. Fourth clutch slipping.

Clutch Slippage In Third Gear Only (740D units)

1. Third clutch slipping.

Clutch Slippage In Second Gear Only (740D units)

1. Second clutch slipping.

Clutch Slippage In Third Gear Only (750 CRD, DRD units)

1. Third clutch slipping.

Clutch Slippage In Third Gear Only (750 CRD, DRD units)

1. Second clutch slipping.

Clutch Slippage In Second Gear Only (750 CRD units)

1. First clutch slipping.

Clutch Slippage In Second and Reverse Gears Only (750 CRD units)

1. First clutch slipping.

Clutch Slippage In Fifth and Reverse Gears Only (750 CRD, DRD units)

1. Fourth clutch slipping.

Clutch Slippage In First Gear Only (750 DRD units)

1. Low clutch slipping.

Vehicle Moves in Neutral

1. Range selector linkage out of adjust-

AUTOMATIC TRANSMISSIONS

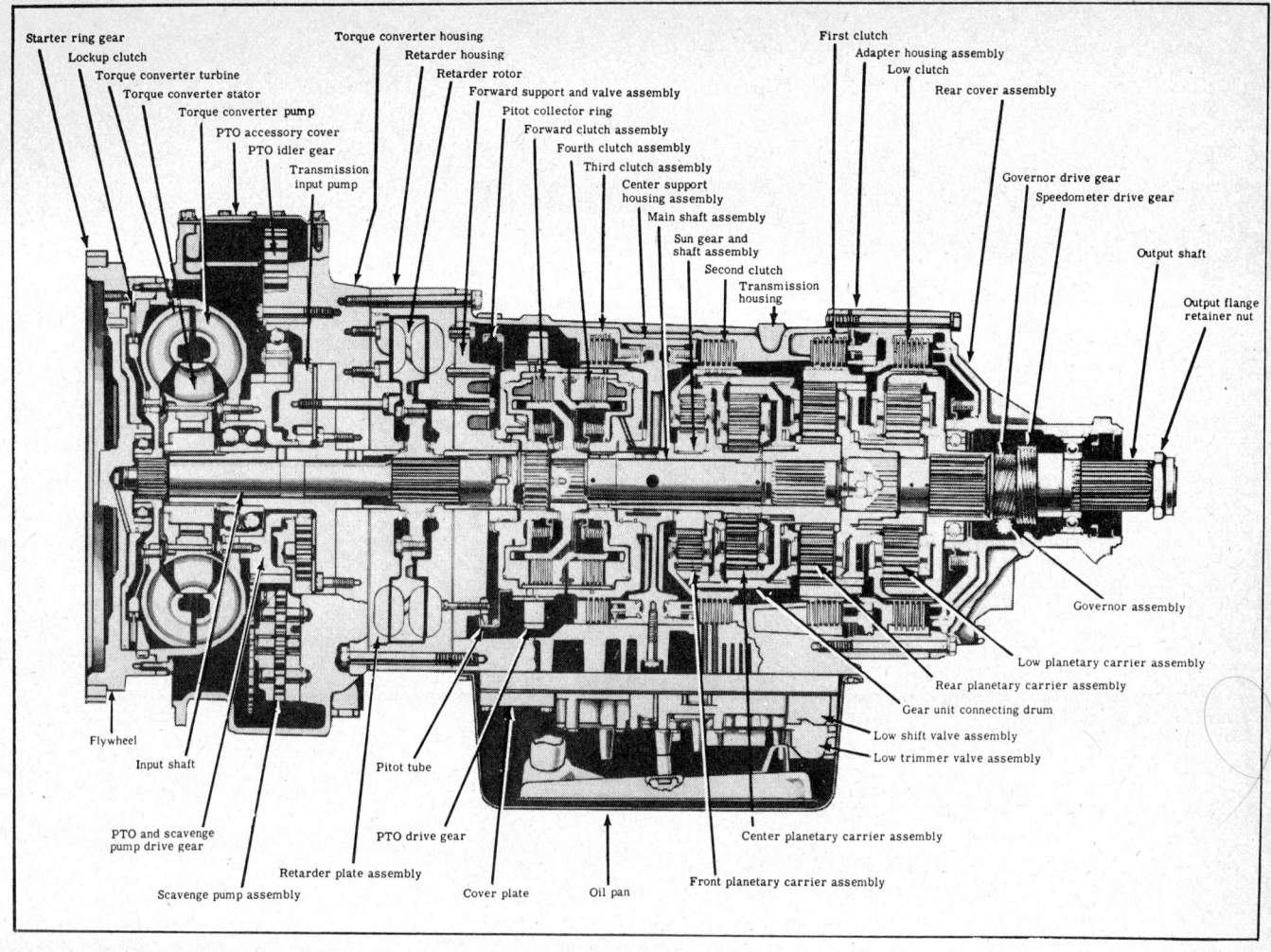

Fig. 3 HT-750 DRD transmission

ment.
2. Forward or fourth clutch will not release.

Oil Thrown From Filler Tube

1. Loose dipstick.
2. Oil level too high.
3. Clogged breather.
4. Worn dipstick gasket.
5. Improper dipstick marking.

MAINTENANCE

Oil Level

The transmission oil level should be checked every 1000 miles. Oil should be added only when the level is below the ADD mark. The safe operating level is from the ADD mark to the FULL mark. One quart of oil changes the level about 1/2" on the dipstick.

In order to check the oil level, the transmission must be at operating temperature (160° to 200° F). Shift the transmission through all ranges to fill all cavities and passages. Vehicle must be level and transmission in Neutral when checking oil.

Changing Oil

Oil should be changed each 50,000 miles or 12 months for on highway vehicles and 25,000 miles, 800 hours or 6 months for off highway vehicles. Internal filter should be changed at first oil change and each 500,000 miles thereafter if equipped with external oil filter. On models less external oil filter, change internal filter at each oil change. External oil filter should be changed after first 5000 miles and each 50,000 miles for on highway vehicles or 25,000 for off highway vehicles thereafter. The transmission should be at operating temperature when oil is drained. This will insure quicker and better drainage.

Remove fill tube from oil pan on early models or drain plug on late models and allow oil to drain. On all models, unfasten the oil pan and replace the internal oil filter. Replace the pan gasket with a new one when installing the pan. Only Dexron fluid is recommended for us in this transmission.

AUTOMATIC TRANSMISSIONS

Allison
Powermatic • Reomatic • Torqmatic • Transmatic

DESCRIPTION

This transmission, Fig. 1, is a hydraulically-operated automatic transmission with six forward gear ratios and one reverse ratio. It is made in two versions, a lighter unit for medium duty trucks and a heavier one for heavy duty trucks. The two models differ chiefly in the hydraulic control system.

The transmission consists basically of a torque converter, a planetary gear train and a hydraulic control system for shifting gears.

The torque converter operates as a hydraulic torque multiplier and a fluid coupling between the truck's engine and the gear train. The torque multiplying phase of the converter operates when the truck starts moving from a standstill and when a heavy load slows down the truck. When no torque multiplication is needed, the fluid coupling phase starts operating automatically.

If the truck should slow down and the converter turbine resists turning, such as when climbing hills or driving in stop-and-go traffic, the converter operation automatically changes from a fluid coupling phase to a torque multiplication phase. This phase occurs after the gears have shifted into third gear ratio (when driving in Drive or Intermediate ranges) or first gear ratio (when in Low range).

At certain engine speeds when the action of the torque converter is no longer needed, an automatic lockup clutch in the converter locks the engine directly to the gear train for greater efficiency. The hydraulic system which operates the lockup clutch automatically disengages the clutch each time an automatic or manual upshift or downshift is being made.

A pedal-operated hydraulic retarder in the transmission assists the service brakes in controlling the truck's speed during long downhill braking or when slowing down in stop-and-go traffic. When the retarder pedal is depressed and the retarder valve opens, transmission fluid flows into the retarder cavity located between the converter and transmission housings. The cavity contains a rotor, which is connected to the turbine output shaft, and stationary reaction vanes on both

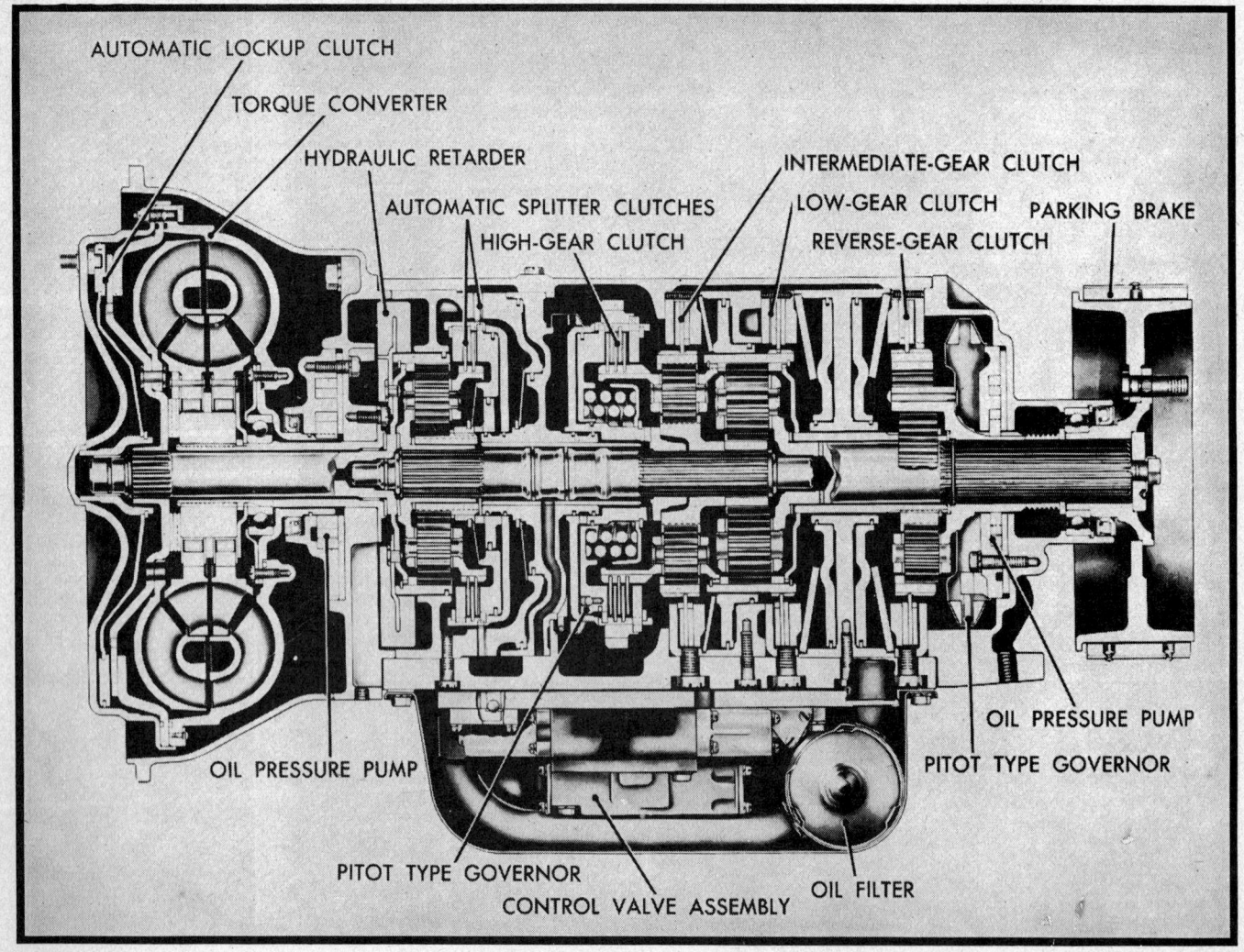

Fig. 1 Sectional view of Allison six-speed automatic transmission

AUTOMATIC TRANSMISSIONS

sides of the rotor. When the fluid fills the cavity, it churns against the reaction vanes and slows down the rotor. The retarding effort is transmitted to the drive line and slows down the truck.

The retarder will continue to operate as long as the retarder pedal is depressed. However, heat is generated in the fluid by the retarder action, and the fluid temperature may rise faster than it can be cooled if the retarder is operated continuously. A warning light on the instrument panel indicates that the retarder operation should be discontinued until the fluid cools and the warning light goes out. When the pedal is released and the retarder valve closes, the fluid in the cavity automatically discharges and permits the rotor to turn without drag.

The transmission gear train contains four sets of constant-mesh planetary gears which are operated by hydraulically-actuated clutches. All forward gear shifts, except the upshift and downshift between second and third gear ratios, are fully automatic and are controlled, through a system of hydraulic valves, by throttle position and truck speed.

The four planetaries are arranged in series to permit one of them to become a "splitter" for the others. The splitter planetary, located between the torque converter and the range gears, has two ratios that are used when the low, intermediate or high clutch is applied. A reduction ratio, or low splitter, operates in neutral, first, third, fifth and reverse gears. A direct drive ratio, or high splitter, is used in second, fourth and sixth gears.

Two separate fluid-velocity governors in the transmission provide the fluid pressures needed to operate the hydraulic control system and make the shifts.

Two regular duty power take-off openings are located at the sides of the transmission housing.

DRIVING INSTRUCTIONS

The manual controls needed to operate the transmission are a range selector lever, an accelerator pedal, and a pedal for the hydraulic retarder.

A neutral position (N), three forward speed positions (Dr, Int and Lo) are provided for the range selector lever to control the various automatic gear ratio shifts in the transmission.

The selector lever must be at N to start the engine. When the lever is at Dr, the transmission can be operated in 3rd, 4th, 5th and 6th gear ratios. The Int (intermediate range) position permits the use of only 3rd and 4th gear ratios. When the lever is in Lo (low range) the transmission will operate only in 1st and 2nd gear ratios. The reverse gear ratio can be used when the selector lever is at R.

"Rocking" Out of Deep Ruts

To "rock" the truck out of deep ruts, move the selector lever back and forth between Lo and R while keeping the engine running at a steady speed. Time the movement of the lever to take advantage of the "rocking" momentum of the truck.

Pushing or Towing To Start The Engine

If the truck has to be pushed or towed to start the engine, place the selector lever at N and turn on the ignition switch. When the truck's speed reaches about 25 mph, move the selector lever to Dr and hold the accelerator pedal about halfway down. If the truck is being towed, be careful not to run into the towing truck when the engine starts.

Operating The Hydraulic Retarder

The hydraulic retarder is not a substitute for the service brakes but is designed only to slow down the truck. It assists the brakes and relieves them from excessive use and wear during long downhill braking and when slowing down in stop-and-go traffic.

To slow down the truck, push down and hold the hydraulic retarder pedal. The retarder operates most effectively in the intermediate and low ranges at engine speeds of 2800–3500 rpm.

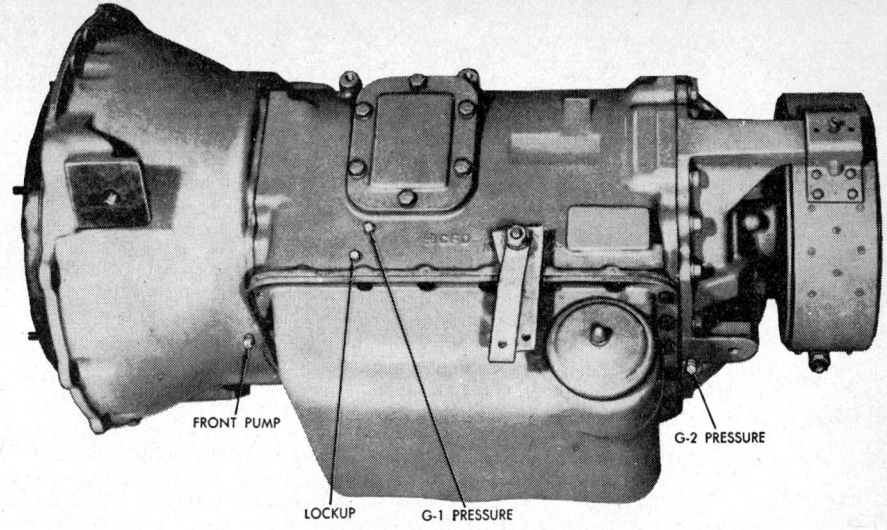

Fig. 2 Pressure check point locations

TROUBLE SHOOTING

Shift Points High on 1st and 2nd and all Lockup Shifts

1. G-1 Pressure insufficient.
2. Lube pressure low.
3. Anchor bolts holding diaphragm in housing loose.
4. G-1 circuit leakage.
5. Front fluid velocity governor damaged.
6. Front pitot tube loose or damaged.

Lockup Shift Points High and Transmission Won't Shift to 2nd Gear

1. G-1 pressure insufficient.
2. Lube pressure low.
3. G-1 circuit leakage.
4. Lockup shift valve sticking.
5. Anchor bolts holding high range clutch diaphragm in housing loose.
6. Front fluid velocity governor damaged.
7. Front pitot tube loose or damaged.

Low-Main Pressure In All Ranges

1. Air leak at oil transfer tubes or seals in oil pan.
2. Oil filter element clogged.
3. Main pressure regulator valve primary and secondary springs weak or improper.
4. TV pressure low at full throttle; normal at closed throttle.
5. TV spring weak or broken.
6. Range selector valve body leakage.
7. Oil transfer plate gasket blown or damaged.
8. Rear pump ball not in range selector valve body.
9. Valves sticking.
10. Front pump worn or damaged.

Low Main Pressure In Low Range

1. Low range circuit of range selector valve body leaking.
2. Leakage between low range piston housing and transmission housing.
3. Excessive leakage at low range piston seals.
4. Gasket at oil transfer plate leaking.

Misses 2nd Gear On Downshift to Low Range

1. Shifting manually at too low vehicle speed.
2. G-1 pressure insufficient.
3. Rear oil pump malfunctioning.

Transmission Will Not Shift to 4th Gear In Int or Dr Ranges

1. G-2 pressure insufficient.
2. Rear pitot tube loose.
3. Rear pitot (G-2) splitter plug sticking.
4. Rear fluid velocity governor damaged.
5. Rear oil pump malfunction or orifice in pump housing clogged.
6. Rear pitot tube damaged or improperly installed.

All Shift Points Too Low At Full Throttle

1. TV pressure low at full throttle.
2. Throttle valve spring weak or broken.
3. Main pressure leaking into governor circuit.

All Shift Points Too High Except Lockup and 1st and 2nd Shift At Part Throttle

1. G-2 pressure insufficient.

AUTOMATIC TRANSMISSIONS

2. Rear pitot tube loose.
3. Rear fluid velocity governor damaged.
4. Rear pitot tube damaged.

Buzzing Noise Occurring Intermittently

1. Low oil level.
2. Oil filter element clogged.
3. Air leak at oil transfer tubes or seals in oil pan.

Insufficient G-2 Pressure

1. Rear pitot tube loose.
2. Rear fluid velocity governor damaged.
3. Rear pitot tube damaged or improperly installed.
4. Rear oil pump malfunction.
5. Oil transfer plate gasket blown or damaged.

Insufficient G-1 Pressure

1. Lube pressure low.
2. G-1 circuit leak or obstruction.
3. Anchor bolts holding high range clutch diaphragm in housing loose.
4. Front fluid velocity governor damaged.
5. Front pitot tube damaged or loose.

Low Lube Pressure

1. Oil lines restricted.
2. Cooler lines or fittings leaking.
3. Lube regulator valve ball or spring in hydraulic retarder control valve body faulty.
4. Oil filter element clogged.
5. Pump overage regulator malfunction.
6. Front oil pump malfunction.
7. Converter pressure regulator valve ball malfunction.
8. Oil level low.

Oil Leakage Into Converter Housing

1. Engine crankshaft rear oil seal leaking.
2. Torque converter seals leaking.
3. Front oil pump lip-type seal faulty or seal drain restricted.
4. Hook-type seal ring on converter pump hub broken.
5. Drive studs in converter pump cover loose.
6. O-type seal ring at front oil pump leaking.

Transmission Heating Up In All Ranges

1. Oil level low.
2. Oil level high.
3. Engine cooling system malfunction.
4. Oil cooler lines restricted.
5. Hydraulic retarder partially applied.
6. Bushing on converter ground sleeve worn.

Lockup Clutch Will Not Engage

1. G-1 pressure insufficient.
2. Lockup shift valve or lockup cut-off valve sticking.
3. Hook-type seal rings on splitter shaft or turbine shaft broken.
4. Lockup clutch piston seal ring leaking.
5. Excessive internal leakage.

No Response to Movement of Shift Lever

1. Oil filter clogged.
2. Oil level low.
3. Range selector linkage defective.
4. Main pressure low.
5. Low splitter clutch failure.
6. Clutch piston seals leaking.

High Stall Speed

1. Oil level low.
2. Clutch pressure low.
3. Converter pressure low.
4. Range clutches failure.
5. Low splitter clutch failure.

Low Stall Speed

1. Engine not performing efficiently.
2. Converter stators functioning improperly due to improper assembly or failure of components.

Rough Shifting

1. Manual selector linkage out of adjustment.
2. Throttle valve linkage out of adjustment.
3. Valves sticking.

Engine Overspeeds On Full Throttle Shift Out of Low Range

1. Downshift timing valve sticking.
2. Seals on intermediate range clutch piston excessively worn.

Loss of Hydraulic Retarder Braking Effect

1. Oil level low.
2. Hydraulic retarder valve linkage out of adjustment.
3. Oil filter element clogged.
4. Air leaks at oil transfer tubes or seals in oil pan.
5. Lube regulator valve in hydraulic retarder valve body failure.
6. Hook-type seal ring on outside diameter of splitter ring gear faulty.

Excessive Slippage and Clutch Chatter In 1st and 2nd Lockup Only

1. Low range clutch failure.
2. Excessive leakage of low range clutch piston seals.

Excessive Slippage and Clutch Chatter In 1st, 3rd and 5th Gear Lockup Only

1. Low splitter clutch failure.
2. Anchor bolts holding high range clutch diaphragm in housing loose.
3. Excessive leaking of low splitter clutch piston seals.

Excessive Slippage and Clutch Chatter In 2nd, 4th and 6th Gear

1. High splitter clutch slipping.
2. Anchor bolts holding high range clutch diaphragm in housing loose.
3. Excessive leaking of high splitter clutch piston seals.

Excessive Slippage In 3rd and 4th Gear Lockup Only

1. Intermediate range clutch failure.
2. Intermediate range clutch piston seals leaking excessively.

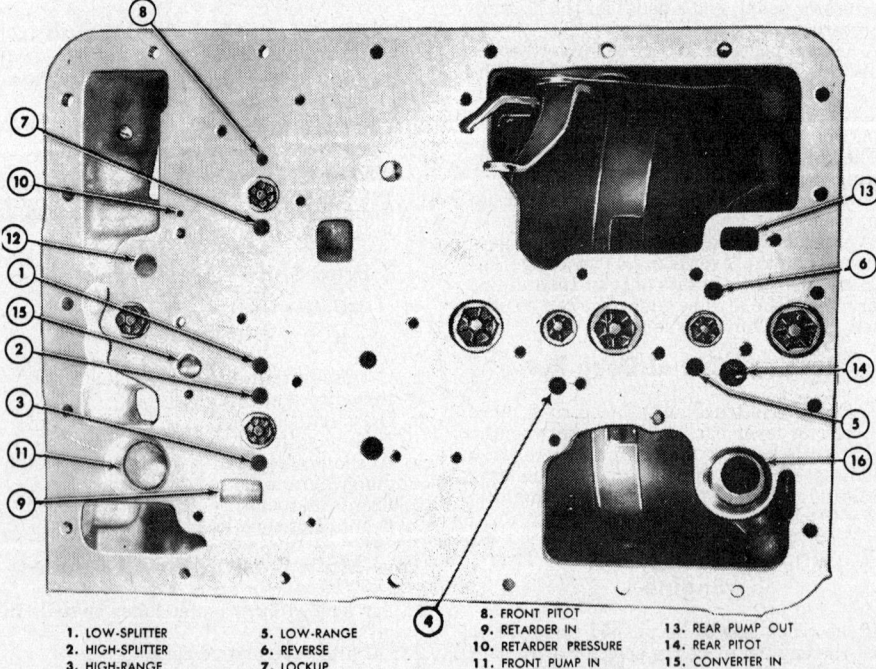

CLUTCH APPLY PASSAGES
1. LOW-SPLITTER
2. HIGH-SPLITTER
3. HIGH-RANGE
4. INTERMEDIATE-RANGE
5. LOW-RANGE
6. REVERSE
7. LOCKUP

OTHER PASSAGES
8. FRONT PITOT
9. RETARDER IN
10. RETARDER PRESSURE
11. FRONT PUMP IN
12. FRONT PUMP OUT
13. REAR PUMP OUT
14. REAR PITOT
15. CONVERTER IN
16. REAR PUMP IN

Fig. 4 Transmission housing fluid passage holes

AUTOMATIC TRANSMISSIONS

Dirty Oil

1. Failure to change at specified interval.
2. Oil filter element faulty.
3. Excessive heat.
4. Clutch failure.

Slippage In 5th and 6th Gear Lockup Only

1. High range clutch slippage.
2. High range clutch piston seals leaking excessively.

Slippage In All Gears

1. Oil level low.
2. Clutch pressure low.
3. Lockup clutch slipping.

Excessive Slippage In Reverse Range Lockup Only

1. Reverse range clutch failure.
2. Reverse range clutch piston seals leaking excessively.

Vehicle Moves Forward In Neutral

1. Range selector linkage out of adjustment.
2. Range clutch failure or dragging.
3. Insufficient range clutch clearances.

Vehicle Moves Backward In Neutral

1. Range selector linkage out of adjustment.
2. Reverse range clutch failure or dragging.

Vehicle Will Not Push Start

1. Engine trouble.
2. Oil level low.
3. Rear oil pump malfunction.
4. Also refer to troubles concerning excessive clutch slippage and failure of vehicle to move when engine is running and selector is shifted to forward ranges.

Throws Oil Out of Transmission Filler Tube

1. Dipstick loose.
2. Breather line clogged, disconnected or pinched.
3. Oil level too high.

Oil Leak At Rear Bearing Retainer

1. Bearing retainer bolts loose.
2. Retainer gasket blown.
3. Gasket of improper thickness installed.

OIL PRESSURE CHECKS

Plugged holes are provided for checking oil pressures, Fig. 2. These plugs can be removed for the installation of oil pressure gauges.

CAUTION: *Do not install any gauges while the engine is running. By using these oil pressure check points, abnormal oil pressures that will cause malfunction of the hydraulic-controlled components can be found. The following data applies to the medium duty unit. Full throttle pressures for the heavy duty unit are 10% higher.*

Gear	Operation	P.S.I.*
1st	Converter	
	closed throttle	185
	full throttle	220
	Lockup	
	closed throttle	70
	full throttle	82
2nd	Lockup	
	closed throttle	70
	full throttle	82
3rd	Converter	
	closed throttle	185
	full throttle	220
	Lockup	
	closed throttle	85
	full throttle	100
4th	Lockup	
	closed throttle	70
	full throttle	82
5th	Lockup	
	closed throttle	70
	full throttle	82
6th	Lockup	
	closed throttle	70
	full throttle	82
Reverse	Converter	
	closed throttle	185
	full throttle	220
	Lockup	
	closed throttle	70
	full throttle	82

*The above data are for medium duty units; full throttle operation on heavy duty units are 10% higher.

AIR PRESSURE CHECKS

Compressed air may be used to check the operation of the various clutches in the transmission and to find leaks that may be caused by broken, damaged or omitted seals.

To make the air pressure checks, remove the oil pan, valve body and oil transfer plate from the transmission. Then apply 80–100 lbs. (psi) air pressure at the appropriate holes in the mounting pad at the bottom of the transmission housing, Figs. 2 and 3.

When compressed air is applied as directed, listen for the noise that occurs when the clutch is applied. If no clutch application noise is heard, a leak may exist in the hydraulic system. Refer to the fluid leakage data below to determine the cause of the leaks at any of the check points.

Low Splitter Clutch

1. Leak between diaphragm and case:—Bottom two anchor bolts loose or not drawing diaphragm to case.

High Splitter Clutch

1. Leak between diaphragm and case:—Bottom two anchor bolts loose or not drawing diaphragm to case.
2. Leak at piston I.D.:—Broken or omitted hook-type oil seal.
3. Leak at piston O.D.:—Broken, nicked or omitted synthetic seal.
4. Air comes out of lube hole in retarder valve body pad:—Front hub hook-type seal ring broken or omitted.
5. Air comes out of retarder feed:—Rear hub hook-type seal ring broken or omitted.

High Range Clutch

1. Leak between diaphragm and case:—Bottom two anchor bolts loose or not drawing diaphragm to case.
2. Air escapes at front pitot hole (8) or at lube hole in retarder valve body pad:—Inner hook-type seal ring on rear hub broken or omitted.
3. Air escapes at lube hole in retarder valve body pad:—Rear hook-type seal ring on rear hub broken or omitted.
4. Air may escape around clutch piston spring:—Hook-type seal ring for clutch I.D. broken or omitted.
5. Air may escape around high range clutch hub:—Synthetic seal at piston O.D. broken, nicked or omitted.

Intermediate Range Clutch

1. Leak between case and intermediate clutch piston housing:—Anchor bolts loose. Intermediate clutch housing not tight against hole in case.
2. Leak at piston I.D.:—Hook-type ring broken or omitted.
3. Air escapes around low range clutch plate:—Hook-type ring broken or omitted.
4. Leak at piston O.D.:—Synthetic seal at piston O.D. broken, nicked or omitted.

Low Range Clutch

1. Leak between case and low-reverse piston housing:—Anchor bolt loose. Low-reverse clutch housing not tight against case.
2. Leak at piston I.D.:—Hook-type seal broken or omitted.
3. Air escapes around clutch I.D.:—Hook-type seal broken or omitted.
4. Leak at piston O.D.:—Synthetic seal broken, nicked or omitted.

Reverse Clutch

1. Leak between case and low-reverse piston housing:—Anchor bolt loose. Low-reverse clutch housing not tight against case.
2. Leak at piston I.D.:—Hook-type seal broken or omitted.
3. Air escapes around clutch I.D.:—Hook-type seal broken or omitted.
4. Leak at piston O.D.:—Synthetic seal broken, nicked or omitted.

Lockup Clutch

1. Leak at piston I.D.:—Synthetic seal broken, nicked or omitted.
2. Leak at O.D. of converter cover:—Synthetic seal between reaction plate and cover, or between plate and converter pump flange damaged or omitted.
3. Leak at turbine shaft:—Broken or omitted hook-type rings at front end of turbine shaft, front end of splitter shaft, or center of splitter shaft.

MAINTENANCE

Adding Fluid

The oil level should be checked every 1000 miles and oil added as necessary as outlined below:

1. Transmission oil should be at normal operating temperature of 150 to 200°.
2. Apply hand brake and service brakes securely. *Do not apply the hydraulic retarder while checking the oil level.* Applying the hydraulic retarder while in a stalled condition will aerate the oil, making an accurate oil level check impossible.

AUTOMATIC TRANSMISSION

3. Place range selector lever in Dr range and run engine at normal idle speed.
4. Before removing dipstick clean the area around the dipstick opening as a precaution against dirt entering transmission.
5. The oil level should be at the "Full" mark on the dipstick. If the oil level it at the "Add" mark, or below it, add enough oil to bring the level up to the "Full" mark. If the oil level is higher than the level specified above, drain the oil back to the correct level.
6. Securely seat the dipstick in the filler tube.

Changing Fluid

The oil should be changed every 5000 miles under normal operating conditions for off-highway or urban operation. The oil should be changed at 10,000 mile intervals for normal highway operation. Replace the oil filter at each change.
1. Drain oil immediately after operation while the oil is still warm.
2. Loosen the transmission oil filter cover and allow oil to drain thoroughly. Do not completely remove the cover until drainage is complete.
3. Remove cover and filter and install new filter.
4. Pour eight quarts of Hydraulic Transmission Fluid "Type A" or Automatic Transmission Fluid "Type C" into the transmission.
5. Apply parking brake and position range selector in N and start engine.
6. Move range selector lever to Dr.
7. Run engine at normal idle speed and add sufficient oil to bring the level up to the "Add" oil mark on the dipstick.
8. With service brakes applied, shift the transmission through all ranges. Continue to run the engine until normal operating temperature of the transmission is attained. Then add oil, if necessary, to bring the level up to the "Full" mark.

Oil Cooler

The oil cooler (heat exchanger), through which the transmission oil is circulated before returning to the oil pan, dissipates the heat created by normal operation of the torque converter, transmission and hydraulic retarder. The cooling medium is the engine coolant.

When a clutch failure or other internal trouble has occurred in the transmission, any metal particles or clutch plate material that may have been carried into the oil cooler should be removed from the system by flushing the cooler before the transmission is put back into service. Foreign matter in the oil cooler could block off the front pitot feed hole, get into various gears and clutches, or block off the output shaft bushing lubrication orifice in the splitter shaft.
1. Disconnect both oil cooler lines at the fittings in the hydraulic retarder valve body.
2. Back-flush the oil cooler and lines with clean solvent and compressed air. *Do not exceed 100 psi air pressure*. An engine desludge gun may be used for flushing.
3. Remove all remaining solvent from the system with compressed air.
4. Flush the system again with Automatic Transmission Fluid. If, after the final flushing, there is no flow through the cooler, or if the flow is restricted, replace the radiator.

GMC POW-R-FLO & Chevrolet Powerglide

DESCRIPTION

This Powerglide is essentially a torque converter coupled to a two-speed transmission. The gear portion of the transmission is a two-speed compound planetary gear set, permitting a gear reduction of 1.82 to 1 on the light duty version and 1.76 to 1 on the heavy duty version. The shift from low gear to direct drive is automatic, and the vehicle speed at which the shifts occur is determined by the interaction of a governor driven by the output shaft and a throttle valve controlled by the accelerator pedal. Thus, the transmission starts both the torque converter and the gear box multiplying torque. As vehicle speed increases, the gear box section upshifts to direct drive, leaving only the torque converter for any speed-torque changes required. The torque multiplication ability of the converter multiplied by the planetary gear reduction allows an overall torque multiplication of approximately 4.55 to 1.

TROUBLE SHOOTING GUIDE

Oil Forced Out Filler Tube

1. Oil level too high; aeration and foaming caused by planet carrier runnig in oil.
2. Water in oil.
3. Leak in pump suction circuits.

Oil Leaks

1. Transmission case and extension: extension oil seal, shifter shaft oil seal, speedometer driven gear fitting, pressure taps, oil cooler pipe connections, vacuum modulator and case, transmission oil pan gasket.
2. A very smoky exhaust indicates a ruptured vacuum modulator diaphragm.
3. Converter cover pan; front pump attaching bolts, pump seal ring, pump oil seal, plugged oil drain in front pump, porosity in transmission case.

No Drive In Any Position

1. Low oil level.
2. Clogged oil suction screeen.
3. Defective pressure regulator valve.
4. Front pump defective.
5. Input shaft broken.
6. Front pump priming valve stuck.

Erratic Operation and Slippage— Light to Medium Throttle

1. Low oil level.
2. Clogged oil suction screen.
3. Improper band adjustment.
4. Band facing worn.
5. Low band apply linkage disengaged or broken.
6. Servo apply passage blocked.
7. Servo piston ring broken or leaking.
8. Converter stator not holding (rare).

Engine Speed Flares On Upshift

1. Low oil level.
2. Improper band adjustment.
3. Clogged oil suction screen.
4. High clutch partially applied—blocked feed orifice.
5. High clutch plates worn.
6. High clutch seals leak.
7. High clutch piston hung up.
8. High clutch drum relief ball not sealing.
9. Vacuum modulator line plugged.
10. Vacuum modulator defective.

Will Not Upshift

1. Maladjusted manual valve lever.
2. Throttle valve stuck or maladjusted.
3. No rear oil pump output caused by stuck priming valve, sheared drive pin or defective pump.
4. Defective governor.
5. Stuck low-drive valve.

Harsh Upshifts

1. Throttle valve linkage improperly adjusted.
2. Vacuum modulator line broken or disconnected.
3. Vacuum modulator diaphragm leaks.
4. Vacuum modulator valve stuck.
5. Hydraulic modulator valve stuck.
6. Improper low band adjustment.

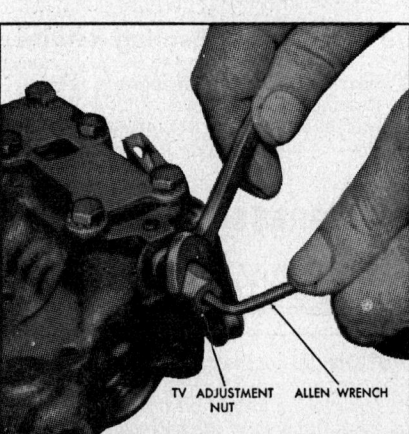

Fig. 1 Adjusting throttle pressure (on bench)

AUTOMATIC TRANSMISSION

Harsh Closed Throttle (Coast) Downshifts

1. High engine idle speed.
2. Improper band adjustment.
3. Vacuum modulator line broken or disconnected.
4. Modulator diaphragm ruptured.
5. Sticking hydraulic modulator valve, pressure regulator valve or vacuum modulator valve.
6. Downshift timing valve malfunction.

No Downshift (Direct-to-Low) Accelerator Floored

1. Throttle control linkage improperly adjusted.
2. Sticking shifter valve or throttle and detent valve.

Truck Creeps In Neutral

1. Manual control linkage improperly adjusted.
2. High clutch or low band not released.

No Drive In Reverse

1. Manual control linkage improperly adjusted.
2. Reverse clutch piston stuck.
3. Reverse clutch plates worn out.
4. Reverse clutch leaking excessively.
5. Blocked reverse clutch apply orifice.

Improper Shift Points

1. Throttle valve linkage improperly adjusted.
2. Incorrectly adjusted throttle valve.
3. Defective governor.
4. Rear pump priming valve stuck.

Unable To Push Start

1. Rear pump drive gear not engaged with drive pin on output shaft.
2. Drive pin sheared off or missing.
3. Rear pump priming valve not sealing.
4. Rear pump defective.

MAINTENANCE

Oil Level

The transmission oil level should be checked every 1000 miles. Oil should be added only when the level is near the "Add" mark on the dipstick with oil hot or at operating temperature.

In order to check oil level accurately, the engine should be idled with the transmission oil hot and the control lever in neutral "N" position.

It is important that the oil level be maintained no higher than the "Full" mark on the oil level gauge. *Do not overfill, for when the oil level is at the full mark on the dipstick, it is just slightly below the planetary gear unit. If additional oil is added, bringing the level above the full mark, the planetary unit will run in the oil, foaming and aerating the oil. This aerated oil carried through the various oil pressure passages may cause malfunction of the transmission assembly, resulting in cavitation noise in the converter and improper band or clutch application.*

Changing Oil

Periodic draining of the oil pan when equipped with a drain plug is recommended every 12,000 miles under normal operating conditions and more frequently under extreme service usage. It is realized that only a portion of the total transmission fluid can be drained at the oil pan. However, the addition of even this volume of fresh fluid will replenish the additives in the remaining fluid sufficiently to increase transmission durability.

THROTTLE VALVE, ADJUST

No provision is made for checking TV pressures. However, if operation of the transmission is such that some adjustment of the throttle valve is indicated, pressures may be raised or lowered by adjusting the position of the jam nut on the throttle valve assembly, Fig. 1.

To raise TV pressure 3 psi, back off the jam nut one full turn. This increases the dimension from the jam nut to the TV valve stop. Conversely, tightening the jam nut one full turn lowers TV pressure 3 psi.

A difference of 3 psi in TV pressure will cause a change of approximately 2 to 3 mph in the wide open throttle upshift point. Smaller pressure adjustments can be made by partial turns of the jam nut. The end of the TV adjusting screw has an allen head so the screw may be held stationary while the jam nut is moved. *Use care when making this adjustment since no pressure tap is provided to check TV pressure.*

LOW BAND, ADJUST

Low band adjustment should be performed at 12,000 mile intervals, or sooner if operating performance indicates low band slippage.

1. Raise vehicle and place selector lever in Neutral.
2. Remove protective cap from transmission adjusting screw.
3. Loosen adjusting screw locknut 1/4 turn and hold in this position with a wrench, Fig. 2.
4. Using a suitable inch-pound torque wrench as shown, adjust band to 70 inch-lbs and back off four complete turns for a band that has been in operation for 6000 miles or more, or three turns for one in use less than 6000 miles.

CAUTION: Be sure to hold the locknut at 1/4 turn loose during the adjusting procedure.

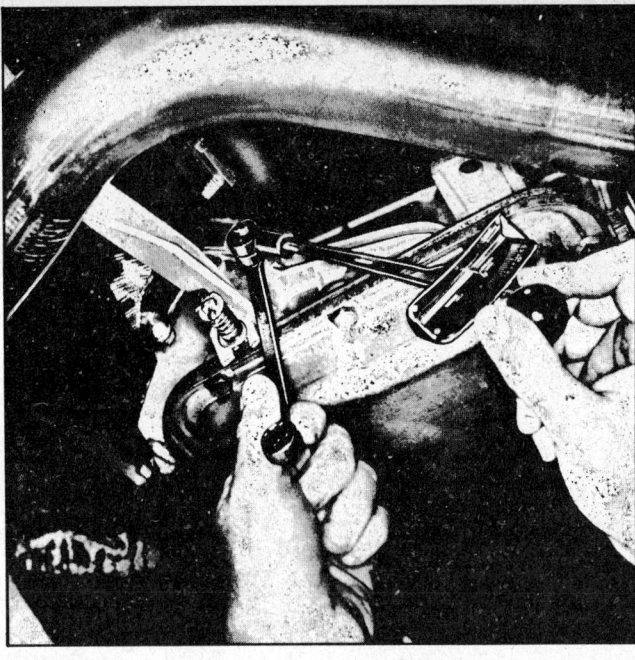

Fig. 2 Adjusting low band

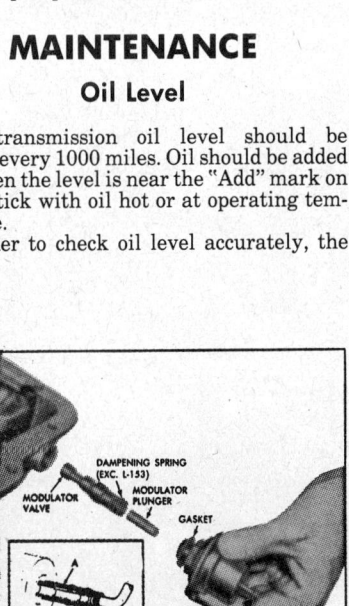

Fig. 3 Vacuum modulator, gasket & valve

Fig. 4 Detent guide plate installation

AUTOMATIC TRANSMISSION

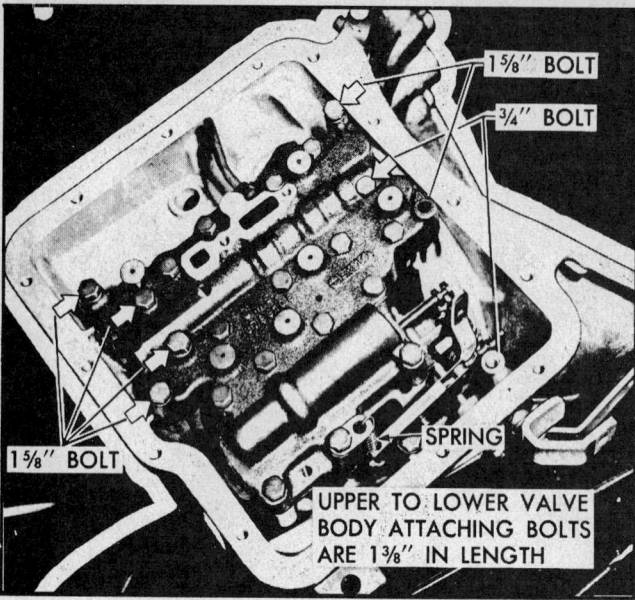

Fig. 5 Control valve assembly installation

Fig. 6 Inner control levers, marking pawl & bracket

Then tighten locknut. The amount of back off is not an approximate figure; it must be exact.

VACUUM MODULATOR VALVE

1. To remove, disconnect line from vacuum modulator, Fig. 3.
2. Unscrew vacuum modulator from oil pan.
3. Remove vacuum modulator, gasket and valve.
4. Reverse removal procedure to install.

LOW SERVO

1. Remove servo cover and gasket (3 screws).
2. Remove cover oil seal, servo piston and return spring.
3. Reverse removal procedure to install.

NOTE: *If low servo is not functioning properly, overhaul servo as directed in the repair section of this chapter.*

VALVE BODY

1. To remove control valve, remove vacuum modulator valve as outlined above.
2. Remove oil pan and gasket.
3. Remove two bolts attaching detent guide plate to valve body and transmission case. Remove guide plate and range selector detent roller spring, Fig. 4.
4. Remove remaining control valve bolts, Fig. 5.

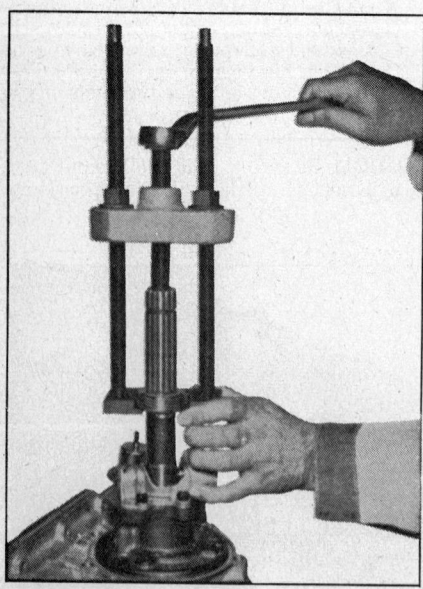

Fig. 7 Removing speedometer drive gear

Fig. 8 Removing governor valve & shaft

AUTOMATIC TRANSMISSIONS

5. Carefully remove valve body and gasket, disengaging servo apply tube from transmission case as valve body is removed.
6. Reverse removal procedure to install valve body, being sure range selector detent lever is in position shown in Fig. 5 and that pin on parking lock and range selector inner lever is engaged in slot in manual valve.

MANUAL LEVERS & OIL SEAL, REPLACE

1970-71

On these models valve body removal is not necessary to remove the above parts. The revised procedure is as follows:
1. Raise vehicle and drain transmission.
2. Remove oil pan and clean.
3. Disconnect T.V. and shift linkage. *Before removing T.V. and shift inner levers, notice position of shaft to inner lever for easier reassembly.*
4. Remove T.V. lever and shift lever.
5. Remove oil seal.
6. Reverse procedure to install.

PARKING PAWL

After removing the control valve assembly as outlined above, remove the parking pawl, bracket and inner control levers. To make the installation, proceed as follows:
1. Install parking lock pawl and shaft. Install a new "E" ring on shaft.
2. Install parking lock pawl pull-back spring over its boss to rear of pawl. Short leg of spring should locate in hole in parking pawl, Fig. 6.
3. Install parking lock pawl reaction bracket (2 bolts). Fit actuator assembly between parking lock pawl and bracket.
4. Insert outer shift lever into case, making sure to pick up inner shift lever and parking lock assembly. Tighten Allen head nut.
5. Insert outer TV lever and shaft special washer and O-ring seal into case and pick up inner TV lever. Tighten Allen head nut.
6. Install selector lever detent roller.
7. Install valve body as directed above.

EXTENSION HOUSING SEAL

1. Disconnect propeller shaft from transmission.
2. Use a suitable puller to remove extension rear oil seal.
3. With a suitable installer, drive new seal into bore of extension. Sealing cement should be used at outer diameter of seal to prevent leakage. Wipe off excess cement. Reconnect propeller shaft.

EXTENSION BUSHING

1. Remove extension oil seal as outlined above. Then, using a suitable remover tool, pull bushing from rear of extension.
2. Place new bushing in pilot end of a suitable installer and drive bushing into bore of extension. Install rear oil seal.

SPEEDOMETER DRIVEN GEAR

1. Disconnect speedometer drive cable fitting. Remove cap screw and retainer clip holding driven gear in extension and remove gear.
2. Reverse removal procedure to install.

EXTENSION CASE

1. Disconnect propeller shaft from transmission output shaft.
2. Disconnect speedometer cable fitting.
3. Install transmission lift to support transmission and engine.
4. Unfasten extension from support crossmember (2 studs).
5. Unfasten extension from transmission case (5 bolts).

NOTE: *Remove any shims found between extension and crossmember. Tie shims together as it is vital that exactly the same number of shims be used when the extension is reinstalled as these shims affect the drive line angle.*

6. Reverse removal procedure to install.

SPEEDOMETER DRIVE GEAR

1. Remove extension case as outlined above. Remove speedometer drive gear from output shaft, Fig. 7.

NOTE: Later units use a nylon gear retained on the shaft by a clip.

2. Using a suitable installer, install gear on output shaft and replace extension case.

GOVERNOR

1. Remove extension case and speedometer drive gear as outlined above.
2. Remove "C" clip from governor shaft on weight side of governor.
3. Remove shaft and governor valve from opposite side of governor, Fig. 8. Remove two Belleville springs.
4. Loosen governor drive screw and lift governor from output shaft.
5. Reverse removal procedure to install governor. However, be sure concave side of Belleville springs are against transmission output shaft.

FORD C4 Dual Range Unit

DESCRIPTION

The main control incorporates a manually selective first and second gear range. The transmission features a drive range that provides for fully automatic upshifts and downshifts, and manually selected low and second gears.

The transmission consists essentially of a torque converter, a compound planetary gear train, two multiple disc clutches, a one-way clutch and a hydraulic control system, Fig. 1.

For all normal driving the selector lever is moved to the green dot under "Drive" on the selector quadrant on the steering column or on the floor console. As the throttle is advanced from the idle position, the transmission will upshift automatically to intermediate gear and then to high.

With the throttle closed the transmission will downshift automatically as the car speed drops to about 10 mph. With the throttle open at any position up to the detent, the downshifts will come in automatically at speeds above 10 mph and in proportion to throttle opening. This prevents engine lugging on steeping hill climbing, for example.

When the selector lever is moved to "L" with the transmission in high, the transmission will downshift to intermediate or to low depending on the road speed. At speed above 25 mph, the downshift will be from high to intermediate. At speeds below 25 mph, the downshift will be from high to low. With the selector lever in the "L" position the transmission cannot upshift.

TROUBLE SHOOTING GUIDE

The items to check for each trouble symptom are arranged in a logical sequence that should be followed for quickest results.

Rough Initial Engagement in D1 or D2

1. Engine idle speed.
2. Vacuum diaphragm unit or tubes restricted, leaking or maladjusted.
3. Check control pressure.
4. Pressure regulator.
5. Valve body.
6. Forward clutch

1-2 or 2-3 Shift Points Erratic

1. Check fluid level.
2. Vacuum diaphragm unit or tubes restricted, leaking or maladjusted.
3. Intermediate servo.
4. Manual linkage adjustment.
5. Governor.
6. Check control pressure.
7. Valve body.

525

Automatic Transmissions

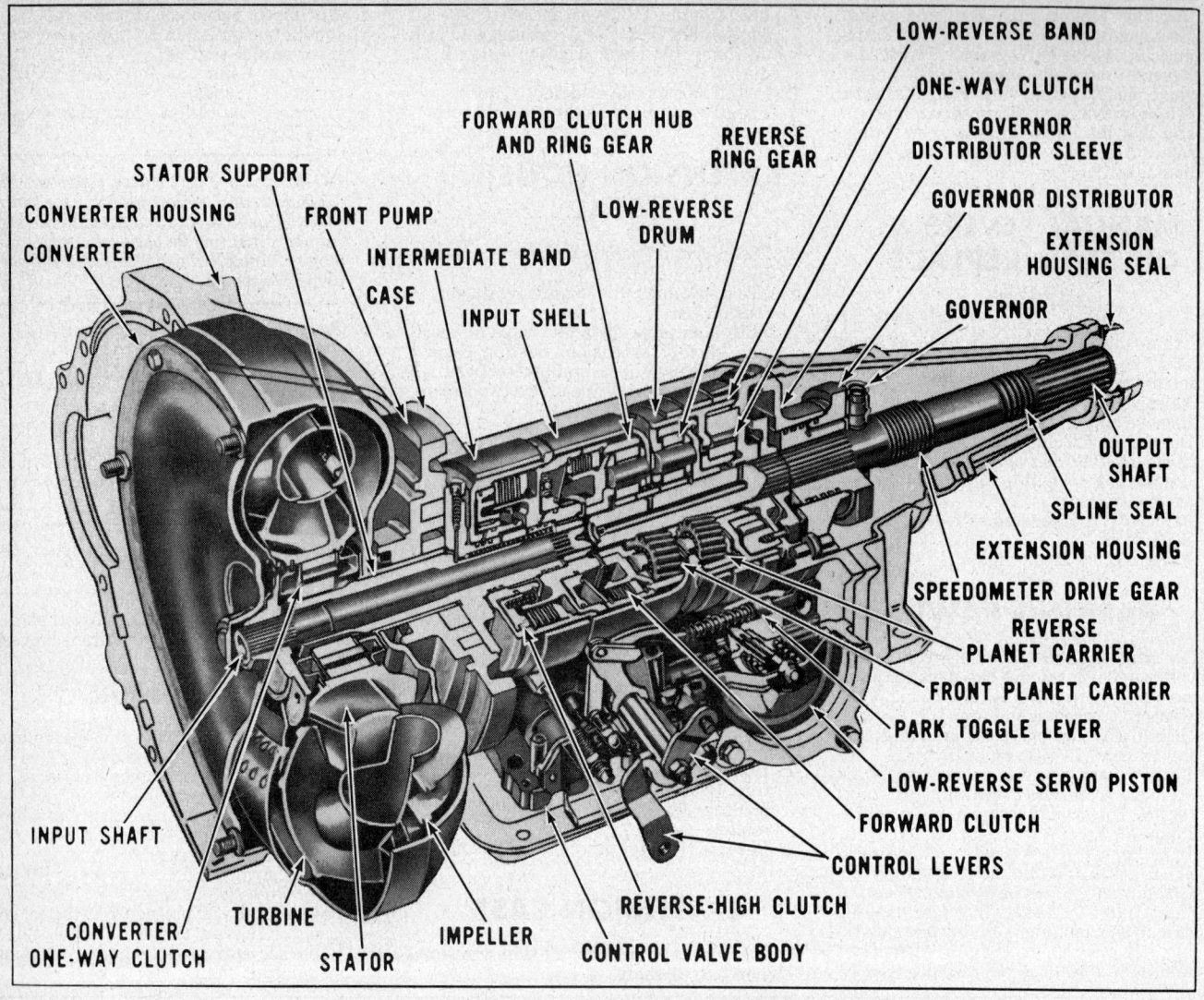

FIG. 1 C4 dual range automatic transmission

8. Make air pressure check.

Rough 1-2 Upshifts

1. Vacuum diaphragm unit or tubes restricted, leaking or maladjusted.
2. Intermediate servo.
3. Intermediate band.
4. Check control pressure.
5. Valve body.
6. Pressure regulator.

Rough 2-3 Upshifts

1. Vacuum diaphragm unit or tubes restricted, leaking or maladjusted.
2. Intermediate servo.
3. Check control pressure.
4. Pressure regulator.
5. Intermediate band.
6. Valve body.
7. Make air pressure check.
8. Reverse-high clutch.
9. Reverse-high clutch piston air bleed valve.

Dragged Out 1-2 Shift

1. Check fluid level.
2. Vacuum diaphragm unit or tubes restricted, leaking or maladjusted.
3. Intermediate servo.
4. Check control pressure.
5. Intermediate band.
6. Valve body.
7. Pressure regulator.
8. Make air pressure check.
9. Leakage in hydraulic system.

Engine Overspeeds on 2-3 Shift

1. Manual linkage.
2. Check fluid level.
3. Vacuum diaphragm unit or tubes restricted, leaking or maladjusted.
4. Reverse servo.
5. Check control pressure.
6. Valve body.
7. Pressure regulator.
8. Intermediate band.
9. Reverse-high clutch.
10. Reverse-high clutch piston air bleed valve.

No 1-2 or 2-3 Shift

1. Manual linkage.
2. Downshift linkage, including inner lever position.
3. Vacuum diaphragm unit or tubes restricted, leaking or maladjusted.
4. Governor.
5. Check control pressure.
6. Valve body.
7. Intermediate band.
8. Intermediate servo.
9. Reverse-high clutch.
10. Reverse-high clutch piston air bleed valve.

No 3-1 Shift in D1 or 3-2 Shift in D2

1. Governor.
2. Valve body.

No Forced Downshifts

1. Downshift linkage, including inner lever position.
2. Valve body.
3. Vacuum diaphragm unit or tubes restricted, leaking or maladjusted.

Runaway Engine on Forced 3-2 Downshift

1. Check control pressure.

AUTOMATIC TRANSMISSIONS

2. Intermediate servo.
3. Intermediate band.
4. Pressure regulator.
5. Valve body.
6. Vacuum diaphragm unit or tubes restricted, leaking or maladjusted.
7. Leakage in hydraulic system.

Rough 3–2 or 3–1 Shift at Closed Throttle

1. Engine idle speed.
2. Vacuum diaphragm unit or tubes restricted, leaking or maladjusted.
3. Intermediate servo.
4. Valve body.
5. Pressure regulator.

Shifts 1–3 in D1 and D2

1. Intermediate band.
2. Intermediate servo.
3. Vacuum diaphragm unit or tubes restricted, leaking or maladjusted.
4. Valve body.
5. Governor.
6. Make air pressure check.

No Engine Braking in 1st Gear —Manual Low

1. Manual linkage.
2. Reverse band.
3. Reverse servo.
4. Valve body.
5. Governor.
6. Make air pressure check.

Slips or Chatters in 1st Gear—D1

1. Check fluid level.
2. Vacuum diaphragm unit or tubes restricted, leaking or maladjusted.
3. Check control pressure.
4. Press regulator.
5. Valve body.
6. Ford clutch.
7. Leakage in hydraulic system.
8. Planetary one-way clutch.

Slips or Chatters in 2nd Gear

1. Check fluid level.
2. Vacuum diaphragm unit or tubes restricted, leaking or maladjusted.
3. Intermediate servo.
4. Intermediate band.
5. Check control pressure.
6. Pressure regulator.
7. Valve body.
8. Make air pressure check.
9. Forward clutch.
10. Leakage in hydraulic system.

Slips or Chatters in R

1. Check fluid level.
2. Vacuum diaphragm unit or tubes restricted, leaking or maladjusted.
3. Reverse band.
4. Check control pressure.
5. Reverse servo.
6. Pressure regulator.
7. Valve body.
8. Make air pressure check.
9. Reverse-high clutch.
10. Leakage in hydraulic system.
11. Reverse-high piston air bleed valve.

No Drive in D1 Only

1. Check fluid level.
2. Manual linkage.
3. Check control pressure.

Fig. 2 Intermediate band adjustment

4. Valve body.
5. Make air pressure check.
6. Planetary one-way clutch.

No Drive in D2 Only

1. Check fluid level.
2. Manual linkage.
3. Check control pressure.
4. Intermediate servo.
5. Valve body.
6. Make air pressure check.
7. Leakage in hydraulic system.
8. Planetary one-way clutch.

No Drive in L Only

1. Check fluid level.
2. Manual linkage.
3. Check control pressure.
4. Valve body.
5. Reverse servo.
6. Make air pressure check.
7. Leakage in hydraulic system.
8. Planetary one-way clutch.

No Drive in R Only

1. Check fluid level.
2. Manual linkage.
3. Reverse band.
4. Check control pressure.
5. Reverse servo.
6. Valve body.
7. Make air pressure check.

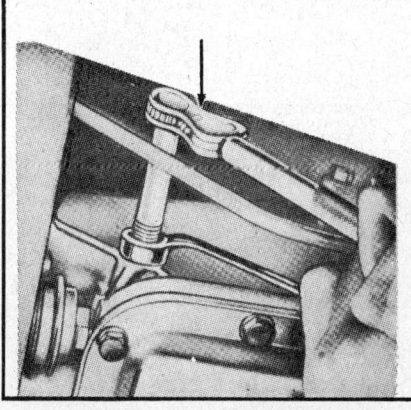

Fig. 3 Low-reverse band adjustment

8. Reverse-high clutch.
9. Leakage in hydraulic system.
10. Reverse-high clutch piston air bleed valve.

No Drive in Any Selector Position

1. Check fluid level.
2. Manual linkage.
3. Check control pressure.
4. Pressure regulator.
5. Valve body.
6. Make air pressure check.
7. Leakage in hydraulic system.
8. Front pump.

Lockup in D1 Only

1. Reverse-high clutch.
2. Parking linkage.
3. Leakage in hydraulic system.

Lockup in D2 Only

1. Reverse band.
2. Reverse servo.
3. Reverse-high clutch.
4. Parking linkage.
5. Leakage in hydraulic system.
6. Planetary one-way clutch.

Lockup in L Only

1. Intermediate band.
2. Intermediate servo.
3. Reverse-high clutch.
4. Parking linkage.
5. Leakage in hydraulic system.

Lockup in R Only

1. Intermediate band.
2. Intermediate servo.
3. Forward clutch.
4. Parking linkage.
5. Leakage in hydraulic system.

Parking Lock Binds or Does Not Hold

1. Manual linkage.
2. Parking linkage.

Maximum Speed Too Low, Poor Acceleration

1. Engine performance.
2. Brakes bind.
3. Converter one-way clutch.

Noisy in N or P

1. Check fluid level.
2. Pressure regulator.
3. Front pump.
4. Planetary assembly.

Noisy in All Gears

1. Check fluid level.
2. Pressure regulator.
3. Planetary assembly.
4. Forward clutch.
5. Front pump.
6. Planetary one-way clutch.

Car Moves Forward in N

1. Manual linkage.
2. Forward clutch.

AUTOMATIC TRANSMISSIONS

MAINTENANCE

Checking Oil Level

1. Make sure car is on a level floor.
2. Apply parking brake firmly.
3. Run engine at normal idle speed. If transmission fluid is cold, run engine at a fast idle until fluid reaches normal operating temperature. When fluid is warm, slow engine to normal idle speed.
4. Shift selector lever through all positions, then place lever at "P". Do not shut down engine during fluid level checks.
5. Clean all dirt from dipstick cap before removing dipstick from filler tube.
6. Pull dipstick out of tube, wipe it clean and push it all the way back in tube.
7. Pull dipstick out of tube again and check fluid level. If necessary, add enough fluid to raise the level to the "F" mark on dipstick. Do not overfill.

Drain & Refill

NOTE: The Ford Motor Company recommends the use of an automatic transmission fluid with Qualification No. M2C-33F, type F, for 1970-79 models and M2C-138-CJ or Dextron II for 1980 models (on container). The recommended fluid is said to have a greater coefficient of friction and greater ability to handle maximum engine torques without band or clutch slippage.

Normal maintenance and lubrication requirements do not necessitate periodic fluid changes. If a major failure has occurred in the transmission, it will have to be removed for service. At this time the converter and transmission cooler must be thoroughly flushed to remove any foreign matter.

When filling a dry transmission and converter, install five quarts of fluid. Start engine, shift the selector lever through all ranges and place it a R position. Check fluid level and add enough to raise the level in the transmission to the "F" (full) mark on the dipstick.

When a partial drain and refill is required due to front band adjustment or minor repair, proceed as follows:

1. Loosen and remove all but two oil pan bolts and drop one edge of the pan to drain the oil.
2. Remove and clean pan and screen.
3. Place a new gasket on pan and install pan and screen.
4. Add three quarts of fluid to transmission.
5. Run engine at idle speed for about two minutes.
6. Check oil level and add oil as necessary.
7. Run engine at a fast idle until it reaches normal operating temperature.
8. Shift selector lever through all ranges and then place it in R position.
9. Add fluid as required to bring the level to the full mark.

BANDS, ADJUST

Intermediate Band

1. Loosen lock nut several turns.
2. With tool shown in Fig. 2 tighten adjusting screw until tool handle clicks. *This tool is a pre-set torque wrench which clicks and overruns when the torque on the adjusting screw reaches 10 ft-lbs.*
3. Back off adjusting screw exactly 1 3/4 turns.
4. Hold adjusting screw from turning and tighten lock nut.

Rear Band

1. Loosen lock nut several turns.
2. Tighten adjusting screw until tool handle clicks, Fig. 3. *Tool shown is a pre-set torque wrench which clicks and overruns when the torque on the* adjusting screw reaches 10 ft-lbs.
3. Back off adjusting screw exactly 3 full turns.
4. Hold adjusting screw from turning and tighten lock nut.

FORD FMX Cast Iron Case

DESCRIPTION

This transmission, Fig. 1, is a three speed unit which provides automatic upshifts and downshifts. First and second gears may be selected manually. This unit consists of a torque converter, planetary gear train, multiple disc clutches and hydraulic control system.

TROUBLE SHOOTING GUIDE

Rough Initial Engagement

1. Idle speed.
2. Vacuum unit or tubes.
3. Front band.
4. Check control pressure.
5. Pressure regulator.
6. Valve body.

Shift Points High, Low or Erratic

1. Fluid level.
2. Vacuum unit or tubes.
3. Manual linkage.
4. Governor.
5. Check control pressure.
6. Valve body.
7. Downshift linkage.

Rough 2-3 Shift

1. Manual linkage.
2. Front band.
3. Vacuum unit or tubes.
4. Pressure regulator.
5. Valve body.
6. Front servo.

Engine Overspeeds, 2-3 Shift

1. Vacuum unit or tubes.
2. Front band.
3. Valve body.
4. Pressure regulator.

No 1-2 or 2-3 Shifts

1. Governor.
2. Valve body.
3. Manual linkage.
4. Rear clutch.
5. Front band.
6. Front servo.
7. Leakage in hydraulic system.
8. Pressure regulator.

No Forced Downshifts

1. Downshift linkage.
2. Check control pressure.
3. Valve body.

Rough 3-2 or 3-1 Shifts

1. Engine idle speed.
2. Vacuum unit or tubes.
3. Valve body.

Slips or Chatters in 2nd

1. Fluid level.
2. Vacuum unit or tubes.
3. Front band.
4. Check control pressure.
5. Pressure regulator.
6. Valve body.
7. Front servo.
8. Front clutch.
9. Leakage in hydraulic system.

Slips or Chatters in 1st

1. Fluid level.
2. Vacuum unit or tubes.
3. Check control pressure.
4. Pressure regulator.
5. Valve body.
6. Front clutch.
7. Leakage in hydraulic system.
8. Fluid distributor sleeve in output shaft.
9. Planetary one-way clutch.

Slips or Chatters in Reverse

1. Fluid level.
2. Rear band.
3. Check control pressure.
4. Pressure regulator.
5. Valve body.
6. Rear servo.
7. Rear clutch.
8. Vacuum unit or tubes.
9. Leakage in hydraulic system.
10. Fluid distributor sleeve in output shaft.

No Drive in D or D2

1. Valve body.
2. Make air pressure check.
3. Manual linkage.
4. Front clutch.
5. Leak in hydraulic system.
6. Fluid distributor sleeve in output shaft.

AUTOMATIC TRANSMISSIONS

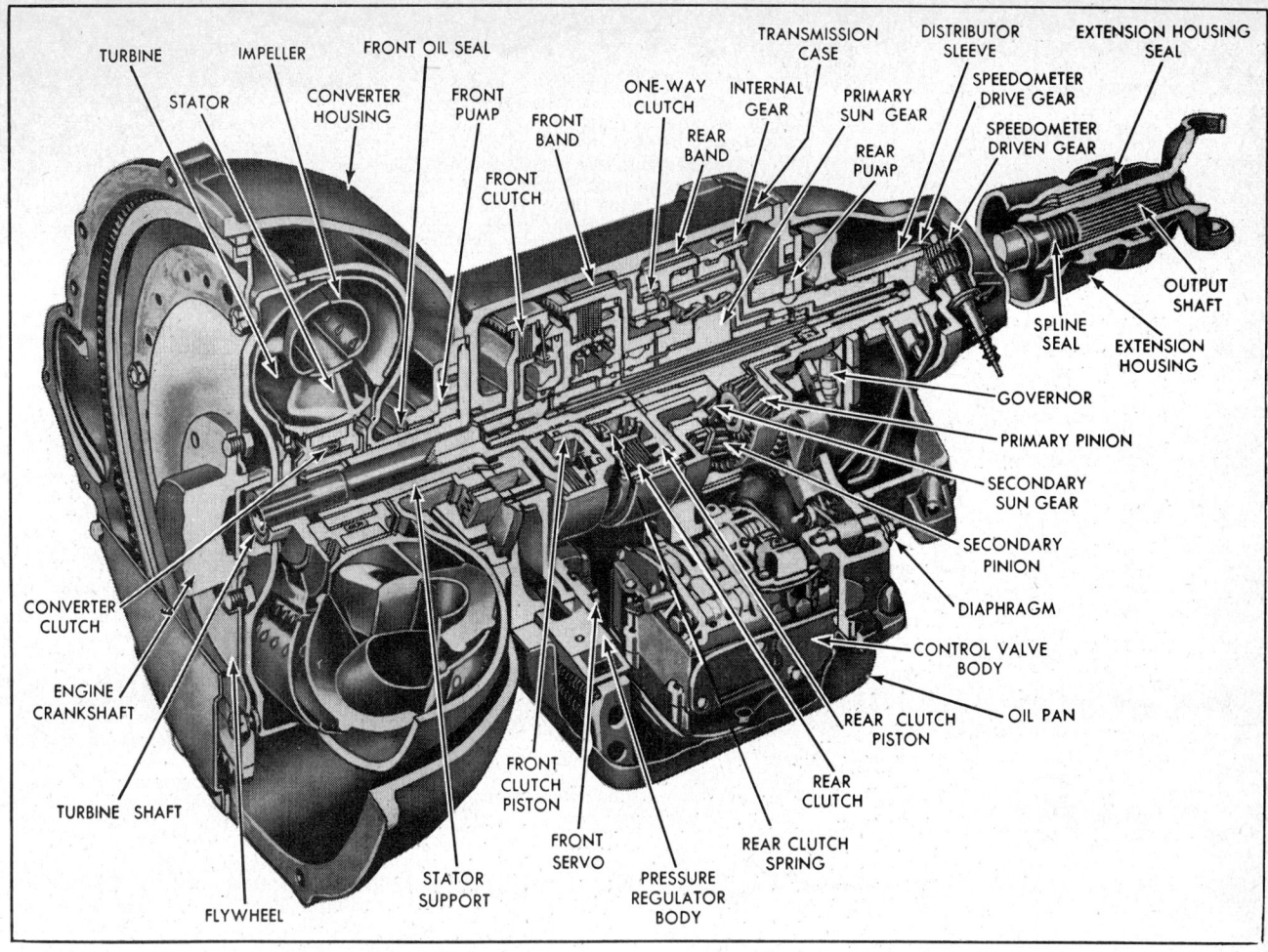

Fig. 1 Ford FMX three speed transmission with cast iron case. Note that the rear pump is not used after 1967.

No Drive in D1

1. Manual linkage.
2. Valve body.
3. Planetary one-way clutch.

No Drive in L

1. Manual linkage.
2. Front clutch.
3. Valve body.
4. Make air pressure check.
5. Leak in hydraulic system.
6. Fluid distributor sleeve in output shaft.

No Drive in R

1. Rear band.
2. Rear servo.
3. Valve body.
4. Make air pressure check.
5. Rear clutch.
6. Leak in hydraulic system.
7. Fluid distributor sleeve in output shaft.

No Drive in Any Range

1. Fluid level.
2. Manual linkage.
3. Check control pressure.
4. Pressure regulator.
5. Valve body.
6. Make air pressure check.
7. Leak in hydraulic system.

Lockup in D or D1

1. Manual linkage.
2. Rear servo.
3. Front servo.
4. Rear clutch.
5. Parking linkage.
6. Leak in hydraulic system.

Lockup in D2

1. Manual linkage.
2. Rear band.
3. Rear servo.
4. Rear clutch.
5. Parking linkage.
6. Leak in hydraulic system.
7. Planetary one-way clutch.

Lockup in R

1. Front band.
2. Front servo.
3. Front clutch.
4. Parking linkage.
5. Leak in hydraulic system.

Lockup in L

1. Front band.
2. Pressure regulator.
3. Valve body.
4. Rear clutch.
5. Parking linkage.

6. Leak in hydraulic system.

Parking Lock Binds or Won't Hold

1. Manual linkage.
2. Parking linkage.

Unable to Push Start

1. Fluid level.
2. Manual linkage.
3. Pressure regulator.
4. Valve body.
5. Rear pump.
6. Leak in hydraulic system.

Transmission Overheats

1. Oil cooler and connections.
2. Pressure regulator.
3. Converter one-way clutch.

Engine Runaway on Forced Downshift

1. Front band.
2. Pressure regulator.
3. Valve body.
4. Front servo.
5. Vacuum unit or tubes.
6. Leak in hydraulic system.

AUTOMATIC TRANSMISSIONS

Maximum Speed Below Normal, Acceleration Poor

1. Converter one-way clutch.

No 3–1 Downshift

1. Engine idle speed.
2. Vacuum unit or tubes.
3. Valve body.

Noise in Neutral

1. Pressure regulator.
2. Front clutch.
3. Front pump.

Noise in 1–2–3 or R

1. Pressure regulator.
2. Planetary assembly.
3. Front clutch.
4. Rear clutch.
5. Front pump.

Noise in Reverse

1. Pressure regulator.
2. Front pump.

Noise on Coast in Neutral

1. Rear pump.

MAINTENANCE

Adding Fluid

The fluid level in the transmission should be checked at 1000-mile intervals. Make sure that the car is standing level, and firmly apply the parking brake.

Run the engine at normal idle speed. If the transmission fluid is cold, run the engine at fast idle speed until the fluid reaches normal operating temperature. When the fluid is warm, slow the engine down to normal idle speed, shift the transmission through all ranges and then place the lever or button at P.

Clean all dirt from the transmission fluid dipstick cap before removing the dipstick from the filler tube. Pull the dipstick out of the tube, wipe it clean and push it all the way back into the tube.

Pull the dipstick out again and check the fluid level. If necessary, add enough Type F Automatic Transmission Fluid to the transmission to raise the fluid level to the F (full mark) on the dipstick.

Changing Fluid

The transmission fluid should be changed at 24,000-mile intervals. The procedure for changing fluid is as follows:

1. Remove cover from lower front side of converter housing.
2. Remove one of the converter drain plugs. Then rotate the converter 180 deg. and remove the other plug. *Do not attempt to turn the converter with a wrench on the converter stud nuts as there is danger of stripping threads as well as skinning your knuckles on the bell housing.*
3. When all fluid has drained, remove and clean the oil pan and screen.
4. Using a new pan gasket, install screen and pan.
5. Connect filler tube to oil pan and tighten fitting securely.
6. Install both converter drain plugs.
7. Install converter housing cover.
8. Install 5 quarts of Automatic Transmission Fluid.
9. Run engine at idle speed for about 2 minutes; then add the additional quantity of oil required for the particular transmission being serviced.
10. Run engine at a fast idle until it reaches normal operating temperature.
11. Shift the transmission through all positions; then place it at P and check fluid level. If necessary, add enough fluid to bring the level to the F mark on the dipstick.

BAND ADJUSTMENTS

The front and rear bands of the transmission should be adjusted at 15,000 mile intervals or as operation of the transmission dictates.

Front Band

1970–77
1. Drain fluid from transmission, remove and clean oil pan and screen.
2. Loosen front servo adjusting screw locknut.
3. Pull back on actuating rod and insert a 1/4 inch spacer between adjusting screw and servo piston stem.
4. Tighten adjusting screw to 10 inch-lbs. torque. Remove spacer and tighten adjusting screw an additional 3/4 turn. Hold adjusting screw stationary and tighten locknut securely.
5. Install oil pan with new gasket and add fluid to transmission.

Rear Band

NOTE: On all 1970–77 models, there is no access hole in the floor pan to adjust the rear band. With the use of special tools this band can be adjusted externally as follows:
1. Loosen rear bank adjusting screw locknut. A special tool is required to gain access in limited space.
2. Tighten adjusting screw until special tool clicks. It is preset to overrun when torque reaches 10 ft. lbs.
3. Back off adjusting screw 1 1/2 turns. **NOTE:** Severe damage may result if the adjusting screw is not backed off exactly 1 1/2 turns.
4. Hold adjusting screw stationary and tighten locknut securely.

OIL PRESSURE REGULATOR

Remove oil pan and screen. Maintain constant pressure on spring retainer to prevent damage to springs and remove retainer from bosses on oil pressure regulator body. Remove springs and pilots. Remove the three pipes. Unfasten and remove the oil pressure regulator from the transmission case.

CONTROL VALVE

To remove the assembly, loosen the adjustment on the front and rear bands 5 or 6 turns. Loosen front servo attaching screws. Remove cap screws and washers which attach control valve to case. Align throttle and manual levers to permit removal of control valve. Disengage front servo tubes from control valve and lift valve assembly from case.

FRONT & REAR SERVOS

To remove the front servo, remove the cap screw which holds it to the case. Hold the actuating lever strut with one hand and lift the servo from the case.

To remove the rear servo, take out the attaching cap screws. Then hold the anchor strut and lift the servo from the case.

EXTENSION HOUSING SEAL

After removing the drive shaft and telescopic shield, the seal may be pulled out of the extension housing.

Before installing the new seal, inspect the sealing surface of the universal joint yoke for scores. If scores are evident, replace the yoke. Inspect the counterbore in the housing for burrs. Polish all burrs with crocus cloth.

To install the new seal, position it in the bore of the extension housing with the felt side of the seal to the rear. The seal may be driven into the housing with a special tool designed for the purpose.

OIL DISTRIBUTOR

With Bolted Distributor & Sleeve

After removing the extension case remove the spacer from the transmission output shaft and slide the distributor toward the rear of the transmission. Note that the tube spacer is located in the center tube.

Remove the three tubes and spacer from the distributor. Remove the screws which attach the distributor to the sleeve and separate these parts.

Inspect the distributor and sleeve for burrs on the mating surfaces and obstructed fluid passages. Check the fit of the tubes in the distributor. Inspect the distributor sleeve for wear and scores in the sleeve bore.

To assemble, align the distributor and sleeve and install the cap screws. Install the tubes in the distributor with the spacer installed on the center tube.

With One Piece Distributor & Sleeve

After removing the extension housing, remove the distributor drive gear snap ring. Remove distributor gear, taking care not to lose the gear drive ball. Remove distributor sleeve and pipes from the transmission. Inspect the 4 seal rings on the output shaft for wear or breakage, and replace if necessary. Inspect the distributor sleeve for wear and the tubes for proper alignment and fit into the distributor sleeve.

With tubes installed in the distributor sleeve, install distributor on output shaft (chamfer forward) sliding the distributor over the seal rings and at the same time guiding tubes into the case. Install speedometer drive ball and gear and install snap ring.

GOVERNOR

Remove the governor inspection cover from the extension housing. Rotate the drive shaft to bring the governor body in line with the inspection hole. Remove the two screws which attach the governor body to the counterweight, and remove the body.

AUTOMATIC TRANSMISSIONS

Remove the valve from the new governor body. Lubricate the valve with automatic transmission fluid. Install the valve in the body, making sure the valve moves freely in the bore. Install the body in the counterweight making sure the fluid passages in the counterweight and body are aligned.

Ford C6 Dual Range Unit

DESCRIPTION

As shown in Fig. 1, the transmission consists essentially of a torque converter, a compound planetary gear train controlled by one band, three disc clutches and a one-way clutch, and a hydraulic control system.

TROUBLE SHOOTING GUIDE

No Drive In Forward Speeds

1. Manual linkage adjustment.
2. Check control pressure.
3. Valve body.
4. Make air pressure check.
5. Forward clutch.
6. Leakage in hydraulic system.

Rough Initial Engagement in D, D1, D2 or 2

1. Engine idle speed too high.
2. Vacuum diaphragm unit or tubes restricted, leaking or maladjusted.
3. Check control pressure.
4. Valve body.
5. Forward clutch.

1–2 or 2–3 Shift Points Incorrect or Erratic

1. Check fluid level.
2. Vacuum diaphragm unit or tubes restricted, leaking or maladjusted.
3. Downshift linkage, including inner lever position.
4. Manual linkage adjustment.
5. Governor defective.
6. Check control pressure.
7. Valve body.
8. Make air pressure check.

Rough 1–2 Upshifts

1. Vacuum diaphragm unit or tubes restricted, leaking or maladjusted.
2. Intermediate servo.
3. Intermediate band.
4. Check control pressure.
5. Valve body.

Rough 2–3 Shifts

1. Vacuum diaphragm or tubes restricted leaking or maladjusted.
2. Intermediate servo.
3. Check control pressure.
4. Intermediate band.
5. Valve body.
6. Make air pressure check.
7. Reverse-high clutch.
8. Reverse-high clutch piston air bleed valve.

Dragged Out 1–2 Shift

1. Check fluid level.
2. Vacuum diaphragm unit or tubes restricted, leaking or maladjusted.
3. Intermediate servo.
4. Check control pressure.
5. Intermediate band.
6. Valve body.
7. Make air pressure check.
8. Leakage in hydraulic system.

Engine Overspeeds on 2–3 Shift

1. Manual linkage adjustment.
2. Check fluid level.
3. Vacuum diaphragm unit or tubes restricted, leaking or maladjusted.
4. Intermediate servo.
5. Check control pressure.
6. Valve body.
7. Intermediate band.
8. Reverse-high clutch.
9. Reverse-high clutch piston air bleed valve.

No 1–2 or 2–3 Shift

1. Manual linkage adjustment.
2. Downshift linkage including inner lever position.
3. Vacuum diaphragm unit or tubes restricted, leaking or maladjusted.
4. Governor.
5. Check control pressure.
6. Valve body.
7. Intermediate band.
8. Intermediate servo.
9. Reverse-high clutch.
10. Leakage in hydraulic system.

No 3–1 Shift In D1, 2 or 3–2 Shift In D2 or D

1. Governor.
2. Valve body.

No Forced Downshifts

1. Downshift linkage, including inner lever position.
2. Check control pressure.
3. Valve body.

Runaway Engine on Forced 3–2 Shift

1. Check control pressure.
2. Intermediate servo.
3. Intermediate band.
4. Valve body.
5. Vacuum diaphragm unit or tubes restricted, leaking or maladjusted.
6. Leakage in hydraulic system.

Rough 3–2 Shift or 3–1 Shift at Closed Throttle

1. Engine idle speed.
2. Vacuum diaphragm unit or tubes restricted, leaking or maladjusted.
3. Intermediate servo.
4. Check control pressure.
5. Valve body.

Shifts 1–3 in D, D1, 2, D2

1. Intermediate band.
2. Intermediate servo.
3. Valve body.
4. Governor.
5. Make air pressure check.

No Engine Braking in 1st Gear—Manual Low Range

1. Manual linkage adjustment.
2. Low-reverse clutch.
3. Valve body.
4. Governor.
5. Make air pressure check.
6. Leakage in hydraulic system.

Creeps Excessively

1. Engine idle speed too high.

Slips or Chatters In 1st Gear, D1

1. Check fluid level.
2. Vacuum diaphragm unit or tubes restricted, leaking or maladjusted.
3. Check control pressure.
4. Valve body.
5. Forward clutch.
6. Leakage in hydraulic system.
7. Planetary one-way clutch.

Slips or Chatters In 2nd Gear

1. Check fluid level.
2. Vacuum diaphragm unit or tubes restricted, leaking or maladjusted.
3. Intermediate servo.
4. Intermediate band.
5. Check control pressure.
6. Valve body.
7. Make air pressure check.
8. Forward clutch.
9. Leakage in hydraulic system.

Slips or Chatters In Reverse

1. Check fluid level.
2. Vacuum diaphragm unit or tubes restricted, leaking or maladjusted.
3. Manual linkage adjustment.
4. Low-reverse clutch.
5. Check control pressure.
6. Valve body.
7. Make air pressure check.
8. Reverse-high clutch.
9. Leakage in hydraulic system.
10. Reverse-high clutch piston air bleed valve.

No Drive In D1 or 2

1. Manual linkage adjustment.
2. Check control pressure.
3. Valve body.
4. Planetary one-way clutch.

No Drive In D, D2

1. Check fluid level.
2. Manual linkage adjustment.

AUTOMATIC TRANSMISSIONS

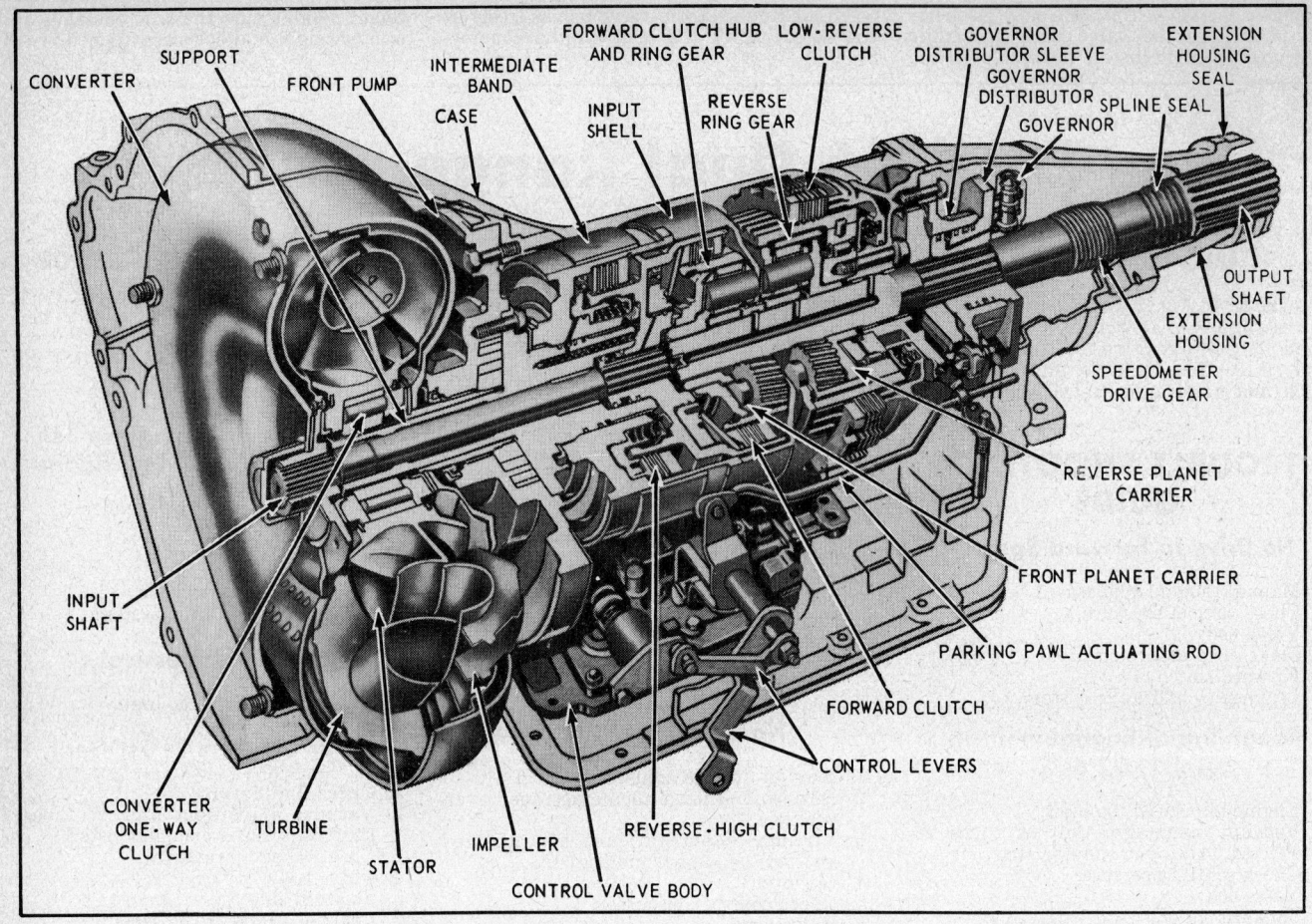

Fig. 1 C6 dual range automatic transmission

3. Check control pressure.
4. Intermediate servo.
5. Valve body.
6. Make air pressure check.
7. Leakage in hydraulic system.

No Drive In L or 1

1. Check fluid level.
2. Check control pressure.
3. Valve body.
4. Make air pressure check.
5. Leakage in hydraulic system.

No Drive In R Only

1. Check fluid level.
2. Manual linkage adjustment.
3. Low-reverse clutch.
4. Check control pressure.
5. Valve body.
6. Make air pressure check.
7. Reverse-high clutch.
8. Leakage in hydraulic system.
9. Reverse-high clutch piston air bleed valve.

No Drive In Any Selector Position

1. Check fluid level.
2. Manual linkage adjustment.
3. Check control pressure.
4. Valve body.
5. Make air pressure check.
6. Leakage in hydraulic system.
7. Front pump.

Lockup In D1 or 2

1. Valve body.
2. Parking linkage.
3. Leakage in hydraulic system.

Lockup In D2 or D

1. Low-reverse clutch.
2. Valve body.
3. Reverse-high clutch.
4. Parking linkage.
5. Leakage in hydraulic system.
6. Planetary one-way clutch.

Lockup In L or 1

1. Valve body.
2. Parking linkage.
3. Leakage in hydraulic system.

Lockup In R Only

1. Valve body.
2. Forward clutch.
3. Parking linkage.
4. Leakage in hydraulic system.

Parking Lock Binds or Does Not Hold

1. Manual linkage adjustment.
2. Parking linkage.

Transmission Overheats

1. Oil cooler and connections.
2. Valve body.
3. Vacuum diaphragm unit or tubes restricted, leaking or maladjusted.
4. Check control pressure.
5. Converter one-way clutch.
6. Converter pressure check valves.

Maximum Speed Too Low, Poor Acceleration

1. Engine performance.
2. Car brakes.
3. Forward clutch.

Transmission Noisy In N and P

1. Check fluid level.
2. Valve body.
3. Front pump.

Noisy In 1st, 2nd, 3rd or Reverse

1. Check fluid level.
2. Valve body.
3. Planetary assembly.
4. Forward clutch.
5. Reverse-high clutch.
6. Planetary one-way clutch.

Car Moves Forward In N

1. Manual linkage adjustment.
2. Forward clutch.

AUTOMATIC TRANSMISSIONS

Fluid Leak

1. Check fluid level.
2. Converter drain plugs.
3. Oil pan gasket, filler tube or seal.
4. Oil cooler and connections.
5. Manual or downshift lever shaft seal.
6. 1/8" pipe plugs in case.
7. Extension housing-to-case gasket.
8. Extension housing rear oil seal.
9. Speedometer driven gear adapter seal.
10. Vacuum diaphragm unit or tubes.
11. Intermediate servo.
12. Engine rear oil seal.

MAINTENANCE

Checking Oil Level

1. Make sure car is on a level floor.
2. Apply parking brake firmly.
3. Run engine at normal idle speed. If transmission fluid is cold, run engine at a fast idle until fluid reaches normal operating temperature. When fluid is warm, slow engine to normal idle speed.
4. Shift selector lever through all positions, then place lever at "P." Do not shut down engine during fluid level checks.
5. Clean all dirt from dipstick cap before removing dipstick from filler tube.
6. Pull dipstick out of tube, wipe it clean and push it all the way back in tube.
7. Pull dipstick out of tube again and check fluid level. If necessary, add enough fluid to raise the level to the "F" mark on dipstick. Do not overfill.

Drain & Refill

NOTE: The Ford Motor Company recommends the use of an automatic transmission fluid with Qualification No. M2C-33F for 1970-76 models and M2C-138-CJ or Dextron II for 1977-80 models (on container). The recommended fluid is said to have a greater coefficient of friction and greater ability to handle maximum engine torques without band or clutch slippage.

Normal maintenance and lubrication requirements do not necessitate periodic fluid changes. If a major failure has occurred in the transmission, it will have to be removed for service. At this time the converter and transmission cooler must be thoroughly flushed to remove any foreign matter.

1. To drain the fluid, loosen pan attaching bolts and allow fluid to drain.
2. After fluid has drained to the level of the pan flange, remove pan bolts working from rear and both sides of pan to allow it to drop and drain slowly.
3. When fluid has stopped draining, remove and clean pan and screen. Discard pan gasket.
4. Using a new gasket, install pan.
5. Add 3 quarts of recommended fluid to transmission through filler tube.
6. Run engine at idle speed for 2 minutes, and then run it at a fast idle until it reaches normal operating temperature.
7. Shift selector lever through all positions, place it at "P" and check fluid level.
8. If necessary, add enough fluid to transmission to bring it to the "F" mark on the dipstick.

BAND ADJUSTMENT

NOTE: When making the intermediate band adjustment, the lock nut must be discarded and a new one installed each time the band is adjusted.

1. Loosen the locknut on the adjusting screw several turns.
2. Torque the screw to 10 ft.-lbs., or until the adjuster wrench overruns.
3. Back the screw off exactly 1½ turns.
4. Hold the adjustment and torque the locknut to the 35-45 ft.-lbs.

OIL PAN & CONTROL VALVE

Removal

1. Raise truck on hoist or jack stands.
2. Loosen and remove all but two oil pan bolts from front of case and drop rear edge of pan to drain fluid. Remove and clean pan and screen.
3. Unfasten and remove valve body.

Installation

1. Position valve body to case, making sure that selector and downshift levers are engaged, then install and torque attaching bolts to specifications.
2. Using a new pan gasket, secure pan to case and torque bolts to specifications.
3. Lower truck and fill transmission to correct level with specified fluid.

INTERMEDIATE SERVO

Removal

1. Raise truck and remove engine rear support-to-extension housing bolts.
2. Raise transmission high enough to relieve weight from support.
3. Remove support (1 bolt).
4. Lower transmission.
5. Place drain pan beneath servo.
6. Remove servo cover-to-case bolts.
7. Loosen band adjusting screw locknut.
8. Remove servo cover, piston, spring and gasket from case, *screwing band adjusting screw inward as piston is removed. This insures that there will be enough tension on the band to keep the struts properly engaged in the band end notches while the piston is removed.*

Replacing Seal

1. Apply air pressure to port in servo cover to remove piston and stem.
2. Remove seals from piston.
3. Remove seal from cover.
4. Dip new seals in transmission fluid.
5. Install seals in piston and cover.
6. Dip piston in transmission fluid and install in cover.

Installation

1. Position new gasket on servo cover and spring on piston stem.
2. Insert piston stem in case. Secure cover with bolts, taking care to back off band adjusting screw while tightening cover bolts. Make sure that vent tube retaining clip is in place.
3. Raise transmission high enough to install engine rear support. Secure support to extension housing. Lower transmission as required to install support-to-crossmember bolt.
4. Remove jack and adjust band.
5. Lower truck and replenish fluid as required.

EXTENSION HOUSING & GOVERNOR

Removal

1. Raise truck and drain transmission.
2. Disconnect parking brake cable at equalizer.
3. Remove torque plate.
4. Disconnect drive shaft from rear axle flange and remove from transmission.
5. Disconnect speedometer cable from extension housing.
6. Remove two nuts that secure engine rear mount to crossmember.
7. Raise transmission with a jack just high enough to relieve weight from crossmember. Remove crossmember.
8. Remove engine rear support.
9. Lower transmission to permit access to extension housing bolts. Remove bolts and slide housing off output shaft.
10. Disconnect governor from distributor (4 bolts) and slide governor off output shaft.

Installation

1. Secure governor to distributor flange.
2. Position new gasket on transmission.
3. Secure extension housing to case.
4. Secure engine rear support to case.
5. Install crossmember.
6. Lower transmission and remove jack. Then install and torque engine rear support-to-extension housing bolts.
7. Install speedometer cable, connect parking brake cable to equalizer and install drive shaft.
8. Install torque plate to floor pan.
9. Replenish transmission fluid.

AUTOMATIC TRANSMISSIONS
Chrysler Corp. Loadflite & A-345

DESCRIPTION
Loadflite

These transmissions, Figs. 1 and 2, combine a torque converter with a fully automatic three speed gear system. The converter housing and transmission case are an integral aluminum casting. The transmission consists of two multiple disc clutches, an overrunning (one-way) clutch, two servos and bands and two planetary gear sets to provide three forward speeds and reverse.

The common sun gear of the planetary gear sets is connected to the front clutch by a driving shell that is splined to the sun gear and to the front clutch retainer.

The hydraulic system consists of a single oil pump and a valve body that contains all the valves except the governor valve.

Venting of the transmission is accomplished by a drilled passage through the upper part of the front pump housing.

The torque converter is attached to the engine crankshaft through a flexible driving plate. The converter is cooled by circulating the transmission fluid through an oil-to-water type cooler located in the radiator lower tank. The converter is a sealed assembly that cannot be disassembled.

A-345

This transmission, Figs. 2 and 3 except for the compounder, lower valve body and lack of an internal parking mechanism, is basically the same as the Loadflite A-727, and may be serviced as such except for the following procedures described in this chapter.

This transmission consists of a sealed torque converter, a fully automatic four speed transmission, four multiple disc clutches, two overrunning clutches, two servos and bands, three planetary gear sets and a hydraulic system.

TROUBLE SHOOTING GUIDE

Harsh Engagement In D-1-2-R

1. Engine idle speed too high.
2. Hydraulic pressures too high or too low.
3. Low-reverse band out of adjustment.
4. Accumulator sticking, broken rings or spring.
5. Low-reverse servo, band or linkage malfunction.
6. Worn or faulty front and/or rear clutch.

Delayed Engagement In D-1-2-R

1. Lower fluid level.
2. Incorrect manual linkage adjustment.
3. Oil filter clogged.
4. Hydraulic pressures too high or low.
5. Valve body malfunction or leakage.
6. Accumulator sticking, broken rings or spring.
7. Clutches or servos sticking or not operating.
8. Faulty front oil pump.
9. Worn or faulty front and/or rear clutch.
10. Worn or broken input shaft and/or reaction shaft support seal rings.
11. Aerated fluid.

Runaway or Harsh Upshift and 3-2 Kickdown

1. Low fluid level.
2. Incorrect throttle linkage adjustment.
3. Hydraulic pressures too high or low.
4. Kickdown band out of adjustment.
5. Valve body malfunction or leakage.
6. Governor malfunction.
7. Accumulator sticking, broken rings or spring.
8. Clutches or servos sticking or not operating.
9. Kickdown servo, band or linkage malfunction.
10. Worn or faulty front clutch.
11. Worn or broken input shaft and/or reaction shaft support seal rings.

No Upshift

1. Low fluid level.
2. Incorrect throttle linkage adjustment.
3. Kickdown band out of adjustment.
4. Hydraulic pressures too high or low.
5. Governor sticking.
6. Valve body malfunction or leakage.
7. Accumulator sticking, broken rings or spring.
8. Clutches or servos sticking or not operating.

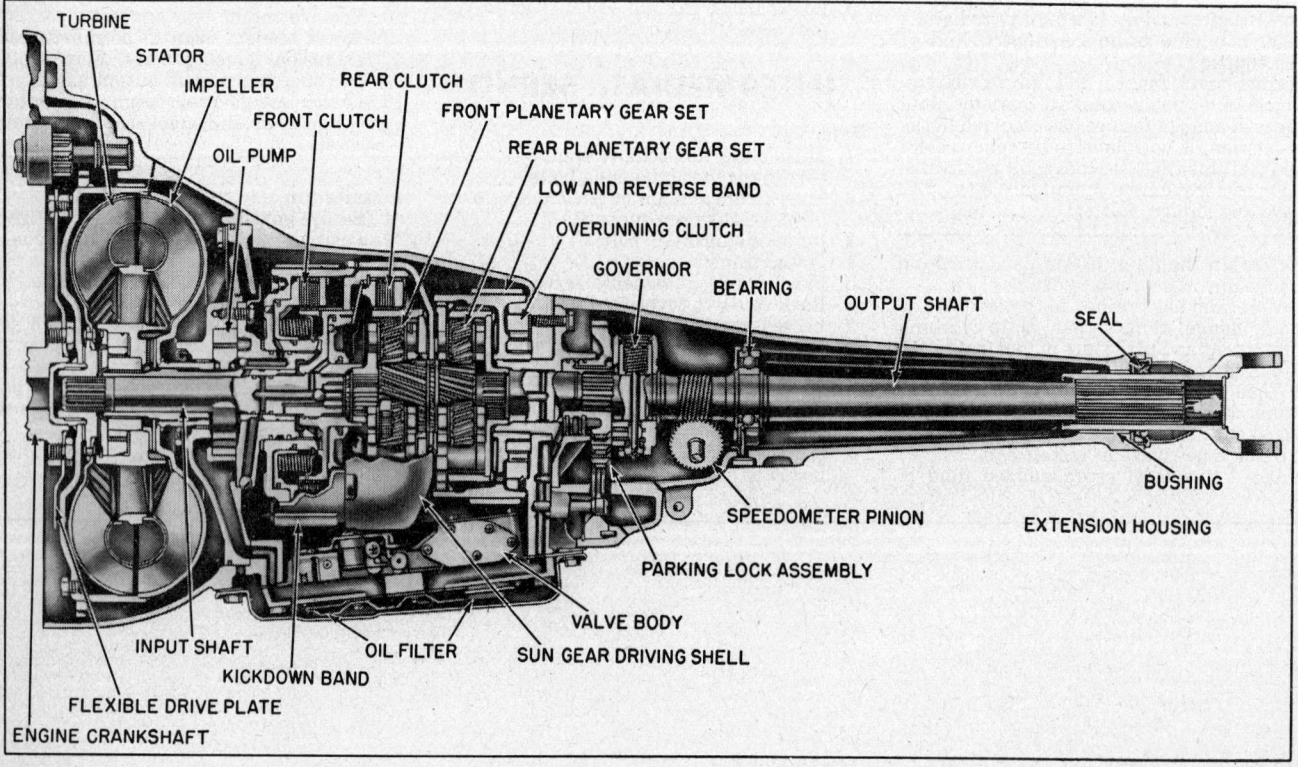

Fig. 1 Model A-727 Loadflite transmission. (Typical)

AUTOMATIC TRANSMISSIONS

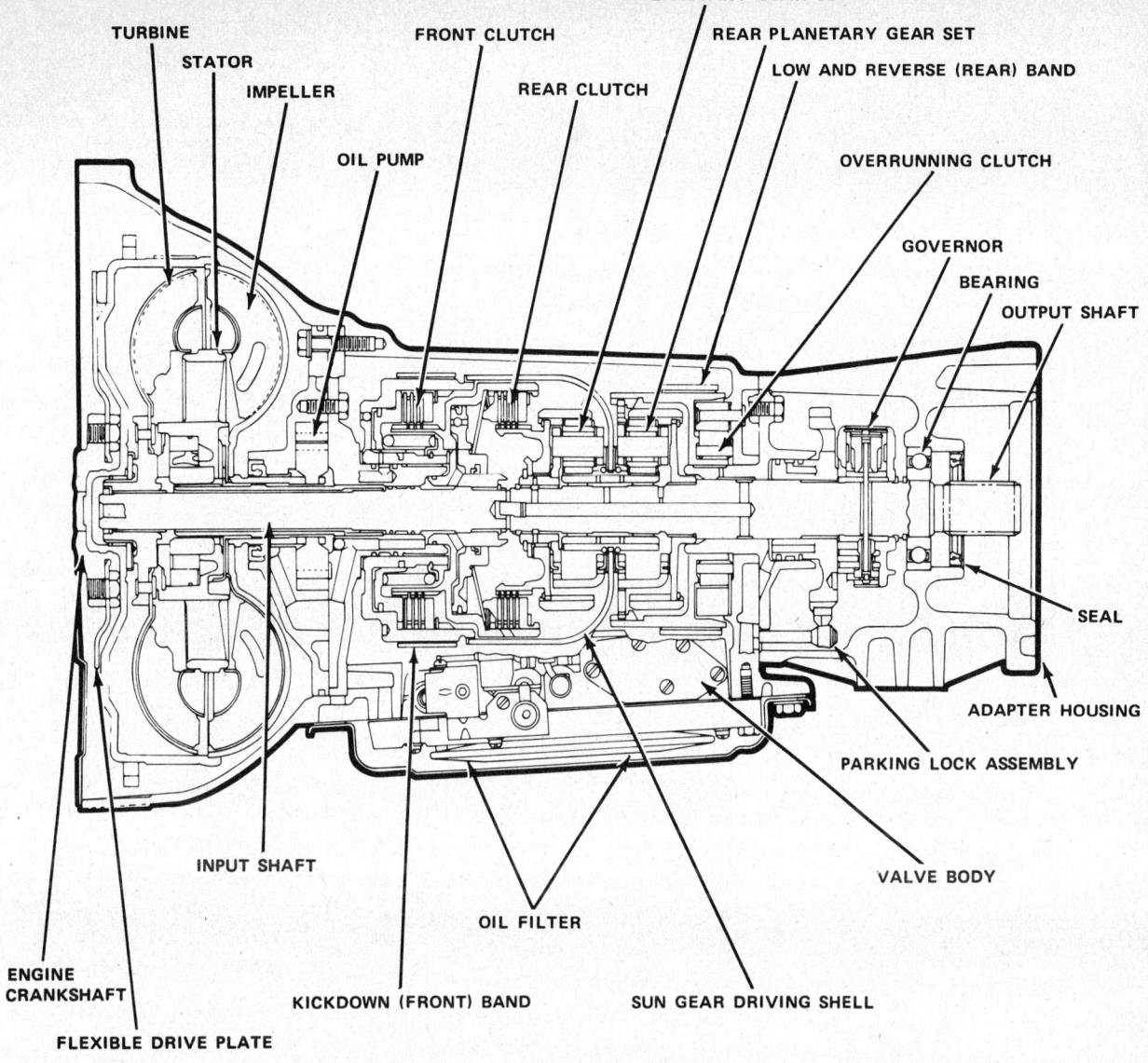

Fig. 2 Model 999 Loadflite transmission.

9. Faulty on pump.
10. Kickdown servo, band or linkage malfunction.
11. Worn or faulty front clutch.
12. Worn or broken input shaft and/or reaction shaft support seal rings.

No Kickdown or Normal Downshift

1. Incorrect throttle linkage adjustment.
2. Incorrect gearshift linkage adjustment.
3. Kickdown band out of adjustment.
4. Hydraulic pressure too high or low.
5. Governor sticking.
6. Valve body malfunction or leakage.
7. Accumulator sticking, broken rings or spring.
8. Clutches or servos sticking or not operating.
9. Kickdown servo, band or linkage malfunction.
10. Overrunning clutch not holding.

Erratic Shifts

1. Low fluid level.
2. Aerated fluid.
3. Incorrect throttle linkage adjustment.
4. Incorrect gearshift control linkage adjustment.
5. Hydraulic pressures too high or low.
6. Governor sticking.
7. Oil filter clogged.
8. Valve body malfunction or leakage.
9. Clutches or servos sticking or not operating.
10. Faulty oil pump.
11. Worn or broken input shaft and/or reaction shaft support seal rings.

Slips In Forward Drive Positions

1. Low oil level.
2. Aerated fluid.
3. Incorrect throttle linkage adjustment.
4. Incorrect gearshift control linkage adjustment.
5. Hydraulic pressures too low.
6. Valve body malfunction or leakage.
7. Accumulator sticking, broken rings or spring.
8. Clutches or servos sticking or not operating.
9. Worn or faulty front and/or rear clutch.
10. Overrunning clutch not holding.
11. Worn or broken input shaft and/or reaction shaft support seal rings.

Slips In Reverse Only

1. Low fluid level.
2. Aerated fluid.
3. Incorrect gearshift control linkage adjustment.
4. Hydraulic pressures too high or low.
5. Low-reverse band out of adjustment.
6. Valve body malfunction or leakage.
7. Front clutch or rear servo sticking or not operating.
8. Low-reverse servo, band or linkage malfunction.
9. Faulty oil pump.

AUTOMATIC TRANSMISSIONS

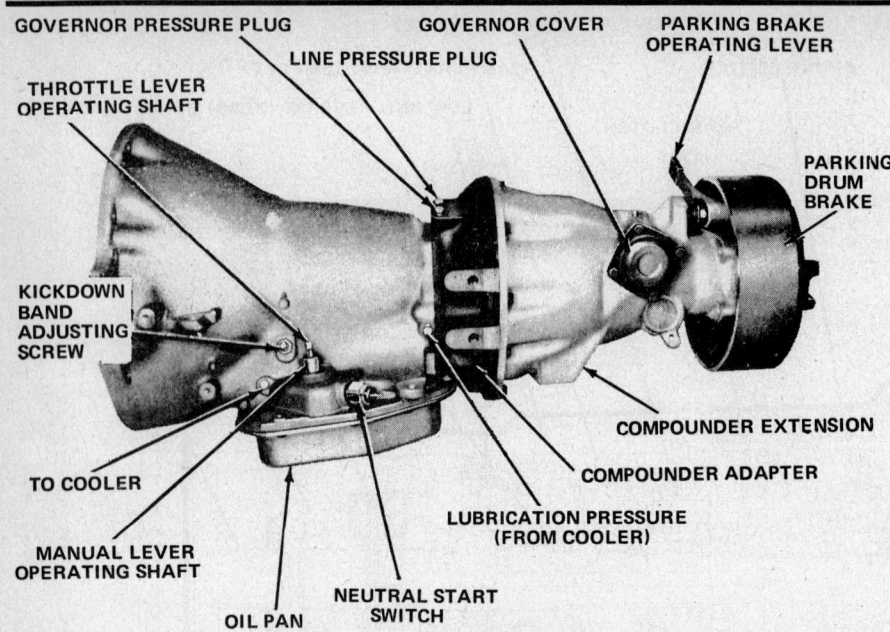

Fig. 3 A-345 transmission assembly. Left side

Slips In All Positions

1. Low fluid level.
2. Hydraulic pressures too low.
3. Valve body malfunction or leakage.
4. Faulty oil pump.
5. Clutches or servos sticking or not operating.
6. Worn or broken input shaft and/or reaction shaft support seal rings.

No Drive In Any Position

1. Low fluid level.
2. Hydraulic pressures too low.
3. Oil filter clogged.
4. Valve body malfunction or leakage.
5. Faulty oil pump.
6. Clutches or servos sticking or not operating.

No Drive In Forward Drive Positions

1. Hydraulic pressures too low.
2. Valve body malfunction or leakage.
3. Accumulator sticking, broken rings or spring.
4. Clutches or servos, sticking or not operating.
5. Worn or faulty rear clutch.
6. Overrunning clutch not holding.
7. Worn or broken input shaft and/or reaction shaft support seal rings.

No Drive In Reverse

1. Incorrect gearshift control linkage adjustment.
2. Hydraulic pressures too low.
3. Low-reverse band out of adjustment.
4. Valve body malfunction or leakage.
5. Front clutch or rear servo sticking or not operating.
6. Low-reverse servo, band or linkage malfunction.
7. Worn or faulty front clutch.

Drives In Neutral

1. Incorrect gearshift control linkage adjustment.
2. Incorrect control cable adjustment.
3. Valve body malfunction or leakage.
4. Rear clutch inoperative.

Drags or Locks

1. Kickdown band out of adjustment.
2. Low-reverse band out of adjustment.
3. Kickdown and/or low-reverse servo, band or linkage malfunction.
4. Front and/or rear clutch faulty.
5. Planetary gear sets broken or seized.
6. Overrunning clutch worn, broken or seized.

Grating, Scraping or Growling Noise

1. Kickdown band out of adjustment.
2. Low-reverse band out of adjustment.
3. Output shaft bearing and/or bushing damaged.
4. Governor support binding or broken seal rings.
5. Oil pump scored or binding.
6. Front and/or rear clutch faulty.
7. Planetary gear sets broken or seized.
8. Overrunning clutch worn, broken or seized.

Buzzing Noise

1. Low fluid level.
2. Pump sucking air.
3. Valve body malfunction.
4. Overrunning clutch inner race damaged.

Hard to Fill, Oil Flows Out Filler Tube

1. High fluid level.
2. Breather clogged.
3. Oil filter clogged.
4. Aerated fluid.

Transmission Overheats

1. Low fluid level.
2. Kickdown band adjustment tight.
3. Low-reverse band adjustment too tight.
4. Faulty cooling system.
5. Cracked or restricted oil cooler line or fitting.
6. Faulty oil pump.
7. Insufficient clutch plate clearance in front and/or rear clutches.

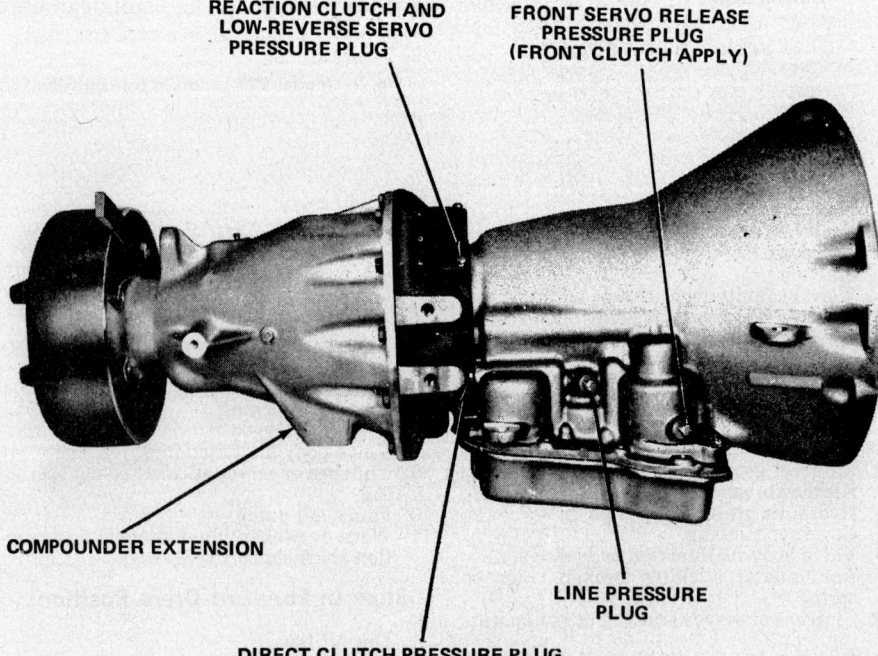

Fig. 4 A-345 transmission assembly. Right side

AUTOMATIC TRANSMISSIONS

Starter Will Not Energize In Neutral or Park

1. Incorrect gearshift control linkage adjustment.
2. Faulty or incorrectly adjusted neutral starting switch.
3. Broken lead to neutral switch.

MAINTENANCE

Service Note

It has been found that an occasional "no-drive" condition, generally occurring after making the first stop when a vehicle is cold can be caused by incorrect transmission oil level. In cases where this condition is encountered, it is essential that the transmission oil level be checked and corrected as outlined below.

On 1970-71 models, oil should be at the "Add 1 Pint" mark when *cold* and between the "Full" and "Add 1 Pint" mark when *hot*.

If the no-drive condition still exists with the correct oil level, the push button cable adjustment should be checked.

After the above corrections have been made, if the no-drive condition still exists, it is suggested that the transmission be removed and the front pump disassembled for inspection before attempting any further repairs. Inspect the pump inner rotor and front support for wear, especially where the pinion rubs the support. The clearance specified for the front pump rotors and the face of the housing is .001" to .0025". If this clearance is increased in any way, such as wear, out-of-flatness, foreign objects between housing and support, the clearance will increase and the front pump will not be able to maintain capacity.

Adding Oil

To check the oil level, apply the parking brake and operate the engine at idle speed. Move selector lever into each position ending in the neutral position. A properly filled transmission should read near the "add one pint" mark when the fluid temperature is 70° F., and near but not over the "full" mark at 180° F. which is normal operating temperature. Then add oil as necessary to bring the oil to the prescribed level.

Changing Oil

Oil should be changed every 32,000 miles. Vehicles that operate continuously with abnormal loads should have more frequent periodic maintenance. Transmission should not be idled in gear for long periods. When refilling, use only fluids labeled Dextron II.

1. Remove drain plug (if equipped) from transmission oil pan and allow oil to drain.

NOTE: *If the oil pan does not have a drain plug, loosen pan bolts and tap pan with a soft mallet to break it loose, permitting fluid to drain.*

2. On 1970-77 models, remove flywheel access plate, remove torque converter drain plug and allow to drain. Replace plug.
3. Remove transmission oil pan, clean intake screen and pan, and reinstall.
4. Add 6 quarts on 1970-77 or 4 quarts on 1978-79 units of automatic transmission fluid through filler tube.
5. Start engine and add approximately one quart while engine is idling.
6. Allow engine to idle for about two minutes. Then with parking brake applied, depress each push button momentarily, ending with the "N" button pushed in.
7. Add oil as necessary to bring to proper level.

BANDS, ADJUST

Kickdown Band

The kickdown band adjusting screw is located on the left side of the transmission case near the throttle lever shaft.

1. Loosen lock nut and back off approximately five turns. Check adjusting screw for free turning in transmission case.
2. Using an inch-pound torque wrench, tighten the band adjusting screw to a reading of 72 inch lbs.
3. On A-345 units, backoff adjusting screw 2 turns. On Loadflite units, backoff adjusting screw the number of turns listed in Fig. 5.
4. While holding adjusting screw in position, tighten lock nut.

Low and Reverse Band

1. Raise vehicle, drain transmission and remove oil pan.
2. Loosen adjusting screw lock nut and back off nut approximately five turns. Check adjusting screw for free turning in the lever.
3. Using an inch-pound torque wrench, tighten band adjusting screw to a reading of 72 inch lbs.
4. On Dodge and Plymouth models, backoff adjusting screw 2 turns. On 1972-79 International models, backoff adjusting screw 2¼ turns. On 1980 Jeep CJ-7 models (model 999 transmission), backoff adjusting screw 4 turns. On 1980 Jeep Cherokee, Wagoneer and Truck (model 727 transmission), backoff adjusting screw 2 turns. On all models, while holding adjusting screw in position, tighten lock nut.
5. Install oil pan and fill transmission with fluid.

Model	Year	Engine	Number of Turns
DODGE & PLYMOUTH			
B100-300, CB, MB300-400 & Voyager	1970-79	6 Cyl.	2½
		V8	2
Ramcharger & Trail Duster	1974-79	Except V8-440	2½
		V8-440	2
D, P, S & W 100-800	1970-71	All	2
	1972-73	6 Cyl.	2½
		V8	2
	1974-77	Except V8-440	2½
		V8-440	2
	1978-79	Except 6-243 Diesel & V8-440	2½
		6-243 Diesel & V8-440	2
M300-600 & RM300-400	1970-79	V8-318 & 360	2½
		V8-413 & 440	2
INTERNATIONAL			
All	1972-79	All	2¼
JEEP			
CJ-7	1980	All	2
Cherokee, Wagoneer & Truck	1980	All	2½

Fig. 5 Kickdown band adjustment chart

AUTOMATIC TRANSMISSIONS

Turbo Hydra-Matic 400 & 475

DESCRIPTION

This transmission, Fig. 1, is a fully automatic unit consisting primarily of a three-element hydraulic torque converter and a compound planetary gear set. Three multiple-disc clutches, two one-way clutches, and two bands provide the friction elements required to obtain the desired functions of the planetary gear set.

NOTE: The two one-way clutches mentioned above consist of an intermediate sprag and a roller clutch.

Beginning with 1971 units, the intermediate sprag clutch was replaced by an intermediate roller clutch.

The torque converter, the multiple-disc clutches and the one-way clutches couple the engine to the planetary gears through oil pressure, providing three forward speeds and reverse. The torque converter, when required, supplements the gears by multiplying engine torque.

Torque Converter

The torque converter is of welded construction and is serviced as an assembly. The unit is made up of two vaned sections, or halves, that face each other in an oil-filled housing. The pump half of the converter is connected to the engine and the turbine half is connected to the transmission.

When the engine makes the converter pump revolve, it sends oil against the turbine, making it revolve also. The oil then returns in a circular flow back to the converter pump, continuing this flow as long as the engine is running.

Stator

The convertor also has a smaller vaned section, called a stator, that funnels the oil back to the converter pump through smaller openings, at increased speed. The speeded up oil directs additional force to the engine-driven converter pump, thereby multiplying engine torque. In other words, without the stator, the unit is nothing more than a fluid coupling.

The stator assembly in some transmissions is a variable pitch unit. The stator blades are operated at either of two positions: maximum or high angle, and minimum or low angle.

Maximum or high angle means greater redirection of the oil and increased engine speed, and torque multiplication for maximum performance. At engine idle, it reduces the converter's efficiency, reducing "creep". Minimum or low angle results in a more efficient converter for cruising operation.

TROUBLE SHOOTING GUIDE

Oil Pressure High

1. Vacuum line or fittings clogged or leaking.
2. Improper engine vacuum.
3. Vacuum leak in vacuum operated accessory.
4. Vacuum modulator.
5. Modulator valve.
6. Water in modulator.
7. Pressure regulator.
8. Oil pump.
9. Governor.
10. Malfunction in detent downshift system. Check for shorted detent wiring, detent solenoid stuck open, detent feed orifice in spacer plate blocked or restricted, loose detent solenoid, damaged detent valve bore plug or detent regulator valve pin too short.

Oil Pressure Low

1. Low oil level.
2. Defective vacuum modulator.
3. Filter blocked or restricted, or incorrect filter assembly.
4. O-ring seal on intake pipe and/or grommet omitted or damaged.
5. Split or leaking oil intake pipe.
6. Malfunction in oil pump. Check for stuck pressure regulator and/or boost valve, weak pressure regulator valve spring, insufficient spacers in pressure regulator, excessive gear clearance, gears damaged, worn or incorrectly installed, pump cover-to-body gasket mispositioned, defective or mismatched pump body-to-pump cover.
7. Internal circuit leakage.
8. Case porosity.
9. Intermediate clutch cup plug leaking or mispositioned.
10. Low-reverse check ball mispositioned or missing. This will cause no reverse and no overrun braking in low range.

No Drive In Drive Range

1. Low oil level (check for leaks).
2. Manual control linkage not adjusted properly.
3. Low oil pressure. Check for blocked strainer, defective pressure regulator, pump assembly or pump drive gear. See that tangs have not been damaged by converter.
4. Check control valve assembly to see if manual valve has been disconnected from manual lever pin.
5. Forward clutch may be stuck or damaged. Check pump feed circuits to forward clutch, including clutch drum ball check.
6. Sprag or roller clutch assembled incorrectly.

1-2 Shift At Full Throttle Only

1. Detent switch may be sticking or defective.
2. Detent solenoid may be stuck open, loose or have leaking gasket.
3. Control valve assembly may be leaking, damaged or incorrectly installed.
4. Third-to-second shift valve stuck.
5. Case porosity.

1st Speed Only—No 1-2 Shift

1. Governor valve may be sticking.
2. Driven gear in governor assembly loose, worn or damaged.
3. The 1-2 shift valve in control valve assembly stuck closed. Check governor feed channels for blocks, leaks, and position. Also check control valve body gaskets for leaks and damage.
4. Intermediate clutch plug in case may be leaking or blown out.
5. Check for porosity between channels and for blocked governor feed channels in case.
6. Center support oil rings missing, or damaged. Orifice plug missing.
7. Intermediate clutch piston seals missing, incorrectly installed or damaged.

No 2-3 Shift—1st & 2nd Only

1. Detent solenoid may be stuck open.
2. Detent switch may not be properly adjusted.
3. Control valve assembly may be stuck, leaking, damaged, or incorrectly installed.
4. Control valve body gaskets leaking, damaged or incorrectly installed.
5. Check direct clutch case center support for broken, leaking or missing oil rings.
6. Check clutch piston seals and piston ball check in clutch assembly.

Moves Forward In Neutral

1. Manual control linkage improperly adjusted.
2. Manual valve disconnected or broken.
3. Inside detent lever pin broken.
4. Transmission oil pressure leaking into forward clutch apply passage.
5. Burned forward clutch plates.
6. Forward clutch does not release.

No Drive In Reverse or Slips In Reverse

1. Check oil level.
2. Manual control linkage improperly adjusted.
3. Vacuum modulator assembly may be defective.
4. Vacuum modulator valve sticking.
5. Strainer may be restricted or leaking at intake.
6. Regulator or boost valve in pump assembly may be sticking.
7. Low oil pressure.
8. Rear servo and accumulator may have damaged or missing servo piston seal ring.
9. Reverse band burned out or damaged. Determine that apply pin or anchor pins engage properly.
10. Direct clutch may be damaged or may have stuck ball check in piston.
11. Forward clutch does not release.
12. Low-reverse ball check missing from case.
13. Control valve body malfunctioning. Check for leaking, damaged or incorrectly installed gaskets, 2-3 shift valve stuck open, or restricted reverse feed passage.

Slips In All Ranges & On Starts

1. Check oil level.
2. Vacuum modulator defective.
3. Modulator valve sticking.
4. Strainer assembly plugged or leaking at neck.
5. Pump assembly regulator or boost valve

AUTOMATIC TRANSMISSIONS

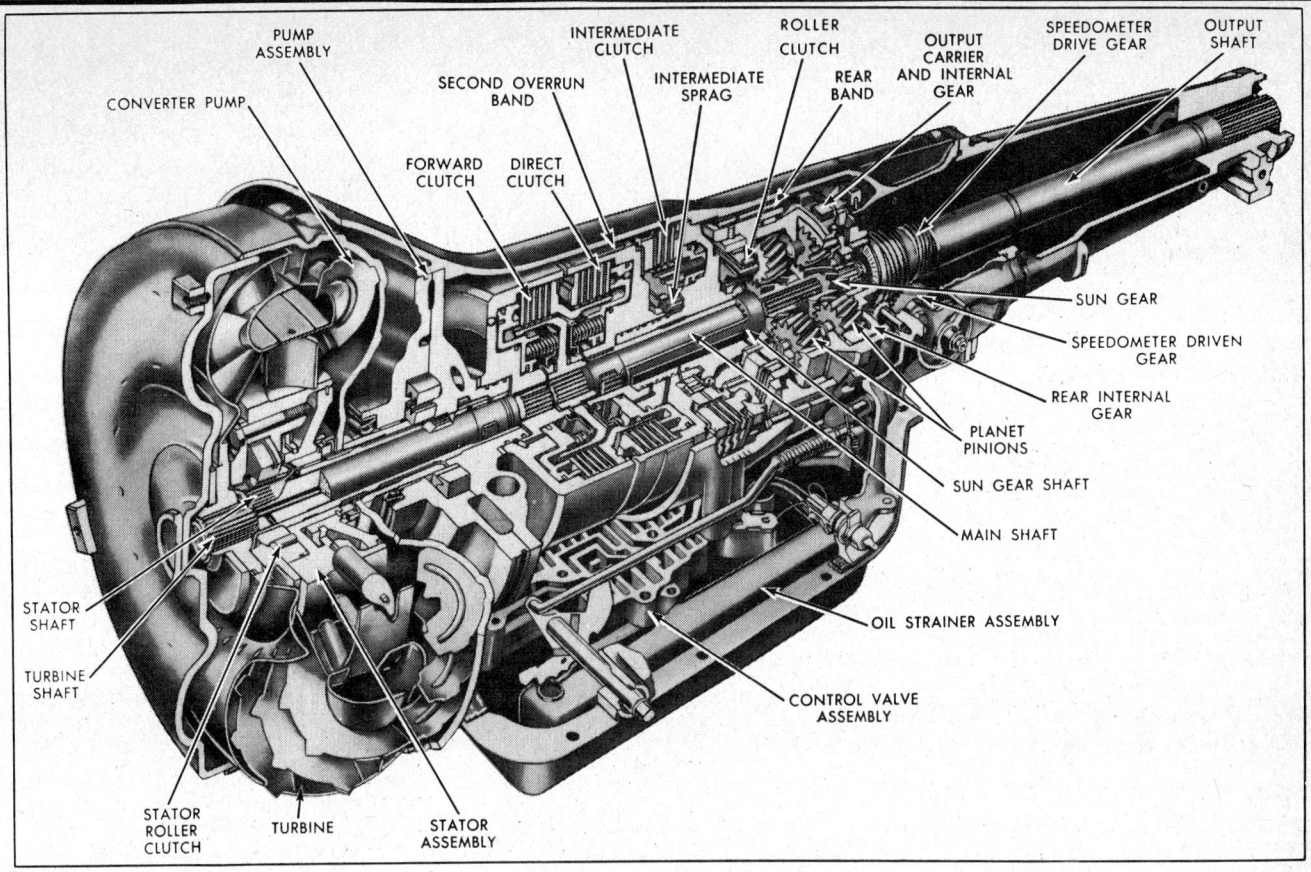

Fig. 1 Turbo-hydra-Matic "400 & 475" transmission

sticking.
6. Leaks from damaged gaskets or cross leaks from porosity of case.
7. Forward and direct clutches burned.
8. Low oil pressure.

Slips 1–2 Shift

1. Incorrect oil level.
2. Vacuum modulator valve sticking.
3. Vacuum modulator defective.
4. Pump pressure regulator valve defective.
5. Porosity between channels in case.
6. Control valve assembly.
7. Pump-to-case gasket may be mispositioned.
8. Intermediate clutch plug in case may be missing or leaking excessively.
9. Intermediate clutch piston seal missing or damaged.
10. Intermediate clutch plates burned.
11. Front or rear accumulator oil ring may be damaged.
12. Leak in center support feed circuit, excessive leak between center support tower and bushing, blocked center support orifice bleed plug hole, center support bolt not properly seated.
13. Raised ridge around case center support bolt not allowing control valve assembly to seat properly.
14. Low oil pressure.

Slips 2–3 Shift

1. Items 1 through 6 under Slips 1-2 Shift will also cause 2-3 shift slips.
2. Direct clutch plates burned.

3. Oil seal rings on direct clutch may be damaged permitting excessive leaking between tower and bushing.

Rough 1–2 Shift

1. Modulator valve sticking.
2. Modulator assembly defective.
3. Pump pressure regulator or boost valve stuck or inoperative.
4. Control valve assembly loosened from case, damaged or mounted with wrong gaskets.
5. Intermediate clutch ball missing or not sealing.
6. Porosity between channels in case.
7. Rear servo accumulator assembly may have oil rings damaged, stuck piston, broken or missing spring or damaged bore.

Rough 2–3 Shift

1. Items 1, 2 and 3 under Rough 1-2 Shift will also cause rough 2-3 shift.
2. Front servo accumulator spring broken or missing. Accumulator piston may be sticking.

No Engine Braking In Second Speed

1. Front servo or accumulator oil rings may be leaking.
2. Front band may be broken or burned out.
3. Front band not engaged on anchor pin and/or servo pin.

No Engine Braking In Low Range

1. Low-reverse check ball may be missing from control valve assembly.
2. Rear servo may have damaged oil seal ring, bore or piston; leaking, apply pressure.
3. Rear band broken, burned out or not engaged on anchor pins or servo pin.

No Part Throttle Downshifts

1. Vacuum modulator assembly.
2. Modulator valve.
3. Regulator valve train.
4. Control valve assembly has stuck 3-2 valve or broken spring.

No Detent Downshifts

1. Detent switch needs fuse, connections tightened or adjustment.
2. Detent solenoid may be inoperative.
3. Detent valve train in control valve assembly malfunctioning.

Low or High Shift Points

1. Oil pressure. Check vacuum modulator assembly, vacuum line connections, modulator valve, and pressure regulator valve train.
2. Governor may have sticking valve or feed holes that are leaking, plugged or damaged.
3. Detent solenoid may be stuck open or loose.
4. Control valve assembly. Check detent, 3-2, and 1-2 shift valve trains, and check

AUTOMATIC TRANSMISSIONS

spacer plate gaskets for positioning.
5. Check case for porosity, missing or leaking intermediate plug.

Won't Hold In Park

1. Manual control linkage improperly adjusted.
2. Internal linkage defective; check for chamfer on actuator rod sleeve.
3. Parking pawl broken or inoperative.
4. Parking pawl return spring missing, broken or incorrectly installed.

Noisy Transmission

1. Pump noises caused by high or low oil level.
2. Cavitation due to plugged strainer, porosity in intake circuit or water in oil.
3. Pump gears may be damaged.
4. Gear noise in low gear of Drive Range - transmission grounded to body.
5. Defective planetary gear set.
6. Clutch noises during application can be worn or burned clutch plates.

Forward Clutch Plates Burned

1. Check ball in clutch housing damaged, stuck or missing.
2. Clutch piston cracked, seals damaged or missing.
3. Low line pressure.
4. Manual valve mispositioned.
5. Restricted oil feed to forward clutch.
6. Pump cover oil seal rings missing, broken or undersize; ring groove oversize.
7. Case valve body face not flat or porosity between channels.
8. Manual valve bent and center land not properly ground.

Intermediate Clutch Plates Burned

1. Constant bleed orifice in center support missing.
2. Rear accumulator piston oil ring damaged or missing.
3. 1-2 accumulator valve stuck in control valve assembly.
4. Intermediate clutch piston seal damaged or missing.
5. Center support bolt loose.
6. Low line pressure.
7. Intermediate clutch plug in case missing.
8. Case valve body face not flat or porosity between channels.
9. Manual valve bent and center land not ground properly.

Direct Clutch Plates Burned

1. Restricted orifice in vacuum line to modulator.
2. Check ball in direct clutch piston damaged, stuck or missing.
3. Defective modulator bellows.
4. Center support bolt loose.
5. Center support oil rings or grooves damaged or missing.
6. Clutch piston seals damaged or missing.
7. Front and rear servo pistons and seals damaged.
8. Manual valve bent and center land not cleaned up.
9. Case valve body face not flat or porosity between channels.
10. Intermediate sprag clutch installed backwards.
11. 3-2 valve, 3-2 spring or 3-2 spacer pin installed in wrong location in 3-2 valve bore.

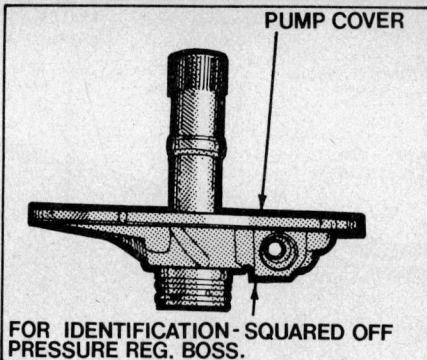

Fig. 2 Pressure regulator identification

MAINTENANCE
Checking & Adding Fluid

Fluid level should be checked at every engine oil change. The full ("F") and "ADD" marks on the transmission dipstick are one pint apart and determine the correct fluid level at normal operating temperature (180°F.). *Careful attention to transmission oil temperature is necessary as proper fluid level at low operating temperatures will be below the "ADD" mark on the dipstick. Proper fluid level at higher operating temperatures will rise above the "F" mark.*

Fluid level must always be checked with the car on a level surface, and with the engine running to make certain the converter is full. To determine proper fluid level, proceed as follows:

1. Operate engine at a fast idle for about 1½ minutes with selector lever in park ("P") position.
2. Reduce engine speed to slow idle and check fluid level.
3. With engine running, add fluid as required to bring it to the proper level.

NOTE: Beginning with 1973, Chevrolet and GMC models are using a revised type Dexron fluid. An early change to a darker color from the usual red color or a strong odor that is usually associated with overheated fluid is normal, and should not be treated as a positive sign of needed maintenance or unit failure.

The normal maintenance schedule for drain and refill of this type fluid remains unchanged at 24,000 miles under normal service and 12,000 miles under severe operating conditions.

CAUTION: *Do not overfill as foaming might occur when the fluid heats up. If fluid level is too low, especially when cold, complete loss of drive may result after quick stops. Extremely low fluid level will result in damage to transmission.*

Draining Bottom Pan Only

1. Disconnect filler tube at bottom pan and allow fluid to drain. Remove and discard filler tube O-ring.
2. Use a new O-ring on filler tube and install tube on pan.
3. Lower car and add three quarts of transmission fluid through filler tube when replacing intake pipe and strainer assembly. When just draining bottom pan, add only two quarts.
4. Operate engine at a fast idle for about 1½ minutes with selector lever in park ("P") position.
5. Reduce engine speed to slow idle and check fluid level. Then add fluid as required to bring it to the proper level.

Adding Fluid to Fill Dry Transmission & Converter

1. Add seven quarts of fluid through filler tube.
2. Operate engine at a fast idle for about 1½ minutes with selector lever in park ("P") position.
3. Reduce engine speed to slow idle and add three more quarts of fluid.
4. Check fluid level and add as required to bring it to the proper level.

IN VEHICLE REPAIRS
Pressure Regulator Valve

NOTE: A solid type pressure regulator valve must be used only in a pump cover with a "Squared Off" (machined) pressure regulator boss, Fig. 2. A pressure regulator valve with oil holes and an orifice cup plug may be used with either type pump.

1. Remove bottom pan and strainer.
2. Using a screwdriver or steel rod, compress regulator boost valve bushing against pressure regulator spring.

CAUTION: Pressure regulator spring is under extreme pressure and will force valve bushing out of bore when snap ring is removed if valve bushing is not held securely.

3. Continue to exert pressure on valve bushing and remove snap ring. Gradually release pressure on valve bushing until spring force is exhausted.
4. Carefully remove regulator boost valve bushing and valve, and pressure regulator spring. Be careful not to drop parts as they will fall out if they are not held.
5. Remove pressure regulator valve and spring retainer. Remove spacers if present.
6. Reverse procedure to install.

Control Valve Body

1. Remove bottom pan and strainer.
2. Disconnect pressure switch lead wire.
3. Remove control valve body attaching screws and detent roller spring assembly. *Do not remove solenoid attaching screws.*
4. Remove control valve body and governor pipes. If care is used in removing control valve body, the six check balls will stay in place above spacer plate.
5. Remove governor pipes and manual valve from control valve body.
6. Reverse procedure to install.

Governor

1. Remove governor cover and discard gasket.
2. Withdraw governor from case.

AUTOMATIC TRANSMISSIONS

3. Reverse procedure to install, using a new gasket.

Modulator & Modulator Valve

1. Remove modulator attaching screw and retainer.
2. Remove modulator assembly from case and discard O-ring seal.
3. Remove modulator valve from case.
4. Reverse procedure to install, using a new O-ring seal.

Parking Linkage

1. Remove bottom pan and oil strainer.
2. Unthread jam nut holding detent lever to manual shaft.
3. Remove manual shaft retaining pin from case.
4. Remove manual shaft and jam nut from case.
5. Remove O-ring seal from manual shaft.
6. Remove parking actuator rod and detent lever assembly.
7. Remove parking pawl bracket, pawl return spring and pawl shaft retainer.
8. Remove parking pawl shaft, O-ring seal and parking pawl.
9. Reverse procedure to install, using new seals and gasket.

Rear Seal

1. Remove propeller shaft.
2. Pry out seal with screwdriver.
3. Install new seal with a suitable seal driver.
4. Install propeller shaft.

Turbo Hydra-Matic 200

Description

The Turbo Hydra-Matic 200 transmission, Fig. 1, is fully automatic and consists of a three element torque converter and a compound planetary gear set. Three multiple disc clutches, a roller clutch and a band provide the required friction elements to obtain the desired function of the planetary gear set.

The Turbo Hydra-Matic 200C, incorporates a converter clutch assembly consisting of a three element torque converter, and a converter clutch, Fig. 2. The converter clutch is splined to the turbine assembly and when operated, applies against the converter cover providing a mechanical direct drive coupling of the engine to the planetary gears. When the converter clutch is released, the assembly operates as a normal torque converter. The converter clutch is applied only when transmission is in third gear, vehicle speed is above 30 mph, engine coolant temperature is above 130° F, engine vacuum is above 3 in. Hg. and brake pedal is released.

TROUBLE SHOOTING GUIDE

No Drive in Drive Range

1. Low oil level.
2. Manual linkage maladjusted.
3. Low oil pressure due to:
   a. Restricted or plugged oil screen.
   b. Oil screen gasket improperly installed.
   c. Oil pump pressure regulator.

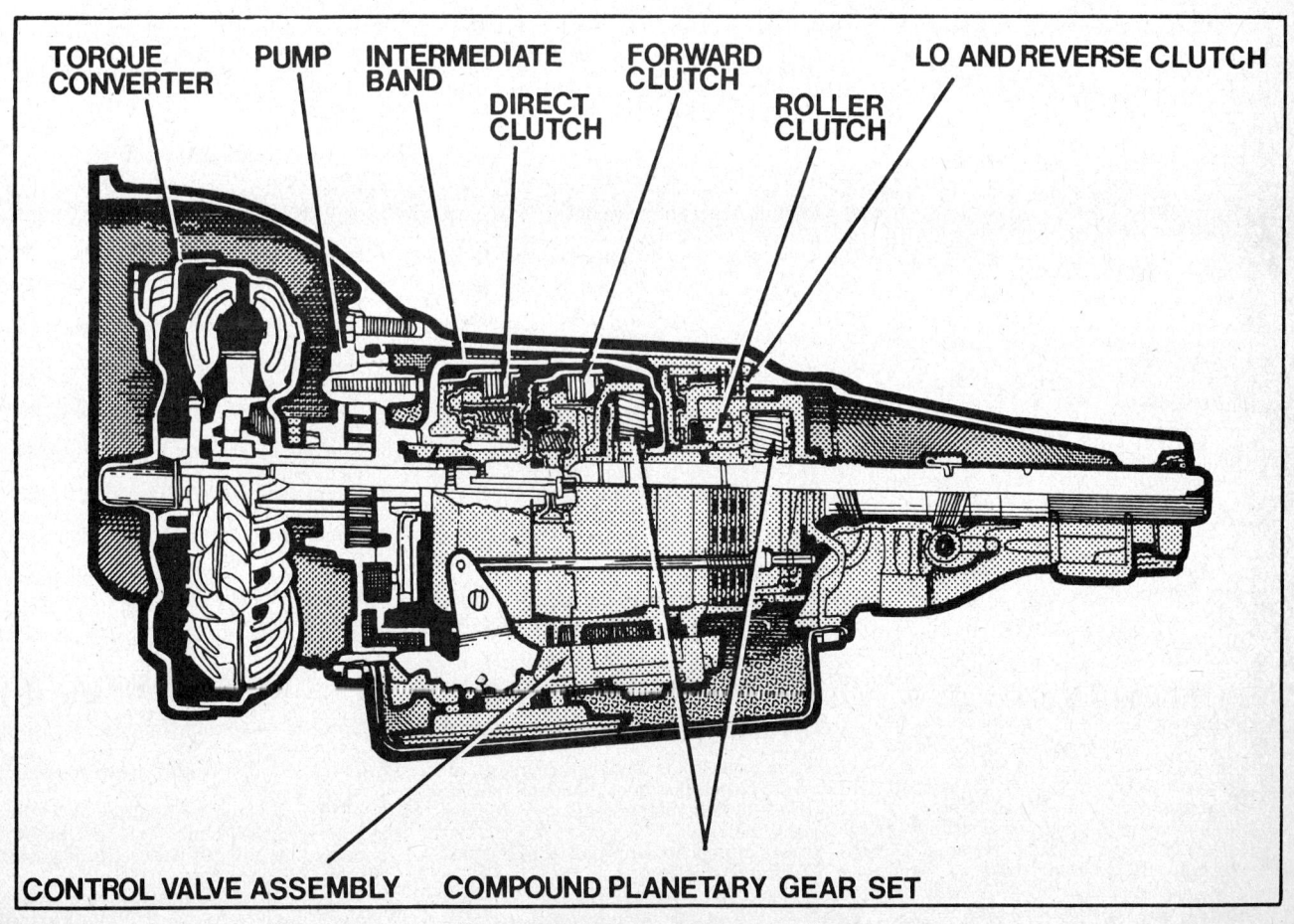

Fig. 1 Turbo-Hydramatic 200 transmission

AUTOMATIC TRANSMISSIONS

    d. Pump drive gear tangs damaged by converter.
    e. Case porosity in intake bore.
4. Forward clutch malfunctioning due to:
    a. Forward clutch not applying due to cracked piston, damaged or missing seals, burned clutch plates, snap ring not in groove.
    b. Forward clutch seal rings damaged or missing on turbine shaft, leaking feed circuits due to damaged or mispositioned gasket.
    c. Clutch housing check ball stuck or missing.
    d. Cup plug leaking or missing from rear of turbine shaft in clutch apply passage.
    e. Incorrect forward clutch piston assembly or incorrect number of clutch plates.
5. Roller clutch malfunctioning due to missing rollers or springs or possibly galled rollers.

Oil Pressure High Or Low

1. Throttle valve cable maladjusted, binding, disconnected or broken.
2. Throttle lever and bracket improperly installed, disconnected or binding.
3. Throttle valve shift valve, throttle valve or plunger binding.
4. Pressure regulator valve and spring malfunctioning due to:
    a. Binding valve.
    b. Incorrect spring.
    c. Oil pressure control orifice in pump cover plugged, causing high oil pressure.
    d. Pressure regulator bore plug leaking.
5. Manual valve disconnected.
6. Intermediate boost valve binding, causing oil pressures to be incorrect in 2nd and low ranges.
7. Orifice in spacer plate at end of intermediate boost valve plugged.
8. Reserve boost valve binding, causing pressure to be incorrect in reverse only.
9. Orifice in spacer plate at end of reverse boost valve plugged.

1–2 Shift At Full Throttle Only

1. Throttle valve cable maladjusted, binding, disconnected or broken.
2. Throttle lever and bracket assembly binding or disconnected.
3. Throttle valve exhaust ball lifter or number 5 check ball binding, mispositioned or disconnected.

NOTE: If number 5 ball is fully seated, it will cause full throttle valve pressure regardless of throttle valve position.

4. Throttle valve and plunger binding.
5. Valve body gaskets leaking, damaged or incorrectly installed.
6. Porous control valve assembly.

First Speed Only, No 1–2 Shift

1. Due to governor and governor feed passages:
    a. Plugged governor oil feed orifice in spacer plate.
    b. Plugged orifice in spacer plate that feeds governor oil to the shift valves.
    c. Balls missing in governor assembly.
    d. Governor cover O-ring missing or leaking. If governor cover O-ring leaks, an external oil leak will be present and there will be no upshift.
    e. Governor shaft seal missing or damaged.
    f. Governor driven gear stripped.
    g. Governor weights binding.
    h. Governor assembly missing.
2. Control valve assembly 1-2 shift valve or 1-2 throttle valve stuck in downshift position.
3. Porosity in case channels or undrilled 2nd speed feed holes.
4. Excessive leakage between case bore and intermediate band apply ring.
5. Intermediate band anchor pin missing or disconnected from band.
6. Missing or broken intermediate band.
7. Due to intermediate servo assembly:
    a. Servo to cover oil seal ring damage or missing.
    b. Porous servo cover or piston.
    c. Incorrect intermediate band apply pin.
    d. Incorrect cover and piston.

1st & 2nd Only, No 2–3, Shift

1. 2-3 shift valve or 2-3 throttle valve stuck in downshift position.
2. Direct clutch feed orifice in spacer plate plugged.
3. Valve body gaskets leaking, damaged or incorrectly installed.
4. Porosity between case passages.
5. Pump passages plugged or leaking.
6. Pump gasket incorrectly installed.
7. Rear seal on pump cover leaking or missing.
8. Direct clutch oil seals missing or damaged.
9. Direct clutch piston or housing cracked.
10. Direct clutch plates damaged or missing.
11. Direct clutch backing plate snap ring out of groove.
12. Intermediate servo to case oil seal broken or missing on intermediate servo piston.
13. Intermediate servo exhaust hole in case between servo piston seals plugged or undrilled.

Moves Forward In Neutral

1. Manual linkage maladjusted.
2. Forward clutch does not release.
3. Cross leakage between pump passages.
4. Cross leakage to forward clutch through clutch passages.

No Drive in Reverse or Slips in Reverse

1. Throttle valve cable binding or maladjusted.
2. Manual linkage maladjusted.
3. Throttle valve binding.
4. Reverse boost valve binding in bore.
5. Low overrun clutch valve binding in bore.
6. Reverse clutch piston cracked, broken or has missing seals.
7. Reverse clutch plates burned.
8. Reverse clutch has incorrect selective spacer ring.
9. Porosity in passages to direct clutch.
10. Pump to case gasket improperly installed or missing.
11. Pump passages cross leaking or restricted.
12. Pump cover seals damaged or missing.
13. Direct clutch piston or housing cracked.
14. Direct clutch piston seals cut or missing.
15. Direct clutch housing ball check, stuck, leaking or missing.
16. Direct clutch plates burned.
17. Incorrect direct clutch piston.
18. Direct clutch orifices plugged in spacer plate.
19. Intermediate servo to case seal cut or missing.

Slips 1–2 Shift

1. Aerated oil due to low level.
2. 2nd speed feed orifice in spacer plate partially blocked.
3. Improperly installed or missing spacer plate gasket.
4. 1-2 accumulator valve stuck, causing low 1-2 accumulator pressure.
5. Weak or missing 1-2 accumulator valve spring.
6. 1-2 accumulator piston seal leaking or spring missing or broken.
7. Leakage between 1-2 accumulator piston and pin.
8. Incorrect intermediate band apply pin.
9. Excessive leakage between intermediate band apply pin and case.
10. Porous intermediate servo piston.
11. Servo cover to servo seal damaged or missing.
12. Incorrect servo and cover.
13. Throttle valve cable improperly adjusted.
14. Shift throttle valve or throttle valve binding.
15. Intermediate band worn or burned.
16. Case porosity in 2nd clutch passages.

Rough 1–2 Shift

1. Throttle valve cable improperly adjusted or binding.
2. Throttle valve or plunger binding.
3. Shift throttle or 1-2 accumulator valve binding.
4. Incorrect intermediate servo pin.
5. Intermediate servo piston to case seal damaged or missing.
6. 1-2 accumulator oil ring damaged piston stuck, bore damaged or spring broken or missing.

Slips 2–3 Shift

1. Low oil level.
2. Throttle valve cable improperly adjusted.
3. Throttle valve binding.
4. Direct clutch orifice in spacer plate partially blocked.
5. Spacer plate gaskets improperly installed or missing.
6. Intermediate servo to case seal damaged.
7. Porous direct clutch feed passages in case.
8. Pump to case gasket improperly installed or missing.
9. Pump passages cross feeding, leaking or restricted.
10. Pump cover oil seal rings damaged or missing.
11. Direct clutch piston or housing cracked.
12. Direct clutch piston seals cut or missing.
13. Direct clutch plates burned.

Rough 2-3 Shift

1. Throttle valve cable improperly installed or missing.
2. Throttle valve or throttle valve plunger binding.
3. Shift throttle valve binding.
4. Intermediate servo exhaust hole undrilled or plugged between intermediate servo piston seals.
5. Direct clutch exhaust valve number 4 check ball missing or improperly installed.

AUTOMATIC TRANSMISSIONS

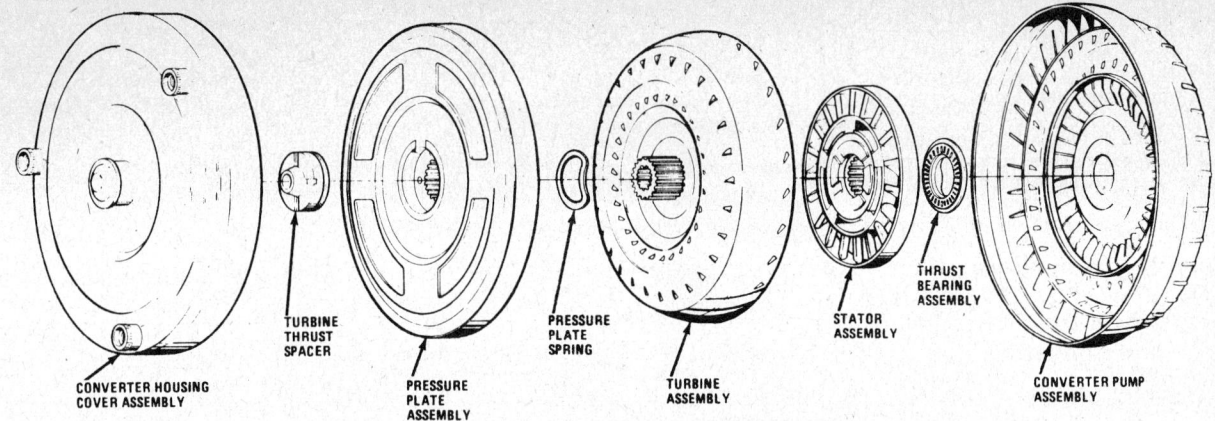

Fig. 2 Torque converter clutch. T.H.M. 200C

No Engine Braking In 2nd Speed

1. Intermediate boost valve binding in valve body.
2. Intermediate-Reverse number 3 check ball improperly installed or missing.
3. Shift throttle valve number 3 check ball improperly installed or missing.
4. Intermediate servo to cover seal missing or damaged.
5. Intermediate band off anchor pin, broken or burned.

No Engine Braking In 1st Speed

1. Low overrun clutch valve binding in valve body.

NOTE: The following conditions will also cause no reverse.

2. Low-reverse clutch piston seals broken or missing.
3. Porosity in low-reverse piston or housing.
4. Low-reverse clutch housing snap ring out of case.
5. Cup plug or rubber seal missing or damaged between case and low-reverse clutch housing.

No Part Throttle Downshift

1. Throttle plunger bushing passages obstructed.
2. 2-3 throttle valve bushing passages obstructed.
3. Valve body gaskets improperly installed or damaged.
4. Spacer plate hole obstructed or undrilled.
5. Throttle valve cable maladjusted.
6. Throttle valve or shift throttle valve binding.

Low or High Shift Points

1. Throttle valve cable binding or disconnected.
2. Throttle valve or shift throttle valve binding.
3. Number 1 throttle shift check ball improperly installed or missing.
4. Throttle valve plunger, 1-2 or 2-3 throttle valves binding.
5. Valve body gaskets improperly installed or missing.
6. Pressure regulator valve binding.

7. Throttle valve exhaust number 5 check ball and lifter, improperly installed, disconnected or missing.
8. Throttle lever binding, disconnected or loose at valve body mounting bolt or not positioned at the throttle valve plunger bushing pin locator.
9. Governor shaft to cover seal broken or missing.
10. Governor cover O-rings broken or missing.

NOTE: Outer ring will leak externally and the inner ring will leak internally.

11. Case porosity.

Will Not Hold In Park

1. Manual linkage maladjusted.
2. Parking pawl binding in case.
3. Actuator rod or plunger damaged.
4. Parking pawl damaged.
5. Parking bracket loose or damaged.
6. Detent lever nut loose.
7. Detent lever hole worn or damaged.
8. Detent roller to valve body bolt loose.
9. Detent roller or pin damaged, incorrectly installed or missing.

Converter Clutch Applied In All Ranges, Engine Stalls When Transmission Is Put In Gear (T.H.M. 200C)

1. Converter clutch valve in pump sticking in apply position.

Converter Clutch Applies Erratically (T.H.M. 200C)

1. Vacuum switch malfunction.
2. Release orifice at pump blocked or restricted.
3. Damaged turbine shaft O-ring.
4. Converter malfunctioning, clutch pressure plate warped.
5. O-ring damaged at solenoid.
6. Solenoid bolts loose.

Converter Clutch Applies At A Very Low or High 3rd Speed Gear (T.H.M. 200C)

1. Governor switch malfunction.
2. Governor malfunction.

3. High line pressure.
4. Converter clutch valve sticking or binding.
5. Solenoid inoperative or shorted to case.

MAINTENANCE

To check fluid, drive vehicle for at least 15 minutes to bring fluid to operating temperature (200° F). With vehicle on a level surface and engine idling in Park and parking brake applied, the level on the dipstick should be at the "F" mark. To bring the fluid level from the ADD mark to the FULL mark requires 1 pint of fluid. If vehicle cannot be driven sufficiently to bring fluid to operating temperature, the level on the dipstick should be between the two dimples on the dipstick with fluid temperature at 70° F.

If additional fluid is required, use only Dexron or Dexron II automatic transmission fluid.

NOTE: An early change to a darker color from the usual red color and or a strong odor that is usually associated with over-heated fluid is normal and should not be considered as a positive sign of required maintenance or unit failure.

CAUTION: When adding fluid, do not overfill, as foaming and loss of fluid through the vent may occur as the fluid heats up. Also, if fluid level is too low, complete loss of drive may occur especially when cold, which can cause transmission failure.

Every 60,000 miles, the oil should be drained, the oil pan removed, the screen cleaned and fresh fluid added. For vehicles subjected to more severe use such as heavy city traffic especially in hot weather, prolonged periods of idling or towing, this maintenance should be performed every 15,000 miles.

Draining Bottom Pan

1. Remove front and side oil pan attaching bolts, then loosen the rear oil pan attaching bolts.
2. Carefully pry oil pan loose and allow fluid to drain into a suitable container.
3. Remove the oil pan and gasket, then remove the screen attaching bolts and remove screen.
4. Thoroughly clean oil screen and oil pan

AUTOMATIC TRANSMISSIONS

with solvent.
5. Install oil screen using a new gasket and torque attaching bolts to 6–10 ft. lbs., then install oil pan using a new gasket and torque attaching bolts to 10–13 bolts.
6. Add 3 quarts of fluid, then with engine idling and parking brake applied, move selector lever through each range and return selector lever to PARK.
7. Check fluid level and add fluid as required to bring level between the two dimples on the dipstick.

Adding Fluid To Dry Transmission and Converter

1. Add 4½ quarts of fluid.
2. With transmission in PARK and parking brake applied, start the engine and place carburetor on fast idle cam.
3. Move shifter lever through each range, then with transmission in PARK, add additional fluid as required to bring the level between the two dimples on the dipstick.

IN VEHICLE REPAIRS

Valve Body Assembly

1. Drain transmission fluid, then remove oil pan and screen.
2. Remove detent cable retaining bolt and disconnect cable.
3. Remove throttle lever and bracket assembly. Use care to avoid bending throttle lever link.
4. Remove detent roller and spring assembly.
5. Support valve body and remove retaining bolts, then while holding manual valve, remove valve assembly, spacer plate and gaskets as an assembly to prevent dropping the five check balls.

NOTE: After removing valve body assembly, the intermediate band anchor band pin, and reverse cup plug may be removed.

6. To install control valve reverse removal procedure and torque all valve body bolts to 8 ft. lbs.

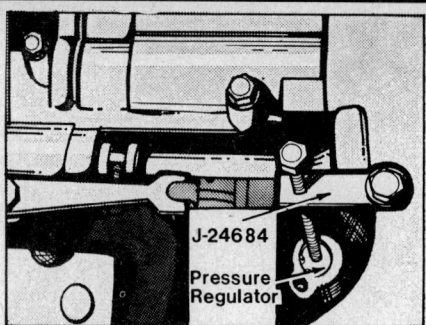

Fig. 3 Removing or installing pressure regulator

CAUTION: Assure that intermediate band anchor pin is located on intermediate band prior to installation of valve body, as damage will result.

Governor

1. Disconnect battery ground cable and remove cleaner.
2. On vehicles with air conditioning, remove the five heater core cover screws, then disconnect the electrical connectors and position heater core aside.
3. Disconnect exhaust pipe and allow to hang down.
4. Support transmission, then remove transmission rear support bolts and propeller shaft and lower transmission until enough clearance is obtained to remove governor.
5. Remove governor retainer ring and cover, then remove governor and washer.

NOTE: If governor to case washer falls into transmission, use a small magnet to remove it. If it cannot be easily removed, replace the washer with a new one.

6. To install governor, reverse removal procedure.

CAUTION: Do not attempt to hammer governor assembly into case, as damage to governor, case or cover may result.

Pressure Regulator Valve

1. Drain transmission fluid, then remove oil pan and screen.
2. Using a small screwdriver or tool J-24684, Fig. 3, compress regulator spring.
3. Remove retaining ring and slowly release spring tension.
4. Remove pressure regulator bore plug, valve, spring and guide.
5. To assemble, install pressure regulator spring, guide and valve with stem end first and bore plug with hole side out.
6. Using a small screwdriver or tool J-24684, Fig. 3, compress regulator spring and install retaining ring.

TRANSMISSION REPLACE

1. Disconnect battery ground cable.
2. Disconnect detent cable from carburetor and remove dipstick.
3. Raise and support vehicle, then remove converter housing cover, starter and propeller shaft.

NOTE: Install plug on rear end of transmission to prevent oil leakage.

4. Remove exhaust pipe bracket and disconnect shift linkage and speedometer cable.
5. Loosen nuts retaining oil cooler lines to transmission, then remove clips retaining lines and move lines away to prevent damage when transmission is removed.
6. Remove the three nuts and bolts retaining converter to flex plate and the three nuts and bolts retaining frame bracket to transmission mount.
7. Using a suitable jack, raise engine and transmission, then remove the four bolts retaining frame bracket to crossmember and remove transmission mount.
8. Remove transmission to engine bolts, then lower and remove transmission.

CAUTION: Use care to avoid dropping converter.

9. Reverse procedure to install, making sure that converter rotates freely before torquing nuts and bolts to 30 ft. lbs.

Turbo Hydra-Matic 250 & 350

DESCRIPTION

The Turbo Hydra-Matic 250, 350, Figs. 1 and 2, are fully automatic three speed transmissions consisting of a three element torque converter and a compound planetary gear set. The Turbo Hydra-Matic 250C and 350C, also incorporate a torque converter clutch, Fig. 3. The Turbo Hydra-Matic 350 transmission has four multiple-disc clutches, two roller clutches and a band to provide the required friction elements to obtain the desired function of the planetary gear set. The Turbo Hydra-Matic 250 transmission uses an adjustable intermediate band in place of the intermediate clutch found in the Turbo Hydra-Matic 350. Also, the Turbo Hydra-Matic 250 has three multiple-disc clutches and one roller clutch.

The friction elements couple the engine to the planetary gears through oil pressure, providing three forward speeds and one reverse.

The three element torque converter is of welded construction and is serviced as an assembly. The unit consists of a pump or driving member, a turbine or driven member and a stator assembly. When required, the torque converter supplements the gears by multiplying engine torque.

The Turbo Hydra-Matic 250C and 350, the converter clutch assembly consist of a three element torque converter, with the addition a converter clutch, Fig. 3. The converter clutch is splined to the turbine assembly and when operated, applies against the converter cover providing a mechanical direct drive coupling of the engine to the planetary gears. When the converter clutch is released, the assembly operates as a normal torque converter. The converter clutch is applied only when transmission is in third gear, vehicle speed is above 30 mph, engine coolant temperature is above 130°F, engine vacuum is above 3 in. Hg. and brake pedal is released.

AUTOMATIC TRANSMISSIONS

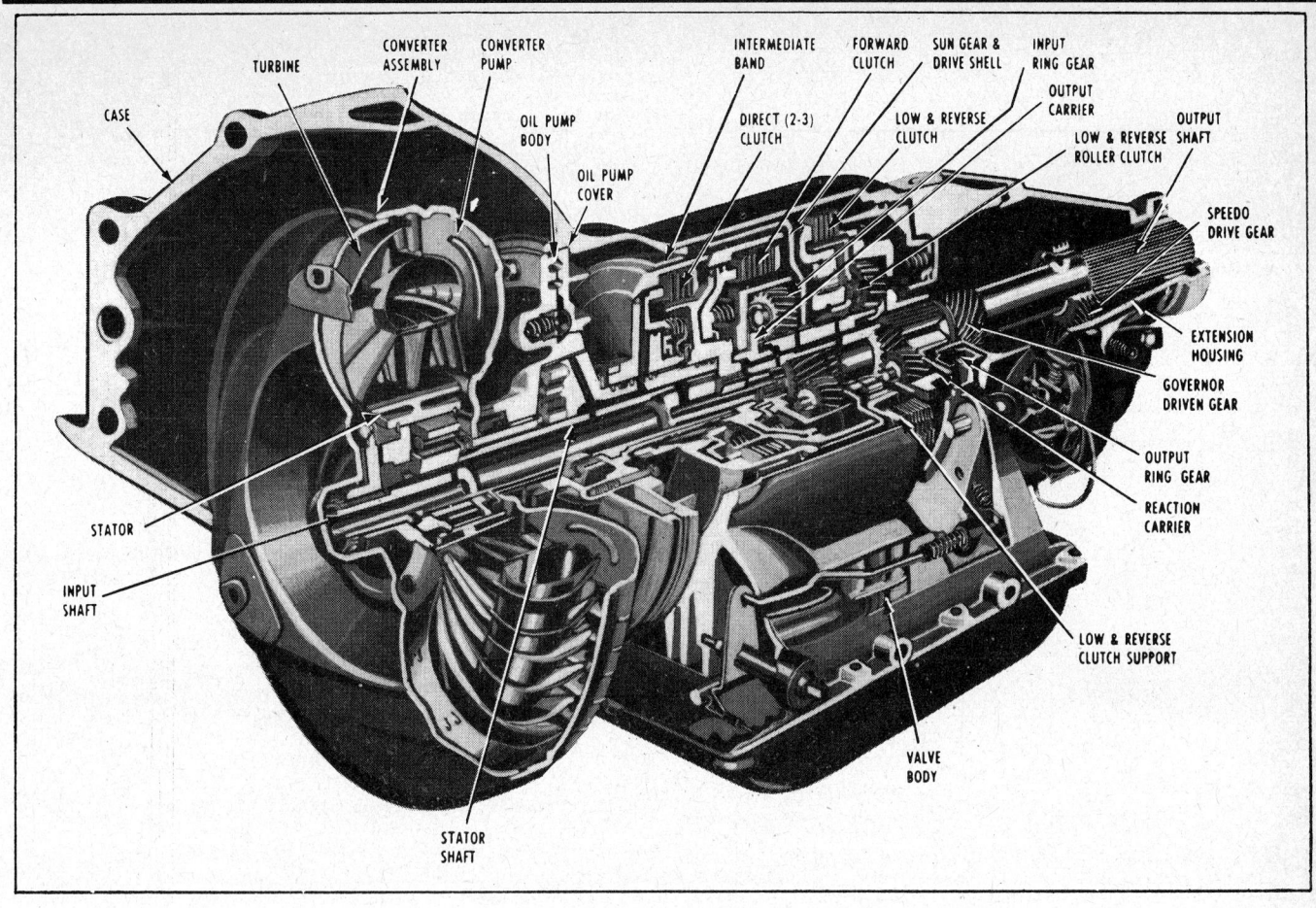

Fig. 1 Turbo Hydra-Matic "250" transmission

TROUBLE SHOOTING GUIDE

No Drive In Drive Range

1. Low oil level (check for leaks).
2. Manual control linkage improperly adjusted.
3. Low oil pressure due to blocked strainer, defective pressure regulator, pump assembly or pump drive gear. See that tangs have not been damaged by converter. Check case for porosity in intake bore.
4. Check control valve assembly to be sure manual valve has not been disconnected from inner lever.
5. Forward clutch may be stuck or damaged. Check pump feed circuits to forward clutch, including clutch drum ball check.
6. Roller clutch assembly broken or damaged.

Oil Pressure High or Low

High Pressure:
1. Vacuum line or fittings leaking.
2. Vacuum modulator.
3. Modulator valve.
4. Pressure regulator.
5. Oil pump.

Low Pressure:
1. Vacuum line or fittings obstructed.
2. Vacuum modulator.
3. Modulator valve.
4. Pressure regulator.
5. Governor.
6. Oil pump.

1-2 Shift At Full Throttle Only

1. Detent valve may be sticking or linkage may be misadjusted.
2. Vacuum line or fittings leaking.
3. Control valve body gaskets leaking, damaged or incorrectly installed. Detent valve train or 1-2 valve stuck.
4. Check case for porosity.

First Speed Only, No 1-2 Shift

T.H.M. 250 & 350
1. Governor valve may be sticking.
2. Driven gear in governor assembly loose, worn or damaged. If driven gear shows damage, check output shaft drive gear for nicks or rough finish.
3. Control valve governor feed channel blocked or gaskets leaking 1-2 shift valve train stuck closed.
4. Check case for blocked governor feed channels or for scored governor bore which will allow cross pressure leak. Check case for porosity.
5. Intermediate clutch or seals damaged.
6. Intermediate roller clutch damaged.

T.H.M. 250
1. Intermediate servo piston seals damaged, missing or installed improperly.
2. Intermediate band improperly adjusted.
3. Intermediate servo apply rod broken.

1st & 2nd Only, No 2-3 Shift

1. Control valve 2-3 shift train stuck. Valve body gaskets leaking, damaged or improperly installed.
2. Pump hub-to-direct clutch oil seal rings broken or missing.
3. Direct clutch piston seals damaged. Piston ball check stuck or missing.

No First Speed

T.H.M. 250
1. Intermediate band adjusted too tightly.
2. 1-2 shift valve stuck in upshift position.

T.H.M. 350
1. Excessive number of clutch plates in intermediate clutch pack.
2. Incorrect intermediate clutch piston.

Moves Forward In Neutral

1. Manual linkage misadjusted.
2. Forward clutch not releasing.

No Drive In Reverse or Slips In Reverse

1. Low oil level.
2. Manual linkage misadjusted.
3. Modulator valve stuck.
4. Modulator and reverse boost valve stuck.
5. Pump hub-to-direct clutch oil seal rings broken or missing.

545

AUTOMATIC TRANSMISSIONS

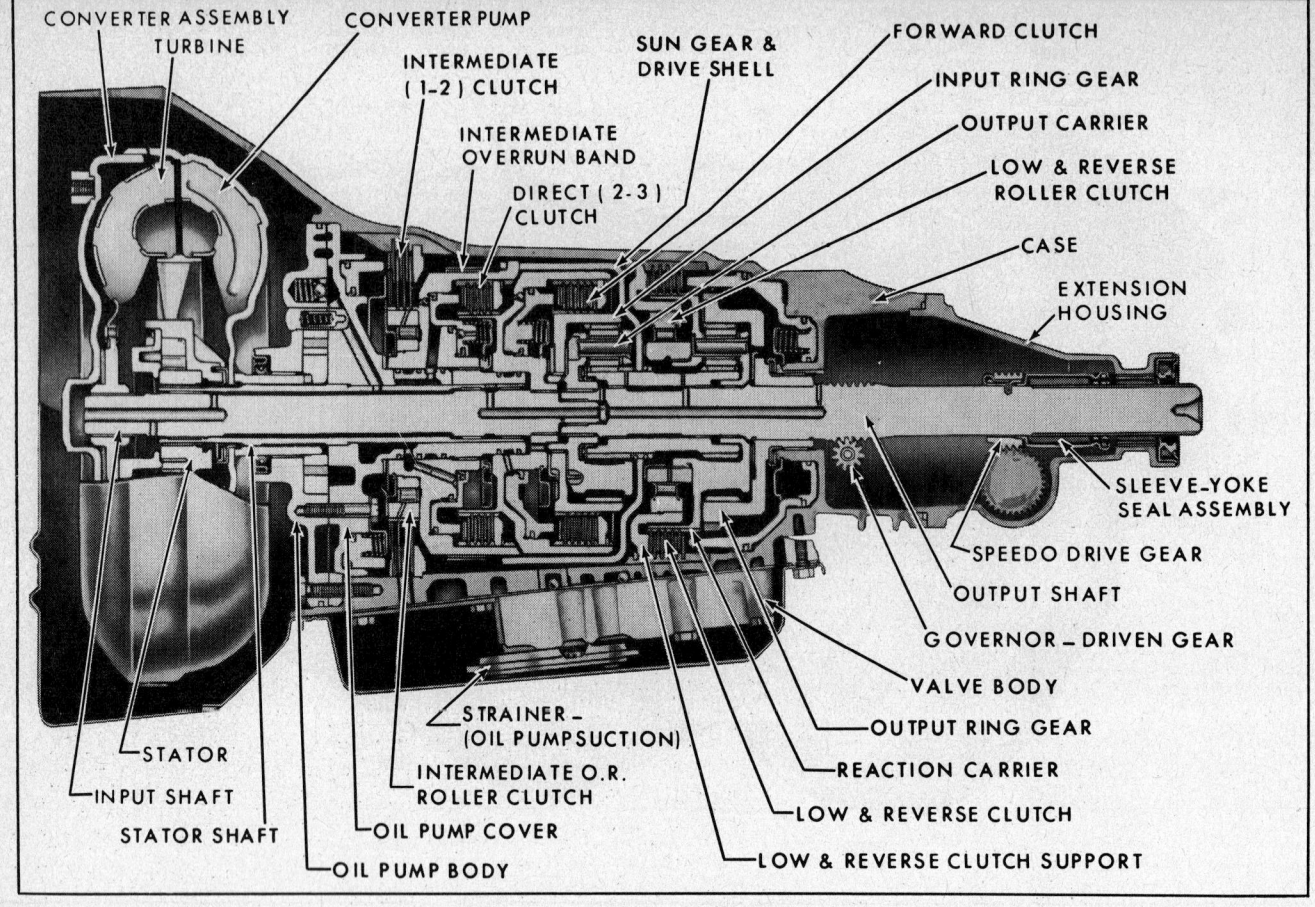

Fig. 2 Turbo Hydra-Matic "350" transmission

6. Direct clutch piston seal cut or missing.
7. Low and reverse clutch piston seal cut or missing.
8. Number 1 check ball missing.
9. Control valve body gaskets leaking or damaged.
10. 2-3 valve train stuck in upshifted position.
11. 1-2 valve train stuck in upshifted position.
12. Intermediate servo piston or pin stuck so intermediate overrun band is applied.
13. Low and reverse clutch piston out or seal damaged.
14. Direct clutch plates burned—may be caused by stuck ball check in piston.
15. Forward clutch not releasing.

Slips In All Ranges

1. Low oil level.
2. Vacuum modulator valve defective or sticking.
3. Filter assembly plugged or leaking.
4. Pressure regulator valve stuck.
5. Pump to case gasket damaged.
6. Check case for cross leaks or porosity.
7. Forward clutch slipping.

Slips 1-2 Shift

T.H.M. 250 & 350
1. Low oil level.
2. Vacuum modulator assembly defective.
3. Modulator valve sticking.
4. Pump pressure regulator valve defective.
5. 2-3 accumulator oil ring damaged or missing. 1-2 accumulator oil ring damaged or missing. Case bore damaged.
6. Pump to case gasket mispositioned or damaged.
7. Check for case porosity.
8. Intermediate clutch piston seals damaged. Clutch plates burned.

T.H.M. 250
1. Intermediate servo piston seals damaged or missing.
2. Burned intermediate band.

T.H.M. 350
1. 2-3 accumulator oil ring damaged or missing.

Rough 1-2 Shift

T.H.M. 250 & 350
1. Vacuum modulator, check for loose fittings, restrictions in line or defective modulator assembly.
2. Modulator valve stuck.
3. Valve body regulator or boost valve stuck.
4. Pump to case gasket mispositioned or damaged.
5. Check case for porosity.
6. Check 1-2 accumulator assembly for damaged oil rings, stuck piston, broken or missing spring, or damaged case bore.

T.H.M. 250
1. Intermediate band improperly adjusted.
2. Improper or broken servo spring.

T.H.M. 350
1. Burned intermediate clutch plates.
2. Improper number of intermediate clutch plates.

Slips 2-3 Shift

1. Low oil level.
2. Modulator valve or vacuum modulator assembly defective.
3. Pump pressure regulator valve or boost valve; pump to case gasket mispositioned.
4. Check case for porosity.
5. Direct clutch piston seals or ball check leaking.

Rough 2-3 Shift

1. High oil pressure. Vacuum leak, modulator valve sticking or pressure regulator or boost valve inoperative.
2. 2-3 accumulator piston stuck, spring broken or missing.

No Engine Braking In Second Speed

1. Intermediate servo or 2-3 accumulator oil rings or bores leaking or accumulator piston stuck.
2. Intermediate overrun band burned or broken.
3. Low oil pressure: Pressure regulator and/or boost valve stuck.

No Engine Braking In 1st Speed

1. Manual low control valve assembly stuck.

AUTOMATIC TRANSMISSIONS

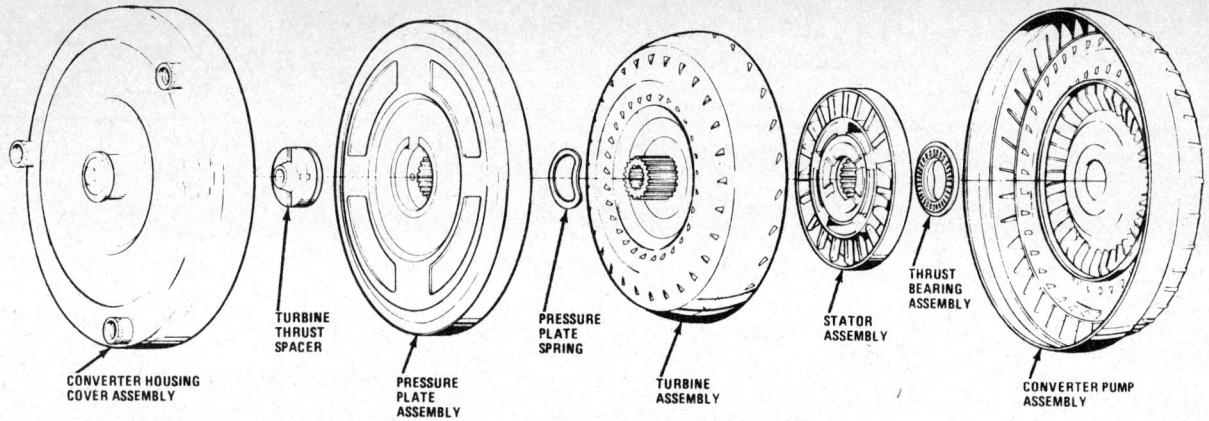

Fig. 3 Torque converter clutch. T.H.M. 250C & 350C

2. Low oil pressure: Pressure regulator and/or boost valve stuck.
3. Low and reverse clutch piston inner seal damaged.

No Part Throttle Downshift

1. Oil pressure: Vacuum modulator assembly, modulator valve or pressure regulator valve train malfunctioning.
2. Detent valve and linkage sticking, disconnected or broken.
3. 2-3 shift valve stuck.

No Detent Downshifts

1. 2-3 valve stuck.
2. Detent valve and linkage sticking, disconnected or broken.

Low or High Shift Points

1. Oil pressure: Check engine vacuum at transmission end of modulator pipe.
2. Vacuum modulator assembly vacuum line connections at engine and transmission, modulator valve, pressure regulator valve train.
3. Check governor for sticking valve, restricted or leaking feed holes, damaged pipes or plugged feed line.
4. Detent valve stuck open.
5. 1-2 or 2-3 valve train sticking.
6. Check case for porosity.

Won't Hold In Park

1. Manual linkage misadjusted.
2. Parking brake lever and actuator assembly defective.
3. Parking pawl broken or inoperative.

Burned Forward Clutch Plates

1. Check ball in clutch drum damaged, stuck or missing.
2. Clutch piston cracked, seals damaged or missing.
3. Low line pressure.
4. Pump cover oil seal rings missing, broken or undersize; ring groove oversize.
5. Transmission case valve body face not flat or porosity between channels.

Burned Intermediate Clutch Plates

T.H.M. 350
1. Intermediate clutch piston seals damaged or missing.
2. Low line pressure.

3. Transmission case valve body face not flat or porosity between channels.

Burned Intermediate Band

T.H.M. 250
1. Intermediate servo piston seals damaged or missing.
2. Low line pressure.
3. Transmission case valve body face not flat or porosity between channels.

Burned Direct Clutch Plates

1. Restricted orifice in vacuum line to modulator.
2. Check ball in clutch drum damaged, stuck or missing.
3. Defective modulator.
4. Clutch piston cracked, seals damaged or missing.
5. Transmission case valve body face not flat or porosity between channels.

Noisy Transmission

NOTE: Before checking transmission for noise, ensure noise is not coming from water pump, alternator or any belt driven accessory.

Park, Neutral & All Driving Ranges

1. Low fluid level.
2. Plugged or restricted screen.
3. Damaged screen to valve body gasket.
4. Porosity in valve body intake area.
5. Transmission fluid contaminated with water.
6. Porosity at transmission case intake port.
7. Improperly installed case to pump gasket.
8. Pump gears are damaged.
9. Driving gear assembled backwards.
10. Crescent interference in pump.
11. Damaged or worn oil pump seals.
12. Loose converter to flywheel bolts.
13. Damaged converter.

1st, 2nd And/Or Reverse Gear

1. Planetary gears or thrust bearings damaged.
2. Damaged input or output ring gear.

Acceleration in any Gear

1. Transmission case or transmission oil cooler lines contacting underbody.
2. Broken or loose engine mounts.

Squeal At Low Vehicle Speed

1. Speedometer driven gear shaft seal requires lubrication or replacement.

Converter Clutch Applied In All Ranges; Engine Stalls When Transmission Is Put In Gear

T.H.M. 250C & 350C
1. Converter clutch valve in pump sticking in apply position.

Converter Clutch Applies Erratically

T.H.M. 250C & 350C
1. Vacuum switch malfunction.
2. Release orifice at pump blocked or restricted.
3. Damaged turbine shaft O-ring.
4. Converter malfunctioning, clutch pressure plate warped.
5. O-ring damaged at solenoid.
6. Solenoid bolts loose.

Converter Clutch Applies At A Very Low or High 3rd Speed Gear

T.H.M. 250C & 350C
1. Governor switch malfunction.
2. Governor malfunction.
3. High line pressure.
4. Converter clutch valve sticking or binding.
5. Solenoid inoperative or shorted to case.

MAINTENANCE

Fluid should be checked every 6,000 miles with engine idling, selector lever in neutral position, parking brake set and transmission at operating temperature. Use only General Motors Dexron transmission fluid when adding oil. Do not overfill.

Every 24,000 miles, remove drain plug in transmission oil pan and drain transmission oil sump. Add 1½ quarts after replacing plug, check fluid and add enough fluid to bring level to the Full mark.

NOTE: Beginning with 1973, Chevrolet and

AUTOMATIC TRANSMISSIONS

GMC models are using a revised type Dexron fluid. An early change to a darker color from the usual red color and or a strong odor that is usually associated with overheated fluid is normal, and should not be treated as a positive sign of needed maintenance or unit failure.

The normal maintenance schedule for drain and refill of this type fluid remains unchanged at 24,000 miles under normal service and 12,000 miles under severe operating conditions, such as trailer towing.

Valve Body Assembly

1. Remove oil pan and strainer.
2. Remove retaining pin to disconnect downshift actuating lever bracket, remove valve body attaching bolts and detent roller and spring assembly.
3. Remove valve body assembly while disconnecting manual control valve link from range selector inner lever.

CAUTION: Do not drop valve.

4. Remove manual valve and link from valve body assembly.
5. Reverse procedure to install.

Governor

1. Where necessary, remove shift linkage and transmission to crossmember bolts.
2. Raise transmission with jack and remove crossmember. Lower transmission enough to remove governor.
3. Remove governor cover retainer and cover.
4. Remove governor.

Intermediate Clutch Accumulator Piston Assembly

1. Remove two oil pan bolts adjacent to accumulator piston cover, install compressor on oil pan lip and retain with these two bolts.
2. Compress intermediate clutch accumulator piston cover and remove retaining ring piston cover and O ring from case.
3. Remove spring and intermediate clutch accumulator piston.

Vacuum Modulator & Modulator Valve Assembly

1. Disconnect vacuum hose from modulator stem and remove vacuum modulator screw and retainer.
2. Remove modulator and its O ring.
3. Remove modulator valve from case.

Extension Housing Oil Seal

1. Remove propeller shaft.
2. Pry out lip seal with screwdriver or small chisel.

Manual Shaft, Range Selector Inner Lever & Parking Linkage Assemblies

1. Remove oil pan and strainer.
2. Remove manual shaft to case retainer and unthread jam nut holding range selector inner lever to manual shaft.
3. Remove jam nut and remove manual shaft from range selector inner lever and case. *Do not remove manual shaft lip seal unless replacement is required.*
4. Disconnect parking pawl actuating rod from range selector inner lever and remove bolt from case.
5. Remove bolts and parking lock bracket.
6. Remove pawl disengaging spring.
7. If necessary to replace pawl or shaft, clean up bore in case and remove shaft retaining plug, shaft and pawl.

Turbo Hydra-Matic 425

DESCRIPTION

This transmission is a fully automatic unit used for front wheel drive applications, Fig. 1. It consists primarily of a three-element hydraulic torque converter, dual sprocket and chain link assembly, compound planetary gear set, three multiple disc clutches, a sprag clutch, a roller clutch, two band assemblies, and a hydraulic control system.

Torque Converter

The torque converter consists of a pump or driving member, a turbine or driven member and a stator or reaction member.

The stator is mounted on a one-way roller clutch which allows it to overrun when not used as a reaction member.

The torque converter couples the engine to the planetary gear set through the use of a drive sprocket, a chain link assembly, and a driven sprocket. Clockwise engine torque turns the drive sprocket clockwise. This, in turn, drives the driven sprocket in a clockwise direction. This in effect is a reverse in the direction of engine torque due to the side mounting of the gear unit.

Planetary Gear Set

The gear set provides three forward ratios and reverse.

TROUBLE SHOOTING GUIDE

NOTE: In many of the following diagnosis procedures, it is recommended that air pressure be applied to help in determining if the seal, rings or pistons are stuck, missing or damaged. Therefore, when air is applied, listen carefully for escaping air and piston action as air is applied to a particular area.

No Drive In "D" Range

1. Low oil level. Check for external leaks or vacuum modulator diaphragm leaking.
2. Manual linkage maladjusted. Correct alignment in manual lever shift quadrant.
3. Low oil pressure.
4. Oil strainer O-ring seal missing or damaged, neck weld leaking, strainer blocked.
5. Oil pump pressure regulator stuck or inoperative. Pump drive gear tangs damaged by converter.
6. Case porosity in intake bore.
7. Control valve. Manual valve disconnected from manual lever pin. (Other shift lever positions would also be affected.)
8. Forward clutch does not apply. Piston cracked; seals missing or damaged. These defects can be checked by removing the valve body and applying air pressure to the drive cavity in the case valve body face. Missing, damaged or worn oil rings on driven support housing can also be checked in this manner at the same time because they can also cause the forward clutch not to apply. Clutch plates burned.
9. Roller clutch inoperative. Rollers worn, damaged springs, or damaged races. May be checked by placing selector lever in "L" range.

No Drive In "R" or Slips In Reverse

1. Low oil level.
2. Manual linkage.
3. Oil pressure. Vacuum modulator defective, modulator valve sticking.
4. Restricted strainer, leak at intake pipe or O-ring seal. Pressure regulator or boost valve sticking.
5. Control valve body gaskets leaking or damaged (other malfunctions may also be indicated). Low-reverse check ball missing from case (this will cause no overrun braking in low range). The 2-3 valve train stuck open (this will also cause 1-3 upshifts in drive range). Reverse feed passage not drilled; also check case passages. Apply air to reverse passage in case valve body face.
6. Rear servo and accumulator. Servo piston seal ring broken or missing. Apply air pressure to drilled hole in intermediate clutch passage of case valve body face to check for piston operation and excessive leakage. Band apply pin too short (this may also cause no overrun braking or slip in overrrun braking in low range).
7. Rear band burned, loose lining, apply pin or anchor pin not engaged; band broken.
8. Direct clutch outer seal damaged or missing. Clutch plates burned (may be caused by stuck ball check in piston).
9. Forward clutch does not release (will also cause drive in neutral range).

Drive In Neutral

1. Manual linkage maladjusted.
2. Forward clutch does not release (this condition will also cause no reverse).

1st Speed Only—No 1-2 Upshift

1. Governor valve sticking; driven gear loose, damaged or worn. If driven gear

AUTOMATIC TRANSMISSIONS

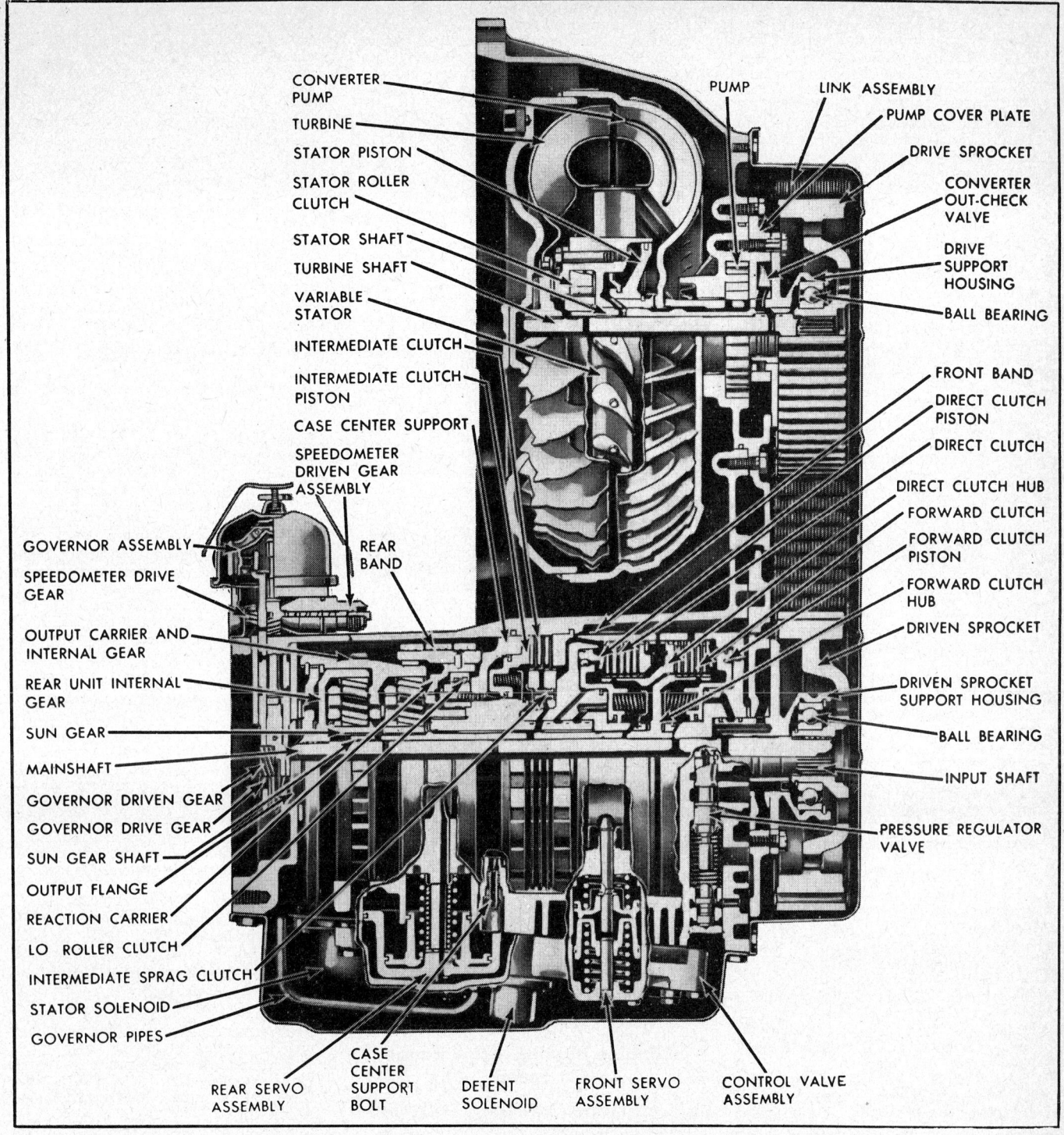

Fig. 1 General Motors front wheel drive Turbo Hydra-Matic transmission

shows signs of water or damage, check output flange drive gear for nicks or rough finish.
2. Control valve. The 1-2 shift valve train stuck closed. Dirt, chips or damaged valve in 1-2 shift valve train. Governor feeds channels blocked or leaking; pipes out of position. Valve body gaskets leaking or damaged. Case porosity between oil channels. Governor feed passage blocked.
3. Intermediate clutch. Case center support oil rings missing, broken or defective. Clutch piston seals missing, improperly assembled, cut or damaged. Apply air to intermediate clutch passage located in case valve body face to check for these defects.

1-2 Shift Obtained Only At Full Throttle

1. Detent switch sticking or defective.
2. Detent solenoid loose, gasket leaking, sticks open, electrical wire pinched between cover and casting.
3. Control valve body gasket leaking or damaged. Detent valve train stuck.

1st & 2nd Speeds Only No 2-3 Shift

1. Detent solenoid stuck open (the 2-3 shift would occur at very high speeds) may be diagnosed as no 2-3 shift.

549

AUTOMATIC TRANSMISSIONS

2. Detent switch sticking or defective.
3. Control valve body. The 2-3 valve train stuck with dirt or foreign material. Valve body gaskets leaking or damaged.
4. Direct clutch. Case center support oil rings missing or broken. Clutch piston seals missing, improperly assembled, cut or damaged; piston ball check stuck or missing. Apply air to direct clutch passage in case valve body face to check these conditions.

Slips In All Ranges

1. Oil level incorrect.
2. Low oil pressure. Vacuum modulator defective or valve sticking. Oil strainer plugged or leaks at neck; O-ring (case to strainer) missing or damaged. Pressure regulator or boost valve sticking.
3. Case cross channel leaks; porosity.
4. Forward, intermediate and direct clutches slipping. Clutch plates burned. Always look for a primary defect that would cause clutch plates to burn. (Missing feed holes, seals and oil rings, etc., are primary defects).
5. Roller clutch rollers worn; springs or cage damaged, and worn or damaged races (operates normally in low and reverse ranges).

Slips 1-2 Shift

1. Oil level incorrect.
2. Low oil pressure. Look for defective vacuum modulator or valve sticking. Pump Pressure regulator valve stuck.
3. Front servo accumulator piston cracked or porous, oil rings damaged or missing.
4. Control valve. The 1-2 accumulator valve train (may cause a slip-bump shift). Porous valve body or case valve body face.
5. Rear servo accumulator oil ring missing or damaged; case bore damaged; piston cracked or damaged.
6. Case porous between oil passages.
7. Intermediate clutch lip seals missing, cut or damaged. Apply air pressure to intermediate clutch passage in case valve body face to check. Clutch plates burned. Case center support leaks in feed circuits (oil rings damaged or grooves damaged) or excessive leak between tower and bushing.

Rough 1-2 Shift

1. Oil pressure. Check vacuum modulator for loose fittings, restrictions in line; defective vacuum modulator. Modulator valve stuck. Pressure regulator boost valve stuck.
2. Control valve. 1-2 accumulator valve train; valve body-to-case bolts loose; gaskets inverted, off location, or damaged.
3. Case. Intermediate clutch passage check ball missing or not seating. Case porous between channels.
4. Rear servo accumulator piston stuck. Apply air pressure to 1-2 accumulator passage in case valve body face(you should hear the servo piston move). Broken or missing spring; bore scored or damaged.

Slips 2-3 Shift

1. Oil level high or low.
2. Low oil pressure. Modulator defective or valve sticking. Pump pressure regulator valve or boost valve sticking.
3. Control valve. Accumulator piston pin leak at valve body end.
4. Direct clutch piston seals leaking. Case center support oil seal rings damaged or excessive leak between tower and bushing. Apply air to direct clutch passage in case valve body face. If air comes out intermediate passage, center support is defective.

Rough 2-3 Shift

1. Oil pressure high. Vacuum modulator defective or valve sticking. Pump pressure regulator valve or boost valve stuck or inoperative.
2. Front servo accumulator spring missing or broken; accumulator piston stuck.

Shifts Occur at Too High or Too Low Car Speed

1. Oil pressure. Vacuum modulator defective or valve sticking. Leak in vacuum line (engine to transmission). Vacuum modulator line fitting on carburetor blocked. Pump pressure regulator valve or boost valve train stuck.
2. Governor valve stuck or sticking. Feed holes restricted or leaking; pipes damaged or mispositioned.
3. Detent solenoid stuck open or loose on valve body (will cause late shifts).
4. Control valve. Detent valve train sticking; 3-2 valve train sticking; 1-2 shift valve stuck; 1-2 detent valve sticking open (will probably cause early 2-3 shift).
5. Spacer plate gaskets inverted or mispositioned; orifice holes missing or blocked; check balls missing or mislocated.
6. Case porous in channels or foreign material blocking channels.

No Detent Downshift

1. Detent switch mispositioned or electrical connections loose.
2. Solenoid defective or electrical connections loose.
3. Control valve detent valve train stuck.

No Engine Braking—Super Range 2nd Speed

1. Front servo or accumulator piston rings broken or missing. Case or valve body bores worn oversize, causing excessive leakage.
2. Front band worn or burned (check for cause); band end lugs broken or damaged; band lugs not engaged on anchor pins or servo apply pin (check for cause).

No Engine Braking—Low Range 1st Speed

1. Control valve low-reverse check ball missing from case.
2. Rear servo oil ring damaged or missing; piston damaged or porous, causing a leak in apply pressure.
3. Rear band lining worn or burned (check for cause); band end lugs broken; band ends not engaged on anchor pin or servo apply pin. These items will also cause slip in reverse or no reverse.

Will Not Hold Car In Park Position

1. Manual linkage maladjusted (external).
2. Parking brake lever and actuator rod assembly defective (check for proper actuator spring action). Parking pawl broken or inoperative.

Poor Performance or Rough Idle

1. Stator switch defective or maladjusted.
2. Stator solenoid defective or wire ground to solenoid housing; electrical connection loose; stator valve train stuck (located in valve body); oil feed circuit to stator restricted or blocked (check feed hole in stator shaft); converter-out check valve broken or missing (reed valve located in cover plate under drive support housing).
3. Turbine shaft converter return passage not drilled; oil seal rings broken, worn or missing.
4. Case porous in feed circuit channels or foreign material blocking feed circuit.
5. Converter assembly defective.

Transmission Noise

1. Pump noise. Oil level high or low; water in oil, driving gear assembled upside down; driving or driven gear teeth damaged.
2. Gear noise (1st gear drive range). Check planetary pinions for tooth damage. Check sun gear and front and rear internal gears for tooth finish or damage.
3. Clutch noise during application. Check clutch plates.
4. Sprocket and chain link assembly. Chain link too long (sounds similar to popcorn popping). There will be a rough burr along teeth or drive sprocket if chain link is too long; replace chain link and drive sprocket. Drive or driven sprocket teeth damaged. Engine mounts worn or damaged.

Burned Forward Clutch Plates

1. Check ball in clutch housing damaged, stuck or missing.
2. Clutch piston cracked, seals damaged or missing.
3. Low line pressure.
4. Manual valve mispositioned.
5. Restricted oil feed to forward clutch.
6. Pump cover oil seal rings missing, broken or undersize or ring groove oversize.
7. Case valve body face not flat or porosity between channels.
8. Manual valve bent and center land not ground properly.

Burned Intermediate Clutch Plates

1. Rear accumulator piston oil ring damaged or missing.
2. 1-2 accumulator valve stuck in control valve assembly.
3. Intermediate clutch piston seals damaged or missing.
4. Center support bolt loose.
5. Low line pressure.
6. Intermediate clutch plug in case missing.
7. Case valve body face not flat or porosity between channels.
8. Manual valve bent and center land not ground properly.

Burned Direct Clutch Plates

1. Restricted orifice in vacuum line to modulator.
2. Check ball in direct clutch piston damaged, stuck or missing.
3. Defective modulator bellows.
4. Center support bolt loose.

AUTOMATIC TRANSMISSIONS

5. Center support oil rings or grooves damaged or missing.
6. Clutch piston seals damaged or missing.
7. Front and rear servo pistons and seals damaged.
8. Manual valve bent and center land not cleaned up.
9. Case valve body face not flat or porosity between channels.
10. Intermediate sprag clutch installed backwards.

MAINTENANCE
Adding Oil

The fluid level should be checked at every engine oil change interval, and should be changed at 12,000 mile intervals. The fluid level should be checked with the selector lever in PARK position, engine running at the idle speed and vehicle on a level surface. *The filler tubes comes out from the final drive housing but it is for the transmission.*

Changing Oil

When changing transmission oil, first add 4 quarts, start the engine, and add oil to bring the fluid level to the FULL mark on the dipstick. Total capacity after overhaul is 10 quarts. Use on Dexron automatic transmission oil.

NOTE: Beginning with late 1973 models, General Motors is using a revised type Dexron fluid. An early change to a darker color from the usual red color and or a strong odor that is usually associated with over-heated fluid is normal, and should not be treated as a positive sign of needed maintenance or unit failure.

The normal maintenance schedule for drain and refill of this type fluid remains unchanged at 12,000.

ANTI-SKID BRAKE SYSTEMS

INDEX

	Page No.
A/C (General Motors) System	559
Eaton	557
International Harvester Adaptive System	551
Kelsey-Hayes	557
Rockwell-Standard Skid-Trol System	553

INTERNATIONAL ADAPTIVE BRAKE SYSTEM

This system is designed to prevent any wheel from locking up during brake applications above a speed of about 5 mph. The system reduces skid potential of a locked wheel and still maintains brake pressure for maximum stopping effort. The end result is to improve directional control and steerability of the vehicle, and in many cases to reduce the distance required to bring the vehicle to a stop.

The major components of this system are shown in Fig. 1. These include a mechanically driven speed sensor at each rear wheel, an electronic control unit located on the dash panel left side in the passenger compartment and a pressure modulator in the left side of the engine compartment.

The speed sensors incorporate a stationary permanent magnet and coil in one case and a tone wheel, Fig. 2, which are attached to a mounting bracket. Part of the mounting bracket forms a spring to hold the tone wheel knurled shaft in contact with the rubber drive band pressed into the drive ring. The drive ring, located between the axle flange and drum, rotates with the rear wheel.

The pressure modulator, Fig. 3, incorporates a vacuum chamber, bypass tube, end plate, air valve, bypass valve and pressure modulator switch. Engine vacuum is applied to the modulator. The hydraulic circuit for the rear brakes is routed from the master cylinder, through the brake warning light switch to the pressure modulator and on to the rear brakes.

Operation

Engine Running—Vehicle Not In Motion

The wheel sensors do not generate any signals for transmission to the electronic control unit when the vehicle is not in motion. Hence, the electronic control unit sends no commands to the pressure modulator.

Engine Running—Vehicle In Motion

With the vehicle in motion, alternating current voltage is generated at each rear wheel sensor and sent to the electronic control unit. The electronic control unit processes the signals received from the rear wheel sensors to sample the speed of each rear wheel. If the brakes are not applied or if they are applied lightly, the electronic control unit does not send any commands to the pressure modulator.

When the brakes are applied with greater force, the electronic control unit, based on wheel sensor signals, determines the rate at which each rear wheel is decelerating. If the rate is great and might produce wheel slippage or lockup, the electronic control unit sends a command to the modulator that controls the braking for the rear wheel or wheels concerned.

Exercise Cycle

If the engine is started with the brake pedal depressed, the pressure modulator goes through an exercise cycle. When the ignition switch is turned from OFF to START the modulator cycles once. This cycle insures that the system is working properly. The cycle can be heard under some conditions, but should not be a cause for concern.

Warning System

This anti-skid system includes a secondary system to warn the driver of certain types of failures in the system. The warning system uses the brake warning light. The warning light will be on under the following conditions:
1. If the pressure modulator is activated in the absence of a brake light signal.
2. If the electronic control unit sends a signal to open the air valve on a modulator in the absence of a signal to open the bypass valve.

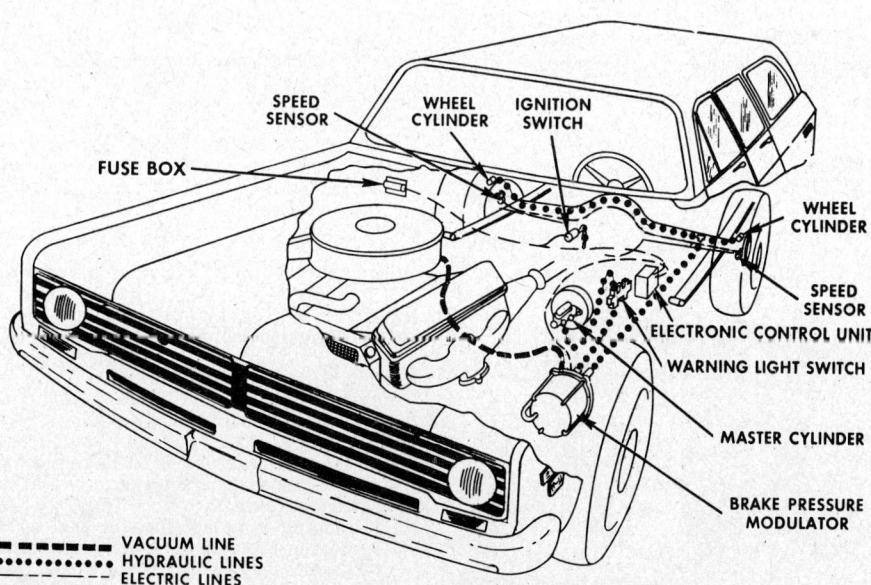

Fig. 1 International Harvester anti-skid brake system components

ANTI-SKID BRAKE SYSTEMS

3. If the electrical continuity of the air valve lead wire is broken.
4. If a blown fuse, loose connection or open circuit occurs between the ignition switch and the electronic control unit.

Disabling Anti-Skid System

If necessary parts or service is not available, the system should be disabled. The brakes will then function the same as those on trucks without this system. Proceed as follows:

Disconnect the electronic control unit (all three connectors), Fig. 4, and the vacuum supply hose at the manifold fitting, Fig. 5. The fitting and the hose to the modulator should be plugged to prevent entry of foreign material.

An additional step may be necessary to disable the system for one type of failure that can occur. If the modulator diaphragm plate sticks in the retracted position, hydraulic pressure is cut off from the rear brakes. To determine if this malfunction is present, have a helper depress the brake pedal and open a rear brake bleeder screw. If the fluid runs freely, the shut-off valve is open. If not, the valve is closed and the modulator must be bypassed. This can be accomplished as follows:

Disconnect both hydraulic lines from modulator, bend lines slightly and connect the two lines using an adapter and a union. This is done in conjunction with disconnecting the electrical and vacuum systems.

Trouble-Shooting

Brake Warning Lamp (Red) Test

1. Turn ignition switch to "Start" position, if warning lamp does not light when engine cranks, replace lamp bulb or repair warning circuit as necessary.
2. If warning lamp remains lit after bulb is replaced or circuit repaired, proceed to next step to determine if malfunction is in anti-skid system or basic brake system. If warning lamp is lit while engine cranks and goes out when engine starts, proceed to "Electrical Circuit Tests."
3. To determine if malfunction is in anti-skid system or basic brake system when warning lamp remains "On", disconnect electrical lead from brake warning switch. If warning lamp goes out, malfunction is in basic brake system and must be repaired. If warning lamp remains lit, proceed to "Electrical Circuit Tests".

Anti-Skid Brake Cycling Indicator Lamp (Green) Test

1. Disconnect cycling lamp connector, Fig. 4, and connect a jumper wire from the battery positive terminal to lamp side of connector. If lamp does not light, replace bulb and socket assembly.
2. If lamp lights in step 1, remove jumper wire and connect cycling lamp connector. Check anti-skid system by road testing vehicle on gravel or similar surface at a reasonable speed but at a minimum of 20 MPH. Apply sufficient brake pedal pressure to normally lock wheels and observe cycling lamp. If cycling lamp flickers and rear wheels appear to roll at low speed then lock, the anti-skid brake system is

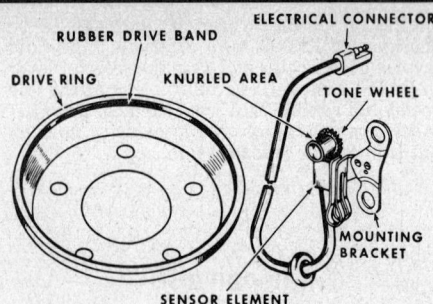

Fig. 2 Speed sensor & drive ring assembly

satisfactory. If not, proceed to "Electrical Circuit Tests".

Electrical Circuit Tests

Step 1: Checks at Electronic Control Unit

Make measurements listed in Fig. 6 at the Electronic Control Unit connectors, Fig. 7. The connectors should be disconnected except those measurements indicated with a double asterisk (**). All readings must be obtained from the terminals on the side of the connector attached to the brake harness modulator cable assembly and speed sensor assembly. If any reading is not within specifications, refer to indicated step for additional measurements or repairs.

Step 2: Modulator Switch Circuit

NOTE: Make measurements in sequence of steps listed below to identify faulty components. When faulty component has been identified, reconnect all connectors except A, B and C at ECU, Fig. 4. Repeat measurement in Step 1 which produced incorrect reading. This repeat measurement is necessary to insure malfunction still exists prior to replacing any component.

a. Disconnect connector D, Fig. 4, and on modulator lead side of connector, measure resistance between Pin 3 and the ground. If zero ohms is indicated, replace modulator cable. If any reading above zero ohms is obtained, modulator or modulator switch is faulty and modulator must be replaced.

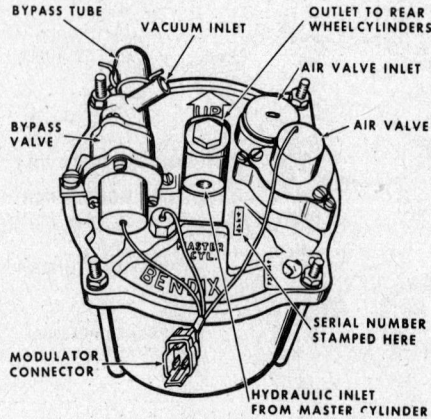

Fig. 3 Pressure modulator

Step 3: Air Valve & Bypass Valve Circuits

Refer to NOTE under "Step 2; Modulator Switch Circuit" and proceed as follows:
a. With connector D, Fig. 4, disconnected, measure resistance between pin which had incorrect reading and the ground. If reading obtained is 3 to 5 ohms, replace modulator cable assembly. If reading obtained is not within specifications, replace modulator.

Step 4: Electronic Control Unit Ground Circuit

a. Disconnect body ground wire from under instrument panel, clean wire end eye and ground point on body where eye is secured and reconnect the ground wire.
b. Measure resistance between Pin 2 on brake harness side of connector B and the ground. If zero ohms is indicated, the ground connection was unsatisfactory and the malfunction has been corrected. If any reading above zero ohms is obtained, replace brake harness.

Step 5: Power Supply Circuit

Refer to NOTE under "Step 2: Modulator Switch Circuit" and proceed as follows:
a. Check for blown 10 amp fuse in-line between ignition switch and connector and replace if necessary. If fuse is satisfactory, ensure circuit is properly connected to ignition switch and battery voltage is present at ignition switch terminal.
b. If fuse and circuit connections are satisfactory and battery voltage is present at switch terminal but not at Pin 4, connector B with ignition switch "On", replace brake harness.

Step 6: Stop Light to Electronic Control Unit Circuit

Refer to NOTE under "Step 2: Modulator Switch Circuit" and proceed as follows:
a. Measure DC voltage between output side of stop light switch and the ground with the brakes applied. If battery voltage is obtained, replace brake harness. If reading obtained is below battery voltage, measure DC voltage between battery side of stop light switch and the ground. If battery voltage is obtained, adjust stop light switch position or replace switch as necessary. If reading is below battery voltage, check wiring to stop light switch and repair as necessary.

Step 7: Voltage Feedback

Refer to NOTE under "Step 2: Modulator Switch Circuit" and proceed as follows:
a. Check stop lamp operation and correct if necessary. Repeat measurement which produced incorrect reading. If reading is still above zero volts, check tail light-stop light assemblies for proper ground connections and repair as necessary.

Step 8: Electronic Control Unit Circuits

If reading obtained is not within specifications, the electronic control unit is faulty, requiring replacement.

Step 9: Warning Light Circuit

Refer to NOTE under "Step 2: Modulator Switch Circuit" and proceed as follows:
a. Separate connectors E and F, Fig. 8, then on the speed sensor side of the connectors, repeat measurement which produced incorrect reading.
b. If reading is as specified in Fig. 6, the speed sensor cable is defective and must be replaced. If reading is not within specifications, disconnect speed sensor connector in line with connector which had faul-

ANTI-SKID BRAKE SYSTEMS

ty reading. Measure resistance between the two terminals and between each terminal and the ground.

c. If all readings are correct, replace rear axle sensor harness. If any reading is not within specifications, the corresponding speed sensor is faulty, requiring replacement.

Modulator Test

a. With engine operating, disconnect connector D, Fig. 4, and on modulator side of connector, measure resistance between Pin 3 and the ground.
b. If reading obtained is above zero ohms, replace modulator.

Vacuum & Hydraulic Tests

Step 1: Vacuum Supply Check
a. Ensure all vacuum hose connections are proper, start engine and check for vacuum leaks. Repair as necessary.
b. Connect a vacuum gauge between modulator vacuum hose and modulator inlet. Gauge should indicate normal engine vacuum. If not, check for vacuum leak or tune engine as necessary.

Step 2: Air Valve & Bypass Valve Operation
a. With connector D, Fig. 4, disconnected, start engine and observe vacuum reading.

NOTE: Air valve and bypass valve should not be energized for more than two minutes with a five minute cooling-off period between since valve solenoids may be damaged by excessive heat.

b. Connect a jumper wire between battery positive terminal and Pin 1 on modulator side of connector. Vacuum reading should drop. If not, replace modulator.
c. Connect a second jumper wire from the battery positive terminal and Pin 2 on the connector, leaving the first jumper wire in place. The vacuum reading should increase to reading previously noted in step a. If not, replace modulator. If vacuum reading does increase, proceed to Step 3.

Step 3: Hydraulic Shut-Off Valve
a. Install a suitable hydraulic pressure gauge in modulator output and bleed air from system and gauge.
b. Start engine and apply brake pedal to obtain a 500-600 PSI reading.

NOTE: The air and bypass valves should not be energized for more than two minutes with a five minute cooling-off period between since the valve solenoids may be damaged by excessive heat.

c. With brake pedal still depressed, connect jumper wires between battery positive terminal and Pins 1 and 2 on modulator side of connector D. The hydraulic pressure should drop to zero and if not, replace modulator.
d. Hold brake pedal depressed and keep jumper wires connected for a two minute period. Hydraulic pressure should not rise during this period. If the pressure did rise, replace modulator.

Step 4:
If results of all three steps are normal, the electronic control unit is faulty, requiring replacement.

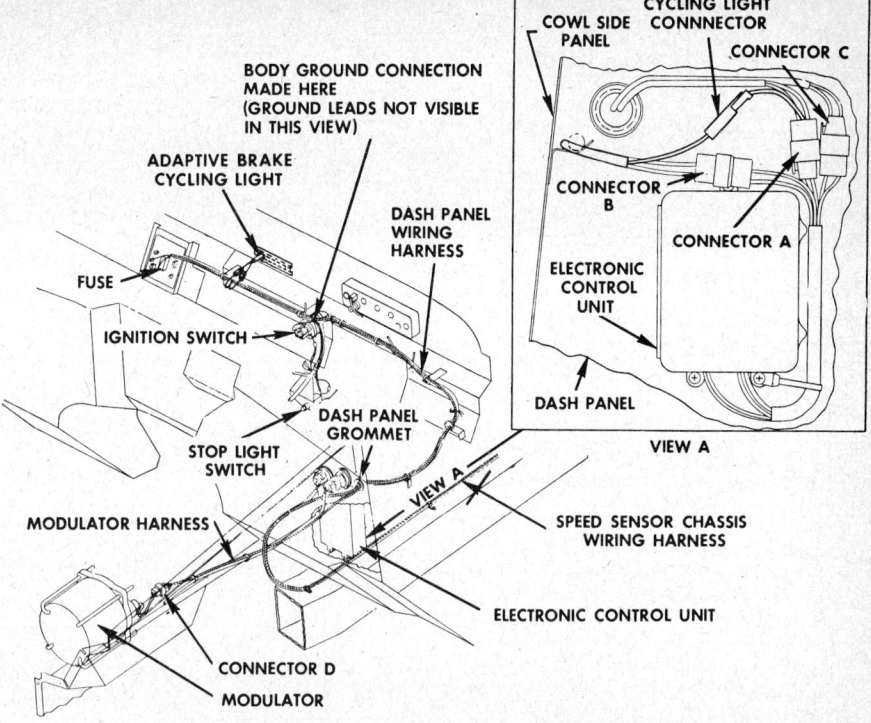

Fig. 4 Anti-skid brake system body & cab wiring schematic

Hydraulic Output Test

a. Connect a suitable hydraulic pressure gauge in modulator output and bleed air from system and gauge.
b. Disconnect connector D, Fig. 4, and connect a jumper wire between battery positive terminal and Pin 2 on modulator side of connector D.

NOTE: Air and bypass valves should not be energized for more than two minutes with a five minute cooling-off period between since the valve solenoids may be damaged by excessive heat.

c. Start engine and depress brake pedal to obtain a pressure of 600 PSI. If hydraulic pressure does not rise when brake pedal is depressed, replace modulator.

False Cycling Test

Step 1: Speed Sensor Inspection
a. Remove rear wheel and drum and ensure sensor mounting bracket holds sensor knurled wheel against drive ring rubber drive band. Remove drive ring.
b. Check tone wheel teeth, sensor mounting bracket and sensor lead for damage. Ensure sensor wheel can be easily turned.
c. Inspect rubber drive band pressed into drive ring for slippage inside ring or for damage. Replace drive ring if necessary.
d. Inspect sensor knurled wheel for deposits of foreign material. If deposits are excessive, clean knurled area with a knife.
e. Install drive ring, drum and wheel.

Step 2: Functional Check
a. Drive over a rough road (gravel road, brick road or similar surface) with light pressure on brake pedal until the false cycling occurs. Keep speed under 15 MPH.
b. Connect a jumper wire between Pins 1 and 3 of connector C with the connector joined.
c. Disconnect one speed sensor at a time and drive over same area and under same conditions which produced false cycling.
d. When false cycling stops, replace disconnected speed sensor. Remove jumper wire from connector C.
e. If both speed sensors function properly, the electronic control unit is defective, requiring replacement.

ROCKWELL-STANDARD SKID-TROL

Computer/Control Valve

The computer/control valve assembly, Figs. 9 and 10, functions as a normal brake relay valve and as a solenoid operated modulative valve. During normal operation, the valve supplies air to the brake chambers. This air pressure is equal to the pressure supplied from the treadle (brake) valve. Air pressure from the treadle valve is transmitted through

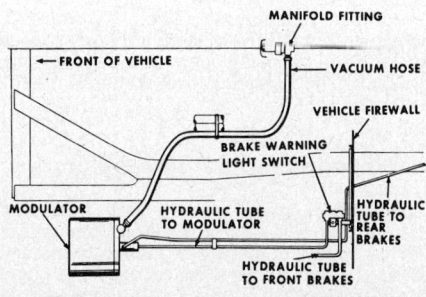

Fig. 5 Vacuum & hydraulic system routing

553

ANTI-SKID BRAKE SYSTEMS

Between	and	Measure	Ignition Switch	Brake Pedal	Reading Should Be	If not, refer to
Connector A-3 Pin						
Pin 1	Ground	Ohms	Off	Released	3.0-5.0	Step 3
Pin 2	Ground	Ohms	Off	Released	3.0-5.0	Step 3
Pin 3	Ground	Ohms	Off	Released	0	Step 2
Pin 2**	Ground	DC Volts	On	Applied	0	Step 8
Pin 1**	Ground	DC Volts	On	Applied	0	Step 8
Connector B-4 Pin						
Pin 1	Ground	DC Volts	Off	Applied	12*	Step 6
Pin 1***	Ground	DC Volts	Off	Released	0 w/Headlights ON	Step 7
Pin 2**	Pin 2 Connector C	Ohms	Off	Released	0	Step 8
Pin 3	Ground	DC Volts	On	Released	12*	Step 9
Pin 2	Ground	Ohms	Off	Released	0	Step 4
Pin 4	Ground	DC Volts	On	Released	12*	Step 5
Connector C-3 Pin						
Pin 1	Ground	Ohms	Off	Released	Above 50,000	Step 10
Pin 1	Pin 2	Ohms	Off	Released	250-350	Step 10
Pin 2	Ground	Ohms	Off	Released	Above 50,000	Step 10
Pin 3	Ground	Ohms	Off	Released	Above 50,000	Step 10
Pin 3	Pin 2	Ohms	Off	Released	250-350	Step 10

*Should be same as battery voltage.
**Make measurements with all connectors connected.
***Make measurements with headlights on.

Fig. 6 Circuit checks at electronic control unit

the solenoid to the top of the diaphragm, in turn, forcing the diaphragm downward, opening the poppet valve and permits supply air to flow through the delivery ports to the brake chamber.

When Skid-Trol action is initiated by the computer which has sensed imminent wheel lock, the air pressure transmitted to the brake chambers is modulated through solenoid action. When the solenoid is energized by the computer, air pressure from the treadle valve is blocked off and the existing air is directed to exhaust. The diaphragm then moves upward, in turn, closing the poppet supply seat, opening the exhaust seat and directs brake chamber air to exhaust.

The computer is a fully solid state unit encased in the control valve body and is totally sealed. The computer circuitry operates on either positive or negative ground and includes provisions for two wheel speed sensor inputs, a solenoid input a 12 volt D.C. power input and a failure warning indication circuit. The wheel speed sensors send velocity information to the computer. The computer, in turn, processes this data and directs the control valve to provide the necessary corrective action to adjust brake pressure. The internal failure sensing circuitry monitors the system for proper functioning. When a failure is detected, this failure sensing circuitry causes an internal fuse to open and returns the brakes on the affected axle to standard manual control.

Wheel Speed Sensors & Rotors

The wheel speed sensors used with this system are self-generating electromagnetic devices which generate a signal frequency directly proportional to wheel speed. A pulse is generated each time a tooth of the slotted rotor passes the sensor. The sensor consists of a permanent magnet, two coils and an output cable placed in the adjusting spring and into the housing Fig. 11. The sensor is automatically adjusted to the proper position when the rotor pushes against the sensor as the hub and drum assembly is installed.

The rotor is mounted against the inner surface of the brake drum in place of the grease slinger. The assembly rotates with the wheel and drum with the minimum allowable radial and axial runout. The radial runout of the rotor depends on the concentricity between the wheel bearings and axle spindle. Also, if the total axial runout of the rotor exceeds .020 inch, the output signal generated by the sensor will be affected, in turn, feeding an incorrect pulse to the computer.

Diagnosis & Testing

To properly diagnose and test the Skid-Trol

ANTI-SKID BRAKE SYSTEMS

System, the use of Service Aid Tester, tool C-4368, is required. However, the following tests may be performed without the tester:

System Failure Warning Lamp Test

With the engine cranking, the system failure warning lamp should light. If not, check for burned out lamp bulb and wiring for proper connections. If lamp bulb and wiring are satisfactory, perform relay test.

Axle System Failure Test

This test is performed to determine which axle system has failed when the system failure warning lamp is lit.
1. With an ohmeter, check resistance across the relay terminals with the following color coded wires:
   Relay No. 1—Light green wire & brown wire
   Relay No. 2—Dark blue wire & green wire
   Relay No. 3—Dark green wire & tan wire
2. Any relay producing an infinite reading indicates the axle system that has failed. If no infinite reading is obtained at any relay, one relay may be defective. Perform relay test to determine defective relay.

Relay Test

1. With ignition "Off", note location of wiring connectors, then disconnect the connectors.
2. With an ohmmeter, check resistance between the terminals which had the red wire and purple wire connected. Resistance reading should be zero. If not, replace relay.
3. Check resistance between the two remaining terminals. Resistance should be 50 ohms or less. If not, replace relay.

Computer Voltage Test

1. Check battery voltage and note reading.
2. Disconnect computer power cable and turn ignition switch to "Run".
3. Check voltage between black wire and white wire of the disconnected power cable. If voltage obtained is not within one volt of battery voltage, check the 10 amp circuit breaker and the red and white wires for opens, shorts and proper connections.

Relay Voltage Tests

Relay Coil Wire Test
1. Note battery voltage and with computer power cable connected, disconnect the following wires from the relays:
   Relay No. 1—Light green wire & brown wire
   Relay No. 2—Dark blue wire & green wire
   Relay No. 3—Dark green wire & tan wire
2. Turn ignition switch to "Run".
3. Check voltage across the disconnected wires of each relay. Voltage reading should be within one volt of battery voltage. If not, check wiring for opens, shorts and proper connections.

NOTE: If the following wires are shorted to ground, the computer fuse will blow:

Relay No. 1—Light green wire
Relay No. 2—Green wire
Relay No. 3—Tan wire

Relay Contact Wire Test
1. Note battery voltage and disconnect red

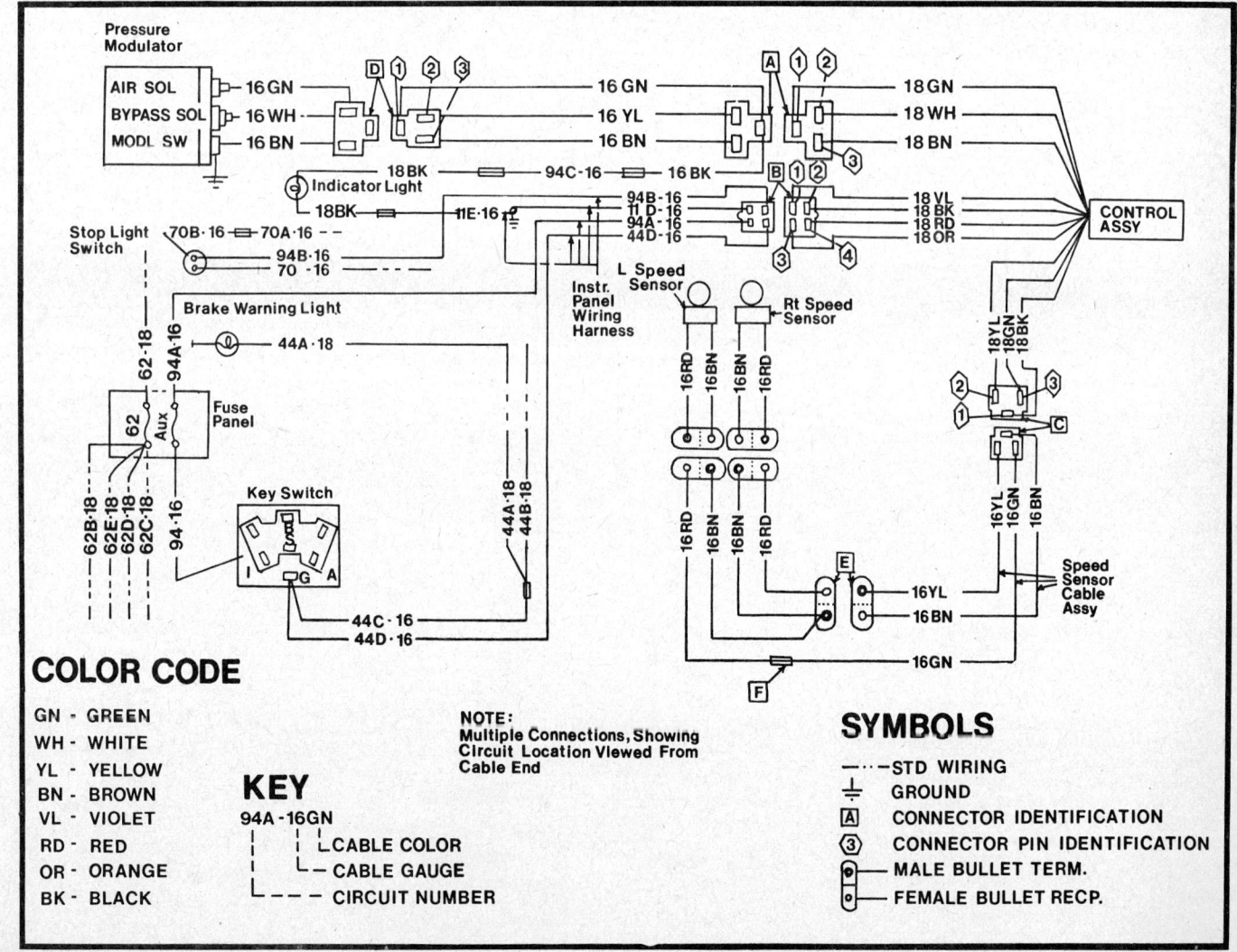

Fig. 7 Anti-skid brake system wiring diagram

ANTI-SKID BRAKE SYSTEMS

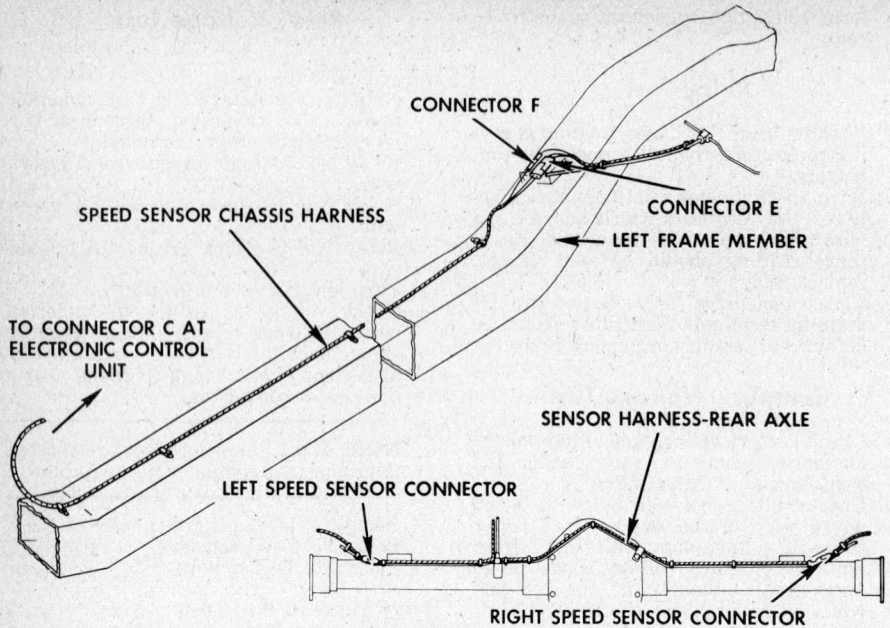

Fig. 8 Anti-skid brake system axle & chassis wiring schematic

4. Remove sensor and adjusting spring from housing by prying out spring, Fig. 13.

Installation
1. Slide new spring over back and sides of sensor.
2. Inspect rubber support caps and replace, if necessary.
3. Install sensor and spring over pins and press until spring engages side of housing.
4. The initial sensor setting is approximately $7/16$ (0.44 inch) inch from housing, Fig. 14. The sensor may be inserted to this setting or a plastic stop can be installed over the pins. If plastic stop is used, remove stop prior to hub and drum installation.
5. Insert connector through hole in brake spider or dust shield and install grommet.
6. Route sensor cable along air delivery hose. Ensure cable does not interfere with any brake component or the hub. Secure cable to air delivery hose at 8 inch intervals.
7. When the wheel is installed, the sensor should be positioned to the maximum setting in the housing. As the wheel nuts are torqued, the rotor acting on the sensor face, forces the sensor back to the correct setting. Ribs, located on the sensor face, will wear slightly during the first few wheel revolutions until clearance is obtained between sensor and rotor.

Rotor Service
1. Raise vehicle and remove hub, drum and tire.
2. Assemble tools on hub and drum, Figs. 15 and 16.
3. Zero dial indicator and using the cone clamp handle, pivot dial indicator around rotor surface, Fig. 17.
4. If runout exceeds .020 inch, replace rotor as follows:
   a. Remove screws and washers securing rotor to brake drum, then the rotor.
   b. Apply a suitable seal to rotor and brake drum contact surfaces.
   c. Install rotor on brake drum and tighten screws.

and purple wires from relays.
2. Turn ignition switch to "Run".
3. Check voltage between disconnected red and purple wires of each relay. Voltage readings should be within one volt of battery voltage. If not, check red and purple wires for opens, shorts and proper connections.

Service

Computer Or Control Valve, Replace

Removal
1. Disconnect vehicle power source and relieve air pressure from reservoir supplying axle system.
2. Remove computer cover to upper housing screws and pull computer and cover assembly from housing. If replacing computer, disconnect power and sensor connectors from cover, Fig. 10.
3. Disconnect solenoid leads from computer, Fig. 12, and position computer aside or remove from vehicle.
4. Disconnect all air lines from control valve, Fig. 10, then remove screws securing control valve and the control valve from vehicle.

Installation
1. Install control valve and attaching screws.
2. Connect air lines to valve. Recharge sully reservoir and check air lines for leaks.
3. Inspect computer cover gasket for damage and replace, if necessary. Use a suitable adhesive to bond gasket to cover.
4. Connect computer solenoid leads.
5. Install computer and cover assembly into upper housing and loosely install attaching screws. Ensure solenoid leads are not pinched between cover and upper housing.
6. Check valve for proper operation by applying brake and observing brake action. No audible leakage should be noted during application and air pressure should rapidly relieve when the brakes are released.
7. Connect power cable connector, if necessary.
8. Torque computer cover screws to 100 inch lbs.
9. Connect sensor connectors, if necessary.

Wheel Sensor, Replace

Removal
1. Cut nylon tie straps securing sensor cable to air delivery hose, however, only up to the inline connector.
2. Disconnect sensor to computer cable at inline connector. Do not twist connector.
3. Slide sensor cable and connector through hole in spider or dust shield.

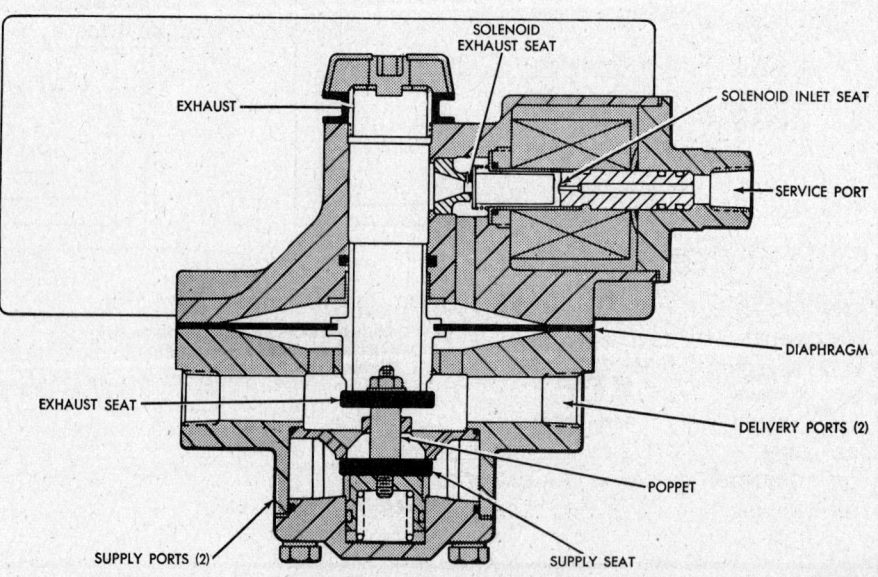

Fig. 9 Cross-sectional view of computer/control valve

ANTI-SKID BRAKE SYSTEMS

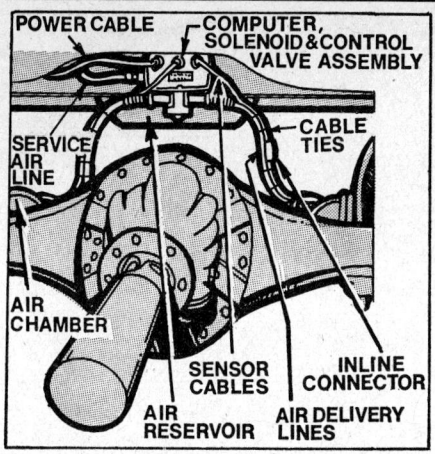

Fig. 10 Computer/Control Valve location

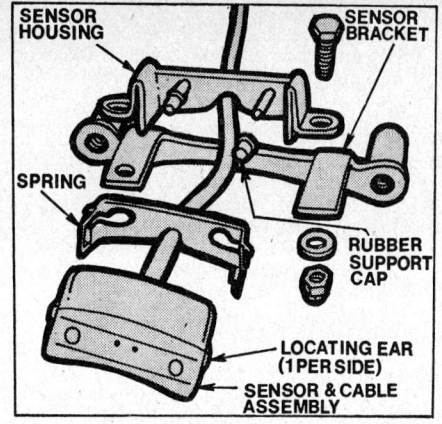

Fig. 11 Sensor components

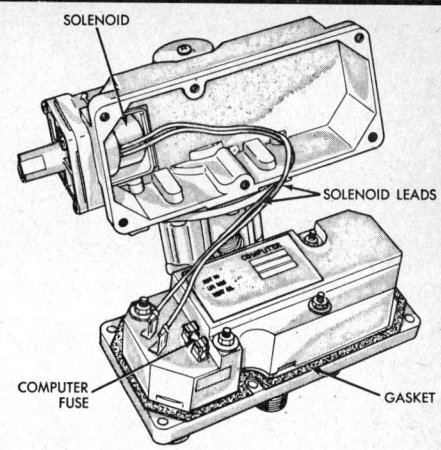

Fig. 12 Solenoid lead connections

EATON & KELSEY-HAYES ANTI-SKID

These two anti-skid systems are basically similar in design and operation, however, the individual system components are not interchangeable, except for the disc assemblies. If a specific system is used on one axle of a truck, that system must be used on all axles. The computer module on the Eaton system is color coded black and gold. The Kelsey-Hayes computer module is color coded blue. Both systems incorporate the following components:

Sensor

The sensor assembly is comprised of the sensor and mounting bracket. On wheels equipped with disc brakes, the sensor is mounted inside one of the bolts securing the brake adapter to the wheel spindle, Fig. 18. On wheels equipped with drum brakes, the sensor is mounted on the brake backing plate, Fig. 19.

The Eaton sensor is mounted on the bracket with spring loaded screw packs and contains a magnet and two coils. The Kelsey-Hayes sensor is friction-fitted in the bracket.

The sensor transmits a voltage to the computer as the notches in the disc assembly "Excite" the sensor. The voltage frequency is directly proportional to wheel speed.

Disc Assembly

On drum brakes, the disc assembly is mounted inside the drum with attaching bolts. On disc brakes, the disc assembly is pressed inside the brake rotor. A ring of notches on the disc are used to "Excite" the sensor as the wheel rotates, Fig. 20.

Monitor Assembly & Warning Lamp

The monitor assembly is an electronic unit that receives signals from the axle modulators, in turn activating the warning lamp in event of a system failure. The warning lamp, mounted on the dash panel, is used to indicate a malfunction in the skid control system.

The warning lamp should light momentarily when the ignition switch is turned "ON". If the lamp stays lit for more than a few seconds, a malfunction is indicated. The bulb and lamp circuit should be checked if the lamp fails to light when the ignition switch is turned "On".

Warning Lamp & Power Relays

The warning lamp relay is used to activate the warning lamp if no power is available to the system. The power relay provides power to the modulators and the monitor assembly. The power relay may be installed specifically for the skid-control system or may be an accessory relay already mounted in the truck.

Modulator Assembly

Anti-Lock Valve Assembly

The anti-lock valve assembly is a combined relay and solenoid valve. The relay valve applies and releases the brakes, responding to foot valve application. The solenoid valve exhausts the air pressure to release the brakes, when the computer determines from the sensor signals that a wheel is locking up.

Computer Assembly

The Solid-state computer determines if a wheel is locking up by receiving sensor signals which are directly the wheel deceleration rate. If a wheel lock-up is sensed, the computer energizes the solenoid valve momentarily, relieving brake pressure, in turn releasing the brakes. The system can cycle up to eight.

Testing & Diagnosis

Modulator Operation & Leak Test

1. Chock wheels and fully charge air brake system.
2. Apply brakes several times and check brake operation at all wheels.
3. With a soap solution, leak test exhaust port under the valve. Slight leakage is permitted as follows:
   a. Brakes applied—a one inch bubble in 3 seconds.
   b. Brakes released—a one inch bubble in 5 seconds.
4. On Eaton systems, separate computer from valve, then leak test solenoid mounting with soap solution. With the brakes fully applied, no leakage is permitted.
5. Replace valve if excessive leakage is noted or if it functions improperly.

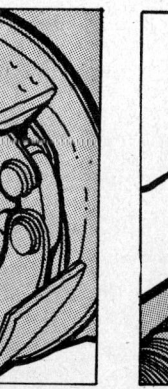

Fig. 13 Sensor removal

Fig. 14 Sensor installation

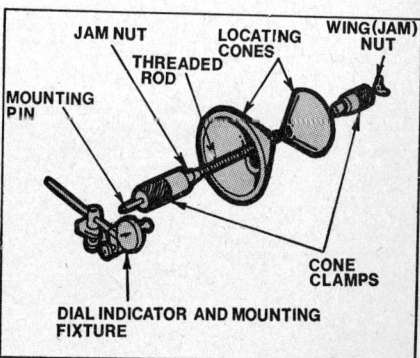

Fig. 15 Rotor runout tools

ANTI-SKID BRAKE SYSTEMS

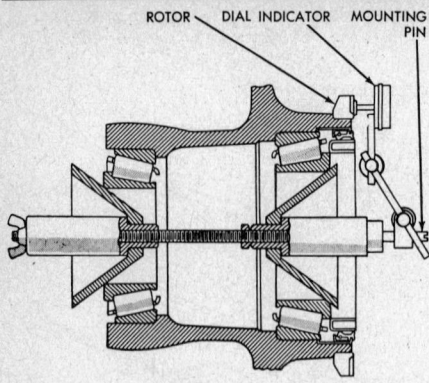

Fig. 16 Rotor runout tools positioned in hub

2. Remove screw packs, Fig. 26 and pull sensor from bracket.
3. Disconnect leads from junction block or modulator and remove sensor from vehicle.

Installation
1. Inspect gauge blocks for wear and replace, if necessary, Fig. 27.
2. Connect sensor leads to junction block.
3. Install sensor on bracket, then the screw packs. Ensure screw pack and lower body fully engage sensor slot.
4. Slide sensor to outermost position on bracket and torque screw packs to 35–50 inch lbs.
5. Install brake drum and wheel. When installing brake drum, avoid rocking drum into position. Use the bearings and spindle nut to position drum. The disc assembly will position and wear the sensor until the proper clearance is obtained.

Kelsey-Hayes Sensor W/Drum Brake, Replace

Removal
1. Remove wheel and brake drum.
2. Remove bracket attaching bolts and separate bracket from brake backing plate, Fig. 19.
3. Push sensor from bracket and disconnect leads from junction block.
4. Remove sensor from vehicle.

Installation
1. Connect sensor leads to junction block.
2. Insert sensor in bracket and place sensor in outermost position in bracket.
3. Install bracket and mounting screws.
4. Install brake drum and wheel. When installing brake drum, avoid rocking drum into position. Use the bearings and spindle nut to position drum. The disc assembly will properly position sensor.

Kelsey-Hayes Sensor W/Disc Brakes, Replace

Removal
1. Disconnect sensor leads at junction block.
2. Remove sensor lead bracket from spindle, Fig. 18.
3. Unscrew sensor from adapter and spindle.
4. Push sensor from bolt.

Installation
1. Insert sensor into bolt and push sensor

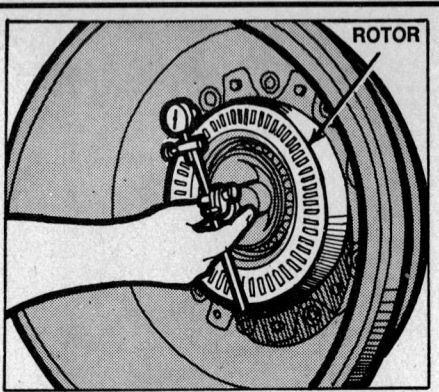

Fig. 17 Checking rotor runout

out to contact disc when bolt and sensor assembly is installed. Then, install the assembly.
2. Install sensor lead bracket on spindle.
3. Connect sensor leads to junction block.

Disc Assembly, Replace

The disc assembly is serviceable only on wheel with drum brakes.

Removal
1. Remove wheel and brake drum.
2. Remove screws securing disc assembly to brake drum, Fig. 19, then the disc assembly.

Installation
1. Attach disc assembly to brake drum.
2. Reposition sensor as outlined under the "Sensor, Replace" procedures.
3. Install brake drum and wheel.

Monitor Assembly, Replace
1. Disconnect wiring connectors from monitor assembly.
2. Remove monitor assembly mounting screws and the monitor assembly.
3. Reverse procedure to install.

Modulator Assembly, Replace

Removal
1. Chock wheels and ensure vehicle will not roll when brakes are released.
2. Drain air system reservoir.
3. Remove cover from computer module or terminal housing.
4. Note location of all electrical connections to computer module, then disconnect the electrical connections.
5. Note location of all air lines to modulator, then disconnect the air lines.
6. Remove modulator mounting bolts and the modulator.

NOTE: It may be necessary to remove the modulator mounting bracket from frame.

Installation
1. Replace damaged air lines.
2. Install modulator on mounting bracket.
3. Connect electrical leads and air lines to modulator.
4. Perform "Modulator Operation & Leak Test" as outlined under "Testing and Diagnosis".

Eaton Computer, Replace
1. Remove through bolts from front of com-

Warning Lamp Operation Test

1. Turn ignition switch to "On" and observe warning lamp. Lamp should light for 2–4 seconds and go out. If lamp remains on, the cause may be the warning relay powering the warning lamp circuit, axle system malfunction or a defective warning monitor assembly.
2. If lamp flashes on and off in step 1, a loose connection is indicated.
3. If lamp fails to light in step 1, replace bulb and recheck. If lamp still does not light, check for proper ground and power to lamp. If voltage is present at the monitor "P" terminal and no voltage at the "W" terminal for 2–4 seconds after turning the ignition switch "On", replace monitor assembly.

Electrical Diagnosis

Refer to the following Figures for electrical diagnostic procedures:
Fig. 21—Kelsey-Hayes monitor assembly diagnosis.
Fig. 22—Kelsey-Hayes modulator and sensor diagnosis.
Fig. 23—Eaton or Kelsey-Hayes power supply diagnosis.
Fig. 24—Eaton monitor assembly diagnosis.
Fig. 25—Eaton modulator and sensor diagnosis.

Service

Eaton Sensor, Replace

Removal
1. Remove wheel and brake drum.

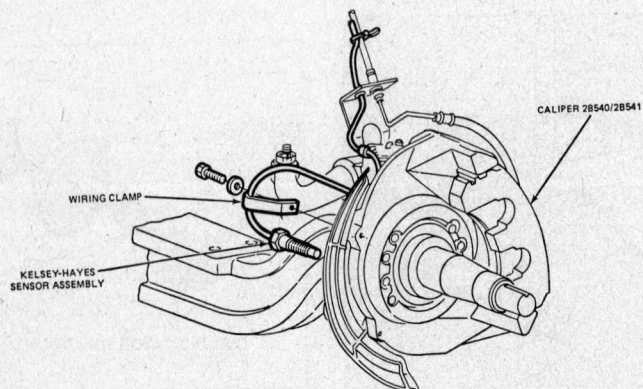

Fig. 18 Sensor installation with disc brakes.

ANTI-SKID BRAKE SYSTEMS

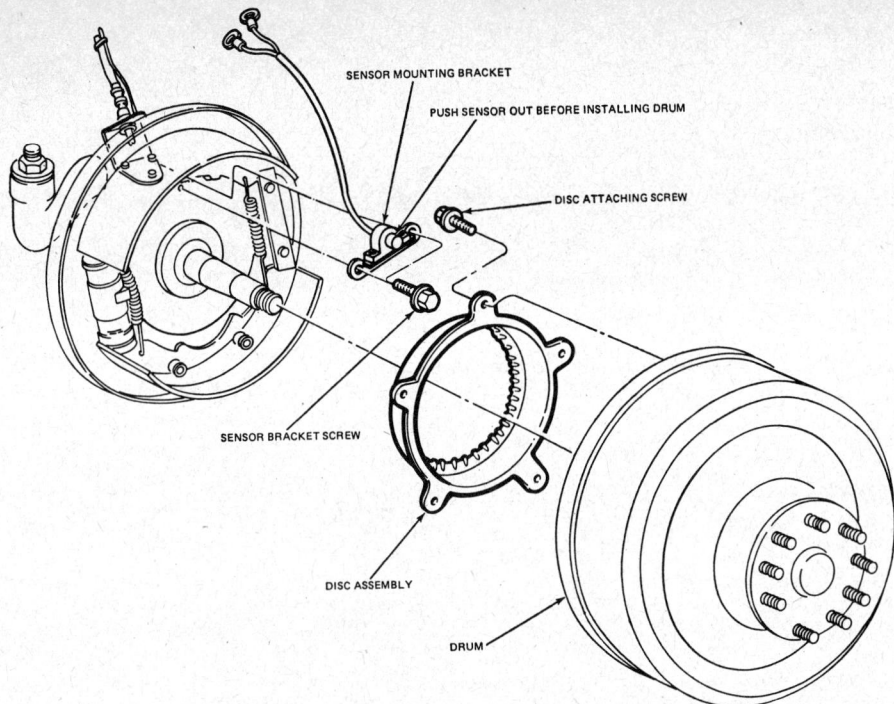

Fig. 19 Sensor installation with drum brakes (Typical)

puter module.
2. Separate computer from valve and disconnect solenoid leads, Fig. 28.
3. Note wiring connections inside computer housing, then disconnect the wiring.
4. Remove spring clip and separate harness from computer housing.
5. Reverse procedure to install.

Kelsey-Hayes Computer, Replace

1. Remove bolts securing computer to valve, Fig. 29.
2. Separate computer from valve, using caution not to stretch solenoid wires.
3. Disconnect solenoid leads and pull dust cover over solenoid leads, Fig. 30.
4. Remove screw securing computer mounting plate to valve.
5. Reverse procedure to install. When installing mounting bolts, the longer bolts are installed at the top of the valve. Torque mounting bolts to 50 inch lbs.

AC (GENERAL MOTORS) ANTI-SKID

This anti-skid control system is an axle by axle system in which both wheel brakes on a single axle are modulated simultaneously. The main components incorporated in the system are the wheel speed sensors, modulator, electrical cables and connectors, and a cab warning unit. Each axle has a modulator and each wheel assembly has a wheel speed sensor. The modulator is the logic center for each axle for the operation of the axle wheel lock control components. The modulator analyzes signals from the wheel speed sensors, in turn signaling the solenoid to release air brake pressure is wheel lock-up is imminent.

If a malfunction occurs in an axle system, the malfunction has no effect on other axle systems. The affected axle system will then function as a normal air brake. The cab warning lamp will be lit for the specific malfunction.

This system incorporates an external wheel speed sensor, mounted on a bracket bolted to the axle housing or to the brake spider. The brake drum has notched teeth on the outer edge. When the wheel assembly rotates, AC voltage is generated in the wheel sensor which is then transmitted to the modulator. This AC voltage is dependent upon the rate of change of the magnetic field. The magnetic field is altered three factors: clearance between the sensor and drum, wheel speed and the width of the teeth on the brake drum.

Logic Component Operation, Fig. 31

The wheel speed sensors (A and B) transmit AC electrical signals to the logic center. The logic center incorporates a self check circuit (E) which checks both wheel speed sensors, the battery power source (C) and the condition of the brake release solenoid (N). If a malfunction is present, a signal is transmitted to the cab warning lamp (D) and the release solenoid (N) so brake release cannot occur (G).

The wheel speed signals are then combined (F) after the self check and this combined signal is continuously analyzed to determine if wheel lock control is necessary. When the speed indicates that the wheels are decelerating (H), this deceleration rate is transmitted to a companion circuit (J). If the deceleration rate is too great, the logic "OR" (L) signals the solenoid (N) to energize and release air brake pressure until the deceleration rate is acceptable. Simultaneously, the combined wheel

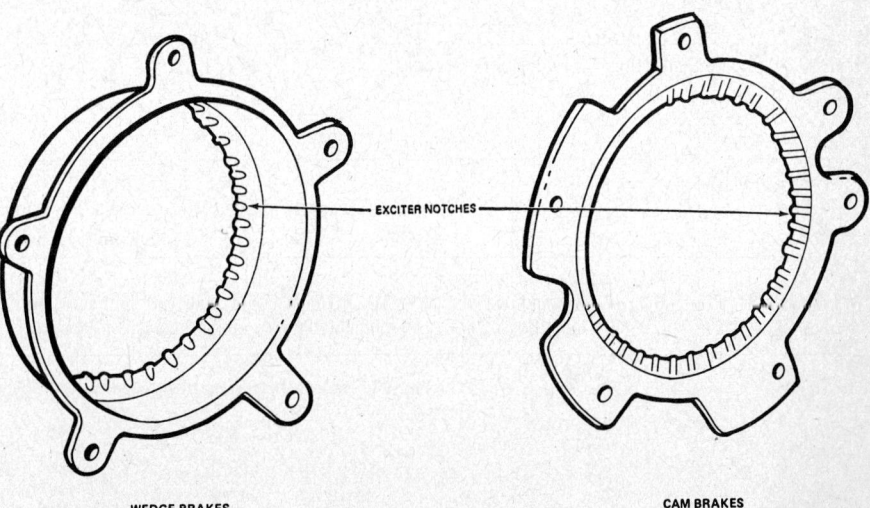

Fig. 20 Disc assembly

ANTI-SKID BRAKE SYSTEMS

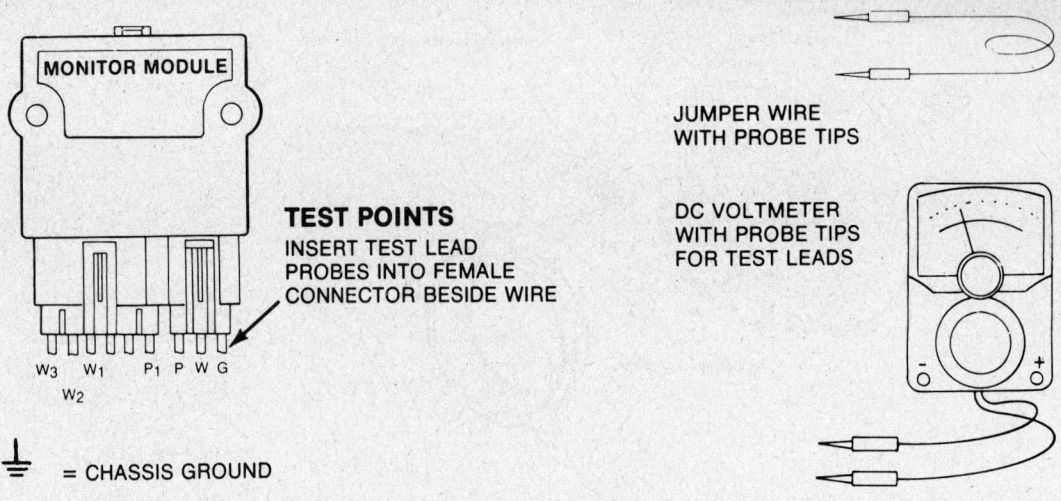

TEST	PROCEDURE	RESULTS
A. Power to Monitor	1. Voltmeter: + to P − to ⏚ 2. Ignition on 3. 11-14 Volts required	Not Okay — check power supply circit (Fig. 20) and blue wire to relay. Okay — check monitor ground (B).
B. Monitor Ground	1. Voltmeter: + to P − to G 2. Ignition on 3. 11-14 volts required	Not Okay — repair ground and check warning light. Okay — check power out (C).
C. Power Out to Warning Relay	1. Voltmeter: + to P1 − to ⏚ 2. Ignition on 3. 11-14 volts required	Not Okay — replace monitor assembly. Okay — check for warning signal in (D).
D. Warning Signal In	1. Ingition on 2. Jumper from P (or any hot terminal) to W1, W2, W3 in turn. 3. Drive vehicle 15 mph or faster if vehicle speed is involved. 4. Light should go out for terminal receiving a warning signal	Warning Light out — test modulator sending warning signal. Light stays on — check warning signal out (D1).
D1. Warning Signal Out	1. Ignition 2. Voltmeter: + to W − to ⏚ 3. Zero volts required	Voltage out — replace monitor Okay (no voltage) — check warming relay (E).
E. Warning Relay	1. Ignition on 2. Volmeter: + to green wire terminal of relay − to ⏚	Okay — check relay ground. Repair ground or replace relay. Not Okay — repair green wire from monitor PI to relay.
NOTE: Replace monitor assembly if: (1) Warning relay and W1, W2, W3 signals are okay, but light stays on. (2) Light doesn't come on momentarily with ignition on (see "Warning Lamp Operation Test").		

Fig. 21 Kelsey-Hayes monitor assembly diagnosis

ANTI-SKID BRAKE SYSTEMS

TEST POINTS

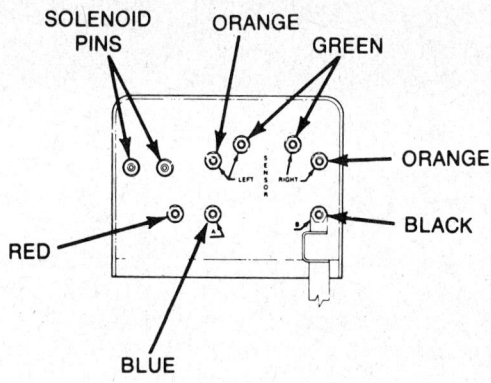

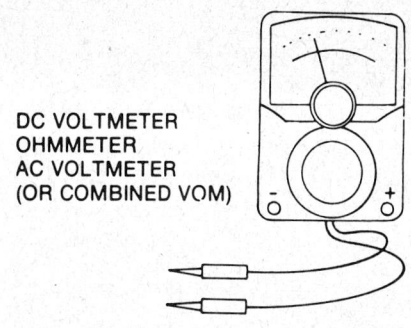

DC VOLTMETER
OHMMETER
AC VOLTMETER
(OR COMBINED VOM)

⏚ = CHASSIS GROUND

NOTE: VOLTAGES ARE DC UNLESS SPECIFIED AC

TEST	PROCEDURE NOTE: Voltages are DC unless specified AC	RESULTS
F. Warning Signal Out	1. Remove red wire 2. Voltmeter: + to FAIL − to CHASSIS 3. Ignition on 4. Okay signal is 6-14 volts	Less than 6 volts — check power in to modulator (G). Okay — repair red wire from modulator to monitor and check warning light.
G. Power in to Modulator	1. Ignition on 2. Voltmeter: + to HOT − to ⏚ 3. 11-14 volts required	Okay — check ground (H). Not Okay — repair blue wire to splice in harness (if other modulators OK) or check out power supply (Fig. 20).
H. Modulator Ground	1. Ignition on 2. Voltmeter: + to HOT − to CHASSIS 3. 11-14 volts required	Okay — check solenoid resistance (I). Not Okay — repair ground.
I. Solenoid Resistance	1. Ohmmeter leads to solenoid pins 2. 4-6 ohms required	Not Okay — replace valve assembly. Okay — check sensor output voltage (J).
J. Sensor Output Voltage (Test both Sensors)	1. Jack up wheels and release brakes. Ignition off. 2. AC Voltmeter: + to ORANGE − to GREEN 3. Turn wheel 30 rpm (one turn every 2 seconds) 4. 0.2 volts AC required	Not Okay — check sensor resistance (K). Okay — check for sensor short (L).
K. Sensor Resistance (Test Low-Output Sensor)	1. Remove orange and green wires 2. Ohmmeter leads to wire eyelets. 3. 4000Ω to 6000Ω required	Okay — remove wheel and reposition sensor. Not Okay — repair open sensor wire or replace sensor.
L. Short Sensor or Wire	1. Ohmmeter leads: sensor wire and ⏚ 2. High resistance (10,000Ω) required	Okay — replace computer module if all other tests are okay. Not Okay — repair shorted sensor wire. If not shorted, replace sensor.

Fig. 22 Kelsey-Hayes modulator & sensor diagnosis

ANTI-SKID BRAKE SYSTEMS

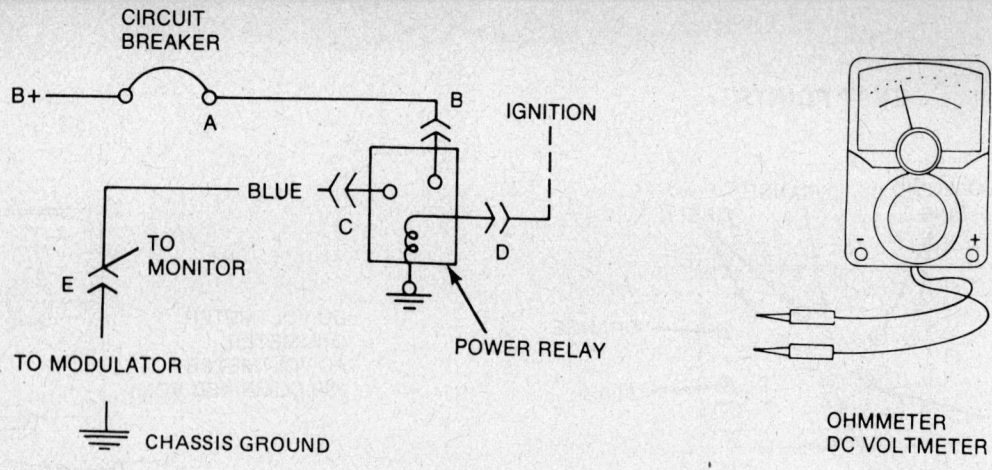

TEST	PROCEDURE	RESULTS
M. Power out of Breaker	1. Voltmeter: + to A – to ⏚ 2. 12-14 volts required.	Okay — check for power from relay (O). Not Okay — check for short to ground.
N. Short to Ground	1. Circuit breaker open 2. Ohmeter leads: A and ⏚ 3. Should be infinite resistance	Okay — replace breaker. Zero Resistance — trace and repair short circuit.
O. Power out from Relay	1. Ignition on 2. Voltmeter: + to C – to ⏚ 3. 11-14 volts required	Okay — check blue wiring to monitor and modulators; tests A and G. Not Okay — check battery power in (P).
P. B+ Power in to Relay	1. Voltmeter: + to B – to ⏚ 2. 11-14 Volts required	Okay — check ignition power in (Q). Not Okay — repair circuit between relay and breaker.
Q. Ignition Power in to Relay	1. Ignition on 2. Voltmeter: + to D – to ⏚ 3. 12-14 volts required	Okay — check relay ground. If okay, replace relay and recheck warning lamp. Not Okay — locate and repair open ignition power circuit.
NOTE: Refer to wiring schematics for connector locations.		

Fig. 23 Eaton or Kelsey-Hayes power supply diagnosis

speed signal is analyzed by the slip level detector (I). If the wheel slip is too great, a decision in the companion circuit (K) is made the logic "OR" (L) again signals the solenoid (N) to release the air brake pressure.

The logic "OR" (L) will signal for a brake release if either the wheel deceleration level or the wheel slip level is too great since either condition will cause wheels to lock up without the wheel lock control. When wheel speed recovers, the brake release signal is removed and the brakes are re-applied until a release condition is detected.

Diagnosis & Testing

Refer to Figs. 32 through 54 for diagnosis procedures. Procedures for both volt-ohmmeter and AC test plug are outlined.

Service

Wheel Sensor, Replace

1. Loosen sensor jam nut, then remove sensor from mounting bracket, Fig. 55.
2. Remove clips and ties from wiring harness, then disconnect harness connector and remove sensor.
3. Connect harness connector to sensor and install harness clips and ties, then position sensor in mounting bracket.
4. If original is to be installed, assemble sensor to bracket so that sensor is in contact with drum edge, then back sensor out one turn. This should provide a sensor to drum clearance of .040 to .060 inch. Torque jam nut to 30 to 40 ft. lbs.
5. If a new sensor is to be installed, assemble sensor to mounting bracket so that sensor is contact with drum edge, then torque jam nut to 30 to 40 ft. lbs. New sensors incorporate a fiber spacer which is removed within the first few revolutions of the drum, leaving the proper sensor to drum clearance.

Modulator, Replace

1. Block wheels, then drain air system.
2. Disconnect air lines and electrical connections from modulator.
3. Remove mounting nuts and bolts and modulator.
4. Reverse procedure to install, torque modulator attaching bolts to 25 to 30 ft. lbs.

Modulator Disassemble

1. Remove four outer cover attaching screws, Fig. 56, using tools J-25360-5, 9.
2. Using a rubber mallet, separate controller and cover assembly from lower casting.

NOTE: Use care not to damage sealing surfaces of casting.

3. Disconnect two solenoid leads from controller terminals, then remove controller and cover assembly.
4. Remove four lower cover to valve assembly attaching screws using tools J-25360-5, 9.

NOTE: It is not necessary to remove lower

ANTI-SKID BRAKE SYSTEMS

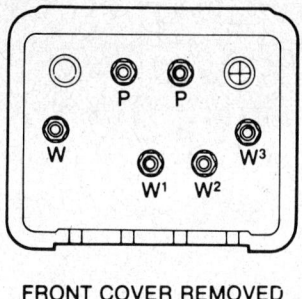

FRONT COVER REMOVED

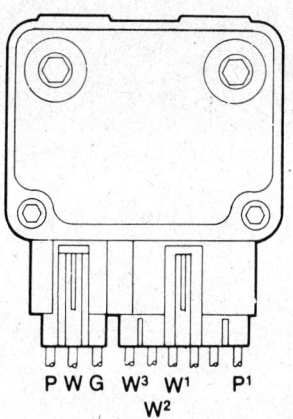

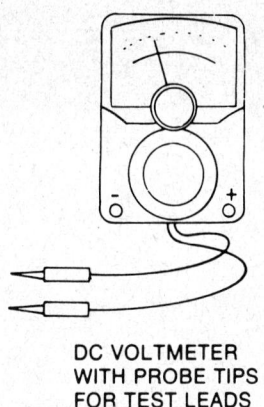

DC VOLTMETER WITH PROBE TIPS FOR TEST LEADS

TEST POINTS

INSERT TEST LEAD PROBES INTO FEMALE CONNECTOR BESIDE PLUG OR REMOVE COVER TO EXPOSE TEST POINTS.

⏚ = CHASSIS GROUND

TEST	PROCEDURE	RESULTS
A. Power to Monitor	1. Voltmeter: + to P — to ⏚ 2. Ignition on 3. 11-14 volts required	Not Okay — check power supply circuit (Fig. 20) and blue wire to power relay. Okay — check ground (B).
B. Monitor Ground	1. Voltmeter: + to P — to G 2. Ingition on 3. 11-14 volts required	Not Okay — ground monitor and recheck warning lamp. Okay — check power out (C).
C. Power out to Warning Relay	1. Voltmeter: + to PI — to ⏚ 2. Ignition on 3. 11-14 volts required	Not Okay — replace monitor assembly. Okay — check for warning signal in.
D. Warning Signal In	1. Ignition on 2. Voltmeter: + to W1, W2, W3 — to ⏚ 3. 3-8 volts required for OK signal	Not Okay — test modulator sending not-okay signal. Okay — check warning signal out (D1).
D1. Warning Signal Out	1. Ignition on 2. Voltmeter: + to W — to ⏚ 3. Zero volts required	Voltage Out — replace monitor. Okay (no voltage) — check warning relay (E).
E. Warning Relay	1. Ignition on 2. Voltmeter: + to green wire terminal of relay — to ⏚ 3. 11-14 volts required	Okay — check relay ground. Repair ground or replace relay. Not Okay - repair green wire from monitor PI to relay.
NOTE: Replace monitor assembly if: (1) Warning relay and W1, W2, W3 signals are okay, but light stays on. (2) Light doesn't come on momentarily with ignition on (see "Warning Lamp Operation Test").		

Fig. 24 Eaton monitor assembly diagnosis

ANTI-SKID BRAKE SYSTEMS

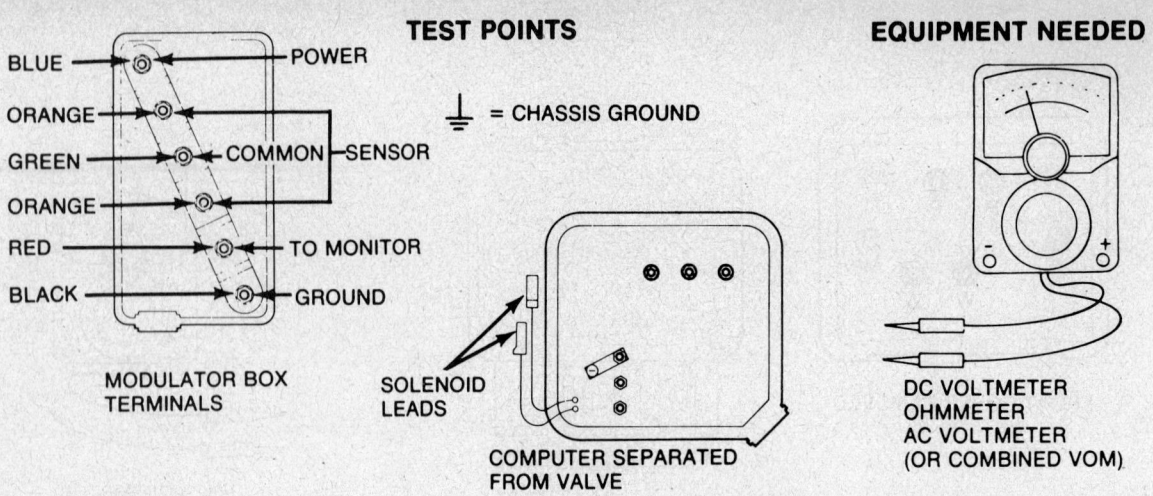

TEST	PROCEDURE NOTE: Voltages are DC unless specified AC	RESULTS
F. Warning Signal Out	1. Ignition on 2. Voltmeter: + to RED – to ⏚ 3. 3-8 volts required for okay	Okay — repair red wire to monitor and check warning light. Not Okay — check power in (G).
G. Power in to Modulator	1. Ignition on 2. Voltmeter: + to BLUE – to ⏚ 3. 11-14 volts required	Okay — check modulator ground (H). Not Okay — repair blue wire to splice in harness (if other modulators okay) or check out power supply (Fig. 20).
H. Modulator Ground	1. Ignition off 2. Ohmmeter leads to computer and ⏚ 3. Zero ohms required.	Okay — check solenoid resistance (I) and solenoid terminal resistance (I1). Not Okay — Repair ground.
I. Solenoid Resistance	1. Separate computer from valve 2. Ohmmeter to solenoid terminals 3. 4-6 ohms required	Okay — check lead resistance (I1). Not Okay — replace valve assembly.
I1. Solenoid Lead Resistance (In Computer)	1. Solenoid leads off 2. Ohmmeter: to solenoid leads on computer 3. 10,000 ohms or higher required	Okay — check sensor output voltage (J). Not Okay — reverse ohmmeter leads and recheck Still Not Okay — replace computer module.
J. Sensor Output Voltage (Test both Sensors)	1. Jack up wheels and release brakes. Ignition off. 2. AC voltmeter: + to ORANGE – to GREEN 3. Turn wheel (43 rpm for 20-inch; 56 rpm for 15 inch) 4. 0.3 volts AC required	Okay — check for shorted sensor (L). Not Okay — check sensor resistance (K).
K. Sensor Resistance (Test Low-Output Sensor)	1. Remove orange and green leads 2. Ohmmeter: to wire eyelets 3. 500-1500 ohms required	Okay — remove wheel and re-position sensor. Not Okay — repair open sensor wire or replace sensor.
K1. Computer Sensor Terminal Resistance	1. Green wire off terminal. 2. Ohmmeter: open terminal and ⏚ 3. 10,000 ohms required	Okay — check for shorted sensor or wire (L). Not Okay — replace computer module.
L. Shorted Sensor or Wire	1. Ohmmeter: GREEN wire and ⏚ 2. Both sensors connected 3. 3000 ohms required	Okay — replace computer module if all tests above are okay. Not Okay — repair shorted sensor wire. If not shorted, replace sensor.

Fig. 25 Eaton modulator & sensor diagnosis

ANTI-SKID BRAKE SYSTEMS

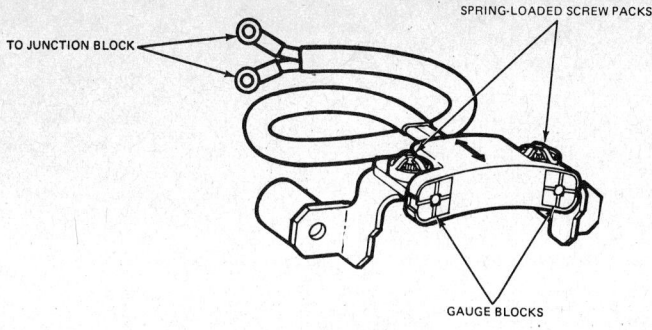

Fig. 26 Eaton sensor assembly

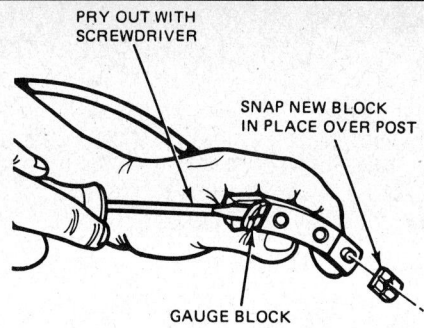

Fig. 27 Replacing Eaton sensor gauge blocks

cover assembly unless entire valve assembly is to be replaced.

5. Using a rubber mallet, separate lower cover from valve assembly.

NOTE: Use care not to damage sealing surfaces of casting.

6. Remove two long and two short bolts attaching solenoid valve body and relay valve body.
7. Separate relay valve body from solenoid valve body, then remove O ring seal from between valve bodies and discard.
8. Using suitable pliers remove flow restrictor from relay valve body.
9. Remove O ring from flow restrictor and discard.
10. Pull relay valve piston from valve body.
11. Remove conical spring and O ring from piston and discard.
12. Remove screw retaining seal to piston, then separate components and discard molded rubber valve assembly.
13. Remove snap ring and washer, then pull out exhaust valve body, spring and modulation tube.
14. Remove and discard exhaust valve body and modulation tube O rings and spring.
15. Remove seal retainer from modulation tube and discard seal.

NOTE: Use care not to damage distort seal retainer.

16. Remove screw from exhaust valve body then separate components and discard exhaust diaphragm.
17. Remove allen head screw from solenoid valve body.
18. Remove solenoid using tool No. J-25360-1.
19. Remove three check valve cover to solenoid valve body attaching screws, then separate cover from valve body.
20. Remove spring and button check valve, then using a small screw driver carefully pry out metal valve seat retainer and remove spring and check valve.
21. Using a screw driver through check valve

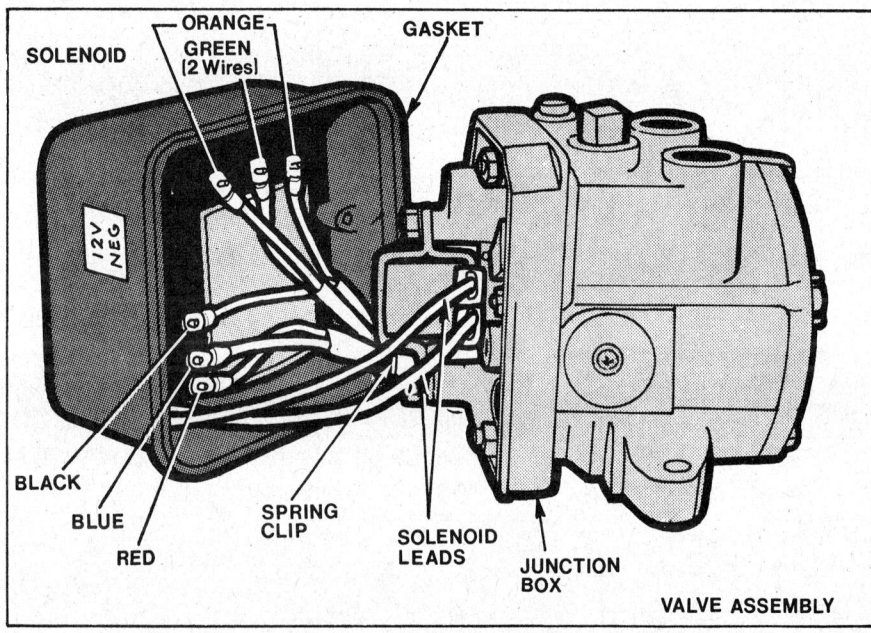

Fig. 28 Eaton computer replacement

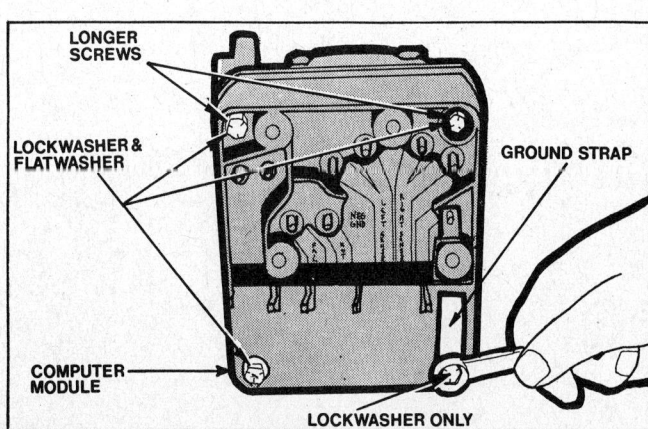

Fig. 29 Kelsey-Hayes computer replacement

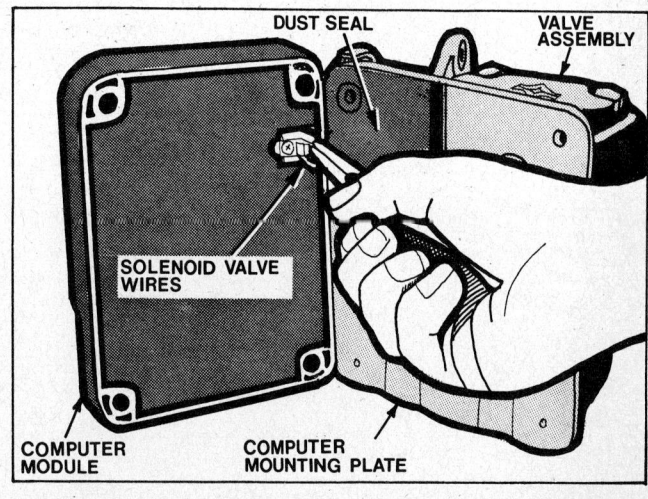

Fig. 30 Kelsey-Hayes computer solenoid lead connections

565

ANTI-SKID BRAKE SYSTEMS

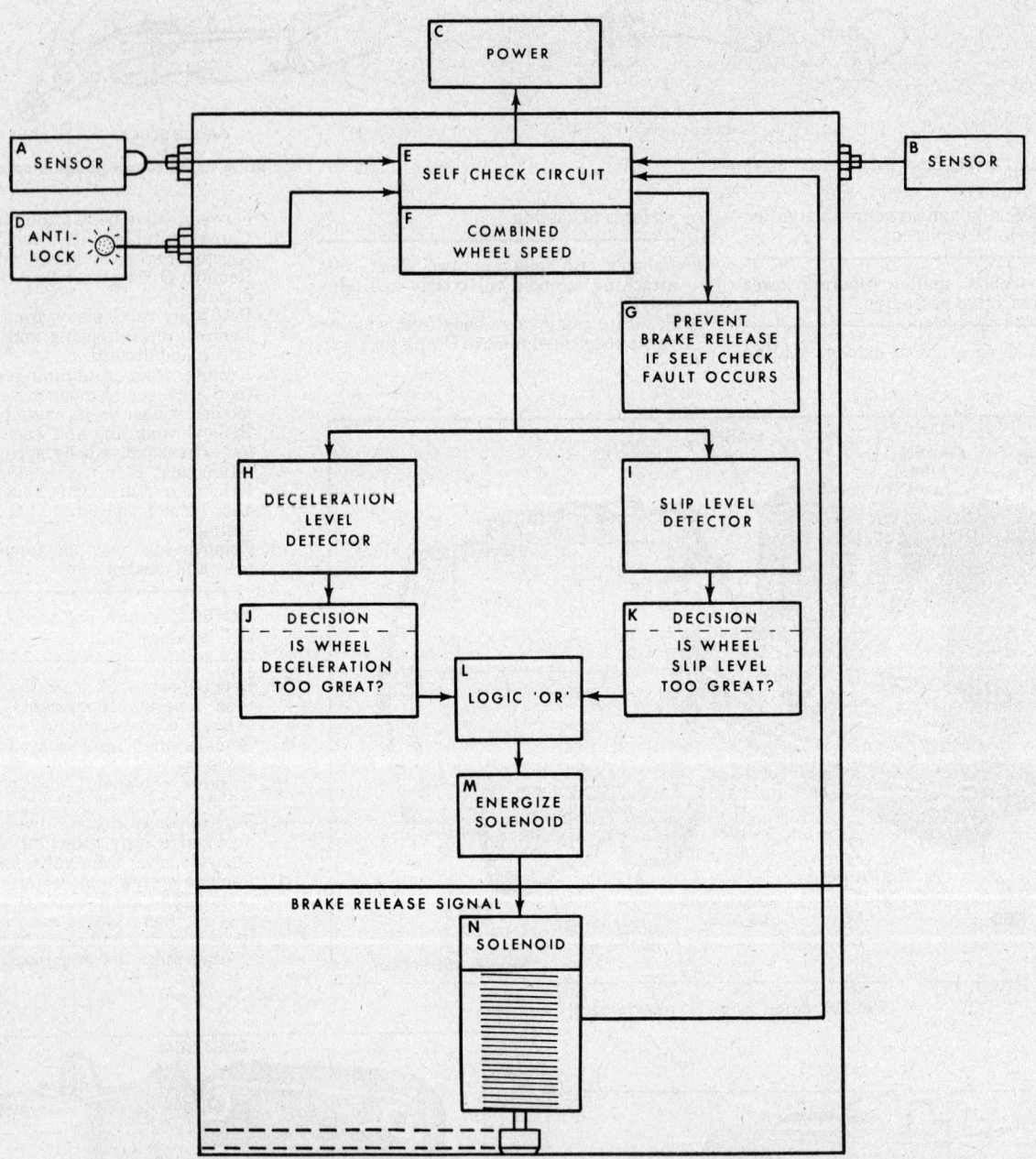

Fig. 31 AC logic component operation

ANTI-SKID BRAKE SYSTEMS

PROBLEM

WARNING LIGHT COMES ON AND STAYS ON

WARNING LIGHT LOCATED IN THE INSTRUMENT PANEL, OPERATES WHEN THE IGNITION SWITCH IS "ON" OR POWER IS APPLIED TO THE WHEEL LOCK CONTROL SYSTEM.

WARNING LIGHT COMES ON FOR UP TO 5 SECONDS WHEN IGNITION SWITCH IS TURNED ON TO CHECK BULB AND WARNING CIRCUIT.

WARNING LIGHT IS NORMALLY "OFF" WHEN SYSTEMS ARE FUNCTIONAL.

VOLT-OHMMETER METHOD

WARNING LIGHT COMES ON AND STAYS ON WHEN A PROBLEM IS DETECTED IN ONE OR MORE AXLE SYSTEMS.

TROUBLE SHOOTING PROCEDURE LOCATES FAULTY AXLE SYSTEM/SYSTEMS AND ISOLATES PROBLEM TO WARNING LIGHT, POWER CABLE, SENSOR CABLE, SENSOR, MODULATOR, HARNESS ADAPTER, OR VEHICLE WIRING.

	STEP	PROCEDURE	WARN LIGHT	RESULTS	NEXT STEP
LOCATE FAULTY AXLE	1	TURN IGNITION SWITCH "ON". DISCONNECT POWER CABLE FROM EACH MODULATOR ASSEMBLY, ONE AT A TIME, UNTIL WARNING LIGHT GOES "OFF". (DO NOT RECONNECT CABLES UNLESS INSTRUCTED.)	OFF	WARNING LIGHT WILL GO "OFF" WHEN A FAULTY SYSTEM IS DISCONNECTED. CONTINUE TROUBLESHOOTING THAT AXLE SYSTEM.	2
		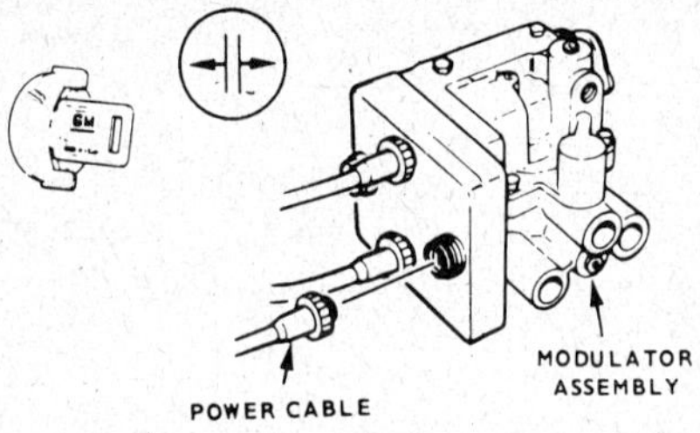	ON	IF WARNING LIGHT STAYS "ON" WHEN ALL SYSTEMS ARE DISCONNECTED, PROBLEM IS IN WARNING LIGHT CIRCUIT.	1A
	1A	DISCONNECT POWER CABLES AT WIRING HARNESS ADAPTER, ONE AT A TIME, UNTIL THE WARNING LIGHT GOES "OFF".	OFF	WARNING LIGHT GOES "OFF" WHEN POWER CABLE IS DISCONNECTED, PROBLEM IS IN THAT POWER CABLE.	1B
		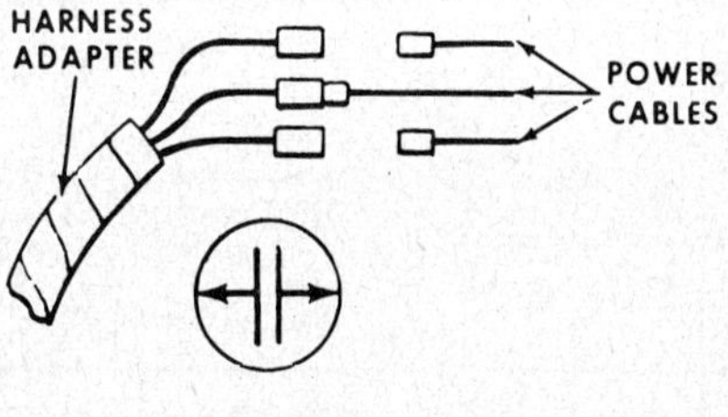	ON	IF ALL POWER CABLES HAVE BEEN DISCONNECTED AND WARNING LIGHT IS STILL "ON", PROBLEM IS SHORT TO NEGATIVE IN WIRING HARNESS ADAPTER, CAB WIRING, OR WARNING LIGHT.	1C
	1B	REPLACE POWER CABLE. RECONNECT POWER CABLES AT WIRING HARNESS ADAPTER, ONE AT A TIME, MAKING SURE THE WARNING LIGHT REMAINS "OFF".	OFF	WARNING LIGHT CIRCUIT IS "OK."	5
			ON	IF WARNING LIGHT COMES "ON" WHEN A POWER CABLE IS RECONNECTED, PROBLEM IS IN THAT POWER CABLE.	(1B)
	1C	DISCONNECT INSTRUMENT PANEL (I/P) CONNECTOR FROM WIRING HARNESS ADAPTER.	OFF	WARNING LIGHT GOES "OFF" WHEN I/P LEAD IS DISCONNECTED, PROBLEM IS IN WIRING HARNESS ADAPTER.	1D
		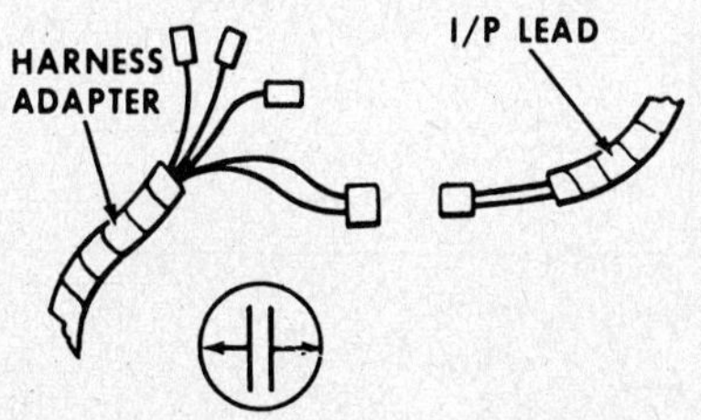	ON	WARNING LIGHT REMAINS "ON", PROBLEM IS IN WARNING LIGHT OR CAB WIRING BETWEEN INDICATOR LIGHT AND HARNESS ADAPTER.	1E

Fig. 32 AC anti-skid diagnosis and testing

ANTI-SKID BRAKE SYSTEMS

	STEP	PROCEDURE	WARN LIGHT	RESULTS	NEXT STEP
LOCATE FAULTY AXLE	1D	REPLACE WIRING HARNESS ADAPTER. RECONNECT I/P LEAD. RECONNECT POWER CABLES AT ADAPTER ONE AT A TIME, MAKING SURE THE WARNING LIGHT REMAINS "OFF".	OFF	WARNING LIGHT CIRCUIT IS "OK."	5
			ON	IF WARNING LIGHT COMES "ON" WHEN ADAPTER IS CONNECTED, PROBLEM IS IN ADAPTER.	(1D)
	1E	DISCONNECT WARNING LIGHT FROM CAB WIRING.	OFF	PROBLEM IS IN CAB WIRING BETWEEN INDICATOR LIGHT AND ADAPTER HARNESS.	1F
			ON	WARNING INDICATOR LIGHT IS PROBLEM.	1G
	1F	REPLACE OR REPAIR WIRING. RECONNECT I/P LEAD AND POWER CABLES AT ADAPTER ONE AT A TIME, MAKING SURE THE WARNING LIGHT REMAINS "OFF".	OFF	WARNING LIGHT CIRCUIT IS "OK".	5
			ON	IF WARNING LIGHT COMES "ON" WHEN LAMP IS CONNECTED TO CAB WIRING, PROBLEM REMAINS IN WIRING.	1F
	1G	REPLACE WARNING INDICATOR LIGHT. RECONNECT I/P LEAD AND POWER CABLES AT ADAPTER ONE AT A TIME, MAKING SURE THE WARNING LIGHT REMAINS "OFF."	OFF	WARNING LIGHT CIRCUIT IS "OK".	5
			ON	IF WARNING LIGHT COMES "ON" WHEN I/P LEAD IS CONNECTED, PROBLEM IS IN WARNING LIGHT.	(1G)
POWER CABLE	2	MEASURE D.C. VOLTAGE AT POWER CABLE TERMINALS AS SHOWN.	—	VOLTAGE GREATER THAN 10 V.D.C. MODULATOR IS GETTING POWER. PROBLEM IN SENSOR, SENSOR CABLES, OR MODULATOR.	3
			—	VOLTAGE LESS THAN 10 V.D.C. MODULATOR IS NOT GETTING POWER. PROBLEM IS IN POWER CABLE, POWER CABLE CONNECTIONS TO CAB WIRING, OR CAB WIRING.	2A
	2A	TO INVESTIGATE FURTHER, MEASURE D.C. VOLTAGE AT CAB END OF POWER CABLE AS SHOWN. (DO NOT DISCONNECT POWER CABLE FROM WIRING HARNESS ADAPTER).		VOLTAGE GREATER THAN 10 V.D.C. PROBLEM IS IN POWER CABLE	2B
				VOLTAGE LESS THAN 10 D.C.V. PROBLEM IS IN CAB OR VEHICLE WIRING.	2C

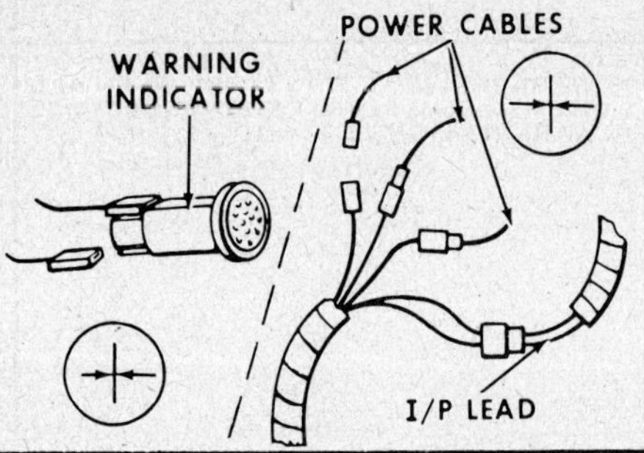

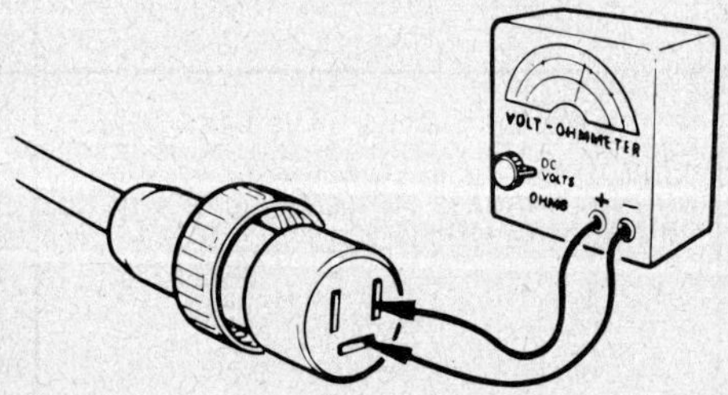

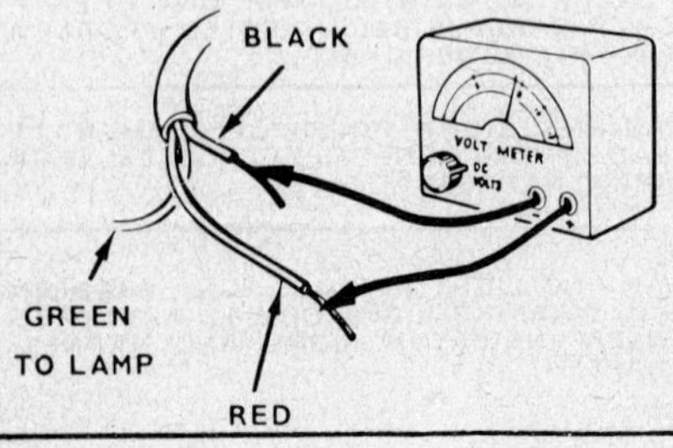

Fig. 33 AC anti-skid diagnosis and testing

ANTI-SKID BRAKE SYSTEMS

	STEP	PROCEDURE	WARN LIGHT	RESULTS	NEXT STEP
POWER CABLE	2B	REPLACE POWER CABLE AND CHECK VOLTAGE PER STEP 2 PROCEDURE. IF VOLTAGE IS LESS THAN 10 V.D.C. THERE IS STILL A POWER CABLE PROBLEM REPAIR OR REPLACE. IF VOLTAGE IS GREATER THAN 10 V.D.C. RECONNECT POWER CABLE TO MODULATOR. 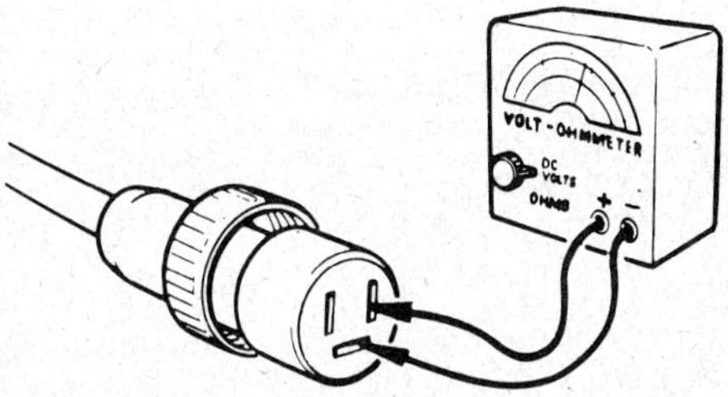	OFF	SYSTEM IS OK.	5
			ON	POWER CABLE PROBLEM HAS BEEN CORRECTED. ——————————————— OTHER PROBLEM IS IN SENSORS, SENSOR CABLES OR MODULATOR.	3
LOCATE FAULTY AXLE	2C	CHECK AND REPAIR TRUCK ELECTRICAL SYSTEM INCLUDING FUSE OR CIRCUIT BREAKER, BATTERY, AND BATTERY TERMINALS AND ALTERNATOR OR GENERATOR. AFTER REPAIRING PROBLEM IN VEHICLE ELECTRICAL SYSTEM, RECONNECT POWER CABLE TO MODULATOR. 	OFF	SYSTEM IS "OK".	5
			ON	THERE IS STILL A PROBLEM WITH THE AXLE BEING EVALUATED.	2
SENSOR & SENSOR CABLE	3	DISCONNECT SENSOR CABLES FROM BOTH SENSORS. MEASURE RESISTANCE OF EACH SENSOR AS SHOWN: 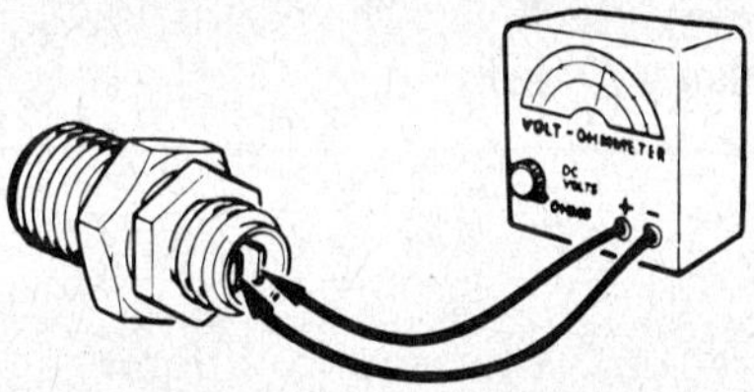	—	RESISTANCE BETWEEN 1000 & 2000 OHMS.	3A
			—	RESISTANCE **NOT** BETWEEN 1000 & 2000 OHMS. SENSOR IS FAULTY – REPLACE & RECHECK PER THIS STEP.	(3)
	3A	MEASURE RESISTANCE OF EACH SENSOR FROM SENSOR TERMINAL TO SENSOR BODY AS SHOWN. 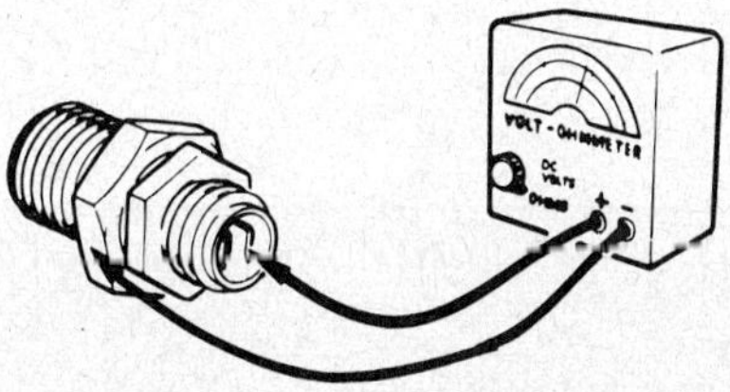	—	RESISTANCE GREATER THAN 100,000 OHMS. SENSOR IS GOOD.	3B
			—	RESISTANCE LESS THAN 100,000 OHMS. SENSOR IS FAULTY – REPLACE & RECHECK PER STEP 3.	3

Fig. 34 AC anti-skid diagnosis and testing

ANTI-SKID BRAKE SYSTEMS

	STEP	PROCEDURE	WARN LIGHT	RESULTS	NEXT STEP
SENSOR & SENSOR CABLE	3B	RECONNECT SENSOR CABLES TO BOTH SENSORS. DISCONNECT BOTH SENSOR CABLES FROM MODULATOR & MEASURE RESISTANCE AT TERMINALS OF **BOTH** SENSOR CABLES AS SHOWN:	—	BOTH CABLES HAVE A RESISTANCE BETWEEN 1000 & 2000 OHMS.	3C
		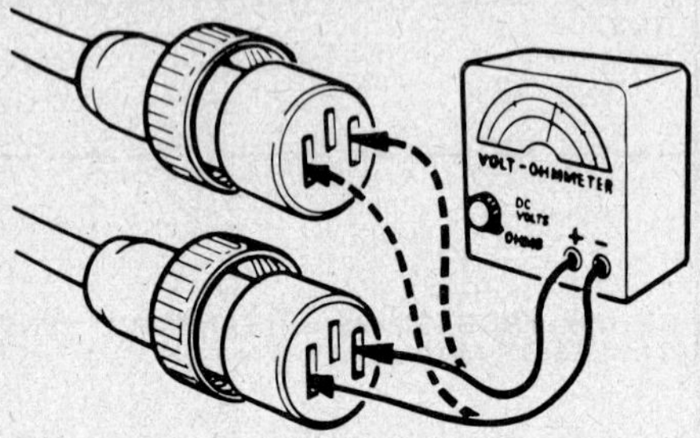	—	RESISTANCE OF ONE CABLE (OR BOTH CABLES) IS NOT BETWEEN 1000 & 2000 OHMS. RECHECK CONNECTION BETWEEN SENSOR & SENSOR CABLE. IF RESISTANCE IS STILL NOT BETWEEN 1000 & 2000 OHMS, SENSOR CABLE IS FAULTY REPLACE CABLE & RECHECK PER THIS STEP.	(3B)
	3C	MEASURE RESISTANCE AT TERMINALS OF **BOTH** SENSOR CABLES AS SHOWN.	—	BOTH CABLES HAVE A RESISTANCE GREATER THAN 100,000 OHMS. SENSOR & SENSOR CABLES ARE GOOD.	3D
		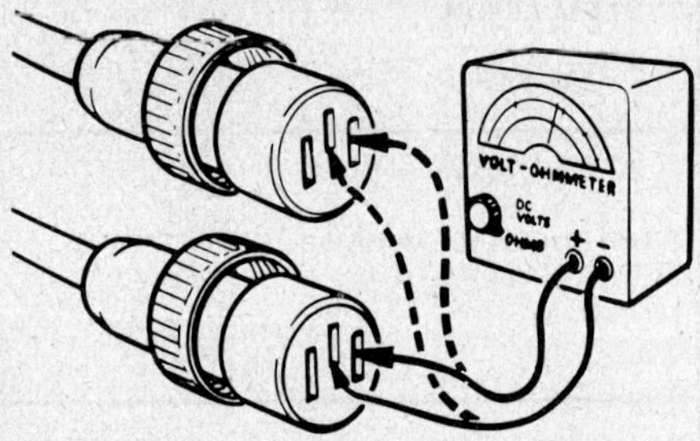	—	RESISTANCE OF ONE CABLE (OR BOTH CABLES) IS LESS THAN 100,000 OHMS. SENSOR CABLE IS FAULTY — REPLACE CABLE AND RECHECK PER STEP 3B.	3B
	3D	RECONNECT BOTH SENSOR CABLES TO THE MODULATOR. ALSO RECONNECT THE POWER CABLE. (CONNECT SENSOR CABLES BEFORE CONNECTING POWER CABLE).	OFF	SYSTEM IS "OK"	5
		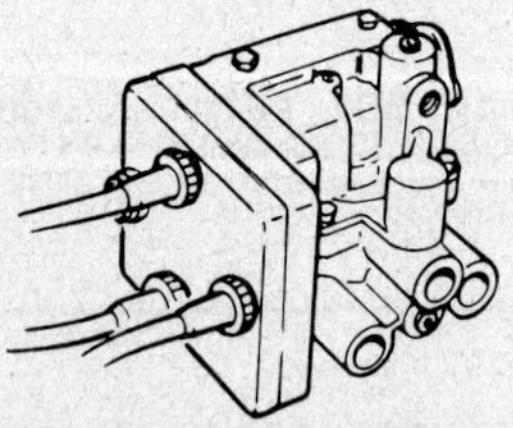	ON	SENSOR & SENSOR CABLES HAVE BEEN CHECKED AND FOUND GOOD. PROBLEM MUST BE IN MODULATOR.	4
REPLACE MODULATOR	4	REPLACE MODULATOR ASSEMBLY, DISCONNECT AND RECONNECT ALL HOSES AND CABLES PROPERLY.	OFF	SYSTEM IS "OK"	5
		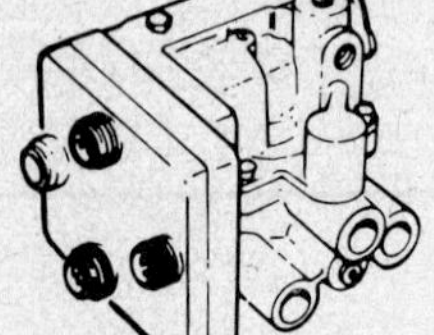	ON	THERE IS STILL A PROBLEM WITH THE SYSTEM ON THIS AXLE. CONTINUE TROUBLE-SHOOTING.	3

Fig. 35 AC anti-skid diagnosis and testing

ANTI-SKID BRAKE SYSTEMS

	STEP	PROCEDURE	WARN LIGHT	RESULTS	NEXT STEP
LOCATE OTHER FAULTY AXLES	5	PLUG IN REMAINING POWER CABLES TO OTHER AXLE/S, ONE AT A TIME, AND CHECK THE WARNING LIGHT AFTER EACH CABLE IS PLUGGED IN. 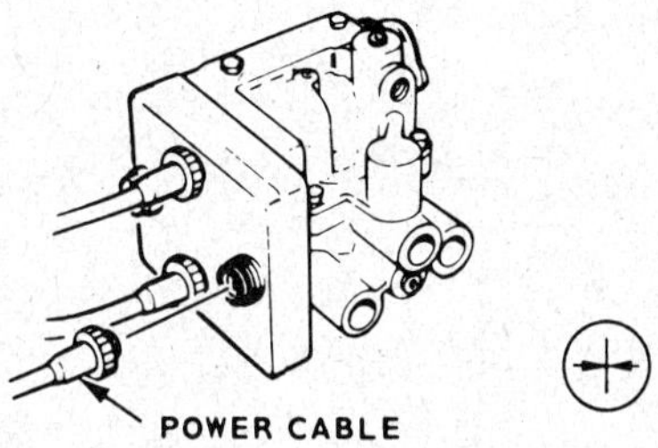	OFF	SYSTEM IS "OK".	—
			ON	IF WARNING LIGHT COMES ON AND STAYS ON AFTER PLUGGING IN POWER CABLE, THER IS SOMETHING WRONG WITH THAT AXLE SYSTEM ALSO.	2

PROBLEM

"WARNING LIGHT OFF" & "NO BULB-CHECK"

WARNING LIGHT COMES ON FOR UP TO 5 SECONDS WHEN IGNITION SWITCH IS TURNED ON TO CHECK BULB AND WARNING CIRCUIT. THIS IS NORMAL AND IS CALLED THE "BULB–CHECK" WHEN THERE IS NO "BULB–CHECK", TROUBLESHOOTING IS REQUIRED.

VOLT-OHMMETER METHOD

WHEN THERE IS NO "BULB–CHECK", THE MOST PROBABLE CAUSE IS A LOOSE OR BURNED-OUT WARNING LAMP. IF THE LAMP CIRCUIT IS FUNCTIONAL, EVERY AXLE SYSTEM HAS A PROBLEM IN THE POWER CABLE AND/OR MODULATOR.

	STEP	PROCEDURE	WARN LIGHT	BULB CHECK	RESULT	NEXT STEP
IN-LINE FUSE	1	CHECK IN-LINE 3 AMP FUSE. REPLACE IF NECESSARY. TURN ON IGNITION AND OBSERVE FOR "BULB-CHECK."	—	OFF	"BULB-CHECK" IS FUNCTIONAL. RETURN VEHICLE TO SERVICE.	—
			—	OFF	NO "BULB-CHECK", CONTINUE TROUBLESHOOTING.	2
			—	ON	SEE PROCEDURE "WARNING LIGHT COMES ON AND STAYS ON."	—

Fig. 36 AC anti-skid diagnosis and testing

ANTI-SKID BRAKE SYSTEMS

STEP	PROCEDURE	WARN LIGHT	BULB CHECK	RESULT	NEXT STEP
2 — WARNING LAMP & CAB WIRING TEST	DISCONNECT I/P CONNECTOR FROM ADAPTER: JUMPER FROM GROUND TO GREEN WIRE IN I/P CONNECTOR. 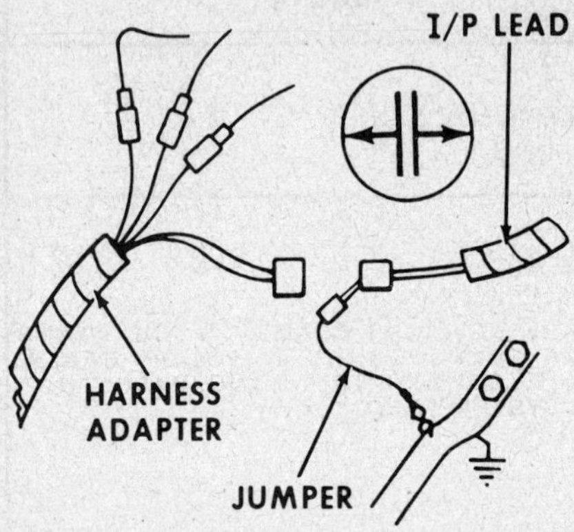	OFF	—	PROBLEM IS IN LAMP, LAMP SOCKET OR CAB WIRING.	2A
		ON	—	LAMP AND LAMP WIRING OK. EVERY AXLE SYSTEM HAS A PROBLEM IN THE POWER CABLE AND/OR MODULATOR.	3
3 — AXLE SYSTEM TEST	REPEAT THIS STEP FOR EVERY AXLE SYSTEM. DISCONNECT POWER CABLES FROM ALL MODULATORS. MEASURE D.C. VOLTAGE AT POWER CABLE AS SHOWN — OBSERVE POLARITY.	ON	—	VOLTAGE GREATER THAN 10 V.D.C. POWER CABLE IS OK. PROBLEM IS IN MODULATOR.	3A
		OFF	—	PROBLEM IS IN POWER CABLE REGARDLESS OF VOLTAGE MEASURED.	3B
	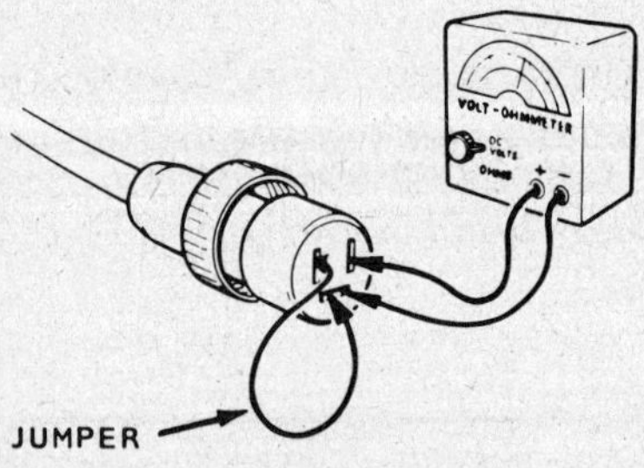	ON OR OFF	—	METER POINTER DEFLECTS DOWNSCALE (INDICATING REVERSE POLARITY) PROBLEM IS **REVERSE POLARITY** IN POWER CABLE OR IN CAB WIRING.	3C
2A — WARNING LAMP & CAB WIRING	CORRECT WARNING LAMP AND/OR CAB WIRING PROBLEM BY REPAIRING OR REPLACING FAULTY COMPONENTS. TURN IGNITION "ON" AND LOOK FOR "BULB-CHECK".	—	YES	"BULB-CHECK" IS FUNCTIONAL. RETURN VEHICLE TO SERVICE.	—
		—	NO	CONTINUE TROUBLESHOOTING.	2

Fig. 37 AC anti-skid diagnosis and testing

ANTI-SKID BRAKE SYSTEMS

STEP	PROCEDURE	WARN LIGHT	BULB CHECK	RESULT	NEXT STEP
3A REPLACE MODULATOR	REPLACE MODULATOR. DISCONNECT AND RE-CONNECT ALL HOSES AND CABLES PROPERLY. TURN ON IGNITION AND LOOK FOR "BULB-CHECK".	—	YES	THIS AXLE SYSTEM OK. CONTINUE TROUBLESHOOTING NEXT AXLE.	3
				IF THIS IS FINAL AXLE SYSTEM, RECONNECT ALL POWER CABLES AND RETURN VEHICLE TO SERVICE.	—
		—	NO	PROBLEM IS STILL IN MODULATOR.	(3A)
3B POWER CABLE	REPLACE POWER CABLE AND RECONNECT TO MODULATOR. TURN IGNITION "ON" AND LOOK FOR "BULB-CHECK".	—	YES	THIS AXLE SYSTEM IS OK. CONTINUE TROUBLESHOOTING NEXT AXLE.	3
				IF THIS IS FINAL AXLE SYSTEM, RECONNECT ALL POWER CABLES AND RETURN VEHICLE TO SERVICE.	—
		—	NO	CONTINUE TROUBLESHOOTING THIS AXLE.	3
3C CAB WIRING	CORRECT REVERSE POLARITY PROBLEM IN POWER CABLE OR IN CAB WIRING, AND RECONNECT POWER CABLE TO MODULATOR. TURN IGNITION "ON" AND LOOK FOR "BULB-CHECK".	—	YES	THIS AXLE SYSTEM IS OK. CONTINUE TROUBLESHOOTING NEXT AXLE.	3
				IF THIS IS FINAL AXLE SYSTEM, RECONNECT ALL POWER CABLES AND RETURN VEHICLE TO SERVICE.	—
		—	NO	CONTINUE TROUBLESHOOTING THIS AXLE.	3

Fig. 38 AC anti-skid diagnosis and testing

ANTI-SKID BRAKE SYSTEMS

AIRBRAKE – WLC MODULATOR ELECTRICAL SERVICE PROCEDURE
("SOLENOID" AND/OR "CONTROLLER & COVER ASSEMBLY" ONLY)

VOLT-OHMMETER METHOD

	STEP	INSTRUCTIONS	NEXT STEP
DISASSEMBLY	1	REMOVE CONTROLLER & COVER ASSEMBLY & DISCONNECT SOLENOID LEADS. 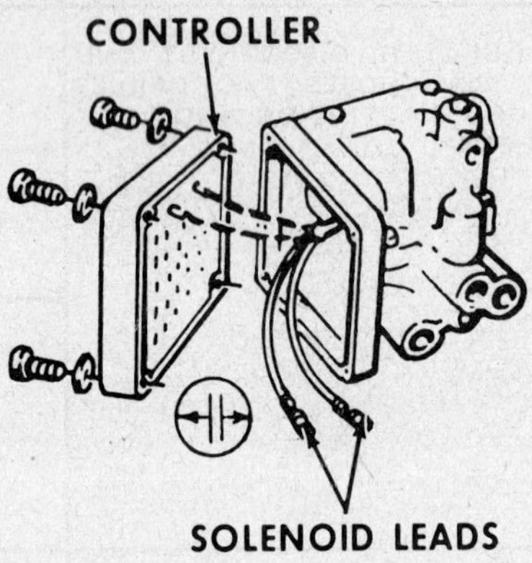	2
SOLENOID	2	TAKE SOLENOID LEADS AND MOMENTARILY CONNECT THEM TO A 12 VOLT BATTERY. 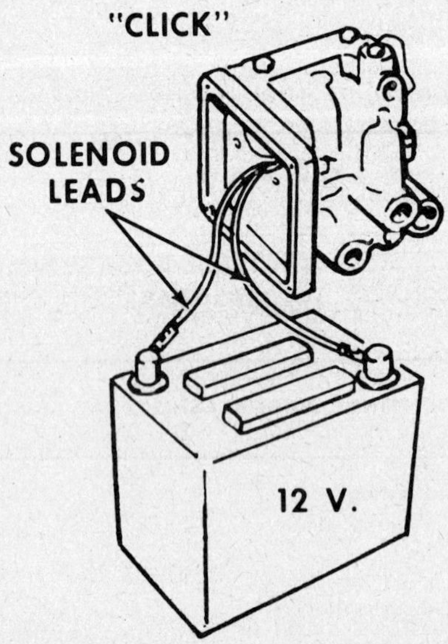	SOLENOID IS OK IF YOU HEAR A "CLICK" WHEN LEADS ARE CONNECTED AND ANOTHER "CLICK" WHEN THEY ARE DISCONNECTED. PROBLEM IS IN THE CONTROLLER & COVER ASSEMBLY. → 5
			IF "CLICKS" ARE NOT HEARD, PROBLEM IS IN SOLENOID. → 3

Fig. 39 AC anti-skid diagnosis and testing

ANTI-SKID BRAKE SYSTEMS

	STEP	INSTRUCTION		NEXT STEP
SOLENOID	3	REPLACE THE SOLENOID.	CONTINUE WITH NEXT STEP —	4
SOLENOID	4	TEST NEW SOLENOID IN SAME MANNER AS SHOWN IN STEP NO. 2.	SOLENOID IS OK IF A "CLICK" IS HEARD WHEN LEADS ARE CONNECTED AND ANOTHER "CLICK" WHEN THEY ARE DISCONNECTED. REASSEMBLE THE CONTROLLER & COVER ASSEMBLY AND RETEST MODULATOR.	6
SOLENOID	4	TEST NEW SOLENOID IN SAME MANNER AS SHOWN IN STEP NO. 2.	IF NO "CLICKS" ARE HEARD, PROBLEM IS STILL IN SOLENOID.	3
CONTROLLER	5	INSTALL NEW CONTROLLER & COVER ASSEMBLY.		6
TESTING REPAIRED MODULATOR ASSEMBLY	6	TEST THE REPAIRED MODULATOR BY SIMULATING A VEHICLE INSTALLATION ON THE BENCH AS FOLLOWS: CONNECT TWO SPEED SENSORS, TWO SPEED SENSOR CABLES, A BATTERY, AND A 12 VOLT TROUBLE LIGHT AS SHOWN. 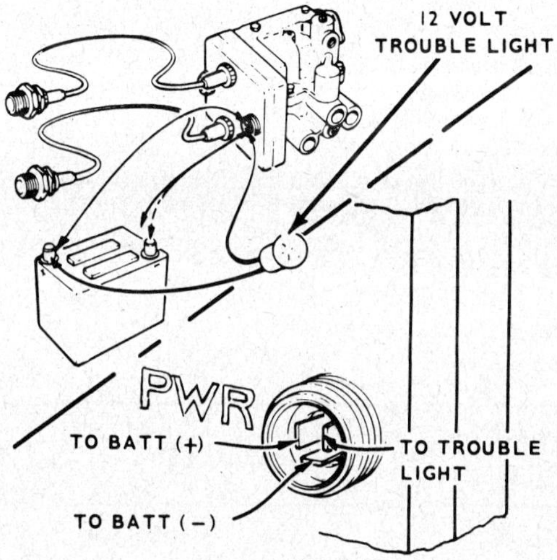 WHEN THE LEAD IS CONNECTED TO THE NEGATIVE TERMINAL OF THE BATTERY, A NORMAL "BULB-CHECK" SHOULD OCCUR.	NORMAL BULB — CHECK IS OBSERVED. (THE TROUBLE LIGHT COMES ON FOR UP TO 5 SECONDS AND THEN GOES OFF.)	7
TESTING REPAIRED MODULATOR ASSEMBLY	6		NO "BULB-CHECK" IS OBSERVED OR TROUBLE LIGHT REMAINS ON. DOUBLE CHECK ALL ELECTRICAL CONNECTIONS. IF THE LIGHT REMAINS ON, THERE IS STILL A PROBLEM IN THE MODULATOR ASSEMBLY.	1
TESTING REPAIRED MODULATOR ASSEMBLY	7	DISCONNECT ONE SENSOR CABLE FROM MODULATOR TO SIMULATE A FAULT.	IF THE TROUBLE LIGHT COMES "ON" AND STAYS ON, THE WARNING SYSTEM HAS CORRECTLY DETECTED THE FAULT.	8
TESTING REPAIRED MODULATOR ASSEMBLY	7	DISCONNECT ONE SENSOR CABLE FROM MODULATOR TO SIMULATE A FAULT.	IF THE TROUBLE LIGHT DOES NOT COME "ON", THE WARNING CIRCUIT IS NOT OPERATING.	5

Fig. 40 AC anti-skid diagnosis and testing

ANTI-SKID BRAKE SYSTEMS

	STEP	INSTRUCTION		NEXT STEP
TESTING REPAIRED MODULATOR ASSEMBLY	8	RECONNECT THE SENSOR CABLE TO THE MODULATOR.	IF THE TROUBLE LIGHT GOES "OFF", THE MODULATOR IS OPERATING PROPERLY AND MAY BE RETURNED TO SERVICE.	—
			IF THE TROUBLE LIGHT REMAINS "ON", DOUBLE CHECK ALL TEST CONNECTIONS. IF LIGHT REMAINS "ON", THERE IS A PROBLEM IN THE CONTROLLER & COVER ASSEMBLY.	5

PROBLEM

WARNING LIGHT COMES ON AND STAYS ON

TRACTOR WARNING LIGHT LOCATED IN THE INSTRUMENT PANEL, OPERATE WHEN THE IGNITION SWITCH IS "ON" OR POWER IS APPLIED TO THE WHEEL LOCK CONTROL SYSTEM.

WARNING LIGHT COMES ON FOR UP TO 5 SECONDS WHEN IGNITION SWITCH IS TURNED ON TO CHECK BULB AND WARNING CIRCUIT.

WARNING LIGHT IS NORMALLY "OFF" WHEN SYSTEMS ARE FUNCTIONAL.

TEST PLUG METHOD

WARNING LIGHT COMES ON AND STAYS ON WHEN A PROBLEM IS DETECTED IN ONE OR MORE AXLE SYSTEMS.

TROUBLE SHOOTING PROCEDURE LOCATES FAULTY AXLE SYSTEM/SYSTEMS AND ISOLATES PROBLEM TO WARNING LIGHT, POWER CABLE, SENSOR CABLE, SENSOR, MODULATOR, HARNESS ADAPTER OR VEHICLE WIRING.

	STEP	PROCEDURE	WARN LIGHT	RESULTS	NEXT STEP
LOCATE FAULTY AXLE	1	TURN IGNITION SWITCH "ON", DISCONNECT POWER CABLE FROM EACH MODULATOR ASSEMBLY, ONE AT A TIME, UNTIL WARNING LIGHT GOES "OFF". (DO NOT RECONNECT CABLES UNLESS INSTRUCTED.)	OFF	WARNING LIGHT WILL GO "OFF" WHEN A FAULTY SYSTEM IS DISCONNECTED. CONTINUE TROUBLESHOOTING THAT AXLE SYSTEM.	2
			ON	IF WARNING LIGHT STAYS "ON" WHEN ALL SYSTEMS ARE DISCONNECTED, PROBLEM IS IN WARNING LIGHT CIRCUIT.	1A

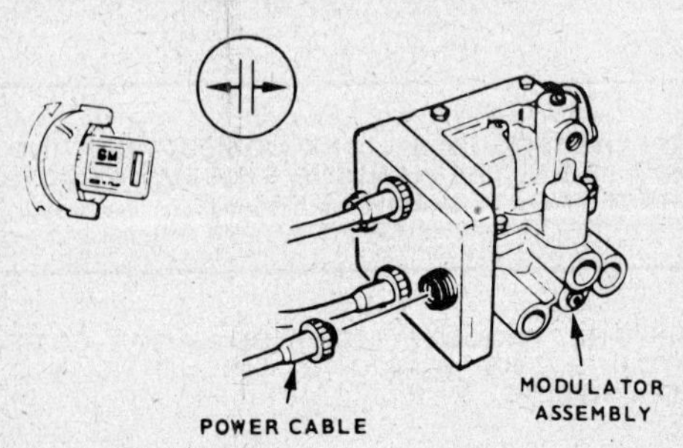

Fig. 41 AC anti-skid diagnosis and testing

ANTI-SKID BRAKE SYSTEMS

	STEP	PROCEDURE	WARN LIGHT	RESULTS	NEXT STEP
LOCATE FAULTY AXLE	1A	DISCONNECT POWER CABLES AT WIRING HARNESS ADAPTER ONE AT A TIME, UNTIL THE WARNING LIGHT GOES "OFF". 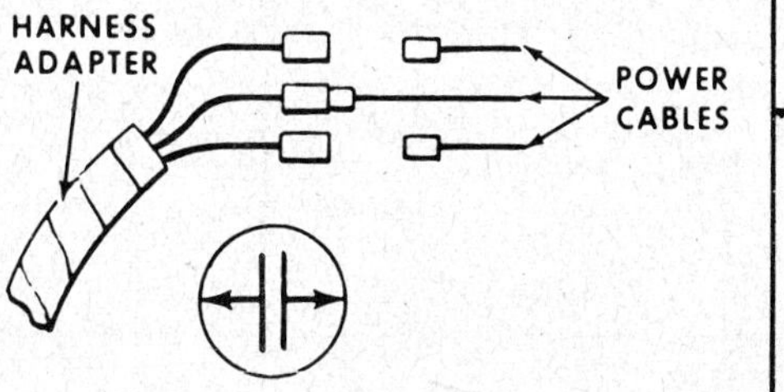	OFF	IF WARNING LIGHT GOES "OFF" WHEN POWER CABLE IS DISCONNECTED, PROBLEM IS IN THAT POWER CABLE.	1B
			ON	IF ALL POWER CABLES HAVE BEEN DISCONNECTED AND WARNING LIGHT IS STILL "ON", PROBLEM IS SHORT TO NEGATIVE IN WIRING HARNESS ADAPTER, CAB WIRING, OR WARNING LIGHT.	1C
	1B	REPLACE POWER CABLE. RECONNECT POWER CABLES AT WIRING HARNESS ADAPTER, ONE AT A TIME, MAKING SURE THE WARNING LIGHT REMAINS "OFF".	OFF	WARNING LIGHT CIRCUIT IS "OK".	5
			ON	IF WARNING LIGHT COMES "ON" WHEN A POWER CABLE IS RECONNECTED, PROBLEM IS IN THAT POWER CABLE.	(1B)
	1C	DISCONNECT INSTRUMENT PANEL (I/P) CONNECTOR FROM WIRING HARNESS ADAPTER. 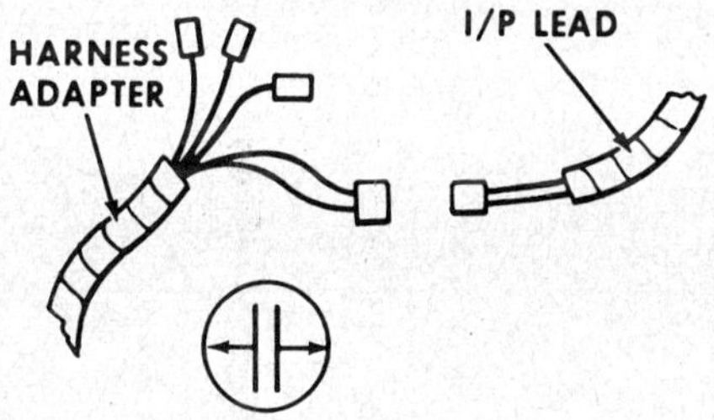	OFF	WARNING LIGHT GOES "OFF" WHEN I/P LEAD IS DISCONNECTED, PROBLEM IS IN WIRING HARNESS ADAPTER.	1D
			ON	WARNING LIGHT REMAINS "ON", PROBLEM IS IN WARNING LIGHT OR CAB WIRING BETWEEN INDICATOR LIGHT AND HARNESS ADAPTER.	1E
	1D	REPLACE WIRING HARNESS ADAPTER. RECONNECT I/P LEAD. RECONNECT POWER CABLES AT ADAPTER ONE AT A TIME, MAKING SURE THE WARNING LIGHT REMAINS "OFF".	OFF	WARNING LIGHT CIRCUIT IS "OK".	5
			ON	IF WARNING LIGHT COMES "ON" WHEN ADAPTER IS CONNECTED, PROBLEM IS IN ADAPTER.	(1D)
	1E	DISCONNECT WARNING LIGHT FROM CAB WIRING.	OFF	PROBLEM IS IN CAB WIRING BETWEEN INDICATOR LIGHT AND ADAPTER HARNESS.	1F
			ON	WARNING INDICATOR LIGHT IS PROBLEM.	1G
	1F	REPLACE OR REPAIR WIRING. RECONNECT I/P LEAD AND POWER CABLES AT ADAPTER ONE AT A TIME, MAKING SURE THE WARNING LIGHT REMAINS "OFF".	OFF	WARNING LIGHT CIRCUIT IS "OK".	5
			ON	IF WARNING LIGHT COMES "ON" WHEN LAMP IS CONNECTED TO CAB WIRING, PROBLEM REMAINS IN WIRING.	(1F)

Fig. 42 AC anti-skid diagnosis and testing

ANTI-SKID BRAKE SYSTEMS

	STEP	PROCEDURE	WARN LIGHT	RESULTS	NEXT STEP
LOCATE FAULTY AXLE	1G	REPLACE WARNING INDICATOR LIGHT. RECONNECT I/P LEAD AND POWER CABLES AT ADAPTER ONE AT A TIME, MAKING SURE THE WARNING LIGHT REMAINS "OFF". 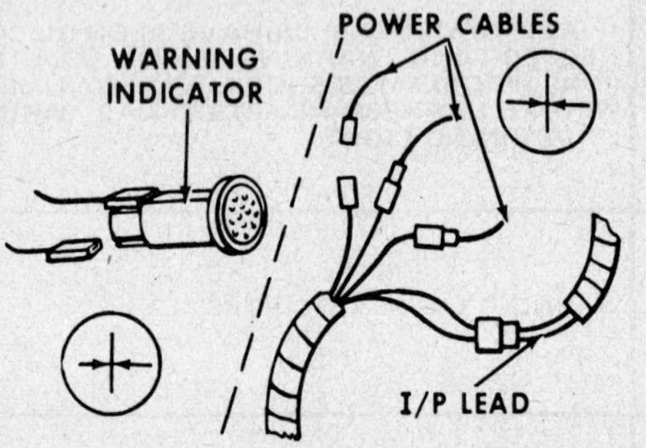	OFF	WARNING LIGHT CIRCUIT IS "OK".	5
			ON	IF WARNING LIGHT COMES "ON" WHEN I/P LEAD IS CONNECTED, PROBLEM IS IN WARNING LIGHT.	(1G)
POWER CABLE TEST	2	TAKE POWER CABLE AND CONNECT IT TO POWER PLUG FROM SERVICE TOOL KIT. 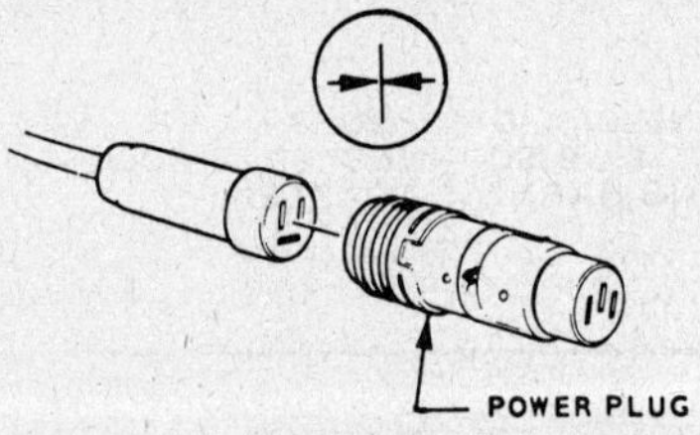	—	IF GREEN LIGHT IN POWER PLUG COMES "ON", MODULATOR IS GETTING POWER. PROBLEM IS IN THE SENSOR, SENSOR CABLES, OR MODULATOR.	3
			—	IF GREEN LIGHT IN POWER PLUG IS "OFF", MODULATOR IS NOT GETTING POWER. PROBLEM IS IN POWER CABLE, POWER CABLE CONNECTIONS TO CAB WIRING, OR CAB WIRING.	2A
POWER CABLE	2A	TO INVESTIGATE FURTHER, TAKE POWER PLUG AND PLUG IT TOGETHER WITH POWER ADAPTER PLUG. TOUCH RED PIN TO RED WIRE AND BLACK PIN TO BLACK WIRE AT OTHER END OF POWER CABLE (IN CAB). 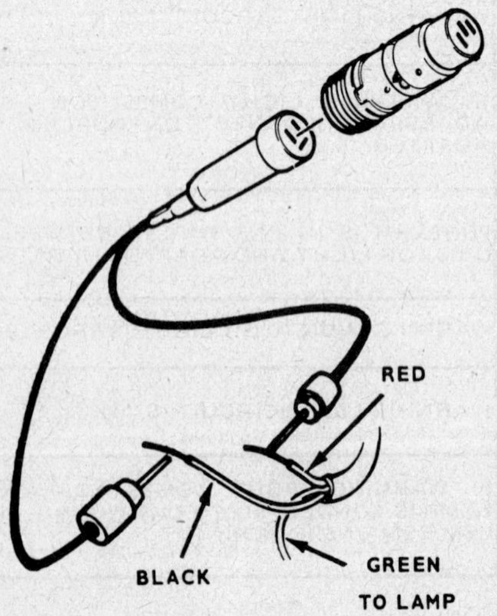	—	IF GREEN LIGHT IN POWER PLUG COMES "ON", PROBLEM IS IN POWER CABLE.	2B
			—	IF GREEN LIGHT IN POWER PLUG IS "OFF", PROBLEM IS IN CAB OR VEHICLE WIRING.	2C

Fig. 43 AC anti-skid diagnosis and testing

ANTI-SKID BRAKE SYSTEMS

	STEP	PROCEDURE	WARN LIGHT	RESULTS	NEXT STEP
POWER CABLE	2B	REPLACE POWER CABLE. INSTALL POWER PLUG IN MODULATOR END OF NEW POWER CABLE TO MAKE SURE POWER WILL NOW BE AVAILABLE TO MODULATOR. (GREEN LIGHT IN POWER PLUG SHOULD BE "ON". IF IT ISN'T, THERE IS STILL A POWER CABLE PROBLEM. REPAIR OR REPLACE.) REMOVE POWER PLUG AND CONNECT POWER CABLE TO THE MODULATOR. 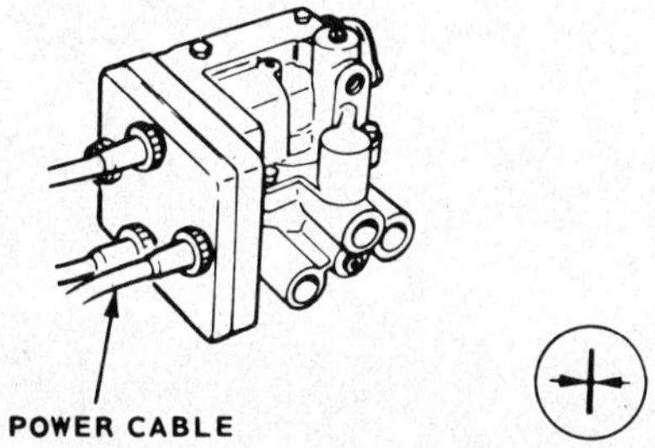	OFF	SYSTEM IS "OK".	5
			ON	PROBLEM IS IN SENSORS, SENSORS CABLES, OR MODULATOR.	3
	2C	CHECK AND REPAIR TRUCK ELECTRICAL SYSTEM INCLUDING FUSE OR CIRCUIT BREAKER, BATTERY, AND BATTERY TERMINALS AND ALTERNATOR OR GENERATOR. AFTER REPAIRING PROBLEM IN VEHICLE ELECTRICAL SYSTEM, RECONNECT POWER CABLE TO MODULATOR. 	OFF	SYSTEM IS "OK".	5
			ON	THERE IS STILL A PROBLEM WITH THE AXLE BEING EVALUATED.	2
SENSOR TEST	3	RECONNECT POWER CABLE AND DISCONNECT BOTH SENSOR CABLES FROM MODULATOR. TAKE BOTH BLUE SENSOR PLUGS FROM SERVICE TOOL KIT AND PLUG INTO SENSOR TERMINALS ON MODULATOR. (CYCLE IGNITION KEY "OFF-ON" TO PREVENT LATCHING OF WARNING LIGHT.) 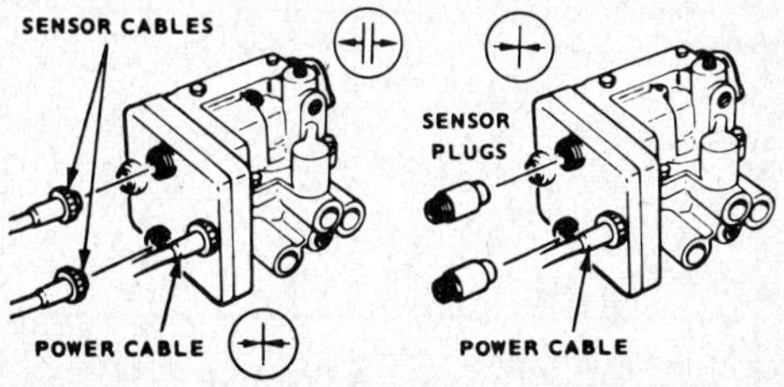	OFF	PROBLEM IS IN SENSORS OR SENSOR CABLES.	3A
			ON	CONTINUE WITH NEXT STEP –	4

Fig. 44 AC anti-skid diagnosis and testing

ANTI-SKID BRAKE SYSTEMS

STEP	PROCEDURE	WARN LIGHT	RESULTS	NEXT STEP
3A	REMOVE ONE BLUE SENSOR PLUG AND RECONNECT LEFT SENSOR CABLE. 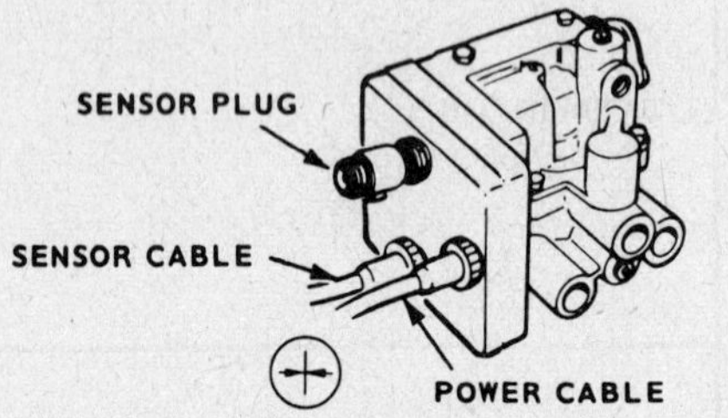	OFF	LEFT SENSOR AND SENSOR CABLE ARE OK. PROBLEM IS IN RIGHT SENSOR OR SENSOR CABLE.	3B
		ON	PROBLEM IS IN LEFT SENSOR OR SENSOR CABLE.	3F
3B	REMOVE REMAINING BLUE SENSOR PLUG AND RECONNECT RIGHT SENSOR CABLE TO MODULATOR. (NOT NECESSARY IF PREVIOUS STEP WAS 3J). DISCONNECT RIGHT SENSOR CABLE FROM SENSOR AND CONNECT IT TO BLUE SENSOR PLUG. 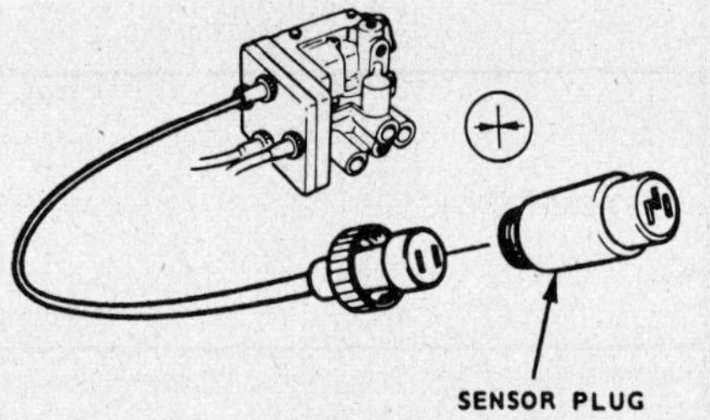	OFF	PROBLEM IS IN RIGHT SENSOR.	3C
		ON	PROBLEM IS IN RIGHT SENSOR CABLE.	3D
3C	REPLACE RIGHT SENSOR. REMOVE BLUE SENSOR PLUG (NOT NECESSARY IF PREVIOUS STEP WAS 3E). AND REINSTALL SENSOR CABLE TO SENSOR.	OFF	SYSTEM IS "OK".	5
		ON	PROBLEM IS STILL IN RIGHT SENSOR OR CABLE CONNECTIONS. REPAIR OR REPLACE.	(3C)
3D	REPLACE RIGHT SENSOR CABLE. REINSTALL BLUE SENSOR PLUG IN END OF CABLE. 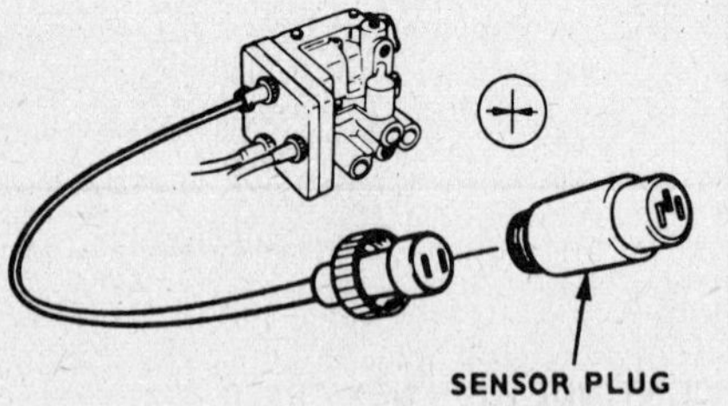	OFF	NEW RIGHT SENSOR CABLE IS "OK".	3E
		ON	PROBLEM IS STILL IN RIGHT SENSOR CABLE OR CABLE CONNECTIONS. REPAIR OR REPLACE.	(3D)
3E	REMOVE BLUE SENSOR PLUG AND RECONNECT NEW RIGHT SENSOR CABLE TO RIGHT SENSOR.	OFF	SYSTEM IS "OK".	5
		ON	PROBLEM IS IN RIGHT SENSOR.	3C

Fig. 45 AC anti-skid diagnosis and testing

ANTI-SKID BRAKE SYSTEMS

	STEP	PROCEDURE	WARN LIGHT	RESULTS	NEXT STEP
SENSOR & SENSOR CABLES (CONTINUED)	3F	DISCONNECT LEFT SENSOR CABLE FROM SENSOR AND CONNECT IT TO BLUE SENSOR PLUG. 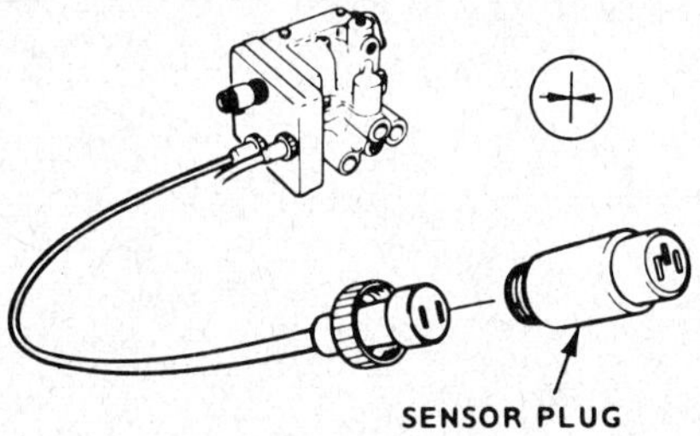	OFF	PROBLEM IS IN LEFT SENSOR.	3G
			ON	PROBLEM IS IN LEFT SENSOR CABLE.	3H
	3G	REPLACE LEFT SENSOR. REMOVE BLUE SENSOR PLUG (NOT NECESSARY IF PREVIOUS STEP WAS 3D and REINSTALL SENSOR CABLE TO SENSOR.	OFF	LEFT SENSOR AND SENSOR CABLE "OK".	3J
			ON	PROBLEM IS STILL IN LEFT SENSOR OR CABLE CONNECTIONS. REPAIR OR REPLACE.	(3G)
	3H	REPLACE LEFT SENSOR CABLE. REINSTALL BLUE SENSOR PLUG IN END OF CABLE. 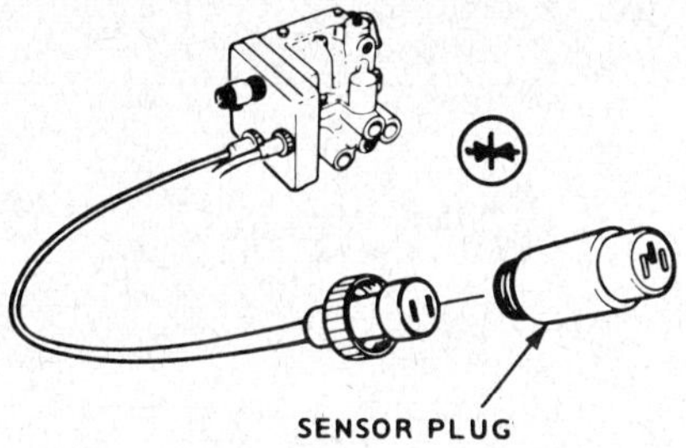	OFF	NEW LEFT SENSOR CABLE IS "OK".	3I
			ON	PROBLEM IS STILL IN LEFT SENSOR CABLE OR CABLE CONNECTIONS. REPAIR OR REPLACE.	(3H)
	3I	REMOVE BLUE SENSOR PLUG AND CONNECT NEW LEFT SENSOR CABLE TO LEFT SENSOR.	OFF	LEFT SENSOR AND SENSOR CABLE ARE "OK".	3J
			ON	PROBLEM IS IN LEFT SENSOR.	3G
	3J	REMOVE BLUE SENSOR PLUG FROM MODULATOR AND REINSTALL RIGHT SENSOR CABLE. 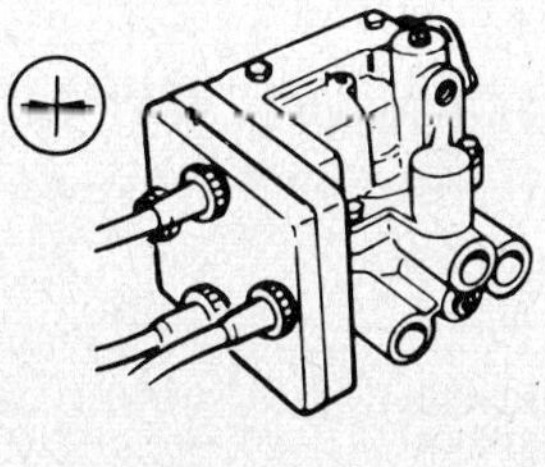	OFF	SYSTEM IS "OK".	5
			ON	PROBLEM IS IN RIGHT SENSOR OR SENSOR CABLE.	3B

Fig. 46 AC anti-skid diagnosis and testing

ANTI-SKID BRAKE SYSTEMS

	STEP	PROCEDURE	WARN LIGHT	RESULTS	NEXT STEP
REPLACE MODULATOR	4	REPLACE MODULATOR ASSEMBLY, DISCONNECT AND RECONNECT ALL HOSES AND CABLES PROPERLY. 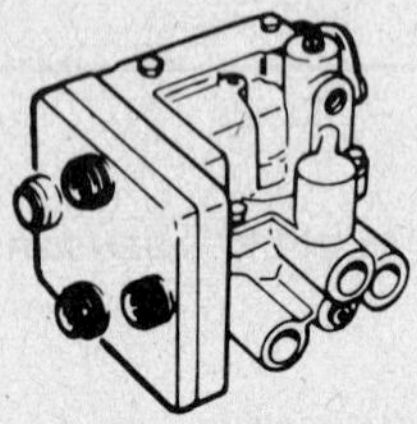	OFF	SYSTEM IS "OK".	5
REPLACE MODULATOR	4		ON	THERE IS STILL A PROBLEM WITH THE SYSTEM ON THIS AXLE. CONTINUE TROUBLE-SHOOTING.	3
LOCATE OTHER FAULTY AXLES	5	PLUG IN REMAINING POWER CABLES TO OTHER AXLE/S, ONE AT A TIME, AND CHECK THE WARNING LIGHT AFTER EACH CABLE IS PLUGGED IN. 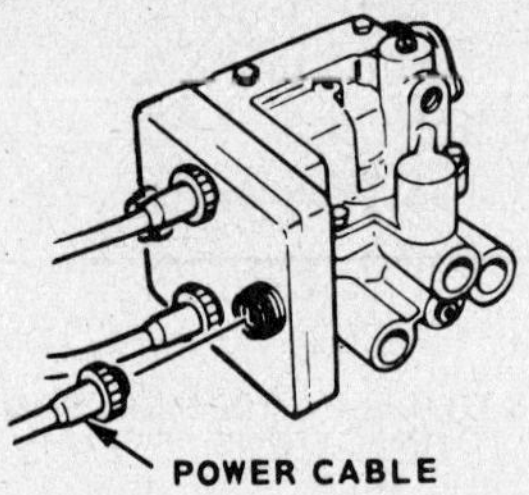 	OFF	SYSTEM IS "OK".	—
LOCATE OTHER FAULTY AXLES	5		ON	IF WARNING LIGHT COMES ON AND STAYS ON AFTER PLUGGING IN POWER CABLE, THERE IS SOMETHING WRONG WITH THAT AXLE SYSTEM ALSO.	2

POWER CABLE

PROBLEM

"WARNING LAMP OFF" & "NO BULB-CHECK"

WARNING LIGHT COMES ON FOR UP TO 5 SECONDS WHEN IGNITION SWITCH IS TURNED ON TO CHECK BULB AND WARNING CIRCUIT. THIS IS NORMAL AND IS CALLED THE "BULB-CHECK". WHEN THERE IS NO "BULB-CHECK", TROUBLE-SHOOTING IS REQUIRED.

TEST PLUG METHOD

WHEN THERE IS NO "BULB-CHECK", THE MOST PROBABLE CAUSE IS A LOOSE OR BURNED-OUT WARNING LAMP, IF THE LAMP CIRCUIT IS FUNCTIONAL, EVERY AXLE SYSTEM HAS A PROBLEM IN THE POWER CABLE AND/OR MODULATOR.

	STEP	PROCEDURE	WARN LIGHT	BULB CHECK	RESULT	NEXT STEP
IN-LINE FUSE	1	CHECK IN-LINE 3 AMP FUSE. REPLACE IF NECESSARY. TURN ON IGNITION AND OBSERVE FOR "BULB-CHECK". 	—	OFF	"BULB-CHECK" IS FUNCTIONAL. RETURN VEHICLE TO SERVICE.	
IN-LINE FUSE	1		—		NO "BULB-CHECK", CONTINUE TROUBLE-SHOOTING.	2
IN-LINE FUSE	1		—	ON	SEE PROCEDURE "WARNING LIGHT COMES ON AND STAYS ON".	—

Fig. 47 AC anti-skid diagnosis and testing

ANTI-SKID BRAKE SYSTEMS

STEP	PROCEDURE	WARN LIGHT	BULB CHECK	RESULT	NEXT STEP
2 — WARNING LAMP & CAB WIRING TEST	DISCONNECT I/P CONNECTOR FROM ADAPTER: JUMPER FROM GROUND TO GREEN WIRE IN I/P CONNECTOR. 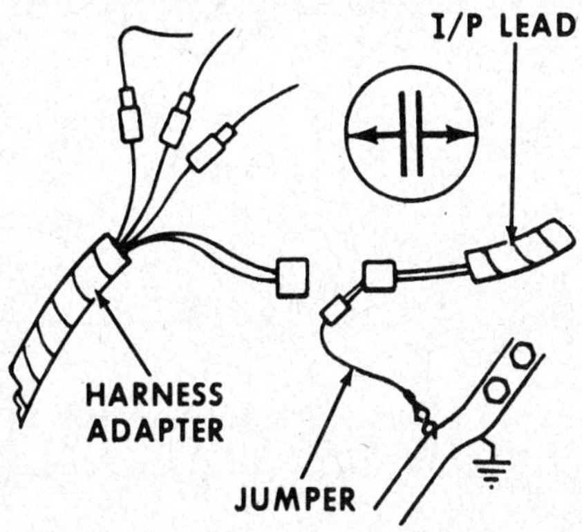 (I/P LEAD, HARNESS ADAPTER, JUMPER)	OFF	—	PROBLEM IS IN LAMP, LAMP SOCKET, OR CAB WIRING.	2A
		ON	—	LAMP AND LAMP WIRING OK, EVERY AXLE SYSTEM HAS A PROBLEM IN THE POWER CABLE AND/OR MODULATOR.	3
3 — AXLE SYSTEM TEST	REPEAT THIS STEP FOR EVERY AXLE SYSTEM. DISCONNECT POWER CABLES FROM ALL MODULATORS. CONNECT THE POWER PLUG (FROM THE SERVICE TOOL KIT) TO THE POWER CABLE OF THE AXLE SYSTEM YOU ARE TROUBLESHOOTING. 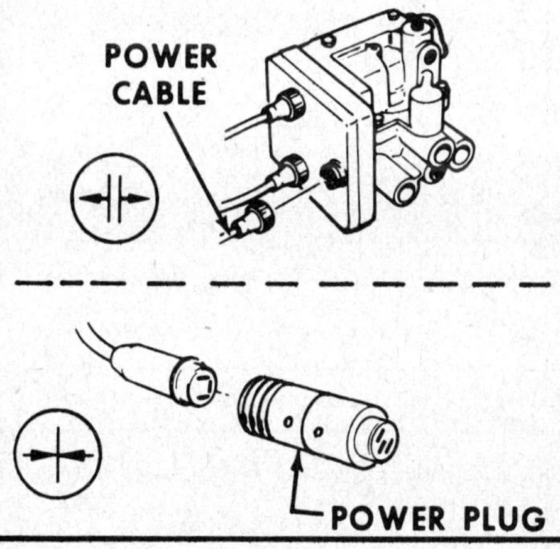 (POWER CABLE, POWER PLUG)	ON	—	IF GREEN LIGHT IN POWER PLUG IS "ON", POWER CABLE IS OK. PROBLEM IS IN MODULATOR.	3A
		OFF	—	IF GREEN LIGHT IN POWER PLUG IS "ON", OR BOTH POWER PLUG LIGHTS ARE "OFF", PROBLEM IS IN POWER CABLE.	3B
		ON OR OFF	—	IF RED LIGHT IN POWER PLUG IS "ON" PROBLEM IS REVERSE POLARITY IN CABLE OR IN CAB WIRING.	3C
2A — WARNING LAMP & CAB WIRING	CORRECT WARNING LAMP AND/OR CAB WIRING PROBLEM BY REPAIRING OR REPLACING FAULTY COMPONENTS. TURN IGNITION "ON" AND LOOK FOR "BULB-CHECK".	—	YES	"BULB-CHECK" IS FUNCTIONAL. RETURN VEHICLE TO SERVICE.	—
		—	NO	CONTINUE TROUBLESHOOTING.	2

Fig. 48 AC anti-skid diagnosis and testing

ANTI-SKID BRAKE SYSTEMS

STEP	PROCEDURE	WARN LIGHT	BULB CHECK	RESULT	NEXT STEP
3A REPLACE MODULATOR	REPLACE MODULATOR. DISCONNECT AND RE-CONNECT ALL HOSES AND CABLES PROPERLY. TURN ON IGNITION AND LOOK FOR "BULB-CHECK".	—	YES	THIS AXLE SYSTEM OK. CONTINUE TROUBLESHOOTING NEXT AXLE.	3
				IF THIS IS FINAL AXLE SYSTEM, RECONNECT ALL POWER CABLES AND RETURN VEHICLE TO SERVICE.	—
		—	NO	PROBLEM IS STILL IN MODULATOR.	(3A)
3B POWER CABLE	REPLACE POWER CABLE AND RECONNECT TO MODULATOR. TURN IGNITION "ON" AND LOOK FOR "BULB-CHECK".	—	YES	THIS AXLE SYSTEM IS OK. CONTINUE TROUBLESHOOTING NEXT AXLE.	3
				IF THIS IS FINAL AXLE SYSTEM, RECONNECT ALL POWER CABLES AND RETURN VEHICLE TO SERVICE.	—
		—	NO	CONTINUE TROUBLESHOOTING THIS AXLE.	3
3C CAB WIRING	CORRECT REVERSE POLARITY PROBLEM IN POWER CABLE OR IN CAB WIRING, AND RECONNECT POWER CABLE TO MODULATOR. TURN IGNITION "ON" AND LOOK FOR "BULB-CHECK".	—	YES	THIS AXLE SYSTEM IS OK. CONTINUE TROUBLESHOOTING NEXT AXLE.	3
				IF THIS IS FINAL AXLE SYSTEM, RECONNECT ALL POWER CABLES AND PUT VEHICLE BACK IN SERVICE.	—
		—	NO	CONTINUE TROUBLESHOOTING THIS AXLE.	3

Fig. 49 AC anti-skid diagnosis and testing

ANTI-SKID BRAKE SYSTEMS

AIR BRAKE – WHEEL LOCK CONTROL MODULATOR – ELECTRICAL SERVICE PROCEDURE

("Solenoid" and/or "Controller and Cover Assembly" only)

TEST PLUG METHOD

	STEP	PROCEDURE	NEXT STEP
DISASSEMBLY	1	REMOVE CONTROLLER AND COVER ASSEMBLY AND DISCONNECT SOLENOID LEADS.	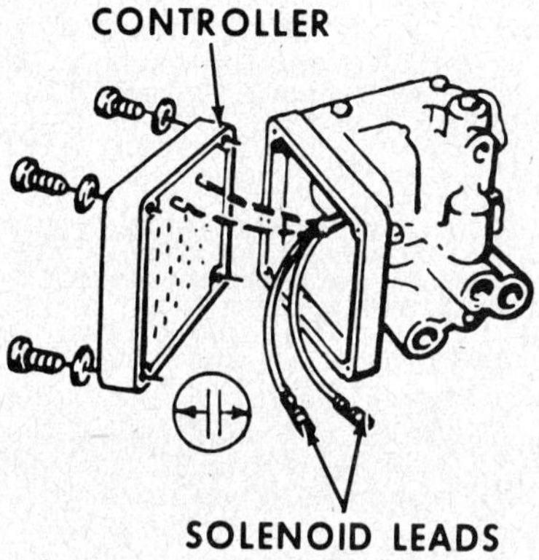 2
SOLENOID	2	TAKE SOLENOID LEADS AND MOMENTARILY CONNECT THEM TO A 12 VOLT BATTERY. 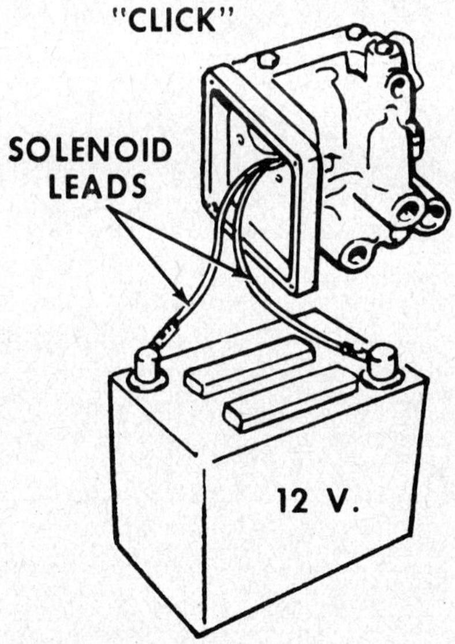 SOLENOID IS OK IF YOU HEAR A "CLICK" WHEN LEADS ARE CONNECTED AND ANOTHER "CLICK" WHEN THEY ARE DISCONNECTED. PROBLEM IS IN CONTROLLER AND COVER ASSEMBLY.	5
SOLENOID		IF "CLICKS" ARE NOT HEARD – PROBLEM IS IN SOLENOID.	3
SOLENOID	3	REPLACE THE SOLENOID. CONTINUE WITH NEXT STEP –	4
SOLENOID	4	TEST NEW SOLENOID IN SAME MANNER AS DESCRIBED IN STEP 2. SOLENOID IS OK IF A "CLICK" IS HEARD WHEN LEADS ARE CONNECTED AND ANOTHER "CLICK" WHEN THEY ARE DISCONNECTED. REASSEMBLE THE CONTROLLER AND COVER ASSEMBLY AND RETEST MODULATOR.	6
SOLENOID		IF NO "CLICKS" ARE HEARD, PROBLEM IS STILL IN SOLENOID.	3

Fig. 50 AC anti-skid diagnosis and testing

ANTI-SKID BRAKE SYSTEMS

	STEP	PROCEDURE		NEXT STEP
CONTROLLER	5	REPLACE THE CONTROLLER AND COVER ASSEMBLY.		6
TESTING REPAIRED MODULATOR ASSEMBLY	6	TEST THE REPAIRED ASSEMBLY BY INSTALLING TWO "SENSOR" PLUGS (FROM TROUBLESHOOTING KIT) INTO SENSOR TERMINALS AND "MODULATOR TEST" PLUG INTO POWER TERMINAL. USE "POWER" AND "POWER ADAPTER" PLUGS FROM THE KIT TO SIMULATE TRACTOR WARNING LIGHT. CONNECT LEADS AS SHOWN BELOW — A NORMAL "BULB-CHECK" SHOULD BE OBSERVED WHEN THE CIRCUIT IS COMPLETED BY CONNECTING BLACK LEAD TO NEGATIVE TERMINAL OF BATTERY. 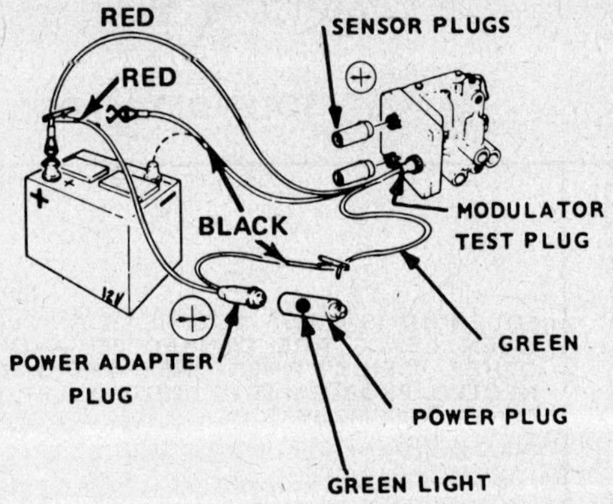	NORMAL "BULB-CHECK" IS OBSERVED (THE GREEN LIGHT IN THE POWER PLUG COMES ON FOR 2-5 SECONDS AND THEN GOES OFF.	7A
			NO "BULB-CHECK", OR — LAMP IN POWER PLUG REMAINS "ON". CHECK ALL TEST PLUGS AND OTHER ELECTRICAL CONNECTIONS. IF LAMP REMAINS "ON", THERE IS STILL A PROBLEM IN MODULATOR ASSEMBLY.	1
	7	REMOVE ONE SENSOR PLUG TO SIMULATE A FAULT.	GREEN LAMP SHOULD GO "ON" INDICATING A FAULT. THIS IS NORMAL.	8
			GREEN LAMP DOES NOT COME "ON" INDICATING SELF-CHECK CIRCUIT IS NOT OPERATING. REMOVE CONTROLLER AND COVER ASSEMBLY PER STEP 1 AND REPLACE PER STEP 5.	5
	8	REINSTALL SENSOR PLUG BACK ON SENSOR TERMINAL.	GREEN LAMP SHOULD GO "OFF". THIS IS NORMAL AND INDICATES MODULATOR ASSEMBLY IS OPERATIONAL — RETURN TO SERVICE.	—
			GREEN LAMP REMAINS "ON". DOUBLE CHECK ALL TEST PLUGS AND OTHER ELECTRICAL CONNECTIONS. IF LAMP IS STILL "ON", REPEAT MODULATOR SERVICE PROCEDURE.	1

Fig. 51 AC anti-skid diagnosis and testing

ANTI-SKID BRAKE SYSTEMS

AC WHEEL LOCK CONTROL
SERVICE TOOL KIT CHECKOUT

SERVICE TOOL KIT COMPONENTS ARE FUNCTIONAL IF THE FOLLOWING REQUIREMENTS ARE MET. IF THE REQUIREMENTS ARE NOT MET, REPLACE THE COMPONENT.

TEST	PROCEDURE	REQUIREMENTS
SENSOR PLUGS	MEASURE RESISTANCE AT BOTH ENDS OF EACH SENSOR PLUG AS SHOWN 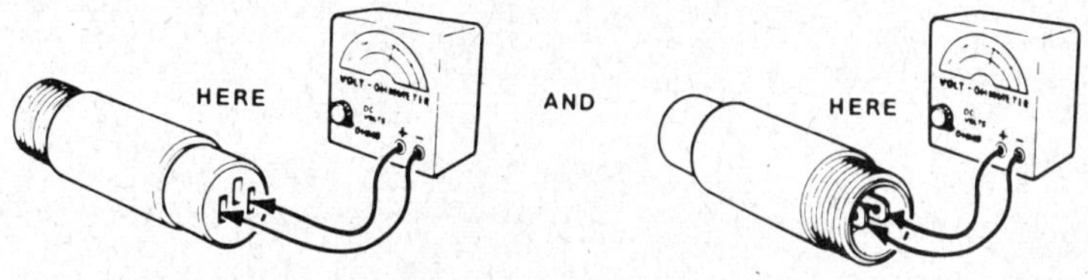 — HERE AND HERE	RESISTANCE SHOULD BE BETWEEN 1000 AND 2000 OHMS
POWER ADAPTOR PLUG	MEASURE RESISTANCE OF POWER ADAPTOR PLUG IN TWO PLACES AS SHOWN 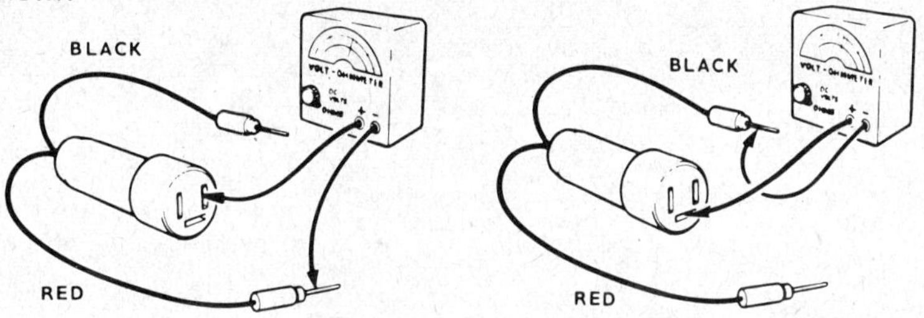 (BLACK / RED)	RESISTANCE SHOULD BE LESS THAN 1.0 OHM
POWER PLUG	CONNECT 12 VOLTS TWO PLACES ONE AT A TIME AS SHOWN 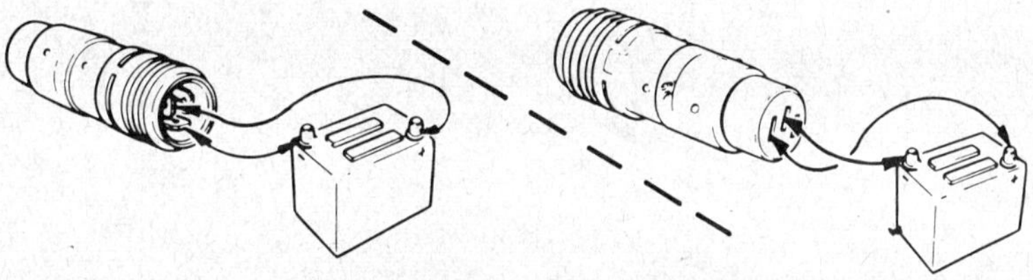	GREEN LIGHT SHOULD BE "ON"; RED LIGHT SHOULD BE "OFF"
POWER PLUG	CONNECT 12 VOLTS TWO PLACES ONE AT A TIME AS SHOWN 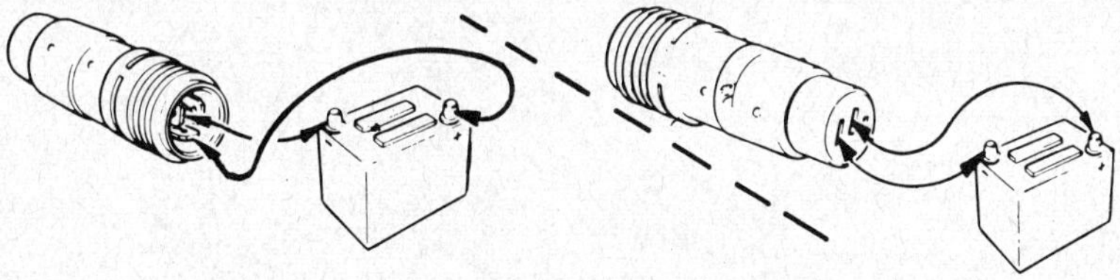	RED LIGHT SHOULD BE "ON"; GREEN LIGHT SHOULD BE "OFF"
	MEASURE RESISTANCE AS SHOWN 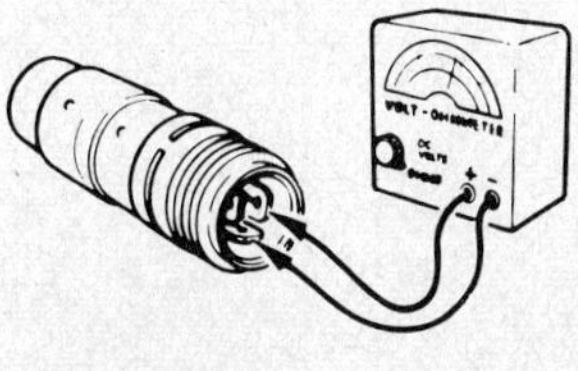	RESISTANCE SHOULD BE LESS THAN 1.0 OHM

Fig. 52 AC anti-skid diagnosis and testing

ANTI-SKID BRAKE SYSTEMS

TEST	PROCEDURE	REQUIREMENTS
SENSOR ADAPTOR PIGTAIL	MEASURE RESISTANCE OF EACH WIRE IN PIGTAIL AS SHOWN 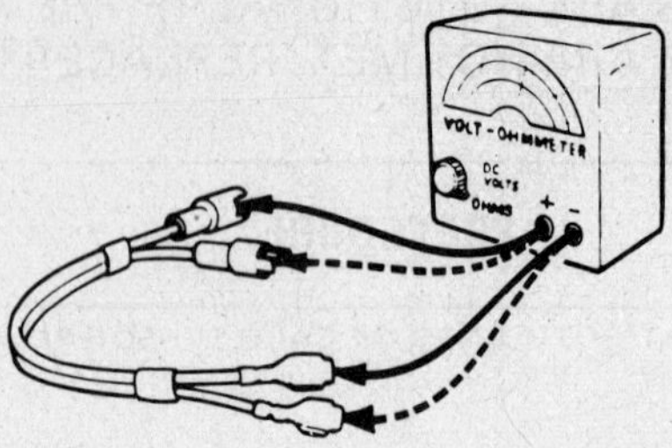	RESISTANCE SHOULD BE LESS THAN 1.0 OHM
MODULATOR TEST PLUG	MEASURE RESISTANCE OF MODULATOR TEST PLUG THREE PLACES AS SHOWN 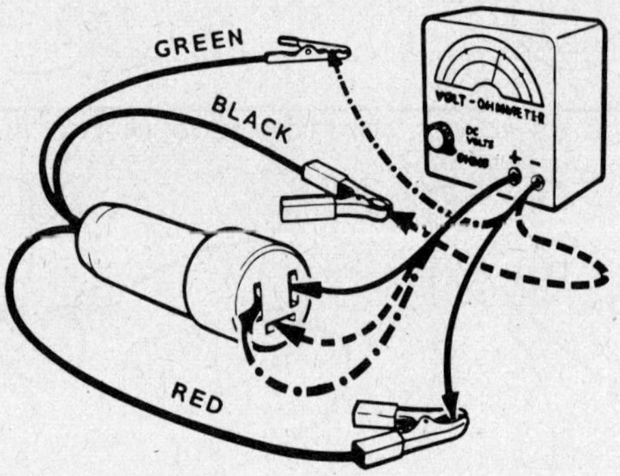 (GREEN, BLACK, RED)	RESISTANCE SHOULD BE LESS THAN 1.0 OHM

MODULATOR PNEUMATIC CHECKOUT PROCEDURE

	STEP	PROCEDURE	RESULT	NEXT STEP
CHARGE AIR	1	BLOCK VEHICLE AND FULLY CHARGE AIR BRAKE SYSTEM	PRESSURE SHOULD BE SUFFICIENT TO REMOVE SPRING BRAKES.	2
BRAKE APPLICATION	2	MAKE SEVERAL BRAKE APPLICATIONS 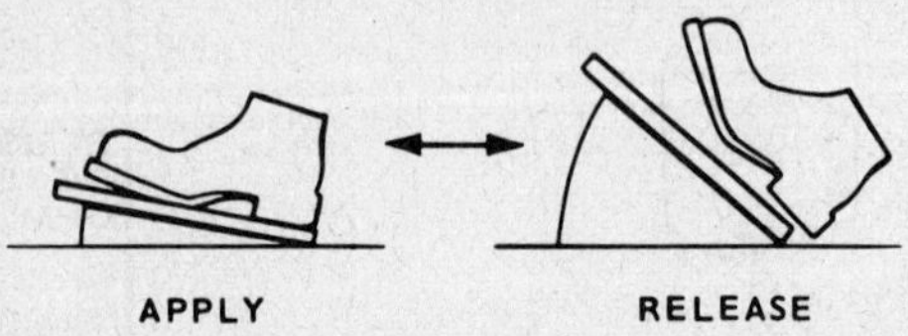 (APPLY / RELEASE)	BRAKE CHAMBERS SHOULD APPLY AND RELEASE AT ALL WHEELS.  (APPLY / RELEASE)	3
			VALVE DOES NOT FUNCTION	6

Fig. 53 AC anti-skid diagnosis and testing

ANTI-SKID BRAKE SYSTEMS

	STEP	PROCEDURE	RESULT	NEXT STEP
RELEASE LEAKAGE	3	RELEASE THE BRAKES. COAT EXHAUST PORT OF VALVE WITH SOAP SOLUTION. 	A 1 INCH DIAMETER BUBBLE IN 5 SECONDS IS ACCEPTABLE.	4
			EXCESSIVE LEAKAGE	6
APPLICATION LEAKAGE	4	MAKE AND HOLD A SERVICE BRAKE APPLICATION. COAT THE EXHAUST PORT OF VALVE WITH SOAP SOLUTION. 	A 2 INCH DIAMETER BUBBLE IN 3 SECONDS IS ACCEPTABLE.	5
			EXCESSIVE LEAKAGE	6
VALVE LEAKAGE	5	MAKE AND HOLD A SERVICE BRAKE APPLICATION. COAT THE RELAY-SOLENOID VALVE MATING SURFACE WITH A SOAP SOLUTION. 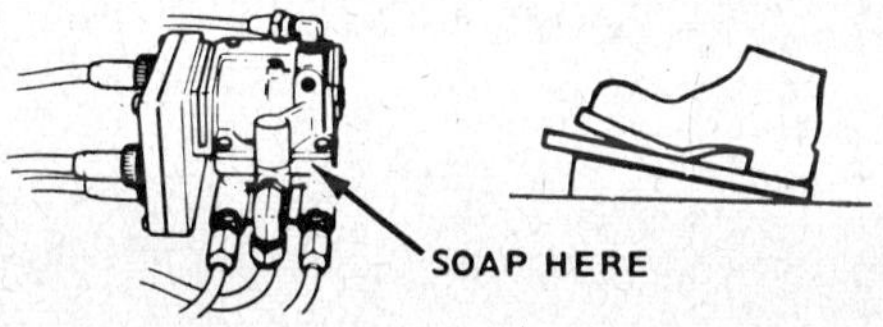	NO LEAKAGE. PNEUMATIC SYSTEM OK.	—
			LEAKAGE	6
OVERHAUL VALVE	6	REMOVE MODULATOR FROM VEHICLE AND OVERHAUL PER VALVE OVERHAUL PROCEDURE. REINSTALL ON VEHICLE.	REPEAT MODULATOR PNEUMATIC CHECKOUT PROCEDURE	1

Fig. 54 AC anti-skid diagnosis and testing

opening, press on flat surface of seat and remove solenoid valve components.
22. Pull out metal retainer and remove rubber solenoid exhaust valve.
23. Using suitable pliers, remove restriction piston from solenoid valve body, then remove O ring and discard.

Modulator Assemble

NOTE: Lubricate all new seals and O rings with Dow Corning No. 33 silicone grease or equivalent.

1. Install O rings on restriction piston, then press either end of piston into solenoid valve body until piston bottoms, Fig. 56.
2. Position rubber solenoid exhaust in metal retainer, then press retainer and exhaust in until retainer snaps into place.
3. Install O rings on valve body and press small end into solenoid valve body through solenoid bore until seated.
4. Install O rings on solenoid valve stem and cage, then install spring on valve stem.
5. Install valve stem end without spring through open end of valve cage, then install diaphragm seal on end of stem protruding from other side of cage.
6. Install cage and valve stem into solenoid bore, Fig. 57.
7. Place rubber button check valve on small end of conical spring, then insert large end of spring into large diameter check valve bore.
8. Install O ring on metal valve seat retainer, then press open end of retainer into large diameter check valve bore until fully seated.
9. Insert button check valve into long spring, then install rounded end of check valve into small diameter check valve bore in solenoid valve body.
10. Install O ring on check valve cover, then position spring on cover boss and install cover. Torque attaching screws to 55 to 65 in. lbs.
11. Install O ring on solenoid, then thread solenoid into solenoid valve body using tool No. J-25360-1. Torque solenoid to 66 to 96 in. lbs.
12. Place tension ball into solenoid valve body hole and install allen head screw. Torque screw to 20 to 30 in. lbs.
13. Position washer over screw with concave side facing screw head, then install diaphragm on exhaust valve body and torque attaching screw to 20 to 25 in. lbs.
14. Install seal and retainer on modulation

ANTI-SKID BRAKES

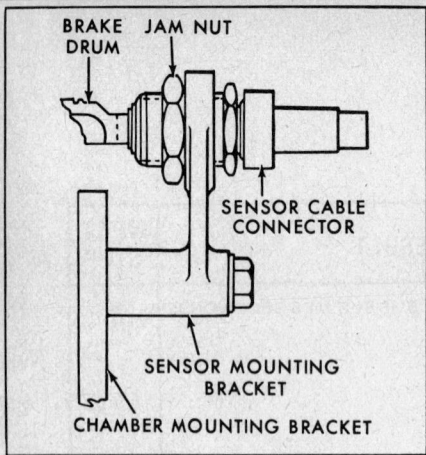

Fig. 55 Wheel speed sensor

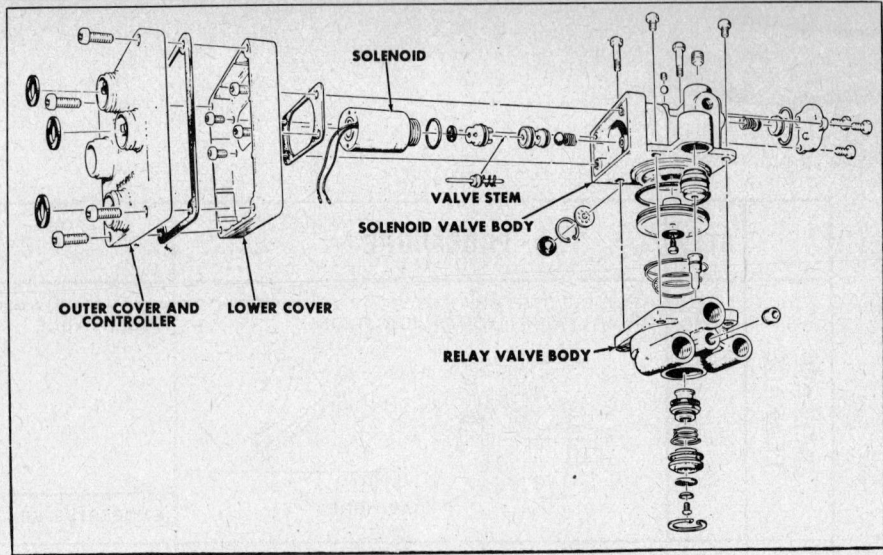

Fig. 56 AC modulator disassembled

tube.
15. Install O rings on modulation tube and valve body.
16. Install modulation tube, seal and first, into relay valve body, then position spring over tube.
17. Press exhaust valve body into relay valve body until fully seated, then install washer and snap ring, Fig. 58.
18. Position molded rubber valve assembly inside of relay piston with rib against piston, then install and torque retaining screw to 70 to 80 in. lbs.
19. Install O ring on relay piston.
20. Position small end of conical spring over lugs in piston cavity in relay valve body, then press relay piston into bore.
21. Install O ring on flow restrictor, then press flow restrictor into bore on relay valve body.
22. Install O ring on solenoid valve body, position relay and solenoid valve bodies to align rate control valve restriction bores and attaching bolt holes. Press valve bodies together until seated and install four attaching screws. Torque attaching screws to 110 to 130 in. lbs.
23. Insert solenoid leads through lower cover gasket and large oval hole in cover with concave side of cover facing away from valve assembly.
24. Install cover on valve body and install and torque attaching screws to 140 to 160 in. lbs. using tools 25360-5, 9.
25. Position gasket on cover and controller assembly, then connect two stator leads to controller terminals.
26. Carefully position excess solenoid leads inside lower cover and place controller and cover assembly on valve assembly. Assemble with Aux stamp on cover closest to modulator mounting surface.
27. Install attaching screws and torque to 16 to 20 ft. lbs. using tools J-25360-5, 9.

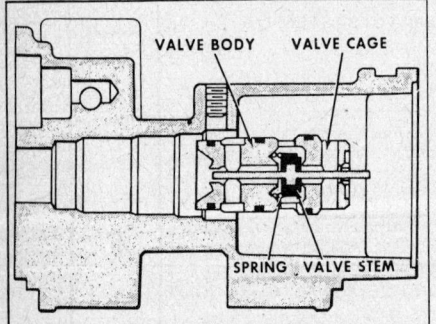

Fig. 57 Solenoid valve, stem and cage installation

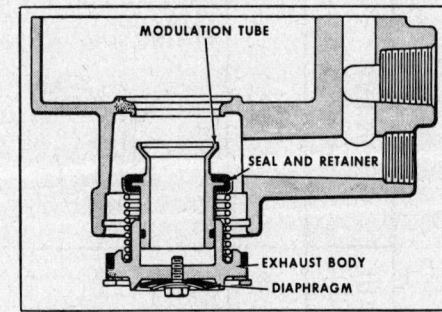

Fig. 58 Modulator tube and exhaust valve installation

BRAKE ADJUSTMENTS

INDEX

Page No.

BENDIX BRAKES
Duo-Servo Type 590
Uni-Servo Type 591
Non-Servo Type 591

TIMKEN (ROCKWELL) BRAKES
DH Model 591
FSH Model 592
H Model 592
T Model 593

P Model 593
P Model, Heavy Duty 594
Stopmaster 594

WAGNER BRAKES
Non-Servo Type 595
F Model 597
FA Model 597
Twin Action Type 598

BENDIX DUO-SERVO BRAKE

This type brake, Fig. 1, is self-energizing in both forward and reverse. Each brake has one wheel cylinder mounted at the top of the backing plate below the single anchor pin. The anchor pin holds the wheel cylinder in place, being inserted through a flange on the wheel cylinder casting. Shoe return springs hold the upper end of the shoes against the pin with the brakes released. A guide plate, installed on the anchor pin outside of the shoe webs, holds the upper end of the shoes in alignment. Brake shoe lower guides, riveted to the backing plate, are also used on some models.

Brake adjustment is made at the adjusting screw in the adjusting link assembly. The link spring holds the shoe ends in place in the link ends. The link spring also serves as a lock for the notched adjusting screw.

Each brake shoe is held against three bear-

BRAKE ADJUSTMENTS

ing surfaces on the backing plate by the hold-down pins and springs. Lining on the secondary (rear) shoe is longer than the lining on the primary (front) shoe.

Unless the vehicle has a transmission parking brake, the rear brake assemblies have a parking brake lever attached by a cable to the secondary shoes. A strut between the primary and secondary shoes assures braking action by both shoes. Parking brake action is entirely mechanical and operates independently of the hydraulic brake system.

Adjustment, Fig. 1

Before attempting to make any adjustments, be sure the wheel bearings are properly adjusted and that the brake backing plates are tight.
1. Jack up wheels clear of floor and release parking brake.
2. Remove adjusting hole covers.
3. Insert screwdriver or special adjusting tool in slot of backing plate to engage star wheel adjusting screw.
4. Move outer end of tool toward axle, expanding brake shoes to a point where the wheel can just be turned by hand.
5. Parking brake cable (if used) adjustment should be made at this time. With brake shoes still expanded, disconnect parking brake cable at intermediate lever end. With parking brake lever applied approximately one inch from fully released position, pull cables by hand to remove all slack. Then adjust cables as required at yoke ends so that clevis pins can be inserted.
6. Back off star wheel adjusting screw until brake drums turn freely. It may be necessary to tap the backing plate lightly to permit brake shoes to assume a central position.
7. Pull parking brake lever back until rear wheel can just be turned by hand. Check rear wheels for equal brake drag. If drag is unequal, loosen the tight brake until drag is equal on both rear wheels.

Anchor Pin Adjustment

On some models, an adjustable anchor pin is provided for when brakes have been relined or when brake action is unequal or severe. Some vehicles have the adjustable anchor on all four brake assemblies while others have it on the front wheels only.
1. Loosen nut on anchor pin at inner side of backing plate, then retighten nut 1/4 turn beyond finger-tight.
2. Remove adjusting hole cover from backing plate and turn star wheel adjuster to expand brake shoes until a heavy drag is felt when turning the brake drum by hand.
3. While continuing to expand shoes, periodically tap backing plate adjacent to the anchor pin to cause the anchor pin to center itself. When brake drag can no longer be relieved by tapping on the backing plate, hold anchor pin and tighten lock nut securely.

BENDIX UNI-SERVO BRAKE

This type brake, Fig. 2, is essentially the same as the duo-servo type except that a single end wheel cylinder is used instead of the double end type shown in Fig. 1. Adjustments are also the same as outlined for the duo-servo type.

It should be noted that some models of this type brake had the wheel cylinder mounted on the side of the assembly instead of the top as shown in Fig. 2.

BENDIX NON-SERVO BRAKE

This type brake, Fig. 3, has the upper end of the shoes extending through the wheel cylinder boots and contacting inserts in the wheel cylinder pistons. The shoe ends are held firmly against the pistons by the brake shoe return springs. The lower end of the shoes are held against a fixed anchor plate by the anchor spring. A hold-down spring at the center of each shoe holds the shoes in alignment. An eccentric adjustment located near the center of each shoe provides a means of compensating for lining wear and is the only shoe adjustment required.

Adjustment

1. With wheels raised clear of floor and hand brake released, turn forward shoe adjusting cam until a heavy drag occurs. Then turn the cam in the opposite direction until the drum is just free of drag.
2. Repeat with the rear shoe.

TIMKEN (ROCKWELL) "DH" BRAKE

This brake, Fig. 4, commonly referred to as the Duplex Brake, is an hydraulically-actuated dual primary assembly. It features identical shoe and liner assemblies and four identical return springs which simplify assembly and disassembly, Fig. 5.

Adjustment

Brake is adjusted from the back face of the backing plate at the slotted holes. Insert screwdriver through slotted hole against ratchet lugs of adjusting bolts and move end of handle up or down as a lever, depending on rotation desired.

Shoe liners should be brought out against the brake drum until a slight drag can be felt while the drum is in rotation. Adjusting bolt should then be backed off until drum can rotate freely. Brake shoes should be adjusted individually.

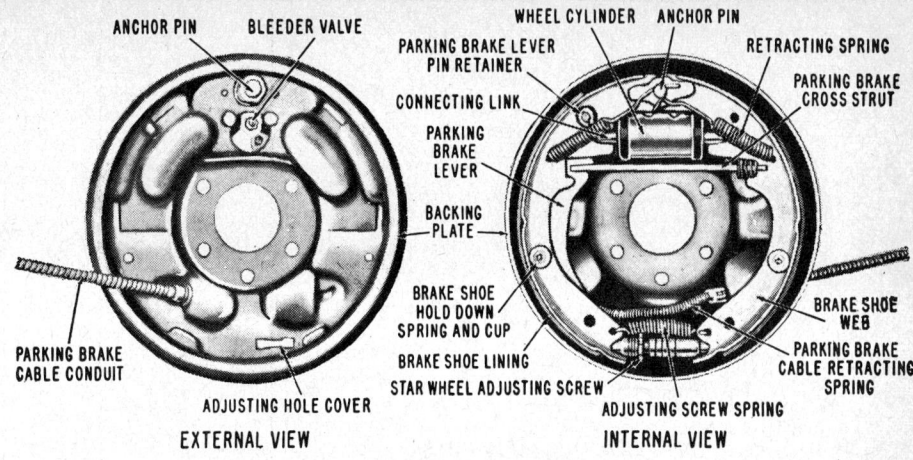

Fig. 1 Bendix duo-servo single anchor brake with star wheel adjustor

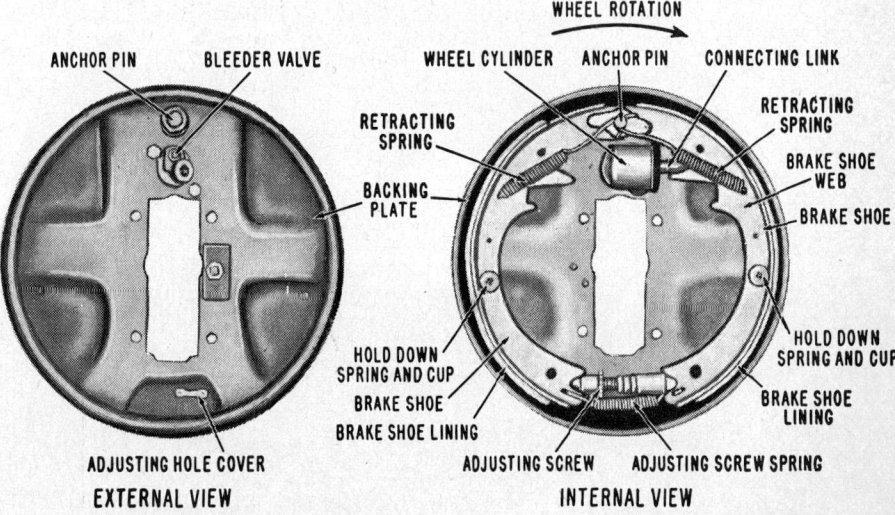

Fig. 2 Bendix uni-servo single anchor brake with star wheel adjuster

BRAKE ADJUSTMENTS

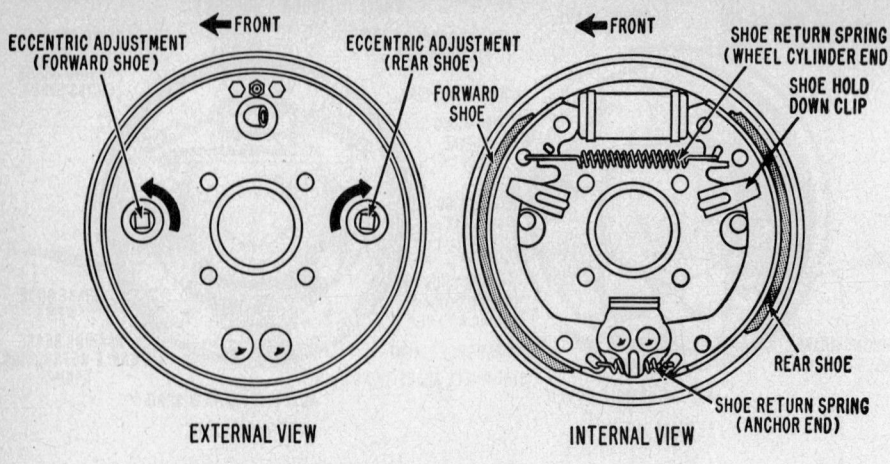

Fig. 3 Bendix non-servo breake of the floating shoe type with an eccentric cam adjustment for each shoe

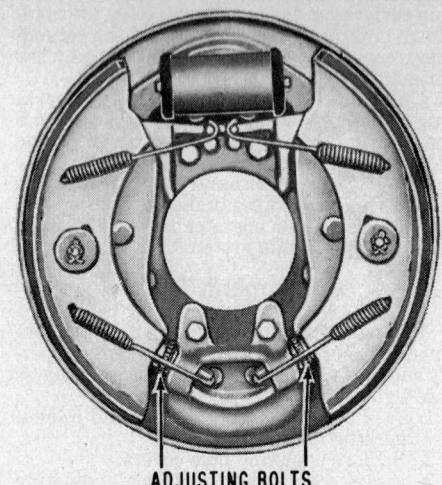

Fig. 4 Timken (Rockwell) "DH" series brake

TIMKEN (ROCKWELL) "FSH" BRAKE

This brake, Fig. 6, is a floating shoe hydraulic assembly. Actuation permits the shoes to center themselves in the drum with equal effectiveness in either direction. This brake is supplied either with or without a built-in mechanical parking brake.

This brake is also built with automatic adjustment for use on special applications. On the automatic type, one actuation of the foot pedal sets the automatic adjustment. No further adjustment of the brake is required during the life of the brake lining. Fig. 7 shows the components that make up the assembly.

Adjustment

The adjustable type brake has two eccentric cams that may be adjusted with a wrench on the adjusting bolts at the back face of the backing plate.

Upon reassembly, first actuate the brake to center the shoes in the drum. Then adjust the liners out until a slight drag can be felt while the drum is in rotation. Back off the adjusting bolt until the drum can rotate freely.

Subsequent adjustments to compensate for lining wear may be made by moving the shoe in or out by turning the eccentric cam in the required direction.

TIMKEN (ROCKWELL) "H" BRAKE

The brake, Fig. 8, is a light duty, two shoe type mounted on the backing plate which also serves as a dust shield. Adjustable anchor pins provide a means of centering the brake shoe arc in relation to the drum. Secondary or minor adjustments are made by rotating the eccentric cam which bears on the brake shoe flange or pin in the shoe web.

Adjustment

Following overhaul or when new linings are installed, the initial adjustment should be carefully made to locate properly the curvature of the lining to the drum and to obtain the proper clearance.

Each shoe must be adjusted to center the brake shoe arc in relation to the drum. Back off on both anchor pins and cams and adjust each shoe individually.

Adjust cam to bring lining into contact with drum and rotate anchor in enough to relieve drag. Repeat until additional rotation of anchor pin will no longer relieve drag, Fig. 9. Lock anchor pin lock nut and back off cam just enough to permit wheel to turn freely.

Subsequent adjustments to compensate for lining wear are made with the eccentric cam only. Turn cam to bring lining into contact with drum. Then back off just enough to permit free rolling drum. Repeat on opposite shoe.

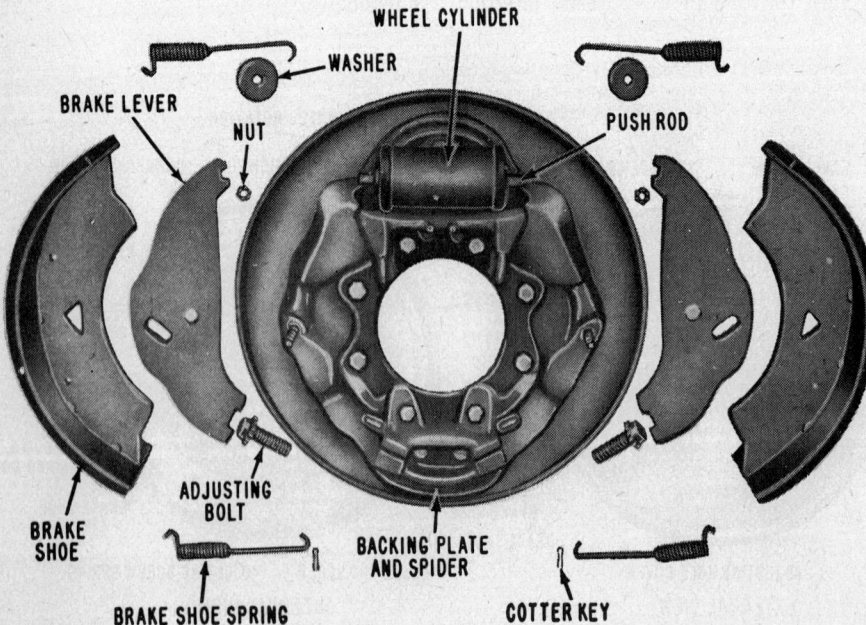

Fig. 5 Timken (Rockwell) "DH" series brake components

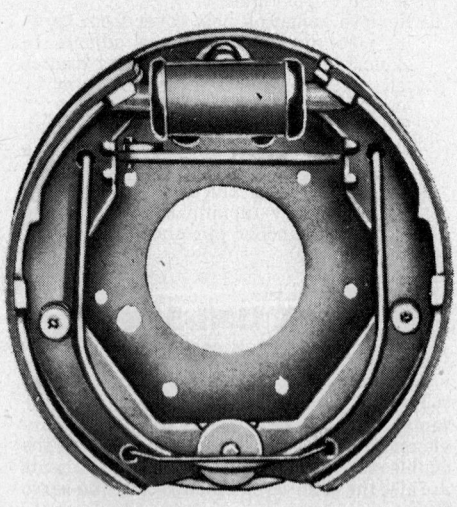

Fig. 6 Timken (Rockwell) "FSH" series brake

BRAKE ADJUSTMENTS

TIMKEN (ROCKWELL) "T" BRAKE

The "T" series brake, Fig. 10, is an air actuated two shoe brake, each shoe employing a one piece liner of uniform thickness. These brakes are either unit mounted with all component parts assembled on a backing plate or spider, or have inboard cam supports where operation warrants locating the air chambers toward the axle centers.

Some sizes of "T" brakes employ fabricated shoes with hardened steel cam roller followers Fig. 10, while other sizes employ either heat-treated malleable cast shoes with hardened cam follower wear pads, Fig. 11, or cam roller followers. Anchor pins of two different designs are used in various sizes of "T" series brakes. Some sizes use eccentric pins while others use fixed anchor pins.

The "T" series brakes are equipped with enclosed adjustable levers when shoe liner thickness does not exceed 3/8". The enclosed adjustable lever on these will permit the maximum liner wear. "T" series brakes with thicker liners, up to and including 1/2", are equipped with slack adjusters. Fig. 12 illustrates the component parts of the assembly.

Adjustment

On the "T" Fabricated Steel Brake, each shoe must be adjusted to center the brake shoe arc with the drum.
1. Rotate both anchor pins to the full release position.
2. Adjust cam to bring the liners in with drum and rotate anchor pins just enough to relieve drag. Repeat until additional rotation of anchor pins will no longer free drag.
3. Tighten anchor pin lock nuts and back off cam to minimum running clearance. To compensate for liner wear on both the fabricated steel and the cast assemblies, adjust cam at cam lever adjusting bolt to bring liners in contact with drum and back off to minimum running clearance.

TIMKEN (ROCKWELL) "P" BRAKE

The automotive "P" series brake is an air actuated two shoe brake, each shoe employing two 3/4" tapered block liners, Fig. 13. These shoes are fabricated steel, mounted on individual anchor pins and supported by open type spiders. The air chamber mounts on a bracket that bolts directly to the spider, thus making the brake completely unit mounted.

Automotive "P" series brakes may also be equipped with inboard cam supports where operation or axle design requires mounting the air chambers toward the axle centers. Dust shields are available for use when protection becomes desirable.

The "P" series brakes are actuated by "S" type constant lift cams which are forged integrally with shaft and supported in nylon bushings. Cam pressure is applied by cam roller followers. Fig. 14 shows the brake components.

Adjustment

New liners should be circle ground to .070" less than drum diameter. Adjust cam as required to obtain 80% contact.

Adjust slack adjusters or levers to obtain 3/4" travel at 60 lbs. pressure. When travel increases to 1 1/2" due to wear, readjust to 3/4".

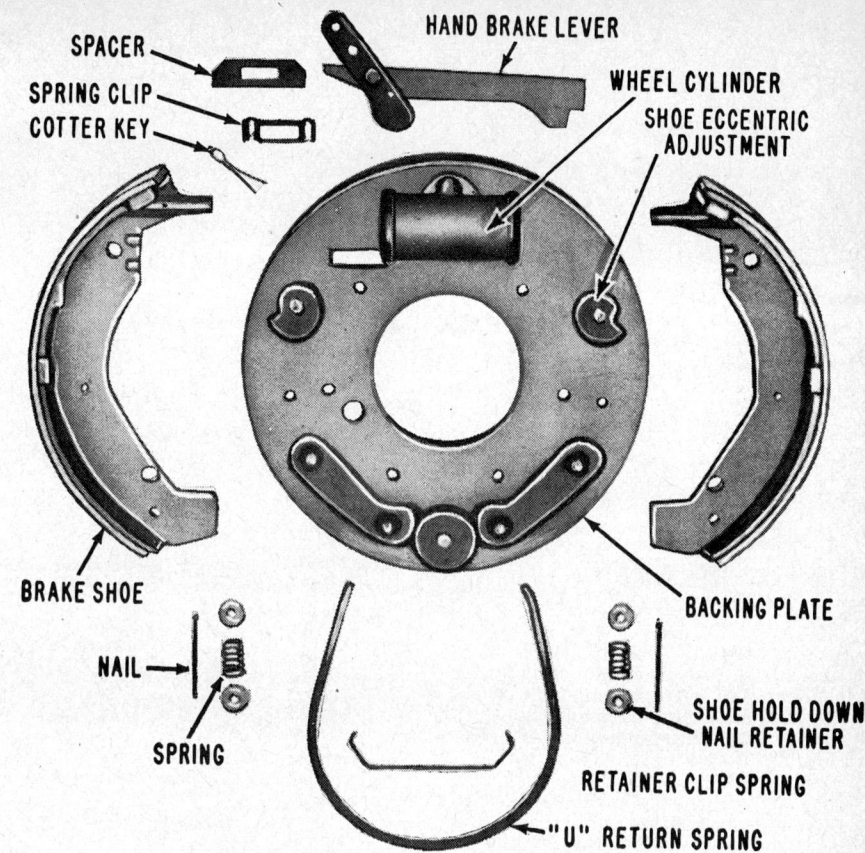

Fig. 7 Timken (Rockwell) "FSH" series brake components. When equipped with the parking lever feature, an upper coil spring is generally used rather than the "U" spring

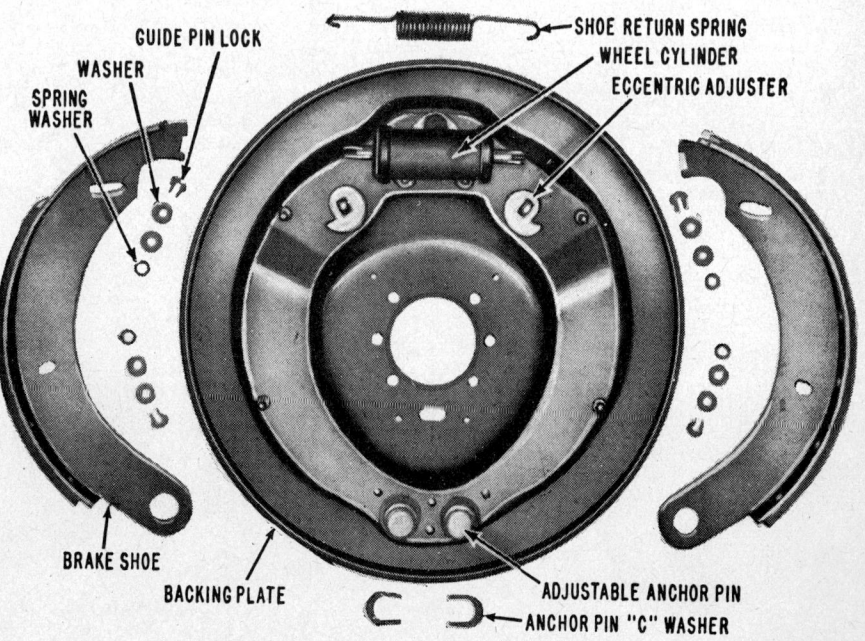

Fig. 8 Timken (Rockwell) "H" series brake

BRAKE ADJUSTMENTS

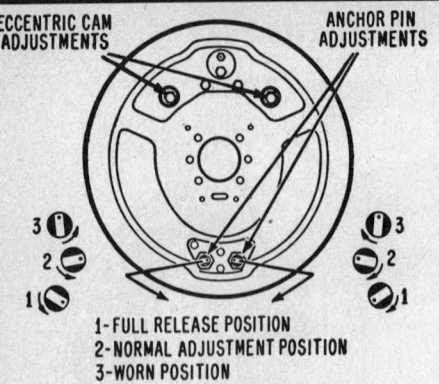

1—FULL RELEASE POSITION
2—NORMAL ADJUSTMENT POSITION
3—WORN POSITION

Fig. 9 (Rockwell) Timken "H" series brake adjustments

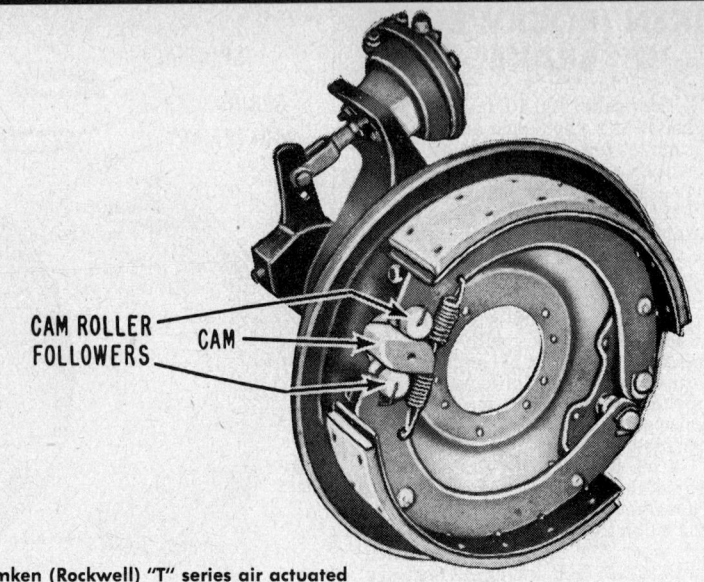

Fig. 10 Timken (Rockwell) "T" series air actuated brake with cam roller followers

TIMKEN (ROCKWELL) HEAVY DUTY "P" BRAKE

The Heavy Duty "P" series brake, Fig. 15, is an air actuated two shoe brake designed for heavy duty and special equipment where greater shoe and drum areas are necessary. This heavy duty series ranges from 18" to 22" and in width from 4" to 7".

The shoes are of heat treated malleable castings mounted on open spiders by individual anchor pins. Each shoe has hardened cam pressure pads and employs two 3/4" tapered block liners.

The camshaft and air chamber support bracket is mounted directly on the brake spider, making the assembly complete as a unit. However, the heavy duty brake may also be equipped with inboard cam supports where operation or axle design requires mounting the air chambers toward the axle centers.

Cam pressure is applied to the shoe hardened wear pads through the double "S" cam which is supported in needle bearings. Fig. 16 illustrates the component parts of the brake assembly.

Adjustment

New liners should be circle ground to .070" less than the drum diameter. Adjust cam as required to obtain 80% contact.

Adjust slack adjusters or levers to obtain 3/4" travel at 60 lbs. pressure. When travel increases to 1 1/2" due to wear, readjust to 3/4".

TIMKEN (ROCKWELL) STOPMASTER BRAKE

The Stopmaster Brake is a wedge actuated brake. The brake power units can be either air chambers or hydraulic cylinders. They can also be equipped with Fail-Safe units to provide parking and emergency braking. The brake power unit forces a wedge between two rollers and two plungers. This causes the plungers to spread apart and push the brake shoes against the brake drum.

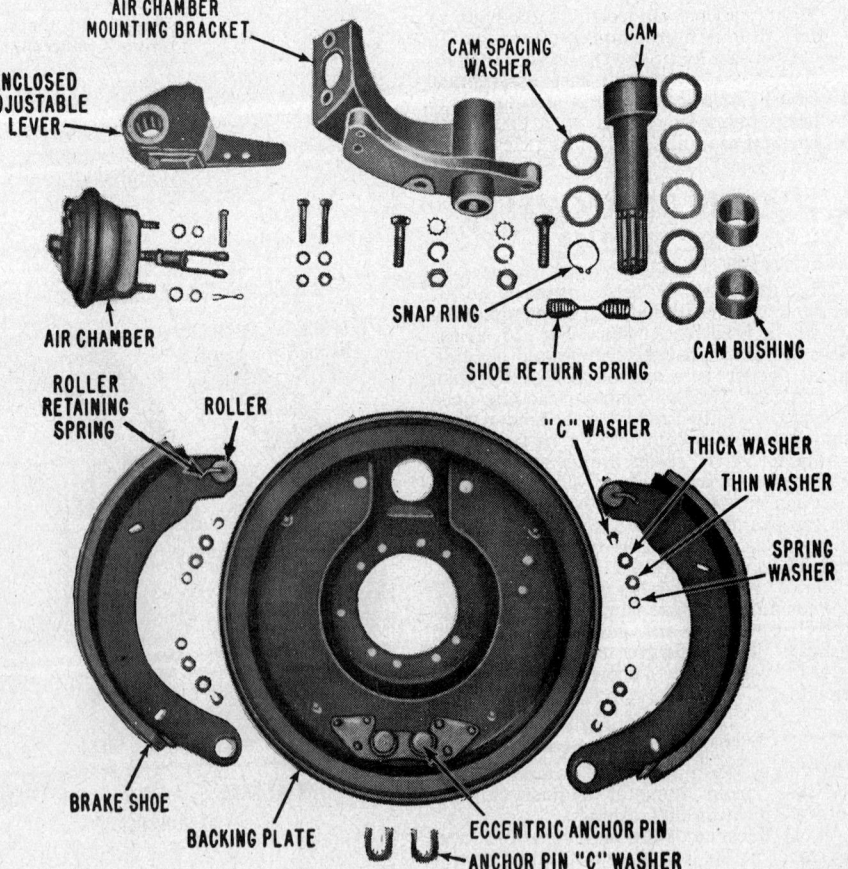

Fig. 11 Timken (Rockwell) "T" series air actuated brake with cam follower wear pads

Fig. 12 Timken (Rockwell) "T" series brake components

BRAKE ADJUSTMENTS

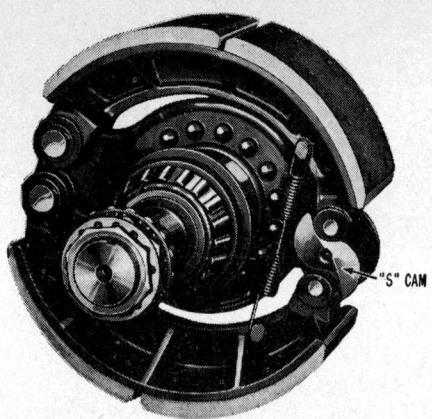

Fig. 13 Timken (Rockwell) "H" series brake adjustments

There are several variations of Stopmaster Brakes in use. Some have two power units per brake and others only one. Where two power units are used, there may be a Fail-Safe unit on one or both. The brake support may be either a cast spider or a stamped backing plate. On the cast spiders, the plunger housings may be either integral or bolted on. Brake shoe adjustment may be either manual or automatic.

Adjustment

Manual Adjusters
1. Hoist vehicle free of ground.
2. Remove cover from adjusting slot (two places on each brake).

NOTE: On RS type brakes the adjusting slots are above and below the single power unit. On RD type brakes the adjusting slots are below the forward and above the rear power unit. If star-wheel adjusting bolts are not found at these positions, the brake has been assembled on the wrong side of the vehicle.

3. Adjusting bolts have right-hand threads. With an adjusting spoon, turn star-wheel until heavy drum drag is developed. Then back off the bolt to a very light drag of the drum. Repeat for other brake shoe.
4. Replace dust covers in adjusting slots. Repeat for other brakes.

Automatic Adjusters
Check drum to lining clearance with feeler gauge. If clearance is more than .060", adjust brake manually (same as above) and schedule the vehicle for brake service.

WAGNER NON-SERVO BRAKE

This type brake, Fig. 17, has an adjustable anchor pin and an eccentric cam for each shoe. Note that the brake shown has a stepped type hydraulic cylinder with one end smaller than the other. However, other models have both ends of the cylinder the same diameter.

Minor Adjustment
1. With wheels raised clear of floor and hand brake in released position, rotate cam "A" outward until front shoe contacts drum and a definite drag is felt when wheel is turned by hand. Then back off adjustment until wheel is free.
2. Repeat procedure with cam "B".

Major Adjustment
1. With wheels and drums installed, rotate cam "A" until there is a brake drag felt when wheel is turned by hand.
2. Turn shoe anchor "C" in the direction of forward rotation of the wheel until a definite brake drag is felt. Note position of the anchor. Turn anchor "C" back in the opposite direction until the same amount of brake drag is felt and again note the position of the anchor. The turn anchor "C" back until it is halfway between the two extremes, producing a free wheel. This will indicate that the shoe is roughly centralized.

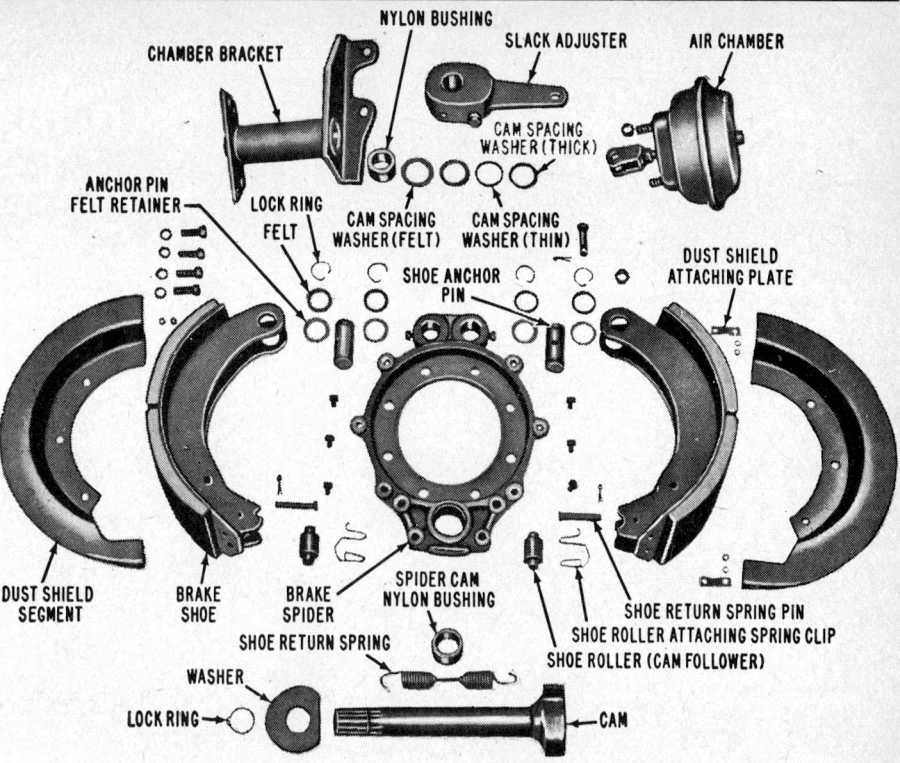

Fig. 14 Timken (Rockwell) "P" series brake components

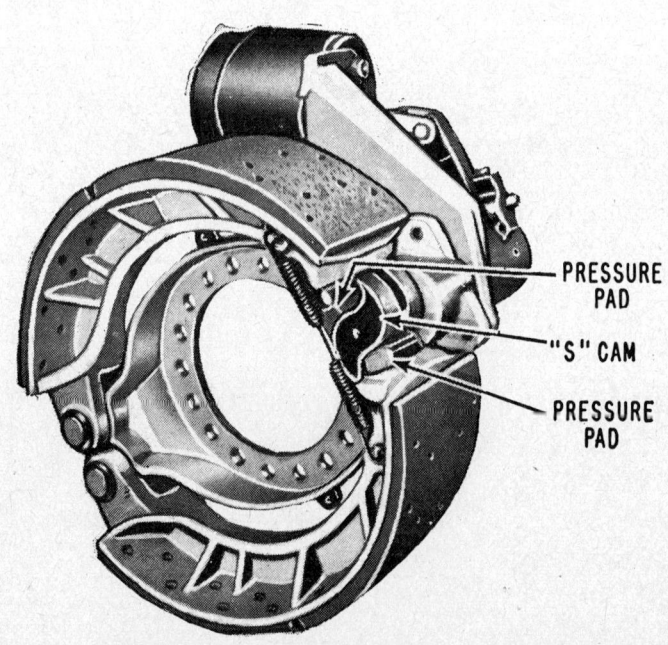

Fig. 15 Timken (Rockwell) "P" series heavy duty brake

BRAKE ADJUSTMENTS

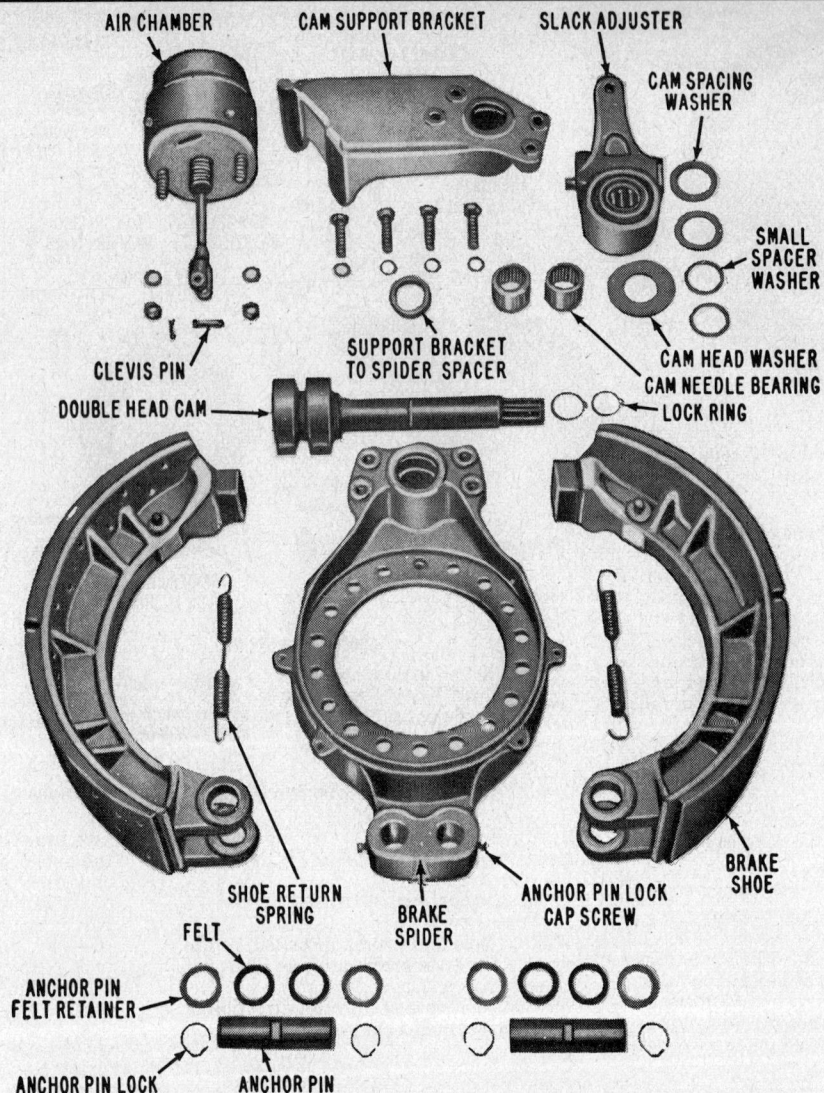

Fig. 16 Timken (Rockwell) heavy duty "P" series brake components

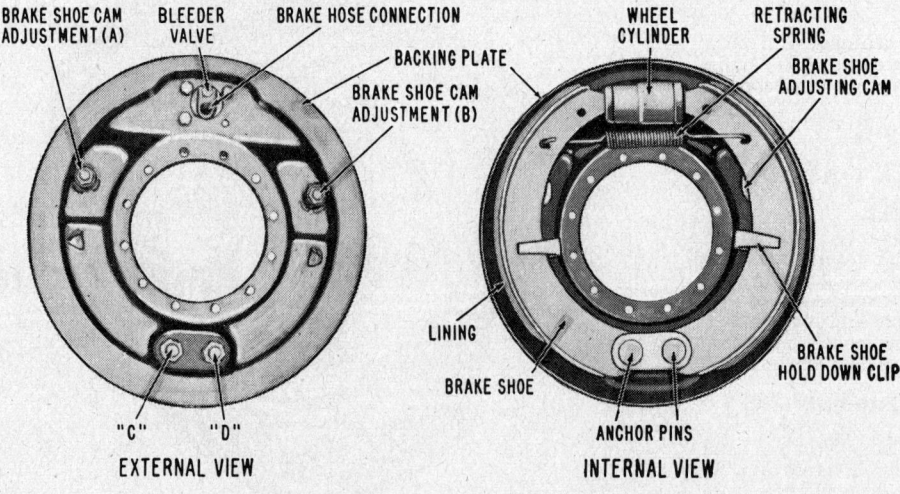

Fig. 17 Wagner brake with two adjustable anchor pins and an eccentric came adjustment for each shoe

BRAKE ADJUSTMENTS

3. Check both toe and heel of the shoe with a feeler gauge to determine the next steps to be taken in moving the adjustments.
4. Adjust cam "A" and anchor "C" until a clearance of .005" is obtained at the heel and a clearance of .010" is obtained at the toe end of the shoe as measured about 1½" from ends of lining.
5. Tighten lock nut on anchor "C" securely. Recheck clearances at shoe ends to make sure adjustments have not altered.
6. Repeat the foregoing operations on the rear shoe by adjusting cam "B" and anchor "D", substituting the word reverse for the word forward.

WAGNER "F" BRAKE

This type brake, Fig. 18, is self-centering and has two identical brake shoes arranged on the backing plate so that their toes are diagonally opposite. Two single end hydraulic cylinders are arranged so that one cylinder is mounted between each shoe toe and the opposite shoe heel.

The two hydraulic cylinder pistons apply equal amounts of hydraulic force to each shoe toe. Each cylinder body is shaped to provide an anchor block for the opposite shoe heel. Each cylinder anchor block serves as a shoe stop centering point and provides the fulcrum around which the shoe heel pivots when the brakes are applied.

Adjustment

1. With wheels jacked clear of floor, place wrench on one adjusting cam stud to adjust one shoe. Rotate wrench in the direction of forward wheel rotation until lining drags on drum.
2. Move wrench slightly in opposite direction until wheel is free to turn; then move wrench an additional 7 to 10 degrees to provide running clearance (7 to 10 degrees is equal to 1" to 1½" of travel at end of an 8-inch wrench).
3. Place wrench on opposite adjusting cam stud and adjust second shoe in the same manner.

WAGNER "FA" BRAKE

The type brake, Fig. 19, has two single end wheel cylinders per wheel. The closed ends have slotted anchor surfaces which supports the opposite brake shoe. Brake shoes are identical and are all energized by forward rotation.

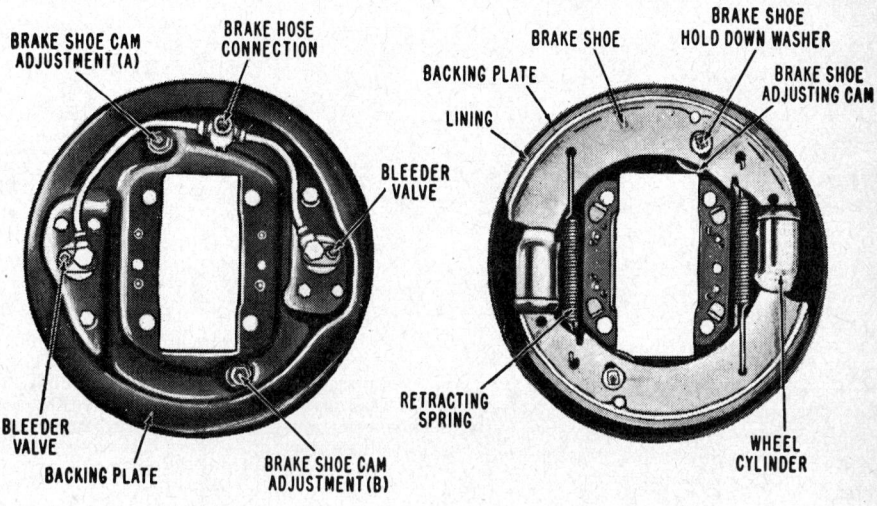

Fig. 18 Wagner "F" type brake. It should be noted that some models have the wheel cylinders mounted near the top and bottom of the assembly with the adjusting cams located at the sides

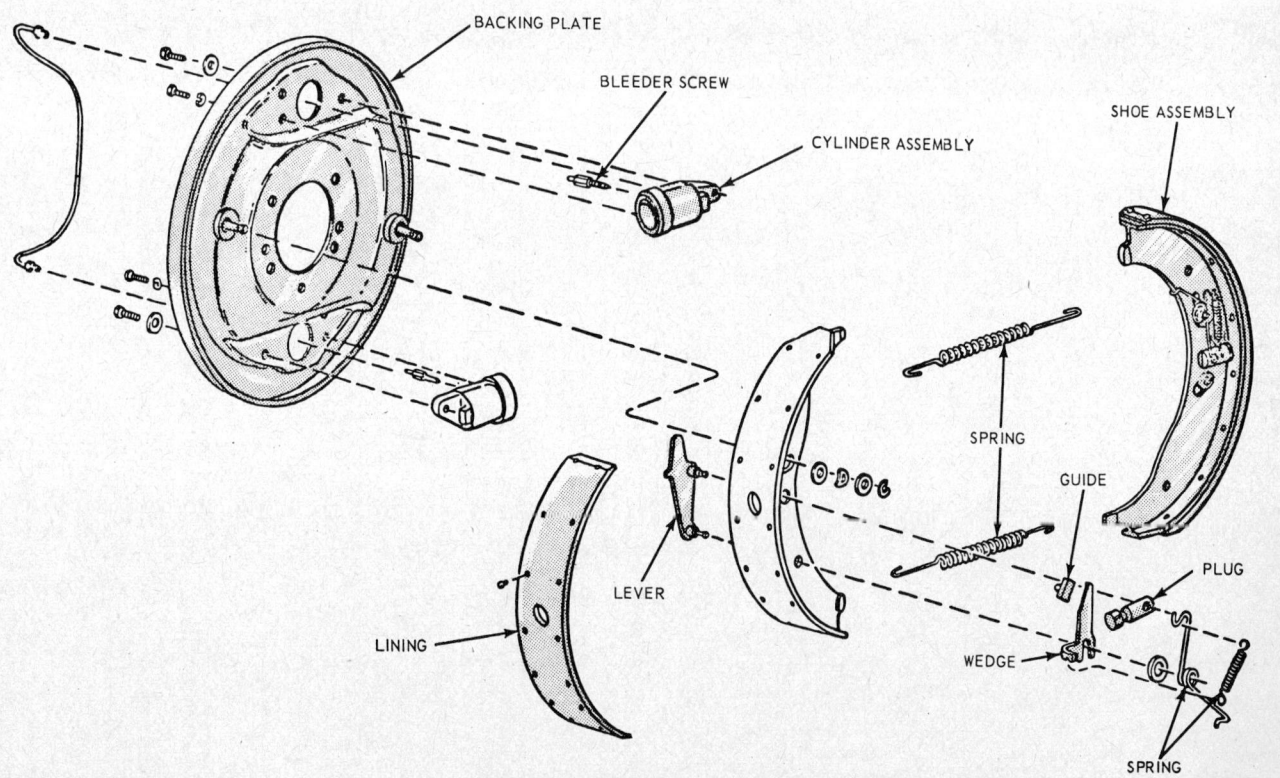

Fig. 19 Wagner "FA" self-adjuster front wheel brake

BRAKE ADJUSTMENTS

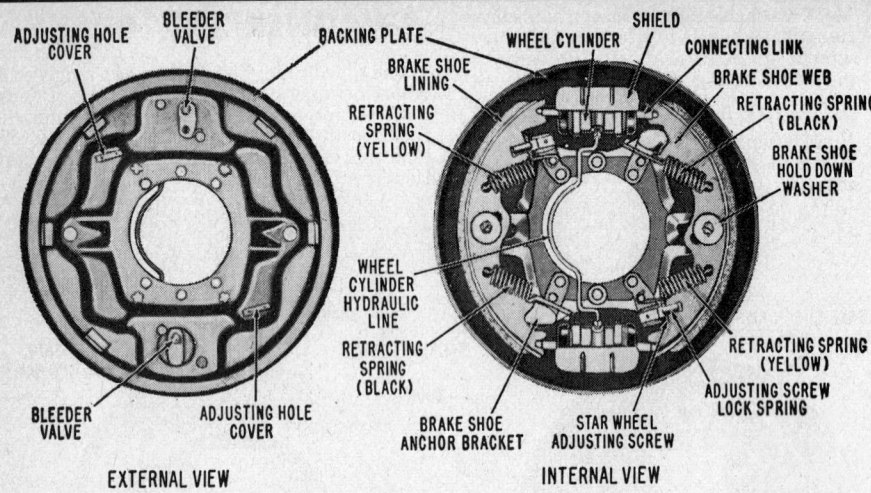

Fig. 20 Wagner twin action brake. Some models have the wheel cylinders mounted at approximately 5 and 11 o'clock positions. Also, some have brake shoe retracting springs of unequal lengths

Manual Adjustment

Brake shoes may be manually expanded by two $5/8''$ hex-head, friction spring locked studs, which are exposed on the backcam located under the shoe table. Torque limit for manual adjustment should not exceed 120 in. lbs.

Automatic Adjustment

On each shoe an automatic adjuster lever is pivot-pinned to the inner side of the shoe web and rests against the manual adjuster cam. A drum contact plug in the center of the shoe tables has a shank pinned to the automatic adjuster lever on the outside of the web.

A spring loaded serrated wedge slides on the lever pivot pin, between a washer and the shoe web, under the shank of the drum contact plug entering the space between the plug pin and the wedge guide which is also pinned to the shoe. An adjuster torsion spring is hooked over the plug pin, lever pivot pin and the edge of the shoe table.

As brake lining wears, the drum depresses the drum contact plug which swings the adjuster lever away from the shoe table. Thereupon, the spring loaded wedge moves to keep the gap between the plug pin and the wedge guide closed, holding the lever and shoe in adjusted position. At maximum lining wear, the drum contact plug pin bottoms in the slot in the shoe web, stopping the automatic adjusting process.

WAGNER TWIN ACTION BRAKE

This type brake, Fig. 20, is equipped with two double end hydraulic cylinders which apply hydraulic pressure to both the toe and heel of two identical, self-centering shoes. The shoes anchor at either toe or heel, depending upon the direction of drum rotation. Brake anchor supports and backing plates are riveted to the axle housing flange. The supports have slotted anchor pins at the shoe heels, and adjusting screws at the shoe toes. The adjusting screws act as anchors in the reverse direction of rotation. Each adjusting screw is threaded into or out of its support by means of an adjusting wheel. The adjusting wheels are accessible through slots in the backing plate.

Adjustment

1. With wheels raised clear of floor, remove adjusting holes covers from backing plate.
2. Use a screwdriver or special adjusting tool through opening in backing plate and turn rear adjusting screw until a light drag is felt as wheel is turned. Then back off until drum turns freely.
3. Repeat adjustment at front adjusting screw. Install adjusting hole covers. Fig. 21 shows the twin action brake that employs a self-adjuster.

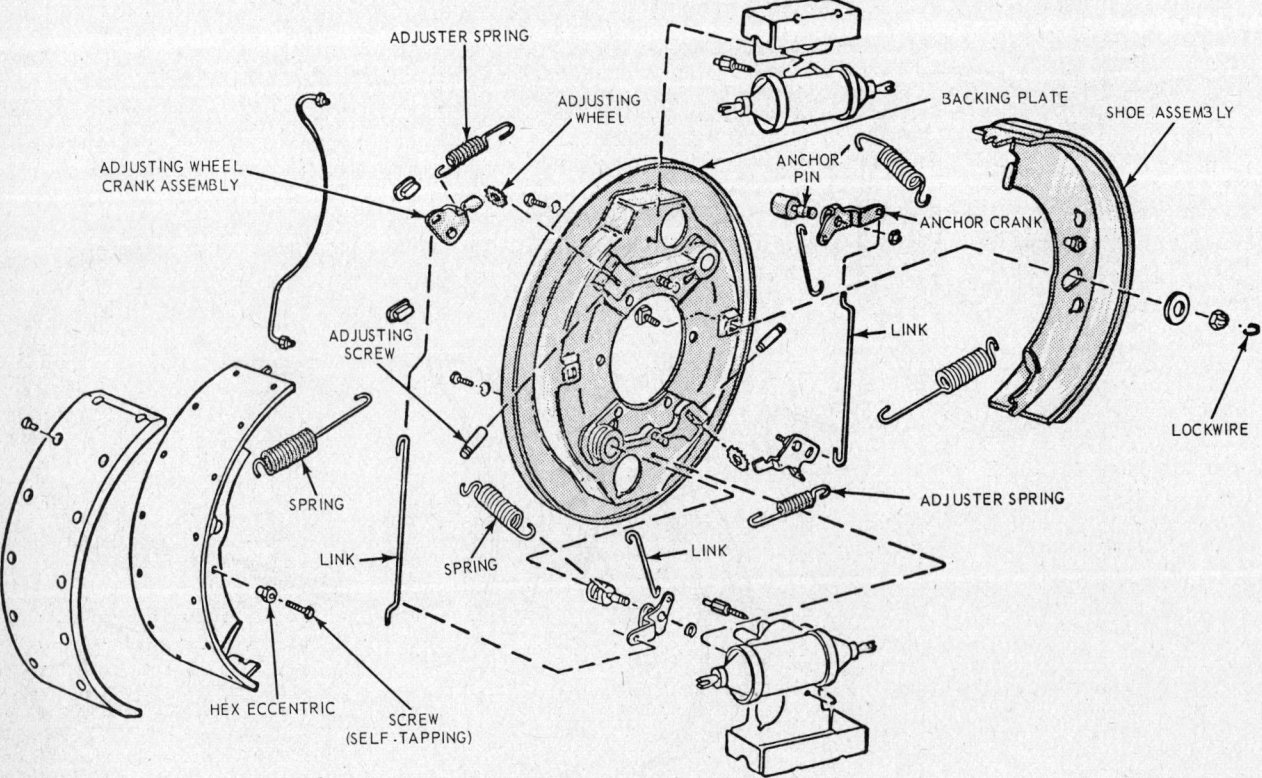

Fig. 21 Wagner twin action self-adjuster brake

STOPMASTER BRAKES

INDEX

	Page No.
Description	599
Actuating Systems	599
Adjustable Plungers	599
Power Unit Adjustment	600
Wedge Alignment	600
Fail-Safe Units	600

Servicing Components

Trouble Shooting Guide	601
Brake Adjustments	601
Power Unit Service	601
Fail-Safe Unit Service	604
Removing Power Unit	605
Air Chamber Service	605
Hydraulic Cylinder Service	605
Wedge Service	605
Installing Power Unit	606
Plunger Housing	606
Installing Plungers	606
Fail-Safe Manifolding	607

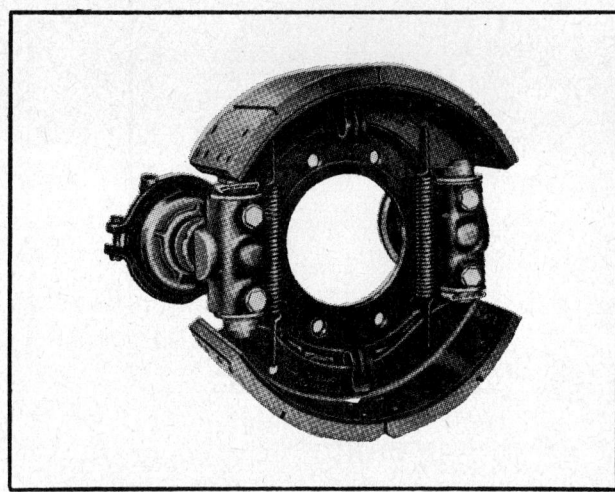

Fig. 1 Stopmaster FDA brake with bolted on spider and integral plunger housings

Fig. 2 Stopmaster RSA brake, backing plate mounted and bolted on plunger housing

DESCRIPTION

The Stopmaster Brake is a wedge actuated brake. The brake power units can be either air chambers or hydraulic cylinders. They can also be equipped with Fail-Safe units to provide parking and emergency braking. The brake power unit forces a wedge between two rollers and two plungers. This causes the plungers to spread apart and push the brake shoes against the brake drum.

There are several variations of Stopmaster Brakes in use. Some have two power units per brake and others only one. Where two power units are used, there may be a Fail-Safe unit on one or both. The brake support may be either a cast spider or a stamped backing plate. On the cast spiders, the plunger housings may be either integral or bolted on. Brake shoe adjustment may be either manual or automatic.

The basic Stopmaster Brakes are identified as model RDA, RDH, RSA or RSH with letters denoting the following: R—Stopmaster Brake; S—Single Actuated; A—Air operated; H—Hydraulic operated. Figs. 1, 2, 3 and 3A illustrate four types of brakes.

Stopmaster Actuating System

Fig. 4 shows one of the actuating systems of an air-operated, double-actuated Stopmaster RDA brake. All parts are shown in the off position.

This system has an air chamber power unit threaded into the wedge bore of the plunger housing. The socket in the end of the diaphragm push rod connects the air chamber to the wedge rod. The wedge retracting spring acts as the return spring for both the wedge and the diaphragm. A pair of rollers are held in place on the wedge head by a retaining cage. The rollers are also engaged in corresponding slots in the inner ends of the plungers. The unslotted portions of the inner ends of the plungers are resting on abutments in the plunger housing. The outer ends of the plungers are engaged with and supporting the brake shoes.

On a double-actuated brake, each of the two actuating systems has one anchor (solid) plunger and one adjustable plunger (as illustrated). On a single actuated brake the one actuating system would have two adjustable plungers. All of the plungers are retained in the housings and the roller slots are kept in proper alignment by means of guide screws that engage slots in the side of the plungers. A hydraulic brake would have a hydraulic cylinder threaded into the plunger housing (in place of air chamber). The hydraulic piston would connect with the wedge rod.

When the brake is actuated, the air chamber pushes the wedge head deeper in between the rollers. This spreads the rollers and plungers apart and pushes the brake shoes outward. Initially all the plungers are lifted off of the plunger abutments and momentarily suspended. As the brake shoes contact the drums, the drum drags the shoes and the suspended plungers around with it. This causes the plunger at the trailing end of each shoe to reseat on its abutment and thus absorb and transfer the brake torque to the brake support. When the brake is released, the wedge spring returns the wedge and diaphragm to the off position. At the same time, the shoe return springs push the raised plungers back to the abutments.

Adjustable Plungers

Two types of adjustable plungers are in use—manual and automatic. The manually adjusted plunger has an adjusting bolt threaded into the plunger itself. The bolt head is scalloped to facilitate adjustment and carries a detent arrangement that engages the brake shoe web and prevents accidental rotation of the bolt.

On the automatically adjusted plunger, Fig.

STOPMASTER BRAKES

Fig. 3 Stopmaster RDA brake with welded on spider and bolted on plunger housings

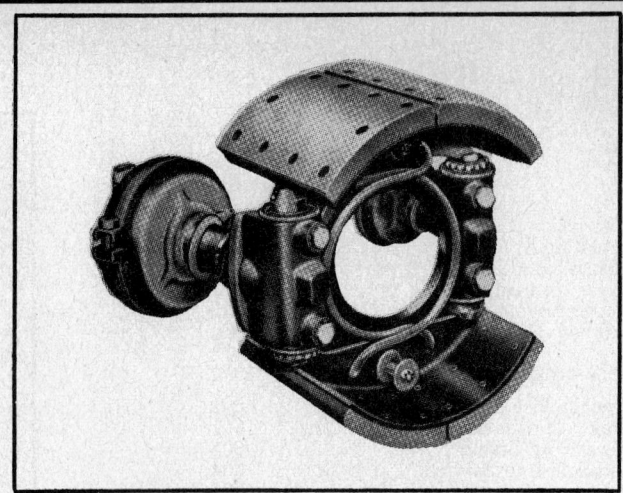

Fig. 3A Stopmaster RDA brake with welded on spider and bolted on plunger housings

5, the adjusting bolt is threaded into an adjusting sleeve which in turn is free-fitted inside the plunger itself. The plunger guide screw is replaced by a hollow cap screw, a spring and an adjusting pawl which also serves as the plunger guide. The end of the adjusting pawl has saw-tooth type teeth which engage corresponding helical teeth on the outside of the adjusting screws.

As the brake is actuated, the plunger, sleeve and bolt move outward and the sloping face of the teeth on the adjusting sleeve lifts the adjusting pawl against the spring. When the brake is released, all the parts return to their starting points. As the lining wears, the plunger stroke and resulting pawl lift gradually increases until the pawl climbs over and drops into the next tooth space. This time, when the brake is released and the plunger is pushed back into its bore, the upright face of the pawl teeth causes the adjusting sleeves to rotate and advance the adjusting bolt. This reduces the lining clearance and the cycle starts over again. The automatic adjuster operates only in forward vehicle direction.

Power Unit Adjustment

The air chamber (or hydraulic cylinder) should be screwed into the wedge bore of the plunger housing to such a depth that the wedge is ready to lift the plungers off of the abutment seats at the first movement of the diaphragm (or piston). This provides the least lost motion and maximum useful chamber (or piston) stroke.

Current power units are designed to "bottom out" in the wedge bore and provide this optimum adjustment automatically. (The bottoming type units have a short unthreaded portion on the leading end, Fig. 6.) Earlier power units must be adjusted manually by screwing the power unit into the wedge bore deep enough for the wedge to spread the plungers so they can be pushed back and forth in the plunger housing. Then the power unit is backed out until the back and forth plunger movement disappears. *The newer bottoming type units can be used as replacements for the earlier units to obtain the bottoming feature.*

Wedge Alignment

When the power unit is removed from the brake, the wedge assembly may also become dislodged. Before reinstalling the power unit, reposition the wedge assembly so that the rollers and roller cage are engaged in the plunger slots, Fig. 7. On newer brake assemblies this is accomplished automatically by simply aligning the two ears on the wedge spring retainer with corresponding grooves in the wedge bore of the plunger housing. On older assemblies, the wedge head must be aligned manually so that the rollers engage the plunger slots properly. In either case, proper alignment can be checked by pushing on the wedge rod while visually checking for shoe and plunger lift.

Fail-Safe Units

The Fail-Safe unit is a spring powered brake actuator that assembles piggy-back on the air chamber. As shown in Fig. 8, Fail-Safe units are produced in three types, Custom,

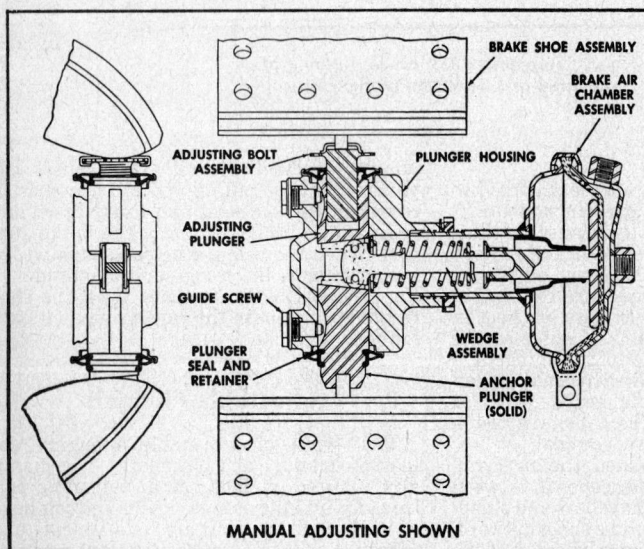

Fig. 4 Actuating system of air operated RDA brake (3/4" stroke wedge assembly shown)

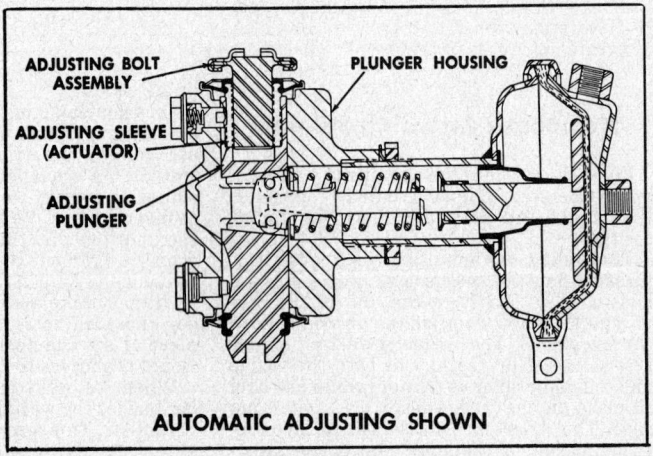

Fig. 5 Actuating mechanisms with automatically adjusted plunger (1 3/4" stroke wedge assembly shown)

STOPMASTER BRAKES

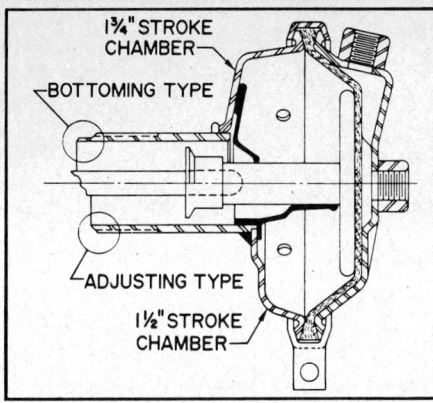

Fig. 6 Power unit adjustment

TROUBLE SHOOTING

If Brakes are Poor or Do Not Apply
Check system pressure at source and at brakes for possible restriction or leak in brake lines, valves, etc. Brakes out of adjustment. Leaking diaphragm or wheel cylinder cup.

Uneven Braking or Lining Wear
Check for ruptured diaphragm. Wedge rod out of push rod socket. Rollers and cage out of plunger socket. Corroded or frozen plungers. Brakes out of adjustment. Grease on lining. Glazed lining. Shoes installed backward.

Automatic Adjusters Not Working
Adjusting pawl installed backward. Pawl spring collapsed or missing. Bolt frozen in adjusting sleeve. Detent damaged, allowing bolt to rotate with sleeve. Adjusting plunger in wrong position (should be at leading end of shoe).

Fail-Safe Unit Not Holding
Power spring not fully released (uncaged). Brakes out of adjustment. Hold-off air not releasing fully. Power spring broken.

Brake Dragging
Low Fail-Safe holding air pressure (need 70 psi minimum). Improper connection of emergency line at Fail-Safe. Leaking lines or Fail-Safe seals.

BRAKE ADJUSTMENTS

Refer to "Brake Adjustments" section located elsewhere in this manual.

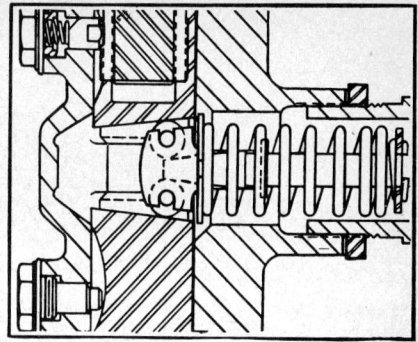

Fig. 7 Wedge alignment

POWER UNIT SERVICE

Air Chamber Diaphragm

The following procedures are used to replace the diaphragm and boot with the non-pressure housing on the brake assembly.
1. Cage power spring if Fail-Safe unit is used.
2. Remove air lines and tag emergency line.
3. Remove clamp ring nuts, bolts and Fail-Safe warning tag, and bottoming chamber tags, if used.
4. Spread clamp ring. Hold diaphragm on non-pressure half and remove pressure half or Fail-Safe head.

Standard and Super. When 70 psi or more air pressure is applied against the piston, the spring will be held in a compressed position. When the air pressure is removed, the spring will push the piston against the diaphragm plate and apply the brake.

On the Super Fail-Safe units an internal venting system working in conjunction with a one-way breathing arrangement on the cap allows system air to fill the vacuum behind the system when the Fail-Safe is actuated and keeps the seal from direct atmospheric contamination.

All types of Fail-Safe units are equipped with manual caging bolts to permit safe handling for service work. These bolts are sealed and prevented from rotating due to vibration.

Safety Precaution
When the brakes are equipped with Fail-Safe units (or other auxiliary spring power units), cage the power springs before starting any disassembly or removal of wheels and drums. After parts are all reassembled and in place, uncage the power springs before returning the vehicle to service. When a vehicle is disabled due to low or lost air pressure, block wheels and cage the power springs before moving the vehicle.

Caging and Uncaging Fail-Safe Units
On Custom units, the head of the caging bolt is exposed at all times beyond the plastic cap. However, the cap should be backed off three turns before turning caging bolt, otherwise the bolt may damage the cap.

On Standard units, first loosen the boot clamp screw and remove the rubber boot (if one is used). Then loosen the caging bolt-lock screws and swing the lock out of the way.

The power spring on both types is caged (compressed) by turning the caging bolt clockwise approximately 18 full turns. Do not force the bolt beyond its normal stop. Uncaging (releasing) the spring is accomplished by reversing the procedure—again do not force the bolt beyond its normal stop. If desired, both the caging and uncaging operation can be made easier by applying air pressure to the Fail-Safe chamber to take the spring load off the caging bolt.

On Custom units, after uncaging the spring, retighten the plastic cap by hand. On Standard units, after uncaging the spring, swing bolt-lock back and secure in place. Clean cap and boot and install boot with vent slot at bottom.

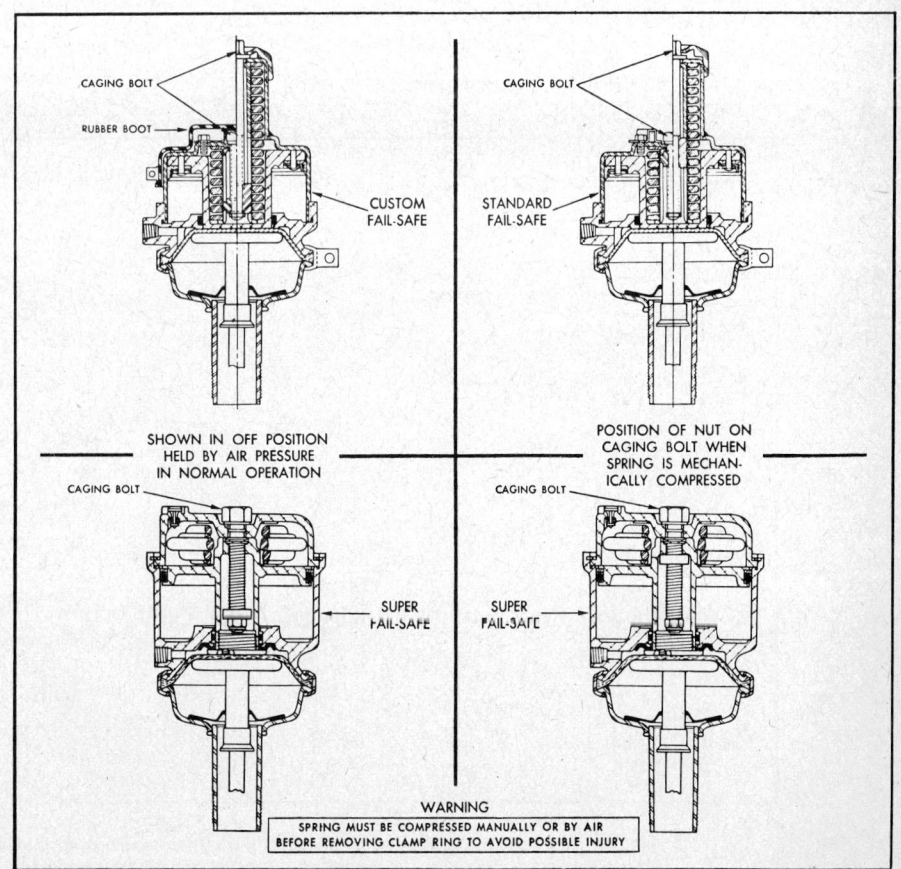

Fig. 8 Fail-Safe units

601

STOPMASTER BRAKES

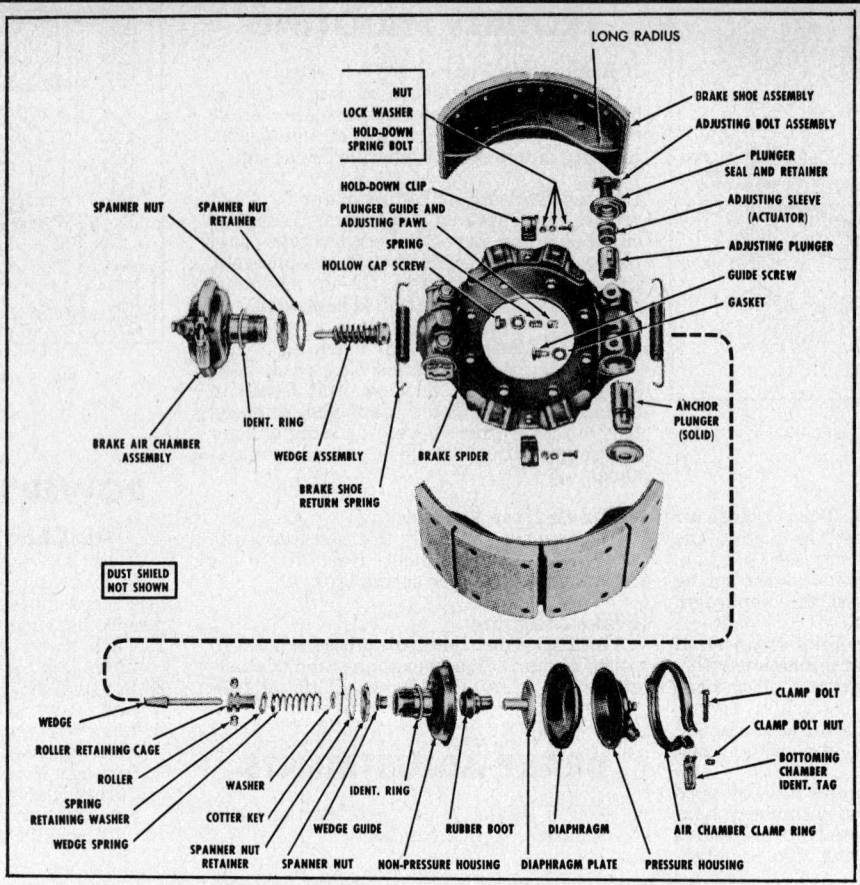

Fig. 9 The RDA brake shown, with integral plunger housings, employs a cast spider mounting that bolts to a flange on the axle housing. Adjusters may be manual or automatic (automatic shown)

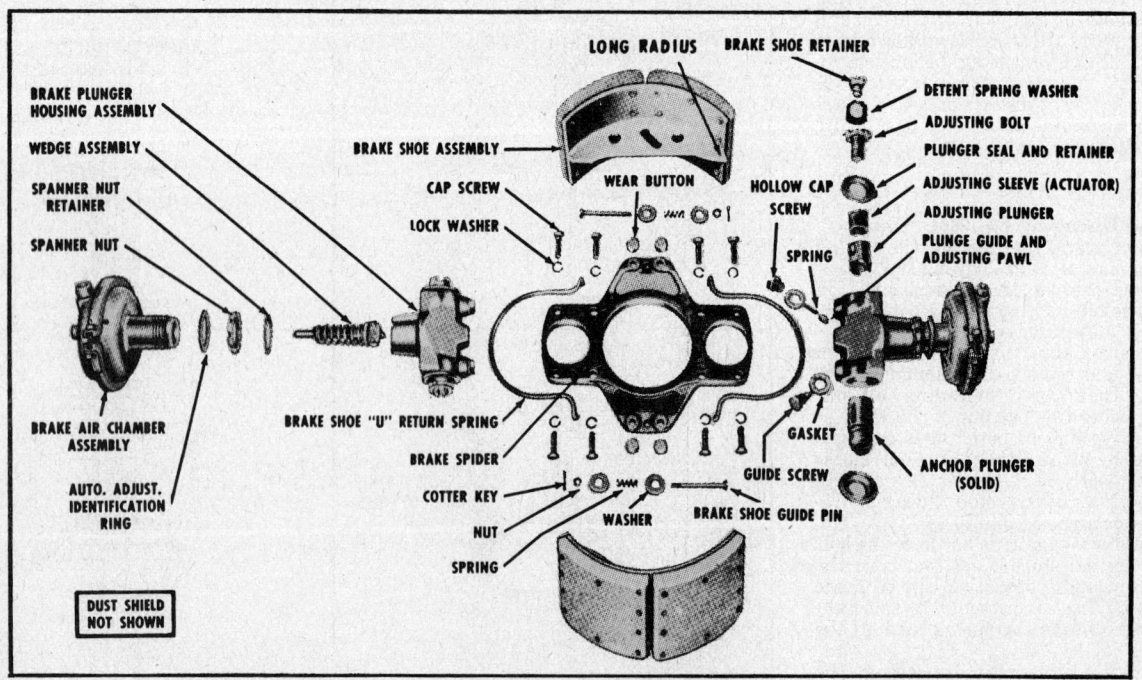

Fig. 10 The RDA brake shown, with separate plunger housings, employs a cast closed end spider that is welded to the axle. The actuation system is removed by removing four capscrews and brake air chamber assembly. This is 12¼" diameter trailer brake and employs an automatic adjuster

STOPMASTER BRAKES

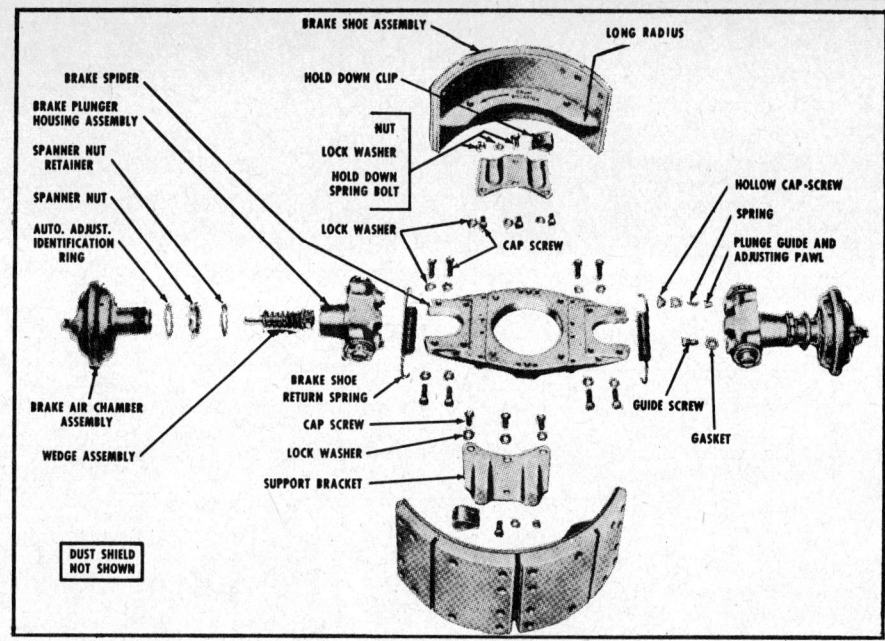

Fig. 11 The RDA brake shown, with separate plunger housings, employs a cast open end spider that is welded to the axle. The open end spider permits removal of the complete actu-action system at disassembly. This brake employs automatic adjusters

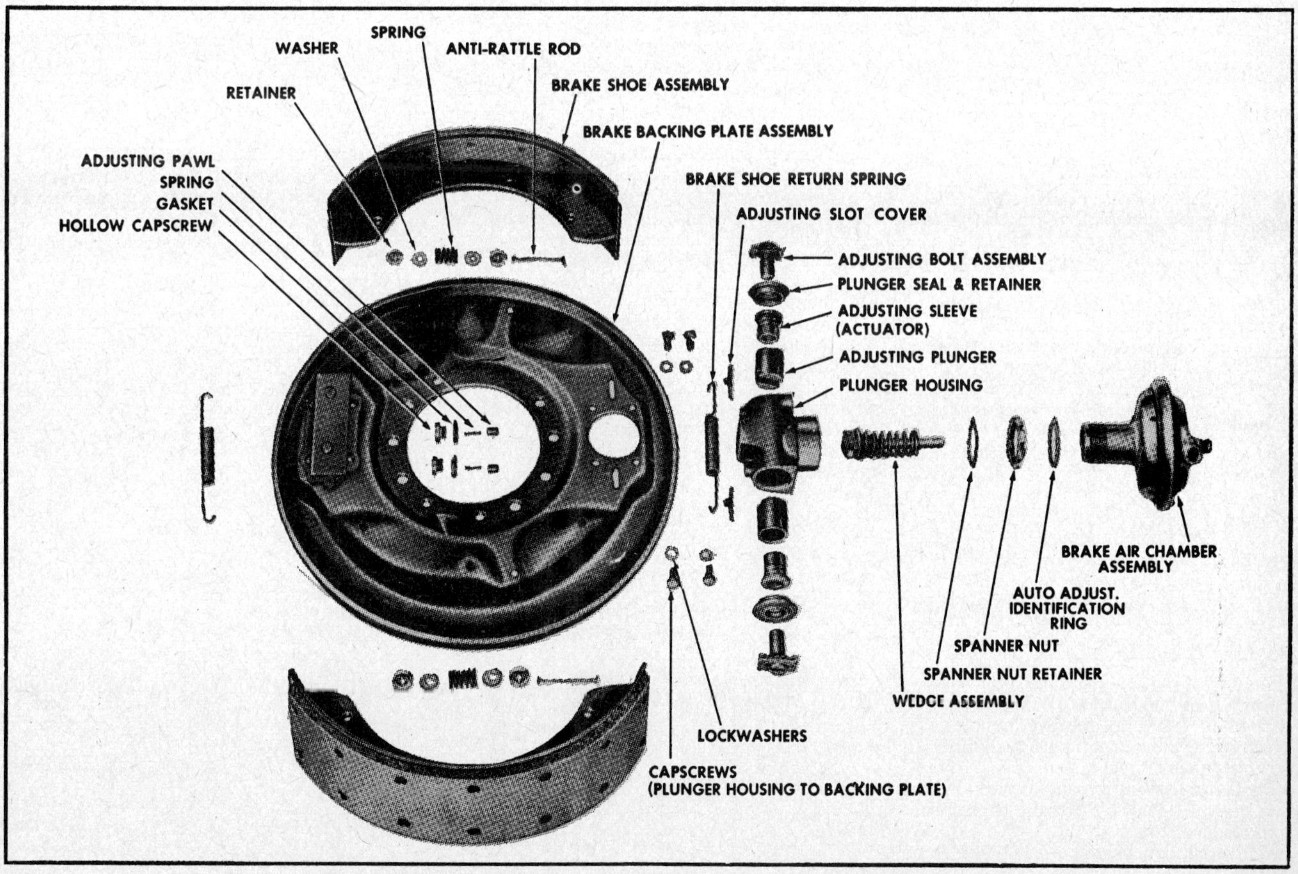

Fig. 12 The RSA brake shown, with separate plunger housing, has a stamped backing plate that bolts to a flange on the axle housing. Adjuster may be manual or automatic (automatic shown)

STOPMASTER BRAKES

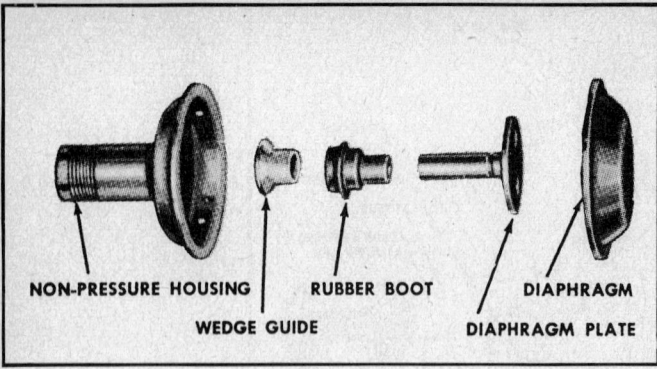

Fig. 13 Air chamber diaphragm parts layout

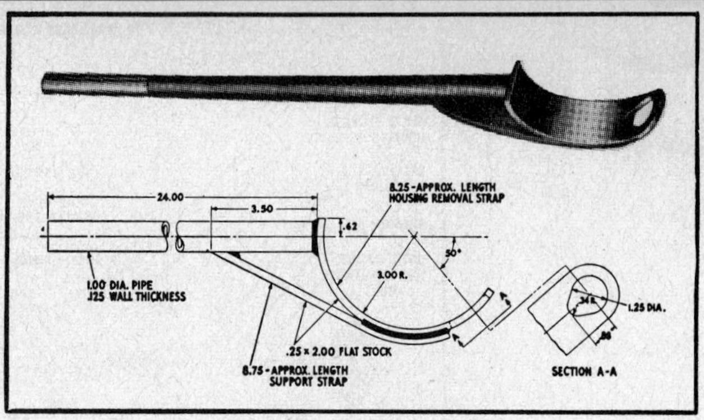

Fig. 14 Special wrench for removal of Fail-Safe unit housing

5. Carefully remove diaphragm while holding diaphragm plate against wedge rod. This will prevent wedge assembly from coming out of engagement with the plungers.

NOTE: If wedge assembly backs out of plunger anytime during the entire procedure, remove non-pressure housing from brake to replace diaphragm.

6. Continue to hold plate and inspect boot. If boot is torn or not attached to housing, strip old boot from housing and carefully remove plate assembly off wedge rod and out of non-pressure housing tube. (Boot and wedge guide will remain on plate push rod.)
7. Remove wedge guide and old boot from push rod. Inspect guide for wear and replace if necessary.

Reassemble, Fig. 13
1. Install new boot on diaphragm plate push rod and press wedge guide all the way on to end of push rod.
2. Clean non-pressure housing with cement thinner or similar material in area where boot is to be cemented.
3. Apply cement to housing around tube end. Position plate push rod assembly into tube. Carefully engage wedge rod so as not to pull it out of plungers.
4. While holding plate against wedge, press boot into position for cementing.
5. Install new diaphragm over plate and onto non-pressure housing while pushing plate against wedge. Assemble pressure half and clamp ring in reverse manner of disassembly.
6. Connect air lines to proper chamber and Fail-Safe ports. Make a full pressure brake application and check for air leaks. Road test for brake performance.

FAIL-SAFE UNIT SERVICE

Disassemble—Standard & Custom
1. Remove air chamber diaphragm.
2. Secure Fail-Safe unit by hexagon part of cap in a vise and remove housing by unscrewing it from cap with a spanner or strap wrench, Fig. 14.
3. Pull piston assembly out of cap. Piston can be pushed out by turning caging bolt and release spring.
4. Remove rubber washer and O-ring from Fail-Safe unit (use small screwdriver or other pointed tool.)

NOTE: Do not disassemble the cap and spring assembly or the piston assembly. If parts are damaged, the complete assembly must be replaced.

Assemble, Fig. 15
1. Inspect and check for worn parts that may need replacement. Inspect threads, bore, and end of cap and spring assembly carefully for nicks or scratches that would affect sealing. Clean all parts. DO NOT use solvent to clean leather piston seal, rubber boot or plastic cap (Custom units). Use hot soapy water.
2. Wipe internal parts clean with a soft cloth and re-grease thoroughly with recommended grease. The power spring and all mating parts should be packed with grease.
3. Install rubber washer and O-ring seal in proper grooves in Fail-Safe housing. The rubber washer must fit completely and squarely in its groove.
4. Install piston and seal assembly halfway into the cap.
5. Clamp hexagon part of cap securely in a vise and place Fail-Safe housing onto piston and seal assembly. Push housing down to engage threads on cap.
6. To start threads, turn housing counter-clockwise until thread engagement is felt. Then turn housing at least three turns clockwise to insure proper thread engagement.
7. Tighten housing onto cap until it bottoms, using wrench used for disassembly.

Disassemble—Super Fail-Safe Unit
Follow steps 1 to 4 under diaphragm replacement covered previously and then proceed as follows:

1. Referring to Fig. 15A, release foot set screw and unscrew foot from piston. Remove piston seal and sealing compound from joint at cap and housing.
2. Take out lock ring and separate cap, spring and piston assembly from housing. Remove rubber seal from housing, if used.
3. Remove hex nut and snap ring from release bolt. Secure cap, spring and piston assembly in arbor press or clamping fixture.
4. Turn release bolt until square nut falls free, release pressure of press or fixture until spring is unloaded. Assembly can now be removed from press or fixture. Separate cap from spring and piston.
5. Remove back-up ring and "O" ring from piston groove.
6. Remove two small back-up rings and "O" ring from I.D. in bottom of housing and the two bearing spring washers, located at top of piston and inside top of cap.
7. Take out cotter pin or snap ring from release bolt. This permits removal of inner washer from release bolt.
8. Take release bolt out of cap. Remove "O" ring from groove of bolt and take off outer flat washer.
9. Reverse removal procedure to assemble.

Bench Test for Leaks
Plug one Fail-Safe port and apply air pressure (150 psi maximum) to other Fail-Safe port. Apply soapy water to check for leaks in three places. Bubbles at release bolt indicate leakage at leather piston seal, and bubbles at piston plunger indicate leakage at O-ring. These leaks can generally be corrected by cycling the piston (with spring uncaged) by applying and releasing air pressure. Bubbles

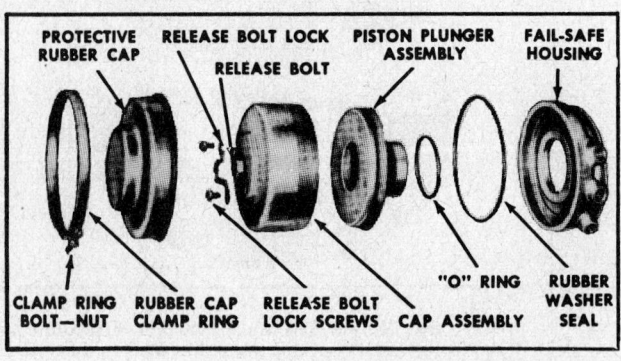

Fig. 15 Standard and Custom Fail-Safe unit disassembled

STOPMASTER BRAKES

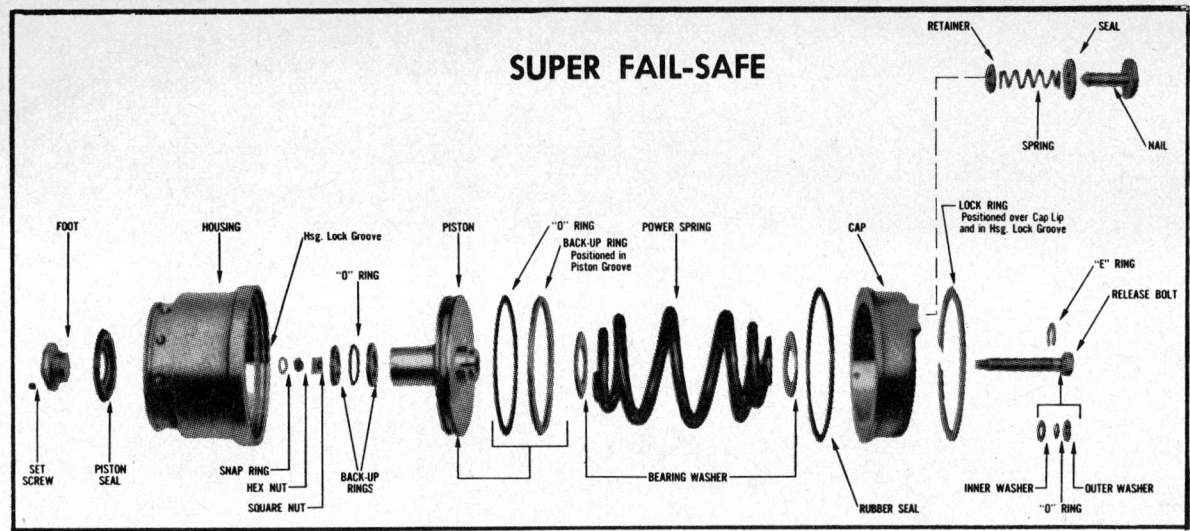

Fig. 15A Super Fail-Safe unit disassembled

at the cap threads indicate leakage past the rubber washer. This leakage is corrected by reassembling the cap and housing and properly installing the rubber washer.

When leak test is completed, install Fail-Safe unit onto non-pressure half of power unit in reverse order of disassembly.

REMOVING POWER UNIT FROM BRAKE

To remove either an air or hydraulic power unit from the brake assembly, proceed as follows:
1. If Fail-Safe unit is used, cage the power spring.
2. Remove brake lines and tag emergency line.
3. Determine type of power unit used, bottoming or adjusting type. Bottoming air chambers have an identification tag fastened to the clamp ring bolt and bottoming hydraulic cylinders have the word "bottoming" cast on housing.
4. If adjusting type unit is used, carefully mark the position of the assembly on the first exposed thread on the housing tube with a scribe or punch and hammer to aid reassembly.
5. Using a drift and hammer, straighten retainer and then loosen spanner nut.

NOTE: On welded-on spider-mounted brakes with open ends, the entire actuation system can be taken off at this time as one assembly, if desired, by removing four spider-to-plunger housing capscrews. However, the hub and drum and dust shield will have to be taken off before removing the actuation system.

6. Unscrew power unit from plunger housing. At this time, remove and inspect wedge assembly, and repair as necessary.

AIR CHAMBERS

To service an air chamber, follow the procedure covered under *Air Chamber Diaphragm*, disregarding wedge assembly precautions. Note that adjusting type non-pressure housing is interchangeable with bottoming type housing and may be converted at this time.

HYDRAULIC CYLINDERS

Disassemble, Fig. 16
1. After removing cylinder from brake, remove bleeder screw and drain all fluid.
2. Place threaded end of cylinder on a cloth or wood surface and push internal parts out with air pressure. If parts are frozen, hydraulic pressure may be necessary.
3. Remove piston, cup, seal, and ball spacer from cylinder. Early piston design use a post to retain the cup seal and act as a spacer. To service, remove the piston post extension.

Assemble, Fig. 16.
1. Clean all parts in hydraulic fluid. If cylinder bore is corroded, scored or scratched, it must be replaced. Inspect piston for nicks, scoring or corrosion and polish with crocus cloth. Inspect end of bleeder screw for marks that would prevent it from sealing.
2. Lubricate cylinder bore with clean hydraulic fluid that is to be used with this system.
3. Install ball spacer in bottom of cylinder.
4. Install cup seal into cylinder, carefully entering lip of cup seal into cylinder bore, with flat end of cup out.
5. Install piston (flat end first) into cylinder and push piston and cup down to bottom of bore. Then install bleeder screw.

WEDGE ASSEMBLY

Disassemble, Fig. 17
1. Remove wedge from plunger housing by pulling it straight out.
2. Remove cotter key or "E" washer (earlier design) from wedge shaft while holding spring compressed by hand.
3. Remove wedge retainer washer, wedge spring and retainer.
4. Insert a thin-bladed screwdriver between one flat of the wedge head and roller retainer cage. Spread cage open just far enough to remove rollers.

IMPORTANT: Do not attempt to drive wedge through the rollers and cage or force the rollers through the slightly closed slots of the cage. This will perma-

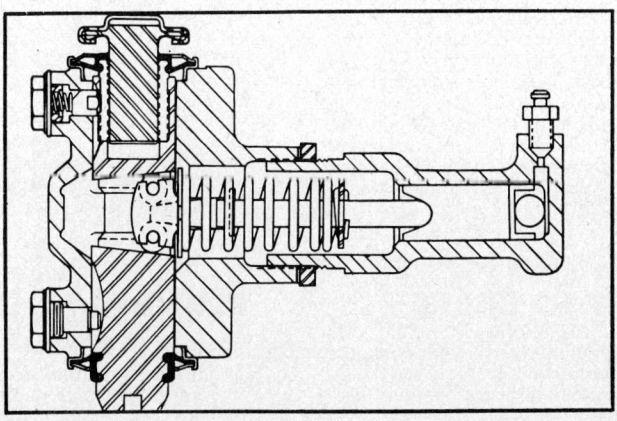

Fig. 16 Hydraulic cylinder

STOPMASTER BRAKES

Fig. 17 Wedge assembly

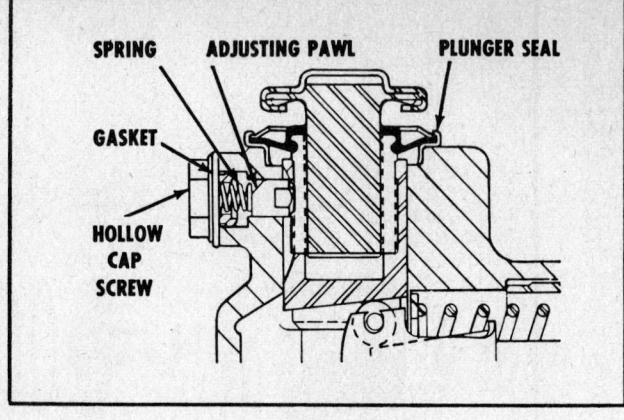

Fig. 18 Plunger Housing

nently damage the cage.

5. Remove roller retainer cage by sliding it off wedge shaft.

Assemble, Fig. 17
1. Clean all parts thoroughly and inspect. Check angled faces of wedge to see that they are free from pits or marks. If "E" washer type lock is used, inspect wedge shaft lock groove to see that it is sharp and clean. Inspect roller retainer cage to make sure it will contain rollers properly, and inspect the spring for marks that would cause breakage.
2. Insert wedge shaft into roller retainer cage so angled faces of wedge head are exposed.
3. Insert a thin-bladed screwdriver between flat of wedge head and roller retainer cage. Spread cage open just far enough to insert roller (journal hub into cage slot). Tip roller into cage and position other journal hub into slot of retainer. Install other roller in same manner and remove screwdriver. *Do not force rollers through ends of cage slots.*
4. Install spring retainer over wedge shaft and position centrally over cage and roller assembly.

NOTE: Current production and service replacement use a spring retainer that has two tabs or protrusions on the O.D. These tabs serve to align the wedge assembly as it is installed into the plunger housing by engaging grooves in the wedge bore. If the plunger housing is not equipped with such grooves, remove the tabs at the break-off marks and file the O.D. of the retainer smooth.

5. Install wedge spring over wedge shaft (large coil first). Add spring washer and compress spring by hand far enough to expose cotter key hole or "E" lock groove and install cotter or "E" lock.
6. Install wedge assembly into plunger housing. Check for correct roller-plunger engagement by first pushing on wedge rod by hand while checking for plunger and shoe lift; second, measure standout of wedge rod from end of threaded housing bore. When properly assembled, wedge standout is $2\frac{1}{4}''$.

INSTALLING POWER UNIT TO BRAKE

Check position of plunger housing to make certain wedge assembly is properly seated. Be sure to replace automatic adjusting identification ring (if used) on power unit tube. Thread spanner nut onto power unit tube and install spanner nut retainer.

Bottoming Type Power Unit
1. Screw power unit into plunger housing until it bottoms (spanner nut loose).
2. Align connection ports with brake lines, if necessary, unscrewing power unit not more than one full turn.
3. Connect brake lines.
4. Make and hold a full pressure brake application. At this time position spanner nut retainer so it will engage plunger housing slot and drive spanner nut with a drift and hammer until it is tight against the retainer and plunger housing. Release brake pressure.
5. Using a drift and hammer, peen section of retainer into one slot of spanner nut.
6. Check for leaks at all connections.
7. Bleed hydraulic brakes (if used).
8. After installing drums, uncage Fail-Safe units.

Power Unit with Depth Mark
1. Screw power unit into plunger housing several turns. Turn spanner nut toward plunger housing so depth mark on threads is just exposed. Continue turning power unit into plunger housing until it bottoms on spanner nut and retainer.
2. Continue procedures 3 to 6 for bottoming type power units.

Units Without Depth Mark
1. Screw power unit into plunger housing until it bottoms. This will push wedge assembly between plungers and lift them off their seats inside the housing. By pushing on one shoe or plunger, second shoe or plunger will be seen to move.
2. Unscrew power unit one turn. Push on one shoe or plunger and then the other alternately, observing movement of opposite plunger. If there is movement of the opposite plunger, unscrew power unit another turn and continue this procedure until no plunger movement can be detected. This point is usually two or three turns from the bottomed position.
3. Follow Steps 3 to 6 for bottoming type units.

PLUNGER HOUSING

Disassemble
1. With brake shows removed, remove guide screws and gaskets from plunger housing. If brake is automatic adjusting, remove hollow capscrew, gasket, spring and adjusting pawl, Fig. 18.

2. Pry plunger seals loose and remove anchor (solid) plungers, adjusting plungers, adjusting sleeves (actuator), and adjusting bolt. If a four-piece adjusting bolt is used it should also be disassembled.

Assemble
1. Inspect and clean all parts, including housing plunger and seal bores and shoe rest pads. DO NOT solvent clean any rubber parts. Wire brush plunger parts and adjusting bolt threads to remove caked-on dirt or corrosion.
2. Carefully inspect plunger seals and gaskets for tears, cuts or deterioration and replace as required. Also check the angled plunger roller faces for pits, grooves or nicks and replace if necessary.

NOTE: RD spider mounted brakes have one adjusting plunger and one anchor (solid) plunger per plunger housing. The anchor plungers are marked on the shoe slot end— "R" for right-hand brakes and "L" for left-hand brakes. Do not mix.

Assemble Seals On Plungers
1. Apply film of grease to inside surfaces of seals.
2. On anchor plungers, inspect nose for burrs. Mask brake show web slot in plunger nose with masking tape to protect seals.
3. Carefully push double lip seal onto plunger, stretching outer seal lip over plunger nose end until inner seal lip is completely in the second plunger groove and the outer seal lip is in the first plunger groove. Remove masking tape. *Brakes employing single grooved plungers and single lip seals are assembled in the same manner except masking tape is not used.*
4. On manual adjusting plungers, push inner seal lip over threaded hole end of plunger until lip completely enters plunger seal groove.

INSTALLING PLUNGERS

RD Brakes
1. Coat all plunger bores with grease.
2. Make sure anchor plungers marked "L" and "R" are installed in left-hand and right-hand brakes, respectively.
3. Coat entire plunger with grease, packing cavity behind seal, and insert plunger and seal into housing with key-way slot aligned with guide screw hole. Make cer-

STOPMASTER BRAKES

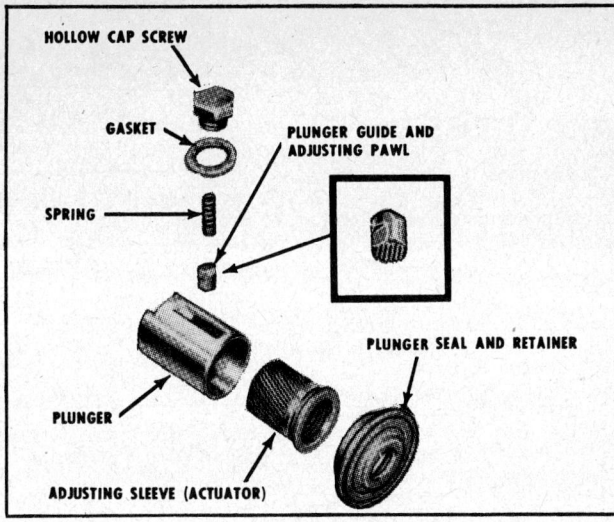

Fig. 19 Automatic adjusting plunger

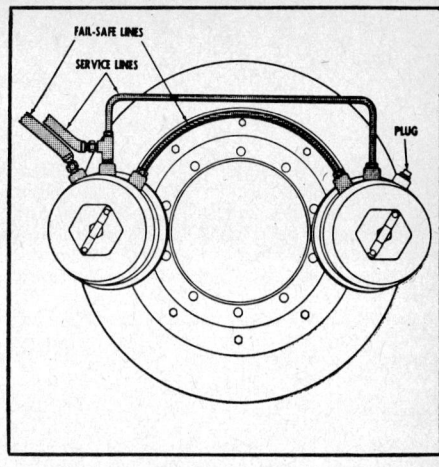

Fig. 20 Manifolding of Fail-Safe chambers

tain plunger goes all the way into plunger bore and seats on bosses on bottom.
4. Make certain guide screw end enters plunger key-way slot so plunger can slide freely in housing bore. Tighten guide screws to 15-20 ft-lbs torque.

RS Brake With Manual Adjust Plungers

1. Apply grease to outside of plunger and install plunger and seal into housing in same manner described for anchor plungers. Also follow procedures for seating plunger seal and assembling gasket and guide screw.
2. Coat adjusting bolt threads with grease and turn bolt into adjusting plunger by working it through hole in outer seal flap, being careful not to pinch seal on threads. Turn adjusting bolt in just short of seal. DO NOT bottom bolt on seal.

NOTE: If four-piece adjusting bolt is used, assemble parts in the following manner after adjusting bolt has been installed into plunger. A. Install detent washer on retainer, making sure flats are aligned, then install spring ring in groove in retainer. B. Turn open end of spring ring so that it faces dimple in detent washer. C. Install detent and retainer so that open end of spring ring and detent dimple engages the bolt last. Push assembly into bolt with thumb pressure only. DO NOT FORCE as it will damage spring ring.

RS Brake with Automatic Adjust Plungers

1. Grease inside and outside surfaces of both adjusting plunger and adjusting sleeve, Fig. 19. Place plunger into housing, aligning plunger key-way slot with guide hole and assemble adjusting pawl, gasket, spring, and hollow capscrew into plunger housing. Turn capscrew in one or two turns.

NOTE: The adjusting pawl has teeth and flats on one end and a chamfered edge on the other end. Coat pawl with grease and insert it into guide hole, teeth first, and with chamfer toward brake shoe. This aligns pawl and sleeve teeth and flats with keyway slot.

2. Assemble plunger seal onto adjusting sleeve. Insert sleeve into plunger, wiggling it so pawl and sleeve teeth mesh. If necessary, back off capscrew to enable meshing of pawl and sleeve teeth. Push sleeve into plunger until it bottoms.
3. Seat seal into plunger housing and hand-tighten capscrew into plunger housing.
4. Proper meshing of pawl and sleeve teeth can be checked at this point. Grease adjusting bolt threads and thread it into adjusting sleeve after working it through seal flap hole, being careful not to pinch seal in threads. Thread adjuster bolt into sleeve until it bottoms. A clicking sound and a ratcheting feel will indicate meshing of teeth. Turn bolt out three turns; if there is no clicking sound or ratcheting feel, this indicates proper meshing.
5. Tighten hollow capscrew to a torque of 15-20 ft-lbs.
6. Coat adjusting bolt with grease and thread it into the sleeve after working it through the seal flap hole, being careful not to pinch the seal on the threads. Turn bolt in just short of the seal. DO NOT bottom it on the seal. Pull the bolt outward slightly against the seal to insure entry of seal lip in sleeve groove. Push bolt and sleeve back into plunger.

NOTE: On earlier models of front brakes (backing plate mounted) a finger spring type of adjusting bolt lock was used. To assemble, first install plunger parts, press in seal, turn bolt into plunger or adjusting sleeve and then install finger spring and guide bolt. Lock guide bolt by peening lock plate to bolt boss and head.

The installation of plungers with single lip seals is the same as for double lip seals except with automatic adjusters. The single lip is installed on the adjusting sleeve first. Grease the sleeve, seal and adjusting plunger and install in the plunger housing. Then assemble the adjusting pawl, spring and hollow capscrew with gasket. Drive the seal into the housing. Screw the adjusting bolt into the sleeve until it bottoms and perform the check for adjusting pawl tooth mesh as outlined previously. Then back the bolt out about $1/2$ turn.

MANIFOLDING

For all tandem axle applications, four Standard Fail-Safe chambers on one axle of the tandem or four Custom Fail-Safe chambers located one (per brake) at each corner of the tandem is recommended, Fig. 20.

Any single Fail-Safe chamber configuration, either Standard, Custom or Super, requires automatic show adjustment to work within the range of the lift provided by single wedge.

Before operating the vehicle, the caging bolt must be turned counter-clockwise as far as it will go (about 18 turns) to release the Fail-Safe spring. This allows the Fail-Safe unit to function in the event of air pressure failure.

BENDIX TWINPLEX BRAKES

DESCRIPTION

The Twinplex brake, Fig. 1, is a wedge actuated mechanical brake. The torque spider, Fig. 2, is the basic foundation of the unit and includes guide pads, guide bosses and the two actuators which are integral with the spider. A service brake air chamber or spring brake chamber is mounted on each actuator. The actuator, Fig. 3, is comprised of an adjusting piston assembly, anchor piston and a wedge and roller assembly.

The adjusting piston incorporates the piston, adjusting nut, adjusting screw, adjusting screw link and automatic adjuster parts. The adjusting screw link has a slot for the shoe web and on the opposite end, a machined ramp to accept the wedge roller. A boot, boot protector and protector retainer are installed in the adjusting piston end of the actuator.

The anchor piston, Fig. 4, has a machined ramp for the wedge roller, a groove for the dust boot and a slot for the shoe web. An indexing pin is pressed into each piston and the pistons are identified right hand and left hand and are not interchangeable.

The wedge and roller cannot be disassembled and must be replaced as an assembly. The wedge, made from hardened steel and chrome plated, is available in angles of 10°, 12°, 14° or 18°, depending upon application. The wedge angle is stamped on the side of the wedge for identification.

The brake shoes have an anchor end and an adjusting end which is marked "ADJ END" and is installed in the adjusting screw link slot. Both shoes are self-energizing during forward or reverse braking and are held in contact against the adjusting screw links and anchor pistons by shoe-to-shoe springs.

OPERATION

When the brakes are applied, air pressure enters the service brake chamber, Fig. 3, and actuates the diaphragm and push rod. The wedge shaft, bottomed in the push rod, is pushed between the adjusting and anchor pistons, causing the pistons to ride outward on the rollers and forcing the brake shoes against the brake drum. If air pressure is lost, the spring brake chamber mechanically applies the wedge brake.

The adjusting piston incorporates an adjusting nut, adjusting screw and adjusting nut cap. An overload spring secures the adjusting nut cap to the adjusting nut. The adjusting screw is coupled with the adjusting nut and a slotted link is mated with the brake shoe web. A detent spring prevents the adjusting screw from turning during automatic adjuster operation.

When the brakes require an adjustment, the pistons will move far enough outward for the adjuster levers to pick up the next tooth on the adjuster cap, Fig. 5. When the brakes are released and the shoes retract, the pistons are pressed back into the actuator, causing the adjuster lever to pivot downward on the adjuster lever pin. This pivoting action rotates the adjuster nut cap and the adjuster nut one tooth. The adjuster screw does not rotate with the adjuster nut, therefore, moves outward when the adjuster nut rotates. The brake shoes are expanded .001 inch when the adjuster nut rotates one tooth position.

BRAKE SHOES
Removal

If air pressure is present in the system, ensure that service brakes are not applied and air pressure is not applied to the service brake air chamber. If air pressure is removed from the system and the brakes are equipped with spring brake chambers, release spring brakes, permitting the shoes to retract, thereby providing clearance from drum removal.

1. Remove wheel and tire assemblies, then the hub and drum. To retract brakes, if necessary, remove dust shield and back off star wheel at each adjusting screw.
2. Remove brake shoe return springs with a suitable tool, then the brake shoes from the torque spider.

Installation

1. Lubricate adjusting screw link shoe slots with a suitable lubricant. Also, lubricate anchor piston slots and the torque spider guide pads and brackets with lubricant.
2. Install shoes on torque spider, then the shoe return springs. Install a spring damper over each return spring.

NOTE: If brake drum is resurfaced .080 inch over original drum diameter, the standard adjusting screws must be replaced with service adjusting screws (P/N 323128).

3. Install drum and hub, then the wheel and tire assemblies.

NOTE: If oversized linings are installed and the linings are too thick for drum installation, the linings may be ground on the vehicle using an axle attached grinding tool. Grind linings .020 to .030 inch under drum diameter.

4. Rotate wheel in a forward direction and apply the brakes 25 to 30 times, thereby adjusting brakes.

PISTONS, WEDGE & ROLLER ASSEMBLIES
Disassembly

1. Disconnect air hose from service brake air chamber. It is permitted to separate air chamber halves in place of disconnecting air hose.
2. Straighten edges of air chamber tube lockwasher, then loosen check nut on air chamber tube.
3. Unscrew air chamber from actuator.

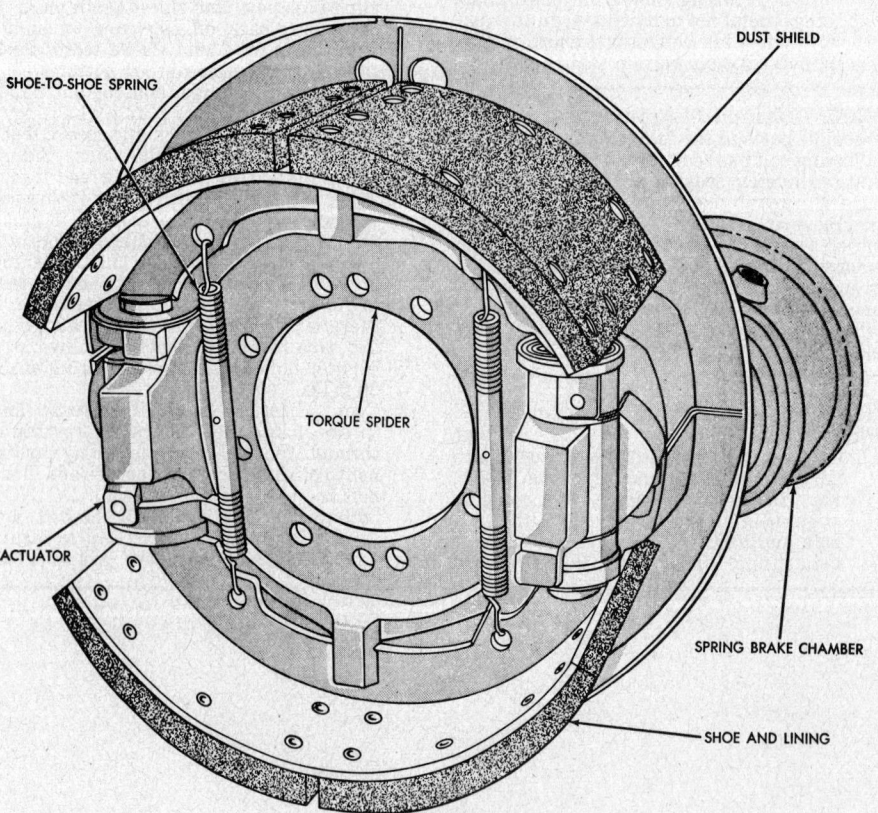

Fig. 1 Twinplex brake assembly

BENDIX TWINPLEX BRAKES

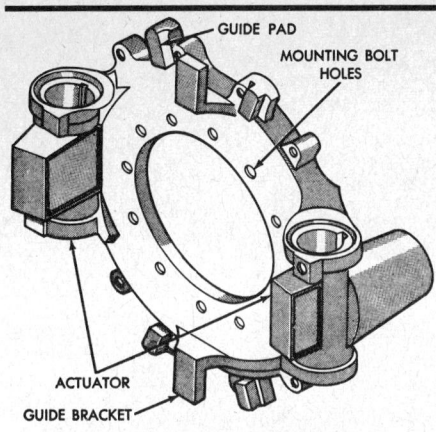

Fig. 2 Torque spider

4. Remove wedge and roller assembly from actuator housing, Fig. 6.

   NOTE: The wedge and roller is not disassembled for service. If any part is worn or damaged, replace complete assembly.

5. Remove boot protector retainer and boot protector from actuator.
6. Unseat adjusting piston boot from actuator and pull adjusting piston assembly from actuator bore.
7. Unseat anchor piston boot from actuator bore, then pull anchor piston from actuator bore, then remove dust boot from piston.
8. Remove adjuster lever and spring from actuator, Fig. 7.
9. Remove adjusting screw and nut assembly from adjusting piston, then unscrew nut from screw.
10. Remove automatic adjuster overload spring from top of adjusting nut and cap assembly and separate nut from cap.
11. Pry adjusting screw link from adjusting screw.

Assembly

1. If removed, press a new adjuster lever pin in place, ensuring new pin fits snugly in actuator hole.
2. If removed, install a new roller stop spring in actuator, Fig. 3.
3. Assemble adjuster nut cap and adjuster nut and align slots. Install a small drill

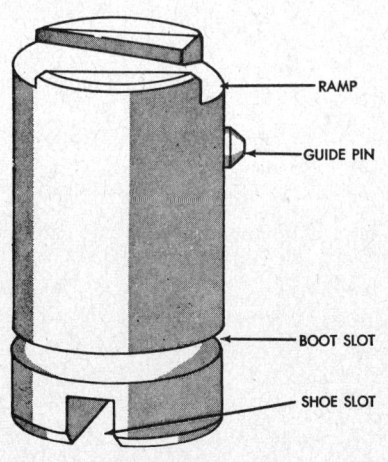

Fig. 4 Anchor piston

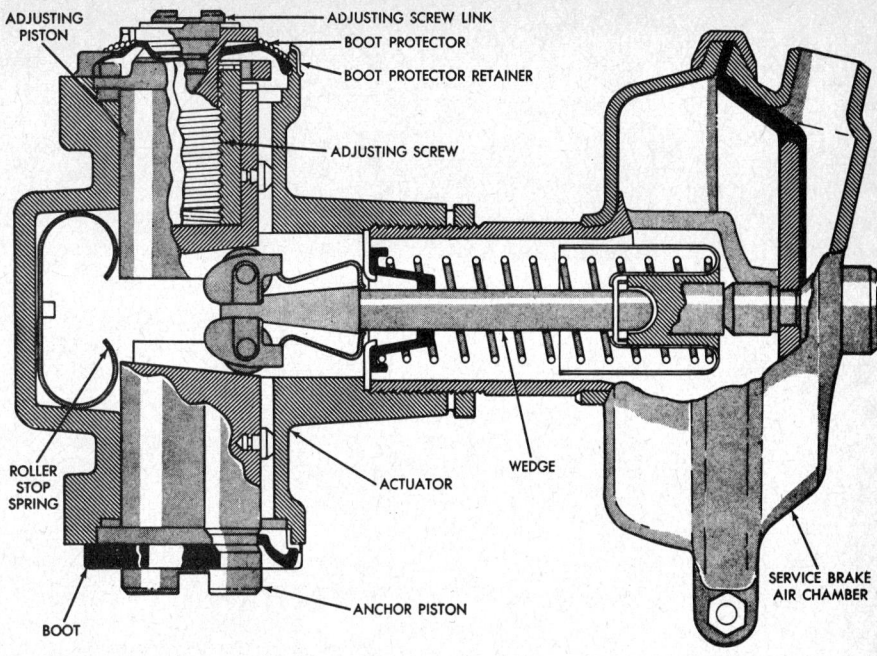

Fig. 3 Brake actuator & air chamber

bit or rod through alignment holes in cap and nut for proper alignment when installing overload spring.

4. Install overload load spring in slots of adjuster nut and cap with open end of spring toward alignment hole, Fig. 8. To check overload spring action, hold adjuster nut with overload spring upward and turn adjuster nut cap clockwise. The cap should slightly rotate clockwise, against the overload spring, but not counter-clockwise.
5. Install retaining ring in adjuster screw link groove.
6. Install detent spring on adjuster screw link so detent will engage star wheel teeth when link is pressed into adjuster screw, Fig. 9.
7. Lubricate adjuster screw hollow end with suitable lubricant and install screw link into adjuster screw, ensuring link is fully pressed into the screw.
8. Install boot on adjuster screw and adequately lubricate adjuster screw and adjuster nut threads with suitable lubricant.
9. Rotate adjuster screw into nut until bottomed, then back screw out one full turn.
10. Lubricate outside surface of adjuster nut and inside surface of adjuster piston, then install adjuster nut assembly into adjuster piston.
11. Install dust boot in anchor piston groove, using caution not to damage boot.
12. Insert adjuster lever spring hook into hole of adjuster lever, Fig. 7. Coat spring and lever with suitable lubricant. Install adjuster spring into actuator well, then the adjuster lever on the lever pin.
13. Adequately lubricate adjuster piston outside diameter, ramp on piston bottom, and actuator bore with suitable lubricant, then install adjuster piston into actuator bore, aligning piston guide pin with slot in bore.
14. Adequately lubricate anchor piston outside diameter, ramp on piston bottom, and ramp end of actuator bore

with suitable lubricant, then install anchor piston into actuator bore, aligning piston guide pin with slot in bore.

15. Place boot on actuator and, using a $1\frac{5}{8}$ inch socket or similar tool and a mallet, seat metal ring of boot in actuator. Ensure boot is not damaged and that it is fully seated.
16. Install boot protector on adjuster piston boot and press boot retainer over boot protector.
17. Lubricate wedge and roller assembly with suitable lubricant and install assembly into actuator.
18. Some air chambers have a collet check nut, Fig. 10. If air chamber has a collet nut and the actuator inside diameter is not chamfered, assemble collet nut and lockwasher so flat side of nut is against the actuator, Fig. 11. If actuator bore is chamfered, install nut so flat side faces toward air chamber. If old type check nut,

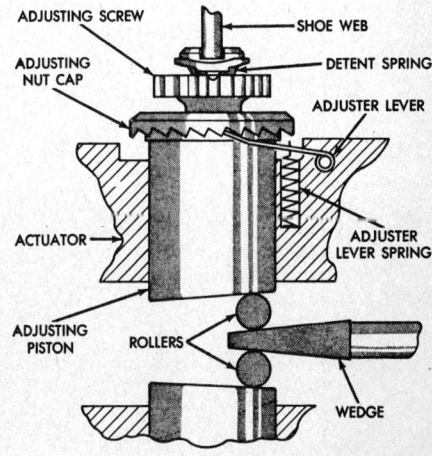

Fig. 5 Automatic adjuster

BENDIX TWINPLEX BRAKES

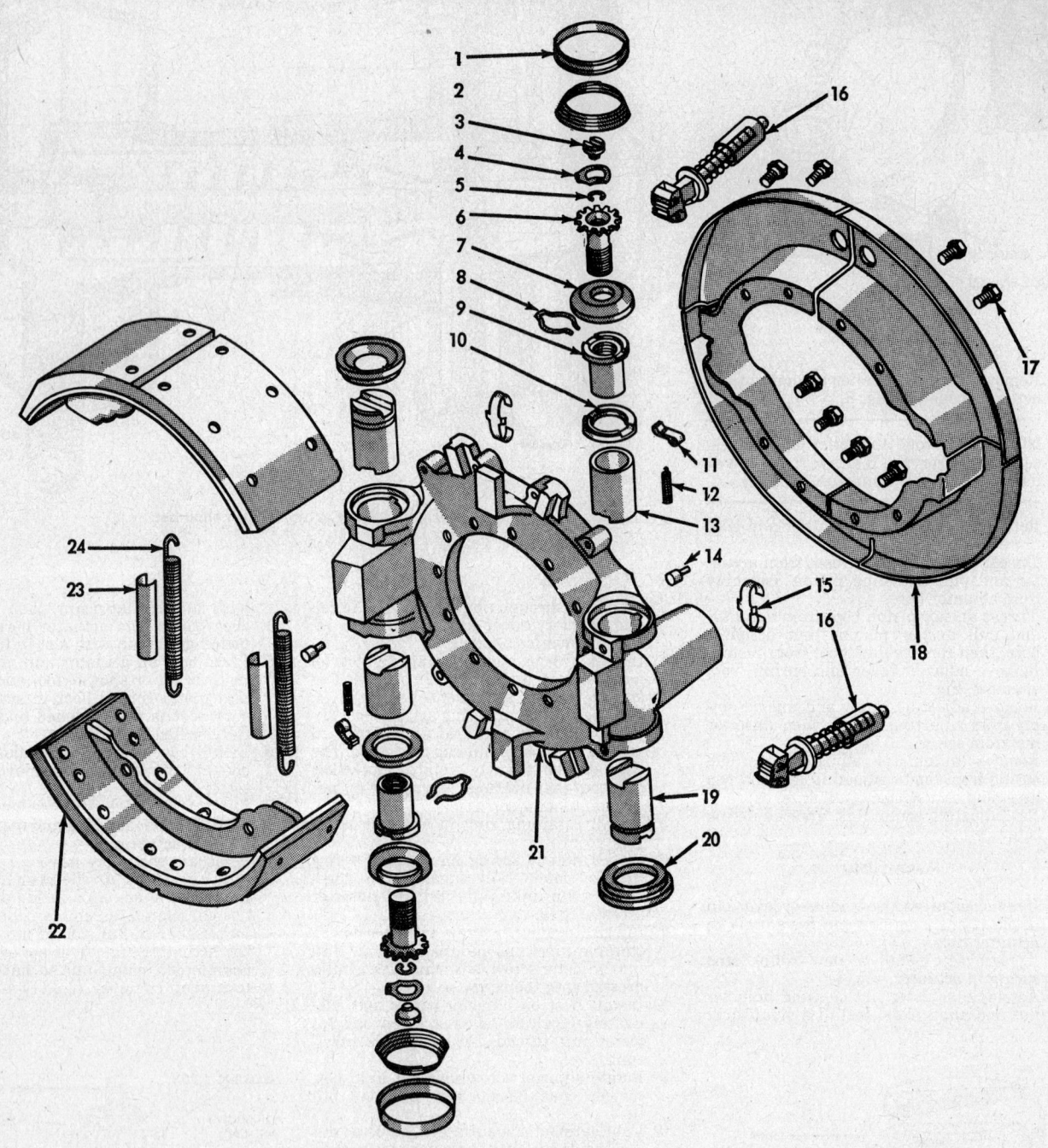

1. Boot Protector Retainer
2. Boot Protector
3. Adjusting Screw Link
4. Detent Spring
5. Link Retainer
6. Adjusting Screw
7. Adjusting Piston Boot
8. Automatic Adjuster Overload Spring
9. Adjusting Nut
10. Adjusting Nut Cap
11. Automatic Adjuster Lever
12. Adjuster Lever Spring
13. Adjusting Piston
14. Adjusting Lever Pin
15. Roller Stop Spring
16. Wedge and Roller Assembly
17. Dust Shield Screw
18. Dust Shield
19. Anchor Piston
20. Anchor Piston Boot
21. Spider
22. Shoe and Lining
23. Spring Damper
24. Shoe-to-Shoe Spring

Fig. 6 Twinplex brake, disassembled

BENDIX TWINPLEX BRAKES

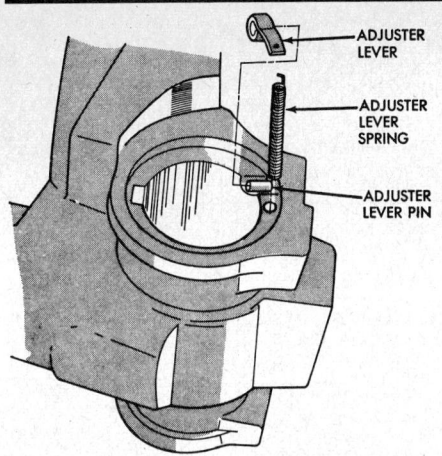

Fig. 7 Adjuster lever & spring

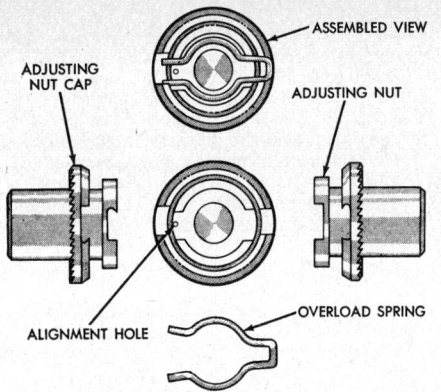

Fig. 8 Adjuster nut, cap & overload spring

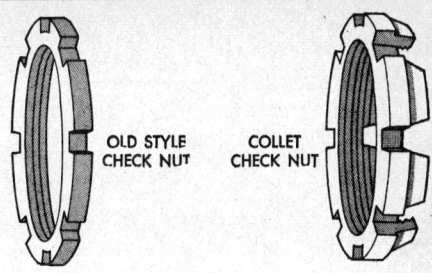

Fig. 10 Air chamber tube check nut identification

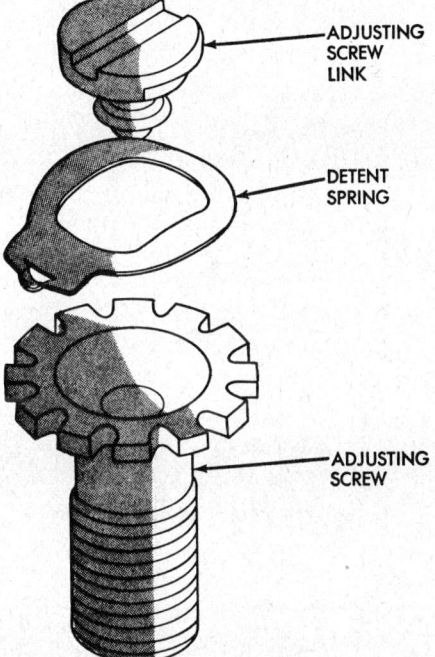

Fig. 9 Adjuster screw link & detent spring

Fig. 10, is installed a lockwasher is required.
19. Install check nut and lockwasher, if required, on air chamber tube, then screw air chamber tube into actuator until tube is tight against wedge stop washer. Ensure wedge shaft end is properly seated in air chamber diaphragm push rod.
20. Torque air chamber tube check nut to 150 ft. lbs. against lockwasher or actuator. Bend lockwasher outer edge, if used, into check nut notches.
21. Connect air hose to air chamber.

NOTE: Do not back air chamber tube out of actuator to align hose connection. Loosen clamp ring securing chamber halves and rotate inner chamber to align hose connection. Use care not to crimp or turn air chamber diaphragm.

BRAKE AIR CHAMBERS
Removal & Disassembly

CAUTION: Park vehicle on level surface and chock wheels. Also, exhaust air pressure from system.

1. Disconnect air hose from brake air chamber.
2. Straighten edges of air chamber tube lockwasher, then loosen check nut on air chamber tube.
3. Unscrew air chamber from actuator housing.
4. Remove clamp ring and separate chamber halves, Fig. 12.
5. Remove diaphragm, diaphragm plate and boot from chamber.

NOTE: It is recommended to install a new boot and diaphragm when an air chamber is disassembled.

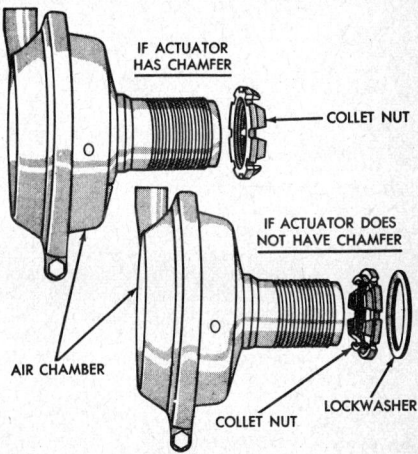

Fig. 11 Air chamber tube collet check nut installation

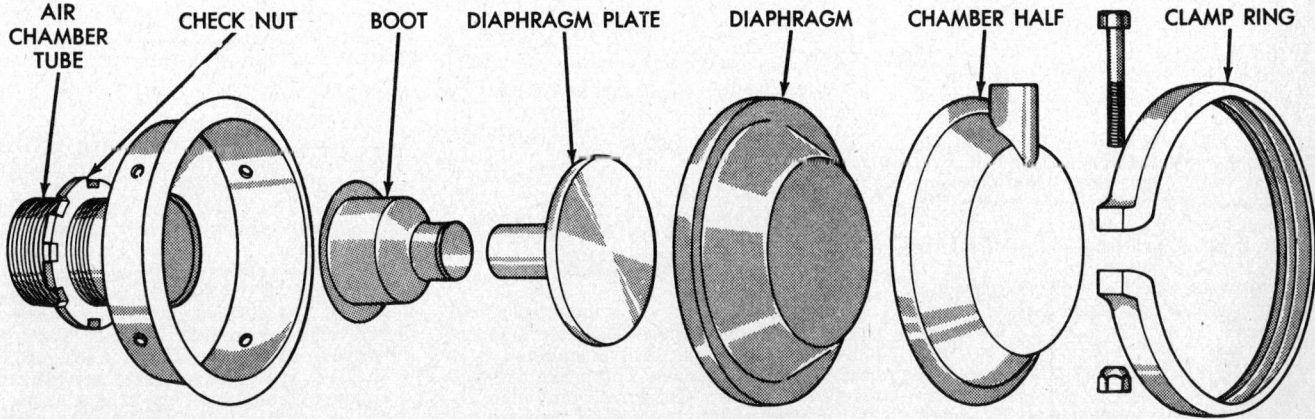

Fig. 12 Brake air chamber

611

BENDIX TWINPLEX BRAKES

Assembly & Installation

NOTE: The diaphragm must be glued to the diaphragm plate and the boot be glued to that portion of the air chamber with a suitable adhesive.

1. Lubricate hollow end of diaphragm plate push rod with suitable lubricant and insert push rod through boot.
2. Ensure diaphragm lip is properly positioned around chamber edge and install other chamber half.
3. Install and tighten clamp ring and ensure ring is fully seated.
4. Apply air pressure to the chamber and check for leaks using a soap and water solution.
5. Some air chambers have a collet check nut, Fig. 10. If air chamber has a collet check nut and the actuator inside diameter is not chamfered, assemble collet nut and lockwasher so flat side of nut is against the actuator, Fig. 11. If actuator bore is chamfered, install nut so flat side faces toward air chamber. If old type check nut, Fig. 10, is installed, a lockwasher is required.
6. Install check nut and lockwasher, if required, on air chamber tube, then screw air chamber tube into actuator until tube is tight against wedge stop washer. Ensure wedge shaft end is properly seated in air chamber diaphragm push rod.
7. Torque air chamber tube check nut to 150 ft. lbs. against lockwasher or actuator. Bend lockwasher outer edge, if used, into check nut notches.

NOTE: Do not back air chamber tube out of actuator to align hose connections. Loosen clamp ring securing chamber halves and rotate inner chamber to align hose connections. Use care not to crimp or turn air chamber diaphragm.

PARKING BRAKES

EXTERNAL CONTRACTING BAND TYPE

This type brake, Fig. 1, operates on a drum mounted on the companion flange at the rear of the transmission mainshaft. The brake band is anchored to a bracket that is attached to the transmission case. The linkage is so arranged that both ends of the brake band are contracted equally. The braking effort is equalized to each wheel through the differential.

Disassembly

1. Remove hand brake lever.
2. Remove brake adjusting screw after removing nuts from screw.
3. Remove jam nuts, adjusting bolt washer and spring from bottom of adjusting bolt.
4. Remove cam lever pin from spacer links, cam levers and adjusting bolt.
5. Remove adjusting bolt, release springs and cam operating shoe.
6. Remove anchor adjusting screw.
7. Remove brake band assembly, also anchor clip spring.

Reassembly

1. Reline brake band with proper lining.
2. Insert anchor clip spring into anchor support and install brake band assembly.
3. Install anchor adjusting screw.
4. Insert adjusting bolt through cam operating shoe, upper brake band bracket, upper release spring, locating bracket hole, lower release spring and lower brake band bracket.
5. Install cam lever pin through spacer links, cam levers, and adjusting bolt hook end. Secure with new cotter pin.
6. Install adjusting spring, washer and jam nuts on lower end of adjusting bolt.
7. Insert adjusting screw into locating bracket and through lower brake band bracket and install nuts.
8. Install draw rod end and secure with clevis pin and cotter pin.
9. Adjust hand brake as directed below and secure anchor adjusting screw with lock wire.

Adjustment

1. Three places are provided for adjustment. Where the band is supported by a bracket

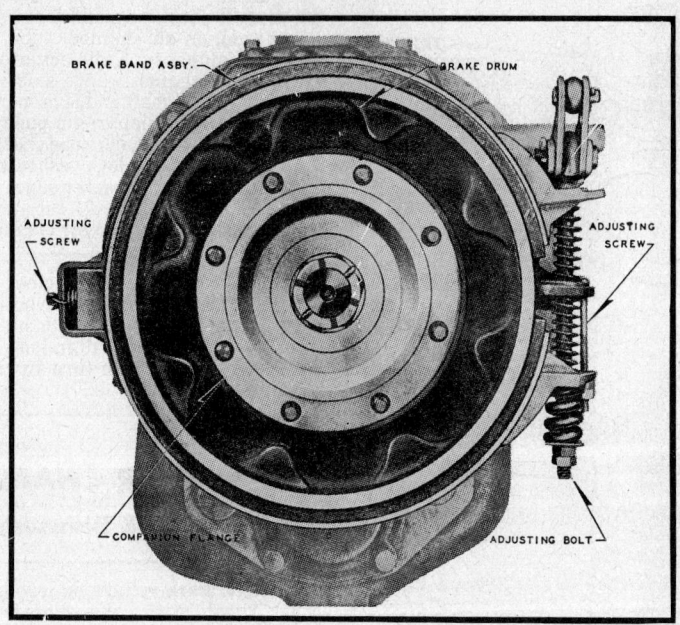

Fig. 1 External contracting band type parking brake

is a screw to adjust the band clearance at this point. Turning the screw to the right moves band and lining toward drum. Proper clearance is 1/32". After adjustment is completed, lock with wire.
2. Pull up lower half of band with bolt holding end of band to brake support. Allow 1/32" clearance and lock this adjustment with the locknut on the bolt.
3. Adjust clearance for upper half of band by means of the jam nuts at the bottom of the brake adjusting bolt and lock the two jam nuts together.

INTERNAL EXPANDING TYPE BRAKE

This type brake, Fig. 2, is mounted at the rear of the transmission. The brake support plate is attached to the transmission rear bearing cap or retainer. The brake drum is mounted between universal joint flanges. At the start of braking action, brake shoes are forced out against the drum by a lever-operated cam. The self-energizing action of both shoes then completes brake application.

Adjustment

A brake adjustment should be made before it becomes necessary to pull the hand brake lever to the limit of its travel to obtain full brake application.

1. Jack up at least one wheel. Block wheels and release hand brake.
2. Remove clevis pin connecting pull rod and relay lever. This will assure freedom for full shoe release.
3. Rotate drum to bring an access hole into line with adjusting screw at bottom of shoes.
4. Expand shoes by rotating adjusting screw with screwdriver inserted through hole in drum, Fig. 3. Move outer end of screwdriver away from drive shaft. Continue adjustment until a snug fit is obtained on a .010" feeler gauge placed between the drum and adjusting end of each shoe.
5. Place parking lever in fully release position. Take up slack in brake linkage by

PARKING BRAKES

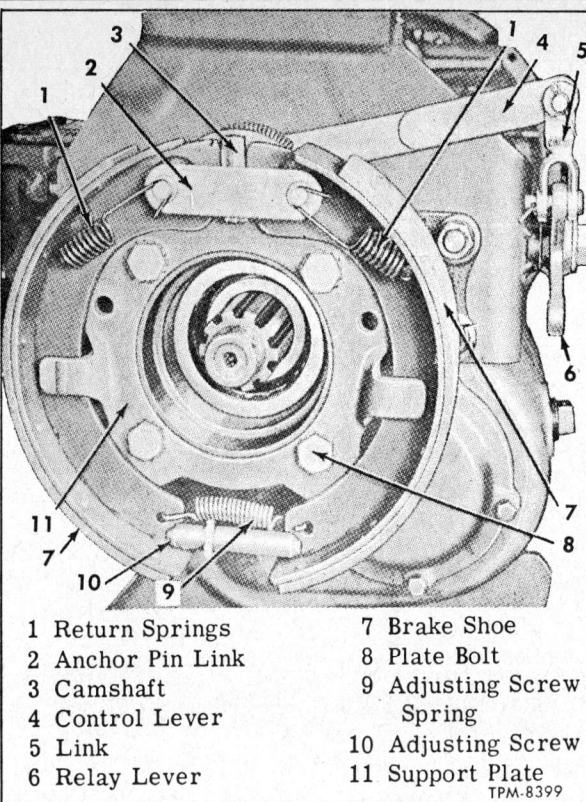

1 Return Springs
2 Anchor Pin Link
3 Camshaft
4 Control Lever
5 Link
6 Relay Lever
7 Brake Shoe
8 Plate Bolt
9 Adjusting Screw Spring
10 Adjusting Screw
11 Support Plate

TPM-8399

Fig. 2 Internal expanding type brake installed

pulling back on control lever just enough to overcome spring tension. Adjust clevis of pull rod to line up with hole in relay lever. Insert clevis pin and cotter pin, then tighten clevis lock nut.

Brake Shoe Service

NOTE: Fig. 3 illustrates the brake with the output shaft flange removed. It is not neces-

Fig. 3 Internal expanding type brake adjustment

sary to remove the flange to remove brake shoes. The flange is removed for clarity of illustration.

1. Jack up at least one wheel. Block wheels and release parking brake.
2. Disconnect U-joint at brake drum.
3. Unfasten and remove yoke flange.
4. Lift off brake drum.
5. Remove shoe return springs and anchor pin link from cam ends of brake shoes far enough to permit removal of support plate. Remove shoes, then separate by removing adjusting screw and spring.
6. After shoes have been relined, position brake shoes on lever arms and install brake shoe pins, retainers and capscrews.
7. Place spring and washers on tie rod. Swing rear lever arm forward and insert tie rod through hole in bottom of arm.
8. Move lever to released position and install tension spring.
9. Install adjusting nut and lock nut and adjust brakes as outlined above.

DISC TYPE BRAKE
All Exc. Tru-Stop

The disc type parking brake, Figs. 4 and 5, consists of a spider and spacers located between two disc plates and brake shoe assemblies. The disc assembly is mounted to the drive line between the companion flange and universal joint. The spider and spacers separate the disc plates and insure adequate cooling and prevent warping during continuous heavy duty operation. When the brake is applied, a squeezing action of the brake shoes against the discs provides the braking effort needed.

Disassembly
1. Disconnect brake cable at brake lever.
2. Remove locking and adjusting nuts from adjusting rod.
3. Remove clevis pin from lower end of operating arm.
4. Remove operating lever and adjusting rod from brake shoe levers.
5. Remove brake lever spring and washers from between brake shoe levers.
6. Remove small brake shoe retracting

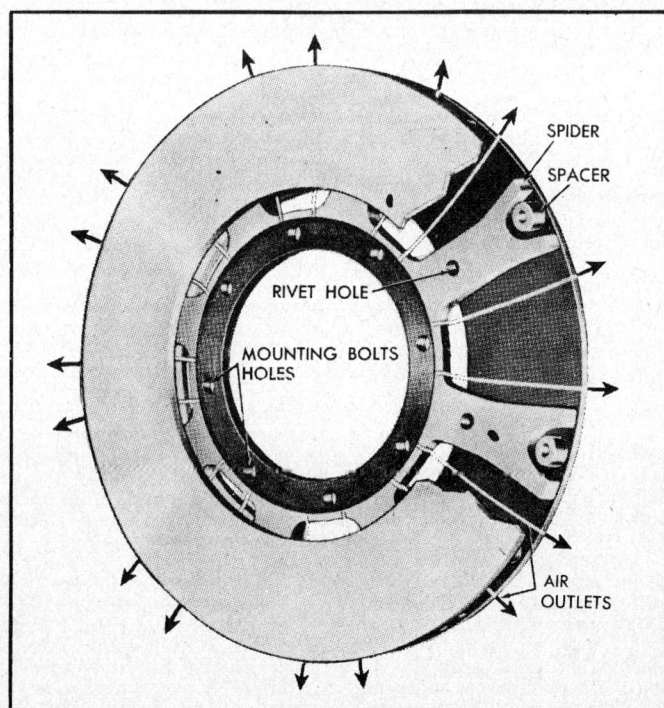

Fig. 4 Cutaway view of a typical disc assembly

613

PARKING BRAKES

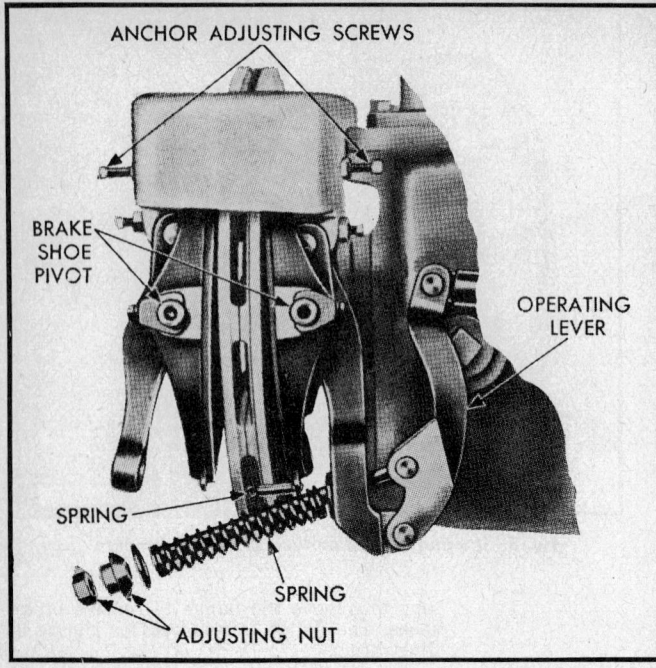

Fig. 5 Disc type parking brake, exc. Tru-Stop

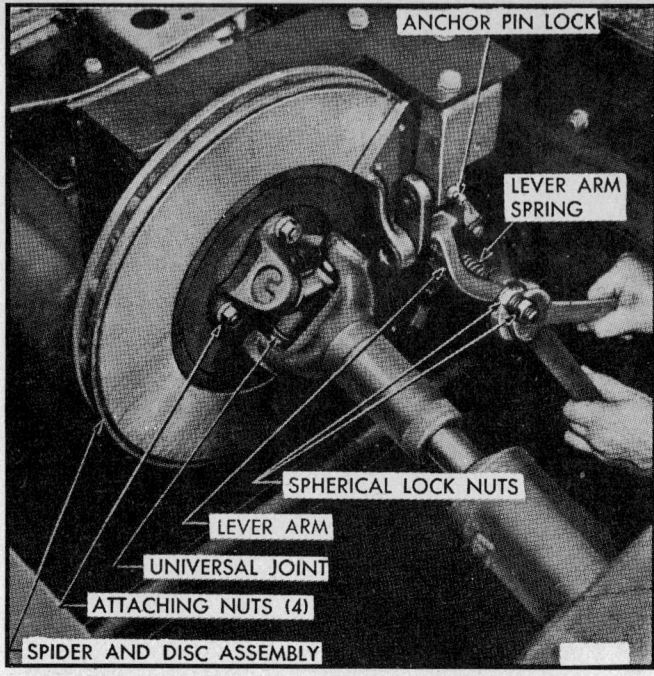

Fig. 6 Adjusting disc type parking brake, exc. Tru-Stop

spring.
7. Remove rear brake shoe pivot locking bolt and clamp.
8. Remove rear brake shoe pivot pin and brake shoe from lever assembly.
9. Remove front brake shoe pivot locking bolt and clamp.
10. Remove front brake shoe pivot pin and brake shoe.

Reassembly
Clean all moving parts with solvent and air dry for inspection. Inspect all linkage for worn parts. If inspection reveals worn pins or bushings, replace both pin and bushing.
1. Install front brake shoe, pivot pin, clamp and lock screw.
2. Install rear brake shoe, pivot pin, clamp and lock screw.
3. Install brake shoe retracting spring.
4. Install spring and washers between brake shoe operating levers.
5. Install adjusting rod through front lever spring and rear brake shoe lever.
6. Install spherical nut and lock nut on adjusting rod.
7. Install clevis pin and cotter pin in operating linkage and lever.
8. Connect cable and operating lever.

Adjustment
1. Disconnect cable from operating lever.
2. Disconnect U-joint from flange so disc is free to turn.
3. Adjust both brake anchor screws, Fig. 6, so that a slight drag may be felt when passing a .030" feeler gauge between top end of brake shoe and disc.
4. Leaving the feeler gauge in place, tighten spherical adjusting nut until a slight drag may be felt on a .030" feeler gauge inserted at lower end of both brake shoes.
5. While holding adjusting nut, tighten lock nut.
6. Remove all feeler stock and revolve brake disc and check for dragging.
7. Install U-joint.

Tru-Stop
This disc type parking brake, Fig. 6A, is mounted between the propeller shaft flange and the auxillary transmission shaft companion flange. The ventilated brake disc is located between the brake shoes and when the brake is applied, the shoes are forced against the disc.

Brake Shoe Removal
1. Remove tie rod locknut and adjusting nut, then the tension spring.
2. Place in-cab parking brake lever to the applied position so rear lever arm can be swung clear of tie rod, then remove tie rod washers and spring.
3. Remove brake shoe pin retainer screws, retainers, brake shoe pins and brake shoes.

Brake Shoe Installation
1. Place brake shoes on lever arms and install brake shoe pins, pin retainers and screws.
2. Install spring and washers on tie rod, then swing rear lever arm forward and insert tie rod through hole in arm.
3. Place in-cab parking brake lever in released position and install tension spring, adjusting nut and locknut.

Adjustment
1. Disconnect brake cable or rod clevis from brake lever.
2. Tighten adjusting nut until spring pressure forces lever against front lever arm.
3. Install a $1/32$ inch shim between rear brake shoe and disc, then tighten adjusting nut until front brake shoe firmly contacts disc, however, still allowing for shim removal.
4. Ensure tension spring is properly installed and adjust parallel adjusting screws until front and rear shoes are parallel with disc surfaces. This adjustment provides $1/64$ inch clearance between front and rear brake shoes and disc at all points.
5. Ensure in-cab parking brake lever is in fully released position and install clevis on brake lever. Adjust clevis on cable or rod so clevis can be installed without changing position of lever.

MGM SHORTSTOP BRAKE

This type brake, Fig. 7, is used on tandem axle trucks equipped with Bendix Twinplex wedge-type air brakes. Shortstop brake units provide mechanical spring actuation of the Twinplex wedge brakes whenever air pressure fails. During normal operation, the Shortstop power spring is held compressed by air pressure under the piston in the unit. When air pressure fails, the power spring forces the piston inward. This motion is transmitted by the release bolt to the push rod and pressure plate to move the piston assembly in the non-pressure air chamber, applying the wedge in the service brakes. The release bolt permits releasing the service brakes if normal air pressure cannot be restored.

Two of the three inlets on the Shortstop unit transmit air pressure to the service brake air chamber for normal service brake application. The third inlet in the center transmits air pressure to the piston chamber to compress the power spring. If air pressure fails in the Shortstop piston chamber, the power spring applies the brakes and, unless pressure can be reestablished, the service brakes must be released as follows in order to move the truck:
1. Referring to Fig. 7, remove bolt and nut holding cap and filter to the housing and remove cap and filter.
2. Using a deep socket wrench, unscrew release bolt until it turns freely. The brake shoe pressure is now released. Follow this procedure until all Shortstop units are released.
3. When air pressure has been restored,

PARKING BRAKES

1. Brake Support Bracket
2. Parallel Adjusting Screws
3. Front Lever Arm Pin
4. Pin Retaining Screw
5. Brake Cable Clevis
6. Brake Lever
7. Brake Shoe Pin Retainer
8. Brake Shoe Pin
9. Front Brake Shoe
10. Rear Brake Shoe
11. Front Lever Arm
12. Brake Disc
13. Tension Spring
14. Spring
15. Rear Lever Arm
16. Adjusting Nut
17. Tie Rod

Fig. 6A Tru-Stop disc type parking brake

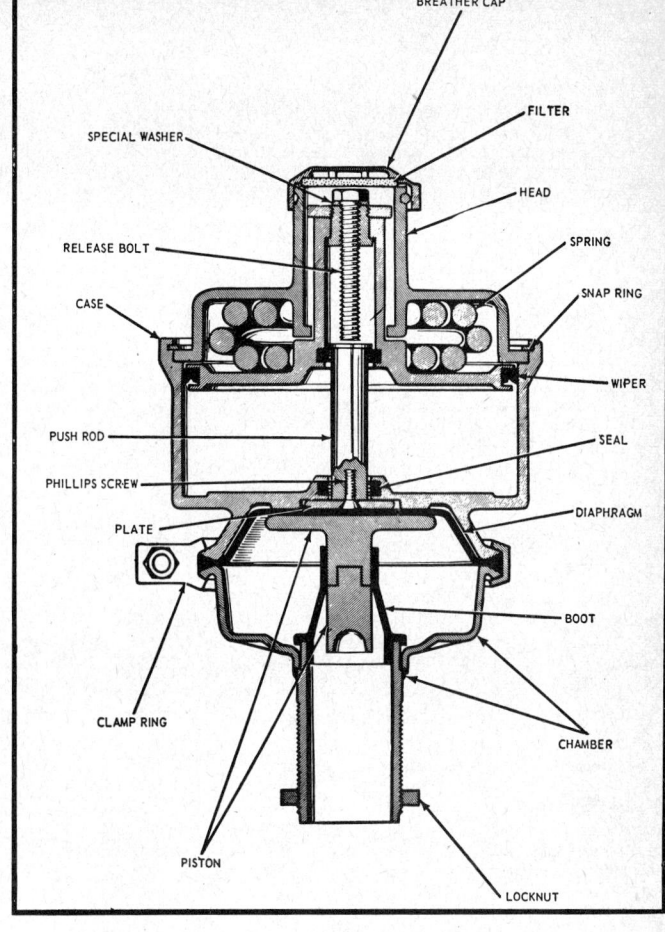

Fig. 7 MGM Shortstop emergency and parking brake

screw the release bolt in until the lockwasher holds it securely. This MUST be done to regain Shortstop protection.

Parking Operation

For parking operation, a control valve is provided in the cab. Pulling the valve knob out will release the air from the Shortstop pressure chamber, allowing the spring pressure to apply the brakes. The spring will be compressed again and the brakes released as soon as the parking valve is pushed in and/or system air pressure is restored by the compressor.

Shortstop Unit, Replace

1. Disconnect all air lines to unit.
2. Remove breather cap and filter, then unscrew release bolt completely, using a deep socket wrench.
3. Remove clamp ring fastening Shortstop unit to service brake chamber and remove Shortstop unit.
4. To install, first make sure release bolt is completely unscrewed.
5. Position Shortstop unit to service brake chamber and install clamp ring.
6. Connect air lines, charge Shortstop chamber with air and screw release bolt in tight. Install cap and filter.

Shortstop Unit, Overhaul

1. Referring to Fig. 8, use a sharp thin-bladed penknife or screwdriver to remove the solder from the head of the Phillips screw.
2. Position Phillips head screwdriver and seat it in screw slot with aid of a light hammer.
3. Remove Phillips head screw and pressure plate.
4. Remove release bolt and washer and insert a screwdriver through release bolt hole. Hold screwdriver firmly against top of push rod and charge the spring brake piston chamber with air (70 psi minimum).
5. Remove screwdriver and unscrew guide washer, using a drift punch and hammer.
6. Exhaust the air pressure. Remove sealant covering and snap ring between head and case.
7. Place spring brake assembly in an arbor press prior to final disassembly. Press must have a 6" stroke remaining after unit is placed in press.
8. Take up slight tension on press. Do not attempt to press head into case.
9. Using a screwdriver, remove snap ring from groove in case.
10. Relax press slowly. The spring will push head out of case. When spring is free, remove entire assembly from press.
11. Remove head and spring from case.
12. Grasp piston by its hub and pull it straight out of case.
13. Wash all parts in suitable non-oily solvent.
14. Inspect all parts for wear or damage. Replace with new parts or refinish with emery or crocus cloth, if necessary.

Reassembly

1. With all parts perfectly clean, apply a low temperature moly-type lubricant to all inside surfaces.
2. Lightly lubricate seal groove in piston, also collar seal and push rod seal.
3. If removed from piston, the push rod is installed by working the flanged end through the seal in the center of the piston.
4. Install piston assembly in the case, starting at a 45° angle. Slowly bring piston hub to 90° and install push rod in seal.
5. Install spring on piston and head on spring.
6. Place assembly in an arbor press and slowly compress spring. Use care, making

615

PARKING BRAKES

sure piston hub enters head opening correctly. Continue to compress assembly, making sure lip of head seats against shoulder of case correctly.
7. Install snap ring, tapping both ends to insure complete seating.
8. Relax press pressure and remove assembly from press.
9. Using a screwdriver through release bolt hole, press down firmly on push rod while charging the cylinder with air (70 psi minimum).
10. Remove screwdriver and install guide washer on insert in piston hub. Tighten washer to 30 ft-lbs minimum, and check for air leaks as follows:

Checking for Air Leaks

1. Charge unit with air. Apply oil around guide washer. If bubbles appear, replace the main seal.
2. With unit charged with air, apply oil around push rod in diaphragm end of case. If bubbles appear, replace push rod seal.
3. Install pressure plate on push rod. Use emery cloth to smooth burrs off head of Phillips head screw, if present.
4. Clean snap ring groove area with solvent and apply a sealant to cover the snap ring. If possible, allow sealant to dry overnight before installing unit on truck.

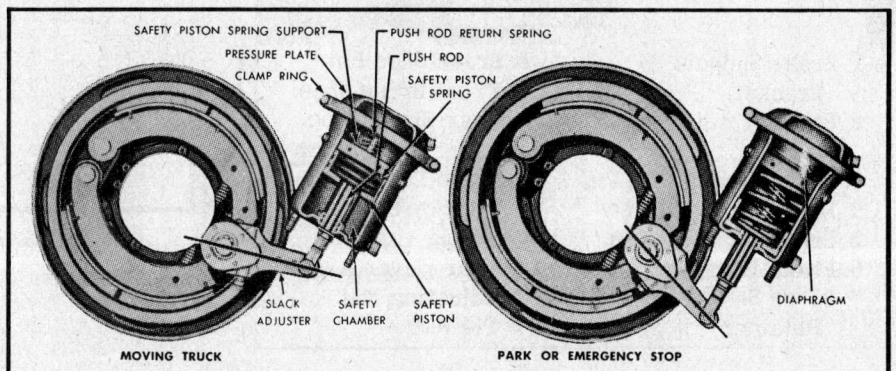

Fig. 8 Shortstop brake unit disassembled

MAXIBRAKE

This device, Fig. 9, is available on vehicles with full air brakes for emergency stops or parking. The air brake chamber (used on rear axle brakes only) is much like the conventional brake chamber; it differs only in that it contains an independently spring-loaded piston which, when released due to low air pressure, will apply the service brakes.

Normal air pressure applied to the safety chamber and piston keeps the piston spring compressed, while the service brakes continue to operate normally.

A manual control valve, located in the cab, exhausts the air from the safety chamber so that the safety piston spring pressure can be used for emergency stops.

Fig. 9 Maxibrake operation

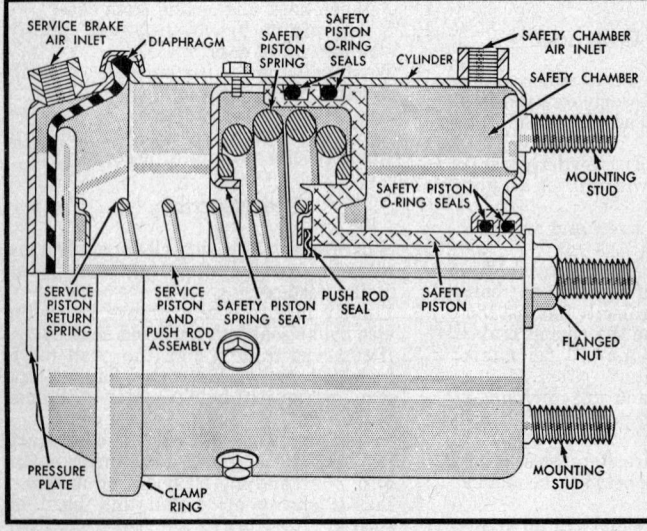

Fig. 10 Maxibrake air brake chamber (sectional view)

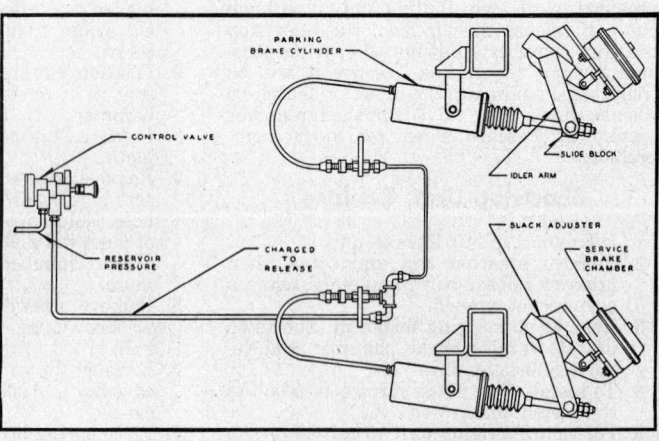

Fig. 11 MGM spring-type parking brake system

PARKING BRAKES

Remove & Install

Release all air from the system and then disconnect air lines from brake chamber. Disconnect push rod yoke from slack adjuster. Remove mounting nuts and take off brake chamber.

To install, position brake chamber on mounting bracket and install retaining nuts. Connect push rod yoke to slack adjuster. Connect air lines to brake chamber and build up the air pressure.

Disassembly

1. Referring to Fig. 10, first mark both the pressure plate and cylinder with relation to clamping ring and air line fittings so that unit can be reassembled in the same position.
2. Remove clevis yoke and flanged nut from push rod and install a 3/4" OD × 5/8" ID flat washer and a 5/8" nut on push rod. Tighten nut until plate end of push rod is seated on safety piston spring support. *It is necessary to compress push rod return spring and safety piston spring so the unit may be disassembled safely without being hampered by spring pressure.*
3. Remove clamp ring, pressure plate and diaphragm from cylinder.
4. Unfasten safety piston spring support from cylinder body and remove complete inner assembly (8 screws).
5. Place push rod and piston assembly on work bench and remove nut and washer used to compress springs. With spring tension removed, disassemble push rod, return spring, safety piston, spring and seat.
6. Remove push rod seal from bore of piston and O-ring seals from piston and cylinder.

Reassembly, Fig. 10

NOTE: Always be sure that the correct return spring is used in any brake chamber. Also be sure that the brake chamber on the opposite side of the axle has the same return spring, otherwise uneven braking will result.

If a new diaphragm is installed in the brake chamber on one side of the axle, a new one should be installed in the corresponding brake chamber on the opposite side also, otherwise uneven braking will result.

1. Coat safety piston and inside of cylinder with Lubriplate or other suitable lubricant.
2. Rest push rod upright on a flat surface and assemble in order: push rod return spring, safety piston spring seat and spring, and safety piston. Compress push rod and springs by installing nut and flat washer used in disassembly procedure.
3. Install push rod seal in piston bore and install O-ring seals on piston and in cylinder.
4. Position piston and spring assembly in cylinder. Align threaded holes in piston spring support with holes in side of cylinder, and install retaining capscrews.
5. Position diaphragm and pressure plate with clamp ring to cylinder; align marks made prior to disassembly and tighten clamp ring.
6. Remove nut and washer used to compress springs. Connect air lines to brake chamber and build up air pressure.
7. With safety chamber under pressure, and safety piston in retracted position, run flange nut up snug on push rod and install clevis yoke.

NOTE: Maintain distance of 2 13/16" between centerline of clevis pin holes in yoke and mounting flats of cylinder. Tighten flange nut against yoke to lock it in place.

TROUBLE SHOOTING AIR SYSTEM

Slow Pressure Build-Up In Reservoirs

1. Leaking application valves, check valve or relief valve.
2. Leaking compression discharge valves.
3. Leaking lines or connections.
4. Weak unloader piston return springs.
5. Clogged compressor air cleaner.
6. Worn compressor pistons and rings. Carbon in discharge line.
7. Bent or kinked line.
8. Insufficient discharge valve travel.

Quick Loss of Reservoir Pressure when Engine is Stopped

1. Leaking relief valve.
2. Leaking compression discharge valves.
3. Leaking tubing or connections.
4. Leaking application valves or check valve.
5. Leaking governor.

Compressor Not Unloading

1. Unloader pistons leaking or sticking.
2. Restriction in passages from governor to unloader.
3. Governor not operating properly.

Slow Brake Application, Slow Release or Inefficient Brakes

1. Low system pressure.
2. Brake chamber push rod travel excessive.
3. Restriction in line.
4. Leaking brake chamber diaphragm.
5. Poor brake lining or drum condition.
6. Leaking brake valve or weak rubber spring in valve.
7. Binding cam or camshafts.
8. Quick release valve leaking or sticking.

MGM SPRING BRAKE

This parking brake mechanism, Fig. 11, utilizes spring pressure as a separate power medium to apply the service brakes on the driving rear axle. The system is completely self-contained, with an individual cylinder applied to two or more rear wheel brakes in the service brake system. It complements the basic brake system but does not replace it. The cylinders are held inactive by the same compressed air source used to apply the service brakes. Approximately 90 psi is required to hold this brake in the fully released position, thereby assuring that the vehicle is not put into operation with insufficient service brake air pressure.

Operation

Two or four wheel brakes on the rear driving axle are provided with a springloaded air cylinder, connected to the slack adjuster through an idler arm with slide block, Fig. 11. Air pressure applied to the cylinders by a driver controlled valve, compresses the springs in the cylinders holding the piston rods in the extended position, thereby allowing the service brake system to function independently. When a normal foot brake application is made and the service brake chambers actuate the slack adjuster, the idler arm and slide block ride freely on the extended piston rod.

Control Valve

The parking brake control valve, located in the cab, is both manual and automatic. The control valve knob should be pushed "in" for park and pulled "out" for drive. In the case of an air loss, detected by the driver, the control valve knob can be pushed in, exhausting the air pressure in the cylinder, allowing the springs to retract the piston rod and apply the brakes. Even through this brake is primarily installed a parking brake, an emergency brake application will automatically occur any time the system pressure drops below a safe level, whether or not the control valve knob is pushed in. If the system pressure is exhausted while the vehicle is parked, it will be necessary to build pressure up to 90 psi before pulling out the control valve knob to release the brakes.

Brake Cylinder

Each parking brake cylinder is attached to a gimbal hanger bracket with two trunnion bolts. The trunnion bolts pass through the gimbal bracket and pilot into nylon bushings that are pressed into the bosses on each side of the cylinder housing. This allows the cylinder to oscillate, as required, when piston and rod are in operation. A piston, fitted with a neoprene seal is installed in the cylinder bore. Coiled springs, compressed between the piston rear face and cylinder head, provide the necessary energy for applying the parking brake. A rubber boot, covering the piston rod opening in the cylinder head, prevents the entrance of dirt and water into the cylinder.

Two springs are in the position shown in Fig. 12 when there is no air pressure in the parking brake system due to either a manual or an automatic brake application. When air pressure in the cylinder is reduced to approximately 80 psi the piston rod moves one-half inch. Air in the cylinder must be reduced to approximately 70 psi in order for the rod to move 1 1/2 inches. With normal service brake adjustment it is at this point that the brake shoes contact the drum. Brakes are fully applied when cylinder pressure drops to approximately 40 psi.

Maintenance

This brake system requires very little maintenance other than periodic visual inspection. It is important to see that the rubber boot, covering the piston rod opening in the cylinder head, is in place on the retainer and in good condition. If boot becomes torn or deteriorated it must be replaced. Failure to replace a defective boot will allow dirt and foreign matter to work its way into the cylinder, scoring the polished cylinder wall. Badly pitted or scored walls will damage the piston seal, permitting air to leak past the piston and cause the brakes to drag.

The other important inspection point is the nylon bushings, pressed into the cylinder housing bosses, and the trunnion bolts. If excessive wear develops, replace bushings and trunnion bolts. Failure to do so will cause the bosses to break due to vibration, and render the parking brake inoperative.

PARKING BRAKES

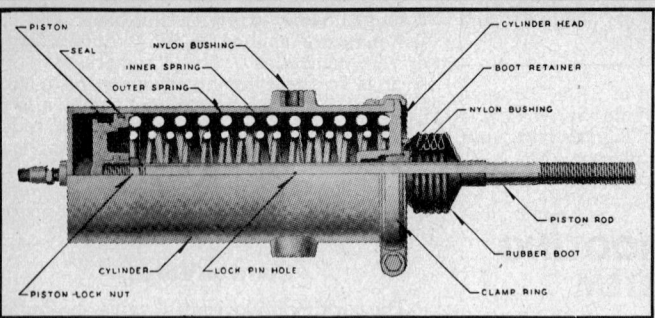

Fig. 12 Parking brake cylinder

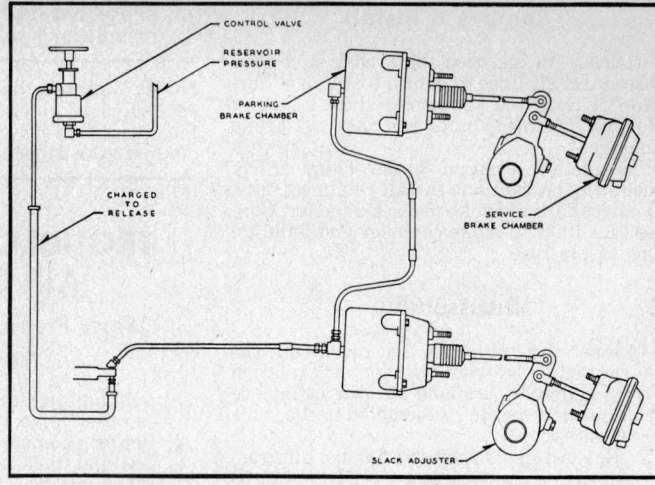

Fig. 13 Berg "Airo-Mech" spring-type parking brake system

Adjustment

The parking brake cylinder should be charged with air to move the piston and rod to the fully released or "drive" position before adjustment is made. Loosen and back off the two 3/4" nuts on end of piston rod. Adjust the service brakes through the slack adjusters. Then tighten the two 3/4" nuts with fingers until the large nut rests firmly against the slide block in the idler arm, then lock the jam nut.

NOTE: Adjustment to compensate for brake lining wear should be made at the slack adjusters—never by tightening the nuts on the end of the piston rod.

Lubrication

Every six months fill cylinders with air and insert lock pin in piston rod, Fig. 12. Remove air hose and pour one ounce of S.A.E. 10 engine oil through the tapped hole. Replace the air hose, fill cylinder with air and remove lock pin. Turn piston rod 1/4 turn by using a wrench on the 3/4" nuts at end of rod. Do not use pipe wrench to turn rod.

Keep piston rod clean and lightly lubricate it with Lubriplate or equivalent to prevent slide block from binding when service brakes are in operation.

BERG "AIRO-MECH" SPRING BRAKE

The parking brake control valve handle is pulled up to park and pushed down to release. The parking brake mechanism utilizes spring pressure as a separate power medium to apply the service brakes on the driving axle. It is released by the same compressed air source used to apply the service brakes, Fig. 13. At least 40 psi is required for complete release, thereby assuring that the vehicle is not put into operation with insufficient service brakes.

Parking brake spring tension is sufficient to hold a fully loaded vehicle on maximum grades permitted on modern highways, provided brake drums and lining are in good condition and shoes are properly adjusted.

Each brake on the driving axle is provided with a spring-loaded air chamber, connected to the slack adjuster by a flexible cable. Air pressure applied to the chambers by a driver-controlled valve, compresses the springs, thereby releasing the brakes. Although the parking brake chambers are connected to the slack adjusters, the parking brake system operates independently of the service brakes. The control valve is so designed that it is both manual and automatic. In case of an air loss below a safe level, the air in the chambers is exhausted and the brakes are automatically applied.

Brake Chamber, Fig. 14

Each brake chamber is mounted on a bracket which is clamped to a special rear spring shackle bolt. A piston, fitted with an O-ring to form an air-tight seal, is installed in the chamber bore. Three coil springs, compressed between the piston rear face and chamber cover, provide the necessary energy for applying the parking brake. A flexible cable, connecting the piston rod and slack adjuster, transmits the spring pressure to the brake cam.

The springs are in the position shown in Fig. 14 (720 lbs. pressure) when there is no air pressure in the parking brake system due to either a manual or an automatic brake application. When air pressure in the system reaches approximately 25 psi, the piston begins to move and compress the springs. At 50 psi the piston has reached the end of its travel (contacting shoulder on cover); springs are fully compressed and brakes are fully released.

Control Valve, Fig. 15

The parking brake control valve is both manual and automatic. It serves as a manual control for releasing and applying the parking brake and also automatically applies the

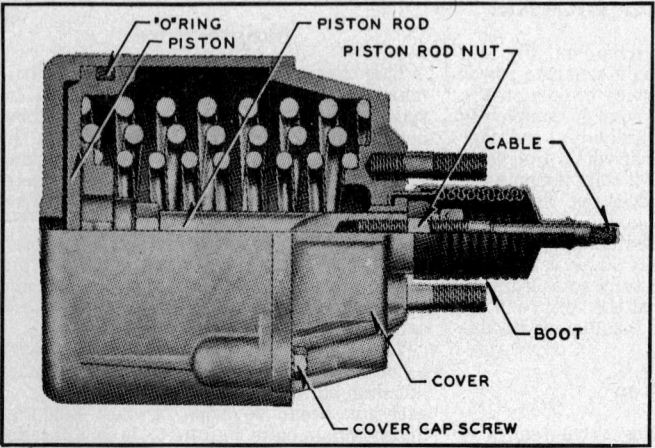

Fig. 14 Parking brake chamber

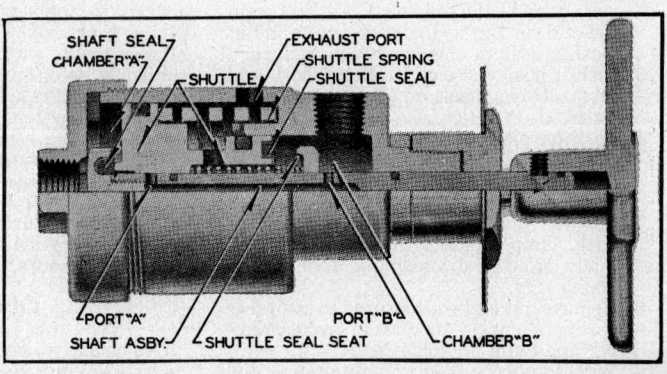

Fig. 15 Hand control valve

PARKING BRAKES

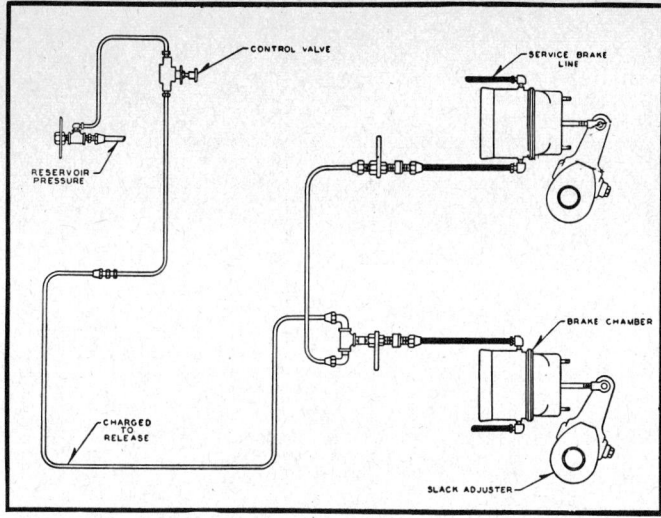

Fig. 16 Berg "Shur-Brake" spring-type parking brake system

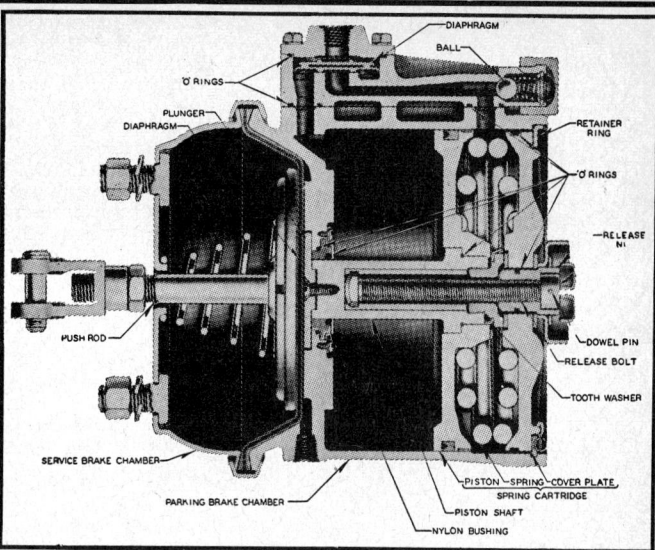

Fig. 17 Brake chamber with quick release valve

brakes in case of emergency.

When sufficient tractor air pressure is built up, the shuttle moves, compressing the shuttle spring. The shaft seal, which is attached to the shaft assembly, and held in contact with the shuttle by the shaft spring, moves the shuttle valve, thus containing the air pressure in chamber "A".

The operator then pushes the handle downward, causing the shuttle seal seat (integral with shaft) to contact the shuttle seal and unseat the shaft seal. Air pressure is then permitted to enter the hollow shaft through port "A" and pass through port "B", entering the air lines leading to the brake chambers and releasing the parking brakes.

The air pressure in chambers "A" and "B" is now equal as they are directly connected by the ports in the hollow shaft. Air pressure in the entire brake system is now the same. If pressure anywhere in the parking or service brake system drops to approximately 35 psi, the shuttle spring in the control valve expands and moves the shuttle, unseating the shuttle seal seat, thereby permitting the air to escape through the exhaust port and apply the brakes.

In a manual brake application the operator lifts the handle which draws the shuttle seal seat away from the shuttle seal in order to permit the air pressure to exhaust. In an automatic brake application the shuttle spring forces the shuttle away from the seal seat.

Adjustment

Each cable should have a small amount of slack in it to eliminate the possibility of a partial brake application due to the rise and fall of the axle on rough surfaces.

Service brakes should be properly adjusted and the parking brake chambers charged with air to the "released" position before adjustment can be made. Adjustment to compensate for lining wear should be made at the slack adjusters—not on the cables. No general lubrication of the parking brake system is required.

BERG "SHUR-BRAKE" SPRING BRAKE

This parking brake is the spring-applied air-release type which acts in conjunction with the rear wheel brake shoes, Fig. 16. The parking brake control valve handle is pulled out to park and pushed in to relase.

This system operates in a similar manner to the Berg Airo-Mech type described above. At least 45 psi is required for complete release, thereby assuring that the vehicle is not put into operation with insufficient service brake air supply.

Fig. 18 Exploded view of quick release valve

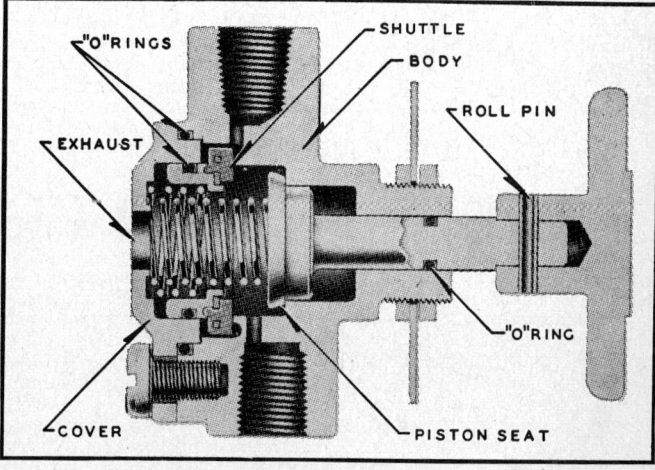

Fig. 19 Hand control valve

619

PARKING BRAKES

Brake Chambers, Fig. 17

Each unit contains two separate air tight chambers, the parking brake chamber and service brake chamber, each supplied by its own air pressure source. A barrel-shaped coil spring, compressed between the piston's rear face and the spring plate, provides the necessary energy for applying the spring brake. A piston shaft, passing through an air-tight nylon bushing in the chamber separation wall and bearing on the pressure face of the service brake diaphragm, transmits the spring pressure to the slack adjuster through the service brake rod and clevis assembly. A rubber boot (not used when the brake is equipped with a quick release valve) is fitted over the rear lip of the brake chamber cylinder to prevent dirt and water entering the unit.

Quick Release Valve, Fig. 18

Mounted to the parking brake chamber, an integral quick release valve is used on some brake chamber assemblies to control the flow of air pressure within the chamber.

A function of the valve is to equalize air pressure within the unit to that of the vehicle's system pressure. In doing so, the excess chamber pressure is exhausted to the atmosphere through the valve's exhaust port. Being a normal function of the unit, it should not be confused with spring brake malfunction.

At least once a year, the quick release valve should be removed from the parking brake chamber and disassembled. Check valve diaphragm and rubber-coated ball check. If tears or nicks are present, replace. Pay particular attention to the feather edge around the outer circumference of the diaphragm. A repair kit is available to recondition the valve.

Hand Control Valve, Fig. 19

The parking brake control valve is both manual and automatic. It serves as a manual control for releasing and applying the parking brakes and also automatically applies the brakes in case of emergency (vehicle air pressure below 38 psi).

When sufficient pressure is built up, the operator pushes the control valve knob in, causing the piston seat to move in, sealing the shuttle and closing the air passage from the outlet port to exhaust. Further inward movement of the knob unseats the shuttle from the valve body seat, permitting the air pressure on the inlet side to pass through the valve to the outlet port and hence to the parking brake chambers. A minimum pressure of 40 psi must be available at the inlet port to counteract the spring pressure and thus hold the piston in against the shuttle.

Should the inlet pressure fall below 40 psi, the spring force acting on the piston seat will move the piston assembly and knob outward, causing the shuttle spring to follow the piston seat until the shuttle contacts the valve body seat. Further movement of the piston results in losing contact with the shuttle and opens the air passage from the outlet port to exhaust, thus evacuating the pressure from the brake chambers and allowing the full force and effect of the springs to act on the slack adjusters through the service brake linkage.

Adjustment

The parking brakes must be placed in the "released" position and the service brakes adjusted in the normal manner. Other than service brake adjustment, no adjustment of the parking brake system is required. No general lubrication of the parking brake system is required.

AIR BRAKES

INDEX

	Page No.
Air Compressor	620
Governors	620
Brake Valves	624
Double Check Valve and Stop Light Switch	626
Stop Light Switch	626
Hand Control Valve	627
Brake Relay Valve	627
Relief Valve	627
Quick Release Valve	628
Limiting Quick Release Valve	628
Two-Way Valve	628
Tractor Protection Valve	629
Control Valve	630
Check Valve	631
Low Pressure Indicator	631
Brake Chambers	631
Slack Adjusters	631
Reservoir and Drain Cocks	631
Tubing, Hose and Fittings	631
Brake Assemblies	631

Air brake equipment on trucks and truck tractors provides a means of controlling the brakes through the medium of compressed air. The equipment consists of a group of devices as shown in Fig. 1. Some of these devices maintain a supply of compressed air, some direct and control the flow of compressed air, and others transfer the energy of compressed air into the mechanical force and motion necessary to apply the brakes.

Different sizes and types of devices are in use on different types of vehicles to meet operating requirements. Following are the devices comprising a typical air brake system with a brief description of the function of each device along with service requirements.

AIR COMPRESSOR

The compressor supplies the compressed air to operate the brakes. Two types are in general use, the piston type and the rotary type. Both types run continuously while the engine is operating.

In the piston type, Figs. 2 and 3, the actual compression of air is controlled by the governor which, acting in conjunction with the unloading mechanism in the compressor cylinder block, starts and stops the compression of air by loading or unloading the compressor when the pressure in the air brake system reaches the desired minimum of 95–105 pounds or maximum of 110–120 pounds.

In the rotary type, Figs. 4 and 5, the actual compression of air is regulated by the control valve (governor) which starts or stops air compression by "loading" or "unloading" the compressor as required. This action establishes an intermittent pumping cycle which keeps reservoir tank pressure within the desired range.

B-W GOVERNORS

The compressor controls the air pressure in the reservoir by actuating the unloading mechanism in the compressor when the compressor reaches the maximum limit of 120 psi. It permits compression of air to continue when reservoir pressure falls below the 95 psi minimum.

The governor is mounted on the compressor by a bracket. A passage in the bracket carries the air pressure from the governor to the compressor unloading mechanism. *On some applications the governor is mounted directly on the compressor.*

B-W TYPE D GOVERNOR

Operation

As air pressure increases, the diaphragm and stem assembly moves against the pressure setting spring, Fig. 6. When reservoir pressure reaches the governor cutout point (120 pounds) the exhaust valve is seated and the inlet valve is opened, permitting air pressure to flow to the air compressor unloading mechanism. As reservoir pressure is reduced to 95 pounds, the inlet valve closes and the exhaust valve opens, thus allowing the compression of air to be resumed.

Adjustment

Normal cut-out pressure of the governor is 110 to 120 pounds and normal cut-in pressure is 95 to 105 pounds. Cut-in and cut-out pressures may be adjusted by removing the cap nut, cotter pin and then turning the adjusting nut. Turn nut clockwise to raise the setting, and counterclockwise to lower the setting. *The range between cut-out and cut-in pressures is fixed at approximately 20 pounds and cannot be adjusted.*

Service

Prior to reassembly lightly coat the valve parts, valve bores and O-rings with recommended grease (B-W 240176).
1. Install new O-ring seals on cap nuts, inlet valve seat, diaphragm stem, and in groove of exhaust stem bore of body.

AIR BRAKES

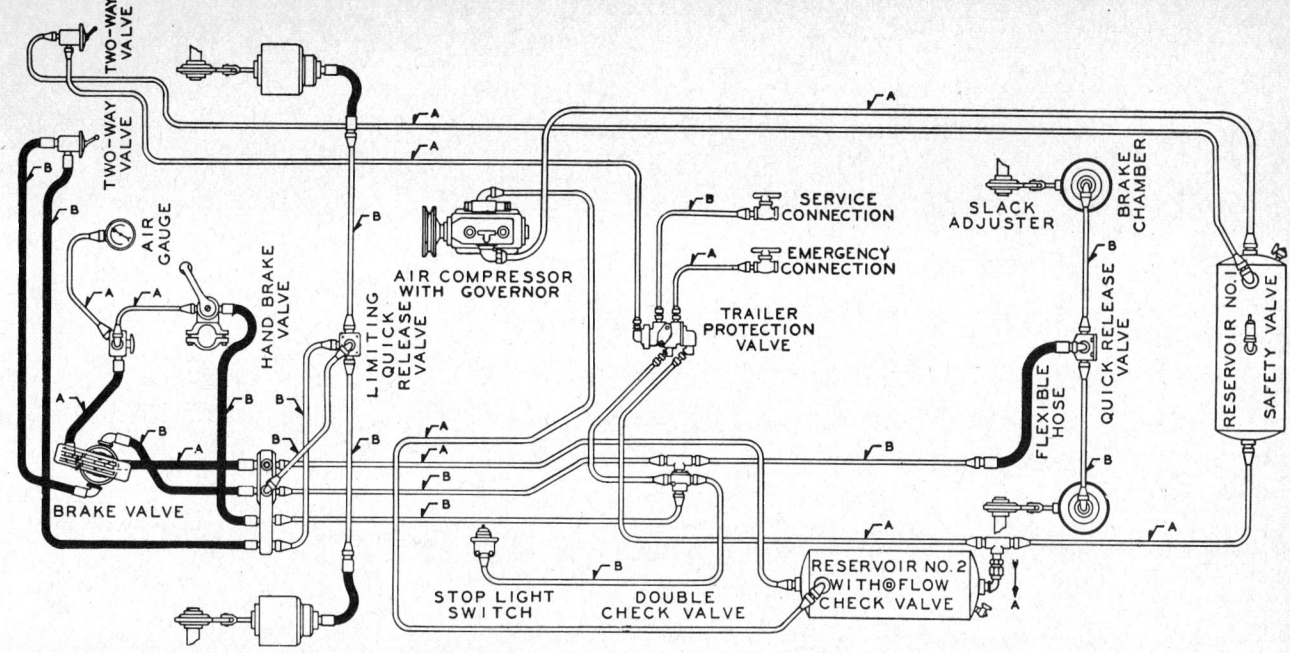

Fig. 1 Typical air brake system with breakaway valve

Grease lightly before installing.
2. Install conical spring and exhaust stem in body.
3. Install diaphragm on stem, making sure that bevelled side of each follower face diaphragm. Fasten in place with nut and cotter pin.
4. Install diaphragm and stem assembly. Fasten body and spring cage together with four screws.
5. Install cylindrical filters.
6. Install and tighten filter cap nuts. Make certain O-rings and rubber washers are in place.

NOTE: Attach a dial indicator to flanges of body and spring cage with indicator stem contacting end of exhaust stem. Pull diaphragm stem outward as far as possible and set indicator at zero. Then push diaphragm stem inward to limit of its travel and note reading on indicator. Total travel should be within .060″ to .098″. Install shims, inlet valve seat and valve and repeat procedure with dial indicator zeroed on end of inlet valve. Add or remove shims under inlet valve seat until travel is .030″ to .040″.

7. Install valve and seat retaining springs. Then install body cap nut with O-ring.
8. Install spring and spring seat and assemble nut on stem.

NOTE: Mount governor on suitable test bench or on vehicle and build up reservoir

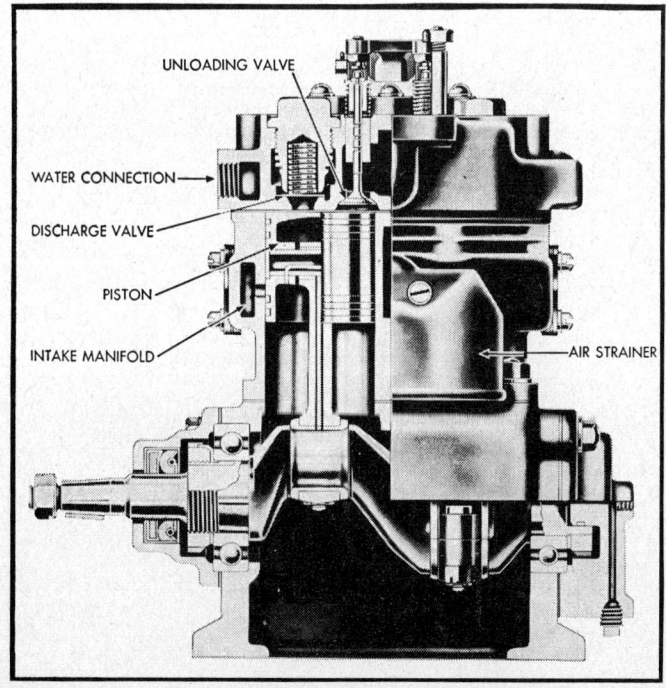

Fig. 2 Piston type air compressor (Typical)

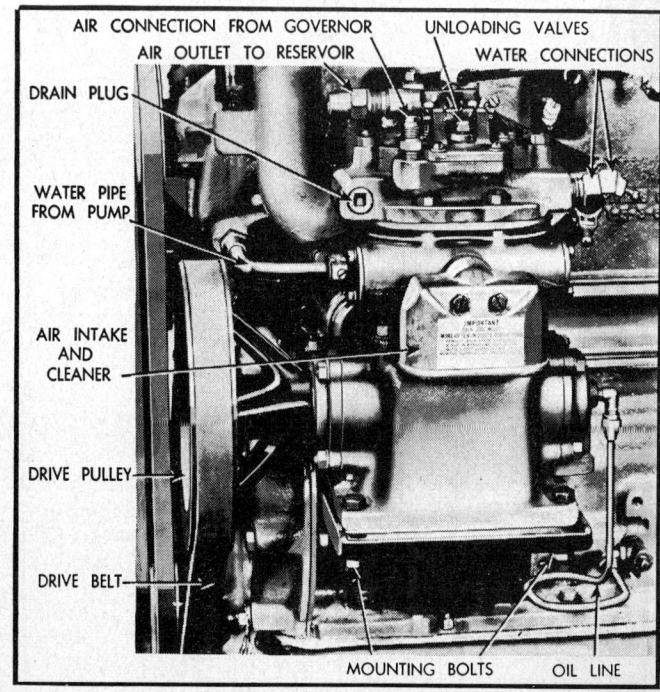

Fig. 3 Side-mounted piston type air compressor

AIR BRAKES

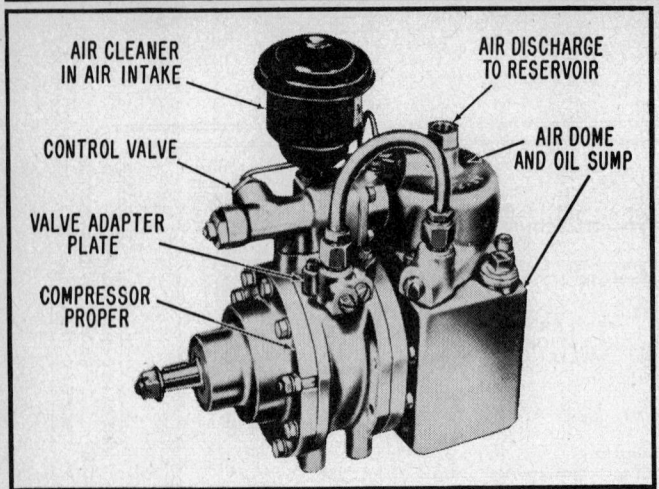

Fig. 4 Rotary type air compressor

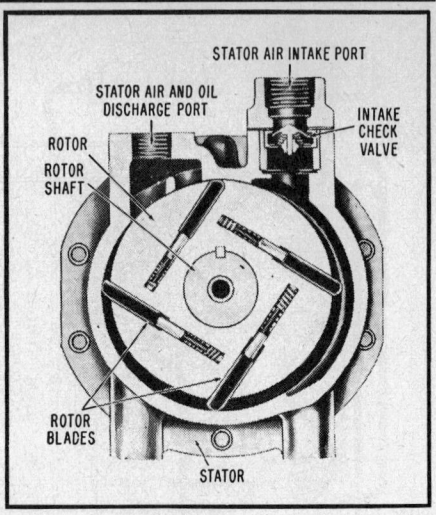

Fig. 5 Rotor and stator of rotary type air compressor

pressure from zero. Note pressure at which air starts to escape from spring cage. If pressure is below 110 pounds, turn adjusting nut clockwise; if pressure is above 120 pounds, turn counterclockwise. After final adjustment, leakage should start at 110–120 pounds. Lock with new cotter pin.

9. Install spring cage cap nut with O-ring in place.

B-W TYPE D-2 GOVERNOR

Operation

Referring to Fig. 7, reservoir air pressure exerts force on bottom of piston and inlet-exhaust valve. Piston movement is prevented by the adjusting screw and spring assembly as long as reservoir pressure does not exceed the spring pressure above piston.

When reservoir pressure does exceed spring pressure, the piston lifts. The exhaust stem does not move since it butts against the head of the stationary adjusting screw. The inlet-exhaust valve moves with the piston until it contacts exhaust stem (closing exhaust passage in stem). Continued piston movement unseats inlet-exhaust valve from its seat in piston.

Air pressure is then permitted to pass around inlet-exhaust valve, through passage in piston, and out unloader port to unloading mechanism in compressor. Spring pressure above piston forces piston downward when reservoir pressure becomes less than spring pressure. As piston moves downward, it contacts inlet-exhaust valve, closing air inlet. Continued downward movement unseats the inlet-exhaust valve from the exhaust stem, permitting air in unloader to escape and compression of air to resume.

Service

Coat parts with B-W 240176 grease and reassemble governor as follows:
1. Install O-ring in counterbore in piston. Install retaining washer and stake securely.
2. Install exhaust stem spring in piston.
3. Install exhaust stem in piston bore by passing it through spring and O-ring.
4. Install inlet-exhaust valve in piston.
5. Install inlet-exhaust valve spring against valve and snap outer end in groove provided.
6. Install O-rings in piston grooves. Be sure they are not twisted.
7. Install piston in housing bore with exhaust stem up.
8. Install adjusting screw and spring assembly. Then install snap ring.

NOTE: If pressure adjustment is necessary, loosen lock nut and turn adjusting screw clockwise to decrease and counterclockwise to increase reservoir air pressure. When satisfactory, tighten lock nut and install dust cover.

M-R GOVERNORS

These governors are available in three different designs: original design, intermediate design and the present design, Fig. 7A. The governor, working in conjunction with the air compressor unloader mechanism, automatically maintains a pre-set air pressure in the air system. The operation of all governors is basically the same.

With the engine off and no air pressure in the system, the governor spring maintains the plunger in the down position, thereby seating the inlet valve on the body.

With the engine operating, air pressure

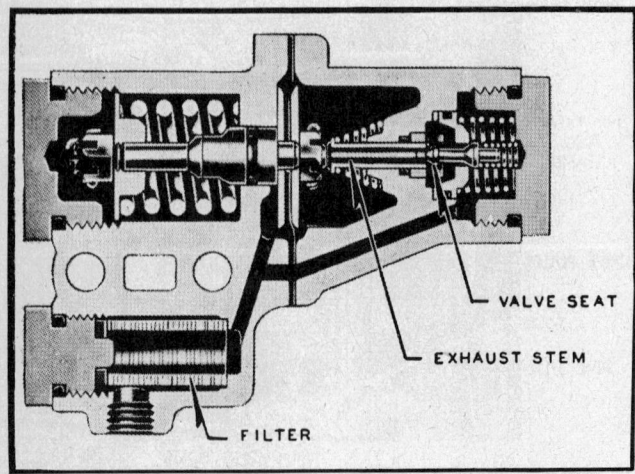

Fig. 6 Type D compressor governor

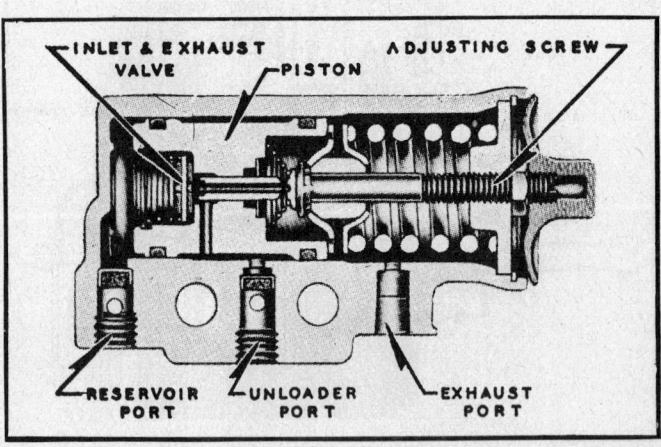

Fig. 7 Type D-2 compressor governor

AIR BRAKES

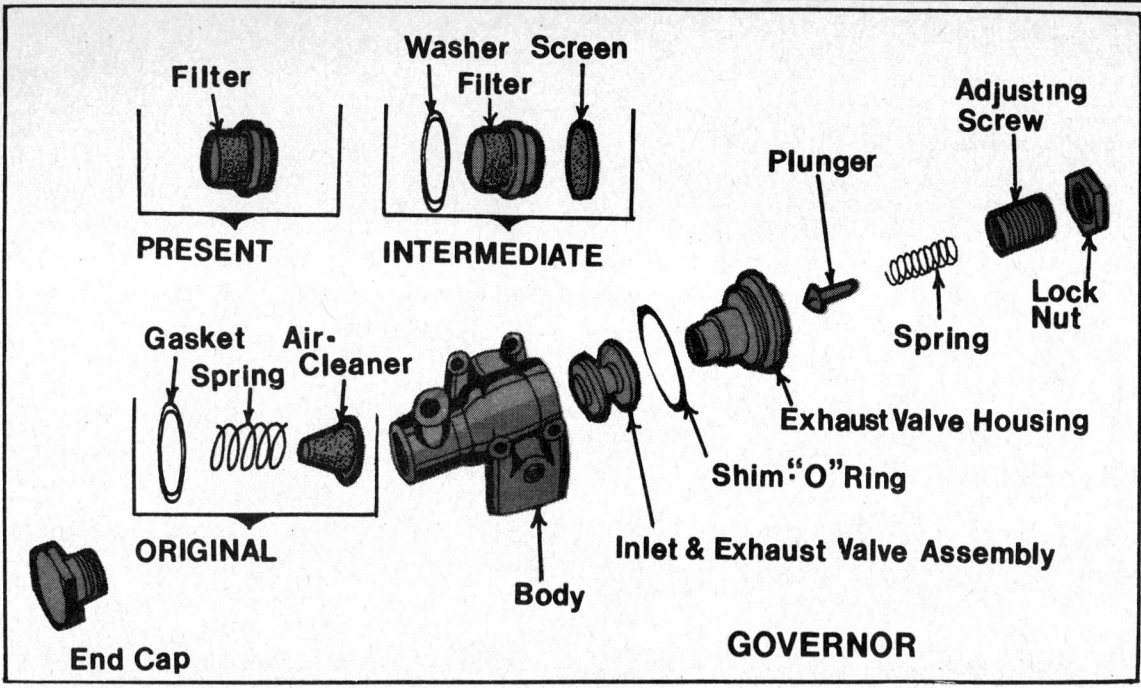

Fig. 7A M-R compressor governor

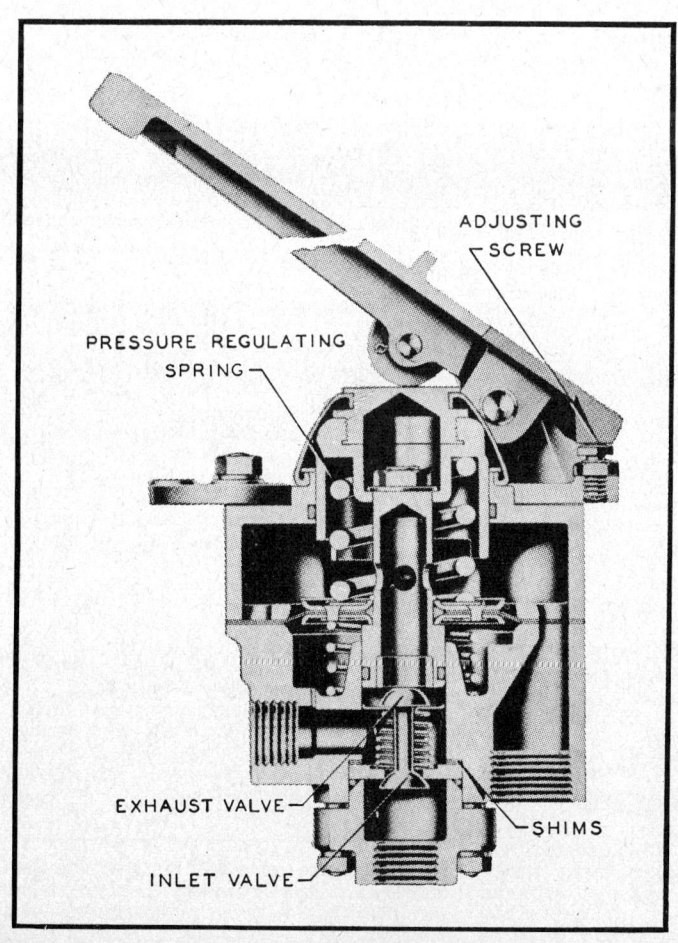

Fig. 8 Type D-1 brake application valve

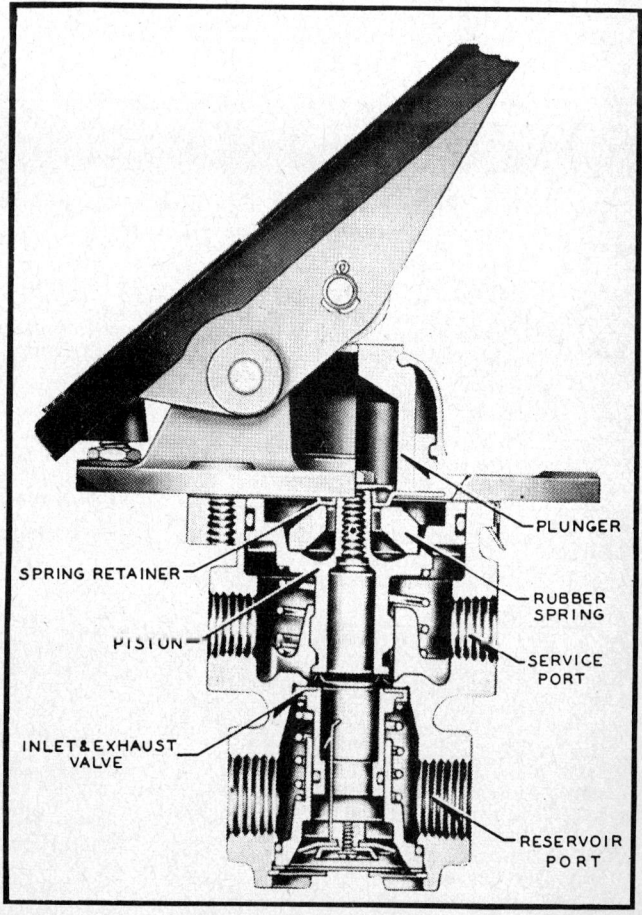

Fig. 9 Type E-3 brake valve

AIR BRAKES

passes from the reservoir to the governor port. As air pressure increases, the inlet valve is slowly raised from the seat until maximum or cut-out pressure is reached. The inlet valve then snaps to full open, raising the plunger and compressing the spring, in turn seating the exhaust valve. The reservoir pressure is passed through the inlet valve orifice and around the exhaust valve, filling the center cavity of the governor and passing through the connecting tube to the upper cavity of the unloader assembly.

When reservoir air pressure decreases to minimum or cut-in pressure, the inlet valve is seated by governor spring pressure acting against the plunger and also unseats the exhaust valve. This action permits air pressure in the unloader and governor to exhaust through a port in the adjusting screw.

Service

Original & Intermediate Design

1. Install inlet and exhaust valves or the assembly (intermediate design) into body, Fig. 7A.
2. Install plunger and governor spring.
3. Place three shims on exhaust valve housing and install housing by turning housing into body until tight.
4. Rotate adjusting screw inward nine complete turns while holding valve housing secure and loosely install adjusting screw lock nut.

NOTE: Adjusting screw should protrude approximately $3/8$ inch from exhaust valve housing.

5. Install screen or air cleaner into body. Assemble filter (intermediate design), washer and end cap, then install the assembly into body.
6. Mount governor on a suitable test bench and build reservoir pressure to 115 PSI. If governor cuts-out before 115 PSI is reached, turn adjusting screw clockwise one complete turn and repeat this step.
7. Slowly rotate adjusting screw counter-clockwise until governor cuts out.
8. Bleed air from reservoir until governor cuts in. Cut-in pressure should be 93–98 PSI.
9. If cut-in pressure is not within specifications, remove exhaust valve housing, adjusting screw, lock nut and shims. If cut-in pressure was below 93 PSI, add shims to the assembly. If cut-in pressure was above 98 PSI, remove shims. The addition or removal of one shim is equal to a range change of approximately 4 PSI. Install exhaust valve housing, adjusting screw and lock nut.

NOTE: Pressure differential between cut-in and cut-out must not be less than 15 PSI. Recheck cut-out pressure and adjust if necessary.

Present Design

1. Install valve assembly into valve body, Fig. 7A, then the plunger and spring.
2. Lubricate exhaust valve housing "O" ring and install on housing. Turn exhaust valve housing into body until bottomed on valve assembly, then turn back $3/4$ turn and loosely install locknut on exhaust valve housing.
3. Turn adjusting screw in nine complete turns.

NOTE: Adjusting screw should protrude approximately $3/8$ inch from exhaust valve housing.

4. Assemble filter and end cap, then install in body.
5. Mount governor on a suitable test bench and build reservoir pressure to 115 PSI. If governor cuts-out before 115 PSI is reached, turn adjusting screw clockwise one complete turn and repeat this step.
6. Slowly rotate adjusting screw counter-clockwise until governor cuts out.
7. Bleed air from reservoir until governor cuts in. Cut-in pressure should be 93–98 PSI.
8. If cut-in pressure is below 93 PSI, hold adjusting screw stationary and rotate exhaust valve housing approximately $1/6$ turn counter-clockwise. If cut-in pressure is above 98 PSI, rotate exhaust valve housing $1/6$ turn clockwise. Rotating exhaust valve housing $1/6$ turn results in a range change of approximately 5 PSI.

NOTE: Pressure differential between cut-in and cut-out must not be less than 15 PSI. Recheck cut-out pressure and adjust if necessary.

9. Tighten exhaust valve housing and adjusting screw lock nuts.

B-W TYPE D-1 BRAKE VALVE

This brake valve, Fig. 8, is actuated by a brake treadle. Operation of the brake treadle regulates the movement of an inlet valve and an exhaust valve which, in turn, control the air pressure being delivered to or released from the brake chambers.

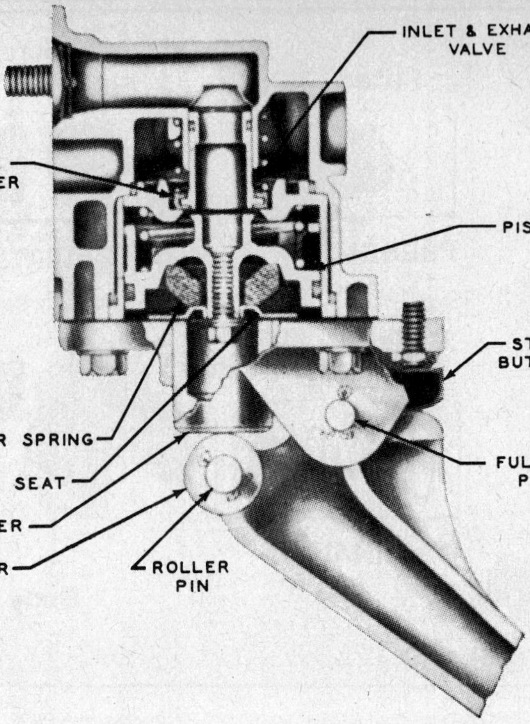

Fig. 9A Type E-5 brake valve

Adjustment

If brake valve does not release promptly or does not fully release, it indicates exhaust valve is not opening sufficiently. This can be caused by improper adjustment of the adjusting screw (screw being turned out too far, causing lever roller to exert too much force against spring cage when lever is in released position) or by insufficient shims being used between intake valve seat and body of valve.

If brake valve does not apply promptly, it indicates intake valve is not opening sufficiently. This can be caused by too many shims being used between intake valve seat and brake valve body. To adjust, proceed as follows:

1. Make sure intake valve is seated.
2. Place a depth gauge against intake valve by inserting gauge through reservoir supply port in intake valve body.
3. Apply brake valve and measure maximum intake valve travel which should be .148" to .156". Add shims between intake valve seat and body of brake valve to decrease travel. Remove shims to increase travel.
4. Turn adjusting screw until roller on lever just barely contacts top of spring cage. *Make sure spring cage is up as far as it will go.* Then lock adjusting screw.
5. Test adjustment by placing a .109" thickness gauge between roller and spring cage with brake released. The air pressure delivered by the brake valve should be from two to seven pounds.

NOTE: If brake valve does not graduate the delivered pressure properly, check to make sure bleed hole to cavity immediately below diaphragm is not restricted.

AIR BRAKES

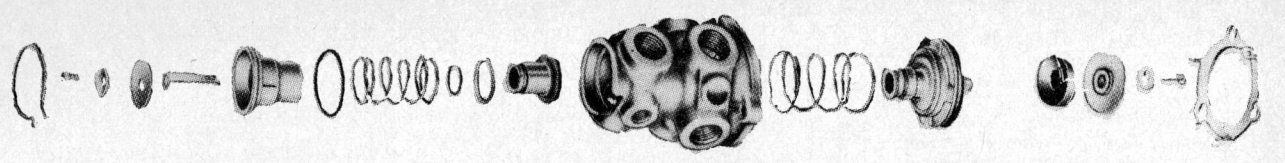

Fig. 10 Exploded view of E-3 brake valve

B-W TYPE E BRAKE VALVES

E-2 and E-3 brake valves have an insert type combination inlet-exhaust valve that can easily be removed for service without disconnecting any air lines or removing the valve. A diaphragm type exhaust check valve in the bottom of the inlet-exhaust valve prevents entry of dirt at the exhaust port, Fig. 9.

The supply ports in the lower portion of the valve are charged with reservoir pressure whereas the delivery ports in the upper portion of the valve are charged with air pressure at application only.

The E-5 brake valve, Fig. 9A, is a suspended pedal operated type.

Service

Type E-2 & E-3

Prior to reassembly, lightly coat valve parts, valves bores and O-rings with B-W 240176 grease. Reassemble as follows, referring to Fig. 10.

1. Position rubber spring in piston with concave side down.
2. Place retainer on rubber spring.
3. Center flat washer on rubber spring retainer.
4. Pass capscrew through flat washer and install in piston. Tighten to 50 ft-lbs torque.
5. Install O-ring in piston groove.
6. Place piston return spring in valve body.
7. Install piston assembly with care so that O-ring is not damaged or twisted in the process.
8. Install retainer and snap ring prongs in place while depressing piston.
9. Attach adapter plate to valve body with three screws.
10. Position preload spring in exhaust check valve seat.
11. Install exhaust diaphragm so that it is seated on hub against bottom of preload spring. Install diaphragm washer, lockwasher and screw.
12. Install O-ring on body of exhaust check valve seat.
13. Install O-ring on inlet-exhaust valve.
14. Install inlet-exhaust valve spring on shoulder of exhaust valve seat. Position spring seat washer on inlet-exhaust valve.
15. Slide inlet-exhaust valve into exhaust check valve seat so that prong of preload spring snaps over shoulder in inlet-exhaust valve.
16. Install insert in inlet-exhaust valve.
17. Install identification ring.
18. Install snap ring.
19. Place boot on plunger and install plunger in adapter bore after coating outside of plunger with B-W 239377 grease. Slip boot over hub of adapter plate.

Type E-5

1. Install exhaust check diaphragm in valve body.
2. Install inlet valve stem "O" ring and retainer, then install "O" rings on inlet valve seat.
3. Assemble piston by installing rubber spring, spring seat, washer cap screw and "O" ring.
4. Install inlet and exhaust valve, inlet valve seat with tab on seat aligning with valve body slot, and piston assembly, then install valve retainer, ensuring tabs snap into position.

Installation

After attaching valve to mounting bracket, check to see that roller contacts plunger. Loosen locknut behind rubber stop button and turn adjusting screw, if necessary.

Connect wires to stop light switch, and air lines to valve fittings. After reservoir pressure is built up, check air line connections for leakage with soap suds.

NOTE: Rebuilt valves should be tested before putting vehicle into service. Connect an air gauge into service line and note pressure at all treadle positions during both application and release. Pressure should remain steady. Approximately full reservoir pressure should register at full application. Coat exhaust port with soap suds and check for leakage. In both fully applied and fully released positions, leakage should not exceed a one-inch soap bubble in one second.

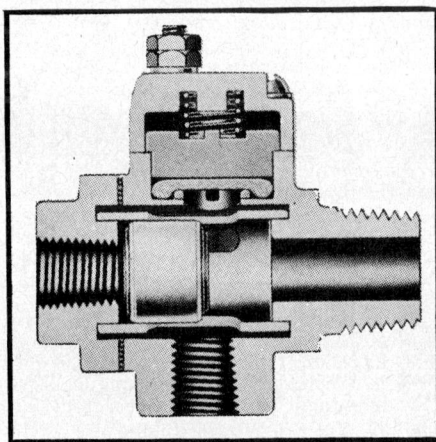

Fig. 11 Double check valve and stop light switch

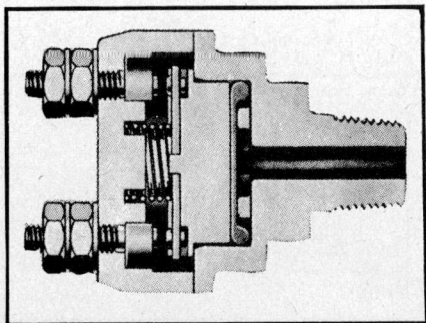

Fig. 12 Stop light switch

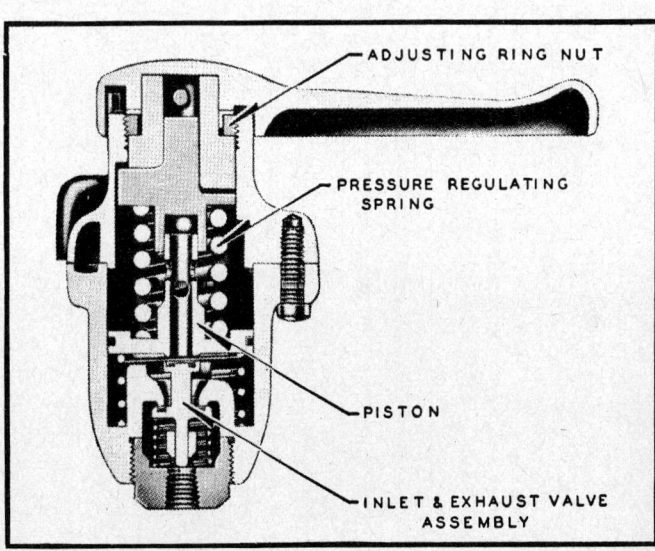

Fig. 13 TC hand control valve

AIR BRAKES

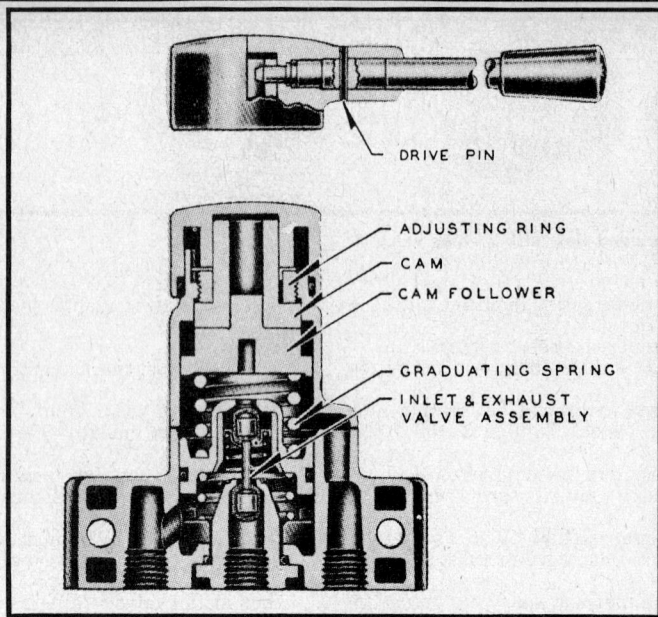

Fig. 14　TC-2 hand control valve

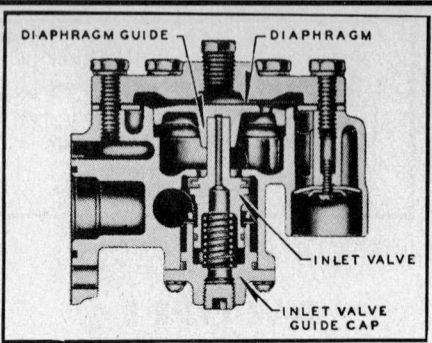

Fig. 15　Brake relay valve (R-5)

Testing

Periodically test the serviceability of the valve by applying and releasing the brake valve and noting that the brakes apply and release on both the tractor and trailer. Apply and release the hand control valve, noting that the brakes apply and release on the trailer only. When the treadle valve is applied, there should be no leakage at the exhaust port of the hand control valve, or at the exhaust port of the treadle valve when the hand control valve is applied.

Service

The double check valve and stop light switch should be serviced when the brake valve is removed from the vehicle.

Remove end cap, cap gasket and shuttle. If the shuttle guide or the sealing ends of shuttle show excessive wear, service by replacement. If valve seats in cap or housing are corroded or pitted excessively, replace valve. *Do not lubricate double check valve.*

B-W DOUBLE CHECK VALVE & STOP LIGHT SWITCH

The shuttle type double check valve portion of this combination valve provides a means for making a separate trailer brake application. The left end, Fig. 11, is attached to a service port of the brake valve. A service line from the hand control valve is connected to the opposite end. A service line leading to the trailer brakes is connected to the outlet port. The stop light switch is mounted on top of the valve opposite the outlet port.

Entry of air from the treadle valve causes the shuttle to seal the opposite inlet port and direct air to the trailer brakes. Simultaneously, another service line leading from the brake valve actuates the tractor brakes. When the hand control valve is applied, the shuttle seals the inlet port leading from the treadle valve and directs air to the trailer only. In either case, air pressure actuates the stop light switch.

NOTE: A leaking double check valve would cause an air loss during brake applications due to air escaping through the open exhaust port of the valve connected to the opposite inlet port. Service air from the treadle valve would escape through the exhaust port of the hand control valve or vice versa.

B-W STOP LIGHT SWITCH

The stop light switch shown in Fig. 12 is used mainly in truck applications and is similar to the switch that is combined with the double check valve. Both type switches are actuated by air pressure and complete the stop light circuit each time a brake application is made.

As the switch should make contact at three to seven pounds air pressure, it is important that the contacts are clean and that the diaphragm is not worn and permitting leakage. The diaphragm can be removed from the switch body (without removing switch from vehicle) by making a slight brake application.

When reassembling the switch, be sure the diaphragm faces as shown in Fig. 12, and that the contact strip is installed on the piston so that the round side of contacts face the termi-

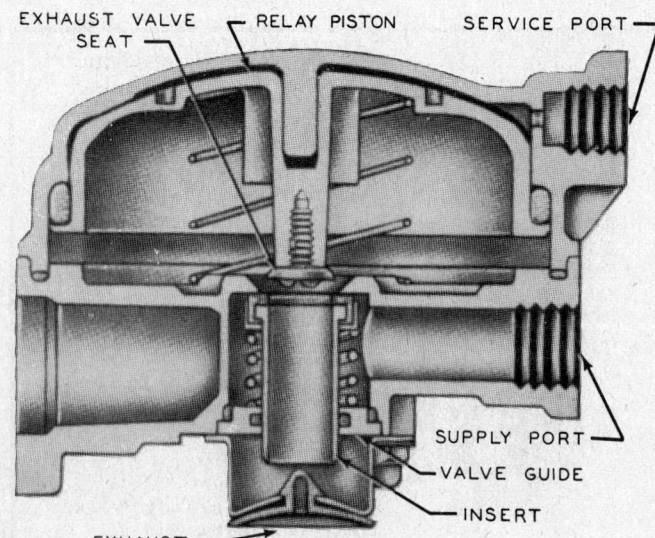

Fig. 15A　Brake relay valve (R-6)

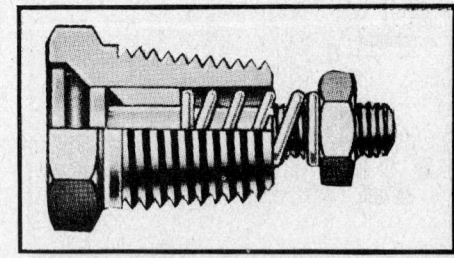

Fig. 16　Relief valve

AIR BRAKES

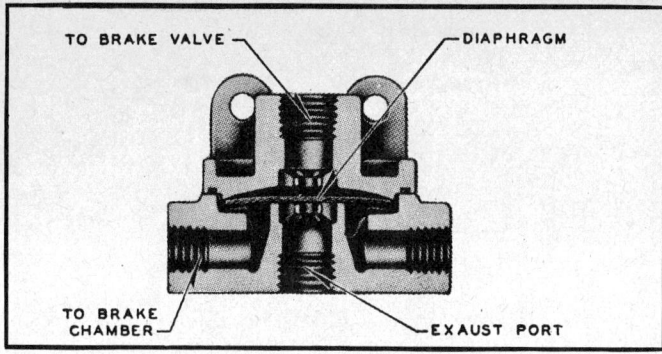

Fig. 17 Quick release valve (not required on rear axle when relay valve is used)

nal cover. Lubricate diaphragm, piston and body bore with B-W 239377 grease.

HAND CONTROL VALVE

Either of two types of hand control valves have been used. One, model TC, is shown in Fig. 13, and the other, model TC-2, is shown in Fig. 14. Adjusting rings are provided in both types for adjusting delivery pressure.

Like the E-2 foot brake valve, the TC and TC-2 valves are designed for convenient servicing of the inlet-exhaust valve. This portion of the hand control valve can be removed from the bottom by disconnecting the supply line only—without removing the valve itself.

Service—TC Valve

Prior to reassembling the valve, lightly coat the internal parts with B-W 240176 grease.
1. If adjusting ring is removed, install with marks in alignment.
2. Install adjusting ring lock.

NOTE: If pressure adjustment is necessary, do not install adjusting ring lock and handle until adjustment has been made. Valve should deliver 75 to 85 pounds. Turn adjusting ring clockwise to increase pressure, and counterclockwise to decrease it.

3. Align either groove with lock plunger and install cam follower.
4. Install cam. Rotate cam follower so that cam will be at its lowest point ("OFF" position).
5. Position piston return spring in valve body.
6. Place new O-ring in groove and install piston.
7. Position graduating spring on cam.
8. Attach valve cover to body (4 screws).
9. Position handle on cam follower with pin holes in alignment. Install Allen head pin.
10. Place O-ring in position in valve body and install inlet valve screw cap together with inlet valve spring and inlet-exhaust valve.

Service—TC-2 Valve

Prior to reassembling valve, lightly coat internal parts with B-W 240176 grease.
1. Position piston return spring in valve body.
2. Slide piston into valve body after installing O-ring on it.
3. Install adjusting ring in cover and align marks that should have been made before removing.
4. Install adjusting ring lock.
5. Install cam follower.
6. Install cam. Rotate follower to permit cam to seat on it.
7. Position graduating spring on piston.
8. Position gasket on valve body.
9. Attach cover to valve body with two special capscrews. Make sure gasket is positioned properly.
10. Position O-ring on valve cover.
11. Install valve head on follower (with handle holes in alignment) and over valve cover. Carefully push O-ring under valve head.
12. Slide valve handle into valve head and follower after installing O-ring on handle. Install drive pin.

NOTE: If pressure adjustment is necessary, do not install drive pin until adjustment has been made. Remove adjusting ring lock and turn ring clockwise to increase delivery pressure, and counterclockwise to decrease. Valve should deliver 75 to 85 pounds pressure.

13. Slide inlet-exhaust valve into valve body after installing O-ring. Install screws and lockwashers.
14. Test valve for leakage in same manner as testing foot brake valve.

Fig. 19 Two-way valve

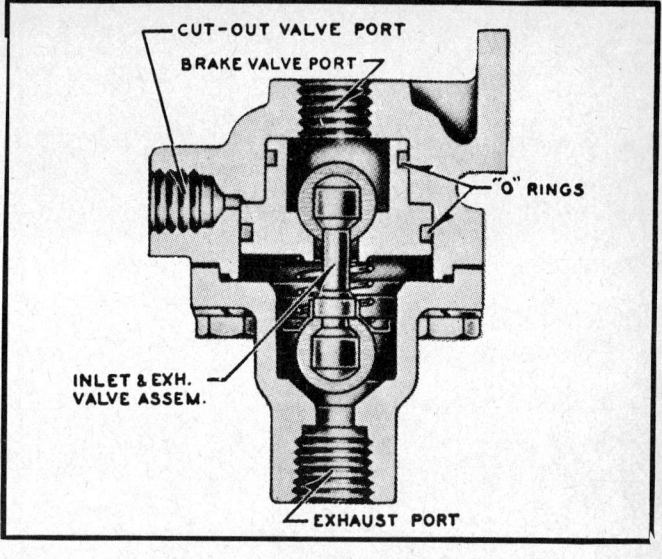

Fig. 18 Limiting quick release valve

R-5 & R-6 BRAKE RELAY VALVE

The relay valve, Figs. 15 & 15A, used on tandem vehicles, is designed to speed up the application and release of the rear brakes by shortening the length of tubing through which air from the brake valve must pass. It is, in reality, a separate application valve connected directly to the air tanks and actuated by air pressure from the brake application valve.

A feature of this valve is its use of an insert type inlet valve assembly which can easily be removed for service or replacement without removing the valve from the vehicle.

Service

At least once a year the relay valve should be disassembled and cleaned. All rubber parts subject to wear should be replaced if unserviceable. The inlet valve assembly (insert) should be removed for cleaning and inspection. Remove the four screws from the inlet valve guide cap and slide the insert through the bottom of the valve. The insert is disassembled by removing the retaining ring from the inlet valve guide cap.

The relay cover, diaphragm and diaphragm ring can be detached from the valve body by removing the cover capscrews. *Maintenance Kit 859785 contains all parts* necessary to recondition the R-5 Relay Valve.

Prior to reassembly, lightly lubricate the diaphragm guide bore, the bore of the inlet valve guide cap and all O-rings with B-W 240176 grease. After reinstalling valve, test it for leakage as follows:
1. Fully charge brake system.
2. Make several brake applications and check for prompt response at all wheels both at application and release.
3. Coat exhaust port of relay valve with soap suds. Leakage should not exceed one-inch soap bubble in two seconds in either the fully released or fully applied positions.

RELIEF VALVE

The pressure relief or safety valve, Fig. 16, protects the air brake system against excessive pressure. The relief valve is installed in

AIR BRAKES

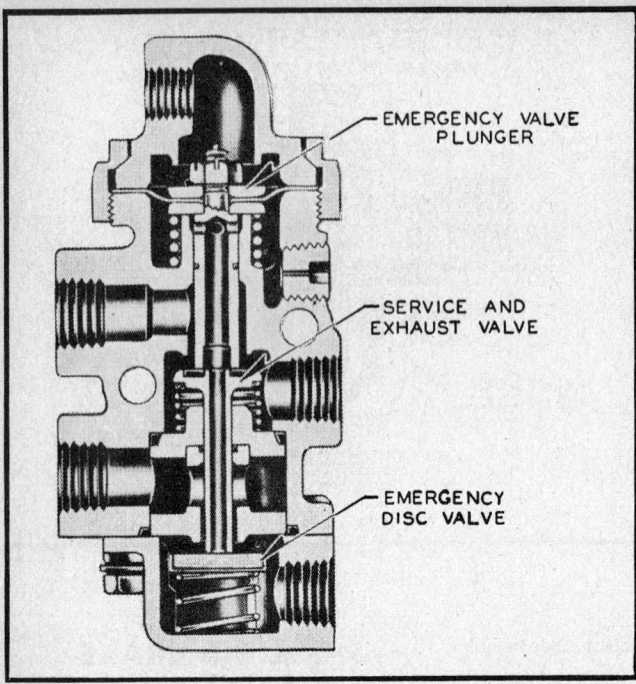

Fig. 20 Tractor protection valve

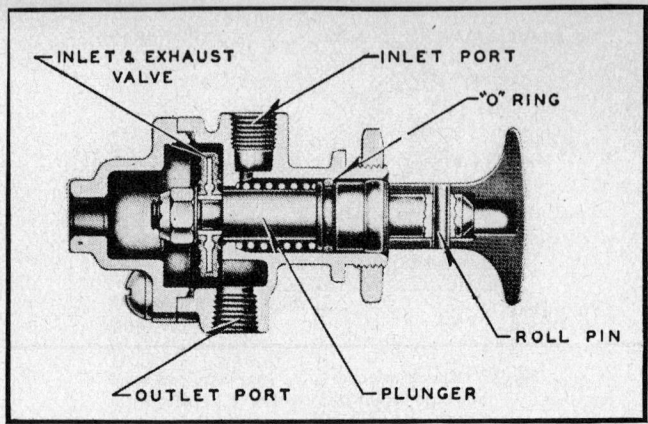

Fig. 21 Control valve

the reservoir and resembles a pipe plug in appearance. It has a hex head, and consists of a brass body, a poppet type valve, an O-ring, a pressure spring and an adjusting nut. The valve is pre-set to open at 140–150 psi.

Should the brake system pressure rise to about 140 pounds (usually resulting from a malfunctioning or improperly adjusted governor, or an inoperative compressor unloading mechanism) the pressure within the reservoir overcomes spring pressure. The valve is then unseated and air pressure in excess of the spring setting is exhausted.

Service

At least once a year, remove, disassemble and clean the relief valve. Replace unserviceable parts or the entire valve, if necessary.

Reset the valve to release at 145 psi. Pressure setting is adjusted by turning the adjusting screw. Turning in a clockwise direction with raise setting, and turning counterclockwise will lower setting. After installing valve, check for leakage.

QUICK RELEASE VALVE

These valves, Fig. 17, are used to hasten the release of air pressure from the front and rear wheel brake chambers.

When the brakes are applied, air entering at the top deflects the diaphragm and passes to the brake chambers, closing the exhaust port seat. In release, the pressure on the top of the diaphragm is released by the brake valve, whereupon the brake chamber pressure deflects the diaphragm upward, opening the exhaust port so that the chamber pressure passes to the atmosphere. This speeds up the release and saves time which, without the release valve, would be expended in passing the brake chamber pressure up to the brake valve for release.

Service

With the brakes applied, cover the exhaust port with soap suds to determine leakage at seat. A three-inch soap bubble in three seconds is permissible. Replace diaphragm about once a year. No lubrication is required.

LIMITING QUICK RELEASE VALVE

A limiting quick release valve, Fig. 18, is used in conjunction with the two-way valve shown in Fig. 19. It is used on air brake systems where driver-controlled front wheels brakes are desired.

The design of the limiting quick release valve is such that it reacts according to the setting of the two-way valve by admitting one-half treadle valve delivery pressure to the front wheel brake chambers when the two-way valve is set for slippery road. Front wheel brakes receive full delivery pressure when the two-way valve is set for dry road.

The limiting quick release valve is usually mounted on a frame front crossmember. A service line from the treadle valve is connected to the inlet port of the two-way valve. Another service line is connected to the inlet port (top) of the limiting quick release valve. The service line from the output port of the two-way valve is connected to the limiting quick release valve at the port facing the rear. The two side ports of the limiting quick release valve are connected to the front brake chambers.

The limiting quick release valve is usually mounted on a frame front crossmember. A service line from the treadle valve is connected to the inlet port of the two-way valve. Another service line is connected to the inlet port (top) of the limiting quick release valve. The service line from the output port of the two-way valve is connected to the limiting quick release valve at the port facing the rear. The two side ports of the limiting quick release valve are connected to the front brake chambers.

The limiting quick release valve, beside providing for one-half reduction of front wheel braking pressures, also serves as the front axle quick release valve.

Service

Once a year, the valve should be disassembled, cleaned and inspected. The gasket, piston O-rings, and inlet and exhaust valves should be replaced. The inlet and exhaust valves are identical and are a snap fit over the ends of the stem.

Slightly pitted bores can be reconditioned by polishing. If bores or valve seats are deeply pitted, service is by replacement of body, cover and piston, as required. Prior to reassembly, lubricate valve with B-W 240176 grease.

TWO-WAY VALVE

The two-way valve, Fig. 19, is an "OFF" (released) and "ON" (applied) valve used to

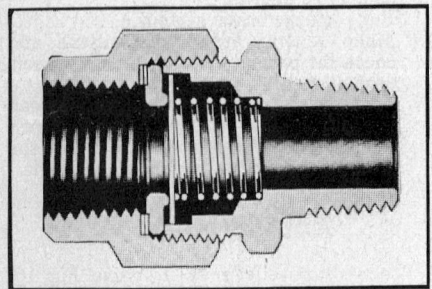

Fig. 22 Check valve (B-W)

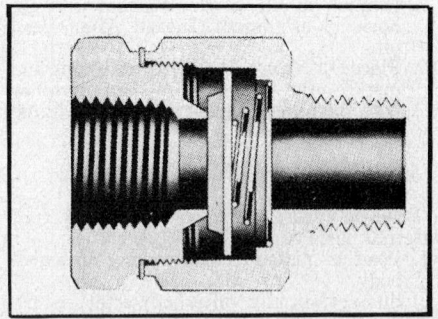

Fig. 23 Check valve (Midland)

AIR BRAKES

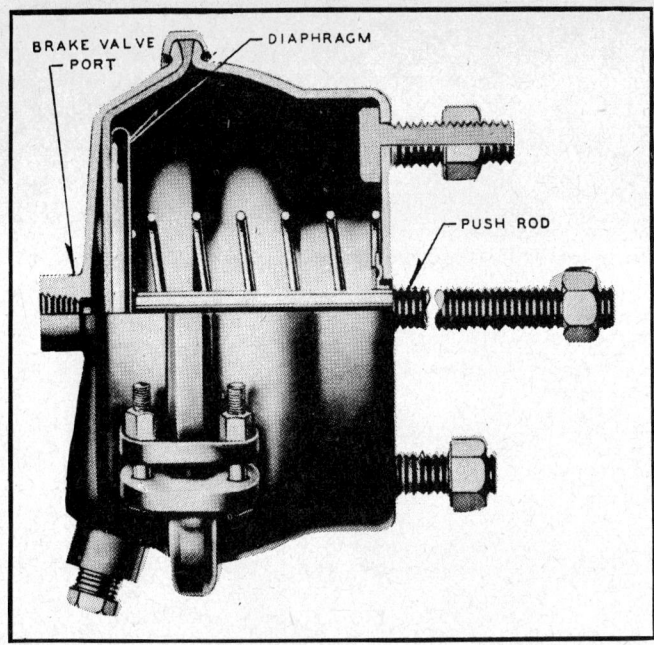

Fig. 24 Diaphragm type brake chamber

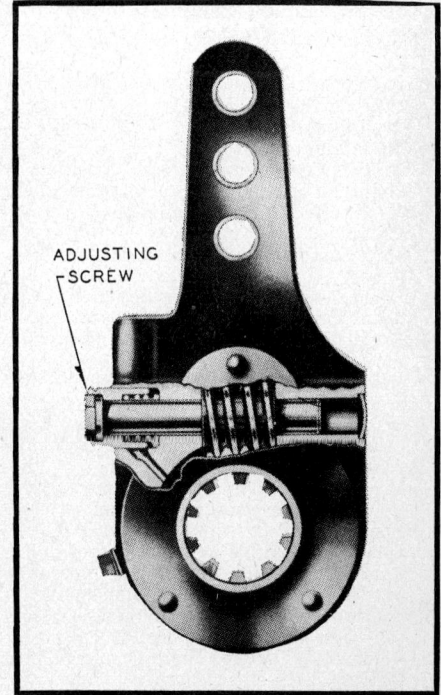

Fig. 25 Piston type brake chamber

manually control other air devices as the limiting quick release valve and tractor protection valve.

Either of two types of two-way valves are used to control the limiting quick release valve. The lever type, Fig. 19, is mounted on the dash, whereas the cable-operated type is mounted on the left frame rail and remotely controlled from the cab.

The valve shown in Fig. 19 is also used with the tractor protection valve. On some applications, it is used in place of the control valve shown in Fig. 21, and provides manual control only.

The operation of the two-way valve in conjunction with the limiting quick release valve is explained above. When the two-way valve is used with the tractor protection valve, the released ("OFF") position is for "emergency," and the applied ("ON") position is for "normal."

Service

At least once each year the valve should be disassembled, cleaned and inspected. Replace O-rings and inlet valve. Lubricate valve with B-W 240176 grease.

After reassembling valve, test for leakage in both applied and released positions by coating the exhaust opening with soap suds. Leakage should not exceed one-inch soap bubble in five seconds.

TRACTOR PROTECTION VALVE

This valve provides a means of preserving air pressure in sufficient amount to stop the tractor in the event of a trailer breakaway. The system also provides for an automatic trailer brake application if an air loss in the tractor or trailer system is undetected by the operator. (The operator is normally forewarned by the low pressure indicator before this happens).

The tractor protection valve, Fig. 20, in effect, is a set of remotely controlled cut-out cocks with both manual and automatic controls. The valve is manually controlled by a push-pull control valve, Fig. 21, which is connected to the tractor reservoir. When the control valve is set in the "charge" position, air pressure is admitted to the control port of the tractor protection valve, thereby opening the service and emergency lines to the trailer.

When the control valve is set in the "emergency" position, air pressure in the emergency lines between the control valve and tractor protection valve, and also between the tractor protection valve and the trailer relay emergency valve is exhausted. The emergency features of the trailer relay emergency valve then cause a trailer brake application.

The control valve should be set in the "emergency" position when disconnecting a trailer and in the "charge" position immediately after connecting one.

Service

At least once a year the tractor protection valve should be disassembled and cleaned.

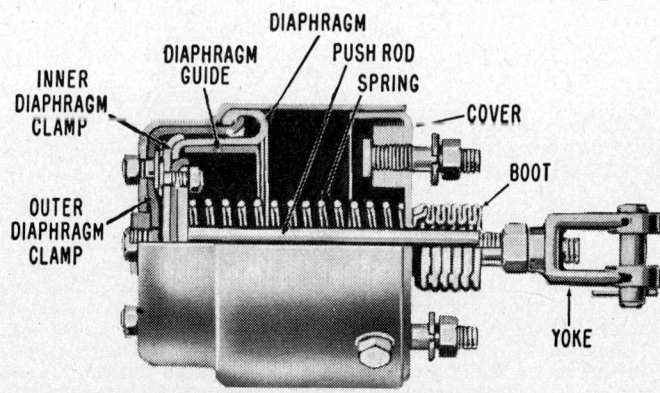

Fig. 26 Roto brake chamber

Fig. 27 Slack adjuster

AIR BRAKES

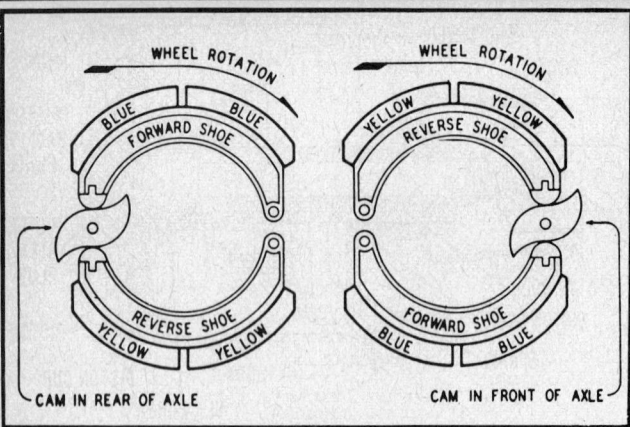

Fig. 28 Combination lining installation

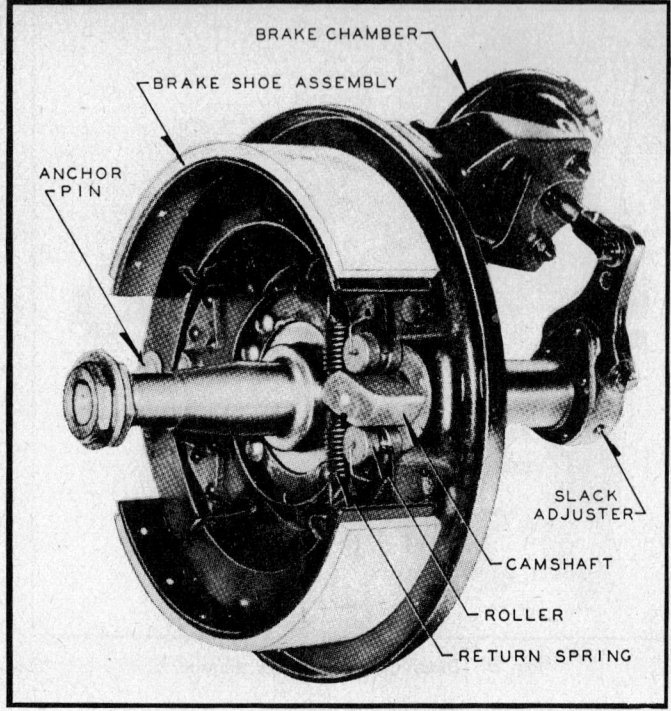

Fig. 29 Typical front brake

Rubber parts and others subject to wear should be replaced as required. Prior to reassembly coat all internal parts (except springs and diaphragm) with B-W 240176 grease.
1. Position O-ring in valve body bore.
2. Install disc valve seat as an assembly with service and exhaust valve guide, service and exhaust valve spring, and the small O-ring.
3. Install O-ring in counterbore at bottom of valve body.
4. Install emergency disc valve spring in cover.
5. Position disc valve on its spring with rubber side away from spring.
6. Install cover.
7. Position exhaust plunger spring in valve body.
8. Install exhaust valve plunger assembly in body after installing followers, diaphragm, nut, and plunger stem O-ring.
9. Position control cap on body with control port facing same as exhaust port. Install and tighten cap nut securely to prevent leakage.

Testing Valve—With Two-Way Valve

1. Block vehicle wheels to prevent vehicle from moving.
2. Drain brake system.
3. Close drain cocks.
4. Set two-way valve in "normal" position.
5. Connect a test gauge in tractor protection valve service port or trailer service line coupling.
6. Start engine to build up air pressure in system.
7. When system pressure reaches 30–40 psi, make and hold a brake application. Note pressure on test gauge. A full application should show full or nearly full reservoir pressure. A partial application should be proportional to it.
8. Release brakes. No air should be passing through emergency line until system pressure reaches 45–55 psi.
9. Set two-way valve in "emergency" position and remove test gauge from service line and connect it into emergency line.
10. Set two-way valve in "normal" position. Continue to build up reservoir pressure until it reaches maximum. Stop engine.
11. Set two-way valve in "emergency" position. Test gauge should drop to zero.
12. Remove test gauge. There should be no leakage at the emergency line. Make and hold a brake application. There should be no leakage at the service line. Release brake.
13. Reconnect test gauge to emergency line and set control valve in "charge" position. Test gauge should register reservoir pressure.
14. Turn on ignition key and open reservoir drain cock. Low pressure buzzer should be activated at about 60 psi. Tractor protection valve should vent the emergency line at 30–40 psi which would actuate trailer relay emergency valve if trailer was connected.
15. Disconnect test gauge. Make and hold a brake application. There should be no noticeable leakage at either the service or emergency ports of the tractor protection valve below 25 psi system pressure.

CONTROL VALVE

The push-pull type tractor protection control, Fig. 21, is basically an "on" and "off" valve, but differs from the two-way valve in that it also has an automatic pressure release.

This particular control valve releases automatically at approximately 20 psi. The valve has three pipe ports—one supply and two delivery (only one delivery port is used). The unthreaded port at the bottom is the exhaust.

The shank of the control button has a red warning ring that is visible when the valve is set in the "emergency" position.

Operation

A line from the reservoir is connected to the supply port. When the system pressure reaches about 50 pounds, the operator pushes the control button in (charge position). Reservoir air pressure then flows through the valve and out the delivery port. The button will automatically stay in after 50 pounds of pressure has been built up.

To apply the valve the operator pulls the button out. The inlet seat seals off the supply of air and the exhaust opens, exhausting the air in the line between the push-pull control valve and tractor protection valve.

If a drop in system pressure takes place that is unnoticed by the operator, and the tractor protection valve fails to vent, the control valve will automatically exhaust when system pressure drops to approximately 20 psi. The tractor protection valve will then seal off the service and emergency lines to the trailer.

Service

Every six months the control valve should be removed, disassembled, cleaned and inspected. Worn parts should be replaced as required.

To remove the valve from the cab, first block vehicle wheels and bleed off brake system. Drive the roll pin out of the valve button and plunger. Remove button and mounting nut. Remove valve from cab.

Disassemble valve by removing two screws and separate cover and body. Remove plunger nut, washer and inlet and exhaust valve. Slide plunger out of valve body. Remove O-ring from plunger and spring from valve body.

When reassembling the valve, tighten plunger nut to 30–40 inch-lbs torque. Lubricate O-ring and bearing surfaces with Barium base grease (B-W 240176).

Testing Valve

With system pressure at zero, build up the pressure and hold the control valve plunger in. The control valve plunger should remain in when system pressure is above 50 psi. With the system pressure built up, pull the control valve plunger out and note that the delivery air is exhausted through the exhaust port of the control valve. Then push the button in and note that air is again delivered through the

AIR BRAKES

valve.

With the control valve plunger out and the red indicator on the button showing, check the exhaust port for leakage past the inlet valve. With system pressure above approximately 70 psi and the control button in (colored indicator not visible) check the exhaust port for leakage by the exhaust valve. Check around the plunger for leakage by the plunger grommet. Also check for gasket leakage between cover and body.

CHECK VALVE

The single check, or one-way valve, Figs. 22 and 23, is installed in the line between the two compartments of the reservoir tank and permits flow of air in one direction only.

The check valve is opened by air passing from the wet tank compartment to the dry tank compartment. If pressure in the wet tank falls below that of the dry tank, the check valve remains closed, thereby preserving air pressure in the dry tank.

Periodically the valve should be removed, disassembled, cleaned and inspected. Worn parts should be replaced as necessary. Do not lubricate valve.

Test the valve by applying air pressure in the direction opposite normal flow and check for leakage. Valve should hold a pressure of 200 psi.

LOW PRESSURE INDICATOR

The low pressure indicator consists of a pressure switch and an audible buzzer. It is a safety device designed to give the operator an automatic warning when the reservoir air pressure is (or when it drops) below a safe limit for continuous braking operation.

The switch is electrically connected in series with the buzzer and ignition switch. The electrical circuit is closed until there is at least 60 psi air pressure in the reservoirs. The device is inoperative when the ignition switch is off.

Service

If the indicator fails to operate, by-pass the switch with a jumper wire to determine whether the switch or buzzer is faulty. Service is by replacement only as adjustments to either are not recommended.

BRAKE CHAMBERS

A typical diaphragm type brake chamber is shown in Fig. 24. A piston type, Fig. 25, and a Rotochamber, Fig. 26, are also used. They all convert the energy of compressed air into the mechanical force necessary to expand the brake shoes against the brake drums.

Air pressure delivered to the brake chambers by the brake valve moves the diaphragm (or piston) and push rod outward, applying the brake. As the brake pedal is released, air pressure is exhausted from the brake chambers and the springs return the diaphragms (or pistons) and push rods to their released position, releasing the brakes.

SLACK ADJUSTERS

The slack adjuster, Fig. 27, is an adjustable lever, including a worm and gear, so arranged that it not only serves as a regular brake lever during normal brake application but also

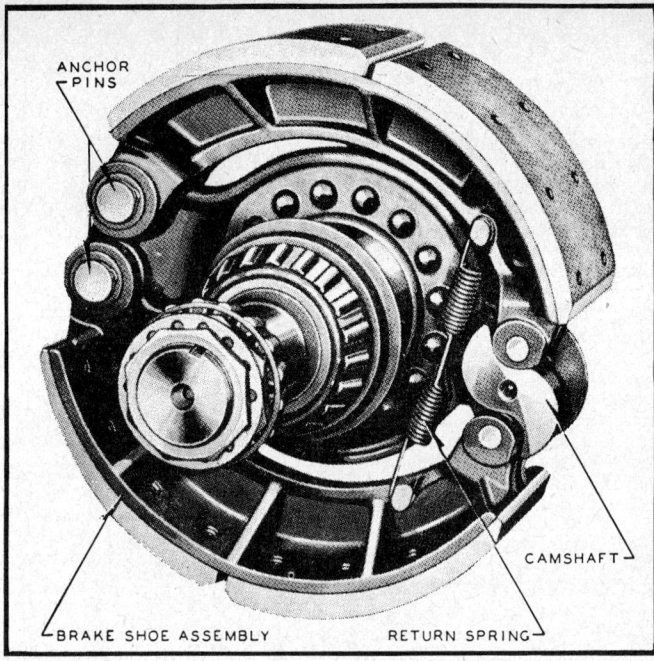

Fig. 30 Typical rear brake

provides a quick and easy method of brake adjustment.

In normal braking, the entire slack adjuster operates as a unit, rotating bodily with the brake camshaft as the brakes are applied or released. The splined end of the slack adjuster is mounted on the brake camshaft and the other end is connected to the push rod of the brake chamber.

Service

The slack adjuster requires no attention other than periodic inspection of the bronze bushing fitted in the hole in the slack adjuster arm. If worn excessively, replace the bushing.

Sufficient lubrication is provided when initially assembled and, therefore, lubrication of the slack adjuster should be confined only to such a time as is necessary to service or overhaul the entire unit.

RESERVOIR & DRAIN COCKS

Either of two types of air tanks may be used. The dual type tank consists of one tank having two separate compartments of equal size, whereas two individual tanks are used with the second type.

The front section (or wet tank) of the dual type tank and the rear tank of the individual type are connected to the air compressor and serve to provide a place where the air, heated during compression, may cool, and oil and water vapors condense. The rear section (or dry tank) of the dual type tank and the front tank of the individual type are charged from the wet tank by external piping and supply the air brake system—and any other air devices used. A one-way check valve in the line between the two tanks prevents air loss in case of leakage between the wet tank and compressor.

Each air tank is equipped with a drain cock. On the dual type tank, the upper one is for the front (wet) tank and the other is for the rear (dry) tank. Both type tanks should be drained regularly—the frequency depending on local humidity and the condition of the compressor. In many cases, daily draining will be necessary.

TUBING, HOSE & FITTINGS

Every 20,000 miles cover the tubing, hose and fittings with soap suds. If leakage is evident, the tubing should be repaired or replaced. Hose must be replaced. Leakage at fittings should be stopped by tightening the connections.

BRAKE ASSEMBLIES

IMPORTANT: The procedure which follows outlines the general procedure for disassembling and reassembling of brakes and for brake adjustments. For details on the various types of brakes in use, refer to the *Brake Adjustment Chapter*.

Disassembly

1. To remove shoes and replace lining, first raise vehicle until wheels are free to rotate.
2. Release hand brake.
3. Loosen slack adjusters to free shoes in drum.
4. Remove wheel or hub.
5. Remove pull-back spring or springs.
6. Remove brake shoe assemblies from anchor pins after locks, anchor plate, lock screws or whatever method is used to hold them in place, is removed. After removal the shoes may be relined or replaced.

Reassembly

1. Install brake shoe assemblies and lock in

AIR BRAKES

place on anchor pins.
2. Install pull-back spring or springs.
3. Install wheel or hub.
4. Adjust wheel bearings.
5. Adjust brake and lower vehicle.

Combination Linings

Combination type linings, having a different coefficient of friction for forward (primary) and reverse (secondary) shoes, are frequently used. For ready identification primary linings are usually painted blue on the edge and secondary linings are painted yellow. When applying new brake linings it is important to establish correctly the forward and reverse shoes for each brake assembly, and then apply the linings as indicated in Fig. 28.

To identify the forward or reverse shoe, each brake must be considered as a separate unit. If the camshaft is behind the axle, the top shoe is the forward acting shoe. If the camshaft is ahead of the axle, the bottom shoe is the forward acting shoe.

Brake Adjustments

NOTE: As covered in the *Brake Adjustment Chapter* several different types of service brakes are used and the methods of adjustment vary slightly as outlined in the following.

Before making any brake adjustments, always check wheel bearing adjustment. Raise the vehicle until wheels are free to rotate. Release hand brake and proceed as follows:

Front Brakes
1. Referring to Fig. 29, tighten slack adjusters until brake shoes are tight against drum.
2. Back off slack adjuster until wheel turns freely without brake drag.
3. Loosen the two anchor pin lock nuts and turn eccentric anchor pin until there is .005" clearance between brake drum and heel of each shoe, measured with a feeler gauge.
4. Clearance between drum and toe of each shoe should measure .010". Adjust slack adjuster to obtain this clearance.

NOTE: Where the clearance is greater on one shoe than the other, loosen the camshaft bracket bolts and tap the camshaft up or down as required to equalize this clearance.

5. Following the adjustment outlined in Step 4, it may be necessary to reset the drum-to-heel adjustment.
6. When adjustment is completed, tighten anchor pin lock nuts, being sure to hold the anchor pin stud with a wrench to prevent altering the adjustment.

Rear Brakes
1. Referring to Fig. 30, tighten brakes with slack adjusters until shoes are tight against drum.
2. Back off slack adjuster until wheel turns freely without brake drag.

NOTE: Adjustment of the brakes before operating the vehicle should be made as follows: With the system charged to normal operating pressure, connect a test gauge to any convenient point in the brake chamber line and test the delivered pressure by depressing the brake treadle to the floor. This pressure should not be appreciably less than the reservoir pressure.

Check brake chamber push rods to be certain that each is fully released. A positive method is to remove the clevis pin from the push rod yoke and check alignment of holes in yoke and slack adjuster arm. If necessary, make adjustment so that slack adjuster arm and brake chamber push rod form an angle of 90 degrees at the mid-point of slack adjuster travel. In released position, angle formed should be greater than 90 degrees. All slack adjusters on the vehicle should be mounted at the same angle and have the same amount of travel. All brake chambers and slack adjusters should be of the same size and type.

HYDRAULIC BRAKE SYSTEMS

SINGLE MASTER CYLINDER SYSTEM

Depressing the brake pedal moves the master cylinder push rod and piston, forcing hydraulic fluid out through a check valve, Fig. 1. This fluid flows through the hydraulic lines into the wheel cylinders, forcing the wheel cylinder pistons outward from the center of the cylinder and expanding the brake shoes and linings against the brake drums.

When the brake pedal is quickly released, the master cylinder piston returns to the released position faster than fluid returns from the lines. Holes in the piston head allow fluid to pass from the rear to the front of the piston head, past the primary cup to fill the space.

At the same time (when the pedal is released) the brake shoe return springs force the wheel cylinder pistons to return toward the center of the wheel cylinder (released position). Fluid forced out of the wheel cylinders by this action returns to the master cylinder by overcoming the pressure of the master cylinder piston spring which holds the check valve closed. As this fluid returns, the excess portion will return to the reservoir through the compensating port which is uncovered when the master cylinder piston is in the released position. The piston spring will close the check valve when the pressure in the lines is reduced to 8 to 12 lbs, maintaining a slight pressure in the lines at all times. The purpose of this pressure is to keep the wheel cylinder cups from leaking fluid and to reduce the possibility of air entering the system.

DUAL MASTER CYLINDER SYSTEM

When the brake pedal is depressed, both the primary (front brake) and the secondary (rear brake) master cylinder pistons are moved simultaneously to exert hydraulic fluid pressure on their respective independent hydraulic system. The fluid displacement of the two master cylinders is proportioned to fulfill the requirements of each of the two independent hydraulic brake systems, Figs. 2 and 3.

If a failure of the rear (secondary) brake system should occur, initial brake pedal movement causes the unrestricted secondary piston to bottom in the master cylinder bore. Primary piston movement displaces hydraulic fluid in the primary section of the dual master cylinder to actuate the front brake system.

Should the primary (front) system fail, initial brake pedal movement causes the unrestricted primary piston to bottom out against the secondary piston. Continued downward movement of the brake pedal moves the secondary piston to displace hydraulic fluid in the rear brake system to actuate the rear brakes.

The increased pedal travel and the increased pedal effort required to compensate for the loss of the failed portion of the brake system provides a warning that a partial brake system failure has occurred. When the ignition switch is turned on, a brake warning light on the instrument panel provides a visual indication that one of the dual brake systems has become inoperative.

Should a failure of either the front or rear brake hydraulic system occur, the hydraulic fluid pressure differential resulting from pressure loss of the failed brake system forces the valve toward the low pressure area to light the brake warning switch.

Brake Warning Light Switches

There are three basic types of brake warning light switches as shown in Figs. 4, 5 and 6, and usually they form a common electrical circuit with the parking brake light.

When a pressure differential occurs between the front and rear brake systems, the valves will shuttle toward the side with the low pressure.

As shown in Fig. 4, movement of the differential valve forces the switch plunger upward over the tapered shoulder of the valve to close the switch contacts and light the dual brake warning lamp, signaling a brake system failure.

In Fig. 5, the valve assembly consists of two valves in a common bore that are spring-loaded toward the centered position. The spring-loaded switch contact plunger rests on top of the valves in the centered position (right view). When a pressure differential occurs between the front and rear brake systems, the valves will shuttle toward the side with the low pressure. The spring-loaded switch plunger is "triggered", and the ground circuit for the warning light is completed, lighting the lamp (left view).

In Fig. 6, as pressure fails in one system the other system's normal pressure forces the piston to the inoperative side, contacting the switch terminal, causing the warning light on the instrument panel to glow.

HYDRAULIC BRAKE SYSTEMS

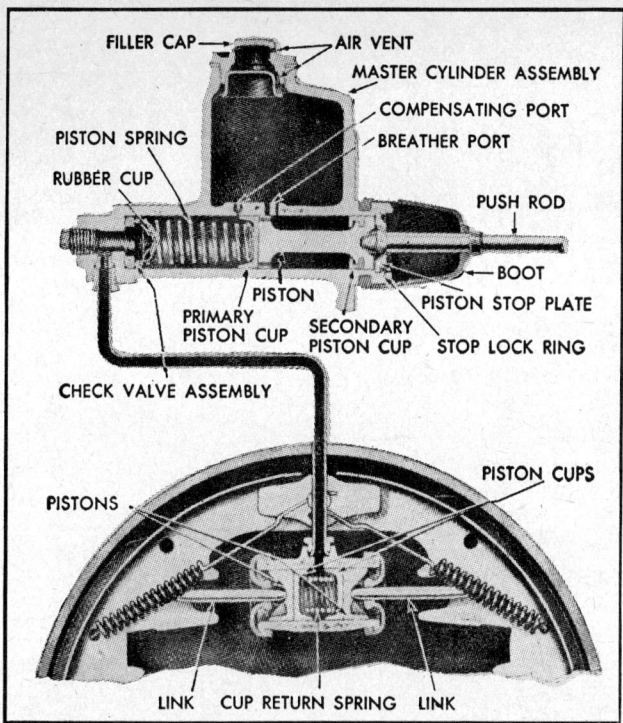

Fig. 1 Diagram of a typical hydraulic brake system

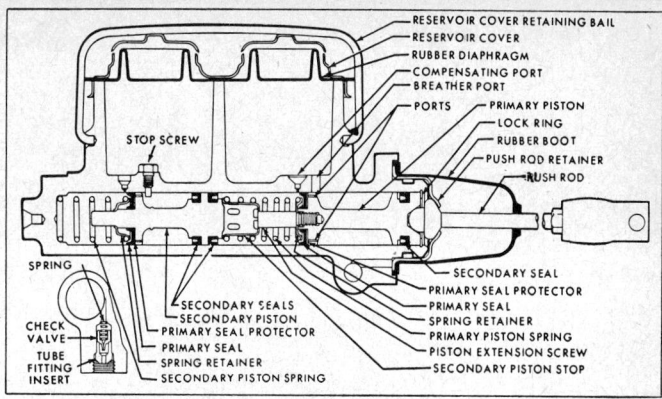

Fig. 2 Delco-Moraine dual master cylinder (typical)

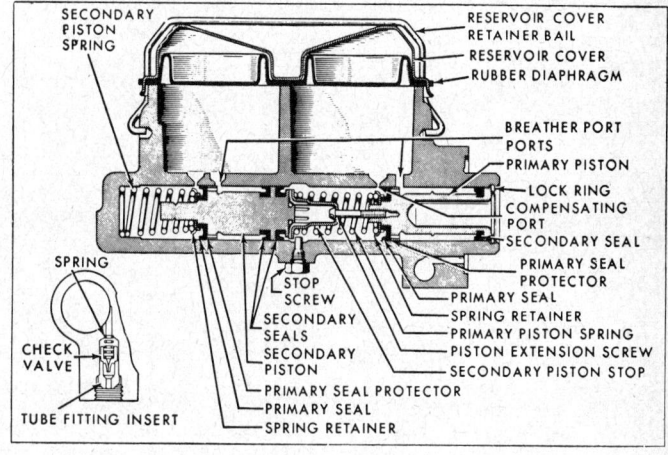

Fig. 3 Bendix dual master cylinder (typical)

Testing Warning Light System

If the parking brake light is connected into the service brake warning light system, the brake warning light will flash only when the parking brake is applied with the ignition switch ON. The same light will also glow should one of the two service brake systems fail when the brake pedal is applied.

To test the system, turn the ignition ON and apply the parking brake. If the lamp fails to light, look for a burned out bulb, disconnected socket, a broken or disconnected wire at the switch.

Fig. 7 is an exterior view of one of these switches. They are usually mounted on the left frame side rail or on the brake pedal bracket.

To test the brake warning system, raise the vehicle and open a wheel bleeder valve while a helper depresses the brake pedal and observes the warning light on the instrument panel. If the bulb fails to light, look for a burned out bulb, disconnected socket, or a broken or disconnected wire at the switch. If the bulb is not burned out, and the wire continuity is proven, replace the brake warning switch.

COMBINATION VALVE

The combination valve, Fig. 8, is a metering valve, failure warning switch, and a proportioner in one assembly and is used on disc brake applications. The metering valve delays front disc braking until the rear drum brake shoes contact the drum. The failure warning switch is actuated in event of front or rear brake system failure, in turn activating a dash warning lamp. The proportioner balances front to rear braking action during rapid deceleration.

Metering Valve

When the brakes are not applied, the metering valve permits the brake fluid to flow through the valve, thus allowing the fluid to expand and contract with temperature changes.

When the brakes are initially applied, the metering valve stem moves to the left, preventing fluid to flow through the valve to the front disc brakes. This is accomplished by the smooth end of the metering valve stem contacting the metering valve seal lip at 4 to 30 PSI, Fig. 9. The metering valve spring holds the retainer against the seal until a predetermined pressure is produced at the valve inlet port which overcomes the spring pressure and permits hydraulic pressure to actuate the front disc brakes, Fig. 10. The increased pressure into the valve is metered through the valve seal, to the front disc brakes, producing an increased force on the diaphragm. The diaphragm then pulls the pin, in turn pulling the retainer and reduces the spring pressure on the metering valve seal. Eventually, the pressure reaches a point at which the spring is pulled away by the diaphragm pin and retainer, leaving the metering valve unrestricted, permitting full pressure to pass through the metering valve.

Failure Warning Switch

If the rear brake system fails, the front system pressure forces the switch piston to the right, Fig. 11. The switch pin is then forced up into the switch, completing the electrical circuit and activates the dash warning lamp.

When repairs are made and pressure returns to the system, the piston moves to the left, resetting the switch. The detent on the piston requires approximately 100 to 450 PSI to permit full reset of the piston. In event of front brake system failure, the piston moves to the left and the same sequence of events are followed as for rear system failure except the piston resets to the right.

Proportioner

During rapid deceleration, a portion of the vehicle's weight is transferred to the front wheels. This resultant loss of weight at the rear wheels must be compensated for to avoid early rear wheel skid. The proportioner reduces the rear brake system pressure, delaying rear wheel skid. The pressure developed within the valve acts against the large end of the piston, overcoming the spring pressure and moves the piston to the left, Fig. 12. The piston then contacts the stem seat and proportions (restricts) line pressure through the valve.

During normal braking action, the proportioner is not functional. Brake fluid flows into the proportioner between the piston center hole and the valve stem, through the stop plate and to the rear brakes. Spring pressure loads the piston, during normal braking, causing it to rest against the stop plate, Fig. 13.

Master Cylinder Service

Figs. 14 to 17 show an array of dual and single master cylinders. With cylinder re-

633

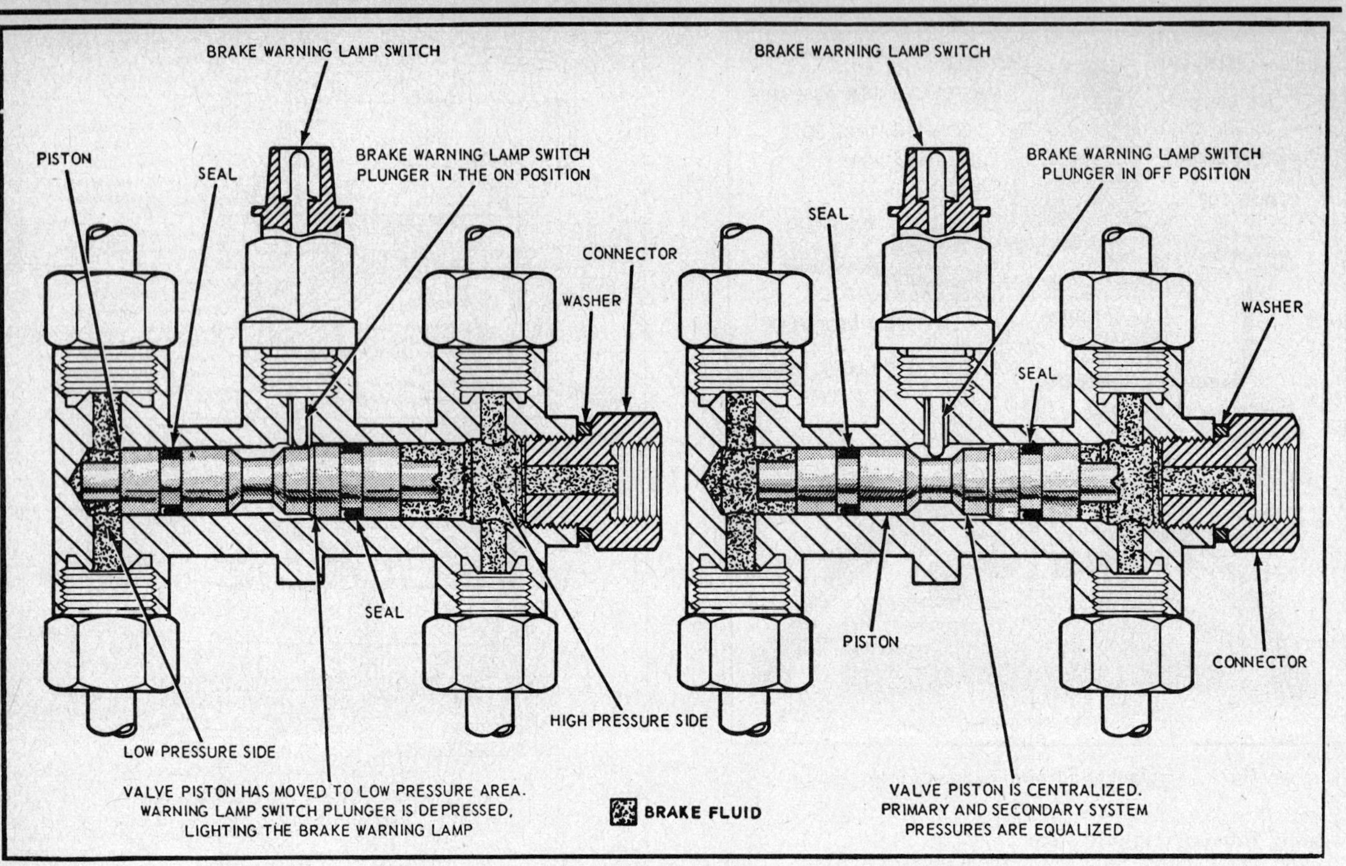

HYDRAULIC BRAKE SYSTEMS

Fig. 4 Pressure differential valve and brake warning light switch

moved from vehicle, and from brake booster if so equipped, remove the covers and disassemble the unit as suggested by the illustration of the unit being serviced.

When disassembled, wash all parts in alcohol ONLY. Use an air hose to blow out all passages, orifices and valve holes. Air dry and place parts on clean paper or lint-free cloth. Inspect master cylinder bore for scoring, rust, pitting or etching. Any of these conditions will require replacement of the housing. Inspect master cylinder pistons for scoring, pitting or distortion. Replace piston if any of these conditions exist.

If either master cylinder housing or piston is replaced, clean new parts with alcohol and blow out all passages with air hose.

Examine reservoirs for foreign matter and check all passages for restrictions. If there is any suspicion of contamination or evidence of corrosion, completely flush the hydraulic system as outlined below.

When overhauling a master cylinder, use all parts contained in the repair kit. Before starting reassembly, dip all cups, seals, pistons, springs, check valves and retainers in alcohol and place in a clean pan or on clean paper. *Wash hands with soap and water to prevent contamination of rubber parts from oil, kerosene or gasoline.* During assembly, dip all parts in clean, heavy duty brake fluid.

Inspect through side outlet of dual master cylinder housing to make certain cup lips do not hang up on edge of hole or turn back, which would result in faulty operation. A piece of 3/16" rod with an end rounded off will be helpful in guiding cups past hole.

BLEEDING BRAKES

NOTE: Pressure bleeding is recommended for

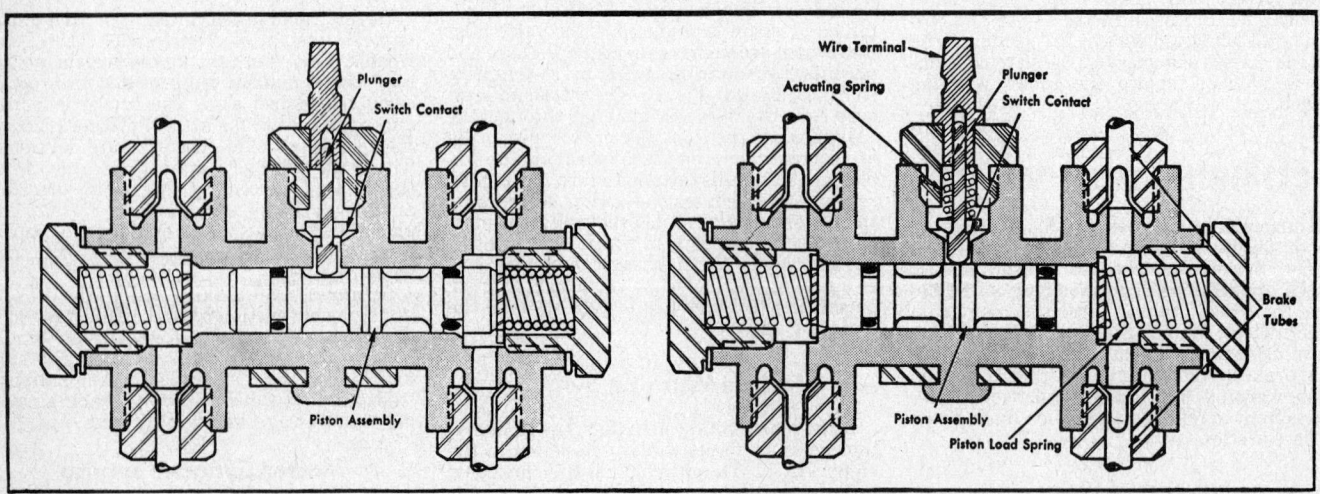

Fig. 5 Pressure differential valve and brake warning light switch

HYDRAULIC BRAKE SYSTEMS

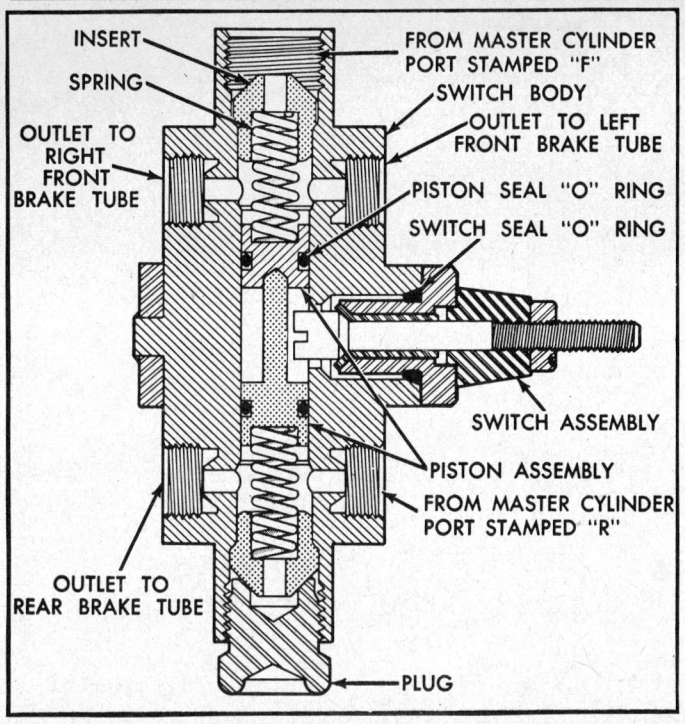

Fig. 6 Pressure differential valve and brake warning light switch

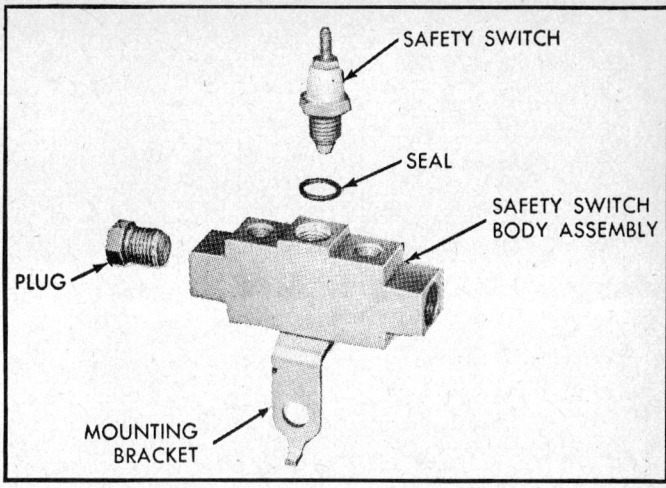

Fig. 7 Typical pressure valve and brake warning light switch. These switches are usually mounted on left frame side rail

all hydraulic brake systems.

The bleeding operation itself is fairly well standardized. First step in all cases is cleaning the dirt from the filler cap before removing it from the master cylinder. This should be done thoroughly.

Pressure bleeding is fastest because the master cylinder doesn't have to be refilled several times, and the job can be done by one man. Pressure bleeding equipment of the diaphragm type is recommended. If using equipment which is not of the diaphragm type, make sure to prevent air from the pressure tank from entering the lines, do not shake the tank while air is being added to the tank or after it has been pressurized. Set the tank in the required location, bring the air hose to the tank, and do not move it during the bleeding operation. The tank should be kept at least one-third full.

NOTE: On vehicles equipped with disc brakes, the brake metering valve or combination valve must be held in its position, using the recommended tool, (C-4121 for Chrysler Corp., J-22742 for Ford Motor Co. and J-23709 or J-23770 for General Motors).

If air does get into the fluid, releasing the pressure will cause the bubbles to increase in size, rise to the top of the fluid, and escape.

Pressure should not be greater than about 35 lb. per sq. in.

NOTE: On vehicles equipped with plastic reservoirs, do not exceed 25 psi. bleeding pressure.

When bleeding without pressure, open the bleed valve three-quarters of a turn, depress the pedal a full stroke, then close bleeder screw and allow pedal to return slowly to its released position. Repeat this operation several times until expelled brake fluid flows in a solid stream without air bubbles. On vehicles

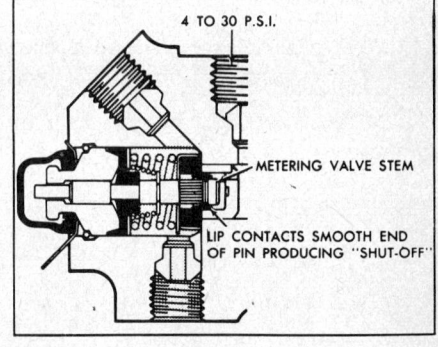

Fig. 9 Metering valve, initial braking

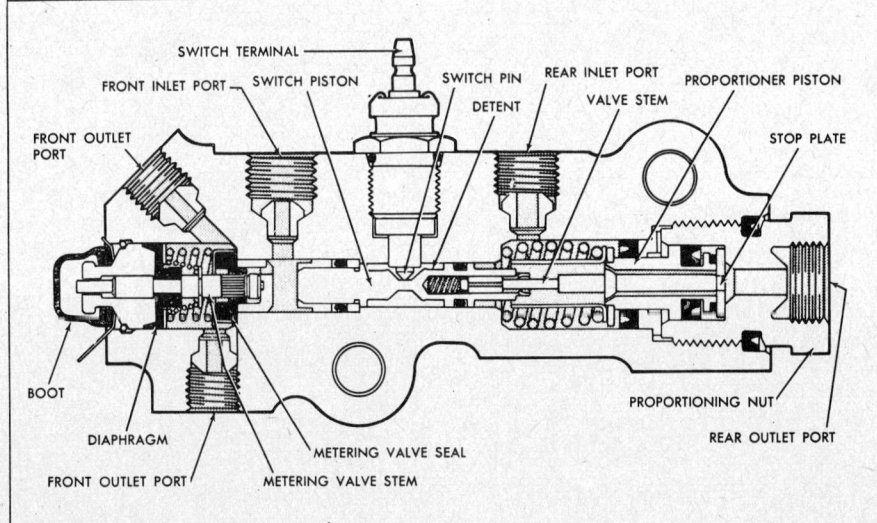

Fig. 8 Combination valve

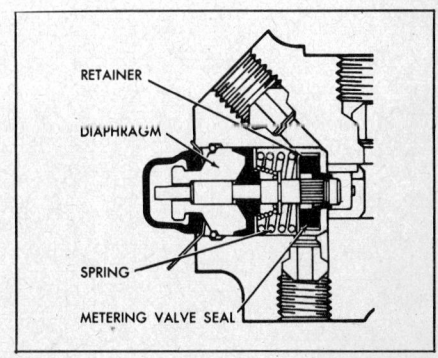

Fig. 10 Metering valve, continued braking

HYDRAULIC BRAKE SYSTEMS

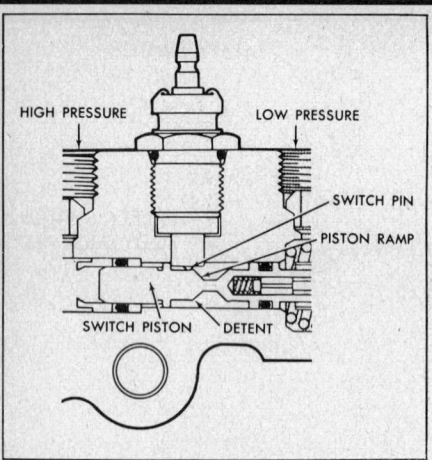

Fig. 11 Failure warning switch, rear system failure

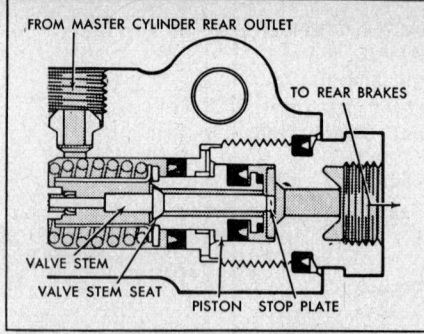

Fig. 12 Proportioner, rapid deceleration

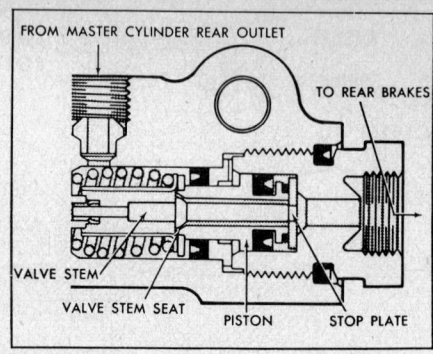

Fig. 13 Proportioner, normal braking

with power brakes, first reduce the vacuum in the power unit to zero by pumping the brake pedal several times with the engine off before starting to bleed the system.

Pressure bleeding, of course, eliminates the need for pedal pumping. Chrysler Corp. suggests that, when pressure is used, the bleeder valve should be opened and closed intermittently at about four-second intervals. This gives a whirling action to the fluid in the wheel cylinder, and helps expel the air.

At one time, some makers recommended that a clean container be used for the drained fluid, so that the fluid could be reused. All now agree that drained fluid should be discarded. Care should be taken not to spill brake fluid, since this can damage the finish of the vehicle.

Flushing is essential if there is water, mineral oil or other contaminants in the lines, and whenever new parts are installed in the hydraulic system. Fluid contamination is usually indicated by swollen and deteriorated cups and other rubber parts.

Bleeding is necessary on all four wheels if air has entered the system because of low fluid level, or the line or lines have been disconnected. If a line is disconnected at any one wheel cylinder, that cylinder only need be bled. Of course, on brake reline jobs, bleeding is advisable to remove any air or contaminants.

Master cylinders equipped with bleeder valves should be bled first before the wheel cylinders are bled. In all cases where a master cylinder has been overhauled, it must be bled. Where there is no bleeder valve, this can be done by leaving the line (or lines) loose, actuating the brake pedal to expel the air and then tightening the line (or lines).

NOTE: After overhauling a dual master cylinder used in conjunction with disc brakes, it is advisable to bleed the cylinder before installing it on the vehicles. The reason for this recommendation is that air may be trapped between the master cylinder pistons because there is only one residual pressure valve (check valve) used in these units.

The recommended precedure for Chrysler Line vehicles is as follows:
1. Clamp master cylinder in a vise and attach the special Bleeding Tubes (Tool No. C4029) Fig. 17A. *Be sure that the residual pressure valve is on the end of the tube in the large capacity reservoir as shown. This keeps the brake fluid from being syphoned out of the reservoir while bleeding.*
2. Fill both reservoirs with approved brake fluid.
3. Using a wooden stick or dowel (vehicles with power brakes) depress push rod slowly and allow the pistons to return under pressure of the springs. Do this several times until all air bubbles are expelled.
4. Remove bleeding tubes from cylinder and install cover and gasket.
5. Install master cylinder on vehicle and bleed wheel cylinders, preferably with a pressure bleeder.

Alternate Method
1. Support assembly in a vise and fill both reservoirs with brake fluid.
2. Loosely install a plug in each outlet port of the cylinder. Depress push rod several times until air bubbles cease to appear in the brake fluid.
3. Tighten plugs and attempt to depress the piston. Piston travel should be restricted after all air is expelled.
4. Install master cylinder on vehicle and bleed wheel cylinders, preferably with a

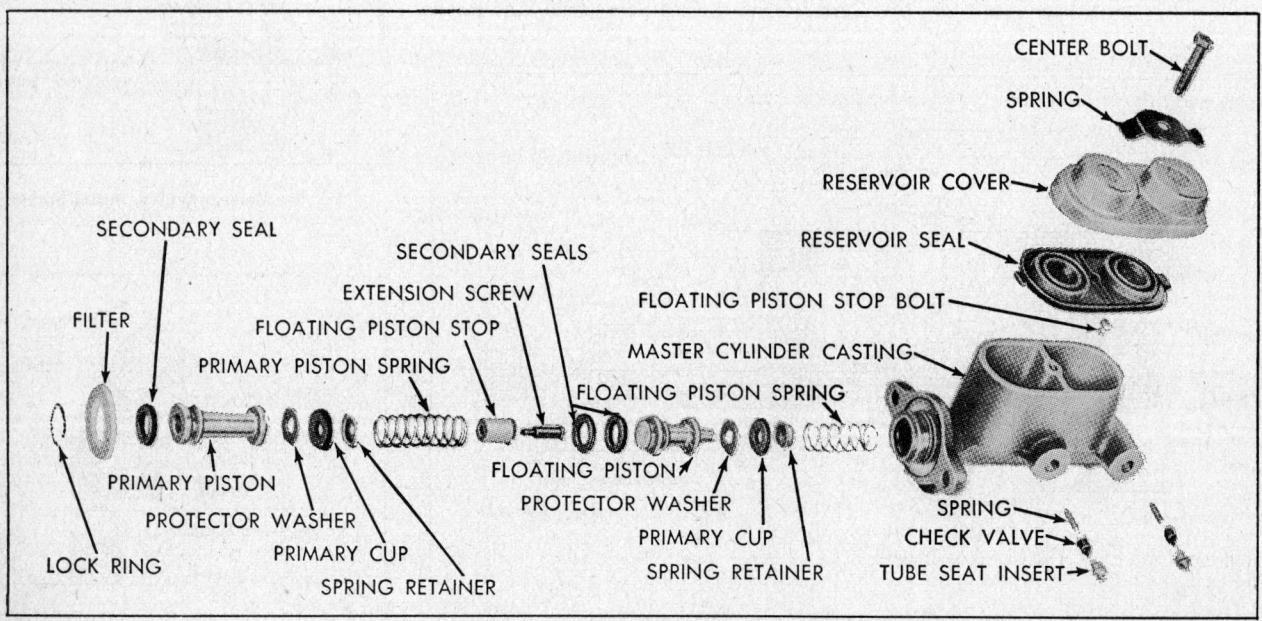

Fig. 14 Disassembled view of a typical Delco-Moraine dual master cylinder

HYDRAULIC BRAKE SYSTEMS

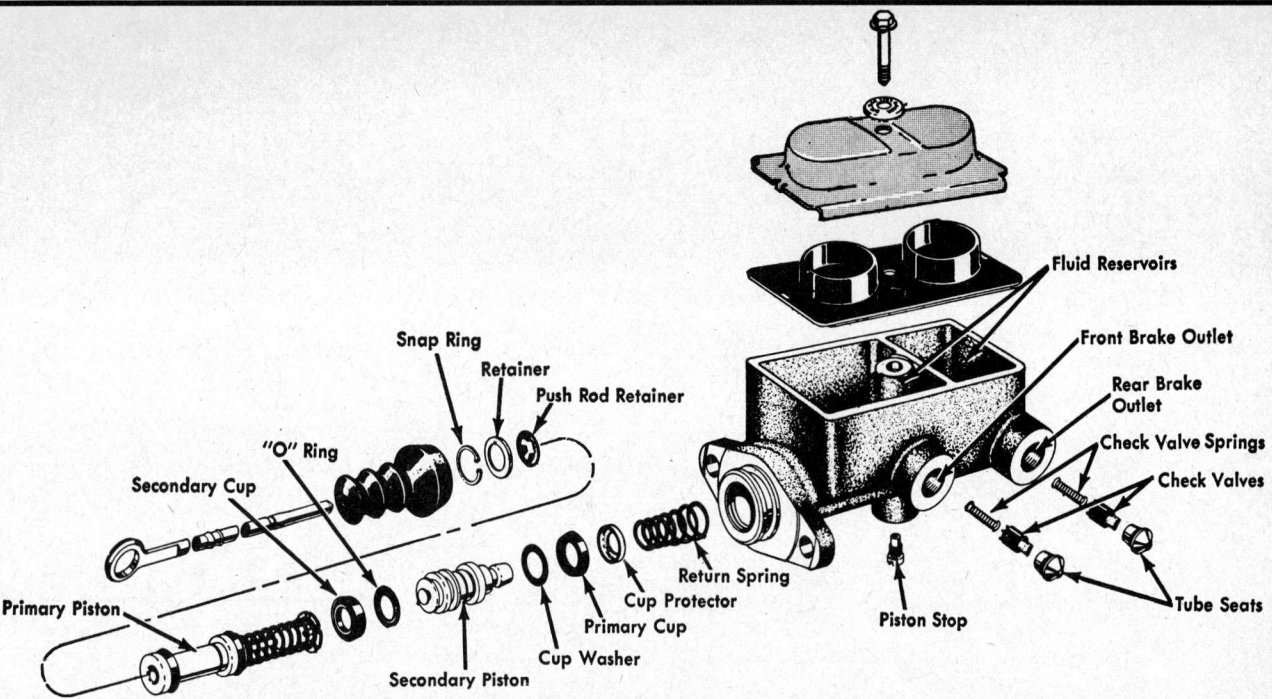

Fig. 15 Disassembled view of a typical Bendix dual master cylinder

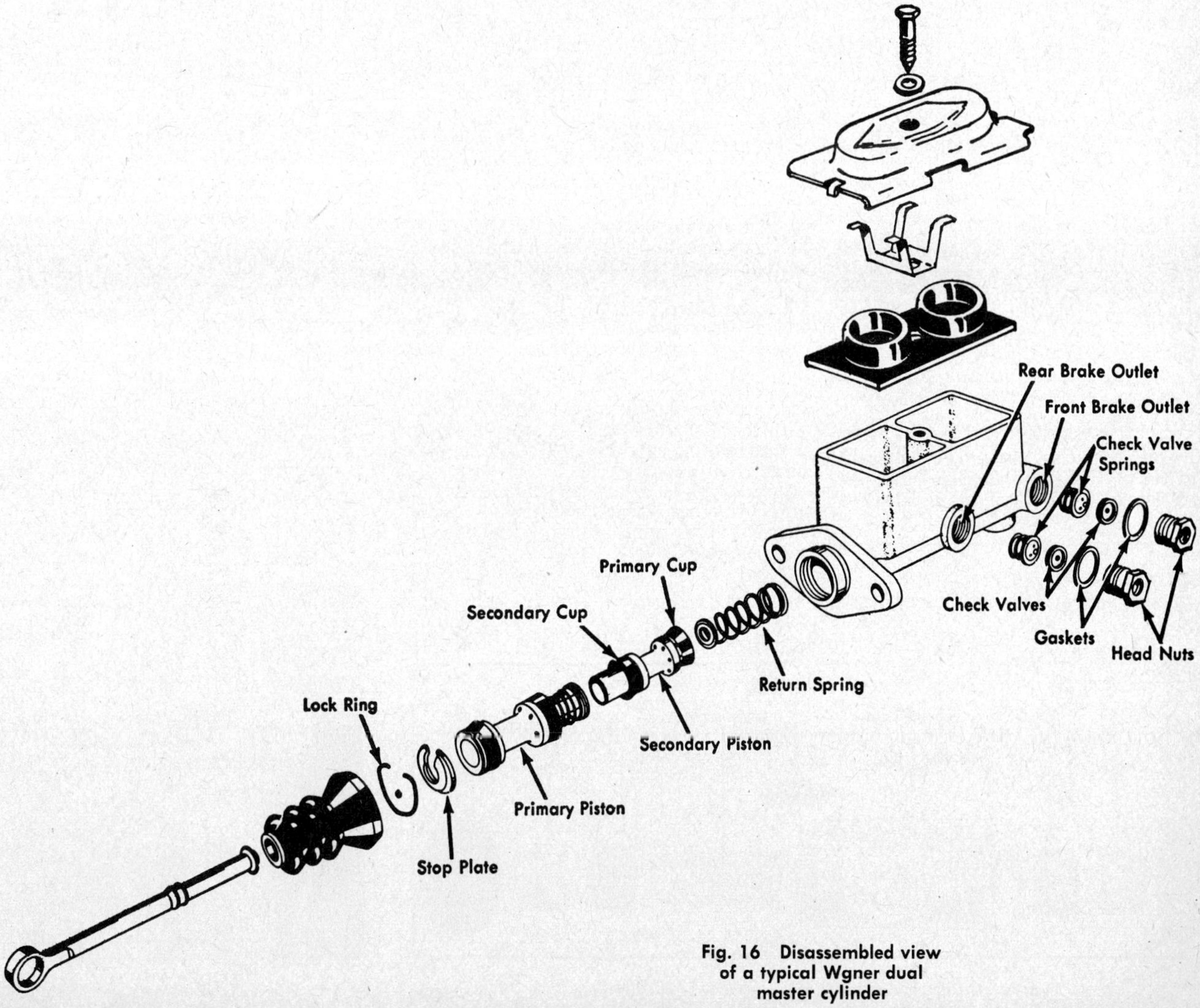

Fig. 16 Disassembled view of a typical Wgner dual master cylinder

HYDRAULIC BRAKE SYSTEMS

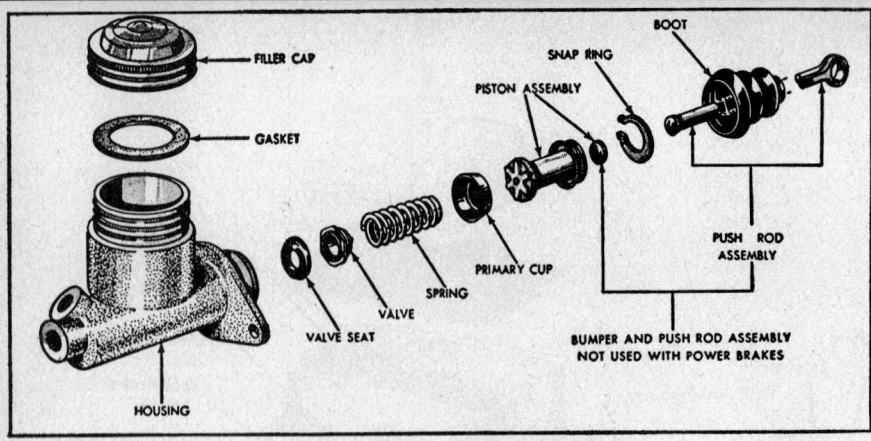

Fig. 17 Typical single brake master cylinder

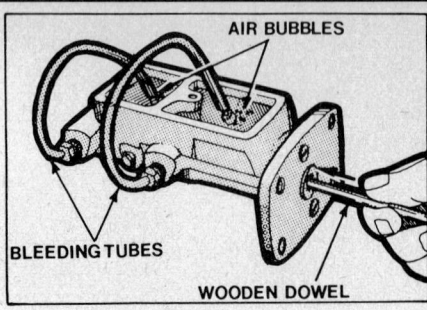

Fig. 17A Bleeding master cylinder used in conjunction with disc brakes

pressure bleeder.

Testing Dual Master Cylinders

Be sure that master cylinder compensates in both ports. This can be done by applying the brake pedal lightly (engine running with power brakes), and observing for brake fluid squirting up in the reservoirs. This may only occur in the front chamber. To determine if the rear compensating port is open, pump up the brakes rapidly and then hold the pedal down. Have an observer watch the fluid in the rear reservoir while the pedal is raised. A disturbance in the fluid indicates that the compensating port is open.

Wheel Bleeding Sequence

Difference of opinion as to whether the longest or shortest line should be bled first still exists. To be safe, use the sequence given below, recommended by the vehicle manufacturers:

Chrysler Corp.	RR-LR-RF-LF
Ford Company	RR-LR-RF-LF
General Motors	LF-RF-LR-RR
American Motors	RR-LR-RF-LF

Dual Master Cylinder Bleeding Notes

Ford Motor Co.

NOTE: Some vehicles use a self-centering valve. After any bleeding operation, turn ignition switch to ACC or ON position and depress brake pedal. Valve will center itself.

General Motors

On vehicles equipped with combined drum and disc brakes, the pressure differential valve must be held in its open position while bleeding the brakes using a pressure type bleeder. This is done by depressing the plunger and holding it in place using a special tool. When using pressure bleeding equipment follow the recommendations of the manufacturer.

American Motors

Before bleeding brakes, disconnect the switch terminal wire and remove nylon switch terminal, contact plunger actuating spring, and nylon plunger with contact.

In the event the valve has "triggered", the valve centering spring pressure may hold the switch plunger. If this happens, apply a slight amount of brake pedal pressure while releasing the plunger from the valve body.

After the bleeding operation, assemble the plunger spring and install valve with contact down. Install the nylon terminal and connect warning light wire to valve terminal. In the event brake fluid leaks from the center terminal body opening when the terminal is removed, replace the valve assembly.

Chrysler Corp.

Some Chrysler built vehicles with disc brakes are equipped with front disc brake pressure metering valves.

The purpose of the metering valve is to provide a better match of the front disc brakes with the rear drum brakes, resulting in improved braking balance *in light pedal applications*.

Gravity bleed and pedal methods are not affected by the presence of the metering valve. However, pressure bleeding is influenced by the metering valve.

Bleed pressure, which is normally about 35 psi, is high enough to cause the metering valve to close, which stops the flow of fluid to the front brakes. However, the valve can be held open manually by depressing the pressure release plunger (located at the bottom of the valve) in its uppermost position by hand or secured with masking tape while bleeding the brakes.

CAUTION: Under no conditions should a rigid clamp, wedge or block be used to secure the plunger as this can cause an internal failure in the valve. It should be noted that the pressure release plunger of the valve is already in its uppermost position when there is no pressure present.

WHEEL CYLINDERS

1. Remove wheel, drum and brake shoes.
2. Disconnect hydraulic line at wheel cylinder. *Do not pull metal line away from cylinder as the cylinder connection will bend metal line and make installation difficult. Line will separate from cylinder when cylinder is moved away from brake backing plate.*
3. Remove screws holding cylinder to brake plate and remove cylinder.

Overhaul

1. Referring to Fig. 18 as a guide, remove boots, pistons, springs and cups from cylinder.
2. Place all parts, except cylinder casting, in alcohol. Wipe cylinder walls with alcohol.
3. Examine cylinder bore. A scored bore may be honed providing the diameter is

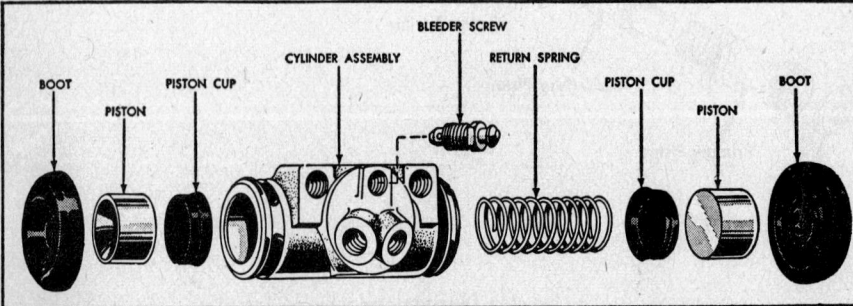

Fig. 18 Disassembled view of a typical wheel cylinder

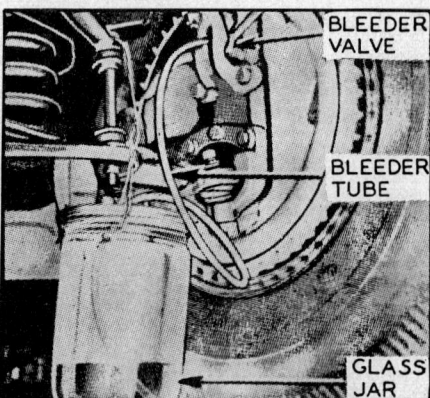

Fig. 19 Bleeding wheel cylinder

HYDRAULIC BRAKE SYSTEMS

not increased more than .005". Replace worn or damaged parts from the repair kit.
4. Before assembling, wash hands with soap and water only as oil, kerosene or gasoline will contaminate rubber parts.
5. Lubricate cylinder wall and rubber cups with brake fluid.
6. Install springs, cups, pistons and boots in housing.
7. Wipe end of hydraulic line to remove any foreign matter.
8. Place hydraulic cylinder in position. Enter tubing into cylinder and start connecting fitting.
9. Secure cylinder to backing plate and then complete tightening of tubing fitting.
10. Install brake shoes, drum and wheel.
11. Bleed system as outlined previously, and adjust brakes.

FLUSHING SYSTEM

It may sometimes become necessary to flush out the system due to the presence of mineral oil, kerosene, gasoline, etc., which will cause swelling of rubber piston cups and valves so they become inoperative. The procedure is as follows:
1. Attach bleeder tube and open bleeder valve at left front wheel, Fig. 19.
2. Flush out system thoroughly with clean alcohol, pumping the fluid from the master cylinder and out of the wheel cylinder bleeder valve.
3. Repeat Steps 1 and 2 at remaining wheel cylinders. To insure thorough flushing, about a 1/2 pint of alcohol should be bled through each wheel cylinder.
4. Replace all rubber parts in master and wheel cylinders. Thoroughly clean cylinders and pistons in alcohol before installing new parts.
5. After installing parts, fill system with recommended brake fluid and flush system of cleaning solution and then bleed brakes. In doing this, pump brake fluid from wheel chylinder bleeder valves until clear brake fluid flows from bleeder tube and then, if necessary, continue until no air bubbles emerge from bleeder tube.

HYDRAULIC TUBING

Steel tubing is used to conduct hydraulic pressure to the brakes. All fittings, tubing and hose should be inspected for rusted, damaged or defective flared seats. The tubing is equipped with a double flare or inverted seat to insure more positive seating in the fitting. To repair or reflare tubing, proceed as follows:
1. Using the tool shown in Fig. 20 or its equivalent, cut off the damaged seat or damaged tubing.
2. Ream out any burrs or rough edges showing on inside edges of tubing. This will make the ends of the tubing square and insure better seating of the flared end. *Before flaring tubing, place a compression nut on tubing.*
3. Open handles of flaring tool and rotate jaws of tool until mating jaws of tubing size are centered in the area between vertical posts.
4. Slowly close handles with tubing inserted in jaws but do not apply heavy pressure to handle as this will lock tubing in place.
5. Referring to Fig. 20, place gauge on edge over end of tubing and push tubing through jaws until end of tubing contacts recessed notch of gauge matching size of tubing.
6. Squeeze handles of flaring tool and lock tubing in place.
7. Place proper size plug of gauge down in end of tubing. Swing compression disc over gauge and center tapered flaring screw in recess in disc.
8. Lubricate taper of flaring or screw and screw in until plug gauge has seated in jaws of flaring tool. This action has started to invert the extended end of tubing.
9. Remove gauge and apply lubricant to tapered end of flaring screw and continue to screw down until tool is firmly seated in tubing.
10. Remove tubing from flaring tool and inspect the seat. If seat is cracked, cut off cracked end and repeat flaring operation.

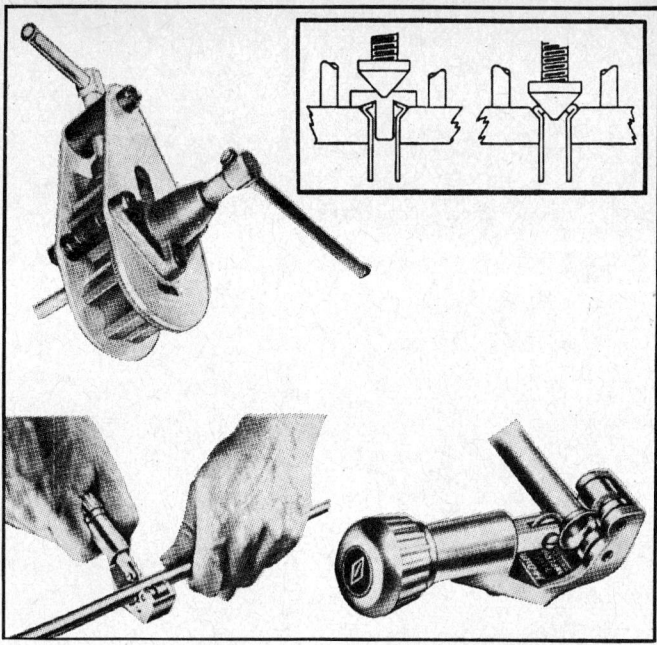

Fig. 20 Cutting and flaring hydraulic brake tubing

BRAKE BOOSTERS

INDEX

	Page No.
Booster Bleeding Procedures	640

BENDIX BOOSTERS

	Page No.
Air-Pak Power Unit	644
Duo-Vac	651
Hydro Boost	654

Hydrovac

	Page No.
Piston Type	640
Single Diaphragm Type	645, 647, 648
Tandem Diaphragm Type	
Dash Mounted	648
Frame Mounted	642, 650

MIDLAND-ROSS BOOSTERS

	Page No.
Double Diaphragm Type	659
Hy-Power Diaphragm Type	657
Single Diaphragm Type	
Dash Mounted	656
Frame Mounted	657

BRAKE BOOSTERS

BOOSTER BLEEDING

Bleeding hydraulic brake systems which include a brake booster requires that the booster be bled first before proceeding with the operation on the wheel cylinders. (Bleeding instructions are given in the *Hydraulic Brake System* chapter.)

As shown in the illustrations, Figs. 1 to 6, all boosters have a bleed screw on the control valve (screw No. 1) and some have another bleed screw on the hydraulic cylinder (screw No. 2). Start the bleeding operation with the control valve bleed screw, then the hydraulic cylinder screw and, finally, bleed the wheel cylinders.

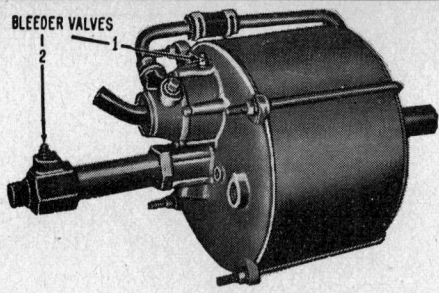

Fig. 2 Single 6¾" Hydrovac

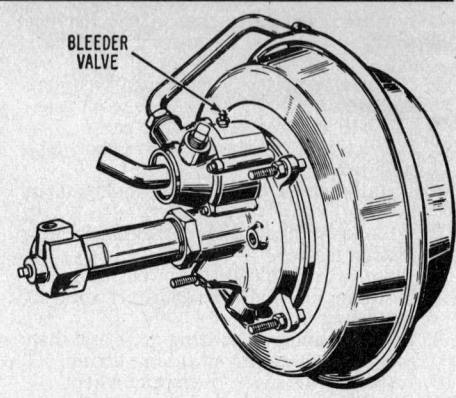

Fig. 5 Diaphragm type power cylinder. Note that only one bleeder valve is used

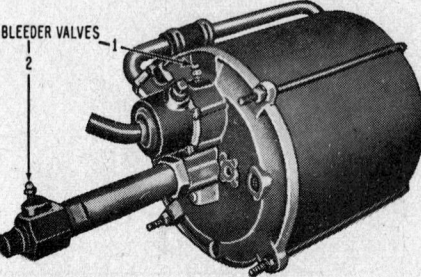

Fig. 3 Single 9½" Hydrovac

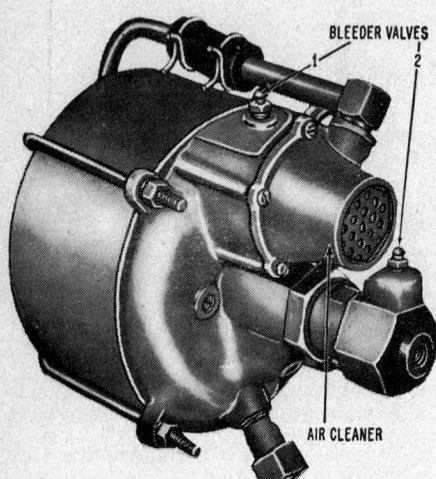

Fig. 1 Single 6¾" diameter Hydrovac with integral air cleaner

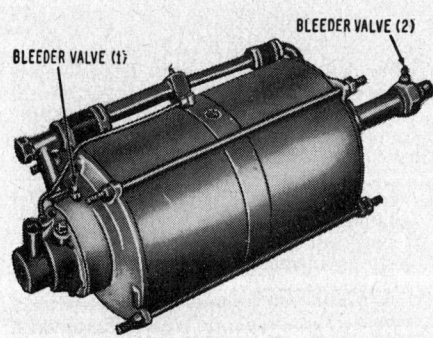

Fig. 4 Tandem 9½" Hydrovac

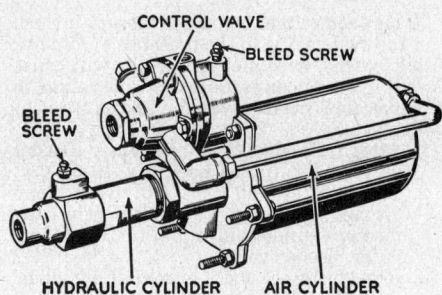

Fig. 6 Air-Pak power cylinder

Bendix Brake Boosters

PISTON TYPE HYDROVAC

Disassembly Notes

1. Before separating the main components of the booster, scribe a line across the cylinder shell and end plate so these parts can be reassembled in their original position.
2. Before separating the vacuum piston from the end plate, use hook-type clamps to hold the spring compressed.
3. Always use a repair kit and install all parts contained in the kit regardless of the condition of the old parts.

Reassembly

1. Press push rod leather seal into end plate with lip of seal toward hydraulic cylinder side of end plate, Fig. B1.
2. Assemble push rod seal parts into end plate as shown. Install stop washer with chamfered side toward end plate, the seal cup with lip of cup away from stop washer, retainer washer with flat side next to cup and small end of spring as shown. Place washer against spring and assemble snap ring into groove. Install new cylinder end seal.
3. Assemble hydraulic control valve piston retainer ring and stop washer into the fitting, Fig. B1.
4. Dip piston cups in brake fluid and assemble them on piston. On 6¾" diameter boosters, assemble one piston cup, spacer and the other cup on the piston and secure with the C-washer. Pinch ends of C-washer together. Lip of both piston cups must point *toward* C-washer end of piston. On 9½" units, assemble piston cups into grooves of piston. Cups must be assembled with their lips pointing *away* from each other. Insert piston and cups into the fitting, with the hole end of piston next to stop washer.
5. Place new rubber gasket over threaded end of fitting, thread fitting into end plate, and tighten fitting securely.
6. Thread nut on guide tube to limit of threads, Fig. B2.
7. Assemble reinforcing plate and seal over threads of guide tube. *Use care not to damage seal.*
8. Position guide tube and reinforcing plate assembly against cylinder shell. From inside shell, install and thread nut onto guide tube until it is flush with end of tube. Stake nut securely in two places, and tighten tube nut against reinforcing plate to insure a good seal between guide tube and cylinder shell.

640

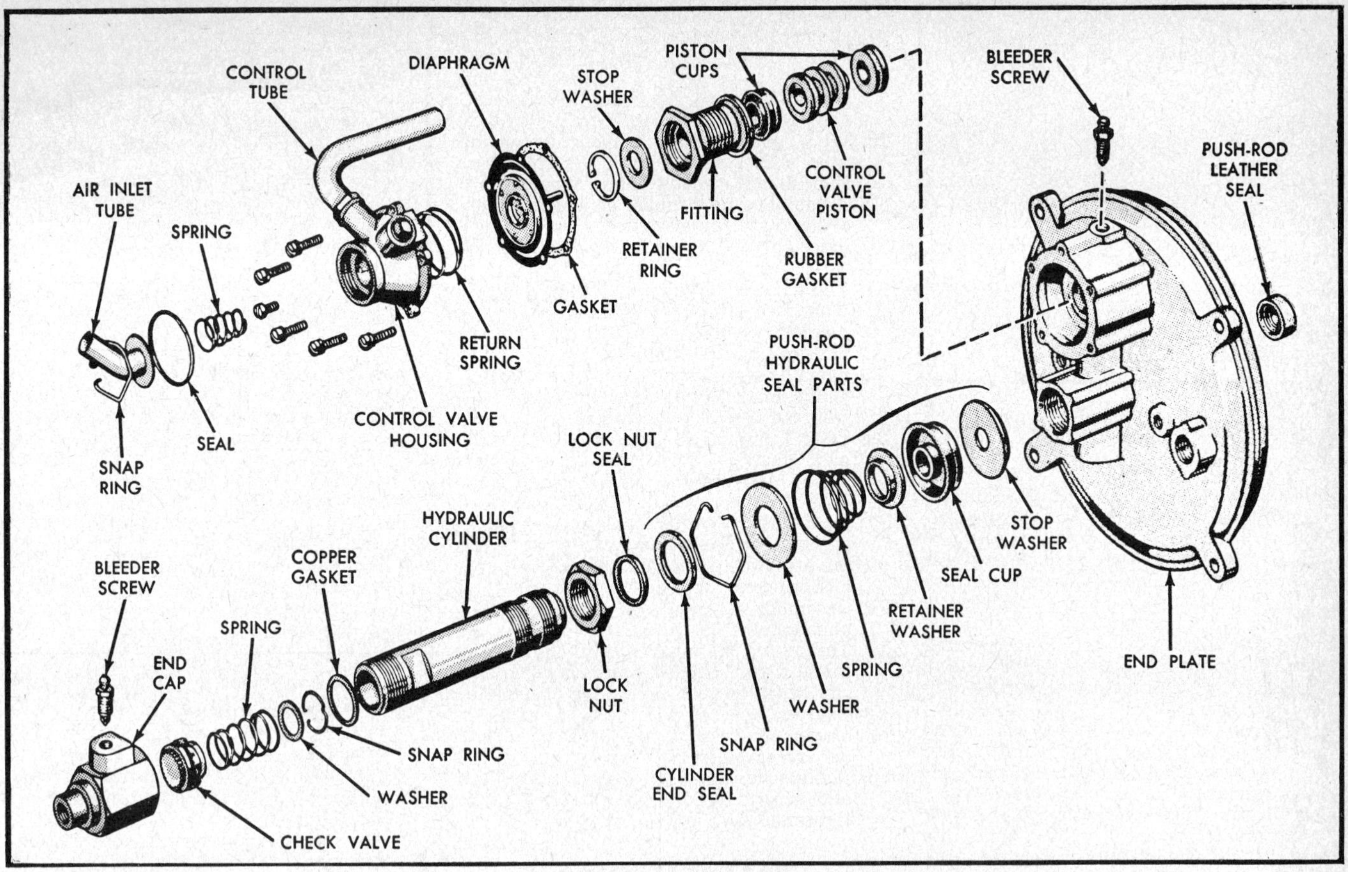

BRAKE BOOSTERS

Fig. B1 End plate disassembled. Piston type Hydrovac

9. Fabricate a vacuum piston ring by cutting a one-inch section from an old cylinder shell of correct size. Place assembly ring, Fig. B3, on bench and assemble vacuum piston parts in the assembly ring. Install larger diameter piston plate with chamfered side of hole up. Lip of packing should be *up* on $6\frac{3}{4}''$ units and *down* on $9\frac{1}{2}''$ units. The seal ring and small diameter piston plate is installed with chamfered side of hole down.
10. Cut wicking to required length and assemble it against inner face of piston packing lip.
11. Position expander ring inside wicking with gripper points up and notch at loop end of expander ring under clip near opposite end of expander ring.
12. Assemble retainer plate with cut-out portion over loop of expander ring.
13. Hold guide in vertical position and assemble flat washer over threaded end.
14. With assembly ring still in position over vacuum piston, turn piston and ring upside down and assemble them into guide. To prevent damage to seal ring, remove larger diameter piston plate while guiding seal ring over threads.
15. Replace piston plate and assemble nut onto guide. Tighten nut securely and stake in two places. *Do not remove assembly ring until piston is installed in cylinder shell.*
16. On $9\frac{1}{2}''$ units, clamp hexagonal section of guide firmly in a vise. Assemble push rod attaching parts over beveled end of push rod, Fig. B4, starting with lock ring. Use care in assembling snap ring in groove at lower end of push rod to avoid distorting lock ring.
17. On $9\frac{1}{2}''$ units, insert end of push rod in recess at end of guide. Attach push rod to guide by compressing spring and inserting lock ring in groove of guide. Be sure lock ring is firmly seated in groove.
18. Assemble check valve parts in end cap, Fig. B1, and secure with lock ring. Be sure lock ring is firmly seated in groove.
19. Place a new copper gasket in end cap. Thread hydraulic cylinder into end cap with milled flats next to end cap. Tighten cylinder securely.
20. Install bleeder screw into end cap. Thread

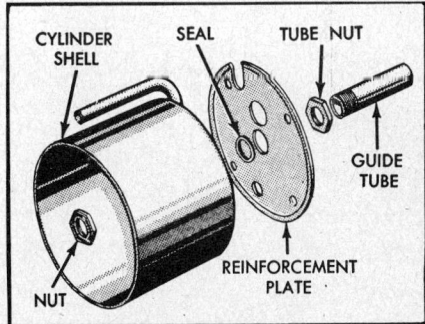

Fig. B2 Cylinder shell and guide tube disassembled

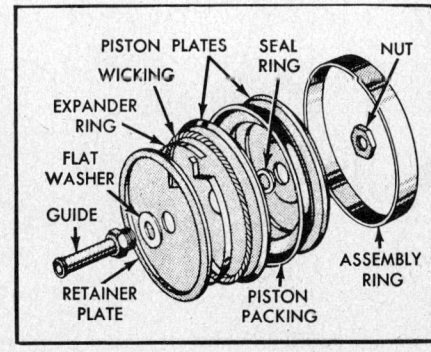

Fig. B3 Vacuum piston disassembled

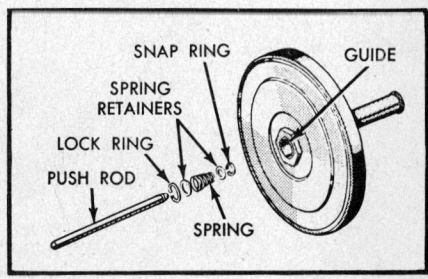

Fig. B4 Push rod parts

BRAKE BOOSTERS

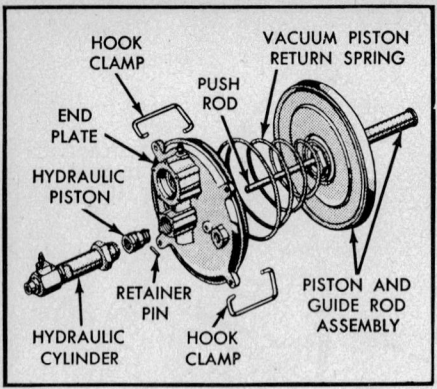

Fig. B5 Vacuum piston, end plate and hydraulic cylinder

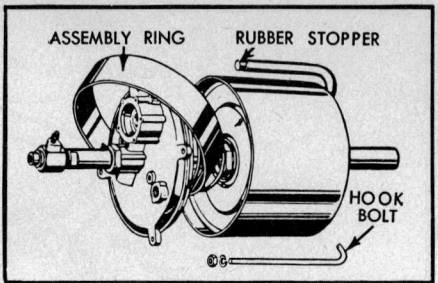

Fig. B6 Assembly ring removal

lock nut on cylinder to limit of thread. Position a new lock nut seal over two sections of thread.

21. Mount vacuum piston and guide in vise at hex portion of guide. Place piston return spring over push rod with small end of spring next to piston, Fig. B5.
22. Carefully guide push rod through leather seal of end plate. Compress spring and install hook clamps to hold spring compressed.
23. Position hydraulic piston on push rod and secure with retainer pin. Slide retainer spring over hole in piston to hold retainer pin in place.
24. Carefully guide hydraulic cylinder over lip of piston cup, and thread cylinder into end plate (hand tight). Remove hook clamps and unit from vise.
25. Mount cylinder shell in vise (at guide tube nut) with cylinder shell in vertical position.
26. Insert rubber stopper into control line tube, Fig. B6.
27. With top face of vacuum piston flush with top edge of assembly ring, line up assembly ring with cylinder shell and guide vacuum piston into shell. On $9\frac{1}{2}''$ units, if vacuum piston is permitted to tip slightly, vacuum piston guide will not enter guide tube.
28. As soon as guide has entered tube, lift assembly ring to permit inspection of piston packing. If leather packing has started to enter cylinder shell without any part of packing folded back, remove rubber stopper, press vacuum piston into cylinder shell about 2" and replace rubber stopper. If inspection reveals that any part of packing has been folded back, repeat above operation.
29. With rubber stopper still in control line tube, slide assembly ring over end plate, Fig. B6, and remove rubber stopper.
30. Assemble a new rubber gasket in groove of end plate and align end plate with cylinder shell at scribe marks. Install hook bolts and tighten uniformly.
31. The use of guide pins threaded into end plate will simplify assembly of spring, diaphragm, gasket and control valve housing, and will reduce possibility of damaging diaphragm during assembly. Guide pins may be made by cutting heads from $8-32 \times 2\frac{1}{2}''$ machine screws.
32. Install guide pins. Position a new gasket over pins and install diaphragm, return spring and control valve housing, Fig. B1.
33. Hold control valve housing and parts against end plate and remove one guide pin at a time, replacing with a screw and lock washer. Tighten screws securely.
34. Assemble vacuum hose on control tube and tighten hose clamp.
35. Thread hydraulic cylinder into end plate (hand tight). Align bleeder screw in end cap with bleeder screw in end plate. Tighten lock nut securely. *Do not use a wrench when tightening hydraulic cylinder in end plate.*
36. Make sure that all bolts, nuts, washers and screws are in place and securely tightened.

TANDEM TYPE PISTON HYDROVAC

NOTE: When disassembling, refer to the illustrations and observe the following: After removing the hydraulic cylinder and seal, place booster in an arbor press and insert a brass drift through atmospheric port in rear end plate. Press vacuum cylinder piston until hydraulic piston is exposed at hydraulic cylinder opening in end plate. Compress push rod pin retaining spring (on hydraulic piston), remove retaining pin and hydraulic piston from push rod. Disassemble hydraulic piston and remove booster from vise.

After disassembling the end plates, cylinder shells and center plate, force the center plate and rear vacuum piston together. Then insert a rod through the hole in the piston rod to hold the piston return spring in the compressed position. Fabricate two assembly rings from an old cylinder. Place assembly ring over front piston and remove nut securing front piston to rod. Then, remove piston rod nut, push rod retainer pin and push rod. Remove front piston, but keep parts assembled in assembly ring.

Reassembly, Fig. B7

1. Assemble rear vacuum piston by installing nut on rear vacuum piston end of piston rod with flat side of nut upward, Fig. B8.
2. Position larger diameter piston plate on piston rod with chamfered side of hole at the top. Guide rubber seal ring over threads of piston rod.
3. Place assembly ring on flat surface and install leather packing with lip side upward. Then position smaller diameter piston plate, with chamfered side of hole downward, in the ring.
4. Cut a new piece of wick to the required length. Then place it against inner face of leather packing lip. Assemble wick retainer (with gripper points upward) against wick and hook notched end of retainer under clip near opposite end of ring.
5. Position cut-out of retainer plate over loop of wick retainer.
6. Hold piston parts in assembly ring, as-

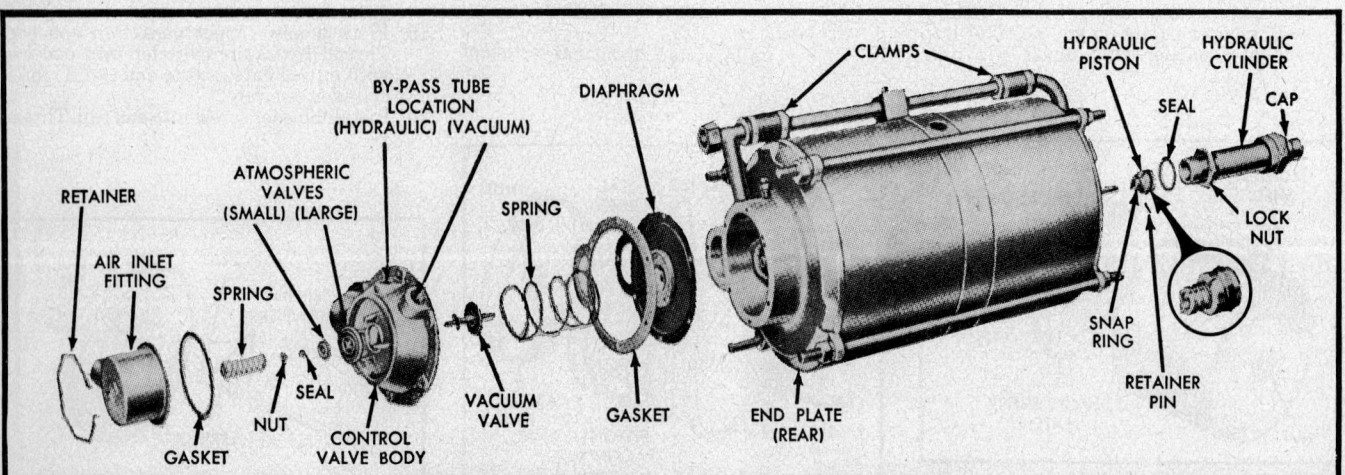

Fig. B7 Tandem piston type Hydrovac

BRAKE BOOSTERS

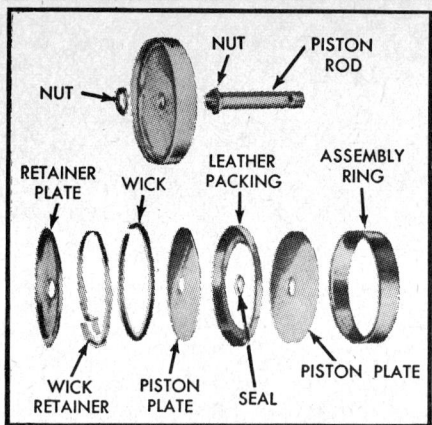

Fig. B8 Rear vacuum piston and rod assembly

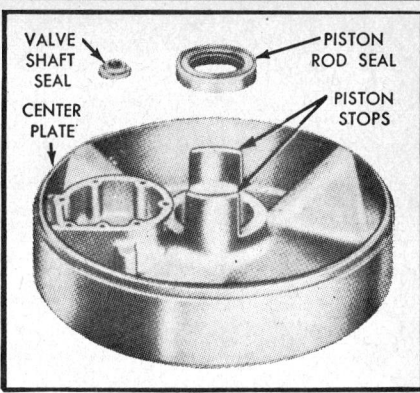

Fig. B9 Fast application valve and piston rod seals

semble them on end of piston rod, then install nut on top of piston assembly. Tighten nut until it is flush with end of piston rod. Stake nut securely in two places. Clamp staked nut firmly in vise. Then tighten nut on opposite side of piston plate solidly against piston plate.

7. Place fast application valve shaft and rod seals, Fig. B9, into center plate. Piston valve shaft seal must be flush with bottom of hole. Piston rod seal should rest against shoulder of center plate.
8. Position center plate as shown in Fig. B10. Then place return spring on top of seal with small end at top. Install a bullet-nosed tool on threaded end of valve shaft and insert valve shaft through seal. Position gasket on center plate.
9. Place valve seat plate (with seat side downward) on gasket and install screws and lockwashers.
10. Turn center plate over. Place lower diaphragm plate (rounded edge up) on valve shaft. Then place diaphragm gasket on top of plate, Fig. B11. Position diaphragm on top of gasket so that screw holes and by-pass hole index with identical holes in center plate. Install other diaphragm plate with rounded edge facing diaphragm.
11. Install nut on valve shaft. Use a screwdriver to prevent shaft from turning and tighten nut. Stake nut securely at two opposite points.
12. Position gasket and valve cover on center plate then install screws and lockwashers.
13. Place return spring over piston rod with small end of spring at bottom, Fig. B12.
14. Carefully guide piston rod through seal in center plate with piston stop flanges of center plate facing upward. Press center plate down against spring and insert a rod in the piston rod.
15. Assemble large end of push rod in end of piston rod and install pin.
16. Thread nut on piston rod with flat side of nut upward to limit of threads.
17. If front piston was disassembled to replace leather piston packing, cotton wicking or other parts, assemble piston parts in assembly ring in same order as rear piston, Fig. B8. Hold parts in ring and turn assembly ring over. Remove large diameter piston plate and seal. With assembly ring still in place, guide remaining piston parts over end of push rod and against piston rod nut, Fig. B13. Carefully install seal over threads of piston rod. Place larger diameter piston plate on piston rod with chamfered side of hole toward seal.
18. Install piston rod nut (flat side downward) on end of piston rod. Tighten nut until it is flush with face of piston rod. Stake nut securely at opposite points.
19. Hold piston rod nut in a vise or with a wrench and tighten inner nut securely against piston. *Use care when tightening inner nut to prevent retainer plate from shifting.*
20. Remove assembly ring. Then remove rod holding return spring compressed.
21. Hold end cap in a vise and assemble parts as shown in Fig. B14. Small end of spring must be placed inside check valve clips.
22. Install new copper gasket in end cap. Hydraulic cylinder must be assembled with milled flats next to end cap. Tighten hydraulic cylinder solidly in end cap and thread lock nut on hydraulic cylinder up to limit of threads.
23. Install lock nut seal (if used) in groove of cylinder tube. Install bleeder screw in cap.
24. Press leather seal into hydraulic cylinder bore of front end of plate (from inner side of plate) with lip of seal toward outer end of plate, Fig. B15.
25. Install push rod seal and related parts in order shown in Fig. B15. Chamfered side of washer is down, lip of push rod seal is up, flat side of flange washer is next to seal. Install retaining washer.
26. Install snap ring in inner groove of end plate.
27. Place rear end plate on holding fixture, Fig. B16, and install stop washer with flat side in valve fitting. Install retainer.
28. Dip hydraulic piston cups in brake fluid. Assemble cups on pistons with lips of cups positioned away from each other.
29. Insert piston into valve fitting with open end of piston toward stop washer.
30. Install new gasket on stop fitting. If fitting has no groove install copper gasket; if fitting has a groove use rubber seal gasket.
31. Install valve fitting in end plate. Tighten fitting equipped with rubber gasket firmly. Torque fitting equipped with copper gasket to 325–330 ft-lbs.
32. Assemble vacuum control valve parts in control body in sequence shown in Fig. B7. Install a new lead washer.
33. Install tee fitting and tubes on center plate. Small diameter pipe on vacuum tee should be toward front end plate.
34. Dip front piston leather packing and wicking in vacuum cylinder oil and allow excess oil to drain off.
35. Position a new gasket on front edge of center plate. Install front cylinder to center plate, Fig. B17. Coat interior of cylinder with vacuum oil. Carefully guide push rod through seal in front end plate. At same time, align vacuum tube in end plate with vacuum tube on center plate.
36. Position new gasket on front end plate and place on front cylinder.
37. Slide hose in place to connect two vacuum tubes.
38. Position a new gasket on outer edge of center plate, Fig. B18. Coat interior of rear cylinder with vacuum cylinder oil. Then tip front cylinder and end plate assembly at a 45-degree angle to prevent damage to rear piston leather packing. Carefully push rear cylinder over rear piston and onto center plate.
39. Place a new gasket on rear end plate. Then install end plate on rear cylinder, aligning end plate vacuum tube and center plate vacuum tube.
40. Install cylinder studs and tighten nuts securely.
41. Position vacuum hoses on tubes and tighten clamps.
42. Connect hydraulic by-pass tube to front and rear end plates. Install tube clip and screw to center plate.
43. To assembly hydraulic piston parts, place large end of spring in retainer cup and install check ball in piston body behind spring.
44. Dip new piston cup in brake fluid. Install cup on piston with lip of cup toward check ball.
45. Place booster assembly in arbor press. Insert a brass drift through atmospheric port in rear end plate. Press hydraulic

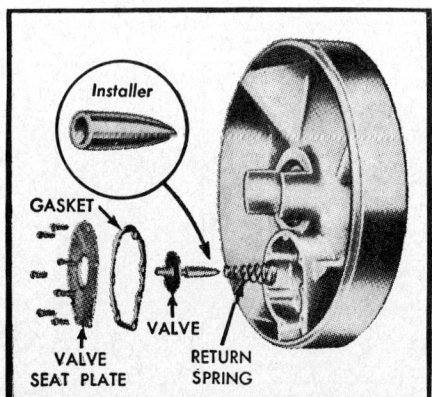

Fig. B10 Fast application valve and seal

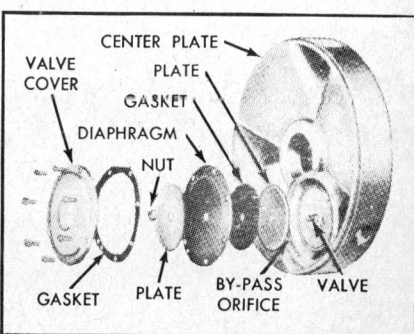

Fig. B11 Fast application valve and diaphragm

BRAKE BOOSTERS

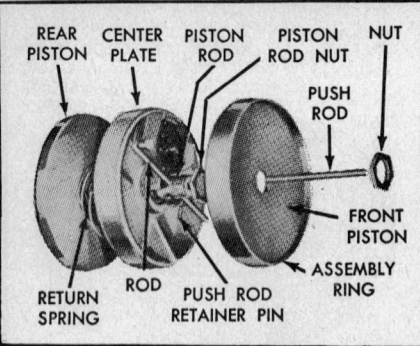

Fig. B12 Push rod piston and center plate

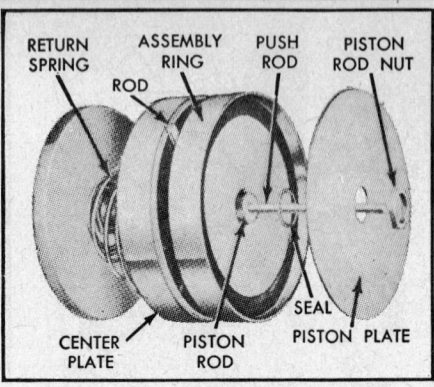

Fig. B13 Rear vacuum piston, return spring and outer plate assembly

der end cap to the facing surface of the end plate varies according to the size of the Air-Pak. Therefore, before disassembling the unit, make a note of this dimension (see Fig. B24) so it can be adjusted properly when the unit is reassembled.

1. Before separating the main components of the unit, Fig. B20, scribe a line on end plate and control body and also on the end plate and booster control body to assure proper alignment of these parts during reassembly.
2. Disassemble the unit as suggested by the illustrations, observing the following:
3. To disengage push rod from hydraulic piston, place piston over booster return spring, Fig. B21. Compress return spring by pressing toward end plate to move push rod forward. Remove pin retaining hydraulic piston to push rod. Remove hydraulic piston.
4. When removing booster piston, return spring and push rod from end plate, a hook clamp may be used to hold return spring in compressed position while removing pin, Fig. B21. Clamp should hook through one of the end plate holes and over end of booster piston. Clamp may be fabricated to dimensions shown in Fig. B21.
5. To remove push rod seal and gasket from end plate, thread a 1/4" pipe tap into the seal. Drive seal out from booster body end of end plate, using a short piece of rod against pipe tap.
6. With special tool, Fig. B22, remove control valve cylinder from end plate.
7. To disassemble booster piston, use a holding fixture to prevent damaging piston. Dimensions for fabricating fixture are shown in Fig. B23.

Reassembly

NOTE: Always use a repair kit when servicing an Air-Pak unit, and use all parts contained in the kit regardless of the condition of the old parts. Do not allow any of the parts to come in contact with mineral oil or grease.

1. To aid in reassembling the booster piston, make an assembly ring from an old booster body of the same diameter as the one being serviced. Fig. B25 shows a sample assembly ring.
2. With assembly ring flat on work bench, insert a new packing leather inside ring with lip up, Fig. B23. Place packing retainer over packing leather with cupped edge pointing toward packing leather.
3. Cut a new wick to proper length and dip it in vacuum cylinder oil. Assemble wick against inner lip of packing leather.
4. Position a new expander ring on inner side of wick (gripping points up). Engage notch at loop end of ring with hook near opposite end of ring.
5. Position retainer over expander ring with cut-out in retainer lining up with loop in expander ring.
6. Place assembly ring with assembled parts over threaded boss of booster piston. Install packing retainer nut finger tight.
7. Clamp piston holding fixture in vise. Place booster piston and assembly ring on holding fixture. Tighten packing retainer nut securely. *Do not remove assembly ring from piston until assembly is to be inserted into booster body.*
8. Remove piston assembly and holding fixture from vise.

HYDRAULIC CYLINDER END CAP
1. Clamp end cap in vise.
2. Insert check valve, spring (with small end inside tabs of check valve) and retaining washer in cap bore. Compress spring and insert a new snap ring. Be sure snap ring is engaged in its recess.

HYDRAULIC CYLINDER
1. Place new copper gasket in end cap. Screw hydraulic cylinder into end cap and tighten.
2. Screw lock nut onto inner threaded portion of cylinder. Dip a new gasket in brake fluid and place it between threaded portions of cylinder.
3. Install bleeder screw.
4. Remove end cap and hydraulic cylinder from vise.

CONTROL VALVE CYLINDER
1. Dip a new control valve piston, hydraulic

cylinder piston until piston rod is exposed at front end plate. Assemble hydraulic piston on push rod and install retaining pin. Remove booster from press. Install seal on hydraulic cylinder.
46. Carefully guide hydraulic cylinder over piston cup and thread cylinder into end plate. Align bleeder screw in end cap with bleeder screw in control valve. Adjust hydraulic cylinder to the dimension given for the unit being serviced, Fig. B19, plus or minus 1/2 turn.
47. Install 5 guide pins (made from 8-32 x 2 1/2" machine screws with heads cut off) in rear end plate.
48. Install air inlet fitting gasket and spring in control valve body, then install retainer.
49. Install diaphragm, inserting its stem into piston hole. Place diaphragm spring, gasket and control valve body on top of diaphragm.
50. Remove guide pins one at a time, and replace each with an attaching screw and new lock washer. Tighten screws progressively and firmly.
51. Install hydraulic and vacuum by-pass tubes.
52. See that all bolts, nuts, screws and plugs are in place, and that all tubes, clamps and fittings are firmly tightened.
53. Remove lube plugs from end and center plates. Add vacuum cylinder oil to level of filler plug holes. Install and tighten plugs.

BENDIX AIR-PAK POWER UNIT

Disassembly Notes

CAUTION: The length of the hydraulic cylinder, measured from the outer end of the cylin-

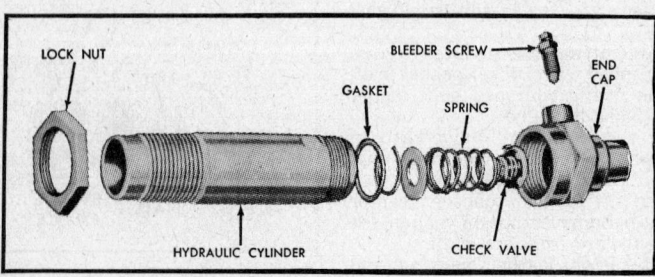

Fig. B14 Hydraulic cylinder, check valve and end cap

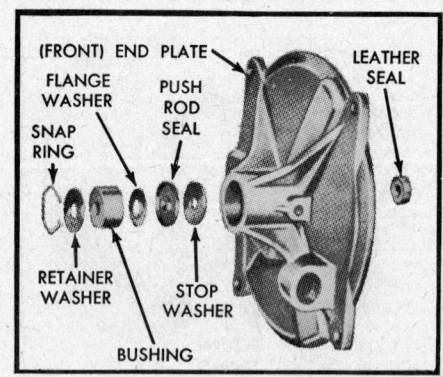

Fig. B15 Hydraulic cylinder push rod seals

BRAKE BOOSTERS

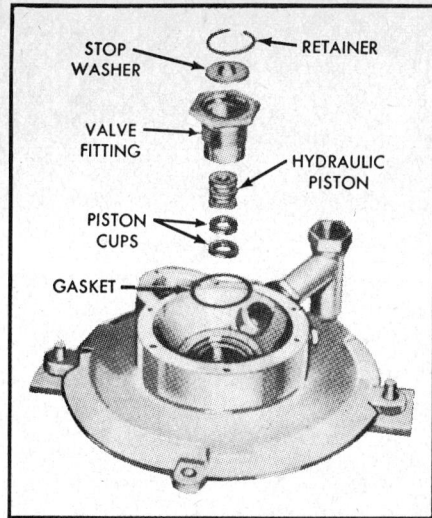

Fig. B16 Hydralic control valve piston and fitting

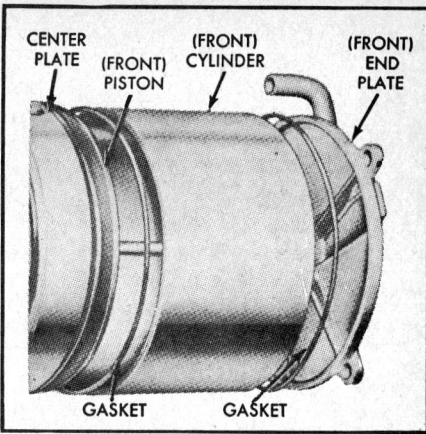

Fig. B17 Front cylinder and end plate

cup and air seal cup in brake fluid. Assemble hydraulic cup in recess of valve piston (at chamfered end of piston). Lip of hydraulic cup must be pointing toward chamfered end of piston.
2. Assemble air seal (identified by red dot) in other recess of valve piston with lip pointing opposite to that of hydraulicc cup.
3. Insert retainer into recess in notched end of control valve cylinder.
4. Place piston assembly into valve cylinder from opposite side of retainer ring groove, with hole end of piston next to retainer.

DIAPHRAGM
1. Place a new diaphragm over threaded end of stem with concave side of diaphragm toward threaded end.
2. Place flat side of washer facing nut. Screw diaphragm nut over threaded end of stem finger tight.
3. Clamp diaphragm nut in a vise. Tighten assembly by using a drift in one of the adapter holes.
4. Remove diaphragm assembly from vise and stake nut.

END PLATE
1. Clamp flange of end plate in vise.
2. Position a new seal gasket and a leather push rod seal into recess in end of base of end plate with push rod seal lip pointing toward seal gasket.

3. Seat push rod seal in recess by using a length of 7/8″ or 15/16″ rod and tapping rod with fiber mallet. Insert a new fiber stop washer with chamfered side toward push rod seal.
4. Dip a new cup in brake fluid and place it against washer with lip of cup pointing away from stop washer.
5. Position seal retainer and spacer in bore with counterbore of retainer next to cup, Fig. B22. Install spring and washer.
6. Hold assembled parts in place by installing stop ring into its recess in end plate bore. Dip new O-ring in brake fluid and insert it in recess in bore of end plate.
7. Dip a new control valve cylinder seal in brake fluid and install it in recess of control valve cylinder.
8. Screw control valve cylinder into end plate. Tighten cylinder using tool shown in Fig. B22.
9. Install bleeder screw, fitting bolts and gasket.
10. Dip hydraulic piston in brake fluid. Lip of cup must point toward hydraulic cylinder end cap.
11. Slide push rod with booster return spring through end plate seals and cup.
12. Place booster piston with assembly ring over end of push rod and spring retainer.
13. Compress booster return spring and slide hydraulic piston assembly onto other end of push rod, Fig. B21. Line up hydraulic piston, pull back piston spring, and install pin in push rod hole. Release pressure on booster return spring and remove booster piston assembly.

NOTE: The hook clamp, Fig. B21, may be used to hold booster return spring in compressed position while installing pin. Clamps should hook through one side of holes in end plate and over end of booster piston.

14. Carefully guide hydraulic cylinder and end cap over lip of hydraulic piston cup. Then thread cylinder into end plate finger tight.
15. Remove end plate from vise.

BOOSTER BODY
1. Insert a new booster body seal in groove of end plate. Make sure seal is properly seated.
2. Apply a light coat of vacuum cylinder oil to inner walls of booster body. *Do not use engine oil.*
3. Insert booster piston into booster body (wick end first) being careful not to damage or roll over leather lip. Remove assembly ring.
4. Assemble booster body to end plate by placing body over return spring. Line up scribed marks on body and end plate. Secure body to end plate, using two short bolts at each upper end of body.
5. Install remaining bolts, tightening each evenly and uniformly.
6. Adjust length of hydraulic cylinder to its original position as measured before unit was disassembled, Fig. B25.
7. Align bleeder screw on hydraulic cylinder end fitting with bleeder screw on end plate. Tighten lock nut securely.
8. Install fitting bolt and gasket into end of hydraulic cylinder end cap.

BOOSTER CONTROL BODY
1. Place a new seal on adapter. Position small end of spring in body bore over poppet valve stem and install adapter.

2. Remove body from vise.
3. Place diaphragm washer in recess in end plate, with flat side facing outward.
4. Position diaphragm return spring and diaphragm in booster control body.
5. Position booster control body on end plate. Align diaphragm holes and control body-to-end plate alignment marks. Install bolts and lockwashers and tighten bolts securely.
6. Install a new seal on control body end of air control tube. Connect air control tube to booster control body and to booster body.

SINGLE DIAPHRAGM TYPE HYDROVAC

NOTE: Before disassembling the booster, scribe a line across the two halves of the diaphragm chamber and also across the end plate and control valve housing so that these parts can be reassembled in their original position. When reassembling use all the parts contained in the repair kit regardless of the condition of the old parts.

Reassembly, Fig. B26

1. If the push rod and diaphragm were disassembled, thread the push rod nut on the rod to the limit of the thread. Flat side of nut should face diaphragm. Position guide washer and diaphragm plate on

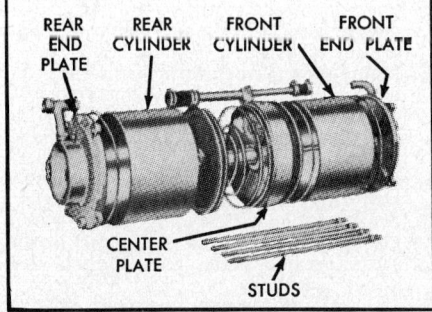

Fig. B18 Power cylinder

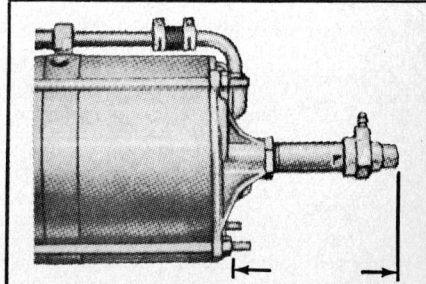

Fig. B19 Hydraulic cylinder adjustment
Atlast models .... 7 3/16″
Modul models .... 8 13/16″
Dreadnaught models .... 10 5/8″

645

BRAKE BOOSTERS

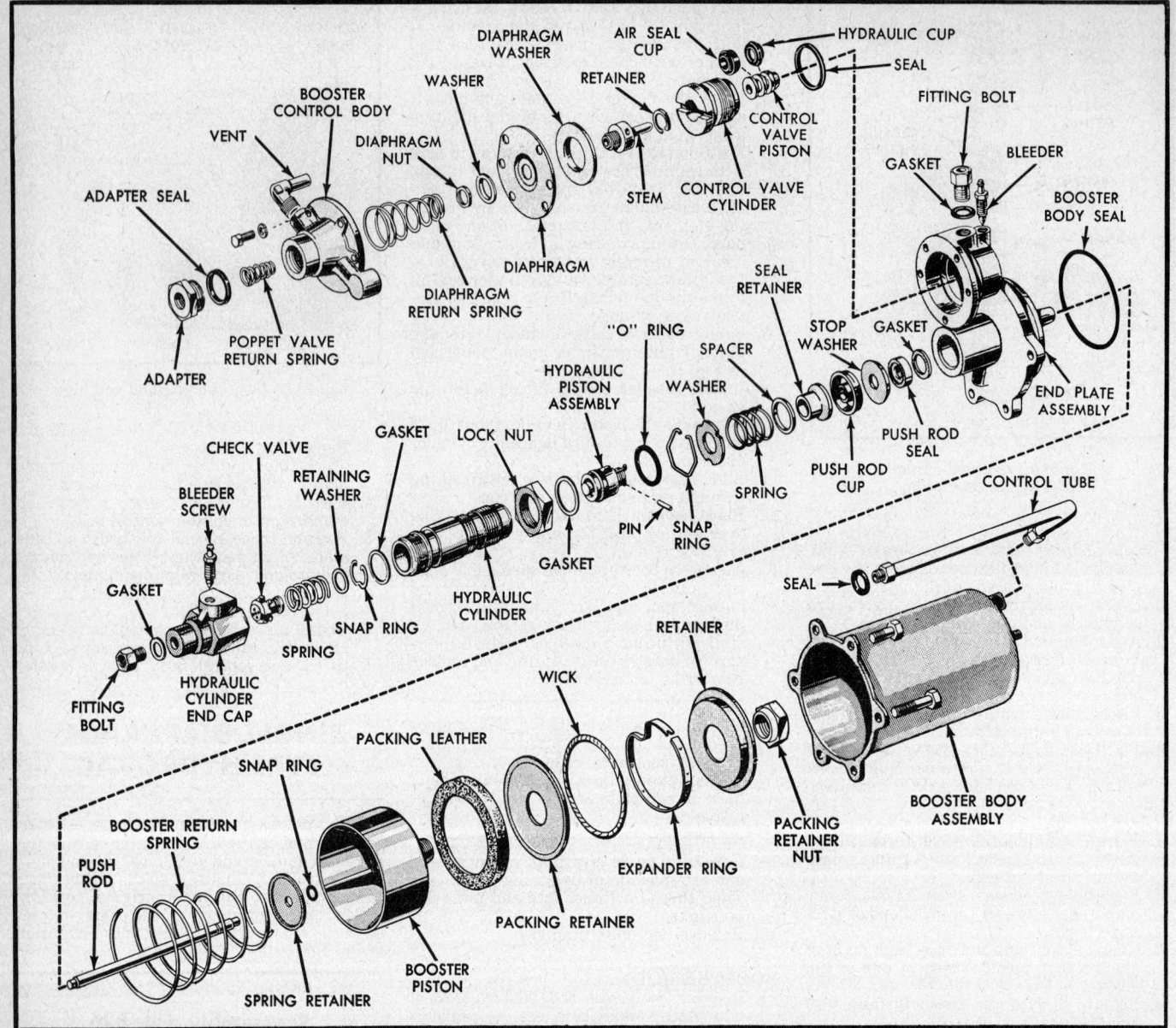

Fig. B20 Air-Pak power unit

push rod. Position diaphragm and cupped washer with concave side of washer next to diaphragm. Install and stake nut in place.
2. If front diaphragm shell bolts were removed, installed bolts, using rubber seals. Stake bolts to shell. Place rear shell on bench. Position push rod and diaphragm on shell. Install front shell and align front and rear shells to scribed mark and to bead on diaphragm. Install clamp band over rim of two shells and tighten securely.
3. Dip control valve piston cup and seal in brake fluid and position cup with lip away from hole end of piston. Position seal on piston with lip flare opposite that of cup flare.
4. Insert piston into fitting. Place seal on fitting, then install fitting on end plate. Install washer and lock ring.
5. Position gasket, diaphragm and spring on end plate.
6. Position control valve housing over spring. Align scribed marks on control valve housing and end plate. Install capscrews and tighten securely.
7. Position spring in valve housing with small end toward valve housing. Install gasket cover and lock ring.
8. Install a new ring seal in groove of end plate.
9. Place small end of return spring over guide washer of diaphragm.
10. Position end plate over return spring and align scribed marks located on end plate and diaphragm chamber. Install nuts and lockwashers and tighten nuts uniformly.
11. Slide hose over control tube and tighten clamp.
12. Install check valve, spring, washer, snap ring, spring retainer and second snap ring in end cap.
13. Install lock nut and new seal on hydraulic cylinder.
14. Dip piston cup in brake fluid. Position cup on piston with lip of cup toward small diameter end of piston.
15. Position return spring over small end of piston. Insert spring and piston into hydraulic cylinder.
16. Install stop washer with chamfered edge toward diaphragm. Install push rod seal with flared edge toward hydraulic cylinder, then the spacer with chamfered edge toward seal, the spring, and guide bearing with serrated end outward. Install snap ring and a new seal in end plate.
17. Screw cylinder into end plate. Align bleeder screw on end cap with bleeder screw on end plate, then tighten lock nut.
18. Position a new copper washer in end cap on check nut and screw hydraulic cylinder into end cap. Tighten cylinder se-

BRAKE BOOSTERS

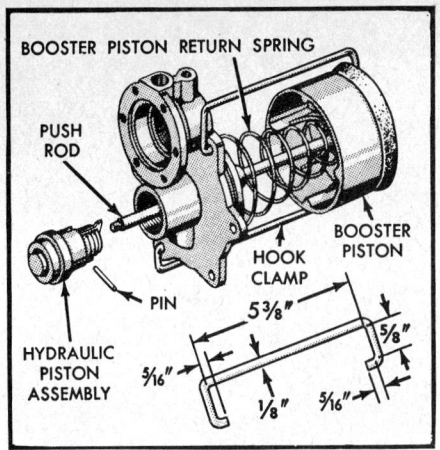

Fig. B21 Push rod pin removal

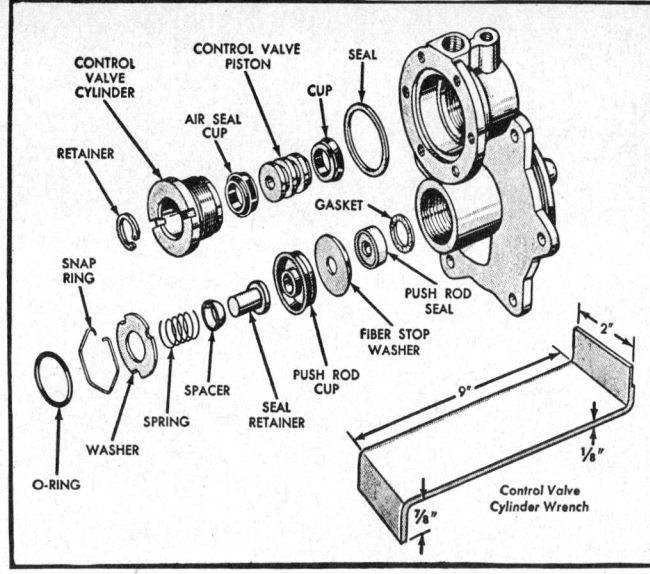

Fig. B22 End plate disassembled

SINGLE DIAPHRAGM TYPE HYDROVAC

NOTE: Before disassembling unit, scribe marks across front and rear shells, across flange of hydraulic cylinder and across flanges of valve body and housing. Diaphragm assembly should be removed only if damaged parts are to be replaced.

Reassembly, Fig. B27

1. Install check valve, spring, washer and snap ring on end fitting, then assemble O-ring and end fitting on hydraulic cylinder.
2. Install cups, back to back on control valve piston, then assemble piston, diaphragm retainer and valve diaphragm.

   NOTE: Make certain that inner bead of diaphragm is seated in piston groove.

3. If removed, install small coil end of poppet spring over valve poppet and install parts in valve body. Assemble valve seal (flat side facing up) and poppet retainer on stem of valve poppet. Invert valve body and rest valve poppet on a small wood block. Using a soft hammer, tap small retainer lightly until retainer snap locks on stem. Assemble plastic cover in valve body.
4. Install spring retainer (flange facing down) on spring in valve body then place piston and diaphragm on spring retainer and press outer bead of diaphragm into groove of valve body.
5. Coat control valve piston with brake fluid and assemble piston in control valve cylinder. Align scribe marks on valve body, install and tighten screws.
6. Place new seal on clean wood block with rubber side facing down. Rest push rod vertically on seal stem and strike threaded end of push rod with soft hammer to seat stem in push rod.

   NOTE: Make certain that shoulders of push rod and seal are in contact.

7. Install onto push rod the snap ring, retainer, washer, guide bearing with O-ring in groove, seal cup and seal retainer on push rod.
8. Install piston onto push rod and secure with retaining pin and ring. Coat cup with brake fluid and install it on piston.
9. Assemble nut, washer, diaphragm plate, diaphragm, washer and nut on push rod.
10. Install the gasket in groove in flange of hydraulic cylinder, aligning the cut-out in front shell with port in hydraulic cylinder, install and tighten screws.
11. Install large coil end first of return spring against diaphragm plate. Coat hydraulic cylinder bore with brake fluid and work piston, cups and seal into cylinder bore.
12. Roll back outer edge of diaphragm and press against diaphragm to compress return spring. Guide parts on push rod into cylinder bore and secure with snap ring.

NOTE: Make certain that snap ring is securely seated before relieving pressure on spring.

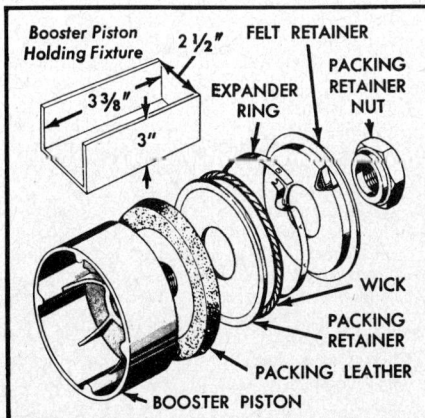

Fig. B23 Booster piston disassembled

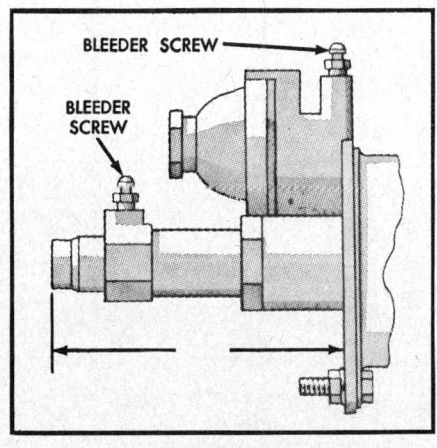

Fig. B24 Hydraulic cylinder length setting

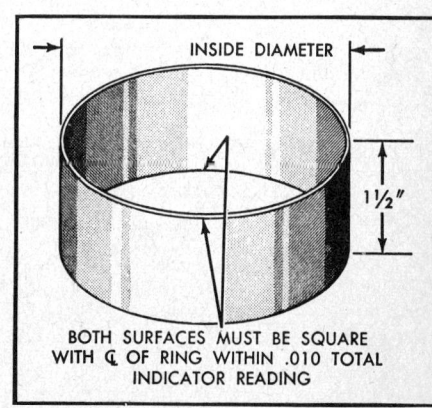

Fig. B25 Assembly ring made from old booster body

647

BRAKE BOOSTERS

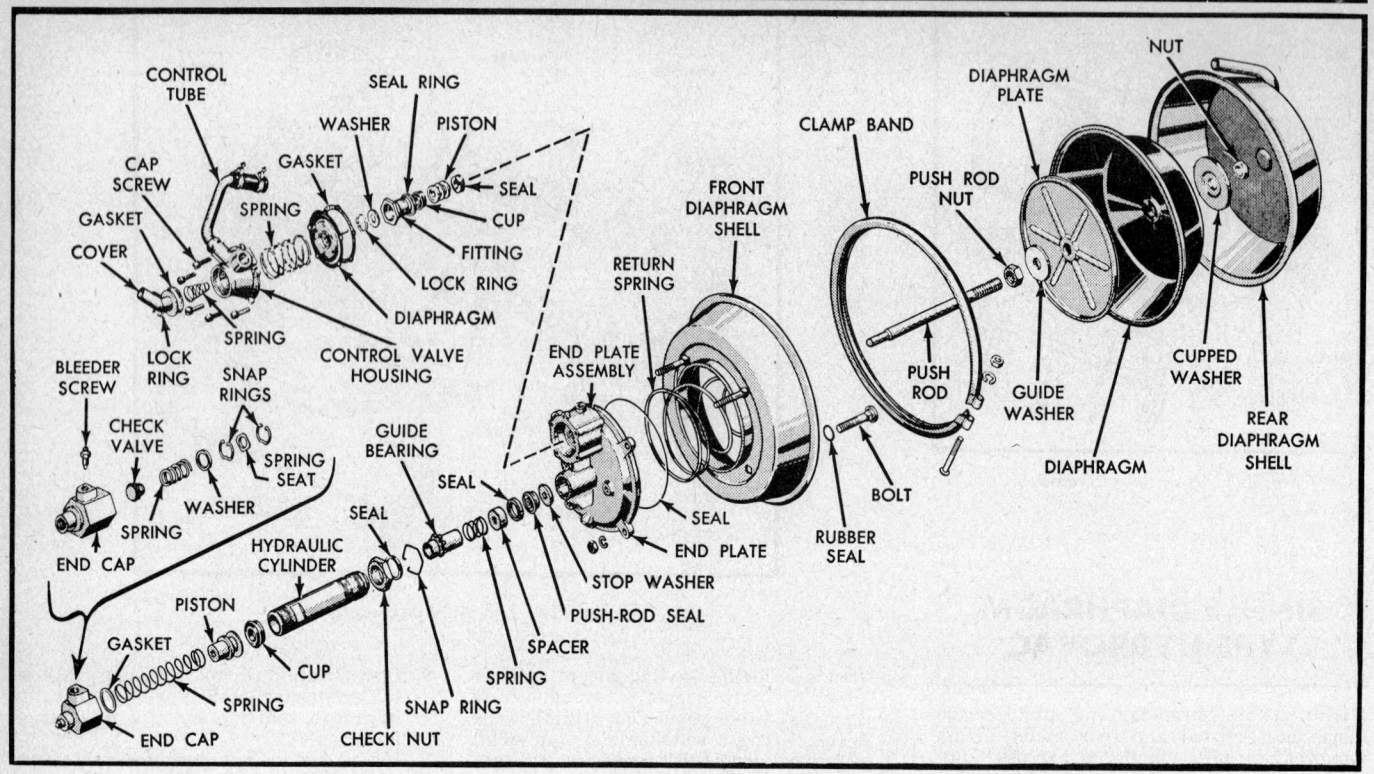

Fig. B26 Diaphragm type Hydrovac disassembled

13. Lightly coat both sides of diaphragm with silicone lubricant or talcum powder then align scribe marks on front and rear shells and press rear shell flange and diaphragm bead into place against front shell flange.
14. Install band clamp nut and bolt. Tap band lightly with a rawhide mallet while torquing nut to 30-40 in. lbs.
15. Install a new seal on vacuum tube and install tube and hose on real shell tube and torque tube nut to 80-120 in. lbs.

SINGLE DIAPHRAGM TYPE

NOTE: Before disassembling unit, scribe marks on rear diaphragm housing, clamp band and front housing, on front diaphragm housing and hydraulic cylinder and on control valve housing and hydraulic cylinder body.

CAUTION: When removing diaphragm and plate assembly, be very careful as outer edge of diaphragm plate is very sharp and can cause serious cuts if not handled properly.

Reassembly, Fig. B28

1. Place control valve spring on body and install in housing, then install valve seat from other end and secure it with valve cap (press fit).
2. Install seal ring and retainer in housing and secure with snap ring, then assemble diaphragm retainer, diaphragm, diaphragm washer, control piston and cup seal.
3. Install control valve diaphragm assembly in cylinder body and place control valve diaphragm return spring into housing.
4. Install housing and spring on cylinder body and tighten the four bolts alternately.
5. Install block vee on piston and valve insert in valve body, then assemble valve body, piston and push rod and secure with snap ring.
6. Install spacer and O-ring on push rod and vee block in bushing, then install bushing and washer (where required) on push rod.
7. Install push rod, piston and bushing assembly in hydraulic cylinder body. Secure with snap ring or retainer (torque retainer to 15-20 ft. lbs.) and retaining ring.
8. Place gasket, front housing and reinforcement plate on hydraulic cylinder body and tighten the two bolts.
9. Install diaphragm return spring, spacer, diaphragm, plate assembly and lock nut on push rod.
10. Install tube and nut assembly on control valve and install O-ring.
11. Position rear housing against front housing and secure with clamp band, then install mounting bracket on hydraulic cylinder body (or check valve end cap, if used).

DASH MOUNTED, TANDEM DIAPHRAGM TYPE

NOTE: Before disassembling unit, scribe marks across front and rear shells of power section and across mounting bracket.

Reassembly, Fig. B29

1. Place rear shell on wood blocks, with studs down, and press new seal, with plastic bearing face first, into rear shell.

NOTE: The top outside flange of seal should be pressed in .305 inch (about 5/16 inch) below flat shell surface next to seal cavity.

2. Place front diaphragm on front plate. Apply a light film of silicone lubricant on outside surface of front plate hub and liberally on center plate bore seal, then install large O-ring seal on the center plate and press O-ring against the four bosses around outside diameter of center plate.
3. Carefully guide center plate and seal assembly (seal side first) onto front plate hub. Apply a light coat of silicone lubricant on front and rear bearing surfaces of valve plunger, avoiding the rubber grommet inside plunger. Assemble valve plunger around rubber bumper and set spring and plunger assembly in recess of front plate hub, with grommet side facing up.
4. With vacuum seal firmly placed against shoulder on outside of front plate hub, set rear plate with threaded bore facing down, over the valve plunger and screw rear plate into front plate hub. Place a 1 1/16 inch hex stock bar in vise and place plate assembly with front plate down, on hex bar. Using air channel slot or rear plate edges, torque plates to 120-180 in. lbs.
5. Remove plate assembly from vise and install rear diaphragm onto rear plate and over lip of center plate. Assemble

BRAKE BOOSTERS

rear diaphragm spring retainer over rear diaphragm and lip of center plate, then press retainer onto center plate until it seats against shoulder of center plate.

6. Coat inside wall of rear shell with talcum powder and liberally apply silicone lubricant to bearing seal in rear shell and to the scalloped cut-outs on edge of front shell.

NOTE: When assembling diaphragm and plate assembly in rear shell, the rear diaphragm and center plate lugs must be aligned between lances on rear shell.

7. With valve rod eyelet clamped in a vise, carefully guide valve housing sleeve through bearing seal inside of the rear shell, maintaining diaphragm and plates in correct alignment. Ease outer rim of front diaphragm into rear shell until outer rim of front diaphragm is under each of the retaining lances on rear shell.

8. Place large end of a diaphragm spring over front plate hub and position rear shell onto spring so that scribe marks will be aligned when the shells are twist-locked together (use a flat bar on rear shell to turn shells).

NOTE: Make certain that cut-outs on front shell are aligned with retaining lances on rear shell.

9. Guide rim of front shell into rear shell and press firmly downward on rear shell until edge of front shell clears the lances on rear shell, then twist the rear shell clockwise in relation to front shell until contact's with stops. Remove unit from vise.

10. Liberally apply silicone lubricant to entire surface of rubber reaction disc and to piston end of hydraulic push rod, then place reaction disc on piston end of push rod. Apply a light coat of silicone lubricant on rod of push rod, keeping lubricant away from threads.

NOTE: Do not allow lubricant on the adjustment screw or threads.

11. Install push rod with reaction disc on piston end into front plate hub cavity, then twist push rod to make sure that reaction disc is seated in front plate hub and air bubbles are eliminated between hub, disc and push rod piston.

12. Assemble seal (support plate side first) over adjustment screw end of push rod, then press seal into front shell recess until seal bottoms against shell. If vacuum check valve was removed, coat a new grommet with alcohol and press it into front shell, making certain that grommet is seated in shell.

13. Coat shoulder of check valve and inside of grommet with alcohol and press check valve into grommet until entire circumference of check valve flange bears against grommet.

14. Coat poppet valve with alcohol and assemble it into valve housing with small end of poppet first, then coat the poppet retainer with alcohol and assemble it into the housing with flange facing out. Press in against retainer to make certain that shoulder on the retainer is positioned inside poppet.

15. Assemble retainer, valve silencers and filters and valve return spring over ball end of valve rod, then coat rubber grommet and ball end of valve rod with alcohol. Guide the spring, filters and silencers into valve housing and assemble the ball end of valve rod in valve plunger. Using a soft mallet, tap end of valve rod to lock ball end of rod in valve plunger grommet, then press filters into place and assemble retainer on end of valve housing, being careful not to chip the plastic.

16. Coat small diameter of dust guard with alcohol and assemble over valve rod eye, using care not to damage the guard. Press guard against valve housing and seat large diameter end of guard over scalloped flange of rear flange.

17. Using gauge shown in Fig. B30, check

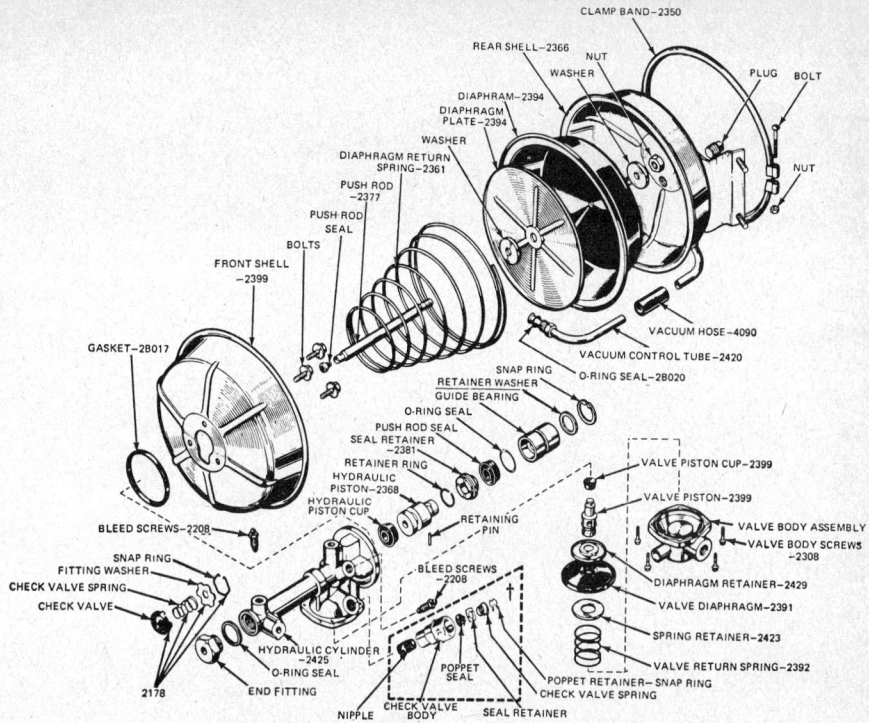

Fig. B27 Frame mountd single diaphragm type, disassembled

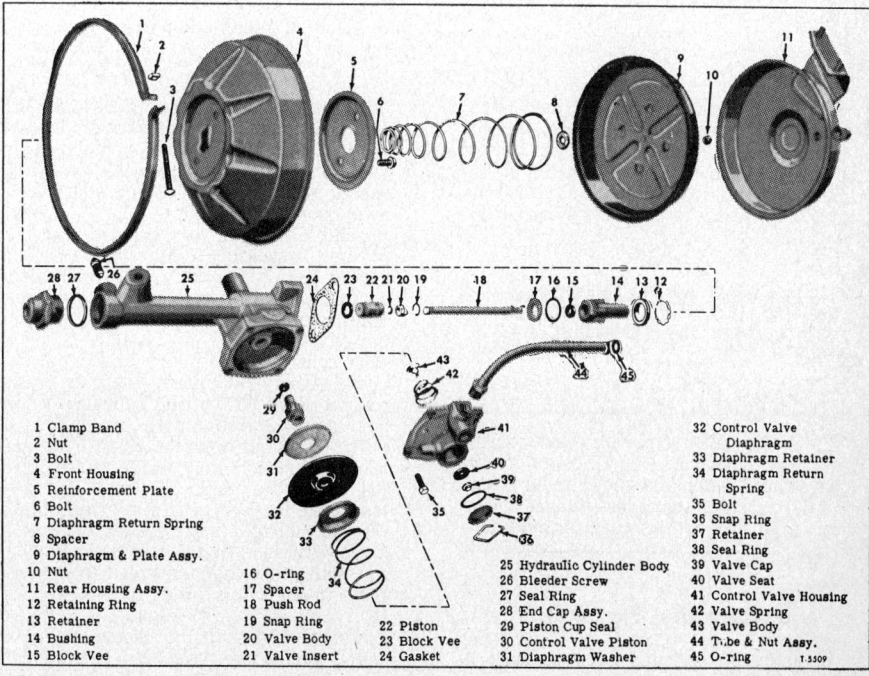

Fig. B28 Frame mounted single diaphragm type, disassembled

BRAKE BOOSTERS

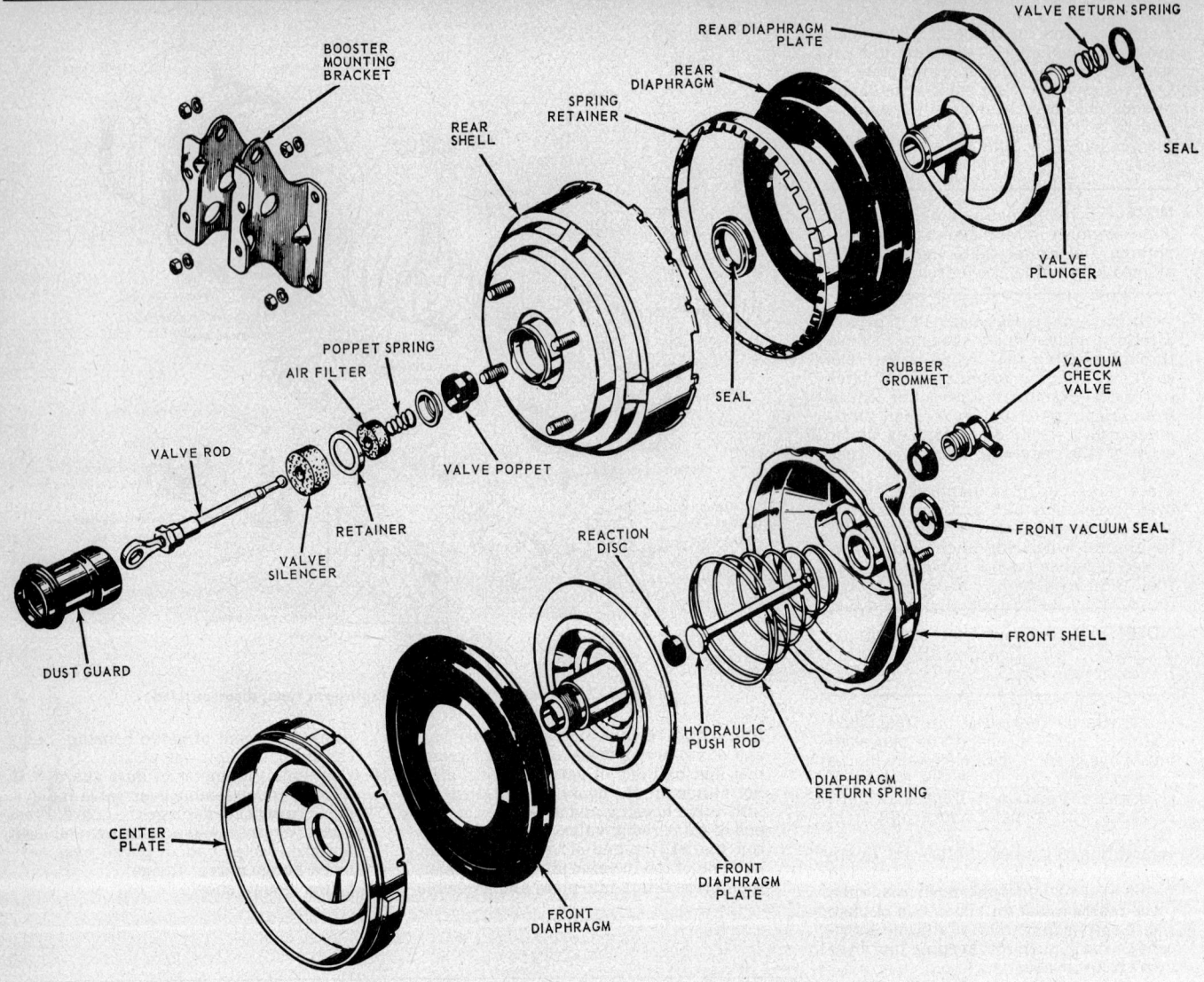

Fig. B29 Dash mounted tandem diaphragm type, disassembled

distance from end of hydraulic push rod to master cylinder mounting face of front shell. If this distance is not within .880–.895 inch, hold the serrated end of the push rod with pliers and turn the adjusting screw to obtain the correct dimension.

FRAME MOUNTED TANDEM DIAPHRAGM TYPE

NOTE: Before disassembling unit, scribe marks across both clamping rings, on shells, across top surface of hydraulic cylinder flange and onto front shell and across flanges of control valve housing below hydraulic cylinder.

Reassembly, Fig. B31

1. Assemble piston cups back to back in grooves of control valve piston.
2. Slide diaphragm retainer (flange side first) onto other end of control valve piston. Coat inside diameter of diaphragm with alcohol then slide it over end of piston and seat it against retainer. Assemble spring retainer with flange side facing away from diaphragm.
3. Assemble control valve piston and diaphragm assembly onto valve return spring, then place spring into valve body around vacuum poppet guides and press diaphragm bead firmly into groove on flange of body.
4. Coat control valve piston and cups with brake fluid and insert them into the control valve bore of the hydraulic cylinder. Align scribe marks on flanges of valve body and housing. Install the four retaining screws and torque to 40–60 in. lbs.
5. Assemble washer, rear diaphragm plate, rear diaphragm and washer on end of shaft with hole. Install nut on shaft. Grip nut with a vise then insert a drift through holes in shaft and torque nut to 10–15 ft. lbs.
6. Install O-ring seal into groove in hub of center shells, then coat seal, bearing surface and outside of rear shaft with silicone lubricant.
7. Install rear shaft through bearing hub and seal of center shell, then assemble washer, front diaphragm and diaphragm plate on end of shaft, install and torque nut to 10–15 ft. lbs.
8. To install a new seal on push rod, place seal on wood block with rubber side facing down. Rest end of push rod vertically over seal stem and using a rawhide mallet, strike end of push rod to seat the seal.

NOTE: Make certain that shoulders of seal and rod are in contact.

9. Coat push rod, push rod bearing and all hydraulic parts with brake fluid, then install support plate and piston stop assembly, push rod bearing with O-ring installed in its groove, push rod cup and seal retainer onto push rod.
10. Install snap ring on piston, but not into its groove, then connect piston to the push rod using valve plunger pin and slide piston snap ring into its groove to cover the plunger pin hole. Coat piston cup with brake fluid and install it onto the piston.
11. Install residual check valve, check valve

BRAKE BOOSTERS

spring and washer into the end fitting then install end fitting and washer on hydraulic cylinder and torque to 50–85 ft. lbs.
12. Place ring seal in groove around flange of hydraulic cylinder and slide small diameter end of diaphragm spring over piston end of push rod and coat hydraulic cylinder bore and piston with brake fluid.
13. Bottom small coil end of return spring against spring retainer on push rod and place large coil end of spring inside front shell with hydraulic piston inserted through hole in shell.
14. Slightly compress return spring, then guide hydraulic piston, seal retainer, push rod cup and push rod bearing into cylinder bore, then seat hydraulic cylinder flange against the front shell with ring seal in place.
15. Place support plate and stop assembly on other side of shell and install the three bolts that retain stop assembly and the front shell to the hydraulic cylinder. Relieve pressure on spring.
16. Using talcum powder or silicone lubricant, lightly coat both sides of front and rear diaphragm beads, then guide rear shaft onto push rod and align scribe marks on shell flanges next to front diaphragm. Press shells together to seat bead of front diaphragm in shell flanges around the circumference.
17. Install clamping ring, bolt and nut on shell flanges, then using a rawhide mallet, lightly tap ring while torquing nut to 30–40 in. lbs.
18. With scribe marks aligned on rear shells and rear diaphragm bead in shell flanges around the circumference, press rear shells together and install the clamping ring onto the shell flanges. Torque nut in same manner as in previous step.
19. Connect hose tee to control tube on rear shell and onto hose nipple on center shell using hose clamps, then assemble ring seal on end of control tube to hose tee with a hose clamp. Connect tube nut into control valve body and torque tube nut to 80–120 in. lbs.
20. If pipe plug was removed, install it in rear shell and torque to 12–20 ft. lbs. If bleeder screws were removed, install them into hydraulic cylinder and torque to 10–15 ft. lbs.

NOTE: Tube seat inserts in input and output hydraulic ports should not be removed, except if replacing a damaged tube seat.

DUO-VAC DUAL DIAPHRAGM TYPE

Disassembly Notes Fig. B32

1. Scribe one mark across left and fitting outlet adapter and hydraulic cylinder in front of bleed screw. Scribe another mark on top of hydraulic cylinder flange and on front shell. Finally, scribe one mark on top of front shell across clamp band onto center shell.
2. Mark opposite half of power unit in same places as above, using two scribe marks instead of one at each location.
3. If control valve is to be disassembled, scribe a mark across air inlet tube base plate and flange of valve cover, across flanges of valve cover, body and across flange and bosses of mounting bracket and valve body.

NOTE: Do not disassemble power diaphragm, or push rod assembly unless required for replacement of damaged parts.

Reassembly, Fig. B32

Control Valve

1. Install mounting bracket onto the control valve with scribe marks aligned, then place control valve mounting bracket in vise with bore facing up.
2. Coat cups with brake fluid, assemble them in pairs and back to back onto pistons. Coat control valve bore with silicone lubricant then coat piston and cups with brake fluid and install them into bore, (either end first). Insert cups into bore and press piston to the bottom.
3. Coat other piston with brake fluid and install it flat end first into bore until it bottoms against first piston. Install stop washer and secure with a snap ring.
4. Install poppet assembly in valve cover through the air inlet side. Install small coil end of conical spring around top of metal stem of small atmospheric poppet. Install large return spring (light blue) on large atmospheric poppet.
5. Coat gasket with powdered graphite and install it against shoulder of air inlet opening. Seat air inlet tube and plate assembly on plate and valve cover. Secure tube and plate with snap ring.

NOTE: Make certain that all corners of snap ring are seated in groove.

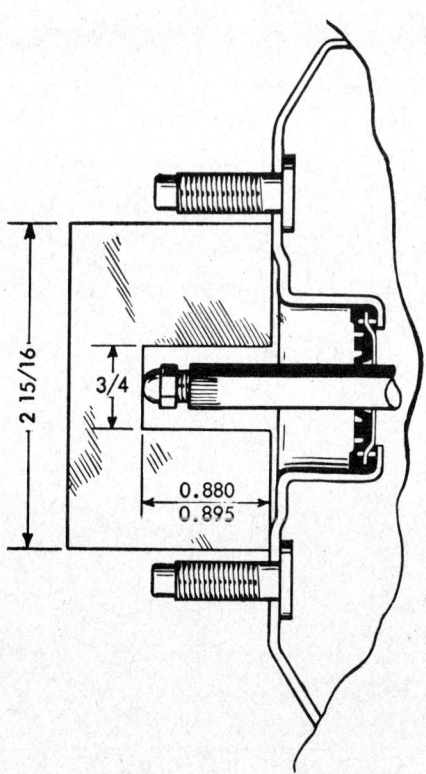

Fig. B30 Push rod gauge dimension and adjustment

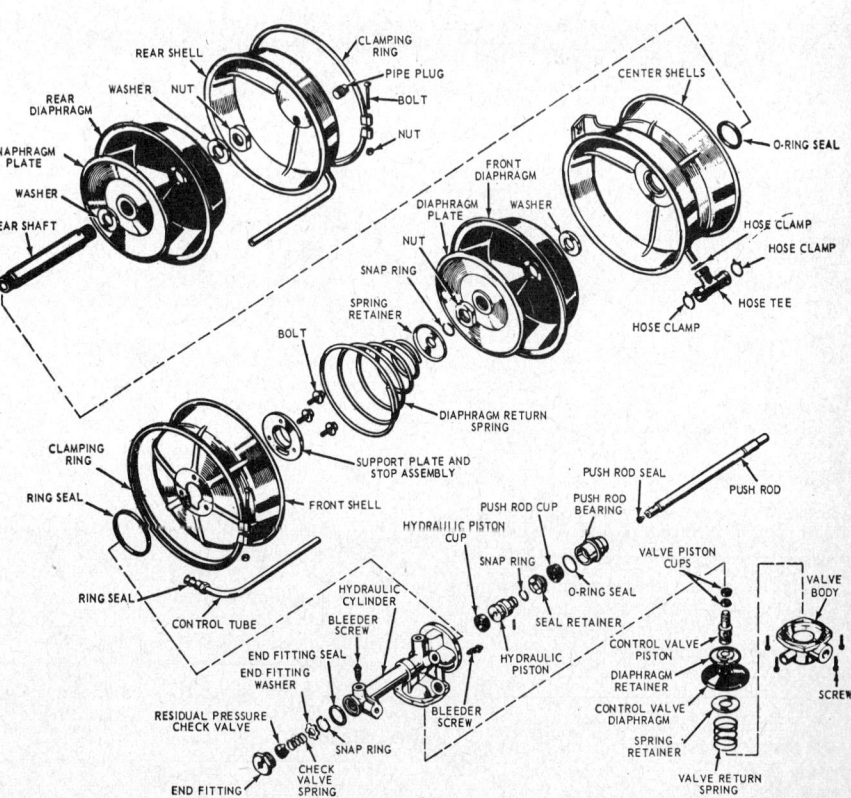

Fig. B31 Frame mounted tandem diaphragm type, disassembled

BRAKE BOOSTERS

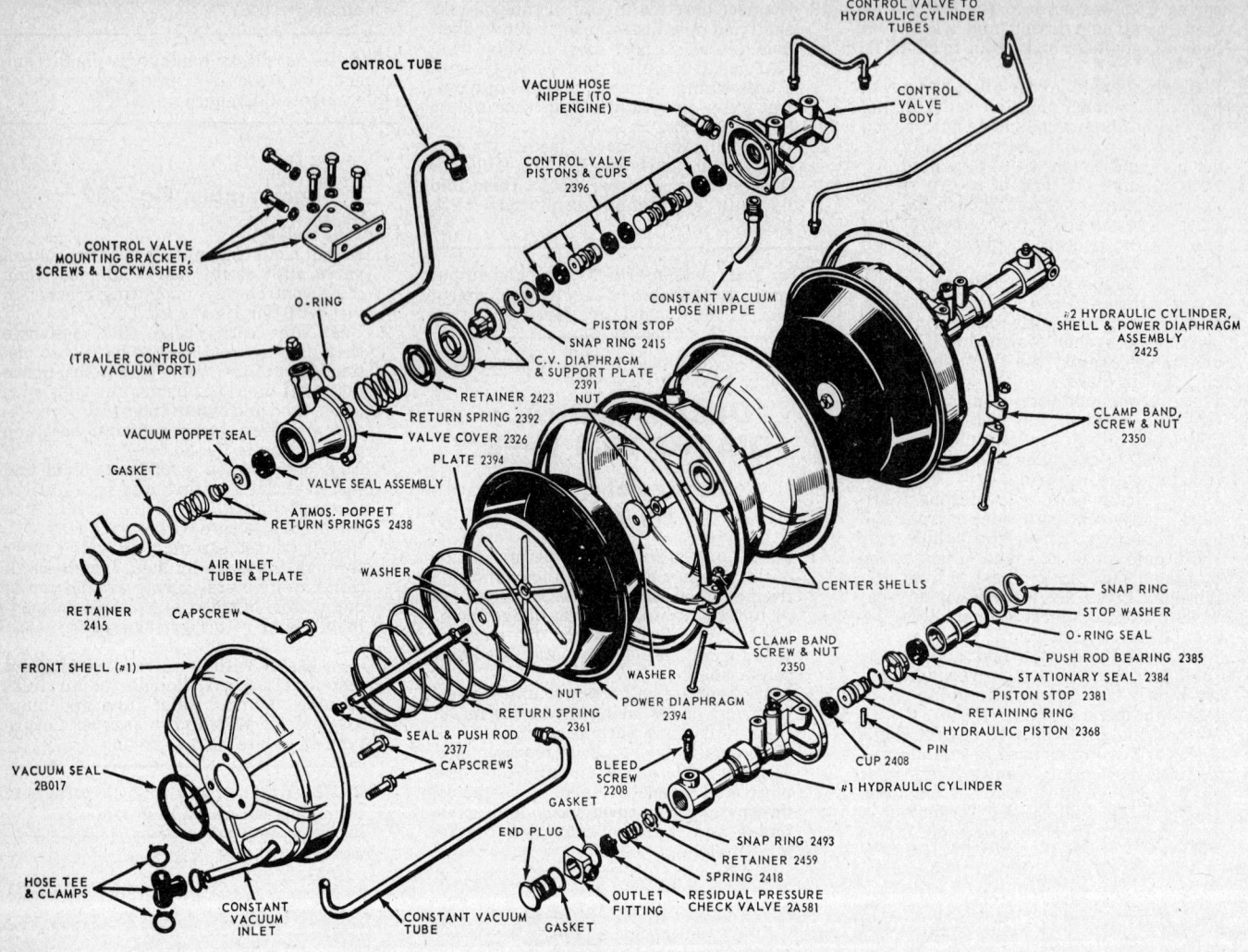

Fig. B32 Frame mounted Duo-Vac dual diaphragm type, disassembled

6. Coat inside diameter of control valve with brake fluid and slide diaphragm onto hub of plastic plate. Both heads of diaphragm should be facing up with stem of plate facing down. Install metal diaphragm and spring retainer onto hub with retainer flanges facing up and bottom of retainer holding inner bead of diaphragm in groove around plate hub.
7. Coat outer bead of diaphragm with brake fluid and slide diaphragm return spring (orange) onto hub of plate. Bottom spring in metal retainer and install diaphragm, plate, retainer and spring assembly into control valve cover spring end first. Seat bead of diaphragm in groove around cover flange, install four cover to valve body screws and torque to 60–90 in. lbs.

NOTE: Make certain that stem of plastic diaphragm plate bottoms in cavity in front control valve piston and that scribe marks on flanges of cover and body are aligned.

8. Remove assembly from vise and install O-ring seal in groove of control tube port.

Hydraulic Cylinder
1. Install new push rod seal if removed. Place seal on wood block with rubber side of seal facing down. Hold push rod above seal with hole in push rod resting on stem of seal. Tap threaded end of push rod with soft mallet until end of push rod bottoms against shoulder of seal.
2. If removed, assemble power diaphragm parts on push rod, screw the thick nut (if used) with undercut side first onto push rod, until it bottoms on threads. Install washer, support plate (curled flange side first), power diaphragm, washer and nut on push rod. Grip nut or flat on push rod and torque end nut to 160–200 in. lbs.
3. Coat hydraulic piston and bearing parts with brake fluid and install them onto push rod from the seal end in the following order; snap ring, stop washer, push rod guide bearing with O-ring in its outer groove and seal cavity end last. Followed by the, bottom (flat side) of stationary seal in guide bearing, piston stop with grooved side last, retainer ring and the hydraulic piston and cup assembly.

NOTE: The lips of seal and piston cup must face the hydraulic piston end of the push rod.

4. Install pin through holes in piston and push rod, secure pin with retainer ring. Seat ring securely in groove around hydraulic piston.
5. Install new square vacuum seal into groove around hydraulic cylinder flange, then align front shell with scribe marks on hydraulic cylinder flange. Install three retaining screws and torque to 130–230 in. lbs.
6. Coat bore of hydraulic cylinder, piston, seal and bearing parts with brake fluid. Grip hydraulic cylinder collar in vise with bleed screw facing up, cylinder horizontal and hub facing out. Install large coil end first, of power diaphragm return spring over hydraulic piston and push rod and seat spring against diaphragm support plate.
7. Lift assembly, then seat small end of spring against front shell and carefully guide hydraulic piston assembly, piston stop, stationary seal and push rod guide bearing with O-ring into bore of hydraulic cylinder. Press firmly against diaphragm to compress diaphragm return spring, then seat stop washer against push rod guide bearing and secure it with snap ring inside groove in hub of hydraulic cylinder.

NOTE: Before releasing pressure on diaphragm, make certain that snap ring is properly seated to avoid personal injury

BRAKE BOOSTERS

and damage to parts.

8. Install residual pressure check valve, spring and retainer into end fitting and secure with snap ring, then install end of spring inside check valve against metal disc and bottom rubber face of valve in the fitting. Place retainer washer with indented center flange inside outer spring coil and seat snap ring securely into groove.
9. Slide new copper gasket on end fitting followed by correctly marked (1 or 2 scribe marks) side outlet adapter and a second new copper gasket. Install end fitting assembly into output end of hydraulic cylinder, aligning the scribe marks on outlet and cylinder, torque the fitting to 50-85 ft. lbs.
10. Repeat above steps, to reassemble the other hydraulic cylinder.

Complete Unit

1. With diaphragm facing up, grip hydraulic cylinder collar and front shell assembly in vise. Lightly coat bead of diaphragm, flanges of front shell and center shell with talcum powder or silicone lubricant.
2. Press diaphragm bead into front shell flange and seat flange of center shell against it.

NOTE: Make certain that bead is fully seated around circumference against both shell flanges.

3. Align matching scribe marks on shell flanges, clamp band, screw, part number tag and nut, As viewed from end fitting of hydraulic cylinder with bleed screw at 12 o'clock. The opening in clamp band must be at 7 o'clock, the vacuum inlet tube on front shell must be at 4:30 o'clock and the control vacuum inlet port (atmospheric inlet) on center shell must be next to the clamp band. Torque clamp nut to 30-40 in. lbs., then using a rawhide mallet, tap on band at three points 90 degrees apart and retorque clamp nut to 30-40 in. lbs.

NOTE: If vacuum ports and tubes are not in locations described above, disassemble shells and remove hydraulic cylinder. Rotate shell to correct position and repeat steps 1, 2 and 3. If a vertical position of unit makes assembly of #2 hydraulic cylinder difficult, reposition unit, by positioning collar of #1 cylinder in a horizontal position or by positioning collar of #2 cylinder in a vertical position.

4. Coat bead of #2 diaphragm and shell flanges as described above and assemble #2 hydraulic cylinder to center shell with bead of diaphragm fully seated against both shell flanges around circumferences and with matching scribe marks aligned on shell flanges.
5. Install clamp band with opening aligned with the other clamp band opening and torque clamp nut to 30-40 in. lbs. tap on band as in step 3 and retorque clamp nut to 30-40 in. lbs.
6. Install control valve assembly, bolt and washer onto the #1 hydraulic cylinder.

NOTE: The valve must be on same side as the 12 inch vacuum tube extending from #1 front shell.

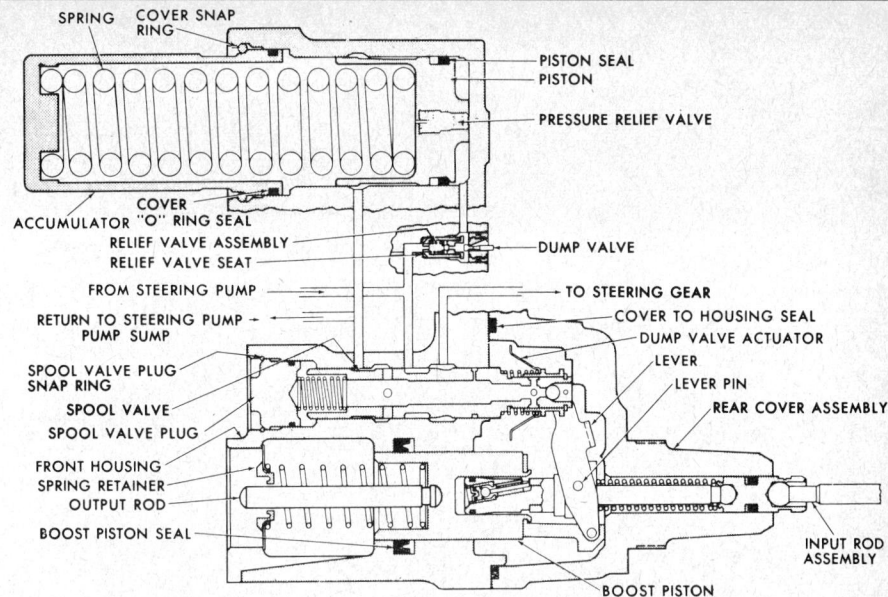

Fig. B33 Sectional view of Bendix Hydro-Boost with spring type accumulator

7. Connect short piece of 14 inch hydraulic tubing from top rear port (next to front shell) of control valve body with the input port on top of #1 hydraulic cylinder. Torque both tube nuts to 135-150 in. lbs.
8. Connect long piece of 14 inch hydraulic tubing from top front port of control valve body with the input port on top of #2 hydraulic cylinder. Torque tube nuts to 135-150 in. lbs.
9. Connect the 58 inch tube to control tube port of valve cover, sliding end of tube through O-ring. Connect tube end with control vacuum port on top of center shell and torque tube nut to 100-140 in. lbs.
10. Install short part of 12 inch tube with tube seated in port on bottom of control valve body. Torque tube nut to 80-120 in. lbs. Install hose tee and hose clamp on this tube and the 12 inch tube extending from front shell. Secure hose tee with clamps.
11. Connect the longer piece of the 12 inch tube into hose tee and secure with clamp. Attach tube nut end to the vacuum port on #2 shell and torque tube nut to 80-120 in. lbs.

NOTE: If any tubing does not reach from

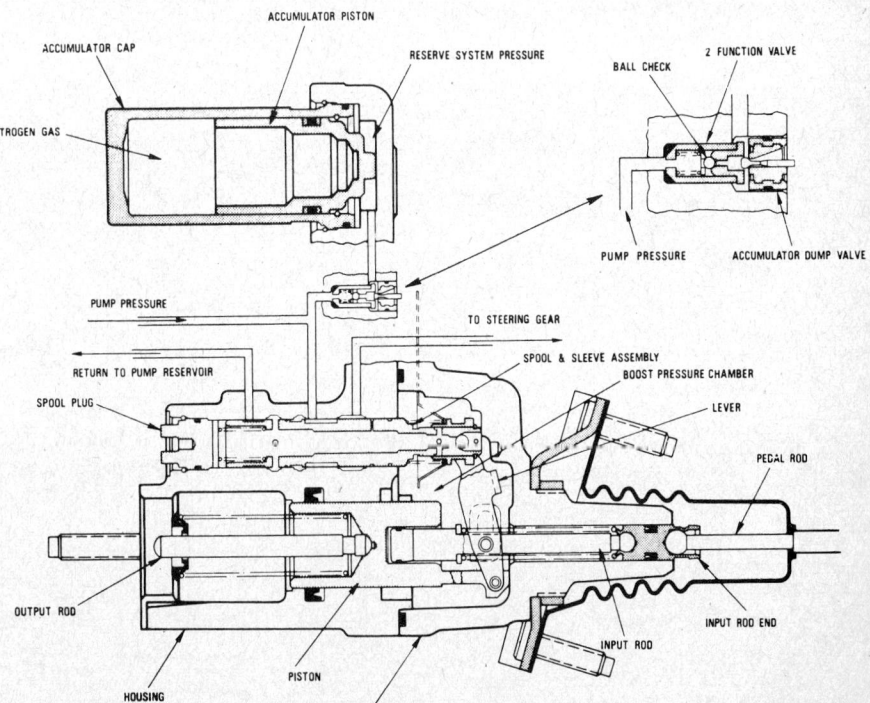

Fig. B34 Sectional view of Bendix Hydro-Boost with pneumatic type accumulator

653

BRAKE BOOSTERS

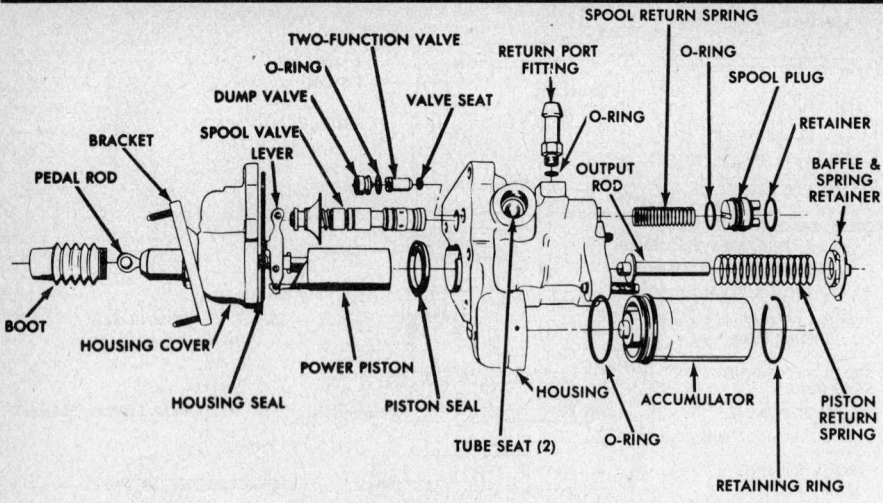

Fig. B35 Hydro-Boost unit disassembled

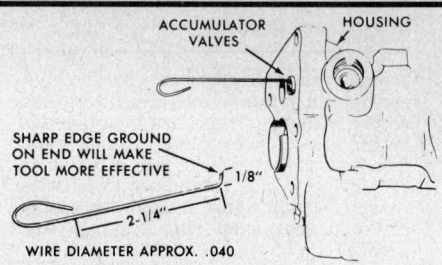

Fig. B36 Removing accumulator valves

control valve ports to power unit ports, check steps 1 through 6 to determine whether shell or control valve parts must be repositioned.

HYDRO-BOOST

Description

The Hydro-Boost system, Figs. B33 and B34, provides an additional cylinder in the brake system. This cylinder contains no brake fluid. The Hydro-Boost cylinder is hydraulically operated, by pressurized fluid from the power steering pump, providing power assist to operate a dual master cylinder brake system.

The booster is composed of two sections; the linkage section and the power section, Fig. B34.

On early units, a spring accumulator incorporated in the Hydro-Boost, Fig. B33, stores sufficient fluid under pressure, to provide several power assisted stops in the event that pressure fluid from the power steering pump is stopped for any reason (such as a ruptured line). On late units, a pneumatic accumulator is used, Fig. B34.

The booster is designed so that if a total absence of power assist occurs, the brakes can be applied manually, but somewhat greater pressure on the brake pedal is required.

Booster Disassemble, Fig. B35

1. Secure booster mounting bracket in a vise with pedal rod facing downward.
2. With a small screwdriver, disengage tabs of baffle and spring retainer from ledge inside opening near master cylinder mounting flange of the booster. Remove retainer piston return springs and output rod from opening.
3. Position drain pan under booster housing, then remove five housing to housing cover attaching bolts.
4. Carefully lift housing from cover, leaving spool valve and power piston assembly attached to housing cover.

NOTE: If accumulator is to be serviced, refer to Accumulator Service.

5. Remove power piston seal from housing bore.
6. Remove seal from housing cover.
7. If accumulator valve is to be removed, fabricate tool from .040 in. diameter wire as shown in Fig. B36. Remove dump valve by catching tool under pin guide near center of valve, then remove two function valve and seat, Fig. B37.
8. Remove hose fitting O-ring, if necessary.
9. Remove spool valve and spring from power piston assembly by rotating valve out of lever arm. Refer to Fig. B38, and inspect spool valve. If spool valve is found to be defective, the valve assembly must be replaced.
10. Inspect power piston. If scratches can be felt with finger nail, replace power piston.
11. Using diagonal cutters, cut off end of connecting pin, then push pin out using a suitable punch and remove piston.
12. If necessary, remove spool valve plug retaining ring and spool valve plug.

Cleaning and Inspection

1. Clean all parts in a suitable solvent being careful to avoid losing small parts.
2. Inspect valve spool and valve spool bore in booster housing for corrosion, nicks, scoring or other damage. Discoloration of the spool or bore, particularly in the grooves is not harmful.
3. If the valve spool or the spool bore has nicks or scoring that can be felt with a fingernail, particularly on the lands, the spool and housing should be replaced as an assembly, Fig. B38.

NOTE: The clearance between the valve spool and the spool bore of the housing is important. Because of this, the spool and housing make are made as a selective assembly and therefore can only be replaced as an assembly.

4. Inspect the input rod and piston assembly for corrosion, nicks, scoring or excessive wear. If the piston is damaged, the input rod and piston assembly should be replaced.
5. Inspect piston bore in booster housing for corrosion, nicks, scoring or other damage. If the bore is damaged, the valve spool and housing should be replaced as an assembly.

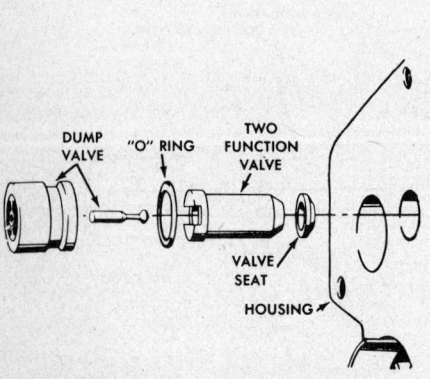

Fig. B37 Accumulator valves

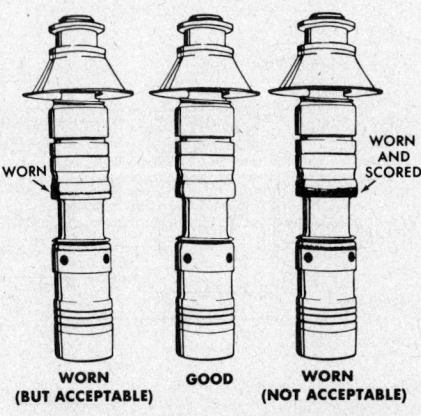

Fig. B38 Spool valve inspection

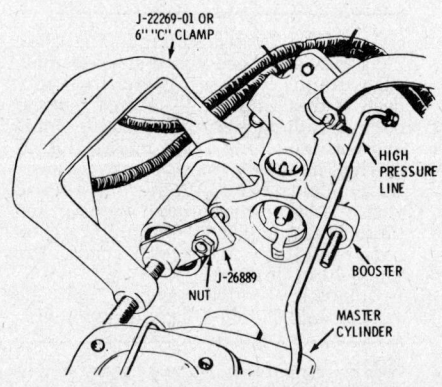

Fig. B41 Removing pneumatic type accumulator

BRAKE BOOSTERS

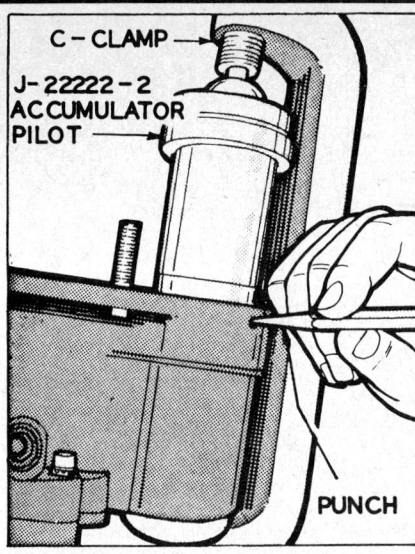

Fig. B39 Unseating accumulator retaining snap ring. Spring type units

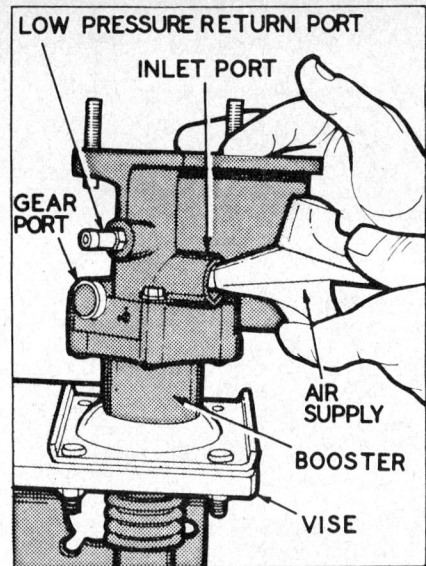

Fig. B40 Removing accumulator piston with compressed air. Spring type units

Booster Assemble, Fig. B35

CAUTION: Be sure to keep all parts clean until reassembly. Re-wash at reassembly if there is any occasion to doubt cleanliness. Lubricate all seals and metal friction parts with power steering fluid. Whenever the booster is disassembled, all seals, spiral snap rings, check valve and ball should be replaced. All of these parts are included in a seal kit.

1. If removed, install spool valve and O-ring, then push spool valve in and install snap ring.
2. Slide connecting bracket on piston into small yoke in lever and push pin through hole.
3. Using tool No. J-26410, mushroom end of pin. Ensure lever moves freely with no binding.
4. Secure booster mounting bracket in a vise with pedal rod facing downward.
5. Install housing seal in groove on housing cover.
6. Install power piston seal in housing with flat side facing toward master cylinder mounting flange.
7. If removed, install O-ring and return hose fitting.
8. If removed, install accumulator valve seat with cup side facing upward, Fig. B37. The seat can be forced to the bottom of the bore by installing the two function valve. Insert dump valve over two function valve making certain that dump valve plunger is held in position until installation is completed.
9. Insert spool valve spring and spool valve assembly into housing bore.
10. Pull upward on power piston and extend lever to accept sleeve on spool valve, then push seal protector onto power piston until it seats.
11. While holding lever extended, position housing with spool valve assembly directly over rear cover and slide lever pins into slot on sleeve.
12. Center power piston in bore and lower housing down onto rear cover. Push housing and cover together, then remove tool No. J-25083.
13. Install housing to cover attaching bolts. Torque bolts to 20 ft. lbs.
14. Install output rod, spring and spring retainer.
15. Secure baffle and spring retainer using a 7/8 in. deep socket.
16. If removed, install accumulator as described under Accumulator Service.

Accumulator Service

Spring Type Accumulator
1. Secure booster mounting bracket to a vise with pedal rod facing downward.
2. Pump pedal rod several times to ensure accumulator is depleted.
3. Using a suitable C-clamp and tool J-22222-2, depress accumulator spring cap and insert a punch into small hole in front housing to unseat retainer ring, Fig. B39. Remove retainer ring.
4. Slowly and carefully back off C-clamp until spring tension on cap is relieved, then remove clamp, spring cap and accumulator spring.
5. Plug gear and return ports, then while holding hand over accumulator piston, pressurize booster with compressed air through the inlet port, Fig. B40. Piston will back out of housing bore. If compressed air is not available, use a hook fabricated from a stiff piece of wire. Engage hook in piston inlet hole, then using a suitable tool for leverage, wrap wire around tool and pry against housing to remove piston from bore.
6. Disassemble booster as described under Booster Disassemble.
7. Using a small diameter wire hook, remove charging valve and seat.
8. Reverse procedure to assemble. Lubricate components with clean power steering fluid. If piston cannot be seated in bore, pump pedal rod several times to relieve trapped air pressure below piston. Use care not to disturb relief valve when installing accumulator spring in piston.

Pneumatic Accumulator

NOTE: Do not attempt to repair or apply heat to the accumulator. Before discarding an inoperative accumulator, drill a 1/16 in. in diameter hole through the end of the accumulator pan. Do not drill through the piston end. Always wear safety glasses when performing service on the accumulator.

1. Pump pedal rod several times to ensure accumulator is depleted.
2. Secure brake booster mounting bracket in a vise with pedal rod facing downward.
3. Place tool No. J-26889 over master cylinder stud and install retaining nut.
4. Using a C-clamp, depress accumulator can, then insert a punch into hole in housing to unseat retaining ring, Fig. B41. Remove ring from housing using a small screwdriver.

NOTE: If can cannot easily be depressed approximately .10 in., the accumulator is still charged. This indicates an internal problem with the accumulator valves and the brake booster must be disassembled.

5. Slowly back off C-clamp until tension is relieved, then remove C-clamp, retaining cap and accumulator.
6. Reverse procedure to assemble. Lubricate accumulator can seal with power steering fluid. Ensure accumulator can retaining ring is completely seated in housing groove.

BRAKE BOOSTERS

Midland-Ross Brake Boosters

DASH-MOUNTED DIAPHRAGM TYPE

Disassembly Notes

CAUTION: The booster push rod is provided with an adjustment screw to maintain the correct relationship between booster control valve plunger and master cylinder piston. Failure to maintain this relationship will prevent the master cylinder piston from completely releasing hydraulic pressure and can cause the brakes to drag. Therefore, inasmuch as the adjustment varies between one vehicle and another, measure and note for future reference the distance between master cylinder mounting surface and end of screw. Master cylinder must be removed to gain access to push rod (see Fig. M7).

1. Disassemble the booster as suggested by Fig. M1.
2. Scribe a line across booster body and end plate before separating these parts to ensure proper alignment on reassembly.
3. Do not remove valve operating rod from control valve plunger unless plunger or rod is to be replaced. To remove, hold rod firmly and force plunger off rod, breaking plastic retainer. Remove all pieces of broken plastic retainer from groove in plunger if plunger is to be used again with replacement rod.
4. Always use a repair kit when reassembling, and use all parts contained in the kit regardless of condition of old parts.

Reassembly, Fig. M1

1. If valve operating rod was removed from plunger, assemble new plastic retainer to end of rod, Fig. M1. Insert rod into plunger so that retainer engages groove in plunger.
2. Install "Block Vee" type seal and O-rings on valve plunger, Fig. M2.
3. Insert control valve plunger into control valve hub from rear of hub, Fig. M3.
4. Assemble atmospheric valve, return spring and reaction load ring to valve plunger and hub.
5. Push control valve plunger forward and reaction load ring backward against return spring in order to install retainer in groove of plunger.
6. Install O-ring in groove at front side of diaphragm. Assemble valve plunger and hub to diaphragm so that operating rod and small diameter end of hub enter front side of diaphragm and protrude from rear side.
7. Install "Block Vee" type seal in hub rear seal adapter, with sealing lip toward rear. Slide seal and adapter over rear end of valve hub so that large diameter side of adapter bears against diaphragm.
8. Install two plastic plunger guides in their grooves on valve plunger, Fig. M4.
9. Install rubber reaction ring in valve hub so that ring locating knob indexes in notch in hub with ring tips toward front, Fig. M4.
10. Assemble reaction lever and ring, then install assembly in valve hub, Fig. M4.
11. Assemble reaction cone and cushion ring

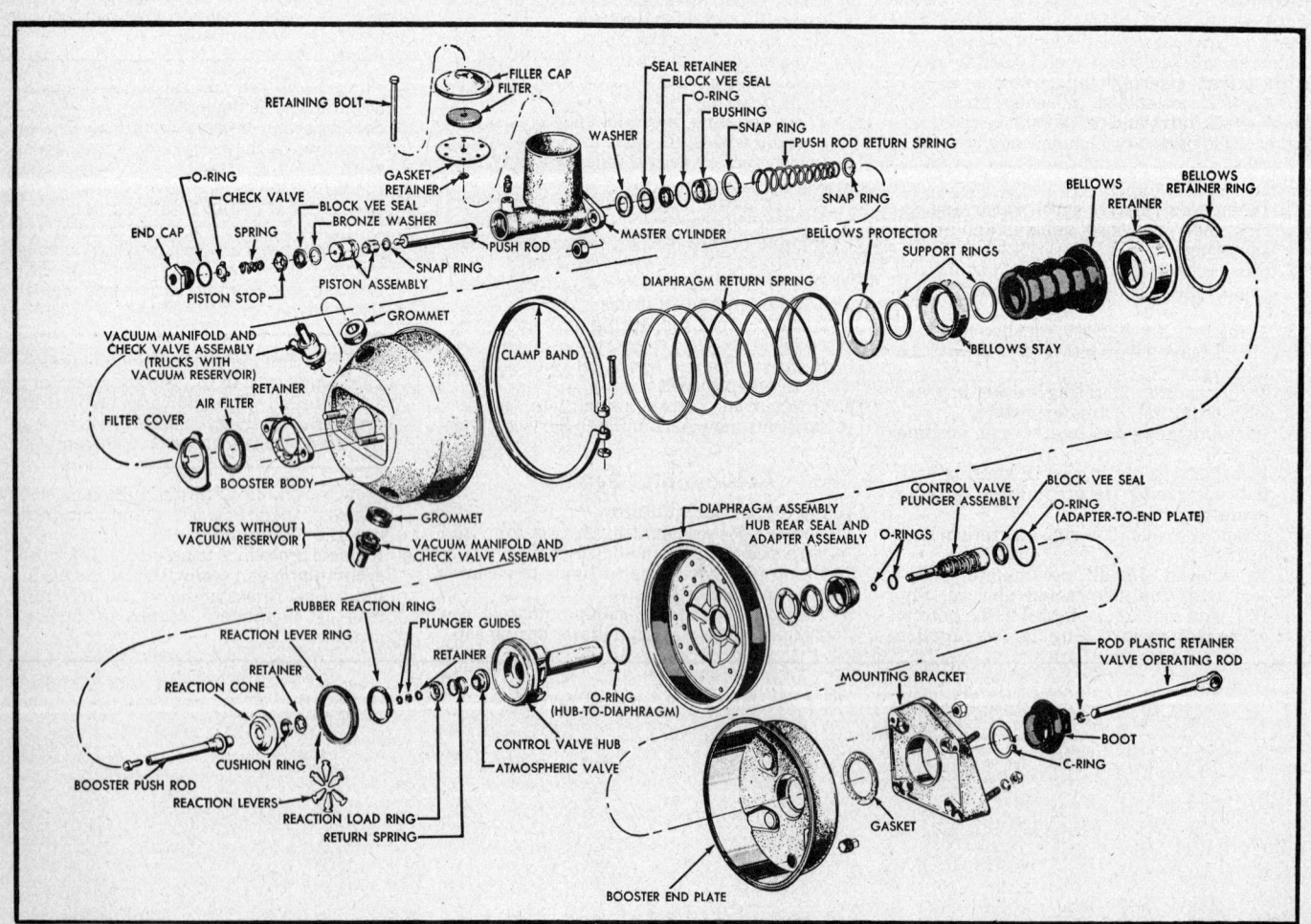

Fig. M1 Midland dash-mounted diaphragm type booster

BRAKE BOOSTERS

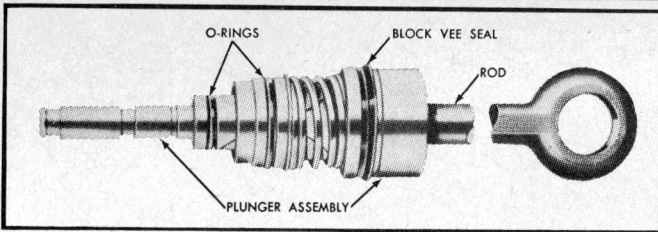

Fig. M2 Valve operating rod end plunger assembly

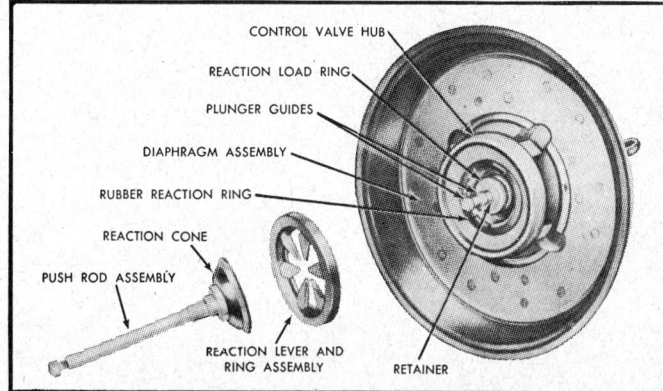

Fig. M4 Reaction components and push rod to valve hub

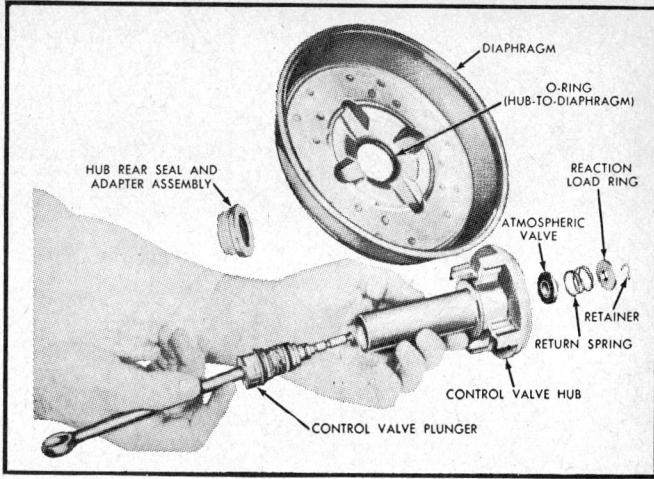

Fig. M3 Control valve components to hub and diaphragm

to push rod and secure to rod with retainer, Fig. M1. Install push rod to valve hub so that valve plunger indexes in push rod, Fig. M4.
12. Assemble bellows retainer to rear fold of bellows. Install bellows stay and two support rings. Plastic stay is located in center fold of bellows with support ring in fold at each side of stay, Fig. M1. Assemble bellows protector to front fold.
13. Position bellows over push rod against front side of diaphragm. Secure bellows to diaphragm by installing retaining ring, Fig. M5. Make sure retaining ring is fully seated.
14. Install O-ring in groove at front side of end plate. Assemble bellows, control valve and diaphragm to end plate by inserting valve hub through front side of end plate with small diameter side of seal adapter protruding from rear side of end plate, Fig. M1.
15. Install large C-ring to rear seal adapter at rear side of end plate.
16. Install diaphragm return spring in booster body, and assembly end plate to booster body so that scribed marks are aligned. *Be sure that lip of diaphragm is evenly positioned between retaining flanges of booster body and end plate.* Secure booster body, diaphragm and end plate together with clamp band and tighten clamp bolt and nut.
17. Pull front lip of bellows through booster body and position it around outer face of booster body, Fig. M6.
18. Place gasket on end plate, slide mounting bracket over end plate studs and install retaining nuts, Fig. M1.
19. Slide rubber boot over valve operating rod and engage boot with groove on mounting bracket.
20. Install rubber grommet in vacuum port in booster body. Large diameter side of grommet should be to outside of booster. Force vacuum manifold and check valve through grommet. Do not push grommet into vacuum chamber.
21. Install air filter cover, filter and retainer on booster body.
22. Check booster push rod adjustment and, if necessary, adjust to same dimension measured before unit was disassembled, Fig. M7.

FRAME MOUNTED, SINGLE DIAPHRAGM TYPE

Disassembly Notes

1. Before separating the major components of the unit, mark both halves of the diaphragm body with a scriber. Also mark the flanges of the control valve body and slave cylinder body so these parts can be reassembled in their original positions.
2. Scribe a line on the side of valve body cover and valve body before removing cover.
3. Always use a repair kit when servicing these units, and use all parts in the kit regardless of the condition of the old parts.

Reassembly, Fig. M8

1. Install control rod diaphragm, by-pass valve, atmospheric and vacuum springs and diaphragm pressure plate assembly.

NOTE: When replacing rod in diaphragm assembly, hold push rod in radius blocks as close to ring groove as possible. Use sealant on threads making sure that proper length rod and proper size diaphragm is used.

2. Install seals on push rod bushing with lip of seals facing slave cylinder body.

NOTE: If rear chamber is dented, it must be replaced as brakes will not release.

3. Place slave cylinder body in a vise and install gasket, then insert piston rod housing through front half of booster body and into slave cylinder body. Tighten securely.
4. Place diaphragm and press plate assembly in rear chamber, then insert push rod into slave cylinder and clamp chambers together with clamp strap making certain to align scribe marks.
5. Insert gauge C-13456 firmly against rod bushing and make certain that push rod length is within indications on gauge.
6. Install slave cylinder piston with open end facing chamber body and install piston cup with lip of cup toward end plug.
7. Install spring retainer and return springs using a new copper gasket and tighten plug.
8. Lubricate piston cups with brake fluid and install control valve piston.
9. Install diaphragm return spring with small coil toward diaphragm, then install control valve body making certain that scribe marks are aligned.

HY-POWER DIAPHRAGM TYPE

Disassembly Notes

1. Before separating the major components of the unit, mark both halves of the diaphragm body with a scriber. Also mark the flanges of the control valve body and slave cylinder body so these parts can be reassembled in their original positions, Fig. M9.
2. Scribe a line on the side of valve body cover and valve body before removing cover.
3. Always use a repair kit when servicing these units, and use all parts in the kit regardless of the condition of the old parts.

BRAKE BOOSTERS

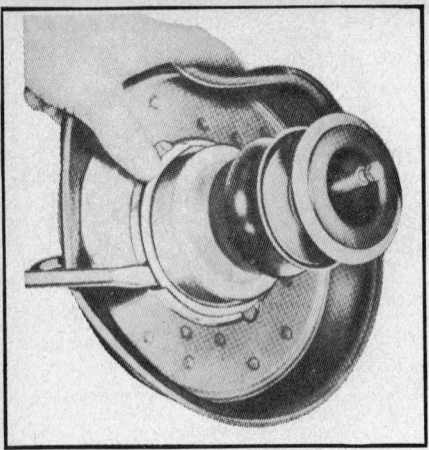

Fig. M5 Bellows installation

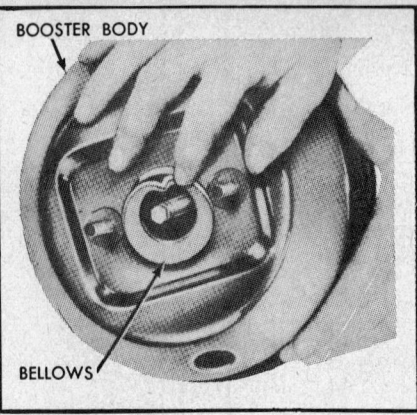

Fig. M6 Bellows-to-booster body engagement

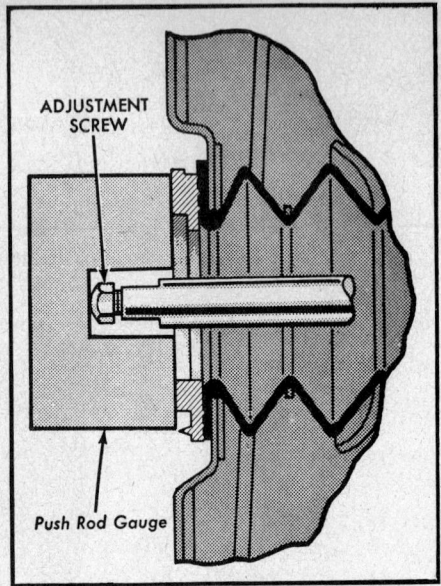

Fig. M7 Push rod adjustment. Measure adjustment before disassembly of booster to be sure it is correct when booster is installed

Reassembly, Fig. M9

1. Position a new seal in control valve body. Assemble spring and spacer in valve body and secure with screw and lock washer. Tighten screw securely.
2. Position control valve diaphragm and plate and secure with retainer nut.
3. Install seal on control valve piston.
4. Insert check valve spring, valve and retainer in hydraulic piston. Be sure check valve floats freely and does not bind in bore.
5. Install transfer bushing, rubber seal and gasket on front body of slave cylinder body.

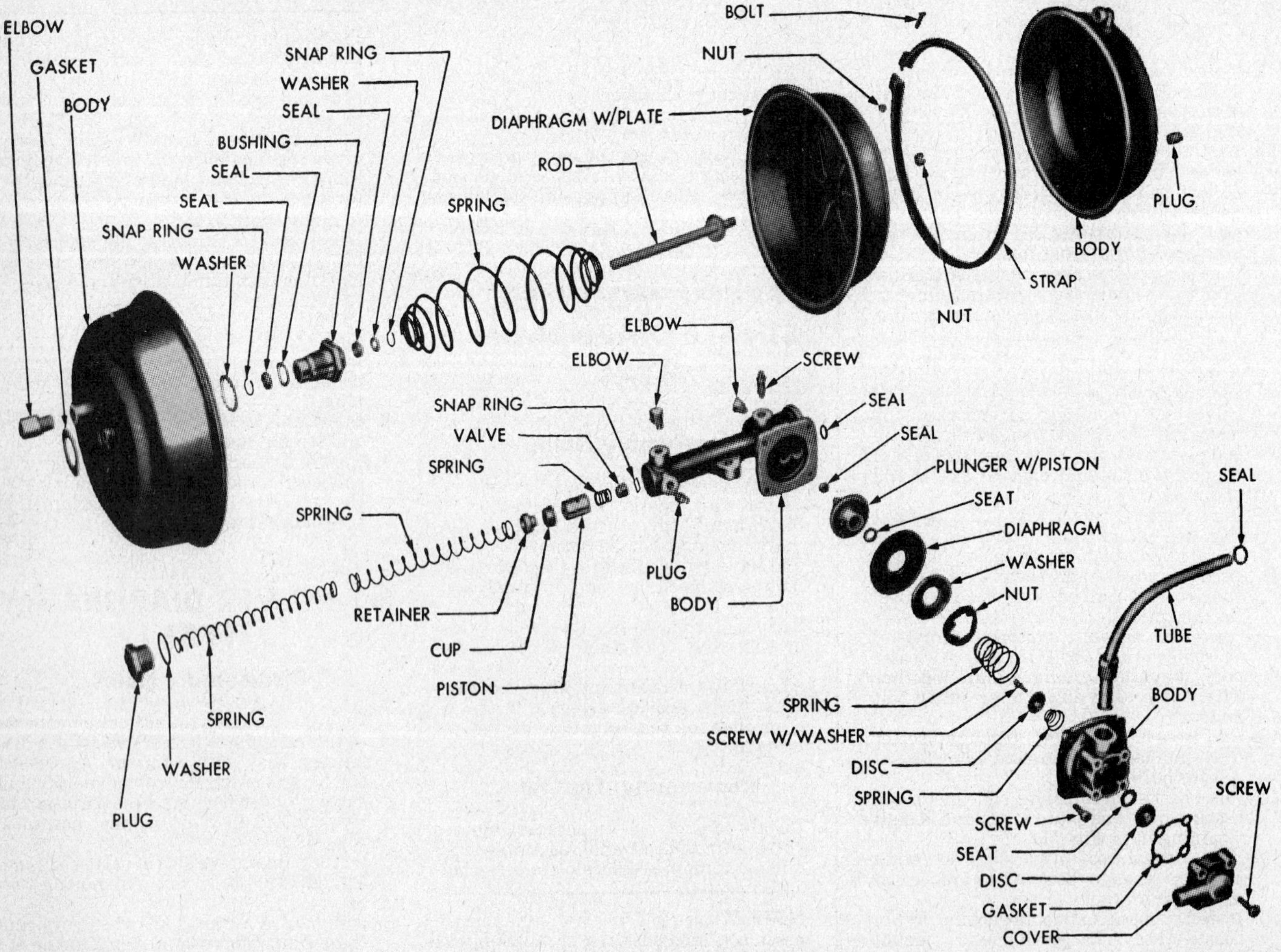

Fig. M8 Frame mounted single diaphragm type, disassembled

BRAKE BOOSTERS

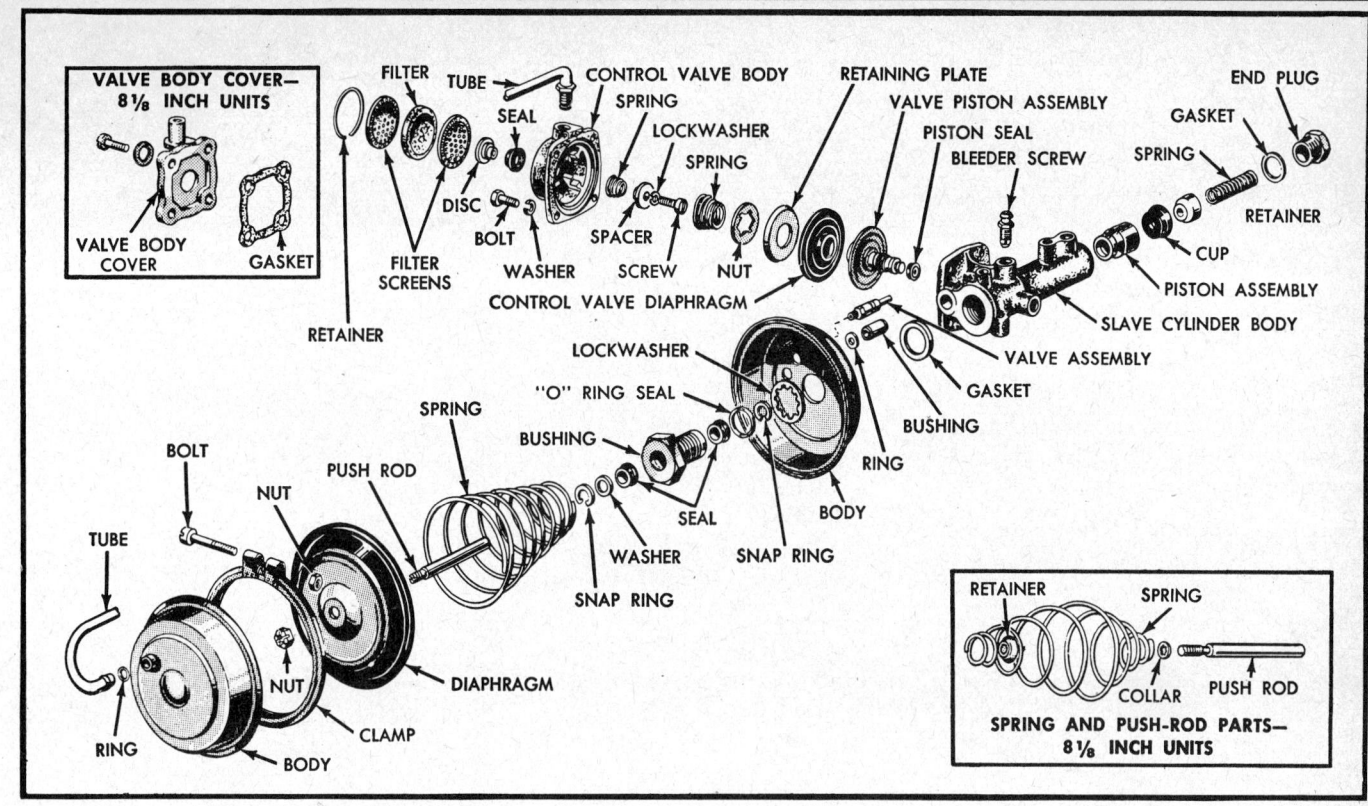

Fig. M9 Hy-Power vacuum booster disassembled

6. Install push rod seals, washer and snap rings in push rod bushing. Both push rod seals should be installed with open end of seal facing slave cylinder body. Install lock washer over end of bushing, and install bushing seal.
7. Mount slave cylinder body in a vise. Position front body over end of slave cylinder, inserting transfer bushing with proper hole in front body.
8. Thread push rod bushings in place. Be sure front body seats squarely on slave cylinder body, and tighten bushing securely.
9. Coat piston bores in slave cylinder body with brake fluid. Dip hydraulic cylinder piston, seals, spring retainer and spring in brake fluid.
10. Install hydraulic piston in slave cylinder bore with recessed end (large bore of piston) toward push rod bushing. Carefully position piston cup with recessed end toward large spring, spring retainer and spring on top of piston. *On frame-mounted booster, install spring seat in spring coils.*
11. Position new copper gasket on end plug and screw plug in slave cylinder. Tighten plug securely.
12. Dip control valve piston and diaphragm in brake fluid. Position control valve spring on diaphragm with small end of spring over piston boss.
13. Position control valve body over spring align scribe marks, install valve body on slave cylinder body and secure with attaching bolts and lock washers. Tighten bolts securely.
14. Position new gasket on control valve body. Place valve body cover over gasket and secure cover with attaching bolts and lock washers.
15. Position collar over threaded end of push rod. Place spring retainer in spring as shown in insert of Fig. M9. Insert push rod and collar in coils of spring and through retainer. Place diaphragm over threaded end of push rod and secure with push rod nut. After nut is tightened, coat threads of push rod with shellac to prevent leakage. Coat push rod with brake fluid.
16. Place return spring over push rod bushing.
17. Place rear body on top of diaphragm with scribed marks on rear body aligned with mark on front body. Compress return spring and install and tighten clamp, making certain diaphragm bead is properly positioned between two halves of body.
18. Install by-pass tube.

DOUBLE DIAPHRAGM TYPE

Disassembly Notes

1. Before separating main components, scribe marks on front and rear vacuum chambers to assist in aligning parts on reassembly.
2. Always use a repair kit, and use all the parts contained in the kit regardless of the condition of the old parts.

Reassembly, Fig. M10

1. Install outer seal in groove in slave cylinder piston with lip of seal toward small end of piston.
2. Install spring and valve in end of piston and hook piston onto end of front push rod.
3. Insert round end of rear push rod into rear end of front push rod. Place two halves of collar in front push rod and install snap ring.
4. Install seal in flange end of push rod guide bushing, with lip of seal pointing inward. Install washer over seal and secure with snap ring.
5. Install seal in bore in other end of bushing, with lip of seal pointing outward.
6. Install O-ring in groove in guide bushing.

VACUUM CHAMBER ASSEMBLY

1. Install piston rod guide bushing in intermediate vacuum chamber. Insert bushing through vacuum chamber from external control line tee-fitting port side. Clamp a socket in vise and set hex head of guide bushing in socket. Install nut on guide bushing and tighten firmly, using another socket. Stake nut at bushing threads at three points after tightening.
2. Install snap ring in groove in rear end of piston rod, then install collar on rod with chambered side of hole over snap ring. Install rear diaphragm over piston rod, then thread nut onto end of rod. Clamp nut in vise and use 1/4" bar stock through holes in piston rod to tighten rod into nut. After tightening, stake edge of nut into threads on piston rod at three points.
3. Install large end of diaphragm return spring under clips on rear diaphragm plate.
4. With piston rod near nut still clamped in vise, install intermediate vacuum chamber over piston rod with piston rod guide bushing inside small end of diaphragm

BRAKE BOOSTERS

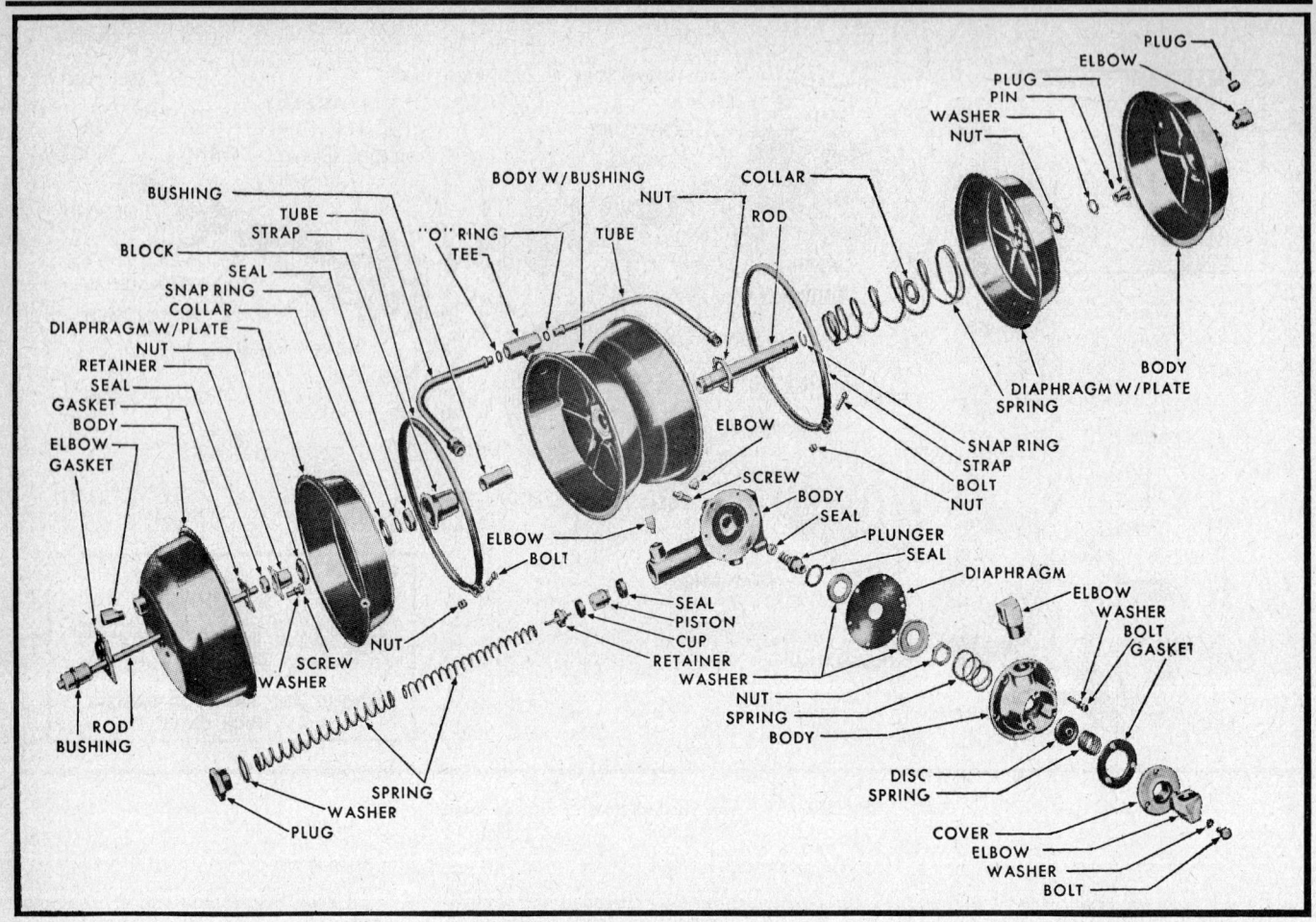

Fig. M10 Double diaphragm booster disassembled

spring. Press down on intermediate vacuum chamber, compressing spring to expose snap ring groove in piston rod. Install snap ring, collar, front diaphragm and nut. Tighten nut firmly and stake in place at three points.

5. Mount slave cylinder body in vise with outer end down. Outer end must be exposed so that piston and push rods can be inserted later.
6. Place slave cylinder piston stop washer in slave cylinder bore. Make sure washer seats against shoulder in cylinder bore.
7. Place front vacuum chamber to slave cylinder gasket on slave cylinder body, with all holes aligned. Position front vacuum chamber on slave cylinder and install cap screw with lock washer. *Do not tighten cap screw.*
8. Place guide bushing gasket on front vacuum chamber. Then insert guide bushing through vacuum chamber and into slave cylinder bore. Cut-out of guide bushing flange must be positioned at vacuum passage in vacuum chamber. Attach piston rod guide to slave cylinder with four socket head screws. Tighten these screws and the one cap screw previously installed loosely.
9. Place intermediate vacuum chamber on front vacuum chamber with front diaphragm bead positioned between cupped flange of vacuum chambers, and with scribed marks aligned. Install front clamp strap and tighten clamp nut firmly. Install external control tube tee in intermediate vacuum chamber. When tee is firmly tightened, it must be at right angle to vacuum chamber with small diameter end to rear.
10. With rear push rod, front push rod and slave cylinder piston assembled as previously directed, insert push rods up through slave cylinder bore. Rear push rod must enter vacuum chamber piston rod as slave cylinder piston enters slave cylinder bore. Use a wood screwdriver handle to push piston up into slave cylinder bore.
11. Press down on rear diaphragm plate, compressing diaphragm spring, to expose end of rear push rod. Place washer on piston rod end plug. Place end plug over end of push rod and install pin. Thread end plug into piston rod and tighten firmly.
12. Position rear vacuum chamber over rear diaphragm, aligning scribed marks made earlier. Install rear clamp strap and tighten nut securely.
13. Place O-ring over end of rear control tube and insert tube into tee. Install rubber elbow on rear control tube and in opening in rear vacuum chamber.

CONTROL VALVE

1. Install new piston seal on small end of control valve piston with lip of seal toward small end of piston.
2. Install diaphragm on control valve piston with bead at inner diameter seated in groove in piston. Place diaphragm washer over piston against diaphragm with cupped side away from diaphragm. Place new diaphragm nut over piston and press down firmly against washer.
3. Insert metering wire through hole in side of piston. Both ends of wire must be bent over so wire cannot fall out, but must be free to move in hole.
4. Insert piston into bore in slave cylinder body, using care not to damage lips of piston seals.
5. Place valve spring over stem on vacuum valve disc (small end first). Insert stem of valve disc through opening in control valve body from inner side, making sure large end of spring seats squarely against body. Place atmosphere valve disc over valve stem (seal side first), then install O-ring on valve stem.
6. Place small end of control valve piston return spring over outer end of control valve piston. Install control valve body, making sure control valve spring seats squarely in body, and that groove around outer edge of body engages bead on diaphragm. Attach body to slave cylinder with capscrews.
7. Install cover and gasket on control valve body and attach with screws.
8. Insert end of control tube into rubber elbow or tee in vacuum chamber, and insert other end into control tube port in control valve body. Thread control tube nut into valve body and tighten firmly.
9. Install end cap with gasket in end of slave cylinder and tighten firmly.
10. Install bleeder screws in top of slave cylinder body.
11. Cover all openings to prevent entrance of dirt during installation.

DISC BRAKES

INDEX

	Page No.
Bendix—Sliding Caliper	674
Delco Moraine	663
Ford	
Sliding Caliper (Single Piston)	666
Sliding Caliper (Dayton, Dual Piston)	675
Floating Caliper (Dayton)	666
Kelsey-Hayes—Floating Caliper	668
Kelsey-Hayes—Sliding Caliper	
Single Piston	670
Dual Piston	672

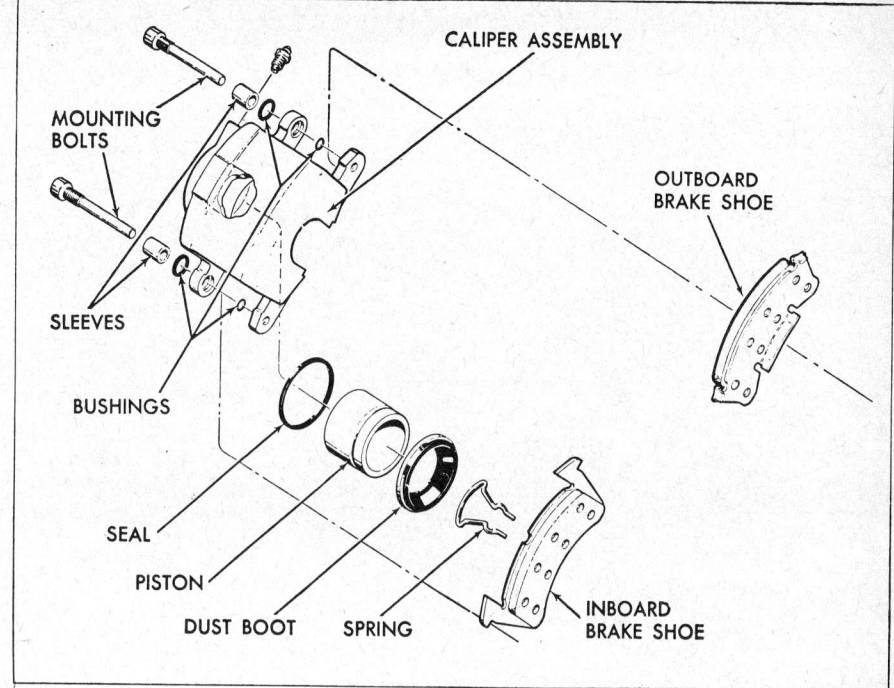

Fig. 1 Single piston caliper. Exploded

TROUBLE SHOOTING

Excessive Pedal Travel

1. Shoe and lining knock back after violent cornering or rough road travel.
2. Piston and shoe and lining assembly not properly seated or positioned.
3. Air leak or insufficient fluid in system or caliper.
4. Loose wheel bearing adjustment.
5. Damaged or worn caliper piston seal.
6. Improper booster push rod adjustment.
7. Shoe out of flat more than .005".
8. Rear brake automatic adjusters inoperative.
9. Improperly ground rear brake shoe and lining assemblies.

Brake Roughness or Chatter; Pedal Pumping

1. Excessive lateral run-out of rotor.
2. Rotor excessively out of parallel.

Excessive Pedal Effort

1. Frozen or seized pistons.
2. Brake fluid, oil or grease on linings.
3. Shoe and lining worn below specifications.
4. Proportioning valve malfunction.
5. Booster inoperative.
6. Leaking booster vacuum check valve.

Pull, Uneven or Grabbing Brakes

1. Frozen or seized pistons.
2. Brake fluid, oil or grease on linings.
3. Caliper out of alignment with rotor.
4. Loose caliper attachment.
5. Unequalized front tire pressure.
6. Incorrect front end alignment.
7. Lining protruding beyond end of shoe.

Brake Rattle

1. Excessive clearance between shoe and caliper or between shoe and splash shield.
2. Shoe hold-down clips missing or improperly positioned.

Heavy Brake Drag

1. Frozen or seized pistons.
2. Operator riding brake pedal.
3. Incomplete brake pedal return due to linkage interference.
4. Faulty booster check valve holding pressure in hydraulic system.
5. Residual pressure in front brake hydraulic system.

Caliper Brake Fluid Leak

1. Damaged or worn caliper piston seal.
2. Scores in cylinder bore.
3. Corrosion build-up in cylinder bore or on piston surface.
4. Metal clip in seal groove.

No Braking Effect When Pedal is Depressed

1. Piston and shoe and lining assembly not properly seated or positioned.
2. Air leak or insufficient fluid in system or caliper.
3. Damaged or worn caliper piston seal.
4. Bleeder screw open.
5. Air in hydraulic system or improper bleeding.

Rear Brakes Locking On Application

On brake system equipped with a proportioning or rear pressure regulator valve, should the valve malfunction rear brakes may receive excess pressure, resulting in wheel lock-up.

SERVICE PRECAUTIONS

Brake Lines & Linings

Remove one of the front wheels and inspect the brake disc, caliper and linings. (The wheel bearings should be inspected at this time and repacked if necessary).

Do not get any oil or grease on the linings. If the linings are worn to within .030" of the surface of the shoe, replace both sets of shoe and lining assemblies. It is recommended that both front wheel sets be replaced whenever a respective shoe and lining is worn or damaged. Inspect and, if necessary, replace rear brake linings also.

If the caliper is cracked or fluid leakage through the casting is evident, it must be replaced as a unit.

Shoe & Lining Wear

If visual inspection does not adequately determine the condition of the lining, a physical check will be necessary.

To check the amount of lining wear, remove a wheel from the car, the caliper from the steering knuckle, and the shoe and lining assemblies. Three thickness measurements should be taken (with a micrometer) across the middle section of the shoe and lining; one reading at each side and one reading in the center.

When a shoe and lining assembly has worn to a thickness of .180", it should be replaced. If shoes do not require replacement, reinstall

DISC BRAKES

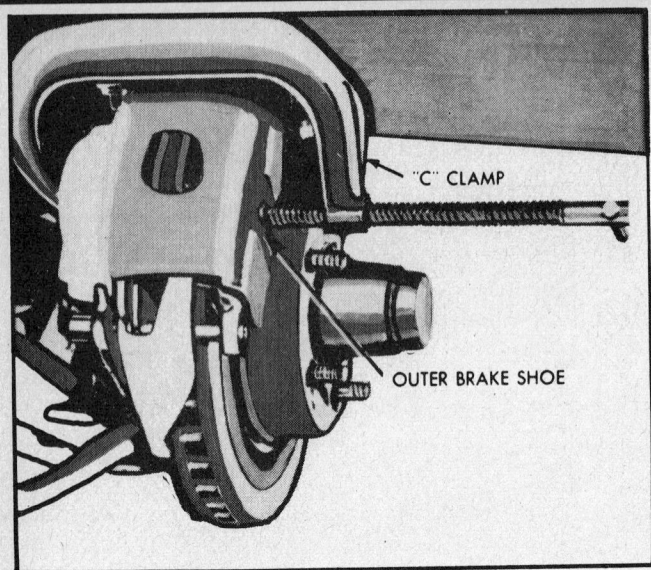

Fig. 2 Compressing piston and shoes with "C" clamp

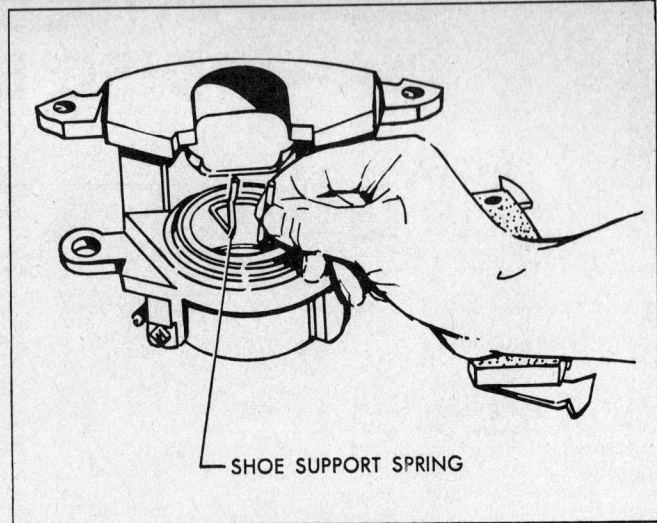

Fig. 3 Installing support spring

them in their original inner and outer positions.

Brake Roughness

The most common cause of brake chatter on disc brakes is a variation in thickness of the disc. If roughness or vibration is encountered during highway operation or if pedal pumping is experienced at low speeds, the disc may have excessive thickness variation. To check for this condition, measure the disc at 12 points with a micrometer at a radius approximately one inch from edge of disc. If thickness measurements vary by more than .0005", the disc should be replaced with a new one.

Excessive lateral runout of braking disc may cause a "knocking back" of the pistons, possibly creating increased pedal travel and vibration when brakes are applied.

Before checking the runout, wheel bearings should be adjusted. The readjustment is very important and will be required at the completion of the test to prevent bearing failure. Be sure to make the adjustment according to the recommendations given.

Brake Disc Service

Servicing of disc brakes is extremely critical due to the close tolerances required in machining the brake disc to insure proper brake operation. In manufacturing brake discs, tolerances of the rubbing surfaces for flatness is .001" and usually for parallelism .0005". Lateral runout of the faces should not exceed .004 to .005" in most cases although the limit on Ford Company products is only .002".

The maintenance of these close controls of the shape of the rubbing surfaces is necessary to prevent brake roughness. In addition, the surface finish must be non-directional and maintained at a micro inch finish. This close control of the rubbing surface finish is necessary to avoid pulls and erratic performance and promote long lining life and equal lining wear of both left and right brakes.

In light of the foregoing remarks, refinishing of the rubbing surfaces should not be attempted unless precision equipment, capable of measuring in micro inches (millionths of an inch) is available.

To check runout of a disc, mount a dial indicator on a convenient part (steering knuckle, tie rod, disc brake caliper housing) so that the plunger of the dial indicator contacts the disc at a point one inch from the outer edge. If the total indicated runout exceeds specifications, install a new disc.

General Precautions

1. Grease or any other foreign material must be kept off the caliper, surfaces of the disc and external surfaces of the hub, during service procedures. Handling the brake disc and caliper should be done in a way to avoid deformation of the disc and nicking or scratching brake linings.
2. If inspection reveals rubber piston seals are worn or damaged, they should be replaced immediately.
3. During removal and installation of a wheel assembly, exercise care so as not to interfere with or damage the caliper splash shield, the bleeder screw or the transfer tube.
4. Front wheel bearings should be adjusted to specifications.
5. Be sure vehicle is centered on hoist before servicing any of the front end components to avoid bending or damaging the disc splash shield on full right or left wheel turns.
6. Before the vehicle is moved after any brake service work, be sure to obtain a firm brake pedal.
7. The assembly bolts of the two caliper housings should not be disturbed unless the caliper requires service.

Inspection of Caliper

Should it become necessary to remove the caliper for installation of new parts, clean all parts in alcohol, wipe dry using lint-free cloths. Using an air hose, blow out drilled passages and bores. Check dust boots for punctures or tears. If punctures or tears are evident, new boots should be installed upon reassembly.

Inspect piston bores in both housings for scoring or pitting. Bores that show light scratches or corrosion can usually be cleaned with crocus cloth. However, bores that have deep scratches or scoring may be honed, provided the diameter of the bore is not increased more than .002". If the bore does not clean up within this specification, a new caliper housing should be installed (black stains on the bore walls are caused by piston seals and will do no harm).

When using a hone, be sure to install the hone baffle before honing bore. The baffle is used to protect the hone stones from damage. Use extreme care in cleaning the caliper after honing. Remove all dust and grit by flushing the caliper with alcohol. Wipe dry with clean lint-less cloth and then clean a second time in the same manner.

Bleeding Disc Brakes

NOTE: Chrysler Corp. recommends only pressure bleeding for all models.

The disc brake hydraulic system can be bled manually or with pressure bleeding equipment (except as noted above). On vehicles with disc brakes the brake pedal will require more pumping and frequent checking of fluid level in master cylinder during bleeding operation.

Never use brake fluid that has been drained from hydraulic system when bleeding the brakes. Be sure the disc brake pistons are returned to their normal positions and that the shoe and lining assemblies are properly seated. Before driving the vehicle, check brake operation to be sure that a firm pedal has been obtained.

Testing Proportional Valve

When a premature rear wheel slide is obtained on a brake application, it usually is an indication that the fluid pressure to the rear wheels is above the 50% reduction ratio for the rear line pressure and that a malfunction has occurred within the proportioning valve.

To test the valve, install gauge set in brake line between master cylinder and proportioning valve, and at output end of proportioning valve and brake line. Be sure all joints are fluid tight.

Have a helper exert pressure on brake pedal (holding pressure). Obtain a reading on master cylinder output of approximately 800

DISC BRAKES

psi. While pressure is being held as above, reading on valve outlet should be 530–570 psi. If the pressure readings do not meet these specifications, the valve should be removed and a new valve installed.

DELCO-MORAINE SINGLE PISTON

The caliper assembly used on all models except Vega, Fig. 1, slides on its mounting bolts whereas the caliper on Vega models, the caliper assembly slides on mounting sleeves which are secured by two mounting pins. Upon brake application, fluid pressure against the piston forces the inboard shoe and lining assembly against the inboard side of the disc. This action causes the caliper assembly to slide until the outboard lining comes into contact with the disc. As pressure builds up, the linings are pressed against the disc with increased force.

All Exc. Vega

Caliper Removal

1. Siphon enough brake fluid out of the master cylinder to bring fluid level to 1/3 full to avoid fluid overflow when the caliper piston is pushed back into its bore.
2. Raise vehicle and remove front wheels.
3. Using a "C" clamp, as illustrated in Fig. 2, push piston back into its bore.
4. Remove two mounting bolts and lift caliper away from disc.

Brake Shoe Removal

1. Remove caliper assembly as outlined above.
2. Remove inboard shoe. Dislodge outboard shoe and position caliper on the front suspension so the brake hose will not support the weight of the caliper.
3. Remove shoe support spring from piston.
4. Remove two sleeves from inboard ears of the caliper.
5. Remove four rubber bushings from the grooves in each of the caliper ears.

Brake Shoe Installation

1. Lubricate new sleeves, rubber bushings, bushing grooves and mounting bolt ends with Delco Silicone Lube or its equivalent.
2. Install new bushings and sleeves in caliper ears.

NOTE: Position the sleeve so that the end toward the shoe is flush with the machined surface of the ear.

3. Install shoe support spring in piston cavity, Fig. 3.
4. Position inboard shoe in caliper so spring ends centrally contact shoe edge. Initially, this will place the shoe on an angle. Push upper edge of shoe down until shoe is flat against backing plate. When properly seated, spring ends will not extend past shoe more than .100".
5. Position outboard shoe in caliper with shoe ears over caliper ears and tab at bottom of shoe engaged in caliper cutout.
6. With shoes installed, lift caliper and rest bottom edge of outboard lining on outer edge of brake disc to be sure there is no clearance between outboard shoe tab and caliper abutment.
7. Using a 1/4" × 1" × 2 1/2" metal bar to bridge caliper cutout, clamp outboard shoe to caliper with a "C" clamp.
8. Bend both ears of outboard shoe over caliper until clearance between shoe ear and caliper (measured at both the edge and side of the caliper) is .005" or less, Fig. 4.
9. Remove "C" clamp and install caliper.

Disassembling Caliper

1. Remove caliper as outlined above.
2. Disconnect hose from steel line, remove U shaped retainer and withdraw hose from frame support bracket.
3. After cleaning outside of caliper, remove brake hose and discard copper gasket.
4. Drain brake fluid from caliper.
5. Pad caliper interior with clean shop towels and use compressed air to remove piston, Fig. 5.

NOTE: Use just enough air pressure to ease piston out of bore. Do not blow piston out of bore.

CAUTION: Do not place fingers in front of piston in an attempt to catch or protect it when applying compressed air. This could result in serious injury.

6. Carefully pry dust boot out of bore.
7. Using a small piece of wood or plastic, remove piston seal from bore.

NOTE: Do not use a metal tool of any kind to remove seal as it may damage bore.

8. Remove bleeder valve.

Assembling Caliper

1. Lubricate caliper piston bore and new piston seal with clean brake fluid. Position seal in bore groove.
2. Lubricate piston with clean brake fluid and assemble a new boot into the groove in the piston so the fold faces the open end of the piston, Fig. 6.
3. Using care not to unseat the seal, insert piston into bore and force the piston to the bottom of the bore.
4. Position dust boot in caliper counterbore and install, Fig. 7.

NOTE: Check the boot installation to be sure the retaining ring moulded into the boot is not bent and that the boot is installed below the caliper face and evenly all around. If the boot is not fully installed, dirt and moisture may enter the bore and cause corrosion.

5. Install the brake hose in the caliper using a new copper gasket.
6. Install shoes and re-install caliper assembly.

Caliper Installation

1. Position caliper over disc, lining up holes in caliper with holes in mounting bracket. If brake hose was not disconnected during removal, be sure not to kink it during installation.
2. Start mounting bolts through sleeves in inboard caliper ears and the mounting bracket, making sure ends of bolts pass under ears on inboard shoe.

NOTE: Right and left calipers must not be interchanged.

3. Push mounting bolts through to engage holes in the outboard ears. Then thread mounting bolts into bracket.
4. Torque mounting bolts to 30-40 ft. lbs.
5. If brake hose was removed, reconnect it and bleed the calipers.

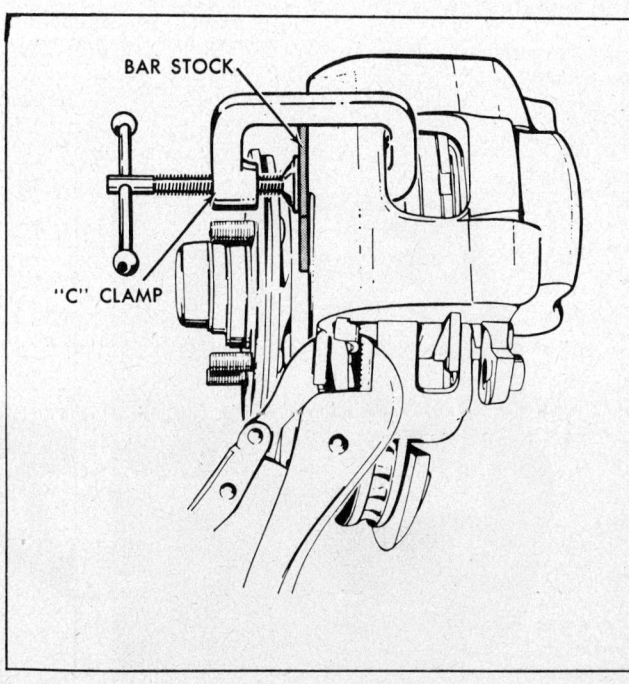

Fig. 4 Fitting shoe to caliper

DISC BRAKES

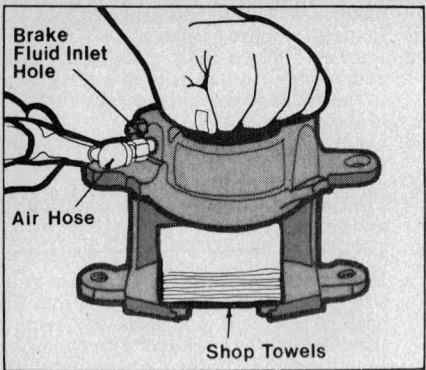

Fig. 5 Removing piston from caliper

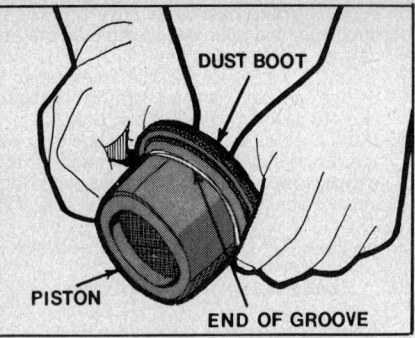

Fig. 6 Installing boot to piston

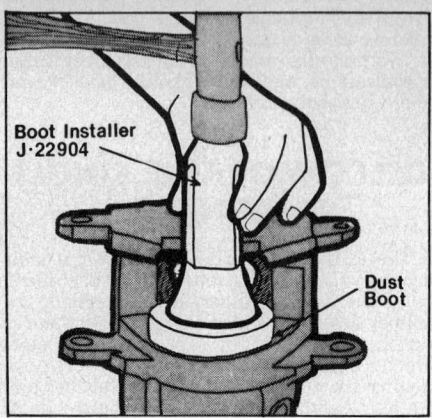

Fig. 7 Installing boot to caliper

6. Replace front wheels, lower vehicle and add brake fluid to master cylinder to bring level to 1/4" from top.

NOTE: Before moving vehicle, pump brake pedal several times to be sure it is firm. Do not move vehicle until a firm pedal is obtained.

VEGA

Lining Removal

1. Support vehicle on hoist and remove wheel assembly.
2. Remove the two mounting pin stamped nuts, Fig. 8, and slide out the mounting pins, Fig. 9.
3. Lift caliper off disc and support caliper from suspension using wire.
4. Slide inboard and outboard shoes past mounting sleeve openings and remove mounting sleeves and bushing assemblies.
5. If caliper is to be removed, disconnect brake line.

Lining Installation

1. Install new sleeves with bushings on caliper grooves, Fig. 10.

NOTE: The "shouldered end" of sleeve must be installed toward outside.

2. Install inner shoe on caliper and slide shoe ears over sleeve, Fig. 10. Install the outer shoe in the same manner.

CAUTION: If pads are being re-used, they must be installed in same location as when removed.

3. Mount caliper on rotor. If brake line was disconnected, reconnect and torque bolt to 22 ft. lbs.

NOTE: To avoid overflow, it may be necessary to remove half of brake fluid capacity from master cylinder.

4. Install mounting pins from outside in and install stamped nuts, Fig. 11. Nuts should be pressed on as far as possible using a suitable size socket that just seats on outer edge of nut.
5. Install wheel assembly and lower vehicle.
6. Add brake fluid to within 1/4 inch from top of master cylinder and test brake operation to insure a firm brake pedal before moving vehicle.

Caliper Disassembly

1. Remove caliper as described under "Lining Removal".
2. Drain brake fluid from caliper and clean exterior of caliper using clean brake fluid.
3. Using clean towels, pad interior of caliper and remove piston by applying just enough compressed air to fluid inlet port to ease piston out of bore.

CAUTION: Do not place fingers in front of piston in an attempt to catch or protect it when applying compressed air.

4. Carefully using a screwdriver so as not to scratch piston bore, pry dust boot out of piston bore, Fig. 12.
5. Using a piece of wood or plastic so as not to damage bore, remove piston seal from its groove in caliper bore.
6. Remove bleeder screw.

Cleaning & Inspection

1. Clean all metal parts in clean brake fluid,

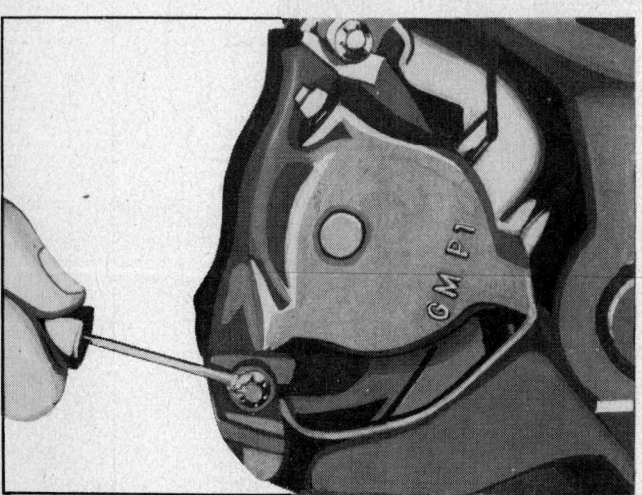

Fig. 8 Removing stamped nuts from mounting pins

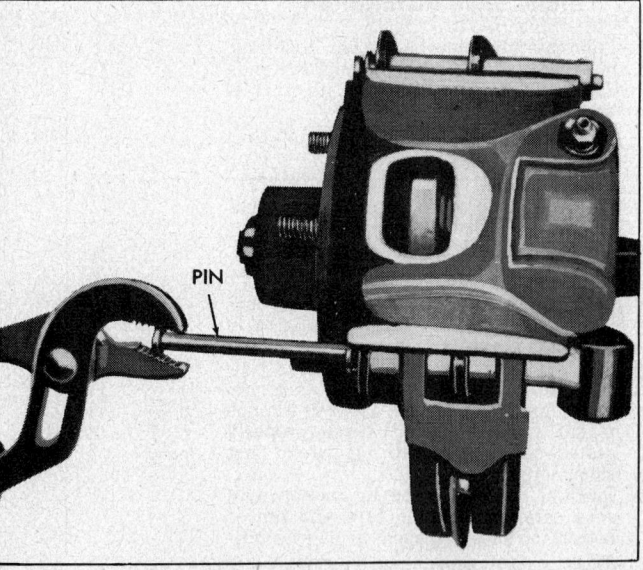

Fig. 9 Removing mounting pins

DISC BRAKES

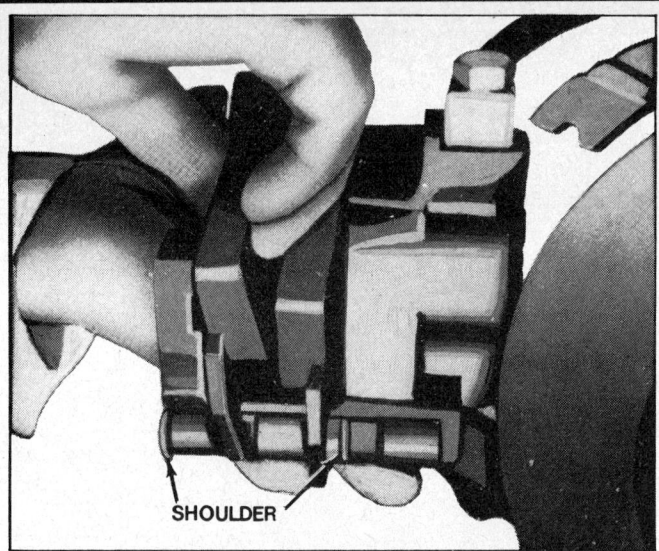

Fig. 10 Mounting sleeves and brake shoe installation

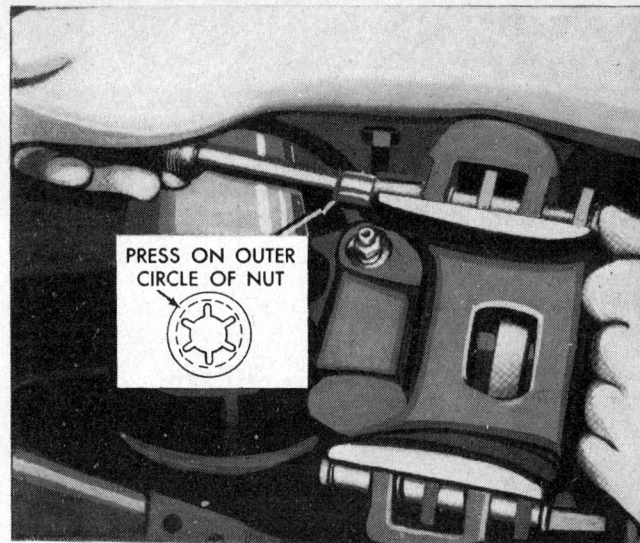

Fig. 11 Installing stamped nuts on mounting pins

then using clean filtered air, dry parts and blow out all passages in caliper and bleeder valve.

NOTE: Always use clean brake fluid to clean caliper parts. Never use mineral base cleaning solvents as they can cause rubber parts to deteriorate and become soft and swollen, also the use of lubricated compressed air will leave a film of oil on metal parts that may damage rubber parts when they come in after reassembly.

2. Inspect piston surface for scoring, nicks, corrosion and worn or damaged plating. If any surface defects are detected, replace piston.

CAUTION: The piston outside surface is the primary sealing surface in the caliper. It is manufactured and plated to close tolerances, therefore refinishing by any means or the use of any abrasive is not recommended.

3. Check caliper bore for same defects as piston. The piston bore is not plated and stains or minor corrosion may be polished with crocus cloth.

CAUTION: Do not use emery cloth or any other form of abrasive and thoroughly clean caliper after use of crocus cloth. If caliper cannot be cleaned up in this manner, replace caliper.

Caliper Assembly

NOTE: The dust boot and piston seal are to be replaced each time that the caliper is disassembled.

1. Lubricate piston bore and new piston seal with clean brake fluid, then position seal in caliper bore groove.
2. Lubricate piston with clean brake fluid and assemble a new boot into groove in piston, Fig. 13.
3. Install piston into bore using care not to unseat seal, then force piston to bottom of bore.

NOTE: Approximately 50–100 pounds of force are required to push piston to bottom of bore.

4. Position dust boot in caliper counterbore and seat boot using tool shown in Fig. 14.

NOTE: Check boot installation to make sure that retaining ring moulded into boot is not bent and that boot is installed evenly all around. If boot is not fully installed, dirt and moisture may enter bore.

5. Install caliper as described under "Caliper Installation".

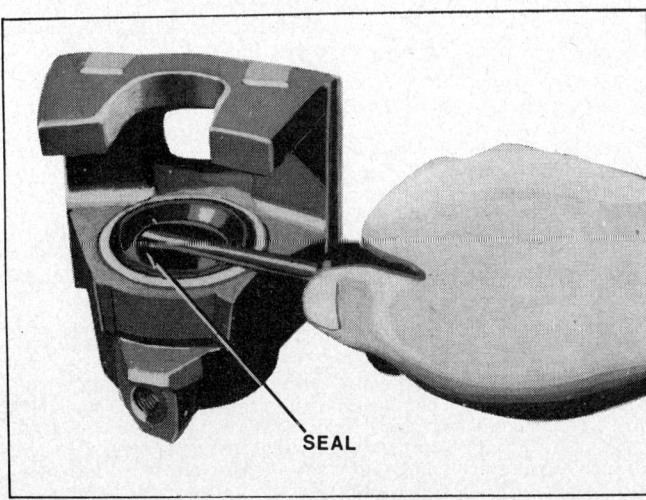

Fig. 12 Dust boot seal removal

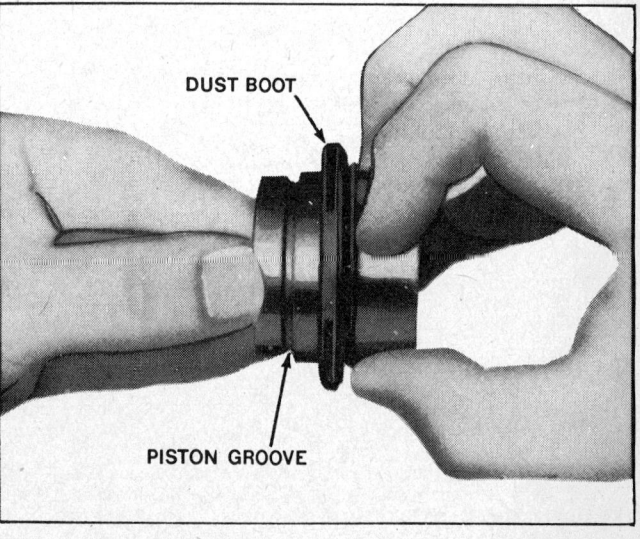

Fig. 13 Installing piston on boot

665

DISC BRAKES

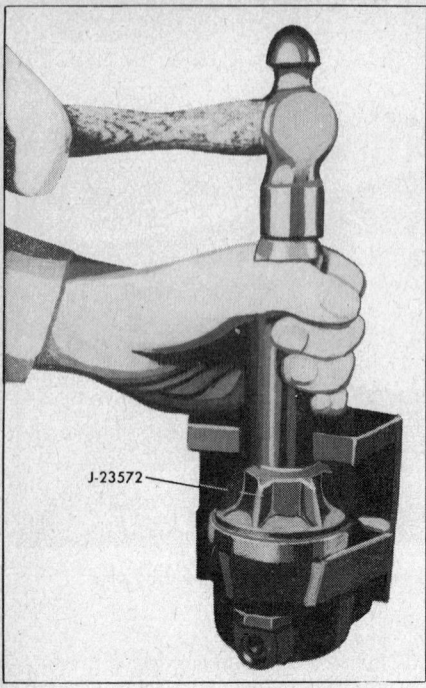

Fig. 14 Sealing dust boot in caliper

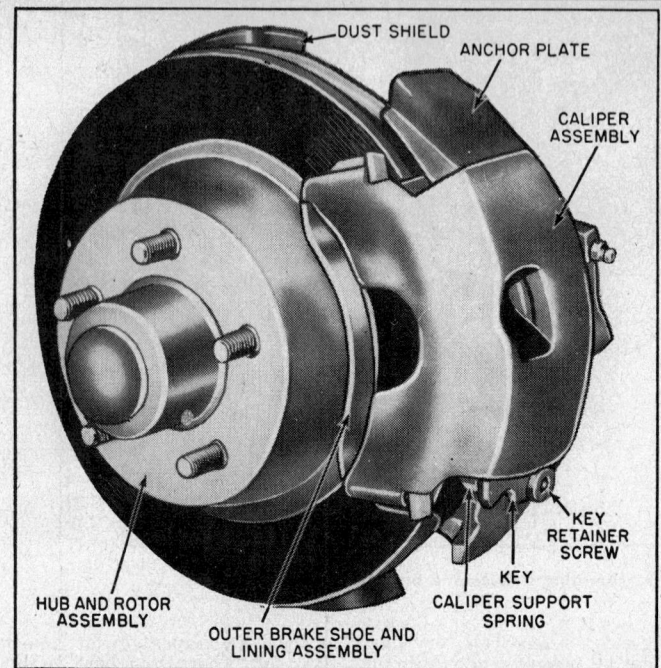

Fig. 15 Ford single piston sliding caliper disc brake

FORD SINGLE PISTON SLIDING CALIPER

The caliper assembly is made up of a sliding caliper housing assembly and an anchor plate, Fig. 15.

The anchor plate is bolted to the wheel spindle arm. Two angular machined surfaces on the upper end of the caliper housing contact mating machined surfaces of the anchor plate. A steel, plated key and a caliper support spring is fitted between the angular machined surfaces of the lower end of the caliper and the machined surface of the anchor plate. The key is held in position with a retaining screw. The caliper is held in position against the mating surfaces of the anchor plate by means of the caliper support spring. A brake shoe anti-rattle spring clip is provided on the anchor plate at the lower end of the inner brake shoe and lining assembly. The inner and outer brake shoe assemblies are not interchangeable.

The sliding caliper contains a single cylinder and a piston with a molded dust boot to seal the cylinder bore from contamination. A square section rubber piston seal is positioned in a groove in cylinder bore to provide sealing between cylinder and piston.

Caliper Removal

1. Raise car and support with safety stands. Block both rear wheels if a jack is used.
2. Remove wheel and tire assembly from hub.
3. Disconnect brake hose from caliper.
4. Remove retaining screw from caliper retaining key, Fig. 15.
5. Slide caliper retaining key and support spring either inward or outward from anchor plate. Use hammer and drift, if necessary, to remove the key and caliper support spring. Use care to avoid damaging the key.
6. Lift caliper assembly away from anchor plate by pushing caliper down against anchor plate and rotate upper end upward out of anchor plate, Fig. 16.
7. Remove inner shoe and lining from anchor plate. The brake shoe anti-rattle clip (inner shoe only) may become displaced at this time and if so, reposition it on anchor plate. Fig. 17. Tap lightly on outer shoe and lining to free it from caliper.
8. Clean caliper, anchor plate and rotor assemblies and inspect them for signs of fluid leakage, wear or damage. If either lining is worn to within 1/32" of any rivet head, both shoe and lining assemblies must be replaced. Also, if necessary to replace shoes and lining on one wheel, they must be replaced on both wheels to maintain equal brake action.

Caliper Installation

1. If new shoe and lining assemblies are to be installed, use a 4" C-clamp and a block of wood 1 3/4" × 1" and about 3/4" thick to seat the caliper piston in its bore. This must be done to provide clearance for the caliper to fit over new shoes when installed.
2. Be sure brake shoe anti-rattle clip is in place on lower inner brake shoe support on anchor plate with pigtail of clip toward inside of anchor plate. Position inner shoe and lining on anchor plate with lining toward rotor, Fig. 17.
3. Install outer shoe and lining with lower flange ends against the caliper leg abutments and the brake shoe upper flanges over the shoulders on caliper legs. The shoe upper flanges fit tightly against the shoulder machined surfaces. If the same brake shoes and linings are to be used, be sure they are installed in their original positions.
4. Remove C-clamp if used, from the caliper (the piston will remain seated in its bore).
5. Position caliper housing lower V groove on anchor plate lower abutment surface, Fig. 18. Refer to Figs. 18 and 19 to complete assembly following steps shown. Connect brake hose, bleed brakes and replace wheel.

Brake Shoe & Lining, Replace

The procedure to replace the shoe and lining assemblies is the same as the caliper removal discussed previously with the exception that it is not necessary to disconnect the brake hose. Use care to avoid twisting or stretching the brake hose.

Hub & Rotor, Remove

1. Remove caliper and shoes as previously described. If no repairs are necessary on the caliper it is not necessary to disconnect the brake hose. The caliper can be temporarily secured to the upper suspension arm. Do not remove the anchor plate and be careful not to stretch or twist the brake hose.
2. Remove grease cap from wheel spindle and remove cotter pin and nut lock from wheel bearing adjustment nut.
3. Remove wheel bearing adjusting nut and grasp the hub and rotor and pull it out far enough to loosen the washer and outer wheel bearing. Then push it back in and remove the washer, outer wheel bearing and remove the hub and rotor.

FORD (DAYTON) FLOATING CALIPER

The disc brake, Fig. 20, is the floating caliper design with two pistons on one side of the rotor. It is a two piece unit consisting of the caliper and cylinder housing. The caliper is mounted to the anchor plate on two mounting pins and bushings in the anchor plate. The bushings and pins are protected by boot type seals.

DISC BRAKES

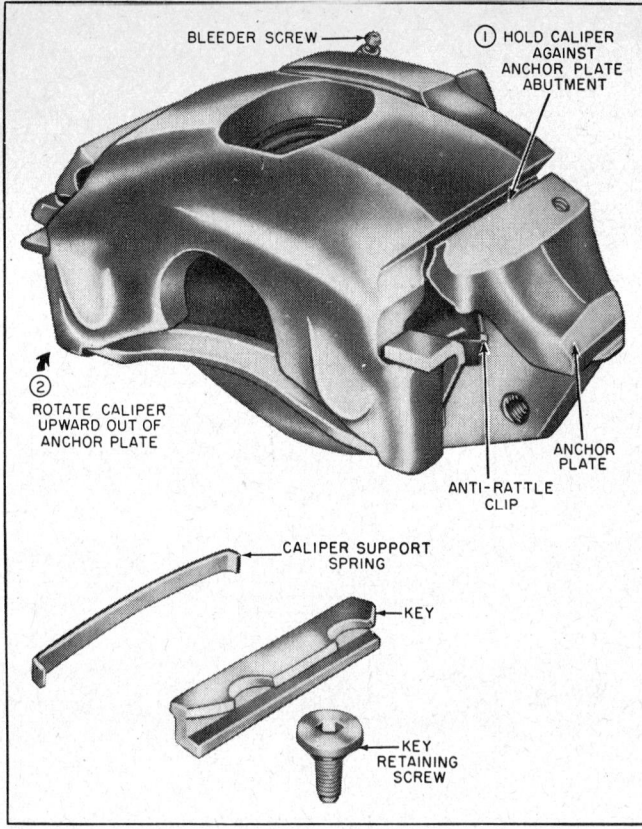

Fig. 16 Removing caliper assembly

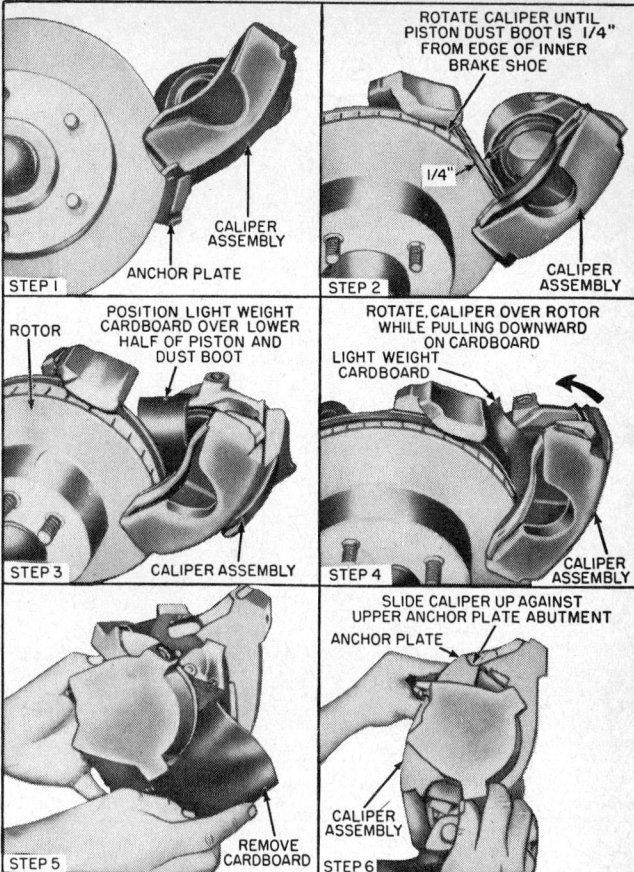

Fig. 18 Installing caliper assembly

Two brake shoe and lining assemblies are used in each caliper, one on each side of the rotor. The shoes are identical and are attached to the caliper with two mounting pins.

The cylinder housing contains the two pistons which, on 1970–72 units, are fitted with an insulator on the front and a seal on the back lip. Also, on 1970–72 units, a friction ring is attached to the back of the piston with a shouldered cap screw. The pistons and cylinder bores are protected by boot seals which are fitted to a groove in the piston and attached to the cylinder housing with retainers. The cylinder assembly is attached to the caliper with two cap screws and washers.

The anchor plate is bolted directly to the spindle. It positions the caliper assembly over the rotor forward of the spindle.

Removal, Shoe & Lining, Replace
Replace shoe and lining assemblies when worn to a minimum of $1/16''$ thickness. Combined thickness of shoe and lining $1/4''$ minimum.
1. Remove the shoe and lining mounting pins, anti-rattle springs and old shoe and lining assemblies.

Installation
1. Remove master cylinder cover.

2. Loosen piston housing to caliper mounting bolts sufficiently to allow installation of new shoes. Do not move pistons.
3. Install new shoes, shoe mounting pins and anti-rattle springs. Be sure spring tangs are located in holes provided in shoe plates.

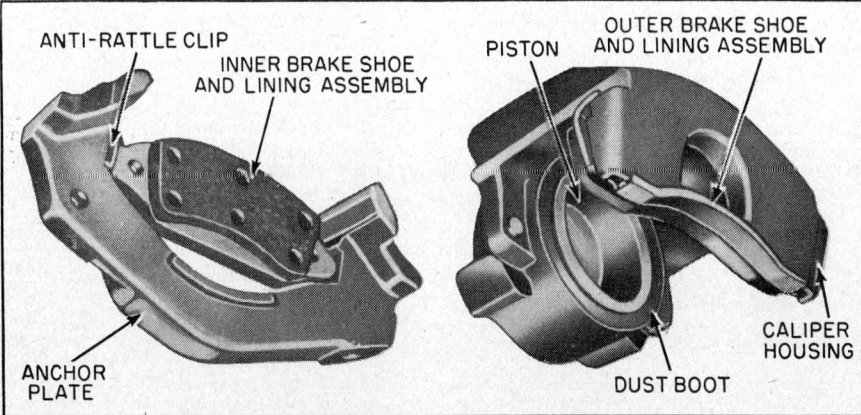

Fig. 17 Caliper and outer shoe removed from anchor plate

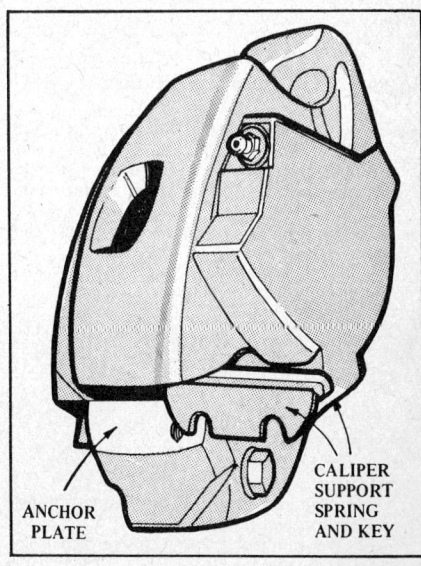

Fig. 19 Installing caliper support spring and retaining key

DISC BRAKES

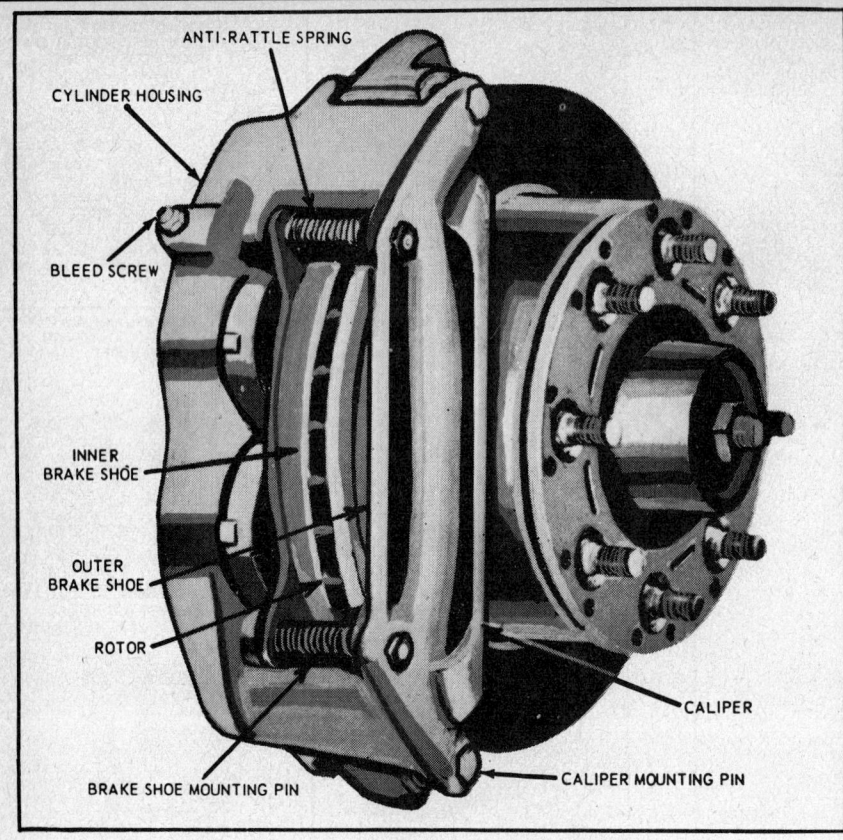

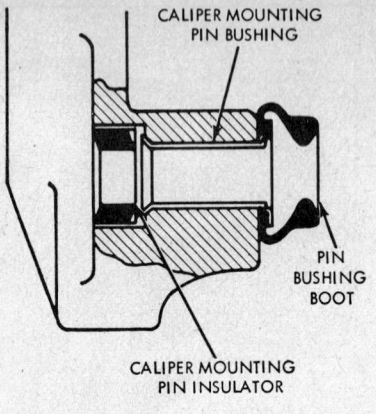

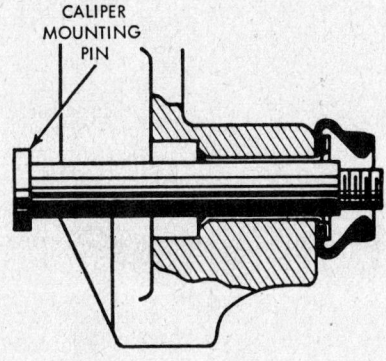

Fig. 20 Floating caliper disc brake

Fig 21 Caliper mounting pin bushing

4. Tighten shoe mounting pins to 17–23 ft. lbs.
5. Reset pistons to correct location in cylinders by placing shims or feeler gauge of .023–.035" between shoe plate of outboard shoe and the caliper. Then retighten piston housing to caliper mounting bolts. Keep cylinder housing square with caliper. Check master cylinder for fluid overflow.
6. Loosen housing to caliper mounting bolts and remove shims. Tighten mounting bolts to 155–185 ft. lbs.
7. Check master cylinder fluid level and replace cover.

Caliper Removal

1. Raise front of vehicle and remove wheel cover.
2. Remove wheel and tire assembly.
3. Remove pins and nuts retaining caliper to anchor plate.
4. Disconnect brake hose from caliper and remove caliper.
5. Reverse procedure to install and bleed brakes.

Caliper Mounting Pin Bushing

Removal
1. Crimp chamfered end of bushing and remove it from anchor plate boss with a pair of pliers.

Installation
1. Assemble pin bushing boot onto caliper mounting pin bushing.
2. Insert pin bushing into anchor plate boss, Fig. 21.
3. Peen end of bushing to conform to chamfered end of anchor plate boss. Use a large ball bearing or similar object.
4. Insert caliper mounting pin into bushing from chamfered end and tap lightly around circumference of pin with a rubber mallet to insure that bushing conforms to anchor plate boss and pin is free in bushing.
5. Insert caliper mounting pin insulator into large end of anchor plate boss.
6. Lubricate bushing with chassis lubricant.

Caliper Service

If caliper is leaking, the piston assemblies must be removed from the housing and replaced, Fig. 22. If cylinder bores are scored, corroded or excessive wear is evident, the piston housing must be replaced. Do not hone the cylinder bores as piston assemblies are not available for oversize bores. The piston housing must be removed from the caliper for replacement.

Disc Hub & Rotor Removal

1. Remove caliper as outlined previously.
2. Remove the dust cap, cotter pin, nut, washer and outer bearing and remove rotor from spindle.
3. Remove inner bearing cone and seal.
4. Reverse procedure to install.

KELSEY-HAYES FLOATING CALIPER

This type brake is a floating caliper, single piston, ventilated unit, actuated by the hydraulic system, Fig. 23. The caliper assembly, Fig. 24, is made up of a floating caliper assembly and an anchor plate. The anchor plate is bolted to the wheel spindle arm by two bolts. The caliper is attached to the anchor plate through two spring steel stabilizers. The caliper slides on two guide pins which also attach to the stabilizers. A single piston is used. The cylinder bore contains a piston with a molded rubber dust boot to seal the cylinder bore from contamination and also to return the piston to the released position when hydraulic pressure is released. Also a rubber piston seal is used to provide sealing between cylinder and piston.

Service Precautions

In addition to the precautions described at the beginning of this chapter, the following must be observed.
1. If the piston is removed for any reason the piston seal must be replaced.
2. During removal and installation of a wheel assembly, use care not to interfere with and damage the caliper splash shield or the bleeder screw fitting.
3. Be sure the vehicle is centered on the hoist before servicing any front end components to avoid bending or damaging the rotor splash shield on full right or left wheel turns.
4. The proportioning valve should not be disassembled or adjustments attempted on it.
5. The wheel and tire must be removed separately from the brake rotor.
6. The caliper assembly must be removed from the spindle prior to removal of shoe and lining assembly.
7. Do not attempt to clean or restore oil or grease soaked brake linings. When contaminated linings are found, linings must be replaced in complete axle sets.

DISC BRAKES

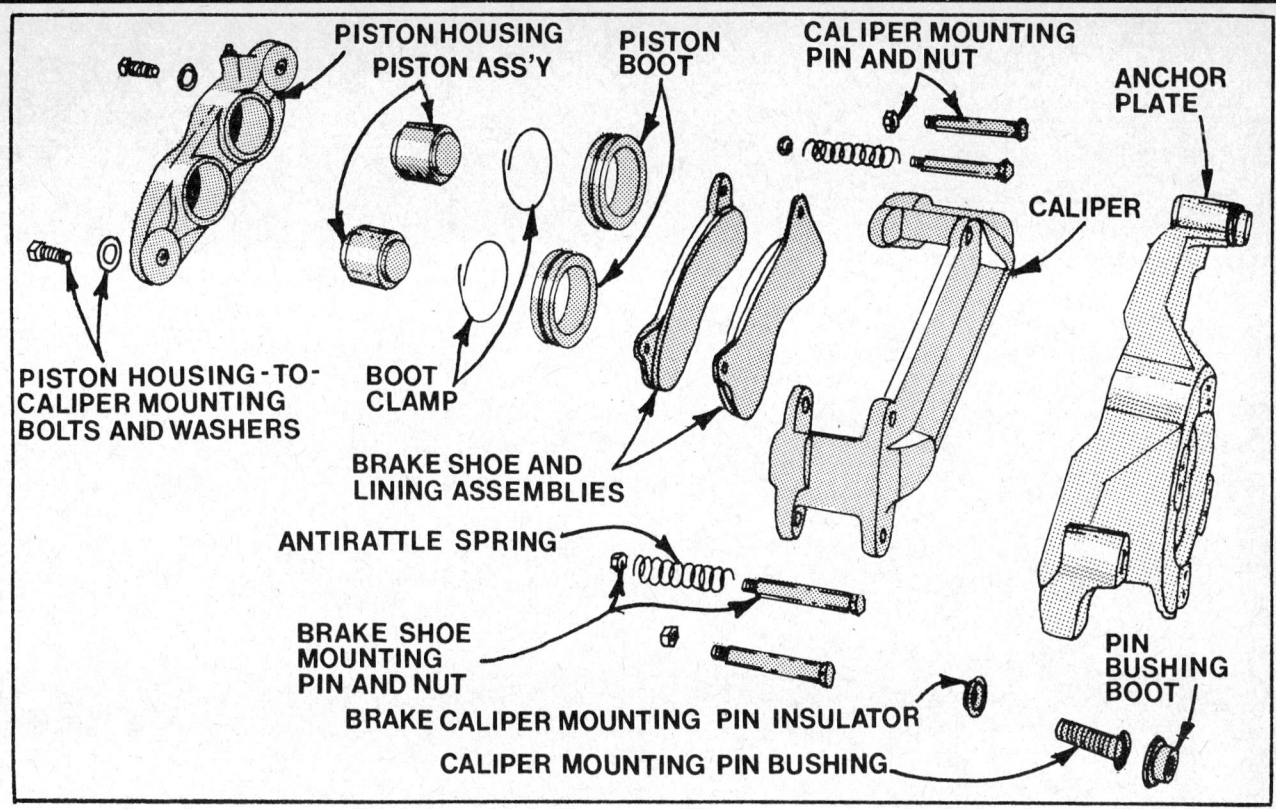

Fig. 22 Ford (Dayton) floating caliper disc brake disassembled (Typical)

Remove & Disassemble Caliper

1. Raise vehicle and remove front wheels.
2. Remove inboard shoe hold down clips and slide outer retaining clips from shoe retaining pins, Fig. 25.
3. Disconnect brake line.
4. Remove guide pins and bolts, if necessary, and remove caliper assembly from stabilizer.
5. Lift caliper away from disc.
6. Slide shoes and lining assemblies out of caliper.
7. Remove guide pin insulators from anchor plate.

NOTE: If necessary to remove the piston, apply air pressure to the fluid port in the caliper, Fig. 26, to remove the piston. Place a cloth over the piston to prevent damage to the piston. If the piston is seized and cannot be forced from the caliper, tap lightly around the piston before applying air pressure. Care should be taken because the piston can develop considerable force due to pressure build-up.

8. Remove dust boot from caliper.
9. Remove rubber piston seal from cylinder and discard it.

Assemble & Install Caliper

1. Apply a film of clean brake fluid to the new caliper piston seal and install it in cylinder bore. Be sure seal does not become twisted and that it is seated fully in the groove.
2. Install a new dust boot by setting the flange squarely in the outer groove of the caliper bore.
3. Coat piston with brake fluid and install in cylinder bore. Spread dust boot over piston as it is installed. Seat dust boot in piston groove.
4. Position inner brake shoe so that ears of shoe rests on top of anchor plate bosses and beneath hold-down springs.
5. Install new caliper guide pin insulators in anchor plate.
6. Position caliper on anchor plate.
7. Install guide pins loosely in anchor plate, being sure guide pins are free of oil, grease or dirt.
8. Install caliper on spindle.

Brake Shoes & Linings, Install

NOTE: When new shoe and lining assemblies are being installed to replace worn linings it will be necessary to push the piston all the way into the caliper bore. This will displace fluid from the caliper into the master cylinder reservoir. Check the primary (front) brake system reservoir level and remove fluid to approximately half full before replacing brake shoes. This will prevent overflow. Do not re-use the removal fluid.

1. Install new caliper guide pin insulators in anchor plate.
2. Position caliper in anchor plate.
3. Install caliper guide pins loosely in anchor plate, being sure they are free of oil, grease or dirt.
4. Position outer brake shoe on caliper and install two retaining pins and clips.
5. Install inner brake shoe so that ears of shoe are on top of anchor plate bosses and under shoe hold-down springs.
6. Position shoe and lining assemblies so that caliper can be placed over rotor. Rotate hammer handle between linings to provide proper clearance.
7. Install caliper over rotor and on spindle. Install and tighten the two caliper bolts, tightening the upper bolt first. Install safety wire and twist ends at least five turns. With moderate pressure applied to brake pedal, tighten stabilizer attaching screws and caliper guide pins.

Fig. 23 Single piston disc brake (typical)

DISC BRAKES

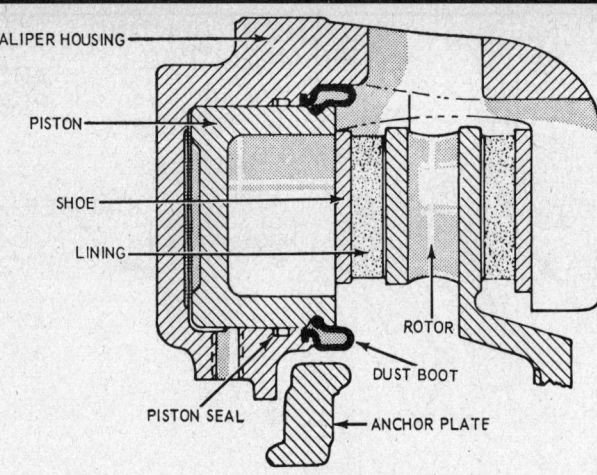

Fig. 24 Single piston disc brake caliper (typical)

KELSEY-HAYES SINGLE PISTON SLIDING CALIPER

This sliding caliper single piston system uses a one piece hub and is actuated by the hydraulic system and disc assembly, Fig. 27. Alignment and positioning of the caliper is achieved by two machined guides or "ways" on the adaptor, while caliper retaining clips allow lateral movement of the caliper, Fig. 28. Outboard shoe flanges are used to position and locate the shoe on the caliper fingers, Fig. 29, while the inboard shoe is retained by the adaptor, Fig. 30. Braking force applied onto the outboard shoe is transferred to the caliper, while braking force applied onto the inboard shoe is transferred directly to the adaptor.

A square cut piston seal provides a hydraulic seal between the piston and the cylinder bore, Fig. 27. A dust boot with a wiping lip installed in a groove in the cylinder bore and piston, prevents contamination in the piston and cylinder bore area. Adjustment between the disc and the shoe is obtained automatically by the outward relocation of the piston as the inboard lining wears and inward movement of the caliper as the outboard lining wears.

Caliper Removal

1. Raise the vehicle and remove front wheel.
2. Remove caliper retaining clips and anti-rattle springs, Fig. 28.
3. Remove caliper from disc by slowly sliding caliper assembly out and away from disc.

NOTE: Use some means to support caliper. Do not let caliper hang from hydraulic line.

Brake Shoe Removal

1. Remove caliper assembly as outlined above.
2. Remove outboard shoe by prying between the shoe and the caliper fingers, Fig. 31, since flanges on outboard shoe retain caliper firmly.

NOTE: Caliper should be supported to avoid damage to the flexible brake hose.

3. Remove inboard brake shoe from the adaptor, Fig. 30.

Brake Shoe Installation

NOTE: Remove approximately 1/3 of the brake fluid out of the reservoir to prevent overflow when pistons are pushed back into the bore.

1. With care, push piston back into bore until bottomed.
2. Install new outboard shoe in recess of caliper.

NOTE: No free play should exist between brake shoe flanges and caliper fingers, Fig. 32.

If up and down movement of the shoe shows free play, shoe must be removed and flanges bent to provide a slight interference fit, Fig. 29. Reinstall shoe after modification, if shoe can not be finger snapped into place, use light "C" clamp pressure, Fig. 33.

3. Position inboard shoe with flanges inserted in adaptor "ways," Fig. 30.
4. Carefully slide caliper assembly into adaptor and over the disc while aligning caliper on machined "ways" of adaptor.

NOTE: Make sure dust boot is not pulled out from groove when piston and boot

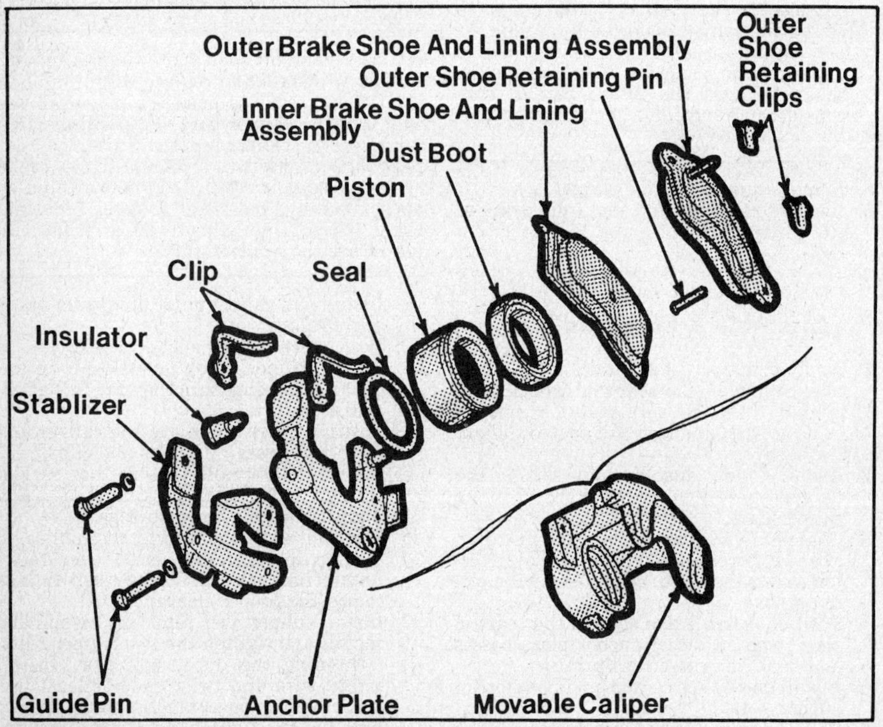

Fig. 25 Single piston disc brake caliper disassembled (typical)

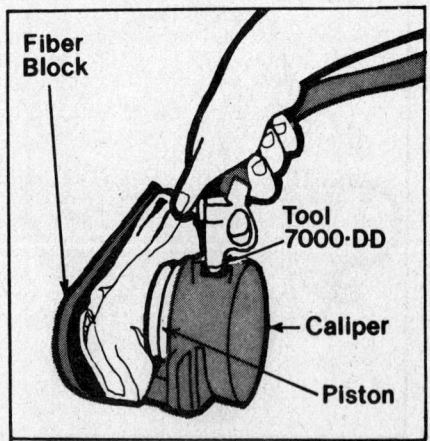

Fig. 26 Removing piston with air pressure

DISC BRAKES

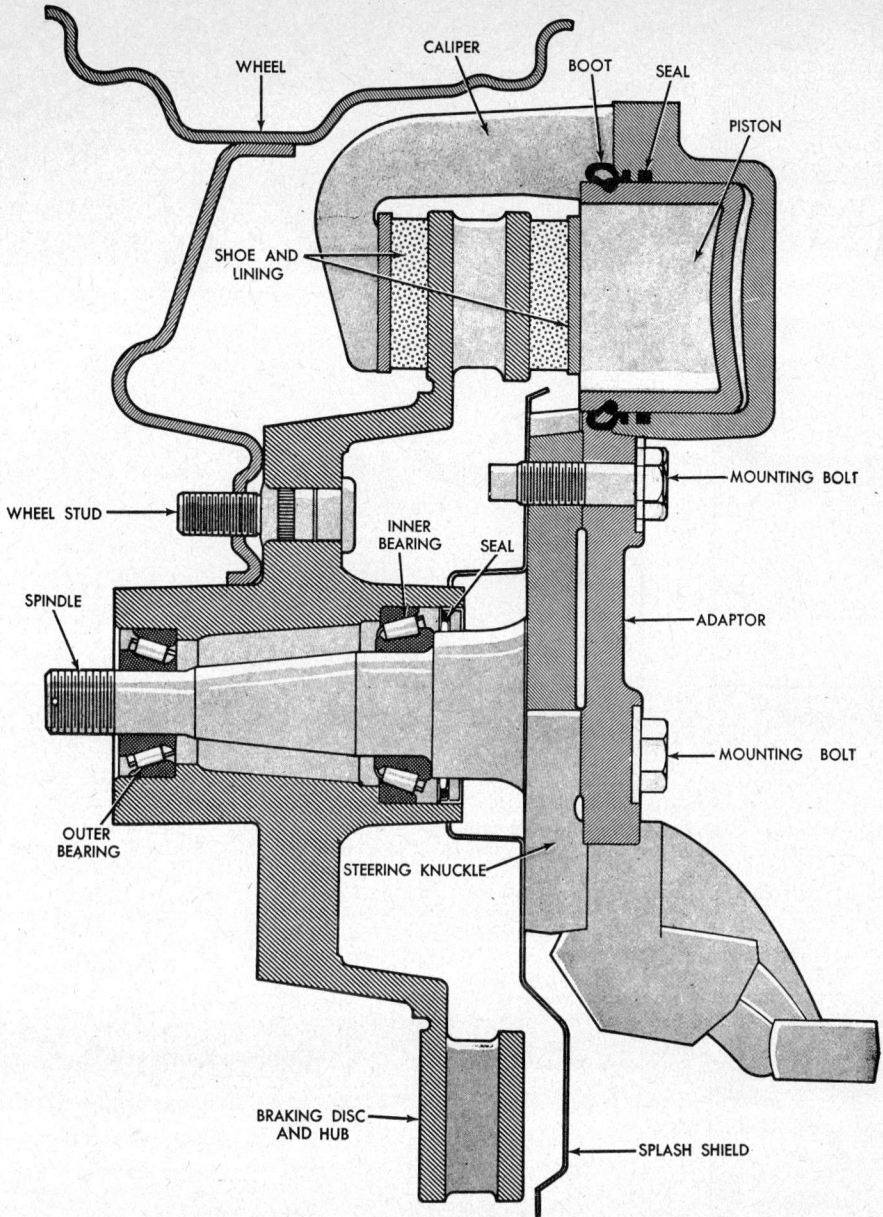

Fig. 27 Sectional view or Kelsey-Hayes single pistong sliding caliper disc brake

4. Mount caliper in a vise equipped with protector jaws.

CAUTION: Excessive vise pressure will distort caliper bore.

5. Remove the dust boot, Fig. 34.
6. Insert a suitable tool such as a small, pointed wooden or plastic object between the cylinder bore and the seal and work seal out of the groove in the piston bore.

NOTE: A metal tool such as a screwdriver should not be used since it can cause damage to the piston bore or burr the edges of the seal groove.

Caliper Assembly

1. Before installing the new piston seal in groove of bore, dip seal in Ucon LB1145Y24 lubricant or equivalent. Work seal gently into the groove (using clean fingers) until seal is properly seated, make sure that seal is not twisted or rolled.

NOTE: Old seals should never be reused.

2. With new piston boot lubricated generously with Ucon LB1145Y24 or equivalent. Using finger pressure, install into caliper by pushing into outer groove of the caliper bore. When properly positioned in groove boot will snap into place. Double check to make sure boot is properly installed and seated by running finger around the inside of the boot.
3. Plug high pressure inlet to caliper and bleeder screw hole and coat piston with a generous amount of lubricant. Spread boot with finger and work piston into boot while pressing down on piston. As piston is depressed, entrapped air below piston will force boot around piston and into its groove.
4. Remove the plug and apply uniform force to the piston (avoid cocking piston) until piston bottoms in bore.
5. Install caliper and shoes as described under "Brake Shoe Installation."

slide over the inboard shoe.

5. Install anti-rattle springs and retaining clips and torque retaining screws to 180 inch-pounds.

NOTE: The inboard shoe anti-rattle spring is to be installed on top of the retainer spring plate, Fig. 28.

Caliper Disassembly

1. With caliper and shoes removed as described previously, place the caliper onto the upper control arm and slowly depress brake pedal, in turn hydraulically pushing piston out of bore.

NOTE: Some 1975 vehicles use plastic caliper pistons. These pistons can be interchanged with the 3.1 bore caliper assembly. However, do not attempt to pry the piston from the caliper, as this may damage the dust boot groove in the piston, and lead to subsequent brake fluid leakage and corrosion of the caliper bore.

2. Support pedal below first inch of pedal travel to prevent excessive fluid loss.
3. To remove piston from the opposite caliper, disconnect flexible brake line at frame bracket, from vehicle side where piston has been removed previously and plug tube to prevent pressure loss. By depressing brake pedal this piston can also be hydraulically pushed out.

CAUTION: Air pressure should never be used to remove piston from bore.

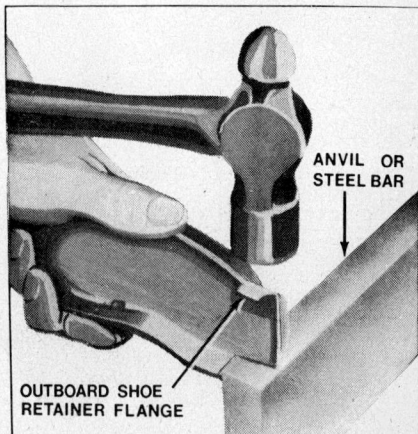

Fig. 29 Fitting outboard shoe retaining flange

671

DISC BRAKES

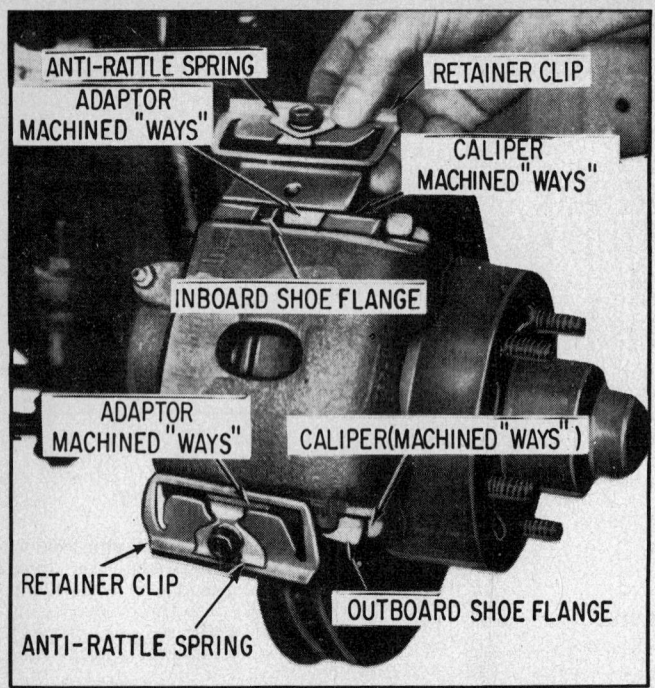

Fig. 28 Caliper mounted "ways" & assembly retention

Fig. 30 Replacing inboard shoe

KELSEY-HAYES DUAL PISTON SLIDING CALIPER

This sliding caliper dual piston system uses a one piece hub and is actuated by the hydraulic system and disc assembly Fig. 35. Alignment and positioning of the caliper is achieved by two machined guides or "ways" on the torque plate, while the caliper retaining clips allow lateral movement of the caliper. Outboard shoe flanges are used to position and locate the shoe on the caliper fingers while the inboard shoe is retained by the torque plate, Fig. 36. However, on some applications, the outboard shoe and lining assembly is retained by a hold-down spring, pin and cup. Braking force applied onto the outboard shoe is transferred to the caliper, while braking force applied onto the inboard shoe is transferred directly to the torque plate.

A square cut piston seal provides a hydraulic seal between the piston and the cylinder bore. A dust boot with a wiping lip installed in a groove in the cylinder bore and piston, prevents contamination in the piston and cylinder bore area. Adjustment between the disc and the shoe is obtained automatically by the outward relocation of the piston as the inboard lining wears and inward movement of the caliper as the outboard lining wears.

Caliper Removal

1. Remove brake fluid from master cylinder to bring fluid level to 1/3 full.
2. Raise vehicle and remove front wheel.
3. Remove retaining plate mounting screws, then the retaining plates and springs,

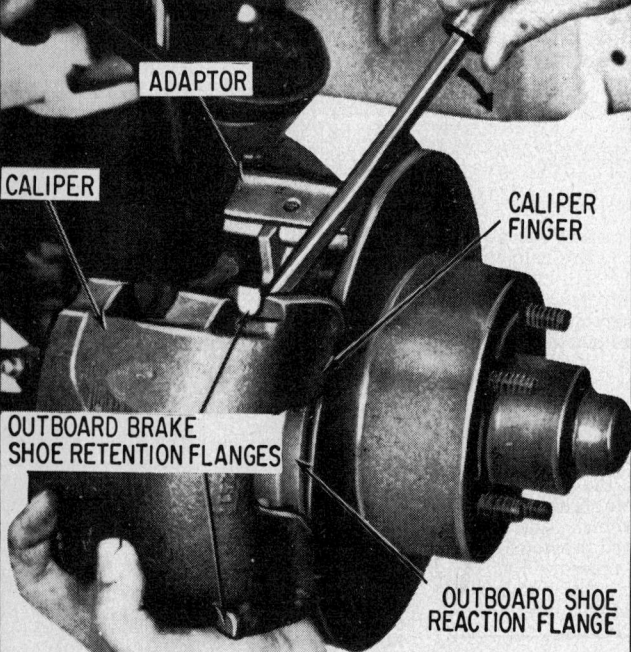

Fig. 31 Removing outboard shoe

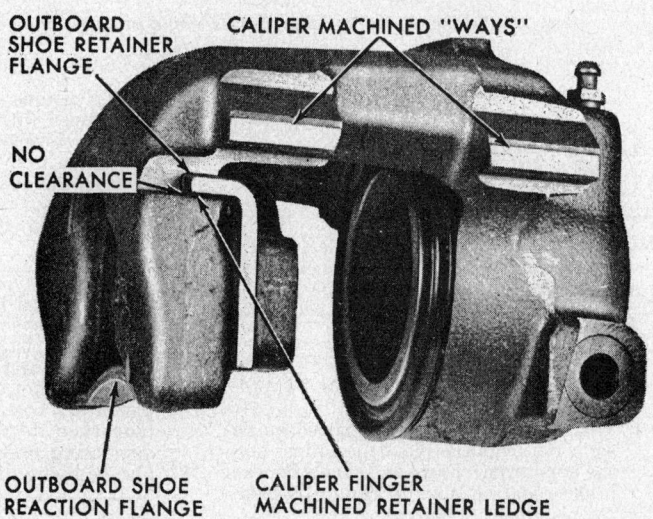

Fig. 32 Positioning outboard shoe onto caliper finger machined retainer ledge

DISC BRAKES

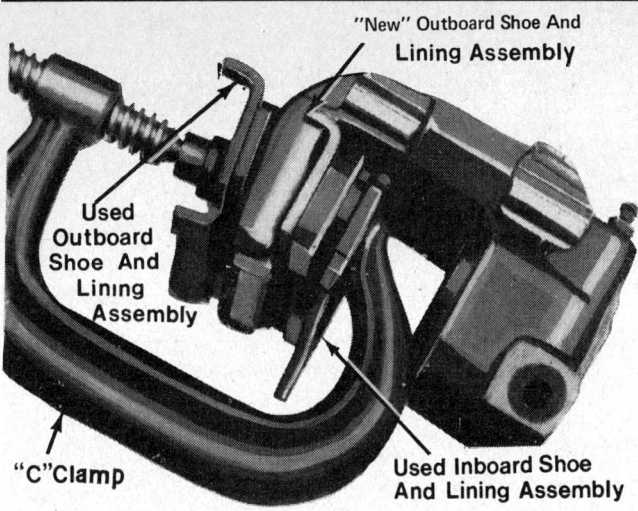

Fig. 33 Installing outboard shoe using "C" clamp

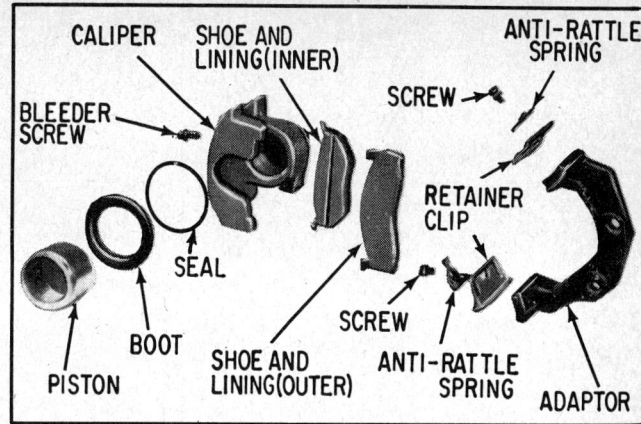

Fig. 34 Exploded view of a Kelsey-Hayes single piston sliding caliper disc brake

Fig. 37.
4. Remove caliper from disc by slowly sliding caliper assembly out and away from disc.

NOTE: Use some means to support caliper. Do not let caliper hang from hydraulic line.

Brake Shoe Removal

1. Remove caliper assembly outlined above.
2. Remove inboard brake shoe from anchor plate, Fig. 38.
3. Tap lightly on outboard brake shoe to free from caliper. The brake shoe may be pried from the caliper using a suitable tool.

NOTE: On some applications, remove the outboard shoe and lining assembly hold-down spring, pin and cup.

Brake Shoe Installation

1. Install new inboard brake shoe into torque plate.
2. Push pistons back into bore until bottomed using a "C" clamp and block of wood, Fig. 39.
3. Install outboard brake shoe with lower flange ends against caliper leg abutments and upper flanges over shoulder over caliper legs. Then secure brake shoe by crimping in position using vise grips, Fig. 40.

NOTE: On some applications, install the outboard shoe and lining assembly hold-down spring, pin and cup.

4. Install caliper onto torque plate.
5. Install retaining plate springs and retaining plate and torque mounting screws to 17-22 ft. lbs.

Caliper Disassembly

1. Remove caliper and brake shoes as previously outlined.
2. To remove pistons, apply air pressure to the fluid port of the caliper to ease pistons from bore, Fig. 41. Use a block of wood and a shop towel to protect pistons from damage.

NOTE: Use just enough air pressure to ease pistons from bores since they may be damaged if violently blown out. Also, do not attempt to catch pistons with fingers since this could result in personal injury.

3. Remove piston boots, Fig. 35.
4. Insert a suitable tool such as a small, pointed wooden or plastic object between the cylinder bore and the seal and work seal out of groove in piston bore.

NOTE: A metal tool such as a screwdriver

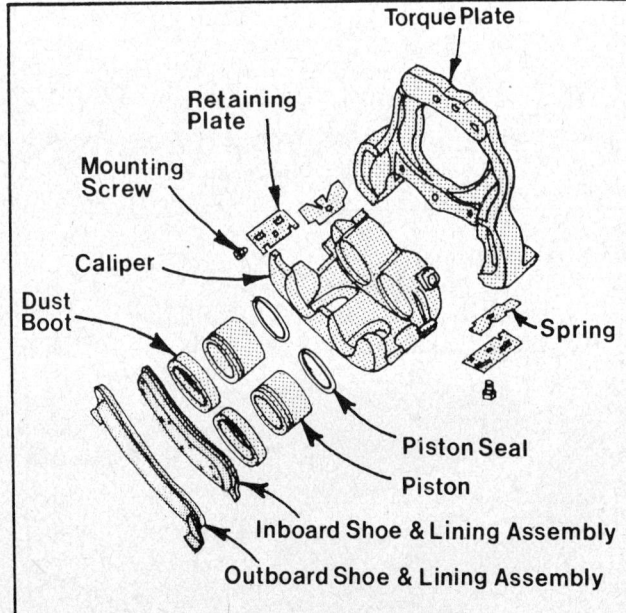

Fig. 35 Exploded view of a Kelsey-Hayes dual piston sliding caliper disc brake

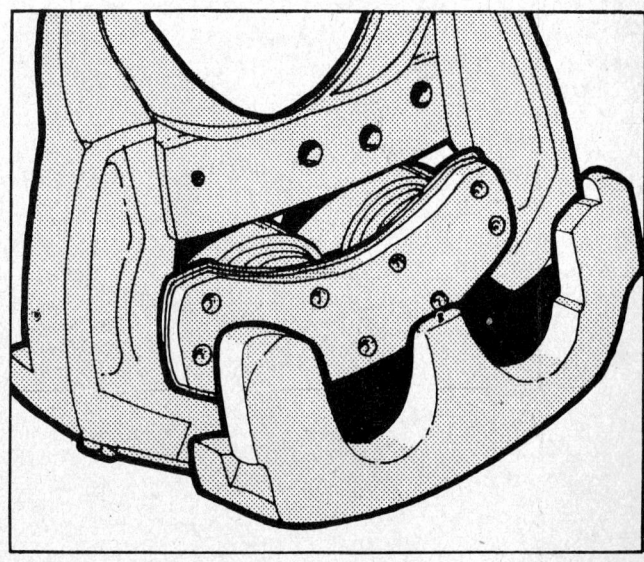

Fig. 36 Inboard brake shoe

673

DISC BRAKES

Fig. 37 Removing retaining plate screws

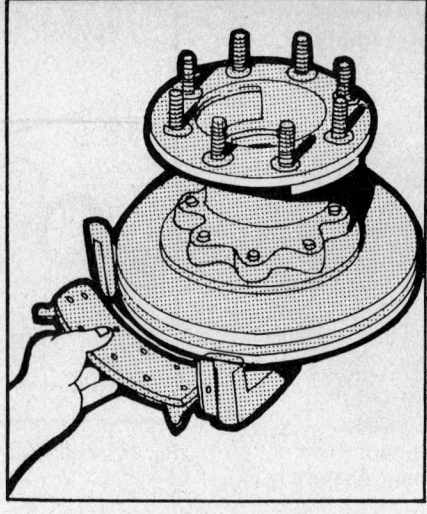

Fig. 38 Removing inboard brake shoe

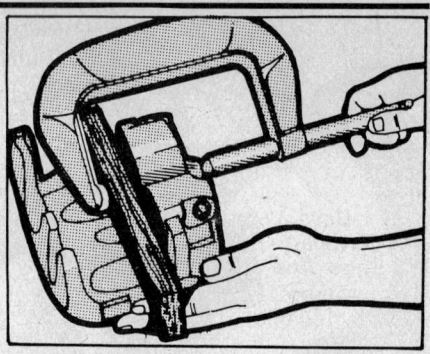

Fig. 39 Installing pistons with "C" clamp

should not be used since it can cause damage to the piston bore or burr the edges of the seal groove.

Caliper Assembly

1. Before installing new piston seal in groove of bore, dip in clean brake fluid. Work seal gently into groove (using clean fingers) until seal is properly seated and ensure seal is not twisted or rolled, Fig. 42.
2. Install dust boot in cylinder groove in similar manner as piston seal described previously.
3. Coat pistons with clean brake fluid and install pistons into bore. Work dust boot around piston using a small flat plastic tool.
4. Press piston straight into caliper bore until bottomed. The dust boot should slide up the piston and enter its groove in the piston.

NOTE: Apply uniform force to piston to avoid cocking piston in bore.

5. Install caliper and brake shoes as described under "Brake Shoe Installation".

BENDIX SLIDING CALIPER DISC BRAKE SERVICE

The Bendix sliding caliper disc brake is used on trucks utilizing the Hydro-Boost power brake system with both the front disc brakes and the 4-wheel disc brakes.

NOTE: On the 4-wheel disc brakes the front & rear systems are identical.

The sliding caliper attaches to and slides on the steering knuckle. The caliper assembly is held in place with a support key and spring Fig. 43. A screw prevents the key from sliding on the steering knuckle. The linings are riveted to the brake shoes. The inboard and outboard brake shoes are not interchangeable.

Caliper Removal

1. Siphon two-thirds of brake fluid from master cylinder reservoir serving front disc brakes.
2. Raise vehicle, support on jackstands and remove front wheels.
3. Bottom the caliper piston in bore. Insert a screwdriver between inboard shoe and piston, then pry piston back into bore. The piston can also be bottomed in the bore with a large "C" clamp, Fig. 44.
4. Remove support key retaining screw.
5. Drive caliper support key and spring from steering knuckle with a suitable drift and hammer, Fig. 45.
6. Lift caliper from anchor plate and off rotor, Fig. 46. Hang caliper from coil spring with wire. Do not allow caliper to hang from brake hose.
7. Remove inboard brake shoe from steering knuckle, then the anti-rattle spring from the brake shoe.
8. Remove outboard brake shoe from caliper, it may be necessary to loosen the brake shoe with a hammer to permit shoe removal.

Caliper Disassembly

1. Drain brake fluid from caliper.
2. Position caliper with shop cloths, Fig. 47, and apply compressed air to fluid inlet port to ease piston from bore.

NOTE: Do not attempt to catch piston or

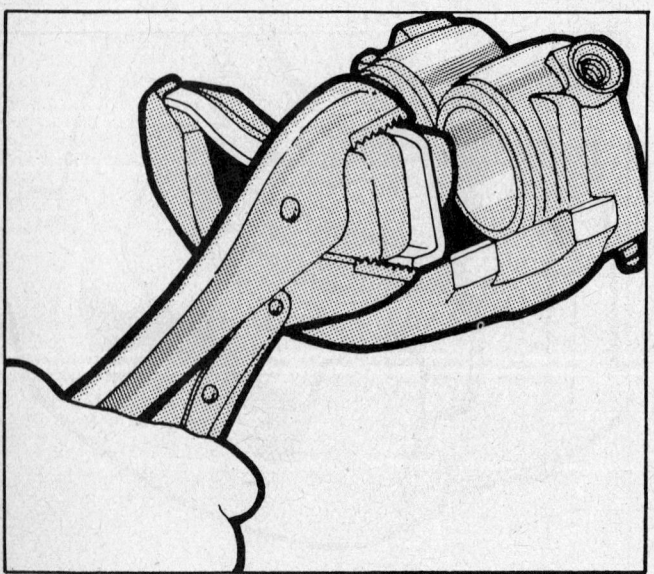

Fig. 40 Securing outboard brake shoe

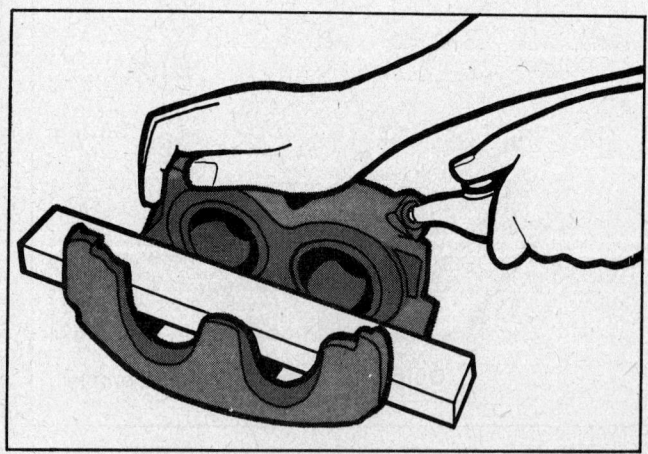

Fig. 41 Removing pistons with air pressure

DISC BRAKES

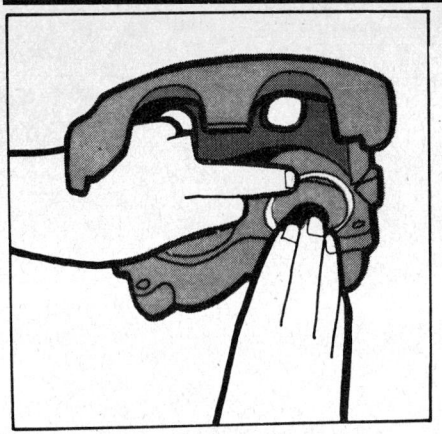

Fig. 42 Piston seal installation

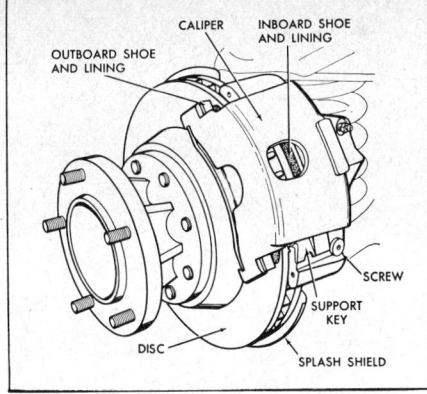

Fig. 43 Bendix sliding caliper disc brake

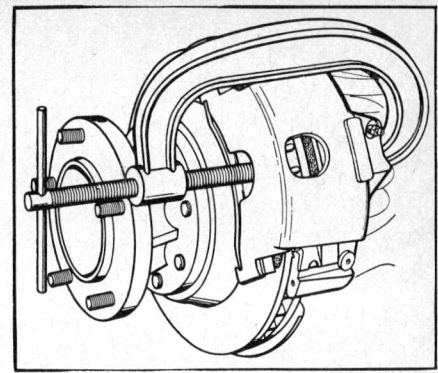

Fig. 44 Bottoming piston in bore

to protect it when applying compressed air since personal injury is possible.

3. Remove boot from piston, then the piston seal from bore, Fig. 48. Use wooden or plastic tool to remove piston seal since metal tools may damage piston.
4. Remove bleeder screw.

Caliper Assembly

1. Coat square cut piston seal with clean brake fluid, then install seal into piston bore. Work seal into groove with clean fingers.
2. Install and torque bleeder screw to 100 inch lbs.
3. Lubricate boot and tool J-24548 with clean brake fluid, then place dust seal on tool, allowing 1/4 inch of tool to extend past small lip of boot Fig. 49.
4. Place dust seal and boot over piston bore, then work large lip of boot into seal groove, Fig. 50. Ensure dust seal is fully seated.
5. Lubricate caliper piston and insert through tool. Center piston in bore and use a hammer handle to apply pressure to install piston halfway into bore, Fig. 50.
6. Remove tool J-24548 and seat small lip of boot in caliper piston groove, then bottom piston in bore.

Brake Shoe & Lining, Replace

The procedures to remove & install the brake shoe and lining assemblies are outlined under "Caliper Removal" and "Caliper Installation". It is not necessary to disconnect the brake hose, however, use caution not to twist or kink hose.

Caliper Installation

1. Clean and lubricate sliding surfaces of caliper and the anchor plate with Delco Silicone Lube, P/N 5459912, or equivalent.
2. Install inboard brake shoe anti-rattle spring on brake shoe rear flange, ensure looped section of clip is facing away from rotor.
3. Install inboard brake shoe in steering knuckle.
4. Install outboard brake shoe in caliper. Ensure the shoe flange is seated fully into outboard arms of caliper. It may be necessary to use a "C" clamp to seat the shoe.
5. Place caliper assembly over rotor and position in steering knuckle. Ensure dust boot is not torn or mispositioned by inboard brake shoe during caliper installation.
6. Align caliper with steering knuckle abutment surfaces, then insert support key and spring between abutment surfaces at the trailing end of caliper and steering knuckle. With a hammer and brass drift, drive caliper support key and spring into position, then install and torque support key retaining screw to 12–18 ft. lbs.
7. Refill master cylinder to within one inch of rim. Press brake pedal several times to seat shoes.
8. Install front wheels and lower vehicle.

FORD (DAYTON) DUAL PISTON SLIDING CALIPER

This disc brake, Fig. 51, is of the sliding caliper design with two pistons on one side of the rotor. The caliper which slides on the anchor plate is retained by a key and spring. A key retaining screws maintains the key and spring in proper position. Two brake shoes and lining assemblies, one on each side of the rotor, are used and are not identical. The brake shoes slide on the caliper bridge and one anti-rattle clip is used on both shoes. The cylinder housing contains the two pistons. The pistons and caliper bores are protected by boot seals fitted to a piston groove and attached to the cylinder housing. The cylinder assembly is attached to the caliper with cap

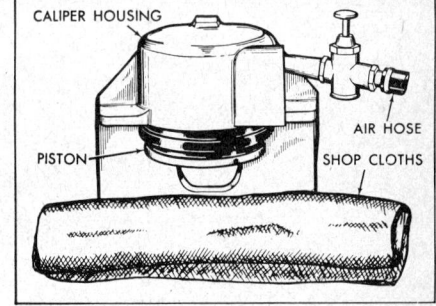

Fig. 47 Removing caliper piston

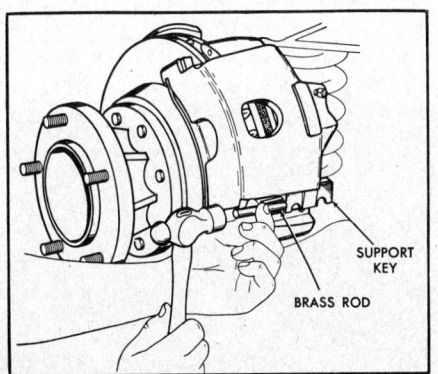

Fig. 45 Removing caliper support key

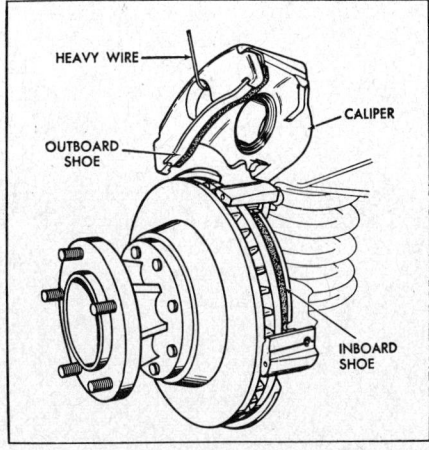

Fig. 46 Removing caliper from disc

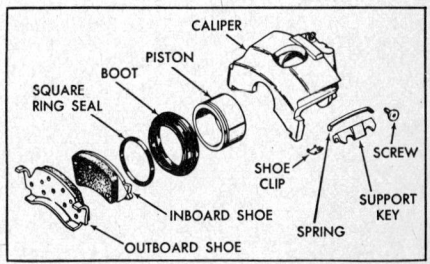

Fig. 48 Caliper, disassembled

675

DISC BRAKES

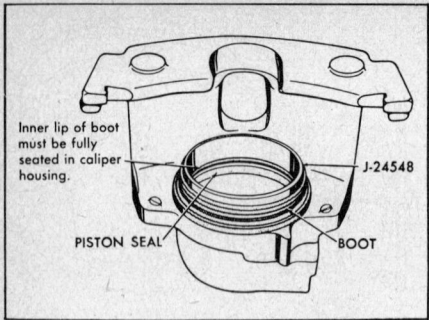

Fig. 49 Installing caliper piston boot

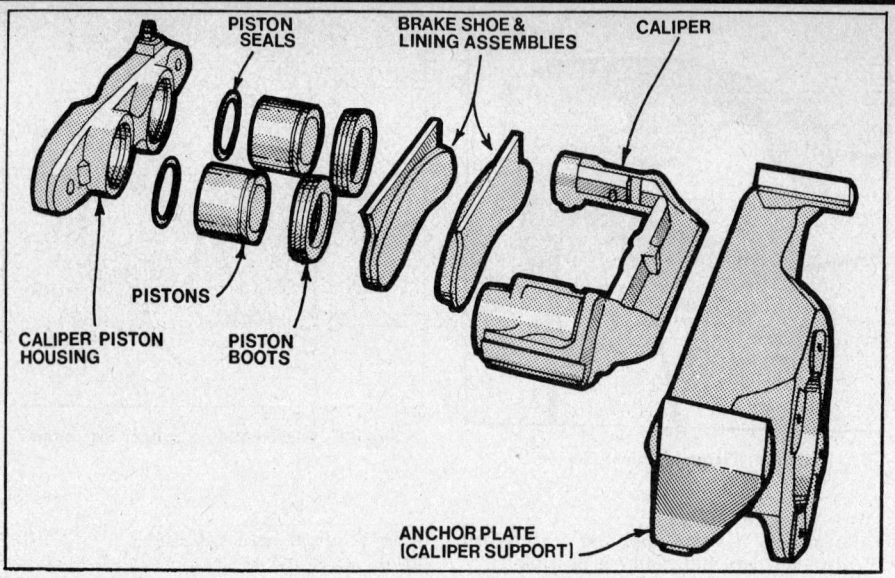

Fig. 51 Ford (Dayton) Dual Piston Sliding Caliper disc brake

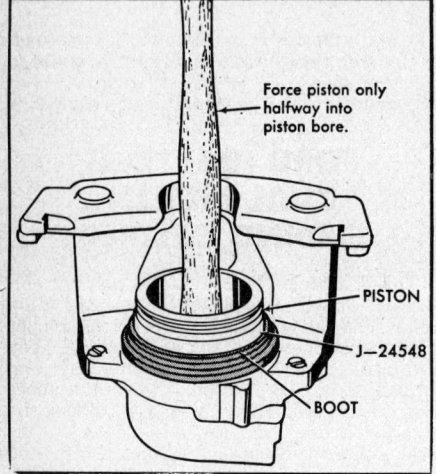

Fig. 50 Installing piston in caliper

screws and washers. The anchor plate and shield are bolted to the spindle. The anchor plate positions the caliper over the rotor forward of the spindle.

Brake Shoe & Lining, Replace

Removal

1. To avoid fluid overflow when pistons are pushed into caliper, remove some brake fluid from master cylinder.
2. Raise vehicle and remove wheel assembly.
3. Remove key retaining screw, Fig. 52, then using a brass drift and hammer, drive out the key and spring, Fig. 53.
4. Remove caliper and its support by rotating the key and spring end out and away from the rotor. Slide opposite end of caliper clear of the slide in the support and off the rotor. Place caliper on tie rod or axle.

NOTE: Do not allow the brake hose to support weight of caliper, as this can damage the hose.

5. Remove caliper brake shoe anti-rattle spring and inner and outer shoe and lining assemblies.
6. Clean and inspect caliper assembly. Thoroughly clean areas of caliper and support that contact during the sliding action of the caliper.

Installation

1. Place used inner lining and shoe assembly over the pistons, then place a C-clamp on the caliper housing midway between the two pistons over the lining and shoe assembly, Fig. 54. Tighten the clamp until pistons are bottomed in caliper, then remove C-clamp and lining and shoe assembly.
2. Install the new inner and outer shoe and lining assemblies, and the anti-rattle spring.
3. Position caliper rail into the slide on the support and rotate the caliper onto rotor.
4. Position the key and spring, Fig. 55, then install the sub-assembly between the caliper and support. Note that the spring is between the key and caliper and that spring tangs overlap the ends of the key.
5. If necessary use a screwdriver to hold caliper against support assembly, then using a hammer, drive the key and spring into position aligning the correct notch with the existing hole in the support.
6. Install the key to support retaining screw and torque to 12–20 ft. lbs.
7. Install wheel assembly and lower vehicle. Check brake fluid level and add as neces-

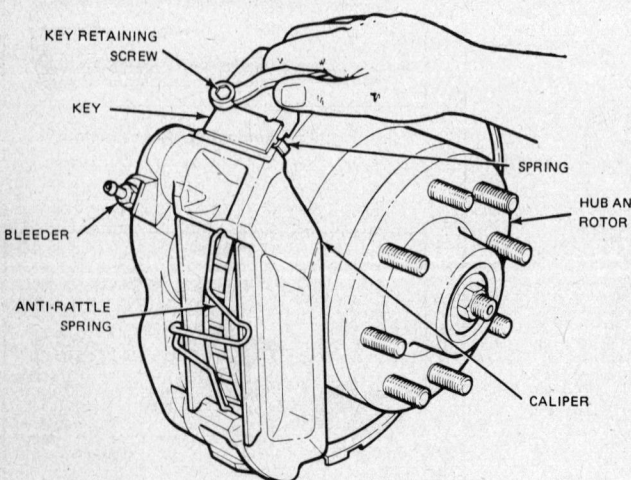

Fig. 52 Removing key retaining screw

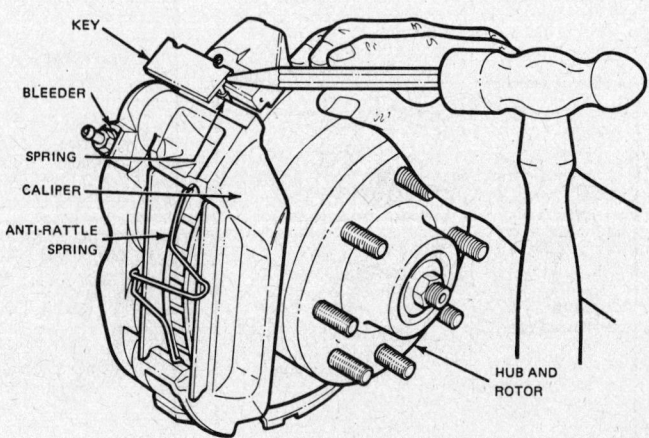

Fig. 53 Removing spring and key

DISC BRAKES

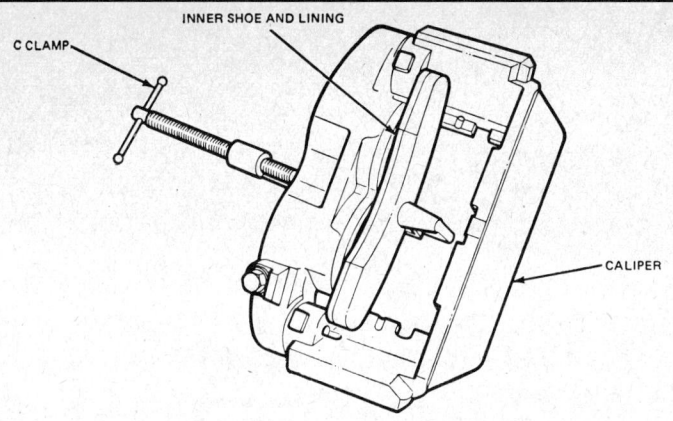

Fig. 54 Bottoming caliper pistons

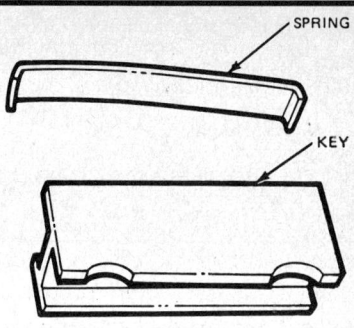

Fig. 55 Caliper spring and key

sary with heavy duty brake fluid.
8. Depress brake pedal several times to seat linings on rotor. Do not move vehicle until a firm brake pedal has been obtained.

Caliper, Replace

Removal
1. Perform steps 1 to 5 outlined under "Brake Shoe & Lining, Replace" Removal procedure.
2. Disconnect flexible hose from caliper.
3. Remove caliper assembly.

Installation
1. Perform steps 1 and 2 outlined under "Brake Shoe & Lining, Replace" installation procedure.
2. Connect flexible hose to caliper.
3. Perform steps 3 to 6 outlined under "Brake Shoe & Lining, Replace" installation procedure, then after bleeding brakes, proceed with the remainder of the procedure.

Caliper Overhaul

Disassembly
1. Drain brake fluid from caliper.
2. Remove brake shoe and lining assemblies.
3. To remove pistons, apply air pressure to the caliper fluid port to ease the pistons from the bores. Use a block of wood and a shop towel to protect pistons from damage.
4. Remove cylinder housing to caliper attaching bolts and separate housing from caliper.
5. Remove piston seals.

Assembly
1. Lubricate cylinder bores and new piston seals with clean brake fluid.
2. Install piston seals in cylinder bore grooves.
3. Lubricate dust boot retaining lips with clean brake fluid and install retaining lips in the boot retaining grooves in the cylinder bores.
4. Lubricate piston with clean brake fluid and insert pistons into dust boots. Start pistons into cylinders until located beyond the piston seals.
5. Place a block of wood over one piston and press piston into cylinder using caution not to damage the piston seals or piston. Press the second piston into the bore.
6. Place piston housing on caliper and install and torque mounting bolts to 155–185 ft. lbs.

BLUE OX COMPRESSION BRAKE

INTRODUCTION

The compression brake is basically a butterfly valve fitted into exhaust pipe between manifold and muffler, which restricts exhaust and causes a build up of 30 to 45 pounds of pressure in the exhaust manifold. The compression brake transforms the engine into a low pressure air compressor, driven by the wheels, which slows down or retards the vehicle. The butterfly is controlled by an air or vacuum switch mounted in the cab. A valve actuated by the accelerator pedal linkage releases the compression brake the instant the engine is accelerated. The compression brake causes a pressure build up in the cylinder during the exhaust stroke when activated.

ADJUSTMENTS

Throttle Valve

Striker arm on accelerator rod should push throttle valve arm when accelerator linkage is in idle position. Throttle valve arm must

Fig. 1 Compression brake adjustments

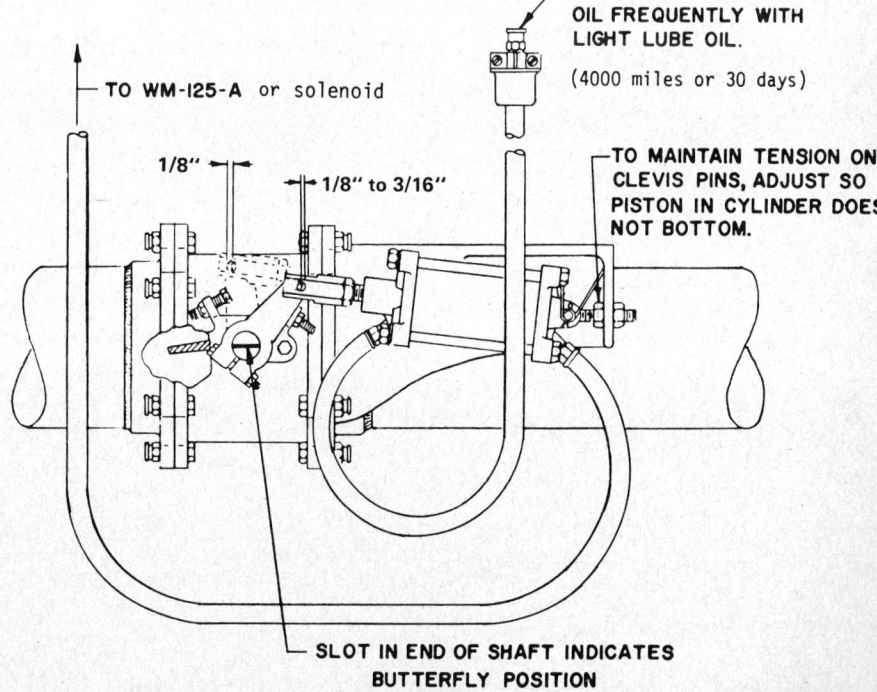

BLUE OX COMPRESSION BRAKE

release at first movement of accelerator linkage to a higher RPM. This movement causes air in brake operating cylinder to be exhausted through exhaust port of throttle valve.

Butterfly Setting

1. Remove clevis pin from piston rod, then move butterfly shaft lever to the forward position.

NOTE: Notch on end of shaft indicates butterfly position. If shaft does not rotate freely, disassemble unit and clean as necessary.

2. Rotate shaft back and forth to ensure butterfly is not loose on shaft.

NOTE: If butterfly is loose on shaft, install new butterfly attaching nuts and bolts. Special heat resistant stainless steel nuts and bolts must be used.

3. Loosen forward step screw, then rotate shaft to closed position.
4. Adjust lever stop screw so that screw contacts stop slightly before butterfly stops in housing.

Cylinder

1. With clevis pin removed from piston rod, place dash control switch on.
2. Check to see that clevis pin hole in piston rod is moving slightly farther than pin hole in lever. The travel of the piston should be 1/8 inch greater than travel of lever, Fig. 1. Adjust lever stop screw as specified.
3. Relieve air pressure and check to ensure that piston moves back freely and completely into cylinder.
4. Check to ensure piston is not bottomed, if piston is bottomed return spring should be checked and replaced if necessary.
5. Place control lever in off position.
6. Clevis pin hole in piston rod should be 1/8 to 3/16 inch closer to cylinder than hole in lever with lever against stop, Fig. 1. Adjust stop screw to obtain specified clearance.
7. Pull piston rod out of cylinder and insert clevis pin.

Final Adjustment

1. With engine operating at idle speed observe RPM, then place compression brake into full on position.
2. A maximum drop of 50 to 75 RPM is allowable.

NOTE: Engine should idle without laboring excessively. If engine does not labor slightly, check for burned butterfly, leaking exhaust gaskets or warped exhaust manifold.

3. If RPM drop is above maximum, adjust lever stop screw to open butterfly slightly.

JACOBS ENGINE BRAKE

MODEL APPLICATION CHART

Cummins Diesel Engines

Model 20
NHC-4	NH-220	NTE-235
NH-180	NHS-6	NTO-6
NHE-180	NHRS-6	NRT-6
NH-195	NT-4	NRTO-6
NHE-195	NT-6	NTF-6

Models 25 & 25A
NHE-220	NHE-225	NH-250
NT-280	NT-335	NT-380
NTC-260, 335	NHC-225, 250	NHCT-240, 270

Model 25B
N-927	NH-250	NHE-220, 225
NHCT-270	NHD-230	NT-280, 300
NHF-240, 265	NHTF-295	NT-335, 380
NTA-370, 420	NTC-290	NTC-335-350
NTF-295, 365	NHC-290	NHC-225, 250

Model 59
V6-140	V6-155	V8-185
V8-210	V8-225	

Model 903
V-903	VT-903

Detroit Diesel Engines

Model 53A
3-53	4-53	6V-53	8V-53

Model 71
4-71	6V-71	12V-71
6-71	8V-71	16V-71

Mack Diesel Engines

Models 67 & 675
673	675	711

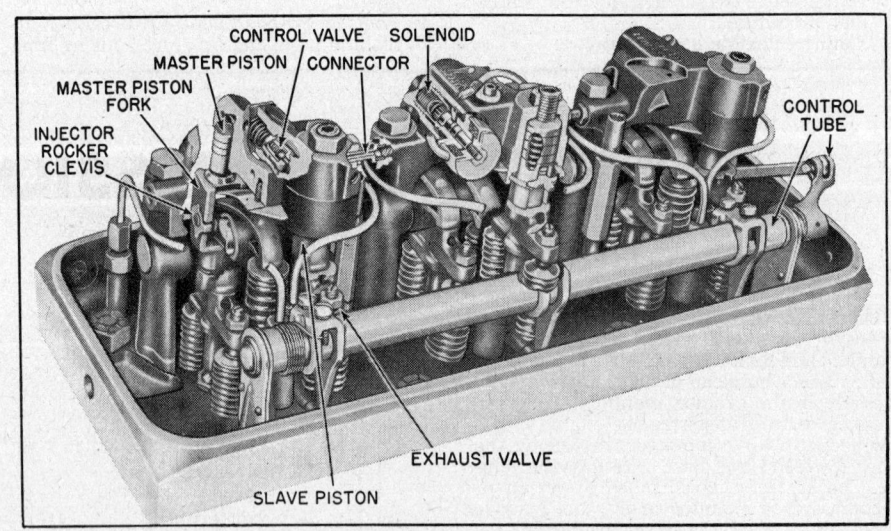

Fig. 1 Jacobs engine brake. Typical

INTRODUCTION

The Jacobs Engine Brake, Fig. 1, is a device which, when energized, effectively converts a power producing diesel engine into a power absorbing air pump. This transfer of motion is accomplished when desired through a master-slave piston arrangement which opens the exhaust valves near the top of the compression stroke, releasing the compressed cylinder charge to exhaust.

The blowdown of compressed air to atmospheric pressure prevents the return of energy to the piston on the expansion stroke, the effect being a net energy loss since the work done in compressing the charge is not returned during the expansion process.

ADJUSTMENTS

Slave Piston, Model 20

1. Loosen and back off locknut.
2. Using Allen wrench, back off slave piston adjusting screw until piston spring "lets go" of adjusting screw (valve piston will move up into housing under influence of its spring until it seats in its bore, remov-

JACOBS ENGINE BRAKE

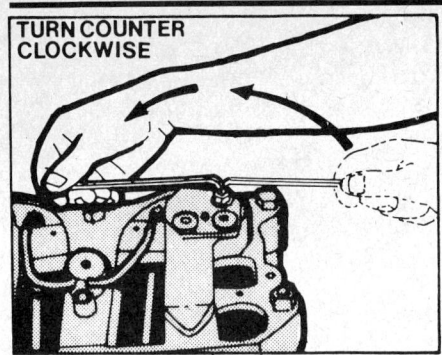

Fig. 2 Slave piston adjustment. Model 20

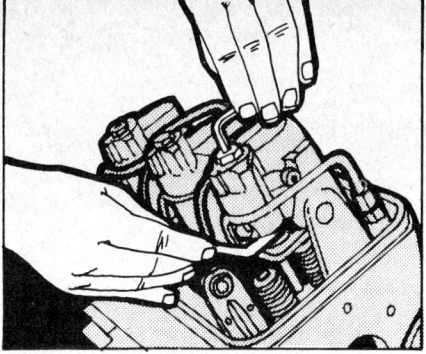

Fig. 3 Slave piston adjustment Models 25, 25A, 25B, 59 & 71 (typical)

Fig. 4 Slave piston adjustment. Models 25, 25A & 25B

ing spring load from adjusting screw.)
3. With engine at operating temperature and idling at 550 RPM, turn adjusting screw down slowly until slave piston contacts crosshead as indicated by the twitch in the handle of the Allen wrench.

NOTE: Do not attempt to make this adjustment by holding the locknut and turning the adjusting screw through both the locknut and the brake housing.

4. Back adjusting screw out exactly 1/2 turn and tighten locknut, Fig. 2.

Slave Piston Models 25, 25A & 25B

NOTE: Adjustment is made statically with engine cold or warm.

1. Loosen locknuts and with an Allen wrench, back slave piston adjusting screws out of housing until the slave pistons seat in the bores.
2. Rotate engine until "1-6 V.S." mark on accessory drive pulley aligns with the timing mark on gear case cover.
3. The exhaust valves on No. 1 and 6 cylinders are now closed. Adjust clearance between slave piston and crosshead to .018 inch on these cylinders, Fig. 3.
4. Rotate engine until the exhaust valves of No. 2 and 5 cylinders are closed and adjust clearance between slave piston and crosshead to .018 inch.
5. Continue to rotate engine until the exhaust valves of No. 3 and 4 cylinders are closed and adjust clearance between slave piston and crosshead to .018 inch.

Slave Piston, Model 53A

With exhaust valves fully closed and the injector spring fully depressed, adjust clearance between the exhaust valve bridge and the exhaust valve stems to .002 inch, Fig. 4. Then, back off adjusting screw 1 1/2 turns. This provides approximately .064 inch operating clearance.

Slave Piston, Model 59

With exhaust valves closed, adjust clearance between crosshead and slave piston to .038 inch, Fig. 3.

Slave Piston, Model 71

NOTE: Before making adjustment, ensure exhaust valves are closed and injector is in the delivery position.

On standard timed engines, the slave piston clearance is .066 inch. On advanced timed engines, the slave piston clearance is .071 inch. Determine type of engine timing before attempting adjustment.
2 valve engines: Insert correct size feeler gauge between slave piston foot and valve stem cap and adjust to specified clearance, Fig. 3.
4 valve engines: Insert correct size feeler gauge between slave piston foot and exhaust valve bridge and adjust to specified clearance, Fig. 3.

Slave Piston, Models 67 & 675

With exhaust valves fully closed, turn slave piston adjusting screw in until zero clearance is obtained between exhaust valve stem cap and slave piston foot. Then back off adjusting screw 3/4 turn.

Slave Piston, Model 903

Install a dial indicator so plunger rests on back side of slave piston, Fig. 5. With exhaust valves closed and the crosshead loose, drive slave piston down with adjusting screw until fingers of piston contact the lug on bottom of crosshead. Zero the dial indicator and back off the adjusting screw until dial indicator measures .023 ± .001 inch.

Buffer Screw Adjustment, Models 53A & 71

With engine running, adjust buffer screw to stop governor "hunt" at idle speed, Fig. 6. Do not increase engine speed above normal idle by forcing buffer screw past point where governor hunt has been eliminated. Tighten locknut. On Model 71, attach buffer switch to buffer screw and position switch to clear other engine components, Fig. 7.

Buffer Switch Adjustment, Model 71

This adjustment is to be made only with tool #2859. Switches are factory set and should not be disturbed except for switch or diode replacement.
1. Insert threaded portion of buffer screw into open end of tool so that buffer spring is close to, but does not touch the plung-

Fig. 5 Slave piston adjustment. Model 903

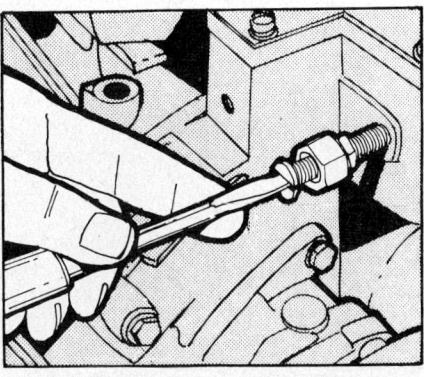

Fig. 6 Adjusting buffer screw. Models 53A & 71 (typical)

Fig. 7 Installing buffer switch. Model 71

679

JACOBS ENGINE BRAKE

2. Tighten lock nut so tool is tight on buffer screw.
3. Push plunger in so it rests on buffer spring and tighten wing screw on plunger.
4. Move micro switch in until it clicks on then back out until it clicks off. Hold this position and tighten switch mounting screws.
6. With switch in this position, a .010" feeler gauge inserted between switch plunger and switch actuator should actuate the switch.

If, after the above adjustment the engine brake does not operate correctly (in the no fuel range only) check fuel rack, idle speed and buffer screw adjustments.

TROUBLE SHOOTING

Engine Fails To Start

1. Solenoid valves stuck in on position.

Sudden Drop In Engine Lube Oil Pressure

1. Oil inlet supply seal missing or damaged.
2. Upper solenoid valve seal missing or damaged.
3. Fuel pipe leakage.

One Or Two Cylinders Fail To Brake

1. Slave piston control valve stuck in "OFF" position.
2. Slave piston control valve failure.
3. Slave piston adjustment incorrect.
4. Engine brake housing oil connectors or seals leaking.

Solenoids Won't Control Brake Operation

1. Center solenoid valve seal missing or damaged.

Solenoids Will Not Energize

1. Blown fuse.
2. Automatic switches fail to close.
3. Incorrect electrical power source.

Engine Brake Slow To Operate

1. Lube oil cold and/or too thick.
2. Lower solenoid valve seal missing or damaged.
3. Solenoid valve filter screen clogged.
4. Control valves binding in housing.
5. Switch operation sluggish.

One Or More Cylinders Fail To Stop Braking Or Engine Stalls

1. One or more slave piston control valves stuck in "ON" position.
2. Solenoid valve sticking in on position.
3. Center solenoid valve seal missing or damaged.
4. Solenoid valve exhaust plugged.
5. Switch stuck in "ON" position or misadjusted.
6. Back or beefer switch set too tight.

No Engine Braking

1. Blown fuse.
2. Low engine oil pressure.
3. Switches misadjusted or defective.

Engine Misses Or Loses Power

1. Slave piston adjustment too tight.

Control Valve Covers Broken Or Bent—Models 20 & 25A

1. Slave piston control valve ball check in adjoining cylinder (same cylinder) leaking or dirty.
2. Control valve under bent or broken cover malfunctioning.

Excessive Lube Oil Consumption, Model 20

1. Solenoid exhaust oil entering intake manifold from vent hole in rocker box.

MANUAL STEERING GEARS
Saginaw Recirculating Ball Worm & Nut Gear

DESCRIPTION

As shown in Fig. 1, the worm on the lower end of the steering shaft and the ball nut which is mounted on the worm have mating spiral grooves in which steel balls circulate to provide a low friction drive between worm and nut.

Two sets of balls are used, ranging in number from approximately 20 to 30 to a set, depending upon the size of the gear unit. Each set of balls operate independently of the other. The circuit through which each set of balls circulates includes the grooves in the worm and ball nut and a ball return guide attached to the outer surface of the nut.

When the wheel and steering shaft turn to the left, the ball nut is moved downward by the balls which roll between the worm and nut. As the balls reach the outer surface of the nut, they enter the return guides which direct them across and down into the ball nut where they enter the circuit again.

When a right turn is made the ball nut moves upward and the balls circulate in the reverse direction.

The teeth of the ball nut engage teeth on the sector which is forged integral with the pitman shaft, Fig. 2. The teeth on the ball nut are made so that a "high point" or tighter fit

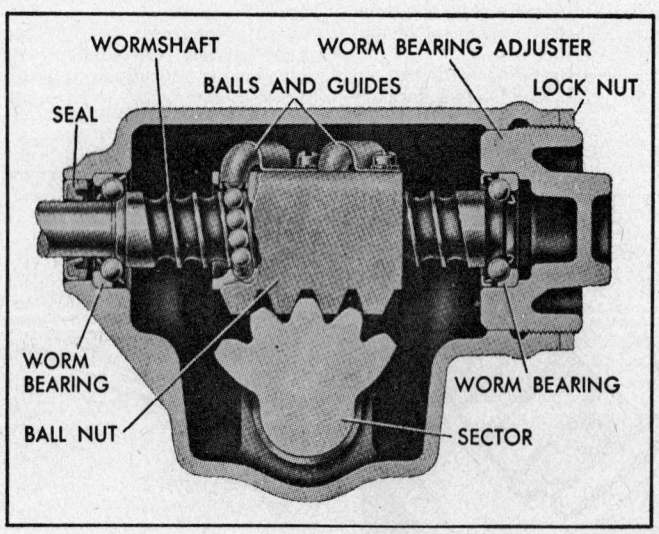

Fig. 1 Recirculating ball-worm and nut steering gear (typical)

MANUAL STEERING GEARS

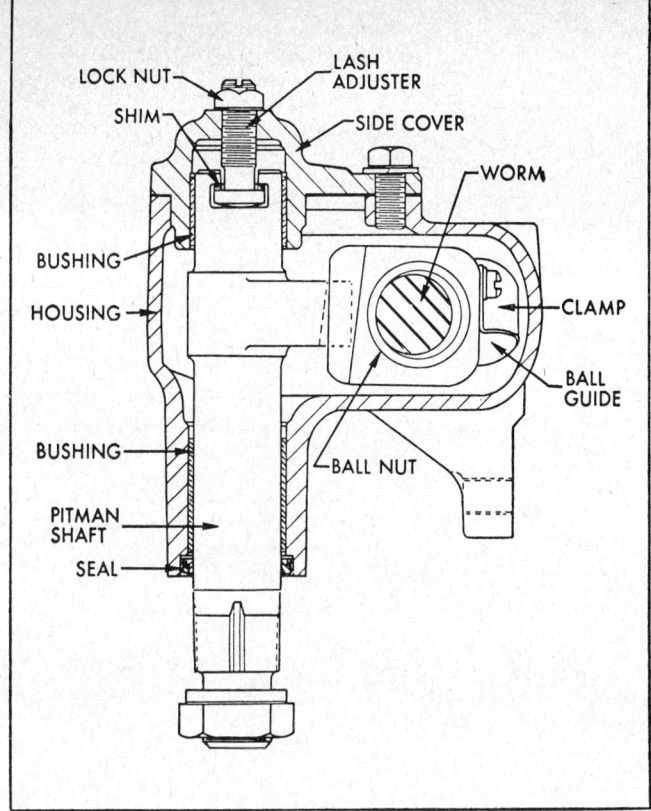

Fig. 2 Recirculating ball-worm and pitman (cross) shaft

exists between the ball nut and pitman shaft sector teeth when the front wheels are in the straight-ahead position. The teeth on the sector are tapered slightly so that a proper lash may be obtained by moving the pitman shaft endwise by means of a lash adjuster screw which extends through the gear housing side cover.

The head of the last adjuster and the selectively fitted shim fit snugly into a T-slot in the end of the pitman shaft so that the screw also controls end play of the shaft. The screw is locked by an external lock nut.

GEAR ADJUSTMENTS

There are two adjustments on the steering gear: worn bearing preload and pitman shaft overcenter preload, Fig. 3.

IMPORTANT

Never attempt to adjust the steering gear while it is connected to the steering linkage. The gear must be free of all outside load in order properly to make any steering gear adjustment.

Preliminary

1. Tighten steering gear mounting bolts.
2. Disconnect steering linkage from steering arm or gear.
3. Turn wheel slowly from one extreme to the other.

CAUTION: Never turn the wheel hard against the stopping point in the gear as damage to the ball nut assembly may result.

4. Steering wheel should turn freely and smoothly throughout its entire range.

NOTE: Roughness indicates faulty internal parts requiring disassembly of the gear unit. Hard pull or binding indicates an excessively tight adjustment of the worm bearings, or excessive misalignment of the steering shaft. Any excessive misalignment must be corrected before the gear can be properly adjusted.

Checking Worm Bearing Preload

1. Turn steering wheel gently in one direction until it stops. This positions gear away from "high point" load.
2. With a spring scale, Fig. 4, measure the pull at the rim of the wheel which is

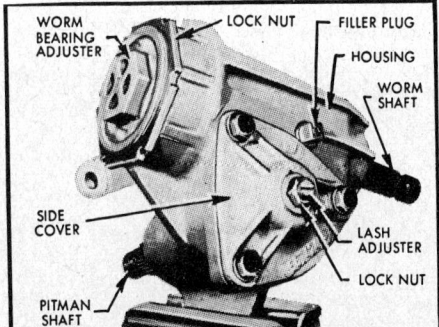

Fig. 3 Steering gear adjustments

required to keep the wheel in motion. This should be between $1/2$ and $3/4$ pounds on light duty gears and $1\frac{1}{2}$ to 2 pounds on heavy duty gears. If the pull necessary to move the wheel is not within these limits, adjustment of worm bearings is necessary.

Adjust Worm Bearing Preload

1. Loosen worm bearing adjuster lock nut, using a drift, Fig. 3.
2. Turn bearing adjuster as required to bring adjustment within specified limits.
3. Tighten lock nut and recheck preload.

Checking Pitman Shaft Overcenter Preload

1. Turn steering wheel from one extreme to the other while counting the total turns, then turn wheel back $1/2$ the number of turns. This positions steering gear on "high point" where a preload should exist between ball nut and pitman shaft teeth.
2. Check pull at wheel rim with spring scale as before, taking highest reading on scale as wheel is turned through center position. This should be between $7/8$ and $1\frac{1}{2}$ pounds on light duty models and $2\frac{3}{4}$ to $3\frac{1}{4}$ pounds on heavy duty gears.
3. If adjustment is not satisfactory, adjust as follows:

Adjust Pitman Shaft Overcenter Preload

1. Loosen lock nut and turn pitman shaft lash adjuster screw as required to bring adjustment within proper limits.
2. After tightening lock nut, rotate steering wheel back and forth through the "high point" and through the entire range to check for tight spots.

NOTE: If lash cannot be removed at the "high point" or if gear load varies greatly and feels rough, the gear should be removed for inspection of internal parts.

3. Attach linkage to steering gear when adjustments have been completed.

STEERING GEAR REPAIRS

Disassemble

1. Referring to Fig. 5, loosen adjusting screw lock nut and remove housing side cover by removing adjusting screw.
2. Loosen lock nut and back off worm bearing adjuster several turns, then remove housing end cover and gasket.
3. Remove lower thrust bearing, steering shaft and upper bearing from housing.
4. Remove ball return guide clamps and guides from ball nut. Turn ball nut over and remove ball nut from steering shaft worm.

Inspection of Parts

1. Clean and inspect all ball and roller bearings and races, including race in housing.
2. Inspect pitman shaft bushings in gear housing and end cover. If bushings are worn excessively, replace bushings.
3. It is advisable to replace pitman shaft

MANUAL STEERING GEARS

Fig. 4 Checking adjustment with spring scale

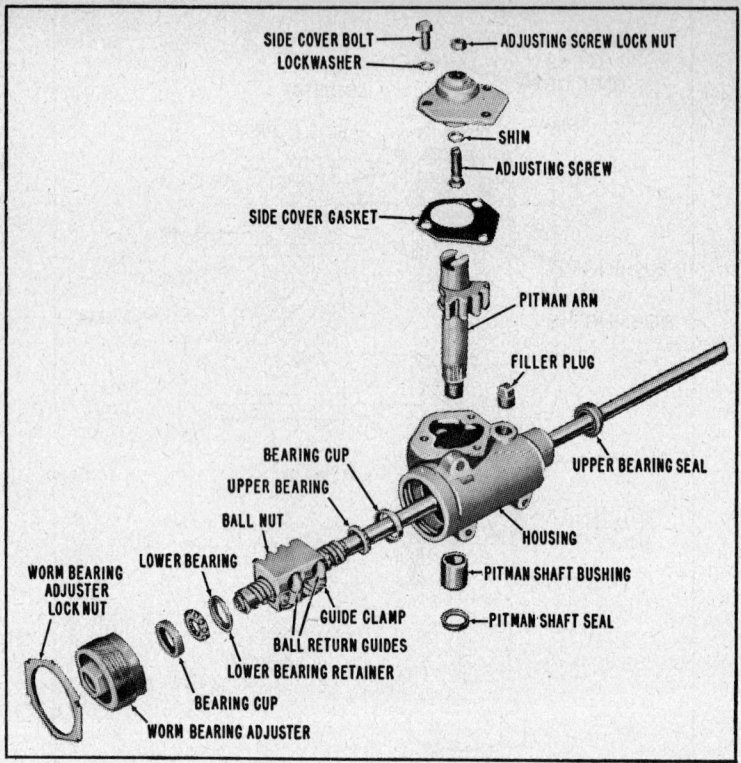

Fig. 5 Steering gear disassembled

grease seal in housing to avoid possible leakage of lubricant. Seal must be installed with feather edge toward inside of housing.
4. Inspect pitman shaft for wear or pits in bearing races, which would require replacement of shaft.
5. Check shaft for straightness.
6. Inspect teeth of ball nut and pitman shaft. If scored or excessively worn it is advisable to replace both parts to insure proper mating of teeth.
7. Check serrations of pitman shaft; if twisted replace shaft.
8. Check fit of pitman shaft adjusting screw and shim in slot in end of pitman shaft. With shim in place, screw head must be free to turn in slot with zero to .002" end play. If end play is excessive, selectively fit a new shim, which are available in four different thicknesses.

Reassemble

NOTE: Lubricate all seals, bushings, bearings and gears with multi-purpose gear lube prior to installation.

1. Position ball nut over worm shaft so that deep side of teeth will be toward side cover when installed in gear housing.
2. Install exactly 1/2 the number of balls in each circuit, rocking worm shaft slightly to aid in installing balls.
3. Place about six balls in each return guide, using grease to hold balls in place.
4. Install return guides, clamp and screw.
5. Rotate worm through its complete travel several times to be sure balls are installed correctly and rotate freely.
6. Place upper bearing on worm shaft and slide worm shaft assembly into housing.
7. Place lower bearing in worm bearing adjuster and install bearing retainer.
8. Install adjuster assembly and lock nut in housing. Tighten adjuster only enough to hold worm bearings in place. Final adjustment will be made later.
9. Turn worm shaft until center groove in ball nut lines up with center of pitman shaft bushing.
10. Install pitman shaft and lash adjuster with shim so that center tooth meshes with center groove in ball nut.
11. Install side cover with gasket on lash adjuster by turning adjuster counter-clockwise.
12. Install side cover bolts and washers.
13. Turn lash adjuster so that teeth on shaft and ball nut engage but do not bind.
14. Install lash adjuster lock nut loosely.
15. To protect pitman shaft seal from damage, cover shaft splines with masking tape. Slide new seal into place and seat it against shoulder in housing.
16. Install new worm shaft seal flush with surface of housing.
17. Fill gear housing with multi-purpose lubricant and adjust gear assembly as outlined previously.

Gemmer or Ross Worm & Roller Gear

DESCRIPTION

In this type steering gear, Fig. 6, the worm is integral with the steering shaft and is supported on each end by opposed tapered roller bearings. The triple tooth roller is attached to the roller shaft by means of a steel shaft. Two needle bearing assemblies are installed between this shaft and the roller.

The roller shaft is mounted in the steering gear housing on two needle bearing assemblies which are pressed into the housing. The housing cover is attached to the housing by four cap screws. An adjustment screw, mounted in the cover, controls roller shaft end play and worm and roller mesh adjustment.

The steering wheel and roller shaft arm (pitman arm) are splined to the steering shaft and roller shaft respectively. Both the pitman arm and steering wheel have master splines to insure correct installation.

ADJUSTMENTS

Worm End Play, Adjust

1. Free the steering gear of all load by disconnecting the linkage and loosening the steering column braces.
2. Loosen the four cover screws about 1/8".
3. Use a knife to separate the top shim, passing the blade all the way around between the shims, being careful not to damage the remaining shims.
4. Remove one shim at a time between inspections to remove the end play.
5. The adjustment is correct when there is not end play and no stiffness in the steering gear throughout the complete range of its travel.

Roller Shaft End Play, Adjust

1. Turn the steering gear to either extreme and back off 1/8 of a turn.
2. Gripping the pitman arm at the hub, the roller shaft should rotate freely without a

MANUAL STEERING GEARS

particle of end play.
3. If end play exists, adjust as required by means of the roller shaft adjusting screw in the side cover.
4. Be sure to tighten the lock nut securely and inspect for end play and free rotation throughout the entire range of steering gear travel.

Worm & Roller Mesh, Adjust

1. Loosen the roller shaft adjusting screw lock nut.
2. With the steering gear in its central position (linkage disconnected) tighten the roller shaft adjusting screw just enough to remove play between the roller shaft roller tooth and worm.
3. Check this by the amount of play felt at the pitman arm. It is better to leave a slight amount of play at this point than to tighten too much.
4. If tightened beyond the point where the lash is removed, serious results will occur which will cause poor steering operation.
5. Tighten the adjusting screw lock nut.

GEAR REPAIRS

1. Referring to Fig. 7, use a suitable puller to remove gear oil seal from housing. If shaft is corroded or dirty, clean the portion between oil seal and serrations to avoid binding in bearings.
2. Place a suitable arbor over cross shaft threads while withdrawing cross shaft, following with the arbor. The arbor will keep bearing rollers from dropping out of their cages.
3. Remove cross shaft adjusting screw lock nut. Remove cover and shims from bottom cover gasket and cross shaft.
4. Remove shaft-worm, bearings and cups.
5. If necessary, drive needle bearings from housing.
6. Clean all parts and inspect for wear.
7. Assemble parts without lubrication. Lubrication should be done after adjustments are completed.
8. If either of the worm thrust bearings is damaged, replace both bearings. Use new oil seals.

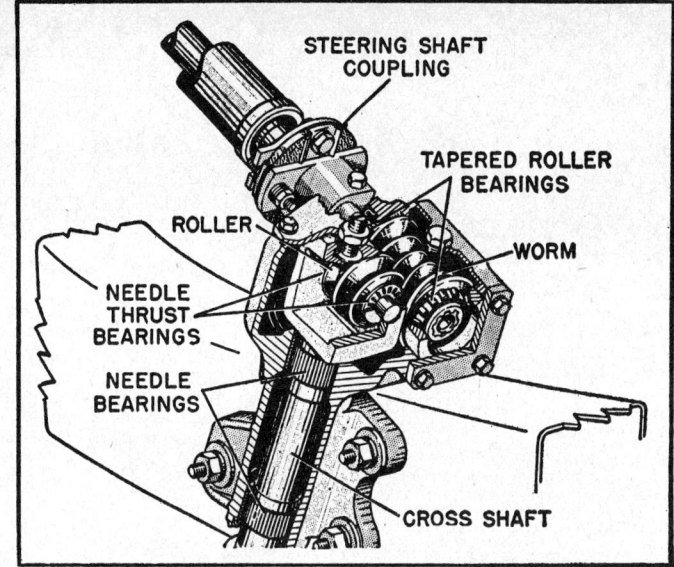

Fig. 6 Worm and roller steering gear (typical)

Fig. 7 Worm and roller gear unit disassembled

Ross Cam & Lever Gear

DESCRIPTION

These steering gears, Figs. 8 to 11, are of the cam and lever type in which the cam is mounted on ball bearings and the lever shaft turns on steel backed bronze bushings.

As the cam is turned by the wheel tube, the follower stud or studs are pulled along the cam groove causing the lever arm to rotate the lever shaft. As an aid to easy steering the lever shaft stud or studs which engage the cam are mounted on tapered roller bearings, Figs. 10 and 11. The groove in the cam is cut shallower in the straight-ahead driving position to provide closer adjustment between the studs and cam where most of the steering action occurs.

Cam End Play, Adjust

Free the steering gear of all load by disconnecting the linkage and loosening the steering column braces. Then adjust as follows:
Shim Adjustment Type—Loosen the lock nut and adjusting screw in the side cover to free the studs in the cam groove. Remove the upper cover stud nuts and raise the housing upper cover to permit removal of adjusting shims, which are .002", .003" and .010" thickness. Clip and remove one thin shim, tighten down the cover and check the adjustment. There should be a slight drag but the steering wheel should turn freely with the thumb and forefinger lightly gripping the rim. If necessary, remove or replace shims until the adjustment is correct.

Plug Adjustment Type—Loosen the housing side cover adjusting screw to free the stud in the cam groove. Turn down the cam adjusting plug, located at the top of the gear housing, until there is a barely perceptible drag so that the steering wheel can be turned freely with the thumb and forefinger lightly gripping the rim.

Lever Shaft Backlash, Adjust

1. Centralize the steering gear by turning the wheel all the way to the right. Then starting from this point count the number of turns required to reach the end of travel to the left. Turn the wheel back half this number of turns to the mid-position.

683

MANUAL STEERING GEARS

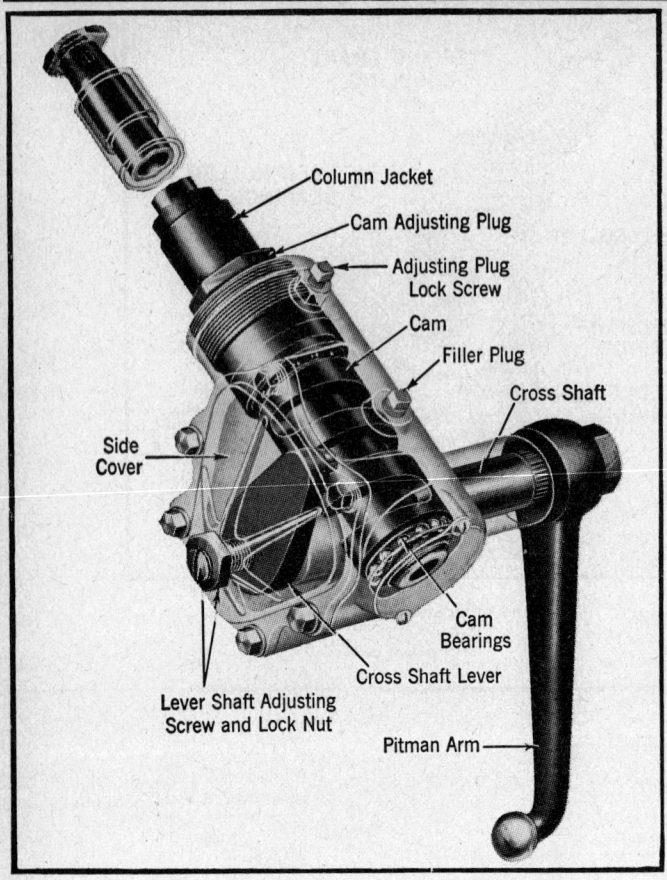

Fig. 8 Cam and single lever steering gear

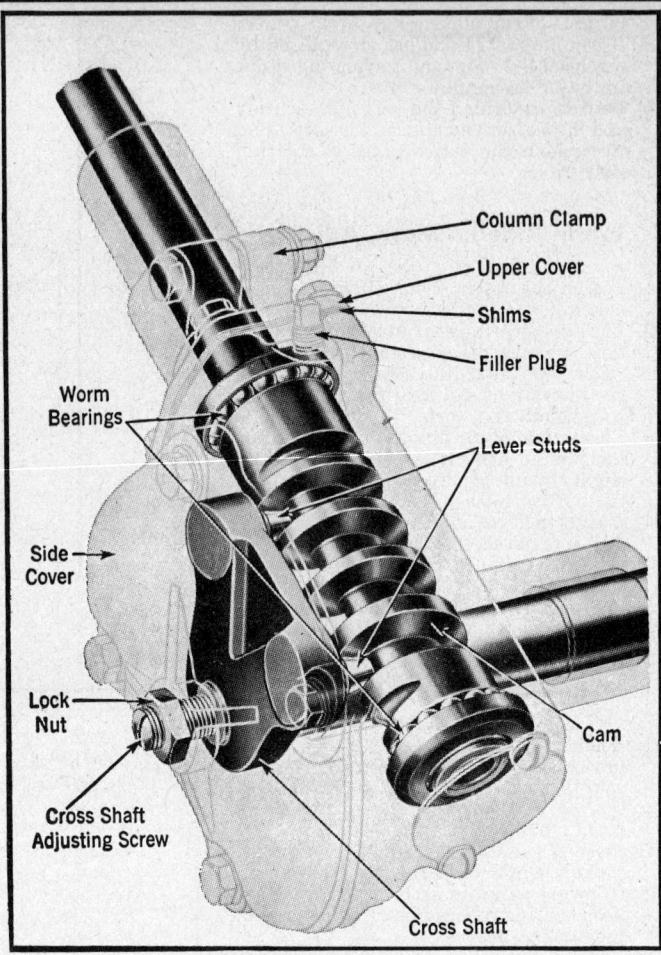

Fig. 9 Cam and twin lever steering gear

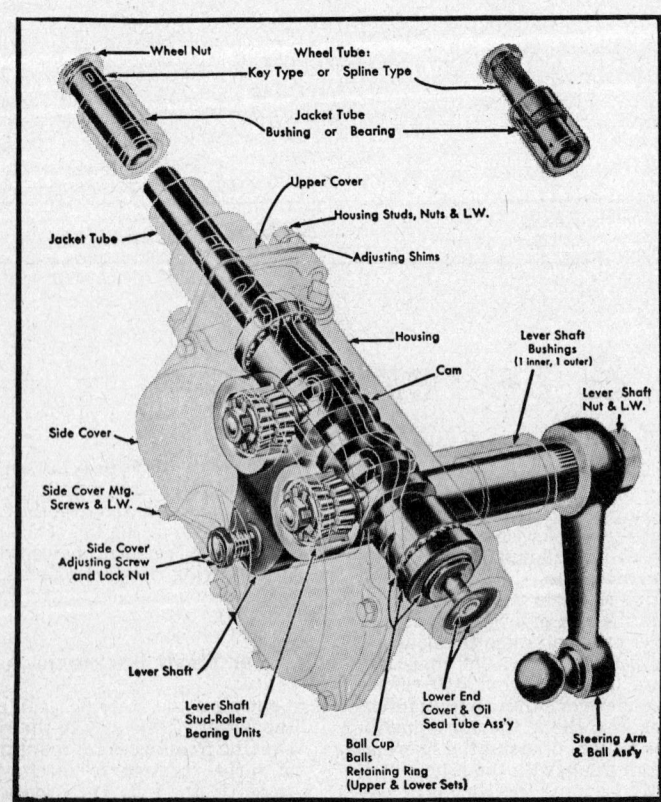

Fig. 11 Twin lever gear unit with roller mounted studs

2. Tighten the side cover adjusting screw until a very slight drag is felt through the mid-position when turning the steering wheel slowly from one side to the other. The gear should not bind in any position but a slight drag should be felt in the mid-position only.
3. After proper adjustment is secured, tighten the lock nut and give the gear a final check for binding.

Stud Roller Bearing, Adjust

In most cases the foregoing adjustments will be adequate but it is sometimes necessary to adjust the stud roller bearing units as they should be preloaded at all times. A heavy drag should be felt when revolving the studs by hand. If a torque wrench is available the bearings should be adjusted so that the torque required to revolve the stud is as follows:

Lever Shaft Dia.	Torque, In. Lb.
1 3/8″	3 to 4
1 1/2″	3 to 4
1 5/8″	4 to 8
1 3/4″	5 to 11

1. To adjust, remove lever shaft from housing, wash the bearings in solvent and blow dry with compressed air, using care not to spin the bearings. Lubricate the bearings with light oil.
2. Straighten out the prong of the locking washer to release the stud nut. Remove the nut and install a new locking washer.
3. While holding the stud nut from turning

MANUAL STEERING GEARS

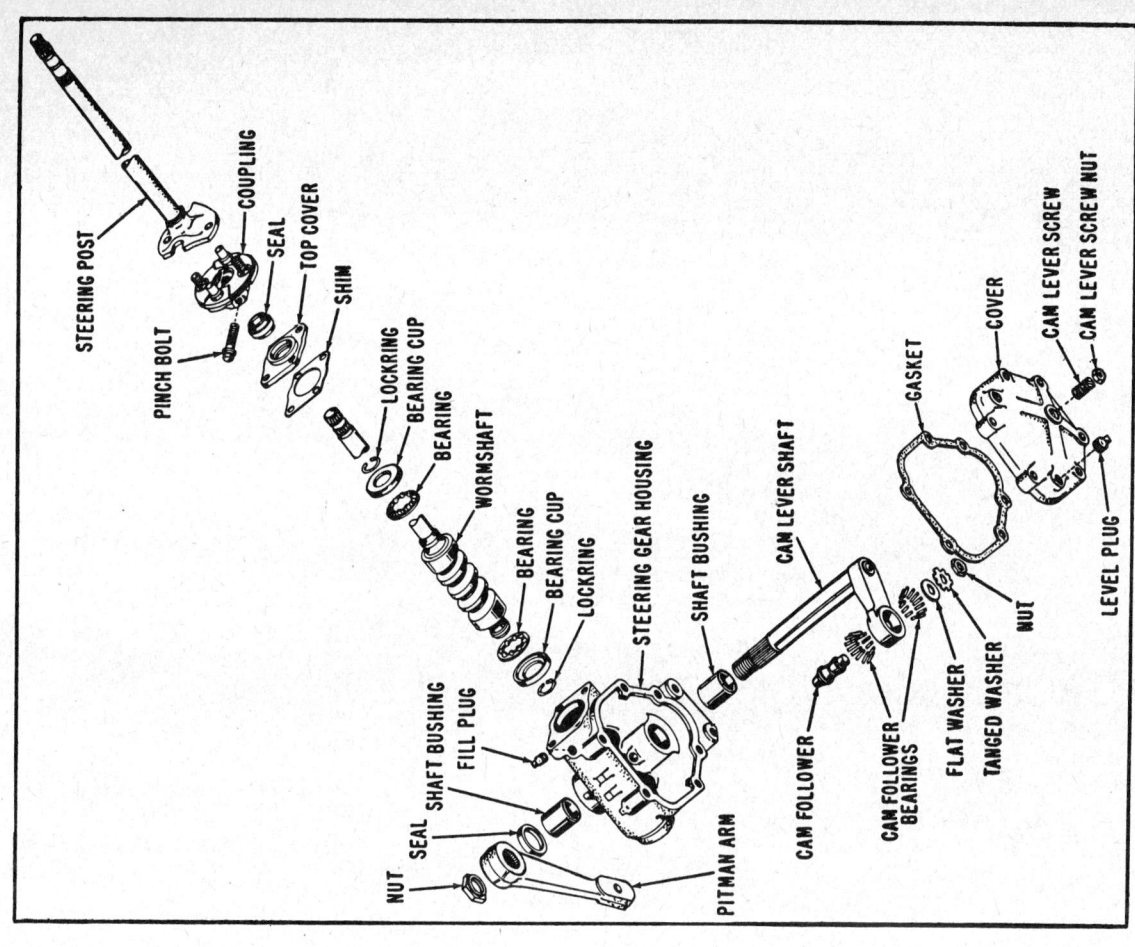

Fig. 12 Single lever gear unit disassembled (typical)

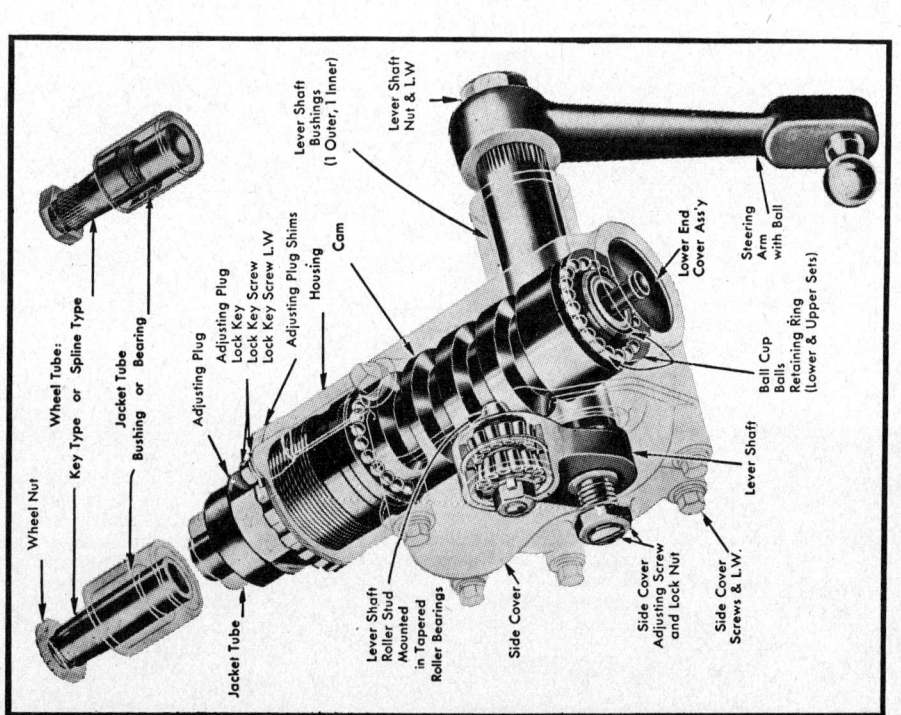

Fig. 10 Single lever gear unit with roller mounted stud

MANUAL STEERING GEARS

with a spanner wrench on the locking washer, tighten the nut as required to revolve the stud in accordance with the table above.
4. When proper adjustment has been secured, bend the prong of the washer against a side of the nut to keep it from turning.
5. Lubricate the bearings with gear oil and assemble the lever shaft in the steering gear housing.

GEAR REPAIRS

Disassemble

1. Using Fig. 12 as a guide, loosen lock nut and back off adjusting screw.
2. Remove side cover and gasket.
3. Clean serrated end of cam lever shaft to prevent seal and/or bushing damage. Then pull cam lever shaft assembly from housing.
4. Remove top cover and adjusting shims (or unscrew adjusting plug) from housing. Then remove steering post and cam assembly.
5. Remove lower cam bearing retainer ring and slip lower bearing cup and ball retainer assembly off shaft. Remove upper bearing in same manner.
6. Remove cam lever shaft oil seal from gear housing. If cam lever bushings are to be replaced, use a suitable arbor and press inner and outer bushings from housing.
7. Remove cam follower from lever shaft by bending down locking tang. Then remove tanged washer and retainer washer and slip bearings and stud out of lever.

Reassemble

1. If cam lever bushings were removed from housing, install new bushings, using an arbor press and a suitable arbor. The bushings should then be line-reamed to fit the cam lever shaft. Use a suitable arbor and install a new cam lever shaft oil seal.
2. Place the inner set of bearing rollers around cam follower stud. Hold rollers in place with heavy grease.
3. Carefully insert stud and assembled rollers into lever and assemble outer set of rollers, using heavy grease. Then install retainer washer, a new tanged lock washer and nut.
4. Adjust gear as outlined above and fill gear housing with specified lubricant.

POWER STEERING GEARS

CONTENTS

	Page No.
Trouble Shooting	686
Maintenance	686
HYDRAULIC PUMPS	
Rotor Type	687
Roller Type	688
Slipper Type	690
Sleeve Type	693
Vane Type	692
Borg Warner	695
Eaton	695
Mack-Scania	695
Pesco	696
TRW	696
Vickers V-200	697
Vickers Exc. V-200	697
POWER CYLINDERS	698
CONTROL VALVES	703
IN LINE BOOSTERS	708
POWER GEARS	
Chrysler	710
Ford	714
Ross	717
Saginaw	726
Sheppard	742

TROUBLE SHOOTING

Hard Steering

HYDRAULIC FLUID OVERFLOW

1. Reservoir too full.
2. Filter out of place.

STANDING OR PARKING

1. Fluid level too low.
2. Loose or glazed pump belt.
3. Check tires: Pressure, wear, alignment, balance.
4. External leakage.
5. Linkage loose, tight, binding, friction.
6. Check entire hydraulic system.

AT ALL TIMES

1. Fluid level low.
2. Pump belt loose or glazed.
3. Check tires: Pressure, wear, alignment, balance.
4. External leakage.
5. Mechanical linkage loose, tight, binding, friction.
6. Check entire hydraulic system.

PART OF THE TIME

1. Fluid level low.
2. Pump belt loose or glazed.
3. Check tires: Pressure, wear, alignment, balance.
4. External leakage.
5. Mechanical seal loose, tight, binding, friction.
6. Steering gear needs adjustment.
7. Interference.
8. Check entire hydraulic system.

"LUMPY" EFFECT OR SHIMMY

1. Fluid level too low.
2. External leakage.
3. Mechanical linkage loose, tight, binding, friction.
4. Defective pump.

JERKS OR SURGES

1. Pump belt loose or glazed.

WHEN TRYING TO STEER "FAST"

1. Fluid level too low.
2. Pump belt loose or glazed.
3. Check tires: Pressure, wear, alignment, balance.
4. External leakage.
5. Check entire hydraulic system.

IN ONE DIRECTION

1. Gear out of adjustment.
2. Interference.
3. Defective control valve.

AT CERTAIN HAND WHEEL POSITIONS

1. Steering gear out of adjustment.
2. Interference.

WITH ABNORMAL NOISES

1. Fluid level too low.
2. Pump belt loose or glazed.
3. Defective pump.

WANDER, DRIFT, "DIVE", "DART"

1. Check tires: Pressure, wear, alignment, balance.
2. Mechanical linkage loose, tight, binding, friction.

LACK OF RECOVERY

1. Mechanical linkage loose, tight, binding, friction.
2. Gear out of adjustment.
3. Interference.
4. Check entire hydraulic system.
5. Defective control valve.

MAINTENANCE

Filling Hydraulic System

1. Fill reservoir with recommended fluid to indicated level and replace cap.
2. Start engine and idle, turning wheels from one extreme to the other three times. Shut off engine and refill reservoir.
3. Continue with Step 2 until system maintains its proper indicated oil level.
4. Run engine at faster speed and continue turning wheels slowly from one extreme to the other and back again for about five minutes to check for leaks. This will bleed the system of air. Again refill the reservoir to the indicated level.

Belt Tension

Pump belt tension is usually obtained by

Power Steering Gears

loosening an adjusting screw and moving the pump upward and outward. The proper tension is obtained when the belt can be depressed about 3/8" halfway between the two pulleys. Tighten pump mounting bolts securely after the adjustment is made.

Power Steering Pump Section

ROTOR TYPE PUMP

This unit, Fig. 1, consists of the reservoir, pressure relief valve, filter element, and the rotating pump gearing. The pump reservoir illustrated has a filler cap with a fluid level checking gauge.

Disassemble

1. Remove reservoir filler cap.
2. Loosen reservoir mounting bolt and remove cover.
3. Remove filter element.
4. Drain oil from reservoir.
5. Remove return stud from body, Fig. 2.
6. Remove reservoir-to-body mounting screws.
7. Remove reinforcement plate and reservoir.
8. Remove four O-ring seals, Fig. 3.
9. Remove intake O-ring seal retainer.
10. Remove cover-to-body mounting screws and separate body from cover, Figs. 4 and 5.
11. Remove gasket, and O-ring seal from body, Fig. 5.
12. Scribe a line on inner and outer rotors for reassembly purposes, Fig. 6.
13. Remove outer and inner rotors.
14. Remove inner rotor drive pin from shaft.
15. Remove bearing retaining ring with snap ring pliers.
16. Remove shaft and bearing from body.
17. Press bearing from shaft.
18. Remove seal from body, using a suitable puller.
19. To remove the combination flow control and relief valve in the pump cover, remove the spring retainer car fitting and circular section rubber O-ring seal and discard seal, Fig. 7.
20. Lift out flow control valve spring.
21. Tap cover on wooden block to remove combination flow control and relief valve.
22. To remove pressure relief valve and spring from flow control valve body, place valve in vise. Place punch against relief valve and remove spring pressure. Remove retaining ring, Fig. 8, using internal snap ring pliers. Then remove relief valve and spring, Fig. 9.

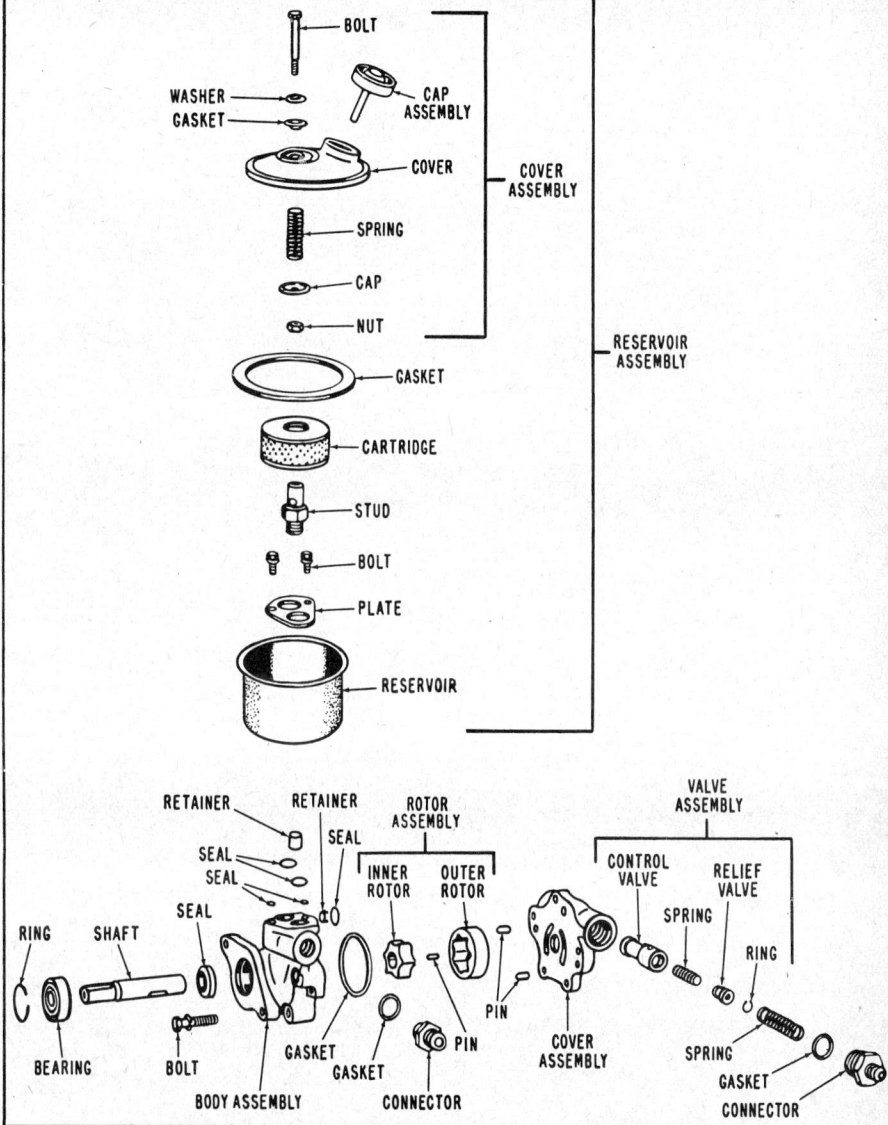

Fig. 1 Rotor type power steering pump disassembled

Reassembly

Clean all parts and air dry only. Coat all parts with a light film of oil as assembly progresses. This will assure initial lubrication of parts.

1. The relief valve spring weight should be checked with a spring tester before preassembling the flow control valve. The spring load is usually between 14 and 16 pounds when compressed to a length of 1 3/16".
2. Preassemble the flow control valve as shown in Figs. 8 and 9.
3. Install flow control valve in pump cover.
4. Install flow control valve spring.
5. Install new O-ring seal on flow control valve cap fitting and install into pump cover.
6. Install new seal with lip toward rotor into pump body, using a suitable seal driver.
7. Press bearing onto shaft until bearing seats against shoulder on shaft.
8. Install shaft and bearing into pump body.
9. Install bearing retaining ring.
10. Install inner rotor drive pin in shaft groove.
11. Install inner rotor, making sure scribe line is facing upward.
12. Install outer rotor, making sure scribe

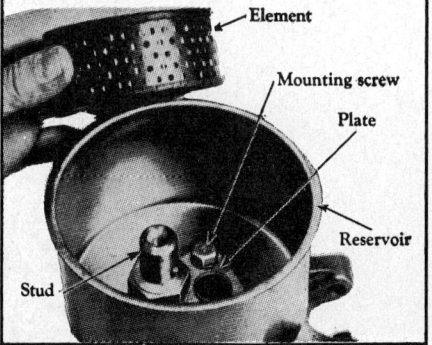

Fig. 2

687

POWER STEERING GEARS

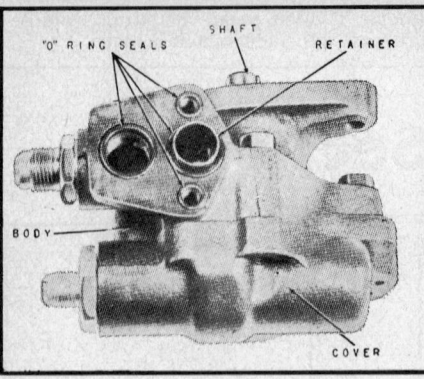

Fig. 3

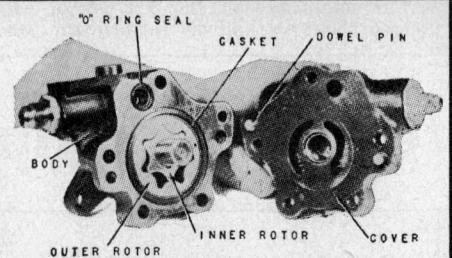

Fig. 5

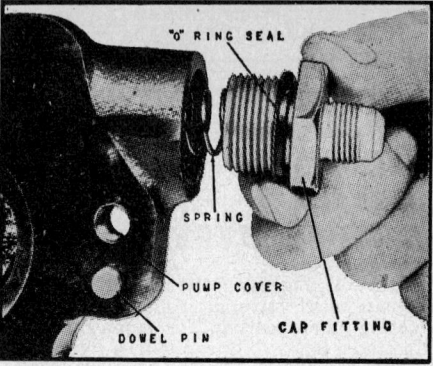

Fig. 7

Fig. 4

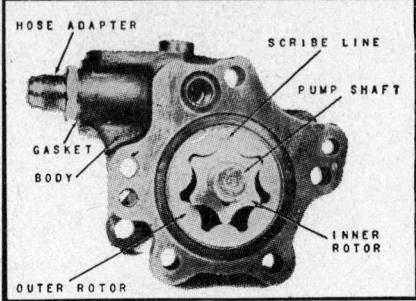

Fig. 6

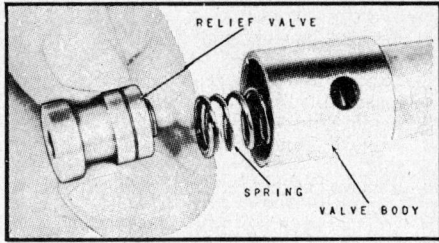

Fig. 8

line is facing upward.
13. After rotors have been nested in pump body, the tooth nose clearance should be checked with a feeler gauge as shown in Fig. 10. If the clearance exceeds .008", replace rotors with a new set. Also the end clearance should be checked as shown in Fig. 11, and in the event that it exceeds .0025", the rotors must be replaced with a new set.
14. Install new O-ring seal in body.
15. Install new body-to-cover gasket.
16. Position cover on body and torque cover screws to 20–25 ft-lbs.
17. Rotate pump shaft and check for free rotation.
18. Install O-ring seal retainer into body.
19. Position four new O-ring seals on pump body to mount reservoir.
20. Position reservoir over the four O-ring seals and pump body.
21. Place reservoir reinforcing plate into position.
22. Secure reservoir and plate to body with two screws and lockwashers.
23. Install pump return stud in body.
24. Install new filter element.
25. Install new cover gasket with cover and tighten securely.

ROLLER TYPE PUMP

This type pump, Fig. 12, consists of reservoir, pressure relief valve, filter element, and the rotating pump cam.

Thoroughly clean exterior of pump and reservoir, using care so that dirt does not enter pump or reservoir upon disassembly. During all assembly operations, extreme caution must be used to prevent any dirt from entering pump. All parts should be lightly oiled during reassembly to provide initial lubrication.

Disassembly

1. Remove reservoir cover, gasket, filter element spring, spring seat and filter element.
2. Remove 5/16" stud with stud puller or two nuts, Fig. 13.

Fig. 9

3. Remove stud that retains filter element support, Fig. 14.
4. Remove reinforcing plate and reservoir.
5. Remove four O-ring seals between reservoir and pump body and discard seals, Fig. 15.
6. Remove cover-to-body mounting screws and studs, Fig. 16. Separate cover from body, Fig. 17, lifting cover vertically from body to prevent internal parts from falling out.
7. Remove O-ring seals from grooves in pump housing, Fig. 17, and discard

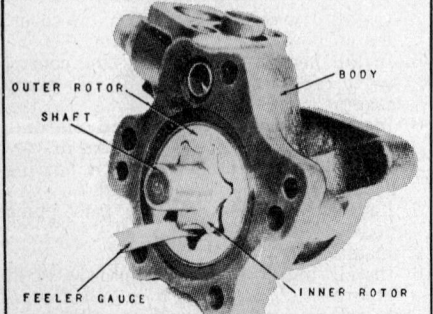

Fig. 10

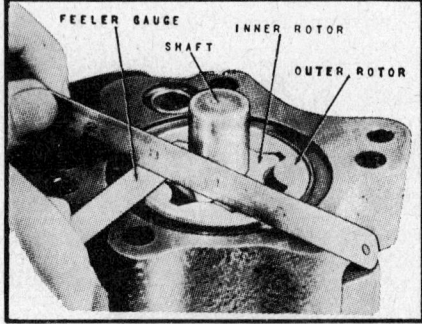

Fig. 11

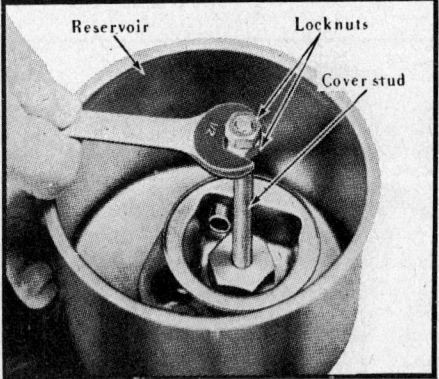

Fig. 13

Power Steering Gears

seals.

8. Before removing carrier, mark a line across the carrier and cam, Fig. 18. This will permit correct reassembly as the carrier has a drive side and must be installed as shown. Do not scratch surfaces when making marks.
9. Remove rollers, carrier and drive pin from shaft. Then lift out cam and cam retaining pin, Fig. 19.
10. Remove bearing retaining ring. Remove shaft and bearing from body, and press bearing from shaft.
11. Remove seal from body, using a suitable seal puller.
12. To remove combination flow control and relief valve in pump cover, Fig. 20, remove spring retainer cap and O-ring seal; discard seal.
13. Lift out flow control valve spring.
14. Tap cover on wooden block to remove combination flow control and relief valve, Fig. 21. *The relief valve is an internal part of the flow control valve and is not to be disassembled.*

Reassembly

1. Install flow control valve into pump cover, making sure exposed ball enters bore first.
2. Install flow control valve spring.
3. Install new O-ring seal on flow control valve retainer cap and install into pump cover. Torque retainer cap to 30–35 ft-lbs.
4. Install new seal with lip toward carrier into pump body, using a suitable seal driver.
5. Press bearing onto pump shaft until bearing seats against shoulder on shaft.
6. Install shaft and bearing into body.
7. Install bearing retainer ring in groove in body, making sure ring is seated properly.
8. Install cam retaining pin into body.
9. Install cam into body, making sure notch in cam indexes with retaining pin and cam is seated firmly in pocket.
10. Install carrier drive pin into groove in pump shaft.
11. Install carrier into pump body, making sure line previously marked on carrier indexes with line marked on cam.
12. Install rollers into pockets of carrier.
13. After the cam, carrier and rollers have been placed in pump body, the end clearance of carrier and rollers in body should be checked, Fig. 22. If end clearance exceeds .002", replace carrier or rollers.
14. Install new O-ring seals in body.

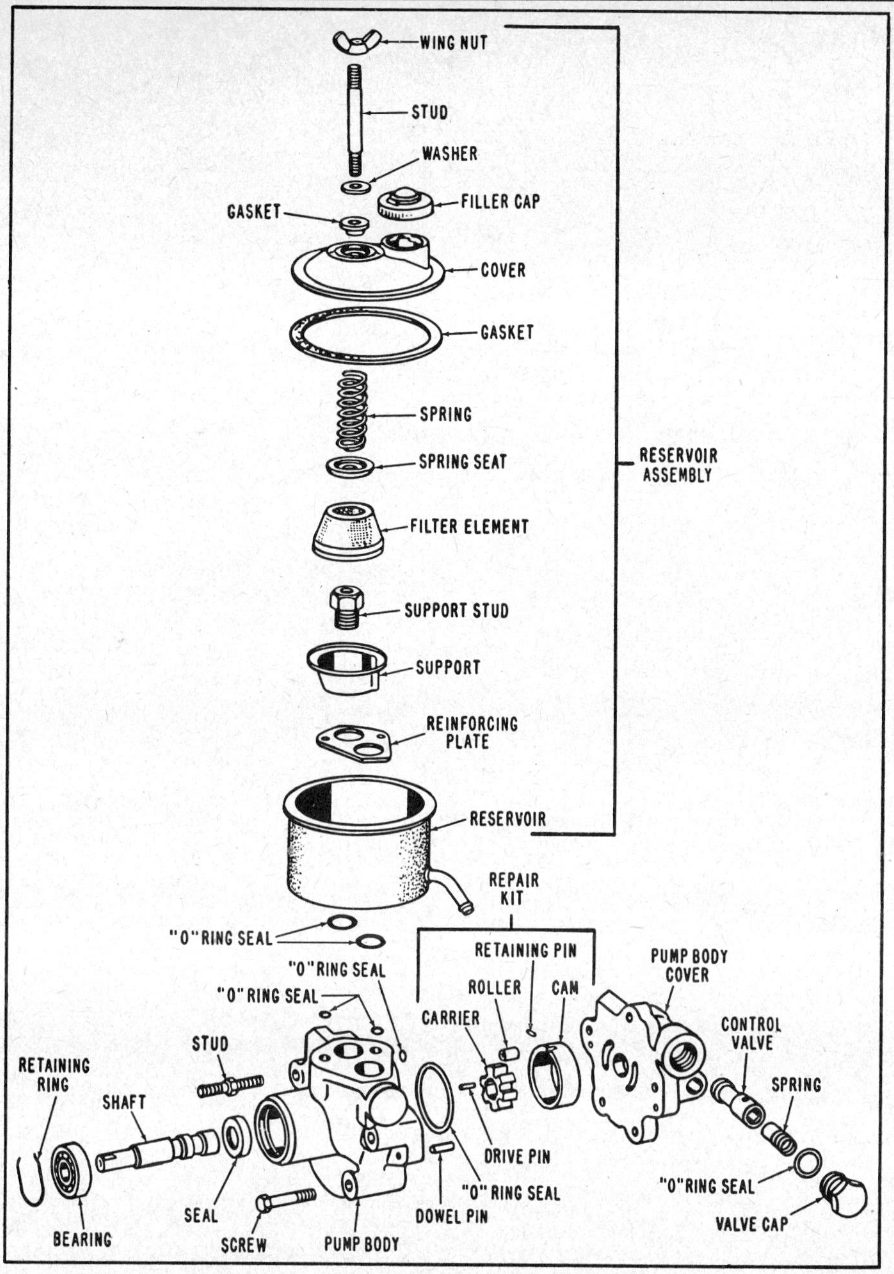

Fig. 12 Roller type power steering pump disassembled

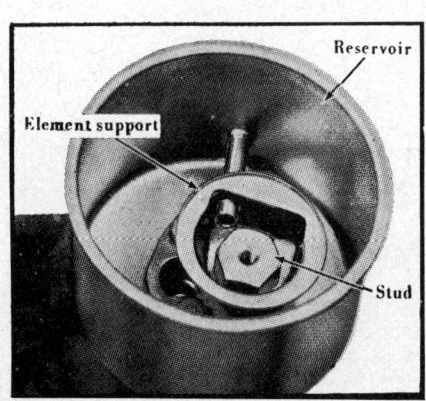

Fig. 14

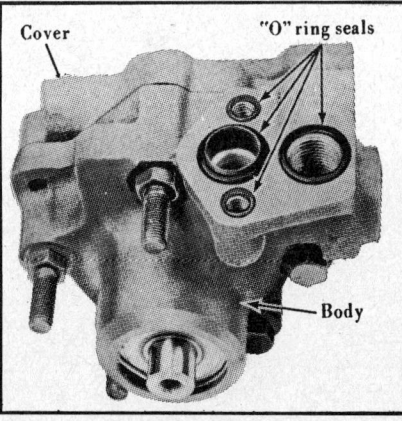

Fig. 15

Fig. 16

Power Steering Gears

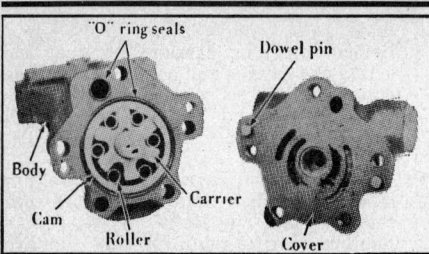

Fig. 17

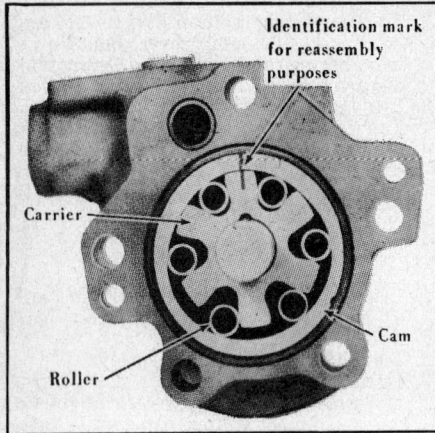

Fig. 18

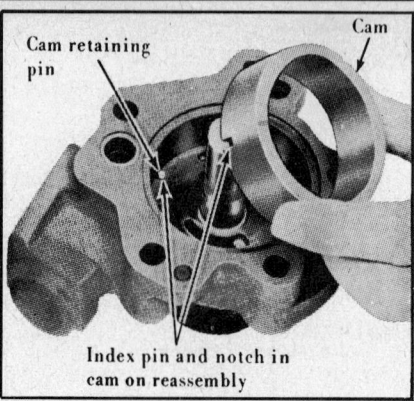

Fig. 19

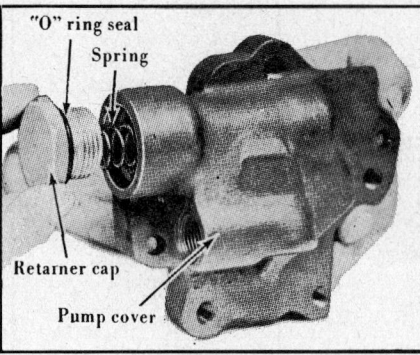

Fig. 20

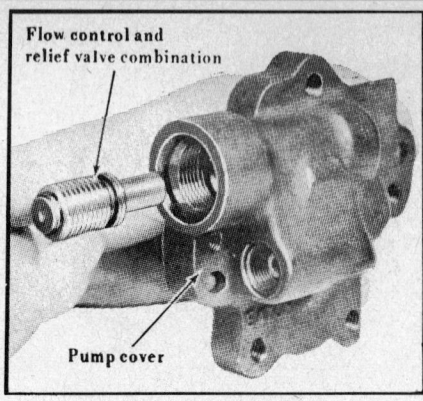

Fig. 21

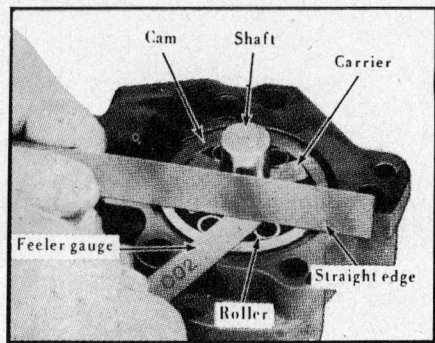

Fig. 22

15. Position cover on body and torque screws and studs to 20–25 ft-lbs. Rotate pump shaft and check for free rotation.
16. Position four new O-ring seals on pump body to mount reservoir.
17. Position reservoir over four O-ring seals and body.
18. Secure reservoir and reinforcing plate and torque screws to 30–35 ft-lbs.
19. Install filter element support and torque stud to 30–35 ft-lbs.
20. Install 5/16" stud into support stud and torque to 40–60 inch-lbs.
21. Place new filter element on support. Position spring seat on top of filter. Install spring over stud and onto spring seat.

Install reservoir cover with new gasket. Install reservoir cap.

SLIPPER TYPE PUMP

NOTE: *Disassembly of the slipper type pump, Fig. 23, is not recommended as the internal parts of the pump are not serviced separately. The only parts that are serviced are the pump assembly, filler cap, reservoir, O-ring and gasket, pump shaft oil seal, flow control plug and O-ring, snap ring and relief valve.*

Disassembly

1. Clean exterior of pump.
2. Remove filler cap and drain reservoir.
3. Remove brackets, reservoir screws, gas-

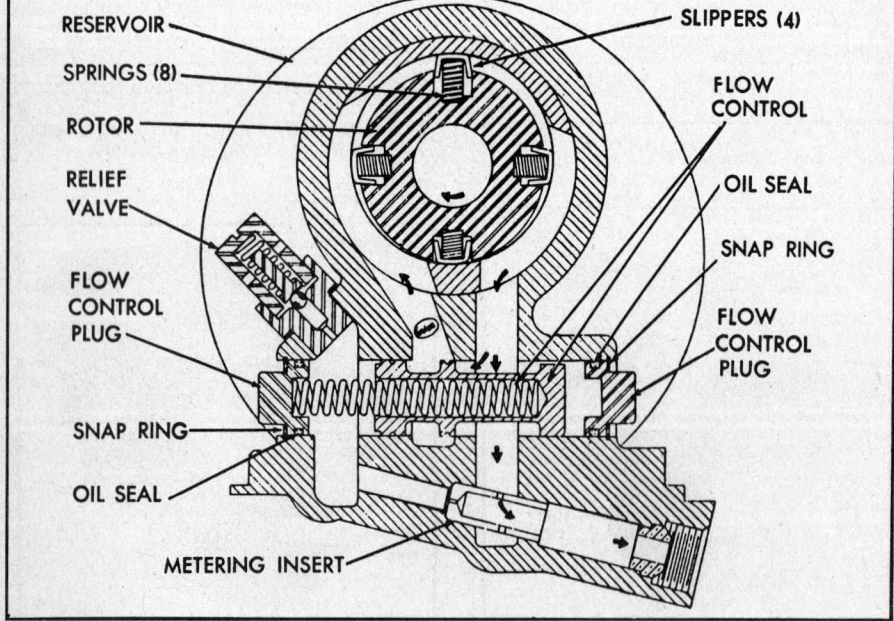

Fig. 23 Slipper type power steering pump

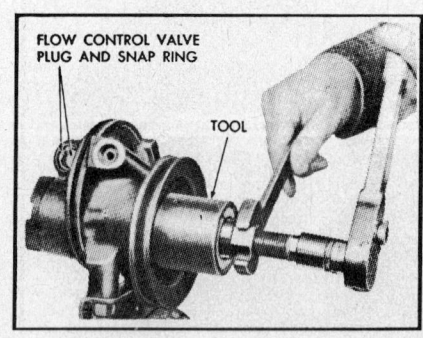

Fig. 24 Removing pump pulley

Power Steering Gears

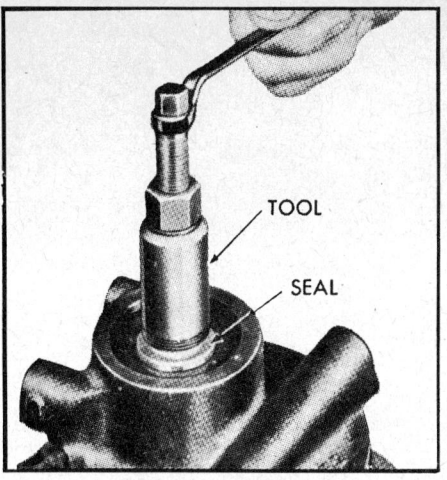

Fig. 25 Removing pump oil seal

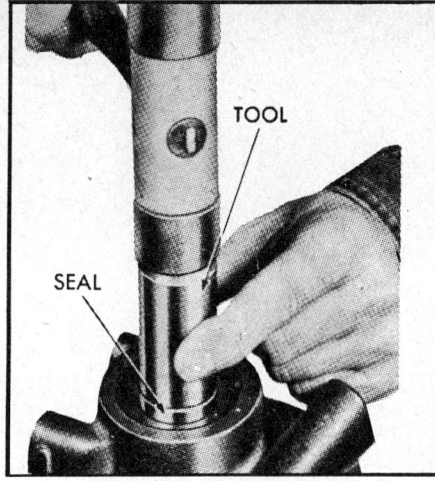

Fig. 26 Installing oil seal

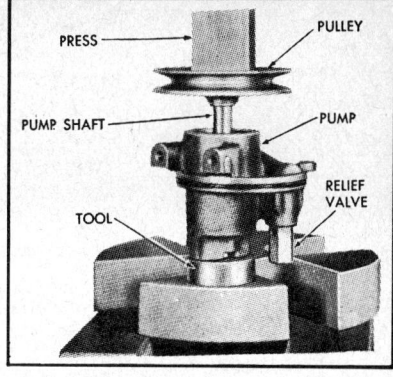

Fig. 27 Installing pump pulley

4. Using spacer washers between front bracket and pump, reinstall front bracket for use as a holding fixture. Clamp bracket in a vise.
5. Use a suitable puller to remove pulley, Fig. 24.
6. Remove relief valve and gasket.
7. Remove flow control valve plug snap ring.
8. Remove flow control valve plug and O-ring by gripping end of plug with needle nose pliers.

CAUTION: *The valve is spring loaded.*

9. Remove oil seal by threading a suitable tool far enough to engage metal portion of seal. Then by turning the center puller screw while holding the tool body will force the seal from the pump, Fig. 25.

Inspection

Clean parts in mineral spirits or other suitable solvent. Discard body-to-reservoir O-ring and flow control valve plug O-ring. Pump shaft should turn freely and should be smooth at seal contact area. Flow control valve bore and valve should be smooth, free of scores or scratches. Valve must operate freely in bore.

NOTE: *Small scratches can be removed with crocus cloth. Do not round off the square edges on the valve as they are vitally important to this type of valve. The housing bore should not be honed. If the bore is scratched or worn, the pump should be replaced.*

Reassembly

1. Install flow control valve spring and valve. Lubricate and assemble a new O-ring on the flow control valve plug and install plug.
2. Install snap ring in bore.
3. Install new oil seal with lip of seal toward pump.
4. Install pressure relief valve and gasket. Tighten plug to 30 ft-lbs torque.
5. Remove front bracket. Support pump body on a holding fixture, Fig. 26. Pump must be supported in the manner shown when installing the seal so that all pressing force will be applied to the shaft only; otherwise the pump body and rotor will be damaged.
6. Install pulley with a heavy duty arbor press, Fig. 27. Press on pulley hub only

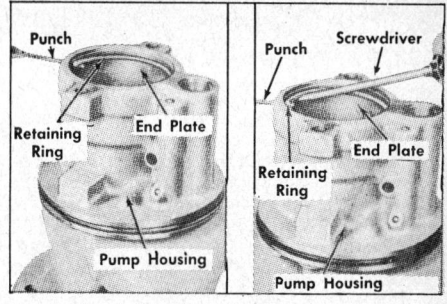

Fig. 29 Removing end plate retaining ring

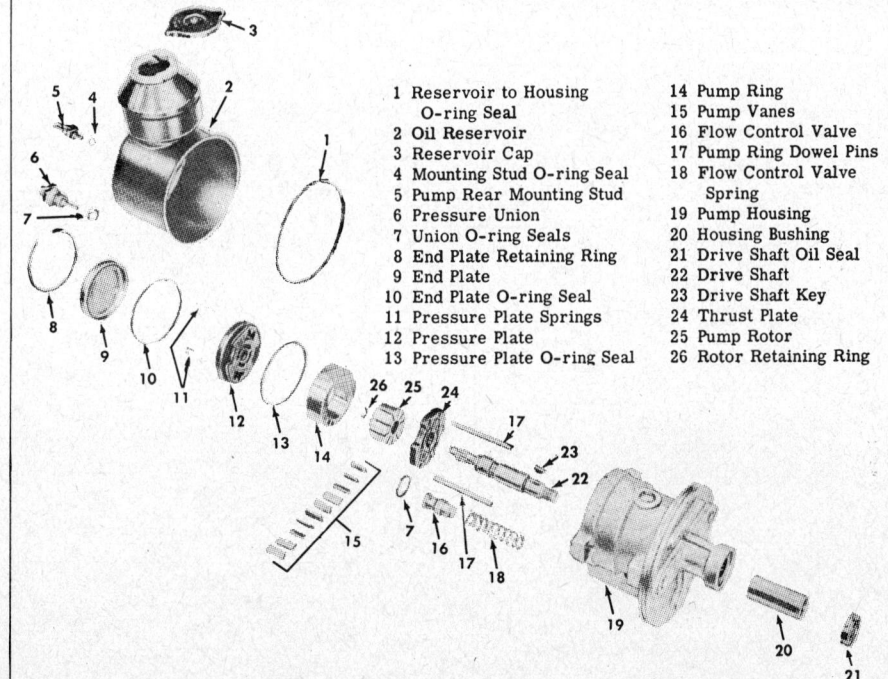

1. Reservoir to Housing O-ring Seal
2. Oil Reservoir
3. Reservoir Cap
4. Mounting Stud O-ring Seal
5. Pump Rear Mounting Stud
6. Pressure Union
7. Union O-ring Seals
8. End Plate Retaining Ring
9. End Plate
10. End Plate O-ring Seal
11. Pressure Plate Springs
12. Pressure Plate
13. Pressure Plate O-ring Seal
14. Pump Ring
15. Pump Vanes
16. Flow Control Valve
17. Pump Ring Dowel Pins
18. Flow Control Valve Spring
19. Pump Housing
20. Housing Bushing
21. Drive Shaft Oil Seal
22. Drive Shaft
23. Drive Shaft Key
24. Thrust Plate
25. Pump Rotor
26. Rotor Retaining Ring

Fig. 28 Vane type power steering pump disassembled

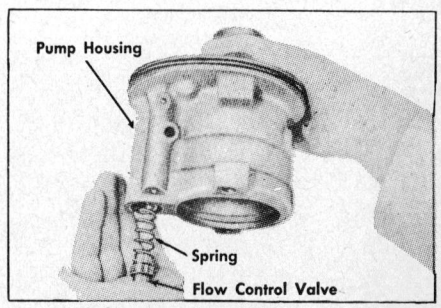

Fig. 30 Removing flow control valve and spring

POWER STEERING GEARS

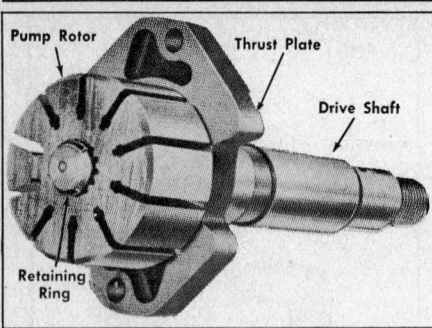

Fig. 31 Thrust plate and rotor installed on drive shaft

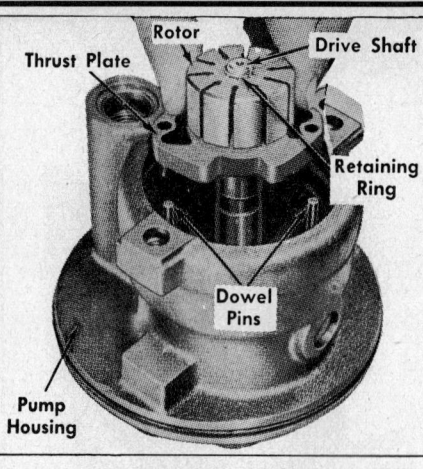

Fig. 32 Installing drive shaft assembly

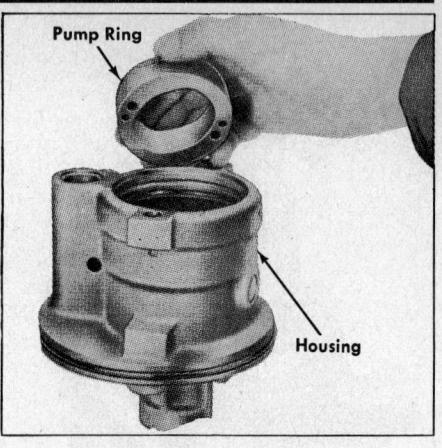

Fig. 33 Installing pump ring

until hub is flush with end of pump shaft.
7. Lubricate large O-ring and reservoir cap screw gasket and install both on pump body.
8. Install reservoir and pump brackets. Torque screws to 10 ft-lbs.

VANE TYPE PUMP

Disassembly

1. Referring to Fig. 28, carefully mount pump in vise with soft jaws and remove reservoir cap.

NOTE: *When clamping pump in vise, do not exert excessive force on front hub as this may distort drive shaft bushing in housing.*

2. Remove rear pump mounting stud and O-ring seal, pressure union and O-ring seal.
3. Remove reservoir, and second pressure union O-ring seal.
4. Using a small punch, depress end plate retaining ring enough to allow removal from groove. Use the 1/8″ diameter hole in housing, Fig. 29. Then remove retaining ring with screwdriver.
5. Remove end plate which is spring loaded and will usually sit above housing level. If end plate sticks, a slight rocking action should free it. If rocking action fails to free plate, use a magnet.
6. Remove two pressure springs from pump housing.
7. Remove flow control valve and spring by inverting housing. Do not disassemble flow control valve as it is serviced as a unit and pre-set at the factory, Fig. 30.
8. Remove drive shaft key from slot in shaft. Then with end of shaft pointed downward, press down until shaft is free.
9. Turn assembly over and remove drive shaft and rotary group.
10. Remove rotor retaining ring from groove in drive shaft. Remove rotor and thrust plate from shaft, Fig. 31.
11. Remove and discard O-ring seals from pump housing. Remove drive shaft oil seal only if inspection shows necessity for replacement.

Inspection

1. Clean all parts except the drive shaft oil seal in cleaning fluid. The seal will be damaged if immersed in cleaning fluid.
2. Check fit of vanes in slots of rotor for tightness or excessive looseness. Vanes must fit snugly but slide freely in slots in rotor. Tight fit of vanes in rotor can usually be corrected by thorough cleaning. Replace rotor if excessive looseness exists between rotor and vanes. Replace vanes if worn or scored.
3. Examine machined surfaces of pump ring for roughness or wear. Replace ring if roughness cannot be corrected with crocus cloth.
4. Inspect thrust plate, pressure plate and end plate for wear, scores or other damage.
5. Inspect pump housing for cracks or damage. Check housing for evidence of wear or scoring.
6. Check all springs for free length, distortion or collapsed coils.
7. Inspect located dowel pins for distortion.
8. Examine outer diameter of flow control valve for scoring or roughness. Slight damage may be cleaned up with crocus cloth. Check valve assembly for freedom of movement in bore of pump housing.
9. Check all oil passages in pump parts for obstruction. Use a piece of tag wire to clean out holes.
10. Check bushing in pump housing for wear or damage.

Reassembly

1. Lubricate new O-ring seals with vaseline and place in pump housing.
2. If drive shaft oil seal was removed during disassembly, lubricate new seal with vaseline. Then install seal in pump body front hub, using a suitable seal driver.
3. Position thrust plate and rotor on drive shaft. Then install rotor retaining ring in groove of drive shaft, Fig. 31.
4. Place pump housing on work bench as shown in Fig. 32 and install two pump ring dowel pins in bore of housing.
5. Install drive shaft in housing, making sure shaft seats properly.
6. Install pump ring in housing over two

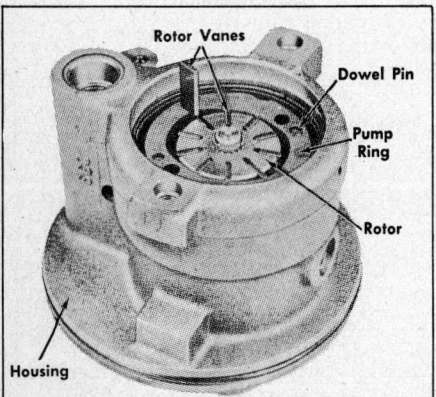

Fig. 34 Installing rotor vanes

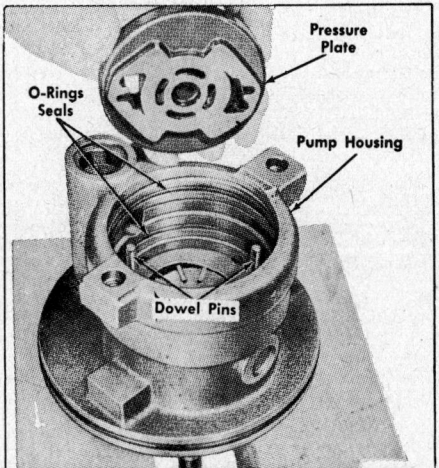

Fig. 35 Installing pressure plate

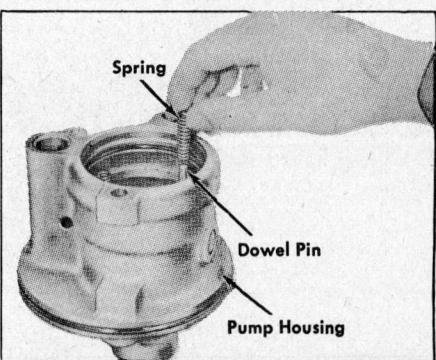

Fig. 36 Installing pressure plate springs

692

Power Steering Gears

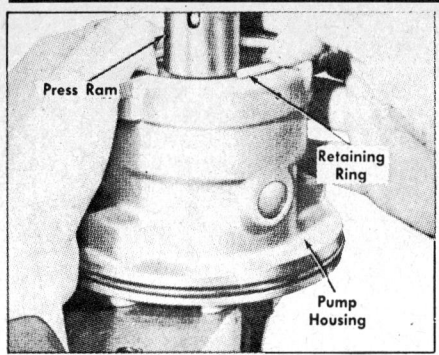

Fig. 37 Installing end plate and retaining ring

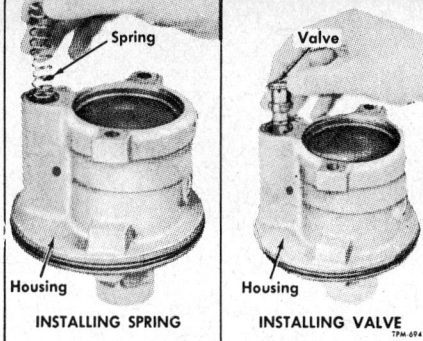

Fig. 38 Installing flow control valve and spring

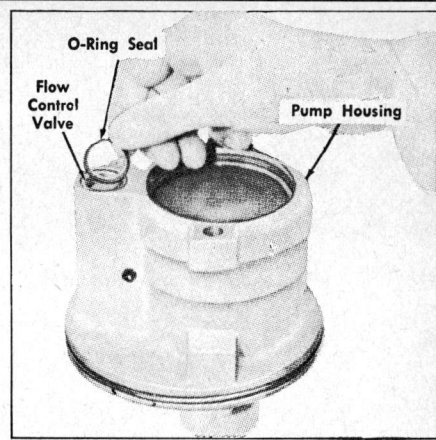

Fig. 39 Installing pressure union O-ring seal

dowel pins with rotation arrow on ring to rear of pump housing, Fig. 33.

NOTE: *Arrow on outer edge of pump ring points in direction of pump rotation (counterclockwise when viewed from rear of pump).*

7. Install rotor vanes in slots of pump rotor, with radius edge of vanes toward outside of rotor, Fig. 34.
8. Position pump housing on two wood blocks and push parts down into place as shown in Fig. 35.
9. Lubricate outside diameter and chamfer of pressure plate with vaseline to insure against damage to O-ring seals in housing. Then install pressure plate in housing over dowel pins.

NOTE: *Ported face of pressure plate goes toward pump ring, Fig. 35.*

10. Using a 2 3/4" diameter sleeve to apply pressure to outer edge of pressure plate only, press pressure plate into seat.

NOTE: *Pressure plate will travel about 1/16" to seat. Do not press or hammer on center of pressure plate as to do so will cause permanent distortion resulting in pump failure.*

11. Install two pressure plate springs, one over each dowel pin in pump housing, Fig. 36.
12. Lubricate outside diameter and chamfer of end plate with vaseline to insure against damage to O-ring seal in housing. Then press end plate into housing. While holding end plate down in housing, install end plate retaining ring. Be sure end plate is completely and solidly seated in groove of housing, Fig. 37.
13. Remove assembly from press and place on work bench. Install flow control spring and valve in bore of housing. Make sure hex head screw goes into housing bore, Fig. 38.
14. Position pressure union O-ring seal in bore of housing over flow control valve, Fig. 39.
15. Mount pump housing in vise with soft jaws and install reservoir.
16. Install pressure union and new O-ring seal in reservoir. Tighten union.
17. Install mounting stud and new O-ring seal in reservoir. Tighten stud.
18. Install drive shaft key in slot in shaft. Support shaft on opposite side while installing key. Install reservoir cap.

SLEEVE TYPE PUMP

Disassembly, Fig. 40

1. Drain oil from pump and reservoir. Cap discharge and return line fittings to exclude dirt from pump.
2. Clean pump and mount it in a vise.
3. Remove reservoir.
4. Loosen capscrews at inlet end cap.
5. Remove flow valve spring retainer fitting.

CAUTION: *Flow and plunger springs are under pressure. Use care when removing cap and retainer to prevent spring and fitting from escaping due to spring force.*

6. Remove flow valve and spring.
7. Remove and disassemble both end caps from inlet cap body and pump housing. Plunger spring will tend to push cylinder blocks out of body. Use care when disassembling.
8. The cylinder blocks will push out of body slightly due to pressure of plunger spring between blocks. Remove cylinder drive blocks and sleeves from pump body as well as cylinder plunger spring.
9. Remove ball bearing retainer ring from housing, using snap ring pliers.
10. Remove shaft and bearing.

Inspection

1. Wipe bearing and shaft assembly with clean, lint-free cloths. Do not soak in cleaning solvent as the lubricants sealed in the bearing may become diluted by solvent.
2. Inspect shaft for wear and bearing for roughness or noisy operation.
3. If bearing must be replaced, remove shaft key and press bearing from shaft away from splined or serrated end of shaft.
4. Examine retaining ring groove in housing.
5. If ball bearing is to be replaced, support bearing on its inner race and press shaft through bearing until retaining ring stops against inner race of bearing. Retaining ring must always be placed between bearing and splined or serrated end of shaft.
6. Check fit of sleeves in cylinder block bores. Sleeves must slide freely.
7. Examine mating surfaces of sleeves and bores. Heavy scoring, if present, can im-

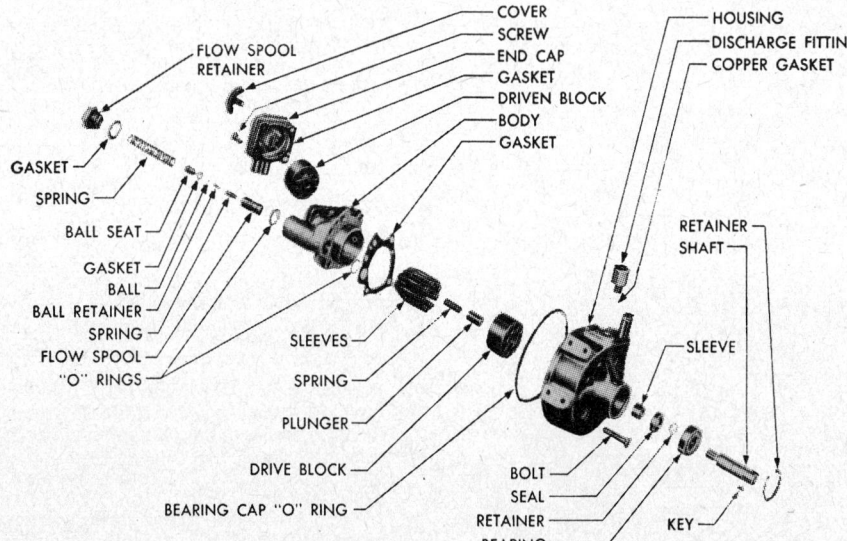

Fig. 40 Sleeve type power steering pump

693

POWER STEERING GEARS

Fig. 41 Drive block assembling fixture

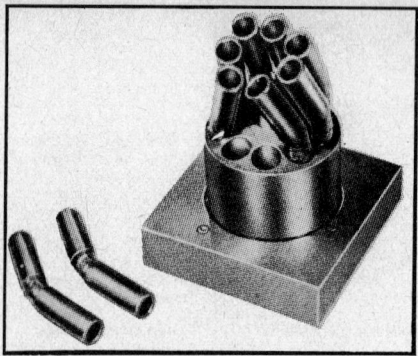

Fig. 42 Assembling sleeves in drive cylinder

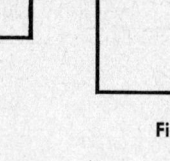

Fig. 43 Installing drive block

pair pump efficiency. Cylinder blocks showing such scoring must be replaced. Hairline markings seen on sleeves are normal.

8. Examine flow valve spool and valve liner. Slight hairline scratches are permissible. Burrs from heavy gouges or scratches which may cause flow spool to stick must be removed. This may be done by polishing with a smooth stone.

CAUTION: *Do not break sharp edges of spool or liner.*

9. Insert flow valve body. By means of a pencil or other such rod which will not mar internal diameter of valve liner, move flow spool back and forth to inspect. On each pass, rotate spool slightly. Spool must slide freely. If spool sticks or drags, remove it from liner. Remove dirt, nicks or burrs, using above caution and check by repeating procedure.

10. Examine shaft seal in bearing cap; if worn or damaged, replace seal.

NOTE: *Lips of seal must point toward casting. Examine running surfaces of bearing cap and inlet end cap. If heavy scratches or gouges are present or if port edges are damaged, the part should be replaced.*

11. Press seal in until shoulder stops against bearing cap casting. Care must be used to see that seal is properly aligned. This operation should be performed in an arbor press.

12. Check pressure relief valve which is located in flow valve spool. The valve must not leak at any pressure below 850 psi. Evidence of leakage will be seen at small holes in side of flow spool. If relief valve leaks, disassemble by removing valve seat and checking for dirt or nicks.

13. Clean all valve parts and reassemble, replacing valve seat if nicked or damaged. Check pressure again. If pressure still falls below minimum requirement, disassemble valve again and replace pressure relief spring or place a $1/32''$ washer between spring and ball retainer. To correct pressures exceeding the maximum requirement, remove valve seat and place a $1/32''$ washer between valve seat and flow spool body.

14. Examine pump body for signs of unusual wear or damage.

Reassembly, Fig. 40

1. Press drive shaft and bearing into bearing cap. Check rotation of shaft to make certain it turns freely. Use a sleeve which bears against outer race of ball bearing and press sub-assembly in place.

CAUTION: *Make certain that the shaft bearing sub-assembly are properly aligned, otherwise the shaft may push sleeve bearing out of bearing cap or may scratch or mar inside diameter of sleeve bearing.*

2. Using assembly fixture (C-3602) shown in Fig. 41, place driven cylinder block (without spline or serration) on fixture.
3. Lubricate (light oil) and insert plunger spring, plunger and seven sleeves in drive block, Fig. 42.
4. Place pump body, square end down, over cylinder drive block and fixture locating pins. Use a pointed probe to align sleeves to a uniform spacing and install remaining sleeves.
5. Position drive splined block with serration over sleeves. Sighting through bores in drive block for alignment, lower cylinder block until it engages the two sleeves in the forward position.
6. Again use a pointed probe slightly smaller in diameter than the sleeve bores, Fig. 43, and correct the alignment of sleeves in the 5 and 7 o'clock positions, at the same time guiding cylinder block downward. Continue this procedure to the 4 and 8 o'clock positions until all sleeves are aligned and engaged. The block is then pushed in all the way.

CAUTION: *Do not force the cylinder block in place. Proper alignment of the block and sleeves will allow the block to be pushed easily into place without excessive pressure. Tighten body to housing.*

7. Remove body and cylinder block from fixture, using care to see that blocks are not forced out of body by plunger spring.
8. Assemble a new end cap gasket on pump body. Install end cap on body and tighten capscrews finger tight.
9. Insert a new O-ring in counterbore at flow valve liner in body. Install a new bearing cap gasket, and assemble bearing cap to body.

1 — Cap Screw
2 — Washer
3 — Rear Cover
3A — Control Valve
4 — "O" Ring
5 — Pump Body
6 — Rear Bearing
6A — Front Bearing
7 — Driven Gear
8 — Drive Gear
9 — Pressure Loading Seal
10 — Pressure Loading Seal
11 — "O" Ring
12 — Front Cover
13 — Shaft Seal
14 — Orifice Plug

Fig. 44 Borg Warner pump, disassembled

POWER STEERING GEARS

NOTE: *It may be necessary to exert hand pressure on bearing cap to get drive block down into body after bearing cap is seated.*

10. Tighten capscrews finger tight. Grip end of pump shaft in vise and rotate pump. Pump should rotate freely without binding. After making sure pump rotates freely, tighten capscrews uniformly to 25 ft-lbs. Check pump again for rotation.
11. Mount pump in vise in vertical position, gripping on bearing hub.
12. Install flow valve spool with the 3/16" land down.
13. Place flow valve spring on top of spool. Replace O-ring on flow spring retainer fitting. Compress flow spring with fitting and screw fitting into place. Tighten to 20 ft-lbs.
14. Install and align a new reservoir O-ring on bearing cap. Lubricate O-ring for ease in assembling reservoir. Align reservoir and push it into place, applying force around its outside diameter.

CAUTION: *Do not attempt to align or pull reservoir into place on the angular boss with the 1/4" capscrews.*

15. Install shaft key and pulley. Tighten pulley attaching bolt to 20 ft-lbs.
16. Refill pump with proper fluid.

BORG WARNER PUMP

Disassembly, Fig. 44

1. Clamp pump in a vise with soft jaws and remove Woodruff key.
2. Remove front and rear covers from pump body by removing cap screws.
3. Slide bearings, drive and driven gears from pump body and remove "O" rings from both covers.
4. Remove pressure loading seals and with a brass drift, drive seal from front cover.
5. Remove control valve and orifice plug from rear cover.

Control Valve, Fig. 45

1. Remove snap ring and slide spool and spring from control valve.
2. Unscrew relief valve seat and remove ball, spring guide and spring.
3. Tap shims from spool bore.
4. Reverse procedure to assemble control valve.

Reassembly, Fig. 44

1. Apply light coat of Permatex No. 3 to front cover bore and press in new seal.
2. Clamp front cover into vise with outside face downward and install new "O" ring and pressure loading seals.
3. Place body on front cover and install front bearings, drive and driven gears, and rear bearings.
4. Install control valve and orifice plug in rear cover.
5. Place new "O" ring on rear cover, assemble rear cover to pump body and install cap screws.
6. Install Woodruff key.

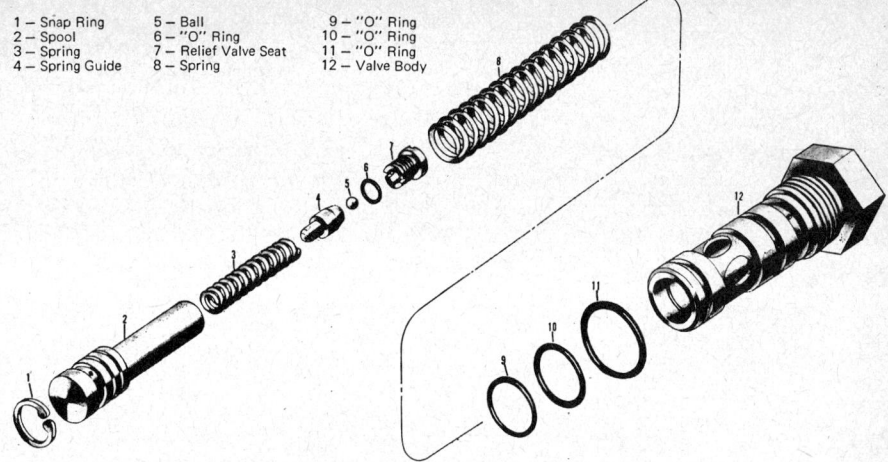

1 – Snap Ring
2 – Spool
3 – Spring
4 – Spring Guide
5 – Ball
6 – "O" Ring
7 – Relief Valve Seat
8 – Spring
9 – "O" Ring
10 – "O" Ring
11 – "O" Ring
12 – Valve Body

Fig. 45 Borg Warner pump flow control valve

EATON PUMP

Disassembly, Fig. 46

1. Remove coupling assembly from pump shaft.
2. Clamp pump in a vise with soft jaws and remove cover, "O" ring and "O" ring retainer.
3. Remove pump shaft, key, snap ring and inner rotor from pump body.
4. Turn body over and tap outer rotor out of body.
5. Remove oil seal from body and flow control valve from pump cover.

Reassembly, Fig. 46

1. Install new oil seal and inner rotor and shaft assembly into pump body.
2. Install outer rotor and "O" rings in body and thrust washer in cover.
3. Install cover on pump body and flow control valve into cover.
4. Install coupling assembly onto shaft.

MACK-SCANIA PUMP

Disassembly, Fig. 47

1. Remove cover from housing.
2. Remove housing "O" ring, lock pin from shaft and rotor assembly from housing.
3. Remove key and shaft, then with a suitable puller remove oil seal from housing.
4. Remove connector and flow control spring from valve body.

NOTE: Use care when removing connector from valve body as it is spring loaded

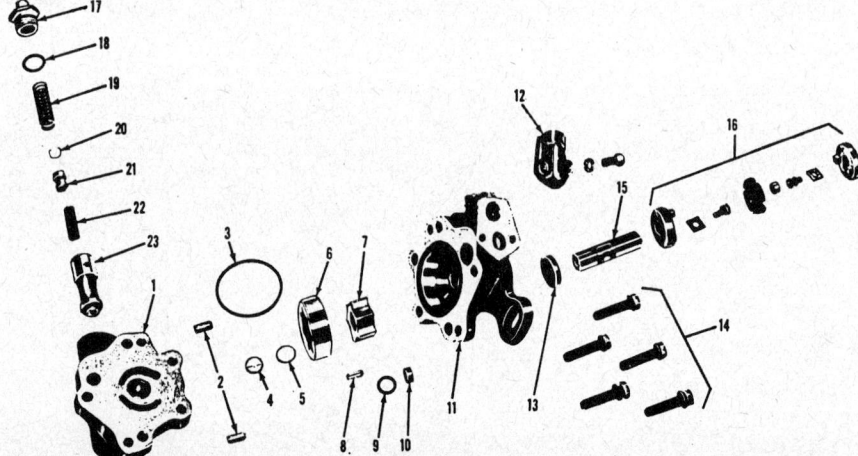

1. Cover
2. Cover Dowel
3. Body O-Ring
4. Thrust Washer
5. Snap Ring
6. Outer Rotor
7. Inner Rotor
8. Drive Pin
9. Bypass O-Ring
10. Bypass O-Ring Retainer
11. Body
12. Outlet Adapter
13. Oil Seal
14. Cover Screws
15. Pump Shaft
16. Coupling Assembly
17. Hose Connector
18. Connector O-Ring
19. Flow Control Valve Spring
20. Valve Retainer Snap Ring
21. Relief Valve
22. Relief Valve Spring
23. Flow Control Valve

Fig. 46 Eaton pump, disassembled

Power Steering Gears

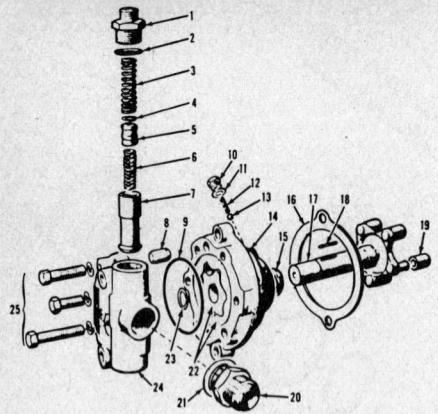

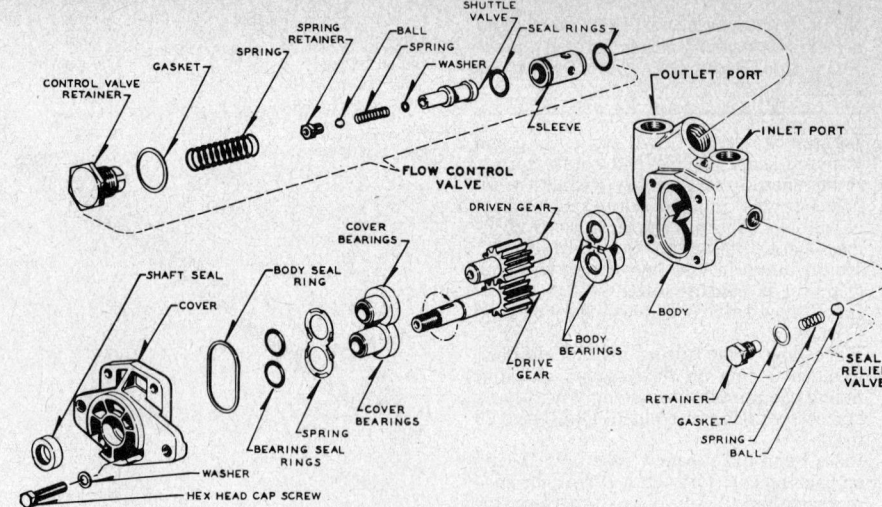

1. Connector
2. O-Ring
3. Flow Control Valve Spring
4. Lock Ring
5. Pressure Regulator Piston
6. Pressure Regulator Spring
7. Flow Control Valve
8. Dowel
9. Housing O-Ring
10. Valve Plug
11. Gasket
12. Spring
13. Valve Ball
14. Housing
15. Oil Seal
16. Gasket
17. Pump Shaft
18. Key
19. Rubber Bushing
20. Connector
21. Connector Gasket
22. Rotor Assembly
23. Pump Shaft Lock Ring
24. Cover
25. Cover Screws

Fig. 47 Mack-Scania pump, disassembled

by the flow control spring.

5. Turn cover over and tap valve assembly out.
6. Remove lock ring, piston and spring from valve body.

Reassembly, Fig. 47

1. Install spring, piston and lock ring into valve body.
2. Install valve body, spring, "O" ring and connector into cover.
3. Install new oil seal, rotor and shaft into housing, aligning keyway on shaft with slot in rotor, then install key and lock ring.
4. Install new "O" ring on housing, then install cover.

PESCO PUMP

Disassembly, Fig. 48

1. Remove hex head cap screws and cover from pump body.
2. Press shaft seal from cover and remove cover bearings, body and bearing seal rings and spring.
3. Remove drive and driven gears and body bearings.
4. Remove flow control valve retainer, gasket and spring, then shuttle valve assembly from body.
5. Remove sleeve from body, then "O" rings from sleeve.
6. Remove seal relief valve retainer, gasket, spring and ball from body.

Reassembly, Fig. 48

1. Install seal relief valve ball, spring, gasket and retainer into body.

Fig. 48 Pesco pump, disassembled

2. Install new "O" rings on sleeve, then sleeve into body.
3. Insert shuttle valve, spring, gasket and control valve retainer into sleeve and body.
4. Install body bearings, drive and driven gears and cover bearings.
5. Place spring on cover bearings, ensuring lips of springs face bearing flanges, and install bearing seal and body seal rings.
6. Apply light coat of Permatex No. 3 to cover bore, then press new shaft seal into cover.
7. Install cover and secure with hex head cap screws.

TRW PUMP

Disassembly, Fig. 49

1. Using suitable puller, remove pulley from shaft.
2. Remove reservoir mounting bolt and gasket from rear of pump. Pry reservoir from pump and discard O-ring.
3. If necessary, remove relief valve and gasket.

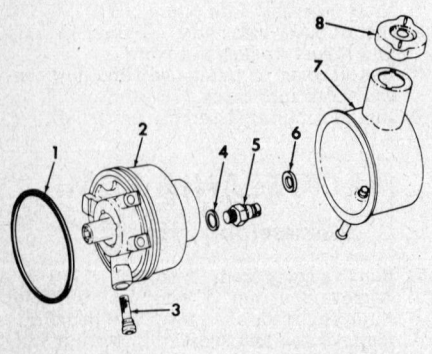

1 SEAL, O-RING
2 PUMP, ASM.
3 SCREEN
4 GASKET
5 VALVE, RELIEF
6 GASKET
7 RESERVOIR
8 CAP, W/GASKET

Fig. 49 TRW pump disassembled

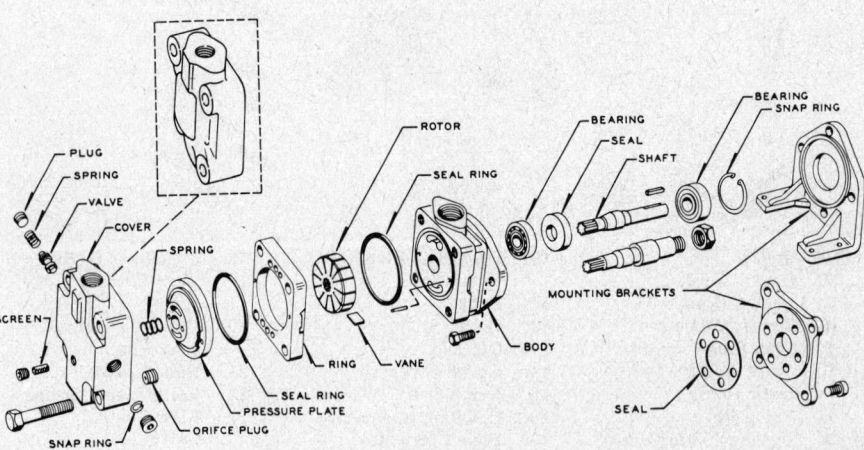

Fig. 50 Vickers V-200 pump, disassembled

Power Steering Gears

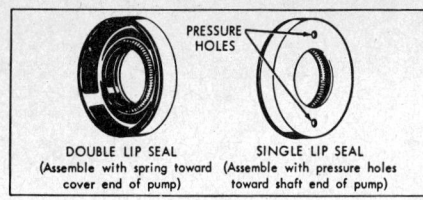

Fig. 51 Vickers V-200 pump, shaft seal installation

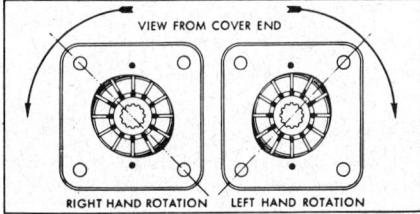

Fig. 52 Vickers, V-200 pump, elliptical ring positioning

Reassembly, Fig. 49

1. Using new gasket, install relief valve in pump body and torque to 20-25 ft. lbs.
2. Install pulley onto shaft as follows:
   a. Position pump on press with rear end supported on a 5/8 inch socket.

CAUTION: If rear end of pump is not

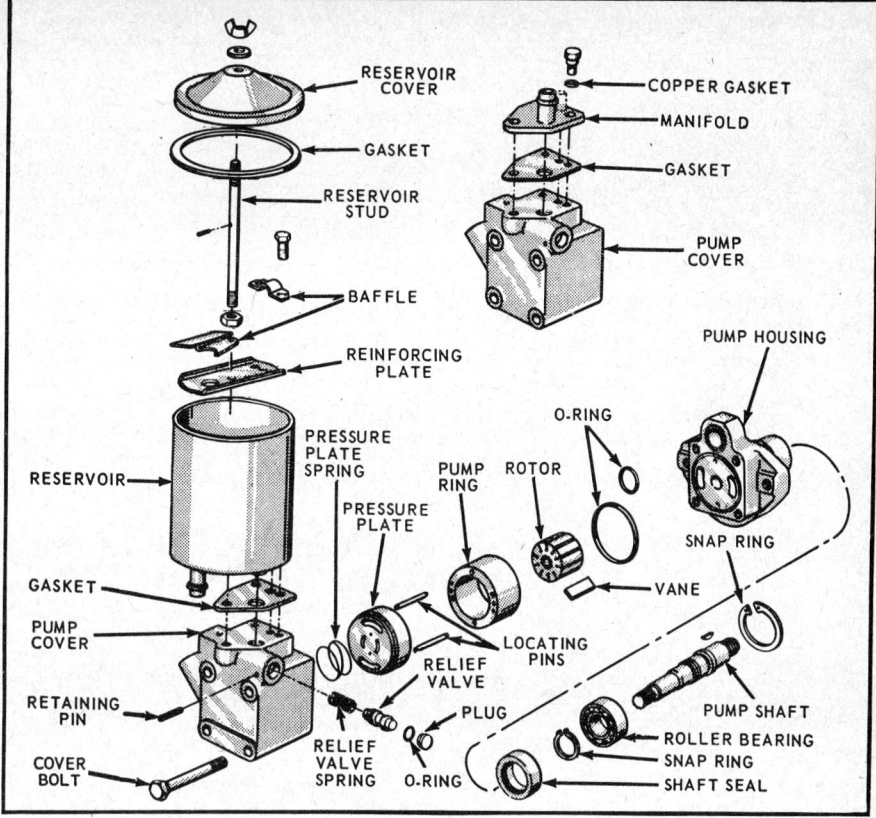

Fig. 53 Vickers power steering pump exc. V-200 pump disassembled

supported, damage to internal pump parts will result when pulley is pressed onto shaft.

b. For 6-258 engines, press pulley until flush with shaft.
c. For DV-550B engines, press pulley until shaft is recessed 5/32 inch from pulley. To obtain this dimension, place two 3/4 inch outside diameter by 5/32 inch thick flat washers on shaft end. Washers will position pulley so that shaft is recessed the specified 5/32 inch.
3. Lightly coat new O-ring with petroleum jelly or power steering fluid and install O-ring into pump body groove.
4. Install reservoir onto pump body and secure with mounting bolt and copper washer.

VICKERS V-200 PUMP

Disassembly, Fig. 50

1. Remove mounting flange and clamp pump body in a vise with cover end up.
2. Note location of cover port, then remove cover and "O" ring.
3. Remove spring, pressure plate and elliptical ring.
4. Remove vanes from rotor, then rotor from shaft.
5. Remove shaft key and outer bearing snap ring and tap shaft from body.
6. Press outer bearing from shaft, remove shaft seal and press inner bearing from body.

Reassembly, Fig. 50

1. Press outer bearing onto shaft and inner bearing into body.
2. Correctly install shaft seal into pump body, Fig. 51.
3. Slide shaft into body until bearing is fully seated and install snap ring.
4. Install new "O" rings in pump body and cover.
5. Install elliptical ring in proper position, Fig. 52.
6. Install rotor on shaft and insert vanes in slots with radius edges facing cam ring.
7. Install pressure plate, spring, cover and cover screws.
8. Turn shaft to check for internal binding and install key and mounting flange.

VICKERS EXC. V-200 PUMP

Disassemble, Fig. 53

1. Clamp pump mounting flange in a vise with soft jaws.
2. If pump is equipped with a reservoir proceed as follows: Remove wing nut, washer, reservoir cover and gasket. Remove the stud and nut from the reservoir. Remove two screws, lock washers, and baffle from the reservoir. Separate reservoir and gasket from pump.
3. If pump is not equipped with a reservoir proceed as follows: Remove three manifold attaching screws and the copper washer and separate the manifold and gasket from the pump.

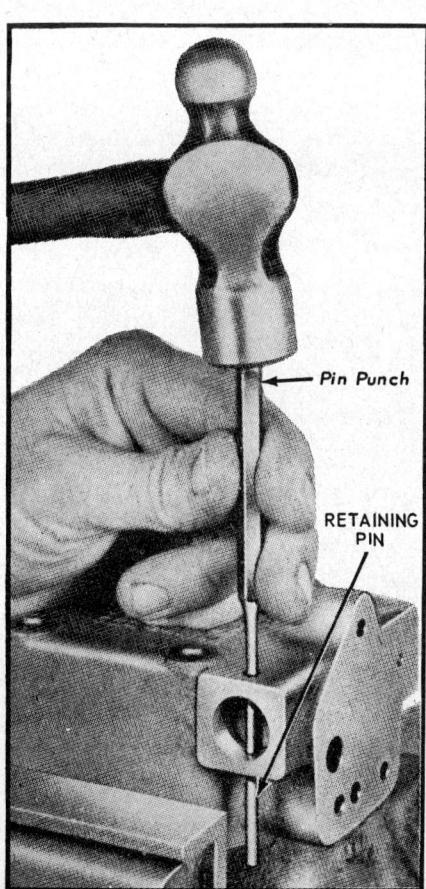

Fig. 54 Removing relief valve retaining pin

POWER STEERING GEARS

4. With pump clamped in a soft jaw vise, remove four cover attaching screws and separate the cover and pressure plate spring from pump body.
5. Hold the pump ring and remove the pressure plate from pump body.
6. Remove the pump ring, locating pins, rotor and vanes, and the two "O" rings from the pump body.
7. Remove the snap ring from the shaft end of pump housing.
8. Press the shaft and needle bearing out of housing.
9. Remove shaft seal from the housing.
10. If the bearing is worn or damaged, remove the snap ring from the shaft and press the shaft from the bearing.
11. Place the pump cover in a soft jaw vise and drive the retaining pin from the cover with a pin punch, Fig. 54. Do not allow the relief valve and plug to fall out of the cover and become damaged.
12. Remove the plug, relief valve and spring from the cover. The relief valve can be pushed from the cover through a hole inside the cover. Remove the pressure fitting from the cover.

Reassembly, Fig. 53

During assembly, immerse all parts in clean hydraulic oil and replace all seals, gaskets and "O" rings.
1. Position the shaft seal to the pump body, being careful not to damage the seal.

Fig. 55 Vane installation

Press the seal in until it engages the shoulder in the body.
2. Install the small snap ring on the pump shaft and press the bearing on the shaft.
3. Install the shaft and bearing in the pump body and install the snap ring.
4. Install the two pump ring locating pins in the valve body and install the pump ring.

NOTE: The pump ring must be installed with the arrow on the outside diameter of the ring pointing in the direction of pump rotation. This is important because the direction of pump rotation varies with engine usage.

5. Install the rotor with the chamfered edge of the splined hole toward the pump body.
6. Install the vanes with their radius edge toward the center of the rotor, Fig. 55.
7. Install the pressure plate and "O" rings.
8. Install the pressure plate spring and cover and tighten screws to 25–30 ft. lbs.
9. Position the relief valve spring in the bore. Insert the relief valve in the bore with the hex toward the spring.
10. Install the plug with the "O" ring in the bore and install a new retaining pin.
11. If equipped with a reservoir, install same in the reverse order of removal.
12. If not equipped with a reservoir install the manifold in the reverse order of removal.
13. Rotate the pump shaft to check for free operation and install the pressure fitting in the pump cover.

NOTE: *The following material covers a miscellaneous collection of power cylinders to be found on all types of trucks. When necessary to service a unit, first identify it by the exploded views furnished with the test. During the overhaul procedure, remove and discard all O-rings and seals, using new ones upon reassembly. Lubricate all O-rings and seals with light engine oil before installation.*

Power Cylinder Section

TYPE A POWER CYLINDER

Disassembly, Fig. 1

1. Drain hydraulic fluid by running piston rod from end to end.
2. Use a suitable spanner wrench to loosen cover about 1/8 of a turn. This will bend out the staked portion of outer cylinder. The cylinder should then be tapped lightly with a mallet in the staked area to straighten out the threads.
3. Unscrew cover and remove from cylinder barrel and piston rod.
4. Remove seal from piston rod.
5. Remove spring retainer and spring.
6. Loosen packing from around bearing and remove.
7. Remove bearing from cylinder barrel and piston rod.
8. Remove rings from piston.

Reassembly, Fig. 1

1. Install rings to piston and rod.
2. Using a piston installer sleeve, insert piston rod in barrel.
3. Slide bearing onto piston rod and into barrel.
4. Using new packing, position into barrel and around bearing.
5. Install spring with large diameter next to bearing, making sure it rests in its seat.
6. Insert spring retainer into spring.
7. With a suitable thimble positioned on threaded end of rod and over wrench flats,

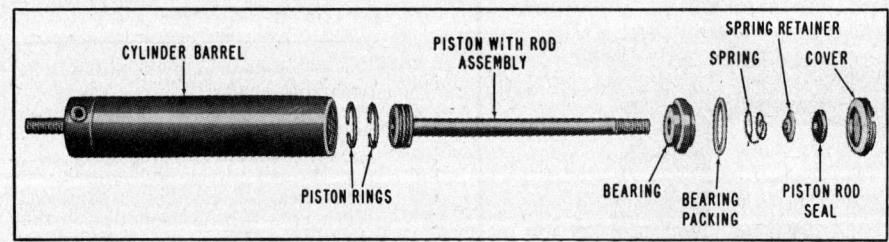

Fig. 1 Type A power cylinder mounted on tie rod

install a new piston rod seal, making sure the side on which is molded "this side out" is started on the rod.
8. Install cover, using spanner wrench to tighten securely. The face of the cover should now be flush with the end of the outer cylinder barrel.
9. Stake outer cylinder barrel into a wrench slot in the cover, using a blunt nosed tool. Select a point on the cylinder not previously staked. Minor leakage may occur around cylinder threads. However, this will stop as the packing swells after contacting the oil.

TYPES B & C POWER CYLINDERS

These cylinders have the bearing welded to the cylinder barrel. Also the cylinder shown in Fig. 3 has a socket welded to the head end of the cylinder. The only components that are serviced are the piston rod seals, socket seats, spring and plug.

Disassembly, Figs. 2 & 3

1. Drain fluid by running piston rod from end to end.
2. Remove internal snap ring from bearing.
3. Pull piston rod outward to disengage seals from cylinder bearing. In the event the seals remain in the bearing bore, an awl may be used to pry the seals out. However, when using this method, care must be taken not to scratch the piston rod.
4. Remove seals, back-up ring, and retaining rings from piston rod.
5. Remove socket plug seats and spring from opposite end of cylinder.
6. Wash socket seats and spring in cleaning solvent and inspect for damage or wear.

Power Steering Gears

Reassembly, Figs. 2 & 3

1. Install spring seat in socket end of cylinder.
2. Install inner seat into socket with concave side facing outward.
3. Position outer seat with concave side facing inward into socket.
4. Loosely assembly plug into socket.
5. Cover threaded end of piston rod with cellophane or plastic tape to prevent damage to seals during installation.
6. Install O-ring seal over piston rod. Then slip on the back-up ring, small retaining ring, large retaining ring, seal, large retaining ring. Secure assembled parts with snap ring.

TYPES D, E, F POWER CYLINDERS

Disassembly, Figs. 4, 5, 6

1. Drain hydraulic fluid by running piston rod from end to end.
2. Remove cover.
3. Using a drift punch and hammer, work around the bearing, tapping it lightly into the cylinder barrel inner edge of snap ring. (This item does not apply to Figs. 4 and 5.)
4. Insert punch in hole along side cylinder barrel to disengage lock ring from its groove, and remove lock ring.
5. Pull on piston rod end to remove rod and internal parts from cylinder barrel. When removing the parts from the piston rod, slide them off the piston end of the rod.
6. Remove piston rod nut, piston and rings.
7. Remove bearing.
8. Remove O-ring seal and back-up ring from bearing.
9. Remove piston seal and inner O-ring seal from bearing.
10. Wash all parts in cleaning solvent and inspect for damage or wear.

Reassembly, Figs. 4, 5, 6

NOTE: *As all parts are machined to very close limits, use extreme care in handling. Damaged sealing edges or burrs will not permit the unit to function them properly. The by-pass valve is an internal part of the piston assembly and in the event it does not function properly, it will be necessary to replace the piston assembly as components of the by-pass valve are not supplied separately. To prevent damage to any of the parts, it is recommended that assembly be made from the piston end of the rod.*

1. Assemble inner O-ring seal and piston rod seal in bearing.
2. Assemble back-up ring and O-ring seal to bearing and slide over piston rod down toward threaded end of rod.
3. Assemble rings on piston, then install piston to rod.
4. Install piston nut and torque to 225–230 ft-lbs. If tightening nut without use of torque wrench, be careful of over-tightening as this may cause piston to swell and prevent assembly in barrel.
5. Using a piece of shim stock .010" thick wrapped around piston and rings, slide complete piston rod assembly into cylinder barrel. Push assembly into cylinder as far as possible.
6. Insert bearing into cylinder barrel, taking precautions not to damage bearing O-ring seal against hydraulic line fitting hole in cylinder. To assist in pushing O-ring past this hole, use a piece of wood having a round edge to work the O-ring past the edge.
7. Working around the bearing with a drift punch and hammer, move the bearing past the inner edge of the snap ring groove in the cylinder barrel. This applies only to cylinder shown in Fig. 6.
8. Install lock ring in its groove.
9. Pull back on piston rod until bearing contacts edge of snap ring.
10. Install end plate and secure with lockwashers and screws.

TYPE G POWER CYLINDER

Disassembly, Fig. 7

1. Drain hydraulic fluid by running piston rod from end to end.
2. Remove cover.
3. Using a punch and hammer, work around bearing, tapping it lightly into cylinder barrel to permit snap ring removal.
4. Insert punch in hole along side of cylinder barrel to disengage snap ring from its groove; remove snap ring.

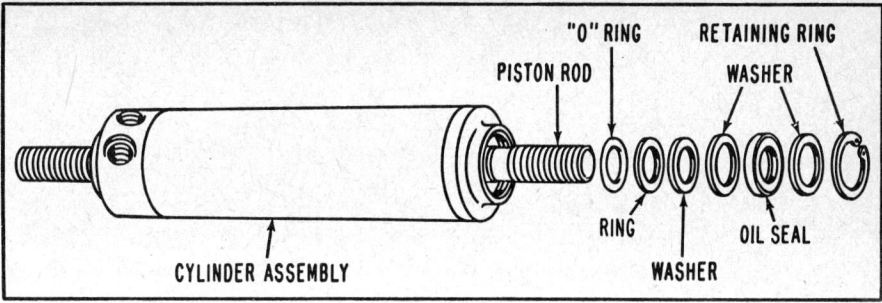

Fig. 2 Type B power cylinder mounted on tie rod

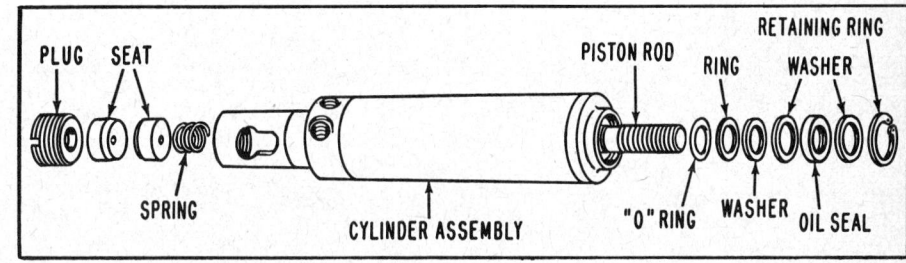

Fig. 3 Type C power cylinder mounted on the rod

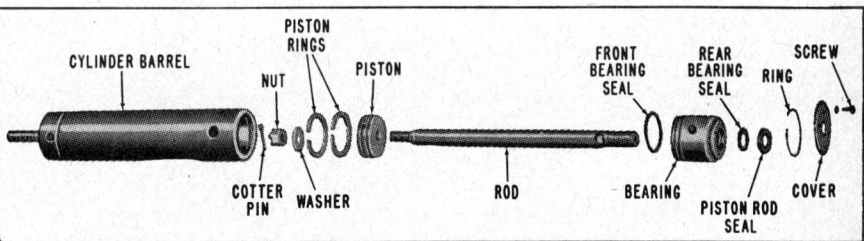

Fig. 4 Type D power cylinder mounted on tie rod

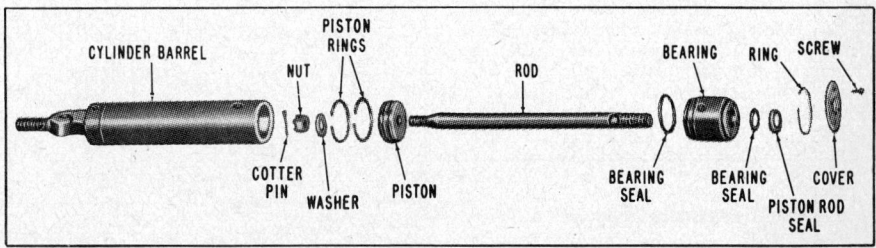

Fig. 5 Type E power cylinder mounted on frame side rail

POWER STEERING GEARS

5. Pull on piston rod end to remove rod and internal parts from cylinder barrel. When removing parts from piston rod, slide them off piston end of rod.
6. Remove piston rod nut, piston and rings.
7. Remove bearing.
8. Remove O-ring seal and back-up ring from bearing.
9. Remove snap ring from front of bearing.
10. Remove retaining ring, seal, washers, back-up ring and O-ring from bearing.
11. Remove socket plug seats and spring from opposite end of cylinder.
12. Wash all parts and inspect for damage or wear.

Reassembly, Fig. 7

NOTE: *As all parts are machined to very close limits, use extreme care in handling them. Damaged sealing edges or burrs will not permit the unit to function properly. To prevent damage to any of the parts, assembly should be made from the piston end of the rod.*

1. Assemble O-ring, back-up ring, washers, seal (lip toward front of bearing) and retaining ring.
2. Install snap ring in bearing groove.
3. Install back-up ring and O-ring to rear of bearing.
4. Slide bearing over piston rod down threaded end of rod.
5. Assemble seal and piston rings to piston, then install piston to rod.
6. Install piston nut and tighten securely.
7. Slide complete piston rod assembly into cylinder barrel. Push assembly into cylinder as far as possible.
8. Insert bearing into cylinder barrel, taking precautions not to damage bearing O-ring against edge of cylinder barrel.
9. Working around bearing with a drift punch and hammer, move bearing past inner edge of snap ring groove in cylinder barrel.
10. Install lock ring in its groove.
11. Pull back on piston rod until bearing contacts edge of snap ring.
12. Install end plate and secure with lockwashers and screws.
13. Install seat spring in socket end of cylinder.
14. Install inner seat into socket with concave side facing outward.
15. Position outer seat with concave side facing inward into socket.
16. Loosely assemble socket plug into socket.

TYPE H CHEVROLET & GMC POWER CYLINDER

NOTE: *This power cylinder, Fig. 8, is used on all models of the above truck makes when equipped with Saginaw Rotary Valve and Spool Valve Power Steering Gears. The piston rod end of the cylinder is attached to the steering relay tie rod, idler lever and tie rod, or drag link, depending on the truck application. The opposite end of the cylinder is attached to a bracket which is bolted to the frame or front axle.*

Disassembly, Fig. 8

NOTE: *The only parts that can be replaced are the piston rod seals and the socket end ball stud seats and adjuster screws.*

1. Remove adjuster screw and ball stud seats from both ends of power cylinder.
2. Loosen clamp bolt on outside of socket end assembly.
3. Using a wide blade screwdriver to keep the piston from turning, unthread socket end from piston rod.
4. Force piston rod in and out of power cylinder to drain remaining fluid.
5. Remove scraper retainer snap ring from groove in piston rod guide assembly.
6. Apply air pressure to retraction port in guide assembly while at the same time holding a finger over the extension port. This will dislodge wiper ring assembly, scraper retainer, O-ring seal, and piston rod seal from guide.
7. Clean all parts with cleaning solvent and dry with compressed air. Replace all parts that are not in first class condition.

Reassembly, Fig. 8

1. Lubricate lip of piston rod seal with a thin layer of grease containing zinc oxide #3, and insert it into guide assembly with the "U" of the cup toward bottom of opening in guide.
2. Install scraper retainer O-ring seal.
3. Install scraper retainer in guide with "U" side pointing out.
4. Insert wiper ring assembly. Then install retaining snap ring. Make sure ring is well seated in groove of guide.
5. Thread socket end assembly on piston rod

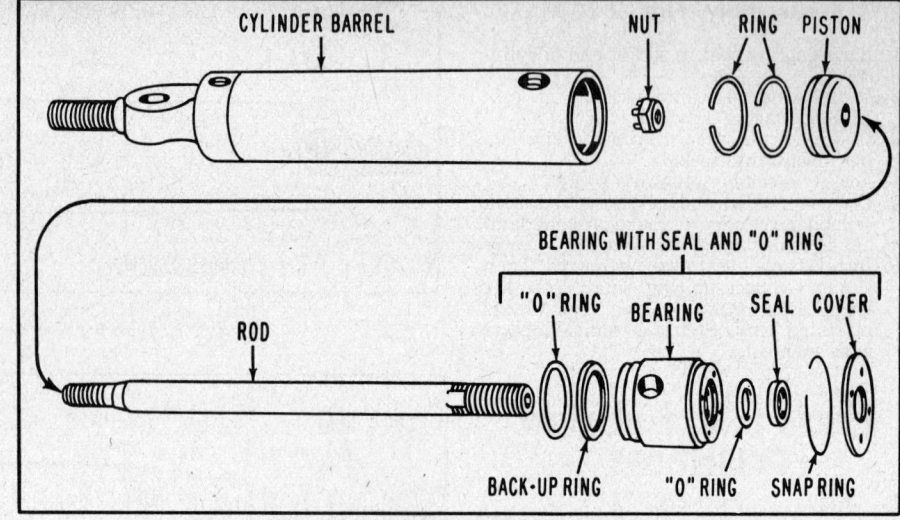

Fig. 6 Type F power cylinder mounted on frame side rail

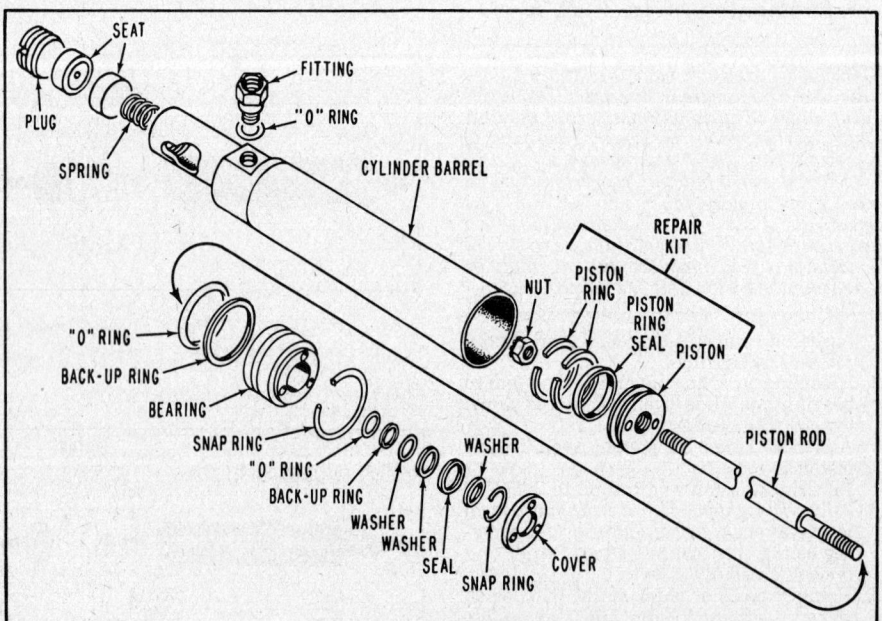

Fig. 7 Type G power cylinder mounted on frame side rail and connected to pitman arm or to a steering arm

POWER STEERING GEARS

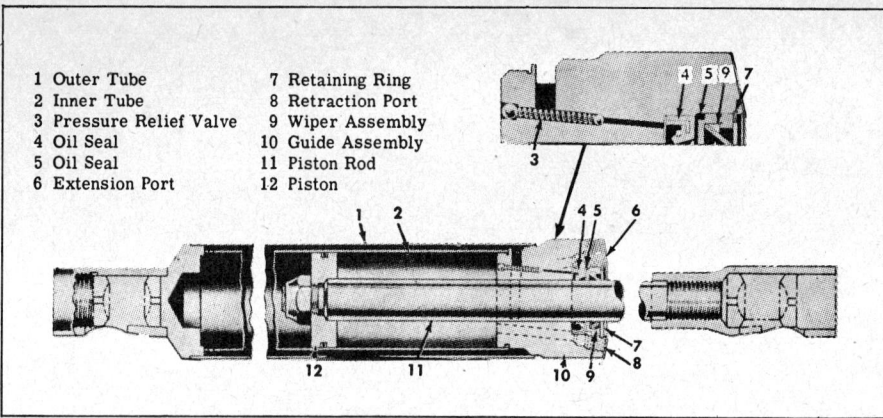

Fig. 8 Type H power cylinder used on Chevrolet and GMC trucks equipped with Saginaw Rotary and Spool Valve power steering gears

1 Outer Tube
2 Inner Tube
3 Pressure Relief Valve
4 Oil Seal
5 Oil Seal
6 Extension Port
7 Retaining Ring
8 Retraction Port
9 Wiper Assembly
10 Guide Assembly
11 Piston Rod
12 Piston

until it shoulders against rod.
6. Tighten clamp bolt securely.
7. At both ends of power cylinder, install ball seats. Then thread adjuster screws into the sockets loosely. Adjust after installed on vehicle.

TYPE 1 CHEVROLET & GMC POWER CYLINDER

NOTE: *This type power cylinder, Fig. 9, is used on the above truck makes with linkage type power steering. There are only two units that can be disassembled: They are the piston rod seal assembly and the ball stud assembly.*

Disassembly, Fig. 9

1. Remove snap ring at piston rod end of power cylinder.
2. Pull piston rod out of cylinder, being careful not to spray oil out of cylinder ports.
3. Remove piston rod seal, scraper, washer, and scraper element from piston rod.
4. Depress plug. Then remove snap ring from groove in ball stud housing.
5. Remove plug, spring, spring seat, and ball stud. Remove grease fitting.
6. If necessary to remove ball stud seat from housing, seat will have to be pressed out.

Inspection

1. Clean all parts except seals in solvent and dry with compressed air.
2. Check seat spring for free length, distortion or collapsed coils.
3. Check all parts for wear or damage and replace any that are not in first class condition.

Reassembly, Fig. 9

1. If previously removed, press new ball stud seat in housing.
2. Position ball stud, spring seat, spring, and plug in housing. Depress plug and install snap ring in housing groove.
3. At opposite end of power cylinder, position seal, scraper, washer and scraper element on piston rod.
4. Move parts into position in cylinder. Then install retaining snap ring.

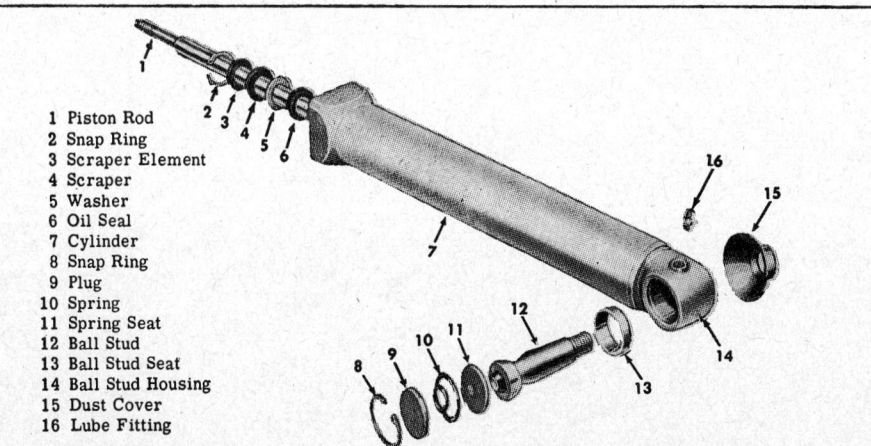

1 Piston Rod
2 Snap Ring
3 Scraper Element
4 Scraper
5 Washer
6 Oil Seal
7 Cylinder
8 Snap Ring
9 Plug
10 Spring
11 Spring Seat
12 Ball Stud
13 Ball Stud Seat
14 Ball Stud Housing
15 Dust Cover
16 Lube Fitting

Fig. 9 Type I power cylinder used on Chevrolet and GMC trucks equipped with linkage type power steering

TYPE J DODGE POWER CYLINDER

NOTE: *This type power cylinder, Fig. 10, is used with trucks having linkage type power steering. Service procedure is limited to replacement of the seals only.*

1. To disassemble refer to Fig. 10 and loosen clamp on vertical ball stud.
2. Place wrench on flats, located on end of piston rod, and remove vertical ball stud.
3. Remove retaining ring with snap ring pliers.
4. Remove scraper washer, dust seal, seal back-up washer and "V" block seal.

NOTE: *If dust seal or "V" block seal have surface breaks or cuts they should be replaced. The scraper washer should be a close fit (.001–.0035") on the piston rod.*

5. Reverse foregoing procedure to assembly cylinder.

TYPE K DODGE POWER CYLINDER

NOTE: *This type power cylinder, Fig. 11 is used in conjunction with the Ross power steering gear with built-in concentric control valve. Service on the latter unit is given further on.*

Disassembly, Fig. 11

1. Loosen socket clamp at steering gear arm end and remove socket from piston rod.

NOTE: *Socket is threaded on piston rod. Scribe a mark on the piston rod to insure that socket will be reassembled on piston rod to maintain proper power piston rod adjustment.*

2. Remove four screws attaching cylinder end cover to cylinder bearing.
3. Remove bushing retaining snap ring.
4. Remove hose connector.
5. Lubricate area around retaining ring groove with a liberal amount of light engine oil. Then carefully remove bearing with leather back-up ring and O-ring. Rotate bearing slightly while slowly pulling outward on bearing.
6. Carefully withdraw piston rod and piston with rings. Rotate piston rod slowly when approaching bearing retainer groove in cylinder so that piston rings will drop into retainer groove.
7. Remove piston retaining lock nut from piston rod and remove piston assembly.

NOTE: *If ball socket or springs require replacement, scribe a mark on plugs and sockets to maintain proper ball socket adjustment upon reassembly.*

Inspection

1. Clean all parts and air dry.
2. Inspect cylinder and piston for excessive

Power Steering Gears

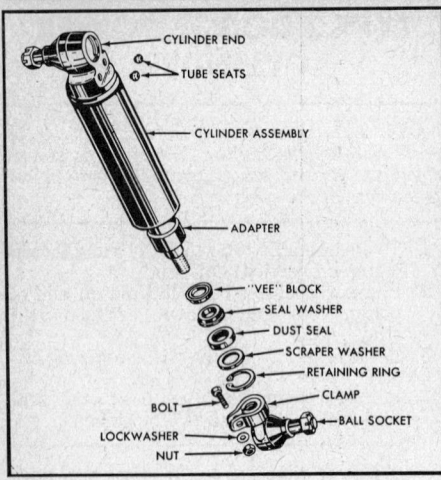

Fig. 10 Type J power cylinder used on Dodge trucks with linkage type power steering

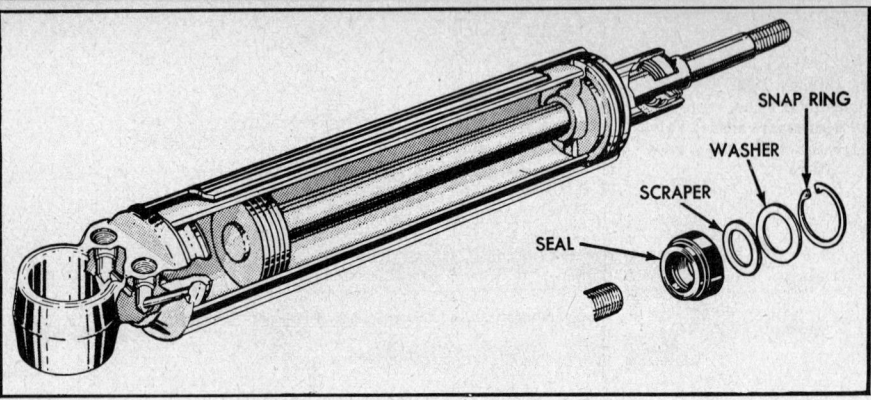

Fig. 12 Type L power cylinder used on Ford trucks with linkage type power steering

wear.
3. Cylinder bore size for the 2¾" bore cylinder is 2.747–2.750". For the 2¼" bore cylinder the bore size is 2.247–2.250". Piston ring gap should be .003–.005".
4. Make sure piston poppet works freely in piston.
5. Inspect piston rod for wear or damage.
6. Inspect bushing for wear in bearing bore. Replace all seals.

Reassembly, Fig. 11

1. Install piston on piston rod and install lock nut. Torque nut to 100–125 ft-lbs for the 2¾" bore cylinder and 60–55 ft-lbs for the 2¼" bore cylinder.
2. Install piston rings and space gaps 15 degrees apart.
3. Lubricate piston and rings liberally with automatic transmission fluid.
4. Install piston and piston rod assembly into cylinder bore.

NOTE: *Enter piston carefully to clear bushing retainer ring groove. Use four pieces of .0015" feeler stock to assist in installation of piston assembly.*

5. Position piston until it bottoms in cylinder.
6. Install back-up washer and O-ring on bearing.
7. For the 2¾" bore cylinder install the O-ring and seal in bushing with lip of seal toward bushing. For the 2¼" bore cylinder, install O-ring seal, back-up leather washer, flat washer, steel retaining ring, oil seal, seal retaining ring and snap ring in that order.
8. Lubricate bushing and seals and carefully install bushing over piston rod and insert it in cylinder.
9. Install bushing retaining ring, making sure it is seated properly in cylinder groove.
10. Install cylinder cover and attaching screws.
11. Install socket clamp on steering gear arm socket.
12. Thread socket to scribe marks made at disassembly.
13. Install clamp screw, lockwasher and nut and tighten nut to 40 ft-lbs.
14. Install spring retainer, ball seats and plugs.
15. Install spring, ball seat, support bracket ball, ball seat and plug.
16. Lubricate ball and seats and tighten plug until ball moves freely and without any bind.

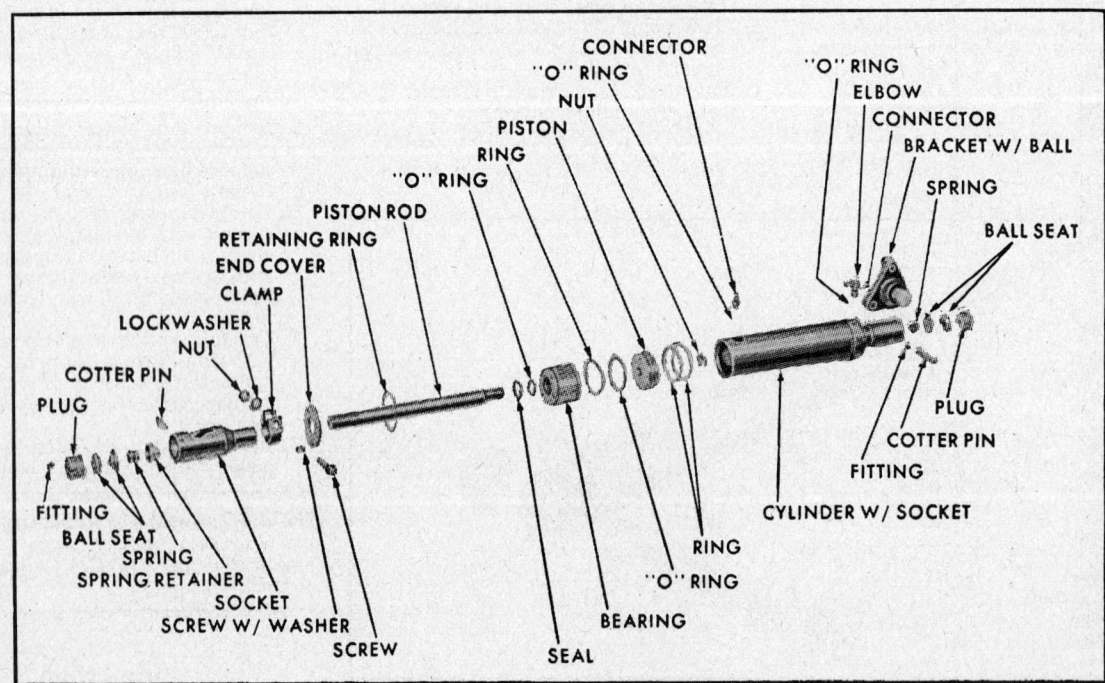

Fig. 11 Type K power cylinder used on Dodge trucks in conjunction with Ross power steering gear with built-in concentric control valve

Power Steering Gears

TYPE L FORD POWER CYLINDER

NOTE: *This type power cylinder is used on trucks having a separately mounted hydraulic control valve. The only service required is to replace the seal.*

1. Referring to Fig. 12, remove snap ring from end of cylinder.
2. Pull piston out all the way to remove retainer washer, bronze scraper washer and oil seal.
3. After lubricating seal with automatic transmission fluid, position bronze scraper washer in seal.
4. Position seal and retainer washer on piston, and install seal and washer in cylinder, using suitable deep socket.
5. Install retaining snap ring.

TYPE M POWER CYLINDER

Disassembly, Fig. 13

1. Remove cylinder head snap ring, push cylinder head in and remove cylinder tube snap ring.
2. Pull rod, head and piston assembly from housing.
3. Remove snap ring, washer, seal assembly, washer and cylinder head.
4. Remove piston nut, piston and copper seal.

Inspection

1. Clean all parts and air dry.
2. Inspect cylinder and piston for wear. Replace piston rings as necessary.
3. Inspect seal assembly for broken or notched edges and replace as necessary.
4. Inspect pin and universal block for wear. Pin should fit snugly in cylinder base and universal block.

Reassembly

1. Install copper seal, piston and piston nut on rod.
2. Compress piston rings and install piston and rod into body.

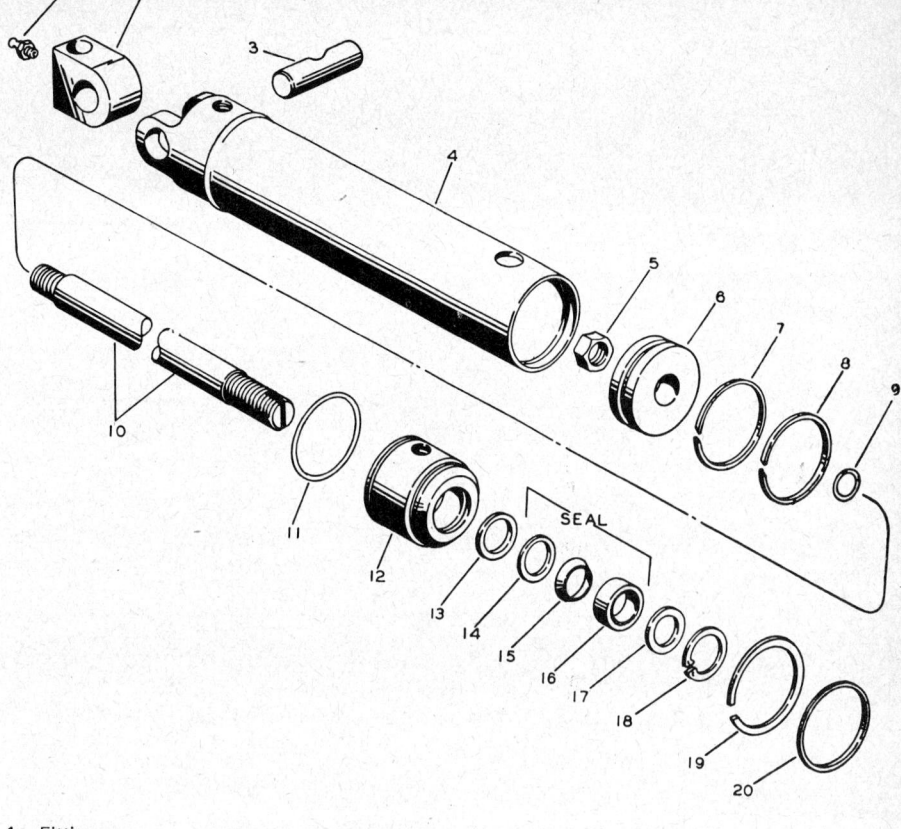

1 — Fitting
2 — Universal Block
3 — Pin
4 — Body
5 — Piston Nut
6 — Piston
7 — Piston Ring
8 — Piston Ring
9 — Copper Seal
10 — Rod
11 — "O" Ring
12 — Cylinder Head
13 — Snap Ring
14 — Neoprene Seal
15 — Nylon Wedge Seal
16 — Seal
17 — Washer
18 — Snap Ring
19 — Cylinder Tube Snap Ring
20 — Cylinder Head Snap Ring

Fig. 13 Type M power cylinder used on White trucks

3. Install washers and seal assembly into cylinder head and secure with snap ring.
4. Lubricate and install "O" ring on cylinder head and secure with snap ring.
5. Install snap ring in body and pull rod outward, forcing the head against snap ring, then install the cylinder head snap ring.

Control Valve Section

This section covers service procedures on the three general types of control valves which are:

1. Type used with linkage type power steering but mounted separately from the power cylinder.
2. Type used with linkage type power steering but mounted in combination with the power cylinder. This design is commonly known as an "In Line Booster."
3. Type built into the steering gear itself.

NOTE: *Since the major parts of the valve are machined to very close limits, they should be handled carefully to prevent damage to the sealing edges. Damaged or burred edges will prevent the valve from functioning properly.*

Cleanliness throughout the entire servicing procedure cannot be over-emphasized. Parts should be cleaned with a suitable solvent, washed and dried. Always use new O-ring seals when reassembling. Lubricate all seals and O-rings with light engine oil during reassembly.

TYPES A, B, C, D CONTROL VALVES

Disassembly, Figs. 1, 2, 3, 4

1. Remove dust seal.
2. Using a screwdriver or chisel, unlock end cover caps by straightening lock ring tabs.
3. Unscrew and remove both end covers from valve body.

NOTE: *Use extreme care so as not to damage mating surfaces on valve body when removing caps. Also the use of a strap wrench will prevent damage to the exterior finish of the caps.*

4. Remove lock rings from each end of valve body assembly.
5. Remove gland and spring from valve body by slightly pushing on threaded end of valve spool.

POWER STEERING GEARS

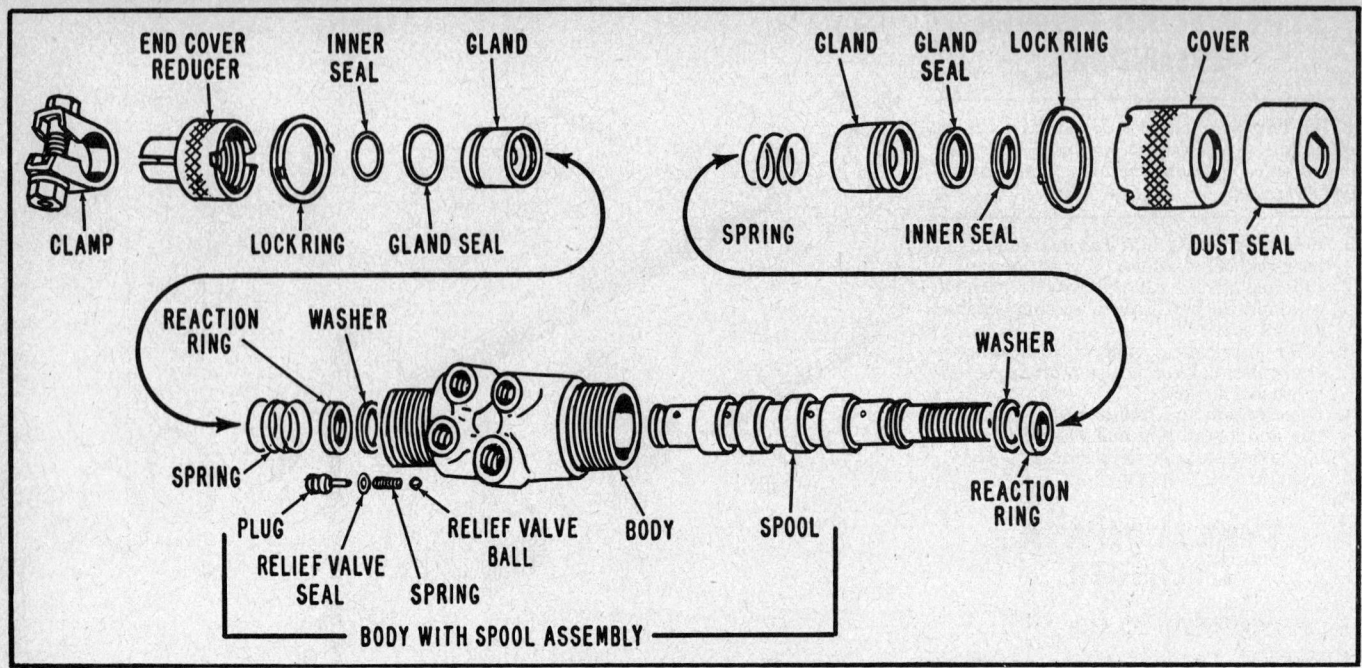

Fig. 1 Type A control valve mounted between pitman arm and steering gear

NOTE: *On the valve shown in Fig. 4, it will be necessary to remove the "C" washer and plain washer before the O-ring, gland and spring can be removed.*

6. On valve shown in Fig. 2, remove ring.
7. Remove O-ring from end of valve spool (end from which gland was removed).
8. Remove gland and spring from opposite end of valve by pulling on threaded end of valve spool. When removing spool, one reaction ring and spacing washer (if used) will probably remain in valve body which can easily be removed. The other ring and spacing washer (if used) will remain on the spool.

NOTE: *Check the relation of the threaded end of valve spool to ports in valve body before removing spool. This is important for reassembly.*

9. Remove remaining O-ring and reaction ring from valve spool. Match reaction rings with their respective glands.
10. Remove O-rings from glands.
11. Components of the relief valve unit should not require servicing except for

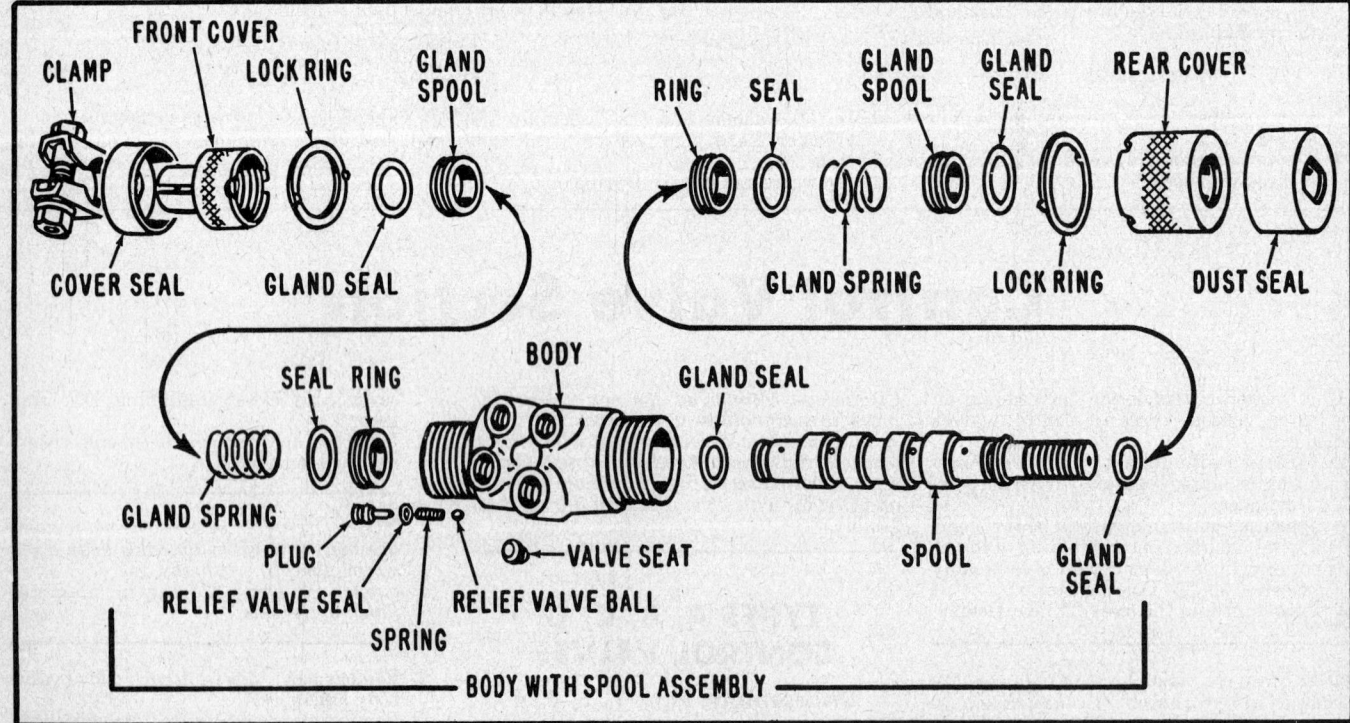

Fig. 2 Type B controlve valve mounted between pitman arm and steering gear

Power Steering Gears

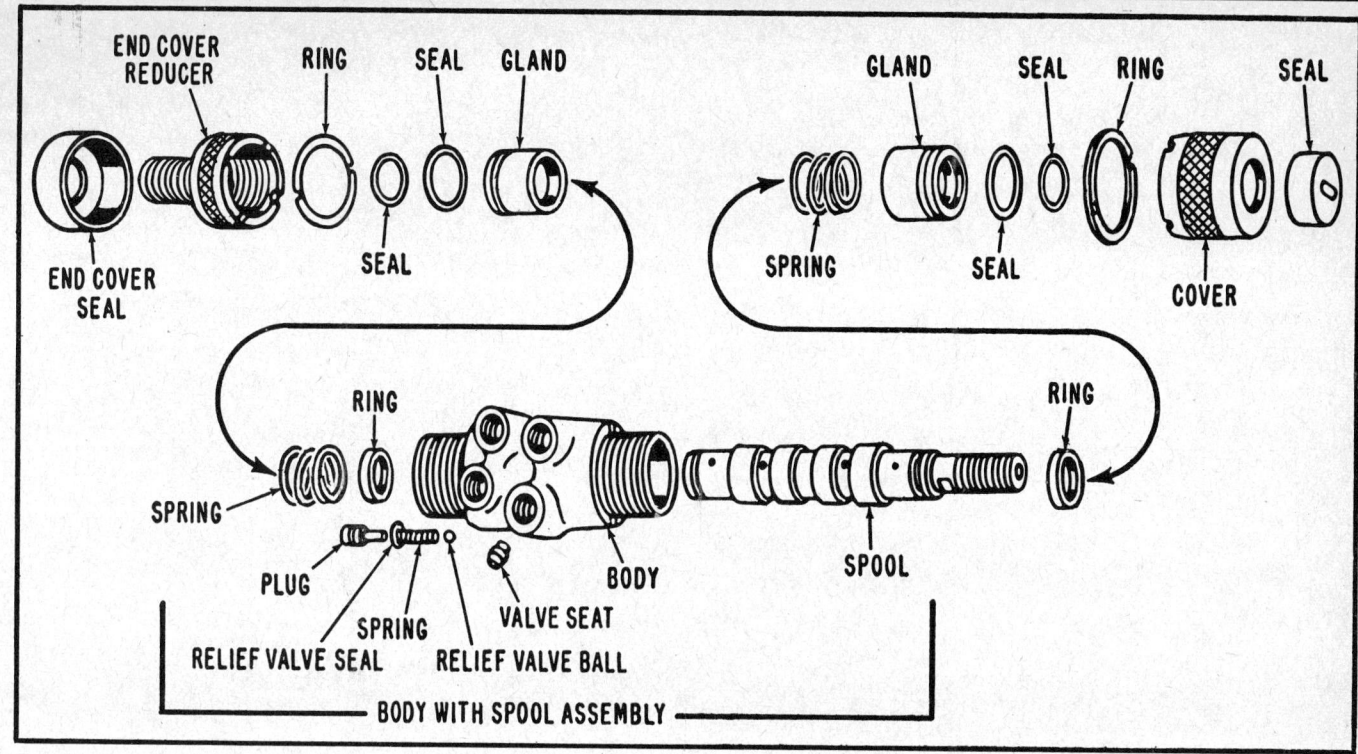

Fig. 3 Type C control valve mounted on frame side rail

possible replacement of the small O-ring should leakage be evident. Remove relief valve plug. Remove O-ring seal from plug. Remove relief valve spring and steel ball.

Reassembly

NOTE: *Since very little wear takes place in these valves, the only parts that need replacing in addition to the O-rings are the centering springs, lock rings, and occasionally an end cover or clamp assembly. Inspect the valve spool bore for nicks, burrs or scoring. Slight score marks may be removed with crocus cloth provided it is used carefully. When using on valve spool, use extreme care not to round off the sharp edge portion as this is vitally important to this type of valve.*

1. Assemble steel ball into relief valve bore in valve body, then slide in spring.
2. Assemble new O-ring seal to plug assembly and insert into valve body. Press plug in until it is flush with outside surface of valve body. After the valve has been completely assembled, the relief valve is held in place by the end cover lock ring.
3. Slide spool in valve body. Be sure spool is inserted in same position it was in before disassembly. Use care to prevent damage to sealing edges. After spool has been pushed through valve body, assemble one reaction ring and one O-ring on spool.
4. Assemble remaining reaction ring and O-ring seal on spool.
5. Assemble springs on each end of spool.
6. Assemble O-ring seals on glands.
7. Install glands (as matched to the respective reaction rings) to each end of spool.
8. Install lock rings over threaded end of valve body, inserting lugs of ring into milled slots of valve body.
9. Assemble end caps until a tight fit has been obtained. Lock end caps by driving lock ring tabs into one of milled slots of caps and valve body.
10. Assemble dust seal.

TYPE E CONTROL VALVE
Disassembly, Fig. 5

1. Pry dust cover out of valve housing.
2. Remove lock nut from end of valve shaft.
3. Remove two valve housing-to-adapter housing bolts.
4. Lift valve housing and valve spool from adapter housing.
5. Lift valve spool and "V" block seal out of valve housing. Remove "V" block seal from groove in valve spool and discard.
6. Remove valve adjustment spring, reaction spool, spring thrust washer, reaction spring, spring retainer and annulus seal from valve shaft. Discard annulus seal.
7. Remove O-ring seal from groove in valve

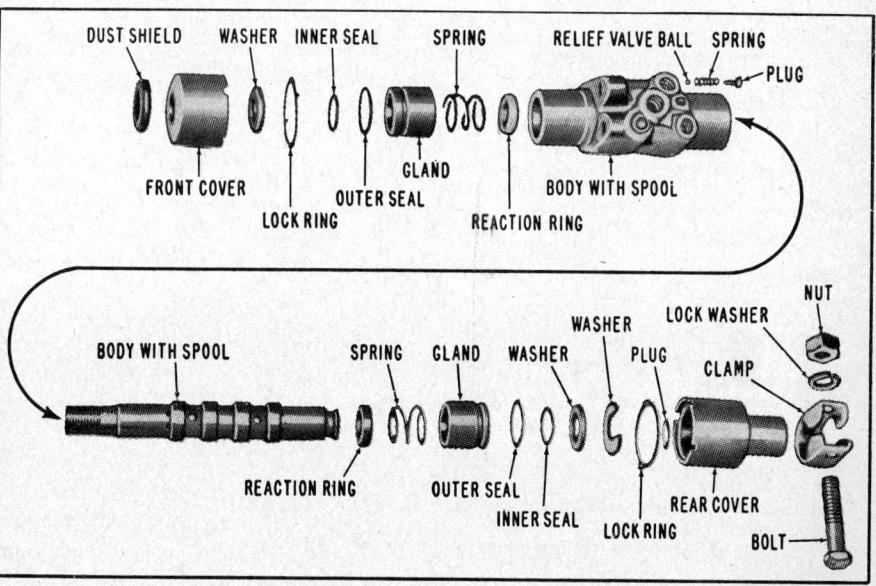

Fig. 4 Type D control valve mounted on frame side rail

Power Steering Gears

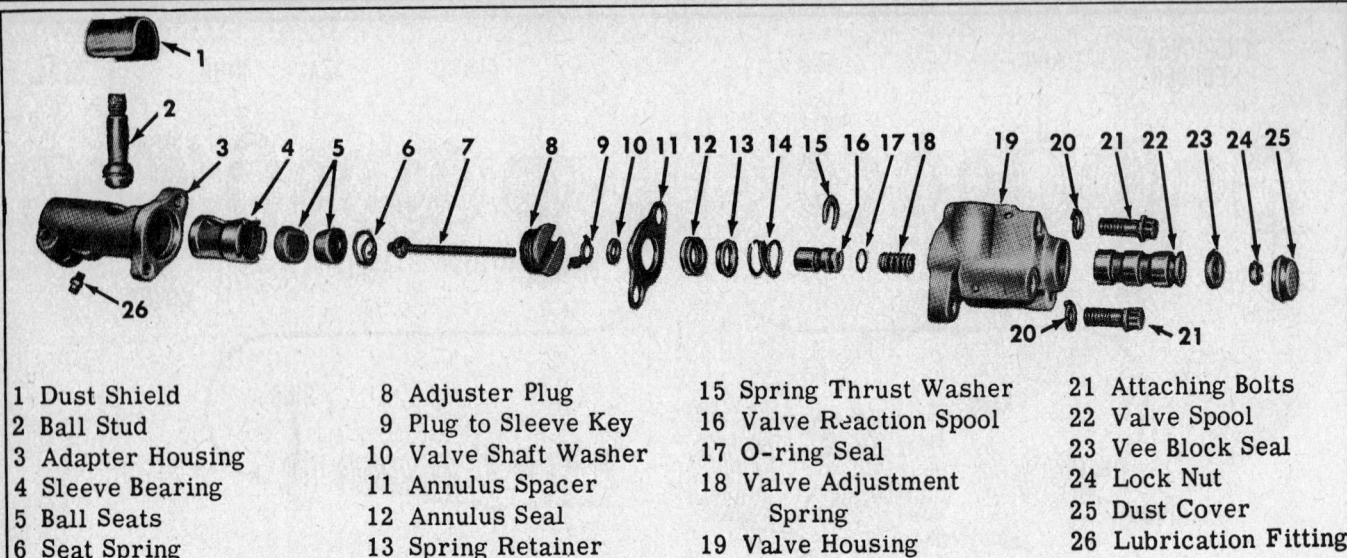

1 Dust Shield	8 Adjuster Plug	15 Spring Thrust Washer
2 Ball Stud	9 Plug to Sleeve Key	16 Valve Reaction Spool
3 Adapter Housing	10 Valve Shaft Washer	17 O-ring Seal
4 Sleeve Bearing	11 Annulus Spacer	18 Valve Adjustment Spring
5 Ball Seats	12 Annulus Seal	19 Valve Housing
6 Seat Spring	13 Spring Retainer	20 Lock Washers
7 Valve Shaft	14 Valve Spring	21 Attaching Bolts
		22 Valve Spool
		23 Vee Block Seal
		24 Lock Nut
		25 Dust Cover
		26 Lubrication Fitting

Fig. 5 Type E control valve used on Chevrolet and GMC trucks with linkage type power steering

reaction spool. Remove spring thrust washer from groove in reaction spool. Discard O-ring seal.

8. Remove annulus spacer, shaft washer and plug-to-sleeve key from valve shaft.
9. Using a screwdriver, turn ball stud adjuster plug out of adapter housing. Remove plug and valve shaft. Use care not to nick top surface of adjuster plug.
10. Remove spring and one ball seat from adapter housing.
11. Remove ball stud, second ball seat and sleeve bearing from adapter housing.

Inspection

1. With all parts clean and dry, check valve spring, adjustment spring and seat spring for free length, distortion or collapsed coils.
2. Inspect adapter housing and valve housing for cracks or other damage.
3. Inspect all threads for crossed or stripped condition.
4. Discard all seals and replace all parts not in first class condition.

Reassembly, Fig. 5

1. Install sleeve bearing and first ball seat in adapter housing.
2. Install ball stud, second ball seat and spring seat in adapter housing. Note that small coil of spring goes down.
3. With adapter housing mounted in a vise, insert valve shaft through slot in adjuster plug. Then install shaft and plug in adapter housing.
4. Turn adjuster plug in tight. Then back it off until slot lines up with notches in sleeve bearing.
5. Install plug-to-sleeve key on valve shaft. Be sure small tangs on end of key engage notches in sleeve bearing.
6. Position annulus spacer over valve shaft and on adapter housing.
7. Position new O-ring seal in groove of valve reaction spool.
8. Install new annulus seal (lip up) on valve shaft.
9. Position spring retainer, valve spring, valve reaction spool and valve adjustment spring on valve shaft in that order.
10. Install spring thrust washer in groove of valve reaction spool. Side of washer with chamfer should be up.
11. Position new "V" block seal in groove of valve spool with lip down. Then install spool and seal in valve housing, being careful not to jam spool in housing.
12. Position valve housing and spool on adapter housing. Be sure side ports of housing are on same side as ball stud in adapter. Attach housing to adapter and tighten securely.
13. Depress valve spool and turn lock nut on valve shaft about four turns.
14. Using a plastic hammer, tap new dust cover into bore of valve housing.

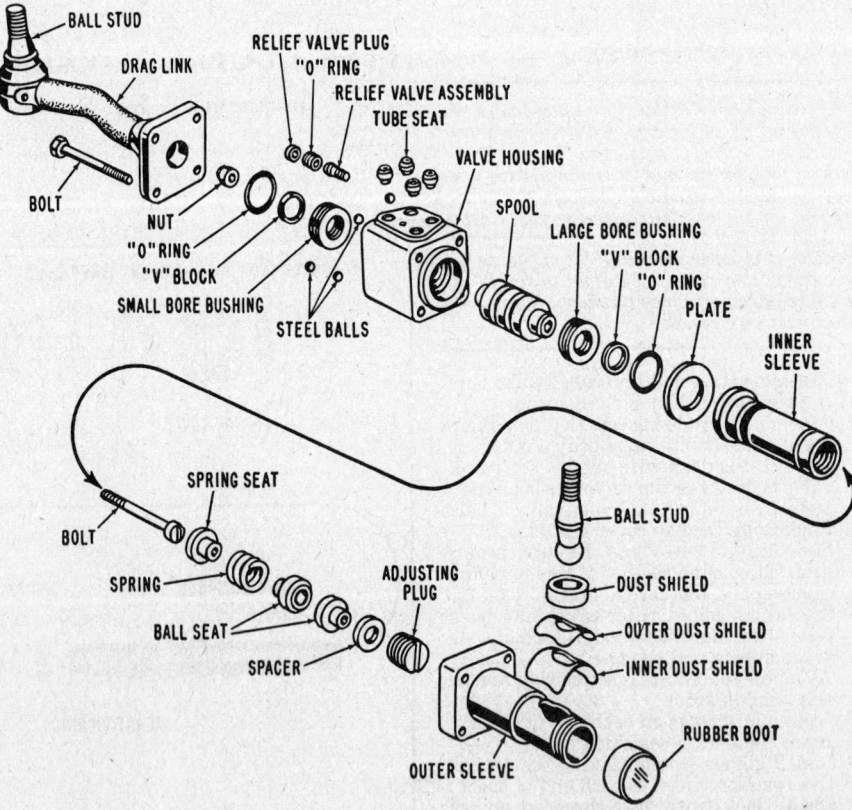

Fig. 6 Type F control valve used on Dodge trucks with linkage type power steering

POWER STEERING GEARS

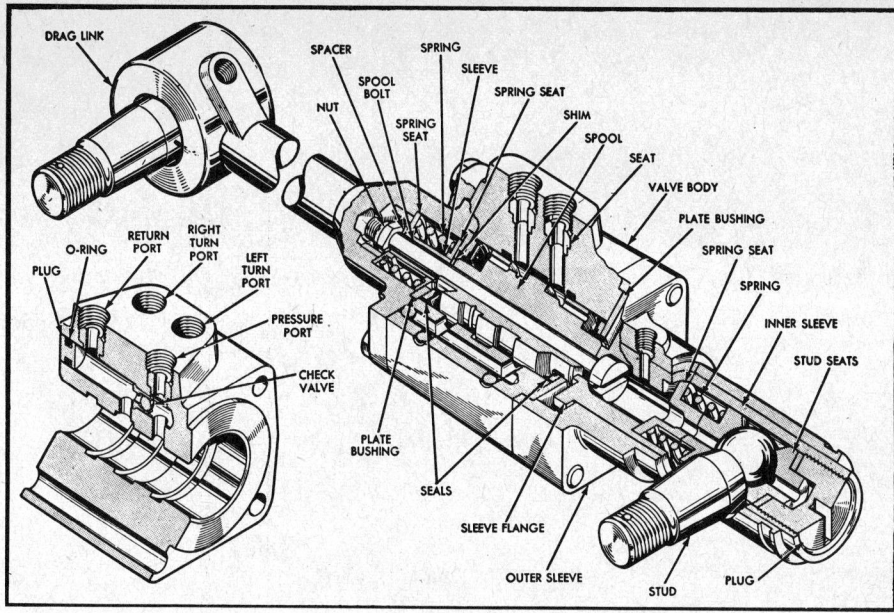

Fig. 7 Type G control valve used on Ford C and H Series trucks

TYPE F CONTROL VALVE

Disassembly, Fig. 6

1. Remove bolts attaching drag link to valve assembly. If the drag link ball stud is exceptionally loose, the entire drag link assembly must be replaced.
2. Remove sliding sleeve boot and adjusting plug from inner sleeve.
3. Remove ball seal dust shields, ball stud, ball seal, spacer, spring and spring seat.
4. Hold head of spool bolt with screwdriver in slotted head and remove lock nut from spool bolt. Then remove bolt, inner sleeve and plate.
5. Remove spool bushings by pressing on alternate ends of spool projections by hand enough to expose seals which are assembled in large and small bore bushings. If external seals and spool projection seals show wear or surface breaks, they should be replaced.
6. Remove spool, using care to protect spool edges and bore of valve housing from damage.

CAUTION: *Do not clean spool or valve housing with cloth. Remove foreign matter with dry compressed air.*

Reassembly, Fig. 6

1. Carefully assemble valve spool into valve housing bore with the large projection end of spool facing sliding sleeve and small projection end facing drag link.
2. Assemble large bore bushing and small bore bushing with their respective "V" block and O-ring seals inserted in their respective ends of valve housing.
3. Install inner sleeve into outer sleeve and install spool bolt in hole at flange end of sliding sleeve.
4. Place stop plate over spool bolt and insert bolt in spool and install lock nut. Make sure stop plate is positioned between sliding sleeve and valve housing.
5. Tighten lock nut and back it off about 1/4 turn until spool can be rotated without any bind.
6. Position drag link with ball stud on same side as valve ports and install four through bolts. Tighten bolts securely and install lock wire.
7. Install sliding sleeve spring seat, spring ball seat, ball stud, ball seat, spacer and adjusting plug in that order.
8. Install tube seats.
9. Tighten adjusting plug and back off just enough to align holes in outer sleeve with seat in adjusting plug and secure with cotter pin.
10. Install rubber boot and lock wire.
11. Install sliding sleeve inner dust shield, outer dust shield and stud outer dust shield.

TYPE G CONTROL VALVE

Disassemble, Fig. 7

1. Remove four housing bolts and drag link assembly.
2. After unthreading ball stud plug, remove outer seat and spacer, ball stud, and inner seat, spring and spring seat.
3. After removing and discarding nut from spool bolt, remove spacer washer, centering spring seats, spring and sleeve, bushing seal plate and shim. *Note that spacer washer and shim are not identical and note their relative positions.*
4. Separate valve housing from outer sleeve and remove plate bushing.
5. Remove spool bolt and inner sleeve from outer sleeve.
6. Press spool to free seals from housing and remove seal and spool. Remove spool carefully to avoid nicks or scratches.
7. If necessary to replace check valve or its O-ring, remove plug by means of a piece of brass rod inserted through return port.

Reassembly, Fig. 7

1. After lubricating spool seals and spool with automatic transmission fluid, carefully position spool in valve body. *Grooved valley between lands must be toward drag link.*
2. Position seals. Inner lip of each seal should be toward valve body.
3. Position spool bolt and inner sleeve in outer sleeve.
4. Position plate bushing in outer sleeve and place valve body next to outer sleeve.

NOTE: *Note that the valve body face has a shoulder that mates with outer sleeve face.*

5. Position shim (ground surface toward spool), bushing seal plate, sleeve, spring, spring seats and spacer washer on spool

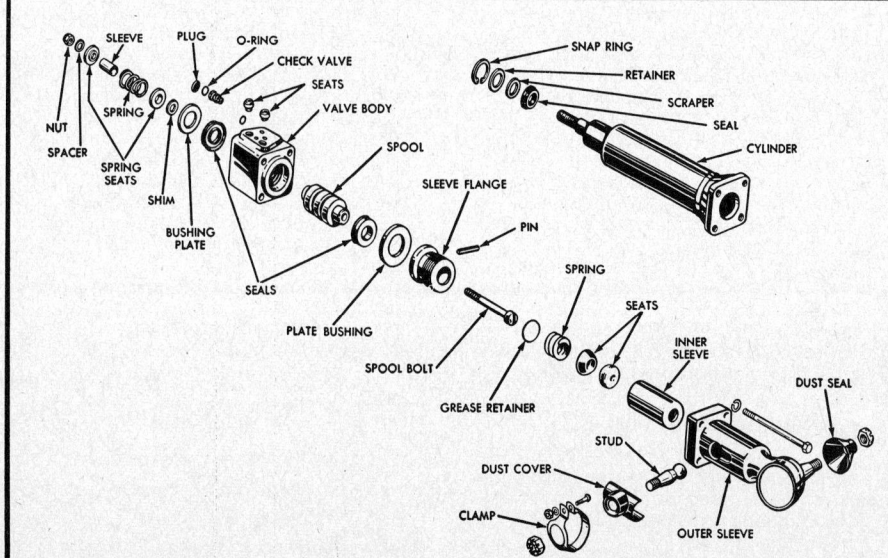

Fig. 8 Type H control valve used on Ford E and T Series trucks. This is an "In Line Booster" consisting of a combined power cylinder and control valve

707

POWER STEERING GEARS

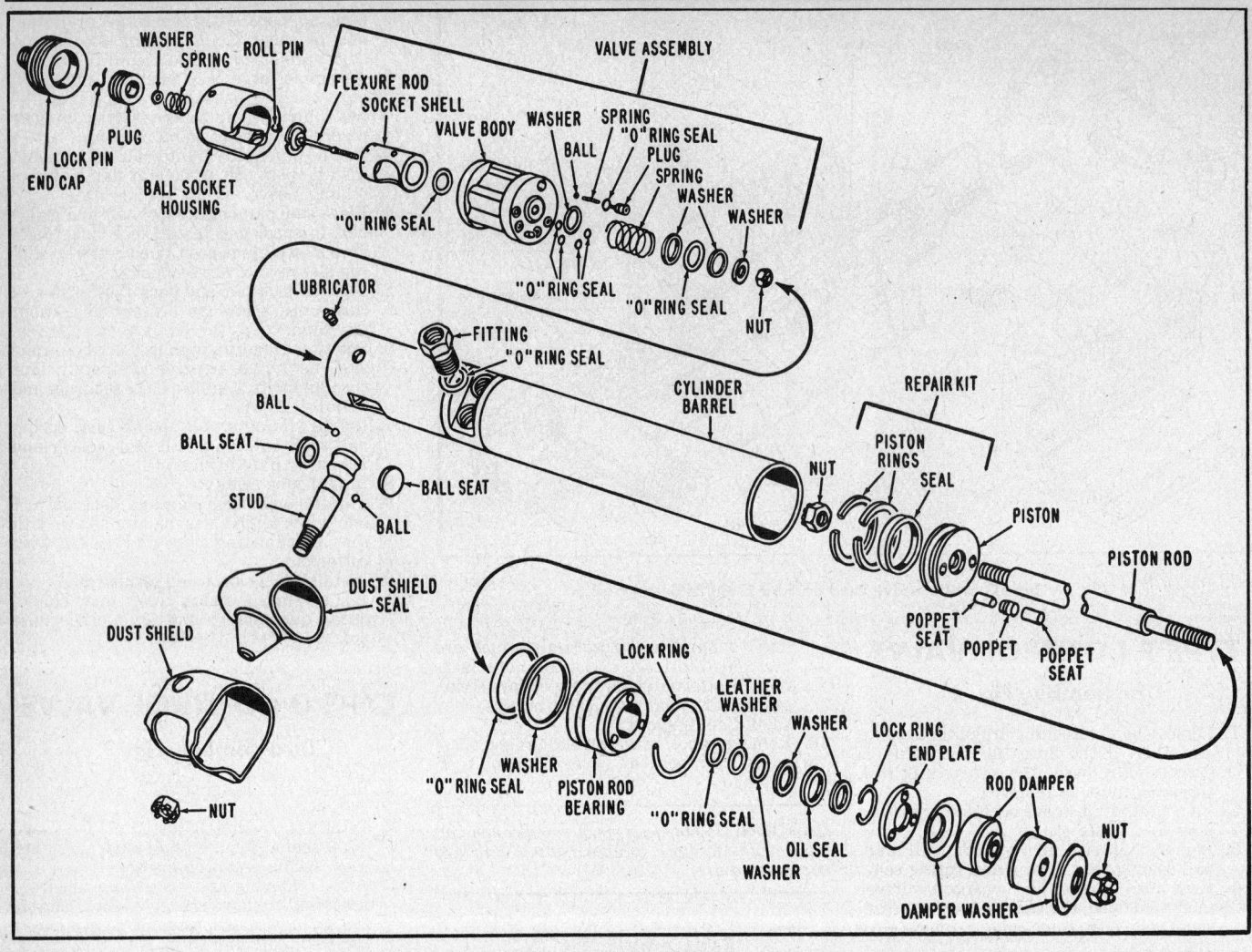

Fig. 9 Type I "In Line Booster" used on International and other trucks

bolt. Install a new nut.
6. Position ball stud and its seat components in inner sleeve.
7. Tighten ball stud plug until spring is fully compressed, then back it off to the nearest cotter pin hole and insert cotter pin.
8. Position drag link against valve body and install housing bolts.

TYPE H CONTROL VALVE

"In Line Booster" Combining Control Valve with Power Cylinder Disassembly, Fig. 8

1. After removing dust cover clamp, remove four valve body bolts and separate cylinder assembly from valve body.
2. After removing and discarding nut from spool bolt, remove spacer washer, outer spring seat, spring, sleeve, inner spring seat, bushing plate and shim.

NOTE: *Note that spacer washer and shim are identical, and note their relative position.*

3. Separate valve body from outer sleeve and remove plate bushing.
4. Pull out sleeve bolt as far as possible, and remove lock pin from sleeve plate.
5. Unthread sleeve plate from inner sleeve, and remove stud, its seat and spring assembly, and the inner sleeve.
6. Press on spool to free spool seals from housing, and remove seals and spool. Remove spool carefully to avoid nicks and scratches.
7. If necessary to replace check valve or plug O-ring, remove plug by means of an appropriately bent brass rod inserted through return port.
8. Before removing any part of cylinder piston seal assembly, carefully clean area and remove snap ring.
9. Use air pressure applied at one of the ports in the mounting face of the cylinder to dislodge seal, scraper and retainer.

Reassembly, Fig. 8

1. Lubricate new seal with automatic transmission fluid and install seal, scraper and retainer, using a deep socket.
2. Install snap ring.
3. After lubricating spool seals and spool with automatic transmission fluid, carefully position spool in valve body. *The larger diameter bearing surface of spool must be next to cylinder.*
4. Position seals. Inner lip of each seal must be toward valve body.
5. Position inner sleeve, stud and its seat, and spring in outer sleeve.
6. Completely thread sleeve plate (with spool bolt) into inner sleeve, and then back off plate to nearest aligning holes for lock pin. Insert pin.
7. Position plate bushing in housing. Then position valve body next to outer sleeve. *Note that the valve body face has a shoulder that mates with outer sleeve face.*
8. Position shim (ground surface toward spool), bushing plate, inner spring seat, sleeve, spring, outer seat and spacer washer on spool bolt in that order. Install and tighten a new nut.
9. Position cylinder against valve body, install and tighten bolts.

TYPE I CONTROL VALVE

"In Line Booster" Combining Control Valve with Power Cylinder Disassembly of Power Cylinder, Fig. 9

1. Drain oil from cylinder and valve by

708

Power Steering Gears

moving piston rod in and out from one extreme end of its travel to the other.
2. Disassemble cylinder parts on threaded end of piston rod by removing slotted nut, cushion retainers and cushions.
3. Remove end plate.
4. Using a drift and hammer, work around bearing, tapping it lightly into cylinder barrel about 1/4".
5. Insert punch in hole along side of cylinder barrel to disengage lock ring from its groove. Remove lock ring.
6. Pull on piston rod end to remove internal parts from cylinder. When removing parts from piston rod, slide them off piston end of rod.
7. Remove piston rod nut. Hold rod by the two wrench flats just above outer threaded end to prevent damage to finish on rod O.D.
8. Slide off piston and remove ring and seal.
9. Check action of poppet valve for leakage. If defective, replace piston assembly.
10. With bearing removed from rod, remove O-ring and back-up washer from O.D. of bearing.
11. Remove sealing parts in bearing by first removing lock ring, then retainer washer, oil seal, spacing washers, leather back-up washer and O-ring.

Disassembly of Control Valve, Fig. 9

1. With slotted nut removed from ball stud, remove dust seal cover and dust seal.
2. Straighten out the one staked place and remove end cap.
3. Remove lock pin and unscrew adjusting plug.
4. From inside plug remove spring and washer.
5. Remove outer ball seat.
6. Remove ball stud and inner ball stud seat. Do not lose steel balls.
7. Unscrew grease fitting.
8. Pull out valve sub-assembly, using care not to damage threads in outer end of valve housing when pulling this assembly. As this sub-assembly is removed, the four small O-rings may or may not remain in counterbores on end of valve body. If not they will be found on face of cylinder head.
9. To simplify disassembling of flexure rod, socket shell, valve body and spool subassembly, reassemble ball stud against inner ball seat, install outer ball seat in socket shell and screw adjusting plug in. This will tend to keep flexure rod from turning when unscrewing elastic nut.
10. After above disassembling has been completed, remove ball stud, seats and adjusting plug from socket shell.
11. After elastic nut has been removed, washer, centering washers, seal, spring, washer, socket shell and flexure rod can be disassembled.
12. Remove spool from valve body by pushing out from end opposite counterbore O-ring seats in valve body.
13. Remove plug assembly.

Reassembling Power Cylinder, Fig. 9

1. Lubricate all seals and O-rings with light engine oil before installing.
2. Assemble O-ring to inside of bearing, then leather back-up ring and steel spacing washers. Assemble oil seal with its lip toward outside. Assemble retainer washer and secure oil seal parts with lock ring.
3. Assemble back-up ring on O.D. of bearing, then O-ring on pressure side of bearing.
4. To prevent damage to rod seal, assemble bearing to rod from piston end of rod. Slide bearing over piston rod toward outer end of rod.
5. Assemble seal in piston ring groove of piston and rings over seal.
6. Assemble piston to end of rod and secure with nut.
7. Slide piston into cylinder barrel. Push assembly into cylinder halfway, and assemble bearing into cylinder, taking care not to damage O-ring as it slides past retaining ring groove in cylinder.
8. Lock bearing in place with retaining ring in cylinder groove.
9. Check for freedom of binding by moving piston rod back and forth.
10. Assemble end plate and tighten screws securely.
11. Install inner cushion retainer with cup side out. Assemble inner and outer rubber cushions, then outer cushion retainer with cup side in. Secure assembly with slotted nut.

Reassembly of Valve, Fig. 9

1. Assemble O-ring to groove in spool and insert spool in valve body from end opposite the four small O-ring seats. This will prevent O-ring from being cut by sharp inner edges of body.
2. If by-pass unit has been removed, place new O-ring on plug. Stand body on end and drop ball into hole. Place spring over plug stem and insert in hole until flush with end face of valve body.
3. To assist easier assembly of centering washers, spring, seal, washer and elastic nut, assemble flexure rod to socket shell, and assemble in socket shell the inner ball seat, ball stud, outer ball seat and adjusting plug. Tighten securely. Place this assembly in a vise, holding at threaded end of socket shell.
4. Slide valve body and spool assembly over flexure rod, being sure the four counterbored holes are on top.
5. Assemble centering washer, O-ring centering washer and heavy washer. Press into valve body carefully until elastic nut can be started on threaded end of flexure rod. Using a box wrench push down on top of washer, while at the same time rotating valve body back and forth until O-ring and outer centering washer enter valve body completely.
6. As this is being done, tighten elastic nut until parts seat solidly. To assure all parts are correctly aligned, hold valve body in hand with threaded end of flexure rod against a solid object and push to check freedom of valve spool.
7. Disassemble ball stud, seats, and adjusting plug from socket shell.
8. Assemble four O-rings to valve body.
9. Slide valve body with flexure rod into cylinder housing. *Roll pin assembled in valve body must fit in dowel hole in face of cylinder head.*
10. Assemble socket housing over socket shell, aligning slotted opening in socket housing with rectangular opening in cylinder housing.

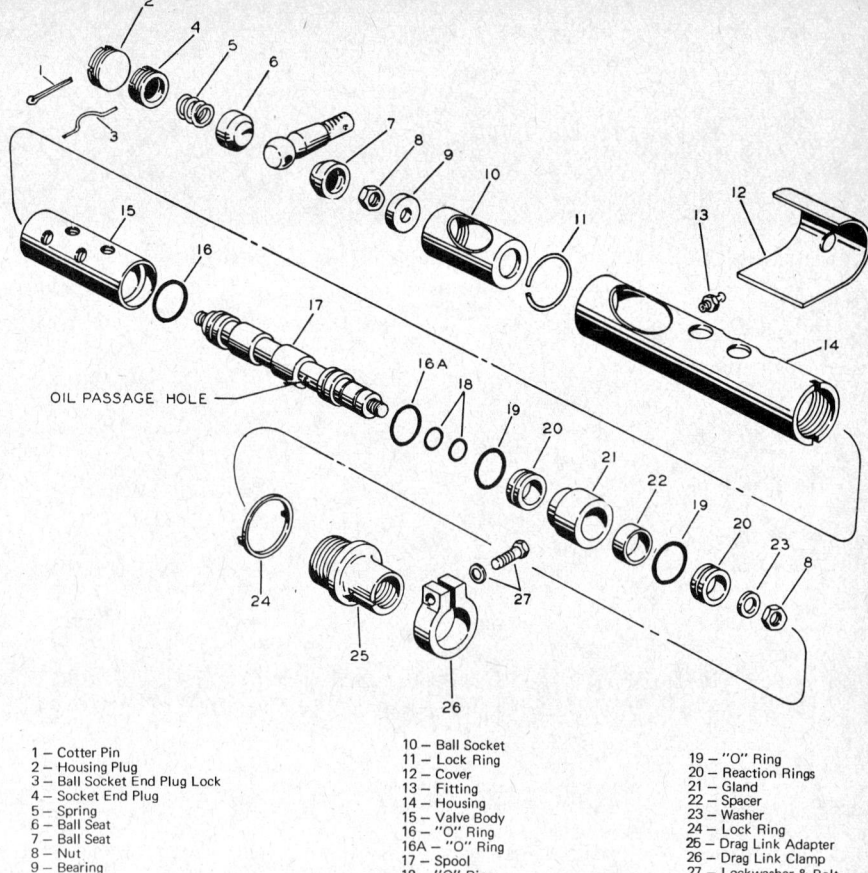

1 — Cotter Pin
2 — Housing Plug
3 — Ball Socket End Plug Lock
4 — Socket End Plug
5 — Spring
6 — Ball Seat
7 — Ball Seat
8 — Nut
9 — Bearing
10 — Ball Socket
11 — Lock Ring
12 — Cover
13 — Fitting
14 — Housing
15 — Valve Body
16 — "O" Ring
16A — "O" Ring
17 — Spool
18 — "O" Ring
19 — "O" Ring
20 — Reaction Rings
21 — Gland
22 — Spacer
23 — Washer
24 — Lock Ring
25 — Drag Link Adapter
26 — Drag Link Clamp
27 — Lockwasher & Bolt

Fig. 10 Type I control valve disassembled

709

POWER STEERING GEARS

11. Align socket shell with opening described in Step 10.
12. Install inner ball seat.
13. Apply a small amount of heavy cup grease to the two small holes in socket shell and insert the steel balls.
14. Carefully insert ball stud into socket shell through rectangular opening in cylinder housing and ball socket housing. Use care to see that balls remain in position in groove in ball stud as ball stud rests against inner ball seat.
15. Install outer ball seat.
16. Assemble washer and spring into opening of adjusting plug.
17. Screw adjusting plug into threaded end of socket shell. Tighten plug by hand, then back off to the nearest aligning hole for lock. Ball stud should be firm but move freely.
18. Install lock pin and snap in place.
19. Install end cap and tighten. Secure assembly by crimping cylinder housing at one place as provided for in cap.
20. Install grease fitting.
21. Assemble rubber dust seal, then metal dust seal cover.

TYPE J CONTROL VALVE
Fig. 10

1. Remove cotter pin, housing plug, ball socket end plug lock, socket end plug, spring and ball seats.
2. With control valve held in a vise, straighten crimped lock ring in notch of drag link adapter, then remove adapter.
3. Insert a drift into spool oil passage, preventing spool rotation, remove spool nut, ball socket and bearing.
4. Remove nut from pool gland end, then washer, gland, reaction rings and spacer.

NOTE: Some units incorporate a spring instead of the spacer.

5. Slide spool toward gland end of body and remove "O" ring seal, then move spool toward ball stud side and remove the other "O" ring.
6. Remove spool from gland end of body, then remaining "O" rings.
7. Reverse procedure to reassemble.

Chrysler Constant Control Power Steering Section

The Constant Control Full Time Power Steering consists of a hydraulic pressure pump, a power steering gear and connecting hoses. The power steering gear consists of a gear housing, containing a gear shaft and sector shaft; a power piston with gear teeth milled into the side of the piston which is in constant mesh with the gear shaft sector teeth; and a worm shaft which connects the steering wheel to the power unit piston through a coupling.

Steering Gear Repairs

Prior to disassembly, clean the gear assembly thoroughly in a suitable solvent. Crocus cloth may be used to remove small nicks and burrs provided it is used carefully. When used on the steering gear valve, use extreme care not to round off the sharp edge portions of the two lands located between the valve drilled holes. Remove and discard all "O" ring seals, using new ones lubricated with fluid when reassembling.

Disassemble

1. Drain steering gear by rotating wormshaft from stop to stop.
2. Remove valve body and three "O" rings, Fig. CC1.
3. Remove valve lever by prying under spherical head, Fig. CC2. *Use care not to collapse slotted end of valve lever as this will destroy bearing tolerances of head.*
4. Remove gear shaft cover nut, Fig. CC3.
5. Rotate wormshaft to position sector shaft teeth at center of piston travel, then loosen power train nut.
6. Install tool C-3786 on sector shaft threaded end and slide tool into housing until tool and shaft engages bearings.
7. Rotate wormshaft to left stop, compressing power train components, then remove power train nut and housing head tang washer. Using a screwdriver, pry on piston teeth to remove complete power train, Fig. CC6.

NOTE: The cylinder head, center race and spacer assembly and the housing head must be kept in close contact since the reaction rings may become disengaged from grooves in cylinder head and housing. Also, the center spacer may separate from center race and jam in the housing, in turn damaging the spacer and/or housing when removing the power train.

8. Remove worm shaft upper oil seal, Fig. CC7, and disassemble column jacket support. Reaction seal may be removed from groove in face of jacket support by blowing air pressure into ferrule chamber. Make sure passage from ferrule chamber to upper reaction chanber is unobstructed.

Column Jacket Support, Assemble

Install worm shaft upper oil seal with sealing lip toward bearing, Fig. CC8. Tool C-3650 should be used to drive seal until tool bottoms on casting to obtain proper compression of rubber seal. Lubricate reaction seal and install in groove in face of column jacket support with flat side of seal out.

Cylinder Head

Disassemble—Remove two "O" rings in outer grooves in head. Remove "O" ring in groove in face of cylinder head with air pressure into oil hole located in groove between two "O" ring grooves, Fig. CC9. Replace cylinder head seal if necessary, Fig. CC10. Check oil passage in ferrule for obstruction. Check lands of cylinder head for burrs.

Assemble—Lubricate and install two large "O" rings in grooves on head. Install lower reaction seal in groove in face of head. The small "O" ring for ferrule groove should be installed after worm shaft bearing preload has been established, otherwise "O" ring will be damaged by reaction springs.

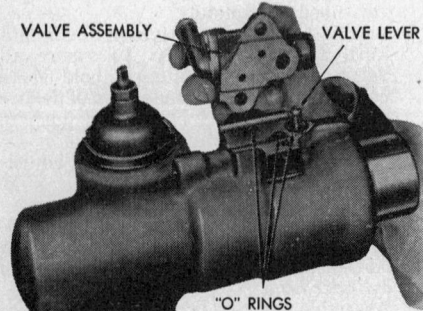

Fig. CC1 Removing or installing valve body assembly

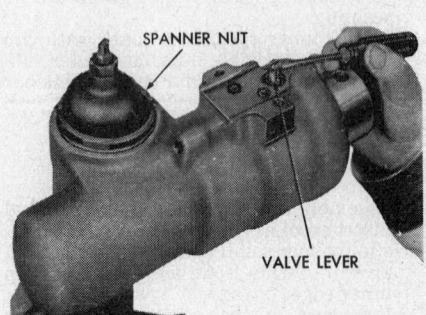

Fig. CC2 Removing valve lever

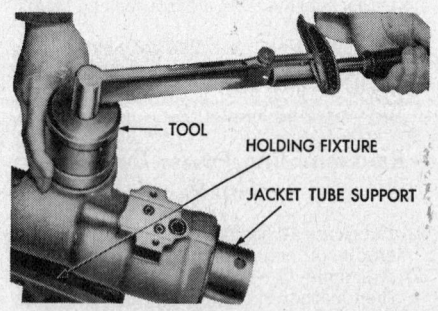

Fig. CC3 Removing or installing gear shaft cover nut

POWER STEERING GEARS

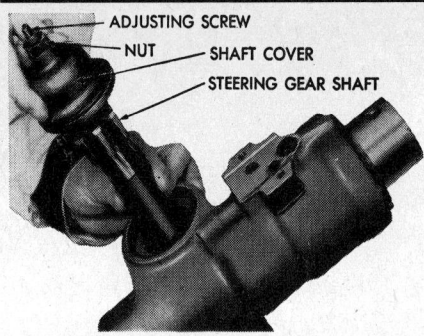

Fig. CC4 Removing or installing gear shaft & cover

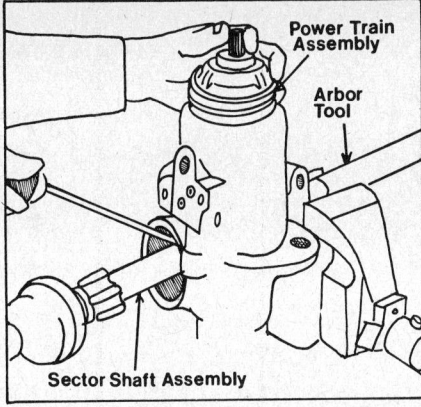

Fig. CC6 Removing or installing power train

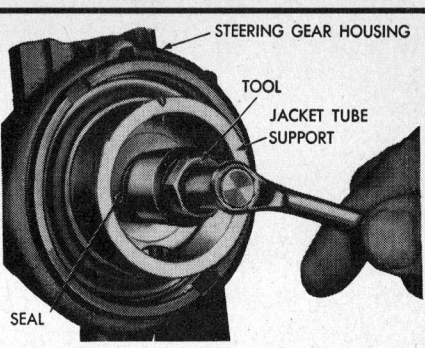

Fig. CC7 Removing worm shaft upper oil seal

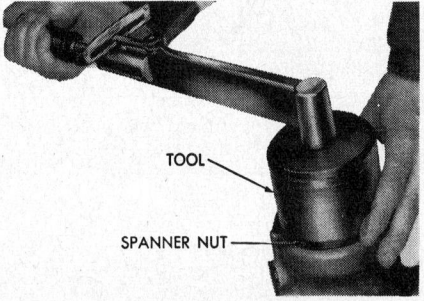

Fig. CC5 Removing steering column support nut

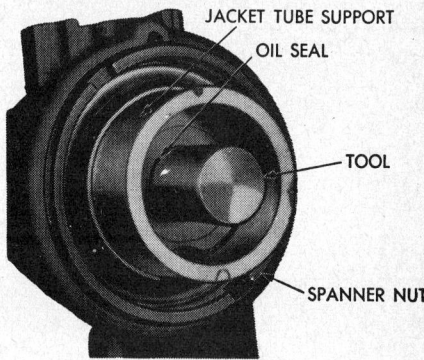

Fig. CC8 Installing worm shaft upper oil seal

valve body to steering valve body and torque attaching screws to 95 inch lbs. Install new copper sealing gasket and fitting in threaded hole on top of valve body and torque to 30 lb. ft.

Gear Shaft

Disassemble—Remove adjusting screw lock nut and unscrew cover from adjusting screw. Remove screw and washer from "T" slot in end of gear shaft. Remove date tag gasket from top of cover and large "O" ring from base of cover.

Assemble—Place adjusting screw washer over screw and slide both into "T" slot of shaft. Screw cover into adjusting screw until gear shaft bottoms in cover. Install date tag gasket over adjusting screw into position at top of cover. Install lock nut on adjusting screw but do not tighten. Install large "O" ring in groove on lower face of gear cover.

Steering Gear Housing

Disassemble—The equipment shown in Fig. CC12 should be used for this operation. After removing the oil seal snap ring and back-up ring, remove the oil seal by sliding the threaded portion of the tool's adapter over end of gear shaft and install nut section of tool (C-3350) on shaft. Maintain pressure on adapter with nut of tool while turning adapter, forcing it into seal until it has bottomed in seal. Apply two half rings and retainer over both portions of tool. As hex nut is removed from shaft seal will be pulled from housing.

Steering Valve

Disassemble—Remove outlet fitting, spring, valve piston and cushion spring. Remove valve body (2 screws) from steering valve. Shake out valve piston. If spool valve or valve housing is damaged, replace complete valve assembly. Do not remove valve end plug unless inspection indicates a leak at seal.

Assemble—Fig. CC11. Install steering valve in housing. Valve lever hole should align with steering gear valve lever opening in bottom of valve housing. Valve must fit smoothly in housing without striking or binding. If valve end plug was removed installed new seal and tighten plug to 25 lb. ft. torque. Install cushion spring, then lubricate and install valve piston, nose end first, into valve body. Install spring on top of piston and outlet plug and torque to 20 ft. lbs. Assemble control

Assemble—Install gear shaft oil seal in housing (lip of seal toward needle bearing) using Tool C-3350. Place adapter against seal and tool nut on threaded end of gear shaft. Tighten tool nut until adapter shoulder contacts housing, Fig. CC13. Install oil seal back-up ring, oil seal and snap ring.

Power Train, Assemble

Fig. CC14. Position piston assembly on bench with worm shaft up. Slide cylinder head (ferrule up) on worm shaft and against piston flange, making sure gap on worm shaft ring is closed to avoid breaking ring. Lubricate and install in the following order:
1. Lower thrust bearing race (thick).
2. Lower thrust bearing.

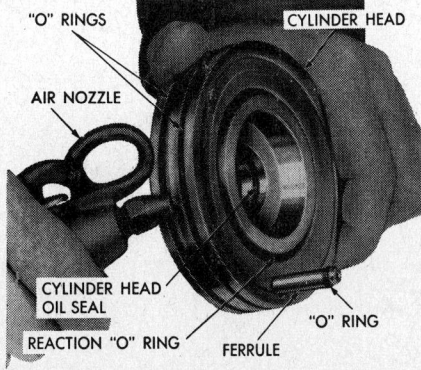

Fig. CC9 Removing reaction ring from cylinder head

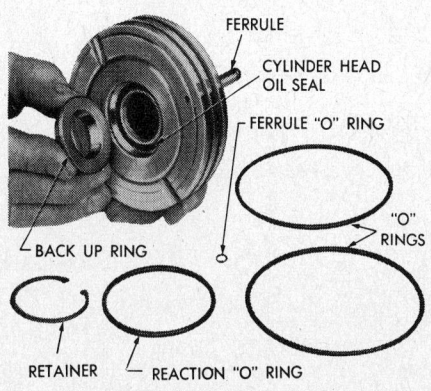

Fig. CC10 Removing cylinder head set

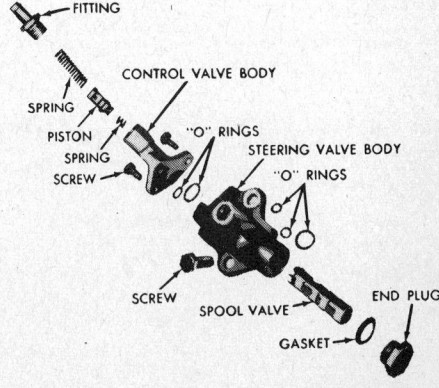

Fig. CC11 Control valve disassembled

Power Steering Gears

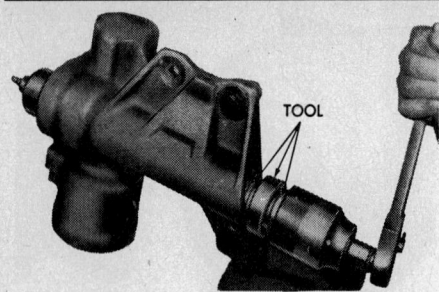

Fig. CC12 Removing gear shaft oil seal

5. Center bearing race, indexing control hole with hole in center bearing race.
6. Install upper thrust bearing, upper thrust bearing race (thin) and new worm shaft thrust bearing nut.
7. Tighten nut as follows: Turn worm shaft clockwise 1/2 turn and hold shaft in this position while tightening nut to 50 lb. ft. torque.

NOTE: *If worm shaft is turned more than 1/2 turn cylinder head seal will clear oil ring on worm shaft.*

8. Always check position of worm shaft oil ring before bottoming cylinder head against worm piston shoulder to avoid damaging oil ring.
9. Loosen worm bearing adjusting nut.
10. Retighten worm bearing adjusting nut to give a bearing torque of 16 to 24 oz. Check by placing rounds of cord around center bearing race. Make a loop in one end and hook the loop of a spring scale in the cord loop. Pulling on cord will cause bearing race to rotate, Fig. CC15.
11. If adjusting nut is tightened properly, reading on scale will be 16 to 24 oz. Stake flange of adjusting nut into depression in worm shaft to lock securely.
12. Stake upper part of adjusting nut into wormshaft knurled area in four places, 90° apart. Check bearing preload after first staking operation and adjust, if necessary, by tapping the adjusting nut with a mallet.
13. Apply a torque of 20 ft. lbs. to the adjusting nut in both directions. The nut should not move, ensuring nut was properly staked.
14. Install center bearing spacer over bearing race to engage dowel pin with slot in center bearing race.

NOTE: *Make sure valve lever hole in center bearing race and center spacer are properly aligned.*

Steering Gear, Assemble

1. With steering gear housing fastened in holding fixture, lubricate power train housing bore with fluid and install power train assembly, Fig. CC5. Face piston teeth to the right and valve lever hole in center race and spacer in "Up" position.

NOTE: *Ensure cylinder head is bottomed against housing shoulder.*

2. With valve lever hole in center bearing race and spacer aligned with valve level hole in gear housing, install valve lever (double bearing end first) into center bearing race and spacer, ensuring valve lever slots are parallel to wormshaft, Fig. CC16. It may be necessary to gently tap end of valve lever to seat lower pivot point

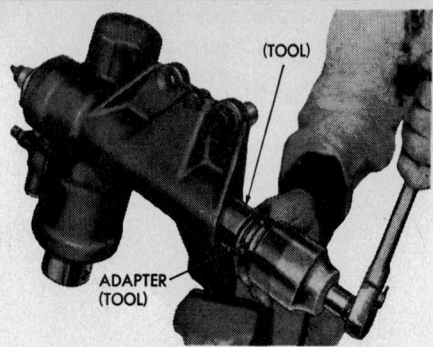

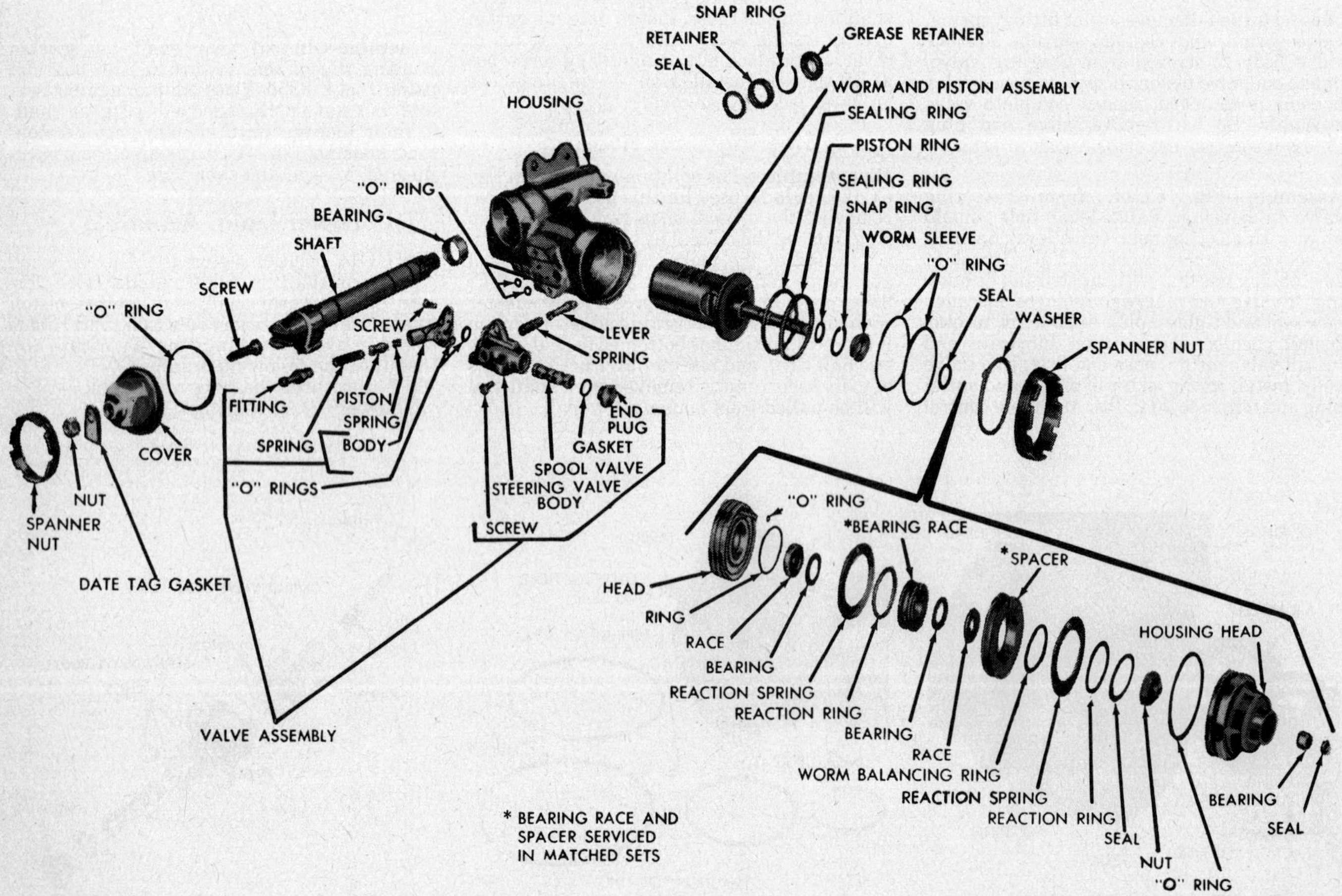

Fig. CC13 Installing gear shaft oil seal

Fig. CC14 Steering gear disassembled

Power Steering Gears

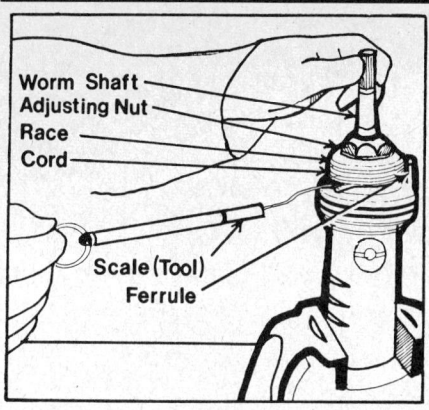

Fig. CC15 Checking worm shaft bearing preload

TROUBLE SHOOTING

Hard Steering

1. Tires not properly inflated.
2. Low oil level in reservoir.
3. Loose pump belt.
4. Oil on pump belts.
5. Steering linkage needs lubrication.
6. Power steering pump output low.
7. Cross shaft adjustment too tight.
8. Pressure control valve stuck in closed position.
9. External oil leaks.
10. Defective or damaged valve lever.
11. Dirt or chips in steering gear.
12. Damaged column support worm shaft bearings.
13. Damaged thrust bearings or excessive preload adjustment.
14. Rough or hard to turn worm and piston assembly.
15. Excessive internal leakage.

Poor Recovery From Turns

1. Tires not properly inflated.
2. Steering linkage binding.
3. Improper wheel alignment.
4. Damaged or defective steering tube bearings.
5. Steering column jacket and steering gear not properly aligned.
6. Improper cross shaft mesh adjustment.
7. Pressure control valve piston stuck open.
8. Column support spanner nut loose.
9. Defective or damaged valve lever.
10. Improper worm thrust bearing adjustment.
11. Burrs or nicks in reaction ring grooves in cylinder head or column support.
12. Defective or damaged cylinder head worm shaft seal ring.
13. Dirt or chips in steering gear unit.
14. Rough or catchy worm and piston assembly.

Self-Steering or Leads to Either Side

1. Tires not properly inflated.
2. Improper wheel alignment.
3. Steering wheel off center when car is traveling straight ahead.
4. Valve body out of adjustment.
5. Valve lever damaged.
6. Column support spanner nut loose.
7. Return turn reaction seal damaged.
8. Column coupling bottomed.

Temporary Increase In Effort When Turning Steering Wheel

1. Low oil level.

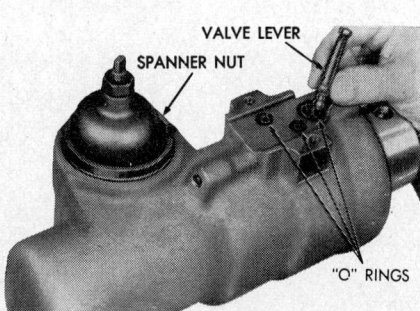

Fig. CC16 Installing valve lever

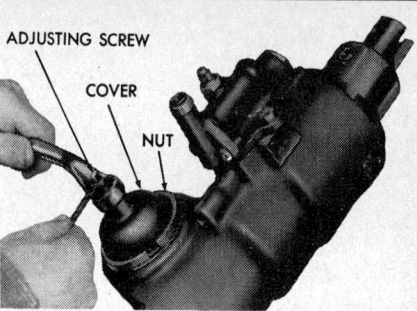

Fig. CC17 Adjusting sector shaft backlash

2. Loose pump belt.
3. Oil on pump belts.
4. Binding steering linkage.
5. Engine idle too slow.
6. Defective power steering pump.
7. Air in system.
8. External adjustment.
9. Improper cross shaft adjustment.
10. Excessive internal leakage.

Excessive Steering Wheel Free Play

1. Improper cross shaft adjustment.
2. Column support spanner nut loose.
3. Improper worm thrust bearing adjustment.
4. Improper front wheel bearing adjustment.

Lack of Assistance in One Direction

1. Oil leaking past worm shaft cast iron seal ring or ferrule "O" ring.

Lack of Assistance in Both Directions

1. Broken "O" ring on worm piston.
2. Piston end plug loose.
3. Pump belt slipping.
4. Pump output low.

Noises

1. Buzzing noise in neutral only is caused by sticking pressure control valve.
2. Noisy power pump.
3. Damaged hydraulic lines.
4. Pressure control valve sticking.
5. Improper sector shaft adjustment.
6. Air in system.

Lack of Effort, Left Turn

1. Left turn reaction seal "O" ring missing, damaged or worn.
2. Left turn reaction oil passage not drilled in housing or cylinder head.
3. Left turn reaction ring sticking in cylinder head.

Lack of Effort, Right Turn

1. Right turn U-shaped reaction seal missing, damaged or worn.
2. Right turn reaction oil passage not drilled in housing head or ferrule pin.
3. Right turn reaction ring sticking in housing head.

Lack of Effort in Both Directions

1. Improper sector shaft adjustment.
2. Pressure plates installed on wrong side of reaction rings.

---

in center race.

3. Install housing head tang washer, indexing with groove in housing, and steering column support nut and torque nut to 150–200 ft. lbs. Ensure valve lever remains centered in housing hole by rotating wormshaft until piston bottoms in both directions and observe valve lever action. The valve lever must be in center of hole and return to the center position when wormshaft torque is relieved.
4. Install valve lever spring (small end first), position power piston at center of travel and install sector shaft and cover assembly, indexing sector teeth with piston rack teeth. Ensure sector shaft cover "O" ring is installed properly.
5. Install and torque cover nut to 110–200 ft. lbs.
6. Install valve body onto housing with valve lever entering hole in valve spool. Ensure "O" rings are installed properly, then install and torque valve retaining screws to 7 ft. lbs.

Tests and Adjustments

1. Fill reservoir to level mark.
2. Connect test hoses to hydraulic pump on car with pressure gauge installed between pump and steering gear to register pressures.
3. Start engine and operate at idle to bring steering gear to normal operating temperature.
4. Center the valve until unit is not self-steering. Tap valve body retaining screw heads to move valve body up on steering housing or end plug to move valve body down.
5. Rotate wormshaft through range of travel to bleed air from system, then refill reservoir.
6. With steering gear on center, tighten sector shaft adjusting screw until backlash is removed from steering arm, Fig. CC17. If the power train was removed, tighten adjusting screw an additional 1¼ turns, then tighten locknut.
7. Operate unit through several cycles, aligning piston rack and sector teeth.
8. With gear on center, readjust sector shaft backlash. Loosen adjusting screw until backlash is present, then tighten adjusting screw until backlash is removed. Tighten adjusting screw an additional ⅜ to ½ turn and torque locknut to 28 ft. lbs.
9. Recenter valve body.

POWER STEERING GEARS

Ford Torsion Bar Power Steering

DESCRIPTION

The power steering unit, Figs. F1, F2 & F3, is a torsion bar type of hydraulic-assisted system. This system furnishes power to reduce the amount of turning effort required at the steering wheel. It also reduces road shock and vibrations.

The unit includes a worm and one piece rack-piston which is meshed to the gear teeth on the steering sector shaft. The unit also includes a hydraulic valve, valve actuator, input shaft and torsion bar assembly which are mounted on the end of the worm shaft and operated by a twisting action of the torsion bar.

The spool valve type gear, Fig. F2, is designed with the one piece rack-piston, worm and sector shaft in the one housing and the valve spool in an attaching housing. The Rotary Valve type gear, Fig. F3, uses a one piece rotary valve and sleeve assembly. Therefore no centering shims are used and no adjustment is possible. This makes possible internal fluid passages between valve and cylinder, thus eliminating all external lines and hoses except the pressure and return hoses between pump and gear.

The power cylinder is an integral part of the gear housing. The piston is double acting in that fluid pressure may be applied to either side of the piston.

A selective metal shim, used only on the spool valve type gear, Fig. F2, is located in the valve housing of the gear is for the purpose of tailoring the steering gear efforts. If efforts are not satisfactory they can be changed by increasing or decreasing shim thickness as follows:

Efforts heavy to the left—increase shim thickness. Efforts light to the left—decrease shim thickness. A change of one shim size will increase or decrease steering efforts approximately 1½ inch lbs. on 1966–71 models and 2 inch lbs. on 1972–74 models. Shims are available in the following selective thicknesses:

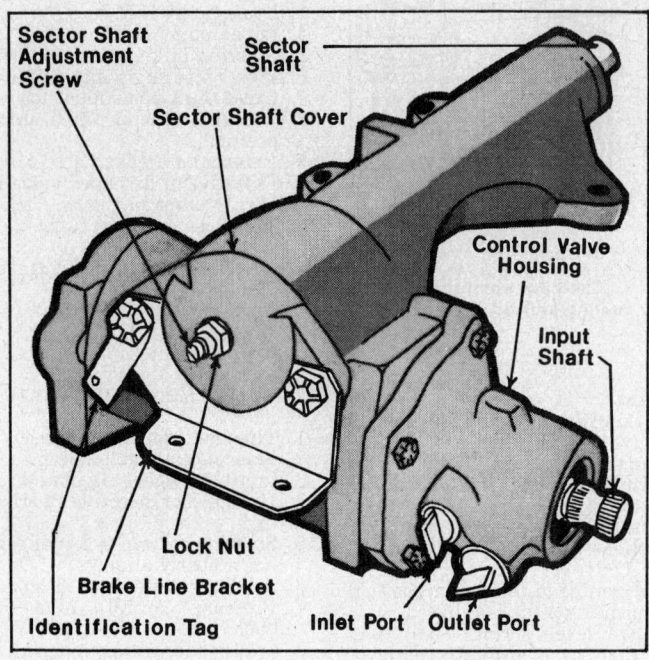

Fig. F1   Ford torsion bar power steering gear

.0057 to .0063"
.0077 to .0083"
.0097 to .0103"
.0117 to .0123"
.0137 to .0143"

Operation

The operation of the hydraulic control valve spool is governed by the twisting of a torsion bar. All effort applied to the steering wheel is transmitted directly through the input shaft and torsion bar to the worm and piston. Any resistance to the turning of the front wheels results in twisting of the bar. The twisting of the bar increases as the front wheel turning effort increases. The control valve spool, or the rotary valve sleeve actuated by the twisting of the torsion bar, directs fluid to the side of the piston where hydraulic assistance is required.

As the torsion bar twists, its radial motion is transferred into axial motion by helical threads. Thus, the valve is moved off center, and fluid is directed to one side of the piston or the other.

IN-VEHICLE ADJUSTMENTS & REPAIRS

Valve Spool Or Rotary Valve Centering Check

1. Install a 2000 psi pressure gauge in pressure line between pump outlet port and steering gear inlet port. *Make sure that valve on gauge is in fully open position.*
2. Check fluid level in reservoir and replen-

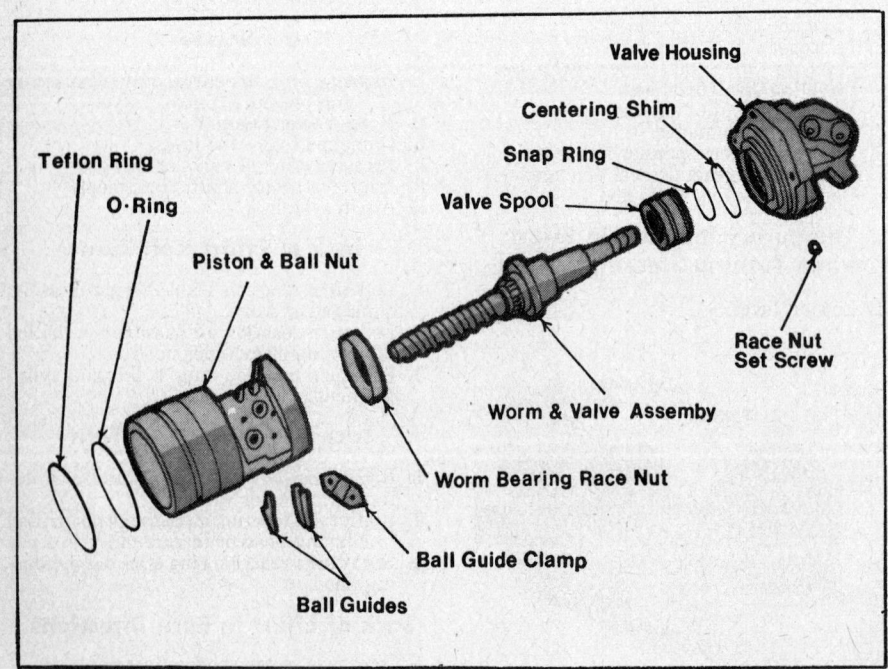

Fig. F2   Ball nut & valve housing disassembled. Spool valve type

POWER STEERING GEARS

ish as required.
3. Start engine and cycle steering wheel from stop-to-stop to bring steering lubricant up to normal operating temperature. Stop engine and recheck reservoir. Add fluid as necessary.
4. With engine running at a fast idle speed (1000 rpm) and steering wheel centered, attach an inch-pound torque wrench to steering wheel retaining nut. Apply sufficient torque to wrench in each direction (either side of center) to get a gauge reading of 250 psi.
5. *Valve Spool type gear*
The torque reading should be the same in both directions. If the difference between readings exceeds 4 inch lbs, remove steering gear from vehicle and change thickness of valve centering shim. On 1966–71 units, use only one shim and on 1972–74 units, use as many shims as necessary, not exceeding .030 inch total thickness. If steering effort is heavy to the left, increase shim thickness and if steering effort is light to the left, decrease shim thickness.
Rotary Valve type gear
The torque reading should be the same in both directions. If the difference between readings exceeds 4 inch lbs., remove steering gear from vehicle and replace the shaft and control assembly.

NOTE: The "out-of-vehicle" procedure for centering check is the same as for the "in-vehicle" except the torque and simultaneous pressure reading must be made at the right and left stops instead of either side of center.

Steering Gear Adjustments

Preload (thrust bearing adjustment) and worm-to-rack preload cannot be changed in service. The only adjustment that can be performed is the total overcenter position load to eliminate excessive lash between sector and rack teeth.
1. Disconnect pitman arm from sector shaft.
2. Disconnect fluid return line at reservoir and cap reservoir return line pipe.
3. Place end of return line in a clean container and cycle steering wheel in both directions as required to discharge fluid from gear.
4. Remove ornamental cover from wheel hub and turn steering wheel 45° from left stop.
5. Using an inch-lb torque wrench on steering wheel nut, determine torque required to rotate shaft slowly through an approximately 1/8 turn from the 45° position.
6. Turn steering gear back to center, then determine torque required to rotate shaft back and forth across center position.
7. Loosen adjuster nut and turn adjusting screw until reading is 11 to 12 inch lbs. greater than torque measured 45° from stop. Hold screw in place and tighten locknut.
8. Recheck readings and replace pitman arm and steering wheel.
9. Connect fluid return line and replenish reservoir.

STEERING GEAR REPAIRS

Disassembly

1. Hold steering gear over drain pan in an inverted position and cycle input shaft six times to drain remaining fluid from gear.
2. Remove lock nut and brass thrust washer from adjusting screw.
3. Turn input shaft to either stop, then turn it back approximately 1 3/4 turns to center the gear.
4. Remove two sector shaft cover studs, brake line bracket and identification tag.
5. Tap lower end of sector shaft with a soft-faced hammer to loosen it, then lift cover and shaft from housing as a unit. Discard O-ring.
6. Turn sector shaft cover counterclockwise off adjuster screw.
7. Remove four valve housing attaching bolts. Lift valve housing from gear housing while holding piston to prevent it from rotating off worm shaft. Remove valve housing and lube passage O-rings and discard.
8. Stand valve body and piston on end with piston end down. Rotate input shaft counterclockwise out of piston, allowing balls to drop into piston.
9. Place a cloth over open end of piston and turn it upside down to remove balls.
10. Remove ball guide clamp screws from ball nut and remove clamp and guides, Figs. F2 & F3.
11. Hold valve body in a fixture and loosen the Allen head race nut screw from the valve housing and remove the worm bearing race nut.
12. Carefully slide input shaft, worm and valve out of valve housing.

CAUTION: Do to the close diametrical

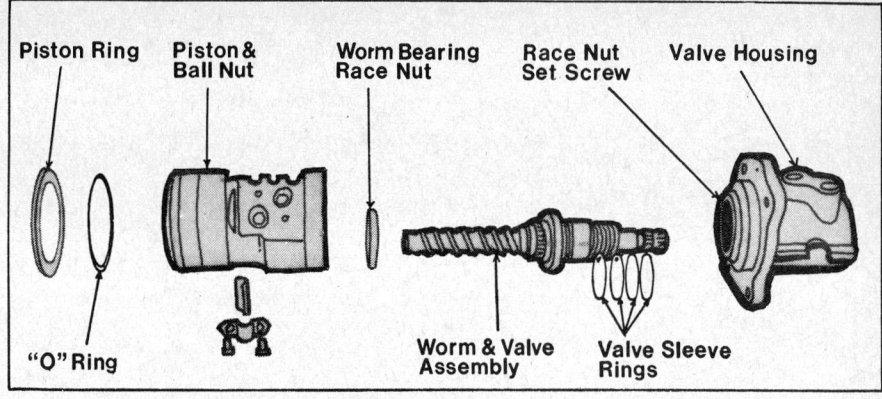

Fig. F3 Ball nut & valve housing disassembled. Rotary valve type

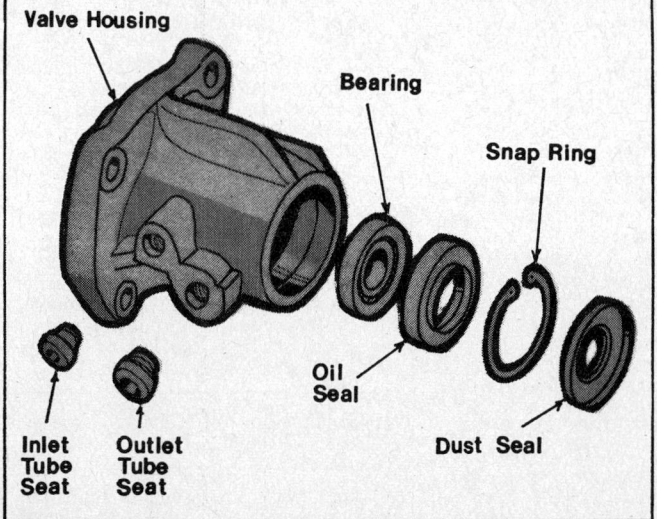

Fig. F4 Valve housing disassembled

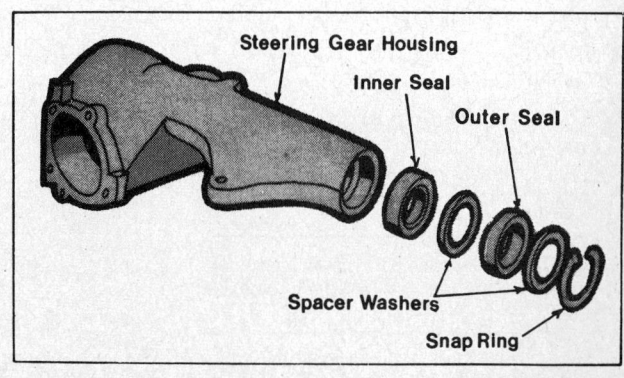

Fig. F5 Steering gear housing disassembled

POWER STEERING GEARS

clearance between valve spool and housing, the slightest cocking of the spool may cause it to jam in housing.

13. Remove shim from valve housing if disassembling the spool valve type gear, Fig. F2.

Reassembly

1. On 1966-74 units, place required thickness valve spool centering shim in housing, (spool valve type gear only), Fig. F2.
2. Install worm and valve in housing.
3. Install race nut in housing and torque to 55-65 ft-lbs.
4. On 1966-69 units, install race nut and torque to 20-30 ft. lbs. On 1970-73 units, install race nut set screw and torque to 20-25 in. lbs. On 1974-76 units, install race nut set screw and torque to 15-25 in. lbs.
5. Place piston on bench with ball guide holes facing up. Insert worm shaft into piston so that first groove is in alignment with hole nearest to center of piston, Fig. F6.
6. Place ball guide into piston. Place 27 to 29 balls in guide, (depending on piston design), turning worm clockwise (viewed from input end of shaft). If all balls have not been fed into guide upon reaching right stop, rotate input shaft in one direction and then in the other while installing remaining balls. After balls have been installed, do not rotate input shaft or piston more than 3½ turns off the right stop to prevent balls from falling out of circuit.
7. Secure guides to ball nut with clamp.
8. Position new lube passage O-ring in counterbore of gear housing.
9. Apply vaseline to teflon seal.
10. Place a new O-ring on valve housing.
11. Slide piston and valve into gear housing, being careful not to damage teflon seal.
12. Align lube passage in valve housing with one in gear housing, and install but do not tighten attaching bolts at this time.
13. Rotate ball nut so that teeth are in same plane as sector teeth. Torque four valve housing attaching bolts to 35 to 45 ft-lbs.
14. Position sector shaft cover O-ring in gear housing. Turn input shaft as required to center piston.
15. Apply vaseline to sector shaft journal, then position sector shaft and cover into gear housing. Install the brake line bracket, identification tag and air conditioner line mounting bracket (if so equipped) and sector shaft cover bolts, torquing them to 55-70 ft-lbs.
16. Attach an inch lb. torque wrench to input shaft and adjust mesh load as outlined previously.

Valve Housing, Replace

1. Referring to Fig. F4, remove dust seal and snap ring.
2. Invert housing and from opposite seal end, gently tap bearing and seal out of housing.

CAUTION: Exercise care when inserting and removing tool to prevent damage to valve bore in housing.

3. Remove oil inlet and outlet tube seats with "EZ-out" if damaged.
4. Coat tube seats with vaseline and position them in housing. Install and tighten tube nuts to press seats to proper location.
5. Coat bearing and seal surface in housing with a film of vaseline.
6. Position bearing in valve housing. Seat bearing in housing with tool T65P-3524-A1 making sure that bearing rotates freely.
7. Dip new oil seal in gear lube. Then seal facing outward. Drive seal into housing until outer edge of seal does not quite clear snap ring.
8. Place snap ring in housing. Then drive on ring with tool T65P-3524-A1 until snap ring seats in its groove to locate seal properly.
9. Place dust seal in housing with dished side (rubber side) facing out. Drive dust seal in place so that it is located behind undercut in input shaft when it is installed.

Worm & Valve (Valve Sleeve), Replace

Spool Valve Type Gear
1. Remove snap ring from actuator.
2. Slide control valve spool off worm shaft, Fig. F2.
3. Install valve spool evenly and slowly with a slight oscillating motion into flanged end of valve housing with valve identification groove between spool lands outward. Check for freedom of valve movement within housing working area. Spool should enter housing bore freely and fall by its own weight.
4. If valve spool is not free, check for burrs at outward edges of working lands in housing and remove with a hard stone.
5. Check valve for burrs and, if necessary, stone valve in a radial direction only.
6. Remove valve spool from housing.
7. Slide spool onto worm shaft, making sure that the beveled ID of the snap ring is away from the spool.
8. Install snap ring to retain spool.
9. On 1971 gear units, check clearance between spool and snap ring, which should be .0005 to .0035. If not within these limits select a snap ring that will allow .002" clearance.

Rotary Valve Type Gear
1. Remove valve sleeve rings, Fig. F3, from sleeve by inserting the blade of a small pocket knife carefully under them and cutting them off, without scratching the valve sleeve.
2. With the worm end of the worm and valve sleeve assembly mounted into a soft-jawed vise, install mandrel tool T75L-3517-A1 over the sleeve and slide one valve sleeve ring over the tool.
3. Slide the pusher tool T75L-3517-A2 over the mandrel then rapidly push down on the pusher tool, forcing the ring down the ramp and into the fourth groove of the valve sleeve. Repeat this step three more times, each time adding one of the spacers, tool T75L-3517-A3, under the mandrel tool.

NOTE: Adding the spacer each time will align the mandrel tool with the next groove of the valve sleeve.

4. After installing all four valve sleeve rings, apply a light coat of gear lubricant to the sleeve and rings.
5. Slowly install the sizing tube tool T75L-3517-A4, over the sleeve valve end of the worm shaft and onto the valve sleeve rings.

NOTE: Make sure that the rings turn freely in the grooves.

Piston & Ball Nut, Replace

1. Remove teflon ring and O-ring from piston and ball nut, Figs. F2 & F3.
2. Dip a new O-ring in gear lube and install on piston and ball nut.
3. Install new teflon ring on piston and ball nut, being careful not to stretch it any more than necessary.

Gear Housing, Replace

1. Remove snap ring and spacer washer, Fig. F5, from lower end of gear housing.
2. Remove lower seal from housing and life spacer washer from housing.
3. Remove upper seal in same manner.

NOTE: Some housings have only one seal and one spacer.

4. Dip both sector shaft seals in gear lube.
5. Position sector shaft inner seal (widest one) into housing with lip facing inward. Press into place with tool T65P-3576-B.

Fig. F6 Assembling piston on worm shaft

POWER STEERING GEARS

Place a 0.090 inch spacer washer on top of seal.
6. Place outer seal in housing with lip facing inward and press into place. Place a 0.090 inch spacer washer on top of seal and apply more lubricant.
7. Position snap ring in housing and press it in place to properly locate seals and engage snap ring in the groove.

TROUBLE SHOOTING

Hard Steering

1. Low or uneven tire pressure.
2. Improper gear adjustment.
3. Improper wheel alignment.
4. Low fluid level.
5. Twisted or bent suspension parts, frame and linkage components.
6. Tight wheel bearings.
7. Steering spindle bent.
8. Pump belt out of adjustment.
9. Pump output low.
10. Air in system.
11. Valve spool or rotary valve out of adjustment.
12. Valve spool or rotary valve sticking.
13. Steering linkage binding.

Hard Steering, Straight Ahead

1. Steering adjustment too tight.
2. Steering gear shaft binding.

Hard Steering While Turning or Parking

1. Oil level low.
2. Pump pressure low.
3. Pressure loss in steering gear due to leakage past "O" rings.
4. Pressure loss between valve spool and sleeve (valve spool type gear only.)
5. Pressure loss past piston ring or scored housing bore.

Loose Steering

1. Loose wheel bearings.
2. Loose tie rod ends or linkage.
3. Worn ball joints.
4. Worn suspension parts.
5. Insufficient mesh load.
6. Insufficient worm bearing preload.
7. Valve spool or rotary valve out of adjustment.

Erratic Steering

1. Oil or brake fluid on brake lining.
2. Out of round brake drums.
3. Improperly adjusted brakes.
4. Under-inflated tires.
5. Broken spring or other details in suspension system.
6. Improper caster adjustment.
7. Fluid level low.

Binding or Poor Recovery

1. Steering gear shaft binding.
2. Steering gear out of adjustment.
3. Steering linkage binding.
4. Valve spool or rotary valve binding due to dirt or burred edges.
5. Valve spool or rotary valve out of adjustment.
6. Interference at sector shaft and ball stud.

Loss of Power Assist

1. Pump inoperative.
2. Hydraulic lines damaged.
3. Power cylinder damaged.
4. Valve spool or rotary valve out of adjustment.

Loss of Power Assist In One Direction

1. Valve spool or rotary valve out of adjustment.

Noisy Pump

1. Air being drawn into pump.
2. Lines touching other parts of car.
3. Oil level low.
4. Excessive back pressure caused by obstructions in lines.
5. Excessive wear of internal parts.

Poor Return of Steering Gear to Center

1. Valve spool or rotary valve sticking.
2. Valve spool or rotary valve out of adjustment.
3. All items given under "Binding or Poor Recovery."

Steering Wheel Surge While Turning

1. Valve spool or rotary valve sticking.
2. Excessive internal leakage.
3. Belt slippage.

Ross Power Steering Section

SEMI-INTEGRAL GEAR

These power steering gears, Figs. R1, R2 and R3, are of the semi-integral type with either a built-in or externally mounted hydraulic control valve on or within the steering gear. The steering is then teamed with a fluid reservoir, power steering pump, and either an axle or frame mounted cylinder to provide a power assist for the steering system. Effort applied to the steering wheel actuates the control valve which directs fluid from the pump to the power cylinder. Fig. R4 illustrates the operation of built-in concentric control valve.

NOTE: *There is no adjustment to make on the control valve. The steering gear itself, however, is adjusted in the same manner as the comparable mechanical steering gear.*

Removal of Gear

Because of the different kinds of steering columns used on various model trucks, some variation in the removal procedure can be expected. However, before removing the gear, regardless of type, always note the hook-up of the hydraulic lines. Identify them by tagging connecting lines and marking the valve ports into which each connects. The general procedure which follows can be adapted to both the solid and jointed type steering columns. However, where a jointed column is being used, it is not necessary to remove the steering wheel and column.

1. On solid type columns, remove steering wheel. On jointed column models, loosen nut on steering shaft collar and remove steering column shaft from gear.
2. Use a puller to remove pitman arm.
3. Disconnect hydraulic lines at control valve. Plug all openings to keep out dirt.
4. Unfasten gear from its mounting and remove from chassis.

EXC. HPS-70

Disassembly

1. Loosen lock nut and unscrew lever shaft adjusting screw a few turns.
2. Remove gear housing side cover.
3. Slide lever shaft from housing after making sure that there are no burrs on outer end of shaft to damage bushings and seal in housing.
4. To remove control valve, identify position and face of valve next to housing with a point file or punch.
5. Remove lower end cover.
6. Remove adjusting nuts by straightening bent prong of lock washer. Remove tongued spacer washer. Remove bearings and O-rings, noting especially the position of each part of bearing.
7. Remove control valve. Do not damage any polished surfaces or the edges of the lands on spool and body while handling. Protect all internal surfaces and parts by covering valve. Any small dirt particle will affect proper operation of unit.
8. Remove upper bearings and O-rings in same manner as lower ones, noting their position.
9. Remove steering gear upper cover and gasket and pull cam and shaft from housing.

Inspection

Inspect the steering gear in the usual manner as one would the manual steering gear.

NOTE: *The control valve spool and valve are selectively fitted. The spool has identifying grooves in one end. Mark the valve body end where the identifying groove in the spool was positioned. If this is not done, maximum efficiency of the valve cannot be expected.*

1. Handle valve parts carefully to avoid damage. Note the condition of the edges of lands on spool and body. If edges are damaged, leakage will result.
2. When removing spool, plungers and springs, place parts on lint-free cloth.

POWER STEERING GEARS

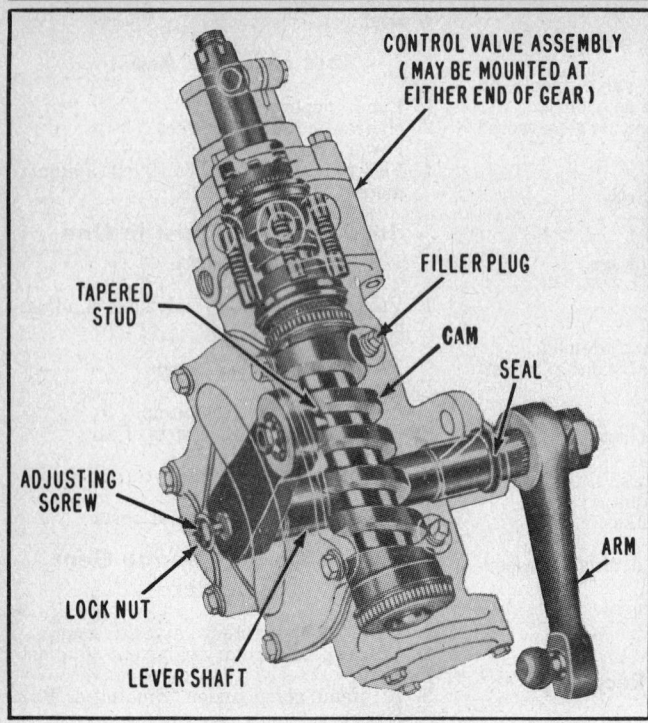

Fig. R1 Ross power steering gear with a built-in concentric type control valve

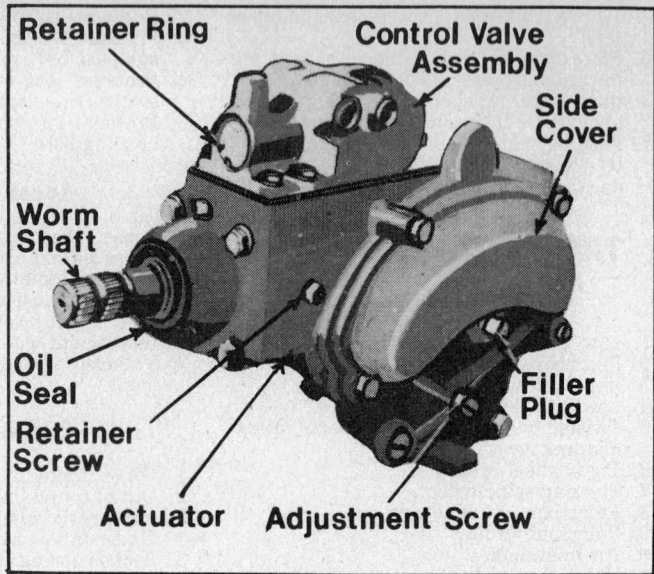

Fig. R2 Ross model HPS-70 semi-integral power steering gear with externally mounted control valve (Typical of Dodge)

Cover to protect from dust and dirt.
3. Inspect all other parts carefully, giving special attention to spline in steering arm and steering arm ball. Replace all defective parts.

Reassembly, Fig. R5

1. Slide cam with bearings assembled into housing. Be sure unit turns freely without binding.
2. Install new gasket and upper cover.
3. Assemble shim pack to lever shaft and install shaft in housing. Do not damage oil seal in end of housing trunnion. A cut seal lip will permit lubricant to leak out.
4. Assemble gasket and side cover, but do not adjust at this time.
5. Install thrust washer, thrust bearing and bearing race over lower end of camshaft. Be certain that bearing race is installed so that O-ring side faces toward control valve. Position O-ring seals.
6. Assemble control valve unit on end of gear, making sure plungers and springs do not fall out. Note that valve is positioned properly relative to port openings and as previously marked before disassembly. Plug valve port openings to prevent entrance of dirt.
7. Assemble lower O-rings and bearings.
8. Slide on washer with internal lug and new lock washer with eight external lugs. Assemble adjusting nut and adjust as covered below under "Adjustments".
9. Install lower end cover and new gasket and secure with bolts and lock washers.

MODEL HPS-70

Steering Gear, Fig. R6

1. Loosen cross shaft adjusting screw lock-

nut and back off adjusting screw a few turns, then remove housing side cover and gasket.
2. Slide levershaft from steering gear housing. First make certain that there are no burrs on outer end of shaft which may damage levershaft bushings. Keep shim pack intact.

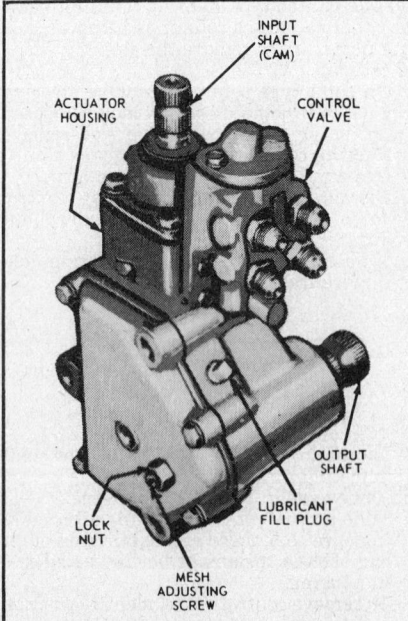

Fig. R3 Ross model HPS-70 semi-integral power steering gear with externally mounted control valve (Typical of Ford)

3. Remove control valve and spool assembly, attaching screws and valve as an assembly, then remove actuator housing gasket and actuator lever.
4. Remove upper cover and actuator housing attaching screws and slide cover from cam and tube assembly.
5. Remove actuator retaining screw and slide actuator housing from actuator. Remove actuator and cam tube as an assembly, then remove steering gear end cover and gasket.
6. Remove valve actuator and cam tube as an assembly, then remove steering gear end cover and gasket.
7. Remove cam and tube bearing and bearing retaining ring.

Valve Actuator and Cam Disassembly

1. Place lower end of cam and tube assembly in a soft jawed vise.
2. Straighten adjusting lockwasher tangs and remove adjusting nut and lockwasher.
3. Remove tongued spacer washer, upper thrust washers and thrust bearing.
4. Remove upper centering washer from end of actuator.
5. Remove actuator, using care not to lose centering screws that are in actuator.
6. Remove lower centering washer, thrust washer and thrust bearing.

Control Valve, Disassembly

CAUTION: The major parts of the control valve are precision machined to close tolerences. The body and spool are selectively fitted and are not separately replaceable. If either part needs replacing, the control valve must be replaced as a unit. Sealed edges of the valve sleeve and spool should not be broken as excessive leakage and reduced hydraulic power will result. Use care when handling parts to prevent damage.

Power Steering Gears

1. Remove retainer ring, cover plate and O-ring seal.
2. Remove valve body housing end cover and O-ring seals from valve body.
3. Remove elastic stop nut and washer from end of clevis rod assembly and pull rod out of spool.
4. Push spool out in same direction to permit removal of centering washers, O-ring and centering spring.
5. Using care not to damage seal, remove O-ring from spool using a pointed tool.
6. If necessary, remove by-pass valve parts, plug assembly, spring and ball.
7. Inspect spool and valve body for scoring by dirt. Wear should be negligible because spool operates in circulating.

Control Valve, Reassembly Fig. R7

NOTE: Refer to caution under "Control Valve, Disassembly."

1. Install O-ring on spool, then lubricate spool using SAE 10 oil and assemble spool into valve body being sure end with O-ring is towards clevis end of valve.

   NOTE: When assembling spool into valve body, a twisting motion applied to the spool will aid in assembly. Before assembly, make certain that all parts are thoroughly cleaned.

2. Install centering washer, spring, centering washer, O-ring, and centering washer into control valve body.
3. Install clevis rod into spool and assemble washer and lock nut onto rod. Torque nut to 125–150 inch lbs.
4. If by-pass valve parts were removed, replace O-ring on by-pass plug before installing plug in body, then install steel ball, spring, and by-pass plug into control valve body.

Steering Gear and Valve Actuator, Reassembly Fig. R6

NOTE: Replace all gaskets and seals.

1. If removed, install needle bearings and retainers into end of steering gear housing, being careful not to press bearing too hard against bearing retaining ring.
2. Install tube and cam in a soft jawed vise and assemble lower thrust bearing over tube, seating bearing against upper end of cam.
3. In order, install the following parts; thrust washer, centering washer, actuator, actuator centering springs, centering washer, thrust washer, thrust bearing, thrust washer, tongued washer, new lockwasher (pronged with 13 external lugs) and adjusting nut.
4. To adjust thrust bearing, torque adjusting nut to 75 inch lbs. and rotate cam in relation to actuator. Back off adjusting nut to next tang of pronged lockwasher. Torque required to rotate cam in relation to actuator should be $1/2$ to 3 inch lbs.

   NOTE: This adjustment is similar to a wheel bearing adjustment and should provide a light preload of needle thrust bearings without lash or heavy drag.

5. Assemble cam and tube with actuator assembly in housing, making certain that cam rotates and oscillates freely in housing.
6. Position actuator gasket and install actuator housing over actuator.
7. Position actuator housing and assemble actuator retainer screw and seal washer. Make certain that screw engages horizontal slot in actuator.
8. Position actuator housing upper cover gasket, then fasten upper cover and actuator housing, using the four long mounting screws.
9. Assemble shim pack onto levershaft and install levershaft into steering housing, using care not to damage oil seal in end of housing trunnion.
10. Position side cover gasket and install side cover, then install lever shaft adjusting screw and lock nut.
11. Adjust lever stud in cam groove as follows:
    a. Tighten side cover adjusting screw until a slight drag (high spot) is felt when turning gear through mid-position. If high spot cannot be felt, remove shims from shim pack until it can be felt.

    NOTE: This is a delicate and important adjustment, therefore, remove only enough shims to permit feel of high spot.

    b. When adjusting to a high spot, back off adjusting screw $1/16$ turn and lock adjustment with lock nut.
    c. If high spot can be felt without removal of shims, additional shims may be needed in shim pack. A positive way of checking is to add shims until high spot cannot be felt, then remove shims until high spot can be felt.
    d. After lock nut has been tightened, check adjustment by turning gear through its full travel (from extreme left to extreme right).
    e. Install actuator lever into actuator housing, making sure stud end of lever seats in groove of actuator and position slot in other end of lever so that

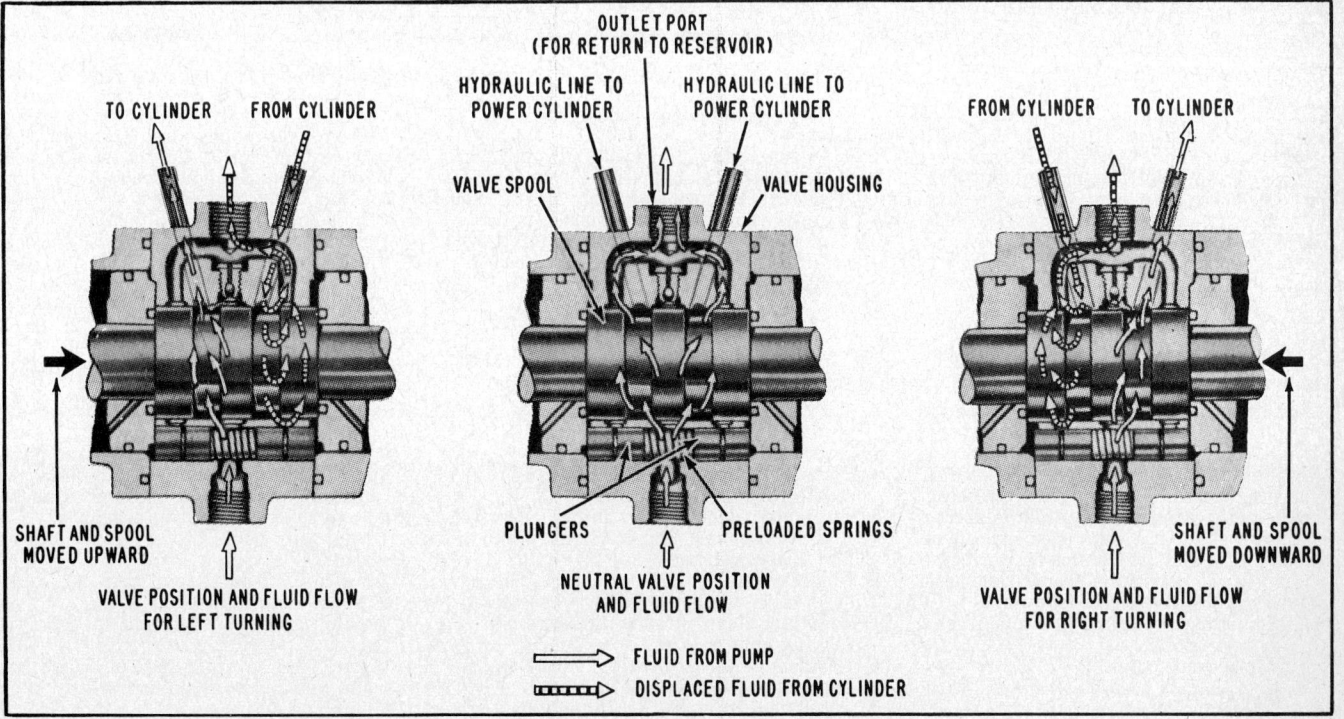

Fig. R4 Ross built-in concentric control valve operation

Power Steering Gears

pin in clevis of flexure rod will fit freely into lever when mounting valve on actuator housing.

f. Mount gasket and control valve on actuator housing making certain clevis pin fits freely into slot of actuator lever. Start all four mounting screws and tighten lightly in rotation before finally torquing to 10–15 ft. lbs.

NOTE: Overtorquing may cause valve spool to be pulled off center by actuator level interference with clevis pin.

g. Be sure spool actuates (moves axially in both directions) before installing end covers. This can be done by placing steering gear arm on lever shaft, then turning worm shaft to move steering arm against a stop and applying sufficient force to actuate valve spool. Reverse arm against an opposite stop to actuate valve spool in either direction.
h. Assemble O-ring on end of control valve body and install valve housing end cover and tighten screws securely.
i. Assemble O-ring, cover plate and retaining ring into clevis rod end of control valve housing.

12. Install end cover gasket and end cover.

Adjustments, All Models

Thrust Bearing Adjustment
1. Turn gear off its center position to free stud in cam groove.
2. Remove upper cover.
3. Remove adjusting nut and spacer washer.
4. Test freedom of nut on camshaft by running it on camshaft without the eight-lug washer in place until the nut seats firmly against thrust bearing using only the fingers to run the nut. If this cannot be done, the threads are fouled and must be cleared with a thread file or other means.
5. Reassemble parts, using the tongued spacer washer (with internal lug) and eight-pronged lock washer.
6. Turn on adjusting nut and tighten to 10 ft-lbs. Back off nut 10 to 20 degrees, which can be done by moving the nut relative to the washer approximately the width of one of the lugs. Observe the lugs nearest in alignment with a pair of flats and bend lugs tightly against flats.
7. Install upper cover.

Stud in Cam Groove Adjustment
1. Tighten side cover. Adjust screw until a slight drag is felt when slowly turning gear through mid-position. No drag is actually necessary. It is suggested as a positive means of knowing that the backlash is removed. The drag should be very slight.
2. A shim pack is used between lever and housing to prevent taper pin from being pulled into cam groove by external forces on lever shaft. The shim pack consists of .003", .010" and .020" shims between two washers. To determine proper thickness of shim pack, proceed as follows:
   a. Adjust high spot and then place gear on high spot.
   b. Remove side cover.
   c. Hold shaft in position with hand with tapered pin pressed in cam groove.
   d. If shim pack can be turned with fingers, add shims until pack cannot be turned and then remove one .003" shim.
   e. Reassemble side cover and adjust as per Step "a" above. If high spot cannot be felt, remove one shim at a time until desired adjustment is obtained.
3. Lock the adjustment. While holding adjusting screw, tighten lock nut. Recheck adjustment through full travel of steering gear.

Cam & Actuator Assembly Thrust Bearings Adjustment, Model HPS-70
1. Turn gear off its center position to free stud in cam groove, then remove upper cover retaining screws and remove cover. Place 3/8 inch spacers on screws and reinstall screws without cover.
2. Straighten lockwasher prong, remove nut, lockwasher, upper thrust washers and thrust bearing.
3. Finger tighten nut on camshaft making sure there is no thread interference. If necessary clean threads to insure a free turning nut.
4. Reassemble thrust bearing, thrust washers, tongued lockwasher and nut.
5. Torque adjusting nut to 75 inch lbs.
6. Rotate cam with respect to actuator and back off adjusting nut to first locking tang.
7. Measure torque required to rotate cam with respect to actuator. If torque exceeds 3 inch lbs., back off adjusting nut to next locking tang and recheck torque. Final torque should be 1/2 to 3 inch lbs.
8. Bend lockwasher tang and reinstall cover and retaining screws.
9. Connect steering column joint and drag link.

Stud Roller Bearing Adjustment, Model HPS-70
The preceding adjustments should be sufficient in nearly every instance, but in some cases it may be necessary to adjust stud roller bearing lever in unit shaft. In order to make this adjustment, steering gear must be removed and shaft removed from gear.
1. Break off bent prong from locking washer.
2. Lubricate all parts with SAE 90 Multi-Purpose Gear Lubricant.
3. Tighten stud adjusting nut to 4–6 inch lbs.
4. Rotate stud several times in both directions and back off adjusting nut, then tighten adjusting nut to 1 1/2 inch lbs.
5. Lock adjusting nut by bending unused prong of locking washer over nut.

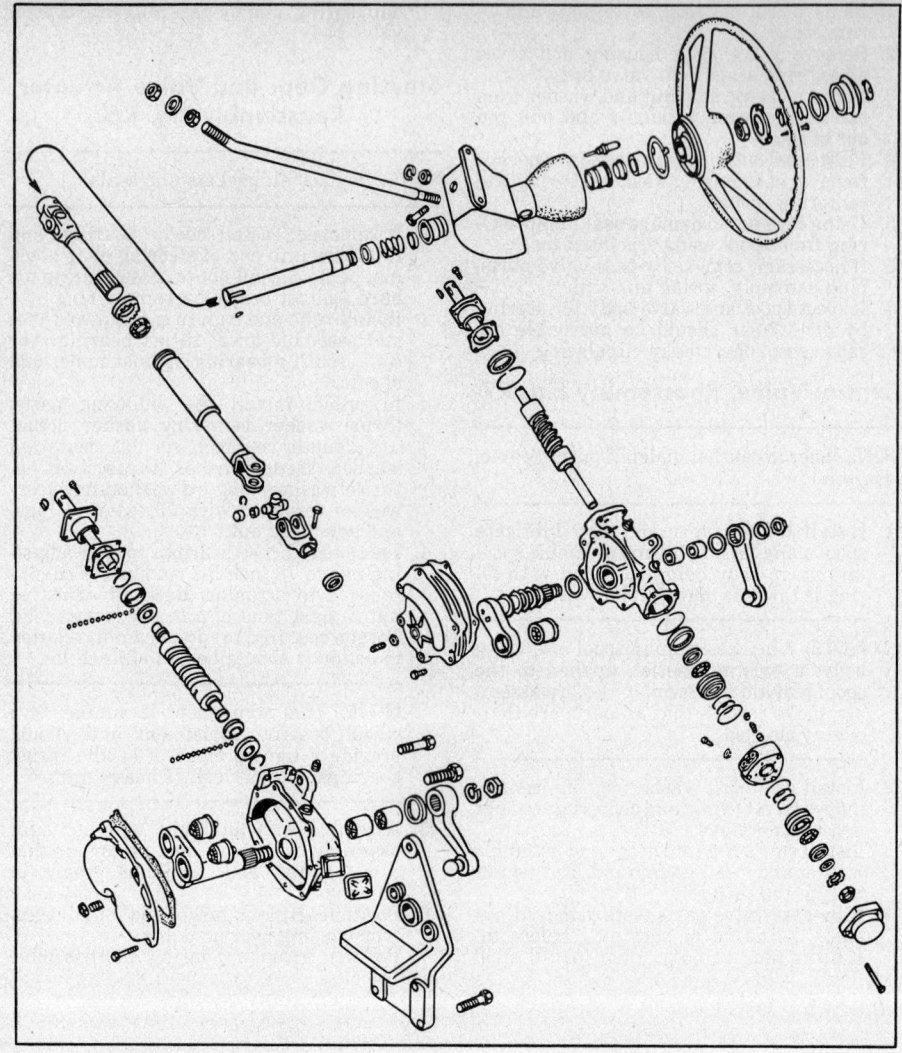

Fig. R5 Disassembled view of Ross steering gear with concentric control valve

Power Steering Gears

POWER STEERING WITH TOGGLE TYPE CONTROL VALVE

This steering gear, Fig. R8, a standard Ross cam and lever type incorporating a hydraulic toggle type valve. Steering effort applied to the steering wheel actuates the valve which, in turn, directs hydraulic fluid from a pump to a power cylinder located in the steering linkage. Fig. R9 illustrates the operation of the control valve.

NOTE: *Steering gear adjustments are similar to that outlined for the Ross steering gear with the concentric type control valve. There is no adjustment on the control valve. However, when clamped to the actuator housing the valve spool must not be pulled off center.*

Control Valve Removal

1. Loosen lock nut and unscrew lever shaft adjusting screw a few turns.
2. Remove housing side cover.
3. Slide lever shaft from housing, having first made sure that there are no burrs on the outer end of shaft to damage bushing and seal in housing. Keep shim pack intact.
4. Remove screws holding valve to actuator housing and remove valve.

Control Valve Disassembly

The major parts of the valve, which are the body and spool, are machined to very close limits and with precision machined edges. The spool and valve body are selectively fitted according to size of O.D. of spool and I.D. of body. Therefore, these two parts are not supplied separately. If either needs replacing, the entire valve assembly must be replaced.

1. Remove retainer ring, cover plate and O-ring seal.
2. Remove end cover and O-ring seals from valve body.
3. Remove elastic stop nut and washer from end of flexure rod and pull flexure rod out of spool.
4. Push spool out in same direction to permit removal of centering washers, O-ring and centering spring.
5. Remove O-ring from spool. Use pointed instrument but be careful not to damage seal.
6. By-pass valve parts, plug assembly, spring and ball may be removed if desired.
7. Inspect spool. Inspect body internally. Check for scoring due to dirt in system.

Reassemble Steering Gear, Fig. R10

1. If needle bearings in ends of housing have been removed, replace them. Take care not to press bearing too hard against retaining ring.
2. Pre-assemble actuator assembly on cam and stub shaft as follows:
   a. First be sure that threads of nut and camshaft are free of interference by running nut onto camshaft with finger pressure only. If nut cannot be turned all the way with the fingers, the threads are fouled and must be cleaned with a thread file or other means.
   b. Assemble needle bearing over stub shaft and seat against upper end of cam.
   c. Assemble actuator in sequence shown in Fig. R10.
   d. Adjust thrust bearing as outlined for the gear with concentric control valve.
3. Assemble cam in housing, being sure cam rotates and oscillates freely in housing.
4. Assemble gasket to top of housing.
5. Assemble actuator housing over actuator.
6. Position actuator housing for location of valve mounting. Assemble retainer screw and washer. Be sure screw engages horizontal slot in actuator.
7. Assemble gasket to actuator housing.
8. Assemble upper cover.
9. Fasten upper cover and actuator housing

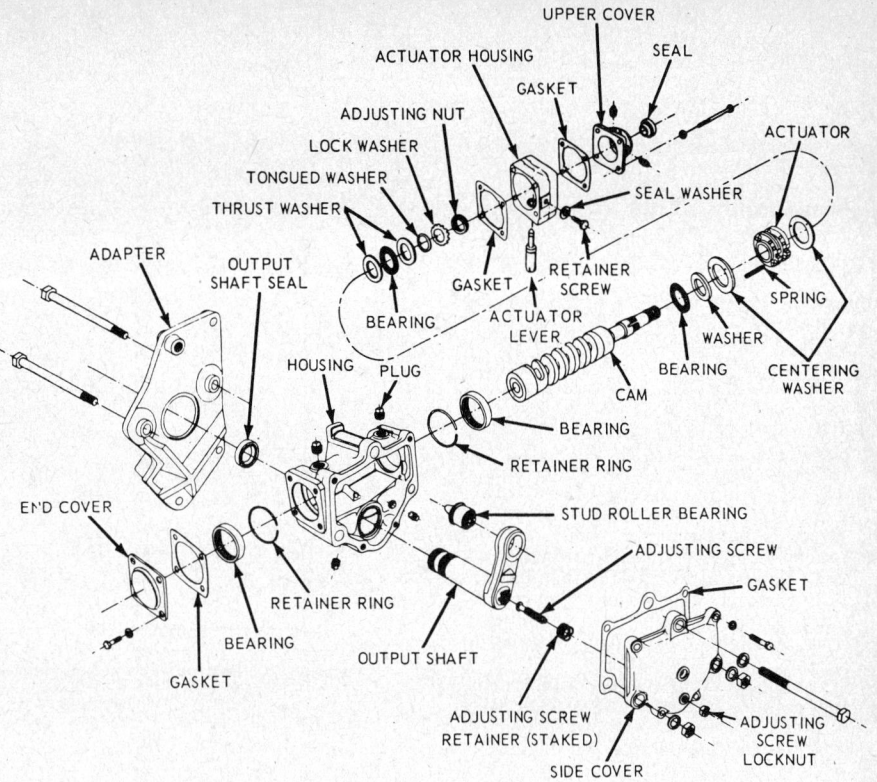

Fig. R6 Disassembled view of Ross model HPS-70 power steering gear

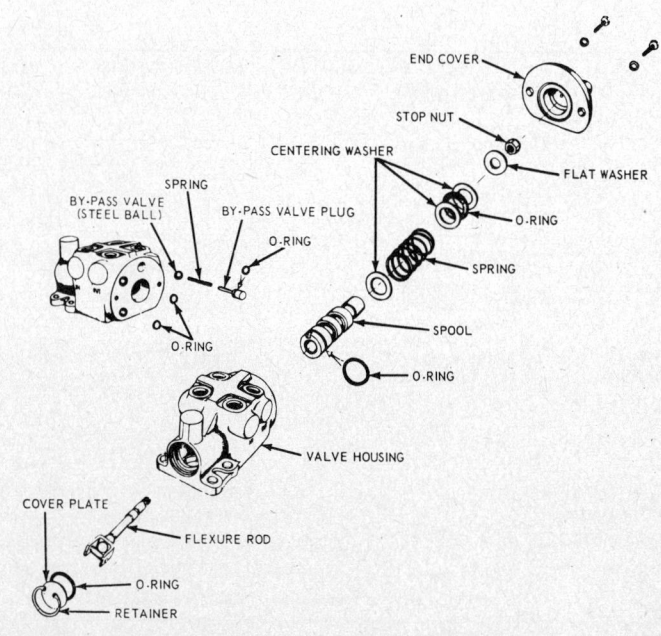

Fig. R7 Control valve housing

721

POWER STEERING GEARS

to gear housing.
10. Assemble shim pack to lever shaft and install shaft in housing.
11. Assemble gasket and side cover to housing.
12. Assemble adjusting screw and lock nut.
13. Adjust screw in side cover as outlined for gear with concentric control valve.

Reassemble Control Valve, Fig. R10

1. Assemble O-ring on spool.
2. Assemble spool in valve body, being sure end with O-ring is toward clevis end of valve. When assembling spool in body, a twisting motion applied to the spool will be helpful. Before reassembling, be sure all parts are thoroughly clean. Light engine oil should be applied to spool and O-rings.
3. Assemble into valve body the centering washer, spring, centering washer, O-ring and centering washer in that order.
4. Assemble flexure rod in spool.
5. Assemble washer and nut to flexure rod and tighten nut to 125-150 inch-lbs.
6. If by-pass valve parts were removed, replace O-ring on plug before assembling in body. Assemble ball, spring and plug in body.
7. Assemble actuator lever in actuator housing, making sure stud end of lever seats in groove of actuator and position slot in other end of lever so that pin in clevis of flexure rod will fit freely into it when mounting valve.
8. Place gasket on actuator housing and mount valve, making sure clevis pin fits freely into slot of actuator lever.
9. Start mounting screws and tighten lightly in rotation before applying the final tightening torque of 10-15 ft-lbs. *Careless tightening may cause valve spool to be pulled off center by actuator lever interference with clevis pin.*
10. Be sure spool moves freely in both directions before assembling end covers as follows: Place steering gear arm on lever shaft. Move steering arm against stop. Apply sufficient effort to actuate spool. Reverse arm against opposite stop to actuate spool in other direction.

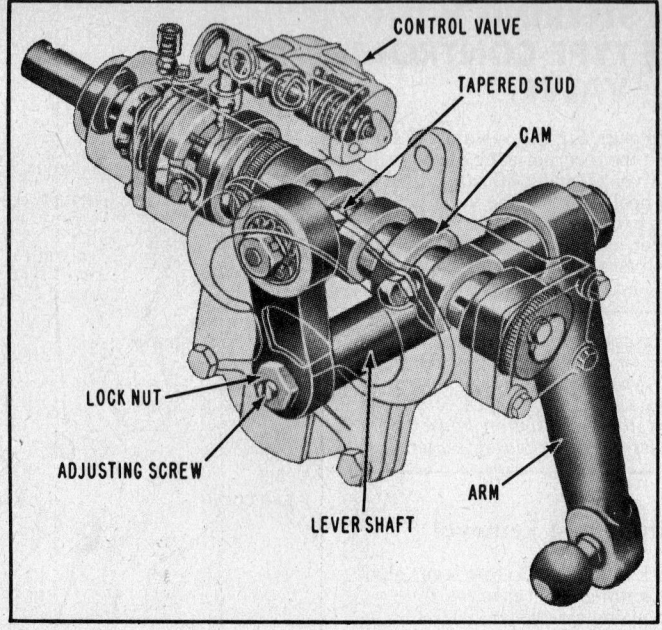

Fig. R8 Ross power steering gear with an integral toggle type control valve

11. Assemble O-rings on end of body and install end cover and tighten to valve body.
12. Assemble O-ring, cover plate and retaining ring.

HF54 & HF64 INTEGRAL TYPE GEARS

These fully integral steering gears incorporate a hydraulic control valve and power cylinder, Figs. R11 and R12. Power is transmitted to the output shaft by gear teeth on the rack piston mating with the sector gear. Fluid flow from the pump is directed to the power cylinder by the control valve which is concentric with the input shaft. Fig. R8 illustrates the operation of the concentric control valve.

Disassembly

1. Rotate input shaft to position sector shaft index mark perpendicular to centerline of gear (straight ahead position).
2. Remove side cover attaching screws, tap end of sector shaft with a mallet to disengage side cover seal and allow gear housing to drain. Remove side cover and sector shaft as an assembly.
3. Remove sector shaft seal adapter screws and adapter from housing.
4. Remove control valve adapter screws and the control valve and rack piston assembly from housing.
5. Remove sector shaft adjusting screw lock

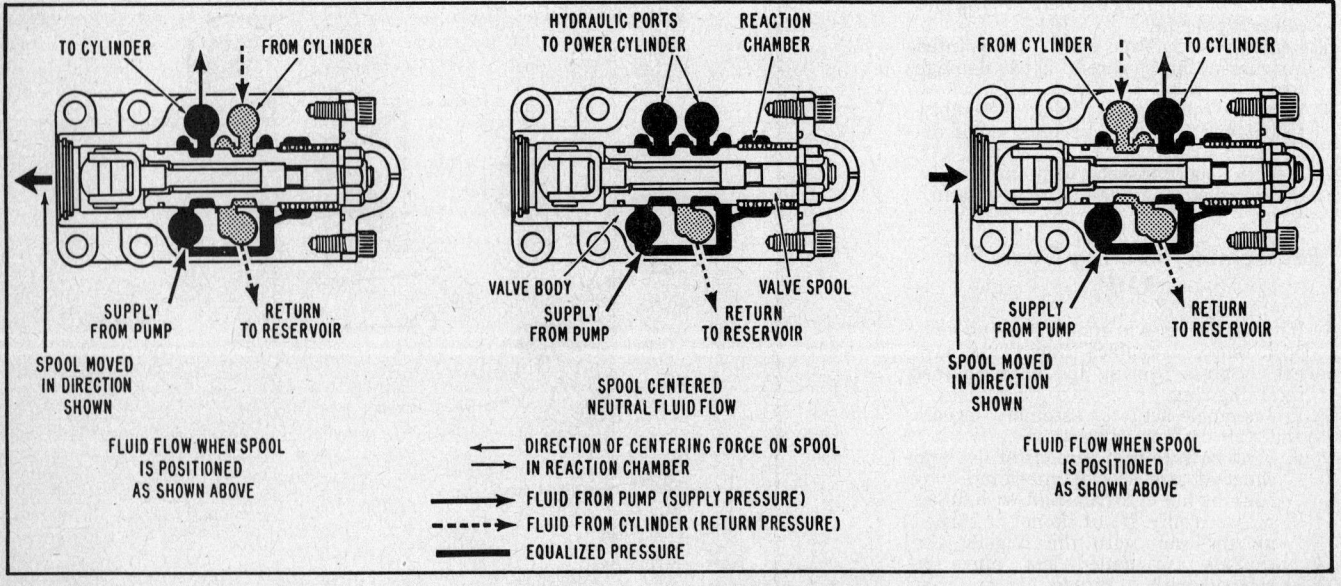

Fig. R9 Toggle type control valve operation

POWER STEERING GEARS

nut and rotate adjusting screw clockwise to remove from side cover.
6. Remove unloader valve retainer, unloader valves, rod and spring from rack piston.
7. Inspect rack piston assembly for damage and, if damage is not evident, do not disassemble rack piston assembly. If rack piston assembly is damaged, disassemble as follows:
   a. Remove ball guide retainer, guide and balls. Tilt rack piston over a clean pan and rock worm shaft to empty all the balls.
   b. Remove worm shaft from rack piston.
8. Clamp input shaft in a soft-jawed vise and remove snap ring, washer, bronze washer, cup, seal and washer. Cut teflon cup from shaft, if necessary.
9. Remove valve cover dirt and water seal, valve cover screws and valve cover from control valve.
10. Unstake adjuster nut lock washer and remove adjuster nut.
11. Remove lock washer, internal tang washer, small bearing race, thrust bearing and large bearing race. Remove control valve and adapter from input shaft.
12. Remove spiral lock ring, seal and washer from valve cover adapter counterbore.
13. The valve should not be disassembled since the body and spool are machined to close tolerances with precision edges. If the valve body or spool is worn or damaged, replace the complete valve assembly. However, if during gear disassembly, the valve parts drop out, reassemble the valve as follows:
   a. Clean all parts with a petroleum-base solvent and blow dry. Do not wipe dry with a cloth since lint may cause binding and sticking of valve components.
   b. Insert spool into valve with machined identification groove in ID of spool facing toward gear housing, Fig. R13.
   c. Insert the six solid centering plunger sets with reaction springs into body with small hole in each plunger facing outward.

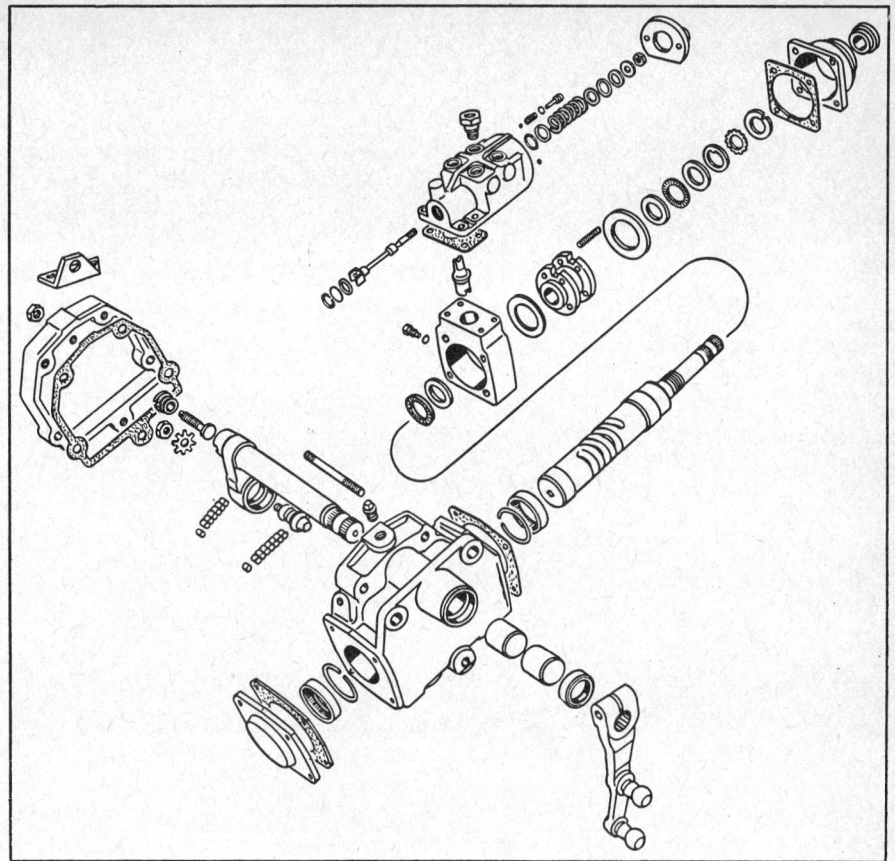

Fig. R10 Disassembled view of a Ross power steering gear with an integral toggle type control valve

Assembly

1. On HF-54 gears, if sector shaft bearing was removed, install snap ring in gear housing outboard side.
2. On all gears, press sector shaft bearing, if removed, into housing until outer surface is flush with housing.
3. Lubricate unloader valve pressure adjusting screw "O" ring and slide into groove on non-threaded end of adjusting screw.
4. Thread adjusting screw into housing lower end until approximately 7/8 inch of the screw protrudes from housing. Install and tighten adjusting screw lock nut.
5. Secure input shaft in a soft-jawed vise, permitting access to either end of shaft.
6. On HF-54 gears, install large thrust race, thrust bearing, control valve with cylinder ports facing toward the shoulder, small bearing race, internal tang washer, lock washer and thrust bearing adjustment nut.
7. On HF-64 gears, install thrust bearing race washer, spacer, control valve with cylinder ports facing toward shoulder, needle thrust bearing, thrust bearing race washer, tang washer, lock washer and thrust bearing adjustment nut.
8. On all gears, torque adjustment nut to 20 ft. lbs., then loosen one-half to one lock washer prongs. Bend one prong into adjustment nut slot. Control valve should rotate freely on input shaft with a torque of 2–3 1/2 in. lbs. and without any end play.
9. Install new washer, seal and spiral lock ring in valve cover adapter counterbore with lip of seal facing toward spiral lock ring.
10. Lubricate valve cover seal and cylinder port seals, then place seals into control valve cover adapter recesses on the surface adjacent to control valve.
11. Reposition input shaft in vise to secure serrated end.
12. Slide adapter over input shaft, align cylinder port seals with control valve ports and install one attaching bolt finger tight.
13. Assemble steel washer, rubber seal, teflon cup with lip facing toward seal, bronze washer and retaining washer. Compress washer and seal and install snap ring on input shaft end, ensuring snap ring is fully seated in groove and recessed area of retaining washer.
14. Clamp rack piston in a soft-jawed vise with ball guide holes facing upward.
15. Expand piston ring and install in piston groove.
16. On HF-54 gears, clean unloader valve threads and install valve into rack piston. Clean seat threads and apply a drop of Lock-tite. Assemble seat with lock washer and torque to 10–15 ft. lbs., then bend lock washer against one flat of seat.
17. On all gears, lubricate input shaft seal and install input shaft into rack piston bore.
18. Install sixteen balls into ball guides while rotating input shaft counterclockwise. Alternate black spacer balls and polished steel balls. Coat ball return guides with grease and install six remaining balls. Secure guide retaining clip to rack piston and torque screws to 8–10 ft. lbs. Bend prong of lock washer against flat of screw.
19. (continued as above — numbering follows)
20. Lubricate sector shaft adjusting screw and place screw head in end slot of sector shaft, then install screw retainer. Tighten retainer to permit rotation of screw with noticeable end play. Stake retainer and check rotational effort.
21. Press new pressure relief plug, if removed or damaged, into side cover until flush with surface.
22. On HF-64 gear, install snap ring into side cover, then on all gears install steel washer with taper facing toward snap ring, leather washer and two piece seal. Ensure the words "Oil Side" are visible on seal after installation.
23. Thread sector shaft adjusting screw and sector shaft assembly into side cover. On HF-54 gears, ensure that the shaft seal has not been mispositioned.
24. On all gears, install outer seal on seal adapter, then the leather washer and inner seal, ensuring the words "Oil Side" are visible on seal after installation.
25. Press input shaft needle bearing, if removed, into control valve cover. Press bearing from part number end to a depth of 1 1/8 inch from valve cover face. Ensure rollers are free to rotate.
26. Install control valve cover seal with lip

723

Power Steering Gears

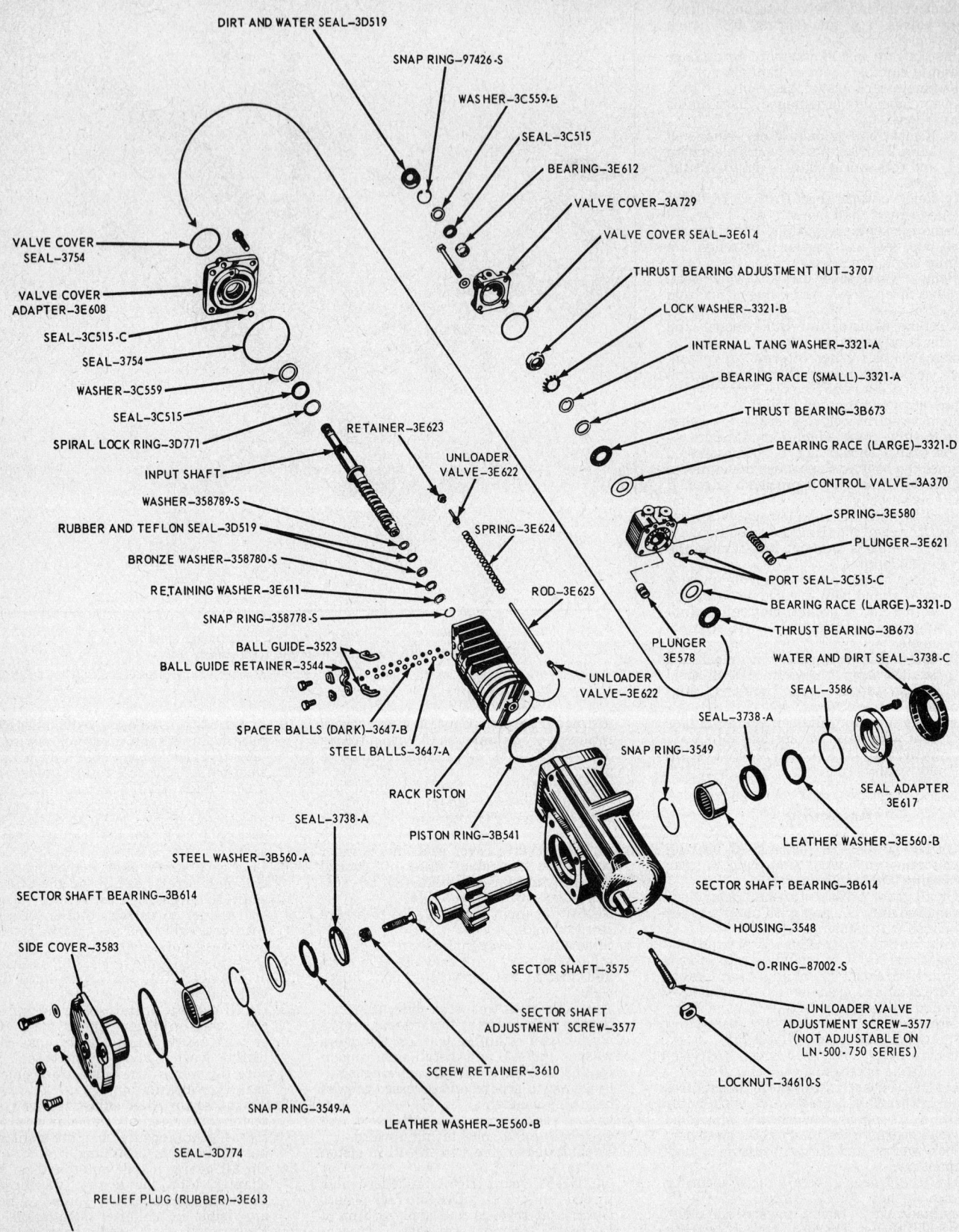

Fig. R11 Disassembled view of Ross model HF-54 integral power steering gear

Power Steering Gears

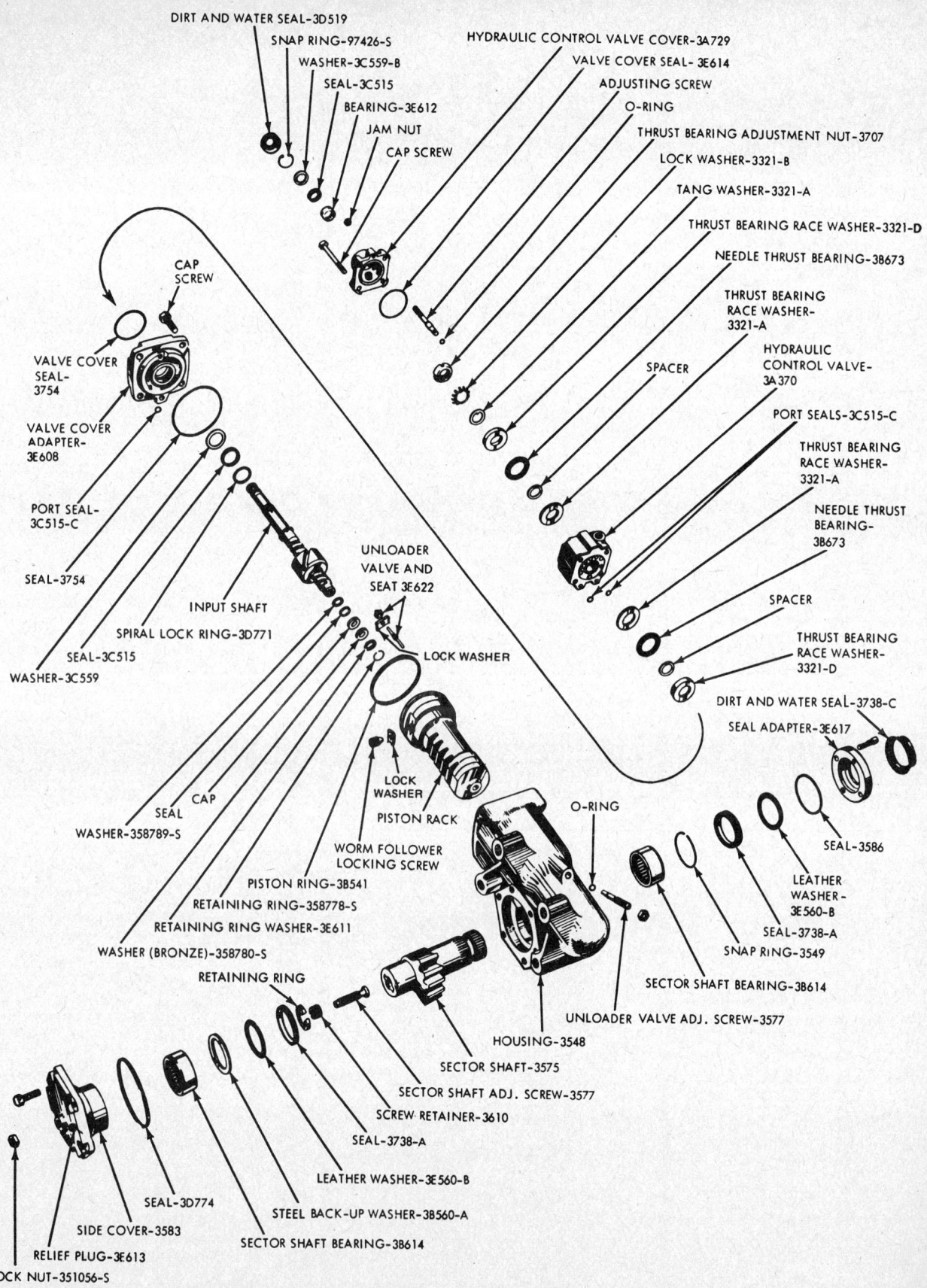

Fig. R12 Disassembled view of Ross model HF-64 integral power steering gear

POWER STEERING GEARS

facing toward needle bearing. Lubricate washer and install on cover, then the snap ring, thereby securing seal and washer.

27. Fill new dirt and water seal with a suitable lubricant and install on control valve cover.
28. Lubricate gear housing bore and start rack piston into bore. Compress ring and move piston into position so piston teeth are visible through side cover opening. Install adapter to housing bolts and remove bolt installed in step 12.
29. Lubricate and install new valve cover seal into valve cover recess, then slide valve cover onto input shaft and install attaching bolts.
30. Rotate input shaft to align rack piston center tooth (marked tooth) with side cover opening.
31. Lubricate and install new side cover "O" ring on cover, then install side cover and sector shaft assembly onto gear housing, ensuring center tooth meshes with center space (marked space). Install and torque side cover screws to 45–55 ft. lbs. on HF-54 gears or 150–170 ft. lbs. on HF-64 gears.
32. Cover sector shaft serrations with tape to protect adapter seal and install adapter over sector shaft and onto gear housing.
33. Pack adapter outer seal with suitable lubricant and install seal on adapter.

Adjustments

Sector Shaft
1. Disconnect drag link from pitman arm.
2. Center steering wheel and check for free movement between sector shaft and rack piston. If the pitman arm moves freely, remove gear from vehicle to adjust.
3. Loosen sector shaft adjusting screw lock nut.
4. Rotate input shaft through full travel at least five times and torque sector shaft adjusting screw to 15–20 in. lbs. while rotating input 90 degrees each side of center.
5. Loosen adjusting screw one turn and measure the torque required to rotate input shaft 90 degrees each side of center.

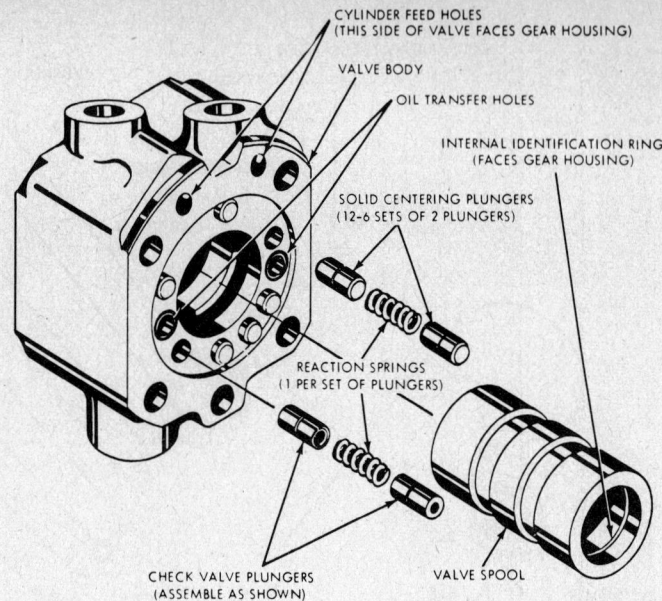

Fig. R13 Hydraulic control valve assembly

Tighten adjusting screw lock nut until snug, then tighten adjusting screw to provide an increased rotating torque of 2–4 in. lbs. 45 degrees each side of center. Torque adjusting screw lock nut to 20–25 ft. lbs.

NOTE: The input torque of the assembled gear with hydraulic oil drained should not exceed 15 in. lbs. for full travel of the output shaft.

Unloader Valve
This adjustment is made for right turn only on HF-54 gears and both turns on HF-64 gears.
1. Install a suitable pressure gauge between pump and steering gear pressure port.
2. Idle engine, turn steering to right stop and note pressure reading.
3. Loosen unloader valve adjusting screw lock nut and turn adjusting screw clockwise to obtain a pressure reading 400 psi below reading noted above.

NOTE: Do not hold steering in extreme position longer than 15 seconds since heat damage may occur to the pump.

4. On HF-64 gears, repeat procedure for left turn.
5. On HF-54 gears, torque adjusting screw lock nut to 17–22 ft. lbs. On HF-64 gears, torque upper adjusting screw lock nut to 15–20 ft. lbs. and the lower adjusting screw lock nut to 20–25 ft. lbs.
6. Remove pressure gauge.

Saginaw Power Steering Gear Section

NON-INTEGRAL ROTARY VALVE TYPE

This power steering system, Fig. S1, consists primarily of three units used in conjunction with a conventional steering gear. They are the control valve, power cylinder and hydraulic pump.

The power cylinder is actuated by the operation of the control valve which supplies hydraulic pressure on either side of the power cylinder piston as required, depending on the position of the valve. The pressure used to operate this system is supplied by a vane-type pump. (The power cylinder and pump are covered elsewhere in this chapter).

Disassembly

In most cases, complete disassembly of the steering gear will not be necessary. It is suggested that only those assemblies which are faulty be disassembled. As in repairing any hydraulically operated unit, cleanliness is of the utmost importance. Therefore, the bench, tools and parts must be kept clean at all times. Thoroughly clean the exterior of the steering gear with a suitable solvent, and when necessary, drain as much of the hydraulic fluid as possible from the unit.

Clamp Yoke Removal
1. With the gear assembly removed from the vehicle, drain as much fluid from the unit as possible. This is not necessary if only the yoke is being replaced.
2. If not previously removed, mark the stub shaft and clamp yoke before removing the yoke so they can be assembled in the same position when the gear is reassembled.
3. Remove bolt and clamp yoke from stub shaft.

Adjuster Plug, Fig. S2
REMOVAL
1. Turn stub shaft to turn pitman arm counterclockwise until ball nut reaches end of its travel at the top.
2. Loosen and remove adjuster plug lock nut.
3. Remove adjuster plug with spanner wrench.
4. Remove upper thrust bearing from steering gear top cover.

DISASSEMBLY
1. Remove O-ring seal.
2. Remove stub shaft oil seal retaining ring and back-up washer.
3. Remove stub shaft oil seal by prying out with screwdriver.
4. Do not remove stub shaft bearing unless inspection shows necessity.

POWER STEERING GEARS

5. Replace all seals, and other parts not in first class condition.

REASSEMBLY
1. Position adjuster plug on wood block.
2. If previously removed, install needle bearing through thrust bearing end of plug. Press against identification end of bearing until end of bearing is flush with bottom surface of stub shaft seal bore.
3. Lubricate new stub shaft oil seal with automatic transmission fluid. Then install seal with lip toward inside of plug and back-up washer far enough into bore of plug to provide clearance for retainer ring.
4. Install oil seal retaining ring, being sure it is seated properly in groove.
5. Lubricate new O-ring seal with vaseline and install on plug.

Rotary Valve Assembly, Fig. S3

The complete valve assembly is a precision unit with selectively fitted parts and is hydraulically balanced at the factory. Only those parts which are marked as service items are replaceable. If replacement of any non-serviceable parts is necessary, the complete rotary valve assembly must be replaced.

The valve assembly rarely requires service with the possible exception of replacing the valve spool dampener O-ring. Do not disassemble the valve unless absolutely necessary since this may result in damage to the assembly. If the valve spool dampener O-ring requires replacement, remove the valve spool only. Replace the O-ring and reinstall spool immediately. Do not disassemble further.

REMOVAL
1. Remove clamp yoke and adjuster plug as outlined above.
2. Remove valve assembly by grasping stub shaft and pulling straight out. It may be necessary to use pliers to aid in removal but use care not to damage stub shaft splines.

DISASSEMBLE
1. Remove spool spring by prying on small coil with screwdriver. Do not pry against valve body as this may result in a sticky valve. Work spring onto bearing diameter of stub shaft, then slide spring off shaft.
2. The diametral clearance between valve and spool may be as little as .0004". The slightest cocking of spool may jam it in valve body. To remove the spool, hold the valve assembly in both hands with stub shaft pointing down and tap stub shaft gently against wood block. It may be necessary to push lightly on valve spool with a pencil or small brass rod by inserting pencil or rod through openings in valve cap until spool is far enough out of valve so it can be grasped by hand, Fig. S4. Withdraw spool with a steady oscillating pull to prevent jamming, Fig. S5.

NOTE: *If a slight sticking occurs, make a gentle attempt to reverse withdrawal procedure. If this does not free spool, it has become cocked in the valve body bore. Do not attempt to force spool in or out of valve body. If such is the case, continue to disassemble valve assembly and return to the spool as outlined later.*

3. Remove stub shaft, torsion bar and valve cap by holding valve in both hands as before, except with thumbs on valve body. Tap torsion bar slightly against work bench. This will dislodge cap from valve body-to-cap pin. The stub shaft, torsion bar and valve cap can then be removed from valve body.

4. If valve spool has become cocked as mentioned above, it can now be freed. By visual inspection on a flat surface, it can be determined in which direction the spool is cocked. A very few light taps with a small soft-faced hammer should align the spool in the bore and free it. *Do not tap the spool with anything metallic. If spool can be rotated it can be removed.*
5. Remove dampener O-ring seal from spool.
6. Do not remove valve rings or ring back-up seals unless inspection shows necessity.

INSPECTION
1. If valve leaks around torsion bar, the entire valve must be replaced.
2. If valve rings and back-up seals show evidence of excessive wear, carefully cut rings and seals and remove them.
3. Check pin in valve body which engages cap. If badly worn, cracked or broken, entire valve should be replaced.
4. Check worm pin groove in valve body

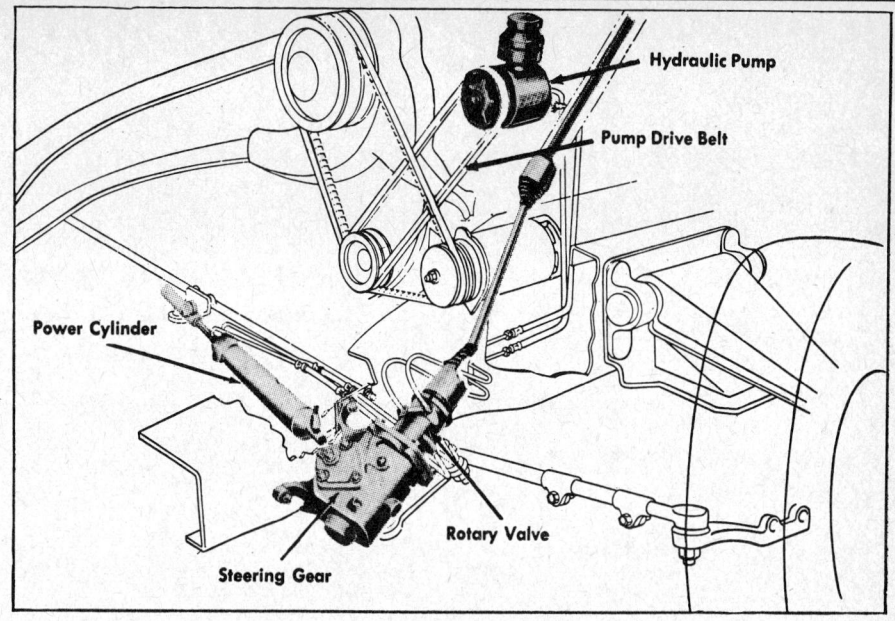

Fig. S1 Saginaw rotary valve power steering gear used on Chevrolet and GMC trucks

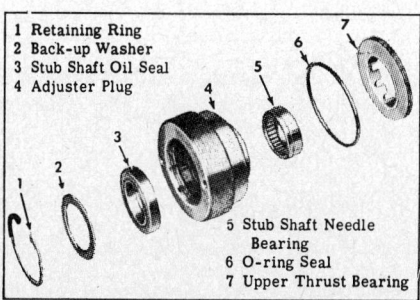

1 Retaining Ring
2 Back-up Washer
3 Stub Shaft Oil Seal
4 Adjuster Plug
5 Stub Shaft Needle Bearing
6 O-ring Seal
7 Upper Thrust Bearing

Fig. S2 Adjuster plug components and upper thrust bearing

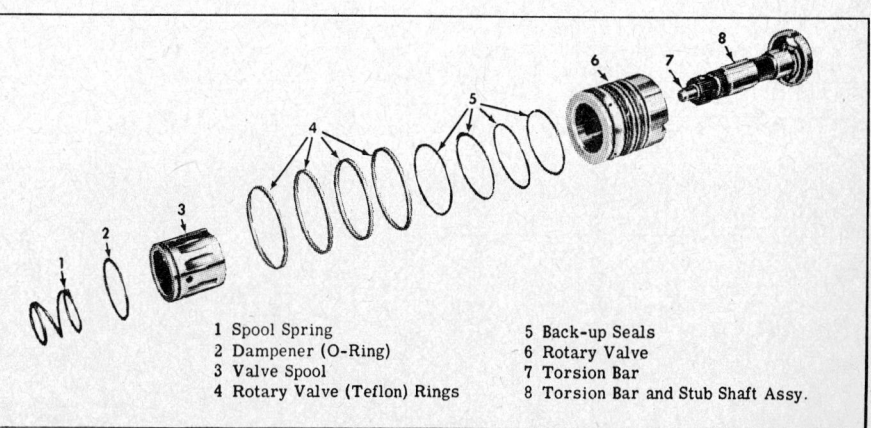

1 Spool Spring
2 Dampener (O-Ring)
3 Valve Spool
4 Rotary Valve (Teflon) Rings
5 Back-up Seals
6 Rotary Valve
7 Torsion Bar
8 Torsion Bar and Stub Shaft Assy.

Fig. S3 Rotary valve components disassembled

POWER STEERING GEARS

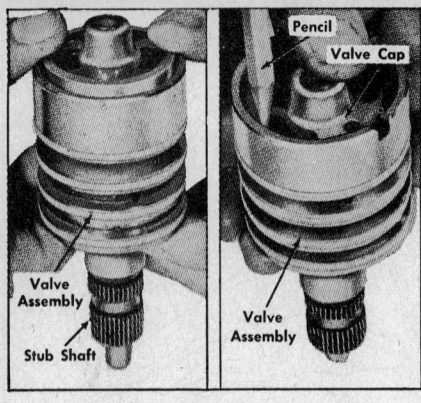

Fig. S4 Loosening valve spool

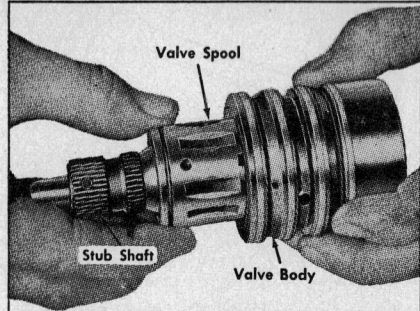

Fig. S5 Removing valve spool

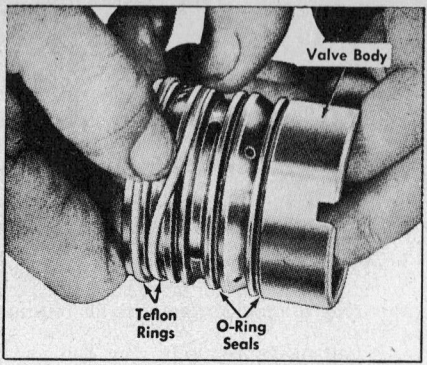

Fig. S6 Installing valve rings

(smaller of two). If worn badly, entire valve should be replaced.
5. Check spool drive pin stub shaft if badly worn replace entire valve.
6. Examine outside diameter of spool for nicks, burrs or bad wear spots. If found, replace entire valve. A slight polish is normal on valve surfaces.
7. If nicks, burrs or bad wear spots are evident on valve, replace entire valve assembly. As on the spool a slight polish is normal on valving surfaces.
8. Check fit of spool in valve body bore without spool dampener O-ring seal and lubricant. Spool should rotate smoothly without binding or catching. If either occurs, entire valve must be replaced. A small burr on the spool or in the valve body can usually be removed with a very fine hone.
9. Check valve spool spring for free length, distortion or collapsed coils. Free length should be .82"; if it measures .79" or less, spring should be replaced.

REASSEMBLY
1. Lubricate four new valve body (Teflon) rings and four new back-up O-ring seals with automatic transmission fluid. Assemble rings and seals on valve body, Fig. S6.

NOTE: *Do not allow seals to become twisted.*

2. Install new spool dampener O-ring seal in spool groove. Lubricate seal with automatic transmission fluid.
3. Assemble stub shaft in valve body, aligning groove in valve cap with pin in valve body. Tap lightly on cap with plastic hammer until cap is against shoulder in valve body with pin in cap groove.

NOTE: *Make sure groove and pin are in line before tapping on cap. Hold these parts together during balance of assembly procedure.*

4. Lubricate valve spool with automatic transmission fluid. Slide spool over stub shaft with notch toward valve body. Align notch with spool drive pin in stub shaft and carefully engage spool in valve body bore.

NOTE: *Because the clearance between spool and valve body is very small, extreme care must be taken when assembling these parts. Push the tool evenly and slowly with a slight oscillating motion until spool reaches drive pin. Rotate spool slowly with pressure until notch engages pin. Before pushing spool completely in, make sure spool dampener O-ring seal is evenly distributed in spool groove. Slowly push spool completely in, using extreme care not to cut or pinch O-ring seal.*

5. Position seal protector, Fig. S7, or equivalent over stub shaft. Slide valve spool spring over seal protector and work spring down until it is seated in undercut part of stub shaft. Take care not to scratch sealing surface of stub shaft.

NOTE: *If during assembly, stub shaft and cap assembly is allowed to slip out of engagement with valve body pin, spool will be permitted to enter valve body too far. Dampener O-ring seal will expand into valve body oil grooves, preventing withdrawal of spool. Attempt to withdraw spool with slight pull and much rotary motion. If this does not free spool after several tries, make sure spool is free to rotate. Then place valve body on a flat surface with notched end up and tap spool with wooden or plastic rod until O-ring seal is cut and spool can be removed. Replace dampener O-ring seal with new part and proceed with assembly as described*

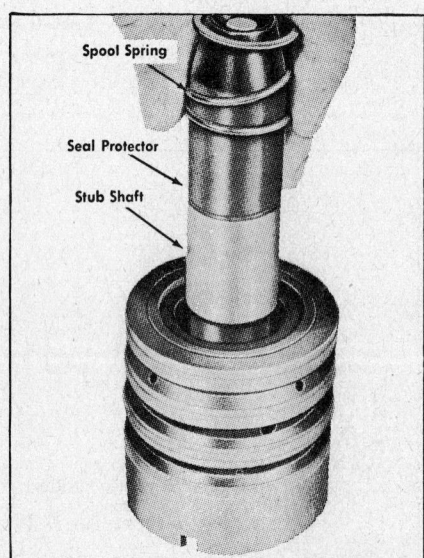

Fig. S7 Installing valve spool spring

above.

STEERING GEAR
Removal

1. Mark clamp bolt on intermediate or lower shaft and steering gear stub shaft so gear can be installed in the same position.
2. Disconnect linkage from pitman arm.
3. Unfasten steering gear shaft from stub shaft.
4. Raise shaft and clamp yoke off stub shaft.
5. On some vehicles it may be necessary to remove lower or intermediate shaft to provide clearance for steering gear removal.
6. Drain as much fluid from gear as possible.
7. Disconnect control valve-to-pump tubes.
8. Unfasten gear from frame and remove.

Disassemble, Fig. S8

1. Remove top cover with worm and ball nut as a unit. Remove lower worm thrust bearing. Hold assembly as shown in Fig. S9 with hand holding ball nut from turning and top cover from dropping.
2. Try action of ball nut on worm shaft. Nut must rotate freely with no evidence of binding or roughness. Tape shaft worm at both ends of ball nut to keep nut from running up or down on shaft.
3. Remove top cover from shaft worm.

CAUTION: *Do not hold worm shaft and ball nut in a vertical position as ball nut will travel by its own weight to end of shaft. If ball nut sharply strikes either end of shaft worm, ball guides will be damaged.*

4. Using a screwdriver and hammer, remove worm seal and back-up washer from top cover.
5. Further disassembly should be confined to that found necessary as a result of inspection.

Reassembly, Fig. S8

1. Position seal back-up washer in top cover over bearing.
2. Lubricate worm seal and press it in to seat against back-up washer. Seal should be positioned so its lip faces away from back-up washer.
3. Insert worm through top cover.
4. Mount gear housing in vise so that top

728

POWER STEERING GEARS

cover opening is up.
5. Lubricate lower worm thrust bearing and position it in cup in lower end of gear housing. Install bearing retainer.
6. Position new top cover gasket on gear housing.
7. Remove tape from worm shaft and rotate ball nut so it reaches end of shaft.
8. Lift top cover, worm and ball nut by grasping top cover and worm. Turn shaft into a vertical position so that ball nut is at bottom. Guide assembly into gear housing until end of shaft contacts lower thrust bearing. In so doing, rotate worm so ball nut return guide clamp faces back-up adjuster opening in housing.
9. Bolt top cover to gear housing and torque to 35-45 ft-lbs.
10. Install pitman shaft and side cover.
11. Align valve body drive pin on worm shaft with narrow pin slot in valve body.

CAUTION: *Do not push against stub shaft as this may cause stub shaft and cap to push out of valve body, allowing valve spool dampener seal to slip in valve body oil grooves. Valve assembly should be pushed in by pressing against body with fingers. Be sure valve body is properly seated before installing and adjusting the adjuster plug. Return port in valve housing should be fully visible when valve body is properly seated.*

Adjustments

THRUST BEARING PRELOAD
1. Install seal protector over end of stub shaft, Fig. S10.
2. Install adjuster plug.
3. Tighten adjuster plug up snugly with spanner wrench, Fig. S11, then back off 1/4 turn.
4. Attach inch-pound torque wrench to stub shaft and measure rotary valve drag, Fig. S11.
5. Adjust bearing so that preload is one to three inch-pounds torque in excess of rotary valve drag while swinging torque wrench back and forth through a 60-degree arc.

NOTE: *Due to the low torque adjustment and because it would be difficult to get an accurate reading on wrench, do not use a torque wrench having a maximum torque reading over 100 inch-pounds. When taking torque readings, take the reading while pulling torque wrench to the right and a reading pulling to the left. Total both readings and take one-half of this total as the average torque.*

6. Using a suitable wrench, install adjuster plug lock nut and tighten to 50-65 ft-lbs. torque.
7. Recheck thrust bearing preload. Total adjustment plus seal drag must not exceed 8 inch-pounds.
8. Install pitman shaft seal so that lips of seal face inside of gear housing.

ADJUSTING BACK-UP ADJUSTER
On gears having a back-up adjuster, install adjuster in gear housing. Then tighten adjuster until it bottoms against ball nut return guide clamp. Back off 1/8 to 1/4 turn and secure in place with adjuster lock nut.

ADJUST PITMAN SHAFT PRELOAD
After steering gear is completely assembled, find center or straight-ahead position of worm by rotating worm through full travel, counting the number of turns and reversing one-half the number of turns counted.

When taking the following torque readings, take a reading pulling the torque wrench to the right and a reading pulling to the left. Total both readings and take one-half of the total as the average torque.

Using the equipment shown in Fig. S12, adjust lash adjuster so that torque is between four and eight inch-pounds in excess of the total bearing preload and valve drag readings previously recorded. The pitman shaft preload reading should be taken with the gear on center and while rotating the steering shaft through an arc of not more than 10 degrees.

Tighten lash adjuster nut to 25-35 ft-lbs. The final over-center reading, which represents the total of the valve and seal drag, worm bearing preload, and lash adjuster preload, should not exceed 16 inch-pounds.

SPOOL VALVE POWER STEERING GEAR

This steering gear is a recirculating ball bearing, worm and sector nut type. A spool type control valve, Fig. S13, is mounted concentrically on the worm shaft and bolted to the lower end of the steering gear housing.

The spool valve is held in neutral position by ten centering plungers and five springs in the valve housing which bear against the thrust bearing and at the same time against the adapter and valve covers.

Removal
1. Remove steering wheel.
2. Disconnect all control linkage, horn parts and brackets attached to steering column.
3. Remove hydraulic connections to control valve. Cover or plug exposed tubes and ports to prevent dirt entering into hydraulic system.
4. Remove pitman arm with a suitable puller.
5. Remove steering gear from vehicle.

Spool Valve Removal, Fig. S13
1. Scribe a mark on valve cover, valve body,

Fig. S8 Saginaw rotary valve power steering disassembled

1 Lock Nut
2 Bolt
3 Lock Washer
4 Side Cover
5 Side Cover Gasket
6 Needle Bearing
7 Pitman Shaft and Sector Gear
8 Lash Adjuster
9 Needle Bearing
10 Oil Seal
11 Lock Washer
12 Nut
13 Steering Gear Housing
14 Drain Plug
15 Expansion Plug
16 Lock Nut
17 Back-up Adjuster
18 Bearing Cup
19 Lower Thrust Bearing
20 Thrust Bearing Cone
21 Stop
22 Ball Nut
23 Needle Bearing
24 Top Cover Gasket
25 Top Cover
26 Back-up Washer
27 Filler Plug
28 Worm Oil Seal
29 Worm Shaft
30 Top Cover Bolt
31 Connectors
32 Lock Washer
33 Worm Balls
34 Ball Return Guides
35 Screw
36 Return Guide Clamp
37 Torsion Bar and Stub Shaft Assembly
38 Rotary Valve
39 Back-up Seals
40 Rotary Valve (Teflon) Rings
41 Valve Spool
42 Dampener O-ring
43 Spool Spring
44 Upper Thrust Bearing
45 O-ring Seal
46 Adjuster Plug
47 Stub Shaft Needle Bearing
48 Stub Shaft Oil Seal
49 Back-up Washer
50 Retaining Ring
51 Lock Nut
52 Valve Body Drive Pin

729

POWER STEERING GEARS

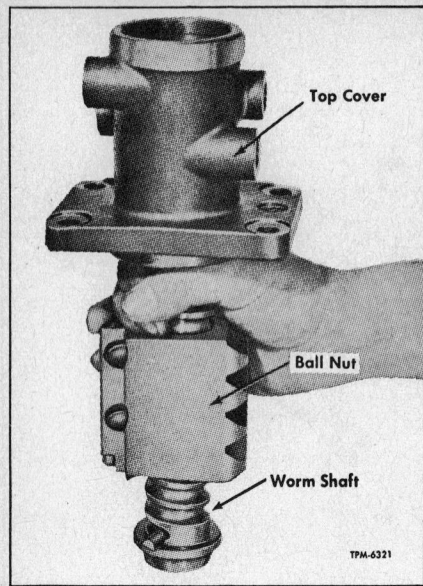

Fig. S9 Top cover, worm and ball nut

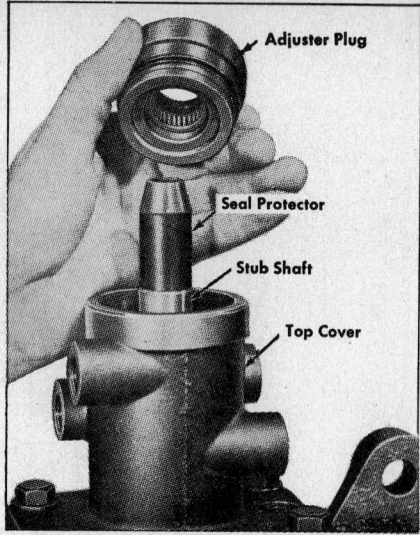

Fig. S10 Installing adjuster plug

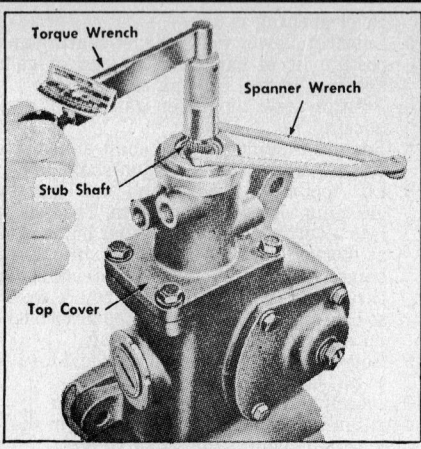

Fig. S11 Adjusting thrust bearing preload

adapter, and steering gear housing to insure proper positioning of parts upon reassembly.
2. Remove valve cover.
3. Remove control valve worm bearing adjuster nut.
4. Remove valve spool preload spring from worm shaft.
5. Remove lower small bearing race, bearing and large bearing race. Keep these parts together so they can be reinstalled together upon reassembly.
6. Remove valve housing, spool, plungers and centering springs as a unit.
7. Remove upper large bearing race, bearing and small bearing race, keeping these parts together so they can be reinstalled together upon reassembly.
8. Remove adapter from gear housing and from worm shaft.

Spool Valve, Disassembly, Fig. S13

1. Remove valve centering plungers and springs from valve body.
2. Remove valve spool from valve housing, noting which end of spool has a groove or counterbore on the I.D. so parts can be reassembled properly.

Spool Valve, Reassemble, Fig. S13

1. Coat valve centering plungers and valve spool with grease containing zinc oxide #1.
2. Install valve spool in valve body with groove or counterbore at same end in relation to valve body as noted upon disassembly.
3. Do not force spool into valve body. When spool is properly aligned it will drop into place. Forcing spool will damage both spool and valve bore.
4. Install valve centering springs into their bores in valve body.
5. Install a plunger at each end of centering springs.

Steering Gear

The procedure for disassembling and reassembling the steering gear is similar to that for the mechanical gear of the same design. However, adjustments are somewhat different, the procedure for which follows:

Adjustments

Before adjusting the steering gear, be sure to check the following important items:
1. The thrust bearings have small races away from valve faces.
2. Scribed marks on valve body, adapter and steering gear housing are aligned.
3. Install valve spool preload spring on worm shaft.
4. Install a new adjuster plug nut finger tight.
5. Install valve clamping ring and valve end cover-to-adapter bolts. Tighten bolts to 15–20 ft-lbs.

NOTE: *A valve clamping ring, Fig. S14,*

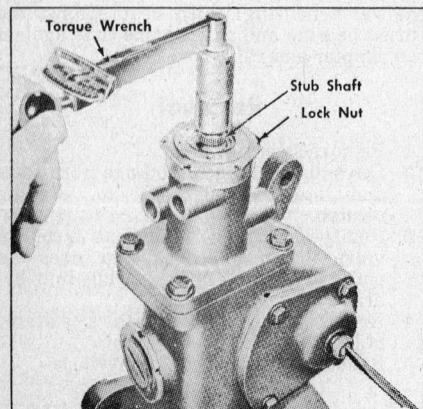

Fig. S12 Adjusting pitman shaft preload

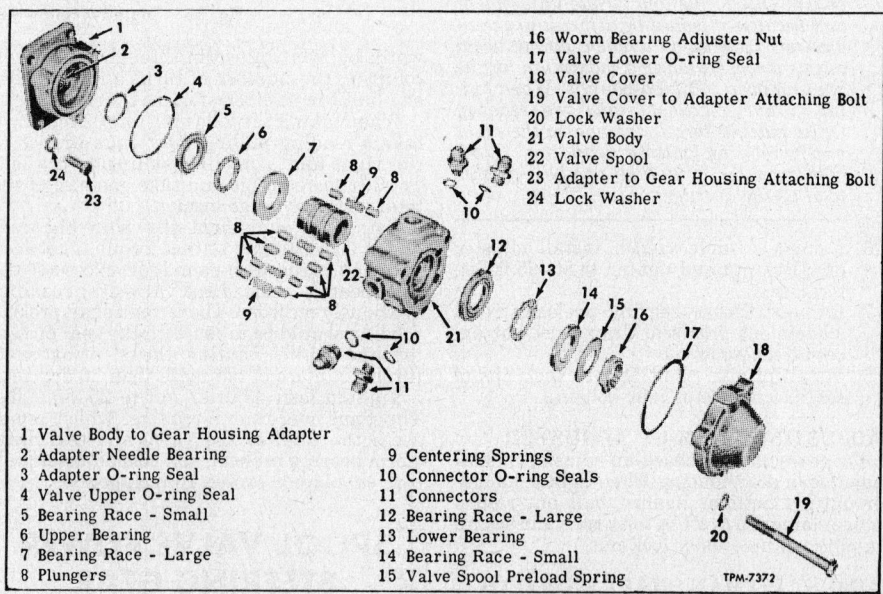

Fig. S13 Spool valve components disassembled

1 Valve Body to Gear Housing Adapter
2 Adapter Needle Bearing
3 Adapter O-ring Seal
4 Valve Upper O-ring Seal
5 Bearing Race - Small
6 Upper Bearing
7 Bearing Race - Large
8 Plungers
9 Centering Springs
10 Connector O-ring Seals
11 Connectors
12 Bearing Race - Large
13 Lower Bearing
14 Bearing Race - Small
15 Valve Spool Preload Spring
16 Worm Bearing Adjuster Nut
17 Valve Lower O-ring Seal
18 Valve Cover
19 Valve Cover to Adapter Attaching Bolt
20 Lock Washer
21 Valve Body
22 Valve Spool
23 Adapter to Gear Housing Attaching Bolt
24 Lock Washer

Power Steering Gears

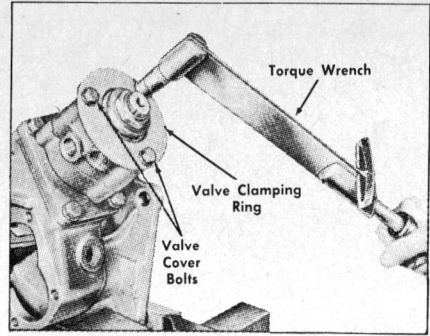

Fig. S14 Adjusting worm bearing preload

can be made from a valve cover by cutting out the middle portion and leaving outer ring only.

6. Install steering wheel. Hold wheel on center and tighten adjuster nut firmly to remove all end play of valve spool.
7. Back off nut and retighten lightly. Release steering wheel, making sure nut exerts light pressure against spring loaded plungers, Fig. S14.
8. Tighten nut until a load of 1/2 to 1 lb. is measured with a spring scale on the rim of the 18" steering wheel. Stake nut in place.
9. Remove valve clamping ring and position valve cover with marks scribed previously with related parts.
10. Install attaching bolts and torque to 15–20 ft-lbs.
11. With lash adjuster screw and shim in place in slotted end of pitman shaft, start side cover over end of shaft. Insert screwdriver into hole in side cover to engage slot in screw.
12. Turn steering shaft until ball nut is in approximate center of shaft worm. Center tooth of pitman shaft sector gear must enter center tooth space of ball nut rack.
13. Insert pitman shaft into housing, meshing teeth as described.
14. Turn lash adjuster to pull cover over end of shaft. Back off adjuster screw to permit lash between sector and ball nut.
15. Install and tighten side cover bolts.
16. With gear on center, adjust pitman shaft adjuster screw so that pull on the 18" diameter steering wheel is 1¼ to 2 pounds through a 20-degree arc over center. Tighten lock nut.
17. Total pull on 18" wheel for all adjustments should be 1⅛ to 2 pounds over center.
18. Install pitman shaft oil seal.

INTEGRAL ROTARY VALVE TYPE, SINGLE PISTON

This type power steering gear, Fig. S15, operates entirely by displacing oil to provide hydraulic pressure assists only when turning. As the entire gear assembly is always filled with oil, all internal components of the gear are immersed in oil, making periodic lubrication unnecessary. In addition this, oil acts as a cushion to absorb road shocks that may be transmitted to the driver.

The steering shaft, hydraulic valve, worm and rack piston nut are all in line, making a compact and space saving steering gear. All oil passages are internal except the pressure and return hoses between gear and pump.

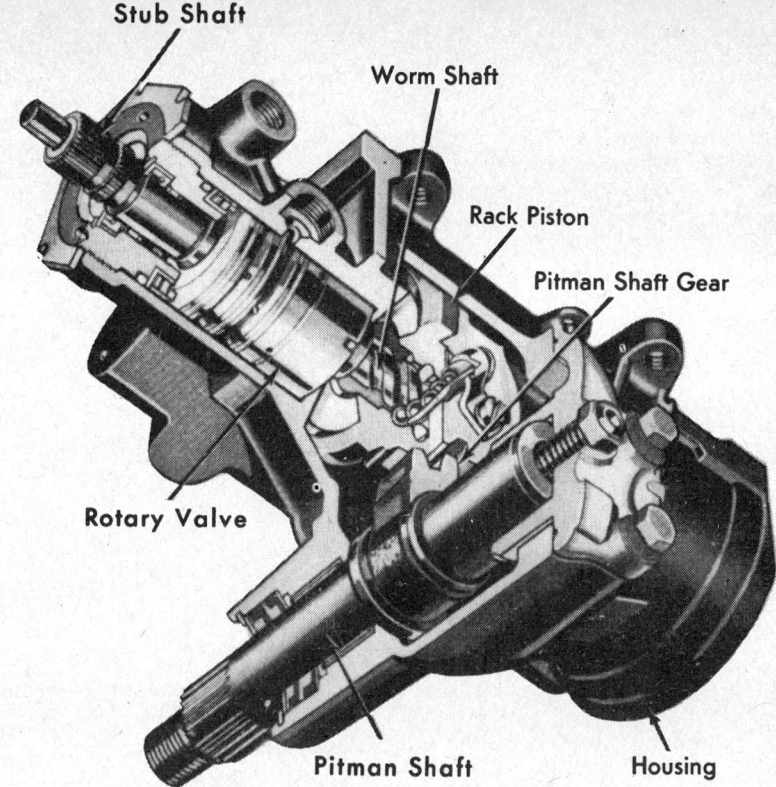

Fig. S15 Integral rotary valve power steering gear, single piston

MAINTENANCE

Four factors affect power operation of the steering system: fluid level and condition, drive belt tension, pump pressure and steering gear adjustment. These should always be checked before any major service operations are performed.

Conditions such as, hard or loose steering, road shock or vibrations are not always due to steering gear or pump, but are often related instead to such factors as low tire pressure and front end alignment. These factors should be checked and corrected before any adjustment of the steering gear is made.

Checking Fluid Level

1. Run engine to normal operating temperature, then shut it off. Remove reservoir filler cap and check oil level on dipstick. Level should be up to "Full" mark on dipstick.
2. If level is low, add power steering fluid to proper level on dipstick and replace filler cap.

NOTE: *When adding less than one pint of fluid, it is permissible to use automatic transmissioin fluid. When adding larger quantities or when making a complete fluid change, it is recommended that special power steering fluid be used.*

3. When checking fluid level after system has been serviced, air must be bled from the system as follows:

Bleeding System

1. With wheels turned all the way to the left, add the recommended fluid to the "Add" mark on dipstick.
2. Start engine. While running at fast idle, recheck fluid level and, if necessary, add fluid to the "Add" mark on dipstick.
3. Bleed system by turning wheels from side to side without hitting stops. Maintain fluid level just above internal pump casting. Fluid with air in it will have a light tan appearance. This air must be eliminated from fluid before normal steering action can be obtained.
4. Return wheels to center position and continue to run engine for two or three minutes, then shut it off.
5. Road test vehicle to make sure steering functions normally and is free from noise.
6. Recheck fluid level, making sure level is at the "Full" mark.

GEAR ADJUSTMENTS ON VEHICLE

When the steering gear is thought to be out of adjustment, a quick check can be made by moving the steering wheel back and forth with short slow motions at the "on-center" position with engine shut off. Excessive looseness felt or heard indicates that either the pitman shaft or the thrust bearing requires adjustment.

NOTE: In vehicle steering gear adjustments are not recommended for 1974–76 Dodge, Jeep, Plymouth and 1975–76 Chevrolet and GMC vehicles. Steering gear adjustments for

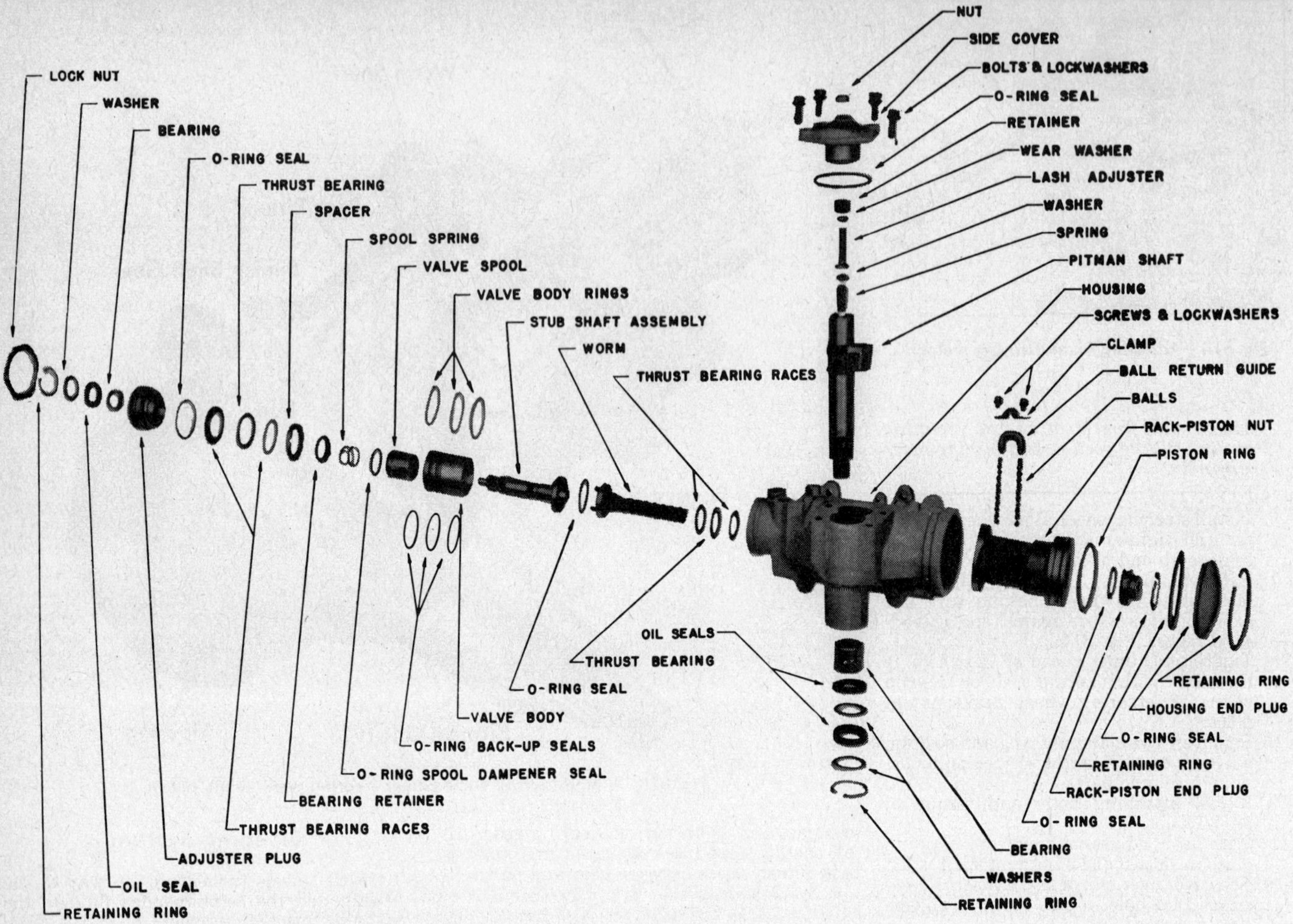

Power Steering Gears

Fig. S16 Integral rotary valve power steering gear disassembled

these vehicles are made with the steering gear removed from the vehicle as outlined under "Bench Adjustments."

Over-Center Adjustment

1. Disconnect pitman arm from pitman shaft.
2. Loosen pitman shaft adjusting screw locknut, back adjusting screw out to limit of travel, then turn screw inward 1/2 turn.
3. Locate center of steering wheel travel and using an inch pound torque wrench connected to the steering shaft nut, rotate wheel through center of travel and note torque reading (combined ball and thrust bearing preload).
4. Tighten adjusting screw until torque reading is 3-6 in. lbs. on Chevrolet and GMC or 6 in. lbs. on Ford and Jeep more than the combined ball and thrust bearing preload noted in the above step. Total steering gear preload must not exceed 14 in. lbs. on Chevrolet and GMC trucks. Tighten locknut and recheck preload.
5. Connect pitman arm to pitman shaft.

STEERING GEAR

Disassemble

1. Referring to Fig. S16, position gear in vise with gear housing end plug facing up.
2. Rotate gear housing end plug retaining ring so that one end of ring is over hole in housing. Spring one end of ring with a punch to allow screw-driver to be inserted to lift ring out, Fig. S17.
3. Rotate coupling flange counterclockwise

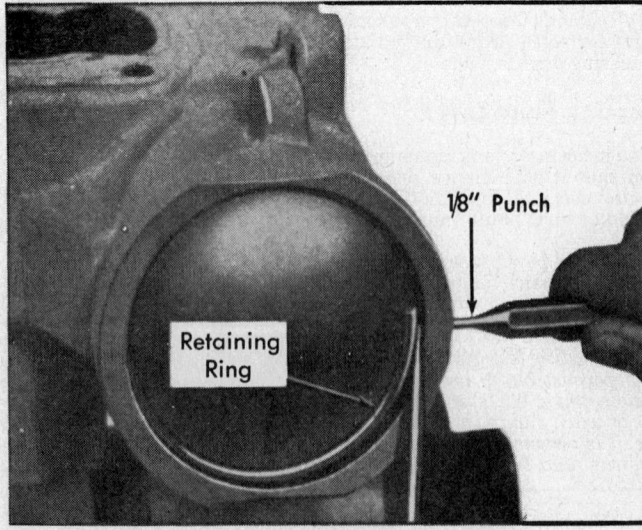

Fig. S17 Removing end plug retaining ring

POWER STEERING GEARS

Fig. S18 Installing rack-piston arbor & ring compressor

Fig. S19 Removing adjuster plug

until rack-piston just forces end plug out of housing. Remove plug from housing.

CAUTION: *Do not rotate any further than necessary or balls will fall out of their circuit and pitman shaft teeth and rack-piston will become disengaged.*

4. Remove rack-piston end plug, using a 1/2" square drive.

NOTE: *To make removal easier, tap rack-piston end plug with a plastic mallet to unseat threads. This is important as end plug is tightened to 75–80 ft. lbs. during assembly and could break during removal if not handled carefully.*

5. Remove lock nut from pitman shaft adjuster screw and discard.
6. Remove four side cover retaining screws and washers from cover.
7. Rotate pitman shaft adjuster screw with an Allen wrench until side cover is lifted free of housing.
8. Separate side cover from pitman shaft; discard side cover O-ring seal.
9. Turn coupling flange until pitman shaft teeth are centered in housing.
10. Tap end of pitman shaft with a soft mallet and slide pitman shaft out of housing.
11. Remove housing end plug O-ring seal and discard.
12. Insert Rack-Piston Arbor into rack-piston against end of worm, Fig. S18. Turn coupling flange counterclockwise, while holding tool tightly against worm, to force rack-piston onto arbor, and remove rack-piston from gear housing.
13. Remove stub shaft-to-coupling flange retaining screw and remove flange.
14. Remove adjuster plug lock nut by breaking it loose with hammer and punch, and remove lock nut from housing.
15. Loosen adjuster plug and remove from housing, Fig. S19.
16. Remove valve assembly by grasping stub shaft and pulling out.
17. Remove worm, lower thrust bearing and races from upper end of housing.

Replacing Valve Spool Dampener "O" Ring (Only If Gear Squawks)

NOTE: *The rotary valve assembly includes the valve body, valve spool and stub shaft assembly. All these parts are precision units and are hydraulically balanced at the factory. Under no circumstances are parts in this unit to be replaced or interchanged with other parts or units. If unit parts are scored or damaged the entire rotary valve assembly is to be replaced.*

1. To replace the valve spool dampener "O" ring, work spool spring into bearing diameter of stub shaft and remove spool spring.
2. Tap end of stub shaft gently against workbench to remove valve spool. *The diametrical clearance between the valve body and spool may be as low as .0004". The slightest cocking of the spool may jam it in the valve body.*
3. Remove valve spool dampener "O" ring.
4. Install new "O" ring in valve spool groove, then lubricate seal in automatic transmission fluid. Do not allow seal to twist in groove.
5. With notch end of spool towards valve body, install spool, aligning spool notch with pin in stub shaft, Fig. SR6.
6. *Because of the small clearance between spool and valve body, extreme care must be taken when assembling these parts. Push spool evenly and slowly with a slight oscillating motion until spool reaches drive pin. Before pushing spool completely in, make sure dampener "O" ring seal is evenly distributed in spool groove. Slowly push spool completely in, with extreme care taken not to cut or pinch "O" ring seal.*
7. Slide spool spring over stub shaft and work spring into position.

Disassemble Rotary Valve

1. If used, work spool spring onto bearing diameter of stub shaft and remove spool spring.
2. Tap end of stub shaft gently against workbench to remove valve spool.

NOTE: *Because of the slight clearance between valve body and spool, the slightest cocking of spool may jam it in valve body. If slight cocking occurs, make a gentle attempt to reverse removal procedure. If this does not free spool, it has become cocked in valve body bore and may be removed later.*

3. Remove and discard valve spool dampener "O" ring.
4. Remove stub shaft, torsion bar (small diameter bar extending through stub shaft) and valve cap by tapping end of torsion bar lightly with a plastic hammer. This will dislodge cap from valve body cap pin, Fig. S20. Do not disassemble stub shaft as these parts are pinned together and serviced only as an assembly.
5. If valve spool has become cocked as mentioned above, first inspect parts to determine in which direction the spool is cocked. A few very light taps with a plas-

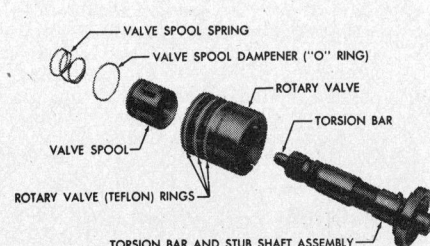

Fig. S20 Rotary valve disassembled

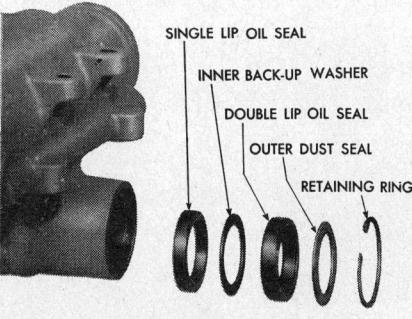

Fig. S21 Pitman shaft seals & washers

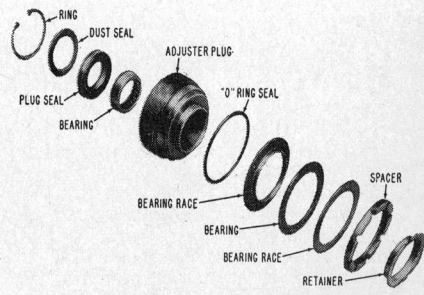

Fig. S22 Adjuster plug disassembled

POWER STEERING GEARS

Fig. S23 Loading rack-piston nut

tic hammer should align and free the spool in the bore. Remove and discard "O" ring dampener seal from spool.
6. Carefully remove valve body Teflon rings and ring back-up "O" ring seals.

Disassemble Housing

1. Remove pitman shaft outer dust seal retaining ring, Fig. S21.
2. Remove outer dust seal.
3. Remove seal (double lip) by inserting off-set screwdriver between seal and back-up washer and prying out of housing.
4. Remove back-up washer.
5. Remove seal (single lip) by cutting and collapsing seal.
6. Remove pitman shaft needle bearings (if necessary) with a suitable driver.
7. If connectors are to be removed, tap threads in holes of connectors using 5/16-18 NF tap. Remove connectors by using threaded bolt into tapped holes with washer and nut as extractor.

ASSEMBLE SUB-ASSEMBLIES

Refer to Fig. S16 and lubricate all parts as they are assembled.
1. Screw lash adjuster through side cover until cover bottoms on pitman shaft gear. Install lash adjuster lock nut while holding lash adjuster with 7/32" Allen wrench.
2. Mount adjuster plug in vise with soft jaws.
3. If it has been removed, assemble needle bearing by pressing towards thrust bearing end of adjuster plug against identification end of bearing. End of bearing to be flush with bottom surface of stub shaft seal bore.
4. Install stub shaft far enough to provide clearance for dust seal and retaining ring. Install new dust seal with rubber surface outward. Install new retaining ring.
5. Assemble large thrust bearing race, thrust bearing, small race and spacer (with grooves up) on adjuster plug, Fig. S22, and secure with retainer.

Assembly Rotary Valve

1. Assemble one valve body Teflon ring back-up "O" ring seal in each groove in valve body, being sure seals do not become twisted.
2. Assemble valve Teflon rings in ring grooves over "O" ring seals by carefully slipping rings over valve body. The rings may appear loose or twisted in the grooves but the heat of the oil during subsequent operation will cause them to straighten.

3. Install valve spool dampener "O" ring seal in valve spool groove, being sure it is not twisted.
4. Insert stub shaft through valve spool, engaging spool locking pin.
5. Pull valve spool and stub shaft assembly into valve body, aligning stub shaft notch and valve body pin.
6. If used, slide spool spring over stub shaft and place into position.
7. Lubricate cap-to-worm "O" ring and install in valve body. *During assembly of the valve, if the stub shaft and cap is allowed to slip out of engagement with the valve body pin, the spool will be permitted to enter the valve body too far. The dampener "O" ring seal may expand into valve body oil grooves, preventing removal of spool. If this happens, remove spool spring and disassemble rotary valve. Press on spool until "O" ring seal is cut and can be removed. Install new "O" ring and reassemble.*

Assemble Housing

1. With stamped end of needle bearing facing outward, drive bearing into bore from outside of housing until flush. Make sure bearings rotate freely.
2. Lubricate cavity between lips of pitman shaft (double lip) seal with power steering fluid.
3. Lubricate and install pitman shaft seals as shown in Fig. S21. Make sure seal lips are properly positioned, retaining ring is seated.
4. If connectors were removed, install new ones by driving them into place.

Assemble Rack-Piston and Worm

1. Lubricate and install new ring back-up seal and Teflon piston ring on rack-piston nut, being careful ring and seal do not

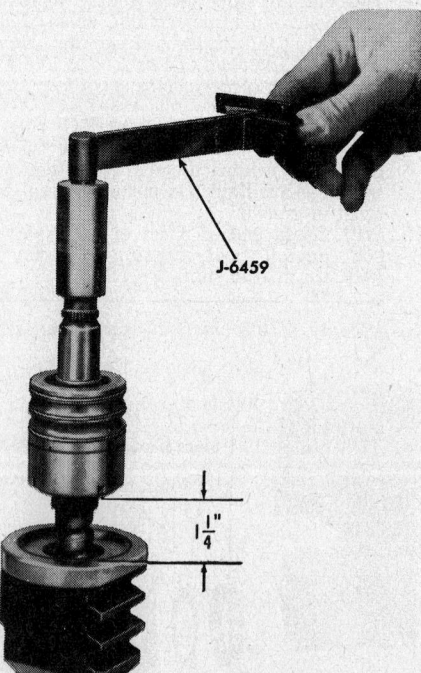

Fig. S24 Checking worm preload

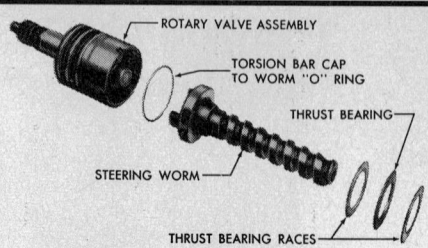

Fig. S25 Worm shaft & rotary valve disassembled

twist during installation.
2. Insert worm into rack-piston nut to bearing shoulder.
3. Align ball return guide holes with worm groove. On Ford, International Harvester and Jeep units, load 16 balls into guide hole nearest Teflon piston ring. On Dodge and Plymouth units load 17 balls into guide hole nearest teflon piston ring. On Chevrolet and GMC gears, load 15 balls on 1969–70 units or 17 balls on 1971–76 units into guide hole nearest teflon piston ring. Slowly rotate worm to left when loading balls into circuit, Fig. S23. If balls are installed properly, the worm should turn out of the rack-piston nut.

NOTE: Install black and silver balls alternately as black balls are .0005 inch smaller than silver balls.

4. Fill one-half of ball return guide with remaining balls. Place other guide over balls and plug each end with heavy grease to prevent balls from falling out when installing guides into rack-piston nut.
5. Insert guides into guide holes of rack-piston nut. Make sure black ball in guide is installed next to white ball in rack piston. Guides should fit loosely.

Check Worm Preload

The worm groove is ground with a high point in the center. When the rack-piston nut passes over this high point, a preload of a 1 to 4 inch pounds torque should be obtained.
1. With worm pointing up, clamp rack-piston nut in a vise with soft jaws (do not hold rack-piston nut in area of Teflon ring).
2. Place valve on worm, engaging worm drive pin.
3. Rotate worm until it extends 1¼" from rack-piston nut to thrust bearing face, Fig. S24. This is the center position.
4. Attach an inch pound torque wrench with socket on stub shaft, Fig. S24. Oscillate wrench through a total arc of approximately 60° in both directions several times and take a reading. The highest reading obtained with worm rotating should be between 1 and 4 inch pounds. Take a torque reading pulling the torque wrench to the right and a reading pulling the wrench to the left. Total both readings and take one-half of this total as the average torque. *Do not use a torque wrench having maximum torque reading of more than 100 inch pounds.*

Refitting Rack-Piston Balls

Do not refit balls unless the steering is loose. If such is the case, a thrust adjustment

POWER STEERING GEARS

Fig. S26 Installing adjuster plug

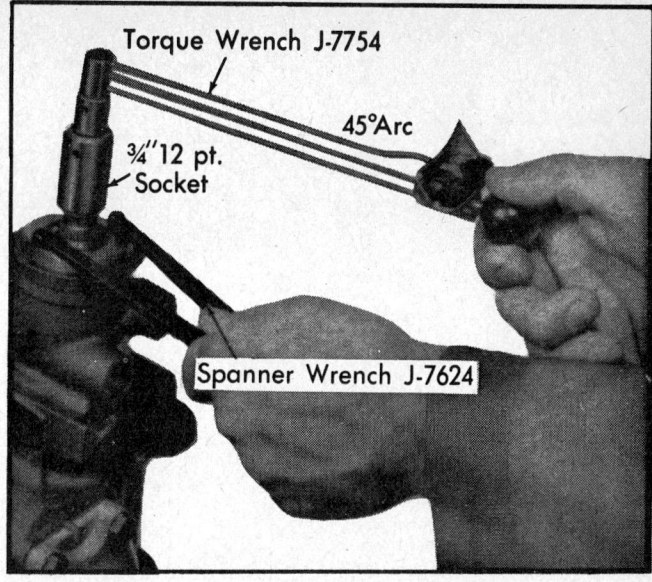

Fig. S29 Thrust bearing preload adjustment, units equipped with flat thrust races

and over-center adjustment should correct the problem if it lies in the steering gear. If balls are pitted or rough, then select the proper ball size for proper adjustment.

If the torque reading obtained above is too high or too low (on new balls only), disassemble and reassemble, using the next size smaller (or larger) balls and recheck worm preload.

A rack-piston nut with a ball size of 7 does not have a number stamped on the flat surface. For ball sizes other than 7, the ball size is stamped on the flat surface of the rack-piston nut. Ball sizes are numbered from 6 to 11, with 6 being the smallest and 11 the largest. Ball sizes are graduated in increments of .00008" from .28117" to .28157".

STEERING GEAR, ASSEMBLE

Install Rack-Piston Worm and Valve

1. Install valve and worm in housing as a unit, Fig. S25.
2. Install new "O" rings on adjuster plug.
3. Install adjuster plug on stub shaft in gear housing finger tight, Fig. S26.
4. Holding a suitable Teflon ring compressor sleeve tightly against shoulder of gear housing, insert rack-piston nut and arbor into housing, holding arbor until it contacts worm end, Fig. S18.
5. Holding arbor tight against worm, turn stub shaft flange and worm to draw ball nut onto worm and into housing until arbor is free. Be certain that no balls drop out.
6. Remove arbor and sleeve.

Install Rack-Piston Nut End Plug

1. Install new "O" ring seal on end plug, being careful not to allow seal to twist in groove.
2. Install end plug in rack-piston nut by pressing into place.
3. Install end plug retaining ring, being sure ring is bottomed in its groove.

Install Housing Lower End Plug

1. Install new housing end plug "O" ring seal.
2. Insert end plug into gear housing and seat against "O" ring. Slight pressure may be necessary to seat end plug properly.
3. Install end plug retainer ring so end of ring extends over and at least 1/2" beyond ring removal assist hole.

Install Pitman Shaft Gear and Side Cover

1. Install stub shaft flange and turn steering worm until center groove of rack-piston is aligned with center of pitman shaft needle bearings.
2. Install new side cover "O" ring.
3. Install pitman shaft gear so that center tooth of gear meshes with center groove of rack-piston. Make sure side cover "O" ring is in place before pushing cover against housing.
4. Install and torque side cover screws to 25-30 ft. lbs. torque.

Install Stub Shaft Flange

Rotate stub shaft slightly over two complete turns from either extreme right or left turn. This will place gear in center position, which will place torsion bar pin through stub shaft in a straight up and down position.

Rotate flange so the bolt with the large

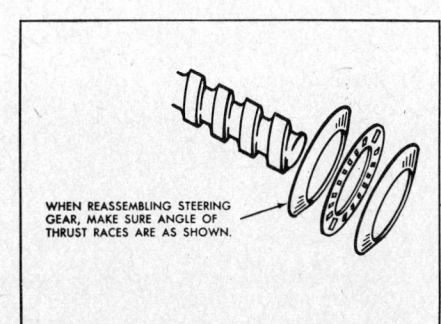

Fig. S27 Conical type thrust races

head is in top position. Visually align the block tooth in the serrations of the flange with the torsion bar pin and install flange of stub shaft. Tighten flange clamping bolt to a torque of 25-30 ft. lbs.

SUB-ASSEMBLIES, INSTALL

1. Position gear housing in vise with adjuster plug end facing up.
2. Lubricate worm shaft, lower thrust bearing and races with power steering fluid, then position thrust bearing and races on worm.

NOTE: Some 1974-77 steering gear assemblies may incorporate conical type thrust races, Fig. S27. When servicing a steering gear equipped with the flat type thrust races, it is recommended that the flat thrust races are replaced with the new conical type. The thrust bearing for these units remains unchanged.

3. Align valve body drive pin on worm with narrow pin slot on valve body. Be sure O-ring seal between valve body and worm head is installed.
4. Position valve body and worm shaft in housing as a unit.

CAUTION: *Do not push against stub shaft as this might cause stub shaft and cap to pull out of valve body, allowing spool seal to slip into valve body oil grooves. Valve assembly can be installed by pushing on outer diameter of valve body housing with the fingers of both hands. Make certain that Teflon rings are not binding on inside of housing. Valve is properly seated when oil return hole in gear housing is fully visible.*

5. Place a suitable seal protector over end of stub shaft, Fig. S26.
6. Lubricate new adjuster plug O-ring seal with power steering fluid and install in

735

POWER STEERING GEARS

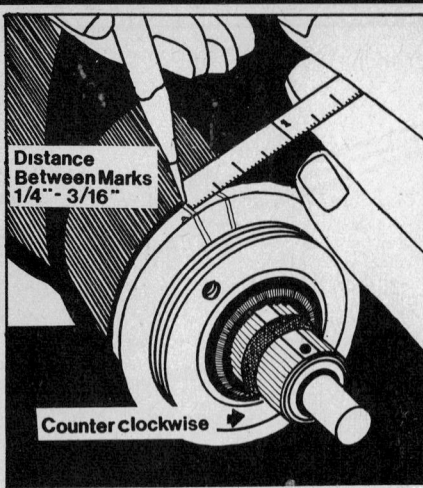

Fig. S28 Thrust bearing preload adjustment, units equipped with conical thrust races

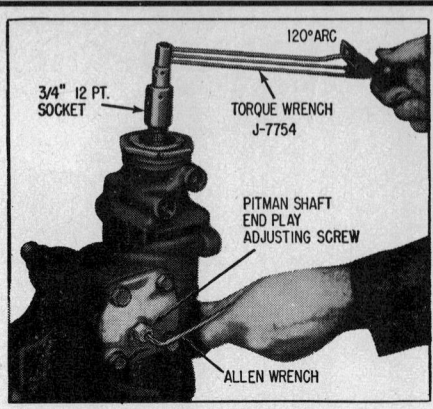

Fig. S30 Over-center preload adjustment

groove on adjuster plug.
7. Install adjuster plug over end of stub shaft and tighten just enough to make certain that all parts are properly seated in gear housing. Remove seal protector.
8. Install adjuster plug lock nut loosely on adjuster plug.
9. Install seal compressor in gear housing, holding it tightly against shoulder in housing, Fig. S18.
10. Insert rack-piston into housing until arbor engages worm. Turn stub shaft clockwise, using a 3/4" wrench, to draw rack-piston into housing. When piston ring is in housing bore, arbor and seal compressor can be removed.
11. Turn stub shaft as necessary until middle rack groove in rack-piston is aligned with center of pitman shaft needle bearing.
12. Lubricate new side cover O-ring seal and install in groove in face of side cover.
13. Assemble side cover on pitman shaft by screwing cover onto adjusting screw until cover bottoms on pitman shaft.
14. Install pitman shaft so that center tooth in sector meshes with center groove of rack-piston. Make sure side cover O-ring is in place before pushing side cover down on gear housing.
15. Install side cover screws and lockwashers and tighten to 30 ft-lbs.
16. Hold adjuster screw with Allen wrench and install new adjuster lock nut halfway on adjuster screw.
17. Install rack-piston end plug in rack-piston and tighten plug to 75–80 ft-lbs.
18. Lubricate new housing end plug O-ring seal with power steering fluid and install in gear housing.
19. Insert end plug into gear housing and seat against O-ring seal. Slight tapping with a mallet may be necessary to seat end plug properly.
20. Snap end plug retainer ring into place with fingers. Slight tapping may be required to bottom ring in housing securely. Install coupling flange.

BENCH ADJUSTMENTS
Thrust Bearing Preload

NOTE: If thrust race usage is unknown (flat or conical races), perform adjustment outlined under the "Units with Conical Thrust Races" procedure. If preload measured is less than 4 inch pounds or greater than 10 inch pounds, use the adjustment procedure outlined for the particular model steering gear.

Units with Conical Thrust Races

1. Tighten adjuster plug until plug and thrust bearing bottoms.
2. Draw a line on gear housing aligning with one adjuster plug hole. Draw a second line on gear housing 1/4 to 3/16 inch from first line in the counter-clockwise direction, Fig. S28.
3. Turn adjuster plug counter-clockwise until hole aligns with second line, then tighten locknut while holding adjuster plug securely to prevent plug rotation.
4. Rotate stub shaft to right stop, then back 1/4 turn. Using an inch pound torque wrench to rotate stub shaft, measure preload. Reading should be between 4 and 10 inch pounds.

Units with Flat Thrust Races

1975–77 Jeep
1. Tighten adjuster plug snugly, then back off 1/2 turn.
2. Measure drag torque using an inch pound torque wrench to rotate stub shaft. Fig. S29.
3. While rotating stub shaft with torque wrench, tighten or loosen adjuster plug to obtain a torque reading of 4 in. lbs. above drag torque.
4. Tighten adjuster plug locknut and recheck preload.

1974–77 Dodge D100-800, Ramcharger & Plymouth Trail Duster
1. Tighten adjuster plug snugly, then back off 1 turn.
2. Rotate stub shaft to right stop, then back 1/4 turn.
3. Measure drag torque using an inch pound torque wrench to rotate stub shaft, Fig. S29.
4. Tighten adjuster plug snugly, then while rotating stub shaft with the torque wrench, loosen adjuster plug until torque reading obtained is 3 to 4 inch pounds greater than drag torque.
5. Tighten locknut and recheck preload.

1973 Chevrolet, GMC, 1974 Jeep & 1975–77 Ford
1. Tighten adjuster plug snugly, then back off 1/4 turn.
2. Measure drag torque using an inch pound torque wrench to rotate stub shaft, Fig. S29.
3. While rotating stub shaft with the torque wrench, tighten adjuster plug until torque reading obtained is 3 to 4 inch pounds greater than drag torque.
4. Tighten locknut and recheck preload.

International Harvester, 1970–77 Dodge Motor Home Chassis, 1970–72 Chevrolet & GMC, 1970–74 Ford & 1971–73 Jeep
1. Tighten adjuster plug snugly, then back off 1/8 turn.
2. Rotate stub shaft to right stop, then back 1/2 turn.
3. Measure drag torque using an inch pound torque wrench to rotate stub shaft, Fig. S29.
4. Tighten adjuster plug while rotating stub shaft with torque wrench until torque reading is 1–3 in. lbs. greater than drag torque on Ford, International Harvester and Jeep units. On Chevrolet and GMC gears, torque reading should be 1/2–2 in. lbs. on 1970 units, 2 in. lbs. on 1971–72 units and 3–4 in. lbs. on 1973–74 units greater than the drag torque. On 1970–77 Dodge Motor Home Chassis gears, the torque reading should be 2 in. lbs. greater than the drag torque.
5. Tighten lock nut and recheck preload.

Over-Center Preload

1. Rotate stub shaft from stop to stop, counting number of turns, then turn back exactly 1/2 number of turns to locate center of travel.
2. Measure combined ball and thrust bearing preload on Dodge, Ford, International Harvester, Jeep, Plymouth and 1974–77 Chevrolet and GMC units. On 1970–73 Chevrolet and GMC gears, the torque reading should be 3–6 in. lbs. greater than combined ball and thrust bearing preload.

TROUBLE SHOOTING
Hard Steering

1. Frozen steering shaft bearings.
2. Lower coupling flange rubbing against adjuster.
3. Steering adjustment tight.
4. Low oil level in pump.
5. Loose pump belt.
6. Insufficient oil pressure.
7. Improper tire inflation.
8. Flow control valve sticking.
9. Pump leaking internally.
10. Steering gear leaking internally.

Poor Return of Steering

1. Frozen steering shaft bearings.
2. Lower coupling flange rubbing against adjuster.
3. Tires not inflated properly.
4. Incorrect caster and toe-in.
5. Tight steering linkage.
6. Steering gear misalignment.
7. Tight suspension ball joints.
8. Steering adjustment tight.
9. Thrust bearing adjustment right.
10. Tight sector-to-rack piston adjustment.
11. Rack piston nut and worm preload too tight.

Power Steering Gears

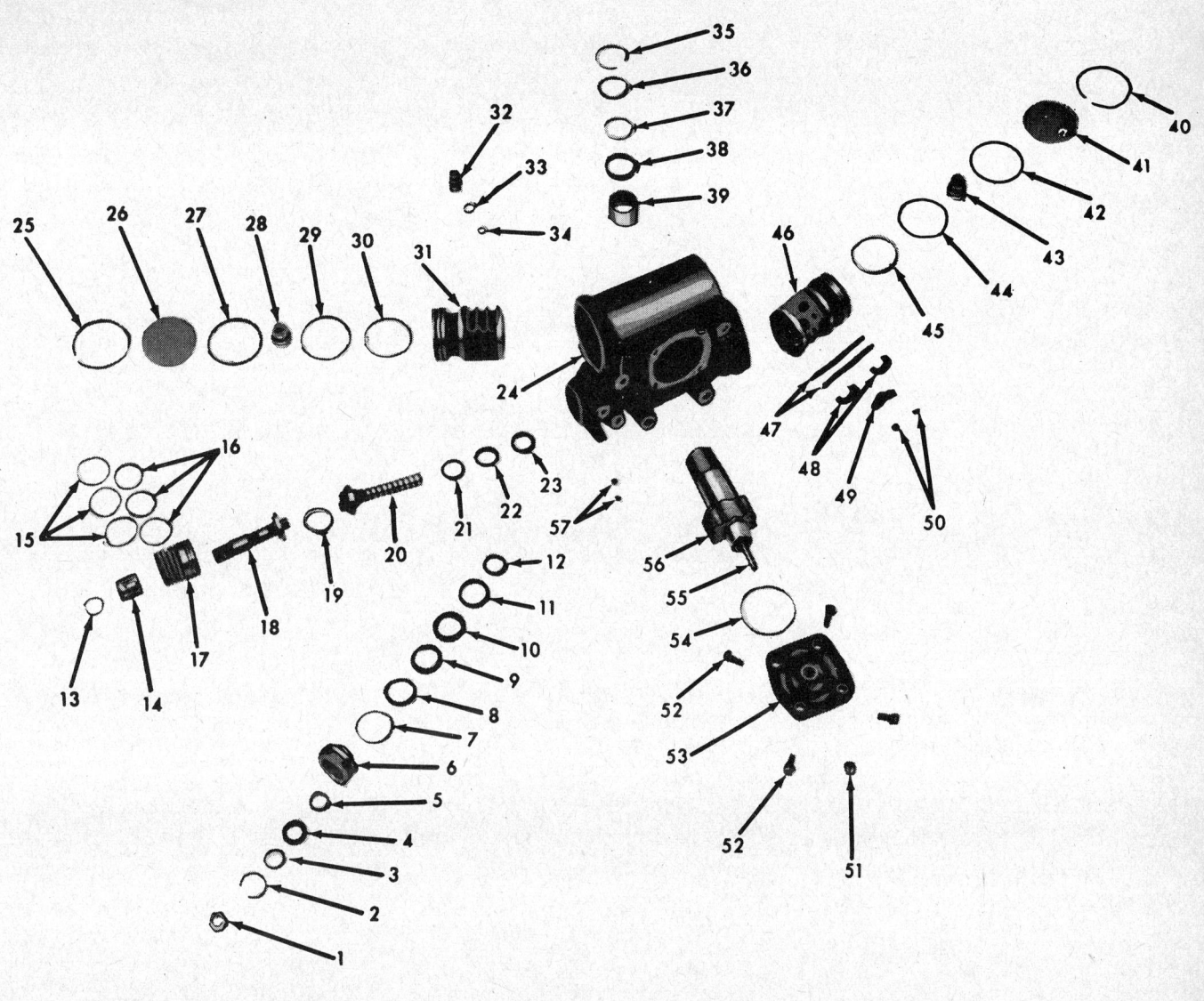

1. Locknut
2. Retaining Ring
3. Back-Up Washer
4. Stub Shaft Seal
5. Needle Bearing
6. Adjuster Plug
7. "O" Ring
8. Thrust Race (Upper)
9. Thrust Bearing
10. Thrust Race
11. Spacer
12. Retainer
13. Dampener "O" Ring
14. Valve Spool
15. Teflon "O" Rings
16. Back-Up "O" Rings
17. Valve Body
18. Stub Shaft
19. Cap to Body "O" Ring
20. Steering Worm
21. Thrust Bearing Race
22. Thrust Bearing
23. Thrust Bearing Race
24. Housing
25. Retaining Ring
26. Housing End Plug
27. End Plug "O" Ring
28. Rack Piston End Plug
29. Teflon "O" Ring
30. Back-Up "O" Ring
31. Rack Piston
32. Relief Valve
33. "O" Ring
34. "O" Ring
35. Retaining Ring
36. Dust Seal
37. Back-Up Washer
38. Oil Seal
39. Needle Bearing
40. Retaining Ring
41. Housing End Plug
42. End Plug "O" Ring
43. Rack Piston End Plug
44. Teflon "O" Ring
45. Back-Up "O" Ring
46. Rack Piston
47. Balls
48. Ball Return Guides
49. Clamp
50. Lockwasher & Screw Assemblies
51. Lock-Nut
52. Side Cover Bolts
53. Side Cover
54. Side Cover "O" Ring
55. Preload Adjuster Screw
56. Sector Shaft
57. Connectors

Fig. S31 Integral dual piston power steering gear disassembled

POWER STEERING GEARS

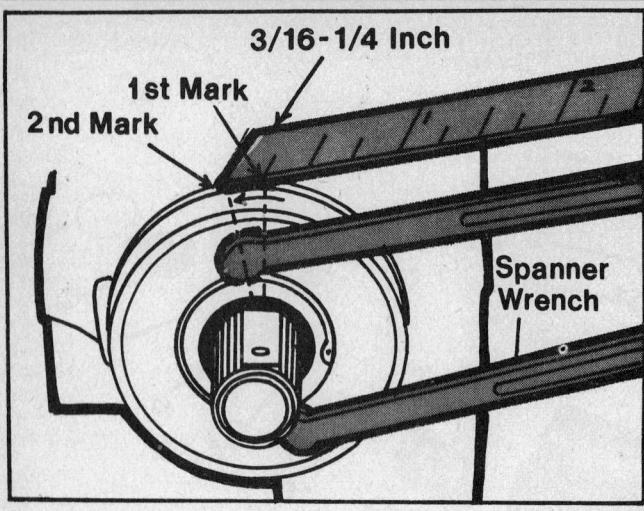

Fig. S32 Thrust bearing adjustment

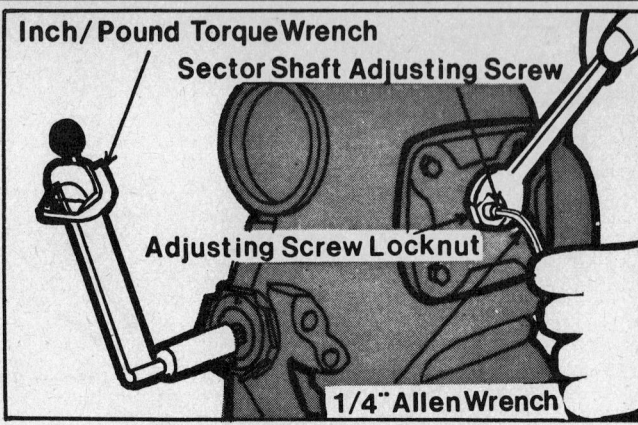

Fig. S33 Over-center adjustment

12. Sticky valve spool.
13. Lack of lubricant in suspension joints and steering linkage.
14. Steering wheel rubbing against directional signal housing.
15. Rubber spacer in shift tube is rubbing steering shaft.

Car Leads to One Side

1. Front end misalignment.
2. Unbalanced or badly worn valve.
3. Improper tire inflation.

Momentary Increase In Effort When Turning Wheel Fast

1. Low oil level in pump.
2. Pump belt slipping.
3. High internal leakage.

External Oil Leaks

1. Loose hose connections.
2. Damaged hose.
3. Side cover O-ring seal.
4. Pitman shaft seals.
5. Housing end plug seal.
6. Adjuster plug seals.
7. Torsion bar seal.
8. Defective housing.

Steering Gear Noise

1. A rattle or chuckle noise caused by loose over-center adjustment.
2. A hissing sound caused by gear being loose on frame.

Excessive Wheel Kickback or Loose Steering

1. Lash in steering linkage.
2. Air in system.
3. Excessive lash between pitman shaft sector and rack piston.
4. Loose thrust bearing adjustment.
5. Ball nut and worm preload.
6. Steering gear loose on frame.
7. Steering linkage worn.
8. Improper front wheel bearing adjustment.
9. Poppet valve worn.

Wheel Surges or Jerks

1. Loose pump belt.
2. Fluid level low.
3. Steering linkage hitting engine oil pan at full turn.
4. Sticky flow control valve.

Hard Steering When Parking

1. Loose pump belt.
2. Low oil level in reservoir.
3. Lack of lubrication in linkage or front suspension.
4. Tires not properly inflated.
5. Insufficient oil pressure.
6. Low oil pressure due to restriction in hoses.
7. Low oil pressure due to worn piston ring or scored housing bore.
8. Pressure loss due to leakage at valve rings, valve body-to-worm seal or rack piston end plug seal.
9. Pressure loss due to loose fit of spool in valve body or leaky valve body.

Valve Squawk

1. Cut or worn dampener ring on valve spool.
2. Loose or worn rotary valve parts.
3. Loose belt.
4. Glazed belt.
5. Flow control valve sticking or binding.

No Effort Required to Turn

1. Broken torsion bar.

INTEGRAL DUAL PISTON GEAR

Description

This power steering gear is a recirculating ball type, Fig. S31, and incorporates a dual cylinder system in which a double geared sector shaft is actuated by two rack-pistons moving in opposite directions. The primary rack-piston contains the worm gear assembly.

The open center rotary type four-way control valve directs oil to either side of the rack-pistons. The valve is operated by a torsion bar, attached to the valve body at one end and to the valve spool through the stub shaft at the

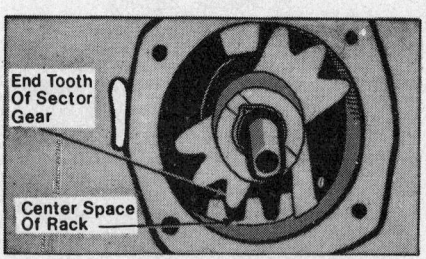

Fig. S34 Indexing sector shaft to clear rack teeth

Fig. S35 Sector shaft end tooth aligned with rack center space

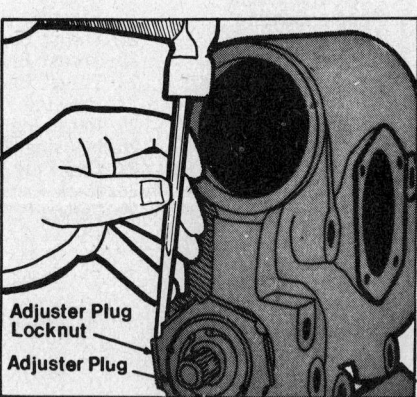

Fig. S36 Adjuster plug locknut removal

POWER STEERING GEARS

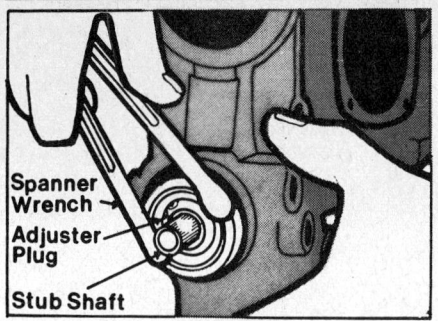

Fig. S37 Adjuster plug removal

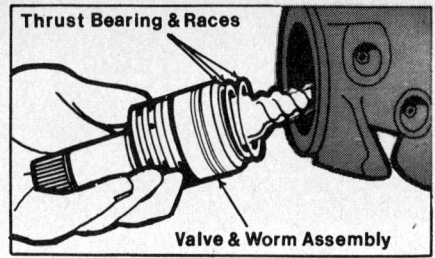

Fig. S38 Worm & valve assembly removal

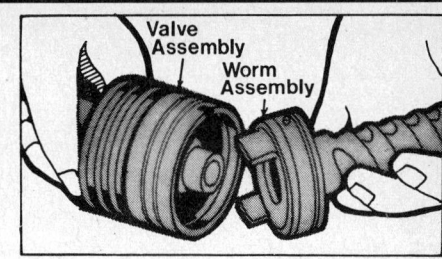

Fig. S39 Separating worm from valve

other. When the torsion bar twists, the valve spool is displaced in relation to the valve body, thereby operating the valve.

Adjustments

In-vehicle adjustments of this power steering gear is not recommended since the hydraulic fluid may cause a variable in the adjustment. For proper adjustment, remove steering gear from vehicle, drain fluid and mount in a suitable vise.

Thrust Bearing Adjustment

1. Remove adjuster plug locknut and rotate adjuster plug clockwise until plug and thrust bearing are firmly bottomed.
2. Mark gear housing in-line with a hole in adjuster plug, Fig. S32. Measure 3/16 to 1/4 inch counter-clockwise and place a second mark on gear housing.
3. Rotate adjuster plug counter-clockwise until hole in plug aligns with second mark.
4. Install and tighten adjuster plug lock-nut while maintaining adjuster plug position.
5. With an inch pound torque wrench, rotate stub shaft to right stop, then back 1/4 turn, noting rotating torque. The reading should be between 4 and 10 in. lbs., if not, repeat procedure.

Over-Center Adjustment

1. With steering gear centered, loosen sector shaft adjuster screw locknut, tighten adjuster screw and re-tighten locknut.
2. Measure over-center torque at stub shaft by rotating shaft with an inch pound torque wrench through a 180 degree arc either side of center and note torque reading when passing over-center, Fig. S33.
3. Adjust over-center preload until torque reading is 4–8 in. lbs. greater than reading obtained in above step on new gear assemblies or 4–5 in. lbs. greater on used gear assemblies.
4. Total over-center preload on new gears should not exceed 18 in. lbs. or 14 in. lbs. on used gears.

NOTE: Total over-center preload includes thrust bearing, over-center and drag torques.

Steering Gear Disassembly

1. Position end plug retaining ring so gap is approximately 1/4 inch from hole in housing on both primary and secondary cylinders. Then, using a small punch inserted through housing hole to dislodge retaining ring, pry ring from housing groove.
2. Rotate stub shaft counter-clockwise until end cover is forced from primary cylinder.

NOTE: Do not rotate stub shaft any farther than necessary for cover removal since the rack-piston balls may drop into the piston chamber.

3. Remove end cover "O" ring from housing groove.
4. Remove rack-piston end plug by first loosening plug using a brass drift and a hammer, then rotate end plug out of rack-piston with a 1/2 inch square drive.
5. Remove sector shaft adjuster screw locknut, side cover bolts and, using a 1/4 inch Allen wrench, rotate adjuster screw clockwise until side cover separates from sector shaft.
6. Rotate stub shaft counter-clockwise until sector shaft teeth are disengaged from rack-piston.

NOTE: If the secondary piston end cover is free, proceed to step 8.

7. Index sector shaft so it clears rack-piston completely, Fig. S34. Then, rotate stub shaft clockwise until rack-piston bottoms in gear housing and slowly turn stub shaft counter-clockwise to engage sector shaft end tooth with center tooth space of primary rack, Fig. S35. Continue turning stub shaft until the leading tooth of sector shaft forces the secondary rack against end cover, in turn pushing the end cover from housing.
8. Remove secondary cylinder rack-piston. Do not remove end plug unless plug is to be replaced.
9. Rotate stub shaft clockwise until sector shaft teeth are disengaged from rack-piston, then index sector shaft so it clears rack completely, allowing free movement of rack.
10. Insert ball retaining tool into rack-piston bore with tool pilot seated into end of worm. Rotate stub shaft counter-clockwise, holding tool firmly against worm, to force rack-piston onto tool. Remove rack-piston and the ball retaining tool from gear housing.
11. Index sector shaft teeth to clear housing, then remove sector shaft.
12. Remove adjuster plug locknut, Fig. S36, and adjuster plug, Fig. S37.
13. Remove valve and worm assembly, ensuring both races and thrust bearing are removed from gear housing, Fig. S38, then separate worm from valve, Fig. S39.

Sub-Assembly Service
Adjuster Plug Disassembly

1. If oil seal only is to be replaced, install adjuster plug into housing finger tight. Remove retaining snap ring, Fig. S40, back-up washer and pry oil seal from adjuster plug bore, Fig. S41.
2. If thrust bearing only is to be placed, pry thrust bearing retainer from plug bore, Fig. S42, and remove spacer, washer,

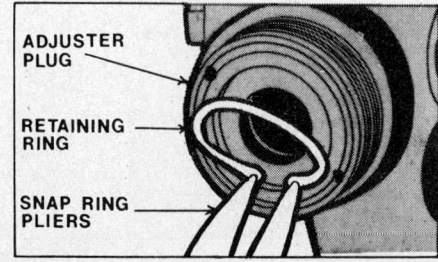

Fig. S40 Adjuster plug snap ring removal

Fig. S41 Adjuster plug oil seal removal

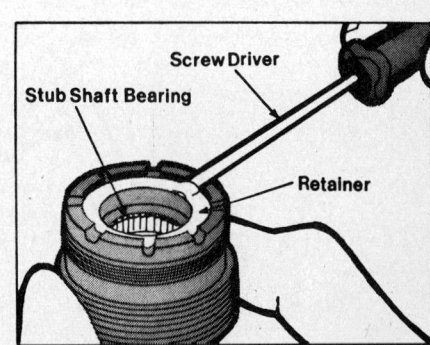

Fig. S42 Adjuster plug thrust bearing retainer removal

Power Steering Gears

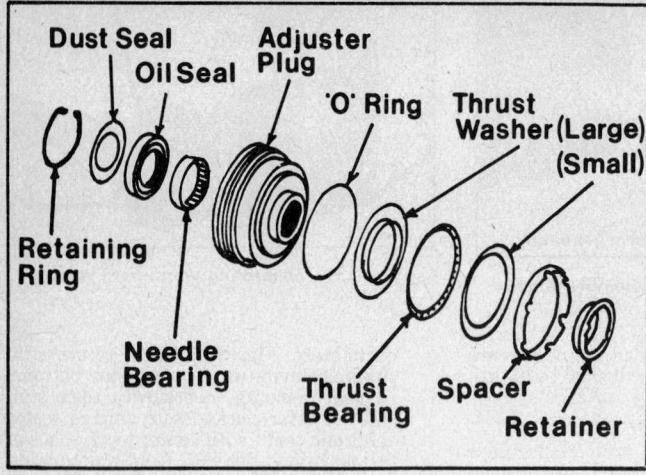

Fig. S43 Adjuster plug disassembled

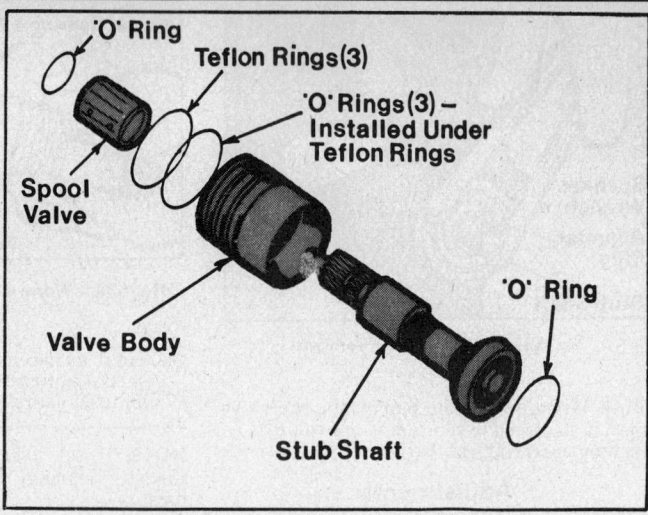

Fig. S44 Valve & stub shaft assembly

bearing and second washer.
3. With thrust bearing assembly remove from plug, drive needle bearing, oil seal, and dust seal from adjuster plug, Fig. S43.

Valve & Stub Shaft Disassembly

1. Remove cap to wormshaft "O" ring, Fig. S44.
2. Hold valve assembly with stub shaft facing downward, then tap stub shaft lightly against work bench until cap is free from valve body approximately 1/4 inch, Fig. S45.

NOTE: If shaft assembly is pulled out too far, the valve spool may become cocked and bind in the valve body.

3. Disengage shaft pin, Fig. S46, and remove spool by rotating it while removing, Fig. S47. If binding occurs, realign valve spool, then remove.
4. Remove damper "O" ring.

NOTE: The teflon rings generally do not require replacement unless severely worn or damaged. However, when replacing the teflon rings, replace the "O" rings also.

Primary Rack-Piston Disassembly

1. Remove ball return guide clamp screws, then the guide, arbor tool and recirculating balls.

Hose Connector Replacement

NOTE: This procedure may be performed on or off the vehicle.

1. Using a 5/16 × 18 tap, cut threads into connector seat. Only cut two or three threads to prevent check valve damage.
2. Using a 5/16 × 18 bolt, nut and flat washer, thread the bolt into the threaded connector. Hold the bolt stationary and turn the nut to bear against the flat washer. The washer will lodge against the gear housing, causing the bolt to move out, pulling the connector seat from the housing.
3. Clean gear housing and ensure no metal chips or dirt remain.
4. Remove and discard poppet check valve and spring from pressure port.
5. Install new check valve spring in pressure port with large end facing downward. Ensure spring is properly seated in pressure port counterbore.
6. Install new check valve over spring with tangs facing downward and valve centered on small end of spring.
7. Using grease to hold connector seat on check valve, drive the seat into place.

Sector Shaft Needle Bearing & Seals Replacement

1. If seals only are to be replaced, remove snap ring retainer and outer steel washer. Pry dust seal from housing, remove inner steel washer, then pry out inner seal.
2. To remove needle bearing and seals, press bearing and seals from housing, using a

Fig. S46 Shaft pin disengaged

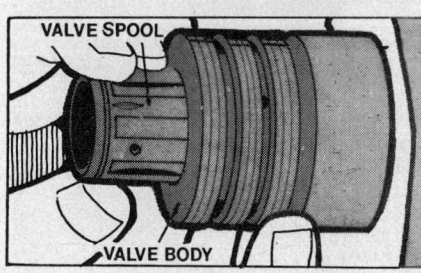

Fig. S47 Valve spool removal

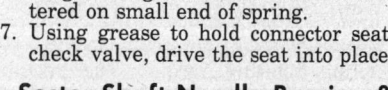

Fig. S45 Freeing valve body from stub shaft

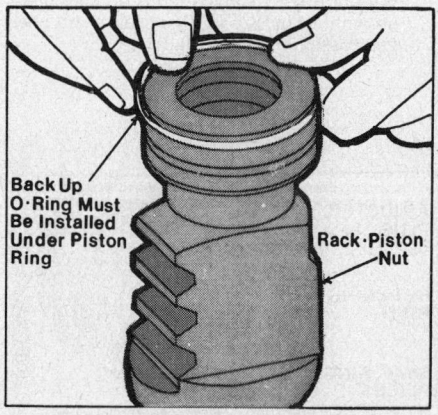

Fig. S48 Rack-piston teflon seal & "O" ring installation

Power Steering Gears

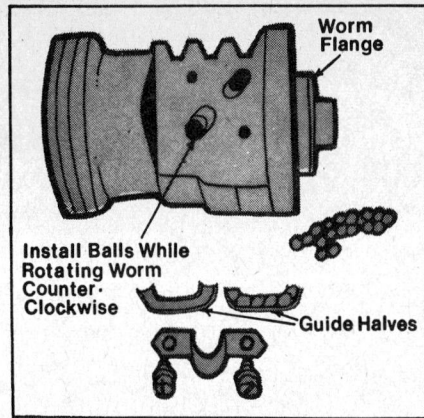

Fig. S49 Installing balls into rack-piston

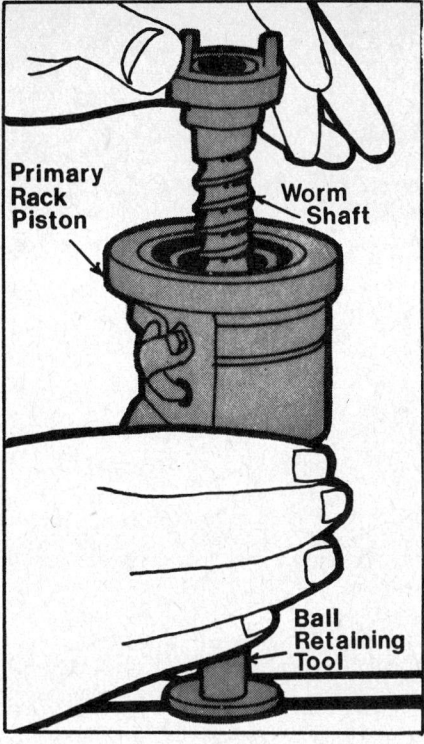

Fig. S50 Ball retaining tool installation

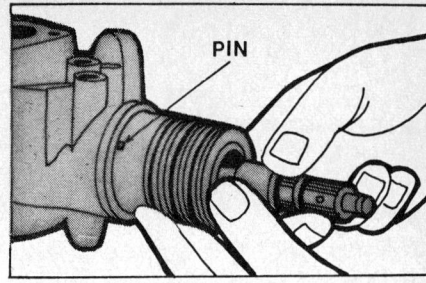

Fig. S53 Valve to wormshaft alignment

Fig. S54 Valve body properly seated

suitable tool to apply pressure from cover side of housing.
3. Lubricate needle bearing, then using tool J-24654, press bearing into housing until tool bottoms on housing hub.
4. Lubricate inner double lipped seal and place seal on tool J-24656 with seal identification facing toward tool handle. Drive seal into bore until tool bottoms.
5. Install back-up washer into bore and place dust seal onto tool J-24656 with sealing lip facing toward tool handle, then press seal into bore until seal just clears snap ring groove.
6. Install snap ring retainer into bore groove, ensuring snap ring is properly seated in groove.

Primary Rack Piston Assembly

1. Lubricate and install new teflon seal and "O" ring into rack-piston groove, Fig. S48, if removed.
2. Slide wormshaft into rack-piston and rotate worm to align worm groove with ball return guide hole nearest piston ring.
3. Lubricate balls and while rotating wormshaft clockwise, load 28 balls into guide hole nearest piston ring, Fig. S49. Alternately install the black and silver balls since the black balls are .0005 inch smaller than the silver balls.
4. Place the remaining six balls into the ball return guide, using the same alternate sequence as in the previous step. Retain balls with a suitable grease and install the ball guide into rack-piston holes, then the ball guide clamp and torque retaining screws to 6 ft. lbs.
5. Remove wormshaft while installing the ball retaining tool, Fig. S50 as described under "Steering Gear Disassembly".

Secondary Rack-Piston Assembly

1. Lubricate and install new teflon seal and "O" ring into rack-piston groove, Fig. S48, if removed.
2. Slide wormshaft into rack-piston and rotate worm to align worm groove with ball return guide hole nearest piston ring.
3. Lubricate balls and while rotating wormshaft clockwise, load 28 balls into guide hole nearest piston ring, Fig. S49. Alternately install the black and silver balls since the black balls are .0005 inch smaller than the silver balls.
4. Place the remaining six balls into the ball return guide, using the same alternate sequence as in the previous step. Retain balls with a suitable grease and install the ball guide into rack-piston holes, then the ball guide clamp and torque retaining screws to 6 ft. lbs.
5. Remove wormshaft while installing the ball retaining tool, Fig. S50 as described under "Steering Gear Disassembly".

Secondary Rack-Piston Assembly

1. Lubricate and install new teflon ring and "O" ring into rack-piston groove, if removed.

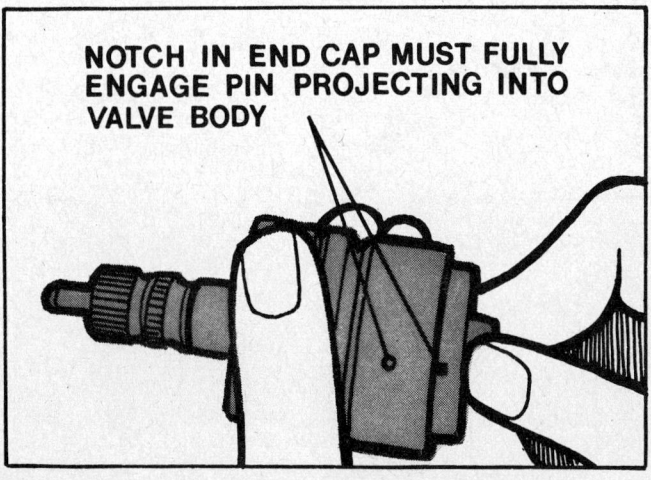

Fig. S51 Notch & pin alignment

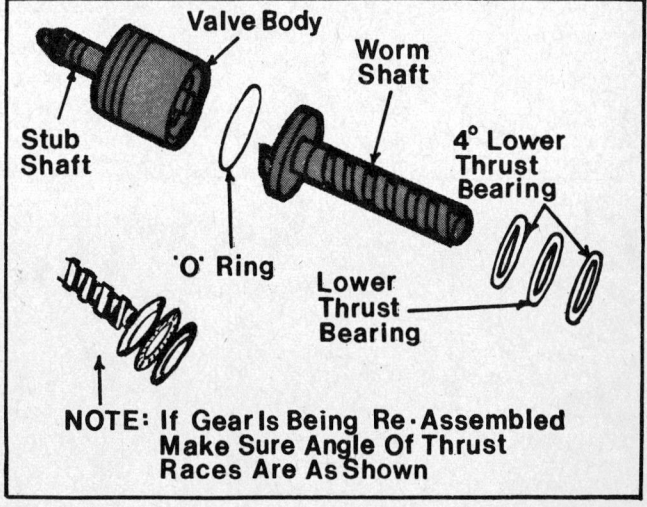

Fig. S52 Worm & valve body with thrust washers

POWER STEERING GEARS

Valve & Stub Shaft Assembly

1. Lubricate and install new valve body teflon rings and "O" rings into valve body grooves, if removed.
2. Lubricate and install valve spool damper "O" ring over valve spool.
3. Lubricate valve spool and body and rotate spool slightly while pushing spool into valve body, until shaft pin hole is visible from opposite end.
4. Slide stub shaft into spool until shaft pin can be inserted into valve spool hole.
5. Align notch in shaft cap with pin in valve body, Fig. S51, then press valve spool and shaft assembly into valve body.

NOTE: The valve body pin must mate with the cap notch prior to valve body installation.

6. Install new "O" ring in valve body shaft cap end.

Adjuster Plug Assembly

1. Press needle bearing into adjuster plug with tool J-8524-1 until tool bottoms in plug.
2. Using tool J-85241, seat new oil seal into plug with sealing lip facing away from tool. Install the dust seal using the same tool, then the snap ring retainer.
3. Lubricate and install new adjuster plug "O" ring in plug groove. Place large thrust washer with flat side facing toward plug on plug hub, then install thrust bearing, small thrust washer with flange side facing away from plug and the spacer with grooves facing away from bearing.
4. Install bearing retainer by tapping lightly on flat surface of retainer.

NOTE: Projections must not extend beyond spacer when seating retainer. Also, the spacer must be free to rotate.

STEERING GEAR REASSEMBLY

1. Lubricate worm, thrust bearing and washers with power steering fluid.
2. Install thrust washer, bearing and second thrust washer over end of worm, Fig. S52. Note position of conical thrust races, if equipped.
3. Lubricate valve body, teflon rings and new cap to body "O" ring, then install "O" ring in valve body, seated against lower shaft cap.
4. Align narrow notch in valve body with pin in worm and install valve and shaft assembly into gear housing, Fig. S53. The valve body is installed properly when housing oil return hole is completely uncovered, Fig. S54.
5. Seat adjuster plug against valve body in housing and adjust thrust bearing preload as outlined under "Adjustments".
6. To install rack-pistons:
   a. Lubricate rack-piston teflon ring with power steering fluid and with ball retaining tool in place, push rack-piston into housing with rack teeth facing toward sector shaft opening until the tool bottoms against worm.
   b. Using a 3/4 inch 12 point socket, rotate stub shaft clockwise to thread rack-piston onto worm with ball retaining tool held against worm. Remove ball retaining tool and center the rack teeth in sector shaft opening.
   c. Install secondary rack-piston in opposite cylinder with end plug facing outward and rack teeth facing toward sector shaft opening. Align center tooth space with primary rack-piston.
7. To install sector shaft and side cover:
   a. Install sector shaft into housing with tapered teeth of sector shaft engaging primary rack-piston teeth.
   b. Install new side cover "O" ring, then place side cover on housing. Insert a 1/4 inch allen wrench through side cover hole and into sector shaft adjuster screw. Turn screw counter-clockwise to thread screw through side cover until cover bottoms on housing.
   c. Install and torque side cover bolts to 35 ft. lbs.
8. Install and torque rack-piston end plug to 75 ft. lbs.
9. Install end covers with new "O" rings, then the retaining rings.

Sheppard Integral Power Steering Section

DESCRIPTION

This system is of the integral type and incorporates the steering shaft, power cylinder and control valve into a single assembly, Fig. SH1. The actuating shaft is geared to the control valve, housed within the piston. When the shaft is turned, the control valve moves axially, directing oil flow to either piston end, in turn forcing the piston through the cylinder. The piston rack rotates the pinion, output shaft and the Pitman arm.

DISASSEMBLY, FIG. 1

1. Remove pitman arm using a suitable puller.

NOTE: The pitman arm may be retained by two socket head retaining set screws, a self-locking nut or by a split nut and cap screw.

2. Scribe reference marks between bearing cap, cylinder head and housing for proper reassembly.

NOTE: The cylinder and bearing cap will fit either end of housing.

3. Remove pinion gear cover to housing attaching bolts.

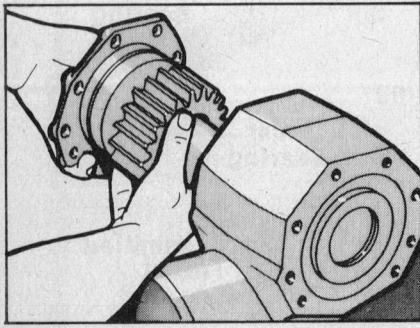

Fig. 2 Output shaft pinion gear removal

Fig. 3 Bearing cap & actuating shaft removal

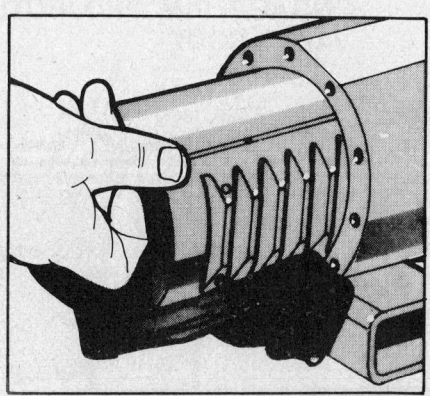

Fig. 4 Piston assembly removal

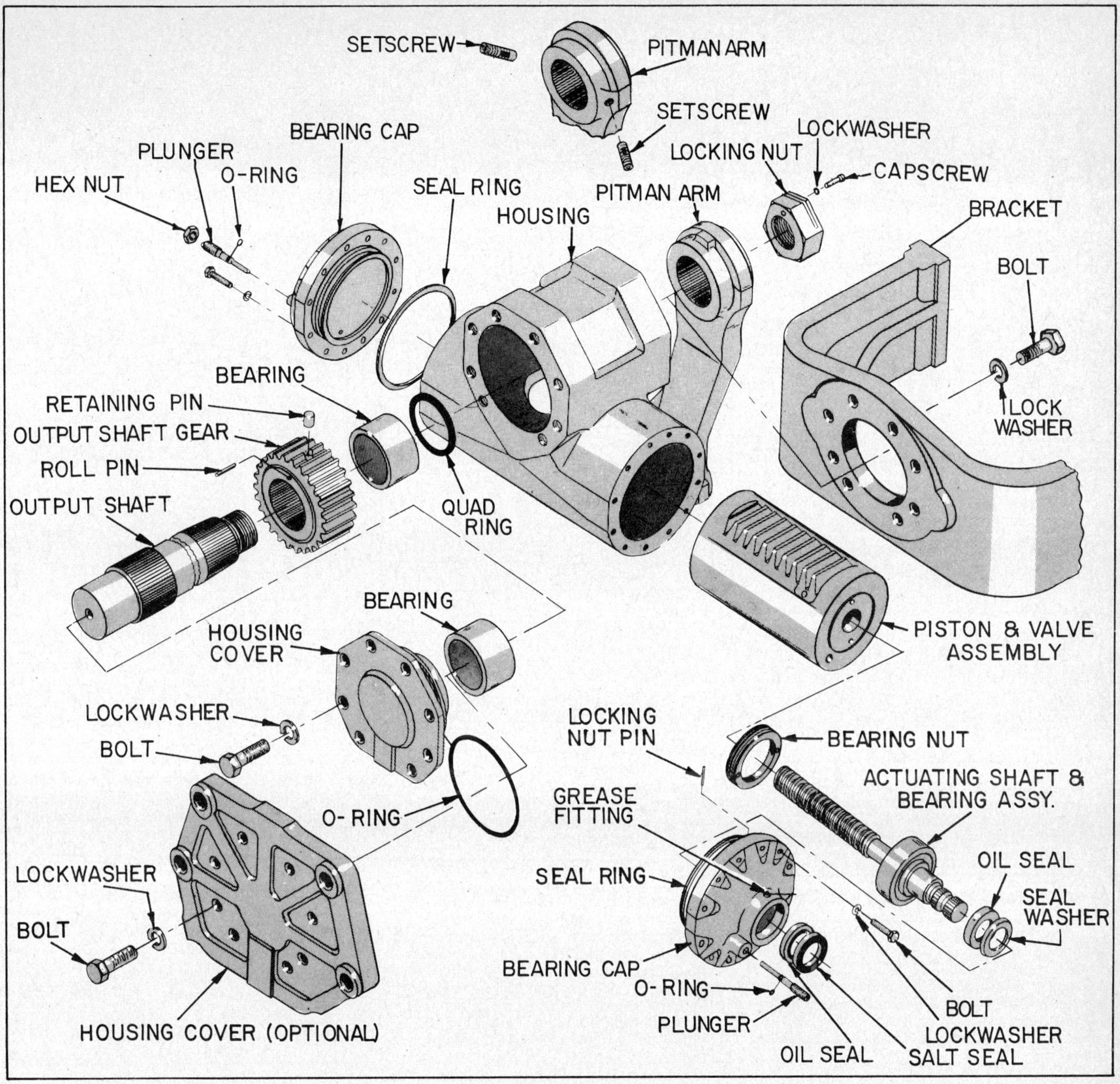

POWER STEERING GEARS

Fig. 1 Sheppard power steering gear, disassembled

4. Clean the exposed part of the output shaft to prevent bearing damage, then using a mallet, tap end of output shaft to loosen cover.
5. Slide output shaft pinion gear and cover assembly from housing, Fig. 2.
6. Pull output shaft from cover. Remove and discard cover "O" ring.
7. Loosen relief valve plunger jamb nuts and remove plungers from cylinder head and bearing cap. Remove and discard square ring seals or gaskets.

NOTE: Late production units may have slotted and recessed relief plungers.

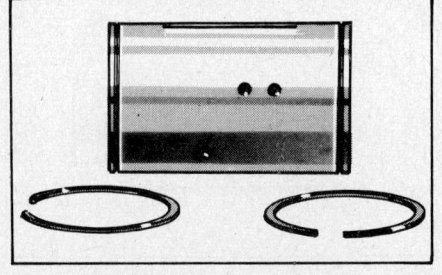

Fig. 5 Piston assembly, early production units

These plungers are removed or adjusted using a straight bladed screwdriver.

8. Remove bolts from bearing cap. Then rotate actuating shaft to free bearing cap from piston and housing.
9. While supporting bearing cap, rotate actuating shaft until shaft is free from piston, Fig. 3. Remove and discard gasket or seal ring. Some units use square ring seals in place of gaskets on cylinder head and bearing cap.
10. Remove cylinder head and discard gasket or seal ring.
11. Slide piston assembly from housing bore, Fig. 4.

743

POWER STEERING GEARS

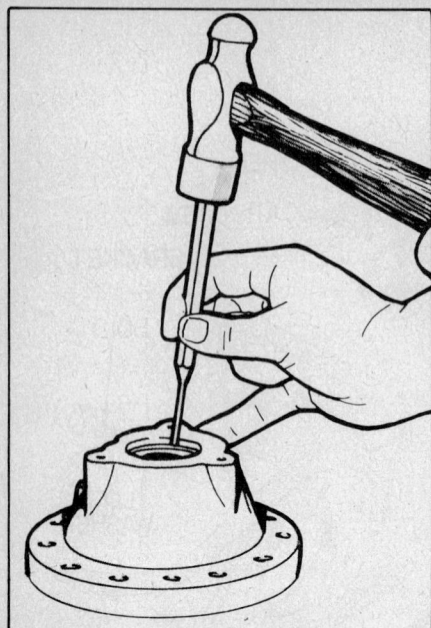

Fig. 6 High pressure seal removal

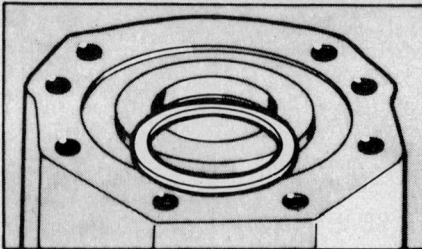

Fig. 7 Quad ring removal

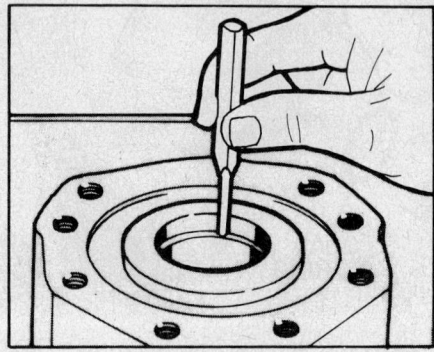

Fig. 8 Bronze bearing removal

Fig. 9 Piston top adjusting nut removal

Fig. 10 Piston top reversing spring removal

NOTE: Early production units may utilize piston rings, Fig. 5. If so, remove and discard piston rings since the rings are no longer required. However, the 372/382 series steering gears with the step bore housing and piston flange will use the piston ring.

12. Pull locking pin from housing, then using a suitable spanner wrench, remove bearing retaining nut from cap.
13. Drive actuating shaft and bearing from bearing cap using a mallet or press.

NOTE: The actuating shaft and bearing are serviced as an assembly. Also, the actuating shaft may be of several types. The thread may be a machine cut thread or a rolled thread. The rolled thread may appear rough and flaky or have a split in the thread. This is a normal condition for a rolled thread.

14. The standard and short series bearing caps utilize three seals for high pressure sealing and actuating shaft protection. The high pressure seal is protected by a dirt and a salt seal. The grease cavity between the dirt and salt seals are filled with chassis lube to prevent the entry of dirt and salt. Flush the cavity by forcing grease through the cavity with a low pressure grease gun.
15. Press the three seals from the bearing cap by pressing the seals toward the inside of the bearing cap.

NOTE: The back-up washers will also be removed and should be retained for reinstallation with the new seals. Also, early production units use two seals in the bearing cap and the back-up washer is machined into the bearing cap. Use a screwdriver to pry the dirt seal from the bearing cap on these units, then using a suitable punch placed through the access holes, drive the high pressure seal from the bearing cap, Fig. 6.

16. On standard high pressure, short series and 372/382 series units, remove the pinion gear roll pin, then drill out the retaining pin. Press pinion gear from shaft.

NOTE: If the retaining pin cannot be drilled out, it can be sheared with approximately 10 tons of pressure. Drive half of the pin out of the pinion gear and drill out the remaining half from the shaft.

17. On low pressure units, remove the two pinion gear cap screws with an allen wrench and rotate pinion gear retaining

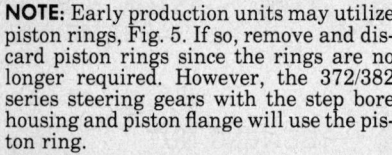

Fig. 11 Actuating valve removal

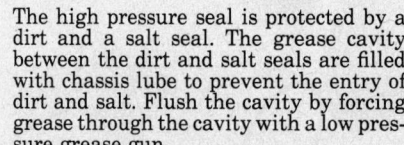

Fig. 12 Piston relief ball assembly removal

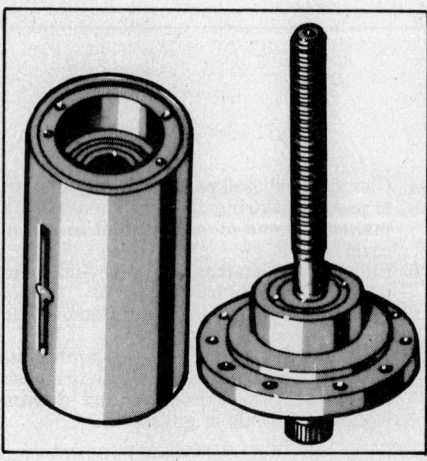

Fig. 13 Bearing cap & piston assembly, short series

POWER STEERING GEARS

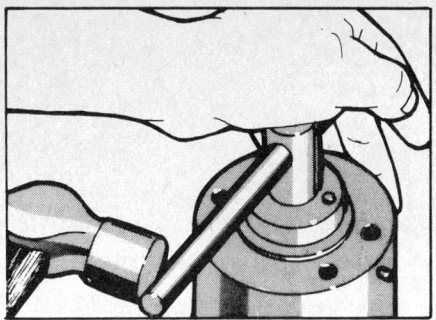

Fig. 14 Bottom piston plug removal, short series

nut counter-clockwise to remove. Then, press pinion gear from shaft.
18. On all units, remove and discard Quad ring oil seal from the gear housing, Fig. 7.
19. With a suitable punch, drive bronze bushing from housing, Fig. 8.
20. Remove bronze bearing with a suitable tool.

Standard Piston, Disassembly

1. Make an alignment mark between the top adjustment nut and piston so the nut can be installed in the original position.
2. Remove pin securing adjustment nut to piston.
3. With a suitable spanner wrench, remove top adjustment nut from piston, Fig. 9.

NOTE: The bottom adjustment nut, located inside the piston, should not be removed.

4. Remove the top reversing spring from the nose of the actuating valve, Fig. 10, then pull the actuating valve from piston, Fig. 11.

NOTE: Do not force the valve from the piston bore. The actuating valve and piston are serviced as an assembly due to critical tolerances.

5. Remove actuating valve positioning pin from piston.

NOTE: The positioning pin on late production units incorporate an "O" ring oil seal. Also, the reversing springs are the only

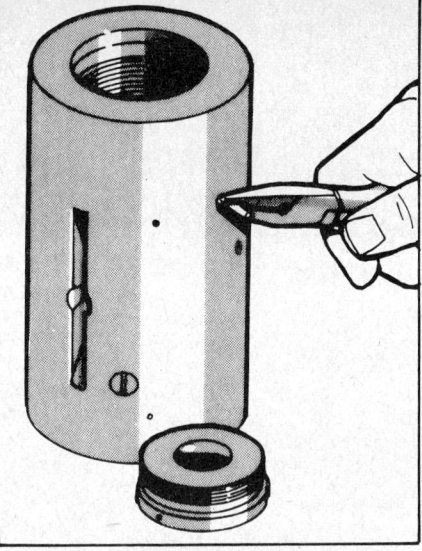

Fig. 15 Valve adjusting nut locking pin removal, short series

servicable components of the piston assembly.

6. Using a suitable allen wrench, remove relief ball seats, relief balls and spring, Fig. 12.

NOTE: The balls are under spring tension. Use caution when removing to prevent loss or personal injury.

7. In event of severe oil contamination, remove and clean piston bottom plug. On reinstallation, the plug must be pinned.

Short Series Piston, Disassembly

NOTE: The short series units use an inverted bearing cap and the piston is machined to permit the bearing to travel inside the top of the piston, Fig. 13. Also, the top adjusting nut is factory adjusted and must not be removed.

1. Remove bottom plug locking pin. The pin may be drilled out or may be sheared when removing the plug. Using a suitable spanner wrench, remove bottom plug from piston, Fig. 14.
2. Pry adjusting nut locking pin through piston and pull out with a suitable pair of pliers, Fig. 15.

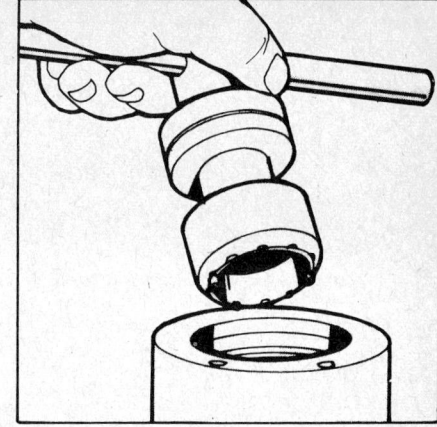

Fig. 16 Valve adjusting nut removal, short series

3. Mark position of adjusting nut and piston so the nut can be installed in original position.
4. Using a suitable spanner wrench, remove valve adjusting nut, Fig. 16.
5. Remove the double reversing springs, then pull actuating valve from piston bore.
6. Remove valve positioning pin with a suitable screwdriver. Remove and discard "O" ring.
7. Remove the two bottom reversing springs, Fig. 17.
8. Using a suitable allen wrench, remove relief ball seats, relief balls and spring from piston.

372-382 Series Piston (Step Bore), Disassembly, Fig. 18

These pistons are disassembled in the same manner as the standard piston except the piston ring flange is factory located and installed and must not be removed. Also, the piston is replaceable.

ASSEMBLY

1. Press new bushings into gear housing and cover. The bushing should be installed so the inside face of the bushing is flush with the inside face of the gear housing. Also, the bushing face must be flush with the cover except on model 592

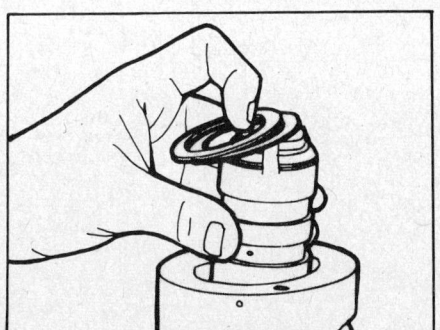

Fig. 17 Bottom reversing spring removal, short series

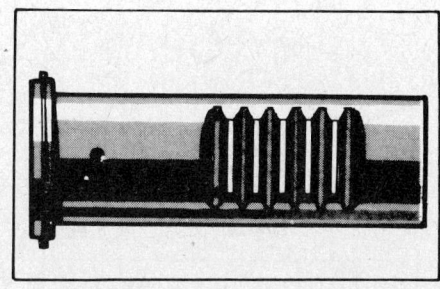

Fig. 18 372-382 step bore piston

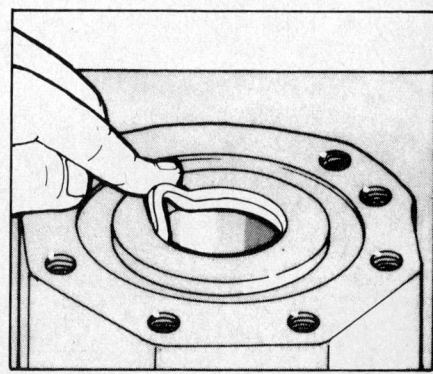

Fig. 19 Quad ring installation

POWER STEERING GEARS

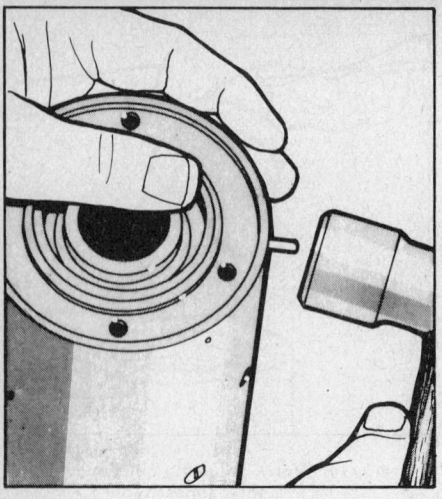

Fig. 20 Valve positioning pin installation

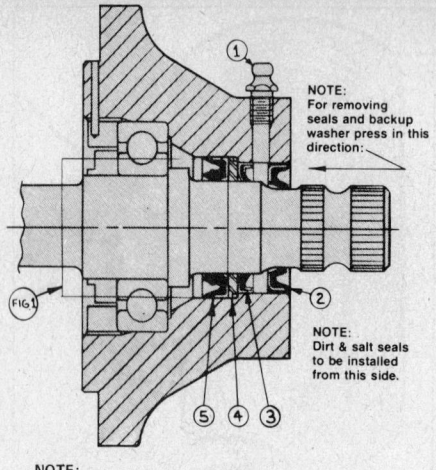

NOTE: Backup washer and the high pressure oil seal installed from this side.

Fig. 21 Bearing cap seal installation

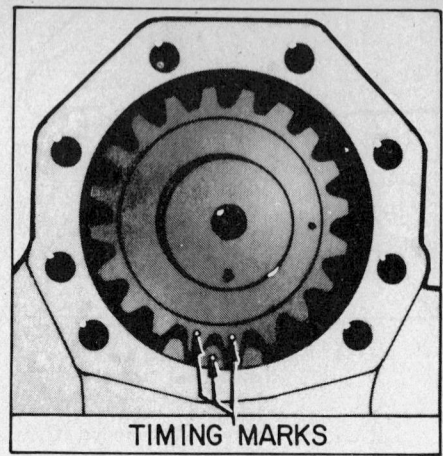

Fig. 22 Pinion gear timing marks aligned

units and 392/492 units. On model 592 units, the bushing should be recessed 5/16 inch from the cover and face on 392/492 units, the bushing should be recessed 1/2 inch from the cover face.

NOTE: When installing the bushing in the output shaft bore of the housing and the bushing is easily installed, encountering little press resistance, remove the bushing. Then, clean the bushing of all oil and grease and the housing bore of foreign material by scraping with a brass sheet. Coat the housing bore and the outside diameter of the bushing with Loctite High Strength Retainer Compound and reinstall the bushing. Allow a minimum of 6 hours curing time, then remove excess compound with naphtha.

The bronze bushings are presized and boring or honing is not required.

2. Install a new Quad ring into gear housing groove, Fig. 19.

3. Install the relief valve spring and one relief ball into valve bore, then install one of the valve seats. The valve seat must be tight and flush with or slightly below the end surface of the piston. Install the second relief ball and seat.
4. Place one of the reversing springs in bottom of valve bore. The spring should be centered since the valve must enter the inside diameter of the spring.
5. Install the valve positioning pin into the piston, Fig. 20. Rotate the pin inward with a screwdriver until the pin is below the surface of the piston. The flats must enter into the piston 1/4 inch to engage the mating slot in the valve.
6. Slide actuating valve into piston so the slot on end of valve is positioned over the pin.

7. Place reversing spring onto shoulder of valve end.
8. Install valve adjustment nut. Rotate nut clockwise into the piston until the nut is against the spring. Align the marks made during disassembly on nut and piston. Install the locking pin and ensure that the pin is below the outside edge of the piston.
9. On short series pistons, install piston plug and the locking pin. If the piston plug enters farther into the unit than the original locking pin hole, drill a new hole 180° opposite original pin position and install pin.
10. Install bearing cap seals. Press the seals into position as shown in Fig. 21.

NOTE: On early production steering gears, the high pressure seal is installed with the lip facing inside and the dirt seal with the lip toward the outside.

11. Adequately lubricate the seals.
12. Press actuating shaft assembly into the bearing cap.
13. Install bearing retaining nut. Insert the locking pin through the hole in the bearing cap and into hole in nut. If a new nut is used, drill a 3/32 inch diameter hole in nut. The nut must be in place to drill the hole. Drill through the locking pin hole in the bearing cap and 3/16 inch into the nut.

Fig. 23 Miter gear timing marks, miter gearbox

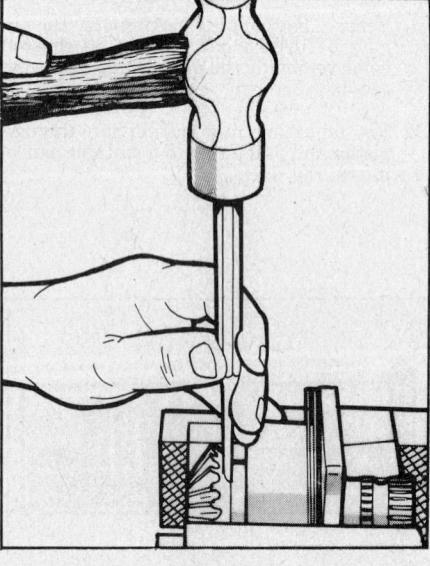

Fig. 24 Miter gear roll pin removal, miter gearbox

Fig. 25 Miter gear removal, miter gearbox

POWER STEERING GEARS

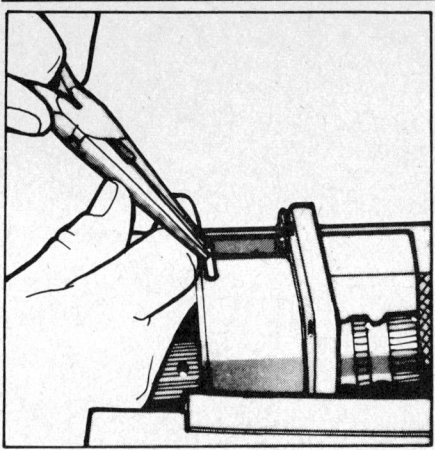

Fig. 26 Cover locking pin removal, miter gearbox

Fig. 27 Bearing retaining nut removal, miter gearbox

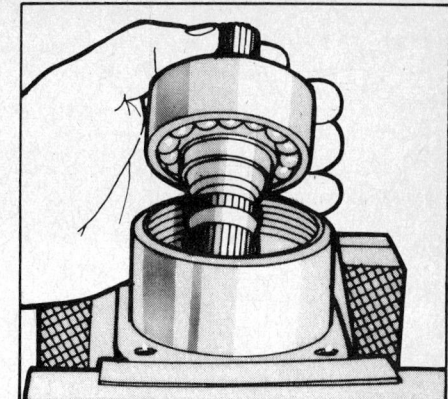

Fig. 28 Bearing & actuating shaft removal, miter gearbox

14. Align the timing mark on the pinion gear with marked spline on output shaft, Fig. 22. Press gear onto shaft, if necessary. Install the gear retaining nut. The nut must be tight against the output shaft gear. Install capscrews into retaining nut. If holes do not align, back off retaining nut until the holes align.

    NOTE: On high pressure units, align shaft and gear retaining pin holes and press gear onto shaft.

15. Install retaining pin through gear and seat into shaft, then install roll pin.
16. Lightly coat cylinder bore with engine oil.
17. Install piston into cylinder bore with the opening for the actuating shaft facing toward the bearing cap end of housing.
18. Align timing mark on piston rack with center of pinion gear housing.
19. Lubricate the housing bearing and Quad ring, then slide output shaft through housing. Align timing marks on pinion gear with timing mark on rack.
20. Install cylinder head with new gasket or seal. Align marks made during disassembly and tighten bolts.
21. Using a new gasket or seal on bearing cap, thread actuating shaft into valve. Align punch marks on gear housing and bearing cap. Rotate shaft until the cap is positioned on end of cylinder. Check the plunger hole alignment with valve seat in

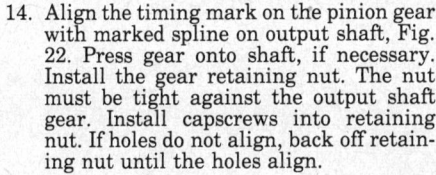

Fig. 29 Inside housing bolt removal, miter gearbox

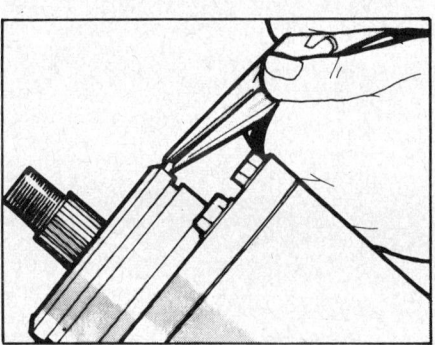

Fig. 31 Bearing cap locking pin removal, miter gearbox

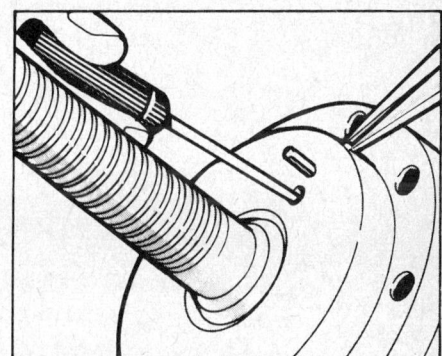

Fig. 33 High pressure seal removal, late production miter gearbox

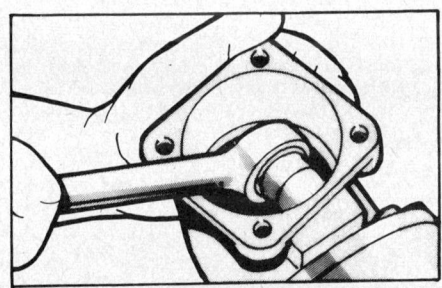

Fig. 30 Bearing cap "O" ring removal, miter gearbox

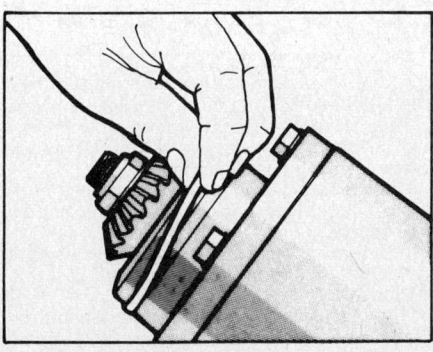

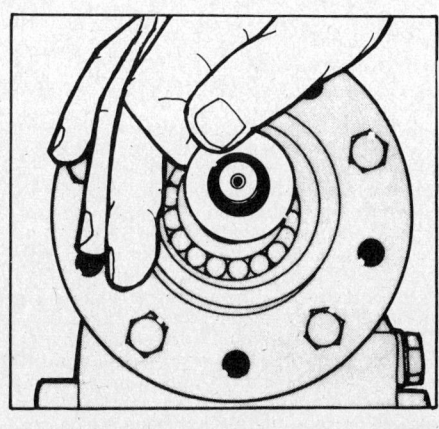

Fig. 32 Shim replacement, miter gearbox

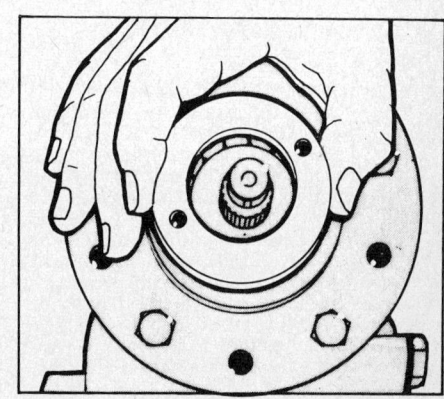

Fig. 34 Bearing retaining nut installation, miter gearbox

POWER STEERING GEARS

the piston. Install and tighten bearing cap bolts.
22. Place a new "O" ring on housing cover, then install cover assembly. It may be necessary to use a mallet to tap cover into place. Install and torque cover bolts.
23. Install new "O" rings on relief valve plungers. Install plunger and turn plungers inward approximately six turns.
24. Install pitman arm onto output shaft.

MITER GEARBOX SERVICE

Disassembly

1. Remove cover bolts and lock washers, then the cover from housing.
2. Note timing marks on shaft and gear, then drive roll pin from miter gear, Fig. 23, Fig. 24.
3. Pull miter gear from actuating shaft, Fig. 25
4. Remove locking pin from cover, Fig. 26.
5. Rotate the bearing retaining nut counter-clockwise from cover, Fig. 27, then remove bearing and actuating shaft assembly from cover, Fig. 28.
6. Drive actuating shaft from bearing with a mallet.
7. If replacement is necessary, remove seal from cover.
8. Remove grease fitting from housing.
9. Remove bolt from inside housing, Fig. 29.
10. Remove bolts and lock washers securing housing to bearing cap.
11. Tap housing from bearing with a mallet.
12. If replacement is necessary, remove "O" ring from bearing cap groove, Fig. 30.
13. Remove retaining nut and washer from actuating shaft.
14. Pull miter gear from actuating shaft.
15. Remove locking pin from bearing cap, Fig. 31. Place a mark on the lock nut to indicate proper pin hole location.
16. Place an alignment mark between lock nut and housing, then remove lock nut from bearing cap.
17. Remove shims from top of bearing, Fig. 32.
18. Remove housing bolts and lock washers.
19. Remove bearing cap and shaft assembly, turning the shaft from the valve. Note the timing marks on shaft and valve for reassembly.
20. Remove actuating shaft and bearing assembly from bearing cap, using either a mallet or a press, if necessary.
21. If damaged, remove locking pin, then the fixed plunger from bearing cap.
22. If replacement is required, remove high pressure oil seal from bearing cap.

NOTE: On early production units, the seal must be pried from bearing cap. On late production units, two holes are drilled in the bearing cap to facilitate the use of a pin punch for seal removal, Fig. 33.

Assembly

1. If removed, press new oil seal into bearing cap.
2. If removed, install fixed plunger into bearing cap. Install locking pin so the pin is positioned slightly below bearing cap surface.
3. Press bearing onto actuating shaft.
4. Install actuating shaft and bearing assembly into bearing cap. It may be necessary to use a press. Avoid damaging oil seal when installing the assembly.
5. Rotate actuating shaft into valve and align timing marks between shaft and valve.
6. Install bearing cap to housing lock washers and bolts.
7. Place shims on upper bearing surface, Fig. 32.
8. Install bearing retaining nut into bearing cap, Fig. 34.
9. Align mark on lock nut with pin hole and install locking pin through bearing cap into bearing retaining nut.
10. Install miter gear on actuating shaft, with marks aligned, Fig. 23, then the washer and retaining nut.
11. Install new "O" ring in bearing cap groove, if removed.
12. Install housing into bearing cap. Use a mallet to tap into position.
13. Install housing to bearing cap lockwashers and bolts.
14. Install the bolt inside housing.
15. Install grease fitting into housing.
16. If removed, install seal into cover.
17. With a mallet, drive actuating shaft into bearing. Use a press, if necessary.
18. Install bearing and actuating assembly into cover. Use a press, if necessary.
19. Rotate bearing retaining nut clockwise into cover.
20. Install locking pin through cover into bearing retaining nut.
21. Position miter gear on actuating shaft, aligning marks on gear and shaft.
22. Install miter gear roll pin.
23. Install cover assembly onto housing.
24. Install cover to housing lock washers and bolts.
25. Fill miter box housing with Fiske Magic ball bearing lubricant.

ADJUSTMENTS

Relief Valve Plungers, Adjust

1. Install pitman arm onto output shaft with marks aligned. Install drag link, if removed.
2. Rotate bearing cap plunger and cylinder head plunger into the gear until bottomed.
3. Start engine and operate at fast idle speed.
4. With full weight of vehicle on the wheels, turn steering wheel until the bearing cap plunger opens the relief valve. Do not force the wheel.
5. Adjust bearing cap plunger outward and continue to turn steering wheel until 1/8 inch clearance is maintained at the wheel stops. Then, lock the plunger with jam nut.
6. Repeat steps 4 and 5 to adjust cylinder head plunger.

CRANKCASE VENTILATION SYSTEMS

CRANKCASE VENTILATION

Crankcase ventilation has an important function in controlling sludge and keeping the engine lubricating system in good condition. Ineffective or inoperative crankcase ventilators are responsible for lubricating troubles serious enough in some cases to cause engine failure.

In order to control smog, the manifold vacuum system of crankcase ventilation is used on all vehicles, Fig. 1. The correct operation of this system depends upon a free flow of air from the carburetor air cleaner through the oil filler tube and engine to the control valve mounted on the intake manifold, Fig. 1. The arrows indicate the direction of the flow of air.

The system sucks crankcase vapors into the intake manifold to be burned in the combustion chamber. The flow of the vapors is controlled by the ventilator valve. The valve is actuated by engine vacuum working against spring tension. The high vacuum at engine idle provides minimum ventilation; low vacuum at road speeds provides maximum ventilation.

Servicing the system consists of checking the valve, the tubing and the air intake. The valve should be removed and checked for proper operation and for harmful deposits.

Remove the tubing and blow out any deposits with compressed air. When reinstalling the valve and tubing, make sure all connections are tight to prevent air leaks.

On some engines, the system air intake is a hose from the air cleaner to the oil filler tube. Make sure the hose is in good condition, and all connections are air tight. Check the oil filler tube cap to be sure it makes an air tight seal on the tube. Air leaks can easily be checked for by squirting kerosene at the connections.

On other engines, the system air intake is a filter type oil filler tube cap. Check the cap filter to be sure it is free of dirt. Clean it in solvent if necessary.

NOTE: If idle speed is slow, unstable, rolling with frequent stalling, breather backflow and oily engine compartment, the ventilator valve may be completely clogged or the valve may be stuck in the open position.

A valve stuck in the closed position is indicated by breather backflow and oily engine compartment.

If the valve is stuck in the intermediate position, it will be indicated by rough fast idle and stalling.

The ventilation valve assembly should be cleaned every six months or 6000 miles (whichever comes first) and more frequently in service such as extensive engine idling during cold weather.

CRANKCASE VENTILATION SYSTEMS

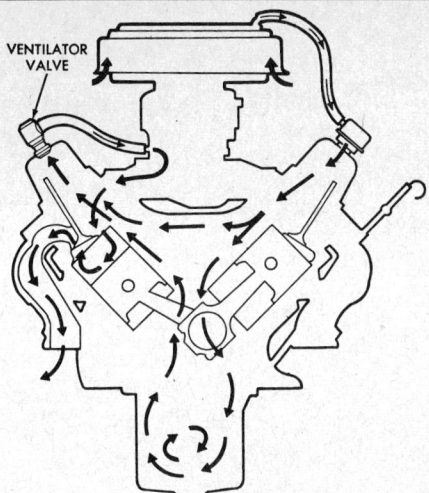

Fig. 1 Typical crankcase ventilation system

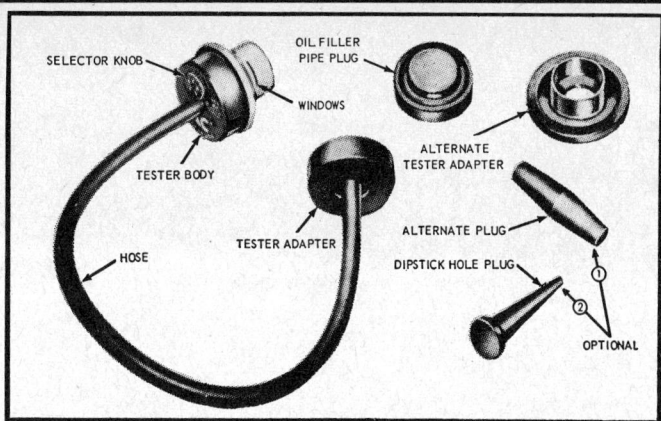

Fig. 2 AC positive crankcase ventilation system tester

When the valve assembly is removed for cleaning, place a finger over the open end of the hose or tube and have the engine started. If the ventilator hose and carburetor passages are open and operating normally, a strong suction will be felt and there will be a large change in engine idling quality when the end of the hose is uncovered. If these conditions are not observed, the carburetor passages and/or ventilator hose are clogged and must be cleaned.

PCV SYSTEM TESTS

If a condition of rough or loping engine idle speed is evident, do not attempt to compensate for this idle condition by disconnecting the crankcase ventilation system and making carburetor adjustments. The removal of the system from the engine will adversely affect the fuel economy and engine ventilation with resultant shortening of engine life.

To determine whether the loping or rough idle condition is caused by a malfunctioning crankcase ventilation system, perform either of the following tests.

Regulator Valve Test

1. Install a regulator valve known to be good in the crankcase ventilation system.
2. Start engine and compare engine idle condition to the prior idle condition.
3. If the loping or rough idle condition remains when the good regulator valve is installed, the crankcase ventilation system is not at fault. Further engine component diagnosis will have to be made to find the cause of the malfunction.
4. If the idle condition proves satisfactory, replace the regulator valve and clean hoses, fittings, etc.

AC Tester (Air Intake)

This test uses the AC positive crankcase ventilation tester, Fig. 2, which is operated by the engine vacuum through the oil filler opening.

1. With engine at normal operating temperature, remove oil filler cap and dipstick.
2. Connect one end of the hose to the tester body and connect the other end of the hose to the tester adapter.
3. Use the dipstick hole plug to plug the opening in the dipstick tube.
4. Insert the tester adapter in the filler cap opening and turn the selector knob to No. 2 (Fig. 2).
5. If the vehicle has a system with the tube from the air cleaner going into the oil filler cap, disconnect the tube at the filler cap and plug the tube.
6. Start engine and let it idle.
7. With plugs secure and tube free of kinks, hold tester body upright and note color in the tester windows. Following lists the various colors and probable cause or related condition of the system.

Fig. 3 Ford positive crankcase ventilation system tester

GREEN: System operating properly.

GREEN & YELLOW
1. Regulator valve or system partially plugged.
2. Slight kink in tester hose.
3. Slight engine blow-by.
4. Plugs from kit or engine vacuum lines are not properly sealed.
5. Tester knob improperly set.

YELLOW
1. Regulator valve or system partially plugged.
2. Tester hose kinked or blocked.
3. Blow-by at maximum capacity of regulator valve.
4. Plugs from kit or engine vacuum lines are not properly sealed.
5. Tester knob improperly set.

YELLOW & RED
1. Regulator valve or system partially or fully plugged.
2. More engine blow-by than regulator valve can handle.
3. Vent hose plugged or collapsed.

RED
1. Regulator valve or system fully plugged or stuck.
2. Vent hose plugged or collapsed.
3. Extreme blow-by.

Ford Tester

1. With engine at operating temperature, remove oil filler cap and install tester C8AZ6B627-A into cap opening. Ensure tester forms an air tight seal with valve cover preventing air leakage causing apparent tester failure or inaccurate readings.
2. If tester settles into the green (good) area, the system functions properly, Fig. 3. If tester ball settles into the red (repair) area, clean or replace system components as needed.

EMISSION CONTROL SYSTEMS

This section will deal with system descriptions, operations, visual inspections and maintenance procedures not requiring special training and sophisticated testing equipment. The testing and maintenance requiring special knowledge and equipment will be covered at the end of this section.

INDEX

Domestic Truck Systems
	Page No.
Catalytic Converters	777
Electric Assist Choke	750
Fuel Evaporative Controls	778

AMERICAN MOTORS
	Page No.
Air Guard	751
Engine Mod.	755
Exhaust Gas Recirculation	755
Thermostatic Air Cleaner	756
Vacuum Throttle Modulating System	756
Trans. Controlled Spark	754

CHRYSLER CORP.
	Page No.
Air Injection	751
Cleaner Air Package	763
Cleaner Air System	764
Coolant Control EGR System	767
Exhaust Gas Recirculation	767
EGR Time Delay System	768
Ignition	766
NOx System	765
Orifice Spark Advance Control	766
Temperature Operated Vacuum By-Pass	766
Vacuum Throttle Positioner	767

FORD MOTOR CO.
	Page No.
Auto Therm Air Cleaner	756
Cold Start Spark Advance	774
Cold Start Spark Hold	775
Cold Temperature Activated Vacuum	774
Delay Vacuum By-Pass	773
Distributor Vacuum Vent Valve	775
Dual-Area Diaphragm	773
Dual Signal Spark Advance System	776
Electronic Distributor Modulator	769
Electronic Spark Control	770
Exhaust Gas Recirculation	771
High Speed EGR Modulator Sub-System	770
Improved Combustion	768
Spark Delay Valve	771
Temperature Activated Vacuum	773
Thermactor	751
Trans. Regulated Spark	770
Trans. Regulated Spark +1	770
Vacuum Operated Exhaust Heat Control Valve	774
Wide Open Throttle Load Control Valve	776

GENERAL MOTORS CORP.
	Page No.
Air Injection Reactor	751
Combined Emission Control	761
Controlled Combustion System	757
Early Fuel Evaporation	763
Exhaust Gas Recirculation	761
Speed Controlled Spark	761
Thermostatic Controlled Air Cleaner	756
Throttle Return Control System	763
Trans. Controlled Spark	759

ELECTRIC ASSIST CHOKE

Most 1973-79 American Motors Jeep, Chrysler and Ford and 1976-79 General Motors vehicles with 6 cylinder and V8-454 engine, are equipped with an electric assist choke. This device aids in reducing the emissions of hydrocarbon (HC) and carbon monoxide (CO) during starting and warmup (choke on) period. The electric assist choke is designed to give a more rapid choke opening at temperatures of about 60° to 65° F. or greater and a slower choke opening at temperatures of about 60° to 65° F. or below.

The electric assist choke system does not change any carburetor service procedures and cannot be adjusted. If system is found out of calibration the heater control switch and/or choke unit must be replaced.

American Motors & Ford
Fig. 1—The electric choke system consists of a choke cap, thermostatic spring, a bimetal temperature sensing disc (switch), and a ceramic positive temperature coefficient (PTC) heater. The choke is powered from terminal or tap of the alternator. Current is constantly supplied to the ambient temperature switch. The system is grounded through a ground strap connected to the carburetor body. At temperatures below approximately 60 degrees, the switch opens and no current is supplied to the ceramic heater located within the thermostatic spring. Normal thermostatic spring choking action then occurs. At temperatures above approximately 60-65 degrees, the temperature sensing switch closes and current is supplied to the ceramic heater. As the heater warms, it causes the thermostatic spring to pull the choke plates open within 1–1½ minutes.

Chrysler

NOTE: The wattage of the choke heater is part of the choke calibration and may change from year to year.

Fig. 2—The control switch is connected to the ignition switch from which electrical power is obtained and transfered through electrical connection to the control switch. The 1973 switch serves two purposes.
1. Above 63° F. the control switch will energize the choke heater.
2. After a period of time, the control switch will de-energize the choke heater. The shut-down will result after the control switch warms to about 110° F. by engine heat and a small electrical heater within the switch. Since the heater control switch is mounted to the engine and near the carburetor, some winter operation may energize the choke heater. This could happen after the choke has opened without benefit of electric heat. If this happens it will have no adverse effect on

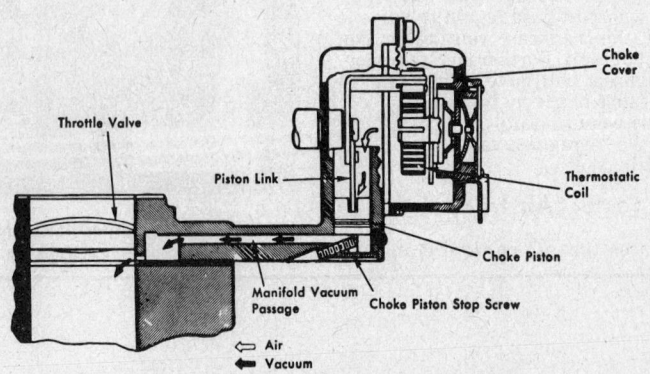

Fig. 1 American Motors & Ford electric assist choke

EMISSION CONTROL SYSTEMS

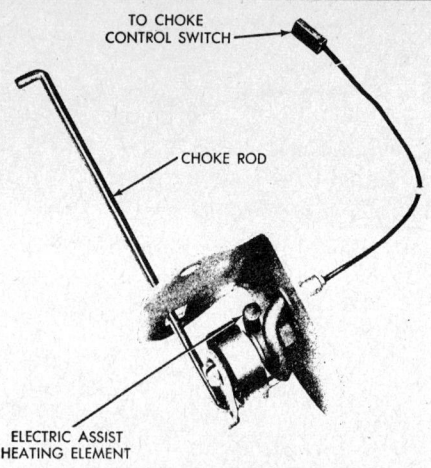

Fig. 2 Chrysler electric assist choke

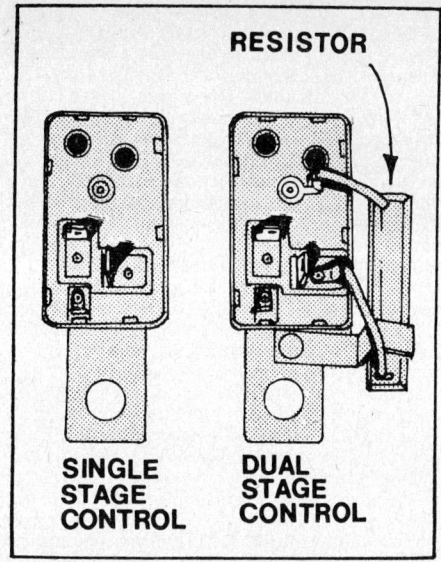

Fig. 3 Choke control unit. 1975-76 Chrysler Corp.

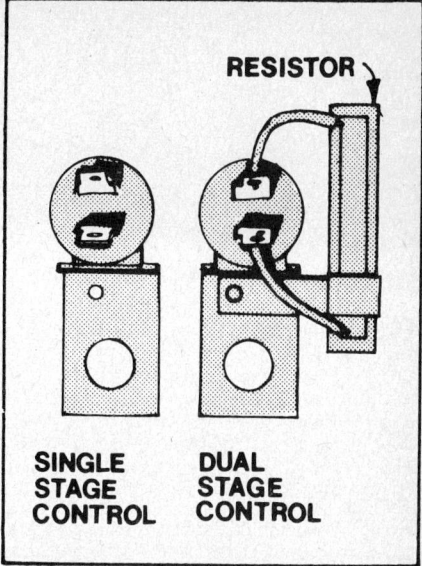

Fig. 4 Choke control unit. 1977-79 Chrysler Corp.

engine operation, and will soon be turned off.

The 1974 switch serves three purposes:
1. Below 58° F. the control switch will partially energize the choke heater.
2. Above 58° F. the control switch will fully energize the choke heater.
3. The control switch will de-energize the choke heater at approximately 110° F. During winter operations, engines will experience three stages of choke heat; partial heat during engine warmup, full heat after engine warm-up and no heat well after engine warm-up. Engine starts during summer temperatures will not experience the partial heat stage.

Two different control switches are used on 1975-79 vehicles, a single stage unit and a dual stage unit, Figs. 3 and 4.

The 1975-76 single stage control switch serves two purposes:
1. Above 68° F., the control switch will energize the choke heater.
2. At about 130° F., the control switch will de-energize the choke heater.

Since the control switch is engine mounted, some cold engine operation may energize the choke heater, especially if the choke valve has been opened without electric heat. This condition which has no adverse effect on engine operation, will return to normal.

The 1977-79 single stage control switch shortens choke duration only above 80° F. Below 55° F, electric heat is not available until the engine is at normal operating temperature. Normal engine heat will then warm the control and energize the choke heater, but only after the choke has opened by engine heat.

The 1975-76 dual stage control switch serves four purposes:
1. Below 58° F., the control switch will partially energize the choke heater.
2. Between 58-68° F., the control switch will either partially energize or fully energize the choke heater.
3. Above 68° F., the control switch will fully energize the choke heater.
4. At about 130° F., the control switch will de-energize the choke heater.

The 1977-79 dual stage control switch shortens choke duration above 80° F and stabilizes choke duration during cold weather operation. During hot weather operation, electric assist heat is hotter than during cold weather operation assist level.

Cold weather heat levels are regulated by an electrical resistor connected to both terminals of the control. Below 55° F, electrical power is reduced by the resistor. Above 80° F, the resistor is bypassed by a switch inside the control to supply full power.

Engines started during cold weather conditions will experience two levels of choke heat, low during engine warm-up and high after engine warm-up. High heat levels occur after the choke is open to insure an open choke condition under all driving conditions and minimize choking action which can occur after short stops during cold weather operation.

Engines started in hot weather conditions will not experience low choke heat levels. Engines started hot will only experience high heat because the switch is normally warmer than 80° F.

NOTE: The heating element should not be exposed to or immersed in any fluid for any purpose. An electric short in the wiring to the heater or within the heater will be a short of the ignition system.

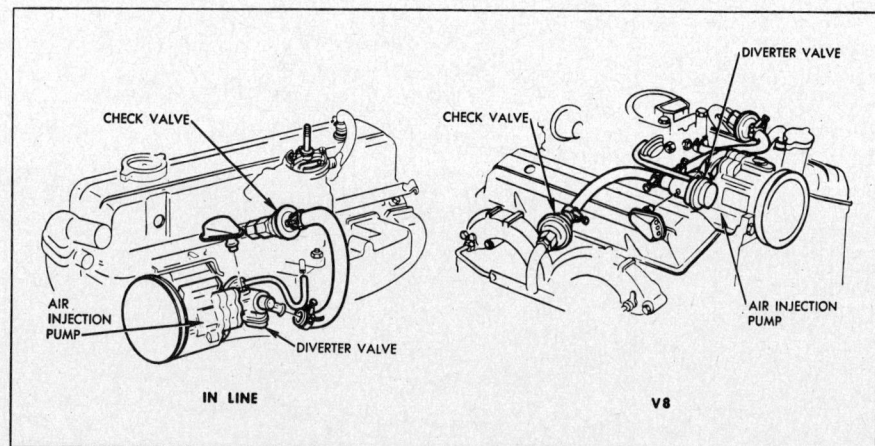

Fig. 5 Typical installation of an air pump system with a diverter valve, otherwise known as an air bypass valve. 1970-79

AIR PUMP SYSTEMS

Chrysler Air Injection
Jeep Air Guard
GM Air Injection Reactor (A.I.R.) and Ford Thermactor

All air pump systems, Fig. 5, consist of an air injection pump, air injection tubes (one for each cylinder), a diverter or air by-pass valve, check valves (one for In Line engines, two for V8s), air manifolds, tubes and hoses necessary to connect the various components.

Carburetors and distributors for engines with an air pump system are designed particularly for these engines. Therefore, they should not be interchanged with or replaced by a carburetor or distributor designed for an engine without an air pump system.

The air injection pump, Figs. 6 and 7, compresses the air and injects it through the air manifolds, hoses and injection tubes into the

EMISSION CONTROL SYSTEMS

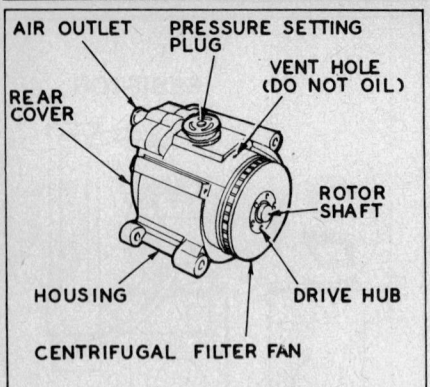

Fig. 6 Air injection pump with integral centrifugal air filter & pressure relief valve

exhaust system in the area of the exhaust valves. The fresh air ignites and burns the unburned portion of the exhaust gases in the exhaust system, thus minimizing exhaust contaminations.

The diverter or air by-pass valve, Figs. 8 and 9, when triggered by a sharp increase in manifold vacuum, shuts off the injected air to the exhaust port areas and prevents backfiring during this richer period. On engine overrun the total air supply is dumped through the muffler or the diverter or air by-pass valve. At high engine speeds the excess air is dumped through the pressure relief valve when the pressure relief valve is part of the air pump, Fig. 6, and through the diverter or air by-pass valve when the pressure relief valve is part of the diverter or air by-pass valve, Fig. 9.

1975-79 Ford Motor Co. trucks use three different types of by-pass valves, depending on the application.

The timed air by-pass valve, Fig. 10, prevents backfiring during engine deceleration when larger amounts of unburned gases flow into the exhaust manifold which causes rapid burning when mixed with fresh air. To prevent this backfiring, the by-pass valve momentarily diverts air from the pump to atmosphere. During normal operation, vacuum is equalized on both sides of the diaphragm. The return spring holds the valve closed, thus allowing fresh air to flow to the exhaust port. During deceleration, the sudden rise of intake manifold vacuum under the diaphragm overcomes spring pressure and pulls the valve downward. Air is then momentarily diverted to atmosphere because vacuum is quickly equalized on both sides of the diaphragm through a small orifice in the diaphragm.

The normally closed timed by-pass valve, Fig. 11, is used on vehicles with a catalytic converter. During normal operation, engine manifold vacuum applied through the vacuum differential valve holds the valve upward, allowing thermactor air to flow to the exhaust manifolds and blocking the vent port. When intake manifold vacuum rises or drops sharply, the vacuum differential valve operates and momentarily cuts off the vacuum to the by-pass valve. The spring pulls the stem down, seating the valve to cut off pump air to the exhaust manifolds, causing the dump valve to momentarily divert the air to atmosphere. If air pump pressure becomes excessive or there is a restriction in the system, the excess pressure will unseat the valve in the lower portion of the by-pass valve and allow a partial flow of pump air to the atmosphere, while at the same time, the valve in the upper part of the by-pass is still unseated and allows a partial flow of pump air to the exhaust manifold to meet system requirements.

The timed and vented by-pass valve, Fig. 12, functions as a timed valve until vented, then it will continuously by-pass as long as signal vacuum is four or more inches Hg.

The check valve or valves prevent exhaust gases from entering and damaging the air injection pump, as back flow can occur even under normal operating conditions.

When properly installed and maintained, the system will effectively reduce exhaust emissions. However, if any system component or any engine component that operates in conjunction with the air pump system should malfunction, the exhaust emissions might be increased.

Vacuum Differential Valve (VDV)

On 1975-79 Ford vehicles with the Thermactor system and catalytic converters, a VDV Fig. 13, is used to control the operation of the air bypass valve. Under normal operation, vacuum applied through the VDV holds the valve upward, blocking the vent port and allowing Thermactor air flow. During acceleration or deceleration or in case of system failure, the VDV momentarily cuts off vacuum flow to the bypass valve, diverting the Thermactor air flow to atmosphere. In case of excessive pressure or system restriction, the

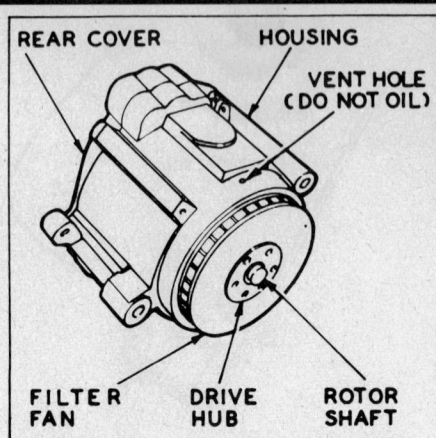

Fig. 7 Air injection pump with centrifugal air filter without pressure relief valve

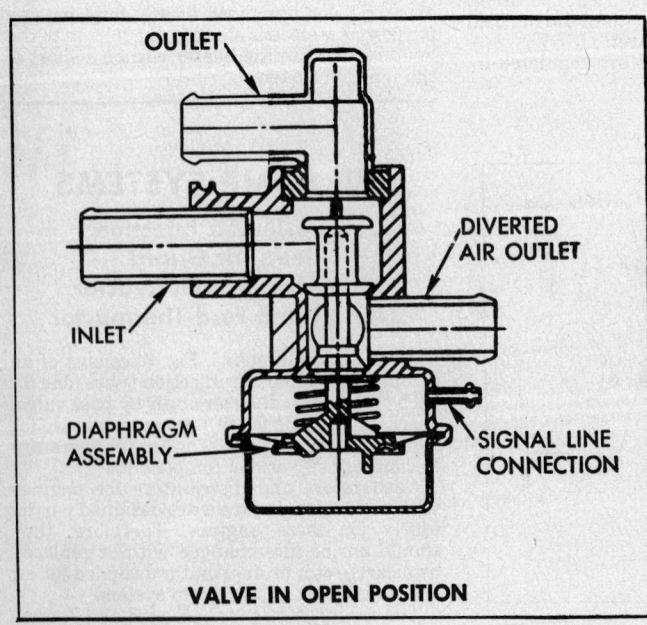

Fig. 8 Typical diverter or air by-pass valve

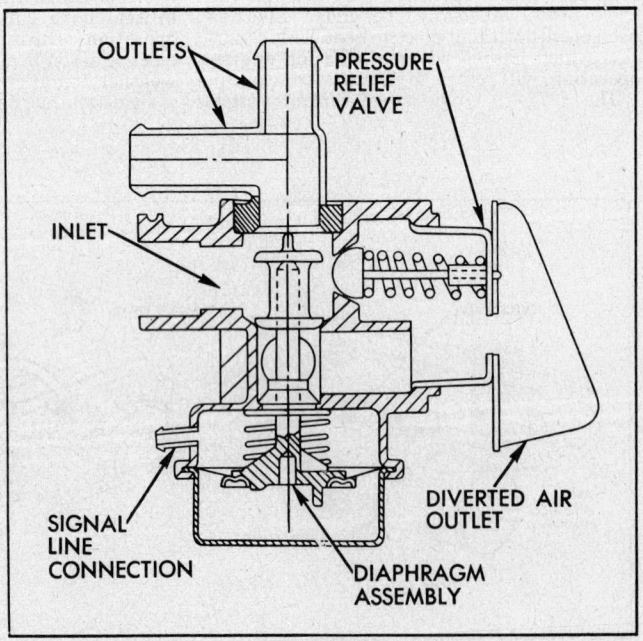

Fig. 9 Typical diverter or air by-pass valve with integral pressure relief valve

EMISSION CONTROL SYSTEMS

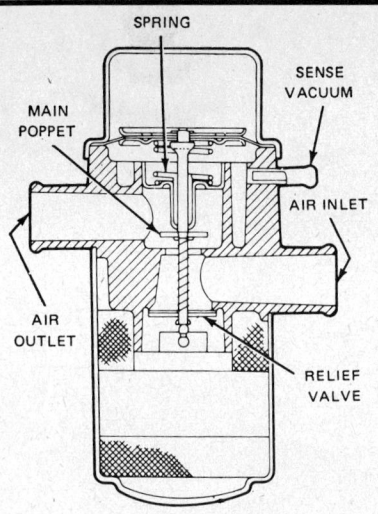

Fig. 10 Timed air by-pass valve. Ford Motor Co.

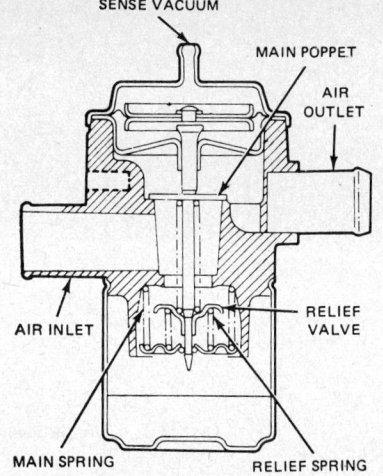

Fig. 11 Normally closed air by-pass valve. Ford Motor Co.

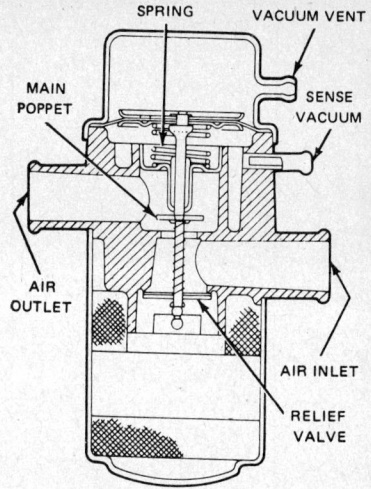

Fig. 12 Timed & vented air by-pass valve. Ford Motor Co.

excess pressure will unseat the valve in the lower part of the bypass valve, allowing a partial flow of air to atmosphere. At the same time, the valve in the upper part of the valve remains unseated allowing a partial flow of air to the exhaust manifold.

The VDV valve used on some 1978-79 General Motors vehicles equipped with V6-231, is similar in appearance and operation as the one described previously for Ford Motor Co. vehicles.

Maintenance

Because of the relationship between "Engine Tune Up" and "Unburned Exhaust Gases", the condition of the engine tune up should be checked whenever the air pump system seems to be malfunctioning. Particular care should be taken in checking items that affect fuel-air ratio, such as the crankcase ventilation system (PCV), the carburetor and carburetor air cleaner.

Because of the similarity of many parts, typical illustrations and procedures are given in the following test.

Air Manifold, Hose and Tube, Fig. 14
1. Inspect all hoses for deterioration or holes.
2. Inspect all tubes for cracks or holes.
3. Check all tube and hose routing as interference may cause wear.
4. Check all hose and tube connections.
5. If a leak is suspected on the pressure side of the system, or any tubes and/or hoses have been disconnected on the pressure side, the connections should be checked for leaks with a soapy water solution. With the pump running, bubbles will form is a leak exists.
6. To replace any hose or tube, note the routing, then remove the hose(s) or tube(s) as required.

CAUTION: The hoses used with this system are made of special material to withstand high temperature. No other type hose should be substituted.

Check Valves
1. Check valves should be inspected whenever the hose is disconnected from the check valve or whenever check valve failure is suspected.

NOTE: An air pump that has shown any indications of having exhaust gases in the pump would indicate check valve failure.

2. Orally blow through the check valve (toward air manifold) then attempt to suck back through the check valve. Flow should be in one direction only (toward air manifold).
3. To replace a check valve, disconnect pump outlet hose at check valve. Remove check valve from air manifold, being careful not to bend or twist the air manifold.

Diverter or Air By-Pass Valve
1. Check condition and routing of all lines,

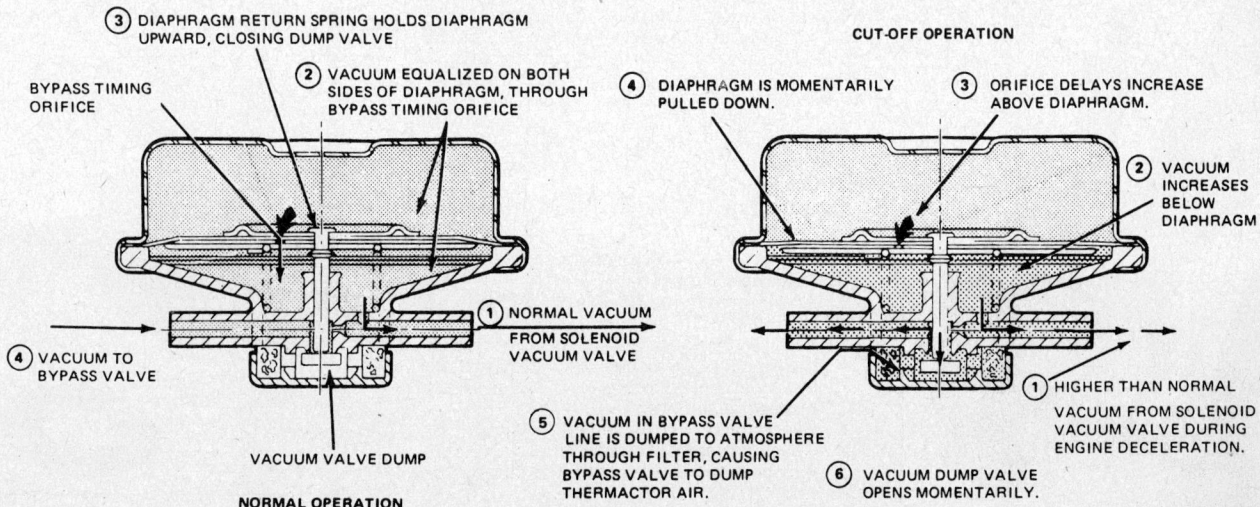

Fig. 13 Vacuum differential valve. 1975-79 Ford with Thermactor & catalytic converter

753

EMISSION CONTROL SYSTEMS

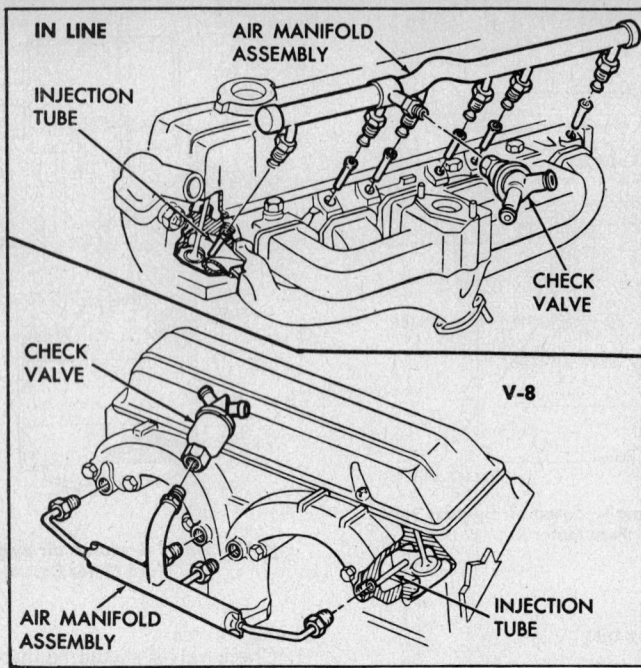

Fig. 14 Typical air manifold installations

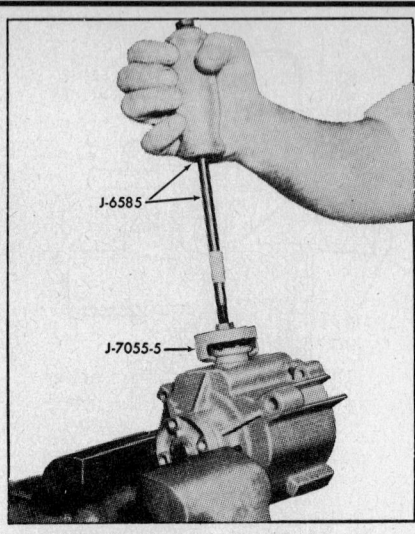

Fig. 15 Removing pressure relief valve with slide hammer tool shown

especially the signal line. All lines must be secure without crimps and not leaking.
2. Disconnect signal line at valve. A vacuum signal must be available with engine running.
3. With engine warmed up to operating temperature and carburetor at curb idle, no air should be escaping through the valve's muffler. Manually open and quickly close the throttle; a momentary blast of air should discharge through the valve's muffler for at least one second. Defective valve should be replaced.

CAUTION: Although sometimes similar in appearance, these valves are designed to meet particular requirements of various engines; therefore, be sure to install the correct valve for the engine being serviced.

4. To replace a valve, disconnect vacuum signal line and valve exhaust hose or hoses.
5. Remove diverter or air by-pass valve from pump; also muffler from valve assembly, noting angle of attachment.
6. Install muffler to new valve at angle previously noted.
7. Install diverter or air by-pass valve to pump or bracket with new gasket.
8. Install outlet and vacuum lines and check system for leaks.

Air Injection Tube

There is no periodic service or inspection for air injection tubes. However, whenever the cylinder head is removed from In Line engines, or whenever exhaust manifolds are removed from V8 engines, inspect the tubes for carbon build-up and warped or burnt tubes. Remove any carbon build-up with a wire brush. Warped or burnt tubes must be replaced.
1. To replace a tube, remove carbon from tubes and, using penetrating oil, work tubes out of cylinder head or exhaust manifold.
2. Install new tubes in cylinder head or manifold.

Air Injection Pump

1. Accelerate engine to about 1500 rpm and observe air flow from hose or hoses. If air flow increases as engine is accelerated, the pump is operating satisfactorily. If air flow does not increase or is not present, proceed as follows:
2. Check for proper drive belt tension.
3. Check for leaky pressure relief valve. Air may be heard leaking with the pump running.

NOTE: The air pump system is not completely noiseless. Under normal conditions noise rises in pitch as engine speed increases. To determine if excessive noise is the fault of the system, operate the engine with the pump drive belt removed. If excessive noise does not exist with the belt removed, proceed as follows:

4. Check for seized air pump.
5. Check hoses, tubes, air manifolds and all connections for leaks and proper routing.
6. Check carburetor air cleaner for proper installation.
7. Check air pump for proper mounting.
8. If none of the above conditions exist and the air pump has excessive noise, remove and replace the pump unit.
9. To replace the pump, disconnect hoses at pump and remove pump pulley.
10. Unfasten and remove pump.
11. Install pump with mounting bolts loose.
12. Install pump pulley and drive belt.
13. Adjust drive belt tension and connect hoses at pump.

Pressure Relief Valve

When the pressure relief valve is incorpo-

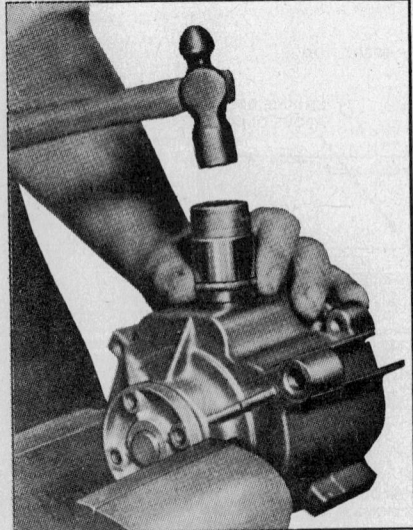

Fig. 16 Installing pressure relief valve

Fig. 17 Removing centrifugal type pump air filter

EMISSION CONTROL SYSTEMS

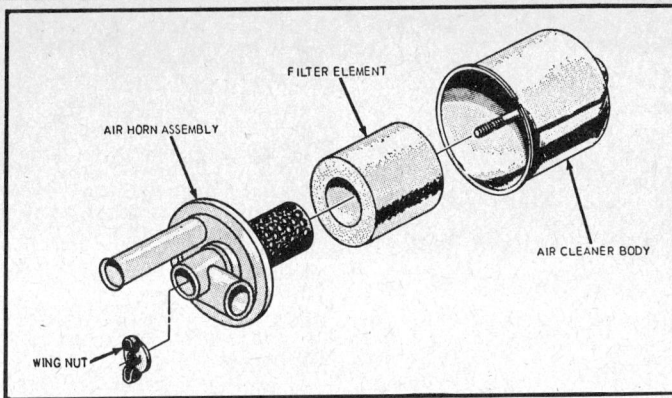

Fig. 18 Conventional type pump air filter

rated in the diverter or air by-pass valve the complete valve must be replaced. If the relief valve is in the pump, proceed as follows:
1. Pull relief valve from pump, Fig. 15.
2. Using a 15/16" socket, Fig. 16, tap relief valve into housing until valve shoulders on housing. Use extreme care to avoid distorting housing.

NOTE: Various length pressure setting plugs designed for the particular requirements of the vehicle being serviced determine the pressure required to open the relief valve. Usually, the pressure setting plugs are color-coded. To remove the pressure setting plug, carefully unlock the legs from the inside surface of the relief valve with a small screwdriver. To install the plug, carefully push it into the relief valve until the legs lock. If a pressure setting plug is to be reused be sure the leg angles are sufficient for the plug to lock in place.

Centrifugal Pump Filter
1. To replace the centrifugal type, Fig. 17, remove drive belt and pump pulley. Pry loose outer disc of filter fan, being careful to prevent fragments from entering the air intake hole.
2. Install the new filter by drawing it on with the pulley and pulley bolts. Do not attempt to install a filter by hammering it or pressing it on.
3. Draw the filter down evenly by alternately tightening the bolts. Make certain that the outer edge of the filter slips into the housing. The slight amount of interference with the housing bore is normal.

Conventional Type Filter, Fig. 18
Remove and replace the air filter element as suggested by the illustration. The filter element is not cleanable; it must be replaced. Position the assembled air horn and filter element in the air cleaner body, being sure the tang is fitted into the slot.

JEEP "ENGINE MOD" SYSTEM

This system controls exhaust emission levels by using composition cylinder head gaskets instead of steel gaskets and a special carburetor and distributor calibration. The carburetor incorporates idle limiters. The distributor centrifugal advance is calibrated to provide best performance and economy in the driving range and ignition timing is retarded only at idle speed (T.D.C.) to reduce exhaust emission levels at this slow engine speed. These engine modifications will result in a more complete combustion. Thermostatically controlled air cleaners are also used on most units to speed up engine warm-up.

JEEP EXHAUST GAS RECIRCULATION (EGR)

The EGR system consists of a diaphragm actuated flow control valve (EGR valve), coolant temperature override switch, low temperature vacuum signal modulator, high temperature vacuum signal modulator and connecting hoses.

The purpose of the EGR system is to limit the formation of oxides of nitrogen (NOx) by diluting the fresh intake charge with a metered amount of exhaust gas, thereby reducing the peak temperatures of the burning gases in the engine combustion chambers.

EGR Valve
The EGR valve is mounted on a machined surface at the rear of the intake manifold on V8 engines and on the side of the intake manifold on six cylinder engines. The valve used with an automatic transmission is calibrated differently than the valve used with a manual transmission.

The valve is held in a normally closed position by a coiled spring located above the diaphragm. A special fitting is provided at the carburetor to route ported (above throttle) vacuum through hose connections to a fitting on the valve which is located above the diaphragm. A passage in the intake manifold directs exhaust gas from the exhaust crossover passage (V8 engine) or from below the riser area (six cylinder engine) to the EGR valve. When the diaphragm is actuated by vacuum, the valve opens and meters exhaust gas through another passage in the intake manifold to the floor of the manifold below the carburetor.

Coolant Temperature Override Switch
This switch is located at the coolant passage of the intake manifold (adjacent to oil filler tube) on a V8 engine or at the left side of the engine block (formerly the drain plug location) on a six cylinder engine. The outer part of the switch is open and not used. The inner port is connected by a hose to the EGR fitting at the carburetor. The center port is connected to the EGR valve.

When the coolant temperature is below 115° F (160° F on some vehicles), the center port of the switch is closed and no vacuum signal is applied to the EGR valve, therefore, no exhaust gas will flow through the valve. When the coolant temperature reaches 115° F (160° F on some vehicles), both the center and inner port of the switch are open and a vacuum signal is applied to the EGR valve. However, the vacuum signal to the EGR valve is subject to regulation by low and high temperature signal modulators.

Low Temperature Vacuum Signal Modulator
This unit is located at the left side of the front upper crossmember, just ahead of the radiator, on the same mounting bracket as the TCS ambient temperature override switch and is connected to the EGR vacuum signal

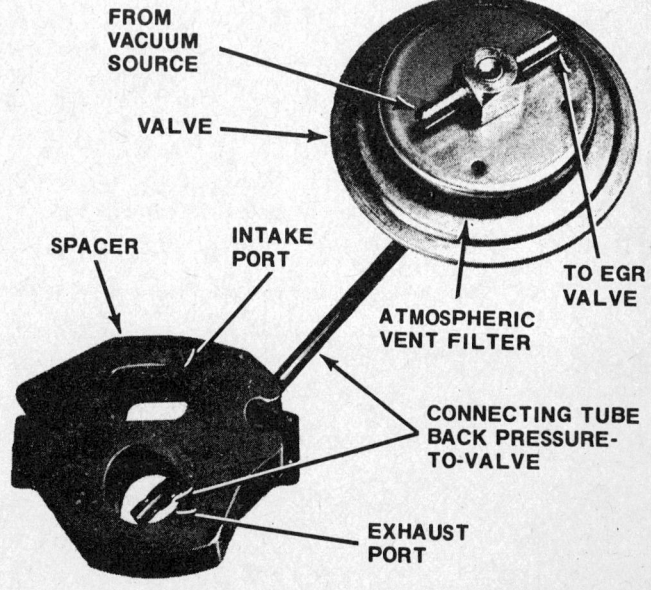

Fig. 19 Jeep Exhaust Back-Pressure Sensor

755

EMISSION CONTROL SYSTEMS

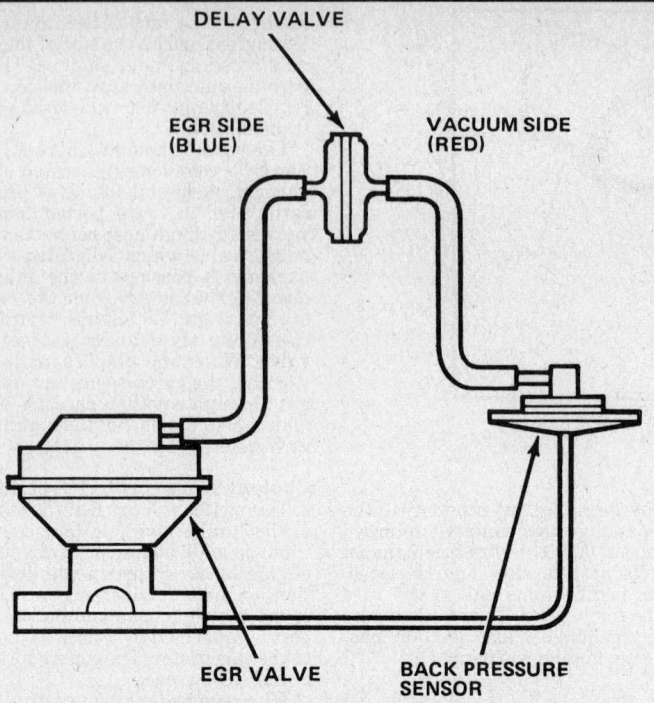

Fig. 20 EGR delay valve. 1977–79 American Motors Jeep

hose. The modulator is open when ambient temperatures are below 60° F. This causes a weakened vacuum signal to the EGR valve and a resultant decrease in the amount of exhaust gas being recirculated.

High Temperature Vacuum Signal Modulator

This unit is located at the rear of the engine compartment and is connected to the EGR vacuum signal hose. The modulator opens when the underhood air temperature reaches 115° F and causes a weakened vacuum signal to the EGR valve. As a result, the amount of exhaust gas being recirculated is decreased.

Exhaust Back-Pressure Sensor

1974 California light duty vehicles equipped with V8-360 engines and automatic transmission and 1975–79 heavy duty vehicles equipped with V8-360 and 401 engines, are required to have an exhaust back-pressure transducer, Fig. 19. This device consists of a diaphragm valve, a spacer, and a metal tube. The EGR valve is mounted to the sensor spacer and is modulated by the sensor.

The EGR system, when equipped with a back-pressure sensor, obtains a vacuum signal at the carburetor spark port and not the EGR port. The vacuum signal passes through the EGR CTO (Coolant Temperature Override) switch (when coolant temperature exceeds 115° F with black CTO switch or 160° F with yellow CTO switch) to the valve portion of the sensor where it is modulated by exhaust back-pressure.

When exhaust back-pressure is relatively high, as during acceleration and some cruising conditions, exhaust back-pressure traveling through the metal tube overcomes spring tension on the diaphragm within the back-pressure sensor valve, and closes the valve atmospheric vent.

With the back-pressure sensor valve no longer vented to atmosphere, the vacuum signal now passes through the back-pressure sensor valve, and the EGR valve. When vacuum signals the EGR valve, exhaust gas recirculation commences.

When exhaust back-pressure is too low to overcome diaphragm spring tension, the vacuum signal is vented to atmosphere and does not pass through to the EGR valve. With no vacuum signal applied to the EGR valve, exhaust gas does not recirculate.

The back-pressure sensor is not serviceable and must be replaced if defective.

EGR Delay Valve

This valve is used on 1976–79 V8-360, 401 engines with 4 barrel carburetor. The delay valve is installed between the EGR valve and back-pressure sensor, Fig. 20, and delays the vacuum signal to the EGR valve to prevent hesitation on initial acceleration. The delay valve is color coded to prevent improper installation. The red side of the valve connects to the back-pressure sensor and the blue side connects to the EGR valve.

VACUUM THROTTLE MODULATING SYSTEM

This system (VTM), which is used to reduce hydrocarbon emissions during coasting, consists of a decel valve located at the right front side of the intake manifold and a throttle modulating diaphragm located at the carburetor base.

During coasting, when manifold vacuum reaches about 21–22 inches Hg., the decel valve opens to allow vacuum to operate the throttle modulating diaphragm. The throttle modulating diaphragm holds the throttle valve slightly open, thereby allowing more air to enter the combustion chambers to lean out the overrich mixture and reduce hydrocarbon emissions.

THERMOSTATIC CONTROLLED AIR CLEANER, TAC & AUTO-THERM AIR CLEANER SYSTEMS

Jeep Six & All Ford

Temperature Controlled

Carburetor air temperature is thermostati-

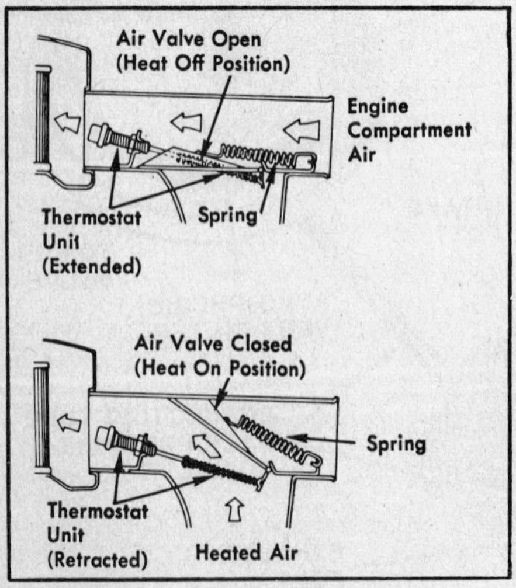

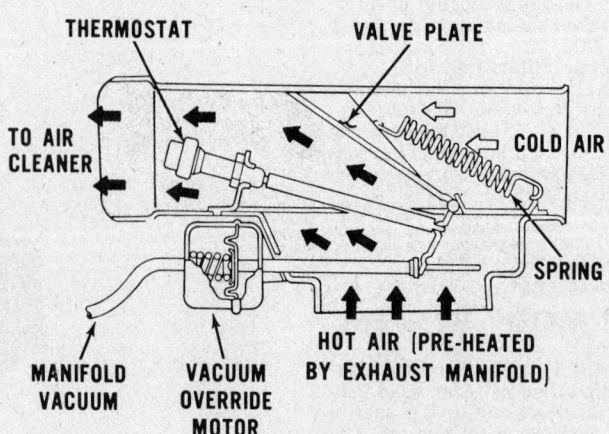

Fig. 21 Temperature operated duct and valve assembly

Fig. 22 Duct and valve assembly with vacuum override motor

EMISSION CONTROL SYSTEMS

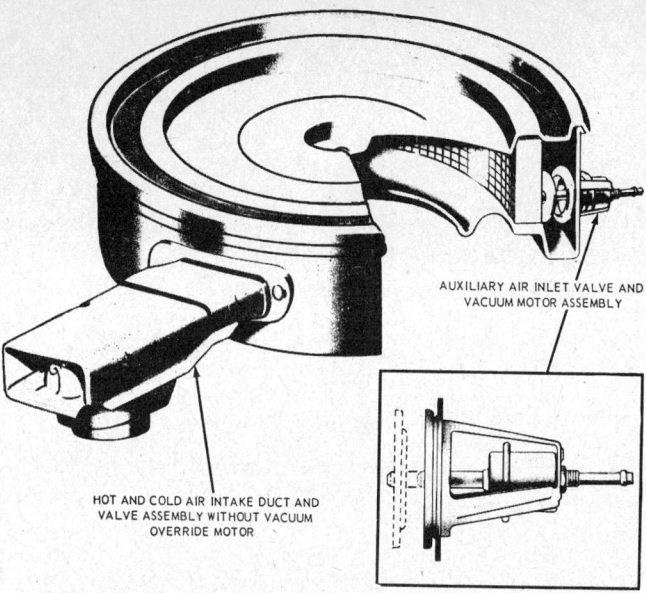

Fig. 23 Air cleaner with auxiliary air inlet valve and vacuum motor

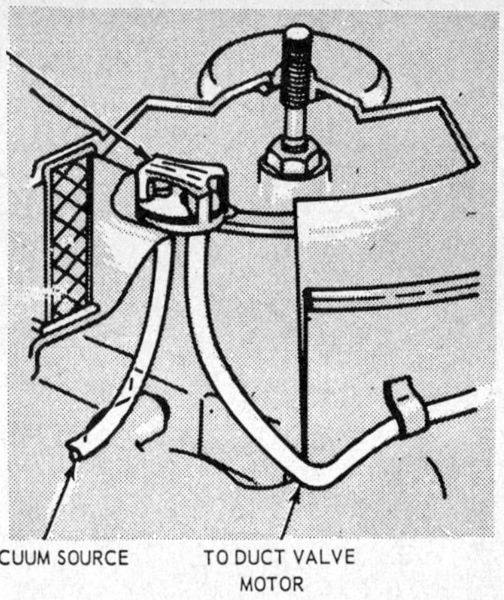

Fig. 24 Vacuum operated duct and valve assembly

cally controlled by the air duct and valve assembly. Air from the engine compartment, or heated air from the shrouded exhaust manifold is supplied to the engine Fig. 21.

During the engine warm-up period when the air temperature entering the air duct is less than 105° F, the thermostat is in the retracted position and the air valve is held in the closed position by the air valve spring, thus shutting off the air from the engine compartment. Air is then drawn from the shroud at the exhaust manifold.

As the temperature of the air passing the thermostat unit rises, the thermostat starts to open and pull the air valve down. This allows cooler air from the engine compartment to enter the air cleaner. When the temperature of the air reaches 130° F, the air valve is in the open position so that only engine compartment air is allowed to enter the air cleaner.

Vacuum Controlled

Some Ford systems incorporate a vacuum override motor, Fig. 22. This motor during cold acceleration periods provides additional air to carburetor. The decrease in intake manifold vacuum during acceleration causes the vacuum override motor to override the thermostat control, opening the system to both engine compartment air and heated air from the exhaust manifold shroud.

Yet another Ford application of same system uses a vacuum motor, Fig. 23, installed on the perimeter of the air cleaner to take the place of the vacuum override motor. When the manifold vacuum is low, during heavy engine loading or high speed operation, a spring in the vacuum motor opens the motor valve plate into the air cleaner. This provides the maximum air supply for greater volumetric efficiency.

Thermostatically Controlled Vacuum Operated

A vacuum operated duct valve with a thermostatic bi-metal color, Fig. 24, is used on some installations. The valve in the duct assembly is in an open position when the engine is not operating. When the engine is operating at below normal operating temperature, manifold vacuum is routed through the bi-metal switch to the vacuum motor to close the duct valve allowing only heated air to enter the air cleaner. When the engine reaches normal operating temperature the bi-metal switch opens an air bleed which eliminates the vacuum and the duct valve opens allowing only cold air to enter the air cleaner. During periods of acceleration the duct valve will open regardless of temperature due to the loss of manifold vacuum.

American Motors V8 & All General Motors

Figs. 25 thru 28—Carburetor air temperature is controlled by a pair of doors, located in the air cleaner snorkel, which channel either pre-heated or under hood air to the carburetor.

Pre-heated air is obtained by passing under hood air through ducts surrounding the exhaust manifold, causing it to pick up heat from the manifold surface. The heated air is then drawn up through a pipe to the air cleaner snorkel.

Underhood air is picked up at the air cleaner snorkel in the conventional manner.

The two air mixing doors work together so that as one opens, the other closes and vice versa. When underhood temperature is below approximately 90 deg. F., the cold air door closes, causing the hot air door to open. Hot air from the exhaust manifold stove is then drawn into the carburetor. As the underhood temperature increases, the cold air door begins to open until the temperature reaches approximately 115° to 130 deg. F, at which time the cold air door is fully open and the hot air door is fully closed.

The doors are controlled by a vacuum motor mounted on the air cleaner snorkel. This motor, in turn, is controlled by a sensor inside the air cleaner which regulates the amount of vacuum present in the vacuum motor according to air cleaner temperature. Whenever manifold vacuum drops below 5–8 inches, depending on the unit, the diaphragm spring in the motor will open the cold air door wide in order to provide maximum air flow.

The vacuum motor and control door assembly in the left snorkel on outside air induction units does not have a sensor and is controlled only by manifold vacuum. This snorkel remains closed until full throttle is obtained. With manifold vacuum at 6–8 inches, the door will open, allowing maximum air flow.

GENERAL MOTORS CCS
Controlled Combustion System

The CCS system, Fig. 25, uses a special calibrated carburetor and distributor, related hoses, plus the component parts of the closed P.C.V. system.

Exhaust emissions are controlled at idle by using a double acting vacuum advance unit to retard the spark. The retard side of the unit is connected to a spark port in the carburetor throttle flange below the throttle plate. When the throttle is opened beyond idle position, vacuum from above the throttle plate is ported to the advance side of the unit which then functions in the normal manner (spark advances).

Exhaust emissions are held below the maximum allowable level under all other operating conditions without the use of the complete A.I.R. system.

The CCS system is designed to keep the air entering the carburetor at approximately 100 deg. F. When the underhood temperature is less than 100 deg. F. By keeping the temperature at 100 deg. F. or above, the carburetor can be calibrated to operate more efficiently without affecting engine performance, provide improved fuel economy, eliminate carburetor icing and improve engine warm-up.

Operation, Figs. 25 thru 28

During engine warm-up period, with engine compartment temperatures below 85 to 128 deg. F., the temperature sensor is closed. This allows engine vacuum to be directed to the vacuum motor, closing the valve plate to outside air. With the valve closed, the cool air will flow through the holes in the left side of the shroud where it is heated. The heated air then flows up through the hot air pipe and connector into the air cleaner.

As the temperature inside of the air filter element reaches approximately 128 deg. F., the bi-metal temperature sensor bleeds off vacuum to the right vacuum motor, causing the valve to open, allowing underhood air to be mixed with the heated air as needed to keep the air temperature at approximately 128 deg. F.

Under full throttle or below 6 to 8 inches of vacuum, the vacuum motor will no longer hold the valve open to hot air. Therefore, the

757

EMISSION CONTROL SYSTEMS

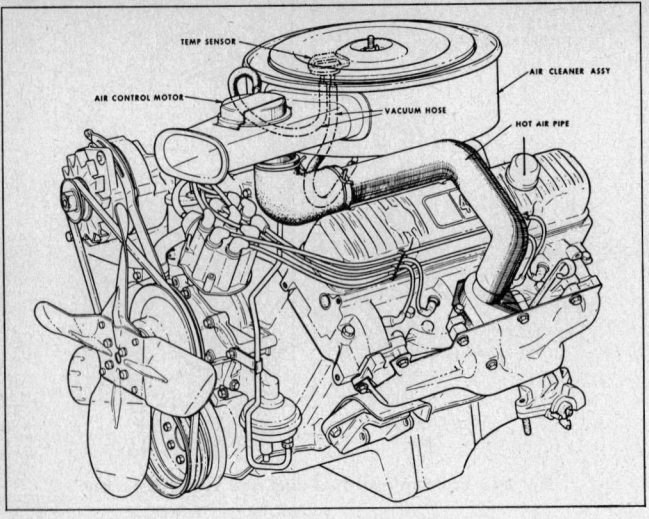

Fig. 25 Controlled Combustion System installed on a V8 engine

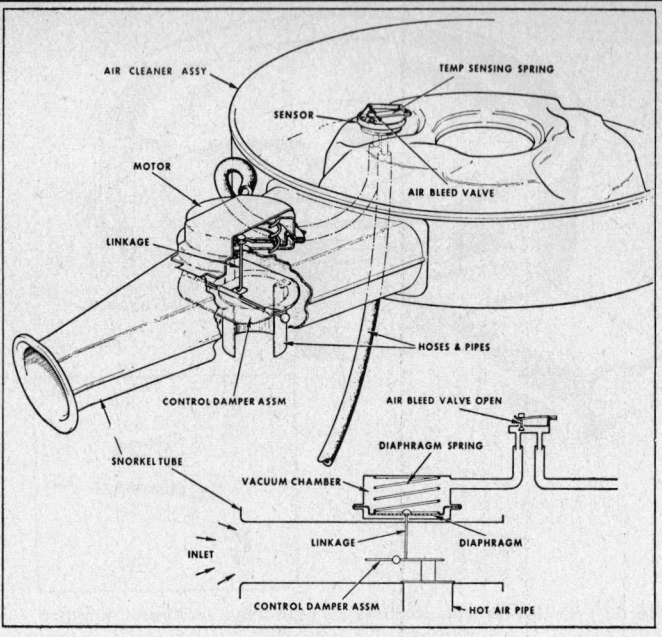

Fig. 26 Cold air door open

hot air pipe is closed off, allowing only underhood air to enter the air cleaner.

The vacuum motor and valve plate in the left snorkel (when used) is controlled only by intake manifold vacuum. Therefore, this snorkel is always closed until full throttle is desired, allowing maximum air flow into the air cleaner.

Thermo Vacuum Switch

Because of the increased possibility of engine overheating at idle with the C.C.S. calibration, the thermo vacuum switch Fig. 29 is added to the system on some engines. This switch senses engine coolant temperature and, if temperature reaches 220 deg. F., the switch valve moves to allow manifold vacuum to reach the distributor to advance the timing and allow the engine to run cooler.

Idle Stop Solenoid

Most vehicles equipped with the Controlled Combustion System (CCS), have an idle stop solenoid mounted on the carburetor, Fig. 30. The purpose of this solenoid is to prevent engine operation after the ignition is shut off, a condition known as "dieseling." Dieseling is prevalent with the CCS system, especially when the vehicle has an automatic transmission, for the following reasons:

With the Controlled Combustion System for exhaust emission reduction, the ignition timing is slightly retarded and idle rpm is slightly higher. Also engine operating temperature is higher—195°F.

With automatic transmissions, idle speed is set with the transmission in Drive. When the driver is about to turn off the ignition, the selector lever is shifted to Park or Neutral position. Since the load of the transmission is removed in these ranges, idle rpm rises into the 700 rpm range.

With the engine running at this rpm, plus other factors, such as higher operating temperature, regular fuel and slightly retarded spark, "dieseling" may be encountered. The solenoid eliminates this dieseling possibility by closing the throttle valve(s) when the ignition is turned off.

As shown, the solenoid is mounted on the carburetor and acts upon the throttle valve(s) in the same manner as an idle set screw. When the ignition switch is turned on, the solenoid coil is activated and the plunger is driven to its full extended position. The plunger acts on the throttle valve lever and sets the throttle valve(s) in a position to

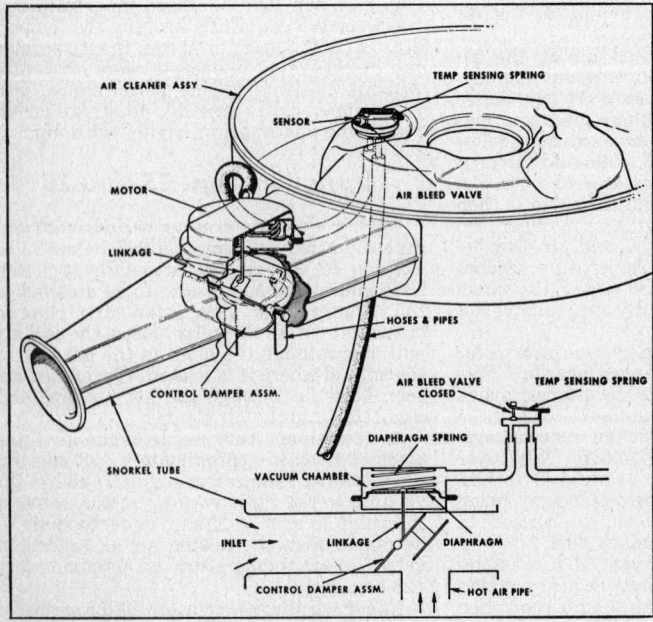

Fig. 27 Hot air door open. CCS

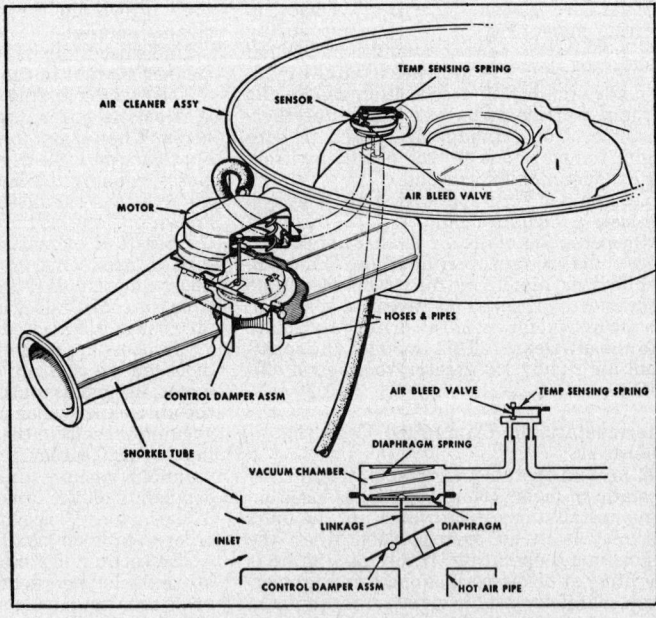

Fig. 28 Cold and hot air doors both partially open. CCS

EMISSION CONTROL SYSTEMS

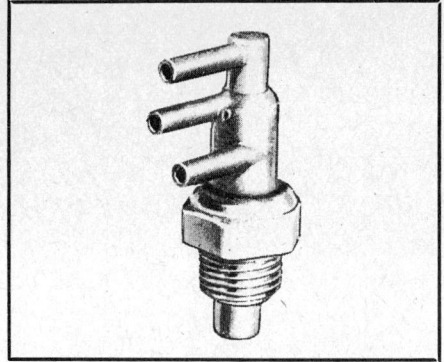

Fig. 29 Thermo vacuum switch. Typical of General Motors CCS, Ford IMCO and Chrysler NOx, OSAC (temperature sensing valve)

Fig. 30 Idle stop solenoid

achieve the specified rpm.

When the ignition switch is turned off, the solenoid is de-energized and the plunger retracts into the solenoid. The throttle valve(s) closes to a position controlled by the low idle adjusting screw. At this point the throttle valve(s) is opened only enough to allow the engine to run at a much lower rpm. This lower setting keeps the throttle valve(s) from completely closing and scuffing the throttle bore(s).

The lower idle speed setting just mentioned is achieved with a set screw when the solenoid is electrically disconnected. The setting for normal idle speed is adjusted with solenoid energized, through the hex screw in the plunger and/or by repositioning the solenoid in its mounting clamp.

NOTE: To set the solenoid while starting a hot engine, the accelerator pedal must be depressed approximately one-third of its travel.

When starting a cold engine, however, the accelerator pedal must be fully depressed to set both the choke and the idle stop solenoid.

TRANSMISSION CONTROLLED SPARK (TCS)

American Motors

This system is designed to provide vacuum spark advance during high gear operation and certain engine conditions. The resultant is a lower peak combustion pressure and temperature during the power stroke, significantly reducing exhaust emissions.

Basically the system incorporates an ambient temperature override switch, solenoid vacuum valve, solenoid control switch and in some systems a coolant temperature override switch.

The ambient temperature override switch, senses ambient temperatures and completes the electrical circuit from the battery to the solenoid vacuum valve when ambient temperatures are above 63° F.

The solenoid vacuum valve is attached to the intake manifold. When the valve is energized, carburetor ported vacuum is blocked and the distributor vacuum line is vented to atmosphere through a port in the valve, resulting in no vacuum advance. When the valve is de-energized, ported vacuum is applied to the distributor resulting in normal vacuum advance.

The solenoid control switch, located at the transmission, opens or closes in relation to car speed automatic transmission equipped cars or gear range manual transmission equipped. At speeds above 34 MPH on automatic transmission equipped cars, high gear on manual transmission equipped cars, the switch opens and breaks the ground circuit to the solenoid vacuum valve. At speeds under 25 MPH automatic transmission equipped cars, lower gear

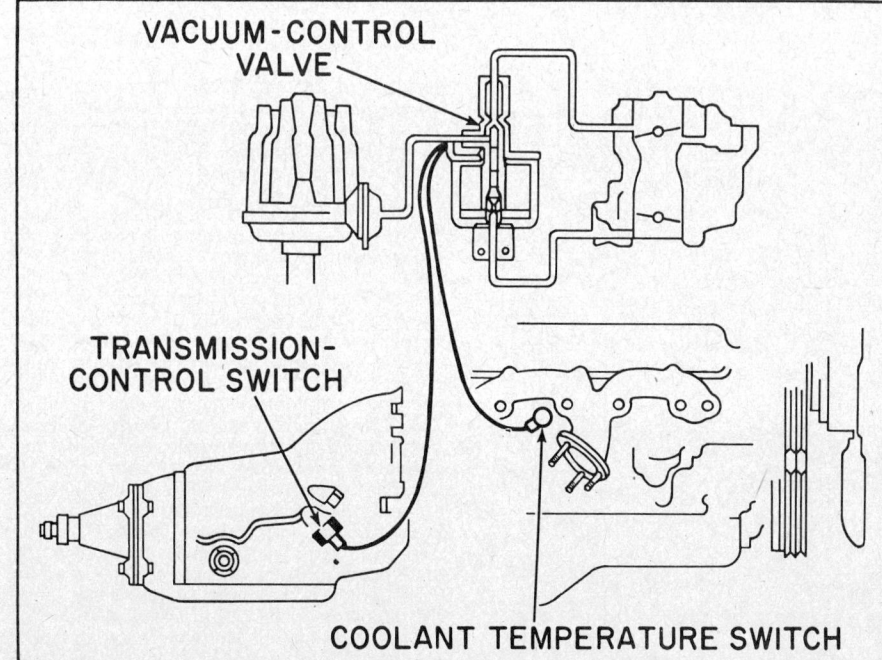

Fig. 31 Typical T.C.S. emission control

EMISSION CONTROL SYSTEMS

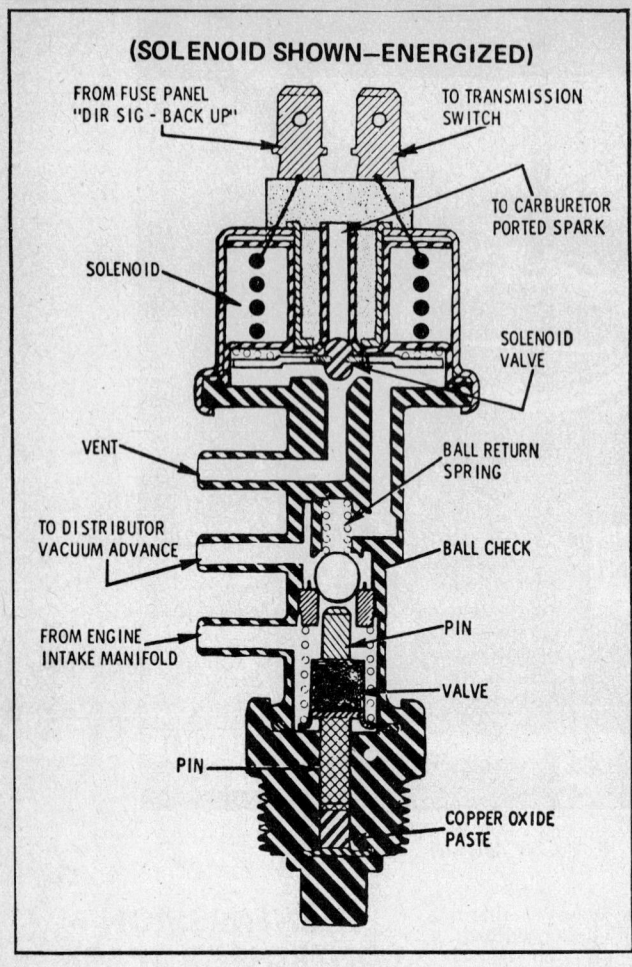

Fig. 32 TVS-TCS combination valve

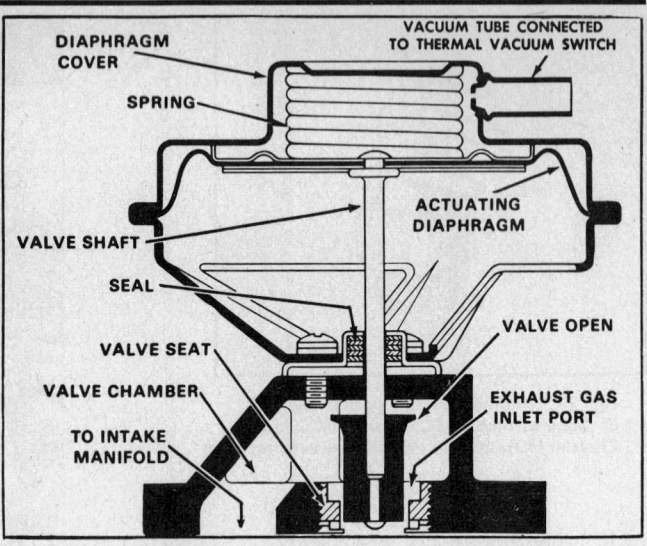

Fig. 33 Single diaphragm E.G.R. valve cross section

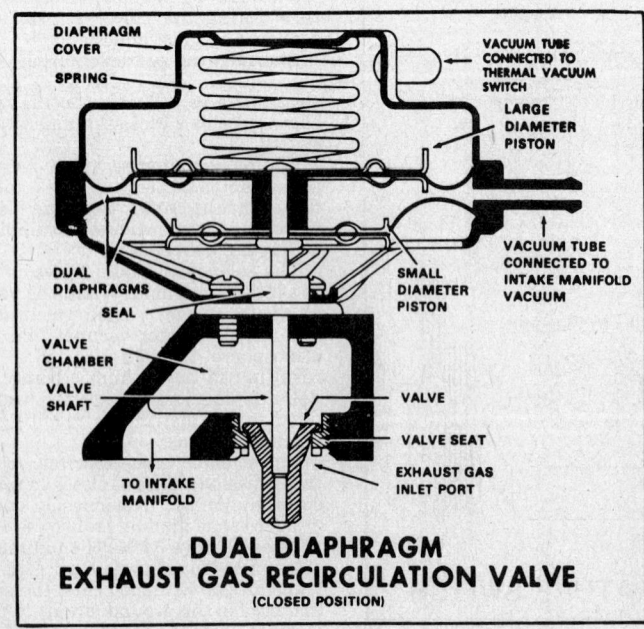

Fig. 34 Dual diaphragm E.G.R. valve cross section

ranges manual transmission equipped, the switch closes and completes the ground circuit to the solenoid vacuum valve.

On automatic transmission equipped vehicles, the switch is automatically operated by the speedometer gear speed while on manual transmissions, the switch is manually operated by the shifter shaft.

The coolant temperature override switch, is threaded into the thermostat housing and is used on all V8 and some 6 cylinder engines. It is also used in conjunction with TCS systems. Its purpose is to improve driveability during the warm-up period by providing full distributor vacuum advance until the engine coolant temperature has reached 160° F. The switch incorporates a thermal unit which reacts to coolant temperatures to route either intake manifold or carburetor ported vacuum to the distributor vacuum advance diaphragm.

General Motors

This system is designed to provide vacuum spark advance during high gear operation only. The resulting ignition timing in the lower gears significantly reduces exhaust emissions.

Basically, the T.C.S. system consists of a vacuum control valve, transmission control switch and a coolant temperature switch. The valve controls the vacuum signal to the distributor vacuum advance unit in response to a signal from either switch, Fig. 31.

The vacuum control valve is of solenoid design and is installed in the vacuum line between the carburetor and the distributor. When energized by the transmission control switch, the valve blocks the vacuum source and vents the advance unit through the carburetor air horn.

When the engine is cold, and in some units when the engine temperature exceeds 210° F, the coolant temperature switch overrides the system and provides full manifold vacuum to the advance unit, advancing timing in turn lowering engine operating temperature. This switch operates through a relay mounted on the fire wall. Some systems use combination TVS-TCS valve, Fig. 32, to provide system over-riding vacuum to the advance unit.

A Distributor Vacuum Spark Thermal Valve, sensing air-fuel mixture temperature, provides full advance in any gear when the mixture temperature is below 62° F. When the air-fuel mixture temperature rises above 62° F, the thermal valve closes, shutting off vacuum in turn, to provide vacuum advance, the distributor must be energized, depending on condition, by the TCS switch, Cold Feed Switch or the Hot Coolant Switch.

The TCS switch grounds the distributor solenoid in high gear only when the Cold Feed Switch is closed. The Cold Feed Switch depending on application closes when cylinder

EMISSION CONTROL SYSTEMS

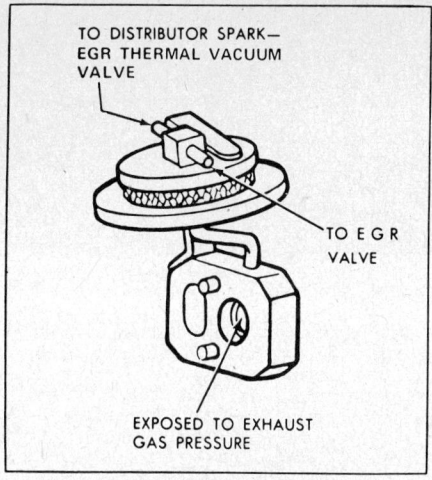

Fig. 35 Exhaust back pressure transducer valve

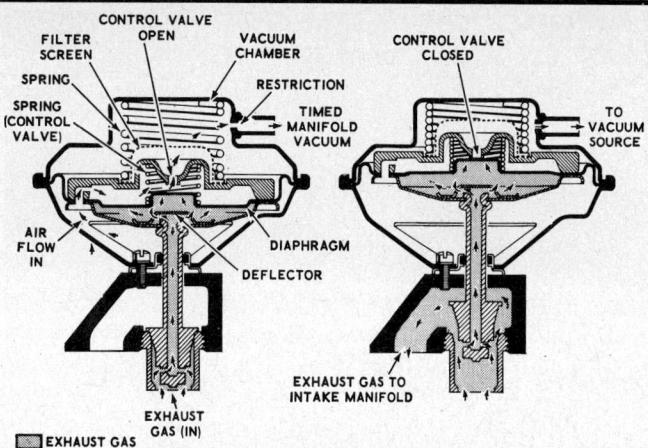

Fig. 36 Integral back pressure EGR valve. General Motors

head temperature reaches 125°, 149° or 155° F. Regardless of TCS switch position, the Hot Coolant Switch grounds the distributor solenoid when coolant temperature is over 240° F.

On some models, a Distributor Vacuum Spark Delay Valve is installed between the distributor solenoid and distributor. This valve restricts the rate of initial vacuum supplied to the distributor, full vacuum will be supplied gradually.

GENERAL MOTORS CEC

Combined Emission Control System

This system is designed to provide vacuum spark advance during high gear operation only, as does the T.C.S. system, but the C.E.C. solenoid vacuum switch also regulates curb idle and high gear deceleration throttle positions, further reducing emissions.

The C.E.C. system consists of a vacuum control solenoid valve, transmission control switch, coolant temperature switch and a time-delay relay.

When the solenoid is in the non-energized position, vacuum to the distributor vacuum advance unit is shut off and the distributor is vented to the atmosphere through a filter at the opposite end of the solenoid. When the solenoid is energized by one of the switches or the relay, the vacuum port is uncovered and the plunger is seated at the opposite end, shutting off the clean air vent. This routes vacuum to the distributor. The solenoid is energized in high gear by the transmission switch. The coolant temperature switch over-rides the transmission switch to energize the solenoid and provide vacuum advance below 82° F., for 1970-72 vehicles and 93° for 1973-74 vehicles. The time-delay relay is incorporated into the circuit to energize the solenoid for approximately 15 seconds on 1970-72 vehicles and 20 seconds on 1973-74 vehicles, after the ignition key is turned on.

When the solenoid plunger is in the nonenergized position, it allows the throttle to close to the curb idle setting. When the solenoid plunger is in the energized position, it keeps the throttle open to the high gear deceleration position which controls hydrocarbon emission.

GENERAL MOTORS SCS

Speed Controlled Spark

This system is essentially the same as the T.C.S. system except that here the vacuum spark advance is controlled by the vehicles speed rather than the gear position of the transmission.

The S.C.S. system consists of a vacuum advance solenoid valve, a speed sensing switch and a temperature switch. The vacuum control valve is installed in the vacuum line between the carburetor and the distributor. When energized, this valve cuts off vacuum to the distributor. The speed sensing switch de-energizes the vacuum control valve at speeds above 38 mph allowing normal vacuum spark advance. Abnormal operating temperatures (below 85 degrees F and above 220 degrees F) will cause the temperature switch to de-energize the vacuum control valve, over-riding the speed sensing switch.

Testing

To test the S.C.S. system, leave the distributor vacuum hose connected, be certain the engine temperature is between 95 and 230 degrees F, and proceed as follows:
1. Raise the rear wheels.
2. Start engine and shift into Drive.
3. Accelerate engine while watching the timing mark on the harmonic balancer. Timing should advance when the car speed exceeds 38 mph.

Trouble Shooting

Full Vacuum Advance at all Speeds:
1. Blown fuse.
2. Wire disconnected at vacuum control valve.
3. Wire disconnected at speed sensor.
4. Faulty speed sensor.
5. Faulty temperature switch.

No Vacuum Advance at Speeds Over 38 mph:
1. Vacuum lines reversed at vacuum control valve.
2. Foreign matter in vacuum control valve.
3. Distributor vacuum line broken or disconnected.
4. Faulty vacuum control valve.
5. Speed sensor switch or wire shorted.

GENERAL MOTORS EGR

Exhaust Gas Recirculation

Figs. 33 and 34—This system is used to reduce oxides of nitrogen emissions at the engine's exhaust. This is accomplished by introducing exhaust gases into the intake manifold at throttle positions other than idle. It consists of an E.G.R. valve mounted on a special intake manifold. The exhaust gas intake port of the E.G.R. valve is connected to the intake manifold exhaust crossover channels where it can pick up exhaust gases.

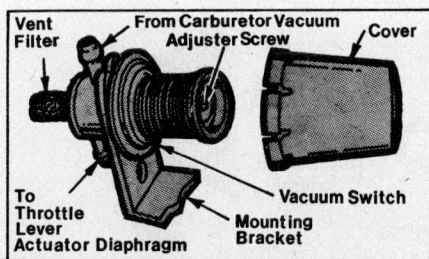

Fig. 37 Throttle return control valve. General Motors

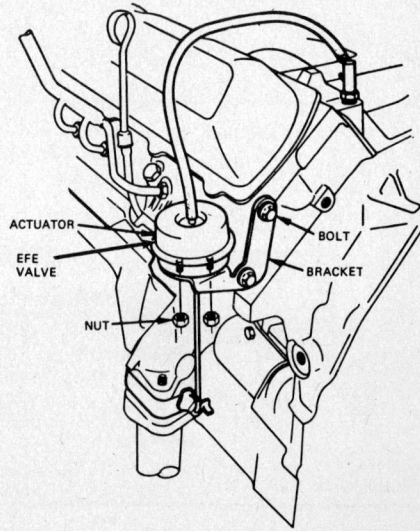

Fig. 38 Typical EFE valve installation. General Motors

EMISSION CONTROL SYSTEMS

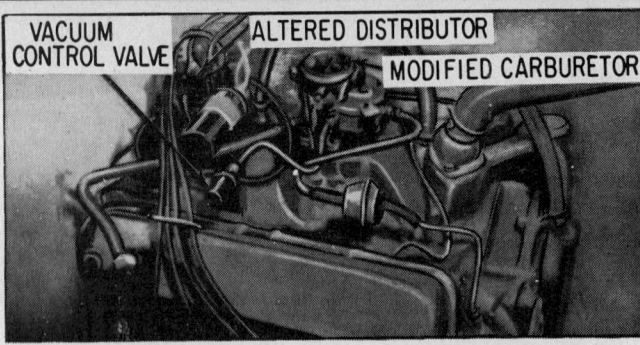

Fig. 39 Chrysler's Cleaner Air Package (CAP). Unlike the others this system uses no air pump

As the throttle valves are opened and the engine speeds up, vacuum is applied to a vacuum diaphragm in the E.G.R. valve through a connecting tube. When the vacuum reaches approximately 3" hg., the diaphragm moves upward against spring tension and is in the full-up position at approximately 7" to 8" hg. of vacuum. This diaphragm is connected by a shaft to a valve which closes off the exhaust gas port. As the diaphragm moves up, it opens the valve in the exhaust gas port which allows exhaust gas to be pulled into the intake manifold and enter the cylinders. The exhaust gas port must be closed during idle as the mixing of exhaust gases with the fuel air mixture at this point would cause rough running.

The dual diaphragm EGR valve, Fig. 34, is designed to provide increased exhaust gas recirculation rates when engine loads increase.

NOTE: Manifold vacuum is used as the signal to indicate the engine load.

The valve is similar to the single diaphragm valve except that a second diaphragm has been added to the valve and is connected to the upper diaphragm, with a spacer thus both diaphragms move together. A manifold vacuum signal is applied to the volume between the two diaphragms. The upper diaphragm has a larger diameter piston than the lower diaphragm, therefore the load caused by the manifold vacuum between the two diaphragms aids the spring load. Thus as the engine load increases and manifold vacuum decreases the combined load of the spring and the vacuum chamber are reduced allowing the valve to open further for a given EGR vacuum signal.

Therefore, for high intake manifold vacuums (such as cruising), the opening is less than for low manifold vacuums obtained during accelerations. The valve now is capable of providing more recirculation on accelerations where loads are higher and the tendency to produce NOx is greater.

Exhaust Back Pressure Transducer Valve

Fig. 35.—This valve, used on some 1974–76 California vehicles, modulates EGR flow according to engine load. The device consists of a diaphragm valve, a spacer and a metal tube.

The EGR system, when equipped with a back pressure transducer valve, obtains a vacuum signal at the carburetor spark port and not at the EGR port. This vacuum is modulated by the transducer and, in turn activates the EGR valve.

When exhaust back-pressure is relatively high, as during acceleration and some cruising conditions, exhaust back-pressure traveling through the metal tube overcomes spring tension on the diaphragm within the back-pressure transducer valve, and closes the valve atmospheric vent.

With the back-pressure transducer valve no longer vented to atmosphere, the vacuum signal now passes through the back-pressure transducer valve, and the EGR valve. When vacuum signals the EGR valve, exhaust gas recirculation commences.

When exhaust back-pressure is too low to overcome diaphragm spring tension, the vacuum signal is vented to atmosphere and does not pass through to the EGR valve. With no vacuum signal applied to the EGR valve, exhaust gas does not recirculate.

The E.G.R. valve cannot be disassembled and no actual service is required on it. However, it can be checked for proper operation as follows:

EGR System Test

1. Check the exhaust gas valve shaft for movement by opening the throttle to 2000 rpm. The shaft should move upward and return to its original position when the engine speed is allowed to drop to idle.
2. An outside vacuum source can be connected to the vacuum supply port in the top of the E.G.R. valve. The valve shaft should reach the top of its travel at 7" to 10" hg. of vacuum and the vacuum should not leak down.
3. If the E.G.R. valve does not operate correctly, it must be replaced.

Integral Back Pressure Transducer Valve

Fig. 36—This valve is used on 1977–79 light duty emissions California and high altitude 6 cylinder and V8 engines, and regulates the EGR flow according to engine load.

A small diaphragm controlled valve inside the EGR valve assembly acts as a pressure regulator. The control valve receives an exhaust back pressure signal through the hollow shaft which exerts a force on the bottom of the control valve diaphragm, opposed by light spring pressure. A metal deflector plate prevents hot exhaust gases from flowing directly on the diaphragm.

Vacuum is applied to the EGR valve from the carburetor spark port, to assure no exhaust gas recirculation during idle. During off-idle operation, manifold vacuum is applied to the vacuum chamber through a restriction in the signal tube. When engine load is light, and back pressure is low, the control valve is open, allowing air to flow from the bleeds in the diaphragm plate, through the control valve orifice, and into the vacuum chamber. The air bleeds off vacuum, decreasing the signal trying to open the EGR valve. If back pressure does not close the control valve, sealing off the air flow, there will not be any vacuum build-up to open the EGR valve for exhaust gas recirculation.

When power demands are made on the engine, and exhaust gas recirculation is required, exhaust back pressure increases, closing the control valve, thereby shutting off air flow through the valve. Vacuum builds up in the vacuum chamber until the spring force

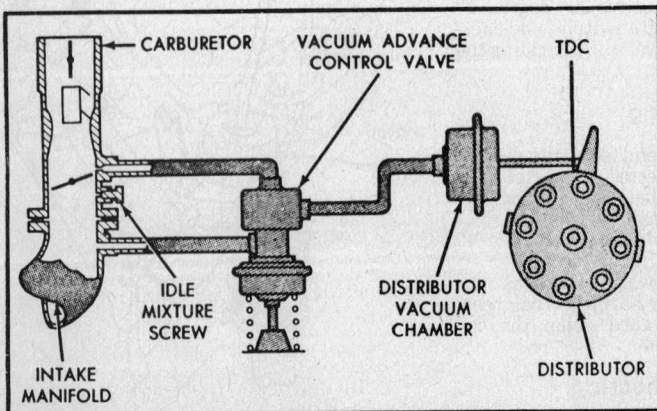

Fig. 40 Relationship of carburetor, vacuum advance control valve and distributor

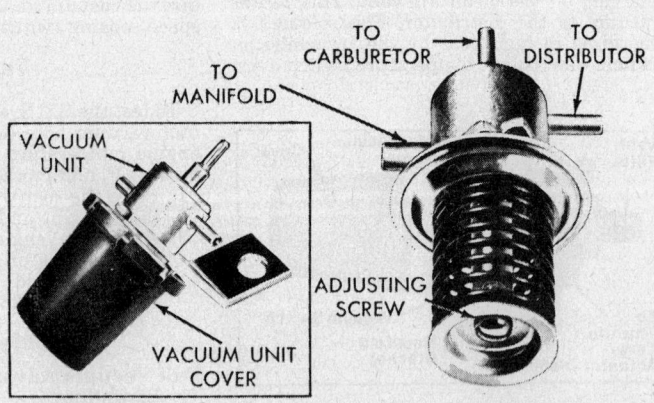

Fig. 41 Distributor vacuum advance control valve, deceleration valve

EMISSION CONTROL SYSTEMS

holding the EGR valve closed is overcome.

When the EGR valve opens, the exhaust pressure decreases because some of the exhaust gas is flowing into the intake manifold through the EGR passage. In actual operation, the system will reach a balanced condition providing maximum EGR operation.

Any increase in engine load will momentarily increase the exhaust signal, causing the control valve to close, allowing a stronger vacuum signal. The system will then stabilize at a greater EGR flow.

At maximum engine load, when manifold vacuum is nearly zero, there will be no EGR flow momentarily. This is due to the insufficient vacuum required to pull the valve open, even though high exhaust back pressure has closed the control valve.

GM THROTTLE RETURN CONTROL SYSTEM

This system (TRC), is used on some California vehicles. During coasting, the control valve, Fig. 37, opens to allow vacuum to operate the throttle lever actuator. The throttle actuator lever holds the throttle valve slightly open, thereby allowing more air to enter the combustion chambers to lean out the overrich mixture and reduce hydrocarbon emissions. When manifold vacuum drops below a predetermined value, the control valve closes, allowing the throttle actuator to return the throttle valve to normal idle.

GM EARLY FUEL EVAPORATION (EFE)

This system is used on some 1975–79 vehicles to provide a source of rapid heat for quick induction system warm-up during cold engine operation. Rapid heat is more desirable because it provides for better fuel evaporation and a more uniform mixture.

The vacuum operated EFE heat control valve mounted between the exhaust manifold and pipe, Fig. 38, directs a portion of the exhaust gases through the intake manifold and to the base of the carburetor during engine warm-up. A thermal vacuum switch (TVS) is used to regulate the EFE valve at or below a predetermined temperature. Refer to chart.

6-250	150° F.
V8-350	180° F.
V8-454	100° F.
V8-455	120° F.

When engine coolant is at or below the specified temperature, the TVS will cause vacuum to flow to the EFE control valve, diverting the exhaust gases through the intake manifold to the base of the carburetor. At temperatures above those specified, the TVS closes off vacuum to the EFE control valve, stopping the flow of exhaust gases through the intake manifold.

CHRYSLER CAP

Cleaner Air Package

The Cleaner Air Package is in addition to the Positive Crankcase Ventilation (PCV). The PCV device is designed to control the emission of hydrocarbon vapors from the crankcase, whereas the Cleaner Air Package controls the emission of hydrocarbon vapors (unburned gasoline) and carbon monoxide in the vehicle exhaust.

The Cleaner Air Package is engineered to continuously control carburetion and ignition at the best settings for performance and combustion during all driving conditions. These adjustments keep unburned gasoline and carbon monoxide in the exhaust at a minimum concentration.

Only three special components are involved in the CAP installation, Fig. 39. The carburetor and distributor have been re-designed and a new component—the Vacuum Advance Control Valve—has been added. In addition, some cooling system components have been changed to handle the increased heat rejection at idle and low speed.

Special Carburetor and Ignition

The carburetor is specially calibrated to provide learner mixtures at idle and low speed operation. The distributor is designed to give retarded timing at idle. The vacuum advance control valve, in conjunction with the distributor, provides advance timing during deceleration.

CAP idle timing for all engines is retarded instead of advanced. Exhaust emission is reduced at idle by using leaner air/fuel mixtures, increased engine speed, and retarded ignition timing. The higher air flow at this

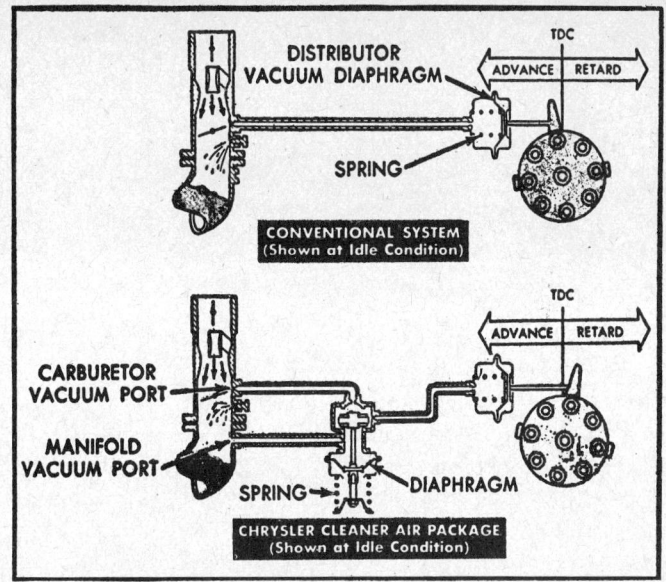

Fig. 42 Engine idle condition

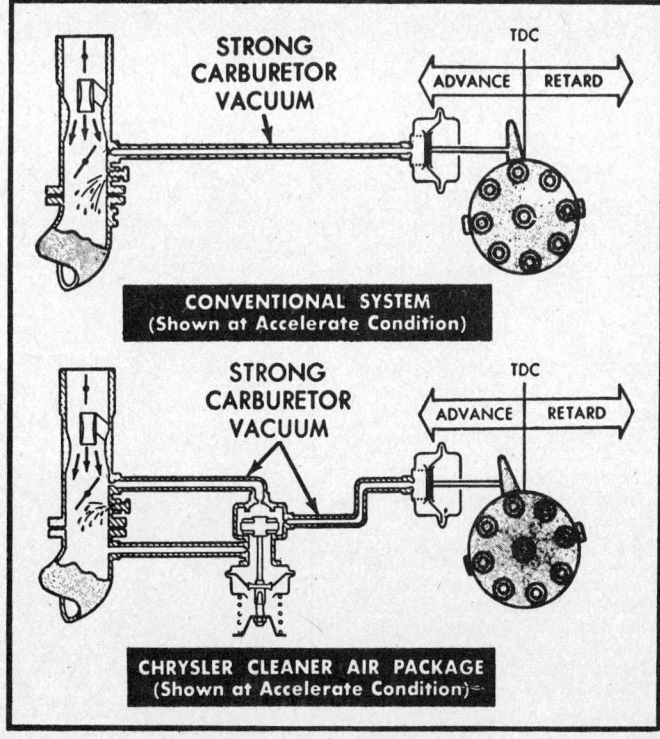

Fig. 43 During acceleration

EMISSION CONTROL SYSTEMS

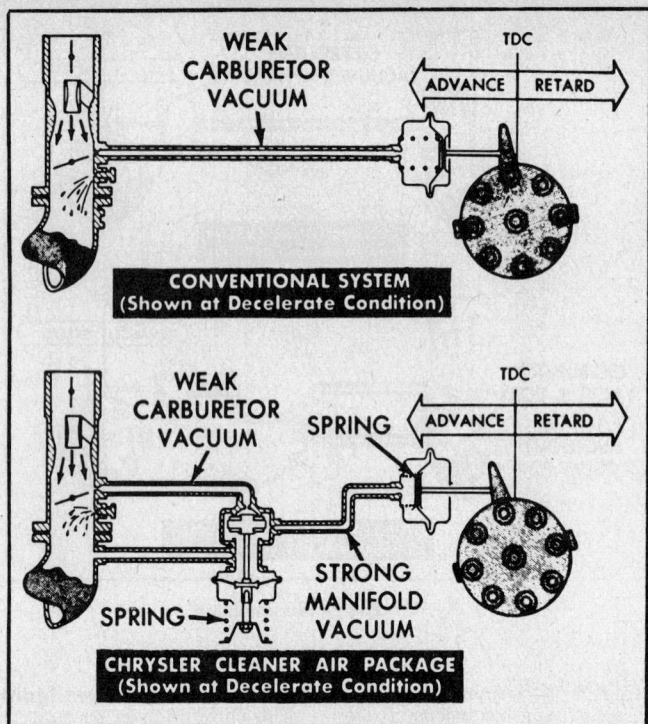

Fig. 44 During deceleration

idle condition approximates the desirable conditions of cruise. CAP, therefore, is designed to operate with late timing during idle, and with conventional spark advance during acceleration and cruise.

Vacuum Advance Control Valve

Early ignition of the air/fuel mixture is needed during deceleration to provide the most efficient combustion and reduced exhaust emissions. The vacuum advance control valve provides the additional spark advance during deceleration. The vacuum advance control valve is connected by vacuum hoses to the carburetor, to the intake manifold, and to the distributor vacuum chamber, Figs. 40 and 41.

Carburetor vacuum and manifold vacuum act on the vacuum advance control valve. From these two signals, the vacuum advance control valve senses engine speed and load conditions, and relays a vacuum signal to the distributor to vary spark timing when necessary to reduce emissions to an acceptable level.

Engine Idle, Fig. 42

The initial idle timing is retarded as much as 15 degrees from conventional timing. The vacuum advance control valve does not effect timing at idle because the distributor vacuum chamber receives the same vacuum signal as in the conventional system, namely, carburetor vacuum. At idle it is not strong enough to overcome the distributor vacuum diaphragm spring.

Manifold vacuum acts on the vacuum control valve diaphragm, but is not strong enough to overcome the vacuum control valve spring. So the spring holds the vacuum control valve closed to manifold vacuum and open to the low carburetor vacuum.

Acceleration, Fig. 43

During acceleration and cruise, manifold vacuum is not strong enough to actuate the CAP control valve. Thus the CAP system operates in the same manner as the conventional system. The throttle plate opens enough to permit the distributor vacuum advance to function, and spark timing is advanced according to the amount of vacuum created by the pumping action of the pistons.

Deceleration, Fig. 44

The conventional system provides the highest emissions under deceleration conditions. Carburetor vacuum is too weak to overcome the distributor advance diaphragm spring.

Manifold vacuum is at its strongest under deceleration conditions. Therefore, the CAP system uses manifold vacuum rather than carburetor vacuum to control spark timing.

Manifold vacuum is strong enough to overcome the vacuum advance control valve spring and the distributor vacuum diaphragm spring, moving spark timing to the maximum advance condition.

CHRYSLER CAS

Cleaner Air System

This system uses higher inlet air temperature, higher idle speeds, retarded ignition timing, leaner carburetor mixtures and built in modifications such as lower compression ratios, increased overlap camshafts and redesigned intake manifolds and combustion chambers.

Heated Air System, Fig. 45

This system uses a thermostatically controlled air cleaner to maintain a predetermined air temperature entering the carburetor when underhood temperatures are less than 100° F. By maintaining this temperature, the carburetor can be calibrated leaner, improve engine warm-up and minimize carburetor icing. Temperature is controlled by intake manifold vacuum, a temperature sensor and a vacuum diaphragm which operates the heat control door in the air cleaner snorkel.

During engine warm-up, air is heated by a shroud surrounding the exhaust manifold, then the air is piped to the air cleaner snorkel and into the carburetor. The vacuum diaphragm controls the air control valve which is closed to outside air. Therefore all air entering the carburetor is heated.

During normal operation, as the air entering the air cleaner increases, the air control valve opens to allow heated air to mix with cold air to keep the air entering the carburetor at about 100° F.

During wide-open throttle operation or at

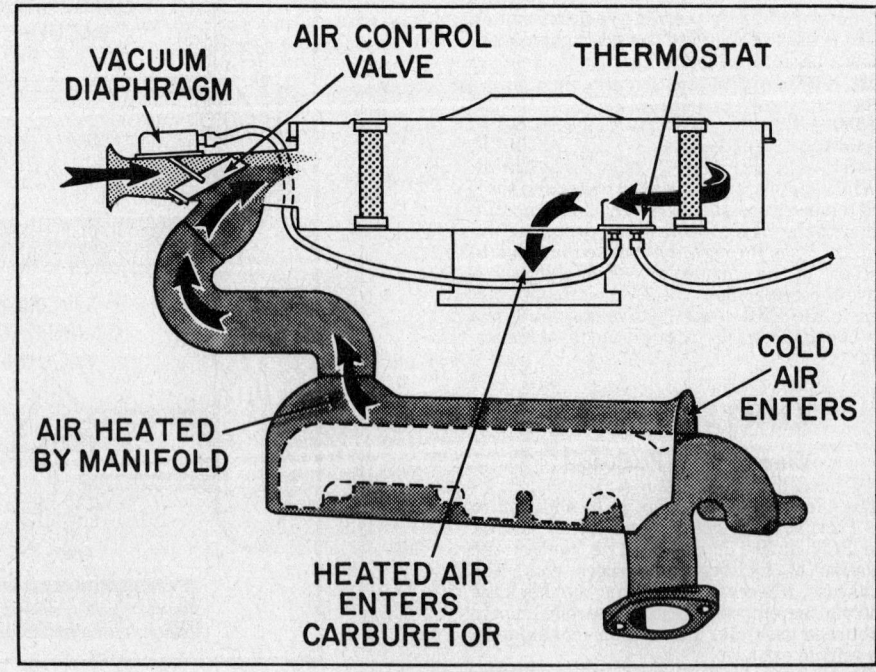

Fig. 45 Chrysler Corp. Heated Air Inlet system

EMISSION CONTROL SYSTEMS

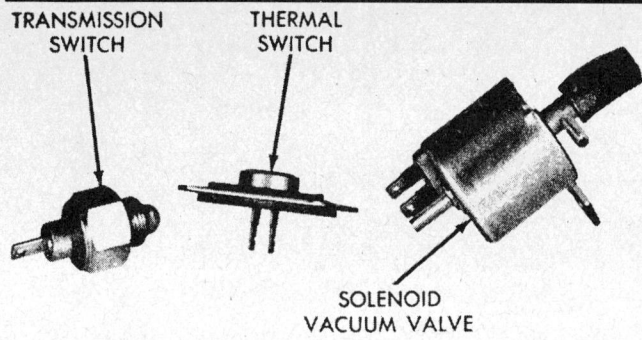

Fig. 46 NOx system components. Manual trans.

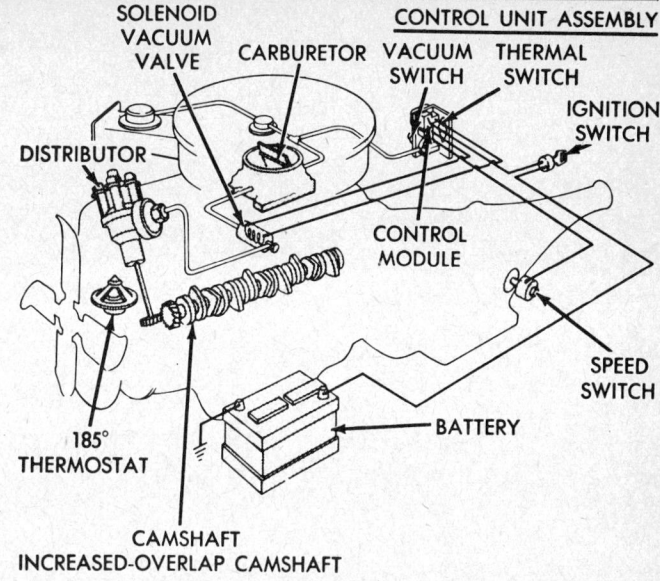

Fig. 47 NOx system components. Automatic trans.

any time engine vacuum is below 4–6 inches Hg., the hot air duct is closed off allowing only cold air to enter the carburetor.

Idle Speed Solenoid

Because of the high idle speeds used on some engines, these engines have an electrical solenoid throttle stop which holds the throttle at the correct idle position when energized but de-energizes when the ignition is turned off, allowing the throttle blades to close more completely, thereby eliminating the possibility of "afterrun" or "dieseling."

Distributor Solenoid

Some engines have a solenoid incorporated in the distributor vacuum advance mechanism to retard the ignition timing when the throttle is closed. At closed throttle, and with the idle adjusting screw in the closed position, electrical contacts on the carburetor throttle stop cause the distributor solenoid to energize. This retards the ignition timing to reduce emissions during hot idle conditions. Cold or part throttle starting is not penalized because the distributor solenoid is not energized unless the hot idle adjusting screw is against the throttle stop contact.

NOTE: Ignition timing must be set at closed throttle to give accurate setting.

Lower Compression Ratios

Compression ratios have been lowered by various modifications in the piston head design and in the quench height. This reduction in compression ratios permits the engine to operate satisfactorily on lower octane fuel, thereby achieving a slight reduction in HC and NOx emission levels.

Combustion Chamber Design

The combustion chamber is designed to eliminate pockets and close clearance spaces which have a tendency to quench the flame before all of the air-fuel mixture is burned. By increasing the quench heights, more complete burning of the air-fuel mixture is achieved, thereby substantially reducing the HC emission levels.

Increased Overlap Camshaft

The increased valve overlap produced by the camshaft causes some dilution of the incoming air-fuel mixture. This dilution lowers the peak combustion temperature which results in lowered NOx emission levels.

Redesigned Intake Manifold

Intake manifolds have been redesigned to promote rapid fuel vaporization during engine warm-up. The exhaust crossover floor of the intake manifold between the inlet gases and exhaust gases has been thinned out with improved thickness control, thereby reducing the time required to get the heat from the exhaust manifold gases into the inlet gases. By adding this additional heat, fuel vaporizes quicker, and leaner air-fuel mixtures can be used, resulting in lower CO emission levels.

CHRYSLER NOx
Oxides of Nitrogen

The NOx system controls nitrogen oxides emissions by allowing vacuum spark advance only in high gear (manual transmission), or above 30 mph (automatic transmission), and with the use of an increased overlap camshaft and a 185 degree F coolant thermostat. Vacuum to the distributor is controlled by a solenoid vacuum valve mounted in the line between the carburetor vacuum port and the distributor. When the solenoid is energized the plunger shuts off vacuum to the distributor and vents it to the atmosphere. When it is de-energized the plunger opens allowing normal vacuum spark advance. There are two separate systems employed to control the solenoid vacuum valve, one for vehicles equipped with manual transmissions and the other for those having automatic transmissions.

Manual Transmission

The NOx system for manual transmissions consists of a solenoid vacuum valve, transmission switch and in the 1971 system a thermal switch, Fig. 46. The solenoid vacuum valve is mounted and operates as explained above. The transmission switch is mounted on the transmission housing and is used to sense the transmission gear position. It remains closed ("on") in any gear below high which energizes the solenoid thereby preventing vacuum spark advance. It opens when the top gear is selected permitting normal vacuum spark advance. The thermal switch is mounted on the fire wall and senses ambient air temperature. If the temperature is below 70 degrees F, this switch will be open. This breaks the cir-

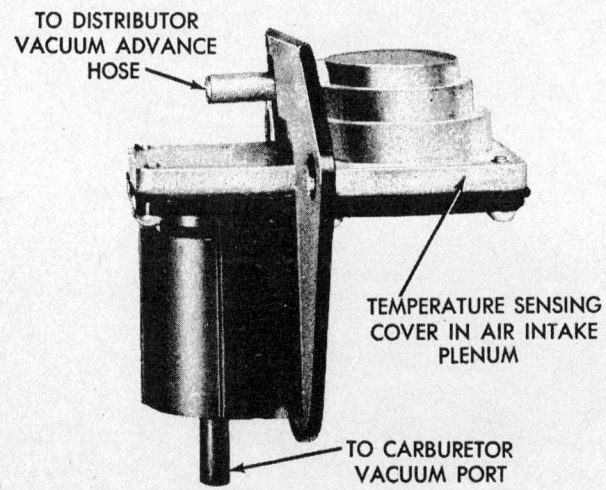

Fig. 48 Chrysler OSAC valve

EMISSION CONTROL SYSTEMS

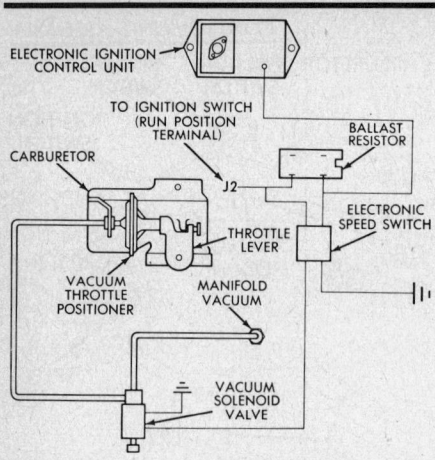

Fig. 49 Throttle positioner system. 1975-79

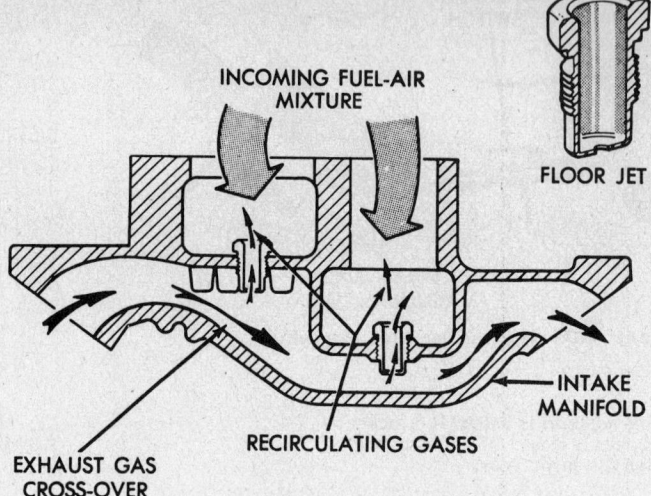

Fig. 50 EGR floor jets V8 configuration

cuit between the transmission switch and the solenoid valve leaving the NOx system inoperative and allowing normal vacuum spark advance in all gears.

Automatic Transmission

The NOx system for automatic transmission equipped vehicles consists of a solenoid vacuum valve, a speed switch and a control unit assembly, Fig. 47. The solenoid vacuum valve is mounted and operates as explained above. The speed switch senses the vehicle speed and is mounted in line with the speedometer cable. The control unit assembly mounts on the fire wall. It contains three parts, the control module, the thermal switch and the vacuum switch. It senses ambient temperature and manifold vacuum. These components work together for one purpose, to prevent vacuum spark advance under following conditions:
1. Temperature above 70 degrees F.
2. Speeds below 30 mph.
3. Acceleration necessary on 1971 vehicles only.

Whenever all conditions are present, the solenoid vacuum valve will be energized shutting off vacuum to the distributor.

CHRYSLER IGNITION

Electronic Ignition

A better control of exhaust emissions is achieved through the use of the "Electronic Ignition". By eliminating the breaker points, engine misfiring and increased emissions caused by worn or misadjusted breaker points is eliminated.

Distributor Solenoid, 1972-73

A start only solenoid is used on some distributors to provide additional spark advance during engine starting. The solenoid is located in the vacuum unit attached to the distributor housing and operates only while the ignition switch is in start position.

Use of the solenoid provides improved starting characteristics while maintaining a low level of hydrocarbon and carbon monoxide emissions at idle.

CHRYSLER ORIFICE SPARK ADVANCE CONTROL (OSAC)

Fig. 48—The OSAC system is used on all 1973-79 engines, to aid in the control of NOx (Oxides of Nitrogen). The system controls the vacuum to the vacuum advance actuator of the distributor.

A tiny orifice is incorporated in the OSAC valve which delays the change in ported vacuum to the distributor by about 17 seconds when going from idle to part throttle. When going from part throttle to idle, the change in ported vacuum to the distributor will be instantaneous. The valve will only delay the ported vacuum signal when the ambient temperature is about 60° F. or above. Vacuum is obtained by a vacuum tap just above the throttle plates of the carburetor. This type of tap provides no vacuum at idle, but provides manifold vacuum as soon as the throttle plates are opened slightly. Proper operation of this valve depends on air tight fittings and hoses and on freedom from sticking or plugging due to deposits.

TEMPERATURE OPERATED VACUUM BY-PASS VALVE

A vacuum by-pass valve, Fig. 29, is used on some engine applications to reduce the possibility of engine overheating under extremely high temperature operating conditions. When engine coolant temperature at idle reaches 225° F., the valve opens automatically and applies manifold vacuum directly to the distributor for normal vacuum spark advance. This will by-pass the NOx or OSAC system.

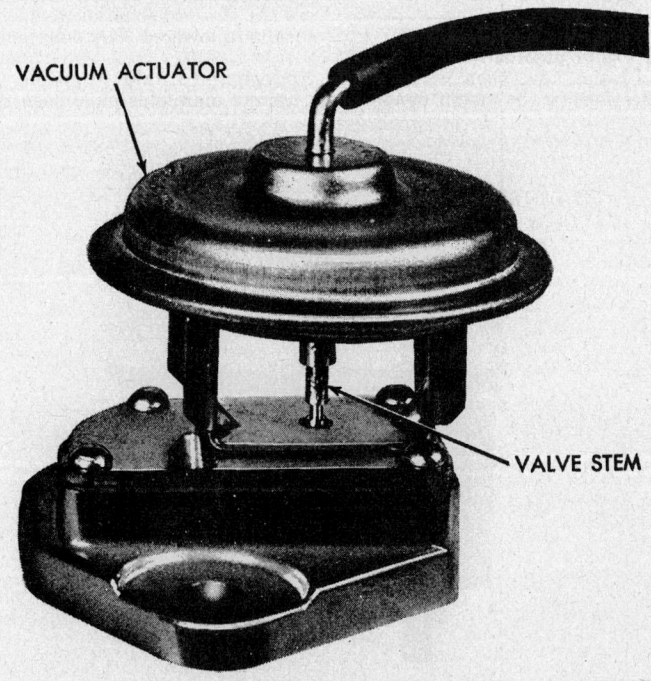

Fig. 51 Chrysler EGR control valve

EMISSION CONTROL SYSTEMS

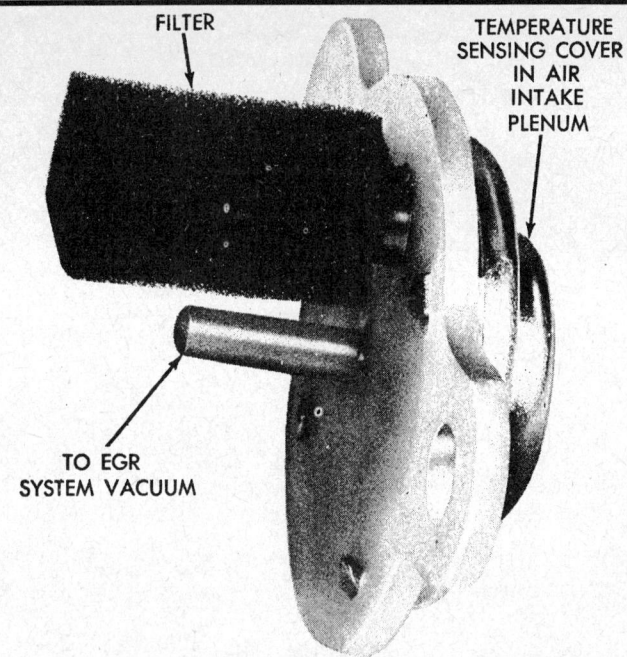

Fig. 52 Chrysler EGR temperature control valve

Fig. 53 Dual diaphragm vacuum advance valve

This increases engine idle speed and provides additional engine cooling. When the engine has cooled to normal operating temperature, the NOx or OSAC system is restored to normal operation.

CHRYSLER VACUUM THROTTLE POSITIONER

Some 1975–79 vehicles are equipped with a throttle positioner system to prevent unburned hydrocarbon emissions through the exhaust system when the engine is decelerated from a high rpm. This system consists of an electronic speed switch, an electrically controlled vacuum solenoid valve and a vacuum actuated throttle positioner, Fig. 49.

The electronic speed switch senses ignition pulses from the 5 ohm ballast resistor terminal connected to the ignition control unit. When engine speed exceeds 2000 rpm, the speed switch allows vacuum to energize the throttle positioner. When the positioner is energized, a throttle stop provided, will prevent the engine from returning to the idle position. When the throttle is released, it will return the idle to 1750 rpm. As the engine decelerates, the electronic speed switch senses when the engine speed drops below 2000 rpm and de-energizes the throttle positioner. This permits the throttle to return to the normal idle stop position and the engine will continue to decelerate to the idle speed. This operation positions the throttle partially open (1750 rpm) whenever the engine decelerates from a speed above 2000 rpm to a speed just below 2000 rpm, thus providing sufficient air flow through the engine to dilute the air/fuel mixture.

CHRYSLER EXHAUST GAS RECIRCULATION (EGR)

In this system, exhaust gases are circulated to dilute the incoming fuel air mixture. Dilution of the incoming mixture lowers peak flame temperatures during combustion and thus limits the formation of NOx.

Floor Jet Exhaust Gas System 1972–73

In this system the exhaust gases are introduced into the intake manifold through jets in the floor below the carburetor, Fig. 50. An orifice in each jet allows a controlled amount of exhaust gas to be drawn through by engine vacuum to dilute incoming fuel and air. In eight cylinder engines, exhaust gases are taken from the intake manifold exhaust crossover passage. While in six cylinder engines, gases are taken from the exhaust manifold "plenum" chamber located at the "hot spot" below the carburetor riser.

NOTE: In 1973–79 two additional systems are used to control the rate of exhaust gas recirculation, depending on engine model. These systems are: Ported Vacuum Control System and Venturi Vacuum Control System.

Both systems use the same type exhaust gas recirculation (EGR) control valve, Fig. 51, only the method of controlling the valve is different. The valve is a vacuum actuated, poppet type unit used to modulate exhaust gas flow from the exhaust gas crossover into the incoming air fuel mixture.

Venturi Vacuum Control System

The venturi vacuum control system utilizes a vacuum tap at the throat of the carburetor venturi to provide a control signal. This vacuum signal is amplified to the level required to operate the EGR control valve. Elimination of recycle at wide open throttle is accomplished by a dump diaphragm which compares venturi and manifold vacuum to determine when wide open throttle is achieved. At wide open throttle, the internal reservoir is "dumped", limiting output to the EGR valve to manifold vacuum. The valve opening point is set above the manifold vacuums available at wide open throttle.

NOTE: This system is dependent primarily on engine intake airflow as indicated by the venturi signal, and is also affected by intake vacuum and exhaust gas back pressure.

Ported Vacuum Control System

The ported vacuum control system utilizes a slot type port in the carburetor throttle body which is exposed to an increasing ratio of manifold vacuum as the throttle plate opens. This throttle bore port is connected through an external nipple directly to the EGR valve. The flow rate is dependent on three variables, 1) manifold vacuum, 2) throttle position, and 3) exhaust gas back pressure. Recycle at wide open throttle is eliminated by calibrating the valve opening point above manifold vacuums available at wide open throttle as port vacuum cannot exceed manifold vacuum. Elimination of wide open throttle recycle provides maximum performance.

Temperature Control Valve

The plenum mounted temperature control valve, Fig. 52, is utilized on the ported vacuum control system and the venturi vacuum control system. The valve reduces the recycle rate at low ambient temperature for improved driveability. The unit contains a temperature sensitive bimetal disc which senses plenum air temperature. The snap action of the disc unplugs a calibrated orifice to provide the bleed air. Calibration is protected by an air filter unit.

Coolant Control Exhaust Gas Recirculation (CCEGR)

1974–79 engines using EGR are equipped with a CCEGR valve mounted in the radiator top tank. When coolant temperature in the top tank reaches 65° F, the valve opens so that vacuum is applied to open the EGR valve. On some 1974–79 engines, a similar CCEGR valve set for 90° F. is mounted in the thermostat housing.

Coolant Controlled Engine Vacuum Switch (CCEVS)

This switch is used on 1977–79 vehicles to improve hot driveability by preventing opera-

EMISSION CONTROL SYSTEMS

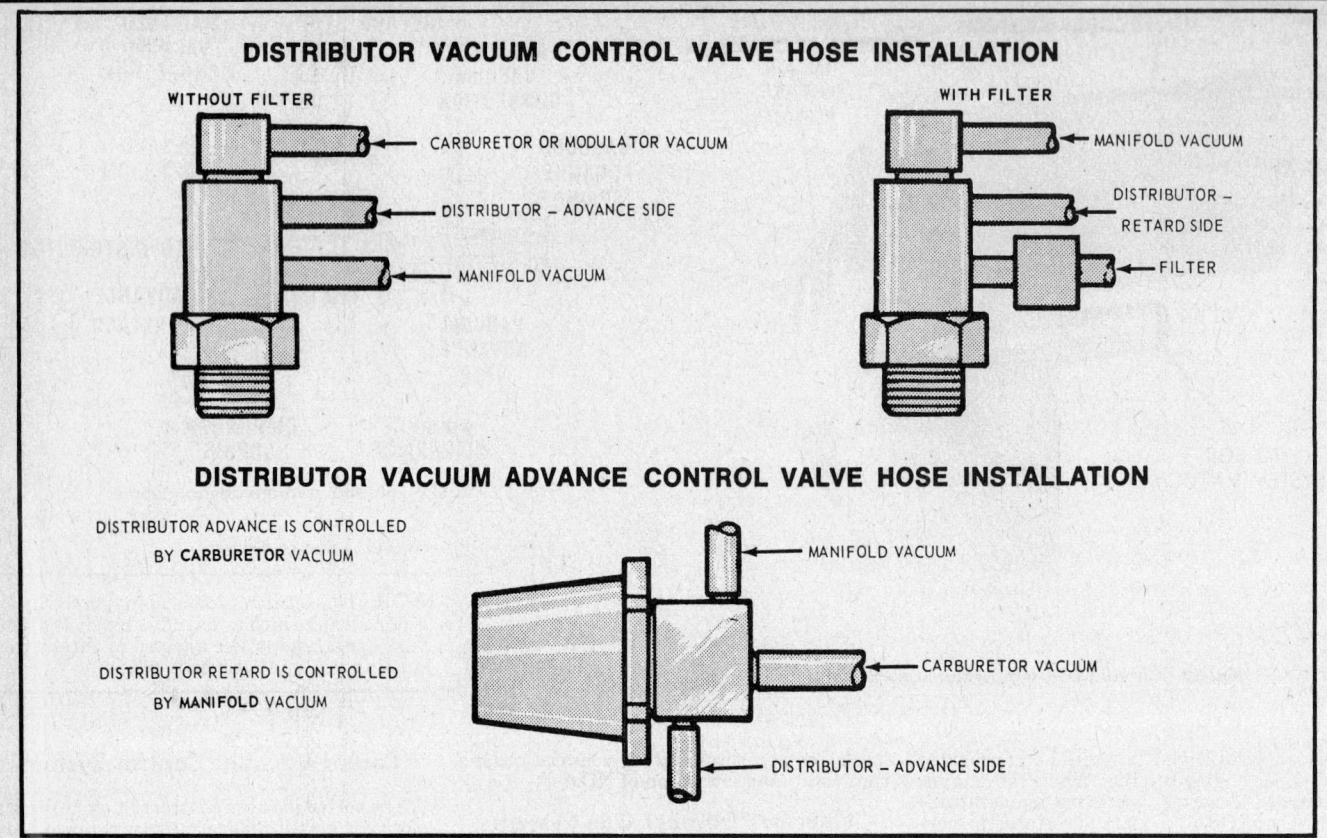

Fig. 54 Distributor vacuum control valve and distributor vacuum advance control valve

tion of the Idle Enrichment System, Power Heat Valve System and Air Injection Switching System after the coolant temperature has reached a predetermined temperature. When the engine coolant temperature is below 86° F (green), 108° F (orange) or 138° F (neutral), the valve opens allowing manifold vacuum to operate one or more of the systems previously mentioned.

Charge Temperature Switch (CTS)

This switch, used on all 1979 vehicles, is installed in the intake manifold where it is exposed to the incoming air fuel mixture charge. When the charge temperature is below 60° F., the CTS will be closed permitting no EGR valve operation. When the charge temperature is above 60° F., the CTS will open, permitting the EGR time delay device to count down and resume normal EGR operation.

The EGR time delay device used with this system is unique and not interchangeable with those of previous years.

EGR Time Delay & Idle Enrichment System

On most 1974-79 vehicles, a time-delay device is used in the EGR system which works in conjunction with the idle enrichment system to improve engine starting and performance. This system consists of an electronic timer and either one or two vacuum solenoids. The electronic timer energizes the solenoid(s) during starting and for 35 seconds thereafter. When the solenoid(s) energizes, vacuum to the EGR amplifier is cut off, thereby stopping exhaust gas recirculation. At the same time, vacuum is applied to the idle enrichment system through the solenoid and/or a block coolant valve when the engine block temperature is below 98° F. for California vehicles or 150° F. for all other vehicles. On 1974-76 Calif. and 1977-79 all except V8-360, idle enrichment is controlled only by engine coolant temperature. The system used on V8-318 engines except California, functions basically in the same manner except that it uses two vacuum solenoids, one controlling the EGR system, the other controlling the idle enrichment system. Thirty-five seconds after engine start-up, the solenoid(s) de-energize, allowing normal EGR operation and stopping idle enrichment.

FORD IMCO SYSTEM

Improved Exhaust Emission Control System

This system combines a thermostatically controlled air cleaner and higher engine operating temperature with leaner carburetor calibration and later ignition timing under closed throttle operating conditions.

Dual Diaphragm Distributor

Fig. 53—In addition to the conventional centrifugal and vacuum advance control units, this unit uses a separate diaphragm to retard the spark timing under closed throttle conditions. The advance diaphragm is connected to the carburetor above the throttle plate(s) so that when the throttle is opened, the timing is advanced. The retard diaphragm is connected to the intake manifold so that during closed throttle operation, when manifold vacuum is high, the timing is retarded to provide more complete combustion.

Distributor Vacuum Control Valve

This valve, Fig. 54, is exposed to cooling system temperature and when coolant temperature exceeds normal limits during long idle periods, the valve opens a vacuum passage to the advance diaphragm of the distributor which speeds up the engine idle lowering the temperature.

To test the valve, proceed as follows:
1. With engine at operating temperature, connect a tachometer to the engine.
2. Note engine idle rpm with transmission in neutral.
3. Disconnect the vacuum hose from the intake manifold at the temperature sensing valve and plug the hose.
4. If idle speed does not change when hose is disconnected, the valve is acceptable to this point. If idle drops 100 rpm or more, valve must be replaced.
5. Reinstall vacuum line then cover radiator sufficiently to raise engine coolant temperature above thermostat setting.

NOTE: Be sure all-season coolant is up to specification and exercise caution so that the engine does not become unduly overheated.

6. Continue to run the engine until the high temperature lamp comes on or the temperature gauge reaches the high end of the band. At this point, the engine idle speed should increase by approximately 100 rpm. If it has not, the valve is defective and must be replaced.

EMISSION CONTROL SYSTEMS

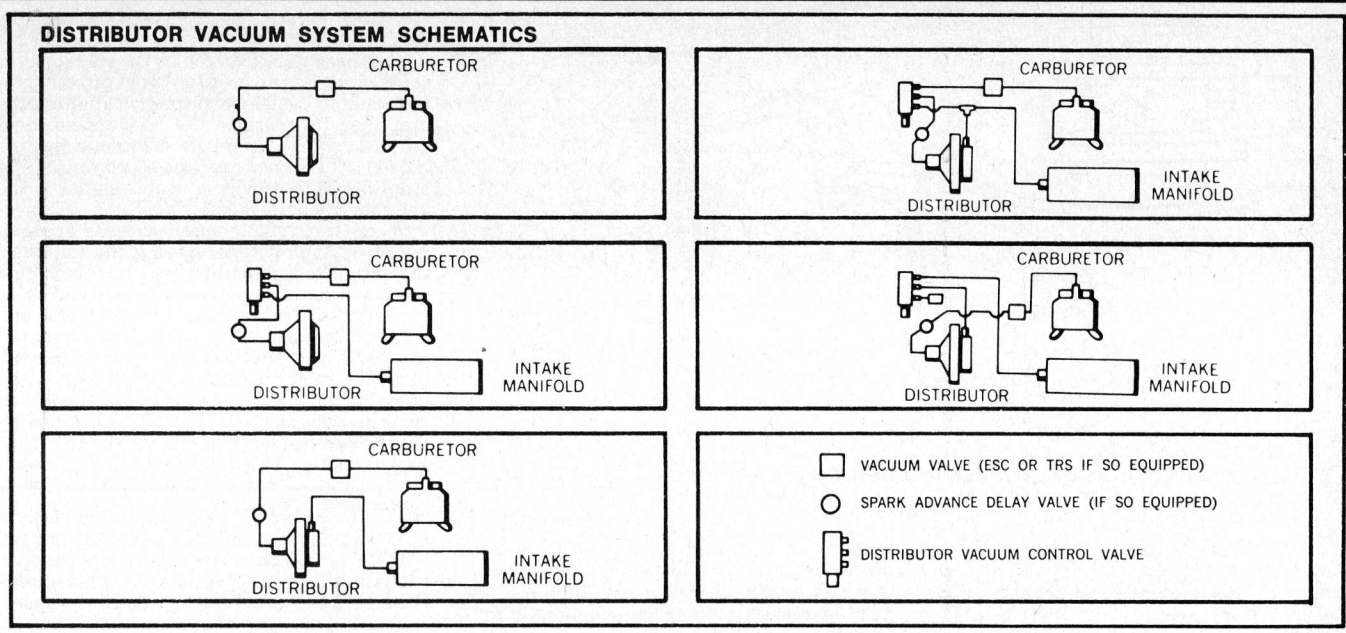

Fig. 55 Ford distributor vacuum system schematics

Distributor Vacuum Advance Control Valve

This valve, Figs. 41 and 54, provides the necessary ignition advance during acceleration periods to provide the most efficient combustion and reduce emissions. To check the valve, proceed as follows:

1. With engine at operating temperature and idle speed correctly set, connect a tachometer to the engine.
2. Remove cover from valve and slowly turn the adjusting screw counterclockwise without exerting any inward pressure. After five and no more than six turns, the idle speed should suddenly increase to approximately 1000 rpm.

NOTE: Any more than six turns out will release the compressed spring and washer.

3. If idle speed does not increase after the sixth turn, push inward on the end of the spring and release. Idle speed will increase.
4. After valve has been triggered to the higher rpm, slowly turn the adjusting screw clockwise until idle speed drops back down to proper level. Turn screw one additional turn clockwise.
5. Increase engine speed to 2000 rpm and hold for approximately five seconds then release throttle. The engine should return to idle within four seconds. If not, check return time with dashpot backed off so it does not contact the throttle lever.
6. If the engine still will not return to idle within four seconds, turn the adjusting screw clockwise in one-quarter turn increments until throttle return is satisfactory.
7. If throttle does not return after four one-quarter turn adjustments, the valve is defective and must be replaced.

NOTE: Application of the distributor vacuum control valve and the dual-diaphragm vacuum advance mechanism will vary from vehicle to vehicle, Fig. 55.

FORD ELECTRONIC DISTRIBUTOR MODULATOR

Description

This system operates to prevent spark advance below 23 mph on acceleration and below approximately 18 mph on deceleration. Control by the modulator is canceled out if the outside air temperature is below 58 deg. F, allowing the distributor to operate through the standard vacuum control system, Fig. 56.

The modulator system consists of four components: speed sensor, thermal switch, and electrical control amplifier-solenoid valve. The control amplifier and solenoid valve are combined in one assembly and mounted in the passenger compartment on the dash panel. The speed sensor is connected to the speedom-

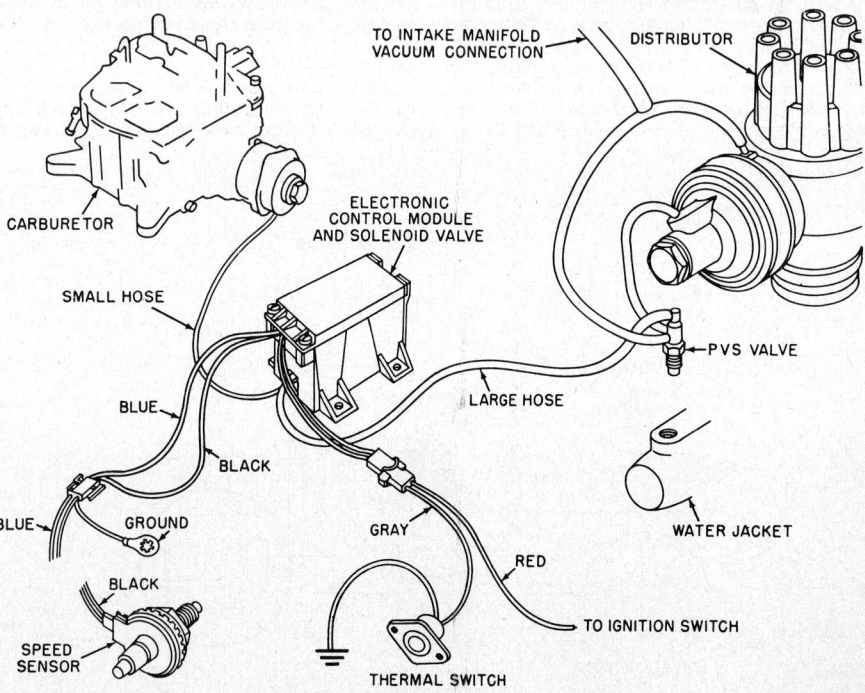

Fig. 56 Electronic Distributor Modulator

769

EMISSION CONTROL SYSTEMS

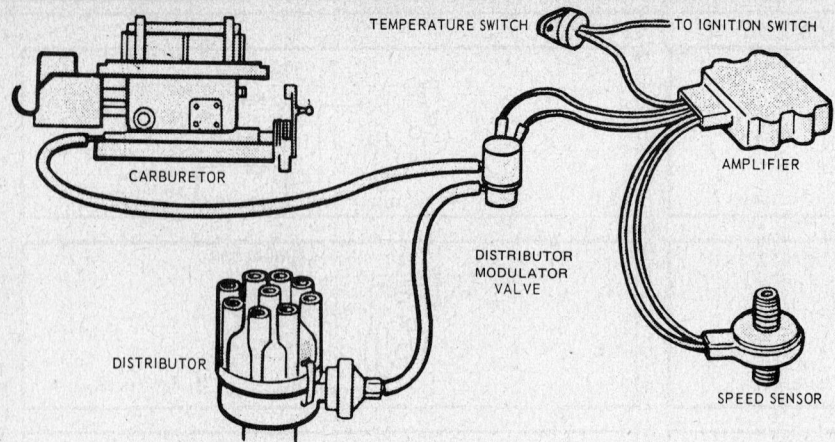

Fig. 57 Ford Electronic Spark Control system

eter cable. The thermal switch is mounted near the front door hinge pillar on the outside of the cowl panel. It may be mounted on either the right or left side.

FORD ESC SYSTEM

Electronic Spark Control System

This system, Fig. 57, reduces the exhaust emissions of an engine by providing vacuum spark advance only at speeds above 24 to 33 mph (depending on the engine application). It consists of a speed sensor, an electronic amplifier, an outside air temperature switch and a vacuum control valve. The vacuum control valve is inserted between the carburetor vacuum advance port and the distributor primary advance connection. This valve is normally open, but when energized electrically by the electronic amplifier it closes to cut off vacuum to the primary vacuum advance unit on the distributor thus preventing vacuum spark advance. The temperature switch, which is mounted in either the right or left A-pillar, senses outside air temperature. A temperature below 49 degrees F will cause the switch contacts to open, thereby de-energizing the vacuum valve and allowing normal vacuum advance at all speeds. A temperature of 60 degrees plus or minus 5 degrees F causes the contacts to close, thereby cutting off vacuum to the advance side of the distributor at speeds below 24 to 33 mph. On deceleration the vacuum advance cut-out speed is approximately 18 mph.

On some applications the vacuum hose connections between the carburetor and distributor may route through a PVS valve. This valve serves as a by-pass or safety override switch. When the coolant temperature reaches 230 degrees F, manifold vacuum is applied directly to the primary (advance) side of the distributor advancing the timing and thereby lowering operating temperature.

FORD HIGH SPEED EGR MODULATOR SUB-SYSTEM

The high speed EGR modulator sub-system used on some V8 engines, Fig. 58, is basically the same in operation as the ESC system described previously. This system cuts off exhaust gas recirculation flow by stopping vacuum flow from the EGR port to the EGR valve at speeds above 64 mph, in turn improving driveability.

The vacuum solenoid valve installed in the vacuum line is normally open (not energized), allowing vacuum flow from the EGR port to the EGR valve. The EGR system remains functional when the valve is not energized.

The speed sensor driven by the speedometer cable, produces an electric signal directly proportional to vehicle road speed, signalling the amplifier to energize the vacuum solenoid valve at which time the electronic module receives the signal from the speed sensor and amplifies it to provide a usable signal to the vacuum solenoid valve.

When the vehicle speed exceeds approximately 64 mph (trigger speed of the amplifier) the circuit to the ignition switch is completed and the normally open vacuum solenoid valve is energized. The plunger moves upwards and shuts off the EGR port vacuum and the vent at the bottom of the vacuum valve is opened, bleeding vacuum from the EGR valve and hose. Spring force closes the EGR valve which remains non functional until the vacuum solenoid valve is de-energized, at speeds below approximately 64 mph.

NOTE: There is a continuous internal vacuum bleed provided by the vent at the top of EGR valve. Whether the valve is in a closed or open position, this vent purges the vacuum supply hose from carburetor of any gasoline vapor.

FORD TRS SYSTEM

Transmission Regulated Spark Control System

This system, Fig. 59, reduces the exhaust emissions of an engine by providing vacuum spark advance only in high gear. It consists of a vacuum control valve, an outside air temperature switch, and a transmission switch. The vacuum control valve is inserted between the carburetor vacuum advance port and the distributor primary advance connection. This valve is normally open, but when energized electrically by the transmission switch it closes to cut off vacuum to the primary vacuum advance unit on the distributor thus preventing vacuum spark advance. The temperature switch, which is mounted in either the right or left A-pillar senses outside air temperature. A temperature below 49 degrees F will cause the switch contacts to open, thereby de-energizing the vacuum valve and allowing normal vacuum advance in all gears. A temperature of 60 degrees plus or minus 5 degrees F causes the contacts to close, thereby cutting off vacuum to the advance side of the distributor in all but high gear.

FORD TRS + 1

Transmission Regulated Spark + 1

Fig. 60—The TRS+1 system consists of two separate vacuum control systems, that are electrically controlled by input information from a manual transmission gear selector switch, and an outside ambient air temperature switch. The TRS function of the TRS+1 system is identical to the function performed by the 1972 TRS system. The plus 1 system of the TRS+1, controls the selection of the carburetor vacuum source for the vehicle EGR system. The EGR vacuum supply source can be either carburetor spark port, or carburetor EGR port depending upon the manual transmission gear selected, and the outside ambient air temperature.

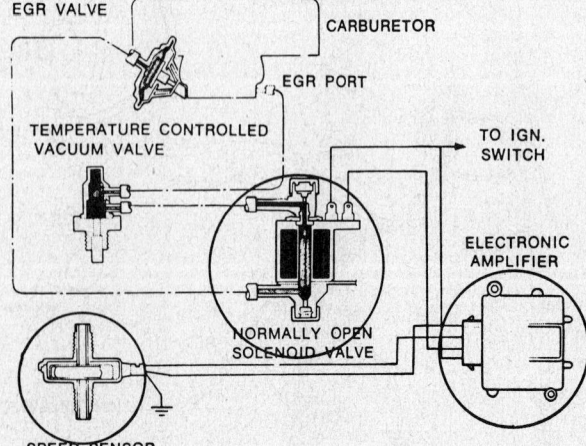

Fig. 58 Ford high speed EGR modulator sub-system components

EMISSION CONTROL SYSTEMS

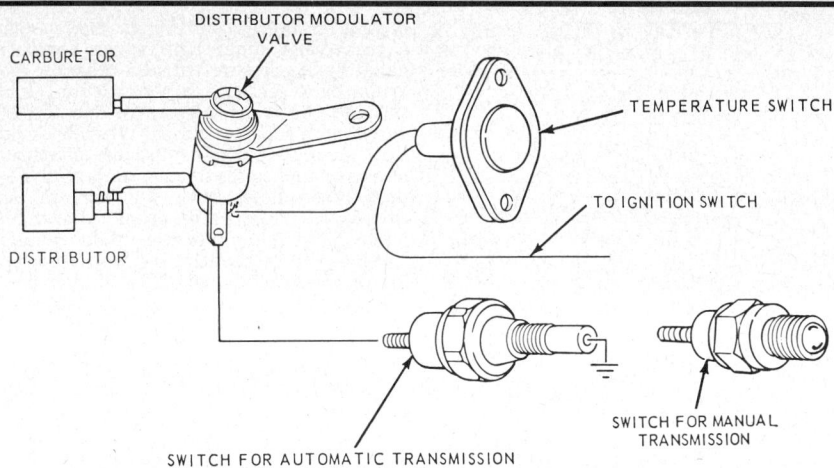

Fig. 59 Ford TRS system

FORD SPARK DELAY VALVE

This unit is used in conjunction with some of the other Ford systems. Its purpose is to further reduce emissions by delaying the spark advance during rapid acceleration and by cutting off advance immediately upon deceleration.

This plastic disc-shaped valve is installed in the carburetor vacuum line at the distributor advance diaphragm. It is a one way valve and will not operate if installed backwards. The black side of the valve must be toward the carburetor. This valve cannot be repaired or checked for proper operation.

NOTE: On all systems which employ the dual diaphragm distributor the line which has high vacuum at idle (normal operating temperature) is connected to the secondary (retard) side of the distributor vacuum advance unit. This is the connection closest to the distributor cap.

FORD EGR SYSTEM
Exhaust Gas Recirculation

In this system the exhaust gases are metered through the EGR valve to a passage in the carburetor spacer, or on some 1974 eight cylinder engines, through two drilled passages in the floor of the intake manifold riser under the carburetor therefore diluting the air fuel mixture entering the combustion chambers. Dilution of the incoming mixture lowers peak flame temperatures during combustion and thus limits the formation of nitrogen oxides (NOx).

Most eight cylinder engines use the "Spacer Entry" EGR System which has the EGR valve mounted on the rear of the carburetor spacer, Fig. 61. The exhaust gases are taken from a drilled passage in the exhaust crossover of the intake manifold. The exhaust gas is then routed through a metered EGR valve to a passage in the carburetor spacer and fed into the primary bore. Some 1974 eight cylinder engines use the "Floor Entry" EGR system, which has the EGR valve mounted on the rear of the intake manifold. The EGR valve controls the exhaust gases that enter specially cast passages in the manifold from the exhaust crossover passage. When the valve opens, the exhaust crossover is then opened to the two drilled passages in the floor of the intake manifold riser under the carburetor, Fig. 62.

On six cylinder models, the EGR system is basically the same as eight cylinder vehicles except that the exhaust gas is routed directly from the exhaust manifold.

Two variables control the operation of the EGR system, 1) engine coolant temperature and 2) carburetor vacuum. When engine coolant temperature is below the specified level the EGR system is locked out by a temperature controlled vacuum switch. This vacuum switch is installed in series with the EGR valve. This valve receives vacuum from a port in the carburetor body. When the valve is closed due to lower coolant temperature, no vacuum is applied to the EGR valve and no exhaust gas is fed to the air-fuel mixture. When the engine coolant temperature reaches the specified level, the valve opens allowing vacuum to be applied to the EGR valve. Exhaust gas is then fed to the air-fuel mixture.

The second factor controlling EGR operation is carburetor vacuum. The location of the EGR port in the carburetor determines at what point vacuum is sent to the EGR valve. Vacuum should be fed to the EGR vacuum control valve when the primary throttle plate reaches a position corresponding to a road speed of approximately 20 mph under light acceleration.

A Venturi Vacuum Amplifier, Fig. 63, used in 1974–79, uses a weak venturi vacuum signal to produce a strong intake manifold vacuum to operate the EGR valve, thereby achieving an accurate, repeatable and almost exact proportion between venturi airflow and EGR flow. This assists in controlling oxides of nitrogen with minimal sacrifice in driveability.

There are three types of EGR valves, the poppet type, modulating type and the tapered stem type.

NOTE: If the tapered stem valve is plugged or causes rough idle due to leakage, it should be replaced.

The poppet type valve, Fig. 64, consists of

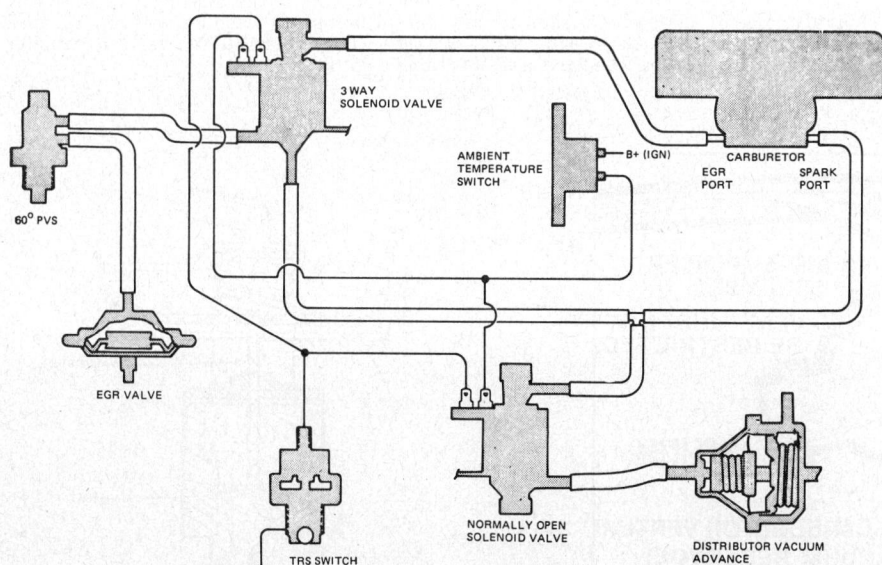

Fig. 60 Ford transmission regulated spark one system—TRS+1

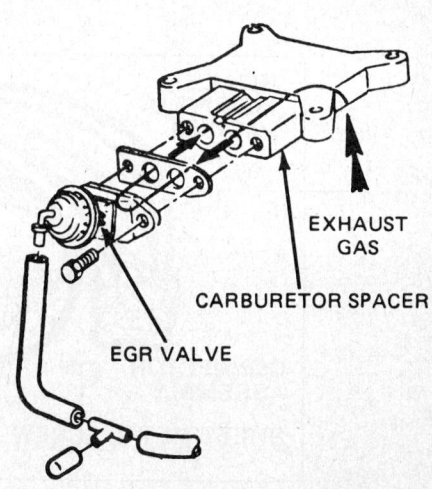

Fig. 61 Ford V8 EGR valve hook up

EMISSION CONTROL SYSTEMS

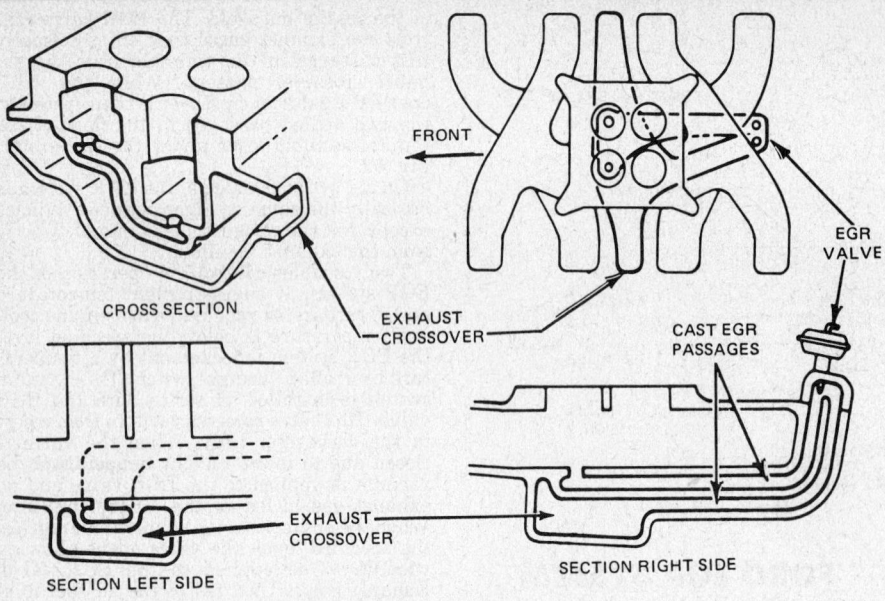

Fig. 62 Ford Floor Entry EGR System

springloaded diaphragm, and a valve stem and valve operating in an enclosed valve body. At approximately 3 inch Hg of vacuum, the valve begins to open. The valve stem is pulled forward unseating the valve and allowing exhaust gas to flow into the valve chamber. Venturi vacuum will then pull the gas from the chamber into the air-fuel flow and then into the combustion chambers. Once the valve has been unseated the only means of limiting exhaust gas flow is the size of the flow restrictor placed in the inlet port of the valve body. The size of the restrictor will vary according to engine application.

On the modulating type valve, Fig. 65, an additional disc has been added to the valve stem below the main valve. The modulating valve operates exactly like the poppet valve when vacuum is between approximately 3 in Hg and 10.5 in Hg. When vacuum reaches approximately 10.5 inches, the lower disc (high vacuum flow restrictor) approaches the shoulders of the valve seat and restricts the flow of exhaust gas. The purpose of the modulation of gas flow is to improve driveability on certain engine models.

NOTE: The EGR valve and vacuum control valve cannot be repaired and must be replaced if damaged.

EGR Non-Integral Back Pressure Transducer

Used on some 1976–79 EGR systems, the back pressure transducer is connected to an adapter between the EGR valve and intake manifold. The transducer modulates EGR flow by varying vacuum signal to EGR valve according to exhaust back pressure. Exhaust back pressure is sensed in pressure cavity of transducer spacer, Fig. 66.

EGR Integral Back Pressure Transducer

This valve, Fig. 67, performs the same function as the non-integral back pressure transducer used on some systems. The valve assembly has an internal exhaust gas chamber with a transducer diaphragm which senses exhaust back pressure through a hollow stem. When back pressure is low, vacuum is bled through the transducer valve and the EGR valve stem remains closed. When back pressure increases, the transducer diaphragm moves up and closes the transducer valve vacuum bleed hole. With the vacuum bleed closed, the EGR valve opens, allowing exhaust gas to flow into the intake manifold. Because the EGR outlet is always exposed to manifold vacuum and EGR gas inlet flow is restricted by an orifice, back pressure at the transducer drops when the EGR valve opens. When the back pressure drops, the vacuum bleed hole opens, closing the EGR valve and allowing pressure to build up again. The cycle is continually repeated, modulating the flow of exhaust gas into the intake manifold.

Cold Start Cycle

The EGR/CSC System regulates both distributor advance and EGR valve operation according to coolant temperature by sequentially switching vacuum signals. The major system components are, a 95° F EGR-PVS (Ported Vacuum Switch) valve, a SDV (Spark Delay Valve) and a vacuum check valve, Fig. 68.

When engine coolant temperature is below 82° F, the EGR-PVS valve admits carburetor EGR port vacuum (at about 2500 RPM) directly to the distributor advance diaphragm, through the one way check valve. At the same time, the EGR-PVS valve shuts off carburetor EGR vacuum to the EGR valve and transmission diaphragm.

When engine coolant temperature is 95° F and above, the EGR-PVS valve is actuated and directs carburetor EGR vacuum to the EGR valve and transmission diaphragm instead of the distributor. At temperatures between 82° and 95° F, the EGR-PVS valve may be open, closed or in mid position.

The Spark Delay Valve (SDV) delays carburetor vacuum to the distributor advance by restricting the vacuum signal through the SDV for a predetermined time. During normal acceleration, little or no vacuum is admitted to the distributor advance diaphragm until acceleration is completed and engine coolant temperature is 95° F or higher.

The check valve blocks off vacuum signal from the SDV to the EGR-PVS valve so that carburetor spark vacuum will not be dissipated when the EGR-PVS valve is actuated above 95° F.

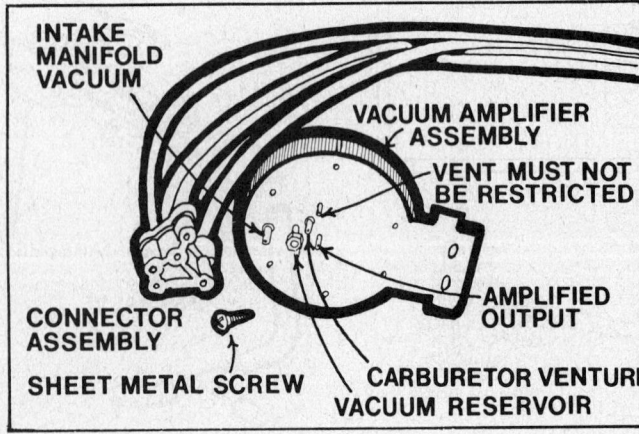

Fig. 63 Venturi Vacuum Amplifier

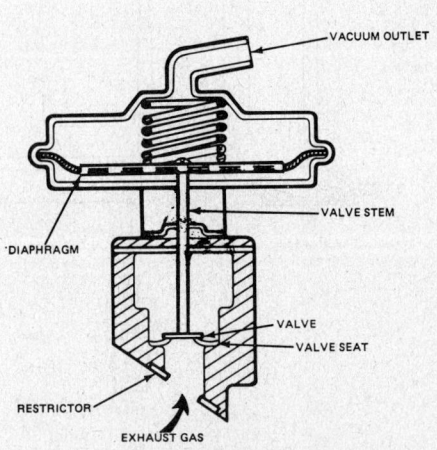

Fig. 64 Ford poppet-type EGR valve

EMISSION CONTROL SYSTEMS

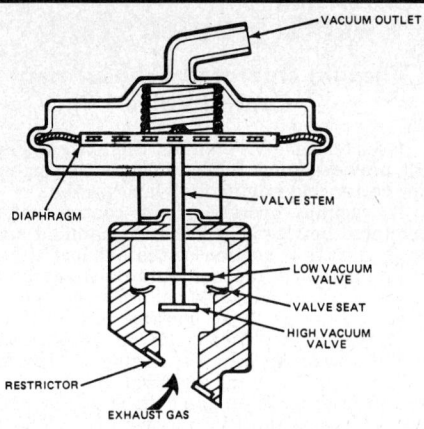

Fig. 65 Ford modulating type EGR valve

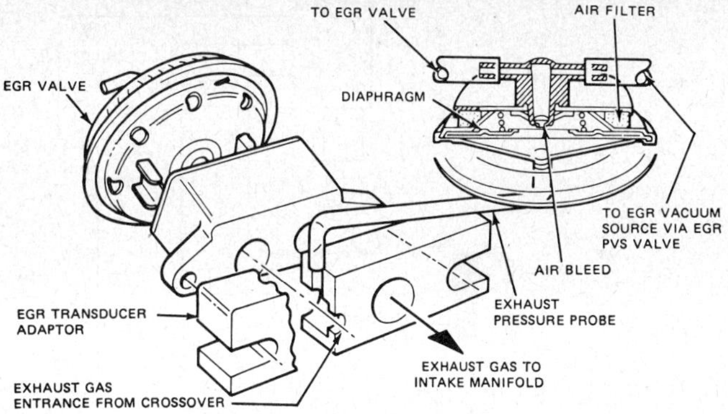

Fig. 66 EGR valve non-integral exhaust back pressure transducer. Ford Motor Co.

The 235° F PVS valve which is not part of the EGR-PVS system is connected to the distributor vacuum advance to prevent engine overheating as on previous models.

DUAL-AREA DIAPHRAGM

On 1973-79 vehicles, new dual-area diaphragms are used, Fig. 69. These diaphragms offset effects of engines using the EGR system and equipped with automatic transmissions. The new diaphragms permit vehicles to function with satisfactory shift spacing and shift feel.

To test, remove the vacuum diaphragm and test unit using an outside vacuum source. Set regulator on tester to 18 in. Hg with end of vacuum hose blocked off then connect vacuum hose to vacuum diaphragm unit. If unit does not hold 18 in. Hg reading, the diaphragm is leaking and must be replaced.

FORD DVB SYSTEM

Delay Vacuum By-Pass System

This system is designed to delay distributor vacuum advance under varying ambient temperatures and vehicle speeds. The system consists of a solenoid vacuum valve (SV), spark delay valve (SDV), and a check valve (one-way valve), Fig. 70.

The spark delay valve SDV is a two-way flow device used for controlling distributor vacuum advance. It delays the flow of vacuum in one direction through a sintered metal restrictor, yet permits an instantaneous flow in the other direction through a one-way check valve.

When the vehicle is accelerating, the direction of air flow is from the distributor toward the carburetor through the restrictor.

The check valve is held closed by the pressure differential between the SDV inlet and outlet connections. After a specified time period, (depending on restrictor porosity) the vacuum will bleed through the restrictor and equalize the pressure at both connections.

When the vehicle decelerates, the pressure differential is reversed, the direction of air flow is reversed, and the check valve opens, to instantly equalize air pressure across the valves.

Since different vehicle engine and transmission combinations require different time delay periods to effectively meet emission requirements, five different type SDV valves are used in the various vehicle engine applications. Each type is color coded.

Since the SDV is not affected by ambient air temperature changes, it would act to retard the distributor spark advance during cold weather when exhaust emissions can be met normally without the retarding action. For this reason, the DVB system is also connected between the vacuum source at the carburetor spark port and the distributor primary diaphragm in parallel with the SDV system.

At temperatures of 60 degrees F and above, the normally open solenoid vacuum valve receives battery voltage from the ambient temperature switch whenever the ignition switch is on closing the solenoid valve and shutting off vacuum to the distributor. The temperature switch is open at temperatures of 49 degrees F and below and no signal is sent to the solenoid valve. Thus, the solenoid valve will remain open admitting carburetor spark port vacuum to the distributor primary vacuum diaphragm directly through the open solenoid valve.

NOTE: The DVB system is energized only when the weather is warm and allows no direct flow of vacuum through the solenoid valve.

The DVB system check valve prevents the outlet of the SDV valve from being vented to the atmosphere to cause a loss of vacuum to the distributor resulting in no distributor advance when the DVB is energized. The check valve must be installed in the vacuum line as shown or the SDV valve will not permit the check valve to close.

FORD TAV SYSTEM

Temperature Activated Vacuum

This system selects either the carburetor spark port vacuum, or the carburetor EGR port vacuum as a function of outside ambient air temperature.

The EGR system can be used in addition to the TAV system, although systems work independently of each other.

The TAV system, Fig. 71, consists of an ambient temperature switch, a three-way vacuum valve, and an external inline vacuum

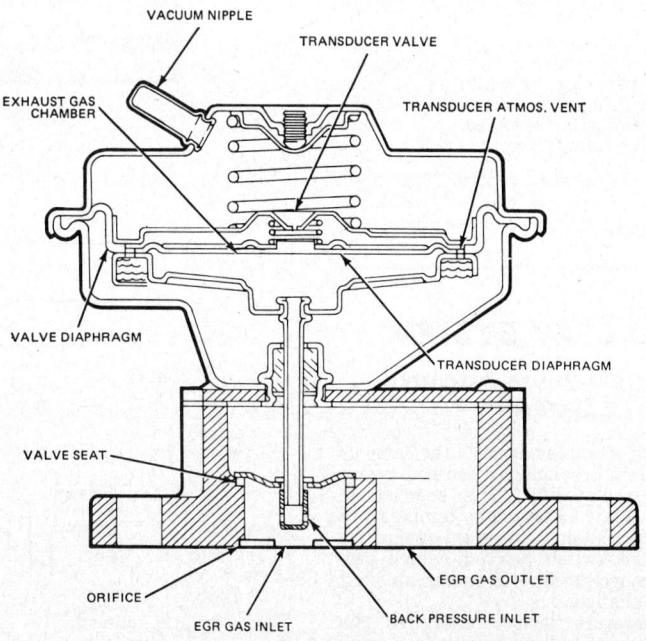

Fig. 67 EGR integral back pressure transducer. Ford Motor Co.

EMISSION CONTROL SYSTEMS

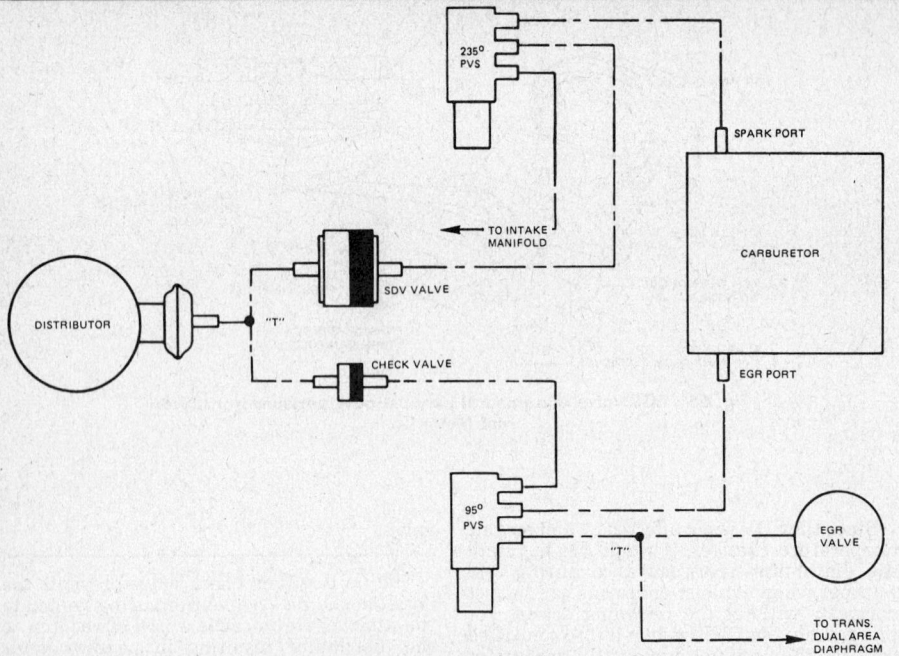

Fig. 68 Ford EGR/CSC System

FORD HCV SYSTEM

Vacuum Operated Exhaust Heat Control Valve

Used on some V8 engines, this system, Fig. 73, provides quick induction system warm-up for better cold engine fuel vaporization.

A vacuum operated heat control valve mounted between the exhaust manifold and pipe, directs a portion of the exhaust gases through the intake manifold during engine warm-up. On cold starts, manifold vacuum is directed to the heat control valve (HCV) through the top two ports in HCV PVS (ported vacuum switch), closing the HCV. When engine coolant temperature reaches a predetermined value, the PVS closes off vacuum and vents the PVS allowing the HCV to close under spring tension. The three PVS valves used may be identified as follows:

PVS Body Color	Opening Temp. (° F.)
Black	92–98
Blue	125–131
Purple	157–163

COLD START SPARK ADVANCE (CSSA)

Used on some 1975–79 engines, this system, Figs. 74 and 75, is added to the distributor control to provide manifold vacuum when engine coolant is below 125° F. by providing vacuum from the intake manifold, through the Distributor Retard Control Valve (DRCV), the CSSA PVS and to the distributor. At 125° F. and above, the vacuum flows

bleed. The three-way vacuum valve is used to select the carburetor vacuum source that is supplied to the distributor vacuum advance mechanism. The ambient temperature switch provides the switching circuit to determine which vacuum source will be selected as a function of outside air temperature. The in-line vacuum bleed function is to purge the vacuum line in the TAV system of any excessive gasoline vapors.

The basic difference between a TAV system and the standard IMCO system is the selective control feature provided by TAV system for distributor vacuum advance as a function of outside air temperature.

When the ambient air temperature is above 60 degrees F the three-way vacuum valve is energized, therefore the EGR vacuum is controlling the distributor advance. When the ambient air temperature is below 49 degrees F the three-way vacuum valve is de-energized, therefore the spark port vacuum is controlling the distributor advance.

NOTE: The TAV system controls spark advance below 49 degrees F, while the EGR system controls spark advance above 60 degrees F.

When ambient temperature is below 49° F, the system is inoperative and the distributor diaphragm and EGR valve receives vacuum directly from its respective carburetor ports.

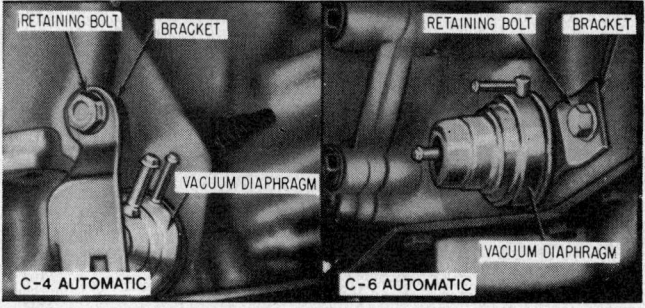

Fig. 69 Dual diaphragm vacuum modulator

FORD CTAV SYSTEM

Cold Temperature Activated System

This system operates basically the same as the TAV system previously discussed except that a latching relay, Fig. 72, has been added. The latching relay, activated by temperature switch closing remains energized regardless of temperature switch position which prevents system cycling due to minor ambient temperature changes.

The temperature switch energizes the three-way vacuum valve and latching relay when ambient temperature is above 65° F.

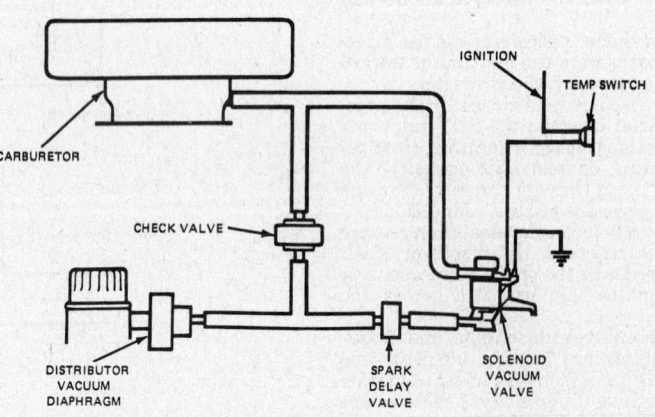

Fig. 70 Ford delay vacuum by-pass system—DVB

EMISSION CONTROL SYSTEMS

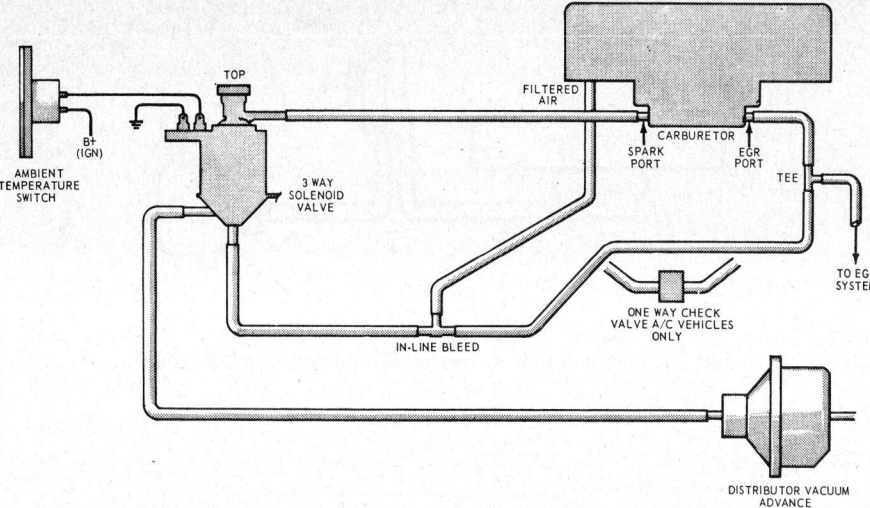

Fig. 71 Ford temperature activated vacuum system—TAV

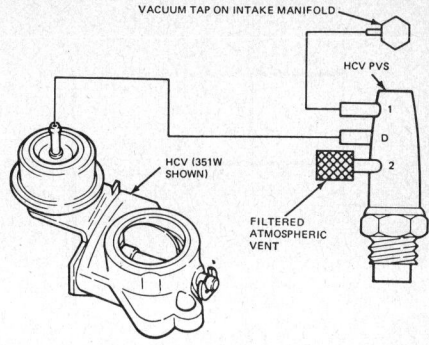

Fig. 73 Heat Control Valve (HCV) System. 1975-76 Ford

from the carburetor spark port, through the cooling PVS, the SDV, the CSSA PVS and to the distributor. Above 235° F., the vacuum flows through the SDV and CSSA PVS to the distributor. If engine overheats at idle, increased vacuum will flow to the distributor to increase engine speed. When engine coolant temperature decreases, spark advance will be controlled by the carburetor spark port.

COLD START SPARK HOLD (CSSH)

This system provides momentary spark advance hold during acceleration when the engine is cold, to provide improved cold engine acceleration.

When engine coolant temperature is less than 128° F, the CSSH PVS is closed and the distributor vacuum signal travels through the restrictor, Fig. 76.

When the engine is started cold, high vacuum acts on the vacuum advance unit to provide maximum advance. During acceleration, the high vacuum in the vacuum advance unit is slowly bled down through the restrictor, providing a modified vacuum advance during the initial stage of acceleration.

DISTRIBUTOR VACUUM VENT VALVE

This valve, Fig. 77, is used on some 1977-79 Ford Motor Co. vehicles equipped with a variable venturi carburetor. The primary functions of this valve are to control exhaust emissions, to prevent fuel migration to the distributor and act as a delay valve.

This valve controls exhaust emissions by

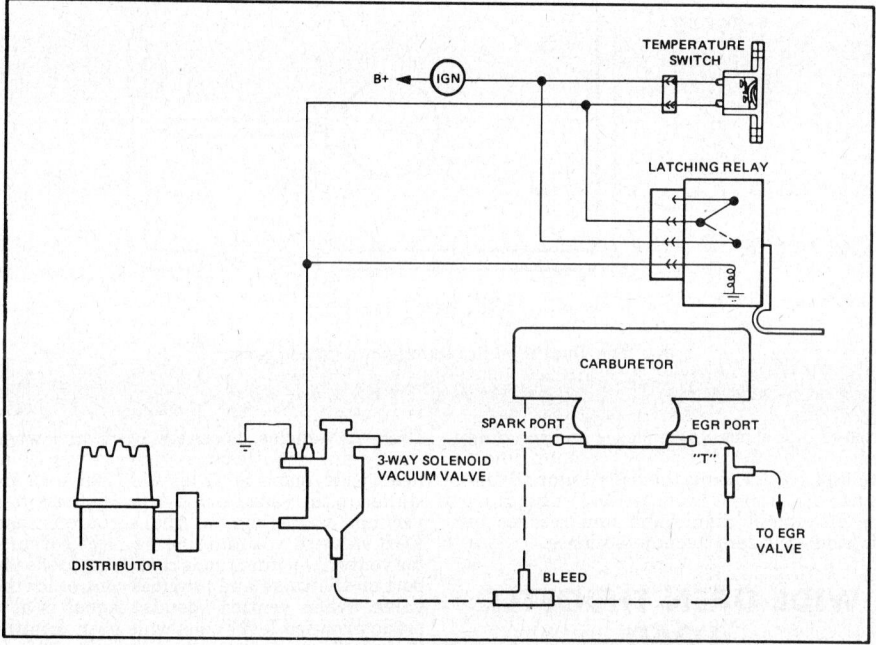

Fig. 72 Ford cold temperature activated vacuum system—CTAV

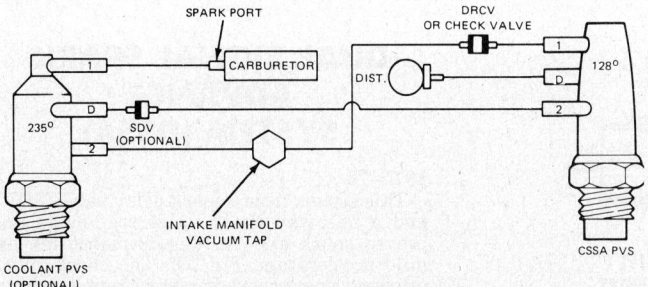

Fig. 74 Cold start spark advance system. 1975-76 Ford

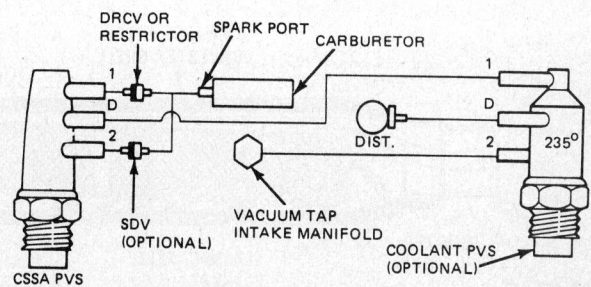

Fig. 75 Cold start spark advance system. 1977-79 Ford

EMISSION CONTROL SYSTEMS

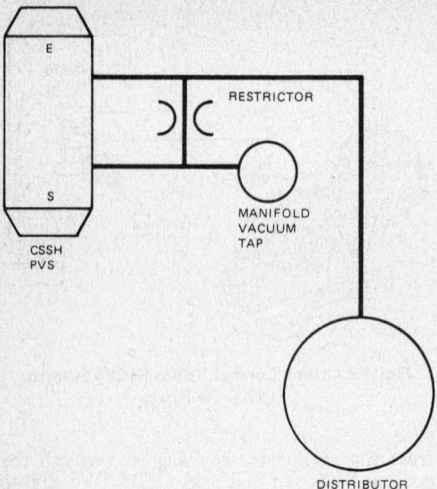

Fig. 76 Cold start spark hold (CSSH) system. Ford

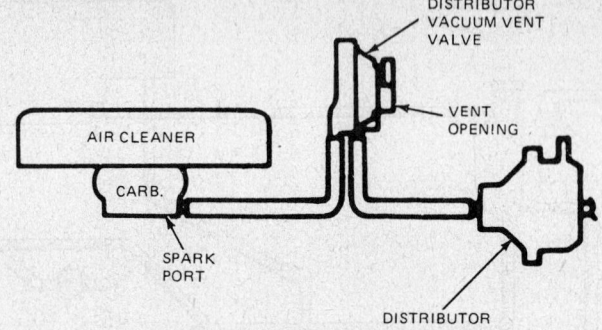

Fig. 77 Typical distributor vent valve installation. 1977–79 Ford

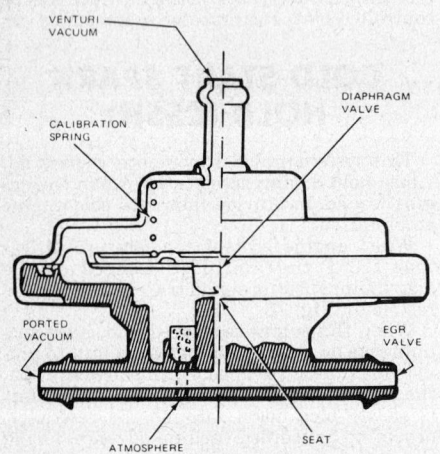

Fig. 78 EGR load control valve

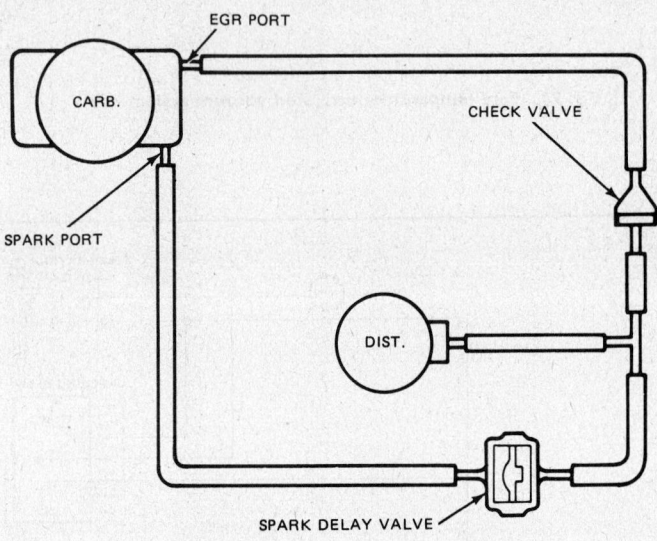

Fig. 79 Dual signal spark advance (DSSA) system

delaying vacuum spark advance during light acceleration and eliminating vacuum spark advance during heavy acceleration, deceleration and idle.

When spark port vacuum is applied to the vent valve, the dump valve closes, the check valve opens and the distributor vacuum advance unit begins to evacuate through the sintered metal restrictor which acts as a spark delay valve. When spark port vacuum decreases, the check valve closes and the dump valve opens the distributor vacuum line to atmosphere. Venting the distributor vacuum line to atmosphere prevents fuel migration to the distributor diaphragm and returns the distributor to zero vacuum advance.

WIDE OPEN THROTTLE LOAD CONTROL VALVE

This valve, Fig. 78, which is used on some 1978–79 vehicles, closes the EGR valve when the engine requires maximum power at or near wide open throttle. This valve is installed in the vacuum line between the ported vacuum connection on the carburetor and EGR valve. A vacuum line from the carburetor venturi vacuum tap is connected to the top port on the valve and provides control for the valve. When venturi vacuum signal is at a predetermined level near wide open throttle, it is strong enough to overcome the calibration spring pressure and unseat the diaphragm valve, diverting EGR source vacuum to the atmosphere and causing the EGR valve to close. Normal EGR flow is resumed when there is a reduction in engine load from the wide open throttle position.

DUAL SIGNAL SPARK ADVANCE SYSTEM (DSSA)

1975–76

This system uses a spark delay valve (SDV) and a one way check valve to provide improved spark and EGR performance during mild acceleration, Fig. 79. The check valve prevents spark port vacuum from reaching EGR and causing excessive EGR flow. The valve also prevents EGR port vacuum from

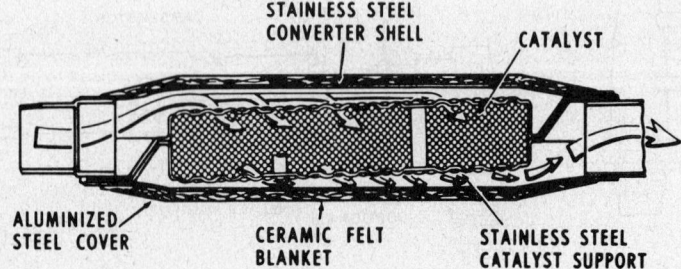

Fig. 80 American Motors and General Motors catalytic converter

EMISSION CONTROL SYSTEMS

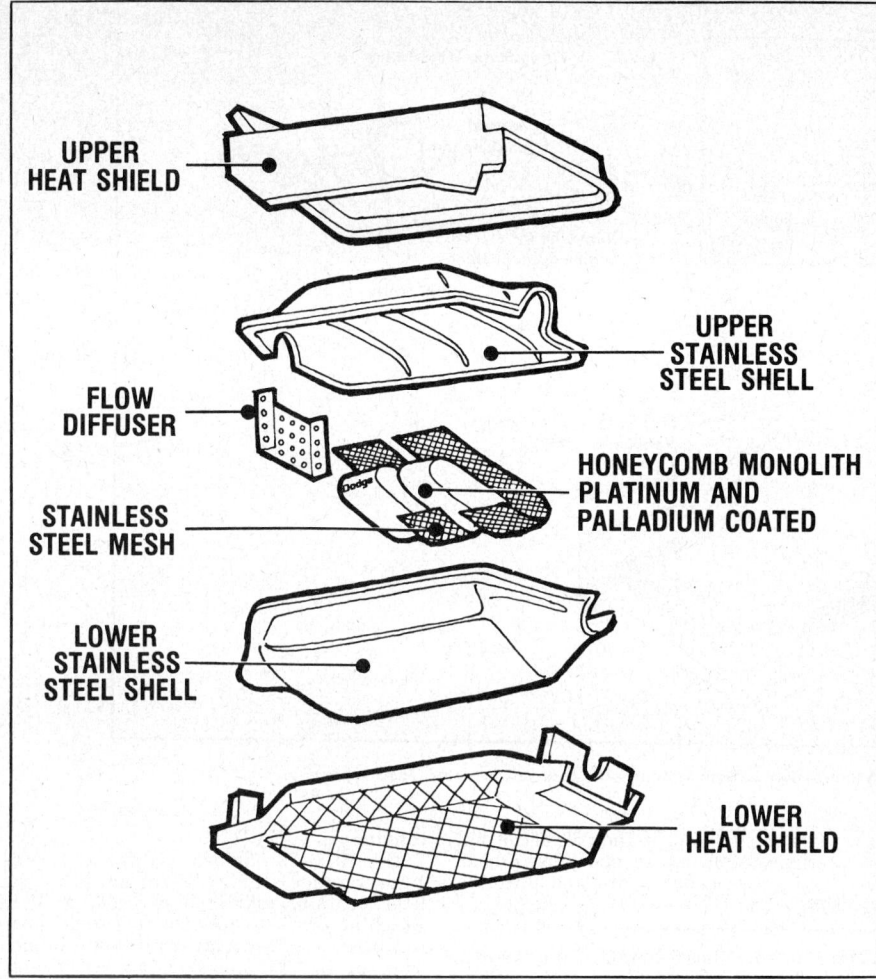

Fig. 81 Chrysler Corp. catalytic converter

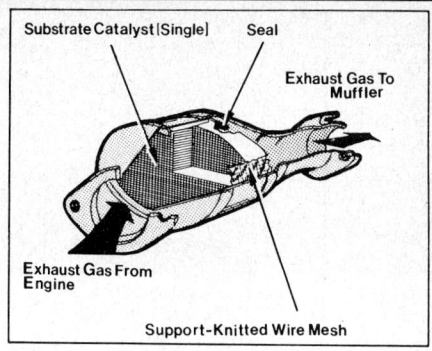

Fig. 82 Ford catalytic converter with single substrate catalyst

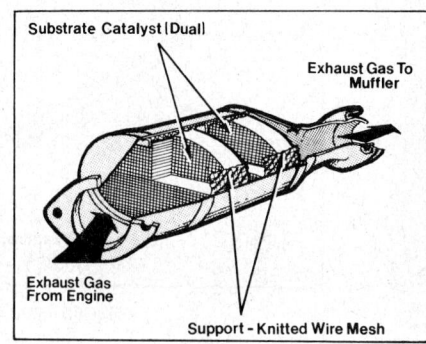

Fig. 83 Ford catalytic converter with dual substrate catalyst

CATALYTIC CONVERTERS

The catalytic converter serves two purposes: it permits a faster chemical reaction to take place and although it enters into the chemical reaction, it remains unchanged, ready to repeat the process. The catalytic converter combines hydrocarbons (HC) and carbon monoxide (CO) with oxygen to form water (H_2O) and carbon dioxide (CO_2).

The catalyst is structured in the form of pellets, Fig. 80 (General Motors & American Motors), or a honeycomb monolithic composition, Figs. 81 (Chrysler Corp.) 82 and 83 (Fords). The catalyst consists of a porous substrate of an inert material, coated with platinum and other noble metals, the catalytically active materials.

This device, located in the exhaust system between the exhaust manifold and muffler, requires the use of heat shields, in some cases, due to its high operating temperatures. The heat shields are necessary to protect chassis

diluting spark port vacuum which could result in improper spark advance. The SDV permits application of full EGR vacuum to distributor vacuum advance during mild acceleration. During cruise conditions, EGR port vacuum is applied to EGR valve and spark port vacuum is applied to distributor vacuum advance.

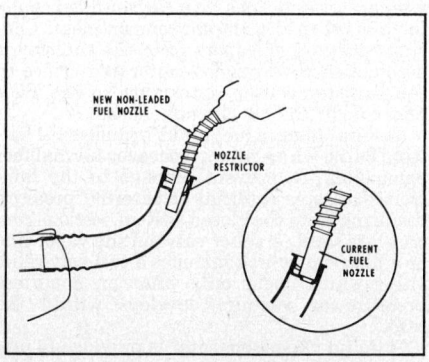

Fig. 84 Fuel tank filler safety neck for all vehicles equipped with catalytic converters (Typical)

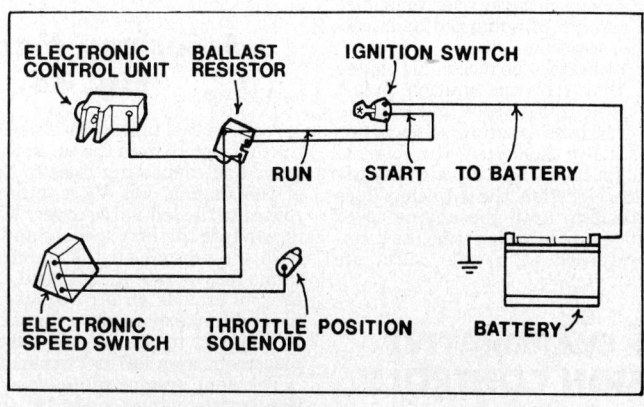

Fig. 85 Chrysler Corp. throttle control systems for all vehicles equipped with catalytic converters

777

EMISSION CONTROL SYSTEMS

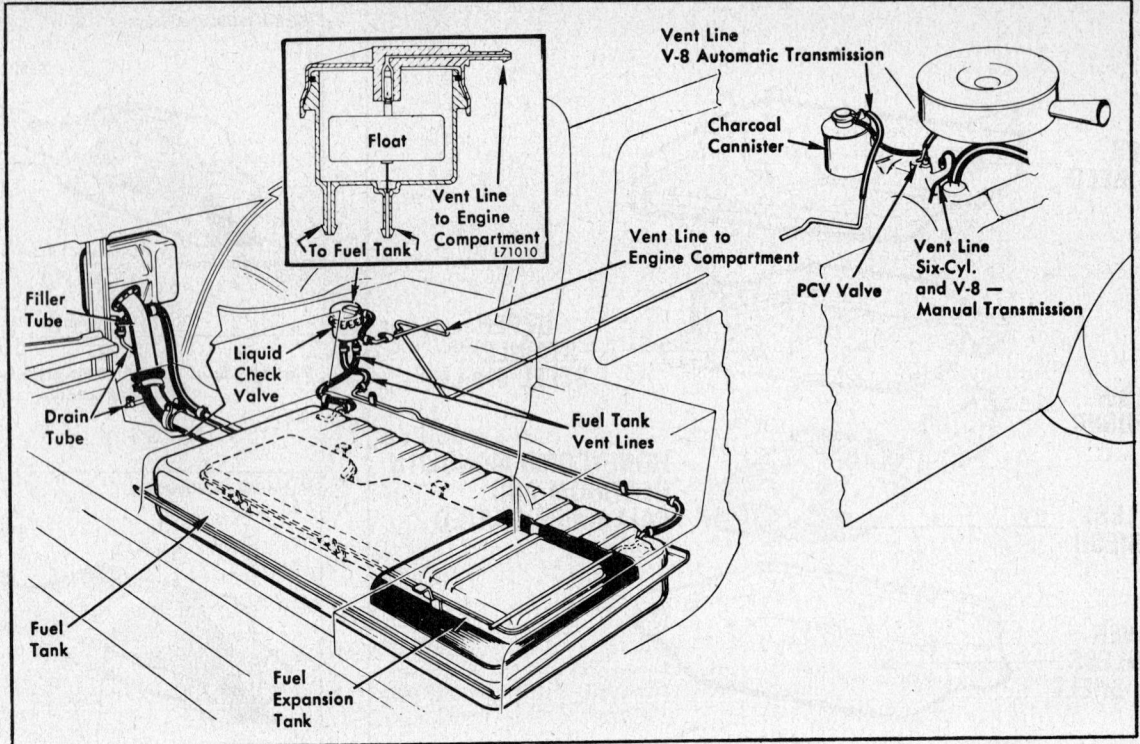

Fig. 86 Evaporative emission control system with charcoal canister. Jeep typical

components, passenger compartment and other areas from heat related damage.

A smaller diameter fuel tank filler tube neck is incorporated to prevent the larger service station pump nozzle, used for leaded fuels, being inserted into the filler tube, thereby preventing system contamination, Fig. 84.

CAUTION: Since the use of leaded fuels contaminates the catalysts, deteriorating its effectiveness, the use of unleaded fuels is mandatory in vehicles equipped with catalytic converters. The catalytic converter can tolerate very small amounts of leaded fuels without permanently reducing the catalyst effectiveness.

Some Chrysler Corp. vehicles equipped with catalytic converters, have a Catalyst Protection System, Fig. 85, which prevents overheating of the converter during high speed deceleration. This overheating condition occurs when the catalyst tries to oxidize the increased amount of unburned hydrocarbons during deceleration.

This system consists of an electronic engine speed switch that receives ignition pulses from the electronic control unit and a carburetor mounted throttle position solenoid. At engine speeds above 2000 rpm, the solenoid will energize to hold the throttle slightly open. During deceleration, the throttle will be held in this position until the engine speed drops below 2000 rpm at which time the throttle will be returned to normal curb idle speed.

FUEL EVAPORATIVE EMISSION CONTROLS

CAUTION: The utmost care should be exercised when using a torch in the area of the fuel evaporation system as an open flame near these hoses may cause a fire and ultimate explosion.

NOTE: Vapor line hoses used in these systems are made from a special rubber material. Bulk service hoses are available for service and will be marked "EVAP". Ordinary fuel hoses should not be used as they are subject to deterioration and may clog system.

CAUTION: Installation of a fill cap from a non-emission fuel tank will render the system inoperative, since the non-emission fill cap is vented and the system must be sealed to function properly. Also if a non-vented fill cap is installed on a conventional tank, the result will be a serious deformation or a total collapse of the fuel tank.

American Motors, Fig. 86

A closed fuel tank vent is used which routes the fuel vapors from the tank, through a check valve and connecting lines to the valve cover of the engine. On V8 engines, the line is routed to the left valve cover. Vapors are then drawn into the PCV system and burned along with the normal air-fuel mixture. Most fuel tanks incorporate an integral fuel expansion tank to provide an air displacement area for normal fuel expansion, unless the tank itself is designed to provide an adequate air displacement area for fuel expansion.

The vent system routes raw fuel vapor to the engine valve cover. A check valve is included to prevent the flow of liquid fuel to the valve cover under all operating conditions.

The 1971–79 engines incorporate a "Fuel Vapor Storage (Charcoal) Canister". This canister contains activated charcoal granules which absorb and store the fuel tank vapors until they are drawn into the intake manifold through the PCV system on six cylinder engines or the carburetor air cleaner on V8 engines.

The filler cap includes a two-way relief valve which is closed to atmosphere under normal operating conditions and opens only when an abnormal pressure or vacuum develops within the tank. It is normal to occasionally encounter an air pressure release when removing the filler cap.

General Motors, Fig. 87

Fuel vapor is drawn from the tank, through a separator and lines, to a carbon-filled canister located in the engine compartment. Constant purging of vapors from the canister is accomplished through a calibrated orifice in the canister center connection to the PCV hose and/or the air cleaner snorkel.

General Motors fuel tanks include a fill limiting baffle which allows space for normal fuel expansion. To prevent damage to the tank from excessive internal or external pressure resulting from the closed system, various controls are used. A relief valve in the vapor line or a filler cap which includes a two-way relief valve which opens only when an abnormal pressure or vacuum develops within the tank.

A liquid vapor separator is provided to prevent liquid fuel from entering the system. Liquid fuel entering the separator is spilled back into the tank while raw fuel vapor is passed into the lines.

Emission Control Systems

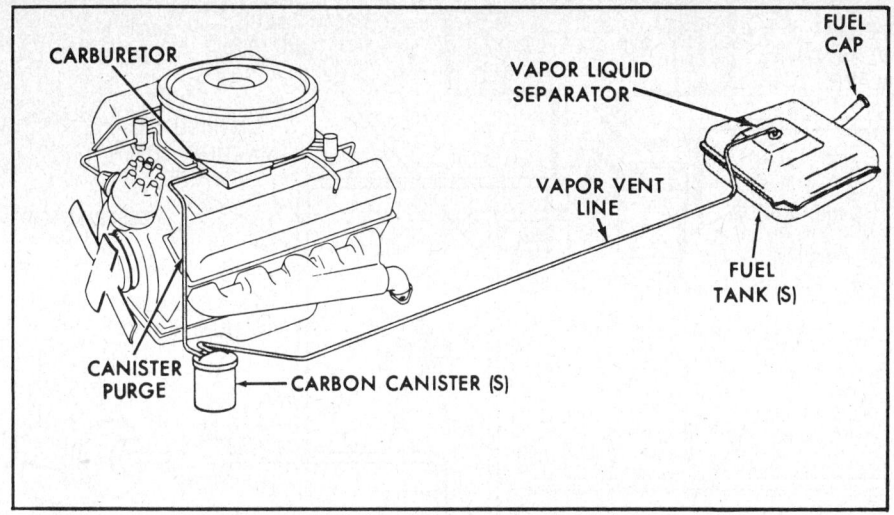

Fig. 87 Evaporative emission control system. General Motors typical

The carbon canister provides a storage place for the raw fuel vapor when the engine is not running. When the engine is running, vapors are drawn from the canister into the engine.

Maintenance:
The only service required is that the filter mounted at the bottom of the canister be replaced every 2 years, or 24,000 miles with heavy duty emissions or 30,000 miles with light duty emissions.

NOTE: The purge valve (used on some applications), can be repaired without replacing complete vapor canister, using repair kit, part No. 7041344. The service is NOT a routine maintenance item and should be performed if damage or parts are missing.

Chrysler Corp.

1970–71 System, Fig. 88

This is a closed system venting fuel vapors through lines to the engine crankcase by way of the crankcase inlet air cleaner. With the engine running, the vapors are purged from the crankcase with the normal crankcase vapor.

The fuel tank incorporates an expansion tank to provide space for air displacement during normal fuel expansion. The filler cap is a special unit which incorporates a relief valve.

A liquid vapor separator is included between the tank and the vapor line to insure against liquid fuel entering the system. Liquid fuel is spilled back into the tank while raw fuel vapor is admitted into the vapor line.

1972–79 System, Figs. 89 & 90

In this system when the fuel tank is filled to the base of the filler tube, vapors can no longer escape, they become trapped above the fuel. Vapor flow through the vent line is blocked by the limiting valve; and the filler tube is blocked by fuel preventing more fuel to enter the tank. At any time pressures in the

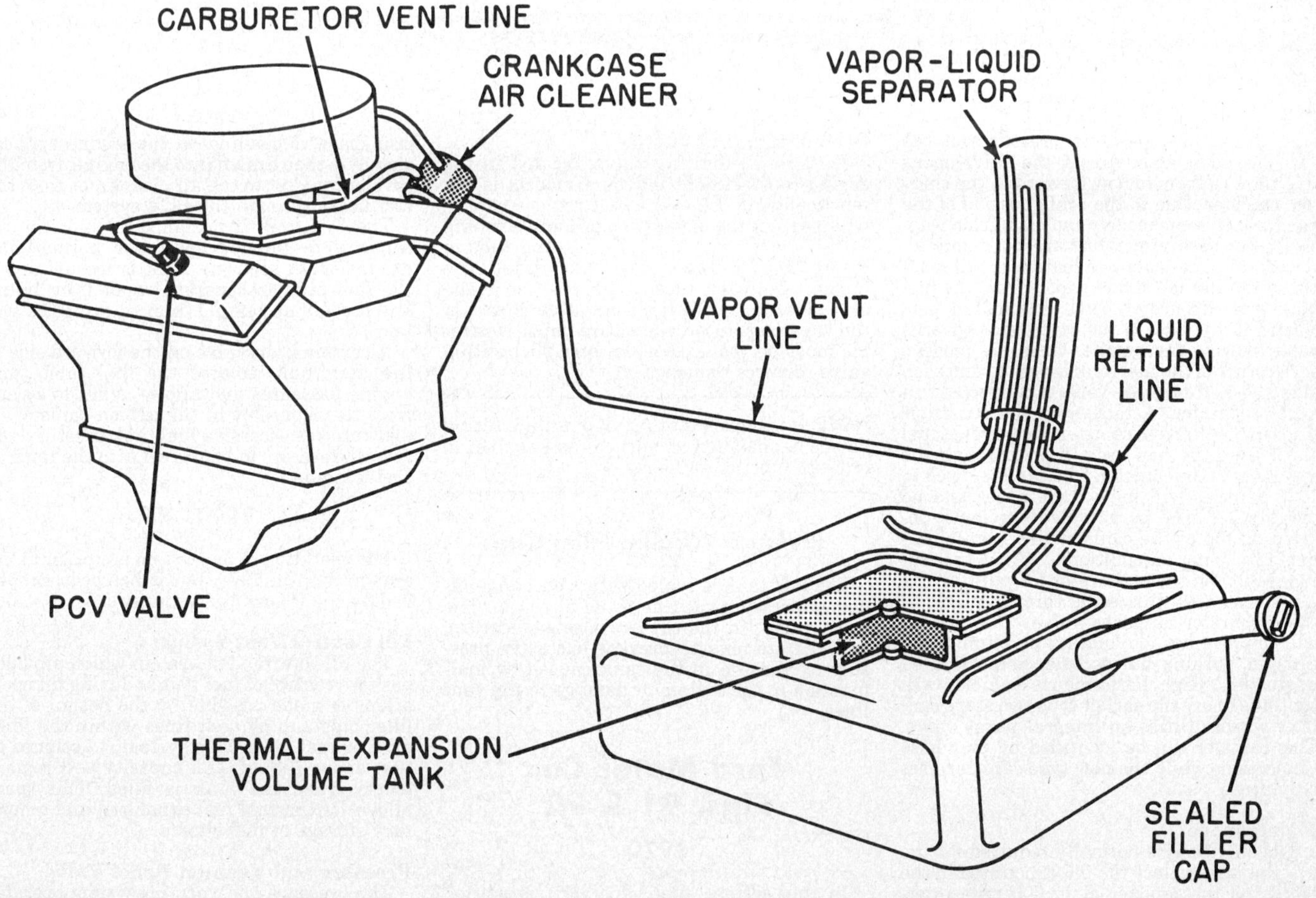

Fig. 88 Evaporative emission control system. Chrysler Corp., 1970–71. Typical

EMISSION CONTROL SYSTEMS

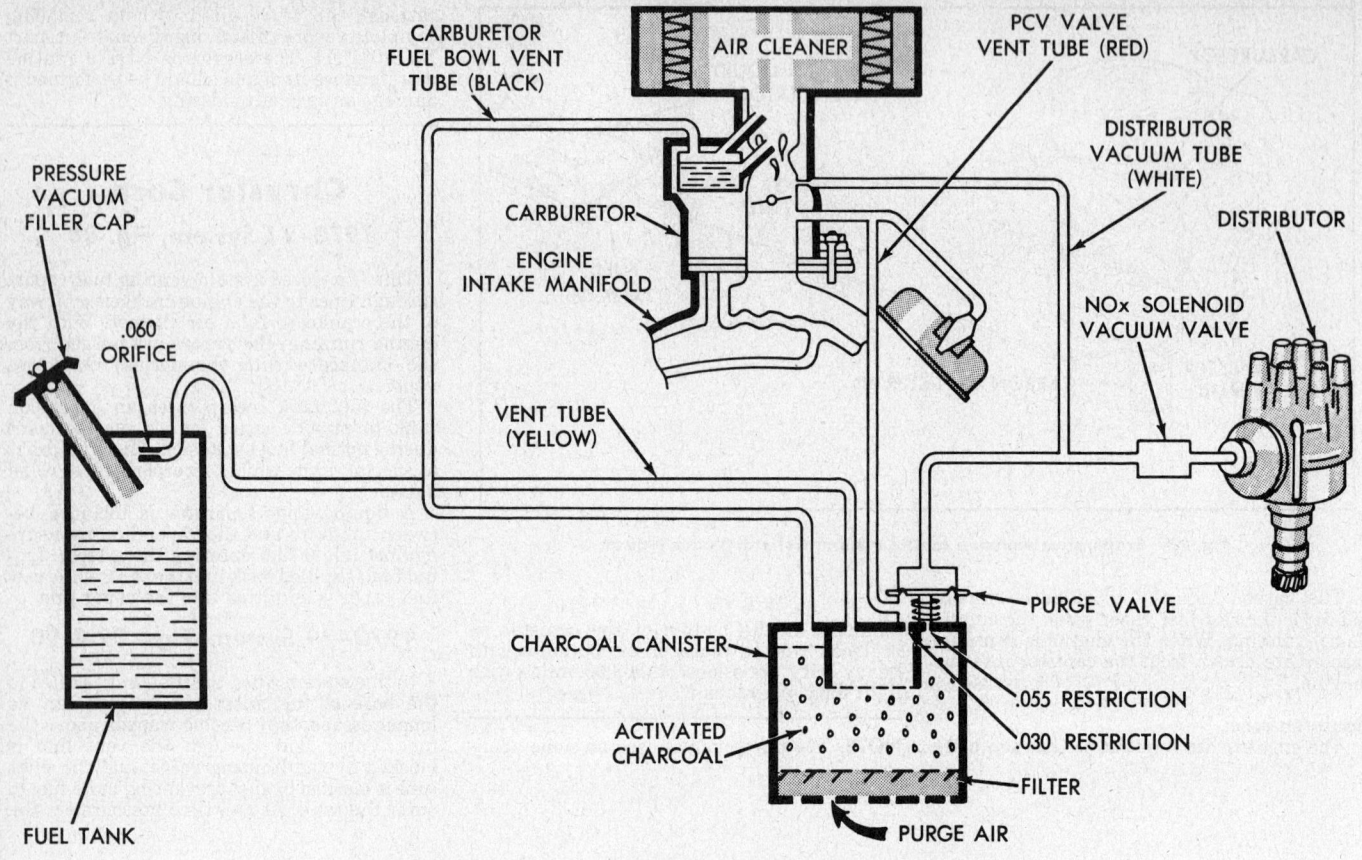

Fig. 89 Evaporative emission control system. Chrysler Corp., typical of Dodge Vans & Motor Homes 1972-74

tank rise above operating pressures of the limiting valve, about 1/2 psi the valve opens and allows vapors to flow forward to the charcoal canister. Due to the configuration of the fuel tank on some models and all station wagons, vapor separator tanks are not required. The charcoal canister is a feature on all models for the storage of fuel vapors from the fuel tank and carburetor bowl. A vacuum port located in the base of the carburetor governs vapor flow to the engine. On some models, each corner of the fuel tank is vented and each of the hoses from these vents is connected to a vapor separator. A tube from the separator leads to the charcoal canister. Evaporated fuel vapor from the fuel tank, flows through the separator to the canister. The canister used in 1973 vehicles will have three hoses and no purge valve. The purge valve previously located on top of the canister has been eliminated by using an additional ported vacuum connection on the carburetor for purging the canister. This utilizes the throttle plates of the carburetor as purge valve. This system will improve hot idle quality by eliminating canister purging during idle. Some limited production, High Performance vehicles will continue to use the earlier type two stage canister which utilizes an integral purge valve. This canister can be identified by four hose connections while the new type canister uses only three.

Maintenance

The only service normally required for the system, is to replace the filter mounted in the bottom of the canister at 12,000 mile intervals.

Overfill Limiting Valve

The overfill limiting valve, located in the engine compartment on some models is not serviceable, in the event that replacement is required, cut the old valve out using a tubing cutter. Flare the end of the existing tube to insure a good vapor seal and install the replacement valve in the same position as the old valve. If overfill limiting valve is part of the vapor separator, the entire vapor separator must be replaced if the overfill limiting valve requires replacement.

NOTE: It is important that all overfill limiting valves be installed as vertical as possible, in order to function properly.

Pressure-Vacuum Filler Cap

The fuel tank is sealed with a special engineered pressure vacuum relief filler cap. The relief valves in the cap are a safety feature, and operate only to prevent excessive pressure or vacuum in the tank caused by malfunction in the system or damage to the vent lines.

Ford Motor Co. Figs. 91 & 92

1970

In this system, fuel vapor is transported either to a carbon canister or the engine crankcase, depending on the engine application. It is then drawn into the engine, from the carbon canister to the air cleaner, or from the crankcase through the PCV system.

The fuel tank is designed to limit the fill capacity to provide space for normal fuel expansion. A separate tank is located above the fuel tank to separate vapor from liquid and prevent any liquid from entering the system.

A combination valve on the forward side of the fuel tank isolates the fuel tank from engine pressures and allows vapor to escape from the separator to the carbon canister. It also relieves excessive fuel tank pressure and allows fresh air to be drawn into the tank as fuel is used.

1971-77

The operation of the system is similar to the system used in 1970, but it has been simplified by the following modifications:

Fill Control Vent System

The fill control vent system which provides positive control of fuel height during fill operations is made possible by the design of the filler pipe and by vent lines within the filler neck or fuel tank. This system is designed so that about 10% of tank capacity will remain empty when the tank is filled. This space allows for thermal fuel expansion and temporary storage of fuel vapors.

Pressure and Vacuum Relief Valve

The pressure and vacuum system operates through the use of a sealed fill cap with a

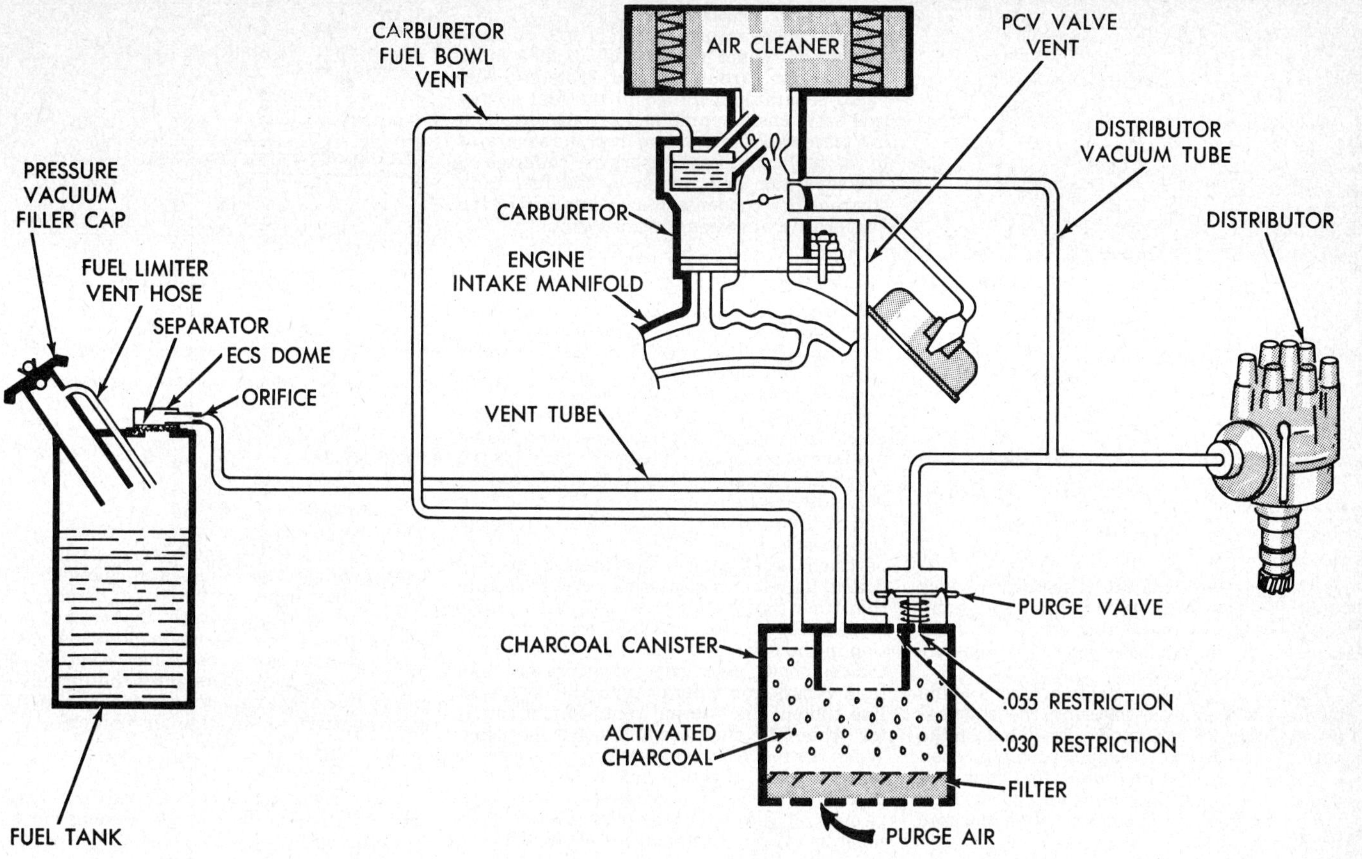

EMISSION CONTROL SYSTEMS

Fig. 90 Evaporative emission control system. Chrysler Corp., exc. Dodge Vans & Motor Homes 1972–79. Typical

built-in pressure and vacuum relief valve. Under normal operating conditions, the valve opens to relieve pressure when it exceeds 3/4 to 1 1/4 psi. When fuel tank vacuum reaches 1/2 inch mercury maximum, the valve opens allowing air to enter the system.

Vapor Vent and Storage System
This system, on vertically mounted fuel tanks consists of a vapor separator, Fig. 93, mounted on the uppermost surface of the tank. The empty space at the top of the tank provides adequate breathing space for the vapor separator. Horizontally mounted fuel tanks use a raised mounting section for the

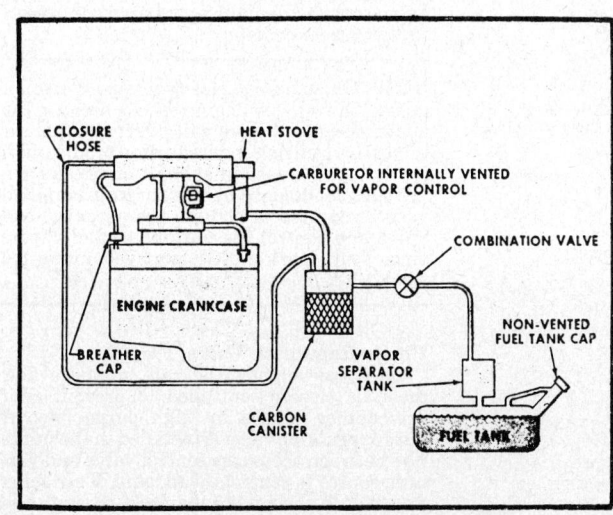

Fig. 91 Evaporative emission control system. Ford carbon storage type

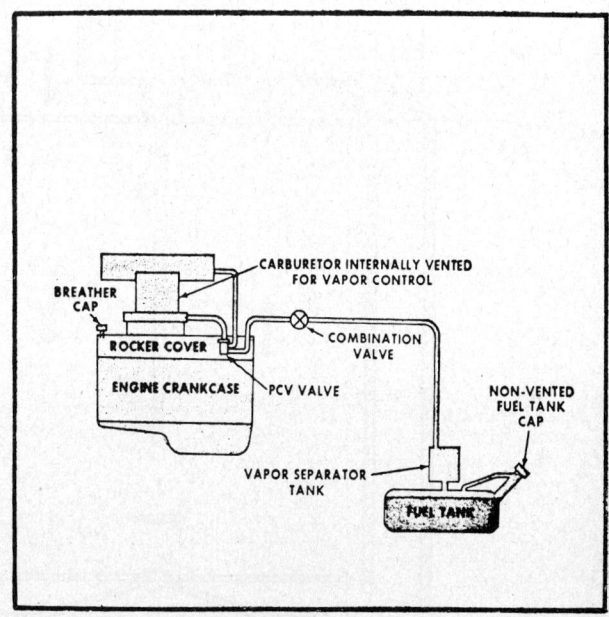

Fig. 92 Evaporative emission control system. Ford crankcase storage type

781

EMISSION CONTROL SYSTEMS

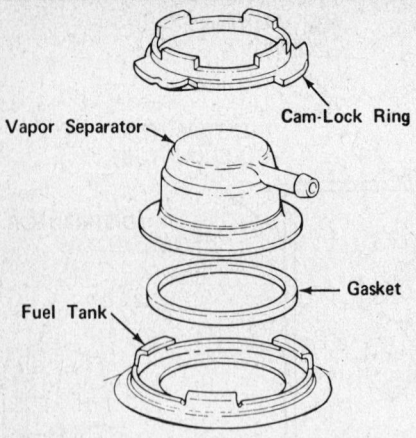

Fig. 93 Tank mounted vapor separator

Fuel Vapor Return System

A fuel vapor return system is used on some engines to reduce the amount of fuel vapor entering the carburetor. It consists of a fuel vapor separator installed in the fuel supply line between the pump and carburetor and a one piece vapor return line from the separator to the fuel tank. Fuel vapors are collected in the separator and routed to the fuel tank where they recondense or are contained by the evaporative emission control system.

1978-79

These models use a manifold purge system. The charcoal canister media has been changed with a more efficient carbon, and a purge control valve situated atop the charcoal canister controls the evaporative system.

The purge signal (EGR port, spark port or manifold vacuum), actuates the purge valve to allow purging of the canister through the purge line. When the engine is off, the purge valve directs fuel vapors from the fuel tank and carburetor bowl to the canister. An exception to this would be when the engine compartment is below the temperature where sufficient gasoline vaporization occurs. During this time the thermal vent valve (on some models) closes, stopping flow in either direction in the bowl vent line. The purpose of the thermal bowl vent valve is to prevent fuel tank vapors from migrating up the bowl vent line and out the internal vent of the carburetor when the fuel bowl is not vaporizing. When the fuel bowl is vaporizing, the thermal valve is open, allowing flow to the canister. Also, the internal fuel bowl vent valve must be open (at idle) and/or the solenoid vent valve must be open (ignition off) to allow flow into

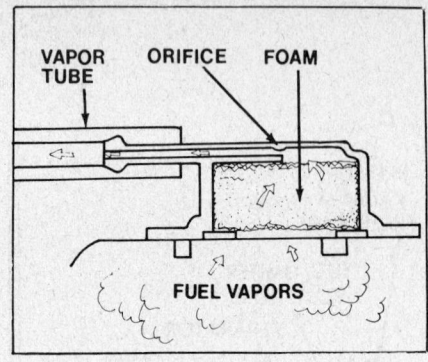

Fig. 94 Vapor separator cross section

the canister.

Carbon Canister, Fig. 95

The carbon canister is a carryover design of the one used in previous years, except that routing of the vapors has been changed. The carbon has been improved to handle the increased demands which the system has placed on it. The vapors in previous years were fed to the carbon bed from the bottom up. On 1978-79, the vapors enter the top of the purge side of the canister and travel in a "U" shape pattern to the fresh air vent side.

Purge Control Valve, Fig. 96

The valve is installed on the carbon canister and controls the flow of fuel vapors during various engine operating modes. The control is provided by a vacuum signal from either the spark port, EGR port or intake manifold and opens or closes the valve accordingly.

When the engine is off, the vapors from the fuel tank and carburetor fuel bowl are routed through the purge control valve and into the carbon canister for storage.

During normal cruise conditions, spark port or EGR vacuum is strong enough to open the orifice in the purge control valve to allow fuel vapors to flow from the carburetor canister through the purge line to a connection in the PCV tube or into the carburetor spacer. At the same time, the vapors from the fuel tank are also directed into the purge line.

At idle and low speed cruise conditions, spark port or EGR port vacuum is not strong enough to open the orifice in the purge control valve so that the fuel vapors are then routed to the carbon canister.

NOTE: On some vehicles fuel vapors are not purged during low engine speeds because the additional fuel vapors will affect the fuel air mixture, resulting in a reduction of idle quality and an increase in exhaust emissions. On vehicles not affected by this purging, manifold vacuum is used to actuate the purge control valve and control the purging of fuel vapors since spark port or EGR port vacuum is too weak.

Purge Regulator Valve, Fig. 97

On some vehicles the rate of purge flow must be closely controlled to prevent poor driveability caused by high purge flow. A purge regulator valve is installed in the purge line between the purge control valve and vacuum source to control the amount of air being drawn into the intake manifold through the canister. The valve must be mounted in an upright position.

The purge regulator valve contains a

vapor separator. This raised section provides additional breathing space for the vapor separator since the space allowed for thermal expansion of fuel is not as deep as it is on vertically mounted tanks.

The vapor separator which acts as a baffle to prevent fuel from entering the charcoal canister, Fig. 94, consists of a small hole in the outlet connected to the vapor tube plus open cell foam to separate liquid fuel and fuel vapors. The fuel vapors in the tank go through the opening in the vapor separator and into the vapor tube.

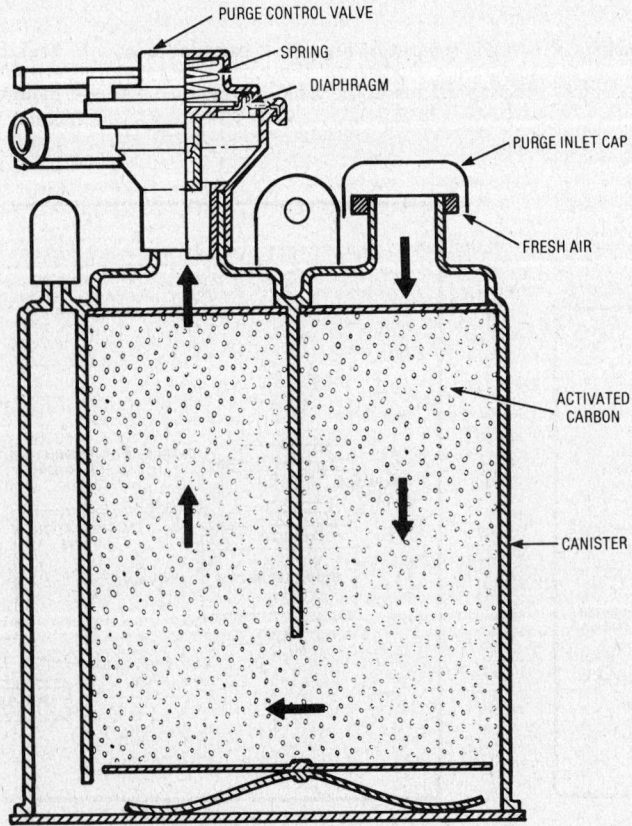

Fig. 95 Charcoal Canister. 1978-79 Ford Motor Co.

EMISSION CONTROL SYSTEMS

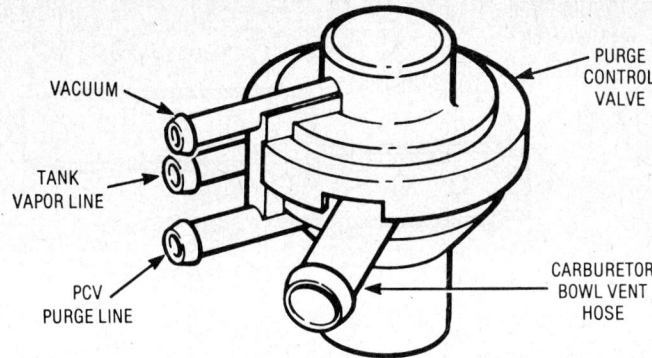

Fig. 96 Purge control valve. 1978–79 Ford Motor Co.

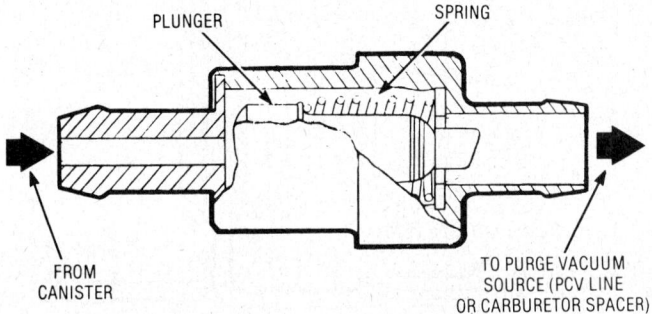

Fig. 97 Purge regulator valve. 1978–79 Ford Motor Co.

plunger and spring which functions in the same manner as a PCV valve. High vacuum draws the plunger up against the calibrated spring, closing the orifice to control the air flow. When vacuum drops, the spring pushes the plunger down to reduce air flow restriction.

Air Cleaner Vapor Dam, Fig. 98

A vapor dam is installed in the air cleaner at the zip tube opening. It traps most of the fuel vapors emitted by the carburetor while the vehicle is not in operation. The heavier than air vapors lie in the bottom of the air cleaner tray and are purged when the engine is started.

Solenoid Vent Valve, Fig. 99

The purpose of this valve is to close off the fuel bowl vent line when the engine is operating. It is a normally open valve located in the fuel bowl vent to canister line. This valve is on carburetors which do not have a built-in fuel bowl vent valve.

When the ignition switch is turned on, the coil energizes and the plunger is pulled against the valve seat to the closed position to prevent purge vacuum from reaching the carburetor fuel bowl and upsetting the balanced air pressure.

When the ignition switch is turned off, the coil de-energizes and spring pressure unseats the plunger to allow fuel vapors to flow to the carbon canister where they are stored until purged when the engine is started.

NOTE: If vacuum from the purge control valve does reach the fuel bowl vent line, the resultant low air pressure in the bowl will cause a lean fuel mixture condition. When diagnosing a driveability problem associated with a lean fuel mixture, check the solenoid vent valve and/or the built-in fuel bowl vent. The vent valves must be closed when the engine is operating.

Thermal Vent Valve, Fig. 100

The valve is used on some vehicles and is located in the fuel bowl vent to canister line. This valve is normally closed.

When underhood temperatures are low, the bi-metal contracts to close the valve. This prevents fuel tank vapors from venting through the carburetor fuel bowl during periods of fuel tank heat build-up.

When underhood temperatures are high, the bi-metal expands to open the valve and allow fuel bowl vapors to flow through the thermal vent valve. Also, the engine must be turned off so that the solenoid vent valve is open to allow this passage of fuel vapors through the thermal vent valve.

PVS Valve

The PVS (ported vacuum switch) valve allows vacuum to open the purge control valve as the engine warms up. The purge control valve closes as soon as the engine is turned off and vacuum drops off.

The evaporative emission system may be equipped with either a 2 or 4 port PVS. The 4 port PVS valve is actually two vacuum valves in one, and performs the same function as two 2 port valves.

Auxiliary Fuel Bowl Vent Tube, Fig. 101

Used on some vehicles, this auxiliary vent tube is teed into the primary fuel bowl vent tube to vent the fuel bowl when the internal vent is closed (external vent is closed) and the solenoid or thermal vent valves are closed. This tube is vented to the air cleaner.

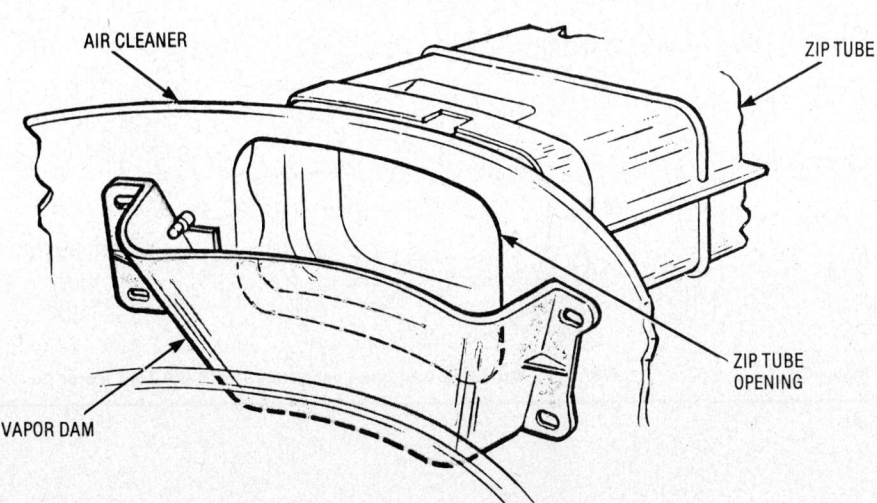

Fig. 98 Air cleaner vapor dam. 1978–79 Ford Motor Co.

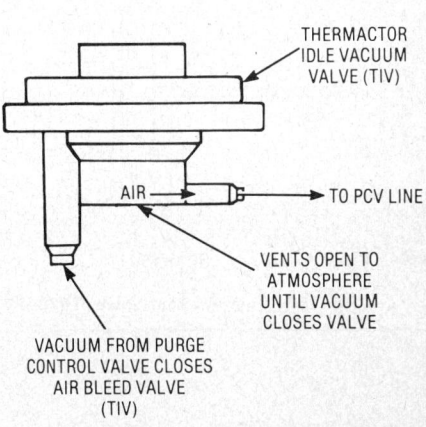

Fig. 102 Thermactor idle vent valve. 1978–79 Ford Motor Co.

EMISSION CONTROL SYSTEMS

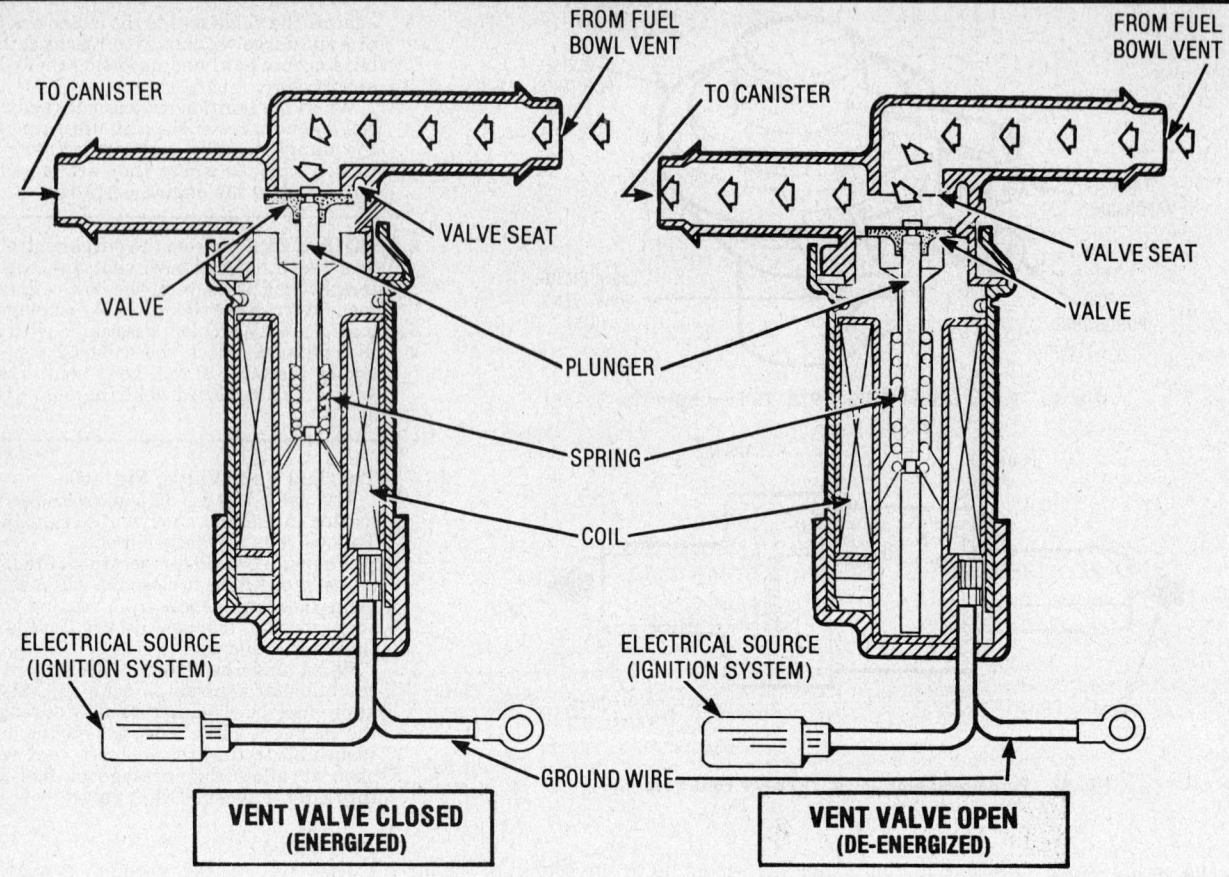

Fig. 99 Solenoid vent valve. 1978-79 Ford Motor Co.

Thermactor Idle Vacuum Valve (TIV), Fig. 102

This valve is used on some vehicles to improve hot idle. When the engine is at normal operating temperature, the system is activated and purge air is drawn from the canister through the PCV line and into the induction system through the carburetor spacer. The purge air flow into the carburetor is taken into consideration when the idle air-fuel mixture is calibrated and set. However, under warm start conditions the purge control valve is closed and the choke is off which creates an overly rich idle mixture condition, resulting in poor idle. This condition continues only for a few seconds after a warm engine start because actuation of the purge control valve is delayed by the retard delay valve and by the time required to evacuate the vacuum reservoir.

To overcome this condition, the TIV valve is used as an air bleed valve. The TIV valve bleeds air into the PCV line to lean out the idle fuel mixture until the purge control valve opens. The same vacuum that opens the purge control valve closes the TIV valve.

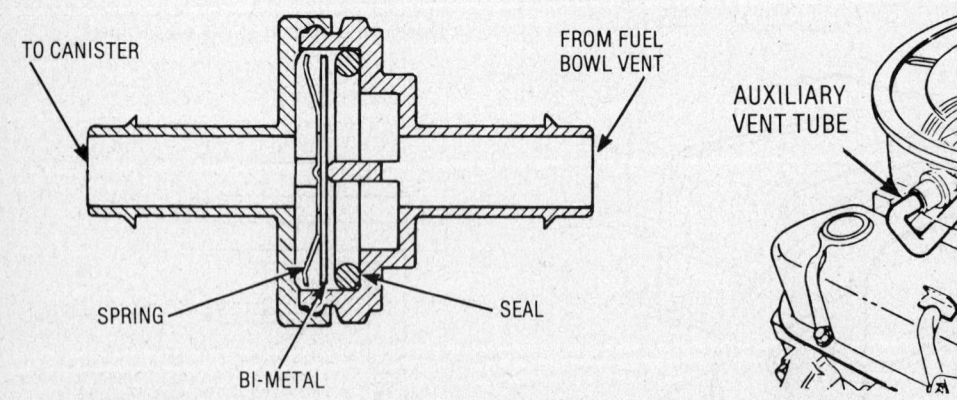

Fig. 100 Thermal vent valve. 1978-79 Ford Motor Co.

Fig. 101 Auxiliary fuel bowl vent tube. 1978-79 Ford Motor Co.

EMISSION CONTROL SYSTEMS

Emission System Servicing

INDEX

Page No.

Catalytic Converters	797
Electric Assist Choke	785

AMERICAN MOTORS

Exhaust Gas Recirculation	787
Thermostatic Air Cleaner	787
Trans. Controlled Spark	788
Vacuum Throttle Modulating System	787

CHRYSLER CORP.

Catalyst Protection System	798
Cleaner Air Package	791
Cleaner Air System	792
Coolant Control EGR	794
Exhaust Gas Recirculation	793
Idle Enrichment System	794
Ignition	792
NOx System	792
Orifice Spark Advance Control	793
Temperature Operated Vacuum By-Pass Valve	793
Vacuum Throttle Positioner	793

FORD MOTOR CO.

Auto-Therm Air Cleaner	787
Cold Start Spark Advance	796
Cold Temperature Activated Vacuum	796
Delay Vacuum By-Pass	795
Electronic Distributor Modulator	794
Electronic Spark Control	794
Evaporative Emission System	798
High Speed EGR Modulator Sub-System	795
Spark Delay Valve	796
Temperature Activated Vacuum	796
Trans. Regulated Spark	795

GENERAL MOTORS CORP.

Combined Emission Control	791
Thermostatic Controlled Air Cleaner	787
Throttle Return Control System	790
Trans. Controlled Spark	788

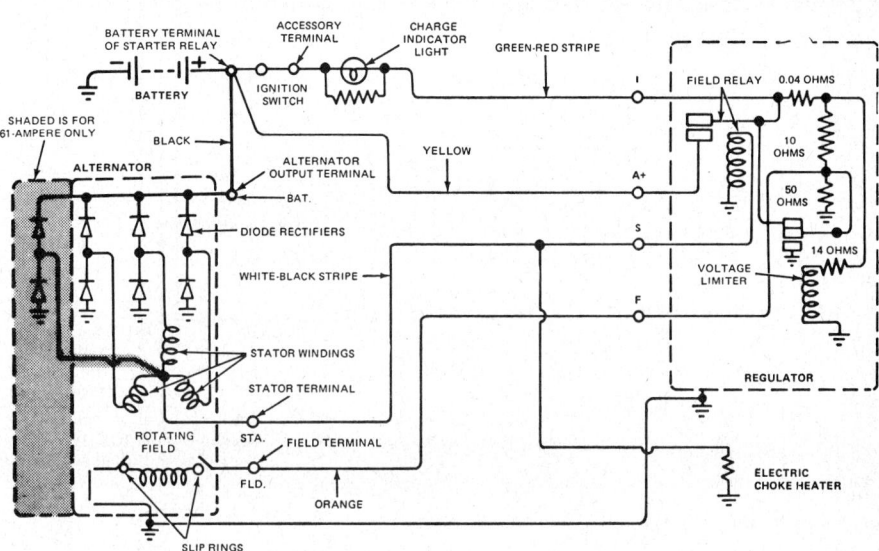

Fig. 1 Ford electric choke wiring schematic (Typical)

ELECTRIC ASSIST CHOKE

1973 American Motors & Ford

If the system, Fig. 1, operates at stabilized temperatures below 55 degrees either the temperature sensing disc is broken or the switch contact points have become welded at the heater.

If the system does not operate at stabilized temperatures above 110 degrees the problem is either dirt in the switch area, improper plating on the heater contact points or a broken temperature sensing disc. If the choke does not release within the specified time, check to be sure the bi-metal spring is connected to the choke lever tang. Also check to be sure the ceramic heater is bonded in the choke cap.

NOTE: If damage occurs to any part of the

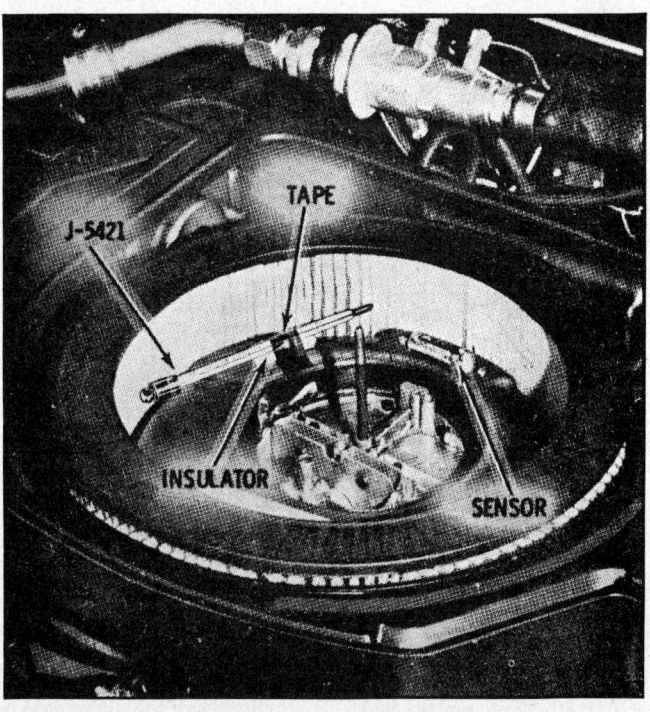

Fig. 2 Checking temperature sensor with thermometer. CCS System

EMISSION CONTROL SYSTEMS

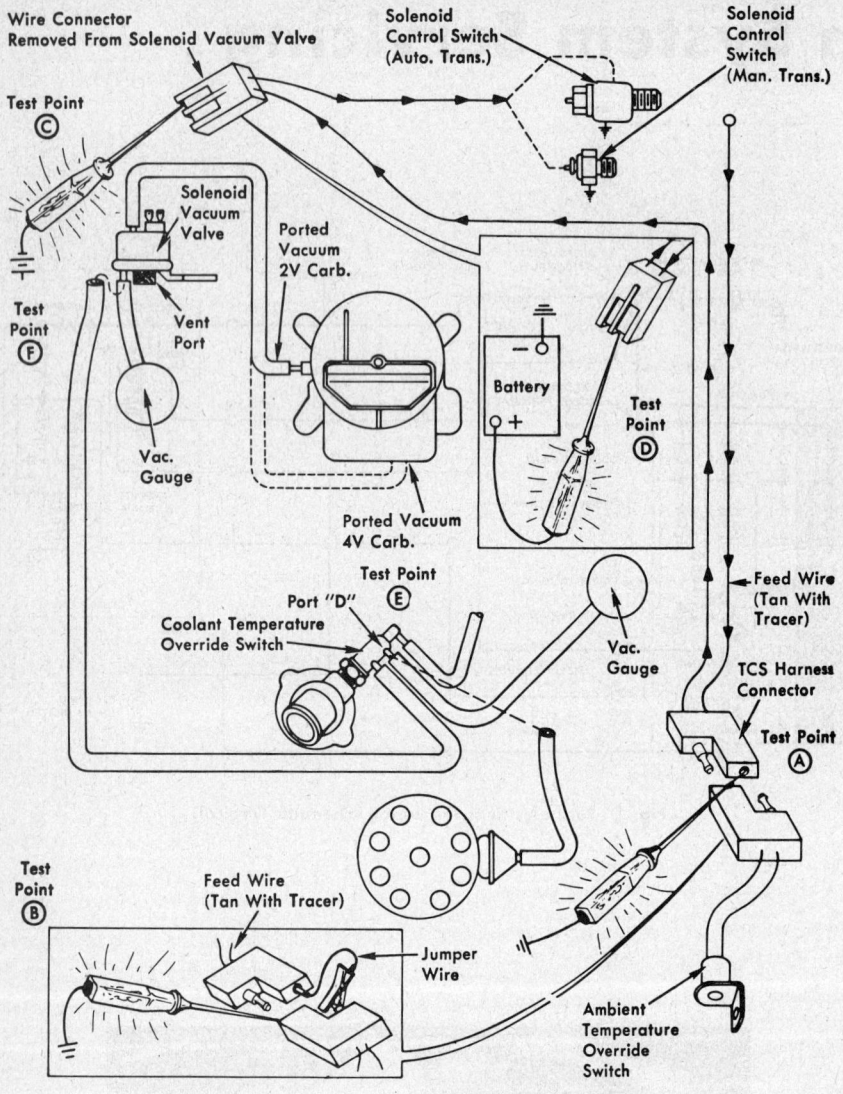

Fig. 3 American Motors TCS system test connections

electric choke cap, the entire cap must be replaced as an assembly.

1974-79 American Motors

1. Disconnect electrical lead from choke housing, then connect a test lamp between choke housing terminal and electrical lead.
2. Disconnect choke heat tube from choke housing and start engine.
3. Using a small thermometer, position thermometer bulb end inside heat tube passage in choke housing, then read thermometer and observe test lamp.
4. Lamp should be out between 60–80° F and should be on at temperatures below or above these temperatures.

NOTE: If test lamp did not light, check 7 volt source from alternator. If test lamp did light within 60–80° F, replace choke cover.

Chrysler
Choke Control Switch

1. Check test light by connecting it to battery and carefully noting intensity of light.
2. Before starting engine, disconnect both electrical connectors from the control switch on 1973 vehicles, "BAT" connector from the control switch on 1974–76 vehicles and ignition harness electrical connector from control switch on 1977–79 vehicles.
3. Connect test light to the load (small) terminal of the control switch and to ground.
4. Start engine and allow it to reach normal operating temperature.
5. Apply 12 volts to "BAT" terminal of control switch. The test light must light and have the same intensity as noted in step 1, if not the control unit is defective. Also the test light may go on for a few seconds or it may remain on for a longer duration but must not remain on for more than 5 minutes. If the above does not occur, the control switch is defective and must be replaced.

Choke Heating Element Test

1. Disconnect electric heating element at the control switch.
2. Connect an ohmmeter lead to the crimped junction of this wire at the choke end.

NOTE: Do not connect to the steel heater casing.

3. Hold the other ohmmeter lead against the choke housing or engine manifold.
4. Electrical resistance of 4–6 ohms for 1973 and 4–12 ohms for 1974–79 units is normal. Meter readings indicating an open or a short, replace choke assembly.

NOTE: The electric assist choke system does not change any carburetor service procedures and cannot be adjusted. However, the choke linkage and shaft must move freely hot or cold.

If the system is found out of calibration, a new heater control switch or choke unit must be installed.

1974-77 Ford

1. Remove air cleaner and make certain that it was not interfering with the choke plate, then check linkages and fast idle cam for freedom of operation.

NOTE: If delay valve is used, make certain it is operating properly.

2. On all vehicles, disconnect hot air supply tube from choke housing, then using Choke Tester LRE-34618 or equivalent, check for correct operation of choke.
3. Disconnect stator lead and connect a 0–3 amp ammeter between choke lead connector and stator lead, then start engine and observe reading.
4. On all vehicles, cool choke until temperature is less than 55° F. If current flow is noted, cap is defective.
5. At about 5 minutes of engine operation, a current reading of .3–1 amps should be noted.
6. If no current draw is noted, check for proper operation of alternator before replacing choke housing.

1978-79 Ford

1. Disconnect stator lead at connector leading from choke cap and connect a test light in series with stator lead and ground.
2. With engine running, test light should glow.
3. If light does not glow, repair or replace either the alternator or choke wire.
4. With engine running at normal operating temperature, place test light in series with choke terminal and alternator lead. If light does not glow, replace choke cap assembly.

General Motors

1. Allow choke to cool so that choke plate fully closes when throttle is opened.

NOTE: This test must be performed with engine off and ambient temperature at 60° F. to 80° F.

EMISSION CONTROL SYSTEMS

2. Start engine and determine amount of time for choke blade to fully open.
3. If choke plate fails to open within 3.5 minutes, proceed testing procedure.
4. With engine running, check voltage at choke heater connection. If voltage is 12-15 volts, replace electric choke unit.
5. If voltage is low or zero, check all connections and wires.

NOTE: If any connections in the oil pressure switch circuit are faulty or if oil pressure switch failed in the open position, the oil pressure warning light will be on with the engine running. Repair wires as required.

6. If all wiring and connections are good, replace oil pressure switch.

AMERICAN MOTORS EXHAUST GAS RECIRCULATION (EGR)

The EGR valve on the intake manifold must be removed, cleaned and inspected at the mileage intervals as specified. The exhaust gas passages in the intake manifold also should be inspected and cleaned as required.

After cleaning, open the EGR valve manually by pressing down on the pintle, then release.

NOTE: If the valve does not return to the fully closed position, it must be replaced.

Inspect the exhaust gas inlet and discharge passages of the intake manifold for any restriction caused by carbon or lead deposits.

On six cylinder engines, lead or carbon deposits build up rapidly in the exhaust gas discharge passage upper hole. If the deposits cannot be removed a 9/16 inch drill bit may be used.

Testing
1974-76

With engine idling at operating temperature, manually depress EGR diaphragm, lifting the pintle off its seat. A sudden drop of about 200 RPM should be noticed, indicating that the EGR valve is closing off exhaust from the intake passages. If there is no change in engine RPM and the engine idles properly, the EGR passage to the intake manifold is blocked. If engine idles poorly and lifting the pintle off its seat does not improve idle RPM, the EGR valve is sticking open, defective or there is a flaw in the intake manifold.

Connect a tee in the EGR vacuum signal line near the EGR valve, then connect a vacuum gauge to the tee. Place fingers against EGR valve diaphragm, then slowly accelerate engine and notice amount of vacuum indicated when EGR valve diaphragm begins to move. Refer to the following table for correct values as indicated by part number.

Part Number	Vacuum Required	
	Start Open	Max. Open
7030881	2.8-3.2	6.9-7.3
7040176	2.8-3.2	5.3-5.7
7043589	1.8-2.2	5.0
17050471	1.8-2.2	5.5
17050472	1.8-2.2	3.8-4.2

Continue to accelerate engine until vacuum required to achieve maximum recirculation is obtained. Diaphragm should be deeply depressed with no leakage indicated.

1977-79

With engine idling at normal operating temperature, accelerate engine to 1500 rpm and release throttle. A definite movement should be noticed in the EGR diaphragm. If diaphragm does not move, check for leaking vacuum lines, faulty vacuum signal to EGR valve, defective EGR valve or back pressure sensor.

With engine idling at normal operating temperature, manually depress EGR valve diaphragm. Engine speed should drop immediately, indicating proper operation of the EGR valve during engine idling. If there is no change in engine speed and the engine is idling properly, exhaust gases are not reaching the combustion chamber, and the probable cause is a plugged passage between the EGR valve and the intake manifold. If the engine idles poorly and the speed is not greatly affected when the EGR valve diaphragm is closed, the EGR valve is not stopping the flow of exhaust gases to the combustion chambers. Check for defective hoses, incorrectly routed hoses or defective EGR valve.

American Motors EGR CTO Switch Test

NOTE: Engine coolant temperature should be below 100° F.

1. Check vacuum lines for leaks and correct routing.
2. On 1974-76 vehicles disconnect vacuum lines at back pressure sensor and connect a vacuum gauge. On 1977-79 vehicles, disconnect vacuum line at EGR valve and connect a vacuum gauge.
3. Operate engine at approximately 1500 rpm, no vacuum should be indicated on gauge.

NOTE: If vacuum is indicated, replace EGR CTO switch.

4. Idle engine until coolant temperature exceeds 115° F (black color coded) or 160° F (yellow color coded).
5. Operate engine at 1500 rpm, ported carburetor vacuum should be indicated on gauge.

NOTE: If vacuum is not indicated, replace EGR CTO switch.

American Motors Exhaust Back Pressure Sensor

1. Inspect all EGR vacuum lines for leaks and correct routing.

NOTE: On 1974-76 models, make certain vacuum line from EGR CTO is connected to nipple with .030 inch restriction.

2. Using a tee fitting, connect a vacuum gauge in line between EGR valve and exhaust back pressure sensor.
3. With engine idling there should be no vacuum indicated on gauge.

NOTE: If vacuum is indicated at idle speed, check for correct vacuum line connections. Make certain manifold vacuum is not being used as a vacuum source. If carburetor is providing vacuum, check for partially open throttle plate which could be providing premature ported vacuum to back pressure sensor.

4. Accelerate engine to 2000 rpm and check vacuum gauge for the following:
   a. There should be no vacuum reading if coolant temperature is below 115° F.
   b. Ported vacuum should be indicated if coolant temperature is above 115° F (black CTO switch) or 160° F (yellow CTO switch).
5. If no vacuum was indicated during test, make certain vacuum is being applied to inlet side of back pressure sensor. If vacuum connections are correct, remove back pressure sensor and inspect spacer port and tube for restrictions. Deposits caused by carbon or lead deposits can be removed using a spiral wire brush. If no vacuum is obtained, replace back pressure sensor.

American Motors Delay Valve

NOTE: Bypass the back-pressure sensor when testing, as the sensor has a bleed which may give false readings.

1. Install a tee fitting in vacuum line between red side of delay valve and vacuum source.
2. Connect vacuum gauge to tee fitting, then while observing EGR valve operation, increase engine speed until 3 to 10 inches of vacuum are indicated on the gauge. It should take from 18 to 32 seconds for the vacuum signal to reach the EGR valve.
3. Replace delay valve if it takes less than 18 seconds or more than 32 seconds for vacuum signal to reach the EGR valve.
4. While maintaining 3 to 10 inches of vacuum, disconnect vacuum line from delay valve on 1976 models, or from CTO switch line to delay valve on 1977-79 models. EGR valve should close within .5 second or less. If valve does not seat within this time, replace delay valve.

VACUUM THROTTLE MODULATING SYSTEM

1. With engine off and idle speed previously set, position throttle lever against curb idle adjusting screw.
2. Measure clearance between throttle modulating diaphragm plunger and throttle lever. Clearance should be 1/16 inch. (.062 inch).
3. To adjust, loosen jam nut and turn diaphragm assembly as required.

TAC, THERMOSTATIC CONTROLLED AIR CLEANER & AUTO-THERM AIR CLEANER SYSTEM

American Motors

Mechanically Controlled
1. Remove air cleaner top and immerse

787

EMISSION CONTROL SYSTEMS

snorkel in cold water making sure that thermostat unit is covered.
2. Place a thermometer in water and observe temperature while slowly heating water. With water temperature at 105° F for 1974–76 and 1977–79 except Calif. and 75° F for 1977–79 Calif. or less, the air valve must be in closed position (heat on).
3. Heat water until temperature reaches 130° F for 1974–76, 1977–79 except Calif. and 90° F for 1977–79 Calif., air valve must be in fully open position (heat off).

Vacuum Controlled
1. Remove air cleaner assembly from engine and allow to cool to ambient temperature.
2. After cooling, observe position of air valve. It should be fully open to outside air.
3. Install air cleaner assembly and reconnect hot air hose and vacuum line, then start engine and observe position of air valve. It should be fully closed to outside air.
4. Move throttle rapidly to 1/2 to 3/4 opening and release. Air valve should open and then close again.
5. After engine has reached operating temperature, the air valve should be open to outside air.

NOTE: If air valve does not close at room temperature with vacuum applied, check for a mechanical bind in the snorkel, vacuum motor linkage disconnected, vacuum leaks in hoses or connections at vacuum motor, thermal sensor or intake manifold. If air valve mechanism operates freely and no vacuum leaks are detected, connect a hose from intake manifold vacuum to vacuum motor. If air valve now closes, the thermal sensor is defective. If air valve does not close, vacuum motor is defective.

Ford

Immerse the air cleaner snorkel in a container of cold water. Make certain the thermostat unit is covered by the water. Place a thermometer in the water and observe the temperature while heating the water slowly. With the water temperature at 105 degrees F. or less, the air valve must be in the closed (heat on) position.
With water temperature at 130 degrees F., the air valve must be fully open (heat off) position. If the air valve does not open and close at the temperatures specified, check the valve and spring mechanism for a binding condition. If the valve mechanism is in satisfactory condition, the thermostat unit is defective and the complete assembly must be replaced.

General Motors Functional Checks

Vacuum Motors
1. With engine off, look into left and right snorkel to be sure the valve plates are open. *On the smaller engines the left snorkel will be blocked closed and will not operate.*
2. Start engine and observe valve plates with engine idling. If equipped, the left plate will close immediately, regardless of temperature.
3. If the temperature in the air cleaner is below 90 deg. F., the right valve plate will also close to outside air. With temperatures above approximately 100 deg. F., the valve will remain open.

4. If vacuum motors fail to operate with vacuum directly applied, replace motor.

Temperature Sensor
1. With engine temperature below 85 deg. F., tape a thermometer in air cleaner, Fig. 2.
2. Install air cleaner cover and start engine.
3. When cold air door starts to open, remove air cleaner cover and check temperature. If temperature is below approximately 85 deg. F., sensor must be replaced.

NOTE: If hoses have been removed from connectors for any reason, it is very important that they be correctly positioned for proper operation.

TRANSMISSION CONTROLLED SPARK SYSTEM (TCS)

American Motors

1973

A vacuum gauge and a probe type current tester can be used to check for proper operation of the TCS system and the coolant temperature override switch with ambient temperature above 63 degrees F. Check all vacuum hose connections for proper routing. Begin tests with engine coolant temperature below 160 degrees F.

Test
1. Turn ignition switch on. Disconnect the TCS harness connector. Connect the tester wire lead to a good ground and touch the probe to the disconnected feed wire, Fig. 3, "Test Point A." The tester bulb should light, if not, check the ignition feed circuit through the main harness connector fuse.
2. Use a jumper wire to temporarily connect the ignition feed wire (female terminal) to the male terminal of the ambient temperature override switch wire. Ground tester wire lead and touch the probe to the open female terminal of the ambient temperature override switch wire, Fig. 3, "Test Point A." The tester bulb should light, if not, there is a defect in the ambient temperature switch or switch wires.
   To check switch operation below 63 degrees F., place a wet cloth over the bracket end of the switch. The light should go out within a short time. If not, the switch is defective.

NOTE: Freon gas may also be used to cool the switch.

3. Disconnect the wire connector from the solenoid vacuum valve. Ground the test lead and touch the probe first to one terminal of the wire connector and then to the other, Fig. 3, "Test Point C." The tester bulb should light at one of the terminals, if not, the ignition feed wire connected to the TCS connector is defective.

CAUTION: Do not touch the tester probe to the terminals of the solenoid vacuum valve with the wires connected because the solenoid control switch located at the transmission will be damaged.

4. With lead connected to the positive battery cable, touch the probe to the solenoid vacuum valve ground wire, Fig. 3, "Test Point D." The tester bulb should light, if not, the solenoid control switch at the transmission or the switch wire is defective.
5. V8 engines only: Disconnect coolant temperature override switch port "D." Connect a vacuum gauge to this port, Fig. 3, "Test Point E." Start the engine; it should indicate manifold vacuum. When the engine coolant temperature reaches 160 degrees F. the vacuum reading should drop approximately 4–6 inches. When running a cold engine if the gauge does not indicate manifold vacuum or if the vacuum reading does not drop when the coolant temperature reaches 160 degrees F., the coolant temperature override switch is defective.
6. Disconnect the vacuum hose from the front port, Fig. 3, "Test Point F" and connect vacuum gauge. Raise the vehicle rear wheels off the floor. On manual transmission equipped vehicles, place the gear selector in high gear and run the engine above idle speed. Carburetor ported vacuum should be indicated on the vacuum gauge. On automatic transmission equipped vehicles, place the gear selector in "Drive" and slowly increase engine speed while observing the vacuum gauge. When the speedometer needle reaches approximately 34 mph, the needle of the vacuum gauge indicates carburetor ported vacuum. If no vacuum is indicated, the solenoid vacuum valve is defective or no carburetor ported vacuum is being applied to the valve.

1974–79

1975–76 Test and Adjustment, Exc. Calif.
1. Disconnect wire from solenoid control switch and connect a 12 volt test lamp in series between switch wire and terminal.
2. Raise and support vehicle so that rear wheels are free to rotate.
3. Observe speedometer and test lamp. At speeds between 33–37 mph, the lamp should go off. If test lamp remains on above this range, the solenoid control switch can be adjusted by turning the 1/16 inch allen head screw clockwise to increase opening speed and counterclockwise to decrease opening speed. Fig. 4. Adjust switch opening speed to 35 mph.

CTO Switch Test

1975–76 Except Calif. Models
1. Connect a vacuum gauge to center port of CTO switch.
2. Manifold vacuum should be indicated when coolant temperature is below 160° F.
3. Ported carburetor vacuum should be indicated when coolant temperature is 160° F.

TCS System & CTO Switch Test

1975–76 Calif. Models & 1977 All
Test 1
1. Disconnect vacuum lines from center port and inner port of CTO switch and connect a vacuum gauge to center port.
2. Start engine; manifold vacuum should be indicated on gauge.
3. Operate engine until coolant temperature is above 160° F. No vacuum should be indicated on gauge.

NOTE: If CTO switch does not function as

EMISSION CONTROL SYSTEMS

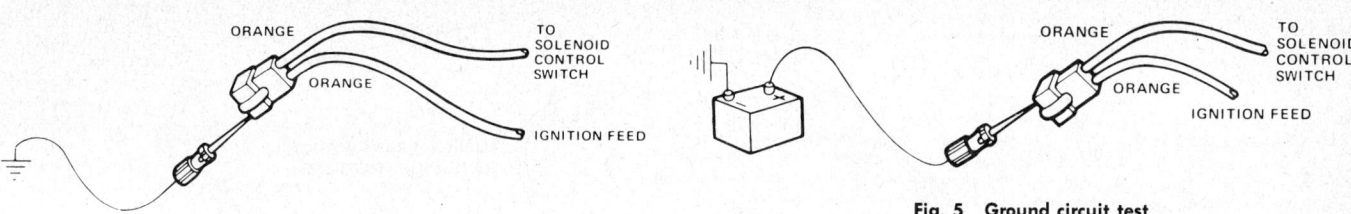

Fig. 4 Current supply test

Fig. 5 Ground circuit test

described, it should be replaced.

4. On 1977 vehicles:
   a. Stop engine and disconnect vacuum gauge from CTO.
   b. Disconnect hose from vacuum port 2 and connect vacuum gauge to it.
   c. Move manifold vacuum hose from port 1 to port D and start engine.
   d. If coolant temperature is above 160° F for all except V8-360 Calif., or 115° F for V8-360 Calif., manifold vacuum should be indicated on gauge. If not, CTO switch is defective.

Test 2
1. Turn ignition switch to on position.
2. Disconnect wire connector from solenoid valve.
3. Using a test lamp, check each connector terminal.

NOTE: Test lamp should light at one terminal only; if not, ignition feed portion of TCS system is defective.

Test 3

NOTE: Vehicles with manual transmission must be in neutral.

1. Connect wire lead of test lamp to battery positive terminal.
2. Disconnect two wire connector at solenoid vacuum valve. Touch probe end of test lamp to solenoid vacuum valve ground wire terminal at connector. If test lamp lights, proceed to step 3, if not proceed as follows:
   a. Disconnect wire connector at solenoid control switch on transmission, then connect a jumper wire from connector to ground.
   b. If test lamp lights solenoid control switch is defective. If test lamp does not light, solenoid control switch wiring is defective.
3. On vehicles equipped with manual transmission, position gear selector in high gear. Test lamp should go out, if not solenoid control switch is defective.
4. On vehicles equipped with automatic transmission proceed as follows:
   a. Raise vehicle and support so that rear wheels are free to rotate.
   b. Adjust switch opening to 35 mph, if test lamp does not go out at any speed, replace solenoid control switch.
5. Stop engine and lower vehicle.
6. Connect wire connector to solenoid vacuum valve, then proceed as follows:
   a. Disconnect solenoid control switch wire connector.
   b. Connect test lamp lead to switch terminal and touch probe to wire connector.
   c. Start engine. Test lamp should light, if not solenoid control switch is defective.
   d. Accelerate engine to 33 to 37 mph; test lamp should go out.
   e. If test lamp does go out at a speed of 33 to 37 mph, adjust switch.
7. To adjust switch, rotate 1/16 in. allen head adjusting screw clockwise to increase and counterclockwise to decrease switch opening.

Test 4
1. Disconnect vacuum line from vent side of solenoid valve and connect a vacuum gauge to solenoid valve port.
2. Disconnect wire connector from solenoid valve.
3. On vehicles with manual transmission, position gear selector in neutral.
4. On all models, operate engine, ported vacuum should be indicated on gauge.
5. Connect wire connector to solenoid valve and operate engine, no vacuum should be indicated on gauge.

NOTE: If solenoid vacuum valve does not function as described, it should be replaced.

TCS System Test
1978–79 MODELS

Test 1—Current Supply Test, Fig. 4
1. Turn ignition switch on, then disconnect connector from solenoid vacuum valve.
2. Connect wire lead of test lamp to ground.
3. Touch probe end of test lamp to each terminal of connector. Test lamp should light at terminal of orange ignition feed wire. If not, ignition feed to TCS system is defective.

Test 2—Ground Circuit Test (Manual Trans.), Fig. 9
1. Place gearshift lever in Neutral and connect test lamp wire to battery positive terminal.
2. Touch test lamp probe to orange solenoid switch wire terminal in solenoid connector. Test lamp should light.
3. Shift transmission to each gear except high. Test lamp should remain on.
4. Shift transmission to high gear. Test lamp should go out.

NOTE: If test lamp does not light at all, proceed to Test 4.

Test 3—Ground Circuit Test (Auto Trans.), Fig. 5
1. Raise and properly support vehicle so that drive wheels are off the ground.
2. Connect test wire lamp to battery positive terminal, then disconnect wire connector from solenoid vacuum valve and insert probe of test lamp into orange solenoid switch wire terminal.
3. Start engine and place transmission in Drive. While observing test lamp, note speed at which test lamp goes out. Slowly decelerate engine and note speed at which test lamp goes on.
4. Test lamp should go out above 37 mph and should go on below 33 mph. If operation is not as specified, adjust switch using a 1/16 inch allen wrench in switch terminal and turning clockwise to increase opening speed or counterclockwise to decrease opening speed, Fig. 7.

NOTE: If test lamp does not light at all, proceed to Test 4.

Test 4—Solenoid Control Switch Test, Fig. 6

NOTE: Perform this test if test lamp did not light when connected to orange wire as described in Test 2 or 3.

1. Disconnect wire from solenoid control switch at transmission (manual) or rear of engine (automatic).
2. Connect jumper wire from disconnected wire to ground.

NOTE: If test lamp now lights as described in Test 2 or 3, control switch is defective.

Test 5—Solenoid Vacuum Valve Test

NOTE: Engine must be warm before performing this test.

1. Apply parking brake, then place manual transmission in Neutral, or automatic transmission in Park.
2. Disconnect distributor vacuum advance line at solenoid valve, then connect a vacuum gauge to solenoid vacuum valve where distributor line was disconnected.
3. Start engine and run at 1000–1500 rpm. No vacuum should be indicated.
4. Maintain engine speed and disconnect two-wire connector from solenoid. Vacuum gauge should indicate ported vacuum. Connect and disconnect wire connector several times to verify operation.
5. Replace valve if defective.

Vacuum Spark Control Check Valve Test
1978–79 Models
1. Disconnect hose from vacuum advance

EMISSION CONTROL SYSTEMS

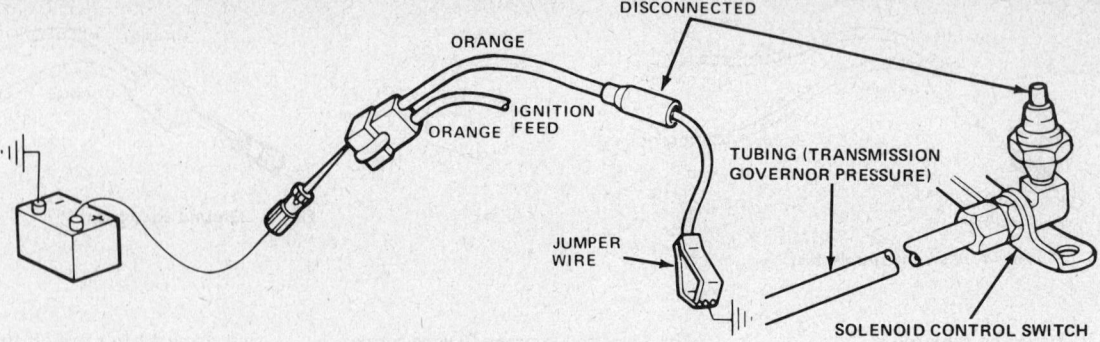

Fig. 6 Solenoid control switch test

unit, and connect gauge to disconnected hose.
2. Start engine. Gauge should indicate manifold vacuum.
3. Stop engine and observe gauge. If vacuum drops off rapidly, the check valve is defective.

NOTE: A very gradual loss of vacuum is normal because of slight leakage in the CTO switch.

Thermal Vacuum Switch (TVS)

1. Cool air cleaner to below the TVS calibration point of 40 to 50° F.
2. Disconnect vacuum lines from TVS and connect a vacuum gauge to one port and a vacuum pump to the other port.
3. Apply vacuum to TVS. There should be no vacuum reading indicated on the gauge when TVS temperature is below its calibration point. If there is, replace the TVS.
4. Start engine and allow temperature of TVS to reach 40 to 50° F. Vacuum should be indicated through TVS. If not, replace TVS.

Non-Linear Vacuum Regulator (NLVR)

1979 Models
1. Connect a vacuum gauge to distributor port (Dist.) of NLVR.
2. With engine idling, a vacuum reading of 7 in. Hg. should be indicated.
3. Gradually, open throttle. As engine speed increases, ported vacuum from the carburetor should be indicated on the vacuum gauge.

General Motors
System Functional Checks

T.C.S. can be checked for proper operation by connecting a vacuum gauge into the vacuum line between the distributor and the vacuum control valve.
There should be full vacuum only when the transmission is in high gear with the engine at operating temperature. The vacuum check should be made during a road test.

Trouble Shooting

Full Vacuum in All Gears:
1. Blown fuse.
2. Wire disconnected at vacuum control valve.
3. Wire disconnected at transmission control valve.
4. Faulty transmission control switch.
5. Energized coolant temperature switch.

No Vacuum in High Gear:
1. Vacuum lines reversed at vacuum control valve.
2. Foreign matter in vacuum control valve.
3. Faulty vacuum control valve.
4. Distributor vacuum line broken or disconnected.
5. Transmission control switch or wire shorted.

Solenoid & Valve Test

1. Disconnect hoses and electrical connector.
2. Connect a hose to the carburetor port on top of the solenoid and blow through hose. Air should come out distributor center port.
3. Plugging distributor center port should shut off air flow through solenoid if valve is functioning properly.
4. Connect one electrical terminal to a 12 volt source and ground other terminal with a jumper.
5. Remove hose from carburetor on top of the solenoid and connect to distributor center port.
6. Blow through hose. Air should come out the top vent port. If not, valve is defective.
7. Plug the top vent port of valve and blow into hose. Air should be blocked off. If air comes out the bottom engine intake manifold port or the carburetor port on top of the solenoid, the valve is defective.

Temperature Vacuum Switch Test

The temperature vacuum switch section should be tested with the engine running at fast idle, at normal temperature, valve closed. Connect a vacuum gauge to the distributor vacuum port. A zero reading for a duration of one-minute or longer would indicate a properly functioning valve.

NOTE: Vacuum control hoses must be in good condition, correctly installed and fit tightly.

Transmission Control Switch Test

This switch should be tested by removing hoses and electrical connections and installing a test hose at the distributor port. Air blown into the test hose should come out of the vacuum port. A similar test made by energizing the unit solenoid with a jumper wire, should divert air to the vent port. If either test fails, valve is defective.

THROTTLE RETURN CONTROL SYSTEM

General Motors
Checking Control Valve
1. Disconnect valve to carburetor hose at carburetor and connect to an external vacuum source equipped with a vacuum gauge, then disconnect valve to actuator hose at actuator and connect to a vacuum gauge.
2. Firmly place finger over end of bleed fitting (foam filter does not have to be removed), then apply a minimum of 23 inches Hg. vacuum to control valve and seal off vacuum source. If the gauge on the actuator side does not read the same as the vacuum source gauge, the valve needs adjustment. If vacuum drops off on either gauge (bleed fitting still covered), the valve is leaking and must be replaced.
3. With a minimum of 23 inches Hg. vacuum still applied to control valve, uncover bleed fitting. The vacuum reading on the actuator side will drop to zero and the reading of the vacuum source gauge will drop to a value designated as the "valve set point". If this value is not within .50 inches Hg. vacuum of the specified value listed under "Adjusting Control Valve", the valve must be adjusted.

Adjusting Control Valve
1. Disconnect valve to carburetor hose at carburetor and connect to an external vacuum source equipped with a vacuum gauge, then disconnect valve to actuator hose at actuator and connect to vacuum gauge.
2. Firmly place finger over end of bleed fitting and apply minimum of 23 inches Hg. vacuum to the control valve. Seal off the vacuum source, then uncover the bleed fitting. The vacuum reading on the actuator side will drop off to zero and the reading on the vacuum source gauge will drop to a value designated as the "valve set point". If this value is not 21.5 ± .50 inches Hg. for V8-350 and 400 or 21 ± .50 inches Hg. for V8-454, or 22 inches Hg. for V8-455, the valve must be adjusted as follows:
3. To adjust the valve, pry off the plastic

EMISSION CONTROL SYSTEMS

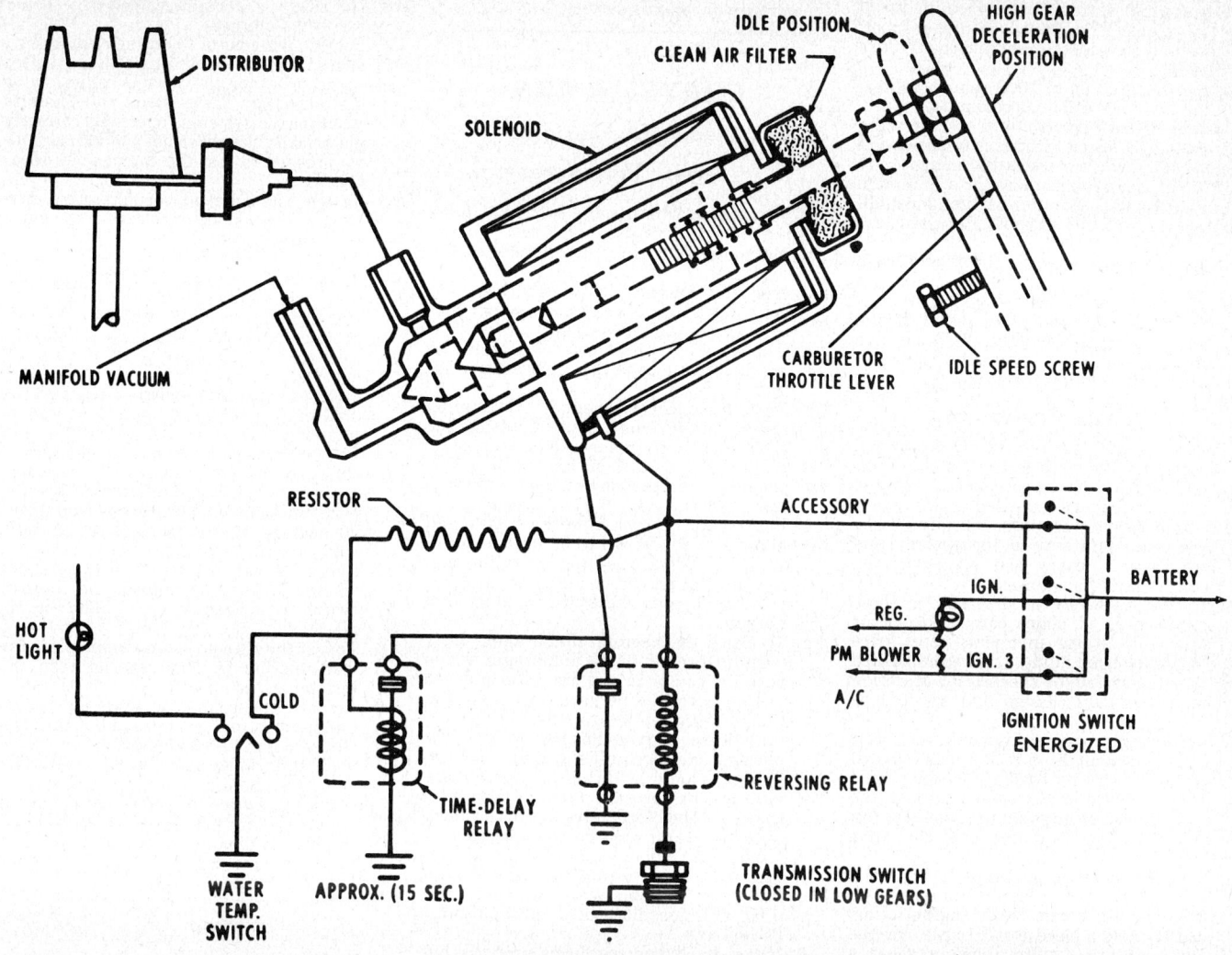

Fig. 7 General Motors C.E.C. system schematic

cover and turn the screw clockwise to raise the set point or counterclockwise to lower the set point and recheck setting. If the valve cannot be adjusted, it must be replaced.

Checking Throttle Lever Actuator

1. Disconnect valve to actuator at valve and connect to an external vacuum source equipped with a vacuum gauge, then apply 20 inches Hg. vacuum to actuator and seal off vacuum source. If vacuum reading drops, the actuator is leaking and must be replaced.
2. To check actuator, proceed as follows:
   a. Check throttle lever, shaft and linkage for freedom of operation.
   b. Run engine until operating temperature is reached and idle is stabilized with transmission in neutral or park. Note idle speed.
   c. Apply 20 inches Hg. vacuum to actuator, then open throttle slightly and allow to close against extended actuator plunger. Note engine speed.
   d. Release and reapply 20 inches Hg. vacuum and note the rpm to which engine speed increases. If speed is not within 150 rpm, the actuator plunger may be binding or the actuator diaphragm may be defective. If binding condition does not exist or cannot be corrected, the actuator must be replaced.
   e. Release vacuum. If engine speed does not return to within 50 rpm of the speed noted in step 2b, the actuator plunger may be binding. If binding problem cannot be corrected, then actuator must be replaced.
3. If engine rpm noted in step 2c is not within the specified TRC range, listed under "Adjusting Throttle Lever Actuator", the throttle lever actuator must be adjusted.

Adjusting Throttle Lever Actuator

1. Disconnect valve to actuator hose at valve and connect to an external vacuum source equipped with a vacuum gauge.
2. Check throttle lever, shaft and linkage for freedom of operation.
3. Run engine until operating temperature is reached and idle is stabilized with transmission in neutral or park.
4. Apply 20 inches Hg. vacuum to actuator, then open throttle slightly and allow to close against extended actuator plunger. Note engine speed.
5. If speed noted above is not within 1475-1525 rpm for V8-350 and 400 engines, or 1375-1425 rpm for V8-454 engines, turn the actuator screw in or out as necessary to obtain the desired TRC speed range and repeat step 4, and readjust if necessary.
6. On V8-455, adjust actuator by rotating until plunger tips contacts throttle lever.

GENERAL MOTORS CEC

Combined Emission Control System
Functional Checks

The C.E.C. system, Fig. 7, is tested in the same manner as the T.C.S. system.

CHRYSLER CAP

Cleaner Air Package

Vacuum Advance Control Valve Adjustment

1. With engine idle and ignition timing set correctly and engine at operating temperature, connect a tachometer to the engine.
2. Using a tee connector, connect a vacuum

791

EMISSION CONTROL SYSTEMS

gauge into the distributor vacuum line. If the engine is equipped with a dashpot, adjust it so it does not contact the throttle lever.
3. Speed engine up to 2000 rpm in neutral and hold speed for approximately 5 seconds. Release throttle and observe vacuum gauge. When throttle is released, distributor vacuum should increase to 16"Hg. and remain there for a minimum of 1 second. Distributor vacuum must fall to 6"Hg. within 3 seconds after throttle is released.
4. If necessary, remove cover and turn spring end adjusting screw counterclockwise to increase the period vacuum remains above 6"Hg. One turn will change setting by approximately 1/2"Hg. If valve cannot be adjusted, it must be replaced.
5. If necessary, readjust dashpot.

Service Procedure

Periodic servicing of the system is required to maintain good engine performance and prevent malfunction of the system because of the combustion products deposited in the valve, hose and carburetor passages. Every six months clean and service the system, and replace the valve every year. To service the systems, proceed as follows:
1. In cases of severe service, such as those experienced in police cars, taxicabs, or other operations involving short trips with prolonged idling, it is recommended that the system be checked for operation with every oil change and serviced as required.
2. With engine idling, remove ventilator valve assembly from rocker arm cover. If valve is working freely, a hissing noise will be heard as air passes through the valve, and a strong vacuum should be felt when a finger is placed over the valve inlet.
3. If valve is working properly, reinstall ventilator valve assembly and remove oil filler breather cap. With engine idling, loosely hold a piece of stiff paper over the oil filler pipe. After allowing about a minute for crankcase pressure to reduce, the paper will be drawn against the filler pipe with noticeable force. If this occurs, a final check should be made to be certain the valve shuttle is free.
4. Shut off engine, remove valve and shake it vigorously. A clicking noise should be heard if valve shuttle is free. If noise is heard, valve is satisfactory and no further service is necessary.
5. If valve does not click when shaken, or the paper is not drawn against the filler pipe with noticeable force, replace valve and recheck the system.

NOTE: Do not attempt to clean the valve. Replace it with a new one that has a black end washer.

6. Remove ventilator valve hose from cap and carburetor. Inspect for deposits and clean if necessary.
7. Remove breather cap and wash it thoroughly in kerosene or other suitable solvent to remove old oil and dirt. Reoil filter element.
8. Service air cleaner element.
9. Remove carburetor. Hand turn a suitable drill through the passages to dislodge foreign particles.

CAUTION: Use a drill that will clean the passages without removing any metal. Blow passages clean. It is not necessary to disassemble the carburetor for this service.

CHRYSLER CAS
Cleaner Air System
Service Procedure

To determine whether the system is functioning properly, proceed as follows:
1. Make sure all vacuum hoses and the stove to air cleaner flexible connector are properly attached and in good condition.
2. With engine cold, and ambient temperature in the engine compartment below 100 deg. F, the heat control door in the snorkel should be in the up (heat on) position.
3. With the engine warmed up and running, check the air temperature entering the snorkel or at the sensor. When temperature is 105 deg. F or higher, the door should be in the down (heat off) position.
4. Remove air cleaner from the engine and allow it to cool down to 90 to 95 deg., F. With 20"Hg. vacuum applied to the sensor, the door should be in the up (heat on) position. If not, check the vacuum diaphragm.
5. To check the vacuum diaphragm, apply vacuum directly to the diaphragm with a vacuum gauge in the line and a bleed valve to control the vacuum inserted in the line between the gauge and the vacuum source. Apply 20" Hg. to the diaphragm and close off the line. The diaphragm should hold this vacuum for five minutes. Release the vacuum then with the use of the bleed valve; build the vacuum slowly and observe the operation of the door. The door should lift off the bottom of the snorkel at 5"Hg. and reach the full open position with no more than 9"Hg. If it does not, the diaphragm must be replaced.
6. If the diaphragm performs properly but proper temperature is not maintained, replace the sensor and repeat the temperature checks.

CHRYSLER NOx
Oxides of Nitrogen
Manual Transmission

To test the NOx system on a manual transmission equipped vehicle, be certain that the plenum chamber temperature is well above 70 degrees F and proceed as follows:
1. Place the transmission in Neutral.
2. Turn on the ignition switch.
3. Disconnect the wire from the B+ connector of the ballast resistor while holding

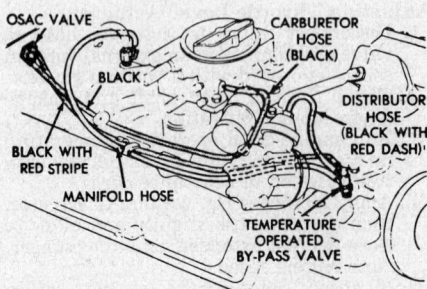

Fig. 8 Chrysler by-pass valve hose routing

the solenoid vacuum valve. You should feel it de-energize.
4. Select high gear of the transmission. You should feel no energizing of the solenoid valve, whether the wire is connected or disconnected. These steps will indicate whether the system is operating correctly electrically. If it does not operate normally, proceed to test the components separately.
5. To test the solenoid vacuum valve, first remove the connector to expose the valve blade terminals.
6. Jump the piggy back connector on the ballast resistor to one of the solenoid vacuum valve blade terminals. Jump the other blade terminal on the valve to ground. With the ignition switch on, the solenoid should energize. If it does not energize, it should be replaced.
7. To test the thermal switch, disconnect the dual plug from it and use a short wire to jump the plug and make a circuit.
8. Place the transmission in Neutral and turn the ignition switch on. The solenoid vacuum valve should energize. If the plenum chamber temperature is well above 70 degrees F and the solenoid vacuum valve does not energize when the thermal switch is connected but does energize when the plug is jumped, the thermal switch is defective and should be replaced.
9. To test the transmission switch, place the transmission in Neutral and turn the ignition switch on.
10. Remove the connector from the switch and jump it to a good ground. If the solenoid vacuum valve functions when this is done, the transmission switch is probably defective. Before replacing it, however, check the switch for proper torque in the transmission housing. This should be 180 in. lbs. to insure proper grounding. If proper torque does not relieve the problem, replace the switch.

Automatic Transmission

To test the NOx system on an automatic transmission equipped vehicle, be certain that the plenum chamber temperature is well above 70 degrees F and proceed as follows:
1. Raise the rear wheels.
2. Use a tee fitting, place a vacuum gauge between the distributor and the solenoid vacuum valve.
3. Disconnect and plug the vacuum line at the vacuum switch on the control unit assembly.
4. Start the engine and run it at a fast idle (above 850 rpm). The vacuum gauge should read zero.
5. Remove the electrical lead from the control unit "T" connector and the vacuum gauge should register vacuum. Reconnect the wire and the gauge should drop to zero.
6. Reconnect the vacuum line to the vacuum switch and disconnect the single wire lead from the control unit to the speed switch. The gauge should register vacuum.
7. Place the transmission in Drive. Sharp acceleration will cause the vacuum gauge to drop to zero suddenly.
8. Limit the speed to 40 mph and as the rpm stabilizes, the gauge should suddenly register vacuum.
9. Reconnect speed switch lead. Disconnect and plug the vacuum line at the vacuum switch. The gauge should register zero.
10. Accelerate the engine to above 30 mph. The gauge should register normal vacu-

EMISSION CONTROL SYSTEMS

um.
11. If the solenoid vacuum switch itself is found to be in proper operating condition and yet no solenoid action occurred in the foregoing steps, replace the control unit assembly.

CHRYSLER IGNITION

Refer to Electronic Ignition chapter for system trouble shooting.

CHRYSLER ORIFICE SPARK ADVANCE CONTROL (OSAC)

Test

NOTE: Ambient temperature in area of vehicle must be above 68 degrees F. for this test.

Inspect hose connections. Replace any hoses that may allow air leakage. Check operation of valve. With engine running at 2000 rpm in neutral, disconnect hose at the OSAC valve leading to distributor and attach a vacuum gauge to this port. If very gradual increase in vacuum is observed, approximately 15 seconds to a stabilized level, the valve is operating properly (some variations between engines). If vacuum immediately goes up to manifold vacuum or there is no vacuum, the OSAC valve is not operating properly and must be replaced.

CHRYSLER TEMPERATURE OPERATED VACUUM BY-PASS VALVE & THERMAL IGNITION CONTROL VALVE

Tests

1. Check vacuum hose routing and installation, Fig. 8. Check coolant level.
2. Attach a tachometer to engine.
3. Bring engine to normal operating temperature with choke wide open.
4. Adjust idle to 600 rpm. (For testing purposes only).
5. Disconnect the hose from manifold vacuum port and plug hose.
6. Check engine idle speed; no change indicates valve is holding, if idle speed drops 100 rpm or more, the valve is defective.
7. Re-install the manifold vacuum port hose.
8. Cover radiator to increase engine coolant temperature.

NOTE: Do not overheat engine.

9. Idle engine until temperature is approximately 225 degrees F. If engine idle speed has not increased 100 rpm or more before gauge indicator reaches top of normal indication on temperature gauge, the valve is defective.

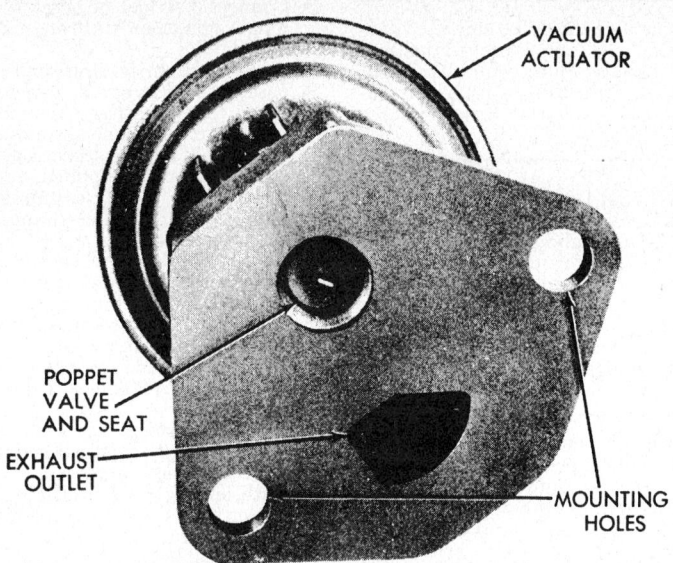

Fig. 9 Chrysler EGR control valve

CHRYSLER VACUUM THROTTLE POSITIONER

Adjustment

1. Start engine and allow to idle in neutral, then accelerate engine to above 2000 rpm to make sure that throttle positioner operates and can maintain its position when a hand load is applied. If not, determine cause of malfunction and correct as necessary as described under "Testing" procedure before proceeding further.
2. Accelerate engine to about 2500 rpm, then loosen positioner adjustment lock nut and rotate positioner assembly until it just contacts throttle lever.
3. Release throttle and adjust positioner to decrease engine speed until a sudden drop in speed occurs (over 1000 rpm). Continue adjusting positioner in decreasing direction 1/4 turn and tighten lock nut.
4. Accelerate engine to about 2500 rpm and release throttle. If engine speed returns to normal idle, throttle positioner is properly adjusted.

Testing

1. Check all hose connections and wiring harness of system.
2. Using an external vacuum source, apply vacuum to actuator. If actuator does not operate, it should be replaced. If actuator operates, pinch off supply hose and observe actuator. If actuator remains in operating position for one minute or more it is operating properly.
3. Using an external vacuum source, apply vacuum to manifold supply hose connection on solenoid valve. Disconnect electrical connector from solenoid and ground terminal of solenoid. Apply 12 volts to other terminal and note vacuum actuator operation. If actuator does not operate when 12 volts are applied, replace solenoid. If actuator operates normally, replace speed switch.

CHRYSLER EXHAUST GAS RECIRCULATION

Service

Every 12,000 miles or 12 months, the complete EGR system should be inspected and tested. To assure proper operation of this system all passages and moving parts must operate properly free of deposits. Hoses and connections must be free from leaks.

NOTE: Ambient temperature in the area of the vehicle must be above 68 degrees F. for this test.

Warm up engine and allow the engine to idle in neutral with the carburetor throttle closed. Abruptly accelerate the engine to approximately 2000 rpm, but not over 3000 rpm. Visible movement of the EGR valve stem should occur during this operation; this can be determined by change in the relative position of the groove on the EGR valve stem. This operation should be repeated several times to confirm movement. Movement of the stem indicates that the control system is functioning correctly.

If control system is functioning properly, the valve and passages may be checked for exhaust gas flow by applying a vacuum of at least 10 inches Hg directly to the EGR control valve with the engine warm and idling in neutral. Idle speed should drop 150 rpm or more when vacuum is applied. This reduction in idle speed confirms that exhaust gas recirculation is taking place. If the speed change does not occur or is less than the specified, exhaust deposits in the EGR valve or intake manifold EGR passages are indicated.

EGR Control Valve Service

The EGR valve should be inspected for deposits with particular attention to the poppet and seat area, Fig. 9. If deposits exceed a thin film condition, the EGR valve should be cleaned. If wear of the stem or other moving components is noted, the valve should be replaced.

EMISSION CONTROL SYSTEMS

NOTE: Extreme care should be exercised during the cleaning operation to prevent spilling of solvent on the valve diaphragm, as this will cause diaphragm failure. Do not push on diaphragm to operate valve, use vacuum source only.

Floor Jet Exhaust Gas System

Every 12,000 miles of operation inspect the floor jets for deposit buildup. With engine off and carburetor air cleaner removed, hold choke and throttle valves open. Using a suitable light, inspect the floor jets visually through the carburetor. If there is an open path through the orifice the jets are satisfactory. If a jet is plugged, remove jet, clean and reinstall.

NOTE: Floor jet is non-magnetic, stainless steel material. Caution should be taken so that jets will not fall into intake manifold ports during removal and installation.

Coolant Control Exhaust Gas Recirculation (CCEGR) Valve

The CCEGR valve can be tested for proper operation by placing it in ice and cooling it to below 40° F. Using vacuum pump and gauge tool C-4207 or equivalent, apply a vacuum of at least 10 inches of mercury to the valve nipple corresponding to the blue striped hose. If vacuum reading drops off more than 1 inch in one minute, the valve should be replaced.

Charge Temperature Switch (CTS)

1. No EGR operation with engine warm:
   a. Check hose routing and EGR solenoid operation.
   b. Remove center connector from CTS and wait 90 seconds.
   c. If EGR operation now resumes, replace CTS.
2. EGR operation with engine cold:
   a. Check hose routing and EGR solenoid operation.
   b. Remove center connector from CTS and check for 10 ohms resistance between center terminal of CTS and ground.
   c. If ohmmeter indicates an open circuit, replace CTS.
   d. If ohmmeter does not indicate an open circuited CTS, check for open circuit in the CTS to engine ground wire.

NOTE: When replacing CTS switch, do not torque more than 60 inch lbs. Overtorquing will break off the nylon threads in the intake manifold.

CHRYSLER IDLE ENRICHMENT SYSTEM

Testing

Idle Enrichment System
1. Warm engine to normal operating temperature, then remove air cleaner.

NOTE: Do not cap any fittings opened by hose removal as leakage is needed for testing.

2. Disconnect hose from idle enrichment diaphragm at plastic connector and remove connector from hose.
3. Connect 3-4 feet of hose to enrichment diaphragm, then start engine and run at slow idle.
4. Apply vacuum to other end of hose and observe engine speed change. If engine speed changes when vacuum is applied, the idle enrichment system is operating properly. If engine speed does not change when vacuum is applied, replace valve assembly on Holley carburetors, or proceed to steps 5 and 6 if equipped with Carter carburetor.
5. Cover air inlet passage and observe engine speed change. If speed changes, the diaphragm is leaking or the air valve is stuck open. If speed does not change, the air valve is stuck closed.
6. Clean valve and repeat step 4. If not operating properly, replace diaphragm.

Time Delay System
1. Check wiring for proper connections and correct as necessary.
2. With ignition switch off, disconnect connector from time delay solenoid valve.
3. Connect a test light across connector terminals.
4. Start engine. Test light should go on and remain on for 35 seconds on 1975-76 vehicles and black color coded valves, 60 seconds for orange color coded valves, or 90 seconds for red color after engine starts.
5. If light does not go on, remains on indefinitely, or does not remain on the amount of time specified in step 4, replace timer.

NOTE: In order to avoid overloading of timer, the tester current draw should not exceed .5 amps.

CHRYSLER COOLANT CONTROLLED ENGINE VACUUM SWITCH (CCEVS)

1. Check vacuum hoses for proper routing and make sure that valve is properly installed. Also make sure that engine coolant is at proper level.
2. Disconnect molded connector from valve and connect a 1/8 inch inside diameter hose to bottom port of valve.
3. With engine coolant at 75° F. or less, blow air through hose. If air does not flow freely, replace valve.
4. Start engine and warm to normal operating temperature, then using an external vacuum source, apply 10 inches Hg to valve. If vacuum level drops more than one inch in 15 seconds, replace valve.

FORD ELECTRONIC DISTRIBUTOR MODULATOR

Testing

1. Connect a vacuum gauge to the large hose connection of the electronic module.
2. Elevate the rear wheels of the vehicle.
3. Start the engine. With the transmission in neutral, the vacuum gauge should read zero.
4. With transmission in gear, slowly accelerate to approximately 35 mph.
5. Vacuum should cut in between 21 to 31 mph. Vacuum reading should be at least 6" Hg. at 25 mph.
6. Allow vehicle to coast down from 25 to 15 mph. At some speed in this range, the vacuum should drop to zero and remain there.
7. With the transmission in neutral and engine running, chill the thermal switch and place the engine on fast idle, approximately 1500 rpm. There should be a vacuum reading. If unit checks out at this point, it is operating properly. If not, proceed as follows.
8. Check supply voltage at the red wire of the quick disconnect (female end) with ignition switch on the On position. Meter should read battery voltage.
9. If meter reads zero, check the fuse and wiring from the ignition switch.
10. Check the thermal switch by disconnecting the yellow quick disconnect and inserting an ohmmeter from the gray wire (female end) to ground.
11. Place one hand on the thermal switch and allow switch to warm up. Switch should now be open. Chill the switch and it should close.
12. Leave plug disconnected and, using a jumper, connect the two red wires together. Connect a jumper from the gray wire of the male plug. Do not connect the other end of this wire to anything at this time.
13. Run the engine at approximately 1500 rpm.
14. Connect a vacuum gauge at the carburetor spark port vacuum connection and record the reading. Reconnect vacuum line to the carburetor.
15. Connect vacuum gauge at the large hose connection of the solenoid valve.
16. There should be no vacuum reading.
17. Ground gray jumper wire. Vacuum reading should now match that of step 14. If not, replace the module.
18. Remove jumper wire from thermal switch. Leave switch disconnected.
19. With vehicle on hoist and running at 30 mph, vacuum gauge should show a reading.
20. Check speed sensor continuity. Resistance of the sensor is 40-60 ohms at room temperature. Resistance of the sensor to ground should be infinite. If not, replace the sensor.

FORD ESC SYSTEM

Electronic Spark Control System

Testing

To test the E.S.C. system, proceed as follows:
1. Raise the rear wheels.
2. Disconnect the vacuum hose at the distributor primary advance diaphragm and connect it to a vacuum gauge.
3. Ensure that the temperature switch is above 55 degrees F by warming it with the hand or a hot sponge.
4. Start the engine and put the transmission in drive.
5. The vacuum gauge should register zero until the appropriate 23, 28 or 33 mph speed is attained, at which point it should register at least 6" Hg.
6. If there is no vacuum in any case at over 33 mph, there are four possible causes:
   a. No vacuum at the carburetor vacuum advance port. With the transmission in Park or Neutral, block open the

EMISSION CONTROL SYSTEMS

throttle to about 1500 rpm and determine if there is vacuum at carburetor vacuum advance port. Repair as necessary.
   b. Pinched, blocked, misrouted or disconnected hoses. Follow vacuum hose from carburetor to PVS valve and through the PVS valve to the ESC vacuum control valve.
   c. Inoperative ESC control system. Disconnect one or both electrical leads at ESC vacuum control valve and follow vacuum to the gauge at the distributor.
   d. Throttle down the engine.
   e. If there is no vacuum in step c, reconnect the ESC vacuum control valve.
7. If there is vacuum below the cut-in speeds, trouble exists in the ESC system which prevents the valve from being energized. Therefore, it is necessary to test the individual system components:
   a. Temperature Switch Test: This test can be made in the vehicle or on the bench. Disconnect the multiple plug and connect an ohmmeter to both wire terminals from the switch. Place the switch in the palm of the hand and allow sufficient time to warm it. If the ohmmeter registers a reading with the switch at 60 degrees F or higher, the switch is good.
   To test the switch at low temperature, chill it with ice or water which is below 49 degrees F. At this temperature the switch should be open and no reading should register on the ohmmeter. If the switch is good, check the power supply.
   b. Power Supply Test: Ground the lead on a test lamp and check for voltage at the temperature switch connector of the instrument panel wiring (circuit No. 640-red-yellow-hash). With ignition on, the lamp should light. If no voltage is present at the terminal, replace or repair the wiring to the ignition switch or replace the ignition switch. If the previous steps have not located the problem, replace the electronic amplifier.
   c. Speed Sensor Test: Disconnect the speed sensor at the multiple plug and check the sensor for continuity using an ohmmeter. Resistance of the speed sensor at room temperature is 40–60 ohms.
   Also, check the resistance of the speed sensor to ground. There should be no continuity between the black wire and the case. Replace the speed sensor if the resistance readings are incorrect.

FORD HIGH SPEED EGR MODULATOR SUB-SYSTEM

Testing

1. Disconnect vacuum hose from EGR valve and install a "tee" fitting and connect a vacuum gauge with a long hose into the vacuum line.
2. Raise front and rear wheels off ground, with vacuum gauge visible from the driver's seat.
3. Start engine and allow to run at fast idle for about 3 to 4 minutes. At curb idle speed the vacuum gauge should read zero.
4. Place transmission in third gear for manual transmission and in drive for automatic transmission. Observe the speedometer and vacuum gauge. Increase engine speed. The vacuum reading should increase. At about 67 mph the vacuum reading should drop to zero, indicating that the EGR High-Speed Modulator sub-system is functioning properly.
5. If system is not functioning properly check the vacuum solenoid valve. Disconnect the electrical leads from the valve to isolate it from the electronic amplifier.

CAUTION: Never connect any test jumper or test light to the valve unless it is isolated from the amplifier, as severe damage to the amplifier will result.

6. Connect jumper wires from the valve terminals to the battery and to a ground, operate engine in neutral at about 3000 rpm. The valve should close when power is applied. If there is a vacuum reading replace the valve.
7. If there is no vacuum reading with the valve energized, check for power at the amplifier connector using a self powered test light. If there is no power, check and repair the ignition switch circuit. If there is power check ground connection. If grounded properly, check speed sensor for continuity with an ohmmeter placed across sensor. The resistance should be 40 to 60 ohms. If the speed sensor is functioning properly, replace the amplifier.

FORD TRS SYSTEM

Transmission Regulated Spark Control System
Testing

Manual Transmission

With a vacuum gauge connected to the T.R.S. system, Fig. 10, between the vacuum control valve and the distributor advance unit, and the temperature switch known to be above 55 degrees F, proceed as follows:
1. Start the engine in Neutral. No vacuum should be indicated on the gauge (circuit energized).
2. Disengage the clutch and increase engine speed to 1000 to 1500 rpm. The vacuum indication should still remain at zero.
3. Disengage the clutch then place the transmission in high gear. With the engine running between 1000–1500 rpm and the clutch disengaged, a vacuum of at least 6 inches of mercury should be indicated on the gauge. Make sure the engine is stopped before engaging the clutch.
4. To test transmission switch, proceed as follows: Disconnect both wires from the vacuum control valve. Connect the transmission switch lead from the valve blade terminal in series with a test light to the positive terminal of the battery. With the engine and ignition off, move the gear selector through all positions. The light should stay on in all but high gear. If the light stays on in high gear, the circuit is grounded or the switch is inoperative. If the light does not go on in any gear, the circuit is open or again the switch is inoperative.
5. To test the temperature switch, proceed as follows: Disconnect both wires from the vacuum control valve. Connect the temperature switch lead from the blade terminal of the vacuum control valve in series with a test light to ground. Turn on the ignition switch and warm the temperature switch with the palm of the hand or a hot sponge. The light should go on when the temperature of the switch exceeds 65 degrees F. Cool the switch with an aerosol spray (such as starting fluid) or ice until its temperature is below 49 degrees F and the light should go out. If the light does not go on when warmed, the circuit is open or grounded or the switch is inoperative. If it does not go out when cooled, either the cooling process was not sufficient or the switch is inoperative.

Automatic Transmission

With a vacuum gauge connected to the T.R.S. system, Fig. 10, between the vacuum control valve and the distributor advance unit, and the temperature switch known to be above 65 degrees F, proceed as follows:
1. Start the engine (Park or Neutral). No vacuum should be indicated on the gauge (circuit energized).
2. With foot brake applied firmly, shift into reverse.
3. Disconnect one wire from the vacuum control valve to de-energize the circuit, Fig. 11. Shift into neutral and increase engine speed from 1000 to 1500 rpm. Vacuum should be indicated on the gauge. Reconnect the wire to the valve after the test is made.

NOTE: Malfunction of the electrical circuit affects the vacuum, but the vacuum portion has no effect on the electrical. Therefore, in the event of no vacuum, disconnect both hoses at the valve and connect both hoses together with a nipple, and then repeat step 3.

4. To test transmission switch, proceed as follows: Disconnect both wires from the vacuum control valve. Connect the transmission switch lead from the valve blade terminal in series with a test light to the positive terminal of the battery. Start the engine, apply foot brake and move shift lever through all positions. The light should go out in the reverse position. If the light stays on in all positions, the circuit is grounded or the switch is faulty. If the light does not go on at all, the circuit is open or the switch is again inoperative.
5. To test the temperature switch, follow the procedure outlined in step 5 under "Manual Transmission."

FORD DVB SYSTEM

Delay Vacuum By-Pass

Tests
1. Disconnect the ignition feed wire to the DVB vacuum valve.
2. Connect a vacuum gauge to the distributor primary vacuum hose.
3. Start the engine, vacuum should be present as the engine speed increases. The vacuum should fluctuate in direct response to the throttle setting.
4. Connect the ignition feed wire to the DVB vacuum valve.
5. Repeat step 3. The vacuum gauge should show a much slower response to throttle change. The vacuum supply is now being controlled by the SDV valve restrictor.
6. Refer to Fig. 12, for proper DVB temperature switch activation and spark advance path.

NOTE: When servicing the SDV valve, replace

EMISSION CONTROL SYSTEMS

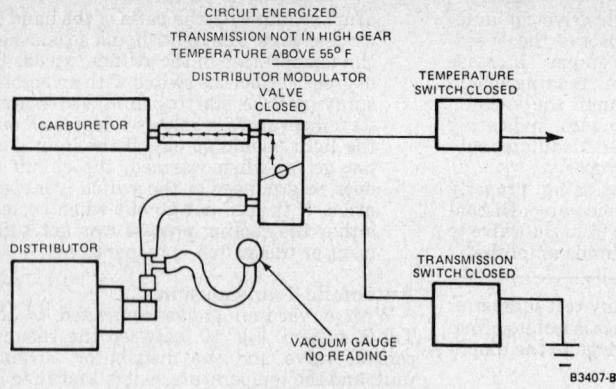

Fig. 10 TRS circuit energized

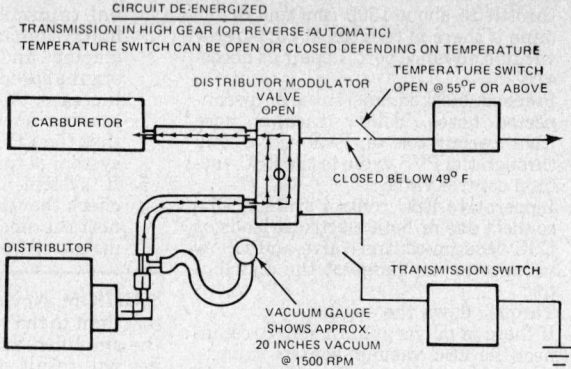

Fig. 11 TRS circuit de-energizer

with proper color coded valve, Fig. 13.

CAUTION: The vacuum hose and wiring connections for a DVB system must be connected properly, or the system will not function.

FORD TAV SYSTEM

Temperature Activated System

System Checks

The TAV system vacuum hoses and wiring connection must be connected properly, or the system will not function.
1. The EGR and spark port vacuum must be connected to the correct inlet of the three-way vacuum valve.
2. The TAV system three-way vacuum valve must be adequately grounded to the cylinder block.
3. The TAV system three-way vacuum valve must be energized when the ignition switch is in the run position, and the ambient temperature is above 65 degrees F. Check power to the valve with a test light connected between the b+ terminal of the valve and chassis ground. The light should be lit, if the above conditions are present.
4. A false vacuum reading may be present at the distributor vacuum inlet if the vehicle is equipped with a PVS valve. The PVS valve may leak manifold vacuum back into the system. If vacuum is present when the vehicle engine is at idle, check the PVS valve for leakage.

NOTE: A check valve is installed in the EGR vacuum supply line on all vehicles equipped with air conditioning to prevent vacuum feed back into the EGR system. If there is feed back into EGR system replace check valve.

FORD CTAV SYSTEM

Cold Temperature Activated System

NOTE: Prior to performing any test on this system, insure that temperature switch is above 65° F.

Vacuum System Test
1. With a tachometer connected, disconnect three-way solenoid vacuum valve ground lead. Connect a vacuum gauge to distributor end of hose running from solenoid vacuum valve and if no vacuum reading is observed at 1500 RPM, check vacuum source back to carburetor spark port.
2. If a vacuum reading of approximately 15 inches Hg was observed in above check, reconnect solenoid vacuum valve ground lead. If a vacuum reading is still noted, check solenoid vacuum valve ground and electrical leads back to ignition switch.
3. If after reconnecting solenoid vacuum valve ground lead, vacuum is low or non-existant, run engine at 3000 RPM and if no vacuum is observed, check vacuum source back to carburetor EGR port.
4. If a vacuum reading of approximately 9 inches Hg was observed at 3000 RPM, system is functioning normally.

Electrical System Test
1. Disconnect temperature switch connector and connect a test lamp between the solenoid vacuum valve ground terminal and the ground. Turn ignition "On." If lamp lights, the latching relay is defective, requiring replacement.
2. If lamp does not light in above check, reconnect temperature switch connector. If lamp still does not light, check temperature switch and wiring back to ignition switch.
3. If lamp lights in above check, again disconnect temperature switch connector. If lamp goes out, replace latching relay. If lamp remains lit, connect the test lamp to temperature switch connector and cool temperature switch to below 49° F. If lamp lights, the temperature switch is faulty, requiring replacement.
4. If lamp does not light when temperature switch is cooled to below 49° F, the system is operating normally.

FORD CSSA SYSTEM

Cold Start Spark Advance System

NOTE: If engine is pinging, perform steps 1 thru 4

1. Connect tachometer and start engine.

CAUTION: Do not leave transmission in drive for more than 15 seconds while performing steps 2 and 4.

2. With parking brake applied, brake pedal depressed and transmission in drive, accelerate engine and observe rpm at which spark knock or pinging occurs.
3. Place transmission in neutral and accelerate engine to 1500 rpm to allow transmission to cool. Repeat this step three times.
4. Disconnect and plug vacuum advance line from distributor. Repeat step 2 to recorded rpm.
5. If spark knock or pinging reoccurred, stop engine and proceed to next step. If spark knock or pinging did not reoccur, the CSSA PVS and or retard delay valve (if used) is faulty. Repair or replace as necessary.
6. Remove spark delay valve (SDV), or vacuum check valve, or spark delay valve and check as described further on.
7. Using a tee fitting, connect a vacuum gauge to distributor advance hose, disconnect and plug vacuum hose from bottom port of Cold Start PVS.
8. With engine idling at normal operating temperature, there should be no vacuum reading. If vacuum is obtained, the Cold Start PVS should be replaced.
9. Reconnect hose to bottom port of Cold Start PVS and disconnect and plug hose from top port of Cold Start PVS.
10. On vehicles with a cooling PVS, check vacuum at distributor with engine at normal idle. If reading is still greater than specified, the cooling PVS should be replaced.
11. With engine idling in neutral, momentarily open the throttle half way.
12. Observe vacuum gauge for a quick rise and fall as throttle is opened and closed. If vacuum is obtained, the spark advance system is operating properly. If no vacuum is obtained, check vacuum line for leakage or obstruction and correct as necessary.

FORD (SDV)

Spark Delay Valve

NOTE: To perform the following procedure, an external vacuum source capable of maintaining a minimum constant 10 inches Hg. is required.

Mono Delay Valve
1. Set external vacuum source to 10 inches

EMISSION CONTROL SYSTEMS

Temperature	Temperature Switch	Spark Advance Path
49° F. or Below	Open	DVB – Direct
49° F. – 60° F.	Open or Closed	DVB or SDV
60° F. or Above	Closed	SDV – Delayed

Fig. 12 Ford DVB system operating temperatures

Color	Number Value
White	5
Yellow	10
Blue	15
Green	20
Red	30

Fig. 13 Ford SDV valve color code chart

Hg. and connect black side of delay valve to vacuum source.
2. Connect a vacuum gauge with a 24 inch hose to colored side of delay valve.
3. Apply 10 inches Hg. vacuum and observe time in seconds for gauge to read 0–8 inches Hg. The minimum and maximum time for gauge to read 8 inches Hg. should be as follows:

Color	I.D. No.	Time in Seconds	
		Min.	Max.
Black and Gray	1	1	4
Black and Brown	2	2	5
Black and White	5	4	12
Black and Yellow	10	5.8	14
Black and Blue	15	7	16
Black and Green	20	9	20
Black and Orange	30	13	24
Black and Red	40	15	28

Dual Delay Valve

1. Set external vacuum source to 10 inches Hg. and connect vacuum gauge with a 24 inch hose to DIST nipple of delay valve.
2. Connect black side of delay valve and CARB nipple of delay valve to vacuum source.

NOTE: Avoid applying vacuum to CARB nipple while applying vacuum to black side of valve.

3. Apply 10 inches Hg. of vacuum and observe time in seconds for gauge to read from 0–8 inches Hg. The minimum and maximum time for gauge to read 8 inches Hg. should be as follows:

Color	I.D. No.	Time in Seconds	
		Min.	Max.
Black and White	5	4	12
Black and Yellow	10	5.8	14
Black and Blue	15	7	16
Black and Green	20	9	20
White and Brown	2	2	2
White and Green	20	9	20

Retard Delay Valve

1. Set external vacuum source to 10 inches Hg. and connect colored side of delay valve to vacuum source.
2. Connect a vacuum gauge with a 24 inch hose to white side of delay valve.
3. Apply 10 inches Hg. of vacuum and observe time in seconds for gauge to read from 0–8 inches Hg. The minimum and maximum time for gauge to read 8 inches Hg. should be as follows:

Color	I.D. No.	Time in Seconds	
		Min.	Max.
White/Brown	2	2	5
White/Green	20	9	20
Black/White	5	4	12
Black/Yellow	10	5.8	14
Black/Blue	15	7	16
Black/Green	20	9	20

CATALYTIC CONVERTER SYSTEM

American Motors & General Motors

Catalyst Removal

1. Install aspirator, Fig. 14, and connect an air line to aspirator, creating a vacuum in the converter, thereby holding pellets in place when fill plug is removed.
2. Using a 3/4 inch Allen wrench or tool J-25077-3, Fig. 15, remove converter fill plug.
3. Install vibrator, Fig. 16, and empty catalyst container to converter.
4. Disconnect air line from aspirator and reconnect line to vibrator. Catalyst will now drain from converter, Fig. 17.
5. When all catalyst has been drained from converter, remove container and discard the used catalyst.

Catalyst Installation

1. Fill container with recommended replacement catalyst and install fill tube extension to fixture.
2. Connect air line to aspirator and vibrator, then secure catalyst container to the fixture, Fig. 17.
3. When catalyst stops flowing, disconnect air line from vibrator and ensure catalyst has filled converter flush with fill plug hole. Add catalyst, if necessary.
4. Apply a suitable anti-seize compound to fill plug threads, then install and torque fill plug to 50 ft. lbs.
5. Disconnect air line from aspirator, then

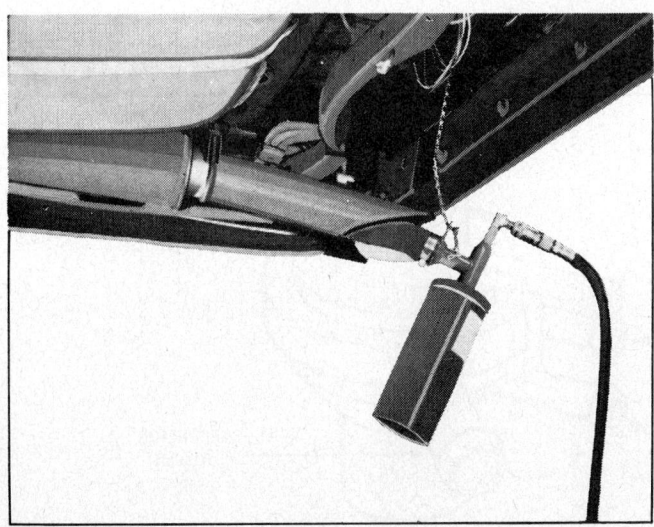

Fig. 14 Aspirator installation

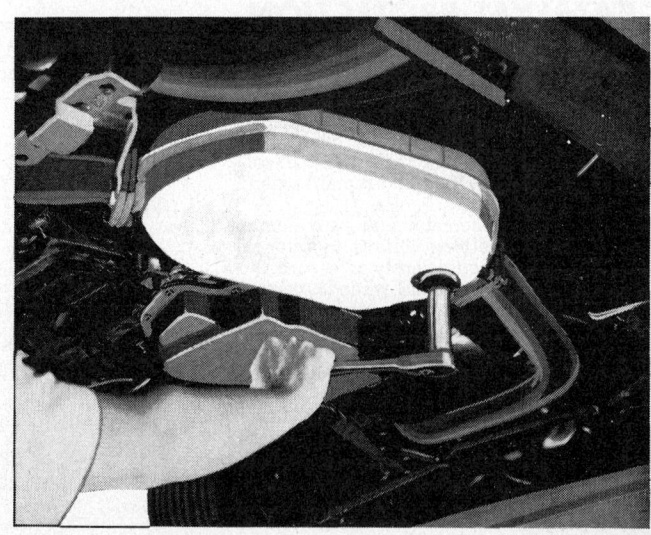

Fig. 15 Catalytic converter fill plug removal and installation

EMISSION CONTROL SYSTEMS

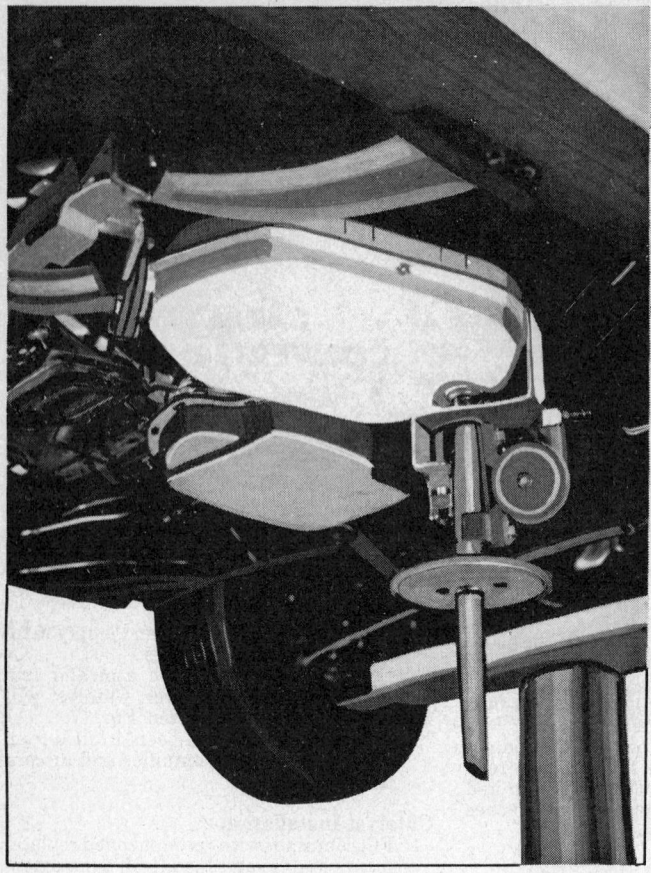

Fig. 16 Vibrator installation

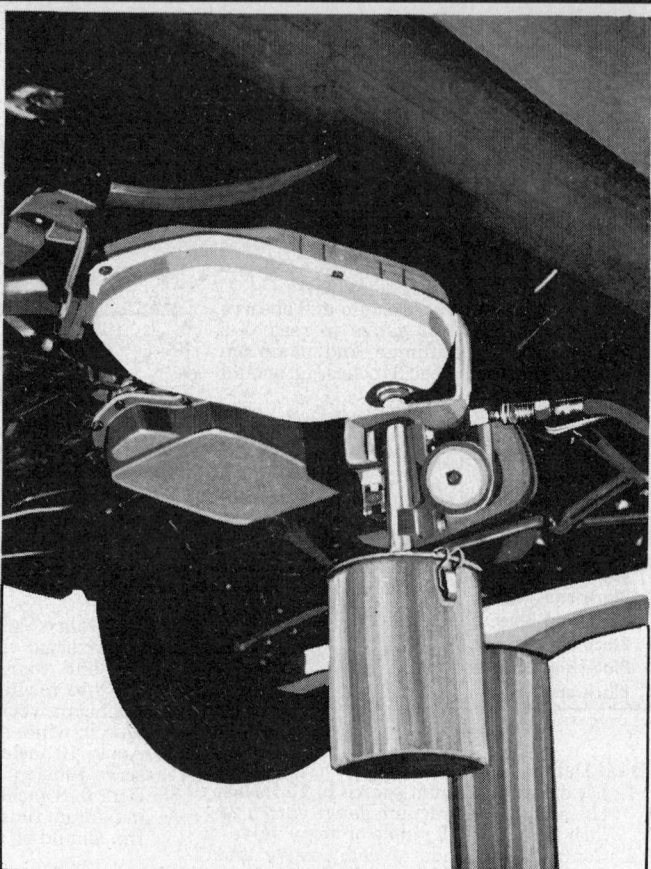

Fig. 17 Draining and refilling catalytic converter

remove aspirator.

Chrysler Corp. & Ford

The catalytic converters used in these vehicles are not serviceable. After determining that the catalyst has lost its effectiveness, the catalytic converter assembly must be replaced.

CATALYST PROTECTION SYSTEM

Chrysler

1. Disconnect wire from throttle position solenoid and hold throttle wide open. Apply battery voltage to solenoid. If solenoid does not extend and remain extended, replace unit.
2. Connect a tachometer and start engine, then apply battery voltage to solenoid. Open throttle sufficiently to assure that solenoid fully extends when current is applied. With solenoid energized, engine speed should be 1500 rpm ± 50 rpm. Adjust to specifications as required. Allow time for OSAC to provide vacuum and engine speed to stabilize.
3. Disconnect solenoid wire from battery voltage and reconnect it to electronic speed switch.
4. Slowly accelerate engine from idle. As engine speed passes approximately 2000 rpm, the solenoid should extend and remain extended. Slowly decelerate engine. At or before engine speed reaches 1800 rpm, the solenoid should deactivate. If solenoid does not respond properly, the speed switch must be replaced.

1978–79 FORD MOTOR CO. EVAPORATIVE EMISSION SYSTEM

System Diagnosis

NOTE: If engine will not start, proceed to step 1. If it does start and run, proceed to step 2.

1. Disconnect purge line, Fig. 18A, from purge control valve and plug line, then attempt to start engine. If engine does not start, the problem is not in the evaporative control system.
2. With engine idling, disconnect vacuum signal line, Fig. 18A, from purge control valve and plug hose, then remove valve from canister. If a strong hissing sound is heard at purge control valve, replace valve.

NOTE: A slight hissing sound is normal due to small orifice in valve.

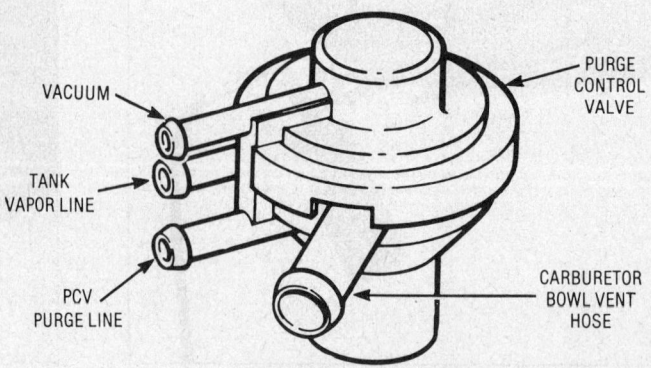

Fig. 18 Purge control valve line connections. 1978 Ford Motor Co.

EMISSION CONTROL SYSTEMS

3. Reconnect vacuum signal line, Fig. 18, to purge control valve which remains separated from canister, then accelerate engine to about 2000 rpm so that ported vacuum is applied to purge control valve. If strong hissing sound is heard at purge control valve, system is performing properly. Proceed to step 4. If not, check for vacuum at source port, and operation of PVS valve, PCV valve, and retard delay valve (s). Repair or replace components as necessary.
4. Return engine to idle. Strong hissing sound at purge control valve should stop if there is a port vacuum signal at valve. If strong hissing sound does not stop, check for vacuum at source port and check operation of retard delay valve(s). Repair or replace components as necessary.
5. Reconnect purge control valve to canister.

NOTE: Make sure that carburetor fuel bowl vent line has a continuous downward slope to the carbon canister.

AUTOCAR

INDEX OF SERVICE OPERATIONS

	Page No.
AXLES, DRIVING	
Eaton Axle Service	204
Spicer Axle Service	239
Timken Axle Service	241
Locking Differentials	192
Front Wheel Locking Hubs	505
BRAKES	
Adjustments	590
Air Brake Service	620
Anti-Skid Brakes	551
Bendix Twinplex Brake	608
Brake Booster Service	639
Hydraulic System Service	632
Parking Brake Service	612
Stopmaster Brake Service	599
CLUTCHES	
Air-Hydraulic Control	468
Clutch Service	429
COOLING SYSTEM	
Cooling System Capacity	801

	Page No.
Variable Speed Fans	10
ELECTRICAL	
Alternator Service	52
Dash Gauge Service	179
Distributor Service	141
Electronic Ignition	152
Generator Service	11
Ignition Coils and Resistors	7
Starting Motor Service	29
Starter Switch Service	21
Tune Up Service	2
FUEL & EXHAUST	
Blue Ox Compression Brake	677
Crankcase Ventilation	748
Emission Controls	750
Fuel Pump Service	183
Jacobs Engine Brake	678
L.P.G. Carburetion	190
Turbochargers	187
SPECIFICATIONS	
Cooling System Capacity	801

	Page No.
Crankcase Capacity	801
Crankshaft and Bearings	①
Generator and Regulator	800
Piston, Pin and Rings	①
Starting Motor	801
Wheel Alignment	801
①—See White Chapter.	
STEERING GEARS	
Manual Steering	680
Power Steering	686
TRANSFER CASES	469
TRANSMISSIONS	
Allison AT-540, 543	510
Allison MT-640, 643, 644, 650	512
Allison HT-740, 750	514
Allison 6 Speed	518
Clark	275
Fuller	289
New Process	329
Spicer	346
Warner	406

GENERATOR & REGULATOR SPECIFICATIONS

★ To polarize generator, reconnect leads to regulator; then momentarily connect a jumper wire from the "Gen" to the "Bat" terminals of the regulator.

	Generator					Regulator					
							Cutout Relay				
Gen. No.	Rotation ①	Brush Spring Tension, Oz.	Rated Cap. Amps.	Gen. Field Ground Location★	Field Current	Reg. No.	Closing Voltage	Arm. Air Gap, In.	Voltage Setting	Current Setting	Current & Voltage Reg. Arm. Air, Gap, In.
1106665	CC	23	31	External	1.13–1.27②	1118328	12.8	.020	14.3	31	.075
1106801	C	20	40	External	1.37–1.50②	1118338	12.8	.020	14.3	40	.075
1106805	CC	20	50	External	1.37–1.50②	1118880	12.8	.020	14.5	50	.075
1106808	C	20	50	External	1.37–1.50②	1118838	12.8	.020	14.3	50	.075
1106815	CC	20	50	External	1.37–1.50②	1118368	12.8	.020	14.3	50	.075
1106816	CC	20	40	External	1.37–1.50②	1118337	12.8	.020	14.3	40	.075
1106821	C	20	40	External	1.37–1.50②	1118886	12.8	.020	14.5	40	.075
1106822	C	20	50	External	1.37–1.50②	1118880	12.8	.020	14.5	50	.075
1106849	CC	20	50	External	1.37–1.50②	1118838	12.8	.020	14.5	50	.075
1106850	CC	20	40	External	1.37–1.50②	1118886	12.8	.020	14.5	40	.075
1106909	CC	20	50	External	1.37–1.50②	1118881	12.6	.020	14.6	50	.075

①—As viewed from drive end; C—Clockwise. CC—Counterclockwise. ②—At 12 volts.

AUTOCAR

MODEL INDEX & ENGINE APPLICATION

ENGINE IDENTIFICATION—Autocar Service Parts Identification Plate is located inside of truck cab. Stamped on the plate is the model of the engine, transmission, auxiliary transmission, rear axle and front axle. This data represents only the equipment on the vehicle when it was shipped from the factory. Prior to Autocar's assimilation by The White Motor Company, identification plates were attached to engines and transmissions.

Model	Engine Make	Basic Engine Model ②	Crankcase Refill Capacity, Qts.	Cooling System Capacity, Qts.
Diesel Engines				
A42B, F	Cummins	NH-230	—	—
A42TB	Cummins	NTC-230	—	—
A64B, F	Cummins	NH-230	—	—
A64TB	Cummins	NTC-230	—	—
C9364B	Cummins	NTC-230	—	—
C9364U	Cummins	NTC-230	—	①
CK64	Cummins	NH-230	28	①
CK64B, F	Cummins	NH-230	—	—
DC87T	Cummins	NH-230	28	①
DC87TU	Cummins	NTC-230	—	①
DC7366	Cummins	NH-230	28	①
DC9364, B	Cummins	NH-230	28	①
DC9364U	Cummins	NTC-230	—	—
DC9964	Cummins	NH-230	28	①
DC9964U	Cummins	NTC-230	—	—
DC9966	Cummins	NH-230	28	①
DC10364U	Cummins	NTC-230	—	—
DC10364, B	Cummins	NH-230	28	①
DC10366	Cummins	NH-230	28	①
DD9964	Cummins	NH-230	—	—
KK9364, B	Cummins	NH-230	28	①
KL64	Cummins	NTC-230	—	—
KM42, 64	Cummins	NTC-230	—	—
KS42, 64	Cummins	NTC-230	—	—
S42, A42	Cummins	NH-230	28	①
S42B	Cummins	NH-230	—	—
S42TB	Cummins	NTC-250	—	—
S64, A64	Cummins	NH-230	28	①
S64TB	Cummins	NTC-230	—	—
WFT6342T	Cummins	NTC-290	—	—
WFT6364	Cummins	NTC-290	—	—
WFT7564T	Cummins	NTC-290	—	—

①—Cooling system capacity varies depending on engine and radiator installed.
②—Optional engines available in most Diesel models.

WHEEL ALIGNMENT SPECIFICATIONS

Front Axle Model	Caster, Deg.	Camber, Deg.	Toe-In, Inch	Kingpin Inclination, Deg.
DCAS	①	1	3/32	0
FD-900, FE-900	①	1	3/32	5 1/2
FE-18	①	1	3/32	0
FF921	①	1	3/32	5 1/2
FG-900	①	0	3/32	8
FU-900	①	1	3/32	0
FH-901, FL-901	①	1	3/32	5 1/2
FCA	①	1	3/32	0
F3-140	①	②	3/32	③
F3W-120, 140	①	②	3/32	③
F233, F235	5	0	1/4	0
FDS-1600	①	0	—	0
F-7900	①	—	—	—
FDS-1800	①	0	3/32	0
27642	①	0	3/32	8

①—Caster angle varies with each chassis due to model, springs and suspension, steering gear, etc.
②—Right side 1/4°. Left side 1/2°.
③—Right side 6 3/4°. Left side 6 1/2°.

STARTING MOTOR SPECIFICATIONS

| Unit Part No. | Rotation ① | Brush Spring Tension, Oz. | No Load Test | | | Torque Test | | |
			Amperes	Volts	R.P.M.	Amperes	Volts	Torque Ft. Lb.
1107671	C	35	112	10.6	3240	320–385	3.5	—
1108605	C	24–28	75	11.25	6000	615	5.85	29
1108607	C	24–28	75	11.25	6000	615	5.85	29
1108840	C	36–40	115	11.60	7000	570	2.30	20
1108863	C	36–40	100	23.00	8000	525	3.00	32

Continued

AUTOCAR

STARTING MOTOR SPECIFICATIONS—Continued

Unit Part No.	Rotation ①	Brush Spring Tension, Oz.	No Load Test			Torque Test		
			Amperes	Volts	R.P.M.	Amperes	Volts	Torque Ft. Lb.
1108872	C	36–40	100	23.00	8000	525	3.00	32
1108956	C	36–40	65	11.30	5500	675	4.00	30
1109510	C	36–40	65	11.40	6000	725	5.00	44
1109173	C	36–40	65	11.40	6000	725	5.00	44
1113641	C	—	75–105①	9	6000	—	—	—
1113658	C	—	130–160①	9	6000	—	—	—
1113664	C	—	130–160①	9	6000	—	—	—
1113670	C	—	130–160①	9	6000	—	—	—
1113678	C	—	130–160①	9	6000	—	—	—
1113708	C	35–40	100	23.00	8000	500	3.00	28
1113800	C	35–40	100	23.00	8000	500	3.00	28
1113818	C	80	60–90②	23	7000–10000	500	3.5	26
1113842	C	80	60–90②	23	7000–10000	500	3.5	26
1113851	C	80	60–90②	23	7000–10000	500	3.5	26
1113872	C	80	60–90②	23	7000–10000	500	3.5	26
1113876	C	80	60–90②	23	7000–10000	500	3.5	26
1113882	C	80	60–90②	23	7000–10000	500	3.5	26
1114052	C	—	120–150①	9	3750	—	—	—
1114055	C	—	140–190①	9	5500	—	—	—
1114058	C	80	140–190②	9	5500	700	1.5	15
1114070	C	—	140–190①	9	5500	—	—	—
1114072	C	80	140–190②	9	5500	700	1.5	15
1114077	C	—	120–150①	9	3750	—	—	—
1114078	C	—	120–150①	9	3750	—	—	—
1114082	C	80	90–130②	11.5	7600	600	2.5	16.5
1114086	C	80	140–190②	9	5500	700	1.5	15
1114087	C	80	115–170②	11.0	9500	700	1.5	15
1114088	C	80	140–190②	9	5500	700	1.5	15
1114096	C	—	120–150①	9	3750	—	—	—
1114098	C	80	115–170②	11.0	9500	700	1.5	15
1114110	C	—	140–190①	9	5500	—	—	—
1114128	C	—	140–190①	9	5500	—	—	—
1114129	C	—	140–190①	9	5500	—	—	—
1114132	C	80	115–170②	11.0	9500	700	1.5	15
1114135	C	—	120–150①	9	3750	—	—	—
1114137	C	—	120–150①	9	3750	—	—	—
1114143	C	—	140–190①	9	5500	—	—	—
1114144	C	—	140–190①	9	5500	—	—	—
1114145	C	—	140–190①	9	5500	—	—	—
1114154	C	—	120–150①	9	3750	—	—	—
1114157	C	—	140–190①	9	5500	—	—	—
1114158	C	—	140–190①	9	5500	—	—	—
1114159	C	—	140–190①	9	5500	—	—	—
1114161	C	—	140–190①	9	5500	—	—	—
1114163	C	—	140–190①	9	5500	—	—	—
1114193	C	—	140–190①	9	5500	—	—	—
1114720	C	—	140–190①	9	5500	—	—	—

①—As viewed from drive end: C—Clockwise.
CC—Counterclockwise.
②—Includes solenoid.

BROCKWAY

INDEX OF SERVICE OPERATIONS

	Page No.
AXLES, DRIVING	
Eaton Axle Service	204
Spicer Axle Service	239
Timken Axle Service	241
Locking Differentials	192
Front Wheel Locking Hubs	505
BRAKES	
Adjustments	590
Air Brake Service	620
Anti-Skid Brakes	551
Bendix Twinplex Brake	608
Brake Booster Service	639
Hydraulic System Service	632
Parking Brake Service	612
Stopmaster Brake Service	599
CLUTCHES	
Air-Hydraulic Control	468
Clutch Service	429
COOLING SYSTEM	
Cooling System Capacity	803
Variable Speed Fans	10

	Page No.
ELECTRICAL	
Alternator Service	52
Dash Gauge Service	179
Distributor Service	141
Electronic Ignition	152
Generator Service	11
Ignition Coils and Resistors	7
Starting Motor Service	29
Starter Switch Service	21
Tune Up Service	2
FUEL & EXHAUST	
Blue Ox Compression Brake	677
Crankcase Ventilation	748
Emission Controls	750
Fuel Pump Service	183
Jacobs Engine Brake	678
L.P.G. Carburetion	190
Turbochargers	187
SPECIFICATIONS	
Cooling System Capacity	803
Crankcase Capacity	803
Crankshaft and Bearings	806

	Page No.
Distributor	806
Generator and Regulator	807
Piston, Pin and Rings	806
Starting Motor	807
Tune Up	805
Valve	805
Wheel Alignment	807
STEERING GEARS	
Manual Steering	680
Power Steering	686
TRANSFER CASES	469
TRANSMISSIONS	
Allison AT-540, 543	510
Allison MT-640, 643, 650, 653, 653 CR	512
Allison HT-740, 750	514
Allison 6 Speed	518
Clark	275
Fuller	289
New Process	329
Spicer	346
Warner	406

MODEL INDEX & ENGINE APPLICATION

ENGINE IDENTIFICATION—Engine model is stamped on plate attached to engine. Transmissions also have identification plates attached to them which gives the transmission manufacturers name and model of unit.

Truck Model	Standard Engine			Crankcase Refill Capacity Qts.	Cooling System Capacity Qts.	Truck Model	Standard Engine			Crankcase Refill Capacity Qts.	Cooling System Capacity Qts.
	Make	Mfg's. Model	Brockway Model				Make	Mfg's. Model	Brockway Model		
TRACTOR MODELS						N360T	Detroit	NH-230	—	—	—
147T	Continental	M6363	41BD	7	31	E360T	Detroit	671N	—	—	—
155T	Continental	B6427	42BXD	8	32	F360T	CAT	1674	—	—	—
158T	Continental	L478	44BD	—	36	K360T	Detroit	8V71N	—	—	—
C158T	Cummins	C-160	C-160	—	30	V360T	Cummins	V903	—	—	—
257T	Continental	R6572	48BD	14	44	N361T	Cummins	NH-230	—	—	—
N257T	Cummins	NH-220	NH-220	—	40	E361T	Detroit	671N	—	—	—
258T	Continental	R6572	48FD	14	40	F361T	CAT	1674	—	—	—
N258T	Cummins	NH-220	NH-220	—	42	K361T	Detroit	8V71N	—	—	—
260T	Continental	R6572	48BD	14	40	V361T	Cummins	V903	—	—	—
N260T	Cummins	NH-220	NH-220	—	42	N457T	Cummins	NH-230	—	—	—
C358T	Cummins	C-180	—	—	—	E457T	Detroit	671N	—	—	—
J358T	Cummins	V555	—	—	—	F457T	CAT	1674	—	—	—
T358T	Detroit	V8185	—	—	—	K459T	Detroit	8V71N	—	—	—
N358T	Cummins	NH-230	—	—	—	V459T	Cummins	V903	—	—	—
N359T	Cummins	NH-230	—	—	—	E527T	Detroit	671N	—	—	—
E359T	Detroit	671N	—	—	—	J527T	Cummins	V555	—	—	—
K359T	Detroit	8V71N	—	—	—	N527T	Cummins	NH230	—	—	—
V359T	Cummins	V903	—	—	—	T527T	Cummins	V8-210	—	—	—

Continued

BROCKWAY

MODEL INDEX & ENGINE APPLICATION—Continued

Truck Model	Standard Engine			Crankcase Refill Capacity Qts.	Cooling System Capacity Qts.	Truck Model	Standard Engine			Crankcase Refill Capacity Qts.	Cooling System Capacity Qts.
	Make	Mfg's. Model	Brockway Model				Make	Mfg's. Model	Brockway Model		
CHASSIS & CAB MODELS						158LQ	Continental	L478	44BD	—	36
128L	Continental	M6330	40BD	7	31	C158LL	Cummins	C-160	C-160	—	30
147L	Continental	M6363	41BD	7	31	C158LQ	Cummins	C-160	C-160	—	30
148L	Continental	B6427	42BXD	8	32	260LF	Continental	R6572	48BD	14	44
158L	Continental	L478	44BD	—	36	N260LF	Cummins	NH-220	NH-220	—	42
260L	Continental	R6572	48BD	14	44	260LQ	Continental	R6572	48BD	14	44
776LL	CAT	3208	—	—	—	N260LQ	Cummins	NH-220	NH-220	—	42
C158L	Cummins	C-160	C-160	—	30	C358LL	Cummins	C-180	—	—	—
J358L	Cummins	V555	—	—	—	J358LL	Cummins	V555	—	—	—
N260L	Cummins	NH-220	NH-220	—	42	N358TL	Cummins	NH-230	—	—	—
C358L	Cummins	C-180	—	—	—	N358LL	Cummins	NH-230	—	—	—
T358L	Detroit	V8185	—	—	—	T358LL	Detroit	V8185	—	—	—
N358L	Cummins	NH-230	—	—	—	E359LL	Cummins	NH-230	—	—	—
N359L	Cummins	NH-230	—	—	—	E359TL	Detroit	671N	—	—	—
E359L	Detroit	671N	—	—	—	K359LL	Detroit	8V71N	—	—	—
K359L	Detroit	8V71N	—	—	—	K359TL	Detroit	8V71N	—	—	—
V359L	Cummins	V903	—	—	—	N359LL	Cummins	NH-230	—	—	—
N360L	Detroit	NH-230	—	—	—	N359TL	Cummins	NH-230	—	—	—
E360L	Detroit	NH-130	—	—	—	V359LL	Cummins	V903	—	—	—
F360L	CAT	1674	—	—	—	V359TL	Cummins	V903	—	—	—
K360L	Detroit	8V71N	—	—	—	E360LL	Detroit	671N	—	—	—
V360L	Cummins	V903	—	—	—	E360TL	Detroit	671N	—	—	—
N361L	Detroit	NH-230	—	—	—	F360LL	CAT	1674	—	—	—
E361L	Detroit	671N	—	—	—	F360TL	CAT	1674	—	—	—
F361L	CAT	1674	—	—	—	H360TL	Detroit	12V71N	—	—	—
K361L	Detroit	8V71N	—	—	—	K360LL	Detroit	8V71N	—	—	—
V361L	Cummins	V903	—	—	—	K360TL	Detroit	8V71N	—	—	—
E527L	Detroit	671N	—	—	—	N360LL	Cummins	NH-230	—	—	—
J527L	Cummins	V555	—	—	—	N360TL	Cummins	NH-230	—	—	—
N527L	Cummins	NH230	—	—	—	V360LL	Cummins	V903	—	—	—
T527L	Cummins	V8-210	—	—	—	V360TL	Cummins	V903	—	—	—
A550L, T	Detroit	6V-53N	—	—	—	U360LL	Detroit	12V71N	—	—	—
B550L, T	CAT	3306	—	—	—	U360TL	Detroit	12V71N	—	—	—
E550L, T	Detroit	671N	—	—	—	E361LL	Detroit	671N	—	—	—
J550L	Cummins	V555	—	—	—	E361TL	Detroit	671N	—	—	—
N550L, T	Cummins	NTC230	—	—	—	F361LL	CAT	1674	—	—	—
A758L, T	Detroit	6V53N	—	—	—	F361TL	CAT	1674	—	—	—
N758L, T	Cummins	NTC230	—	—	—	K361LL	Detroit	8V71N	—	—	—
E759L, T	Detroit	671N	—	—	—	K361TL	Detroit	8V71N	—	—	—
N759L, T	Cummins	NTC230	—	—	—	N361LL	Cummins	NH-230	—	—	—
E761L, T	Detroit	671N	—	—	—	N361TL	Cummins	NH-230	—	—	—
F761L, T	CAT	1674	—	—	—	V361LL	Cummins	V903	—	—	—
K761T	Detroit	8V71N	—	—	—	V361TL	Cummins	V903	—	—	—
N761L, T	Cummins	NTC230	—	—	—	E457TL	Detroit	671N	—	—	—
V761L, T	Cummins	VT903	—	—	—	F457TL	CAT	1674	—	—	—
A776L, T	Detroit	6V53N	—	—	—	H457TL	CAT	1693TA	—	—	—
C776L, T	CAT	3208	—	—	—	N457TL	Cummins	NH-230	—	—	—
E776L, T	Detroit	671N	—	—	—	K459TL	Detroit	8V71N	—	—	—
L776L, T	Detroit	6V92T	—	—	—	U459TL	Detroit	12V71N	—	—	—
N776L, T	Cummins	NTC230	—	—	—	V459TL	Cummins	V903	—	—	—
TANDEM AXLE MODELS						E527TL	Detroit	671N	—	—	—
148LL	Continental	B6427	42BXD	8	32	J527LL	Cummins	V555	—	—	—
158LL	Continental	L478	44BD	—	36	N527LL	Cummins	NH230	—	—	—
						N527TL	Cummins	Sup. 250	—	—	—

Continued

BROCKWAY

MODEL INDEX & ENGINE APPLICATION—Continued

Truck Model	Standard Engine Make	Mfg's. Model	Brockway Model	Crankcase Refill Capacity Qts.	Cooling System Capacity Qts.	Truck Model	Standard Engine Make	Mfg's. Model	Brockway Model	Crankcase Refill Capacity Qts.	Cooling System Capacity Qts.
T527LL	Cummins	V8-210	—	—	—	E761LL, TL	Detroit	671N	—	—	—
A550LL	Detroit	6V-53N	—	—	—	F761LL, TL	CAT	1674	—	—	—
B550LL, TL	CAT	3306	—	—	—	K761LL, TL	Detroit	8V71N	—	—	—
E550LL, TL	Detroit	671N	—	—	—	N761LL	Cummins	NTC230	—	—	—
J550LL	Cummins	V555	—	—	—	N761TL	Cummins	NTC250	—	—	—
N550LL	Cummins	NTC230	—	—	—	V761LL, TL	Cummins	VT903	—	—	—
N550TL	Cummins	NTC250	—	—	—	H762LL, TL	CAT	1693TA	—	—	—
A758LL	Detroit	6V53N	—	—	—	U762LL, TL	Detroit	12V71N	—	—	—
N758LL	Cummins	NTC230	—	—	—	A776, LL	Detroit	6V53N	—	—	—
N758TL	Cummins	NTC250	—	—	—	E776LL, TL	Detroit	671N	—	—	—
E759LL, TL	Detroit	671N	—	—	—	L776LL, TL	Detroit	6V92T	—	—	—
K759LL, TL	Detroit	8V71N	—	—	—	N776LL	Cummins	NTC230	—	—	—
N759LL	Detroit	NTC230	—	—	—	N776TL	Cummins	NTC250	—	—	—
N759TL	Cummins	NTC250	—	—	—	**OFF-HIGHWAY MODELS**					
V759LL, TL	Cummins	VT903	—	—	—	260LFOH	Continental	R6572	48BD	14	44
F760LL, TL	CAT	1674	—	—	—	260LROH	Continental	R6572	48BD	14	44
K760TL	Detroit	8V71N	—	—	—	N260LROH	Cummins	NH-220	NH-220	H	42
N760LL	Cummins	NTC230	—	—	—	N260LFOH	Cummins	NH-220	NH-220	—	42
N760TL	Cummins	NTC250	—	—	—						
V760TL	Cummins	VT903	—	—	—						

GENERAL ENGINE SPECIFICATIONS

Engine Model	No. Cyls. & Valve Location	Bore & Stroke	Piston Displacement, Cu. In.	Compression Ratio①	Maximum Brake H.P. @ R.P.M.①	Maximum Torque, Ft. Lb. @ R.P.M.①	Normal Oil Pressure, Lbs.
38B	6 In Block	3³/₄ × 4³/₈	290	6.3	104 @ 3200	212 @ 1250	60
41BD	6 In Block	4 × 4¹³/₁₆	363	6.7	150 @ 3200	293 @ 1600	60
42BD	6 In Block	4⁵/₁₆ × 4⁷/₈	427	6.4	165 @ 3000	352 @ 1600	60
42BX	6 In Block	4⁵/₁₆ × 4⁷/₈	427	6.7	142 @ 3000	332 @ 1200	60
46B	6 In Head	4¹/₂ × 5³/₈	513	5.9	180 @ 2800	400 @ 1300	60
46BD	6 In Head	4¹/₂ × 5³/₈	513	6.2	220 @ 2800	412 @ 1400	60
46FD	6 In Head	4¹/₂ × 5³/₈	513	6.2	220 @ 2800	412 @ 1400	60
48BD	6 In Head	4³/₄ × 5³/₈	572	6.3	230 @ 2800	484 @ 1400	60
48FD	6 In Head	4³/₄ × 5³/₈	572	6.3	230 @ 2800	484 @ 1400	60
49BD	6 In Head	4⁷/₈ × 5³/₈	602	6.3	232 @ 2800	482 @ 1200	60

①—Current production.

TUNE UP & VALVE SPECIFICATIONS

Engine Model	Firing Order	Spark Plugs Type①	Spark Plugs Gap	Ignition Timing Timing Mark	Ignition Timing Location	Cylinder Head Torque, Ft. Lb.	Valve Seat Angle, Degrees	Valve Clearance H—Hot C—Cold Intake	Valve Clearance H—Hot C—Cold Exhaust	Valve Spring Pressure Lb. @ In. Length
38B	153624	D14	.025	1/2" BTDC	Flywheel	70–75	②	.022C	.024C	119 @ 1¹/₂
40BD	153624	D10	.025	1/2" BTDC	Flywheel	70–75	②	.020H	.022H	119 @ 1¹/₂
41BD	153624	D14	.025	5/16" BTDC	Flywheel	70–75	②	.016H	.024H	119 @ 1¹/₂
42BX	153624	D10	.030	5/8" BTDC	Flywheel	70–75	②	.016H	.022H	144 @ 1.316
42BD	153624	D10	.025	3/16" BTDC	Flywheel	70–75	②	.016H	.024H	144 @ 1.316
46B	153624	D10	.025	1" BTDC	Flywheel	85–95	②	.020H	.024H	①
46BD	153624	D10	.025	5/8" BTDC	Flywheel	85–95	②	.023C	.033C	①

Continued

BROCKWAY

TUNE UP & VALVE SPECIFICATIONS—Continued

Engine Model	Firing Order	Spark Plugs Type ①	Spark Plugs Gap	Ignition Timing Timing Mark	Ignition Timing Location	Cylinder Head Torque, Ft. Lb.	Valve Seat Angle, Degrees	Valve Clearance H–Hot C–Cold Intake	Valve Clearance H–Hot C–Cold Exhaust	Valve Spring Pressure Lb. @ In. Length
46FD	153624	D10	.025	5/8" BTDC	Flywheel	85–95	②	.023C	.030H	①
48BD③	153624	D10	.025	1/2" BTDC	Flywheel	85–95	②	.020H	.030H	①
48FD③	153624	D10	.025	1/2" BTDC	Flywheel	85–95	②	.020H	.030H	①
48BD④	153624	D10	.020	TDC	Flywheel	85–95	②	.023C	.033C	①
48FD④	153624	D10	.020	TDC	Flywheel	85–95	②	.023C	.033C	①
49BD	153624	D10	.025	1/2" BTDC	Flywheel	85–95	②	.020H	.030H	①

①—Champion.
②—Intake 30°, exhaust 45°.
③—Gasoline.
④—LPG.

DISTRIBUTOR SPECIFICATIONS

Unit Part No. ①	Rotation ②	Cam Angle, Degrees	Breaker Gap, In.	Condenser Capacity, Mfds.	Breaker Arm Spring Tension, Oz.	Centrifugal Advance Deg. @ R.P.M. of Dist. Advance Starts	Centrifugal Advance Deg. @ R.P.M. of Dist. Full Advance	Vacuum Advance Inches of Vacuum to Start Plunger Movement	Vacuum Advance Inches of Vacuum for Full Plunger Travel	Vacuum Advance Maximum Vacuum Advance, Dist. Degrees
1GC-5001-B	CC	39	.020	.25–.28	17–20	1 @ 275	15 @ 1200	None	None	None
1GC-6002-1AE	CC	39	.020	.25–.28	17–20	1 @ 400	9 @ 1250	None	None	None
1GC-6002-1AF	CC	39	.020	.25–.28	17–20	1 @ 475	6 @ 1425	None	None	None
1GC-6002-1AG	CC	39	.020	.25–.28	17–20	1 @ 425	8 @ 1425	None	None	None
1GC-6002-1E	CC	39	.020	.20–.25	17–20	1 @ 390	9 @ 1250	None	None	None
1GC-6002-1R	CC	39	.020	.20–.25	17–20	1 @ 400	8 @ 1420	None	None	None
1GC-6002-1S	CC	39	.020	.20–.25	17–20	1 @ 475	6 @ 1420	None	None	None
1GC-6010-1B	CC	39	.020	.20–.25	17–20	1 @ 465	6 @ 1415	None	None	None
1GC-6010-1C	CC	39	.020	.20–.25	17–20	1 @ 285	14 @ 1600	None	None	None
1GC-6010-1D	CC	39	.020	.25–.28	17–20	1 @ 300	14 @ 1600	None	None	None
1GC-6010-1E	CC	39	.020	.25–.28	17–20	1 @ 325	12 @ 1400	None	None	None

①—Distributor number stamped on plate riveted to housing.
②—As viewed from top, CC—Counterclockwise.

PISTON, PIN, RING, CRANKSHAFT & BEARING SPECIFICATIONS

Engine Model	Wristpin Diameter	Piston Clearance, Inch②	Ring End Gap, In. (Minimum) Comp.	Ring End Gap, In. (Minimum) Oil	Crank Pin Diameter, Inch	Rod Bearing Clearance, In.	Rod Bolt Torque, Lb. Ft.	Main Bearing Journal Diameter, In.	Main Bearing Clearance, Inch	Main Bolt Torque, Lb. Ft.
38B	1.109	.005	.008	.008	2.248–2.249	.001–.0028	70–75	2.623–2.624	.0015–.0037	①
40BD	1.109	.005	.008	.008	2.248–2.249	.001–.0028	70–75	2.624–2.625	.0015–.0037	①
41BD	1.109	.002	.008	.008	2.248–2.249	.001–.0028	70–75	2.624–2.625	.0015–.0037	①
42BD	1.250	.003	.008	.008	2.498–2.499	.001–.003	100–110	2.873–2.874	.0015–.0037	100–110
42BX	1.250	.005	.008	.008	2.498–2.499	.001–.003	100–110	2.873–2.874	.0015–.0037	100–110
46B	1.500	.005	.013	.013	2.999–3.000	.001–.003	85–95	3.249–3.250	.0022–.004	85–95
46BD	1.500	.005	.013	.013	2.999–3.000	.001–.003	85–95	3.249–3.250	.0022–.004	85–95
46FD	1.500	.005	.013	.013	2.999–3.000	.001–.003	85–95	3.249–3.250	.0022–.004	85–95
48BD	1.500	.005	.013	.013	2.999–3.000	.001–.003	85–95	3.249–3.250	.0022–.004	85–95
48FD	1.500	.005	.013	.013	2.999–3.000	.001–.003	85–95	3.249–3.250	.0022–.004	85–95
49BD	1.500	.005	.013	.013	2.999–3.000	.001–.003	85–95	3.249–3.250	.0022–.004	85–95

①—1/2" 100–110, 9/16" 130–140.
②—Pistons removed from above.

BROCKWAY

GENERATOR & REGULATOR SPECIFICATIONS

★ To Polarize Generator: For internally grounded systems, disconnect field lead from regulator and momentarily flash this lead to the regulator battery terminal. For externally grounded systems, reconnect leads to regulator; then momentarily connect a jumper wire from the "Arm" to the "Bat" terminals of the regulator.

	Generator					Regulator					
Gen. No.①	Rotation ⑤	Brush Spring Tension, Oz.	Rated Cap. Amps.	Gen. Field Ground Location★	Field Current	Reg. No.	Cutout Relay		Voltage Setting	Current Setting	Current & Voltage Reg. Arm. Air Gap, In.
							Closing Voltage	Arm. Air Gap, In.			
GCH-4612B-1	C	23–26	50	Internal	5.8–6.4②	VRC-4101B	6.5	.060	7.2	50	④
GCH-4613A-1	C	23–26	50	Internal	5.8–6.4②	VRC-4101B	6.5	.060	7.2	50	④
GDJ-4829A	C	36–60	55	Internal	5.9–7.7③	VRH-4102A	13.0	.060	14.1	55	④
GDJ-4844A	C	36–60	55	Internal	1.1–1.3③	VRH-4102A	13.0	.060	14.1	55	④
GEB-6001A	C	64–68	32	External	3.7–4.3②	VRP-4004C	6.3	.031	7.2	32	.048
GEB-6001C	C	64–68	32	External	3.7–4.3②	VRP-4004C	6.3	.031	7.2	32	.048

①—Generator number stamped on plate riveted to housing.
②—At 5 volts.
③—At 10 volts.
④—Voltage unit .040", current unit .047".
⑤—As viewed from drive end; C—Clockwise.

STARTING MOTOR SPECIFICATIONS

Unit Part No. ①	Rotation ②	Brush Spring Tension, Oz.	No Load Test			Torque Test		
			Amperes	Volts	R.P.M.	Amperes	Volts	Torque Lb. Ft.
MAB-4071	C	42–53	60	5	3600	390	2	9.2
MAS-4102	C	42–53	40	10	3900	340	4	13.2
MAW-4042	C	42–53	65	5	4300	335	2	6.0
ML-4301	C	38–49	65	5	2250	370	2	10.3
ML-4303	C	42–53	65	5	2250	370	2	10.3
ML-4318	C	42–53	65	5	2250	370	2	10.3

①—Starter number stamped on plate riveted to housing.
②—As viewed from drive end; C—Clockwise.

WHEEL ALIGNMENT

Axle Model	Caster	Camber	Toe-In
32350①	1	1	1/16–1/8
FD-901①	1	1	1/16–1/8
FE-10A-43②	2	1	1/16–1/8
FG-900③	2	1	1/16–1/8

①—Kingpin angle 5½°.
②—Kingpin angle 0°.
③—Kingpin angle 8°.

CHEVROLET

> **NOTE:** See the GMC Truck Chapter for service procedures on V6-305C, 379, 401, 432, 478 & V8-637 engines

INDEX OF SERVICE OPERATIONS

AXLES, DRIVING

	Page No.
Own Make Axle Service	909
Dana Spicer Series 60	910
Eaton Axle Service	204
Spicer Axle Service	239
Timken Axle Service	241
Locking Differentials	192
Front Wheel Locking Hubs	505
Front Wheel Drive	916

BRAKES

Adjustments	590
Air Brake Service	620
Anti-Skid Brakes	551
Bendix Twinplex Brake	608
Brake Booster Service	639
Disc Brakes	661
Hydraulic System Service	632
Parking Brake Service	612
Stopmaster Brake Service	599

CLUTCHES

Clutch Pedal, Adjust	888
Clutch Service	429
Air-Hydraulic (Air-Pak)	468
Hydraulic Controls	888

COOLING SYSTEM

Cooling System Capacity	809
Variable Speed Fans	10
Water Pumps	847

ELECTRICAL

Alternator Service	52
Dash Gauge Service	179
Distributors, Standard	141
Electronic Ignition	152
Generator Service	11
Ignition Coils and Resistors	7
Starting Motor Service	29
Starter Switch Service	21
Tune Up Service	2

ENGINE (Overhead Cam) 847

ENGINE (Overhead Valve)

	Page No.
Camshaft and Bearings	843
Crankshaft Rear Oil Seal	845
Cylinder Head, Replace	839
Hydraulic Lifters	841
Main Bearings	844
Pistons	844
Piston and Rod, Assemble	844
Push Rods	840
Rocker Arms	840
Rocker Arm Studs	840
Rod Bearings	844
Timing Case Cover	841
Timing Gears	842
Timing Chain	843
Valves, Adjust	839
Valve Arrangement	839
Valve Guides	841
Valves, Remove	840

ENGINE OILING

Crankcase Capacity	809
Oil Pan, Replace	846
Oil Pump	846

FRONT SUSPENSION

Coil Spring Suspension	918
Front Wheel Locking Hubs	505
Wheel Alignment, Adjust	918

FUEL & EXHAUST

Carburetor Adjustments	852
Crankcase Ventilation	748
Emission Controls	750
Fuel Pump Service	183
L.P.G. Carburetion	190
Turbochargers	187

SPECIFICATIONS

Alternator and Regulator	832
Carburetor Adjustments	852
Crankshaft and Bearing	836
Distributor	825
Engine Tightening Torque	835
General Engine Data	812
Piston, Pin and Ring	836

	Page No.
Starting Motor	830
Tune Up	816
Valve	824
Wheel Alignment	837

STEERING

Steering Gear, Replace	935
Manual Steering Gear Service	680
Power Steering Gear Service	686

TRANSFER CASES 469

TRANSMISSIONS, Manual

Clark	275
Fuller	289
Muncie 3 Speed	890
Muncie 4 Speed	896
New Process	327
Saginaw 3 Speed	890
Saginaw 4 Speed	900
Spicer	346
Tremec 3 Speed	890
Vega (1971-72)	894, 895
Vega (1973-75)	892, 900
Warner	406

TRANSMISSIONS, Automatic

Allison AT540, 543	510
Adjustments	904
Replace	903
Allison MT640, 643, 644, 650, 653, 654CR	512
Adjustments	904
Replace	903
Allison HT-740, 750	514
Allison Powermatic	518
Adjustments	903
Replace	903
Powerglide	522
Adjustments	906
Replace	904
Turbo Hydra-Matic 200	541
Adjustments	907
Replace	907
Turbo Hydra-Matic 250	544
Adjustments	907
Replace	907
Turbo Hydra-Matic 350	544
Adjustments	908
Replace	907
Turbo Hydra-Matic 400, 475	538
Adjustments	908
Replace	908

CHEVROLET

TRUCK MODELS & ENGINE APPLICATION

IDENTIFICATION PLATE: Located inside driver's compartment. Engine identification and other unit data on plate represents only the equipment in the vehicle when shipped from the factory.

Models	Year	Engine Make	Standard Engine Model	Crankcase Refill Capacity, Qts.	Cooling System Capacity, Qts.
BLAZER					
6 Cyl.	1970–73	Own	6-250	4	12.6
V8	1970–73	Own	V8-307	4	15.8
6 Cyl.	1974–80	Own	6-250	4	15
V8	1977–79	Own	V8-305	4	18
V8	1974–79	Own	V8-350	4	18
EL CAMINO					
V8	1970	Own	V8-283	4	17
13380-580	1970–72	Own	6-250	4	12.2
1AC80, AD80	1974–77	Own	6-250	4	12½
13480-680	1970–72	Own	V8-307	4	15
1AC80, AD80	1973	Own	V8-307	4	15
1AC80, AD80	1976	Own	V8-305	4	18
1AC80, AD80	1974–77	Own	V8-350	4	18
1AW80, 215	1978–79	Own	V6-200	4	15
1AW80	1980	Own	V6-229	4	18.5
1AW80	1980	Own	V8-305	4	19
1AW80, 215	1978–79	Own	V8-305, 350	4	18
1AW80	1979	Buick	V6-231	4	—
1AW80	1979	Own	V8-267	4	—
VEGA					
14105	1971–72	Own	4-140	4	—
1HV05	1973	Own	4-140	4	—
1HV05	1974–75	Own	4-140	4	—
CONVENTIONAL GASOLINE					
CS10	1970–71	Own	6-250	4	12
CE10	1970–71	Own	V8-307	4	15.8
CS10	1972	Own	6-250	4	12.1
CE10	1972	Own	V8-307	4	15.5
C10	1973	Own	6-250	4	14.6
C10	1973	Own	V8-307	4	17.8
C10	1974–80	Own	6-250	4	15
C10	1980	Own	V8-305	4	17.5
C10	1974–79	Own	V8-350	4	18
CS20	1970–71	Own	6-250	4	12.2
CE20	1970–71	Own	V8-307	4	15.8
CS20	1972	Own	6-250	4	12.1
CE20	1972	Own	V8-307	4	15.8
C20	1973	Own	6-250	4	14.6
C20	1973	Own	V8-307	4	17.7
C20	1974–80	Own	6-250	4	15
C20	1975–80	Own	6-292	5	15
C20	1977–79	Own	V8-305	4	18
C20	1974–79	Own	V8-350	4	18
CS30	1970–72	Own	6-250	4	12.2
CE30	1970–72	Own	V8-307	4	15.8
C30	1973–79	Own	6-250	4	14.6
CONVENTIONAL GASOLINE—Continued					
C30	1973	Own	V8-307	4	17.8
C30	1974–79	Own	6-250	4	15
C30	1975–80	Own	6-292	5	15
C30	1974–79	Own	V8-350	4	18
C5D042	1979	Own	V8-350	5	21
C6D042	1979	Own	V8-350	5	21
C6D062①	1979	Own	V8-366	6	33
C7D042	1979	Own	V8-366	6	33
C7D064②	1979	Own	V8-366	6	33
CS40	1970–71	Own	6-250	4	16.1
CE40	1970–71	Own	V8-350	4	20.4
CS40	1972	Own	6-250	4	16
CE40	1972	Own	V8-350	4	21
CS50	1970–72	Own	6-292	5	16.5
CS50	1973–74	Own	6-250	4	16
CS50	1975–78	Own	6-292	5	17
CE50	1970–71	Own	V8-350	6	20.4
CE50	1972	Own	V8-350	4	20
CE50	1973–78	Own	V8-350	5	21
CM50	1972	Own	V6-305	8	36
CE60	1970–71	Own	V8-366	6	31.2
CE60	1972	Own	V8-366	6	33.1
CE60	1973	Own	V8-350	4	20
CE60	1974–78	Own	V8-350	5	21
CM60	1972	Own	V6-351	8	34
CM60	1973–74	Own	V6-305	8	36
CS60	1973	Own	6-292	5	16.5
CS60	1974–78	Own	6-292	5	17
HM80	1970–71	GMC	V6-401	10	37
HM80	1972	GMC	V6-401	9	37
HM80	1973–74	Own	V6-432	10	37
HE80	1975–77	Own	V8-427	6	37
HE90	1972	GMC	V8-637	20	51
J8C042	1979	Own	V8-427	8	36.5
J8C064②	1979	Own	V8-427	8	36.5
CE65	1973–77	Own	V8-366	6	36
CM65	1973–74	Own	V6-379	10	34.5

①—6 × 2 Tandem Series
②—6 × 4 Tandem Series

FOUR-WHEEL DRIVE

Models	Year	Engine Make	Standard Engine Model	Crankcase Refill Capacity, Qts.	Cooling System Capacity, Qts.
KS10	1970–71	Own	6-250	4	12.2
KE10	1970–71	Own	V8-307	4	15.8
KS10	1972	Own	6-250	4	12.1
KE10	1972	Own	V8-307	4	16.2
K10	1973	Own	6-250	4	14.6
K10	1973	Own	V8-307	4	17.8
K10	1973	Own	V8-350	4	17.8
K10	1974–80	Own	6-250	4	15
K10	1974–79	Own	V8-350	4	18
K10	1978	Own	V8-305	4	18

Continued

CHEVROLET

TRUCK MODELS & ENGINE APPLICATION—Continued

IDENTIFICATION PLATE: Located inside driver's compartment. Engine identification and other unit data on plate represents only the equipment in the vehicle when shipped from the factory.

Models	Year	Engine Make	Standard Engine Model	Crankcase Refill Capacity, Qts.	Cooling System Capacity, Qts.
KS20	1970–71	Own	6-250	4	12.2
KS20	1972	Own	6-250	4	12.1
K20	1973	Own	6-250	4	14.6
K20	1973	Own	V8-307	4	17.8
K20	1973	Own	V8-350	4	17.8
K20	1974	Own	6-250	4	15
K20	1975–79	Own	6-292	5	14.8
K20	1974–76	Own	V8-350	4	18
K20	1980	Own	V8-350	4	18
K20	1978–79	Own	V8-305	4	18
K30	1977–80	Own	6-292	5	15
KE20	1970–72	Own	V8-307	4	16.1
TANDEM SERIES					
ME50	1970	Own	V8-350	5	20.4
ME60	1970–72	Own	V8-366	6	33
ME65	1973–79	Own	V8-366	6	33
MM65	1974	Own	V6-432	10	36
JM80	1970–72	GMC	V6-401	10	37
JM80	1973–74	Own	V6-432	10	37
JE80	1975–79	Own	V8-247	6	37
JE90	1972	GMC	V8-637	20	51
STEP-VAN & FORWARD CONTROL SERIES					
GS10	1970–71	Own	6-250	4	12½
GE10	1970–71	Own	V8-307	4	18.5
GS10	1972	Own	6-250	4	12.6
GE10	1972	Own	V8-307	4	15.9
G10	1973	Own	6-250	4	12.8
G10	1973	Own	V8-307	4	15.8
G10	1974–80	Own	6-250	4	17
G10	1974–76	Own	V8-350	4	18
PS10	1970–71	Own	6-250	4	10
PS10	1972	Own	6-250	4	10.5
P10	1973	Own	6-250	4	11.5
P10	1974	Own	6-250	4	13
P10	1975–80	Own	6-292	5	13.6
GS20	1970–71	Own	6-250	4	12½
GE20	1970–71	Own	V8-307	4	15.8
GE20	1971	Own	V8-350	4	17.3
GS20	1972	Own	6-250	4	12.6
GE20	1972	Own	V8-350	4	16.1
G20	1973	Own	6-250	4	12.6
G20	1973	Own	V8-350	4	16.1
G20	1974	Own	6-250	4	13
G20	1975–78	Own	6-292	5	14.8
G20	1979–80	Own	6-250	4	17
G20	1974–76	Own	V8-350	4	18
PS20	1970–71	Own	6-250	4	12.5
PE20	1970–71	Own	V8-307	4	18.7
PS20	1972	Own	6-250	4	11.1
PE20	1972	Own	V8-307	4	15.2

Models	Year	Engine Make	Standard Engine Model	Crankcase Refill Capacity, Qts.	Cooling System Capacity, Qts.
STEP-VAN & FORWARD CONTROL SERIES—Continued					
P20	1973	Own	6-250	4	11.5
P20	1973	Own	V8-307	4	14.9
P20	1974	Own	6-250	4	13
P20	1975–79	Own	6-292	5	13.6
P20	1974–76	Own	V8-350	4	17
GS30	1971	Own	6-250	4	13.8
GE30	1971	Own	V8-350	4	17.3
GS30	1972	Own	6-250	4	12.6
GE30	1972	Own	V8-350	4	16.1
G30	1973	Own	6-250	4	12.6
G30	1973	Own	V8-350	4	16.1
G30	1974	Own	6-250	4	13
G30	1975–78	Own	6-292	5	14.8
G30	1974–76	Own	V8-350	4	18
G30	1978–80	Own	V8-350	4	18
G30	1979	Own	6-250	4	—
P30	1970	Detroit	3-53N	12	20¼
PS30	1970	Own	6-250	4	12.5
PE30	1970–71	Own	V8-307	4	18.7
PE30	1971–72	Own	V8-350	4	22.5
PE30	1972	Own	V8-307	4	15.2
PE30	1972	Own	V8-350	4	22.5
P30	1973	Own	6-250	4	11.5
P30	1973	Own	V8-307	4	14.9
P30	1973	Own	V8-350	4	18.3
P30	1974	Own	6-250	4	13
P30①	1975–79	Own	6-292	5	13.6
P30	1974–76	Own	V8-350	4	17
P30②	1977–80	Own	V8-350③	4	19
P30②	1977–80	Own	V8-464④	6	25
PT30	1970	Detroit	3-53N	12	20¼
P40	1971	Own	6-250	4	—
P4T042	1979	Own	6-292	4	17
PS40	1970	Own	6-250	4	13

①—Except Motor Home Chassis
②—Motor Home Chassis
③—125", 137" and 158" wheelbase
④—178" wheelbase

TILT CAB SERIES					
TS50	1970–71	Own	6-292	4	17
TE50	1970–71	Own	V8-350	4	28.1
TE50	1972	Own	V8-350	4	24.6
TE60	1970–71	Own	V8-366	6	35.2
TE60	1972	Own	V8-366	6	33.7
TE60	1973–79	Own	V8-350	5	28.1
TE65	1974–79	Own	V8-366	6	35.2
TM60	1973	Own	V6-305	8	45
TM60	1974	Own	V6-305	8	46.6

Continued

CHEVROLET

TRUCK MODELS & ENGINE APPLICATION—Continued

IDENTIFICATION PLATE: Located inside driver's compartment. Engine identification and other unit data on plate represents only the equipment in the vehicle when shipped from the factory.

Models	Year	Engine Make	Standard Engine Model	Crankcase Refill Capacity, Qts.	Cooling System Capacity, Qts.
TM65	1973-74	Own	V6-379	8	45
TM80	1970-72	GMC	V6-401	10	46.7
TM80	1973	Own	V6-432	10	46.7
TM80	1973	GMC	V6-478	8	47.4
TM80	1974	Own	V6-432	10	47
W6N042	1979	Own	V8-350	5	28
W7N042	1979	Own	V8-366	6	35
WM80	1972	GMC	V6-401	11	46.7
WM80	1973-74	Own	V6-432	10	47
TE90	1972	GMC	V8-637	20	53.9

SCHOOL BUS SERIES

Models	Year	Engine Make	Standard Engine Model	Crankcase Refill Capacity, Qts.	Cooling System Capacity, Qts.
B6P042	1979	Own	V8-350	5	25
SS40	1970-71	Own	6-250	4	16
SS50	1970-71	Own	6-292	4	16 1/2
SE50	1970-71	Own	V8-350	4	20.4
SM50	1972	Own	V6-305	8	36
SS60	1973	Own	6-292	4	16.5
SS60	1974	Own	6-292	5	17
SM60	1973-74	Own	V6-305	8	36
SE60	1973-79	Own	V8-350	5	20
SG60	1973-74	GMC	DH478	10	29
RM80	1972	GMC	V6-401	11	40.7
RM80	1973	Own	V6-432	10	40 3/4

CONVENTIONAL DIESELS

Models	Year	Engine Make	Standard Engine Model	Crankcase Refill Capacity, Qts.	Cooling System Capacity, Qts.
C10	1978-80	Olds	V8-350	6	18
CD50	1970-71	Detroit	4-53N	14	20
CG50	1970	GMC	D478	10	29 3/4
CG60	1974	GMC	DH478	10	29
HV70	1970-71	Detroit	6V-53N	14	36
HV70	1972-78	Detroit	6V-53N	14	36.5
HY70	1975-77	Catpl'r	3208	12	50 1/2
HY70	1978	Catpl'r	3208	10	44
JV70	1970	Detroit	6V-53N	16	37
JV70	1971	Detroit	6V-53N	14	36
JV70	1972-78	Detroit	6V-53N	14	36.5
JY70	1975-77	Catpl'r	3208	12	50 1/2
JY70	1978	Catpl'r	3208	10	44
HC90	1971	Cum'ins	NHCT270	36	54.4
HC90	1973	Cum'ins	NTC270E	28	54.4
HC90	1973-78	Cum'ins	NTC290	28	61.5
HH90	1971-73	Detroit	8V-71N	24	55.7
HH90	1974	Detroit	8V-71N	24	80
HH90	1975-78	Detroit	8V-71N	27	80
HI90	1970-73	Detroit	6-71N	19	45
HI90	1974	Detroit	6-71N	19	51.2
HI90	1975-78	Detroit	6-71N	22	51 1/4
HN90	1970-71	Cum'ins	NHC-250	20	48 1/2
HN90	1972	Cum'ins	NHC250	24	53
HN90	1973-74	Cum'ins	NHC250	24	52.9

Models	Year	Engine Make	Standard Engine Model	Crankcase Refill Capacity, Qts.	Cooling System Capacity, Qts.
JB90	1972	Cum'ins	V8-903	26	61
JB90	1973	Cum'ins	V8-903	26	61
JC90	1971	Cum'ins	NHCT270	36	54.4
JC90	1972	Cum'ins	NTC270E	28	54.4
JC90	1973	Cum'ins	NTC290	28	61.5
JC90	1975-78	Cum'ins	NTC-290	28	61 1/2
JH90	1971-74	Detroit	8V-71N	24	55.7
JH90	1975-78	Detroit	8V-71N	27	80
JI90	1970-72	Detroit	6-71N	19	45
JI90	1973	Detroit	6-71N	19	54.7
JI90	1974-78	Detroit	6-71N	22	51 1/4
JJ90	1977	Detroit	6V-92TT	—	—
JN90	1970-71	Cum'ins	NHC-250	20	48 1/2
JN90	1972	Cum'ins	NHC250	20	53
JN90	1973	Cum'ins	NHC250	20	52.9
J9C042	1979	Detroit	8V-71N	22	60
J9C064 ①	1979	Detroit	8V-71N	22	60
MB90	1972-73	Cum'ins	V8-903	26	61
MC90	1972-73	Cum'ins	NTC-350	28	63.5
MI90	1970-71	Detroit	6-71N	19	45
MH90	1970-72	Detroit	8V-71N	24	56
MH90	1975-76	Detroit	8V-71N	27	73
NI-9005	1977-78	Detroit	6-71N	22	50
NH-9005	1977-78	Detroit	8V-71N	23	92
NJ-9005	1977-78	Detroit	6V-92N	18	80
NC-9005	1977-78	Detroit	NTC290	28	72
N9E042	1979	Detroit	8V-71N	23	92
N9E064 ①	1979	Detroit	8V-71N	23	92
N9F042	1979	Detroit	8V-71N	23	92
N9F064 ①	1979	Detroit	8V-71N	23	92
MH-9005	1977-78	Detroit	8V-71N	23	92
MC-9005	1977-78	Cum'ins	NTC290	28	72
MK-9005	1977-78	Detroit	8V-92N	27	92

①—Tandem Series

TILT DIESELS

Models	Year	Engine Make	Standard Engine Model	Crankcase Refill Capacity, Qts.	Cooling System Capacity, Qts.
TG50	1972	GMC	DH478	11	38.3
TG60	1973-74	GMC	DH478	11	38.3
TV70	1970-71	Detroit	6V-53N	14	34 1/2
TV70	1972	Detroit	6V-53N	14	31.9
TV70	1973-74	Detroit	6V-53N	14	31.5
WV70	1972-74	Detroit	6V-53N	16	31.5
FB90	1972-74	Cum'ins	V8-903	26	61
FI90	1970-71	Detroit	6-71N	19	48 1/2
FI90	1972-74	Detroit	6-71N	19	51.2
FI90	1975-78	Detroit	6-71N	22	51 1/4
FJ90	1975-78	Detroit	6V-92	18	57
FN90	1970-71	Cum'ins	NHC-250	24	48 1/2
FC90	1970-71	Cum'ins	NHCT270	36	48 1/2
FC90	1972	Cum'ins	NTC270E	28	55
FC90	1974-78	Cum'ins	NTC-290	28	55

Continued

CHEVROLET

TRUCK MODELS & ENGINE APPLICATION—Continued

IDENTIFICATION PLATE: Located inside driver's compartment. Engine identification and other unit data on plate represents only the equipment in the vehicle when shipped from the factory.

Models	Year	Engine Make	Standard Engine Model	Crankcase Refill Capacity, Qts.	Cooling System Capacity, Qts.
FH90	1970–71	Detroit	8V-71N	24	60½
FH90	1972–74	Detroit	8V-71N	24	73
FH90	1975–78	Detroit	8V-71N	27	73
FN90	1972–74	Cum'ins	NHC-250	20	53
DB90	1972–74	Cum'ins	V8-903	26	61
DB90	1975–76	Cum'ins	VT-903	18	62
DC90	1970–71	Cum'ins	NHCT270	36	48½
DC90	1972	Cum'ins	NTC270E	28	55
DC90	1974–78	Cum'ins	NTC-290	28	55
DH90	1970–71	Detroit	8V-71N	24	60½
DH90	1972–74	Detroit	8V-71NE	24	73
DH90	1975–77	Detroit	8V-71N	27	73
DI90	1970–71	Detroit	6-71N	19	48½
DI90	1972–74	Detroit	6-71N	19	51.2
DI90	1975–78	Detroit	6-71N	22	51
DJ90	1975–78	Detroit	6V-92	18	57
DK90	1975–78	Detroit	8V-92	27	74
DN90	1970–71	Cum'ins	NHC-250	24	48½
DN90	1972–74	Cum'ins	NHC-250	20	53
DP90	1972–74	Detroit	12V-71	38	98
DP90	1975–78	Detroit	12V-71N	34	98
DL90	1977–78	Cum'ins	KT450	—	71
DR90	1977–78	Catpl'r	3406	34	69
D9K042	1979–80	Detroit	8V-71N	23	72
D9K064①	1979–80	Detroit	8V-71N	23	72
D9L042	1979–80	Detroit	8V-71N	23	72
D9L064①	1979–80	Detroit	8V-71N	23	72
TW90	1973	Detroit	6V-71N	—	54

①—Tandem Series

GENERAL ENGINE SPECIFICATIONS

Year	Engine Model	Carb. Type	Bore & Stroke	Comp. Ratio	Horsepower @ R.P.M.	Torque Lbs. Ft. @ R.P.M.	Governed Speed R.P.M. No Load	Normal Oil Pressure Lbs.
1970	6-250	1 Bore	3.875 × 3.53	8.5	155 @ 4200	235 @ 1600	4000	40–60
	6-292	1 Bore	3.875 × 4.125	8.0	170 @ 4000	275 @ 1600	3900	40–60
	V8-307, 200 H.P.	2 Bore	3.875 × 3.25	9.0	200 @ 4600	300 @ 2400	4100	30
	V8-350, 215 H.P.	2 Bore	4.00 × 3.48	8.0	215 @ 4400	320 @ 2400	4000	30
	V8-350, 250 H.P.	2 Bore	4.00 × 3.48	9.0	250 @ 4800	345 @ 2800	—	50–65
	V8-350, 255 H.P.	4 Bore	4.00 × 3.48	9.0	255 @ 4600	355 @ 3000	—	30
	V8-350, 300 H.P.	4 Bore	4.00 × 3.48	10.25	300 @ 4800	380 @ 3200	—	50–65
	V8-366	4 Bore	3.937 × 3.76	8.0	235 @ 4000	345 @ 2600	4000	50–75
	V8-396	4 Bore	4.094 × 3.76	9.0	310 @ 4800	400 @ 3200	—	50–75
	V8-427	4 Bore	4.25 × 3.76	8.0	260 @ 4000	405 @ 2600	4000	50–75
	V6-401M	2 Bore	4.87 × 3.58	7.5	237 @ 4000	372 @ 1600	3400	60
	V6-478M	2 Bore	5.125 × 3.86	7.5	254 @ 3700	442 @ 1400	3200	60
1971	4-140, 90 H.P.	1 Bore	3.50 × 3.625	8.0	90 @ 4600	136 @ 2400	—	40
	4-140, 110 H.P.	2 Bore	3.50 × 3.625	8.0	110 @ 4800	138 @ 3200	—	40
	6-250, 145 H.P.	1 Bore	3.875 × 3.53	8.5	145 @ 4200	230 @ 1600	4000	40–60
	6-250, 155 H.P.	1 Bore	3.875 × 3.53	8.5	155 @ 4200	235 @ 1600	4000	40–60
	6-292, 165 H.P.	1 Bore	3.875 × 4.125	8.0	165 @ 4000	270 @ 1600	3900	40–60
	6-292, 170 H.P.	1 Bore	3.875 × 4.125	8.0	170 @ 4000	270 @ 1600	3900	40–60
	V8-307, 200 H.P.	2 Bore	3.875 × 4.25	8.5	200 @ 4600	300 @ 2400	4000	30
	V8-307, 215 H.P.	2 Bore	3.875 × 4.25	8.5	215 @ 4800	305 @ 2800	4000	30
	V8-350, 245 H.P.	2 Bore	4.00 × 3.48	8.5	245 @ 4800	350 @ 2800	4000	30
	V8-350, 255 H.P.	4 Bore	4.00 × 3.48	9.0	255 @ 4600	355 @ 3000	4000	30
	V8-350, 270 H.P.	4 Bore	4.00 × 3.48	8.5	270 @ 4800	360 @ 3200	4000	30
	V8-350, 250 H.P.	4 Bore	4.00 × 3.48	8.5	250 @ 4600	350 @ 3000	4000	30
	V8-350, 215 H.P.	2 Bore	4.00 × 3.48	8.0	215 @ 4000	335 @ 2800	4000	30
	V8-366	4 Bore	3.937 × 3.76	8.0	235 @ 4000	345 @ 2600	4000	—
	V8-400④	4 Bore	4.126 × 3.76	8.5	300 @ 4800	400 @ 3200	—	—
	V8-427	4 Bore	4.25 × 3.76	8.0	260 @ 4000	405 @ 2600	4000	—
	V8-454, 365 H.P.	4 Bore	4.251 × 4.00	8.5	365 @ 4800	465 @ 3200	—	—

Continued

CHEVROLET

GENERAL ENGINE SPECIFICATIONS—Continued

Year	Engine Model	Carb. Type	Bore & Stroke	Comp. Ratio	Horsepower @ R.P.M.	Torque Lbs. Ft. @ R.P.M.	Governed Speed R.P.M. No Load	Normal Oil Pressure Lbs.
	V8-454, 425 H.P.	4 Bore	4.251 × 4.00	9.0	425 @ 5600	475 @ 4000	—	—
	V6-478M	2 Bore	5.125 × 3.86	7.5	254 @ 3700	442 @ 1400	3200	60
	V8-637	2 Bore	5.125 × 3.86	7.5	275 @ 2800	600 @ 1600	2800	60
1972	4-140, 80 H.P.③	1 Bore	3.50 × 3.625	8.0	80 @ 4400	121 @ 2800	—	40
	4-140, 90 H.P.③	2 Bore	3.50 × 3.625	8.0	90 @ 4800	121 @ 3200	—	40
	6-250③	1 Bore	3.875 × 3.53	8.5	110 @ 3800	185 @ 1600	4000	40–60
	6-292, 125 H.P.③	1 Bore	3.87 × 4.12	8.0	125 @ 3600	225 @ 2400	3900	40–60
	6-292, 135 H.P.③	1 Bore	3.87 × 4.12	8.0	135 @ 3800	240 @ 2000	3900	40–60
	V8-307, 130 H.P.③	2 Bore	3.875 × 3.25	8.5	130 @ 4000	230 @ 2400	—	30
	V8-307, 135 H.P.③	2 Bore	3.875 × 3.25	8.5	135 @ 4000	230 @ 2400	—	30
	V8-350, 155 H.P.③	2 Bore	4.00 × 3.48	8.0	155 @ 4000	265 @ 2400	4000	50–65
	V8-350, 165 H.P.③	2 Bore	4.00 × 3.48	8.5	165 @ 4000	280 @ 2400	—	50–65
	V8-350, 175 H.P.③	4 Bore	4.00 × 3.48	8.5	175 @ 4000	280 @ 2400	—	50–65
	V8-366③	4 Bore	3.937 × 3.76	8.0	200 @ 4000	295 @ 2800	4000	40–55
	V8-400, 210 H.P.③④	4 Bore	4.126 × 3.76	8.5	210 @ 4000	320 @ 2800	—	45–55
	V8-400, 240 H.P.③④	4 Bore	4.126 × 3.76	8.5	240 @ 4400	345 @ 3200	—	40
	V8-427③	4 Bore	4.25 × 3.76	8.0	230 @ 4000	360 @ 2400	4000	40–55
	V8-454③	4 Bore	4.251 × 4.00	8.5	270 @ 4000	390 @ 3200	—	40
	V6-401③	2 Bore	4.87 × 3.58	7.5	175 @ 3400	298 @ 1600	3400	60
	V6-478③	2 Bore	5.125 × 3.86	7.5	192 @ 3200	371 @ 1400	3200	60
	V8-637③	2 Bore	5.125 × 3.86	7.5	219 @ 2800	478 @ 1600	2800	60
1973	4-140, 72 H.P.③	1 Bore	3.50 × 3.62	8.0	72 @ 4400	100 @ 2000	—	40
	4-140, 85 H.P.③	2 Bore	3.50 × 3.62	8.0	85 @ 4800	115 @ 2400	—	40
	6-250③	1 Bore	3.87 × 3.53	8.25	100 @ 3600	175 @ 1600	—	40–60
	6-250③	1 Bore	3.87 × 3.53	8.5	100 @ 3600	175 @ 2000	—	40–60
	6-292③	1 Bore	3.87 × 4.12	8.0	120 @ 3600	215 @ 2000	—	40–60
	6-292③	1 Bore	3.87 × 4.12	8.0	130 @ 3600	225 @ 2000	—	40–60
	V6-305C③	2 Bore	4.250 × 3.58	7.75	148 @ 4000	238 @ 1600	—	57
	V6-305③	2 Bore	4.25 × 3.58	7.75	148 @ 4000	238 @ 1600	—	57
	V8-307③	2 Bore	3.87 × 3.25	8.5	115 @ 3600	205 @ 2000	—	30
	V8-307③	2 Bore	3.87 × 3.25	8.5	130 @ 4000	220 @ 2000	—	30
	V8-350③	2 Bore	4.00 × 3.48	8.5	145 @ 4000	255 @ 2400	—	40
	V8-350③	4 Bore	4.00 × 3.48	8.5	175 @ 4000	260 @ 2800	—	40
	V8-350③	4 Bore	4.00 × 3.48	8.5	155 @ 4000	255 @ 2400	—	40
	V8-350③	2 Bore	4.00 × 3.48	8.0	160 @ 4000	265 @ 2400	—	30
	V8-366③	4 Bore	3.937 × 3.76	8.0	200 @ 4000	310 @ 2800	—	40–55
	V6-379③	2 Bore	3.562 × 3.86	7.5	170 @ 3600	280 @ 1600	—	57
	V8-427③	4 Bore	4.25 × 3.76	8.0	230 @ 4000	360 @ 2800	—	40–55
	V6-432③	2 Bore	4.875 × 3.86	7.5	190 @ 3200	331 @ 1600	—	60
	V8-454③	4 Bore	4.25 × 4.00	8.25	245 @ 4000	375 @ 2800	—	40
	V8-454③	4 Bore	4.25 × 4.00	8.25	240 @ 4000	355 @ 2800	—	40
	V8-454③	4 Bore	4.25 × 4.00	8.25	250 @ 4000	365 @ 2800	—	40
	V6-478③	2 Bore	5.125 × 3.86	7.0	192 @ 3200	371 @ 1400	—	60
	V8-637③	2 Bore	5.125 × 3.86	—	—	—	—	—
1974	4-140③	2 Bore	3.50 × 3.62	8.2	75 @ 5000	88 @ 3000	—	64
	4-140③	1 Bore	3.50 × 3.62	8.0	75 @ 4400	115 @ 2400	—	40
	4-140③	2 Bore	3.50 × 3.62	8.0	85 @ 4400	122 @ 2400	—	40
	6-250③	1 Bore	3.87 × 3.53	8.25	100 @ 3600	175 @ 1800	—	40–60
	6-292③	1 Bore	3.87 × 4.12	8.0	120 @ 3600	215 @ 2000	—	40–60
	V6-305C③	2 Bore	4.250 × 3.58	—	148 @ 4000	238 @ 1600	—	57
	V8-350③	2 Bore	4.00 × 3.48	8.5	145 @ 3800	250 @ 2200	—	40
	V8-350③	4 Bore	4.00 × 3.48	8.5	160 @ 3800	255 @ 2400	—	40
	V8-350③	4 Bore	4.00 × 3.48	8.5	160 @ 3800	245 @ 2400	—	40

Continued

CHEVROLET

GENERAL ENGINE SPECIFICATIONS—Continued

Year	Engine Model	Carb. Type	Bore & Stroke	Comp. Ratio	Horsepower @ R.P.M.	Torque Lbs. Ft. @ R.P.M.	Governed Speed R.P.M. No Load	Normal Oil Pressure Lbs.
	V8-366③	4 Bore	3.937 × 3.76	—	200 @ 4000	310 @ 2800	—	40–55
	V6-379③	2 Bore	3.562 × 3.86	—	170 @ 3600	280 @ 1600	—	57
	V8-400③	2 Bore	4.126 × 3.76	8.5	150 @ 3200	290 @ 2000	—	40
	V8-400③	4 Bore	4.126 × 3.76	8.5	180 @ 3800	290 @ 2400	—	40
	V6-432③	2 Bore	4.875 × 3.86	—	190 @ 3200	331 @ 1600	—	60
	V8-427③	4 Bore	4.25 × 3.76	—	230 @ 4000	360 @ 2800	—	40–55
	V8-454③	4 Bore	4.25 × 4.00	8.25	230 @ 4000	350 @ 2800	—	40
	V8-454③	4 Bore	4.25 × 4.00	8.25	245 @ 4000	365 @ 2800	—	40
	V8-454③	4 Bore	4.25 × 4.00	8.25	235 @ 4000	360 @ 2800	—	40
	V6-478③	2 Bore	5.125 × 3.86	—	192 @ 3200	371 @ 1400	—	60
1975	4-140③	1 Bore	3.50 × 3.625	8.0	78 @ 4200	120 @ 2000	—	40
	4-140③	2 Bore	3.50 × 3.625	8.0	87 @ 4400	122 @ 2800	—	40
	4-140③⑤	2 Bore	3.50 × 3.625	8.0	80 @ 4400	116 @ 2800	—	40
	6-250③⑥	1 Bore	3.87 × 3.53	8.25	105 @ 3800	185 @ 1200	—	40–60
	6-250③⑥	1 Bore	3.87 × 3.53	8.25	100 @ 3600	175 @ 1800	—	40–60
	6-292③	1 Bore	3.875 × 4.12	8.0	120 @ 3600	215 @ 2000	—	40–60
	6-292③	1 Bore	3.875 × 4.12	8.0	130 @ 3600	225 @ 2000	4000	40–60
	V8-350③	2 Bore	4.00 × 3.48	8.5	145 @ 3800	250 @ 2200	—	40
	V8-350③	4 Bore	4.00 × 3.48	8.5	160 @ 3800	250 @ 2400	—	40
	V8-350③	4 Bore	4.00 × 3.48	8.5	160 @ 4000	265 @ 2400	—	40
	V8-366③	4 Bore	3.937 × 3.76	8.0	195 @ 4000	290 @ 2800	4000	40–55
	V8-366③	4 Bore	3.937 × 3.76	8.0	200 @ 4000	305 @ 2800	4000	40–55
	V8-400③	4 Bore	4.126 × 3.76	8.5	175 @ 3600	290 @ 2800	—	40
	V8-427③	4 Bore	4.25 × 3.76	7.8	220 @ 4000	360 @ 2400	4000	40–55
	V8-455③	4 Bore	4.25 × 4.00	8.15	215 @ 4000	350 @ 2400	—	40
	V8-455③	4 Bore	4.25 × 4.00	8.15	245 @ 4000	355 @ 3000	—	40
	V8-454 Calif. H.D.③	4 Bore	4.25 × 4.00	8.15	245 @ 4000	375 @ 2800	—	40
1976	6-250③⑧	1 Bore	3.875 × 3.53	8.25	100 @ 3600	175 @ 1800	—	40–60
	6-250③⑨	1 Bore	3.875 × 3.53	8.25	105 @ 3800	185 @ 1200	—	40–60
	6-292③	1 Bore	3.87 × 4.12	8.0	120 @ 3600	215 @ 2000	—	40–60
	V8-350③	2 Bore	4.0 × 3.48	8.5	145 @ 3800	250 @ 2200	—	40
	8-350③⑦	2 Bore	4.0 × 3.48	8	160 @ 4000	265 @ 2400	—	30
	V8-350③	4 Bore	4.0 × 3.48	8.5	165 @ 3800	260 @ 2400	—	40
	V8-350③⑩	4 Bore	4.0 × 3.48	8.5	165 @ 3800	255 @ 2800	—	40
	8-366③⑦	4 Bore	3.937 × 3.76	8	195 @ 4000	290 @ 2800	—	40–55
	V8-400③⑪	4 Bore	4.125 × 3.75	8.5	175 @ 3600	290 @ 2800	—	40
	V8-400③⑫	4 Bore	4.125 × 3.75	8.5	175 @ 3600	305 @ 2000	—	40
	8-427③⑦	4 Bore	4.25 × 3.76	8	220 @ 4000	360 @ 2400	—	40–55
	V8-454③⑨	4 Bore	4.251 × 4.0	8.25	245 @ 3800	365 @ 2800	—	40
	V8-454③⑧	4 Bore	4.251 × 4.0	8.15	240 @ 3800	370 @ 2800	—	40
	V8-454 Calif.③	4 Bore	4.251 × 4.0	8.15	250 @ 3800	385 @ 2800	—	40
1977	6-250③⑤⑫	1 Bore	3.87 × 3.53	8.25	90 @ 3600	180 @ 1600	—	40–60
	6-250③⑫⑬	1 Bore	3.87 × 3.53	—	110 @ 3800	195 @ 1600	—	40–60
	6-250③⑧	1 Bore	3.87 × 3.53	8.25	100 @ 3600	175 @ 1800	—	40–60
	6-250③⑨	1 Bore	3.87 × 3.53	8.25	110 @ 3800	195 @ 1600	—	40–60
	6-292③⑧	1 Bore	3.87 × 4.12	8	120 @ 3600	215 @ 2000	—	40–60
	6-292③⑦	1 Bore	3.87 × 4.12	8	130 @ 3600	225 @ 2000	—	40–60
	V8-305③⑨	2 Bore	3.74 × 3.48	8.5	145 @ 3800	245 @ 2400	—	40
	V8-305③⑧	2 Bore	3.74 × 3.48	8.5	140 @ 3800	235 @ 2000	—	40
	V8-350③⑦	2 Bore	4.00 × 3.48	8	160 @ 4000	265 @ 2400	—	30
	V8-350③⑨⑬	4 Bore	4.00 × 3.48	8.5	165 @ 3800	260 @ 2400	—	40
	V8-350③⑧	4 Bore	4.00 × 3.48	8.5	165 @ 3800	255 @ 2800	—	40
	V8-350③⑤	4 Bore	4.00 × 3.48	8.5	160 @ 3800	260 @ 2400	—	40

Continued

CHEVROLET

GENERAL ENGINE SPECIFICATIONS—Continued

Year	Engine Model	Carb. Type	Bore & Stroke	Comp. Ratio	Horsepower @ R.P.M.	Torque Lbs. Ft. @ R.P.M.	Governed Speed R.P.M. No Load	Normal Oil Pressure Lbs.
	V8-366③⑭	4 Bore	3.937 × 3.76	8	200 @ 4000	305 @ 2800	—	40–55
	V8-366③⑮	4 Bore	3.937 × 3.76	8	195 @ 4000	290 @ 2800	—	40–55
	V8-400③	4 Bore	4.125 × 3.75	8.5	175 @ 3600	290 @ 2800	—	40
	V8-427③	4 Bore	4.25 × 3.76	8	220 @ 4000	360 @ 2400	—	40–55
	V8-454③⑨	4 Bore	4.25 × 4.00	8.15	245 @ 3800	365 @ 2800	—	40
	V8-454③⑧⑬	4 Bore	4.25 × 4.00	8.15	240 @ 3800	370 @ 2800	—	40
	V8-454③⑤	4 Bore	4.25 × 4.00	8.15	250 @ 3800	385 @ 2800	—	40
1978	V6-200③⑤	2 Bore	3.5 × 3.48	8.2	105 @ 3800	180 @ 2000	—	40–60
	V6-200③⑬	2 Bore	3.5 × 3.48	8.2	95 @ 3800	160 @ 2000	—	40–60
	V6-231③	2 Bore	3.80 × 3.40	8.0	105 @ 3400	185 @ 2000	—	37
	6-250③⑧⑬	1 Bore	3.87 × 3.53	8.2	100 @ 3600	175 @ 1800	—	40–60
	6-250③⑨⑬	1 Bore	3.87 × 3.53	8.2	115 @ 3800	195 @ 1800	—	40–60
	6-250③⑯	1 Bore	3.87 × 3.53	8.2	100 @ 3800	185 @ 1600	—	40–60
	6-292③⑪	1 Bore	3.87 × 4.12	8.1	120 @ 3600	215 @ 2000	—	40–60
	6-292③㉗	1 Bore	3.87 × 4.12	8.0	130 @ 3600	225 @ 2000	—	40–60
	V8-305③⑫⑬	2 Bore	3.74 × 3.48	8.5	145 @ 3800	245 @ 2400	—	40
	V8-305③⑤⑫	2 Bore	3.74 × 3.48	8.5	135 @ 3800	240 @ 2000	—	40
	V8-305③⑨①	2 Bore	3.74 × 3.48	8.5	140 @ 3800	235 @ 2000	—	40
	V8-305③⑧⑰	2 Bore	3.74 × 3.48	8.5	145 @ 3800	245 @ 2400	—	40
	V8-350③㉗	2 Bore	4.00 × 3.48	8.0	160 @ 4000	265 @ 2400	—	30
	V8-350③⑨⑬	4 Bore	4.00 × 3.48	8.5	165 @ 3800	260 @ 2400	—	40
	V8-350③⑧⑬	4 Bore	4.00 × 3.48	8.5	165 @ 3800	255 @ 2800	—	40
	V8-350③⑯	4 Bore	4.00 × 3.48	8.5	155 @ 3800	250 @ 2400	—	40
	V8-350③	4 Bore	4.00 × 3.48	8.2	170 @ 3800	270 @ 2400	—	40
	V8-350③⑤	4 Bore	4.00 × 3.48	8.2	160 @ 3800	260 @ 2400	—	40
	V8-366③㉗	4 Bore	3.937 × 3.76	8.0	200 @ 4000	305 @ 2800	—	40–55
	V8-400③⑧⑬	4 Bore	4.125 × 3.75	8.5	175 @ 3600	290 @ 2800	—	40
	V8-400③⑨⑬	4 Bore	4.125 × 3.75	8.5	165 @ 3600	290 @ 2000	—	40
	V8-427	4 Bore	4.25 × 3.76	8.0	220 @ 4000	360 @ 2400	—	40–55
	V8-454③⑨⑬	4 Bore	4.25 × 4.00	8.15	205 @ 3600	335 @ 2800	—	40
	V8-454③⑧⑬	4 Bore	4.25 × 4.00	8.15	240 @ 3800	370 @ 2800	—	40
	V8-454③⑯⑤	4 Bore	4.25 × 4.00	8.15	205 @ 3600	335 @ 2400	—	40
	V8-454③	4 Bore	4.25 × 4.00	8.15	250 @ 3800	385 @ 2800	—	40
1979	V6-200③	2 Bore	3.5 × 3.48	8.2	94 @ 4000	154 @ 2000	—	40–60
	V6-231③	2 Bore	3.80 × 3.40	8.0	115 @ 3800	190 @ 2000	—	37
	6-250③⑬	2 Bore	3.87 × 3.53	8.1	130 @ 3800	210 @ 2400	—	40–60
	6-250③⑤⑱	2 Bore	3.87 × 3.53	8.1	125 @ 4000	205 @ 2000	—	40–60
	6-250③⑤⑲	2 Bore	3.87 × 3.53	8.1	130 @ 4000	205 @ 2000	—	40–60
	6-292③⑪	1 Bore	3.87 × 4.12	8.1	115 @ 3400	215 @ 1600	—	40
	6-292③㉘	1 Bore	3.87 × 4.12	7.8	120 @ 3600	215 @ 2000	—	40–60
	6-292③㉙	1 Bore	3.87 × 4.12	7.8	125 @ 3600	225 @ 1600	—	40–60
	V8-267③	2 Bore	3.5 × 3.48	8.2	125 @ 3800	215 @ 2400	—	45
	V8-305③⑫⑬	4 Bore	3.74 × 3.48	8.4	160 @ 4000	235 @ 2400	—	40
	V8-305③⑤⑫	2 Bore	3.74 × 3.48	8.4	155 @ 4000	225 @ 2400	—	40
	V8-305③⑬⑯	2 Bore	3.74 × 3.48	8.4	140 @ 4000	240 @ 2000	—	40
	V8-350③㉗	2 Bore	4.00 × 3.48	8.0	160 @ 3600	275 @ 2400	—	30
	V8-350③⑳	4 Bore	4.00 × 3.48	8.2	165 @ 3800	255 @ 2800	—	40
	V8-350③⑤㉑	4 Bore	4.00 × 3.48	8.2	155 @ 3600	260 @ 2000	—	40
	V8-350③⑬㉑	4 Bore	4.00 × 3.48	8.2	165 @ 3600	270 @ 2000	—	40
	V8-350③⑬㉒	4 Bore	4.00 × 3.48	8.2	165 @ 3600	270 @ 2000	—	40
	V8-350③㉒㉓	4 Bore	4.00 × 3.48	8.2	155 @ 3600	260 @ 2000	—	40
	V8-366③⑮	4 Bore	3.937 × 3.76	7.6	180 @ 4000	290 @ 2400	—	40–55
	V8-366③⑭	4 Bore	3.937 × 3.76	7.6	190 @ 4000	305 @ 2400	—	40–55

Continued

CHEVROLET

GENERAL ENGINE SPECIFICATIONS—Continued

Year	Engine Model	Carb. Type	Bore & Stroke	Comp. Ratio	Horsepower @ R.P.M.	Torque Lbs. Ft. @ R.P.M.	Governed Speed R.P.M. No Load	Normal Oil Pressure Lbs.
	V8-427③	4 Bore	4.25 × 3.76	7.5	220 @ 4000	360 @ 2400	—	40–55
	V8-454③㉖	4 Bore	4.25 × 4.00	8.0	205 @ 3600	335 @ 2800	—	40
	V8-454③㉕	4 Bore	4.25 × 4.00	7.9	210 @ 3800	340 @ 2800	—	40
	V8-454③㉗	4 Bore	4.25 × 4.00	7.6	245 @ 4000	380 @ 2500	—	40–55
1980	V6-229③	2 Bore	3.736 × 3.48	8.6	115 @ 4000	175 @ 2000	—	45
	V6-231③	2 Bore	3.80 × 3.48	8.0	110 @ 3800	190 @ 1600	—	45
	6-250	2 Bore	3.87 × 3.53	—	—	—	—	—
	V8-267③	2 Bore	3.50 × 3.48	8.3	120 @ 3600	215 @ 2000	—	45
	6-292㉘	1 Bore	3.88 × 4.12	7.8	115 @ 3400	215 @ 1600	—	40–60
	6-292㉙	1 Bore	3.88 × 4.12	7.8	125 @ 3600	225 @ 1600	—	40–60
	V8-305③⑬	4 Bore	3.74 × 3.48	8.6	155 @ 4000	240 @ 1600	—	45
	V8-305③⑤	4 Bore	3.74 × 3.48	8.6	155 @ 4000	230 @ 2400	—	45
	V8-350③㉗	2 Bore	4.0 × 3.48	8.0	161 @ 3800	275 @ 2400	4000	30
	V8-366③②⑮	4 Bore	3.937 × 3.76	7.6	180 @ 4000	290 @ 2400	4000	40–55
	V8-366③㉗⑭	4 Bore	3.937 × 3.76	7.6	190 @ 4000	305 @ 2400	4000	40–55
	V8-427③⑮	4 Bore	4.25 × 3.76	7.5	195 @ 3800	340 @ 2400	4000	40–55
	V8-427③⑭	4 Bore	4.25 × 3.76	7.5	210 @ 3800	350 @ 2400	4000	40–55
	V8-454③	4 Bore	4.25 × 4.00	7.6	225 @ 4000	365 @ 2400	4000	40–55
	V8-454③⑤㉔	4 Bore	4.25 × 4.00	—	250 @ 3800	385 @ 2800	—	40
	V8-454③⑬㉔	4 Bore	4.25 × 4.00	—	240 @ 3800	370 @ 2800	—	40
	V8-454③㉕	4 Bore	4.25 × 4.00	—	210 @ 3800	340 @ 2800	—	40
	V8-454③㉖	4 Bore	4.25 × 4.00	—	205 @ 3600	335 @ 2800	—	40

①—California only Light Medium Duty Emissions up to 8500 GVWR.
②—Bus chassis models.
③—Ratings are NET—as installed in vehicle.
④—Marketed as 400 cu. in., but actually 402 cu. in.
⑤—California.
⑥—Light Duty.
⑦—Heavy Duty.
⑧—Heavy duty emissions, GVWR 6001 lbs. & above.
⑨—Light duty emissions, GVWR 6000 lbs. & under.
⑩—Rated when GVWR is over 6000 lbs.
⑪—Series 10-30.
⑫—El Camino.
⑬—Exc. Calif.
⑭—Dual exhaust.
⑮—Single exhaust.
⑯—Exc. El Camino.
⑰—California only Heavy Duty Emissions 8501 GVWR and Above.
⑱—10 Series.
⑲—20-30 Series.
⑳—Exc. Van & Suburban models.
㉑—Suburban models.
㉒—Van models.
㉓—Calif. & Hi Alt.
㉔—Motor Home.
㉕—Step Van, FC chassis & Pick Up models with heavy duty emissions.
㉖—Suburban & Pick Up models with light duty & medium duty emissions.
㉗—Medium & heavy duty models.
㉘—P4T042 models.
㉙—C5D042 & C6D042 models.

TUNE UP SPECIFICATIONS

The following specifications are published from the latest information available. This data should be used only in the absence of a decal affixed in the engine compartment.

★ When using a timing light, disconnect vacuum hose or tube at distributor and plug opening in hose or tube so idle speed will not be affected.

● When checking compression, lowest cylinder must be within 80 percent of highest.

▲ Before removing wires from distributor cap, determine location of the No. 1 wire in cap, as distributor position may have been altered from that shown at the end of this chart.

Year & Engine	Spark Plug		Ignition Timing BTDC①★				Curb Idle Speed②		Fuel Pump Pressure
	Type	Gap	Firing Orders Fig.▲	Man. Trans.	Auto. Trans.	Location	Man. Trans.	Auto. Trans.	
1980									
V6-229	R45TS	.045	A	8°	12°	Damper	700/800	600/675D	4½–6
V6-231 Exc. Calif.	R45TSX	.060	B	—	15°	Damper	—	560/670D	3 Min.
V6-231 Calif.	R45TSX	.060	B	—	15°	Damper	—	600D	3 Min.
6-250 Exc. Calif.	R46TS	.035	C	10°	10°	Damper	450/750	450/650D	4½–6
6-250 C&G-10 Calif.	R46TS	.035	C	10°	10°	Damper	425/750	425/600D	4½–6

Continued

CHEVROLET

TUNE UP SPECIFICATIONS—Continued

The following specifications are published from the latest information available. This data should be used only in the absence of a decal affixed in the engine compartment.

★ When using a timing light, disconnect vacuum hose or tube at distributor and plug opening in hose or tube so idle speed will not be affected.

● When checking compression, lowest cylinder must be within 80 percent of highest.

▲ Before removing wires from distributor cap, determine location of the No. 1 wire in cap, as distributor position may have been altered from that shown at the end of this chart.

Year & Engine	Spark Plug Type	Gap	Firing Orders Fig.▲	Ignition Timing BTDC①★ Man. Trans.	Auto. Trans.	Location	Curb Idle Speed② Man. Trans.	Auto. Trans.	Fuel Pump Pressure
6-250 C&G-20 Calif.	R46TS	.035	C	10°	8°	Damper	425/750	425/600D	4½–6
6-292	R44T	.035	C	8°	8°	Damper	700	700N	4–5
V8-267	R45TS	.045	D	—	4°	Damper	—	500/600D	7½–9
V8-305 El Camino Exc. Calif.	R45TS	.045	D	4°	4°	Damper	700	500/600D	7½–9
V8-305 El Camino Calif.	R45TS	.045	D	—	4°	Damper	—	550/650D	7½–9
V8-305 Series 10-30	R45TS	.045	D	㊸	8°	Damper	600/700	500/600D	④
V8-350 2 Barrel Carb. B, C, P & W-4, 5, 6	R44T	.045	D	4°㊹	4°㊹	Damper	700	700N	7–9
V8-350 4 Barrel Carb.⑦	R45TS	.045	D	8°㊺	8°㊺	Damper	700	500/600D	④
V8-350 4 Barrel Carb. Exc. Calif.⑧	R44T	.045	D	4°	4°	Damper	700	700N	④
V8-350 4 Barrel Carb. Calif.⑧	R44T	.045	D	6°	6°	Damper	700	700N	④
V8-366	R43T	.045	D	8°	8°	Damper	700	700N	7–9
V8-400 G-20	R45TS	.045	D	—	4°	Damper	—	500/600D	④
V8-400 K-20 & G, K-30 Exc. Calif.	R44T	.045	D	—	4°	Damper	—	700N	④
V8-400 K-20 & G, K-30 Calif.	R44T	.045	D	—	6°	Damper	—	700N	④
V8-427	R42T	.045	D	8°	8°	Damper	700	700N	7–9
V8-454 C-20 & C, P-30	R44T	.045	D	4°	4°	Damper	700	700N	7½–9
V8-454 C7D	R42T	.045	D	8°	8°	Damper	700	700N	7–9
1979									
V6-200	R45TS	.045	A	8°	12°	Damper	700/800	600/700D	4¼–5¾
V6-231 Exc. Calif. & High Alt.	R45TSX	.060	B	—	15°	Damper	—	③	3 Min.
V6-231 Calif. & High Alt.	R45TSX	.060	B	—	15°	Damper	—	600D	3 Min.
6-250 C, G & K-10	R46TS	.035	C	10°	10°	Damper	425/750	425/600D	4½–6
6-250 C-20 & G-20, 30 Exc. Calif.	R46TS	.035	C	10°	10°	Damper	425/750	425/600D	4½–6
6-250 C-20 & G-20, 30 Calif.	R46TS	.035	C	6°	8°	Damper	425/750	425/600D	4½–6
6-292	R44T	.035	C	8°	8°	Damper	700	700N	4½–6
V8-267	R45TS	.045	D	4°	8°	Damper	600/700	500/600D	7½–9
V8-305 Exc. High Alt.⑤	R45TS	.045	D	4°	4°	Damper	700	500/600D	7½–9
V8-305 High Alt.	R45TS	.045	D	—	8°	Damper	—	600/650D	7½–9
V8-305 C, G, K-10 & C-20	R45TS	.045	D	6°	6°	Damper	600/700	500/600D	④
V8-350 2 Barrel Carb. B, C, P & W-4, 5, 6	R44T	.045	D	4°	4°	Damper	700	700N	—
V8-350 4 Barrel Carb.⑤	R45TS	.045	D	—	8°	Damper	—	600/650D	7½–9
V8-350 4 Barrel Carb.⑦	R45TS	.045	D	8°	8°	Damper	700	500/600D	④
V8-350 4 Barrel Carb.⑧	R44T	.045	D	4°	4°	Damper	700	700N	④
V8-366	R43T	.045	D	—	4°	Damper	700	700N	6
V8-400 K-10, 20 & C-20, 30	R45TS	.045	D	—	4°	Damper	—	500/600D	④
V8-400 G, K-30	R44T	.045	D	4°	4°	Damper	700	700N	④
V8-427	R42T	.045	D	8°	8°	Damper	700	700N	6

Continued

817

CHEVROLET

TUNE UP SPECIFICATIONS—Continued

The following specifications are published from the latest information available. This data should be used only in the absence of a decal affixed in the engine compartment.

★ When using a timing light, disconnect vacuum hose or tube at distributor and plug opening in hose or tube so idle speed will not be affected.

● When checking compression, lowest cylinder must be within 80 percent of highest.

▲ Before removing wires from distributor cap, determine location of the No. 1 wire in cap, as distributor position may have been altered from that shown at the end of this chart.

Year & Engine	Spark Plug Type	Spark Plug Gap	Firing Order Fig.▲	Ignition Timing BTDC①★ Man. Trans.	Ignition Timing BTDC①★ Auto. Trans.	Location	Curb Idle Speed② Man. Trans.	Curb Idle Speed② Auto. Trans.	Fuel Pump Pressure
V8-454⑦	R45TS	.045	D	8°	8°	Damper	700	550/600D	7½–9
V8-454⑧	R44T	.045	D	4°	4°	Damper	700	700N	7½–9
V8-454 C-7D	R42T	.045	D	8°	8°	Damper	700	700N	6
1978									
V6-200	R45TS	.045	A	8°	8°	Damper	700	600D	4¼–5¾
V6-231	R46TSX	.060	B	15°	15°	Damper	600/800	600/670D	3 Min.
6-250 Exc. Calif. & High Alt.⑦	R46TS	.035	C	8°	8°	Damper	425/750	⑨	4–5
6-250 Calif.⑦	R46TS	.035	C	8°	10°	Damper	425/750	425/600D	4–5
6-250 High Alt.⑦	R46TS	.035	C	8°	12°	Damper	425/750	425/600D	4–5
6-250⑧	R46T	.035	C	6°	6°	Damper	450/600	450/600N	4–5
6-292⑧	R44T	.035	C	8°	8°	Damper	450/600	450/600N	4–5
6-292⑥	R44T	.035	C	8°	8°	Damper	600	600N	4–5
V8-305 Exc. Calif.⑤⑦	R45TS	.035	D	4°	4°	Damper	600	500D	7½–9
V8-305 Calif.⑤	R45TS	.035	D	—	6°	Damper	—	500/600D	7½–9
V8-305⑧	R44T	.045	D	6°	6°	Damper	700	700N	7½–9
V8-350 2 Barrel Carb.⑥	R44T	⑩	D	4°	4°	Damper	600	700N	7½–9
V8-350 4 Barrel Carb.⑤⑪	R45TS	.045	D	6°	6°	Damper	700	500/600D	7½–9
V8-350 4 Barrel Carb. Calif.⑤	R45TS	.045	D	—	8°	Damper	—	500/650D	7½–9
V8-350 4 Barrel Carb. High Alt.⑤	R45TS	.045	D	—	8°	Damper	—	500/600D	7½–9
V8-350 4 Barrel Carb.⑦	R45TS	.045	D	8°	8°	Damper	⑫	500/600D	7½–9
V8-350 4 Barrel Carb. Exc. Calif.⑧	R44T	.045	D	8°	8°	Damper	700	700N	7½–9
V8-350 4 Barrel Carb. Calif.⑧	R44TX	.060	D	2°	2°	Damper	700	700N	7½–9
V8-366 Exc. Calif.	R43T	.045	D	8°	8°	Damper	700	700N	8¼
V8-366 Calif.	R43TX	.060	D	8°	8°	Damper	700	700N	8¼
V8-400 Exc. Calif.⑧	R44T	.045	D	4°	4°	Damper	700	700N	7½–9
V8-400 Calif.⑧	R44T	.045	D	2°	2°	Damper	700	700N	7½–9
V8-400 Calif.⑦	R45TS	.045	D	—	4°	Damper	—	500/600D	7½–9
V8-427 Exc. Calif.	R42T	.045	D	8°	8°	Damper	700	700N	8¼
V8-427 Calif.	R42TX	.060	D	8°	8°	Damper	700	700N	8¼
V8-454⑦	R45TS	.045	D	8°	8°	Damper	700	500/600D	7½–9
V8-454⑧	R44T	.045	D	8°	8°	Damper	700	700N	7½–9
1977									
6-250 Exc. Calif. & High Alt.⑤	R46TS	.035	C	6°	8°	Damper	⑬	⑨	4–5
6-250 Calif.⑤	R46TS	.035	C	—	6°	Damper	—	425/550D	4–5
6-250 High Alt.⑤	R46TS	.035	C	—	10°	Damper	—	425/600D	4–5
6-250 Exc. Calif. & High Alt.⑦	R46TS	.035	C	8°	12°	Damper	425/750	⑨	4–5
6-250 Calif.⑦	R46TS	.035	C	6°	10°	Damper	425/850	425/600D	4–5
6-250 High Alt.⑦	R46TS	.035	C	—	12°	Damper	—	425/600D	4–5
6-250⑧	R46T	.035	C	6°	6°	Damper	450/600	450/600N	4–5
6-292 Series 10-30	R44T	.035	C	8°	8°	Damper	450/600	450/600N	4–5

Continued

CHEVROLET

TUNE UP SPECIFICATIONS—Continued

The following specifications are published from the latest information available. This data should be used only in the absence of a decal affixed in the engine compartment.

★ When using a timing light, disconnect vacuum hose or tube at distributor and plug opening in hose or tube so idle speed will not be affected.

● When checking compression, lowest cylinder must be within 80 percent of highest.

▲ Before removing wires from distributor cap, determine location of the No. 1 wire in cap, as distributor position may have been altered from that shown at the end of this chart.

Year & Engine	Spark Plug Type	Spark Plug Gap	Firing Order Fig. ▲	Ignition Timing BTDC①★ Man. Trans.	Ignition Timing BTDC①★ Auto Trans.	Location	Curb Idle Speed② Man. Trans.	Curb Idle Speed② Auto. Trans.	Fuel Pump Pressure
6-292 Series 40-60	R44T	.035	C	8°	8°	Damper	600	600N	4½–5½
V8-305 Exc. Calif.⑤⑦	R45TS	.045	D	8°	8°	Damper	600/700	500/650D	7½–9
V8-305 Exc. Calif.⑧	R44T	.045	D	6°	6°	Damper	700	700N	7½–9
V8-350 2 Barrel Carb.⑥	R44T	.035	D	4°	4°	Damper	600	600N	7½–9
V8-350 4 Barrel Carb.⑤	R45TS	.045	D	—	8°	Damper	—	⑭	7½–9
V8-350 4 Barrel Carb.⑦⑪	R45TS	.045	D	8°	8°	Damper	700	500/650D	7½–9
V8-350 4 Barrel Carb. Calif.⑦	R45TS	.045	D	6°	6°	Damper	700	500/650D	7½–9
V8-350 4 Barrel Carb. High Alt.⑦	R45TS	.045	D	—	6°	Damper	—	600/650D	7½–9
V8-350 4 Barrel Carb. Exc. Calif.⑧	R44T	.045	D	8°	8°	Damper	700	700N	7½–9
V8-350 4 Barrel Carb. Calif.⑧	R44TX	.060	D	2°	2°	Damper	700	700N	7½–9
V8-366 Exc. Calif.	R43T	.045	D	8°	8°	Damper	700	700N	7½–9
V8-366 Calif.	R43TX	.060	D	8°	8°	Damper	700	700N	7½–9
V8-400 Exc. Calif.⑧	R44T	.045	D	—	4°	Damper	700	700N	7½–9
V8-400 Calif.⑧	R44T	.045	D	—	2°	Damper	700	700N	7½–9
V8-427 Exc. Calif.	R42T	.035	D	8°	8°	Damper	700	700N	7½–9
V8-427 Calif.	R42TX	.060	D	8°	8°	Damper	700	700N	7½–9
V8-454⑦	R45TS	.045	D	—	4°	Damper	—	600D	7½–9
V8-454⑧	R44T	.045	D	8°	8°	Damper	700	700N	7½–9
1976									
6-250⑤	R46TS	.035	C	6°	6°	Damper	425/850	⑮	3½–4½
6-250 Exc. Calif.⑦	R46TS	.035	C	⑯	10°	Damper	425/900	425/550D	3½–4½
6-250 Calif.⑦	R46TS	.035	C	6°	10°	Damper	425/1000	425/600D	3½–4½
6-292 Series 10-30	R44T	.035	C	8°	8°	Damper	450/600	450/600N	4–5
6-292 Series 40-60 Less H.E.I.⑰	R44T	.035	E	8°	8°	Damper	800	600D	4–5
6-292 Series 40-60 w/H.E.I.	R44T	.035	C	8°	8°	Damper	800	600D	4–5
V8-305 El Camino	R45TS	.045	D	6°	8°	Damper	800	600D	7–8½
V8-305 Series 10-20	R44T	.045	D	6°	6°	Damper	800	600D	7–8½
V8-350 2 Barrel Carb.⑤⑦	R45TS	.045	D	2°	6°	Damper	800	600D	7–8½
V8-350 2 Barrel Carb. Less H.E.I.⑥⑱	R44T	.035	F	4°	4°	Damper	600	600N	7½–9
V8-350 2 Barrel Carb. w/H.E.I.⑥	R44T	.035	D	4°	4°	Damper	600	600N	7½–9
V8-350 4 Barrel Carb. Exc. Calif.⑤⑦	R45TS	.045	D	8°	8°	Damper	800	600D	7–8½
V8-350 4 Barrel Carb. Calif.⑤⑦	R45TS	.045	D	6°	6°	Damper	800	600D	7–8½
V8-350 4 Barrel Carb. Exc. Calif.⑧	R44TX	.060	D	8°	8°	Damper	700	700N	7–8½
V8-350 4 Barrel Carb. Calif.⑧	R44TX	.060	D	2°	2°	Damper	700	700N	7–8½
V8-366 Exc. Calif. Less H.E.I.⑱	R43T⑲	.035	F	8°	8°	Damper	700	700N	7½–9

Continued

819

TUNE UP SPECIFICATIONS—Continued

The following specifications are published from the latest information available. This data should be used only in the absence of a decal affixed in the engine compartment.

★ When using a timing light, disconnect vacuum hose or tube at distributor and plug opening in hose or tube so idle speed will not be affected.

● When checking compression, lowest cylinder must be within 80 percent of highest.

▲ Before removing wires from distributor cap, determine location of the No. 1 wire in cap, as distributor position may have been altered from that shown at the end of this chart.

Year & Engine	Spark Plug		Ignition Timing BTDC①★				Curb Idle Speed②		Fuel Pump Pressure
	Type	Gap	Firing Order Fig.▲	Man. Trans.	Auto Trans.	Location	Man. Trans.	Auto. Trans.	
V8-366 Exc. Calif. w/H.E.I.	R43T⑲	.035	D	8°	8°	Damper	700	700N	7½–9
V8-366 Calif.	R43TX⑳	.060	D	8°	8°	Damper	700	700N	7½–9
V8-400⑤	R45TS	.045	D	—	8°	Damper	—	600D	7–8½
V8-400⑧	R44TX	.060	D	—	4°	Damper	—	700N	7–8½
V8-427 Exc. Calif. Less H.E.I.⑱	R42T㉑	.035	F	8°	8°	Damper	700	700N	7½–9
V8-427 Exc. Calif. w/H.E.I.	R42T㉑	.035	D	8°	8°	Damper	700	700N	7½–9
V8-427 Calif.	R42TX㉒	.060	D	8°	8°	Damper	700	700N	7½–9
V8-454⑦	R45TS	.045	D	—	㉓	Damper	—	600D	7–8½
V8-454⑧	R44T	.045	D	8°	8°	Damper	700	700N	7–8½
1975									
4-140 1 Barrel Carb.	R43TSX	.060	G	8°	10°	Damper	700/1200	550/750D	3–4½
4-140 2 Barrel Carb.	R43TSX㉔	.060	G	10°	12°	Damper	㉕	600/750D	3–4½
6-250 Exc. Calif.⑤	R46TX	.060	C	10°	10°	Damper	425/850	425/550D	3½–4½
6-250 Calif.⑤	R46TX	.060	C	—	10°	Damper	—	425/600D	3½–4½
6-250 Series 10-30	R46TX	.060	C	10°	10°	Damper	425/900	425/550D	3½–4½
6-292 Series 10-30	R44TX	.060	C	8°	8°	Damper	450/600	450/600N	3½–4½
6-292 Series 40-60⑰	R44T	.035	E	8°	8°	Damper	600	600N	4–5
V8-350 2 Barrel Carb.⑤⑦	R44TX	.060	D	6°	6°	Damper	800	600D	7–8½
V8-350 2 Barrel Carb.⑥⑱	R44T	.035	F	4°	4°	Damper	㉖	550N	7½–9
V8-350 4 Barrel Carb.⑤⑦	R44TX	.060	D	6°	㉗	Damper	800	600D	7–8½
V8-350 4 Barrel Carb. Exc. Calif.⑧	R44TX	.060	D	8°	8°	Damper	600	600N	7–8½
V8-350 4 Barrel Carb. Calif.⑧	R44TX	.060	D	2°	2°	Damper	700	700N	7–8½
V8-366 Exc. Calif.⑱	R43T⑲	.035	F	8°	8°	Damper	700	700N	7½–9
V8-366 Calif.	R43TX	.060	D	8°	8°	Damper	700	700N	7½–9
V8-400 El Camino	R44TX	.060	D	—	8°	Damper	—	600D	7–8½
V8-400 Exc. Calif.⑧	R44TX	.060	D	4°	4°	Damper	700	700N	7–8½
V8-400 Calif.⑧	R44TX	.060	D	2°	2°	Damper	700	700N	7–8½
V8-427 Exc. Calif.⑱	R42T⑲	.035	F	8°	8°	Damper	700	700N	7–9½
V8-427 Calif.	R42TX	.060	D	8°	8°	Damper	700	700N	7–9½
V8-454 Exc. Calif.⑤⑦	R44TX	.060	D	—	16°	Damper	—	㉘	7–8½
V8-454 Exc. Calif.⑧	R44TX	.060	D	8°	8°	Damper	500/700	500/700N	7–8½
V8-454 Calif.⑧	R44TX	.060	D	8°	8°	Damper	600	600N	7–8½
1974									
4-140⑰	R42TS	.035	H	10°	12°	Damper	700	750D	3–4½
6-250 Light Duty⑰	R46T	.035	E	8°	8°	Damper	850	600D	4–5
6-250 Heavy Duty⑰	R46T	.035	E	6°	6°	Damper	600	600	4–5
6-292⑰	R44T	.035	E	8°	8°	Damper	600	600	4–5
V6-305C⑰	CR44NS	.035	I	7½°	7½°	Damper	600	600	5–7
V8-350, 145 H.P.⑱	R44T	.035	F	TDC	8°	Damper	900	600D	7–8½
V8-350, Light Duty⑱	R44T	.035	F	8°	8°	Damper	900	600D	7–8½
V8-350, Light Duty, Exc. El Camino⑱	R44T	.035	F	㉙	12°	Damper	900	600D	7–8⅛
V8-350, Light Duty, Calif.⑱	R44T	.035	F	4°	㉙	Damper	900	600D	7–8½

Continued

CHEVROLET

TUNE UP SPECIFICATIONS—Continued

The following specifications are published from the latest information available. This data should be used only in the absence of a decal affixed in the engine compartment.

★ When using a timing light, disconnect vacuum hose or tube at distributor and plug opening in hose or tube so idle speed will not be affected.

● When checking compression, lowest cylinder must be within 80 percent of highest.

▲ Before removing wires from distributor cap, determine location of the No. 1 wire in cap, as distributor position may have been altered from that shown at the end of this chart.

Year & Engine	Spark Plug Type	Gap	Firing Order Fig.▲	Ignition Timing BTDC①★ Man. Trans.	Auto. Trans.	Location	Curb Idle Speed② Man. Trans.	Auto. Trans.	Fuel Pump Pressure
V8-350 Heavy Duty⑱	R43T	.035	F	4°	4°	Damper	600	600	7–8½
V8-366⑱	R43T	.035	F	8°	8°	Damper	600	600	7–9
V6-379⑰	R43T	.035	I	6°	6°	Damper	575	575	5–7
V8-427⑱	R42T	.035	F	8°	8°	Damper	600	600	7–9
V6-432⑰	R43T	.035	I	6°	6°	Damper	525	525	5–7
V8-454 Light Duty⑱	R44T	.035	F	10°	10°	Damper	800	600D	7–8½
V8-454 Heavy Duty⑱	R44T	.035	F	8°	8°	Damper	700	700	7–8½
V6-478⑰	R43T	.035	I	7½°	7½°	Damper	525	525	5–6½
1973									
4-140 Exc. Calif.⑰	R42TS	.035	H	10°	12°	Damper	㉚	750D	3–4½
4-140 Calif.⑰	R42TS	.035	H	8°	8°	Damper	㉚	750D	3–4½
6-250 Light Duty⑰	R46T	.035	E	6°	6°	Damper	700	600	3½–4½
6-250 Heavy Duty⑰	R46T	.035	E	4°	4°	Damper	700	700	3½–4½
6-292 Exc. Calif.⑰	R44T	.035	E	4°	4°	Damper	700	700	3½–4½
6-292 Calif.⑰	R44T	.035	E	8°	8°	Damper	600	600	3½–4½
V6-305C⑰	CR44NS	.040	I	7½°	—	Damper	550	—	5–7
V8-307 Light Duty⑱	R44T	.035	F	4°	8°	Damper	900	600	5–6½
V8-307 Heavy Duty⑱	R44T	.035	F	TDC	TDC	Damper	600	600	5–6½
V8-350 Light Duty⑱	R44T	.035	F	㉛	12°	Damper	900	600	7–8½
V8-350 Heavy Duty⑱	R44T	.035	F	4°	4°	Damper	600	600	7–8½
V8-366 Exc. Calif.⑱	R44T	.035	F	8°	8°	Damper	550	550	7–9
V8-366 Calif.⑱	R44T	.035	F	8°	8°	Damper	750	750	7–9
V6-379⑰	R43T	.035	I	8°	—	Damper	550	—	5–7
V8-427 Exc. Calif.⑱	R44T	.035	F	8°	8°	Damper	550	550	7–9
V8-427 Calif.⑱	R44T	.035	F	8°	8°	Damper	750	750	7–9
V6-432⑰	R43T	.035	I	8°	—	Damper	575	—	5–6½
V8-454 Light Duty⑱	R44T	.035	F	10°	10°	Damper	800	600	7–8½
V8-454 Heavy Duty Exc. Calif.⑱	R44T	.035	F	10°	10°	Damper	700	700	7–8½
V8-454 Heavy Duty Calif.⑱	R44T	.035	F	5°	8°	Damper	700	700	7–8½
V6-478⑰	CR43N	.035	I	7½°	—	Damper	575	—	5–6½
V8-637⑱	CR42N	.035	J	5°	—	Damper	475	—	7½–9
1972									
4-140, 80 H.P.⑰	R42TS	.035	H	6°㉜	6°	Damper	㉝	700D	3–4½
4-140, 90 H.P.⑰	R42TS	.035	H	8°	8°	Damper	㉝	700D	3–4½
6-250⑰	R44T	.035	E	4°㉞	4°㉞	Damper	700	600D	3½–4½
6-292⑰	R44T	.035	E	4°	4°	Damper	550	500D	3½–4½
V8-307⑱	R44T	.035	F	4°	㉟	Damper	㊱	600D	5–6½
V8-350⑱	R44T	.035	F	4°	8°	Damper	900	700D	7–8⅛
V6-351C⑰	CR43N	.035	I	7½°	—	Damper	650	—	5–6½
V8-366⑱	R43T	.035	F	8°	—	Damper	550	—	7½–9
V6-401⑰	CR43N	.035	I	7½°	—	Damper	525	—	5–6½
V8-402⑱	R44T	.035	F	8°	8°	Damper	750	600D	7–8½
V8-427⑱	R42T	.035	F	8°	—	Damper	550	—	7½–9
V8-454⑱	R44T	.035	F	8°	8°	Damper	750	600	7–8½
V6-478⑰	CR43N	.035	I	7½°	—	Damper	525	—	5–6½

Continued

821

CHEVROLET

TUNE UP SPECIFICATIONS—Continued

The following specifications are published from the latest information available. This data should be used only in the absence of a decal affixed in the engine compartment.

★ When using a timing light, disconnect vacuum hose or tube at distributor and plug opening in hose or tube so idle speed will not be affected.

● When checking compression, lowest cylinder must be within 80 percent of highest.

▲ Before removing wires from distributor cap, determine location of the No. 1 wire in cap, as distributor position may have been altered from that shown at the end of this chart.

Year & Engine	Spark Plug Type	Spark Plug Gap	Ignition Timing BTDC①★ Firing Order Fig.▲	Ignition Timing BTDC①★ Man. Trans.	Ignition Timing BTDC①★ Auto. Trans.	Location	Curb Idle Speed② Man. Trans.	Curb Idle Speed② Auto. Trans.	Fuel Pump Pressure
V8-637⑱	CR42N	.035	J	5°	—	Damper	475	—	7½-9
1971									
4-140, 90 H.P.⑰	R42TS	.035	H	6°	6°	Damper	850	650D	3-4½
4-140, 110 H.P.⑰	R42TS	.035	H	6°	10°	Damper	㊲	650D	3-4½
6-250, 145 H.P.⑰	R46T	.035	E	4°	4°	Damper	550	500D	3½-4½
6-250, 155 H.P.⑰	R46T	.035	E	TDC	4°	Damper	750	600D	3½-4½
6-292⑰	R44T	.035	E	4°	4°	Damper	550	500D	3½-4½
V8-307, 200 H.P. Exc. G 10-30⑱	R45TS	.035	F	4°	8°	Damper	600	550	5-6½
V8-307, 200 H.P. Exc. C, K, P 10-30⑱	R45	.035	F	2°	2°	Damper	700	600	5-6½
V8-307, 215 H.P.⑱	R45TS	.035	F	4°	4°	Damper	550	500	5-6½
V8-350, 215 H.P.⑱	R44	.035	F	4°	4°	Damper	500	500	7-8½
V8-350, 245 H.P.⑱	R45TS	.035	F	2°	6°	Damper	600	550D	7-8½
V8-350, 250 H.P.⑱	R44TS	.035	F	4°	8°	Damper	600	550D	7-8½
V8-350, 255 H.P.⑱	R44	.035	F	TDC	4°	Damper	700	600D	7-8½
V8-350, 270 H.P.⑱	R45TS	.035	F	4°	8°	Damper	600	550D	7-8½
V8-366⑱	R43T	.035	F	8°	8°	Damper	500	500D	5-6½
V8-400㊳⑱	R44TS	.035	F	8°	8°	Damper	600	550D	7-8½
V6-401⑰	CR43N	.035	I	10°	—	Damper	525	—	5-6½
V8-427⑱	R42T	.035	F	8°	8°	Damper	500	500D	5-6½
V8-454, 365 H.P.⑱	R42TS	.035	F	8°	8°	Damper	600	600D	7-8½
V8-454, 425 H.P.⑱	R42TS	.035	F	8°	12°	Damper	600	600D	7-8½
V6-478⑰	CR43N	.035	I	10°	—	Damper	525	—	5-6½
V8-637⑱	CR42N	.035	J	10°	—	Damper	425	—	7½-9
1970									
6-250㊴⑰	R46T	.035	E	TDC	4°	Damper	750㊵	600D㊵	3½-4½
6-250㊶⑰	R46T	.035	E	TDC	4°	Damper	550	500	3½-4½
6-292㊴⑰	R44T	.035	E	TDC	4°	Damper	700㊵	600D㊵	3½-4½
6-292㊶⑰	R44T	.035	E	TDC	4°	Damper	550	500	3½-4½
V8-307㊴⑱	R45	.035	F	2°	8°	Damper	700㊵	600D㊵	5-6½
V8-350, 215 H.P.㊷⑱	R44	.035	F	4°	4°	Damper	500	500	7-8½
V8-350, 255 H.P.⑱	R44	.035	F	TDC	4°	Damper	700	600	7-8½
V8-366⑱	CR42N	.035	F	6°	6°	Damper	500	500	5-6½
V8-396⑱	R44T	.035	F	4°	4°	Damper	600	500	7-8½
V6-401⑱	CR43N	.035	I	7.5°	—	Damper	525	—	5-6½
V8-427⑱	CR42N	.035	F	6°	6°	Damper	500	500	5-6½
V6-478⑱	CR43N	.035	I	7.5°	—	Damper	525	—	5-6½
V8-637⑱	CR42N	.035	J	5°	—	Damper	475	—	7½-9

①—B.T.D.C.—Before top dead center.
②—Idle speed on Man. Trans. vehicles is adjusted in Neutral & on Auto. Trans. vehicles is adjusted in Drive (D) or Neutral (N) as specified. Where two idle speeds are listed, the higher speed is with the A/C or idle solenoid energized.
③—Less A/C, 550D RPM; with A/C, 560/670 RPM.
④—With vapor return line, 5½-7 psi.; less vapor return line, 7½-9 psi.
⑤—El Camino.
⑥—Series 40-60.
⑦—Series 10-30 light duty emissions, GVWR 6000 lbs. & under.
⑧—Series 10-30 heavy duty emissions, GVWR 6001 lbs. & above.
⑨—Less A/C, 425/550 RPM; with A/C, 425/600D RPM.
⑩—Except Calif., .035"; Calif., .045".
⑪—Except Calif. & high altitude.
⑫—Except Calif., 600 RPM; Calif., 700 RPM.
⑬—Less A/C, 425/750 RPM; with A/C, 425/800 RPM.
⑭—Except high altitude, 500/650 RPM; high altitude, 600/650 RPM.
⑮—Except Calif., 425/550 RPM; California,

425/600D RPM.
(16)—Models w/ 3 spd. man. trans., 6° BTDC; models w/4 spd. man. trans., 10° BTDC.
(17)—Breaker point gap, new .019", used .016"; dwell angle, 31–34°.
(18)—Breaker point gap, new .019", used .016"; dwell angle, 30°.
(19)—For predominately urban driving where spark plug fouling may occur, use R44T.
(20)—For predominately urban driving where spark plug fouling may occur, use R44TX.
(21)—For predominately urban driving where spark plug fouling may occur, use R43T or R44T.
(22)—For predominately urban driving where spark plug fouling may occur, use R43TX or R44TX.
(23)—Models less catalytic converter, 8° BTDC; Models w/catalytic converter, 12° BTDC.
(24)—If cold weather starting problems are encountered, use R43TS gapped at .035."
(25)—Exc. Calif., 700 RPM; Calif., 700/1200 RPM.
(26)—Models less governor, 450 RPM; models w/ governor, 550 RPM.
(27)—El Camino except Calif., 8° BTDC; El Camino California models & all Series 10-30 models, 6° BTDC.
(28)—El Camino, 500/600D RPM; Series 10-30, 500/650D RPM.
(29)—Exc. Suburban, 8°; Suburban, 6°.
(30)—1 barrel carb, 1000 RPM; 2 barrel carb, 1200 RPM.
(31)—Exc. C-20 Suburban, 8°; C-20 Suburban, 2°.
(32)—Calif, 4°.
(33)—2 barrel carb. and Calif. 4-speed, 1200; all others 850.
(34)—TDC on Calif. K-20 Suburban.
(35)—Series 10, 8°; all others 4°.
(36)—Calif. C, K, G, 950; all others 900.
(37)—3 speed, 850; 4 speed, 1200.
(38)—Marketed as 400, but actually 402.
(39)—W/Evap., C.C.S.g T.C.S. Series 10.
(40)—With solenoid disconnected, 400.
(41)—With C.C.S.
(42)—Air Injection Reactor System.
(43)—Distributor model No. 1103381, set at 8° BTDC; distributor model No. 1103369, set at 6° BTDC.
(44)—Non-governed California models, set at 2° BTDC.
(45)—C-10 & 20 series with distributor models No. 1103339, set at 6° BTDC.

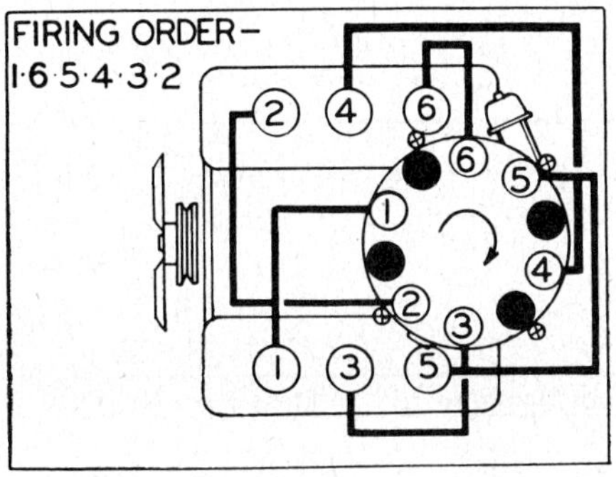

Fig. A

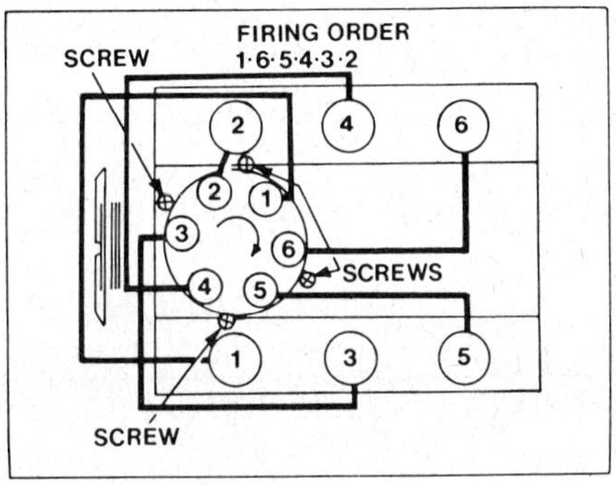

Fig. B

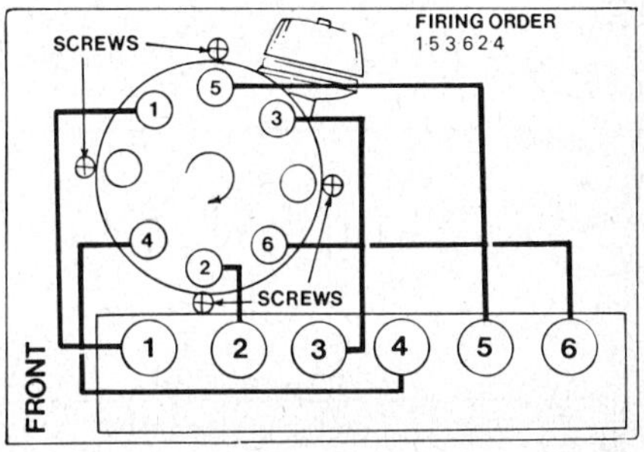

Fig. C

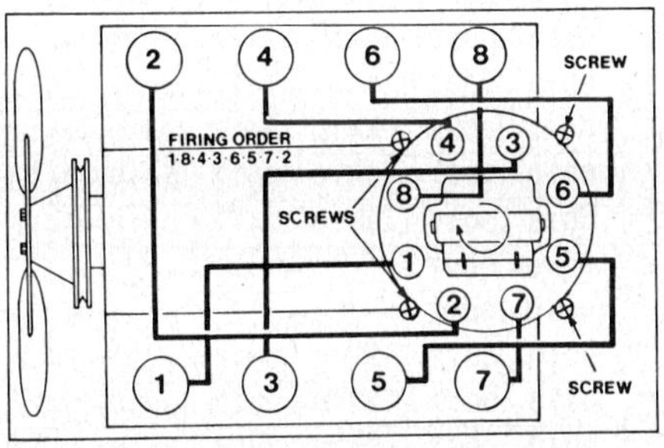

Fig. D

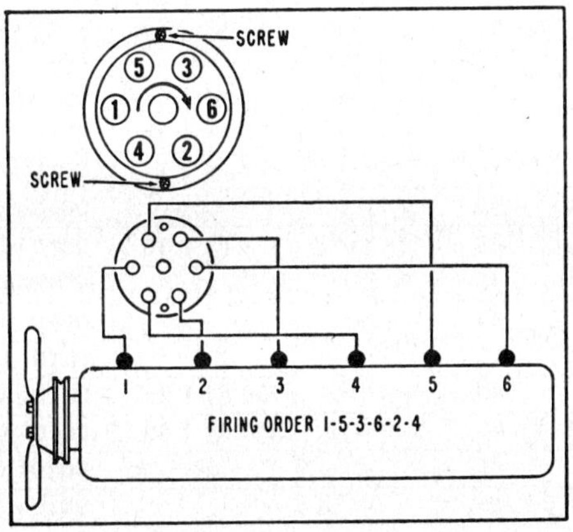

Fig. E

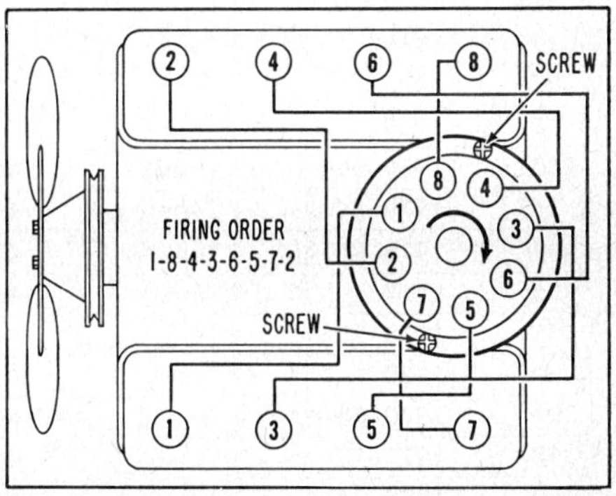

Fig. F

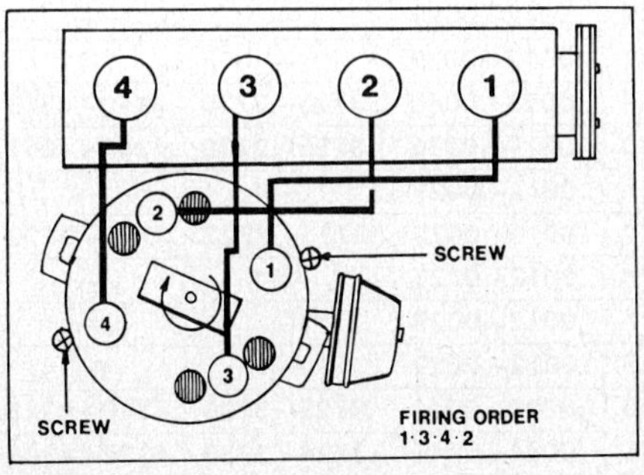

Fig. G

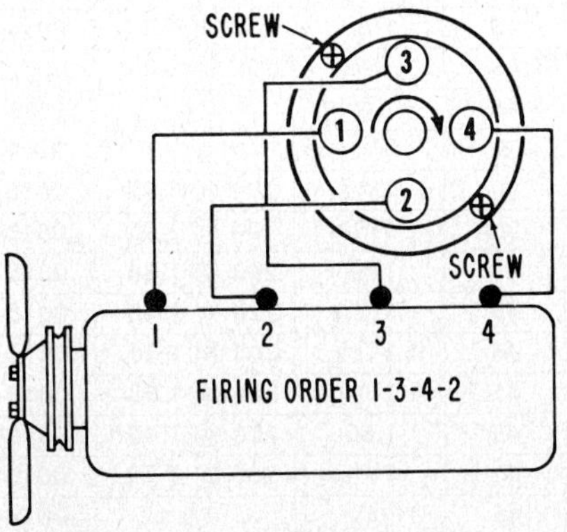

Fig. H

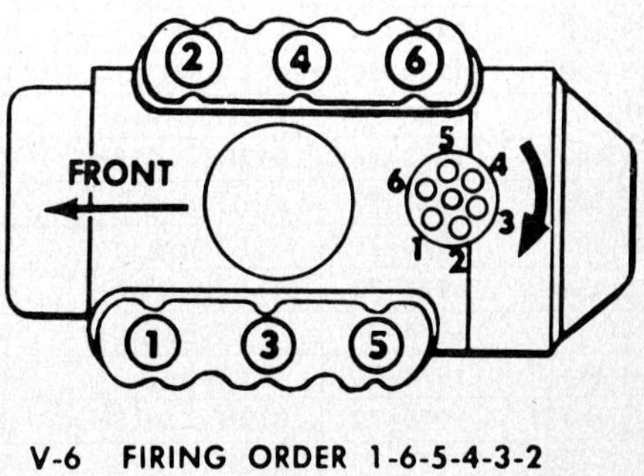

V-6 FIRING ORDER 1-6-5-4-3-2

Fig. I

CHEVROLET

TUNE UP NOTES—Continued

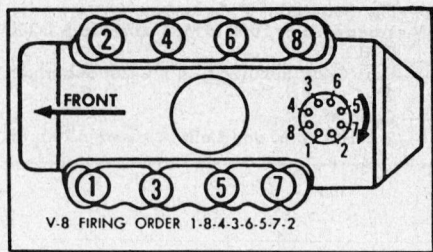

Fig. J

VALVE SPECIFICATIONS

Engine Model	Year	Valve Lash		Valve Angles		Valve Springs		Valve Stem Clearance		Stem Diameter, Std.	
		Int.	Exh.	Seat	Face	Installed Height	Pressure Lbs. @ In.	Intake	Exhaust	Intake	Exhaust
4-140 1BB1.	1971-75	.015C	.030C	46	45	1 3/4	186 @ 1.29	.0010-.0027	.0010-.0027	.3410-.3417	.3410-.3417
4-140	1971-75	.015C	.030C	46	45	1 3/4	190 @ 1.31	.0010-.0027	.0010-.0027	.3410-.3417	.3410-.3417
V6-200	1978-79	1 Turn③		46	45	1 45/64	200 @ 1.25	.0010-.0027	.0010-.0027	.3410-.3417	.3410-.3417
V6-229	1980	1 Turn③		46	45	1 45/64	①	.0010-.0027	.0010-.0027	.3410-.3417	.3410-.3417
V6-231	1978-79	—		45	45	1 23/32	168 @ 1.327	.0015-.0032	.0015-.0032	.3402-.3412	.3405-.3412
V6-231	1980	—		45	45	1 23/32	182 @ 1.34	.0015-.0035	.0015-.0035	.3402-.3412	.3405-.3412
6-250	1970-80	1 Turn③		46	45	1 21/32	186 @ 1.27	.0010-.0027	.0015-.0032	.3410-.3417	.3410-.3417
V8-267	1979-80	1 Turn③		46	45	1 45/64	⑤	.0010-.0027	.0010-.0027	.3410-.3417	.3410-.3417
6-292	1970-80	1 Turn③		46	45	1 5/8	179 @ 1.30	.0010-.0027	.0015-.0032	.3410-.3417	.3410-.3417
8-305	1977	1 Turn③		46	45	⑩	⑪	.0010-.0027	.0010-.0027	—	—
8-305	1978-79	1 Turn③		46	45	⑫	⑬	.0010-.0027	.0010-.0027	—	—
V8-305	1980	1 Turn③		46	45	1.7	④	.0010-.0027	.0010-.0027	.3410-.3417	.3410-.3417
8-307	1970-73	1 Turn③		46	45	1 23/32	200 @ 1.25	.0010-.0027	.0010-.0027	.3410-.3417	.3410-.3417
8-350	1970-73	1 Turn③		46	45	1 23/32	200 @ 1.25	.0010-.0027	.0010-.0027	.3410-.3417	.3410-.3417
8-350	1974-76	1 Turn③		46	45	⑧	⑨	.0010-.0027	.0010-.0027	.3410-.3417	.3410-.3417
8-350	1977	1 Turn③		46	45	⑩	⑪	.0010-.0027	.0010-.0027	—	—
8-350	1978-80	1 Turn③		46	45	⑫	⑬	.0010-.0027	.0010-.0027	—	—
V6-351C	1970-72	.012H	.018H	②	②	1 59/64	204 @ 1.92	.0020-.0030	.0025-.0040	.3725-.3730	.4340-.4345
8-366	1970-79	1 Turn③		46	45	1 13/16	220 @ 1.40	.0010-.0027	.0012-.0029	.3715-.3722	.3713-.3720
8-396	1970	1 Turn③		46	45	1 7/8	240 @ 1.38	.0017-.0020	.0019-.0022	.3415-.3722	.3713-.3720
8-400	1970-76	1 Turn③		46	45	1 23/32	200 @ 1.25	.0010-.0027	.0012-.0027	.3410-.3417	.3410-.3417
8-400	1977	1 Turn③		46	45	⑩	⑪	.0010-.0027	.0012-.0029	—	—
8-400	1978-80	1 Turn③		46	5	⑫	⑬	.0010-.0027	.0012-.0029	—	—
V6-401	1970-72	.012H	.018H	②	②	1 59/64	204 @ 1.92	.0015-.0030	.0025-.0040	.3725-.3730	.4340-.4345
V6-432	1973-74	.012H	.018H	②	②	1 59/64	204 @ 1.92	.0015-.0030	.0019-.0036	.3725-.3730	.4344-.4351
8-402	1971-72	1 Turn③		46	45	1 7/8	240 @ 1.38	.0010-.0027	.0012-.0029	—	—
8-427	1970-79	1 Turn③		46	45	1 13/16	220 @ 1.40	.0010-.0027	.0019-.0022	.3715-.3722	.3713-.3720
8-454	1971-73	1 Turn③		46	45	1 7/8	300 @ 1.38	.0010-.0027	.0012-.0027	—	—
8-454	1974-77	1 Turn③		46	45	1 7/8	300 @ 1.38	.0010-.0027	.0012-.0029	—	—
8-454	1978-80	1 Turn③		46	45	1.80	220 @ 1.40	.0010-.0027	.0012-.0029	—	—
V6-478	1970-72	.012H	.018H	②	②	1 59/64	204 @ 1.92	.0015-.0030	.0025-.0040	.3725-.3730	.4340-.4345
V8-637	1971-72	.010H	.018H	45	45	⑥	⑦	.0014-.0031	.0024-.0041	.3724-.3730	.4339-.4346

CHEVROLET

VALVE SPECIFICATIONS—NOTES—Continued

①—Intake, 175 @ 1.25; Exhaust, 190 @ 1.25.
②—Intake 30, exhaust 45.
③—Tight from zero lash point.
④—Intake, 175 @ 1.25; Exhaust, 184 @ 1.16.
⑤—Intake, 180 @ 1 1/4; Exhaust, 190 @ 1 5/32.
⑥—Inner spring 1 57/64; outer spring 2 3/32.
⑦—Inner spring—70 @ 1.397 inch; outer spring—154 @ 1.595.
⑧—Intake 1 23/32", exhaust 1 5/8".
⑨—Intake 200 @ 1.25"; exhaust 189 @ 1.20.
⑩—Intake 1 23/32; Exhaust 1 19/32.
⑪—Intake 194-206 @ 1.25; Exhaust 194-206 @ 1.16.
⑫—Intake, 1.70; exhaust, 1.61.
⑬—Intake, 180 @ 1.25; exhaust, 190 @ 1.16.

DISTRIBUTOR SPECIFICATIONS

Year	Model	Distributor Number	Rotation ①	Breaker Gap (New)	Dwell Angle Deg.	Breaker Arm Spring Tension	Centrifugal Advance Degrees @ R.P.M. of Distributor		Vacuum Advance	
							Advance Starts	Full Advance	Inches of Vacuum To Start Plunger	Max. Adv. Dist. Deg. @ Vacuum
1970	6-230	1110459	C	.019	31–34	19–23	0 @ 500	18 @ 2300	7	11 1/2 @ 16
	6-230	1110460	C	.019	31–34	19–23	0 @ 500	16 @ 2300	7	11 1/2 @ 16
	6-230, 250	1110465	C	.019	31–34	19–23	0 @ 450	16 @ 2100	7	11 1/2 @ 16
	6-230, 250	1110466	C	.019	31–34	19–23	0 @ 450	14 @ 2100	7	11 1/2 @ 16
	6-250	1110463	C	.019	31–34	19–23	0 @ 450	16 @ 2100	7	11 1/2 @ 16
	6-250	1110464	C	.019	31–34	19–23	0 @ 450	14 @ 2100	7	11 1/2 @ 16
	6-292	1110467	C	.019	31–34	19–23	0 @ 450	16 @ 2100	7	11 1/2 @ 16
	6-292	1110468	C	.019	31–34	19–23	0 @ 450	16 @ 2100	7	11 1/2 @ 16
	8-307	1111481	C	.019	28–32	19–23	0 @ 500	14 @ 2150	6	7 1/2 @ 12
	8-307	1110912	C	.019	28–32	19–23	0 @ 400	12 @ 2150	8	17 @ 10
	8-350	1111338	C	.019	28–32	19–23	0 @ 450	16 @ 2500	—	—
	8-350	1111495	C	.019	28–32	19–23	0 @ 375	14 @ 2050	8	7 1/2 @ 15 1/2
	8-350	1111500	C	.019	28–32	19–23	0 @ 450	14 @ 2100	8	7 1/2 @ 15 1/2
	8-350	1111955	C	.019	28–32	19–23	0 @ 450	16 @ 2050	7	6 1/2 @ 17
	8-366, 427	1111337	C	.019	28–32	19–23	0 @ 450	18 @ 2200	—	—
	8-366, 427 Trans. Ign.	1111346	C	—	28–32	—	0 @ 575	14 @ 2200	—	—
	8-396	1111500	C	.019	28–32	19–23	0 @ 450	14 @ 2100	8	7 1/2 @ 15 1/2
	V6-401, 478M	1110478	C	.019	31–34	14–23	0 @ 510	12 @ 1750	3–5	7 1/2 @ 8 1/4
	V6-478SN	1110451	C	—	31–34	—	0 @ 450	12 @ 1800	7–9	5 @ 14.7
1971	6-250	1110489	C	.019	31–34	19–23	0 @ 465	12 @ 2050	8	11 1/2 @ 16
	6-292 10–30 Ser.	1110486	C	.019	31–34	19–23	0 @ 430	14 @ 2000	8	9 @ 16
	6-292 40–60 Ser.	1110491	C	.019	31–34	19–23	0 @ 500	15 @ 2100	6–8	11 1/2 @ 16
1971–72	4-140	1110435	C	.019	31–34	19–23	0 @ 475	11 @ 2000	7	12 @ 15
	4-140	1110492	C	.019	31–34	19–23	0 @ 590	12 @ 2000	7	12 @ 15
	8-307 10 Ser.	1112040	C	.019	29–31	19–23	0 @ 340	10 @ 2100	8	10 @ 17
	8-307 10 Ser.	1112041	C	.019	29–31	19–23	0 @ 400	12 @ 2150	8	10 @ 17
	8-307 20, 30 Ser.	1112043	C	.019	29–31	19–23	0 @ 400	10 @ 2100	8	7 1/2 @ 15 1/2
	8-350 10–30 Ser.	1112046	C	.019	29–31	19–23	0 @ 400	12 @ 2150	8	7 1/2 @ 15 1/2
	8-350 10–30 Ser.	1112047	C	.019	29–31	19–23	0 @ 430	9 @ 2100	8	7 1/2 @ 15 1/2
	8-350 40–60 Ser.	1112048	C	—	28–32	—	0 @ 600	10 @ 1900	7–9	8 @ 15 1/2
	8-350 40–60 Ser.	1111364	C	—	28–32	—	0 @ 550	10 @ 1900	—	—
	8-366, 427	1111365	C	—	28–32	—	0 @ 625	13 @ 2200	—	—
	V6-401, 478M	1110478	C	.016	31–34	—	0 @ 510	12 @ 1750	3.5	7 1/2 @ 8 1/4
	8-402	1112064	C	.019	29–31	19–23	0 @ 465	15 @ 2200	8	10 @ 17
	8-454	1112052	C	.019	28–32	19–23	0 @ 428	11 @ 1950	8	10 @ 17
	V6-478SN	1110451	C	.016	31–34	—	0 @ 450	12 @ 1800	7–9	5 @ 14.9
	8-637	1111985	C	—	28–32	—	1 @ 550	14 @ 1600	3–5	9 @ 7.3
1972	6-250, Exc. G Ser.	1110489	C	.019	31–34	19–23	0 @ 465	12 @ 2050	8	11 1/2 @ 16
	6-250, G Ser.	1110493	C	.019	31–34	19–23	0 @ 465	12 @ 2050	8	11 1/2 @ 16
	6-250, 20–30 Ser.	1110498	C	.019	31–34	19–23	0 @ 465	12 @ 2050	8	8 @ 13
	6-292	1110486	C	.019	31–34	19–23	0 @ 430	14 @ 2000	8	9 @ 16
	V6-351C	1110478	C	.019	31–34	—	0 @ 510	11 @ 1750	3–5	7 1/2 @ 6 1/4

Continued

CHEVROLET

DISTRIBUTOR SPECIFICATIONS—Continued

Year	Model	Distributor Number	Rotation ①	Breaker Gap (New)	Dwell Angle Deg.	Breaker Arm Spring Tension	Centrifugal Advance Degrees @ R.P.M. of Distributor		Vacuum Advance	
							Advance Starts	Full Advance	Inches of Vacuum To Start Plunger	Max. Adv. Dist. Deg. @ Vacuum
1973	4-140	1110496	C	.019	31–34	—	0 @ 800	11 @ 2400	7	12 @ 15
	6-250, 10 Ser. Exc. G	1110499	C	.019	31–34	—	0 @ 465	12 @ 2050	7	6 @ 15
	6-250, 10 Ser. G	1110500	C	.019	31–34	—	0 @ 465	12 @ 2050	7	6 @ 15
	6-250, 20-30 Ser. Exc. G	1110489	C	.019	31–34	19–23	0 @ 465	12 @ 2050	8	11½ @ 16
	6-250, 20-30 Ser. G	1110493	C	.019	31–34	19–23	0 @ 465	12 @ 2050	8	11½ @ 16
	6-292, Exc. NB-2	1110486	C	.019	31–34	—	0 @ 430	10 @ 2000	9	9 @ 13
	6-292 NB-2	1110518	C	.019	31–34	—	0 @ 465	7 @ 2050	10	5 @ 13
	V6-305C, 379, 432, 478M	1110478	C	.016	31–34	—	1 @ 510	11 @ 1250	4	½ @ 7.2
	V6-432, 478M, K-19	1112674	C	.016	31–34	—	1 @ 510	11 @ 1250	—	—
	V6-478SN	1110451	C	.016	31–34	—	1½ @ 450	11 @ 1800	8	5 @ 14.8
	8-307 10 Ser.	1112102	C	.019	29–31	—	0 @ 500	10 @ 2100	6	7½ @ 12
	8-307 10 Ser.	1112227	C	.019	29–31	—	0 @ 500	12 @ 2150	6	7½ @ 12
	8-307 20–30 Ser.	1112096	C	.019	29–31	—	0 @ 550	12 @ 2100	10	5 @ 15
	8-350 Std. Trans.③	1112093	C	.019	29–31	—	0 @ 550	9 @ 2100	6	7½ @ 14
	8-350 Auto. Trans.③	1112094	C	.019	29–31	—	0 @ 550	7½ @ 21	6	7½ @ 14
	8-350 20–30 Ser.	1112097	C	.019	29–31	—	0 @ 550	11 @ 2100	8	5 @ 13
	8-350 Exc. Calif.	1111364	C	—	28–32	—	1 @ 550	10 @ 1900	—	—
	8-350 Exc. Calif.	1111369	C	—	29–31	—	1 @ 600	10 @ 1900	—	—
	8-350 Calif.	1112048	C	—	28–32	—	1 @ 600	10 @ 1900	8	8 @ 17
	8-350 Calif.	1113171	C	—	29–31	—	1 @ 600	10 @ 2100	—	—
	8-350 Calif.	1112092	C	—	29–31	—	1 @ 600	10 @ 2100	—	—
	8-350 Calif.	1111372	C	—	29–31	—	1 @ 600	10 @ 2100	—	—
	8-366, 427	1111365	C	.016	28–32	—	1 @ 625	13 @ 2200	—	—
	8-366	1111370	C	—	29–31	—	1 @ 600	13 @ 2200	—	—
	8-454 Exc. 20 Suburban	1112113	C	.019	29–31	—	0 @ 550	7½ @ 2100	6	10 @ 15
	8-454 20 Suburban	1112504	C	.019	29–31	—	0 @ 550	7½ @ 2100	8	7½ @ 15½
1974	4-140	1110496	C	.019	31–34	19–23	0 @ 800	11 @ 2400	7	12 @ 15
	6-250, 10 Ser. Exc. G	1110499	C	.019	31–34	19–23	0 @ 550	12 @ 2050	7	12 @ 15½
	6-250, 10 Ser. G	1110500	C	.019	31–34	19–23	0 @ 500	12 @ 2050	7	12 @ 15½
	6-250, 20-30 Ser. Exc. G	1110520	C	.019	31–34	19–23	0 @ 550	12 @ 2050	13	5 @ 13½
	6-250, 20–30 Ser. G	1110525	C	.019	31–34	19–23	0 @ 550	12 @ 2050	13	5 @ 13½
	6-292, 20–30 Ser.	1110518	C	.019	31–34	19–23	0 @ 500	12 @ 2100	10	5 @ 13½
	V6-305C, 379, 432, 478	1112674	C	—	31–34	19–23	0–2 @ 510	10–12 @ 1750	—	—
	V8-350 40–60 Ser.⑨	1111364	C	—	28–32	19–23	0–2 @ 550	9–11 @ 1900	—	—
	V8-350 40–60 Ser.	1112149	C	—	28–32	19–23	0–2 @ 450	9–11 @ 1900	—	—
	V8-350 40–60 Ser.	1111373	C	—	29–31	19–23	0–2 @ 550	9–11 @ 1900	—	—
	8-350, C, K10, Suburban	1112093	C	.019	29–31	19–23	0 @ 550	9 @ 2100	6	7½ @ 14
	8-350, G10-30	1112847	C	.019	29–31	19–23	0 @ 550	9 @ 2100	3	7 @ 8½
	8-350 Auto. Trans. (Calif.)④	1112847	C	.019	29–31	19–23	0 @ 550	9 @ 2100	3	7 @ 8
	8-350, C, K, G	1112543	C	.019	29–31	19–23	0 @ 500	11 @ 2100	6	7½ @ 14
	8-350 Auto. Trans.③	1112848	C	.019	29–31	19–23	0 @ 450	7 @ 2100	3	7 @ 8½
	8-350 Std. Trans.③	1112844	C	.019	29–31	19–23	0 @ 500	10 @ 2100	3	7 @ 8½
	8-350 Std. Trans.⑤	1112844	C	.019	29–31	19–23	0 @ 500	10 @ 2100	3	7 @ 8½
	8-350 Std. Trans.⑥	1112849	C	.019	29–31	19–23	0 @ 500	11 @ 2100	3	7 @ 8½
	8-350 G, P-30	1112097	C	.019	29–31	19–23	0 @ 600	11 @ 2100	8	5 @ 13½
	8-366, 427	1111365	C	—	28–32	19–23	0–2 @ 625	12–14 @ 2200	—	—

Continued

CHEVROLET

DISTRIBUTOR SPECIFICATIONS—Continued

Year	Model	Distributor Number	Rotation ①	Breaker Gap (New)	Dwell Angle Deg.	Breaker Arm Spring Tension	Centrifugal Advance Degrees @ R.P.M. of Distributor		Vacuum Advance	
							Advance Starts	Full Advance	Inches of Vacuum To Start Plunger	Max. Adv. Dist. Deg. @ Vacuum
	V8-366 Auto. Trans.	1111374	C	—	29–31	19–23	0–2 @ 625	12–14 @ 2200	—	—
	8-454, C, K-10	1112113	C	.019	29–31	19–23	0 @ 550	9 @ 2100	6	10 @ 15.7
	8-454, C, K, Suburban	1112504	C	.019	29–31	19–23	0 @ 550	9 @ 2100	8	8 @ 16
	8-454 C, K20-30	1112105	C	.019	29–31	19–23	0 @ 550	10 @ 2100	6	12 @ 14.3
1975	4-140	1112862	C	—	—	—	0 @ 810	11 @ 2400	5	12 @ 12
	6-250	1112863	C	—	—	—	0 @ 550	8 @ 2100	4	9 @ 12
	6-250 Calif.	1110650	C	—	—	—	0 @ 550	8 @ 2100	4	7 @ 12
	6-292	1112887	C	—	—	—	0 @ 550	12 @ 2100	10	5 @ 13
	6-292⑩	1110516	C	.019	31–34	—	0 @ 650	13 @ 2050	9	5 @ 13.25
	8-350	1112880	C	—	—	—	0 @ 600	11 @ 2100	4	9 @ 12
	8-350	1112888	C	—	—	—	0 @ 550	8 @ 2100	4	9 @ 12
	8-350	1112940	C	—	—	—	0 @ 600	10 @ 2100	8	7½ @ 15½
	8-350, 400 Calif.	1112884	C	—	—	—	0 @ 575	11 @ 2100	8	5 @ 13
	8-350⑨⑩	1111364	C	—	28–32	—	0 @ 550	11 @ 1900	—	—
	8-350⑩⑪	1112149	C	—	28–32	—	0 @ 450	11 @ 1900	—	—
	8-350⑩⑫	1111373	C	—	29–31	—	0 @ 550	11 @ 1900	—	—
	8-366⑬	1111378	C	—	28–32	—	0 @ 625	14 @ 2200	—	—
	8-366⑫⑬	1111379	C	—	29–31	—	0 @ 625	14 @ 2200	—	—
	8-366⑭	1112890	C	—	—	—	0 @ 600	14 @ 2200	—	—
	8-400	1112941	C	—	—	—	0 @ 500	9½ @ 1725	8	5 @ 13
	8-427⑬	1111378	C	—	28–32	—	0 @ 625	14 @ 2200	—	—
	8-427⑭	1112890	C	—	—	—	0 @ 600	14 @ 2200	—	—
	8-454 L.D.⑦	1112886	C	—	—	—	0 @ 900	6 @ 2100	4	9 @ 7
	8-454 L.D.⑧	1112943	C	—	—	—	0 @ 550	9 @ 2100	6	10 @ 15
	8-454 H.D.	1112869	C	—	—	—	0 @ 550	10 @ 2100	6	10 @ 15
	8-454 H.D.	1112494	C	—	—	—	0 @ 550	10 @ 2100	10	7 @ 17
1976	6-250 Std. Trans.	1110666	C	—	—	—	0 @ 500	10 @ 2100	4	12 @ 15
	6-250	1112863	C	—	—	—	0 @ 550	8 @ 2100	4	9 @ 12
	6-250 Calif. Std. Trans.	1110667	C	—	—	—	0 @ 500	10 @ 2100	4	7½ @ 12
	6-250 Calif. Auto. Trans.	1110650	C	—	—	—	0 @ 550	8 @ 2100	4	7½ @ 12
	6-250⑬⑮	1110666	C	—	—	—	0 @ 500	10 @ 2100	4	12 @ 15
	6-250, 292⑬	1112887	C	—	—	—	0 @ 550	12 @ 2050	10	5 @ 13
	6-292⑩	1110516	C	.019	31–34	—	0 @ 650	13 @ 2050	9	5 @ 13.25
	6-292 Calif.	1110664	C	—	—	—	0 @ 550	12 @ 2050	10	5 @ 13
	8-350 2 BBl.	1112880	C	—	—	—	0 @ 600	11 @ 2100	4	9 @ 12
	8-350 4 BBl.	1112888	C	—	—	—	0 @ 550	8 @ 1200	4	9 @ 12
	8-350 4 BBl.	1112940	C	—	—	—	0 @ 600	10 @ 2100	8	7½ @ 15½
	8-350 Calif. 4 BBl.	1112905	C	—	—	—	0 @ 600	11 @ 2100	6	7½ @ 12
	8-350, 400 Calif.	1112884	C	—	—	—	0 @ 575	11 @ 2100	8	5 @ 13
	V8-350⑨⑩	1111364	C	—	28–32	—	0 @ 550	11 @ 1900	—	—
	V8-350⑪⑩	1112149	C	—	28–32	—	0 @ 450	11 @ 1900	—	—
	V8-350⑫⑩	1111373	C	—	28–32	—	0 @ 550	11 @ 1900	—	—
	V8-366⑬⑩	1111378	C	—	29–31	—	0 @ 625	14 @ 2200	—	—
	V8-366⑫⑬⑩	1111379	C	—	28–32	—	0 @ 625	14 @ 2200	—	—
	V8-366⑭⑩	1112890	C	—	—	—	0 @ 600	14 @ 2200	—	—
	8-400	1112941	C	—	—	—	0 @ 500	9½ @ 1725	8	5 @ 13
	V8-427⑬⑩	1111378	C	—	18–32	—	0 @ 625	14 @ 2200	—	—
	V8-427⑭⑩	1112890	C	—	—	—	0 @ 600	14 @ 2200	—	—
	8-454⑦	1112886	C	—	—	—	0 @ 650	6 @ 2100	4	9 @ 7
	8-454⑧	1112494	C	—	—	—	0 @ 550	10 @ 2100	10	7½ @ 17
	8-454 Calif.	1112869	C	—	—	—	0 @ 550	10 @ 2100	6	10 @ 15

Continued

CHEVROLET

DISTRIBUTOR SPECIFICATIONS—Continued

Year	Model	Distributor Number	Rotation ①	Breaker Gap (New)	Dwell Angle Deg.	Breaker Arm Spring Tension	Centrifugal Advance Degrees @ R.P.M. of Distributor		Vacuum Advance	
							Advance Starts	Full Advance	Inches of Vacuum To Start Plunger	Max. Adv. Dist. Deg. @ Vacuum
1977	6-250 ⑬⑮⑰	1110678	C	—	—	—	0 @ 500	10 @ 2100	4	12 @ 15
	6-250 ⑫⑬⑰	1110674	C	—	—	—	0 @ 550	8 @ 2100	4	9 @ 12
	6-250 ⑭⑬⑰	1110692	C	—	—	—	0 @ 550	10 @ 2100	4	7½ @ 12
	6-250 ⑫⑭⑰	1110682	C	—	—	—	0 @ 550	8 @ 2100	4	9 @ 12
	6-250, 292 ⑬⑯	1110679	C	—	—	—	0 @ 550	12 @ 2050	10	5 @ 13
	6-292 ⑭⑯	1110680	C	—	—	—	0 @ 550	12 @ 2050	10	5 @ 13
	V8-305 ⑰	1103252	C	—	—	—	0 @ 500	10 @ 1900	4	9 @ 12
	V8-305 ⑯	1103237	C	—	—	—	0 @ 500	10 @ 1900	8	5 @ 13
	V8-350 ⑬⑰⑱	1103253	C	—	—	—	0 @ 550	11 @ 2300	4	9 @ 12
	V8-350 ⑰⑲	1103246	C	—	—	—	0 @ 600	11 @ 2100	4	9 @ 12
	V8-350 ⑭⑰	1103254	C	—	—	—	0 @ 600	11 @ 2100	6	7½ @ 12
	V8-350 ⑬⑯	1103274	C	—	—	—	0 @ 600	10 @ 2100	6	7½ @ 12
	V8-350 ⑭⑯	1103250	C	—	—	—	0 @ 575	11 @ 2100	8	5 @ 13
	V8-350 ⑩	1103251	C	—	—	—	0 @ 500	10 @ 1900	—	—
	V8-366	1103241	C	—	—	—	0 @ 550	13 @ 2200	—	—
	V8-400 ⑬	1103249	C	—	—	—	0 @ 500	9½ @ 1725	6	7½ @ 12
	V8-400 ⑭	1103250	C	—	—	—	0 @ 575	11 @ 2100	8	5 @ 13
	V8-427	1103241	C	—	—	—	0 @ 550	13 @ 2200	—	—
	V8-454 ⑬	1103238	C	—	—	—	0 @ 550	10 @ 2100	10	7½ @ 17
	V8-454 ⑭	1103240	C	—	—	—	0 @ 550	10 @ 2100	6	10 @ 15
1978	V6-200 ㉒⑬⑰	1110696	C	—	—	—	0 @ 500	10 @ 1900	3	8 @ 6.5
	V6-231 ㉒⑬⑰	1110695	C	—	—	—	0 @ 1000	9 @ 1800	7	12 @ 13
	V6-231 ㉒⑭⑰	1110731	C	—	—	—	0 @ 1000	9 @ 1800	4	8 @ 9
	6-250 ③⑬⑰	1110717	C	—	—	—	0 @ 550	12 @ 2050	4	9 @ 12
	6-250 ⑬⑭⑲⑮⑰	1110715	C	—	—	—	0 @ 500	10 @ 2100	4	9 @ 12
	6-250 ⑬⑭⑲⑫⑰	1110719	C	—	—	—	0 @ 550	8 @ 2100	4	9 @ 12
	6-250 ⑯⑬⑥	1110720	C	—	—	—	0 @ 550	12 @ 2050	10	5 @ 13
	6-292 ⑯⑬③	1110720	C	—	—	—	0 @ 550	12 @ 2050	10	5 @ 13
	6-292 ⑭⑯③	1110721	C	—	—	—	0 @ 550	12 @ 2050	10	5 @ 13
	V8-305 ⑯⑬④	1103237	C	—	—	—	0 @ 500	10 @ 1900	8	5 @ 13
	V8-305 ㉒②⑬⑰	11103281	C	—	—	—	0 @ 500	10 @ 1900	4	9 @ 12
	V8-305 ㉒⑰	11103282	C	—	—	—	0 @ 500	10 @ 1900	4	10 @ 10
	V8-305 ③⑬⑰	1110338	C	—	—	—	0 @ 500	10 @ 1900	5	12 @ 12
	V8-350 ㉒⑬⑰	1103337	C	—	—	—	0 @ 550	8 @ 1200	4	12 @ 10
	V8-350 ㉒⑭⑰	1103285	C	—	—	—	0 @ 600	11 @ 2100	4	5 @ 8
	V8-350 ③⑬⑲⑰	1103286	C	—	—	—	0 @ 550	11 @ 2300	4	9 @ 12
	V8-350 ⑭③⑰	1103302	C	—	—	—	0 @ 550	11 @ 2300	6	7.5 @ 12
	V8-350 ⑭⑥⑰	1103339	C	—	—	—	0 @ 550	11 @ 2300	4	5 @ 8
	V8-350 ⑭⑯③	1103250	C	—	—	—	0 @ 575	11 @ 2100	8	5 @ 13
	V8-350 ⑨⑬⑭⑯	1103251	C	—	—	—	0 @ 500	10 @ 1900	—	—
	V8-350 ⑬⑯③	1103274	C	—	—	—	0 @ 600	10 @ 2100	6	7.5 @ 13
	V8-366 ⑨⑬⑭⑯	1103241	C	—	—	—	0 @ 550	13 @ 2200	—	—
	V8-400 ⑯③⑬	1103249	C	—	—	—	0 @ 500	9.5 @ 1725	6	7.5 @ 12
	V8-400 ⑯③⑭	1103250	C	—	—	—	0 @ 575	11 @ 2100	8	5 @ 13
	V8-400 ⑭⑰③	1103301	C	—	—	—	0 @ 500	9.5 @ 1725	4	5 @ 8
	V8-427 ⑨⑬⑭⑯	1103241	C	—	—	—	0 @ 550	13 @ 2200	—	—
	V8-454 ⑯⑬③	1103238	C	—	—	—	0 @ 550	10 @ 2100	10	7.5 @ 17
	V8-454 ⑯⑭③	1103240	C	—	—	—	0 @ 550	10 @ 2100	6	10 @ 15
	V8-454 ⑬⑭⑰④	1103240	C	—	—	—	0 @ 550	10 @ 2100	6	10 @ 15
	V8-454 ④⑭⑰	1103358	C	—	—	—	0 @ 550	10 @ 2100	4	7.5 @ 10
1979	V6-200 ㉒⑬⑮	1110696	C	—	—	—	0 @ 500	10 @ 1900	2	8 @ 7.5
	V6-200 ㉒⑬⑫	1110756	C	—	—	—	0 @ 700	7 @ 1900	2	12 @ 10
	V6-231 ㉒⑬⑳	1110766	C	—	—	—	0 @ 1000	7.5 @ 1800	4	12 @ 12

Continued

CHEVROLET

DISTRIBUTOR SPECIFICATIONS—Continued

Year	Model	Distributor Number	Rotation ①	Breaker Gap (New)	Dwell Angle Deg.	Breaker Arm Spring Tension	Centrifugal Advance Degrees @ R.P.M. of Distributor		Vacuum Advance	
							Advance Starts	Full Advance	Inches of Vacuum To Start Plunger	Max. Adv. Dist. Deg. @ Vacuum
	V6-231㉒⑭	1110767	C	—	—	—	0 @ 1000	7.5 @ 1800	3	10 @ 12
	6-250⑰③⑬	1110717	C	—	—	—	0 @ 550	12 @ 2050	4	9 @ 12
	6-250⑰③⑭	1110749	C	—	—	—	0 @ 550	8 @ 2100	4	5 @ 8
	V8-267㉒⑬⑮	1103371	C	—	—	—	0 @ 500	11 @ 2200	3	12 @ 10
	V8-267㉒⑬⑫	1103370	C	—	—	—	0 @ 650	8 @ 2100	3	12 @ 10
	6-292	1110753	C	—	—	—	0 @ 550	12 @ 2050	4	5 @ 8
	V8-305㉒⑬⑲⑫⑮	1103282	C	—	—	—	0 @ 500	10 @ 1900	4	10 @ 11
	V8-305㉒⑫⑬	1103379	C	—	—	—	0 @ 500	10 @ 1900	3	10 @ 8.5
	V8-305㉒⑫⑭	1103368	C	—	—	—	0 @ 500	10 @ 1900	4	5 @ 8
	V8-305⑰⑬⑮	1103381	C	—	—	—	0 @ 600	10 @ 2100	3	10 @ 7.5
	V8-305⑰⑫⑬⑮	1103374	C	—	—	—	0 @ 600	10 @ 2100	4	8 @ 7.5
	V8-305⑰⑬⑮	1103369	C	—	—	—	0 @ 600	10 @ 2100	3	8 @ 6.5
	V8-350㉒⑲⑫③	1103353	C	—	—	—	0 @ 500	11 @ 2300	4	10 @ 11
	V8-350⑯⑬⑭	1103375	C	—	—	—	0 @ 575	11 @ 2100	4	5 @ 8
	V8-350③⑬⑮⑰	1103372	C	—	—	—	0 @ 550	11 @ 2300	4	7 @ 8
	V8-350⑭⑮③⑰	1103302	C	—	—	—	0 @ 550	11 @ 2300	6	7.5 @ 12
	V8-350⑫⑬⑭⑮⑰	1103339	C	—	—	—	0 @ 550	11 @ 2300	4	5 @ 8
	V8-350⑬⑫⑰	1103353	C	—	—	—	0 @ 550	11 @ 2300	4	10 @ 10
	V8-350⑫③⑰	1103302	C	—	—	—	0 @ 550	11 @ 2300	6	7.5 @ 12
	V8-350⑫⑭⑥⑰	1103286	C	—	—	—	0 @ 550	11 @ 2300	4	9 @ 12
	V8-350②	1103378	C	—	—	—	—	—	—	—
	V8-366②	1103377	C	—	—	—				
	V8-400⑫⑬⑭⑰	1103375	C	—	—	—	0 @ 575	11 @ 2100	4	5 @ 8
	V8-400⑫⑬⑭⑰	1103301	C	—	—	—	0 @ 500	9.5 @ 1725	4	5 @ 8
	V8-427②	1103377	C	—	—	—	—	—	—	—
	V8-454②	1103377	C	—	—	—				
	V8-454⑫⑬⑭⑮⑯	1103376	C	—	—	—	0 @ 550	10 @ 2100	8	5 @ 13
	V8-454⑬⑬⑭⑰	1103240	C	—	—	—				
	V8-454⑫⑬⑭⑰	1103358	C	—	—	—				
1980	V6-229㉒⑬⑮	1110696	C	—	—	—	0 @ 500	5 @ 1900	2	8 @ 75
	V6-229㉒⑫⑬	1110756	C	—	—	—	0 @ 700	7 @ 1900	2	12 @ 10
	V6-231㉒⑫⑬	1110766	C	—	—	—	0-2 @ 1000	7.5-8.5 @ 1800	4	12 @ 12
	V6-231㉒⑫⑭	1110767	C	—	—	—	0-2 @ 1000	7.5-8.5 @ 1800	3	10 @ 12
	6-250⑫⑬	1110717	C	—	—	—	0 @ 550	12 @ 2050	4	9 @ 12
	6-250⑭⑮	1110747	C	—	—	—	0 @ 550	12 @ 2050	4	7.5 @ 12
	6-250⑫⑭	1110749	C	—	—	—	0 @ 550	8 @ 2100	4	5 @ 8
	6-250⑬⑮	1110755	C	—	—	—	0 @ 550	12 @ 2050	5	8 @ 11.5
	6-292	1110753	C	—	—	—	0 @ 550	12 @ 2050	4	5 @ 8
	V8-267⑫⑬㉒	1103371	C	—	—	—	0 @ 500	11 @ 2200	3	12 @ 10
	V8-305⑬⑮㉒	1103282	C	—	—	—	0 @ 500	10 @ 1900	4	10 @ 11
	V8-305⑫⑭㉒	1103368	C	—	—	—	0 @ 500	10 @ 1900	4	5 @ 8
	V8-305⑬	1103369	C	—	—	—	0 @ 600	10 @ 2100	3	8 @ 6.5
	V8-305⑫⑬㉒	1103379	C	—	—	—	0 @ 500	10 @ 1900	3	10 @ 8.5
	V8-305⑬⑮	1103381	C	—	—	—	0 @ 600	10 @ 2100	3	5 @ 6.5
	V8-350⑫	1103339	C	—	—	—	0 @ 550	11 @ 2300	4	5 @ 8
	V8-350㉓	1103372	C	—	—	—	0 @ 550	11 @ 2300	4	7 @ 8
	V8-350⑬⑮	1103375	C	—	—	—	0 @ 575	11 @ 2100	4	5 @ 8
	V8-350⑭	1103420	C	—	—	—	0 @ 900	12 @ 2000	10	5 @ 13
	V8-350⑫⑭	1103423	C	—	—	—	0 @ 500	9.5 @ 1725	4	7.5 @ 10
	V8-350	1103435	C	—	—	—	0 @ 550	11 @ 2300	3	8 @ 6.5
	V8-350	1103436	C	—	—	—	0 @ 550	11 @ 2300	3	10 @ 7.5

Continued

CHEVROLET

DISTRIBUTOR SPECIFICATIONS—Continued

Year	Model	Distributor Number	Rotation ①	Breaker Gap (New)	Dwell Angle Deg.	Breaker Arm Spring Tension	Centrifugal Advance Degrees @ R.P.M. of Distributor		Vacuum Advance	
							Advance Starts	Full Advance	Inches of Vacuum To Start Plunger	Max. Adv. Dist. Deg. @ Vacuum
	V8-350 ⑫⑬	1103439	C	—	—	—	0 @ 500	9.5 @ 1725	4	7 @ 8
	V8-400 ⑫⑬	1103375	C	—	—	—	0 @ 575	11 @ 2100	4	5 @ 8
	V8-400 ⑫⑭	1103420	C	—	—	—	0 @ 900	12 @ 2000	10	5 @ 13
	V8-400 ⑫⑭	1103423	C	—	—	—	0 @ 500	9.5 @ 1725	4	7.5 @ 10
	V8-400 ⑫⑬	1103439	C	—	—	—	0 @ 500	9.5 @ 1725	4	7 @ 8
	V8-454	1103376	C	—	—	—	0 @ 550	10 @ 2100	8	5 @ 12

①—As viewed from top; C, clockwise; CC, counterclockwise.
②—Medium & Heavy Duty Truck
③—C-K 10, C-K 20 Suburban, G 10-20, G 30 Sport Van.
④—C, K 10-20, Exc. Suburban.
⑤—C10 Suburban (Calif.).
⑥—C, K10, Exc. Suburban G10-30.
⑦—With catalytic converter.
⑧—Without catalytic converter.
⑨—With governor.
⑩—Heavy duty.
⑪—Without governor.
⑫—With auto. trans.
⑬—Exc. Calif.
⑭—Calif.
⑮—Std. trans.
⑯—Heavy duty emissions, GVWR6001 & above.
⑰—Light duty emissions, GVWR 6000 & below.
⑱—Exc. high altitude engines.
⑲—High altitude engines.
⑳—High Altitude, auto. trans. & manual trans. Exc. Calif.
㉑—Auto. trans. Exc. High Altitude.
㉒—El Camino.

STARTING MOTOR SPECIFICATIONS

Starter Model	Year	Brush Spring Tension ①	Free Speed Test			Resistance Test ③	
			Amperes	Volts	R.P.M.	Amperes	Volts
1107371	1970	40	72②	11.8	6025①	295-365	3.5
1107375	1970	35	55-80②	9	3500-6000	300-360②	3.5
1107376	1970	—	55-85②	9	6700-9500	—	—
1107586	1970	—	50-80②	9	5500-9000	—	—
1107550	1973	—	50-80②	9	5500-9000	—	—
1108195, 196	1971-74	—	50-75②	9	6500-10000	—	—
1108338	1970-73	35	55-80②	9	3500-6000	300-360②	3.5
1108350	1970-71	35	35-75②	9	6000-9000	295-365	3.5
1108357	1970-71	35	35-75②	9	6000-9000	—	—
1108360	1970-76	35	55-80②	9	3500-6000	—	—
1108361	1970	35	55-80②	9	3500-6000	300-360②	3.5
1108362	1970-73	35	55-80②	9	3500-6000	—	—
1108363	1970	35	35-75②	9	6000-9000	—	—
1108364	1970-71	35	35-75②	9	6000-9000	—	—
1108365, 367	1970-74	35	50-80②	9	5500-10500	—	—
1108368	1970-73	35	50-80②	9	5500-10500	—	—
1108369	1970-72	35	35-75②	9	6000-9000	—	—
1108370	1970	35	35-75②	9	6000-9000	—	—
1108372	1970-72	35	35-75②	9	6000-9000	—	—
1108385	1972	—	65-95②	9	7500-10000	—	—
1108418	1970-73	—	65-95②	9	7500-10500	—	—
1108425	1970-73	—	35-75②	9	6000-9000	—	—
1113184	1970-74	80	50-70②	9	—	—	—
1113202	1970	80	50-70②	9	—	500	3.4
1113686	1970-74	80	130-160②	9	5000-7000	—	—
1107586	1970-72	—	50-80②	9	5500-9000	—	—
1108427	1973-74	—	55-80②	9	3500-6000	—	—
1108430	1973-74	—	65-95②	9	7500-10500	—	—
1108479	1973	—	50-80②	9	5500-10500	—	—
1108480	1973-74	—	50-80②	9	5500-10500	—	—
1108483	1972-73	—	55-80②	9	3500-6000	—	—
1108484	1970-73	—	35-75②	9	6000-9000	—	—
1108485, 486	1972-76	—	35-75②	9	6000-9000	—	—
1108487	1972-76	—	35-75②	9	6000-9000	—	—

Continued

CHEVROLET

STARTING MOTOR SPECIFICATIONS—Continued

Starter Model	Year	Brush Spring Tension ①	Free Speed Test			Resistance Test ③	
			Amperes	Volts	R.P.M.	Amperes	Volts
1108488	1973	—	35–75②	9	6000–9000	—	—
1108502	1973–74	—	65–95②	9	7500–10500	—	—
1109146	1973	—	50–80②	9	5500–9000	—	—
1113171	1970–73	—	50–70②	9	3500–5500	—	—
1113397	1973	—	130–150②	9	5000–7000	—	—
1114070, 074	1970	—	115–170②	11	6300–9500	—	—
1114101	1970–80	—	120–150②	9	3000–4500	—	—
1114105	1970	—	120–150②	9	3000–4500	—	—
1114121	1970	—	120–150②	9	3000–4500	—	—
1114135	1970	—	120–150②	9	6300–9500	—	—
1114143	1970–79	—	140–190②	9	4000–7000	—	—
1114161	1970–79	—	140–190②	9	4000–7000	—	—
1114163	1970	—	120–150②	9	3000–4500	—	—
1114178	1970–80	—	120–150②	9	3000–4500	—	—
1119631	1970–73	—	95–120②	20	5500–7500	—	—
1108771, 772	1975	—	50–75②	9	6500–10000	—	—
1108744, 778	1975–78	—	50–80②	9	5500–10500	—	—
1108746, 779	1975–76	—	50–80②	9	5500–10500	—	—
1108747, 780	1975–76	—	50–80②	9	3500–6000	—	—
1108748, 781	1975–76	—	65–90②	9	7500–10500	—	—
1108502, 782	1975–76	—	65–90②	9	7500–10500	—	—
1108752	1975–76	—	65–95②	9	7500–10500	—	—
1108753	1975–76	—	65–92②	9	7500–10500	—	—
1108754	1975–76	—	65–95②	9	7500–10500	—	—
1108783	1975–76	—	55–80②	9	3500–6000	—	—
1108784	1975–76	—	55–80②	9	3500–6000	—	—
1108785	1975–76	—	55–80②	9	3500–6000	—	—
1108787	1975–76	—	35–75②	9	6000–9000	—	—
1108788	1975–76	—	65–95②	9	7500–10500	—	—
1108792	1975–76	—	35–75②	9	6000–9000	—	—
1109631	1975–80	—	95–120②	20	5500–7500	—	—
1109772	1975–79	—	95–120②	20	5500–7500	—	—
1113184	1975–76	—	50–70②	9	3500–5500	—	—
1114086	1975–80	—	140–190②	9	4000–7000	—	—
1114101	1975–80	—	120–150②	9	3000–4500	—	—
1114733	1975–79	—	140–190②	9	4000–7000	—	—
1108793	1977	—	55–80②	9	3500–6000	—	—
1109030	1977	—	55–80②	9	3500–6000	—	—
1109032	1977	—	35–75②	9	6000–9000	—	—
1109033	1977	—	65–95②	9	7500–10500	—	—
1109034	1977	—	65–95②	9	7500–10500	—	—
1109035	1977	—	65–95②	9	7500–10500	—	—
1113243	1977	—	50–70②	9	3500–5500	—	—
1109056	1977–80	—	50–80②	9	7500–10500	—	—
1109798	1977–80	—	50–80②	9	5500–10500	—	—
1109052	1977–80	—	65–95②	9	7500–10500	—	—
1108776	1977–80	—	65–95②	9	7500–10500	—	—
1108780	1977–80	—	50–80②	9	3500–6000	—	—
1108779	1977–80	—	50–80②	9	5500–10500	—	—
1108799	1978	—	50–80②	9	5500–10500	—	—
1109075④	1978–79	—	35–75②	9	6000–9000	—	—
1109075⑤	1978–79	—	65–95②	9	7500–10500	—	—
1109076	1978–80	—	65–95②	9	7500–10500	—	—
1109077	1978–79	—	65–95②	9	7500–10500	—	—
1109078	1978–79	—	55–80②	9	3500–6000	—	—

Continued

CHEVROLET

STARTING MOTOR SPECIFICATIONS—Continued

Starter Model	Year	Brush Spring Tension ①	Free Speed Test			Resistance Test ③	
			Amperes	Volts	R.P.M.	Amperes	Volts
1109079	1978–79	—	55–80②	9	3500–6000	—	—
1109086	1978	—	95–120②	9	4000–7000	—	—
1114141	1978–80	—	140–215②	9	4000–7000	—	—
1114161	1978–80	—	140–215②	9	4000–7000	—	—
1114733	1978	—	140–215②	9	4000–7000	—	—
1109059	1978–79	—	65–95②	9	7500–10500	—	—
1108774	1979	—	60–88②	9	6500–10100	—	—
1108778	1979–80	—	50–80②	9	5500–10500	—	—
1109061	1979–80	—	60–85②	9	6800–10300	—	—
1109524	1980	—	50–80②	9	7500–11400	—	—
1114773	1980	—	140–215	9	4000–7000	—	—

①—Minimum
②—Includes solenoid.
③—Check capacity of motor by using a 500 ampere meter and a carbon pile rheostat to control voltage. Apply volts listed across motor with armature locked. Current should be as listed.
④—Except heavy duty starter.
⑤—Heavy duty starter.

ALTERNATOR & REGULATOR SPECIFICATIONS

Year	Alternator					Regulator						
	Model	Field Current @ 80° F. 12 Volts	Cold Output @ 14 Volts		Rated Hot Output Amperes	Model	Field Relay			Voltage Regulator		
			Amperes @ 2000 R.P.M.	Amperes @ 5000 R.P.M.			Air Gap	Point Gap	Closing Voltage	Air Gap	Point Gap	Volts @ 125° F.
1970–71	37 Amp.	2.2–2.6	25	35	37	1119515	.015	.030	2.3–3.7	.067	.014	13.5–14.4
	42 Amp.	2.2–2.6	28	40	42	1119515	.015	.030	2.3–3.7	.067	.014	13.5–14.4
	61 Amp.	2.2–2.6	33	58	61	1119515	.015	.030	2.3–3.7	.067	.014	13.5–14.4
	62 Amp.	4.1–4.6	20①③	55②③	62	1116378	.015	.025	2.5–3.5	—	—	13.5–14.4
	130 Amp.	4–4.5	—	110	100	9000590	.015	.030	2.3–3.7	—	—	13.5–14.4
	61 Amp.	4–4.5	—	58	61	Integral	—	—	—	—	—	—
	42 Amp.	4–4.5	—	37	42	Integral	—	—	—	—	—	—
1971	32 Amp.	4–4.5	—	31	32	—	—	—	—	—	—	—
	55 Amp.	4–4.5	—	50	55	—	—	—	—	—	—	—
1972	1102440	2.2–2.6	25	35	37	1119515	.015	.030	1.5–3.2	.067	.014	13.5–14.4
	1102452	2.2–2.6	25	35	37	1119515	.015	.030	1.5–3.2	.067	.014	13.5–14.4
	1102453	2.2–2.6	25	35	37	1119515	.015	.030	1.5–3.2	.067	.014	13.5–14.4
	1102455	2.2–2.6	33	58	61	1119515	.015	.030	1.5–3.2	.067	.014	13.5–14.4
	1102456	2.2–2.6	25	35	37	1119515	.015	.030	1.5–3.2	.067	.014	13.5–14.4
	1102458	2.2–2.6	28	40	42	1119515	.015	.030	1.5–3.2	.067	.014	13.5–14.4
	1102459	2.2–2.6	28	40	42	1119515	.015	.030	1.5–3.2	.067	.014	13.5–14.4
	1102463	2.2–2.6	33	58	61	1119515	.015	.030	1.5–3.2	.067	.014	13.5–14.4
	1100487	2.2–2.6	33	33	61	Integral	—	—	—	—	—	—
	1100838	2.2–2.6	25	35	37	1119515	.015	.030	1.5–3.2	.067	.014	13.5–14.4
	1100842	2.2–2.6	28	40	42	1119515	.015	.030	1.5–3.2	.067	.014	13.5–14.4
	1100842	2.2–2.6	28	40	42	1119507	.015	.030	3.8–7.2	.067	.014	13.5–14.4
	1100849	2.2–2.6	33	58	61	1119515	.015	.030	1.5–3.2	.067	.014	13.5–14.4
	1100849	2.2–2.6	33	58	61	1119507	.015	.030	3.8–7.2	.067	.014	13.5–14.4
	1117128	2.2–2.4	40①	126②	130	9000590④	.010	.020	7.0–9.0	—	—	13.7–14.3
	1117275	4.1–4.5	—	77	75	Integral	—	—	—	—	—	—
	1117754	4.1–4.6	20①	55②	62	1116374	—	—	4.5–8.0	—	—	13.6–14.3
	1117754	4.1–4.6	20①	55②	62	1116378	—	—	2.0–3.0	—	—	13.6–14.3
	1117756	4.1–4.6	20①	55②	62	9000590④	.010	.020	7.0–9.0	—	—	13.7–14.3
	1117782	4.1–4.6	20①	55②	62	1116778	—	—	2.3–3.0	—	—	13.6–14.3

Continued

CHEVROLET

ALTERNATOR & REGULATOR SPECIFICATIONS—Continued

Year	Alternator					Regulator						
	Model	Field Current @ 80° F. 12 Volts	Cold Output @ 14 Volts		Rated Hot Output Amperes	Model	Field Relay			Voltage Regulator		
			Amperes @ 2000 R.P.M.	Amperes @ 5000 R.P.M.			Air Gap	Point Gap	Closing Voltage	Air Gap	Point Gap	Volts @ 125° F.
1972-73	1100547	4.0-4.5	—	37	42	Integral	—	—	—	—	—	—
	1100548	4.0-4.5	—	55	61	Integral	—	—	—	—	—	—
	1117141	4.0-4.5	—	110	100	Integral	—	—	—	—	—	—
	1117143	4.0-4.5	—	150	145	Integral	—	—	—	—	—	—
1973	1101022	4.0-4.5	—	74	80	Integral	—	—	—	—	—	—
	1102349	4.0-4.5	—	37	42	Integral	—	—	—	—	—	—
	1102350	4.0-4.5	—	55	61	Integral	—	—	—	—	—	—
	1102352	4.0-4.5	—	55	61	Integral	—	—	—	—	—	—
1973-74	1117225	4.1-4.5	—	77	75	Integral	—	—	—	—	—	—
	1117231	4.1-4.5	—	77	75	Integral	—	—	—	—	—	—
	1100497	4.4-4.9	—	36⑤	37	Integral	—	—	—	—	—	—
	1102346	4.0-4.5	—	37	42	Integral	—	—	—	—	—	—
	1102347	4.0-4.5	—	55	61	Integral	—	—	—	—	—	—
	1100573	4.0-4.5	—	37	42	Integral	—	—	—	—	—	—
	1100597	4.0-4.5	—	55	61	Integral	—	—	—	—	—	—
	1100547	4-4.5	—	37	42	Integral	—	—	—	—	—	—
	1100548	4-4.5	—	55	61	Integral	—	—	—	—	—	—
	1101022	4-4.5	—	74	80	Integral	—	—	—	—	—	—
	1102352	4-4.5	—	55	61	Integral	—	—	—	—	—	—
	1117141	4-4.5	—	110	105	Integral	—	—	—	—	—	—
	1117143	4-4.5	—	150	145	Integral	—	—	—	—	—	—
	655988	3	—	97②	105	Integral	—	—	—	—	—	—
	1100838	2.2-2.6	25	35	37	1119515	.015	.030	1.5-3.2	.067	.014	13.5-14.4
	1100842	2.2-2.6	28	40	42	1119507	.015	.030	3.8-7.2	.067	.014	13.5-14.4
	1100842	2.2-2.6	28	40	42	1119515	.015	.030	1.5-3.2	.067	.014	13.5-14.4
	1100849	2.2-2.6	33	58	61	1119507	.015	.030	3.8-7.2	.067	.014	13.5-14.4
	1100849	2.2-2.6	33	58	61	1119515	.015	.030	1.5-3.2	.067	.014	13.5-14.4
	1117756	4.1-4.6	20①	55②	62	9000590⑥	.012	.020	7-8	—	—	13.7-14.3
	1117781	4.1-4.6	20①	55②	62	9000590⑥	.012	.020	7-8	—	—	13.7-14.3
	1117782	4.1-4.6	20①	55②	62	1116374	—	—	4.5-6.5	—	—	13.6-14.3
	1117782	4.1-4.6	20①	55②	62	1116378	—	—	2-3	—	—	13.6-14.3
	1117787	4.1-4.6	20①	55②	62	1116374	—	—	4.5-6.5	—	—	13.6-14.3
	1100934	4.4-4.5	—	36⑤	37	Integral	—	—	—	—	—	—
1974	1100080	—	54	73	80	Integral	—	—	—	—	—	—
	1100081	—	48	61	65	Integral	—	—	—	—	—	—
	1102382	4.0-4.5	—	37	42	Integral	—	—	—	—	—	—
	1102383	4.0-4.5	—	55	61	Integral	—	—	—	—	—	—
	1100575	4.0-4.5	—	50	55	Integral	—	—	—	—	—	—
1974-75	1100545	4.0-4.5	—	31	32	Integral	—	—	—	—	—	—
	1100546	4.0-4.5	—	50	55	Integral	—	—	—	—	—	—
	1100559	4.0-4.5	—	31	32	Integral	—	—	—	—	—	—
	1100560	4.0-4.5	—	50	55	Integral	—	—	—	—	—	—
1975	1100497	4.4-4.9	—	33	37	Integral	—	—	—	—	—	—
	1100575	4.0-4.5	—	50	55	Integral	—	—	—	—	—	—
	1100597	4.0-4.5	—	55	61	Integral	—	—	—	—	—	—
	1102346	4.0-4.5	—	38	42	Integral	—	—	—	—	—	—
	1102347	4.0-4.5	—	55	61	Integral	—	—	—	—	—	—
	1102483	4.0-4.5	—	33	37	Integral	—	—	—	—	—	—
	1102493	4.0-4.5	—	38	42	Integral	—	—	—	—	—	—
	1102500	4.0-4.5	—	50	55	Integral	—	—	—	—	—	—
	1102856	4.0-4.5	—	33	37	Integral	—	—	—	—	—	—
1975-76	1102497	4.0-4.5	30	57	61	Integral	—	—	—	—	—	—

Continued

CHEVROLET

ALTERNATOR & REGULATOR SPECIFICATIONS—Continued

Year	Model	Alternator Field Current @ 80° F. 12 Volts	Cold Output @ 14 Volts Amperes @ 2000 R.P.M.	Amperes @ 5000 R.P.M.	Rated Hot Output Amperes	Regulator Model	Field Relay Air Gap	Point Gap	Closing Voltage	Voltage Regulator Air Gap	Point Gap	Volts @ 125° F.
	1102499	4.0–4.5	25	38	42	Integral	—	—	—	—	—	—
	1102943	2.2–2.6	25	35	37	1119515	—	—	—	—	—	—
	1102944	2.2–2.6	28	40	42	1119515	—	—	—	—	—	—
	1100081	4.4–4.9	45	57	65	Integral	—	—	—	—	—	—
	1102945	2.2–2.6	33	58	61	1119507	—	—	—	—	—	—
	1117225	4.1–4.5	—	77	75	Integral	—	—	—	—	—	—
	1117782	4.1–4.6	20⑦	55⑦	62	1116374	—	—	—	—	—	—
	1117231	4.1–4.5	—	77	75	1116378	—	—	—	—	—	—
	1117481	3.6–4.3	68	86	90	Integral	—	—	—	—	—	—
	1102498	2.2–2.6	33	58	61	Integral	—	—	—	—	—	—
	1101029	4.4–4.9	55	76	80	Integral	—	—	—	—	—	—
	1117147	4.0–4.5	80	110	105	Integral	—	—	—	—	—	—
	711925⑧	2.8	81	105	105	Integral	—	—	—	—	—	—
1976	1102394	4.0–4.5	—	33	37	Integral	—	—	—	—	—	—
	1102478	4.0–4.5	—	51	55	Integral	—	—	—	—	—	—
	1102479	4.0–4.5	—	51	55	Integral	—	—	—	—	—	—
	1102480	4.0–4.5	—	57	61	Integral	—	—	—	—	—	—
	1102489	4.0–4.5	—	38	42	Integral	—	—	—	—	—	—
	1102490	4.0–4.5	—	57	61	Integral	—	—	—	—	—	—
	1102491	4.4–4.9	—	33	37	Integral	—	—	—	—	—	—
	1102841	4.0–4.5	—	38	42	Integral	—	—	—	—	—	—
1977–78	1102499	4.0–4.5	25	38	42	Integral	—	—	—	—	—	—
	1102497	4.0–4.5	30	57	61	Integral	—	—	—	—	—	—
	1101029	4.4–4.9	55	76	80	Integral	—	—	—	—	—	—
	1101020	4.4–4.9	63	97	100	Integral	—	—	—	—	—	—
	711925⑧	2.8	81	105	105	Integral	—	—	—	—	—	—
	2009386⑧	5–6	85	130	130	Integral	—	—	—	—	—	—
1977–80	711925⑧	2.8	81	105⑤	105	Integral	—	—	—	—	—	—
	1100080	4.4–4.9	52	72	80	Integral	—	—	—	—	—	—
	1100081	4.4–4.9	46	58	65	Integral	—	—	—	—	—	—
	1101016	4–4.5	—	76	80	Integral	—	—	—	—	—	—
	1101020	4.4–4.9	63	97	100	Integral	—	—	—	—	—	—
	1101028	4–4.5	—	76	80	Integral	—	—	—	—	—	—
	1101029	4.4–4.9	55	76	80	Integral	—	—	—	—	—	—
	1101030	4.4–4.9	55	76	80	Integral	—	—	—	—	—	—
	1102394	4–4.5	—	33	37	Integral	—	—	—	—	—	—
	1102480	4–4.5	—	57	61	Integral	—	—	—	—	—	—
	1102485	4–4.5	—	38	42	Integral	—	—	—	—	—	—
	1102486	4–4.5	—	57	61	Integral	—	—	—	—	—	—
	1102491	4–4.5	—	33	37	Integral	—	—	—	—	—	—
	1102497	4–4.5	30	57	61	Integral	—	—	—	—	—	—
	1102499	4–4.5	25	38	42	Integral	—	—	—	—	—	—
	1102841	4–4.5	—	38	42	Integral	—	—	—	—	—	—
	1102886	4–4.5	—	57	61	Integral	—	—	—	—	—	—
	1102887	4–4.5	—	38	42	Integral	—	—	—	—	—	—
	1102888	4–4.5	—	57	61	Integral	—	—	—	—	—	—
	1102889	4–4.5	—	33	37	Integral	—	—	—	—	—	—
	1103046	4–4.5	32	60	63	Integral	—	—	—	—	—	—
	1117241	4.1–4.5	—	77	75	Integral	—	—	—	—	—	—
	1117244	4.1–4.5	—	77	75	Integral	—	—	—	—	—	—
	1117481	3.6–4.3	68②	86⑩	90	Integral	—	—	—	—	—	—
	1117732	3.6–4.3	72②	90⑩	90	Integral	—	—	—	—	—	—
	2009386⑧	5–6	85	130⑪	130	Integral	—	—	—	—	—	—

Continued

CHEVROLET

ALTERNATOR & REGULATOR SPECIFICATIONS—Continued

Year	Model	Alternator Field Current @ 80° F. 12 Volts	Cold Output @ 14 Volts Amperes @ 2000 R.P.M.	Cold Output @ 14 Volts Amperes @ 5000 R.P.M.	Rated Hot Output Amperes	Regulator Model	Field Relay Air Gap	Field Relay Point Gap	Field Relay Closing Voltage	Voltage Regulator Air Gap	Voltage Regulator Point Gap	Voltage Regulator Volts @ 125° F.
	5148785⑧	—	15⑨	75⑪	75	Integral	—	—	—	—	—	—
1980	1101042	4–4.6	55	70	70	Integral	—	—	—	—	—	—
	1101044	4–4.5	—	—	70	Integral	—	—	—	—	—	—
	1101066	4–4.5	—	—	70	Integral	—	—	—	—	—	—
	1101071	4–4.5	—	—	70	Integral	—	—	—	—	—	—
	1103043	4–4.5	—	—	42	Integral	—	—	—	—	—	—
	1103044	4–4.5	—	—	63	Integral	—	—	—	—	—	—
	1103069	4–5	32	42	42	Integral	—	—	—	—	—	—
	1103070	4–5	—	60	63	Integral	—	—	—	—	—	—
	1103085	4–4.5	—	—	55	Integral	—	—	—	—	—	—
	1103088	4–4.5	—	—	55	Integral	—	—	—	—	—	—
	1103091	4–4.5	—	—	63	Integral	—	—	—	—	—	—
	1103092	4–4.5	—	—	55	Integral	—	—	—	—	—	—
	1103100	4–4.5	—	—	55	Integral	—	—	—	—	—	—
	1103102	4–4.5	—	—	63	Integral	—	—	—	—	—	—
	1103118	4–4.5	—	—	37	Integral	—	—	—	—	—	—
	1103122	4–4.5	—	—	63	Integral	—	—	—	—	—	—
	1103161	4–4.5	—	—	37	Integral	—	—	—	—	—	—
	1103162	4–4.5	—	—	37	Integral	—	—	—	—	—	—
	1103169	4–4.5	—	—	63	Integral	—	—	—	—	—	—
	1117180	6.5–7.5	54	85	85	Integral	—	—	—	—	—	—

①—At 1100 R.P.M.
②—At 2500 R.P.M.
③—If output is checked without a regulator, output should be 5 to 10% higher than value given.
④—Requires field relay 1116972.
⑤—At 7000 R.P.M.
⑥—Requires field relay 1115481.
⑦—If the output is checked without a regulator, the output is 5–10 amperes higher than the value given.
⑧—Leece-Neville alternator.
⑨—At 600 R.P.M.
⑩—At 6500 R.P.M.
⑪—At 6000 R.P.M.

ENGINE TIGHTENING SPECIFICATIONS★

★ Torque specifications are for clean and lightly lubricated threads only. Dry or dirty threads produce increased friction which prevents accurate measurement of tightness.

Engine	Spark Plugs Ft. Lbs.	Cylinder Head Bolts Ft. Lbs.	Intake Manifold Ft. Lbs.	Exhaust Manifold Ft. Lbs.	Rocker Arm Shaft Bracket Ft. Lbs.	Rocker Arm Studs Ft. Lbs.	Connecting Rod Cap Bolts Ft. Lbs.	Main Bearing Cap Bolts Ft. Lbs.	Flywheel to Crankshaft Ft. Lbs.	Vibration Damper or Pulley Ft. Lbs.
4-140	15	60	30	30	—	—	35	65	60	80
6-250	25④	95③	①	①	—	—	35	65	60	60
6-292	25④	95③	①	①	—	—	40	65	110	60
V6-200	④	65	30	20	—	—	45	70	60	60
V6-229	22	65	30	20	—	—	45	70	60	60
V6-231	20	80	45	25	30	—	40	100	60	175
V8-267	22	65	30	20	—	—	45	70	60	60
V8-283	25	65	30	20	—	—	35	80	60	—
V6-305②	32	63	20	18	23	—	60	175⑩	105	190
V8-305⑫	15④	65	30	20	—	—	45	70	60	60
V8-305⑬	15④	65	30	20	—	—	45	⑨	60	60
V8-307	25④	65	30	20⑦	—	—	45	70⑪	60	—
V8-327	25	65	30	20	—	—	35	80	60	—
V8-350⑫	25④	65	30	20⑦	—	—	45	70	60	60
V8-350⑬	25④	65	30	20⑦	—	—	45	⑨	60	60
V8-366	25④	80⑧	30	20	—	50	50⑭	110	65	85

Continued

CHEVROLET

ENGINE TIGHTENING SPECIFICATIONS★—Continued

★ Torque specifications are for clean and lightly lubricated threads only. Dry or dirty threads produce increased friction which prevents accurate measurement of tightness.

Engine	Spark Plugs Ft. Lbs.	Cylinder Head Bolts Ft. Lbs.	Intake Manifold Ft. Lbs.	Exhaust Manifold Ft. Lbs.	Rocker Arm Shaft Bracket Ft. Lbs.	Rocker Arm Studs Ft. Lbs.	Connecting Rod Cap Bolts Ft. Lbs.	Main Bearing Cap Bolts Ft. Lbs.	Flywheel to Crankshaft Ft. Lbs.	Vibration Damper or Pulley Ft. Lbs.
V6-379②	15	95	20	18	23	—	60	175⑩	105	190
V8-396	25④	80⑧	30	20	—	50	50	⑤	65	85
V8-400	15④	65	30	20	—	—	45	70⑪	60	60
V8-402	25④	80⑧	30	20	—	50	50	110	65	85
V6-401②	25	68	20	18	23	—	68	140⑥	103	140
V8-427	25④	80⑧	30	20	—	50	50⑭	110	65	85
V6-432②	32	95	27	17	22	—	60	175⑩	105	—
V8-454	25④	80⑧	30	20	—	50	50	110	65	85
V6-478②	25	68	20	18	23	—	68	140⑥	103	140
V8-637②	32	132	27	17	22	—	60	175	105	—

①—Outer clamp 20 ft. lbs., others 30 ft. lbs.
②—See GMC Truck chapter for service procedures.
③—Left Hand Front Bolt, 85 ft. lbs.
④—1970-78 5/8", 15 ft. lbs.; 1979-80 5/8", 22 ft. lbs.
⑤—Two-bolt caps 95 ft.-lbs., four-bolt caps 115 ft. lbs.
⑥—Rear (7/16") 90 ft. lbs.
⑦—Inside bolts 30 ft. lbs.
⑧—Aluminum head short bolts 65 ft. lbs., long bolts 75 ft. lbs.
⑨—1970-76, 70 ft. lbs., outer bolts on engines w/4 bolt caps 65 ft. lbs.; 1977-80, 80 ft. lbs., outer bolts on engines w/4 bolt caps 70 ft. lbs.
⑩—Rear (1/2") 95 ft. lbs.
⑪—1977-80 engines, 80 ft. lbs.
⑫—El Camino.
⑬—Exc. El Camino.
⑭—7/16" bolts, 70 ft. lbs.

PISTON, PIN, RING, CRANKSHAFT & BEARING SPECIFICATIONS

Engine Model	Year	Piston Clearance	Ring End Gap① Comp.	Ring End Gap① Oil	Piston Pin Diam.	Rod Bearings Shaft Diameter	Rod Bearings Bearing Clearance	Main Bearings Shaft Diameter	Main Bearings Bearing Clearance	Thrust Bearing No.	Shaft End Play
4-140	1971-72	.0018-.0028	.009	.010	.9271	1.999-2.000	.0007-.0027	2.2983-2.9993	.003-.0029	4	.002-.007
4-140	1973	.0018-.0028	.009	.010	.9271	1.999-2.000	.0007-.0008	2.2993	.0003-.0027	4	.002-.007
4-140	1974-75	.0018-.0028	㉒	.010	.9271	1.999-2.000	.0007-.0038	2.2983-2.2993	㉓	4	.004-.012
V6-200	1978-79	.0007-.0017	.010	.015	.9272	2.0986-2.0998	.0013-.0035	②	③	4	.002-.006
V6-229	1980	.0007-.0017	.010	.015	.9272	2.0986-2.0998	.0013-.0035	②	③	4	.002-.006
V6-231	1978-79	.0008-.0020	.010	.015	.9392	1.999-2.000	.0005-.0026	2.4995	.0004-.0015	2	.004-.008
V6-231	1980	.0008-.0020	.010	.015	.9392	2.2487-2.2495	.0005-.0026	2.4995	.0004-.0017	2	.004-.008
6-250	1970-78	.0005-.0015	.010	.015	.9271	1.999-2.000	.0007-.0027	2.2983-2.2993	.0003-.0029	7	.002-.006
6-250	1979-80	.001-.002	.010	.015	.9271	1.999-2.000	.0010-.0026	2.2979-2.2994	㉕	7	.002-.006
6-292	1972	.0025-.0031	.010	.015	.9271	1.999-2.100	.0007-.0028	2.2983-2.2993	.0008-.0034	7	.002-.006
6-292	1979-80	.0026-.0036	.010	.015	.9271	2.099-2.100	.0010-.0026	2.2979-2.2994	㉕	7	.002-.006
6-292	1975-78	.0026-.0036	.010	.015	.9271	2.099-2.100	.0007-.0027	2.2983-2.2993	.0008-.0034	7	.002-.006
8-267	1979-80	.0007-.0017	.010	.015	.9271	2.0986-2.0998	.0013-.0035	②	③	5	.002-.006
8-305	1976-77	.0007-.0017	.010	.015	.9271	2.099-2.100	.0013-.0035	②	③	5	.002-.006
8-305	1978-80	.0007-.0017	.010	.015	.9271	2.098-2.099	.0013-.0035	②	③	5	.002-.006
8-307	1970-73	.0005-.0011	.010	.015	.9272	2.099-2.100	.0007-.0028	⑥	⑨	5	.002-.006
8-350	1970-72	.0012-.0022	.010	.015	.9272	2.099-2.100	.0007-.0028	⑤	⑨	5	.002-.006
8-350	1973	.0007-.0013	.010	.015	.9272	2.099-2.100	.0013-.0035	⑯	⑰	5	.002-.006
8-350	1974-76	.0007-.0013	⑧	.015	.9272	2.099-2.100	.0013-.0035	⑯	⑰	5	.002-.006
8-350	1977-80	.0007-.0017	.010	.015	.9272	2.099-2.100	.0013-.0035	②	③	5	.002-.006
8-366	1970-79	.003-.004	.010	.010	.9896	2.199-2.200	.0014-.0030	⑩	⑪	5	.006-.010
8-396	1970-71	.0018-.0026	.010	.010	.9896	2.199-2.200	.0009-.0025	⑫	⑬	5	.006-.010
8-400	1974-76	.0014-.0020	.010	.015	.9272	2.099-2.100	.0013-.0035	㉔	⑰	5	.002-.006
8-400	1977-80	.0014-.0024	.010	.015	.9270	2.199-2.200	.0013-.0035	㉔	④	5	.002-.006
8-402	1970-72	.0018-.0026	.010	.015	.9897	2.199-2.200	.0009-.0300	—	⑬	5	.006-.010
8-427	1970-79	.0034-.0044	.010	.010	.9896	2.199-2.200	.0014-.0030	⑩	⑪	5	.006-.010

Continued

CHEVROLET

PISTON, PIN, RING, CRANKSHAFT & BEARING SPECIFICATIONS—Continued

Engine Model	Year	Piston Clearance	Ring End Gap①		Piston Pin Diam.	Rod Bearings		Main Bearings			
			Comp.	Oil		Shaft Diameter	Bearing Clearance	Shaft Diameter	Bearing Clearance	Thrust Bearing No.	Shaft End Play
8-454	1970–72	.0024–.0034	.010	.015	.9897	2.199–2.200	.0009–.0025	⑭	⑮	5	.006–.010
8-454	1973–76	.0018–.0028	.010	.010	.9897	2.1985–2.1995	.0009–.0025	㉑	⑮	5	.006–.010
8-454	1977–80	.0014–.0024 ㉖	.010	.015	.9897	2.1985–2.1995	.0009–.0025	㉑	⑮	5	.006–.010
V6-401	1970–72	.0033–.0039	⑱	—	2.2399	2.8112–2.8122	.0010–.0031	⑳	.0013–.0039	—	.003–.008
V6-478	1970–72	.0039–.0045	⑲	.024	1.2399	2.8112–1.8122	.0010–.0031	⑳	.0013–.0039	—	.003–.008

① —Fit rings in tapered bores to the clearance listed in tightest portion of ring travel.
② —No. 1, 2.4484–2.4493; No. 2, 3, 4, 2.4481–2.4490. No. 5, 2.4479–2.4488.
③ —No. 1, .0008–.0020; No. 2, 3, 4, .0011–.0023. No. 5, .0017–.0032.
④ —No. 1, 2.4484–2.4493; No. 2 & 3, 2.4481–2.4490; No. 4, 2.4479–2.4488.
⑤ —Rear bearing .0008–.0024″, all others .0003–.0019″.
⑥ —Rear 2.4479–2.4488, all others 2.4484–2.4493″.
⑦ —Rear .001–.006″, all others .0008–.0024″.
⑧ —Top ring .010″, second ring .013.
⑨ —Front .0003–.0015″, rear .0008–.0023″, all others .0006–.0018″.
⑩ —Rear 2.7473–2.7483″, all others 2.7481–2.7490.
⑪ —Rear .0029–.0045″, all others .0013–.0025″.
⑫ —Nos. 1 & 2, 2.7487–2.7496″. Nos. 3 & 4, 2.7481–2.7490, No. 5, 2.7478–2.7488″.
⑬ —No. 1, .0007–.0019″. No. 5, .0024–.004″. All others, .0013–.0025
⑭ —No. 1, 2.7485–2.7495″. Nos. 2, 3, 4, 2.7481″. No. 5, 2.7478–2.7488″.
⑮ —Nos. 1, 2, 3, 4, .0013–.0025″. No. 5, .0024″–.0040″.
⑯ —No. 1, 2, 3, 4, 2.4484–2.4493; No. 5 2.4479–2.4488″.
⑰ —No. 1 .0008–.0020″; No. 2, .0011–.0023″, No. 5 .0017–.0033″.
⑱ —Top ring .029″; second and third rings, .020″.
⑲ —Top ring, .031; second and third ring, .022″.
⑳ —All exc. rear, 3.1247–3.1237″; rear, 3.1239–3.1229″.
㉑ —No. 1, 2.7485″–2.7494″. Nos. 2, 3, 2.7481″–2.7490″. No. 5, 2.7478″–2.7488″.
㉒ —Top ring .015, second ring .009.
㉓ —No. 1, .0003–.0020; all others .0003–.0027.
㉔ —No. 1, 2, 3, 4, 2.6484–2.6493; No. 5, 2.6479–2.6488.
㉕ —Nos. 1 thru 6, .0010–.0024. No. 7, .0016–.0035.
㉖ —1980, .003–.004 inch.

WHEEL ALIGNMENT SPECIFICATIONS

Model	Year	Caster, Deg.	Camber, Deg.	Toe-In, In.	Kingpin Inclination, Deg.	Model	Year	Caster, Deg.	Camber, Deg.	Toe-In, In.	Kingpin Inclination, Deg.
C10, 20, 30	1975–78	①	①	3/16	—	CA, PA, 10-30	1972–74	①	+1/4	3/16	—
C-10, 20, 30	1979–80	①	+.2	3/16	—	GA 10-30	1972–74	①	+1/4	3/16	—
K10, 20, 30	1975–78	①	①	0	—	KA 10, 20	1972–74	①	+1 1/2	3/16 ③	—
K10, 20	1979–80	①	+1°	0	—	Vega	1971–74	−3/4	+1/4	3/16–5/16	—
K30	1979–80	①	+1/2°	0	—	El Camino	1971–72	−1	+3/4	1/8–1/4	—
G10, 20, 30	1975–78	①	①	3/16	—	C-P 10	1972	①	①	3/16	—
G-10, 20	1979–80	①	+1/2°	3/16	—	C-P 20-30	1971	①	①	3/16	—
G30	1979–80	①	+.2°	3/16	—	K 10-20	1971	①	①	3/16	—
P10, 20, 30	1975–78	①	—	3/16	—	El Camino	1970	−1/2	+1/2	1/8–1/4	—
P-10, 20, 30	1979–80	①	+.2	3/16	—	C-P10	1970	0	+1/4	1/8–1/4	—
Motor Home	1975–78	①	①	5/16	—	C-P20, 30	1970	0	+1/4	1/8–1/4	—
Motor Home	1979–80	①	+.2	5/16	—	G10, 20	1970	+3 1/4	+1	3/32–3/16	7 1/4
El Camino④	1978–80	+1	+1/2	1/8	—	G10, 20, 30	1971	0	+1/4	1/8–1/4	8 1/2
El Camino⑤	1978–80	+3	+1/2	1/8	—	K10, 20	1970	+3 1/4	+1	3/32–3/16	8 1/2
El Camino④	1977	+1	⑥	0–1/8	—	B6	1979	−2	+1 1/2°	1/8–1/4⑱	7 1/6
El Camino⑤	1977	⑰	⑥	0–1/8	—	C5-6-7	1979	+2	+1 1/2	1/8–1/4⑱	7 1/6
El Camino④	1975–76	+1	⑥	0–1/8	—	D9	1979	0	+1/4	1/8–1/4	5 3/4
El Camino⑤	1975–76	+2	⑥	0–1/8	—	J8-9	1979	+1 1/2	⑮	1/8–1/4⑱	⑯
Vega	1975	−3/4	+1/4	0–1/4	—	N9	1979	0	+1/4	1/8–1/4	5 3/4
El Camino④	1973–74	+1	⑥	0–1/8	—	P4	1979	+2 1/2	+1 1/2	1/8–1/4⑱	7 1/6
El Camino⑤	1973–74	0	⑥	0–1/8	—	W6-7	1979	+4	+1 1/2	1/8–1/4⑱	7 1/6

Continued

CHEVROLET

WHEEL ALIGNMENT SPECIFICATIONS—Continued

Model	Year	Caster, Deg.	Camber, Deg.	Toe-In, In.	Kingpin Inclination, Deg.	Model	Year	Caster, Deg.	Camber, Deg.	Toe-In, In.	Kingpin Inclination, Deg.
C40	1971-72	+2½	+1	1/8-3/16	7¼	WM80	1972	②	⑮	1/8-1/4	⑯
C50	1973	+2½	+1	1/8-3/16	7¼	DB, DP 90	1972-73	+1	⑮	1/8-1/4	⑯
C50	1974	2½	+1	1/16-1/8	7¼	FB, J90	1972-73	+1	⑮	1/8-1/4	⑯
C50, 60, 65	1975-78	+2½	+1½	1/8-1/4⑱	7 1/6	HC, HE90	1972-73	+1	⑮	1/8-1/4	⑯
T50, 60	1971-72	+1¼	+1½	1/8-1/4	7	HH, HM90	1972-73	+1	⑮	1/8-1/4	⑯
T60, 65⑫	1973	+1¼	+1½	1/8-1/4	7	MB, MC 90	1972-73	+1	⑮	1/8-1/4	⑯
T60, 65	1974	1¼	+1½	1/16-1/8	7	RM80	1971-73	+3	⑮	1/8-1/4	⑯
T60, 65⑬⑨	1973-74	+1¼	⑮	1/8-1/4	⑯	TE90	1971-72	②	⑮	1/8-1/4	⑯
T60, 65	1975-78	+4	+1½	1/8-1/4⑱	7 1/6	HJ70	1971	+2 13/16	+1½	1/8-1/4	7
CM60	1971-72	+2½	+1	3/32-3/16	7¼	JM70	1971	+1	⑮	1/8-1/4	⑯
CM65⑫	1973	+2½	+1	3/32-3/16	7¼	JV80	1971	+1	⑮	1/8-1/4	⑯
CM65⑬⑨	1973	+2½	⑮	1/8-7/32	⑯	JV80	1973	+1	+1	1/8-1/4	5½
CM65⑧	1974	2½	1	1/16-1/8	7¼	JE90	1971	+1	⑮	1/8-1/4	⑯
CM65	1974	2½	⑮	1/8-1/4	⑯	HV70	1970-72	+2 13/16	+1½	1/8-1/4	7
P40⑩	1970	+1½	+1	1/8-3/16	7¼	HV70⑫	1973	+2 4/5	+1½	1/8-1/4	7
C-P40⑪	1970	+2½	+1	3/32-3/16	7¼	HV70⑬⑨	1973	+1	⑮	1/8-1/4	⑯
P40, 45	1974	½	1	1/16-1/8	7¼	JV70	1970-73	+1	⑮	1/8-1/4	⑯
P40, 45	1975-78	+2½	+1½	1/8-1/4⑱	7 1/6	TV70	1970-73	+1¼	+1½	1/8-1/4	7
C-S50⑪	1970-73	+2½	+1	3/32-3/16	7¼	TV70⑬⑨	1973	+1¼	⑮	1/8-1/4	⑯
SC-60	1974	2½	1	1/16-1/8	7¼	HM80	1970-72	+2 13/16	+1½	1/8-1/4	7
S60	1975-78	+2½	+1½	1/8-1/4⑱	7 1/6	HM80⑫	1973	+2 3/10	+1½	1/8-1/4	7
M65	1975-78	+2½	+1½	1/8-1/4⑱	7 1/6	HM⑬⑨	1973	+1	⑮	1/8-1/4	⑯
HV70, 75	1975-78	+1 2/5	+1½	1/8-1/4⑱	7 1/6	JM80	1970-73	+1	⑮	1/8-1/4	⑯
HY70, 75	1975-78	+1	+¼	1/8-1/4⑱	⑯	TM80, A	1970-72	②	⑮	1/8-1/4	⑯
H90, 95	1975-78	+1	⑦	1/8-1/4⑱	⑯	TM80, A⑬⑨	1973	0	⑮	1/8-1/4	⑯
J70, 80, 90	1975-78	+1	⑦	1/8-1/4⑱	⑯	TM80, V⑫	1973	+1¼	+1½	1/8-1/4	7
MH90, 95	1975-78	+1	⑦	1/8-1/4⑱	⑯	TM80, V⑬⑨	1973	+1¼	⑮	1/8-1/4	⑯
D90	1975-78	+1	+¼	1/8-1/4⑱	⑯	HI, HN90	1970-73	+1	⑮	1/8-1/4	⑯
F90	1975-78	+1	+¼	1/8-1/4	⑯	MH90	1970-73	+1	⑮	1/8-1/4	⑯
S531⑫	1970	+1¾	+1	3/32-3/16	7¼	DC, DH90	1970-73	+1	⑮	1/8-1/4	⑯
M50	1970	+2½	+1	3/32-3/16	7¼	DI, DN90	1970-73	+1	⑮	1/8-1/4	⑯
C-S60	1970-73	+2½	+1	3/32-3/16	7¼	FC, FH90	1970-73	+1	⑮	1/8-1/4	⑯
T50, 60⑫	1970	+1¾	+1	3/32-3/16	7¼	FI, FN90	1970-73	+1	⑮	1/8-1/4	⑯
C-M-T60⑬⑭	1970	+2½	⑮	1/8-7/32	⑯	JI, MI90	1970-71	+1	⑮	1/8-1/4	⑯
WV70	1972	+1	+1	1/8-1/4	5½	TW, WW90	1973	+1¼	+¼	1/8-1/4	⑯
WV70	1973	+1	⑮	1/8-1/4	7	JN90	1970	+1	⑮	1/8-1/4	⑯

① — Refer to front suspension section of this chapter for specifications.
② — Manual steering, +½°; power steering, 0°.
③ — With full time four wheel drive 0".
④ — Manual steering.
⑤ — Power steering.
⑥ — Left, +1°; right, +½°.
⑦ — Left, −¼; right, +¼.
⑧ — F-070 axle.
⑨ — Rated capacity 12,000 lbs.
⑩ — Rated capacity 4000 lbs.
⑪ — Rated capacity 5000 lbs.
⑫ — Rated capacity 7000 lbs.
⑬ — Rated capacity 9000 lbs.
⑭ — Rated capacity 11000 lbs.
⑮ — Left side +¼°, right side −¼°.
⑯ — Left side 5¾°, right side 6¼°.
⑰ — Radial Tires, +2°; Exc. Radial Tires, +1°.
⑱ — Steel belted radial tires, zero toe in.

CHEVROLET

Overhead Valve Engine Section

See page 847 for 4 cylinder Overhead Cam Engine
See GMC Truck Chapter for Service on V6-305C, 379, 401, 432, 478 & V8-637 Engines

CYLINDER HEAD, REPLACE

NOTE: A new exhaust valve part No. 336771 has been released for service on all 1974 V8-427 truck engines. This valve is of the sodium filled/hollow stem type previously utilized in the GMC V6.

CAUTION: Sodium cooled valves must not be discarded with other scrap metal. If a sodium-cooled valve is accidentally broken, the sodium will react violently with water, resulting in fire and explosion due to the chemical reaction. Also, serious burns will result if sodium or its oxide comes in contact with the skin.

6-250, 292

1. Remove necessary access covers depending on vehicle being serviced.
2. Drain cooling system and remove air cleaner and air compressor.
3. Disconnect choke cable, accelerator pedal rod at bellcrank on manifold, and fuel and vacuum lines at carburetor.
4. Disconnect exhaust pipe at manifold flange, then remove manifolds and carburetor as an assembly.
5. Disconnect wire harness from temperature sending unit and coil, leaving harness clear of clips on rocker arm cover.
6. Disconnect radiator hose at water outlet housing and battery ground strap at cylinder head.
7. Remove spark plugs. On 6-cylinder engines, remove coil.
8. Remove rocker arm cover. Back off rocker arm nuts, pivot rocker arms to clear push rods and remove push rods.
9. Unfasten and remove cylinder head.
10. Reverse removal procedure to install and tighten head bolts to the specified torque and in the sequence shown in Fig. 1.

V6-200, 229 & 231

1. Drain cooling system and engine block.
2. Remove intake and exhaust manifolds.
3. Remove alternator lower mounting bolt and position alternator aside.
4. If equipped with A/C, remove compressor and forward mounting bracket and position aside.
5. Remove rocker arm cover, rocker arms and push rods.

NOTE: Keep rocker arm, rocker arm balls and push rods in order so they can be installed in the same position.

6. Remove cylinder head bolts and cylinder head.
7. Reverse procedure to install. Tighten cylinder head and intake manifold bolts in sequence shown in Figs. 2, 3, 4 and 5.

All V8 Engines

1. Remove intake and exhaust manifolds and air compressor.
2. Remove valve mechanism.
3. Drain coolant from block.
4. Unfasten and remove cylinder head.

Installation:

The gasket surfaces on both head and block must be clean of any foreign material and free of nicks or heavy scratches. Cylinder bolt threads in the block and threads on the head bolts must be clean as dirt will affect bolt torque.

1. On engines using a steel gasket, coat both sides of a new gasket with a good sealer. One method of applying the sealer that will assure the proper coat is with the use of a paint roller. Too much sealer may hold the gasket away from the head or block.

CAUTION: Use no sealer on engines using a composition steel asbestos gasket.

2. Place gasket in position over the dowel pins with the head up.
3. Carefully guide cylinder head into place over dowel pins and gasket.
4. Coat threads of cylinder head bolts with sealing compound and install bolts finger tight.
5. Tighten each bolt a little at a time in the sequence shown in Figs. 6 and 7 until the specified torque is reached (see *Engine Tightening Specifications* chart).
6. Install and tighten intake manifold bolts in sequence shown in Figs. 8 and 9.
7. Install and adjust valve mechanism as outlined further on.

VALVE ARRANGEMENT
Front to Rear

Inline Six	E-I-I-E-I-I-E-E-I-I-E
V6-231	E-I-I-E-I-E
V8's Except below	E-I-I-E-E-I-I-E
V8-366, 396, 427, 454	E-I-E-I-E-I-E-I

VALVES, ADJUST
V8 Engines With Hydraulic Lifters

NOTE: After the engine has been thoroughly warmed up, the valves may be adjusted with the engine shut off as follows: With engine in position to fire No. 1 cylinder the following valves may be adjusted: Exhaust 1-3-4-8, intake 1-2-5-7. Then crank the engine one more complete revolution which will bring No. 6 cylinder to the firing position at which time the following valves may be adjusted: Exhaust 2-5-6-7, intake 3-4-6-8.

The following procedure, performed with the engine running should be done only in case readjustment is required.
1. After engine has been warmed up to operating temperature, remove valve cover and install a new valve cover gasket on cylinder head to prevent oil from running out.
2. With engine running at idle speed, back off valve rocker arm nut until rocker arm starts to clatter.
3. Turn rocker arm nut down slowly until the clatter just stops. This is the zero lash position.
4. Turn nut down 1/4 additional turn and pause 10 seconds until engine runs smoothly. Repeat additional 1/4 turns, pausing 10 seconds each time, until nut has been turned down the number of turns listed in the *Valve Specifications*

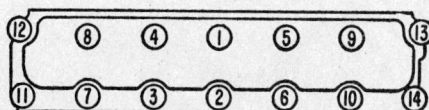

Fig. 1 Cylinder head tightening sequence. 6-250, 292

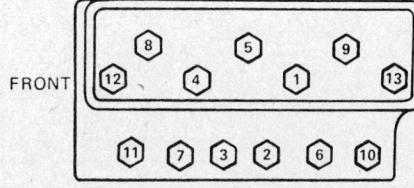

Fig. 2 Cylinder head tightening sequence. V6-200, 229

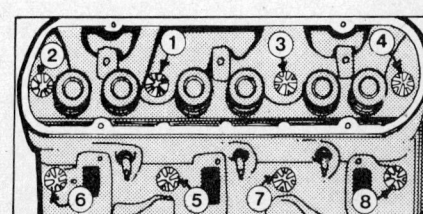

Fig. 3 Cylinder head tightening sequence. V6-231

CHEVROLET

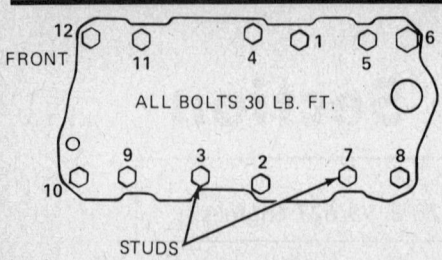

Fig. 4 Intake manifold tightening sequence. V6-200, 229

Chart from the zero lash position.

NOTE: The preload adjustment must be done slowly to allow the lifter to adjust itself to prevent the possibility of interference between the valve head and top of piston, which might result in internal damage and/or bent push rods. Noisy lifters should be replaced.

Mechanical Lifters

With the engine warmed to operating temperature as described above, turn rocker arm stud nut or adjusting screw as required to obtain the clearances given in the *Valve Specifications* table.

NOTE: To be sure that the valves and lifters function perfectly, it is strongly recommended that a vacuum gauge be used when making the adjustment on hydraulic lifter jobs. With vacuum gauge connected and engine idling, tighten each rocker arm nut until the *highest and steadiest vacuum is indicated on the gauge.*

ROCKER ARMS

V6-231

A nylon retainer is used to retain the rocker arm. Break them below their heads with a chisel, Fig. 10, or pry out with channel locks. Production rocker arms can be installed in

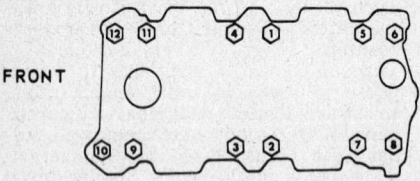

Fig. 8 Intake manifold tightening sequence. V8-267, 283, 305, 307, 327, 350, 400 engines

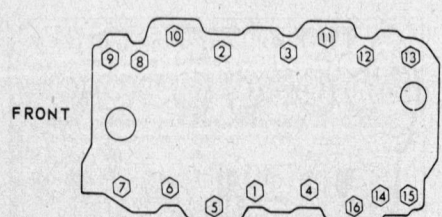

Fig. 9 Intake manifold tightening sequence. V8-366, 396, 402, 427, 454 engines

Fig. 5 Intake manifold tightening sequence. V6-231

any sequence since the arms are identical.
Replacement rocker arms for all engines are identified with a stamping, right (R) and left (L), Fig. 11 and must be installed as shown in Fig. 12.

ROCKER ARM STUDS

Except V6-231

Rocker arm studs that have damaged threads may be replaced with standard studs. Loose studs should be replaced with .003" or .013" oversize studs which are available for replacement.
Remove the old stud by placing a suitable spacer over the stud, Fig. 13. Install a nut and flat washer on the stud and pull out the stud by turning the nut. After reaming the hole for an oversize stud, coat the press-fit area of the new stud with rear axle lubricant. Install the stud by driving it in until it protrudes from the head the same distance as the other studs, Fig. 14

NOTE: On V8-366, 396, 402, 427 & 454 the rocker arm studs are threaded into the cylinder head. Coat threads on cylinder head end of stud before assembling to head.

PUSH RODS

NOTE: When a replacement push rod has a

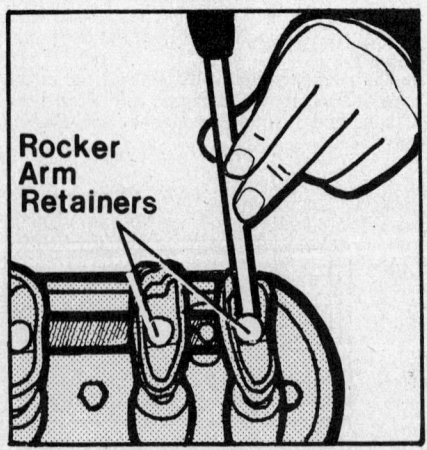

Fig. 10 Removing nylon retainer. V6-231

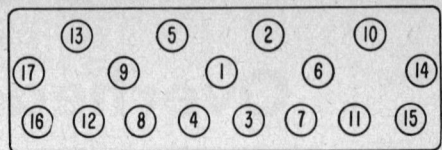

Fig. 6 Cylinder head tightening sequence. V8-267, 283, 305, 307, 327, 350, 400 engines

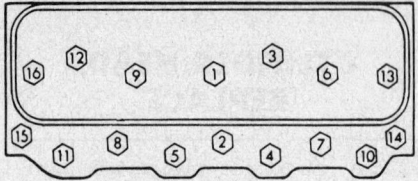

Fig. 7 Cylinder head tightening sequence. V8-366, 396, 402, 427, 454

paint stripe at one end, this painted end must be installed in contact with the rocker arm. To provide durability a hardened insert is incorporated in the rocker arm end of these push rods.

VALVES, REMOVE

CAUTION: Some V8-427 engines are equipped with exhaust valves filled with sodium for cooling purposes. When handling these valves, follow these precautions:
1. Never cut open an old valve and be extremely careful when removing a broken valve from an engine. Otherwise, the metallic sodium in the valve may contact and burn the skin.
2. Bury discarded sodium-cooled valves in some inaccessible place to prevent other persons from handling them. *Never immerse one of these valves in water.*

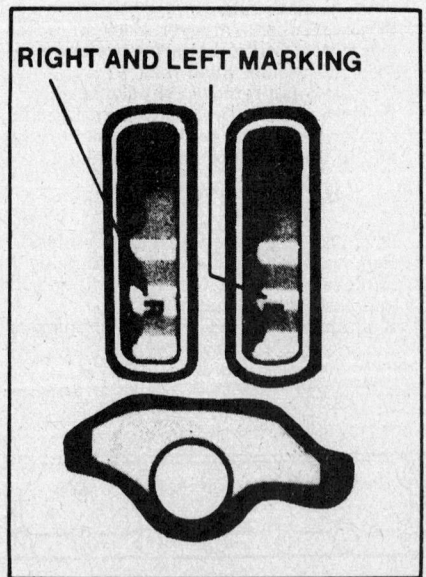

Fig. 11 Service rocker arms identification. V6-231

CHEVROLET

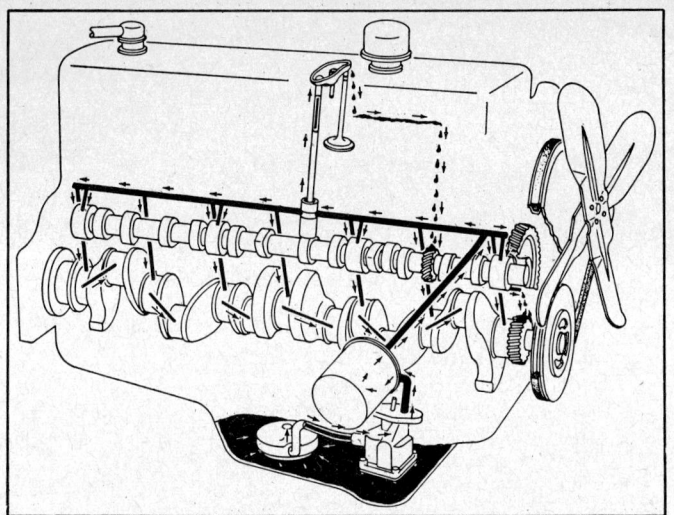

Engine oiling system. 6-250, 292 engines

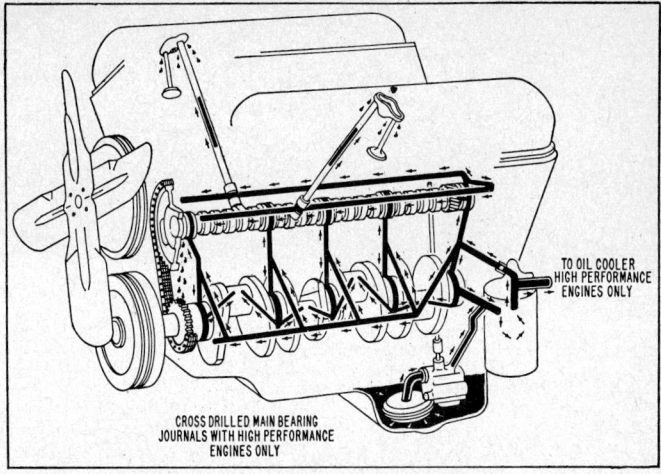

Engine lubrication. V8-366, 396, 402, 427, 454 engines

VALVE GUIDES
All Engines

Valves operate in guide holes bored directly in the cylinder head. When valve stem-to-guide clearance becomes excessive, valves with oversize stems are available for service replacement.

Check the valve stem clearance of each valve (after cleaning) in its respective valve guide. If the clearance exceeds the service limits of .004" on the intake or .005" on the exhaust, ream the valve guide to accommodate the next oversize diameter valve stem.

HYDRAULIC LIFTERS

The hydraulic valve lifters, Fig. 15, are simple in design, readjustments are not necessary and servicing them requires that care and cleanliness be exercised in the handling of parts.

Disassemble & Assemble

1. Hold plunger down with push rod and, using a small screw driver or awl, remove plunger retainer.
2. Remove parts from lifter body.
3. Clean all parts and inspect for damage. If any parts are damaged, the entire lifter assembly should be replaced. The inertia valve in the plunger for rocker arm lubrication should move when the plunger is shaken.
4. To reassemble, invert plunger and set ball into hole in plunger. Place ball check valve retainer over ball and on plunger. Place check valve retainer spring over retainer. Assemble body over plunger assembly. Turn assembly over and install push rod seat. Compress plunger with push rod and install retainer.
5. Compress plunger to open oil holes and fill plunger with SAE 10 oil. Work plunger up and down and refill.

TIMING CASE COVER
6-250, 292

1. To remove cover, remove radiator.
2. Remove vibration damper.
3. Remove oil pan.
4. Unfasten and remove cover.
5. Pry oil seal out of cover with a large screwdriver. Install new seal with open side of seal inside of cover and drive or press seal into place.
6. If oil nozzle is to be replaced, remove it with pliers as shown in Fig. 16. Drive new nozzle in place, using a suitable light plastic or rubber hammer.
7. Clean gasket surfaces.

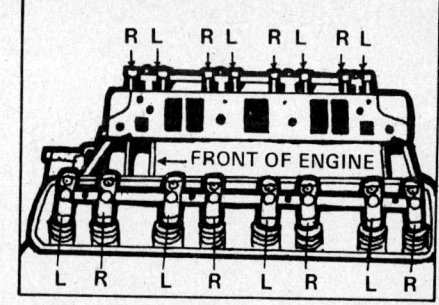

Fig. 12 Service rocker arm installation. V6-231

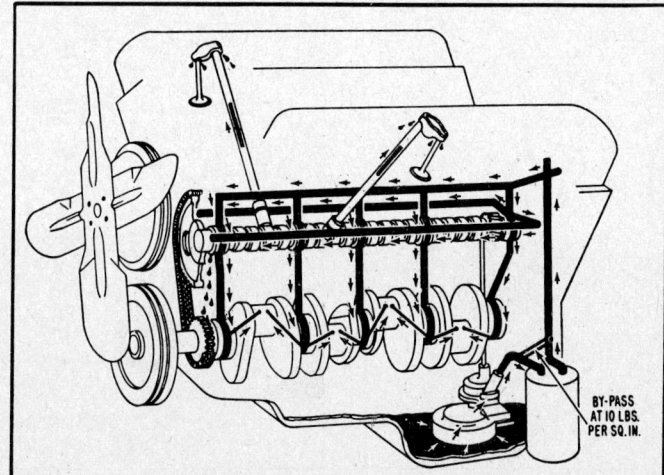

Engine oiling system. V8-267, 283, 305, 307, 327, 350, 400 engines

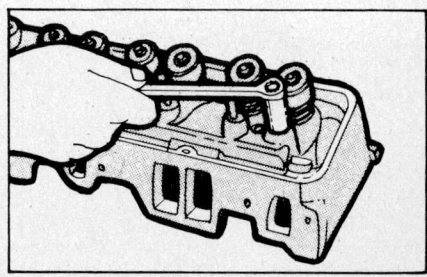

Fig. 13 Removing valve rocker stud

CHEVROLET

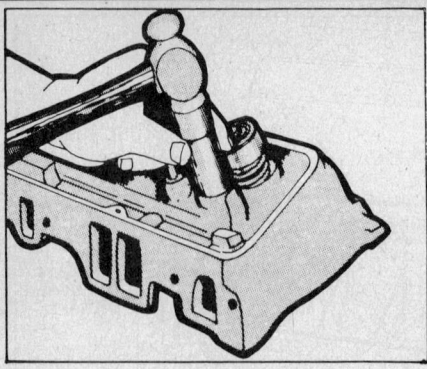

Fig. 14 Installing valve rocker stud

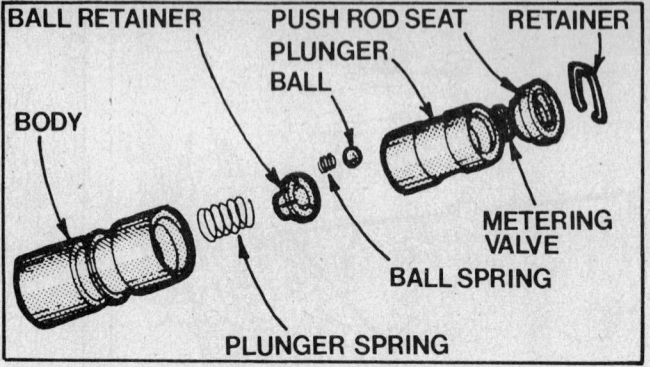

Fig. 15 Hydraulic valve lifter

8. Install a suitable centering tool over end of crankshaft.
9. Coat gasket with light grease and stick it in position on block.
10. Install cover over centering tool, Fig. 17, and install cover screws, tightening them to 6 to 8 ft. lbs. *It is important that the centering tool be used to align the cover so the vibration damper installation will not damage the seal and position seal evenly around damper hub surface.*

V6-200, 229 & All V8 Engines

To remove the cover, take off vibration damper and remove oil pan. Remove heater hose from water pump, and water pump from cylinder block. Unfasten and remove cover from engine.

When installing the cover, make certain that the oil slinger is in place against the crankshaft sprocket. Coat the oil seal with light grease and, using a new cover gasket, install cover and gasket over dowel pins in cylinder block.

V6-231

1. Drain cooling system and remove radiator.
2. Remove fan, pulleys and belts.
3. Remove crankshaft pulley and reinforcement.
4. If equipped with power steering, remove any pump bracket bolts attached to timing chain cover and loosen and remove any other bolts necessary that will allow pump and brackets to be moved out of the way.
5. Remove fuel pump.
6. Remove Delcotron and brackets.
7. Remove distributor cap and pull spark plug wire retainers off brackets on rocker arm cover. Swing distributor cap with wires attached out of the way. Disconnect distributor primary lead.
8. Remove distributor. *If chain and sprockets are not to be disturbed, note position of distributor rotor for installation in the same position.*
9. Loosen and slide clamp on thermostat by-pass hose rearward.
10. Remove bolts attaching chain cover to block.
11. Remove two oil pan-to-chain cover bolts and remove cover.
12. Reverse procedure to install, noting data shown in Fig. 18.

NOTE: Remove the oil pump cover and pack the space around the oil pump gears completely full of vaseline. There must be no air space left inside the pump. Reinstall the cover using a new gasket. This step is very important as the oil pump may lose its prime whenever the pump, pump cover or timing chain cover is disturbed. If the pump is not packed it may not begin to pump oil as soon as the engine is started.

TIMING GEARS

Inline Six & V8 Engines With Timing Gears

When necessary to install a new camshaft gear, the camshaft will have to be removed as the gear is a pressed fit on the shaft. The camshaft is held in position by a thrust plate which is fastened to the crankcase by two capscrews which are accessible through two holes in the gear web.

Use an arbor press to remove the gear and when doing so, a suitable sleeve, Fig. 19, should be employed to support the gear properly on its steel hub.

Before installing a new gear, assemble a new thrust plate on the shaft and press the gear on just far enough so that the thrust plate has practically no clearance, yet is free to turn. The correct clearance is from .001" to .005". Fig. 20.

The crankshaft gear can be removed by utilizing the two tapped holes in conjunction with a gear puller, Fig. 21.

When the timing gears are installed, be sure the punch-marks on both gears are in mesh, Fig. 22 and 23. Backlash between the gears should be from .004" to .006", Fig. 24. Check the run-out of the gears, Fig. 25, and if the camshaft gear run-out exceeds .004" or the

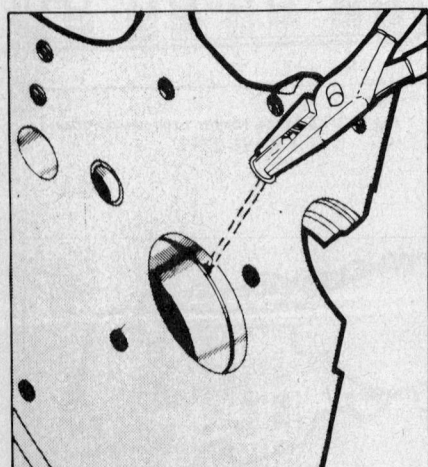

Fig. 16 Timing gear oil nozzle removal. 6-250, 292

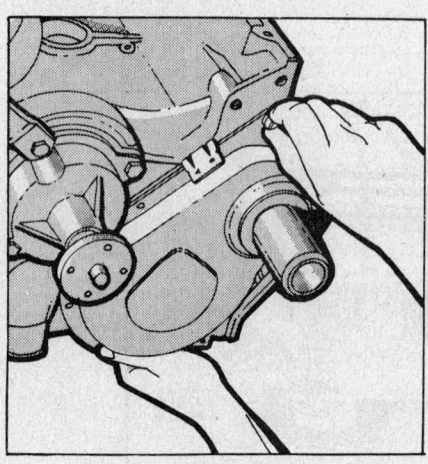

Fig. 17 Installing time case cover. 6-250, 292

Fig. 18 Timing chain cover installation. V6-231

CHEVROLET

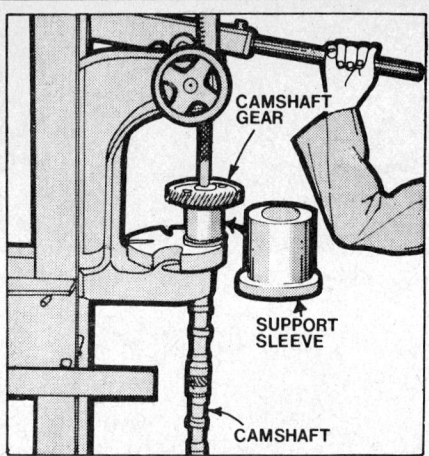

Fig. 19 Removing camshaft gear. 6 cylinder and V8 engines with timing gears

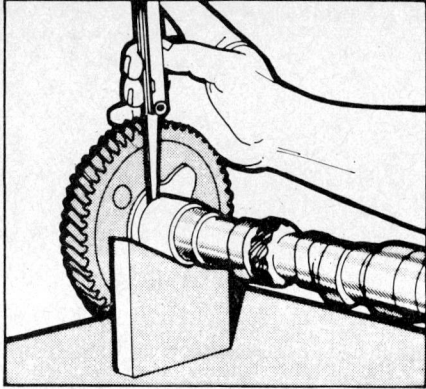

Fig. 20 Checking camshaft end play. 6 cylinder and V8 engines with timing gears

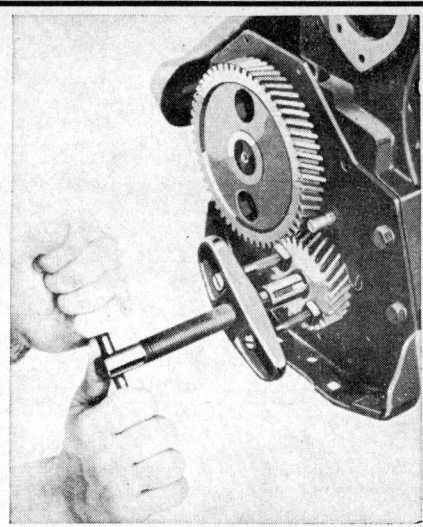

Fig. 21 Using puller to remove crankshaft gear. 6 cylinder and V8 engines with timing gears

crank gear run-out is in excess of .003", remove the gear (or gears) and examine for burrs, dirt or some other fault which may cause the run-out. If these conditions are not the cause, replace the gear (or gears).

TIMING CHAIN

V6-200, 229 & V8 Engines With Timing Chain

1. Remove timing chain cover as outlined previously.
2. Remove crankshaft oil slinger.
3. Crank engine until "O" marks on sprockets are in alignment, Fig. 26.
4. Remove three camshaft-to-sprocket bolts.
5. Remove camshaft sprocket and timing chain together. Sprocket is a light press fit on camshaft for approximately $1/8"$. If sprocket does not come off easily, a light blow with a plastic hammer on the lower edge of the sprocket should dislodge it.
6. If crankshaft sprocket is to be replaced, remove it with a suitable gear puller. Install new sprocket, aligning key and keyway.
7. Install chain on camshaft sprocket. Hold sprocket vertical with chain hanging below and shift around to align the "O" marks on sprockets.

8. Align dowel in camshaft with dowel hole in sprocket and install sprocket on camshaft. *Do not attempt to drive sprocket on camshaft as welch plug at rear of engine can be dislodged.*
9. Draw sprocket onto camshaft, using the three mounting bolts. Tighten to 20 ft. lbs. torque.
10. Lubricate timing chain and install cover.

V6-231

1. With the timing case cover removed as outlined previously, temporarily install the vibration damper bolt and washer in end of crankshaft.
2. Turn crankshaft so sprockets are positioned as shown in Fig. 27. Use a sharp rap on a wrench handle to start the vibration damper bolt out without disturbing the position of the sprockets.

3. Remove oil pan and oil slinger.
4. Remove camshaft distributor drive gear and fuel pump eccentric.
5. Use two large screwdrivers to alternately pry the camshaft sprocket then the crankshaft sprocket forward until the camshaft sprocket is free. Then remove camshaft sprocket and chain, and crankshaft sprocket off crankshaft.
6. To install, assemble chain on sprockets and slide sprockets on their respective shafts with the "O" marks on the sprockets lined up as shown.
7. Complete the installation in the reverse order of removal. Torque sprocket bolts to 22 ft. lbs.

CAMSHAFT

Inline Six

To remove the camshaft, remove radiator, grille, push rods, valve lifters, oil pan, vibration damper and timing case cover. Then pull out camshaft and gear assembly.

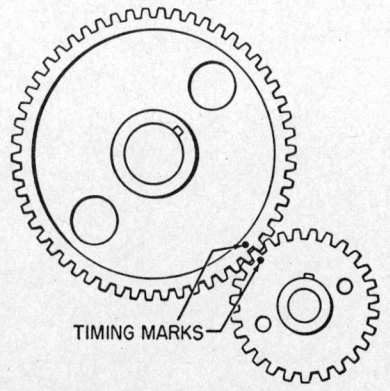

Fig. 22 Valve timing 6 cylinder

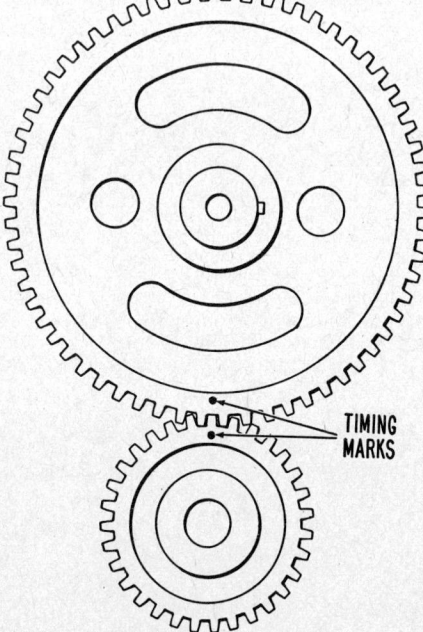

Fig. 23 Valve timing. V8 engines with timing gears

Fig. 24 Checking timing gear backlash 6 cylinder and V8 engines with timing gears

843

CHEVROLET

Fig. 25 Checking runout of timing gears with dial indicator. 6 cylinder and V8 engines with timing gears

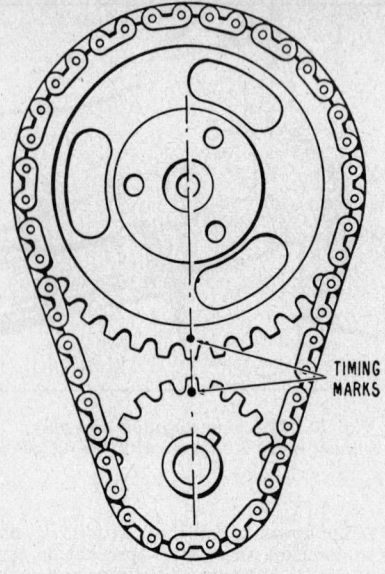

Fig. 26 Valve timing. V6-200, 229 & V8 engines with timing chain

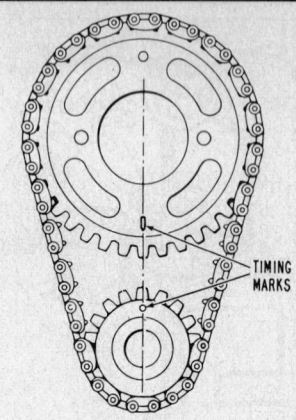

Fig. 27 Valve timing marks. V6-231

If necessary to replace bearings, the engine will have to be removed from the chassis. Then remove camshaft, flywheel and crankshaft. Drive out the expansion plug at the rear of the rear camshaft bearing and use suitable equipment to remove and replace the bearings.

V6-200, 229 & All V8 Engines

To remove the camshaft, remove valve lifters, fuel pump and its push rod, radiator, timing chain and camshaft sprocket. Install two $5/16''$-18 × 4'' bolts in two camshaft bolts holes. Using these bolts as a puller, remove camshaft from engine.

NOTE: When a new camshaft is installed, make certain that it is the correct part for the type of valve mechanism in the engine. Use of a camshaft designed for an engine with hydraulic valve lifters, or vice-versa, will result in extremely rough and noisy engine operation.

V6-231

NOTE: If engine is in the vehicle, the radiator, grille and A/C components will have to be removed. If engine is out of car, proceed as follows:

1. To remove camshaft, remove intake manifold, rocker arm shaft assemblies, push rods and valve lifters.
2. Remove timing chain and sprockets.
3. Slide camshaft out of engine, using care not to mar the bearing surfaces.

PISTON & ROD, ASSEMBLE

Assemble pistons to connecting rods as shown in Figs. 28 through 36.

PISTONS

Exc. V6-231

A .001'' oversize piston is available for service use so that proper clearances can be obtained for slightly worn cylinder bores requiring only light honing to clean up the bores. In addition, oversizes of .020'', .030'' and .040'' are available. If the cylinders have less than .005'' taper or wear they can be reconditioned with a hone and fitted with the .001'' oversize piston.

V6-231

Pistons are available in standard sizes and oversizes of .005, .010 and .030 inch.

ROD BEARINGS

Exc. V6-231

Connecting rod bearing inserts are available in standard size and undersizes of .002'', .010'', .020'' and .030''. The bearings can be replaced without removing the rod assembly by removing the cap and replacing the upper and lower halves of the bearing.

V6-231

Rod bearings are available in standard sizes and undersizes of .001, .002 and .010 inch. Refer to Fig. 37, for undersize markings on bearing.

MAIN BEARINGS

Inline Six

NOTE: The rear main bearing journal has no oil hole drilling. To remove the upper bearing half (bearing half with oil hole) proceed as follows after cap is removed:

1. Use a small drift punch and hammer to start the bearing rotating out of the block.

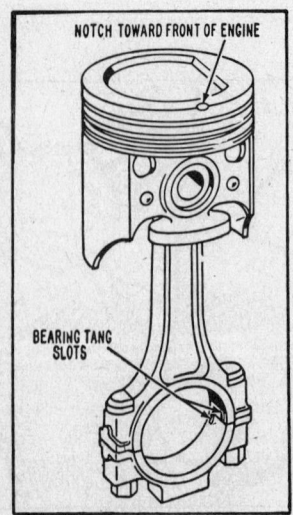

Fig. 28 Piston and rod assembly. 6-250 engine

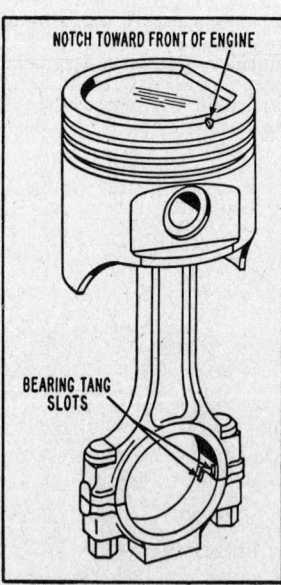

Fig. 29 Piston and rod assembly. 6-292 engine

CHEVROLET

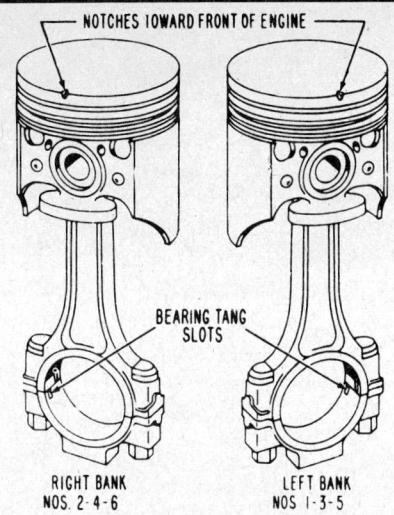

Fig. 30 Piston and rod assembly. V6-200, 229

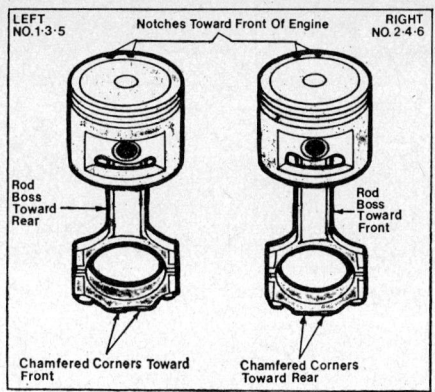

Fig. 31 Piston and rod assembly. V6-231

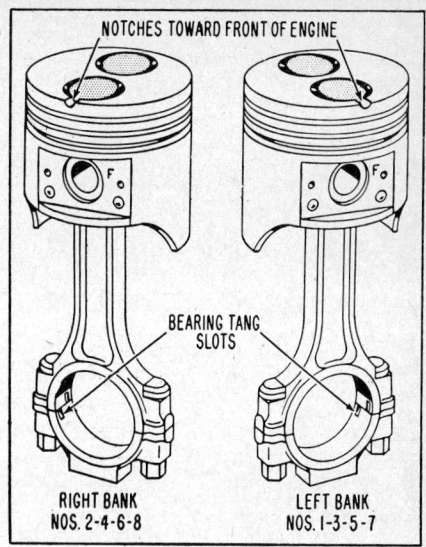

Fig. 32 Piston and rod assembly. V8-267, 305, 307, 350, 400 engines (also see Fig. 33)

2. Use a pair of pliers (tape jaws) to hold the bearing thrust surface to the oil slinger and rotate the crankshaft to pull the bearing out.
3. To install, start the bearing (side not notched) into side of block by hand, then use pliers as before to turn bearing half into place.
4. The last 1/4" movement may be done by holding just the slinger with the pliers or tap in place with a drift punch.

V6-200, 229 & V8 Engines

Shell type bearings are used, and if worn more than .004" should be replaced. No attempt should be made to shim, file or otherwise take up worn bearings.

CRANKSHAFT REAR OIL SEAL

Inline Six

Both halves of the seal, Fig. 38 can be removed without removal of the crankshaft. Always replace upper and lower seal as a unit.
1. Remove oil pan and rear main bearing cap.
2. Remove seal from groove, prying from bottom with a small screwdriver.
3. Clean crankshaft surface. Then insert a new seal, well lubricated with engine oil, in bearing cap groove. *Keep oil off parting line surface as this surface is treated with glue.*
4. Gradually push with a hammer handle until seal is rolled into place.
5. To replace upper half of seal, use a small hammer and brass pin punch to tap one end of seal until it protrudes far enough to be removed with pliers. Install the new seal.
6. Install bearing cap and oil pan.

V6-200, 229 & V8

A neoprene seal is used in the rear main bearing cap in these engines. To change the seal (engine in vehicle) proceed as follows:
1. Remove rear bearing cap.
2. Remove oil seal from groove, prying from bottom, using a small screwdriver.
3. Clean crankshaft surface.
4. Install new seal well lubricated on lip only with engine oil and, with lip facing front of engine, with finger and thumb, roll seal in place. *Keep oil off parting line surface of seal as this is treated with glue.*
5. To replace upper half of seal, use a small hammer and tap a brass pin punch to one end of seal until it protrudes far enough to be removed with pliers.

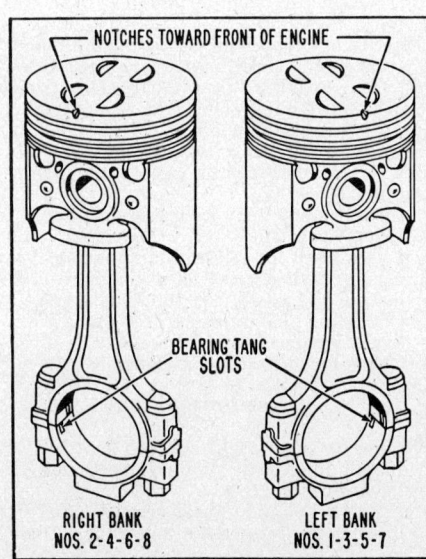

Fig. 33 Piston and rod assembly. V8-267, 305, 307, 350, 400 engines (also see Fig. 32)

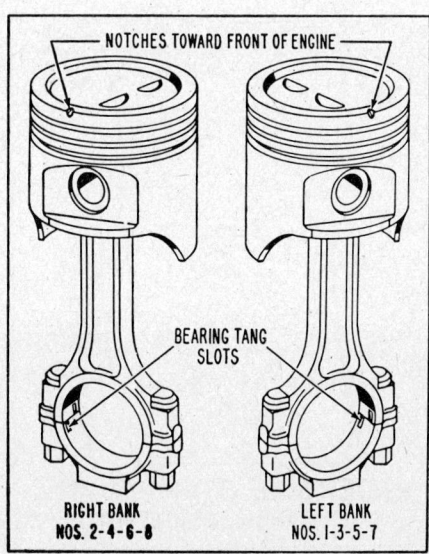

Fig. 34 Piston and rod assembly. V8-327 engine

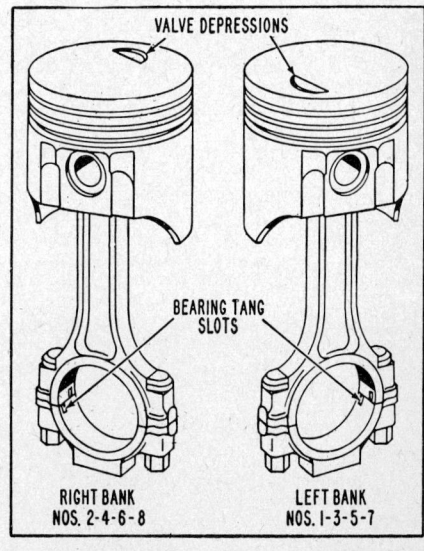

Fig. 35 Piston and rod assembly. V8-366, 427 engines

CHEVROLET

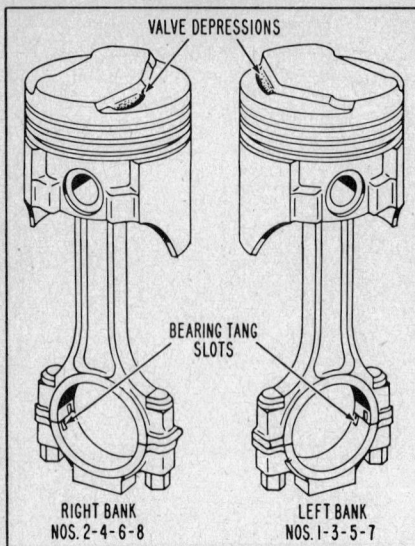

Fig. 36 Piston and rod assembly. V8-396 and 454 engines

engine enough to insert 2″ × 4″ wood blocks between engine mount and frame brackets.
4. Drain engine oil, remove oil pan, gaskets and seals.
5. Reverse procedure to install.

1976-80 Exc. 1978-80 G Models
1. Disconnect battery ground cable.
2. Raise and support vehicle. Drain oil pan and remove starter.
3. Remove flywheel splash shield of converter underpan as applicable.
4. Remove front engine mount through bolts, raise front of engine and reinstall bolts, then lower engine.
5. Remove oil pan bolts and oil pan.
6. Reverse procedure to install.

1978-80 'G' Models
1. Disconnect battery ground cable. Remove engine cover.
2. Remove air cleaner and studs. Remove fan shroud and radiator upper support brackets.
3. Raise and support vehicle.
4. On models equipped with a manual transmission:
   a. Disconnect clutch cross shaft from motor mount bracket.
   b. Remove transmission to bell housing upper bolt.
   c. Remove transmission rear mount bolts and install two 7/16 × 3 inch bolts.
   d. Raise transmission and install 2 inch block between mount and crossmember.
5. On all models, remove starter and drain oil.
6. Remove front engine mount through bolts, raise engine and install wood blocks between engine mounts and cross member brackets.
7. Remove flywheel splash shield or con-

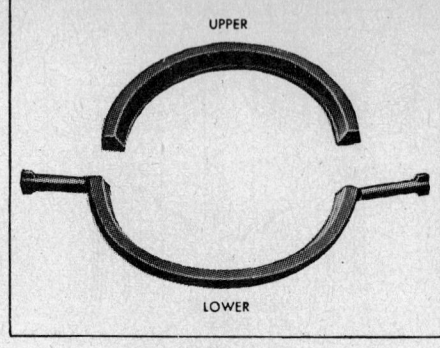

Fig. 38 Crankshaft rear oil seal. 6-250, 292

verter cover as applicable.
8. Remove oil pan bolts and lower pan.
9. Reverse procedure to install.

OIL PUMP

Inline Six

The pumps used in these engines are of the positive gear type. After disassembling the pump, examine the shaft and gears for excessive wear and replace where necessary, or better still, install a new pump. When assembling the pump, be sure the ground side of the idler gear is toward the cover.

The gasket used between the pump cover and the body is special in that it controls the clearance in the pump. If the relief valve parts show wear, install new parts. Be sure that the tapered set screw which holds the pump in place is fully seated and locked with its lock nut.

V6-200, 229 & V8 Engines

The oil pump consists of two gears and a pressure relief valve enclosed in a two-piece housing. Inasmuch as the pump is serviced on an exchange basis no repair operations other than disassembly, cleaning and inspection are covered here.

After removing the oil pan, unfasten pump from rear main bearing cap. Disconnect pump shaft from extension by removing clip from collar. Remove pump cover and take out idler gear, drive gear and shaft.

Should any of the following conditions be found, it is advisable to replace the pump assembly.
1. Inspect pump body for cracks or wear.
2. Inspect gears for wear or damage.
3. Check shaft for looseness in housing.
4. Check inside of cover for wear that would permit oil to leak past the ends of gear.
5. Check oil pick-up screen for damage to screen, by-pass valve or body.
6. Check for oil in air chamber.

Assembly
1. Place drive gear and shaft in body.
2. Install idler gear so its smooth side is toward cover.
3. Install cover and tighten screws to 6–9 ft. lb. and check to see that shaft turns freely.
4. Install pick-up screen on pipe and bend float travel control tang back in place.
5. Assemble collar end of extension shaft over pump drive shaft, aligning tang of

6. Be careful of seal retainer tang while inserting a new seal so that it doesn't cut the seal.
7. Insert a new seal well lubricated with engine oil in groove. Gradually push with hammer handle until seal is rolled into place. *Keep oil off parting line surface as this surface is treated with glue.* Install bearing cap.

OIL PAN, REPLACE

1970-80 V8s, V6-200, 229

1. Drain engine oil and remove dipstick and tube.
2. If equipped remove exhaust crossover pipe.
3. With automatic transmission, remove converter housing under pan.
4. Remove starter brace and inboard bolt and swing starter aside.
5. On 1970-72 CE 10-20-30 models, remove engine front mount bolts (frame bracket-to-mount). Using a suitable jack with a flat piece of wood to prevent damage to oil pan, raise engine enough to insert 2″ × 4″ wood blocks between engine mounts and frame brackets.
6. On K models, remove strut rods if equipped.
7. On 1973 models, support engine and remove front engine mount through bolts.
8. On 1980 El Camino with V6-229, remove upper half of fan shroud. Loosen left engine front mount through bolt and remove right bolt. Raise engine and reinstall bolt. Do not tighten.
9. Remove oil pan and discard gaskets and seals.
10. Reverse procedure to install.

Inline Six

1970-75
1. Disconnect battery ground cable.
2. Remove starter motor.
3. On CS 10-20-30, remove engine front mount bolts (frame bracket-to-mount). Using a suitable jack with a flat piece of wood to prevent damage to oil pan, raise

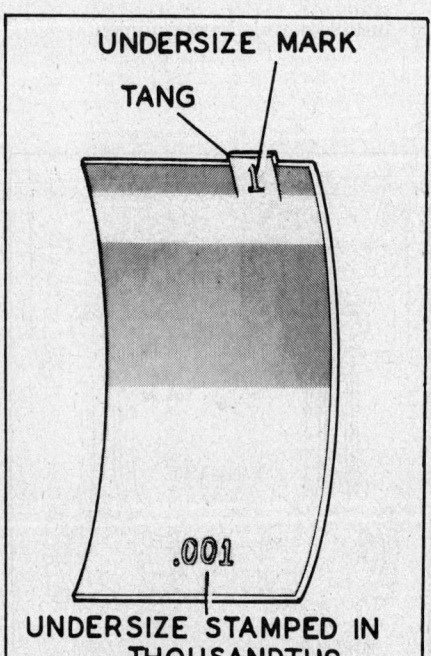

Fig. 37 Location of undersize mark on main and rod bearing sheel. V6-231

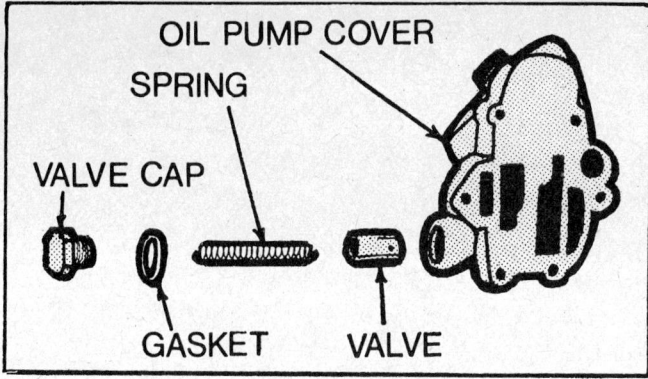

Fig. 39 Oil pump cover and by-pass valve. V6-231

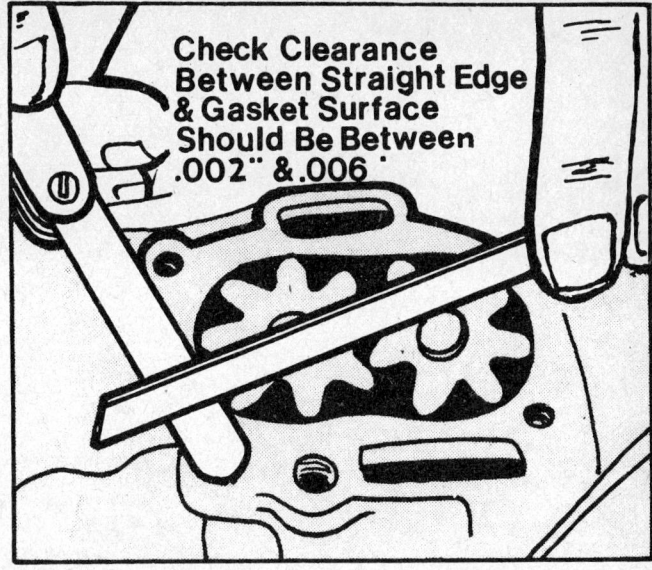

Fig. 40 Checking oil pump gear end clearance. V6-231

extension shaft with slot in end of pump drive shaft. Install retaining clip with flat end in groove of drive shaft.
6. Assemble pump and extension shaft to rear main bearing cap, aligning slot on top end of extension shaft with drive tang on lower end of distributor drive shaft.
7. Install pump to rear main bearing cap bolt and tighten to 45–50 ft. lb.
8. Install oil pan.

V6-231

1. To remove pump, take off oil filter.
2. Disconnect wire from oil pressure indicator switch in filter by-pass valve cap (if so equipped).
3. Remove screws attaching oil pump cover to timing chain cover. Remove cover and slide out pump gears. Replace any parts not serviceable.
4. Remove oil pressure relief valve cap, spring and valve, Fig. 39. Remove oil filter by-pass valve cap, spring and valve. Replace any parts of valve not serviceable.
5. Check relief valve in its bore in cover. Valve should have no more clearance than an easy slip fit. If any perceptible side shake can be felt, the valve and/or cover should be replaced.
6. The filter by-pass valve should be flat and free of nicks and scratches.

Assembly & Installation

1. Lubricate and install pressure relief valve and spring in bore of pump cover. Install cap and gasket. Torque cap to 30–35 ft. lbs.
2. Install filter by-pass valve flat in its seat in cover. Install spring, cap and gasket. Torque cap to 30–35 ft. lbs.
3. Install pump gears and shaft in pump body section of timing chain cover to check gear end clearance. Check clearance as shown in Fig. 40. If clearance is less than .0020", check timing chain cover for evidence of wear.
4. If gear end clearance is satisfactory, remove gears and pack gear pocket *full* of vaseline, not chassis lube.
5. Reinstall gears so vaseline is forced into every cavity of gear pocket and between teeth of gears. *Unless* pump is packed with vaseline, it may not *prime itself when engine is started.*
6. Install cover and tighten screws alternately and evenly. Final tightening is 10–15 ft-lbs. torque. Install filter on nipple.

WATER PUMP, REPLACE

1. Drain cooling system.
2. Remove fan belt and fan.
3. Disconnect all hoses from water pump.
4. Remove pump attaching bolts and remove water pump. On 6-250 engines, pull pump straight out of block to prevent damage to impeller.
5. Reverse procedure to install.

4 Cylinder Overhead Cam Engine Section

ENGINE, REPLACE

1. Raise hood to fully open position and install a bolt through the hood hold-open link to hold hood in wide open position, Fig. 1.
2. Disconnect battery positive cable at battery and negative cable at engine block (except on air conditioned vehicles).
3. Drain cooling system and disconnect hoses at radiator. Disconnect heater hoses at water pump and at heater inlet (bottom hose).
4. Disconnect emission system hoses: PCV at cam cover; canister vacuum hose at carburetor; PCV vacuum at inlet manifold and bowl vent at carburetor.
5. Remove radiator panel or shroud and remove radiator, fan and spacer.
6. Remove air cleaner, disconnecting vent tube at base of cleaner.
7. Disconnect electrical leads at: Delcotron, ignition coil, starter solenoid, oil pressure switch, engine temperature switch, transmission controlled spark switch at transmission, transmission controlled spark solenoid and engine ground strap at cowl.
8. Disconnect: Automatic transmission throttle valve linkage at manifold mounted bellcrank, fuel line at rubber hose to rear of carburetor, transmission vacuum modulator and air conditioning vacuum line at inlet manifold, accelerator cable at manifold bellcrank.
9. On air conditioned cars, disconnect compressor at front support, rear support, rear lower bracket and remove drive belt from compressor.
10. Move compressor slightly forward and allow front of compressor to rest on frame forward brace, then secure rear of compressor to engine compartment so it is out of way.
11. Disconnect power steering pump, if equipped, and position it out of way.
12. Raise car on a hoist and disconnect ex-

CHEVROLET

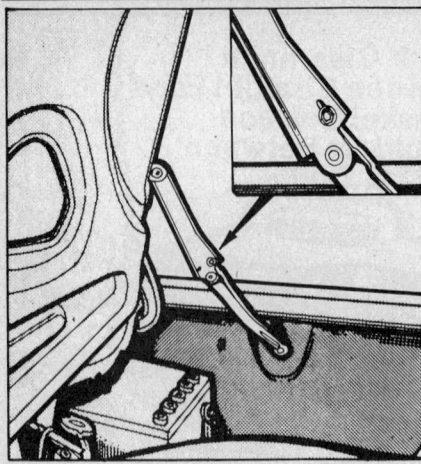

Fig. 1 Hood hold-open bolt installed

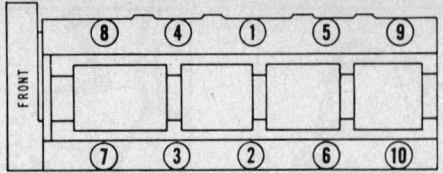

Fig. 2 Cylinder head tightening sequence

Fig. 3 Adjusting valve lash

haust pipe at manifold.
13. Remove engine flywheel dust cover or converter underpan.
14. On automatic transmission cars, remove converter-to-flywheel retaining bolts and nuts and install converter safety strap.
15. Remove converter housing or flywheel housing-to-engine retaining bolts.
16. Loosen engine front mount retaining bolts at frame attachment and lower vehicle.
17. Install floor jack under transmission.
18. Install suitable engine lifting equipment and raise engine slightly to take weight from engine mounts and remove engine front mount retaining bolts.
19. Remove engine and pull forward to clear transmission while slowly lifting engine from car.
20. Reverse procedure to install.

CYLINDER HEAD, REPLACE

1. Remove engine front cover and camshaft cover as outlined further on.
2. Remove timing belt and camshaft sprocket.
3. Remove intake and exhaust manifolds.
4. Disconnect hose at thermostat housing.
5. Remove cylinder head bolts and with the aid of an assistant, lift head and gasket from engine. Place head on two blocks of wood to prevent damage to valves.
6. Reverse procedure to install and tighten head bolts in sequence shown in Fig. 2.

VALVES, ADJUST

1. To adjust valves, the tappet must be on the base circle of the cam lobe. Do this as follows:
   a. Rotate camshaft timing sprocket to align timing mark on sprocket with inverted "V" notch on timing belt upper cover. The following valves can be adjusted with cam in this position (number one firing).
      Number one cylinder—Intake and Exhaust
      Number two cylinder—Intake
      Number three cylinder—Exhaust
   b. Use a feeler gauge and measure clearance between tappet and cam lobe. Adjust clearance by turning adjusting screw in tappet, Fig. 3.

NOTE: It is mandatory that the adjusting screw, Fig. 4, be turned one complete revolution to maintain proper stem-to-screw relationship. Each revolution of screw alters clearance by .003".

   c. Rotate camshaft timing sprocket 180 degrees so timing mark is at 12 o'clock position and in line with notch on timing belt upper cover. The following valves can be adjusted with camshaft in this position (number four firing).
      Number two cylinder—Exhaust
      Number three cylinder—Intake
      Number four cylinder—Intake and Exhaust

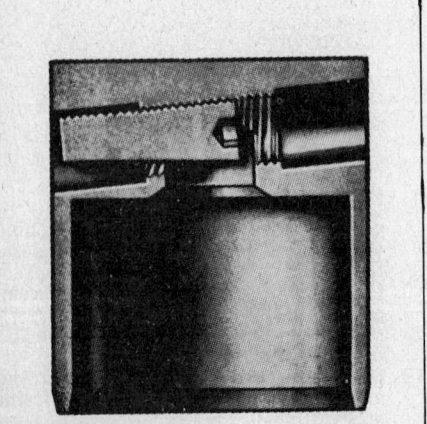

Fig. 4 Tappet and adjusting screw assembly. Screw is threaded in all areas except in valve stem contact surface

VALVE ARRANGEMENT
Front to Rear

4-cylinder .... I-E-I-E-I-E-I-E

CAMSHAFT COVER, REPLACE

1. Raise hood to fully open position and install bolt through the hood hold-open link, Fig. 1.
2. Disconnect battery negative cable at battery.
3. Remove air cleaner wing nut. Disconnect ventilation tube at camshaft cover or at air cleaner; then remove air cleaner.
4. Remove PCV valve from grommet at front of cover.
5. Remove cover-to-cylinder head screws and withdraw cover from head.
6. Reverse procedure to install.

CAMSHAFT, REPLACE

1. Remove hood.
2. Remove camshaft timing sprocket.
3. Remove timing belt upper cover, cam retainer and seal assembly.
4. Remove camshaft cover.
5. Disconnect fuel line at carburetor and remove idle solenoid from bracket.
6. Remove carburetor choke coil, cover and rod assembly.
7. Remove distributor.

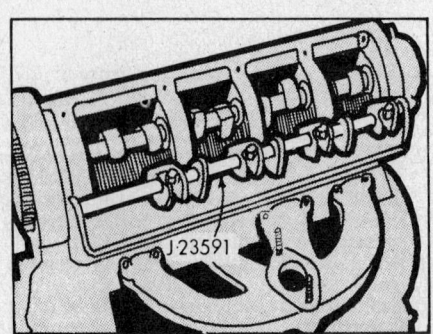

Fig. 5 Camshaft removal tool installed

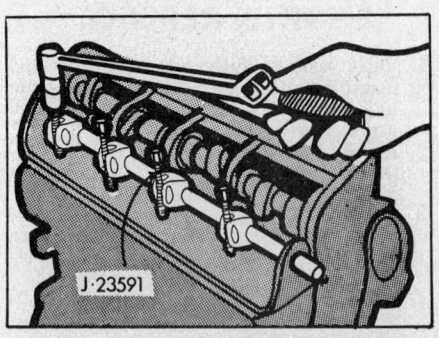

Fig. 6 Depressing valve tappets

CHEVROLET

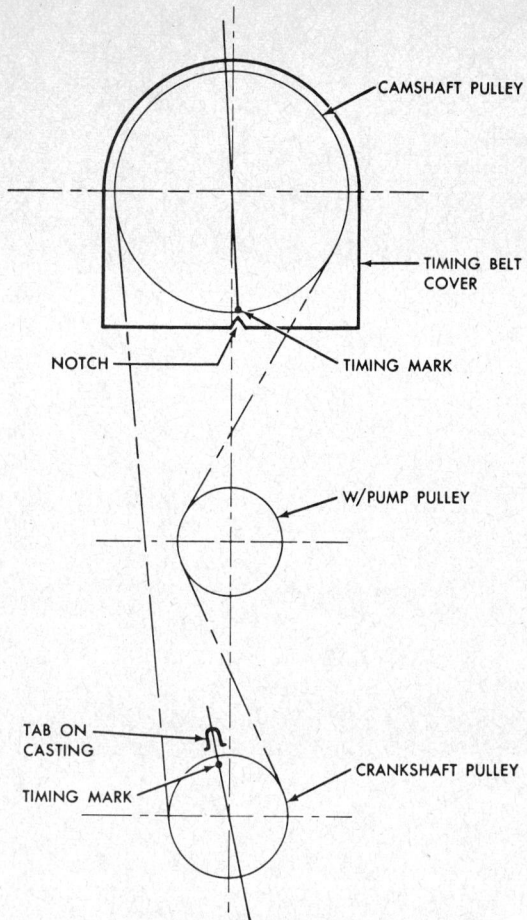

Fig. 7 Sprocket alignment marks

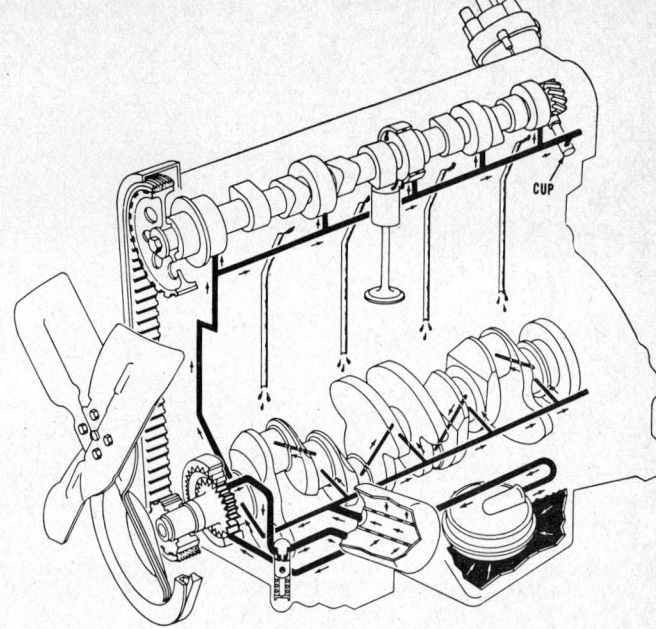

Engine oiling system. 4-140 engine

8. Raise vehicle on a hoist, disconnect engine front mounts at body attachment, raise front of engine and install wood blocks, about 1½" thick, between engine mounts and body. Lower vehicle.
9. Install camshaft removal tool as shown in Fig. 5, to cylinder head as follows:
   a. Position tool to cylinder head so attaching holes align with cam cover lower attaching holes.
   b. Align tappet depressing levers on tool so each lever will depress both intake and exhaust valve for their respective cylinder. Lever should fit squarely in notches adjacent to valve tappets.
   c. With tool aligned, make sure screws in bottom of tool are backed off so they do not make contact with bosses beneath tool.
   d. Install hardened screws supplied with tool, to attach tool to head. Torque screws securely.
   e. Turn screws in bottom of tool downward until they just seat against corresponding bosses on head.
   f. Apply a heavy body lubricant to ball end of lever depressing screws and proceed to tighten screws to depress tappets, Fig. 6.

NOTE: Use a torque wrench to tighten screws the final few turns. About 10 ft. lbs. is required to depress tappets.

10. At this point the camshaft can be removed by sliding it forward from the head.
11. Reverse procedure to install.

CAMSHAFT BEARINGS

After removal of the camshaft as described previously, the bearings can be removed without removing the camshaft end plug.

CAM LOBE LIFT SPECS.

90 H.P.	1971	.4199	.4301
100 H.P.	1971	.4365	.4365
80 H.P.①	1972	.4199	.4302
80 H.P.②	1972	.4367	.4379
90 H.P.	1972	.4367	.4379
72 H.P.	1973	.4199	.4302
85 H.P.	1973	.4369	.4379
75 H.P.	1974	.4199	.4302
85 H.P.	1974	.4367	.4379
78 H.P.	1975	.4199	.4302
87 H.P.	1975	.4367	.4379

①—Except California vehicles.
②—California vehicles.

VALVE TIMING

Intake Open Before TDC

90 H.P.	1971	22
100 H.P.	1971	25

Intake Open Before TDC

80 H.P.①	1972	22
80 H.P.②	1972	28
90 H.P.	1972	28
72 H.P.	1973	22
85 H.P.	1973–74	28
75 H.P.	1974	22
78 H.P.	1975	22
87 H.P.	1975	28

①—Except California vehicles.
②—California vehicles.

VALVE GUIDES

On all engines, valves operate in guide holes bored in the cylinder head. If clearance becomes excessive, use the next oversize valve and ream the bore to fit. Valves with oversize stems are available in .003, .015 and .030".

ENGINE FRONT COVER, REPLACE

1. Raise hood to fully open position and install hood hold-open bolt.
2. Disconnect battery ground cable at battery.
3. Remove fan and spacer.
4. Loosen, but do not remove, the two cover lower screws. Cover is slotted to permit easy removal.
5. Remove the two cover upper retaining screws and remove cover.
6. Reverse procedure to install.

TIMING BELT & WATER PUMP, REPLACE

1. Remove engine front cover as previously described.
2. Remove accessory drive pulley or damper.

CHEVROLET

Fig. 8 Checking sprocket alignment, 1972-75

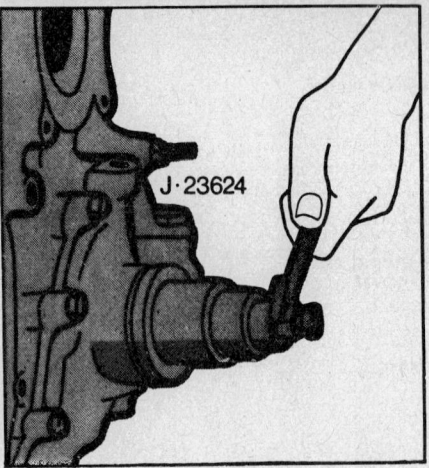

Fig. 9 Installing crankshaft front seal

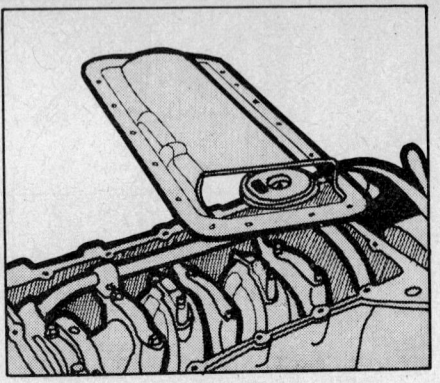

Fig. 10 Removing oil pan baffle

3. Drain coolant and loosen water pump bolts to relieve tension on belt.
4. Remove timing belt lower cover, then remove belt from sprockets.
5. Remove water pump outlet hose and water pump bolts, then the water pump.
6. Reverse procedure to install.

CAMSHAFT SPROCKET, REPLACE

After removal of timing belt, the camshaft sprocket can be removed as follows:
1. Align one hole in sprocket with bolt head behind sprocket, then using a socket on bolt head to prevent cam from turning, remove sprocket retaining bolt and withdraw sprocket from camshaft.
2. When installing, be sure timing marks are aligned as in Fig. 7.

NOTE: For 1972-75 a simplified method is provided for checking camshaft and crankshaft alignment. Proper alignment is assured by making sure hold in left rear of the timing belt upper cover is in line with the corresponding hole in the camshaft sprocket with engine at TDC compression stroke. Check alignment by inserting a pencil or other similar tool through the hole in cover. If alignment is correct, tool will also enter small hole in cam gear, Fig. 8.

CRANKSHAFT SPROCKET, REPLACE

1. Remove engine front cover, accessory drive pulley, timing belt and timing belt lower cover.
2. Install suitable puller to crankshaft sprocket and remove sprocket.

OIL PUMP (CRANKCASE FRONT COVER) SEAL, REPLACE

1. Remove engine front cover, accessory drive pulley, timing belt and timing belt lower cover and crankshaft sprocket.
2. Pry old seal from front cover, being careful not to damage seal housing or seal lip contact surfaces.
3. Coat seal with light engine oil and apply an approved sealing compound to outside diameter of seal.
4. Position seal closed end outward onto crankshaft. Then install seal into bore using tool J-23624, Fig. 9.

PISTONS & RODS, ASSEMBLE

The "F" on the front of the piston must face the front of the engine when the piston and rod assembly is installed in its proper cylinder.

Piston Oversizes

Oversize pistons are not available since bore reconditioning is not recommended. Production pistons are available in four size ranges so pistons can be select fitted to the bores. Cylinder bore repairs, such as glaze busting, honing or reboring will destroy the electro-chemically treated finish necessary for proper piston-to-bore operation. Therefore, if cylinder bores are unserviceable, a new cylinder case and piston assembly should be installed.

MAIN & ROD BEARINGS

Undersizes

Bearings are available in .001, .002, .010 and .020" undersizes.

NOTE: If for any reason main bearing caps are replaced, shimming may be necessary. Laminated shims for each cap are available for service. Shim requirement will be determined by bearing clearance.

OIL PAN, REPLACE

1. Raise vehicle on a hoist and drain engine oil.
2. Support front of engine so weight is off front mounts, and remove frame crossmember and both front crossmember braces.
3. Disconnect idler arm at frame side rail.

NOTE: On air conditioned vehicles, disconnect idler arm at relay rod.

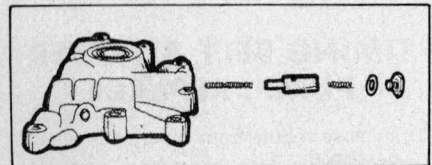

Fig. 11 Oil pump pressure regulator

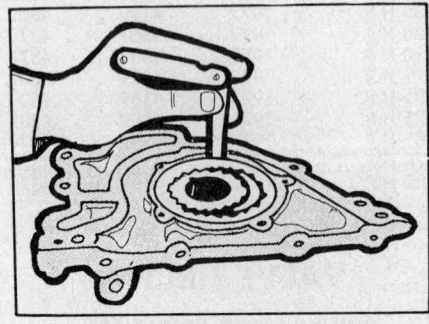

Fig. 12 Checking driven gear-to-housing clearance

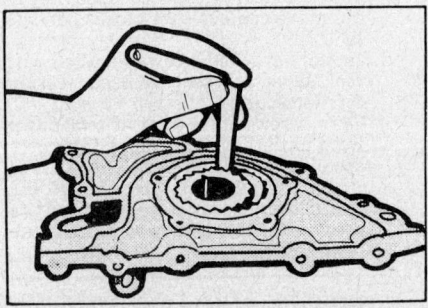

Fig. 13 Checking drive gear-to-cresent clearance

CHEVROLET

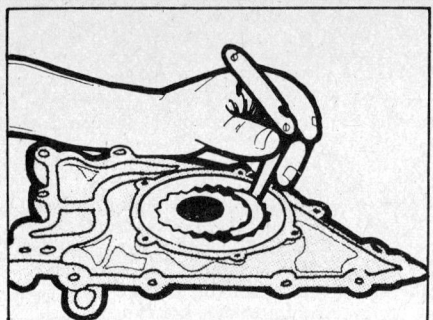

Fig. 14 Checking driven gear-to-cresent clearance

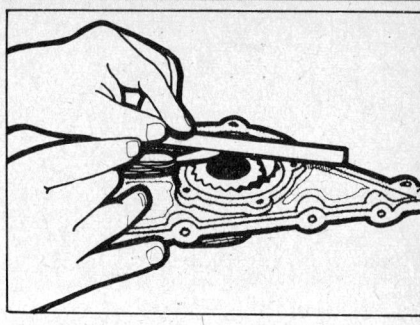

Fig. 15 Checking gear end clearance

er cover and crankshaft sprocket.
2. Raise vehicle on a hoist and remove oil pan and baffle.
3. Remove bolts and stud securing oil pump to cylinder case.

Inspection
1. Clean gasket surfaces, then wash parts in approved solvent and blow out all passages.
2. Check pressure regulator for free operation, Fig. 11.
3. Inspect pump gears for nicks, broken parts and other damage.
4. Check clearance between outside diameter of driven gear and pump. Clearance should be .0038–.0068″, Fig. 12
5. Check clearance between outside diameter of drive gear and cresent. Clearance should be .0023–.0093″, Fig. 13
6. Check clearance between inside diameter of driven gear and pump crescent. Clearance should be .0068–.0148″, Fig. 14.
7. Check gear end clearance. It should be .0009–.0023″, Fig. 15.

NOTE: The pump gears and body are not serviced separately. If pump gears or body are worn, replacement of the entire assembly is necessary.

4. Mark relationship of steering linkage pitman arm to steering gear pitman shaft and remove pitman arm.

NOTE: Do not rotate steering gear pitman shaft while arm is disconnected as this will change steering wheel alignment.

5. Remove flywheel cover or converter underpan.
6. Remove oil pan to cylinder case screws, tap pan lightly to break sealing bond and remove oil pan.
7. Remove pick up screen to baffle support bolts, then remove support from baffle.
8. Remove bolt securing oil pan drain back tube to baffle. Then rotate baffle 90 degrees towards left side of car and remove baffle from pick up screen, Fig. 10.
9. Reverse procedure to install.

OIL PUMP (CRANKCASE FRONT COVER)

1. Remove engine front cover, accessory drive pulley, timing belt, timing belt low-

WATER PUMP, REPLACE

1. Raise hood to fully open position and install hold-open bolt.
2. Disconnect battery ground cable at battery.
3. Remove engine fan and spacer.
4. Loosen, but do not remove, the two cover lower screws. Cover is slotted to permit easy removal.
5. Remove the two cover upper retaining screws and remove cover.
6. Drain coolant and loosen water pump bolts to relieve tension in timing belt.
7. Remove radiator lower hose and heater hose at water pump.
8. Unfasten and remove water pump.
9. Reverse procedure to install.

TIMING BELT TENSION, ADJUST

1. Drain coolant at engine block and remove fan and extension.
2. Remove engine front cover.
3. Remove water pump retaining bolts, clean gasket surfaces on block and pump. Install new gasket and loosely install water pump bolts.

NOTE: Apply an approved anti-seize compound to the water pump bolts before installation.

4. Position tool J-23564 in gauge hole adjacent to left side of pump, Fig. 16.
5. Apply 15 ft. lbs. of torque to water pump as shown in Fig. 17. Tighten water pump bolts while maintaining torque on side of pump.
6. Reinstall front cover, fan, extension and fill cooling system.

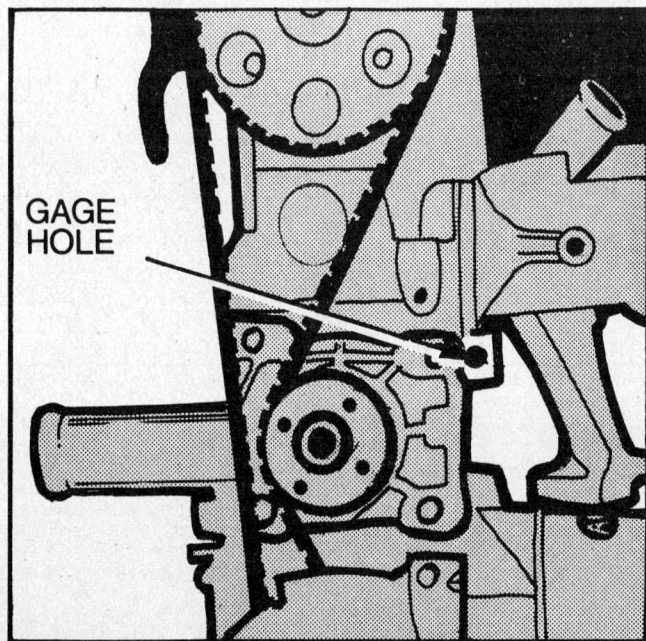

Fig. 16 Tensioning adapter locating hole

Fig. 17 Adjusting timing belt

CHEVROLET

FUEL PUMP, REPLACE

Removal
1. Disconnect battery ground cable.
2. Disconnect meter and pump wires at rear wiring harness connector.
3. Raise vehicle on hoist and drain fuel tank.
4. Disconnect fuel line hose at gauge unit pick up line.
5. Disconnect tank vent lines to vapor separator.
6. Remove gauge ground wire screw at underbody floorpan.
7. Remove tank straps bolts and lower tank carefully.
8. Unscrew retaining ring using spanner wrench J-22554, Fig. 18, and remove pump-tank unit assembly.

Replacement
1. Remove flat wire conductor from plastic clip on fuel tube.
2. Squeeze clamp and pull pump straight back about 1/2 inch.
3. Remove two nuts and lockwashers and conductor wires from pump terminals.
4. Squeeze clamp and pull pump straight back to remove it from tank unit. Take care to prevent bending or circular support bracket.
5. Slide replacement pump through circular support bracket until it rests against rubber coupling. Make sure pump has rubber isolator and saran strainer attached.
6. Attach two conductor wires to pump terminals using lockwashers and nuts being certain flat conductor is attached to terminal located on side away from float arm.
7. Squeeze clamp and push pump into rubber coupling.
8. Replace flat wire conductor in plastic clip on fuel pick up tube.
9. Install unit into tank and replace fuel tank.

Fig. 18 Removing fuel pump and gauge unit

Carburetor Adjustments

5210 CARB. ADJUSTMENT SPECIFICATIONS

See Tune Up Chart for hot idle speeds.

Year	Carb. Part No.	Carb. Model	Float Level (Dry)	Float Drop	Pump Position	Fast Idle Cam Index	Vacuum Plate Pulldown	Fast Idle Setting	Choke Setting
CHEVROLET VEGA									
1973	R-6477A	5210	.420	1"	#3	.140	.300	2000	1 Rich
	R-6478A	5210	.420	1"	#2	.140	.300	2200	2 Rich
	R-6580A	5210	.420	1"	#2	.140	.300	2200	2 Rich
	R-6581A	5210	.420	1"	#3	.140	.300	2000	1 Rich
1974	338168	5210-C	.420	1"	#2	.140	.400	2200	3½ Rich
	338170	5210-C	.420	1"	#2	.140	.400	2200	3½ Rich
	338179	5210-C	.420	1"	#3	.140	.300	2000	2½ Rich
	338181	5210-C	.420	1"	#3	.140	.300	2000	2½ Rich
1975	348659	5210-C	.420	1"	—	—	.325	1600	3 Rich
	348660	5210-C	.420	1"	#2	.110	.300	1600	4 Rich
	348661	5210-C	.420	1"	—	—	.275	1600	3 Rich
	348662	5210-C	.420	1"	#2	.110	.275	1600	4 Rich
	348663	5210-C	.420	1"	—	—	.325	1600	3 Rich
	348664	5210-C	.420	1"	#2	.110	.300	1600	4 Rich
	348665	5210-C	.420	1"	—	—	.275	1600	3 Rich
	348666	5210-C	.420	1"	#2	.110	.275	1600	4 Rich

MODEL 5210

The Holley 5210 two-barrel carburetor, Figs. 1 and 2, has a number of unique features. An automatic choke system activated by a water heated bi-metal thermostatic oil and a primary venturi smaller in size than the secondary venturi.

An Exhaust Gas Recirculation (EGR) system is used on all applications with the EGR valve located in the intake manifold.

Float Adjustment

Fig. 3—With the air horn inverted and the float tang resting lightly on the spring loaded fuel inlet needle, measure the clearance between the bowl cover and the end of each float. Refer to Holley 5210 Specifications Chart. Adjust by bending the float tang as required.

Fast Idle Cam Index Adjustment

Fig. 4—Place the fast idle screw on the second

CHEVROLET

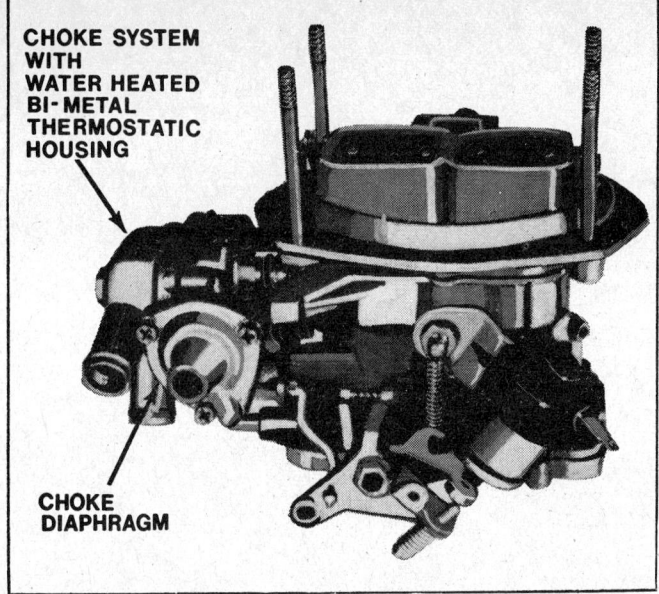

Fig. 1 Holley 5210 2 barrel carburetor

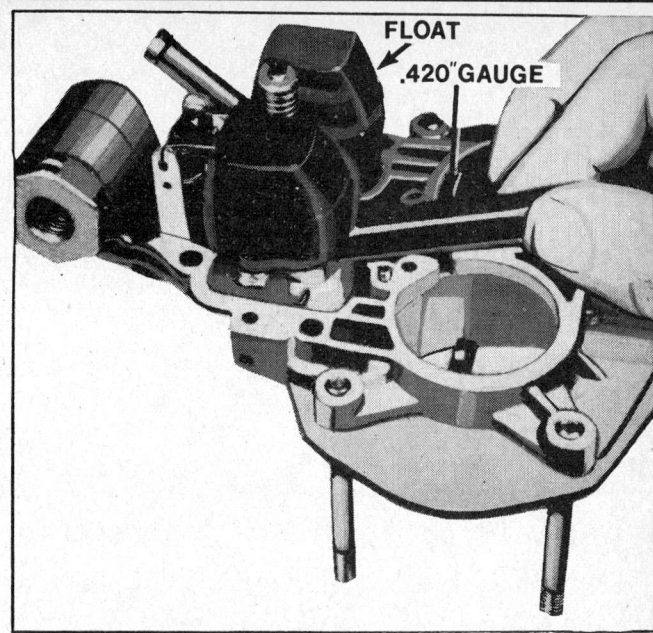

Fig. 3 Checking float level on 5210 carburetor

step of the fast idle cam and against the shoulder of the first step. Place a drill or gauge on the down stream side of the choke plate. Refer to *5210 Specifications Chart*. Adjust by bending the choke lever tang.

NOTE: The dechoke is automatically set when the fast idle cam index is adjusted.

Vacuum Plate Pulldown Adjustment

Fig. 5—Remove the three hex headed screws and ring retaining the choke bi-metal cover. Do not remove the choke water housing screw if adjusting on the car. Pull the choke water housing and bi-metal cover assembly out of the way. With a screwdriver or suitable tool, push the diaphragm stem back against the stop. Place drill or gauge on the down stream side of the primary choke plate. Take all the slack out of the linkage refer to *5210 Specifications Chart*. Adjust by turning adjusting screw in or out with an 5/32 inch Allen wrench.

Secondary Throttle Plate Adjustment

Fig. 6—Back out the secondary throttle stop screw, until the secondary throttle plate seats in the carburetor bore. Turn screw in until it makes contact with tab on the secondary throttle lever, then turn screw in an additional 1/4 turn.

Fast Idle Adjustment

Fig. 7—With the engine at operating temperature, position the fast idle screw on the second step of the fast idle cam against the shoulder of the first step and adjust by turning the fast idle screw in or out. Refer to *5210 Specifications Chart*.

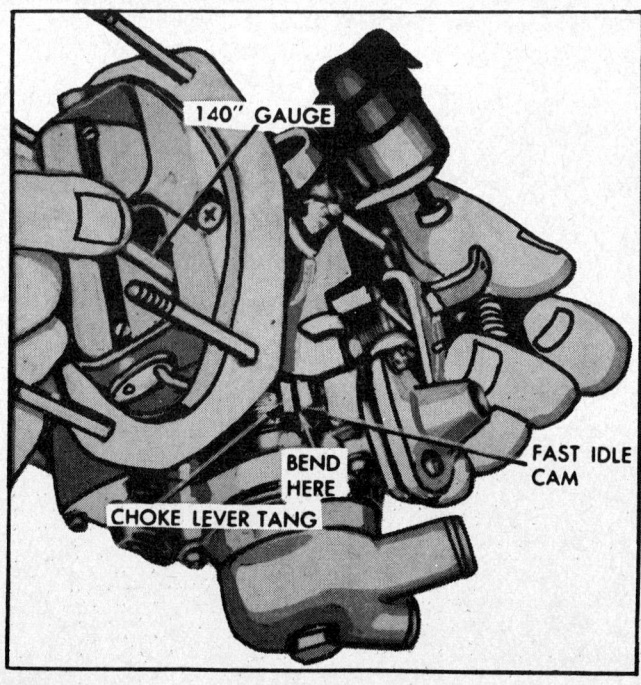

Fig. 4 Fast idle cam index adjustment 5210 Holley carburetor

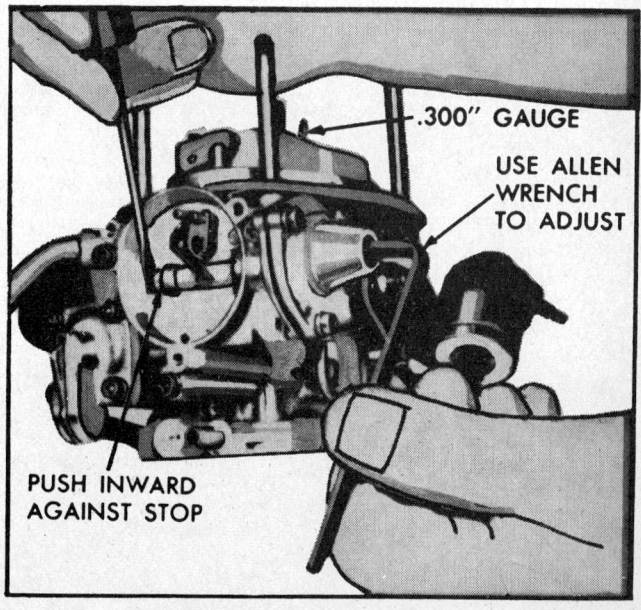

Fig. 5 Vacuum pull down adjustment 5210 Holley carburetor

853

CHEVROLET

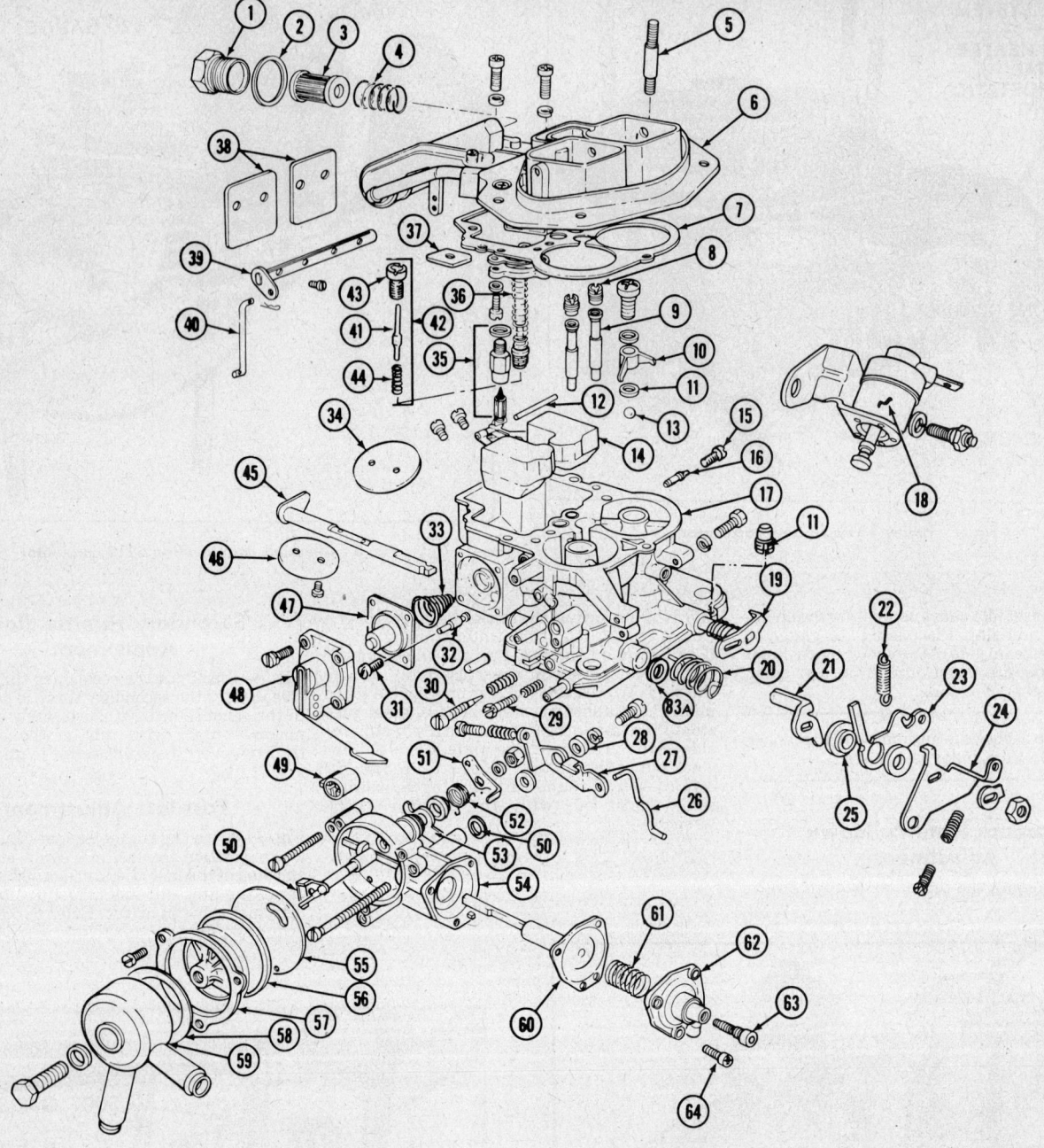

1. Fuel Inlet Nut
2. Gasket
3. Filter
4. Spring
5. Studs, Air Cleaner Attachment
6. Air Horn
7. Gasket
8. High Speed Bleed
9. Main Well Tube
10. Pump Discharge Nozzle
11. Gasket
12. Float Shaft
13. Discharge Check Ball
14. Float
15. Retainer
16. Secondary Idle Jet
17. Carburetor Body Assembly
18. Idle Stop Solenoid
19. Secondary Throttle Lever
20. Throttle Return Spring
21. Idle Lever
22. Secondary Operating Lever Return Spring
23. Secondary Operating Lever
24. Throttle Lever
25. Bushing
26. Fast Idle Rod
27. Fast Idle Lever
28. Bushing
29. Low Idle Screw
30. Fuel Mixture Screw
31. Retainer
32. Primary Idle Jet
33. Return Spring
34. Secondary Throttle Plate
35. Fuel Inlet Needle and Seat Assembly
36. Power Valve Economizer Assembly
37. Choke Rod Seal
38. Choke Plates
39. Choke Shaft and Lever
40. Choke Rod
41. Power Valve
42. Power Valve Assembly
43. Seat
44. Spring
45. Primary Throttle Shaft and Lever Assembly
46. Primary Throttle Plate
47. Accelerator Pump
48. Accelerator Pump Cover
49. Mixture Screw Limiter Cap
50. Choke Housing Shaft
51. Choke Lever
52. Fast Idle Cam Spring
53. Fast Idle Cam
54. Choke Housing
55. Gasket
56. Thermostatic Housing
57. Retainer
58. Gasket
59. Water Cover
60. Diaphragm and Shaft
61. Return Spring
62. Choke Diaphragm Cover
63. Hex Head Screw
64. Cover Screw

Fig. 2 Exploded view of typical Holley 5210 carburetor

CHEVROLET

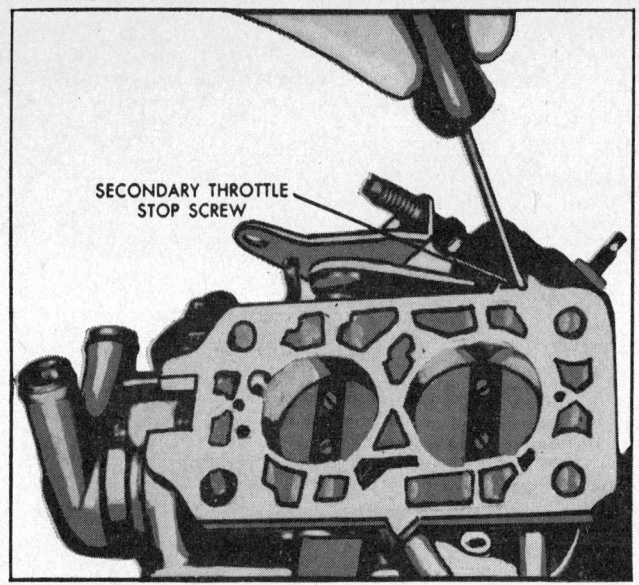

Fig. 6 Secondary throttle plate adjustment

Fig. 7 Fast idle adjustment 5210 Holley carburetor

ROCHESTER 2G, 2GC, 2GV CARBURETOR ADJUSTMENT SPECIFICATIONS

See Tune-Up Chart for Hot Idle Speeds.

★Located on Tag attached to or stamped on Carburetor.

Carb. Part No. ★	Year	Float Level	Float Drop	Pump Rod	Idle Vent	Vacuum Break	Automatic Choke	Choke Rod	Choke Unloader	Fast Idle Speed
7040012	1971	1/4	—	—	—	—	—	—	—	2400
7041105	1971	21/32	1 3/4	1 3/64	—	.080	—	.040	.215	—
7041111	1971	21/32	1 3/4	1 3/64	—	.080	—	.040	.215	—
7041123	1971	23/32	1 3/4	1 5/32	.025	—	—	—	—	—
7041125	1971	21/32	1 3/4	1 3/64	—	.080	—	.040	.215	—
7041126	1971	21/32	1 3/4	1 3/64	—	.080	—	.040	.215	—
7041138	1971	23/32	1 1/4	1 5/32	—	.170	—	.100	.325	—
7041139	1971	23/32	1 1/4	1 5/32	—	.180	—	.100	.325	—
7041181	1971	5/8	1 3/4	1 3/8	—	.120	—	.080	.180	2400
7041182	1971	5/8	1 3/4	1 3/8	—	.120	—	.080	.180	2400
7030699	1972	23/32	1 9/32	—	.025	—	—	—	—	2400
7042102	1972	21/32	1 9/32	1 5/16	—	.080	—	.040	.210	—
7042103	1972	21/32	1 9/32	1 5/16	—	.110	—	.075	.210	—
7042104	1972	21/32	1 9/32	1 5/16	—	.080	—	.040	.210	—
7042105	1972	21/32	1 9/32	1 5/16	—	.110	—	.075	.210	—
7042106	1972	19/32	1 7/8	1 1/16	—	.100	—	.060	.215	2400
7042107	1972	19/32	1 7/8	1 1/16	—	.100	—	.060	.215	2400
7042108	1972	25/32	1 9/32	1 1/2	—	.170	—	.100	.325	—
7042109	1972	25/32	1 9/32	1 1/2	—	.180	—	.100	.325	—
7042123	1972	23/32	1 9/32	1 1/2	—	—	—	—	—	—
7042124	1972	23/32	1 9/32	1 1/2	—	—	—	—	—	—
7042134	1972	23/32	1 9/32	—	.025	—	—	—	—	—
7042822	1972	21/32	1 9/32	1 5/16	—	.080	—	.040	.210	—
7042823	1972	21/32	1 9/32	1 5/16	—	.110	—	.075	.210	—
7042824	1972	21/32	1 9/32	1 5/16	—	.080	—	.040	.210	—
7042825	1972	21/32	1 9/32	1 5/16	—	.110	—	.075	.210	—
7042826	1972	19/32	1 7/8	1 1/16	—	.100	—	.060	.215	2400
7042827	1972	19/32	1 7/8	1 1/16	—	.100	—	.060	.215	2400

Continued

CHEVROLET

ROCHESTER 2G, 2GC, 2GV CARBURETOR ADJUSTMENT SPECIFICATIONS—Continued

See Tune-Up Chart for Hot Idle Speeds.

★Located on Tag attached to or stamped on Carburetor.

Carb. Part No. ★	Year	Float Level	Float Drop	Pump Rod	Idle Vent	Vacuum Break	Automatic Choke	Choke Rod	Choke Unloader	Fast Idle Speed
7043103	1973	21/32	19/32	1 5/16	—	.080	—	.150	.215	1600
7043105	1973	21/32	19/32	1 5/16	—	.080	—	.150	.215	1600
7043108	1973	25/32	19/32	1 7/16	—	.140	—	.200	.250	1600
7043123	1973	23/32	19/32	1 7/16	—	—	—	—	—	—
7043124	1973	23/32	19/32	1 7/16	—	—	—	—	—	—
7043424	1973	23/32	19/32	1 7/16	—	—	—	—	—	—
7044113	1974	19/32	19/32	1 9/32	—	.140	—	.200	.250	1600
7044114	1974	19/32	19/32	1 3/16	—	.130	—	.245	.325	1600
7044123	1974	19/32	19/32	1 9/32	—	.140	—	.200	.250	1600
7044124	1974	19/32	19/32	1 3/16	—	.130	—	.245	.325	1600
7044133	1974–78	19/32	19/32	1 9/16	—	—	—	—	—	—
7044134	1974–78	19/32	19/32	1 7/16	—	—	—	—	—	—
7044434	1974–76	19/32	19/32	1 7/16	—	—	—	—	—	—
7045115	1975	21/32	31/32	1 5/8	—	.130	—	.400	.350	—
7045116	1975	21/32	31/32	1 5/8	—	.130	—	.400	.350	—
7045123	1975	21/32	31/32	1 5/8	—	.130	—	.400	.350	—
7045124	1975	21/32	31/32	1 5/8	—	.130	—	.400	.350	—
17056115	1976	21/32	19/32	1 11/16	—	.130	Index	.260	.325	—
17056116	1976	21/32	19/32	1 11/16	—	.130	1 Rich	.260	.325	—
17056117	1976	9/16	13/16	1 21/32	—	.130	Index	.260	.325	—
17056119	1976	9/16	13/16	1 21/32	—	.130	Index	.260	.325	—
17056123	1976	21/32	19/32	1 11/16	—	.130	Index	.260	.325	—
17056124	1976	21/32	19/32	1 11/16	—	.130	1 Rich	.260	.325	—
17056137	1977	19/32	19/32	1 21/32	—	.190	Index	.260	.325	—
17056433	1977	19/32	19/32	1 9/16	—	—	—	—	—	—
17056434	1977	19/32	19/32	1 7/16	—	—	—	—	—	—
17057108	1977	19/32	19/32	1 21/32	—	.130	Index	.260	.325	—
17057110	1977	19/32	19/32	1 21/32	—	.130	Index	.260	.325	—
17057111	1977	19/32	19/32	1 21/32	—	②	Index	.260	.325	—
17057112	1977	19/32	19/32	1 21/32	—	②	Index	.260	.325	—
17057113	1977	19/32	19/32	1 21/32	—	②	Index	.260	.325	—
17057114	1977	19/32	19/32	1 21/32	—	②	Index	.260	.325	—
17057121	1977	19/32	19/32	1 21/32	—	②	Index	.260	.325	—
17057123	1977	19/32	19/32	1 21/32	—	②	Index	.260	.325	—
17057408	1977	21/32	19/32	1 21/32	—	③	1/2 Lean	.260	.325	—
17057410	1977	21/32	19/32	1 21/32	—	③	1/2 Lean	.260	.325	—
17057412	1977	21/32	19/32	1 21/32	—	③	1/2 Lean	.260	.325	—
17057414	1977	21/32	19/32	1 21/32	—	③	1/2 Lean	.260	.325	—
17058102	1978	15/32	19/32	1 17/32	—	④	Index	.260	.325	—
17058103	1978	15/32	19/32	1 17/32	—	④	Index	.260	.325	—
17058104	1978	15/32	19/32	1 21/32	—	⑤	Index	.260	.325	—
17058105	1978	15/32	19/32	1 21/32	—	④	Index	.260	.325	—
17058107	1978	15/32	19/32	1 17/32	—	⑤	Index	.260	.325	—
17058108	1978	19/32	19/32	1 21/32	—	④	Index	.260	.325	—
17058109	1978	15/32	19/32	1 17/32	—	④	Index	.260	.325	—
17058110	1978	19/32	19/32	1 21/32	—	④	Index	.260	.325	—
17058111	1978	19/32	19/32	1 17/32	—	④	Index	.260	.325	—
17058112	1978	19/32	19/32	1 21/32	—	④	Index	.260	.325	—
17058113	1978	19/32	19/32	1 17/32	—	④	Index	.260	.325	—
17058114	1978	19/32	19/32	1 21/32	—	④	Index	.260	.325	—
17058116	1978	19/32	19/32	1 17/32	—	④	Index	.260	.325	—
17058118	1978	19/32	19/32	1 17/32	—	④	Index	.260	.325	—
17058123	1978	19/32	19/32	1 17/32	—	④	Index	.260	.325	—

Continued

CHEVROLET

ROCHESTER 2G, 2GC, 2GV CARBURETOR ADJUSTMENT SPECIFICATIONS—Continued

See Tune-Up Chart for Hot Idle Speeds.

★Located on Tag attached to or stamped on Carburetor.

Carb. Part No. ★	Year	Float Level	Float Drop	Pump Rod	Idle Vent	Vacuum Break	Automatic Choke	Choke Rod	Choke Unloader	Fast Idle Speed
17058126	1978	19/32	19/32	1 17/32	—	⑤	Index	.260	.325	—
17058127	1978	19/32	19/32	—	—	.190	Index	.260	.325	—
17058128	1978	19/32	19/32	1 17/32	—	⑤	Index	.260	.325	—
17058404	1978	1/2	19/32	1 21/32	—	⑥	1/2 Lean	.260	.325	—
17058405	1978	1/2	19/32	1 21/32	—	⑥	1/2 Lean	.260	.325	—
17058408	1978	21/32	19/32	1 21/32	—	⑥	1/2 Lean	.260	.325	—
17058410	1978	21/32	19/32	1 21/32	—	⑥	1/2 Lean	.260	.325	—
17058412	1978	21/32	19/32	1 21/32	—	⑥	1/2 Lean	.260	.325	—
17058414	1978	21/32	19/32	1 21/32	—	⑥	1/2 Lean	.260	.325	—
17058120	1979	11/16	19/32	1 15/32	—	—	—	—	—	—
17059119	1979	17/32	19/32	1 15/32	—	—	—	—	—	—
17059120	1979	17/32	19/32	1 15/32	—	—	—	—	—	—
17059126	1979	5/8	19/32	1 21/32	—	—	—	—	—	—
17059127	1979	17/32	19/32	1 15/32	—	—	—	—	—	—
17059129	1979	5/8	19/32	1 21/32	—	.130	—	.245	.250	—
17059420	1979	17/32	19/32	1 15/32	—	—	—	—	—	—
17059423	1979	5/8	19/32	1 21/32	—	—	—	—	—	—
17059424	1979	17/32	19/32	1 15/32	—	—	—	—	—	—

①—Bottom of rod should be even with top of hole with choke closed.
②—Before 22500 miles, .130; above 22500 miles, .160.
③—Before 22500 miles, .140; above 22500 miles, .160.
④—.130, reset to .150 at first tune up.
⑤—.130, reset to .160 at first tune up.
⑥—.140, reset to .160 at first tune up.

MODEL 2G, 2GC, 2GV, FIG. 1

Float Level, Fig. 2

With air horn inverted and air horn gasket installed, measure distance from top of air horn gasket to lower edge (sharp edge or lip) of float at outer end of float pontoon. To adjust, bend float arm at rear as shown in inset.

Float Drop, Fig. 3

With air horn assembly held upright and float suspended freely, measure dimension from air horn gasket to bottom of float pontoon. Adjust to specified dimension by bending tang that contacts seat at rear of float arm.

Pump Rod, Fig. 4

Back out idle stop screw and completely close throttle valve in bore. Place gauge on top of air horn ring. Bend pump rod at lower angle to obtain specified dimension to top of pump rod.

Adjust Idle Vent, 1970–74

NOTE: Always make pump adjustment before checking and adjusting idle vent valve.

With choke held in fully open position and idle screw adjusted to specifications on low step of cam, measure opening of idle vent valve and seat at its widest point. Bend tang on accelerator outer lever to adjust.

Adjust Choke Rod, (Fast Idle) Fig. 5

Turn stop screw in until it just contacts bottom step of fast idle cam. Then turn screw in

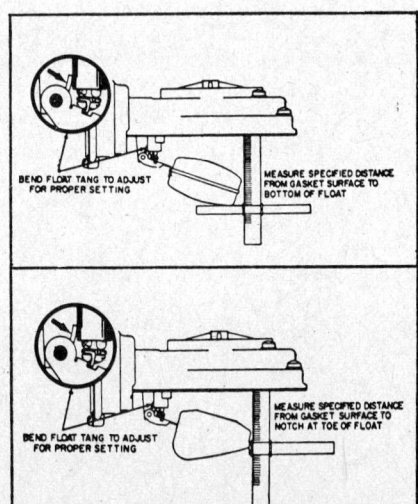

Fig. 2 Float level adjustment. Upper view for brass float and lower view for nitrophyl float

Fig. 3 Float drop adjustment. Upper view for brass float and lower view for nitrophyl float

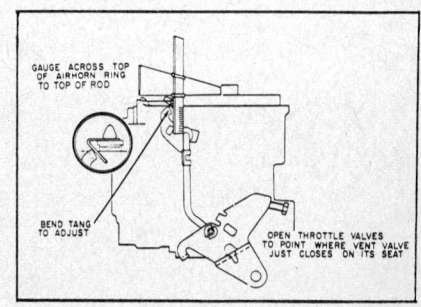

Fig. 4 Pump rod adjustment. Model 2G and 2GC

CHEVROLET

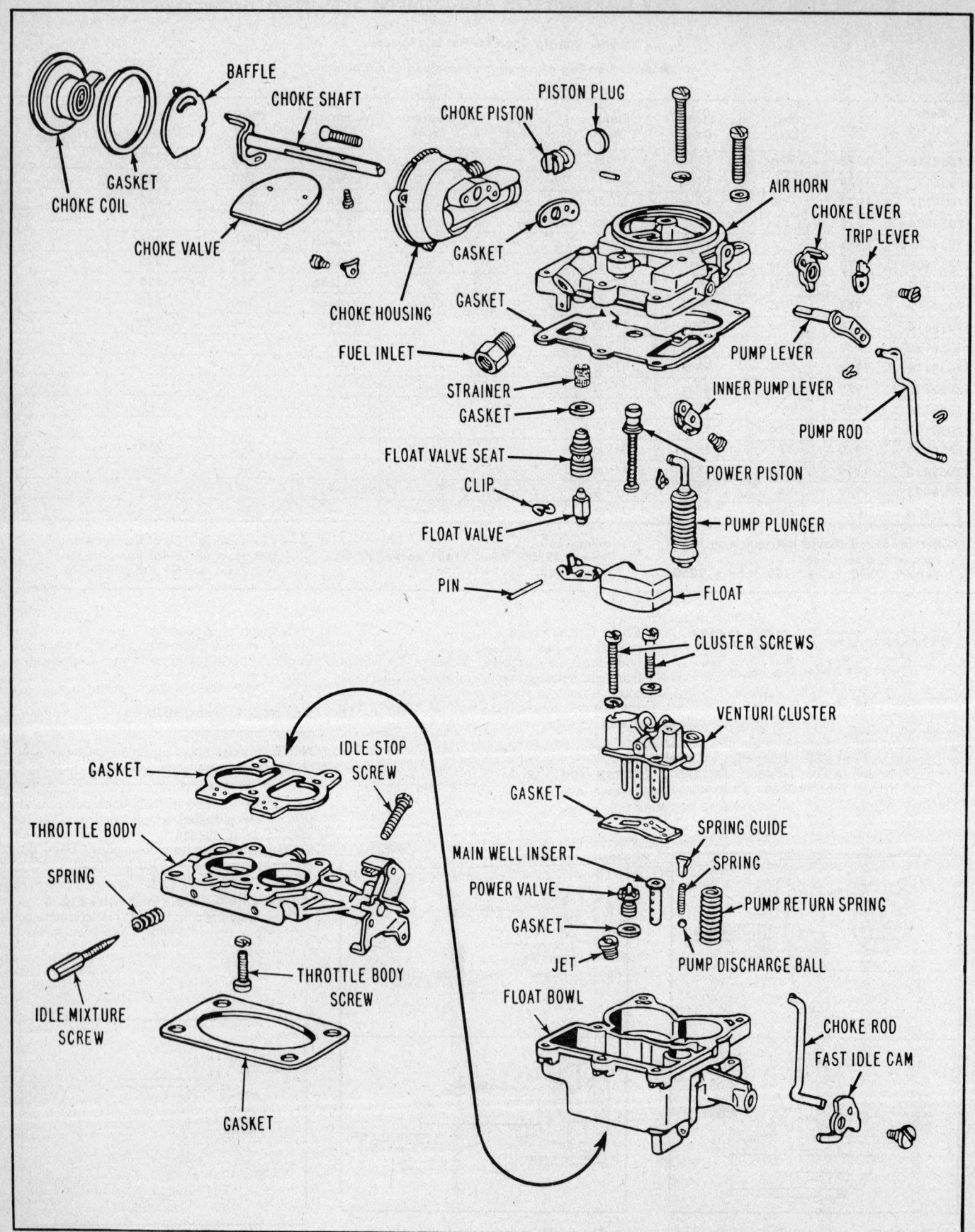

Fig. 1 Rochester Model 2GC carburetor (Typical)

CHEVROLET

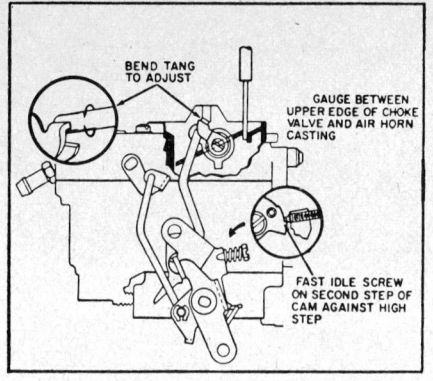

Fig. 5 Choke rod (fast idle) adjustment

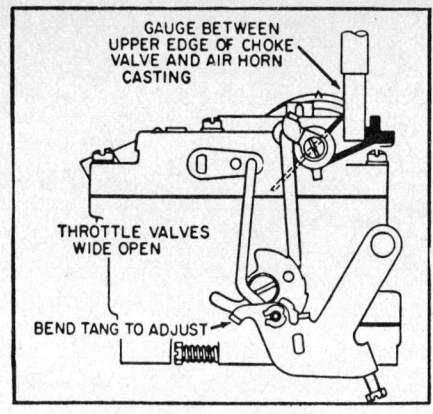

Fig. 6 Choke unloader adjustment

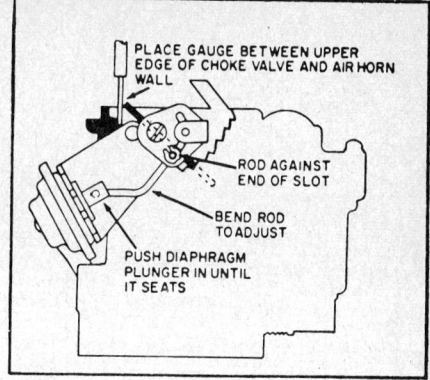

Fig. 7 Choke vacuum break adjustment

one full turn. Place idle screw on second step of fast idle cam against shoulder of high step. With screw in this position, hold choke valve toward closed position with a rubber band and check clearance between upper edge of choke valve and air horn wall. Adjust to specified dimension by bending tang on choke lever and collar assembly.

Adjust Choke Unloader, Fig. 6
With the throttle valves held wide open and the choke valve held toward the closed position with a rubber band, bend the unloader tang on the throttle lever to obtain specified clearance between the upper edge of the choke valve and air horn wall.

Adjust Choke Vacuum Break, Fig. 7
Push the vacuum break diaphragm plunger in until seated. Hold the choke valve toward closed position with a rubber band. Bend vacuum break line so that the specified gauge will fit between the upper edge of the choke valve and inside wall of the air horn. Recheck adjustment with carburetor on engine and engine running.

ROCHESTER MONOJET M, MV, ME ADJUSTMENT SPECIFICATIONS

See Tune Up Chart for Hot Idle Speeds.

Year	Carb. Part No. ①	Initial Idle Mix Screw Turns Open	Float Level	Metering Rod	Idle Vent	Fast Idle Off Car	Choke Rod	Vacuum Break	Unloader	Fast Idle R.P.M.
1970	7040011, 12	4	1/4	.070	.050	.100	.150	—	—	2400
	7040002	4	1/4	.070	.050	.100	.190	.230	.350	2400
	7040021	4	1/4	.070	—	.100	.190	.230	.350	2400
	7040025	4	1/4	.070	.050	.100	.180	.260	.350	2400
	7040022	4	1/4	.070	.050	.100	.275	.350	.350	2400
	7040026	4	1/4	.070	.050	.100	.245	.350	.350	2400
	7040008	4	1/4	.080	.050	.100	.200	—	—	2400
	7040014	4	1/4	.070	.050	.110	.170	.200	.350	2400
	7040017	4	1/4	.090	.050	.100	.190	.225	.350	2400
1971	7041014	—	1/4	.080	—	.100	.160	.200	.350	—
	7041017	—	1/4	.080	—	.100	.180	.230	.350	—
	7041021	—	1/4	.080	—	.100	.180	.230	.350	2400
	7041022	—	1/4	.070	—	.100	.300	.350	.350	2400
	7041023	—	1/16	—	—	.110	.120	.200	.350	2400
	7041024	—	1/16	—	—	.110	.080	.140	.350	2400
	7041025	—	1/4	.070	—	.100	.180	.260	.350	2400
	7041026	—	1/4	.070	—	.100	.275	.350	.350	2400
1972	7042011, 12	—	1/4	.070	—	—	.150	—	—	2400
	7042014	—	1/4	.080	—	—	.125	.190	.500	2400
	7042017	—	1/4	.078	—	—	.150	.225	.500	2400
	7042021	—	1/4	.078	—	—	.150	.225	.500	2400
	7042022	—	1/4	.079	—	—	.125	.190	.500	2400
	7042023	—	1/8	—	—	.110	.130	—	.375	2400
	7042024	—	1/16	—	—	.110	.070	—	.375	2400
	7042025	—	1/4	.070	—	—	.180	.260	.500	2400

Continued

CHEVROLET

ROCHESTER MONOJET M, MV, ME ADJUSTMENT SPECIFICATIONS—Continued

See Tune Up Chart for Hot Idle Speeds.

Year	Carb. Part No. ①	Initial Idle Mix Screw Turns Open	Float Level	Metering Rod	Idle Vent	Fast Idle Off Car	Choke Rod	Vacuum Break	Unloader	Fast Idle R.P.M.
	7042026	—	1/4	.070	—	—	.275	.350	.500	2400
	7042984	—	1/4	.078	—	—	.125	.190	.500	2400
	7042987	—	1/4	.076	—	—	.150	.225	.500	2400
	7042991	—	1/4	.076	—	—	.150	.225	.500	2400
	7042992	—	1/4	.078	—	—	.125	.190	.500	2400
	7042993	—	1/8	—	—	.110	.130	—	.375	2400
	7042994	—	1/16	—	—	.110	.070	—	.375	2400
1973	7043014	—	1/4	.080	—	—	.245	.300	.500	1800
	7043017	—	1/4	.080	—	—	.275	.350	.500	1800
	7043021	—	1/4	.080	—	—	.275	.245	.500	2400
	7043022	—	1/4	.080	—	—	.245	.275	.500	2400
	7043023	—	1/16	—	—	—	.110	.140	.375	2000
	7043024	—	1/16	—	—	—	.085	.120	.375	2200
	7043025	—	1/4	.070	—	—	.350	.290	.600	2400
	7043326	—	1/4	.070	—	—	.375	.290	.600	2400
	7043033	—	1/4	—	—	—	.110	.140	.375	2000
	7043034	—	1/4	—	—	—	.085	.120	.375	2200
	7043323	—	1/4	—	—	—	.110	.140	.375	2000
	7043324	—	1/4	—	—	—	.085	.120	.375	2200
	7043333	—	1/4	—	—	—	.110	.140	.375	2000
	7043334	—	1/4	—	—	—	.085	.120	.375	2000
1974	7044021	—	19/64	.080	—	—	.275	.350	.500	1800
	7044022	—	19/64	.080	—	—	.245	.300	.500	1800
	7044321	—	19/64	.080	—	—	.300	.375	.500	1800
	7044025	—	1/4	.070	—	—	.245	.300	.521②	2400
	7044026	—	1/4	.070	—	—	.275	.350	.521②	2400
	7044023, 33	—	1/16	—	—	—	.080	.130	.375	2000
	7044024, 34	—	1/16	—	—	—	.080	.130	.375	2200
	7044323	—	1/16	—	—	—	.080	.130	.375	2000
	7044324	—	1/16	—	—	—	.080	.130	.375	2200
	7044433	—	1/16	—	—	—	.080	.130	.375	2000
	7044434	—	1/16	—	—	—	.080	.130	.375	2200
	7044014	—	.295	.079	—	—	.230	.275	.500	1800
	7044017	—	.295	.072	—	—	.275	.350	.500	1800
	7044314	—	.295	.073	—	—	.245	.300	.500	1800
1974–76	7044011, 12	—	1/4	.070	—	—	.150	—	—	—
1975	7045002	—	11/32	.080	—	—	.260	③	.325	1800
	7045003, 5	—	11/32	.080	—	—	.275	③	.325	1800
	7045004	—	11/32	.080	—	—	.245	④	.325	1800
	7045008	—	—	—	—	—	—	—	—	—
	7045012	—	11/32	.080	—	—	.160	⑪	.215	—
	7045013	—	11/32	.080	—	—	.275	⑫	.275	—
	7045024, 28	—	1/8	—	—	—	.080	.100	.375	2000
	7045025, 29	—	1/8	—	—	—	.080	.100	.375	2200
	7045302	—	11/32	.080	—	—	.245	④	.275	1800
	7045303	—	11/32	.080	—	—	.275	⑥	.275	1800
	7045304	—	11/32	.080	—	—	.245	③	.325	1800
	7045305	—	11/32	.080	—	—	.275	⑤	.325	1800
	7045314	—	11/32	.080	—	—	.230	⑬	.275	—
1976	17056002	—	11/32	.080	—	—	.130	⑦	.335	—
	17056003	—	11/32	.080	—	—	.145	⑧	.335	—
	17056004	—	11/32	.080	—	—	.130	⑦	.335	—

Continued

CHEVROLET

ROCHESTER MONOJET M, MV, ME ADJUSTMENT SPECIFICATIONS—Continued

See Tune Up Chart for Hot Idle Speeds.

Year	Carb. Part No. ①	Initial Idle Mix Screw Turns Open	Float Level	Metering Rod	Idle Vent	Fast Idle Off Car	Choke Rod	Vacuum Break	Unloader	Fast Idle R.P.M.
	17056006	—	1/4	.080	—	—	.130	.165	.270	—
	17056007	—	1/4	.070	—	—	.130	.165	.275	—
	17056008	—	1/4	.070	—	—	.150	.190	.275	—
	17056009	—	1/4	.070	—	—	.150	.190	.275	—
	17056012	—	11/32	.084	—	—	.090	⑭	.265	—
	17056013	—	11/32	.082	—	—	.090	⑭	.265	—
	17056014	—	11/32	.080	—	—	.090	⑭	.265	—
	17056015	—	11/32	.080	—	—	.090	⑭	.265	—
	17056016	—	11/32	.080	—	—	.115	⑮	.265	—
	17056018	—	11/32	.084	—	—	.090	⑭	.265	—
	17056302	—	11/32	.080	—	—	.155	⑨	.325	—
	17056303	—	11/32	.080	—	—	.180	⑩	.325	—
	17056308	—	1/4	.070	—	—	.150	.190	.275	—
	17056309	—	1/4	.070	—	—	.150	.190	.275	—
1977	17057001	—	3/8	.080	—	—	.125	.150	.325	2100
	17057002	—	3/8	.080	—	—	.110	.135	.325	2100
	17057004	—	3/8	.080	—	—	.110	.135	.325	2100
	17057005	—	3/8	.080	—	—	.125	.180	.325	2100
	17057006	—	5/16	.070	—	—	.150	.180	.275	2400
	17057007	—	5/16	.070	—	—	.150	.180	.275	2400
	17057008	—	5/16	.065	—	—	.150	.180	.275	2400
	17057009	—	5/16	.065	—	—	.150	.180	—	2400
	17057010	—	3/8	.080	—	—	.110	.180	.325	2100
	17057011	—	1/4	.065	—	—	.150	—	—	2400
	17057013	—	3/8	.070	—	—	.100	.125	.325	2000
	17057014	—	3/8	.070	—	—	.085	.125	.325	2000
	17057015	—	3/8	.070	—	—	.100	.125	.325	2000
	17057016	—	3/8	.070	—	—	.095	.015	.325	2000
	17057018	—	3/8	.070	—	—	.085	.120	.325	2000
	17057020	—	3/8	.070	—	—	.085	.125	.325	2000
	17057302	—	3/8	.080	—	—	.110	.135	.275	2100
	17057303	—	3/8	.090	—	—	.125	.150	.325	2100
	17057308	—	5/16	.065	—	—	.150	.180	.275	2400
	17057309	—	5/16	.065	—	—	.150	.180	.275	2400
	17057310	—	3/8	.070	—	—	—	—	—	1800
	17057312	—	3/8	.070	—	—	—	—	—	1800
	17057314	—	3/8	.070	—	—	.100	.110	.225	1800
	17057318	—	3/8	.070	—	—	.100	.110	.225	1800
1978	17058006	—	5/16	.070	—	—	.275	.275	.520	2400
	17058007	—	5/16	.070	—	—	.275	.275	.520	2400
	17058008	—	5/16	.065	—	—	.275	.275	.520	2400
	17058009	—	5/16	.065	—	—	.275	.275	.520	2400
	17058013	—	3/8	.080	—	—	.190	.200	.500	2000
	17058014	—	5/16	.100	—	—	.180	.200	.500	2100
	17058020	—	5/16	.100	—	—	.180	.200	.500	2100
	17058021	—	5/16	—	—	—	.200	.250	.450	2100
	17058022	—	5/16	—	—	—	.200	.250	.450	2100
	17058024	—	5/16	—	—	—	.200	.250	.450	2100
	17058081	—	5/16	—	—	—	.200	.250	.450	2100
	17058082	—	5/16	—	—	—	.200	.250	.450	2100
	17058084	—	5/16	—	—	—	.200	.250	.450	2100

Continued

CHEVROLET

ROCHESTER MONOJET M, MV, ME ADJUSTMENT SPECIFICATIONS—Continued

See Tune Up Chart for Hot Idle Speeds.

Year	Carb. Part No. ①	Initial Idle Mix Screw Turns Open	Float Level	Metering Rod	Idle Vent	Fast Idle Off Car	Choke Rod	Vacuum Break	Unloader	Fast Idle R.P.M.
	17058308	—	5/16	.065	—	—	.275	.275	.520	2400
	17058309	—	5/16	.065	—	—	.275	.275	.520	2400
	17058310	—	5/16	.080	—	—	.190	.250	.600	2100
	17058311	—	5/16	.100	—	—	.190	.250	.600	2100
	17058312	—	5/16	.080	—	—	.190	.250	.600	2100
	17058313	—	5/16	.100	—	—	.190	.250	.600	2100
	17058314	—	3/8	.100	—	—	.190	.245	.400	2000
	17058320	—	5/16	.080	—	—	.190	.250	—	—
	17058322	—	5/16	.080	—	—	.190	.250	.600	—
	17058323	—	5/16	.100	—	—	.190	.250	.600	—
	17058358	—	5/16	.065	—	—	.275	.275	.520	2400
	17058359	—	5/16	.065	—	—	.275	.275	.520	2400
1979	17058009	—	5/16	.065	—	—	.275	.325	.520 ②	2400
	17058011	—	5/16	.065	—	—	.150	—	—	2400
	17059009	—	3/8	.090	—	—	.275	.400	.520 ②	2400
	17059012	—	5/16	.095	—	—	.180	.200	.500	—
	17059013	—	3/8	.100	—	—	.180	.200	.400	1800
	17059014	—	3/8	.100	—	—	.180	.200	.400	2000
	17059020	—	3/8	.100	—	—	.180	.200	.400	2000
	17059023	—	5/16	.095	—	—	.180	.200	.500	—
	17059309	—	3/8	.090	—	—	.275	.400	.520 ②	2400
	17059314	—	3/8	.100	—	—	.190	.245	.400	2000
	17059359	—	3/8	.090	—	—	.275	.400	.520 ②	2400
1979–80	17058011	—	5/16	.065	—	—	.150	—	—	2400
1980	17080009	—	11/32	.090	—	—	.275	.400	.520	—
	17080309	—	11/32	.090	—	—	.275	.400	.520	—
	17080359	—	11/32	.090	—	—	.275	.400	.520	—

① —Located on tag attached to carburetor.
② —Measured at top of choke blade.
③ —Primary .300; auxiliary .290.
④ —Primary .300; auxiliary .150.
⑤ —Primary .350; auxiliary .290.
⑥ —Primary .350; auxiliary .170.
⑦ —Primary .165; auxiliary .265.
⑧ —Primary .180; auxiliary: wide open.
⑨ —Primary .190; auxiliary: wide open.
⑩ —Primary .225; auxiliary: wide open.
⑪ —Primary .200; auxiliary .215.
⑫ —Primary .350; auxiliary .312.
⑬ —Primary .275; auxiliary .312.
⑭ —Primary .110; auxiliary .215.
⑮ —Primary .140; auxiliary: wide open.

MODELS M, MV & ME

Description

This carburetor, Fig. 1, is a single barrel unit with a triple venturi in conjunction with a plain tube nozzle. The fuel flow in the main metering system is controlled by mechanical and vacuum means.

A conventional idling system is used in conjunction with the main metering system. A hot idle compensator is available, where necessary, to maintain smooth engine idle during periods of extreme hot engine operation. The off-idle discharge port is of a vertical slot design which gives good transition between

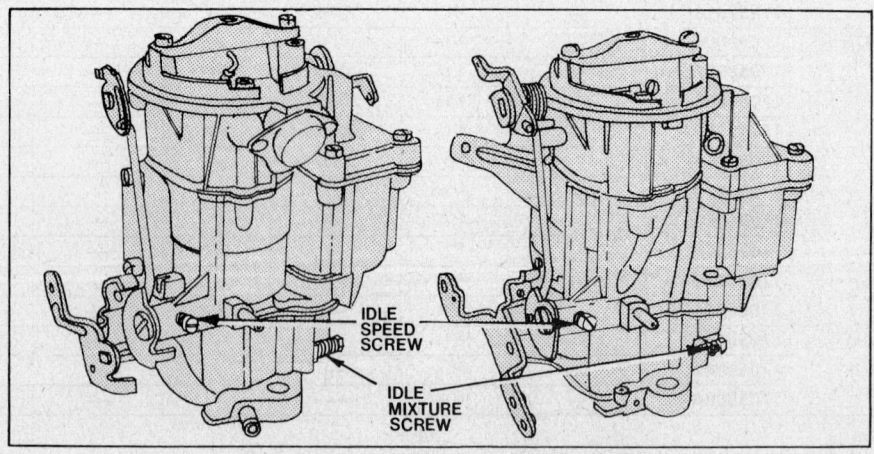

Fig. 1 Rochester Monojet carburetor. Model M

CHEVROLET

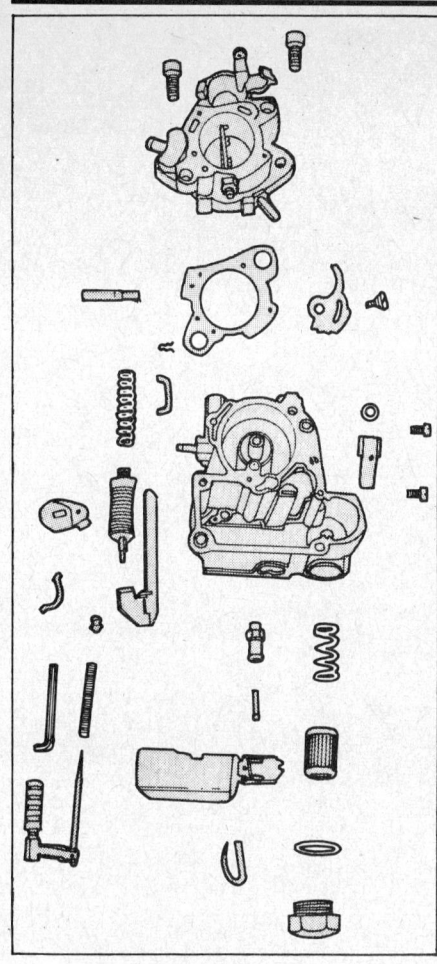

Fig. 2 Float bowl and throttle body. Model M

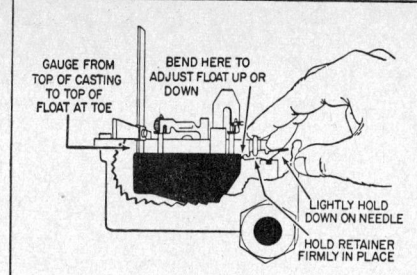

Fig. 3 Float level adjustment. Model M

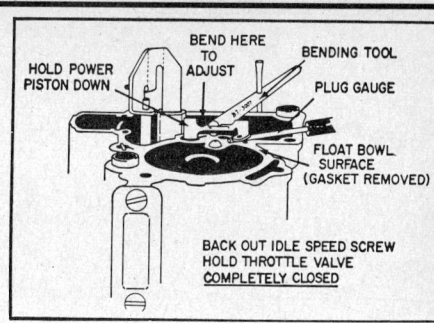

Fig. 4 Monojet metering rod adjustment

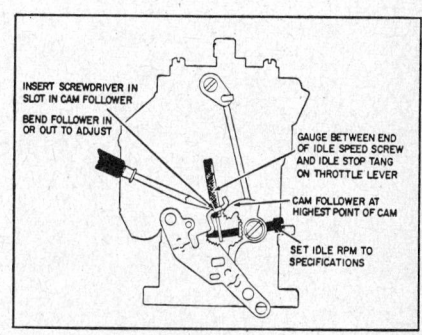

Fig. 5 Fast idle adjustment. Model M

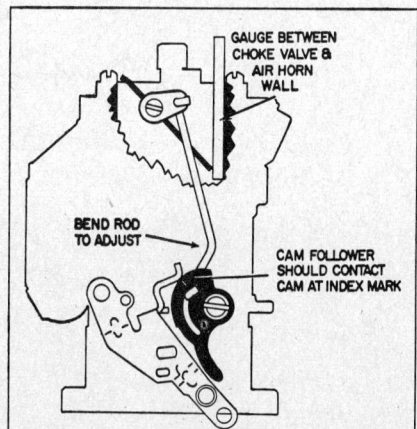

Fig. 6 Choke rod adjustment. Model M

idle and main metering system operations.

Other features of the Monojet include an aluminum throttle body for decreased weight and improved heat transfer, and a thick throttle body-to-bowl insulator gasket to keep excessive engine heat from the float bowl. The carburetor has internally balanced venting through a vent hole in the air horn. Fig. 2 shows an exploded view of the float bowl and throttle body parts.

M & MV Adjustments

Float Level, Adjust, Fig. 3
1. Hold float retaining pin firmly in place and float arm against top of float needle.
2. With adjustable T-scale, measure distance from top of float (at toe) to float bowl gasket surface (gasket removed). Measurement should be made at a point 1/16" in from end of flat surface at float toe (not on radius).
3. Bend float pontoon up or down at float arm junction to adjust.

Metering Rod, Adjust, Fig. 4
1. To check adjustment, back out idle adjusting screw to be sure throttle valve is closed. Rotate fast idle cam so that cam follower is not contacting cam (if installed).
2. With throttle valve completely closed, apply pressure to hanger directly above power piston and hold piston down against its stop.
3. Holding downward pressure on power piston, swing metering rod holder over flat surface of bowl casting unit metering rod rests lightly against inside edge of bowl.
4. Use specified gauge of size listed and insert between bowl casting and lower surface of metering rod holder against metering rod gauge; there should be a sliding fit between surfaces as shown.
5. To adjust, carefully bend metering rod holder up or down at point shown.
6. Install air horn gasket on float bowl by carefully sliding slit portion of gasket over metering rod holder. Then align gasket with dowels provided on top of bowl casting and press gasket firmly in place.
7. Before installing air horn, check operation of entire mechanism, metering rod and accelerator pump for free operation from closed to wide open position.

Initial Idle Speed Screw Setting
1. Hold choke valve wide open so fast idle cam follower clears cam.
2. Adjust idle speed screw until it just contacts lever tang.
3. Adjust idle speed screw an additional 1 1/4 turns with automatic transmission and 2 turns with manual transmission.

Fast Idle, Adjust, Fig. 5
1. Set normal engine idle speed initially by turning idle speed screw 1 1/2 turns in from closed throttle valve position.
2. Place fast idle cam follower tang on highest step of cam.
3. With tang held against cam, check clearance between end of slow idle screw and idle stop tang on throttle lever.
4. To adjust, insert end of screwdriver in slot provided in fast idle cam follower tang and bend inward (toward cam) or outward to obtain specified dimension.

Choke Rod, Adjust, Fig. 6
1. With fast idle adjustment completed, hold fast idle cam follower firmly against cam. Index mark on side of cam should be lined up with contact point of cam follower tang.
2. Rotate choke valve toward closed position by applying force to choke lever.
3. Bend choke rod at point indicated to give specified opening between lower edge of choke valve (at center of valve) and inside air horn wall.

Vacuum Break Adjustment, Fig. 7, 4-140
1. Open throttle valve so cam follower on throttle lever clears fast idle cam.
2. Rotate choke valve toward closed position (use rubber band or spring to keep choke valve in closed position).
3. Seat diaphragm by pushing plunger inward with needle nose pliers.
4. Position gauge between lower edge of choke valve and air horn wall.
5. Bend tang to adjust.

Vacuum Break Adjustment, Fig. 8, 6-250, 292
1. Use outside vacuum source to seat diaphragm.
2. Place gauge between lower edge of choke valve and air horn wall.
3. Bend rod to adjust.

Unloader Adjustment, Fig. 9
1. Hold down on choke valve with rod in end of slot.
2. Hold throttle valve wide open.
3. Position gauge between lower edge of choke valve and air horn wall.
4. Bend tang to adjust.

863

CHEVROLET

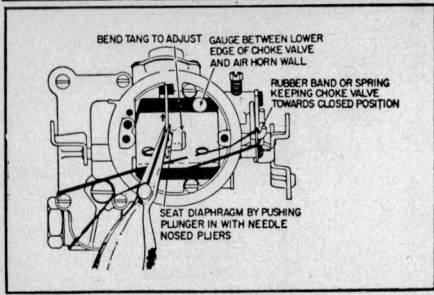

Fig. 7 Vacuum break adjustment. 4-140

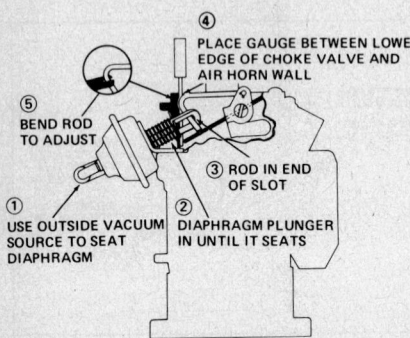

Fig. 8 Vacuum break adjustment. 6-250, 292

Choke Coil Rod Adjustment, Fig. 10, 4-140
1. Hold choke valve wide open.
2. Push down on rod against stop.
3. Top edge of rod should be even with bottom of hole. Bend rod to adjust.

NOTE: On 1972 calif., a swivel is used on end of choke coil rod. Adjust swivel until top of pin on swivel is even with bottom of hole on lever.

Choke Coil Rod Adjustment, Fig. 11, 6-250, 292
1. Hold choke valve closed.
2. Pull upward on coil rod to end of travel.
3. Bottom of rod end which slides into hole in choke lever should be even with top of hole.

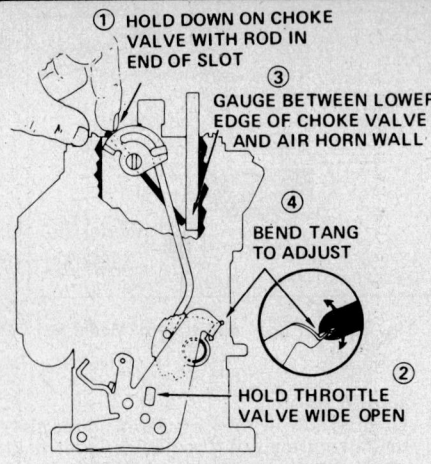

Fig. 9 Unloader adjustment

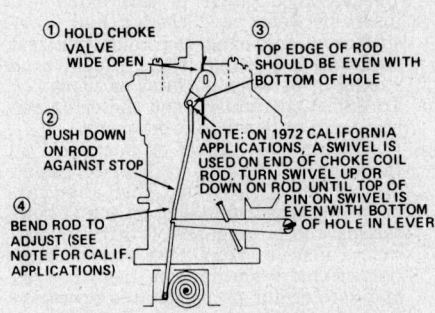

Fig. 10 Choke coil rod adjustment. 4-140

4. Bend choke coil rod at bend to adjust.
5. Connect coil rod to choke lever and install retaining clip.
6. Ensure complete freedom of operation from full open to full closed choke.

On Vehicle Adjustments
Final slow idle, fast idle and idle vent settings should be made on the vehicle using a tachometer. Idle speed and mixture settings must be made with air cleaner on. Warm engine to normal operating temperature; thermostatic air cleaner valve must be in full open position. Slow idle setting must follow procedure shown on decal, which is to adjust mixture screw in to obtain a 20 rpm drop (lean roll), then adjust screw out 1/4 turn.

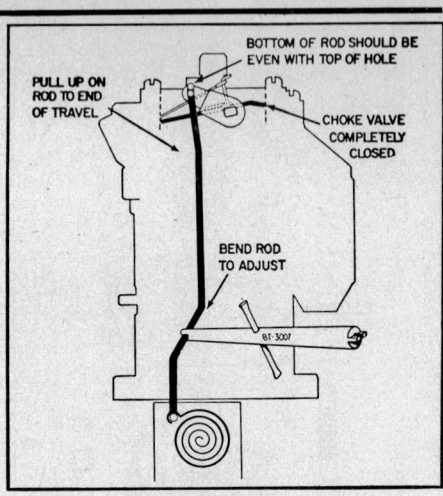

Fig. 11 Choke coil adjustment. 6-250, 292

ME Adjustments

Float Level, Adjust, Fig. 12
1. Hold float retaining pin firmly in place and float arm against top of float needle by pushing downward on float arm at point between needle seat and hinge pin as shown.
2. With adjustable T-scale, measure distance from top of float at toe to float bowl gasket surface (gasket removed). Measurement should be made at a point 1/16" in from end of flat surface at float toe (not on radius).
3. Bend float pontoon up or down at float arm junction to adjust.

Metering Rod Adjustment, Fig. 13
1. Remove metering rod by holding throttle valve wide open. Push downward on metering rod against spring tension, then slide metering rod out of slot in holder and remove from main metering jet.
2. To check adjustment, back out slow idle screw and rotate fast idle cam so that fast idle cam follower is not contacting steps on cam.
3. With throttle valve completely closed, apply pressure to top of power piston and hold piston down against its stop.
4. While holding downward pressure on power piston, swing metering rod holder over flat surface of bowl casting next to carburetor bore.
5. Use specified size drill and insert between bowl casting sealing bead and lower surface of metering rod holder. Drill should

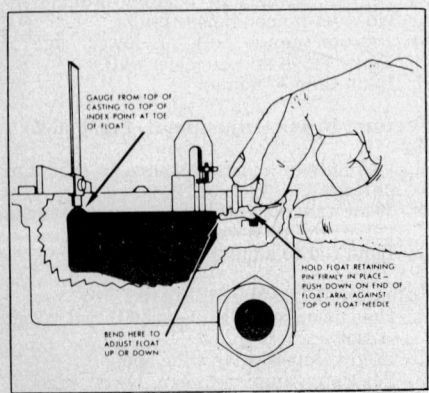

Fig. 12 Float level adjustment. Model ME

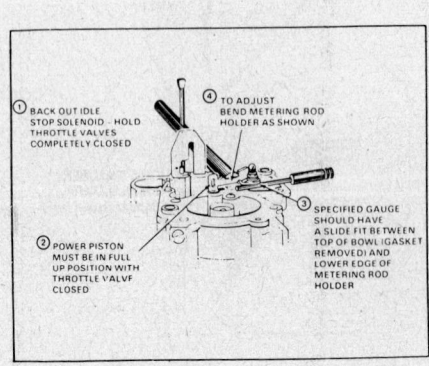

Fig. 13 Metering rod adjustment. Model ME

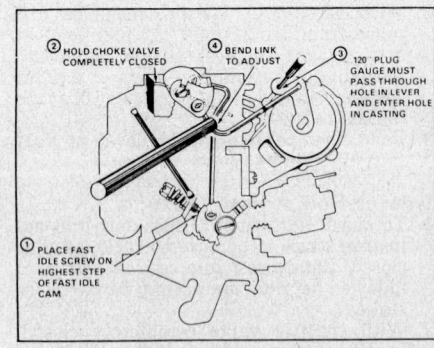

Fig. 14 Choke coil adjustment. Model ME

CHEVROLET

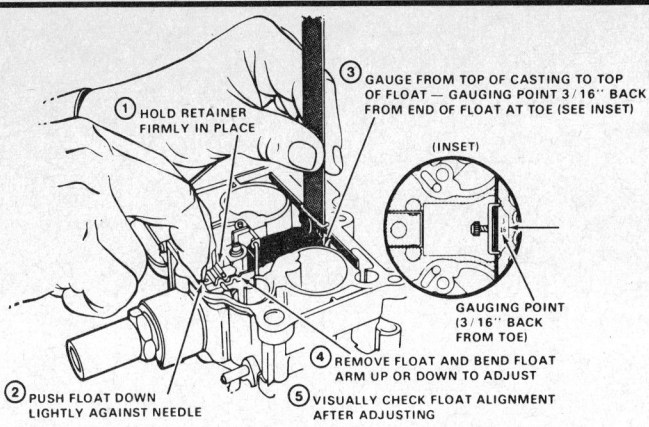

Fig. 1 Float level adjustment. Model M2ME 210

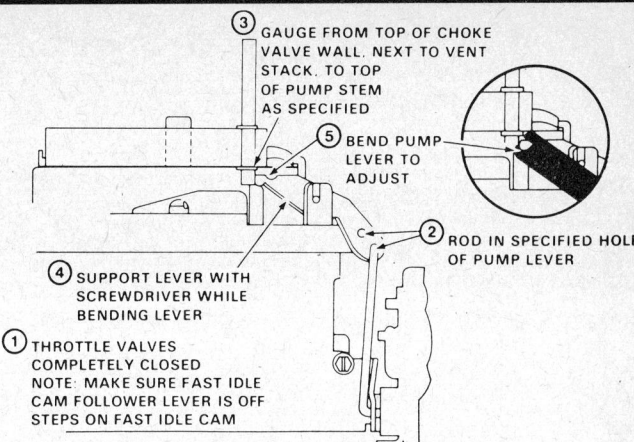

Fig. 2 Pump rod adjustment. Model M2ME 210

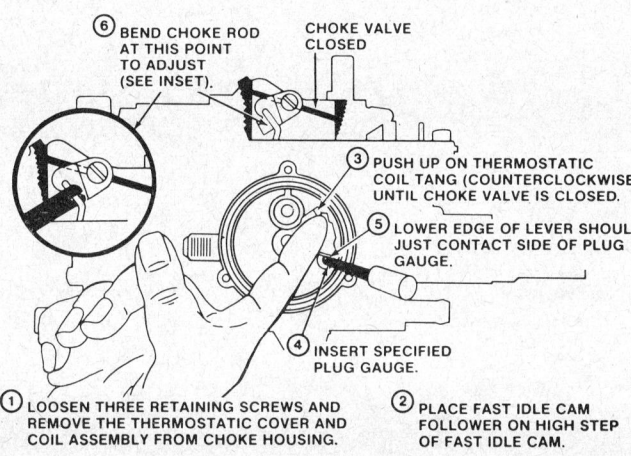

Fig. 3 Choke coil lever adjustment. M2ME 210

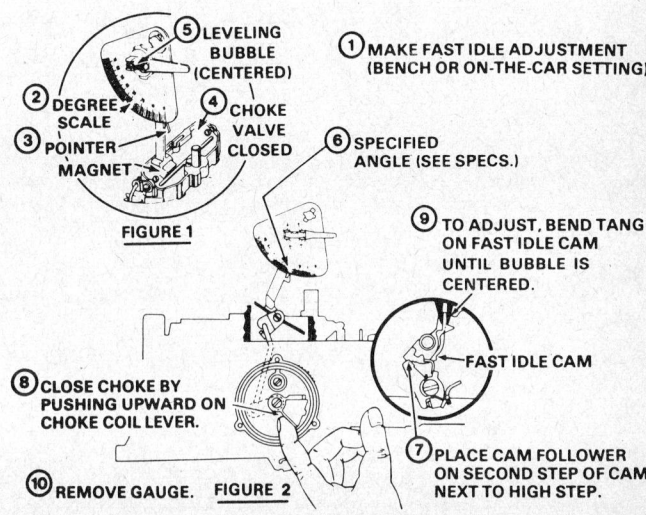

Fig. 4 Choke rod adjustment. Model M2ME 210

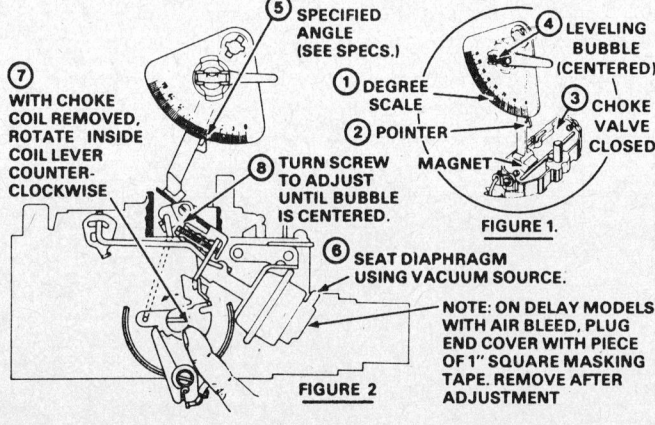

Fig. 5 Vacuum break adjustment. Model M2ME 210

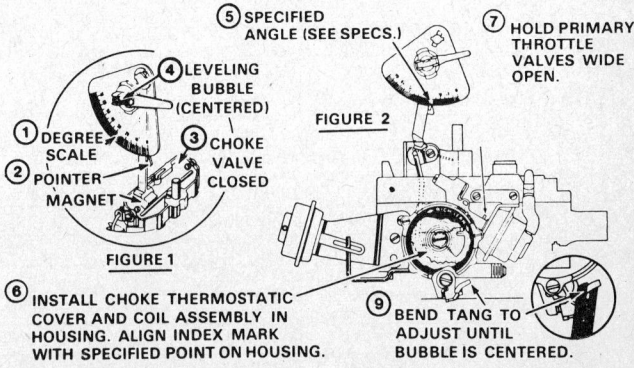

Fig. 6 Choke unloader adjustment. Model M2ME 210

CHEVROLET

tions Chart into choke housing hole. The lower edge of choke coil lever should just contact gauge. To adjust, bend choke rod as required.

Choke Rod, Adjust, Fig. 4

With fast idle adjustment made, and cam follower on second step of fast idle cam and against the high step, push upward on choke coil lever until choke valve closes. Dimension between upper edge of choke valve and air horn wall should be as specified in the *Specifications Chart*. Adjust by bending tang on intermediate choke lever.

Vacuum Break Adjustment (Gauge Method), Fig. 5

Rotate degree scale until zero is opposite pointer, then with choke valve completely closed, place gauge on top of choke valve and rotate bubble until it is centered. Refer to *Specifications Chart* and rotate gauge to degrees specified. Using an external vacuum source, seat choke vacuum diaphragm, then remove choke coil and rotate inside coil lever counterclockwise. To make final adjustment, turn screw in or out until bubble is centered.

NOTE: On delay models with air bleed, remove rubber cover over filter element and plug small bleed hole in vacuum tube with tape. On models with air bleed in end cover, plug cover with 1 inch masking tape. Remove tape after adjustment.

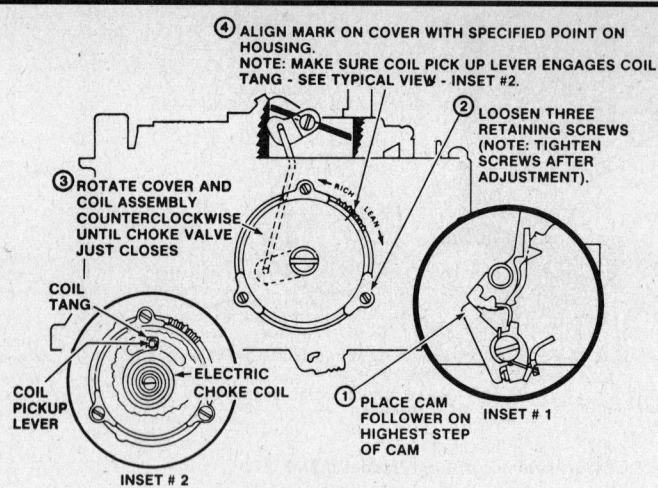

Fig. 7 Choke coil adjustment. Model M2ME 210

Choke Coil, Adjust, Fig. 6

With choke valve held closed by means of a rubber band on vacuum break lever, open throttle valves fully. With valves in this position, dimension between lower edge of choke valve and air horn wall should be as specified. To adjust, bend tang on fast idle lever.

Choke Coil, Adjust, Fig. 7

Place the fast idle cam follower on the highest step of the fast idle cam. Rotate choke cover and coil assembly counterclockwise until the choke valve just closes and the index point on cover aligns with the specified index point on the choke housing.

ROCHESTER 2SE ADJUSTMENT SPECIFICATIONS

See Tune Up chart for curb and fast idle speeds.

Year	Carb. Production No.	Float Level	Accel. Pump	Choke Coil Lever	Choke Rod	Vacuum Break Primary	Vacuum Break Secondary	Air Valve Rod	Choke Setting	Unloader	Secondary Lockout
1979	17059640	1/8"	9/16"	.085	17°	20°	37°	.040	1 Rich	49°	.025
	17059641	1/8"	9/16"	.085	17°	23.5°	37°	.040	1 Rich	49°	.025
	17059642	1/8"	9/16"	.085	17°	20°	37°	.040	1 Rich	49°	.025
	17059643	1/8"	9/16"	.085	17°	23.5°	37°	.040	1 Rich	49°	.025
	17059740	1/8"	9/16"	.085	17°	20°	37°	.040	1 Rich	49°	.025
	17059741	1/8"	9/16"	.085	17°	20°	37°	.040	1 Rich	49°	.025
	17059742	1/8"	9/16"	.085	17°	20°	37°	.040	1 Rich	49°	.025
	17059764	1/8"	9/16"	.085	17°	20°	37°	.040	1 Rich	49°	.025
	17059765	1/8"	9/16"	.085	17°	23.5°	37°	.040	2 Rich	49°	.025
	17059767	1/8"	9/16"	.085	17°	23.5°	37°	.040	1 Rich	49°	.025
1980	17059774	3/16"	15/32"	.085	18°	19°	—	2°	—	32°	.025
	17059775	—	—	.085	—	—	—	—	—	—	.025
	17059776	3/16"	15/32"	.085	18°	19°	—	2°	—	32°	.025
	17059777	—	—	.085	—	—	—	—	—	—	.025
	17080621	1/8"	9/16"	.085	17°	22°	35°	2°	—	41°	.025
	17080622	1/8"	9/16"	.085	17°	22°	35°	2°	—	41°	.025
	17080623	1/8"	9/16"	.085	17°	22°	35°	2°	—	41°	.025
	17080626	1/8"	9/16"	.085	17°	22°	35°	2°	—	41°	.025
	17080674	3/16"	1/2"	.085	18°	19°	—	2°	—	32°	.025
	17080675	3/16"	1/2"	.085	18°	21°	—	2°	—	32°	.025
	17080676	3/16"	1/2"	.085	18°	19°	—	2°	—	32°	.025
	17080677	3/16"	1/2"	.085	18°	21°	—	2°	—	32°	.25
	17080720	1/8"	9/16"	.085	17°	20°	35°	2°	—	41°	.025

Continued

CHEVROLET

ROCHESTER 2SE ADJUSTMENT SPECIFICATIONS—Continued

See Tune Up chart for curb and fast idle speeds.

Year	Carb. Production No.	Float Level	Accel. Pump	Choke Coil Lever	Choke Rod	Vacuum Break Primary	Vacuum Break Secondary	Air Valve Rod	Choke Setting	Unloader	Secondary Lockout
	17080721	1/8"	9/16"	.085	17°	23.5°	35°	2°	—	41°	.025
	17080722	1/8"	9/16"	.085	17°	20°	35°	2°	—	41°	.025
	17080723	1/8"	9/16"	.085	17°	23.5°	35°	2°	—	41°	.025

MODEL 2SE

Adjustments

The Varajet model 2SE, Fig. 1, is a two barrel, two stage, down draft design carburetor. Aluminum die castings are used for the air horn, float bowl and throttle body. A heat insulator gasket is used between the throttle body and float bowl to reduce heat transfer to the float bowl.

The primary stage has a triple venturi, with a small 35mm bore, resulting in good fuel metering control during idle and part throttle operation. The secondary stage has a 46mm bore, providing sufficient air capacity for engine power requirements. An air valve is used in the secondary stage with a single tapered metering rod.

The float chamber is internally vented through a vertical vent cavity in the air horn. The float chamber is also externally vented through a tube in the air horn. A hose connects this tube directly to a vacuum operated vapor vent valve located in the vapor canister. When the engine is not running, the canister vapor vent valve is open, allowing fuel vapor from the float chamber to pass into the canister where the vapor is stored until normally purged.

An adjustable part throttle screw is used in the float bowl to aid emission control. This screw is factory pre-set and a plug is installed to prevent further adjustment or fuel leakage. The plug should not be removed or the screw setting disturbed. If float bowl replacement is required, the service float bowl will include a factory pre-set and plugged adjustable part throttle screw.

A hot idle compensator is used on some models and is located in the air horn. The opening and closing of the hot idle compensator valve is controlled by a bi-metal strip that is calibrated to a specific temperature. When the valve opens, additional air is allowed to bypass the throttle valves and enter the intake manifold to prevent rough idle during periods of hot engine operation.

The idle mixture screw is recessed in the throttle body and is sealed with a hardened steel plug to prevent alteration of the factory pre-set mixture setting. The plug should not be removed and the mixture screw readjusted unless required by major carburetor overhaul or throttle body replacement.

Float Level Adjustment

Fig. 2
1. Hold float retainer firmly in place and push float lightly against needle.
2. With an adjustable T-scale, measure distance between float bowl gasket surface (gasket removed) and float toe.
3. To adjust, remove float and bend float arm.
4. Check float alignment after adjustment.

Pump Adjustment

NOTE: The pump adjustment should not be altered from the specified setting.

Fig. 3
1. Close throttle valves and ensure that fast idle screw is not contacting fast idle cam steps.
2. Measure distance between air horn casting surface and top of pump stem.
3. To adjust, remove pump lever retaining screw and the pump lever. Place the lever in a vise and bend lever end. Do not bend lever in a twisting motion.

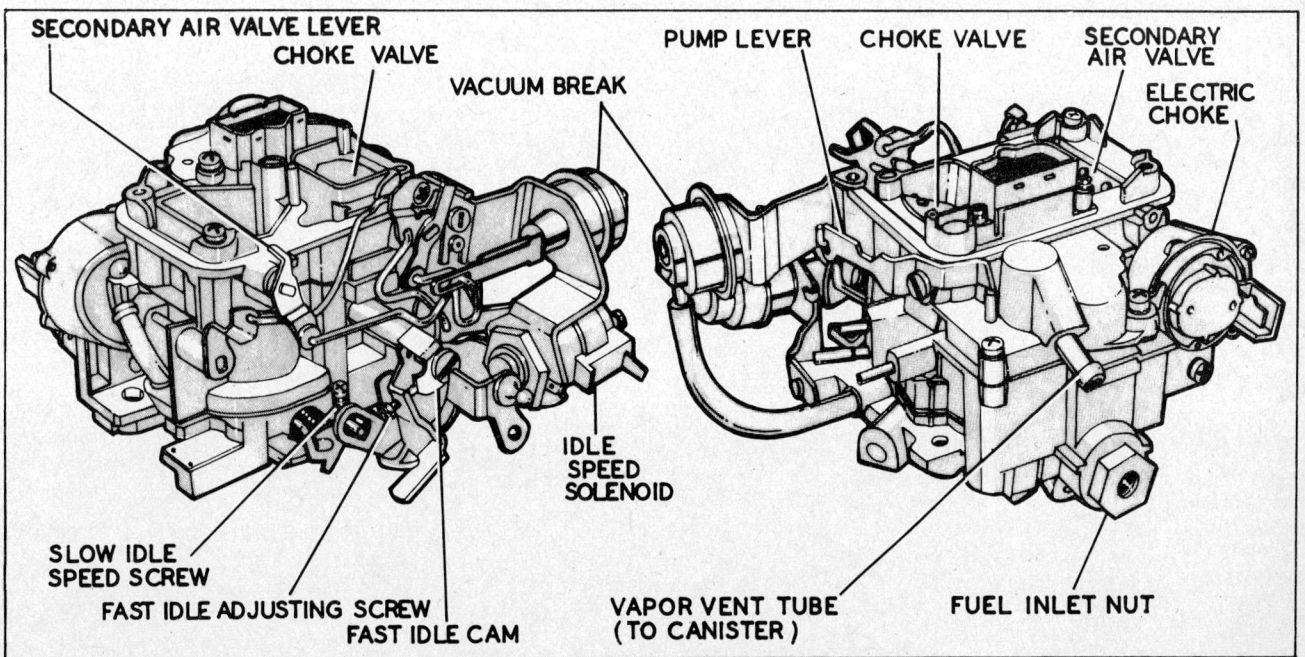

Fig. 1 Varajet 2SE carburetor

CHEVROLET

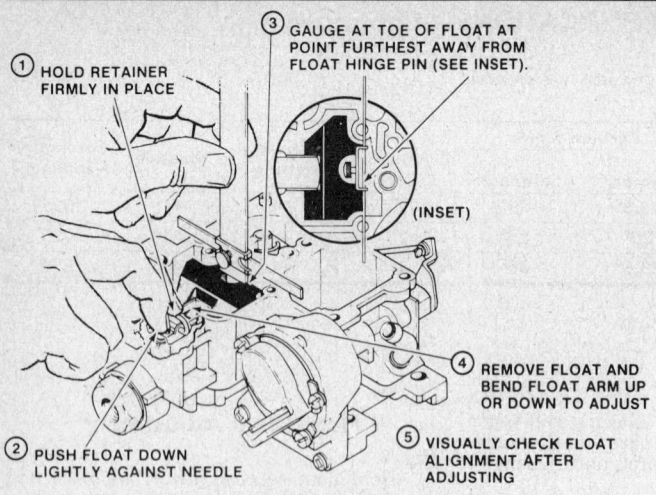

Fig. 2 Float level adjustment

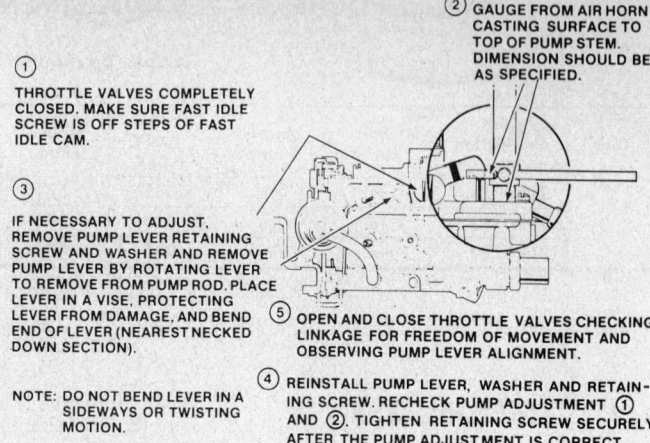

Fig. 3 Pump adjustment

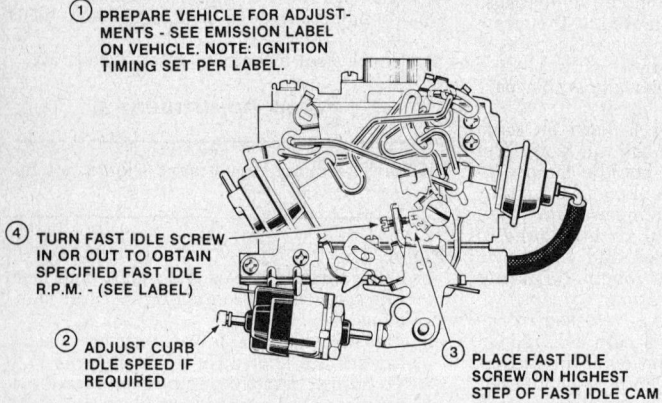

Fig. 4 Fast idle adjustment

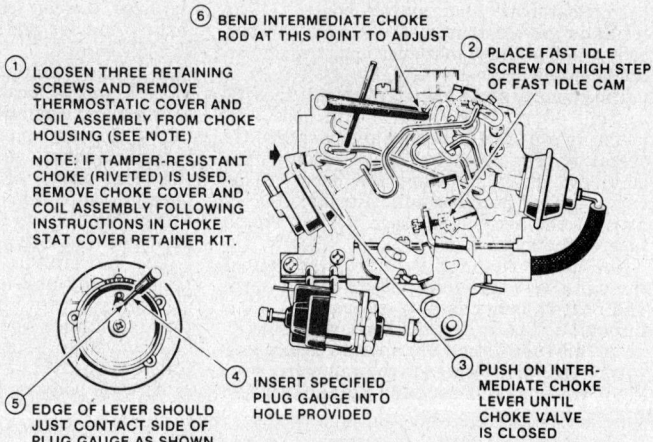

Fig. 5 Choke coil lever adjustment

4. Install pump lever and retaining screw. Recheck pump adjustment.
5. Operate throttle valves to check for freedom of movement and pump lever alignment.

Fast Idle Adjustment
Fig. 4
1. Adjust curb idle speed, if necessary.
2. Place fast idle screw on highest step of cam.
3. Turn fast idle screw to obtain specified fast idle speed.

Choke Coil Lever Adjustment
Fig. 5
1. Loosen choke cover retaining screws, then the cover and coil assembly from

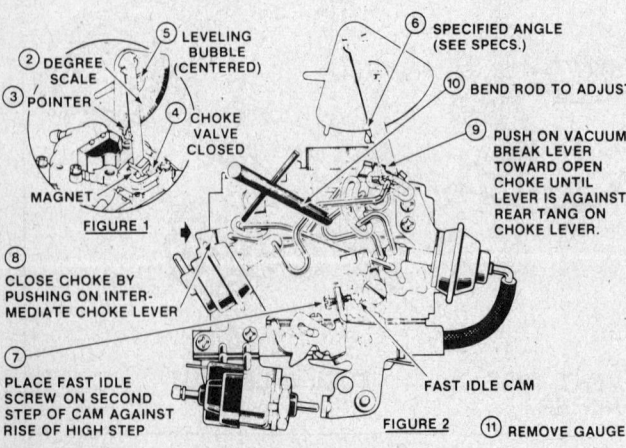

Fig. 6 Choke rod adjustment

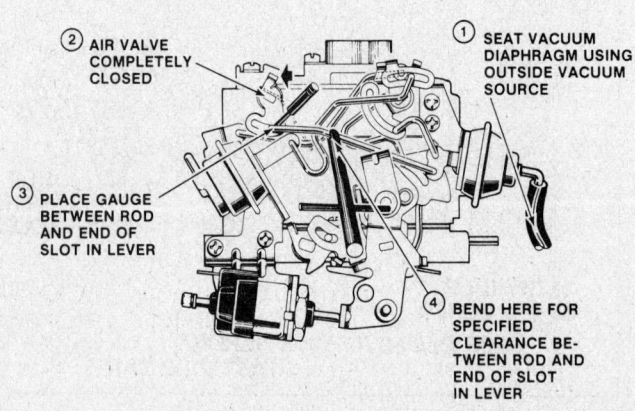

Fig. 7 Air valve rod adjustment

CHEVROLET

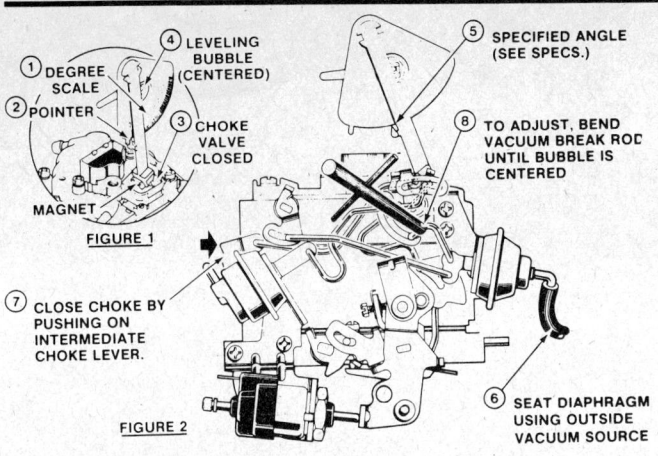

Fig. 8 Primary vacuum break adjustment

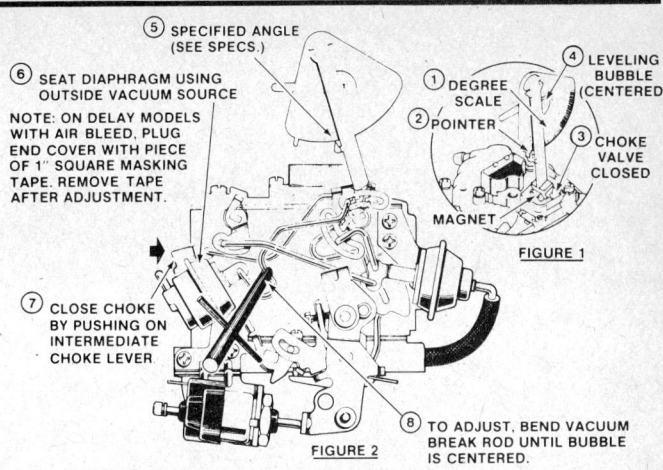

Fig. 9 Secondary vacuum break adjustment

choke housing. If a riveted choke cover is used, remove choke cover and coil assembly as outlined in the choke cover retainer kit.
2. Place fast idle screw on high step of cam.
3. Push the intermediate choke lever until the choke valve closes.
4. Insert specified gauge into hole provided in choke housing. The edge of the lever should just contact gauge.
5. To adjust, bend intermediate choke rod.

Choke Rod Adjustment

NOTE: The choke coil lever and fast idle adjustments must be made before performing this adjustment.

Fig. 6
1. Rotate degree scale until zero is opposite pointer, then with choke valve completely closed, place magnet on top of choke valve and rotate bubble until centered.
2. Rotate scale so specified degree for adjustment is opposite pointer.
3. Place fast idle screw on second step of cam against shoulder of high step.
4. Close choke by pushing intermediate choke lever.
5. Push vacuum break lever toward open choke position until lever contacts rear tang on choke lever.
6. To adjust, bend fast idle cam rod until bubble is centered.

Air Valve Rod Adjustment

Fig. 7
1. Seat vacuum diaphragm with an external

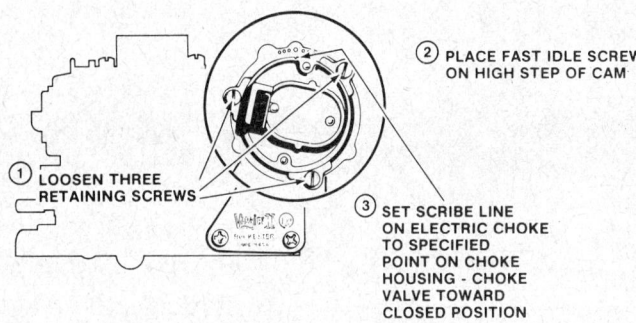

Fig. 10 Choke setting adjustment

vacuum source.
2. Close air valve completely.
3. Place specified gauge between rod and end of lever in slot.
4. To adjust, bend air valve rod.

Primary Vacuum Break Adjustment

Fig. 8
1. Rotate degree scale until zero is opposite

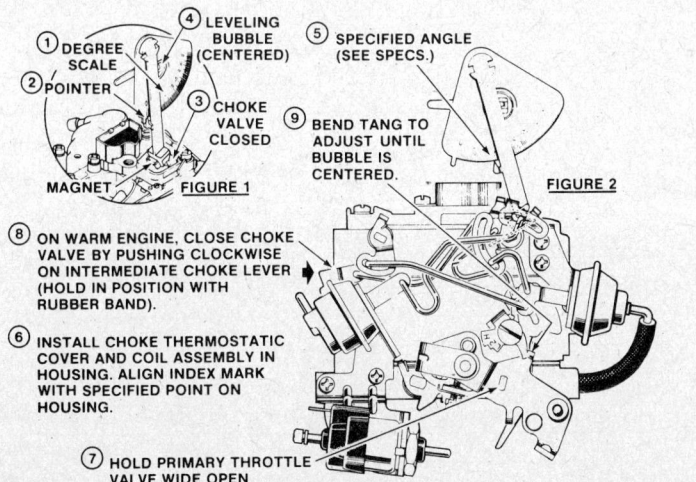

Fig. 11 Unloader adjustment

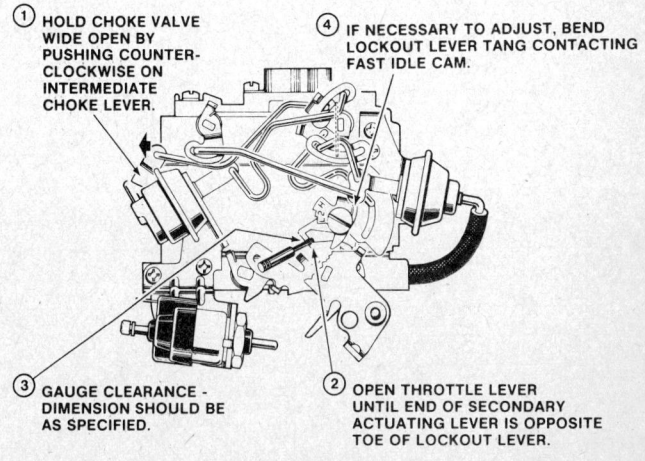

Fig. 12 Secondary lockout adjustment

871

CHEVROLET

pointer, then with choke valve completely closed, place magnet on top of choke valve and rotate bubble until centered.
2. Rotate degree scale so specified degree for adjustment is opposite pointer.
3. Seat vacuum diaphragm with an external vacuum source.
4. Hold choke valve toward closed position by pushing on intermediate choke lever.
5. To adjust, bend vacuum break rod as shown until bubble is centered.

Secondary Vacuum Break Adjustment
Fig. 9
1. Rotate degree scale until zero is opposite pointer, then with choke valve completely closed, place magnet on top of choke valve and rotate bubble until centered.
2. Rotate scale so specified degree for adjustment is opposite pointer.
3. Seat vacuum diaphragm with an external vacuum source.
4. Hold choke valve toward closed position by pushing on intermediate choke lever. Ensure that bucking spring, if used, is compressed and seated.
5. To adjust, bend vacuum break rod as shown until bubble is centered.

Choke Setting
Fig. 10
1. Loosen choke cover retaining screws.
2. Place fast idle screw on high step of cam.
3. Align scribe line on choke cover with specified point on housing. Rotate cover toward closed choke position.
4. Tighten choke cover retaining screws.

Unloader Adjustment
Fig. 11
1. Rotate degree scale until zero is opposite pointer, then with choke valve completely closed, place magnet on top of choke valve and rotate bubble until centered.
2. Rotate degree scale so specified degree for adjustment is opposite pointer.
3. With choke setting properly adjusted, hold primary throttle valve wide open.
4. On warm engines, close choke valve by pushing on intermediate choke lever and hold in position with a rubber band.
5. To adjust, bend tang on throttle lever until bubble is centered.

Secondary Lockout Adjustment
Fig. 12
1. Hold choke valve wide open by pulling on intermediate choke lever.
2. Position throttle lever until end of secondary actuating lever is opposite toe of lockout lever.
3. Insert specified gauge between throttle lever and secondary lockout lever toe.
4. To adjust, bend lockout lever tang contacting fast idle cam.

ROCHESTER QUADRAJET 4MV ADJUSTMENT SPECIFICATIONS

See Tune Up Chart for hot idle speeds.

Carb. Model	Year	Float Level	Pump Rod Hole	Pump Rod Adj.	Idle Vent	Choke Coil Lever	Fast Idle (Bench)	Choke Rod	Vacuum Break	Air Valve Dashpot	Choke Unloader	Air Valve Lockout	Secondary Metering Rods	Air Valve Spring Wind-Up
7040200	1970	1/4	Inner	5/16	—	—	2 Turns	.100	.245	.020	.450	—	—	13/16
7040201	1970	1/4	Inner	5/16	—	—	2 Turns	.100	.275	.020	.450	—	—	13/16
7040202	1970	1/4	Inner	5/16	—	—	2 Turns	.100	.245	.020	.450	—	—	7/16
7040203	1970	1/4	Inner	5/16	—	—	2 Turns	.100	.275	.020	.450	—	—	7/16
7040204	1970	1/4	Inner	5/16	—	—	2 Turns	.100	.245	.020	.450	—	—	13/16
7040205	1970	1/4	Inner	5/16	—	—	2 Turns	.100	.275	.020	.450	—	—	13/16
7040207	1970	1/4	Inner	5/16	—	—	2 Turns	.100	.275	.015	.450	—	—	13/16
7040500	1970	1/4	—	5/16	—	—	2 Turns	.100	.245	.020	.450	—	—	13/16
7040501	1970	1/4	—	5/16	—	—	2 Turns	.100	.275	.020	.450	—	—	13/16
7040502	1970	1/4	—	5/16	—	—	2 Turns	.100	.245	.020	.450	—	—	7/16
7040503	1970	1/4	—	5/16	—	—	2 Turns	.100	.275	.020	.450	—	—	7/16
7040504	1970	1/4	—	5/16	—	—	2 Turns	.100	.245	.020	.450	—	—	13/16
7040505	1970	1/4	—	5/16	—	—	2 Turns	.100	.275	.020	.450	—	—	13/16
7040507	1970	1/4	—	5/16	—	—	2 Turns	.100	.275	.015	.450	—	—	13/16
7029223	1969	7/32	Inner	5/16	3/8	—	2 Turns	.100	.245	.015	.450	.015	7/16	7/16
7040511	1970	1/4	Inner	5/16	—	—	2 Turns	.100	.245	.020	.450	—	—	7/16
7040513	1970	1/4	Inner	5/16	—	—	2 Turns	.100	.275	.020	.450	—	—	7/16
7040208	1970	1/4	Inner	5/16	—	—	2 Turns	.100	.245	.020	.450	—	—	7/16
7040509	1970	1/4	Inner	5/16	—	—	2 Turns	.100	.275 ①	.020	.450	—	—	13/16
7040206	1970	1/4	Inner	5/16	—	—	2 Turns	.100	.245	.020	.450	—	—	13/16
7041200	1971	1/4	—	—	—	—	—	.100	.260	.020	—	—	—	—
7041201	1971	1/4	—	—	—	—	—	.100	.275	.020	—	—	—	—
7041202	1971	1/4	—	—	—	—	—	.100	.260	.020	—	—	—	—
7041203	1971	1/4	—	—	—	—	—	.100	.275	.020	—	—	—	—
7041204	1971	1/4	—	—	—	—	—	.100	.260	.020	—	—	—	—
7041205	1971	1/4	—	—	—	—	—	.100	.275	.020	—	—	—	—
7041206	1971	1/4	—	—	—	—	—	.100	.260	.020	—	—	—	—
7041208	1971	1/4	—	—	—	—	—	.100	.260	.020	—	—	—	—
7041209	1971	11/32	—	—	—	—	—	.100	.260	.020	—	—	—	—
7041211	1971	1/4	—	—	—	—	—	.100	.260	.020	—	—	—	—
7041212	1971	1/4	—	—	—	—	—	.100	.260	.020	—	—	—	—
7041213	1971	1/4	—	—	—	—	—	.100	.275	.020	—	—	—	—
7042202	1972	1/4	—	—	3/8	—	—	.100	.215	.020	.450	—	—	—

Continued

CHEVROLET

ROCHESTER QUADRAJET 4MV ADJUSTMENT SPECIFICATIONS—Continued

See Tune Up Chart for hot idle speeds.

Carb. Model	Year	Float Level	Pump Rod Hole	Pump Rod Adj.	Idle Vent	Choke Coil Lever	Fast Idle (Bench)	Choke Rod	Vacuum Break	Air Valve Dash-pot	Choke Unloader	Air Valve Lockout	Secondary Metering Rods	Air Valve Valve Spring Wind-Up
7042203	1972	1/4	—	3/8	—	—	—	.100	.215	.020	.450	—	—	—
7042206	1972	7/32	—	13/32	—	—	—	.100	.250	.020	.450	—	—	—
7042207	1972	5/16	—	13/32	—	—	—	.100	.250	.020	.450	—	—	—
7042208	1972	3/16	—	3/8	—	—	—	.100	.260	.020	.450	—	—	—
7042210	1972	3/16	—	3/8	—	—	—	.100	.215	.020	.450	—	—	—
7042211	1972	3/16	—	3/8	—	—	—	.100	.215	.020	.450	—	—	—
7042215	1972	1/4	—	3/8	—	—	—	.100	.250	.020	.450	—	—	—
7042216	1972	1/4	—	3/8	—	—	—	.100	.250	.020	.450	—	—	—
7042217	1972	1/4	—	3/8	—	—	—	.100	.250	.020	.450	—	—	—
7042218	1972	1/4	—	3/8	—	—	—	.100	.250	.020	.450	—	—	—
7042219	1972	5/16	—	3/8	—	—	—	.100	.260	.010	.450	—	—	—
7042220	1972	1/4	—	3/8	—	—	—	.100	.250	.020	.450	—	—	—
7042902	1972	1/4	—	3/8	—	—	—	.100	.215	.020	.450	—	—	—
7042903	1972	1/4	—	3/8	—	—	—	.100	.215	.020	.450	—	—	—
7042910	1972	3/16	—	3/8	—	—	—	.100	.215	.020	.450	—	—	—
7042911	1972	3/16	—	3/8	—	—	—	.100	.215	.020	.450	—	—	—
7043200	1973	1/4	Inner	13/22	—	—	—	.430	.250	—	.450	—	—	11/16
7043201	1973	1/4	Inner	13/32	—	—	2 Turns	.430	.250	—	.450	—	—	11/16
7043202	1973	7/32	Inner	13/32	—	—	—	.430	.215	—	.450	—	—	1/2
7043203	1973	7/32	Inner	13/32	—	—	—	.430	.215	—	.450	—	—	1/2
7043207	1973	1/4	Inner	13/32	—	—	—	.430	.250	—	.450	—	—	11/16
7043208	1973	5/16	Inner	13/32	—	—	—	.430	.215	—	.450	—	—	1/2
7043210	1973	7/32	Inner	13/32	—	—	—	.430	.215	—	.450	—	—	1/2
7043211	1973	7/32	Inner	13/32	—	—	—	.430	.215	—	.450	—	—	1/2
7043212	1973	1/4	Inner	13/32	—	—	2 Turns	.430	.215	—	.450	—	—	3/4
7043213	1973	1/4	Inner	13/32	—	—	2 Turns	.430	.215	—	.450	—	—	3/4
7043215	1973	5/16	Inner	13/32	—	—	—	.430	.215	—	.450	—	—	1/2
7043216	1973	1/4	Inner	13/32	—	—	—	.430	.250	—	.450	—	—	11/16
7043507	1973	3/8	Inner	13/32	—	—	—	.430	.275	.015	.450	—	—	11/16
7044201	1974	3/8	Inner	13/32	—	—	2 Turns	.430	.250	.015	.450	—	—	7/16
7044202	1974	1/4	Inner	13/32	—	—	—	.430	.230	—	.450	—	—	7/8
7044203	1974	1/4	Inner	13/32	—	—	—	.430	.230	—	.450	—	—	7/8
7044206	1974	1/4	Inner	13/32	—	—	2 Turns	.430	.230	.015	.450	—	—	7/8
7044207	1974	1/4	Inner	13/32	—	—	2 Turns	.430	.230	.015	.450	—	—	7/8
7044208	1974	1/4	Inner	13/32	—	—	2 Turns	.430	.230	.015	.450	—	—	1 Turn
7044209	1974	1/4	Inner	13/32	—	—	2 Turns	.430	.230	.015	.450	—	—	1 Turn
7044210	1974	1/4	Inner	13/32	—	—	2 Turns	.430	.230	.015	.450	—	—	1 Turn
7044211	1974	1/4	Inner	13/32	—	—	2 Turns	.430	.230	.015	.450	—	—	1 Turn
7044212	1974	.375	Inner	13/32	—	—	—	.430	.230	—	.450	—	—	7/16
7044213	1974	11/32	Inner	13/32	—	—	—	.430	.215	—	.450	—	—	7/8
7044214	1974	11/32	Inner	13/32	—	—	—	.430	.215	—	.450	—	—	7/8
7044215	1974	11/32	Inner	13/32	—	—	—	.430	.215	—	.450	—	—	7/8
7044216	1974	11/32	Inner	13/32	—	—	—	.430	.215	—	.450	—	—	7/8
7044217	1974	.375	Inner	13/32	—	—	—	.430	.230	—	.450	—	—	7/16
7044218	1974	1/4	Inner	13/32	—	—	—	.430	.215	—	.450	—	—	7/8
7044219	1974	1/4	Inner	13/32	—	—	—	.430	.215	—	.450	—	—	7/8
7044221	1974	3/8	Inner	13/32	—	—	2 Turns	.430	.250	.015	.450	—	—	7/16
7044223	1974	.375	Inner	13/32	—	—	—	.430	.220	—	.450	—	—	7/8
7044224	1974	11/32	Inner	13/32	—	—	—	.430	.215	—	.450	—	—	7/8
7044225	1974	3/8	Inner	13/32	—	—	2 Turns	.430	.220	.015	.450	—	—	7/16
7044226	1974	1/4	Inner	13/32	—	—	2 Turns	.340	.230	.015	.450	—	—	3/4
7044227	1974	.375	Inner	13/32	—	—	—	.430	.220	—	.450	—	—	7/8

Continued

CHEVROLET

ROCHESTER QUADRAJET 4MV ADJUSTMENT SPECIFICATIONS—Continued

See Tune Up Chart for hot idle speeds.

Carb. Model	Year	Float Level	Pump Rod Hole	Pump Rod Adj.	Idle Vent	Choke Coil Lever	Fast Idle (Bench)	Choke Rod	Vacuum Break	Air Valve Dash-pot	Choke Unloader	Air Valve Lockout	Secondary Metering Rods	Air Valve Valve Spring Wind-Up
7044500	1974	.375	Inner	13/32	—	—	—	.430	.250	—	.450	—	—	7/16
7044502	1974	1/4	Inner	13/32	—	—	—	.430	.230	—	.450	—	—	7/8
7044503	1974	1/4	Inner	13/32	—	—	—	.430	.230	—	.450	—	—	7/8
7044505	1974	3/8	Inner	—	—	—	2 Turns	.430	.230	.015	.450	—	—	7/16
7044506	1974	1/4	Inner	13/32	—	—	2 Turns	.430	.230	.015	.450	—	—	7/8
7044507	1974	1/4	Inner	13/32	—	—	2 Turns	.430	.230	.015	.450	—	—	7/8
7044508	1974	3/8	Inner	13/32	—	—	2 Turns	.430	.250	.015	.450	—	—	7/16
7044509	1974	1/4	Inner	13/32	—	—	2 Turns	.430	.230	.015	.450	—	—	7/8
7044512	1974	.375	Inner	13/32	—	—	—	.430	.215	—	.450	—	—	7/8
7044513	1974	11/32	Inner	13/32	—	—	—	.430	.215	—	.450	—	—	7/8
7044514	1974	11/32	Inner	13/32	—	—	—	.430	.215	—	.450	—	—	7/8
7044515	1974	11/32	Inner	13/32	—	—	—	.430	.215	—	.450	—	—	7/8
7044516	1974	11/32	Inner	13/32	—	—	—	.430	.215	—	.450	—	—	7/8
7044517	1974	.375	Inner	13/32	—	—	—	.430	.230	—	.450	—	—	7/16
7044518	1974	1/4	Inner	13/32	—	—	—	.430	.215	—	.450	—	—	7/8
7044519	1974	1/4	Inner	13/32	—	—	—	.430	.215	—	.450	—	—	7/8
7044520	1974	.375	Inner	13/32	—	—	—	.430	.250	—	.450	—	—	7/16
7044526	1974	1/4	Inner	13/32	—	—	2 Turns	.430	.230	.015	.450	—	—	3/4
7045212	1975	3/8	Inner	.275	—	—	—	.430	.225	.015	.450	—	—	7/16
7045213	1975	11/32	Inner	.275	—	—	—	.430	.210	.015	.450	—	—	7/8
7045214	1975	11/32	Inner	.275	—	—	—	.430	.215	.015	.450	—	—	7/8
7045215	1975	11/32	Inner	.275	—	—	—	.430	.215	.015	.450	—	—	7/8
7045216	1975	11/32	Inner	.275	—	—	—	.430	.210	.015	.450	—	—	7/8
7045217	1975	3/8	Inner	.275	—	—	—	.430	.225	.015	.450	—	—	7/16
7045225	1975	11/32	Inner	.275	—	—	—	.430	.200	.015	.450	—	—	3/4
7045229	1975	15/32	Inner	.275	—	—	—	.430	.200	.015	.450	—	—	3/4
7045583	1975	11/32	Inner	.275	—	—	—	.430	.230	.015	.450	—	—	7/8
7045584	1975	11/32	Inner	.275	—	—	—	.430	.230	.015	.450	—	—	7/8
7045585	1975	11/32	Inner	.275	—	—	—	.430	.230	.015	.450	—	—	7/8
7045586	1975	11/32	Inner	.275	—	—	—	.430	.230	.015	.450	—	—	7/8
7045588	1975	11/32	Inner	.275	—	—	—	.430	.230	.015	.450	—	—	3/4
7045589	1975	11/32	Inner	.275	—	—	—	.430	.230	.015	.450	—	—	3/4
17056212	1976–77	3/8	Inner	9/32	—	—	—	.290	.155	.015	.295	—	—	7/16
7045213	1976	11/32	Inner	9/32	—	—	—	.290.	.145	.015	.295	—	—	7/8
7045214	1976	11/32	Inner	9/32	—	—	—	.290	.145	.015	.295	—	—	7/8
7045215	1976	11/32	Inner	9/32	—	—	—	.290	.145	.015	.295	—	—	7/8
7045216	1976	11/32	Inner	9/32	—	—	—	.290	.145	.015	.295	—	—	7/8
17056217	1976–77	3/8	Inner	9/32	—	—	—	.290	.155	.015	.295	—	—	7/16
7045225	1976	11/32	Inner	9/32	—	—	—	.290	.138	.015	.295	—	—	3/4
7045229	1976–77	11/32	Inner	9/32	—	—	—	.290	.138	.015	.295	—	—	3/4
7045583	1976–77	11/32	Inner	9/32	—	—	—	.290	.155	.015	.295	—	—	7/8
7045584	1976	11/32	Inner	9/32	—	—	—	.290	.155	.015	.295	—	—	7/8
7045585	1976–77	11/32	Inner	9/32	—	—	—	.290	.155	.015	.295	—	—	7/8
7045586	1976–77	11/32	Inner	9/32	—	—	—	.290	.155	.015	.295	—	—	7/8
7045588	1976	11/32	Inner	9/32	—	—	—	.290	.155	.015	.295	—	—	3/4
7045589	1976	11/32	Inner	9/32	—	—	—	.290	.155	.015	.295	—	—	3/4
17057213	1977	11/32	Inner	9/32	—	—	—	.220	.115	.015	.205	—	—	7/8
17057215	1977	11/32	Inner	9/32	—	—	—	.220	.115	.015	.205	—	—	7/8
17057216	1977	11/32	Inner	9/32	—	—	—	.220	.115	.015	.205	—	—	7/8
17057229	1977	11/32	Inner	9/32	—	—	—	.220	.110	.015	.205	—	—	7/8
17057514	1977	11/32	Inner	9/32	—	—	—	.220	.120	.015	.225	—	—	7/8
17057525	1977	11/32	Inner	9/32	—	—	—	.220	.120	.015	.225	—	—	3/4

Continued

CHEVROLET

ROCHESTER QUADRAJET 4MV ADJUSTMENT SPECIFICATIONS—Continued

See Tune Up Chart for hot idle speeds.

Carb. Model	Year	Float Level	Pump Rod Hole	Pump Rod Adj.	Idle Vent	Choke Coil Lever	Fast Idle (Bench)	Choke Rod	Vacuum Break	Air Valve Dash-pot	Choke Unloader	Air Valve Lockout	Secondary Metering Rods	Air Valve Valve Spring Wind-Up
17057529	1977	11/32	Inner	9/32	—	—	—	.220	.110	.015	.205	—	—	7/8
17058212	1978	7/16	Inner	9/32	—	—	—	②	③	.015	⑦	—	—	7/8
17058213	1978	15/32	Inner	9/32	—	—	—	②	④	.015	⑦	—	—	7/8
17058215	1978	15/32	Inner	9/32	—	—	—	②	④	.015	⑦	—	—	7/8
17058229	1978	15/32	Inner	9/32	—	—	—	②	④	.015	⑦	—	—	7/8
17058513	1978	15/32	Inner	9/32	—	—	—	②	③	.015	⑥	—	—	7/8
17058514	1978	15/32	Inner	9/32	—	—	—	②	③	.015	⑥	—	—	7/8
17058515	1978	15/32	Inner	9/32	—	—	—	②	③	.015	⑥	—	—	7/8
17058525	1978	7/16	Inner	9/32	—	—	—	②	③	.015	—	—	—	3/4
17058529	1978	15/32	Inner	9/32	—	—	—	②	⑤	.015	—	—	—	7/8

①—.245 with auto. trans.
②—With angle gauge set to 42°.
③—With angle gauge set to 26.5°.
④—With angle gauge set to 22°.
⑤—With angle gauge set to 25°.
⑥—With angle gauge set to 43°.
⑦—With angle gauge set to 40°.

MODEL 4MV

The primary side of the carburetor has small bores and a triple venturi for fine fuel control in the idle and economy ranges. The secondary side has large bores and an air valve for high air capacity, Fig. 1.

See Figs. 2 to 14 for adjustment procedures and the specifications chart for adjustments specifications.

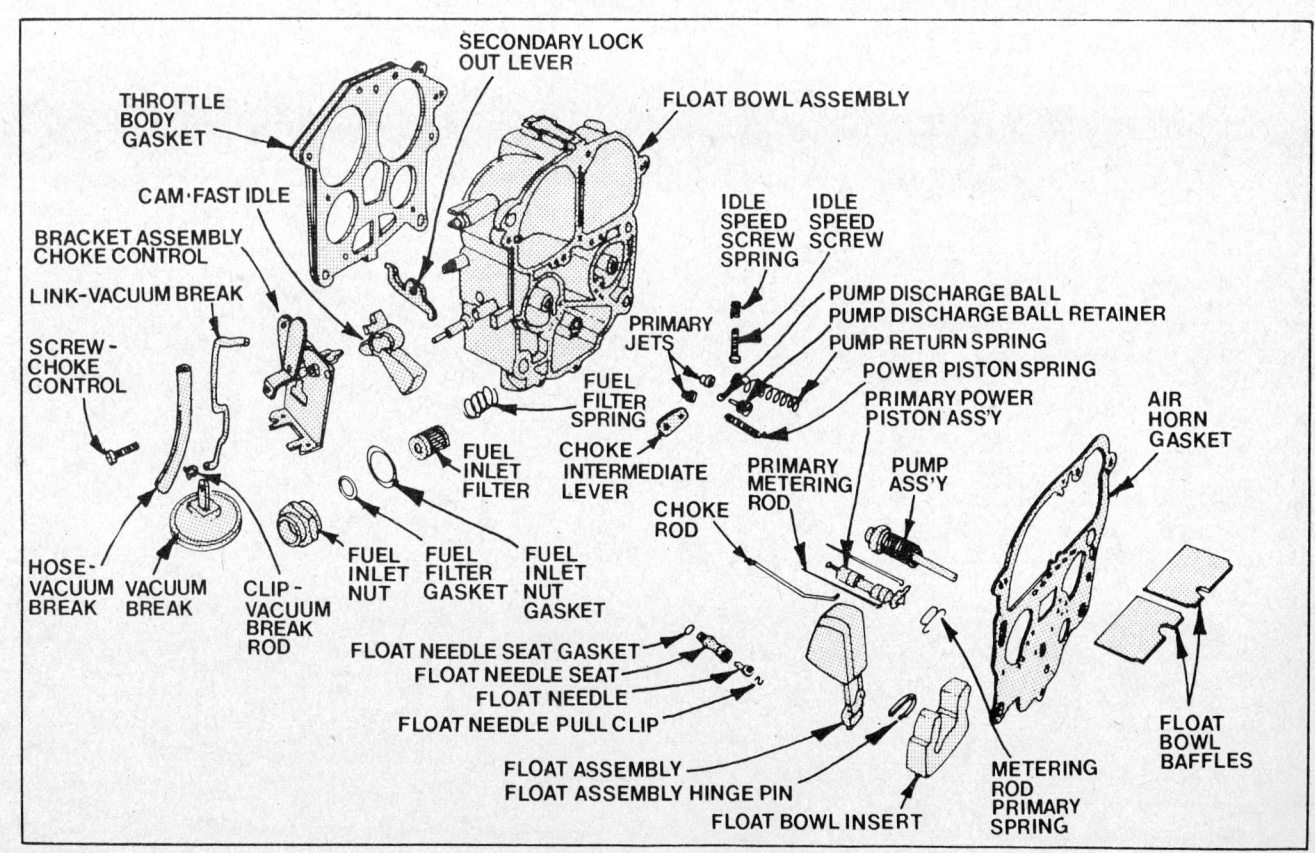

Fig. 1 Rochester Model 4MV carburetor float bowl components

CHEVROLET

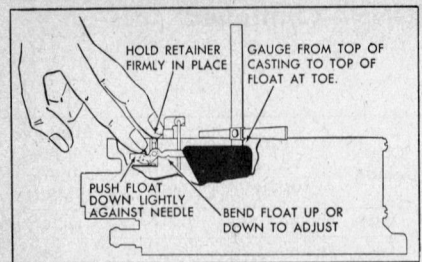

Fig. 2 Float level adjustment. 4MV

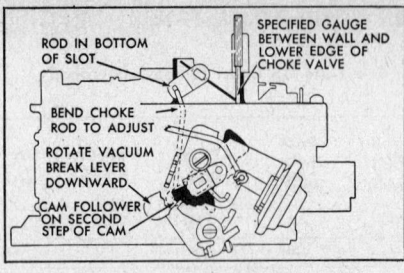

Fig. 6 Choke rod adjustment. 1970–77 Model 4MV

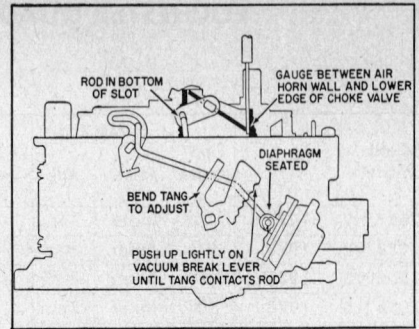

Fig. 8 Vacuum break adjustment. 1970–1977 Model 4MV

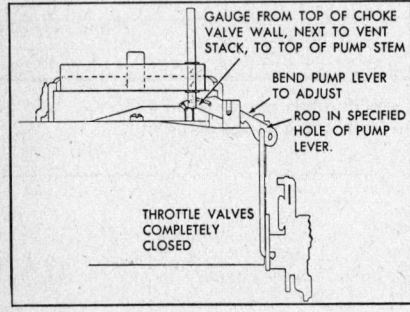

Fig. 3 Pump rod adjustment. 4MV

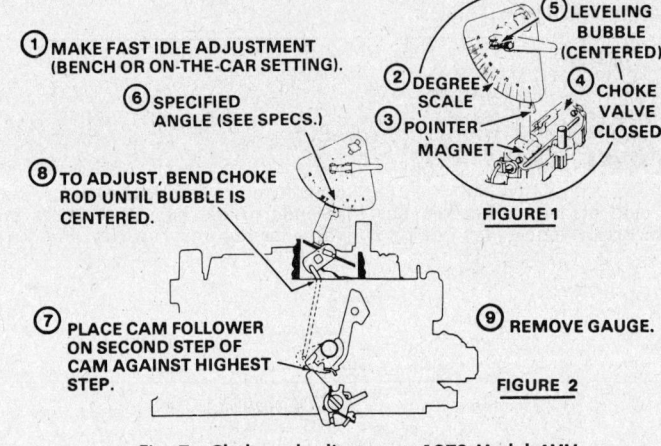

Fig. 7 Choke rod adjustment. 1978 Model 4MV

Fig. 4 Idle vent adjustment. 4MV

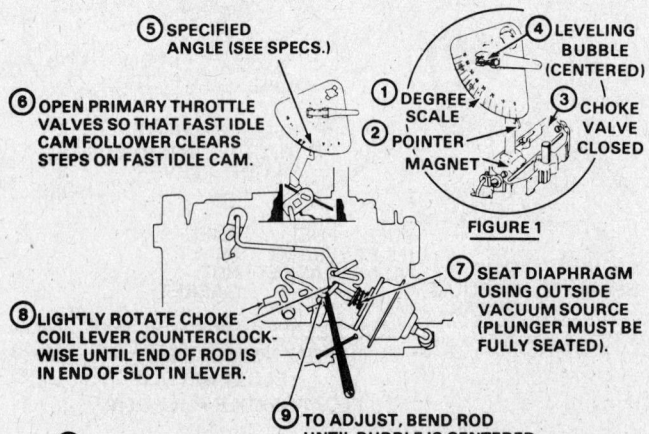

Fig. 5 Preliminary Fast Idle adjustment. 4MV

Fig. 9 Vacuum break adjustment. 1978 Model 4MV

CHEVROLET

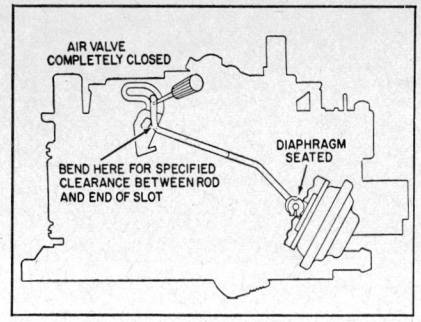

Fig. 10 Air valve dashpot adjustment. 4MV

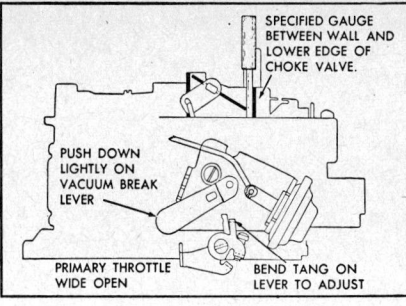

Fig. 11 Unloader adjustment. 1970-77 Model 4MV

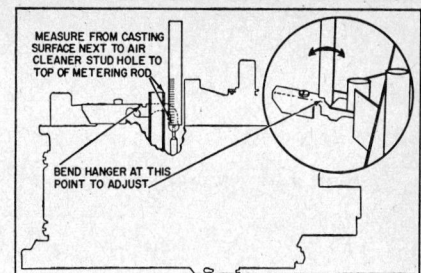

Fig. 13 Secondary metering rod adjustment. Model 4MV

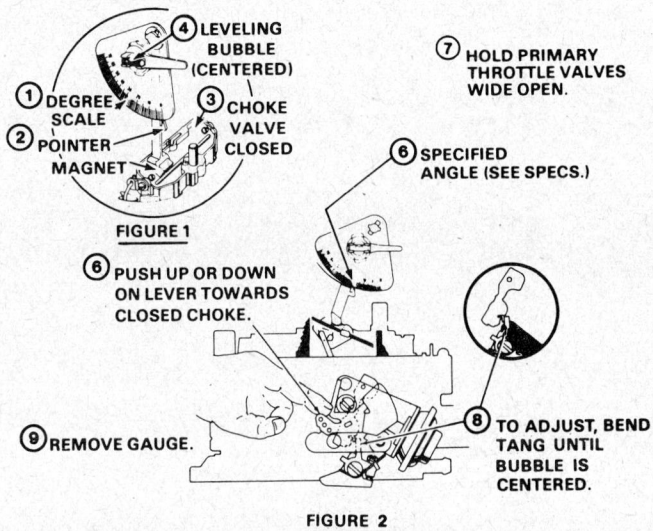

Fig. 12 Unloader adjustment. 1978 Model 4MV

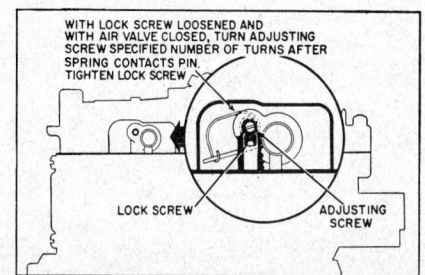

Fig. 14 Air valve spring adjustment. 4MV

QUADRAJET M4M SERIES ADJUSTMENT SPECIFICATIONS

See Tune Up Chart for hot idle speeds.

Year	Carb. Model	Float Level	Pump Rod Hole	Pump Rod Adj.	Bowl Vent	Fast Idle (Bench)	Choke Coil Lever	Choke Rod	Vacuum Break Front	Vacuum Break Rear	Air-Valve Dash-Pot	Choke Setting	Choke Unloader	Air-Valve Valve Spring Wind-Up
1975	7045200	17/32	Inner	.275	—	3 Turns	.120	.300	.200	.550	.015	Index	.325	9/16
	7045202	15/32	Inner	.275	—	3 Turns	.120	.300	.180	.170	.015	—	.325	7/8
	7045203	15/32	Inner	.275	—	3 Turns	.120	.300	.180	.170	.015	—	.325	7/8
	7045206	15/32	Inner	.275	—	3 Turns	.120	.300	.180	.170	.015	Index	.325	7/8
	7045207	15/32	Inner	.275	—	3 Turns	.120	.300	.180	.170	.015	Index	.325	7/8
	7045208	15/32	Inner	.275	—	3 Turns	.120	.300	.180	.170	.015	Index	.325	7/8
	7045209	15/32	Inner	.275	—	3 Turns	.120	.300	.180	.170	.015	Index	.325	7/8
	7045210	15/32	Inner	.275	—	3 Turns	.120	.300	.180	.170	.015	Index	.325	7/8
	7045211	15/32	Inner	.275	—	3 Turns	.120	.300	.180	.170	.015	Index	.325	7/8
	7045218	15/32	Inner	.275	—	3 Turns	.120	.325	.180	.170	.015	—	.325	3/4
	7045219	15/32	Inner	.275	—	3 Turns	.120	.325	.180	.170	.015	—	.325	3/4
	7045220	17/32	Inner	.275	—	3 Turns	.120	.300	.200	.550	.015	—	.325	9/16
	7045222	15/32	Inner	.275	—	3 Turns	.120	.300	.180	.170	.015	Index	.325	7/8

Continued

CHEVROLET

QUADRAJET M4M SERIES ADJUSTMENT SPECIFICATIONS—Continued

See Tune Up Chart for hot idle speeds.

Year	Carb. Model	Float Level	Pump Rod Hole	Pump Rod Adj.	Bowl Vent	Fast Idle (Bench)	Choke Coil Lever	Choke Rod	Vacuum Break Front	Vacuum Break Rear	Air-Valve Dash-Pot	Choke Setting	Choke Unloader	Air-Valve Valve Spring Wind-Up
	7045223	15/32	Inner	.275	—	3 Turns	.120	.300	.180	.170	.015	Index	.325	7/8
	7045224	15/32	Inner	.275	—	3 Turns	.120	.325	.180	.170	.015	Index	.325	3/4
	7045228	15/32	Inner	.275	—	3 Turns	.120	.325	.180	.170	.015	Index	.325	3/4
	7045502	15/32	Inner	.275	—	3 Turns	.120	.300	.180	.170	.015	Index	.325	7/8
	7045503	15/32	Inner	.275	—	3 Turns	.120	.300	.180	.170	.015	Index	.325	7/8
	7045504	15/32	Inner	.275	—	3 Turns	.120	.300	.180	.170	.015	Index	.325	7/8
	7045506	15/32	Inner	.275	—	3 Turns	.120	.300	.180	.170	.015	Index	.325	7/8
	7045507	15/32	Inner	.275	—	3 Turns	.120	.300	.180	.170	.015	Index	.325	7/8
	7045512	17/32	Inner	.275	—	3 Turns	.120	.300	.180	.550	.015	—	.325	9/16
	7045517	17/32	Inner	.275	—	3 Turns	.120	.300	.180	.550	.015	—	.325	9/16
1976	17056200	13/32	Inner	9/32	—	3 Turns	.120	.190	.240	.160	.015	Index	.270	7/8
	17056202	13/32	Inner	9/32	—	3 Turns	.120	.325	.185	—	.015	2 Lean	.325	7/8
	17056203	13/32	Inner	9/32	—	3 Turns	.120	.325	.185	—	.015	3 Lean	.325	7/8
	17056206	13/32	Inner	9/32	—	3 Turns	.120	.325	.185	—	.015	2 Lean	.325	7/8
	17056207	13/32	Inner	9/32	—	3 Turns	.120	.325	.185	—	.015	3 Lean	.325	7/8
	17056208	①	Inner	9/32	—	3 Turns	.120	.325	.185	—	.015	2 Lean	.325	7/8
	17056209	①	Inner	9/32	—	3 Turns	.120	.325	.185	—	.015	3 Lean	.325	7/8
	17056210	13/32	Inner	9/32	—	3 Turns	.120	.325	.185	—	.015	2 Lean	.325	1
	17056211	13/32	Inner	9/32	—	3 Turns	.120	.325	.170	—	.015	2 Lean	.325	1
	17056218	5/16	Inner	9/32	—	3 Turns	.120	.325	.185	—	.015	2 Lean	.325	7/8
	17056219	5/16	Inner	9/32	—	3 Turns	.120	.325	.185	—	.015	3 Lean	.325	7/8
	17056221	7/16	Inner	9/32	—	3 Turns	.120	.300	—	.160	.015	2 Rich	.325	7/8
	17056226	13/32	Inner	9/32	—	3 Turns	.120	.325	.185	—	.015	2 Lean	.325	3/4
	17056228	13/32	Inner	9/32	—	3 Turns	.120	.325	.185	—	.015	2 Lean	.325	7/8
	17056502	13/32	Inner	9/32	—	3 Turns	.120	.325	.185	—	.015	2 Lean	.325	7/8
	17056503	13/32	Inner	9/32	—	3 Turns	.120	.325	.185	—	.015	2 Lean	.325	7/8
	17056506	13/32	Inner	9/32	—	3 Turns	.120	.325	.185	—	.015	2 Lean	.325	7/8
	17056507	13/32	Inner	9/32	—	3 Turns	.120	.325	.185	—	.015	2 Lean	.325	7/8
	17056508	①	Inner	9/32	—	3 Turns	.120	.325	.185	—	.015	2 Lean	.325	7/8
	17056509	①	Inner	9/32	—	3 Turns	.120	.325	.185	—	.015	2 Lean	.325	7/8
	17056512	7/16	Inner	9/32	—	3 Turns	.120	.325	.185	—	.015	Index	.275	7/8
	17056517	7/16	Inner	9/32	—	3 Turns	.120	.325	.185	—	.015	Index	.275	7/8
	17056518	5/16	Inner	9/32	—	3 Turns	.120	.325	.185	—	.015	2 Lean	.325	7/8
	17056519	5/16	Inner	9/32	—	3 Turns	.120	.325	.185	—	.015	2 Lean	.325	7/8
	17056528	13/32	Inner	9/32	—	3 Turns	.120	.325	.185	—	.015	2 Lean	.325	3/4
1977	17057202	15/32	Inner	9/32	—	—	.120	.325	.160	—	.015	2 Lean	—	—
	17057203	15/32	Inner	9/32	—	—	.120	.325	.160	—	.015	3 Lean	.280	7/8
	17057204	15/32	Inner	9/32	—	—	.120	.325	.160	—	.015	2 Lean	.280	7/8
	17051210	15/32	Inner	9/32	—	—	.120	.325	.180	—	.015	2 Lean	.280	1
	17057211	15/32	Inner	9/32	—	—	.120	.325	.180	—	.015	3 Lean	.280	1
	17057218	15/32	Inner	9/32	—	—	.120	.325	.160	—	.015	2 Lean	.280	7/8
	17057219	7/16	Inner	9/32	—	—	.120	.325	.165	—	.015	3 Lean	.280	7/8
	17057221	3/8	Inner	9/32	—	—	.120	.325	—	.160	.015	2 Rich	.325	7/8
	17057222	7/16	Inner	9/32	—	—	.120	.325	.160	—	.015	2 Lean	.280	7/8
	17057228	13/32	Inner	9/32	—	—	.120	.325	.180	—	.015	2 Lean	.280	1
	17057502	15/32	Inner	9/32	—	—	.120	.325	.165	—	.015	2 Lean	.280	7/8
	17057503	15/32	Inner	9/32	—	—	.120	.325	.165	—	.015	1 Lean	.280	7/8
	17057504	15/32	Inner	9/32	—	—	.120	.325	.165	—	.015	2 Lean	.280	7/8
	17057510	15/32	Inner	9/32	—	—	.120	.325	.180	—	.015	2 Lean	.280	7/8
	17057512	7/16	Inner	9/32	—	—	.120	.285	.165	—	.015	Index	.240	7/8
	17057517	7/16	Inner	9/32	—	—	.120	.285	.165	—	.015	Index	.240	7/8

Continued

CHEVROLET

QUADRAJET M4M SERIES ADJUSTMENT SPECIFICATIONS—Continued

See Tune Up Chart for hot idle speeds.

Year	Carb. Model	Float Level	Pump Rod Hole	Pump Rod Adj.	Bowl Vent	Fast Idle (Bench)	Choke Coil Lever	Choke Rod	Vacuum Break Front	Vacuum Break Rear	Air-Valve Dash-Pot	Choke Setting	Choke Unloader	Air-Valve Valve Spring Wind-Up
	17057518	7/16	Inner	9/32	—	—	.120	.325	.165	—	.015	2 Lean	.280	7/8
	17057519	7/16	Inner	9/32	—	—	.120	.325	.165	—	.015	1 Lean	.280	7/8
	17057522	7/16	Inner	9/32	—	—	.120	.325	.165	—	.015	2 Lean	.280	7/8
	17057528	15/32	Inner	9/32	—	—	.120	.325	.180	—	.015	2 Lean	.280	7/8
	17057582	15/32	Outer	9/32	—	—	.120	.325	.180	—	.015	2 Lean	.280	7/8
	17057584	15/32	Outer	9/32	—	—	.120	.325	.180	—	.015	2 Lean	.280	7/8
	17057586	7/16	Outer	9/32	—	—	.120	.325	.180	—	.015	2 Lean	.280	7/8
	17057588	7/16	Outer	9/32	—	—	.120	.325	.180	—	.015	2 Lean	.280	7/8
1978	17058201	15/32	Inner	9/32	—	—	.120	46°	28.5°	—	.015	3 Lean	42°	7/8
	17058202	15/32	Inner	9/32	—	—	.120	.314	②	—	.015	2 Lean	.277	7/8
	17058203	15/32	Inner	9/32	—	—	.120	.314	②	—	.015	2 Lean	.277	7/8
	17058204	15/32	Inner	9/32	—	—	.120	.314	②	—	.015	2 Lean	.277	7/8
	17058210	15/32	Inner	9/32	—	—	.120	.314	③	—	.015	2 Lean	.277	—
	17058211	15/32	Inner	9/32	—	—	.120	.314	③	—	.015	2 Lean	.277	—
	17058218	7/16	Inner	9/32	—	—	.120	46°	27°	—	.015	2 Lean	42°	7/8
	17058219	7/16	Inner	9/32	—	—	.120	46°	28.5°	—	.015	3 Lean	42°	7/8
	17058222	7/16	Inner	9/32	—	—	.120	46°	27°	—	.015	2 Lean	42°	7/8
	17058228	15/32	Inner	9/32	—	—	.120	.314	③	—	.015	2 Lean	.277	7/8
	17058500	3/8	Inner	9/32	—	—	.120	46°	28°	—	.015	3 Lean	42°	7/8
	17058501	3/8	Inner	9/32	—	—	.120	46°	28°	—	.015	3 Lean	42°	7/8
	17058502	15/32	Inner	9/32	—	—	.120	.314	④	—	.015	2 Lean	.277	7/8
	17058503	15/32	Inner	9/32	—	—	.120	46°	30°	—	.015	1 Lean	42°	7/8
	17058504	15/32	Inner	9/32	—	—	.120	.314	④	—	.015	2 Lean	.277	7/8
	17058506	15/32	Inner	9/32	—	—	.120	46°	30°	—	.015	1 Lean	42°	7/8
	17058508	15/32	Inner	9/32	—	—	.120	46°	30°	—	.015	1 Lean	42°	7/8
	17058509	15/32	Outer	11/32	—	—	.120	46°	30°	—	.015	2 Lean	42°	7/8
	17058510	15/32	Outer	11/32	—	—	.120	46°	30°	—	.015	2 Lean	42°	7/8
	17058512	13/32	Inner	9/32	—	—	.120	46°	30°	—	.015	Index	40°	7/8
	17058518	15/32	Inner	9/32	—	—	.120	46°	30°	—	.015	1 Lean	42°	7/8
	17058519	15/32	Inner	9/32	—	—	.120	46°	30°	—	.015	1 Lean	42°	7/8
	17058520	3/8	Inner	9/32	—	—	.120	46°	28°	—	.015	3 Lean	42°	7/8
	17058521	3/8	Inner	9/32	—	—	.120	46°	28°	—	.015	3 Lean	42°	7/8
	17058522	15/32	Inner	9/32	—	—	.120	46°	30o	—	.015	1 Lean	42°	7/8
	17058523	15/32	Inner	9/32	—	—	.120	46°	30°	—	.015	1 Lean	42°	7/8
	17058524	15/32	Inner	9/32	—	—	.120	46°	30°	—	.015	1 Lean	42°	7/8
	17058527	15/32	Inner	9/32	—	—	.120	46°	30°	—	.015	1 Lean	42°	7/8
	17058528	15/32	Inner	9/32	—	—	.120	46°	30°	—	.015	1 Lean	42°	7/8
	17058582	15/32	Inner	9/32	—	—	.120	.314	③	—	.015	2 Lean	.277	7/8
	17058584	15/32	Inner	9/32	—	—	.120	.314	③	—	.015	2 Lean	.277	7/8
	17058586	15/32	Outer	11/32	—	—	.120	46°	30°	—	.015	2 Lean	42°	7/8
	17058588	15/32	Outer	11/32	—	—	.120	46°	30°	—	.015	2 Lean	42°	7/8
1979	17059061	15/32	Inner	9/32	—	—	.120	46°	—	23°	.015	Index	42°	7/8
	17059062	15/32	Inner	1/4	—	—	.120	38°	28°	—	.015	1 Lean	38°	7/8
	17059064	15/32	Inner	1/4	—	—	.120	38°	28°	—	.015	1 Lean	38°	7/8
	17059065	15/32	Inner	9/32	—	—	.120	46°	—	23°	.015	1 Lean	42°	7/8
	17059066	15/32	Inner	9/32	—	—	.120	46°	—	23°	.015	1 Lean	42°	7/8
	17059068	15/32	Inner	9/32	—	—	.120	46°	—	23°	.015	1 Lean	42°	7/8
	17059069	15/32	Inner	9/32	—	—	.120	46°	—	23°	.015	1 Lean	42°	7/8
	17059076	15/32	Inner	9/32	—	—	.120	46°	—	23°	.015	1 Lean	42°	7/8
	17059077	15/32	Inner	9/32	—	—	.120	46°	—	23°	.015	1 Lean	42°	7/8
	17059201	15/32	Inner	9/32	—	—	.120	46°	—	23°	.015	Index	42°	7/8

Continued

CHEVROLET

QUADRAJET M4M SERIES ADJUSTMENT SPECIFICATIONS—Continued

See Tune Up Chart for hot idle speeds.

Year	Carb. Model	Float Level	Pump Rod Hole	Pump Rod Adj.	Bowl Vent	Fast Idle (Bench)	Choke Coil Lever	Choke Rod	Vacuum Break Front	Vacuum Break Rear	Air-Valve Dash-Pot	Choke Setting	Choke Unloader	Air-Valve Valve Spring Wind-Up
	17059205	15/32	Inner	9/32	—	—	.120	46°	—	23°	.015	1 Lean	42°	7/8
	17059206	15/32	Inner	9/32	—	—	.120	46°	—	23°	.015	1 Lean	42°	7/8
	17059207	15/32	Inner	1/4	—	—	.120	38°	27°	—	.015	2 Lean	38°	7/8
	17059208	15/32	Inner	9/32	—	—	.120	46°	—	23°	.015	1 Lean	42°	7/8
	17059209	15/32	Inner	9/32	—	—	.120	46°	—	23°	.015	1 Lean	42°	7/8
	17059212	3/8	Inner	9/32	—	—	.120	46°	24°	—	.015	1 Rich	40°	3/4
	17059213	3/8	Inner	9/32	—	—	.120	37°	23°	—	.015	1 Rich	40°	1
	17059215	3/8	Inner	9/32	—	—	.120	37°	23°	—	.015	1 Rich	40°	1
	17059216	15/32	Inner	1/4	—	—	.120	38°	27°	—	.015	1 Lean	38°	7/8
	17059217	15/32	Inner	1/4	—	—	.120	38°	27°	—	.015	1 Lean	38°	7/8
	17059222	15/32	Inner	9/32	—	—	.120	38°	28°	—	.015	2 Lean	38°	7/8
	17059226	15/32	Inner	9/32	—	—	.120	46°	—	23°	.015	1 Lean	42°	7/8
	17059227	15/32	Inner	9/32	—	—	.120	46°	—	23°	.015	1 Lean	42°	7/8
	17059229	3/8	Inner	9/32	—	—	.120	37°	23°	—	.015	1 Rich	40°	1
	17059363	15/32	Inner	9/32	—	—	.120	46°	—	26°	.015	1 Lean	42°	7/8
	17059366	15/32	Inner	9/32	—	—	.120	46°	—	26°	.015	1 Lean	42°	7/8
	17059368	15/32	Inner	9/32	—	—	.120	46°	—	26°	.015	1 Lean	42°	7/8
	17059377	15/32	Inner	9/32	—	—	.120	46°	—	23°	.015	1 Lean	42°	7/8
	17059378	15/32	Inner	9/32	—	—	.120	46°	—	23°	.015	1 Lean	42°	7/8
	17059501	3/8	Inner	9/32	—	—	.120	46°	28°	—	.015	3 Lean	42°	7/8
	17059502	15/32	Inner	1/4	—	—	.120	38°	28°	—	.015	2 Lean	38°	7/8
	17059503	15/32	Inner	9/32	—	—	.120	46°	—	26°	.015	1 Lean	42°	7/8
	17059504	15/32	Inner	1/4	—	—	.120	38°	28°	—	.015	2 Lean	38°	7/8
	17059506	15/32	Inner	9/32	—	—	.120	46°	—	26°	.015	1 Lean	42°	7/8
	17059508	15/32	Inner	9/32	—	—	.120	46°	—	26°	.015	1 Lean	42°	7/8
	17059509	15/32	Outer	11/32	—	—	.120	46°	30°	—	.015	2 Lean	42°	7/8
	17059510	15/32	Outer	11/32	—	—	.120	46°	30°	—	.015	2 Lean	42°	7/8
	17059512	3/8	Inner	9/32	—	—	.120	46°	24°	—	.015	1 Rich	40°	3/4
	17059513	3/8	Inner	9/32	—	—	.120	37°	23°	—	.015	1 Rich	40°	1
	17059515	3/8	Inner	9/32	—	—	.120	37°	23°	—	.015	1 Rich	40°	1
	17059520	3/8	Inner	9/32	—	—	.120	46°	28°	—	.015	3 Lean	42°	7/8
	17059521	3/8	Inner	9/32	—	—	.120	46°	28°	—	.015	3 Lean	42°	7/8
	17059527	15/32	Inner	9/32	—	—	.120	46°	—	23°	.015	1 Lean	42°	7/8
	17059528	15/32	Inner	9/32	—	—	.120	46°	—	23°	.015	1 Lean	42°	7/8
	17059529	3/8	Inner	9/32	—	—	.120	37°	23°	—	.015	1 Rich	40°	1
	17059582	15/32	Outer	11/32	—	—	.120	38°	33°	—	.015	1 Lean	46°	7/8
	17059584	15/32	Outer	11/32	—	—	.120	38°	33°	—	.015	1 Lean	46°	7/8
	17059586	15/32	Outer	11/32	—	—	.120	46°	30°	—	.015	2 Lean	42°	7/8
	17059588	15/32	Outer	11/32	—	—	.120	46°	30°	—	.015	2 Lean	42°	7/8
1980	17080201	15/32	Inner	9/32	—	—	—	46°	—	23°	.025	—	42°	7/8
	17080202	13/32	Inner	1/4	—	3	.120	20°	27°	—	.025	—	38°	7/8
	17080204	13/32	Inner	1/4	—	3	.120	20°	27°	—	.025	—	38°	7/8
	17080205	15/32	Inner	9/32	—	—	—	46°	—	—	.025	—	42°	7/8
	17080206	15/32	Inner	9/32	—	—	—	46°	—	23°	.025	—	42°	7/8
	17080207	13/32	Inner	1/4	—	—	—	20°	27°	—	.025	—	38°	7/8
	17080211	13/32	Inner	9/32	—	—	—	20°	28°	—	.025	—	38°	1
	17080212	3/8	Inner	9/32	—	—	.120	46°	24°	30°	.025	—	40°	3/4
	17080213	3/8	Inner	9/32	—	—	.120	37°	23°	30°	.025	—	40°	1
	17080215	3/8	Inner	9/32	—	—	.120	37°	23°	30°	.025	—	40°	1
	17080224	15/32	Inner	9/32	—	—	.120	46°	—	23°	.025	—	42°	7/8
	17080225	15/32	Inner	9/32	—	—	.120	46°	—	23°	.025	—	42°	7/8

Continued

CHEVROLET

QUADRAJET M4M SERIES ADJUSTMENT SPECIFICATIONS—Continued

See Tune Up Chart for hot idle speeds.

Year	Carb. Model	Float Level	Pump Rod Hole	Pump Rod Adj.	Bowl Vent	Fast Idle (Bench)	Choke Coil Lever	Choke Rod	Vacuum Break Front	Vacuum Break Rear	Air-Valve Dash-Pot	Choke Setting	Choke Unloader	Air-Valve Valve Spring Wind-Up
	17080226	15/32	Inner	9/32	—	—	.120	46°	—	23°	.025	—	42°	7/8
	17080227	15/32	Inner	9/32	—	—	.120	46°	—	23°	.025	—	42°	7/8
	17080228	13/32	Inner	9/32	—	—	.120	20°	25°	—	.025	—	38°	1
	17080229	3/8	Inner	9/32	—	—	.120	37°	23°	30°	.025	—	40°	1
	17080240	3/16	inner	9/32	—	—	.120	14.5°	16°	16°	.025	—	30°	9/16
	17080242	13/32	Inner	9/32	—	—	.120	14.5°	15°	18°	.025	—	35°	9/16
	17080243	3/16	Inner	9/32	—	—	.120	14.5°	16°	16°	.025	—	30°	9/16
	17080274	7/16	Outer	11/32	—	—	—	16°	24°	32°	.025	—	35°	5/8
	17080290	15/32	Inner	9/32	—	—	—	46°	—	26°	.025	—	42°	7/8
	17080291	15/32	Inner	9/32	—	—	—	46°	—	26°	.025	—	42°	7/8
	17080292	15/32	Inner	9/32	—	—	—	46°	—	26°	.025	—	42°	7/8
	17080293	15/32	Inner	9/32	—	—	—	46°	—	26°	.025	—	42°	7/8
	17080295	15/32	Inner	9/32	—	—	—	46°	—	23°	.025	—	42°	7/8
	17080297	15/32	Inner	9/32	—	—	—	46°	—	23°	.025	—	42°	7/8
	17080502	19/32	—	3/8	—	—	.120	20°	26°	30°	.025	—	38°	7/8
	17080503	15/32	Inner	9/32	—	—	—	46°	—	26°	.025	—	42°	7/8
	17080504	19/32	—	3/8	—	3	.120	20°	26°	30°	.025	—	38°	7/8
	17080505	15/32	Inner	9/32	—	—	—	46°	—	26°	.025	—	42°	7/8
	17080506	15/32	Inner	9/32	—	—	—	46°	—	26°	.025	—	42°	7/8
	17080508	15/32	Inner	9/32	—	—	—	46°	—	26°	.025	—	42°	7/8
	17080509	15/32	Outer	11/32	—	—	—	46°	30°	—	.025	—	42°	7/8
	17080510	15/32	Outer	11/32	—	—	.120	46°	30°	—	.025	—	42°	7/8
	17080512	3/8	Inner	9/32	—	—	.120	46°	24°	30°	.025	—	40°	3/4
	17080513	3/8	Inner	9/32	—	—	.120	37°	23°	30°	.025	—	40°	1
	17080515	3/8	Inner	9/32	—	—	.120	37°	23°	30°	.025	—	40°	1
	17080523	15/32	Inner	9/32	—	—	.120	46°	—	23°	.025	—	42°	7/8
	17080524	15/32	Inner	9/32	—	—	.120	46°	—	23°	.025	—	42°	7/8
	17080525	15/32	Inner	9/32	—	—	.120	46°	—	23°	.025	—	42°	7/8
	17080526	15/32	Inner	9/32	—	—	.120	46°	—	23°	.025	—	42°	7/8
	17080527	15/32	Inner	9/32	—	—	.120	46°	—	23°	.025	—	42°	7/8
	17080528	15/32	Inner	9/32	—	—	.120	46°	—	23°	.025	—	42°	7/8
	17080529	3/8	Inner	9/32	—	—	.120	37°	23°	30°	.025	—	40°	1
	17080540	3/8	—	3/8	—	—	.120	14.5	19°	23°	.025	—	38°	9/16
	17080542	3/8	—	3/8	—	—	.120	14.5	19°	23°	.025	—	38°	9/16
	17080543	3/8	—	3/8	—	—	.120	14.5	19°	23°	.025	—	38°	9/16

①—Needle seat with groove at upper edge, 5/16-inch; Needle seat w/o groove at upper edge, 7/16-inch.
②—Below 22500 miles, .157 in.; above 22500 miles, .179 in.
③—Below 22500 miles, .179 in.; above 22500 miles, .203 in.
④—Below 22500 miles, .164 in.; above 22500 miles, .187 in.

MODEL M4M

The M4M Series (M4MC, M4MCA and M4MEA) Quadrajet carburetor, Fig. 1 is similar to the Quadrajet 4MV unit. However, some modifications have been made to the basic Quadrajet design.

An Adjustable Part Throttle (A.P.T.) feature incorporates an adjustable metering rod assembly operating in a fixed jet. On some models, a barometric pressure-sensitive aneroid (Bellows) is an integral part of the A.P.T. metering rod assembly. This provides a close tolerance control of fuel flow to the main metering system, thereby controlling air/fuel ratios during part throttle operation.

Some units use a multiple stage power enrichment system with two power pistons. One piston is an auxiliary power piston with a single metering rod operating in a fixed jet. The primary power piston with two metering rods operates in replaceable metering jets. This system provides sensitive control of the air/fuel ratio during light engine power requirements while providing richer mixtures during moderate to heavy engine loads.

All units use a bowl mounted choke housing with a thermostatic coil assembly. Also, a dual vacuum break system is used to improve cold engine warm-up and drive-away performance.

Float Level Adjustment

Fig. 2—With an adjustable T-scale, measure distance from top of float bowl gasket surface, with gasket removed, to top of float at a point 1/16 inch back from toe. Dimension should be as specified in the M4M Series Specification Chart. To adjust, bend float arm.

A.P.T. Metering Rod Adjustment

NOTE: This adjustment is performed only when the metering rod, filler spool or aneroid is replaced.

CHEVROLET

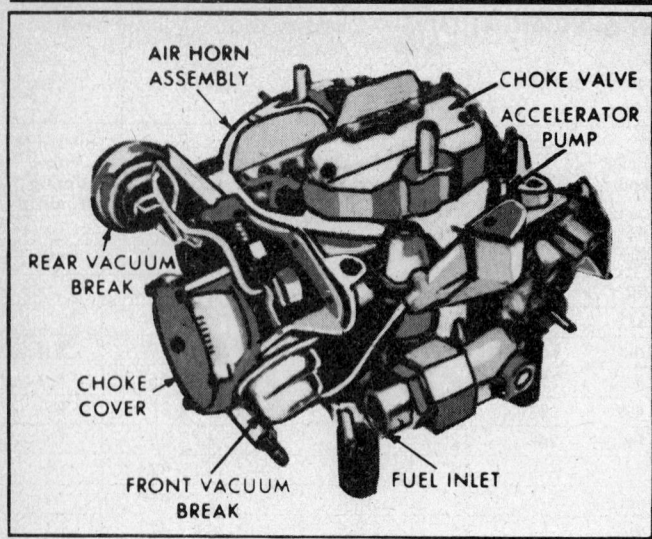

Fig. 1 Quadrajet M4M series carburetor (Typical)

Fig. 3 Quadrajet M4M series A.P.T. metering rod adjustment.

Fig. 3—Mark position of metering rod assembly adjusting screw on cover, then remove cover screws and lift metering rod assembly from float bowl. Rotating the adjusting screw counter-clockwise, count number of turns required to bottom the threaded metering rod assembly in the cover. Note this number for metering rod adjustment.

Remove "E" clip retainer from rod end, then using a small screwdriver, rotate slotted rod clockwise to disengage rod assembly from cover. Use caution when removing the rod assembly since it is spring loaded.

Install tension spring on replacement rod assembly, then thread the assembly into the cover until bottomed. Rotate the adjusting clockwise exactly the same number of turns from adjusting screw alignment mark noted previously. Install "E" clip in rod assembly groove, ensuring clip is securely locked. Place cover and rod assembly in float bowl, aligning cover assembly tab with float bowl tab nearest the fuel inlet nut, then install cover attaching screws.

Pump Rod Adjustment

Fig. 4—With throttle valves completely closed and pump rod in specified hole, measure distance from top of choke valve wall (next to vent stack) to top of pump stem. Dimension should be as specified in the M4M Series Specification Chart. To adjust, bend pump lever.

Bowl Vent Valve Adjustment

Fig. 5—Remove bowl vent valve cover and gasket. With throttle valves completely closed, rotate curb idle screw inward until it contacts throttle lever stop tang, then an additional 1 1/2 turns. Insert the gauge specified in the M4M Series Specification Chart between curb idle screw and throttle lever stop tang. The bowl vent valve should now be closed, then remove the gauge and the valve should open. To adjust, pry out plug located next to pump plunger shaft, then turn bowl vent valve, actuating arm allen head adjusting screw.

Fast Idle Adjustment

Fig. 6—With cam follower on highest step of cam, turn fast idle screw out until primary throttle valve is completely closed. Turn screw in to contact lever, then turn screw in the additional turns listed in the M4M Series Specification Chart.

Choke Coil Lever Adjustment

Fig. 7—With thermostatic coil assembly removed from choke housing, push upward on coil tang to close choke valve. Insert gauge specified in the M4M Series Specification Chart into hole in choke housing. The choke coil lever should contact the gauge. If not, bend choke rod to adjust.

Choke Rod Adjustment
Plug Gauge Method

Fig. 8—With the fast idle adjustment performed, and the cam follower on the second step of the fast idle cam, next to high step, close choke valve by pushing upward on choke lever. Measure dimension between the upper edge of the choke valve and air horn wall. Dimension should be as specified in the M4M Series Specification Chart. To adjust, bend fast idle cam tang.

Angle Gauge Method

Fig. 9—Rotate degree scale until zero is opposite pointer, then with choke valve completely closed, place magnet on top of choke valve and rotate bubble until it is centered. Refer to specifications and rotate gauge to degree specified. Place cam follower on second step of cam next to high step. Close choke by pushing upward on choke coil lever. To adjust bend tang on fast idle cam until bubble is centered, then remove gauge.

Front Vacuum Break Adjustment
Plug Gauge Method

Fig. 10—Place cam follower on highest step of fast idle cam, then using an external vacuum source, seat diaphragm. Push choke coil lever upward until vacuum break lever tang contacts vacuum break plunger stem tang. Measure dimension between upper edge of choke valve and air horn wall. Dimension should be

Fig. 2 Quadrajet M4M series float level adjustment.

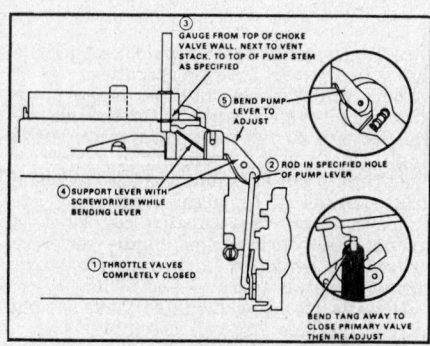

Fig. 4 Quadrajet M4M series pump rod adjustment.

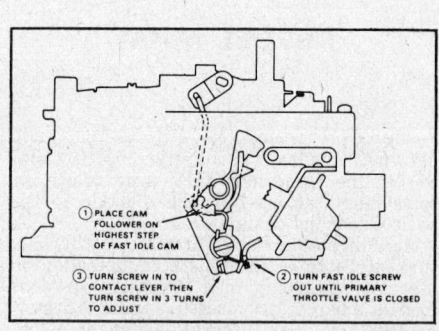

Fig. 6 Quadrajet M4M series fast idle adjustment (Bench).

CHEVROLET

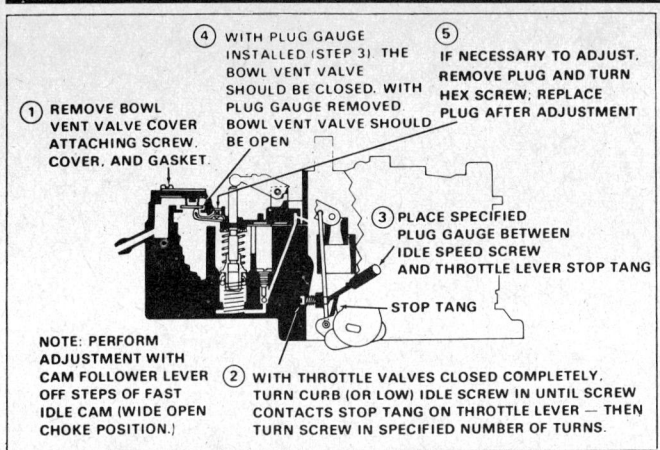

Fig. 5 Quadrajet M4M series bowl vent adjustment.

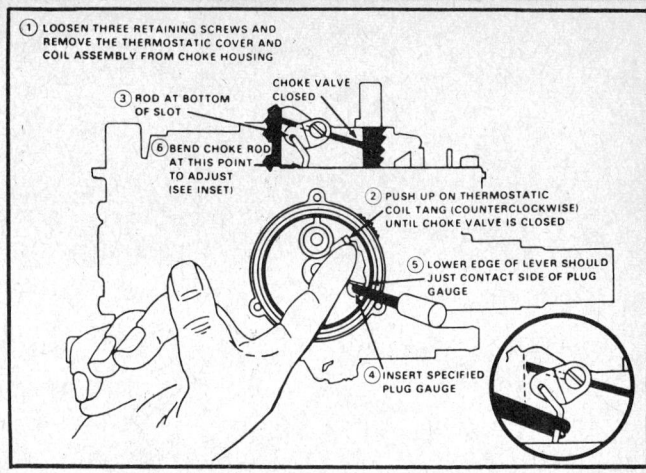

Fig. 7 Quadrajet M4M series choke coil lever adjustment.

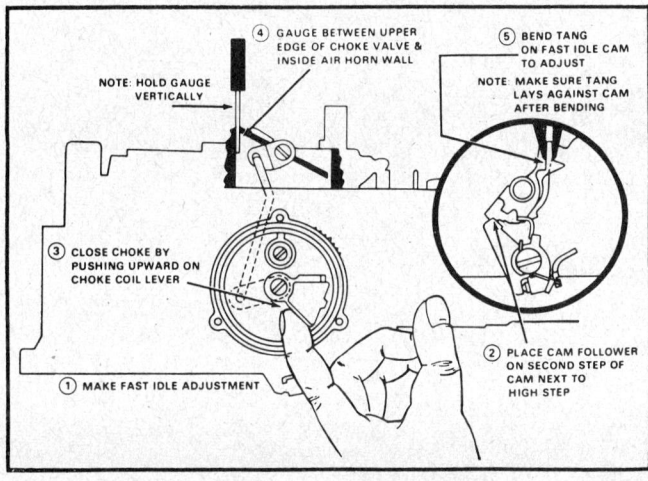

Fig. 8 Quadrajet M4M series choke rod adjustment.

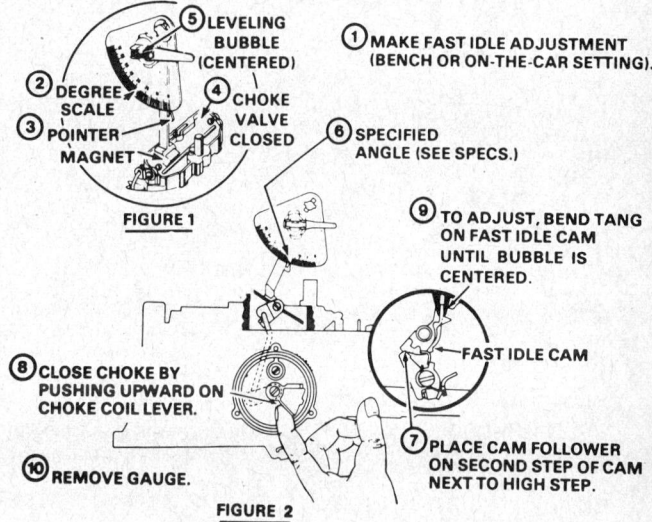

Fig. 9 Choke rod adjustment (angle gauge method). M4M series.

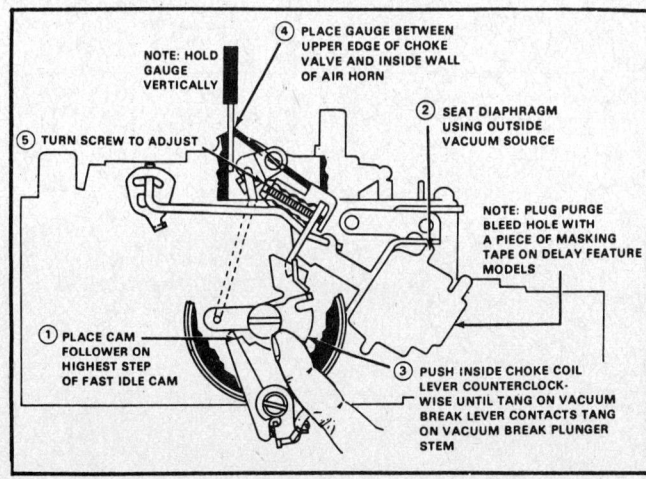

Fig. 10 Quadrajet M4M series front vacuum break adjustment.

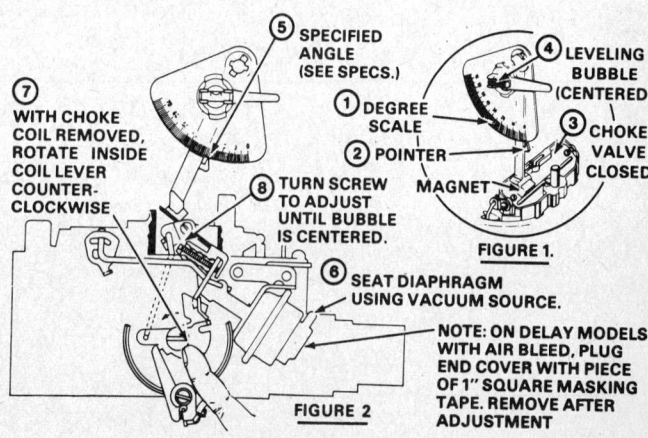

Fig. 11 Front vacuum break adjustment (angle gauge method). M4M series.

CHEVROLET

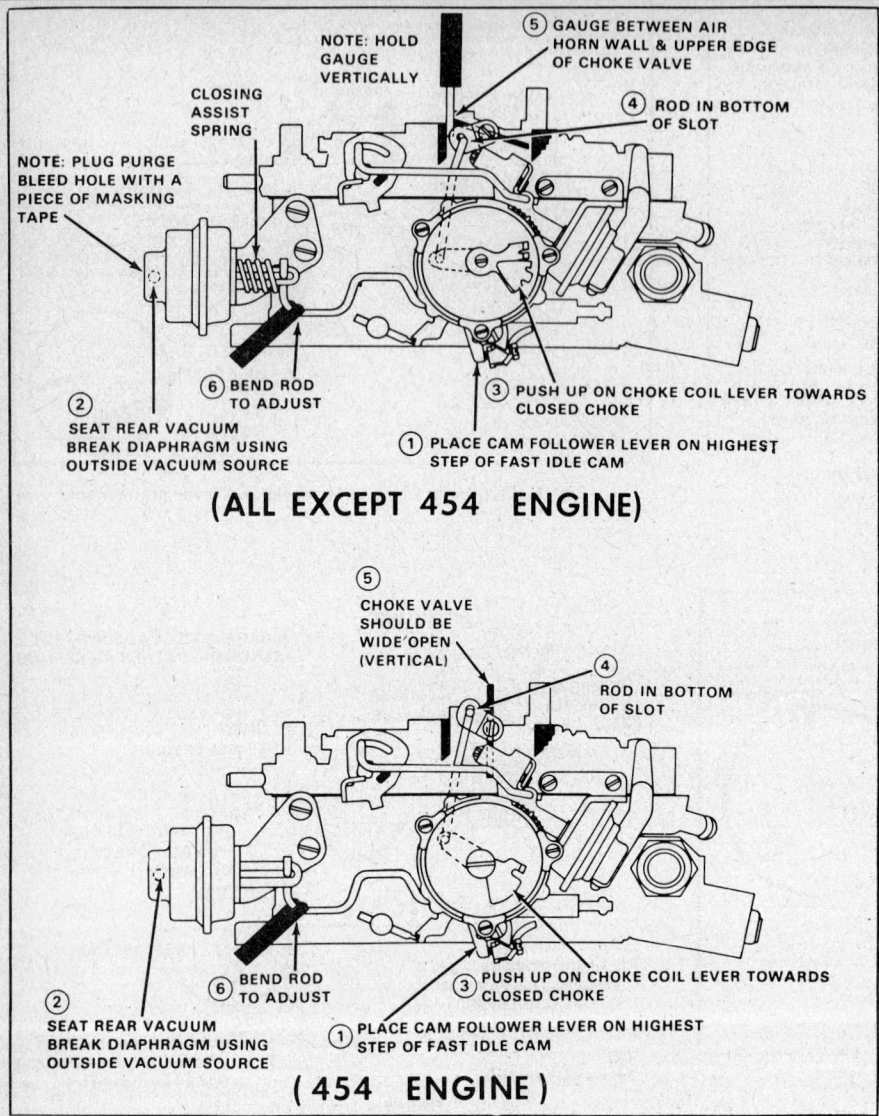

Fig. 12 Quadrajet M4M series rear vacuum break adjustment.

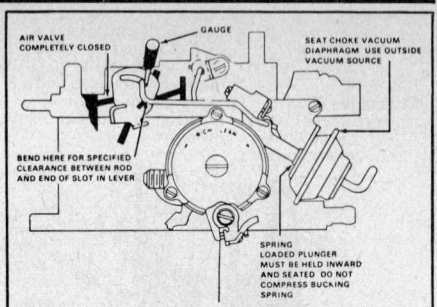

Fig. 13 Quadrajet M4M series air-valve dashpot adjustment.

as specified in the M4M Series Specification Chart. To adjust, turn vacuum break plunger adjusting screw.

Angle Gauge Method

Fig. 11—Rotate degree scale until zero is opposite pointer. With choke valve completely closed, place magnet squarely on top of choke valve, then rotate bubble until it is centered. Refer to specifications and rotate scale so that degree specified is opposite pointer. Seat choke vacuum diaphragm using a vacuum source. Hold choke valve towards the closed position by pushing counter clockwise on inside coil lever. To adjust, turn screw in or out until bubble is centered, then remove gauge.

Rear Vacuum Break Adjustment

Fig. 12—Place cam follower on highest step of fast idle cam, then using an external vacuum source, seat diaphragm. Push upward on choke coil lever toward closed choke position until stem is seated. With choke rod in bottom of slot, insert gauge specified in the M4M Series Specification Chart between upper edge of choke valve and air horn wall on all units except those used on V8-454 engines. On V8-454 units, the choke valve should be wide open (fully vertical position). To adjust, bend vacuum break rod.

Air Valve Dashpot Adjustment

Fig. 13—Using an external vacuum source, seat choke vacuum diaphragm. Then, with the air valve completely closed, place gauge specified in the M4M Series Specification Chart between air valve rod and end of slot in air valve lever. To adjust, bend rod at air valve end.

Choke Coil Adjustment

Fig. 14—Install choke coil and cover assembly. Place fast idle cam follower on

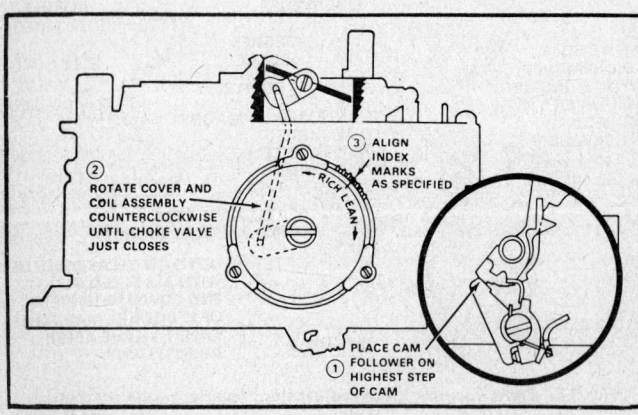

Fig. 14 Quadrajet M4M series automatic choke coil adjustment.

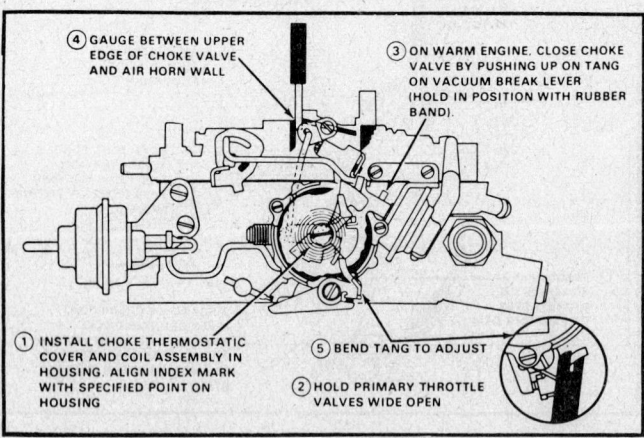

Fig. 15 Quadrajet M4M series choke unloader adjustment.

CHEVROLET

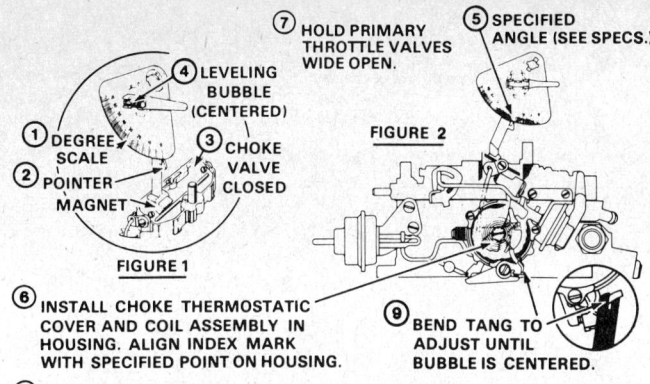

Fig. 16 Unloader adjustment (Angle Gauge Method). M4M series

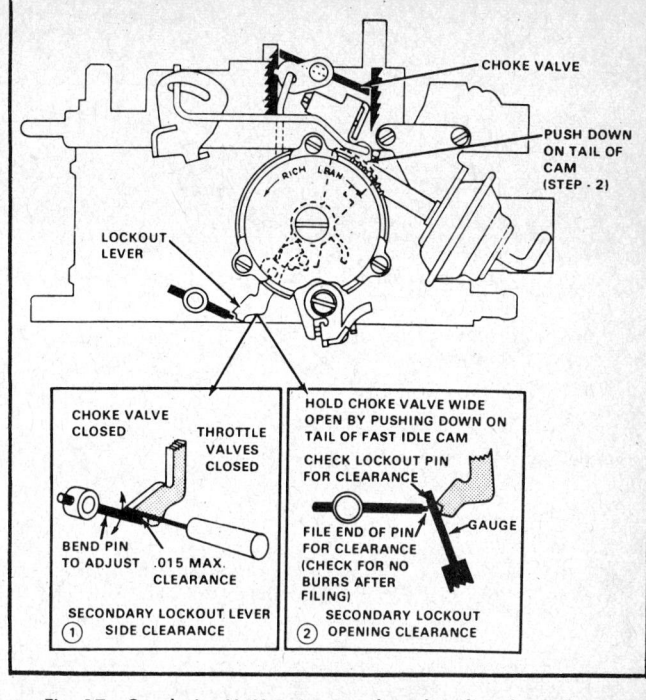

Fig. 17 Quadrajet M4M series econdary throttle valve lockout adjustment.

highest step of fast idle cam. Rotate coil and cover assembly counter-clockwise until choke just closes, then align index mark on choke cover with the specified index mark on choke housing. Refer to the M4M Series Specification Chart.

Choke Unloader Adjustment

Plug Gauge Method

Fig. 15—With the choke coil adjustment performed, close choke, valve and open throttle valve. To close choke valve on a warm engine, push upward on tang of intermediate choke lever that contacts the fast idle cam and hold in place with tha rubber band. Measure dimension between upper edge of choke valve and air horn wall. To adjust, bend tang on fast idle lever.

Angle Gauge Method

Fig. 16—Rotate degree scale until zero is opposite pointer, then with choke valve completely closed, place magnet squarely on top of choke valve. Rotate bubble until it is centered. Refer to specifications and rotate scale until specified degree for adjustment is opposite the pointer. Install choke thermostatic cover and coil assembly in housing. Align index mark with specfied point on housing. Hold primary throttle valve wide open. Close choke valve by pushing up on tang on vacuum break lever. To adjust bend tang on fast idle lever until bubble is centered, then remove gauge.

Secondary Throttle Valve Lockout Adjustment

Lockout-Pin Clearance

Fig. 17—With choke and throttle valves fully closed, measure clearance between lockout-pin and lockout lever. Maximum clearance should not exceed .015 inch. To adjust, bend lockout-pin.

Opening Clearance

Fig. 17—Push downward on fast idle cam tail to open choke valve, then push lock-out lever counter-clockwise so upper end of lever contacts the round pin in fast idle cam. Measure clearance between lockout-pin and lockout lever toe. Clearance should be .015 inch. To obtain proper clearance, file metal from end of lockout-pin.

Secondary Throttle Valves Adjustment

Throttle Closing

Fig. 18—With curb idle speed set, hold choke valve open with cam follower lever off fast idle cam steps. Measure clearance between forward edge of slot in the secondary throttle valve pick-up lever and the secondary actuating rod. On all units except Pontiac, clearance should be .020 inch. On Pontiac units, the clearance is .025 inch. To adjust, bend secondary closing tang on primary throttle lever.

Throttle Opening

Fig. 19—Open primary throttle lever until link lightly contacts secondary lever tang. The bottom end of the link should be in the center of the slot in secondary lever. To adjust, bend tang on secondary lever.

Air Valve Spring Wind-Up Adjustment

Fig. 20—Remove front vacuum break diaphragm unit and air valve dashpot rod. Loosen lock screw and rotate spring adjusting screw counter-clockwise until air valve is partially open. Hold air valve closed, then rotate adjusting screw clockwise specified number of turns after the spring contacts pin. Refer to the M4M Series Specification Chart. Tighten lock screw and install air valve dashpot rod and the front vacuum break diaphragm unit.

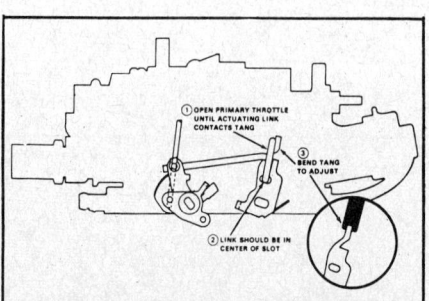

Fig. 18 Quadrajet M4M series secondary throttle valve closing adjustment.

Fig. 19 Quadrajet M4M series secondary throttle valve opening adjustment.

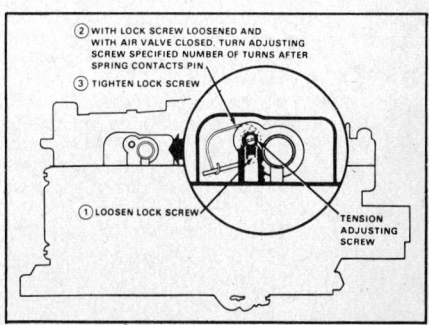

Fig. 20 Quadrajet M4M series air-valve spring wind-up adjustment.

CHEVROLET

HOLLEY 4150 CARBURETOR ADJUSTMENTS

Year	Carb. Part No. ①	Float Level (Dry)	Float Level (Wet)	Pump Lever Clearance	Bowl Vent Clearance	Fast Idle Bench	Fast Idle On Truck (R.P.M.)
1970	R4199A	②	③	.015	.060	.035	2000
	R4200A	②	③	.015	.060	.035	2000
1971	4772-1, 73-1	④	③	.015	.060	.035	2100
1972	R-6292A, 93A	④	③	.015	.060	.035	2100
1973	R-6510A, 11A	④	③	.015	.060	.035	2100
	R-6521A, 22A	④	③	.015	.060	.035	2100
1974	R-6742A, 43A	④	③	.015	.060	.038	2200
	R-6744A, 45A	④	③	.015	.060	.038	2200
1975-76	R-6928A	⑤	③	.015	—	.038	2200
	R-6929A	⑤	③	.015	—	.038	2200
	R-6930A	⑤	③	.015	—	.031	2200
	R-6931A	⑤	③	.015	—	.031	2200
	R-7264A	⑤	③	.015	—	.038	2200
	R-7266A	⑤	③	.015	—	.038	2200
1977	R-7700A	⑥	③	.015	—	.038	2200
	R-7701A	⑥	③	.015	—	.031	2200
	R-7703A	⑥	③	.015	—	.038	2200
	R-7704A	⑥	③	.015	—	.031	2200
1978	R-7923A	⑥	③	.015	.060	.031	2200
	R-7924A	⑥	③	.015	.060	.031	2200
	R-7927A	⑥	③	.015	.060	.031	2200
1979	R-8278A	⑥	③	.015	.060	.031	2200
	R-8279A	⑥	③	.015	.060	.031	2200
	R-8280A	⑥	③	.015	—	.031	2200
	R-8281A	⑥	③	.015	—	.031	2200
	R-8282A	⑥	③	.015	.060	.031	2200
	R-8283A	⑥	③	.015	—	.031	2200
	R-8443A	⑥	③	.015	—	.031	2200
	R-8444A	⑥	③	.015	.060	.031	2200

①—Located on tag attached to carburetor or on casting.
②—Primary .195", secondary .250".
③—Use sight plug in fuel bowl as outlined in text.
④—With bowl inverted, adjust float parallel to bowl floor.
⑤—Primary .197; secondary .166.
⑥—Primary .194; secondary .213.

HOLLEY 4150

The Holley four barrel carburetor, Fig. 1 is a two stage carburetor consisting of eight sub-assemblies. The sub-assemblies are as follows: throttle body, main body, primary and secondary fuel bowls, primary and secondary metering bodies, secondary throttle operating assembly and the governor assembly. The secondary throttle operating assembly controls the secondary stage throttle plates. A vacuum signal to the spring loaded vacuum diaphragm assembly determines the position of the throttle plates.

The governor incorporated on this carburetor provides a better means of controlling engine speed. The throttle lever controls the engine until the governor speed is reached, at this time the governor adjusts the throttle plates to maintain this speed under the various loadings. A clutch arrangement on the throttle body allows the manual control below governing speeds.

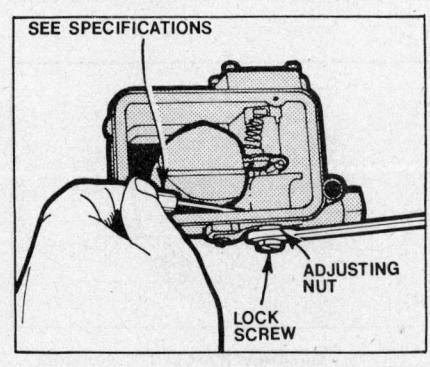

Fig. 2 Float adjustment (dry). Holley 4150

Dry Float Setting, Fig. 2.
1. Invert fuel bowl allowing float to drop to the fully closed position.
2. Using specified gauge pin, check float level setting from lower edge of float bowl to lower edge of float.
3. To adjust float level, turn adjustable needle seat nut. Lock down adjustment with screw.

NOTE: Final adjustment should be made on the vehicle.

Fuel Level Setting
1. Remove air cleaner then remove fuel level sight plugs.
2. With parking brake on and transmission in neutral, start engine and allow it to idle.
3. With car on a level surface, the fuel level should be on a level with the threads at bottom of sight plug port (plus or minus 1/32").
4. If necessary to adjust, loosen inlet needle

CHEVROLET

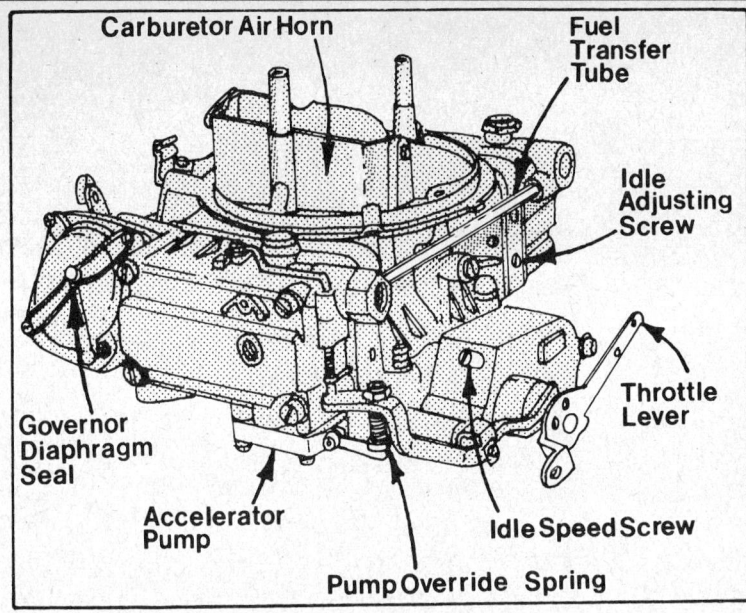

Fig. 1 Holley model 4150G carburetor.

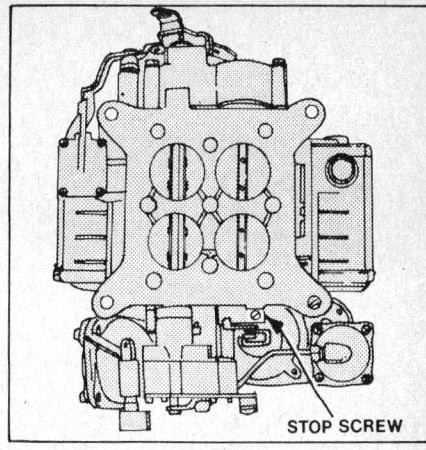

Fig. 3 Secondary throttle stop screw adjustment. Holley 4150

lock screw and turn adjusting nut clockwise to lower on counterclockwise to raise fuel level, then tighten lock screw.

NOTE: 1/6 turn of adjusting nut equals approximately 1/16" fuel level change.

Secondary Throttle Stop Screw Adjustment, Fig. 3
1. Back off on adjustment screw until throttle plates are fully closed.
2. Turn adjustment screw until it just touches the throttle lever and turn one half more to position the valves.

Vent Valve Adjustment, Fig. 4.
1. Back off idle speed screw until throttle plates are fully closed. (Choke valve open and throttle arm off idle screw).
2. Check clearance between choke valve and seat.
3. Bend air vent valve rod to adjust.
4. Turn idle screw in until contact is made with throttle lever, then turn screw in 1 1/2 additional turns for preliminary idle speed setting.

Fast Idle Cam Adjustment, Fig. 5
1. Adjust fast idle screw to provide specified clearance between screw head and fast idle cam.

Adjust Accelerator Pump, Fig. 6
1. Hold throttle lever in wide open position with a rubber band and hold pump lever fully compressed (down), then measure clearance between spring adjusting nut and arm of pump lever.
2. Clearance should be as specified; adjust by turning nut or screw as required while holding opposite end. (The pump operating lever is not threaded.)
3. After adjustment is made, rotate throttle lever to fully closed and partly open again. Any movement of the throttle lever should be noticed at operating lever spring end, indicating correct pump tip-in.

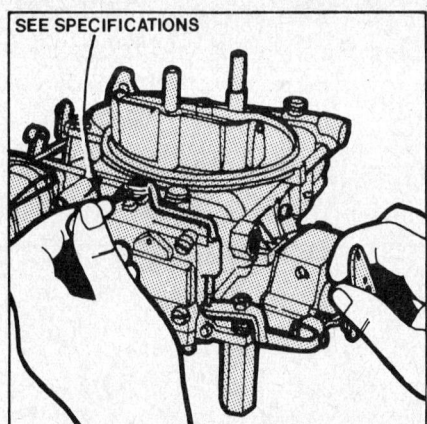

Fig. 4 Vent valve adjustment. Holley 4150

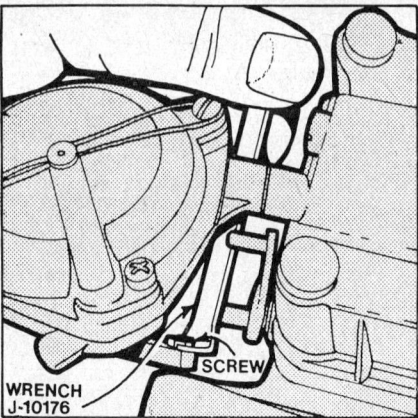

Fig. 5 Fast idle adjustment. Holley 4150

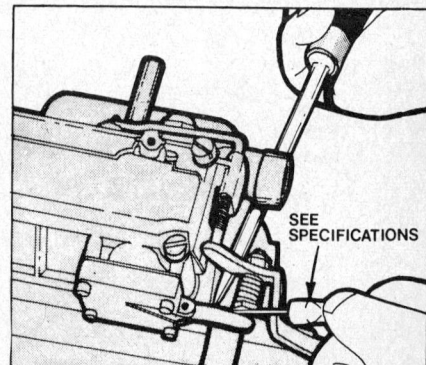

Fig. 6 Accelerator pump adjustment. Holley 4150

CHEVROLET

Clutch Section

HYDRAULIC CONTROLS

Fig. 1 shows a dual master cylinder, one side for clutch operation and the other for brake. A single clutch master cylinder is used in conjunction with air brakes.

When the clutch pedal is depressed, brake fluid is forced from the master cylinder, Fig. 1, into the slave cylinder, Fig. 2, and the slave cylinder push rod moves the clutch release lever. When the clutch pedal is released, fluid from the slave cylinder feeds back to the master cylinder.

A "bleeder" fitting is provided on the slave cylinder and the procedure for bleeding the system is similar to that used on the brake system. Fluid level in the master cylinder should be maintained 1/2" below the top of the cylinder.

Clutch Pedal, Adjust

Two adjustments are necessary: pedal total travel, and pedal free travel. The master cylinder must be filled to 1/2" below the top of the reservoir and the system must be free of air.

Clutch Pedal Total Travel

1. Disconnect clutch fork return spring.
2. Bottom the slave cylinder push rod and piston by pushing the slave cylinder push rod to the front of the vehicle as far as it will go, Fig. 3.
3. Pull clutch fork toward rear of vehicle until the throwout bearing touches the pressure plate release levers.
4. Adjust clearance between slave cylinder push rod fulcrum ("V" block), Fig. 2, by adjusting the nut behind to the clearance given below between fulcrum pivot and clutch fork. This clearance can be checked with the shank of the drill size indicated.

1970	1/2"
1971–74 V6	1/2"
1971 exc. V6	3/16"
1972–73 exc. V6	13/32"
1974–77 V8	13/32"
1974–77 L6	11/32"

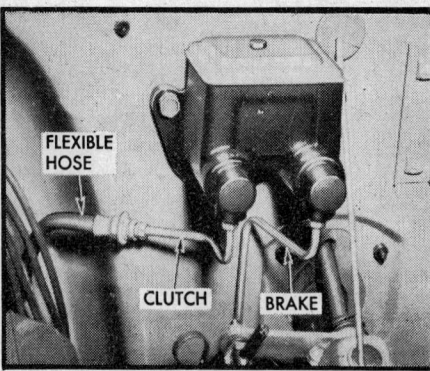

Fig. 1 Dual Master cylinder for clutch and brake operation. (typical)

Clutch Pedal Free Travel

Adjust clutch master cylinder adjustable push rod to obtain free travel between push rod and master cylinder piston. This will amount to 1/8 to 1/4" free pedal travel measured at the center line of the clutch pedal pad just before the clutch push rod touches the master cylinder piston.

CLUTCH PEDAL, ADJUST

Mechanical Linkage

1970–72 Light Duty Exc. El Camino & 1970–80 G Models
1. Disconnect clutch fork return spring at fork.
2. Loosen nut "A", Fig. 4, and back off from swivel about 1/2".
3. Hold clutch fork push rod against fork to move clutch release bearing against clutch fingers (push rod will slide through swivel at cross-shaft).
4. Adjust nut "B" to obtain 3/16 to 1/4" clearance between nut "B" and swivel.
5. Release push rod, connect return spring and tighten nut "A" to lock swivel against nut "B."

6. Check free pedal travel which should be 3/4 to 1 inch on all except 1974–80 G models; and 1 1/4 to 1 1/2 inch on 1974–80 G models.

1973–80 C, K and P Models Except 157" Wheel Base P30 & Motor Home, Fig. 5.
1. Disconnect return spring at clutch fork.
2. Position clutch lever firmly against rubber bumper on brake pedal bracket.
3. Push outer end of fork rearward until release bearing lightly contacts pressure plate.
4. Loosen locknut and adjust rod length so that swivel slips freely into gauge hole. Increase length until all lash is removed from linkage.
5. Reinstall rod into lower hole on lever. Install two washers and cotter pin. Tighten locknut without changing rod length.
6. Reinstall return spring and check pedal travel. Pedal travel should be 1 3/8 to 1 5/8 inch on C-K models; and 1 1/4 to 1 1/2 inch on P models.

1973–80 157 Inch Wheel Base P30, Fig. 5.
1. Disconnect return spring from clutch fork.
2. Loosen nut "G" at swivel.
3. Move clutch fork rod against fork to eliminate play between release bearing and clutch.
4. Position clutch lever against rubber stop on brake pedal bracket.
5. Rotate fork rod until a clearance of 1/4 to 5/8 inch is obtained between shoulder on fork rod and the adjustment nut.
6. Tighten nut "G" against swivel and install return spring.
7. Check free pedal clearance at pedal. Pedal clearance should be 1 3/8 to 1 5/8 inch.

1970 El Camino
1. Disconnect return spring at clutch fork.
2. With clutch pedal against stop, loosen lock nut just far enough to allow the adjusting rod to be turned out of swivel and against fork until release bearing contacts pressure plate fingers lightly.
3. Rotate push rod into swivel three turns and tighten lock nut.

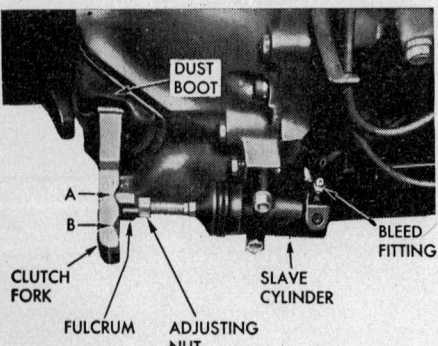

Fig. 2 Slave cylinder and clutch fork. Be sure to note which fulcrum is used ("A" or "B") before disassembly

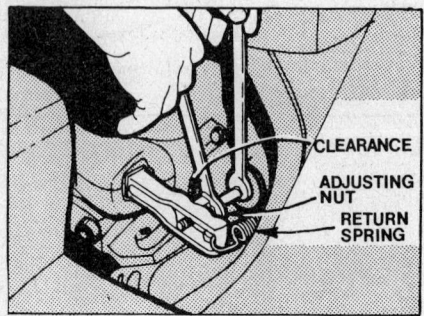

Fig. 3 Adjusting slave cylinder push rod. 1970–77

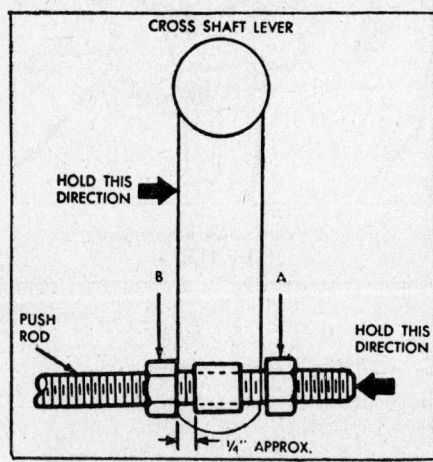

Fig. 4 Clutch pedal free travel adjustment. 1970–80 with typical mechanical linkage

CHEVROLET

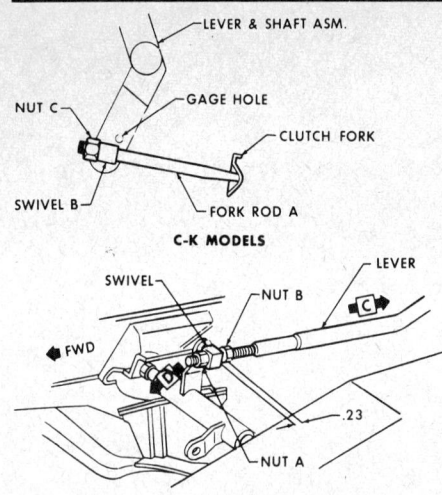

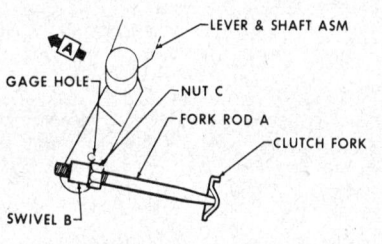

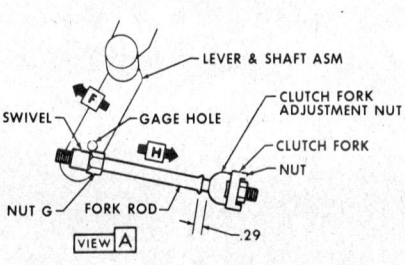

Fig. 5 Clutch pedal adjustment. 1970–80 C-K-P models

4. Install return spring and check clutch pedal free travel. Free travel should be $1^{1}/_{8}$ to $1^{3}/_{4}$ in.

1971–80 El Camino

1. Disconnect return spring at clutch fork.
2. Rotate clutch lever and shaft assembly until pedal is against rubber bumper on dash brace.
3. Push outer end of clutch fork rearward until throwout bearing lightly contacts pressure plate fingers.
4. Install push rod in gauge hole and increase length until all lash is removed, Fig. 6.
5. Remove swivel or rod from gauge hole and insert into lower hole on lever. Install retainer and tighten lock nut using care not to change rod length.
6. Install return spring and check clutch pedal free travel. Free travel should be $3/4$ to $1^{5}/_{16}$ in.

1971–75 Vega

Initial adjustment after clutch and/or cable replacement is made at two points, at the ball stud and the lower end of the cable.

1. Ball stud adjustment is made before attaching the cable as follows: using gauge J-23644, place it so flat end is against the front face of the clutch housing and the hooked end is located at the point of cable attachment on the fork, Fig. 7.
2. Turn ball stud inward until clutch release bearing lightly contacts the clutch spring levers, then install the lock nut and tighten being careful not the change the adjustment. Remove the gauge by pulling outward at the housing end.
3. To adjust the cable, place it through the hole in the fork and pull it until the clutch pedal is firmly against the rubber bumper.
4. Push the clutch fork forward until the throwout bearing lightly contacts the clutch spring levers, then screw the lock pin on the cable until it bottoms out on the fork. Turn it $1/4$ additional clockwise revolution, set pin additional clockwise revolution, set pin into groove in the fork and attach return spring. This procedure will produce .90″ lash at the pedal.

Adjustment for normal clutch wear is accomplished by loosening the lock nut and by turning the clutch fork ball stud counterclockwise until .90″ of free play is obtained at the pedal.

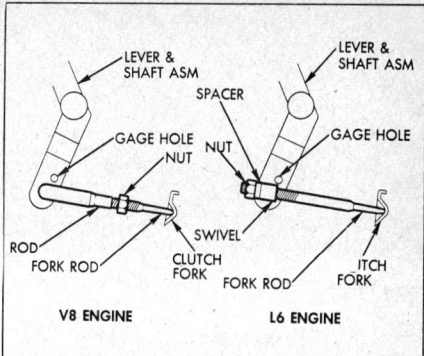

Fig. 6 Clutch pedal adjustment. 1971–80 El Camino

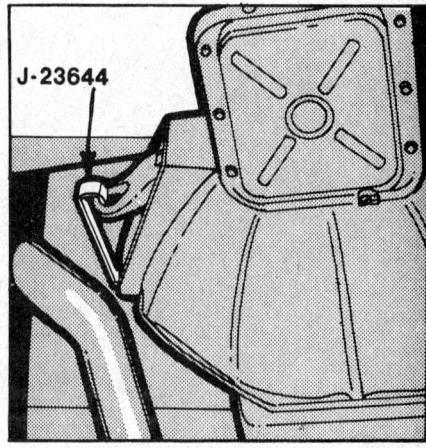

Fig. 7 Clutch adjusting gauge in place. 1971–75 Vega.

CHEVROLET

Manual Shift Transmission Section

NOTE: For Clark, Fuller, New Process, Spicer and Warner transmissions used on Chevrolet trucks, see the "name" chapter for service procedures and lubricant capacities.

Chevrolet Trans. Index & Lube Capacities

Trans. Type	Oil, Pints
3 Speed Muncie	2
3 Speed Saginaw	2
4 Speed	6¼
Power Divider and Auxiliary Trans.	①

①—Fill to bottom of filler plug hole

1976–80 TREMEC 3 SPEED

For service procedures, refer to the Ford Chapter, Transmission Section under "3 SPEED TRANS., 1970–80".

1970–80 MUNCIE 3 SPEED

Disassemble, Fig. 1

1. Remove side cover.
2. Remove clutch gear retainer and gasket.
3. Remove clutch gear bearing-to-gear stem snap ring, then remove bearing by pulling outward on clutch gear until a screwdriver can be inserted between large snap ring and case to complete removal. The bearing is slip fit on the gear and into the case bore.
4. Remove extension to case attaching bolts.
5. Rotate extension to left until groove in extension housing flange lines up with reverse idler shaft. Using a drift, drive reverse idler shaft out of gear and case.
6. Remove clutch gear, mainshaft and extension assembly together through rear case opening. Remove reverse idler gear from case.
7. Remove clutch gear from mainshaft.
8. Expand snap ring in extension housing, tap on end of mainshaft and remove extension from mainshaft.

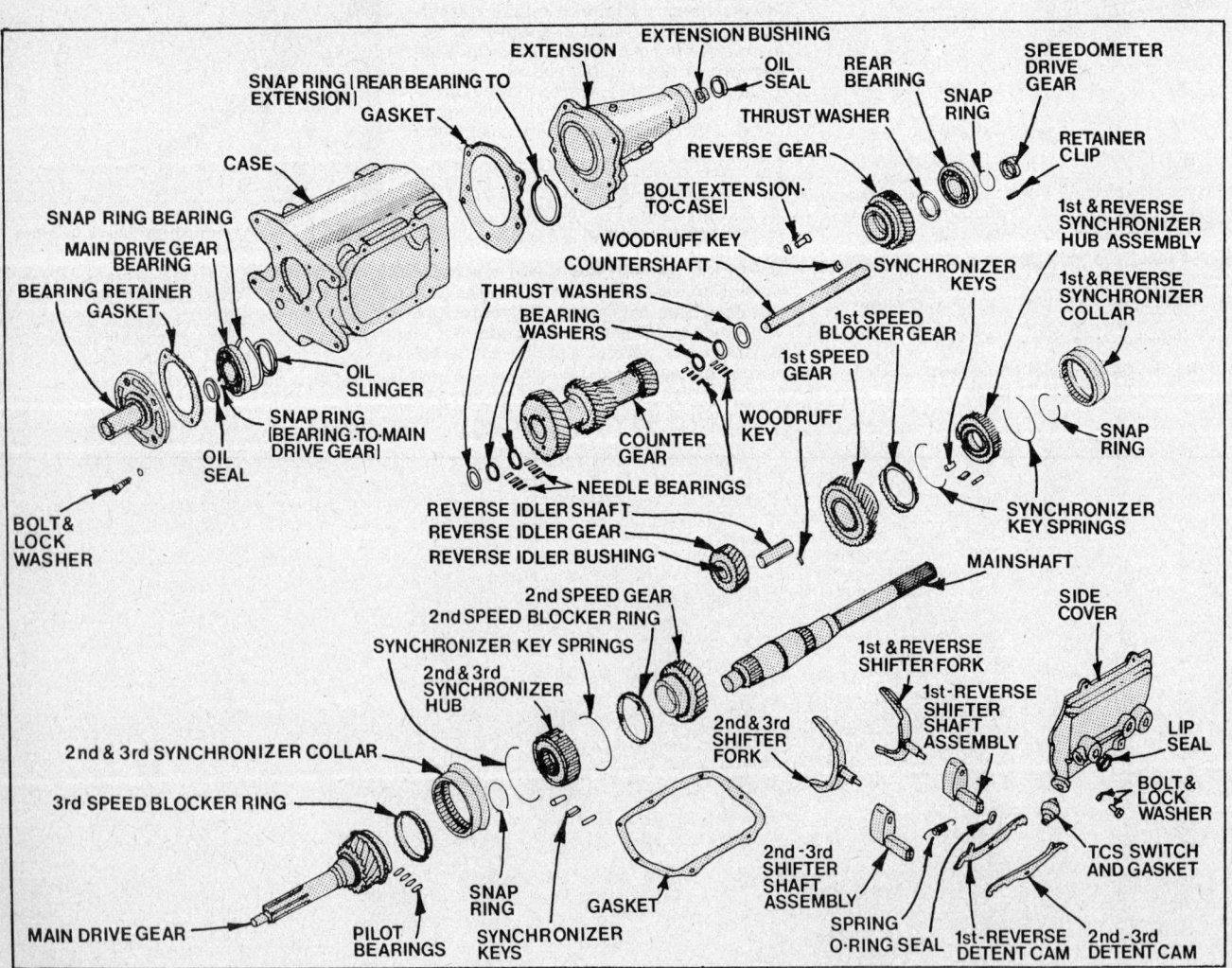

Fig. 1 1970–80 Muncie three-speed transmission. Exploded

CHEVROLET

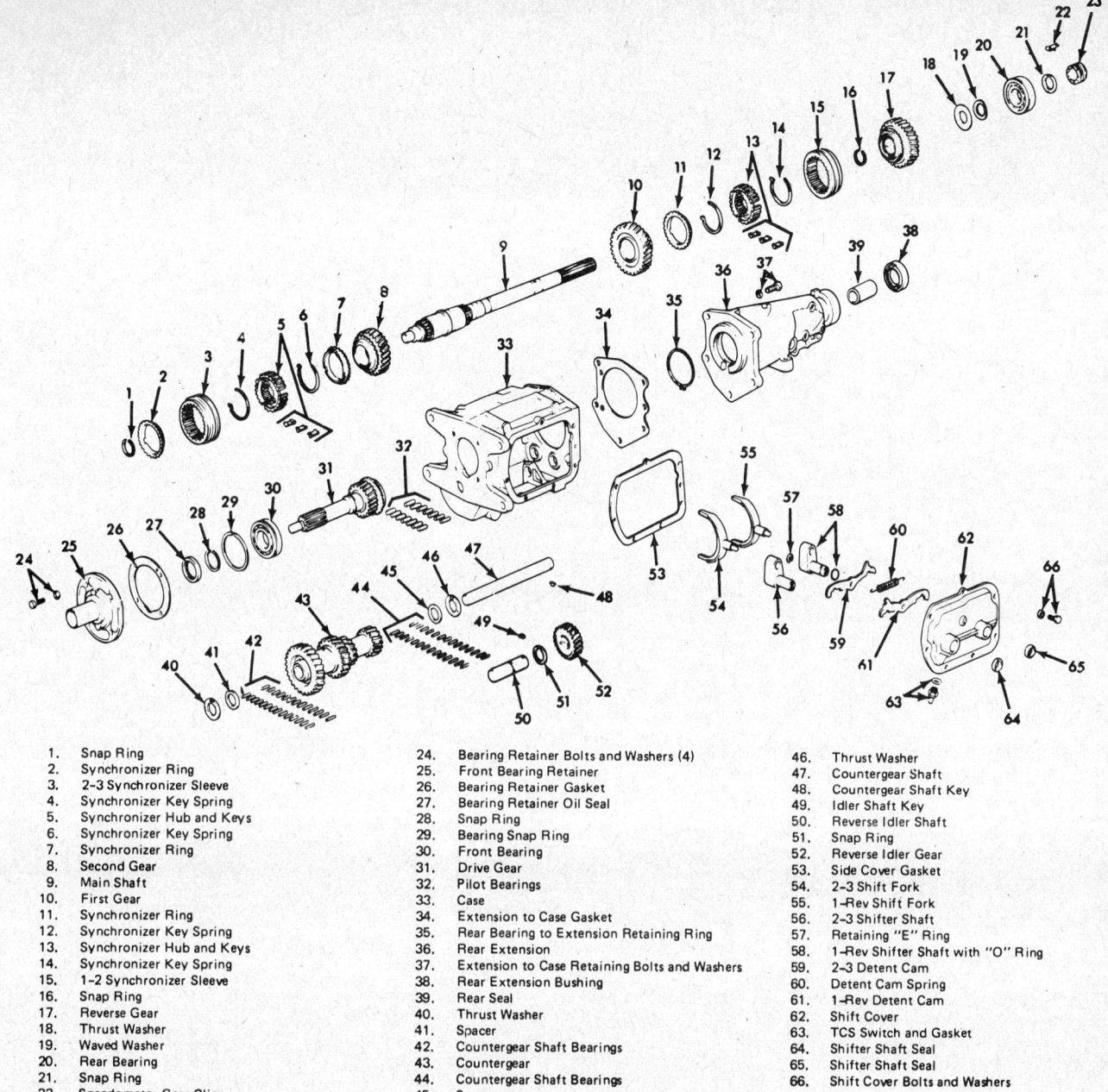

1. Snap Ring
2. Synchronizer Ring
3. 2-3 Synchronizer Sleeve
4. Synchronizer Key Spring
5. Synchronizer Hub and Keys
6. Synchronizer Key Spring
7. Synchronizer Ring
8. Second Gear
9. Main Shaft
10. First Gear
11. Synchronizer Ring
12. Synchronizer Key Spring
13. Synchronizer Hub and Keys
14. Synchronizer Key Spring
15. 1-2 Synchronizer Sleeve
16. Snap Ring
17. Reverse Gear
18. Thrust Washer
19. Waved Washer
20. Rear Bearing
21. Snap Ring
22. Speedometer Gear Clip
23. Speedometer Drive Gear
24. Bearing Retainer Bolts and Washers (4)
25. Front Bearing Retainer
26. Bearing Retainer Gasket
27. Bearing Retainer Oil Seal
28. Snap Ring
29. Bearing Snap Ring
30. Front Bearing
31. Drive Gear
32. Pilot Bearings
33. Case
34. Extension to Case Gasket
35. Rear Bearing to Extension Retaining Ring
36. Rear Extension
37. Extension to Case Retaining Bolts and Washers
38. Rear Extension Bushing
39. Rear Seal
40. Thrust Washer
41. Spacer
42. Countergear Shaft Bearings
43. Countergear
44. Countergear Shaft Bearings
45. Spacer
46. Thrust Washer
47. Countergear Shaft
48. Countergear Shaft Key
49. Idler Shaft Key
50. Reverse Idler Shaft
51. Snap Ring
52. Reverse Idler Gear
53. Side Cover Gasket
54. 2-3 Shift Fork
55. 1-Rev Shift Fork
56. 2-3 Shifter Shaft
57. Retaining "E" Ring
58. 1-Rev Shifter Shaft with "O" Ring
59. 2-3 Detent Cam
60. Detent Cam Spring
61. 1-Rev Detent Cam
62. Shift Cover
63. TCS Switch and Gasket
64. Shifter Shaft Seal
65. Shifter Shaft Seal
66. Shift Cover Bolts and Washers

Fig. 2 1970–80 Saginaw three speed transmission exploded view

Assemble

1. Load double row of roller bearings and thrust washers into each end of countergear. Use heavy grease to hold them in place.
2. Place countergear in case and install countergear shaft and woodruff key from rear of case.

NOTE: Be sure countershaft picks up both thrust washers and that the tangs are aligned in the notches in the case.

3. Position reverse idler in case.
4. Expand snap ring in extension housing and assemble mainshaft and extension.
5. Load rollers into clutch gear bore and assemble 3rd gear blocker ring onto gear with clutching teeth toward gear.
6. Install clutch gear assembly onto mainshaft. Do not install bearing over gear stem as yet.

NOTE: Be sure notches in blocker ring align with keys in the synchronizer assembly.

7. Place gasket on rear of case, and assemble the entire mainshaft-extension to the case as a unit.

NOTE: Be sure clutch gear engages the teeth of the countergear anti-lash plate and that the oil slinger is in place on the clutch gear.

8. Rotate extension and install reverse idler shaft and Woodruff key. Install extension-to-case bolts.
9. With large snap ring on bearing, install clutch gear bearing onto stem of gear and into case bore. Install small snap ring.
10. Install clutch gear bearing retainer with oil return hole at bottom.
11. Install side cover.

CHEVROLET

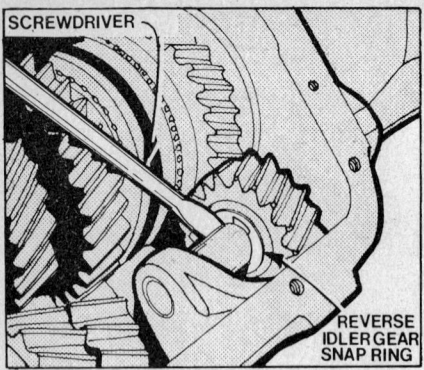

Fig. 3 Removing reverse idler "E" ring

Fig. 4 Removing rear bearing retainer after spring snap ring as shown

1970–80 EL CAMINO, CHEVY VAN & 1973–75 VEGA 3 SPEED

Saginaw

This transmission, Fig. 2, is fully synchronized in that all forward speed changes are accomplished with synchronizer sleeves. The synchronizers permit quicker shifts, greatly reduce gear clash, and permit down shifting from third to second between 40 and 20 mph, and from second to first below 20 mph.

Disassemble

1. Drain lubricant.
2. Remove side cover and gasket.
3. Remove front bearing retainer.
4. Remove front bearing snap ring, pull main drive gear out of case as far as possible and remove bearing.
5. Remove rear bearing retainer-to-case bolts.
6. Remove reverse idler shaft-to-gear "E" ring, Fig. 3.
7. From front of case, remove rear bearing retainer and mainshaft assembly.
8. Remove main drive gear, 14 needle rollers and 3rd speed gear blocking ring from mainshaft.
9. Expand snap ring and remove rear bearing retainer, Fig. 4.
10. Remove countershaft through rear of case, Fig. 5, and remove two tanged thrust washers.
11. Use a long brass drift or punch and drive reverse idler shaft and key through rear of case.
12. Remove reverse idler gear tanged thrust washer.

Disassemble Mainshaft

1. Referring to Fig. 6, remove 2–3 synchronizer sleeve.
2. Remove rear bearing snap ring.
3. Using a ram or arbor press, remove rear bearing, spring washer, thrust washer and reverse gear.
4. Remove speedometer drive gear.
5. Remove first speed synchronizer snap ring. Support first gear on a press and remove first gear and its synchronizer.
6. Remove 2-3 synchronizer snap ring and press off synchronizer and second speed gear.

Synchronizers

NOTE: The synchronizer hubs and sliding sleeves are a selected assembly and should be kept together as originally assembled. The keys and springs may be replaced if worn or broken.

1. Mark hub and sleeve so they can be reassembled in same position.
2. Remove sleeve from hub.
3. Remove keys and springs from hub.
4. Place three keys and two springs in position (one on each side of hub) so all three

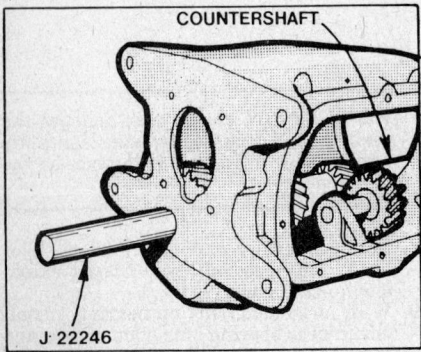

Fig. 5 Removing countershaft, using aligning arbor to hold needle bearings in place

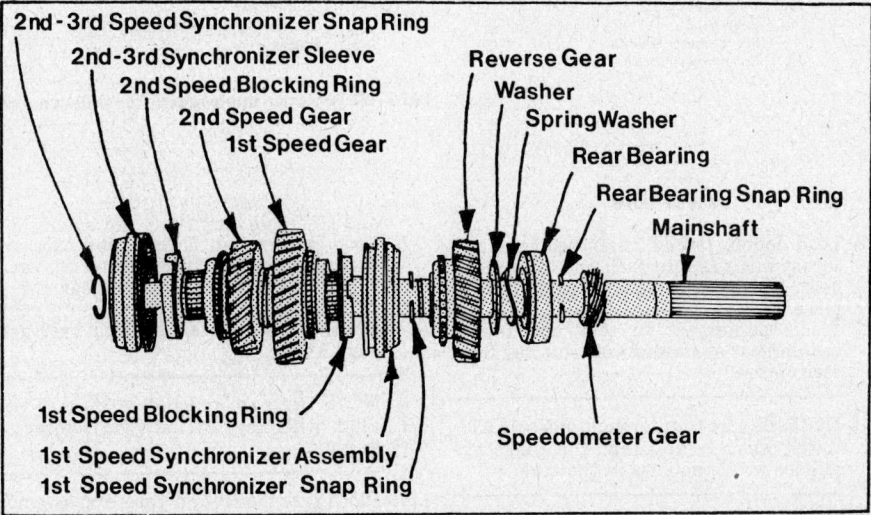

Fig. 6 Mainshaft and related parts assembled loosely to show location of parts

CHEVROLET

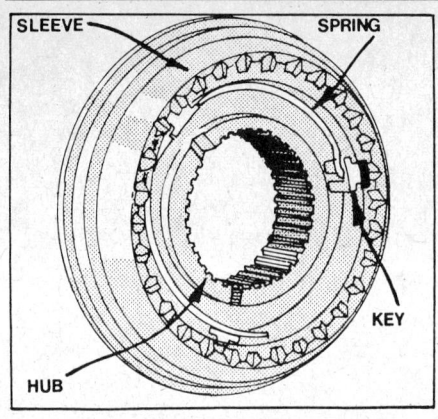

Fig. 7 Synchronizer assembly

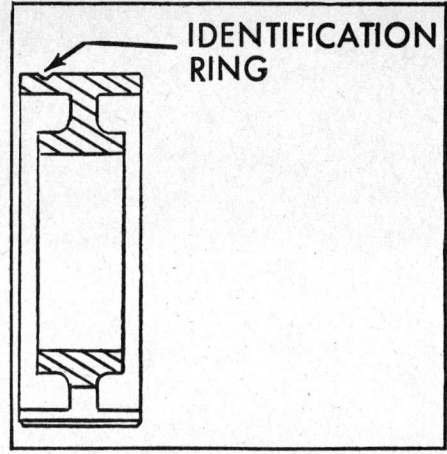

Fig. 8 Identification chamfer around synchronizer hub

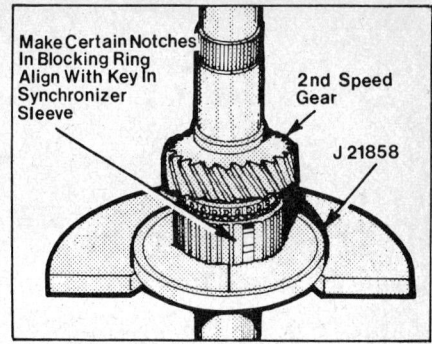

Fig. 9 Installing second speed gear

keys are engaged by both springs, Fig. 7. The tanged end of each synchronizer spring should be installed in different key cavities on either side of hub. Slide sleeve onto hub, aligning marks made before disassembly.

NOTE: A chamfer around outside of synchronizer hub splines identifies end that must be opposite shift fork slot in sleeve, Fig. 8.

Mainshaft, Assemble

1. Install second speed and synchronizer on mainshaft. Using a ram or arbor press, press 2–3 synchronizer (with chamfer toward rear) onto mainshaft, Fig. 9.
2. Install first speed gear and synchronizer on mainshaft, Fig. 10, and install snap ring. *Make certain notches are in blocking ring align with keys.*
3. Install rear bearing retainer. Spread spring washer and rear bearing. Grooves on bearing must be toward reverse gear.
4. Install speedometer drive gear on mainshaft. Press gear until its rear face is 6 inches from rear bearing, Fig. 11.
5. Install 2–3 synchronizer sleeve.

Assemble Transmission

1. Install countergear-to-case thrust washers. Install countergear into case from rear. Make certain woodruff key is in place. Note that antirattle gear is riveted to countergear in four places and is not serviced separately, Fig. 12.
2. Install reverse idler gear tanged steel thrust washer. Install idler gear, shaft and woodruff key. *Reverse idler gear snap ring will be installed after installation of mainshaft.*
3. Install rear bearing retainer. Spread snap ring in retainer to allow snap ring to drop around rear bearing. Press on end of mainshaft until snap ring engages groove in rear bearing.
4. Install 14 needle rollers in main drive gear pocket, using grease to hold them in place. Assemble third gear. Pilot main drive gear and blocking ring over front of mainshaft. Make certain notches in blocking ring align with keys in 2-3 synchronizer.
5. Install rear bearing retainer-to-case gasket.
6. Install rear bearing retainer and mainshaft assembly into case. Torque bearing retainer-to-case bolts to 35-55 ft. lbs. torque.
7. Install bearing on main drive gear. Outer snap ring groove must be toward front of gear. Install snap ring.
8. Install front bearing retainer and gasket.
9. Install reverse idler gear "E" ring.
10. If repairs are required to the side cover, refer to Fig. 13.
11. Install side cover gasket. Place transmission gears in neutral and install side cover. Install bolts and tighten evenly.

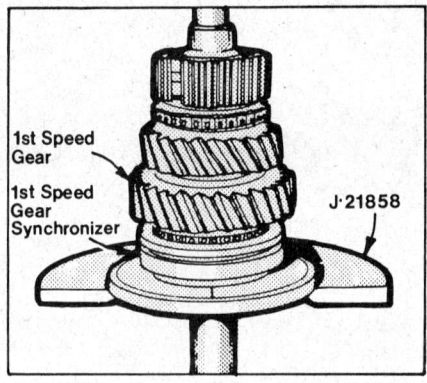

Fig. 10 Installing first speed gear

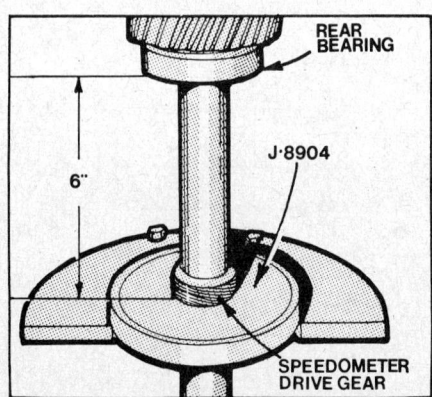

Fig. 11 Installing speedometer drive gear (6" from bearing)

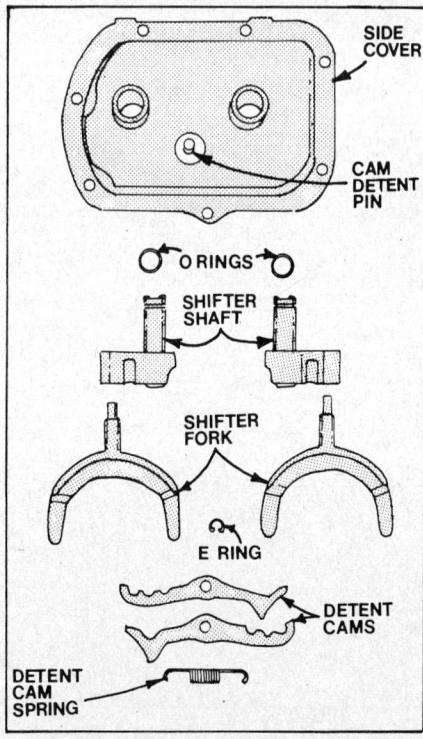

Fig. 13 Disassembled view of side cover

Fig. 12 Anti-rattle gear is riveted to countergear

893

CHEVROLET

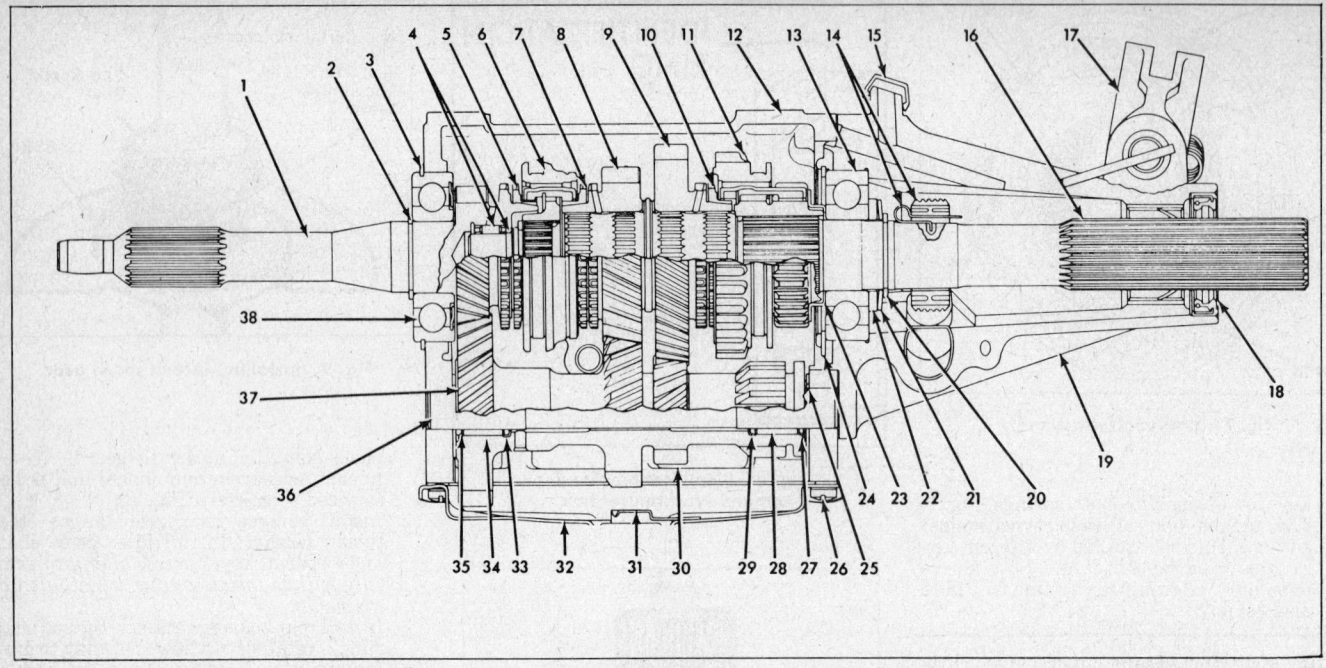

1. Clutch Drive Gear
2. Retaining Ring (Brg.-to-Drive Gear)
3. Retaining Ring (Brg.-to-Case)
4. Pilot Bearing and Spacer Ring
5. 3rd Gear Synchronizer Ring
6. 2-3 Sliding Sleeve and Synchronizer Assembly
7. 2nd Gear Synchronizer Ring
8. 2nd Speed Gear
9. 1st Speed Gear
10. 1st Gear Synchronizer Ring
11. 1st-Rev. Sliding Sleeve and Synchronizer
12. Transmission Case
13. Rear Bearing
14. Speedometer Gear and Retaining Clip
15. Vent Cap
16. Mainshaft
17. Intermediate Shift Lever Assembly
18. Extension Seal
19. Rear Extension
20. Retaining Ring (Brg.-to-Shaft)
21. Belleville Washer
22. Spacer
23. Synchronizer Key Stop Ring
24. Retaining Ring (Brg.-to-Extension)
25. Thrust Washer
26. Cover Screw
27. Spacer
28. Roller Bearing
29. Spacer
30. Countergear
31. Magnet
32. Transmission Cover
33. Spacer
34. Roller Bearing
35. Spacer
36. Countergear Shaft
37. Thrust Washer
38. Clutch Gear Bearing

Fig. 14 Cross section of 3 speed transmission. 1971-72 Vega

1971-72 VEGA 3 SPEED TRANSMISSION

Description

The three speed manual transmission, Fig. 14, is fully synchronized in all forward speeds. The synchronizing mechanism is similar to other Chevrolet transmissions. Shifting is accomplished by a floor mounted shift lever with external linkage connected to a selector shaft which is inside the case.

The engine driven clutch gear drives the countergear through a constant mesh countershaft gear. Forward speed gears on the countergear remain in constant mesh with two non-sliding mainshaft gears giving 1st and 2nd speed. Third speed is a direct drive with the clutch gear engaged directly to the mainshaft. Forward gears are engaged through two sliding synchronizer sleeves mounted on the mainshaft. Engagement of the constant mesh mainshaft gears to the

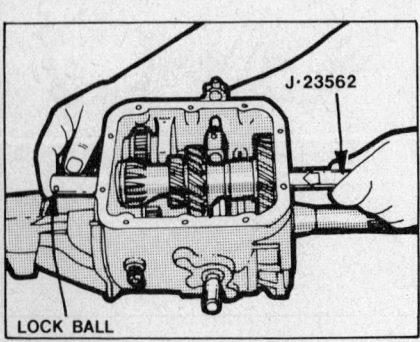

Fig. 16 Removing countergear

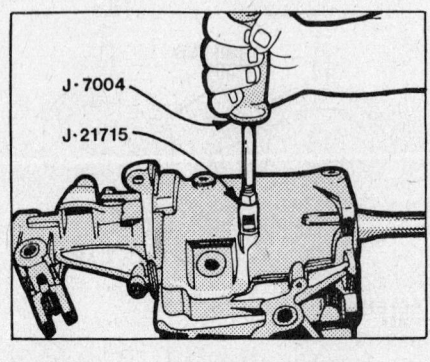

Fig. 17 Removing detent ball plug on 4 speed unit

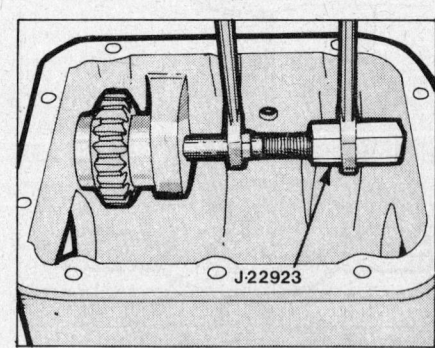

Fig. 18 Removing reverse idler gear

CHEVROLET

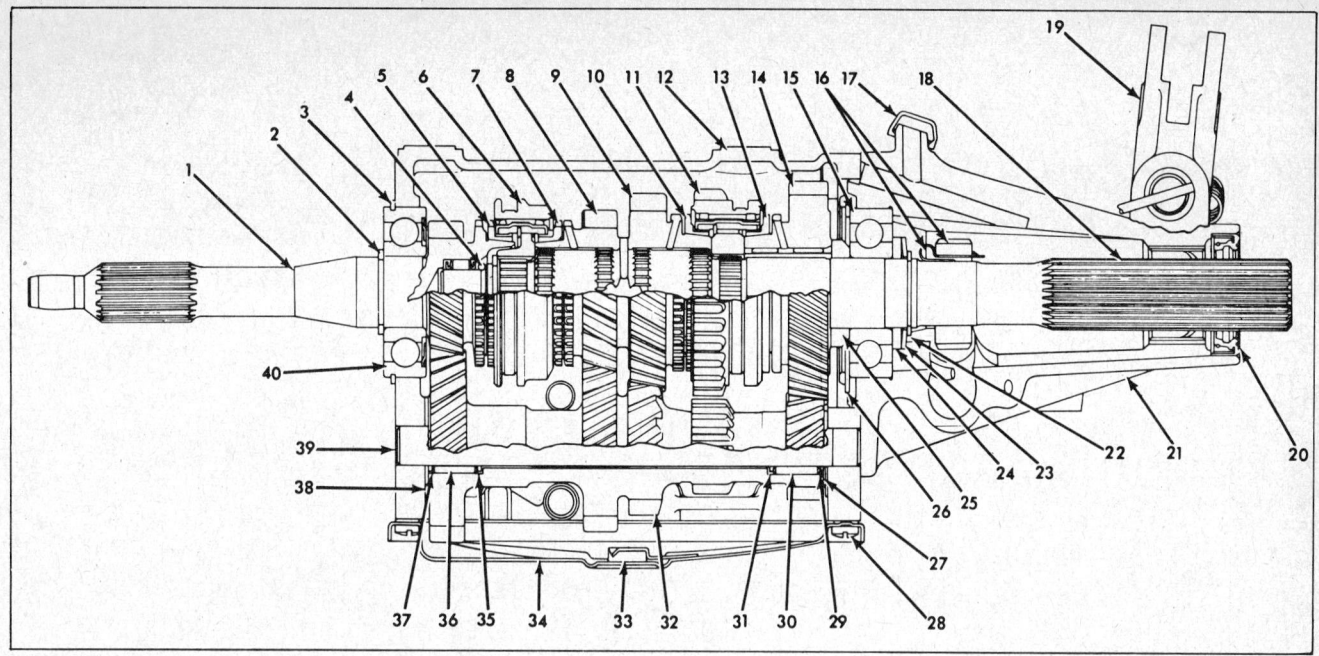

1. Clutch Drive Gear
2. Retaining Ring (Brg.-to-Shaft)
3. Retaining Ring (Brg.-to-Case)
4. Pilot Bearing and Spacer
5. 4th Speed Synchronizer Ring
6. 3-4 Synchronizer Assembly
7. 3rd Speed Synchronizer Ring
8. 3rd Speed Gear
9. 2nd Speed Gear
10. 2nd Speed Synchronizer Ring
11. Sliding Sleeve and Reverse Gear
12. Transmission Case
13. 1st Speed Synchronizer Ring
14. 1st Speed
15. Rear Bearing
16. Speedometer Gear and Clip
17. Vent Cap
18. Mainshaft
19. Intermediate Shift Lever Assembly
20. Rear Seal
21. Rear Extension
22. Retaining Ring (Brg.-to-Shaft)
23. Belleville Washer
24. Spacer
25. Spacer
26. Retaining Ring (Brg.-to-Extension)
27. Thrust Washer
28. Cover Screw
29. Spacer
30. Roller Bearing
31. Spacer
32. Countergear
33. Magnet
34. Cover
35. Spacer
36. Roller Bearing
37. Spacer
38. Thrust Washer
39. Countergear Shaft
40. Clutch Gear Bearing

Fig. 15 Cross section of 4 speed transmission. 1971-72 Vega

mainshaft is accomplished through blocker ring type synchronizers.

The first-reverse synchronizer sleeve has gear teeth on the outside diameter which enables it to function as a first speed synchronizer sleeve and as a reverse gear. The reverse idler gear is in constant mesh with the countergear. When shifting into reverse the first-reverse synchronizer sleeve (reverse gear) is moved to the rearward position which meshes it with the reverse idler gear. This movement ties the reverse gear on the countergear to the mainshaft and causes the mainshaft to rotate in a reverse direction.

1971-72 VEGA 4 SPEED TRANSMISSION

Description

The four speed synchronized transmission, Fig. 15, is similar to the three speed transmis-

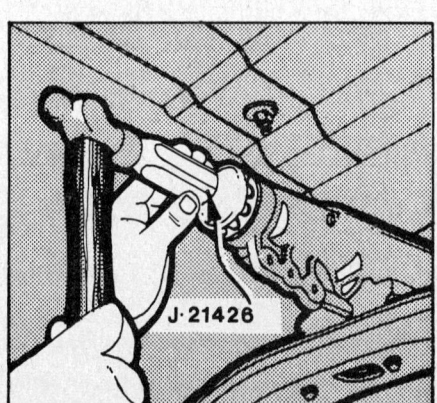

Fig. 19 Installing rear extension seal

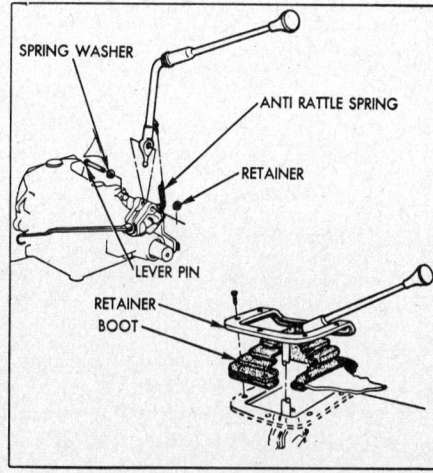

Fig. 20 Gearshift lever installation

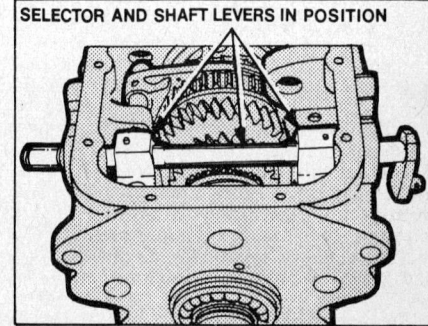

Fig. 21 Shift selector shaft

CHEVROLET

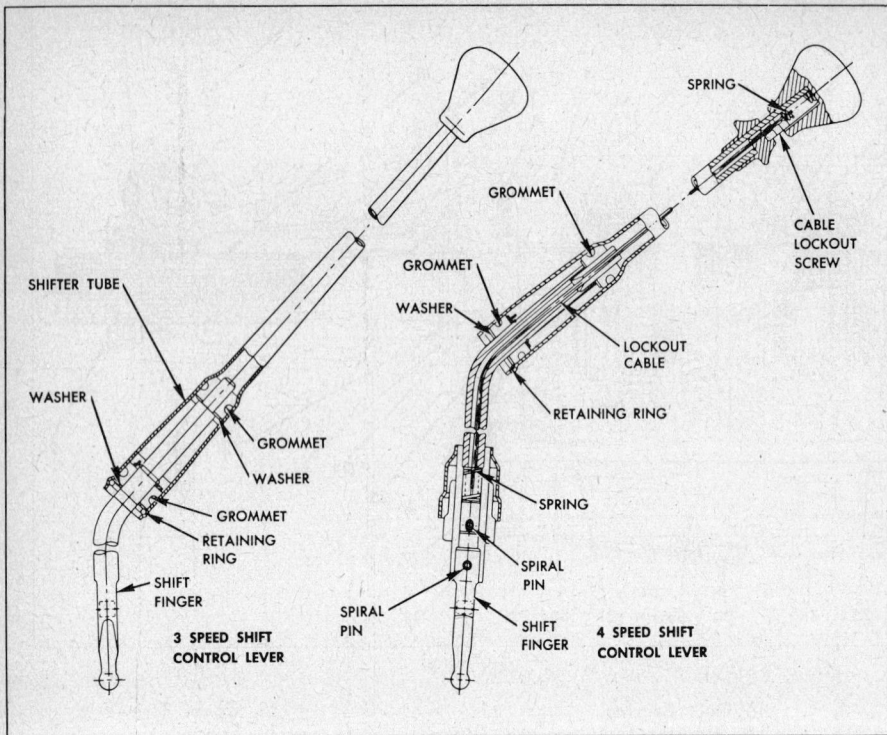

Fig. 22 Shift control lever cross section

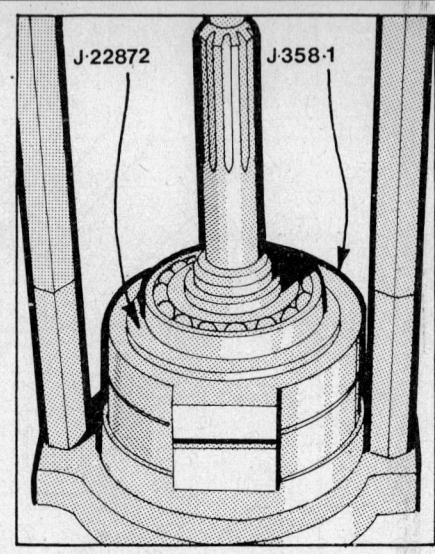

Fig. 24 Removing clutch gear bearing

sion described above. It is fully synchronized in all forward speeds.

The 1st-2nd synchronizer sleeve has gear teeth on the outside diameter which enables it to function as a reverse gear. When shifting into reverse the 1st-2nd sleeve (reverse gear) is in the neutral (center) position. The reverse idler gear (sliding type) is moved forward which simultaneously meshes it with the reverse gears on the mainshaft and countershaft. This causes the mainshaft to rotate in reverse direction.

Transmission Service

NOTE: All integral screws and bolts use metric system threads and cannot be interchanged with other Chevrolet parts now in use. Spiral pins are used to hold all shift forks and intermediate levers in position and cannot be serviced with standard roll pins due to metric sizing.

Disassembly procedures are essentially the same for both transmissions. Access to the internal parts is gained through the bottom cover. The countergear must be removed before the selector and shifter shafts, and the mainshaft assembly. Both transmissions require a countergear needle bearing loading tool (J-23562 and J-22911) to remove or install the countergear, Fig. 16.

During removal of the shifter shafts a special detent ball plug remover tool (J-21715) is needed for the 4 speed unit, Fig. 17. After shifter shaft removal the mainshaft assembly is taken from the case for disassembly. No special tools are needed for its disassembly, however some press operations will be necessary.

The rear extension cannot be removed without first removing countershaft. It is locked to the mainshaft assembly with a locating ring inside the transmission which is the same as Saginaw and Muncie 3 speed units.

A special tool (J-22923) is needed to remove the reverse idler gear shaft, Fig. 18. Shown in Fig. 19, is the rear extension seal installer which may be used either on the bench or in the vehicle.

The shift controls for both transmissions are floor mounted, Fig. 20. The shift selector shaft, Fig. 21, located inside the case with the ends extending through the case perpendicular to the mainshaft, has both side to side and angular movement.

Two intermediate shift levers, which select the gear required, are attached to the selector shaft by means of spiral pins. The side movement of the selector shaft allows the intermediate shift levers to pick up the proper shift shaft. The angular movement positions the shift shaft such that the shift forks (attached to shafts by spiral pins) move the synchronizer sleeves to obtain the required gear.

The 4-speed shift control operation is similar to the 3-speed except for the gear shift lever which has a reverse lockout feature, Fig. 22.

MUNCIE 4 SPEED, 1970-80

Disassemble, Fig. 23

1. Mount transmission in suitable holding fixture and remove transmission cover. If required, insert two 5/16 × 18 screws in cover flange threaded holes and turn evenly to raise cover dowel pins from case.

NOTE: Move reverse shifter fork so that reverse idler gear is partially engaged before attempting to remove cover. Forks must be positioned so rear edge of the slot in the reverse fork is in line with the front edge of the slot in the forward forks as viewed through tower opening.

2. Place transmission in two gears at once to lock gears and remove universal joint flange nut, universal joint front flange and brake drum assembly.
3. Remove parking brake and brake flange plate assembly on models so equipped.
4. Remove rear bearing retainer and gasket.
5. Slide speedometer drive gear off mainshaft.
6. Remove clutch gear bearing retainer and gasket.
7. Remove countergear front bearing cap and gasket.
8. Pry countergear front bearing out by inserting screw drivers into groove at cast slots in case.
9. Remove countergear rear bearing retaining rings from shaft and bearing. With a suitable tool remove countergear rear bearings. This will allow countergear assembly to rest on bottom of case.
10. Remove clutch gear bearing outer race to case retaining ring.
11. Remove clutch gear and bearing by tapping gently on bottom side of clutch gear shaft and prying directly opposite against the case and bearing snap ring groove at the same time. Remove 4th gear synchronizer ring.

CAUTION: Index cut out section of clutch gear in down position with countergear to obtain clearance for removing clutch gear.

12. Remove rear mainshaft bearing snap ring and using a suitable tool remove bearing from case. Slide 1st speed gear thrust washer off mainshaft.
13. Raise rear of mainshaft assembly and push rearward in case bore, then swing front end up and lift from case. Remove synchronizer cone from shaft.
14. Slide reverse idler gear rearward and move countergear rearward until front end is free of case, then lift to remove from case.
15. To remove reverse idler gear, drive re-

CHEVROLET

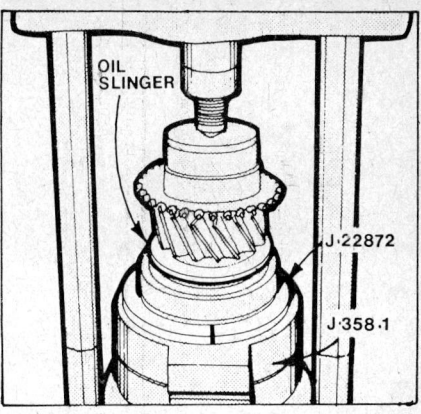

Fig. 25 Replacing clutch gear bearing

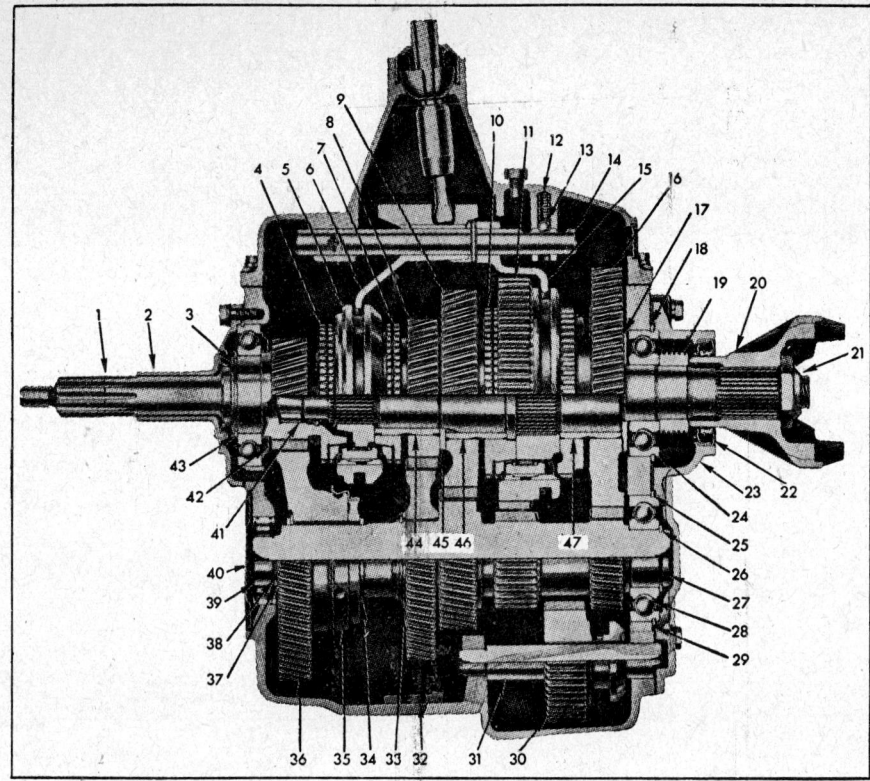

1. Main Drive Clutch Gear	11. Reverse Driven Gear	25. Rear Bearing Snap Ring	39. Front Countershaft Bearing
2. Drive Gear Bearing Retainer	12. Poppet Spring	26. Snap Ring	40. Countergear Front Cover
3. Snap Ring--Outer	13. Poppet Ball	27. Countershaft	41. Pilot Bearing Rollers
4. 3rd and 4th Synchronizer Ring	14. Shift Rail	28. Countershaft Rear Bearing	42. Clutch Gear Oil Slinger
5. 3rd and 4th Synchronizer Collar	15. 1st and 2nd Shift Fork	29. Bearing Snap Ring	43. Snap Ring
6. 3rd and 4th Shift Fork	16. 1st Speed Gear	30. Reverse Idler Gear	44. 3rd Speed Gear Bushing
7. 3rd and 4th Speed Synchronizer Ring	17. Thrust Washer	31. Reverse Idler Shaft	45. Thrust Washer
8. 3rd Speed Gear	18. Bearing Snap Ring	32. Case Magnet	46. 2nd Speed Gear Bushing
9. 2nd Speed Gear	19. Speedometer Drive Gear	33. Snap Ring	47. 1st Speed Gear Bushing
10. 1st and 2nd Synchronizer Assembly	20. Output Yoke	34. Snap Ring	
	21. Flange Nut	35. Damper Assembly	
	22. Rear Bearing Retainer Oil Seal	36. Countergear	
	23. Rear Bearing Retainer	37. Thrust Washer	
	24. Mainshaft Rear Bearing	38. Snap Ring	

Fig. 23 GM CH & SM465 four speed synchromesh transmission. 1970-79

verse idler gear shaft out of case from front to rear using a drift. Remove reverse idler gear from case.

Clutch Gear, Disassemble

1. Removing mainshaft pilot bearing rollers from clutch gear and remove roller retainer. Do not remove snap ring o inside of clutch gear.
2. Remove snap ring securing bearing on stem of clutch gear.
3. Using an arbor press, press gear and shaft out of bearing, Fig. 24.

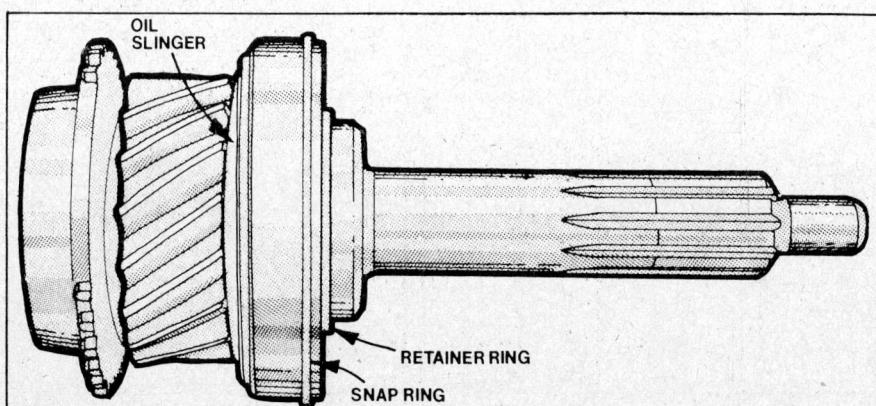

Fig. 26 Clutch gear assembly

Clutch Gear, Inspect

1. Wash all parts in cleaning solvent.
2. Inspect roller bearings for pits and galling.
3. Inspect bearing diameter in shaft recess for galling.
4. Inspect gear teeth for excessive wear.
5. Inspect clutch shaft pilot for excessive wear.
6. Re-oil bearing, then rotate clutch gear bearing slowly and check for roughness.

Clutch Gear, Assemble

1. Press bearing and new oil slinger onto clutch gear shaft, Fig. 25. Slinger should be located flush with bearing shoulder on clutch gear, Fig. 26.
2. Install snap ring to secure bearing on clutch gear shaft.
3. Install bearing retainer ring in groove on O.D. of bearing.

CAUTION: Bearing must turn freely after it is installed on shaft.

4. Install snap ring on I.D. of mainshaft pilot bearing bore in clutch gear.
5. Apply a small amount of grease to bearing surface in shaft recess, install transmission mainshaft pilot roller bearings and install retainer.

NOTE: This roller bearing retainer holds bearings in position and in final transmission assembly is pushed forward into recess by mainshaft pilot.

Mainshaft, Disassemble

1. Remove first speed gear.
2. Remove snap ring in front of 3rd-4th synchronizer assembly.
3. Remove reverse driven gear.
4. Press behind 2nd speed gear to remove 3rd-4th synchronizer assembly, 3rd speed gear and 2nd speed gear along with 3rd gear bushing and thrust washer, Fig. 27.
5. Remove 2nd speed synchronizer ring and keys.
6. Support 2nd speed synchronizer hub at front face and press mainshaft through removing 1st speed gear bushing and 2nd speed synchronizer hub.
7. Split 2nd speed gear bushing with chisel

CHEVROLET

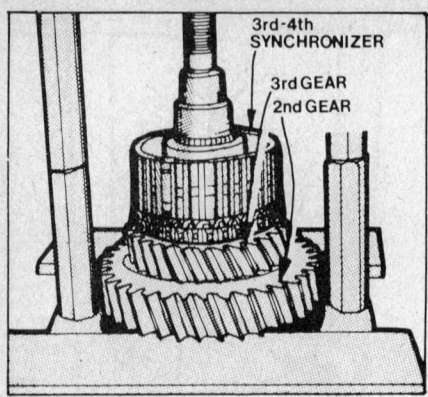

Fig. 27 Disassembly of mainshaft

and remove bushing from shaft.

CAUTION: Exercise care not to damage mainshaft.

Mainshaft, Inspect

1. Wash all parts in cleaning solvent.
2. Inspect mainshaft for scoring or excessive wear at thrust surfaces or splines.
3. Inspect clutch hub and clutch sleeve for excessive wear and make sure sleeve slides freely on clutch hub. Also check fit of clutch hub on mainshaft splines.

NOTE: 3rd and 4th speed clutch sleeve should slide freely on 3rd and 4th speed clutch hub but clutch hub should be snug fit on shaft splines.

4. Inspect 3rd speed gear thrust surfaces for excessive scoring and inspect 3rd speed gear mainshaft bushing for excessive wear.

NOTE: 3rd speed gear must be a running fit on mainshaft bushing and mainshaft bushing should be a press fit on shaft.

5. Check 2nd speed thrust washer for excessive scoring.
6. Inspect 2nd speed gear for excessive wear at thrust surface. Check synchronizer springs for looseness or breakage.
7. Inspect 2nd speed gear synchronizing ring for excessive wear.
8. Inspect bronze synchronizer cone on 2nd speed gear for excessive wear or damage. Also inspect clutch gear synchronizer cone and 3rd speed gear synchronizer cone for excessive wear or damage.

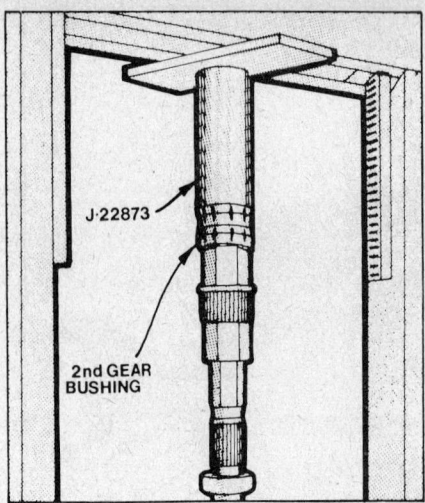

Fig. 28 Installing 2nd speed gear bushing

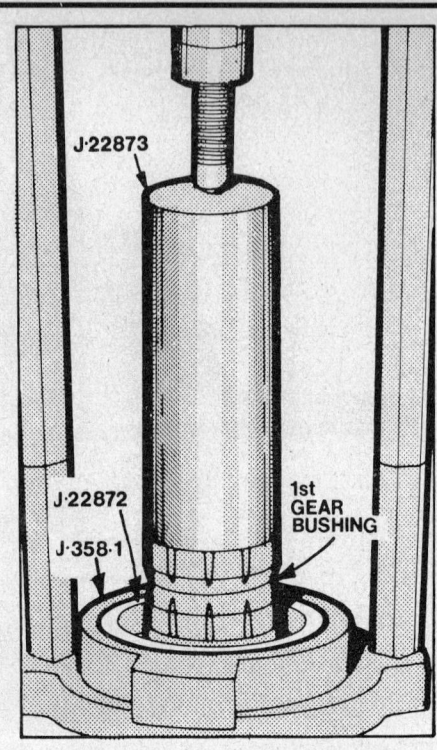

Fig. 29 Installing 1st speed gear bushing

NOTE: 1st and reverse sliding gear must be sliding fit on synchronizer hub and must not have excessive radial and circumferential play. If sliding gear is not free on hub, inspect for burrs which may have rolled up on front ends of half-tooth internal splines and remove by honing.

9. Inspect all gear teeth for excessive wear.

Mainshaft, Assemble

1. Press 2nd speed bushing onto mainshaft until it bottoms against shoulder, Fig. 28.

CAUTION: 1st, 2nd and 3rd speed gear

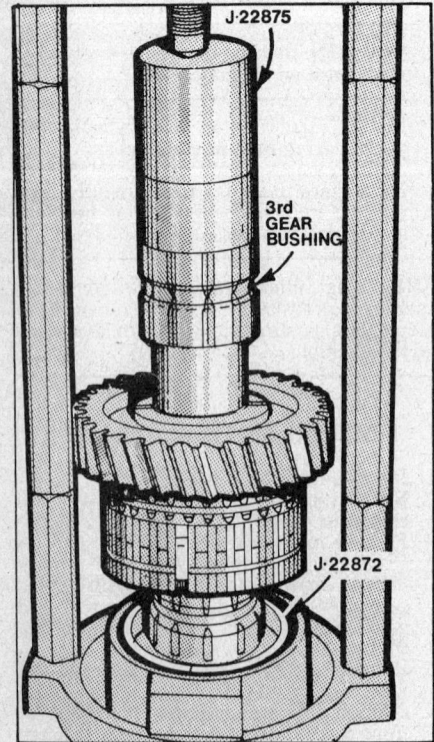

Fig. 30 Installing 3rd speed gear bushing

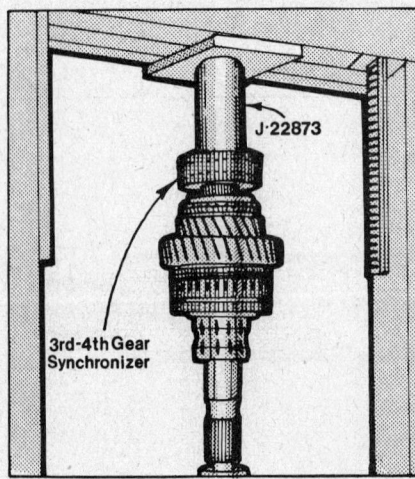

Fig. 31 Installing 3rd and 4th gear synchronizer

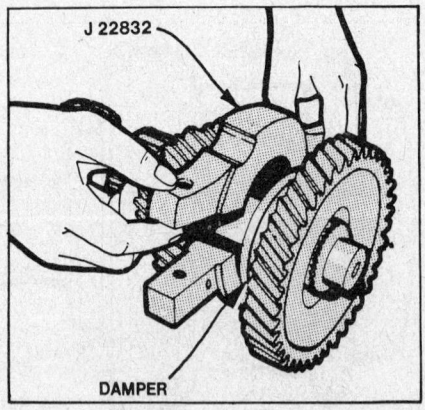

Fig. 32 Positioning Tool J-22832 on countershaft

CHEVROLET

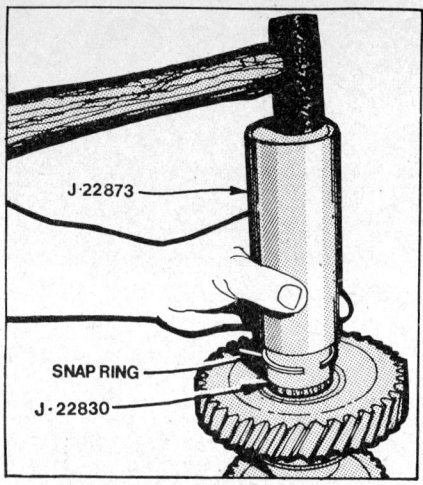

Fig. 33 Installing countergear snap ring

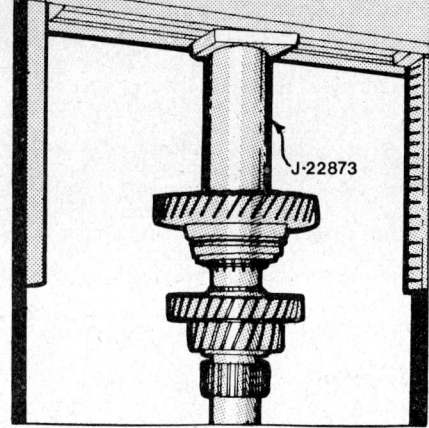

Fig. 34 Installing clutch countergear

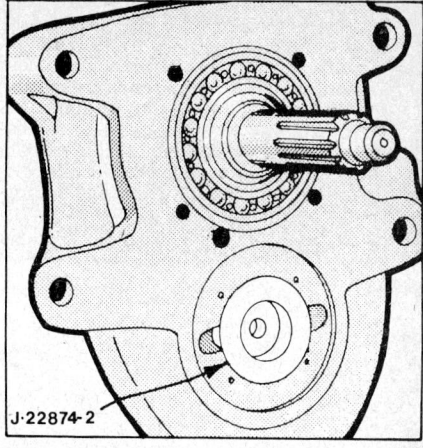

Fig. 36 Countergear front support tool

bushings are sintered iron. Exercise care when installing.

2. Press 1st and 2nd speed synchronizer hub onto mainshaft until it bottoms against shoulder with annulus toward rear of shaft.
3. Install 1st and 2nd synchronizer keys and springs.
4. Press 1st speed gear bushing onto mainshaft until it bottoms against hub, Fig. 29.
5. Install synchronizer blocking ring and 2nd speed gear onto mainshaft and against synchronizer hub. Index synchronizer key slots with keys in synchronizer hub.
6. Install 3rd speed gear thrust washer onto mainshaft with tang or thrust washer in slot on shaft and against 2nd speed gear bushing. Then press 3rd speed gear bushing onto mainshaft until it bottoms against thrust washer, Fig. 30.
7. Install 3rd speed gear synchronizer blocker ring and 3rd speed gear onto mainshaft, against 3rd speed gear thrust washer.
8. Index synchronizer ring key slots with synchronizer assembly keys and drive 3rd and 4th synchronizer assembly onto mainshaft and against 3rd speed gear bushing with thrust face toward 3rd speed gear. Retain synchronizer assembly with snap ring, Fig. 31.
9. Install reverse driver gear with fork groove toward rear.
10. Install 1st speed gear onto mainshaft and against 1st and 2nd synchronizer hub. Install 1st speed gear thrust washer.

Countershaft, Disassemble

1. Remove front countergear snap ring and thrust washer. Discard snap ring.
2. Install Tool J-22832 on countershaft, open side to damper, Fig. 32. Support assembly in arbor press and press countershaft out of clutch countergear assembly.
3. Remove clutch countergear rear retaining ring. Discard snap ring.
4. Remove 3rd speed countergear snap ring. Discard snap ring.
5. Position assembly on an arbor press and press shaft from 3rd speed countergear.

Countershaft, Assemble

1. Position 3rd speed countergear and shaft in arbor press and press gear onto shaft.

NOTE: Install gear with marked surface toward front of shaft.

2. Install new 3rd speed countergear snap ring.
3. Install new clutch countergear rear snap ring as follows: Install Tool J-22830, on end of shaft and position snap ring on tool. Using Tool J-22873, push down on snap ring until it engages groove on shaft. Using snap ring pliers, carefully expand ring until it just slides onto splines, then push ring down on shaft until it engages groove on shaft, Fig. 33.
4. Position clutch countergear on shaft and press countergear onto shaft against snap ring, Fig. 34.
5. Install clutch countergear thrust washer and front snap ring.

Transmission, Assemble

1. Lower countergear into case until it rests

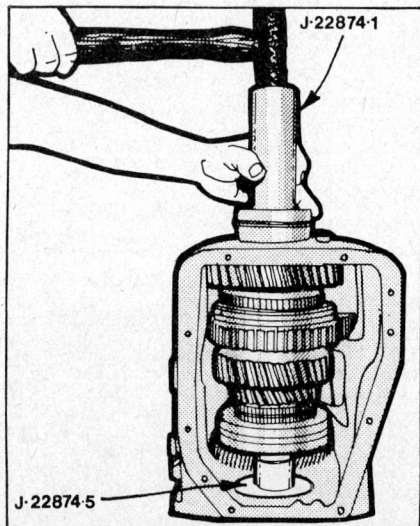

Fig. 35 Installing mainshaft rear bearing

on bottom.

2. Place reverse idler gear in transmission case with gear teeth toward the front. Install idler gear shaft from rear to front, being careful to have slot in end of shaft facing down. Shaft slot face must be at least flush with case.
3. Install mainshaft assembly into case with rear of shaft protruding out rear bearing hole in case. Position Tool J-22874-5 in clutch gear case opening and engaging front mainshaft. Rotate case onto front end, Fig. 35.

NOTE: Install 1st speed gear thrust washer on shaft if not previously installed.

4. Install snap ring on bearing O.D. and position rear mainshaft bearing on shaft. Using Tool J-22874-1 drive bearing onto shaft and into case. Align tangs on snap ring with lube slot of case and slot in tool before driving bearing. Rotate case and remove Tool J-22874-5, Fig. 35.
5. Install synchronizer cone on pilot end of mainshaft and slide rearward to clutch hub.

CAUTION: Make sure three cut-out sections of 4th speed synchronizer cone align with three clutch keys in clutch assembly.

6. Install snap ring on clutch gear bearing O.D. Index cut-out portion of clutch gear teeth to obtain clearance over countershaft drive gear teeth and install clutch gear assembly into case. Raise mainshaft to get clutch gear started and tap bearing outer race with plastic tip hammer.
7. Install clutch gear bearing retainer using a new gasket. Tighten bolts to 15-18 ft. lbs.
8. Install Tool J-22874-2 in countergear front bearing opening in case to support countergear and rotate case onto front end, Fig. 36.
9. Install snap ring on countergear rear bearing O.D., position bearing on countergear and using Tool J-22874-1, drive bearing into place. Rotate case, install snap ring on countershaft at rear bearing and then remove tool, Fig. 37.
10. Tap countergear front bearing assembly into case.
11. Install countergear front bearing cap and

CHEVROLET

gasket.
12. Slide speedometer drive gear over mainshaft to bearing.
13. Install rear bearing retainer and new gasket. Be sure snap ring ends are in lube slot and cut-out in bearing retainer. Install bolts and tighten to 15-18 ft. lbs. Install brake backing plate on models equipped with propeller shaft brake.
14. Install parking brake drum and/or universal joint flange.

NOTE: Apply light coat of oil to seal surface.

15. Lock transmission in two gears at once. Install universal joint flange locknut and tighten to 90-120 ft. lbs.
16. Move all transmission gears to neutral except the reverse idler gear which should be engaged approximately 3/8 of an inch (leading edge of reverse idler gear taper lines up with front edge of 1st speed gear). Install cover assembly. Shifting forks must slide into their proper positions on clutch sleeves and reverse idler gear. Forks must be positioned as in removal.
17. Install cover bolts and tighten to 20-25 ft. lbs.

1975-80 El Camino & 1973-75 VEGA 4 SPEED TRANSMISSION

Saginaw Transmission Disassembly

1. Remove side cover assembly and shift

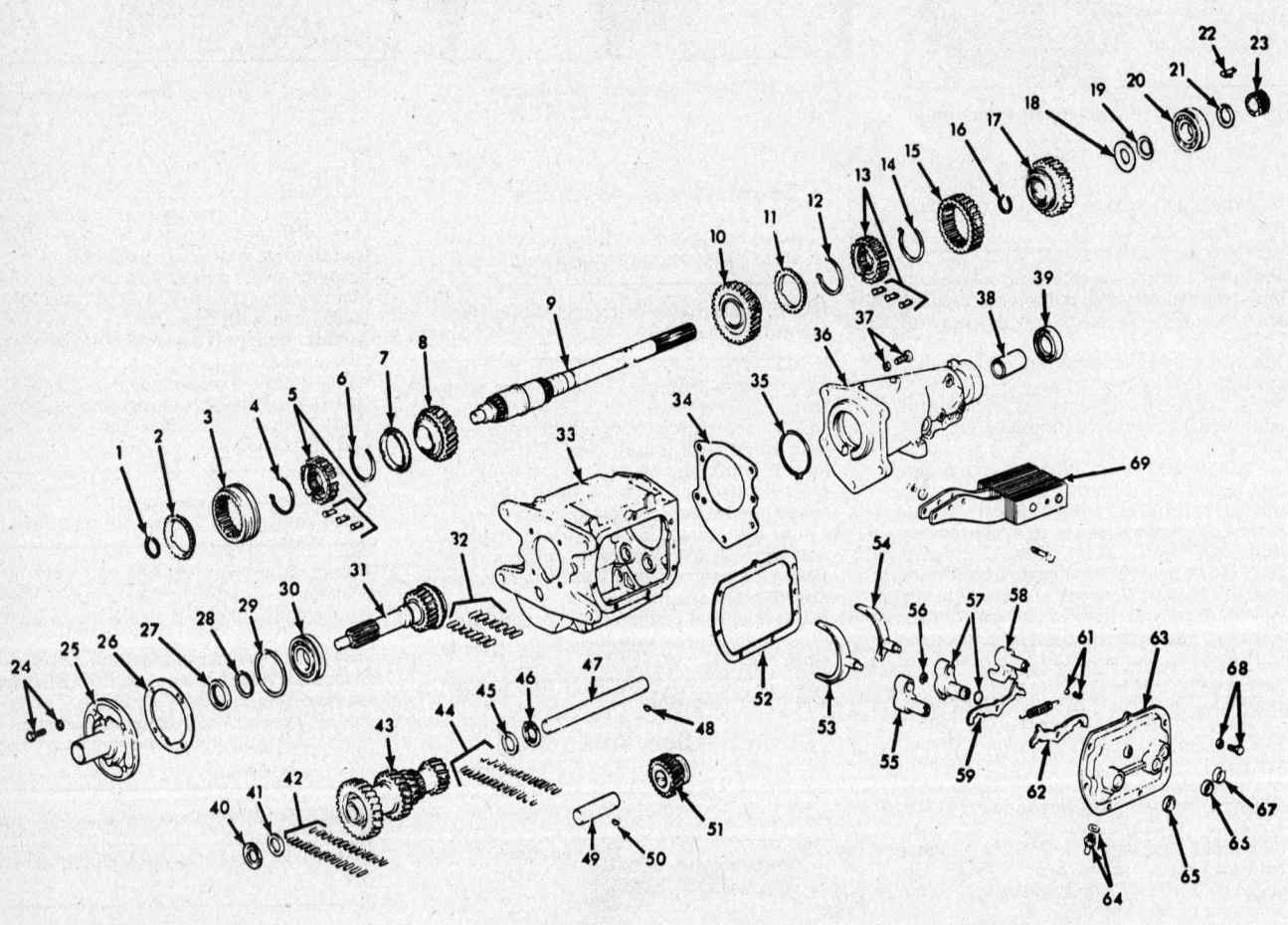

1. Snap ring, Hub to Shaft
2. Synchronizer Ring
3. 3-4 Synchronizer Sleeve
4. Synchronizer Key Spring
5. Synchronizer Hub and Keys
6. Synchronizer Key Spring
7. Synchronizer Ring
8. Third Gear
9. Main Shaft
10. Second Gear
11. Synchronizer Ring
12. Synchronizer Key Spring
13. Synchronizer Hub and Keys
14. Synchronizer Key Spring
15. 1-2 Synchronizer Sleeve & Rev. Gear
16. Snap Ring, Hub to Shaft
17. First Gear
18. Thrust Washer
19. Waved Washer
20. Ring Bearing
21. Snap Ring, Bearing to Shaft
22. Speedometer Gear Clip
23. Speedometer Drive Gear
24. Bearing Retainer Bolts and Washers (4)
25. Front Bearing Retainer
26. Bearing Retainer Gasket
27. Bearing Retainer Oil Seal
28. Snap Ring
29. Bearing Snap Ring
30. Front Bearing
31. Drive Gear
32. Pilot Bearings
33. Case
34. Extension to Case Gasket
35. Rear Bearing to Extension Retaining Ring
36. Rear Extension
37. Extension to Case Retaining Bolts and Washers
38. Rear Extension Bushing
39. Rear Seal
40. Thrust Washer
41. Spacer
42. Countergear Shaft Roller Bearings
43. Countergear
44. Countergear Shaft Roller Bearings
45. Spacer
46. Thrust Washer
47. Countergear Shaft
48. Countergear Shaft Key
49. Reverse Idler Shaft
50. Idler Shaft Key
51. Reverse Idler Gear
52. Side Cover Gasket
53. 3-4 Shift Fork
54. 1-2 Shift Fork
55. 3-4 Shifter Shaft
56. Retaining "E" Ring
57. 1-2 Shifter Shaft with "O" Rings
58. Reverse Shifter Shaft
59. 3-4 Detent Cam
60. Detent Cam Spring
61. Reverse Detent Ball & Spring
62. 1-2 Detent Cam
63. Shift Cover
64. TCS Switch and Gasket
65. Shifter Shaft Seal
66. Shifter Shaft Seal
67. Shift Cover Bolts and Washers
68. Shift Cover Attaching Bolts and Lock Washers
69. Damper Assembly

Fig. 38 Saginaw 4 speed transmission (typical). 1970-80 El Camino & 1973-75 Vega

CHEVROLET

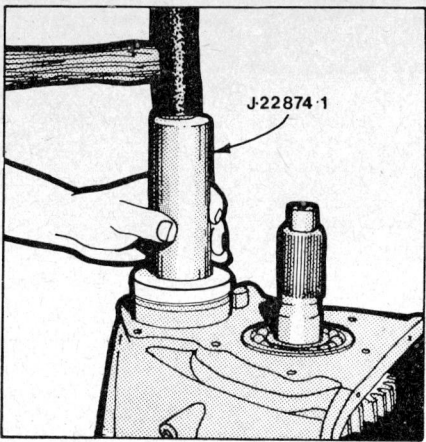

Fig. 37 Installing countergear rear bearing

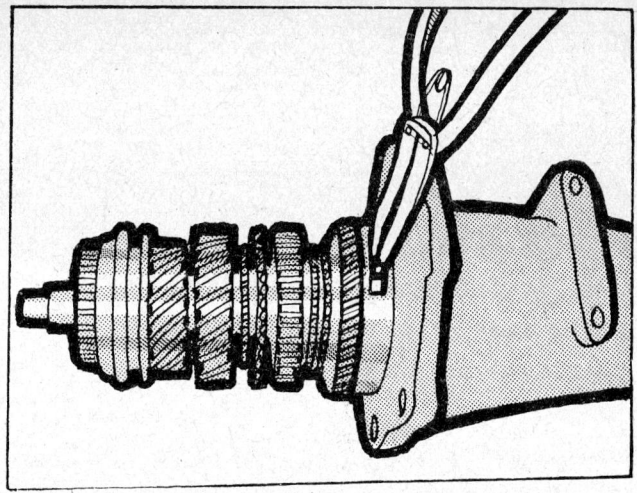

Fig. 40 Removing extension housing

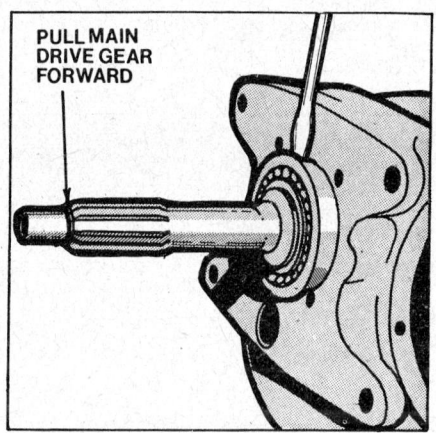

Fig. 39 Removing clutch gear bearing

forks, Fig. 38. Remove damper assembly which is bolted to extension housing.
2. Remove clutch gear bearing retainer.
3. Remove clutch gear bearing to gear stem snap ring, then remove bearing by pulling clutch gear outward until a screwdriver can be inserted between large snap ring and case to complete removal, Fig. 39. Do not remove clutch gear. The bearing is a slip fit on the gear and into the case bore.
4. Remove extension to case bolts and remove clutch gear, mainshaft and extension assembly through rear case opening. Remove clutch gear and blocker ring from mainshaft.
5. Expand extension housing to rear mainshaft bearing snap ring and remove extension, Fig. 40.
6. Using a dummy shaft, drive countershaft and woodruff key out through rear of case, Fig. 41. Dummy shaft will hold roller bearings in position within countergear bore. Remove countergear.
7. Remove reverse idler gear stop ring and, using a long drift, drive idler shaft and woodruff key out through rear of case.

Disassemble Mainshaft

1. Remove snap ring and press 3-4 synchronizer clutch assembly, 3rd speed blocker ring and 3rd gear off mainshaft, Fig. 42.
2. Depress speedometer gear retaining clip and remove gear.
3. Remove rear bearing to mainshaft snap ring, Fig. 43, support 1st gear with press plates and press on rear of mainshaft to remove 1st speed gear, thrust washer, spring washer and rear bearing, Fig. 44.
4. Remove 1-2 sliding clutch hub snap ring, Fig. 45, support 2nd speed gear and press clutch assembly, 2nd speed blocker ring and gear from mainshaft.

Clutch Keys & Springs

NOTE: The clutch hubs and sleeves are a selected assembly and should be kept together as originally assembled, but the keys and springs may be replaced separately.

1. Mark hub and sleeve so they can be matched upon reassembly.
2. Push hub from sliding sleeve and remove keys and springs.
3. Install the three keys and two springs so all three keys are engaged by both springs. The tanged end of each spring should be installed into different key cavities on either side. Slide sleeve onto hub, aligning marks made before disassembly.

NOTE: A groove around the outside of the hub identifies the end that must be opposite the fork slot in the sleeve when assembled. This groove indicates the end of the hub with a .070" greater recess depth.

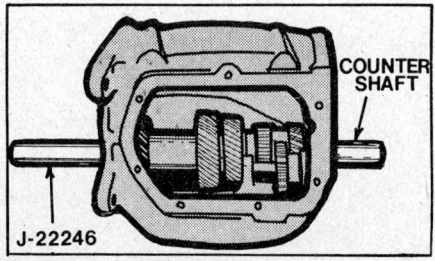

Fig. 41 Removing countershaft

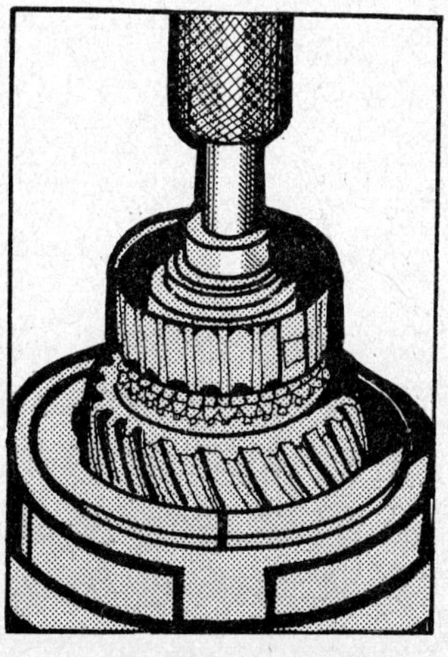

Fig. 42 Removing 3-4 synchronizer assembly

Fig. 43 Removing rear bearing to mainshaft snap ring

901

CHEVROLET

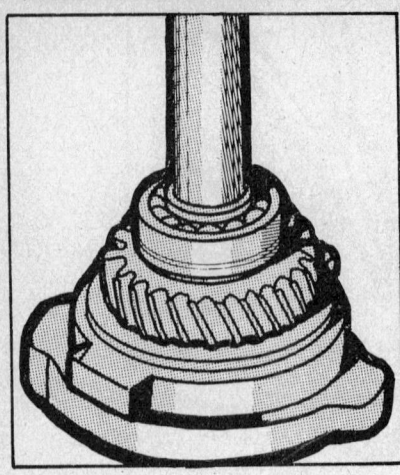

Fig. 44 Removing rear bearing and first speed gear

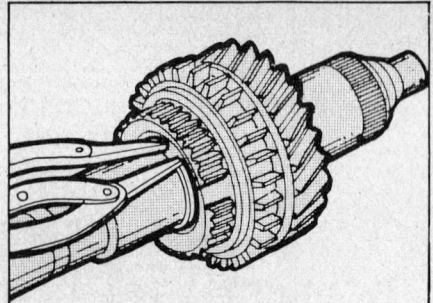

Fig. 45 Removing first and second synchronizer snap ring

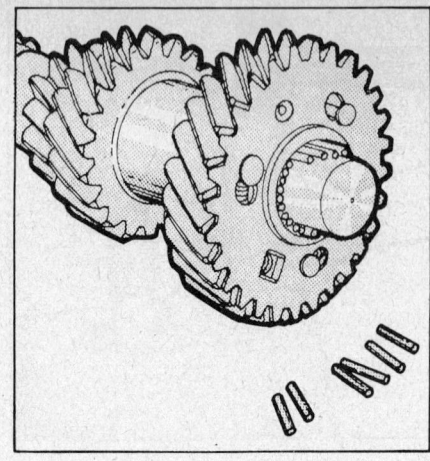

Fig. 46 Loading roller bearings into countergear

Assemble Mainshaft

With front of mainshaft up:
1. Install 3rd speed gear with clutching teeth upward.
2. Install blocker ring with clutching teeth downward over cone of gear. All blocker rings in this unit are identical.
3. Install 3-4 synchronizer assembly with fork slot downward and press it onto mainshaft until it bottoms. *Be sure the notches of the blocker ring align with the keys of the synchronizer assembly.*
4. Install synchronizer hub to mainshaft snap ring. Both synchronizer snap rings are identical.

With rear of mainshaft upward:
5. Install 2nd speed gear with clutching teeth upward.
6. Install a blocker ring with clutching teeth downward over cone of gear.
7. Press 1-2 synchronizer assembly onto mainshaft with fork slot downward. *Be sure notches in blocker ring align with keys of synchronizer assembly.*
8. Install synchronizer hub snap ring.
9. Install a blocker ring with notches downward so they align with the synchronizer keys.
10. Install 1st gear with clutching teeth downward. Install 1st gear thrust washer and spring washer.
11. Press rear bearing onto mainshaft. Install snap ring.
12. Install speedometer drive gear and clip.

Transmission Assembly

1. Load a row of roller bearings and a thrust washer at each end of the countergear, Fig. 46. Use heavy grease to hold them in place.
2. Install countergear through case rear opening with a tanged thrust washer at each end and install countershaft and woodruff key from rear of case. *Be sure countershaft picks up both thrust washers and that the tangs are aligned with their notches in the case.*
3. Install reverse idler gear, shaft and woodruff key from rear of case.
4. Expand extension housing snap ring and assemble extension housing over mainshaft.
5. Load roller bearings into clutch gear bore, using heavy grease to hold them in place, place blocker ring on gear cone with teeth toward gear, and install gear and ring onto mainshaft. Do not install clutch gear bearing at this time. *Be sure notches in blocker ring align with synchronizer keys.*
6. Using new gasket, install mainshaft and extension assembly through rear opening in case. Use sealing cement on bottom bolt.
7. Install large outer snap ring on clutch gear bearing and install bearing onto gear and into case bore. Install gear stem snap ring and bearing retainer.

NOTE: The retainer oil hole should be at the bottom.

8. With transmission in neutral, install cover assembly. *Be sure the shift forks are properly aligned in their grooves in the synchronizer sleeves before attempting to tighten cover bolts.*

WARNER T10 4 SPEED
1970 Chevy Van

For service procedures on this unit, see Warner transmission section in the front of this manual.

WARNER 4 SPEED, 1975-80
El Camino

For service procedures on this transmission refer to GMC Chapter, Manual Shift Transmission Section, Warner 4 Speed, 1975-80 Sprint.

CHEVROLET

Automatic Transmission Section

> For Allison (Powermatic, AT540, MT640, 650), Powerglide and Turbo Hydra-Matic (200, 250, 350, 400, 475) used on Chevrolet, see the "name" chapters for service procedures

POWERMATIC, 1970-71

Transmission, Replace

1. Remove spark plugs and disconnect battery ground strap.
2. Remove filter cartridge from transmission oil pan.
3. Remove control tower.
4. Disconnect throttle valve control rod from lever.
5. Disconnect retarder pedal rod from lever at transmission and unhook return spring from shaft at right side of transmission.
6. Remove oil filler tube and hose.
7. Disconnect oil cooler lines at brake valve body and warning signal wire from sender at top of oil line tee.
8. Disconnect speedometer driven shaft fitting from adapter.
9. Remove propeller shaft and bearing support, and hand brake assembly.
10. Remove flywheel underpan and, turning flywheel as necessary, remove flywheel-to-converter pump cover nuts.
11. Support rear of engine and remove converter housing-to-flywheel housing bolts.
12. Support transmission in suitable cradle and remove transmission mounting bolts.
13. Remove transmission rear support from frame, move transmission to rear slightly and lower from under vehicle.
14. Reverse the foregoing procedure to install the transmission.

Control Linkage, Adjust (Except Tilt Cab)

1. Insert a 1/4" steel pin approximately 3" long through point "A", Fig. 1. This pin must pass through bosses on both sides of lever and a boss on the support bracket.
2. Place carburetor on hot idle stop and position TV rod full rearward against internal stop in transmission. To hold this rod in position a retaining wire must be inserted through the TV lever on the transmission and into a small hole on the transmission pan.
3. Insert swivel "B" on rod "X" into the accelerator control outer lever, then tighten compression nut. *Use the upper hole in the control lever for four barrel carburetor and the lower hole for the two barrel carburetor.*
4. Insert swivel "C" on the TV rod into the accelerator inner lever, then tighten compression nut.
5. If installed, remove the retaining wire from TV lever on transmission. Rotate accelerator control levers through detent. Adjust accelerator pedal rod at "D" so that surface "E" comes in full contact

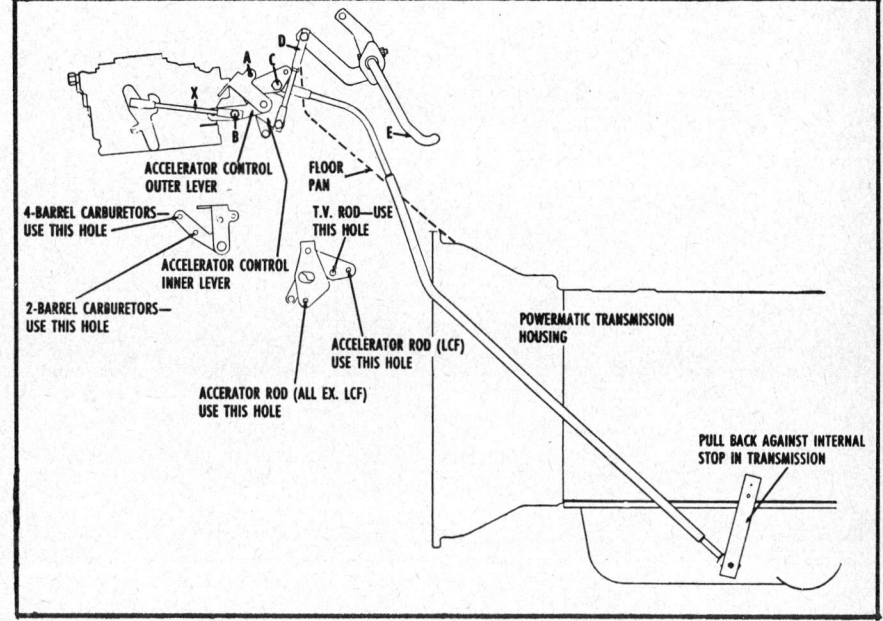

Fig. 1 Linkage adjustment (typical). Powermatic

with floor mat. The L.C.F. accelerator rod attaches at rearmost hole on the inboard arm of the inner lever. All others attach to the lower hole of the outboard arm of the inner control lever. *If engine idles too fast after adjusting, recheck linkage adjustment. Be sure carburetor idle speed screw is fully off the fast idle cam throughout adjustment.*

Hydraulic Retarder Linkage

The adjustment of the hydraulic retarder linkage is fundamentally the same as hydraulic clutch pedal adjustment described in the Clutch Section. However, the hydraulic retarder pedal is adjusted to give 1/8" free pedal travel.

Once the pedal is adjusted, final adjustment of the hydraulic retarder control linkage is completed at the slave cylinder which actuates the hydraulic retarder valve at the Powermatic.

To adjust the slave cylinder, fully depress the slave cylinder push rod into the cylinder, then adjust the clevis on the push rod for free entry to the hydraulic retarder valve lever on the transmission.

Tilt Cab Models

1. Insert a 3" long pin of 1/4" diameter through two holes and notch, Fig. 2, to retain linkage in proper position.
2. With carburetor-to-lever rod clamp nut loose, place carburetor on normal idle stop and tighten clamp nut.
3. With clamp nut loose on transmission throttle valve rod and the TV lever on transmission held fully to the rear, tighten TV rod clamp nut.

Range Selector Linkage

The shift control cable is designed so the only adjustment is on the lower clevis at the transmission shift lever. Place the shift tower shifter lever in full "Lo" position, and the shift on the transmission full rearward. Adjust clevis on cable to insert clevis pin freely in hole in transmission shift lever and secure with cotter pin. Shift slowly a few times to insure that the shift lever is not at the end of its travel at either end of the slot before the detent acts.

AT540, MT640, 650, 654

Transmission, Replace

1. Disconnect battery ground cable and remove spark plugs so that engine can be turned manually.
2. Remove dipstick and drain transmission

CHEVROLET

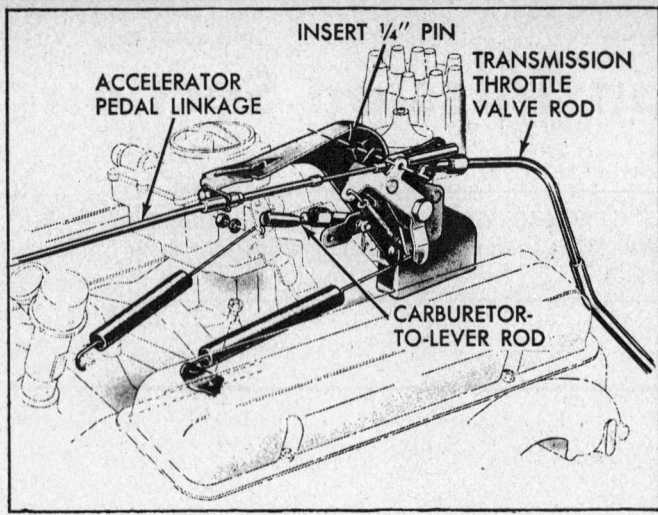

Fig. 2 Powermatic linkage adjustment (typical). Tilt Cab models

fluid.
3. Disconnect oil cooler lines from transmission and disconnect shift cable from transmission shift lever.
4. Disconnect vacuum modulator line, back-up light switch connector, speedometer and parking brake linkage.
5. Remove propeller shaft.
6. Remove the six flex plate-to-converter retaining nuts through access hole in transmission. Rotate flywheel as necessary to gain access to the nuts.
7. Support transmission using a transmission jack (750 lbs. minimum rating), and secure transmission to jack with a safety chain.

NOTE: Position jack so that transmission oil pan will not support weight of transmission.

8. Support engine and remove transmission to crossmember bolts, then raise engine to remove weight from rear engine mounts.
9. Remove transmission to flywheel housing bolts.

NOTE: Inspect transmission and surrounding area to make sure that no lines, hose or wires will interfere with transmission removal.

10. Move transmission rearward, then lower and carefully remove transmission.

NOTE: Keep rear of transmission lower than the front so as not to lose converter.

11. Reverse procedure to install. Torque transmission to flywheel housing bolts to 12–16 ft. lbs., and flex plate to converter bolts to 34–40 ft. lbs.

Control Linkage, Adjust
AT540, MT640, 650

1. Check cable for dimension shown in view A-A, Figs. 3 and 4, and adjust cable as necessary. Make sure that cable is properly secured at point (D, AT540) or (C, MT640, 650).
2. Disconnect clevis (G, AT540) or (D, MT640, 650). Make sure that cable is properly secured at point (F).
3. Place shift lever (B) against stop in "Reverse" position.
4. Place transmission shift lever (H, AT540) or (E, MT640, 650) in "Reverse" position by rotating lever completely counter-clockwise.
5. Adjust clevis (G, AT540) or (D, MT640, 650) so that clevis pin enters transmission shift lever (H, AT540) or (E, MT640, 650) freely. Shorten cable by rotating

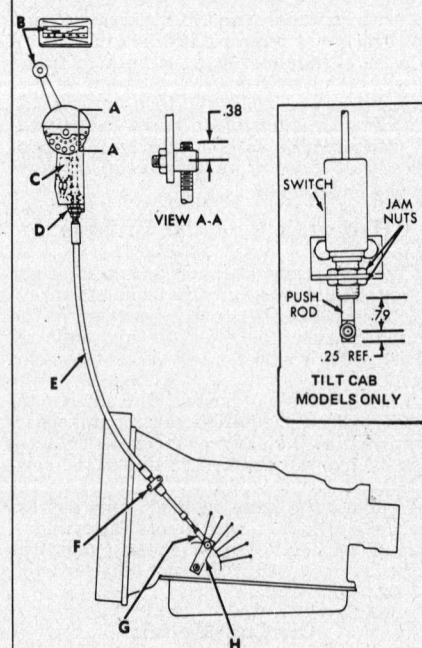

Fig. 3 Linkage adjustment. AT540

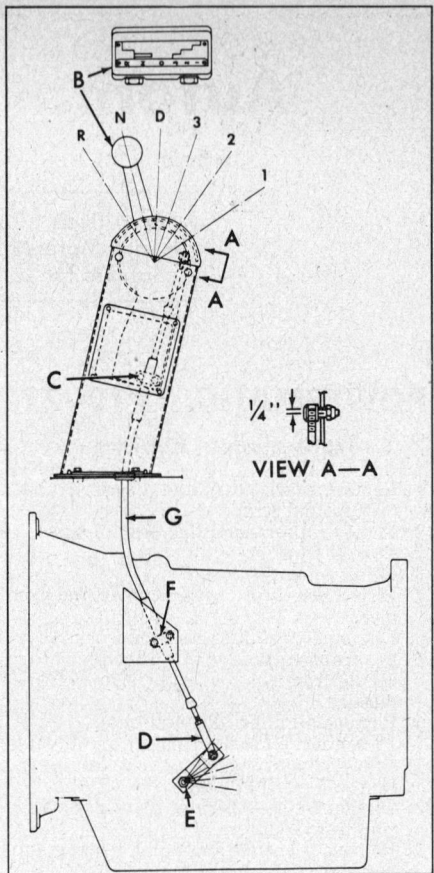

Fig. 4 Linkage adjustment. MT640, 650

clevis two turns clockwise on 1970–73 models; and one turn clockwise on 1974–79 models. Then tighten locknut against clevis, install clevis pin and cotter pin.
6. Check for proper operation of shift lever through all operating ranges.

MT654

NOTE: Before making adjustment, ensure controls are not damaged and operate smoothly.

1. Place range selector lever against stop in "Reverse" position, Fig. 5.
2. Disconnect clevis from transmission lever.
3. Move transmission shift lever fully counterclockwise to "Reverse".
4. Loosen clevis jam nut and adjust clevis until holes on clevis and transmission lever are aligned, then install clevis pin. Adjust clevis 1/2 turn at a time until pin enters freely.
5. Turn clevis one full turn clockwise to allow for cable backlash.
6. Connect clevis to lever and secure with a new cotter pin.
7. Check for proper operation.

POWERGLIDE
Transmission, Replace

Chevy Van
1. Support engine with a jack and remove

CHEVROLET

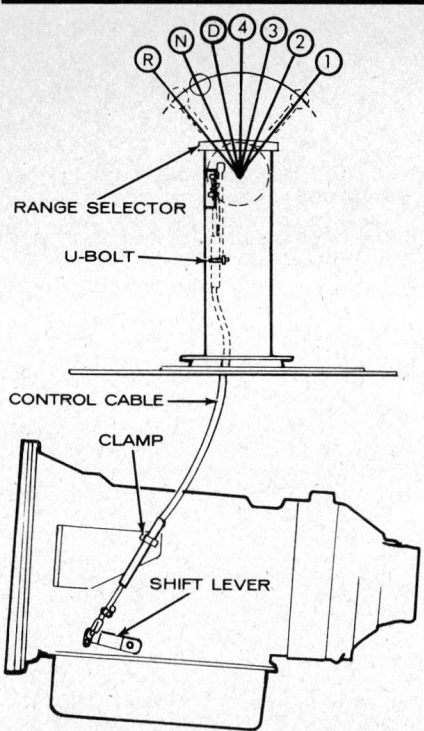

Fig. 5 Shift linkage adjustment. MT654 models

9. Move transmission slightly to rear and downward and out of vehicle.
10. Reverse removal procedure to install transmission. Check for any oil leaks and adjust linkage as required.

Models other than Chevy Van
1. Disconnect vacuum modulator line and speedometer drive cable fitting at transmission. Tie lines out of the way.
2. Disconnect manual and TV control lever rods from transmission.
3. Disconnect propeller shaft from transmission.
4. Support transmission with jack or lift.
5. Disconnect engine rear mount on transmission extension, then remove transmission support crossmember.
6. Remove converter underpan, scribe flywheel-converter relationship, then remove flywheel-to-converter attaching bolts.

NOTE: The "light" side of the converter is noted by a "blue" stripe painted across the ends of the converter cover and housing. This marking should be aligned as closely as possible with the "white" stripe painted on the engine side of the flywheel outer rim (heavy side of engine) to maintain balance during assembly.

7. Support engine at oil pan rail with a jack or other suitable brace capable of supporting engine weight when transmission is removed.
8. Lower rear of transmission slightly so that upper transmission-to-engine bolts can be reached with a universal socket and long extension. Remove upper bolts.

CAUTION: It is best to have a helper observe clearance of upper engine components while transmission rear end is being lowered.

9. Remove remaining transmission attaching bolts.
10. Remove transmission by moving it slight-

propeller shaft.
2. Disconnect control rods from transmission levers, and remove neutral safety switch wire harness.
3. Remove speedometer cable, vacuum line at modulator, and oil cooler lines at transmission.
4. Remove engine rear mount-to-bracket thru bolt.
5. Remove linkage cross shaft from attaching bolts and accelerator linkage at bellcrank before lowering engine. Lower engine enough to allow rear engine mount housing to clear its support bracket.
6. Attach transmission jack or lift to transmission.
7. Remove converter underpan. Scribe flywheel-converter relationship for reassembly, then remove flywheel-to-converter bolts.

NOTE: The "light" side of the converter is denoted by a blue stripe painted across the ends of the converter cover and housing. This marking should be aligned as closely as possible with the white stripe painted on the engine side of the flywheel outer rim (heavy side of engine) to maintain balance during reassembly.

8. Remove transmission-to-engine bolts.

NOTE: Observe converter when moving transmission rearward. If it does not move with transmission, pry it free of flywheel before proceeding. Keep front of transmission upward to prevent converter from falling out. Attach a brace or a length of strong wire to hold converter in position immediately after removal from engine.

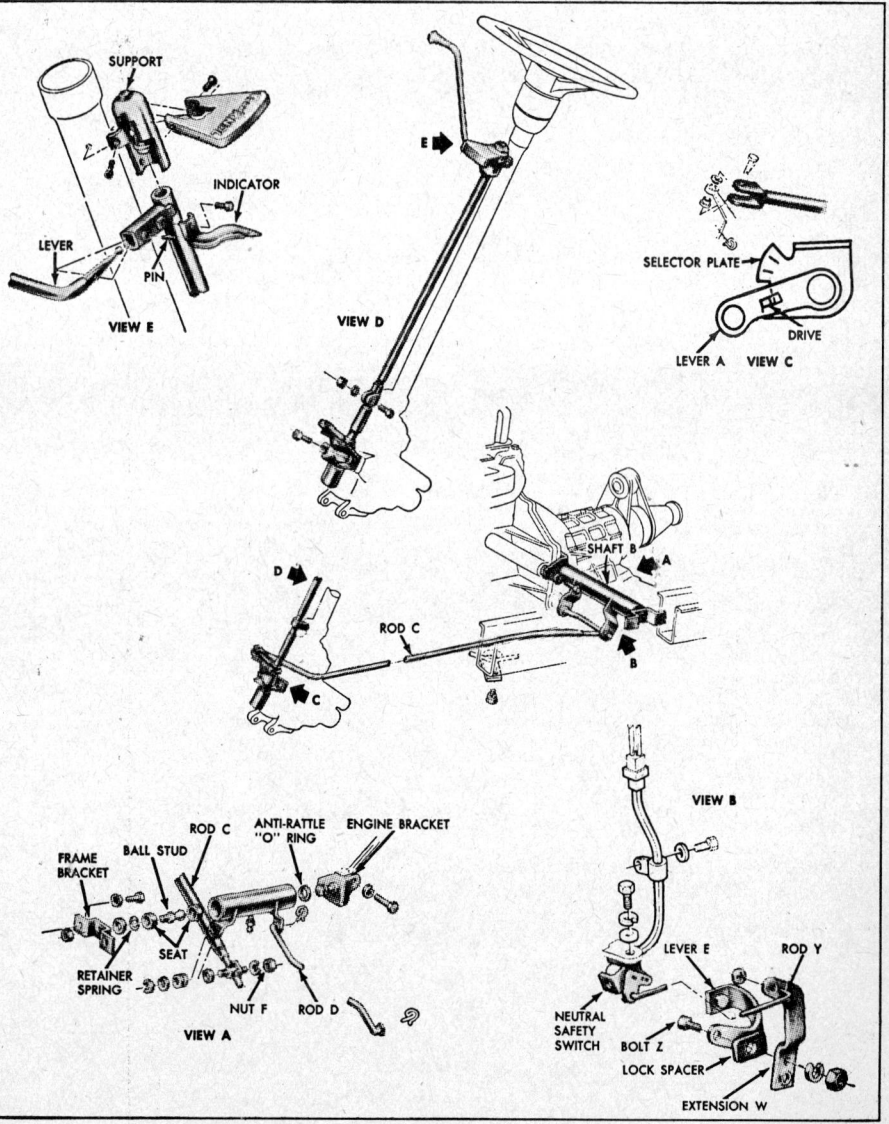

Fig. 6 Powerglide shift control linkage. Chevy Van

CHEVROLET

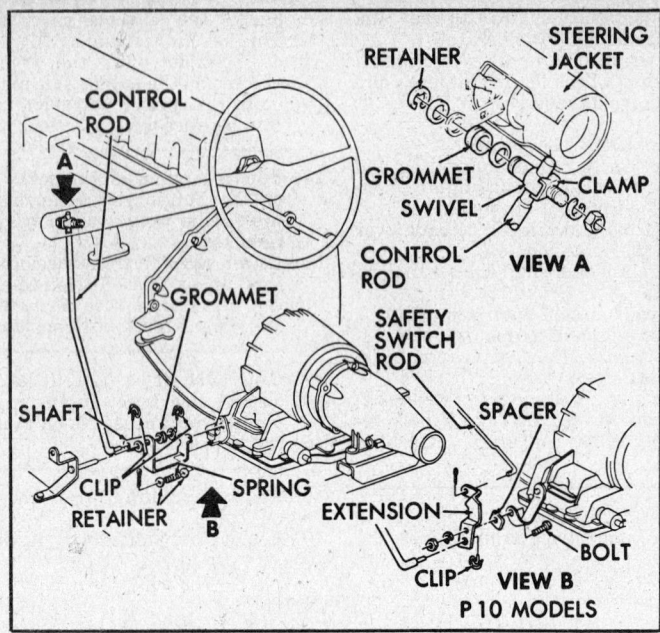

Fig. 7 Aluminum Powerglide shift linkage (typical)

ly to rear and downward, then remove from beneath vehicle.

CAUTION: Keep front of transmission upward to keep converter from falling out. Better still, attach a brace or strong wire across front of converter attached to housing.

11. Reverse removal procedure to install transmission and adjust shift linkage as outlined below.

Shift Linkage, Adjust

Chevy Van

Whenever the linkage has been completely removed, as when replacing the transmission, the following procedure should be strictly adhered to:
1. Referring to Fig. 5, loosely assemble extension (W) to control lever (E), view B.
2. With both transmission and neutral safety switch (pinned) in neutral position, attach switch rod (Y) to neutral switch and lever extension (W). Tighten extension bolt (Z). Then remove pin from neutral switch.
3. Tube and lever (A) must be free in mast jacket. Be certain there is no bind.
4. Set lever (E) in "Drive" position. Obtain drive position by moving transmission lever counterclockwise to low detent, then clockwise one detent to drive.
5. Attach control rod (D) to extension lever (W) and shaft (B) with retainers (view A).
6. Assemble parts shown in view "A" loosely on shaft.
7. Insert control rod (E) in swivel and retainer and attach opposite end of tube and lever (view C).
8. Set tube lever in drive position and tighten nut (F) views A and C.

NOTE: When above procedure is adhered to, the following conditions must be met by manual operation of steering column shift lever: From reverse to drive position travel the transmission detent feel must be noted and related to indicated position on dial. When in Drive and Reverse position, pull lever upward (toward steering wheel) and then release. It must drop back into position with no restriction.

CAUTION: Any inaccuracies in the above adjustment may result in premature failure of the transmission due to operation without controls in full detent. Such operation results in reduced oil pressure and in turn partial engagement of the affected clutches. Partial engagement of the clutches with sufficient pressure to cause apparent normal operation of the vehicle will result in failure of clutches or other internal parts after only a few miles of operation.

Models other than Chevy Van & Vega

1. With engine stopped, lift up on range selector lever and move lever to the position where transmission "Drive" detent is felt.
2. Slowly release lever to feel if shaft lever tang freely enters lock plate.

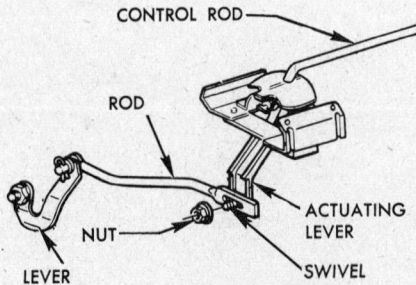

Fig. 8 Shift linkage adjustment. 1973-75 Vega Typical

3. Check "Reverse" range in similar manner.
4. If tang does not freely enter lock plate in both drive and reverse ranges, adjust as follows, referring to Fig. 7.
5. Position range selector lever in driving compartment in "D". Disconnect shift control rod at its swivel attachment to shift control lever on lower end of mast jacket by loosening clamp nut.
6. Place transmission shift control outer lever in Drive position.

NOTE: *Drive detent in transmission is the first clockwise detent position from fully counterclockwise detent or "L" position.*

7. Hold shift control lever (at lower end of mast jacket) against Drive stop of range selector lock plate. With control rod through swivel, tighten clamp nut.
8. Test transmission shifts in all ranges.

1973-75 Vega
1. Place transmission lever in Neutral by rotating lever clockwise to Park, then two detents counter-clockwise to Neutral.
2. Place shift lever in Neutral.
3. Insert flats on swivel into slot in rod and tighten nut to 120 pound inches, Fig. 8.

1971-72 Vega
1. Loosen nut and perform steps 1 and 2 as outlined in the 1973 Vega Console Shift adjustment.
2. Apply rearward force on lever until shift lever contacts detent stop. Install a 0.73 inch spacer between forward nut and swivel and tighten nut against spacer, Fig. 9.
3. Remove spacer and apply a forward force on lever and tighten rearward nut.

Throttle Linkage, Adjust

Chevy Van
1. Referring to Fig. 10, transmission lever (A) must be rotated counter-clockwise against internal transmission stop.
2. Assemble rod (C) to transmission lever.
3. Install swivel (B) on rod, and with accelerator lever in wide open position, adjust swivel on rod to freely enter hole in transmission lever.
4. Lengthen rod by rotating swivel three complete turns and install swivel in transmission lever.

Models other than Chevy Van & Vega

Throttle valve linkage must be adjusted so that when the carburetor throttle valve (or valves) is fully closed (hot idle) the transmission throttle valve lever must be all the way toward the rear of the transmission against its internal stop.

To make the adjustment, first disconnect the throttle linkage at the carburetor to relieve all tension from the rest of the linkage. Then disconnect the throttle rod from the throttle lever at the transmission. Hold the throttle lever back against its stop and adjust the throttle rod clevis, swivel or trunnion (whichever is used) so that the throttle rod can be attached to the throttle lever without moving the lever away from its stop. The throttle linkage at the carburetor can then be adjusted so that the carburetor throttle valve is fully closed (hot idle).

If a road test indicates that the shifts occur too early, shorten the rod a turn or two. If the shifts occur late lengthen the rod a turn or two. Again road test and, if necessary, alter the adjustment as required to obtain the desired result.

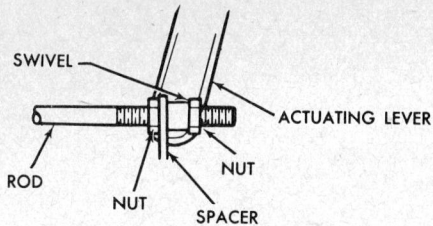

Fig. 9 Shift linkage adjustment. 1971-72 Vega

Vega
1. Place carburetor bell crank in wide open throttle position and transmission lever against internal stop.
2. Align 90 degree rod with hole in lever, Fig. 11, and install retainer through sleeve and rod. Attach clip to lever and rod.

TURBO HYDRA-MATIC "200"

Transmission, Replace

1977-80 El Camino
1. Disconnect battery ground cable.
2. Remove air cleaner and dipstick. Then disconnect detent cable at bracket and carburetor.
3. On models equipped with A/C, remove heater core cover screws, then disconnect wiring connector and position heater core cover with hoses aside.
4. Raise and support vehicle.
5. Remove propeller shaft, then disconnect speedometer cable, oil cooler lines, case electrical connector and shift linkage.
6. Place a suitable jack under transmission and remove transmission rear support to frame side rail bolts.
7. Disconnect catalytic converter bracket from transmission support. Disconnect rear exhaust pipe from catalytic converter, and front pipe from manifold and remove from vehicle.
8. Remove torque converter cover and converter-to-flexplate bolts.
9. Lower transmission until jack is barely supporting it and remove transmission-to-engine bolts.
10. Raise transmission to its normal position. Place a jack under engine and remove transmission rearward from engine and lower from vehicle.

NOTE: Keep front of transmission upward to prevent torque converter from falling out.

11. Reverse procedure to install.

Shift Linkage, Adjust
1. Position shifter assembly in "NEUTRAL", Figs. 11A & 11B.
2. Position transmission shift lever in "NEUTRAL".

NOTE: Obtain "NEUTRAL" position by moving transmission lever clockwise to maximum detent (PARK). Then move lever two detent positions counterclockwise (NEUTRAL).

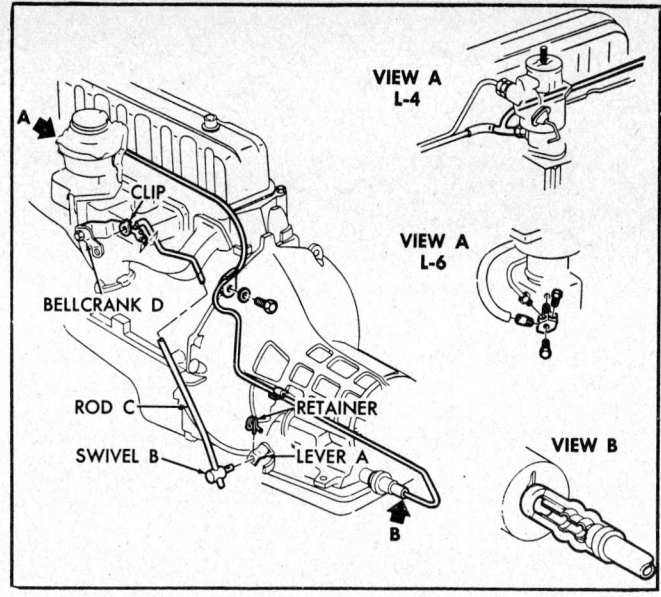

Fig. 10 Powerglide throttle valve linkage. Chevy Van

3. On console shift models, adjust the rod until hole in the rod aligns with shifter pin and install rod on pin.
4. On column shift models, adjust the rod until hold in lever assembly aligns with hole in swivel.
5. On console shift models, install washer and clip. On column shift models, install swivel screw with spring washer.

Detent Cable, Adjust

For detent cable adjustment, refer to the Turbo Hydra-Matic 350 procedure for 1973-80 models.

TURBO HYDRA-MATIC "250"

Transmission, Replace

For transmission replacement, refer to the Turbo Hydra-Matic 350 procedure.

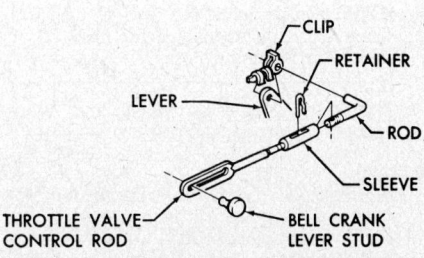

Fig. 11 Throttle linkage adjustment. Vega

Shift Linkage, Adjust

For shift linkage adjustment, refer to the Turbo Hydra-Matic 350 procedure.

Detent Cable, Adjust

For detent cable adjustment, refer to the Turbo Hydra-Matic 350 procedure under 1973-80 models.

TURBO HYDRA-MATIC "350"

Transmission, Replace

1970-72 Blazer
1. Remove floor cover. Remove transfer case shift lever and rod.
2. Raise vehicle and drain transmission.
3. Disconnect vacuum modulator line, speedometer cable and manual linkage.
4. Disconnect front and rear axle drive shafts at transfer case.
5. Remove transmission-to-adapter case bolts and place suitable support under transfer case. Remove transfer case-to-frame bolts and remove transfer case.
6. On V8 units, remove exhaust cross-over pipe.
7. Support transmission with suitable jack and remove crossmember.
8. Remove converter under pan and remove flywheel-to-converter bolts.
9. Support engine at oil pan rail with suitable jack.
10. Carefully lower rear of transmission and remove upper transmission-to-engine bolts. Be sure to observe clearance of upper engine components when lowering transmission.
11. Remove remainder of transmission retaining bolts and remove transmission.

NOTE: Use caution to avoid dropping converter when removing transmission.

CHEVROLET

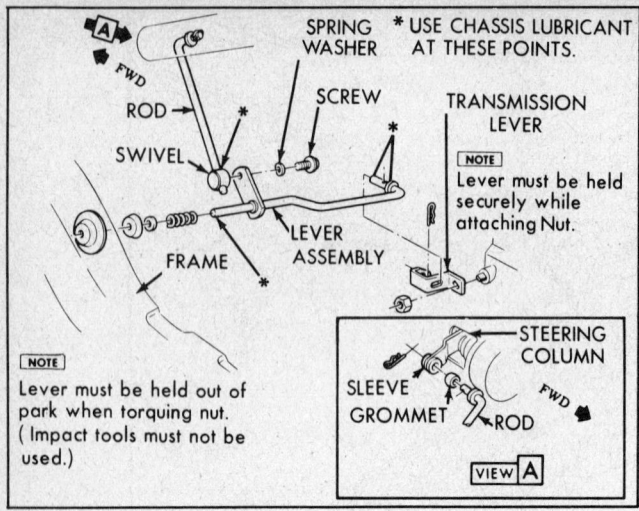

Fig. 11A Shift linkage adjustment. Turbo Hydra-matic 200 with column shift

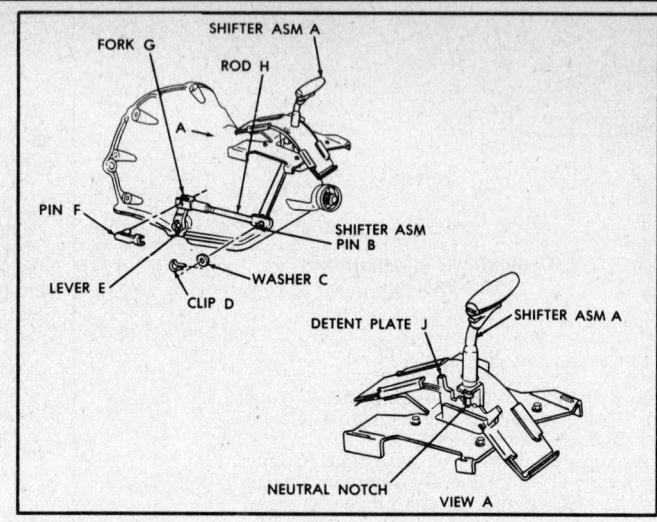

Fig. 11B Shift linkage adjustment. Turbo Hydra-matic 200 with console shift

(Except 1970–72 Blazer & 1973–80 Four Wheel Drive models)
1. Place truck on hoist and drain oil.
2. Disconnect vacuum modulator line and speedometer cable at transmission.
3. Disconnect manual control lever rod and detent cable from transmission.
4. Disconnect propeller shaft from transmission.
5. Install suitable lift equipment and attach on transmission.
6. Disconnect engine rear mount on transmission extension and remove transmission support crossmember. Remove engine rear mount to bracket nut, washer and thru bolt on GA-10, 20 models.
7. Remove converter underpan and mark flywheel-converter relationship for proper assembly, then remove flywheel to converter bolts.
8. Support engine at oil pan rail with a jack of suitable brace to support engine weight when transmission is removed.
9. Lower rear of transmission slightly so upper transmission housing to engine bolts can be reached using a universal socket and a long extension. Remove upper bolts.
10. Remove remaining transmission housing to engine bolts and remove transmission by moving it slightly to the rear and downward.

CAUTION: Keep front of transmission upward to prevent converter from falling out.

1973–80 Four Wheel Drive models
1. Disconnect battery negative cable and the detent cable from carburetor, remove transmission dipstick and drain transmission.
2. Remove transfer case shift lever knob and boot, then raise vehicle.
3. Remove flywheel cover and converter to flywheel bolts.
4. Disconnect shift linkage, speedometer cable, vacuum modulator line, line to filler tube clip, detent cable to filler tube strap and oil cooler lines.
5. Remove crossover pipe to manifold bolts.
6. Remove transfer case adapter to crossmember bolts, raise engine slightly and remove crossmember.
7. Disconnect rear propeller shaft from transfer case, front propeller shaft from front axle, parking brake cable and exhaust system.
8. Support transmission and transfer case with a suitable jack, then remove transfer case to frame bolts and engine to transmission bolts.
9. Remove transmission and transfer case assembly, then separate transfer case from transmission.

Shift Linkage, Adjust
1. Place selector lever in "D".
2. Loosen adjustment swivel at mast jacket lever and rotate the transmission lever until it contacts the drive stop in the steering column.
3. Tighten the swivel and recheck.

Detent Cable, Adjust
Exc. 1973–80
1. Remove air cleaner and loosen detent cable screw.
2. With choke off and accelerator linkage properly adjusted position carburetor lever in wide open throttle position.
3. Pull detent cable rearward until wide open throttle stop in transmission is felt.

NOTE: Cable must be pulled through detent position to reach wide open throttle stop in transmission.

4. Tighten detent cable screw and check linkage for proper operation.

1973–80
Disconnect downshift cable from snap-lock at cable mounting bracket, then position carburetor to wide open throttle and push snap-lock downward until top is flush with remainder of cable.

TURBO HYDRA-MATIC "400", "475"

Transmission, Replace
1. Remove battery ground cable and release parking brake.
2. Raise vehicle on hoist and remove drive shaft.
3. Disconnect speedometer cable, electrical lead to case connector, vacuum line at modulator and oil cooler pipes and shift control linkage.
4. Support transmission with suitable jack and disconnect rear mount from frame crossmember. Remove cross-member.
5. Remove converter under pan, remove converter-to-flywheel bolts.
6. Loosen exhaust pipe to manifold bolts approximately 1/4" and lower transmission until jack is barely supporting it.
7. Remove transmission to engine mounting bolts and remove oil filler tube at transmission.
8. Raise transmission to its normal position, support engine with jack and slide transmission rearward from engine and lower it away from vehicle.

NOTE: Use suitable converter holding tool or be sure to keep rear of transmission lower than front to prevent the converter from sliding off.

Shift Linkage, Adjust

NOTE: Do not use shift indicator pointer as a reference to position the selector lever. When adjusting linkage, the pointer is adjusted last.

1. Place selector lever in Drive (D) position as determined by the transmission detent.
2. Loosen adjustment swivel at the mast jacket and rotate the transmission lever so that it contacts the Drive stop in the steering column.

CHEVROLET

3. Tighten the swivel and recheck adjustment.
4. Readjust indicator pointer if necessary to agree with the transmission detent positions.
5. Readjust neutral safety switch if necessary so the engine will start only in the Park and Neutral positions.

Throttle Linkage, Adjust

Except TE-TE 40-50, 60, GS 100-200, GE 100-200
1. Depress accelerator to the floor.
2. Hold carburetor or governor lever in the wide open throttle position.
3. Adjust swivel on accelerator control rod until it freely enters hole in lever.

TE-TE 40-50-60
1. Depress accelerator to the floor.
2. Hold carburetor throttle lever in the wide open throttle position.
3. Install accelerator cable assembly with sleeve tube nut and ball joint sleeve into ball joint and tighten sleeve tube nut.

GS 100-200, GE 100-200
1. Insert 3/16" diameter gauge pin into hole in lever and accelerator bracket.
2. With carburetor in the wide open throttle position, adjust upper swivel to freely enter hole in lever.
3. Depress accelerator to 1/4" from floor.
4. Install lower rod and adjust lower swivel to freely enter hole in lever.
5. Install clips on swivels and remove gauge pin.

Rear Axle Section

> For Eaton and Timken (Rockwell) driving axles used on Chevrolet trucks, see the "name" chapters for service procedures and lubricant capacities

Chevrolet Axles & Lube Capacities

Axle Type	Rated Lbs. Capacity	Lube Pints
1970–72		
Semi-floating	2400	3 1/2
Semi-floating	2900	4 1/2
Semi-floating	3300	4 1/2
Semi-floating	3500	4 1/2
Full-floating	5200	6 1/2
Full-floating	7200	6 1/2
Full-floating	11000	18
Full-floating	13500	20
Full-floating	15000	19
Full-floating	17000	19
Two-Speed	15000	20
Two-Speed	17000	20
Tandem	28000	19
1973–80		
Semi-floating	1885	2.8
Semi-floating	2700	4.2
Semi-floating	3100	4.2 ①
Semi-floating	3500	4.2 ①
Semi-floating	3750	4.2 ①
Full-floating	5700	5.4
Full-floating	6200	6
Full-floating	7500	5.4
Full-floating	7500	7.2
Full-floating	10000	7.2
Full-floating	11000	14
Full-floating	13500	20
Full-floating	15000	20
Two Speed	15000	18
Full-floating	17000	19 1/2
Two Speed	17000	29 1/2
Two Speed	18500	29 1/2

①—Models with 8 7/8 inch ring gear, 3.5 pts.

CHEVROLET SALISBURY TYPE SEMI-FLOATING AXLE

1970–80

In these rear axles, Figs. 1 & 2, the rear axle housing and differential carrier are cast into an integral assembly. The drive pinion assembly is mounted in two opposed tapered roller bearings. The pinion bearings are preloaded by a spacer behind the front bearing. The pinion is positioned by a washer between the head of the pinion and the rear bearing.

The differential is supported in the carrier by two tapered roller side bearings. These bearings are preloaded by spacers located between the bearings and carrier housing. The differential assembly is positioned for proper ring gear and pinion backlash by varying these spacers. The differential case houses two side gears in mesh with two pinions mounted on a pinion shaft which is held in place by a lock pin. The side gears and pinions

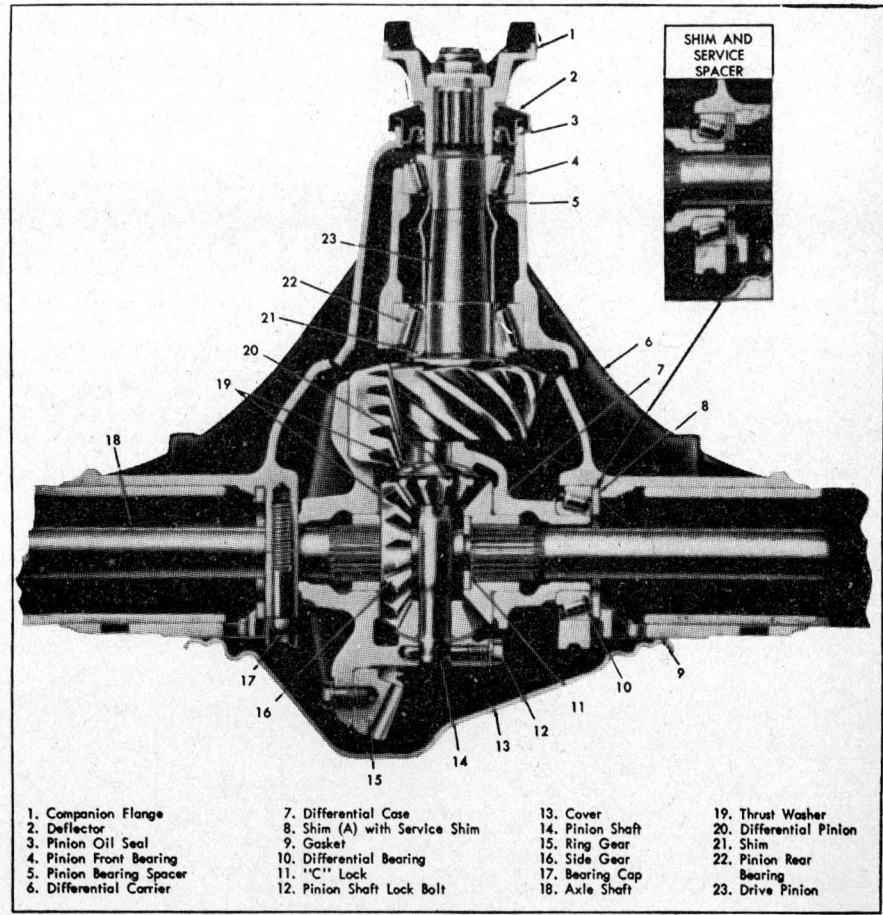

1. Companion Flange
2. Deflector
3. Pinion Oil Seal
4. Pinion Front Bearing
5. Pinion Bearing Spacer
6. Differential Carrier
7. Differential Case
8. Shim (A) with Service Shim
9. Gasket
10. Differential Pinion
11. "C" Lock
12. Pinion Shaft Lock Bolt
13. Cover
14. Pinion Shaft
15. Ring Gear
16. Side Gear
17. Bearing Cap
18. Axle Shaft
19. Thrust Washer
20. Differential Pinion
21. Shim
22. Pinion Rear Bearing
23. Drive Pinion

Fig. 2 Semi floating rear axle of 3300 and 3500 lbs. rated capacity used on 1971–79

CHEVROLET

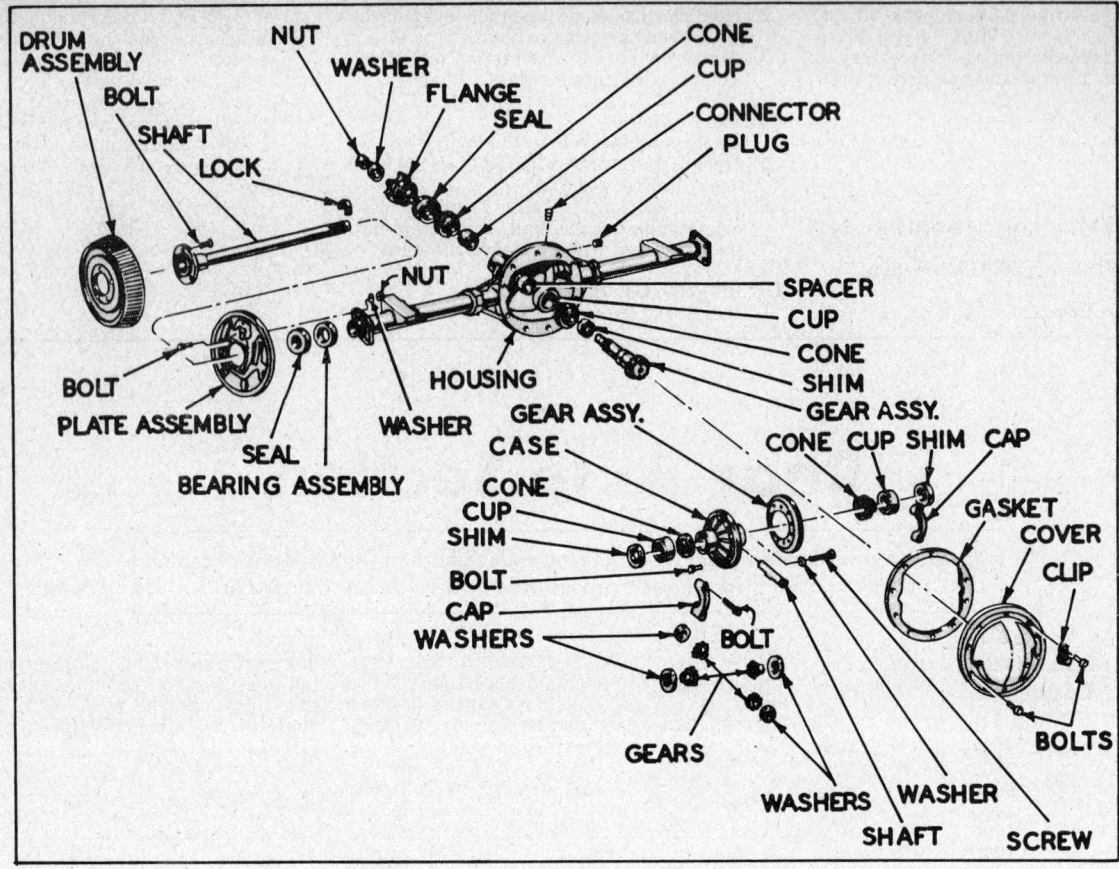

Fig. 1 Salisbury type semi-floating rear axle. 1970-80. Typical

are backed by thrust washers.

Remove & Replace

Construction of the axle assembly is such that service operations may be performed with the housing installed in the vehicle or with the housing removed and installed in a holding fixture. The following procedure is necessary only when the housing requires replacement.
1. Raise vehicle and place stand jacks under frame side rails.
2. Remove rear wheels.
3. Support rear axle assembly with a suitable jack so that tension is relieved in springs and tie rod.
4. Disconnect tie rod at axle housing bracket.
5. Remove trunnion bearing "U" bolts from rear yoke, split universal joint, position propeller shaft to one side and tie it to frame side rail.
6. Remove axle "U" bolt nuts and allow control arm and shock absorbers to hang freely so that they do not interfere with axle. *On K Series trucks, remove spacer from axle housing.*
7. Disconnect hydraulic brake hose at connector on axle housing.
8. Remove brake drum and disconnect parking brake cable at lever and at flange plate.
9. Lower axle and remove from vehicle.
10. Reverse foregoing procedure to install axle assembly.

Axle Shaft, Replace

1. Raise vehicle and remove wheel and brake drum.
2. Drain lube from carrier and remove cover.
3. Remove differential pinion shaft lock screw and remove differential pinion shaft, Fig. 3.
4. Pull flanged end of axle shaft toward center of vehicle and remove "C" lock from button end of shaft.
5. Remove axle shaft from housing, being

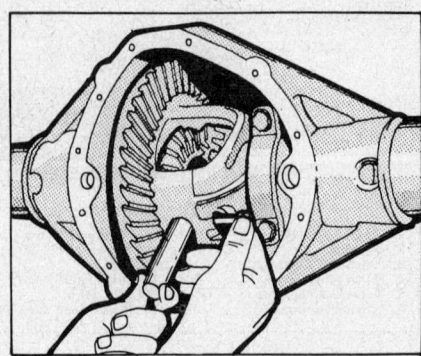

Fig. 3 Removing differential pinion shaft

careful not to damage seal.
6. Reverse foregoing procedure to install the axle shaft.

Wheel Bearing/Oil Seal, Replace

1. Remove axle shaft as previously described.
2. Use a suitable puller to remove bearing and oil seal.
3. Lubricate wheel bearing and cavity between seal lips with wheel bearing lubricant before installation.
4. Reverse procedure to install.

DANA SPICER SERIES 60 AXLE

This axle, Fig. 4, used on 10 Series trucks with V8-396 engines is of the semi-floating design. When used on 20 Series trucks with 396 engine the axle is a full-floating type. The Dana axle is very similar to the Chevrolet Salisbury type axle with the following exceptions:
1. The differential side bearing shims are located between the side bearing cone and roller assembly and the differential case. These bearings are of the tapered roller design and are preloaded. In order to remove the differential case the carrier must be spread but no more than .020".
2. The pinion assembly incorporates an inner and outer bearing shim. The inner

CHEVROLET

shim is used to maintain proper pinion depth while the outer shim is used to maintain proper preload on the pinion bearing. The differential does not employ "C" washers to retain the axle shafts.

Service procedures are otherwise similar to the Salisbury type covered earlier.

CHEVROLET FULL FLOATING AXLES

1970–80 Light Duty Type

The straddle mounted drive pinion is supported at the front by two opposed tapered roller bearings. The pinion rear roller bearing consists of an outer race and roller assembly and a precision ground diameter on the pinion pilot functions as an inner race, Figs. 5 and 6.

On 1970–72 units, Fig. 5, a thrust pad mounted on the end of an adjustable screw in the carrier housing limits deflection of the ring gear under high torque conditions.

On 1973–80 units with a 10½ inch ring gear, Fig. 6, side bearing preload and ring gear to pinion backlash are controlled by side bearing adjusting rings threaded into the carrier. Pinion depth is controlled by a shim located between the pinion bearing retainer assembly and axle housing.

Medium and Heavy Duty Types, Figs. 7, 8

These axles have a straddle-mounted drive pinion which is supported at the rear by a straight roller bearing. The pinion front bearing consists of a double row ball on the medium duty axles and two opposed tapered roller bearings on the heavy duty models. Selective shims placed between front bearing and its seat in the carrier housing provide a means of adjusting pinion depth to attain correct ring gear and pinion tooth contacts.

The differential is a four pinion type. Thrust washers are used between the side gears and case and also between differential pinions and case.

A thrust pad mounted on the end of an adjusting screw threaded into the carrier housing limits deflection of the ring gear under high torque conditions.

Axle Shaft, Replace

7200 Lb. Axles & 1973–80 with 10½" Ring Gear

1. Remove bolts that attach axle shaft flange to wheel hub.
2. On 1970–72 units, install two ½-13 bolts in the threaded holes provided in the axle shaft flange. By turning these bolts alternately the axle shaft may be easily removed from housing, Fig. 9.
3. On 1973–80 units with 10½ inch ring gear, tap on flange with a rawhide mallet to loosen axle shaft, then remove axle shaft by twisting shaft with locking pliers.
4. Thoroughly clean both axle shaft flange and end of wheel hub. *Any lubricant on these surfaces tends to loosen axle shaft flange bolts.*
5. Place a new gasket over axle shaft and position axle shaft in housing so that shaft splines enter differential side gear. Position gasket so that holes are in alignment and install flange-to-hub attaching bolts. Torque bolts to 60 ft. lbs. on 1972–75 Dana 5500 models; 90 ft. lbs. on 1972–75 except Dana 5500; and 115 ft. lbs. on 1976–80 models.

NOTE: To prevent lubricant from leaking through flange holes apply Permatex to bolt threads. Use care in the amount of sealer applied. If the application is too heavy, the sealer may be forced out as the bolt is installed and may destroy the sealing effect of

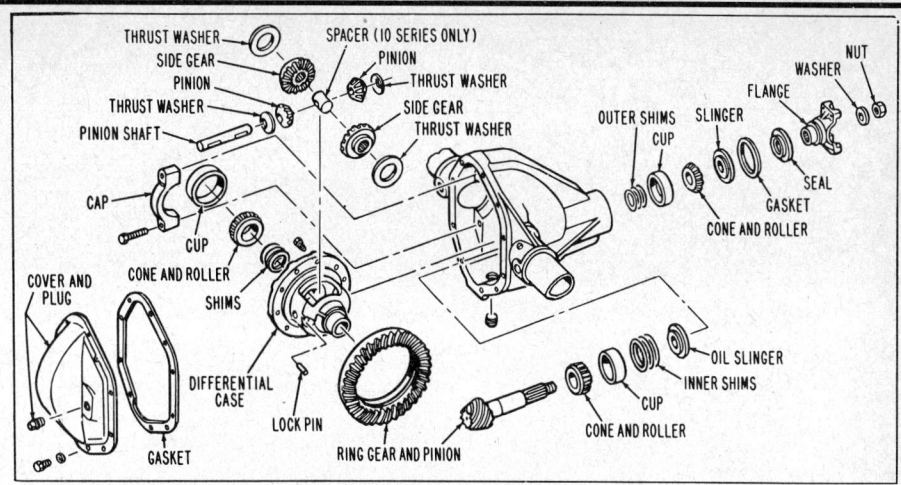

Fig. 4 Dana Spicer Series 60 rear axle

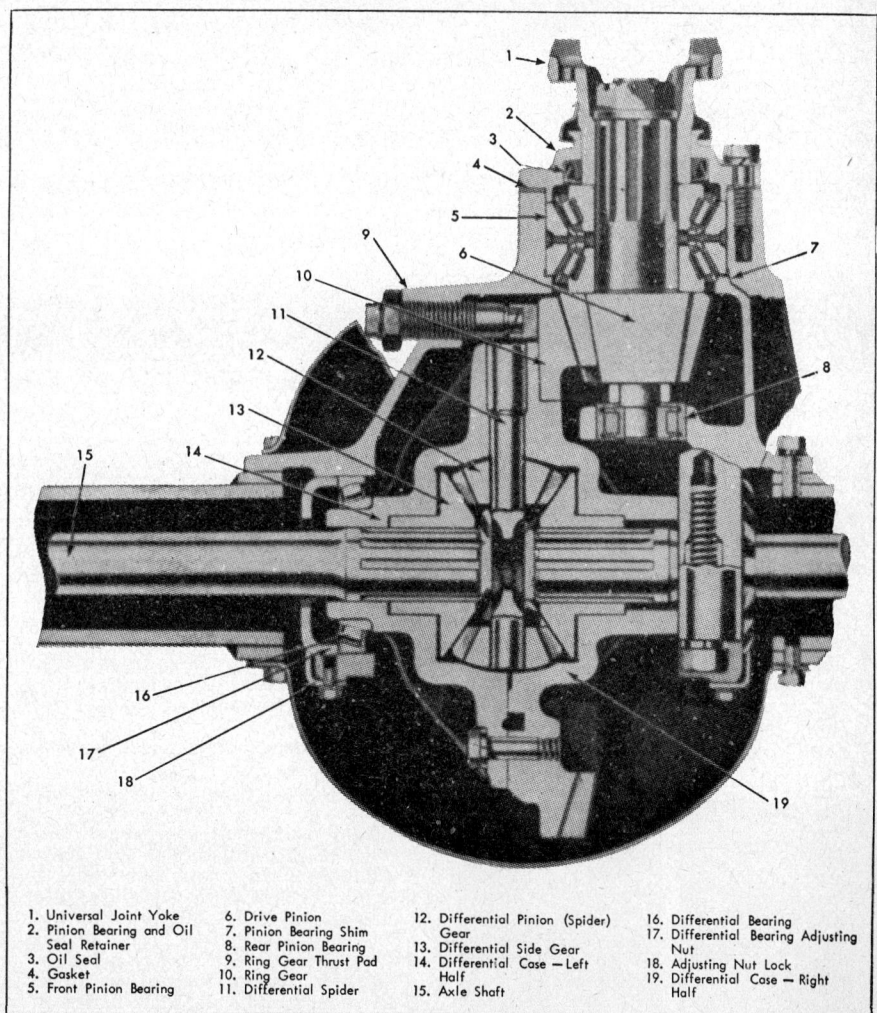

1. Universal Joint Yoke
2. Pinion Bearing and Oil Seal Retainer
3. Oil Seal
4. Gasket
5. Front Pinion Bearing
6. Drive Pinion
7. Pinion Bearing Shim
8. Rear Pinion Bearing
9. Ring Gear Thrust Pad
10. Ring Gear
11. Differential Spider
12. Differential Pinion (Spider) Gear
13. Differential Side Gear
14. Differential Case — Left Half
15. Axle Shaft
16. Differential Bearing
17. Differential Bearing Adjusting Nut
18. Adjusting Nut Lock
19. Differential Case — Right Half

Fig. 5 Full floating rear axle of 5200 and 7200 lbs. rated capacity used on 1970–72

CHEVROLET

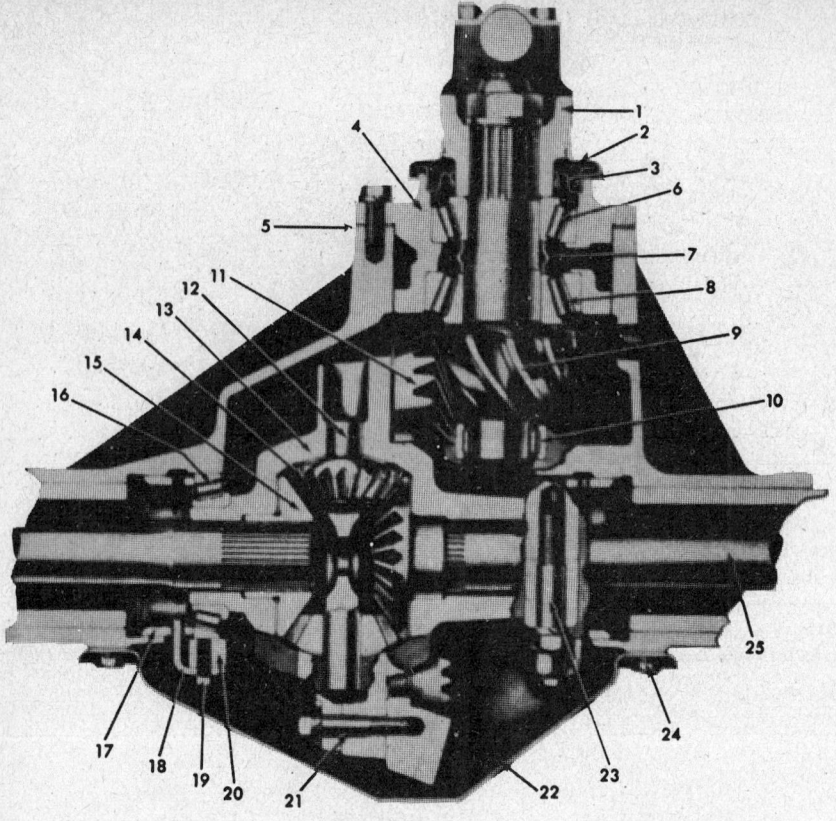

1. Companion Flange
2. Oil Deflector
3. Oil Seal
4. Bearing Retainer
5. Shim
6. Pinion Front Bearing
7. Collapsible Spacer
8. Pinion Rear Bearing
9. Drive Pinion
10. Straddle Bearing
11. Ring Gear
12. Differential Spider
13. Differential Case
14. Differential Pinion
15. Differential Side Gear
16. Side Bearing
17. Side Bearing Adjusting Nut
18. Adjusting Nut Retainer
19. Retainer Screw
20. Bearing Cap
21. Case-to-Ring Gear Bolt
22. Differential Cover
23. Bearing Cap Bolt
24. Cover Screw
25. Axle Shaft

Fig. 6 Full floating rear axle with 10½ inch ring gear used on 1973-80

Wheel Bearings, Replace

Hub & Drum, Remove
1. Remove wheel and axle shaft.
2. Disengage tang of nut lock from slot or flat of lock nut, then remove lock nut from housing tube, using appropriate tool, Fig. 11.
3. Disengage tang of nut lock from slot or flat of adjusting nut and remove nut lock from housing tube.
4. Use appropriate tool, Fig. 11, to remove adjusting nut from housing tube. *On 5200 and 7200 axles, remove thrust washer from housing tube.*
5. Pull hub and drum straight off axle housing, using care on 11,000, 15,000 and 17,000 lb. axles to avoid dropping outer bearing inner race and roller assembly.

NOTE: On 15,000 lb. axle, remove inner bearing race and inner bearing oil seal from axle housing and discard seal.

Bearing Cup, Replace
Replace inner cup (all axles) and outer bearing cup for 17,000 lb. axles as follows:
1. Cut a suitable length of ½" steel bar stock for press-out tool as shown in Fig. 12.
2. Place appropriate press-out tool behind bearing cup, index tool in notches provided, and press out cup with an arbor press.
3. Position bearing cup in hub with thick edge of cup toward shoulder in hub. Then, using applicable cup installer, press cup into hub until it seats on hub shoulder. Make certain cup is not cocked and that it is fully seated against shoulder.

Outer Bearing, Replace
Replace outer bearing on all axles except 17,000 lb. axle as follows. The inner bearing must be removed before attempting to replace the outer bearing.
1. Using a punch of suitable length, tap bearing outer race away from bearing retainer ring, Fig. 13. Then remove retaining ring from hub, Figs. 13 and 14.
2. Press bearing from hub, Figs. 15 and 16.
3. Place axle shaft spacer (11,000 and 15,000 lb. axles) and inner race and roller assembly in hub with larger O.D. of roller assembly toward outer end of hub. Then position bearing cup in hub with thin edge of cup toward outer end of hub. Press cup into hub until clearance is obtained for retainer ring installation.
4. Install retainer ring. Then press bearing cup into positive contact with retainer ring.

NOTE: The bearing cup-to-retainer ring seating procedure is essential to assure that an accurate wheel bearing adjustment will be obtained, and that the ad-

the flange-to-hub gasket.

11,000 & 15,000 Lb. Axles
1. Remove hub cap and install the tool shown in Fig. 10 in tapped hole in shaft flange.
2. Install slide hammer and remove axle shaft.
3. Remove all old gasket material from hub and hub cap. Clean shaft flange and mating surfaces in wheel hub.
4. Install axle shaft so that flange spines index into hub splines. Tap shaft into position.
5. Install new hub cap-to-hub gasket, position cap to hub and install attaching bolts. Torque bolts to 15 ft. lbs.

17,000 Lb. Axles
1. Remove axle shaft flange-to-hub retaining nuts.
2. Strike center of shaft flange with a lead hammer to loosen flange and dowels.
3. Remove tapered dowels from studs and pull axle shaft from housing. It may be necessary to spread dowels to permit removal.
4. Clean old gasket material from wheel hub and axle shaft flange and install a new gasket over hub studs and against hub.
5. Install axle shaft so that splines are aligned with differential side gear and flange holes index over hub studs.
6. Install tapered dowel over each hub stud. Install and tighten ½ inch stud nuts to 50-60 ft. lbs. and ⅝ inch stud nuts to 90-100 ft. lbs.
7. See that clearance exists between face of stud nuts and axle shaft flange. If no clearance exists, it indicates excessive wear at studs, tapered dowels or flange holes. Replace worn part if necessary.

Fig. 9 Removing axle shaft. 5200 and 7200 lb. axles

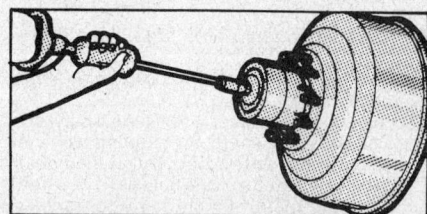

Fig. 10 Removing axle shaft. 11,000 and 15,000 lb. axles

CHEVROLET

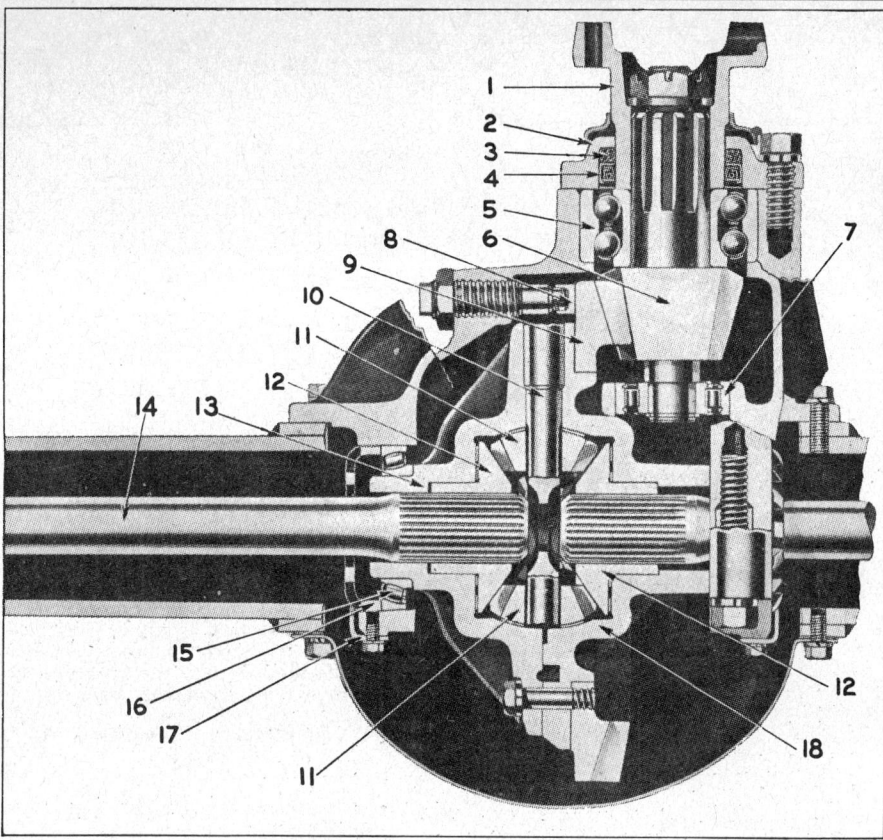

1. Universal Joint Yoke
2. Pinion Bearing Retainer and Oil Seal
3. Oil Seal Packing
4. Oil Seal
5. Front Pinion Bearing
6. Drive Pinion
7. Rear Pinion Bearing
8. Ring Gear Thrust Pad
9. Ring Gear
10. Differential Spider
11. Differential Pinion (Spider) Gear
12. Differential Side Gear
13. Differential Case—Left Half
14. Axle Shaft
15. Differential Bearing
16. Differential Bearing Adjusting Nut
17. Adjusting Nut Lock
18. Differential Case—Right Half

Fig. 7 Full-floating rear axle of 11,000 lbs. rated capacity

4. Install nut lock.
5. Make sure wheel turns freely. Then install lock nut and tighten to specifications given below. Bend tang of nut lock over flat or slot of lock nut.
   a. On 5200 and 7200 lb. axles, tighten lock nut to 175 ft. lbs.
   b. On 11,000 and 15,000 lb. axles, tighten lock nut to a minimum of 250 ft. lbs.
   c. On 17,000 lb. axles, tighten lock nut to 135 ft. lbs.
   d. On axles with 10 1/2 inch ring gear, torque locknut to 65 ft. lbs.
6. Lower vehicle and install axle shaft.

Differential Carrier

Major operations on the differential carrier assembly may be performed without removing the rear axle assembly from the vehicle. After removing the axle shafts, remove the differential carrier assembly from the axle housing.

To facilitate adjusting of pinion depth in the ring gear, there are four shims available for service use. They are .012, .015, .018 and .021".

If the original ring gear and pinion are to be used, it is advisable to replace the same thickness of shims in the carrier housing counterbore that were removed.

If a new ring gear and pinion are used, one .021" shim should be used as a standard starting setup.

Checking Pinion Depth

NOTE: Details on tooth patterns and method of checking ring gear and pinion backlash are given in the Timken and Eaton axle chapters. Backlash between ring gear and pinion in Chevrolet axles are .003–.006" on 5200 lb. axles and .005–.008" on all others.

1. Coat the ring gear teeth lightly with red lead or prussian blue. Then turn the pinion shaft several revolutions in both directions.
2. If the pinion depth is correct, the tooth pattern will be centered on the pitch line and toward the toe of the ring gear.
3. If the pattern is below the pitch line on the ring gear teeth, the pinion is too deep and it will be necessary to remove the pinion assembly and increase the shim thickness between pinion bearing and carrier.
4. If the pattern is above the pitch line on the ring gear teeth, the pinion is too shal-

justment will not loosen up during subsequent vehicle operation.

Wheel Bearings, Adjust

Before checking wheel bearing adjustment, make sure brakes are fully released and do not drag. Check bearing play by grasping tire at top and pulling back and forth or by using a pry bar under tire. If bearings are properly adjusted, movement of brake drum in relation to brake flange plate will be barely noticeable and wheel will turn freely. If movement is excessive, adjust bearings as follows:

1. Remove axle shaft and raise vehicle until wheel is free to rotate.
2. Disengage tang of nut lock from lock nut and remove them from a le housing tube.
3. Using appropriate tool, tighten nut to specifications given below, at the same time rotating hub to make sure that all bearing surfaces are properly seated. Then back off adjusting nut one flat or notch.
   a. On 5200 and 7200 axles, tighten adjusting nut to 50–60 ft. lbs. and back off nut 1/8 turn to align nearest slot with short tang on nut lock.
   b. On 11,000 lb. axle, tighten adjusting nut to 75–100 ft. lbs. and back off nut 1/8 turn to align nearest slot with short tang on nut lock.
   c. On 15,000 lb. axle, tighten adjusting nut to 75–100 ft. lbs. and back it off to align nearest slot with short tang on nut lock.
   d. On 17,000 lb. axle, tighten adjusting nut to 65 ft. lbs. and back it off 1/16" to 1/4 turn to align slot with short tang on nut lock.
   e. On axles with 10 1/2 inch ring gear, torque adjusting nut to 50 ft. lbs.

Fig. 11 Removing bearing adjusting nut lock nut

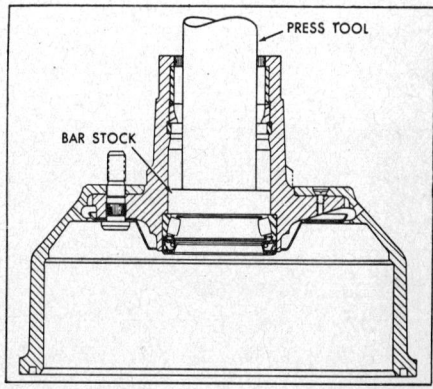

Fig. 12 Removing hub inner bearing cup

913

CHEVROLET

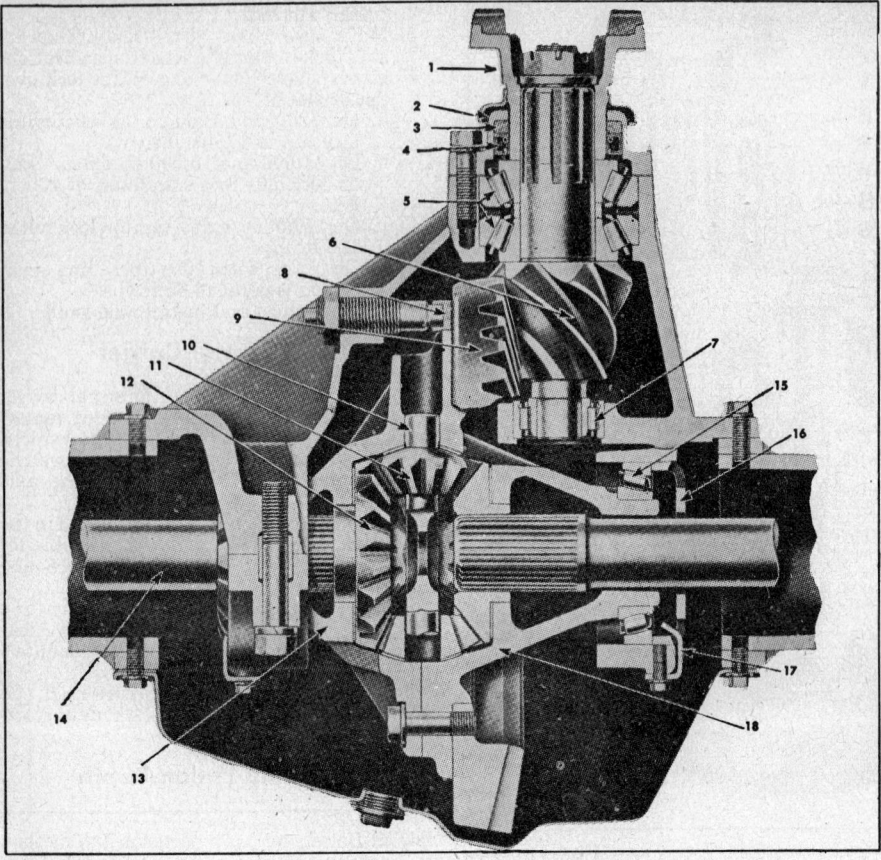

1. Universal Joint Yoke
2. Pinion Bearing Retainer and Oil Seal
3. Oil Seal Packing
4. Oil Seal
5. Pinion Bearing Assembly
6. Drive Pinion
7. Rear Pinion Bearing
8. Ring Gear Thrust Pad
9. Ring Gear
10. Differential Spider
11. Differential Pinion (Spider) Gear
12. Differential Side Gear
13. Differential Case (Left Half)
14. Axle Shaft
15. Differential Bearing
16. Differential Bearing Adjusting Nut
17. Adjusting Nut Lock
18. Differential Case (Right Half)

Fig. 8 Full-floating rear axle 13,500, 15,000 and 17,000 lbs. rated capacity used on 2 and 2½ ton trucks

low and it will be necessary to remove the pinion and decrease the shim thickness between pinion bearing and carrier.

5. Changing the pinion depth will make some change in backlash; therefore, it will be necessary to readjust the backlash.

Ring Gear Thrust Pad, Adjust

After the differential carrier is assembled and properly adjusted, install the thrust pad and tighten the adjusting screw until the bronze tip engages the back of the ring gear while the gear is rotated. Back off the screw 1/12 turn and tighten lock nut, Fig. 17. Make sure screw does not turn during the locking process.

Fig. 13 Removing bearing retainer. 5200 and 7200 lb. axles

CHEVROLET TWO SPEED AXLE

This unit, Fig. 18, is available in 15,000, 17,000 and 18,500 lb. capacity. In low gear, torque is transmitted to the differential case through four planetary pinions. In high range, only the straddle mounted drive pinion and the ring gear operate to produce the high range reduction, the planet and sun gears being locked to revolve with the ring gear.

The electric axle shift unit is mounted on the differential carrier. This unit contains a reversible electric motor, which when energized, shifts the axle into the desired range through mechanism contained in the unit.

Differential Carrier Removal

1. Loosen housing attaching cap screws and drain lubricant.
2. Remove axle shafts and electric or vacuum lines.
3. Disconnect drive shaft and swing it to one side.
4. Remove all carrier attaching cap screws except two at the top. Loosen the top two but leave them installed to prevent the carrier from falling.
5. Tap along the outer edge of the carrier with a soft faced hammer to break carrier loose.

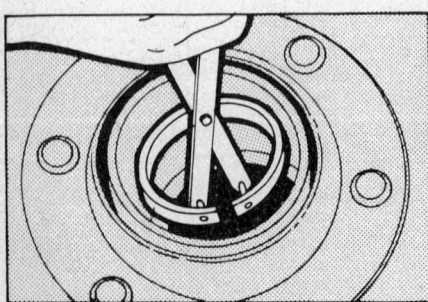

Fig. 14 Removing bearing retainer ring 11,000 and 15,000 lb. axles

Fig. 15 Removing hub outer bearing. 5200 and 7200 lb. axles

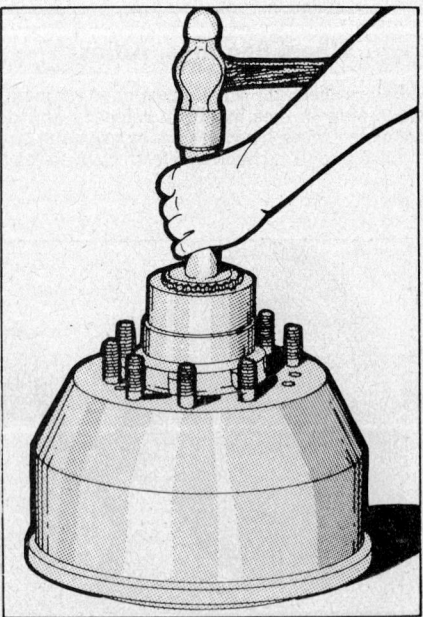

Fig. 16 Removing hub outer bearing. 11,000 and 15,000 lb. axles

CHEVROLET

Fig. 17 Ring gear thrust pad adjustment

6. Support carrier with a suitable jack, remove remaining two cap screws and remove carrier.

Disassembly

1. Remove drive pinion nut and washer. Discard nut and use a new one when reassembling.
2. Remove flange.
3. Remove pinion bearing retainer and pinion. Remove shims from between carrier and retainer. Save shims for readjustment during reassembly.
4. Remove shifter assembly from carrier.
5. Remove shift yoke anchor.
6. Using a drift, drive out shifter yoke shaft.
7. Slide shifter yoke and sleeve to the left, removing the sleeve and yoke from the end of the sun gear.
8. Remove differential bearing adjusting nut lock from each nut and remove locks from both sides.
9. Remove two retaining bolts and withdraw oil trough from carrier.
10. Remove bearing caps and adjusting nuts by tapping on bosses of caps until free of dowels. Remove the differential and planet assembly from the housing.
11. Disassemble pinion.
12. Mark ring gear and differential and planet support case and case cover for alignment by scribing lines on case, cover and gear.
13. Remove cover retaining bolts and remove cover.
14. Mark or tag all gears so they can be reassembled in the same relative position then remove the sun and planet gears.
15. Lift the differential and planet support assembly from the support case.
16. Remove planet support-to-cover bolts and separate the two.
17. Mark or tag all parts for reassembly in the same relative position and remove spider and pinion gears and thrust washers.
18. Remove side gears and thrust washers from each side of the housing.
19. Remove bearings.

Reassembly

Reverse the disassembly procedure to assemble the unit, being careful to align all reference marks made during disassembly.

Ring Gear and Pinion, Adjust

1. Loosen right differential adjusting nut and tighten left adjusting nut.
2. Tighten left adjusting nut until the ring contacts the pinion (zero lash).

Fig. 18 Chevrolet two-speed axle

1. Pinion Flange
2. Dust Deflector
3. Pinion Oil Seal
4. Pinion Front Bearing
5. Pinion Adjusting Shim
6. Pinion Bearing Preload Spacer
7. Pinion Intermediate Bearing
8. Pinion
9. Differential Carrier
10. Pinion Rear Bearing
11. Differential and Planet Support
12. Differential Bearing (Right)
13. Axle Shaft
14. Axle Housing
15. Differential Bearing Adjusting Nut (Right)
16. Oil Baffle
17. Adjusting Nut Lock (Right)
18. Thrust Washers
19. Differential and Planet Support Case Cover
20. Axle Housing Cover (Welded)
21. Differential Pinion
22. Filler Plug
23. Differential Pinion Shaft
24. Differential Side Gear (Left)
25. Magnetic Chip Collector
26. Planet Gears (4)
27. Differential and Planet Support Case
28. Shift Yoke
29. Shift Sleeve
30. Anchor Bolt Lock
31. Anchor
32. Sun Gear
33. Ring Gear
34. Pinion and Bearing Retainer

NOTE: Do not force gears into contact so as to bind them.

3. Back off left adjusting nut approximately two notches to a point where nut lock and nut are aligned. Install nut and lock.
4. Tighten right adjusting nut firmly to force the differential and planet assembly into solid contact with the left adjusting nut. Loosen right adjusting nut until it is free from contact with its bearing, then retighten until nut contacts bearing. Tighten right adjusting nut 1 to 2 additional notches for old bearings and 2 to 3 for new bearings, to a position where nut and lock are aligned and install lock.

NOTE: At this point, the bearings are properly preloaded. Any further adjustment of the ring gear in either direction without a corresponding adjustment of the opposite adjusting nut, will change the bearing preload.

5. With a dial indicator mounted on the housing, measure ring and pinion backlash. Limits are .003″ to .012″ with .005″ to .008″ preferred.

Pinion Depth

1. Paint ring gear teeth with a mixture of red lead and oil to produce a contact pattern.
2. Rotate pinion through several revolutions, applying pressure to the ring gear to develop a definite contact pattern.
3. Pinion depth is controlled by the shim pack between the pinion bearing retainer and the carrier.
4. Changing pinion depth will cause some change in ring gear backlash. After adjusting pinion depth, recheck backlash.

Final Assembly

To install the unit, reverse the removal procedure, being careful to adequately support.

CHEVROLET

Front Wheel Drive

For service procedure on the transfer case used with four-wheel drive trucks, see the Transfer Case Chapter

FRONT AXLE

The front axle is a Spicer unit equipped with steering knuckles, Figs. 1 and 2. To permit the turning and driving of the front wheels, the axle is equipped with steering knuckles and yoke and trunnion type universal joints. 1977-80 K30 series incorporate king pins, while 1970-80 K10 and 20 series incorporate ball joints.

BALL JOINT ADJUSTMENT
1970-80

Ball joint adjustment is generally necessary when there is excessive play in steering, irregular tire wear or persistent loosening of the tie rods.
1. Raise vehicle and support with jack stands placed just inside of front springs.
2. Disconnect drag link and tie rods to permit independent movement of each steering knuckle.
3. On 1970-76 models:
    a. Apply a torque wrench to one of the steering knuckles retaining stud nuts and check torque required to turn steering knuckle. Maximum torque required should be 15 ft. lbs. for 1970-71 or 20 ft. lbs. for 1972-76.

NOTE: Steering knuckle should turn freely without vertical end play.

   b. If torque required is too low, remove upper ball joint cotter pin and locknut, then torque adjusting sleeve to 50 ft. lbs. and reinstall locknut and cotter pin.
   c. Recheck torque required to turn steering knuckle. If torque is still too low, retorque adjusting sleeve to 60 ft. lbs. as described previously.
   d. Recheck torque required to turn steering knuckle. If torque is still to low, replace parts as necessary to bring torque within specifications.
4. On 1977-80 models:
    a. Using a spring scale attached to tie rod mounting hole, determine amount of pull at right angles, required to keep knuckle assembly turning from a straight ahead position.
    b. If pull exceeds 25 lbs., remove upper ball stud nut, and loosen adjusting sleeve as required. Tighten ball stud nut and recheck turning effort.

FRONT AXLE
Remove and Install

1. Disassemble propeller shaft from front axle differential.
2. Raise front of truck and support it with

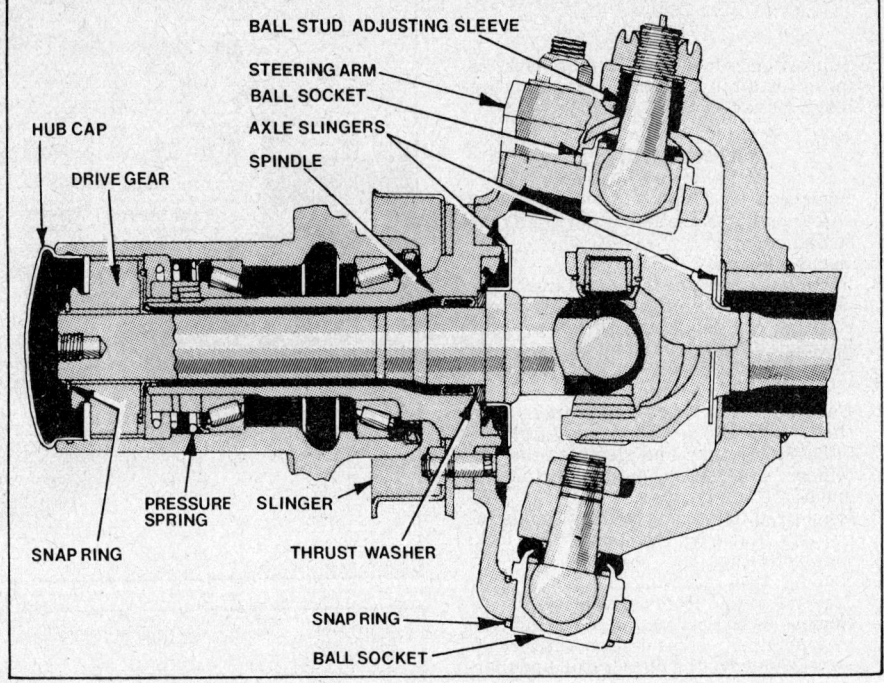

Fig. 1 Steering knuckle and wheel hub. 1970-80 K10, 20 Series Four Wheel Drive front axle

jacks behind front springs.
3. Disconnect drag link from steering arm.
4. Disconnect brake hoses from frame fittings.
5. Disconnect shock absorbers from spring clamp plate or axle brackets.
6. Separate axle from truck springs.
7. Roll front axle from under truck.
8. Install in reverse order of removal.

HUB AND WHEEL BEARING, REPLACE
1970-80

NOTE: On models with Free-Wheeling Hubs, refer to "Front Wheel Locking Hubs" chapter for locking hub removal.

1. Raise and support vehicle.
2. On models with locked hubs, Figs. 1 & 2:
    a. Remove hub cap and snap ring.
    b. Remove drive gear. On K10 and K20 models, remove pressure spring. Place hand over drive gear and pry out using a screwdriver.
3. On all models, remove wheel bearing outer lock nut, lock ring and wheel bearing inner adjusting nut using suitable tool.
4. Remove disc brake caliper and position out of the way.
5. Remove hub-and-disc assembly, outer wheel bearing and spring retainer plate:
    a. Remove inner wheel bearing and oil seal from hub using suitable drift.
    b. Remove inner and outer bearing cups from hub using suitable drift.
6. Reverse procedure to install. Refer to "Wheel Bearings, Adjust" for wheel bearing adjustment.

AXLE SHAFT, REPLACE
1970-80

1. Remove hub and wheel bearing as previously described.
2. Remove spindle attaching nuts, then lightly tap spindle from steering knuckle.
3. Remove thrust washer, then pull axle shaft from axle.
4. Reverse procedure to install. Torque spindle nuts to 45 ft. lbs. on 1970-76 K10 and K20; 25 ft. lbs. on 1977-78 K10 and K20; 60 ft. lbs. on 1977-80 K30; and 33 ft. lbs. on 1979-80 K10 and K20.

CHEVROLET

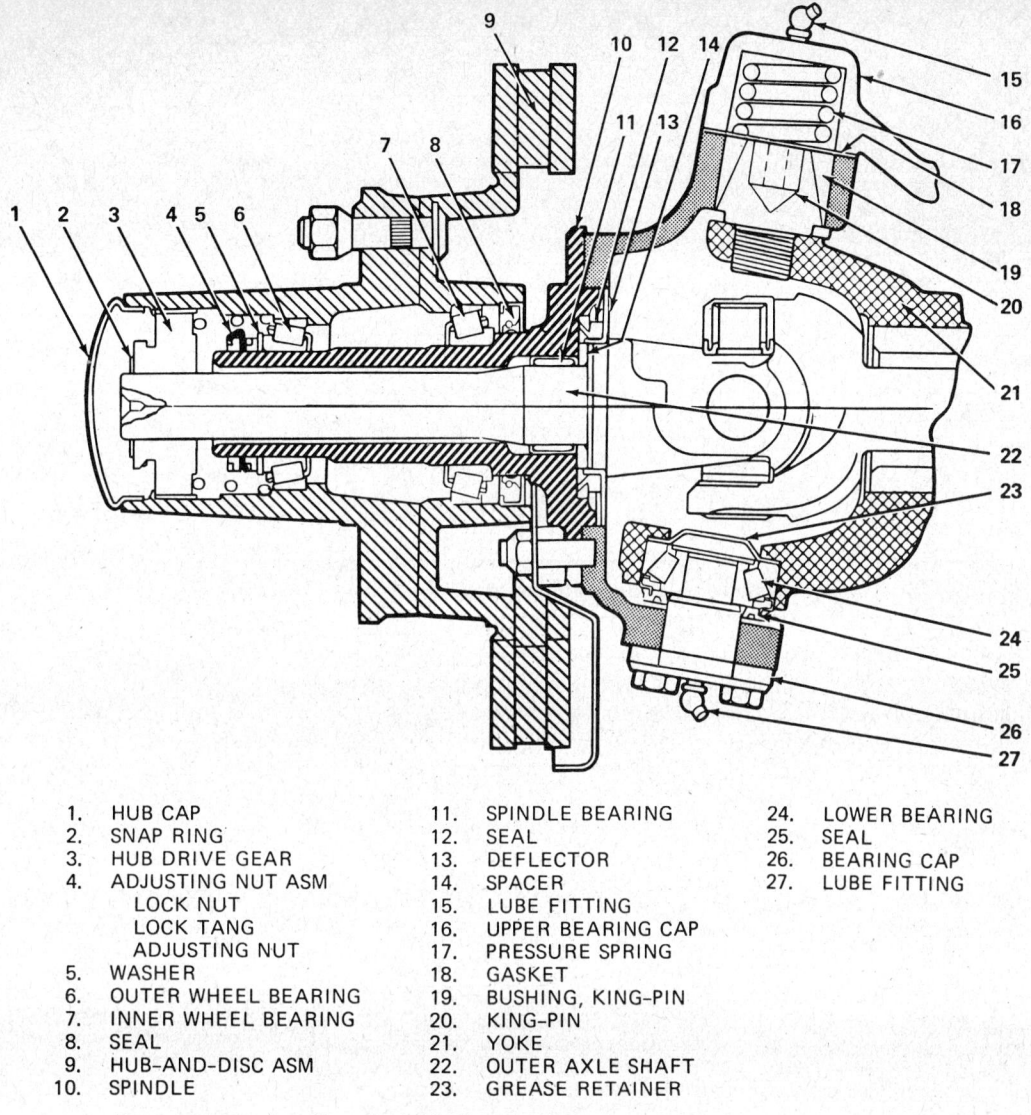

1. HUB CAP
2. SNAP RING
3. HUB DRIVE GEAR
4. ADJUSTING NUT ASM
   LOCK NUT
   LOCK TANG
   ADJUSTING NUT
5. WASHER
6. OUTER WHEEL BEARING
7. INNER WHEEL BEARING
8. SEAL
9. HUB-AND-DISC ASM
10. SPINDLE
11. SPINDLE BEARING
12. SEAL
13. DEFLECTOR
14. SPACER
15. LUBE FITTING
16. UPPER BEARING CAP
17. PRESSURE SPRING
18. GASKET
19. BUSHING, KING-PIN
20. KING-PIN
21. YOKE
22. OUTER AXLE SHAFT
23. GREASE RETAINER
24. LOWER BEARING
25. SEAL
26. BEARING CAP
27. LUBE FITTING

Fig. 2 Steering knuckle and wheel hub. 1977–80 K30 Series Four Wheel Drive front axle

STEERING KNUCKLE, REPLACE

1970–80 with Ball Joints

1. Remove hub and spindle.
2. Disconnect tie rod from steering arm.

CAUTION: If steering arm is removed from knuckle, discard the self-locking nuts and replace with new ones during installation. Tighten nuts to 90 ft. lbs.

3. Remove cotter pin from upper ball joint stud nut, and remove retaining nuts from both ball joints.
4. Separate stud from yoke using suitable ball joint fork at lower joint and repeat at upper joint if required.

CAUTION: Do not remove upper ball joint adjusting sleeve from yoke unless ball joint is being replaced. If it is necessary to loosen the sleeve to remove the knuckle, only loosen the sleeve two threads. The non-hardened threads in the yoke can be easily damaged by the adjusting sleeve.

5. Reverse procedure to install.
6. Torque lower ball joint to 70 ft. lbs., adjusting sleeve to 50 ft. lbs., and upper ball joint to 100 ft. lbs. Tighten tie-rod nut to 45 ft. lbs.

1977–80 K30 with King Pins

1. Remove hub and spindle.
2. Remove upper king pin cap by alternately loosening nuts to unload the compression spring. Withdraw the spring and gasket.
3. Remove the lower bearing cap and king pin.
4. Remove upper king pin tapered bushing and remove and knuckle from yoke. Remove felt king pin seal.
5. Remove upper king pin from yoke using a large breaker bar.
6. Drive lower king pin bearing cup, cone, grease retainer, and seal through bottom of knuckle using suitable tool.
7. Reverse procedure to install.
8. Torque upper king pin to 500–600 ft. lbs., and upper and lower bearing cap nuts to 70–90 ft. lbs.

BALL JOINTS, SERVICE

1970–80 K10 & K20

1. Remove steering knuckle from axle assembly.
2. Remove lower ball joint snap ring.

NOTE: Lower ball joint must be removed before upper ball joint can be serviced.

3. Press lower ball joint from knuckle using suitable tool.
4. Press upper ball joint from knuckle using suitable tool.
5. Press new lower ball joint into knuckle until fully seated. Install snap ring.

NOTE: Lower ball joint does not have a cotter pin hole in stud end.

CHEVROLET

6. Press upper ball joint into knuckle until fully seated.

KING PINS, SERVICE
1977-80 K30

Refer to "Steering Knuckle, Replace" for king pin service.

WHEEL BEARINGS ADJUST
1970-80

1. Remove dust cap or free wheeling hub, lockwasher and outer locknut.
2. Using tool J-6893 and adapter J-23446, torque inner adjusting nut to 50 ft. lbs. while rotating hub. Back off inner adjusting nut and retorque to 35 ft. lbs. while rotating hub.
3. Back off inner adjusting nut 1/4 turn for 1970-72, or 3/8 turn for 1973-80.
4. Assemble lockwasher by turning nut to nearest hole in lockwasher, then install and torque outer locknut to 50 ft. lbs. for all models except 1977-80 K30 series. On 1977-80 K30 series assemble lock washer and outer nut, then torque lock nut to 65 ft. lbs. and bend one ear of lock washer over inner nut and one ear of lock washer over outer nut.

NOTE: Hub assembly should have .001 to .010 inch end play.

5. Install dust cap or free wheeling hub.

Front End & Steering Section

NOTE: Manual and power steering gear repairs are covered in separate chapters. See Index.

CAUTION: On 1979 G-Series and all 1980 models, steering linkage relay rod assemblies will use crimped nuts. Whenever a crimped nut is loosened or removed, it must be replaced with a prevailing torque nut, Fig. 1.

WHEEL ALIGNMENT
1971-75 Vega

The front suspension, Fig. 2, is of the A frame type with short and long control arms. The upper control arm is bolted to the front end sheet metal at each inner pivot point. Rubber bushings are used for mounting.

The lower control arms attach to the front end sheet metal with cam type bolts through rubber bushings. The cam bolts adjust caster and camber.

The upper ball joint is riveted in the upper arm and the lower ball joint is pressed into the lower arm.

Coil springs are mounted between the lower control arms and the shock absorber tower.

Caster

Caster angle is adjusted by loosening the rear lower control arm pivot nut and rotating the cam until proper setting is reached.

NOTE: This eccentric cam action will tend to move the lower control arm fore or aft thereby varying the caster. Hold the cam bolt while tightening the nut.

Camber

Camber angle is adjusted by loosening the front lower control arm pivot nut and rotating the cam until setting is reached.

NOTE: This eccentric cam action will move the lower arm in or out thereby varying the setting. Hold the cam bolt head while tightening the nut.

1970-80 Coil Spring Suspension

Caster and camber adjustments are made by means of shims located between upper control arm shaft and mounting bracket attached to suspension crossmember. A series of convex and concave spacers with flat opposite sides are used. These spacers allow a positive cross shaft-to-bracket attachment regardless of the number of shims used. Shims may be changed at either front or rear to vary caster, or at both points to vary camber.

Caster, 1970-80
1. Measure frame angle at "B", Fig. 3.
2. Check caster on alignment machine.
3. Add angle "B" and caster angle to determine *frame corrected angle*.
4. Measure dimension "A" Fig. 3.
5. Using dimension "A", and the chart for appropriate vehicle, Figs. 4 thru 6 and Caster Specification Chart, find the recommended caster angle.
6. The frame corrected angle should correspond to the recommended angle on the chart within plus or minus 1/4 degree. Make necessary changes to bring caster angle within limits.

Camber, 1970-79
1. Measure camber on alignment machine.
2. Measure dimension "A", Fig. 3.
3. Using dimension "A" and chart for appropriate vehicle, find recommended camber angle.

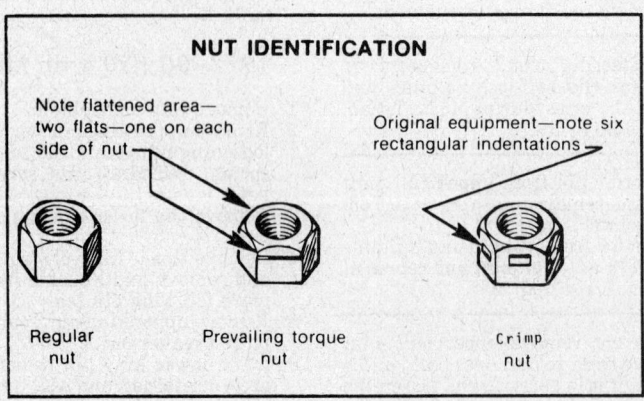

Fig. 1 Crimp nut identification

CHEVROLET

4. If angle in Step 1 does not correspond to the recommended angle in the chart within plus or minus 1/4 degree, make necessary changes.

COIL SPRING SUSPENSION
1970-80

This suspension, Fig. 7, consists of upper and lower control arms pivoting on steel threaded bushings on upper and lower arm shafts which are bolted to the front suspension crossmember and bracket assembly. These control arms are connected to the steering knuckle through pivoting ball joints. A coil spring is located between the lower control arm and a formed seat in the suspension crossmember, thus the lower control arm is the load-carrying member. The double-acting shock absorbers are also attached to the lower control arms and connect with the frame to the rear of the suspension on the upper end.

1970-80 Coil Springs, Replace
All Exc. Vega
1. Raise front of vehicle and place jack stands under frame, allowing control arms to hang free.
2. Disconnect shock absorber and stabilizer bar from lower control arm.
3. Install tool J-23028 or similar tool onto a suitable jack, Fig. 8, place jack under cross-shaft so cross-shaft seats in grooves of tool.
4. Place a safety chain through coil spring and lower control arm, then raise jack, relieving tension from coil spring.
5. Remove cross-shaft to crossmember "U" bolts, lower jack slowly and remove spring.
6. Reverse procedure to install.

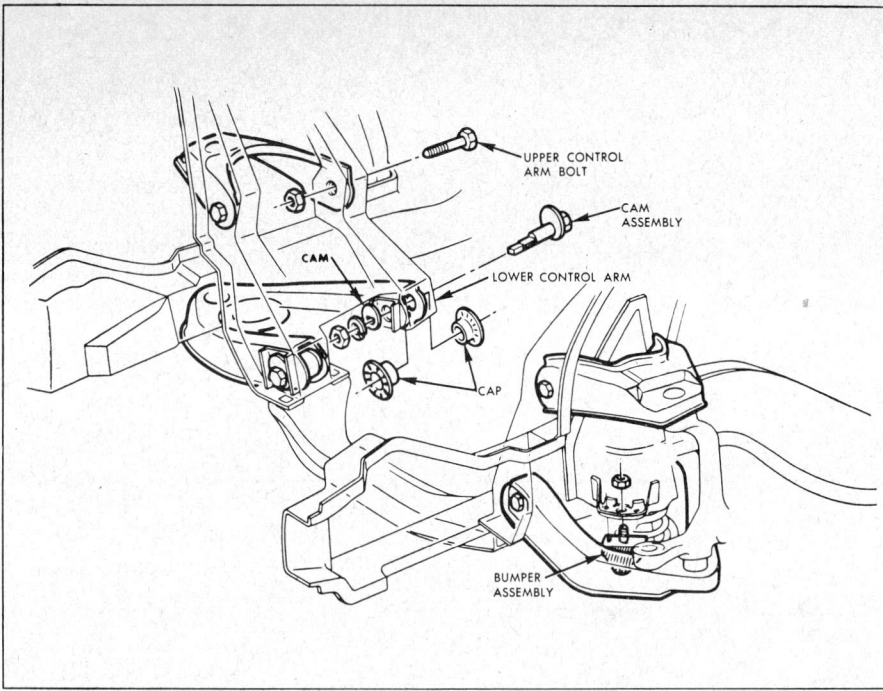

Fig. 2 Front suspension. 1971-75 Vega

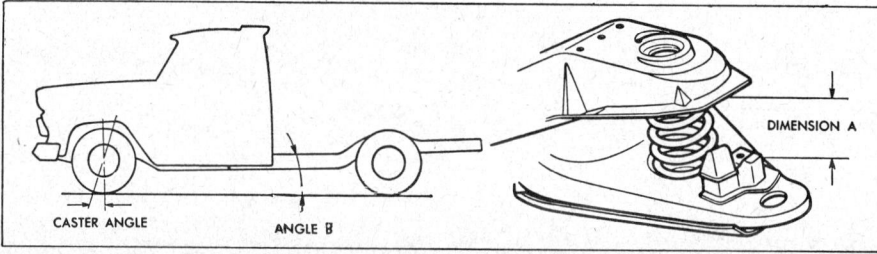

Fig. 3 Caster-camber adjustment. 1970-80 coil spring suspension

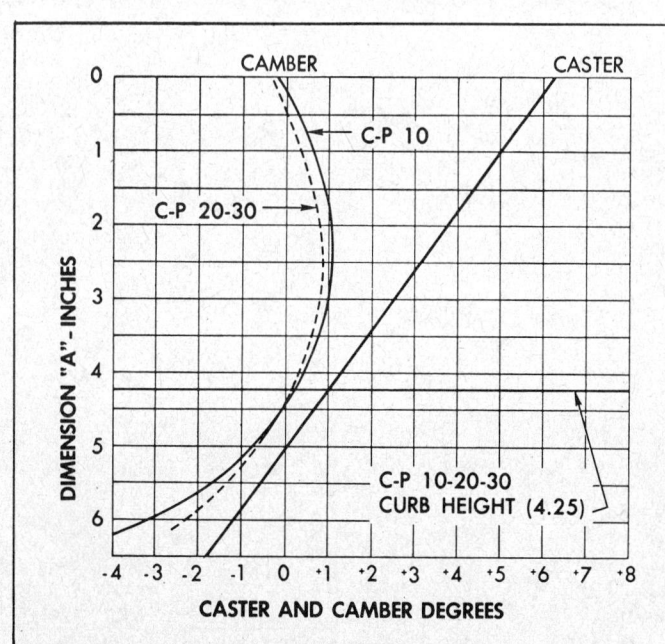

Fig. 4 Caster-camber chart. 1970 coil spring suspension

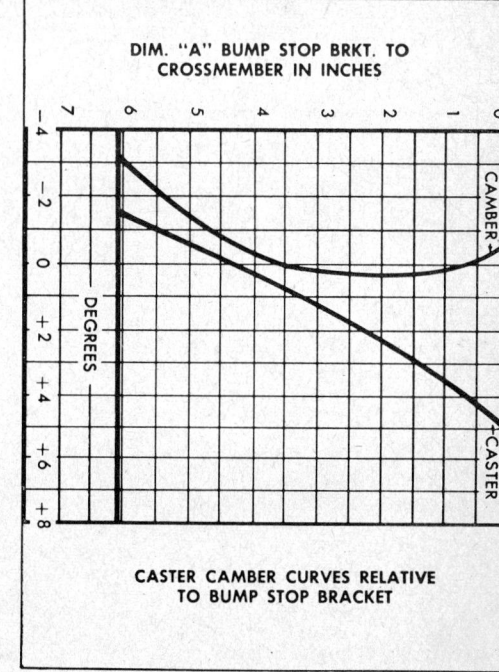

Fig. 5 Caster-camber chart. 1971 Chevy Van and Sportvan

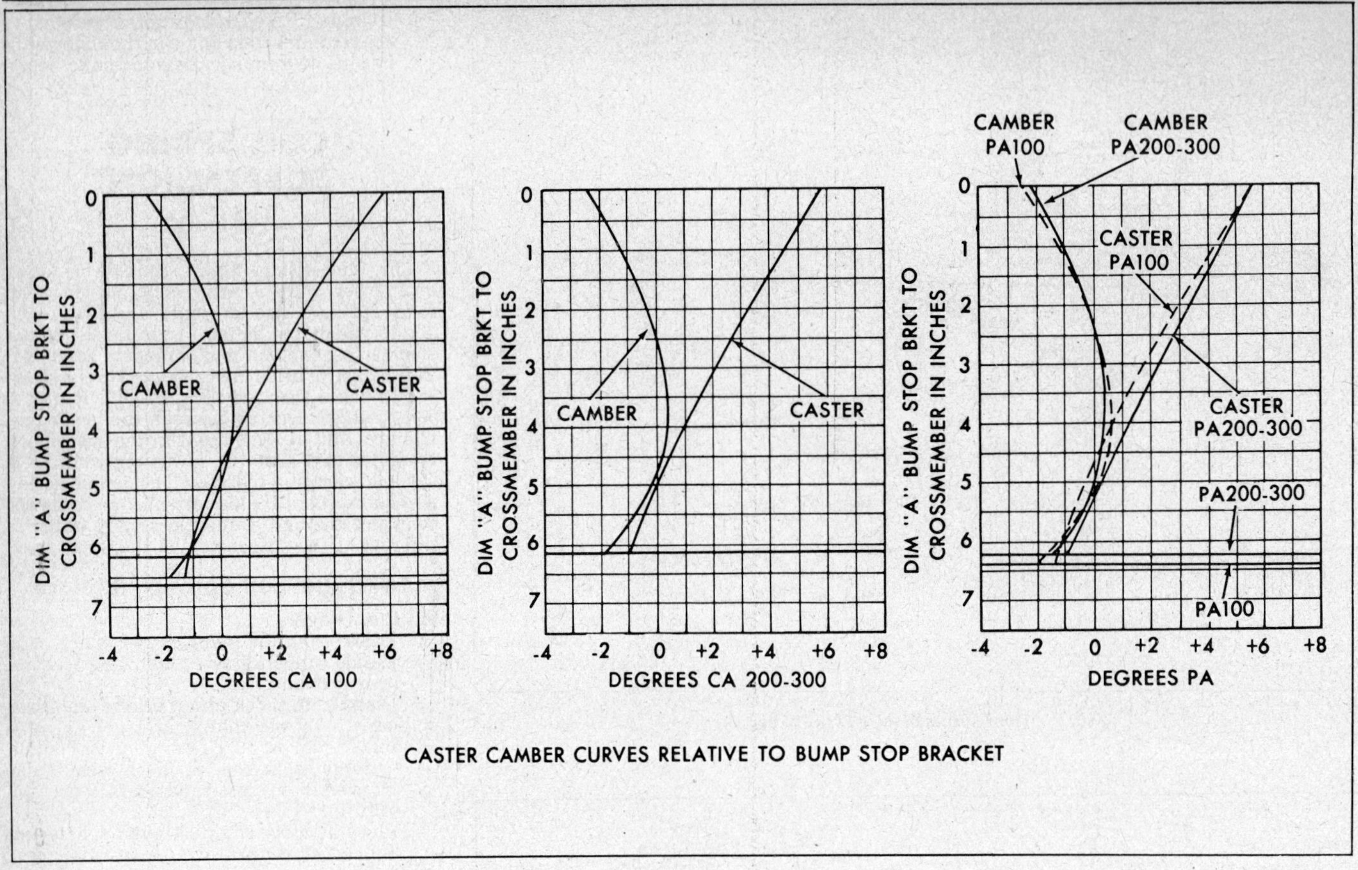

CHEVROLET

Fig. 6 Caster-Camber Chart. 1971 10-30 Series

Vega
1. With shock absorber and stabilizer bar removed, raise vehicle and place jack stands under front braces.
2. Remove wheel and tire assembly.
3. Using a floor jack, support lower control arm. Use a wooden block between jack and lower control arm.
4. Remove the lower ball stud from the knuckle.
5. Remove tie rod end from the knuckle.
6. Slowly lower control arm until spring can be removed.

BALL JOINT INSPECTION
Upper Ball Joint
1. Raise vehicle and support on frame to allow control arms to hang free.
2. Remove wheel assembly.
3. Support lower control arm with adjustable jackstand and disconnect upper ball stud from steering knuckle.
4. Reinstall nut on ball stud and measure

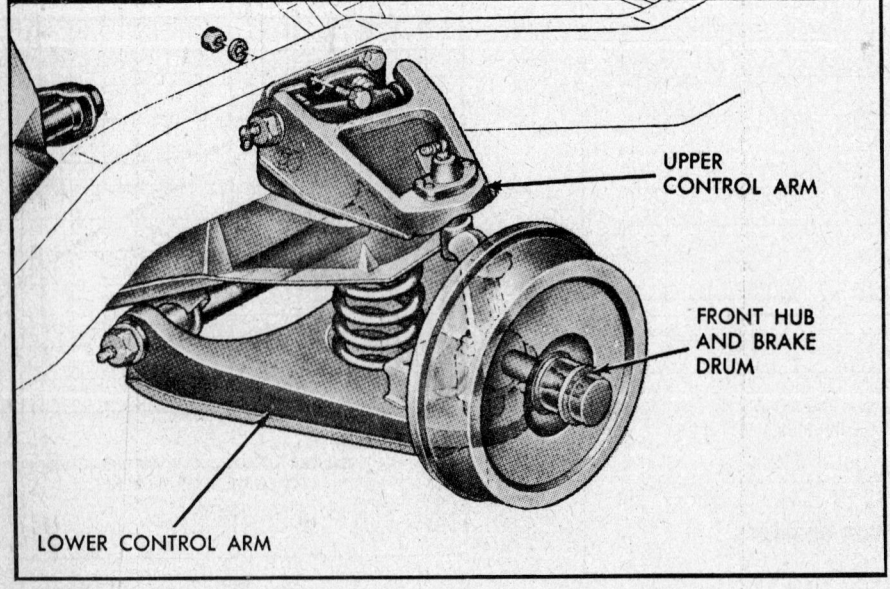

Fig. 7 Coil spring suspension. 1970–80 (typical)

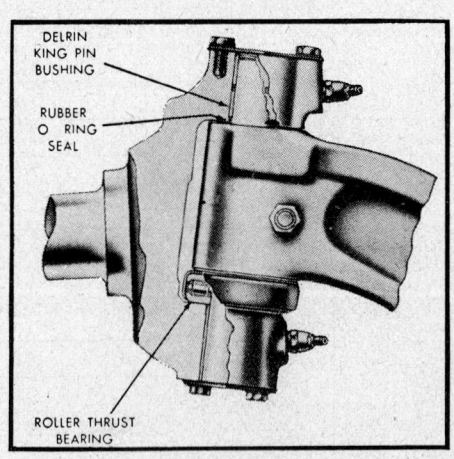

Fig. 12 Steering knuckle. 1970–75 4000, 5000 and 7000 lb. axles

CHEVROLET

WHEEL ALIGNMENT SPECIFICATION CHART

Dimension "A" in Inches Fig. 1A	Caster Angle Degrees														
	2½	2¾	3	3¼	3½	3¾	4	4¼	4½	4¾	5	5¼	5½	5¾	6
1972															
CA, PA, 10	—	—	+2	+1¾	+1½	+1¼	+1	+¾	+½	+¼	0	—	—	—	—
CA, PA 20-30	+2¾	+2½	+2	+1¾	+1½	+1¼	+1	+¾	+½	+¼	0	—	—	—	—
GA 10-20-30	—	+1½	+1	+¾	+½	+¼	0	-¼	-½	-¾	-1	—	—	—	—
K10-20	—	—	—	—	—	+4①	—	—	—	—	—	—	—	—	—
1973															
CA, PA 10	—	—	+2	+1½	+1¼	+1	+¾	+½	+¼	0	-½	—	—	—	—
CA, PA 20-30	+2	+1½	+1¼	+1	+¾	+¼	0	-¼	-½	-¾	-1	—	—	—	—
GA 10-20-30	+2¼	+2	+1½	+1¼	+1	+¾	+½	+¼	0	-¼	-½	—	—	—	—
K10-20	—	—	—	—	—	+4①	—	—	—	—	—	—	—	—	—
1974															
CA 10	—	—	+2	+1½	+1¼	+1	+¾	+½	+¼	0	-½	—	—	—	—
CA 20-30	+1½	+1¼	+1	+¾	+½	+¼	0	-¼	-½	-¾	-1	—	—	—	—
GA 10-30	+2¼	+2	+1½	+1¼	+1	+¾	+½	+¼	0	-¼	-½	—	—	—	—
K10-20	—	—	—	—	—	+4①	—	—	—	—	—	—	—	—	—
P10	—	—	—	+1½	+1¼	+1	+¾	+½	+¼	0	-¼	-½	-¾	-1	-1
P20-30	—	—	—	—	+1¼	+1	+¾	+½	+¼	0	-¼	-½	-¾	-1	-1
P30 (Motor Home)	—	—	+5	+4¾	+4½	+4¼	+4	+3¾	+3½	+3¼	+3	+2¾	+2¾	+2½	+2¼
1975-76															
C10	—	—	+2	+1½	+1¼	+1	+¾	+½	+¼	0	-½	—	—	—	—
C20-30	+1½	+1¼	+1	+¾	+½	+¼	0	-¼	-½	-¾	-1	—	—	—	—
K10-20	—	—	—	—	—	+4①	—	—	—	—	—	—	—	—	—
G10-20-30	+2¼	+2	+1½	+1¼	+1	+¾	+½	0	-¼	-½	—	—	—	—	—
P10-20-30	+2½	+2¼	+2	+1¾	+1½	+1	+¾	+½	+¼	0	-¼	—	—	—	—
Motor Home	+5¾	+5½	+5	+5	+4½	+4¼	+4	+4	+3½	+3¼	+3	—	—	—	—
1977															
C10	—	—	+2	+1½	+1¼	+1	+¾	+½	+¼	0	-½	—	—	—	—
C20-30	+1½	+1¼	+1	+¾	+½	+¼	0	-¼	-½	-¾	-1	—	—	—	—
K10-20-30	—	—	—	—	—	+8①	—	—	—	—	—	—	—	—	—
G10-20-30	+2¼	+2	+1½	+1¼	+1	+¾	+½	+¼	0	-¼	-½	—	—	—	—
P10-20-30	+2½	+2¼	+2	+1¾	+1½	+1	+¾	+½	+¼	0	-¼	—	—	—	—
Motor Home	+5¾	+5½	+5	+5	+4½	+4¼	+4	+4	+3½	+3¼	+3	—	—	—	—
1978															
C10	—	—	+2	+1½	+1¼	+1	+¾	+½	+¼	0	-½	—	—	—	—
C20-30	+1½	+1¼	+1	+¾	+½	+¼	0	-¼	-½	-¾	-1	—	—	—	—
K10-20-30	—	—	—	—	—	+8①	—	—	—	—	—	—	—	—	—
G10-20	+3¼	+3	+2¾	+2½	+2½	+2¼	+2	+2	+1¾	+1½	+1½	—	—	—	—
G30	+2¼	+2	+1½	+1¼	+1	+¾	+½	+¼	0	-¼	-½	—	—	—	—
P10-20-30	+2½	+2¼	+2	+1¾	+1½	+1	+¾	+½	+¼	0	-¼	—	—	—	—
Motor Home	+5¾	+5½	+5	+5	+4½	+4¼	+4	+4	+3½	+3¼	+3	—	—	—	—

Dimension "A" in Inches Fig. 1A	Caster Angle Degrees														
	1½	1¾	2	2¼	2½	2¾	3	3¼	3½	3¾	4	4¼	4½	4¾	5
1979															
C10	—	—	—	—	+2.4	+2.1	+1.8	+1.5	+1.2	+1	+.7	+.5	+.2	+.1	+.3
C20, 30	—	—	—	—	+1.5	+1.2	+.9	+.6	+.3	+.1	0	-.1	-.7	-1.0	-1.2
G10, 20	+2.9	+2.7	+2.3	+2.2	+2	+1.8	+1.6	+1.4	+1.3	+1.1	+.9	+.7	—	—	—
G30	+3.4	+3.0	+2.7	+2.4	+2.1	+1.8	+1.5	+1.3	+1.0	+.7	+.4	+.2	—	—	—
P10	—	—	—	—	+2.3	+2.0	+1.7	+1.5	+1.2	+.9	+.6	+.4	+.1	-.1	-.3
P20, 30	—	—	+2.9	+2.6	+2.3	+2.0	+1.7	+1.4	+1.2	+.9	+.6	+.4	+.2	+.1	—
Motor Home②	—	—	—	—	+5.5	+5.3	+5.0	+4.7	+4.4	+4.1	+3.8	+3.6	+3.3	+3.1	+2.9

Continued

CHEVROLET

WHEEL ALIGNMENT SPECIFICATION CHART—Continued

Dimension "A" in Inches Fig. 1A	Caster Angle Degrees														
	1½	1¾	2	2¼	2½	2¾	3	3¼	3½	3¾	4	4¼	4½	4¾	5
1980															
G10, G20	—	—	—	—	+3.25	+3	+2.75	+2.50	+2.50	+2.50	+2	+2	+1.75	+1.50	+1.50
G30	—	—	—	—	+2.25	+2	+1.50	+1.25	+1	+.75	+.50	+.25	−.25	−.25	−.50

①—No provision for resetting
②—With hydroboost brake system, add .3°.
   With tandem rear wheels, subtract .4°.

Dimension "A" in Inches Fig. 1A	Camber Angle Degrees														
	2½	2¾	3	3¼	3½	3¾	4	4¼	4½	4¾	5	5¼	5½	5¾	6
1975–76															
C10-20-30	—	—	—	—	—	+¼	—	—	—	—	—	—	—	—	—
K10-20	—	—	—	—	—	+1½①	—	—	—	—	—	—	—	—	—
G10-20-30	—	—	—	—	—	+¼	—	—	—	—	—	—	—	—	—
P10	0	0	+¼	+¼	+¼	+¼	+¼	0	0	0	−¼	−½	−¾	—	—
P20-30	0	0	+¼	+¼	+¼	+¼	+¼	+¼	0	0	−¼	+½	−¾	—	—
Motor Home	0	0	+¼	+¼	+¼	+¼	0	0	0	−¼	−½	−¾	−1	—	—
1977–78															
C10-20-30	—	—	—	—	—	+¼	—	—	—	—	—	—	—	—	—
K10-20-30	—	—	—	—	—	①	—	—	—	—	—	—	—	—	—
G10-20-30	—	—	—	—	—	+¼	—	—	—	—	—	—	—	—	—
P10	0	0	+¼	+¼	+¼	+¼	+¼	0	0	0	−¼	−½	−¾	—	—
P20-30	0	0	+¼	+¼	+¼	+¼	+¼	+¼	0	0	−¼	−½	−¾	—	—
Motor Home	0	0	+¼	+¼	+¼	+¼	0	0	0	−¼	−½	−¾	−1	—	—

①—No provision for resetting.

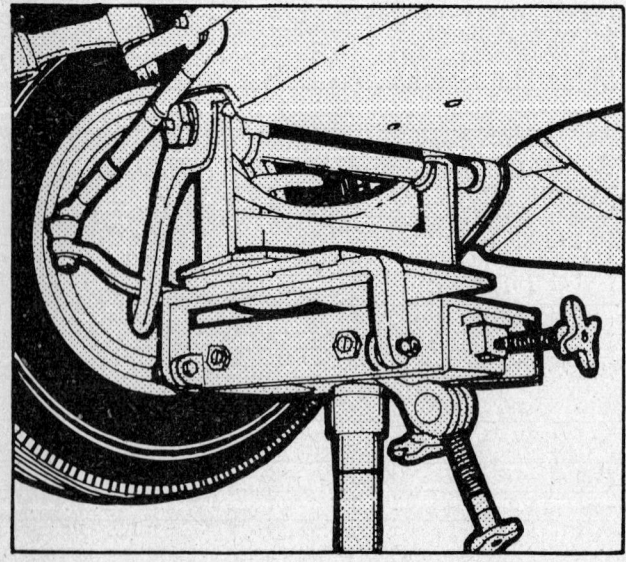

Fig. 8 Coil spring removal. 1970–80 (typical)

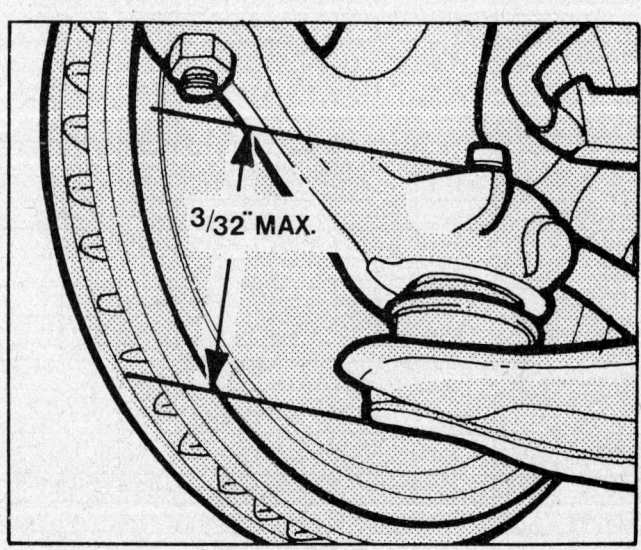

Fig. 9 Checking lower ball joint for wear

CHEVROLET

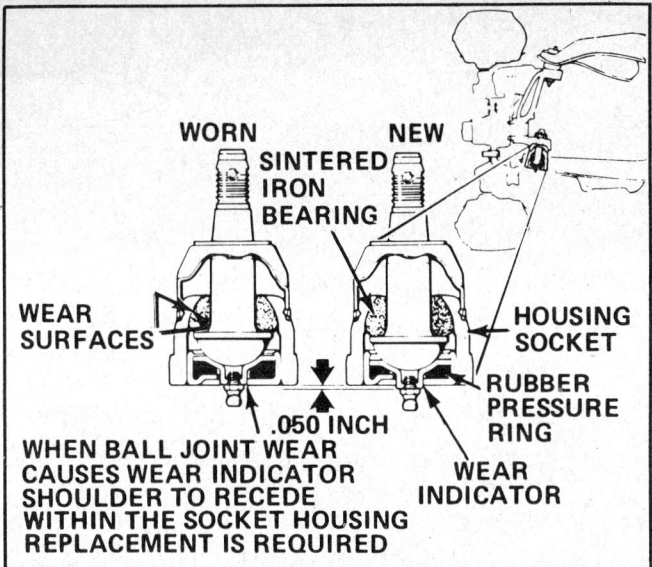

Fig. 10 Lower ball joint wear indicator

torque required to rotate stud with torque wrench. Specified torque for a new ball joint is 2-4 lbs. for Vega, 3-10 for El Camino and 5-10 for all other models. If torque readings are excessively high or low, replace ball joint.

Lower Ball Joint All Exc. 1970-73 El Camino & All Vega Models

NOTE: Lower ball joints are a loose fit when not connected to the steering knuckle. Wear may be checked without disassembling the ball stud as follows:

1. Support weight of control arms at wheel hub and drum.
2. Measure distance between tip of ball stud and tip of grease fitting below ball joint, Fig. 9.
3. Move support to control arm to allow wheel hub and drum to hang free. Measure distance as in Step 2. If difference in measurements exceeds 1/16 inch for El Camino and 3/32 inch for all other models, ball joint is worn and should be replaced.

1970-73 El Camino

Raise car and support lower control arm so spring is compressed in the same manner as if the wheels were on the ground and check axial (up and down) play at ball joint. If play exceeds 1/16", replace the joint.

Another indication of lower ball joint excessive wear is when difficulty is experienced when lubricating the joint. If the liner has worn to the point where the lubrication grooves in the liner have been worn away, then abnormal pressure is required to force lubricant through the joint. Should this condition be evident, replace both lower ball joints.

Vega

The lower ball joint is checked for wear by checking to be sure torque is present. After dislodging ball joint from steering knuckle perform the following:

1. Install the stud nut to the ball stud.
2. Check the torque required to turn the ball stud in the seat.

NOTE: Some torque is required, if zero torque is observed, sufficient wear has taken place for replacement of the ball joint.

1974-80 El Camino & 1975 Vega

These vehicles use lower ball joints incorporating wear indicators. Refer to Fig. 10 to check for wear.

STEERING GEAR, REPLACE

1971-80

1. Place front wheels in straight ahead position.
2. On C-K and El Camino models, remove flexible coupling to steering shaft bolts. On P models, remove lower universal joint pinch bolts and mark position of universal yoke to wormshaft.
3. On all models, mark position of pitman arm to pitman shaft and remove pitman shaft nut or pinch bolt, then pitman arm from shaft with a puller.
4. Unfasten steering gear and remove.
5. On C-K models, remove flexible coupling pinch bolt, then flexible coupling from steering gear wormshaft.

1970

1. Loosen bolt attaching lower end of shaft to steering gear.
2. Disconnect pitman arm from gear.
3. Unfasten steering gear from frame and remove from vehicle.

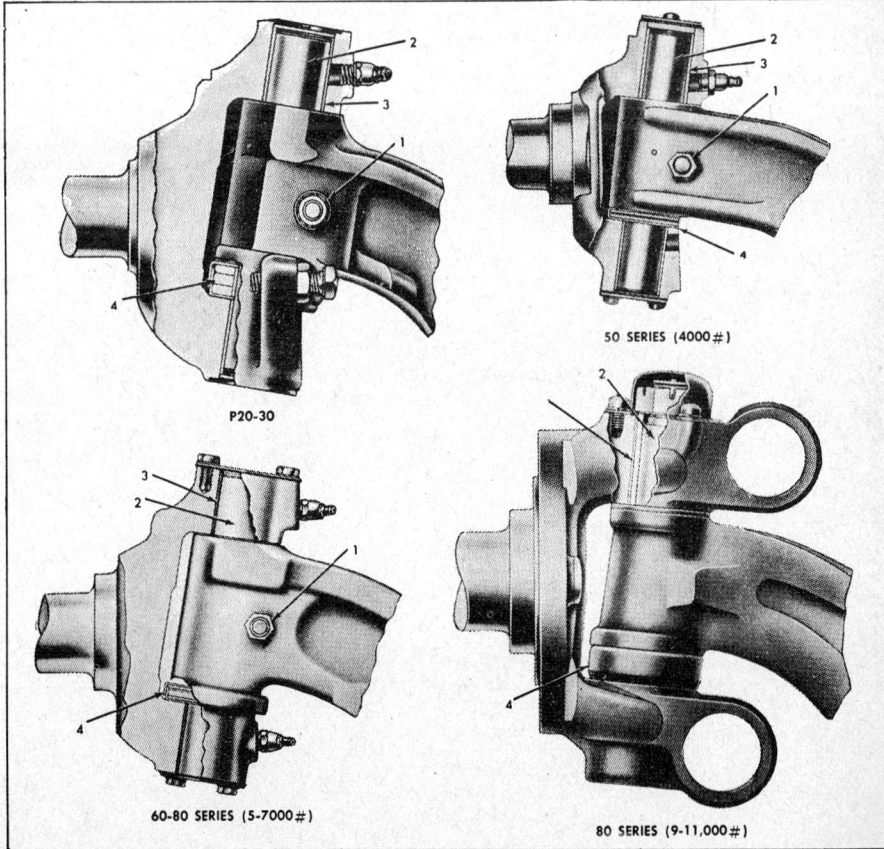

Fig. 11 Steering knuckles and kingpins
1. Kingpin lockpin. 2. Kingpin. 3. Bushing. 4. Thrust bearing.

DIAMOND REO

CONSOLIDATION OF DIAMOND T AND REO TRUCKS

INDEX OF SERVICE OPERATIONS

Page No.

AXLES, DRIVING
Eaton Axle Service	204
Spicer Axle Service	239
Timken Axle Service	241
Locking Differentials	192
Front Wheel Locking Hubs	505

BRAKES
Adjustments	590
Air Brake Service	620
Anti-Skid Brakes	551
Bendix Twinplex Brake	608
Brake Booster Service	639
Hydraulic System Service	632
Parking Brake Service	612
Stopmaster Brake Service	599

CLUTCHES
Air-Hydraulic (Air-Pak)	468
Clutch Service	429

COOLING SYSTEM
Cooling System Capacity	925
Variable Speed Fans	10
Water Pumps	933

ELECTRICAL
Alternator Service	52
Dash Gauge Service	179
Distributors, Standard	141
Electronic Ignition	152
Generator Service	11
Ignition Coils and Resistors	7
Starting Motor Service	29
Starter Switch Service	21
Tune Up Service	2

ENGINE
Camshaft and Bearings	932
Crankshaft End Play	933
Crankshaft Rear Oil Seal	933
Cylinder Head, Replace	932
Cylinder Sleeves	932
Piston and Rod, Assemble	932
Rocker Arms	932
Timing Gears	932
Valve Rotators	932

Page No.

ENGINE OILING
Crankcase Capacity	925
Oil Pump	933

FUEL & EXHAUST
Carburetor Adjustments	933
Crankcase Ventilation	748
Emission Controls	750
Fuel Pump Service	183
L.P.G. Carburetion	190
Turbochargers	187

SPECIFICATIONS
Alternator	929
Carburetor Adjustments	933
Crankshaft and Bearing	931
Distributor	927
Engine Tightening Torque	927
General Engine Data	926
Generator and Regulator	929
Piston, Pin and Ring	931
Starting Motor	928
Tune Up	927
Valve	927
Wheel Alignment	930

STEERING
Manual Steering Gear Service	680
Power Steering Gear Service	686

TRANSFER CASES
TRANSFER CASES	469

TRANSMISSIONS, Manual
Clark	275
Fuller	289
New Process	329
Spicer	346
Warner	406

TRANSMISSIONS, Automatic
Allison MT-640, 643, 644, 650, 653 & 654 CR	512
Allison (6 Speed)	518, 936

DIAMOND REO

MODEL INDEX & ENGINE APPLICATION

Models	Year	Engine Make	Standard Engine Model	Crankcase Refill Capacity, Qts.	Cooling System Capacity, Qts.
CONVENTIONAL TRUCKS					
C-10142	1970	Own	6-130	8	—
C-10142	1971-72	Own	6-145	8	15
C-10142	1973	Own	6-200	—	—
C-10142D	1970-73	Cummins	V8-185	—	12
C-10144	1970-72	Own	6-170	8	15
C-10144	1973	Own	6-200	—	—
C-10144D	1970	Cummins	V8-185	—	12
C-10144D	1973	Cummins	V8-185	—	—
DC-10142	1973	Own	6-170	—	—
DC-10142	1974-75	Own	6-200	—	—
DC-10142D	1973	Cummins	V8-185	—	—
DC-10142D	1974	Cummins	V8-210	—	—
DC-10142D	1975	Cummins	V-555	—	—
DC-10144D	1973	Cummins	V8-185	—	—
DC-10144	1974	Own	6-200	—	—
DC-10144D	1974	Cummins	V8-210	—	—
CONVENTIONAL TANDEMS					
C-10164	1970-72	Own	6-170	8	15
C-10164	1973-75	Own	6-200	—	—
C-10164D	1970-73	Cummins	V8-185	—	12
C-10165	1970-72	Own	6-170	8	15
C-10166	1971-72	Own	6-170	8	—
C-10166	1973	Own	6-200	—	—
C-10166D	1970	Cummins	V8-185	—	12
C-10166D	1971-73	Cummins	V8-210	—	14
C-10186	1972	Own	6-200	8	—
C-10186D	1972	Cummins	C-180	16	—
DC-10164	1973	Own	6-170	—	—
DC-10164	1974-75	Own	6-200	—	—
DC-10164D	1974	Cummins	V8-210	—	—
DC-10164D	1975	Cummins	V-555	—	—
DC-10166	1974	Own	6-200	—	—
DC-10166D	1974	Cummins	V8-210	—	—
90" BBC TRUCKS					
C-9042	1970-71	Own	6-145	8	15
C-9064	1970	Own	8-235	9	19½
C-9064	1971	Own	8-250	—	19½
TILT CAB FORWARD					
CF-5942	1970-71	Own	6-170	8	15
CF-5942T	1970-71	Own	6-170	8	15
CF-5942TD	1970	Cummins	V6-140		
CF-5942D	1970	Cummins	C-180	16	13
CF-5942DDV	1970	Detroit	6V-53N		22
CF-5964	1970	Own	6-170	8	15
CF-5964	1971	Own	6-200	8	15
CF-6542	1972-73	Own	6-200	8	15
CF-6542D	1971-73	Cummins	8-210	—	—
CF-6564	1972-73	Own	6-200	8	15
CF-6564D	1971-73	Cummins	8-210	—	14
CF-5964D	1970	Cummins	C-180	16	13
TILT CAB FORWARD—Continued					
CF-6042	1975	Own	6-200	—	—
CF-6042D	1975	Cummins	V-555	—	—
CF-6064	1975	Own	6-200	—	—
CF-6064D	1975	Cummins	V-555	—	—
CF-6842	1970-71	Chevrolet	8-350	—	—
CF-6842	1970-71	Chevrolet	8-366	—	—
CF-6842D	1970-71	Cummins	V6-140	—	—
CF-8342	1970-71	Own	6-145	8	—
CF-8342D	1970	Perkins	6-354	—	—
CF-8342D	1970-71	Cummins	C-180	16	13
CF-8364	1970-71	Own	6-170	8	—
CF-8364D	1970-71	Cummins	C-180	16	13
CONVENTIONAL DIESEL					
C-11442D	1970	Cummins	NH-220	20	20
C-11442DL	1970	Cummins	NH-220	20	20
C-11442D	1971	Cummins	NH-230	20	20
C-11442DL	1971	Cummins	NH-230	20	20
C-11464D	1970	Cummins	NH-220	20	20
C-11464DL	1970	Cummins	NH-220	20	20
C-11464D	1971	Cummins	NH-230	20	20
C-11464DL	1971	Cummins	NH-230	20	20
C-11642D	1972-73	Cummins	NH-230	20	—
C-11642D	1974-75	Cummins	NTC-290	—	—
C-11642DL	1972-73	Cummins	NH-230	20	—
C-11664DB	1972	Cummins	NTC-270	28	—
C-11664DFLW	1973-74	Cummins	NTC-350	—	—
C-11664DFW	1973-74	Cummins	NTC-350	—	—
C-11664MM	1972	Cummins	NTC-270	28	—
C-11664D	1971-72	Cummins	NTC-335	20	28
C-11664DL	1971-72	Cummins	NTC-335	20	28
C-11664D	1973	Cummins	NH-230	—	—
C-11664D	1974-75	Cummins	NTC-290	—	—
C-11664DL	1973	Cummins	NH-230	—	—
C-11942D	1974-75	Cummins	NTC-290	—	—
C-11942DL	1974	Cummins	NTC-290	—	—
C-11964D	1974-75	Cummins	NTC-350	—	—
C-11964DL	1974	Cummins	NTC-350	—	—
90" BBC DIESEL					
C-9042D	1970-71	Detroit	6-71N	22	18
C-9042D	1970	Cummins	NH-220	20	20
C-9042DL	1970-71	Detroit	6-71N	22	18
C-9042DL	1970	Cummins	NH-220	20	20
C-9042D	1971	Cummins	NH-230	20	20
C-9042DL	1971	Cummins	NH-230	20	20
C-9064D	1970-71	Detroit	6-71N	22	18
C-9064DL	1970-71	Detroit	6-71N	22	18
C-9064D	1971-72	Cummins	NH-230	20	20
C-9064DL	1971	Cummins	NH-230	20	20
C-9242D	1972-73	Cummins	NH-230	20	
C-9242DL	1972-73	Cummins	NH-230	20	

Continued

DIAMOND REO

MODEL INDEX & ENGINE APPLICATION—Continued

Models	Year	Engine Make	Standard Engine Model	Crankcase Refill Capacity, Qts.	Cooling System Capacity, Qts.
90" BBC DIESEL—Continued					
C-9242D	1974–75	Cummins	NTC-290		
C-9242DL	1974	Cummins	NTC-290		
C-9264D	1972–73	Cummins	NH-230	20	
C-9264DL	1972–73	Cummins	NH-230	30	
C-9264D	1974–75	Cummins	NTC-290		
C-9264DL	1974	Cummins	NTC-290		
TILT C.O.E. DIESEL					
CO-5042D	1970	Cummins	NH-220	20	20
CO-5042DL	1970	Cummins	NH-220	20	20
CO-5042D	1971	Cummins	NH-230	20	20
CO-5042DL	1971	Cummins	NH-230	20	20
CO-5064D	1970	Cummins	NH-220	20	20
CO-5064DL	1970	Cummins	NH-220	20	20
CO-5064D	1971	Cummins	NH-230	20	20
CO-5064DL	1971	Cummins	NH-230	20	20
CO-5442D	1974–75	Cummins	NTC-290		
CO-5442DL	1974	Cummins	NTC-290		
CO-5464D	1974	Cummins	NTC-290		
CO-5464D	1975	Cummins	NTC-350		
CO-5464DL	1974	Cummins	NTC-290		
CO-5464DW	1973–74	Cummins	NTC-350		
CO-5464DLW	1973–74	Cummins	NTC-350		
CO-8842D	1974–75	Cummins	NTC-290		
CO-8842DL	1974	Cummins	NTC-290		
CO-8864D	1974	Cummins	NTC-290		
CO-8864D	1975	Cummins	NTC-350		
TILT C.O.E. DIESEL—Continued					
CO-8864DL	1974	Cummins	NTC-290		
CO-8864DW	1973–74	Cummins	NTC-350		
CO-8864DLW	1973–74	Cummins	NTC-350		
TRI-DRIVE					
C-10186	1970–71	Own	6-200	8	15
C-10186D	1970–73	Cummins	V8-210		14
C-9086	1970	Own	8-235	9	
C-11486D	1970	Cummins	NH-220		20
C-11486D	1971–73	Cummins	NH-230		20
C-11686D	1972	Cummins	NH-230	20	
OFF-HIGHWAY VEHICLES					
C-10164-OH	1970–72	Own	6-200	8	15
C-10164D-OH	1972	Cummins	6-200		15
C-10164D-OH	1972	Cummins	C-180	16	
C-9064-OH	1970	Own	8-235	9	
C-9086-OH	1970	Own	8-235	9	
C-11464D-OH	1970–71	Cummins	NH-220		20
C-11486D-OH	1970–71	Cummins	NH-220		20
C-11664D-OH	1972	Cummins	NH-230	20	
C-11664D-OH	1974	Cummins	NTC-290		
C-11686D-OH	1972	Cummins	NH-230	20	
C-11964D-OH	1974	Cummins	NTC-290		
MISCELLANEOUS VEHICLES					
CF-5542	1970–71	Own	6-200	8	15
CF-5542D	1970	Cummins	V8-185	12	12

GENERAL ENGINE SPECIFICATIONS

Year	Engine Model	Number Cylinders & Valve Location	Bore & Stroke	Piston Displ. Cu. In.	Comp. Ratio	Horsepower @ R.P.M.	Torque Lbs. Ft. @ R.P.M.	Governed Speed R.P.M. No Load	Normal Oil Pressure P.S.I.
1970–71	145–145B	6 In Head	4 1/8 × 4 1/8	331	6.73	145 @ 3200	270 @ 1600	3350	35
1970–73	170B	6 In Head	4 1/8 × 4 1/8	331	8.0	170 @ 3400	297 @ 1600	3550①	35
1970–73	200	6 In Head	4 1/4 × 4.7	400	8.0	200 @ 3400	365 @ 1200	3350②	35
1974	6-200	6 In Head	4 1/4 × 4.7	400	7.5	172 @ 3200	345	3200	35
1970–71	235B	8 In Head	4 1/8 × 4 1/8	440	7.3	235 @ 3400	412 @ 2400	3550	35
1970–73	250	8 In Head	4 1/4 × 4 1/8	468	7.50	250 @ 3400	420 @ 2400	3550①	35
1974	8-250	8 In Head	4 1/4 × 4 1/8	468	7.5	228 @ 3400	404	3400	35
1970–71	350	8 In Head	4.0 × 3.48	350	8.0	215 @ 4000	335 @ 2800	4150	50–65
1970–71	366	8 In Head	3.937 × 3.76	366	8.0	235 @ 4000	345 @ 2600	4150	40–55

①—1972–73 3400 governed speed.
②—1972–73 3200 governed speed.

Diamond REO

TUNE UP & VALVE SPECIFICATIONS

Year	Engine Model	Firing Order	Spark Plug Type	Spark Plug Gap	Ignition Timing Mark BTDC	Ignition Timing Location	Valve Angles Seat	Valve Angles Face	Valve Lash Intake	Valve Lash Exhaust	Minimum Valve Spring Pressure Lbs. @ Inch Length
1970-71	145B	153624	J6	.025	6°	Damper①	30	29½	.018C	.018C	64 @ 1.78
1970-73④	170-170B	153624	J6	.025	6°	Damper①	30	29½	.023C	.023C	64 @ 1.78⑤
1970-74⑤	200	153624	J6	.025	6°	Damper①	30	29½	.023C	.023C	64 @ 1.78⑤
1970-71	235B	②	XH-10	.025	6°	Damper①	30	29½	.023C	.023C	64 @ 1.78③
1970-74⑤	250	②	XH-10	.025	⑥	Damper①	30	29½	.023C	.023C	64 @ 1.78③
1970-71	350	②	XJ-6	.035	4°	Damper①	46	45	—	—	76 @ 1.70
1970-71	366	②	N-6	.035	6°	Damper①	46	45	—	—	84 @ 1.80

①—1970 and later engines include flywheel timing marks visible through an opening on left side of flywheel housing. Either may be used depending on ease of viewing.
②—Firing order 15486372. Cylinder numbering (front to rear): Right bank 1-2-3-4, left bank 5-6-7-8.
③—Exhaust springs 63.5 @ 1.583".
④—1973 Calif., electronic ignition.
⑤—1973 Calif. & all 1974, electronic ignition.
⑥—TDC at 400 R.P.M.

ENGINE TIGHTENING SPECIFICATIONS★

★ Torque Specifications are for clean and lightly lubricated threads only. Dry or dirty threads produce increased friction which prevents accurate measurement of tightness.

Year	Engine Model	Spark Plugs Ft. Lbs.	Cylinder Head Bolts Ft. Lbs.	Intake Manifold Ft. Lbs.	Exhaust Manifold Ft. Lbs.	Rocker Arm Shaft Bracket	Connecting Rod Cap Bolts Ft. Lbs.	Main Bearing Cap Bolts Ft. Lbs.	Flywheel to Crankshaft Ft. Lbs.	Vibration Damper or Pulley Ft. Lbs.
1970-71	145B	25-30	110-120①	—	—	—	60-65	110-120	60-67	30-35
1970-71	170B	25-30	110-120①	—	—	—	60-65	110-120	60-67	30-35
1970-71	200	25-30	110-120①	—	—	—	60-65	110-120	60-67	30-35
1970-71	235B	25-30	110-120①	—	—	—	60-65	110-120	65-70	30-35
1970-71	250	25-30	110-120①	—	—	—	60-65	110-120	65-70	30-35
1970-71	350	25-30	110-120①	—	—	—	60-65	110-120	65-70	30-35
1970-71	366	25-30	110-120①	—	—	—	60-65	110-120	65-70	30-35

①—Cylinder head bolts must be retorqued after the first 10 hours of engine operation under a load or the first 500 miles. Back off each bolt ½ turn and tighten to specified torque.

DISTRIBUTOR SPECIFICATIONS

Unit Part No. ①	Rotation ②	Cam Angle, Degrees	Breaker Gap, In.	Condenser Capacity, Mfds.	Breaker Arm Spring Tension, Oz.	Centrifugal Advance Deg. @ R.P.M. of Dist. Advance Starts	Centrifugal Advance Full Advance	Vacuum Advance Inches of Vacuum to Start Plunger Movement	Vacuum Advance Inches of Vacuum for Full Plunger Travel	Maximum Vacuum Advance, Dist. Degrees
1110620	C	26-33	.016	.20-.25	17-21	1 @ 275	14 @ 1200	None	None	None
1110621	C	26-33	.016	.20-.25	17-21	1 @ 325	15 @ 1500	None	None	None
1110623	C	26-33	.016	.20-.25	17-21	1 @ 300	12½ @ 525	None	None	None
1110631	C	26-33	.016	.20-.25	17-21	1 @ 275	15 @ 1200	None	None	None
1110632	C	26-33	.016	.20-.25	17-21	1 @ 325	16 @ 1500	None	None	None
1110633	C	26-33	.016	.20-.25	17-21	1 @ 300	12 @ 525	None	None	None
1111660	C	30	.016	.20-.25	17-21	1 @ 325	16 @ 1500	None	None	None
1111774	C	31-37	.022	.20-.25	17-21	1 @ 275	16 @ 1500	None	None	None
1111779	CC	31-37	.022	.20-.25	17-21	1 @ 325	16 @ 1500	None	None	None
1111806	C	31-37	.022	.20-.25	17-21	1 @ 250	18 @ 1050	None	None	None
1111812	C	31-37	.022	.20-.25	17-21	1 @ 275	15 @ 1150	None	None	None
1111832	C	31-37	.022	.20-.25	17-21	1 @ 225	14 @ 1050	None	None	None
1111854	C	38-45	.016	.20-.25	17-21	1 @ 225	14 @ 1050	None	None	None

Continued

DIAMOND REO

DISTRIBUTOR SPECIFICATIONS—Continued

Unit Part No. ①	Rotation ②	Cam Angle, Degrees	Breaker Gap, In.	Condenser Capacity, Mfds.	Breaker Arm Spring Tension, Oz.	Centrifugal Advance Deg. @ R.P.M. of Dist.		Vacuum Advance		
						Advance Starts	Full Advance	Inches of Vacuum to Start Plunger Movement	Inches of Vacuum for Full Plunger Travel	Maximum Vacuum Advance, Dist. Degrees
1111862	C	31–37	.022	.20–.25	17–21	1 @ 300	11 @ 1200	None	None	None
1111866	C	38–45	.016	.20–.25	17–21	1 @ 275	15 @ 1150	None	None	None
1111905	C	38–45	.016	.20–.25	17–21	1 @ 450	16 @ 1700	None	None	None
1111922	C	38–45	.016	.20–.25	17–21	1 @ 450	13 @ 1375	None	None	None
1111923	C	38–45	.016	.20–.25	17–21	1 @ 425	11 @ 1700	None	None	None
1112355	CC	31–37	.022	.20–.25	17–21	1 @ 250	15 @ 1500	3–5	13–15	7.5
1112365	C	31–37	.022	.20–.25	17–21	1 @ 250	16 @ 1200	None	None	None
1112405	C	31–37	.022	.20–.25	17–21	1 @ 275	15 @ 1150	None	None	None

①—Stamped on plate riveted to housing.
②—As viewed from top! C—Clockwise. CC—Counter-clockwise.

STARTING MOTOR SPECIFICATIONS

Starter Number	Brush Spring Tension, Oz. Minimum	Free Speed Test			Resistance Test①		Lock Torque Test		
		Amperes	Volts	R.P.M.	Amperes	Volts	Amperes	Volts	Torque Ft.-Lbs.
1107224	35	65–100②	10.6	3600–5100	300–360	3.5	—	—	—
1107321	—	55–80②	9	3500–6000	—	—	—	—	—
1107350	—	55–80②	9	3500–6000	—	—	—	—	—
1107506	35	75–100②	10.6	6450–8750	720–870②	5.0	—	—	—
1107542	35	75–100②	10.6	6450–8750	720–870②	5.0	—	—	—
1107578	—	50–80②	9	5500–9000	—	—	—	—	—
1107607	24	75	10.3	6500	—	—	460	5.2	11.5
1107671	35	112	10.6	3240	320–385	3.5	—	—	—
1107681	35	65–100②	10.6	3600–5100	300–360	3.5	—	—	—
1108133	24	70	11.3	6000	—	—	530	6.7	16
1108369	—	35–75②	9	6000–9000	—	—	—	—	—
1108409	24	70	10.0	3000	—	—	490	6.5	28
1108603	24	75	11.25	6000	—	—	615	5.85	29
1108621	24	75	11.25	6000	—	—	615	5.85	29
1108724	36	115	11.6	7000	—	—	570	2.3	20
1108813	36	115	11.6	7000	—	—	570	2.3	20
1108840	36	115	11.6	7000	—	—	570	2.3	20
1108863	36	100	23.0	8000	—	—	525	3.0	32
1108871	36	100	23.0	8000	—	—	525	3.0	32
1108872	36	100	23.0	8000	—	—	525	3.0	32
1108881	36	100	23.0	8000	—	—	525	3.0	32
1108985	36	65	11.3	5500	—	—	675	4.0	30
1109150	36	65	11.4	6000	—	—	725	5.0	44
1113653	—	75–105②	9	5000–7000	—	—	—	—	—
1113658	—	124–185②	9	4700–7600	—	—	—	—	—
1113842	—	75–95②	20	5500–7500	—	—	—	—	—
1114052	—	120–150②	9	3000–4500	—	—	—	—	—
1114058	—	140–190②	9	4000–7000	—	—	—	—	—
1114072	—	140–190②	9	4000–7000	—	—	—	—	—
1114088	—	140–190②	9	4000–7000	—	—	—	—	—
1114089	—	105–135	9	3000–4500	—	—	—	—	—
1114128	—	140–190②	9	4000–7000	—	—	—	—	—
1114145	—	140–190②	9	4000–7000	—	—	—	—	—
1114161	—	140–190②	9	4000–7000	—	—	—	—	—

Continued

DIAMOND REO

STARTING MOTOR NOTES—Continued

①—Check capacity of motor by using a 500 ampere meter and a carbon pile rheostat to control voltage. Apply volts listed across motor with armature locked. Current should be as listed.
②—Includes solenoid.

ALTERNATOR SPECIFICATIONS

| | Alternator | | | | | Regulator | | | |
| | | Rated Output | | Field Current | | | Regulator Test @ 120° F. | | |
Model	Make	Amperes	Volts	Amperes	Volts	Model	Ampere Load	Altern. R.P.M.	Volts
4400JA	Leece-Neville	75	12	—	—	13703RA	—	—	—
6018AC	Leece-Neville	40	12	—	—	13703RA	—	—	—
6218AC	Leece-Neville	53	12	—	—	13703RA	—	—	—
7000AB	Leece-Neville	65	12	—	—	13703RA	—	—	—
7064AA	Leece-Neville	65	12	—	—	13703RA	—	—	—
7500AA	Leece-Neville	85	12	—	—	13703RA	—	—	—
7504AA	Leece-Neville	85	12	—	—	13703RA	—	—	—
7600AA	Leece-Neville	105	12	—	—	13703RA	—	—	—
7604AA	Leece-Neville	105	12	—	—	13703RA	—	—	—
7701AA	Leece-Neville	130	24	—	—	5078RA	—	—	—
1100068	Delco-Remy	52	12	2.2–2.6	12	1119507	—	—	—
1100842	Delco-Remy	42	12	2.2–2.6	12	1119507	—	—	—
1100849	Delco-Remy	61	12	2.2–2.6	12	1119507	—	—	—
1117058	Delco-Remy	85	12	6–6.6	12	9000590	—	—	—
1117089	Delco-Remy	60	12	6–6.6	12	9000590	—	—	—
1117090	Delco-Remy	85	12	6–6.2	12	9000590	—	—	—
1117128	Delco-Remy	130	12	2.22–2.4	12	9000590	—	—	—
1117225	Delco-Remy	75	12	4.1–4.5	12	—	—	—	—
1117753	Delco-Remy	55	12	2.33–2.47	12	①	—	—	—
1117756	Delco-Remy	62	12	4.14–4.62	12	9000590	—	—	—
1117772	Delco-Remy	45	24	3.2–3.5	24	1000591	—	—	—

①—1119507 or 1119605.

GENERATOR & REGULATOR SPECIFICATIONS

★ To Polarize Generator: For internally grounded systems, disconnect field lead from regulator and momentarily flash this lead to regulator battery terminal. For externally grounded systems, reconnect leads to regulator; then momentarily connect a jumper wire from the "Gen" or "Arm" to the "Bat" terminals of the regulator.

| | Generator | | | | | Regulator | | | | | |
| | | | | | | | Cutout Relay | | | | Current & Voltage Reg. Arm. Air Gap, In. |
Gen. No. ①	Rotation and Ground Polarity ③	Brush Spring Tension, Oz.	Rated Cap. Amps.	Gen. Field Ground Location★	Field Current	Reg. No. ②	Closing Voltage	Arm. Air Gap, In.	Voltage Setting	Current Setting	
1100031	C-P	28	40	External	1.87–2.0④	1118842	6.3	.020	7.2	40	.075
1102040	C-N	28	30	External	1.48–1.62⑤	1119001	12.6	.020	14.3	30	.075
1102044	C-N	28	30	External	1.48–1.63⑤	1119001	12.6	.020	14.3	30	.075
1102044	C-P	28	30	External	1.48–1.62⑤	1118839	12.6	.020	14.3	30	.075
1102059	C-N	28	30	External	1.48–1.62⑤	1119001	12.6	.020	14.3	30	.075
1105127	C-N	28	35	External	2.73–3.00	1119604	12.0	.020	14.3	35	.075
1106805	CC-P	20	50	External	1.37–1.50⑤	1118338	12.8	.020	14.3	50	.075
1106808	C-P	20	50	External	1.37–1.50⑤	1118339	12.6	.020	14.2	50	.075
1106821	C	20	40	External	1.37–1.50⑤	1118887	12.7	.020	14.3	40	.075
1106822	C-P	20	50	External	1.37–1.50⑤	1119156	12.6	.020	14.2	50	.075
1106986	C	20	50	External	2.14–2.28	1119606	12.0	.020	14.3	50	.075

Continued

DIAMOND REO

GENERATOR & REGULATOR SPECIFICATIONS—Continued

★ To Polarize Generator: For internally grounded systems, disconnect field lead from regulator and momentarily flash this lead to regulator battery terminal. For externally grounded systems, reconnect leads to regulator; then momentarily connect a jumper wire from the "Gen" or "Arm" to the "Bat" terminals of the regulator.

Generator						Regulator					
Gen. No. ①	Rotation and Ground Polarity ③	Brush Spring Tension, Oz.	Rated Cap. Amps.	Gen. Field Ground Location★	Field Current	Reg. No. ②	Cutout Relay		Voltage Setting	Current Setting	Current & Voltage Reg. Arm. Air Gap, In.
							Closing Voltage	Arm. Air Gap, In.			
1106990	C	20	50	External	2.14–2.28	1119606	12.0	.020	14.3	50	.075
1106991	C	20	55	External	2.14–2.28	1119605	12.0	.020	14.3	55	.075

①—Stamped on plate riveted to housing.
②—Stamped on regulator base.
③—C—Clockwise at drive end.
CC—Counterclockwise at drive end.
P—Positive. N—Negative.
④—At 6 volts.
⑤—At 12 volts.

REO WHEEL ALIGNMENT SPECIFICATIONS

Truck Model	Axle Model	Caster Deg.	Camber Deg.*	Toe-In Inch	Kingpin Angle°†
C, CF & CO Series					
C-90	FC-901	3	1	0–1/8	5 1/2
	FD-901	3	1	0–1/8	5 1/2
	FF-901	3	1	0–1/8	5 1/2
	FH-901	3	1	0–1/8	5 1/2
	FL-901	3	1	0–1/8	5 1/2
	F-901	0①	0	3/16–5/16	0
	FDS-901	0①	0	0–1/8	0
	Model 17	0①	0	0–1/8	0
C-90D	FE-970	3	1	0–1/8	–1
C-101	32550	3	1	0–1/8	5 1/2
C-114D	FE-970	3	1	0–1/8	–1
C-270	31104	2	1	0–1/8	8
	32500	2	1	0–1/8	8
	FC-901	1 1/2	1	0–1/8	5 1/2
C-370	32500	2	1	0–1/8	8
	FC-901	1 1/2	1	0–1/8	5 1/2
	FD-901	1 1/2	1	0–1/8	5 1/2
C-378	FD-900	–1 3/4	1	0–1/8	5 1/2
	FE-900	–1 3/4	1	0–1/8	5 1/2
C-440	F-233	5–7	0	3/16–5/16	0
C-442-OH	F-233	5–7	0	3/16–5/16	0
C-470	32500	2	1	0–1/8	8
	FC-901	1 1/2	1	0–1/8	5 1/2
	FD-901	1 1/2	1	0–1/8	5 1/2
C-478	FD-900	–1 3/4	1	0–1/8	5 1/2
	FE-900	–1 3/4	1	0–1/8	5 1/2
C-536-OH	FG-900	1 1/2	1	0–1/8	5 1/2
C-578	FE-900	–1 3/4	1	0–1/8	5 1/2
CF-83	FC-901	3	1	0–1/8	5 1/2
	FD-901	3	1	0–1/8	5 1/2
	FF-901	3	1	0–1/8	5 1/2
	FH-901	3	1	0–1/8	5 1/2
	FL-901	3	1	0–1/8	5 1/2
	F-235	0①	0	3/16–5/16	0
	FDS-1800	0①	0	0–1/8	0
	Model 17	0①	0	0–1/8	0
C, CF & CO Series—Continued					
CO-50D	FF-901	3	1	0–1/8	5 1/2
	FH-901	3	1	0–1/8	5 1/2
	FFL-901	3	1	0–1/8	5 1/2
CO-78D	FF-901	3	1	0–1/8	5 1/2
	FH-901	3	1	0–1/8	5 1/2
	FL-901	3	1	0–1/8	5 1/2
D Series					
D-478	FD-900	–1 3/4	1	0–1/8	5 1/2
	FE-900	–1 3/4	1	0–1/8	5 1/2
D-632	FE-900	1 1/2	1	0–1/8	5 1/2
D-636	27462	3	1	1/16–1/8	8
D-678	FE-900	–1 3/4	1	0–1/8	5 1/2
D-730	FE-900	1 1/2	1	0–1/8	5 1/2
D-732	27462	3	1	1/16–1/8	8
DC & DCL Series					
DC-101	32550	3	1	0–1/8	5 1/2
DC-403	FD-900	1 1/2	1	0–1/8	5 1/2
	FE-900	1 1/2	1	0–1/8	5 1/2
DC-503	FD-900	1 1/2	1	0–1/8	5 1/2
	FE-900	1 1/2	1	0–1/8	5 1/2
DC-603	FD-900	1 1/2	1	0–1/8	5 1/2
	FE-900	1 1/2	1	0–1/8	5 1/2
DC-633	FD-900	1 1/2	1	0–1/8	5 1/2
	FE-900	1 1/2	1	0–1/8	5 1/2
DCL-633D	FE-900	1 1/2	1	0–1/8	5 1/2
DC-703	FD-900	1 1/2	1	0–1/8	5 1/2
DCL-703D	FE-900	1 1/2	1	0–1/8	5 1/2
DCL-733D	FE-900	1 1/2	1	0–1/8	5 1/2
DF Series					
DF-300	FC-901	1 1/2	1	0–1/8	5 1/2
	FD-901	1 1/2	1	0–1/8	5 1/2
DF-330	FD-901	1 1/2	1	0–1/8	5 1/2
	FE-900	1 1/2	1	0–1/8	5 1/2

①—With wedge.

Continued

DIAMOND REO

REO WHEEL ALIGNMENT SPECIFICATIONS—Continued

Truck Model	Axle Model	Caster Deg.	Camber Deg.*	Toe-In Inch	Kingpin Angle°†	Truck Model	Axle Model	Caster Deg.	Camber Deg.*	Toe-In Inch	Kingpin Angle°†
DF Series						**E Series—Continued**					
DF-400	FC-901	1½	1	0–⅛	5½	E-332	FD-901	1½	1	0–⅛	5½
	FD-901	1½	1	0–⅛	5½	E-400	32500	2	1	0–⅛	8
	FE-900	1½	1	0–⅛	5½	E-402	FC-901	1½	1	0–⅛	5½
DF-430	FD-901	1½	1	0–⅛	5½	E-430	FD-900	1½	1	0–⅛	5½
	FE-900	1½	1	0–⅛	5½	E-432	FE-900	1½	1	0–⅛	5½
	FE-15	1	1	⅛	0	E-436	FL-901	1½	1	0–⅛	5½
DF-500	FD-901	1½	1	0–⅛	5½		FG-900	2	1	0–⅛	8
	FE-900	1½	1	0–⅛	5½	E-500	FD-901	1½	1	0–⅛	5½
DF-530	FE-900	1½	1	0–⅛	5½		FE-900	1½	1	0–⅛	5½
	FE-15	1	1	⅛	0	E-530	FE-900	1½	1	0–⅛	5½
DF-600	FD-901	1½	1	0–⅛	5½	E-630D	FD-901	1½	1	0–⅛	5½
	FE-900	1½	1	0–⅛	5½		FE-901	1½	1	0–⅛	5½
DF-630	FD-901	1½	1	0–⅛	5½		FE-15	1	1	⅛	0
	FE-900	1½	1	0–⅛	5½	E-700D	FD-901	1½	1	0–⅛	5½
	FE-15	1	1	⅛	0		FE-901	1½	1	0–⅛	5½
DF-700	FD-901	1½	1	0–⅛	5½		FE-15	1	1	⅛	0
	FE-900	1½	1	0–⅛	5½	E-730D	FE-900	1½	1	0–⅛	5½
DF-730	FD-901	1½	1	0–⅛	5½		FE-15	1	1	⅛	0
	FE-900	1½	1	0–⅛	5½	E-830D-OH	FE-15	1	1	⅛	0
	FE-15	1	1	⅛	0						
E Series											
E-200	30000	2	1	0–⅛	8						
E-202	32500	2	1	0–⅛	8						
E-300	32500	2	1	0–⅛	8						
E-302	FC-901	1½	1	0–⅛	5½						
E-330	FC-901	1½	1	0–⅛	5½						

*Camber may vary as much as ½° either way from the mean specifications listed.
†Kingpin inclination is built into the axle beam and should not be disturbed.

PISTON, PIN, RING, CRANKSHAFT & BEARING SPECIFICATIONS

Year	Engine Model	Piston Clearance	Ring End Gap Minimum		Piston Pin Dia.	Rod Bearings		Main Bearings			Shaft End Play
			Comp.	Oil		Shaft Diameter	Bearing Clearance	Shaft Diameter	Bearing Clearance	Thrust Bearing	
1970–71	145B	—	.020	.012	—	—	.0010–.0032	—	④	—	.004–.007
1970–71	170B	—	.020	.010	—	—	.0010–.0032	—	①	—	.004–.007
1970–71	200	—	.020	.012	—	—	.0014–.0036	—	①	—	.004–.008
1970–71	235B	—	.020	.012	—	—	.0010–.0032	—	②	—	.006–.010
1970–71	250	—	.020	.012	—	—	.0010–.0032	—	②	—	.006–.010
1970–71	350	—	.015	.015	—	—	.004⑤	—	.004⑤	—	.002–.006
1970–71	366	—	.015	.010	—	—	.004⑤	—	.004⑤	—	.006–.010

① —Front bearing .0014–.0039", others .001–.0035".
② —Front and rear .0012–.0044", others .0012–.0039".
③ —Two thrust plates at front main bearing. Adjust by means of shims at rear of crankshaft timing gear.
④ —Front bearing, .0012–.0037"; all others, .0010–.0035".
⑤ —Maximum.

DIAMOND REO

Engine Section

CYLINDER HEAD, REPLACE

All Engines

When removing a cylinder head a chisel or screw driver should never be used to pry it loose from the cylinder block. Use an eyebolt in the third or fourth spark plug hole (6-cyl. engines), lifting up on the eyebolt while tapping lightly around the edges of the head with a lead or rawhide hammer or mallet. Be sure all the head stud nuts or bolts have been removed before starting to remove the head.

In replacing the head, the stud nuts or bolts at the center of the head should be tightened first and then work outward from side to side and to the ends. Draw the nuts or bolts down evenly until all are normally tight. After the engine has run long enough to warm it up, make a final tightening with a torque wrench to the torque loads given in the *Tune Up & Valve Specifications* table (Figs. 1, 2).

NOTE: Beginning with Engine No. 227579J all V8 engines have been assembled with redesigned rocker arm covers and cylinder heads. Eight bosses were added to the head casting and are drilled and tapped for the cover hold-down bolts. The two studs in each head are positioned at the front and rear corners on the inner edge. *Studs must be used at these four points since the holes are drilled through into the water outlet passages.* If capscrews are used in these tapped holes, water will leak past the threads and into the rocker arm chambers. The other holes are not drilled through.

ROCKER ARM BUSHING

Rocker Arm I.D., Bushing O.D.
(Press fit) 1.1245–1.1255
Bushing I.D., finish after
  assembly .... .9903   .9913
Rocker Arm Shaft O.D. ...... .989   .990
Nominal clearance .... .0013

NOTE: To facilitate assembly of bushing and rocker arm, coat back of bushing with a mixture of white lead and oil before pressing into place.

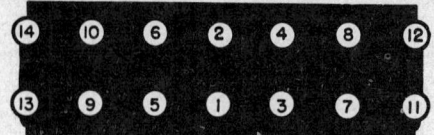

Fig. 1 Cylinder head tightening on 6-cyl. engines

VALVE ROTATORS

Increased exhaust valve service in these engines is accomplished by the use of "Roto Valve" mechanism which is a special valve spring retainer and cap located on the end of the valve stem.

In operation, the rocker arm striking the cap lifts the retainer first, thus taking the spring load off the valve before lifting it from its seat. When the valve is in the raised position, it is free to rotate due to the vibration of the system.

When checking valve clearances, the feeler gauge is placed between the cap and socket as there is no other flat surface in the valve train.

TIMING GEARS

Valve timing is correct when the timing gears are installed so that the timing marks on the gears are meshed. Fig. 3 illustrates the relationship of the parts on V8 engines.

CAMSHAFT & BEARINGS

Camshaft end play is controlled by a thrust plate just behind the camshaft gear. End play should be held to about .005" and can be checked by forcing the shaft back to the limit of its end play and inserting a feeler gauge between the thrust plate and the front end of the shaft. If end play is excessive, install a new thrust plate.

On these engines, steel-backed, lead babbitt-lined split bearings are used.

PISTONS & RODS, ASSEMBLE

If the pistons and the rods have factory markings to indicate their position in the cylinders, assemble and install them according to these marks, or according to the marks made during removal if they were not otherwise marked, Fig. 4.

CYLINDER SLEEVES

Overhead Valve Engines

Whenever piston or ring installation is to be made, check cylinder sleeve bores for scores, out-of-round and taper. If out-of-round .006" or more or if taper wear is .006" or more, sleeve should be replaced. Reboring of sleeves and use of oversize pistons is not recommended. In many cases sleeves can be pulled out by hand to remove from block. When tight, do not drive out by pounding with metal objects as sleeves may be damaged or block distorted.

If rings only are to be installed, prior to

Fig. 2 Cylinder head tightening sequence. V8 engines

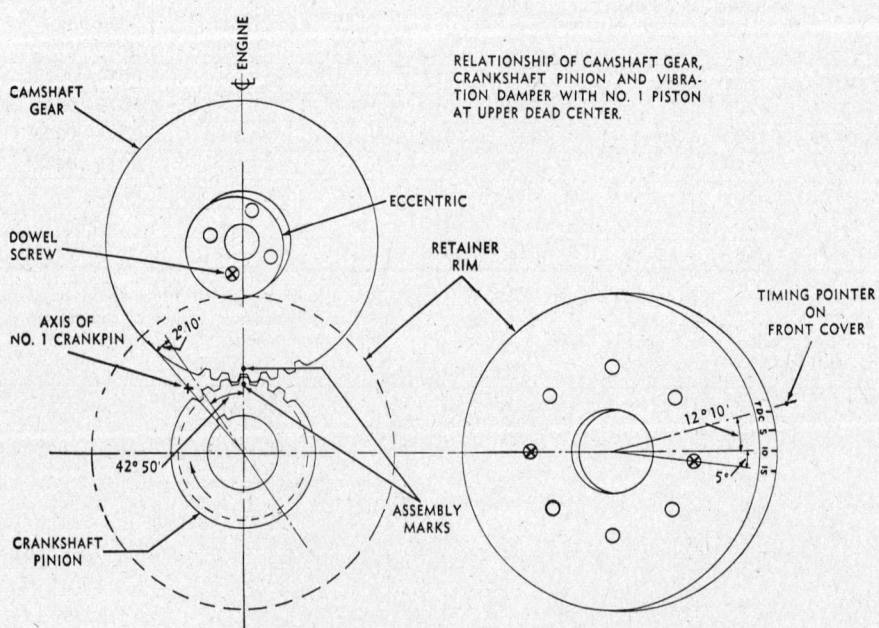

Fig. 3 Relationship of front end components. V8 engines

DIAMOND REO

removing pistons, remove ridge at top of each cylinder wall. When performing this operation, use particular care not to cut beyond the diameter of the cylinder wall. Leave approximately .001" stock at ridge and remove with a hone. Each cylinder should be honed to break the glaze and to provide a better surface for wear-in of the new piston rings.

The cylinder block must be thoroughly cleaned after completion of honing operations.

Drain and dry out block surrounding sleeve area to prevent dripping or seepage of water on bearings. If engine is installed in stand RS-C356, rotating block so that crankshaft is vertical will materially aid in keeping any water or grit off bearing surfaces. If re-ringing is done with engine in chassis, breaking glaze may be omitted due to hazard of grit getting into bearing surfaces.

CAUTION: If engine is rotated to fully inverted position, make certain that any abnormally loose sleeves do not fall out of block.

With sleeves out of block, remove any rough external surfaces with emery cloth *from chamfers only* (above lower "O" ring area). Use only sandpaper to clean other adjacent surfaces of sleeve or block.

CAUTION: Always install new neoprene sealing rings ("O" rings) whenever changing or reinstalling a sleeve. Be particularly careful that "O" rings are installed without a twist, otherwise a leak is likely to develop around "O" ring seam. Coat sealing rings with clean hydraulic fluid or glycerine before installing on sleeve. Be certain top counterbore in block for flange of sleeve is clean before attempting to insert sleeve. Clean the seal lands in block and coat with hydraulic fluid or glycerine before installing sleeve.

Install sleeve and seal assembly in its position in lower diameter of crankcase by allowing sleeve to find its own seat, then with hand pressure on top of flange rotate sleeve right and left and quickly push in place. *Do not force sleeve into block.*

When sleeve is seated check and make sure that top flange, extends .001" to .005" above block. If sleeve flange is below planed surface of block it will not be sealed and held in place by the cylinder head and gasket which may then allow water seepage into the cylinder bore.

Shims of .003" and .006" thickness are available with which sleeve protrusion may be corrected to the allowable tolerance as shown in the following table.

Recommended Schedule for Shim Installation

Height Measured	Add Shim	Height Above Deck
.001" above deck	None	.001"
.000" even	.003"	.003"
.001" Below deck	.003"	.002"
.002" Below deck	.006"	.004"
.003" Below deck	.006"	.003"
.004" Below deck	.006"	.002"
.005" Below deck	.001"	.001"
.006" Below deck	.003" & .006"	.003"
.007" Below deck	.003" & .006"	.002"
.008" Below deck	.003" & .006"	.001"
.009" Below deck	.006" & .006"	.003"
.010" Below deck	.006" & .006"	.002"

Whenever a sleeve height is adjusted by the use of shims, the resulting protrusion should be within .002" of that of the adjacent sleeves if possible.

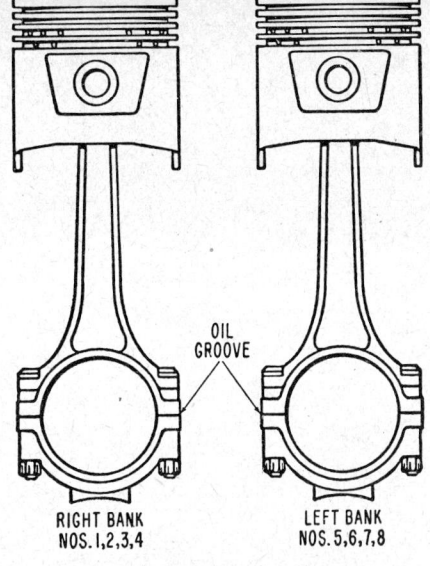

Fig. 4 Correct assembly of pistons and rods. V8 engines

CRANKSHAFT END PLAY, ADJUST

Overhead Valve Engines

On six-cylinder engines crankshaft end thrust is taken up on the front main bearing. On early models it is controlled by flanges on the upper half only of this bearing. Later models have thrust flanges on upper and lower halves.

On V8 engines crankshaft end play is controlled by flanges on the rear main bearing.

A quick check of crankshaft end play can be made by anchoring a dial indicator to the chassis back of the radiator with the indicator on the front of the crankshaft pulley. Throwing the clutch in and out will cause a forward movement of the crankshaft to the extent of its end play. Using a piece of 2 × 4 wood ahead of the pulley, pry the crankshaft back (with foot off clutch pedal).

If check shows end play in excess of .012", immediate correction of the condition is absolutely necessary because if the engine is allowed to run with excessive end play it will destroy the highly polished face of the crankshaft against which the bearing thrust flanges ride. Ultimately, this polished surface will be scored to the extent that a new thrust bearing will wear out in a very few miles. When this condition is reached the only correction is a new crankshaft.

CRANKSHAFT OIL SEAL, REPLACE

Six Cyl. Engines

To replace the rear oil seal it is necessary to remove flywheel, oil pan and oil pan rear arch.

Many cases of oil leakage at the rear of the engine are caused by seals being damaged before and during installation.

In handling this seal, be careful that the inner seal part is not touched by dirt from the hands. Inspect before installing. If it is the least bit dirty or has any grit on it, wash in oleum spirits before installing. Any slight piece of foreign material which might become imbedded in this seal will cause it to leak.

Make sure that the hub of the crankshaft which the seal contacts is absolutely clean, polished and not scored. Invariable when the flywheel is removed, the edge of the crankshaft hub is burred or scratched when freed from the recess where it sets into the flywheel. Be sure and remove all burrs on hub and hub chamfer, eliminating all sharp and jagged edges before fitting seal over crankshaft hub.

As the seal is an expanding fit, be particularly careful not to distort or break the edge when fitting it over the crankshaft hub.

Secure housing or retainer to block from rear with 4 cap screws and tighten. Install rear arch. Secure retainer to arch from front with 3 lower and 2 upper cap screws. First secure all cap screws finger tight. Tighten screws top to opposite bottom alternately. Tighten lower center last.

The rear oil seal lip should be coated with grease (not oil) prior to installation on the crankshaft hub. The grease should be applied to the hub as well as the seal lip in order to avoid wiping the lubricant off the hub when the seal is installed. The purpose of this procedure is to prevent the seal from running with insufficient lubrication and, therefore, becoming excessively hot before crankcase oil can reach it. This grease application will also facilitate sliding the seal over the hub. Use Lubriplate #320, or an equivalent which has a relatively high melting point.

When bolting the housing into place, put Permatex #2 in the cap screw holes to keep internal pressure from forcing oil out between the cap screw and hole threads.

V8 Engines

Oil sealing at the rear main bearing is controlled by a wick-type seal in the same manner as for some side valve engines outlined above.

OIL PUMP REPAIRS

Oil pump is of the rotary type and is assembled to a special machined boss inside the crankcase. As the two rotors are matched at the time of assembly a complete new unit must be installed as rotor repairs are never satisfactory.

Oil pump drive gear is driven from the gear on the camshaft. The gear is pinned to the pump shaft and is replaceable.

WATER PUMP REPAIRS

These engines are equipped with ball bearing pump similar to that used on GC engines. A spring-loaded bellows type carbon seal is used and the shaft is retained by two ball bearings.

In servicing this pump, follow a similar procedure outlined above for GC engines.

CARTER BBR2 CARBURETOR

Model 779S

In this carburetor, Fig. 6, correct air-fuel ratio is provided by a "balance tube" in the air

DIAMOND REO

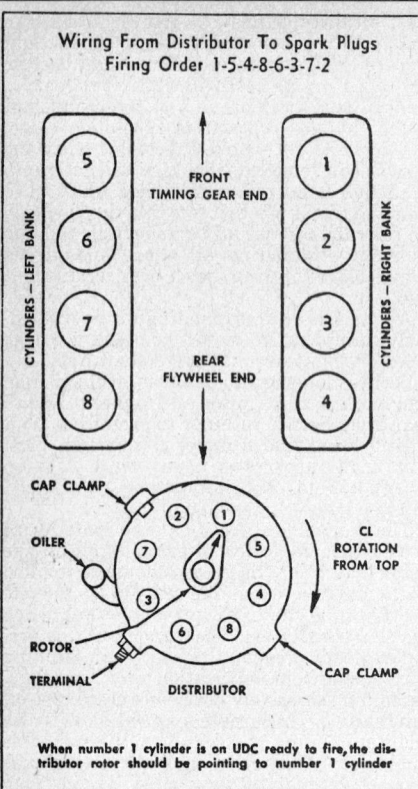

Fig. 5 Ignition details. Reo V8 engines

horn. The balance tube should be checked to see that the passage is open. The object of a balanced carburetor is to provide a constant air-fuel ratio regardless of size, type or condition of the air cleaner. Should the cleaner become clogged, the capacity will be reduced but the air-fuel mixture ratio will not be changed.

Service Note

Excessive richness above 50 mph may be caused by a clogged main vent tube. After removal of the rivet plug beneath the float bowl (use Tool T109-43) the main vent tube can be removed and a new tube inserted with Tool T109-195. Care must be exercised in inserting the new tube which must seat tightly. Use a new rivet to complete the installation.

Idle Adjustment

If the engine stalls while idling, set the throttle lever adjusting screw so the engine does not idle below 450 rpm. Then set the idle adjustment screw from 3/4 to 1 1/4 turns open. If these adjustments to not correct the trouble, remove the idle orifice tube and plug assembly. Clean the tube passages with compressed air.

Float Setting

If the carburetor loads up after considerable service, check the float level as shown in Fig. 7 to a distance of 5/64". Wear on the lip of the float lever will raise the float level. Before adjusting the float, be sure the float lever pin is firmly seated. Reset the float level by bending the lip of the float away from the needle to raise the level, or bend the lip toward the needle to lower the float level. Bend the vertical lip of the float only.

Pump Adjustment

If acceleration is not satisfactory, remove the pump jet and clean with compressed air. However, it is usually advisable to replace the pump jet as its cost is nominal. All jets must be seated gasoline tight. Poor acceleration may be due to damaged or worn plunger leather in the accelerating pump, sediment in the pump cylinder or clogged intake ball check at the bottom of the pump cylinder and discharge ball check in the discharge passage. If the plunger is removed from the cylinder, use care in installing to avoid damage to the plunger leather.

To adjust the pump, remove the air horn assembly, back out the throttle adjusting screw, and place the pump operating link in the center hole of the throttle shaft arm. Place Pump Travel Gauge T109-117S on the edge of the bowl cover so that the lip of the gauge extends over the top of the plunger shaft. Turn the knurled nut of the gauge until the lip contacts the plunger shaft at the closed and wide open throttle positions. The difference in readings obtained at closed and wide open throttle positions should be "30" (30/64") plunger travel. Adjustments can be made by bending the horizontal portion of the pump lifter link.

The pump stroke is adjustable for high or low temperature. Set to the long stroke for cold weather and short stroke for hot weather driving.

CARTER WA1-2542S

Idle Choke Settings

Set idle mixture adjusting screw 1 1/4 to 2 3/4 turns open. For richer mixture turn screw out. Do not idle engine below 500 rpm.
Set automatic choke two points lean.

Float Level Adjustment

The distance from the float (at free end) to tip on lower edge of float chamber cover when needle is seated should be 1/2".

Pump Adjustment

With throttle valve seated, and connector link in upper hole (long stroke) the pump plunger should travel 13/32" from closed to wide open throttle position. Adjust by bending throttle connector rod at the lower angle.

Metering Rod Adjustment

This setting must be made after the pump adjustment or when leaner than standard rod is installed.

Insert Gauge T-109-102 in place of metering rod, seating tapered end of gauge in metering rod jet. Hold gauge vertical to insure seating in jet. With throttle valve seated, press down on piston link directly over piston until it contacts pump arm. There should not be less than .005" clearance between metering rod pin and shoulder in notch in gauge. Gauge must not drag on pin. Adjust by bending lip on piston link. Remove gauge and install metering rod, disc, pin and spring.

Anti-Percolator Adjustment

Open throttle valve .016" by placing drill or Gauge T 109-44 between throttle valve and bore of carburetor (side opposite idle port). Bend rocker arm until there is a clearance of .010" between rocker arm lip and pump arm.

Fast Idle Adjustment

With fast idle cam in normal idle position, tighten throttle lever adjusting screw until it just seats against cam. Hold throttle lever closed and pull cam back until first (or lower) step is against (not on) set screw. There should now be 5/8" clearance between inside wall of air horn and lower edge of choke valve. Adjust by bending fast idle link at offset portion.

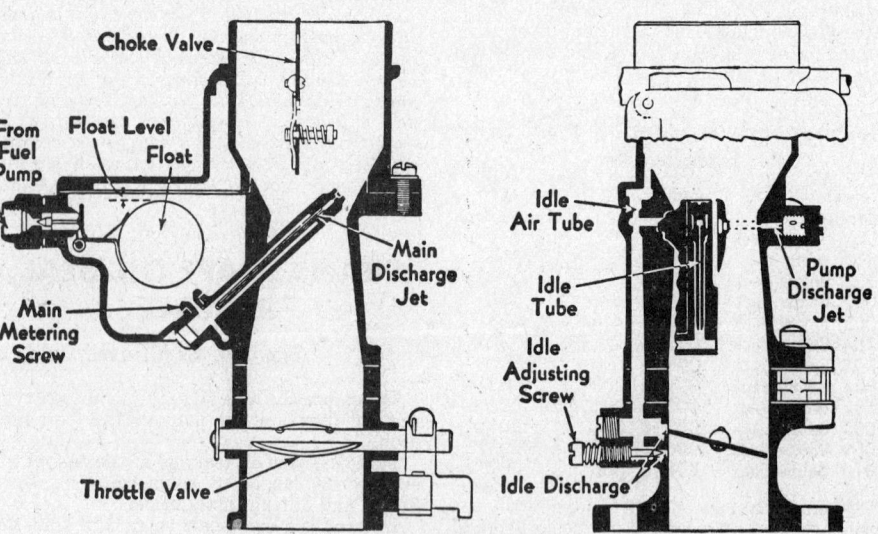

Fig. 6 Carter BBR2 carburetor. Reo OA-255 engine

DIAMOND REO

Unloader Adjustment

With throttle valve wide open there should be 9/16" clearance between lower edge of choke valve and inner wall of air horn. Adjust by bending cam on throttle lever.

CARTER WCFB-2220S, 2265S, 2563S, 2563SA

Idle and Choke Settings

Set idle mixture adjusting screws 3/4 to 1 3/4 (1 1/2 to 2 1/2 on 2220) turns open. For richer mixture turn screws out.
Set automatic choke on "Index" mark.

Float Adjustments, Fig. 8

Vertical Adjustment—With bowl cover assembly inverted and bowl cover gasket removed, check the vertical distance from top of float to cover casting. This distance should be 3/16". Adjust by bending float arms.
Float Drop Adjustment—With bowl cover assembly held in upright position, check distance between center of floats and bowl cover casting (gasket removed). This distance should measure 1/2" (plus or minus 1/16"). Adjust by bending stop tabs on float brackets.
Lateral Adjustment—With metering rods removed, slide the cover assembly into position on the bowl casting. Note any interference between floats and carburetor bowl. If any interference exists, adjust by bending float arms.

Pump Adjustment, Fig. 9

Remove the dust cover from the bowl cover. Back out the fast idle screw and lever set screw until throttle valves seat in bores. With throttle valves seated, the flat on the top of the pump arm should be parallel with the top of the dust cover mounting boss. Adjust by bending the throttle connector rod at lower end. Pump connector link must be in outer hole in pump arm.

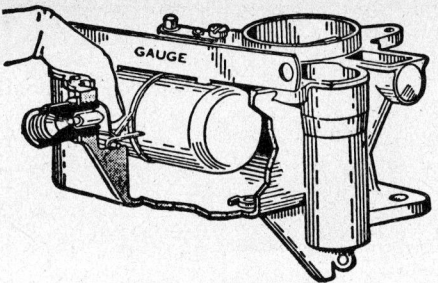

Fig. 7 Float setting. Carter BBR2 carburetor

Metering Rod Adjustment, Fig. 10

This adjustment must always be made after the pump adjustment.
With the idle stop screw backed out and throttle fully closed, loosen the clamp screw on metering rod arm. Then press on vacumeter link until metering rods bottom in bowl. While holding metering rods down and throttle closed, rotate metering rod lift arm until finger on arm contacts lip of vacumeter link and tighten clamp screw in this position.

Vapor Vent Adjustment

This adjustment is to be made after the pump and metering rod adjustments.
With the dust cover and gasket installed and throttle valves wide open, there should be approximately 1/16" clearance between the lower edge of the vent valve and dust cover. Adjust by removing the dust cover and bending the vapor vent arm.

Holley 852-FFG

These carburetors are dual downdraft units incorporating an integral governor. The governor throttle mechanism is part of the carburetor and has been designed to provide the needed power required for moving the throttle to governing speeds as controlled by a separately driven governor rotor. The combination of these two units give instant response and accurate governing.
The carburetor and governor can be cleaned and serviced with ordinary tools and the governor rotor can be serviced independent of the carburetor. *Do not under any circumstances apply compressed air to an assembled carburetor as to do so may rupture the governor diaphragm.*

Fuel & Float Level

When checking the fuel level in an open vessel, under 5 lbs. pump pressure the level should measure 23/32". The measurement is taken below the surface of the float chamber cover (gasket in place) to the level of the fuel. The level may be corrected by bending the float arm, Fig. 11.
The float level can be set when the air horn is off by gauging the distance between the bottom of the float and the flange surface of the air horn, Fig. 12. Holding the air horn upside down and the float in the closed position, measure the distance from the flange surface of the air horn to what would normally be the bottom side of the float (not the soldered seam). The correct distance should measure 1 11/32". Bend the float lever arm as required to correct the float level.

Idle Mixture

The idle mixture is controlled by the idle adjustment needles. Turning these needles in makes a leaner mixture and turning them out makes the mixture richer. Turn the needles in until they just touch the seats and back off one full turn.
When the engine has warmed up to operating temperature, alter the adjustment as required to obtain smooth performance. The range should be between 1 and 1 1/2 turns.

Accelerating Pump

The quantity of the fuel discharged by the accelerating pump can be controlled by changing the position of the pump link in the throttle lever. Of the three different positions (marked 1, 2 and 3) number 2 is the average setting, number 1 is for summer and 3 is for winter operation.

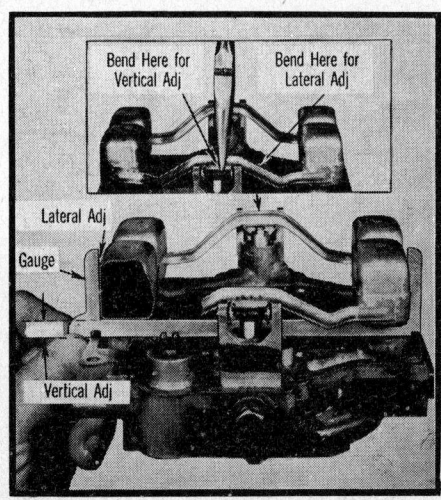

Fig. 8 Float level adjustment. Carter WCFB

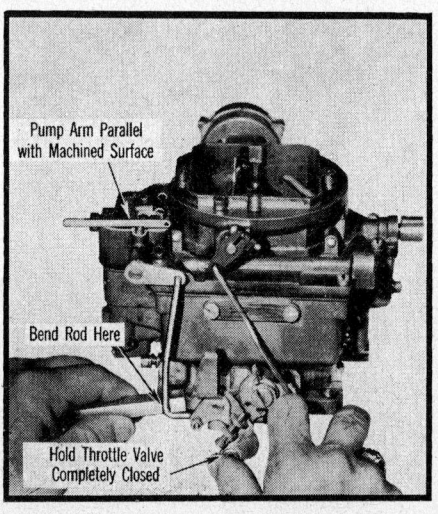

Fig. 9 Pump adjustment. Carter WCFB

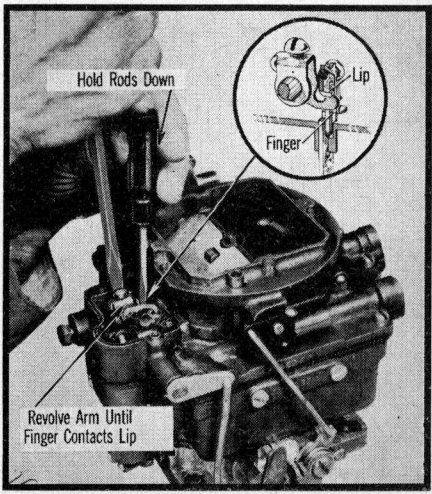

Fig. 10 Metering rod adjustment. Carter WCFB

DIAMOND REO

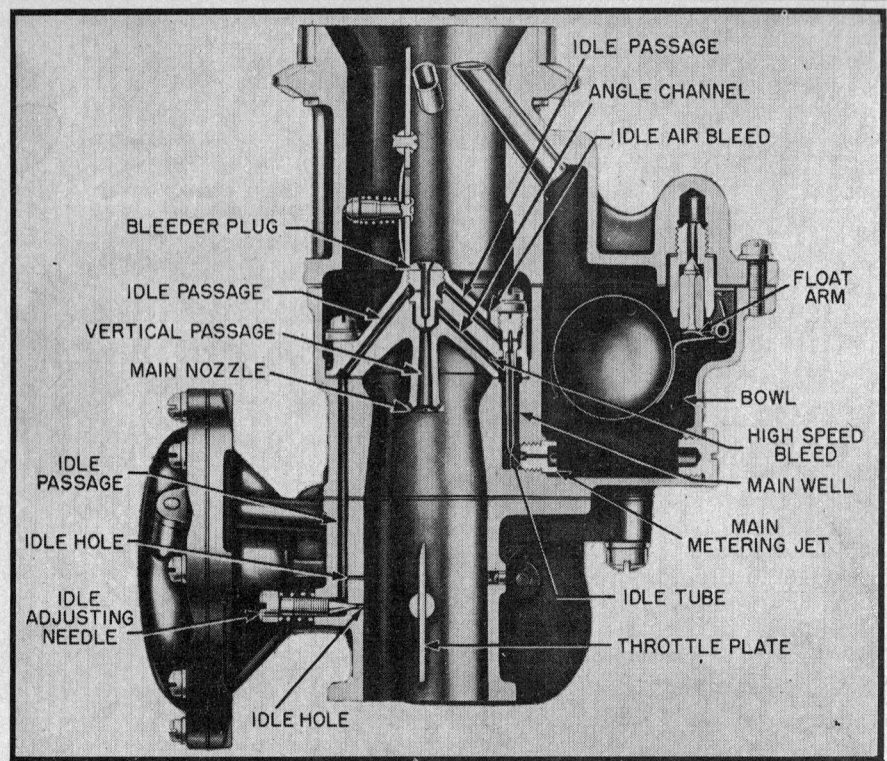

Fig. 11 Holley 852-FFG carburetor

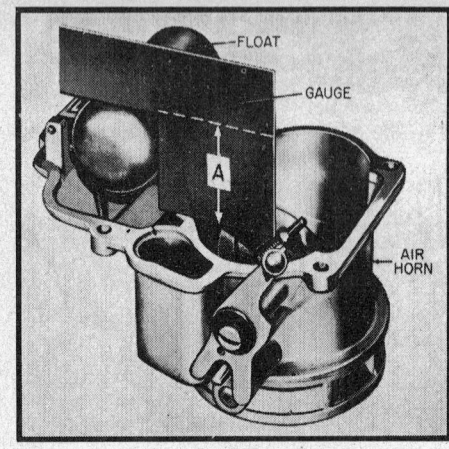

Fig. 12 Float setting Holley 852-FFG carburetor

Transmission & Rear Axles

ALLISON REOMATIC

Range Selector Linkage

1. Move range selector lever from L to R. Six definite detent positions should be felt as the lever moves from front to rear. If not, adjust as follows:
2. Place selector lever at R.
3. At transmission, disconnect range selector cable from transmission control lever.
4. Push control lever (inner lever on transmission) all the way forward and upward.
5. Push control cable up until the selector lever hits the R stop. Adjust threaded clevis so that clevis pin just fits hole in control lever.
6. Assemble clevis to control lever.
7. From driver's seat, again feel for full engagement at each detent position before the lever hits its stop.

Hydraulic Retarder Linkage

The retarder valve, located on the right side of the transmission, must travel a full 1/2" toward the rear just before the retarder pedal hits the stop bolt. When pedal is released, the valve must travel 1/2" to cross shaft to insure full return of pedal. If necessary, adjust as follows:

1. Disconnect hydraulic control rod at transmission end. Pull retarder lever toward rear until the valve is heard and felt to bottom in the retarder valve body. Pull control rod down until pedal contacts its stop bolt.
2. With retarder valve bottomed and pedal against its stop, adjust control rod clevis until the clevis pin just fits into the lever hole.
3. Lengthen control rod by backing off adjusting clevis until there is 1/8" clearance between pedal and its stop bolt at full retarder application.
4. Assemble control rod to lever and recheck adjustment by depressing pedal against the stop bolt. Just before it hits the stop, the retarder valve should be felt to bottom in its body.
5. Check for full release and readjust if necessary.

Throttle Linkage

1. Check engine idle adjustment (475–500 rpm).
2. Disconnect throttle control rod from transmission TV (outer) lever.
3. Depress accelerator pedal down "to detent" (not "through detent"). The carburetor lever should now be against its full throttle stop.
4. Push transmission TV lever forward and upward until it is against its stop inside transmission. With TV lever firmly against the stop, and the accelerator pedal "at detent", adjust throttle control rod clevis so that pin just fits through holes.
5. Remove pin and lengthen control rod by turning clevis out 7 turns counterclockwise.
6. Assemble clevis to control lever.
7. Adjust accelerator stop bolt so that there is a clearance of 1/16" between pedal and bolt head when throttle linkage hits its stop "through the detent". This will provide full travel in the linkage without undue deflection.

Road Test

After making the throttle linkage adjustment outlined above, road test the truck to check the operation of the transmission.

1. If the 3-4 full throttle ("at detent") shift occurs at an engine speed considerably under governed speed, it is probable that the throttle linkage is not properly adjusted. Shorten the throttle control rod at the transmission lever one full turn at a time and repeat the test until the shift occurs at 3100–3300 rpm engine speed.
2. If full throttle 3–4 shift did not occur, and the engine reached governed speed, it is probable that the throttle linkage is too short and should be lengthened one full turn at a time until the shifts occur at 3100–3300 rpm engine speed.
3. Governed speed with the OH-170 engine should be 3400 rpm full load and 3550–3650 rpm no load.

DODGE & PLYMOUTH

INDEX OF SERVICE OPERATIONS

AXLES, DRIVING

	Page No.
Own Make Axle Service	1005
Eaton Axle Service	204
Spicer Axle Service	239
Timken Axle Service	241
Locking Differentials	192
Front Wheel Locking Hubs	505
Front Wheel Drive	1012

BRAKES

Adjustments	590
Air Brake Service	620
Anti Skid Brakes	551
Bendix Twinplex Brake	608
Brake Booster Service	639
Disc Brakes	661
Hydraulic System Service	632
Parking Brake Service	612
Stopmaster Brake Service	599

CLUTCHES

Clutch Pedal, Adjust	991
Clutch, Replace	992
Clutch Service	429
Air-Hydraulic (Air-Pak)	468
Hydraulic Clutch Control	992

COOLING SYSTEM

Cooling System Capacity	938
Variable Speed Fans	10

ELECTRICAL

Alternator Service	52
Dash Gauge Service	179
Distributors, Standard	141
Electronic Ignition	152
Generator Service	11
Ignition Coils and Resistors	7
Starting Motor Service	29
Starter Switch Service	21
Tune Up Service	2

ENGINE

	Page No.
Camshaft and Bearings	962
Crankshaft Rear Oil Seal	963
Cylinder Head, Replace	958
Engine Identification	939
Main Bearings	962
Pistons, Pins and Rings	962
Piston and Rod, Assemble	962
Rocker Arms	958
Rod Bearings	962
Timing Case Cover	961
Timing Gears	962
Timing Chain	961
Valves, Adjust	959
Valve Guides	960
Valve Lifters	960

ENGINE OILING

Crankcase Capacity	938
Oil Pump	963

FRONT SUSPENSION

Front Wheel Locking Hubs	505
Front Axle Construction	1021
Independent Front Suspension	1021

FUEL & EXHAUST

Carburetor Adjustments	964
Crankcase Ventilation	748
Emission Controls	750
Fuel Pump Service	183
L.P.G. Carburetion	190
Turbochargers	187

SPECIFICATIONS

Alternator and Regulator	948, 949
Carburetor Adjustments	985
Crankshaft and Bearing	953
Distributor	950
Engine Tightening Torque	955

	Page No.
General Engine Data	940
Piston, Pin and Ring	953
Starting Motor	949
Tune Up	943
Valve	954
Wheel Alignment	956

STEERING

Manual Steering Gear Service	680
Power Steering Gear Service	686

TRANSFER CASES   469, 1005

TRANSMISSIONS, Manual

Own Make	993
Own Make, Linkage, Adjust	999
Clark	275
Fuller	289
New Process	329
Spicer	346
Warner	406
Transmission, Replace	992

TRANSMISSIONS, Automatic

Allison AT-540, 543	510
Adjustments	1004
Replace	1004
Allison MT-640, 643, 644, 650, 653, 654CR	512
Adjustments	1004
Replace	1004
Loadflite	534
Adjustments	1001
In Vehicle Service	1001
Replace	1000
New Process A-345	534
Adjustments	1002
In Vehicle Service	1002
Replace	1002
Torquematic	518
Adjustments	1003
Replace	1003

DODGE & PLYMOUTH

MODEL INDEX & ENGINE APPLICATION

1970-80

Model	Year	Engine Make	Standard Engine Model	Crankcase Refill Capacity Qts.	Cooling System Capacity Qts.
Compact And Sportsman					
A-100	1970	Own	6-198	4	12
B100	1971-78	Own	6-225	5	13
B100	1979-80	Own	6-225	5	12
B100	1971-72	Own	V8-318	5	18
B100	1973-78	Own	V8-318	5	17
B200	1971-78	Own	6-225	5	13
B200	1980	Own	6-225	5	12
B200	1971-72	Own	V8-318	5	18
B200	1973-78	Own	V8-318	5	17
B200	1979	Own	V8-318	5	16
B300	1971-73	Own	6-225	5	13
B300	1979	Own	6-225	5	12
B300	1971-72	Own	V8-318	5	18
B300	1973-78	Own	V8-318	5	17
B300	1979-80	Own	V8-318	5	16
Dodge Ramcharger					
AW100	1974-78	Own	6-225	5	13
AW100	1974-78	Own	V8-318	5	17
AW100	1979-80	Own	V8-318	5	16
AD100	1974-78	Own	6-225	5	13
AD100	1979-80	Own	6-225	5	12
AD100	1975-78	Own	V8-318	5	17
Plymouth Trail Duster					
PW100	1974-78	Own	6-225	5	13
PW100	1974-78	Own	V8-318	5	17
PW100	1979-80	Own	V8-318	5	16
PD100	1974-78	Own	6-225	5	13
PD100	1979-80	Own	6-225	5	12
PD100	1974-78	Own	V8-318	5	17
Plymouth Voyager					
PB100	1974-78	Own	6-225	5	13
PB100	1979-80	Own	6-225	5	12
PB100	1974-78	Own	V8-318	5	17
PB200	1974-78	Own	6-225	5	13
PB200	1980	Own	6-225	5	12
PB200	1974-78	Own	V8-318	5	17
PB200	1979	Own	V8-318	5	16
PB300	1974-78	Own	6-225	5	13
PB300	1974-78	Own	V8-318	5	17
PB300	1979-80	Own	V8-318	5	16
Tradesman					
B100	1971	Own	6-198	5	13
B100	1972-78	Own	6-225	5	13
B100	1979-80	Own	6-225	5	12
B100	1971-72	Own	V8-318	5	18
B100	1973-78	Own	V8-318	5	17
B200	1971	Own	6-198	5	13
B200	1972-78	Own	6-225	5	13
B200	1980	Own	6-225	5	12
B200	1971-72	Own	V8-318	5	18
B200	1973-78	Own	V8-318	5	17
B200	1979	Own	V8-318	5	16
B300	1971-78	Own	6-225	5	13
B300	1979-80	Own	6-225	5	12
B300	1971-72	Own	V8-318	5	18
B300	1973-78	Own	V8-318	5	17
B300	1979-80	Own	V8-318	5	16
Conventional Cab					
D100	1970-78	Own	6-225	5	13
D100	1979	Own	6-225	5	12
D100	1971-72	Own	V8-318	5	18
D100	1973-78	Own	V8-318	5	17
D100	1979	Own	V8-318	5	16
W100	1970-78	Own	6-225	5	13
W100	1971-72	Own	V8-318	5	18
W100	1973-78	Own	V8-318	5	17
D150	1978	Own	6-225	5	13
D150	1978	Own	V8-318	5	17
D150	1979-80	Own	6-225	5	12
D150	1979-80	Own	V8-318	5	16
W150	1978	Own	6-225	5	13
W150	1978	Own	V8-318	5	17
W150	1979-80	Own	6-225	5	12
W150	1979-80	Own	V8-318	5	16
D200	1970-78	Own	6-225	5	13
D200	1979-80	Own	6-225	5	12
D200	1971-72	Own	V8-318	5	18
D200	1973-78	Own	V8-318	5	17
D200	1979-80	Own	V8-318	5	16
W200	1970-78	Own	6-225	5	13
W200	1971-72	Own	V8-318	5	18
W200	1973-78	Own	V8-318	5	17
W200	1979-80	Own	V8-318	5	16
W200	1979-80	Own	V8-360	5	14½
D300	1970-78	Own	6-225	5	14
D300	1971-72	Own	V8-318	5	18
D300	1973-78	Own	V8-318	5	17
D300	1979-80	Own	V8-360	5	14½
W300	1970-78	Own	6-225	5	14
W300	1971-72	Own	V8-318	5	18
W300	1973-78	Own	V8-318	5	17
W300	1979-80	Own	V8-360	5	14½
D400	1970-71	Own	6-225	5	14
D400	1971	Own	V8-318	5	18
D400	1979-80	Own	V8-360	5	14½
W400	1977-78	Own	V8-360	5	16
W400	1979-80	Own	V8-360	5	14½
D500	1970-74	Own	6-225	5	14
D500	1971-72	Own	V8-318	5	18
D500	1973-78	Own	V8-318	6	19
W500	1970-71	Own	6-225	5	14
W500	1971	Own	V8-318	5	18
D600	1970-72	Own	V8-318	6	25

Continued

DODGE & PLYMOUTH

MODEL INDEX & ENGINE APPLICATION—Continued

Model	Year	Engine Make	Standard Engine Model	Crankcase Refill Capacity Qts.	Cooling System Capacity Qts.
D600	1973–78	Own	V8-318	6	19
W600	1972–78	Own	V8-318	6	19
D700	1970–71	Own	V8-361	8	26
D700	1975	Own	V8-361	8	26
D-700	1976–78	Own	V8-360	6	21
D-800	1970–78	Own	V8-361	8	26
LCF Cab					
C500	1970–71	Own	V8-318	6	25
C600	1970–71	Own	V8-361	8	26
C600	1972–73	Own	V8-318	6	25
C700	1970–71	Own	V8-361	8	27
C800	1970–75	Own	V8-361	8	27
CN800	1974	Catpl'r	1100	—	—
CNT800	1974	Catpl'r	1100	—	—
CN800	1975	Catpl'r	1145	—	—
CNT800	1975	Catpl'r	1145	—	—
CT800	1970–75	Own	V8-361	8	27
CT900	1970–73	Own	V8-413	8	28
CN900	1970–75	Cummins	NH-230	20	41
CNT900	1970–75	Cummins	NH-230	20	41
CN950	1974–75	Cummins	Super 250	28	45½
CNT950	1974–75	Cummins	Super 250	28	45½
C1000	1970–73	Own	V8-413	8	28
Tilt Cab					
L600	1970	Own	6-225	5	18
L700	1970	Own	V8-361	8	27
LN1000	1970–71	Cummins	NH-230	20	44
LNT1000	1970–71	Cummins	NH-230	20	44
LS1000	1972–75	Cummins	NH-230	20	44
LT1000	1972–75	Cummins	NH-230	20	44
LV1000	1970–71	Detroit	8V-71NE	23	56
LVT1000	1970–71	Detroit	8V-71NE	23	56
Forward Control					
P200	1970–72	Own	6-225	5	14
P300	1970–72	Own	6-225	5	14
P400	1970–73	Own	6-225	5	14
Motor Home					
M300	1970–72	Own	V8-318-3	6	22
M300	1975	Own	V8-318-3	6	21
M300	1976–80	Own	V8-360-3	6	21
MB300	1976–78	Own	V8-360	5	16
MB300	1979	Own	V8-360	5	15½
MB300	1980	Own	V8-360	5	14½
MB300	1973–75	Own	V8-318	5	17
RM300	1974	Own	V8-318-3	6	21
MBL300	1975–77	Own	V8-318	5	21
MBL300	1978	Own	V8-318	5	18
MBL300	1979	Own	V8-360	5	15½
MBL300	1980	Own	V8-360	5	14½
MBL400	1979	Own	V8-360	5	15½
MBH300	1977	Own	V8-318	5	17
MBH300	1975–77	Own	V8-360	5	16
MBH300	1978	Own	V8-318	5	18
MBH300	1979	Own	V8-360	5	15½
MBH300	1980	Own	V8-360	5	14½
MBH400	1979	Own	V8-360	5	15½
MBH400	1980	Own	V8-360	5	14½
RM350	1974	Own	V8-318-3	6	21
M375	1970–71	Own	V8-318-3	6	22
M375	1972–73	Own	V8-413-3	6	27
RM400	1974	Own	V8-440-3	6	23
M400	1975	Own	V8-318-3	6	21
M400	1976–80	Own	V8-360-3	6	21
MB400	1976–78	Own	V8-360	5	17
MB400	1979	Own	V8-360	5	15½
MB400	1980	Own	V8-360	5	14½
M500	1975–79	Own	V8-440-3	6	23
M500	1980	Int'l	V8-446	6	24½
M600	1977–79	Own	V8-440-3	6	23
M600	1980	Int'l	V8-446	6	24½
School Bus					
S500	1970–71	Own	6-225	5	14
S500	1971	Own	V8-318	5	—
S600	1970–72	Own	V8-318	6	25
S600	1973–78	Own	V8-318	6	19
S700	1975	Own	V8-361	8	26
S700	1976–78	Own	V8-360	6	21
Kary Van					
CB300	1974–78	Own	6-225	5	13
CB300	1974–78	Own	V8-318	5	17
CB300	1979	Own	V8-360	5	14½
CB300	1980	Own	V8-360	5	14½
CB400	1979	Own	V8-360-3	6	14½
CB400	1980	Own	V8-360-3	6	14½
D500	1974–78	Own	V8-318	6	19
D600	1974–78	Own	V8-318	6	19
D700	1975	Own	V8-361	8	26
D700	1976–78	Own	V8-360	6	21

ENGINE IDENTIFICATION

ENGINE NUMBER LOCATION: The engine serial number location is located on a machined surface on the cylinder block. The engine serial number prefix denotes the series letter, followed by engine model, followed by serial number.

DODGE & PLYMOUTH

GENERAL ENGINE SPECIFICATIONS

Year	Engine Code	Engine Model	Carb. Type	Bore & Stroke	Comp. Ratio	Horsepower @ R.P.M.	Torque Lbs. Ft. @ R.P.M.	Governed Speed R.P.M.	Normal Oil Pressure Lbs.
1970	198	6-198	1 Bore	3.40 × 3.64	8.4	120 @ 4000	182 @ 1600	—	50
	225-1	6-225	1 Bore	3.40 × 4.125	8.4	140 @ 3900	215 @ 1600	3600	50
	225-2	6-225	1 Bore	3.40 × 4.125	8.4	140 @ 3900	215 @ 1600	3600	50
	LA318-1	V8-318	2 Bore	3.91 × 3.31	8.8	210 @ 4000	318 @ 2800	3900	60
	LA318-3	V8-318	2 Bore	3.91 × 3.31	8.0	212 @ 4000	332 @ 2800	3700	70
	361-2	V8-361	2 Bore	4.12 × 3.38	7.5	186 @ 4000	300 @ 2400	3600	70
	361-3	V8-361	2 Bore	4.12 × 3.38	7.5	202 @ 4000	316 @ 2200	3600	70
	361-4	V8-361	2 Bore	4.12 × 3.38	7.5	207 @ 4000	335 @ 2400	3600	70
	383	V8-383	2 Bore	4.25 × 3.38	8.7	258 @ 4400	375 @ 2800	—	60
	413-1	V8-413	2 Bore	4.188 × 3.75	7.5	265 @ 4000	445 @ 2400	—	70
	413-2	V8-413	2 Bore	4.188 × 3.75	7.5	220 @ 3600	386 @ 2200	3600	70
	413-3	V8-413	4 Bore	4.188 × 3.75	7.5	238 @ 3600	407 @ 2000	3600	70
	478①	V8-478	2 Bore	4.50 × 3.75	7.64	234 @ 3600	431 @ 1800	3400	45
	549①	V8-549	4 Bore	4.50 × 4.31	7.6	257 @ 3400	505 @ 2000	3200	45
1971	198	6-198	1 Bore	3.40 × 3.64	8.4	120 @ 4000	182 @ 1600	—	50
	225-1	6-225	1 Bore	3.40 × 4.125	8.4	140 @ 3900	215 @ 1600	3600	50
	225-2	6-225	1 Bore	3.40 × 4.125	8.4	140 @ 3900	215 @ 1600	3600	50
	LA318-1	V8-318	2 Bore	3.91 × 3.31	8.8	210 @ 4000	318 @ 2800	3900	50–70
	LA318-3	V8-318	2 Bore	3.91 × 3.31	8.0	212 @ 4000	322 @ 2800	3700	60–80
	360	V8-360	2 Bore	4.00 × 3.58	8.8	245 @ 4400	350 @ 2400	3900	50–70
	361-2	V8-361	2 Bore	4.12 × 3.58	7.5	186 @ 4000	300 @ 2400	3600	60–80
	361-3	V8-361	2 Bore	4.12 × 3.58	7.5	202 @ 4000	316 @ 2200	3600	60–80
	361-4	V8-361	2 Bore	4.12 × 3.58	7.5	207 @ 4000	335 @ 2400	3600	60–80
	383	V8-383	2 Bore	4.25 × 3.38	8.7	258 @ 4400	375 @ 2800	—	45–65
	413-1	V8-413	4 Bore	4.188 × 3.75	7.5	265 @ 4000	445 @ 2400	—	60–80
	413-2	V8-413	2 Bore	4.188 × 3.75	7.5	220 @ 3600	386 @ 2200	3600	60–80
	413-3	V8-413	4 Bore	4.188 × 3.75	7.5	238 @ 3600	407 @ 2000	3600	60–80
	478①	V8-478	2 Bore	4.50 × 3.75	7.6	234 @ 3600	431 @ 1800	3400	40–50
	549①	V8-549	4 Bore	4.50 × 4.312	7.6	257 @ 3400	505 @ 2000	3200	40–50
1972	225-1	6-225	1 Bore	3.40 × 4.125	8.4	140 @ 3900	215 @ 1600	3600	50
	225-2	6-225	1 Bore	3.40 × 4.125	8.4	140 @ 3900	215 @ 1600	3600	50
	LA318-1	V8-318	2 Bore	3.91 × 3.31	8.8	210 @ 4000	318 @ 2800	3900	50–70
	LA318-3	V8-318	2 Bore	3.91 × 3.31	8.0	212 @ 4000	322 @ 2800	3700	60–80
	LA360	V8-360	2 Bore	4.00 × 3.58	8.7	245 @ 4400	350 @ 2400	3900	50–70
	361-2	V8-361	2 Bore	4.12 × 3.58	7.5	186 @ 4000	300 @ 2400	3600	60–80
	361-3	V8-361	2 Bore	4.12 × 3.58	7.5	202 @ 4000	316 @ 2200	3600	60–80
	361-4	V8-361	2 Bore	4.12 × 3.58	7.5	207 @ 4000	335 @ 2400	3600	60–80
	400	V8-400	2 Bore	4.342 × 3.38	8.2	—	—		45–65
	413-1	V8-413	4 Bore	4.188 × 3.75	7.5	265 @ 4000	445 @ 2400	—	60–80
	413-2	V8-413	2 Bore	4.188 × 3.75	7.5	220 @ 3600	386 @ 2200	3600	60–80
	413-3	V8-413	4 Bore	4.188 × 3.75	7.5	238 @ 3600	407 @ 2000	3600	60–80
	478①	V8-478	2 Bore	4.50 × 3.75	7.6	234 @ 3600	431 @ 1800	3400	40–50
	549①	V8-549	4 Bore	4.50 × 4.31	7.6	257 @ 3400	505 @ 2000	3200	40–50
1973	225-1	6-225	1 Bore	3.40 × 4.125	8.4	110 @ 4000	185 @ 2000	3600	50
	225-2	6-225	1 Bore	3.40 × 4.125	8.4	110 @ 4000	185 @ 2000	3600	50
	LA318-1	V8-318	2 Bore	3.91 × 3.31	8.8	160 @ 4000	265 @ 1600	3900	50–70
	LA318-3	V8-318	2 Bore	3.91 × 3.31	8.0	160 @ 4000	260 @ 2000	3700	60–80
	LA360	V8-360	2 Bore	4.00 × 3.58	8.4	180 @ 4000	295 @ 2400	3900	50–70
	361-2	V8-361	2 Bore	4.12 × 3.38	7.5	150 @ 3600	265 @ 2000	3600	60–80
	361-3	V8-361	2 Bore	4.12 × 3.38	7.5	155 @ 4000	285 @ 2000	3600	60–80
	361-4	V8-361	2 Bore	4.12 × 3.38	7.5	165 @ 4000	310 @ 2000	3600	60–80
	400	V8-400	2 Bore	4.342 × 3.38	8.2	200 @ 4400	320 @ 2400	—	45–65
	413-1	V8-413	4 Bore	4.188 × 3.75	7.5	205 @ 3600	350 @ 2400	—	60–80
	413-2	V8-413	2 Bore	4.188 × 3.75	7.5	180 @ 3200	360 @ 2000	3600	60–80
	413-3	V8-413	4 Bore	4.188 × 3.75	7.5	190 @ 3200	355 @ 2000	3600	60–80

Continued

DODGE & PLYMOUTH

GENERAL ENGINE SPECIFICATIONS—Continued

Year	Engine Code	Engine Model	Carb. Type	Bore & Stroke	Comp. Ratio	Horsepower @ R.P.M.	Torque Lbs. Ft. @ R.P.M.	Governed Speed R.P.M.	Normal Oil Pressure Lbs.
	549①	V8-549	4 Bore	4.5 × 4.31	7.6	230 @ 3200	445 @ 2000	3200	40–50
1974	225-1	6-225②	1 Bore	3.40 × 4.125	8.4	105 @ 4000	180 @ 2000	3600	50
	225-1	6-225③	1 Bore	3.40 × 4.125	8.4	110 @ 4000	175 @ 2000	3600	50
	318-1	V8-318②	2 Bore	3.91 × 3.31	8.6	155 @ 4000	255 @ 2400	3800	50–70
	318-1	V8-318③	2 Bore	3.91 × 3.31	8.6	150 @ 4000	235 @ 2400	3800	50–70
	318-3	V8-318	2 Bore	3.91 × 3.31	7.8	140 @ 4000	250 @ 2000	3700	60–80
	360	V8-360②④	2 Bore	4.00 × 3.58	8.4	185 @ 4000	295 @ 2400	3900	50–70
	360	V8-360②⑤	2 Bore	4.00 × 3.58	8.4	210 @ 4000	285 @ 2400	3900	50–70
	360	V8-360③	2 Bore	4.00 × 3.58	8.4	175 @ 4000	285 @ 2400	3900	50–70
	361-3	V8-361	2 Bore	4.12 × 3.38	7.49	140 @ 3600	260 @ 2000	3600	60–80
	361-4	V8-361	2 Bore	4.12 × 3.38	7.48	155 @ 3200	295 @ 2000	3600	60–80
	400	V8-400②	2 Bore	4.342 × 3.38	8.2	185 @ 4000	305 @ 2400	—	45–65
	400	V8-400③	2 Bore	4.342 × 3.38	8.2	175 @ 4000	305 @ 2400	—	45–65
	413-2	V8-413	2 Bore	4.188 × 3.75	7.54	165 @ 3200	325 @ 2000	3600	60–80
	413-3	V8-413	4 Bore	4.188 × 3.75	7.54	180 @ 3200	335 @ 2000	3600	60–80
	440-1	V8-440②④	4 Bore	4.32 × 3.75	8.12	230 @ 4000	350 @ 3200	—	45–65
	440-1	V8-440②⑤	4 Bore	4.32 × 3.75	8.12	225 @ 4000	345 @ 3200	—	45–65
	440-3	V8-440②	4 Bore	4.32 × 3.75	8.2	235 @ 4000	340 @ 2400	—	45–65
1975	225-1	6-225②	1 Bore	3.40 × 4.125	8.4	95 @ 3600	175 @ 2000	3800	30–80
	225-1	6-225③	1 Bore	3.40 × 4.125	8.4	105 @ 3600	175 @ 2000	3800	30–80
	318-1	V8-318②	2 Bore	3.91 × 3.31	8.6	150 @ 4000	255 @ 2000	3900	30–80
	318-1	V8-318③④	2 Bore	3.91 × 3.31	8.6	150 @ 4000	230 @ 2400	3900	30–80
	318-1	V8-318③⑤	2 Bore	3.91 × 3.31	8.6	155 @ 4000	245 @ 2400	3900	30–80
	318-3	V8-318	2 Bore	3.91 × 3.31	7.8	140 @ 4000	250 @ 2000	3800	30–80
	360	V8-360	2 Bore	4.00 × 3.58	8.4	175 @ 4000	285 @ 2400	3800	30–80
	361	V8-361	2 Bore	4.12 × 3.375	7.5	155 @ 3200	295 @ 2000	3800	30–80
	413	V8-413	4 Bore	4.188 × 3.75	7.5	180 @ 3200	335 @ 2000	3800	30–80
	440	V8-440	4 Bore	4.32 × 3.75	8.2	235 @ 4000	340 @ 2400	—	30–80
1976	225-1	6-225⑥	1 Bore	3.40 × 4.125	8.4	100 @ 3600	170 @ 2000	3600	30–80
	225-1	6-225⑦	1 Bore	3.40 × 4.125	8.4	105 @ 3600	175 @ 2000	3600	30–80
	318-1	V8-318⑥	2 Bore	3.91 × 3.31	8.58	150 @ 4000	255 @ 2000	3900	30–80
	318-1	V8-318④⑦	2 Bore	3.91 × 3.31	8.58	150 @ 4000	230 @ 2400	3900	30–80
	318-1	V8-318⑤⑦	2 Bore	3.91 × 3.31	8.58	155 @ 4000	245 @ 2400	3900	30–80
	318-3	V8-318	2 Bore	3.91 × 3.31	7.8	140 @ 4000	250 @ 2000	3800	30–80
	360-1	V8-360⑥	2 Bore	4.00 × 3.58	8.4	170 @ 4000	280 @ 2400	3800	30–80
	360-1	V8-360④⑦	2 Bore	4.00 × 3.58	8.4	175 @ 4000	285 @ 2400	3800	30–80
	360-1	V8-360⑤⑦	2 Bore	4.00 × 3.58	8.4	185 @ 4000	290 @ 2400	3800	30–80
	360-3	V8-360	2 Type	4.00 × 3.58	8.4	160 @ 4000	260 @ 2000	3800	30–80
	361-4	V8-361	2 Bore	4.12 × 3.38	7.48	150 @ 3200	285 @ 2000	3600	60–80
	400-1	V8-400	2 Bore	4.342 × 3.38	8.2	165 @ 4000	290 @ 2400	—	30–80
	413-3	V8-413	4 Bore	4.188 × 3.75	7.54	175 @ 3200	325 @ 2000	3600	60–80
	440-1	V8-440	4 Bore	4.32 × 3.75	8.2	220 @ 4000	290 @ 2400	—	30–80
	440-3	V8-440	4 Bore	4.32 × 3.75	8.2	225 @ 4000	330 @ 2400	—	30–80
1977	225	6-225⑥	1 Bore	3.40 × 4.125	8.4	100 @ 3600	170 @ 1600	3600	30–80
	225-1	6-225⑦	2 Bore	3.40 × 4.125	8.4	115 @ 3600	175 @ 2000	3600	30–80
	318-1	V8-318⑥	2 Bore	3.91 × 3.31	8.58	150 @ 4000	255 @ 2000	3900	30–80
	318-1	V8-318④⑦	2 Bore	3.91 × 3.31	8.58	150 @ 4000	230 @ 2400	3900	30–80
	318-1	V8-318⑤⑦	2 Bore	3.91 × 3.31	8.58	150 @ 4000	240 @ 2000	3900	30–80
	318-3	V8-318③	2 Bore	3.91 × 3.31	7.8	140 @ 4000	250 @ 2000	—	30–80
	8-360-1	V8-360⑥	2 Bore	4.00 × 3.58	8.4	170 @ 4000	280 @ 2400	3800	30–80
	8-360-1	V8-360④⑦	2 Bore	4.00 × 3.58	8.4	175 @ 4000	285 @ 2400	3800	30–80
	8-360-1	V8-360⑤⑦	2 Bore	4.00 × 3.58	8.4	170 @ 4000	265 @ 2400	3800	30–80
	8-360-3	V8-360④⑦	2 Bore	4.00 × 3.58	8.4	160 @ 4000	260 @ 2400	3800	30–80
	8-360-3	V8-360⑤⑦	2 Bore	4.00 × 3.58	8.4	155 @ 3300	255 @ 2400	3800	30–80
	8-361-4	V8-361③	2 Bore	4.12 × 3.38	7.5	150 @ 3200	285 @ 2000	3600	60–80

Continued

DODGE & PLYMOUTH

GENERAL ENGINE SPECIFICATIONS—Continued

Year	Engine Code	Engine Model	Carb. Type	Bore & Stroke	Comp. Ratio	Horsepower @ R.P.M.	Torque Lbs. Ft. @ R.P.M.	Governed Speed R.P.M.	Normal Oil Pressure Lbs.
	8-400-1	V8-400⑥	2 Bore	4.342 × 3.38	8.2	170 @ 4000	300 @ 2000	—	30-80
	8-400-1	V8-400⑦	2 Bore	4.342 × 3.38	8.2	165 @ 4000	290 @ 2400	—	30-80
	8-413-3	V8-413③	4 Bore	4.18 × 3.75	7.5	175 @ 3200	325 @ 2000	3600	60-80
	8-440-1	V8-440④⑦	4 Bore	4.32 × 3.75	8.2	220 @ 4000	330 @ 2400	—	30-80
	8-440-1	V8-440⑤⑦	4 Bore	4.32 × 3.75	8.2	220 @ 4000	320 @ 2400	—	30-80
	8-440-3	V8-400④⑦	4 Bore	4.32 × 3.75	8.2	225 @ 4000	330 @ 2400	—	30-80
	8-440-3	V8-440⑤⑦	4 Bore	4.32 × 3.75	8.2	225 @ 4000	320 @ 2400	—	30-80
1978	225-1	6-225⑥	2 Bore	3.40 × 4.125	8.4	115 @ 3600	175 @ 1600	—	30-70
	225-1	6-225⑦	2 Bore	3.40 × 4.125	8.4	115 @ 3600	175 @ 2000	—	30-70
	318-1	V8-318⑥	2 Bore	3.91 × 3.31	8.6	145 @ 4000	250 @ 2000	—	30-80
	318-1	V8-318⑦	2 Bore	3.91 × 3.31	8.6	150 @ 4000	230 @ 2400	—	30-80
	360-1	V8-360⑥	2 Bore	4.00 × 3.58	8.5	160 @ 4000	280 @ 2000	—	30-80
	360-1	V8-360⑦	2 Bore	4.00 × 3.58	8.5	175 @ 4000	275 @ 2400	—	30-80
	360-1	V8-360⑤	4 Bore	4.00 × 3.58	8.0	—	—	—	30-80
	360-3	V8-360③	2 Bore	4.00 × 3.58	8.0	160 @ 3600	225 @ 2400	—	30-80
	400-1	V8-400⑥	2 Bore	4.342 × 3.38	8.2	170 @ 4000	300 @ 2000	—	30-80
	400-1	V8-400⑦	2 Bore	4.342 × 3.38	8.2	165 @ 4000	290 @ 2400	—	30-80
	440-1	V8-440⑦	4 Bore	4.32 × 3.75	8.2	220 @ 4000	330 @ 2400	—	30-80
	440-3	V8-440③	4 Bore	4.32 × 3.75	8.1	255 @ 4000	330 @ 2400	—	30-80
1979	225-1	6-225⑥	1 Bore	3.40 × 4.125	8.4	110 @ 3600	175 @ 1600	—	30-70
	225-1	6-225⑦	1 Bore	3.40 × 4.125	8.4	115 @ 3600	175 @ 2000	—	30-70
	225-1	6-225⑤	2 Bore	3.40 × 4.125	8.4	110 @ 3600	—	—	30-70
	318-1	V8-318⑥	2 Bore	3.91 × 3.31	8.7	150 @ 4000	250 @ 2000	—	30-80
	318-1	V8-318⑦	2 Bore	3.91 × 3.31	8.7	150 @ 4000	230 @ 2400	—	30-80
	318-1	V8-318⑤⑥	4 Bore	3.91 × 3.31	8.7	150 @ 3600	—	—	30-80
	318-1	V8-318⑤⑧	4 Bore	3.91 × 3.31	8.7	155 @ 3800	—	—	30-80
	360-1	V8-360⑥	2 Bore	4.00 × 3.58	8.6	160 @ 3600	290 @ 2000	—	30-80
	360-1	V8-360⑦	2 Bore	4.00 × 3.58	8.6	180 @ 3600	270 @ 2000	—	30-80
	360-1	V8-360⑥	4 Bore	4.00 × 3.58	8.6	215 @ 4000	300 @ 3200	—	30-80
	360-1	V8-360⑦	4 Bore	4.00 × 3.58	8.6	175 @ 3600	280 @ 2000	—	30-80
	360-3	V8-360⑦	2 Bore	4.00 × 3.58	8.0	180 @ 3600	260 @ 2400	—	30-80
	360-1	V8-360⑤⑧	4 Bore	4.00 × 3.58	8.6	175 @ 3600	—	—	30-80
	360-1	V8-360⑤⑦	4 Bore	4.00 × 3.58	8.6	180 @ 3600	—	—	30-80
	440-1	V8-440⑦	4 Bore	4.32 × 3.75	8.2	220 @ 4000	320 @ 4000	—	30-80
	440-3	V8-440⑦	4 Bore	4.32 × 3.75	8.1	225 @ 2400	320 @ 2400	—	30-80
1980	225	6-225⑥	1 Bore	3.40 × 4.125	8.4	95 @ 3600	170 @ 1600	—	30-80
	225	6-225⑤⑧	1 Bore	3.40 × 4.125	8.4	90 @ 3600	150 @ 2000	—	30-80
	318	V8-318⑥	2 Bore	3.91 × 3.31	8.7	135 @ 4000	240 @ 2000	—	30-80
	318	V8-318⑥	2 Bore	3.91 × 3.31	8.7	140 @ 4000	240 @ 2400	—	30-80
	318	V8-318⑧	4 Bore	3.91 × 3.31	8.7	160 @ 4000	245 @ 2000	—	30-80
	318	V8-318⑤⑦	4 Bore	3.91 × 3.31	8.0	155 @ 4000	240 @ 2000	—	30-80
	360-1	V8-360⑥	4 Bore	4.00 × 3.58	8.6	170 @ 4000	270 @ 2000	—	30-80
	360-1	V8-360⑧	4 Bore	4.00 × 3.58	8.6	170 @ 4000	270 @ 2000	—	30-80
	360-1	V8-360⑥	4 Bore	4.00 × 3.58	8.6	205 @ 4000	295 @ 3200	—	30-80
	360-1	V8-360⑤⑦	4 Bore	4.00 × 3.58	8.6	175 @ 3600	260 @ 2800	—	30-80
	360-1	V8-360⑦	4 Bore	4.00 × 3.58	8.2	180 @ 3600	270 @ 2000	—	30-80
	360-3	V8-360⑦	4 Bore	4.00 × 3.58	8.0	180 @ 4000	260 @ 2400	—	30-80
	360-3	V8-360⑦	4 Bore	4.00 × 3.58	8.0	210 @ 4000	285 @ 3200	—	30-80
	360-3	V8-360⑤⑦	4 Bore	4.00 × 3.58	8.0	175 @ 3600	260 @ 2800	—	30-80
	360-3	V8-360⑤⑦	4 Bore	4.00 × 3.58	8.0	200 @ 4000	280 @ 3200	—	30-80
	446	V8-446①⑦	4 Bore	4.125 × 4.18	8.0	230 @ 3600	360 @ 2800	—	15-50

①—See International chapter for service on this engine.
②—Light duty.
③—Heavy duty.
④—Exc. Calif.
⑤—Calif.
⑥—Light duty emissions.
⑦—Heavy duty emissions.
⑧—Medium duty emissions.

DODGE & PLYMOUTH

TUNE UP SPECIFICATIONS

The following specifications are published from the latest information available. This data should be used only in the absence of a decal affixed in the engine compartment.

★ When using a timing light, disconnect vacuum hose or tube at distributor and plug opening in hose or tube so idle speed will not be affected.

● When checking compression, lowest cylinder must be within 80 percent of highest.

▲ Before removing wires from distributor cap, determine location of the No. 1 wire in cap, as distributor position may have been altered from that shown at the end of this chart.

Year & Engine	Spark Plug Type	Gap	Firing Order Fig. ▲	Ignition Timing BTDC ①★ Man. Trans.	Auto Trans.	Mark Location	Curb Idle Speed ② Man. Trans.	Auto. Trans.	Fuel Pump Pressure
1980									
6-225 Exc. Calif.	RBL16Y	.035	A	12°	12°	Damper	600	600N	3½–5
6-225 Calif.	RBL16Y	.035	A	12°	12°	Damper	800	800N	3½–5
V8-318 2 Barrel Carb.	RN11Y	.035	B	12°	12°	Damper	600	600N	5–7
V8-318 4 Barrel Carb.③	RN11Y	.035	B	6°	6°	Damper	750	750N	5–7
V8-318 4 Barrel Carb.④	RN11Y	.035	B	8°	8°	Damper	750	750N	5–7
V8-360-1 4 Barrel Carb. Exc. Calif.⑤	RN12Y	.035	B	12°	12°	Damper	650	650N	5–7
V8-360-1 4 Barrel Carb. Exc. Calif.④	RN12Y	.035	B	4°	4°	Damper	700	700N	5–7
V8-360-1 4 Barrel Carb. Calif.	RN12Y	.035	B	10°	10°	Damper	750	750N	5–7
V8-360-3 4 Barrel Carb. Exc. Calif.	RF10	.035	B	4°	4°	Damper	700	700N	5–7
V8-360-3 4 Barrel Carb. Calif.⑥	RF10	.035	B	10°	10°	Damper	750	750N	5–7
V8-360-3 4 Barrel Carb. Calif.⑦	RF10	.035	B	4°	4°	Damper	700	700N	5–7
MV-446	RBN13Y	.035	⑧	5°⑨	5°⑨	Damper	525/575	625/675N	4½–5¾
1979									
6-225 Exc. Calif.	RBL16Y	.035	A	12°	12°	Damper	675	675N	3½–5
6-225 Calif.	RBL16Y	.035	A	8°	8°	Damper	800	800N	3½–5
V8-318 Exc. Calif.	RN12Y	.035	B	12°	12°	Damper	680	680N	5–7
V8-318 Calif.⑩	RN12Y	.035	B	6°	8°	Damper	750	750N	5–7
V8-318 Calif.③	RN12Y	.035	B	6°	6°	Damper	750	750N	5–7
V8-360 2 Barrel Carb. Exc. Calif.⑪	RN12Y	.035	B	10°	10°	Damper	750	750N	5–7
V8-360-3 2 Barrel Carb.⑫	RF10	.035	B	—	TDC	Damper	—	⑬	5–7
V8-360 4 Barrel Carb. Exc. Calif.⑤	RN12Y	.035	B	—	4°	Damper	—	750N	5–7
V8-360 4 Barrel Carb. Calif.③	RN12Y	.035	B	10°	10°	Damper	750	750N	5–7
V8-360 4 Barrel Carb.④	RN12Y	.035	B	4°	4°	Damper	700	700N	5–7
V8-440⑪	OJ11Y	.035	C	—	8°	Damper⑭	—	700N	5–7
V8-440-3⑫	OB69Y	.035	C	—	8°	Damper⑭	—	700N	5–7
1978									
6-225 Exc. Calif.⑩	RBL16Y	.035	A	12°	12°	Damper	750	750N	3½–5
6-225 Exc. Calif.⑮	RBL16Y	.035	A	TDC	TDC	Damper	700	700N	3½–5
6-225 Calif.	RBL16Y	.035	A	8°	8°	Damper	750	750N	3½–5
V8-318 Exc. Calif.⑩	RN11Y	.035	B	12°	12°	Damper	750	750N	5–7
V8-318 Exc. Calif.⑮	RN11Y	.035	B	2°⑯	2°⑯	Damper	750	750N	5–7
V8-318 Calif.	RN11Y	.035	B	12°	12°	Damper	750	750N	5–7
V8-360 2 Barrel Carb. Exc. Calif.⑩	RN12Y	.035	B	6°	6°	Damper	750	750N	5–7
V8-360 2 Barrel Carb. Exc. Calif.⑮	RN12Y	.035	B	4°	4°	Damper	750	750N	5–7

Continued

DODGE & PLYMOUTH

TUNE UP SPECIFICATIONS—Continued

The following specifications are published from the latest information available. This data should be used only in the absence of a decal affixed in the engine compartment.

★ When using a timing light, disconnect vacuum hose or tube at distributor and plug opening in hose or tube so idle speed will not be affected.

● When checking compression, lowest cylinder must be within 80 percent of highest.

▲ Before removing wires from distributor cap, determine location of the No. 1 wire in cap, as distributor position may have been altered from that shown at the end of this chart.

Year & Engine	Spark Plug Type	Gap	Firing Order Fig. ▲	Ignition Timing BTDC①★ Man. Trans.	Auto Trans.	Mark Location	Curb Idle Speed② Man. Trans.	Auto. Trans.	Fuel Pump Pressure
V8-360 2 Barrel Carb. Calif.④	RN12Y	.035	B	TDC	TDC	Damper	700	700N	5–7
V8-360-3 2 Barrel Carb.	RF10	.035	B	—	TDC	Damper	—	⑬	5–7
V8-360 4 Barrel Carb. Exc. Calif.	RN12Y	.035	B	4°	4°	Damper	800	800N	5–7
V8-360 4 Barrel Carb. Calif.	RN12Y	.035	B	6°	6°	Damper	750	750N	5–7
V8-400-1	OJ11Y	.035	C	2°	2°	Damper	700	700N	5–7
V8-440-1 Exc. Calif.	OJ11Y	.035	C	8°	8°	Damper	700	700N	5–7
V8-440-1 Calif.	OJ11Y	.035	C	—	8°	Damper⑭	—	⑰	5–7
V8-440-3	OBL9Y	.035	C	—	8°	Damper⑭	—	700N	5–7
1977									
6-225 Exc. Calif.⑩	RBL15Y	.035	A	2°	2°	Damper	750	750N	3½–5
6-225 Calif.⑩	RBL15Y	.035	A	TDC	2°⑯	Damper	750	750N	3½–5
6-225 Exc. Calif.⑮	RBL11Y	.035	A	TDC	TDC	Damper	700	700N	3½–5
V8-318⑩	RN11Y	.035	B	2°	⑱	Damper	750	750N	5–7
V8-318-1 Exc. Calif.⑮	RN11Y	.035	B	2°⑯	2°⑯	Damper	750	750N	5–7
V8-318-1 Calif.⑮	RN11Y	.035	B	TDC	TDC	Damper	700	700N	5–7
V8-318-3	RF10	.035	B	TDC	TDC	Damper	700	700N	5–7
V8-360⑩	RN12Y	.035	B	—	6°	Damper⑲	—	700N	5–7
V8-360-1 Exc. Calif.⑮	RN12Y	.035	B	⑳	⑳	Damper⑲	750	750N	5–7
V8-360-1 Calif.⑮	RN12Y	.035	B	—	TDC	Damper⑲	—	700D	5–7
V8-360-3	RF10	.035	B	TDC	TDC	Damper⑲	⑬	⑬	5–7
V8-361-4	RN6	.035	C	2½°	2½°	Damper	700	700D	6–7½
V8-400-1	RJ11Y	.035	C	2°	2°	Damper⑭	700	700D	5–7
V8-413-3	RN6	.035	㉑	㉒	㉒	Damper⑭	700	700D	6–7½
V8-440-1	RJ11Y	.035	C	8°	8°	Damper⑭	700	700D	5–7
V8-440-3	BL9Y	.035	C	8°	8°	Damper⑭	700	700D	5–7
1976									
6-225 Exc. Calif.⑩	BL11Y	.035	A	2°	2°	Damper	800	750N	3½–5
6-225 Calif.⑩	BL11Y	.035	A	TDC	TDC	Damper	800	750N	3½–5
6-225-1⑮	BL11Y	.035	A	TDC	TDC	Damper	700	700N	3½–5
V8-318 Exc. Calif.⑩	N11Y	.035	B	2°	2°	Damper	750	750N	5–7
V8-318 Calif.⑩	N11Y	.035	B	TDC	TDC	Damper	750	750N	5–7
V8-318-1⑮	N11Y	.035	B	2°⑯	2°⑯	Damper	750	750N	5–7
V8-318-3 Exc. Calif.	F10	.035	B	TDC	TDC	Damper	700	700N	5–7
V8-318-3 Calif.	F10	.035	B	2°	2°	Damper	700	700N	5–7
V8-360 Exc. Calif.⑩	N12Y	.035	B	—	6°	Damper	700	700N	5–7
V8-360 Calif.⑩	N12Y	.035	B	—	4°	Damper	700	700N	5–7
V8-360-1 Exc. Calif.⑮	N12Y	.035	B	TDC	TDC	Damper	700	700N	5–7
V8-360-1 Calif.⑮	N12Y	.035	B	4°	4°	Damper	700	700N	5–7
V8-360-3	F10	.035	B	TDC	TDC	Damper	⑬	⑬	5–7
V8-361-4	N6	.035	C	2½°	2½°	Damper	700	700N	6–7½
V8-400	J11Y	.035	C	—	8°	Damper⑭	700	700N	5–7

TUNE UP SPECIFICATIONS—Continued

The following specifications are published from the latest information available. This data should be used only in the absence of a decal affixed in the engine compartment.

★ When using a timing light, disconnect vacuum hose or tube at distributor and plug opening in hose or tube so idle speed will not be affected.

● When checking compression, lowest cylinder must be within 80 percent of highest.

▲ Before removing wires from distributor cap, determine location of the No. 1 wire in cap, as distributor position may have been altered from that shown at the end of this chart.

Year & Engine	Spark Plug		Ignition Timing BTDC①★				Curb Idle Speed②		Fuel Pump Pressure
	Type	Gap	Firing Order Fig. ▲	Man. Trans.	Auto Trans.	Mark Location	Man. Trans.	Auto. Trans.	
V8-413-3	N6	.035	㉑	㉒	㉒	Damper	700	700N	6–7½
V8-440-1	J11Y	.035	C	8°	8°	Damper⑭	700	700N	5–7
V8-440-3	BL9Y	.035	C	8°	8°	Damper⑭	700	700N	5–7
1975									
6-225⑩	BL11Y	.035	A	TDC	TDC	Damper	800	750N	3½–5
6-225-1⑮	BL11Y	.035	A	TDC	TDC㉓	Damper	700	700N	3½–5
V8-318 Exc. Calif.⑩	N11Y	.035	B	2°	2°	Damper	750	750N	5–7
V8-318 Calif.⑩	N11Y	.035	B	TDC	TDC	Damper	750	750N	5–7
V8-318-1 Exc. Calif.⑮	N11Y	.035	B	2°⑯	2°⑯	Damper	750	750N	5–7
V8-318-1 Calif.⑮	N11Y	.035	B	TDC	TDC	Damper	700	700N	5–7
V8-318-3 Exc. Calif.	F10	.035	B	TDC	TDC	Damper	700	700N	5–7
V8-318-3 Calif.	F10	.035	B	2°	2°	Damper	700	700N	5–7
V8-360-1 Exc. Calif.	N12Y	.035	B	TDC	TDC	Damper	750	750N	5–7
V8-360-1 Calif.	N12Y	.035	B	4°	4°	Damper	700	700N	5–7
V8-360-3	F10	.035	B	TDC	TDC	Damper	⑬	⑬	5–7
V8-361-4	N6	.035	C	2½°	2½°	Damper	700	700N	6–7½
V8-413-3	N6	.035	㉑	㉒	㉒	Damper	700	700N	6–7½
V8-440-1	J11Y	.035	C	8°	8°	Damper	700	700N	5–7
V8-440-3	BL9Y	.035	C	8°	8°	Damper	700	700N	5–7
1974									
6-225	N11Y	.035	A	TDC㉔	TDC㉔	Damper	800	750N	3½–5
V8-318-1	N11Y	.035	B	TDC㉕	TDC㉕	Damper	750	750N	5–7
V8-318-3	E10	.035	B	TDC	TDC	Damper	700	700N	5–7
V8-360 Exc. Calif.⑩	N12Y	.035	B	2½°	5°	Damper	750	700N	5–7
V8-360 Calif.⑩	N12Y	.035	B	—	2½°	Damper	—	㉖	5–7
V8-360⑮	N12Y	.035	B	TDC	TDC	Damper	750	750N	5–7
V8-361	N6	.035	C	2½°	2½°	Damper	700	700N	6–7½
V8-400⑩	J13Y	.035	C	7½°	7½°	Damper	750	750N	5–7
V8-400⑮	J11Y	.035	C	2½°	2½°	Damper	750	750N	5–7
V8-413-2	N6	.035	㉑	2½°	—	Damper	700	—	6–7½
V8-413-3	N6	.035	㉑	5°	—	Damper	700	—	6–7½
V8-440⑩	J11Y	.035	C	10°㉗	10°㉗	Damper	700	700N	5–7
V8-440-1	J11Y	.035	C	7½°	7½°	Damper	700	700N	5–7
VS-440-3	BL9Y	.035	C	7½°	7½°	Damper	700	700N	5–7
1973									
6-225-1㉚㉛	N11Y	.035	A	TDC	TDC	Damper	750	750N	3½–5
6-225-1㉙	N14Y	.035	A	TDC	TDC	Damper	750	750N	3½–5
6-225-1⑮㉙	N11Y	.035	A	㉞	㉞	Damper	750	750N	3½–5
6-225-2㉙	N6	.035	A	TDC	TDC	Damper	750	750N	3½–5
V8-318-1㉚㉜	N11Y	.035	B	2½°	2½°	Damper	750	700N	5–7
V8-318-1㉙	N11Y	.035	B	2½°	TDC	Damper	750	700N	5–7
V8-318-1⑮㉙	N11Y	.035	B	㉟	㉟	Damper	750	700N	5–7
V8-318-3㉙	F10	.035	B	2½°	2½°	Damper	700	700N	5–7
V8-360㉚㉜	J13Y	.035	B	TDC	TDC	Damper	750	700N	5–7

Continued

DODGE & PLYMOUTH

TUNE UP SPECIFICATIONS—Continued

The following specifications are published from the latest information available. This data should be used only in the absence of a decal affixed in the engine compartment.

★ When using a timing light, disconnect vacuum hose or tube at distributor and plug opening in hose or tube so idle speed will not be affected.

● When checking compression, lowest cylinder must be within 80 percent of highest.

▲ Before removing wires from distributor cap, determine location of the No. 1 wire in cap, as distributor position may have been altered from that shown at the end of this chart.

Year & Engine	Spark Plug Type	Gap	Firing Order Fig. ▲	Ignition Timing BTDC①★ Man. Trans.	Auto. Trans.	Mark Location	Curb Idle Speed② Man. Trans.	Auto. Trans.	Fuel Pump Pressure
V8-360㉙	N13Y	.035	B	TDC	TDC	Damper	750	700N	5–7
V8-361	N6	.035	C	5°	5°	Damper	700	700N	3½–5
V8-400	J11Y	.035	C	㊱	㊱	Damper	700	700N	3½–5
V8-413-2	N6	.035	㉑	5°㊲	—	Damper	600㊳	—	3½–5
V8-413-1, 3	N6	.035	㉑	5°	—	Damper	500	—	3½–5
V8-440-1	J11Y	.035	C	10°	10°	Damper	700	700N	6–7½
V8-440-3	BL9Y	.035	C	7½°	7½°	Damper	750	750N	6–7½
V8-478㉚㉝	UJ6	.035	㉘	10°	—	Damper	425	—	4½
V8-549㉚㉝	UJ6	.035	㉘	10°	—	Damper	425	—	4½
1972									
6-225-1㉚㉛	N11Y	.035	A	TDC	TDC	Damper	㊴	㊴	3½–5
6-225-2㉚㉛	N6	.035	A	TDC	TDC	Damper	700	—	3½–5
V8-318-1㉚㉜	N11Y	.035	B	㊵	㊵	Damper	750	750N	5–7
V8-318-3㉚㉜	F10	.035	B	5°	5°	Damper	700	700N	5–7
V8-318-3㉙	F10	.035	B	—	2½°	Damper	—	700N	5–7
V8-360㉚㉜	J13Y	.035	B	㊶	㊶	Damper	700	700N	5–7
V8-361-2㉚㉜	N6	.035	C	5°	—	Damper	500	—	3½–5
V8-361-3㉚㉜	N6	.035	C	5°	—	Damper	500	—	3½–5
V8-361-4㉚㉜	N6	.035	C	5°	—	Damper	600	—	3½–5
V8-400㉚㉜	J11Y	.035	C	㊶	㊶	Damper	700	700N	3½–5
V8-413-1㉚㉝	N6	.035	㉑	5°	—	Damper	600	—	3½–5
V8-413-1㉙	N6	.035	㉑	—	5°	Damper	—	700N	3½–5
V8-413-2㉚㉝	N6	.035	㉑	5°	—	Damper	600	—	3½–5
V8-413-3㉚㉝	N6	.035	㉑	5°	—	Damper	—	—	3½–5
V8-478㉚㉝	UJ6	.035	㉘	10°	—	Damper	—	—	4–4¾
V8-549㉚㉝	UJ6	.035	㉘	7°	—	Damper	450	—	4–4¾
1971									
6-225-1㉚㉛	N11Y	.035	A	TDC	TDC	Damper	㊺	㊺	3½–5
6-225-2㉚	N6	.035	A	TDC	TDC	Damper	㊺	㊺	3½–5
V8-318-1㉚㉜	N11Y	.035	B	TDC	TDC	Damper	750	750N	5–7
V8-318-3㉚㊸	F10	.030	B	5°	—	Damper	700	—	5–7
V8-360㉚㉜	J13Y	.035	B	—	TDC	Damper	—	750N	5–7
V8-361-2㉚㊸	N6	.035	C	5°	—	Damper	600	—	3½–5
V8-361-3㉚㊸	N6	.035	C	5°	—	Damper	600	—	3½–5
V8-361-4㉚㊸	N6	.035	C	5°	—	Damper	600	—	3½–5
V8-383㉚㊸	J13Y	.035	C	TDC	7½°	Damper	700	600N	3½–5
V8-400㉚㉜	J11Y	.035	C	—	㊶	Damper	—	700N	—
V8-413-2㉚㉝	N6	.035	㉑	—	5°	Damper	—	600N	3½–5
V8-413-3㉚㉝	N6	.035	㉑	5°	—	Damper	500	—	3½–5
V8-478㉚㉝	UJ6	.035	㉘	10°	—	Damper	—	—	4–4¾
V8-549㉚㉝	UJ6	.035	㉘	7°	—	Damper	425	—	4–4¾
1970									
6-198㉚㉝	N11Y	.035	A	TDC	TDC	Damper	700㊷	650N㊷	3½–5
6-225-1㉚㉛	N11Y	.035	A	TDC	TDC	Damper	700㊷	650N㊷	3½–5

Continued

DODGE & PLYMOUTH

TUNE UP SPECIFICATIONS—Continued

The following specifications are published from the latest information available. This data should be used only in the absence of a decal affixed in the engine compartment.

★ When using a timing light, disconnect vacuum hose or tube at distributor and plug opening in hose or tube so idle speed will not be affected.

● When checking compression, lowest cylinder must be within 80 percent of highest.

▲ Before removing wires from distributor cap, determine location of the No. 1 wire in cap, as distributor position may have been altered from that shown at the end of this chart.

Year & Engine	Spark Plug		Ignition Timing BTDC①★				Curb Idle Speed②		Fuel Pump Pressure
	Type	Gap	Firing Order Fig. ▲	Man. Trans.	Auto. Trans.	Mark Location	Man. Trans.	Auto. Trans.	
6-225-2㉚㉛	N6	.035	A	TDC	—	Damper	700㊷	—	3½–5
V8-318-1㉚㉜	N11Y	.035	B	2½°	2½°	Damper	750	700N	5–7
V8-318-1㉚㉜	N11Y	.035	B	5°	5°	Damper	750	700N	5–7
V8-318-3㉚㊸	F10	.030	B	5°	—	Damper	600	—	5–7
V8-361-2㉚㊸	N6	.035	C	5°	—	Damper	600	—	3½–5
V8-361-3㉚㊸	N6	.035	C	5°	—	Damper	600	—	3½–5
V8-361-4㉚㉝	N6	.035	C	5°	—	Damper	500	—	3½–5
V8-383㉚㊸	J13Y	.035	C	TDC	7½°	Damper	700	600N	3½–5
V8-413㉚㉝	N6	.035	㉑	5°	—	Damper	500	—	3½–5
V8-478㉚㊹	UJ6	.035	㉘	10°	—	Damper	450	—	4–4¾
V8-549㉚㊹	UJ6	.035	㉘	7°	—	Damper	450	—	4–4¾

①—B.T.D.C.—Before top dead center.
②—N: Neutral.
③—Medium duty emission, GVWR 6001 to 8500 lbs.
④—Heavy duty emissions, GVWR 8501 lbs. & above.
⑤—Light duty emissions, GVWR, 8500 lbs & under.
⑥—Exc. models with carburetor No. TQ-9261S
⑦—Models with carburetor No. TQ-9261S.
⑧—Cylinder numbering (front to rear), right bank, 1-3-5-7; left bank, 2-4-6-8. Firing order, 1-2-7-3-4-5-6-8
⑨—There are two timing mark plates located on the engine front cover. If the upper timing plate is to be used to check timing, connect timing light to No. 1 cylinder. If the lower timing plate is used to check timing, connect timing light to No. 7 cylinder.
⑩—Light duty emissions, GVWR 6000 lbs. & under.
⑪—Except motor home chassis.
⑫—Motor home chassis.
⑬—Except Calif., 750N RPM; California, 700N RPM.
⑭—On B series, Voyager & motor home chassis models, timing mark located on torque converter.
⑮—Heavy duty emissions, GVWR 6001 lbs. & above.
⑯—A.T.D.C.—After top dead center.
⑰—Medium duty emissions, GVWR 6001 to 8500 lbs., 750N RPM; heavy duty emissions, GVWR 8501 lbs. & above, 700N RPM.
⑱—Except high altitude, 2° BTDC; high altitude, 6° BTDC.
⑲—On B series & Voyager models w/air pump, timing mark located on torque converter.
⑳—Models equipped with Holley 2210 carburetor, TDC; models equipped with Holley 2245 carburetor, 4° BTDC.
㉑—To determine proper firing order diagram it is necessary to observe rotor rotation. Use Fig. C if rotation is counter clockwise & Fig. D if clockwise. This is caused by the fact that some engines use timing gears while others use a timing chain.
㉒—Except school bus, 5° BTDC; TDC.
㉓—California vehicles built after September 11, 1975, set at 2° ATDC.
㉔—Distributor #3755056, 2½° BTDC.
㉕—Distributor #3755201, 2½° BTDC.
㉖—Series 100-800, 750 RPM; except Series, 100-800, 850 RPM.
㉗—California, 5° BTDC.
㉘—Firing order 1-8-7-3-6-5-4-2; cylinder numbering (front to rear): Left bank 1-3-5-7; Right bank 2-4-6-8.
㉙—With electronic ignition.
㉚—Except electronic ignition.
㉛—Point gap, .020"; dwell angle, 41°–46°.
㉜—Point gap, .017"; dwell angle, 30°–34°.
㉝—Point gap, .016"; dwell angle, 28°–32°.
㉞—All except Calif. TDC, California 2½° ATDC.
㉟—All except Calif. 5° BTDC, California, TDC.
㊱—Light duty 10° BTDC, heavy duty 2½° BTDC.
㊲—California, 2½°.
㊳—California, 700 RPM.
㊴—Except Calif., 750 RPM; California, 650 RPM.
㊵—Distributor #3656275, TDC; Distributor # 3656287, 2½°.
㊶—Light duty 5°; heavy duty 2½°.
㊷—With headlights on.
㊸—Point gap, .017"; dwell angle, 30°–35°.
㊹—Point gap, .016"; dwell angle, 25°–29°.
㊺—W/Holley carburetor, 750 RPM; w/Carter carburetor, 800 RPM.

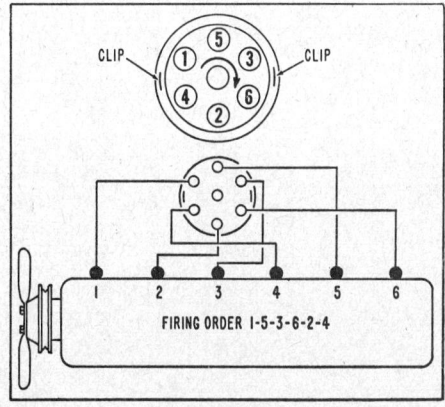

Fig. A

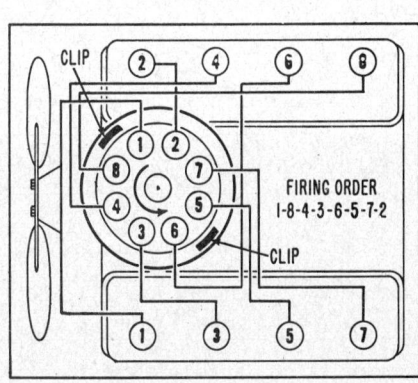

Fig. B

DODGE & PLYMOUTH

TUNE UP NOTES—Continued

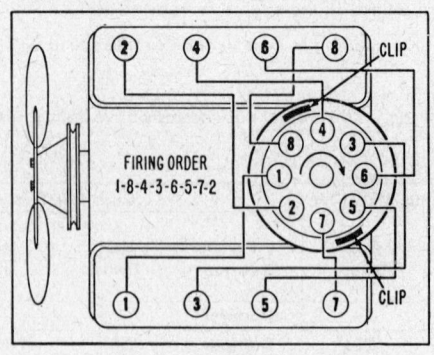

Fig. C

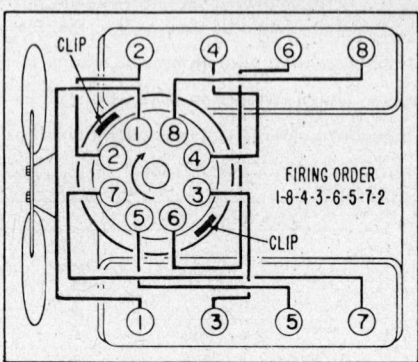

Fig. D

CHRYSLER ALTERNATOR AND REGULATOR SPECIFICATIONS

Unit Number	Ground Polarity	Field Coil Draw Amperes ②	Current Output			Operating Voltage			Voltage Regulator Point Gap	Regulator Armature Air Gap
			Engine R.P.M.	Amperes ③	Volts	Engine R.P.M.	Volts	Voltage @ 117° ①		
2095060	Neg.	2.38–2.75	1250	35	14.6	1250	15	13.5–14.1	.012–.016	.048–.052
2095425	Neg.	2.38–2.75	1250	40	14.6	1250	15	13.5–14.1	.012–.016	.048–.052
2095661	Neg.	2.38–2.75	1250	30	14.6	1250	15	13.5–14.1	.012–.016	.048–.052
2095663	Neg.	2.38–2.75	1250	34	14.6	1250	15	13.5–14.1	.012–.016	.048–.052
2095666	Neg.	2.38–2.75	1250	40	14.6	1250	15	13.5–14.1	.012–.016	.048–.052
2095667	Neg.	2.38–2.75	1250	40	14.6	1260	15	13.5–14.1	.012–.016	.048–.052
2098256	Neg.	2.38–2.75	1250	33.5	15	1250	15	13.5–14.1	.012–.016	.048–.052
2098262	Neg.	2.38–2.75	1250	32.5	15	1250	15	13.5–14.1	.012–.016	.048–.052
2098265	Neg.	2.38–2.75	1250	33.5	15	1250	15	13.5–14.1	.012–.016	.048–.052
2098268	Neg.	2.38–2.75	1250	32.5	15	1250	15	13.5–14.1	.012–.016	.048–.052
2098290	Neg.	2.38–2.75	1250	36.0	15	1250	15	13.5–14.1	.012–.016	.048–.052
2098330	Neg.	2.38–2.75	1250	39.0	15	1250	15	13.5–14.1	.012–.016	.048–.052
2098830	Neg.	2.38–2.75	1250	35.5	15	1250	15	13.5–14.1	.012–.016	.048–.052
2098840	Neg.	2.38–2.75	1250	35.5	15	1250	15	13.3–14.2	.012–.016	.048–.052
2098850	Neg.	2.38–2.75	1250	44	15	1250	15	13.3–14.3	.010–.018	.032–.042
2098855	Neg.	2.38–2.75	1250	33.5	15	1250	15	13.5–14.1	.012–.016	.048–.052
2098860	Neg.	2.38–2.75	1250	32.5	15	1250	15	13.5–14.1	.012–.016	.048–.052
2098865	Neg.	2.38–2.75	1250	37	15	1250	15	13.3–14.3	.012–.016	.048–.052
2098870	Neg.	2.38–2.75	1250	36	15	1250	15	13.4–14.3	.012–.016	.048–.052
2098875	Neg.	2.38–2.75	1250	32.5	15	1250	15	13.5–14.1	.012–.016	.048–.052
2098880	Neg.	2.38–2.75	1250	36	15	1250	15	13.4–14.3	.012–.016	.048–.050
2444897	Neg.	2.38–2.75	1250	51	15	1250	15	13.3–14.3	.012–.016	.048–.052
2444898	Neg.	2.38–2.75	1250	51	15	1250	15	13.3–14.3	.012–.016	.048–.052
2444899	Neg.	2.38–2.75	1250	51	15	1250	15	13.3–14.3	.012–.016	.048–.052
2444900	Neg.	2.38–2.75	1250	51	15	1250	15	13.3–14.3	.012–.016	.048–.052
2642537	Neg.	2.38–2.75	1250	34.5	15	1250	15	13.3–14.3	.010–.018	.032–.042
2875724	Neg.	2.38–2.75	1250	44	15	1250	15	13.3–14.3	.010–.018	.032–.042
2875844	Neg.	2.38–2.75	1250	44	15	1250	15	13.3–14.3	.010–.018	.032–.042
3000010	Neg.	2.38–2.75	1250	51	15	1250	15	13.3–14.3	.010–.018	.032–.042
3438165	Neg.	2.38–2.75	1250	44	15	1250	15	13.3–14.3	.010–.018	.032–.042
3438168	Neg.	2.38–2.75	1250	51	15	1250	15	13.3–14.3	.010–.018	.032–.042
3438173	Neg.	2.38–2.75	1250	44	15	1250	15	13.3–14.3	.010–.018	.032–.042
3438174	Neg.	3.38–2.75	1250	51	15	1250	15	13.3–14.3	.010–.018	.032–.042
3438178	Neg.	2.38–2.75	1250	44	15	1250	15	13.3–14.3	.010–.018	.032–.042
3438180	Neg.	2.38–2.75	1250	51	15	1250	15	13.3–14.3	.010–.018	.032–.042

Continued

DODGE & PLYMOUTH

CHRYSLER ALTERNATOR AND REGULATOR SPECIFICATIONS—Continued

Unit Number	Ground Polarity	Field Coil Draw Amperes ②	Current Output			Operating Voltage			Voltage Regulator Point Gap	Regulator Armature Air Gap
			Engine R.P.M.	Amperes ③	Volts	Engine R.P.M.	Volts	Voltage @ 117° ①		
Red Tag	Neg.	2.5–3.7 ⑤	1250	40	15	1250	15	13.3–14 ④	—	—
Bronze Tag	Neg.	4.5–6.5	1250	40	15	1250	15	13.3–13.9 ④	—	—
Green Tag	Neg.	2.5–3.7 ⑤	1250	47	15	1250	15	13.3–14 ④	—	—
Blue Tag	Neg.	2.5–3.7 ⑤	1250	57	15	1250	15	13.3–14 ④	—	—
Natural Tag ⑥	Neg.	2.5–3.7 ⑤	1250	57	15	1250	15	13.3–14 ④	—	—
Yellow Tag ⑥	Neg.	4.5–6.5	1250	57	15	1250	15	13.3–13.9 ④	—	—
Black Tag	Neg.	2.5–3.7 ⑤	1250	62	15	1250	15	13.3–14 ④	—	—
Yellow Tag ⑦	Neg.	4.75–6.0 ⑨	900	72	13	900	13	13.3–13.9 ④	—	—
Violet Tag	Neg.	4.5–6.5	1250	41	15	1250	15	13.3–13.9 ④	—	—
Natural Tag ⑧⑦	Neg.	4.75–6.0	900	72	13	900	13	13.3–13.9 ④	—	—

①—For each 10° rise in temperature subtract .04 volt; for each 10° drop add .04 volt. Temperature is checked with a thermometer 2 inches from installed voltage regulator cover.
②—Current draw at 12 volts while turning rotor shaft by hand.
③—If output is low, stator or rectifier is shorted.
④—Rated @ 140°.
⑤—1976–77, 4.5–6.5 amps.
⑥—60 amp. alternator.
⑦—1977–78 100 amp. & 1979–80 117 Amp. alternator.
⑧—1978.
⑨—1979–80, 4.5–6.5 amps.

DELCO REMY ALTERNATOR & REGULATOR SPECIFICATIONS

Year	Alternator					Regulator						
	Model	Field Current @ 80° F. 12 Volts	Cold Output @ 14 Volts		Rated Hot Output Amperes	Model	Field Relay			Voltage Regulator		
			Amperes @ 2000 R.P.M.	Amperes @ 5000 R.P.M.			Air Gap	Point Gap	Closing Voltage	Air Gap	Point Gap	Volts @ 125° F.
1970–74	1117089	6.0–6.6	31 ①	58 ②	60	9000590	.010	.015–.025	7–9	—	—	13.7–14.3
	1117756	4.14–4.62	20 ③	55 ②	62	9000590	.010	.015–.025	7–9	—	—	13.7–14.3
	1100072	4.4–4.9	45 ④	57 ⑤	65	—	—	—	—	—	—	—
	1100073	4.4–4.9	54 ④	73 ⑤	80	—	—	—	—	—	—	—
	1117090	6.0–6.6	30 ③	89 ②	85	9000590	.010	.015–.025	7–9	—	—	13.7–14.3
	1117790	6.0–6.6	24 ③	80 ②	85	9000590	.010	.015–.025	7–9	—	—	13.7–14.3

①—At 1000 R.P.M.
②—At 2500 R.P.M.
③—At 1100 R.P.M.
④—At 2000 R.P.M.
⑤—At 5000 R.P.M.

STARTING MOTOR SPECIFICATIONS

Model Number ①	Year	Brush Spring Tension, Oz.	No Load Test			Torque Test		
			Amperes	Volts	R.P.M.	Amperes	Volts	Torque Ft. Lbs.
1114088	1970–74	80	140–190	9	4000–7000	700	1.5	15
1889100	1970–73	32–36	78	11	3800	370	4	8.5
2095150	1970–71	32–48	85	11	1950	475	4	24
2642692	1970–74	32–36	78	11	3800	370	4	8.5
2875560	1970–72	32–36	90	11	1925 Min.	425	4	—
1113167	1970–74	80	50–70	9	3500–5500	230	1.5	6
1114070	1970–71	80	115	11	6300	700	1.5	15
1114058	1970–74	80	140–190	9	4000–7000	700	1.5	15
1113691	1974	—	130–160	9	5000–7000	—	—	—
1114085	1974	—	120–150	9	3000–4500	—	—	—

Continued

DODGE & PLYMOUTH

STARTING MOTOR SPECIFICATIONS—Continued

Model Number ①	Year	Brush Spring Tension, Oz.	No Load Test			Torque Test		
			Amperes	Volts	R.P.M.	Amperes	Volts	Torque Ft. Lbs.
1114128	1974	—	140–190	9	4000–7000	—	—	—
1114161	1974	—	140–190	9	4000–7000	—	—	—
3656575	1974	32–36	90	11	3700–4200	475–550	4	—
3656650	1971–74	32–36	90	11	1925–2600	400–450	4	—
3755900	1974–77	32–36	90	11	3700–4200	475–550	4	—
2642692	1977–78	32–36	78	11	3800	310–445	4	—
4091975	1978–79	32–36	90	11	3700	475–550	4	—
4111855	1980	32–36	90	11	3700	475–550	4	—

①—Stamped on plate riveted to housing.

DISTRIBUTOR SPECIFICATIONS

Distributor Part No. ①	Rotation ②	Breaker Gap	Dwell Angle Deg.	Breaker Arm Spring Tension	Centrifugal Advance Degrees @ R.P.M. of Distributor		Vacuum Advance	
					Advance Starts	Full Advance	Inches of Vacuum To Start Plunger	Max. Adv. Dist. Deg. @ Vacuum
2095270	C	.020	40–45	17–21	1 @ 450	11 @ 2200	4.9	10 @ 12
2095843	C	.017	27–32	17–21	1 @ 600	9 @ 2000	6	11 @ 12
2095844	CC	.017	27–32	17–21	2 @ 425	14 @ 1750	7	11 @ 12
2095845	CC	.017	27–32	17–21	2 @ 425	14 @ 1950	6	11 @ 12
2095846	CC	.017	27–32	17–21	1 @ 440	14 @ 2100	6	11 @ 12
2095957	C	.020	36–42	17–21	2 @ 440	8 @ 1550	5	12 @ 16
2095974	C	.020	40–45	17–21	2 @ 475	14 @ 2200	6	12 @ 12
2095976	C	.020	40–45	17–21	1 @ 475	12 @ 2300	6	7 @ 13
2098665	C	.020	40–45	17–20	1 @ 525	14 @ 2200	8.5	8 @ 10
2098670	C	.020	40–45	17–20	1 @ 560	12 @ 2500	10.5	7 @ 13
2098604	CC	.017	28–33	17–20	2 @ 425	13 @ 1600	9.2	11 @ 12
2098675	C	.020	40–45	17–20	4 @ 475	14 @ 2200	8.5	8 @ 10
2098687	CC	.017	28–33	17–20	2 @ 425	13 @ 2000	9.2	11 @ 12
2098692	C	.020	40–45	17–20	1 @ 540	10 @ 2000	8.5	8 @ 10
2444254	C	.020	40–45	17–20	1 @ 560	12 @ 2500	10.5	7 @ 13
2444255	C	.020	40–45	17–20	1 @ 525	14 @ 2200	9.2	11 @ 12
2444256	C	.020	40–45	17–20	3 @ 475	14 @ 2200	8.5	8 @ 10
2444258	C	.017	28–32	17–20	1 @ 480	11 @ 2300	9	12 @ 16
2444275	CC	.017	28–33	17–20	4 @ 425	13 @ 1600	9.2	11 @ 12
2444276	CC	.017	28–33	17–20	3 @ 425	13 @ 2000	9.2	11 @ 12
2444277	C	.020	36–42	17–21	1 @ 440	8 @ 1550	10	12 @ 16
2444291	C	.017	28–33	17–20	1 @ 450	6 @ 2000	9.2	11 @ 12
2444292	CC	.017	28–33	17–20	2 @ 425	14 @ 1750	9.2	11 @ 12
2444295	C	.020	40–45	17–20	1 @ 540	9 @ 2000	8.5	8 @ 10
2444648	C	.020	40–45	17–20	1 @ 475	12 @ 2200	6	7 @ 13
2444671	C	.020	40–45	17–20	1 @ 475	12 @ 2500	6	8 @ 10
2642234	C	.017	28–32	17–20	1 @ 450	12 @ 1750	6.5	13 @ 13
2642238	C	.017	28–32	17–20	1 @ 475	10 @ 1750	6.5	13 @ 13
2642244	CC	.017	28–32	17–20	1 @ 450	12 @ 2150	6	11 @ 13
2642329	C	.020	40–45	17–20	0–7½ @ 475	17½ @ 2200	7.1	8½ @ 10
2642346	C	.017	28–32	17–20	3 @ 500	17 @ 1900	8	13 @ 15
2642349	C	.020	40–45	17–20	2 @ 500	20 @ 2500	6	11 @ 12
2642352	C	.020	40–45	17–20	3 @ 475	20 @ 2500	6	8 @ 10
2642354	C	.020	40–45	17–20	2 @ 500	17 @ 2200	6	7 @ 13
2642356	C	.017	28–32	17–20	4 @ 500	17 @ 1500	6	13 @ 13
2642371	C	.017	28–32	17–20	2 @ 475	14 @ 2000	6	11 @ 12

Continued

DODGE & PLYMOUTH

DISTRIBUTOR SPECIFICATIONS—Continued

Distributor Part No. ①	Rotation ②	Breaker Gap	Dwell Angle Deg.	Breaker Arm Spring Tension	Centrifugal Advance Degrees @ R.P.M. of Distributor		Vacuum Advance	
					Advance Starts	Full Advance	Inches of Vacuum To Start Plunger	Max. Adv. Dist. Deg. @ Vacuum
2642373	CC	.017	28–32	17–20	4 @ 500	20 @ 2200	5.5	14 @ 14
2642531	CC	.017	28–32	17–20	2 @ 550	17 @ 2200	6	14 @ 16
2642718	C	.017	28–32	17–20	2 @ 525	11 @ 2350	8	13 @ 15
2642721	C	.017	28–32	17–20	1 @ 475	13 @ 2250	8	13 @ 15
2642724	C	.017	28–32	17–20	2 @ 475	19 @ 2350	8	13 @ 16
2642727	CC	.017	28–32	17–20	1 @ 450	11 @ 2150	10	13 @ 16
2642752	C	.020	40–45	17–20	1 @ 475	9 @ 2250	6	8 @ 10
2642755	C	.020	40–45	17–20	0–4½ @ 475	14½ @ 2200	7.1	8.5 @ 10
2642758	C	.020	40–45	17–20	0–2½ @ 525	14½ @ 2200	7.5	10 @ 10½
2642786	C	.020	40–45	17–20	0–3¾ @ 500	19 @ 2200	7.1	11½ @ 12
2642792	C	.020	40–45	17–20	1 @ 500	13 @ 2400	8	7 @ 16
2642795	C	.020	40–45	17–20	2 @ 475	13 @ 2400	6	7 @ 10
2642810	CC	.017	28–32	17–20	2 @ 550	15 @ 2200	12	14 @ 16
2642941	C	.020	40–45	17–20	0–5¾ @ 525	16½ @ 2200	7.1	8½ @ 10
2642949	CC	.017	28–32	17–20	3 @ 525	15 @ 2300	12	14 @ 16
2875199	C	.020	40–45	17–20	0–3¾ @ 500	19 @ 2200	7.1	8½ @ 10
2875202	C	.020	40–45	17–20	0–6¾ @ 500	16 @ 2200	7.1	8½ @ 10
2875206	C	.020	40–45	17–20	0 @ 425	21 @ 2200	6	7 @ 13
2875338	C	.017	28–33	17–20	1 @ 475	14 @ 2250	8	13 @ 15
2875332	C	.020	40–45	17–20	0–2 @ 475	10½ @ 2250	7.1	8½ @ 10
2875340	C	.017	28–33	17–20	0 @ 425	12 @ 2350	8	13 @ 15
2875342	C	.017	28–33	17–20	0 @ 425	19 @ 2350	9	10 @ 15
2875346	CC	.017	28–32	17–20	0 @ 350	14 @ 1750	7	11 @ 12
2875348	CC	.017	28–33	17–20	0 @ 350	13 @ 1600	7	11 @ 12
2875350	CC	.017	28–33	17–20	0 @ 350	13 @ 2000	7	11 @ 12
2875352	CC	.017	28–33	17–20	0 @ 425	19 @ 2200	6.5	10 @ 13
2875354	CC	.017	28–33	17–20	0 @ 425	16 @ 2250	5	8 @ 10
2875364	C	.020	40–45	17–20	0 @ 425	14 @ 2000	8	6 @ 13
2875366	C	.020	40–45	17–20	0 @ 425	14 @ 2000	6	6 @ 8
2875822	C	.020	42–47	17–20	1 @ 550	14 @ 2000	10	7.75 @ 16
2875826	C	.020	42–47	17–20	1 @ 550	14 @ 2000	7	7.75 @ 10
2875838	C	.020	42–47	17–20	1–4 @ 550	12 @ 1900	7.5	8.5 @ 10
2875796	C	.017	30–35	17–20	1 @ 550	19 @ 2400	10.5	10.75 @ 15
2875800	C	.017	30–35	17–20	1 @ 500	14 @ 2150	10.5	11 @ 15
2875804	C	.017	30–35	17–20	½–3½ @ 500	17 @ 2250	9.5	13.5 @ 15
2875653	CC	.016	28–32	17–21	1–4½ @ 500	14.5 @ 1600	7	11.5 @ 12
2875770	CC	.017	30–35	17–21	1–5 @ 500	17 @ 1750	7	11.5 @ 12
2875876	CC	.017	30–35	17–21	1–5 @ 500	17 @ 1750	7	11.5 @ 12
2875742	CC	.017	30–35	17–20	1 @ 550	23 @ 2350	8.5	13.5 @ 13.5
2875747	CC	.017	30–35	17–20	1 @ 500	19 @ 2300	8.5	13.5 @ 13.5
2875655	CC	.016	28–32	17–21	1–4½ @ 500	14.5 @ 1600	7	11.5 @ 12
2875654	CC	.016	28–32	17–21	½–3½ @ 500	14.5 @ 2000	7	11.5 @ 12
2875966	CC	.016	28–32	17–21	½–3½ @ 500	14.5 @ 2000	7½	11.5 @ 12
2959339	CC	.016	28–32	17–21	0 @ 420	12 @ 1600	7	8 @ 11¼
2959396	CC	.016	25–29	17–21	0 @ 320	8 @ 1600	5	8 @ 11.2
3438225	C	.017	30–34	17–20	1 @ 550	16 @ 2100	12	10.5 @ 15
3438227	C	.017	30–34	17–20	1 @ 550	12 @ 2100	10.5	9.75 @ 15
3438237	C	.020	41–46	17–20	0 @ 525	14 @ 1600	7	7.75 @ 10
3438255	C	.017	30–34	17–20	1 @ 550	16 @ 2100	10.5	9.75 @ 15
3498087	CC	.016	28–32	17–21	0–2 @ 340	8 @ 1600	7	8 @ 11¼
3656252	C	.020	41–46	17–20	½–4½ @ 550	14 @ 2000	10	7½ @ 15
3656257	C	.020	41–46	17–20	½–4½ @ 550	14 @ 2000	7	7½ @ 9½
3656260	C	.020	41–46	17–20	½–3½ @ 700	14 @ 2000	10	7½ @ 15
3656266	C	.020	41–46	17–20	½–3½ @ 700	14 @ 2000	7	7½ @ 9½

Continued

DODGE & PLYMOUTH

DISTRIBUTOR SPECIFICATIONS—Continued

Distributor Part No. ①	Rotation ②	Breaker Gap	Dwell Angle Deg.	Breaker Arm Spring Tension	Centrifugal Advance Degrees @ R.P.M. of Distributor		Vacuum Advance	
					Advance Starts	Full Advance	Inches of Vacuum To Start Plunger	Max. Adv. Dist. Deg. @ Vacuum
3656269	C	.020	41–46	17–20	1–4 @ 550	11 @ 1900	7½	8½ @ 10
3656272	C	.017	30–34	17–20	1½–5½ @ 550	16 @ 2100	10	10½ @ 15
3656275	C	.017	30–34	17–20	0–4 @ 600	16 @ 2100	10	10½ @ 15
3656287	C	.017	30–34	17–20	½–3½ @ 550	14 @ 2200	10	10½ @ 16
3656294	C	.017	30–34	17–20	½–4 @ 550	16 @ 2200	10	10½ @ 15
3656329	CC	.017	30–34	17–20	1–5 @ 650	14 @ 2000	10½	10½ @ 15½
3656359	CC	.017	30–35	17–20	1–6 @ 550	16 @ 1750	7	11½ @ 12
3656365	CC	.016	28–32	17–21	½–4 @ 550	14 @ 2000	7	11.5 @ 12
3656373	CC	.017	30–35	17–20	1–6 @ 550	16 @ 1750	7	11½ @ 12
3656375	CC	.016	28–32	17–21	1–6 @ 550	14 @ 1600	7	11½ @ 12
3656377	CC	.016	28–32	17–21	1–5 @ 550	14 @ 1600	7	11½ @ 12
3656379	CC	.016	28–32	17–21	½–4 @ 550	14 @ 2000	7	11.5 @ 12
3656667	C	—	—	—	½–3½ @ 550	16 @ 2200	9½	10 @ 14
3656672	C	—	—	—	½–3½ @ 500	14 @ 2200	10	9½ @ 15
3656678	CC	—	—	—	0–3½ @ 500	16 @ 1700	7	10.5 @ 11½
3656762	C	—	—	—	0–2 @ 500	14 @ 2150	10	9½ @ 14½
3656763	C	—	—	—	0–3½ @ 500	16 @ 2050	9	12 @ 15
3656780	C	—	—	—	0–3½ @ 500	15½ @ 1950	9	12½ @ 15
3656791	CC	—	—	—	½–3½ @ 550	15 @ 1950	10½	10½ @ 15½
3656830	CC	—	—	—	1–5 @ 550	16 @ 1600	9½	9.5 @ 13½
3656839	CC	—	—	—	1–4 @ 550	13½ @ 1900	9½	9½ @ 13½
3656872	CC	—	—	—	1–4½ @ 550	14 @ 2000	9½	9½ @ 13½
3656876	CC	—	—	—	1½–4½ @ 550	14½ @ 1650	7½	11.5 @ 12
3656877	CC	—	—	—	1½–4½ @ 550	14½ @ 1650	7½	11.5 @ 12
3656878	CC	—	—	—	1–3½ @ 550	14 @ 1900	9½	9.5 @ 13½
3755037	C	—	—	—	½–4½ @ 550	14 @ 2000	9½	14 @ 15
3755042	C	—	—	—	½–4½ @ 550	14 @ 2000	7¼	10 @ 11
3755056	C	—	—	—	1–4½ @ 550	14 @ 2200	11	8 @ 12½
3755062	C	—	—	—	½–4½ @ 550	14 @ 2000	10	8 @ 15
3755071	C	—	—	—	½–4½ @ 550	14 @ 2000	7	7½ @ 9½
3755075	C	—	—	—	½–2½ @ 500	12 @ 1900	7	5½ @ 9½
3755150	CC	—	—	—	1½–4½ @ 650	14 @ 2000	10½	10½ @ 15½
3755157	CC	—	—	—	½–3½ @ 650	12 @ 2000	10½	10½ @ 15½
3755160	C	—	—	—	0–3½ @ 500	15½ @ 2000	9½	10 @ 14
3755201	C	—	—	—	½–3 @ 550	14 @ 2150	10	9½ @ 15
3755205	C	—	—	—	1–3½ @ 550	14 @ 1900	7½	10.5 @ 13½
3755467	C	—	—	—	½–3½ @ 550	14 @ 2000	9	10 @ 15½
3755470	C	—	—	—	½–3½ @ 550	14 @ 2000	7	10 @ 11½
3755475	C	—	—	—	½–4 @ 550	14 @ 2000	7	12 @ 12½
3755518	CC	—	—	—	½–3½ @ 650	12 @ 2000	8	11 @ 14
3755520	CC	—	—	—	1–5 @ 550	16 @ 1600	9½	9.5 @ 13½
3755522	CC	—	—	—	½–3 @ 650	10 @ 2000	8	11 @ 14
3755820	C	—	—	—	1–3½ @ 700	13½ @ 2400	9	9½ @ 13
3755821	C	—	—	—	1–4½ @ 600	16 @ 2050	9	12½ @ 15½
3755825	C	—	—	—	½–3½ @ 650	14 @ 2000	9	10 @ 15½
3755841	C	—	—	—	1–4½ @ 650	14 @ 2000	7	12 @ 12½
3755681	CC	—	—	—	1–4.5 @ 650	16 @ 2150	8	11 @ 14
3874082	C	—	—	—	1–4½ @ 600	14 @ 2200	7	10 @ 11½
3874090	C	—	—	—	1½–5½ @ 550	14 @ 2200	7	12 @ 12½
3874101	CC	—	—	—	½–3 @ 600	12 @ 2000	8	11 @ 14
3874115	C	—	—	—	1–3.5 @ 600	12 @ 2000	7	12 @ 12.5
3874302	C	—	—	—	1½–5½ @ 550	14 @ 2200	9	12½ @ 15½

Continued

DODGE & PLYMOUTH

DISTRIBUTOR SPECIFICATIONS—Continued

Distributor Part No. ①	Rotation ②	Breaker Gap	Dwell Angle Deg.	Breaker Arm Spring Tension	Centrifugal Advance Degrees @ R.P.M. of Distributor		Vacuum Advance	
					Advance Starts	Full Advance	Inches of Vacuum To Start Plunger	Max. Adv. Dist. Deg. @ Vacuum
3874323	C	—	—	—	½–3 @ 550	14 @ 2150	11	8 @ 12½
3874596	CC	—	—	—	1½–3½ @ 600	10 @ 2200	10	11 @ 15
3874598	C	—	—	—	1–4½ @ 600	11½ @ 2300	7	10 @ 11½
3874672	—	—	—	—	—	—	—	—
3874876	C	—	—	—	1½–3½ @ 650	4.5 @ 2200	8	12 @ 12½
3874887	CC	—	—	—	1–3.2 @ 650	12 @ 2400	7	8 @ 11½
4091282	C	—	—	—	.8–4.7 @ 500	13½ @ 2400	7	8 @ 13½
4091661	C	—	—	—	1–3 @ 550	13 @ 2000	7	8 @ 15
4091821	CC	—	—	—	½–2½ @ 600	14 @ 2000	10	10½ @ 15½
4091902	C	—	—	—	0–1 @ 650	7 @ 2150	7	12 @ 15
4111487	C	—	—	—	4–6 @ 700	11.5 @ 2200	7	12 @ 15
4111501	C	—	—	—	0–1.5 @ 700	10 @ 2200	7	12 @ 15
4111783	CC	—	—	—	1–2.5 @ 550	13.5 @ 2100	10	9.5 @ 15
4111947	C	—	—	—	1.5–3.5 @ 550	8.5 @ 2200	7	12 @ 15
4111950	C	—	—	—	0.5–2.5 @ 650	10 @ 2200	7	12 @ 15

①—Plate on housing.
②—C: Clockwise; CC: Counterclockwise.

PISTON, PIN, RING, CRANKSHAFT & BEARING SPECIFICATIONS

Year	Engine Model ②	Wristpin Diameter	Piston Clearance, Inch ①	Ring End Gap In. (Minimum)		Crankpin Diameter, Inch	Rod Bearing Clearance, Inch	Main Bearing Journal Diameter, Inch	Main Bearing Clearance, Inch	End Thrust On Bearing No.	Shaft End Play
				Comp.	Oil						
1970–71	6-198	.9008	.0015	.010	.015	2.1865–2.1875	.0005–.0015	2.7495–2.7505	.0005–.0015	3	.002–.007
1970–71	6-225	.9008	.0015	.010	.015	2.1865–2.1875	.0005–.0015	2.7495–2.7505	.0005–.0015	3	.004–.008
1972–73	6-225	.9008	.0015	.010	.015	2.1865–2.1875	.0005–.0015	.27495–2.7505	.0005–.0015	3	.0035–.0085
1974	6-225	.9008	.0015	.010	.015	2.1865–2.1875	.0005–.002	2.7495–2.7505	.0005–.002	3	.002–.007
1975	6-225	.9008	.0015	.010	.015	2.1865–2.1875	.0005–.0015	2.7495–2.7505	.0005–.0015	3	.002–.007
1976	6-225	.9008	.0015	.010	.015	2.1865–2.1875	.0005–.0025	2.7495–2.7505	.0005–.002	3	.002–.009
1977–78	6-225	.9008	.0015	.010	.015	2.1865–2.1875	.0005–.0015	2.7495–2.7505	.0005–.0015	3	.002–.009
1979–80	6-225	.9008	.0015	.010	.015	2.1865–2.1875	.0002–.0022	2.7495–2.7505	.0002–.0022	3	.002–.009
1970–71	8-318	.9842	.0015	.010	.010	2.124–2.125	.0005–.0015	2.4995–2.5005	.0005–.0015	3	.002–.007
1972–73	8-318	.9842	.0015	.010	.015	2.124–2.125	.0005–.0015	2.4995–2.5005	.0005–.002	3	.002–.007
1974	8-318	.9842	.0015	.010	.015	2.124–2.125	.0005–.0025	2.4995–2.5005	.0005–.0025	3	.002–.007
1975	8-318	.9842	.0015	.010	.015	2.124–2.125	.0002–.0022	2.4995–2.5005	.0005–.0015	3	.002–.007
1976	8-318	.9842	.0015	.010	.015	2.124–2.125	.0005–.0015	2.4995–2.5005	.0005–.002	3	.002–.009
1977–78	V8-318-1	.9842	.0015	.010	.015	2.124–2.125	.0002–.0022	2.4995–2.5005	.0005–.0015	3	.002–.007
1979	V8-318	.9842	.0015	.010	.015	2.124–2.125	.0005–.0025	2.4995–2.5005	.0005–.0020	3	.002–.007
1980	V8-318	.9842	.0015	.010	.015	2.124–2.125	.0005–.0025	2.4995–2.5005	⑥	3	.002–.007
1970–71	LA318-3	.9842	.0015	.010	.010	2.1235–2.1245	.001–.002	2.4995–2.5005	.001–.002	3	.002–.007
1972–76	LA318-3	.9842	.0015	.010	.015	2.1235–2.1245	.001–.002	2.4995–2.5005	.001–.002	3	.002–.007
1977–78	V8-318-3	.9842	.0015	.010	.015	2.1235–2.1245	.001–.002	2.4995–2.5005	.0005–.0015	3	—
1971–73	8-360	.9842	.0015	.010	.015	2.124–2.125	.0005–.002	2.8095–2.8105	.0005–.002	3	.002–.007
1974	8-360	.9842	.0015	.010	.015	2.124–2.125	.0005–.0025	2.8095–2.8105	.0005–.0025	3	.002–.007
1975	8-360	.9842	.0015	.010	.015	2.124–2.125	.0005–.0025	2.8095–2.8105	.0005–.0015	3	.002–.007
1976	8-360	.9842	.0015	.010	.015	2.124–2.125	.0005–.0025	2.8095–2.8105	.0005–.002	3	.002–.009
1977–78	V8-360	.9842	.0015	.010	.015	2.124–2.125	.0005–.0025	2.8095–2.8105	.0005–.0015	3	.002–.009
1979	V8-360	.9842	.0015	.010	.015	2.124–2.125	.0005–.0025	2.8095–2.8105	.0005–.0020	3	.002–.009
1980	V8-360	.9842	.0015	.010	.015	2.124–2.125	.0005–.0025	2.8095–2.8105	⑥	3	.002–.009

Continued

DODGE & PLYMOUTH

PISTON, PIN, RING, CRANKSHAFT & BEARING SPECIFICATIONS—Continued

Year	Engine Model ②	Wristpin Diameter	Piston Clearance, Inch ①	Ring End Gap In. (Minimum) Comp.	Ring End Gap In. (Minimum) Oil	Crankpin Diameter, Inch	Rod Bearing Clearance, Inch	Main Bearing Journal Diameter, Inch	Main Bearing Clearance, Inch	End Thrust On Bearing No.	Shaft End Play
1970–71	8-361	1.0936	.0015	.013	.013	2.374–2.375	.001–.002	2.6245–2.6255	.0005–.002	3	.002–.007
1972–76	8-361	1.0936	.0015	.013	.013	2.374–2.375	.001–.002	2.6245–2.6255	.0015–.0025	3	.002–.007
1977–78	V8-361-4	1.0936	.0015	—	—	2.374–2.375	.001–.002	2.6245–2.6255	.0015–.0025	3	.002–.009
1970–71	8-383	1.0936	.0015	.013	.013	2.374–2.375	.0005–.0015	2.6245–2.6255	.0005–.0015	3	.002–.007
1971	8-400	1.0936	.0015	.013	.013	2.374–2.375	.0005–.002	2.6245–2.6255	.0005–.002	3	.002–.007
1972–73	8-400	1.0941	.00125	.013	.013	2.374–2.375	.0005–.0025	2.6245–2.6255	.0005–.002	3	.002–.007
1976	8-400	1.0936	.0013	.013	.015	2.375–2.376	⑤	2.6245–2.6255	.0005–.002	3	.002–.007
1977–78	V8-400	1.0936	.0013	.013	.015	2.376	⑤	2.6245–2.6255	.0005–.002	3	.002–.009
1970–71	8-413	1.0936	.0015	.013	.013	2.374–2.375	.0005–.002	2.7495–2.7505	.0005–.002	3	.002–.007
1972–73	8-413	1.0941	.003④	.013	.013	2.374–2.375	.001–.002	2.7495–2.7505	.0015–.0025	3	.002–.007
1974	8-413	1.0936	.0015	.013	.013	2.374–2.375	.001–.002	2.7495–2.7505	.0015–.0025	3	.002–.007
1975–76	8-413	1.0936	.0013	—	—	2.374–2.375	.001–.002	2.7495–2.7505	.0015–.0025	3	.002–.007
1977–78	V8-413-3	1.0936	.0013	—	—	2.374–2.375	.001–.002	2.7495–2.7505	.0015–.0025	3	.002–.009
1974	440-1	1.0941	.0013	—	—	2.374–2.375	.001–.0025	2.7495–2.7505	.0005–.002	3	.002–.007
1975	440-1	1.0941	.0013	.013	.015	2.374–2.375	.0005–.0015	2.7495–2.7505	.0020–.0022	3	.002–.007
1976	8-440	1.0936	.0013	.013	.015	2.375–2.376	.0005–.003	2.7495–2.7505	.0005–.002	3	.002–.007
1977–78	V8-440	1.0936	.0013	.013	.015	2.376	.0005–.0030	2.7495–2.7505	.0005–.002	3	.002–.009
1979	V8-440	1.0936	.0013	.013	.015	2.375–2.376	.0005–.0030	2.7495–2.7505	.0001–.0022	3	.002–.009
1973–76	440-3	1.0936	.0013	.013	.015	2.374–2.375	.001–.0025	2.7495–2.7505	.0005–.002	3	.002–.007
1980	V8-446③	1.020	.0017	.013	.013	2.498–2.499	.0011–.0036	3.1228–3.1236	.0010–.0036	3	.0025–.0085
1970–71	8-478③	1.3118	.002	.013	.013	2.623–2.624	.0017–.0042	3.123–3.124	.0014–.0044	3	.004–.009
1970–71	8-549③	1.3118	.002	.013	.013	2.623–2.624	.0017–.0042	3.123–3.124	.0014–.0044	3	.004–.009
1974	8-478③	1.3118	.004	.013	.013	2.623–2.624	.002–.004	3.123–3.124	.0015–.0045	3	.004–.009
1974	8-549③	1.3118	.004	.013	.013	2.623–2.624	.002–.004	3.123–3.124	.0015–.0045	3	.004–.009

①—Using a 1/2" wide feeler gauge, a pull of 6 to 9 lbs. should be required to pull feeler gauge past piston. Pistons removed from above.
②—Engine size—cubic inch displacement and number of cylinders.
③—See International chapter for service on this engine.
④—Clearance measured at Piston Pin Centerline.
⑤—2 bbl. Carb. .0005–.0025; 4 bbl. Carb. .0005–.003.
⑥—No. 1, .0005–.0015; Nos. 2, 3, 4 & 5, .0005–.0020.

VALVE SPECIFICATIONS

Engine Model	Year	Valve Lash Int.	Valve Lash Exh.	Valve Angles Seat	Valve Angles Face	Valve Springs Installed Height	Valve Springs Pressure Lbs. @ In.	Valve Stem Clearance Intake	Valve Stem Clearance Exhaust	Stem Diameters, Std. Intake	Stem Diameters, Std. Exhaust
6-198	1970–71	.012H	.024H	45	②	1¹¹⁄₁₆	144 @ 1⁵⁄₁₆	.001–.003	.002–.004	.372–.373	.371–.372
6-225	1970–73	.012H	.024H	45	②	1¹¹⁄₁₆	144 @ 1⁵⁄₁₆	.001–.003	.002–.004	.372–3.73	.371–.372
	1973⑭	.012H	.024H	45	②	⑫	⑦	.001–.003	.002–.004	.372–.373	.371–.372
	1974	.010H	.020H	45	①	1¹¹⁄₁₆	144 @ 1⁵⁄₁₆	.001–.003	.002–.004	.372–.373	.371–.372
	1975	.012H	.024H	45	②	⑫	⑦	.001–.003	.002–.004	.372–.373	.371–.372
6-225-1	1976	.010H	.020H	45	45	1¹¹⁄₁₆	144 @ 1⁵⁄₁₆	.001–.003	.002–.004	.372–.373	.371–.372
6-225	1977–78	.010H	.020H	45	②	1⁵⁹⁄₆₄	144 @ 1⁵⁄₁₆	.001–.003	.002–.004	.372–.373	.371–.372
6-225-1	1977–78	.010H	.020H	45	②	㉔	⑦	.001–.003	.002–.004	.372–.373	.371–.372
6-225	1979–80	.010H	.020H	45	②	1²¹⁄₃₂	144 @ 1⁵⁄₁₆	.001–.003	.002–.004	.372–.373	.371–.372
8-318-3	1970	Zero	Zero	45	45	1¹¹⁄₁₆	⑦	.001–.003	.002–.004	.372–.373	.371–.372
LA-318-1	1970–74	Zero	Zero	45	②	1¹¹⁄₁₆	177 @ 1⁵⁄₁₆	.001–.003	.002–.004	.372–.373	.371–.372
	1975	Zero	Zero	45	45	1²¹⁄₃₂	⑬	.017㉑	.017㉑	.372–.373	.371–3.72
8-318-1	1976	Zero	Zero	45	②	1¹¹⁄₁₆	177 @ 1⁵⁄₁₆	.001–.003	.002–.004	.372–.373	.371–.372
LA-318-3	1970–74	Zero	Zero	45	45	1¹¹⁄₁₆	⑯	.001–.003	.002–.004	.372–.373	.371–.372

Continued

DODGE & PLYMOUTH

VALVE SPECIFICATIONS—Continued

Engine Model	Year	Valve Lash Int.	Valve Lash Exh.	Valve Angles Seat	Valve Angles Face	Valve Springs Installed Height	Valve Springs Pressure Lbs. @ In.	Valve Stem Clearance Intake	Valve Stem Clearance Exhaust	Stem Diameters, Std. Intake	Stem Diameters, Std. Exhaust
8-318-3	1971-73	Zero	Zero	45	②	⑮	⑯	.001-.003	.002-.004	.372-.373	.371-.372
	1974-76	Zero	Zero	45	45	⑲	⑳	.017㉑	.017㉑	.3715	.371-.372
8-318-1	1977-78	Zero	Zero	45	45	1 21/32	⑬	.017㉑	.017㉑	.372-.373	.371-.372
8-318-3	1977-78	Zero	Zero	45	45	㉕	177 @ 1 15/16	.017㉑	.017㉑	.372-.373	.371-.372
8-318	1978-80	Zero	Zero	45	45	㉖	㉗	.001-.003	.002-.004	.372-.373	.371-.372
8-360	1971-73	Zero	Zero	45	②	1 11/16	177 @ 1 5/16	.001-.003	.002-.004	.372-.373	.371-.372
	1974	Zero	Zero	45	②	1 21/32	193 @ 1 1/4	.001-.003	.002-.004	.372-.373	.371-.372
	1975	Zero	Zero	45	②	1 11/16	177 @ 1 5/16	.001-.003	.002-.004	.372-.373	.371-.372
8-360	1976	Zero	Zero	45	②	1 11/16	183 @ 1 5/16	.001-.003	.002-.004	.372-.373	.371-.372
8-360	1977-78	Zero	Zero	45	45	1 21/32	177 @ 1 5/16	.017㉑	.017㉑	.372-.373	.371-.372
8-360	1978-79	Zero	Zero	45	45	㉖	㉗	.001-.003	.002-.004	.372-.373	.371-.372
8-360	1980	Zero	Zero	45	45	㉖	㉘	.001-.003	.002-.004	.372-.373	.371-.372
8-361	1970-71	Zero	Zero	45	45	⑤	⑥	.001-.003	.003-.005	.372-.373	.433-.434
8-361	1972-76	Zero	Zero	45	45	⑨	⑩	.001-.003	.003-.005	.372-.373	.433-.434
8-383	1970-71	Zero	Zero	45	45	1 55/64	195 @ 1 15/32	.001-.003	.002-.004	.372-.373	.371-.372
8-400	1971-74	Zero	Zero	45	45	1 55/64	200 @ 1 7/16	.001-.0027	.001-.0027	.372-.373	.371-.372
8-400	1976-78	Zero	Zero	45	45	1 55/64	200 @ 1 7/16	.0011-.0028	㉒	.3723-.373	㉓
8-413	1970-71	Zero	Zero	45	45	⑤	⑥	.001-.003	.003-.005	.372-.373	.433-.434
8-413-2, 3	1972-76	Zero	Zero	45	45	⑨	⑩	.001-.003	.003-.005	.372-.373	.433-.434
8-413-1	1972-74	Zero	Zero	45	45	⑤	⑥	.001-.003	.003-.005	.372-.373	.433-.434
8-440-1	1974	Zero	Zero	45	45	1 55/64	246 @ 1 23/64	.0016-.0033	.0015-.0032	.3723-.3730	.3718-.3725
	1975	Zero	Zero	45	45	⑰	⑱	.017㉑	.017㉑	.3718-.3725	.3718-.3725
8-440-1	1976-78	Zero	Zero	45	45	1 55/64	200 @ 1 7/16	.0011-.0028	㉒	.3723-.373	㉓
8-440-3	1973-75	Zero	Zero	45	45	⑰	⑱	.0016-.0033	.0015-.0032	.3718-.3725	.371-.372
8-440	1979	Zero	Zero	45	45	1 55/64	200 @ 1 7/16	.0011-.0028	㉒	.3723-.3730	㉓
8-446③	1980	Zero	Zero	45	45	—	188 @ 1.429	.00115-.00285	.00165-.00235	.37215-.37285	.37165-.37235
8-478③	1970-73	Zero	Zero	④	④	⑧	116.5 @ 1 21/32	.0015-.004	.0025-.005	.434-.435	.433-.434
8-478③	1974	Zero	Zero	④	④	⑪	115 @ 1 21/32	.0015-.004	.0025-.005	.434-.435	.433-.434
8-549③	1970-73	Zero	Zero	④	④	⑧	116.5 @ 1 21/32	.0015-.004	.0025-.005	.434-.435	.433-.434
	1974	Zero	Zero	④	④	⑪	115 @ 1 21/32	.0015-.004	.0025-.005	.434-.435	.433-.434

①—Intake 45, exhaust 47.
②—Intake 45, exhaust 43.
③—See International chapter for service on this engine.
④—Intake 15°, exhaust 45°.
⑤—Intake 1 55/64", exhaust 1 47/64".
⑥—Intake 180 @ 1 15/32", exhaust 115 @ 1 3/8".
⑦—Intake 144 @ 1 5/16", exhaust 185 @ 15/32".
⑧—Inner spring 83 @ 1.538"; outer spring 116 1/2 @ 1.663".
⑨—Intake 1 55/64", exhaust 1 3/4".
⑩—Intake 180 @ 1 15/32", exhaust 175 @ 1 21/64".
⑪—Inner spring 83 @ 1 17/32"; outer spring 115 @ 1 21/32".
⑫—Intake 1 11/16", exhaust 1 9/16".
⑬—Intake 185 @ 1 1/4", exhaust 192 @ 1 9/32".
⑭—6-225-2 engine.
⑮—Intake 1 11/16", exhaust 1 35/64".
⑯—Intake 177 @ 1 5/16", exhaust 185 @ 15/32".
⑰—Intake 1 55/64", exhaust 1 47/64".
⑱—Intake 200 @ 1 7/16", exhaust 205 @ 15/16".
⑲—Intake 1 11/16", exhaust 1 31/64".
⑳—Intake 177 @ 1 5/16", exhaust 187 @ 1 1/2".
㉑—Wobble method.
㉒—Hot end, .0021-.0038; Cold end, .0011-.0028.
㉓—Hot end, .3713-.372; Cold end, .3723-.373.
㉔—Intake, 1 59/64"; Exhaust, 1 7/8".
㉕—Seat to retainer, 1 21/32"; with rotators, 1 31/64".
㉖—Intake or Exhaust with rotator; 1 11/16", Exhaust with rotator; 1 31/64".
㉗—Intake or Exhaust without rotator; 177 @ 5/16", Exhaust with rotator; 187 @ 1 5/64".
㉘—Intake, 177 @ 1 5/16; Exhaust with rotator, 189 @ 1 11/16.

ENGINE TIGHTENING SPECIFICATIONS★

★ Torque specifications are for clean and lightly lubricated threads only. Dry or dirty threads produce increased friction which prevents accurate measurement of tightness.

Engine	Spark Plugs Ft. Lbs.	Cylinder Head Bolts Ft. Lbs.	Intake Manifold Ft. Lbs.	Exhaust Manifold Ft. Lbs.	Rocker Arm Shaft Bracket Ft. Lbs.	Rocker Arm Cover Ft. Lbs.	Connecting Rod Cap Bolts Ft. Lbs.	Main Bearing Cap Bolts Ft. Lbs.	Flywheel to Crankshaft Ft. Lbs.	Vibration Damper or Pulley Ft. Lbs.
6-198	30	65	240③	10	25	40③	45	85	55	—
6-225	②	70	240③	10	25	40③	45	85	55	④

Continued

ENGINE TIGHTENING SPECIFICATIONS★—Continued

★ Torque specifications are for clean and lightly lubricated threads only. Dry or dirty threads produce increased friction which prevents accurate measurement of tightness.

Engine	Spark Plugs Ft. Lbs.	Cylinder Head Bolts Ft. Lbs.	Intake Manifold Ft. Lbs.	Exhaust Manifold Ft. Lbs.	Rocker Arm Shaft Bracket Ft. Lbs.	Rocker Arm Cover Ft. Lbs.	Connecting Rod Cap Bolts Ft. Lbs.	Main Bearing Cap Bolts Ft. Lbs.	Flywheel to Crankshaft Ft. Lbs.	Vibration Damper or Pulley Ft. Lbs.
8-318	⑥	⑦	⑧	⑨	①	40③	45	85	⑩	⑪
8-360	⑥	⑯	⑰	20	210③⑮	40③	45	85	55	100
8-361	30	70	⑫	30	25	40③	45	85	⑩	135
8-383	30	70	50	30	30	40③	45	85	60	135
8-400	30	70	40⑭	30	25	40③	45	85	55	135
8-413	30	70	⑫	30	25	40③	45	85	⑩	135
8-440	⑬	70	45	30	25	40③	45	85	55	135
8-446⑤	15	105	—	18	20	6	41	95	—	90
8-478⑤	30	100	—	—	90	—	70	110	100	—
8-549⑤	30	100	—	—	90	—	70	110	100	—

①—1970: LA-318, 15 ft. lbs.; all others, 30 ft. lbs. All 1971–80, 200 in. lbs.
②—1970–74, 30 ft. lbs.; 1975–80, 10 ft. lbs.
③—In. Lbs.
④—Press fit.
⑤—See International chapter for service on this engine.
⑥—14MM plugs, 30; 18MM plugs, 20.
⑦—1970, 85 ft. lbs.; 1971–77, 95 ft. lbs., 1978–80 105 ft. lbs.
⑧—1970, 30 ft. lbs.; 1971–75 & 1977, 35 ft. lbs.; 1976 & 1978–80, 40 ft. lbs.
⑨—1970, 25 ft. lbs.; 1971–80, 20 ft. lbs.
⑩—1970, 60 ft. lbs.; 1971–80, 55 ft. lbs.
⑪—1970, 135 ft. lbs.; 1971–80, 100 ft. lbs.
⑫—1970–74, 40 ft. lbs.; 1975–77, 45 ft. lbs.
⑬—V8-440-1, 30 ft. lbs.; V8-440-3, 10 ft. lbs.
⑭—1977–78, 45 ft. lbs.
⑮—1977–80, 200 in. lbs.
⑯—1970–77, 95 ft. lbs.; 1978–80, 105 ft. lbs.
⑰—1970–77, 35 ft. lbs.; 1978–80, 40 ft. lbs.

WHEEL ALIGNMENT SPECIFICATIONS

Model	Caster, Deg.	Camber, Deg.	Toe-In, Inch	Kingpin Inclination, Deg.
1970 SERIES				
A100	6	1 1/2	0-1/8	4
W100, W200	+1 1/2	+3	0-1/8	7 1/2
W300	+1 1/2	+3 1/2	0-1/8	8
WM300	+1 1/2	+1/2	0-1/8	8
W500	+3/4	+2 1/2	0-1/8	8
D100	+1 1/2-+2 1/2	+1 1/2	0-1/8	4
D200, P200	+1 1/2	+1 1/2	0-1/8	4
D200, Crew Cab	+1 1/2	+2	0-1/8	7
D300, P300, M300	+1 1/2	+2	0-1/8	7
D400, P400, M375	+1 1/2-+2 1/2	+2	0-1/8	7
C500, C600	0-+1⑥	+2	0-1/8	7
C700, C800	0-+1⑥	+1	0-1/8	5 1/2
CT800, C1000	0-+1⑥	+1	0-1/8	5 1/2
CN900, CT900	0-+1⑥	+1	0-1/8	5 1/2
CNT900	0-+1⑥	+1	0-1/8	5 1/2
L600, L700	0-+1⑦	+1	0-1/8	5 1/2
LN1000, LNT1000	0-+1⑥	+1	0-1/8	5 1/2
LV1000, LVT1000	0-+1⑥	+1	0-1/8	5 1/2
1971–72 SERIES				
B100, B200, B300	+1/2⑦	+1/4	1/16-1/8	—
D100, D200, D300	0-+1/2	0-+1/4	1/16-1/8	—
D500, P400	+1 1/2-+2 1/2	+2	0-1/8	7
M300	+4 1/2②	+2	1/16-3/16	7
M375	+5②	+2	0-1/8	—
P200	+1 1/2	+1 1/2	1/16-3/16	4
P300	+1 1/2	+2	1/16-3/16	7
W100, W200	+3	+1 1/2	0-1/8	7 1/2
W300	+3	+1 1/2	0-1/8	8
D600, S600	+1/2-+2	+2	0-1/8	7
W600	+3/4	+2 1/2	0-1/8	8
D800	+4-+5	+1	0-1/8	5 1/2
1973 SERIES				
B100, B200, B300	+1/2⑦	+1/4	1/16-1/8	—
D100, D200, D300	0-+1/2	0-+1/4	1/16-1/8	—
D500, P400	+1 1/2-+2 1/2	+2	0-1/8	7
G400	+1 1/2	+1 1/2	1/16-3/16	4
M300	+4 1/2②	+2	1/16-3/16	7
MBH300, MBL300	+1/2⑦	+1/4	1/16-1/8	—
M375	+5②	+2	0-1/8	—
W100, W200	+3	+1 1/2	0-1/8	7 1/2
W300	+3	+1 1/2	0-1/8	8
D600, S600	+1/2-+2	+2	0-1/8	7
W600	+3/4	+2 1/2	0-1/8	8
D800	+4-+5	+1	0-1/8	5 1/2
CB300	+1/2⑦	+1/4	1/16-1/8	—
C600	+2⑥	2	0-1/8	7
C800, CT800	0-+1⑥	+1	0-1/8	5 1/2
CN900, CT900	0-+1⑥	+1	0-1/8	5 1/2
CNT900, C1000	0-+1⑥	+1	0-1/8	5 1/2
LS1000, LT1000	0-+1⑨	+1	0-1/8	5 1/2
1974 SERIES				
AW-100, PW-100	+3	+1 1/2	0-1/8	—
B100, B200, B300	0-+1⑦	0-+1/2	1/16-1/8	—
MBH300, MBL300, CB300	0-+1⑦	0-+1/2	1/16-1/8	—
PB100, PB200, PB300	0-+1⑦	0-+1/2	1/16-1/8	—
M300, RM300	+1 1/2②⑧	+2	1/16-3/16	—

Continued

DODGE & PLYMOUTH

WHEEL ALIGNMENT SPECIFICATIONS—Continued

Model	Caster, Deg.	Camber, Deg.	Toe-In, Inch	Kingpin Inclination, Deg.
RM350, M375, RM400	+1②⑨	+2	1/16-3/16	—
D100, D200, D300	+1/2	0-+1/2	0-1/8	—
P300	+3②⑧	+2	1/16-3/16	7
P400, D500, D600⑩	+1②⑨	+2	0-1/8	7
S600⑪	+1②⑨	+2	0-1/8	7
S600, D600, D800	+1 1/2②⑧	+1	1/16-3/16	5 1/2
C800, CT800	0-+1⑥	+1	0-1/8	5 1/2
CNT800, CN800	0-+1⑥	+1	0-1/8	5 1/2
CN900, CNT900	0-+1⑥	+1	0-1/8	5 1/2
LS1000, LT1000	0-+1⑥	+1	0-1/8	5 1/2
CN950, LN950	0-+1⑥	+1	0-1/8	5 1/2
1975 SERIES				
AD-100, PD-100⑫	+1/2⑦	+1/4	1/16-1/8	—
AW-100, PW-100⑬	+3	+1 1/2	0	—
B-100, B-200, B-300	+1/2⑦	+1/4	1/16-1/8	—
PB-100, PB-200, PB-300	+1/2⑦	+1/4	1/16-1/8	—
CB-300, MB-300	+1/2⑦	+1/4	1/16-1/8	—
M-300, M-400, M-500⑭	+3①⑬	+2	1/16-3/16	7
M-300, M-400, M-500	+2 1/2①⑯	+2	0-1/8	7
D-100, D-200, D-300	+1/2①	+1/2	1/16-1/8	—
W-100, W-200⑰	+3②	+1 1/2	3/32-11/32	8 1/2
W-200, W-300⑭	+3②	+1/2	0-1/4	8 1/2
W-600⑱	—	—	—	—
W-600⑲	+2 1/2②	+3/4	0-1/8	8
D-500, D-600	+2 1/2①	+2	0-1/8	7
D-600, S-600, D-700, S-700⑳	—	+1	1/16-3/16	7
D-600, S-600, D-700, S-700, D-800	+1 1/2	+1	0-1/8	5 1/2
D-800③	+1/2	+1	0-1/8	5 1/2
1976 SERIES				
AD-100, PD-100	+1/2	+1/4	1/8	—
AW-100, PW-100⑬	+3	+1 1/2	0	—
B-100, B-200, B-300	+1/2⑦	+1/2	1/8	—
CB-300	+1/2⑦	+1/2	1/8	—
MB-300, MB-400	+2 1/4	+1/2	1/8	—
M-300, M-400, M-500	+5 1/2	+2	1/8	—
D-100, D-200, D-300	+1/2	+1/4	1/8	—
W-100, W-200⑬④	+3	+1/2	0	—
W-200, W-300⑬⑭	+3	+1/2	0	—
W-600⑬	+3	—	1/8	—
D-500, D-600, D-700, D-800, S-600, S-700	+2	+1	1/8	—
1977-78 SERIES				
AD-100, PD-100⑫	+1/2	+1/4	1/8	—
AW-100, PW-100⑬	+3	+1/2	0	—

Model	Caster, Deg.	Camber, Deg.	Toe-In, Inch	Kingpin Inclination, Deg.
B-100, B-200, B-300	+1/2⑦	+1/2	1/8	—
PB-100, PB-200, PB-300	+1/2⑦	+1/2	1/8	—
CB-300, MB-300	+1/2⑦	+1/2	1/8	—
MB-400	+2 1/2	+1/2	1/8	—
M-300, M-400, M-500	+5	+2	1/16	—
M-600	+6.41	+1	1/16	—
D-100, D-200, D-300, D-400	+1/2	+1/4	1/8	—
W-100, W-200⑬④	+3	+1 1/2	0	—
W-200, W-300⑬⑭	+3	+1/2	0	—
W-600⑬⑱	+3	+1 1/2	1/16	—
W-600⑬⑲	+3	+1	1/16	—
D-500, D-600, D-700, D-800, S-600, S-700	+2.37	+1	1/16	—
1979 SERIES				
AD-100, PD-100	+1/2	+1/4	1/8	—
AW-100, PW-100⑬	—	—	—	—
B-100, B-200, B-300	+1/2⑦	+1/2	1/8	—
PB-100, PB-200, PB-300	+1/2⑦	+1/2	1/8	—
CB-300, CB-400	+1/2⑦	+1/2	1/8	—
MB-300, MB-400	+1/2⑦	+1/2	1/8	—
M-300	+3	+2	1/8	7
M-400, M-500	+2 1/2	+1	1/16	7
M-600	+2	+1	1/16	7
D-100, D-150, D-200, D-300, D-400	+1/2⑤	+1/4	1/8	—
W-150, W-200②⑬	+3	+1 1/2	0	8 1/2
W-200, W-300, W-400②⑬⑭	+3	+1/2	0	8 1/2

①—Caster should be checked with vehicle loaded. If caster cannot be checked when vehicle is loaded the no load caster is approximately 1° to 2° for manual steering and 5° to 6° for power steering. If vehicle wanders caster should be increased. If steering effort is very high, especially when taking corners, caster should be decreased.
②—No load.
③—9000 lb. axle.
④—3500, 3800 & 4000 lb. axles.
⑤—Loaded.
⑥—Power Steering 4 to 5°.
⑦—Power Steering +2 1/4°.
⑧—Power Steering 4 1/2°.
⑨—Power Steering +4°.
⑩—All D600 except 240" wheel base.
⑪—197" and 221" wheel base.
⑫—Exc. four wheel drive.
⑬—Four wheel drive.
⑭—4500 lb. axle.
⑮—Power steering +6°.
⑯—Power steering +5 1/2°.
⑰—3500 lb. axle.
⑱—6000 lb. axle.
⑲—7500 lb. axle.
⑳—5500 lb. axle.

DODGE & PLYMOUTH

Engine Section

> **NOTE:** Refer to International Chapter for service procedures on V8-446, 478 & 549 engines.

CYLINDER HEAD, REPLACE

V8 Engines

Before an engine is disassembled for valve grinding or major repair work, the operation of the exhaust valve rotators, if so equipped, should be checked by removing the cylinder head covers and observing exhaust valve rotation with the engine running. While the direction of rotation is not important, there should be a large difference in rotation speeds between 1,000 and 3,000 RPM. Improperly functioning rotators should be replaced.

Before installing cylinder heads, clean gasket surfaces of the cylinder block and cylinder heads. Check mating surfaces for flatness using a straightedge and feeler gauge. Use new gaskets and check that all holes are properly punched through. After coating gaskets with a suitable sealer, install cylinder heads ensuring that dowel pins and holes are aligned. Install and torque cylinder head bolts in sequence shown in Figs. 1 and 2. Refer to "Engine Tightening Specifications."

Service Note

V8-318 & 360 U.S. Built Engines

The intake manifold attaching bolts on this engine are tilted upward about 30 degrees at an angle to the manifold-to-cylinder head gasket face. The purpose of this design is to provide more effective sealing at the cylinder block end gaskets. If the intake manifold is removed the installation should be such that the bolt tightening is done evenly and in the sequence shown in Fig. 3.

With gaskets in place start all bolts, leaving them loose. Run bolts 1 through 4 down so the heads just touch manifold. Then tighten these four bolts to 25 foot pound torque. After checking to see that gaskets are properly seated at all surfaces, tighten remaining bolts to 25 foot pounds. Finally tighten all bolts in the sequence shown to 35 foot-pounds.

6-198 & 225

Before an engine is disassembled for valve grinding or major repair work, the operation of the exhaust valve rotators, if so equipped, should be checked by removing the cylinder head cover and observing exhaust valve rotation with the engine running. While the direction of rotation is not important, there should be a large difference in rotation speeds between 1,000 and 3,000 RPM. Improperly functioning rotators should be replaced.

Before installing cylinder head, clean gasket surface of the cylinder block and cylinder head. Check mating surfaces for flatness using a straightedge and feeler gauge. Use a new gasket and check that all holes are properly punched through. After coating gasket with a suitable sealer, install cylinder head ensuring that dowel pins and holes are aligned. Install and tighten cylinder head bolts in sequence, Fig. 4. Repeat procedure and torque bolts in sequence to torque load listed in "Engine Tightening Specifications".

Installation of intake and exhaust manifolds should be performed as follows to avoid breakage due to overtightening and/or expansion:

1. Loosen bolts and nut holding intake manifold to exhaust manifold. After coating with a suitable sealer, position manifold to cylinder head gasket on cylinder head.
2. Install intake and exhaust manifold assembly to cylinder head with cup side of conical washers against manifolds. Snug nuts to approx. 20 in. lbs.
3. Torque intake to exhaust manifold nut to 240 in. lbs. then torque intake to exhaust manifold bolts to 200 in. lbs.
4. Starting from the center and working outward, torque intake and exhaust manifold nuts on cylinder head to 120 in. lbs.

ROCKER ARM SERVICE

NOTE: *When disassembling rocker arms, place all parts on the work bench in their proper sequence to insure correct assembly.*

Clean all sludge and gum formation from the inside and outside of the shafts. Clean oil holes and passages in the rocker arms and shafts. Inspect the shafts for wear.

V8-318 & 360

To provide proper lubrication of the rocker arms, the rocker shafts have a small notch machined at one end. Install rocker arm and shaft assemblies with notch on end of rocker shaft pointing to centerline of engine and toward front of engine on the left bank and to the rear on the right bank. If rocker arms are removed from shaft, care must be taken to ensure proper reassembly. Some exhaust rocker arms have a relieved area on the underside for rotator clearance. Refer to Fig. 5 for proper positioning of rocker arms. Note placement of long stamped steel retainers in the number two and four positions between the rocker arms.

V8-361, 383, 400, 413, 440

The rocker arms are of stamped steel and are arranged on one rocker arm shaft, per cylinder head. The push rod angularity tends to force the pairs of rocker arms toward each other where oilite spacers carry the side thrust at the rocker arms, Fig. 6.

1. Install rocker shafts so that the 3/16" diam-

Fig. 1 Cylinder head tightening sequence. V8-318 & 360

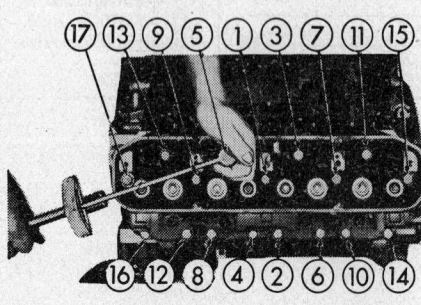

Fig. 2 Cylinder head tightening sequence. V8-361, 383, 400, 413 & 440

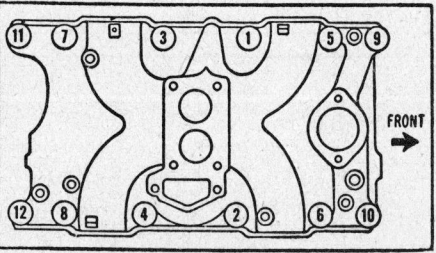

Fig. 3 Intake manifold tightening sequence. V8-318 & 360

DODGE & PLYMOUTH

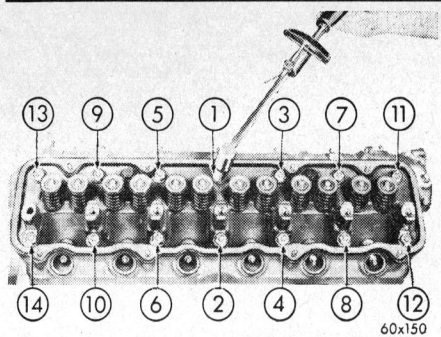

Fig. 4 Head tightening sequence. 6-198 & 225

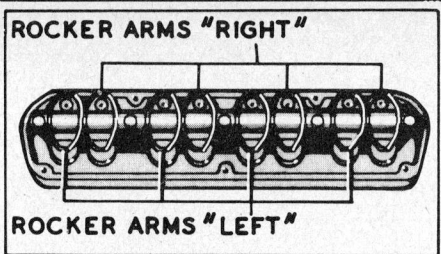

Fig. 5 Rocker arm and shaft assembly installed. V8-318 & 360

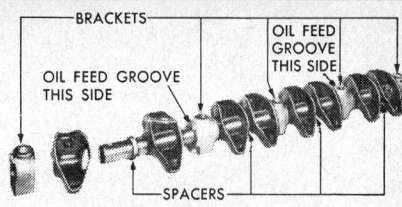

Fig. 6 Rocker arms and shaft. V8-361, 383, 400, 413, 440 (Typical)

eter rocker arm lubrication holes point downward into rocker arm, and so that the 15 degree angle of these holes point outward toward valve end of rocker arm, Fig. 7. The 15 degree angle is determined from the center line of the bolt holes through the shaft which are used to attach the shaft assembly to the cylinder head.

2. On all engines, install rocker arms and shaft assembly, making sure to install long stamped steel retainers in No. 2 and 4 positions.

NOTE: Use extreme care in tightening the bolts so that valve lifters have time to bleed down to their operating length. Bulged lifter bodies, bent push rods and permanent noisy operation may result if lifters are forced down too rapidly.

3. Installation should be as shown in Fig. 8.

6-198 & 225

Positioning rocker arms on rocker shaft requires flat and/or oil hole on rocker shaft to be on top and pointing to front of engine. This ensures proper lubrication of rocker assembly. Install rocker arms with adjusting screw to right side of engine in this order: One rocker arm and one spacer, then two rocker arms and a spacer. Continue this sequence until all rocker arms and spacers are positioned, Fig. 9.

Install rocker assembly to cylinder head in this order:

1. Place a bolt and small retainer in front hole of shaft.
2. Place a bolt and the one wide retainer through the center hole of shaft with six rocker arms on each side of center.
3. Insert remaining bolts and retainers, separating the six pairs of rocker arms. Place long or special bolt and retainer in rear hole of shaft.
4. Locate assembly on cylinder head and position rocker arm adjusting screws in pushrods.
5. Tighten bolts finger tight, bringing retainers in contact with shaft between rocker arms. Retainers must not seat on extended bushing of rocker arm. Torque bolts to specifications listed in "Engine Tightening Specifications".
6. Temporarily set valve lash cold: intake .012 inch (0.304 mm), exhaust .028 inch (0.711 mm). Start and run engine at 550 RPM idle until normal operating temperature is reached. To reduce oil splatter during warm-up, temporarily fit cylinder head cover over rocker assembly.
7. After engine has reached normal operating temperature, adjust valve lash to specifications. Complete installation of remaining parts removed.

VALVES, ADJUST
6-198 & 225

If the cylinder head has been removed it is a good practice to make an initial valve adjustment before starting the engine. Make two chalk marks spaced 120 degrees apart (1/3 of circumference) on the vibration damper so that with the timing mark, the damper is divided into thirds. With the crankshaft at TDC, temporarily set the intake valve lash for No. 1 cylinder at .012 inch and the exhaust at .028 inch. Repeat the procedure for the remaining valves, turning the crankshaft 1/3 turn in the direction of normal rotation while adjusting the valves in the firing order sequence of 1-5-3-6-2-4. For final adjustment, start and run engine at 550 RPM idle until normal operating temperature is reached. Then adjust valve lash to clearance listed in "Valve Specifications".

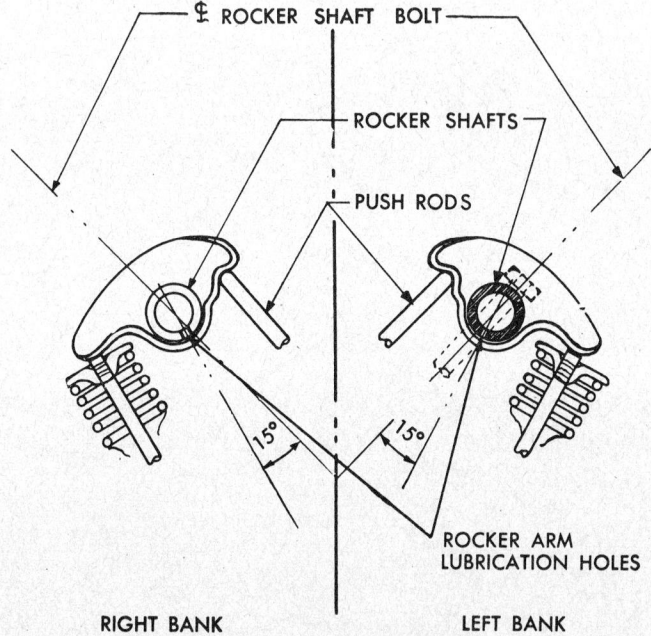

Fig. 7 Rocker arm shaft installation, V8-361, 383, 400, 413 & 440

Fig. 8 Rocker arm installed. V8-361 & 413 (Typical)

959

DODGE & PLYMOUTH

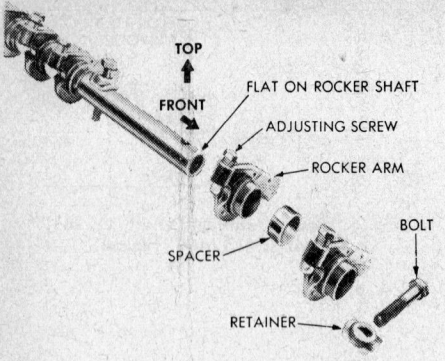

Fig. 9 Rocker arms and shaft. 6-198, 225

VALVE GUIDES
V8-318, 360, 361, 400, 413, 440 & 6-198, 225

These engines do not have removable valve guides, the valves operating in guide holes bored in the cylinder head. Valves with oversize valve stems are available for service replacement when necessary to ream the guide holes.

Standard production reaming of both intake and exhaust valves is .374–.375". When reaming guides for oversize valve stems do not attempt to ream from standard to .030" oversize. If necessary to ream to that size, use the step procedure of .005", .015" and .030". This must be done in order to maintain a true relationship of the guide to the valve seat. The following chart indicates reamer size and valve stem size.

Reamer Oversize	Valve Stem Size
.005"	.379–.380"
.015"	.389–.390"
.030"	.404–.405"

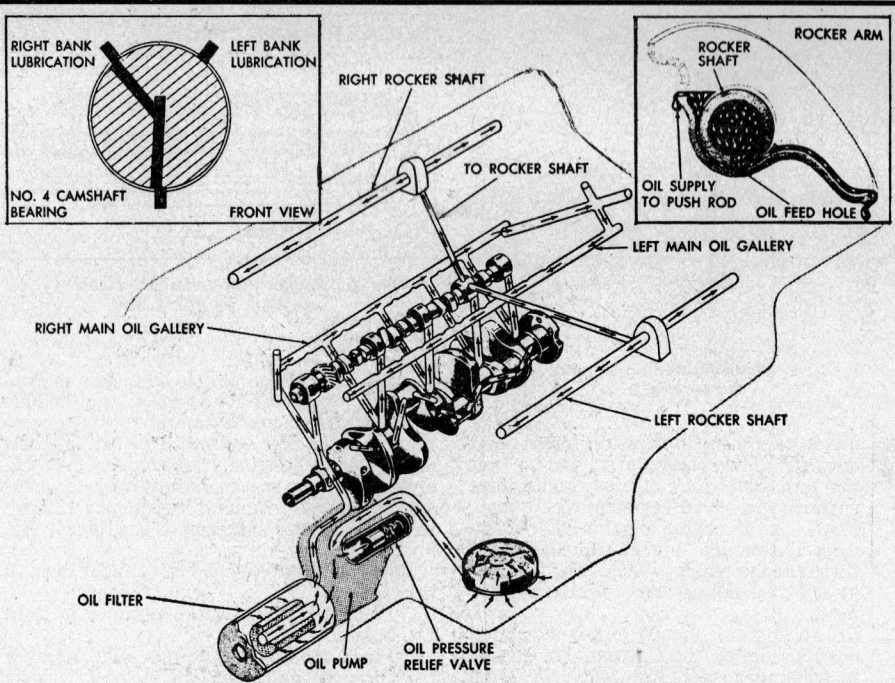

Engine lubrication. V8-361, 383, 400, 413 & 440 (Typical)

If an "I" or an "E" is stamped on the cylinder head at the rocker cover gasket boss, all intake and exhaust valves are oversize in that bank, depending upon what letter is stamped.

HYDRAULIC VALVE LIFTERS

Figs. 10 and 11 illustrate the type of hydraulic valve lifters used. Before disassembling any part of the engine to check for noise,

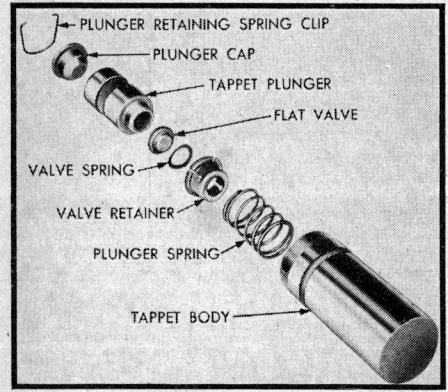

Fig. 10 Hydraulic valve lifter of the flat valve type. V8 engines

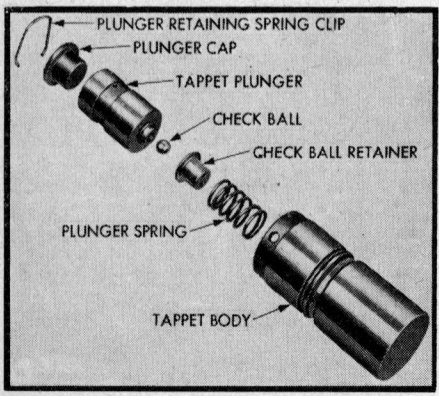

Fig. 11 Hydraulic valve lifter of the ball check type. V8 engines

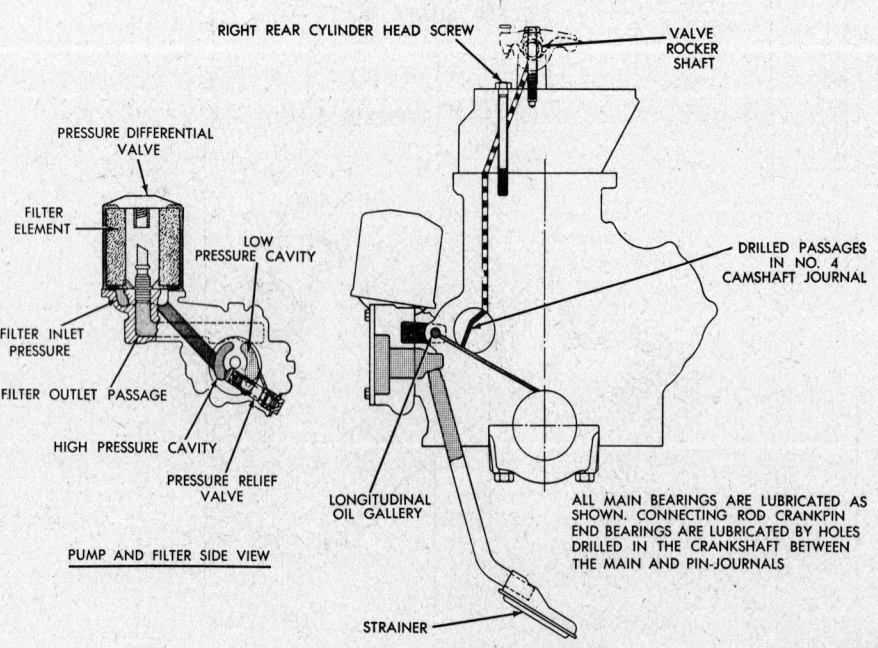

Lubrication diagram 6-198, 225 (Typical)

DODGE & PLYMOUTH

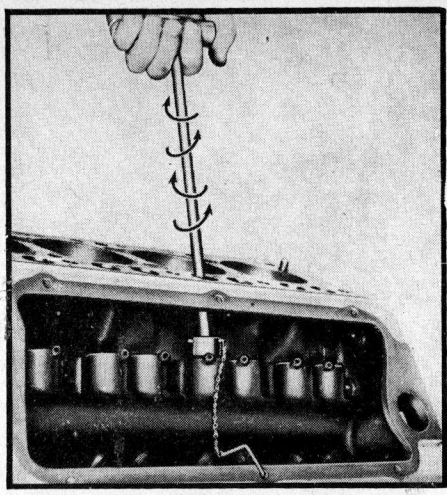

Fig. 12 Removing stuck hydraulic lifter with special tool. V8 engines

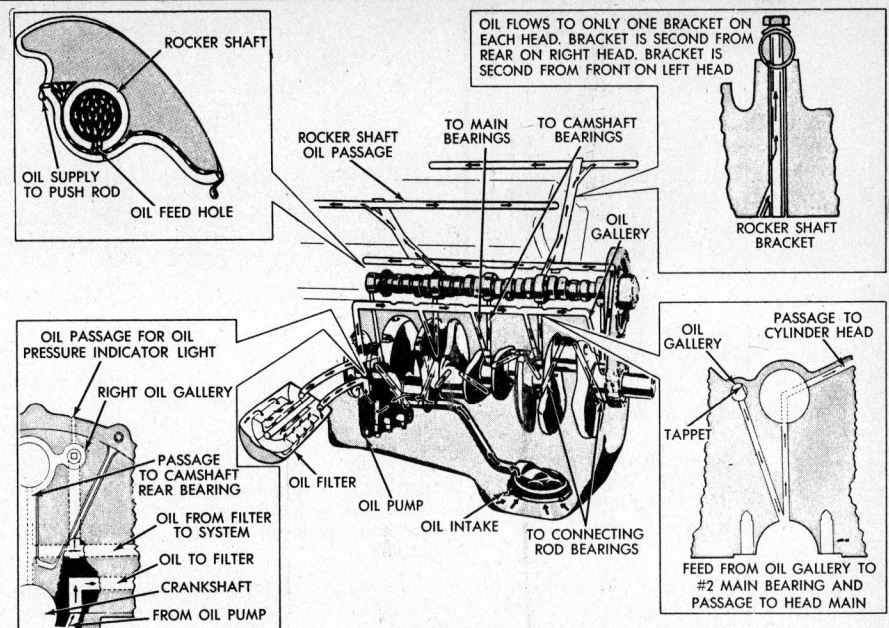

Engine lubrication. V8-318 & 360 (Typical)

check the oil pressure at the gauge and the oil level in the oil pan. The oil level in the pan should *never be above the "full"* mark on the dipstick, *nor below* the "add oil" mark. Either of the two conditions could be responsible for noisy lifters.

Lifter, Replace

Worn valve guides or cocked springs are sometimes mistaken for noisy lifters. Determine which lifter is noisy. If the application of side thrust on the valve spring fails to noticeably reduce the noise, the lifter is probably faulty and should be removed for inspection. Removal of stuck lifters requires a special tool, Fig. 12. When installing hydraulic lifters in the engine, fill them with light engine oil to avoid excessive time required to quiet them during initial operation of engine.

TIMING CHAIN OR GEAR COVER

6-198, 225

1. To remove cover, drain cooling system and remove radiator and fan.
2. Remove vibration damper with a puller.
3. Loosen oil pan bolts to allow clearance and remove chain case cover.

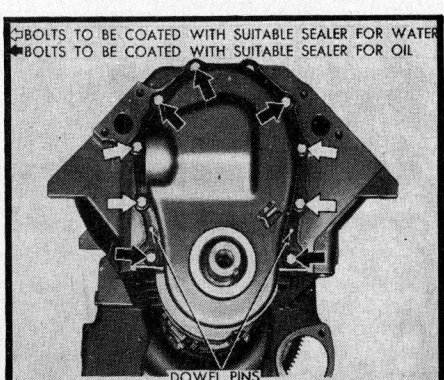

Fig. 13 Installing chain case cover. V8 chain-driven engines

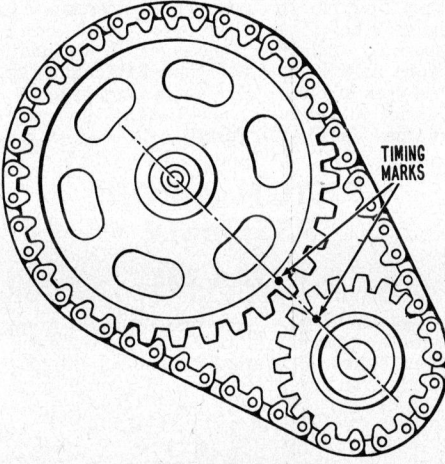

Fig. 14 Valve timing. All six cylinder engines

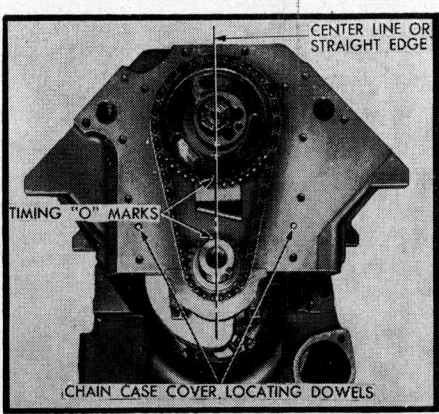

Fig. 15 Valve timing on V8 chain-driven engines

4. Reverse above procedure to install cover.

V8 Engines

To remove cover, first drain cooling system, remove radiator, fan belt and water pump assembly. Then, remove pulley from vibration damper and after removing bolt and washer, use puller to remove damper. Next, remove fuel lines and fuel pump. Loosen oil pan bolts and after removing front bolt at each side, timing cover may be removed. Reverse procedure to install cover, using new oil seal. Fig. 13 shows proper method used to avoid oil and water leaks.

TIMING CHAIN

Chain-Driven Engines

1. After removing timing chain cover as outlined above, remove camshaft sprocket lock bolt, then remove timing chain and sprocket.
2. Clean all parts and inspect chain for broken or damaged links. Inspect sprockets for cracks and chipped, worn or damaged teeth.
3. Turn crankshaft so sprocket timing mark is toward and directly in line with centerline of camshaft.
4. Temporarily install camshaft sprocket. Rotate camshaft to position sprocket timing mark toward and directly in line with centerline of crankshaft; then remove camshaft sprocket.
5. Place chain on crankshaft sprocket and position camshaft sprocket in chain so sprocket can be installed with timing marks aligned and without moving camshaft, Fig. 14.
6. Install remaining components in reverse order of removal.

V8 Engines

To install chain and sprockets, lay both

961

DODGE & PLYMOUTH

Fig. 16 Valve timing on V8 gear-driven engines. View shows fuel pump eccentric being installed

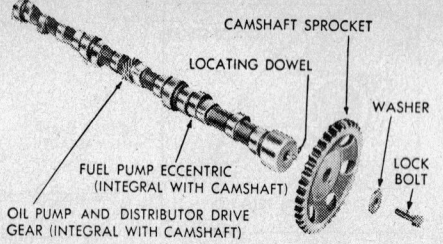

Fig. 17 Camshaft assembly. 6-198, 225

tributor drive gear so that camshaft is prevented from pushing out welch plug. Install camshaft thrust plate and chain oil tab making sure tang of tab is correctly positioned in the lower right hole of thrust plate. After installing timing chain and sprockets, camshaft holding tool may be removed. New lifters must be used if a new camshaft is installed.

6-198 & 225

If camshaft bearings are to be replaced, the engine should be removed from the chassis. Before removing camshaft, remove valve lifters, oil pump and distributor. Slide camshaft out of engine, Fig. 17, then drive out rear welch plug. A special tool is required to remove and install camshaft bearings. When installing new bearings, make certain oil holes in bearings line up exactly with corresponding drilled oil passages in cylinder block. Install a new, well sealed welch plug at the rear of block. Carefully insert properly lubricated camshaft. New lifters must be used if a new camshaft is installed.

PISTON & ROD, ASSEMBLE

6-198 & 225

Piston and rod assemblies must be installed with the notch on the piston head toward the front of the engine, and the oil hole in the connecting rod toward the left side on aluminum

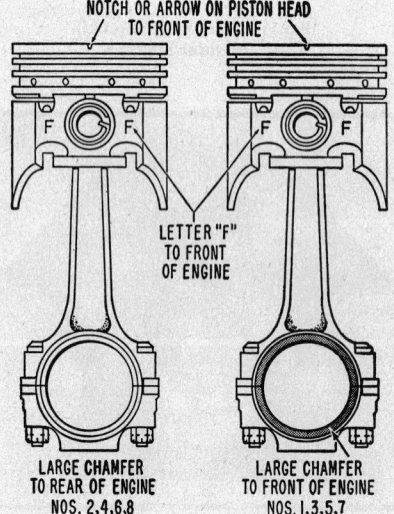

Fig. 19 Correct assembly of pistons and rods. V8 engines

camshaft and crankshaft sprockets on bench. Position sprockets so that the timing marks are next to each other. Place chain on both sprockets, then push sprockets apart as far as the chain will permit. Use a straightedge to form a line through the exact centers of both gears. The timing marks must be on this line.

Slide the chain with both sprockets on the camshaft and crankshaft at the same time, then recheck the alignment, Fig. 15.

NOTE: Use Tool C-3509 to prevent camshaft from contacting welch plug in rear of engine block. Remove distributor and oil pump-distributor drive gear. Position tool against rear side of camshaft gear and attach with distributor retainer plate bolt.

TIMING GEARS

Gear-Driven Engines

For correct valve timing, the timing marks on the camshaft and crankshaft gears should be matched. Fig. 16 shows the installation on V8 engine.

CAMSHAFT & BEARINGS

V8 Engines

If camshaft bearings are to be replaced, the engine should be removed from the chassis and the crankshaft taken out in order that any chips or foreign matter may be removed from the oil passages.

With camshaft removed, drive out rear welch plug. A special tool is required to remove and install camshaft bearings. This tool pulls out all the bearings at once and is also used to install new bearings.

When installing new bearings, be sure oil holes in bearings line up with oil holes in cylinder block. Install new welch plug, with sealer applied, in the rear of block and carefully insert properly lubricated camshaft to within 2 inches of rear welch plug. Position and secure Tool C-3509 with tongue behind dis-

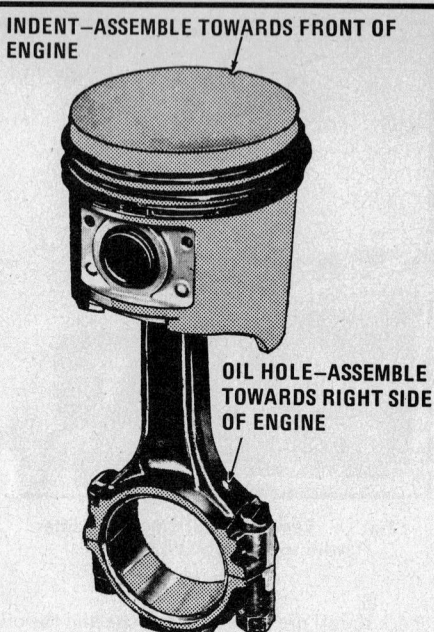

Fig. 18 Piston and rod assembly. 6-198 & 225 engines.

block engines and toward the right side on cast iron block engines, Fig. 18.

All V8 Engines

When installing piston and rod assemblies in the cylinders, the compression ring gaps should be diametrically opposite one another and not in line with the oil ring gap. The oil ring expander gap should be toward the outside of the "V" of the engine. The oil ring gap should be turned toward the inside of the engine "V".

Immerse the piston head and rings in clean engine oil and, with a suitable piston ring compressor, insert the piston and rod assembly into the bore. Tap the piston down into the bore, using the handle of a hammer.

Assemble and install the pistons and rods as shown in Fig. 19.

PISTONS, PINS & RINGS

Pistons are available in standard sizes and the following oversizes: 1970–72 6 cyl. and 1970–77 V8, .005, .020, .040"; 1973–77 6 cyl., .005, .020, .040, .060"; 1978–80 6 cyl., .005, .020"; 1978–80 V8, .020".

Pins are available in the following oversizes: V8-318 & 360, .003, .008". Oversize pins are not available on other engines.

Rings are available in the following oversizes: std. to .009, .020–.029, .040–.049".

MAIN & ROD BEARINGS

Main bearings are furnished in standard sizes and the following undersizes: .001, .002, .003, .010, .012".

Rod bearings are furnished in standard sizes and the following undersizes: .001, .002, .003, .010, .012".

NOTE: Some 1974 V8-400 and V8-440 engines were built with low thrust wall cylinder blocks. These engines require a small thrust wall or flange (No. 3) crankshaft main bear-

DODGE & PLYMOUTH

ing. The dimension "A" in Fig. 20, must be noted if the thrust bearing (No. 3) is to be replaced.

Engines using the small thrust wall (flange) bearing, Fig. 20, can be identified by the yellow "X" painted on the engine identification pad and also engine will be date coded 8-12 on the pad.

All other 1974 V8-400 and V8-440 engines require the large thrust wall bearing.

NOTE: 1972-76 V8-400 and 440 use either forged or cast crankshafts. These engines require that a matching torque converter, short block, damper and connecting rods be used.

If replacement of the crankshaft, torque converter, crankshaft damper or short engine is required, it is important that matching parts are used otherwise severe engine vibration will result. (Consult Chrysler Parts Dept.).

The cast crankshaft engine can be easily identified since it has the letter "E" stamped on the engine numbering pad following the built date.

Also, V8-440 engines built starting January 1975, will have external balance weights at the front damper and torque converter and a clock face will appear on the number 1 counterweight of the cast crankshaft.

6-225 engines built after June 1, 1976 may be equipped with either a cast or forged crankshaft. The following parts are not interchangeable between cast and forged crankshaft engines, crankshaft, crankshaft bearings, connecting rods and bearings and cylinder block. On models equipped with manual transmission, cast crankshaft engine vibration damper is not interchangeable with forged crankshaft engine and requires that a crankshaft screw and washer be used and torqued to 135 ft. lbs. On models equipped with automatic transmission, vibration damper and torque converter are interchangeable between cast and forged crankshaft engines.

CRANKSHAFT OIL SEAL, REPLACE

6-198 & 225

Replacement seals are of two piece rubber

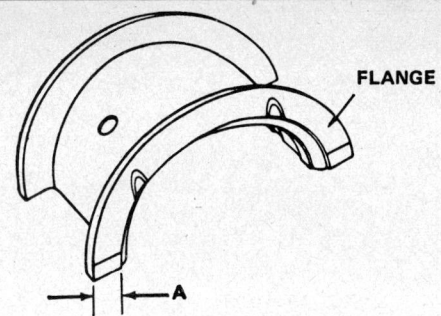

Fig. 20 Main bearing with small thrust wall flange (A)

type composition which make possible the replacement of upper rear seal without removing crankshaft. Both halves must be used. After removing oil pan, rear main bearing cap and seal retainer, pry lower rope seal from retainer with small screwdriver. Screw a special tool into upper rope seal and carefully pull to remove seal while rotating crankshaft. Wipe crankshaft surface clean, then oil lightly before installing new upper seal. After oiling seal lip, hold seal with paint stripe to rear tightly against crankshaft with thumb. Carefully slide seal into groove in block making sure sharp edge does not shave or nick seal. Crankshaft may be rotated to ease seal into groove but sealing lip must not be damaged. Install other half of seal into lower seal retainer again with paint stripe to rear, then install rear main bearing cap and torque to specifications. Before installing seal retainer, apply a small amount of gasket sealer to mating surface of retainer but not on seal ends or seal lip, Fig. 21. Install retainer and torque to 30 ft. lbs.

V8-318 & 360

Replacement of rear main bearing oil seals is similar to procedure given above for 6 cylinder engines. A seal retainer is not found on these engines; lower half of seal is installed into groove in rear main bearing cap.

The 318 engine has capseals in addition to lower seal secured by rear main bearing cap. Cap seal with yellow paint is installed, narrow sealing edge up, into right side with bearing cap in engine position. Cap seals must be flush with shoulder of bearing cap to prevent oil leakage.

The 360 engine requires sealer to be applied adjacent to rear main bearing oil seal as cap seals are not used, Fig. 22. After applying sealer, quickly assemble rear main bearing cap to block and torque to specifications.

V8-361, 383, 400, 413, 440

Replacement seals are of two piece rubber type composition which make possible the replacement of upper rear seal without removing crankshaft. Both halves must be used. After removing oil pan, seal retainer and rear main bearing cap, pry lower rope seal and side seals from lower seal retainer with small screwdriver. Thoroughly clean seal retainer grooves. Screw a special tool into upper rope seal and carefully pull to remove seal while rotating crankshaft. Wipe crankshaft surface clean, then oil lightly before installing new upper seal. After oiling seal lip, hold seal with paint stripe to rear tightly against crankshaft with thumb. Carefully slide seal into groove in block making sure sharp edge does not shave or nick seal. Crankshaft may be rotated to ease seal into groove but sealing lip must not be damaged. Install other half of seal with paint stripe to rear into seal retainer. Install rear main bearing cap and torque to specifications. The side seals used with the rear seal retainer should be installed in the retainer and then into the engine as quickly as possible. These seals are made from a material that expands rapidly when oiled. Apply sealer to mating face of seal retainer but not to side seals or main bearing seal ends, then oil side seals with mineral spirits or diesel fuel. Install seals in seal retainer grooves then quickly install retainer and torque to 30 ft. lbs. Failure to pre-oil seals will result in an oil leak.

OIL PUMP REPAIRS

6-198 & 225

Remove pump from side of engine by first unbolting oil pump cover, Fig. 23. Outer rotor will drop out when cover is removed. Do not allow rotor to be damaged by dropping it. Oil pump can now be unbolted and disassembled for inspection. Press off drive gear, supporting gear to keep load off aluminum body. Inner rotor and shaft can now be removed. Remove oil pressure relief valve plug and lift out spring and plunger. Clean all parts thoroughly. If mating surface of oil pump cover is scratched or grooved, replace pump assembly. Lay a straightedge across pump cover surface. If a .0015 inch feeler gauge can be inserted

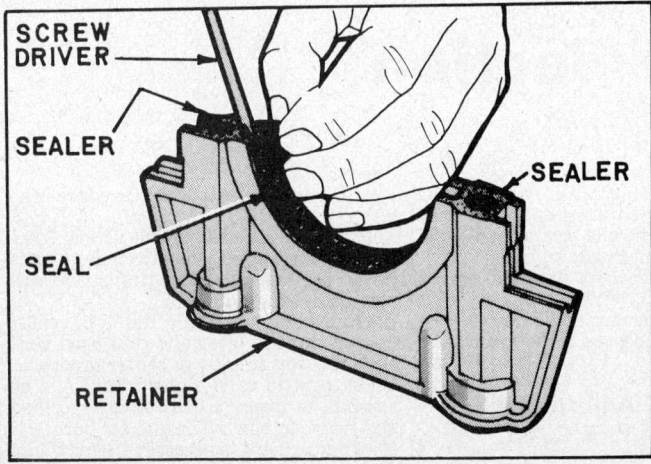

Fig. 21 Lower oil seal and retainer. 6-198 & 225

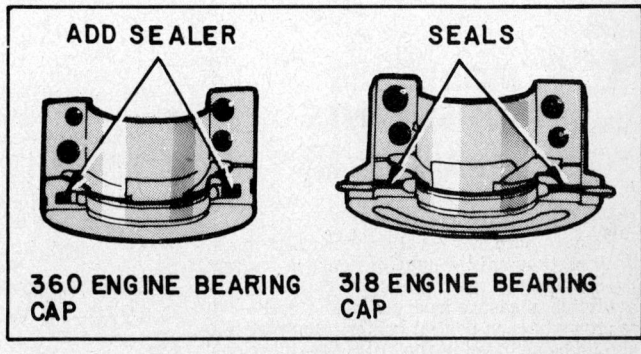

Fig. 22 Rear main bearing caps. V8-318 & 360

963

DODGE & PLYMOUTH

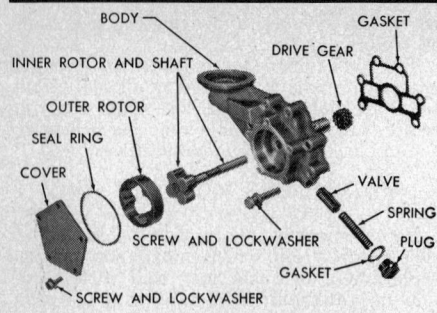

Fig. 23 Oil pump. 6-198 & 225

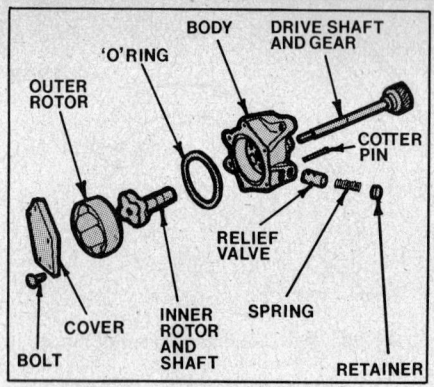

Fig. 24 Oil pump. V8-318 & 360

Fig. 25 Oil pump. V8-361, 383, 400, 413 & 440

between cover and straightedge, replace pump assembly. If outer rotor thickness measures .649 inch or less and the diameter 2.469 inches or less, replace shaft and both rotors. Shaft and both rotors should also be replaced if inner rotor thickness measures .649 inch or less. With outer rotor inserted into pump body, press rotor to one side with fingers. If clearance between rotor and pump body is .014 inch or more, replace oil pump assembly. With inner rotor inserted into pump body, place a straightedge across face between bolt holes. If a feeler gauge of .004 inch or more can be inserted between rotors and straightedge, replace oil pump assembly. Shaft and both rotors should be replaced if tip clearance between inner and outer rotor exceeds .010 inch. Inspect oil pressure relief valve plunger for scoring and free operation in its bore. The relief valve spring has a free length of $2\frac{1}{4}$ inches and should test between 22.3 and 23.3 lbs. when compressed to $1\frac{19}{32}$ inch. Replace spring that fails to meet specifications.

Using new parts as required, assemble pump except for outer rotor and cover. Install oil pump on engine then wet inside of pump with oil to assure priming. Install outer rotor and cover using new seal ring.

V8-318 & 360

Removal of oil pump for servicing requires oil pan to be removed and oil pump unbolted from rear main bearing cap. With pump removed, disassemble pressure relief valve by pulling out cotter pin and drilling a $\frac{1}{8}$ inch hole into center of relief valve retainer cap, Fig. 24. Insert a self-threading sheet metal screw into cap and secure head in vise. While supporting pump body, remove cap by tapping body with soft hammer. Discard retainer cap and remove spring and relief valve. Relief valve spring has a free length of $2\frac{1}{32}$ to $2\frac{3}{64}$ inch and should test between 16.2 and 17.2 lbs. when compressed to $1\frac{11}{32}$ inch. Replace spring that fails to meet specifications. Unbolt oil pump cover and discard oil seal ring. Inner rotor and shaft can now be removed as well as outer rotor. Clean all parts thoroughly and inspect for damage or wear. If mating surface of oil pump cover is scratched or grooved, replace pump assembly. Lay a straightedge across pump cover surface. If a .0015 inch feeler gauge can be inserted between cover and straightedge, replace pump assembly. If outer rotor thickness measures .825 inch or less on 318 engine, .943 inch on 360 engine, replace inner rotor and shaft. With outer rotor inserted into pump body, press rotor to one side with fingers. If clearance between rotor and pump body is .014 inch or more, replace oil pump assembly. With inner rotor inserted into pump body, place a straightedge across face between bolt holes. If a feeler gauge of .004 inch can be inserted between rotors and straightedge, replace oil pump assembly. Shaft and both rotors should be replaced if tip clearance between inner and outer rotor exceeds .010 inch. Using new parts as required, assemble pump. Prime pump before installation by filling rotor cavity with engine oil.

V8-361, 400, 413 & 440

After removing oil filter element unbolt oil pump and filter base assembly. Remove filter base and discard oil seal ring, Fig. 25. Inner rotor and shaft can now be removed as well as outer rotor. Remove pressure relief valve plug and lift out the spring and relief valve plunger. Clean all parts thoroughly and inspect for damage or wear. If mating surface of filter base (oil pump cover) is scratched or grooved, replace filter base. Lay a straight edge across oil pump filter base surface. If a .0015 inch feeler gauge can be inserted between base and straightedge, filter base should be replaced. If outer rotor thickness measures .943 inch or less and diameter measures 2.469 inches or less, replace shaft and both rotors. If inner rotor thickness measures .943 inch or less, replace shaft and both rotors. With outer rotor inserted into pump body, press rotor to one side with fingers. If clearance between rotor and pump body is .014 inch or more, replace pump body. With inner rotor inserted into pump body, place a straightedge across face between bolt holes. If a feeler gauge of .004 inch or more can be inserted between rotors and straightedge, replace pump body. If the top clearance between inner and outer rotor is .010 inch or more, replace shaft and both rotors. Inspect oil pressure relief valve plunger for scoring and free operation in its bore. The relief valve spring has a free length of $2\frac{1}{4}$ inches and should test between 22.3 and 23.3 lbs. when compressed to $1\frac{19}{32}$ inch. Replace spring that fails to meet specifications.

Using new parts as required, assemble pump and fill rotor cavity with engine oil to prime. Before bolting oil pump to engine, install new "O" ring seal on pilot.

Carburetor Section

MODEL BBS ADJUSTMENTS

Float Level Adjustment

Fig. 1

Remove both check balls then invert main body so that only weight of floats is forcing needle against seat. If proper gauge is not available, measure from surface of fuel bowl to crown of each float at center. Float setting should be as listed in the "BBS Specifications Chart". If adjustment is necessary, hold floats on bottom of bowl and bend lip of float lever in or out until correct setting is obtained. Do not allow lip to push against needle as the synthetic rubber tip can be compressed sufficiently to cause a false setting which will affect correct level of fuel in bowl. When float is set correctly, float lip should be perpendicular to or slanted less than 10 degrees away from needle.

Pump & Bowl Vent Adjustment 1970-74 With C.A.P. & C.A.S.

Fig. 2

This adjustment automatically adjusts the accelerator pump as well. The procedure is as follows:

1. Back off idle speed adjusting screw. Open choke valve so that when throttle valve is closed the fast idle adjusting screw will not contact fast idle cam.
2. Be sure pump operating rod is in center hole in throttle lever and that bowl vent clip on pump stem is in center groove.
3. Close throttle valve tightly. It should be possible to insert a drill of the specified size between bowl vent and air horn.
4. If an adjustment is necessary, bend pump operating rod at the lower angle as required to obtain the correct bowl vent

DODGE & PLYMOUTH

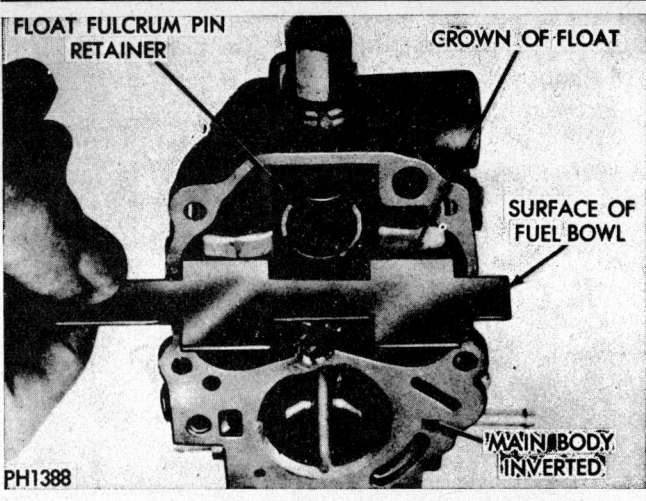

Fig. 1 Checking float level. BBS and BBD carburetors.

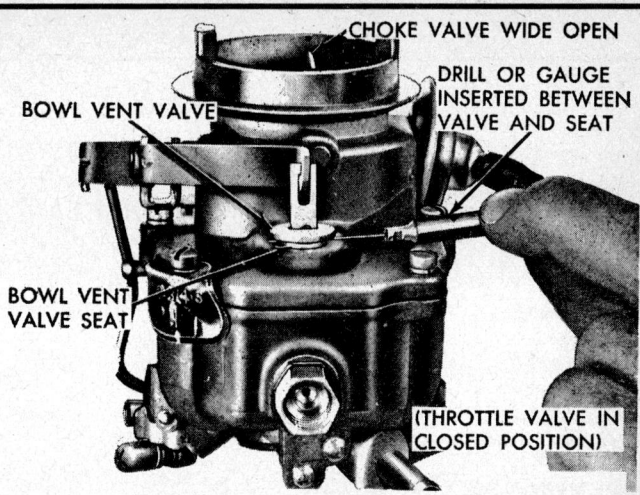

Fig. 2 Checking bowl vent opening. BBS and BBD carburetors

opening.

NOTE: This is an important adjustment since too much lift at the bowl vent will result in considerable loss in low speed fuel economy. If the pump operating rod is moved to either the short or long stroke position, a corresponding change must be made in the location of the bowl vent clip, and the amount of lift of the bowl rechecked and adjusted.

Pump and Bowl Vent Adjustments E.C.S.

On the E.C.S. BBS carburetor, it is necessary to check or set the accelerator pump travel before checking the bowl vent valve opening.

Accelerator Pump Travel Adjustment
1. Be sure the accelerator pump rod is in outer hole (long stroke) of throttle lever.
2. Close throttle valve to curb idle.
3. Using a straight edge placed on flat surface (air cleaner mounting surface), measure distance between straight edge and top of accelerator pump plunger, Fig. 3. Refer to *BBS Specification Chart*.
4. If an adjustment is necessary, bend accelerator pump rod at angle until correct pump travel has been obtained.

Bowl Vent Valve Adjustment
This adjustment to be made after accelerator pump adjustment.
1. With throttle valve at curb idle, measure distance from top of casting to top of bowl vent valve stem, Fig. 4. Refer to *BBS Specifications Chart*.
2. If an adjustment is necessary, bend lower tang on bowl vent valve operating lever (at pivot) until correct opening has been obtained.

Choke Unloader Adjustment

Fig. 5—Hold throttle valve in wide open position. Insert a drill of the specified size between upper edge of choke valve and inner wall of air horn. With a finger lightly pressing against choke valve, a slight drag should be felt as the drill is being withdrawn. If an adjustment is necessary, bend unloader tang to throttle lever as required.

Fast Idle Cam Position
Fig. 6
1. With fast idle speed adjusting screw contacting the second highest step on the fast idle cam, move choke valve toward closed position with light pressure on choke shaft lever.
2. Insert specified drill between choke valve and wall of air horn. If an adjustment is

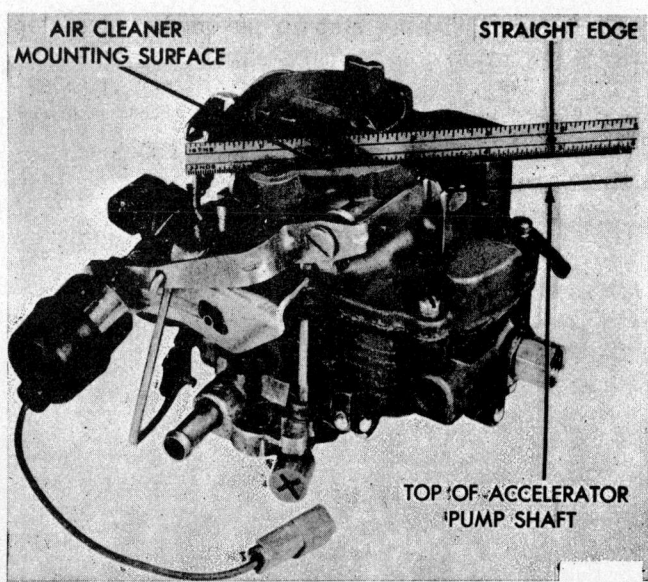

Fig. 3 Checking accelerator pump travel. BBS carburetors with E.C.S.

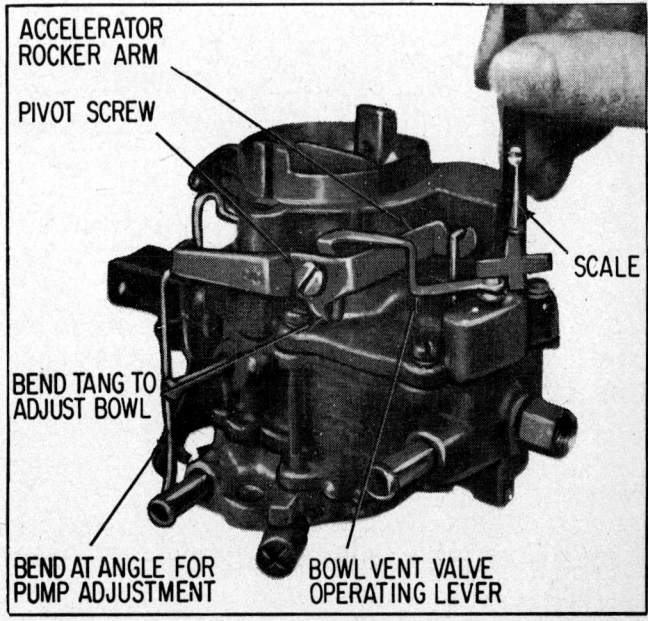

Fig. 4 Bowl vent adjustment. BBS carburetors with E.C.S.

DODGE & PLYMOUTH

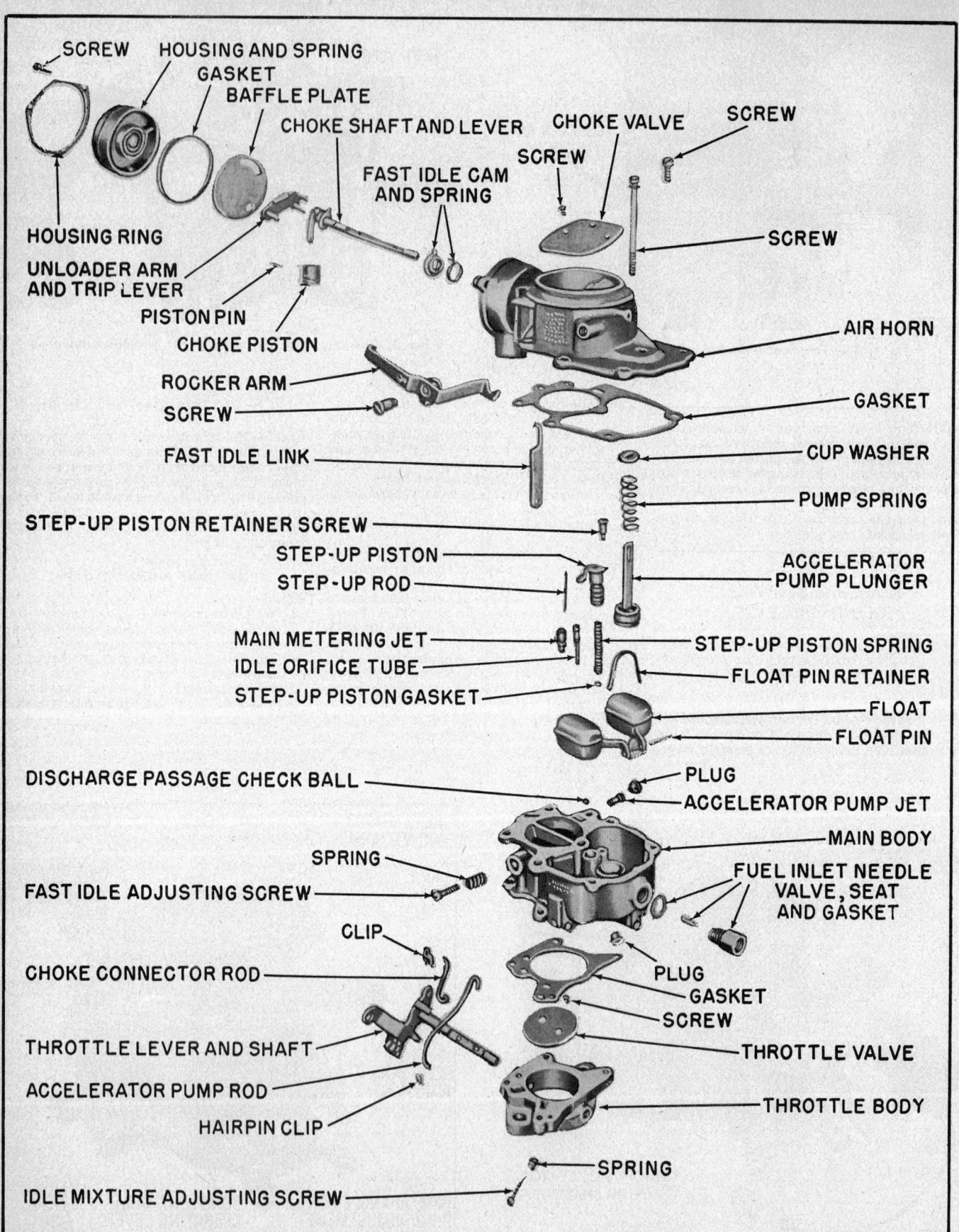

Carter BBS single barrel unit with built-in automatic choke

DODGE & PLYMOUTH

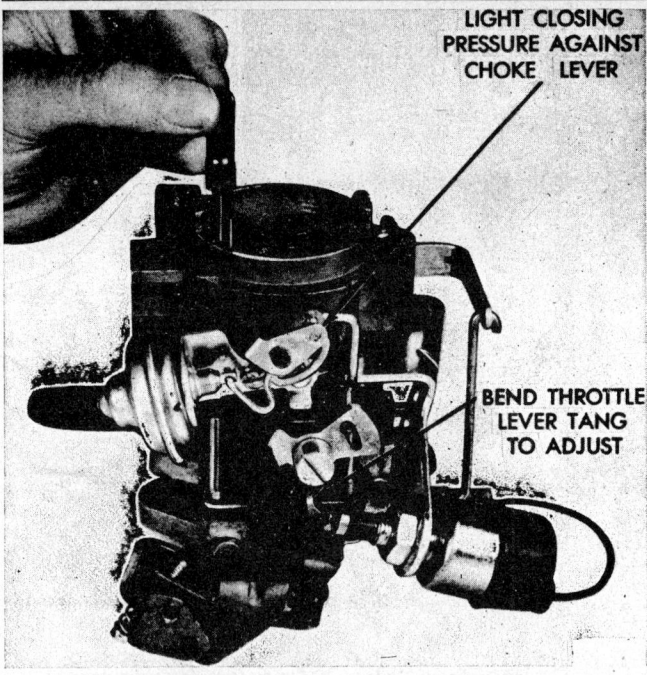

Fig. 5 Checking choke unloader setting (wide open kick). BBS carburetors

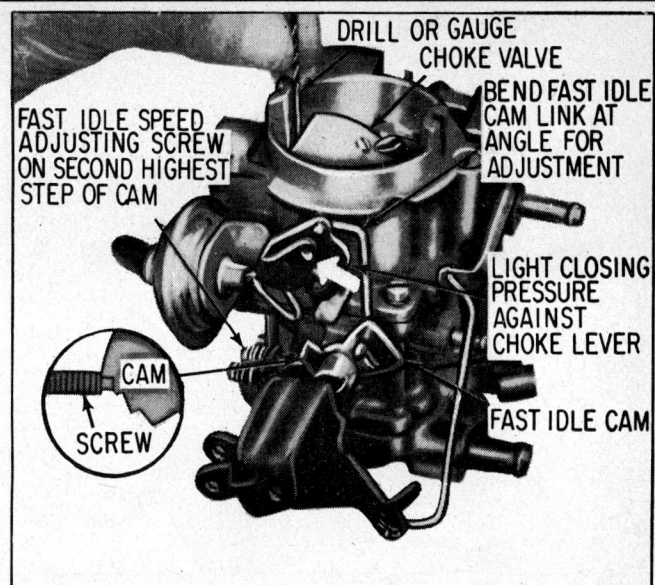

Fig. 6 Fast idle cam position. BBS carburetors

necessary, bend fast idle rod at upper angle until correct valve opening has been obtained.

Vacuum Kick Adjustment

Fig. 7

The choke diaphragm adjustment controls the fuel delivery while the engine is running. It positions the choke valve within the air horn by action of the linkage between the choke shaft and diaphragm. The diaphragm must be energized to measure the vacuum kick adjustment. Use a vacuum source, or vacuum supplied by another vehicle.
Adjust as follows:

1. If adjustment is to be made with the engine running, back off the fast idle speed screw until choke can be closed to the kick position with engine at curb idle. Note the number of screw turns required so that fast idle can be returned to original adjustment. If an auxiliary vacuum source is to be used, open throttle valve (engine not running) and move choke to closed position. Release throttle first, then release choke.
2. When using an auxiliary vacuum source, disconnect vacuum hose from carburetor and connect it to hose from vacuum supply with a small length of tube to act as a fitting. Removal of hose from diaphragm may require forces which change the system. Apply a vacuum of 10 inches or more of mercury.
3. Insert specified drill between choke valve and wall of air horn. Apply sufficient closing pressure on lever to which choke rod attaches to provide a minimum stroke valve opening without distortion of diaphragm link. Note that cylindrical stem of diaphragm will extend as internal spring is compressed. This spring must be fully compressed for proper measurement of vacuum kick adjustment.

4. An adjustment will be necessary if a slight drag is not obtained as drill is being removed. Shorten or lengthen diaphragm link to obtain correct choke opening. Length changes should be made carefully by bending (opening or closing) the bend provided in the diaphragm link. *Do not apply twisting or bending force to diaphragm.*
5. Reinstall vacuum hose on correct carburetor fitting. Return fast idle screw to its original location if disturbed as suggested in Step 1.
6. Check the adjustment as follows: With no vacuum applied to diaphragm, *choke valve should move freely between open and closed positions.* If movement is not free, examine linkage for misalignment or interferences caused by bending operation. Repeat adjustment if necessary to provide proper link operation.

Spring Staged Choke Adjustment

Fig. 8

The spring staged choke is a device incorporated in the choke mechanism that limits the choke blade closing torque when cranking the engine at temperatures below zero. Thus the spring staging of the choke is a better match for the engine's starting mixture requirements at low temperatures.

To check the spring staged choke for correct operating clearance, proceed as follows:
1. Push on hub lever with finger at closed choke position. A small opening should exist between shaft and hub levers as indicated.
2. Using a drill or gauge, measure the opening which should be from .010 to .040".
3. If adjustment is necessary, bend hub lever tang until correct opening is obtained.

Choke Adjustment

Fig. 9—Loosen mounting post lock nut and turn mounting post with screwdriver until index mark on disc is positioned as listed in the *BBS Specifications Chart*. Hold in this position with screwdriver and tighten lock nut.

NOTE: Screwdriver may be held in a vise so that one hand may be used to support housing while tightening nut. After adjustment is completed and coil housing and rod and carburetor are installed on engine, left cover disc and open and close choke valve manually to see if connector rod clears sides of hole in housing cover without binding. If rod does not clear housing cover without binding, replace with a new unit since connecting rod cannot be bent without affecting calibration.

Dashpot Adjustment

Clean Air Carburetors

To adjust the dashpot, have the curb idle speed and mixture properly adjusted, and install a tachometer. Position throttle lever so that actuating tab on lever is contacting stem of dashpot but not depressing it. The tachometer should read 1000 rpm if the setting is correct. If not correct, screw dashpot in or out as required, then tighten lock nut on dashpot against the bracket.

MODEL BBD ADJUSTMENTS

Float Level Adjustment

Fig. 1—With carburetor body inverted so that weight of floats ONLY is forcing needle against its seat, use a T-scale or the tool shown, and check the float level from surface of fuel bowl to crown of each float at center.

If an adjustment is necessary, hold floats on bottom of bowl and bend float lip as required to give the specified dimension.

CAUTION: When bending the float lip, do not

DODGE & PLYMOUTH

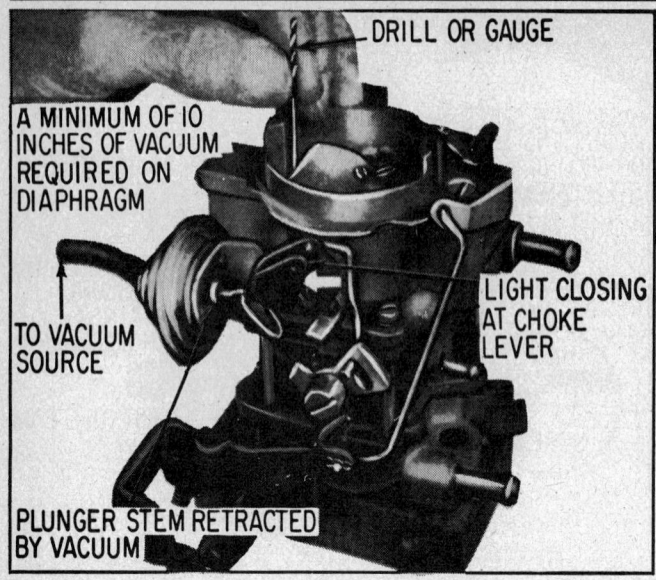

Fig. 7 Vacuum kick adjustment. BBS and BBD carburetors

Fig. 8 Spring staged choke adjustment. BBS carburetors

allow the lip to push against the needle as the synthetic rubber tip (if used) can be compressed sufficiently to cause a false setting which will affect correct level of fuel in bowl. After being compressed, the tip is very slow to recover its original shape.

Accelerator Pump

Except 1¼″ Bore Units, Fig. 10
1. Back off idle adjusting screw. Open choke valve so that fast idle cam allows throttle valves to fully close. Be sure that pump connector rod is installed in outer hole of throttle lever.
2. With throttle valves closed tightly, measure distance between top of air horn and end of pump plunger shaft. If the dimension is not as specified, bend pump connector rod at the angle on the rod until correct setting is obtained.

1974 1¼″ Bore Units & 1975-76 All, Fig. 11
1. Back off curb idle adjusting screw, completely closing throttle valve, then open choke valve, allowing throttle valves to seat in bores. Ensure accelerator pump "S" link is located in outer hole or pump arm.
2. Turn curb idle adjusting screw until screw contacts, stop, then rotate screw two additional turns.
3. Measure distance between air horn surface and top of accelerator pump shaft. Refer to BBD Specifications Chart.
4. Adjust by loosening pump arm adjusting screw and rotating sleeve until proper dimension is obtained. Tighten adjusting screw.

Accelerator Pump and Bowl Vent

C.A.S. Equipped 1¼″ Bore Units, Fig. 2
1. Back off idle speed adjusting screw. Open choke valve so that fast idle cam allows throttle valves to close completely.
2. Be sure pump operating rod is in medium stroke hole in throttle lever, and that bowl vent clip on pump stem is on center notch.
3. With throttle valves closed tightly, it should be just possible to insert the specified gauge or drill size between bowl vent and its seat.
4. If an adjustment is necessary, bend pump operating rod at the angle. On CAP carburetors, bend pump operating rod to give the height of pump plunger stem above bowl cover as specified in the table.

E.C.S. Equipped 1¼″ Bore Units, Fig. 12
1. Back off idle speed adjusting screw to completely close throttle valves. Open

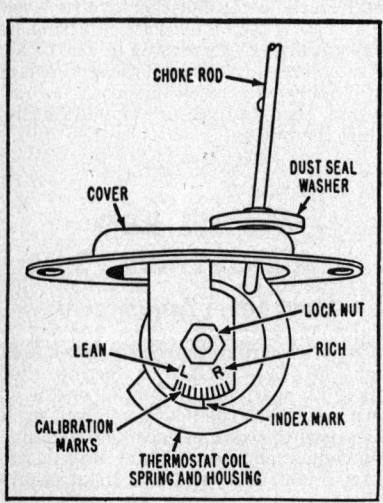

Fig. 9 Well type choke setting. BBS and BBD carburetors

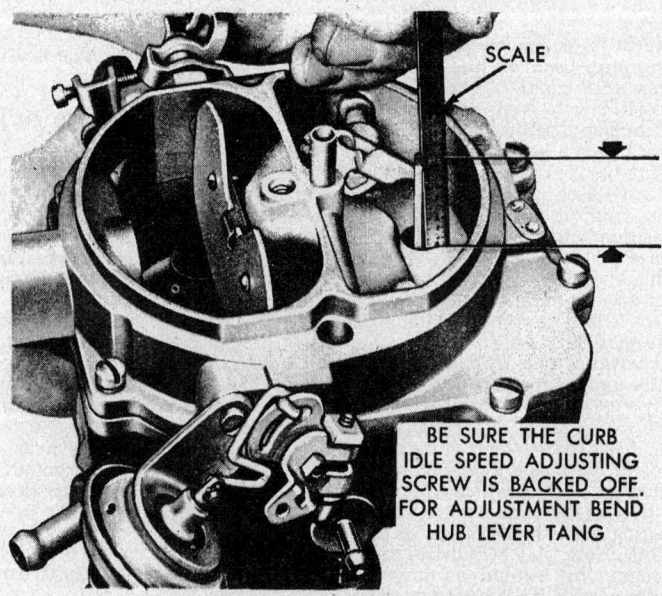

Fig. 10 Checking accelerator pump travel. BBD except 1¼″ bore carburetors

DODGE & PLYMOUTH

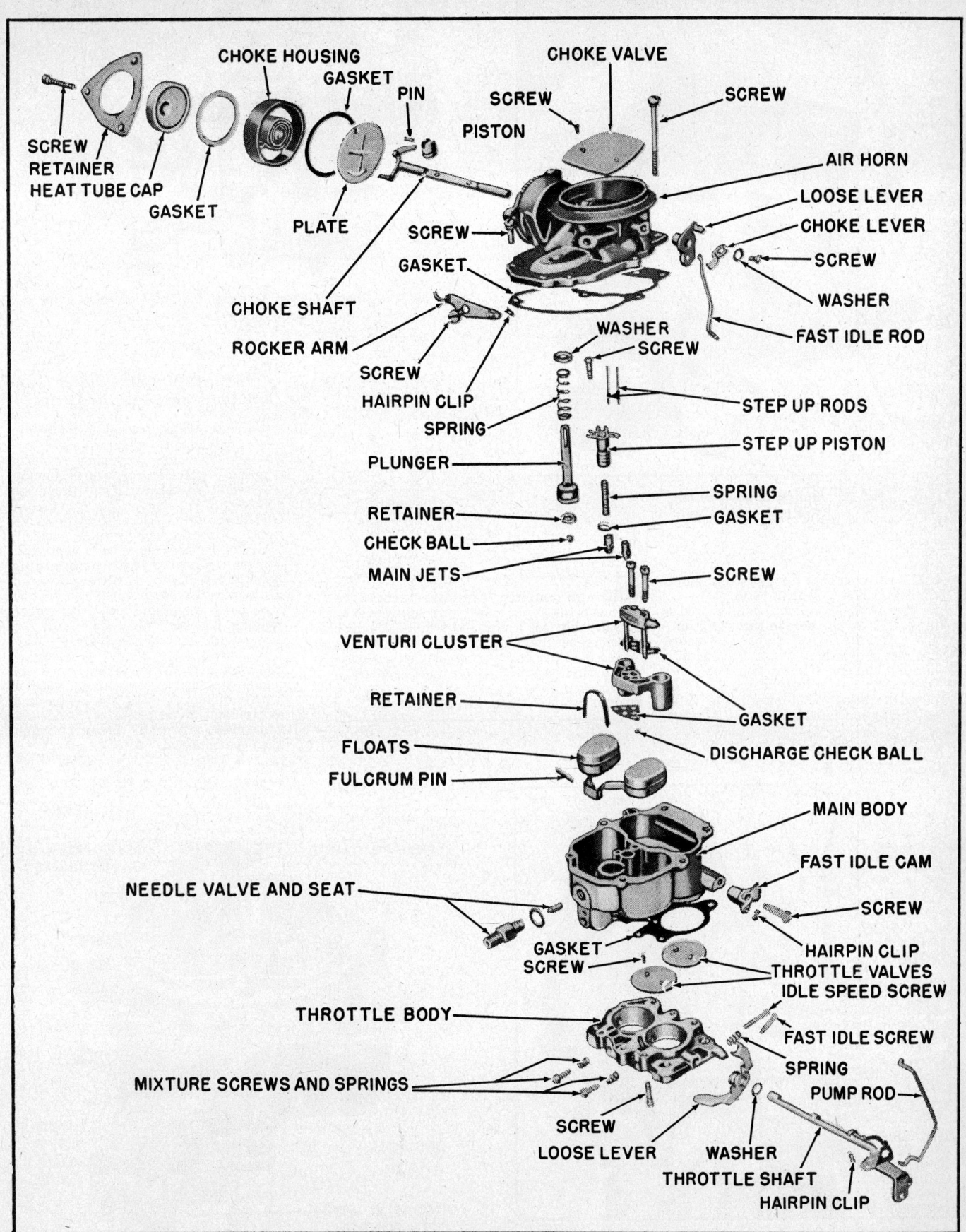

Carter BBD two-barrel unit with built-in automatic choke

DODGE & PLYMOUTH

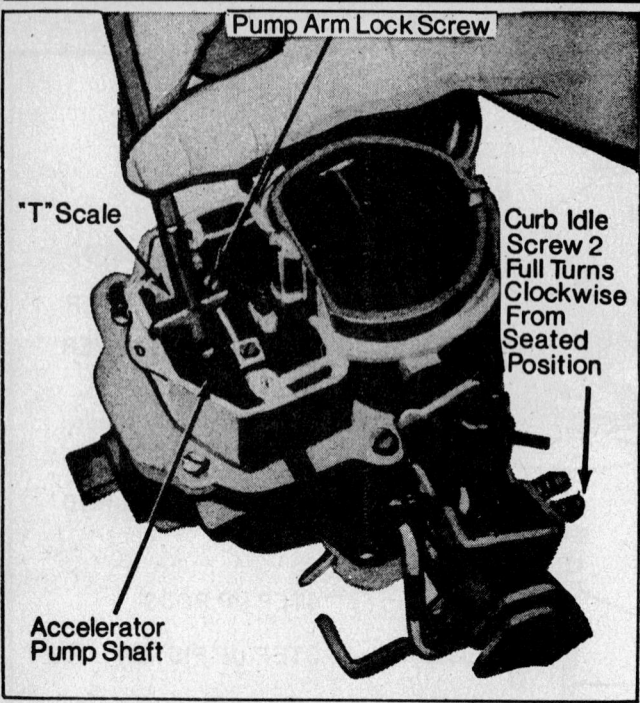

Fig. 11 Accelerator pump setting. 1974 1¼" E.C.S. units and 1975-76 all

Fig. 12 Checking bowl vent opening. BBD 1¼" E.C.S. units

Bowl Vent Adjustment

1½" Bore Units with Separate Pump, Fig. 13

1. Open choke valve so that fast idle cam allows valves to close, curb idle.
2. Be sure that pump operating rod is in long stroke hole in throttle lever. Remove bowl vent valve cover if not previously done.
3. On E.C.S. units, close throttle valves tightly. Using a narrow ruler, measure the distance from top of bowl vent valve (rubber tip) to top of air horn casting. Refer to Specifications Chart. If an adjustment is necessary, bend bowl vent lift arm, using a suitable tool, until correct opening has been obtained. On C.A.S. units, with the throttle valves closed, (curb idle), there should be specified clearance between bowl vent valve and seat on air horn. Measure at outermost or largest dimension with a drill shank. If an adjustment is necessary, bend vent valve lifter arm until correct clearance has been obtained.

choke valve so that fast idle cam allows throttle valves to seat in bores.
2. Be sure accelerator pump operating rod is in medium stroke hole in throttle lever.
3. Close throttle valves tightly. Measure distance between top of vent valve plastic housing and end of pump plunger stem.
4. To adjust pump travel, bend accelerator pump operating rod at lower angle. Refer to BBD Specifications Chart.

NOTE: This is an important adjustment, since too much lift at the bowl vent will result in considerable loss in low speed fuel economy.

Remember that if the pump operating rod is moved to either the short or long stroke position, a corresponding change must be made in the location of the bowl vent clip, and the amount of lift of the bowl vent rechecked.

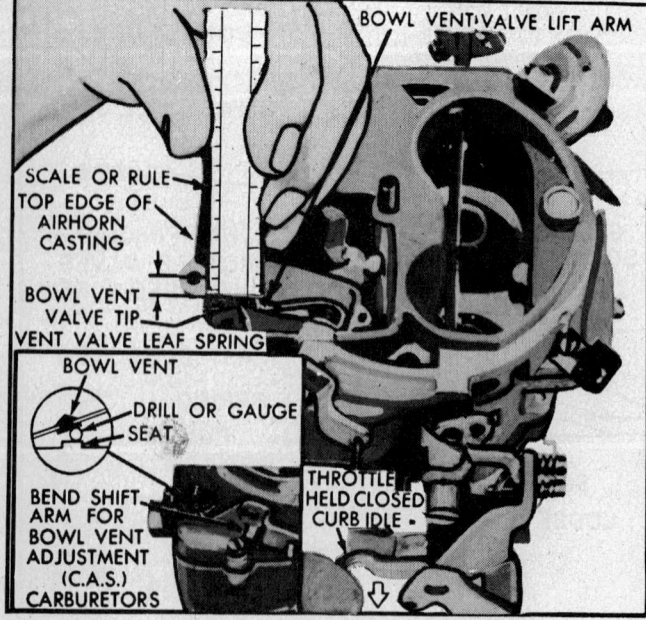

Fig. 13 Measuring bowl vent valve opening. BBD 1½" carburetors

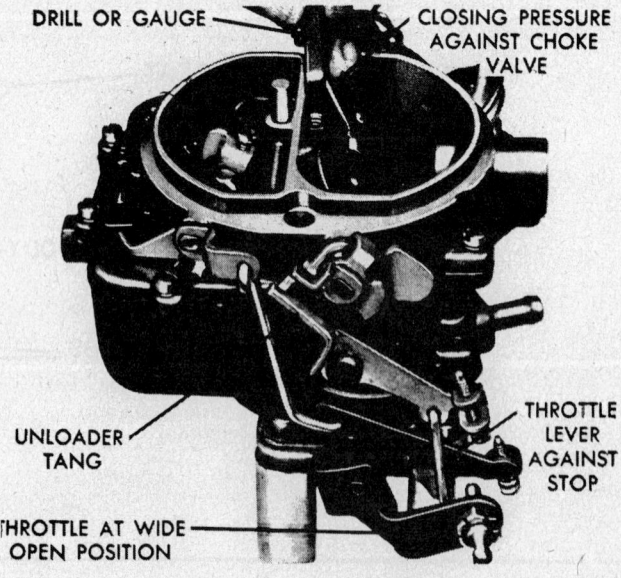

Fig. 14 Choke unloader setting. BBD carburetors

DODGE & PLYMOUTH

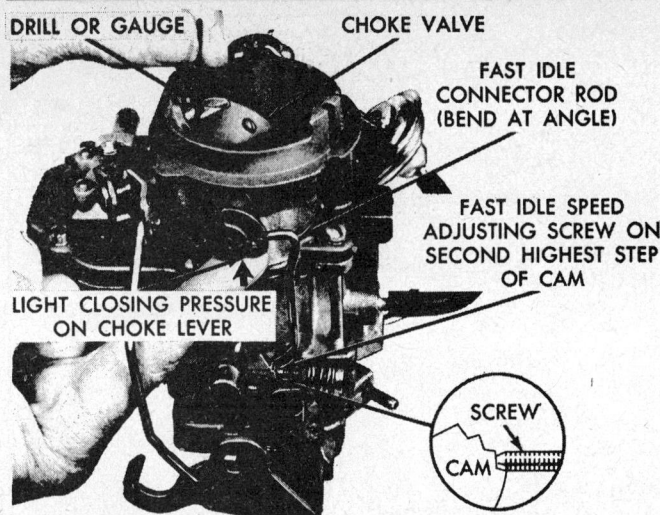

Fig. 15 Fast idle cam position adjustment. BBD 1¼" bore carburetors

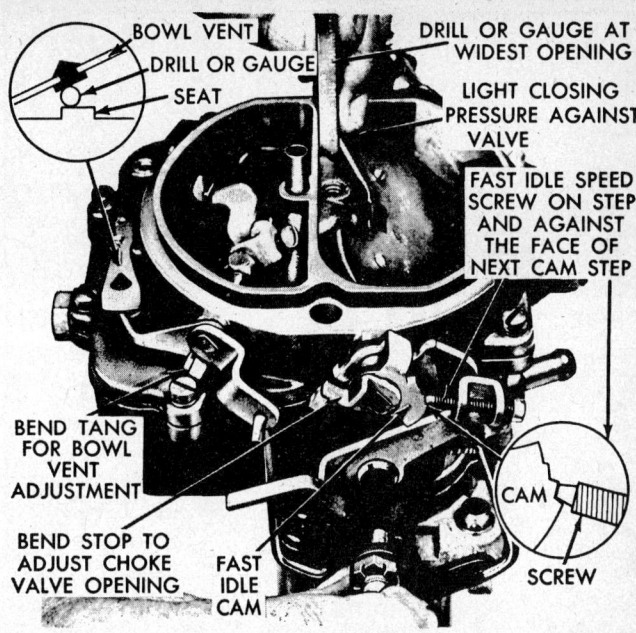

Fig. 16 Fast idle cami position adjustment. BBD except 1¼" bore carburetors

NOTE: Do not bend bowl vent valve leaf spring during bending operation or improper vent valve operation will result.

4. Install bowl vent valve cover and secure with attaching screws.

Choke Unloader Adjustment

Fig. 14—The choke unloader is a mechanical device to partially open the choke valve at wide open throttle. It is used to eliminate choke enrichment during engine cranking. Engines that have been flooded or stalled by excessive choke enrichment can be cleared by the use of the unloader. Adjust as follows:

1. Hold throttle valve in wide open position. Insert the specified drill size between upper edge of choke valve and inner wall of air horn.
2. With a finger lightly pressing against choke valve, a slight drag should be felt as the drill is being withdrawn.
3. If an adjustment is necessary, bend unloader tang on throttle lever until specified opening has been obtained.

Fast Idle Cam Position

Figs. 15 & 16

1. With fast idle adjusting screw contacting second highest step on fast idle cam, move choke valve toward closed position with light pressure on choke shaft lever.
2. Insert the specified size drill between choke valve and air horn wall. An adjustment will be necessary if a slight drag is not obtained as drill is being removed.

Choke Vacuum Kick Adjustment

Figs. 7 & 17

The choke diaphragm adjustment controls the fuel delivery while the engine is running. It positions the choke valve within the air horn by action of the linkage between choke shaft and diaphragm. The diaphragm must be energized to measure the vacuum kick adjustment. Use either a distributor test machine with a vacuum source, or vacuum supplied by another vehicle.

1. If adjustment is to be made with engine running, disconnect fast idle linkage to allow choke to close to kick position with engine at curb idle. If an auxiliary vacuum source is to be used, open throttle valves (engine not running) and move choke to closed position. Release throttle first, then release choke.
2. When using an auxiliary vacuum source, disconnect vacuum hose from carburetor

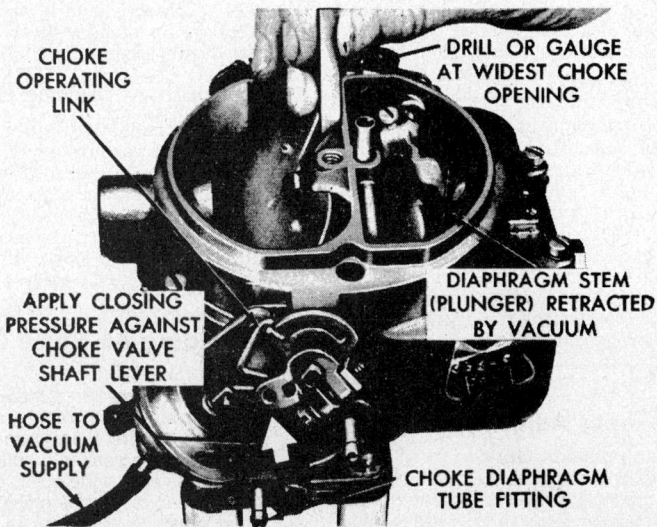

Fig. 17 Choke vacuum kick setting. BBD except 1¼" bore carburetors

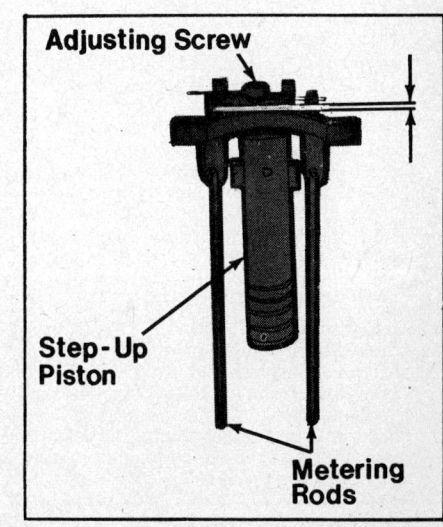

Fig. 18 Step up piston adjustment

DODGE & PLYMOUTH

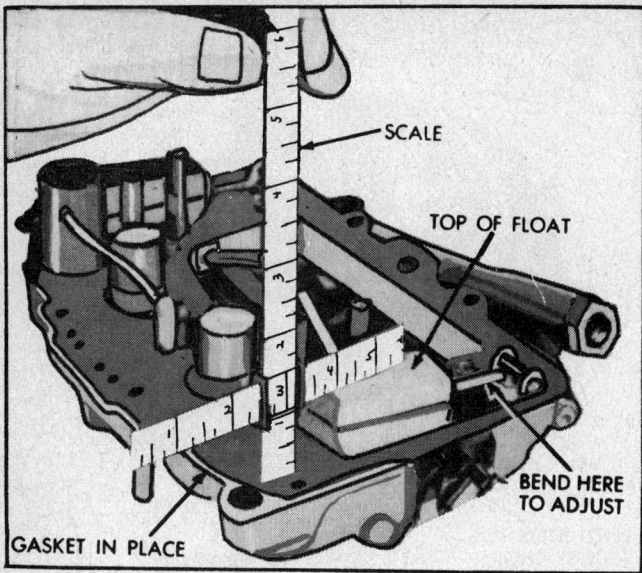

Fig. 19 TQ float setting

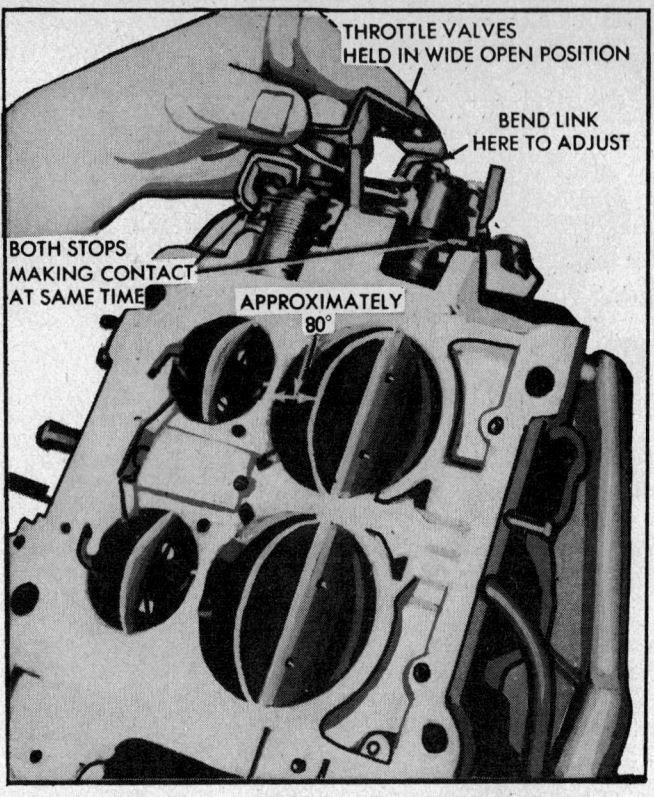

Fig. 20 TQ secondary throttle adjustment

and connect it to hose from vacuum supply with a small length of tube to act as a fitting. Removal of hose from diaphragm may require forces which damage the system. On all 1970-72 units, apply a vacuum of 10 or more inches of mercury and on all 1973-76 units, apply a vacuum of 15 or more inches of mercury.

3. Insert the specified drill size between choke valve and wall of air horn. Apply sufficient closing pressure on lever to which choke rod attaches to provide a minimum choke valve opening without distortion of diaphragm link. Note that the cylindrical stem of diaphragm will extend as internal spring is compressed. This spring must be fully compressed for proper measurement of vacuum kick adjustment.
4. An adjustment will be necessary if a slight drag is not obtained as drill is being removed. Shorten or lengthen diaphragm link to obtain correct choke opening. Length changes should be made carefully by bending (opening or closing) the bend provided in the diaphragm link. *Do not apply twisting or bending force to diaphragm.*
5. Reinstall vacuum hose on correct carburetor fitting. Return fast idle linkage to its original condition if it has been disturbed as in Step 1.
6. Check as follows: With no vacuum applied to diaphragm, choke valve should move freely between open and closed positions. If movement is not free, examine linkage for misalignment or interferences caused by bending operation. Repeat adjustment if necessary.

Step-up Piston Adjustment

1974 1¼" Units & 1975-79 All, Fig. 18
1. Adjust gap in step-up piston to .030 inch on 1974 models and .035 inch on 1975 models by turning allen head screw on top of piston, then install step-up piston assembly into air horn bore, making certain that metering rods are positioned in metering jets.

NOTE: On 1976 units, do not remove or adjust allen head screw on top of vacuum piston.

2. Back off curb idle screw until throttle valves are completely closed. Count number of turns so that screw can be returned to its original setting.
3. Fully depress piston and while applying moderate pressure on rod lifter, tighten rod lifter screw.
4. Release piston and rod lifter and reset curb idle screw.

Well-Type Choke Setting

Fig. 9—Loosen mounting post lock nut and turn mounting post with screwdriver until index mark on disc is positioned as listed in the *BBD Specifications Chart*. Hold in this position with screwdriver and lock nut.

NOTE: Screwdriver may be held in vise so that one hand may be used to support housing while tightening nut. After adjustment is completed and coil housing, rod and carburetor are installed on engine, lift cover disc and open and close choke valve manually to see if connector rod clears sides of hole in housing cover without binding. If rod does not clear housing cover without binding, replace with a new unit since connecting rod cannot be bent without affecting calibration.

Dashpot Adjustment
Manual Transmission Only

To adjust the dashpot, have the curb idle speed and mixture properly adjusted, and install a tachometer. Position throttle lever so that actuating tab on lever is contacting stem of dashpot but not depressing it. Tachometer should read 2500 rpm if the setting is correct. If not correct, screw dashpot in or out as required, then tighten lock nut on dashpot against the bracket.

CARTER TQ ADJUSTMENTS

Float Setting

Fig. 19 With bowl cover inverted, gasket installed and floats resting on seated needle, the dimension of each float from bowl cover gasket to bottom side of float should be as shown in the specifications chart. If adjustment is necessary, bend lever as shown but never allow lip of float lever to be pressed against needle when adjusting.

Secondary Throttle Linkage

Fig. 20 Block choke valve in wide open position and invert carburetor. Slowly open the primary throttle valves until it is possible to measure between lower edge of primary valve and its bore. When dimension is as shown in the specifications chart, the secondary valves should just start to open. If necessary to adjust, bend rod until correct dimension is obtained.

Secondary Air Valve Opening

Fig. 21
1. With air valve in closed position, the opening along air valve at its long side must be at its maximum and parallel with air horn gasket surface.
2. With air valve wide open, the opening of the air valve at the short side and air horn must be as shown in the specifications chart. The corner of air valve is notched for adjustment. Bend the corner

DODGE & PLYMOUTH

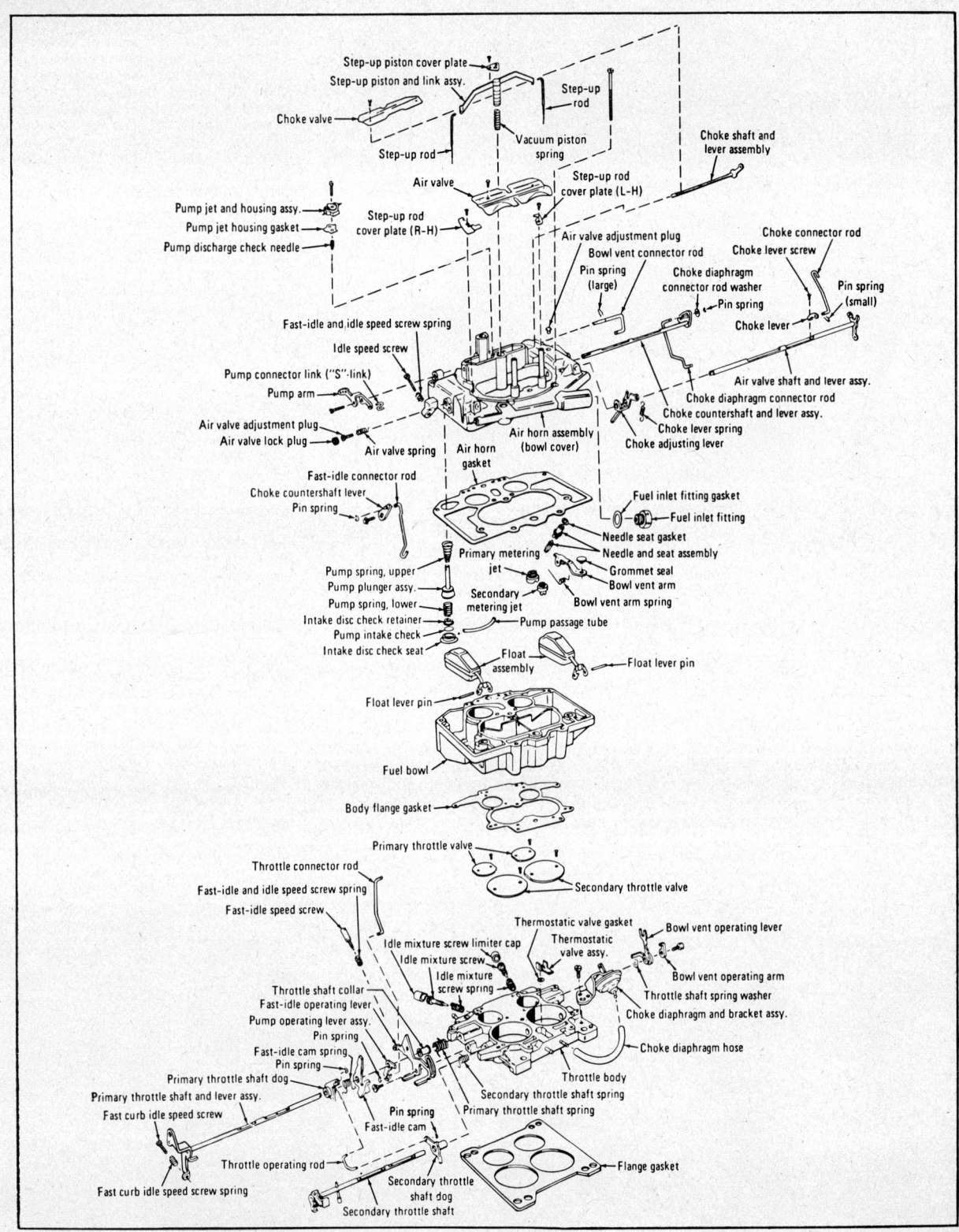

Carter TQ model exploded view

DODGE & PLYMOUTH

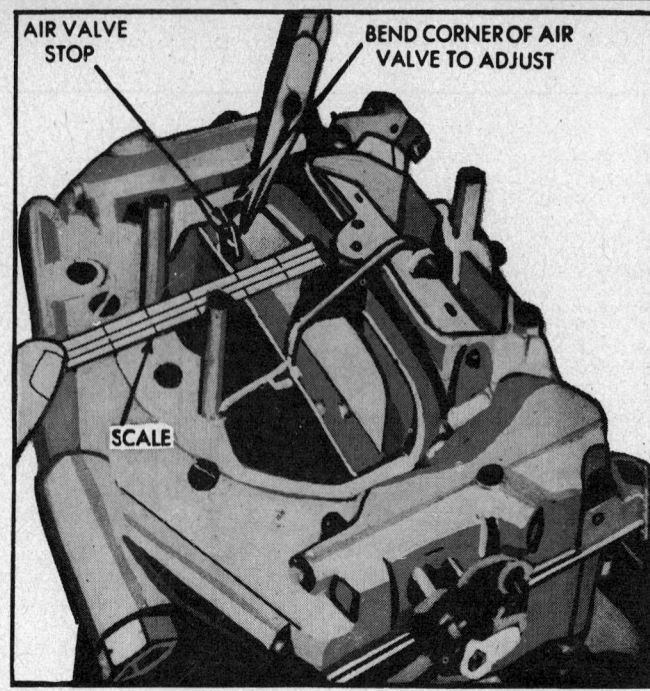

Fig. 21 TQ secondary air valve opening

with a pair of pliers to give proper opening.

Secondary Air Valve Spring Tension

Fig. 22—Loosen air valve lock plug and allow air valve to position itself wide open. With a long screwdriver that will enter center of tool C-4152 positioned on air valve adjustment plug, turn plug counterclockwise until air valve contacts stop lightly, then turn additional turn as specified in the specifications chart. Hold plug with screwdriver and tighten lock plug securely with tool C-4152.

Accelerator Pump Stroke

1973-74
Fig. 23—Move choke valve wide open to release fast idle cam. Back off idle speed adjusting screw until throttle valves are seated in bores. Be sure throttle connector rod is in center hole of pump arm. Close throttle valve tightly and measure distance between top of bowl cover and end of plunger shaft. Dimension should be as shown in the specifications chart. Bend throttle connector rod at lower angle to adjust.

1975-80
Fig. 24—First Stage. Ensure throttle connector rod is in center hole on three hole pump arm or inner hole on two hole pump arm. With idle adjusting screw adjusted to the specified curb idle speed, measure distance from air horn surface to top of accelerator pump plunger. If equipped with an idle stop solenoid the ignition switch must be in the on position. Dimension should be as shown in the specifications chart. Bend throttle connector rod at lower angle to adjust.

Second Stage. With choke in the open position, open throttle until secondary lockout latch is just applied. Plunger downward travel stops at this point. Measure distance from air horn surface to top of accelerator pump plunger. Dimension should be as shown in the specification chart. Bend tang on throttle to adjust.

Choke Control Lever

Fig. 25—Place carburetor on a flat surface and disconnect choke diaphragm rod at diaphragm. Close choke by pushing on choke lever with throttle partly open. Measure vertical distance between top of rod hole in control lever and base of carburetor (flat surface). Dimension should be as shown in the specifications chart. Adjust by bending link connecting the two choke shafts.

If choke control lever adjustment is changed, the vacuum kick, fast idle cam position and choke unloader adjustments must also be reset.

Choke Diaphragm Connector Rod

Fig. 26—Apply a vacuum of 15 or more inches of Mercury to diaphragm to fully depress diaphragm stem. An auxiliary source like a distributor test machine can be used for this purpose. With air valve closed, adjust connector rod to give .040" clearance between air valve and stop.

Vacuum Kick Adjustment

Fig. 27—With engine running, back off fast idle speed screw until choke can be closed to

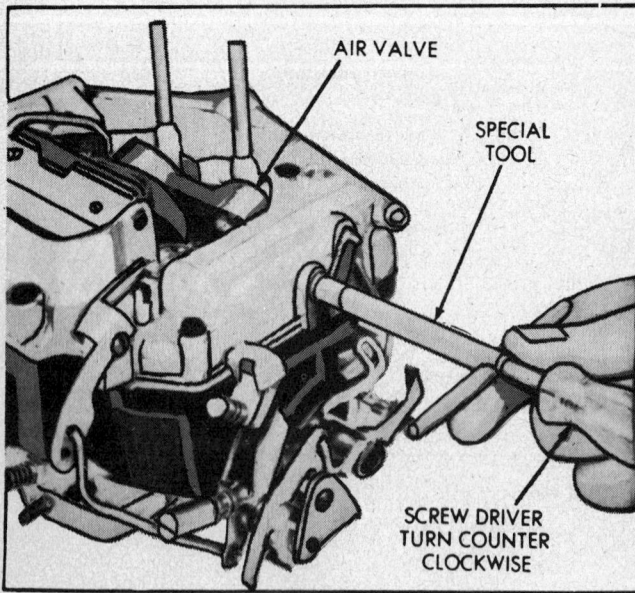

Fig. 22 TQ secondary air valve spring tension

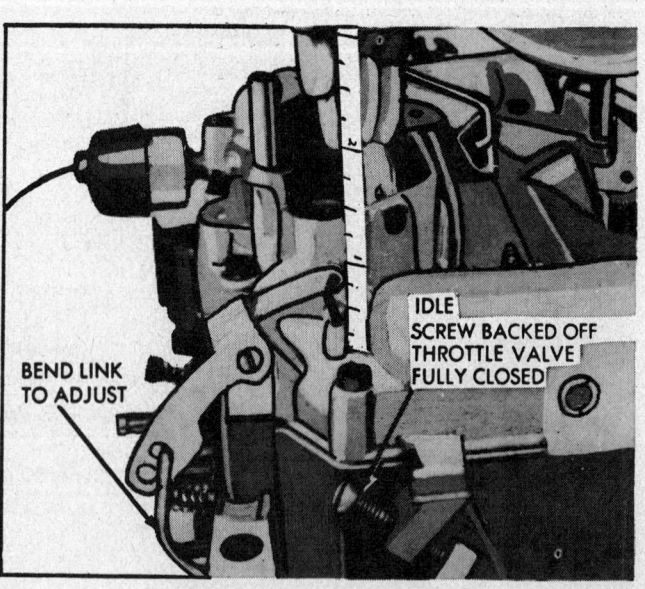

Fig. 23 TQ accelerator pump stroke

DODGE & PLYMOUTH

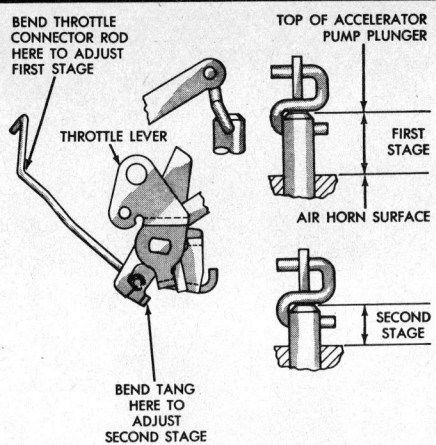

Fig. 24 TQ staged accelerator pump adjustment

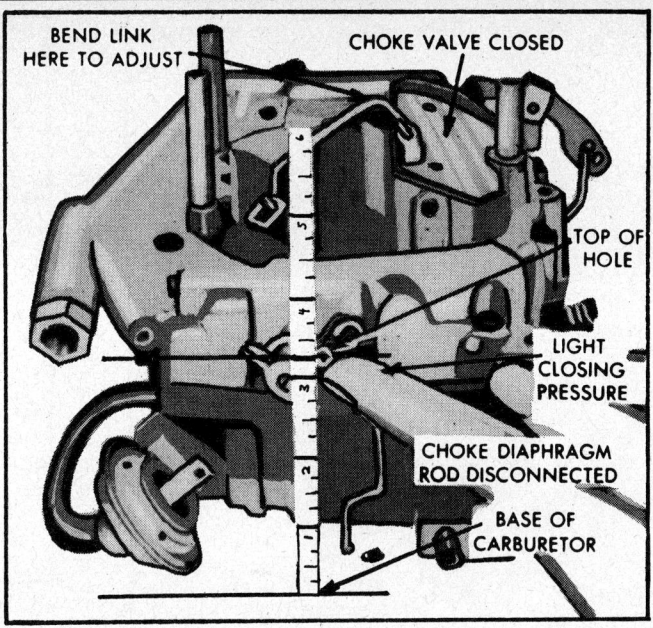

Fig. 25 TQ choke control lever adjustment

kick position at idle. Note number of screw turns so fast idle can be turned back to original adjustment. Insert specified gauge between long side (lower edge) of choke valve and the air horn wall. Apply sufficient pressure on choke control lever to provide a minimum choke valve opening. The spring connecting the control lever to the adjustment lever must be fully extended for proper adjustment. Bend tang as shown to change contact with end of diaphragm rod. Do not adjust diaphragm rod. A slight drag should be felt as gauge is being removed.

Fast Idle Cam & Linkage

Fig. 28—With fast idle adjusting screw on second highest step of fast idle cam, move choke valve towards closed position with light pressure on fast idle cam lever. Clearance between choke valve and air horn wall should be .110 inch on all 1971-73 units, .100 inch on 1974-79 units. Federal 318 engines should have a clearance of .130 inch while California 318 and Federal light duty 360 engines require .100 inch. California light duty 360 engines should have a clearance of .120 inch and all heavy duty 360 engines require .130 inch. If adjustment is necessary, bend fast idle connector rod at angle.

Choke Unloader Adjustment

Fig. 29—Hold throttle valves in wide open position and insert specified drill between long side (lower edge) of choke valve and inner wall of air horn. With finger lightly pressing against choke valve control lever, a slight drag should be felt as drill is withdrawn. Refer to the specification chart for proper drill size or dimension. Adjust by bending tang on fast idle control lever.

Secondary Throttle Lockout

Fig. 30—Move choke control lever to open choke position. Measure clearance between lockout lever and stop. Clearance should be .060-.090 inch. Adjust by bending tang on fast idle control lever.

Bowl Vent Valve Adjustment

Fig. 31—Remove bowl vent valve checking hole plug in bowl cover. With throttle valves

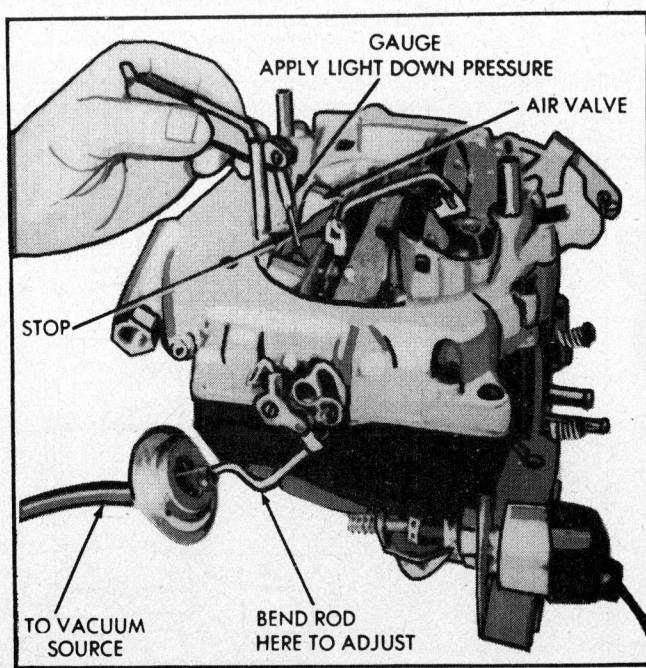

Fig. 26 TQ choke diaphragm connector rod

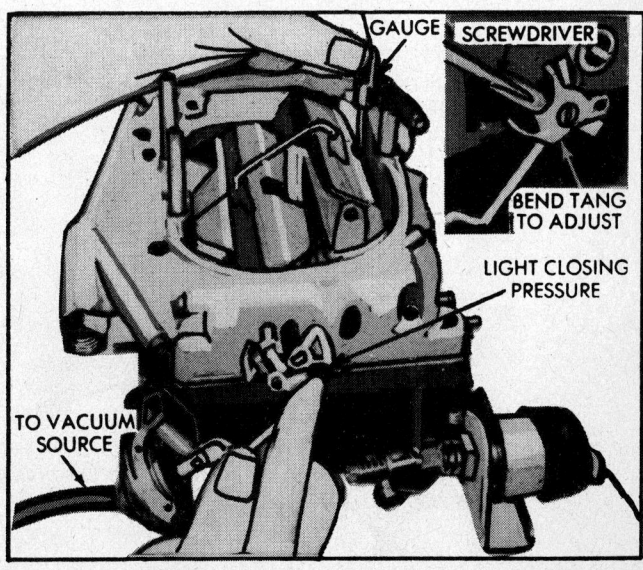

Fig. 27 TQ vacuum kick adjustment

DODGE & PLYMOUTH

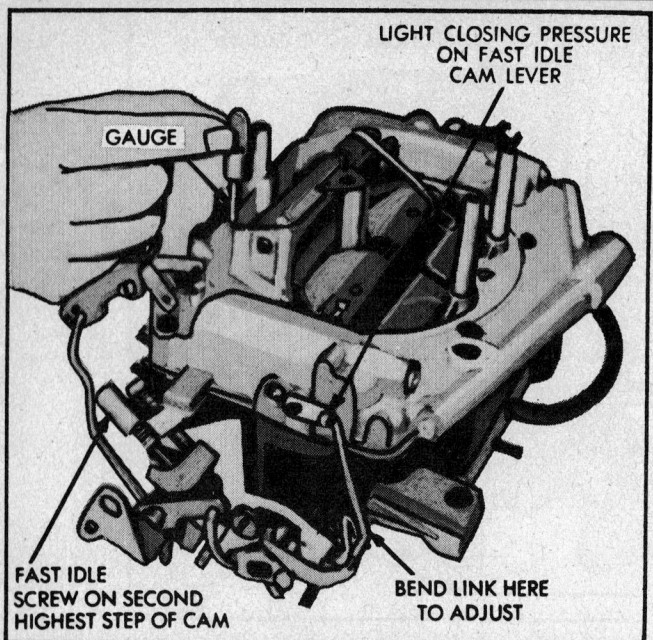

Fig. 28 TQ fast idle cam & linkage adjustment

Fig. 29 TQ choke unloader adjustment

at curb idle, insert a narrow ruler down through hole. Allow ruler to rest lightly on top of valve. Dimension should be .812 inch. Adjust by bending bowl vent operating lever at notch. Install a new plug.

Units with a solenoid bowl vent diaphragm should be tested by removing hose and applying an auxiliary vacuum source of at least 15 inches of Mercury to diaphragm. Viewed through air horn vent tube, valve should move down when vacuum is applied; if it does not, replace leaking diaphragm assembly. Turn ignition switch on and remove auxiliary vacuum source. Valve should remain in down position; if it does not, solenoid or related wiring is defective.

Fast Idle Speed Cam

NOTE: On 1974–75 units, remove air cleaner and plug vacuum fittings to heated air control and OSAC valves.

Fig. 32—With engine off, transmission in neutral and parking brake set, open throttle and close choke. Close throttle to place fast idle speed screw on highest speed step. Turn screw until it drops to second highest speed step. Start engine and determine stabilized speed. Turn fast idle speed screw to obtain speed listed in specifications chart.

HOLLEY EXC. 1945, 2210 & 2245 ADJUSTMENTS

Float Level

Model 1920, Fig. 33

With carburetor inverted, slide float gauge into position and check setting on "touch" leg of gauge. Float should just touch gauge. Reverse gauge and check the "no touch" leg. Float should just clear gauge. To adjust, bend float tab that touches head of fuel inlet needle.

NOTE: Do not allow float tab to contact float needle head while making the adjustment as the rubber tip of the needle can be compressed, giving a false reading.

Models 2300, 4150 & 4160

With fuel bowl inverted, turn adjusting nut in or out until float lever is parallel to floor of float bowl. Tighten lock bolt.

Fuel Level

Model 1920, Fig. 34

With engine running and vehicle on a level floor, measure fuel level through economizer diaphragm opening. Using a 6" scale with a depth gauge as shown, measure distance from

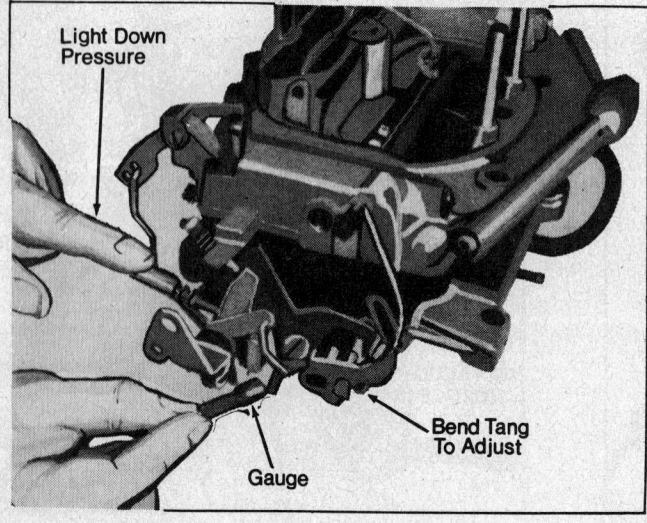

Fig. 30 TQ secondary throttle lockout

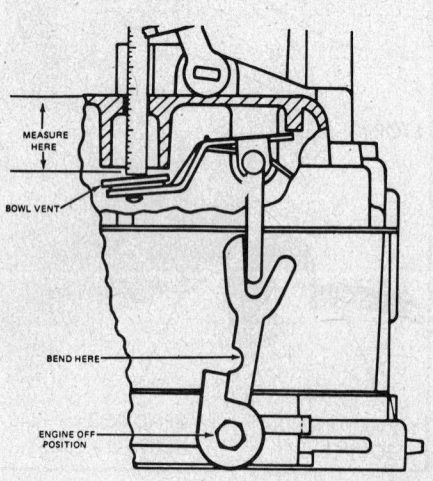

Fig. 31 TQ bowl vent valve adjustment

DODGE & PLYMOUTH

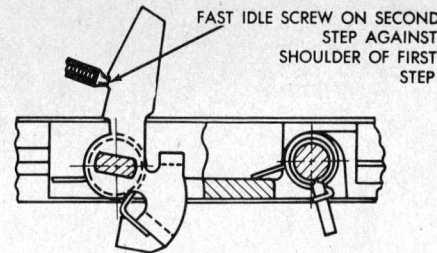

Fig. 32 TQ fast idle speed cam position

machined surface of opening to the exact fuel level. If necessary adjust, proceed as outlined for float level.

Models 2300, 4150 & 4160, Fig. 35

With engine running, remove the sight plug from the fuel bowl and turn adjusting nut up or down until fuel just dribbles out of the sight hole. After correct level has been obtained, tighten the lock screw while holding the adjusting nut.

Fast Idle Cam Position

Model 1920, Fig. 36

With fast idle speed adjusting screw contacting second highest step on fast idle cam, move choke valve toward closed position with light pressure on choke shaft lever. Insert specified drill size between choke valve and air horn wall. If an adjustment is necessary, bend fast idle link at lower angle until correct valve opening is obtained.

NOTE: When the correct fast idle position cam adjustment has been made, the choke unloader (wide open kick) adjustment has also been obtained. No further adjustment is required.

Model 2300, Fig. 37

After setting curb idle speed and with manual control of choke in wide open position, turn fast idle speed screw to obtain clearance of .035 inch between cam and screw head.

Models 4150 & 4160, Fig. 38

Insert specified gauge between top of fast idle cam and choke housing post and apply closing pressure to choke valve. If slight drag is not felt when gauge is withdrawn, adjust by bending choke linkage as indicated.

Bowl Vent

Model 1920, Fig. 39

With throttle valve at curb idle speed, it

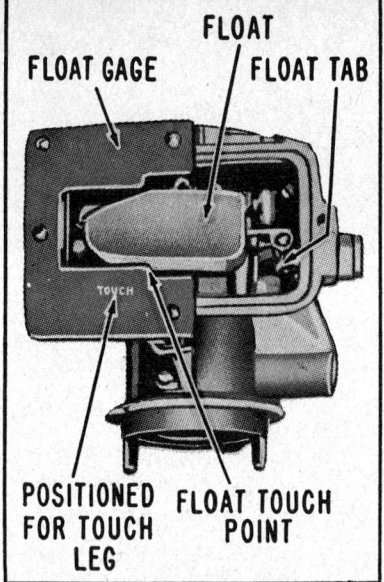

Fig. 33 Float level adjustment. Holley 1920

should be possible to insert a drill of the size specified between bowl vent and the seat. If an adjustment is necessary, bend vent rod at horizontal portion until correct clearance has been obtained. Be sure vent rod does not bind in guide after adjusting.

Dashpot Setting

Model 1920, C.A.P. UNITS, Fig. 40

With curb idle speed and mixture properly set and a tachometer installed, position throttle lever so that actuating tab on lever is contacting stem of dashpot but not depressing it. The tachometer should read 2500 rpm if the setting is correct.

If necessary to adjust the setting, screw the dashpot in or out as required. When the desired setting is obtained, tighten the lock nut on the dashpot against the bracket.

Accelerator Pump Lever Setting

Models 2300, 4150 & 4160, Fig. 41

With throttle valves wide open and pump

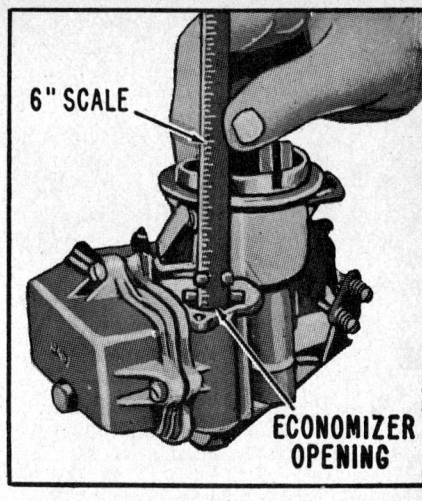

Fig. 34 Checking fuel level. Holley 1920

lever held down, it should be possible to insert a .015" gauge between adjusting nut and lever. Adjust pump override screw to obtain correct clearance.

HOLLEY 1945 ADJUSTMENTS

Dry Float Setting

Fig. 42—Hold float fulcrum retaining pin in position and invert carburetor bowl. Place a straight edge across surface of bowl, contacting float toes. Remove straight edge and measure distance float dropped from surface of fuel bowl. Refer to the specifications chart. Adjust by bending float tang to obtain proper dimension.

Fast Idle Cam Position Adjustment

Fig. 43—With fast idle speed adjusting screw contacting second highest step on fast idle cam, move choke valve toward closed position with light pressure on choke shaft lever.

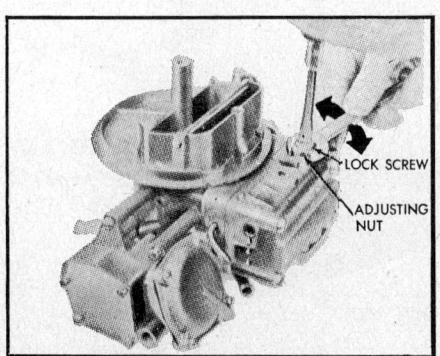

Fig. 35 Adjusting fuel level. Holley 2300, 4150 & 4160

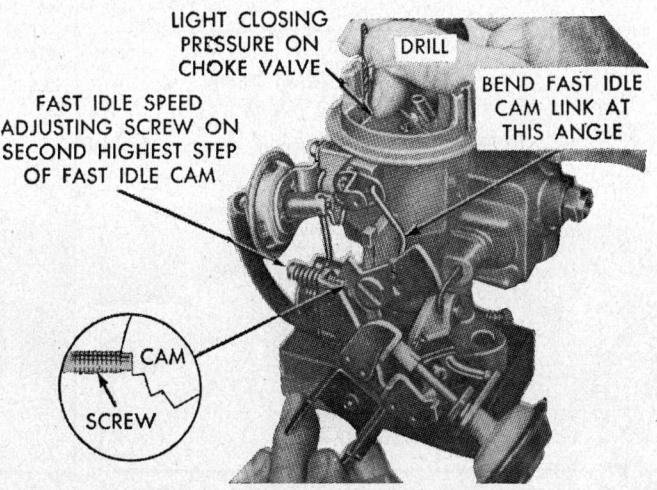

Fig. 36 Fast idle cam position. Holley 1920

DODGE & PLYMOUTH

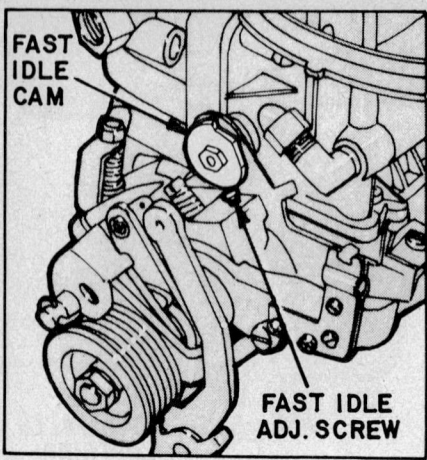

Fig. 37 Fast idle adjustment. Holley 2300

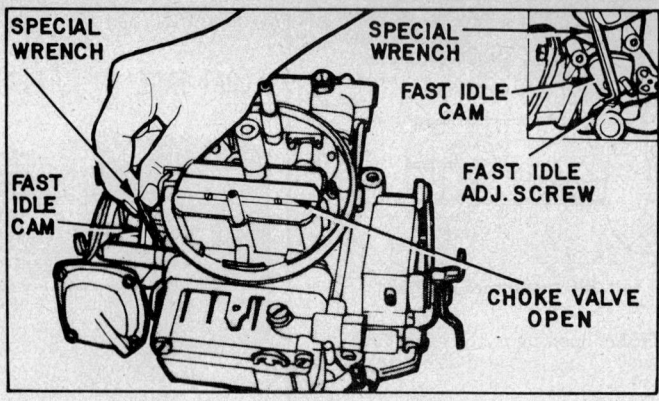

Fig. 38 Fast idle adjustment. Holley 4150

Insert specified gauge between top of choke valve and wall of air horn. Refer to the specifications chart. An adjustment will be necessary if a slight drag is not obtained as drill shank is being removed. Adjust by bending fast idle link at lower angle, until correct valve opening has been obtained.

Choke Vacuum Kick Adjustment

NOTE: Test can be made on or off vehicle.

Fig. 44—If adjustment is to be made with engine running, back off fast idle speed screw until choke can be closed to the kick position with engine at curb idle. (Note number of screw turns required so that fast idle can be returned to original adjustment). If an auxiliary vacuum source is to be used, open throttle valve (engine not running) and move choke to closed position. Release throttle first, then release choke.

When using an auxiliary vacuum source, disconnect vacuum hose from carburetor and connect it to hose from vacuum supply with a small length of tube to act as a fitting. Removal of hose from diaphragm may require forces which damage the system. Apply a vacuum of 15 or more inches of mercury.

Insert gauge between top of choke valve and wall of air horn. Refer to the specifications chart. Apply sufficient closing pressure on lever to which choke rod attaches to provide a minimum choke valve opening without distortion of diaphragm link.

NOTE: The cylindrical stem of diaphragm extends as the internal spring is compressed. This spring must be fully compressed for proper measurement of vacuum kick adjustment.

Adjustment is necessary if slight drag is not obtained when removing the gauge. Shorten or lengthen diaphragm link to obtain correct choke valve opening. Length changes should be made by carefully opening or closing the U-bend provided in the link. Improper bending causes contact between the U-section and the diaphragm assembly.

NOTE: Do not apply twisting or bending force to diaphragm.

After completion of adjustment, reinstall vacuum hose on correct carburetor fitting.

Return fast idle screw to its original location if disturbed. Make following check. With no vacuum applied to diaphragm, the choke valve should move freely between open and closed positions. If movement is not free, examine linkage for misalignment or interferences caused by bending operation.

Choke Unloader (Wide Open Kick) Adjustment

Fig. 45—With throttle valves in wide open position, insert drill gauge between upper edge of choke valve and inner wall of air horn. Refer to the specifications chart. With a finger lightly pressing against shaft lever, a slight drag should be felt as drill is being withdrawn. Adjust by bending unloader tang on throttle lever until correct opening has been obtained.

Accelerator Pump Setting

Fig. 46—With throttle at curb idle position, measure distance from vacuum passage casting to outer edge of hole in pump operating rod. Refer to the specifications chart. Adjust by bending link between throttle lever and pump operating rod.

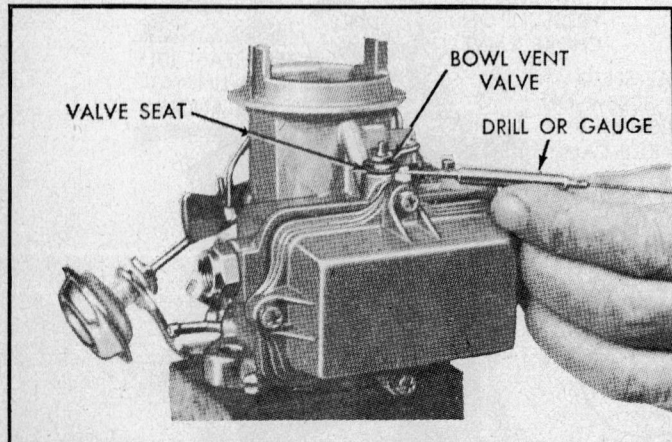

Fig. 39 Checking bowl vent opening. Holley 1920

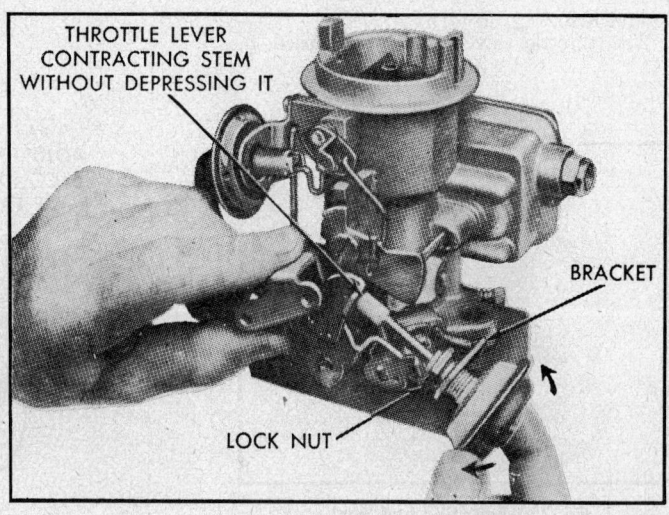

Fig. 40 Adjusting dashpot on C.A.P. units. Holley 1920

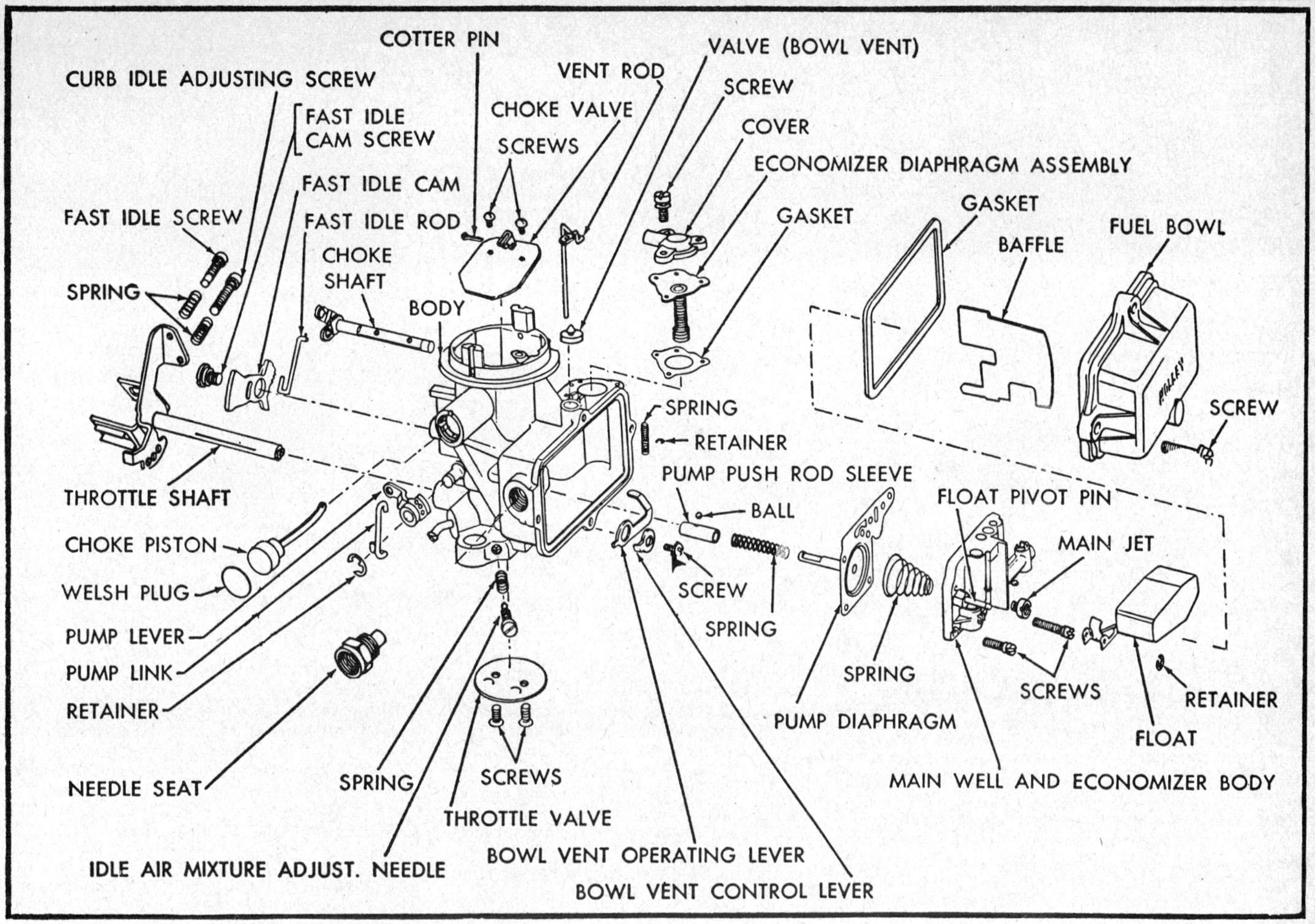

DODGE & PLYMOUTH

Holley Model 1920 single barrel carburetor

HOLLEY 2210 & 2245 ADJUSTMENTS

Float Adjustment

Invert air horn so that weight of float only is forcing needle against seat. Measure the clearance between top of float and float stop, Fig. 47. Be sure drill gauge is perfectly level when measuring. Refer to the specifications chart. Adjust by bending float lip toward or away from needle, using a narrow blade screwdriver, Fig. 48, until correct clearance of setting has been obtained.

Float Drop Adjustment

Check float drop, by holding air horn in an upright position. The bottom edge of float should be parallel to underside surface of air horn, Fig. 49. Adjust by bending tang on float arm until parallel surfaces have been obtained.

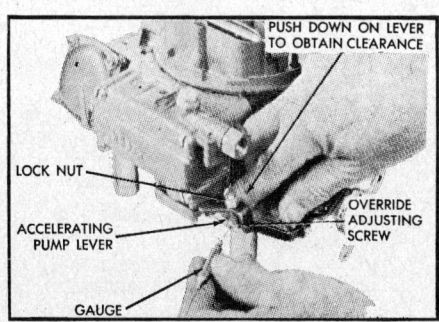

Fig. 41 Accelerator pump lever clearance. Holley 2300, 4150, & 4160

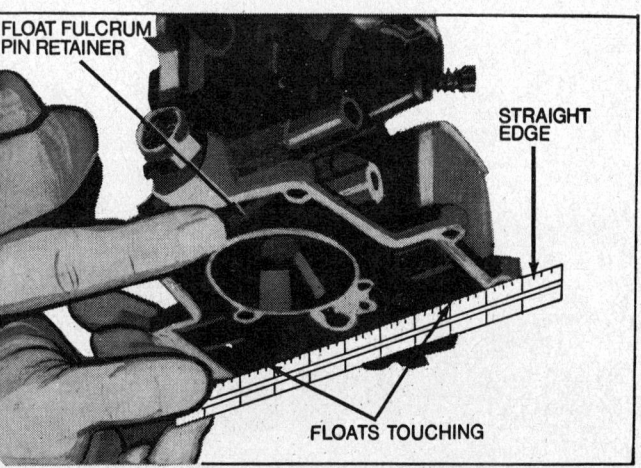

Fig. 42 Measuring float level. 1945 carburetor

DODGE & PLYMOUTH

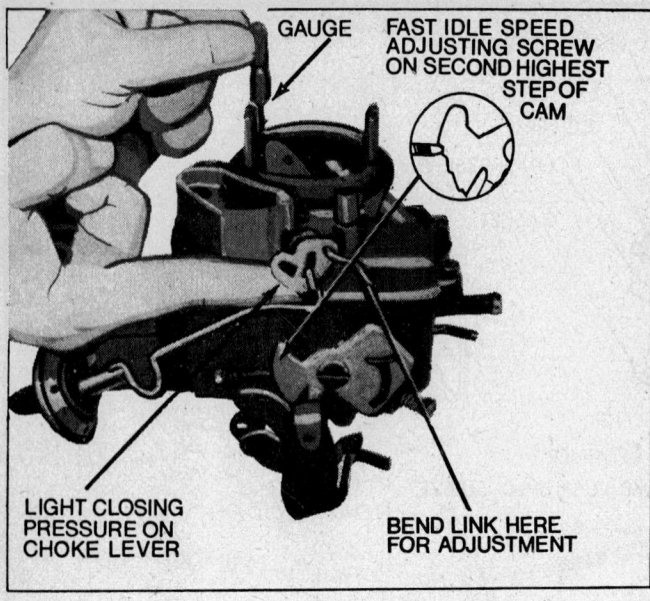

Fig. 43 Fast idle cam position adjustment. 1945 carburetor

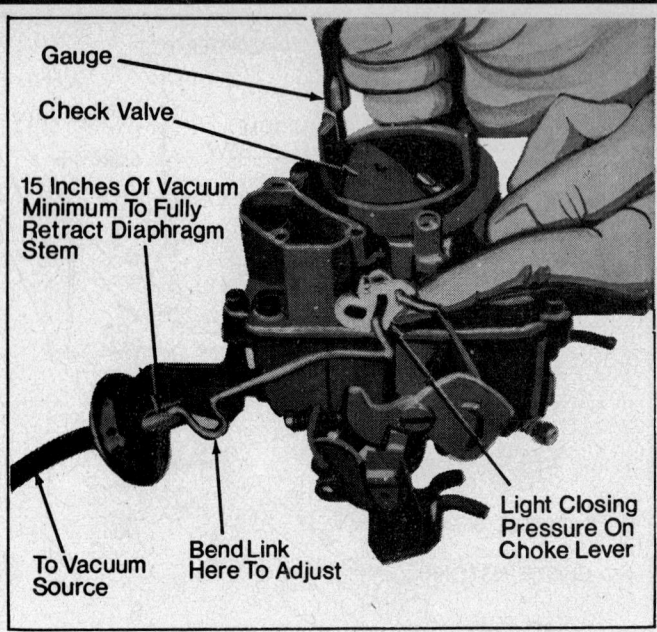

Fig. 44 Choke vacuum kick adjustment. 1945 carburetor

Fast Idle Cam Position Adjustment

Fig. 50—With fast idle speed adjusting screw contacting second highest step on fast idle cam, move choke valve toward closed position with light pressure on choke shaft lever. Insert specified gauge between top of choke valve and wall of air horn. Refer to the specifications chart. An adjustment will be necessary if a slight drag is not obtained as drill shank is being removed. Adjust by bending fast idle link at angle, until correct valve opening has been obtained.

Choke Vacuum Kick Adjustment

NOTE: Test can be made on or off vehicle.

Fig. 51—If adjustment is to be made with engine running, back off fast idle speed screw until choke can be closed to the kick position with engine at curb idle. (Note number of screw turns required so that fast idle can be returned to original adjustment). If an auxiliary vacuum source is to be used, open throttle valve (engine not running) and move choke to closed position. Release throttle first, then release choke.

When using an auxiliary vacuum source, disconnect vacuum hose from carburetor and connect it to hose from vacuum supply with a small length of tube to act as a fitting. Removal of hose from diaphragm may require forces which damage the system. Apply a vacuum of 10 or more inches of mercury.

Insert gauge between top of choke valve and wall of air horn. Refer to the specifications chart. Apply sufficient closing pressure on lever to which choke rod attaches to provide a minimum choke valve opening without distortion of diaphragm link.

NOTE: The cylindrical stem of diaphragm extends as the internal spring is compressed. This spring must be fully compressed for proper measurement of vacuum kick adjustment.

Adjustment is necessary if slight drag is not obtained when removing the gauge. Shorten or lengthen diaphragm link to obtain correct choke valve opening. Length changes should be made by carefully opening or closing the U-bend provided in the link. Improper bending causes contact between the U-section and the diaphragm assembly.

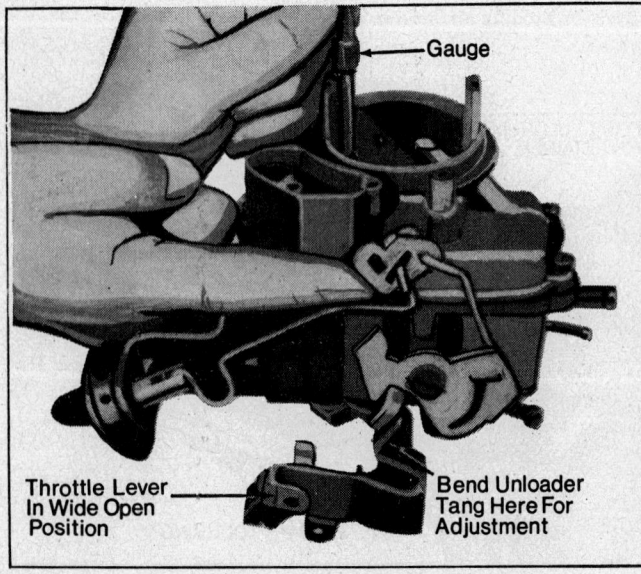

Fig. 45 Choke unloader adjustment. 1945 carburetor

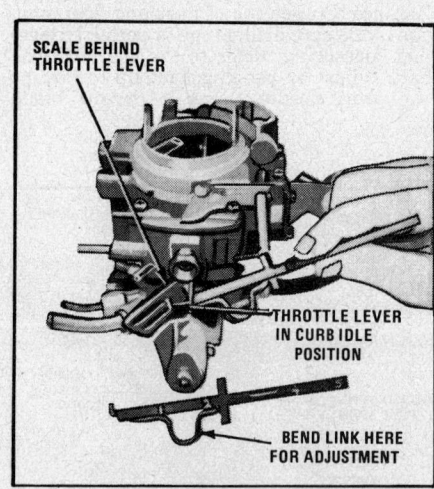

Fig. 46 Accelerator pump adjustment. 1945 carburetor

DODGE & PLYMOUTH

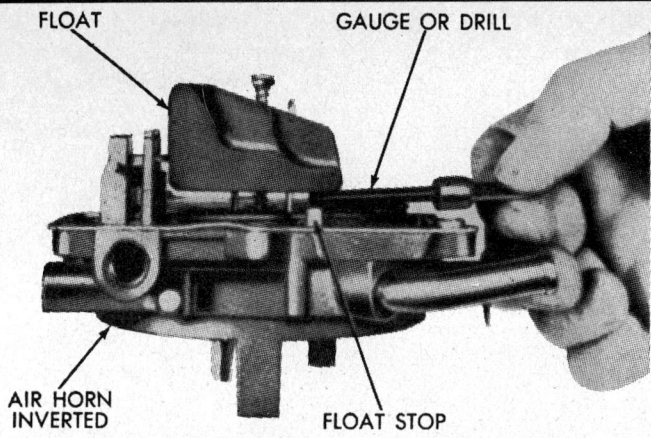

Fig. 47 Measuring float level. 2210 & 2245 carburetors

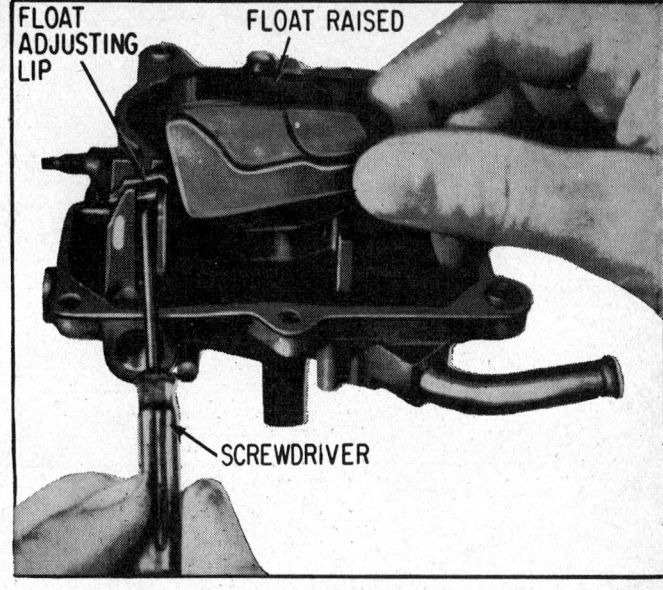

Fig. 48 Float adjustment. 2210 & 2245 carburetors

NOTE: Do not apply twisting or bending force to diaphragm.

After completion of adjustment, reinstall vacuum hose on correct carburetor fitting. Return fast idle screw to its original location if disturbed. Make following check. With no vacuum applied to diaphragm, the choke valve should move freely between open and closed positions. If movement is not free, examine linkage for misalignment or interferences caused by bending operation.

Choke Unloader (Wide Open Kick) Adjustment

Fig. 52—With throttle valves in wide open position, insert drill gauge between upper edge of choke valve and inner wall of air horn. Refer to the specifications chart. With a finger lightly pressing against shaft lever, a slight drag should be felt as drill is being withdrawn. Adjust by bending unloader tang on throttle lever until correct opening has been obtained.

Accelerator Pump Adjustment

Fig. 53—Back off curb idle speed adjusting screw. Open choke valve so that fast idle cam allows throttle valves to be completely seated in bores. Be sure that pump connector rod is installed in correct slot of accelerator pump rocker arm. First slot for manual transmissions next to attaching screw.

Close throttle valves tightly. Measure the distance between top of air horn and end of plunger shaft. Refer to the specifications chart. Adjust pump travel by bending pump operating rod, at loop of rod, until correct setting has been obtained.

Bowl Vent Valve Clearance Adjustment

Fig. 54—With the throttle valves at curb idle, it should be possible to insert an inch gauge between the bowl vent valve plunger stem and operating rod. Refer to the specifications chart. Adjust by bending the tang on pump lever to change arc of contact with throttle lever, until correct clearance has been obtained.

MODEL 2280

This carburetor, Fig. 55, uses four basic metering systems. The basic idle system provides the proper air/fuel mixture for idle and low speed operations. The accelerator pump

Fig. 49 Checking float drop. 2210 & 2245 carburetors

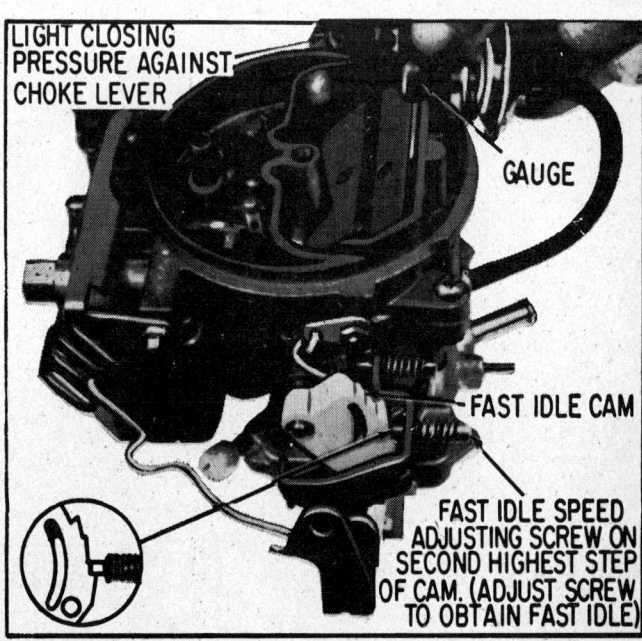

Fig. 50 Fast idle cam position adjustment. 2210 & 2245 carburetors

DODGE & PLYMOUTH

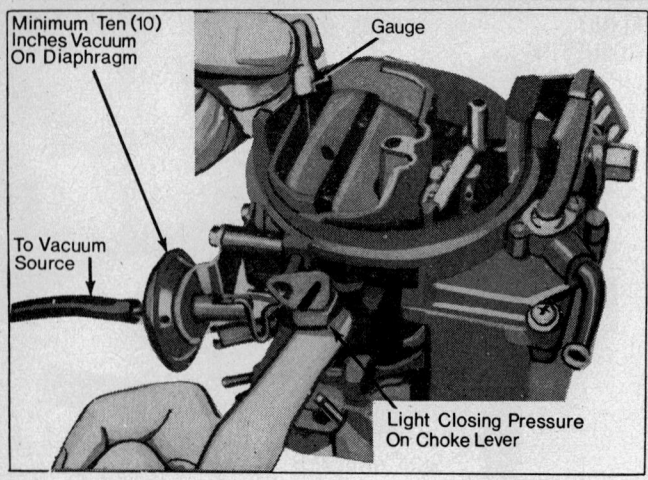

Fig. 51 Vacuum kick adjustment. 2210 & 2245 carburetors

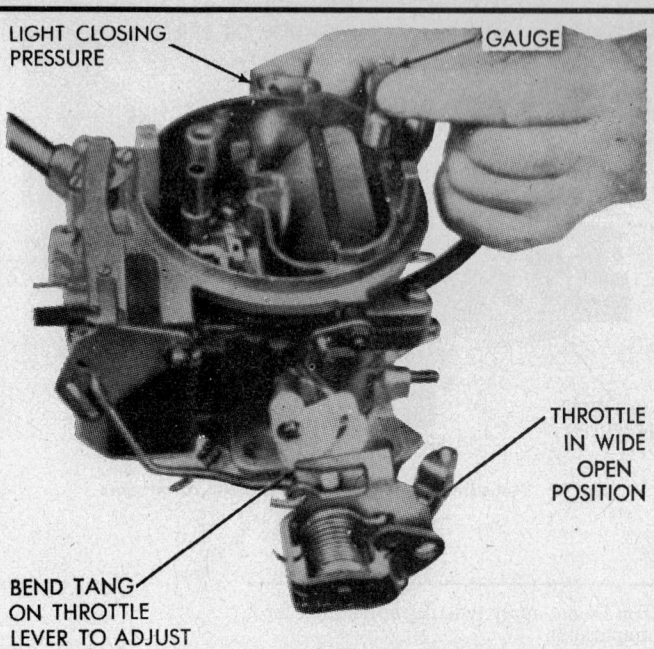

Fig. 52 Choke unloader adjustment. 2210 & 2245 carburetors

system provides additional fuel during acceleration. The main metering system provides the proper air/fuel mixture during normal cruising conditions. The power enrichment system, combining a mechanical and vacuum operated power valve, provides a richer mixture when higher engine power is required.

In addition to the four basic systems, there is a fuel inlet system which supplies fuel to the four basic systems and a choke system which temporarily enriches the mixture to aid in starting and running a cold engine.

Float Adjustment

Fig. 56—Invert main body so the weight of the floats only is forcing the needle against the seat. Hold finger against hinge pin retainer to fully seat in the float hinge cradle. Using a suitable scale, measure distance between the float bowl surface and the toe of each float. To adjust, bend the float tang. If necessary, bend either float arm to equalize individual float positions.

Accelerator Pump Adjustment

Fig. 57—Remove bowl vent cover plate and vent valve spring. Do not dislodge vent valve lever retainer. Ensure that accelerator pump rod is in the inner hole of the pump operating lever and the throttle is at curb idle. Place a straight edge on bowl vent cover surface of air horn over accelerator pump lever. Adjust until lever surface is flush with air horn surface by bending the accelerator pump connector rod. Install vent valve lever spring and bowl vent cover plate.

NOTE: If this adjustment is changed, the bowl vent and mechanical power valve adjustments must be reset.

Choke Unloader Adjustment

Fig. 58—Hold throttle valves in wide open position. Lightly press finger against control lever to move choke valve toward closed position. Insert specified gauge between top of

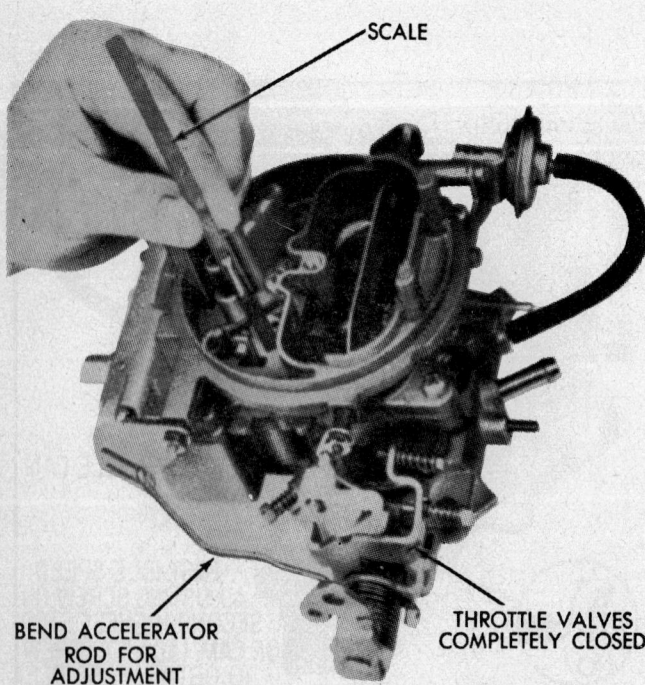

Fig. 53 Accelerator pump adjustment. 2210 & 2245 carburetors

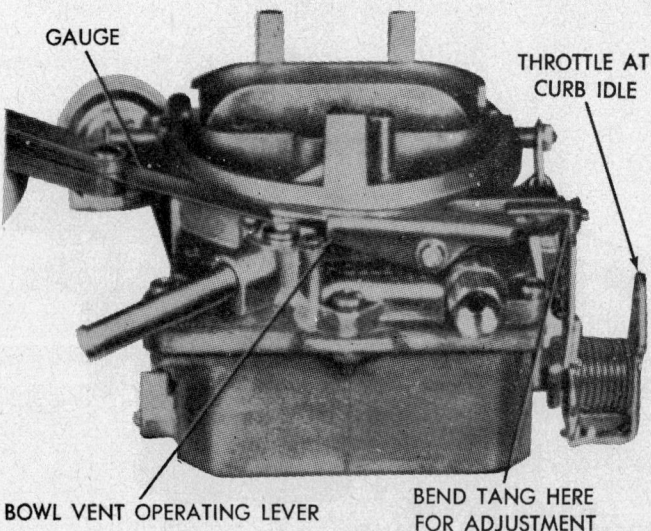

Fig. 54 Bowl vent adjustment. 2210 & 2245 carburetors

DODGE & PLYMOUTH

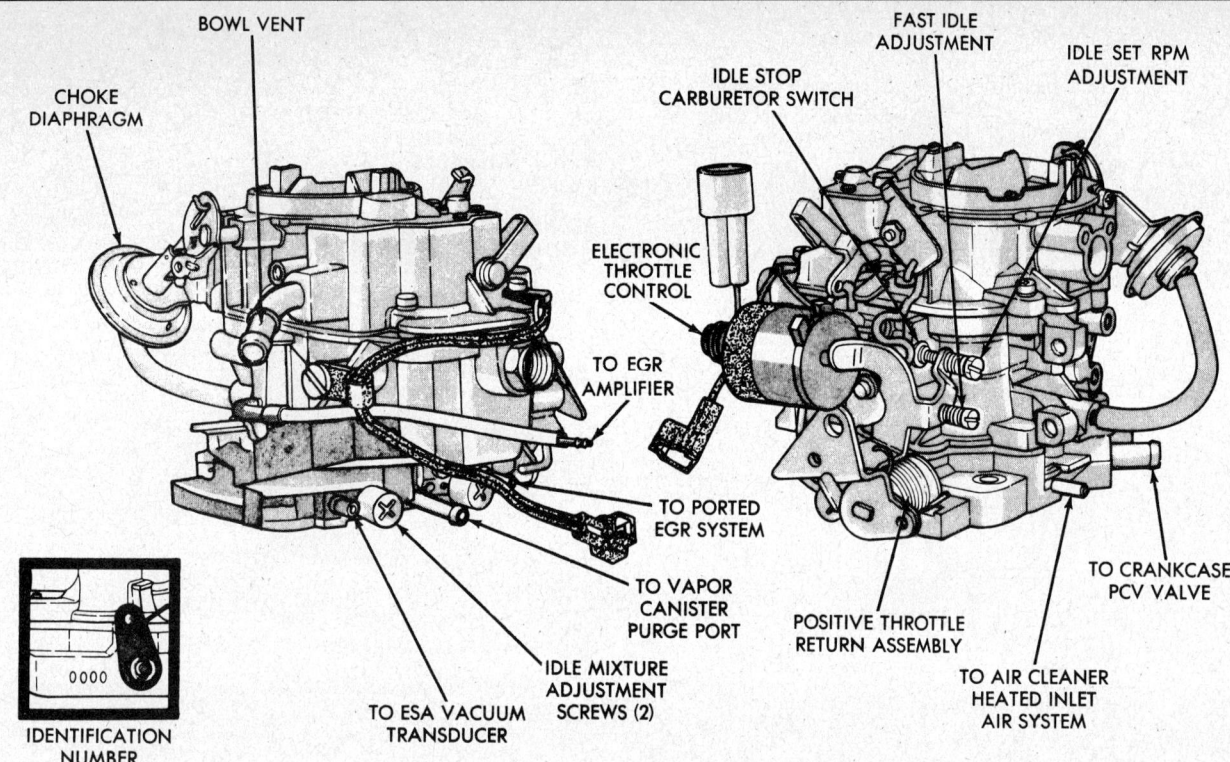

Fig. 55 Holley model 2280 two barrel carburetor

choke valve and air horn wall. To adjust, bend tang on accelerator pump lever.

Choke Vacuum Kick Adjustment

Fig. 59—Open throttle, close choke, then close throttle to trap fast idle cam at closed choke position. Apply approximately 15 inches of vacuum to diaphragm with an external vacuum source. Apply closing pressure on choke lever to completely compress spring in diaphragm stem without distorting linkage. The cylindrical stem of the diaphragm extends to a stop as the spring compresses.

Insert specified gauge between top of choke valve and air horn wall. Adjust by bending diaphragm link at U-bend. Check for free movement between the open and adjusted positions.

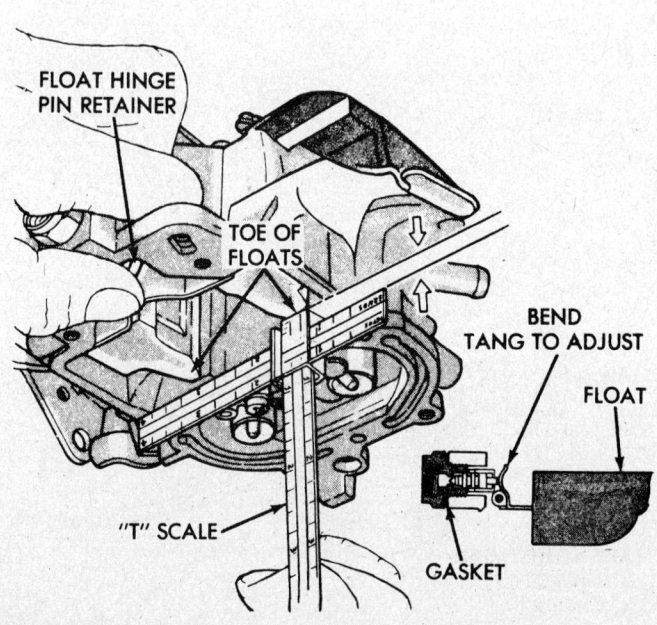

Fig. 56 Float adjustment. 2280 carburetor

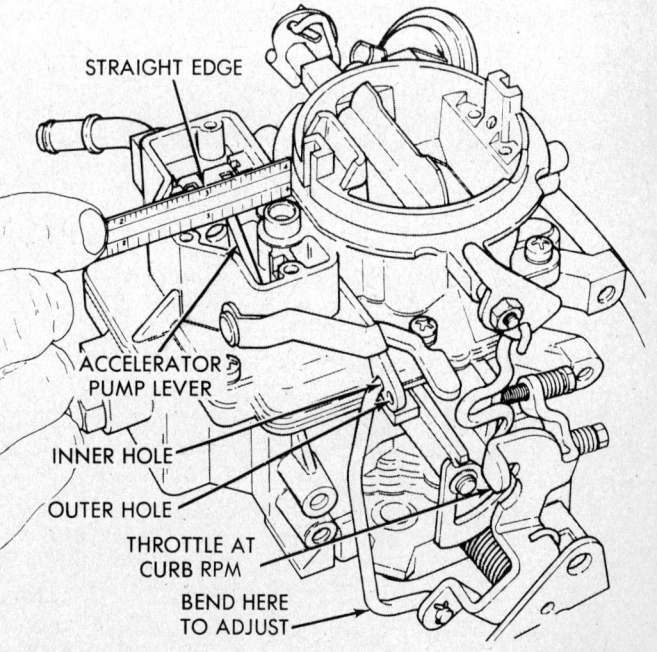

Fig. 57 Accelerator pump adjustment. 2280 carburetor

DODGE & PLYMOUTH

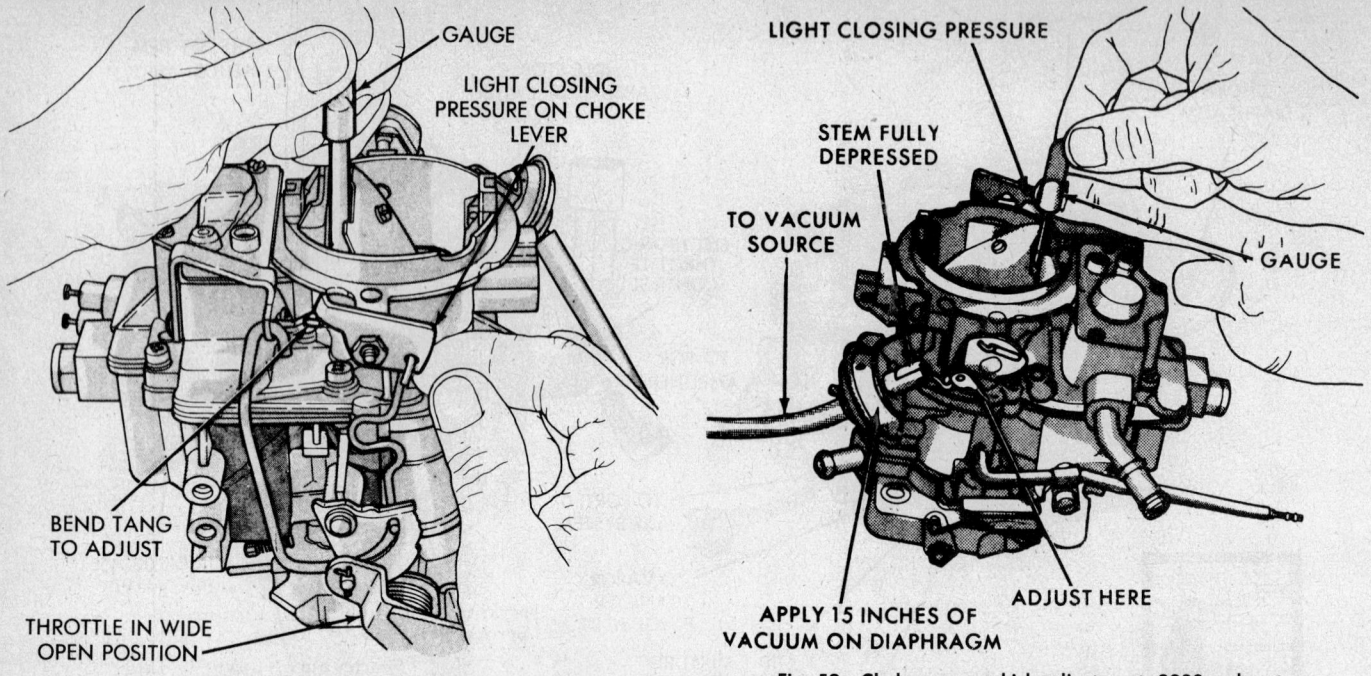

Fig. 58 Choke unloader adjustment. 2280 carburetor

Fig. 59 Choke vacuum kick adjustment. 2280 carburetor

Fast Idle Cam Position Adjustment

Fig. 60—With fast idle speed adjusting screw contacting second highest step of fast idle cam, move choke valve toward closed position with light pressure on choke shaft lever. Insert specified gauge between top of choke valve and air horn wall. To adjust, bend the U-bend in fast idle connector link to obtain proper setting.

Bowl Vent Valve Adjustment

Fig. 61—Remove bowl vent cover plate and vent valve lever spring. Do not dislodge vent valve lever retainer. With throttle at curb idle, press downward on vent valve lever where spring seats. Measure distance between contact surfaces of vent valve tang and vent valve lever. Adjust by bending end of vent valve lever. Install vent valve lever spring and bowl vent cover plate.

Mechanical Power Valve Adjustment

Fig. 62—Remove bowl vent cover plate, vent

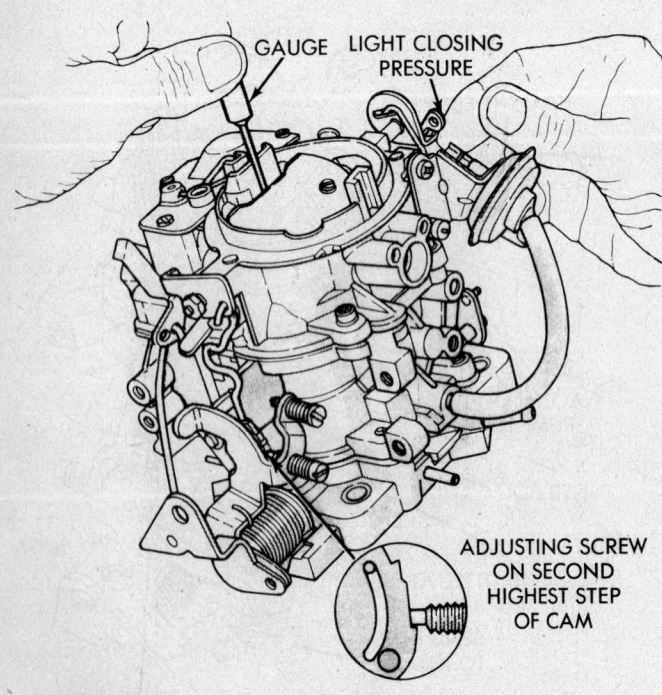

Fig. 60 Fast idle cam position adjustment. 2280 carburetor

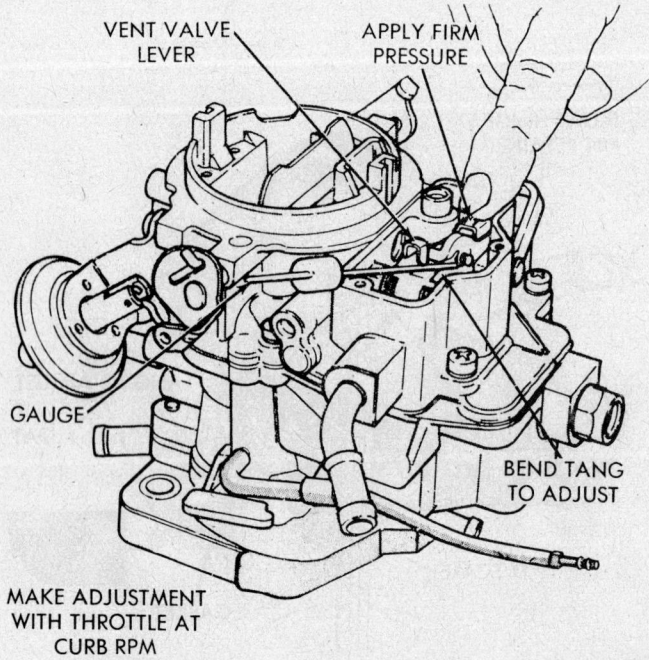

Fig. 61 Bowl vent valve adjustment. 2280 carburetor

DODGE & PLYMOUTH

valve lever spring and retainer, then the vent valve lever and pivot pin. Hold throttle in wide open position. Insert a 5/64 inch allen wrench in mechanical power valve adjustment screw. Push screw downward and release to determine if clearance exists. Turn screw clockwise until zero clearance is obtained. Adjust by turning screw one turn counter-clockwise. Install vent valve lever, pivot pin and retainer, then the vent valve lever spring and bowl vent cover plate.

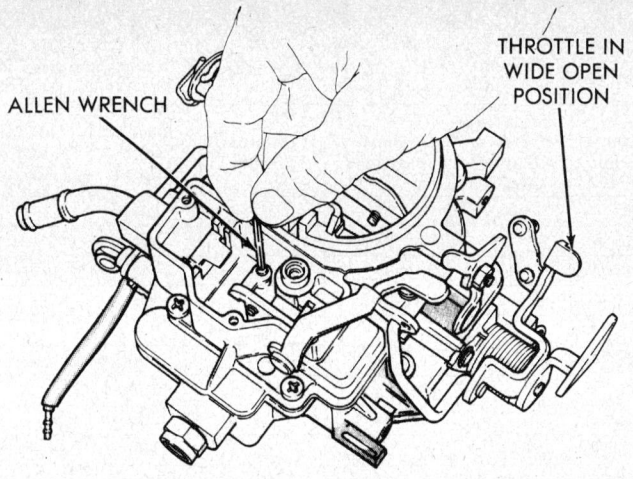

Fig. 62 Mechanical power valve adjustment. 2280 carburetor

CARTER BBS ADJUSTMENT SPECIFICATIONS

See Tune Up Chart for hot idle speed.

Year	Model	Float Level	Pump Setting	Bowl Vent	Choke Unloader	Fast Idle Cam Position	Fast Idle Speed RPM	Choke Vacuum Kick	Automatic Choke Setting
1970–71	4629S	1/4	①	.060	—	—	—	—	—
	4630S	1/4	①	.060	3/16	.076	1550	.110	2 Rich
	4658S	1/4	①	.060	—	—	—	—	—
	4659S	1/4	①	.060	3/16	.076	700②	.110	2 Rich
	4703S	1/4	①	.060	—	—	—	—	—
1970–73	4905S	1/4	①	.060	—	—	—	—	—
	6218S	1/4	5/16	.030	3/16	.076	1800	.110	Fixed
	6219S	1/4	5/16	.030	3/16	.076	2000	.110	Fixed
1972–73	6220S	1/4	5/16	.030	—	—	—	—	—
1973	6395S	1/4	5/16	.030	3/16	.076	2000	.110	Fixed
	6396S	1/4	5/16	.030	3/16	.076	1800	.075	Fixed
1974	7044S	1/4	—	—	3/16	.076	2000	.110	Fixed
	7045S	1/4	—	—	3/16	.076	1800	.075	Fixed

①—Pump is automatically set when bowl vent is properly adjusted.
②—With speed screw on lowest step of cam.

CARTER BBD ADJUSTMENT SPECIFICATIONS

See Tune Up Chart for hot idle speed.

Year	Carb. Model	Idle Mix. Screws Turns Open	Float Setting	Pump Setting	Bowl Vent Adjust	Fast Idle Linkage Adjust	Fast Idle Throttle Valve Clearance	Fast Idle R.P.M.	Choke Unloader Adjust	Choke Diaphragm Linkage Adjust	Choke Setting
BBD MODELS											
1970	4825S	—	1/4	①	1/16	—	—	1500	—	—	—
	4827S	1 1/2	1/4	—	1/16	—	—	1600	1/4	—	2 Rich
	4828S	—	1/4	①	1/32	—	—	1400	—	—	—

Continued

DODGE & PLYMOUTH

CARTER BBD ADJUSTMENT SPECIFICATIONS—Continued

See Tune Up Chart in truck chapters for hot idle speeds.

Year	Carb. Model	Idle Mix. Screws Turns Open	Float Setting	Pump Setting	Bowl Vent Adjust	Fast Idle Linkage Adjust	Fast Idle Throttle Valve Clearance	Fast Idle R.P.M.	Choke Unloader Adjust	Choke Diaphragm Linkage Adjust	Choke Setting
1971	4723S	—	1/4	①	1/32	—	41 Drill ⑤	1600	1/4	20 Drill	Index
	4724S	—	1/4	①	1/32	—	41 Drill ⑤	2000	1/4	20 Drill	Index
	4824S	—	1/4	①	1/32	—	41 Drill ⑤	2000	1/4	20 Drill	Index
	4825S	—	1/4	—	1/32	—	—	1500	—	—	—
	4828S	—	1/4	—	1/32	—	—	1400	—	—	—
	6149S	—	1/4	—	.200	—	—	1700	1/4	—	—
	6150S	—	1/4	—	.200	—	—	1900	1/4	—	—
	6151S	—	1/4	—	.200	—	—	1800	1/4	—	—
	6152S	—	1/4	—	.200	—	—	2000	1/4	—	—
	6169S	1 1/2	1/4	—	1/16	—	—	1600	1/4	—	2 Rich
	6221S	—	1/4	—	1/32	—	—	1700	1/4	—	—
	6222S	—	1/4	—	1/32	—	—	1900	1/4	—	—
	6223S	—	1/4	—	1/32	—	—	1900	—	—	—
	6228S	—	1/4	—	1/32	—	—	1700	—	—	—
1972	6223S	—	1/4	—	1/32	—	—	1900	—	—	—
	6225S	1 1/2	1/4	—	1/16	—	—	1600	1/4	—	2 Rich
1972-73	6228S	—	1/4	—	1/32	—	—	1400	—	—	—
1973	6365S	—	1/4	—	.200	—	—	1500	—	—	—
	6368S	—	1/4	—	.200	—	—	1400	—	—	—
1973-74	6221S	—	1/4	.280	—	.095	—	1700	1/4	—	—
	6222S	—	1/4	.280	—	.095	—	1700	1/4	—	—
	6224S	—	1/4	.340	—	—	—	1900	—	—	—
	6228S	—	1/4	.340	—	—	—	1600	—	—	—
	6229S	—	1/4	.390	—	—	—	1600	—	—	—
	6316S	—	1/4	.280	—	.095	—	1700	1/4	—	—
	6317S	—	1/4	.280	—	.095	—	1700	1/4	—	—
	6343S	—	1/4	.280	—	.095	—	1700	1/4	—	—
	6344S	—	1/4	.280	—	.095	—	1700	1/4	—	—
	6363S	—	1/4	.310	—	.095	—	1600	1/4	—	—
	6364S	—	1/4	.310	—	.095	—	1700	1/4	—	—
	6365S	—	1/4	.340	—	—	—	1900	—	—	—
	6367S	—	1/4	.200	—	.095	—	1800	1/4	—	2 Rich
	6368S	—	1/4	.310	—	—	—	1600	—	—	—
1974	6610S	—	1/4	1/2	—	.095	—	1700	.28	.150	—
	6611S	—	1/4	1/2	—	.095	—	1500	.28	.110	—
	6613S	—	1/4	1/2	—	.095	—	1600	.28	.110	—
	8008S	—	1/4	1/2	—	.095	—	1700	.28	.150	—
1974-76	6537S	—	1/4	1/2	—	.095	—	1500	.31	.110	—
	6540S	—	1/4	1/2	—	.095	—	1700	.25	—	—
	6585S	—	1/4	1/2	—	—	—	1900	—	—	—
	6586S	—	1/4	1/2	—	—	—	1900	—	—	—
1974-77	6536S	—	1/4	1/2	—	.095	—	1700	.28	.150	—
1975-76	8013S	—	1/4	1/2	—	.070	—	1500	.31	.130	—
	8014S	—	1/4	1/2	—	.070	—	1500	.31	.110	—
	8016S	—	1/4	1/2	—	.070	—	1500	.31	.130	—
	8020S	—	1/4	1/2	—	.070	—	1500	.28	.130	—
	8024S	—	1/4	1/2	—	.070	—	1500	.28	.130	—
	8025S	—	1/4	1/2	—	.070	—	1500	.31	.070	—
	8026S	—	1/4	1/2	—	.070	—	1500	.31	.110	—
1977	8081S	—	1/4	1/2	—	.070	—	1500	.310	.150	—
	8082S	—	1/4	1/2	—	.070	—	1500	.280	.130	—
	8085S	—	1/4	1/2	—	.070	—	1500	.280	.130	—
	8108S	—	1/4	1/2	—	.070	—	1500	.310	.150	—

Continued

DODGE & PLYMOUTH

CARTER BBD ADJUSTMENT SPECIFICATIONS—Continued

Year	Carb. Model	Idle Mix. Screws Turns Open	Float Setting	Pump Setting	Bowl Vent Adjust	Fast Idle Linkage Adjust	Fast Idle Throttle Valve Clearance	Fast Idle R.P.M.	Choke Unloader Adjust	Choke Diaphragm Linkage Adjust	Choke Setting
	8110S	—	1/4	1/2	—	.070	—	1500	.280	.095	—
	8112S	—	1/4	1/2	—	.070	—	1500	.310	.110	—
	8113S	—	1/4	1/2	—	.070	—	1500	.310	.130	—
	8115S	—	1/4	1/2	—	.070	—	1500	.280	.130	—
	8121S	—	1/4	1/2	—	.070	—	1500	.310	.070	—
	8146S	—	1/4	1/2	—	.070	—	1500	.310	.070	—
	8147S	—	1/4	1/2	—	.095	—	1700	.280	.150	—
1978	8146S	—	1/4	1/2	—	.070	—	1600	.280	—	—
	8147S	—	1/4	1/2	—	.070	—	1500	.310	.070	—
	8149S	—	1/4	1/2	—	.070	—	1500	.280	.130	—
	8151S	—	1/4	1/2	—	.070	—	1500	.280	.130	—
	8152S	—	1/4	1/2	—	.070	—	1500	.280	.130	—
	8154S	—	1/4	1/2	—	.070	—	1500	.310	.130	—
	8156S	—	1/4	1/2	—	.070	—	1500	.310	.110	—
	8176S	—	1/4	1/2	—	.070	—	⑥	.310	.070	—
	8180S	—	1/4	1/2	—	.070	—	1500	.280	.150	—
1979	8210S	—	1/4	1/2	—	.070	—	1400	.280	.110	—
	8211S	—	1/4	1/2	—	.070	—	1500	.280	.110	—
	8214S	—	1/4	1/2	—	.070	—	1400	.280	.110	—
	8215S	—	1/4	1/2	—	.070	—	1600	.280	.110	—
	8230S	—	1/4	1/2	—	.070	—	1600	.250	.190	—
	8232S	—	1/4	1/2	—	.070	—	1500	.280	.110	—
	8249S	—	1/4	1/2	—	.070	—	1400	.280	.110	—

① —Pump is automatically adjusted when bowl vent is properly adjusted.
② —With fast idle screw on second step and against shoulder of first step of cam.
③ —With speed screw on lowest step of cam.
④ —Automatic transmission, 1400 RPM; manual transmission, 1700 RPM.
⑤ —With fast idle screw on second highest step of cam.
⑥ —Automatic transmission, 1700 RPM; manual transmission, 1600 RPM.

CARTER TQ ADJUSTMENT SPECIFICATIONS

See Tune Up Chart in truck chapters for hot idle speeds.

Year	Carb. Model	Float Setting	Secondary Throttle Linkage	Secondary Air Valve Opening	Secondary Air Valve Spring	Pump Travel @ Curb Idle	Pump Travel @ Secondary Pick-up	Choke Control Lever (Off Vehicle)	Choke Vacuum Kick	Choke Unloader	Fast Idle R.P.M.
1972-73	6446S	1	①	15/32	1 1/4	1/2	—	3 3/8	.160	.190	1700
	6518S	1	①	15/32	1 1/4	1/2	—	3 3/8	.160	.190	1700
1973	6582S	1	①	29/64	1 1/4	1/2	—	3 3/8	.160	.190	1800
1974	9017S	②	①	1/2	1 1/4	1/2	—	3 3/8	.160	.310	1700
	9022S	②	①	1/2	1 1/4	1/2	5/16	3 3/8	.210	.310	1800
	9025S	②	①	1/2	1 1/4	1/2	5/16	3 3/8	.160	.310	1700
1974-76	9036S	②	①	1/2	1 1/4	1/2	5/16	3 3/8	.160	.310	1700
1974-77	6545S	②	①	1/2	1 1/4	1/2	5/16	3 3/8	.160	.310	1700
1975-76	9034S	29/32	①	1/2	1 1/4	1/2	5/16	3 3/8	.160	.310	1700
	9035S	29/32	①	1/2	1 1/4	1/2	5/16	3 3/8	.160	.310	1700
1977	9096S	29/32	①	1/2	1 1/4	1/2	5/16	3 3/8	.100	.310	1700
1978	9116S	29/32	①	1/2	1 1/4	1/2	5/16	3 3/8	.100	.500	1600
	9117S	29/32	①	1/2	1 1/4	1/2	5/16	3 3/8	.100	.310	1700
	9118S	29/32	①	1/2	1 1/4	1/2	5/16	3 3/8	.160	.310	1700
	9123S	29/32	①	1/2	2	1/2	5/16	3 3/8	.150	.500	1600

Continued

DODGE & PLYMOUTH

CARTER TQ ADJUSTMENT SPECIFICATIONS—Continued

See Tune Up Chart in truck chapters for hot idle speeds.

Year	Carb. Model	Float Setting	Secondary Throttle Linkage	Secondary Air Valve Opening	Secondary Air Valve Spring	Pump Travel @ Curb Idle	Pump Travel @ Secondary Pick-up	Choke Control Lever (Off Vehicle)	Choke Vacuum Kick	Choke Unloader	Fast Idle R.P.M.
	9124S	29/32	①	1/2	2	1/2	5/16	3 3/8	.100	.500	1600
	9125S	29/32	①	1/2	2	1/2	5/16	3 3/8	.150	.500	1700
	9126S	29/32	①	1/2	2	1/2	5/16	3 3/8	.100	.500	1600
	9149S	29/32	①	1/2	1 1/2	1/2	5/16	3 3/8	.100	.500	1600
	9173S	29/32	①	1/2	1 1/4	1/2	5/16	3 3/8	.150	.310	1500
1978–79	9150S	29/32	①	1/2	2	1/2	5/16	3 3/8	.100	.500	1400
	9151S	29/32	①	1/2	2	1/2	5/16	3 3/8	.160	.500	1400
1979	9207S	29/32	①	7/16	2	31/64	23/64	3.30	.150	.310	1600
	9208S	29/32	①	7/16	2	31/64	23/64	3.30	.150	.310	1600
	9209S	29/32	①	7/16	2	31/64	23/64	3.30	.150	.310	1600
	9210S	29/32	①	1/2	2	31/64	23/64	3.30	.150	.310	1600
	9211S	29/32	①	1/2	1 1/2	31/64	23/64	3.30	.100	.500	1400
	9212S	29/32	①	1/2	1 1/2	31/64	23/64	3.30	.100	.500	1400
	9223S	29/32	①	1/2	3	11/32	9/64	3.30	.100	.500	1600
	9224S	29/32	①	1/2	3	5/16	3/16	3.30	.100	.500	1600
	9225S	29/32	①	1/2	3	5/16	3/16	3.30	.100	.500	1600
	9226S	27/32	①	1/2	2 5/8	31/64	23/64	3.30	.100	.310	1750
	9228S	29/32	①	1/2	3	11/32	3/16	3.30	.100	.500	1600
	9229S	29/32	①	1/2	3	11/32	3/16	3.30	.100	.500	1600
	9247S	29/32	①	7/16	1 1/2	31/64	23/64	3.30	.100	.500	1400
	9248S	29/32	①	7/16	1 1/2	31/64	23/64	3.30	.100	.500	1400
1980	9251S	29/32	①	7/16	See Text	.340	.190	3 3/8	.150	.310	1600
	9252S	29/32	①	7/16	See Text	.340	.190	3 3/8	.150	.310	1600
	9254S	29/32	①	3/8	See Text	.340	.190	3 3/8	.150	.310	1500
	9261S	29/32	①	7/16	See Text	.340	.190	3 3/8	.130	.310	1600
	9265S	29/32	①	7/16	See Text	.340	.140	3 3/8	.150	.310	1600
	9279S	29/32	①	3/8	See Text	.340	.190	3 3/8	.130	.310	1800
	9281S	29/32	①	3/8	See Text	.340	.190	3 3/8	.180	.310	1800
	9292S	29/32	①	7/16	See Text	.340	.190	3 3/8	.130	.310	1600
	9296S	29/32	①	3/8	See Text	.340	.140	3 3/8	.110	.310	1500
	9300S	29/32	①	3/8	See Text	.340	.190	3 3/8	.180	.310	1800

①—Adjust link so primary & secondary stops both contact at same time.
②—Brass float, 1 inch; cellular plastic float, 29/32 inch.

HOLLEY ADJUSTMENT SPECIFICATIONS

See Tune Up Chart in truck chapters for hot idle speed.

Year	Carb. Model	Carb. Part No.	Idle Mix. Screw Turns Open	Float Level Dry	Fuel Level Wet	Vacuum Kick	Fast Idle Cam Position	Bowl Vent Valve	Fast Idle Speed	Auto. Choke Setting
1970	852	R-4428A	—	1 1/4	5/8	—	—	—	—	—
	2140	R-4430A	—	1/4	1/2	—	—	—	—	—
	2300	R-3652A	1	See Text	See Text	—	.035	—	—	—
	2300	R-3653A	1	See Text	See Text	—	.035	—	—	—
	4150	R-3270A	1	See Text	See Text	—	.066	—	—	—
	4150C	R-4399A	1 1/2	See Text	See Text	.085	#65	—	1900	2 Rich
1971	1920	R-4356A	—	See Text	27/32	39 Drill	52 Drill	3/32	1600①	2 Rich
	1920	R-4357A	—	See Text	27/32	39 Drill	52 Drill	3/32	1600①	2 Rich
	1920	R-4358A	—	See Text	27/32	39 Drill	52 Drill	3/32	1800①	2 Rich

Continued

DODGE & PLYMOUTH

HOLLEY ADJUSTMENT SPECIFICATIONS—Continued

Year	Carb. Model	Carb. Part No.	Idle Mix. Screw Turns Open	Float Level Dry	Fuel Level Wet	Vacuum Kick	Fast Idle Cam Position	Bowl Vent Valve	Fast Idle Speed	Auto. Choke Setting
	1920	R-4359A	—	See Text	27/32	39 Drill	52 Drill	3/32	1800①	2 Rich
	1920	R-4641A	—	See Text	27/32	59 Drill	52 Drill	3/32	1680①	2 Rich
	1920	R-4642A	—	See Text	27/32	39 Drill	52 Drill	3/32	1800①	2 Rich
	1920	R-6371A	—	See Text	27/32	39 Drill	52 Drill	.015	2000	—
	1920	R-6372A	—	See Text	27/32	39 Drill	52 Drill	.015	1900	—
	1920	R-6401A	—	See Text	27/32	39 Drill	52 Drill	.015	2200	—
	1920	R-6402A	—	See Text	27/32	39 Drill	52 Drill	.015	2000	—
	2210	R-6161A	—	.180	—	28 Drill	35 Drill	.015	2000	—
	2210	R-6162A	—	.180	—	30 Drill	35 Drill	.015	2000	—
	2210	R-6163A	—	.180	—	28 Drill	35 Drill	.015	2000	—
	2210	R-6164A	—	.180	—	30 Drill	35 Drill	.015	2000	—
	2210	R-6275A	—	.180	—	28 Drill	35 Drill	.075	2000	—
	2210	R-6276A	—	.180	—	30 Drill	35 Drill	.075	2000	—
	2210	R-6368A	—	.180	—	30 Drill	35 Drill	.015	1900	—
	2210	R-6370A	—	.180	—	30 Drill	35 Drill	.015	2000	—
	2210	R-6373A	—	—	—	28 Drill	35 Drill	.075	2000	—
	2210	R-6374A	—	—	—	30 Drill	35 Drill	.075	2000	—
	2300	R-6277A	1	See Text	See Text	—	—	—	—	—
	2300	R-6278A	1	See Text	See Text	—	—	—	—	—
	4150	R-4399A	1½	See Text	See Text	—	.066	—	1900	2 Rich
	4150C	R6189A	1½	See Text	See Text	.070	#65	.015	1900	2 Rich
1972	2140	R-4430-2	—	¼	½	—	—	—	—	—
	4160	R-6231A	1	See Text	See Text	5 Drill	46 Drill	—	1900	2 Rich
	4160C	R6231A	1½	See Text	See Text	.070	#65	.015	1900	2 Rich
1972-73	2300	R-6277A	1	See Text	See Text	—	.035	—	—	—
	2300	R-6278A	1	See Text	See Text	—	.035	—	—	—
	4150	R-6279A	1	See Text	See Text	—	.066	—	—	—
1973	2140	R-6456	—	¼	½	—	—	—	—	—
	2300	R-6493A	1	See Text	See Text	—	.035	—	—	—
1973-74	1920	R6593A	—	See Text	See Text	.100	.065	.015	2000	—
	1920	R6594A	—	See Text	See Text	.100	.065	.015	1700	—
	1920	R6595A	—	See Text	See Text	.100	.065	.015	2000	—
	1920	R6596A	—	See Text	See Text	.100	.065	.015	1700	—
	2210	R6452A	—	.180	See Text	.150	.110	.015	1900	—
	2210	R6454A	—	.180	See Text	.150	.110	.015	1800	—
	2210	R6472A	—	.180	See Text	.150	.110	.015	1800	—
	2210	R6484A	—	.180	See Text	.160	.110	.015	1900	—
	2210	R6485A	—	.180	See Text	.160	.110	.015	1900	—
	2210	R6486A	—	.180	See Text	.110	.110	.015	1800	—
	2210	R6487A	—	.180	See Text	.160	.110	.015	1800	—
	2210	R6488A	—	.180	See Text	.110	.110	.015	1800	—
	2210	R6575A	—	.180	See Text	.150	.110	.015	1900	—
	2300	R6277A	1	See Text	See Text	—	.035	—	—	—
	2300	R6278A	1	See Text	See Text	—	.035	—	—	—
	4160C	R6495A	1	See Text	See Text	.070	#65 Drill	.015	1800	2 Rich
1974	1945	R6725A	—	See Text	See Text	.140	.080	—	1600	—
	1945	R6921A	—	See Text	See Text	.140	.080	—	1600	—
	1945	R6875A	—	See Text	See Text	.090	.080	—	1800	—
	2210	R6764A	—	.180	See Text	.150	.110	—	1700	—
	2210	R-6765A	—	.180	See Text	.150	.110	—	1800	—
	2210	R6775A	—	.180	See Text	.150	.110	—	1800	—
	2210	R-6886A	—	.180	See Text	.150	.110	—	1800	—
	2210	R-7052A	—	.180	See Text	.160	.110	—	1800	—
	2245	R6762-1A	—	.180	See Text	.150	.110	—	1700	—

Continued

DODGE & PLYMOUTH

HOLLEY ADJUSTMENT SPECIFICATIONS—Continued

Year	Carb. Model	Carb. Part No.	Idle Mix. Screw Turns Open	Float Level Dry	Fuel Level Wet	Vacuum Kick	Fast Idle Cam Position	Bowl Vent Valve	Fast Idle Speed	Auto. Choke Setting
	2245	R6860A	—	.180	See Text	.150	.110	—	1800	—
	2245	R-6990A	—	.180	See Text	.150	.110	.015	1600	—
	2300	R-6769A	1	See Text	See Text	—	.035	—	—	—
	2300	R-6770A	1	See Text	See Text	—	.035	—	—	—
	4150	R-6771A	1	See Text	See Text	—	.066	—	—	—
	4150	R-7138A	—	See Text	See Text	—	.035	—	—	—
1975-76	1945	R-7074A	—	3/64	—	.110	.080	—	1600	—
	1945	R-7076A	—	3/64	—	.090	.080	—	1700	—
	1945	R-7078A	—	3/64	—	.110	.080	—	1600	—
	1945	R-7079A	—	3/64	—	.090	.080	—	1700	—
	1945	R-7080A	—	3/64	—	.110	.080	—	1600	—
	1945	R-7081A	—	3/64	—	.090	.080	—	1700	—
	1945	R-7082A	—	3/64	—	.110	.080	—	1600	—
	1945	R-7083A	—	3/64	—	.090	.080	—	1700	—
	2210	R-6764A	—	.180	See Text	.150	.110	—	1700	—
	2210	R-6765A	—	.180	See Text	.150	.110	—	1800	—
	2245	R-7088A	—	.180	See Text	.150	.110	—	1600	—
	2245	R-7089A	—	.180	See Text	.150	.110	—	1600	—
	2245	R-7090A	—	.180	See Text	.150	.110	—	1600	—
	2245	R-7091A	—	.180	See Text	.150	.110	—	1600	—
	2245	R-7092A	—	.180	See Text	.150	.110	—	1600	—
	2245	R-7103A	—	.180	See Text	.150	.110	—	1600	—
	2245	R-7187A	—	.180	See Text	.150	.110	—	1600	—
	2245	R-7188A	—	.180	See Text	.150	.110	—	1600	—
	2300	R-6769-1A	—	See Text	See Text	—	.035	—	—	—
	2300	R-7137A	—	See Text	See Text	—	.035	—	—	—
	4150	R-6771A	—	See Text	See Text	—	.035	—	—	—
	4150	R-7138A	—	See Text	See Text	—	.035	—	—	—
1977	1945	R-7815A	—	3/64	—	.110	.080	—	1600	—
	1945	R-7816A	—	3/64	—	.110	.080	—	1700	—
	1945	R-7847A	—	3/64	—	.110	.080	—	1600	—
	1945	R-7848A	—	3/64	—	.110	.080	—	1700	—
	1945	R-7849A	—	3/64	—	.110	.080	—	1600	—
	2210	R-6764A	—	.180	—	.150	.110	—	1700	—
	2210	R-6886A	—	.180	—	.150	.110	—	1600	—
	2210	R-6886-1A	—	.180	—	.150	.110	—	1400	—
	2210	R-7870A	—	.180	—	.150	.110	—	1800	—
	2245	R-7088A	—	.180	—	.150	.110	—	1600	—
	2245	R-7091A	—	.180	—	.150	.110	—	1600	—
	2245	R-7092A	—	.180	—	.150	.110	—	1600	—
	2245	R-7103A	—	.180	—	.150	.110	—	1600	—
	2245	R-7403A	—	.180	—	.150	.110	.025	1600	—
	2245	R-7697A	—	.180	—	.150	.110	—	1600	—
	2245	R-7698A	—	.180	—	.150	.110	—	1600	—
	2245	R-7871A	—	.180	—	.130	.110	—	1600	—
	2245	R-8036A	—	.180	—	.150	.110	—	1600	—
1977-78	2300	R-6769-1A	—	See Text	See Text	—	.035	—	—	—
	2300	R-7137A	—	See Text	See Text	—	.035	—	—	—
	4150	R-6771A	—	See Text	See Text	—	.035	—	—	—
	4150	R-7138A	—	See Text	See Text	—	.035	—	—	—
1978	2245	R-6886A	—	.180	—	.150	.110	—	1600	—
	2245	R-6886-1A	—	.180	—	.150	.110	—	1600	—
	2245	R-7088A	—	.180	—	.150	.110	—	1600	—
	2245	R-7871A	—	.180	—	.130	.110	—	1600	—
	2245	R-8026A	—	.180	—	.150	.110	.025	1600	—

Continued

DODGE & PLYMOUTH

HOLLEY ADJUSTMENT SPECIFICATIONS—Continued

Year	Carb. Model	Carb. Part No.	Idle Mix. Screw Turns Open	Float Level Dry	Fuel Level Wet	Vacuum Kick	Fast Idle Cam Position	Bowl Vent Valve	Fast Idle Speed	Auto. Choke Setting
	2245	R-8028A	—	.180	—	.150	.110	—	1600	—
	2245	R-8135A	—	.180	—	.150	.110	.025	1800	—
	2245	R-8453A	—	.180	—	.150	.110	.025	1700	—
	2245	R-8484A	—	.180	—	.150	.110	—	1600	—
1979	1945	R-8593A	—	See Text	See Text	.100	.080	.0625	1600	—
	1945	R-8594A	—	See Text	See Text	.100	.080	.0625	1600	—
	1945	R-8799A	—	See Text	See Text	.100	.080	.0625	1600	—
	1945	R-8800A	—	See Text	See Text	.100	.080	.0625	1600	—
	2245	R-8597A	—	.200	—	.110	.110	.025	1600	—
	2245	R-8598A	—	.200	—	.110	.110	.025	1600	—
	2245	R-8925A	—	.200	—	.110	.110	.025	1600	—
1980	1945	R-8120A	—	See Text	—	.130	.090	.060	1600	—
	1945	R-8721A	—	See Text	—	.130	.090	.060	1700	—
	1945	R-8978A	—	See Text	—	.130	.080	.060	1600	—
	1945	R-8979A	—	See Text	—	.130	.080	.060	1600	—
	2280	R-8999A	—	5/16	—	.130	.070	.030	1600	—
	2280	R-9000A	—	5/16	—	.130	.070	.030	1600	—
	2280	R-9001A	—	5/16	—	.150	.070	.030	1600	—
	2280	R-9209A	—	5/16	—	.150	.070	.030	1600	—

①—Engine hot and screw on lowest step of cam.

Clutch & Manual Transmission Section

NOTE: For Clark, Fuller, New Process, Spicer & Warner transmissions used on Dodge & Plymouth trucks, see the "name" chapter for service procedures and lubricant capacities.

CLUTCH PEDAL, ADJUST (MECHANICAL LINKAGE)

1970 A-100 Compact Models

Shorten or lengthen the clutch release fork rod by turning the adjustment nut until there is 3/16" free play of the clutch fork outer end. This will give the necessary 1" free play at the pedal.

1971-73 "B" Series, 1974-77 Ramcharger & Trailduster

Adjust fork rod by turning self-locking adjusting nut to provide 3/32 inch free movement at end of fork. This movement will provide 1 inch free play at pedal.

1974-77 "B" Series & Voyager; 1978-79 All

Shorten or lengthen clutch release fork rod by turning adjusting nut until there is .187 inch free movement at the clutch fork outer end. This will give the necessary 1 to 1 1/2 inch free play at pedal.

1970-71 All Except "B" Series

Shorten or lengthen clutch release fork by

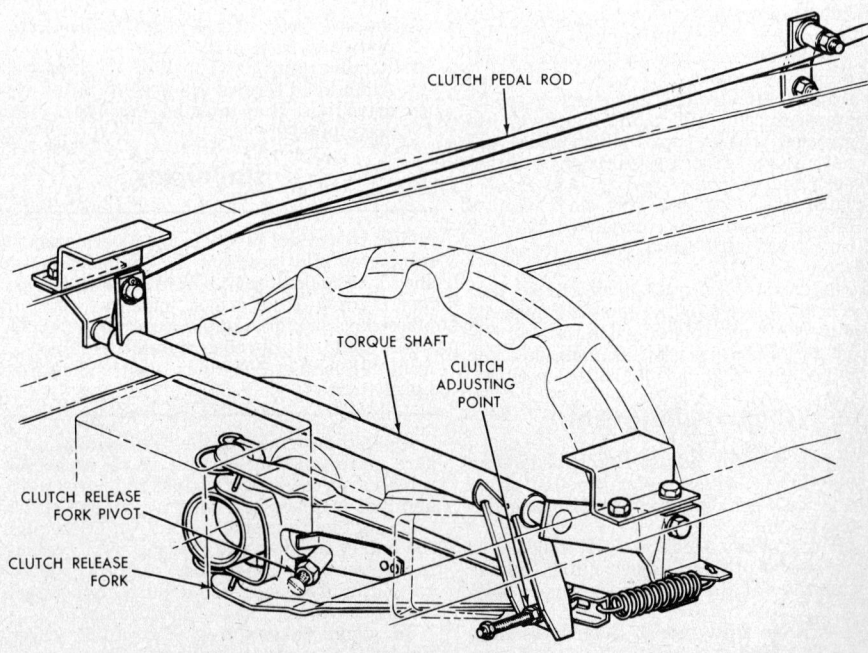

Fig. 1 Clutch linkage & adjusting rod. Medium Duty Tilt Cab

DODGE & PLYMOUTH

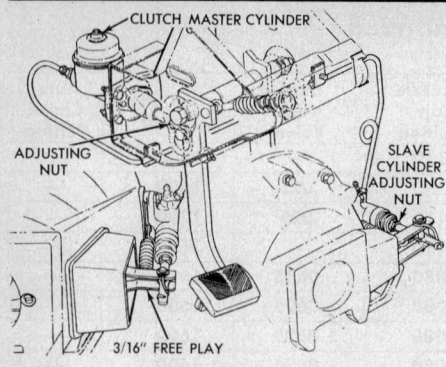

Fig. 2 Hydraulic clutch adjusting points. (Typical)

turning adjusting nut until there is 1/8 inch free play at clutch fork outer end. This provides 1½ inch free play at pedal.

1970-74 Tilt Cab

Adjust fork rod by turning adjusting nut until there is 3/16 inch free play at clutch fork outer end, Fig. 1. This will give the necessary 1 inch free play at pedal.

1975 L, LN, LNT-800 Series W/14 Inch Clutch

Release bearing free play of .069 inch as measured at clutch release shaft lever adjusting screw yields 1 to 1½ inches free play at pedal.

HYDRAULIC CLUTCH

A hydraulic master cylinder and slave cylinder replaces the mechanical linkage. The slave cylinder is connected to and operates the clutch release fork. The master cylinder and slave cylinder are serviced in a similar manner to a brake master cylinder.

When the master cylinder is installed on the dash panel and hydraulic line connected, connect the push rod end to the clutch pedal and adjust as follows:
1. Adjust clutch release over center spring adjusting end nut counterclockwise (to increase tension) until clutch pedal will not return to normal position with 3/4" open end wrench.
2. Turn adjusting end nut clockwise (to reduce tension) approximately 1½ to 2 turns or until good pedal return is achieved.

Adjust master cylinder push rod so that there is .010" free play between the push rod and master cylinder piston when the piston is in the fully returned position and when the clutch pedal is in its normal at rest position.

Clutch Adjustment

1. Inside the cab, adjust clutch pedal free play to 3/16", which is equal to .010" clearance between push rod and master cylinder piston.
2. On Light and Medium Duty models, at the slave cylinder, adjust clutch linkage free play at the clutch fork pivot pin to 3/16", Fig. 2.
3. On Heavy Duty models, adjust the linkage free play at the clutch fork shaft lever to Dimension "A", Fig. 3.

NOTE: On 1970-74 Heavy Duty models, Dimension "A", Fig. 3 is .120 inch.

4. Inside the cab, check clutch pedal reserve which should be a minimum of 1". Pedal reserve is that portion of pedal travel remaining after free play and complete clutch disengagement.

NOTE: If there is not enough pedal reserve, bleed the clutch hydraulic system to make sure there is no air in the system.

CLUTCH, REMOVE

Single Disc-Type

1. Remove the transmission.
2. Remove the clutch housing pan.
3. Remove clutch fork, bearing and sleeve assembly.
4. Mark clutch cover and flywheel to assure proper balance when clutch is installed.
5. Remove clutch cover retaining screws and pull the pressure plate clear of flywheel and, while supporting pressure plate, slide the disc from between flywheel and pressure plate. On some models it may be necessary to rotate the pressure plate to the point of maximum clearance. Then allow plate assembly to drop while tilting the top edge of the clutch cover back to clear the frame crossmember.

Two Plate Type

1. After transmission has been removed, insert two 3/4" blocks of wood between release bearing housing and spring plate. This facilitates removal of clutch-to-flywheel screws and protects the pull-back springs from excessive tension.
2. Remove clutch retaining screws and remove pressure plate and flywheel assembly.
3. Remove rear driven disc, intermediate plate and front driven disc.
4. Remove four drive pins from flywheel. Allen head screws are used to retain the drive pins. They must be removed to clear drive pins.

Installation

NOTE: Heavy duty models use a permanently lubricated pilot bearing. New pilot bushings should be soaked in oil before installing. Pilot bushing requires a grease which will stay in place during high temperature operation. A small amount of grease should be placed in front of bushing and inner surface should be lightly coated.

Clean the surfaces of the flywheel and pressure plate, making certain no oil or grease remains on these parts. Hold the cover plate and disc in place and insert a special clutch aligning tool or a spare clutch shaft through the hub of the disc and into the pilot bearing in the crankshaft. Bolt the clutch cover loosely to the flywheel, being sure that punch marks previously made are lined up.

To avoid distortion of the clutch cover, tighten the cover bolts a few turns each in progression until all are tight.

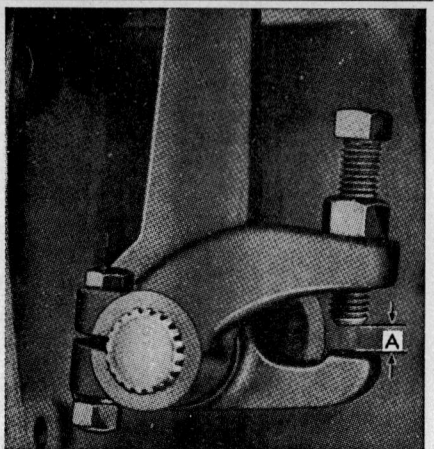

Fig. 3 Heavy duty clutch release bearing adjustment

Guide the transmission into place, using care to see that the driven disc is not bent. Use a floor jack to support the transmission so that the clutch shaft may be guided through the driven disc safely. Finally, adjust the clutch pedal free travel.

TRANSMISSION, REPLACE

Three Speed Units

Disconnect propeller shaft, speedometer cable, speedometer pinion sleeve, gearshift control rods and hand brake cable. Remove transmission-to-clutch housing bolts and pull transmission straight back until input shaft clears clutch disc and release levers before lowering transmission out of truck. Do not disengage clutch or otherwise move clutch or clutch disc unless it is to be removed for service.

Four Speed Overdrive

1. Remove gear shift components, then drain fluid from transmission.
2. Disconnect propeller shaft at rear universal joint, then carefully pull shaft yoke out of transmission housing.
3. Disconnect speedometer cable and back-up light switch.
4. Install engine lifting fixture and raise engine slightly.
5. Using a suitable jack, support transmission, then remove center crossmember.
6. Remove transmission to clutch housing bolts, then slide transmission rearward until drive pinion shaft clears clutch disc.
7. Lower transmission and remove from vehicle.

New Process 4 Speed

Shift gear shift lever into mesh with a drive gear. Disconnect universal joint and loosen yoke retaining nut. Disconnect brake and speedometer cables at transmission. Rotate gearshift lever retainer in a counterclockwise direction and pull up on lever at the same time. Do not lose spring or washer from lever. Remove transmission-to-clutch housing bolts and remove transmission from truck.

DODGE & PLYMOUTH

New Process 5 Speed

Remove gearshift lever, floor mat and floor cover over transmission. Drop center bearing (if equipped). Place jack under transmission and unfasten transmission from clutch housing. Pull transmission with jack straight back about 6 inches. Then lower jack slightly. Move transmission with jack to the left so that clutch shaft will clear clutch housing. Lower transmission out of truck.

Clark & Spicer Units

Remove floor mat and transmission access plate. Disconnect speedometer cable. On models with hand brake assembly, disconnect hand brake lever to hand brake rod or cable. Disconnect clutch control linkage at transmission bell housing. Disconnect propeller shaft and center bearing (if equipped).

If equipped with auxiliary transmission, disconnect transmission-to-auxiliary transmission companion flange. Place transmission jack under transmission and remove clutch housing-to-transmission cap screws. Move transmission back until clutch shaft is clear of clutch housing. Lower transmission from truck.

Spicer Auxiliary Units

Drain transmission lubricant. Shift each shaft to a forward position. Remove clevis pins and then place shafts to neutral position. Disconnect universal joint companion flange next to front of auxiliary transmission. Disconnect emergency brake rod and speedometer cable. *If it is difficult to disconnect speedometer cable, remove brake band.*

Mark sliding yoke and drive shaft with a center punch for proper installation. Position portable hydraulic jack under transmission and remove transmission support bolts. *Observe position of mounting components to assist in proper installation.* Lower transmission and pull sliding yoke from propeller shaft spline. Then remove transmission from truck.

FULLY SYNCHRONIZED 3 SPEED

NOTE: For service procedures on the A–390 model transmission, refer to the "3 SPEED TRANS., 1970–76" in the Ford chapter.

MODEL A–230

Transmission, Disassemble, Fig. 4
1. Shift transmission into 2nd gear for shift fork clearance and remove side cover and shifter assembly.
2. Remove front bearing retainer.

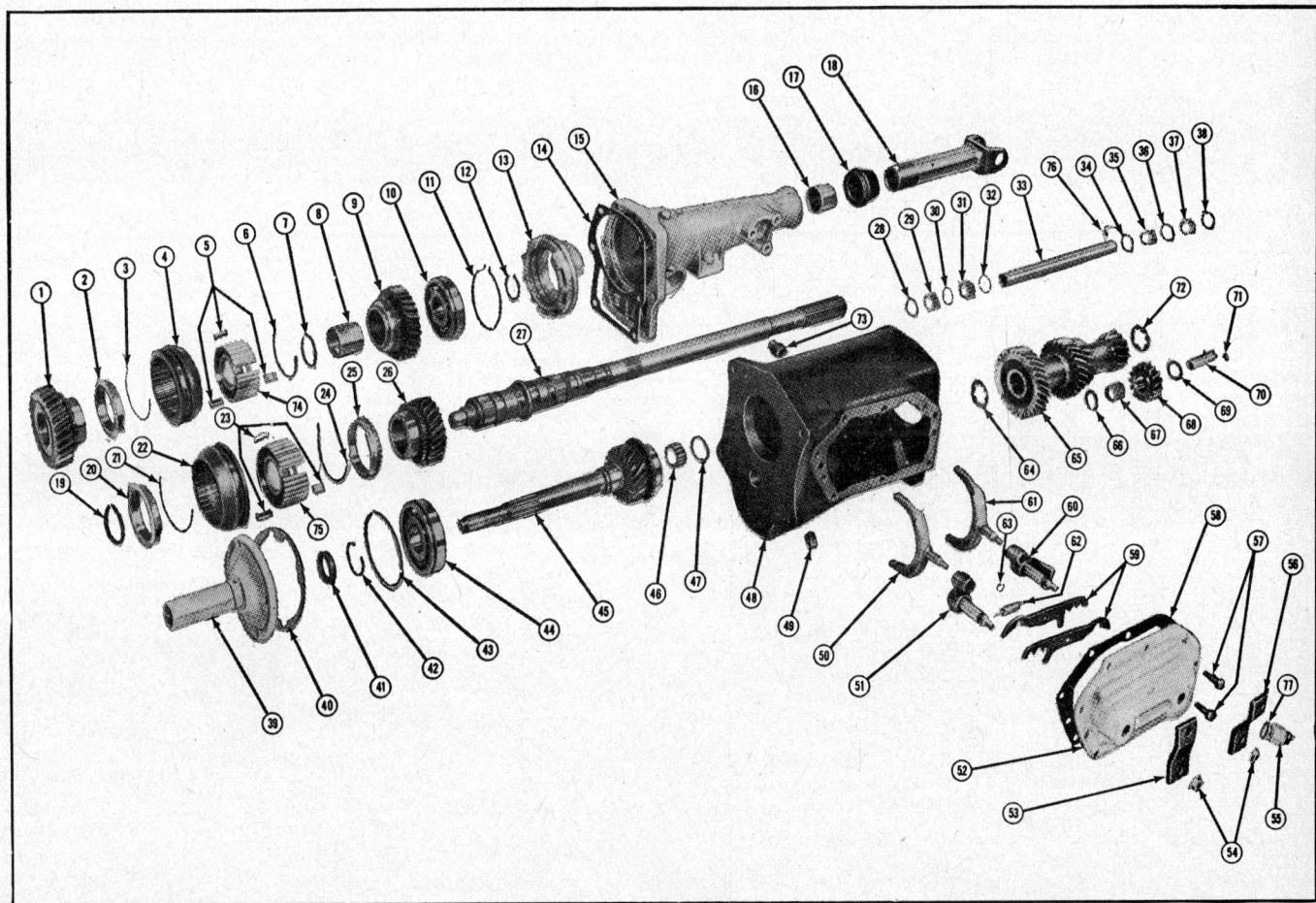

1. Gear, First	14. Gasket	27. Shaft, Output	40. Gasket	53. Lever	66. Washer
2. Ring	15. Extension	28. Washer	41. Seal	54. Nut Locking	67. Roller
3. Spring	16. Bushing	29. Roller	42. Snap Ring	55. Switch	68. Gear, Idler
4. Sleeve	17. Seal	30. Washer	43. Snap Ring	56. Lever	69. Washer
5. Struts (3)	18. Yoke	31. Roller	44. Bearing	57. Bolt	70. Shaft
6. Spring	19. Snap Ring	32. Washer	45. Pinion, Drive	58. Gasket	71. Key
7. Snap Ring	20. Ring	33. Countershaft	46. Roller	59. Lever, Interlock	72. Washer
8. Bushing	21. Spring	34. Washer	47. Snap Ring	60. Lever	73. Plug, Filler
9. Gear, Reverse	22. Sleeve	35. Roller	48. Case	61. Fork	74. Gear, Clutch
10. Bearing	23. Struts (3)	36. Washer	49. Plug, Drain	62. Spring	75. Gear, Clutch
11. Snap Ring	24. Spring	37. Roller	50. Fork	63. Snap Ring	76. Key
12. Snap Ring	25. Ring	38. Washer	51. Lever	64. Washer	77. Gasket
13. Retainer	26. Gear, Second	39. Retainer	52. Housing	65. Gear, Countershaft	

Fig. 4 A-230 fully synchronized three speed transmission

DODGE & PLYMOUTH

Fig. 5 Removing mainshaft assembly

9. Remove mainshaft through rear case opening, Fig. 5
10. Using dummy shaft to retain rollers, tap countershaft out rear of case and lower countergear to bottom of case to permit removal of drive pinion.
11. Remove snap ring from pinion bearing outer race, drive pinion into case and remove through rear case opening.
12. Remove countergear through rear case opening.

Mainshaft

1. Remove 2-3 synchronizer clutch gear retaining ring from front of mainshaft.
2. Slide 2-3 synchronizer and 2nd gear stop ring off of shaft. Remove 2nd gear.
3. Spread snap ring in mainshaft bearing retainer and slide retainer off bearing race.
4. Remove snap ring securing bearing to mainshaft.
5. Support front side of the reverse gear in press and press bearing off shaft. *When bearing clears shaft, do not allow parts to drop through.*
6. Remove 1st-Reverse synchronizer retaining ring and remove synchronizer assembly from mainshaft, Fig. 6
7. Remove 1st gear and stop ring.
8. Reverse procedure to assemble mainshaft.

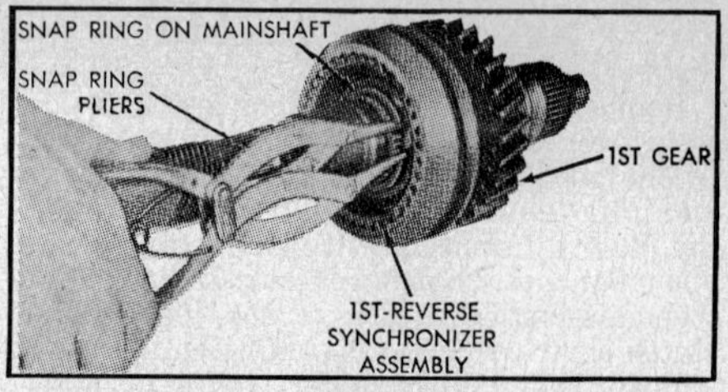

3. Tap drive pinion forward with brass drift as far as possible to provide clearance for mainshaft removal.
4. Rotate cut away part of second gear next to countergear for mainshaft removal clearance. Shift 2-3 synchronizer sleeve forward.
5. Remove speedometer gear.
6. Remove rear extension housing.
7. Using dummy shaft, push reverse idler shaft and key out of case.
8. Remove idler gear with dummy shaft in place to retain rollers. Remove thrust washers.

Fig. 6 Removing 1st-reverse synchronizer snap ring

Transmission, Assemble

1. Using dummy shaft to hold rollers in place and heavy grease to hold thrust washers, carefully place countergear assembly in bottom of case. *Do not finish installation until drive pinion is installed.*
2. Load rollers and retaining ring in drive pinion bore and install drive pinion through rear case opening and into case bore. Install large snap ring on bearing and install front bearing retainer.
3. Align countergear with its shaft bore and install countershaft through gear, driving dummy shaft out as countershaft is installed. Install countershaft key.
4. Carefully tap drive pinion forward to provide mainshaft installation clearance.

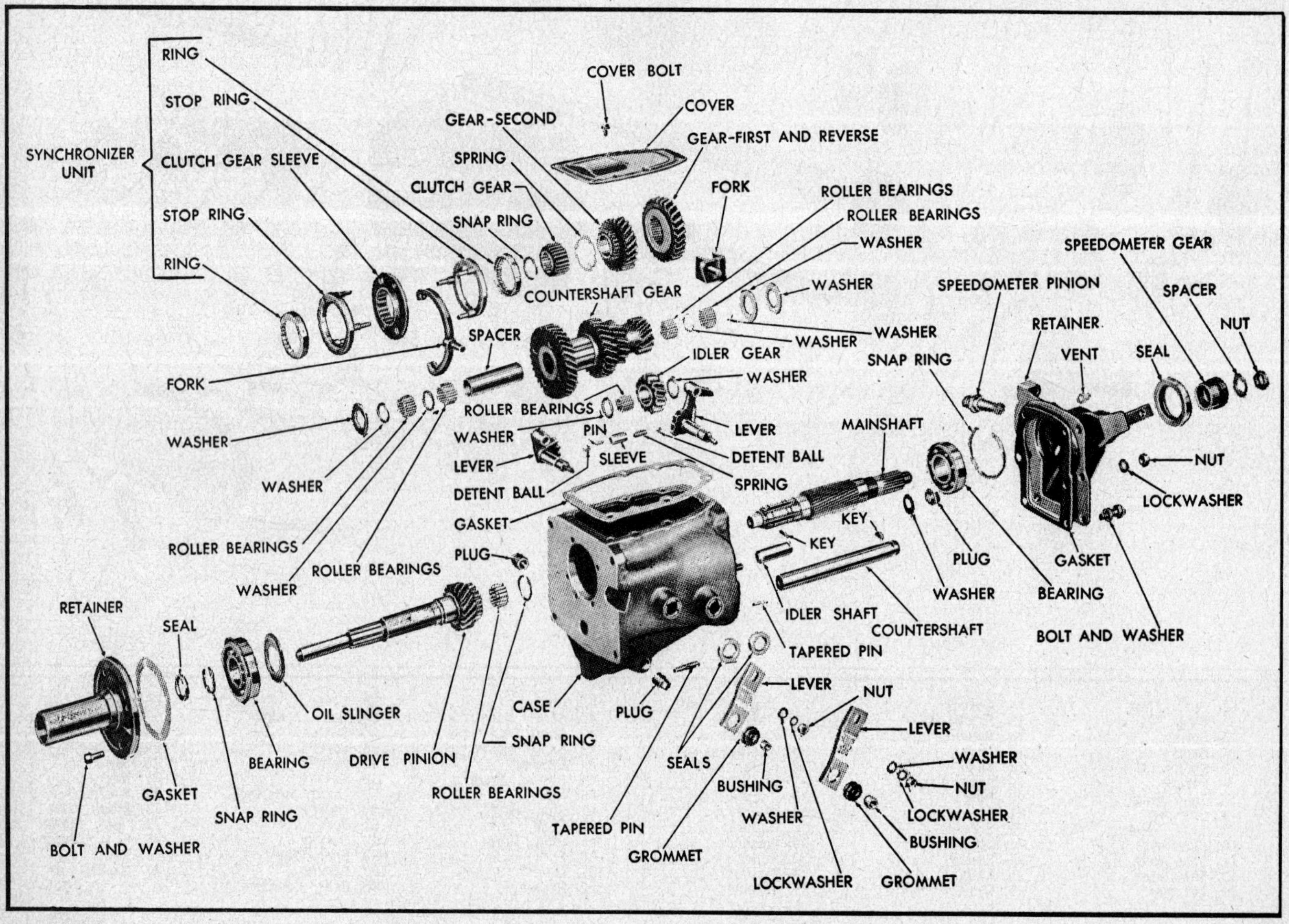

Fig. 7 A-250 three speed transmission 1970-76 (typical)

DODGE & PLYMOUTH

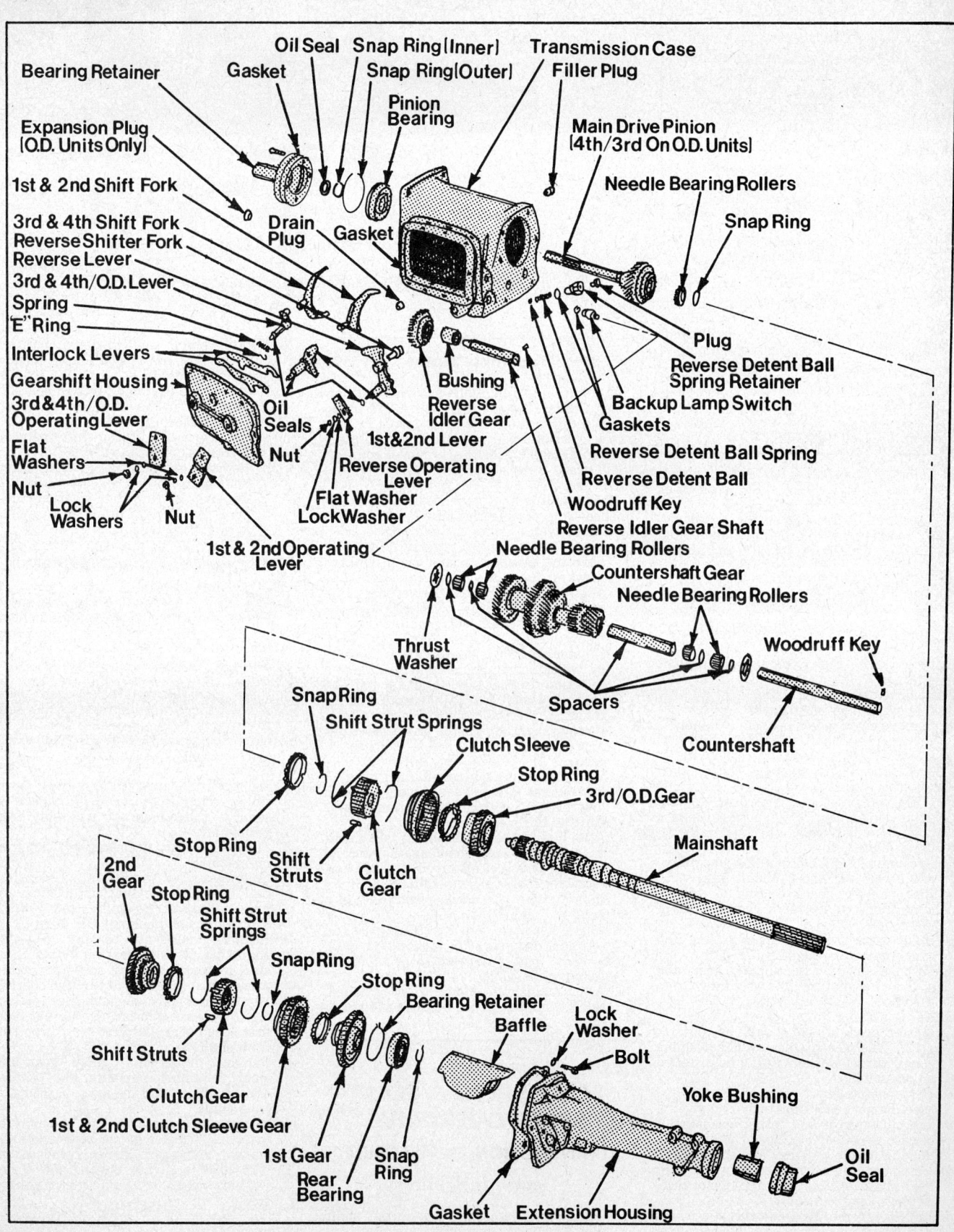

Fig. 8 Four speed overdrive transmission

DODGE & PLYMOUTH

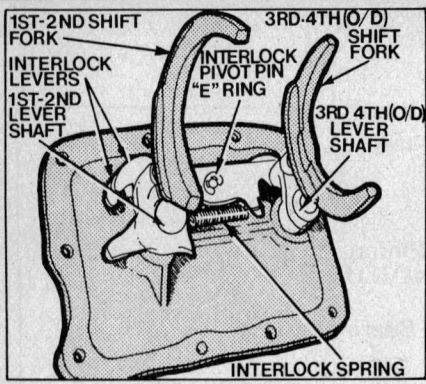

Fig. 9 Gearshift housing assembly. Four speed units

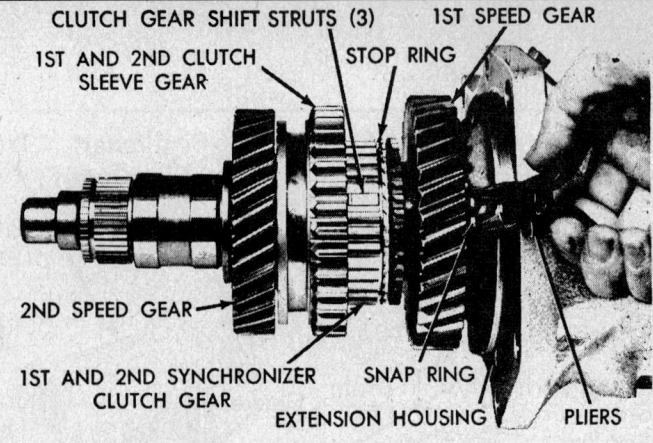

Fig. 10 Compressing center bearing snap ring. Four speed units

5. With 2-3 synchronizer sleeve fully forward and cut out on 2nd gear turned so it is toward countershaft, insert mainshaft assembly through rear case opening.

NOTE: If installation is correct, the bearing retainer will bottom in the case without force. If not, check for out of position strut, roller or stop ring.

6. Using dummy shaft to hold rollers, install reverse idler in case and install idler shaft and key.
7. Install rear extension housing, speedometer gear and with transmission shifted into 2nd gear, install cover and shifter assembly.

MODEL A-250

Transmission, Disassemble, Fig. 7

1. Referring to Fig. 7, remove input shaft retainer.
2. Remove extension housing.
3. Remove transmission cover.
4. Remove clutch shaft bearing retainer.
5. Grasp clutch shaft with hand and pull assembly out of case. *Be careful not to bind inner synchronizer ring on clutch teeth.*
6. With transmission in reverse, remove outer center bearing snap ring, using a hook or a flat blade, then partially remove mainshaft.
7. Cock mainshaft; then remove synchronizer sleeve, rings and 2-3 shift fork.
8. Remove clutch gear snap ring, using snap ring pliers. Slide clutch gear off end of mainshaft.
9. Slide second speed gear, stop ring and synchronizer spring off mainshaft.
10. Remove low-reverse sliding gear and shift fork as mainshaft is withdrawn from case.
11. Using a feeler gauge, check end play of cluster gear, which should be .004" to .012". This measurement will determine if new thrust washers are to be installed at reassembly.
12. Drive countershaft rearward and out of case. Remove key from end of shaft.
13. Lift cluster gear and thrust washers out of case. Disassemble cluster gear by removing needle bearings and spacer.
14. Using a suitable drift, drive reverse idler gear shaft towards rear and out of case. Remove key from shaft.
15. Lift out reverse idler gear, thrust washers and needle bearings out of case. Remove needle bearings from gear.

Assembly Notes

In addition to some outward visual differences, the late model (1975–76) A-250 transmission differs from the early model in that two sets of roller bearings are used to support the countershaft gear. Early model countershaft gears were supported by four sets of roller bearings.

Reassembling the transmission is accomplished by reversing the disassembly procedure. However, observe the following:

1. When installing the reverse idler gear, have the bevelled ends of the gear teeth forward. Raise the idler gear slightly to align with shaft; then drive shaft into case, through thrust washer and gear, until end of shaft is approximately $1/64''$ below surface of case.
2. Cluster gear thrust washers are available in two sizes marked "A" and "B". Make a selection to give .004" to .012" total end play of cluster gear. Make sure tabs on thrust washers slide into grooves in case. Countershaft should be installed until approximately $1/64''$ below surface of case.
3. When installing mainshaft, have offset of low-reverse fork to rear. Engage fork in low-reverse gear, then position in case by shifting in reverse.
4. After sliding the synchronizer clutch gear on mainshaft and down against second speed gear, select a snap ring of the correct thickness and install. *Snap ring should eliminate end play and must be a snug fit.*
5. Check clearance between clutch gear and second speed gear, which should be .003" to .008". *End play in excess of .008" will permit gear "jump out."*
6. After mainshaft is properly positioned, select a snap ring that will be a snug fit at the rear bearing.

FOUR SPEED & FOUR SPEED OVERDRIVE

TRANSMISSION, DISASSEMBLE

Gearshift Housing

1. Remove reverse shift lever from shaft, Fig. 8, then the gearshift housing attaching bolts, Fig. 9.
2. With levers in neutral detent position, pull housing away from case. Remove forks from sleeves.
3. If oil leakage is present around gearshift lever shafts or the interlock levers are cracked, perform the following:
   a. Remove nuts and the shift operating levers from shafts.
   b. Remove gearshift lever shafts from housing.
   c. Remove "E" ring from interlock lever pivot pin, then the interlock levers and spring from housing.

Extension Housing & Mainshaft

Exc. Overdrive Units

1. Remove bolt and retainer securing speedometer pinion adapter in extension housing, then the adapter and pinion from housing.
2. Remove extension housing attaching bolts.
3. Slide third-fourth synchronizer sleeve slightly forward, slide reverse idler gear to center of shaft, then using a mallet, tap extension housing rearward. Slide extension housing and mainshaft assembly from case.
4. Remove snap ring retaining third-fourth synchronizer clutch gear and sleeve assembly, then slide the assembly from mainshaft.
5. Slide third speed gear and stop ring from mainshaft.
6. Compress snap ring retaining mainshaft ball bearing in extension housing and pull mainshaft assembly and bearing from extension housing, Fig. 10.
7. Remove mainshaft bearing retaining snap ring. Remove bearing by installing steel plates on the first speed gear, then press or drive mainshaft through bearing. Use caution not to damage gear teeth.
8. Remove bearing, bearing retainer ring, first speed gear and first speed stop ring from shaft.
9. Remove first-second clutch gear and sleeve assembly snap ring, Fig. 11, then slide assembly and the second speed gear from shaft.
10. Measure countershaft gear end play by inserting a feeler gauge between thrust washer and gear. End play should be .015–.029 in. If not, install new thrust washers when reassembling transmission.

Overdrive Units

1. Remove bolt and retainer securing speed-

DODGE & PLYMOUTH

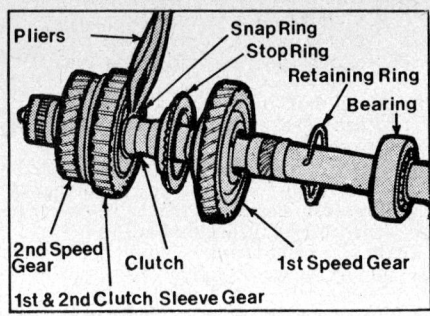

Fig. 11 Removing clutch gear snap ring. Four speed units

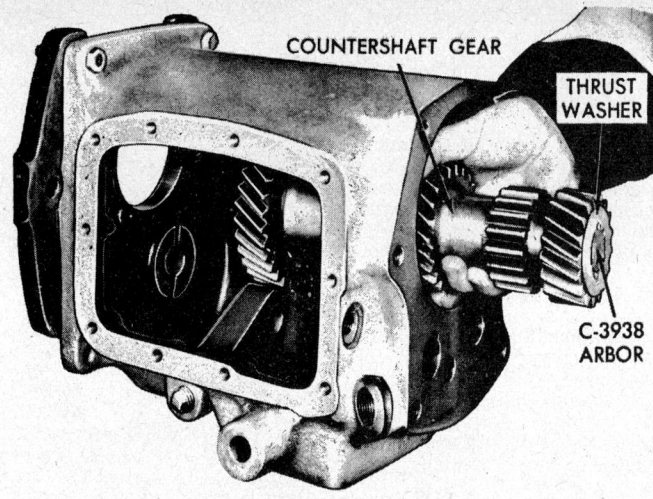

Fig. 12 Replacing countergear. Four speed units

ometer pinion adapter in extension housing, then the adapter and pinion from housing.
2. Remove extension housing attaching bolts.
3. Rotate extension housing on output shaft to expose the rear of countershaft. Clearance is provided on extension housing flange to permit one bolt to be reinstalled to hold the extension housing in the inverted position for access to countershaft.
4. Drill a hole in the countershaft expansion plug at front of case. Then, working through hole, push countershaft rearward until woodruff key is exposed and remove key. Push countershaft forward against expansion plug and, using a brass drift, tap countershaft forward until expansion plug is driven from case.
5. With a dummy shaft, drive countershaft through rear of case, using caution so the countershaft washers do not fall out of position. Lower cluster gear to bottom of case.
6. Rotate extension housing back to normal position.
7. Remove drive pinion bearing retainer attaching bolts, then slide retainer and gasket from pinion shaft. Pry pinion or seal from retainer. Use caution not to nick or scratch seal bore in retainer or the surface on which the seal bottoms.
8. With a brass drift, drive the pinion and bearing assembly through the front of case.
9. Perform steps 3 through 9 as outlined under "Extension Housing & Mainshaft, Except Overdrive Units" procedure.

Drive Pinion & Countershaft Gear

1. Remove pinion bearing inner snap ring, then press pinion from bearing.
2. Remove snap ring and roller bearings from drive pinion cavity.
3. Remove countershaft gear from bottom of case, Fig. 12
4. Remove dummy shaft, needle bearings, thrust washers and spacer from countershaft gear.

Reverse Gear, Lever & Fork

1. Remove reverse gearshift lever detent spring retainer, gasket, plug and detent ball spring from rear of case, Fig. 13.
2. Press reverse idler gear shaft from case and remove woodruff key.
3. If oil leakage is present around the reverse gearshift lever shaft, remove any burrs from shaft. Carefully push reverse gearshift lever shaft inward and remove from case, Fig. 14. Remove detent ball from bottom of case, then the shift fork from shaft and detent plate.

TRANSMISSION, ASSEMBLE

Reverse Gear, Lever & Fork

1. Install new "O" ring on reverse gearshift lever shaft. Lubricate lever shaft and install lever shaft into case bore, then the reverse fork in lever.
2. Install reverse detent spring retainer and gasket and torque to 50 ft. lbs. Insert ball and spring, then install and torque gasket and plug to 24 ft. lbs.
3. Place reverse idler gearshaft in position in end of case and drive into case to position reverse idler gear on the protruding end of shaft with shift slot facing toward rear and engine slot with reverse shift fork.
4. With reverse idler gear properly positioned, drive reverse idler gearshaft into case and install woodruff key. Ensure shaft is flush with surface of case.
5. Install and torque back-up light switch and gasket to 15 ft. lbs. if removed.

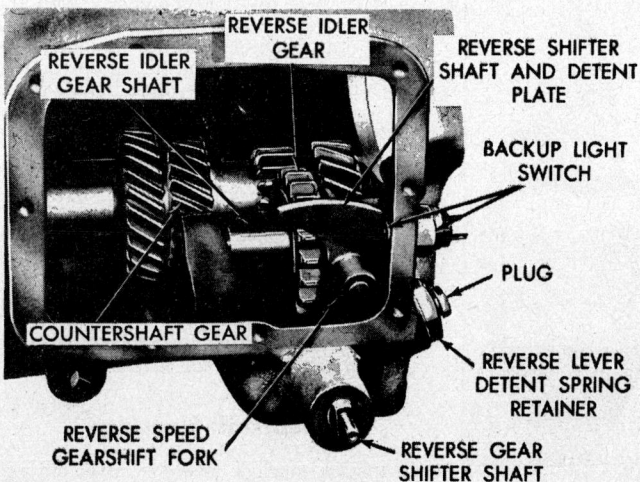

Fig. 13 Reverse gearing and countergear. Four speed units

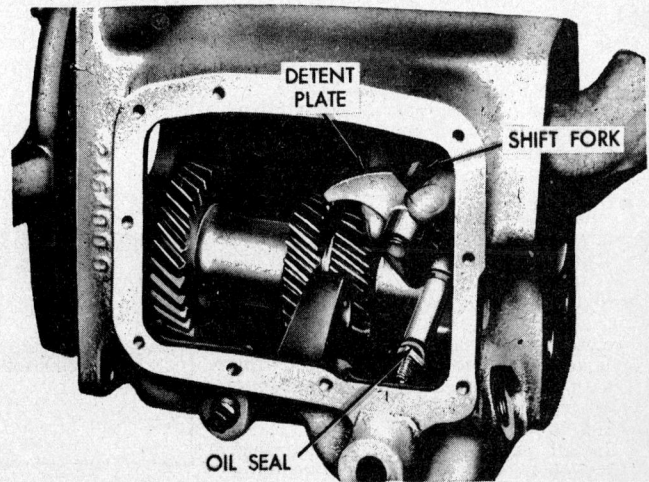

Fig. 14 Removing reverse gear fork and lever. Four speed units

DODGE & PLYMOUTH

Countershaft Gear & Drive Pinion

1. Lubricate countershaft gear bore and install roller bearing spacer with dummy shaft into gear. Center the spacer and dummy shaft.
2. Install 19 rollers, a spacer ring, 19 more rollers and spacer ring into gear.
3. Lubricate and install new thrust washers, if needed, on dummy shaft with tanged side facing toward case boss.
4. Place countershaft gear assembly on bottom of case, Fig. 12
5. Press drive pinion bearing onto pinion shaft with outer snap ring groove facing front of transmission. Fully seat the bearing against gear shoulder.
6. Install new bearing retaining snap ring.
7. With pinion shaft held in a soft jawed vise, install 16 roller bearings in shaft cavity. Cost bearings with heavy grease and install bearing retaining snap ring in groove.
8. On all except overdrive units:
   a. Install drive pinion and bearing assembly through rear of case and position in front bore. Tap into place with a mallet and install outer snap ring in bearing groove.
   b. Insert countershaft in bore at rear of case and raise the countershaft gear until the teeth mesh with drive pinion gear. Ensure thrust washers remain properly positioned.
   c. Align dummy shaft with case bores, then push countershaft into gear. Tap shaft into case until shaft end is flush with case surface. Remove dummy shaft.
9. On all units, install new oil seal in retainer bore.

Extension Housing Bushing, Replace

1. Remove extension housing yoke seal.
2. Drive bushing from housing.
3. Drive new bushing into housing, aligning bushing oil hole with housing oil slot.
4. Install new extension housing yoke seal.

Mainshaft

1. Partially assemble synchronizer components as follows:
   a. Place a stop ring flat on bench, then the clutch sleeve and gear.
   b. Place struts into slots and snap a strut spring into place with the tang inside one strut.
   c. Turn assembly over and install second strut spring with the tang in a different strut.
2. Slide second speed gear onto mainshaft with synchronized cone facing toward rear against shoulder.
3. Slide first-second synchronizer with stop ring lugs indexed in slots onto mainshaft against second gear cone and secure with new snap ring. Slide next stop ring onto shaft and index lugs into clutch hub slots.
4. Slide first speed gear with synchronizer cone facing forward into position against clutch sleeve gear.
5. Install mainshaft bearing retaining ring, then the mainshaft rear bearing. Press bearing into place and install new snap ring to retain bearing.
6. Install partially assembled mainshaft into extension housing and compress bearing retaining ring so mainshaft ball bearing can move inward and bottom against thrust shoulder in extension housing. Release and seat ring in groove in the housing.
7. On all except overdrive units:
   a. Slide third speed gear onto mainshaft with synchronized cone facing forward, then the third gear stop ring.
   b. Install third-fourth synchronizer clutch gear assembly on mainshaft with shift fork slot facing rearward against third speed gear.
   c. Install retaining snap ring, then, with grease, position front stop ring over clutch gear, indexing ring lugs with shift struts.
8. On overdrive units:
   a. Slide overdrive gear onto mainshaft with synchronizer cone facing forward, then the overdrive gear stop ring.
   b. Install third-overdrive synchronizer clutch gear assembly on mainshaft with shift fork slot facing rearward against overdrive gear.

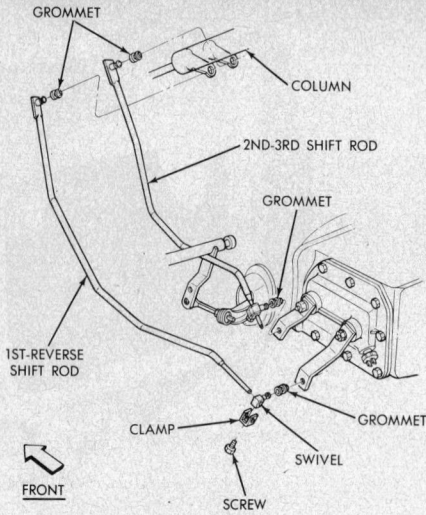

Fig. 15 Disassembled view of gearshift linkage. Except B-Series & Voyager w/A-230 transmission

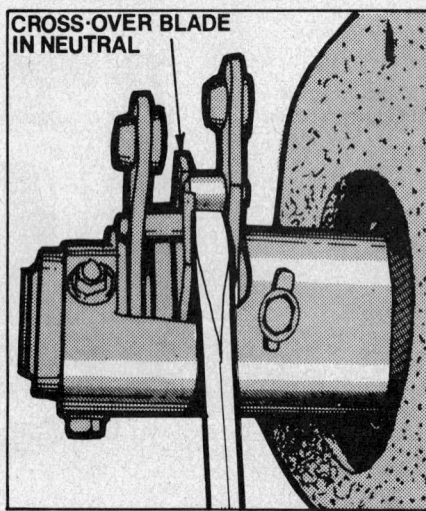

Fig. 16 Gearshift lever adjustments. 1970-79 three speed transmission

c. Install retaining snap ring then, with grease, position front stop ring over clutch gear, indexing ring lugs with shift struts.
9. On all units, coat new extension housing to case gasket with grease, then place gasket on housing.
10. Slide reverse idler gear to center of the shaft, then move the third-fourth synchronizer sleeve or the third-overdrive synchronizer sleeve forward.
11. On all except overdrive units, move drive pinion forward to provide maximum clearance for mainshaft pilot end.
12. On all units, slowly insert mainshaft assembly into case, tilting the shaft as necessary to clear idler and cluster gears. On all except overdrive units, engage the mainshaft with the pilot rollers in the drive pinion gear.
13. On all except overdrive units:
    a. Place third-fourth synchronizer sleeve in neutral position.
    b. If all components are positioned properly the extension housing will bottom on the case without force. If not, check position of struts, pinion rollers and stop rings.
    c. Install and torque extension housing attaching bolts to 50 ft. lbs.
    d. Install drive pinion bearing retainer and gasket. Coat attaching bolt threads with a suitable sealing compound, then install and torque bolts to 30 ft. lbs.
14. On overdrive units:
    a. Place third-overdrive synchronizer sleeve in neutral position.
    b. Rotate extension housing on mainshaft to expose countershaft rear and install one extension housing attaching bolt, holding housing in inverted position and preventing housing from moving rearward.
    c. Install drive pinion and bearing assembly through front of case and into front bore. Install outer snap ring in bearing groove. Tap lightly into position with a mallet. If all components are positioned properly, the bearing outer snap ring will bottom onto case face without force. If not, check position of struts, pinion rollers and stop rings.
    d. Turn transmission upside down while holding countershaft gear assembly to prevent damage.
    e. Lower countershaft gear assembly into position with teeth meshed with drive pinion gear. Ensure thrust washers are positioned properly with the tangs aligned with case slots.
    f. Start countershaft into bore at rear of case and push until approximately halfway into case, then install woodruff key. Push shaft forward until end is flush with case surface. Remove dummy shaft.
    g. Properly align extension housing on case and install and torque extension housing attaching bolts to 50 ft. lbs.
    h. Install drive pinion bearing retainer and gasket. Coat attaching bolt threads with a suitable sealing compound, then install and torque bolts to 30 ft. lbs.
    i. Install new expansion plug in countershaft bore at front of case.

Gearshift Housing

1. Install interlock levers on pivot pin and retain with "E" ring, Fig. 9. Use pliers to install spring on interlock lever hang-

ers.
2. Lubricate and install new "O" rings on shift lever shafts. Lubricate housing bores and push shafts into proper bore.
3. Install operating levers and torque retaining nuts to 18 ft. lbs. Ensure the third-overdrive lever points downward.
4. Rotate shift fork bores to neutral position and install the third-overdrive shift fork in proper bore and under both interlock levers.
5. Position both synchronizer sleeves in neutral and place first-second shift fork in the first-second synchronizer sleeve groove.
6. Lay transmission on its right side and place gearshift housing gasket on case with grease to hold in position.
7. Lower gearshift housing into place, guiding the third-overdrive shift fork into synchronizer groove, and lead the first-second shift fork shaft into the first-second shift lever bore. Raise interlock lever against its spring tension with a screwdriver, allowing first-second shift fork shaft to slip under the levers. The gearshift housing should now seat against case gasket.
8. Install gearshift housing attaching bolts finger tight and shift transmission through all gears to insure proper operation.

NOTE: Eight gearshift housing attaching bolts are shoulder bolts used to accurately locate the mechanism on the transmission. One bolt shoulder is longer and acts as a dowel, passing through the cover and into the case at center of rear flange. Two bolts are of standard design, located at the lower rear of cover.

9. Torque gearshift housing attaching bolts to 15 ft. lbs.
10. The reverse shift lever and the first-second shift lever incorporate cam surfaces which mate in the reverse position to lock the first-second lever, fork and synchronizer in the neutral position. To check, place transmission in reverse, then, while turning input shaft, move first-second lever in each direction. If input shaft lock becomes difficult to turn, the synchronizer is partially engaged, caused by excessive cam clearance. Install a new first-second shift lever of different size. If insufficient cam clearance exists, it is difficult or impossible to shift into reverse.
11. Lubricate reverse shaft and install operating lever, then torque attaching nut to 18 ft. lbs.
12. Install speedometer drive pinion gear and adapter, ensuring range number (indicating number of teeth) is in the six o'clock position.

GEARSHIFT, ADJUST

THREE SPEED

Except A-390 Units

1972-79 Exc. "B" Series & Voyager

1. Disconnect shift rod swivels from transmission levers, then place transmission levers in the neutral position.
2. Move shift lever to align locating slots in column shift housing and bearing housing. Then install a screwdriver or similar tool between cross-over blade and 2-3 shift lever, engaging both lever pins with cross-over blade, Fig. 16.

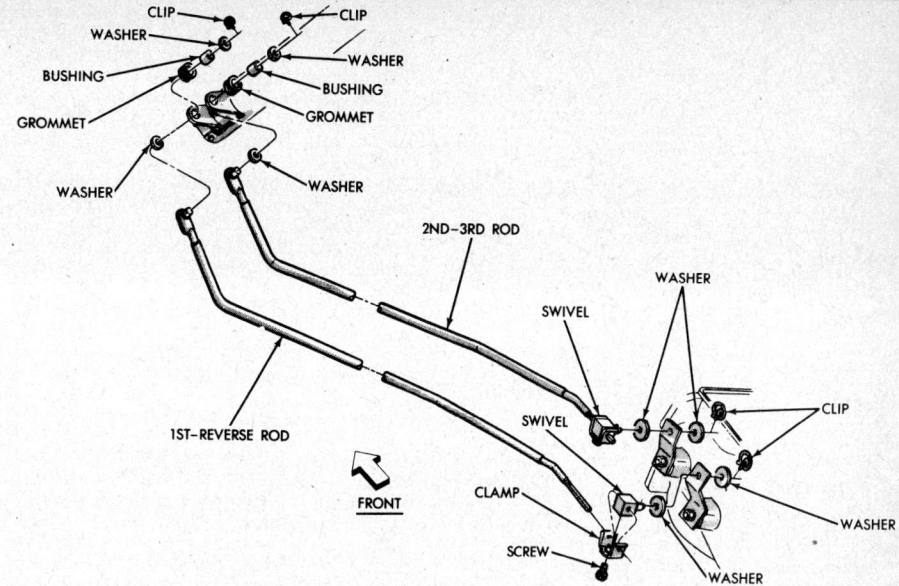

Fig. 17 Disassembled view of column shift linkage. B-Series & Voyager w/A-230 transmission

3. Place transmission 1st-reverse shift lever in reverse position and adjust 1st-reverse rod swivel to enter transmission shift lever and tighten swivel bolt.
4. Remove gearshift housing locating tool and place column lever in neutral position.
5. Adjust 2-3 rod swivel to enter transmission shift lever and tighten swivel bolt.
6. Remove screwdriver or tool from cross-over and check adjustment.

1972-79 "B" Series & Voyager

Adjust length of 2-3 shift rod to properly position shift lever on steering column, then proceed as follows:

1. Install both shift rods and secure at each lever with a clip, then loosen swivel clamp bolts, Fig. 17.
2. Place transmission 2-3 shift lever in 3rd position and place steering column shift lever into a position approximately five degrees above the horizontal position, then tighten swivel clamp bolt.
3. Shift transmission into neutral and install a screwdriver or other suitable tool between cross-over blade and 2-3 lever at steering column, engaging both lever pins and cross-over blade, Fig. 16.
4. Place transmission 1st-reverse lever in neutral position and tighten swivel clamp

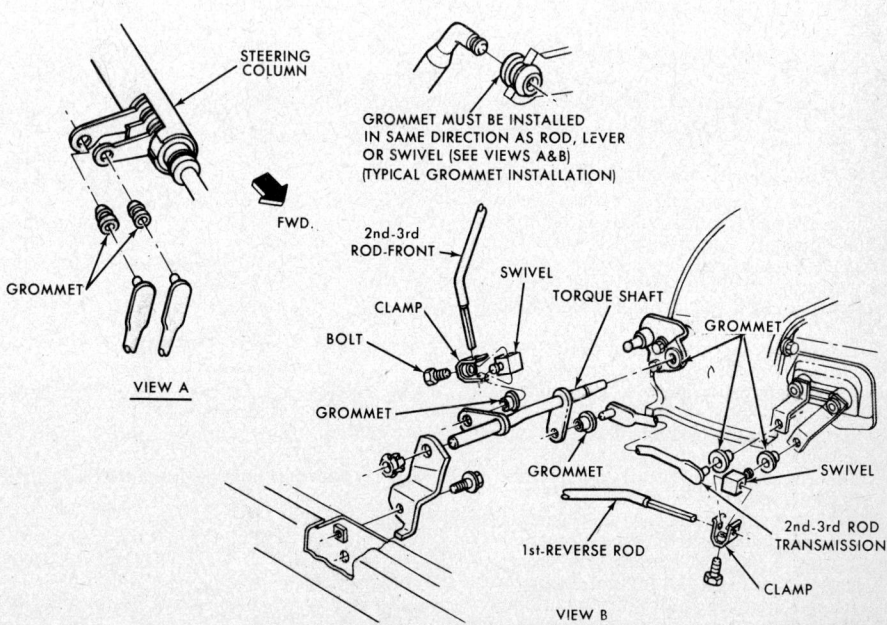

Fig. 18 Disassembled view of column shift linkage. B-Series & Voyager w/A-390 transmission

DODGE & PLYMOUTH

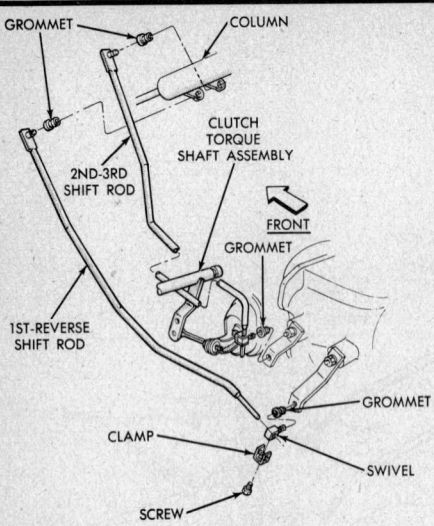

Fig. 19 Disassembled view of gearshift linkage. Except B-Series & Voyager w/A-390 transmission

bolt.
5. Remove screwdriver or tool from cross-1ver and check adjustment.

1970-71

1. Disconnect control rods and place both levers in neutral. The neutral detent balls must be engaged to make this adjustment correctly.

2. Check fore and aft movement of shift levers. If movement exceeds 1/16", loosen and rotate bushing to remove free play. Then retighten screws.
3. Install wedge between cross-over blade and 2-3 lever so that cross-over is engaged with both lever cross-over pins, Fig. 16.
4. Adjust length of 2-3 control rod until stud shaft of control rod or swivel enters hole in levers. During this setting, the 2-3 control rod should be adjusted to position selector lever 10 degrees above horizontal.
5. Adjust 1-Reverse control rod until swivel stub shaft enters hole in lever.
6. Remove wedge and check linkage operation.

A-390 Units

1. Loosen both shift rod swivels, Fig. 18 and 19.
2. Place transmission shift levers in neutral (middle detent) position.
3. Move shift lever to align locating slots in bottom of steering column shift housing and bearing housing. Install a suitable tool into slot.
4. Place a screwdriver or other suitable tool between cross-over blade and 2-3 lever at steering column so both lever pins are engaged by the cross-over blade, Fig. 16.
5. Tighten both shift rod swivel bolts.
6. Remove gearshift housing locating tool.
7. Remove tool from cross-over blade at steering column.
8. Shift through gears to check adjustment and cross-over smoothness.
9. Check for proper operation of steering column lock in reverse. With proper adjust-

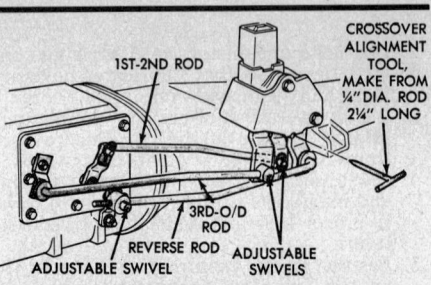

Fig. 20 Gearshift linkage adjustment. Four speed overdrive

ment, the ignition should lock in the reverse position only.

FOUR SPEED OVERDRIVE

1. Install gear shift lever aligning tool, Fig. 20, to hold levers in neutral-cross-over position.
2. With all rods removed from transmission shift levers, place levers in neutral detent position.
3. Adjust threaded shift rod levers so they enter transmission levers freely without any rearward or forward movement.

NOTE: Start with 1-2 shift rod, it may be necessary to pull clip at shifter end to rotate this rod.

4. Install washers and clips, then remove aligning tool and check linkage operation.

Automatic Transmission Section

LOADFLITE TRANSMISSION

Transmission, Replace 1970-79

The transmission and converter must be removed as an assembly; otherwise the converter drive plate, pump bushing and oil seal will be damaged. The drive plate will not support a load; therefore, none of the weight of the transmission should be allowed to rest on the plate during removal. Proceed as follows:

1. Disconnect battery ground cable.
2. On some models it may be necessary to lower exhaust system to provide clearance.
3. Remove engine to transmission struts, if equipped.
4. Disconnect and plug oil cooler lines at transmission.
5. Remove starter motor, oil cooler line bracket and converter access cover.
6. Using a socket wrench on vibration damper bolt, rotate engine clockwise to bring converter drain plug to bottom.
7. Remove plug and drain converter, then loosen transmission oil pan and drain

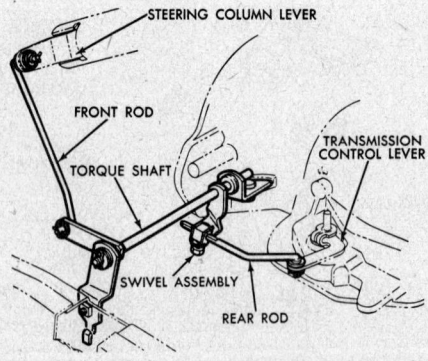

Fig. 1 Gearshift linkage. Loadflite (Typical)

transmission.
8. Mark converter and drive plate to aid in assembly.
9. Remove converter to drive plate attach-

ing bolts, then using a socket wrench on vibration damper bolt, rotate engine clockwise to position bolts.
10. Disconnect propeller shaft at rear universal joint, then carefully pull shaft assembly out of extension housing.
11. Disconnect wire connector from back-up light and neutral start switch.
12. Disconnect gearshift rod and torque shaft assembly from transmission.
13. Disconnect throttle rod from lever at left side of transmission.
14. Remove oil filler tube and disconnect speedometer cable.
15. Support engine at rear, then using a transmission jack raise transmission slightly to relieve load on supports.
16. Remove crossmember, then remove converter housing to engine attaching bolts.
17. Carefully work transmission and converter off engine block dowels and disengage converter hub from end of crankshaft.

NOTE: Attach a small "C" clamp to edge of converter housing to hold converter in place during transmission removal.

18. Lower transmission and remove assem-

DODGE & PLYMOUTH

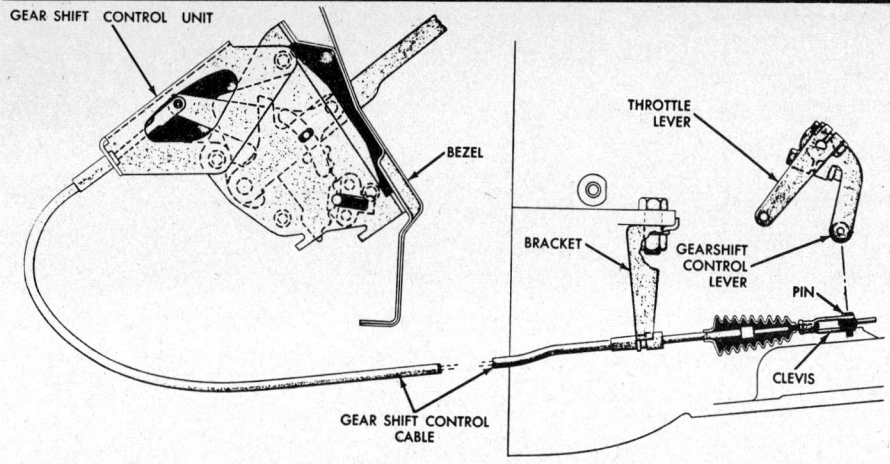

Fig. 2 Gearshift control cable. Loadflite (Typical)

bly from vehicle.
19. Remove "C" clamp and carefully slide converter assembly from transmission.

Gearshift Linkage, Adjust

1. Place gear shift lever in Park position.
2. Move transmission control lever all the way to rear (Park detent), Fig. 1.
3. Adjust rear rod swivel assembly so that swivel can be freely installed in transmission control lever with no load in either direction on linkage.
4. Torque swivel lock bolt to 125 inch pounds, then check adjustment.

Gearshift Control Cable, Adjust

The importance of correct gearshift cable adjustment cannot be over-emphasized. Improper adjustment or a kinked cable can cause erratic shifting or possible front clutch failure. To make the adjustment, proceed as follows:

1. Disconnect control cable from transmission lever, Fig. 2.
2. With selector lever in Park position, check to be sure detent assembly is correctly aligned. If necessary, loosen two mounting screws and align.
3. Place transmission control lever to Park position (fully rearward).
4. With selector lever and control lever both in Park position, adjust cable length with clevis and connect cable to control lever. With correct cable length, clevis pin should be installed without any movement of the control lever.

Extension Housing & Parking Lock Control Rod 1970-79

1. Mark parts for reassembly and remove propeller shaft.
2. Remove speedometer pinion and adapter assembly, then drain about two quarts of fluid from transmission.
3. Remove extension housing to crossmember bolts, then raise transmission with jack and remove crossmember.
4. Remove extension housing to transmission bolts. On console shift models, remove torque shaft lower bracket to extension housing bolts.

NOTE: In the following step, the gearshift must be in "low" therefore positioning the parking lock control rod rearward so it can be disengaged or engaged with the parking lock sprag.

5. Remove two screws, plate and gasket from bottom of extension housing mounting pad, then spread snap ring from output shaft bearing, Fig. 3, and carefully tap extension housing off output shaft bearing.
6. Slide extension housing off shaft to remove parking sprag and spring, then remove snap ring and slide reaction plug and pin assembly out of housing, Fig. 4.
7. To replace parking lock control rod, refer to "Valve Body".

Valve Body

1. Drain transmission and remove oil pan.
2. Loosen clamp bolts and remove throttle and gear selector levers from manual lever.
3. Remove neutral safety switch and oil filter.
4. Place a drain pan under transmission and remove the ten valve body to transmission bolts. Hold valve body in place while removing bolts.
5. Carefully lower valve body while pulling it forward to disengage parking control rod.

NOTE: It may be necessary to rotate output shaft to permit parking control rod to clear sprag.

6. Remove accumulator piston and spring from transmission case. Inspect piston for nicks, scores and wear. Inspect spring for distortion. Inspect rings for freedom in piston grooves and wear or breakage. Replace parts as necessary.

Output Shaft Oil Seal

1. Mark propeller shaft to aid in reassembly and remove propeller shaft being careful not to scratch or nick surface on sliding spline yoke.
2. Using a screwdriver and hammer, drive between extension housing and seal and remove seal.
3. Position new seal and drive it into extension housing using tool C-3995 or C-3972.
4. Carefully install yoke into housing, then align marks made at removal and install propeller shaft.

Governor

1. Remove extension housing, then remove output shaft bearing rear snap ring and remove bearing. On 727 Series, remove remaining snap ring from shaft.
2. Remove snap ring, Fig. 5, from weight end of governor valve shaft and remove valve shaft from governor body.
3. Remove large snap ring from weight end of governor housing, and lift out weight assembly.
4. Remove snap ring from inside governor weight and remove inner weight and spring from outer weight.
5. Remove snap ring from behind governor housing, then slide governor housing and

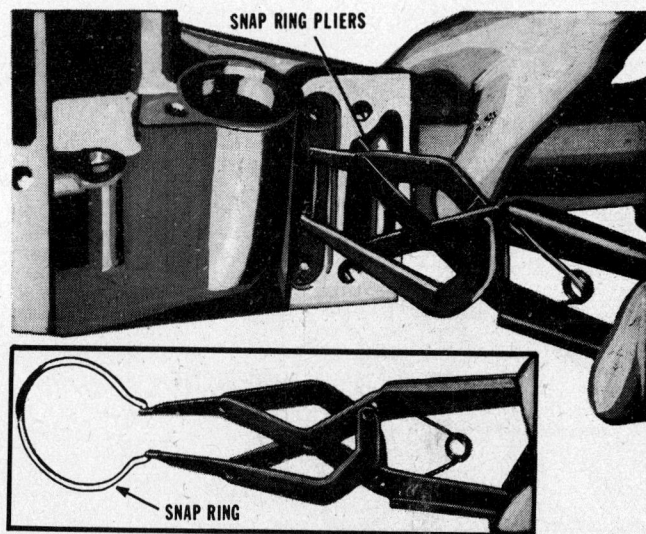

Fig. 3 Removing or installing extension housing snap ring

DODGE & PLYMOUTH

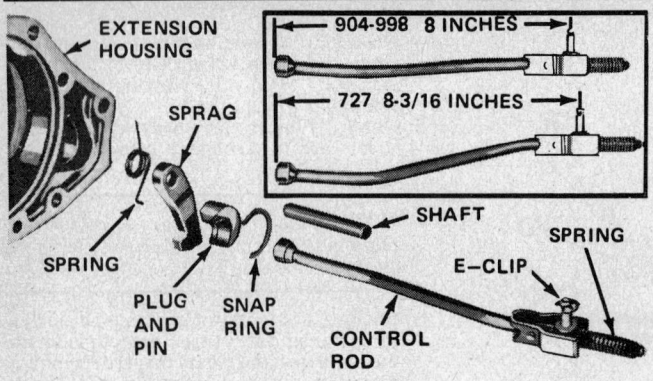

Fig. 4 Parking lock components

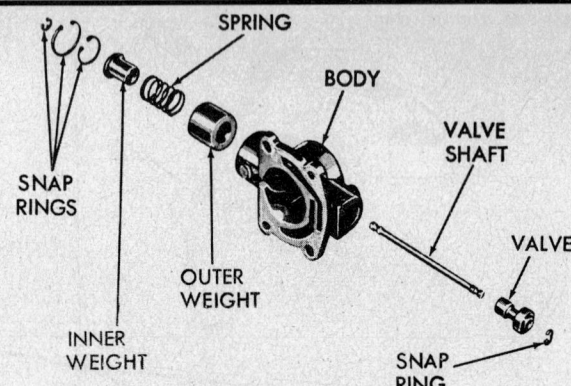

Fig. 5 Governor disassembled

parking brake sprag assembly off input shaft. If necessary, separate governor housing from sprag (4 screws).
6. The primary cause of governor operating failure is due to a sticking governor valve or weights. Rough surfaces may be removed with crocus cloth. Thoroughly clean all parts and check for free movement before assembly.
7. Reverse above operations to assemble and install governor.

NEW PROCESS A-345

Transmission, Replace

NOTE: The compounder, transmission and converter must be removed as an assembly. Do not allow weight of transmission to rest on drive plate during removal, otherwise damage drive plate, pump bushing and oil seal may result.

1. Remove converter access cover.
2. Connect remote control starter switch to starter solenoid so that engine can be rotated from under vehicle, then disconnect high tension lead from ignition coil.
3. Rotate engine using remote starter switch to bring drain plug to 6 o'clock position and drain converter, compounder and transmission.
4. Position a suitable jack under transmission oil pan, raise transmission slightly to relieve weight from mountings.
5. Support rear of engine using a suitable support fixture.
6. Mark converter and drive plate to aid in assembly.

NOTE: Crankshaft flange, converter and inner and outer bolt hole circles of drive plate have one bolt hold offset, so these components can be installed in their original position.

7. Rotate engine using remote starter switch to locate two converter to drive plate attaching bolts at 5 and 7 o'clock positions. Remove both bolts, then rotate engine and remove remaining two bolts.

NOTE: Do not use screwdriver or similar tool to rotate converter or drive plate otherwise drive plate may become distorted. Do not engage starter if drive plate is not attached to converter with at least one bolt or if transmission case to engine attaching bolts have been loosened.

8. Disconnect battery ground cable, then remove starter assembly and transmission oil filler tube.
9. Disconnect oil cooler lines, then plug fittings and case openings.
10. Disconnect wire connector from backup light and neutral start switch.
11. Disconnect gearshift cable, speedometer cable and throttle rod from transmission.
12. Remove crossmember, then disconnect propeller shaft at transmission yoke and tie shaft to frame side rail.
13. Remove converter housing to engine attaching bolts, then carefully work transmission and converter assembly rearward off engine block dowels and disengage converter hub from end of crankshaft.

NOTE: Attach a small "C" clamp to edge of converter housing to hold converter in place during transmission removal.

14. Lower transmission and remove from vehicle.
15. Remove "C" clamp from edge of converter housing, then carefully slide converter out of housing.

Line Pressure, Adjust

Incorrect throttle pressure setting will cause incorrect line pressure readings even though line pressure adjustment is correct. Always inspect and correct throttle pressure adjustment before adjusting line pressure. Line pressure may be adjusted by turning adjusting screw with an allen wrench. Turning adjusting screw counterclockwise in-

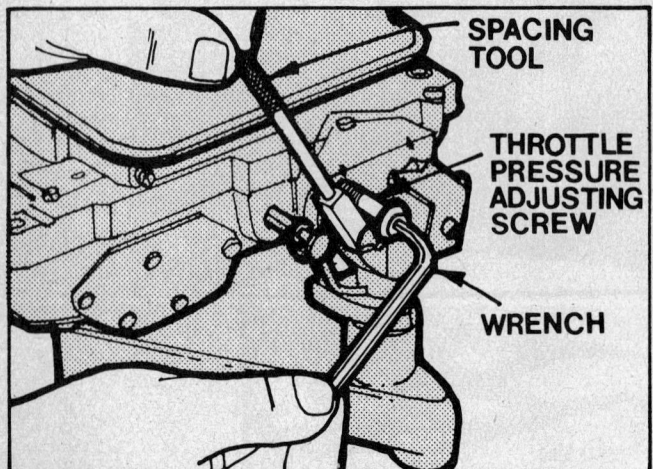

Fig. 6 Throttle pressure adjustment. New Process A-345

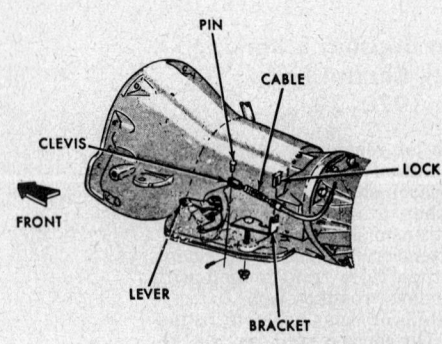

Fig. 7 Gearshift linkage adjustment. New Process A-345

DODGE & PLYMOUTH

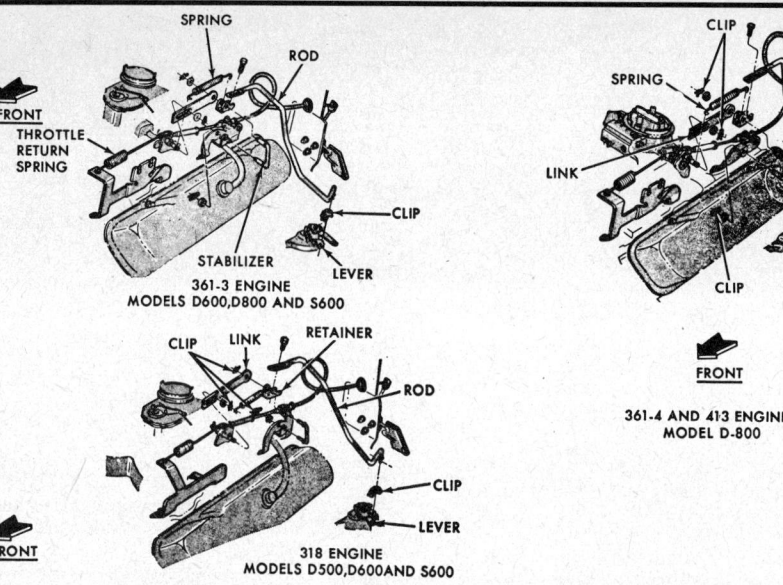
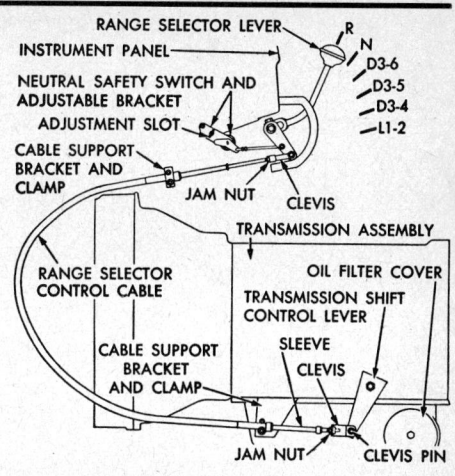

Fig. 8 Throttle linkage adjustment. New Process A-345

Fig. 9 Torqmatic transmission range selector control cable. Typical

creases pressure and clockwise decreases pressure. One complete turn of adjusting screw changes closed throttle line pressure approximately $1\frac{2}{3}$ psi.

Throttle Pressure, Adjust

NOTE: If malfunction is evident, the adjustment should be measured, as throttle pressures cannot be accurately tested.

1. Insert tool C-4233 between throttle lever can and kickdown valve, Fig. 6.
2. Push in on tool and compress kickdown valve against its spring so throttle valve is completely bottomed inside valve body.
3. Exert force to compress spring and turn throttle lever stop screw until head of screw touches throttle lever tang with throttle lever cam touching tool and throttle valve bottomed. Be sure adjustment is made with spring fully compressed and valve bottomed in valve body.

Gearshift Control Linkage, Adjust

1. Disconnect clevis from transmission lever, Fig. 7, then place gear shift selector in neutral and move control lever on transmission two detent positions from rear to neutral.
2. Align clevis hole in transmission lever, then install clevis pin and secure with cotter pin.
3. Recheck adjustment as follows:
   a. Detent position must be close enough to gate stops in neutral and drive to assure that gear shift lever will not remain out of detent position when it is placed against gate and then released.
   b. Engine must start only when gearshift is in neutral. If not, recheck adjustment.
   c. Make certain that vehicle does not move rearward with engine on and gearshift in neutral.

Throttle Linkage, Adjust

1. Operate accelerator to check for throttle opening and closing. If any binding occurs, lubricate linkage and check cable routing or pedal interference with carpet.
2. Disconnect choke rod or block choke valve in full open position, then release fast idle cam by opening throttle and return carburetor to curb idle.
3. Hold transmission throttle lever forward against its stop while adjusting linkage, making certain there is no other force exerted against lower end of rod.
4. Remove spring from stabilizer and retainer and loosen bolt retaining upper end of slotted rod of retainer, Fig. 8.
5. Lightly push rearward on rod, making certain not to disturb throttle lever.
6. Tighten bolt at retainer and install spring at stabilizer and retainer, then connect choke rod or remove blocking and check linkage for correct operation.

TORQMATIC TRANS.

Transmission, Replace

NOTE: On some models it may be necessary to remove air tanks, fuel tanks or special equipment to provide clearance for transmission removal. Converter and transmission must be removed as an assembly.

1. Disconnect battery ground cable.
2. On models with gasoline engine, remove spark plugs so engine can be turned manually. On models with diesel engine, ensure fuel stop knob is pulled all the way out.
3. Loosen transmission oil filter cover and allow transmission oil to drain.
4. After oil has drained, remove oil filter cover, then disconnect range selector cable from shift lever and TV rod from transmission TV lever.
5. Remove oil level gauge, oil filler tube and vent hose assembly.

NOTE: Cover vent hose and oil pan openings to prevent entry of dirt.

6. Disconnect oil cooler line then plug fittings and connections.
7. Disconnect oil temperature switch wire connector.
8. Disconnect speedometer shaft fitting from adapter at rear of transmission.
9. Disconnect propeller shaft from transmission, then disconnect mechanical parking linkage at right side of transmission, if equipped.
10. Remove six bolts attaching flex plate assembly to converter pump cover.

NOTE: Through opening in flywheel housing, use pry bar to manually rotate flywheel to position flex plate to converter pump cover attaching bolts. Do not use wrench on nut or pry against studs on converter cover to rotate flywheel.

11. Support transmission using a suitable jack. Position jack so that oil pan is not supporting weight of transmission. Place safety chain around top of transmission, then attach chain to each side of jack.
12. Support engine at rear, then remove converter housing to frame support bolts. Raise engine slightly to relieve weight from rear mounts.
13. Remove converter housing to flywheel housing attaching bolts.
14. Separate transmission from engine, then carefully lower transmission and converter assembly.

NOTE: When removing transmission, keep rear of transmission lower than front to prevent torque converter from falling out of housing. Ensure converter does not separate from transmission during removal. As soon as transmission is clear of mountings, install a retaining strap across front of converter housing to hold converter in place.

Range Selector Lever Linkage

1. Referring to Fig. 9, place range selector lever in the "R" position.

1003

DODGE & PLYMOUTH

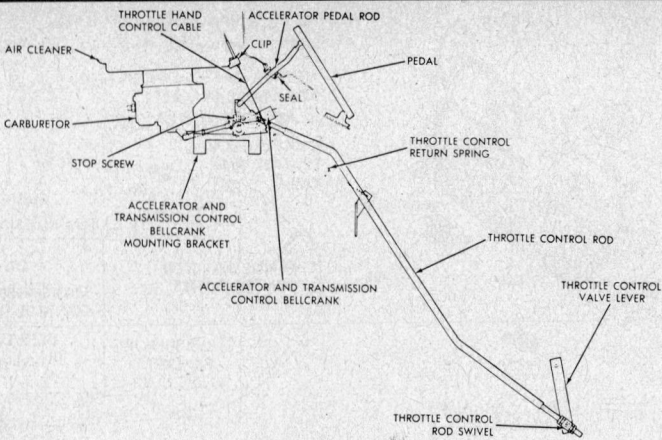

Fig. 10 Torqmatic throttle linkage.

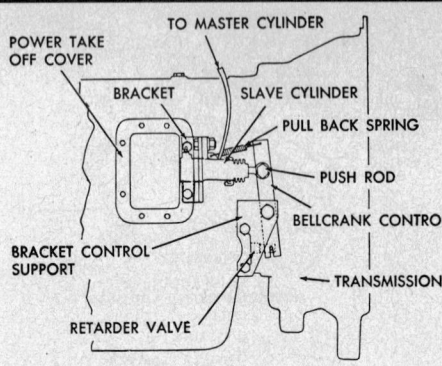

Fig. 11 Retarder linkage.

2. Remove pin from clevis at transmission shift control lever.
3. Move clevis out of the way, then shift control lever all the way forward towards front of truck.
4. Push control cable into its sleeve until selector lever hits the "R" stop. In this position, hole in cable clevis should be aligned with hole in transmission shift control lever.
5. If alignment is not correct, loosen jam nut at clevis and turn clevis in or out until alignment is obtained and clevis pin can be installed easily.
6. Secure clevis pin with cotter pin and tighten jam nut.
7. Test operation of selector lever in all positions.

Neutral Safety Swtich

If necessary to adjust the switch, first loosen the switch bracket screws and rotate the switch clockwise so that the starter circuit is closed when the lever is in neutral. Be sure to tighten mounting screws securely.

Throttle Linkage

1. Referring to Fig. 10 for model being serviced, first remove throttle control return spring and governor floating arm spring. *Do not stretch or distort governor spring in any way as it will throw off the governor calibration.*
2. At transmission, remove transmission throttle control shift rod swivel cotter pin and withdraw swivel from TV lever on transmission.
3. Remove carburetor air cleaner.
4. Place carburetor throttle lever in idle position.
5. Adjust throttle control rod so that accelerator control bellcrank stop is against bracket. Tighten nuts on throttle control rod.
6. Move carburetor throttle lever to wide open position.
7. The wide open throttle stop bolt must be adjusted so that the bolt head contacts the bellcrank when the throttle is in wide open position.
8. With throttle control shaft pushed upwards until travel of rod is stopped by the wide open throttle stop, rotate the transmission throttle control lever (at transmission) forward until the TV lever is firm against the internal stop in the transmission. At this position the swivel pin should freely enter the lower hole in the transmission throttle valve (TV) control lever. Finger tighten front and rear adjusting nuts against swivel.
9. Back off swivel three turns.
10. The through detent pedal stop (located on throttle control bellcrank) must be adjusted so that pedal forces cannot be applied to TV linkage. To do this, adjust stop so that it contacts the bracket bolted to the back of the engine at the same time the TV lever contacts the stop in the transmission. Then turn bolt 1/16 turn further to eliminate any force being applied through the linkage from the stop in the transmission.
11. Reconnect throttle control spring and governor floating arm spring and road test vehicle.
12. After adjustment is complete, failure of the engine to return to the proper idle speed is an indication of too much length in the TV control rod. If engine is properly set at carburetor, this should be corrected by readjusting the TV linkage properly.

Retarder Linkage

Referring to Fig. 11, adjust master cylinder push rod so that there is .010" free play (measured at pedal pad approximately 1/16") between push rod and master cylinder piston, where piston is in its fully returned position. The system must be free of air and master cylinder filled to 1/2" of top. Push rod on slave cylinder should travel 1/2" for full retarder action.

ALLISON AT540, MT640 & 650

Transmission, Replace

NOTE: Transmission and converter must be removed as an assembly.

1. Disconnect battery ground cable.
2. On models with gasoline engine, remove spark plugs so engine can be turned manually. On models with diesel engine, ensure fuel stop knob is pulled all the way out.
3. Disconnect oil filler tube and allow transmission oil to drain.

NOTE: After transmission oil has drained, plug oil pan openings to prevent entry of dirt.

4. Disconnect oil cooler lines, then plug fittings and connections.
5. Disconnect range selector cable from shift lever and vacuum line from modulator.
6. Disconnect speedometer shaft fitting from adapter at rear of transmission.
7. Disconnect propeller shaft from transmission, then disconnect mechanical parking brake linkage at right side of transmission, if equipped.
8. Remove six bolts attaching flex plate assembly to converter cover.

NOTE: Through opening in flywheel cover, use a pry bar to manually rotate flywheel to position flex plate to converter attaching bolts.

9. Support transmission using a suitable jack. Position jack so that oil pan is not supporting weight of transmission. Place safety chain around top of transmission, then attach chain to each side of jack.
10. Support engine at rear, then remove transmission case to crossmember attaching bolts. Raise engine slightly to relieve weight from rear mounting.
11. Remove transmission case to flywheel housing attaching bolts, then inspect transmission and surrounding area to ensure no lines, cables or wires will interfere with transmission removal.
12. Position a jack or sling relative to transmission center of gravity, then separate transmission from engine and lower transmission and converter assembly from vehicle.

NOTE: When removing transmission, keep rear of transmission lower than front to prevent converter from falling out of housing. Ensure converter does not separate from transmission during removal. As soon as transmission is clear of mountings, install a retaining strap across front of converter housing to hold converter in place.

Linkage Adjustments

NOTE: The following general procedure is applicable to most vehicles:

DODGE & PLYMOUTH

1. The shift selector lever should move freely and have a positive detent feel in each position.
2. The shift selector should be adjusted so that the shift tower stops match the transmission detents.
3. With shift linkage correctly adjusted, the shift linkage lever retaining pin should move freely in each range.

CAUTION: Proper installation of external selector lever is important for proper transmission operation. Excessive torque applied to external selector retaining nut may damage internal selector lever.

4. Position selector lever to D or 3rd position and place external lever onto tapered area of selector shaft, then making certain that flats on shaft are adjacent to flats on lever, install retaining nut. Hold lever and torque nut to 15–20 ft. lbs.

NOTE: Do not exceed 20 ft. lbs.

TRANSFER CASE, REPLACE

1. Remove skid plate, if equipped, and drain transfer case.
2. Disconnect speedometer cable and, if equipped with a parking brake assembly, parking brake cable.
3. Disconnect input and output shafts and position shafts aside, properly supported.

NOTE: Some 1978–79 models equipped with a single piece propeller shaft were assembled with the propeller shaft slip yoke positioned toward the rear axle assembly. When servicing these vehicles, the slip yoke should be positioned as assembled in production whether at the rear axle or at the transfer case.

4. Disconnect shift rods and de-clutch rod from transfer case.
5. Support transfer case with a suitable jack.
6. If transfer case is supported by crossmember, or a support bracket, remove crossmember or the support bracket bolts, then lower transfer case from vehicle.
7. If transfer case is secured to an adapter, remove transfer case to adapter mounting bolts. Slide transfer case rearward to disengage front input spline and lower transfer case from vehicle.
8. Reverse procedure to install.

Rear Axle Section

NOTE: For Eaton, Spicer and Timken (Rockwell) driving axles used on Dodge & Plymouth trucks, see the "name" chapters for service procedures and lubricant capacities

DODGE SEMI-FLOATING AXLE ALL EXC. 8 3/8, 9 1/4

In these axles, Figs. 1 & 2, the drive pinion is mounted in two tapered roller bearings, preloaded by a spacer and/or shims.

The differential is supported by two tapered roller side bearings. In the removable type, the differential assembly is positioned for proper ring and pinion back lash and bearing preload by two threaded ring nuts between the bearings and the mounting pedestals. In the integral type, the differential assembly is positioned by shims located between the bearing cone and the hub shoulder of the differential case.

Removal

1. With wheels removed, remove drum retaining clips and brake drum.
2. Through hole in axle shaft flange, remove five nuts from shaft retainer plate. The right hand shaft with adjuster in retainer plate will also have a lock under one of the studs that will be removed at this time.
3. Pull axle shaft assembly with tool.
4. The inner seal should be replaced at this time. Remove seal using Tool C-637, Fig. 3. Install a new seal using Tool C-839, Fig. 4.

Disassembly

1. Install axle shaft in a vise and slide sleeve

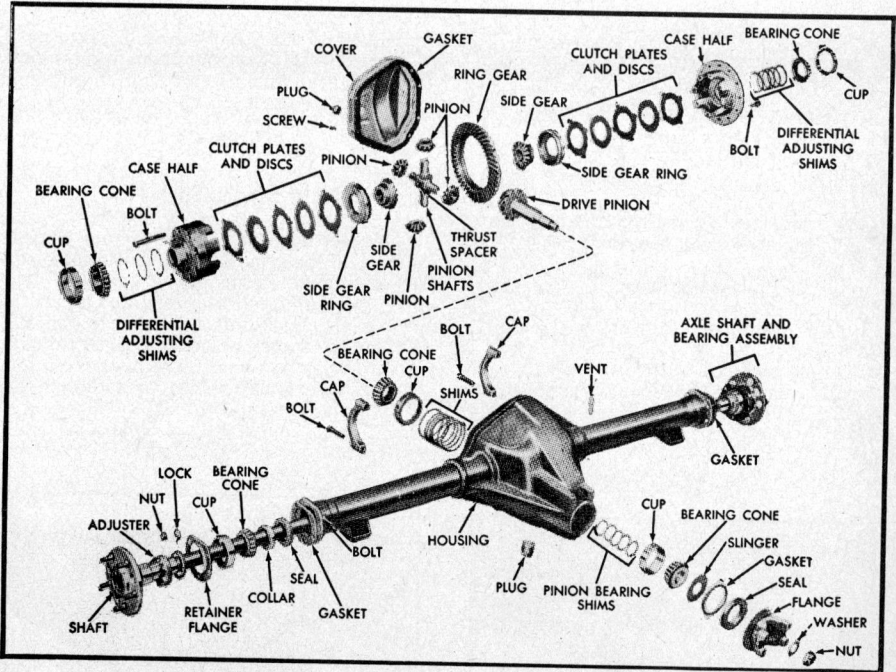

Fig. 2 9 3/4" rear axle assembly. Integral carrier

DODGE & PLYMOUTH

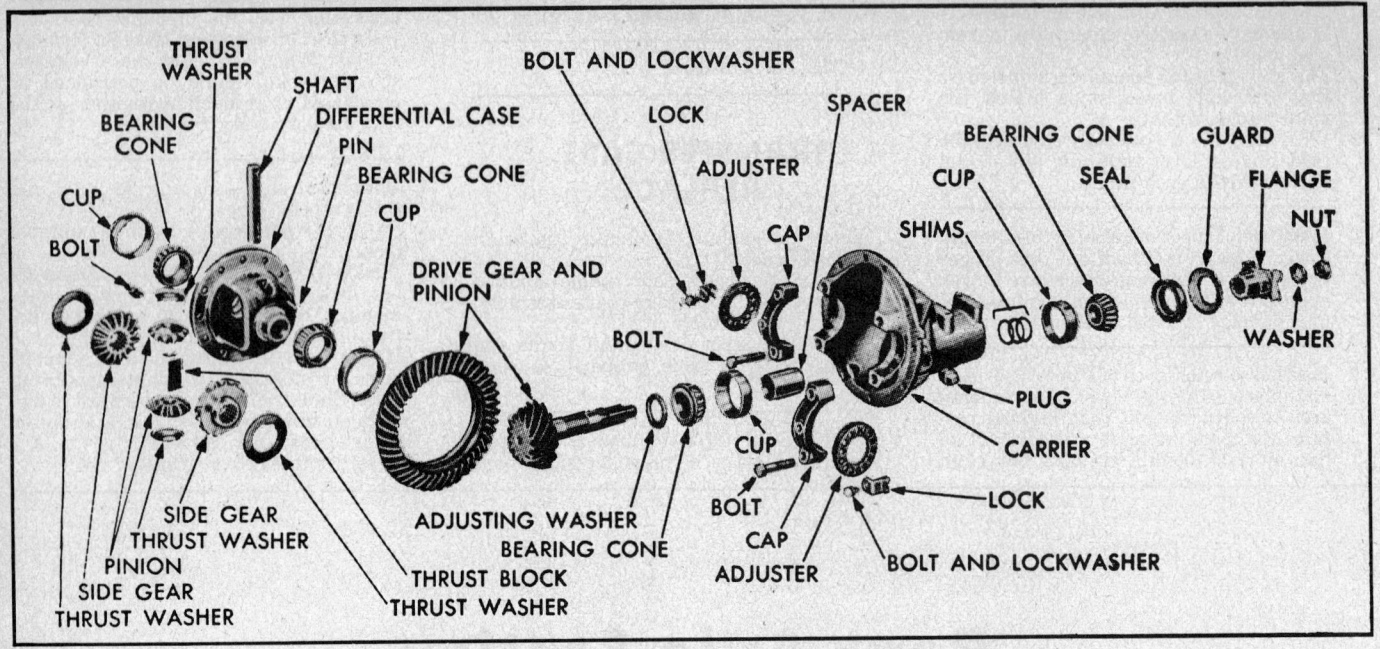

Fig. 1 Differential carrier assembly used with semi-floating axle. Removable type

SP5041 over seal surface of shaft and notch collar, Fig. 5. Slide collar off shaft.
2. Remove roller retainer flange by cutting it off lower edge with a chisel, Fig. 6.
3. Grind a section off flange of inner bearing cone, Fig. 7.
4. Remove bearing rollers from section of flange that was ground away, Fig. 8.
5. Pull roller retainer down as far as possible and cut it with a pair of side cutters and remove from the assembly, Fig. 9.
6. Remove roller bearing cup and protective sleeve from shaft.
7. To avoid scuffing seal journal when bearing cone is being removed, it should be protected by a single wrap of .002" shim stock held in place by a rubber band, Fig. 10.
8. Remove bearing cone with tool set. Tighten bolts of tool alternately until cone is removed, Fig. 11.
9. Remove seal in bearing retainer plate and replace with a new seal.

Assembly

1. Install retainer plate and seal on axle shaft.
2. Install new axle shaft bearing cup, cone and collar on shaft, using tool shown in Fig. 12. Tighten bolts of tool alternately until bearing and collar are seated properly.
3. Inspect axle shaft seal journal for scratches and polish with #600 crocus cloth if necessary.
4. Lubricate wheel bearings.

Installation

1. Install new gasket on left end of housing, add brake backing plate and a second new gasket. Both gaskets are the same on this installation.
2. Slide left axle shaft assembly into position carefully to avoid damaging the new inner seal. Install and tighten retainer plate nuts to 30-35 ft.-lbs.
3. Repeat Step 1 for right side of axle housing.

Axle Shaft End Play

When setting end play both rear wheels must be off the ground, otherwise a false end play setting will occur.
1. Using a dial indicator mounted on a stud or right axle shaft as shown in Fig. 13, turn the adjuster clockwise until there is zero end play. Back off adjuster counterclockwise four notches to establish an axle shaft end play of .013–.023".

2. Tap end of left axle shaft lightly with a plastic mallet to seat right wheel bearing cup against adjuster, and rotate axle shaft several revolutions so that a true end play reading is indicated.
3. Remove one retainer plate nut and install adjuster lock. If tab on lock does not mate with notch in adjuster, turn adjuster slightly until it does. Install nut and torque to 30-35 ft. lbs.
4. Recheck axle shaft end play. If not within prescribed limits, repeat adjustment procedure.
5. Remove dial indicator and install brake drum, drum retaining clips and wheel.

8 3/8 & 9 1/4 INCH INTEGRAL CARRIER TYPE

These axle assemblies, Fig. 14, are of the integral carrier housing hypoid gear type with the centerline of the drive pinion mounted below the centerline of the ring gear. The drive pinion is supported by two preloaded taper roller bearings and the front and rear pinion bearing cones are pressed on the pinion stem. The front and rear pinion bearing cups are pressed against a shoulder that is

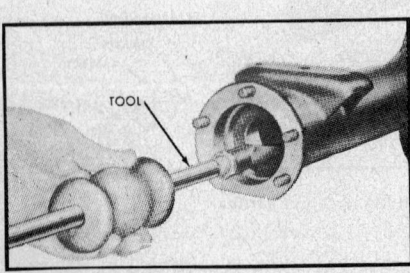

Fig. 3 Removing inner oil seal

Fig. 4 Installing inner oil seal

Fig. 5 Notching bearing retainer collar

DODGE & PLYMOUTH

Fig. 6 Removing roller retainer

Fig. 7 Flange ground off inner bearing cone

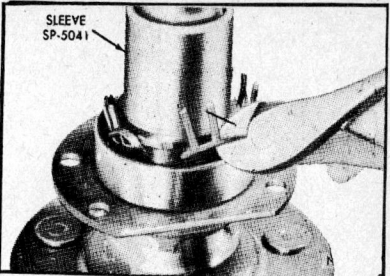

Fig. 9 Cutting out bearing retainer

recessed within the carrier casting. Drive pinion depth of mesh adjustment is controlled by installing metal shims between the rear pinion bearing cup and carrier casting.

AXLE SHAFTS & BEARINGS REPLACE

1. Raise and support vehicle and remove brake drum.
2. Clean area around housing cover, then loosen housing cover and allow lubricant to drain and remove cover.
3. Turn differential case until pinion shaft lock screw is accessible and remove lock screw and pinion shaft, Fig. 15.
4. Push axle shaft inward and remove C-washer locks from axle shaft, Fig. 16, then pull axle shaft from housing being careful not to damage axle shaft bearing.

NOTE: Inspect axle shaft bearing surfaces for signs of spalling or pitting. If any of these conditions exist, both shaft and bearing should be replaced. Normal bearing contact on shaft should be a dull gray and may appear lightly dented.

5. Using tools C-4167 and C-637, remove axle shaft bearing and seal from axle housing, Fig. 17. If bearing shows no sign of excessive wear or damage, it can be reused along with a new seal. Never reuse an axle shaft seal.

NOTE: Remove any burrs that may be present in housing bearing shoulder, as bearing could become cocked during installation.

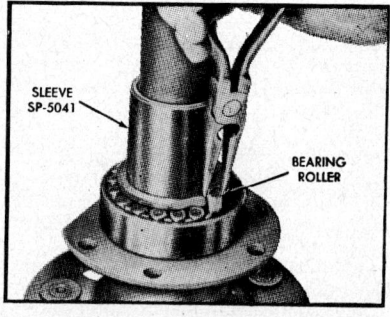

Fig. 8 Removing bearing rollers

6. Using tools C-4198 and C-4171, Fig. 18, install bearing making sure it does not become cocked. Drive bearing until it bottoms against shoulder.

NOTE: Do not use seal to position or bottom bearing as this will damage seal.

7. Using tool C-4130, install axle shaft bearing seal until outer flange of tool bottoms against housing flange face. This will position seal to the proper depth.
8. Reverse disassembly procedure to reassemble axle.

DIFFERENTIAL CASE SERVICE

Removal & Disassembly

1. Remove axle shafts as described previously.
2. Scribe marks on propeller shaft universal joint and pinion flange, then disconnect propeller shaft from differential yoke and secure in an upright position to avoid damage to front universal.
3. Measure and record side play and runout for use during reassembly as follows:
   a. Measure differential side play by positioning a screwdriver or pinch bar between left side of axle housing and differential case, Fig. 19. There should be no side play when differential case is pryed sideways.
   b. Measure drive gear runout by mounting a dial indicator at right angles to back face of drive gear, then rotate drive gear several complete revolutions and note reading. Mark drive gear and differential case at point of maximum runout, this marking will facilitate in determining differential case runout. If total indicated runout is more than .005 inch, the differential case may be damaged. Test for case runout as described further on.
   c. Using an inch pound torque wrench, measure and record pinion bearing preload.
4. Remove drive pinion nut, then using appropriate holding tool, remove pinion flange.
5. Using a screwdriver and hammer, drive pinion oil seal from carrier.
6. Mark axle housing and differential bearing caps for proper relocation during reassembly, Fig. 20, then remove adjuster locks from bearing cap and loosen but do not remove bearing caps.
7. Using tool C-4164 inserted through axle shaft tube, loosen hex adjuster, Fig. 21.
8. Hold differential assembly in place, then using extreme caution, remove bearing caps, adjusters and differential assembly.

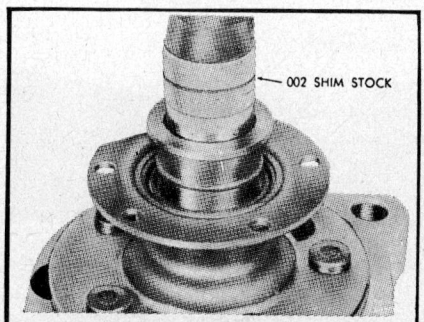

Fig. 10 Seal journal protection

Fig. 11 Removing bearing cone

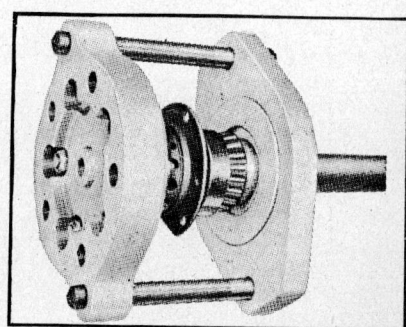

Fig. 12 Installing bearing and collar

1007

DODGE & PLYMOUTH

Fig. 13 Measuring axle shaft end play

Fig. 16 Removing "C" lock washers

case pilot.
13. If drive gear runout exceeded .005 inch in previous check, differential case flange runout should be checked. Install differential case and respective bearing cups and adjusters in housing.
14. Install bearing caps and lightly tighten cap bolts, then using tool C-4164, Fig. 21, tighten both hex adjusters until all side play in bearings has been eliminated.
15. Mount a dial indicator on housing so that pointer on indicator squarely contacts drive gear surface of differential case flange between outer edge of flange and drive gear bolts.
16. Rotate differential case several revolutions and note total indicated runout. If reading is in excess of .003 inch, differential case should be replaced.

NOTE: Differential bearing cups and threaded adjusters must be kept with their respective bearing cones.

9. If necessary to remove drive pinion or front pinion bearing cone, drive pinion stem rearward and out of bearing.

NOTE: This procedure will result in damage to bearing rollers and cups, and both bearing cone and cup must be replaced with new parts. Discard collapsible spacer.

NOTE: If runout does not exceed .003 inch, sometimes it is possible to reduce runout by positioning drive gear 180° from point of maximum runout when reassembling drive gear on differential case.

17. Remove pedestal cap bolts and remove differential case assembly from carrier.
18. Rotate differential side gears until differential pinions appear at differential case window and remove pinions, differential side gears and thrust washers.
19. Using tool C-293-P and adapter plates C-293-44 for 8³/₈ inch units or C-293-47 for the 9¹/₄ inch units and plug SP-3289 for 8³/₈ inch units, or C-293-3 for the 9¹/₄ inch units. Remove differential bearing cones.

10. Using a brass drift and hammer, remove front and rear bearing cups from housing, then remove shim from behind rear bearing cup and record thickness. Discard damaged shim.
11. Using tool C-293-P and adapters C-293-42 for 8³/₈ inch units, or C-293-37 for 9¹/₄ inch units, remove rear bearing cone from drive pinion.

NOTE: Make certain that adapters are located so as not to pull on bearing cage.

12. Mount differential case in a soft jawed vise, then remove drive gear bolts. Note that bolts are left hand threaded. Using a plastic hammer or brass drift, tap drive gear loose and remove from differential

Assembly & Installation

1. Lubricate all components with rear axle lubricant.
2. Install thrust washers on differential side gears, then position gears in counterbores of differential case.
3. Position thrust washers on both differential pinion gears, then mesh the pinion gears making sure pinion gears are exactly 180° apart.
4. Rotate side gears until pinion gears and washers are aligned with differential pinion shaft holes in case.

NOTE: The contact surface of the drive gear and differential case and flange must be clean with all burrs removed.

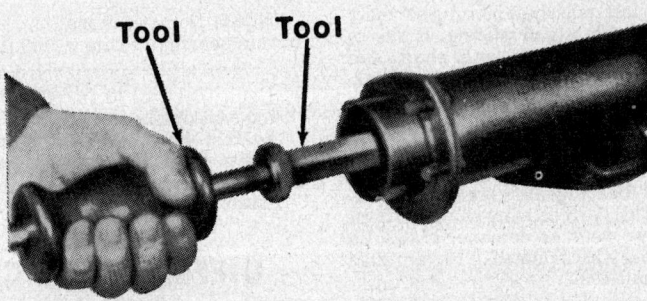

Fig. 17 Removing axle shaft bearing and seal

Fig. 15 Removing differential pinion shaft lock pin

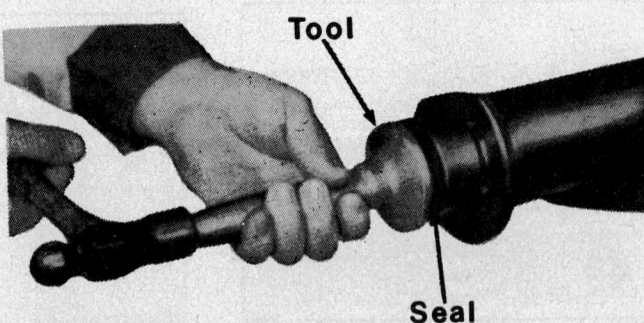

Fig. 18 Installing axle shaft oil seal

DODGE & PLYMOUTH

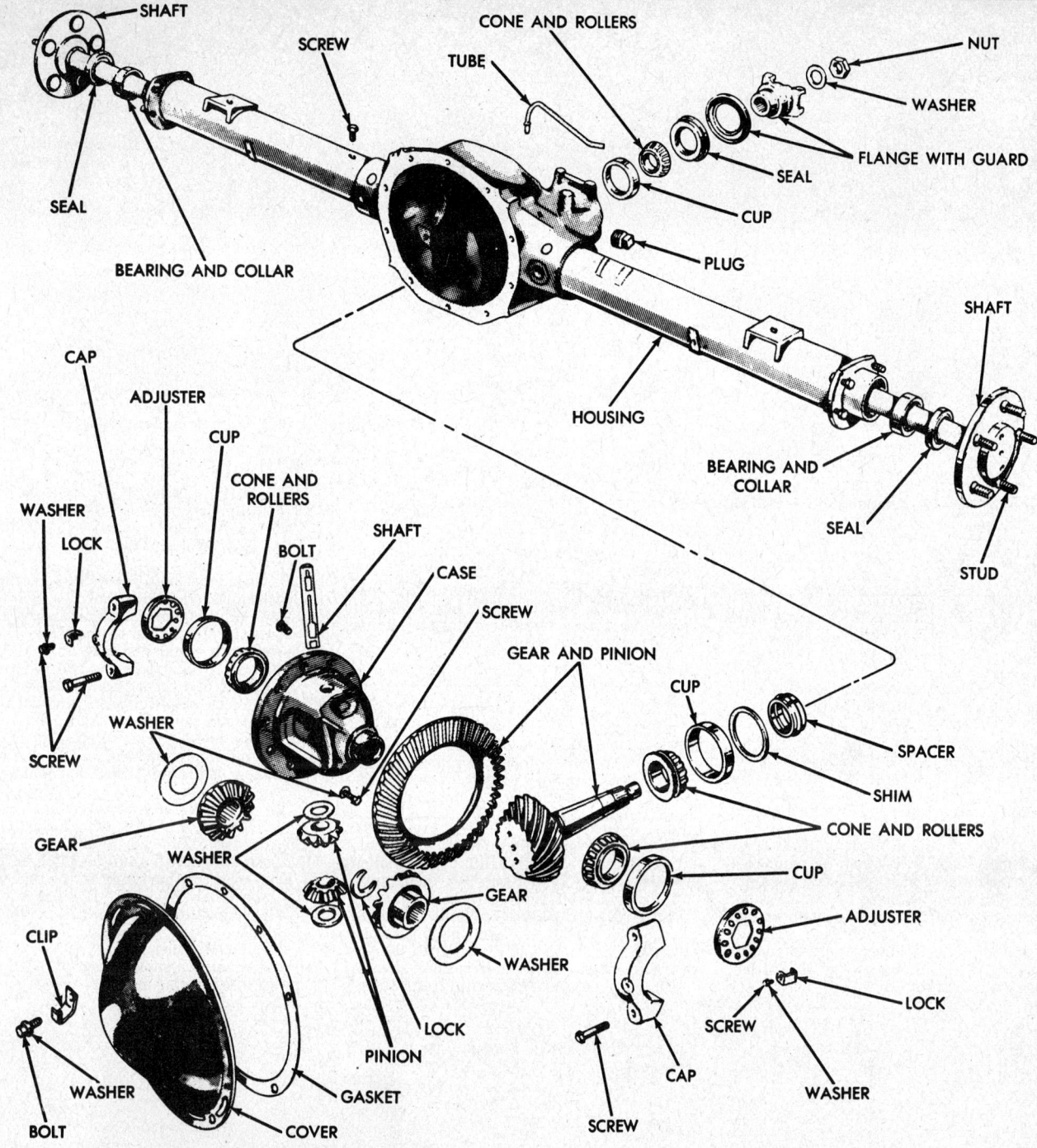

Fig. 14 8³⁄₈″ & 9¹⁄₄″ integral carrier rear axle assembly. The 8³⁄₈ inch unit is equipped with a vent tube mounted on the carrier housing, while the 9¹⁄₄ inch unit has a vent located on the left leg of the housing

5. With an Arkansas stone, relieve the sharp edge of the chamfer on the inside diameter of the ring gear, Fig. 22.

NOTE: If sharp edges are not removed from inside diameter of ring gear, during installation of ring gear on differential case, these edges will remove metal from pilot diameter of case and will imbed between differential case flange and gear. This will cause improper seating of ring gear.

6. Heat ring with a heat lamp or immersing in hot water or oil, with temperatures not exceeding 300° F.

CAUTION: Do not use a torch. It is advisable to use pilot studs equally spaced in three positions to align gear with case.

7. Install unit in a soft jawed vise and alternately torque new drive gear screws (left hand threads) to 70 ft. lbs.

8. Position each differential bearing cone on hub of differential case with taper away from drive gear and using tools C-4107 (for 8³⁄₈ inch units) or C-4213 and C-4171 (for 9¹⁄₄ inch units) install bearing cones. An arbor press may be used in conjunction with installing tool.

CAUTION: Never exert pressure against

1009

DODGE & PLYMOUTH

Fig. 19 Checking differential side play

Fig. 20 Marking bearing caps and housing for proper identification

bearing cage, since bearing damage will result.

9. Install drive pinion bearing cups and using setting gauge tools and adapter sets, Figs. 23 and 24, determine pinion depth of mesh.
10. Start both drive pinion bearing cups into axle housing bores making certain they are not cocked.
11. Assemble spacer SP-5408 for 8 3/8 inch units or SP-6017 for 9 1/4 inch units over tool SP-5385 for 8 3/8 inch units or SP-526 for 9 1/4 inch units followed by the rear pinion bearing cone and insert through rear side of axle carrier.
12. Install front pinion bearing cone over spacer SP-5382 for 8 3/8 inch units, or SP-6022 for the 9 1/4 inch units and position onto stem of tool followed by compression sleeve SP-3194-B for 8 3/8 inch units, or SP-535-A for the 9 1/4 inch units, centralizing washer SP-534 and compression nut SP-3193 for 8 3/8 inch units or SP-533 for the 9 1/4 inch units.
13. While holding compression sleeve from turning with tool C-3281, tighten nut, thereby drawing pinion bearing cups into axle housing bearing cup bores. Permit tool to turn several revolutions while tightening to prevent hardening of bearing cups or cones.

NOTE: The position of the drive gear pinion with respect to the drive gear (depth of mesh) is determined by the location of the bearing cup shoulders in the carrier and by the portion of pinion behind the rear bearing.

14. With main tool remaining in axle housing, loosen nut SP-3193 for 8 3/8 inch units, or SP-533 for the 9 1/4 inch units. Lubricate front and rear pinion bearings with rear axle lubricant and retighten nut to obtain 10–30 inch lbs. of preload for 8 3/8 inch units, or 15–25 inch lbs. for the 9 1/4 inch units. Rotate pinion several complete revolutions to align and lubricate bearing rollers.
15. Install gauge block SP-5383 for 8 3/8 inch units, or SP-6020 for the 9 1/4 inch units on the end of main tool and tighten set screw.
16. Position cross bore arbor SP-5380 for 8 3/8 inch units, or SP-6018 for 9 1/4 inch units into axle housing differential bearing seats. Center arbor to maintain an approximate equal distance at both ends. Position bearing caps and bolts on carrier pedestals and insert a piece of .002 inch shim stock between arbor and each cap. Torque cap bolts to 10 ft. lbs.
17. Using a feeler gauge, select a rear pinion bearing mounting shim which will fit between cross bore and arbor and gauge. This fit must be snug but not too tight. Shims are available in increments of .001 inch from .061–.078 inch for 8 3/8 inch units, or .020–.038 inch for 9 1/4 inch units. To select a shim pack for installation, read the markings on the end of the pinion head (−0, −1, −2, +1, +2 etc). When marking is minus, add that amount to the thickness of shim pack selected. When marking is plus, subtract that amount. Apply other pinion markings in a similar manner.

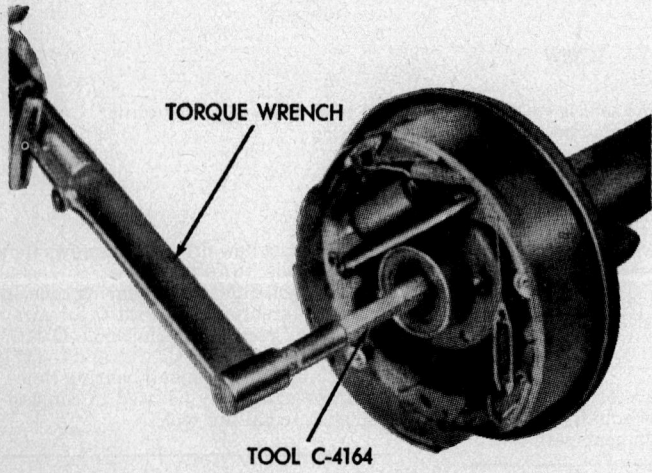

Fig. 21 Loosening or tightening hex adjuster

Fig. 22 Relieving sharp edge on chamfer ring gear

DODGE & PLYMOUTH

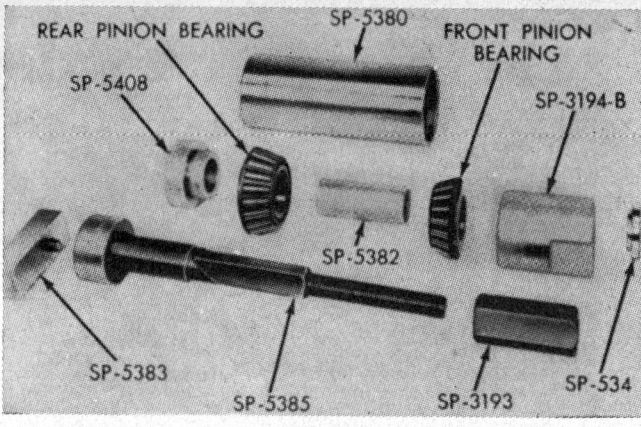

Fig. 23 8³/₈ inch axle pinion setting tools

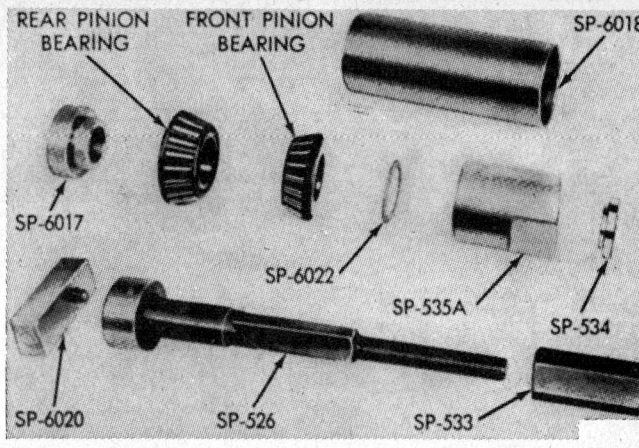

Fig. 24 9¹/₄ inch axle pinion setting tools

18. Remove arbor and tool from axle housing.
19. On 8³/₈ inch units, remove rear pinion bearing cup from casting.
20. Position shim selected previously on pinion followed by rear pinion bearing cone, making certain that pinion head contact surface, bearing cone and shim are clean. Using tool DD-955 press bearing onto pinion stem.
21. Lubricate front and rear pinion bearing cones with rear axle lubricant and insert drive pinion and bearing assembly through axle housing. Install new collapsible spacer over pinion stem and position front pinion bearing cone over pinion stem.
22. Install companion flange using tool C-3718 for 8³/₈ inch units or DD-999 for 9¹/₄ inch units and holding tool C-3281. This is necessary in order to properly install front pinion bearing cone on pinion due to interference fit.

CAUTION: During installation of front pinion bearing cone, be careful not to collapse spacer.

23. Remove tool and flange from pinion stem.
24. Using tool C-4076 for 8³/₈ inch units, or either C-3980 or C-4109 for the 9¹/₄ inch units install drive pinion oil seal. Seal is properly seated when seal flange contacts housing flange face.

NOTE: Outside diameter of seal is coated with a special sealer so no sealing compound is required.

25. While supporting pinion in carrier reinstall companion flange using tools previously described.
26. Remove tools and install Belleville washer with convex side of washer out then the pinion nut.
27. Using holding tool on universal flange, tighten pinion nut to remove end play in pinion, while rotating pinion to insure proper bearing roller seating.
28. Remove holding tool and rotate pinion several revolutions in both directions to permit bearing rollers to seat.
29. Torque pinion nut to 210 ft. lbs. and while rotating pinion, measure pinion bearing preload. The correct bearing preload specifications are 20-35 inch lbs. for new bearings with the pinion nut torqued to 210 ft. lbs. minimum. If when rebuilding axle and the original rear pinion bearing and a new front pinion bearing are used, the correct bearing preload is 10 inch lbs. more than the reading at the time of disassembly with a minimum of 210 ft. lbs. of torque on the pinion nut. If correct preload cannot be obtained at 210 ft. lbs., continue tightening nut in small increments and checking until proper preload is obtained. Bearing preload should be uniform during complete revolution. A preload that varies during rotation indicates a binding condition which must be corrected. The assembly is unacceptable if final pinion nut torque is below 210 ft. lbs. or pinion bearing preload is not within specifications.

CAUTION: The pinion nut should not be backed off to decrease pinion bearings preload. If the desired preload is exceeded for any reason, a new collapsible spacer must be installed and the nut retightened until proper preload is obtained.

30. Coat differential bearing cones, cups and adjusters with axle lubricant and carefully position the entire assembly into housing.
31. Install differential bearing cups on their respective sides, using the marks made during disassembly.
32. Install bearing cap and torque top bolts to 10 ft. lbs. and tighten bottom bolts finger tight until head is just seated on bearing cap.

Differential Bearing Preload & Drive Gear Backlash

The following precautions must be observed when adjusting differential bearing preload and drive gear backlash.

a. Permissible variation is .003 inch. This variation is actually allowable runout. Therefore it is important to index the gears engaging same teeth during all backlash measurements.
b. Also maintain specified adjuster torque to obtain accurate differential bearing preload and drive gear backlash measurements.

NOTE: Excessive torque will produce high bearing load and cause premature bearing failures. Inadequate torque will not support the drive gear load properly, will lead to free play of the differential assembly and excessive drive gear noise.

CAUTION: Differential bearing cups will not always move directly with the adjusters, therefore to insure accurate adjustment changes and to maintain gear mesh index, bearings must be seated by vigorously moving the drive pinion a half turn in each direction five to ten times each time adjusters are moved.

1. Using tool C-4164 turn each hex adjuster, Fig. 23 until bearing free play is eliminated with some drive gear backlash (approximately .010 inch) between drive gear and pinion. Now seat bearings.
2. Install dial indicator and position contact point against drive side of gear tooth. To find point of minimum backlash, check backlash at four positions at approximately 90 degree intervals around drive gear. Rotate gear to position of least backlash. Mark the index so that all backlash readings will be taken with the same teeth in mesh.
3. Loosen right adjuster and tighten left adjuster until the backlash is .003-.004 inch with each adjuster torqued to 10 ft. lbs. Again seat bearings. Torque differential bearing cap bolts to 100 ft. lbs. Using tool C-4164 torque right hex adjuster to 70 ft. lbs. for 8³/₈ inch units and 75 ft. lbs. for the 9¹/₄ inch units. Again seat bearings. Continue to tighten right adjuster and seat rollers until torque remains constant at 70 ft. lbs. for 8³/₈ inch units and 75 ft. lbs. for the 9¹/₄ inch units. Measure backlash. If backlash does not measure between .006-.008 inch, increase torque on right adjuster and seat bearings until correct backlash is obtained. Torque left adjuster to 70 ft. lbs. for 8³/₈ inch units and 75 ft. lbs. for the 9¹/₄ inch units. Seat bearing until torque remains constant.

NOTE: If all previous steps have been properly performed, initial reading on left adjuster will be about 70 ft. lbs. for 8³/₈ inch models and 75 ft. lbs. for the 9¹/₄ inch units. If it is considerably less, complete procedure must be repeated.

4. When adjustments are completed, install adjuster locks. Be sure lock finger is engaged in adjuster hole. Torque lock screws to 90 inch lbs.

DODGE & PLYMOUTH

Front Wheel Drive Section

NOTE: For overhaul procedure on the transfer case used with front-wheel drive trucks, see the Transfer Case chapter.

MODEL 44F

The front axle drive shaft outer end connects through a splined slip joint drive flange to the wheel hub. The inner and outer axle shafts are connected through universal joints which revolve in the steering knuckles. Some service parts replacement can be made without complete removal of the axle assembly. However, it is generally desirable to remove the assembly for complete overhaul.

AXLE ASSEMBLY

Remove and Replace

1. Secure brake pedal in the up position, then raise vehicle.
2. Disconnect front drive shaft at drive pinion yoke.
3. Disconnect drag link at steering knuckle arm (left side only).
4. Disconnect and plug brake line at frame crossmember.
5. Disconnect shock absorbers at lower mounts, then disconnect sway bar assembly from spring plates, if equipped.
6. Remove nuts and washers from "U" bolt spring clips, then remove axle from vehicle.
7. Reverse removal procedure to install axle assembly. Lubricate all fittings, free brake pedal and bleed brakes.
8. Lower vehicle and check front wheel alignment.

Front Drive Axle & Joint Repairs

1. Remove wheel assembly.
2. Remove grease cap from drive flange.
3. Remove bolts and snap ring; then, using a suitable puller, remove drive flange.
4. Remove outer lock nut.
5. Remove nut lock and front wheel bearing adjusting nuts.
6. Remove hub and brake drum.
7. Unfasten brake support and disconnect brake line. If axle is on vehicle, attach brake support with wire to front spring, thus making it unnecessary to disconnect brake lines.
8. Tap end of spindle with soft-head hammer to remove spindle.
9. Inspect spindle for wear and damage.
10. Inspect spindle axle flanged bushing for wear, Fig. 1. If a new bushing is to be installed it requires no reaming. It is so designed that when it is pressed into the spindle, it will be compressed to provide proper running clearance.
11. Remove axle shaft assembly.
12. Disassemble front axle as suggested by Fig. 1.
13. Reverse the removal procedure to install the front axle shaft and joint assembly.

Steering Knuckle Repairs

1. Remove wheel, hub, drum, brake support, spindle and axle shaft, Fig. 2.
2. Disconnect tie rod ends from steering knuckles.
3. Disconnect drag link from steering knuckle arm.
4. Remove steering knuckle felt and oil seal retainers, Fig. 3.
5. Remove lower bearing cap.
6. Unscrew nuts from top of steering knuckle arm. Remove arm, pivot and shims.
7. Remove knuckle housing, felt and oil seal.
8. Remove upper and lower bearing cones.

Assembling Knuckle

1. Place felt and oil seal over end of axle housing.
2. Place original shims on knuckle upper studs, Fig. 3.
3. Install steering knuckle arm and tighten retaining nuts to 35-55 ft. lbs torque.
4. Coat bronze cone with short fiber grease. Insert cone in steering knuckle and install it on knuckle arm pivot. Make sure cone is properly positioned on key.
5. Slide knuckle over yoke, entering upper cone in its cup.
6. Pack lower bearing cone with short fiber grease; tilt bottom of knuckle outward and insert lower cone.
7. Position knuckle over lower cone and install lower bearing cap. Tighten capscrews to 30-50 ft. lbs torque.
8. Check preload of knuckle bearings by hooking a spring scale in the tie rod socket hole, and pulling on scale at right angles to the axle. Preload should be 9 to 25 lbs when in motion without seal attached to Spicer 44F axle. Adjust preload by adding or removing shims under knuckle arm.
9. Attach oiled felt and oil seal to knuckle housing with retainers and screws.
10. Connect tie rod ends and drag link.
11. Install axle shaft, spindle and brake support. Torque to 40 ft. lbs.
12. Install hub, drum and wheel and adjust front wheel bearings as outlined below.
13. Fill steering knuckle joint housing with S.A.E. 140 oil to level of filler plug opening.
14. Check toe-in and adjust if required at the tie rod end. Clamp should be at the bottom for Models W100 and W200.
15. Check turning radius as excessive angle may cause damage to joint assembly. Adjust to 29 degrees turning angle by breaking weld at stop screw lock nut. Secure nut by spot weld after making adjustment.

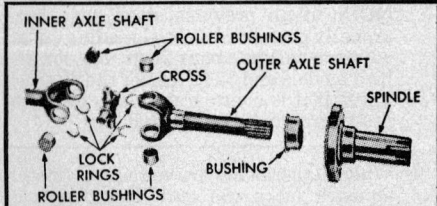

Fig. 1 Universal joint, spindle and bushing assembly. (Typical)

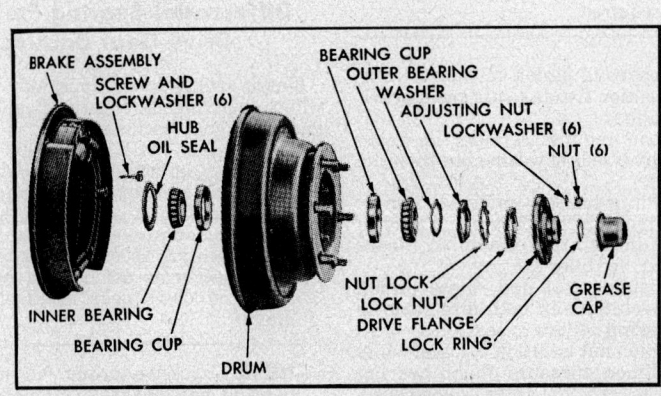

Fig. 2 Brake hub and drum assembly Models W100, W200, W300

DODGE & PLYMOUTH

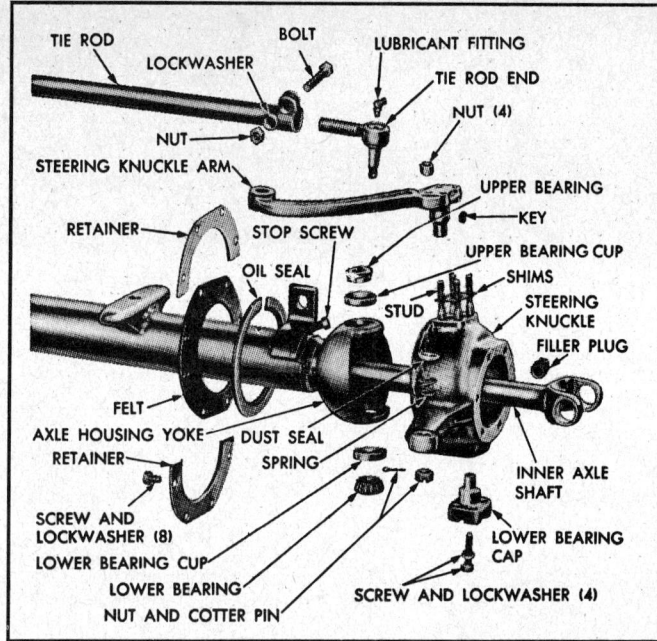

Fig. 3 Spicer 44F axle and steering knuckle assembly. Models W100, W200, Ramcharger & Trailduster. (Typical)

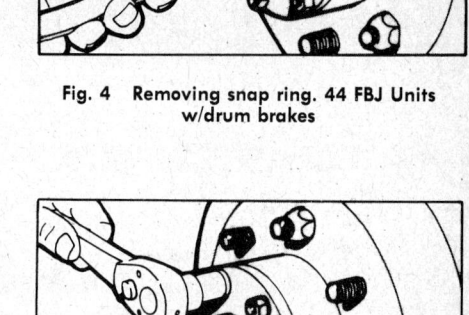

Fig. 4 Removing snap ring. 44 FBJ Units w/drum brakes

Fig. 5 Removing flange nuts. 44 FBJ Units w/drum brakes

Wheel Bearings, Adjust

Tighten bearing adjusting nut while rotating wheel slowly in both directions. Continue tightening until some binding is evident then back off 1/8 turn. Engage lock, then tighten lock nut securely and bend down tabs on lockwasher.

44FBJ, UNITS WITH DRUM BRAKES

Upper or Lower Ball Sockets

Removal
1. Raise and support truck.
2. Remove wheel.
3. Remove hub cap and snap ring, Fig. 4.
4. Remove flange nuts and lock washers, Fig. 5. Remove flange and discard gasket.
5. Using suitable tool, unscrew outer lock nut and remove lock ring, inner lock nut, bearing and brake drum, Fig. 6.
6. Remove nuts from brake support plate then slide brake assembly off spindle and secure out of the way. Do not allow assembly to hang by hydraulic brake hose.
7. Remove spindle, Fig. 7, and bronze spacer from axle shaft.
8. On left side only, remove tie rod from steering knuckle and disconnect steering link from knuckle arm. Unscrew upper steering knuckle arm nuts then remove coned washers and arm, Fig. 8.
9. Remove cotter pin and nut from upper ball socket. Unscrew and discard nut from lower ball socket. Do not reuse lower nut.
10. Remove lower ball socket snap ring, Fig. 9.
11. After securing adapter to knuckle face, Fig. 10, position puller (Tool P-833) and step plate (Tool C-1144) under lower ball socket, Fig. 11, and remove knuckle from yoke.
12. Using suitable tools press ball sockets from yoke and knuckle and discard sockets.
13. Unscrew and discard sleeve from yoke.
14. Clean components thoroughly and inspect. Replace as necessary parts before assembly.

Installation
1. Install upper and lower ball sockets using suitable tools and ensure they are not cocked. Check clearance between sockets and knuckle with .0015 inch feeler gauge. Feeler gauge must not enter at minimum area of contact. Install snap ring on lower ball socket.
2. Using a suitable tool, screw new sleeve into yoke leaving two threads exposed, Fig. 12.
3. Position boots on ball sockets, then assemble knuckle to yoke and finger tighten new nut on lower ball socket.

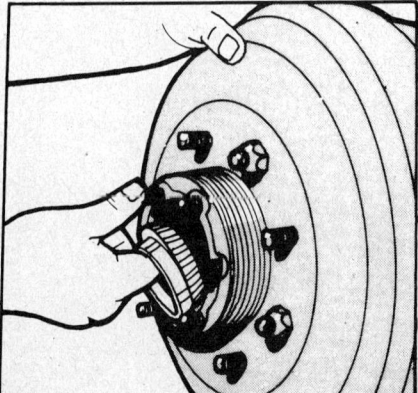

Fig. 6 Removing bearing cone. 44 FBJ Units w/drum brakes

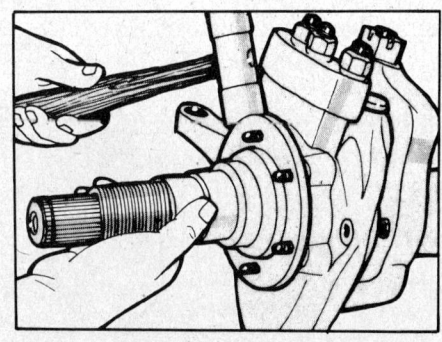

Fig. 7 Removing spindle from knuckle. 44 FBJ Units w/drum brakes

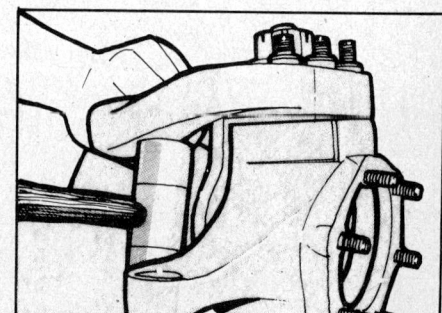

Fig. 8 Removing steering knuckle arm from knuckle. 44 FBJ Units w/drum brakes

DODGE & PLYMOUTH

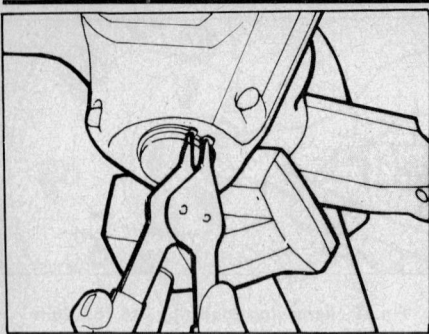

Fig. 9 Lower ball socket snap ring removal. 44 FBJ Units w/drum brakes

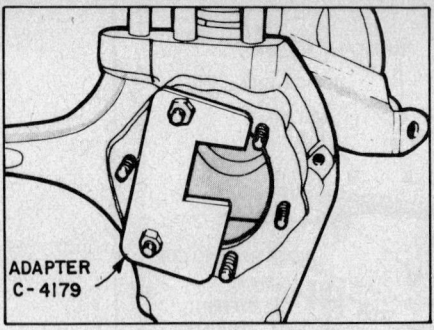

Fig. 10 Adapter tool secured to knuckle. 44 FBJ Units w/drum brakes

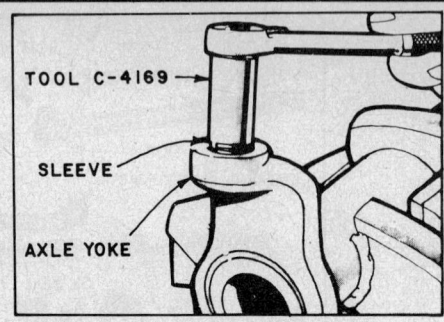

Fig. 12 Yoke sleeve installed. 44 FBJ Units w/drum brakes

4. Seat ball sockets by positioning and tightening proper tools, Fig. 13. Before loosening tools, torque lower socket nut to 80 ft. lbs.
5. After removing tools, tighten adjusting sleeve to 50 ft. lbs. and install upper socket nut. Torque nut to 100 ft. lbs. and install cotter pin if slot in nut and hole in stud are aligned. If not, tighten nut and install pin. Do not loosen.
6. Secure tie rod end to knuckle and torque nut to 45 ft. lbs. On left side only, secure steering knuckle arm to knuckle and torque nuts to 90 ft. lbs. Then assemble steering link to knuckle arm and torque nut to 45 ft. lbs.
7. Carefully slide axle shaft into housing so as not to damage differential seal at side gears. Position bronze spacer on shaft with chamfer inboard and position spindle against knuckle, Fig. 14.
8. Secure brake support plate to knuckle then position brake drum and bearing on spindle and adjust wheel bearings as outlined below.
9. Install new gasket and drive flange. Torque flange nuts to 40 ft. lbs. then install snap ring and hub cap.
10. Install wheel then lower truck and test operation.

Wheel Bearings, Adjust

Tighten bearing adjusting nut while rotat-

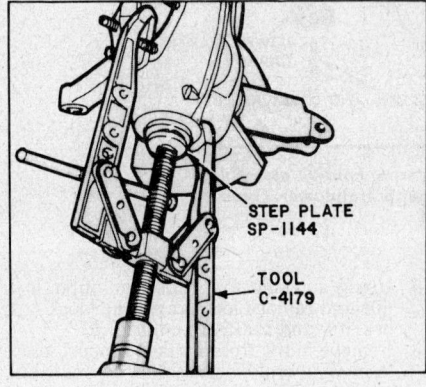

Fig. 11 Using puller to separate knuckle from yoke. 44 FBJ Units w/drum brakes

ing wheel slowly in both directions. Torque nut to 50 ft. lbs. then loosen 1/4 to 1/3 turn and install locknut. Torque outer nut to 50 ft. lbs. Final bearing adjustment should be from .001 inch to .010 inch end play.

44FBJ, UNITS WITH DISC BRAKES

Axle Assembly

Remove and Replace
1. Secure brake pedal in the up position

then raise vehicle.
2. Disconnect front drive shaft at drive pinion yoke.
3. Disconnect drag link at steering knuckle arm (left side only).
4. Disconnect and plug brake line at frame crossmember.
5. Disconnect shock absorbers at lower mounts then disconnect sway bar link assembly, if equipped, from spring plates.
6. Remove nuts and washers from "U" bolt spring clips, then remove axle from vehicle.
7. Reverse procedure to install axle assembly. Lubricate all fittings, free brake pedal and bleed brakes.
8. Lower vehicle and check front wheel alignment.

Servicing Rotor, Hub or Bearings
Removal and Inspection
1. Remove axle shaft cotter pin and loosen outer axle shaft nut.
2. Raise vehicle then remove wheel assembly.
3. After removing caliper retainer and anti-rattle spring assembly, slide caliper out and away from rotor. Hang caliper out of the way. Do not allow caliper to hang by

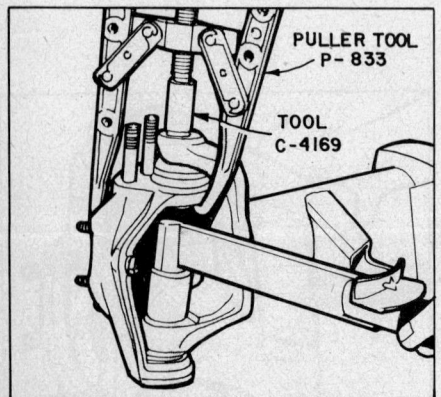

Fig. 13 Tightening lower ball socket nut. 44 FBJ Units w/drum brakes

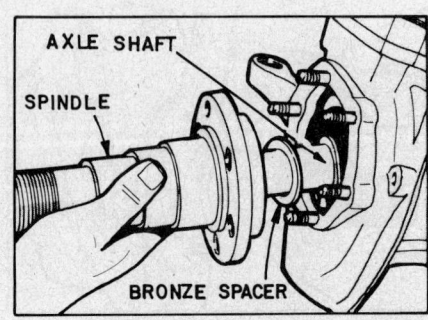

Fig. 14 Installing spindle & spacer to knuckle. 44 FBJ Units w/drum brakes

Fig. 15 Using puller to remove hub & rotor. 44 FBJ Units w/disc brakes

DODGE & PLYMOUTH

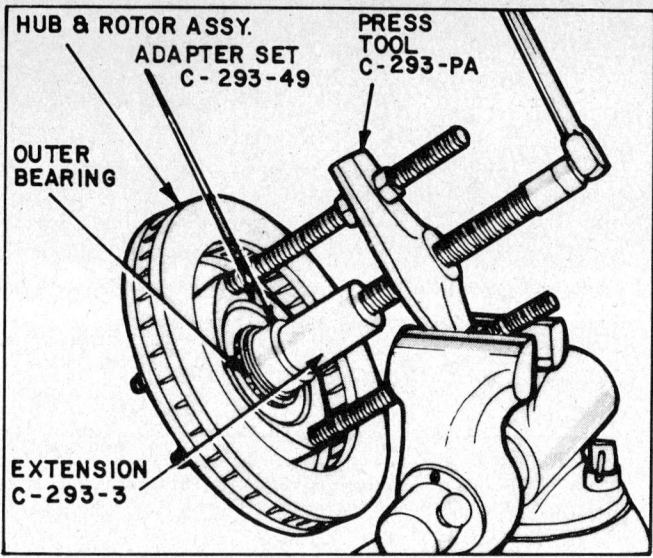

Fig. 16 Removing outer bearing cone. 44 FBJ Units w/disc brakes

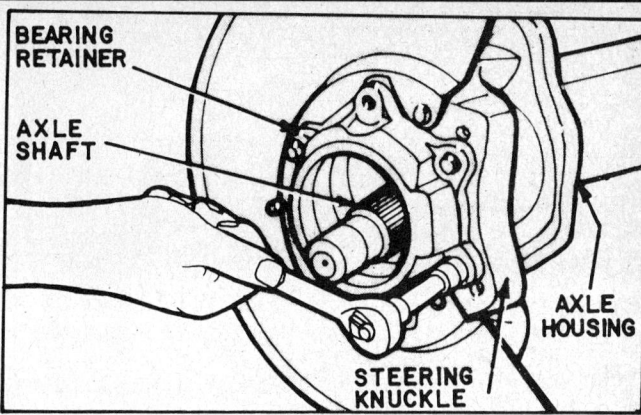

Fig. 17 Removing bearing retainer. 44 FBJ Units w/disc brakes

hydraulic brake hose. Remove inboard brake pad.
4. Remove outer axle shaft nut and washer. Secure a suitable puller to wheel studs and tighten main screw of tool to remove hub and rotor assembly, Fig. 15.
5. Remove puller from hub and rotor assembly.
6. Assemble Modified Bearing Press, Tool C-293-PA, Extension, Tool C-293-3, and Adapters, Tool No. C-293-49, to hub and rotor assembly and position in a vise. Pull outer bearing cone from hub and rotor and discard outer seal, Fig. 16.
7. Remove the six retainer bolts and retainer, Fig. 17, then remove brake caliper adapter from knuckle, if required.
8. Place a pry bar behind inner axle shaft yoke and push bearings out of knuckle, Fig. 18.
9. Remove and discard "O" ring from knuckle, if equipped, then carefully remove axle shaft assembly.

Examine inner seal surface and knuckle bore for wear or damage and replace knuckle if required. If outer axle shaft seal surface is grooved, repair as follows:
a. Measure in from yoke shoulder of axle approximately 3/8 inch. Use a center punch and stake at 1/4 inch intervals around circumference of shaft. This will size shaft and ensure a tight fit of inner seal slinger, Fig. 19.
b. Proper bearing clamp should be checked by installing bearing cups and spacer into knuckle bore and bolting bearing retainer to knuckle, Figs. 20 and 21. If a .004 inch feeler gauge can not be inserted between knuckle and retainer at the six places midway between retainer mounting ears, the knuckle must be replaced, Fig. 22. The brake dust shield may have to be removed to complete this check. If knuckle is serviceable, remove retainer, bearing cups and spacer and install dust shield if removed.

Assembly & Installation
1. Apply RTV sealer or equivalent to seal surface of axle shaft.
2. Using driver, Tool No. C-4398-1, install seal slinger with lip toward splines onto outer axle shaft, Figs. 23 and 24.
3. Carefully insert axle shaft into housing so as not to damage differential seal at side gears. After sliding axle shaft completely in, wedge a pry bar through "U" joint to retain shaft, Fig. 25.
4. Install seal cup using adapter, Tool C-4398-2, and driver, Tool No. C-4398-1. Use a small amount of wheel bearing grease on adapter face to hold cup in position then drive up until bottomed in knuckle, Figs. 26 and 27. Do not remove tool at this time.
5. Using a suitable tool, install new outer seal in retainer plate then locate retainer plate over hub of rotor.
6. Thoroughly pack wheel bearings with Multi-Purpose grease and press outer bearing onto hub using Tool No. C-4246-A and adapters, Fig. 28. Remove tool and place grease coated outer bearing cup over bearing cone followed by spacer, grease coated inner bearing cup and inner bearing cone. Again use Tool Bo. C-4246-A and adapters to press components into position, Fig. 28. Remove tool.
7. Apply a 1/4 inch bead of RTV sealer to retainer face on the chamfer, Fig. 29. This replaces "O" ring discarded during disassembly.
8. Carefully remove seal installing tool from knuckle bore so that outer axle shaft remains centered. If shaft is moved, ensure that lip seal is still riding inside cup.

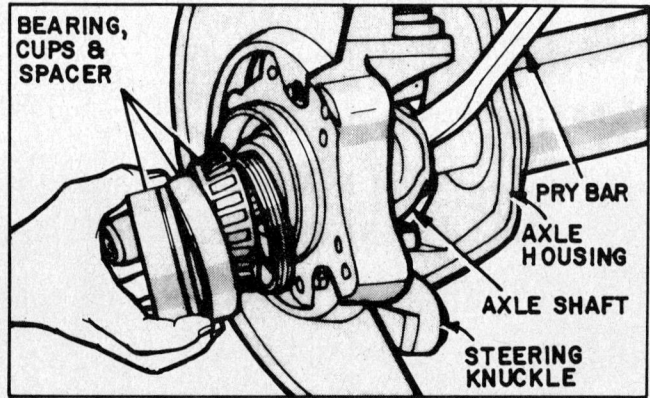

Fig. 18 Using pry bar to remove bearing from knuckle. 44 FBJ Units w/disc brakes

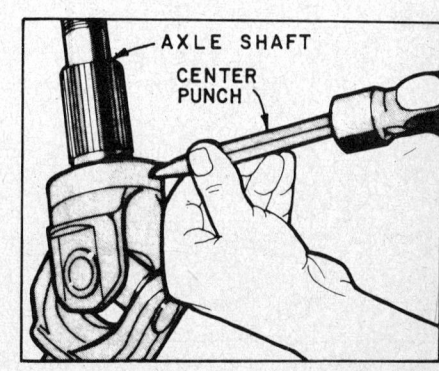

Fig. 19 Sizing axle shaft seal surface. 44 FBJ Units w/disc brakes

DODGE & PLYMOUTH

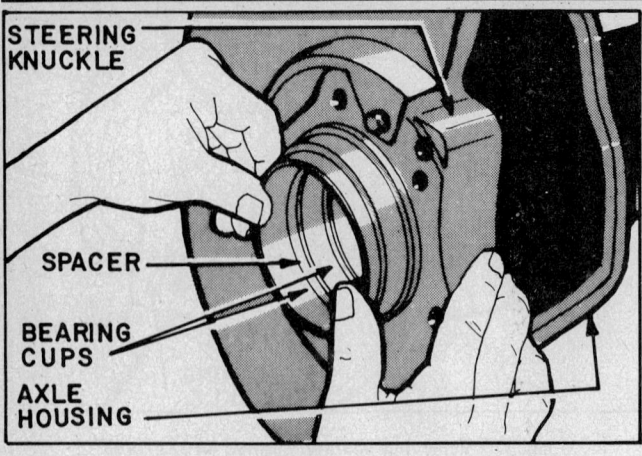

Fig. 20 Installing bearing cups before checking bearing clamp. 44 FBJ Units w/disc brakes

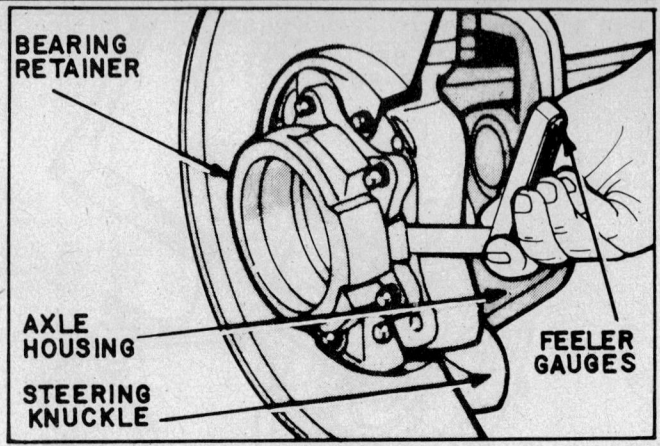

Fig. 22 Checking bearing clamp. 44 FBJ Units w/disc brakes

Correct if necessary.
9. Before assembling hub and rotor to knuckle, position bearing retainer in hub so that grease fitting is facing forward, if equipped. Using a criss-cross method, torque retainer plate bolts to 30 ft. lbs.

NOTE: Bearing retainers that have a grease fitting must be positioned on knuckle so that fitting is facing directly forward, Fig. 30.

10. Install brake adapter and remove pry bar from "U" joint.
11. Install axle shaft washer and nut. Torque nut to 100 ft. lbs. and continue to tighten nut until next slot in nut aligns with help in axle shaft. Install cotter pin.
12. Through the access hole in hub, lubricate fitting in bearing retainer with Multi-Purpose grease until grease flows through new inner seal. Seal may be viewed at the "U" joint area. Spin hub several times and lubricate fitting again. Grease must flow from 1/2 of seal diameter.
13. Replace brake caliper assembly and wheel, then lower truck and test operation.

Steering Knuckle and Ball Joint
Removal and Disassembly
1. Remove axle shaft cotter pin and loosen outer axle shaft nut.
2. Raise vehicle, then remove wheel assembly.
3. After removing caliper retainer and anti-rattle spring assembly, slide caliper out and away from rotor. Hang caliper out of the way. Do not allow caliper to hang by hydraulic brake hose. Remove inboard brake pad.
4. Remove outer axle shaft nut and washer and through access hole in rotor assembly, remove the six bearing retainer bolts.
5. Secure a suitable puller to wheel studs and tighten main screw of tool to remove hub, rotor, bearings, retainer and outer seal as an assembly. Remove puller from rotor.
6. Remove brake caliper adapter from knuckle, then remove and discard "O" ring from knuckle, if equipped.
7. Carefully pull axle shaft assembly out and remove seal and slinger from shaft.

8. Disconnect tie rod from steering knuckle using a suitable tool, Fig. 31, so as not to damage seal.
9. On left side only, disconnect drag link from steering knuckle arm again using a suitable tool to avoid seal damage, Fig. 32.
10. Remove nuts from steering knuckle arm on left side only. Tap arm to loosen tapered dowels. Remove dowels and arm.
11. Remove cotter pin from upper ball joint nut then remove upper and lower ball joint nuts. Discard lower nut.
12. Separate steering knuckle from axle housing yoke using a brass drift and a hammer, then, using a suitable tool, remove and discard sleeve from upper ball joint yoke on axle housing.
13. Secure steering knuckle upside down in a vise and remove snap ring from lower ball joint.
14. Use proper tools to press upper and lower ball joints from steering knuckle. Replace ball joints if any looseness or end play exists.

Assembly and Installation
1. Secure steering knuckle right side up in a vise and press upper and lower ball joints into position using proper tools. Install snap ring on lower joint and new boots on both joints.

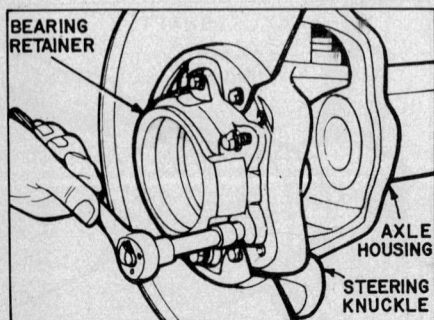

Fig. 21 Installing bearing retainer to check bearing clamp. 44 FBJ Units w/disc brakes

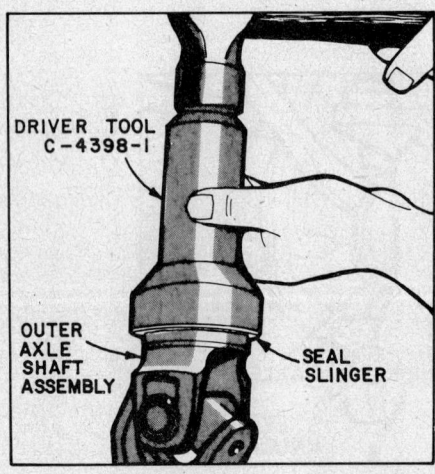

Fig. 23 Installing seal slinger on outer axle shaft. 44 FBJ Units w/disc brakes

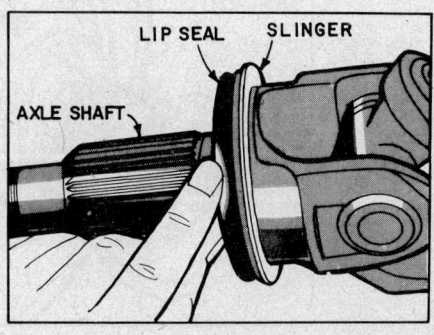

Fig. 24 Installing lip seal on outer axle shaft. 44 FBJ Units w/disc brakes

DODGE & PLYMOUTH

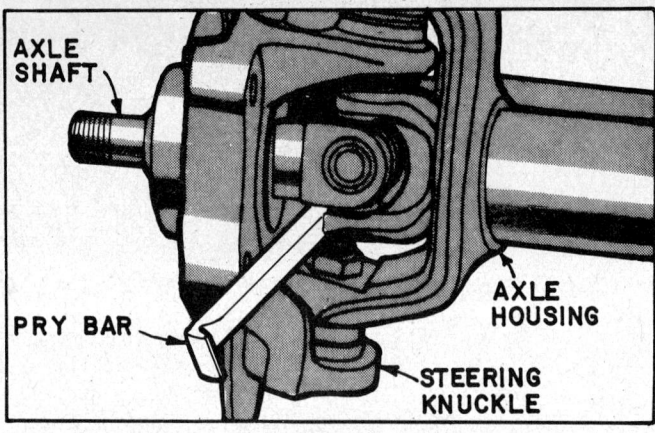

Fig. 25 Using pry bar to retain axle shaft. 44 FBJ Units w/disc brakes

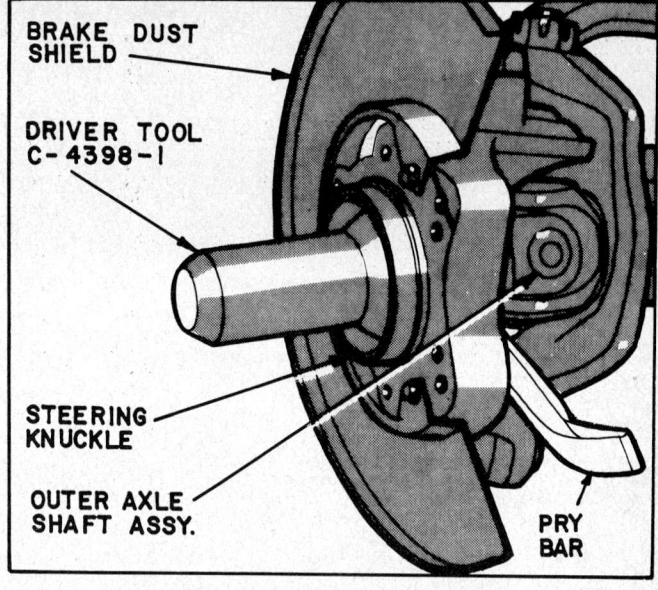

Fig. 27 Tools in place after seal cup is installed. 44 FBJ Units w/disc brakes

2. Thread new sleeve into ball joint yoke on axle housing ensuring that two threads are exposed at the top.
3. Position steering knuckle on axle housing yoke, then install a new lower ball joint nut and torque to 80 ft. lbs.
4. Use Tool No. C-4169 and a torque wrench to torque sleeve in upper ball joint yoke to 40 ft. lbs, then install upper ball joint nut and torque to 100 ft. lbs. Install cotter pin if slot in nuts and hole in stud align. If not, tighten, do not loosen nut to align.
5. On left side only, position steering knuckle arm over studs on steering knuckle. Install tapered dowels and nuts, then torque nuts to 90 ft. lbs. Secure drag link to steering knuckle arm and torque nut to 60 ft. lbs.
6. Secure tie rod end to steering knuckle. Torque nut to 45 ft. lbs.
7. Install brake dust shield, if removed.
8. Inspect outer axle shaft seal surface for grooving. If surface is grooved, repair as described in "Servicing Rotor Hub or Bearings".
9. Apply RTV sealer to seal surface of axle shaft then using driver, C-4398-1, install seal slinger with lip toward splines onto

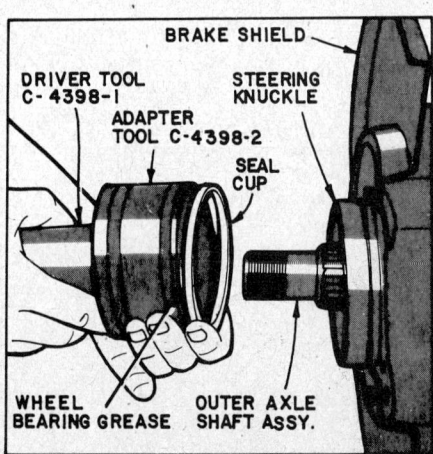

Fig. 26 Using driving & adapter to install seal cup into knuckle. 44 FBJ Units w/disc brakes

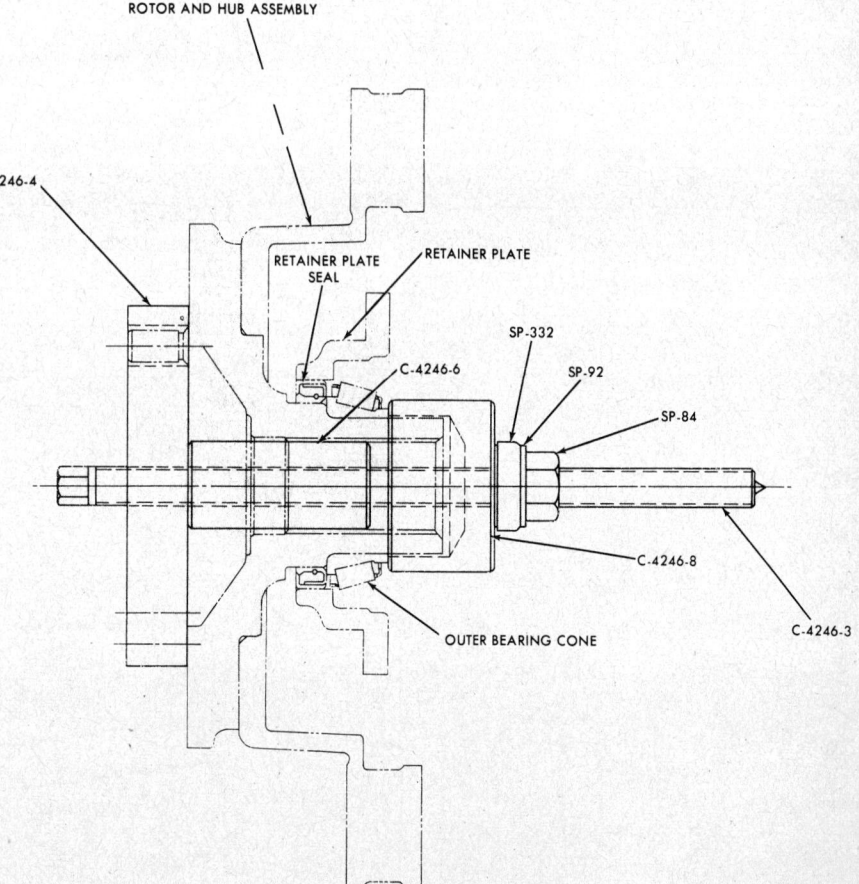

Fig. 28 Tools positioned to press outer bearing onto hub. 44 FBJ Units w/disc brakes

1017

DODGE & PLYMOUTH

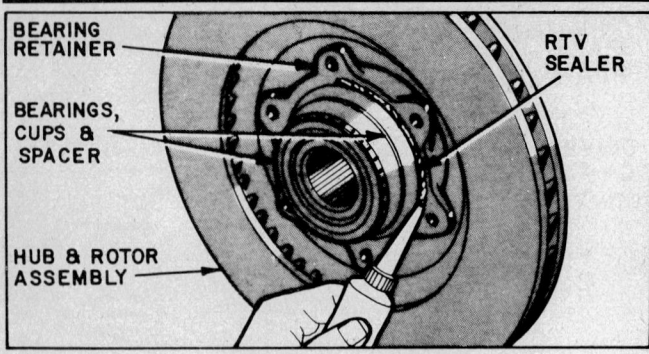

Fig. 29 Forming a seal on bearing retainer face. 44 FBJ Units w/disc brakes

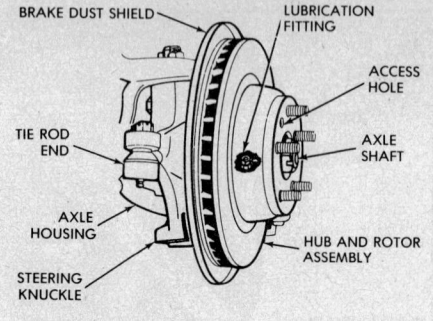

Fig. 30 Bearing retainer positioned with grease fitting facing forward. 44 FBJ Units w/disc brakes

outer axle shaft, Figs. 23 and 24.
10. Carefully insert axle shaft into housing so as not to damage differential seal at side gears. After sliding axle shaft completely in, wedge a pry bar through "U" joint to retain shaft, Fig. 25.
11. Install seal cup using adapter C-4398-2, and driver C-4398-1. Use a small amount of wheel bearing grease on adapter face to hold cup in position, then drive cup until bottomed in knuckle, Figs. 26 and 27. Do not remove tool at this time.
12. Apply a 1/4 inch bead of TRV sealer to retainer face on the chamfer, Fig. 29. This replaces the "O" ring discarded during disassembly.
13. Carefully remove seal installing tool from knuckle bore so that outer axle shaft remains centered. If shaft is moved, ensure that lip seal is still riding inside cup. Correct if necessary.
14. Before installing hub, rotor, retainer and bearing assembly on knuckle, position bearing retainer in hub so that grease fitting is facing forward, if equipped. Use a criss-cross method and torque retainer plate bolts to 30 ft. lbs.

NOTE: Bearing retainers that have a grease fitting must be positioned on knuckle so that fitting is facing directly forward, Fig. 30.

15. Install brake adapter and remove any pry bar from "U" joint.

16. Install axle shaft washer and nut. Torque nut to 100 ft. lbs. and continue to tighten nut until next slot in nut aligns with hole in axle shaft. Install cotter pin.
17. Through the access hole in hub, lubricate fitting in bearing retainer with Multi-Purpose grease until grease flows through new inner seal. Seal may be viewed through "U" joint area. Spin hub several times and lubricate fitting again. Grease must flow from 1/2 of seal diameter.
18. Replace brake caliper assembly and wheel, then lower vehicle and test operation.

60 FRONT AXLE

Axle Shaft, Ball Joint & Steering Knuckle Repairs

Removal & Disassembly
1. Block brake pedal in "Up" position.
2. Raise and support vehicle.
3. Remove wheel.
4. Remove brake caliper from adapter and, using a piece of wire, suspend caliper. Do not hang caliper by brake hose. The inner brake pad will remain on adapter.
5. Remove hub cap and snap ring, Fig. 33.
6. Remove flange nuts and lock washers.
7. Remove drive flange and discard gasket.
8. Straighten tang on lock ring, then remove outer lock nut, lock ring, inner lock nut and outer bearing, Fig. 34. Slide hub and rotor assembly from spindle.
9. Remove inner brake pad from adapter.
10. Remove nuts and washers securing brake splash shield, brake adapter and spindle to steering knuckle.
11. Remove spindle from knuckle. Slide inner and outer axle shaft with bronze spacer, seal and slinger from axle, Fig. 35.
12. Remove cotter key and nut from tie rod. Disconnect tie rod from steering knuckle.
13. On left side only, remove cotter key and nut from drag link. Disconnect drag link from steering knuckle arm. Also, remove nuts and upper knuckle cap. Discard gasket. Removing spring and upper socket sleeve.
14. Remove capscrews from lower knuckle cap and free cap from knuckle and housing.
15. To remove knuckle from housing, swing outward at bottom, then lift up and off upper socket pin.
16. Using a suitable tool, loosen and remove upper socket pin, then the seal, Fig. 36.
17. Press lower ball socket from axle housing with suitable tools.
18. Referring to Fig. 1, disassemble shaft.

Assembly & Installation
1. Lubricate lower ball socket assembly with suitable grease.
2. With suitable tools, press seal and lower bearing cup into axle housing. Then, press lower bearing and seal into axle housing.
3. Using a suitable tool and torque wrench, install and torque upper socket pin to 500–600 ft. lbs, Fig. 36. Install seal over socket pin.
4. Place steering knuckle over socket pin. Fill lower socket cavity with suitable

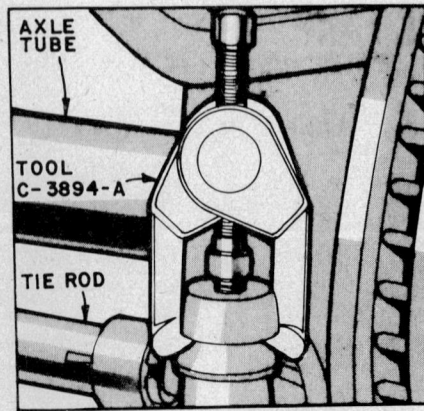

Fig. 31 Using puller to remove tie rod. (Typical)

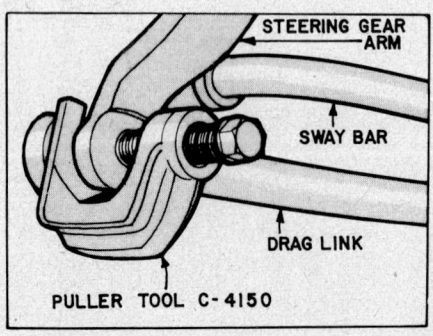

Fig. 32 Using puller to remove drag link from steering arm. (Typical)

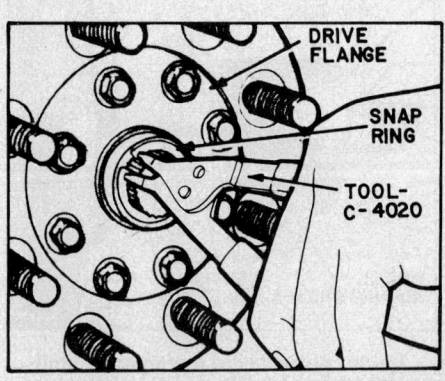

Fig. 33 Removing snap ring. 60 Front Axle

DODGE & PLYMOUTH

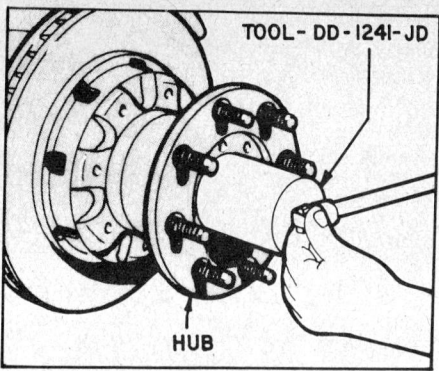

Fig. 34 Removing hub lock nut. 60 Front Axle

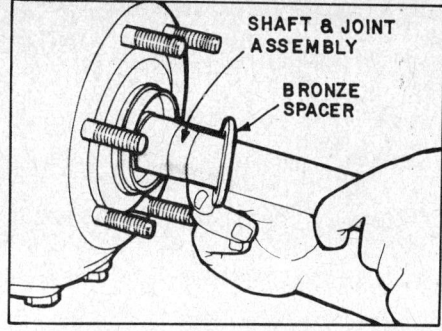

Fig. 35 Removing or replacing axle shaft. 60 Front Axle

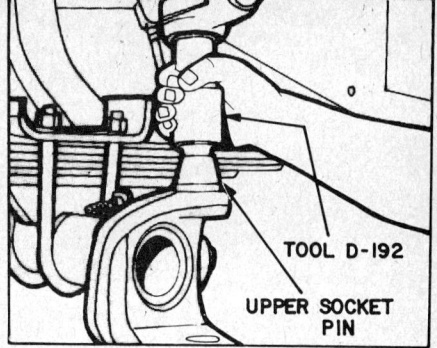

Fig. 36 Removing or replacing upper socket pin. 60 Front Axle

grease. Work lower knuckle cap into place on knuckle and housing. Install capscrews and torque to 70–90 ft. lbs.
5. Lubricate upper socket pin with suitable grease. Align upper socket sleeve in keyway of steering knuckle and slide into position, Fig. 37.
6. Install new gasket over upper steering knuckle studs. Place spring over sleeve. Install cap on left side steering knuckle arm. Install nuts and torque to 70–90 ft. lbs.
7. On left side only, attach drag link to steering knuckle arm and install and torque nut to 60 ft. lbs.
8. Connect tie rod to steering knuckle and install and torque nut to 45 ft. lbs. Install cotter key.
9. Referring to Fig. 1, assemble shaft.
10. Slide axle shaft into position. Place bronze spacer on axle shaft with chamfer facing toward universal joint, Fig. 35.
11. Install spindle, brake adapter and splash shield. Install and torque nuts to 50–70 ft. lbs.
12. Place inner brake pad on adapter.
13. Install hub and rotor assembly onto spindle. Install outer bearing and inner lock nut. Using tool DD-1241-JD and tool C-3952, torque lock nut to 50 ft. lbs. to sat bearings. Then, back off locknut and retorque to 30–40 ft. lbs. while rotating hub and rotor. Back off nut 135 to 150 degrees. Assemble lock ring and outer lock nut. Torque lock nut to 65 ft. lbs. minimum. Bend one tang of lock ring over inner lock nut and another tang over outer lock nut. Bearing end play should be .001–.010 inch.
14. Install new gasket on hub, then the drive flange, lock washers and nuts. Torque nuts to 30–40 ft. lbs. Install snap ring and hub cap, Fig. 33.
15. Position caliper on adapter and torque allen screw to 12–18 ft. lbs.
16. Install wheel and lower vehicle.
17. Remove block from brake pedal.

Wheel Bearing Adjusting Procedure

1. Raise and support truck.
2. Remove outer drive flange snap ring, Fig. 33.
3. Remove flange nuts and lock washers, then remove flange and discard gasket.
4. Straighten tang on lock ring and using suitable tool, remove outer lock nut and lock ring, Fig. 34.
5. To seat bearings, use proper tools to torque inner lock nut to 50 ft. lbs. Then

loosen lock nut and retorque to 30 to 40 ft. lbs. while rotating hub. Back off lock nut 135° to 150°. Install lock ring and torque outer lock nut to at least 65 ft. lbs. Bend one tang of lock ring over outer lock nut and one over inner nut. Final bearing adjustment should be .001 to .010 inch.
6. Install drive flange using new gasket then install snap ring.
7. Lower truck and test operation.

70F FRONT AXLE

Axle Shaft, Ball Joint & Steering Knuckle Repairs

Removal & Disassembly
1. Block brake pedal in "Up" position.
2. Raise and support vehicle.
3. Remove wheel.
4. Remove flange nuts and lock washers.
5. Remove drive flange and discard gasket.
6. Straighten tang on lock ring. Then, remove outer lock nut, lock ring, inner lock nut and outer bearing. Slide hub and drum assembly from spindle.
7. Remove brake support plate attaching nuts and support assembly aside with a piece of wire. Do not hang assembly by

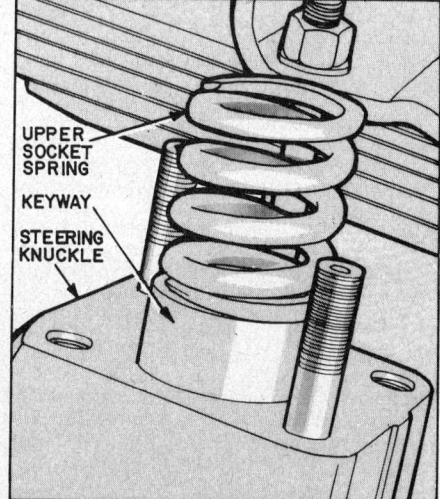

Fig. 37 Correct alignment of upper socket pin to steering knuckle. 60 Front Axle

the brake hose.
8. Remove spindle from steering knuckle by tapping with a mallet to loosen.
9. Inspect spindle for wear and damage. Replace bushing, if necessary. The flanged bushing requires no reaming. When pressed into spindle, it compresses to provide the correct running clearance.
10. Remove axle shaft and joint assembly from axle, Fig. 38.
11. Disconnect tie rod.
12. On left side only, disconnect drag link from steering knuckle arm.
13. Remove capscrews from rear of steering knuckle. Remove the two retainer plates. Discard felt seal and oil seal.
14. Remove capscrews from bottom bearing cap. Pry cap from knuckle and record shim thickness for use at assembly.
15. Lift steering outward and upward off housing to remove. Be sure to retain the lower bearing when removing steering knuckle.
16. Remove capscrews from upper bearing cap.
17. Place steering knuckle upside down in a vise. With a suitable drift and hammer, separate cap or steering knuckle arm from knuckle and bronze bushing. Discard woodruff key. Record thickness of shims for use at assembly.
18. Remove bearing caps from spherical ball on housing. Remove bronze bushing from ball yoke.
19. Referring to Fig. 1, disassemble axle shaft.

Assembly & Installation
1. Lubricate all components with suitable grease.
2. Install bronze bushing into ball yoke and bearing cups into spherical ball on housing with a hammer and a suitable installation tool.
3. Place steering knuckle in a vise.
4. Install .060 inch shim pack on upper cap or steering knuckle. Assemble steering knuckle. Install and torque capscrews to 80–85 ft. lbs.
5. Invert position of steering knuckle in vise.
6. Install new woodruff key. Then, using a hammer and suitable installation tool, tap bronze bearing onto king pin of cap or steering knuckle arm until properly seated. Coat bronze bearing with suitable grease. Pack lower bearing cone with suitable grease.
7. Install new felt seal and oil seal over spherical ball.
8. Assemble steering knuckle to housing.

DODGE & PLYMOUTH

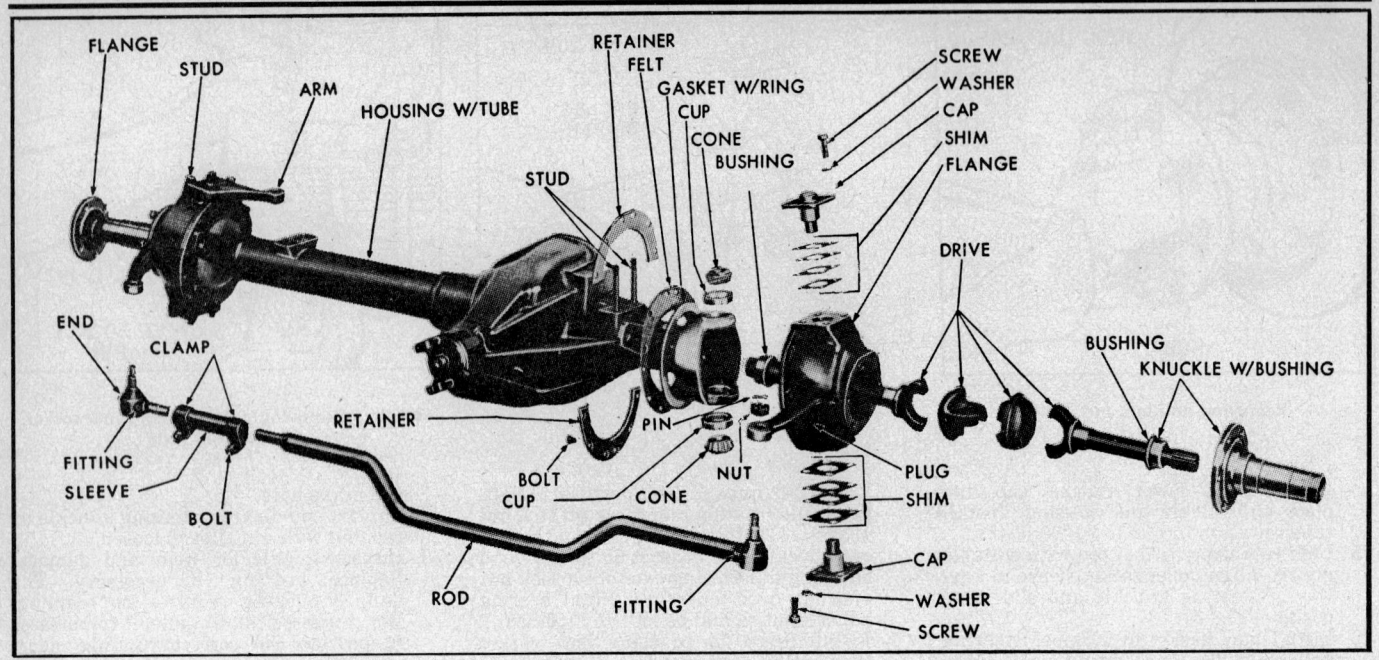

Fig. 38 Spicer 70F axle and steering knuckle assembly. (Typical)

Install lower bearing cone, shim pack, cap and capscrews. Torque capscrews to 80-85 ft. lbs.
9. Place a torque wrench on one of the upper bearing cap capscrews and record torque required to rotate knuckle through complete revolution, not the starting torque. The torque reading should be 20-30 ft. lbs. If preload is too tight, correct by adding shims. If preload is too loose, correct by removing shims. Shims are available in thicknesses of .003, .005, .010 and .030 inch. Note that preload corrections are made to the shim pack under the lower knuckle cap only.
10. Install new oil seal on steering knuckle with split in seal at the top center of the knuckle. Position felt seal against oil seal followed by the two retainer plates. Install and torque capscrews to 20-25 ft. lbs.
11. Connect tie rod to steering knuckle. Install and torque nut to 45-75 ft. lbs. Install cotter key.
12. On left side only, connect drag link to steering knuckle arm. Install and torque nut to 45-75 ft. lbs. Install cotter key.
13. Assemble axle shaft, referring to Fig. 1.
14. Slide axle shaft into axle.
15. Place spindle on steering knuckle followed by the brake support plate assembly. Torque retaining nuts to 85-135 ft. lbs.
16. Install hub and drum assembly on grease coated spindle. Install outer bearing and inner lock nut.
17. Using tool DD-1241-JD and tool C-3952, torque lock nut to 50 ft. lbs. to seat bearings. Then, back off nut and retorque to 30-40 ft. lbs. while rotating hub and drum assembly. Back off nut ¼ turn maximum. Assemble lock ring and outer lock nut. Torque lock nut to 50 ft. lbs. minimum. Bend one tang of lock ring over inner lock nut and another tang over outer lock nut. Bearing end play should be .001-.010 inch.
18. Install new gasket on hub, then the drive flange, lock washers and nuts. Torque nuts to 30-40 ft. lbs.
29. Install wheel and lower vehicle.
20. Remove block from brake pedal.

FDS 75 & 750 FRONT AXLE

Axle Shaft, Ball Joint & Steering Knuckle Repairs

Removal & Disassembly, Fig. 39.
1. Raise and support vehicle.
2. Drain axle lubricant.
3. Remove capscrews securing hub cap to drive flange, then the hub cap.
4. Remove snap ring from end of outer drive shaft.
5. Remove capscrews from drive flange, then the flange from axle shaft and hub.
6. Straighten adjusting lock nut. Remove jam nut, adjusting lock nut, wheel bearing adjusting nut, outer wheel bearing and wheel assembly complete with the hub and drum assembly from spindle.
7. Disconnect and plug hydraulic brake lines. Remove the eight brake support attaching capscrews. Slide oil slinger and brake support from spindle.
8. Remove spindle attaching screw from top of spindle flange. Pull spindle straight out from steering knuckle and outer drive shaft.
9. Pull axle shaft assembly from axle housing.
10. Disconnect tie rod and steering link from steering knuckle.
11. Remove four upper sleeve to steering knuckle capscrews. Disassemble knuckle upper sleeve from steering knuckle. Pull upper sleeve from steering knuckle bore. Upper knuckle bearing cone will remain on the sleeve and is removed at the same time. Remove shim pack and reuse, if not damaged, at assembly.
12. Remove four lower sleeve to steering knuckle capscrews. Disassemble knuckle lower sleeve from steering knuckle. Pull lower sleeve from steering knuckle bore. The lower bearing cone will remain on the sleeve and is removed at the same time. Remove shim pack and reuse, if not damaged, at assembly.
13. Pull knuckle assembly from axle housing. With a suitable tool, remove upper and lower knuckle oil seals from bores in axle housing.
14. Using a suitable sleeve, approximately the same diameter as the socket plug, tap out upper and lower bearing caps and socket plugs.
15. Referring to Fig. 1, disassemble axle shaft.

Assembly & Installation
1. Apply a coat of silastic gasket material or equivalent to mating surface on concave side of socket plugs. Seat plugs with hand pressure in upper and lower bores of axle housing. Remove excess material from plugs and housing.
2. With a suitable sleeve, press upper and lower bearing cups in bores in axle housing. Install upper and lower seals into axle housing, then position steering knuckle over end of axle housing.
3. If bearing cones were removed from upper and lower sleeves, use a suitable diameter sleeve to press cones into position on sleeves.
4. Assemble shim pack to lower knuckle sleeve. The shim pack must not exceed .010 inch thickness. Press sleeve and shim pack through bottom bores of steering knuckle until sleeve bottoms. Install and torque capscrews to 210 ft. lbs.
5. Assemble shim pack to upper knuckle sleeve. Press sleeve and shim pack through upper bores of knuckle and housing until sleeve bottoms. Install and torque capscrews to 210 ft. lbs.
6. Measure and record distance between top grease fitting in upper knuckle sleeve

and the center of the steering arm ball stud. The distance is measured perpendicular to the centerline of the knuckle.

7. Wrap a soft wire or cord around steering arm ball stud and attach a spring scale to wire or cord. Pull spring scale to rotate knuckle. Note number of pounds required to rotate knuckle. Use rotating torque not the starting torque. Rotating torque should be between 11 and 15 pounds. To determine proper preload use the following formulas:

Minimum preload =
$$\frac{11 \text{ ft. lbs} \times 12 \text{ inches}}{\text{Grease Fitting to Ball Stud Dimension}}$$

Maximum preload =
$$\frac{15 \text{ ft. lbs.} \times 12 \text{ inches}}{\text{Grease Fitting to Ball Stud Dimension}}$$

To increase bearing preload, remove shims. To decrease bearing preload, add shims. The adjustment is made at the upper sleeve shim pack.

8. Assemble axle shaft, referring to Fig. 8.
9. Slide axle shaft assembly into axle housing. Position spindle against knuckle mating surface and rotate spindle until countersunk hole in spindle flange aligns with mating hole at top of knuckle. This will align all capscrew holes. Install spindle position screw and torque to 25 ft. lbs. Install felt seal on spindle.
10. Connect tie rod and steering link. Torque tie rod nut to 90 ft. lbs. Install cotter keys. If holes in shafts and slots in nuts are not aligned, continue to tighten nut until cotter key installation is possible.
11. Position brake assembly and oil slinger over spindle. Install and torque capscrews to 70 ft. lbs. Connect hydraulic lines.
12. Place wheel and hub and drum assembly over spindle. Install outer wheel bearing and adjusting nut. Torque nut to 50 ft. lbs. while rotating assembly in both directions to seat bearings. Back off adjusting nut 1/4 to 1/3 turn. Install adjusting lock nut and jam nut. Torque jam nut to 125 ft. lbs. and bend nut lock over nuts.
13. Coat inside hub mating surface with silastic gasket material or equivalent. Coat internal splines of drive flange with wheel bearing grease.
14. Install flange and torque capscrews to 70 ft. lbs.
15. Install snap ring in outer drive shaft groove.
16. Coat inside drive flange mating surface of hub cap with silastic gasket material or equivalent. Assemble cap to drive flange and torque capscrews to 50 ft. lbs.
17. Fill axle assembly with recommended lubricant.
18. Bleed and adjust brakes.
19. Lower vehicle and test operation.

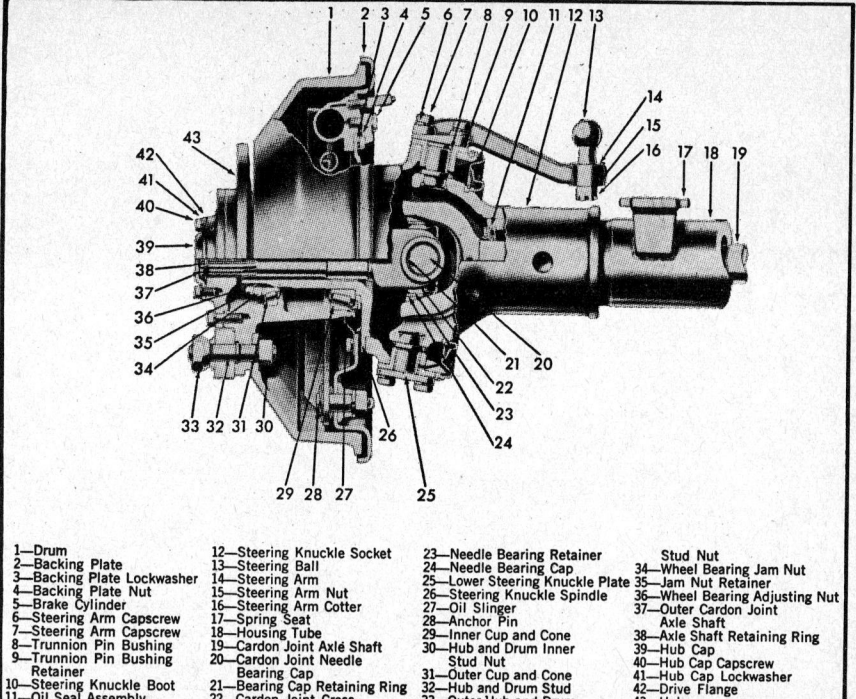

Fig. 39 Detail of housing assembly

1—Drum
2—Backing Plate
3—Backing Plate Lockwasher
4—Backing Plate Nut
5—Brake Cylinder
6—Steering Arm Capscrew
7—Steering Arm Capscrew
8—Trunnion Pin Bushing
9—Trunnion Pin Bushing Retainer
10—Steering Knuckle Boot
11—Oil Seal Assembly
12—Steering Knuckle Socket
13—Steering Ball
14—Steering Arm
15—Steering Arm Nut
16—Steering Arm Cotter
17—Spring Seat
18—Housing Tube
19—Cardon Joint Axle Shaft
20—Cardon Joint Needle Bearing Cap
21—Bearing Cap Retaining Ring
22—Cardon Joint Cross
23—Needle Bearing Retainer
24—Needle Bearing Cap
25—Lower Steering Knuckle Plate
26—Steering Knuckle Spindle
27—Oil Slinger
28—Anchor Pin
29—Inner Cup and Cone
30—Hub and Drum Inner Stud Nut
31—Outer Cup and Cone
32—Hub and Drum Stud
33—Outer Hub and Drum
34—Wheel Bearing Jam Nut
35—Jam Nut Retainer
36—Wheel Bearing Adjusting Nut
37—Outer Cardon Joint Axle Shaft
38—Axle Shaft Retaining Ring
39—Hub Cap
40—Hub Cap Capscrew
41—Hub Cap Lockwasher
42—Drive Flange
43—Hub

Front Axle Construction

INDEPENDENT FRONT SUSPENSION

Description

These vehicles are equipped with a coil spring front suspension system, Figs. 1 through 4. The upper control arms are mounted on longitudinal rails and the lower control arms are mounted on a removable crossmember. Both control arms have replaceable bushings on the inner ends and ball joints on the outer ends. The upper control arms also control caster and camber adjustments through eccentric pivot bolts at the inner ends.

Coil Spring, Replace

1. Raise vehicle on hoist and position jack stands under extreme front ends of longitudinal rails. Lower hoist and remove wheel and tire.
2. Remove shock absorber and upper shock bushing and sleeve. Disconnect sway bar at link if equipped and remove strut.
3. Install spring compressor and remove cotter keys and ball joint nuts.
4. Install ball joint breaker to free lower ball joint and remove breaker.
5. Slowly loosen the coil spring compressor until all tension is relieved and remove the spring.

Lower Ball Joint

1. Remove coil spring as described previously.
2. Unfasten and remove lower control arm.
3. Remove ball joint seal and using a suitable press and sleeve, press ball joint from control arm.

Upper Ball Joint

1. Place jack under outer end of lower control arm and raise vehicle.
2. Remove wheel and tire.
3. Remove ball joint nuts and free upper ball joint using ball joint breaker.
4. Using tool C-3561 unscrew ball joint from control arm.

Wheel Bearings, Adjust

Tighten adjusting nut to 41-54 ft. lbs. while rotating wheel. Stop rotation and loosen nut, then finger tighten adjusting nut and install lock nut and cotter pin. Final bearing adjustment should be from .0001 to .003 inch end play. Clean dust cap, then coat inside with wheel bearing grease but do not fill. Install cap.

DODGE & PLYMOUTH

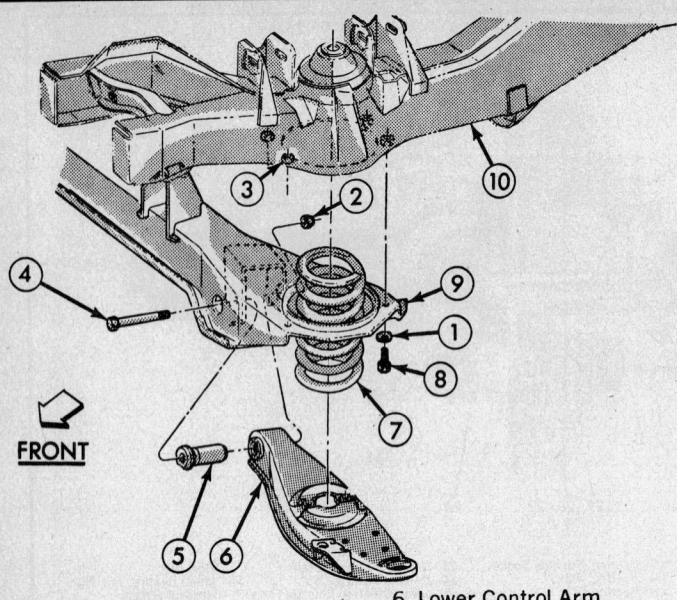

1. Coned Washer
2. Nut
3. Weld Nut
4. Bolt
5. Lower Arm Pivot Bushing
6. Lower Control Arm Assembly
7. Coil Spring
8. Bolt
9. Crossmember Assembly
10. Longitudinal Rail

Fig. 1 Lower control arm and coil spring. "B" Series compacts, Voyager & D100, 20, 300

1. Cam and Bolt Assembly
2. Cam
3. Lock Washer
4. Nut
5. Ball Joint Assembly
6. Ball Joint Assembly
7. Bushing Assembly
8. Lock Nut
9. Upper Control Arm
10. Upper Ball Joint Assembly
11. Bumper Assembly

Fig. 2 Upper control arm, "B" Series compacts, Voyager & D100, 200, 300

5,000, 5,500, 7,000 OR 9,000 LB. FRONT AXLE

Wheel Bearings, Adjust

Torque adjusting nut to 50 ft. lbs. while rotating wheel. Loosen adjusting nut 1/4 to 1/3 turn and install lock ring. Nut should not be more than finger tight. Install lock washer and lock nut, torque to 100–150 ft. lbs., then bend down tabs on lock washer.

Steering Knuckle & Bushings

Removal
1. After removing the wheel and hub, secure brake pedal and remove brake support plate.
2. Secure brake assembly out of the way. Do not allow assembly to hang by hydraulic brake hose.
3. Remove steering knuckle arm from steering knuckle, then remove pivot pin locking screw or pin. Some models have two locking screws.
4. Remove upper pivot pin oil seal plug and drive pivot pin down, pushing lower seal plug from assembly.
5. Pivot thrust bearing is also removed at this time.

NOTE: 9000 lb. axles are equipped and serviced with bronze pivot pin bushings. Lighter axles are equipped with Delrin or Zytel bushings which can distort if steam cleaning equipment is used to clean axle. Service replacement bushings can be the "plastic" type or bronze. Bronze replacement bushings are recommended where severe service is anticipated.

Pivot Pin Bushings

Replace
1. Bronze bushings should be removed and installed using a press or other suitable tool to prevent bushing damage.
2. Ensure grease hole in bushing aligns with grease fitting hole, Fig. 5.
3. Line ream both bronze bushings to insure pivot pin fit. Plastic type bushings do not require line reaming.
4. Fill grease grooves in bushing with Mul-

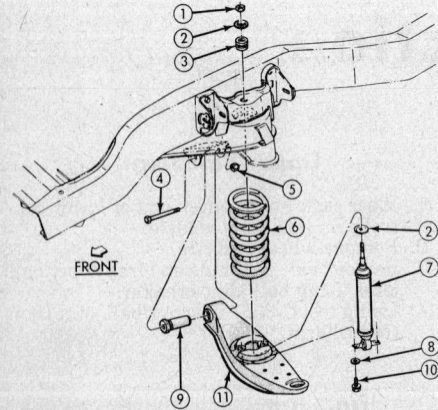

1—Nut
2—Retainer
3—Bushing
4—Bolt
5—Nut
6—Coil Spring
7—Shock Absorber
8—Washer
9—Bushing Assembly
10—Capscrew
11—Lower Control Arm

Fig. 3 Lower control arm and coil spring. D100, D200, D300, Ramcharger & trail-Duster except four wheel drive

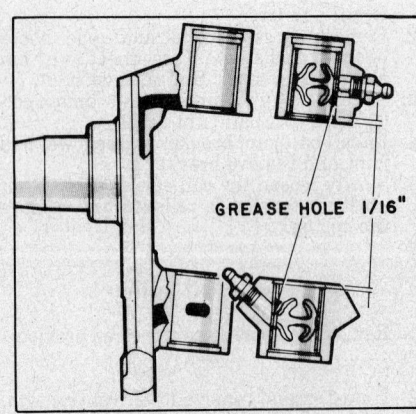

Fig. 5 Pivot pin bushings aligned & installed. (Typical)

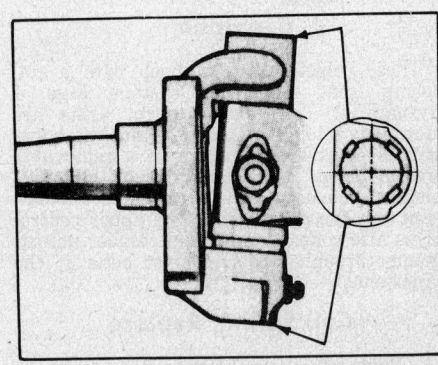

Fig. 6 Grease seal plugs installed & staked. (Typical)

DODGE & PLYMOUTH

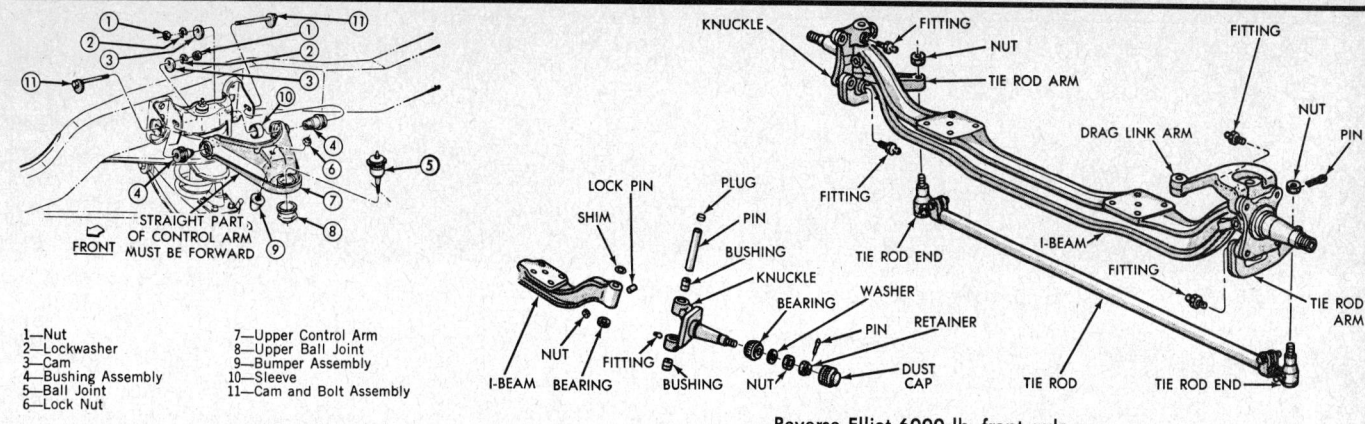

1—Nut
2—Lockwasher
3—Cam
4—Bushing Assembly
5—Ball Joint
6—Lock Nut
7—Upper Control Arm
8—Upper Ball Joint
9—Bumper Assembly
10—Sleeve
11—Cam and Bolt Assembly

Fig. 4 Upper control arm. D100, 200, D300, Ramcharger & Trail Duster except four wheel drive.

Reverse Elliot 6000 lb. front axle

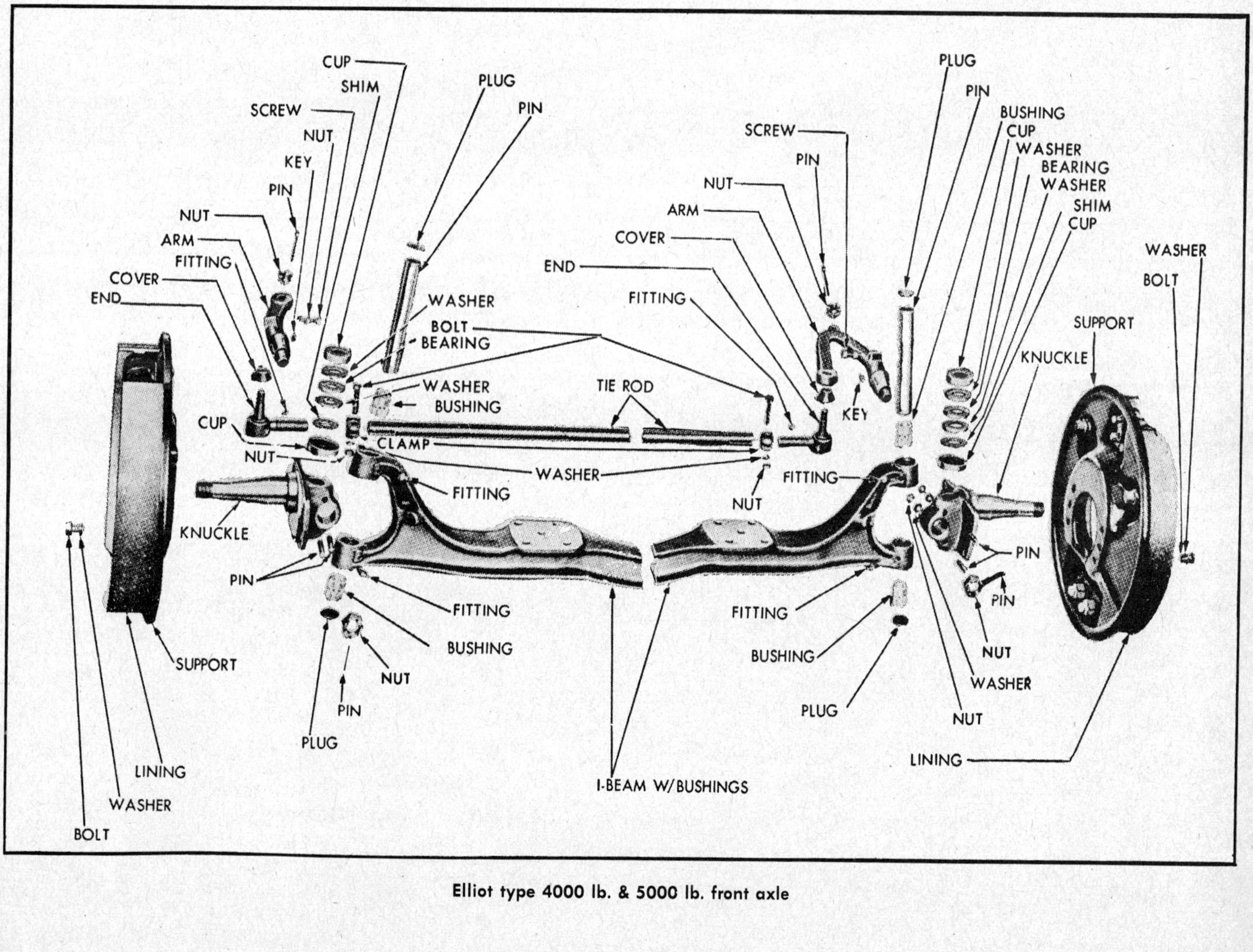

Elliot type 4000 lb. & 5000 lb. front axle

ti-Purpose grease, then check pivot pin for wear or damage.

5. Rough edges of expansion plug mating surfaces should be cleaned for better sealing.

6. Position steering knuckle and pivot pin bushing on axle, then install pivot pin and pivot pin lock.

7. Install expansion plug seals at top and bottom of axle and stake at four points, Fig. 6.

8. Install and tighten steering knuckle arm and brake support plate.

9. Lubricate all fittings, then install hub assembly and wheel, free brake pedal and test operation.

1023

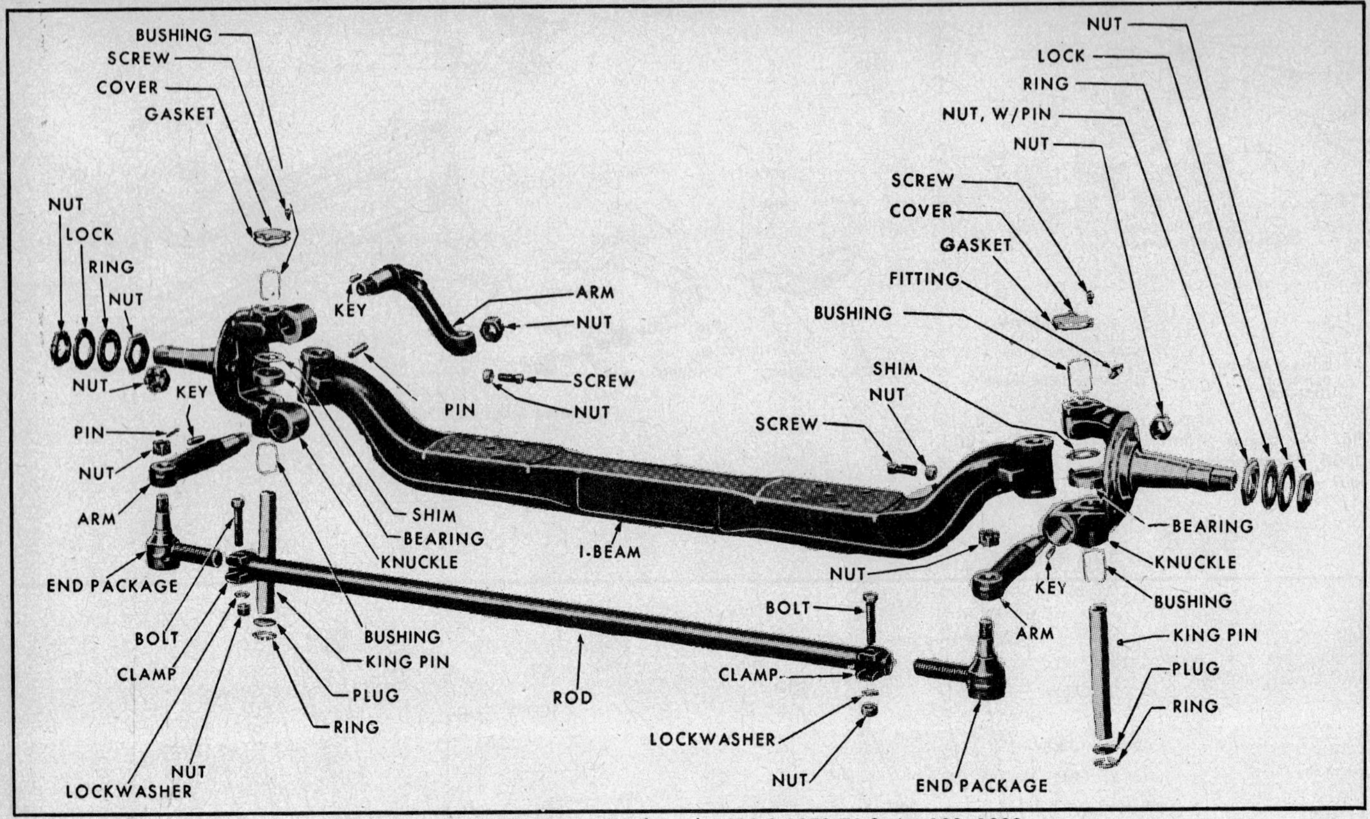

DODGE & PLYMOUTH

Front axle. 1970-76 Series 500 through 1000 & 1972 76 Series 100-1000

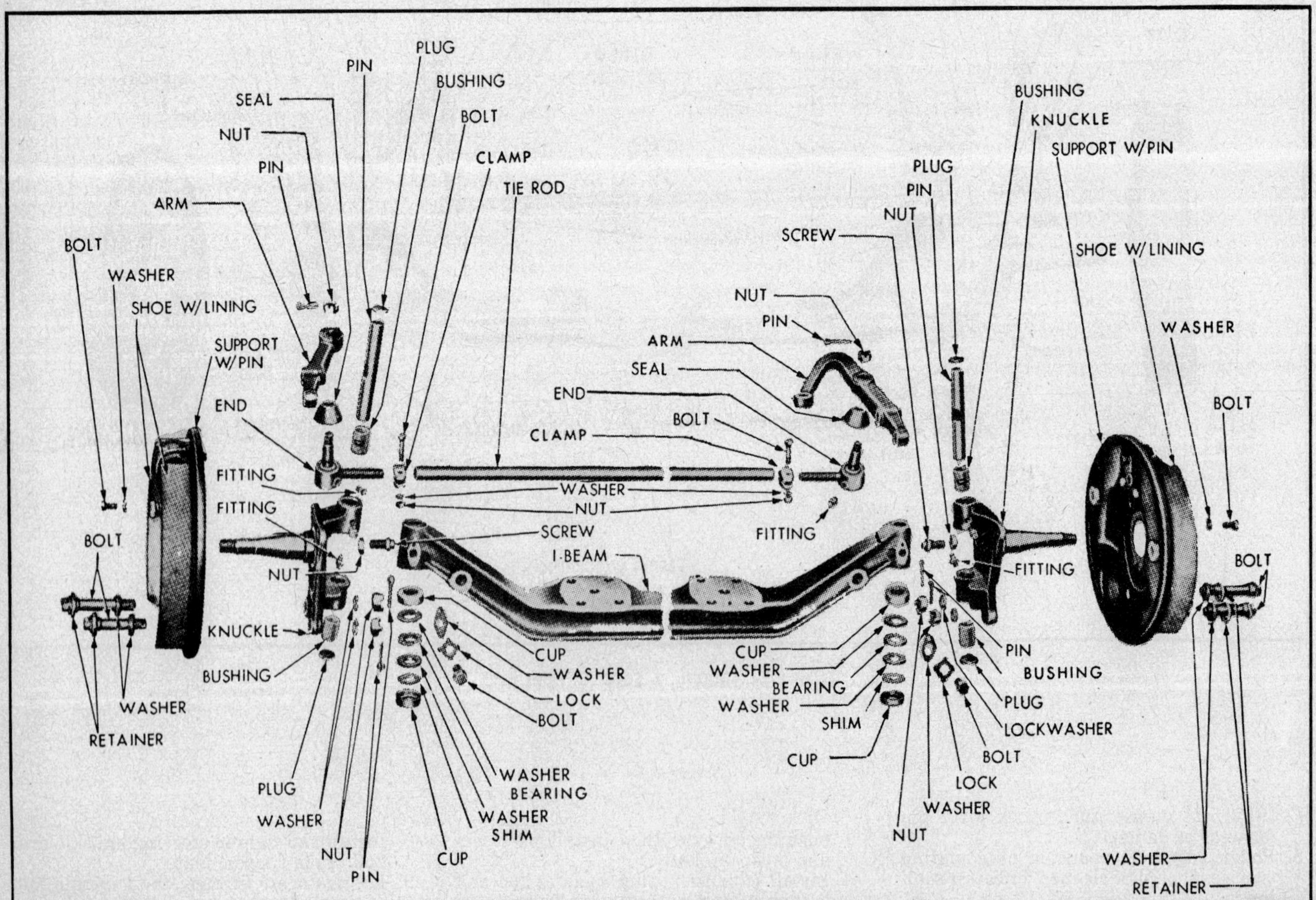

Reverse Elliot 2800 lb. front axle

FORD

INDEX OF SERVICE OPERATIONS

AXLES, DRIVING

	Page No.
Own Make Axle Service	1121
Eaton Axle Service	204
Spicer Axle Service	239, 1120
Timken Axle Service	241
Locking Differentials	192
Front Wheel Locking Hubs	505
Front Wheel Drive	1125

BRAKES

	Page No.
Adjustments	590
Air Brake Service	620
Anti-Skid Brakes	551
Bendix Twinplex Brake	608
Brake Booster Service	639
Disc Brakes	661
Hydraulic System Service	632
Parking Brake Service	612
Stopmaster Brake Service	599

CLUTCHES

	Page No.
Air-Hydraulic (Air-Pak)	468
Clutch Pedal, Adjust	1104
Clutch, Replace	1105
Clutch Service	429
Hydraulic Clutch Release	1104

COOLING SYSTEM

	Page No.
Cooling System Capacity	1026
Variable Speed Fans	10
Water Pumps, Replace	1072

ELECTRICAL

	Page No.
Alternator Service	52
Dash Gauge Service	179
Distributors, Standard	141
Electronic Ignition	152
Generator Service	11
Ignition Coils and Resistors	7
Starting Motor Service	29
Starter Switch Service	21
Tune Up Service	2

ENGINE

	Page No.
Camshaft and Bearings	1069
Crankshaft Rear Oil Seal	1069
Cylinder Head, Replace	1061
Piston and Rod, Assemble	1069
Rocker Arms & Shafts	1066
Rocker Arm Studs	1065
Timing Case Cover	1066
Timing Gears	1068
Timing Chain	1068
Valves, Adjust	1063
Valve Arrangement	1062
Valve Guides	1065
Valve Lifters	1066

ENGINE OILING

	Page No.
Crankcase Capacity	1026
Oil Pan, Replace	1070
Oil Pump, Replace	1072
Oil Pump, Service	1072

FRONT SUSPENSION

	Page No.
Axle Housing Pivot Bushing	1139
Front Spring, Replace	1139
Front Wheel Locking Hubs	505
Radius Arm, Replace	1139
Single I-Beam Axle	1133
Steering Knuckle, Replace	1139
Twin I-Beam Axle	1128
Wheel Bearings, Adjust	1136

FUEL & EXHAUST

	Page No.
Carburetor Adjustments	1073
Crankcase Ventilation	748
Emission Controls	750
Fuel Pump Service	183
L.P.G. Carburetion	190
Turbochargers	187

SPECIFICATIONS

	Page No.
Alternator and Regulator	1056
Carburetor Adjustment Specs.	1073
Crankcase Capacity	1026
Crankshaft and Bearing	1051
Cooling Capacity	1026
Distributor	1045
Engine Tightening Torque	1053
General Engine Data	1028
Generator and Regulator	1056
Piston, Pin and Ring	1051
Starting Motor	1055
Tune Up	1034
Valve	1049
Wheel Alignment	1058

STEERING

	Page No.
Manual Steering Gear Service	680
Power Steering Gear Service	686
Steering Gear, Replace	1139

TRANSFER CASES

	Page No.
	469

TRANSMISSIONS, Manual

	Page No.
Own Make 3 Speed Trans. 1970–80	1108
Own Make 4 Speed Trans. Overdrive	1111
Clark	275
Fuller	289
New Process	329
Spicer	346
Transmission Identification	1106
Warner	406
Tilt Cab Linkage Adjust	1115

TRANSMISSIONS, Automatic

	Page No.
Allison AT-540, 543 Service	510
Replace	1119
Allison MT-640, 650	512
Replace	1119
Allison HT-740, 750	514
Cast Iron 3 Speed	528
Replace	1117
C6	531
Replace	1117
C4	524
Replace	1116
Transmatic	518
Replace	1119

FORD

MODEL INDEX & ENGINE APPLICATION

Model	Year	Engine Make	Standard Engine Model	Crankcase Refill Capacity, Qts.	Cooling System Capacity, Qts.
CONVENTIONAL GASOLINE MODELS					
Bronco	1970–72	Own	6-170	6	9½
	1973–74	Own	6-200	6	9.2
	1975–77	Own	V8-302	5	14.7
	1978–79	Own	V8-351	5	22
	1980	Own	6-300	5	13
	1980	Own	V8-302	5	13
Econoline	1970	Own	6-170	3½	9½
	1970–74	Own	6-240	4	—
	1973	Own	6-300	5	14¼
	1975–79	Own	6-300	5	15
	1980	Own	6-300	5	16
	1980	Own	V8-302	5	16
Ranchero	1970–74	Own	6-250	4	10
	1974	Own	V8-302	4	15
	1975–76	Own	V8-351	4	15.9
	1977–79	Own	V8-302	4	14.3
	1978	Own	V8-351	4	15.4
F-100 (4×4)	1970–74	Own	6-240	5	14
	1975	Own	6-300	5	14
	1976	Own	V8-360	5	22.3
(4×2)	1970–74	Own	6-240	4	13
	1974	Own	V8-360	4	19.6
	1973–79	Own	6-300	5	14½
	1980	Own	6-300	5	13
F-150 (4×2)	1975–79	Own	6-300	5	14.4
	1980	Own	6-300	5	13
(4×4)	1978–79	Own	V8-351	5	15
	1980	Own	6-300	5	13
	1980	Own	V8-302	5	13
F-250 (4×2)	1970–74	Own	6-240	4	14
	1975–79	Own	6-300	5	14.4
	1980	Own	6-300	5	13
(4×4)	1970–74	Own	6-240	5	14
	1975–79	Own	6-300	5	14.4
	1978–79	Own	V8-351	5	20
	1980	Own	6-300	5	13
	1980	Own	V8-302	5	13
F-350	1970–71	Own	6-240	5	14½③
	1973–74	Own	6-300	5	14½③
	1975–79	Own	6-300	5	16.7④
	1975–76	Own	V8-360	5	22.3
	1977–79	Own	V8-351	5	22
(4×2)	1980	Own	6-300	5	13
(4×4)	1980	Own	V8-351	5	15
F-500	1970–71	Own	6-240	5	19
	1973–75	Own	6-300	5	19
	1976–79	Own	6-300	5	18
F-600	1970–75	Own	6-300	6	19
	1976–79	Own	6-300	5	18
	1980	Own	V8-370	8	23.5
(4×4)	1971–75	Own	V8-330	8	26
	1976–78	Own	V8-330	8	24.8
	1979	Own	V8-370	8	24.5
F-700	1970–72	Own	V8-330	9	24
	1973–75	Own	V8-361	8	⑦
	1976–78	Own	V8-361	8	⑧
	1979	Own	V8-370	8	23.5
F-750	1970–74	Own	V8-361	8	24①
	1975	Own	V8-361	8	⑦
	1976–79	Own	V8-361	8	⑧
F-800	1970	Own	V8-361	8	24①
	1979	Own	V8-370	8	—
	1980	Own	V8-429	8	23.8
F-880	1975–79	Own	V8-475	9	46
TILT CAB GASOLINE MODELS					
C-500	1970–71	Own	6-300	6	—
C-600	1970–77	Own	6-300	6	22.5
	1978	Own	V8-330	6	28
	1979	Own	V8-370	8	20.5
	1980	Own	V8-370	8	22
C-700	1970–72	Own	V8-330	8	28
	1973–74	Own	V8-361	8	25
	1975	Own	V8-361	8	29①
	1976–78	Own	V8-361	8	28①
	1979	Own	V8-370	8	20.5
	1980	Own	V8-370	8	24
C-750	1970–74	Own	V8-361	8	28①
	1975	Own	V8-361	8	29①
	1976–78	Own	V8-361	8	28①
C-800	1970–74	Own	V8-361	8	28①
	1975	Own	V8-361	8	29①
	1976–78	Own	V8-361	8	28①
	1979	Own	V8-370	—	—
	1980	Own	V8-429	8	21.8
C-900	1970–75	Own	V8-401	9	52②
	1976–79	Own	V8-477	9	⑪
	1980	Own	V8-477	9	52
TANDEM AXLE GASOLINE MODELS					
CT-800	1970–74	Own	V8-361	8	28①
	1975	Own	V8-389	8	29①
	1976	Own	V8-361	8	28①
	1977–78	Own	V8-389	8	⑨
	1979	Own	V8-370	—	—
	1980	Own	V8-429	8	21.8
CT-900	1971–75	Own	V8-401	9	52②
	1976–79	Own	V8-477	9	⑪
	1980	Own	V8-477	9	52
SCHOOL BUS MODELS					
B-500	1970–71	Own	6-240	5	19
	1973–75	Own	6-300	5	19
	1976–78	Own	6-300	5	18
B-600	1970–75	Own	6-300	6	19
	1976–77	Own	6-300	6	18
	1978	Own	V8-330	8	24
	1979–80	Own	V8-370	8	23.5

Continued

FORD

MODEL INDEX & ENGINE APPLICATION—Continued

Model	Year	Engine Make	Standard Engine Model	Crankcase Refill Capacity, Qts.	Cooling System Capacity, Qts.	Model	Year	Engine Make	Standard Engine Model	Crankcase Refill Capacity, Qts.	Cooling System Capacity, Qts.
B-700	1970–74	Own	V8-330	8	25	LNT-800	1970–71	Own	V8-330	8	—
	1975	Own	V8-330	5	⑦		1973–74	Own	V8-361	8	25½
	1976–77	Own	V8-330	5	⑫		1975	Own	V8-361	8	25½
	1978	Own	V8-361	8	⑭		1976	Own	V8-361	8	⑨
	1979–80	Own	V8-370	8	23.5		1977–78	Own	V8-389	8	⑨
B-750	1970–74	Own	V8-361	8	24①		1979	Own	V8-370	8	24.5
	1975	Own	V8-361	5	⑦		1980	Own	V8-370	8	26.8
	1976–77	Own	V8-361	5	⑧	LTS-800	1971	Own	V8-330	8	—
PARCEL DELIVERY GASOLINE MODELS							1973–74	Own	V8-361	8	25½
P-350	1970–72	Own	6-240	5	19		1975	Own	V8-361	8	25½
	1973–76	Own	6-300	5	18		1976	Own	V8-361	8	⑨
P-400	1970–72	Own	6-240	5	19		1977–78	Own	V8-475	9	⑬
	1973–76	Own	6-300	5	18		1979	Own	V8-429	9	22.5
P-450	1975–76	Own	V8-360	5	—		1980	Own	V8-370	8	26.8
P-500	1970–72	Own	6-240	5	19	LT-880	1972–75	Own	V8-475	9	47
	1973–78	Own	6-300	5	18		1976–78	Own	V8-475	9	45.2
P-550	1975–76	Own	V8-390	5	—	LNT-880	1972–75	Own	V8-475	9	47
P-600	1975–79	Own	6-300	5	18.1		1976–78	Own	V8-475	9	45.2
MOTOR HOME MODELS						L-900	1970–75	Own	V8-401	9	47
M-400	1972–75	Own	V8-360	5	22		1976–80	Own	V8-477	9	47
M-450	1972–76	Own	V8-360	5	22	LN-900	1970–75	Own	V8-401	9	47
M-500	1972–76	Own	V8-390	5	23		1976–80	Own	V8-477	9	47
LOUISVILLE GASOLINE MODELS						LT-900	1971–75	Own	V8-401	9	47
LN-500	1970–71	Own	6-240	5	—		1976–80	Own	V8-477	9	52
LN-600	1970–74	Own	6-300	6	19	LNT-900	1971–75	Own	V8-401	9	47
	1975	Own	V8-330	8	25		1976–80	Own	V8-477	9	52
	1976–78	Own	V8-330	8	⑤	LTS-900	1971–75	Own	V8-401	9	47
	1979	Own	V8-370	8	25		1976–80	Own	V8-477	9	52
LN-700	1970–72	Own	V8-330	8	—	**LOUISVILLE DIESEL MODELS**					
	1973–75	Own	V8-361	8	25	LN-6000	1970–74	Catpl'r	V-150	12	25
	1976–78	Own	V8-361	8	⑥	LN-7000	1970–74	Catpl'r	V-175	12	25
	1979	Own	V8-370	8	25		1975–80	Catpl'r	V-175	10	42
LN-750	1970–74	Own	V8-361	8	25	L-8000	1970–74	Catpl'r	V-175	12	25
	1975	Own	V8-361	8	25		1975	Cummins	V-555	—	28
	1976–78	Own	V8-361	8	⑥		1975–80	Catpl'r	V-175	10	38
L-800	1971–75	Own	V8-361	8	25.5	LN-8000	1970–74	Catpl'r	V-175	12	25
	1976	Own	V8-361	8	⑨		1975	Cummins	V-555	—	28
	1977	Own	V8-330	8	⑫		1975–80	Catpl'r	V-175	10	38
	1978	Own	V8-389	8	24.5	LT-8000	1970–74	Catpl'r	V-175	12	25
	1979	Own	V8-370	8	23.5		1975–80	Catpl'r	V-175	10	38
	1980	Own	V8-370	8	26.8	LTS-8000	1971–74	Catpl'r	V-175	12	25
LN-800	1970–75	Own	V8-361	8	25.5		1975–80	Catpl'r	V-175	10	40
	1976–77	Own	V8-361	8	⑨	LNT-8000	1970–74	Catpl'r	V-175	12	25
	1978	Own	V8-389	8	24.5		1975–80	Catpl'r	V-175	10	38
	1979	Own	V8-370	8	23.5	CL-9000	1978–80	Cummins	NTC-290	28	48
	1980	Own	V8-370	8	26.8	CLT-9000	1978–80	Cummins	NTC-290	28	48
LT-800	1970–71	Own	V8-330	8	—	L-9000	1970–75	Cummins	NH-230	24	47
	1973–74	Own	V8-361	8	25½		1975	Cummins	NTC-250	28	43
	1975	Own	V8-361	8	25½		1976–77	Cummins	NH-230	28	32
	1976	Own	V8-361	8	⑨		1978–80	Cummins	NTC-230	28	52
	1977–78	Own	V8-389	8	⑨	LN-9000	1970–75	Cummins	NH-230	24	47
	1979	Own	V8-370	8	23.5		1975	Cummins	NTC-250	28	43
	1980	Own	V8-370	8	26.8		1976–77	Cummins	NH-230	28	32
							1978–80	Cummins	NTC-230	28	52

Continued

FORD

MODEL INDEX & ENGINE APPLICATION—Continued

Model	Year	Engine Make	Standard Engine Model	Crankcase Refill Capacity, Qts.	Cooling System Capacity, Qts.
LT-9000	1970–74	Cummins	NH-230	24	47
	1975	Cummins	NH-230	28	43
	1976–77	Cummins	NH-230	28	32
	1978–80	Cummins	NTC-230	28	52
LTS-9000	1971–74	Cummins	NH-230	24	47
	1975	Cummins	NH-230	28	43
	1976–77	Cummins	NH-230	28	32
	1978–80	Cummins	NTC-230	28	52
LNT-9000	1970–74	Cummins	NH-230	24	47
	1975	Cummins	NH-230	28	43
	1976–77	Cummins	NH-230	28	32
	1978–80	Cummins	NTC-230	28	52

FORD DIESEL MODELS

Model	Year	Engine Make	Standard Engine Model	Crankcase Refill Capacity, Qts.	Cooling System Capacity, Qts.
C-6000	1970–74	Catpl'r	V-150	12	25
F-6000	1970–74	Catpl'r	V-150	12	25
B-7000	1970	Own	6-363	12	23
	1971–79	Catpl'r	V-175	12	25
C-7000	1970–74	Catpl'r	V-175	12	25
	1975	Catpl'r	V-175	12	32
	1976–80	Catpl'r	V-175	10	44
F-7000	1970–74	Catpl'r	V-175	12	25
	1975–79	Catpl'r	V-175	10	41
C-8000	1970–74	Catpl'r	V-200	12	25

Model	Year	Engine Make	Standard Engine Model	Crankcase Refill Capacity, Qts.	Cooling System Capacity, Qts.
	1975–80	Catpl'r	V-175	10	46
CT-8000	1970–73	Catpl'r	V-175	12	25
	1974	Catpl'r	V-200	12	25
	1975	Catpl'r	V-175	12	32
	1976–79	Catpl'r	V-175	10	46
	1980	Catpl'r	V-200	10	46
W-9000	1970–74	Cummins	NH-230	20	49
	1975	Cummins	NTC-290	28	49
	1976–77	Cummins	NTC-290	28	48
WT-9000	1970–74	Cummins	NH-230	20	49
	1975	Cummins	NTC-290	28	49
	1976–77	Cummins	NTC-290	28	48

① —Add 1½ qts. if equipped with Transmatic transmission.
② —Add 7 qts. if equipped with Transmatic transmission.
③ —Add 2 qts. if equipped with dual rear tires.
④ —Single Rear with Manual Transmission 14.4 quarts.
⑤ —Man. Trans. 20.8 quarts; Auto. Trans. 26.7 quarts.
⑥ —Man. Trans. 24 quarts; Auto. Trans. 26.7 quarts.
⑦ —Man. Trans. 25 quarts; Auto. Trans. 27.6 quarts.
⑧ —Man. Trans. 24.8 quarts; Auto. Trans. 26.8 quarts.
⑨ —Man. Trans. 21.8 quarts; Auto. Trans. 26.6 quarts.
⑩ —Man. Trans. 47 quarts; Auto. Trans. 49 quarts.
⑪ —Man. Trans. 53.2 quarts; Auto. Trans. 59 quarts.
⑫ —Man. Trans. 24.5 quarts; Auto. Trans. 27 quarts.
⑬ —Man. Trans. 45.2 quarts; Auto. trans. 46.9 quarts.
⑭ —Man. trans. 24 quarts; Auto. trans. 30 quarts.

GENERAL ENGINE SPECIFICATIONS

★ See replica of a typical Rating Plate on Index page.

Year	Engine Code On Truck Rating Plate ★	Engine Model	Carb. Type	Bore & Stroke	Comp. Ratio	Horsepower @ R.P.M.	Torque Lbs. Ft. @ R.P.M.	Governed Speed R.P.M. No Load	Normal Oil Pressure Lbs.
1970	F	6-170	1 Bore	3.50 × 2.94	8.7	100 @ 4000	156 @ 2200	—	35–60
	A	6-240	1 Bore	4.00 × 3.18	9.2	150 @ 4000	234 @ 2200	4000	35–60
	L	6-250	1 Bore	3.68 × 3.91	9.1	155 @ 4400	240 @ 1600	—	35–60
	B	6-300	1 Bore	4.00 × 3.98	8.8	165 @ 3600	294 @ 2000	3600	35–60
	F	V8-302	2 Bore	4.00 × 3.00	9.5	210 @ 4400	295 @ 2400	—	35–60
	G	V8-302	2 Bore	4.00 × 3.00	8.6	205 @ 4600	300 @ 2600	—	35–60
	C	V8-330④	2 Bore	3.87 × 3.50	7.4	190 @ 4000	306 @ 2000	3900	35–60
	D	V8-330③	2 Bore	3.87 × 3.50	7.4	190 @ 4000	306 @ 2000	3900	35–60
	H	V8-351	2 Bore	4.00 × 3.50	9.5	250 @ 4600	355 @ 2600	—	35–60
	M	V8-351	4 Bore	4.00 × 3.50	11.0	300 @ 5400	380 @ 3400	—	35–60
	Y	V8-360	2 Bore	4.05 × 3.50	8.4	215 @ 4400	327 @ 2600	—	35–60
	E	V8-361	2 Bore	4.05 × 3.50	7.2	210 @ 4000	345 @ 2000	3800	35–60
	H	V8-390	2 Bore	4.05 × 3.78	8.6	255 @ 4400	376 @ 2600	3800	35–60
	F	V8-391	4 Bore	4.05 × 3.79	7.2	235 @ 4000	372 @ 2000	3800	35–60
	H	V8-401	4 Bore	4.125 × 3.75	7.5	226 @ 3600	343 @ 2000	3400	35–60
	N	V8-429	4 Bore	4.36 × 3.59	11.0	360 @ 4600	476 @ 2800	—	35–60
	C	V8-429CJ	4 Bore	4.36 × 3.59	11.5	345 @ 5800	450 @ 3400	—	35–60
	Z	V8-429 Boss	4 Bore	4.36 × 3.59	10.5	375 @ 5200	450 @ 3400	—	35–60
	K	V8-477	4 Bore	4.50 × 3.75	7.5	253 @ 3400	415 @ 2000	3200	35–60
	L	V8-534	4 Bore	4.50 × 4.20	7.5	266 @ 3200	481 @ 1600	3000	35–60
1971	F	6-170	1 Bore	3.500 × 2.94	8.7	100 @ 4200	148 @ 2600	—	35–60
	—	6-200	1 Bore	3.68 × 3.13	8.7	115 @ 4000	180 @ 2200	—	35–60

Continued

FORD

GENERAL ENGINE SPECIFICATIONS—Continued

Year	Engine Code On Truck Rating Plate	Engine Model	Carb. Type	Bore & Stroke	Comp. Ratio	Horsepower @ R.P.M.	Torque Lbs. Ft. @ R.P.M.	Governed Speed R.P.M. No Load	Normal Oil Pressure Lbs.
	A	6-240	1 Bore	4.000 × 3.18	8.9	140 @ 4000	230 @ 2200	—	35–60
	—	6-250	1 Bore	3.68 × 3.91	9.0	145 @ 4000	232 @ 1600	—	35–60
	B	6-300	1 Bore	4.000 × 3.98	8.8	165 @ 3600	294 @ 2000	—	35–60
	G	V8-302	2 Bore	4.000 × 3.00	8.6	205 @ 4600	300 @ 2600	—	35–60
	F	V8-302	2 Bore	4.00 × 3.00	9.0	210 @ 4600	296 @ 2600	—	35–60
	C	V8-330④	2 Bore	3.87 × 3.50	7.4	190 @ 4400	306 @ 2000	—	35–60
	D	V8-330③	2 Bore	3.87 × 3.50	7.4	190 @ 4400	306 @ 2000	—	35–60
	H	V8-351	2 Bore	4.00 × 3.50	9.0	240 @ 4600	350 @ 2600	—	35–60
	M	V8-351	4 Bore	4.00 × 3.50	10.7	285 @ 5400	370 @ 3400	—	35–60
	Y	V8-360	2 Bore	4.05 × 3.50	8.4	215 @ 4400	327 @ 2600	—	35–60
	E	V8-361	2 Bore	4.05 × 3.50	7.2	210 @ 4000	345 @ 2000	—	35–60
	H	V8-390	2 Bore	4.05 × 3.78	8.6	255 @ 4400	376 @ 2600	—	35–60
	F	V8-391	4 Bore	4.05 × 3.79	7.2	235 @ 4000	372 @ 2000	—	35–60
	H	V8-401	4 Bore	4.125 × 3.75	7.5	226 @ 3600	343 @ 2600	3600⑤	35–65
	K	V8-427	4 Bore	4.500 × 3.75	7.5	253 @ 3400	415 @ 2600	3400⑤	35–60
	C	V8-429	4 Bore	4.36 × 3.59	11.3	370 @ 5400	450 @ 3400	—	30–60
	J	V8-429	4 Bore	4.36 × 3.59	11.5	375 @ 5600	450 @ 3400	—	30–60
	L	V8-534	4 Bore	4.500 × 4.20	7.5	266 @ 3200	481 @ 1800	3200⑤	35–60
1972	F	6-170	1 Bore	3.50 × 2.94	8.4	97 @ 4400	137 @ 2600	—	35
	—	6-200	1 Bore	3.68 × 3.13	8.3	91 @ 4000	154 @ 2200	—	35–60
	A	6-240	1 Bore	4.00 × 3.18	8.5	120 @ 4000	189 @ 2400	—	40–50
	—	6-250	1 Bore	3.68 × 3.91	8.0	95 @ 3600	181 @ 1600	—	35–60
	B	6-300	1 Bore	4.00 × 3.98	8.8	165 @ 3600	294 @ 2000	—	40–50
	F	V8-302	2 Bore	4.00 × 3.00	8.5	143 @ 4200	242 @ 2000	—	30–60
	G	V8-302	2 Bore	4.00 × 3.00	8.2	154 @ 4000	246 @ 2400	—	50–65
	C	V8-330④	2 Bore	3.87 × 3.50	7.4	190 @ 4400	306 @ 2000	—	35–60
	D	V8-330③	2 Bore	3.87 × 3.50	7.4	190 @ 4400	306 @ 2000	—	35–60
	H	V8-351	2 Bore	4.00 × 3.50	8.6	164 @ 4000	276 @ 2000	—	35–85
	Q	V8-351	4 Bore	4.00 × 3.50	8.6	248 @ 5400	299 @ 3800	—	50–70
	Y	V8-360	2 Bore	4.05 × 3.50	8.0	196 @ 4600	291 @ 2400	—	45–55
	E	V8-361	2 Bore	4.05 × 3.50	7.2	210 @ 4000	345 @ 2000	—	35–60
	H	V8-390	2 Bore	4.05 × 3.78	8.2	201 @ 4400	316 @ 2600	—	45–55
	F	V8-391	4 Bore	4.05 × 3.79	7.2	235 @ 4000	372 @ 2000	—	35–60
	S	V8-400	2 Bore	4.00 × 4.00	8.4	168 @ 4200	297 @ 2200	—	35–85
	H	V8-401	4 Bore	4.125 × 3.75	7.5	226 @ 3600	343 @ 2600	3600⑤	35–65
	N	V8-429	4 Bore	4.36 × 3.59	8.5	205 @ 4400	322 @ 2600	—	35–60
	K	V8-477	4 Bore	4.500 × 3.75	7.5	253 @ 3400	415 @ 2600	3400⑤	35–60
	L	V8-534	4 Bore	4.500 × 4.20	7.5	266 @ 3200	481 @ 1800	3200⑤	35–60
1973	T	6-200	1 Bore	3.68 × 3.13	8.3	89 @ 3800	166 @ 2200	—	30–35
	A	6-240④	1 Bore	4.00 × 3.18	8.5	105 @ 3800	175 @ 2400	—	40–60
	A	6-240②	1 Bore	4.00 × 3.18	8.5	109 @ 3600	181 @ 2400	—	40–60
	—	6-250	1 Bore	3.68 × 3.91	8.0	93 @ 3200	197 @ 1400	—	—
	B	6-300②	1 Bore	4.00 × 3.98	8.4	118 @ 3400	226 @ 1800	—	40–60
	B	6-300④	1 Bore	4.00 × 3.98	8.4	114 @ 3400	222 @ 1600	—	40–60
	B	6-300③	1 Bore	4.00 × 3.98	8.4	126 @ 3400	234 @ 1600	—	40–60
	F	V8-302	2 Bore	4.00 × 3.00	8.0	137 @ 4200	230 @ 2200	—	35–60
	G	V8-302	2 Bore	4.00 × 3.00	8.2	139 @ 3800	232 @ 2600	—	40–60
	C	V8-330④	2 Bore	3.87 × 3.50	7.4	137 @ 3200	272 @ 1800	3900	35–60
	D	V8-330③	2 Bore	3.87 × 3.50	7.4	138 @ 3600	250 @ 2400	3800	35–75
	D	V8-330⑥	2 Bore	3.87 × 3.50	7.4	140 @ 3600	253 @ 2400	3800	35–75
	H	V8-351	2 Bore	4.00 × 3.50	8.0	159 @ 4000	250 @ 2400	—	35–60
	Q	V8-351	4 Bore	4.00 × 3.50	8.0	264 @ 5400	264 @ 5400	—	35–60
	Y	V8-360	2 Bore	4.05 × 3.50	8.0	⑭	⑮	—	35–60
	E	V8-361④	2 Bore	4.05 × 3.50	7.2	154 @ 3600	278 @ 2400	3800	35–75
	E	V8-361③	2 Bore	4.05 × 3.50	7.2	153 @ 3600	278 @ 2400	3800	35–75

Continued

1029

FORD

GENERAL ENGINE SPECIFICATIONS—Continued

Year	Engine Code On Truck Rating Plate	Engine Model	Carb. Type	Bore & Stroke	Comp. Ratio	Horsepower @ R.P.M.	Torque Lbs. Ft. @ R.P.M.	Governed Speed R.P.M. No Load	Normal Oil Pressure Lbs.
	E	V8-361⑥	2 Bore	4.05 × 3.50	7.2	156 @ 3600	279 @ 2400	3800	35–75
	H	V8-390	2 Bore	4.05 × 3.78	8.2	161 @ 3600	299 @ 2000	—	35–36
	F	V8-391④	4 Bore	4.05 × 3.79	7.2	181 @ 3600	320 @ 2400	3600⑤	35–75
	F	V8-391③	4 Bore	4.05 × 3.79	7.2	180 @ 3600	320 @ 2400	3600⑤	35–75
	F	V8-391⑥	4 Bore	4.05 × 3.79	7.2	182 @ 3600	321 @ 2400	3600⑤	35–75
	S	V8-400	2 Bore	4.00 × 4.00	8.0	168 @ 3800	310 @ 2000	—	35–60
	H	V8-401	4 Bore	4.125 × 3.75	7.3	173 @ 3400	278 @ 2800	3600⑤	35–60
	N	V8-429	4 Bore	4.36 × 3.59	8.0	201 @ 4400	322 @ 2600	—	35–60
	K	V8-477	4 Bore	4.50 × 3.75	7.2	198 @ 3200	343 @ 2600	3400⑤	35–60
	L	V8-534	4 Bore	4.50 × 4.20	7.3	213 @ 3000	393 @ 1800	3200⑤	35–60
1974	T	6-200	1 Bore	3.68 × 3.13	8.3	85 @ 3800	150 @ 1800	—	35
	A	6-240	1 Bore	4.00 × 3.18	7.9	108 @ 3800	182 @ 2400	4000	40–50
	L	6-250	1 Bore	3.68 × 3.91	8.0	92 @ 3200	234 @ 1600	—	35–55
	B	6-300②	1 Bore	4.00 × 3.98	7.9	126 @ 3400	234 @ 1600	4000	40–50
	B	6-300③	1 Bore	4.00 × 3.98	7.9	126 @ 3400	272 @ 1800	4000	40–50
	㉗	V8-302	2 Bore	4.00 × 3.00	8.0	145 @ 4000	239 @ 2600	—	50–65
	C	V8-330	2 Bore	3.88 × 3.50	7.4	⑦	—	3900	35–55
	D	V8-330③	2 Bore	3.88 × 3.50	7.4	⑧	⑨	3900㉙	㉘
	Q	V8-351	2 Bore	4.00 × 3.50	7.9	163 @ 4200	278 @ 2000	—	50–70
	Q	V8-351	4 Bore	4.00 × 3.50	7.9	254 @ 5600	292 @ 3400	—	50–70
	Y	V8-360	2 Bore	4.05 × 3.50	8.0	⑩	⑪	—	45–55
	E	V8-361③	2 Bore	4.05 × 3.50	7.2	⑫	⑬	3800	45–70
	H	V8-390	2 Bore	4.05 × 3.78	8.2	⑯	⑰	—	45–55
	M	V8-390	4 Bore	4.05 × 3.78	8.2	⑱	⑲	—	45–55
	F	V8-391③	4 Bore	4.05 × 3.79	7.2	⑳	㉑	3800	45–70
	S	V8-400	2 Bore	4.00 × 4.00	8.0	171 @ 3400	329 @ 2000	—	50–70
	H	V8-401㉖	4 Bore	4.125 × 3.75	7.3	171 @ 3400	274 @ 2800	3600⑤	52–62
	J	V8-460	4 Bore	4.36 × 3.850	8.0	㉒	㉓	—	35–65
	J	V8-475	4 Bore	4.50 × 3.75	7.2	㉔	㉕	—	52–62
	K	V8-477㉖	4 Bore	4.50 × 3.75	7.2	198 @ 3200	344 @ 2600	3400⑤	52–62
	L	V8-534㉖	4 Bore	4.50 × 4.20	7.3	213 @ 3000	393 @ 1800	3200⑤	52–62
1975	B	6-300	1 Bore	4.00 × 3.98	7.9	126 @ 3400	234 @ 1600	—	40–50
	B	6-300③	1 Bore	4.00 × 3.98	7.9	126 @ 3400	234 @ 1600	—	40–50
	G	V8-302	2 Bore	4.00 × 3.00	8.0	135 @ 3600	222 @ 2000	—	50–65
	C	V8-330	2 Bore	3.87 × 3.50	7.4	137 @ 3200	272 @ 1800	—	30–55
	D	V8-330③	2 Bore	3.87 × 3.50	7.4	137 @ 3600	250 @ 2400	—	㉘
	M	V8-351	2 Bore	4.00 × 3.50	8.0	—	—	—	
	Y	V8-360	2 Bore	4.05 × 3.50	—	155 @ 3800	263 @ 2000	—	45–55
	E	V8-361③	4 Bore	4.05 × 3.50	7.2	170 @ 3600	284 @ 2400	—	45–70
	F	V8-389③	4 Bore	4.05 × 3.78	7.2	180 @ 3600	302 @ 2700	—	—
	H	V8-390	2 Bore	4.05 × 3.78	—	157 @ 3600	291 @ 1800	—	45–55
	M	V8-390	4 Bore	4.05 × 3.78	—	208 @ 4500	324 @ 2800	—	45–55
	S	V8-400	2 Bore	4.00 × 4.00	8.0	—	—	—	
	H	V8-401㉖	4 Bore	4.125 × 3.75	7.3	171 @ 3400	274 @ 2800	—	52–62
	J	V8-460	4 Bore	4.36 × 3.85	8.0	239 @ 4200	374 @ 2600	—	35–65
	J	V8-475	4 Bore	4.50 × 3.75	7.2	203 @ 3400	341 @ 2600	—	—
	K	V8-477㉖	4 Bore	4.50 × 3.75	7.2	197 @ 3200	341 @ 2600	—	52–62
	L	V8-534㉖	4 Bore	4.50 × 4.20	7.3	212 @ 3000	392 @ 1800	—	52–62
1976	B	6-300㉚	1 Bore	4.00 × 3.98	7.3	㉜	223 @ 1600	—	40–50
	B	6-300㉛	1 Bore	4.00 × 3.98	7.3	㉝	㉞	—	40–50
	B	6-300㉚	1 Bore	4.00 × 3.98	8.0	㉟	㊱	—	40–50
	B	6-300㉛	1 Bore	4.00 × 3.98	8.0	㊲	㊳	—	40–50
	B	6-300③㉚	1 Bore	4.00 × 3.98	7.9	126 @ 3400	234 @ 1600	—	40–50
	B	6-300③㉛	1 Bore	4.00 × 3.98	7.9	127 @ 3600	223 @ 2400	—	40–50
	G	V8-302㉚	2 Bore	4.00 × 3.00	8.0	㊴	㊵	—	50–65

Continued

> # FORD

GENERAL ENGINE SPECIFICATIONS—Continued

Year	Engine Code On Truck Rating Plate	Engine Model	Carb. Type	Bore & Stroke	Comp. Ratio	Horsepower @ R.P.M.	Torque Lbs. Ft. @ R.P.M.	Governed Speed R.P.M. No Load	Normal Oil Pressure Lbs.
	G	V8-302㉛	2 Bore	4.00 × 3.00	8.0	㊶	㊷	—	50–65
	C	V8-330④㉚	2 Bore	3.87 × 3.50	7.4	137 @ 3200	272 @ 1800	—	35–55
	C	V8-330④㉛	2 Bore	3.87 × 3.50	7.4	144 @ 3200	261 @ 2400	—	35–55
	D	V8-330⑥㉚	2 Bore	3.87 × 3.50	7.4	137 @ 3600	250 @ 2400	3600	㉘
	D	V8-330⑥㉛	2 Bore	3.87 × 3.50	7.4	141 @ 3200	255 @ 2400	3600	㉘
	H	V8-351㉚	2 Bore	4.00 × 3.50	8.1	㊸	㊹	—	50–65
	H	V8-351㉛	2 Bore	4.00 × 3.50	8.1	㊺	㊻	—	50–65
	H	V8-351W㉚㊼	2 Bore	4.00 × 3.50	8.0	154 @ 3400	286 @ 1800	—	50–70
	H	V8-351M㊼	2 Bore	4.00 × 3.50	8.0	152 @ 3800	274 @ 1600	—	50–70
	Y	V8-360㉚	2 Bore	4.05 × 3.50	8.0	㊽	㊾	—	45–55
	Y	V8-360㉛	2 Bore	4.05 × 3.50	8.0	㊿	㉛	—	45–55
	E	V8-361㉚	4 Bore	4.05 × 3.50	7.2	170 @ 3600	284 @ 2400	3600	45–70
	E	V8-361㉛	4 Bore	4.05 × 3.50	7.2	166 @ 3600	278 @ 2600	3600	45–70
	F	V8-389㉚	4 Bore	4.05 × 3.78	7.2	178 @ 3400	316 @ 2400	3600	45–70
	F	V8-389㉛	4 Bore	4.05 × 3.78	7.2	175 @ 3400	307 @ 2600	3600	45–70
	H	V8-390㉚	2 Bore	4.05 × 3.78	8.2	156 @ 3400	292 @ 2000	—	45–55
	H	V8-390㉛	2 Bore	4.05 × 3.78	8.2	147 @ 3200	288 @ 2000	—	45–55
	M	V8-390㉚	4 Bore	4.05 × 3.78	8.2	195 @ 4000	312 @ 2400	—	45–55
	M	V8-390㉚㊼	4 Bore	4.05 × 3.78	8.2	190 @ 4000	292 @ 2600	—	45–55
	M	V8-390㉛㊼	4 Bore	4.05 × 3.78	8.2	183 @ 3800	300 @ 2400	—	45–55
	S	V8-400㊼	2 Bore	4.00 × 4.00	8.0	180 @ 3800	336 @ 1800	—	50–70
	J	V8-460㉚	4 Bore	4.36 × 3.85	8.0	53	54	—	35–65
	J	V8-460㉚㊼	4 Bore	4.36 × 3.85	8.0	230 @ 4000	55	—	35–65
	J	V8-460㉛㊼	4 Bore	4.36 × 3.85	8.0	56	57	—	35–65
	J	V8-475㉚	4 Bore	4.5 × 3.75	7.2	203 @ 3400	341 @ 2600	3400	52–62
	J	V8-475㉛	4 Bore	4.5 × 3.75	7.2	215 @ 3400	354 @ 2600	3400	52–62
	K	V8-477㉚	4 Bore	4.5 × 3.75	7.2	197 @ 3200	341 @ 2600	3200	52–62
	K	V8-477㉛	4 Bore	4.5 × 3.75	7.2	208 @ 3200	354 @ 2600	3200	52–62
	L	V8-534㉚	4 Bore	4.5 × 5.2	7.3	212 @ 3000	392 @ 1800	3000	52–62
	L	V8-534㉛	4 Bore	4.5 × 5.2	7.3	218 @ 3000	298 @ 1800	3000	52–62
1977	B	6-300①	1 Bore	4.00 × 3.98	8.9	59	60	—	40–60
	B	6-300㊺㉛	1 Bore	4.00 × 3.98	8.0	37	38	—	40–60
	B	6-300㊺㉚	1 Bore	4.00 × 3.98	8.0	61	62	—	40–60
	B	6-300③㉚	1 Bore	4.00 × 3.98	7.9	126 @ 3400	234 @ 1600	—	40–60
	G	V8-302①	2 Bore	4.00 × 3.00	8.4	63	64	—	40–60
	C	V8-330④㉚	2 Bore	3.88 × 3.50	7.4	137 @ 3200	272 @ 1800	—	35–75
	D	V8-330⑥㉚	2 Bore	3.88 × 3.50	7.4	137 @ 3600	250 @ 2400	3600㊆	35–75
	H	V8-351W①	2 Bore	4.00 × 3.50	8.3	65	66	—	40–65
	H	V8-351M①㉚	2 Bore	4.00 × 3.50	8.0	67	68	—	50–75
	H	V8-351M①㉛	2 Bore	4.00 × 3.50	8.0	69	70	—	50–75
	H	V8-351W㊺	2 Bore	4.00 × 3.50	8.3	71	72	—	40–65
	H	V8-351M㊺	2 Bore	4.00 × 3.50	8.0	73	74	—	50–75
	H	V8-351W㊼	2 Bore	4.0 × 3.50	8.3	135 @ 3200	291 @ 1600	—	40–65
	H	V8-351M㊼	2 Bore	4.0 × 3.50	8.0	161 @ 3600	83	—	50–75
	—	V8-359	2 Bore	4.05 × 3.50	—	—	—	3300㊇	35–75
	E	V8-361㉚	4 Bore	4.05 × 3.50	7.2	170 @ 3600	284 @ 2400	3600㊆	35–75
	E	V8-361㉛	4 Bore	4.05 × 3.50	7.2	166 @ 3600	284 @ 2400	3600㊆	35–75
	F	V8-389㉚	4 Bore	4.05 × 3.78	7.2	178 @ 3400	316 @ 2400	—	35–75
	F	V8-389㉛	4 Bore	4.05 × 3.78	7.2	175 @ 3400	316 @ 2400	—	35–75
	F	V8-391	4 Bore	4.05 × 3.79	—	—	—	3800	35–75
	S	V8-400①	2 Bore	4.00 × 4.00	8.0	75	76	—	50–75
	S	V8-400㊺	2 Bore	4.00 × 4.00	8.0	77	78	—	50–75
	S	V8-400㊼	2 Bore	4.00 × 4.00	8.0	84	85	—	50–75
	J	V8-460㉚	4 Bore	4.36 × 3.85	8.0	79	80	—	40–65

Continued

1031

GENERAL ENGINE SPECIFICATIONS—Continued

Year	Engine Code On Truck Rating Plate	Engine Model	Carb. Type	Bore & Stroke	Comp. Ratio	Horsepower @ R.P.M.	Torque Lbs. Ft. @ R.P.M.	Governed Speed R.P.M. No Load	Normal Oil Pressure Lbs.
	J	V8-460(31)	4 Bore	4.36 × 3.85	8.0	(81)	(82)	—	40–65
	J	V8-460(47)	4 Bore	4.36 × 3.85	8.0	216 @ 4000	366 @ 2600	—	40–65
	J	V8-475	4 Bore	4.50 × 3.75	7.2	212 @ 3400	378 @ 2200	3400(88)	35–60
	K	V8-477	4 Bore	4.50 × 3.75	7.2	206 @ 3200	380 @ 2200	3400(88)	35–60
	L	V8-534	4 Bore	4.50 × 4.20	7.3	218 @ 3100	436 @ 2100	3400(88)	35–60
1978	B	6-300(89)	1 Bore	4.00 × 3.98	8.9	—	—	—	40–60
	B	6-300(90)	1 Bore	4.00 × 3.98	8.0	—	—	—	40–60
	B	6-300(91)(31)	1 Bore	4.00 × 3.98	7.9	126 @ 3400	234 @ 1600	—	40–60
	G	V8-302	2 Bore	4.00 × 3.00	8.4	—	—	—	40–60
	D	V8-330(92)	2 Bore	3.87 × 3.50	7.4	(93)	(94)	3600(86)	—
	D	V8-330(95)	2 Bore	3.87 × 3.50	7.4	(96)	(94)	3600(86)	—
	D	V8-330(97)	2 Bore	3.87 × 3.50	7.4	(98)	(99)	3600(86)	—
	H	V8-351W	2 Bore	4.00 × 3.50	8.3	—	—	—	40–65
	H	V8-351M	2 Bore	4.00 × 3.50	8.0	—	—	—	50–75
	E	V8-361	2 Bore	4.05 × 3.50	7.2	(100)	(101)	3600(87)	—
	E	V8-361(102)	4 Bore	4.05 × 3.50	7.2	(103)	(104)	3600(87)	—
	E	V8-361(105)	4 Bore	4.05 × 3.50	7.2	175 @ 3600	284 @ 2400	3600(87)	—
	E	V8-361(106)	4 Bore	4.05 × 3.50	7.2	(107)	282 @ 2400	3600(87)	—
	E	V8-361(108)	4 Bore	4.05 × 3.50	7.2	167 @ 3600	280 @ 2400	3600(87)	—
	F	V8-389(109)	4 Bore	4.05 × 3.78	7.2	(110)	(111)	3600(87)	—
	F	V8-389(112)	4 Bore	4.05 × 3.78	7.2	(113)	313 @ 2400	3600(87)	—
	F	V8-389(108)	4 Bore	4.05 × 3.78	7.2	175 @ 3400	311 @ 2400	3600(87)	—
	F	V8-389(105)	4 Bore	4.05 × 3.78	7.2	180 @ 3400	318 @ 2400	3600(87)	—
	S	V8-400	2 Bore	4.00 × 4.00	8.0	—	—	—	50–75
	J	V8-460	4 Bore	4.36 × 3.85	8.0	—	—	—	40–65
	J	V8-475(30)	4 Bore	4.5 × 3.75	7.2	(114)	(115)	3400	52–62
	K	V8-477(30)	4 Bore	4.5 × 3.75	7.2	(116)	(117)	3200	52–62
	L	V8-534(30)	4 Bore	4.5 × 4.20	7.3	(118)	(119)	3200	52–62
1979	B	6-300(30)(2)	1 Bore	4.00 × 3.98	7.9	126 @ 3600	234 @ 1800	—	40–60
	B	6-300(31)(2)	1 Bore	4.00 × 3.98	7.9	—	—	—	40–60
	K	6-300(3)(30)	1 Bore	4.00 × 3.98	7.9	117 @ 3600	227 @ 2400	—	40–60
	K	6-300(3)(31)	1 Bore	4.00 × 3.98	7.9	—	—	—	40–60
	G	V8-302	2 Bore	4.00 × 3.00	8.4	—	—	—	40–60
	H	V8-351W	2 Bore	4.00 × 3.50	—	—	—	—	40–65
	H	V8-351M	2 Bore	4.00 × 3.50	—	—	—	—	50–75
	C	V8-370	2 Bore	4.05 × 3.59	8.0	184 @ 3600(120)	302 @ 2800(120)	3600	40–65
	M	V8-370	4 Bore	4.05 × 3.59	8.0	204 @ 3600(120)	311 @ 2800(120)	3600	40–65
	S	V8-400	2 Bore	4.00 × 4.00	—	—	—	—	50–75
	C	V8-429	4 Bore	4.36 × 3.59	8.0	233 @ 4000(120)	369 @ 2700(120)	4000	40–65
	J	V8-460	2 Bore	4.36 × 3.85	—	—	—	—	40–65
	A	V8-460	4 Bore	4.36 × 3.85	—	—	—	—	40–65
	J	V8-475	4 Bore	4.5 × 3.75	7.2	(114)	(115)	3400	35–60
	K	V8-477	4 Bore	4.5 × 3.75	7.2	(116)	(117)	3200	35–60
	L	V8-534	4 Bore	4.5 × 4.20	7.3	(118)	(119)	3200	35–60
1980	E	6-300	1 Bore	4.00 × 3.98					40–60
	F	V8-302	2 Bore	4.00 × 3.00					40–60
	G	V8-351M	2 Bore	4.00 × 3.50					50–75
	W	V8-351W	2 Bore	4.00 × 3.50					40–65
	C	V8-370	2 Bore	4.05 × 3.59					40–70
	A	V8-370	4 Bore	4.05 × 3.59					40–70
	H	V8-370	2 Bore	4.05 × 3.59					40–70
	H	V8-370	4 Bore	4.05 × 3.59					40–70
	Z	V8-400	2 Bore	4.00 × 4.00					50–75
	K	V8-429	4 Bore	4.36 × 3.59					40–70

Continued

FORD

GENERAL ENGINE SPECIFICATIONS—Continued

Year	Engine Code On Truck Rating Plate	Engine Model	Carb. Type	Bore & Stroke	Comp. Ratio	Horsepower @ R.P.M.	Torque Lbs. Ft. @ R.P.M.	Governed Speed R.P.M. No Load	Normal Oil Pressure Lbs.
	L	V8-460	4 Bore	4.36 × 3.85					40–65
	M	V8-477	4 Bore	4.50 × 3.75					35–60
	—	V8-534	4 Bore	4.50 × 4.20					35–60

①—Under 6000 lbs. GVW emissions standard.
②—Light duty.
③—Heavy duty.
④—Medium duty.
⑤—Auto. Trans. 200 R.P.M. higher.
⑥—Extra heavy duty.
⑦—F-500 137 @ 3200; B-500 138 @ 3200.
⑧—F & LN Series Man. Trans. 137 @ 3600, C6 Auto. Trans. 135 @ 3600, Auto. Trans. except C6 131 @ 3600; B-Series Man. Trans. 138 @ 3600, C6 Auto. Trans. 136 @ 3600, Auto. Trans. except C6 132 @ 3600; C Series Man. Trans. 140 @ 3600, Auto. Trans. 128 @ 3800.
⑨—F, LN & B Series Man. Trans. and C6 Auto. Trans. 250 @ 2400, Auto. Trans. except C6 247 @ 2400; C Series Man. Trans. 253 @ 2400, Auto. Trans. 246 @ 2400.
⑩—F-100 4 × 2 Man. Trans. 157 @ 4000, Auto. Trans. 151 @ 3800; F-100 4 × 4 Man. Trans. 153 @ 4000, Auto. Trans. 148 @ 3800; F-250, 350 @ 3600.
⑪—F-100 4 × 2 Man. Trans. 265 @ 2200, Auto Trans. 151 @ 3800; F-100 4 × 4 Man. Trans. 262 @ 2200, Auto. Trans. 256 @ 2200; F-250, 350, 263 @ 2000.
⑫—F-LN-600, 750 Man. Trans. 153 @ 3600, Auto. Trans. 147 @ 3400; B Series & CT-800 Man. Trans. 154 @ 3600; B Series & C-600, 800 Auto. Trans. 148 @ 3400; C-600, 800 Man. Trans. 156 @ 3600; L-Line 800 158 @ 3600.
⑬—F-LN-600, 750 & B Series Man. Trans. 278 @ 2400, Auto. Trans. 275 @ 2400; C-600, 800 & CT-800 Man. Trans. 279 @ 2400; C-600, 800 Auto. Trans. 273 @ 2400; L-Line 800 280 @ 2400.
⑭—F-100 Auto. Trans. 257 @ 2000; F-250-350 Exc. Calif. 148 @ 3800; F-250-350 Calif. 145 @ 3600.
⑮—F-100 Auto. Trans. 161 @ 3600; F-250-350 Exc. Calif. 264 @ 2200; F-250-350 Calif. 263 @ 2000.
⑯—F-100 Auto. Trans. 160 @ 3600; F-250, 350 159 @ 3400.
⑰—F-100 Auto. Trans. 295 @ 2000; F-250, 350 296 @ 2000.
⑱—F-250, 350 Man. Trans. 208 @ 4500, Auto. Trans. 206 @ 4600.
⑲—F-250, 350 Man. Trans. 324 @ 2800, Auto. Trans. 320 @ 2800.
⑳—F-LN-750 Man. Trans. 180 @ 3600, Auto. Trans. 174 @ 3400; B Series Man. Trans. 181 @ 3600; B Series & C-750, 800 Auto. Trans. 175 @ 3400; C-750, 800 Man. Trans. 179 @ 3600; CT-800 177 @ 3600: L-Line 800 182 @ 3600.
㉑—F-LN-750 & B Series Man. Trans. 320 @ 2400, Auto. Trans. 317 @ 2400; C-750, 800 Man. Trans. 318 @ 2400, Auto. Trans. 315 @ 2400; CT-800 317 @ 2400: L-Line 800 182 @ 3600.
㉒—Ranchero 216 @ 4600; F-100 238 @ 4200; F-250, 350 239 @ 4200.
㉓—Ranchero 356 @ 2600; F-100 380 @ 2600; F-250, 350 374 @ 2600.
㉔—LT-880 203 @ 3400: LTN-880 197 @ 3400.
㉕—LT-880 341 @ 2600: LTN-880 336 @ 2600.
㉖—Super Duty.
㉗—Ranchero engine code F, all except Ranchero G.
㉘—With velocity governor 35–55 p.s.i., without velocity governor 45–70 p.s.i.
㉙—Auto. Trans. 100 R.P.M. lower.
㉚—Except California.
㉛—California.
㉜—E-100: 101 @ 3000: F-100: 100 @ 3000.
㉝—E-100: 102 @ 3000: F-100: 100 @ 3000.
㉞—E-100: 225 @ 1600: F-100: 221 @ 1600.
㉟—E-150-350: 118 @ 3400; F-150-350 114 @ 3400: P-350-500; 117 @ 3600.
㊱—E-150-350: 226 @ 1800; F-150-350; 222 @ 1600; P-350-500: 227 @ 1800.
㊲—E-150-350: 124 @ 3600; F-150-350: 118 @ 3600; P-350-500:124 @ 3400.
㊳—E-150-350: 217 @ 2200; F-150-350: 205 @ 2200; P-350-500:222 @ 2200.
㊴—Bronco: 121 @ 3600; F-100: 130 @ 3800.
㊵—Bronco: 217 @ 1800; F-100: 222 @ 2000.
㊶—Bronco: 122 @ 3600; F-100: 134 @ 3600.
㊷—Bronco: 215 @ 1800; F-100: 222 @ 2400.
㊸—E-100: 156 @ 4000; E-150-350: 178 @ 4000.
㊹—E-100: 262 @ 2200; E-150-350: 270 @ 2600.
㊺—E-100: 156 @ 4000; E-150-350: 176 @ 4000.
㊻—E-100: 263 @ 2200; E-150-350: 266 @ 2400.
㊼—Ranchero.
㊽—F-100: 145 @ 3800; F-150-350: 145 @ 3600.
㊾—F-100: 264 @ 2200; F-150-350: 263 @ 2000.
㊿—F-100: 145 @ 3800; F-150-350: 148 @ 3600.
51—F-100: 250 @ 2200; F-150-350: 251 @ 2200.
52—Noise Legislated area engines.
53—E-250-350: 237 @ 4000; F-150-350: 245 @ 4200.
54—E-250-350: 365 @ 2600; F-150-350: 371 @ 2600.
55—E-250-350: 359 @ 2600; F-150-350: 362 @ 2600.
56—E-250-350: 230 @ 4000; F-150-350: 234 @ 4000.
57—E-250-350: 360 @ 2600; F-150-350: 362 @ 2600.
58—Over 6000 lbs. GVW emissions standards.
59—F-100: 119 @ 3200; E-100 exc. Calif. 122 @ 3200; E-100 Calif. 123 @ 3200.
60—F-100: 252 @ 1600; E-100 exc. Calif. 252 @ 1600; E-100 Calif. 253 @ 1600.
61—F-150-350: 114 @ 3200; E-150-350: 120 @ 3400; P-500 117 @ 3600.
62—F-150-350: 227 @ 1800; E-150-350: 229 @ 1400; P-500 227 @ 1800.
63—F-100: 136 @ 3600; Bronco 133 @ 3600; Ranchero: 130 @ 3400.
64—F-100: 245 @ 2000; Bronco exc. Calif. 236 @ 1800: Bronco Calif 235 @ 1800; Ranchero: 243 @ 1800.
65—Exc. Calif.: 141 @ 3200; Calif. auto. trans.: 143 @ 3200; Calif. Man. Trans. 152 @ 3200.
66—Exc. Calif.: 286 @ 1400; Calif. auto. trans.: 287 @ 1600; Calif. Man. Trans.: 286 @ 2000.
67—Non-noise legislated 162 @ 3800; Noise legislated man. trans. 161 @ 3800; Noise legislated auto. trans. 165 @ 3800.
68—Non-noise legislated 282 @ 2000; Noise legislated man. trans. 281 @ 2000; Noise legislated auto. trans. 282 @ 2000.
69—Auto. Trans. 165 @ 3800; Man. Trans., 161 @ 3800.
70—Auto. Trans. 282 @ 2000; Man. Trans. 281 @ 2000.
71—Exc. Calif. 147 @ 3400; Calif. 143 @ 3200.
72—Exc. Calif. Non-noise legislated 276 @ 1800; Exc. Calif. Noise legislated 275 @ 1800; Calif. 272 @ 2000.
73—Exc. Calif. Non-noise legislated 163 @ 3800; Exc. Calif., Noise legislated 162 @ 3800; Calif. 161 @ 3800.
74—Exc. Calif. Non-noise legislated 267 @ 2200; Exc. Calif. Noise legislated 266 @ 2200; Calif. 265 @ 2200.
75—Non-noise legislated 175 @ 3600; Noise legislated 177 @ 3600.
76—Non-noise legislated 326 @ 2000; Noise legislated 325 @ 2000.
77—Exc. Non-noise legislated: 167 @ 3600; Non-noise legislated 169 @ 3600.
78—Exc. Non-noise legislated: 302 @ 2200; Non-noise legislated 303 @ 2200.
79—Non-noise legislated (F-150-350) 245 @ 4200; Noise legislated (F-150-350 & E-250/350) 230 @ 4000: Non-noise legislated (E-250/350) 237 @ 4000.
80—Non-noise legislated (F-150-350) 371 @ 2600; Noise legislated (F-150-350) 362 @ 2600; Non-noise legislated (E-250/350) 365 @ 2600 Noise legislated (E-250/350) 359 @ 2600.
81—F-150-350: 234 @ 4000; E-250/350: 230 @ 4000.
82—F-150-350: 362 @ 2600; E-250/350: 360 @ 2600.
83—Exc. Calif. 285 @ 1800; Calif. 286 @ 1800.
84—Exc. Calif. 173 @ 3800; Calif. 181 @ 4000.
85—Exc. Calif. 326 @ 1600; Calif. 323 @ 1600.
86—3800 W/C-6 Auto. Trans.
87—3400 W/AT-540 Trans.
88—400 W/C6 Auto. trans.
89—E100 & F100.
90—E150-350, F150-350 & P600.
91—F600 & B600.
92—F-LN Series.
93—Auto. trans., exc. C6, 131 @ 3600; C6 135 @ 3800: manual trans.,137 @ 3600.
94—Auto. trans., exc. C6, 247 @ 2400; C6, 250 @ 2400: manual trans. 250 @ 2400.
95—B series.
96—Auto. trans., exc. C6, 132 @ 3600; C6, 136 @ 3800: manual trans., 138 @ 3600.
97—C series.
98—Auto. trans., exc. C6, 128 @ 3600; C6, 139 @ 3800: manual trans.,exc. with velocity governor, 140 @ 3600; with velocity governor 140 @ 3200.
99—Auto. trans., exc. C6, 251 @ 2400; C6, 253 @ 2400: manual trans. exc. with velocity governor, 253 @ 2400: with velocity governor, 275 @ 1800.
100—F-B600/B700, 149 @ 3800; C600, 144 @ 3800.
101—F-B600/B700, 278 @ 2400; C600, 274 @ 2400.

Continued

Ford

GENERAL ENGINE SPECIFICATIONS—NOTES—Continued

- ⑩②—F/B/LN600-700 series.
- ⑩③—Auto. trans., 163 @ 3400: manual trans., exc. Calif., 170 @ 3600: Calif., 166 @ 3600.
- ⑩④—Auto. trans., 280 @ 2400: manual trans., exc. Calif., 280 @ 2400: Calif., 284 @ 2400.
- ⑩⑤—L-line 800 series.
- ⑩⑥—C600-800 series.
- ⑩⑦—Auto. trans., 168 @ 3400: manual trans., 169 @ 3600.
- ⑩⑧—CT800 series.
- ⑩⑨—F/B/LN700, F800 series.
- ⑪⓪—Auto. trans., 171 @ 3400: manual trans., exc. Calif., 178 @ 3400: Calif., 175 @ 3400.
- ⑪①—Auto. trans., 309 @ 2400: manual trans., 316 @ 2400.
- ⑪②—C700-800 series.
- ⑪③—Auto. trans., 176 @ 3400: manual trans. 177 @ 3400.
- ⑪④—F-C 800, 213 @ 3400; L-LT-LTS 800, 212 @ 3400; LN-LNT 800, 210 @ 3400; CT 800, 211 @ 3400.
- ⑪⑤—F 800, 377 @ 2300; L-LT-LTS 800, 380 @ 2200; LN-LNT 800, 375 @ 2200; C 800, 383 @ 2200; CT 800, 382 @ 2200.
- ⑪⑥—L-LT-LTS-LN-LNT 900, 209 @ 3200; C 900, 210 @ 3200; CT 900, 208 @ 3200.
- ⑪⑦—L-LT-LTS 900, 380 @ 2200; LN-LNT 900, 379 @ 2200; C 900, 383 @ 2200; CT 900, 382 @ 2200.
- ⑪⑧—L-LT-LTS 900, 220 @ 3100; LN-LNT 900, 218 @ 3100; C 900, 221 @ 3100; CT 900, 219 @ 3100.
- ⑪⑨—L-LT-LTS 900, 437 @ 2100; LN-LTN 900, 436 @ 2100; C 900, 440 @ 2100; CT 900, 439 @ 2100.
- ⑫⓪—Gross SAE.

TUNE UP SPECIFICATIONS

The following specifications are published from the latest information available. This data should be used only in the absence of a decal affixed in the engine compartment.

★ When using a timing light, disconnect vacuum hose or tube at distributor and plug opening in hose or tube so idle speed will not be affected.

● When checking compression, lowest cylinder must be within 75 percent of highest.

▲ Before removing wires from distributor cap, determine location of the No. 1 wire in cap, as distributor position may have been altered from that shown at the end of this chart.

Year & Engine	Spark Plug		Firing Order Fig. ▲	Ignition Timing BTDC①★		Mark Location	Curb Idle Speed②		Fuel Pump Pressure
	Type	Gap		Man. Trans.	Auto. Trans.		Man. Trans.	Auto. Trans.	
1980									
6-300 Exc. Calif.	BSF-42	.044	⑥②	6°	③	Damper	600/700	550D	5–7
6-300 Calif.	BSF-42	.044	⑥②	6°	10°	Damper	700	550D	5–7
V8-302 E-100, 150 Exc. Calif.	ASF-42	.044	A	8°	10°	Damper	700	575D	6–8
V8-302 E-100 Calif.	ASF-42	.044	A	—	6°	Damper	—	650D	6–8
V8-302 E-150 Calif.	ASF-42	.044	A	—	12°	Damper	—	600D	6–8
V8-302 E-250 Calif.	ASF-42	.044	A	—	10°	Damper	—	575D	6–8
V8-302 F-100, 150 Exc. Calif.④	ASF-42	.044	A	6°	8°	Damper	700	575D	6–8
V8-302 F-100, 150 Calif.④	ASF-42	.044	A	2°	8°	Damper	800	650D	6–8
V8-302 F-150 & Bronco Exc. Calif.⑤	ASF-42	.044	A	8°	⑥⑦	Damper	700	550D	6–8
V8-302 F-150 & Bronco Calif.⑤	ASF-42	.044	A	4°	⑧	Damper	750	575D	6–8
V8-302 F-250 Exc. Calif.	ASF-42	.044	A	⑨	8°	Damper	700	575D	6–8
V8-302 F-250 Calif.	ASF-42	.044	A	—	10°	Damper	—	575D	6–8
V8-351W E-100, 150⑥⑩⑪	ASF-42	.044	B	—	16°	Damper	—	600D	6–8
V8-351W E-100, 150⑥⑩⑫	ASF-42	.044	B	—	14°	Damper	—	600D	6–8
V8-351W E-150⑥⑩⑬	ASF-42	.044	B	—	10°	Damper	—	600D	6–8
V8-351W E-150⑥⑩⑭	ASF-42	.044	B	—	8°	Damper	—	600D	6–8
V8-351M E-250, 350 & F150, 250, 350⑥⑮⑯	ARF-52	.044	B	10°	10°	Damper	600	600D	6–8
V8-351M F-150⑥⑮⑰	ASF-42	.044	B	10°	14°	Damper	650	550/625D	6–8
V8-351M F-150⑥⑮⑱	ASF-42	.044	B	—	8°	Damper	—	550/625D	6–8
V8-351M F-150 & Bronco⑥⑮⑲	ASF-42	.044	B	10°	6°	Damper	650	550/625D	6–8
V8-351M F-150, 250 & Bronco⑥⑮⑳	ASF-42	.044	B	16°	12°	Damper	650	550/625D	6–8
V8-351M F-150 & 250 Calif.⑥⑮㉑	ASF-42	.044	B	10°	—	Damper	800	—	6–8

Continued

FORD

TUNE UP SPECIFICATIONS—Continued

The following specifications are published from the latest information available. This data should be used only in the absence of a decal affixed in the engine compartment.

★ When using a timing light, disconnect vacuum hose or tube at distributor and plug opening in hose or tube so idle speed will not be affected.

● When checking compression, lowest cylinder must be within 75 percent of highest.

▲ Before removing wires from distributor cap, determine location of the No. 1 wire in cap, as distributor position may have been altered from that shown at the end of this chart.

Year & Engine	Spark Plug Type	Gap	Firing Order Fig. ▲	Ignition Timing BTDC①★ Man. Trans.	Auto Trans.	Mark Location	Curb Idle Speed② Man. Trans.	Auto. Trans.	Fuel Pump Pressure
1980—Continued									
V8-351M E & F-250 ⑥⑮㉒	ASF-42	.044	B	—	6°	Damper	—	550/625D	6–8
V8-351M F-250 ⑥⑮㉓	ASF-42	.044	B	—	12°	Damper	—	550/625D	6–8
V8-370 2 Barrel Carb.	ASF-32	.044	㊿	6°	6°	Damper	600	600D	6–8㉔
V8-370 4 Barrel Carb. Exc. Calif.	ASF-32	.044	㊿	6°	6°	Damper	600	600D	6–8㉔
V8-370 4 Barrel Carb. Calif.	ASF-32	.044	㊿	2°	2°	Damper	600	600D	6–8㉔
V8-400 F-150, 250 & Bronco Exc. Calif.	ASF-52	.044	B	6°	3°	Damper	600	600D	6–8
V8-400 F-150, 250 & Bronco Calif.	ASF-52	.044	B	6°	6°	Damper	600	600D	6–8
V8-400 F-350	ASF-42	.044	B	4°	4°	Damper	—	550/625D	6–8
V8-429	ASF-32	.044	㊿	6°	6°	Damper	600	600D	6–8㉔
V8-460	ASF-42	.044	A	—	8°	Damper	—	650D	6–8
V8-477, 534	BYSF-31-4	.040	㊿	10°	10°	Damper	600	600D	6–8㉔
1979									
6-300 E & F-100, 150 & 250	㉕	.044	㊽	6°	10°	Damper	500/700	500/550D	5–7
6-300 E & F-350	㉕	.044	㊽	12°	12°	Damper	500/700	500/550D	5–7
6-300 FB & P-600	㉖	.044	㊽	12°	—	Damper	500/700	—	4–6㉔
V8-302 Ranchero Exc. Calif.	㉗	.050	A	—	8°	Damper	—	600/675D	6–8
V8-302 Ranchero Calif.	㉗	.050	A	—	12°	Damper	—	600/675D	6–8
V8-302 E-100, 150, 250	㉘	.044	A	4°	6°	Damper	700	550/600D㉙	6–8
V8-302 F-100, 150 Exc. Calif.	㉘	.044	A	6°	8°	Damper	700	550/600D	6–8
V8-302 F-100 Calif.	㉘	.044	A	—	8°	Damper	—	550/650D	6–8
V8-302 F-150 Calif.	㉘	.044	A	—	6°	Damper	—	550/600D	6–8
V8-351W Ranchero⑩	㉗	.050	B	—	15°	Damper	—	600/650D	6–8
V8-351W E-100⑩	㉘	.044	B	—	10°	Damper	—	500/600D	6–8
V8-351W E-150 Exc. Calif.⑩	㉘	.044	B	4°	10°	Damper	500/800	500/600D	6–8
V8-351W E-150 Calif.⑩	㉘	.044	B	—	8°	Damper	—	500/650D	6–8
V8-351W E-250⑩	㉘	.044	B	4°	12°	Damper	500/800	500/600D	6–8
V8-351W E-350 & F-800⑩	㉘	.044	B	—	6°	Damper	—	525/650D	6–8
V8-351M Ranchero Exc. Calif.⑮	㉗	.050	B	—	12°	Damper	—	600/650D	6–8
V8-351M Ranchero Calif.⑮	㉗	.050	B	—	14°	Damper	—	600/650D	6–8
V8-351M F-100 Exc. Calif.⑮	⑳	.044	B	10°	6°	Damper	650	550D	6–8
V8-351M F-100 Calif.⑮	㉘	.044	B	—	10°	Damper	—	550D	6–8
V8-351M F-150, 250 & Bronco⑮	㉘	.044	B	㉚	6°	Damper	650	550D	6–8
V8-351M F-350⑮	㉘	.044	B	6°	12°	Damper	600	500/600D	6–8
V8-370 2 Barrel Carb.	㉛	.044	㊿	6°	—	Damper	600	—	6–8㉔
V8-370 4 Barrel Carb.	㉛	.044	㊿	2°	—	Damper	600	—	6–8㉔

Continued

FORD

TUNE UP SPECIFICATIONS—Continued

The following specifications are published from the latest information available. This data should be used only in the absence of a decal affixed in the engine compartment.

★ When using a timing light, disconnect vacuum hose or tube at distributor and plug opening in hose or tube so idle speed will not be affected.

● When checking compression, lowest cylinder must be within 75 percent of highest.

▲ Before removing wires from distributor cap, determine location of the No. 1 wire in cap, as distributor position may have been altered from that shown at the end of this chart.

Year & Engine	Spark Plug Type	Gap	Firing Order Fig. ▲	Ignition Timing BTDC①★ Man. Trans.	Auto. Trans.	Mark Location	Curb Idle Speed② Man. Trans.	Auto. Trans.	Fuel Pump Pressure
1979—Continued									
V8-400 F-150, 250 & Bronco	㉘	.044	B	10°	6°	Damper	650	550D	6–8
V8-400 F-350	㉘	.044	B	3°	3°	Damper	600	600D	6–8
V8-429	㉛	.044	㊿	8°	—	Damper	600	—	6–8㉔
V8-460 E-250	㉘	.044	A	—	14°	Damper	—	650/800D	6–8
V8-460 E-350	㉘	.044	A	—	8°	Damper	—	650D	6–8
V8-475, 477 & 534	㉜	.040	㊽	10°	—	Damper	600	—	6–8㉔
1978									
6-300 E-100	BSF-42	.044	㊷	6°	⑥㉝	Damper	700	550D	5–7
6-300 F-100	BSF-42	.044	㊷	6°	10°	Damper	700	550D	5–7
6-300 E & F-150, 250 Exc. Calif.	BSF-42	.054	㊷	10°	10°	Damper	600	600D	5–7
6-300 E & F-150, 250 Calif.	BSF-42	.044	㊷	6°	8°	Damper	700	550D	5–7
6-300 E & F-350	BSF-42	.054	㊷	10°	10°	Damper	600	600D	5–7
6-300 F, B & P-600	㉞	.054	㊷	10°	—	Damper	600	—	4–6
V8-302 Ranchero	ASF-52	.050	A	—	14°	Damper	—	600D	6–8
V8-302 F-100 Exc. Calif. & High Alt.	ASF-42	.044	A	6°	8°	Damper	700	600D	6–8
V8-302 F-150 Exc. Calif.	ASF-42	.044	A	6°	6°	Damper	750	600D	6–8
V8-302 F-100, 150 Calif.㉟	ASF-42	.044	A	6°	8°	Damper	750	650D	6–8
V8-302 F-150 Calif.㊱	ASF-42	.044	A	—	10°	Damper	—	650D	6–8
V8-302 F-100 High Alt.	ASF-42	.044	A	12°	10°	Damper	800	550D	6–8
V8-330 Exc. Calif.㊲	BSF-31	.030	㊿	6°	—	Damper	550	—	5–7㉔
V8-330 Exc. Calif.㊳	BSF-31	.030	㊿	6°	6°	Damper	600	550D	5–7㉔
V8-330 Calif.㊲	BSF-31	.030	㊿	4°	—	Damper	650	—	5–7㉔
V8-330 Calif.㊳	BSF-31	.030	㊿	8°	—	Damper	650	—	5–7㉔
V8-351W Ranchero⑩	ASF-52	.050	B	—	14°	Damper	—	600/675D	6–8
V8-351W Bronco⑩	ASF-42	.044	B	8°	14°	Damper	650	650D	6–8
V8-351W E-100 Exc. Calif. & High Alt.⑩	ASF-42	.044	B	8°	14°	Damper	600/900	500/600D	6–8
V8-351W E-100 Calif.⑩	ASF-42	.044	B	—	10°	Damper	—	500/700D	6–8
V8-351W E-100 High Alt.⑩	ASF-42	.044	B	—	12°㊴	Damper	—	550D	6–8
V8-351W E-150, 250, 350 Exc. Calif.⑩	㊵	.044	B	6°	8°	Damper	650	550D	6–8
V8-351W E-150, 250 Calif.⑩	ASF-42	.044	B	4°	8°	Damper	650	550D	6–8
V8-351W E-350 Calif.⑩	㊵	.044	B	—	8°	Damper	—	650D	6–8
V8-351M Ranchero Exc. Calif. & High Alt.⑮	ASF-52	.050	B	—	9°	Damper	—	600/675D	6–8
V8-351M Ranchero Calif.⑮	ASF-52	.050	B	—	14°	Damper	—	600/675D	6–8
V8-351M Ranchero High Alt.⑮	ASF-52	.050	B	—	12°㊴	Damper	—	650D	6–8
V8-351M F-100 Exc. Calif. & High Alt.⑮	ASF-42	.044	B	8°	10°	Damper	750	600D	6–8
V8-351M F-100 Calif.⑮	ASF-42	.044	B	—	8°	Damper	—	650D	6–8

Continued

1036

FORD

TUNE UP SPECIFICATIONS—Continued

The following specifications are published from the latest information available. This data should be used only in the absence of a decal affixed in the engine compartment.

★ When using a timing light, disconnect vacuum hose or tube at distributor and plug opening in hose or tube so idle speed will not be affected.

● When checking compression, lowest cylinder must be within 75 percent of highest.

▲ Before removing wires from distributor cap, determine location of the No. 1 wire in cap, as distributor position may have been altered from that shown at the end of this chart.

Year & Engine	Spark Plug		Firing Order Fig. ▲	Ignition Timing BTDC ①★		Mark Location	Curb Idle Speed ②		Fuel Pump Pressure
	Type	Gap		Man. Trans.	Auto Trans.		Man. Trans.	Auto. Trans.	
1978—Continued									
V8-351M F-100 High Alt. ⑮	ASF-42	.044	B	—	14°	Damper	—	650D	6–8
V8-351M F-150, 250, 350, Bronco Exc. Calif. ⑮	ASF-42	.044	B	6°	14°	Damper	650	650D	6–8
V8-351M F-150, 250, Bronco Calif. ⑮	ASF-42	.044	B	6°	8°	Damper	800	650D	6–8
V8-351M F-350 Calif. ⑮	ASF-42	.044	B	10°	10°	Damper	650	650D	6–8
V8-361 Exc. Calif.	BSF-31	.030	㊆	4°	4°	Damper	650	650D	5–7 ㉔
V8-361 Calif.	BSF-31	.030	㊆	6°	6°	Damper	650	650D	5–7 ㉔
V8-391	BSF-31	.030	㊆	4°	4°	Damper	650	650D	5–7 ㉔
V8-400 Ranchero Exc. Calif. & High Alt. ㉟	ASF-52	.050	B	—	13°	Damper	—	575/650D	6–8
V8-400 Ranchero Exc. Calif. & High Alt. ㊱	ASF-52	.050	B	—	14°	Damper	—	600/675D	6–8
V8-400 Ranchero Calif.	ASF-52	.050	B	—	14°	Damper	—	600/675D	6–8
V8-400 Ranchero High Alt.	ASF-52	.050	B	—	8° ㊴	Damper	—	650D	6–8
V8-400 F-100	ASF-42	.044	B	—	6°	Damper	—	600D	6–8
V8-400 F-150, 250, 350, Bronco Exc. Calif.	ASF-42	.044	B	12°	12°	Damper	650	650D	6–8
V8-400 F-150, 250, Bronco Calif.	ASF-42	.044	B	—	8°	Damper	—	650D	6–8
V8-400 F-350 Calif.	ASF-42	.044	B	—	10°	Damper	—	650D	6–8
V8-460 Exc. Calif.	ASF-42	.044	A	—	12°	Damper	—	650D	㊺
V8-460 E-250, F-150, 250 Calif.	ASF-42	.044	A	—	14°	Damper	—	600D	㊺
V8-460 E & F-350 Calif.	ASF-42	.044	A	—	12°	Damper	—	650D	㊺
V8-477, 534	BYSF-31-4	.040	㊿	10°	10°	Damper	600	600D	—
1977									
6-300 E & F-100	BSF-42	.044	㉒	6°	6°	Damper	700	550D	5–7
6-300 E & F-150, 250, 350	BSF-42	.044	㉒	10°	10°	Damper	600	600D	5–7
6-300 P-500	BSF-42	.044	㉒	10°	—	Damper	600	—	4–6
6-300 C-600	BSF-31	.032	㉒	10°	—	Damper	600	—	4–6
V8-302 Ranchero	ARF-52	.050	A	—	2°	Damper	—	500/600D	6–8
V8-302 Bronco Exc. High Alt.	ASF-42	.044	A	⑥㊶	8°	Damper	850	550/650D	6–8
V8-302 Bronco High Alt.	ASF-42	.044	A	8°	8°	Damper	800	550D	6–8
V8-302 E-100 Exc. Calif. & High Alt.	ASF-42	.044	A	㊷	8°	Damper	850	650D	6–8
V8-302 E-100 Calif.	ASF-42	.044	A	6°	—	Damper	800	—	6–8
V8-302 E-100 High Alt.	ASF-42	.044	A	8°	8°	Damper	800	550D	6–8
V8-302 F-100 Exc. Calif. & High Alt.	ASF-42	.044	A	⑥㊸	⑥㊹	Damper	850	650D	6–8
V8-302 F-100 Calif.	ASF-42	.044	A	6°	—	Damper	800	—	6–8
V8-302 F-100 High Alt.	ASF-42	.044	A	8°	8°	Damper	800	550D	6–8
V8-302 F-150	ASF-42	.044	A	6°	6°	Damper	750	650D	6–8
V8-330	BSF-31	.030	㊆	6°	6°	Damper	600	550D	5–7 ㉔

Continued

TUNE UP SPECIFICATIONS—Continued

The following specifications are published from the latest information available. This data should be used only in the absence of a decal affixed in the engine compartment.

★ When using a timing light, disconnect vacuum hose or tube at distributor and plug opening in hose or tube so idle speed will not be affected.

● When checking compression, lowest cylinder must be within 75 percent of highest.

▲ Before removing wires from distributor cap, determine location of the No. 1 wire in cap, as distributor position may have been altered from that shown at the end of this chart.

Year & Engine	Spark Plug		Ignition Timing BTDC(1)★				Curb Idle Speed(2)		Fuel Pump Pressure
	Type	Gap	Firing Order Fig. ▲	Man. Trans.	Auto Trans.	Mark Location	Man. Trans.	Auto. Trans.	
1977—Continued									
V8-351W Ranchero(10)	ARF-52	.050	B	—	4°	Damper	—	625D	6–8
V8-351W E-100 Exc. Calif.(10)	ASF-42	.044	B	(42)	12°	Damper	(42)	550D	6–8
V8-351W E-100 Calif.(10)	ASF-42	.044	B	8°	14°	Damper	900	700D	6–8
V8-351W E-150, 250, 350(10)	ASF-34	.044	B	6°	8°	Damper	650	550D	6–8
V8-351M Ranchero Exc. Calif. & High Alt.(15)(35)	ARF-52	.050	B	—	(6)(45)	Damper	—	650D	6–8
V8-351M Ranchero Exc. Calif. & High Alt.(15)(36)	ARF-52	.050	B	—	8°	Damper	—	500/650D	6–8
V8-351M Ranchero Calif.(15)	ARF-52-6	.060	B	—	(6)(46)	Damper	—	600D	6–8
V8-351M Ranchero High Alt.(15)	ARF-52	.050	B	—	12°	Damper	—	650D	6–8
V8-351M F-100 Exc. Calif. & High Alt.(15)	ASF-42	.044	B	10°	(6)(47)	Damper	800	(6)(48)	6–8
V8-351M F-100 Calif.(15)	ASF-42	.044	B	—	8°	Damper	—	650D	6–8
V8-351M F-100 High Alt.(15)	ASF-42	.044	B	—	10°	Damper	—	650D	6–8
V8-351M F-150, 250, 350 Exc. Calif.(15)	ASF-42	.044	B	12°	(6)(49)	Damper	650	650D	6–8
V8-351M F-150, 250, 350 Calif.(15)	ASF-42	.044	B	—	(6)(50)	Damper	—	650D	6–8
V8-361, F, B, C-600 & B-700 Exc. Calif.(6)(51)	BSF-31	.030	(63)	—	6°	Damper	—	550D	5–7(24)
V8-361F, B, LN, C-600, 700, 750 Exc. Calif.(6)(52)	BSF-31	.030	(63)	—	4°	Damper	—	650D	5–7(24)
V8-361F, B, LN, C-600, 700, 750 Calif.	BSF-31	.030	(63)	—	6°	Damper	—	650D	5–7(24)
V8-361L, LN, LT, LNT, LTS, C, CT-800 Exc. Calif.	BSF-31	.030	(63)	—	4°	Damper	—	650D	5–7(24)
V8-361L, LN, LT, LNT, LTS, C, CT-800 Calif.	BSF-31	.030	(63)	—	6°	Damper	—	650D	5–7(24)
V8-391	BSF-31	.030	(63)	4°	4°	Damper	650	650D	5–7(24)
V8-400 Ranchero Exc. Calif. & High Alt.	ARF-52	.050	B	—	(6)(53)	Damper	—	(6)(54)	6–8
V8-400 Ranchero Calif.	ARF-52-6	.060	B	—	6°	Damper	—	500/600D	6–8
V8-400 Ranchero High Alt.	ARF-52	.050	B	—	10°	Damper	—	650D	6–8
V8-400 F-100	ASF-42	.044	B	—	6°	Damper	—	650D	6–8
V8-400 F-150, 250, 350, Bronco	ASF-42	.044	B	12°	12°	Damper	650	650D	6–8
V8-460 E & F-150, 250, 350	ASF-42	.044	A	—	12°	Damper	—	650D	(65)
V8-477, 534	BYSF-31-4	.040	(64)	—	10°	Damper	—	600D	—
1976									
6-300 E & F-150, 250, 350	BTRF-42	.044	(62)	10°	10°	Damper	600	600D	4–6
6-300 P-350, 400, 500	BTRF-42	.044	(62)	10°	10°	Damper	600	600D	4–6
6-300F, B-500, 600 & C-600 Exc. Calif.(55)	BRF-31	.030	(62)	10°	10°	Damper	600	600D	4–6

Continued

FORD

TUNE UP SPECIFICATIONS—Continued

The following specifications are published from the latest information available. This data should be used only in the absence of a decal affixed in the engine compartment.

★ When using a timing light, disconnect vacuum hose or tube at distributor and plug opening in hose or tube so idle speed will not be affected.

● When checking compression, lowest cylinder must be within 75 percent of highest.

▲ Before removing wires from distributor cap, determine location of the No. 1 wire in cap, as distributor position may have been altered from that shown at the end of this chart.

Year & Engine	Spark Plug		Ignition Timing BTDC①★				Curb Idle Speed②		Fuel Pump Pressure
	Type	Gap	Firing Order Fig. ▲	Man. Trans.	Auto Trans.	Mark Location	Man. Trans.	Auto. Trans.	
1976—Continued									
6-300 F, B-500, 600 Calif.	BRF-31-4	.044	㉒	10°	10°	Damper	600	600D	4–6
V8-302	ARF-42	.044	C	㊷	㊷	Damper	㊷	㊷	6–8
V8-330㊝	BRF-31	.030	㊳	6°	6°	Damper	600	550D	5–7㉔
V8-351W Ranchero⑩	ARF-42	.044	D	—	12°	Damper	—	650D	6–8
V8-351W E-150, 250, 350⑥⑩㊝	ARF-32	.044	D	14°	14°	Damper	650	650D	5–7
V8-351W E-150, 250, 350⑥⑩㊝	ARF-32	.044	D	12°	12°	Damper	650	650D	5–7
V8-351W E-150, 250, 350⑥⑩㊝	ARF-42	.044	D	14°	14°	Damper	650	650D	5–7
V8-351M Ranchero⑮	ARF-42	.044	D	—	8°	Damper	—	650D	6–8
V8-360 Exc. Calif.	BRF-42	.044	㊳	6°	6°	Damper	650	550D	5–7
V8-360 Calif.⑥㊝	BRF-42	.044	㊳	12°	12°	Damper	600	600D	5–7
V8-360 Calif.⑥㊝	BRF-42	.044	㊳	4°	4°	Damper	600	600D	5–7
V8-361 Exc. Calif.㊝	BRF-31	.030	㊳	4°	4°	Damper	650	650D	5–7㉔
V8-361 Calif.㊝	BRF-31	.030	㊳	6°	6°	Damper	650	650D	5–7㉔
V8-390 F-100	BRF-42	.044	㊳	—	12°	Damper	—	650D	5–7
V8-390 F-150, 250, 350 Exc. Calif.	BRF-42	.044	㊳	14°	16°	Damper	650	650D	5–7
V8-390 F-150, 250, 350 Calif.	BRF-42	.044	㊳	14°	14°	Damper	650	650D	5–7
V8-391㊝	BRF-31	.030	㊳	4°	4°	Damper	650	650D	5–7㉔
V8-400 Ranchero Exc. Calif.	ARF-42	.044	D	—	12°	Damper	—	650D	6.7–8.7
V8-400 Ranchero Calif.	ARF-42	.044	D	—	12°	Damper	—	625D	6.7–8.7
V8-460 Ranchero Exc. Calif.	ARF-52	.044	C	—	10°	Damper	—	650D	6.7–8.7
V8-460 Ranchero Calif.	ARF-52	.044	C	—	14°	Damper	—	650D	6.7–8.7
V8-460 F-150, E & F-250, 350	ARF-42	.044	C	—	12°	Damper	—	650D	㊽
V8-477, 534 Exc. Calif.㊝	BRF-31	.030	㊴	6°	6°	Damper	550	550D	—
V8-477, 534 Calif.㊝	BRF-31	.030	㊴	12°	12°	Damper	550	550D	—
1975									
6-300	BTRF-42	.044	㉒	12°	12°	Damper	700	550D	4–6
V8-302	ARF-42	.044	C	㊷	㊷	Damper	㊷	㊷	㊻
V8-330㊝	BRF-31	.030	㊳	㊷	㊷	Damper	㊷	㊷	5–7
V8-351W Ranchero⑩	ARF-42	.044	D	—	12°	Damper	—	650D	5–7
V8-351M Ranchero⑮	ARF-42	.044	D	—	12°	Damper	—	650D	5–7
V8-360 F-100	BRF-42	.044	㊳	6°	㊷	Damper	850	650D	5–7
V8-390 F-100	BRF-42	.044	㊳	—	6°	Damper	—	650D	5–7
V8-391㊝	BRF-31	.030	㊳	㊷	㊷	Damper	㊷	㊷	5–7
V8-400 Ranchero	ARF-42	.044	D	—	12°	Damper	—	650D	5–7
V8-401㊝	BRF-31	.030	㊴	㊷	㊷	Damper	㊷	㊷	—
V8-460 Ranchero	ARF-42	.044	C	—	14°	Damper	—	650D	5.7–7.7
V8-477㊝	BRF-31	.030	㊴	㊷	㊷	Damper	㊷	㊷	—
V8-534㊝	BRF-31	.030	㊴	㊷	㊷	Damper	㊷	㊷	—

Continued

FORD

TUNE UP SPECIFICATIONS—Continued

The following specifications are published from the latest information available. This data should be used only in the absence of a decal affixed in the engine compartment.

★ When using a timing light, disconnect vacuum hose or tube at distributor and plug opening in hose or tube so idle speed will not be affected.

● When checking compression, lowest cylinder must be within 75 percent of highest.

▲ Before removing wires from distributor cap, determine location of the No. 1 wire in cap, as distributor position may have been altered from that shown at the end of this chart.

Year & Engine	Spark Plug Type	Gap	Firing Order Fig. ▲	Ignition Timing BTDC①★ Man. Trans.	Auto Trans.	Mark Location	Curb Idle Speed② Man. Trans.	Auto. Trans.	Fuel Pump Pressure
1974									
6-200, 250	BRF-82	.034	㊷	㊷	㊷	Damper	㊷	㊷	4½–5½
6-240	BRF-42	.034	㊷	㊷	㊷	Damper	㊷	㊷	4–6
6-300 Light Duty Exc. Calif.	BRF-42	.034	㊷	㊷	㊷	Damper	㊷	㊷	4–6
6-300 Light Duty Calif.	BTRF-42	.044	㊷	㊷	㊷	Damper	㊷	㊷	4–6
6-300 Heavy Duty	BRF-31	.030	㊷	㊷	㊷	Damper	㊷	㊷	4–6
V8-302 Ranchero㊿	BRF-42	.034	C	6°	6°	Damper	800	625D	4–6
V8-302 Ranchero㊽	BRF-42	.054	C	6°	6°	Damper	800	625D	4–6
V8-302 Exc. Ranchero㊿	BRF-42	.034	C	㊷	㊷	Damper	㊷	㊷	㊽
V8-302 Exc. Ranchero㊽	BRF-42	.054	C	㊷	㊷	Damper	㊷	㊷	㊽
V8-330㊻	BRF-31	.030	㊽	㊷	㊷	Damper	㊷	㊷	5–6㉔
V8-351W Ranchero⑩㊿	BRF-42	.034	D	—	6°	Damper	—	600D	5–6
V8-351W Ranchero⑩㊽	BRF-42	.034	D	—	6°	Damper	—	600D	5–6
V8-351W Exc. Ranchero⑩	BRF-42	.034	D	㊷	㊷	Damper	㊷	㊷	5–6
V8-351C 2 Barrel Carb. Ranchero㊿㊾	ARF-42	.044	D	—	10°	Damper	—	600D	5–6
V8-351C 2 Barrel Carb. Ranchero㊽㊾	ARF-42	.044	D	—	10°	Damper	—	600D	5–6
V8-351CJ 4 Barrel Carb. Ranchero㊾㊼	ARF-42	.044	D	㊷	㊷	Damper	㊷	㊷	5–6
V8-351C Exc. Ranchero㊾	ARF-42	.044	D	㊷	㊷	Damper	㊷	㊷	5–6
V8-360 Exc. Calif.㊻	BRF-42	.034	㊽	㊷	㊷	Damper	㊷	㊷	5–6
V8-360㊻	BRF-42	.034	㊽	㊷	㊷	Damper	㊷	㊷	5–6
V8-360㊽	BRF-42	.054	㊽	㊷	㊷	Damper	㊷	㊷	5–6
V8-361㊻	BRF-31	.030	㊽	㊷	㊷	Damper	㊷	㊷	5–6㉔
V8-390 Exc. Calif.	BRF-42	.044	㊽	㊷	㊷	Damper	㊷	㊷	5–6
V8-390	BRF-42	.034	㊽	㊷	㊷	Damper	㊷	㊷	5–6
V8-391	BRF-31	.031	㊽	㊷	㊷	Damper	㊷	㊷	5–6㉔
V8-400 Ranchero	ARF-42	.044	D	—	6°	Damper	—	625D	5–6
V8-400 Exc. Ranchero	ARF-42	.044	D	㊷	㊷	Damper	㊷	㊷	5–6
V8-401	BRF-31	.030	㊾	㊷	㊷	Damper	㊷	㊷	—
V8-460 Ranchero	ARF-52	.054	C	—	14°	Damper	—	650D	5–6
V8-460 Exc. Ranchero㊼	ARF-52	.044	C	㊷	㊷	Damper	㊷	㊷	5–6
V8-460 Exc. Ranchero㊽	ARF-42	.044	C	㊷	㊷	Damper	㊷	㊷	5–6
V8-477	BRF-31	.030	㊾	㊷	㊷	Damper	㊷	㊷	—
V8-534	BRF-31	.030	㊾	㊷	㊷	Damper	㊷	㊷	—
1973									
6-200㊀	BRF-82	.034	㊷	6°	6°	Damper	㊷	㊷	4½–5½
6-240㊀	BRF-42	.034	㊷	6°	6°	Damper	㊷	㊷	4–6
6-250㊀	BRF-82	.034	㊷	6°	6°	Damper	750	600D	4½–6½
6-300 Light Duty㊀	BRF-31	.034	㊷	10°	10°	Damper	㊷	㊷	4–6
6-300 Heavy Duty㊀	BRF-31	.034	㊷	10°	10°	Damper	㊷	㊷	4–6
V8-302 Ranchero㊻㊎㊍	BRF-42	.034	C	8°	3°	Damper	800	625D	5–7
V8-302 Ranchero㊻㊎㊌	BRF-42	.034	C	12°	6°	Damper	800	625D	5–7
V8-302 Bronco㊻	BRF-42	.034	C	3°	—	Damper	㊷	—	4½–6½
V8-302 E-100, 200㊻㊎㊋	BRF-42	.034	C	3°	6°	Damper	㊷	㊷	4½–6½

Continued

1040

TUNE UP SPECIFICATIONS—Continued

The following specifications are published from the latest information available. This data should be used only in the absence of a decal affixed in the engine compartment.

★ When using a timing light, disconnect vacuum hose or tube at distributor and plug opening in hose or tube so idle speed will not be affected.

● When checking compression, lowest cylinder must be within 75 percent of highest.

▲ Before removing wires from distributor cap, determine location of the No. 1 wire in cap, as distributor position may have been altered from that shown at the end of this chart.

Year & Engine	Spark Plug		Ignition Timing BTDC①★				Curb Idle Speed②		Fuel Pump Pressure
	Type	Gap	Firing Order Fig. ▲	Man. Trans.	Auto Trans.	Mark Location	Man. Trans.	Auto. Trans.	
1973—Continued									
V8-302 E-100, 200(56)(75)(79)	BRF-42	.034	C	6°	8°	Damper	㊷	㊷	4 1/2–6 1/2
V8-302 F-100(56)	BRF-42	.034	C	6°	6°	Damper	㊷	㊷	4 1/2–6 1/2
V8-330(56)	BRF-31	.030	(63)	6°	6°	Damper	㊷	㊷	4 1/2–6 1/2㉔
V8-351W Ranchero⑩(56)(75)(80)	BRF-42	.034	D	—	6°	Damper	—	625D	5–7
V8-351W Ranchero⑩(56)(75)(81)	BRF-42	.034	D	—	4°	Damper	—	625D	5–7
V8-351C 2 Barrel Carb. Ranchero(56)(70)(75)(82)	ARF-42	.034	D	—	6°	Damper	—	625D	5–7
V8-351C 2 Barrel Carb. Ranchero(56)(70)(75)(83)	ARF-42	.034	D	—	8°	Damper	—	625D	5–7
V8-351C 2 Barrel Carb. Ranchero(56)(70)(75)(84)	ARF-42	.034	D	—	10°	Damper	—	625D	5–7
V8-351CJ 4 Barrel Carb. Ranchero(70)(71)	ARF-42	.034	D	16°	18°	Damper	1000	800D	5–7
V8-360 F-100(56)	BRF-42	.034	(63)	—	3°	Damper	㊷	㊷	4 1/2–6 1/2
V8-360 Exc. F-100(56)	BRF-42	.034	(63)	6°	6°	Damper	㊷	㊷	4 1/2–6 1/2
V8-361(56)	BRF-31	.030	(63)	6°	6°	Damper	㊷	㊷	4 1/2–6 1/2㉔
V8-390(56)	BRF-42	.034	(63)	6°	6°	Damper	㊷	㊷	4 1/2–6 1/2
V8-391(56)	BRF-31	.030	(63)	6°	6°	Damper	㊷	㊷	4 1/2–6 1/2
V8-400 Ranchero(56)(75)(85)	ARF-42	.034	D	—	3°	Damper	—	625D	5–7
V8-400 Ranchero(56)(75)(86)	ARF-42	.034	D	—	6°	Damper	—	625D	5–7
V8-400 Ranchero(56)(75)(87)	ARF-42	.034	D	—	12°	Damper	—	625D	5–7
V8-401(56)	BRF-31	.030	(64)	6°	6°	Damper	㊷	㊷	—
V8-429 Ranchero(56)(75)(88)	ARF-42	.034	C	—	10°	Damper	—	650D	5–7
V8-429 Ranchero(56)(75)(89)	ARF-42	.034	C	—	14°	Damper	—	650D	5–7
V8-429 Ranchero(56)(75)(90)	ARF-42	.034	C	—	11°	Damper	—	650D	5–7
V8-477(56)	BRF-31	.030	(64)	6°	6°	Damper	㊷	㊷	—
V8-534(56)	BRF-31	.030	(64)	6°	6°	Damper	㊷	㊷	—
1972									
6-170(91)	BF-82	.034	(62)	—	6°	Damper	750	—	4 1/2–5 1/2
6-200 Less A/C(91)	BRF-82	.034	(62)	6°	6°	Damper	750	550D	4 1/2–5 1/2
6-200 With A/C(91)	BRF-82	.034	(62)	6°	6°	Damper	800/750	600/550D	4 1/2–5 1/2
6-240 Less Idle Solenoid(91)	BF-42	.034	(62)	6°	6°	Damper	600	550D	4 1/2–5 1/2
6-240 W/Idle Solenoid(91)	BF-42	.034	(62)	6°	6°	Damper	850/500	600/500D	4 1/2–5 1/2
6-250 Less Idle Solenoid(91)	BRF-82	.034	(62)	6°	6°	Damper	550	550D	4–6
6-250 W/Idle Solenoid(91)	BRF-82	.034	(62)	6°	6°	Damper	800/500	600/500D	4–6
6-300(91)	BF-42	.034	(62)	6°	6°	Damper	600	550D	4 1/2–5 1/2
V8-302 Less Idle Solenoid(92)	BRF-42	.034	C	6°	6°	Damper	575	575D	5–7
V8-302 W/Idle Solenoid(92)	BRF-42	.034	C	6°	6°	Damper	800/500	600/500D	5–7
V8-330(92)	BTF-31	.030	(63)	6°	6°	Damper	600	500D	4 1/2–6 1/2㉔
V8-351 2 Barrel Carb. Exc. Calif.(92)	ARF-42	.034	D	6°	6°	Damper	750/500	575/500D	5–7
V8-351 2 Barrel Carb. Calif.(92)	ARF-42	.034	D	—	6°	Damper	—	625/500D	5–7

Continued

FORD

TUNE UP SPECIFICATIONS—Continued

The following specifications are published from the latest information available. This data should be used only in the absence of a decal affixed in the engine compartment.

★ When using a timing light, disconnect vacuum hose or tube at distributor and plug opening in hose or tube so idle speed will not be affected.

● When checking compression, lowest cylinder must be within 75 percent of highest.

▲ Before removing wires from distributor cap, determine location of the No. 1 wire in cap, as distributor position may have been altered from that shown at the end of this chart.

Year & Engine	Spark Plug Type	Gap	Firing Order Fig. ▲	Ignition Timing BTDC ①★ Man. Trans.	Auto. Trans.	Mark Location	Curb Idle Speed ② Man. Trans.	Auto. Trans.	Fuel Pump Pressure
1972—Continued									
V8-351 4 Barrel Carb. Exc. Calif. ㊉	ARF-42	.034	D	16°	16°	Damper	1000/500	700/500D	5–7
V8-351 4 Barrel Carb. Calif. ㊉	ARF-42	.034	D	—	16°	Damper	—	800/500D	5–7
V8-360 ㊈	BF-42	.034	㊈	6°	6°	Damper	650	550D	4½–6½
V8-361 ㊈	BTF-31	.030	㊈	6°	6°	Damper	600	600D	4½–6½㉔
V8-390 ㊈	BF-42	.034	㊈	6°	6°	Damper	650	550D	4½–6½
V8-391 ㊈	BTF-31	.030	㊈	6°	6°	Damper	600	600D	4½–6½㉔
V8-400 Exc. Calif. ㊈	ARF-42	.034	D	—	8°	Damper	—	625/500D	5–7
V8-400 Calif. ㊈	ARF-42	.034	D	—	6°	Damper	—	625/500D	5–7
V8-401 ㊉	BTF-31	.030	㊉	8°	8°	Damper	550	550D	—
V8-429 ㊈	BRF-42	.034	C	—	10°	Damper	—	600/500D	5–7
V8-477, 534 ㊉	BTF-31	.030	㊉	8°	8°	Damper	550	550D	—
1971									
6-170 ㊈	BRF-82	.034	㊈	6°	—	Damper	775㊈	—	4–6
6-200 ㊈	BRF-82	.034	㊈	6°	6°	Damper	750	550D	4–6
6-240 Exc. E-100, 200 & F-100 ㊈	BTF-31	.030	㊈	6°	6°	Damper	850/500	600/500D	4–6
6-240 E-100, 200 & F-100 ㊈	BF-42	.034	㊈	6°	6°	Damper	850/500	600/500D	4–6
6-250 ㊈	BRF-82	.034	㊈	6°	6°	Damper	750/500	600/500D	4–6
6-300 F-100 Exc. Calif. ㊈	BTF-42	.034	㊈	6°	6°	Damper	775/500	550/500D	4–6
6-300 F-100 Calif. ㊈	BF-42	.034	㊈	6°	6°	Damper	775/500	550/500D	4–6
6-300 F-250, 350 ㊈	BTF-31	.034	㊈	6°	6°	Damper	600	550D	4–6
6-300 Exc. F-100, 250, 350 ㊈	BTF-31	.034	㊈	6°	6°	Damper	775	550D	4–6
V8-302 Ranchero ㊈	BRF-42	.034	C	6°	6°	Damper	800/500	㊉㊂	5–7
V8-302 Exc. Ranchero ㊈	BTF-31	.030	C	6°	6°	Damper	800	600D㊂	4½–6½
V8-330 ㊉	BTF-31	.030	㊈	6°	6°	Damper	550	550D	4½–6½㉔
V8-351 2 Barrel Carb. ㊈	ARF-42	.034	C	6°	6°	Damper	750/500	625/500D	5–7
V8-351 4 Barrel Carb. ㊈	ARF-42	.034	C	6°	6°	Damper	825/500	625/500D	5–7
V8-360 F-100 ㊈	BF-32	.034	㊈	6°	6°	Damper	650	500D	4½–6½
V8-360 F-250, 350 ㊉	BF-32	.034	㊈	6°	6°	Damper	650	500D	4½–6½
V8-361 ㊉	BTF-31	.030	㊈	6°	6°	Damper	550	550D	4½–6½㉔
V8-390 F-100 ㊈	BF-32	.034	㊈	6°	6°	Damper	650	500D	4½–6½
V8-390 F-250, 350 ㊉	BF-32	.034	㊈	6°	6°	Damper	650	500D	4½–6½
V8-391 ㊉	BTF-31	.030	㊈	6°	6°	Damper	550	550D	4½–6½㉔
V8-401, 477, 534 ㊉	BTF-31	.030	㊉	10°	10°	Damper	550	500D	—
V8-429 ㊈	BRF-42	.034	C	4°	4°	Damper	700	600D	5–7
1970									
6-170 ㊈	BF-82	.034	㊈	6°	—	Damper	775㊂	—	4–6
6-200 ㊈	BF-82	.034	㊈	6°	6°	Damper	750㊂	550D㊂	4–6
6-240 E-100, 200, 300 & F-100 ㊈	BTF-42	.034	㊈	6°	6°	Damper	850/500㊂	575/500D㊂	4–6
6-240 E-300 Van & F-250, 350 ㊈	BTF-42	.034	㊈	6°	6°	Damper	600㊂	550D㊂	4–6

Continued

1042

TUNE UP SPECIFICATIONS—Continued

The following specifications are published from the latest information available. This data should be used only in the absence of a decal affixed in the engine compartment.

★ When using a timing light, disconnect vacuum hose or tube at distributor and plug opening in hose or tube so idle speed will not be affected.

● When checking compression, lowest cylinder must be within 75 percent of highest.

▲ Before removing wires from distributor cap, determine location of the No. 1 wire in cap, as distributor position may have been altered from that shown at the end of this chart.

Year & Engine	Spark Plug		Ignition Timing BTDC①★				Curb Idle Speed②		Fuel Pump Pressure
	Type	Gap	Firing Order Fig. ▲	Man. Trans.	Auto Trans.	Mark Location	Man. Trans.	Auto. Trans.	
1970—Continued									
6-240 P-350, 400, 500 & F, B, LN-500(96)	BTF-31	.030	(62)	6°	6°	Damper	600(102)	550D(102)	4–6
6-250(96)	BTF-42	.034	(62)	6°	6°	Damper	750/500(102)	600/500D(102)	4–6
6-300 F-100⑨	BTF-42	.034	(62)	6°	6°	Damper	775/500(102)	550/500D(102)	4–6
6-300 F-250, 350(96)	BTF-42	.034	(62)	6°	6°	Damper	600(102)	550D(102)	4–6
6-300 P-350, 400, 500 & F, B, LN-500(96)	BTF-42	.034	(62)	6°	6°	Damper	600(102)	550D(102)	4–6
6-300 C-500, 550, 600(96)	BTF-31	.030	(62)	6°	6°	Damper	600(102)	550D(102)	4–6
V8-302 Ranchero(98)	BF-42	.035	C	6°	6°	Damper	800/500(102)	(102)(103)	4–6
V8-302 Bronco(100)	BF-42	.034	C	6°	—	Damper	675(102)	—	4½–6½
V8-302 E-100, 200 & F-100(100)	BTF-31	.030	C	6°	6°	Damper	800/500(102)	(102)(104)	4½–6½
V8-302 E-300(94)	BTF-31	.030	C	6°	6°	Damper	(102)(105)	(102)(106)	4½–6½
V8-330(94)	BTF-31	.030	(63)	6°	6°	Damper	550	550D	4½–6½㉔
V8-351 2 Barrel Carb.(98)	AF-42	.035	D	6°	6°	Damper	700/500	(102)(106)	5–7
V8-351 4 Barrel Carb.(98)	AF-32	.035	D	6°	6°	Damper	700/500	(102)(106)	5–7
V8-360 F-100(99)	BF-32	.034	(63)	6°	6°	Damper	(102)(107)	(102)(108)	4½–6½
V8-360 F-250, 350(94)	BF-32	.034	(63)	6°	6°	Damper	650(102)	550D(102)	4½–6½
V8-361(94)(101)	BTF-31	.030	(63)	6°	6°	Damper	550(102)	550D(102)	4½–6½㉔
V8-390 F-100(100)	BF-32	.034	(63)	6°	6°	Damper	(102)(107)	(102)(108)	4½–6½
V8-390 F-250, 350(94)(101)	BF-32	.034	(63)	6°	6°	Damper	650(102)	550D(102)	4½–6½
V8-391(94)(101)	BTF-31	.030	(63)	6°	6°	Damper	550(102)	550D(102)	4½–6½㉔
V8-401, 477, 534(94)(101)	BTF-31	.030	(64)	8°	8°	Damper	550(102)	550D(102)	—
V8-429(98)	BF-42	.035	C	6°	6°	Damper	850/500(102)	600D(102)	5–7

①—B.T.D.C.—Before top dead center.
②—Idle speed on man. trans. vehicles is adjusted in Neutral & on auto. trans. vehicles is adjusted in Drive unless otherwise specified. Where two idle speeds are listed, the higher speed is with the A/C or idle solenoid energized.
③—Except E & F-350, 10° BTDC; E & F-350, 12° BTDC.
④—Except 4 wheel drive models.
⑤—4 wheel drive models.
⑥—Refer to engine calibration code on engine identification label, located at rear of left valve cover on V8 engines, on front of valve cover on 6 cylinder engines. The calibration code is located on the label after the engine code number and is preceded by the letter C and the revision code is located below the calibration code and is preceded by the letter R.
⑦—Calibration code 0-54D-R0, T4° BTDC; calibration codes 0-54F-R0 & 0-54M-R0, 8° BTDC.
⑧—Except models w/3.00 axle ratio, 8° BTDC; models w/3.00 axle ratio, 10° BTDC.
⑨—Models w/3 spd. or 4 spd. overdrive man. trans., 6° BTDC; models w/4 spd. man. trans., 8° BTDC.
⑩—Windsor engine.
⑪—Calibration code 0-64A-R0.
⑫—Calibration code 0-64B-R0.
⑬—Calibration code 0-64G-R0.
⑭—Calibration code 0-64H-R0.
⑮—Modified engine.
⑯—Calibration codes, man. trans., 9-71J-R10; auto-trans., 9-72J-R11.
⑰—Calibration codes, man. trans., 0-59G-R0; auto. trans., 0-60A-R0.
⑱—Calibration code, 0-60G-R0.
⑲—Calibration codes, man. trans., 0-59H-R0 & 0-59J-R0; auto. trans., 0-60H-R0 & 0-60J-R0.
⑳—Calibration codes, man. trans., 0-59C-R0; auto. trans., 0-60C-R0.
㉑—Calibration code, 0-59S-R0.
㉒—Calibration code, 0-60D-R0.
㉓—Calibration code, 0-60B-R0.
㉔—Mechanical fuel pump
㉕—BSF-42 or BRF-42.
㉖—BRF-31-4 or BSF-31-4.
㉗—ASF-52 or ARF-52.
㉘—ASF-42 or ARF-42.
㉙—E-100 California models w/2.75 rear axle ratio, set at 500/650D.
㉚—Man. trans., except Calif. models w/3.50 or 3.54 axle ratio 10° BTDC; California models w/3.50 or 3.54 axle ratio, 8° BTDC.
㉛—ASF-32 or ARF-32.
㉜—BYSF-31-4 or BYRF-31-4.
㉝—Except Calibration code 8-52L-R12, 10° BTDC; calibration code 8-52L-R12, 12° BTDC.
㉞—BSF-31-5 or BSF-42.
㉟—Models equipped w/Thermactor pump.
㊱—Models less Thermactor pump.
㊲—Early 1978 models.
㊳—Late 1978 models.
㊴—With dual mode switch disconnected from ignition module.
㊵—ASF-42 or ASF-34.
㊶—Calibration code 7-53H-R0, set at 8° BTDC; calibration code 7-53H-R10, set at 4° BTDC.
㊷—Must refer to engine decal due to running production changes.
㊸—Calibration codes 7-53G-R0, 7-53G-R10 & 7-53G-R11, set at 6° BTDC; calibration code 7-53G-R17, set at 2° BTDC.
㊹—Calibration code 7-54K-R0, set at 8° BTDC; calibration code 7-54K-R15, set at 4° BTDC.
㊺—Calibration code 7-14A-R1, set at 10° BTDC; calibration codes 7-14A-R10, 7-14B-R10 & 7-14C-R11 set at 9° BTDC.
㊻—Calibration codes 7-14N-R0 & 7-14N-R12, set at 8° BTDC; calibration codes 7-14N-R13 & 7-14N-R17, set at 6° BTDC.
㊼—Calibration codes 7-60G-R0 & 7-60G-R10, set at 10° BTDC; calibration code 7-60G-R11, set at 6° BTDC.

Continued

FORD

TUNE UP NOTES—Continued

㊽—Except Calibration code 7-60G-R0, set at 600D RPM; calibration code 7-60G-R0, set at 650D RPM.
㊾—Calibration code 7-72-R0, set at 12° BTDC; calibration code 7-72-R10, set at 14° BTDC.
㊿—Calibration code 7-72J-R0, set at 12° BTDC; calibration codes 7-72J-R1 & 7-72J-R11, set at 10° BTDC.
㉛—Calibration code 7-86C-R0.
㉜—Calibration code 5-86A-R0.
㉝—Calibration codes 7-17B-R1, 7-37A-R0 & 7-37A-R1, 8° BTDC; 7-17B-R15, 12° BTDC; 7-17B-R16, 10° BTDC; 7-17C-R1, 6° BTDC.
㉞—Except calibration codes, 7-37A-R0 & 7-37A-R1, set at 600D RPM; calibration codes 7-37A-R0 & 7-37A-R1, 650D RPM.
㉟—Breaker point gap, .024"; dwell angle, 33°–39°.
㊱—Breaker point gap, .017"; dwell angle, 24°–30.
㊲—Calibration codes except Calif., man. trans. 5-75A-R4, auto. trans. 5-76A-R6; California, man. trans. 5-75J-R6, auto. trans. 5-76J-R8.
㊳—Calibration codes, except Calif., man. trans. 5-75A-R6, auto. trans. 5-76A-R8; California, man. trans. 5-75J-R7, auto. trans. 5-76J-R9.
㊴—Calibration codes, except Calif., man. trans. 5-75A-R3, auto. trans. 5-76A-R5; California, man. trans. 5-75J-R5, auto. trans. 5-76J-R7.
㊵—Calibration codes, man. trans. 5-83J-R3, R4; auto. trans. 5-84J-R7, R8.
㊶—Calibration codes, man. trans. 5-83J-R2; auto. trans. 5-84J-R6.
㊷—Cylinder numbering front to rear, firing order 1-5-3-6-2-4.
㊸—Cylinder numbering (front to rear), right bank 1-2-3-4, left bank 5-6-7-8; firing order 1-5-4-2-6-3-7-8.
㊹—Cylinder numbering (front to rear), right bank 1-2-3-4, left bank 5-6-7-8; firing order 1-5-4-8-6-3-7-2.
㊻—E series, 6–8 psi; F series, 5–7 psi.
㊼—Ranchero, 5–7 psi; F & Bronco, except Calif., 4–6 psi.; California, 5–7 psi.
㊽—Models w/breaker point type ignition, point gap, .017 in.; dwell angle, 26–30°.
㊾—Models w/breakerless ignition.
㊿—F-100 & Bronco except Calif., 4–6 psi; E series & California F-100 & Bronco, 5–6 psi.
⑦⓪—Cleveland engine.
⑦①—Man. trans. models, breaker point gap, both sets .020 in.; dwell angle both sets operating 32–35°. Auto. trans. models, breaker point gap .017 in.; dwell angle, 24–30°.
⑦②—Models w/G.V.W.R. 6000 lbs. & under.
⑦③—Models w/G.V.W.R. 6000 lbs. & above.
⑦④—Breaker point gap, .027 in.; dwell angle, 33–39°.
⑦⑤—Refer to engine calibration code on engine identification label, located at left rear of valve cover.
⑦⑥—Calibration codes, man. tans., 3-10C-R7; auto. trans., 3-11C-R9 & 3-11C-R16.
⑦⑦—Calibration codes, man. trans., 3-10C-R8; auto. trans., 3-11C-R22.
⑦⑧—Calibration codes, man. trans., 3-53C-R3; auto. trans., 3-54C-R3.
⑦⑨—Calibration codes, man. trans., 3-53C-R5; auto. trans., 3-54C-R5.
⑧⓪—Calibration codes, 3-12-R18, R20, R24 & 3-12D-R5.
⑧①—Calibration codes, 3-12-R12 & 3-12D-R3.
⑧②—Calibration code, 3-14C-R9.
⑧③—Calibration code, 3-14C-R14.
⑧④—Calibration codes, 3-14C-R15, R18.
⑧⑤—Calibration code, 3-17-R6.
⑧⑥—Calibration code, 3-17-R15.
⑧⑦—Calibration code, 3-17-R14.
⑧⑧—Calibration code, 3-18-R12.
⑧⑨—Calibration code, 3-18-R14.
⑨⓪—Calibration code, 3-18-R23.
⑨①—Breaker point gap, .027 in.; dwell angle, 35–39°.
⑨②—Breaker point gap, .017 in.; dwell angle, 26–30°.
⑨③—Man. trans. models, breaker point gap .020; dwell angle 26–30°. Auto. trans. models, breaker point gap, .017 in.; dwell angle 26–30°.
⑨④—Breaker point gap, .017 in.; dwell angle, 26–31°.
⑨⑤—Breaker point gap, .027 in.; dwell angle, 35–40°.
⑨⑥—Breaker point gap, .025 in.; dwell angle, 37–42°.
⑨⑦—Single diaphragm dist., point gap .025 in.; dwell angle, 34–37½°. Dual diaphragm dist., point gap .027 in.; dwell angle, 33–38°.
⑨⑧—Single diaphragm dist., point gap .017 in.; dwell angle, 24–29°. Dual diaphragm dist., point gap .021 in.; dwell angle, 26–31°.
⑨⑨—Breaker point gap, .017 in.; dwell angle, 24–29°.
⑩⓪—Breaker point gap, .021 in.; dwell angle 24–29°.
⑩①—If equipped with transistorized ignition, set point gap to .022 in. & dwell angle to 22–24°.
⑩②—With headlights on high beam.
⑩③—Less throttle positioner, 575D RPM; w/throttle positioner, 600/500D RPM.
⑩④—Less A/C, 600D RPM; with A/C, 600/500D RPM.
⑩⑤—Less throttle positioner, 650D RPM; w/throttle positioner, 800/500 RPM.
⑩⑥—Less throttle positioner, 600D RPM; w/throttle positioner, 600/500D RPM.
⑩⑦—Less A/C, 650D RPM; with A/C, 650/500D RPM.
⑩⑧—Less A/C, 550D RPM; with A/C, 550/500D RPM.

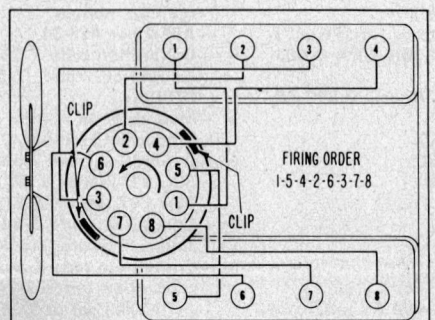

Fig. A

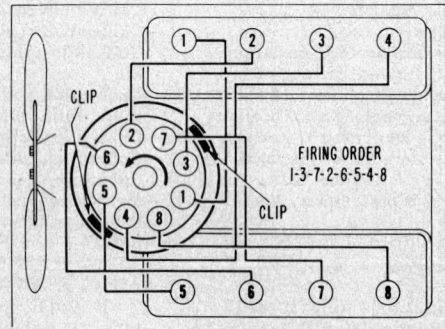

Fig. B

Continued

FORD

TUNE UP NOTES—Continued

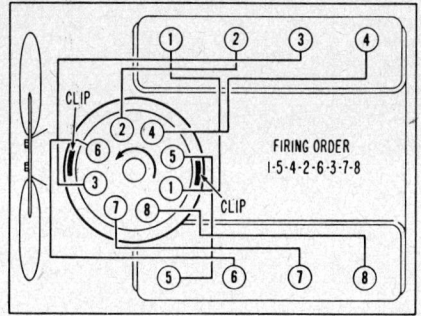

Fig. C

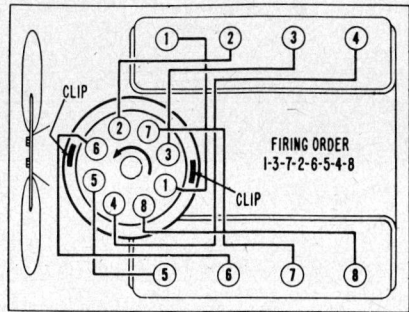

Fig. D

DISTRIBUTOR SPECIFICATIONS

Year	Engine Model	Distributor Number	Breaker Gap, In.	Dwell Angle, Deg.	Breaker Arm Spring Tension Oz.	Centrifugal Advance Deg. @ Dist. R.P.M.		Vacuum Advance Deg. @ In. of Mercury	
						Advance Starts	Maximum Advance	Advance Starts	Maximum Advance
1970	6-170	C8DF-12127A	.027	35-40	17-21	½ @ 350	14 @ 2250	½ @ 5	8 @ 25
	6-170	C9UF-12127F	.027	35-40	17-21	½ @ 350	14 @ 2500	¾ @ 5	6 @ 25
	6-200	D0DF-C	.027	35-40	17-21	½ @ 350	16 @ 2800	1 @ 5	7 @ 25
	6-240①	C8AF-12127	.027	33-38	17-21	½ @ 350	14 @ 2600	¾ @ 5	8 @ 25
	6-240②	C9UF-12127A	.025	34-39	17-21	½ @ 350	14 @ 2600	¼ @ 5	8 @ 25
	6-250	D0OF-A	.027	35-40	17-21	½ @ 350	16 @ 2175	1 @ 5	9 @ 25
	6-300②	C8TF-12127U	.027	35-40	17-21	½ @ 350	11 @ 2275	1½ @ 5	12½ @ 25
	6-300①	C8TF-12127D	.025	37-42	17-21	½ @ 350	11 @ 2400	1 @ 5	12½ @ 25
	8-302 Exc. Bronco②	D0TF-12127G	.017	26-31	17-21	½ @ 350	14 @ 3000	¾ @ 5	8 @ 25
	8-302 Exc. Bronco①	D0TF-12127H	.021	24-29	17-21	½ @ 350	14 @ 3025	¾ @ 5	8 @ 25
	8-302 Bronco①	C8TF-12127F	.021	24-29	17-21	½ @ 250	11 @ 2000	1 @ 5	11½ @ 25
	8-302	D0AF-T	.021	24-29	17-21	¼ @ 350	10¾ @ 2000	⅝ @ 5	11½ @ 25
	8-302	D0AF-Y	.021	24-29	17-21	¼ @ 350	12½ @ 2000	⅜ @ 5	11 @ 25
	8-330②	C7TF-12127D	.017	26-31	17-21	½ @ 350	11 @ 2300	1½ @ 5	9 @ 25
	8-330③	C8TF-12127A	.017	26-31	17-21	½ @ 350	13¼ @ 2000	1¼ @ 5	9 @ 25
	8-351	D0OF-T	.021	24-29	17-21	¼ @ 350	12½ @ 2000	1 @ 5	12½ @ 25
	8-351	D0OF-U	.021	24-29	17-21	¼ @ 350	12¾ @ 2000	½ @ 5	12½ @ 25
	8-351	D0OF-V	.021	24-29	17-21	¼ @ 350	12¾ @ 2000	½ @ 5	10½ @ 25
	8-351	D0OF-Z	.021	24-29	17-21	¼ @ 350	10¼ @ 2000	⅜ @ 5	10½ @ 25
	8-360, 390②	D0TF-12127K	.017	26-31	17-21	½ @ 350	19 @ 2550	1¼ @ 5	9 @ 25
	8-360, 390①	D0TF-12127J	.017	26-31	17-21	½ @ 350	19 @ 2550	1¼ @ 5	9 @ 25
	8-361	C8TF-12127A	.017	26-31	17-21	½ @ 350	13¼ @ 2000	1¼ @ 5	9 @ 25
	8-391	C8TF-12127B	.017	26-31	17-21	½ @ 350	13¼ @ 2000	1¼ @ 5	9 @ 25
	8-401, 477, 534	C3TF-12127L	.017③	26-31④	17-21	½ @ 350	14¼ @ 2000	1 @ 5	8½ @ 25
	8-429	C9AF-Y	.021	24-29	17-21	¼ @ 350	12 @ 2000	½ @ 5	8½ @ 25
	8-429	C9ZF-D	.021	24-29	17-21	¼ @ 350	11 @ 2000	⅜ @ 5	10 @ 25
	8-429	D0AF-M	.021	24-29	17-21	¼ @ 350	13¼ @ 2000	⅜ @ 5	12½ @ 25
	8-429	D0AF-Z	.021	24-29	17-21	¼ @ 350	11½ @ 2000	⅜ @ 5	11 @ 25
	8-429	D0OF-AB	.021	24-29	17-21	¼ @ 350	12½ @ 2000	½ @ 5	8½ @ 25
1971	6-170	C9UF-12127F	.027	33-38	17-21	½ @ 350	14 @ 2500	¾ @ 5	6 @ 25
	6-200	D0DF-C	.027	35-40	17-21	½ @ 350	16 @ 2800	1 @ 5	7 @ 25
	6-200	D1DF-BB	.027	35-40	17-21	½ @ 350	14 @ 2500	1 @ 5	7½ @ 25
	6-200	D1DF-CC	.027	35-40	17-21	½ @ 350	—	1 @ 5	—
	6-240 Auto. Tr.⑤⑥⑦	C8UF-12127D	.027	33-38	17-21	½ @ 350	8¾ @ 2000	½ @ 5	7¾ @ 25
	6-240 Std. Tr.⑧	D1TF-12127CA	.027	34-39	17-21	½ @ 350	14 @ 2800	1 @ 5	8 @ 25

Continued

1045

FORD

DISTRIBUTOR SPECIFICATIONS—Continued

Year	Engine Model	Distributor Number	Breaker Gap, In.	Dwell Angle, Deg.	Breaker Arm Spring Tension Oz.	Centrifugal Advance Deg. @ Dist. R.P.M.		Vacuum Advance Deg. @ In. of Mercury	
						Advance Starts	Maximum Advance	Advance Starts	Maximum Advance
	6-240⑧	C9UF-12127A	.025	34–39	17–21	½ @ 350	14 @ 2600	¾ @ 5	8 @ 25
	6-250 Std. Tr.⑧	D1OF-AB	.027	33–38	17–21	½ @ 350	14 @ 2500	1 @ 5	7½ @ 25
	6-250 Auto. Tr.⑧	D1OF-BB	.027	33–38	17–21	½ @ 350	14 @ 2500	1 @ 5	7½ @ 25
	6-250⑪	D1OF-CA	.027	33–38	17–21	½ @ 350	14 @ 2500	1 @ 5	10 @ 25
	6-300 Std. Tr.⑦	C8TF-12127D	.027	33–38	17–21	½ @ 350	11 @ 2400	1 @ 5	12½ @ 25
	6-300 Std. Tr.①⑧	C8AF-12127A	.027	33–38	17–21	½ @ 350	14 @ 2600	¾ @ 5	8 @ 25
	6-300②	C8TF-12127U	.027	33–38	17–21	½ @ 350	11 @ 2275	1½ @ 5	12½ @ 25
	8-302 Std. Tr.⑨	D0TF-12127M	.021	24–29	17–21	½ @ 350	14 @ 2600	¾ @ 5	10½ @ 25
	8-302 Std. Tr.	D1UF-12127AA	.021	24–29	17–21	½ @ 350	14 @ 2500	1 @ 5	10½ @ 25
	8-302	D0AF-Y	.021	24–29	17–21	¼ @ 350	12½ @ 2000	⅜ @ 5	11 @ 25
	8-302	D0OF-AC	.021	24–29	17–21	¼ @ 350	10¾ @ 2000	½ @ 5	5 @ 25
	8-330⑩	C7TF-12127D	.017	26–31	17–21	½ @ 350	11 @ 2350	1½ @ 5	9 @ 25
	8-330, 361⑪	C8TF-12127A	.017	26–31	17–21	½ @ 350	13¼ @ 2000	1¼ @ 5	9 @ 25
	8-351	D0OF-G	.021	24–29	17–21	¼ @ 350	10¼ @ 2000	½ @ 5	10½ @ 25
	8-351	D0OF-T	.021	24–29	17–21	¼ @ 350	12½ @ 2000	1 @ 5	12½ @ 25
	8-351	D0OF-U	.021	24–29	17–21	¼ @ 350	12¾ @ 2000	½ @ 5	12½ @ 25
	8-351	D0OF-V	.021	24–29	17–21	¼ @ 350	12¾ @ 2000	½ @ 5	10½ @ 25
	8-351	D1OF-GA	.021	24–29	17–21	¼ @ 350	12½ @ 2000	½ @ 5	11 @ 25
	8-351	D1OF-LA	.021	24–29	17–21	¼ @ 350	10¾ @ 2000	½ @ 5	10½ @ 25
	8-360 Std. Tr.⑦	D0TF-12127J	.021	24–29	17–21	½ @ 350	19 @ 2550	1¼ @ 5	9 @ 25
	8-360, 390	D1TF-12127EA	.017	26–31	17–21	½ @ 350	19 @ 2600	1¼ @ 5	9 @ 25
	8-360, 390⑧	D1TF-12127DA	.021	24–29	17–21	½ @ 350	19 @ 2600	1 @ 5	9 @ 25
	8-390 Std. Tr.⑦	D0TF-12127K	.021	24–29	17–21	½ @ 350	19 @ 2550	1¼ @ 5	9 @ 25
	8-391	C8TF-12127B	.017	26–31	17–21	½ @ 350	13¼ @ 2000	1¼ @ 5	9 @ 25
	8-401, 477, 534	C3TF-12127L	.017③	26–31④	17–21	½ @ 350	14¼ @ 2000	1 @ 5	8½ @ 25
	8-401, 477, 534	D1HF-12127AA	.017③	26–31④	17–21	½ @ 350	11 @ 900	1 @ 5	8½ @ 25
	8-429	D0OF-AA	.020	27½–29½	17–21	¼ @ 350	15 @ 2000	⅝ @ 5	8½ @ 25
	8-429	D1AF-NA	.020	27½–29½	17–21	¼ @ 350	14 @ 2000	½ @ 5	8½ @ 25
1972	6-170	D2BF-12127AA	.027	35–39	17–21	½ @ 500	12 @ 2000	½ @ 5	7½ @ 20
	6-200	D2DF-CA	.027	35–39	17–21	½ @ 500	12½ @ 2000	1 @ 5	7 @ 20
	6-200	D2DF-DA	.027	35–39	17–21	1 @ 500	13½ @ 2000	1 @ 5	4 @ 20
	6-200	D2DF-EA	.027	35–39	17–21	½ @ 500	12½ @ 2000	1 @ 5	7 @ 20
	6-200	D2DF-FA	.027	35–39	17–21	½ @ 500	13½ @ 2000	1 @ 5	4 @ 20
	6-240	D2UF-12127AA	.027	35–39	17–21	¼ @ 500	10 @ 2000	½ @ 5	7½ @ 20
	6-240	D2UF-12127CA	.027	35–39	17–21	¼ @ 500	10 @ 2000	½ @ 5	9½ @ 20
	6-240	D2UF-12127DA	.027	35–39	17–21	¼ @ 500	10 @ 2000	½ @ 5	7½ @ 20
	6-250	D2OF-DA	.027	35–39	17–21	1 @ 500	13½ @ 2000	1 @ 5	9½ @ 20
	6-250	D2OF-EA	.027	35–39	17–21	½ @ 500	10½ @ 2000	1 @ 5	9½ @ 20
	6-250	D2OF-PA	.027	35–39	17–21	1 @ 500	10 @ 2000	1 @ 5	9½ @ 20
	6-300	D2TF-12127EA	.027	35–39	17–21	¼ @ 500	10 @ 2000	1¼ @ 5	13½ @ 20
	8-302	D2UF-12127BA	.017	26–30	17–21	¼ @ 500	11½ @ 2000	½ @ 5	5½ @ 20
	8-302	D2UF-12127EA	.017	26–30	17–21	½ @ 500	12 @ 2000	⅝ @ 5	8½ @ 20
	8-302	D2UF-12127FA	.017	26–30	17–21	½ @ 500	10½ @ 2000	¼ @ 5	7½ @ 20
	8-302	D2UF-12127GA	.017	26–30	17–21	½ @ 500	12 @ 2000	½ @ 5	11½ @ 20
	8-302	D2UF-12127LA	.017	26–30	17–21	⅝ @ 500	10½ @ 2000	⅝ @ 5	5½ @ 20
	8-302	D2UF-12127MA	.017	26–30	17–21	¼ @ 500	12 @ 2000	½ @ 5	11½ @ 20
	8-302	D2AF-12127CA	.017	26–30	17–21	¼ @ 500	11 @ 2000	1¼ @ 5	12½ @ 20
	8-302	D2OF-12127RA	.017	26–30	17–21	¼ @ 500	11 @ 2000	1¼ @ 5	5½ @ 20
	8-302	D2ZF-12127LA	.017	26–30	17–21	¼ @ 500	13½ @ 2000	1¼ @ 5	12½ @ 20
	8-330	D2TF-12127FB	.017	26–30	17–21	1 @ 500	10½ @ 2000	⅝ @ 5	9½ @ 20
	8-330	C8TF-12102A4	.017	26–30	17–21	2¼ @ 500	13 @ 2000	¾ @ 5	9 @ 20
	8-351	D2AF-12127KA	.017	26–30	17–21	1½ @ 500	12½ @ 2000	½ @ 5	13 @ 20
	8-351	D2ZF-12127AA	.017	26–30	17–21	¾ @ 500	12½ @ 2000	¾ @ 5	12½ @ 20
	8-351	D2ZF-12127CA	.017	26–30	17–21	½ @ 500	12½ @ 2000	½ @ 5	10 @ 20

Continued

Ford

DISTRIBUTOR SPECIFICATIONS—Continued

Year	Engine Model	Distributor Number	Breaker Gap, In.	Dwell Angle, Deg.	Breaker Arm Spring Tension Oz.	Centrifugal Advance Deg. @ Dist. R.P.M.		Vacuum Advance Deg. @ In. of Mercury	
						Advance Starts	Maximum Advance	Advance Starts	Maximum Advance
	8-351	D2ZF-12127GC	.017	26–30	17–21	1/4 @ 500	11 @ 2000	1 1/4 @ 5	9 1/2 @ 20
	8-351	D22F-12127HA	.017	26–30	17–21	1/2 @ 500	14 1/2 @ 2000	1 1/4 @ 5	9 1/2 @ 20
	8-360, 390	D2TF-12127AA	.017	26–30	17–21	3 @ 500	16 @ 2000	3/4 @ 5	9 1/4 @ 20
	8-360, 390	D2TF-12127JA	.017	26–30	17–21	1/2 @ 500	16 @ 2000	1/2 @ 5	6 1/2 @ 20
	8-360, 390	D2TF-12127KA	.017	26–30	17–21	3 @ 500	16 @ 2000	3/4 @ 5	9 1/4 @ 20
	8-360, 390	D2TF-12127LB	.017	26–30	17–21	1/2 @ 500	16 @ 2000	1/2 @ 5	9 1/4 @ 20
	8-360, 390	D2TF-12127MA	.017	26–30	17–21	1/2 @ 500	16 @ 2000	1 @ 5	9 1/4 @ 20
	8-361	C8TF-12102A	.017	26–30	17–21	2 1/4 @ 500	13 @ 2000	3/4 @ 5	9 @ 20
	8-391	D1HF-12102BA	.017	26–30	17–21	2 1/4 @ 500	13 @ 2000	3/4 @ 5	9 @ 20
	8-400	D2AF-12127RA	.017	26–30	17–21	1 1/2 @ 500	12 @ 2000	1 1/4 @ 5	13 1/2 @ 20
	8-400	DZAF-12127SA	.017	26–30	17–21	1 1/2 @ 500	12 @ 2000	1 1/4 @ 5	13 1/2 @ 20
	8-401, 477, 534	D1HF-12127AA	.017	26–30	17–21	2 5/8 @ 500	11 @ 2000	1/2 @ 5	8 1/2 @ 20
	8-429	D2MF-12127EA	.017	26–30	17–21	1/2 @ 500	9 1/2 @ 2000	1/2 @ 5	11 1/2 @ 20
	8-429	D2MF-12127FA	.017	26–30	17–21	1/2 @ 500	9 1/2 @ 2000	1/2 @ 5	11 1/2 @ 20
1973	6-200	D3BF-12127AA	.027	33–49	17–21	1 1/2 @ 500	11 1/2 @ 2000	3 1/2 @ 5	5 1/2 @ 20
	6-200	D3BF-12127CA	.027	33–49	17–21	1 1/2 @ 500	11 1/2 @ 2000	3 1/2 @ 5	5 1/2 @ 20
	6-240	D3UF-12127BA	.027	33–49	17–21	1/2 @ 500	10 @ 2000	1 @ 5	7 1/4 @ 20
	6-240	D3UF-12127AA	.027	33–49	17–21	1 @ 500	10 1/2 @ 2000	1 @ 5	11 1/2 @ 20
	6-240	D3UF-12127LA	.027	33–39	17–21	1/4 @ 500	10 1/2 @ 2000	1/2 @ 5	7 1/4 @ 20
	6-240	D3UF-12127MA	.027	33–39	17–21	1/4 @ 500	10 1/2 @ 2000	3/4 @ 5	7 1/4 @ 20
	6-250	D30F-12127AA	—	—	—	—	—	—	—
	6-250	D30F-12127BA	.025	33–39	17–21	3/4 @ 500	10 @ 2000	3/4 @ 5	9 1/4 @ 20
	6-250	D30F-12127LA	.025	33–39	17–21	3/4 @ 500	12 @ 2000	3/4 @ 5	9 1/4 @ 20
	6-250	D30F-12127RA	.025	33–39	17–21	3/4 @ 500	10 @ 2000	2 @ 5	9 1/2 @ 20
	6-300	D3TF-12127GA	.027	33–39	17–21	1/2 @ 500	7 1/2 @ 2000	5/8 @ 5	9 1/4 @ 20
	8-302	D3BF-12127BA	.021	24–30	17–21	1/2 @ 500	12 @ 2000	1/2 @ 5	11 1/4 @ 20
	8-302	D3UF-12127GA	.021	24–30	17–21	1 1/4 @ 500	12 1/4 @ 2000	1/2 @ 5	5 1/4 @ 20
	8-302	D30F-12127DA	.017	24–30	17–21	1/2 @ 500	11 @ 2000	5/8 @ 5	5 1/4 @ 20
	8-302	D30F-12127EA	.017	24–30	17–21	1/2 @ 500	11 @ 2000	1 @ 5	5 1/4 @ 15
	8-302	D30F-12127HA	.017	24–30	17–21	1/2 @ 500	12 @ 2000	1/4 @ 5	5 1/4 @ 20
	8-302	D30F-12127JA	.017	24–30	17–21	5/8 @ 500	12 @ 2000	5/8 @ 5	5 1/4 @ 20
	8-302	D30F-12127PA	.017	24–30	17–21	1/2 @ 500	12 1/2 @ 2000	3/4 @ 5	5 1/4 @ 20
	8-302	D3TF-12127RA	.017	24–30	17–21	1/2 @ 500	12 @ 2000	1/2 @ 5	7 1/2 @ 20
	8-302	D3TF-12127TA	—	—	—	—	—	—	—
	8-302	D3UF-12127DA	.017	24–30	17–21	1/4 @ 500	11 @ 2000	1/2 @ 5	9 1/4 @ 20
	8-302	D3UF-12127EA	.017	24–30	17–21	5/8 @ 500	14 1/2 @ 2000	3/4 @ 5	9 1/4 @ 20
	8-302	D3UF-12127HA	.017	24–30	17–21	1/2 @ 500	10 1/2 @ 2000	1/2 @ 5	7 1/4 @ 20
	8-302	D3UF-12127JA	.017	24–30	17–21	3/4 @ 500	10 1/2 @ 2000	1/2 @ 5	7 1/4 @ 20
	8-302	D3UF-12127KA	.017	24–30	17–21	3/4 @ 500	11 @ 2000	1 1/2 @ 5	7 1/4 @ 20
	8-302	D3ZF-12127CA	.017	24–30	17–21	5/8 @ 500	11 1/2 @ 2000	5/8 @ 5	13 1/4 @ 20
	8-330	D3HF-12102BA	.017	24–30	17–21	1/2 @ 500	14 @ 2000	2 @ 5	5 1/2 @ 20
	8-330	D3TF-12102AA	.017	24–30	17–21	1/4 @ 500	14 @ 2000	2 @ 5	5 1/2 @ 20
	8-330	D3TF-12127EA	.017	24–30	17–21	3/4 @ 500	12 1/2 @ 2000	5/8 @ 5	9 1/4 @ 20
	8-351	D30F-12127FA	.020	32–35	17–21	1/2 @ 500	13 @ 2000	1 1/2 @ 5	5 1/2 @ 20
	8-351	D30F-12127GA	.017	24–30	17–21	1/2 @ 500	13 1/2 @ 2000	1 3/4 @ 5	5 1/4 @ 20
	8-351	D3ZF-12127CA	.017	24–30	17–21	5/8 @ 500	11 1/2 @ 2000	5/8 @ 5	13 1/4 @ 20
	8-351	D3ZF-12127GA	.017	24–30	17–21	1/2 @ 500	11 @ 2000	1/2 @ 5	12 1/2 @ 20
	8-359	D3HF-12102DA	.017	24–30	17–21	1/4 @ 500	14 @ 2000	2 @ 5	5 1/2 @ 20
	8-360	D3TF-12127FA	.017	24–30	17–21	5/8 @ 500	13 1/2 @ 2000	1 @ 5	9 1/4 @ 20
	8-360	D3TF-12127HA	.017	24–30	17–21	3/4 @ 500	14 @ 2000	2 @ 5	5 1/4 @ 20
	8-360	D3TF-12127PA	.017	24–30	17–21	3/4 @ 500	13 1/2 @ 2000	1 1/4 @ 5	9 1/4 @ 20
	8-360	D3TF-12127UA	.017	24–30	17–21	3/4 @ 500	13 1/2 @ 2000	3/4 @ 5	9 1/4 @ 20
	8-360	D3TF-12127XA	.017	24–30	17–21	3/4 @ 500	12 1/2 @ 2000	1 1/4 @ 5	13 1/4 @ 20

Continued

FORD

DISTRIBUTOR SPECIFICATIONS—Continued

Year	Engine Model	Distributor Number	Breaker Gap, In.	Dwell Angle, Deg.	Breaker Arm Spring Tension Oz.	Centrifugal Advance Deg. @ Dist. R.P.M.		Vacuum Advance Deg. @ In. of Mercury	
						Advance Starts	Maximum Advance	Advance Starts	Maximum Advance
	8-360	D3TF-12127YA	.017	24–30	17–21	3/4 @ 500	12 1/2 @ 2000	3/4 @ 5	5 1/2 @ 20
	8-361	D3TF-12102CA	.017	24–30	17–21	1/4 @ 500	11 @ 2000	3/4 @ 5	7 1/4 @ 20
	8-390	D3TF-12127BA	.017	24–30	17–21	3/4 @ 500	15 1/2 @ 2000	1 1/8 @ 5	13 1/4 @ 20
	8-390	D3TF-12127HA	.017	24–30	17–21	5/8 @ 500	14 @ 2000	2 @ 5	5 1/4 @ 20
	8-390	D3TF-12127VA	—	—	—	—	—	—	—
	8-390	D3TF-12127XA	.017	24–30	17–21	3/4 @ 500	15 1/2 @ 2000	1 1/4 @ 5	13 1/4 @ 20
	8-391	D3TF-12102BA	.017	24–30	17–21	1/4 @ 500	14 @ 2000	3/4 @ 5	7 1/2 @ 20
	8-400	D3AF-12127BA	.017	24–30	17–21	3/4 @ 500	14 1/2 @ 200	3/4 @ 5	13 1/4 @ 20
	8-400	D3MF-12127GA	.017	24–30	17–21	1/2 @ 500	10 1/2 @ 2000	1/2 @ 5	11 1/4 @ 20
	401, 477, 534	D3HF-12102AA	.017	24–30	17–21	1 1/4 @ 500	14 @ 2000	1/4 @ 5	9 1/2 @ 20
	8-429	D3MF-12127BA	.017	24–30	17–21	1/2 @ 500	11 @ 2000	5/8 @ 5	7 1/4 @ 20
	8-429	D3MF-12127DA	.017	24–30	17–21	1/2 @ 500	10 1/2 @ 2000	1/2 @ 5	11 1/4 @ 20
	8-429	D3SF-12127BA	.017	24–30	17–21	1/2 @ 500	13 1/2 @ 2000	1/2 @ 5	11 1/4 @ 20
	8-429	D3VF-12127CA	.017	24–30	17–21	1/2 @ 500	10 @ 2000	5/8 @ 5	11 1/4 @ 20
1974	6-200	D3BF-12127-CA	—	—	—	3/4 @ 500	12 1/2 @ 2000	5/8 @ 5	7 1/4 @ 20
	6-240	D3UF-12127-BA	—	—	—	1/4 @ 500	10 @ 2000	1/2 @ 5	7 1/4 @ 20
	6-240	D3UF-12127-PA	—	—	—	1/2 @ 500	10 1/2 @ 2000	4 @ 5	5 1/2 @ 20
	6-240	D3UF-12127-RA	—	—	—	1/4 @ 500	10 @ 2000	4 @ 5	5 1/2 @ 20
	6-250	D3DF-12127-FA	—	—	—	3/4 @ 500	10 1/2 @ 2000	1 1/2 @ 5	9 1/4 @ 20
	6-250	D3OF-12127-RA	—	—	—	3/4 @ 500	10 @ 2000	2 @ 5	9 1/4 @ 20
	6-250	D4DE-12127-LA	—	—	—	3/4 @ 500	9 1/2 @ 2000	3/4 @ 5	9 1/4 @ 20
	6-250	D4DE-12127-NA	—	—	—	3/4 @ 500	10 @ 2000	3/4 @ 5	9 1/4 @ 20
	6-250	D4DE-12127-RA	—	—	—	3/4 @ 500	10 1/2 @ 2000	2 @ 5	9 1/4 @ 20
	6-300	D3TF-12127-GA	—	—	—	1/2 @ 500	7 1/4 @ 2000	5/8 @ 5	9 1/4 @ 20
	6-300	D4TE-12127-EA	—	—	—	1/2 @ 500	7 1/4 @ 2000	5/8 @ 5	9 1/4 @ 20
	8-302	D3BF-12127-BA	—	—	—	1/2 @ 500	12 @ 2000	1/2 @ 5	11 1/2 @ 20
	8-302	D3BF-12127-DA	—	—	—	5/8 @ 500	13 1/2 @ 2000	1/2 @ 5	11 1/2 @ 20
	8-302	D3OF-12127-DA	—	—	—	1/2 @ 500	11 @ 2000	5/8 @ 5	5 1/4 @ 20
	8-302	D3OF-12127-HB	—	—	—	3/4 @ 500	13 1/2 @ 2000	3/4 @ 5	11 1/2 @ 20
	8-302	D3UF-12127-EA	—	—	—	5/8 @ 500	14 1/2 @ 2000	3/4 @ 5	9 1/4 @ 20
	8-302	D3UF-12127-FA	—	—	—	3/4 @ 500	14 @ 2000	3/4 @ 5	13 1/4 @ 20
	8-302	D3UF-12127-GA	—	—	—	1/2 @ 500	11 1/2 @ 2000	1/4 @ 5	5 1/4 @ 20
	8-302	D3UF-12127-JA	—	—	—	3/4 @ 500	10 1/2 @ 2000	1/2 @ 5	7 1/4 @ 20
	8-302	D3UF-12127-KA	—	—	—	3/4 @ 500	11 @ 2000	1/2 @ 5	7 1/4 @ 20
	8-302	D4BE-12127-FA	—	—	—	1/4 @ 500	11 1/2 @ 2000	1/4 @ 5	5 1/4 @ 20
	8-302	D4BF-12127-EA	—	—	—	1/4 @ 500	13 1/2 @ 2000	1/4 @ 5	11 1/2 @ 20
	8-302	D4TE-12127-PA	—	—	—	1/4 @ 500	11 1/2 @ 2000	1/2 @ 5	11 1/2 @ 20
	8-302	D4TE-12127-VA	—	—	—	1/4 @ 500	10 @ 2000	1/4 @ 5	11 1/2 @ 20
	8-302	D4UE-12127-FA	—	—	—	1/4 @ 500	11 @ 2000	1/2 @ 5	11 1/2 @ 20
	8-302	D4UE-12127-HA	—	—	—	1/4 @ 500	12 1/2 @ 2000	3/4 @ 5	9 1/4 @ 20
	8-330	D3HF-12102-BA	—	—	—	1/2 @ 500	14 @ 2000	2 @ 5	5 1/2 @ 20
	8-330	D3TF-12127-EA	—	—	—	3/4 @ 500	12 1/2 @ 2000	5/8 @ 5	9 1/4 @ 20
	8-330	DETF-12102-AA	—	—	—	1/4 @ 500	14 @ 2000	2 @ 5	5 1/2 @ 20
	8-351C	D3ZF-12127-GA	—	—	—	1/2 @ 500	11 @ 2000	1/2 @ 5	12 1/2 @ 20
	8-351C	D4AE-12127-AA	—	—	—	1/4 @ 500	10 1/2 @ 2000	1/2 @ 5	12 1/2 @ 20
	8-351CJ	D3OF-12127-FA	—	—	—	1/2 @ 500	13 @ 2000	1 1/2 @ 5	5 1/4 @ 20
	8-351CJ	D3OF-12127-GA	—	—	—	1/2 @ 500	13 1/2 @ 2000	1 3/4 @ 5	5 1/4 @ 20
	8-360	D3TF-12127-HA	—	—	—	5/8 @ 500	14 @ 2000	2 @ 5	5 1/4 @ 20
	8-360	D3TF-12127-PA	—	—	—	3/4 @ 500	17 1/2 @ 2000	1 1/4 @ 5	9 1/4 @ 20
	8-360	D3TF-12127-UA	—	—	—	3/4 @ 500	17 1/2 @ 2000	3/4 @ 5	9 1/4 @ 20
	8-360	D4TE-12127-AA	—	—	—	—	—	—	—
	8-360	D4TE-12127-TA	—	—	—	1/2 @ 500	16 1/2 @ 2000	5 @ 5	7 1/4 @ 20
	8-360	D4TE-12127-YA	—	—	—	1/4 @ 500	13 1/2 @ 2000	3 7/8 @ 5	5 1/4 @ 20
	8-361	D3TF-12102-CA	—	—	—	1 1/4 @ 500	14 @ 2000	1 3/4 @ 5	5 1/2 @ 20

Continued

FORD

DISTRIBUTOR SPECIFICATIONS—Continued

Year	Engine Model	Distributor Number	Breaker Gap, In.	Dwell Angle, Deg.	Breaker Arm Spring Tension Oz.	Centrifugal Advance Deg. @ Dist. R.P.M.		Vacuum Advance Deg. @ In. of Mercury	
						Advance Starts	Maximum Advance	Advance Starts	Maximum Advance
	8-361	D3TF-12102-FA	—	—	—	1¼ @ 500	14 @ 2000	1¾ @ 5	5½ @ 20
	8-361	D4TE-12102-AA	—	—	—	1¼ @ 500	14 @ 2000	1¾ @ 5	5½ @ 20
	8-390	D3TF-12127-HA	—	—	—	⅝ @ 500	14 @ 2000	2 @ 5	5½ @ 20
	8-390	D3TF-12127-VA	—	—	—	¾ @ 500	11 @ 2000	½ @ 5	5½ @ 20
	8-390	D3TF-12127-XA	—	—	—	½ @ 500	15¼ @ 2000	1¼ @ 5	13¼ @ 20
	8-390	D4TE-12127-UA	—	—	—	¼ @ 500	10½ @ 2000	1 @ 5	7½ @ 20
	8-391	D3TF-12102-BA	—	—	—	¼ @ 500	14 @ 2000	¼ @ 5	7½ @ 20
	8-391	D3TF-12102-GA	—	—	—	¼ @ 500	14 @ 2000	¼ @ 5	7½ @ 20
	8-400	D4OE-12127-CA	—	—	—	¼ @ 500	10½ @ 2000	2¼ @ 5	13½ @ 20
	8-460	D4TE-12127-HA	—	—	—	¼ @ 500	11¼ @ 2000	⅝ @ 5	11¼ @ 20
	8-460	D4TE-12127-NA	—	—	—	¼ @ 500	8½ @ 2000	¾ @ 5	9½ @ 20
	8-460	D4VE-12127-CA	—	—	—	¼ @ 500	10½ @ 2000	⅝ @ 5	11¼ @ 20
	8-401, 475, 477, 534	D3HF-12127-AA	—	—	—	1¼ @ 500	14 @ 2000	¼ @ 5	9½ @ 20
1975-80	No longer available								

① —Dual vacuum diaphragm.
② —Single vacuum diaphragm.
③ —Transistor ignition, .020".
④ —Transistor ignition, 22–24°.
⑤ —With Exhaust Emission System.
⑥ —Light duty.
⑦ —Except California.
⑧ —California.
⑨ —With Improved Combustion (IMCO).
⑩ —Medium Duty.
⑪ —Heavy Duty.

VALVE SPECIFICATIONS

Engine Model	Year	Valve Lash①		Valve Angles		Valve Springs		Valve Stem Clearance		Stem Diameter/ Std.	
		Int.	Exh.	Seat	Face	Installed Height	Pressure Lbs. @ In.	Intake	Exhaust	Intake	Exhaust
6-170	1970-72	④		45	44	1 19/32	150 @ 1.222	.0008–.0025	.0010–.0027	.3100–.3107	.3098–.3105
6-200	1970-72	⑤		45	44	1 19/32	150 @ 1.222	.0008–.0025	.0010–.0027	.3100–.3107	.3098–.3105
6-200	1973-74	.079–.129		45	44	1 19/32	⑥	.0008–.0025	.0010–.0027	.3100–.3107	.3098–.3105
6-240	1970-72	⑨		45	44	1 11/16	197 @ 1.3	.0010–.0027	.0010–.0027	.3416–.3423	.3416–.3423
6-240	1973	.124		45	44	⑩	⑪	.0010–.0027	.0010–.0027	.3416–.3423	.3416–.3423
6-240	1974	.100–.150		45	44	⑩	⑪	.0010–.0027	.0010–.0027	.3416–.3423	.3416–.3423
6-250	1970-72	.095–.145⑫		45	44	1 19/32	150 @ 1.222	.0008–.0025	.0010–.0027	.3100–.3107	.3098–.3105
6-250	1973	.095–.145		45	44	1 19/32	⑬	.0008–.0025	.0010–.0027	.3100–.3107	.3098–.3105
6-250	1974	.095–.145		45	44	1 19/32	150 @ 1.18	.0008–.0025	.0010–.0027	.3100–.3107	.3098–.3105
6-300 L.D.	1970-71	.082–.152		45	44	1 37/64	193 @ 1.18	.0010–.0027	.0010–.0027	.3416–.3423	.3416–.3423
6-300 L.D.	1972-75	⑮		45	44	⑩	⑪	.0010–.0027	.0010–.0027	.3416–.3423	.3416–.3423
6-300 L.D.	1976-77	.125–.175		45	44	⑩	㉙	.0010–.0027	.0010–.0027	.3416–.3423	.3416–.3423
6-300 H.D.	1970-71	.082–.152		45	44	⑩	⑪	.0010–.0027	.0010–.0027	.3416–.3423	.3416–.3423
6-300 H.D.	1972-80	⑮		45	44	⑩	⑪	.0010–.0027	.0010–.0027	.3416–.3423	.3416–.3423
8-302	1970-72	⑰		45	44	1 41/64	180 @ 1.23	.0010–.0027	.0010–.0027	.3416–.3423	.3416–.3423
8-302	1973	.090–.140		45	44	1 11/16	200 @ 1.31	.0010–.0027	.0015–.0032	.3416–.3423	.3411–.3418
8-302	1974	.100–.150		45	44	⑩	⑪	.0010–.0027	.0010–.0027	.3416–.3423	.3416–.3423
8-302	1975	.115–.130		45	44	⑱	200 @ 1.31	.0010–.0027	.0015–.0032	.3416–.3423	.3411–.3418
8-302	1976	.115–.165		45	44	⑱	200 @ 1.31	.0010–.0027	.0015–.0032	.3416–.3423	.3411–.3418
8-302	1977-80	.096–.165		45	44	⑱	㉚	.0010–.0027	.0015–.0032	.3416–.3423	.3411–.3418
8-330 M.D.	1970-73	.050–.150		45	44	1 53/64	189 @ 1.42	.0010–.0027	.0028–.0042	.3711–.3718	.3701–.3708
8-330 M.D.	1974	.080–.130		45	44	1 53/64	189 @ 1.42	.0010–.0027	.0020–.0037	.3711–.3718	.3701–.3708
8-330 M.D.	1975-76	.105–.155		45	44	1 53/64	189 @ 1.42	.0010–.0027	.0020–.0040	.3711–.3718	.3701–.3708
8-330 M.D.	1977	.105–.155		45	44	1 53/64	220 @ 1.38	.0010–.0027	.0020–.0037	.3711–.3718	.3701–.3708
8-330 H.D.	1970-73	.050–.150⑲		45	44	1 43/64	185 @ 1.24	.0010–.0027	.0020–.0037	.3711–.3718	.4338–.4348
8-330 H.D.	1974-76	.105–.155		45	44	1 43/64	185 @ 1.24	.0010–.0027	.0020–.0040	.3711–.3718	.4338–.4348
8-330 H.D.	1977-79	.105–.155		45	44	㉒	㉓	.0010–.0027	.0020–.0040	.3711–.3718	.4338–.4348
8-351C-2V	1970-73	.100–.150		45	44	1 53/64	210 @ 1.42	.0010–.0027	.0015–.0032	.3416–.3423	.3411–.3418
8-351C-2V	1974	.100–.150		45	44	1 53/64	226 @ 1.39	.0010–.0027	.0015–.0032	.3416–.3423	.3411–.3418
8-351C-4V	1970-74	.100–.150		45	44	1 53/64	285 @ 1.32	.0010–.0027	.0015–.0032	.3416–.3423	.3411–.3418

Continued

FORD

VALVE SPECIFICATIONS—Continued

Engine Model	Year	Valve Lash① Int.	Valve Lash① Exh.	Valve Angles Seat	Valve Angles Face	Valve Springs Installed Height	Valve Springs Pressure Lbs. @ In.	Valve Stem Clearance Intake	Valve Stem Clearance Exhaust	Stem Diameter, Std. Intake	Stem Diameter, Std. Exhaust
8-351-M	1975–78	.125–.175		45	44	1 53/64	226 @ 1.39	.0010–.0027	.0015–.0032	.3416–.3423	.3411–.3418
8-351M	1979–80	.125		45	44	⑦	226 @ 1.39	.0010–.0027	.0015–.0032	.3416–.3423	.3411–.3418
8-351W	1975–76	.131–.181		45	44	1 51/64	200 @ 1.34	.0010–.0027	.0015–.0032	.3416–.3423	.3411–.3418
8-351W	1977–80	.123–.173		45	44	㉛	㉜	.0010–.0027	.0015–.0032	.3416–.3423	.3411–.3418
8-359, 361	1977	.105–.155		45	44	㉒	㉓	.0010–.0027	.0020–.0040	.3711–.3718	.4338–.4348
8-360	1970–71	.100–.200		45	44	1 53/64	220 @ 1.38	.0010–.0027	.0020–.0034	.3711–.3718	.3711–.3718
8-360	1972–76	.119–.169㉑		45	44	1 53/64	220 @ 1.38	.0010–.0027	.0015–.0032	.3711–.3718	.3706–.3713
8-360 F-100	1973–76	.119–.169㉑		45	44	㉒	㉓	.0010–.0027	.0015–.0032	.3711–.3718	.3706–.3713
8-361	1978	.105–.155		45	44	㉒	㉓	.0010–.0027	.0020–.0040	.3711–.3718	.4338–.4348
8-361, 391	1970–73	.050–.150⑲		45	44	1 43/64	185 @ 1.24	.0010–.0024	.0020–.0037	.3711–.3718	.4338–.4348
8-361, 391	1974–76	.105–.155		45	44	1 43/64	185 @ 1.24	.0010–.0027	.0020–.0040	.3711–.3718	.4338–.4348
8-370③	1979	.100–.150		45	44	㊱	⑳	.0010–.0027	.0020–.0037	.3711–.3718	.3701–.3708
8-370③	1980	.125–.175		45	44	㊱	⑧	.0010–.0027	.0020–.0037	.3711–.3718	.3701–.3708
8-370, 429⑭	1979	.100–.150		45	44	1.72	⑳	.0010–.0027	.0016–.0035	.3711–.3718	.3703–.3712
8-370, 429⑭	1980	.125–.175		45	44	1 23/32	㊲	.0010–.0027	.0015–.0035	.3711–.3718	.3703–.3712
8-389	1975–76	.105–.155		45	44	1 43/64	185 @ 1.24	.0010–.0027	.0020–.0040	.3711–.3718	.4338–.4348
8-389, 391	1977–78	.105–.155		45	44	㉝	㉞	.0010–.0027	.0020–.0040	.3711–.3718	.4338–.4348
8-390	1970–71	.100–.200		45	44	1 53/64	220 @ 1.38	.0010–.0027	.0020–.0034	.3711–.3718	.3711–.3718
8-390	1972–75	.119–.169㉑		45	44	1 53/64	220 @ 1.38	.0010–.0027	.0015–.0032	.3711–.3718	.3706–.3713
8-390 F-100	1973–75	.119–.169㉑		45	44	㉒	㉓	.0010–.0027	.0015–.0032	.3711–.3718	.3706–.3713
8-400	1972–76	.100–.150㉔		45	44	1 53/64	226 @ 1.39	.0010–.0027	.0015–.0032	.3416–.3423	.3411–.3418
8-400	1977–78	—		45	44	1 53/64	226 @ 1.39	.0010–.0027	.0015–.0032	.3416–.3423	.3411–.3418
8-400	1979–80	.175		45	44	⑦	226 @ 1.39	.0010–.0027	.0015–.0032	.3416–.3423	.3411–.3418
8-401	1970–76	.020H②	.020H②	45	44	1 45/64	⑯	.0010–.0026	.0024–.0040	.4349–.4358	.4335–.4344
8-428CJ	1970		.150	㉕	㉖	1 53/64	268 @ 1.32	.0015–.0032	.0015–.0032	.3711–.3718	.3706–.3713
8-429	1970	.125		45	44	1 13/16	253 @ 1.33	.0010–.0027	.0010–.0027	.3416–.3423	.3416–.3423
8-429	1971–72	㉗		45	44	1 13/16	229 @ 1.33	.0010–.0027	.0010–.0027	.3416–.3423	.3416–.3423
8-429	1973	.075–.125		45	44	1 13/16	169 @ 1.39	.0010–.0027	.0010–.0027	.3416–.3423	.3416–.3423
8-460	1973	.105–.155		45	44	1 13/16	169 @ 1.39㉟	.0010–.0027	.0010–.0027	.3416–.3423	.3416–.3423
8-460	1974–80	.100–.150㉘		45	44	1 13/16	253 @ 1.33㉟	.0010–.0027	.0010–.0027	.3416–.3423	.3416–.3423
8-475	1974–79	.020H②	.020H②	45	44	1 45/64	180 @ 1.28	.0010–.0026	.0024–.0040⑯	.4349–.4358	.4335–.4344
8-477, 534	1970–80	.020H②	.020H②	45	44	1 45/64	180 @ 1.28	.0010–.0026	.0024–.0040⑯	.4349–.4358	.4335–.4344

①—On engines with hydraulic lifters, clearance specified is at valve stem tip with lifter collapsed.
②—Mechanical lifters.
③—2 barrel carb.
④—Hydraulic lifters—1970–72, .100–.150.
⑤—Hydraulic lifters—1970, .145; 1971, .079–.144; 1972, .100–.150.
⑥—1973, Intake 146 @ 1.20; Exhaust 153 @ 1.21; 1974–75, Intake 150 @ 1.18; Exhaust 150 @ 1.22.
⑦—Intake 1 53/64; Exhaust 1 45/64.
⑧—Intake 216 @ 1.26; Exhaust 216 @ 1.32.
⑨—1970–71, .082–.152; 1972, .100–.150.
⑩—Intake 1 45/64; Exhaust 1 37/64.
⑪—Intake 197 @ 1.30; Exhaust 192 @ 1.18.
⑫—1972, .100–.150.
⑬—Intake 146 @ 1.20; Exhaust 149 @ 1.18.
⑭—4 barrel carb.
⑮—1972, .100–.150; 1973, .124; 1974, .100–.150; 1975–80, .125–.175.
⑯—1977 .0020–.0042.
⑰—1970–71, .067–.167; 1972, .067–.117.
⑱—Intake 1 11/16; Exhaust 1 19/32.
⑲—1970–71, .100–.200; 1972–73, .100–.150.
⑳—Intake 230 @ 1.26; Exhaust 230 @ 1.32.
㉑—1975, .144–.184.
㉒—Intake 1 53/64; Exhaust 1 43/64.
㉓—Intake 220 @ 1.38; Exhaust 185 @ 1.24.
㉔—1975, .125–.175.
㉕—Intake 30°; Exhaust 45°.
㉖—Intake 29°; Exhaust 44°.
㉗—1971, .155; 1972, .075–.125.
㉘—1974, .075–.125.
㉙—Intake 197 @ 1.30; Exhaust 192 @ 1.80.
㉚—1977–78, Intake 200 @ 1.31; Exhaust 200 @ 1.20; 1979, Intake 202 @ 1.36; Exhaust 200 @ 1.20; 1980, Intake 204 @ 1.36; Exhaust 200 @ 1.20.
㉛—Intake 1 25/32; Exhaust 1 19/32.
㉜—1977–78, Intake 200 @ 1.34; Exhaust 200 @ 1.20; 1979–80, Intake 200 @ 1.36; Exhaust 200 @ 1.20.
㉝—Intake 1 43/64; Exhaust 1 45/64.
㉞—Intake 220 @ 1.38; Exhaust 180 @ 1.28.
㉟—1977–80 229 @ 1.33.
㊱—Intake 1 23/32; Exhaust 1 25/32.

FORD

PISTON, PIN, RING, CRANKSHAFT & BEARING SPECIFICATIONS

Year	Engine Model	Wristpin Diameter	Piston Clearance, Inch①	Ring End Gap, In. (Minimum)		Crank Pin Diameter, Inch	Rod Bearing Clearance, Inch	Main Bearing Journal Diameter, In.	Main Bearing Clearance, Inch	Shaft End Play
				Comp.	Oil					
1970	8-351	.9120	.0014–.0022	.010	.015	2.3103–2.4388	.0008–.0026	2.7484–2.7492	.0013–.0029	.004–.010
	8-429	1.401	.0014–.0022	.010	.010	2.4992–2.5000	.0008–.0028	2.9994–3.0002	.0005–.0025	.004–.008
1970–71	6-250	.912	.0014–.0020	.010	.015	2.1232–2.1240	.0008–.0026	2.3982–2.3990	.0005–.0025	.004–.008
1970–72	6-170, 200	.9121	.0014–.0020⑮	.010	.015	2.1232–2.1240	.0008–.0024	2.2482–2.2490	.0005–.0022	.004–.008
	6-240	⑪	.0014–.0022	.010	.015	2.1228–2.1236	.0008–.0024	2.3982–2.3990	.0005–.0022	.004–.008
	6-300	⑪	.0014–.0022	.010	.015	2.1228–2.1236	.0009–.0027	2.3982–2.3990	.0009–.0028	.004–.008
	V8-289, 302	.912	.0018–.0026	.010	.015	2.1228–2.1236	.0008–.0026	2.2482–2.2490	.0005–.0024	.004–.008
	8-330	.9751	.0017–.0025	.010	.015	2.4380–2.4388	.0008–.0025	2.7484–2.7492	.0011–.0029	.004–.008
	8-330 H.D.	.9751	.0025–.0033	.015	.015	2.4377–2.4385	.0011–.0029	2.7479–2.7487	.0010–.0030	.004–.010
	8-360, 390	.9751	.0015–.0023	.010	.015	2.4380–.24388	.0008–.0026	2.7484–2.7492	.0005–.0024	.004–.010
	8-361	.9751	.0017–.0025	.010	.015	2.4377–2.4385	.0011–.0029	2.7479–2.7487	.0010–.0030	.004–.010
	8-391	.9751	.0017–.0025	.015	.015	2.4377–2.4385	.0011–.0029	2.7472–2.7480	.0010–.0030	.004–.010
	8-401	1.2200	.0028–.0034	②	.013	2.7092–2.7100	.0017–.0035	3.1246–3.1254	.0018–.0036	.004–.008
	8-477	1.2200	.0028–.0034	②	.013	2.7092–2.7100	.0017–.0035	3.1246–3.1254	.0018–.0036	.004–.008
	8-534	1.2200	.0028–.0034	②	.013	2.7092–2.7100	.0017–.0035	3.1246–3.1254	.0018–.0036	.004–.008
1971	8-351	.9120	.0014–.0022	.010	.015	2.3103–2.3111	.0008–.0026	2.7484–2.7492	.009–.0026	.004–.010
	8-429	1.401	.0014–.0022	.010	.015	2.4992–2.5000	.0008–.0028	2.9994–3.0002	.0005–.0025	.004–.008
1972	6-250	.912	.0013–.0021	.008	.015	2.1232–2.1240	.0008–.0024	2.3982–2.3990	.0005–.0022	.004–.008
	8-351	.9121	.0014–.0022	.010	.015	2.3103–2.3111	.0008–.0026	2.7484–2.7492	.0009–.0026	.004–.010
	8-351	.9121	.0014–.0022	.010	.015	2.3103–2.3111	.0011–.0026	2.7484–2.7492	.0011–.0028	.004–.010
	8-400	.9738	.0014–.0022	.010	.015	2.3103–2.3111	.0008–.0026	2.9994–3.0002	.0009–.0026	.004–.010
	8-429	1.401	.0014–.0022	.010	.015	2.4992–2.5000	.0008–.0028	2.9994–3.0002	⑭	.004–.008
1973	6-200	.9121	.0013–.0021	.012	.015	2.1232–2.1240	.0008–.0024	2.2482–2.2490	.0008–.0024	.004–.008
	6-240	.975	.0014–.0022	.010	.015	2.1228–2.1236	.0008–.0024	2.3982–2.3990	.0005–.0022	.004–.008
	6-250	.912	.0013–.0021	.008	.015	2.1232–2.1240	.0008–.0024	2.3982–2.3990	.0008–.0024	.004–.008
	6-300	.9751	.0014–.0022	.010	.015	2.1228–2.1236	.0009–.0027	2.3982–2.3990	.0009–.0026	.004–.008
	6-300 H.D.	.9751	.0014–.0022	.010	.015	2.1228–2.1236	.0009–.0027	2.3982–2.3990	.0009–.0028	.004–.008
	V8-302	.9121	.0018–.0026	.010	.015	2.1228–2.1236	.0008–.0026	2.2482–2.2490	⑬	.004–.008
	V8-330	.9751	.0025–.0033	.010	.015	2.4380–2.4388	.001–.0029	2.7484–2.7492	.001–.0029	.004–.010
	V8-330 H.D.	.9751	.0025–.0033	.010	.015	2.4380–2.4388	.001–.0029	2.7479–2.7487	.001–.0029	.004–.010
	8-351	.9121	.0014–.0022	.010	.015	2.3103–2.3111	.0008–.0026	2.7484–2.7492	.0009–.0026	.004–.010
	8-351	.9121	.0014–.0022	.010	.015	2.3103–2.3111	.0011–.0026	2.7484–2.7492	.0011–.0028	.004–.010
	V8-360, 390	.9751	.0015–.0023	⑫	.015	2.4380–2.4388	.0008–.0025	2.7484–2.7492	.0005–.0025	.004–.010
	V8-361, 391	.9751	.0025–.0033	⑫	.015	2.4377–2.4385	.001–.0029	2.7479–2.7487	.001–.0029	.004–.010
	8-400	.9738	.0014–.0022	.010	.015	2.3103–2.3111	.0008–.0026	2.9994–3.0002	.0009–.0026	.004–.008
	V8-401, 477, 534	1.2200	.0028–.0034	.018	.013	2.7092–2.7100	.0017–.0035	3.1246–3.1254	.0018–.0036	.004–.008
	8-429	1.401	.0014–.0022	.010	.015	2.4992–2.5000	.0008–.0028	2.9994–3.0002	⑭	.004–.008
1974	6-200	.9122	.0013–.0021	.008	.015	2.123–2.124	.0008–.0024	2.248–2.249	.0008–.0024	.004–.008
	6-240	.9751	.0014–.0022	.010	.015	2.1228–2.1236	.0008–.0024	2.3982–2.3990	.0005–.0015	.004–.008
	6-250	.9121	.0013–.0021	.008	.015	2.1232–2.1240	.0008–.0024	2.3982–2.3990	.0008–.0024	.004–.008
	6-300	.9751	.0014–.0022	.010	.015	2.1228–2.1236	.0009–.0027	2.3982–2.3990	.0009–.0026	.004–.008
	6-300 H.D.	.9751	.0014–.0022	.010	.015	2.1228–2.1236	.0009–.0027	2.3982–2.3990	.0009–.0028	.004–.008
	V8-302	.9121	.0018–.0026	.010	.015	2.1228–2.1236	.0008–.0026	2.2482–2.2490	⑬	.004–.008
	V8-330	.9751	.0025–.0033	.010	.015	2.4380–2.4388	.001–.0029	2.7484–2.7492	.001–.0029	.004–.010
	V8-330 H.D.	.9751	.0025–.0033	.010	.015	2.4377–2.4385	.001–.0029	2.7484–2.7492	.001–.0029	.004–.010
	8-351C	.9121	.0014–.0022	.010	.015	2.3103–2.3111	.0008–.0026	2.7484–2.7492	.0009–.0026	.004–.008
	V8-360, 390	.9751	.0015–.0023	⑫	.015	2.4380–2.4388	.0008–.0025	2.7484–2.7492	.0005–.0025	.004–.010
	V8-361, 391	.9751	.0025–.0033	⑫	.015	2.4377–2.4388	.001–.0029	2.7479–2.7487	.001–.0029	.004–.010
	8-400	.9752	.0014–.0022	.010	.015	2.3103–2.3111	.0011–.0026	2.9994–3.0002	.0011–.0028	.004–.008
	V8-401, 475, 477, 534	1.2200	.0028–.0034	②	.013	2.7092–2.7100	.0017–.0035	3.1246–3.1254	.0018–.0036	.004–.008
	V8-460	1.0400	.0022–.0030	.010	.015	2.4992–2.5000	.0008–.0028	2.9994–3.0002	⑭	.004–.008

Continued

FORD

PISTON, PIN, RING, CRANKSHAFT & BEARING SPECIFICATIONS—Continued

Year	Engine Model	Wristpin Diameter	Piston Clearance, Inch①	Ring End Gap, In. (Minimum) Comp.	Ring End Gap, In. (Minimum) Oil	Crank Pin Diameter, Inch	Rod Bearing Clearance, Inch	Main Bearing Journal Diameter, In.	Main Bearing Clearance, Inch	Shaft End Play
1975	6-300	.9752	.0014–.0022	.010	.015	2.1228–2.1236	.0008–.0015	2.3982–2.3990	.0008–.0015	.004–.008
	8-302	.9122	.0018–.0026	.010	.015	2.1228–2.1236	.0008–.0015	2.2482–2.2490	⑯	.004–.008
	8-330	.9752	.0025–.0033	.010	.015	2.4380–2.4388	.0008–.0015	2.7484–2.7492	.0005–.0015	.004–.010
	8-351W	.9122	.0018–.0026	.010	.015	2.3103–2.3111	.0008–.0015	2.9994–3.0002	.0008–.0015	.004–.008
	8-351M	.9752	.0014–.0022	.010	.015	2.3103–2.3111	.0008–.0015	2.9994–3.0002	.0008–.0015	.004–.008
	8-360	.9752	.0015–.0023	⑫	.015	2.4380–2.4388	.0008–.0015	2.7484–2.7492	.0005–.0015	.004–.010
	8-361	.9752	.0025–.0033	⑫	.015	2.4377–2.4385	.0008–.0015	2.7479–2.7492	.0005–.0015	.004–.010
	8-390	.9752	.0015–.0023	⑫	.015	2.4380–2.4388	.0008–.0015	2.7484–2.7492	.0005–.0015	.004–.010
	8-391	.9752	.0025–.0033	⑫	.015	2.4377–2.4388	.0008–.0015	2.7479–2.7492	.0005–.0015	.004–.010
	8-400	.9752	.0014–.0022	.010	.015	2.3103–2.3111	.0008–.0015	2.9994–3.0002	.0008–.0015	.004–.008
	8-401, 477, 534	1.2200	.0028–.0034	②	.013	2.7092–2.7100	.0017–.0025	3.1246–3.1254	.0018–.0025	.004–.008
	8-460	1.0401	.0014–.0022	.010	.015	2.4992–2.5000	.0008–.0015	2.9994–3.0002	⑰	.004–.008
1976	6-300	.9752	.0014–.0022	.010	.015	2.1228–2.1236	.0008–.0015	2.3982–2.3990	.0008–.0015	.004–.008
	8-302	.9121	.0018–.0026	.010	.015	2.1228–2.1236	.0008–.0015	2.2482–2.2490	.0008–.0015	.004–.008
	8-330	.9752	.0025–.0033	.010	.015	2.4380–2.4388	.0008–.0015	2.7484–2.7492	.0005–.0015	.004–.010
	8-351W	.9121	.0018–.0026	.010	.015	2.3103–2.3111	.0008–.0015	2.9994–3.0002	.0008–.0015	.004–.008
	8-351M	.9752	.0014–.0022	.010	.015	2.3103–2.3111	.0008–.0015	2.9994–3.0002	.0008–.0015	.004–.008
	8-360	.9752	.0015–.0023	⑫	.015	2.4380–2.4388	.0008–.0015	2.7484–2.7492	.0005–.0015	.004–.010
	8-361	.9752	.0025–.0033	⑫	.015	2.4377–2.4385	.0008–.0015	2.7479–2.7487	.0005–.0015	.004–.010
	8-389	—	—	—	—	—	—	2.7479–2.7487	—	—
	8-390	.9752	.0015–.0023	⑫	.015	2.4380–2.4388	.0008–.0015	2.7484–2.7492	.0005–.0015	.004–.010
	8-391	.9752	.0025–.0033	⑫	.015	2.4377–2.4385	.0008–.0015	2.7479–2.7487	.0005–.0015	.004–.010
	8-400	.9752	.0014–.0022	.010	.015	2.3103–2.3111	.0008–.0015	2.9994–3.0002	.0008–.0015	.004–.008
	8-401, 477, 534	1.2200	.0028–.0034	②	.013	2.7092–2.100	.0017–.0025	3.1246–3.1254	.0018–.0025	.004–.008
	8-460	1.0401	.0014–.0022	.010	.015	2.4992–2.5000	.0008–.0015	2.9994–3.0002	.0008–.0015	.004–.008
1977	6-300	.9752	.0014–.0022	.010	.010	2.1228–2.1236	.0008–.0015	2.3982–2.3990	.0008–.0015	.004–.008
	8-302	.9122	.0018–.0026	.010	.010	2.1228–2.1236	.0008–.0015	2.2482–2.2490	⑯	.004–.008
	8-330	.9752	.0025–.0033	.010	.010	⑱	.0008–.0015	2.7484–2.7492	.0008–.0015	.004–.010
	8-351W	.9122	.0022–.0030	.010	.010	2.3103–2.3111	.0008–.0015	2.9994–3.0002	.0008–.0015	.004–.008
	8-351M	.9750	.0014–.0022	.010	.010	2.3103–2.3111	.0008–.0015	2.9994–3.0002	.0008–.0015	.004–.008
	8-359	.9752	.0025–.0033	⑫	.015	2.4377–2.4385	.0008–.0015	2.7479–2.7487	.0008–.0015	.004–.010
	8-361	.9752	.0025–.0033	⑫	.015	2.4377–2.4385	.0008–.0015	2.7479–2.7487	.0008–.0015	.004–.010
	8-389	.9752	.0025–.0033	⑫	.015	2.4377–2.4385	.0008–.0015	2.7479–2.7487	.0008–.0015	.004–.010
	8-391	.9752	.0025–.0033	⑫	.015	2.4377–2.4385	.0008–.0015	2.7479–2.7487	.0008–.0015	.004–.010
	8-400	.9750	.0014–.0022	.010	.010	2.3103–2.3111	.0008–.0015	2.9994–3.0002	.0008–.0015	.004–.008
	8-460	1.0401	.0014–.0022	.010	.010	2.4992–2.5000	.0008–.0015	2.9994–3.0002	.0008–.0015	.004–.008
	8-475, 477, 534	1.2200	.0028–.0034	②	.013	2.7092–2.7100	.0019–.0027	3.1246–3.1254	.0019–.0025	.004–.008
1978	6-300	.9752	.0014–.0022	.010	.010	2.1228–2.1236	.0008–.0015	2.3982–2.3990	.0008–.0015	.004–.008
	8-302	.9122	.0018–.0026	.010	.010	2.1228–2.1236	.0008–.0015	2.2482–2.2490	.0008–.0015	.004–.008
	8-330	.9752	.0025–.0033	.010	.010	2.4377–2.4385	.0008–.0015	2.7484–2.7492	.0008–.0015	.004–.010
	8-351M	.9750	.0014–.0022	.010	.015	2.3103–2.3111	.0008–.0015	2.9994–3.0002	.0008–.0015	.004–.008
	8-351W	.9122	.0022–.0030	.010	.010	2.3103–2.3111	.0008–.0015	2.9994–3.0002	.0008–.0015	.004–.008
	8-361	.9752	.0025–.0033	⑫	.015	2.4377–2.4385	.0008–.0015	2.7479–2.7487	.0008–.0015	.004–.010
	8-389	.9752	.0025–.0033	⑫	.015	2.4377–2.4385	.0008–.0015	2.7479–2.7487	.0008–.0015	.004–.010
	8-391	.9752	.0025–.0033	⑫	.015	2.4377–2.4385	.0008–.0015	2.7479–2.7487	.0008–.0015	.004–.010
	8-400	.9750	.0014–.0022	.010	.015	2.3103–2.3111	.0008–.0015	2.9994–3.0002	.0008–.0015	.004–.008
	8-460	1.0401	.0022–.0030	.010	.010	2.4992–2.5000	.0008–.0015	2.9994–3.0002	.0008–.0015	.004–.008
	8-475, 477, 534	1.2200	.0028–.0034	②	.013	2.7092–2.7100	.0019–.0027	3.1246–3.1254	.0019–.0025	.004–.008
1979	6-300	.9752	.0014–.0022	.010	.010	2.1228–2.1236	.0008–.0015	2.3982–2.3990	.0008–.0015	.004–.008
	8-302	.9122	.0018–.0026	.010	.015	2.1228–2.1236	.0008–.0015	2.2482–2.2490	⑯	.004–.008
	8-351W	.9122	.0022–.0030	.010	.015	2.3103–2.3111	.0008–.0015	2.9994–3.0002	.0008–.0015	.004–.008

Continued

FORD

PISTON, PIN, RING, CRANKSHAFT & BEARING SPECIFICATIONS—Continued

Year	Engine Model	Wristpin Diameter	Piston Clearance, Inch①	Ring End Gap, In. (Minimum) Comp.	Ring End Gap, In. (Minimum) Oil	Crank Pin Diameter, Inch	Rod Bearing Clearance, Inch	Main Bearing Journal Diameter, In.	Main Bearing Clearance, Inch	Shaft End Play
	8-351M	.9750	.0014–.0022	.010	.010	2.3103–2.3111	.0008–.0015	2.9994–3.0002	.0008–.0015	.004–.008
	8-370	1.0401	.0018–.0039	.010	—	2.4992–2.5000	.0008–.0015	2.9994–3.0002	.0008–.0026	.004–.008
	8-400	.9750	.0014–.0022	.010	.010	2.3103–2.3111	.0008–.0015	2.9994–3.0002	.0008–.0015	.004–.008
	8-429	1.0401	.0019–.0037	.013	.013	2.4992–2.5000	.0008–.0015	2.9994–3.0002	.0008–.0026	.004–.008
	8-460	1.0401	.0022–.0030	.010	.010	2.4992–2.5000	.0008–.0015	2.9994–3.0002	.0008–.0015	.004–.008
	8-475, 477, 534	1.2200	.0028–.0034	②	.013	2.7092–2.7100	.0019–.0027	3.1246–3.1254	.0019–.0028	.004–.008
1980	6-300	.9752	.0014–.0022	.010	.010	2.1228–2.1236	.0008–.0015	2.3982–2.3990	.0008–.0015	.004–.008
	8-302	.9122	.0018–.0026	.010	.010	2.1228–2.1236	.0008–.0015	2.2482–2.2490	⑯	.004–.008
	8-351W	.9122	.0022–.0030	.010	.010	2.3103–2.3111	.0008–.0015	2.9994–3.0002	.0008–.0015	.004–.008
	8-351M	.9752	.0014–.0022	.010	.010	2.3103–2.3111	.0008–.0015	2.9994–3.0002	.0008–.0015	.004–.008
	8-370	1.0401	.0018–.0039	⑲	⑲	2.4992–2.5000	.0008–.0015	2.9994–3.0002	.0008–.0015	.004–.008
	8-400	.9752	.0014–.0022	.010	.010	2.3103–2.3111	.0008–.0015	2.9994–3.0002	.0008–.0015	.004–.008
	8-429	1.0401	.0019–.0037	.013	.013	2.4992–2.5000	.0008–.0015	2.9994–3.0002	.0008–.0015	.004–.008
	8-460	1.0401	.0022–.0030	.010	.010	2.4992–2.5000	.0008–.0015	2.9994–3.0002	.0008–.0015	.004–.008
	8-477, 534	1.2200	.0028–.0034	②	.013	2.7092–2.7100	.0019–.0027	3.1246–3.1254	.0019–.0028	.004–.008

①—Measured at bottom of skirt.
②—Top ring .018", others .015".
⑤—Medium duty 2.4380–2.4388", heavy duty 2.4377–2.4385".
⑩—Medium duty 2.7484–2.7492", heavy duty 2.7479–2.7487".
⑪—1970–72 Wristpin Diam. .9751.
⑫—Top ring, .015", others .010".
⑬—No. 1 .0001–.0020", others .0005–.0024".
⑭—No. 1 .0004–.0020", others .0012–.0028".
⑮—1972 6-170, .0013–.0026.
⑯—No. 1, .0001–.0015"; others, .0005–.0015".
⑰—No. 1, .0004–.0015"; others, .0009–.0015".
⑱—Medium duty engines 2.4380–2.4388; Heavy duty engines 2.4377–2.4385.
⑲—2 barrel carb, comp. .010; oil .010. 4 barrel carb, comp. .013; oil .013.

ENGINE TIGHTENING SPECIFICATIONS★

★ Torque specifications are for clean and lightly lubricated threads only. Dry or dirty threads produce increased friction which prevents accurate measurement of tightness.

Year	Engine Model	Spark Plug Ft-Lbs.	Cylinder Head Ft-Lbs.	Intake Manifold Ft-Lbs.	Exhaust Manifold Ft-Lbs.	Rocker Shaft Support Ft-Lbs.	Rocker Cover Ft-Lbs.	Conn. Rod Cap Ft-Lbs.	Main Bearing Caps Ft-Lbs.	Flywheel To Crankshaft Ft-Lbs.	Damper or Pulley Ft-Lbs.
1970–71	6-170	15–20	70–75	—	13–18	30–35	3–5	19–24	60–70	75–85	85–100
	6-200	15–20	70–75	—	13–18	30–35	3–5	19–24	60–70	75–85	85–100
	6-240	15–20	70–75	23–28	23–28	⑲	7–9	40–45	60–70	75–85	130–150
	6-250	15–20	70–75	—	13–18	30–35	3–5	21–26	60–70	75–85	85–100
	6-300	15–20	70–75	20–25	20–25	⑲	7–9	40–45	60–70	75–85	130–145
	V8-289, 302	15–20	65–72	20–22	15–20	—	3–5	19–24	60–70	75–85	70–90
	V8-330	15–20	80–90	32–35	18–24	40–45	10–12	40–45	95–105	75–85	②
	V8-351	15–20	95–100	23–25	18–24	—	3–5	40–45	60–70	75–85	70–90
	V8-429	15–20	130–140	25–30	28–33	—	5–6	40–45	95–105	75–85	70–90
	V8-352	15–20	80–90	32–35	12–18	40–45	10–12	40–45	95–105	75–85	70–90
	V8-360, 390	15–20	80–90	32–35	12–18	40–45	10–12	40–45	95–105	75–85	70–90
	V8-361	15–20	80–90	32–35	18–24	40–45	10–12	40–45	95–105	75–85	150–175
	V8-391	15–20	80–90	32–35	18–24	40–45	10–12	40–45	95–105	75–85	150–175
	V8-401	15–20	170–180	23–28	23–28	—	5–7	60–65	130–150	100–110	130–145
	V8-477	15–20	170–180	23–28	23–28	—	5–7	60–65	130–150	100–110	130–145
	V8-534	15–20	170–180	23–28	23–28	—	5–7	60–65	130–150	100–110	130–145
1971	V8-351	15–20	95–105	⑬	12–16	—	3–5	40–45	95–105	75–85	70–90
	V8-429	15–20	130–140	25–30	28–33	—	5–6	40–45	95–105	75–85	70–90
1972	V8-351	15–20	95–105	⑩	12–16	—	3–5	40–45	⑫	75–85	70–90
	V8-400	15–20	95–105	⑩	12–16	—	3–5	40–45	⑫	75–85	70–90
	V8-429	15–20	130–140	25–30	28–33	—	5–6	40–45	95–105	75–85	70–90

Continued

FORD

ENGINE TIGHTENING SPECIFICATIONS—Continued

★ Torque specifications are for clean and lightly lubricated threads only. Dry or dirty threads produce increased friction which prevents accurate measurement of tightness.

Year	Engine Model	Spark Plug Ft-Lbs.	Cylinder Head Ft-Lbs.	Intake Manifold Ft-Lbs.	Exhaust Manifold Ft-Lbs.	Rocker Shaft Support Ft-Lbs.	Rocker Cover Ft-Lbs.	Conn. Rod Cap Ft-Lbs.	Main Bearing Caps Ft-Lbs.	Flywheel To Crankshaft Ft-Lbs.	Damper or Pulley Ft-Lbs.
1972-74	6-250	15-20	70-75	—	13-18	30-35	3-5	21-26	60-70	75-85	85-100
	6-170, 200	15-20	70-75	—	13-18	30-35	3-5	19-24	60-70	75-85	85-100
	6-240, 300	15-20	70-75	28-33	23-28	⑲	4-7	40-45	⑥	75-85	130-150
	8-302	15-20	65-72	⑦	12-16	⑧	3-5	19-24	60-70	75-85	③
	8-330 MD	15-20	80-90	④	18-24	40-45	⑤	40-45	95-105	75-85	70-90
	8-330 HD, 361, 391	15-20	80-90	④	18-24	40-45	⑤	40-45	95-105	75-85	150-175
	V8-351	15-20	⑭	⑩	12-22	—	3-5	40-45	⑫	75-85	70-90
	8-360, 390	15-20	80-90	④	12-18	40-45	⑤	40-45	95-105	75-85	70-90
	V8-400	15-20	95-105	⑬	12-16	—	3-5	40-45	⑫	75-85	70-90
	8-401, 477, 534	15-20	170-180	23-28	23-28		⑤	60-65	150-165	100-110	130-175
	V8-429	15-20	130-140	25-30	28-33	—	5-6	40-45	95-105	75-85	70-90
1974	8-460	15-20	130-140	25-30	28-33	⑨	5-6	40-45	95-105	75-85	70-90
1975	6-250	15-25	70-75	—	18-24	30-35	3-5	21-26	60-70	75-85	85-100
	6-300	15-20	70-85	①	23-28	⑲	4-7	40-45	60-70	75-85	130-150
	8-302	10-15	65-72	23-25	18-24	⑮	3-5	19-24	60-70	75-85	70-90
	8-330	15-20	90	40-45	18-24	40-45	4-7	40-45	95-105	75-85	130-150
	8-351W	10-15	105-112	23-25	18-24	⑮	3-5	40-45	95-105	75-85	70-90
	8-351M	10-15	95-105	⑬	18-24	⑪	3-5	40-45	⑫	75-85	70-90
	8-360, 390	15-20	90	40-45	12-18	40-45	4-7	40-45	95-105	75-85	130-150
	8-361, 391	15-20	90	40-45	18-24	40-45	4-7	40-45	95-105	75-85	150-175
	8-389	15-20	90	40-45	18-24	40-45	4-7	40-45	95-105	75-85	150-175
	8-400	10-15	95-105	⑬	18-24	⑪	3-5	40-45	⑫	75-85	70-90
	8-401	15-25	170-180	—	22-32	—	5-7	60-65	150-165	100-110	130-175
	8-460	10-15	130-140	22-37	28-33	⑨	5-6	40-45	95-105	75-85	70-90
	8-477, 534	15-25	170-180	—	22-32	—	5-7	60-65	150-165	100-110	130-175
1976	6-300	15-20	70-85	①	23-28	⑲	4-7	40-45	60-70	75-85	130-150
	V8-302, 351	10-15	65-70	23-25	18-24	17-23	3-5	19-24	60-70	75-85	70-90
	V8-330, 361	15-20	90	40-45	18-24	40-45	4-7	40-45	95-105	75-85	130-150
	V8-360	15-20	90	40-45	12-18	40-45	4-7	40-45	95-105	75-85	150-175
	V8-390	15-20	90	40-45	12-18	40-45	4-7	40-45	95-105	75-85	130-150
	V8-391	15-20	90	40-45	18-24	40-45	4-7	40-45	95-105	75-85	150-175
	V8-460	—	130-140	—	28-33	—	5-6	40-45	95-105	75-85	70-90
	V8-401, 477, 534	15-25	170-180	—	22-32	—	5-7	60-65	150-165	100-110	35-50
1977	6-300	15-25	70-85	22-32	28-33	⑲	4-7	40-45	60-70	75-85	130-150
	8-302	10-15	65-72	23-25	18-24	⑮	3-5	19-24	60-70	75-85	70-90
	8-330	15-25	90	40-45	18-24	40-45	4-7	40-45	95-105	75-85	⑰
	8-351W	10-15	105-112	23-25	18-24	⑮	3-5	40-45	95-105	75-85	70-90
	8-351M	10-15	95-105	⑯	18-24	⑪	3-5	40-45	95-105	75-85	70-90
	8-359	15-25	90	40-45	18-24	40-45	4-7	40-45	95-105	75-85	⑰
	8-361	15-25	90	40-45	18-24	40-45	4-7	40-45	95-105	75-85	⑰
	8-389	15-25	90	40-45	18-24	40-45	4-7	40-45	95-105	75-85	⑰
	8-391	15-25	90	40-45	18-24	40-45	4-7	40-45	95-105	75-85	⑰
	8-400	10-15	95-105	⑯	18-24	⑪	3-5	40-45	95-105	75-85	70-90
	8-460	10-15	130-140	22-23	28-33	⑪	5-6	40-45	95-105	75-85	70-90
	8-475, 477, 534	10-15	170-180	25-32	22-32	—	5-7	60-65	150-165	100-110	130-175
1978	6-300	15-25	70-85	22-32	28-33	⑲	4-7	40-45	60-70	75-85	130-150
	8-302	10-15	65-72	23-25	18-24	⑱	3-5	19-24	60-70	75-85	70-90
	8-330	15-25	90	40-45	18-24	40-45	4-7	40-45	95-105	75-85	⑰

Continued

FORD

ENGINE TIGHTENING SPECIFICATIONS—Continued

★ Torque specifications are for clean and lightly lubricated threads only. Dry or dirty threads produce increased friction which prevents accurate measurement of tightness.

Year	Engine Model	Spark Plug Ft-Lbs.	Cylinder Head Ft-Lbs.	Intake Manifold Ft-Lbs.	Exhaust Manifold Ft-Lbs.	Rocker Shaft Support Ft-Lbs.	Rocker Cover Ft-Lbs.	Conn. Rod Cap Ft-Lbs.	Main Bearing Caps Ft-Lbs.	Flywheel To Crankshaft Ft-Lbs.	Damper or Pulley Ft-Lbs.
	8-351M	10–15	105	⑯	18–24	⑪	3–5	40–45	95–105	75–85	70–90
	8-351W	10–15	105–112	23–25	18–24	⑱	3–5	40–45	95–105	75–85	70–90
	8-361	15–25	90	40–45	18–24	40–45	4–7	40–45	95–105	75–85	⑰
	8-389	15–25	90	40–45	18–24	40–45	4–7	40–45	95–105	75–85	⑰
	8-391	15–25	90	40–45	18–24	40–45	4–7	40–45	95–105	75–85	⑰
	8-400	10–15	105	⑯	18–24	⑪	3–5	40–45	95–105	75–85	70–90
	8-460	10–15	130–140	22–32	28–33	⑪	5–6	40–45	95–105	75–85	70–90
	8-475, 477, 534	15–25	170–180	25–32	22–32	—	5–7	60–65	150–165	100–110	130–175
1979	6-300	15–25	70–85	22–32	28–33	⑲⑳	4–7	40–45	60–70	75–85	130–150
	8-302	10–15	65–72	23–25	18–24	⑪	3–5	19–24	60–70	75–85	70–90
	8-351W	10–15	105–112	23–25	18–24	⑪	3–5	40–45	95–105	75–85	70–90
	8-351M, 400	10–15	95–105	⑯	18–24	⑪	3–5	40–45	95–105	75–85	70–90
	8-370, 429	5–10	130–140	22–32	28–33	⑪	5–6	45–50	95–105	75–85	150–175
	8-460	5–10	130–140	22–32	28–33	⑪	5–6	40–45	95–105	75–85	70–90
	8-475, 477, 534	—	—	25–32	—	—	—	—	—	—	—
1980	6-300	10–15	85	22–32	28–33	⑲⑳	4–7	40–45	60–70	75–85	130–150
	8-302	10–15	65–72	23–25	18–24	⑪	3–5	19–24	60–70	75–85	70–90
	8-351W	10–15	105–112	23–25	18–24	⑪	3–5	40–45	95–105	75–85	70–90
	8-351M, 400	10–15	95–105	⑯	18–24	⑪	3–5	40–45	95–105	75–85	70–90
	8-370, 429	10–15	130–140	22–32	28–32	⑪	5–7	45–50	95–105	75–85	150–175
	8-460	5–10	130–140	22–32	28–32	⑪	5–6	40–45	95–105	75–85	70–90
	8-477, 534	10–15	170–180	25–32	22–32	170–180	5–7	60–65	150–165	100–110	130–175

①—Intake man. to exhaust man., 28–33; Intake man. to cyl. head, 23–28.
②—Medium duty same as V8-352, heavy duty same as V8-361.
③—1972, 100–130 ft. lbs.; 1973-74, 70–90 ft. lbs.
④—1972, 32–35 ft. lbs.; 1973-74, 40–45 ft. lbs.
⑤—1972, 10–12 ft. lbs; 1973-74, 4–7 ft. lbs.
⑥—1972-73, 60–70 ft. lbs.; 1974, 65–72 ft. lbs.
⑦—1972-73, 23–25 ft. lbs.; 1974, 17–25 ft. lbs.
⑧—Rocker arm stud nut 1970-72, 18–20 ft. lbs.; 1973-78, 17–23 ft. lbs.
⑨—Rocker arm bolt, 18–25 ft. lbs.
⑩—1/4" bolts 6–9 ft. lbs.; 3/8" bolts 22–23 ft. lbs.; 5/16 bolts 25 ft. lbs.
⑪—Rocker arm bolts to cylinder head 18–25.
⑫—3/8" bolts 35–45 ft. lbs.; 1/2" bolts 95–105 ft. lbs.
⑬—5/16" 21–25 ft. lbs., 3/8" 27–33 ft. lbs.
⑭—1972, 95–105 ft. lbs.; 1973-74, 105–112 ft. lbs.
⑮—Rocker arm nut to cylinder head bolt, 17–23 ft. lbs.
⑯—3/8" 22–32 ft. lbs.; 5/16" bolts 19–25 ft. lbs.
⑰—5/8" bolts 130–150 ft. lbs.; 3/4" bolts 150–175 ft. lbs.
⑱—Early 1978 with positive stop nut, 17–23 ft. lbs. Late 1978 with fulcrum and bolt, 18–25 ft. lbs.
⑲—Breakaway torque, 4.5–15 ft. lbs. Refer to "Valves, Adjust" procedure
⑳—Rocker arm stud nut torque, 17–23 ft. lbs. Refer to "Valves, Adjust" procedure.

STARTING MOTOR SPECIFICATIONS

Year	Starter Type	Ampere Draw Normal Load	Engine Cranking Speed R.P.M.	Minimum Stall Torque @ 5 volts Ft. Lbs.	Maximum head Amperes	No Load Ampere @ 12 Volts	Brushes Length Inch	Brushes Wear Limit Inch	Brushes Spring Tension Ounces
1970-73	Ford 4½" Diameter	150–180	250–290	15.5	670	70	.50	.25	40
	Eltra	200	—	17.2	525	60	.47	.25	42–53
	Delco Positive Engagement	150	—	15	700	140	.75	.25	45
	Delco Inertia	200	—	17.5	525	60	.75	.25	24
	Delco 24 Volt	375	—	24	500	60–90	.75	.375	80
1970-74	Prestolite	200	—	17.2	525	60	.47	.25	45–53
1976-80	Prestolite	200	—	17.2	525	80	.47	.25	45–53
1971-77	Ford Solenoid Actuated	180–210	140–170	—	—	70	.50	.25	40
1974	Delco Positive Engagement	150①	—	15②	700	140	.75	.25	45
	Delco Inertia	200	—	17.5	525	60	.75	.25	24

Continued

FORD

STARTING MOTOR SPECIFICATIONS—Continued

Year	Starter Type	Ampere Draw Normal Load	Engine Cranking Speed R.P.M.	Minimum Stall Torque @ 5 volts Ft. Lbs.	Maximum head Amperes	No Load Ampere @ 12 Volts	Brushes Length Inch	Brushes Wear Limit Inch	Brushes Spring Tension Ounces
1974–79	Ford 4″ Diameter	150–200	180–250	9	460	70	.50	.25	40
	Ford 4½″ Diameter	150–180	150–290	15.5	670	70	.50	.25	40③
1975–80	Delco Positive Engagement	150①	—	15②	900	180	.75	.25	45
	Delco Inertia	200	—	17.5	525	60	.75	.25	24
1980	Ford 4″ Diameter	150–200	180–250	—	—	70	.50	.25	40
	Ford 4½″ Diameter	150–180	150–290	—	—	80	.50	.25	80

①—Diesel engines: 650–750 amperes.　　②—At 1.5 volts.　　③—1978–79, 80 ounces.

GENERATOR, ALTERNATOR & REGULATOR SPECIFICATIONS

Year	Unit Make	Rated Output @ 15 Volts Amperes	Field Coil Draw @ 12 Volts Amperes	Voltage Regulation @ 75° F.	Current Limiter Amperes	Current Limiter Air Gap	Voltage Limiter Contact Gap	Voltage Limiter Air Gap	Field Relay Contact Gap	Field Relay Air Gap	Field Relay Closing Voltage
1970–71	Autolite (Purple)	38	2.5	13.5–15.3	—	—	—	—	—	.010–.018	2.0–4.2
	Autolite (Orange)	42	2.9	13.5–15.3	—	—	—	—	—	.010–.018	2.0–4.2
	Autolite (Red)	55	2.9	13.5–15.3	—	—	—	—	—	.010–.018	2.0–4.2
	Autolite (Green)	60	4.6	13.5–15.3	—	—	—	—	—	.010–.018	2.0–4.2
	Autolite (Black)	65	2.9	13.9–14.9	—	—	—	—	Sealed	Sealed	2.0–4.2
	Autolite (Red)	85	2.9	13.9–14.9	—	—	—	—	Sealed	Sealed	2.0–4.2
	Leece Neville	65	2.9	13.9–14.9	—	—	—	—	Sealed	Sealed	2.0–4.2
	Leece Neville	105	3.0	13.9–14.9	—	—	—	—	Sealed	Sealed	2.0–4.2
1972	Motorcraft (Purple)	38	2.5	—	—	—	—	—	—	—	—
	Motorcraft (Orange)	42	2.9	—	—	—	—	—	—	—	—
	Motorcraft (Red)	55	2.9	—	—	—	—	—	—	—	—
	Motorcraft (Green)	61	2.9	—	—	—	—	—	—	—	—
	Motorcraft (Black)	65	2.9	13.9–14.9	—	—	—	—	Sealed	Sealed	2.0–4.2
	Motorcraft (Red)	85	2.9	13.9–14.9	—	—	—	—	Sealed	Sealed	2.0–4.2
	Leece Neville	65	2.9	13.9–14.9	—	—	—	—	Sealed	Sealed	2.0–4.2
	Leece Neville	105	3.0	13.9–14.9	—	—	—	—	Sealed	Sealed	2.0–4.2
1973–75	Motorcraft (Purple)	38	2.5	—	—	—	—	—	—	—	—
	Motorcraft (Orange)	42	2.9	—	—	—	—	—	—	—	—
	Motorcraft (Red)	55	2.9	—	—	—	—	—	—	—	—
	Motorcraft (Green)	61	2.9	—	—	—	—	—	—	—	—
	Motorcraft (Black)	70	2.9	—	—	—	—	—	Sealed	Sealed	2.0–4.2
	Motorcraft (Red)	90	2.9	—	—	—	—	—	Sealed	Sealed	2.0–4.2
	Leece-Neville	70	2.9	—	—	—	—	—	Sealed	Sealed	2.0–4.2
	Leece-Neville	105	2.9	—	—	—	—	—	Sealed	Sealed	2.0–4.2
1976	Motorcraft (Orange)	40	2.9	—	—	—	—	—	—	—	—
	Motorcraft (Green)	60	2.9	—	—	—	—	—	—	—	—
	Motorcraft (Black)	70	2.9	—	—	—	—	—	—	—	—
	Motorcraft (Red)	90	2.9	—	—	—	—	—	—	—	—
	Leece-Neville	70	2.9	—	—	—	—	—	—	—	—
	Leece-Neville	105	2.9	—	—	—	—	—	—	—	—

Continued

FORD

GENERATOR, ALTERNATOR & REGULATOR SPECIFICATIONS—Continued

Year	Unit Make	Rated Output @ 15 Volts Amperes	Field Coil Draw @ 12 Volts Amperes	Voltage Regulation @ 75° F.	Regulation					
					Current Limiter		Voltage Limiter		Field Relay		
					Amperes	Air Gap	Contact Gap	Air Gap	Contact Gap	Air Gap	Closing Voltage
1977	Motorcraft (Orange)	40	2.9	—	—	—	—	—	—	—	—
	Motorcraft (Green)	60	2.9	—	—	—	—	—	—	—	—
	Motorcraft (Black)	70	2.9	—	—	—	—	—	—	—	—
	Motorcraft (Red)	90	2.9	—	—	—	—	—	—	—	—
	Leece-Neville	70	2.9	—	—	—	—	—	—	—	—
	Leece-Neville	105	2.9	—	—	—	—	—	—	—	—
1978	Motorcraft (Orange)	40	2.9	13.5–14.3	—	—	—	—	—	—	—
	Motorcraft (Green)	60	2.9	13.5–14.3	—	—	—	—	—	—	—
	Motorcraft (Green)⑥	60	4.0	13.8–14.6	—	—	—	—	—	—	—
	Motorcraft (Black)	70	2.9	13.5–14.3	—	—	—	—	—	—	—
	Motorcraft (Red)	90	2.9	13.5–14.3	—	—	—	—	—	—	—
	Motorcraft (Red)⑥	90	4.0	13.8–14.6	—	—	—	—	—	—	—
	Leece-Neville	70	2.9	—	—	—	—	—	—	—	—
	Leece-Neville	105	2.9	—	—	—	—	—	—	—	—
1979	Motorcraft (Orange)⑥	40	4.0	13.8–14.6	—	—	—	—	—	—	—
	Motorcraft (Green)⑥	60	4.0	13.8–14.6	—	—	—	—	—	—	—
	Motorcraft (Black)⑥	65	4.0	13.8–14.6	—	—	—	—	—	—	—
	Motorcraft (70 Amp)⑥	70	4.0	13.8–14.6	—	—	—	—	—	—	—
	Motorcraft (100 Amp)⑥	100	4.0	13.8–14.6	—	—	—	—	—	—	—
	Leece-Neville	70	2.9	—	—	—	—	—	—	—	—
	Leece-Neville	105	2.9	—	—	—	—	—	—	—	—
	Leece-Neville	130	5.7	—	—	—	—	—	—	—	—
1980	Motorcraft (Orange)⑥	40	4	—	—	—	—	—	—	—	—
	Motorcraft (Green)⑥	60	4	—	—	—	—	—	—	—	—
	Motorcraft (Black)⑥	65	4	—	—	—	—	—	—	—	—
	Motorcraft (70 Amp)⑥	70	4	—	—	—	—	—	—	—	—
	Motorcraft (100 Amp)⑥	100	4	—	—	—	—	—	—	—	—
	Leece-Neville	70	2.9	—	—	—	—	—	—	—	—
	Leece-Neville	105	2.9	—	—	—	—	—	—	—	—
	Leece-Neville	130	5.7	—	—	—	—	—	—	—	—

①—Lower contacts 0.1 to 0.3 below (listed) upper contact voltage.
②—At 125° F.
③—Econoline.
④—Units w/electro mechanical regulator.
⑤—Units w/transistorized regulator.
⑥—Solid state alternator, these units are marked with blue ink on front of pulley. The electronic voltage regulator used with these units is color coded black for systems w/ warning indicator lamp & blue for systems w/ammeter.

FORD

WHEEL ALIGNMENT SPECIFICATIONS

Truck Model	Front Axle Code	Caster Deg.	Camber Deg.	Toe-In Inch	Kingpin Angle Deg.
1970 MODELS					
Bronco	—	+3½ ⑨	+1½ ⑨	1/8	8½
Econoline	—	+3	+1	1/8	—
Ranchero	—	−3/4	+3/8	1/4	—
F100, F250	—	+3	+1	1/8	4
F100 (4×4)	—	+3½	+1½	1/8	8½
F250 (4×4)	—	+4	+1½	1/8	7½
F350	—	+3	+1½	1/8	4
P350, 3500	—	+4½	+5/8	1/8	4½
P400, 500, 4000, 5000	—	+3½	+1/2	1/8	4½
F-B500 Thru 750	—	+3½ ⑤	+5/8	1/4	4
C500 Thru 750 ①	—	+3	+5/8	1/4	5½
C750 ⑧	—	+3	⑩	1/4	5½
C-CT800 Thru 8000 ⑫	—	+3	⑩	3/8	5½
L Ser. Exc. LN500 ⑥	—	+3¾	+5/8	1/4	5½
L Ser. Exc. LN500 ⑧	—	+4	⑩	3/8	—
LN500	—	+4½ ⑩	⑩	1/4	5½
W-WT9000 ⑫	—	+3	⑩	3/8	—
Center Point Steering	—	+1/2	⑪	1/4	0
1971 MODELS					
Bronco	—	+2½ ⑨	+1½ ⑨	1/8	8½
Econoline, E300	—	+5	+2	3/32	—
Ranchero	—	−3/4	+1/4	1/4	—
E100, E200	—	+3	+2	3/32	—
F100 (4×4)	—	+2½	+1½	1/8	8½
F250 (4×4)	—	+4	+1½	1/8	7½
F600 (4×4)	—	+3	+1	1/8	—
F100, 250	—	+3	+1	3/32	—
F350	—	+3	+1½	3/32	—
P350, 3500	—	+4½	+5/8	1/8	4½
P400, 500, 4000, 5000	—	+3½	⑩	1/8	4½
F-B 500 Thru 750 ⑬	—	+3½	+5/8	1/4	—
F-B 500 Thru 750 ⑭	—	+3½	⑩	1/4	—
C500 Thru 750 ⑥	—	+3	+5/8	1/4	—
C750 ⑧	—	+3	⑩	3/8	—
C-CT 6000, 7000	—	+3	+5/8	1/4	—
C-CT 9000, 12000	—	+3	⑩	3/8	—
C-CT 15000	—	+3	+5/8	3/8	—
L Ser. Exc. LN500-750 ⑥	—	+3¾	+5/8	1/4	—
L Ser. Exc. LN500-750 ⑧	—	+4	+5/8	3/8	—
LN500-750	—	+4½	+5/8	1/4	—
W-WT9000	—	+3½	+3/8	3/8	—
Center Point Steering	—	+1/2	⑪	7/16	—
1972–73 MODELS					
Bronco	—	+3½	+1½ ⑨	1/8	8½
Econoline, E300 1972	—	+5	+2	3/32	—
E300 1973	—	+5	+2	1/32	—
Ranchero 1972	—	+3/4	+3/4	1/4	—
Ranchero 1973	—	+3/4	+3/4	3/8	—
E100, 200 1972	—	+6	+2	3/32	—
E100, 200 1973	—	+4½	+2	1/32	—
F100 (4×4)	—	+3½	+1½ ⑨	1/8	8½
F250 (4×4)	—	+4	+1½ ⑨	1/8	7½
F600 (4×4)	—	+3	+1	1/8	—
F100, 250 1972	—	+6	+1	3/32	—
F100, 250 1973	—	+4½	+1	3/32	—
F350 1972	—	+6	+1½	3/32	—
F-350 1973	—	+4½	+1½	3/32	—
P350, 3500	—	+4½	+5/8	1/8	4½
P400, 500, 4000, 5000	—	+3½	+1/2	1/8	4½
F-B-500 thru 750 ⑬	—	+3½	+5/8	1/4	—
F-B-500 thru 750 ⑭	—	+3½	⑩	3/8	—
C500 thru C750 ⑥	—	+3	+5/8	1/4	—
C750 ⑧	—	+3	⑩	3/8	—
C-CT6000, 7000	—	+3	+5/8	1/4	—
C-CT9000, 12000	—	+3	⑩	3/8	—
C-CT 15000	—	+3	+5/8	3/8	—
L Ser. Exc. LN500-750 ⑥	—	+3¾	+5/8	1/4	—
L Ser. Exc. LN500-750 ⑧	—	+4	+5/8	3/8	—
L Ser. 1200 Conven.	—	+2½	+5/8	1/4	—
LN500-750	—	+4½	+5/8	1/4	—
W-WT9000	—	+3½	⑩	1/4	—
Center Point Steering	1	+1/2	⑪	7/16	—
1974–75 MODELS					
Bronco	—	+3½	+1½ ⑨	5/32	8½
Econoline E300, 350	—	+5	+2	1/32	—
Ranchero 1974	—	+2	⑮	1/8	—
Ranchero 1975	—	+4	⑯	1/8	—
E100, 150, 200, 250	—	+4½	+2	1/32	—
F100 (4×4)	—	+3½	+1½ ⑨	1/8	8½
F250 (4×4)	—	+4	+1½ ⑨	1/8	7½
F600 (4×4)	—	+3	+1	1/8	—
F100, 250	—	+4½	+1	3/32	—
F-350	—	+4½	+1½	3/32	—
P350, 3500	—	+4½	+5/8	1/8	4½
P400, 500, 4000, 5000	—	+3½	+1/2	1/8	4½
F-B-500 thru 750 ⑬	—	+3½	+5/8	1/4	—
F-B-500 thru 750 ⑭	—	+3½	⑩	3/8	—
C500 thru C750 ⑥	—	+3	+5/8	1/4	—
C750 ⑧	—	+3	⑩	3/8	—
C-CT6000, 7000	—	+3	+5/8	1/4	—
C-CT9000, 12000	—	+3	⑩	3/8	—
C-CT15000	—	+3	+5/8	3/8	—
L Ser. Exc. LN500-750 ⑥	—	+3¾	+5/8	1/4	—
L Ser. Exc. LN500-750 ⑧	—	+4	+5/8	3/8	—
L-W-WT Ser. 12000 Conv.	—	+3	+5/8	1/4	—
LN500-750	—	+4½	+5/8	1/4	—
W-WT9000	—	+3½	⑩	1/4	—
Center Point Steering	—	+1/2	⑪	7/16	—
1976 MODELS					
Ranchero	—	+4	⑯	1/8	—
Bronco	—	+4½	+1½	5/32	8½
Econoline E-350	—	+5	+2	1/8	—
E-100, 150, 260	—	+4½	+2	1/8	—
F-100, 250 (4×2)	—	+4½	+1	3/32	—
F-350 (4×2)	—	+4½	+1½	3/32	—
F-100, 150 (4×4)	—	+4½	+1½	5/32	8½
F-250 (4×4)	—	+4	+1½	5/32	7½

Continued

FORD

WHEEL ALIGNMENT SPECIFICATIONS—Continued

Truck Model	Front Axle Code	Caster Deg.	Camber Deg.	Toe-In Inch	Kingpin Angle Deg.
P-350	—	+4 1/2	+5/8	1/8	4 1/2
P-400, 500	—	+3 1/2	+1/2	1/8	4 1/2
F-600 (4×4)	—	+3	+1	1/8	—
F-B-500 thru 750 ⑬	—	+3 1/2	+5/8	1/4	—
F-B-500 thru 750 ⑭	—	+3 1/2	⑩	3/8	—
C-600 thru 750 ⑥	—	+3	+5/8	1/4	—
C-600 thru 750 ⑧	—	+3	⑩	3/8	—
LN-600-750 ⑬	—	+4 1/2	+5/8	1/4	—
LN-600-750 ⑭	—	+4 1/2	⑩	3/8	—
L Ser 800-9000 ⑥	—	+3 3/4	+5/8	1/4	—
L Ser 800-9000 ⑱	—	㉙	+5/8	3/8	—
C Series 800 thru 8000	—	+3	⑩	⑲	—
W-Wt-9000	—	+3	⑩	1/4	—

1977 MODELS

Truck Model	Front Axle Code	Caster Deg.	Camber Deg.	Toe-In Inch	Kingpin Angle Deg.
F-250 ⑳	—	4	1	5/32	—
F-150 ⑳㉑	—	3 1/2	1 1/2	3/16	—
P-500	—	3 1/2	1/2	1/8	—
F-500-600, LN-600 ㉒	—	㉔	5/8	1/4	—
B-500, F-C-B-LN-600-750, LT-LNT-800, LT-880, F-C-LN-6000, F-B-C-7000, L800-900, LN-800 ㉓	—	㉕	5/8	1/4	—
F-600-700, B-LN-600-700, LN-F-B-750, F-B-LN-7000, F-880 ㉒	—	㉖	5/8	3/8	—
F-C-L-LN-750-7000, LT-880, CT-LN-LNT-800, C-L-LT-LTS-800-900 ㉓	—	㉗	㉝	3/8	—
F-LN-750-7000, F-880 ㉒	—	㉙	5/8	3/8	—
L-LT-LN-LNT-800, L-LN-LNT,8000, LNT-9000, L-LN-LNT-900, C-7000, F-LNT-880, L-600-700-750 ㉒	—	㉘	5/8	3/8	—
L-LT-LTS-LN-LNT-800-900-8000-9000, LT-LNT-880, C-750-800-900-7000-8000, CT-800-900-8000 ㉒	—	㉚	5/8	3/8	—
L-LT-LTS-LN-LNT-C-CT-800-900-L-LT-LTS-LN-LNT-8000-9000, LNT-LT-880, C-8000, CT-8000, W-WT-9000 ㉒	—	㉛	5/8	1/4	—
C-900, CT-800-900, CT-8000, LT-800-900, LTS-800-900, LT-LTS-8000-9000, LN-LNT-800-900-8000-9000 ㉒	—	㉜	5/8	3/8	—
F-100/150 (4×2), F-250, 6200-6900 GVW	—	6 1/2	1	1/8	—
F-250, 7800-8000 GVW, F-250 Supercab (4×2)	—	5 7/8	1 5/8	1/8	—
F-350, F-250, F-350 Crew CAB, F-250, 8100 GVW S.C.	—	6 1/8	1 7/8	1/8	—
E-100/150	—	3 7/8	1/2	1/8	—
E-250/350	—	6 1/2	7/8	1/8	—

1978 MODELS

Truck Model	Front Axle Code	Caster Deg.	Camber Deg.	Toe-In Inch	Kingpin Angle Deg.
F-150 ⑳㉑	—	+4	+1 1/2	3/32	8 1/2
F-250 ⑳	—	+8	+1 1/2	3/32	8 1/2
P-600	—	+3 1/2	+1/2	1/8	4 1/2
F-600, LN-600 ㉓	—	㉔	+5/8	1/4	—
B-600, F-C-B-LN-600-700, LT-LNT-800, LT-800, F-C-LN-6000, F-B-C-7000, L-800-900, LN-800 ㉓	—	㉕	+5/8	1/4	—
F-600-700, B-LN-600-700, LN-F-B-700, F-B-LN-700, F-800 ㉒	—	㉖	5/8	3/8	—
F-C-L-LN-700-7000, LT-800, C-L-LT-LTS-800-900, CT-LN-LNT-800 ㉓	—	㉗	㉝	3/8	—
L-LT-LN-LNT-800, L-LN-LNT-8000, LNT-9000, L-LN-LNT-900, F-LT-LNT-800, C-600-700, C-7000 ㉒	—	㉘	5/8	3/8	—
F-LN-700, 7000, F-800 ㉒	—	㉙	5/8	3/8	—
L-LT-LTS-LN-LNT-800-900-8000-9000, LT-LNT-800, C-700-800-900-7000-8000, CT-800-900-8000 ㉒	—	㉚	5/8	3/8	—
L-LT-LTS-LN-LNT-C-CT-800-900, L-LT-LTS-LN-LNT-8000-9000, LNT-LT-800, CT-8000, C-8000 ㉒	—	㉛	5/8	1/4	—
C-900, CT-800-900, CT-8000, LT-800-900, LTS-LN-LNT-8000-9000, LNT-LT-800, CT-8000, C-8000 ㉒	—	㉜	5/8	* 1/4	—
CL-CLT-9000 ㉒	—	3 1/4	5/8	1/4	—
F-100/150/250/350	—	②	②	②	—
E-100/150/250/350	—	②	②	②	—

1979 MODELS

Truck Model	Front Axle Code	Caster Deg.	Camber Deg.	Toe-In Inch	Kingpin Angle Deg.
F-250-350 ⑳	—	+4	+1 1/2	3/32	8 1/2
F-150 ③	—	+4	+1 1/2	3/32	8 1/2
F-150 ⑳㉑	—	+8	+1 1/2	3/32	8 1/2
P-600	—	+3 1/2	+1/2	1/8	4 1/2
F-600, LN-600 ㉓	—	㉔	5/8	1/4	—
B-600, F-C-B-LN-600-700, LT-LNT-800, F-C-LN-6000, F-B-C-7000, L-800, 900, LN-800 ㉓	—	㉕	5/8	1/4	—
F-600-700, B-LN-600-700, LN-F-B-700, F-B-LN-7000, F-800 ㉒	—	㉖	5/8	3/8	—
F-C-L-LN-700-7000, C-L-LT-LTS-800-900, CT-LN-LNT-800 ㉓	—	㉗	㉝	3/8	—

Continued

FORD

WHEEL ALIGNMENT SPECIFICATIONS—Continued

Truck Model	Front Axle Code	Caster Deg.	Camber Deg.	Toe-In Inch	Kingpin Angle Deg.
L-LN-LNT-800-8000, LT-800, LNT-9000, L-LN-LNT-900, F-LT-LNT-800, C-600-700, C-7000㉒	—	㉘	5/8	3/8	—
F-LN-700-7000, F-800㉒	—	㉙	5/8	3/8	—
LT-LTS-LN-LNT-800-900-8000-9000, LT-LNT-800, C-700-800-900-7000-8000, CT-800-900-8000㉒	—	㉚	5/8	3/8	—
LT-LTS-LN-LNT-C-CT-800-900, L-LT-LTS-LN-LNT-8000-9000, LNT-LT-800, C-CT-8000, W-WT-9000㉒	—	㉛	5/8	1/4	—
C-900, CT-800-900, CT-8000, LT-800, 900, LTS-LN-LNT-8000-9000, LNT-LT-800, C-8000, CT-8000㉒	—	㉜	5/8	3/8	—
CL-CLT-9000㉒	—	3 1/4	5/8	1/4	—
F-100-150-250-350	—	②	②	②	—
E-100-150-250-350	—	②	②	②	—

1980 MODELS

Truck Model	Front Axle Code	Caster Deg.	Camber Deg.	Toe-In Inch	Kingpin Angle Deg.
F-100-150-250-350	—	②	②	②	8
E-100-150-250-350	—	②	②	②	—
F-150⑳㉑	—	②	②	②	13
F-250-350⑳	—	②	②	②	13
F-600, LN-600㉓	—	㉔	+5/8	1/4	—
F-C-B-LN-600-700, LT-LNT-800, F-C-LN-6000, C-7000, L-800-900, LN-800㉓	—	㉕	+5/8	1/4	—
F-B-LN-600-700, LN-7000, F-800㉒	—	㉖	+5/8	3/8	—
F-C-L-LN-700-7000, C-L-LT-LTS-800-900, CT-LN-LNT-800㉓	—	㉗	㉝	3/8	—
F-L-LT-LN-LNT-800, LNT-9000, L-LN-LNT-8000, L-LN-LNT-900, C-600-700, C-7000㉒	—	㉘	5/8	3/8	—
F-LN-700, F-800, LN-7000㉒	—	㉙	5/8	3/8	—
L-LT-LTS-LN-LNT-800-900-8000-9000, C-700-800-900-7000-8000, CT-800-900-8000㉒	—	㉚	5/8	3/8	—
L-LT-LTS-LN-LNT-C-CT-800-900, L-LT-LTS-LN-LNT-8000-9000, C-CT-8000, W-WT-9000㉒	—	㉛	5/8	1/4	—
C-900, LT-CT-800-900, CT-8000, LTS-LN-LNT-8000-9000, LNT-LT-800, C-CT-8000㉒	—	㉜	5/8	3/8	—
CL-CLT-9000㉒	—	3 1/4	5/8	1/4	—

①—Left side 3/4°, right 1/4°.
②—Refer to Front End Section of this chapter.
③—Super cab.
④—Power Steering 7 1/2°.
⑤—Power Steering 6 1/2°.
⑥—With 6000 and 7000 lb. capacity axle.
⑦—Power Steering 7°.
⑧—With 9000 and 12000 Lb. capacity axle.
⑨—Designed into axle and not adjustable.
⑩—Left side +3/8, right side −1/8.
⑪—Left side +1/2, right side zero.
⑫—Except center point steering.
⑬—With 5000–7000 lb. capacity axle.
⑭—With 9000 lb. capacity axle.
⑮—Left side +1/2°, right side +1/8°.
⑯—Left side +1/2°, right side +1/4°.
⑰—With 9000 lb. capacity axle +4; with 12000 lb. capacity axle +2 1/2; With 16000, 18000, 20000 lb. capacity axles +3 1/2.
⑱—With 9000, 12000, 16000, 18000, 20000 lb. capacity axles.
⑲—With 7000 lb. capacity axle 1/4; With 9000 lb. capacity axle and above, 3/8.
⑳—4-wheel drive.
㉑—Bronco.
㉒—Air brakes.
㉓—Hydraulic brakes.
㉔—F-B series, 3 1/2°; LN series, 4 1/2°.
㉕—F-B series, 3 1/2°; LN series medium 4 1/2°; L-LN series heavy 3 3/4°; C series, 3°.
㉖—F-B series, 3°; L series, 3 1/2°.
㉗—Exc. C series, 4°; C series, 3°.
㉘—C series w/9.5 frame, 2°51′; C series w/9.76 frame, 4 1/2°; L series exc. drop frame, 5°; LN-LNT series w/drop frame, 3 1/2°.
㉙—F-B series, 3°; LN series, 3 1/2°.
㉚—L series exc. drop frame, 5°; LN-LNT w/drop frame, 3 1/2°; C series w/9.5 frame, 2°51′; C series w/9.76 frame, 4 1/2°.
㉛—C series w/9.5 frame & L-W series w/2° wedge, 3°; L series w/drop frame 3 1/2°; C series w/9.76 frame, 4 1/2°.
㉜—C series w/16000 axle, 3°; all w/16000-18000-20000 axles exc. C series, 3 1/2°.
㉝—C series LH, 3/8°; C series RH, −1/8°; exc. C series, 5/8°.

Ford Engine Section

CYLINDER HEAD, REPLACE

V8-401, 477, 534

1. Remove intake manifold.
2. Remove push rod cover and rocker arm covers.
3. Disconnect muffler inlet pipes at exhaust manifolds.
4. Release spring tension on rocker arms by loosening adjusting screws.
5. Remove rocker arm shaft and oil baffle plate. *Because five cylinder head bolts also serve as pedestals for the rocker arm shaft, each time the rocker arm assembly is removed, a new cylinder head gasket must be installed.*
6. Remove push rods, keeping them in proper sequence so they may be installed in original location.
7. Remove remaining cylinder head bolts and lift off head.
8. Install heads in the reverse order of removal and tighten bolts in the sequence shown in Fig. 1 to the torque given in the *Engine Tightening Chart*.

V8-370, 429, 460

1. Remove intake manifold and disconnect exhaust pipe from exhaust manifold.
2. Loosen air conditioner drive belt (if equipped), then loosen alternator bolts and remove the bolt attaching alternator bracket to cylinder head.
3. If equipped with air conditioning, shut off compressor service valves and remove valves and hoses from compressor then remove compressor and place out of way. Remove compressor upper mounting bracket from cylinder head.
4. If not equipped with air conditioning, remove bolts attaching power steering reservoir bracket to left cylinder head and position reservoir and bracket out of the way.
5. On 1970 V8-429 engines, back off adjusting nuts, turn rocker arms to one side and remove push rods. On V8-370, 460 and 1971-79 V8-429 engines, remove rocker arm bolts, rocker arms, oil deflectors, fulcrums and push rods.

NOTE: Keep all parts in sequence so that they can be reinstalled in their original locations.

6. Remove cylinder head bolts taking note as to the length of each bolt and remove the cylinder head.

NOTE: If necessary to loosen cylinder head gasket seal, pry at forward corners of cylinder head and against casting provided on cylinder block.

7. Install heads in the reverse order of removal and torque cylinder head bolts in three steps and in the sequence shown in Fig. 1. Final tightening should be to the torque listed in the Engine Tightening Table. Torque intake manifold bolts to torque spec given in Engine Tightening Table and in sequence shown in Fig. 1A.

V8-330, 360, 361, 389, 390, 391, 427

1. Remove intake manifold and carburetor as a unit.
2. Disconnect exhaust manifolds at exhaust pipes.
3. If left head is being removed, remove ignition coil.
4. Unfasten and lift off head.
5. Install heads in the reverse order of removal and torque cylinder head bolts in three steps and in the sequence shown in Fig. 1. Final tightening should be to the torque listed in the Engine Tightening Specifications chart. Torque intake manifold bolts to torque specs given in Engine Tightening Specifications chart and in sequence shown in Fig. 1B.

V8-302, V8-351 & 400

1. Remove intake manifold and rocker arm

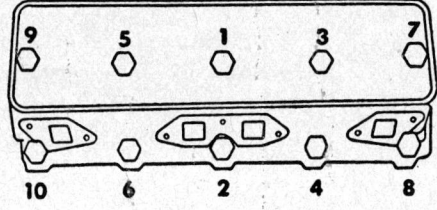

Fig. 1 Cylinder head tightening sequence. V8 engines

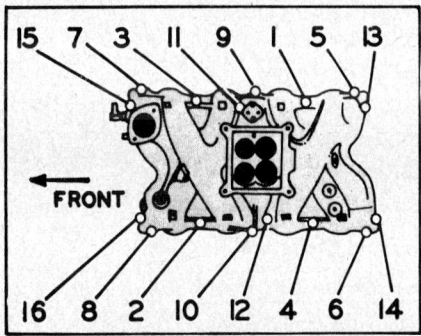

Fig. 1A Intake manifold tightening sequence. V8-370, 429 & 460

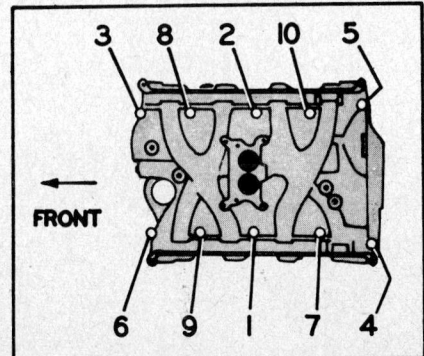

Fig. 1B Intake manifold tightening sequence. V8-330, 360, 361, 389, 390, 391 & 427

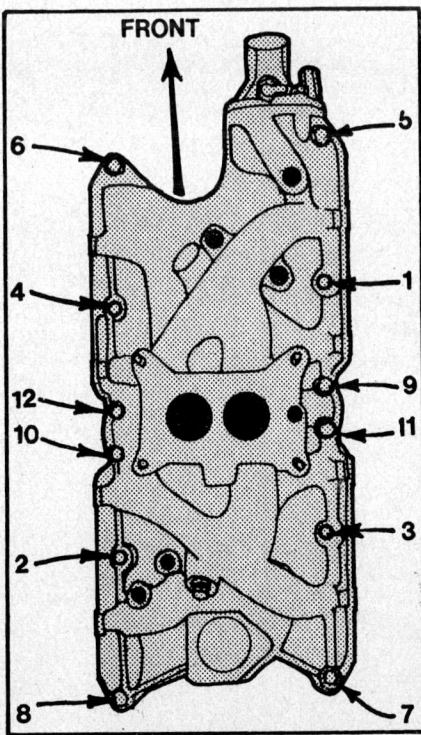

Fig. 1C Intake manifold tightening sequence. V8-302 & 1976-80 V8-351W

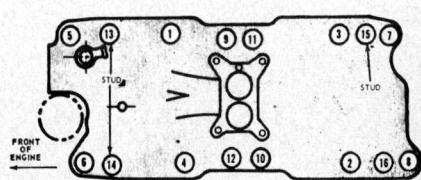

Fig. 1D Intake manifold tightening sequence. 1970-75 V8-351W

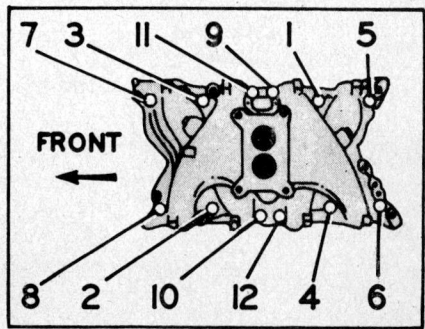

Fig. 1E Intake manifold tightening sequence. V8-351C, 351M & 400

Ford

covers.

2. If removing right cylinder head, loosen alternator adjusting arm and remove alternator mounting bracket and spacer then swing alternator down. On Bronco and Econoline models, remove ignition coil and air cleaner inlet duct from right cylinder head.
3. If removing left cylinder head, remove accelerator shaft assembly from front of cylinder head.
4. Disconnect exhaust pipes from exhaust manifolds.
5. Loosen rocker arm stud nuts or bolts and remove push rods in sequence so that they can be installed in their original locations.
6. On V-8-302, remove exhaust valve stem caps.
7. Remove the cylinder head bolts and cylinder head.
8. Install cylinder heads in the reverse order of removal and torque cylinder head bolts in three steps and in sequence shown in Fig. 1. Final tightening should be to the torque listed in the Engine Tightening Table. Torque intake manifold bolts to torque specs given in Engine Tightening Table and in sequence shown in Figs. 1C, 1D and 1E.

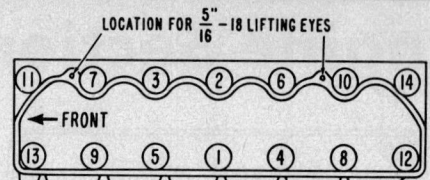

Fig. 2 Cylinder head tightening sequence. 6-240, 300

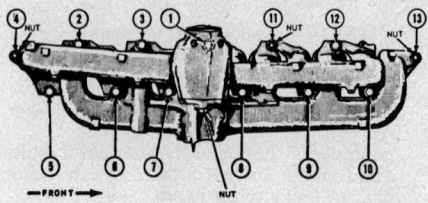

Fig. 2A Intake & exhaust manifold tightening sequence. 6-240 & 300

6-240, 300

1. Drain cooling system. On Econoline, remove right front seat and engine compartment cover.
2. Remove air cleaner.
3. Remove PCV valve from rocker arm cover, and disconnect vent hose at intake manifold inlet tube.
4. Disconnect hoses, wires, carburetor linkage, fuel and vacuum lines as necessary for removal of head.
5. Disconnect exhaust pipe from manifold.
6. Unfasten and position coil to one side.
   a. If equipped with Thermactor, remove air tube and vacuum hose from anti-backfire and intake manifold. Disconnect air pump outlet hoses at air manifold and at anti-backfire valve. Disconnect air pump to air cleaner hose at the pump. Remove the air pump and air manifold assembly from the cylinder head. Remove the air cleaner and mounting bracket assembly, exhaust manifold heat shield, air pump mounting bracket and anti-backfire valve and bracket assembly.
7. Remove valve rocker arm cover.
8. Loosen rocker arm stud nuts so that rocker arms can be rotated to one side.
9. Remove valve push rods, keeping them in proper sequence so they may be installed in their original locations.
10. Remove cylinder head bolts and use a lifting sling to remove cylinder head with manifolds attached.
11. Reverse procedure to install and tighten head bolts in three steps and in the sequence shown in Fig. 2 to the torque listed in the Engine Tightening Table. Torque intake manifold bolts to torque specs given in Engine Tightening Table and in sequence shown in Fig. 2A.

6-170, 200 & 250

1. Drain cooling system.
2. Remove air cleaner.
3. Disconnect upper radiator hose at engine.
4. Disconnect exhaust pipe from manifold.
5. Disconnect accelerator retracting spring choke control cable and accelerator rod at carburetor.
6. Disconnect fuel line and distributor vacuum line at carburetor.
7. Disconnect coolant lines at carburetor spacer.
8. Disconnect distributor vacuum line at distributor and carburetor fuel line at the fuel pump and remove lines as an assembly.
9. Disconnect plug wires at the spark plugs and temperature sending unit wire at the sending unit.
10. Remove PCV valve from rocker arm cover and disconnect vent hose at intake manifold inlet tube.
11. If equipped with Thermactor, remove hoses from Thermactor system as necessary for accessibility.
12. Remove rocker arm cover.
13. Remove the rocker arm shaft support bolts and remove rocker shaft assembly.
14. Remove valve push rods, keeping them in proper sequence so they may be installed in their original locations.
15. Remove cylinder head bolts and remove the cylinder head.
16. Reverse procedure to install head and tighten head bolts in three steps and in the sequence shown in Fig. 3 to the torque listed in the Engine Tightening Table.

VALVE ARRANGEMENT
Front to Rear

6-240, 300	E-I-E-I-E-I-E-I-E-I-E-I
6-170, 200, 250	E-I-I-E-I-E-I-E-I-I-E
V8-302 Left Bank	E-I-E-I-E-I-E-I
V8-302 Right Bank	I-E-I-E-I-E-I-E
V8-330, 361, 391	E-I-E-I-I-E-I-E
V8-351, 400 Right Bank	I-E-I-E-I-E-I-E

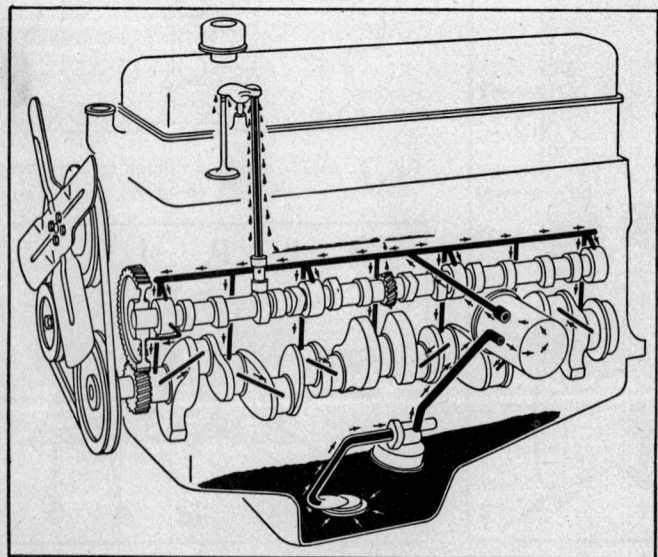

Engine oiling system. 6-240, 6-300

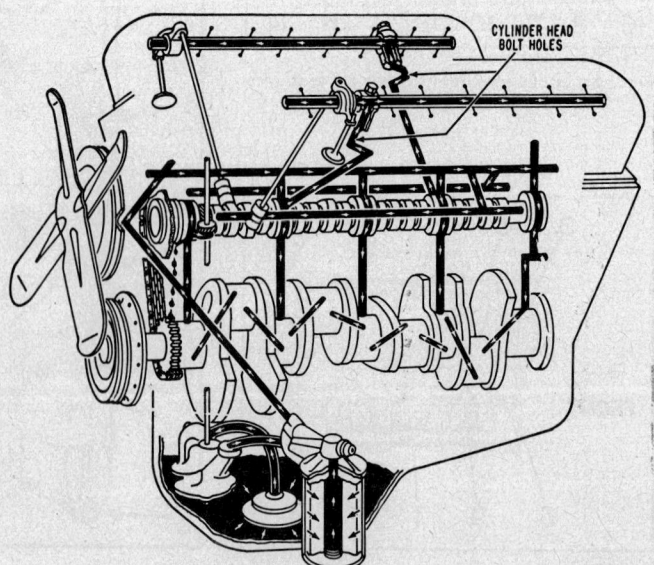

Engine lubrication V8-330, 332, 360, 361, 390, 391, 427

Ford

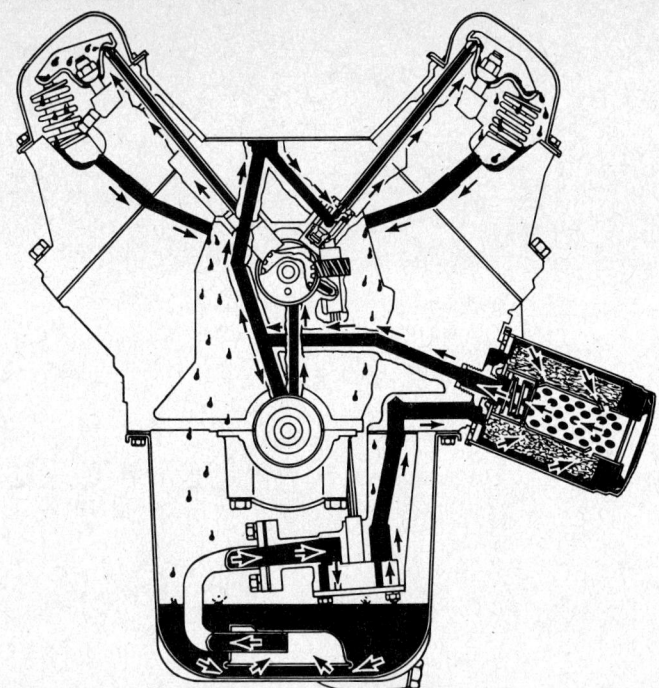
Engine oiling system. V8-302, 351, 400

of 7 ft. lbs. with the oversize screw, replace the rocker arm and adjusting screw assembly.

Non-Adjustable Rocker Arms

The push rod of the non-adjustable rocker arm has a spherical push rod socket instead of an adjusting screw. The push rods are available in standard size, .060" undersize and .060" oversize.

Valve clearance is checked by compressing the push rod end of the rocker arm until the valve lifter plunger is completely bottomed. While holding the lifter in the fully collapsed position, check the available clearance between the rocker arm and valve stem. If the clearance is less than .067", install undersize push rod. If clearance is more than .200", install an oversize push rod.

6-240, 300

1970–78

NOTE: Before adjusting valves, check breakaway torque (torque required to turn nut in a counterclockwise direction) of stud nut. If breakaway torque is less than 4.5–15 ft. lbs., replace the stud nut. If breakaway torque is still not within specifications, replace the stud.

Starting with No. 1 cylinder, position each piston at TDC compression stroke as described previously. With No. 1 piston at TDC compression stroke, adjust intake and exhaust valve clearance for that cylinder by loosening the stud nut until there is clearance between the push rod and rocker arm, then tighten stud nut just enough to remove all rocker arm clearance. This may be determined by rotating and/or moving the push rod as the stud nut is tightened. When clearance has been eliminated, tighten stud nut one additional turn.

Follow the firing order and repeat the above procedure for the remaining valves with piston of cylinder at TDC compression stroke.

1979–80

NOTE: Before adjusting valves, check break-

V8-351, 400 Left Bank	E-I-E-I-E-I-E-I
V8-360, 389, 390, 427	E-I-E-I-I-E-I-E
V8-401, 477, 534	E-I-E-I-I-E-I-E
V8-370, 429, 460 Left Bank	E-I-E-I-E-I-E-I
V8-370, 429, 460 Right Bank	I-E-I-E-I-E-I-E

VALVES, ADJUST

6-170, 200, 250

Rotate crankshaft to place No. 1 piston at TDC of its compression stroke and adjust the following valves:

No. 1 Intake   No. 3 Exhaust
No. 1 Exhaust   No. 4 Intake
No. 2 Intake   No. 5 Exhaust

Rotate crankshaft one full revolution to place No. 6 piston at TDC compression and adjust the remaining valves:

No. 2 Exhaust   No. 5 Intake
No. 3 Intake   No. 6 Intake
No. 4 Exhaust   No. 6 Exhaust

Adjustable Rocker Arms

Turn rocker arm adjusting screw to obtain proper valve adjustment as listed in *Valve Specifications* table.

NOTE: If the torque required to tighten the self-locking adjusting screw is less than 3 ft. lbs., install a new standard or .002" oversize screw. If unable to obtain a minimum torque

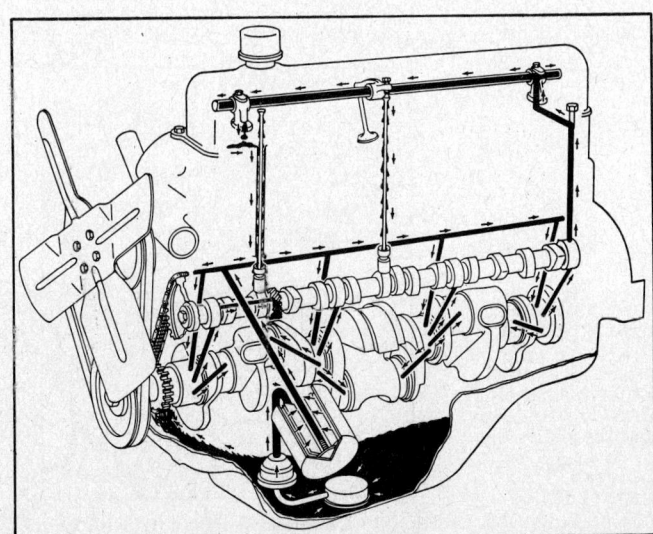
Engine oiling diagram. 170, 200, 250

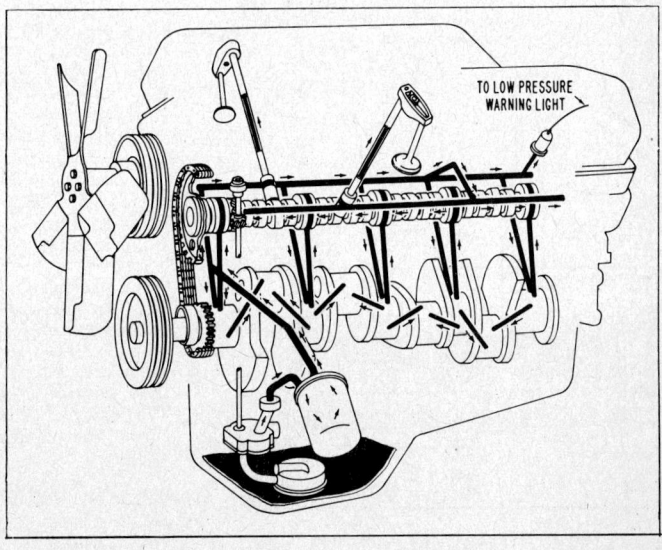
Engine oiling system. V8-429, 460

FORD

away torque (torque required to turn nut in a counterclockwise direction) of stud nut. If breakaway torque is less than 4.5-15 ft. lbs., replace the stud nut. If breakaway torque is still not within specifications, replace the stud nut. Also, for these engines, a .060 inch shorter push rod or .060 inch longer push rod is available to compensate for dimensional changes in the valve mechanism and provide for valve adjustment.

Starting with No. 1 cylinder, position each piston at TDC compression stroke as described previously. With No. 1 piston at TDC compression stroke, install and torque stud nut to 17-23 ft. lbs. Using a suitable tool, Fig. 3A, slowly apply pressure to bleed down the lifter until the plunger is completely bottomed. While holding the lifter in this position, check clearance between rocker arm and valve. If clearance is not as specified in the VALVE SPECIFICATIONS CHART, install a longer or shorter push rod as necessary to bring clearance within specifications.

Follow the firing order and repeat the above procedure for the remaining valves with piston of cylinder at TDC compression stroke.

V8-427

Position the piston of the cylinder being checked at TDC, then using tool 6513 or equivalent, apply pressure to the rocker arm to slowly bleed down the valve lifter until it is fully collapsed. With the lifter fully collapsed, check the valve clearance. If the clearance is not within specifications, turn the adjusting nut as required to obtain the desired clearance.

NOTE: One turn of the adjusting nut will change the valve clearance by about .066 inch.

All V8's With Hydraulic Lifters Exc. V8-427

To provide a means to compensate for dimensional changes in the valve train and provide for valve adjustment, .060 inch shorter or longer push rods are available. If the valve clearance is less than the minimum, the .060 inch shorter push rod should be used. If the clearance is more than the maximum, the longer push rod should be used. To check the valve clearance, proceed as follows:

1970-73 V8-429, 1970-80 V8-302, 351, 400 & 460

1. Mark crankshaft pulley at three locations, with number 1 location at TDC timing mark (end of compression stroke), number 2 location one half turn (180°)

clockwise from TDC and number 3 location three quarter turn clockwise (270°) from position number 2.
2. Turn crankshaft to number 1 location, then compress valve lifter using tool T71P-6513-A or equivalent, Fig. 3A, and check the clearance on the following valves:

V8-302, 351W, 460 & 1970-73 V8-429
No. 1 Intake   No. 1 Exhaust
No. 7 Intake   No. 5 Exhaust
No. 8 Intake   No. 4 Exhaust

V8-351C, 351M, 400
No. 1 Intake   No. 1 Exhaust
No. 4 Intake   No. 3 Exhaust
No. 8 Intake   No. 7 Exhaust

3. Turn crankshaft to number 2 location, then compress valve lifter using tool T71P-6513-A or equivalent, Fig. 3A, and check the clearance on the following valves:

V8-302, 351W, 460 & 1970-73 V8-429
No. 4 Intake   No. 2 Exhaust
No. 5 Intake   No. 6 Exhaust

V8-351C, 351M, 400
No. 3 Intake   No. 2 Exhaust
No. 7 Intake   No. 6 Exhaust

4. Turn crankshaft to number 3 location, then compress valve lifter using tool T70P-6513-A or equivalent, Fig. 3A, and check the clearance on the following valves:

V8-302, 351W, 460 & 1970-73 V8-429
No. 2 Intake   No. 3 Exhaust
No. 3 Intake   No. 7 Exhaust
No. 6 Intake   No. 8 Exhaust

V8-351C, 351M, 400
No. 2 Intake   No. 4 Exhaust
No. 5 Intake   No. 5 Exhaust
No. 6 Intake   No. 8 Exhaust

All V8-330, 359, 360, 361, 370, 389, 390, 391 & 1979 V8-429

1. Turn the engine until number 1 piston is at TDC and at the end of its compression stroke and check the clearance on the following valves after compressing the valve lifter using tool T58P-6565-A, Fig. 3A, or equivalent:

No. 1 Intake   No. 1 Exhaust
No. 3 Intake   No. 4 Exhaust
No. 7 Intake   No. 5 Exhaust
No. 8 Intake   No. 8 Exhaust

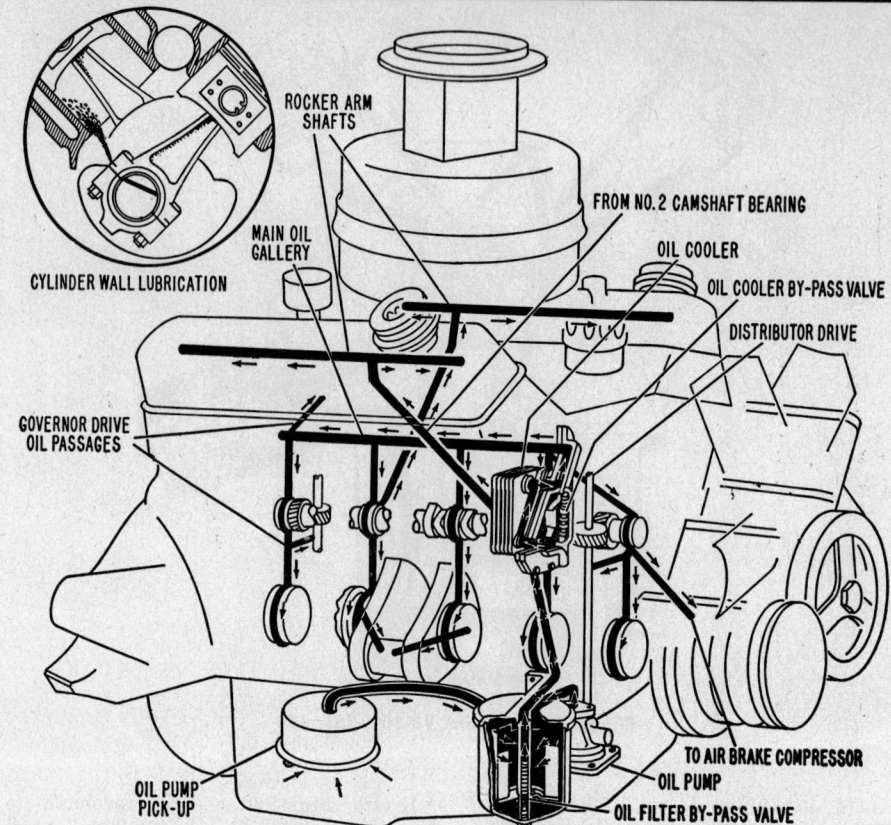

Engine lubrication. V8-401, 477, 534 engines

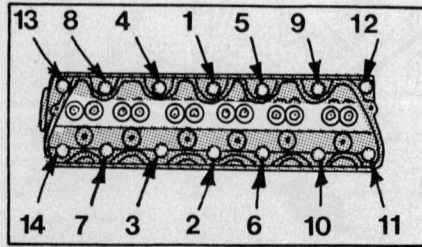

Fig. 3 Cylinder head tightening sequence. 6-170, 200, 250

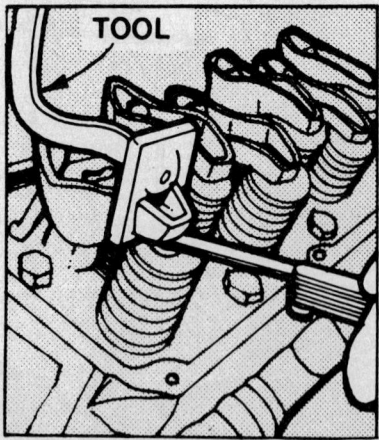

Fig. 3A Compressing valve lifter with tool to check clearance on engines with hydraulic valve lifters.

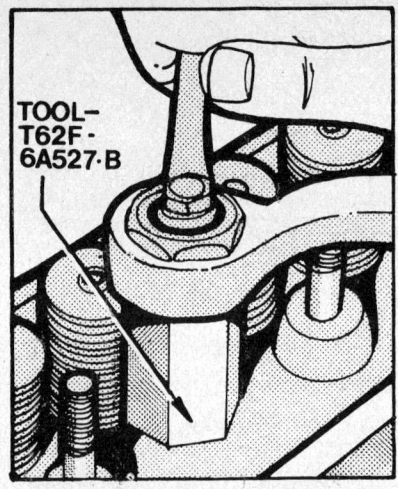

Fig. 4 Rocker arm stud removal.
6-240, 300, V8-302, 1970–77 & Early 1978
V8-302, 1975–77 & Early 1978 V8-351W

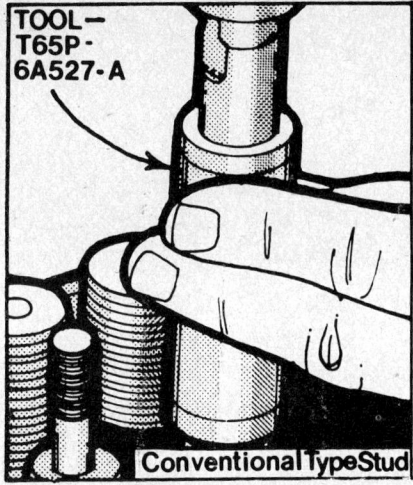

Fig. 5 Rocker arm stud installation. 6-240 300

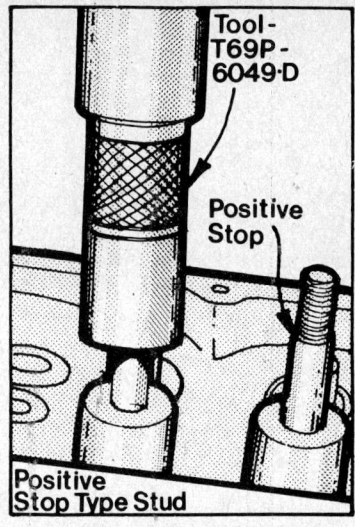

Fig. 6 Rocker arm stud installation.
1970–77 & Early 1978
V8-302, 1975–77 & Early
1978 V8-351W

2. Turn the crankshaft one complete turn (360°) to position number 6 cylinder at TDC and at the end of its compression stroke and check the clearance on the following valves after compressing valve lifter using tool T58P-6565-A, Fig. 3A, or equivalent:

No. 2 Intake   No. 2 Exhaust
No. 4 Intake   No. 3 Exhaust
No. 5 Intake   No. 6 Exhaust
No. 6 Intake   No. 7 Exhaust

V8's With Mechanical Lifters

Make three chalk marks on the vibration damper. Space the marks 90 degrees apart (1/4 of circumference) so that with the timing mark, the damper is divided into four equal parts. Rotate the crankshaft until No. 1 piston is near TDC at the end of the compression stroke and adjust the following valves:

No. 1 intake and exhaust
No. 2 intake
No. 4 exhaust
No. 5 exhaust
No. 7 intake

Rotate the crankshaft 180 degrees (1/2 turn) which puts No. 4 piston on TDC. Then adjust the following valves:

No. 4 intake
No. 5 intake
No. 6 exhaust
No. 8 exhaust

Rotate the crankshaft 270 degrees (3/4 turn), which puts No. 3 piston on TDC. Then adjust the following valves:

No. 2 exhaust
No. 3 intake and exhaust
No. 6 intake
No. 7 exhaust
No. 8 intake

VALVE GUIDES

Valve guides in these engines are an integral part of the head and, therefore, cannot be removed. For service, guides can be reamed oversize to accommodate one of three service valves with oversize stems (.003", .015" and .030").

Check the valve stem clearance of each valve (after cleaning) in its respective valve guide. If the clearance exceeds the service limits of .004" of the intake or .005" on the exhaust, ream the valve guides to accommodate the next oversize diameter valve.

ROCKER ARM STUD

6-240, 300, & V8-302, 351W Exc. Late 1978 & 1979–80

If necessary to replace a rocker arm stud, a rocker arm stud kit is available and contains a stud remover, a stud installer, and two reamers, one .006" and the other .015".

Rocker arm studs that are broken or have damaged threads may be replaced with standard studs. Loose studs in the head may be replaced with .006", .010" or .015" oversize studs which are available for service.

When going from a standard size stud to a .015" oversize stud, always use a .006" reamer and a .010" reamer before finish reaming with a .015" reamer.

If a stud is broken off flush with the stud boss, use an easy-out to remove the broken stud, following the instructions of the tool manufacturer.

Remove stud with tool T62F-6A527-B, Fig. 4. On 6-240-300 and V8-289 and 1968-early 1969 V8-302, install new stud with tool T65P-6A527-A, Fig. 5. On late 1969, 1970–77 and early 1978 V8-302 and all V8-351W, install new stud with tool T69P-6049-D, Fig. 6.

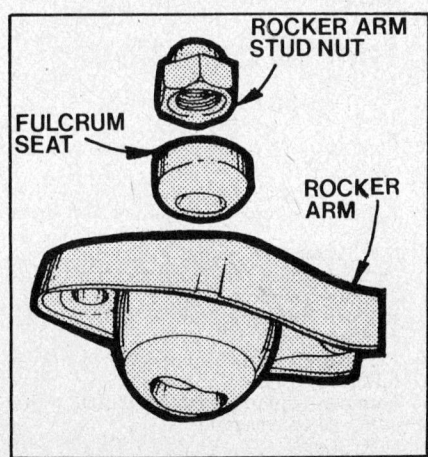

Fig. 7 Rocker arm assembly. 6-240, 300, 1970–71 V8-429, 1970–77 & Early 1978 V8-302, 1975–77 & Early 1978 V8-351W

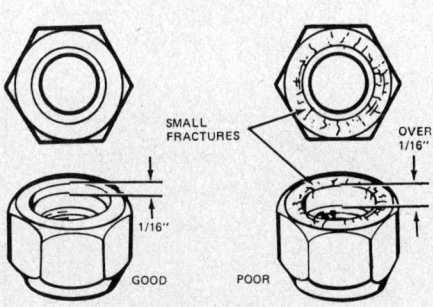

Fig. 7A Inspection of rocker arm stud nut. Except Late 1978 & 1979–80 V8-302 & 351W

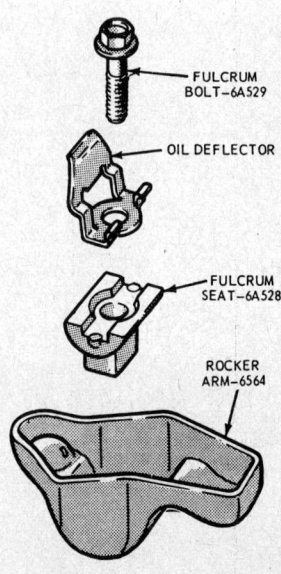

Fig. 8 Rocker arm assembly. V8-351C, 351M, 370, 400, 460, 1972–73 429, 1979 429

FORD

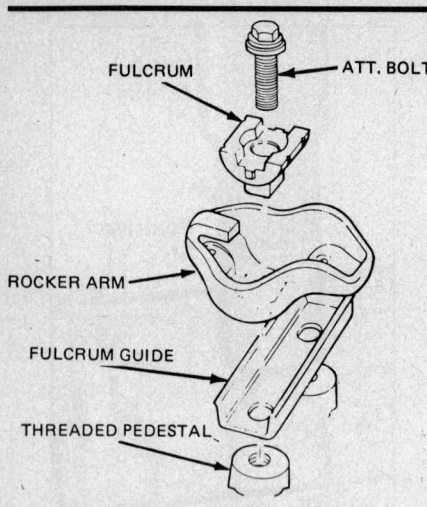

Fig. 8A Rocker arm assembly. Late 1978 & 1979-80 V8-302 & 351W

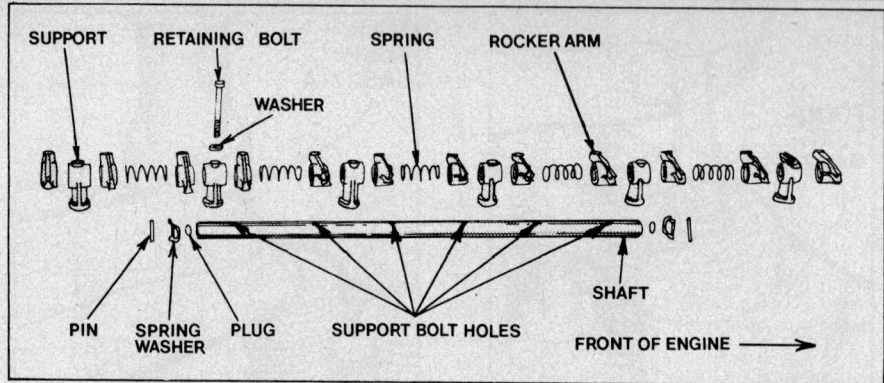

Fig. 9 Rocker arm shaft assembly. 6-170, 200, 250

1970-71 V8-429 & V8-302, 351W Exc. Late 1978 & 1979-80

These engines use a rocker arm stud and nut. To disassemble, remove rocker arm nut, fulcrum seat and rocker arm, Fig. 7. Inspect condition of nut, Fig. 7A, and replace if necessary.

ROCKER ARM & FULCRUM

Late 1978 & 1979-80 V8-302 & 351W, 1972-73 & 1979 V8-429 & All V8-351C, 370, 400 & 460

The rocker arm is supported by a fulcrum bolt which fits through the fulcrum seat and threads into the cylinder head. To disassemble, remove the bolt, oil deflector, fulcrum seat and rocker arm, Figs. 8 and 8A.

ROCKER ARMS & SHAFTS

To disassemble the rocker arms, remove cotter pins from each end of the shaft and remove the flat washers and spring washers. Slide rocker arms, springs and supports off shaft, being sure to identify all parts so they can be assembled in the same position.

If it is necessary to remove the plugs from each end of the shaft, drill or pierce one plug, then insert a steel rod through the plug and knock out the plug on the opposite end. Working from the open end, knock out the remaining plug.

Assemble the rocker arms and related parts as indicated by Figs. 9 to 11.

HYDRAULIC VALVE LIFTERS

Hydraulic Lifters, Fig. 12 Replace

6-170, 200 & 250
1. Remove cylinder head assembly.
2. Using a magnet, remove and install one lifter at a time.

NOTE: If lifters are stuck in their bores by excessive varnish or gum, it may be necessary to use a plier-type tool to remove them. Rotate the lifter back and forth to loosen the gum and varnish which may have formed on the lifter.

6-240, 300
1. Remove valve rocker arm cover.
2. Remove valve push rod cover.
3. Loosen rocker arm stud nuts until rocker arms can be disengaged from push rods.
4. Remove push rods, keeping them in a rack so they may be installed in their original location.
5. Remove valve lifters, using a magnet rod. Place lifters in a rack so they may be installed in their original location.

ALL V8's WITH ROCKER ARM SHAFTS
1. Remove intake manifold.
2. Remove rocker arms and shafts.
3. Remove push rods, keeping them in a rack in sequence so they may be installed in their original location.
4. Remove valve lifters with a magnet rod and place them in a rack in sequence so they may be installed in original location.
5. Reverse procedure to install.

V8-302, 351, 370, 400, 1979 429 & 460
1. Remove intake manifold.
2. Remove rocker arm covers. Loosen rocker arm stud nuts or bolts and rotate rocker arms to the side.
3. Remove push rods in sequence so they can be installed in their original bores.
4. Using a magnet, remove the lifters and place them in a numbered rack so they can be installed in their original bores. If lifters are stuck in their bores, it may be necessary to use a plier-type tool to remove them.
5. The internal parts of each lifter are matched sets. Do not intermix parts.

TIMING CASE COVER

V8-302, 351 & 400

1. Remove air cleaner and intake duct assembly.
2. Drain cooling system and crankcase.
3. Remove radiator, fan, pulley and drive belts.
4. Disconnect fuel pump outlet line from pump. Remove fuel pump retaining bolts and lay the pump to one side.
5. Remove crankshaft pulley and vibration damper.
6. Remove oil pan to cylinder front cover retaining bolts.
7. Remove cylinder front cover and water pump as an assembly.

1970-75 6-240, 6-300

1. Drain cooling system and crankcase.
2. On N Series, remove air cleaner and

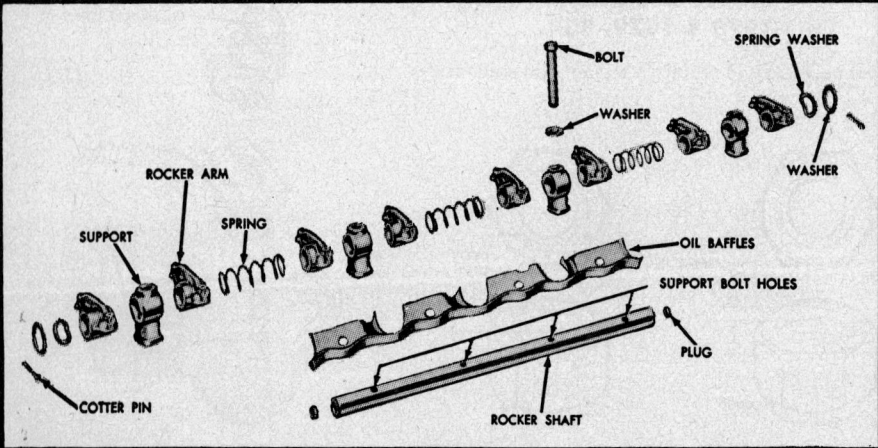

Fig. 10 Layout of rocker arm parts. V8-330, 360, 361, 389, 391, 427

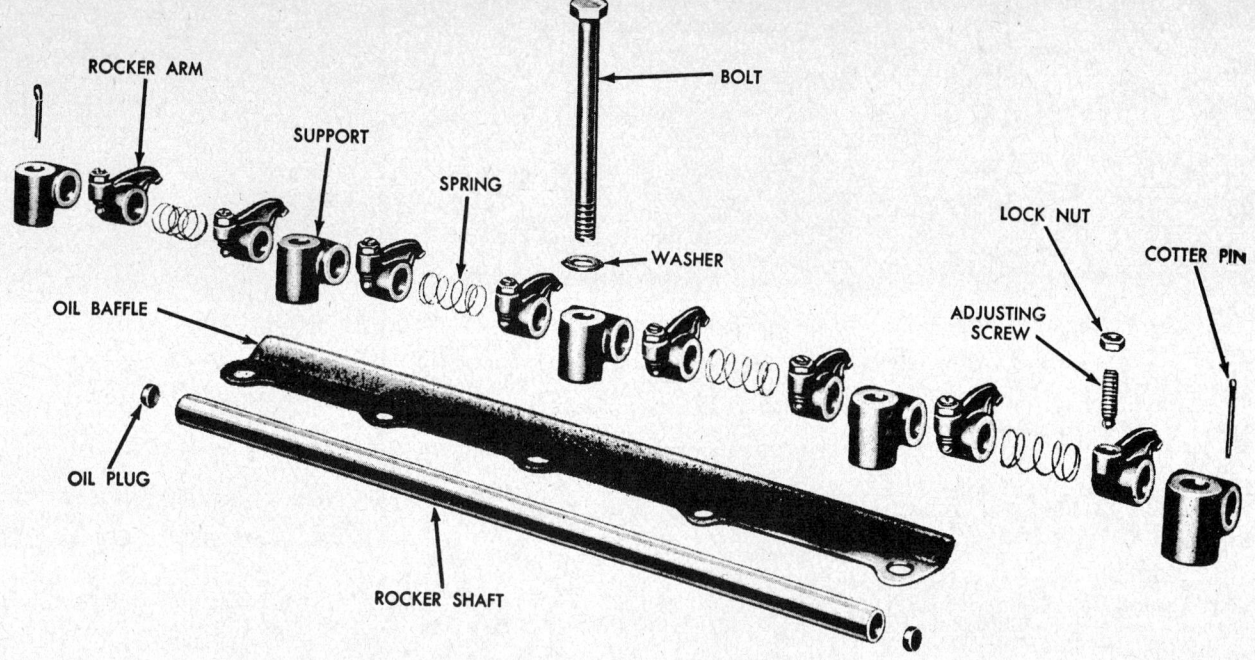

Fig. 11 Layout of rocker arm parts. V8-401, 477, 534 engines

grille.
3. Remove shroud and radiator.
4. Remove fan, drive belts and pulley. It may be necessary to remove air compressor belt and/or power steering pump belt.
5. Remove vibration damper.
6. Remove oil dipstick and oil pan.
7. Remove oil pump screen and inlet tube.
8. Remove timing gear cover.

1976–80 6-300

1. Drain cooling system.
2. Remove shroud and radiator.
3. Remove alternator adjusting arm bolt, loosen drive belt and swing the adjusting arm aside.
4. Remove fan, drive belts, spacer and pulleys.
5. Remove vibration damper.
6. Remove the front oil pan and front cover attaching screw.
7. Remove timing case cover and discard gasket. Replace crankshaft oil seal with new one.
8. Reverse procedure to install.

1970–78 V8-330, 360, 361, 390, 391, 427

1. Drain cooling system and crankcase.
2. Remove air cleaner.
3. Disconnect battery ground cable.
4. Disconnect distributor vacuum line.
5. Disconnect necessary water hose.
6. If equipped, disconnect transmission oil cooler lines.
7. Remove radiator and support. If equipped with automatic radiator shutter, leave it attached to radiator.
8. On high fan installation, remove fan and drive belt.
9. Remove power steering pump and position it to one side, leaving hoses attached.
10. If equipped, remove air compressor.
11. Remove alternator.
12. Remove water pump and fan.
13. On C Series, remove fan from vibration damper.
14. Remove vibration damper.
15. Remove fuel pump and lay it aside with flexible fuel line attached.
16. Remove crankshaft sleeve.
17. Remove front cover, alternator support bracket and adjusting arm bracket, and engine front support bracket.

1970–80 V8-401, 475, 477, 534

1. Drain cooling system and crankcase.
2. Remove fan, shroud, radiator and shutter.
3. Remove alternator, power steering pump and air compressor drive belts.
4. On F, T, L & LT Series, remove front engine support bolts, then lift front of engine about one inch with a floor jack to allow removal of vibration damper.
5. Remove vibration damper.
6. Remove air compressor idler pulley and disconnect alternator adjusting arm at front cover.
7. Remove water pump.
8. Remove engine front support bracket and oil level dipstick.
9. Remove timing cover attaching bolts, then using a thin bladed knife between cover and cylinder block; cut oil pan gasket flush with cylinder block and remove timing gear cover.

NOTE: If oil slinger and crankshaft gear is to be removed on 1966–68 models, it will be necessary to remove oil pan.

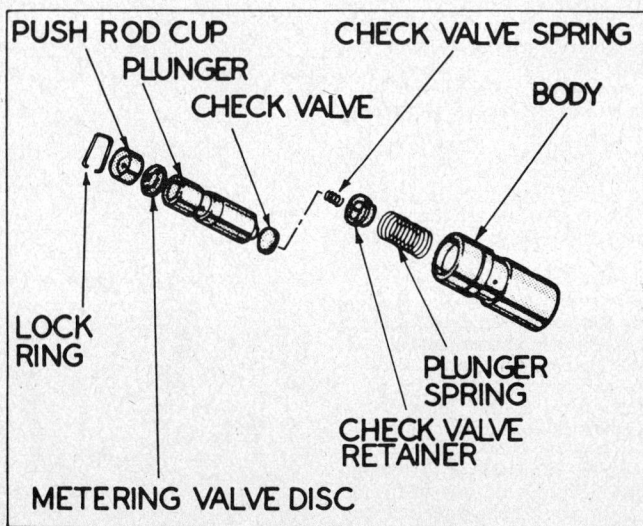

Fig. 12 Hydraulic valve lifter

FORD

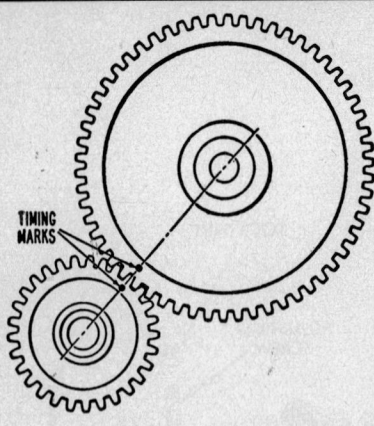

Fig. 13 Valve timing. 6-240, 300

V8-460 & 1970–73 V8-429

1. Drain cooling system and crankcase.
2. Remove radiator fan and shroud, then disconnect upper and lower hoses and oil cooler lines from radiator. Remove radiator upper support and radiator.
3. Loosen alternator attaching bolts and the air conditioning idler pulley, then remove drive belts and water pump pulley.
4. Remove bolts attaching compressor support, water pump and compressor and remove compressor support (if used).
5. Remove crankshaft pulley, then using a puller, remove vibration damper and woodruff key.
6. Loosen by-pass hose from water pump and disconnect heater return hose from water pump.
7. Remove fuel pump and plug fuel lines to prevent entry of dirt.
8. Remove cylinder front cover bolts, then using a thin blade knife, cut oil pan seal between cover and block and remove cover.

1979 V8-370, 429

1. Drain cooling system and crankcase.
2. Remove air cleaner.
3. Disconnect battery ground cable.
4. Disconnect distributor vacuum line.
5. Disconnect necessary water hose.
6. If equipped, disconnect transmission oil cooler lines.

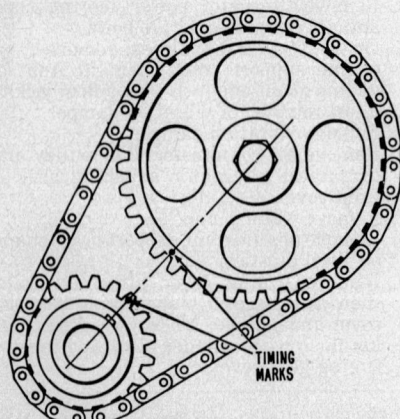

Fig. 15 Valve timing marks. 6-170, 200, 250

7. Remove radiator and support. If equipped with automatic radiator shutter, leave it attached to radiator.
8. On high fan installation, remove fan and drive belt.
9. Remove power steering pump and position it to one side, leaving hoses attached.
10. If equipped, remove air compressor.
11. Remove alternator.
12. Remove water pump and fan.
13. On C Series, remove fan from vibration damper.
14. Remove vibration damper.
15. Remove fuel pump and lay it aside with flexible fuel line attached.
16. Remove front cover and front mount to engine and oil pan attaching bolts. Raise engine slightly, then using a thin bladed knife, cut oil pan gasket flush with cylinder block to oil pan junction before removing the cover and front mount from block.

6-170, 200, 250

1. Remove any front sheet metal that would interfere with the removal of the front cover.
2. Drain the cooling system and the crankcase.
3. Disconnect the radiator upper hose at the outlet housing and the lower hose at the water pump.
4. Remove the radiator, drive belt, fan and pulley.
5. If equipped with Thermactor system, remove the air pump drive belt.
6. If so equipped, remove the accessory drive pulley.
7. Remove the vibration damper.
8. Remove the front cover and the oil pan.

TIMING GEARS
6-240, 6-300

CAUTION: When the crankshaft and camshaft lose their timing relationship through removal of timing gears, interference may occur between crankshaft and cam lobes. Therefore, to prevent possible damage to camshaft lobes, do not rotate crankshaft or camshaft without timing gears installed.

Camshaft Metal Gear
1. With front cover removed, crank engine until timing gear marks are aligned as shown in Fig. 13.
2. Install gear puller and remove gear.
3. Be sure key and spacer are properly installed. Align keyway with key and install gear on camshaft.
4. Check backlash between crank and cam gear, using a dial indicator. Hold gear firmly against block while making check. Backlash should be between .002″ and .004″.

Camshaft Fiber Gear
1. With timing gear cover removed, remove crankshaft oil slinger and camshaft.
2. Press gear off camshaft and remove thrust plate spacer and key.
3. Install camshaft in engine and install spacer and thrust plate on camshaft.
4. Insert key in keyway.
5. Position gear on camshaft with timing marks aligned, Fig. 13. Be sure gear and spacer are tight against shoulder on camshaft and that thrust plate can be moved freely. Install thrust plate screws.

Fig. 14 Valve timing. Typical of V8 engines with timing gears

6. Check gear backlash as outlined above; it should be .002–.004″.

Crankshaft Gear
1. After removing gear cover, remove oil slinger from crankshaft.
2. Use a suitable puller to remove gear.
3. Install key in crankshaft keyway.
4. Install crankshaft gear and oil slinger.

All V8-401, 477, 534

The camshaft gear is a slip-on fit and is retained on the end of the camshaft by a lock plate and three cap screws.

To remove, drain cooling system and crankcase. Remove oil pan, radiator, water pump and front cover. Crank engine until timing marks are aligned as shown in Fig. 14. Remove cap screws and lock plate and take off camshaft gear.

When installing the gear, be sure to have the timing marks lined up as shown.

TIMING CHAIN
6-170, 200, 250 & V8-302, 351, 400

After removing the cover as outlined above,

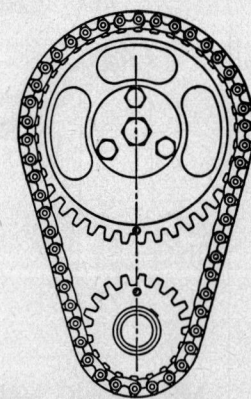

Fig. 16 Valve timing. Typical of V8 engines with timing chain

Ford

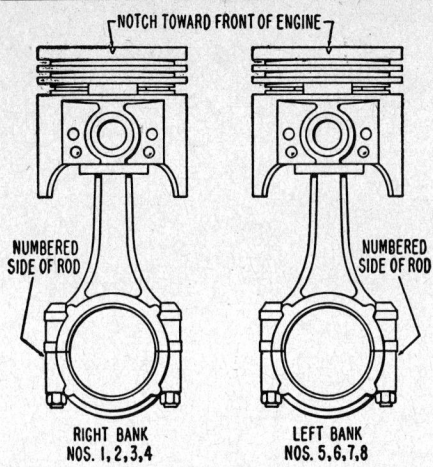

Fig. 17 Piston and rod assembly. V8-390 Light Duty & V8-302, 351, 400, 427, 429, 460

CAMSHAFT & BEARINGS
Six Cylinder

NOTE: On some Econoline models, it is necessary to remove the engine and transmission from the vehicle. Ensure that adequate clearance exists for camshaft removal with the engine in the vehicle.

1. Disconnect battery ground cable.
2. Drain cooling system and oil pan.
3. Remove radiator, valve lifters, front cover, oil pump and the oil pan.
4. Disconnect outlet lines at fuel pump and position fuel pump aside.
5. Remove distributor.
6. Rotate crankshaft to align timing marks, Fig. 13.
7. Remove camshaft thrust plate screws and the camshaft. Use caution not to damage the camshaft lobes when removing camshaft.
8. Reverse procedure to install.

All V8's Exc. V8-401, 477 & 534

1. On V8-370, 1979 V8-429 and Econoline models with V8-302 and 351, remove grille.
2. Drain cooling system, disconnect all hoses and lines from radiator and remove radiator.
3. Remove rocker arm covers, loosen rocker arms and remove pushrods in sequence.
4. Remove intake manifold and remove valve lifters in sequence.
5. Remove cylinder front cover and timing chain as described previously.
6. Remove camshaft thrust plate and carefully remove camshaft by pulling toward front of engine.

NOTE: Use caution to avoid damaging the camshaft bearings.

V8-401, 477 & 534

1. Disconnect battery ground cable.
2. Remove intake manifold and front cover.
3. Rotate crankshaft to follow firing order and loosen valve adjusting screws. Then, slide rocker arm to one side and remove push rods.
4. Remove distributor, governor and push rod cover.
5. Remove valve lifters.
6. Remove crankshaft front oil slinger.
7. Align timing marks, Fig. 14.
8. Remove camshaft thrust plate attaching bolts, then the gear, spacer, thrust plate and camshaft as an assembly.
9. Reverse procedure to install.

PISTON & ROD, ASSEMBLE

Lubricate all parts with light engine oil. Position the connecting rod in the piston and push the pin into place, Figs. 17 to 20. Insert new piston pin retainers (when used) by spiralling them into the piston with the fingers. Do not use pliers.

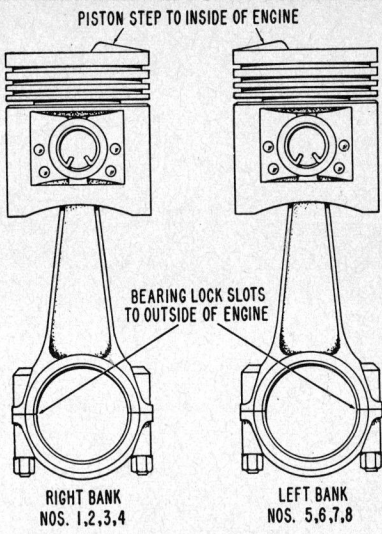

Fig. 18 Assembly of pistons and rods. V8-401, 477, 534

CRANKSHAFT REAR OIL SEAL

A new rubber split-lip rear crankshaft oil seal is released for service. This seal can be installed without removal of the crankshaft and also eliminates the necessity of seal installation tools.

1. Remove oil pan.
2. Remove rear main bearing cap.
3. Loosen remaining bearing caps, allowing crankshaft to drop down about $1/32''$.
4. Remove old seals from both cylinder block and rear main bearing cap. Use a brass rod to drift upper half of seal from cylinder block groove. Rotate crankshaft while drifting to facilitate removal.
5. Carefully clean seal groove in block with a brush and solvent. Also clean seal groove in bearing cap. Remove the oil seal retaining pin from the bearing cap if so equipped. *The pin is not used with the split-lip seal.*

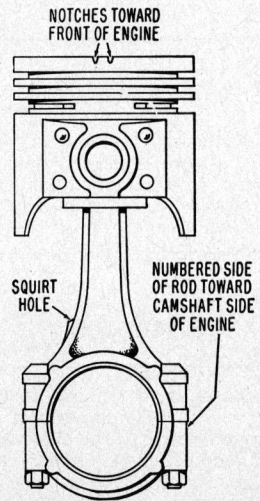

Fig. 20 Piston and rod assembly. 6-170, 200, 250, 240, 300

remove the crankshaft front oil slinger. Crank the engine until the timing marks are aligned as shown in Figs. 15 & 16. Remove camshaft sprocket retaining bolt and washer. Slide sprockets and chain forward and remove them as an assembly. Reverse the order of the foregoing procedure to install the chain and sprockets, being sure the timing marks are properly aligned.

V8-330, 360, 361, 370, 389, 390, 391, 427, 429, 460

To install the chain, align the slotted camshaft spacer with the dowel hole in the camshaft. Position the sprockets and chain on the camshaft and crankshaft. Be sure the timing marks on sprockets are positioned as shown in Fig. 16. Install fuel pump eccentric and camshaft sprocket cap screw.

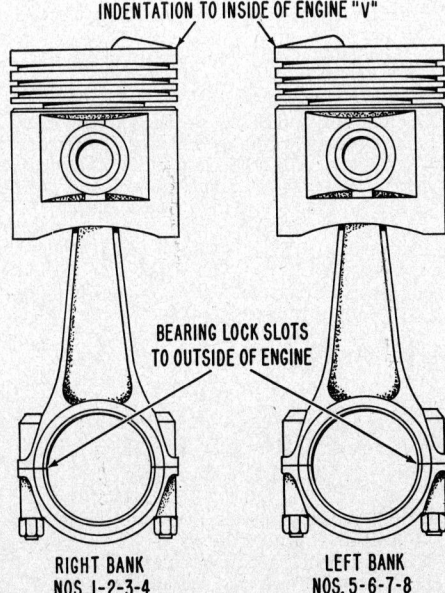

Fig. 19 Piston and rod assembly V8-330, 360, 361, 389, 390 Heavy Duty, 391

Ford

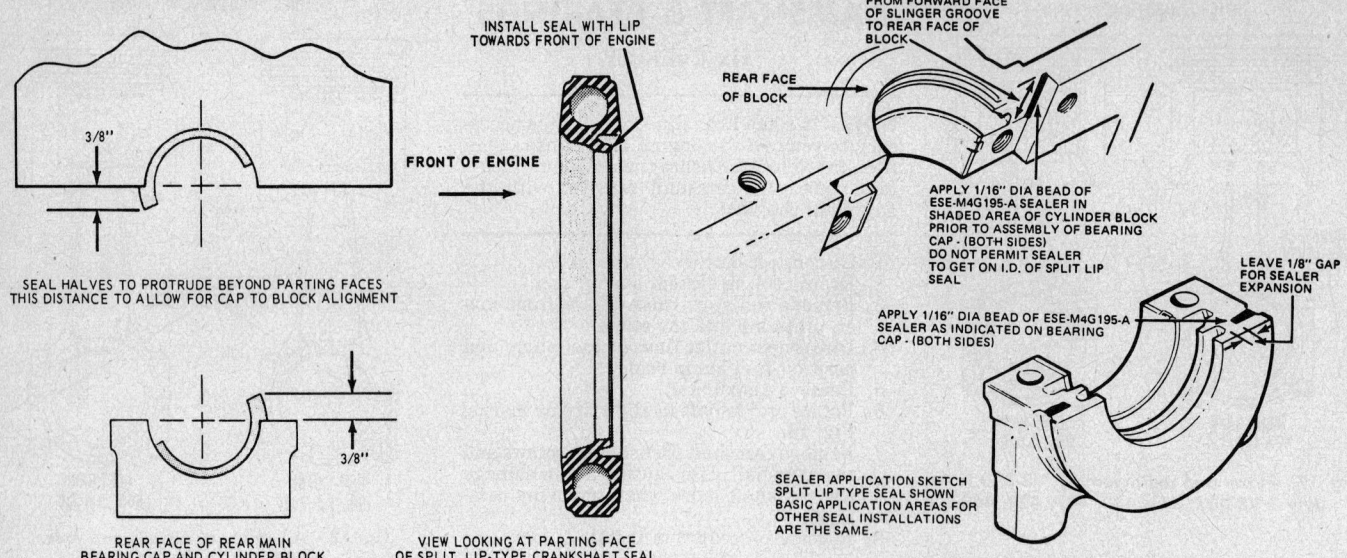

Fig. 21 Crankshaft rear oil seal installation. All exc. 6-240, 300

Fig. 22 Applying sealer to crankshaft rear oil seal. All exc. 6-240 & 300

6. Dip seal halves in clean engine oil.
7. Carefully install upper seal half in its groove with undercut side of seal toward front of engine, Fig. 21, by rotating it on shaft journal of crankshaft until approximately 3/8″ protrudes below the parting surface. *Be sure no rubber has been shaved from outside diameter of seal by bottom edge of groove.*
8. Retighten main bearing caps and torque to specifications.
9. Install lower seal in main bearing cap with undercut side of seal toward front of engine, and allow seal to protrude about 3/8″ above parting surface to mate with upper seal upon cap installation.
10. Apply suitable sealer to parting faces of cap and block, Fig. 22. Install cap and torque to specifications.

NOTE: If difficulty is encountered in installing the upper half of the seal in position, lightly lap (sandpaper the side of the seal opposite the lip side using a medium grit paper). After sanding, the seal must be washed in solvent, then dipped in clean engine oil prior to installation.

SERVICE BULLETIN

A revised crankshaft rear oil seal has been released for service. This new seal may be received when ordering an oil pan gasket kit and is installed in the same manner as described previously, Fig. 23.

6-240, 300

NOTE: If crankshaft rear oil seal replacement is the only operation being performed, it can be done in the vehicle. If the oil seal is being replaced in conjunction with a rear main bearing replacement, the engine must be removed from the vehicle. To replace the seal only, proceed as follows:

1. Remove starting motor.
2. Disconnect transmission from engine and slide it back. On manual shift transmission, remove clutch assembly.
3. Remove flywheel and engine rear cover plate.
4. Use an awl to punch two holes in crankshaft rear oil seal. Punch holes on opposite sides of crankshaft and just above bearing cap-to-cylinder block split line. Insert a sheet metal screw in each hole.
5. Use two large screwdrivers or pry bars and pry against both screws at the same time to remove seal. It may be necessary to place small blocks of wood against cylinder block to provide a fulcrum point for pry bars. Use caution to avoid scratching or otherwise damaging crankshaft oil seal surfaces.

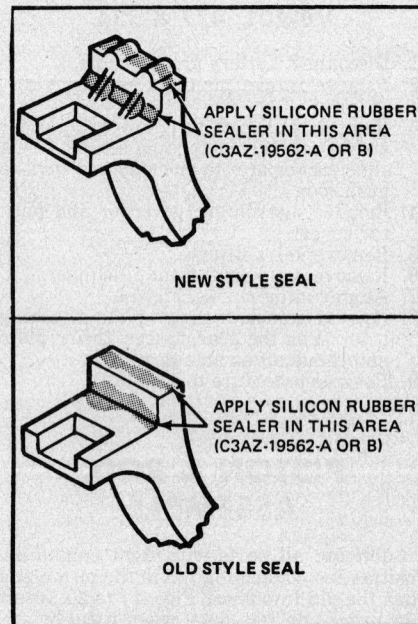

Fig. 23 Revised crankshaft rear oil seal

Installation

1. Clean oil seal recess in cylinder block and rear main bearing cap.
2. Coat new oil seal and crankshaft with a light film of engine oil.
3. Start seal in recess and install it until it is fully seated in seal recess, Fig. 24.
4. Be sure seal was not damaged during installation and reverse the procedure of removal to complete the operation.

OIL PAN, REPLACE

6-170, 200 & 250 Exc. Econoline

1. Drain the crankcase.
2. Remove the dipstick and flywheel housing inspection cover.
3. Remove oil pan and gasket and the oil pump inlet tube and screen assembly.
4. Reverse the procedure to install.

6-240, 300 Exc. Econoline

1. Drain crankcase.
2. On F-100 and F-250, drain cooling system and remove radiator and starter. Remove engine front mounting nuts and raise engine with a transmission jack and wood block. Place one-inch wood blocks between front engine mounts and support brackets. Lower engine and remove jack.
3. On all models, remove oil pan and inlet tube retaining bolts. Remove inlet tube and screen from oil pump and let it lay in oil pan. Then remove oil pan.
4. Reverse procedure to install, Figs. 22 and 25.

1970–74 6-240 & V8-302 Econoline

1. Remove oil dipstick attaching bolts and position it out of the way.
2. Drain crankcase and remove oil filter.
3. Disconnect steering rod at idler arm.
4. Remove nuts and washers retaining front engine supports to crossmember.
5. Position support jack under damper and

Fig. 24 Crankshaft rear oil seal installation. 6-240, 300

raise engine as required.
6. Remove nuts retaining engine support crossmember to side rails and frame. Remove engine support crossmember.
7. Position engine support tools to side rails and front engine supports. Lower support jack.
8. Remove oil pan.

1970–72 6-170 Econoline

1. Drain cooling system and crankcase.
2. Remove fan and water pump pulley.
3. Disconnect upper water hose.
4. Disconnect flexible line at fuel pump.
5. Raise vehicle on hoist and remove air deflector from below radiator.
6. Disconnect radiator lower hose.
7. Remove starter.
8. Remove engine front support bolts.
9. Raise front of engine and place 2" thick wood blocks between front support insulators and support brackets.
10. Remove oil pan bolts and oil pump inlet tube and screen and lay in bottom of pan. Then remove oil pan.
11. Reverse procedure to install, being sure

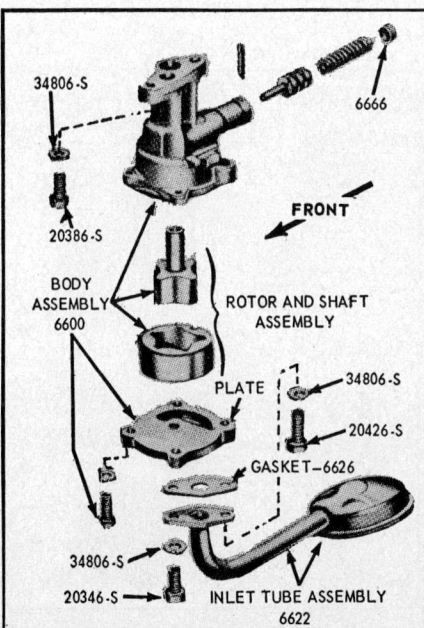

Fig. 26 Oil pump. 6-170, 200 & 250

to first lay inlet tube and screen in pan before placing pan in position.

Bronco V8-302 & 351W

1. Remove air cleaner and duct.
2. Remove oil level dipstick and tube.
3. Remove oil pan attaching bolts and remove oil pan.

1975–79 Econoline V8-302 & 351W

1. Disconnect battery ground cable.
2. Remove engine cover, air cleaner and drain cooling system.
3. If used, disconnect power steering pump and air conditioning pump from their mounts and position the units aside.
4. Remove fan shroud bolts and position shroud over fan, then remove oil filler tube and oil dipstick tube and disconnect upper and lower radiator hoses.
5. Raise and support vehicle and remove alternator splash shield.
6. Disconnect fuel line from pump and exhaust pipes from manifolds, then drain crankcase and remove engine mount to chassis bracket retaining nuts.
7. If equipped with automatic transmission, disconnect oil cooler lines from radiator and remove dipstick and oil filler tube.
8. Disconnect shift linkage from transmission, then remove center driveshaft support and remove driveshaft from transmission.
9. Remove rear crossmember retaining bolts and remove braces, then support transmission and remove crossmember. Remove mount from crossmember then reinstall crossmember and install bolts finger tight.
10. Remove right exhaust pipe heat deflector, then raise engine as far as possible and insert wooden blocks between engine mounts and chassis brackets to support engine.
11. Remove oil pan attaching bolts, then lower oil pan onto crossmember and remove oil pump pickup tube attaching bolts and lower the tube into the oil pan and remove the oil pan.

F-100, 150 V8-302 & 351W

1. Remove the oil level dipstick and tube, then remove the fan shroud attaching bolts and position shroud over the fan.
2. Remove engine mounts to chassis bracket retaining nuts.
3. If equipped with automatic transmission, disconnect the oil cooler line from the left side of the radiator.
4. Raise engine and place wooden blocks between the engine mounts and chassis brackets.
5. Drain the oil pan, then remove the oil pan attaching bolts and lower the oil pan onto the crossmember.
6. Remove the pick tube attaching bolts then lower the pickup tube into the oil pan and remove the oil pan.

V8-302

1. To remove pan, drain oil and remove oil level dipstick.
2. On automatic transmission equipped vehicles, remove converter housing dust cover.
3. On Tilt Cab models, crank engine until No. 1 piston is up on T.D.C.
4. Disconnect oil pump inlet tube at oil pump. Remove "O" ring seal from pump

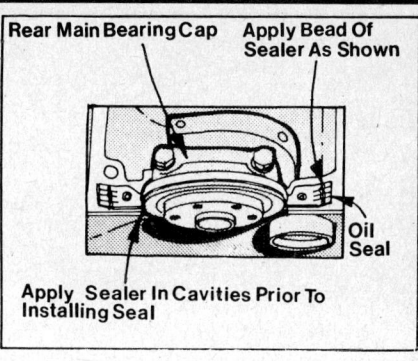

Fig. 25 Oil pan rear seal installation. 6-240, 300

end of tube.
5. Unfasten and remove oil pan.
6. Remove nut securing inlet tube to oil pan; then remove pump and screen from pan.

V8-401, 477, 534

To remove pan, drain oil and remove oil level dipstick. Unfasten and remove oil pan.

V8-330, 360, 361, 370, 389, 390, 391, 427, 1979 429

1. To remove pan and oil pump, drain crankcase and remove oil level dipstick and tube.
2. Unfasten and lower oil pan to axle. Position crankshaft so that counterweight will clear pan.
3. Remove oil pump and inlet tube retaining bolts. Then place pump, screen and intermediate drive shaft in the pan.
4. Remove pan and pump.
5. Reverse removal procedure to install. First place pan on axle. Install pump and screen. Then attach oil pan.

V8-460, 1970–73 V8-429

1. Disconnect battery ground cable, then disconnect radiator shroud and place it over the fan.
2. Support vehicle on hoist and drain crankcase.
3. Remove engine support thru bolts, then place a floor jack under front edge of oil pan with wood block between oil pan and jack.

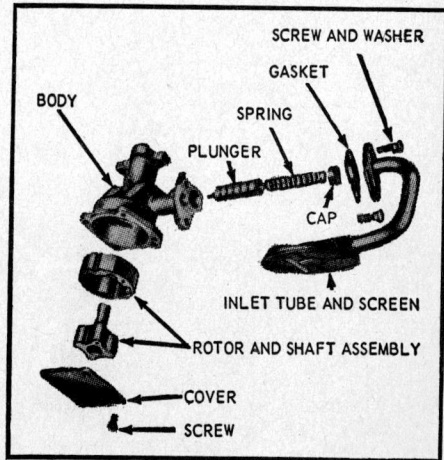

Fig. 27 Oil pump. 6-240, 300

FORD

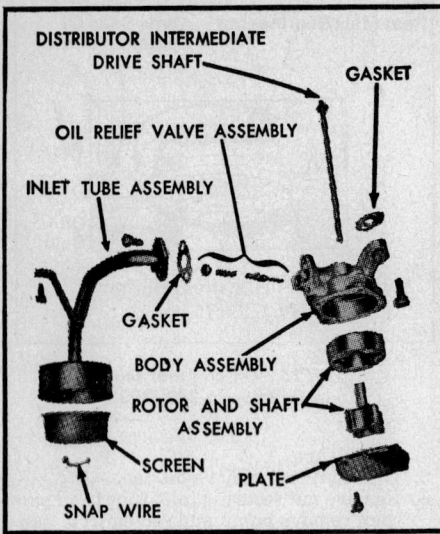

Fig. 28 Oil pump. V8-330, 360, 361, 390, 391

4. Raise engine enough to place 1¼ inch wood blocks between insulators and brackets and remove floor jack.
5. Remove oil filter, then remove oil pan bolts and oil pan.

NOTE: It may be necessary to rotate crankshaft to obtain clearance between the crankshaft throws and oil pan.

OIL PUMP, REPLACE

6-170, 200, 250

1. Remove oil pan as outlined previously.
2. Remove oil pump bolts and remove the pump, gasket and intermediate drive shaft.
3. To install, prime the pump with engine oil.
4. Position the intermediate drive shaft into the distributor socket.
5. Position a new gasket on the pump housing and insert the drive shaft into the pump.
6. Install the pump and shaft as an assembly.

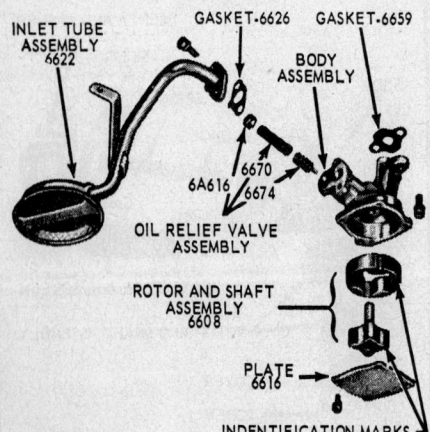

Fig. 30 Oil pump. V8-302, 351W

NOTE: Do not force the pump if it will not seat readily. The drive shaft hex may be misaligned with the distributor shaft. To align, rotate the intermediate shaft into a new position.

7. Install oil pan.

6-240, 6-300

1. After removing oil pan as outlined previously, unfasten and remove oil pump.
2. Prime pump with engine oil.
3. Coat a new pump gasket with oil-resistant sealer and place it on pump.
4. Install pump and oil pan.

V8-330, 360, 361, 370, 390, 391, 1979 429

1. Oil pump is removed together with oil pan as outlined previously.
2. To install, position a new pump inlet tube gasket on pump and install tube.
3. Prime pump with engine oil.
4. Place pump in oil pan and position pan on crossmember.
5. Place a new pump gasket on engine.
6. Insert intermediate drive shaft into pump housing and install pump and shaft as a unit.

NOTE: If pump will not seat readily, the drive shaft hex may be misaligned. To align, rotate shaft into a new position.

7. Install oil pan.

V8-401, 477, 534

1. After removing oil pan, remove pump and pick-up tube. Then remove intermediate drive shaft from engine.
2. To install, place new gasket on pump housing, prime the pump and install pump, shaft and pick-up tube as a unit.

NOTE: If the pump will not seat readily, rotate the shaft into a new position as it may have been misaligned.

3. Install oil pan.

V8-302, 351, 400 427, 460

1. Remove oil pan as described previously.
2. Remove oil pump bolts and oil pump.
3. To install, prime oil pump with engine oil and apply sealant on gasket.
4. Insert distributor intermediate shaft making certain that it is properly seated and install oil pump.

NOTE: Do not force pump into place if it will not seat readily, as the intermediate shaft may be misaligned with distributor shaft. To align, rotate intermediate shaft until pump can be seated without applying force.

5. Install oil pan.

OIL PUMP, SERVICE

Rotor Type Pump

1. To disassemble, Figs. 26 thru 31, remove

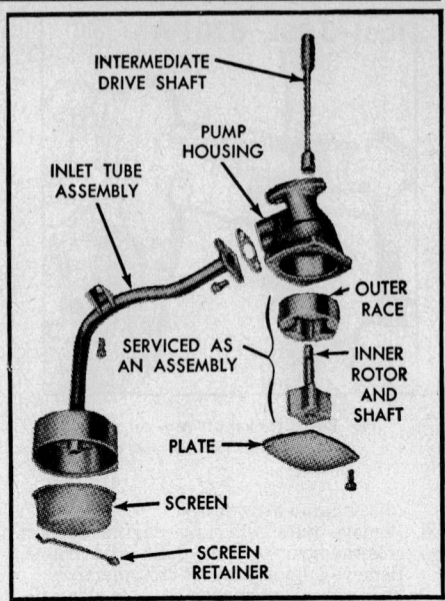

Fig. 29 Oil pump. V8-401, 477, 534

cover, inner rotor and shaft assembly and outer race. Remove staking marks at relief valve chamber cap. Insert a self-threading sheet metal screw of proper diameter into oil pressure relief valve chamber cap and pull cap out of chamber. Then remove spring and plunger.
2. To assemble, install pressure relief valve plunger, spring and a new cap. Stake cap in place. Install outer race, inner rotor and shaft.

NOTE: Be sure identification dimple mark on outer race is facing outward and on the same side as dimple on rotor. Inner rotor and shaft and outer race are furnished only as a unit. One part should not be replaced without replacing the other.

3. Install pump cover.

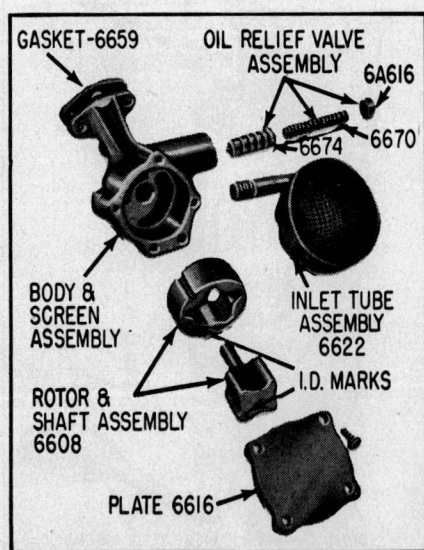

Fig. 31 Oil pump assembly. V8-351C, 351M & 400

Ford

WATER PUMP

NOTE: All water pumps have a sealed bearing integral with water pump shaft. The bearing requires no lubrication. A bleed hole in the pump housing allows water that may leak past the seal to be thrown out by the slinger. This is not a lubrication hole. If the pump is damaged and requires repair, replace it with a new pump or a rebuilt one.

V8-302, 351, 400

1. On Econoline models, remove air cleaner and intake duct assembly.
2. Drain cooling system.
3. On Econoline models, remove radiator.
4. Remove drive belts, fan, spacer and water pump pulley.
5. On Bronco and F-100 models, remove fan shroud if so equipped, and disconnect the lower radiator hose.
6. Loosen alternator pivot bolt and bolt retaining alternator adjusting arm to water pump.
7. On Thermactor engines, remove air pump mounting bolts.
8. Disconnect heater by-pass hoses.
9. Remove bolts securing water pump to cylinder front cover. Remove water pump.

V8-460, 1970–73 V8-429

1. Drain cooling system.
2. Remove fan and shroud and loosen the power steering pump attaching bolts.
3. If equipped with air conditioning, remove the compressor attaching bolts and secure compressor to left fender brace.
4. Remove power steering attaching bolts and place pump aside.
5. If equipped with air conditioning, remove compressor brackets.
6. Disconnect heater, by-pass and radiator lower hose from water pump.
7. Remove water pump attaching bolts and remove water pump.

6-170, 200, 250

1. Drain cooling system.
2. Loosen alternator adjusting arm bolt and remove drive belt. If unit is equipped with an air compressor, remove the compressor belt.
3. Remove the fan and pulley.
4. Disconnect heater hose, lower radiator hose and radiator supply line at the water pump.
5. Unfasten and remove the water pump.

6-240, 6-300

1. To remove pump, drain cooling system and remove alternator drive belt, and air compressor belt (if used).
2. Remove fan and pulley.
3. Disconnect hose as required.
4. Unfasten and remove pump.

V8-330 MD & 427

1. Drain cooling system and remove alternator drive belt.
2. Remove fan, spacer and pulley.
3. Disconnect hose as required.
4. Unfasten and remove pump.

V8-330 HD, 360, 361, 370, 390, 391, 1979 429

1. Drain cooling system and remove drive belts.
2. On engines with water pump mounted fans, remove fan, spacer and pulley. Let fan rest down in shroud. On high fan engines, remove fan and bracket. On low fan engines, remove fan from crankshaft.
3. If equipped with air compressor, unfasten and position compressor on frame rail. Remove compressor mounting bracket.
4. If equipped with power steering, remove steering pump and position it to one side, leaving hoses attached.
5. Disconnect hose as required.
6. Unfasten and remove pump.

V8-401, 477, 534

1. Drain cooling system and disconnect hose as required.
2. Remove fan belts.
3. On F and T Series trucks, remove fan and pulley and lower them into bottom of radiator shroud. Unfasten and remove the pump. On C and H Series trucks, unfasten and remove pump, pulley and gaskets as a unit.

Carburetor Section

1970–80 CARTER YF, YFA ADJUSTMENT SPECIFICATIONS

See Tune Up Chart for hot idle speed.

Year	Carb. Model	Float Level	Fast Idle Cam Setting	Dechoke or Unloader Setting	Pulldown Setting	Choke Setting
1970	C9TF-E	7/32	—	—	—	—
	C9TF-F	7/32	—	—	—	—
	D0BF-A	7/32	.038	.280	.225	Index
	D0TF-E	7/32	—	.280	.225	Index
	D0TF-F	7/32	.031	.280	.265	1 Lean
	D0TF-G	7/32	.039	.280	.265	Index
	D0TF-J	7/32	.036	.280	.225	Index
	D0TF-K	7/32	.031	.280	.265	1 Lean
	D0TF-L	7/32	—	.280	.225	Index
1971	C9TF-E	7/32	—	—	—	—
	C9TF-F	7/32	—	—	—	—
	D1BF-CA	7/32	.105	.280	.200	Index
	D1TF-VA	3/8	.175	.280	.230	Index
	D1TF-XA	3/8	.175	.280	.230	Index
	D1TF-YA	3/8	.175	.280	.230	Index
	D1TF-ZA	7/32	.175	.280	.260	1 Lean
	D1TF-AAA	7/32	.175	.280	.260	Index
	D1TF-ABA	7/32	.175	.280	.260	1 Lean
	D1UF-TA	3/8	.175	.280	.230	Index
	D1UF-UA	3/8	.175	.280	.230	Index

Continued

FORD

1970–80 CARTER YF, YFA ADJUSTMENT SPECIFICATIONS—Continued

See Tune Up Chart for hot idle speed.

Year	Carb. Model	Float Level	Fast Idle Cam Setting	Dechoke or Unloader Setting	Pulldown Setting	Choke Setting
1972	C9TF-E	7/32	—	—	—	—
	C9TF-F	7/32	—	—	—	—
	D2BF-DA	7/32	.105	.280	.200	Index
	D2TF-LA	3/8	.175	.280	.230	1 Lean
	D2TF-MA	3/8	.175	.280	.230	Index
	D2TF-RA	3/8	.175	.280	.230	1 Lean
	D2TF-SA	3/8	.175	.280	.260	1 Lean
	D2TF-VA	3/8	.175	.280	.230	1 Lean
	D2UF-GA	3/8	.175	.280	.230	Index
	D2UF-FA	3/8	.175	.280	.230	1 Lean
1973	D3TF-JA	3/8	.170	.250	.230	Index
	D3UF-HA	3/8	.175	.250	.230	1 Lean
1974	D4TE-YC	3/8	.110	.280	.290	Index
	D4TE-ZA	3/8	.175	.280	.230	1 Lean
	D4TE-ABA	3/8	.120	.120	.260	Index
	D4UE-KB	3/8	.110	.280	.290	Index
	D4UE-LA	3/8	.175	.280	.230	1 Lean
	D4UE-NA	3/8	.175	.280	.290	Index
1975	D4HE-AA	3/8	—	—	—	—
	D4TE-AGA	3/8	—	—	—	—
	D4TE-AUA	3/8	—	—	—	—
	D5TE-ADA	3/8	.110	.280	.290	Index
	D5TE-AFA	3/8	—	—	—	—
	D5TE-AGA	3/8	.110	.280	.230	1 Rich
	D5TE-AJA	3/8	—	—	—	—
	D5TE-AKA	3/8	.110	.280	.290	Index
	D5TE-ALA	3/8	.110	.280	.290	Index
	D5TE-AMA	3/8	.110	.280	.230	1 Rich
	D5TE-ANA	3/8	.110	.280	.230	1 Rich
	D5TE-APA	3/8	.110	.280	.290	Index
1976	D5TE-AFA	3/8	—	—	—	—
	D5TE-AFB	3/8	—	—	—	—
	D5TE-AGA	3/8	.110	.280	.230	1 Rich
	D5TE-AGB	23/32	.110	.280	.230	1 Rich
	D5TE-AJA	3/8	—	—	—	—
	D5TE-AJB	3/8	—	—	—	—
	D5TE-APA	3/8	.110	.280	.290	Index
	D5TE-APB	23/32	.110	.280	.290	Index
	D5TE-CAB	23/32	.110	—	.280	Index
	D5UE-AAB	23/32	.110	.280	.290	Index
	D5UE-EA	3/8	.110	.280	.290	Index
	D5UE-FA	3/8	.110	.280	.290	Index
	D6TE-DA	23/32	.110	.280	.290	Index
	D6TE-HA	23/32	.110	.280	.290	Index
	D6TE-KA	23/32	.110	.280	.290	Index
	D6TE-ZA	23/32	.110	.280	.290	Index
	D6UE-FA	23/32	.110	.280	.290	Index
	D6UE-MA	23/32	.110	.280	.290	Index
1977	D7TE-MA	25/32	.110	.280	.290	Index
	D7TE-PA	25/32	.110	.280	.290	Index
1978	D8TE-AAA	23/32	.110	.280	.230	1 Rich
	D8TE-BUA	25/32	.140	.280	.230	Index

Continued

FORD

1970–80 CARTER YF, YFA ADJUSTMENT SPECIFICATIONS—Continued

See Tune Up Chart for hot idle speed.

Year	Carb. Model	Float Level	Fast Idle Cam Setting	Dechoke or Unloader Setting	Pulldown Setting	Choke Setting
	D8TE-BVA	25/32	.140	.280	.230	Index
	D8TE-BWA	25/32	.140	.280	.230	Index
	D8TE-CDA	23/32	—	—	—	—
	D8TE-CKB	25/32	.140	.280	.230	Index
	D8TE-CNA	25/32	.140	.280	.230	Index
	D8TE-UA	23/32	—	—	—	—
	D8UE-AAA	25/32	.140	.280	.230	Index
	D8UE-EA	25/32	—	—	—	—
	D8UE-ZA	25/32	.140	.280	.230	Index
	D2UE-EA	25/32	—	—	—	—
1979	D9TE-KA	11/16	.140	.280	.230	Index
	D9TE-ZB	11/16	.140	.280	.230	Index
	D9UE-FA	11/16	.140	.280	.230	Index
	D9TE-NA	11/16	.140	.280	.230	Index
	D9TE-LA	11/16	.140	.280	.230	Index
	D9TE-MA	11/16	.140	.280	.230	Index
	D9TE-CA	11/16	.140	.280	.290	Index
	D9TE-VA	11/16	.140	.280	.290	Index
	D9TE-BA	11/16	—	—	—	—
	D9TE-AA	11/16	—	—	—	—
1980	E0TE-ABA	11/16	.140	.280	.290	—
	E0TE-ACA	11/16	.140	.280	.320	—
	E0TE-AEA	11/16	.140	.280	.230	—
	E0TE-AFA	11/16	.140	.280	.230	—
	E0TE-AHA	11/16	.140	.280	.230	—
	E0TE-AKA	11/16	.140	.280	.230	—
	E0TE-ALA	11/16	.140	.280	.230	—
	E0TE-ATA	11/16	.140	.280	.320	—
	E0TE-CA	11/16	.140	.280	.230	—
	E0TE-FA	11/16	.140	.280	.290	—
	E0UE-GA	11/16	.140	.280	.230	—
	E0UE-LA	11/16	.140	.280	.230	—
	E T0E-ARA	11/16	.140	.280	.320	—
	E0UE-KA	11/16	.140	.280	.230	—

1970–80 MODEL 2100, 2150-2V ADJUSTMENT SPECIFICATIONS

See Tune Up Chart for hot idle speeds.

Year	Carb. Model	Float Level (Dry)	Fuel Level (Wet)	Pump Setting Hole No.	Choke Plate Clearance (Pull down)	Fast Idle Cam Linkage Clearance	Dechoke Clearance	Dashpot Setting	Choke Setting
1970	D0AF-C	7/16	13/16	#3	.150	.130	1/16	—	1 Rich
	D0AF-D	7/16	13/16	#2	.150	.130	1/16	.125	1 Rich
	D0AF-U	7/16	13/16	#2	.150	.130	1/16	—	1 Rich
	D0BF-C	17/32	29/32	#3	.160	.140	—	5/64	1 Rich
	D0OF-K	7/16	13/16	#4	.220	.140	1/16	—	Index
	D0OF-L	7/16	13/16	#3	.190	.130	1/16	.125	1 Rich
	D0OF-M	7/16	13/16	#3	.190	.130	1/16	—	1 Rich
	D0TF-A	7/16	13/16	#4	.165	—	—	—	—
	D0TF-B	31/64	7/8	#4	.190	.160	1/16	.125	Index

Continued

FORD

1970–80 MODEL 2100, 2150-2V ADJUSTMENT SPECIFICATIONS—Continued

See Tune Up Chart for hot idle speeds.

Year	Carb. Model	Float Level (Dry)	Fuel Level (Wet)	Pump Setting Hole No.	Choke Plate Clearance (Pull down)	Fast Idle Cam Linkage Clearance	Dechoke Clearance	Dashpot Setting	Choke Setting
	D0TF-C	7/16	13/16	#4	.190	.160	1/16	.125	Index
	D0TF-M	7/16	13/16	#4	.190	.160	1/16	—	Index
	D0TF-N	31/64	7/8	#4	.190	.160	1/16	—	Index
	D0TF-R	7/16	13/16	#4	.190	.160	1/16	.125	Index
	D0TF-S	31/64	7/8	#4	.190	.160	1/16	.125	Index
	D0UF-B	7/16	13/16	#3	.170	.150	1/16	—	2 Rich
	D0UF-C	7/16	13/16	#2	.170	.140	1/16	5/64	Index
	D0UF-E	7/16	13/16	#2	.170	.140	1/16	—	Index
	D0UF-F	7/16	13/16	#2	.170	.140	1/16	5/64	Index
	D0UF-G	7/16	13/16	#3	.170	.150	1/16	5/64	2 Rich
1971	D1AF-BA	7/16	13/16	#2	.150	.130	1/16	—	Index
	D1AF-DA	7/16	13/16	#3	.170	.150	1/16	—	1 Rich
	D1BF-AA	1/2	29/64	#3	.170	.150	1/16	—	1 Rich
	D1OF-PA	7/16	13/16	#3	.230	.190	1/16	—	Index
	D1OF-RA	7/16	13/16	#3	.200	.170	1/16	—	1 Rich
	D1OF-YA	7/16	13/16	#3	.200	.170	1/16	—	1 Rich
	D1OF-ZA	7/16	13/16	#3	.230	.190	1/16	—	Index
	D1OF-ABA	7/16	13/16	#3	.170	.150	1/16	—	1 Rich
	D1TF-AA	7/16	13/16	#4	.165	—	—	—	—
	D1TF-EA	7/16	13/16	#2	.160	.150	1/16	.125	Index
	D1TF-HA	31/64	7/8	#4	.190	.170	1/16	.125	Index
	D1TF-NA	7/16	13/16	#4	.190	.160	1/16	.125	1 Rich
	D1TF-AKA	7/16	13/16	#4	.170	.150	1/16	.125	2 Rich
	D1TF-ALA	31/64	7/8	#4	.190	.160	1/16	.125	2 Rich
	D1TF-AMA	7/16	13/16	#3	.170	.150	1/16	—	Index
	D1UF-AA	7/16	13/16	#3	.160	.140	1/16	—	Index
	D1UF-CA	7/16	13/16	#2	.160	.140	1/16	1/8	Index
	D1UF-DA	7/16	13/16	#2	.160	.140	1/16	—	Index
	D1UF-FA	7/16	13/16	#2	.160	.140	1/16	1/8	1 Rich
	D1UF-SA	7/16	13/16	#3	.160	.140	1/16	1/8	Index
	D1ZF-AA	7/16	13/16	#2	.150	.130	1/16	—	Index
	D1ZF-SA	7/16	13/16	#3	.200	.170	1/16	—	1 Rich
	D1ZF-UA	7/16	13/16	#3	.200	.170	1/16	—	1 Rich
1972	D2AF-UC	7/16	13/16	#3A	.170	.150	1/16	—	Index
	D2BF-AA	1/2	29/64	#3A	.140	.110	1/16	—	1 Rich
	D2GF-AA	7/16	13/16	#2A	.150	.130	1/16	.125	1 Rich
	D2GF-AB	7/16	13/16	#2A	.150	.130	1/16	.125	1 Rich
	D2GF-AC	7/16	13/16	#2A	.150	.130	1/16	.125	1 Rich
	D2GF-BA	7/16	13/16	#2A	.150	.130	1/16	—	1 Rich
	D2GF-BB	7/16	13/16	#2A	.150	.130	1/16	—	1 Rich
	D2GF-BC	7/16	13/16	#2A	.150	.130	1/16	—	1 Rich
	D2MF-FB	7/16	13/16	#4A	.180	.150	1/16	—	Index
	D2MF-FE	7/16	13/16	#4B	.170	.150	1/16	—	Index
	D2MF-FF	7/16	13/16	#4B	.155	.150	1/16	—	Index
	D2OF-KA	7/16	13/16	#2A	.140	.130	1/16	—	1 Rich
	D2OF-KB	7/16	13/16	#2A	.140	.130	1/16	—	1 Rich
	D2OF-UB	7/16	13/16	#3A	.190	.160	.030	—	1 Rich
	D2OF-VA	7/16	13/16	#2A	.150	.130	1/16	—	1 Rich
	D2TF-AA	31/64	7/8	#2A	.160	.160	.160	.125	1 Lean
	D2TF-BA	7/16	13/16	#4A	.165	—	—	—	—
	D2TF-CA	7/16	13/16	#2A	.140	.120	1/16	1/16	2 Rich
	D2TF-DB	7/16	13/16	#2A	.140	.120	.120	1/16	2 Rich
	D2TF-EA	7/16	13/16	#2A	.140	.120	1/16	—	2 Rich

Continued

Ford

1970–80 MODEL 2100, 2150-2V ADJUSTMENT SPECIFICATIONS—Continued

See Tune Up Chart for hot idle speeds.

Year	Carb. Model	Float Level (Dry)	Fuel Level (Wet)	Pump Setting Hole No.	Choke Plate Clearance (Pull down)	Fast Idle Cam Linkage Clearance	Dechoke Clearance	Dashpot Setting	Choke Setting
	D2TF-FC	7/16	7/8	#2A	.160	.160	.140	—	1 Lean
	D2TF-GA	7/16	13/16	#4A	.160	.140	.140	.125	Index
	D2TF-JA	31/64	7/8	#4A	.160	.140	.140	.125	2 Rich
	D2TF-KA	7/16	13/16	#4A	.160	.140	.140	.125	2 Rich
	D2UF-AA	7/16	13/16	#3A	.140	.110	1/16	—	1 Rich
	D2UF-BA	7/16	13/16	#3A	.140	.110	1/16	1/16	1 Rich
	D2UF-CA	7/16	13/16	#2A	.140	.110	1/16	1/16	Index
	D2UF-DA	7/16	13/16	#2A	.140	.110	1/16	—	Index
	D2UF-EA	7/16	13/16	#2A	.140	.110	1/16	1/16	Index
	D2UF-LA	7/16	13/16	#3A	.140	.110	1/16	—	1 Rich
	D2UF-MA	7/16	13/16	#2A	.140	.110	1/16	—	Index
	D2UF-PA	7/16	13/16	#2A	.140	.110	1/16	—	1 Rich
	D2WF-CA	7/16	13/16	#3A	.190	.160	.030	—	2 Rich
1973	D3AF-CE	7/16	13/16	#2	—	—	—	—	2 Rich
	D3AF-DC	7/16	13/16	#3	—	—	—	—	3 Rich
	D3AF-KA	7/16	13/16	#3	—	—	—	—	3 Rich
	D3BF-BE	1/2	29/32	#2A	—	—	—	—	2 Rich
	D3BF-EA	1/2	29/32	#3A	—	—	—	—	2 Rich
	D3GF-AF	7/16	13/16	#2A	—	—	—	—	3 Rich
	D3GF-BB	7/16	13/16	#2A	—	—	—	—	1 Rich
	D3TF-AB	7/16	13/16	#4A	—	—	—	—	—
	D3TF-DD	31/64	7/8	#2A	—	—	—	—	Index
	D3TF-GC	31/64	7/8	#4A	—	—	—	—	Index
	D3TF-HC	7/16	13/16	#4A	—	—	—	—	Index
	D3TF-MC	7/16	13/16	#4A	—	—	—	—	Index
	D3TF-NA	7/16	13/16	#2A	—	—	—	—	2 Rich
	D3UF-AD	7/16	13/16	#3A	—	—	—	—	2 Rich
	D3UF-CD	7/16	13/16	#2A	—	—	—	—	2 Rich
	D3UF-DC	7/16	13/16	#3A	—	—	—	—	2 Rich
	D3UF-EC	7/16	13/16	#3A	—	—	—	—	2 Rich
	D3UF-FC	7/16	13/16	#2A	—	—	—	—	2 Rich
1974	D4AE-DA	7/16	13/16	#2A	—	—	—	—	1 Rich
	D4AE-EA	7/16	13/16	#2A	—	—	—	—	3 Rich
	D4AE-FA	7/16	13/16	#3A	—	—	—	—	3 Rich
	D4AE-GA	7/16	13/16	#3A	—	—	—	—	3 Rich
	D4AE-HB	7/16	13/16	#3A	—	—	—	—	3 Rich
	D4BE-FA	1/2	29/32	#3	—	—	—	—	2 Rich
	D4DE-LA	7/16	13/16	#2	—	—	—	—	2 Rich
	D4DE-NB	7/16	13/16	#2	—	—	—	—	3 Rich
	D4ME-BA	7/16	13/16	#3A	—	—	—	—	3 Rich
	D4OE-CA	—	—	—	—	—	—	—	—
	D4OE-FA	7/16	13/16	#2A	—	—	—	—	3 Rich
	D4OE-GA	7/16	13/16	#2	—	—	—	—	3 Rich
	D4OE-JA	—	—	—	—	—	—	—	—
	D4TE-EA	7/16	13/16	#3	—	—	—	—	2 Rich
	D4TE-GA	31/64	7/8	#3	—	—	—	—	1 Lean
	D4TE-LA	7/16	13/16	#2	—	—	—	—	2 Rich
	D4TE-TA	31/64	7/8	#3	—	—	—	—	Index
	D4TE-AZA	7/16	13/16	#2	—	—	—	—	2 Rich
	D4TE-BAA	31/64	7/8	#3	—	—	—	—	1 Rich
	D4TE-CAA	7/16	13/16	#2	—	—	—	—	2 Rich
	D4TF-AA	1/2	29/32	#3	—	—	—	—	2 Rich
	D4UE-AA	7/16	13/16	#3	—	—	—	—	2 Rich

Continued

FORD

1970–80 MODEL 2100, 2150-2V ADJUSTMENT SPECIFICATIONS—Continued

See Tune Up Chart for hot idle speeds.

Year	Carb. Model	Float Level (Dry)	Fuel Level (Wet)	Pump Setting Hole No.	Choke Plate Clearance (Pull down)	Fast Idle Cam Linkage Clearance	Dechoke Clearance	Dashpot Setting	Choke Setting
	D4UE-BA	7/16	13/16	#2	—	—	—	—	2 Rich
	D4UE-FA	7/16	13/16	#3	—	—	—	—	3 Rich
	D4UE-GA	7/16	13/16	#3	—	—	—	—	2 Rich
	D4UE-HA	7/16	13/16	#2	—	—	—	—	2 Rich
	D4UE-JA	7/16	13/16	#2	—	—	—	—	2 Rich
	D4UE-UA	7/16	13/16	#2	—	—	—	—	2 Rich
	D4UF-AA	7/16	13/16	#3	—	—	—	—	2 Rich
1975	D5AE-AA	7/16	13/16	#3	.125	—	—	—	3 Rich
	D5AE-EA	7/16	13/16	#3	.125	—	—	—	3 Rich
	D5DE-HA	7/16	13/16	#3	.140	—	—	—	3 Rich
	D5DE-UA	7/16	13/16	#2	.140	—	—	—	3 Rich
	D5ME-BA	7/16	13/16	#2	.125	—	—	—	3 Rich
	D5ME-FA	7/16	13/16	#2	.125	—	—	—	3 Rich
	D5OE-AA	7/16	13/16	#2	.140	—	—	—	3 Rich
	D5OE-BA	7/16	13/16	#3	.125	—	—	—	3 Rich
	D5OE-CA	7/16	13/16	#3	.125	—	—	—	3 Rich
	D5OE-DA	7/16	13/16	#2	.140	—	—	—	3 Rich
	D5OE-GA	7/16	13/16	#2	.125	—	—	—	3 Rich
	D5TE-LA	31/64	7/8	#2	.135	—	—	—	Index
	D5TE-PA	31/64	7/8	#2	.160	—	—	—	3 Rich
	D5TE-VA	31/64	7/8	#3	.179	—	—	—	2 Rich
	D5TE-YD	31/64	7/8	#3	.179	—	—	—	3 Rich
	D5TE-ZA	31/64	7/8	#4	.179	—	—	—	3 Rich
	D5TE-AAD	31/64	7/8	#3	.179	—	—	—	3 Rich
	D5TE-ABA	7/16	13/16	#4	—	—	—	—	—
	D5TE-ACB	7/16	13/16	#4	—	—	—	—	—
	D5TE-ASA	31/64	7/8	#4	.179	—	—	—	Index
	D5TE-ATA	31/64	7/8	#4	.179	—	—	—	Index
	D5TE-AUB	31/64	7/8	#3	.179	—	—	—	2 Rich
	D5TE-BCA	31/64	7/8	#2	.179	—	—	—	2 Rich
	D5TE-BCB	31/64	7/8	#2	.179	—	—	—	2 Rich
	D5TE-BDA	31/64	7/8	#2	.179	—	—	—	2 Rich
	D5TE-BDB	31/64	7/8	#2	.179	—	—	—	2 Rich
	D5TE-BEA	31/64	7/8	#3	.179	—	—	—	2 Rich
	D5TE-BFA	31/64	7/8	#3	.179	—	—	—	2 Rich
	D5TE-BFB	31/64	7/8	#3	.179	—	—	—	2 Rich
	D5TE-BGA	31/64	7/8	#3	.179	—	—	—	3 Rich
	D5TE-BHA	31/64	7/8	#2	.135	—	—	—	Index
	D5TE-BJA	31/64	7/8	#2	.160	—	—	—	2 Rich
	D5UE-BA	31/64	7/8	#3	.153	—	—	—	1 Rich
	D5UE-DC	31/64	7/8	#3	.153	—	—	—	3 Rich
	D5UE-JD	31/64	7/8	#3	.160	—	—	—	3 Rich
	D5UE-KD	31/64	7/8	#3	.160	—	—	—	3 Rich
	D5UE-ZA	31/64	7/8	#3	.153	—	—	—	1 Rich
1976	D5TE-PA	31/64	7/8	#2	.160	—	—	—	3 Rich
	D5TE-VA	31/64	7/8	#3	.179	—	—	—	2 Rich
	D5TE-YA	—	—	—	—	—	—	—	—
	D5TE-YF	31/64	7/8	#3	.140	.160	—	—	2 Rich
	D5TE-ZA	31/64	7/8	#3	.179	—	—	—	3 Rich
	D5TE-ZB	31/64	7/8	#3	.140	.160	—	—	2 Rich
	D5TE-AAA	—	—	—	—	—	—	—	—
	D5TE-AAC	31/64	7/8	#4	.160	—	—	—	3 Rich
	D5TE-AAF	31/64	7/8	#3	.140	.160	—	—	3 Rich

Continued

FORD

1970–80 MODEL 2100, 2150-2V ADJUSTMENT SPECIFICATIONS—Continued
See Tune Up Chart for hot idle speeds.

Year	Carb. Model	Float Level (Dry)	Fuel Level (Wet)	Pump Setting Hole No.	Choke Plate Clearance (Pull down)	Fast Idle Cam Linkage Clearance	Dechoke Clearance	Dashpot Setting	Choke Setting
	D5TE-ABA	7/16	13/16	#4	—	—	—	—	—
	D5TE-ACB	7/16	13/16	#4	—	—	—	—	—
	D5TE-ASA	31/64	7/8	#4	.179	—	—	—	Index
	D5TE-ATA	31/64	7/8	#4	.179	—	—	—	Index
	D5TE-AUA	—	—	—	—	—	—	—	—
	D5TE-AUB	31/64	7/8	#3	.179	—	—	—	2 Rich
	D5TE-BCA	31/64	7/8	#2	.179	—	—	—	2 Rich
	D5TE-BCB	31/64	7/8	#2	.179	—	—	—	2 Rich
	D5TE-BDA	31/64	7/8	#2	.179	—	—	—	2 Rich
	D5TE-BDB	31/64	7/8	#2	.179	—	—	—	2 Rich
	D5TE-BEA	31/64	7/8	#3	.179	—	—	—	2 Rich
	D5TE-BEB	31/64	7/8	#3	.140	.160	—	—	2 Rich
	D5TE-BFA	31/64	7/8	#3	.179	—	—	—	2 Rich
	D5TE-BFB	31/64	7/8	#3	.179	—	—	—	2 Rich
	D5TE-BGA	31/64	7/8	#3	.179	—	—	—	3 Rich
	D5TE-BMA	31/64	7/8	#2	.140	.160	—	—	Index
	D5UE-AA	31/64	7/8	#2	.160	.180	—	—	3 Rich
	D5UE-BA	31/64	7/8	#3	.153	—	—	—	1 Rich
	D5UE-CA	1/2	7/8	#2	.160	—	—	—	3 Rich
	D5UE-DA	—	—	—	—	—	—	—	—
	D5UE-DC	31/64	7/8	#3	.153	—	—	—	3 Rich
	D5UE-JA	—	—	—	—	—	—	—	—
	D5UE-JD	31/64	7/8	#3	.160	—	—	—	3 Rich
	D5UE-KA	—	—	—	—	—	—	—	—
	D5UE-KD	31/64	7/8	#3	.160	—	—	—	3 Rich
	D5UE-LA	31/64	7/8	#2	.160	.180	—	—	3 Rich
	D5UE-MA	31/64	7/8	#2	.160	.180	—	—	3 Rich
	D5UE-ZA	31/64	7/8	#3	.153	—	—	—	1 Rich
	D6AE-HA	7/16	13/16	#2	.160	.180	—	—	3 Rich
	D6AE-JA	7/16	13/16	#2	.160	.180	—	—	2 Rich
	D6AE-KA	7/16	13/16	#2	.160	.180	—	—	2 Rich
	D6ME-AA	7/16	13/16	#2	.160	.180	—	—	3 Rich
	D6ME-BA	7/16	13/16	#2	.160	.180	—	—	2 Rich
	D6OE-AA	7/16	13/16	#3	.160	.180	—	—	3 Rich
	D6TE-FA	31/64	7/8	#2	.140	.160	—	—	Index
	D6TE-GA	31/64	7/8	#2	.140	.160	—	—	3 Rich
	D6TE-GB	—	—	—	—	—	—	—	—
	D6TE-RA	31/64	7/8	#2	.179	—	—	—	2 Rich
	D6TE-SA	31/64	7/8	#3	.179	—	—	—	2 Rich
	D6TE-TA	31/64	7/8	#3	.179	—	—	—	2 Rich
	D6TE-VA	31/64	7/8	#2	.135	—	—	—	2 Rich
	D6TE-YA	31/64	7/8	#2	.135	—	—	—	3 Rich
	D6TE-YB	31/64	7/8	#2	.135	—	—	—	3 Rich
	D6TE-AAC	31/64	7/8	#4	.160	—	—	—	3 Rich
	D6UE-HA	—	—	—	—	—	—	—	—
	D6UE-JA	31/64	7/8	#2	.180	.200	—	—	3 Rich
	D6UE-NA	—	—	—	—	—	—	—	—
	D6WE-AA	7/16	13/16	#2	.160	.180	—	—	3 Rich
	D6WE-BA	7/16	13/16	#2	.160	.180	—	—	2 Rich
1977	D7AE-ACA	7/16	13/16	#2	.156	.170	—	—	Index
	D7AE-AHA	7/16	13/16	#3	.179	.189	—	—	Index
	D7AE-AKA	7/16	13/16	#3	.179	.189	—	—	Index
	D7BE-YA	7/16	13/16	#2	.147	.167	—	—	1 Rich
	D7OE-LA	7/16	13/16	#4	.169	.189	—	—	3 Rich

Continued

FORD

1970–80 MODEL 2100, 2150-2V ADJUSTMENT SPECIFICATIONS—Continued
See Tune Up Chart for hot idle speeds.

Year	Carb. Model	Float Level (Dry)	Fuel Level (Wet)	Pump Setting Hole No.	Choke Plate Clearance (Pull down)	Fast Idle Cam Linkage Clearance	Dechoke Clearance	Dashpot Setting	Choke Setting
	D7OE-RA	3/4	3/4	#3	.167	.187	—	—	2 Rich
	D7OE-TA	7/16	13/16	#3	.185	.205	—	—	2 Rich
	D7TE-ABA	31/64	7/8	#2	.140	—	—	—	3 Rich
	D7TE-ACA	31/64	7/8	#2	.140	—	—	—	3 Rich
	D7TE-ADA	31/64	7/8	#3	.140	—	—	—	3 Rich
	D7TE-AFA	31/64	7/8	#2	.140	—	—	—	3 Rich
	D7UE-TA	7/16	13/16	#3	.170	—	—	—	3 Rich
	D7UE-YA	7/16	13/16	#2	.170	—	—	—	3 Rich
	D7UE-ZC	7/16	13/16	#3	.170	—	—	—	Index
	D7UE-ACA	31/64	7/8	#3	.170	—	—	—	1 Rich
	D7UE-ADA	31/64	7/8	#4	.170	—	—	—	2 Rich
	D7UE-AEA	31/64	7/8	#4	.170	—	—	—	1 Rich
	D7UE-ANA	31/64	7/8	#3	.170	—	—	—	2 Rich
	D7TE-AHA	31/64	7/8	#3	.160	—	—	—	Index
	D7TE-AKA	31/64	7/8	#3	.160	—	—	—	Index
	D7TE-ALA	31/64	7/8	#3	.160	—	—	—	1 Rich
	D7TE-AMA	31/64	7/8	#4	.160	—	—	—	3 Rich
	D7TE-ANA	31/64	7/8	#4	.160	—	—	—	3 Rich
	D7TE-APA	31/64	7/8	#4	.160	—	—	—	3 Rich
	D7TE-ARA	31/64	7/8	#4	.160	—	—	—	3 Rich
	D7TE-BEA	31/64	7/8	#3	.160	—	—	—	Index
	D7TE-AKA	31/64	7/8	#3	.160	—	—	—	Index
	D7TE-AUA	31/64	7/8	#4	.160	—	—	—	3 Rich
	D7TE-AYA	31/64	7/8	#4	.160	—	—	—	3 Rich
	D7TE-AZA	31/64	7/8	#4	.160	—	—	—	3 Rich
1978	D8AE-JA	3/8	3/4	#3	.167	—	—	—	3 Rich
	D8BE-ACA	7/16	3/4	#4	.155	—	—	—	2 Rich
	D8BE-ADA	7/16	13/16	#2	.110	—	—	—	3 Rich
	D8BE-AEA	7/16	13/16	#2	.110	—	—	—	4 Rich
	D8BE-AFA	7/16	13/16	#2	.110	—	—	—	4 Rich
	D8DE-HA	1 19/32	13/16	#3	.157	—	—	—	Index
	D8FE-BA	1 19/32	13/16	#2	.128	—	—	—	2 Rich
	D8KE-EA	1 19/32	13/16	#2	.135	—	—	—	3 Rich
	D8ME-BA	7/16	13/16	#2	.135	—	—	—	Index
	D8OE-BA	3/8	3/4	#3	.167	—	—	—	3 Rich
	D8OE-EA	1 19/32	13/16	#2	.136	—	—	—	Index
	D8OE-HA	7/16	13/16	#3	.180	—	—	—	2 Rich
	D8SE-CA	1 19/32	13/16	#3	.150	—	—	—	2 Rich
	D8SE-DA	7/16	13/16	#3	.147	—	—	—	3 Rich
	D8SE-EA	7/16	13/16	#3	.147	—	—	—	3 Rich
	D8SE-FA	3/8	13/16	#3	.147	—	—	—	3 Rich
	D8SE-GA	3/8	13/16	#3	.147	—	—	—	3 Rich
	D8TE-AA	31/64	7/8	#4	.150	—	—	—	—
	D8TE-BA	31/64	7/8	#3	.140	—	—	—	Index
	D8TE-DA	31/64	7/8	#4	.130	—	—	—	Index
	D8TE-GA	31/64	7/8	#2	.130	—	—	—	3 Rich
	D8TE-LA	31/64	7/8	#3	.130	—	—	—	Index
	D8TE-ARA	31/64	7/8	#3	.145	—	—	—	Index
	D8TE-ATA	31/64	7/8	#3	.145	—	—	—	2 Rich
	D8TE-BEA	31/64	7/8	#2	.200	—	—	—	3 Rich
	D8TE-BJA	31/64	7/8	#3	.175	—	—	—	3 Rich
	D8TE-BLA	31/64	7/8	#4	.180	—	—	—	2 Rich
	D8TE-BNA	31/64	7/8	#3	.130	—	—	—	3 Rich

Continued

FORD

1970–80 MODEL 2100, 2150-2V ADJUSTMENT SPECIFICATIONS—Continued

See Tune Up Chart for hot idle speeds.

Year	Carb. Model	Float Level (Dry)	Fuel Level (Wet)	Pump Setting Hole No.	Choke Plate Clearance (Pull down)	Fast Idle Cam Linkage Clearance	Dechoke Clearance	Dashpot Setting	Choke Setting
	D8TE-CCA	31/64	7/8	#2	.130	—	—	—	3 Rich
	D8TE-CGA	31/64	7/8	#2	.130	—	—	—	1 Rich
	D8TE-CHA	31/64	7/8	#2	.130	—	—	—	3 Rich
	D8TE-CPA	31/64	7/8	#3	.185	—	—	—	3 Rich
	D8UE-DA	31/64	7/8	#3	.185	—	—	—	3 Rich
	D8UE-GA	31/64	7/8	#2	.205	—	—	—	1 Rich
	D8UE-HA	31/64	7/8	#2	.215	—	—	—	Index
	D8UE-KA	7/16	13/16	#3	.185	—	—	—	Index
	D8UE-MA	31/64	7/8	#2	.215	—	—	—	Index
	D8UE-SA	31/64	7/8	#3	.180	—	—	—	3 Rich
	D8UE-VA	31/64	7/8	#4	.145	—	—	—	Index
	D8WE-DA	7/16	13/16	#4	.143	—	—	—	1 Rich
	D8WE-TA	3/8	3/4	#4	.135	—	—	—	Index
	D8ZE-UA	3/8	3/4	#4	.135	—	—	—	Index
	D84E-EA	3/8	3/4	#3	.167	—	—	—	3 Rich
1979	D9TE-CRA	31/64	7/8	2	.145	—	—	—	3 Rich
	D9TE-BSB	31/64	7/8	2	.136	—	—	—	1 Rich
	D9TE-BUB	31/64	7/8	3	.140	—	—	—	3 Rich
	D9TE-BTB	31/64	7/8	2	.145	—	—	—	3 Rich
	D9TE-ALB	31/64	7/8	3	.145	—	—	—	Index
	D9TE-AMB	31/64	7/8	3	.145	—	—	—	Index
	D9TE-BPB	31/64	7/8	3	.150	—	—	—	3 Rich
	D9TE-BRB	31/64	7/8	3	.150	—	—	—	3 Rich
	D9TE-CPA	31/64	7/8	3	.145	—	—	—	Index
	D9TE-CTA	31/64	7/8	3	.130	—	—	—	3 Rich
	D9TE-CSA	31/64	7/8	3	.130	—	—	—	3 Rich
	D9TE-BNB	31/64	7/8	2	.145	—	—	—	Index
	D9TE-BJB	31/64	7/8	2	.135	—	—	—	Index
	D8TE-BJA	31/64	7/8	3	.160	—	—	—	3 Rich
	D9UE-DB	7/16	13/16	2	.200	—	—	—	Index
	D9UE-LB	31/64	7/8	3	.140	—	—	—	3 Rich
	D9UE-GA	7/16	13/16	2	.200	—	—	—	Index
	D9UE-KA	31/64	7/8	4	.175	—	—	—	1 Rich
	D9TE-DCB	31/64	7/8	2	.145	—	—	—	2 Rich
	D9UE-EB	7/16	13/16	2	.190	—	—	—	Index
	D9DE-RA	7/16	13/16	2	.125	—	—	—	3 Rich
	D9DE-RB	7/16	13/16	2	.125	—	—	—	3 Rich
	D9DE-SA	7/16	13/16	2	.125	—	—	—	3 Rich
	D9OE-CB	7/16	13/16	3	.132	—	—	—	3 Rich
	D9OE-DB	7/16	13/16	3	.132	—	—	—	3 Rich
	D9AE-AHA	7/16	13/16	3	.147	—	—	—	3 Rich
	D9AE-AJA	7/16	13/16	3	.147	—	—	—	3 Rich
	D9WE-JA	7/16	13/16	3	.150	—	—	—	2 Rich
	D9WE-MB	7/16	13/16	3	.132	—	—	—	1 Rich
	D9WE-NB	7/16	13/16	3	.132	—	—	—	1 Rich
1980	E0TE-BEA	—	13/16	#2	.140	—	.25	—	—
	E0TE-BGA	—	13/16	#2	.135	—	.25	—	—
	E0TE-BHA	—	13/16	#2	.135	—	.25	—	—
	E0TE-BRA	—	7/8	#3	.128	—	.115	—	—
	E0TE-BSA	—	7/8	#2	.140	—	.115	—	—
	E0TE-BYA	—	7/8	#2	—	—	.115	—	—
	E0TE-CFA	—	13/16	#2	.128	—	.25	—	—
	E0TE-CLA	—	7/8	#2	.140	—	.200	—	—

Continued

FORD

1970–80 MODEL 2100, 2150-2V ADJUSTMENT SPECIFICATIONS—Continued

See Tune Up Chart for hot idle speeds.

Year	Carb. Model	Float Level (Dry)	Fuel Level (Wet)	Pump Setting Hole No.	Choke Plate Clearance (Pull down)	Fast Idle Cam Linkage Clearance	Dechoke Clearance	Dashpot Setting	Choke Setting
	EOTE-CVA	—	7/8	#2	.105	—	.25	—	—
	EOTE-CYA	—	13/16	#2	.140	—	.25	—	—
	EOTE-CZA	—	13/16	#2	.140	—	.25	—	—
	EOTE-DBA	—	7/8	#3	.130	—	.25	—	—
	EOTE-DCA	—	7/8	#3	.130	—	.25	—	—
	EOTE-DDA	—	7/8	#3	.128	—	.115	—	—
	EOTE-EAA	—	13/16	#2	.128	—	.25	—	—
	EOUE-AA	—	13/16	#3	.105	—	.25	—	—
	EOUE-ABA	—	13/16	#2	.140	—	.25	—	—
	EOUE-AAA	—	13/16	#3	.195	—	.25	—	—
	EOTE-BLA	—	7/8	#3	.148	—	.25	—	—
	EOTE-BFA	—	7/8	#3	.148	—	.25	—	—
	EOTE-BZA	—	7/8	#3	.148	—	.25	—	—
	EOTE-CCA	—	7/8	#3	.159	—	.25	—	—
	EOTE-CBA	—	7/8	#3	.159	—	.25	—	—
	EOTE-EDA	—	7/8	#4	.155	—	.25	—	—
	EOTE-DGA	—	7/8	#4	.155	—	.25	—	—
	EOTE-EEA, EFA	—	7/8	#4	.160	—	.25	—	—
	EOUE-NA	—	13/16	#3	.105	—	.25	—	—
	EOUE-PA, RA	—	13/16	#4	.185	—	.25	—	—
	EOUE-SA, TA	—	13/16	#3	.195	—	.25	—	—
	EOUE-VA	—	13/16	#4	.185	—	.25	—	—
	EOTE-DEA	—	7/8	#4	.170	—	.25	—	—
	EOTE-DFA	—	7/8	#4	.180	—	.25	—	—
	EOTE-ECA	—	7/8	#4	.175	—	.25	—	—

HOLLEY 2300-2V ADJUSTMENT SPECIFICATIONS

Year	Model	Float Level (Dry)	Float Level (Wet)	Pump Cam Position	Pump Override Spring Adj.	Choke Setting
1970–71	C9HF-A	—	②	#2	.015	—
	C9HF-B	—	②	#2	.015	—
1972	D2HF-AA	①	②	#2	.015	—
	D2HF-BA	①	②	#2	.015	—
	D2HF-CA	①	②	#2	.015	—
1973	D3HF-AA	①	②	#2	.015	—
	D3HF-BA	①	②	#2	.015	—
	D3HF-CA	①	②	#2	.015	—
	D3HF-JA	①	②	#2	.015	—
1974–78	D4TE-AHA	①	②	#2	.015	—
	D4TE-AJA	①	②	#2	.015	—
	D4TE-AKA	①	②	#2	.015	—
	D4TE-AMA	①	②	#2	.015	—
1978	D8TE-AJA	③	②	#2	.015	—
	D8TE-BPA	③	②	#2	.015	—
	D8TE-CEA	③	②	#2	.015	—
1979	D9TE-CUA	①	②	#2	.015	—
1979–80	D9TE-APA	①	②	#2	.015	—
	D9TE-ABC	①	②	#2	.015	—
1980	EOTE-PA	—	②	#1	—	—
	EOTE-BCA	—	②	#1	—	—

①—Parallel with float bowl floor (inverted).   ②—Lower edge of sight plug.   ③—Parallel with float bowl floor (inverted) plus one turn clockwise.

FORD

HOLLEY MODEL 4150, 4160 & 4180-4V ADJUSTMENT SPECIFICATIONS

Year	Carb. Model	Float Level (Dry)	Float Level (Wet)	Pump Cam Position	Pump Override Spring Adjustment	Pulldown Setting	Choke Unloader	Choke Setting
1970–71	C9HF-C	—	②	#2	.015	—	—	—
	D0HF-A	—	②	#2	.015	—	—	—
	D0HF-B	—	②	#2	.015	—	—	—
	D0HF-C	—	②	#2	.015	—	—	—
1972	D2HF-DA	①	②	#2	.015	—	—	—
	D2HF-EA	①	②	#1	.015	—	—	—
	D2HF-FA	①	②	#1	.015	—	—	—
	D1HF-FA	①	②	#1	.015	—	—	—
1973	D3HF-DA	①	②	#2	.015	—	—	—
	D3HF-EA	①	②	#1	.015	—	—	—
	D3HF-FA	①	②	#1	.015	—	—	—
	D3HF-GA	①	②	#1	.015	—	—	—
1974	D4HE-DA	①	②	#1	.015	—	—	—
	D4HE-CA	①	②	#1	.015	—	—	—
	D4HE-BA	—	②	#1	—	—	—	—
	D4TE-ARA	①	②	#1	.015	—	.315	Index
	D4TE-ASA	①	②	#1	.015	—	.315	Index
	D4TE-ANA	—	②	#2	—	—	—	—
1974–75	D4HE-BA	①	②	#1	.015	—	—	—
	D4HE-CA	①	②	#1	.015	—	—	—
	D4HE-DA	①	②	#1	.015	—	—	—
1975	D5TE-BA	①	②	#2	.015	—	—	—
	D5TE-CB	①	②	#2	.015	—	—	—
	D5TE-AA	①	②	#2	.015	—	—	—
	D5TE-BRA	①	②	#2	.015	—	—	—
	D5TE-DA	①	②	#1	.015	.180	.315	Index
	D5TE-EA	①	②	#1	.015	.180	.315	Index
	D5TE-FA	①	②	#1	.015	.180	.315	Index
	D5TE-GA	①	②	#1	.015	.180	.315	Index
	D5HE-BA	①	②	#1	.015	—	—	—
	D5HE-CA	①	②	#1	.015	—	—	—
1975–76	D4HE-CA	①	②	#1	.015	—	—	—
	D4HE-DA	①	②	#1	.015	—	—	—
	D5TE-AA	①	②	#2	.015	—	—	—
	D5TE-BA	①	②	#2	.015	—	—	—
	D5TE-BRA	①	②	#2	.015	—	—	—
	D5TE-CB	①	②	#2	.015	—	—	—
	D5HE-BA	①	②	#1	.015	—	—	—
	D5HE-CA	①	②	#1	.015	—	—	—
	D5TE-DA	①	②	#1	.015	.180	.315	Index
	D5TE-EA	①	②	#1	.015	.180	.315	Index
	D5TE-FA	①	②	#1	.015	.180	.315	Index
	D5TE-GA	①	②	#1	.015	.180	.315	Index
1976	D6HE-CB	①	②	#1	.015	—	—	—
	D6HE-DB	①	②	#1	.015	—	—	—
	D5TE-FB	①	②	#1	.015	.200	.315	2 Lean
	D5TE-GB	①	②	#1	.015	.190	.315	2 Lean
1976–77	D5HE-BA	①	②	#1	.015	—	—	—
	D5HE-CA	①	②	#1	.015	—	—	—
	D5TE-BRA	①	②	#2	.015	—	—	—
	D5TE-AA	①	②	#2	.015	—	—	—
	D5TE-CB	①	②	#2	.015	—	—	—
1977	D6HE-DA	—	②	#1	—	—	—	—
	D6HE-CA	—	②	#1	—	—	—	—
	D4TE-EAA	—	②	#2	—	—	—	—
	D4TE-CA	—	②	#2	—	—	—	—
	D5TE-B	—	②	#2	—	—	—	—

Continued

FORD

HOLLEY MODEL 4150, 4160 & 4180-4V ADJUSTMENT SPECIFICATIONS—Continued

Year	Carb. Model	Float Level (Dry)	Float Level (Wet)	Pump Cam Position	Pump Override Spring Adjustment	Pulldown Setting	Choke Unloader	Choke Setting
	D7HE-CA	—	②	#1	—	—	—	—
	D7HE-RA	—	②	#1	—	—	—	—
1977-78	D5TE-BRA	①	②	#2	.015	—	—	—
	D5TE-CB	①	②	#2	.015	—	—	—
1978	D8TE-AGA	③	②	#2	.015	—	—	—
	D8TE-AHA	③	②	#2	.015	—	—	—
	D8TE-BRA	③	②	#2	.015	—	—	—
	D8TE-BSA	③	②	#2	.015	—	—	—
	D8HE-AA	③	②	#1	.015	—	—	—
	D8HE-CA	③	②	#1	.015	—	—	—
	D8HE-EA	①	②	#1	.015	.375	—	—
	D8HE-BA	③	②	#1	.015	—	—	—
	D8HE-DA	③	②	#1	.015	—	—	—
	D8HE-FA	①	②	#1	.015	.375	—	—
	D8TE-BZA	①	②	#2	.015	—	—	—
	D8TE-CBA	①	②	#2	.015	—	—	—
	D6HE-CB	①	②	#1	.015	.375	—	—
	D6HE-DB	①	②	#1	.015	.375	—	—
1979	D9HE-DA	①	②	#1	—	—	—	—
	D9HE-CA	①	②	#1	.015	—	—	—
	D9HE-FA	①	②	#1	.015	—	—	—
	D9HE-EA	①	②	#1	.015	—	—	—
	D9TE-BKA	①	②	#1	.015	.210	.315	5 Rich
	D9TE-AGA	①	②	#1	.015	.210	.315	5 Rich
	D9TE-AEA	①	②	#1	.015	.210	.315	5 Rich
	D9TE-ACC	①	②	#1	.015	—	—	—
	D9TE-AZA	①	②	#1	.015	—	—	—
	D9TE-AYB	①	②	#1	.015	—	—	—
	D9TE-AHD	①	②	#1	.015	—	—	—
1980	D9TE-AHE	—	②	#2	—	—	—	—
	D9TE-EBA	—	②	#2	—	—	—	—
	D9TE-ETA	—	②	#1	—	—	—	—
	D9TE-EUA	—	②	#1	—	—	—	—
	E0TE-JA	—	②	#1	—	—	—	—
	E0TE-RA	—	②	#1	—	—	—	—

①—Parallel with float bowl floor (inverted).
②—Lower edge of sight plug.
③—Parallel with float bowl floor (inverted) plus one turn clockwise.

1970-78 MODEL 4300/4350-4V ADJUSTMENT SPECIFICATIONS

See Tune Up Chart for hot idle speed.

Year	Carb. Model	Float Level (Dry)	Pump Setting (Hole No.)	Choke Plate Clearance (Pulldown)	Fast Idle Cam Linkage Setting	Auxiliary Inlet Valve Setting	Metering Rod Setting	Dechoke Clearance	Dashpot Setting	Choke Setting
1970	D0AF-AB	25/32	#2	.250	.220	1/16	—	.300	.070	Index
	D0AF-AG	25/32	#2	.220	—	1/16	—	.300	.070	Index
	D0AF-AL	25/32	#2	.250	.220	1/16	—	.300	.070	Index
	D0AF-AM	25/32	#2	.220	—	1/16	—	.300	.070	Index
	D0AF-L	25/32	#2	.250	.220	1/16	—	.300	.070	Index
	D0OF-AA	53/64	#2	.200	.180	—	—	.300	—	Index
	D0OF-AB	53/64	#2	.180	.160	1/16	—	.300	—	Index
	D0OF-AC	53/64	#2	.200	.180	1/16	—	.300	.080	Index
	D0OF-AD	53/64	#2	.200	.180	—	—	.300	—	Index
	D0OF-Y	53/64	#2	.200	.180	—	—	.300	.080	Index

Continued

FORD

1970–78 MODEL 4300/4350-4V ADJUSTMENT SPECIFICATIONS—Continued

See Tune Up Chart for hot idle speed.

Year	Carb. Model	Float Level (Dry)	Pump Setting (Hole No.)	Choke Plate Clearance (Pulldown)	Fast Idle Cam Linkage Setting	Auxiliary Inlet Valve Setting	Metering Rod Setting	Dechoke Clearance	Dashpot Setting	Choke Setting
	D0OF-Z	53/64	#2	.180	.160	—	—	.300	—	Index
1971	D1AF-MA	49/64	#2	.220	—	1/16	—	—	1/16	Index
	D1OF-AAA	13/16	#2	.200	.180	1/16	—	—	—	Index
	D1OF-EA	13/16	#2	.180	.160	1/16	—	—	—	Index
1972	D2AF-AA	49/64	#1	.220	.200	—	—	—	—	2 Rich
	D2AF-AB	49/64	#1	.220	.200	—	—	—	—	2 Rich
	D2SF-BA	49/64	#1	.220	.200	—	—	—	—	2 Rich
	D2SF-BB	49/64	#1	.220	.200	—	—	—	—	2 Rich
	D2ZF-AA	13/16	#1	.200	.200	.030	—	—	—	Index
	D2ZF-BB	13/16	#1	.180	.200	.030	—	—	—	Index
1973	D3AF-HA	49/64	#1	.210	.200	.060	—	—	—	Index
	D3MF-AE	7/16	#3	—	—	—	—	—	—	3 Rich
	D3ZF-AC	53/64	#1	.180	.180	.030	—	—	—	Index
	D3ZF-BC	53/64	#1	.170	.170	.030	—	—	—	1 Rich
1974	D4AE-NA	3/4	#1	.220	.200	1/16	—	—	—	Index
	D4TE-ATA	13/16	#1	.220	.180	1/16	—	—	—	Index
	D4TE-BB	3/4	#1	.220	.200	1/16	—	—	—	Index
	D4VE-AB	3/4	#1	.220	.200	1/16	—	—	—	Index
1975–76	D5AE-CA	31/32	Inner	②	.160	—	.120	.300	—	2 Rich
	D5AE-DA	31/32	Inner	②	.160	—	.120	.300	—	2 Rich
	D5TE-ARC	15/16	#2	.160	.170	1/16	①	.300	—	Index
	D5TE-ARD	1.00	#2	.160	.170	.030	①	.300	—	Index
	D5TE-BBA	15/16	#2	.160	.170	1/16	①	.300	—	Index
	D5TE-BBB	59/64	#2	.160	.170	.060	①	.300	—	Index
	D5TE-BBC	1.00	#2	.160	.170	.030	①	.300	—	Index
	D5UE-NA	15/16	#2	.160	.170	1/16	①	.300	—	Index
	D5UE-NB	59/64	#2	.160	.170	.060	①	.300	—	Index
	D5UE-NC	1.00	#2	.160	.170	.030	①	.300	—	Index
	D5UE-SA	15/16	#2	.160	.170	1/16	①	.300	—	Index
	D5UE-SB	1.00	#2	.160	.170	.030	①	.300	—	Index
	D5VE-AD	15/16	#1	②	.160	1/16	①	.300	—	2 Rich
	D5VE-BA	15/16	#1	②	.160	1/16	①	.300	—	2 Rich
1976	D6AE-CA	1.00	#2	③	.140	.030	①	.300	—	2 Rich
	D6AE-DA	31/32	#2	④	.160	.030	①	.300	—	2 Rich
	D6AE-FA	1.00	#2	③	.140	.030	①	.300	—	2 Rich
	D6UE-KA	1.00	#2	.160	.170	—	—	.300	—	Index
	D6UE-LA	1.00	#2	.160	.170	—	—	.300	—	Index
	D6TE-NA	1.00	#2	.160	.170	—	—	.300	—	Index
	D6TE-UA	1.00	#2	.160	.170	—	—	.300	—	Index
1977	D7UE-AFA	1.00	#2	.160	.170	—	—	.300	—	Index
	D7UE-AGA	1.00	#2	.160	.170	—	—	.300	—	Index
	D7TE-BJA	1.00	#2	.160	.170	—	—	.300	—	Index
	D7TE-BLA	1.00	#2	.160	.170	—	—	.300	—	Index
1978	D8TE-AKA	1.00	#3	.160	.160	—	—	.300	—	Index
	D8UE-AA	1.00	#3	.160	.160	—	—	.300	—	Index
	D7UE-ASA	1.00	#3	.160 ⑤	.160	—	—	.300	—	Index
	DTUE-ASA	1.00	#3	.160 ⑤	.160	—	—	.300	—	Index
	D8UE-AA	1.00	#3	.160	.160	—	—	.300	—	Index
	D8TE-AMA	1.00	#3	.160	.170	—	—	.300	—	Index
	D8UE-CA	1.00	#3	.160	.170	—	—	.300	—	Index

①—Check before disassembling and reset to original setting.
②—Initial setting, .160"; delayed setting, .190".
③—Initial setting, .140"; delayed setting, .190".
④—Initial setting, .160"; delayed setting, .210".
⑤—Delayed setting, .200".

Ford

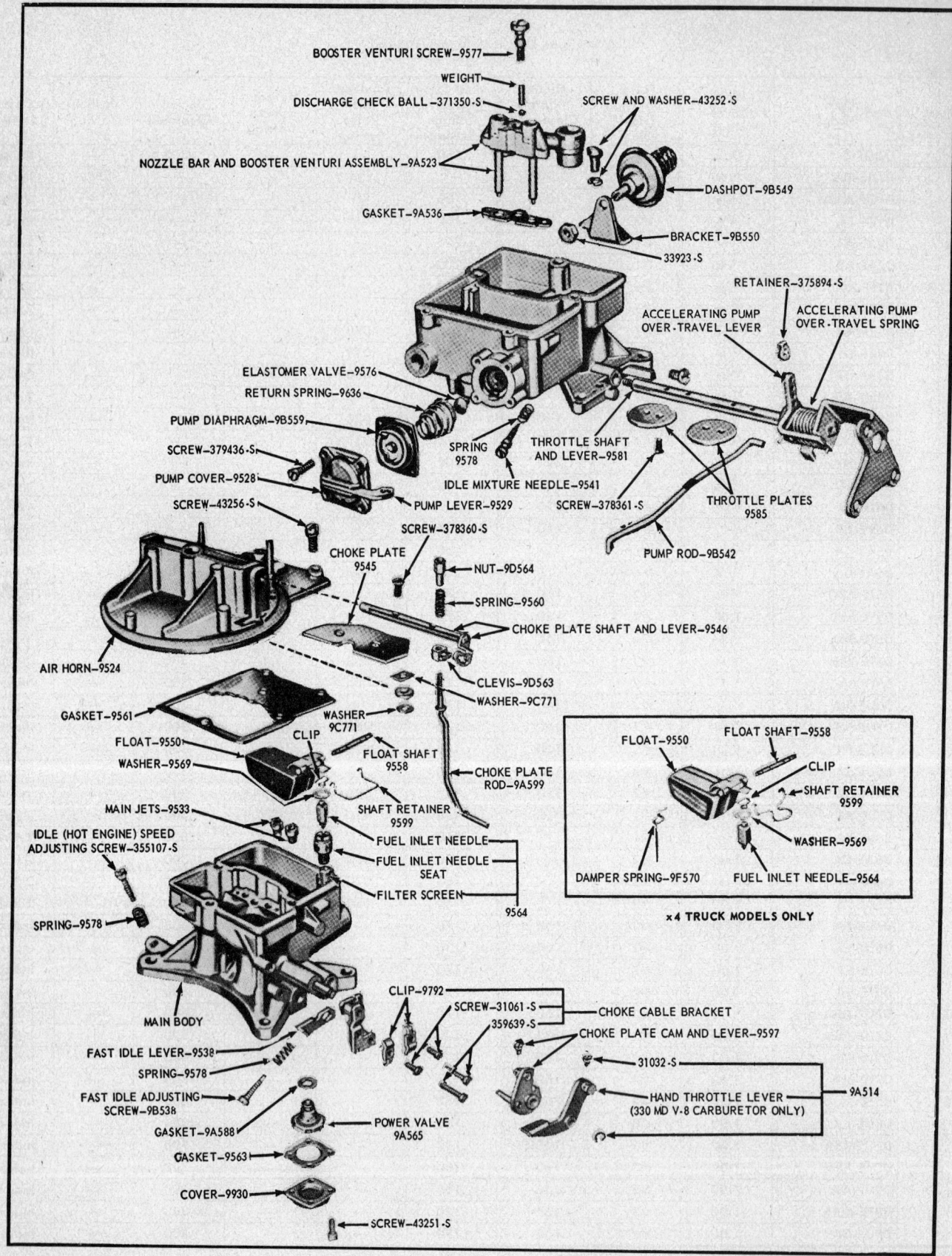

Ford-Autolite/Motorcraft Model 2100, 2150-2V (Typical)

FORD

Fig. 1 Float adjustment. Ford Autolite/Motorcraft 2100, 2150-2V

FORD AUTOLITE/ MOTORCRAFT CARBURETOR ADJUSTMENTS

Model 2100, 2150-2V

Float Adjustment (Dry), Fig. 1

The dry float fuel level adjustment is a preliminary adjustment only. The final adjustment must be made after the carburetor is mounted on the engine.

Remove the air horn. With float raised and fuel inlet needle seated, check distance between top surface of main body and top surface of float. Take measurement at a point $1/8''$ from the free end of the float and $1/8''$ ($5/16''$ metal float) in from side of float adjacent to inside wall of air horn.

If cardboard gauge is used, place gauge in corner of the enlarged end section of fuel bowl as shown. The gauge should touch float near the end but not on the end radius.

Depress the float tab to seat the fuel inlet needle. The float height is measured from the gasket surface of the main body with gasket removed. If necessary, bend float tab to bring setting within specified limits. This should provide the correct fuel level setting.

Fuel Level (Wet), Fig. 2

1. Operate engine to normalize engine temperatures, and place vehicle on a flat surface as near level as possible. Stop the engine.
2. Remove air cleaner and carburetor air horn assembly and gasket.
3. Temporarily place air horn gasket in position on carburetor main body and start engine. Let engine idle for a few minutes, then remove air horn and gasket to provide accessibility to float assembly.
4. While engine is idling, use a standard depth scale to measure vertical distance from top machined surface of carburetor main body to level of fuel in bowl. Measurement must be made at least $1/4''$ away from any vertical surface to insure an accurate reading, because the surface of the fuel is higher at the edges than in the center.
5. If an adjustment is required, stop the engine and bend the flot tab as necessary to bring the fuel level within specifications.

Accelerating Pump Adjustment, Figs. 3 & 4

The primary throttle shaft lever (overtravel lever) has 4 holes and the accelerating pump link has 2 or 4 holes to control the pump stroke for various atmospheric temperatures, operating conditions and specific engine applications.

NOTE: The stroke should not be changed from the specified setting.

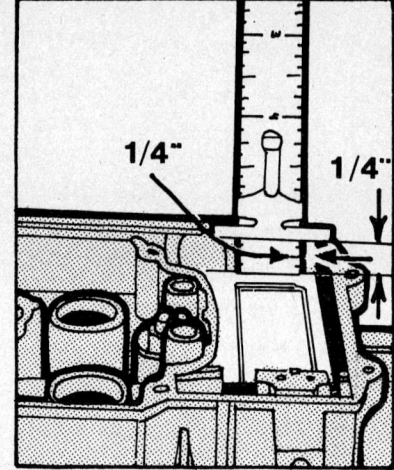

Fig. 2 Fuel level adjustment. Ford Autolite/Motorcraft 2100, 2150-2V

1. To release rod from retainer clip, press tab end of clip toward rod. Then, at the same time, press rod away from clip until it is disengaged.
2. Position clip over specified hole in overtravel lever. Press ends of clip together and insert operating rod through clip and lever. Release clip to engage rod.

Choke Plate Clearance, Manual Choke, Fig. 5

Remove air cleaner. Pull choke cam and lever to full-choke position. Insert the specified drill or gauge between downward side of choke plate and air horn wall. The gauge or drill will open the choke plate against the pull-down spring tension. Adjust the choke operating (pull-down) rod adjusting nut so it just contacts plastic swivel.

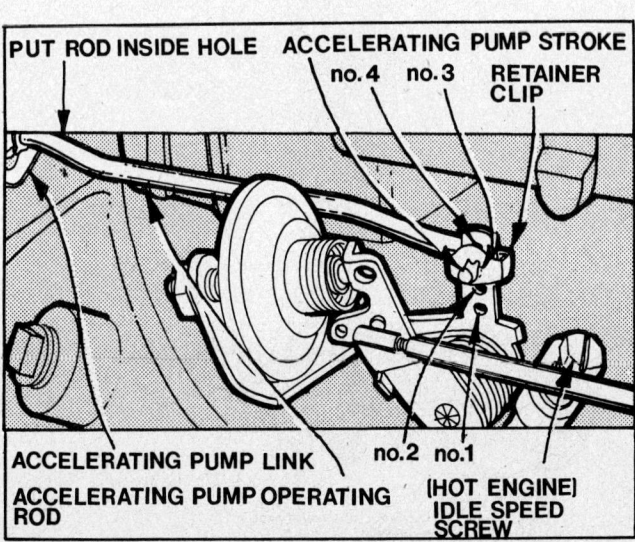

Fig. 3 Pump stroke adjustment, 1970–71. Ford Autolite/Motorcraft 2100-2V

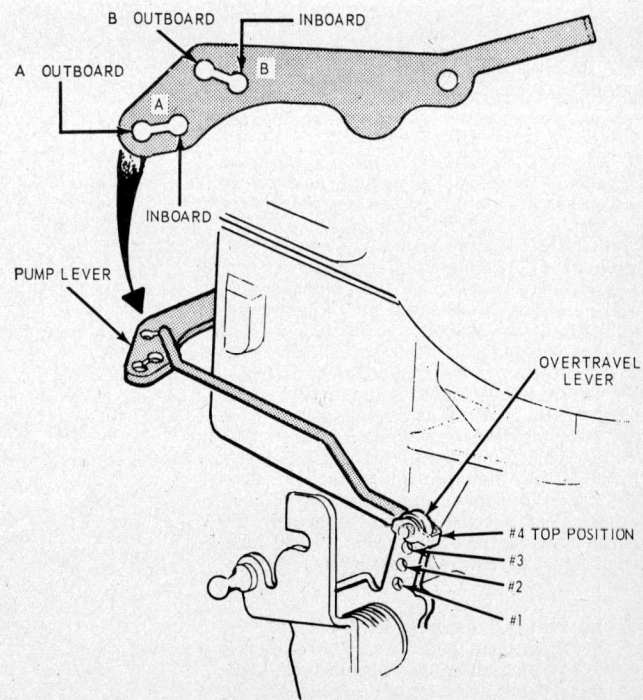

Fig. 4 Pump stroke adjustment, 1972–80. Ford Autolite/Motorcraft 2100, 2150-2V

Ford

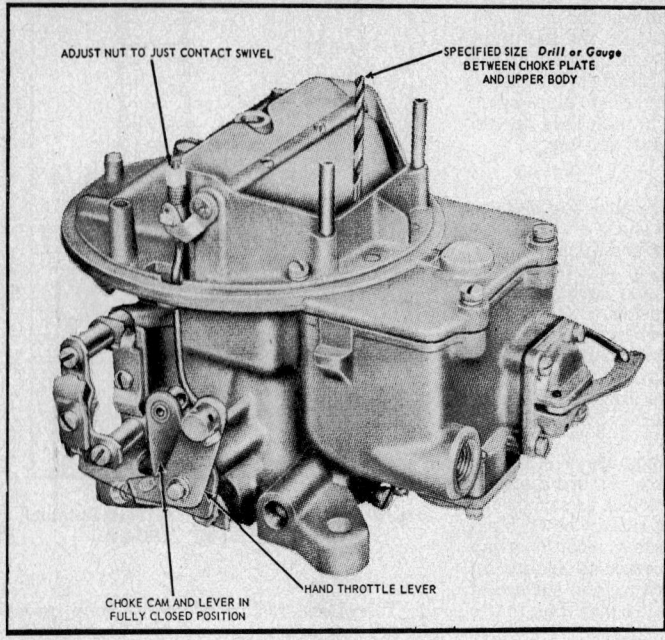

Fig. 5 Choke plate clearance adjustment, manual choke. Ford Autolite/Motorcraft 2100-2V

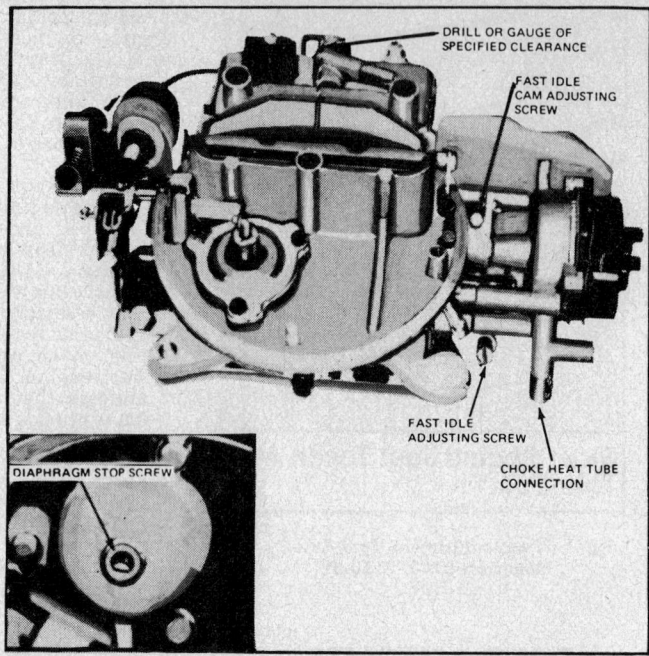

Fig. 6 Choke plate clearance, 1970–72 automatic choke & 1973–74 All. Ford Autolite/Motorcraft 2100-2V

Choke Plate Clearance, Automatic Choke, 1970–72

1. With the engine at normal operating temperature, loosen the choke thermostatic spring housing retainer screws and set the housing 90 degrees in the rich direction.
2. Disconnect and remove the choke heat tube from the choke housing.
3. Turn the fast idle adjusting screw outward one full turn.
4. Start the engine, then check clearance between the lower edge of the choke plate and the air horn wall, Fig. 6. Refer to Specifications Chart.
5. Adjust by turning the diaphragm stop screw located on the underside of the choke diaphragm housing, clockwise to decrease or counterclockwise to increase the clearance, Fig. 6.
6. Connect the choke heat tube and set the choke thermostatic spring housing to specifications. Adjust the fast idle speed.

Choke Plate Clearance, 1973–74 All

Since the choke plate pulldown is set in production by means of an air-fuel meter; no specific clearance is indicated for pulldown adjustment. If the vehicle shows indication of leanness during cold starting, decrease the clearance between the choke plate and the air horn wall by 0.020 inch. If the engine shows signs of an overrich condition during cold starting, increase the pulldown clearance by 0.020 inch. If additional adjustment is required always make the adjustments in steps of 0.020 inch. If the original pulldown adjustment is lost, set the clearance between the choke plate and the air horn to 0.160 inch. Then adjust as required in steps on 0.020 inch, Fig. 6.

Choke Plate Clearance, 1975–80 All

1. Set throttle on fast idle cam top step, Fig. 8, then loosen choke thermostatic housing retaining screws and set housing 90° in rich direction.
2. Activate pulldown motor by manually forcing pulldown control diaphragm link in direction of applied vacuum or by applying vacuum to external vacuum tube.
3. Check clearance between choke plate and center of carburetor air horn wall nearest fuel bowl, Fig. 7. Refer to the Specifications Chart. If clearance is not as specified, reset by adjusting diaphragm stop on end of choke pulldown diaphragm.

Fast Idle Cam Clearance, 1970–74

1. Loosen the choke thermostatic spring housing retainer screws and set the housing 90 degrees in the rich direction.
2. Position the fast idle speed screw at the kickdown step of the fast idle cam. The kickdown step is identified on most units by a V stamped on the cam, Fig. 8. When a two-piece fast idle lever is used, a tang on the top lever will align with the V mark on the cam, Fig. 8.
3. Be sure the cam is at the kickdown position while checking or adjusting the fast idle cam clearance. Check clearance between the lower edge of the choke plate and the air horn wall, Fig. 9. Refer to the Specifications Chart. Adjust clearance by turning the fast idle cam clearance ad-

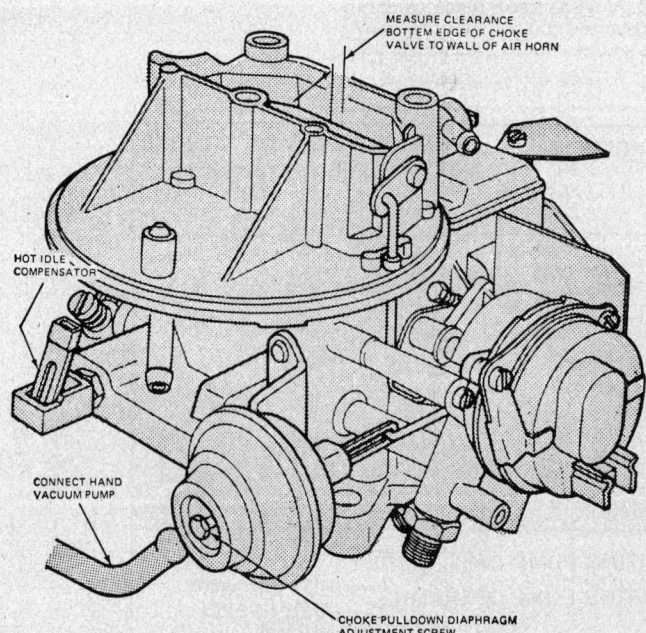

Fig. 7 Choke plate clearance. 1975–79 All. Ford Autolite/Motorcraft 2150-2V

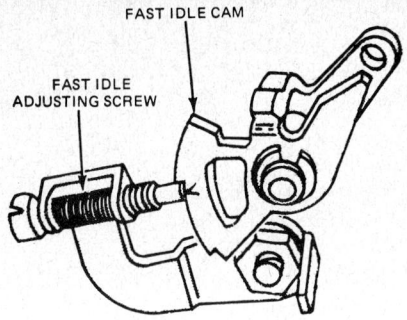

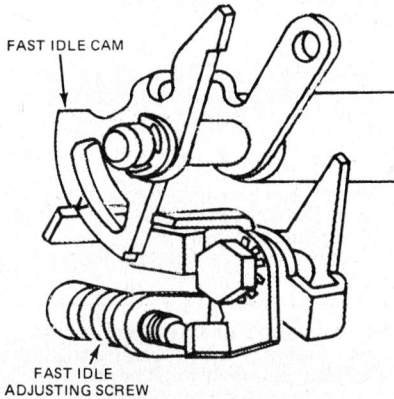

Fig. 8 Fast idle cam assemblies. Ford Autolite/Motorcraft 2100, 2150-2V

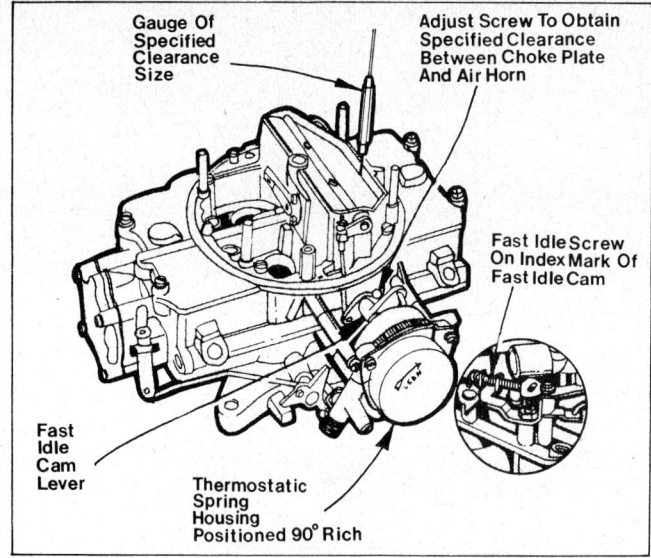

Fig. 9 Fast idle cam linkage adjustment. Ford Autolite/Motorcraft 2100, 2150-2V

justing screw clockwise to increase and counterclockwise to decrease the clearance.
4. Set the choke thermostatic spring housing to specifications, Fig. 12. Adjust the anti-stall dashpot, idle speed and fuel mixture.

Fast Idle Cam Clearance, 1975–80
1. Open and close throttle slightly and observe where fast idle screw contacts cam. The fast idle screw should be set to approximate high cam speed and should strike the second highest step on fast idle cam.

2. After adjusting fast idle cam with fast idle screw, allow choke plate to close. Choke plate should close tightly in air horn.
3. If choke plate is loose, an additional adjustment must be made to pulldown diaphragm rod assembly, by loosening lock nut and tightening turnbuckle until choke plate is tight on airhorn.

Automatic Choke Valve Tension
Turn thermostatic spring cover against spring tension until index mark on cover is aligned with mark specified in the *Specifications Chart* on choke housing, Fig. 10.

Fast Idle Speed, Figs. 8 & 11
The fast (cold engine) idle speed is adjusted with the hand throttle control rod pushed fully inward to prevent contact of the hand (manual) throttle lever with the fast idle pick-up lever during the adjustment procedure.

With the hot idle speed properly adjusted, manually rotate the choke cam and lever until the fast idle adjusting screw rests on the index mark (arrow) on the cam. Turn fast idle adjusting screw in or out as required so that screw just contacts the cam at the index mark to obtain the specified fast idle rpm.

Anti-Stall Dashpot, Fig. 12
With air cleaner removed, and with engine idle speed and mixture properly adjusted, loosen anti-stall dashpot lock nut. Hold throttle in closed position and depress plunger with a screwdriver. Check clearance between throttle lever and plunger tip with a feeler gauge of the specified clearance dimension. Then turn dashpot in its bracket in a direction to provide the specified clearance.

Staged Choke Vacuum Control, 1972

NOTE: This adjustment should be made only if the control unit has been replaced, the carburetor has been overhauled or a choke adjustment has been made.

NOTE: Before performing this adjustment, the choke pulldown and fast idle cam must be adjusted.

1. Close choke plate.
2. Measure the clearance between the forward edge of the choke link and the edge of the slot in the choke vacuum lever, Fig. 13.

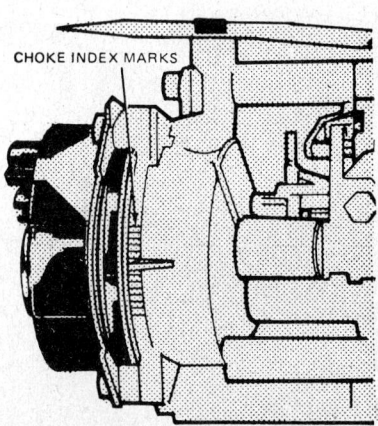

Fig. 10 Automatic choke adjustment. Ford Autolite/Motorcraft 2100, 2150-2V

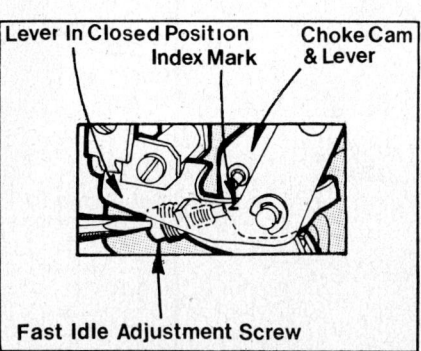

Fig. 11 Fast idle speed adjustment. Ford Autolite/Motorcraft 2100, 2150-2V (Typical)

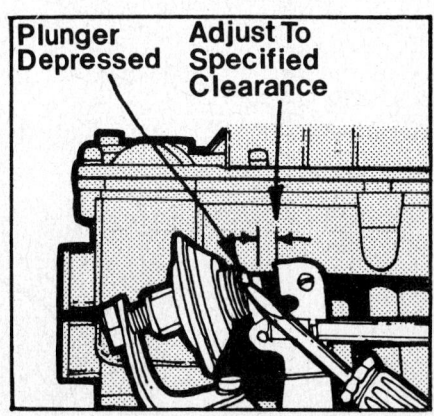

Fig. 12 Dashpot adjustment. Typical of all Ford applications

FORD

Fig. 13 Staged choke vacuum control adjustment, 1972. Ford Autolite/Motorcraft 2100-2V

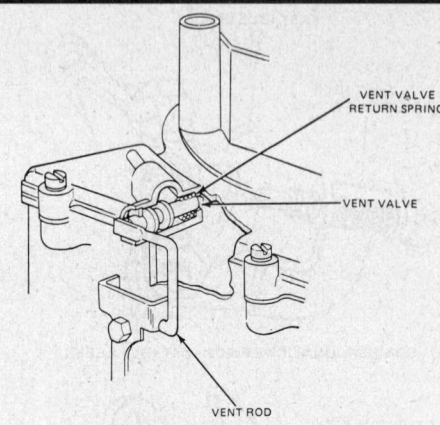

Fig. 14 Bowl vent valve, 1972. Ford Autolite/Motorcraft 2100-2V

NOTE: Place C-clip in a position so that gap is visible.

3. Adjust by inserting a 1/4 inch socket and drive on the nylon adjuster, Fig. 13. Hold the choke link with needlenose pliers to prevent flexing, then turn the adjuster until 1/32 inch clearance is obtained.

Bowl Vent Valve, 1972
1. Fully depress the vent valve into the valve bore.
2. Measure the clearance between the flat on the vent rod and the fully seated valve, Fig. 14.
3. Adjust by bending the vent rod at the point where it contacts the accelerator pump lever until 3/32 inch clearance is obtained.

Model 4300-4V

Float Setting, Figs. 15 & 16
1. Adjust gauge to specified height.
2. Insert gauge into air horn outboard holes as shown.
3. Check clearance and alignment of float pontoons to gauge. Both pontoons should just touch gauge for proper setting. Align pontoons if necessary by slightly twisting pontoons.
4. If it is necessary to adjust float clearance, bend primary needle tab downward to raise float and upward to lower float.

NOTE: To raise float, insert open end of bending tool to *right* side of float lever tab and between needle and float hinge. Raise float lever off needle and bend tab downward.
To lower float, insert open end of bending tool to *left* side of float lever tab, between needle and float hinge. Support float lever and bend tab upward.

Auxiliary Valve Setting, Fig. 17
1. Turn the air horn assembly upright allowing the float to hang freely.
2. Push up on the float until the primary fuel inlet needle lightly contacts its seat.
3. While holding the float in this position, measure the clearance between the float lever auxiliary tab and the auxiliary inlet valve plunger.
4. Adjust by bending the tab. Refer to the *Specifications Chart*.

NOTE: To measure this clearance on a police fleet carburetor with a semi-articulating float, the float assembly must be positioned so that the bottom of both pontoons are same distance from gasket surface of air horn when primary fuel inlet is seated.

Fast Idle Speed Adjustment
The fast idle adjusting screw contacts one edge of the fast idle cam. Each position on the fast idle cam permits a slower idle rpm as engine temperature rises and choking is reduced.

NOTE: Make certain the curb idle speed and mixture are adjusted to specification before attempting to set the fast idle speed.

1. With the engine operating temperature normalized (hot), air cleaner removed and the tachometer attached, manually rotate

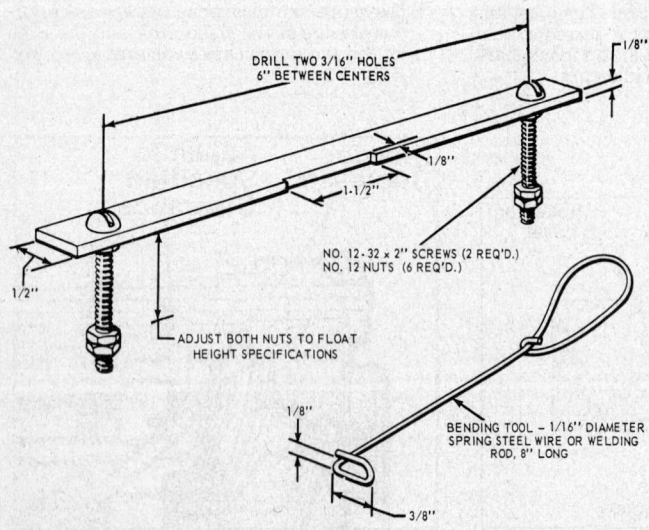

Fig. 15 Float setting gauge & bending tool. Ford Autolite/Motorcraft 4300, 4350-4V

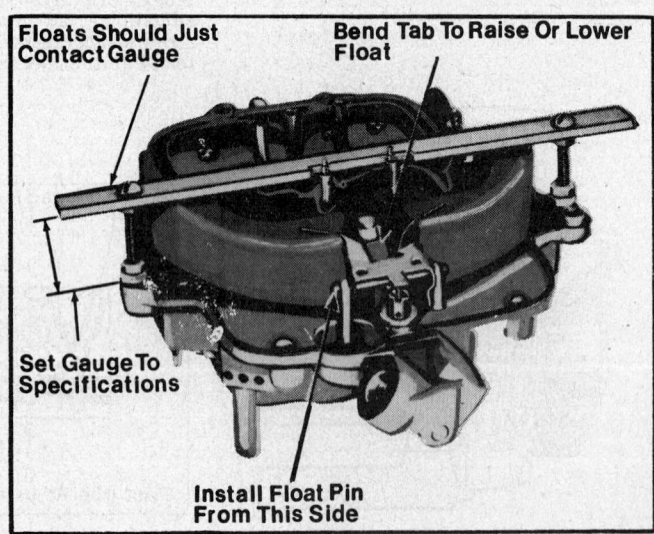

Fig. 16 Float setting. Ford Autolite/Motorcraft 4300, 4350-4V

Ford

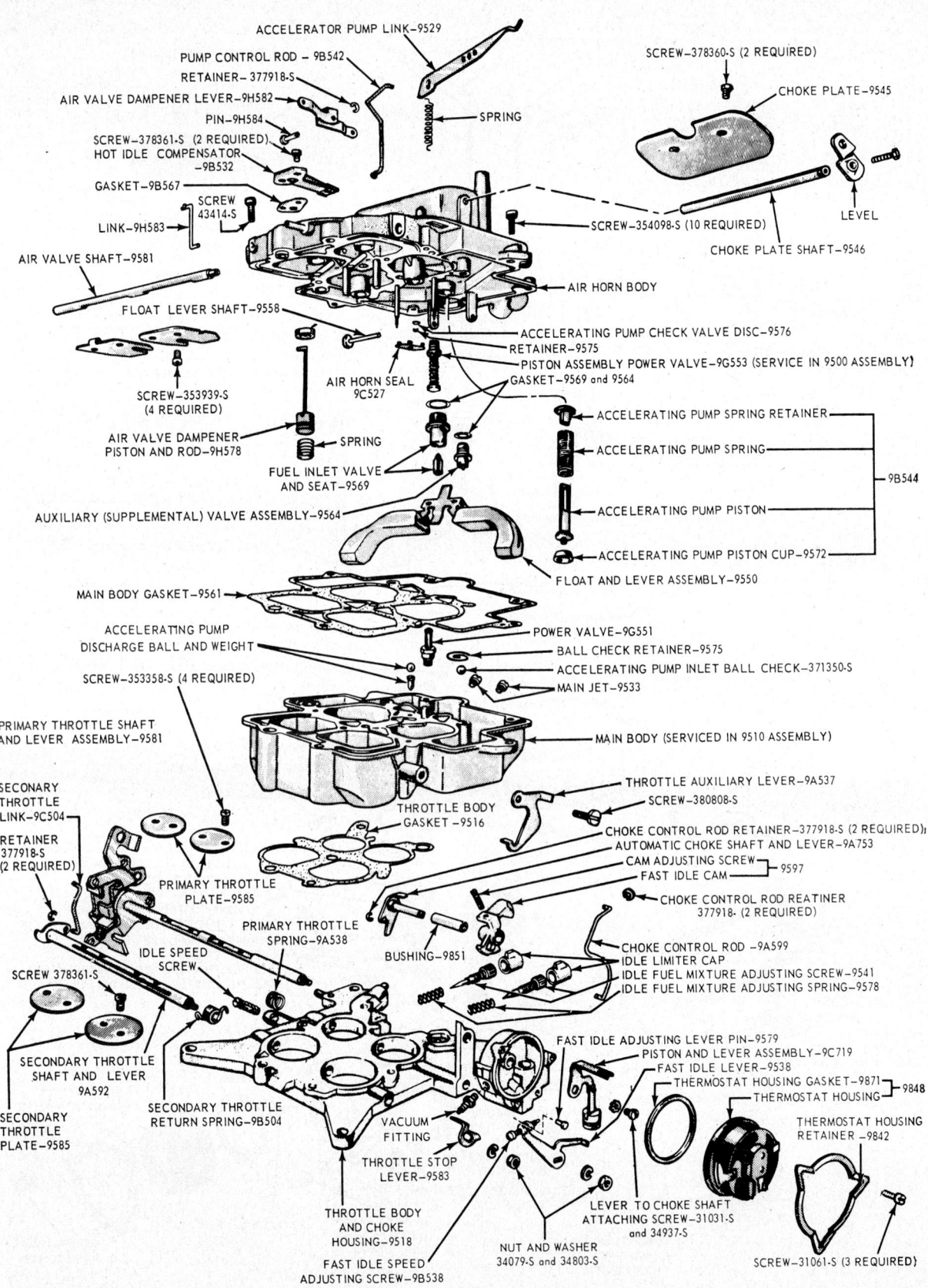

Ford-Autolite/Motorcraft Model 4300-A, 4V (Typical)

Ford

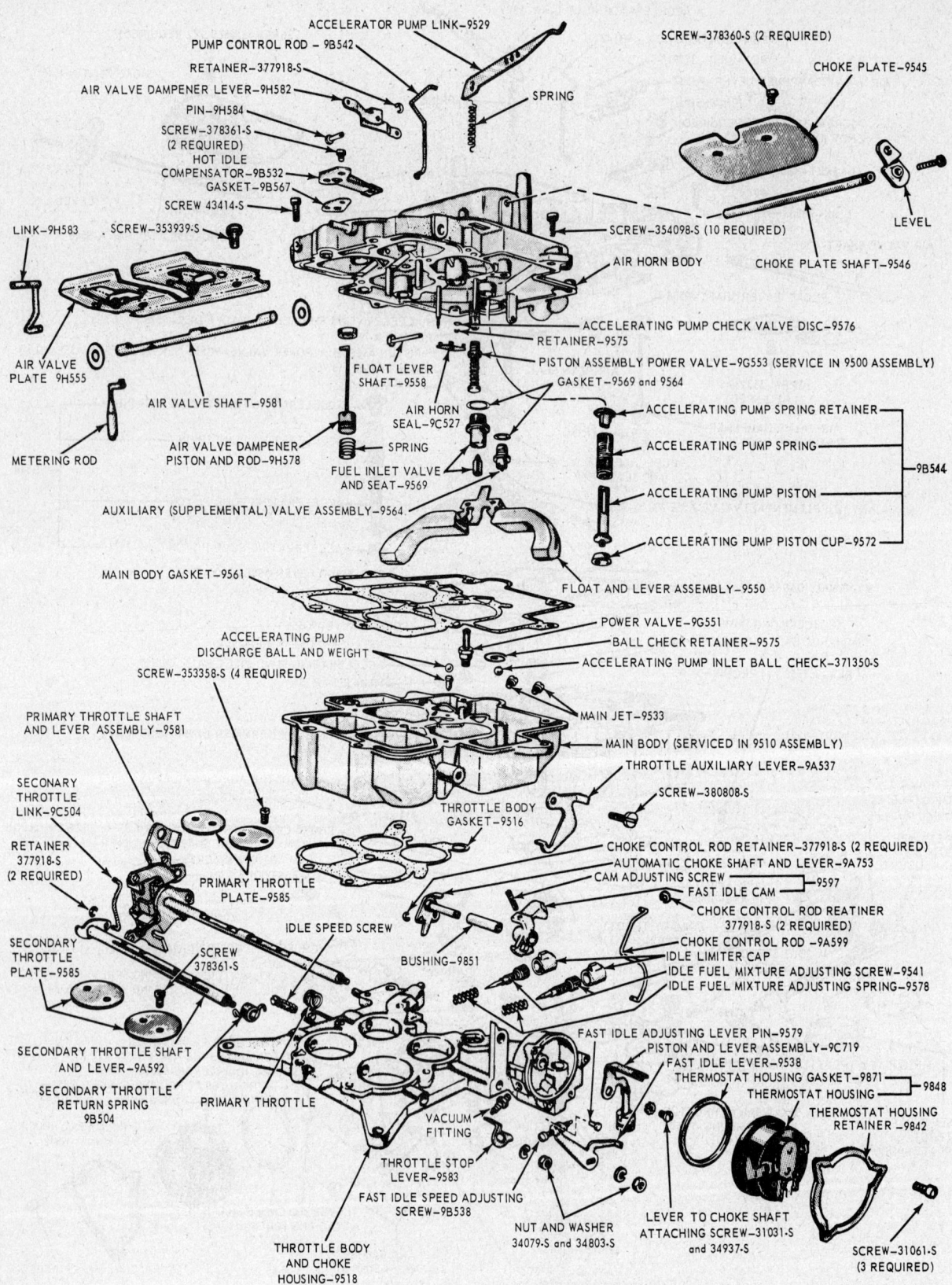

Ford-Autolite/Motorcraft Model 4300-D, 4V (Typical)

FORD

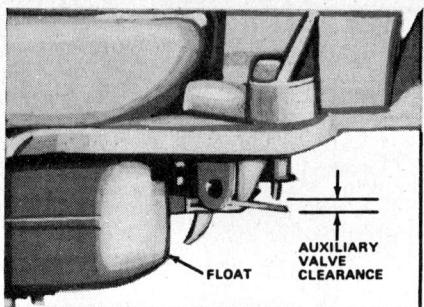

Fig. 17 Auxiliary inlet valve adjustment. Ford Autolite/Motorcraft 4300, 4350-4V

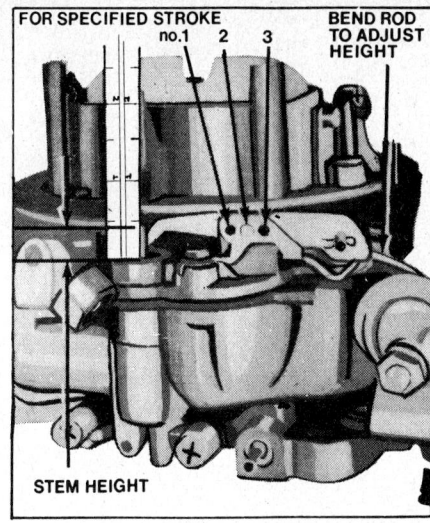

Fig. 18 Pump stroke adjustment. Ford Autolite/Motorcraft 4300-4V

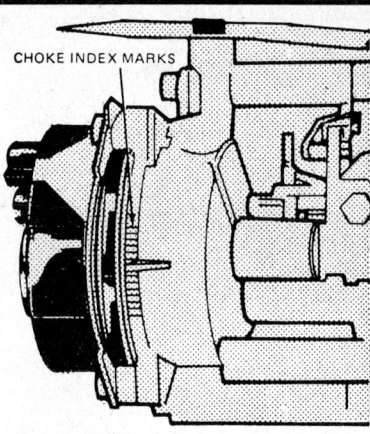

Fig. 19 Automatic choke setting. Ford Autolite/Motorcraft 4300-4V

the fast idle cam until the fast idle adjusting screw rests on the center step of the cam.
2. Adjust by turning the fast idle adjusting screw inward or outward as required. Refer to the *Specifications Chart.*

Accelerator Pump Stroke Adjustment, Fig. 18
The accelerator pump stroke has been calibrated to inject a pre-determined quantity of fuel into the air stream and help keep the exhaust emission level of the engine within the specified limits. The additional holes provided for pump stroke adjustment are for adjusting the stroke for specific engine applications.

NOTE: The stroke should not be changed from the specified setting.

If the pump stroke has been changed from the specified setting, refer to the following instructions to correct the stroke to specification. Before adjusting the accelerator pump stroke, measure the height of the pump piston. Adjust by bending the pump control rod to correct the piston stem height. Refer to *Specifications Chart.*

Automatic Choke Setting, Fig. 19
1. If carburetor is installed on engine, loosen choke heat tube nut.
2. Loosen choke cover retaining screws.
3. Rotate choke cover clockwise to reduce choking action or counterclockwise to increase choking action.
4. Tighten choke cover screws and choke heat tube nut.

Staged Choke Vacuum Control Adjustment
This adjustment should be made only if the control unit has been replaced, carburetor has been overhauled or a choke adjustment has been made.
1. Close choke plate.
2. Back off the adjusting sleeve locknut until it is clear of the adjusting sleeve.
3. Turn the adjusting sleeve inward until the choke plate just begins to move. Scribe a mark on the upper flat of the sleeve, then back off the sleeve one complete turn.
4. Tighten the locknut firmly against the sleeve to set the adjustment.

NOTE: Do not turn the diaphragm stem.

Dechoke Clearance, Fig. 20
1. Open and hold throttle plate to wide open position.
2. Rotate choke plate toward closed position until pawl on fast idle speed lever contacts fast idle cam.
3. Check clearance between lower edge of choke plate and air horn wall.
4. Adjust clearance to specifications by bending pawl on fast idle speed lever forward to increase (backward to decrease) clearance.

Choke Plate Pulldown & Fast Idle Cam, Fig. 21
1. Remove choke cover.
2. Bend a .036" wire gauge at a 90° angle, approximately 1/8" from the end.
3. Insert bent edge of gauge between piston slot and upper edge of right hand slot in choke housing.
4. Rotate automatic choke lever counterclockwise until gauge is snug in piston

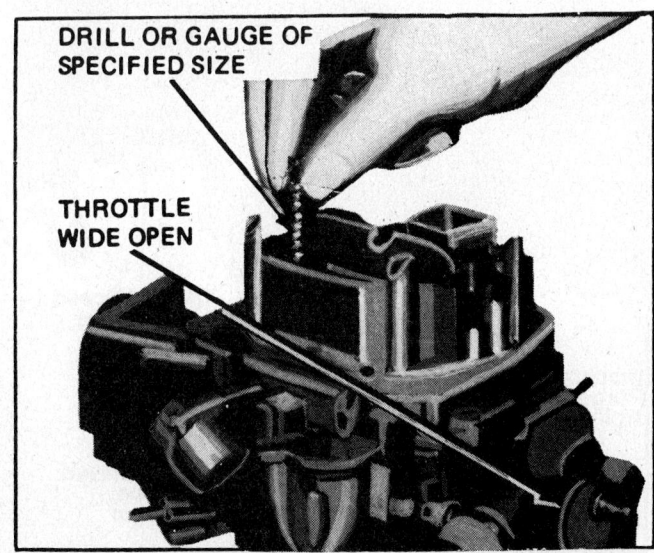

Fig. 20 Dechoke clearance adjustment. Ford Autolite/Motorcraft 4300, 4350-4V

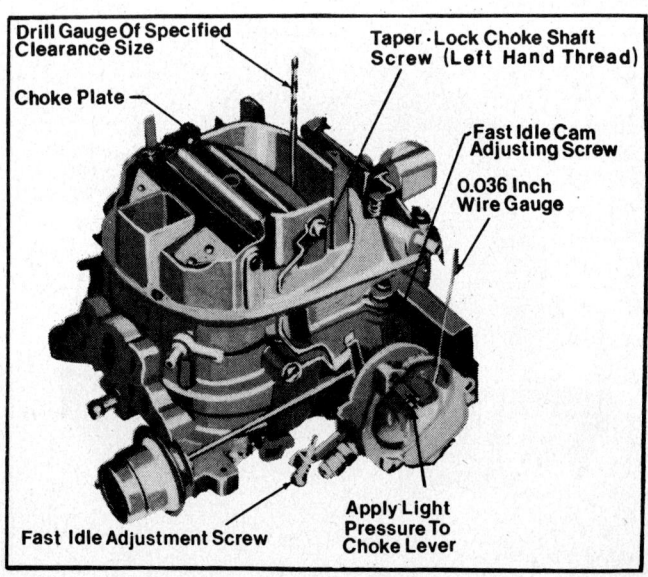

Fig. 21 Choke plate pulldown, Ford Autolite/Motorcraft 4300, 4350-4V. Fast idle cam adjustment, Ford Autolite/Motorcraft 4300-4V.

Ford

Fig. 22 Bowl vent valve adjustment. Ford Autolite/Motorcraft 4300-4V

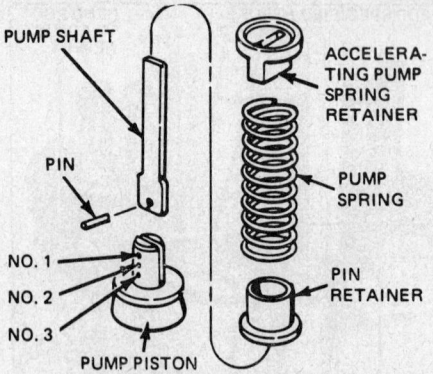

Fig. 23 Accelerator pump stroke adjustment. Ford Motorcraft 4350-4V

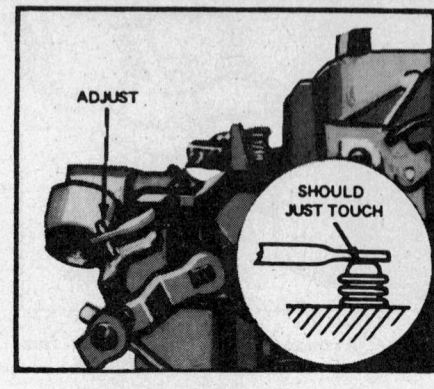

Fig. 24 Mechanical fuel vent valve adjustment. Ford Motorcraft 4350-4V

slot. Exert light pressure on choke lever to hold gauge in place.
5. Using a gauge pin, check pulldown clearance between lower edge of choke plate and air horn wall.
6. Adjust pulldown clearance to specifications by bending adjusting arm on choke shaft lever. Bend downward to increase (upward to decrease) clearance.
7. Remove gauge and install choke cover loosely so it can rotate. Be sure thermostatic spring end is engaged in choke lever slot.
8. Rotate choke cover to 90° rich.
9. Position fast idle adjusting screw end to kickdown step on fast idle cam and hold in this position.
10. Using a gauge pin, check fast idle cam clearance between lower edge of choke plate and air horn wall.
11. Adjust fast idle cam clearance to specifications by turning adjusting screw clockwise to increase (counterclockwise to decrease) clearance.
12. Install choke cover and rotate it to specified setting, then tighten cover.

Bowl Vent Valve, Fig. 22
1. Set throttle plates in closed position.
2. Check clearance between vent valve and valve seat.
3. If clearance is not .070 inch, bend end of vent valve lever downward to decrease and upward to increase.

Model 4350-4V

Accelerator Pump Adjustment

The piston-to-shaft pin position which is the only adjustment, is pre-set to deliver the correct amount of fuel for the engine on which it is installed and should not be changed from the specified setting. Do not attempt to adjust the accelerator pump stroke by turning the vacuum limiter level adjusting nut. This adjustment is pre-set and changing it could affect driveability.
1. Remove air horn assembly, then disconnect accelerator pump from operating lever by depressing spring and sliding arm out of pump shaft slot.
2. Disassemble spring and nylon keeper retaining adjustment pin. Refer to the specifications chart. If pin is not in specified hole, remove it, reposition shaft in specified hole and reinstall pin, Fig. 23.
3. Slide nylon retainer over pin and position spring on shaft; then compress spring on shaft and install pump on arm.

Vent Valve Adjustment
1. With engine at curb idle speed and solenoid throttle positioner (if used) in extended position, adjust vent valve so that arm is just touching valve stem, Fig. 24.
2. With engine off, observe that vent operating linkage pushes down on vent valve stem.

Initial Choke Pulldown
1. Remove choke housing assembly, then open throttle about half-way and position fast idle adjusting screw on high stem of fast idle cam.
2. Bend a .036" wire gauge at 90° angle,

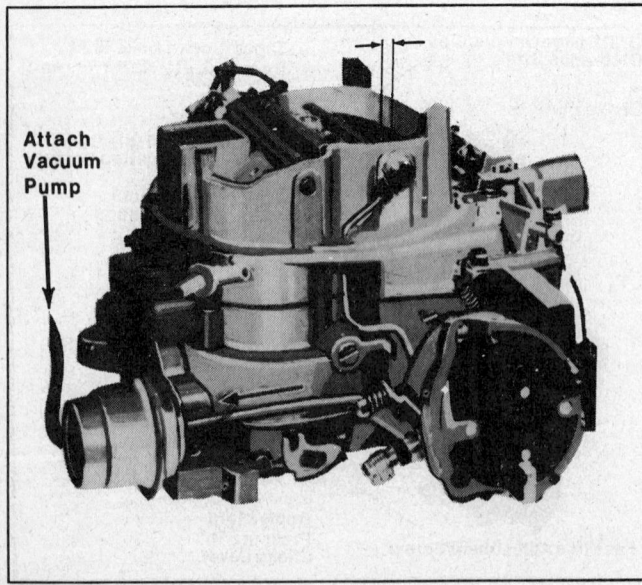

Fig. 25 Choke plate delayed pulldown adjustment. Ford Motorcraft 4350-4V

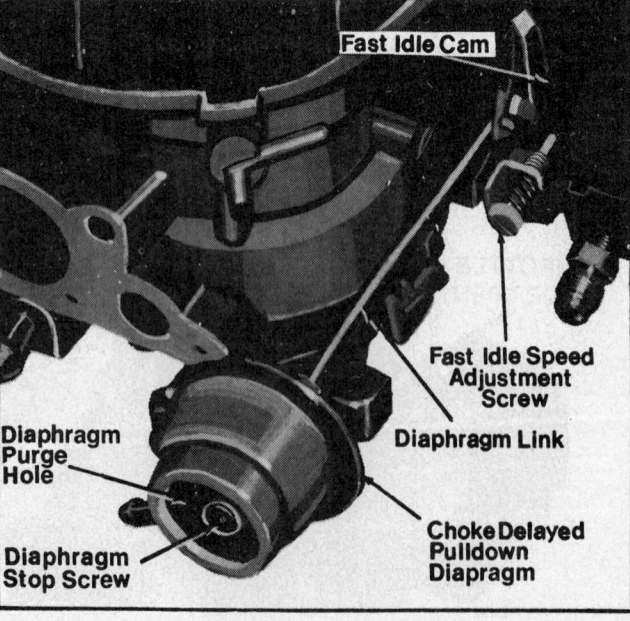

Fig. 26 Choke plate delayed pulldown stop screw adjustment. Ford Motorcraft 4350-4V

Ford

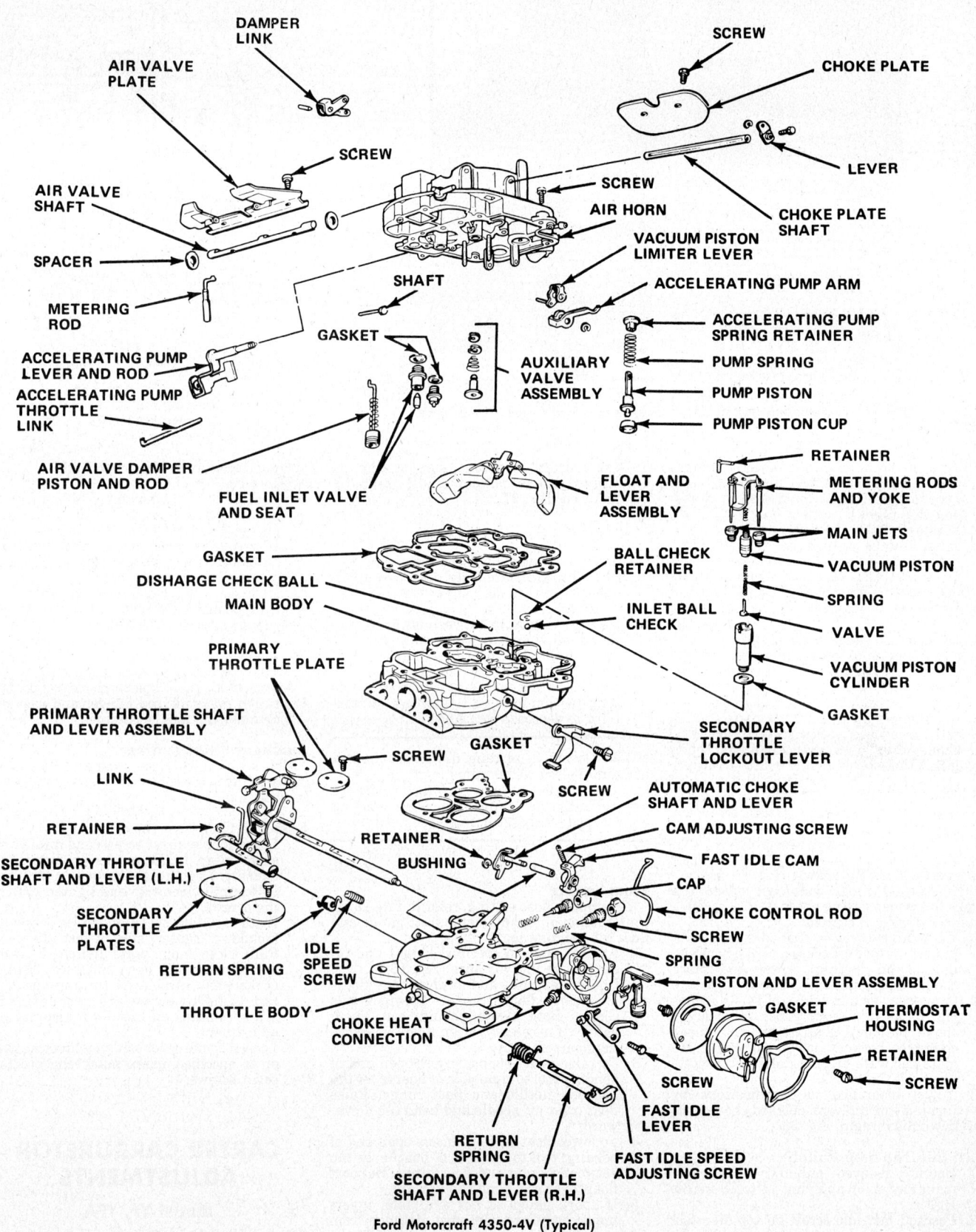

Ford Motorcraft 4350-4V (Typical)

FORD

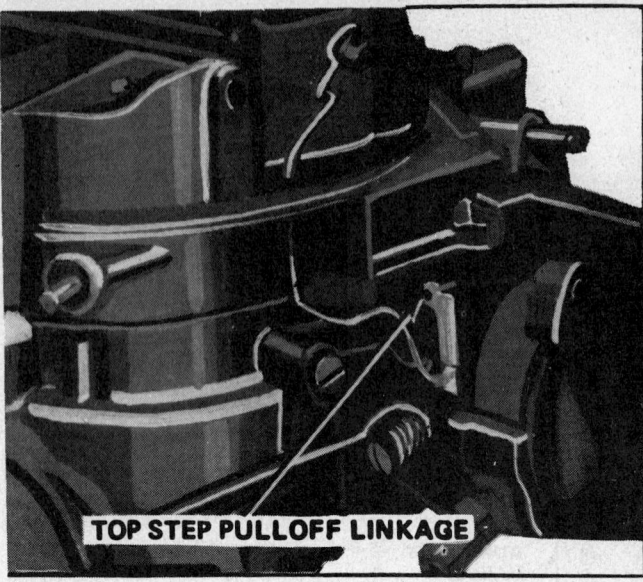

Fig. 27 Fast idle top step pulldown adjustment. Ford Motorcraft 4350-4V

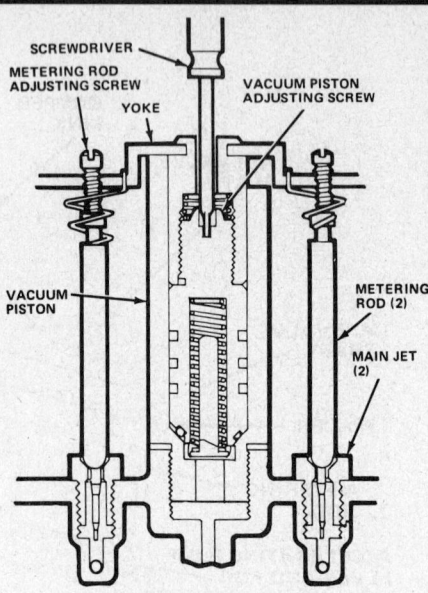

Fig. 28 Metering rod adjustment. Ford Motorcraft 4350-4V

about 1/8" from end, then insert bent end of gauge between choke piston slot and upper edge of right hand slot in choke housing, Fig. 21
3. Rotate choke lever counterclockwise until gauge is snug in piston slot, then apply light force to lever to hold gauge and move top of choke rod away from carburetor while moving bottom of rod toward carburetor to remove end play from linkage.
4. Using a drill gauge or pin of specified size, check clearance between lower edge of choke plate and wall, Fig. 21. Refer to the Specifications Chart.
5. Adjust clearance to specifications, by turning lock screw on choke plate shaft 3 full turns in a clockwise direction. Pry choke lever from shaft to break taper lock. Choke lever should rotate freely on choke shaft.
6. With drill gauge and .036" wire gauge positioned as above, tighten, screw on choke shaft.
7. Install choke housing assembly.

Delayed Choke Pulldown
The delayed choke pulldown opens the choke to a wider setting about 6 to 18 seconds after the engine is started.
1. With throttle set on fast idle cam, note position of index marks on choke housing, then loosen retaining screws and rotate cap 90° in closing (rich) direction.
2. Connect a vacuum source of 14–18 inches Hg. to vacuum supply port of delayed choke pulldown diaphragm and check clearance between lower edge of choke plate and wall, Fig. 25. Refer to the Specifications Chart.
3. Adjust clearance to specifications by turning stop screw on delayed choke pulldown diaphragm, Fig. 26.

Fast Idle Top Step Pulloff
1. Operate delayed pulldown diaphragm manually or by applying 14 to 18 inches Hg.
2. Position fast idle screw on top step fast idle cam with choke plate closed. If necessary, rotate choke housing cap to close choke plate.
3. Observe that fast idle speed adjusting screw drops to second step of cam as delayed choke pulldown diaphragm is operated, Fig. 27.

Dechoke (Unloader) Clearance
1. Hold throttle plate fully open and apply pressure on choke valve toward close position.
2. Measure clearance between lower edge of choke valve and air horn wall, Fig. 20. Refer to the Specifications Chart.
3. Adjust clearance to specifications by bending unloader tang which contacts fast idle cam forward to increase or rearward to decrease clearance.

NOTE: Do not bend tang downward from a horizontal plane. After adjustment, make certain that there is at least .070 inch clearance between unloader tang and choke housing with throttle fully open.

Float Setting
To simplify float setting, refer to Fig. 15 for construction of an adjustable float gauge and float tab bending tool.
1. Adjust gauge to specified height and insert gauge into air horn, Fig. 16.
3. Check clearance and alignment of floats to gauge. Refer to the Specifications Chart. Both floats should just touch gauge. If necessary, align floats by twisting floats slightly.
3. To raise float setting, insert open end of bending tool to right side of float lever tab between needle and float hinge. Raise float lever off needle and bend tab downward.
4. To lower float setting, insert open end of bending tool to left side of float lever tab between needle and float hinge. Support float lever and bend tab upward.
5. If above gauge is not available, invert upper body and measure distance from top of float to gasket surface of upper body. Adjust alignment and height of floats with bending tool as described previously.

Vacuum Piston & Metering Rods Adjustment
1. Remove air horn assembly, then depress metering rod hanger and turn vacuum piston adjusting screw and metering rod adjusting screws until metering rod hanger is fully seated against vacuum cylinder top face, Fig. 28.
2. Hold metering rod hanger in full downward position and turn each metering rod adjusting screw clockwise until the metering rods are now properly positioned in relation to vacuum piston.
3. Turn vacuum piston adjusting screw clockwise until specified clearance between metering rod hanger and vacuum cylinder top face is obtained.

Auxiliary Valve Setting
Check auxiliary valve clearance as shown in Fig. 17. If necessary to adjust clearance, use bending tool, Fig. 15.

Fast Idle Cam
1. Loosen choke cover screws and rotate cover to align index marks on cover and housing. Then, rotate cover an additional 90° counterclockwise and tighten attaching screws.
2. Place fast idle speed adjusting screw on kickdown (center) step of fast idle cam. Fully close choke plate and check clearance between air horn and lower edge of choke plate. Adjust by turning fast idle cam adjusting screw, ensuring adjusting screw remains on kickdown step during adjustment.
3. Loosen choke cover screws and rotate cover to specified index mark and tighten cover screws.

CARTER CARBURETOR ADJUSTMENTS
Model YF, YFA

Float Adjustment, Fig. 29
Invert the air horn assembly, and check the clearance from the top of the float to the bottom of the air horn with the float level gauge.

FORD

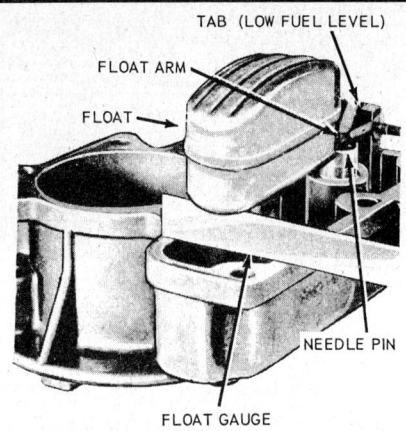

Fig. 29 Float level adjustment. Carter YF, YFA

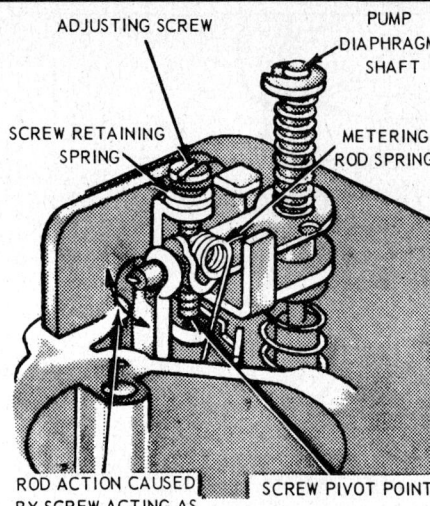

Fig. 30 Metering rod adjustment. Carter YF, YFA

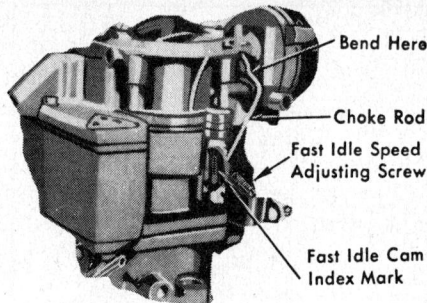

Fig. 31 Fast idle cam linkage adjustment, 1971–78. Carter YF, YFA

Hold the air horn at eye level when gauging the float level. The float arm (lever) should be resting on the needle pin. Do not load the needle when adjusting the float. Bend the float arms as necessary to adjust the float level (clearance). Do not bend the tab at the end of the float arm. It prevents the float from striking the bottom of the fuel bowl when empty.

Pump Adjustment

With throttle valve seated in bore of carburetor, press down on upper end of diaphragm shaft until it reaches its bottom position. The metering rod arm should now contact the pump lifter link at the outer end nearest the springs. Adjust by bending the pump connector link at its lower angle.

Metering Rod Adjustment, Fig. 30

Back out the idle speed adjusting screw until the throttle plate is closed tight in the throttle bore. Press down on upper end of diaphragm shaft until diaphragm bottoms in vacuum chamber. Metering rod should contact bottom of metering rod well, and metering rod should contact lifter link at the outer end, nearest the springs and at supporting lug. For models not equipped with metering rod adjusting screw, adjust by bending lip of metering rod arm to which metering rod is attached, up or down as required. For models equipped with a metering rod adjusting screw, turn the adjusting screw until metering rod just bottoms in the body casting. For final adjustment turn metering rod adjusting screw in (clockwise) one additional turn.

Fast Idle Cam Linkage Adjustment, 1971–78, Fig. 31

Position fast idle screw on second step of fast idle cam and against shoulder of highest step. Using a drill of specified size, check clearance between lower edge of choke plate and bore. Refer to the Specifications Chart. To adjust, bend choke connector rod as required.

Fast Idle Cam Linkage Adjustment, 1970, Fig. 32

Open throttle plate and hold choke plate in fully closed position to allow fast idle cam to return to fast idle position. Using a drill of specified size, check clearance between throttle plate and throttle bore. Refer to the Specifications Chart. To adjust, bend choke connector rod as required.

Choke Unloader Adjustment, Fig. 33

With throttle valve held wide open and choke valve held toward closed position with a rubber band, there should be the clearance listed in the *Specifications Chart* between lower edge of choke valve and inner air horn wall. Adjust by bending unloader lug on choke trip lever.

Choke Plate Pulldown Adjustment

Bend a 0.026 in. diameter wire gauge at a 90 degree angle approximately 1/8-inch from one end. Insert the bent end of the gauge between the choke piston slot and the right hand slot in choke housing. Rotate the choke piston lever counterclockwise until gauge is snug in the piston slot. Exert a light pressure on choke piston lever to hold the gauge in place, then use a drill with a diameter equal to the specified edge of choke plate and carburetor bore to check clearance, Fig. 34.

To adjust the choke plate pulldown clearance, bend the choke piston lever as required to obtain specified setting.

NOTE: When bending the lever, be careful not to distort the piston link. Install the choke thermostatic spring housing and gasket. Set the housing to specifications.

Dechoke Adjustment

Hold the throttle plate fully open and close the choke plate as far as possible without forcing it. Use a drill of specified diameter to check the clearance between choke plate and air horn, Fig. 35. If clearance is not within specification, adjust by bending arm on choke trip lever of the throttle lever. Bending the arm downward will decrease the clearance, bending it upward will increase the clearance.

If the choke plate clearance and fast idle cam linkage adjustment was performed with the carburetor on the engine, adjust the engine idle speed and fuel mixture. Adjust dashpot (if so equipped).

Dashpot Adjustment

With the engine idle speed and mixture properly adjusted, the engine at normal operating temperature, loosen the antistall dashpot lock nut, Fig. 12. Hold the throttle in the curb idle position and depress the dashpot plunger. Measure the clearance between the throttle lever and plunger tip. Turn the antistall dashpot to provide 7/64" ± 1/64" clearance between the tip of the plunger and the throttle lever. Tighten the locknut to secure the adjustment.

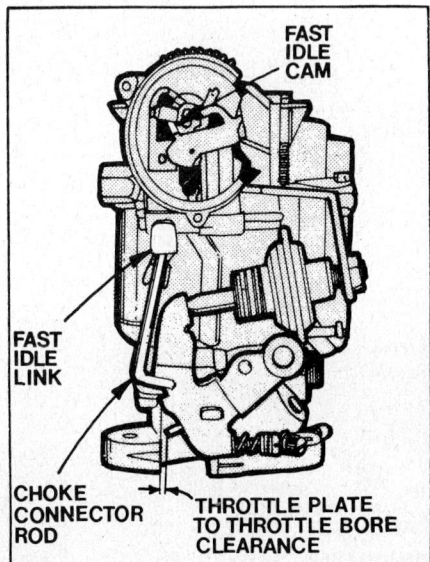

Fig. 32 Fast idle cam linkage adjustment, 1970 Carter YF

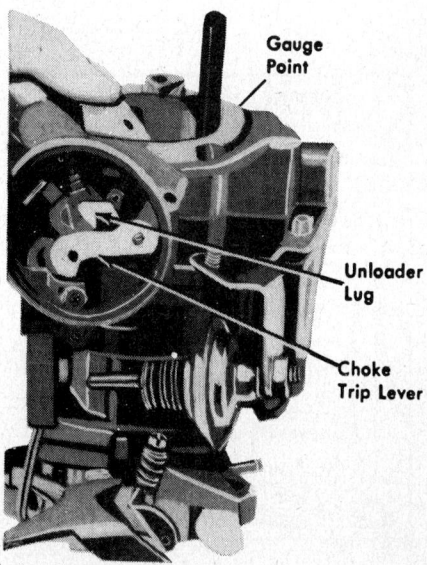

Fig. 33 Choke unloader adjustment. Carter YF

FORD

Fig. 34 Choke plate pulldown adjustment. Carter YF & YFA

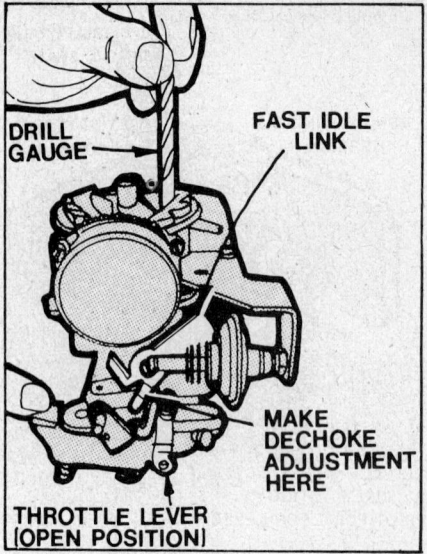

Fig. 35 Dechoke adjustment. Carter YF, YFA

Fig. 36 Float adjustment. Holley 2300-2V & 4150, 4160, 4180-4V

Automatic Choke Adjustment

Loosen choke cover retaining screws and turn choke cover so that line or index mark on cover lines up with the specified mark listed in the *Specifications Chart* on choke housing.

HOLLEY CARBURETOR ADJUSTMENTS

Models 2300-2V & 4150, 4160, 4180-4V

Float Adjustment (Dry), Fig. 36

The dry float adjustment is a preliminary fuel level adjustment only. The final adjustment must be performed after the carburetor is installed on the engine.

With fuel bowl and float removed, adjust the float so that it is parallel to the fuel bowl with the top of the fuel bowl inverted. On four-barrel units, adjust both sides in the same manner.

Fuel Level (Wet) Adjustment, Fig. 37

1. Operate engine to normalize engine temperatures and place the vehicle on a flat surface as near level as possible. Stop engine and remove air cleaner.
2. Check fuel level in each bowl separately. Place a suitable container below the fuel level sight plug in the fuel bowl to collect any spillover of fuel. Carefully remove sight plug and gasket. On a four-barrel unit, check each fuel bowl separately. The fuel level within the bowl should be at the lower edge of the sight plug opening (plus or minus $1/16''$).
3. If the fuel level is too high, drain the bowl and refill it. Check the fuel level again before altering the float setting. Install the bolt removed for draining and sight plug and start engine to fill the fuel bowl. After the engine has stabilized, stop the engine and check the fuel level.
4. If the fuel level is still too high, it should first be lowered below specifications and then raised until it is just at the lower edge of the sight plug opening. To adjust the fuel level, proceed as follows:
5. With engine stopped, loosen lock screw

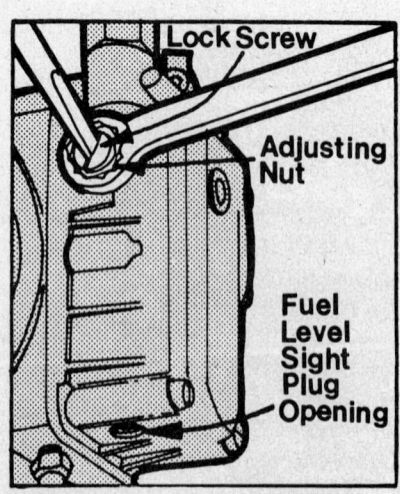

Fig. 37 Fuel level adjustment. Holley 2300-2V & 4150, 4160 4160 4180-4V

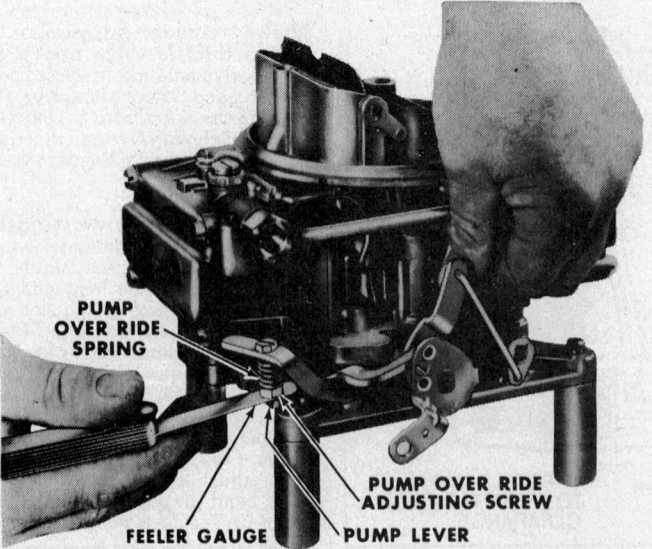

Fig. 38 Accelerator pump lever adjustment. Holley 2300-2V & 4150, 4160, 4180-4V (Typical)

Ford

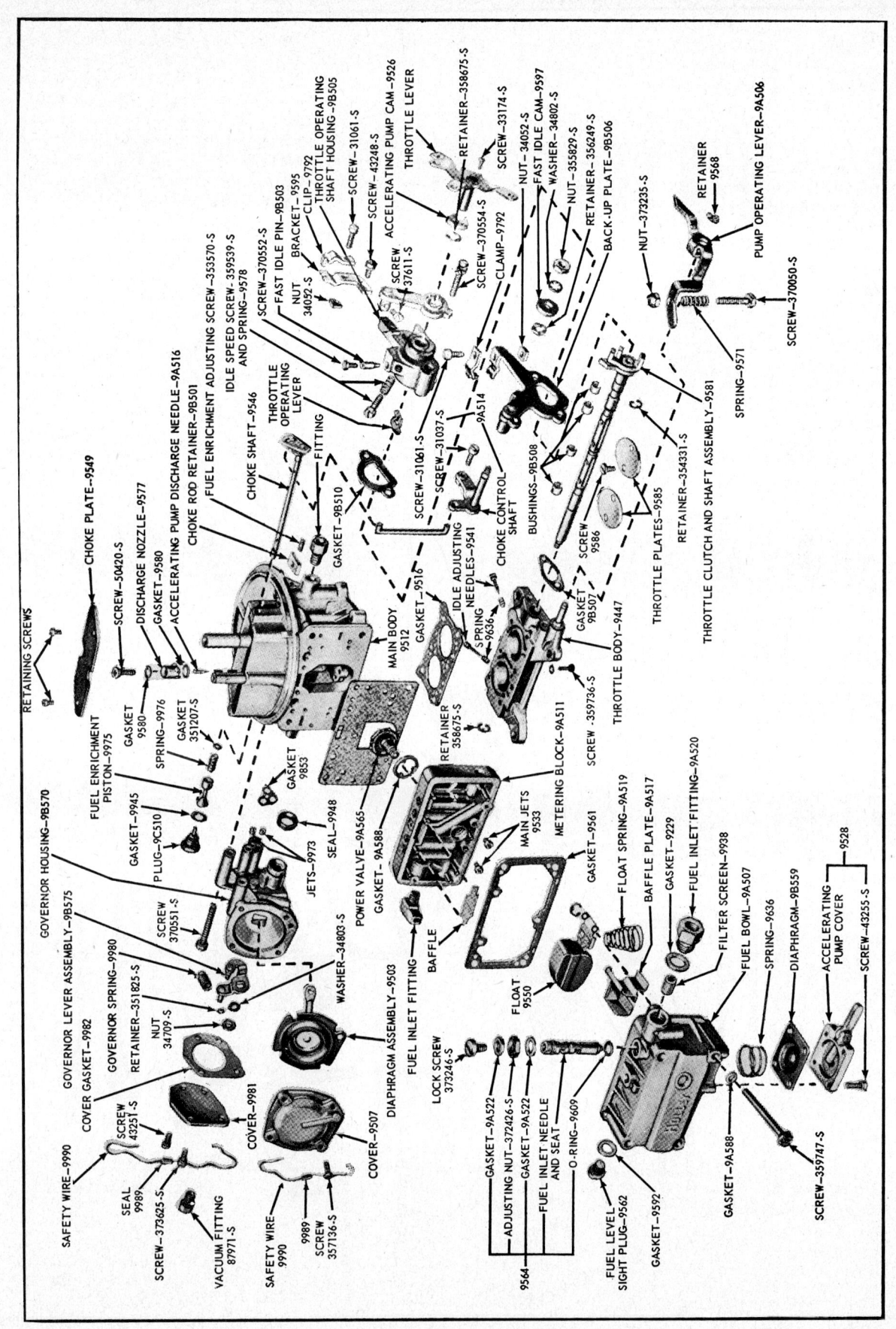

Holley Model 2300-2V (Typical)

Ford

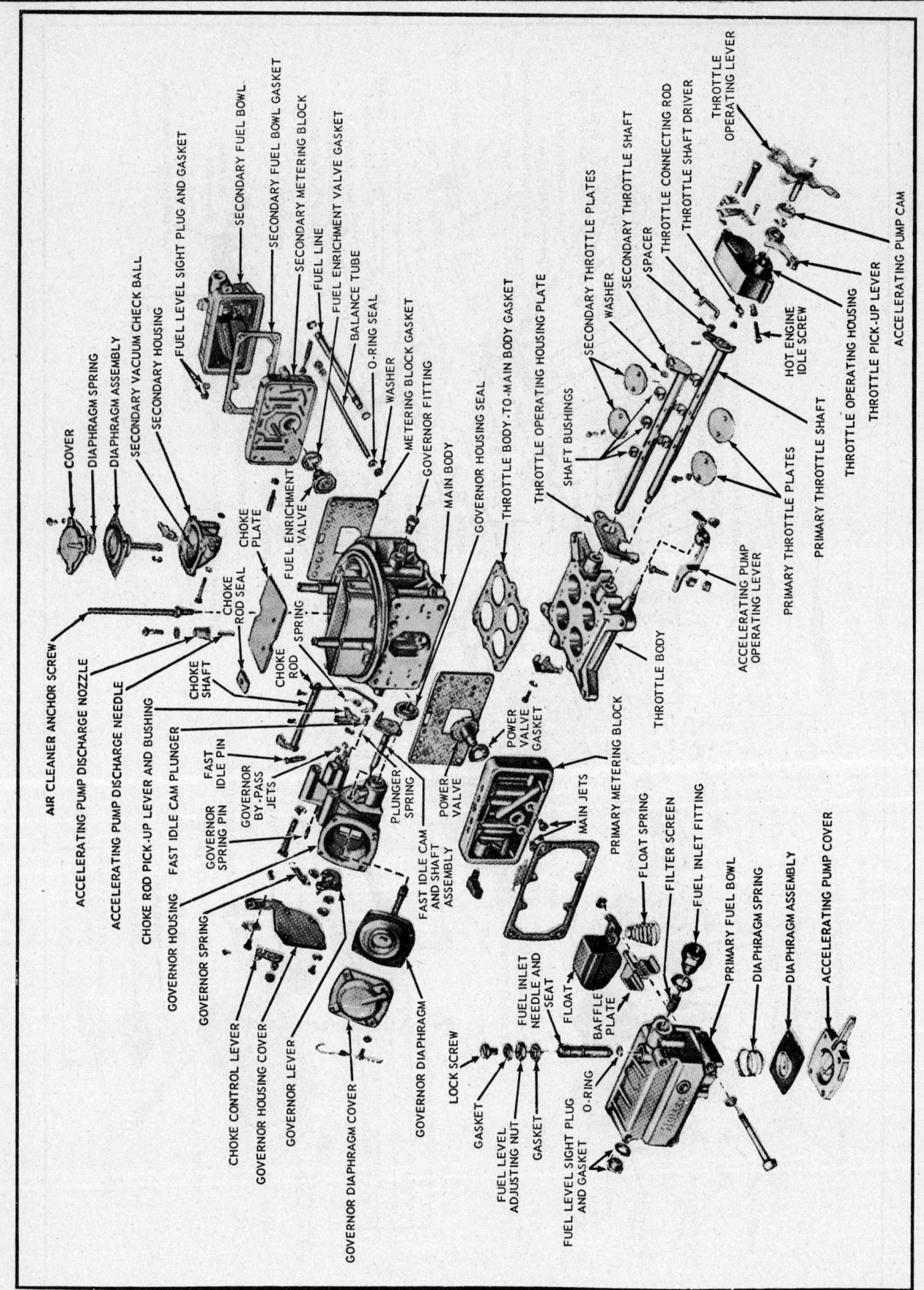

Holley Model 4150-4V (Typical)

Ford

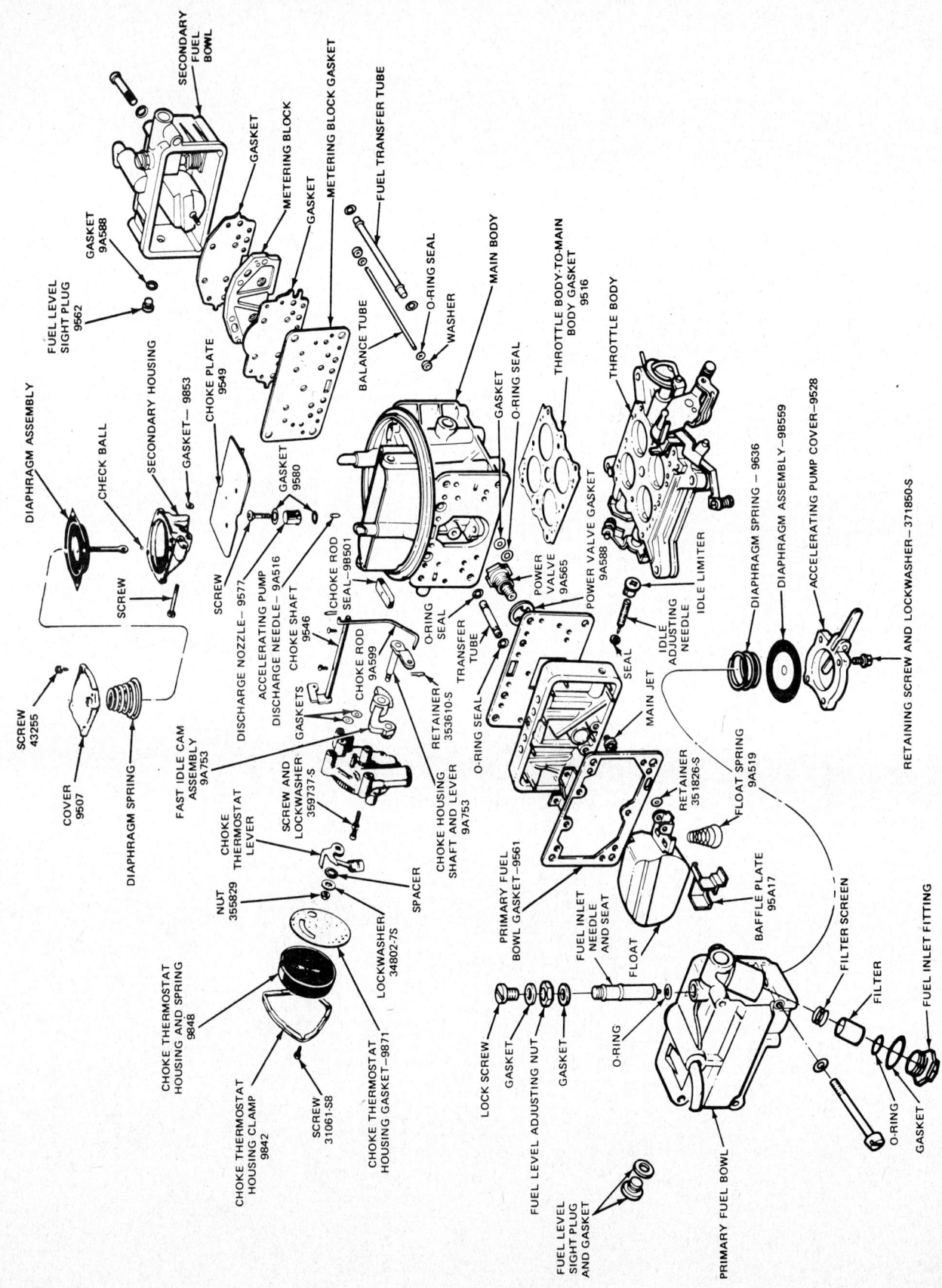

Holley Model 4180-C

Ford

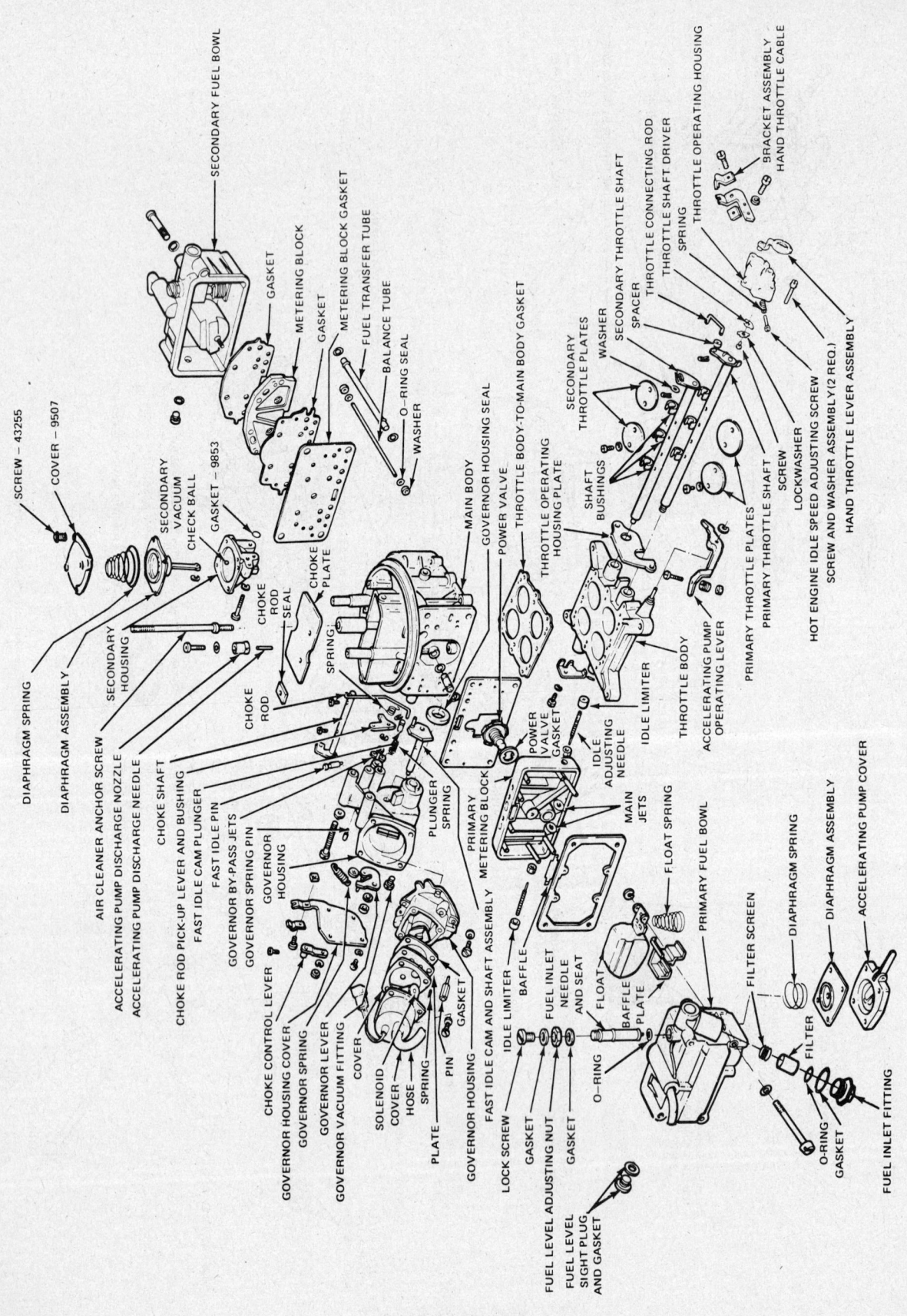

Holley Model 4180-EG

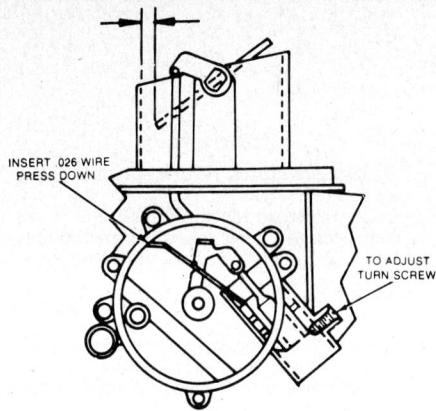

Fig. 39 Choke plate pulldown adjustment. Holley 4180 units

just enough to allow rotation of the adjusting nut underneath. *Do not loosen lock screw or attempt to adjust the fuel level with the sight plug removed and engine running because the pressure in the line will spray fuel out and cause a fire.*

6. Turn adjusting nut approximately 1/2 turn IN to lower the fuel below the sight plug opening (1/6 turn, depending upon direction of rotation, will raise or lower the float at the sight plug opening 3/64"). Tighten lock screw and install sight plug. Start engine and check.
7. If adjustment is not satisfactory, loosen lock screw and turn adjusting nut in increments of 1/6 turn or less until correct fuel level is achieved. After each adjustment, tighten lock screw, install sight plug, start engine and, after fuel is stabilized, check the fuel level at the sight plug opening.

Accelerating Pump Level, Fig. 38

1. Using a feeler gauge and with throttle plates wide open, there should be the specified clearance (minimum) between pump operating lever adjustment screw and pump arm when pump arm is depressed manually.
2. If adjustment is required, loosen lock nut and turn adjusting screw in to increase clearance and out to decrease clearance. One-half turn of screw is equal to approximately .015".
3. When proper adjustment has been made, hold screw in position with a wrench and tighten lock nut.

Accelerating Pump Stroke

To satisfy the requirements in various climates, the pump discharge can be adjusted. The bottom hole (No. 2) in the pump cam and throttle lever provides the maximum pump discharge for extreme cold weather, and the top hole (No. 1) provides the minimum pump discharge for warm weather operation.

If a change in the adjustment is required, make certain the proper hole in plastic pump cam, located behind throttle lever, is properly indexed with the numbered hole in the throttle lever before installing the retaining screw.

Secondary Throttle Plate Adjustment, 4150, 4160 & 4180 Units

With secondary throttle plates closed, rotate secondary throttle shaft lever adjusting screw counter-clockwise until the secondary throttle plates seat in the bores. On all units rotate adjusting screw clockwise until it contacts the secondary lever, then an additional 1/4 turn on 4150 units or 1/2 turn on 4160 units.

Choke Plate Pulldown, 4160 Units

1. Remove choke thermostatic spring housing from carburetor.
2. Block throttle half open so the fast idle cam does not contact the adjusting screw.
3. With a suitable tool, depress choke piston down against the adjusting screw.
4. Check clearance between front edge of choke plate and the air horn wall. The clearance should be as follows: No. D4TE-ARA, .150 inch; No. D4TE-ASA, .180 inch; Nos. D5TE-EA, GA, .190 inch.
5. To adjust clearance, rotate adjusting screw clockwise to decrease clearance or counter-clockwise to increase clearance.
6. Install thermostatic spring housing on carburetor and rotate housing counter-clockwise to align the index mark on spring housing with center index mark on choke housing.

Choke Plate Pulldown, 4180 Units

1. Remove thermostat housing, gasket and retainer.
2. Insert a piece of wire, Fig. 39, into choke piston bore to move the piston down against the stop screw. Maintain light closing pressure on choke plate and measure the gap between the lower edge of the choke plate and air horn wall.
3. To adjust, remove the putty covering the adjustment screw and turn clockwise to decrease gap or counter-clockwise to increase gap setting.
4. Reinstall choke thermostatic housing, gasket and retainer. Do not tighten screws until Fast Idle Cam Set adjustment has been performed.

Dechoke Clearance Adjustment, 4160 Units

1. With throttle held in the wide open position, rotate choke plate toward closed position until pawl on fast idle speed lever contacts fast idle cam.
2. Check clearance between upper edge of choke plate and air horn wall. Clearance

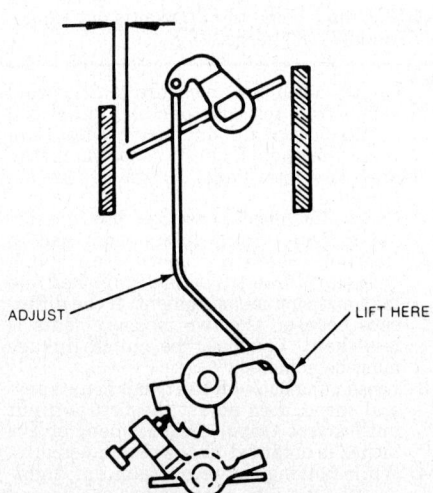

Fig. 41 Fast idle cam adjustment.

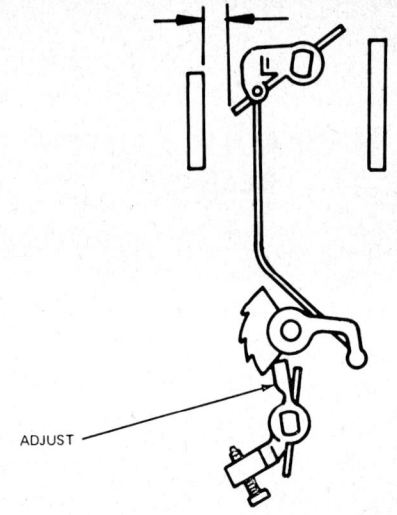

Fig. 40 Dechoke adjustment. Holley 4180 units

should be as follows: D4TE-ARA, ASA, .300 inch; D5TE-EA, GA, .315 inch.
3. To adjust clearance, bend the pawl on the fast idle speed lever forward to increase clearance or rearward to decrease clearance.

Dechoke Clearance, 4180 Units

1. Hold throttle in wide open throttle position.
2. Apply a light closing pressure on the choke plate and measure the gap between the lower edge of the choke plate and air horn wall.
3. To adjust, bend the pawl on the fast idle lever, Fig. 40, forward to increase or backward to decrease the clearance.

Fast Idle Cam Set, 4180 Units

1. Rotate choke cap 45 degrees counter-clockwise to close the choke plate. Tighten screws.
2. Open and close throttle to place fast idle screw on top step of cam, Fig. 41.
3. Place a pulldown gauge between lower edge of choke plate and air horn wall, then open and close the throttle to allow fast idle cam to drop.
4. Press upward on fast idle cam. There should be little or no movement indicating that the fast idle screw is on the kickdown step of the cam, against the first step.
5. To adjust, use bending tool and bend the choke control rod to assure proper fast idle location on the cam, Fig. 41.
6. Loosen screws and reset the choke thermostatic housing to the proper index mark and retighten screws.

Decel Throttle Modulator, 4180 Units

1. With engine at normal operating temperature, apply 19 inches Hg. of vacuum to decel throttle modulator.
2. Loosen decel throttle modulator lock nut and rotate modulator to achieve 1800 rpm.

Choke Thermostatic Spring Adjustment, 4160 & 4180 Units

1. Loosen thermostatic spring housing clamp retaining screws.
2. Rotate spring housing to align index mark on spring housing with center index mark on choke housing.

FORD

Clutch Section

HYDRAULIC CLUTCH RELEASE

When the clutch pedal is depressed, fluid is forced from the master cylinder into a slave cylinder. The slave cylinder push rod moves the clutch release lever which in turn pivots on a trunnion in the flywheel housing, and forces the release bearing against the pressure plate release fingers.

When the clutch pedal is released, the master cylinder return spring and the release lever retracting spring force the fluid from the slave cylinder back to the master cylinder.

The fluid used in this system is the same as that used in the brake system. A bleeder fitting is installed on the slave cylinder and procedures for bleeding are the same as those for brakes. The master cylinder fluid level should be maintained at 1/2" below the top of the master cylinder reservoir.

CLUTCH PEDAL, ADJUST

MECHANICAL RELEASE
Bronco & Econoline

NOTE: For 1975-80 Econoline & 1978-80 Bronco models, refer to 1972-80 under "F-100, 350 Series".

1. Measure total travel of pedal. Travel should be within specifications shown below:
   Bronco
   1970 . . . . 6 11/16–6 43/64"
   1971 . . . . 6 11/16–6 15/16"
   1972-77 . . . . 6 3/4–7"

   Econoline
   1970-74 . . . . 7 1/2–7 3/4"

2. If total pedal travel is not as specified in step 1, adjust clutch pedal stop:
   a. On Bronco models, move clutch pedal and bumper as necessary to obtain desired total pedal travel.
   b. On Econoline models, loosen clutch pedal bumper eccentric bolt and rotate bumper until desired pedal travel is obtained.

3. Check clutch pedal free travel. Travel should be within specifications shown below:
   Bronco
   1970-71 . . . . 1 7/32–1 7/16"
   1972 . . . . 1 1/8–1 5/8"
   1973-77 . . . . 3/4–1 1/2"
   Econoline
   1970-72 . . . . 1 1/8–1 1/2"
   1973-74 . . . . 3/4–1 1/2"

4. On 1970-71 Econoline models, if clutch pedal free travel is not as specified in step 3, loosen locknut and adjust pushrod until it contacts clutch release lever, Insert a .180 inch feeler gauge on 1970-71 models, or a .165 inch feeler gauge on 1972 models between pushrod and locknut and tighten locknut against feeler gauge. Remove feeler gauge and adjust pushrod until it contacts adjusting nut.

5. On Bronco and 1972-74 Econoline models, if clutch pedal free travel is not as specified in step 3, loosen locknut and adjust pushrod as necessary until desired clutch pedal free play is obtained.

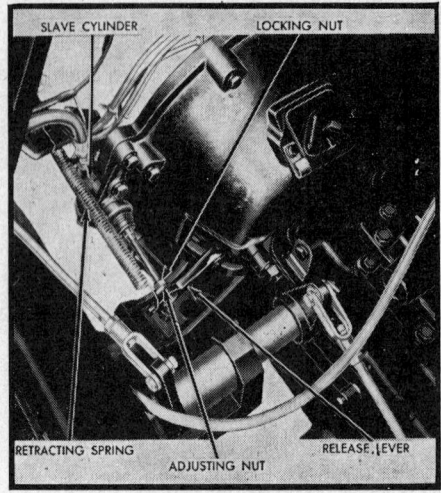

Fig. 1 Slave cylinder push rod adjustment

F-100, 350 Series

1970-71
1. Adjust pedal stop to provide a pedal height of 7 3/8–7 3/4 inches.
2. Disconnect retracting spring and slide release rod extension bullet firmly against release lever to eliminate free play.
3. While holding bullet firmly against release lever, insert a .200 ± .020 inch feeler gauge and finger tighten jam nut against feeler gauge.
4. Turn second jam nut against first jam nut and remove feeler gauge, then using two wrenches, tighten the second jam nut against the first one.
5. Check for 1–1 1/2 inches free pedal travel, and readjust as necessary.

1972-80

NOTE: Clutch pedal total travel is not adjustable on 1973-80 vehicles.

1. On 1972 vehicles, measure clutch pedal height from top edge of clutch pedal pad to bare floor pan. If dimension is less than 7 3/8 inches, adjust clutch pedal bumper to provide a total pedal height of 7 3/8–7 3/4 inches.
2. Check clutch pedal free travel by measuring distance from clutch pedal pad to steering wheel rim, then depress clutch pedal until free travel is diminished and take a second measurement. If the difference between the two measurements is less than 3/4 inches, the clutch linkage must be adjusted.
3. Loosen and back-off the two jam nuts several turns, then adjust the first jam nut until a free travel measurement of 1 1/2 inches is obtained at the clutch pedal.
4. While holding the second jam nut, tighten the first jam nut against the second one.
5. Recheck free pedal travel and readjust as necessary.

Ranchero

1. Disconnect clutch return spring from release lever.
2. Loosen release lever rod lock nut.
3. Move release lever rearward until release bearing lightly contacts clutch pressure plate release fingers.
4. Adjust adapter length until adapter seats in release lever pocket.
5. Insert the proper feeler gauge (see below) against back face of rod adapter, then tighten lock nut finger tight against feeler gauge.
   1972-74 . . . . .194"
   1970-71 . . . . .136"
6. Remove feeler gauge. Hold lock nut in position and tighten adapter against nut.
7. Install release spring and check for free travel of pedal which is 7/8" to 1 1/8".

F, B & LN, N 500-750 Series

1. Adjust clutch pedal stop to obtain total pedal travel of 8 1/16–8 5/16 inches on 1970-71, 7 7/8 inches on 1972-80 except LN and N series, or 13 inches on 1972-80 LN and N Series.
2. Adjust clutch pedal free travel by backing off jam nut and adjusting clearance between spherical nut and release lever. Clearance on gasoline engine models should be 1/4 inch, and clearance on diesel engine models should be 1/8 inch.

NOTE: Retracting spring must be in place when making adjustment.

3. Tighten jam nut.

1970–71 L Series Exc. 500, 750

1. Adjust clutch pedal stop to obtain total pedal travel of 10 15/32 inches as measured from free position to floor mat.
2. Adjust clutch pedal free play to 3/16–3/8 inch.
3. If necessary, readjust pedal stop to maintain specified free pedal play.

LN, LNT-8000, N-1000-D, NT-850, 950-D Series (With NH Series Engine)

1. Adjust clutch pedal stop to obtain total clutch pedal travel of 8 15/32–8 23/32 inches.
2. Insert a 1/4 inch alignment pin into relay rod, then with clutch pedal again stop, adjust vertical rod length to allow free installation of retaining bolt.
3. Install 1/4 inch alignment pins into relay lever and clutch equalizer shaft, then adjust relay to clutch equalizer shaft to allow free installation of retaining bolt.
4. On vehicles equipped with Spicer 6000, 8000, 8312 and Fuller 5H74 and R96 transmission, adjust equalizer shaft to release lever push rod to obtain a clearance of 1/4–5/16 inch between edge of push rod and bottom of groove in clutch release lever. On vehicles equipped with Fuller T-905 or RT-910, adjust clearance to 7/32–15/64 inch.

W SERIES

1. Adjust clutch pedal stop to obtain a total pedal travel of 10 15/32–10 31/32.

2. Adjust clutch pedal overcenter assist spring spherical locknut to provide a spring length of 7¼ inches for 1970-73 with 500 pound clutch, or 7 inches for 1970-73 with 420 pound clutch. Measure distance inside spring ends, and when performing spring adjustment, hold spring retainer from rotating, assuring that assist spring and anchor are aligned at right angles.
3. Adjust vertical tension rod turnbuckle so that lever is perpendicular with top of frame. Make adjustment with cab in locked position and a ¼ inch diameter pin installed in lever. After adjustment, position thin section of turnbuckle toward body sheet metal to provide maximum clearance between sheet metal and radiator side support.
4. Insert another ¼ inch aligning spring through frame bracket and outer equalizer lever, and check inner equalizer to be sure it is perpendicular with top of frame. If lever is not perpendicular, adjust rod length as necessary, then remove the two aligning pins.
5. Adjust length of linkage return spring to 10½ inches on all except W-1000D series with Cummins V8 engine, or 17 inches on W-1000D series with Cummins V8 engine.
6. Disconnect equalizer rod at clutch housing cross shaft lever, then while holding cross shaft lever rearward, adjust length of equalizer rod so that hole in cross shaft and hole in clevis are aligned. Back-off clevis 7½ turns and reconnect equalizer rod at cross shaft lever and tighten locknuts at all clevis connections.

NOTE: The above adjustment should result in a free pedal travel of 1⅜-1½ inches and ⅛ inch free bearing lash at clutch bearing hub.

HYDRAULIC RELEASE CLUTCH PEDAL, ADJUST

Before making any adjustments, be sure that the system is free of air and that the master cylinder fluid is at the specified level.

F, N, NT, T Series
1. Adjust pedal stop to permit total pedal travel of 8¼".
2. Set clutch pedal initial free travel to 3/16" to ⅜" by adjusting the eccentric bolt. This measurement is taken at the centerline of the pedal pad.
3. If necessary, readjust pedal stop to maintain initial specified free travel.
4. To adjust slave cylinder on gasoline engines without SAE flywheel housing, disconnect release lever retracting spring and push slave cylinder push rod toward front of vehicle as far as possible, then pull release lever back until release bearing contacts pressure plate release fingers. Adjust clearance between slave cylinder push rod spherical nut and release lever to ¼ inch on all except super duty engines, and 13/64 inch on super duty engines. Tighten jam nut and reconnect retracting spring.

NOTE: As a result of the above adjustment, free pedal travel should be 2 inches.

5. To adjust slave cylinder on super duty engines with SAE flywheel housing, disconnect release lever retracting spring, then loosen clamp bolt of external release lever and push slave cylinder push rod toward front of vehicle as far as possible. Hold push rod against internal stop, then loosen push rod jam nut and adjust wing nut to obtain 8⅞ inches as measured from flat end of slave cylinder casting to angled edge of wing nut. Tighten jam nut, then loosen outer adjusting arm set screw jam nut and rotate arm clockwise to eliminate release bearing lash. Adjust set screw to obtain ¼ inch clearance between edge of wing nut and notch on external release lever. Tighten set screw and reconnect retracting spring.
6. On vehicles with diesel engines, adjust slave cylinder by pushing push rod against piston and piston against internal cylinder stop. Disconnect retracting spring, then with release lever held against bearing retainer, loosen jam nut and adjust wing nut on push rod to obtain ¼ inch clearance. Tighten jam nut and reconnect retracting spring.

NOTE: Do not adjust slave cylinder to perform subsequent clutch adjustments.

If clearance between push rod wing nut and release lever is reduced to 3/32 inch, internal clutch adjustment must be performed.

C Series
1. Adjust eccentric bolt and pedal stop to give 5/32" to ¼" of initial free travel before master cylinder push rod contacts piston. This measurement is taken at centerline of pedal pad.
2. Disconnect release lever retracting spring. Push slave cylinder push rod the full distance of its travel toward front of truck. Pull release lever toward rear of truck until release bearing touches release fingers.
3. Loosen locknut and adjust conical nut or wing nut until there is ¼ inch clearance between release lever and conical nut or wing nut on all except 1972-79 models with 13 inch clutch, of 13/64 inch on all 1972-79 models with 13 inch clutch.

H and HT Series
1. Adjust clutch pedal height to 10⅜" by moving bumper and its bracket.
2. By means of eccentric bolt, adjust initial free pedal travel ⅛" to ¼".
3. Disconnect release lever retracting spring. Push slave cylinder push rod the full distance of its travel forward, and move release lever to the rear until release bearing touches release fingers.
4. Adjust clearance between slave cylinder push rod spherical nut and release lever to 3/16" to obtain final free travel. As a result of this adjustment, there should be final free travel of approximately 1½". Tighten jam nut.

P SERIES
1970-71
1. Adjust clutch master cylinder push rod extension to give 3/16" to ⅜". This adjustment should be checked with clutch pedal retracting spring attached.
2. Disconnect release lever retracting spring. Adjust clearance between slave cylinder push rod spherical nut and clutch release lever to ¼". As a result of this adjustment, there should be a final free travel of at least 2".

1972-76 350, 400

NOTE: Pedal free play is controlled by the master cylinder and is not adjustable. To adjust slave cylinder, proceed as follows:

1. Bottom slave cylinder push rod against the internal stop.
2. Push clutch release lever back until release bearing contacts clutch fingers.
3. Adjust conical nut to obtain ¼ inch clearance between release lever and conical nut.
4. Tighten jam nut against conical nut.

1972-80 500, 600
1. With retracting spring attached and pedal against stop, adjust master cylinder push rod to obtain ¼ inch free pedal play, then tighten jam nut.
2. Bottom slave cylinder push rod against internal stop, then push clutch release lever back until release bearing contacts clutch fingers.
3. Loosen jam nut and adjust conical nut to obtain ¼ inch clearance between release lever and conical nut.
4. Tighten jam nut against conical nut.

CLUTCH, REPLACE

1. On 1970-71 models, remove the two bolts which attach the slave cylinder to the flywheel housing and remove the slave cylinder push rod from the release lever. Remove release lever rod. Remove transmission from clutch housing. Remove release bearing and hub from release lever.
2. On all models, mark the clutch assembly and flywheel so the parts may be installed in the same relative position.
3. Loosen the clutch-to-flywheel attaching bolts a little at a time until the tension on the clutch springs is relieved. Then unscrew the bolts completely and remove the clutch assembly and driven disc.

Installation

1. Coat pilot bearing bore in flywheel with a small amount of wheel bearing grease. *Avoid using too much grease as it may be thrown on the clutch disc when the clutch revolves.*
2. Install pilot bearing in flywheel. On 12" clutch, install the bearing with its shielded side toward the rear.
3. Install clutch pilot tool in clutch disc and position disc on flywheel so that the pilot tool enters the pilot bearing.
4. Position pressure plate and cover assembly on flywheel and install the retaining cap screws. Tighten the cap screws to a torque of 17-20 ft. lb. If the original clutch is being installed, be sure to align the marks made prior to removal.
5. Position the release bearing and hub on the release lever. Install the transmission. Position release bearing and hub on the release lever. Install adjusting nut and lock nut on release rod. Connect the clutch pedal retracting spring to the release lever and check the clutch pedal free travel.

FORD

Transmission Section

NOTE: For Clark, Fuller, New Process, Spicer and Warner transmissions used on Ford trucks, see the "name" chapter for service procedures and lubricant capacities

TRANSMISSION IDENTIFICATION

Code	Mfr. Name①	Mfr. Model①
1970 Auxiliary Units		
1	Spicer	5831C
2	Spicer	5831D
3	Spicer	7231B
4	Spicer	7231D
5	Spicer	8341A-C
6	Spicer	8031C
7	Spicer	8031G-P
8	Spicer	7041
C	Fuller	3K65
D	Fuller	4E75
1970 100–600 Series		
A	New Process	435
B	Ford	3Spd. O.D.
C	Ford	3 Spd. L.D.
D	Warner	3 Spd. M.D.
E	Warner	3 Spd. H.D.
F	Warner	4 Spd.
G	Ford	Automatic
M	Clark	285-V
O	New Process	542-FL
P	Warner	4 Spd.
T	New Process	542-FO
2	Clark	282-V
4	Clark	280-VO
9	New Process	542-FD
1970-72 700-9000 LN500-9000-C500-900 Series		
A	New Process	435
B	Spicer	8516
C	Fuller	RT-610
D	Clark	387-V
E	Fuller	5H74
F	Fuller	5HA74
G	Clark	380-VO
H	Fuller	RTO-913
K	Spicer	6453A
L	Allison	AT-540
M	Clark	285-V
N	Spicer	6352
O	Fuller	T-905B
O	New Process	542-FL
P	Warner	T-19 4 Spd.
Q	Spicer	5652
R	Spicer	8716
S	Spicer	5756B
T	New Process	542-FO
U	Spicer	6852G
V	Fuller	RT-910
W	Spicer	6352B
X	Allison	MT30
X	Fuller	T-905A
Y	Allison	MT41
Z	Allison	MT40
1	Spicer	8552A
1	Allison	MT42
2	Clark	282-V
3	Fuller	RT-906
4	Clark	280-VO
5	Fuller	RTO-910
6	Fuller	RTO-915
7	Clark	385-V
9	Fuller	RT-915
9	New Process	542-FD

Code	Mfr. Name①	Mfr. Model①
1971–72 100–600 Series		
A	New Process	435
B	Warner O.D.	T-85 3 Spd.
C	Ford	3 Spd.
D	Warner	T-89F 3 Spd.
E	Warner	T-87G 3 Spd.
F	Warner	T-18 4 Spd.
G	Ford	C6 Automatic
1973–74		
A	New Process	435
B	Spicer	8516
B	Spicer	P8516
C	Ford	3 Spd.
C	Fuller	RT-610
D	Clark	387-V
D	Warner	T-19G
E	Fuller	5H74
E	Fuller	5HA74
F	Warner	T-18
G	Ford	C4 Auto.
G	Warner	T-87G
H	Allison	MT650
J	Fuller	RTO-9513
J	Ford	FMX Auto.
K	Spicer	6453A
L	Allison	AT540
M	Clark	285V
N	Spicer	6352
O	New Process	542FL
O	Fuller	T-905B
P	Warner	T-19
P	Ford	C6 Auto.
Q	Spicer	5652
R	Spicer	8716
S	Spicer	5756B
T	New Process	542-FO
T	Fuller	TRO-9509B
U	Spicer	6852G
V	Fuller	RT-910
W	Spicer	6352B
X	Fuller	T-905A
Y	Allison	MT41
Z	Allison	MT40
1	Spicer	8552A
1	Allison	MT42
2	Clark	282V
3	Fuller	RT-906
4	Clark	280VO
5	Fuller	RTO-910
6	Fuller	RTO-915
7	Clark	385V
8	Allison	MT640
9	Fuller	RT-915
9	New Process	542-FD
1974		
G	Spicer	SST 6 + 1
J	Spicer	6453
P	Fuller	RT-613
1975		
A	New Process	435
A	Spicer	SST 10

Code	Mfr. Name①	Mfr. Model①
B	Spicer	RP8516-3B
C	Ford	3 Spd.
C	Fuller	RT-610
D	Clark	387V
E	Spicer	RT12510
E	Warner	T19
F	Spicer	RTO-12-513
F	Warner	T18
G	Ford	Auto.
G	Spicer	SST 6 + 1
H	Allison	MT650
J	Fuller	RTO-9513
J	Ford	FMX Auto.
K	Spicer	6453
L	Allison	AT540
M	Clark	285V
N	Spicer	6352
O	New Process	542FL
O	Fuller	T-905B
P	Warner	T19
P	Fuller	RT-613
Q	Spicer	5652
R	Spicer	P8716-3A
S	Spicer	5756-B
T	New Process	542FO
T	Fuller	TRO-9509-B9
U	Spicer	6852G
V	Fuller	RT-910
W	Spicer	6352B
X	Fuller	T-905A
1	Spicer	8552A
2	Clark	282V
3	Fuller	RT-906
4	Clark	280VO
4	Fuller	RT-9513
5	Fuller	RTO-910
6	Fuller	RTO-915
7	Clark	385V
8	Allison	MT640
9	Fuller	RT-915
9	New Process	542FD
1975 Auxiliary Units		
2	Spicer	5831D
3	Spicer	7231B
4	Spicer	7231D
5	Spicer	8341C
6	Spicer	8031B
8	Spicer	7041
1976		
A	New Process	435
A	Spicer	SST10
B	Spicer	RP8516-3B
C	Ford	3 Spd.
C	Fuller	RT-610
D	Clark	387V
E	Fuller	RT12510
E	Warner	T19
F	Fuller	RTO-12-513
F	Warner	T18
G	Ford	Auto.
G	Spicer	SST1007-2F
G	Warner	T87G
H	Allison	MT650
J	Fuller	RTO-9513
J	Ford	FMX Auto.

FORD

TRANSMISSION IDENTIFICATION—Continued

Code	Mfr. Name①	Mfr. Model①
K	Spicer	6453
L	Allison	AT540
M	Clark	285V
N	Spicer	6352
O	New Process	542FL
O	Fuller	T-905B
P	Warner	T19
P	Fuller	RT-613
P	Ford	C6 Auto.
Q	Spicer	5652
Q	Fuller	RT-1110
R	Spicer	RP8716-3A
S	Spicer	5756-B
T	New Process	542-FO
T	Fuller	RTO-9509-B9
U	Spicer	6852G
V	Fuller	RT-910
W	Spicer	6352B
X	Fuller	RT-910
Z	Clark	397V
1	Spicer	8552A
2	Clark	282V
3	Fuller	RT-906
4	Clark	280-VO
4	Fuller	RT-9513
5	Fuller	RTO-910
6	Fuller	RTO-915
6	Clark	390V
7	Clark	385V
8	Allison	MT640
9	Fuller	RT-915
9	New Process	542FD

1976 Auxiliary Units

Code	Mfr. Name	Mfr. Model
2	Spicer	5831D
3	Spicer	7231B
4	Spicer	7231D
5	Spicer	8341C
6	Spicer	8031B
8	Spicer	7041

1977

Code	Mfr. Name	Mfr. Model
A	New Process	435
A	Spicer	SST10
B	Spicer	CM6052A
C	Ford	3 Spd.
C	Fuller	RT610
D	Spicer	CM5252
E	Fuller	RT12510
F	Warner	T18
F	Fuller	RTO12513
G	Spicer	SST10072A
G	Ford	Auto
H	Allison	MT650
J	Fuller	RTO9513
J	Ford	Auto
K	Spicer	6052B
L	Allison	AT540
M	Clark	285
N	Spicer	CM6052
N	Spicer	6352
O	New Process	542FL
O	Fuller	T905B
P	Warner	T19
P	Fuller	RT613
Q	Spicer	CM5052A
Q	Spicer	5652
Q	Spicer	CM6052A
Q	Fuller	RT1110
R	Spicer	CM6052C
S	Spicer	CM6052B
S	Spicer	5656B
T	New Process	542FO
T	Fuller	RT09509B
U	Spicer	6852G
V	Fuller	RT910
X	Fuller	T905A
Y	Spicer	RP85163A
Z	Clark	397
Z	Ford	Auto
2	Clark	282
3	Fuller	RT906
4	Clark	280
4	Fuller	RT9513
5	Fuller	RT0910
6	Clark	390
7	Spicer	CM5052
8	Allison	MT640
8	Fuller	RT9509A
9	New Process	542

1977 Auxiliary Units

Code	Mfr. Name	Mfr. Model
4	Spicer	7231D
5	Spicer	R8341-2
8	Spicer	7041

1978

Code	Mfr. Name	Mfr. Model
A	New Process	435
A	Spicer	SST-1010
B	Clark	4 Spd. O/D
B	Spicer	CM-6052A
C	Ford	3 Spd.
C	Fuller	RT-610
D	Spicer	CM-5252A
E	Fuller	RT-12510
F	Fuller	RTO-12513
F	Warner	4 Spd.
G	Spicer	SST-1007-2A
G	Ford	C6
H	Allison	MT-650
I	Ford	C6
J	Fuller	RT-12510
K	Spicer	CM-6052B
L	Allison	AT-540
M	Clark	285V
O	New Process	542-FL
P	Fuller	RT-613
P	Warner	T-19
Q	Fuller	RT-1110
S	Spicer	CM-6052C
T	Fuller	RTOF-12513
T	New Process	542-FO
U	Ford	C6
V	Fuller	RT-910
W	Ford	C4
X	Fuller	T-905A
X	Ford	FMX
Y	Spicer	RP-85163A
Z	Clark	397
2	Clark	282V
3	Fuller	RT-906
4	Fuller	RT-9513
4	Clark	280-VO
5	Fuller	RTO-910
6	Clark	390
7	Spicer	CM-5052A
8	Allison	MT-640
8	Fuller	RTO-958LL
9	New Process	542-FD

1978 Auxiliary Units

Code	Mfr. Name	Mfr. Model
4	Spicer	7231D
7	Spicer	R-8341-2
8	Spicer	7041

1979

Code	Mfr. Name	Mfr. Model
A	New Process	435
B	Clark	4 Spd. O/D
B	Spicer	CM-6052B
C	Ford	3 Spd.
C	Fuller	RT-610
D	Spicer	CM-5252A
E	Fuller	RT-12510
F	Warner	4 Spd.
F	Fuller	RT-12513
G	Ford	Auto. Trans.
G	Clark	282-VHD
H	Allison	MT-653
J	Fuller	RTO-9513
K	Spicer	CM-6052C
L	Allison	AT-540
M	Clark	285
M	Clark	285V
N	Clark	285-VHD
O	Fuller	T-905B
O	New Process	542-FL
P	Warner	T-19
P	Fuller	RT-613
Q	Fuller	RT-1110
S	Spicer	CM-6052C
T	Warner	T-19
U	Ford	C6
U	Spicer	SST-10073A
V	Fuller	RT-910
W	Ford	C4
X	Ford	C6
X	Ford	MFX
X	Fuller	T-905A
Y	Spicer	RP-85163A
Z	Clark	397
2	Clark	282
2	Clark	282V
3	Fuller	RT-906
4	Clark	280-VO
4	Fuller	RT-9513
5	Fuller	RTO-910
6	Clark	390
7	Spicer	CM-5052A
8	Allison	MT-643
8	Fuller	RT-9509A
9	New Process	5542-F

1979 Auxiliary Units

Code	Mfr. Name	Mfr. Model
3	Spicer	7231D
4	Spicer	7231D
5	Spicer	7041
6	Spicer	R-8341L
7	Spicer	R-8341L
8	Spicer	7041

1980
F-100-350, E-100-350, Bronco, F & B-600

Code	Mfr. Name	Mfr. Model
A	New Process	4 Spd.
B	Clark	4 Spd. O/D
C	Ford	3 Spd.
D	Spicer	5052A
E	Spicer	5252A
F	Warner	4 Spd.
G	Ford	Auto. Trans.
J	Ford	Auto. Trans.
K	Ford	Auto. Trans.
L	Allison	AT-540
M	Clark	285-V
O	New Process	542-FL
P	Warner	T-19
W	Clark	282 VHD
X	Clark	285 VHD
X	Ford	Auto. Trans.
2	Clark	282-V
9	New Process	542-FD

700 Thru 9000 Series & N600-C600 Parcel

Code	Mfr. Name	Mfr. Model
AA	Allison	AT-540
8	Allison	MT-640

FORD

TRANSMISSION IDENTIFICATION—Continued

Code	Mfr. Name①	Mfr. Model①	Code	Mfr. Name①	Mfr. Model①	Code	Mfr. Name①	Mfr. Model①
AB	Allison	MT-643	FG	Fuller	RTO-910	SC	Spicer	CM-5252A
H	Allison	MT-650	FH	Fuller	RTO-958LL	SD	Spicer	CM-6052A
AC	Allison	MT-653	FI	Fuller	RT-1110	SE	Spicer	CM-6052B
CA	Clark	280	FJ	Fuller	RT-9509A	SF	Spicer	CM-6052C
4	Clark	280-VO	FK	Fuller	RT-9513	SG	Spicer	RP-85163-A
CB	Clark	282	FL	Fuller	RTO-9513	WA	Warner	T-19
CC	Clark	282 VHD	FM	Fuller	RT-12510			
CD	Clark	285	FN	Fuller	RTO-12513			
CE	Clark	285 VHD	T	Fuller	RTOF-12513		**1980 Auxiliary Units**	
CF	Clark	390	NA	New Process	NP-435	3	Spicer	7231D
CG	Clark	397	NB	New Process	NP-542-FD	4	Spicer	7231D
FA	Fuller	RT-610	NC	New Process	NP-542-FL	5	Spicer	7041
FB	Fuller	RT-613	T	New Process	NP-542-FO	6	Spicer	R-8341L
FC	Fuller	T-905A	G	Spicer	SST-1007-2A	7	Spicer	R-8341L
FD	Fuller	T-905B	SA	Spicer	SST-1007-3A	8	Spicer	7041
FE	Fuller	RT-906	A	Spicer	SST-1010			
FF	Fuller	RT-910	SB	Spicer	CM-5052A			

①—See name chapter for repair procedures.

3 SPEED TRANS., 1970–80

Disassembly

1. Remove transmission cover, Fig. 1.
2. Remove extension housing. To prevent mainshaft from following housing (with resultant loss of needle bearings) tap end of mainshaft while withdrawing housing.
3. Remove front bearing retainer.
4. Remove filler plug from right side of case. Then working through plug opening, drive roll pin out of case and countershaft with small punch, Fig. 2.
5. Hold counter gear with a hook and, with a dummy shaft, push countershaft out rear of case until counter gear can be lowered to bottom of case, Fig. 5.
6. Pull main drive gear forward until gear contacts case, then remove large snap ring.

NOTE: On some models, it is necessary to move gear forward to provide clearance when removing mainshaft assembly. On other models, the drive gear is removed from front of case.

7. Remove snap ring and slide speedometer drive gear off mainshaft. Remove lock ball from shaft.
8. Remove snap ring and remove mainshaft rear bearing from shaft and case, Fig. 4.
9. Place both shift levers in neutral (central) position.
10. Remove a set screw that retains detent springs and plugs in case. Remove one spring and plug. Fig. 5.
11. Remove low-reverse set screw and slide shift rail out through rear of case.
12. Rotate low-reverse shift fork upward and lift it from case.
13. Remove 2-3 set screw and rotate 2-3 shift rail 90 degrees with pliers.
14. Lift interlock plug from case with a magnet rod.
15. Tap inner end of 2-3 shift rail to remove expansion plug from front of case. Remove shift rail.
16. Remove 2-3 detent plug and spring from detent bore.
17. Rotate 2-3 shift fork upward and lift from case.
18. Lift mainshaft assembly out through top of case.
19. On some transmissions, push main drive gear into case until bearing is free of bore, then lift gear and bearing through top of case.
20. Working through front bearing opening, drive reverse idler gear shaft out through rear of case with a drift, Fig. 6.
21. Lift reverse idler gear and two thrust washers from case.
22. Lift counter gear and thrust washers from case, Fig. 7. Be careful not to allow dummy shaft and needle bearings to fall out of gear.
23. Remove countershaft-to-case retaining pin and any needle bearings that may have fallen into case.
24. Unfasten and lift shift levers off shafts. Slide each lever and shaft out of case. Discard O-ring seal from each shaft, Fig. 8.
25. Remove snap ring from front end of mainshaft and remove synchronizers, gears and related parts, Fig. 9.
26. If main drive gear is to be disassembled, refer to Fig. 10.

Assembly

Counter Gear

1. Coat bore at each end of counter gear with grease.
2. Hold appropriate dummy shaft in gear and install 25 needle bearings and a retainer washer in each end of gear, Fig. 7.
3. Install counter gear, thrust washers and countershaft in case.
4. Place transmission case in vertical position and check end play with a feeler gauge as shown in Fig. 11. If end play exceeds .018", replace thrust washers as required to obtain .004–.018" end play.
5. Once end play has been established, remove countershaft with dummy shaft.
6. Allow counter gear assembly to remain in case.

Reverse Idler Gear

1. Install idler gear, thrust washers and shaft in case.
2. Make sure that thrust washer with flat side is at the web end, and that the spur gear is toward the rear of case, Fig. 6.
3. Check reverse idler gear end play in same manner and to the same clearance as the counter gear. If end play is within limits of .004–.018" leave gear in case.

Low-Reverse Synchronizer

1. Install an insert spring, Fig. 12, in groove of low-reverse synchronizer hub. Make sure spring covers all insert grooves.
2. Start hub in sleeve, making sure that alignment marks are properly indexed.
3. Position three inserts in hub, making sure that small end is over spring and that shoulder is on inside of hub.
4. Slide sleeve and reverse gear onto hub until detent is engaged.
5. Install other insert spring in front of hub to hold inserts against hub.

Second-Third Synchronizer

1. Install one insert spring, Fig. 13, into a groove of synchronizer hub, making sure that all three insert slots are fully covered.
2. With alignment marks on hub and sleeve aligned, start hub into sleeve.
3. Place three inserts on top of retaining spring and push assembly together.
4. Install remaining insert spring so that spring ends cover same slots as do other spring. Do not stagger springs.
5. Place a synchronizer blocking ring in each end of sleeve.

Main Drive Line

1. Lubricate mainshaft splines and machined surfaces with transmission lube.
2. Slide low-reverse synchronizer, Fig. 9, onto mainshaft with teeth end of gear facing toward rear of shaft. Secure in place with snap ring.
3. Coat tapered machined surface of low gear with grease. Place blocking ring on greased surface.
4. Slide low gear onto mainshaft with blocking ring toward rear of shaft. Rotate gear as necessary to engage the three notches in blocking ring with synchronizer inserts. Secure low gear with thrust washer and snap ring.
5. Coat tapered machined surface of 2nd gear with grease and slide blocking ring onto it. Slide 2nd gear with blocking ring

Ford

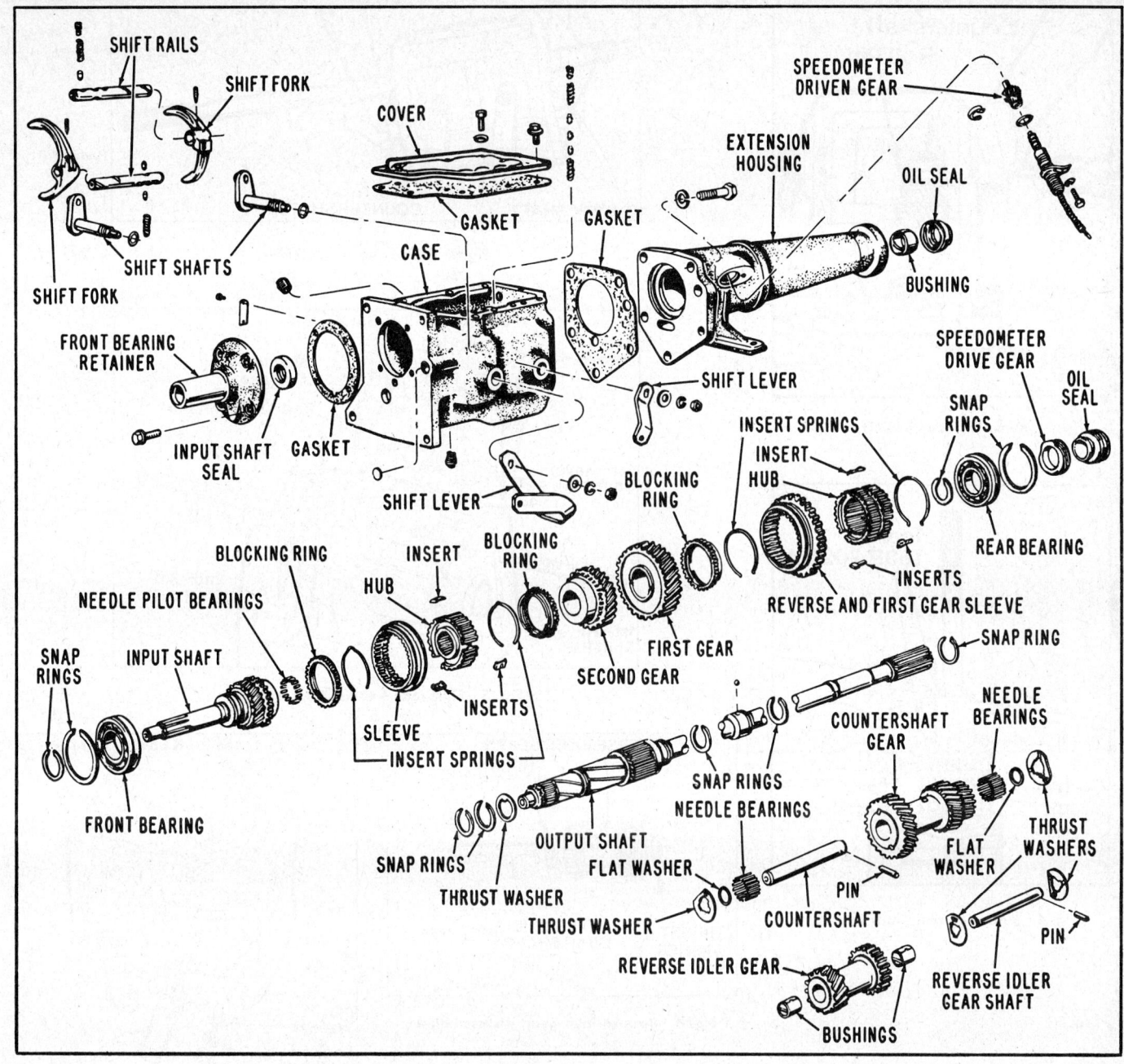

Fig. 1 Exploded view of three-speed transmission. 1970-80

and 2-3 synchronizer onto mainshaft. Tapered machined surface of 2nd gear must be toward front of shaft. Make sure that notches in blocking ring engage synchronizer inserts. Secure synchronizer with snap ring.
6. Install new O-ring on each of two shift lever shafts, Fig. 8. Lubricate shafts with transmission lube and install them in case. Secure each lever on its shaft with a flat washer, lock washer and nut.
7. Coat bore of main drive gear shaft with thick coat of grease. Install 15 needle bearings in gear pocket, Fig. 10.
8. Position drive gear assembly into case.
9. Place a detent spring and plug in case, Fig. 5. Place 2-3 shift fork in synchronizer groove. Rotate fork into position and install 2-3 shift rail. It will be necessary to depress detent plug to enter rail in bore. Move rail inward until detent plug engages center (neutral) notch. Secure fork to shaft with set screw.
10. Install interlock plug in case. If 2-3 shift rail is in neutral position, top of interlock will be slightly lower than surface of low-reverse shift rail bore.
11. Place low-reverse shift fork in groove of synchronizer. Rotate fork into position and install low-reverse shift rail. Move rail inward until center (neutral) notch is aligned with detent bore. Secure fork to shaft with set screw.
12. Install remaining detent plug and spring. Secure spring with slotted head set screw. Turn set screw in until head is flush with case.
13. Install new expansion plug in case.
14. Install large snap ring on drive bearing. Work drive gear into case and onto mainshaft until snap ring is seated against case. Make sure that needle bearings do not fall out of place and that notches in blocking ring engage inserts in synchronizer.

NOTE: The foregoing applies only to transmissions used with V8-390 engines. On all other models, the drive gear is installed through front of case with bear-

Ford

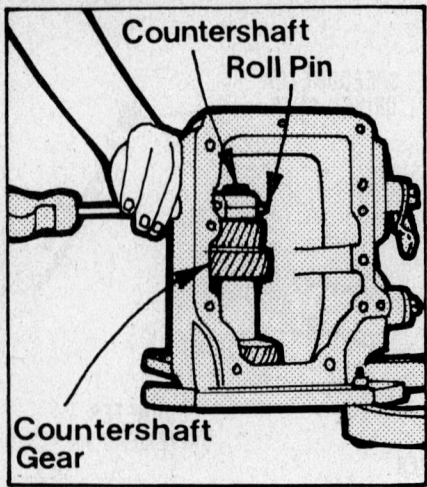

Fig. 2 Removing countershaft roll pin

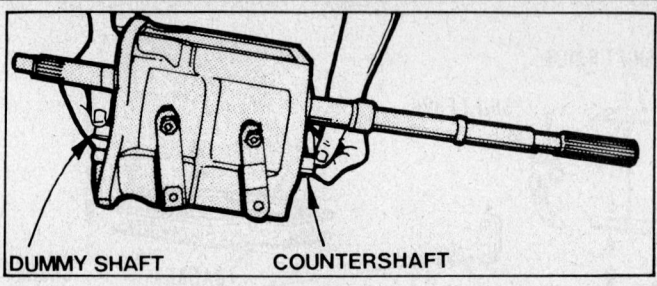

Fig. 3 Removing countershaft

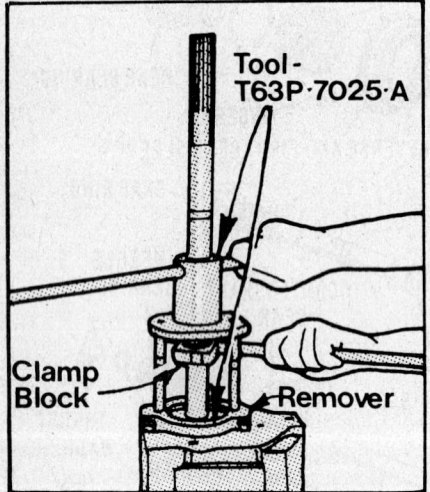

Fig. 4 Removing mainshaft bearing

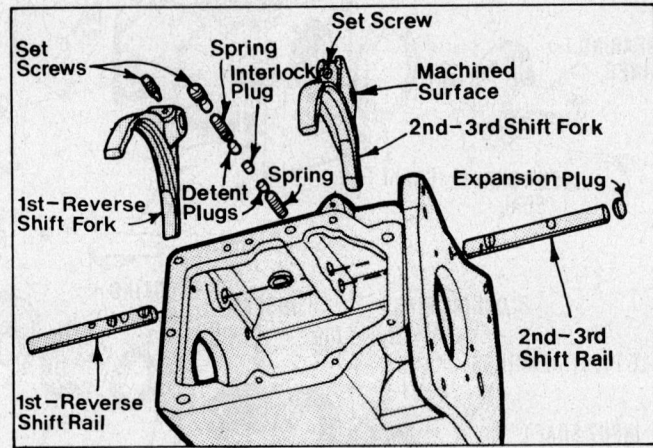

Fig. 5 Shift rods & forks, disassembled

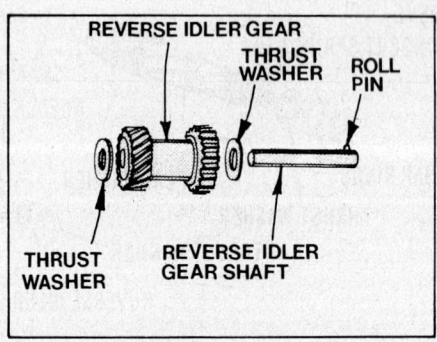

Fig. 6 Reverse idler gear, disassembled

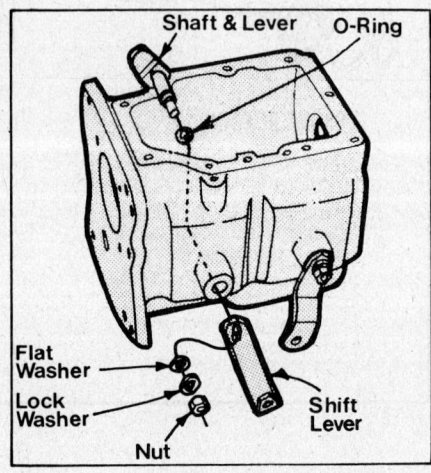

Fig. 8 Shift lever & related components

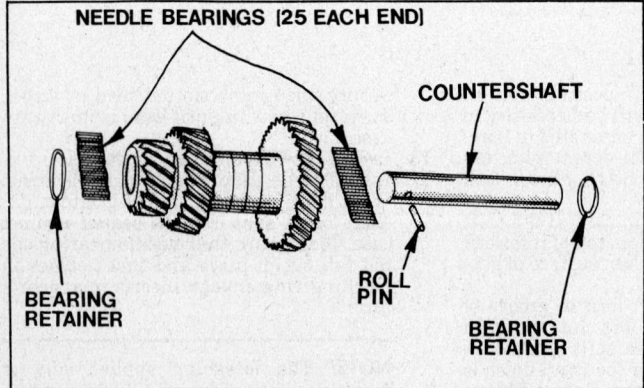

Fig. 7 Countergear, disassembled

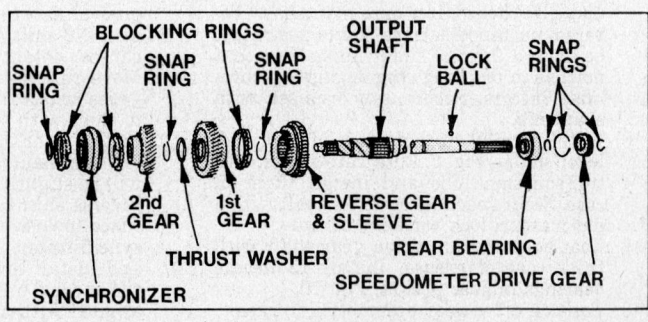

Fig. 9 Mainshaft, disassembled

Ford

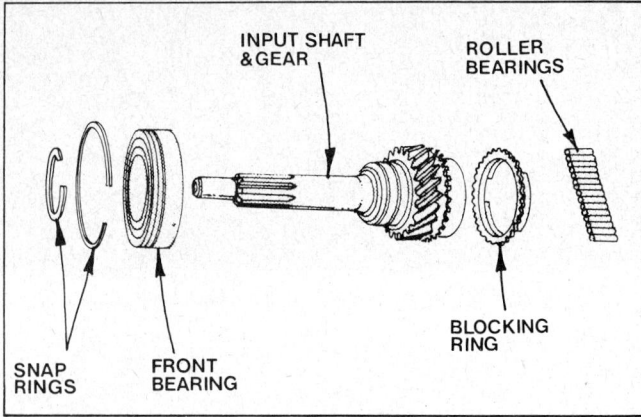

Fig. 10 Main drive gear, disassembled

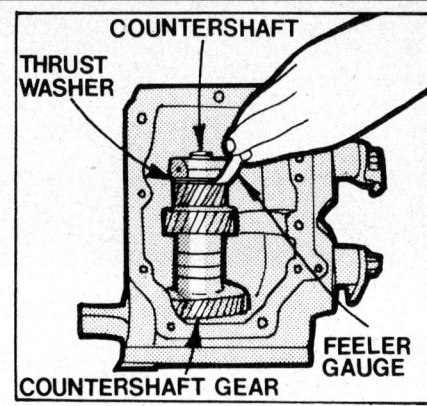

Fig. 11 Checking countergear end play

ing in place on shaft.

15. Position new front bearing retainer gasket on case. Place bearing retainer on case, making sure oil return groove is at the bottom. Install and tighten attaching screws to 30–36 ft-lbs.
16. Install large snap ring on mainshaft rear bearing. Place bearing on mainshaft with snap ring end toward rear of shaft. Press bearing into place and secure with snap ring.
17. Hold speedometer drive gear lock ball in detent and slide gear into place. Secure gear with snap ring.

Final Assembly

1. Place transmission in vertical position. Working through drain hole in bottom of case, align bore of counter gear and thrust washers with bore of case, using a screwdriver.
2. Working through rear of case, push dummy shaft out with countershaft. Before countershaft is completely inserted, make sure the hole that accommodates roll pin is aligned with hole in case.
3. Working through lubricant filler hole, install roll pin (Fig. 2) in case and countershaft.
4. Install filler and drain plugs, making sure magnetic plug is installed in bottom of case.
5. Install extension housing with new gasket and torque attaching cap screws to 42–50 ft-lbs.
6. Place transmission in gear, pour lubricant over entire gear train while rotating input and output shafts.
7. Install cover with new gasket and torque attaching screws to 14–19 ft-lbs. on 1970–76 models, and 20–25 ft-lbs. on 1977–80 models. Coat gasket and cover screws with sealer.

FOUR SPEED OVERDRIVE TRANS.

Disassembly

1. Remove the lower extension housing to case attaching screw to drain lubricant.
2. Remove cover attaching screws and the cover from case.
3. Remove the long spring retaining detent plug in case, then, using a magnet, remove detent plug.
4. Remove extension housing to case screws and the extension housing.
5. Remove input shaft bearing retainer attaching screws and slide retainer from input shaft.
6. Support countershaft gear with a wire hook. Working from front of case, push countershaft out rear of case with a dummy shaft. Lower countershaft gear to bottom of case and remove the wire hook.
7. Remove set screw from first and second speed shift fork, then slide first and second speed shift rail out rear of case, Fig. 13A.
8. With a magnet, remove interlock detent from between the first and second and the third and overdrive shift rails.
9. Shift transmission into overdrive position. Remove set screw from the third and overdrive shift fork. Remove the side detent bolt, detent plug and spring. Rotate the third and overdrive speed shift rail 90 degrees and tap rail out front of case with a suitable punch and hammer.
10. With a magnet, remove interlock plug from top of case.
11. Remove snap ring securing speedometer drive gear to output shaft, then slide gear from shaft. Remove speedometer gear drive ball.
12. Remove output shaft bearing retaining snap ring and the snap ring from outside diameter of output shaft bearing.
13. Remove output shaft bearing.
14. Remove input shaft bearing retaining snap ring and the snap ring from outside diameter of input shaft bearing.
15. Remove input shaft bearing from shaft and case, then the input shaft and blocking ring from front of case.
16. Position output shaft to right side of case

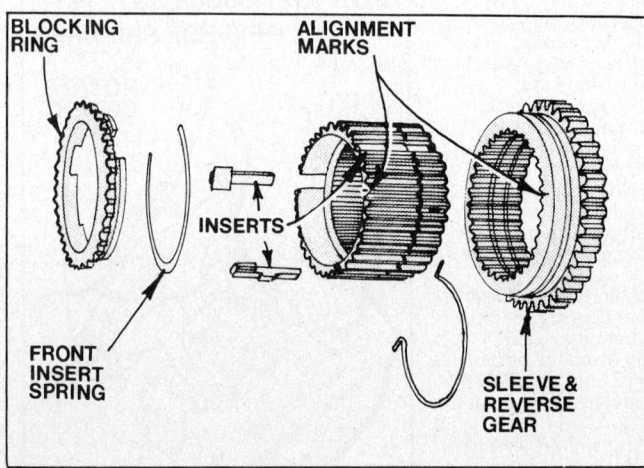

Fig. 12 Low-reverse synchronizer, disassembled

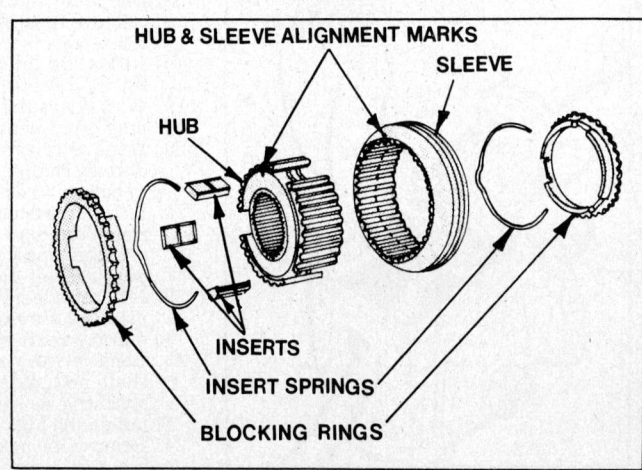

Fig. 13 Second-high synchronizer, disassembled

1111

Ford

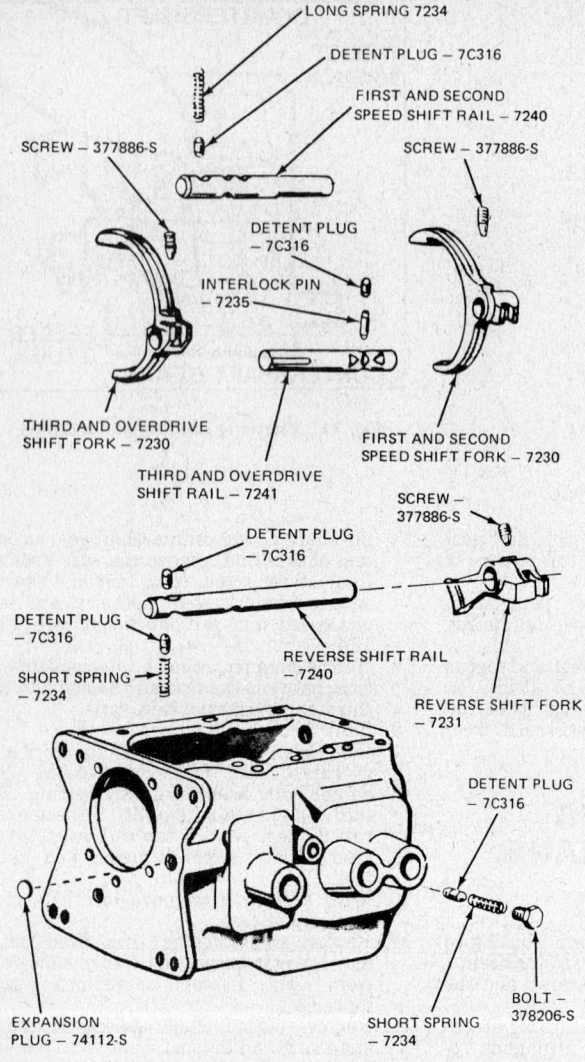

Fig. 13A Shift forks & rails, disassembled

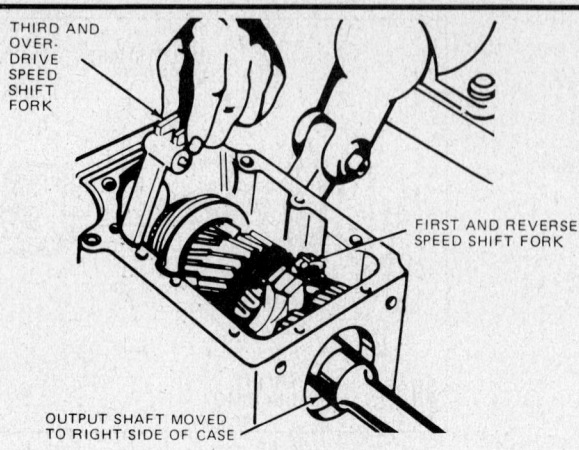

Fig. 13B Removing shift forks

speed gear thrust washer, gear and blocking ring from rear of output shaft.

Sub-Assembly Service

Cam & Shaft Seals

NOTE: To facilitate reassembly, note position of cams and shafts assemblies and levers before removal from transmission case.

1. Remove three shift levers, Fig. 13G.
2. Remove three cams and shafts from inside of case.
3. Remove O-ring from each cam and shaft.
4. Dip new O-rings in gear lubricant and install them on cams and shafts.
5. Slide each cam and shaft into its respective bore in case.
6. Secure each shift lever.

Synchronizers

1. Push synchronizer hub from each sleeve, Fig. 13H.
2. Separate inserts and springs from hubs. Do not mix parts from one synchronizer to another.
3. Position hub in sleeve, being sure that alignment marks are properly indexed.
4. Place three inserts into hub. Install insert springs, making sure that irregular surface (hump) is seated in one of inserts. Do not stagger springs.

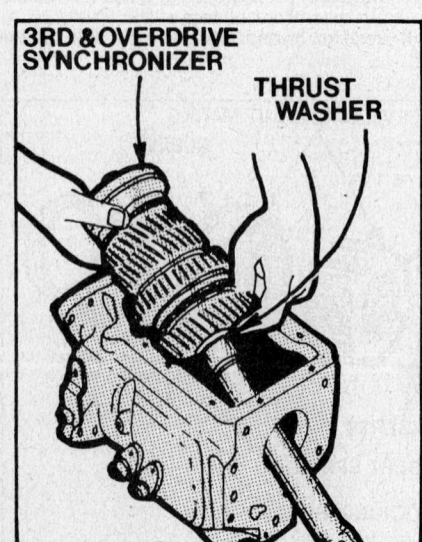

Fig. 13C Replacing output shaft assembly

and remove shift forks, Fig. 13B.
17. Lift output shaft assembly from case, Fig. 13C, support the thrust washer and first speed gear to prevent the washer and gear from sliding from shaft.
18. Remove reverse gear shift fork set screw, rotate reverse shift rail 90 degrees, Fig. 13D, slide shift rail out rear of case and lift the reverse shift fork from case.
19. With a magnet, remove reverse detent plug and spring with a magnet.
20. Remove reverse idler gear shaft with a dummy shaft and lower reverse idler gear to bottom of case, Fig. 13E.
21. Lift countershaft gear and thrust washers from bottom of case, using caution not to drop bearings or the dummy shaft from countershaft gear.
22. Lift reverse idler gear shaft from case, using caution not to drop bearings or the dummy shaft from reverse idler gear.
23. Remove snap ring from front of output shaft and slide the third and overdrive synchronizer, blocking and gear from output shaft, Fig. 13F.
24. Remove the next snap ring and the second speed gear thrust washer, gear and blocking ring from output shaft.
25. Remove the next snap ring and the first

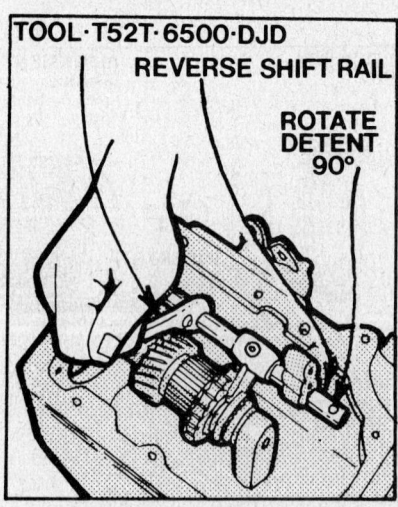

Fig. 13D Replacing reverse shift rail

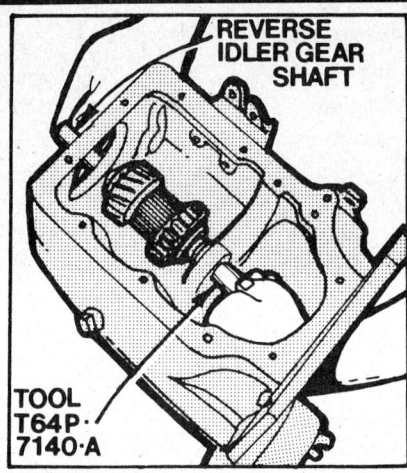

Fig. 13E Removing reverse idler gear shaft

Countershaft Gear Bearings
1. With unit disassembled, coat bore in each end of countergear with grease, Fig. 13I.
2. Hold a suitable dummy shaft in gear and insert 21 rollers and a retainer washer in each end of gear.

Reverse Idler Gear Bearings
1. With unit disassembled, Fig. 13J, coat bore at each end of gear with grease.
2. Hold a suitable dummy shaft in gear and insert 22 rollers and retainer washer at each end of gear.
3. Install sliding gear on reverse idler gear, making sure that shift fork groove is toward front.

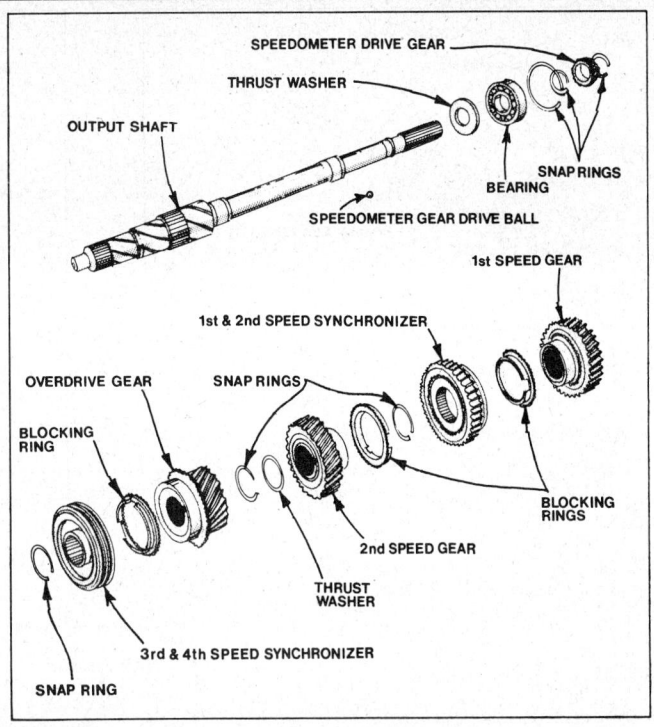

Fig. 13F Output shaft disassembled

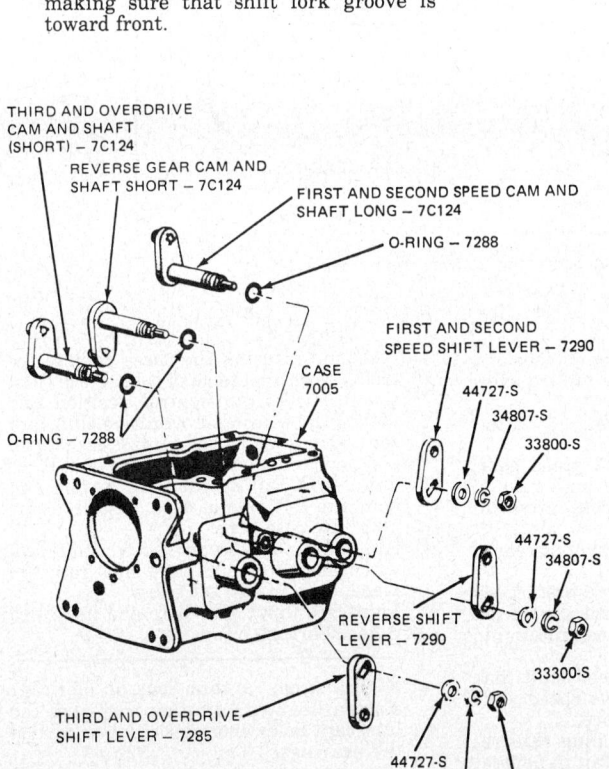

Fig. 13G Cams, shafts & levers

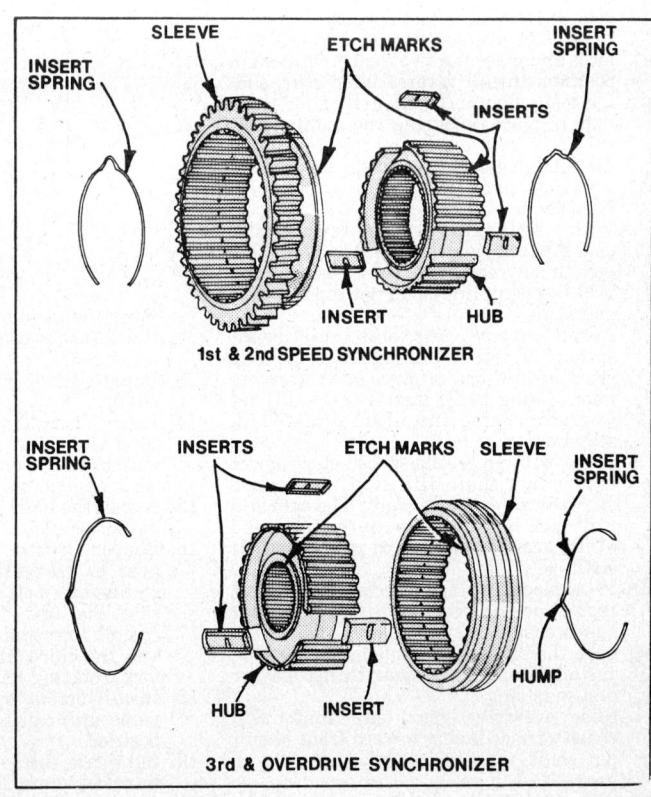

Fig. 13H Synchronizer assemblies, disassembled

FORD

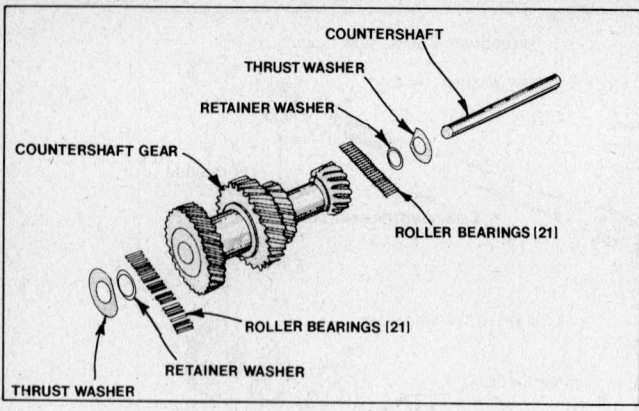

Fig. 13I Countergear, disassembled

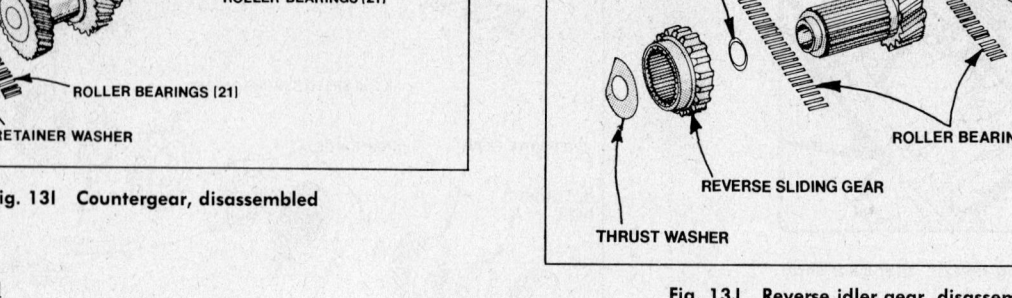

Fig. 13J Reverse idler gear, disassembled

Input Shaft Seal
1. Remove seal from input shaft bearing retainer.
2. Lubricate sealing surface and install new seal.

Transmission Assembly
1. Lubricate countershaft gear thrust surfaces and position a thrust washer at each end of case. Place countershaft gear, dummy shaft and roller bearings in the case.
2. Place case in the vertical position, align gear bore and thrust washers with case bores and install countershaft.
3. Place case in the horizontal position and, with a feeler gauge, check countershaft gear end play which should be .004–.018 inch. If not, replace thrust washers.
4. Reinstall dummy shaft in countershaft gear and place gear at bottom of case.
5. Lubricate reverse idler gear thrust surfaces and place the two thrust washers in position. Install reverse idler gear, sliding gear, dummy shaft and roller bearings in place, ensuring the sliding gear shift fork groove is facing toward front of case. Align gear bore and thrust washers with case bores and install the reverse idler shaft.
6. With a feeler gauge, check reverse idler gear end play which should be .004–.018 inch. If not, replace thrust washers. If end play is within limits, do not remove gear and shaft.
7. Install reverse gear shift rail detent spring and detent plug into case. Holding reverse shift fork in place on the reverse idler sliding gear, install the shift rail from rear of case. Install shift rail to fork set screw.
8. Place first and second speed synchronizer onto output shaft with shift fork groove facing toward rear of shaft. The synchronizer hub is installed with the teeth end of the gear facing toward rear of output shaft.
9. Place blocking ring on second speed gear, then slide the gear onto front of output shaft, ensuring synchronizer inserts engage the blocker ring notches.
10. Install second speed gear thrust washer and snap ring.
11. Slide overdrive gear onto shaft with coned surface facing toward front of output shaft, then install blocking ring on gear.
12. Slide third and overdrive gear synchronizer onto shaft, ensuring synchronizer inserts engage blocking ring notches and the thrust surface is facing toward overdrive gear.
13. Install snap ring at front of output shaft.
14. Place blocking ring on first speed gear, then slide first speed gear onto rear of output shaft, ensuring synchronizer inserts engage blocking ring notches.
15. Install the heavy thrust washer at rear of output shaft.
16. Support thrust washer and first speed gear to prevent washer and gear from sliding off shaft and lower assembly into case, Fig. 13C.
17. Install first and second speed shift fork and the third and overdrive speed shift fork, rotating forks into place.
18. Install detent spring and plug into reverse shift rail, then place rail in neutral position.
19. Lubricate third and overdrive shift rail interlock pin and install in shift rail.
20. Align third and overdrive shift fork with shift rail bores and slide shift rail into position, ensuring the three detents are facing toward outside of case. Place front synchronizer into neutral position and install the third and overdrive shift fork set screw. Place synchronizer in neutral position and install the third and overdrive shift rail detent plug, spring and bolt into left side of case. Install detent plug into case bore.
21. Align first and second speed shift fork with case bores and slide shift rail into place, then install set screw.
22. Lubricate input gear bore and install 15 roller bearings into bore.

NOTE: Apply a thin coat of lubricant since a heavy application may plug the lubricant holes and restrict lubrication of the bearings.

23. Place front blocking ring in the third and overdrive synchronizer.
24. Place a dummy bearing on rear of output shaft to support and align shaft in case.

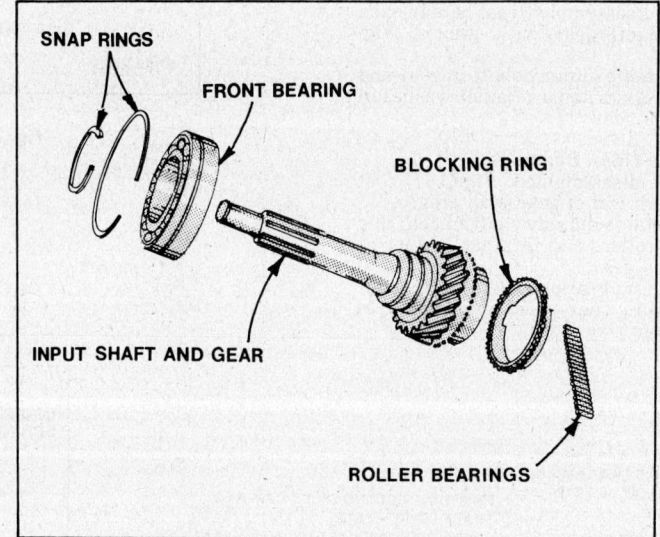

Fig. 13K Input shaft, disassembled

25. Install input shaft gear into case, ensuring output shaft pilot enters roller bearings in input gear pocket.
26. Place input shaft bearing on input shaft and press bearing onto shaft and into case bore, Fig. 13K.
27. Install input shaft and bearing snap rings, Fig. 13K.
28. Place new gasket on input shaft bearing retainer, apply sealer to attaching bolts and install and torque attaching bolts to 19–25 ft. lbs.
29. Remove dummy bearing from output shaft and install output shaft bearing onto shaft and press into case bore.

NOTE: Before pressing bearing onto output shaft, ensure the bearing is aligned with the case bore and the countershaft is not interfering with the output shaft assembly.

30. Install output shaft and bearing snap rings.
31. Place transmission in the vertical position. Align countershaft gear bore and thrust washers with case bore and install countershaft.
32. Install extension housing on case with a new gasket, apply sealer to attaching screws and install and torque to 42–50 ft. lbs.
33. Install filler plug.
34. Pour transmission lubricant over gear train while rotating input shaft.
35. Place each shift fork in all positions to ensure proper operation.
36. Install remaining detent plug in case and the long spring to secure detent plug.
37. Install cover with a new gasket, apply sealer to attaching screws and install and torque attaching screws to 20–25 ft. lbs.
38. Apply sealer to the third and overdrive shift rail plug bore and install new expansion plug.

TILT CAB SHIFT LINKAGE

1970–71 Adjustment

1. Shift transmission into neutral.
2. On 1970–71 models, loosen both turnbuckle bolts, Fig. 14, and rotate turnbuckle until shift lever ball is the specified distance from the instrument panel shown in the table below:

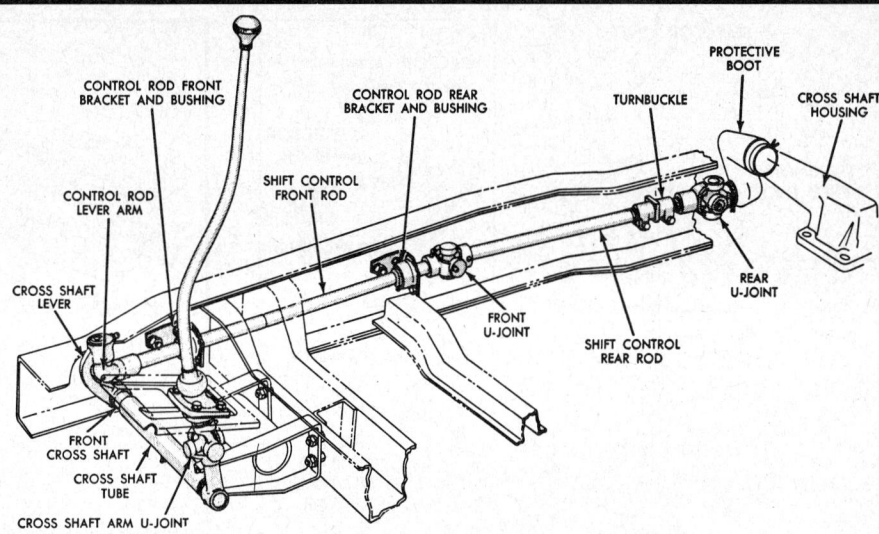

Fig. 14 Tilt cab shift linkage. 1970–71 Typical

Shift Lever Ball to Instrument Panel Clearance

Trans. Model	Clearance
Fuller RTO-510	6.50"–7.00"
Warner T19	7.00"–7.50"
Clark 300, 380	8.25"–8.75"
Clark 280, Spicer 5000	9.25"–9.75"
Spicer 6000	9.75"–10.25"
New Process 435	10.00"–10.50"
New Process 541, Fuller R96	10.50"–11.00"

3. Tilt cab on 1970–71 models.
4. Using a drift or a screwdriver, turn rear U-joint counterclockwise (viewed from rear) until rear cross shaft finger bottoms the plunger (except on Spicer units) in the transmission shift housing. On a Spicer transmission, rotate U-joint until the finger bottoms firmly in the gate.
5. Holding the finger in position, rotate the shift control rear rod until there is the specified distance (see below) between inner surface of cross shaft lever and right-hand end of cross shaft tube.
6. Tighten turnbuckle bolts.
7. On 1970–71 models, lower cab.

Transmission Lever Clearance

Transmission	Distance
Warner T-98	1/4"
New Process 435	3/8"
New Process 540	3/16"
Fuller 8 Speed	3/16"
Clark 5 Speed H.D.	1/4"
Clark 5 Speed M.D.	3/8"
Spicer 5 Speed	7/16"

1972–80 Adjustment

1. Shift transmission into neutral and loosen both turnbuckle nuts, Fig. 14A.
2. Rotate turnbuckle until shift lever is located 6 1/4 inch from instrument panel (view Z), Fig. 14B.
3. Rotate rear universal joint counterclockwise (looking rearward from front of truck) as far as possible.

NOTE: Spring plunger in transmission must be fully compressed on CM50, CM60, QM60, 280, 380, 390, 5000 and

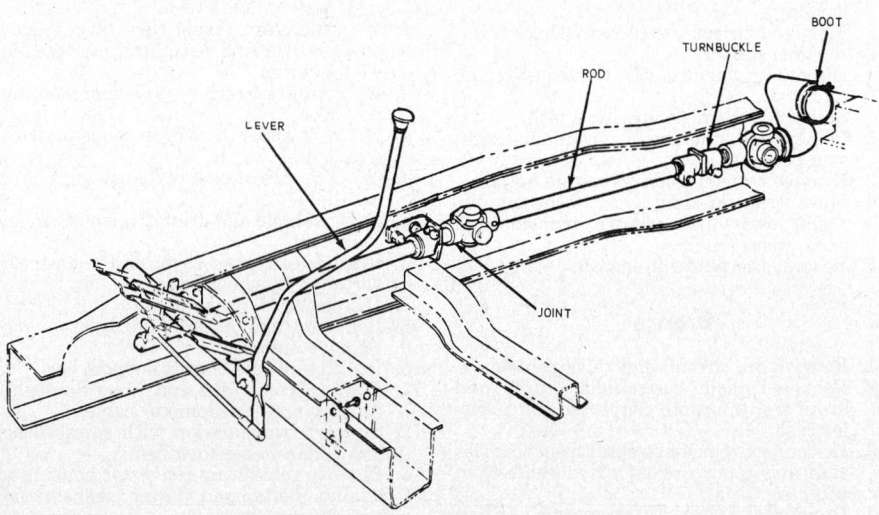

Fig. 14A Tilt cab shift linkage. 1972–80

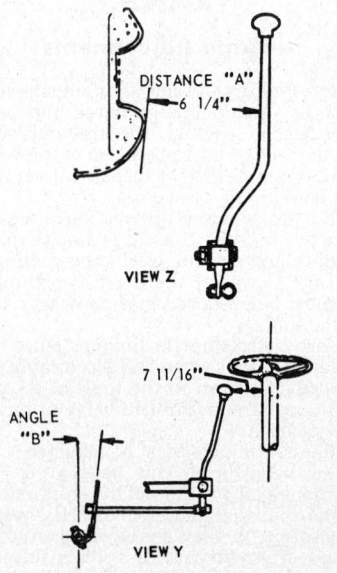

Fig. 14B Shift linkage adjustments. 1972–80 Tilt cab

FORD

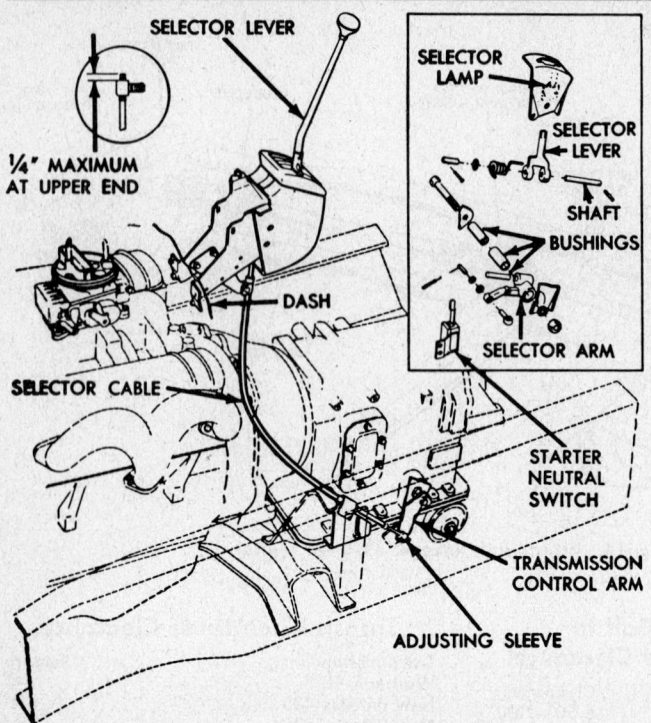

Fig. 15 Transmatic range selector linkage. Conventional cab models

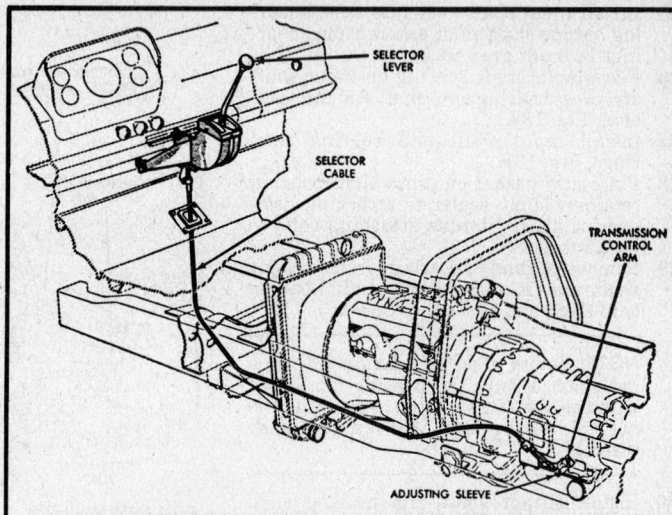

Fig. 16 Transmatic range selector linkage

6000 model transmissions.

4. Position shift arm at 2½° from vertical (angle "B"), Fig. 14B, then tighten turnbuckle nuts.
5. Adjust shift rod to position shift lever ball $7^{11}/_{16}$ inch from steering column (view Y), Fig. 14B, then tighten jam nuts on shift rod. Threads on shift rod must be centered within $1/8$ inch.

FORD AUTOMATIC TRANS.

Linkage Adjustments

Before making any checks or adjustments of the transmission linkage check the performance of the engine. The transmission is often blamed for poor operation of the vehicle when the engine is not tuned to deliver maximum power.

There are so many linkage variations and intricate hook-ups that it is impractical to illustrate and go into specific procedures for each one. However, there are two things to remember when it becomes necessary to adjust the linkage.

1. Carburetor throttle linkage must be so adjusted that when the accelerator pedal is pushed down to the limit of its travel the carburetor throttle valve(s) must be wide open.
2. Manual linkage must be adjusted so that the hand lever can be moved freely through all positions of the shift indicator and that the pointer is directly over the positions as they are selected. And with the carburetor throttle valve(s) fully open the transmission linkage must be adjusted so that the TV lever on the transmission will move to the limit of its travel.

C4 CRUISEOMATIC, REPLACE

Exc. Bronco, Econoline & Ranchero

1. Drain transmission and converter.
2. Remove drive shaft.
3. Disconnect oil cooler lines from transmission.
4. Remove downshift lever return spring from low-reverse servo cover.
5. Disconnect shift rods from transmission levers.
6. Disconnect neutral start switch wiring harness at connectors.
7. Remove speedometer gear from extension housing.
8. Remove four converter-to-flywheel bolts.
9. Remove starter.
10. Disconnect vacuum line from diaphragm unit.
11. Support transmission with a jack.
12. Remove crossmember from under extension housing.
13. Remove transmission-to-engine bolts.
14. Move transmission away from engine. Then lower and remove transmission from under truck.
15. Reverse procedure to install.

Bronco

1. Remove fan shroud and raise vehicle.
2. Remove transfer case shield, if used, and drain transmission, converter and transfer case.
3. Disconnect rear drive shaft from transfer case and remove front drive shaft from vehicle.
4. Disconnect exhaust system and position aside.
5. Remove speedometer gear from transfer case.
6. Disconnect oil cooler lines, shift linkage and neutral start switch wires from transmission.
7. Remove starter.
8. Disconnect vacuum lines from modulator and retaining clip.
9. Remove crossmember-to-transfer case adapter and crossmember-to-frame side support attaching bolts.
10. Raise transmission and transfer case with a suitable jack and remove left side support bracket-to-frame bolts, side support bracket, crossmember and upper crossmember insulators.
11. Raise transmission and transfer case slightly and disconnect shift rod and shift lever bracket from transfer case.
12. Remove converter housing to engine bolts, slide transmission and transfer case rearward and lower assembly from vehicle.
13. Remove transfer case adapter to transmission bolts and slide transmission from transfer case.
14. Reverse procedure to install.

Econoline

1. Working from inside the truck, remove engine cover and disconnect neutral start switch wires.
2. On V8 units, remove air cleaner heat tube flex hose.
3. Remove upper converter housing-to-engine bolts.
4. On V8, disconnect exhaust pipe from manifold.
5. Raise vehicle and drain transmission and converter.
6. Remove converter cover and remove converter-to-flywheel bolts.
7. Disconnect drive shaft.
8. Remove transmission filler tube.
9. Remove starter.
10. Install suitable engine support bar.
11. Disconnect vacuum and cooler lines, shift linkage and speedometer cable.
12. Support transmission with suitable jack and remove crossmember.
13. Remove remaining converter housing-to-engine bolts and lower transmission away from vehicle.
14. Reverse procedure to install.

Ford

Ranchero

1. Disconnect neutral safety switch wires in engine compartment.
2. Raise vehicle and remove converter cover at low front side of converter housing.
3. Drain converter.
4. Remove propeller shaft.
5. Remove vacuum line hose from transmission vacuum unit. Disconnect vacuum line from clip.
6. Remove two extension housing to crossmember bolts.
7. Remove speedometer cable from extension housing.
8. Disconnect exhaust pipe from manifold.
9. Remove parking brake cable from equalizer lever.
10. Loosen transmission oil pan bolts and drain oil at one corner of pan.
11. Disconnect cooler lines from the transmission.
12. Remove the manual and kick down linkage rods from transmission shift levers.
13. Where necessary, disconnect the neutral start switch wires.
14. Remove starter.
15. Remove fluid.
16. Remove four converter-to-flywheel nuts.
17. Support transmission with jack.
18. Remove crossmember.
19. Remove converter housing-to-engine bolts.
20. Lower transmission and remove from vehicle.

C6 CRUISEOMATIC, REPLACE

1970-80 Exc. Ranchero & 1975-76 Econoline

1. Remove two upper converter housing-to-engine bolts and oil filler tube-to-cylinder head bolt.
2. Raise vehicle and drain transmission.
3. Disconnect drive shaft.
4. Disconnect speedometer cable, shift linkage, oil cooler lines and vacuum line.
5. Remove starter.

NOTE: On F-150-250 models with four wheel drive and Bronco, remove the transfer case.

6. Remove four converter-to-flywheel bolts.
7. Support transmission with a suitable jack and remove both crossmembers.
8. Secure transmission to jack, remove remaining converter-to-engine bolts and lower transmission away from vehicle.
9. Reverse procedure to install.

1972-78 Ranchero

NOTE: On models with the neutral safety switch wire harness connected at the dash panel, disconnect the harness before raising the vehicle.

1. Working from engine compartment, remove the two bolts retaining the fan shroud to the radiator. On 1975-78 models, disconnect the battery.
2. Raise vehicle and drain transmission and converter.
3. Remove drive shaft and starter.
4. Remove four converter to flywheel attaching points.
5. Disconnect parking brake front cable from equalizer.
6. Disconnect speedometer cable and transmission linkage.
7. Where necessary, disconnect muffler inlet pipes from exhaust manifold.
8. Support the transmission with a suitable jack, remove parking brake rear cables from the equalizer and remove the crossmember and rear engine support.
9. Lower transmission and remove oil cooler lines, vacuum line and transmission oil filler tube.
10. Secure the transmission to the jack with the chain, remove the converter housing to cylinder block bolts and carefully move the transmission away from the engine, at the same time lowering it to clear the underside of the vehicle.

1970-71 Ranchero

1. Working inside engine compartment, disconnect neutral switch wires from harness connector and clip on dash.
2. Remove bolt that secures filler tube to rear of right cylinder head.
3. Raise car on hoist or stands.
4. Drain converter and oil pan.
5. Remove drive shaft.
6. Disconnect shift rods from transmission levers.
7. Disconnect speedometer cable from extension housing.
8. Disconnect hose from vacuum diaphragm at rear of transmission. Remove vacuum tube from clip at transmission.
9. Remove starter.
10. Lift filler tube from case.
11. Remove four converter-to-flywheel nuts.
12. Remove two nuts that attach engine rear support to crossmember.
13. Raise transmission to take weight off crossmember.
14. Remove crossmember.
15. Remove rear engine support.
16. Lower transmission and disconnect oil cooler lines.
17. Secure transmission to jack with a chain.
18. Remove six converter housing-to-cylinder block bolts.
19. Move jack rearward until transmission clears engine; tip it forward to provide clearance. Lower and remove transmission.
20. Reverse procedure to install.

1975-80 Econoline

1. Working from inside the truck, remove engine cover and disconnect neutral start switch wires.
2. On V8 units, remove air cleaner heat tube flex hose.
3. Remove upper converter housing-to-engine bolts.
4. On V8, disconnect exhaust pipe from manifold.
5. Raise vehicle and drain transmission and converter.
6. Remove converter cover and remove converter-to-flywheel bolts.
7. Disconnect drive shaft.
8. Remove transmission filler tube.
9. Remove starter.
10. Install suitable engine support bar.
11. Disconnect vacuum and cooler lines, shift linkage and speedometer cable.
12. Support transmission with suitable jack and remove crossmember.
13. Remove remaining converter housing-to-engine bolts and lower transmission away from vehicle.
14. Reverse procedure to install.

HEAVY DUTY CRUISEOMATIC

1970-77 Exc. Ranchero

Transmission & Converter

1. Drain converter.
2. Disconnect oil filler pipe.
3. On 1970-77 models, wedge the converter in place.
4. Remove starter.
5. Disconnect oil cooler hoses (if used).
6. Disconnect linkage from transmission.
7. Remove hose from vacuum unit.
8. Disconnect speedometer cable and remove drive shaft.
9. Remove both rear engine support bolts.
10. With transmission jack raise engine and transmission high enough to remove engine rear supports.
11. Lower engine against floor stand or engine support bar so that converter housing is clear of crossmember when all weight is off transmission jack.
12. Remove remaining converter housing-to-engine bolts.
13. Where necessary, loosen and drop the exhaust system to allow converter to clear exhaust pipe.
14. Remove flywheel-to-converter bolts.
15. Move transmission rearward and lower it, leaving flywheel attached to crankshaft. If additional clearance is needed, tilt rear of assembly upright slightly and to the rear enough to allow removal of flywheel-to-crankshaft bolts.
16. Move assembly to rear and remove it.
17. Reverse procedure to install.

1970-80 Ranchero

NOTE: On some models, it is necessary to remove the two upper converter housing to engine bolts before raising vehicle.

1. Raise vehicle and place on jack stands, then drain transmission oil pan.
2. Remove converter access cover and remove converter drain plug.
3. Remove converter to flywheel attaching nuts, reinstall converter drain plugs and converter housing access cover to hold converter in place when transmission is removed.
4. Remove starter and propeller shaft.
5. Where necessary, disconnect exhaust pipes from manifold.
6. Disconnect oil cooler lines, speedometer cable, vacuum hose and manual downshift linkage.
7. Disconnect TRS switch wire, if equipped.
8. Support transmission with suitable jack and remove crossmember.

NOTE: On some models, it is necessary to remove the engine rear support to transmission bolts before crossmember removal.

9. Lower transmission and remove filler tube and dipstick.
10. Remove converter housing-to-engine bolts. On 1970 models, move transmission rearward until it clears the engine, then tip forward to provide clearance during removal. On 1973-79 models, move transmission and jack rearward and lower away from vehicle.
11. Reverse procedure to install.

1117

Ford

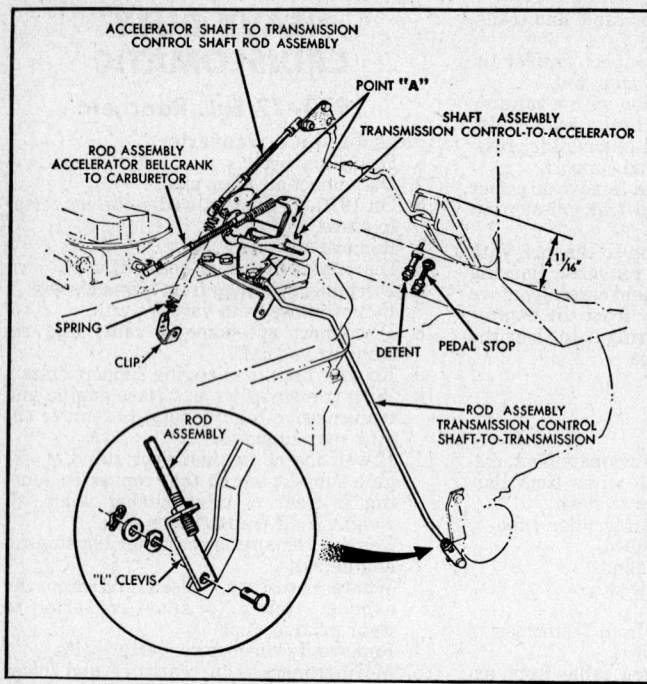

Fig. 17 Transmatic throttle linkage. 1970–71 exc. Super Duty engines. Conventional cab

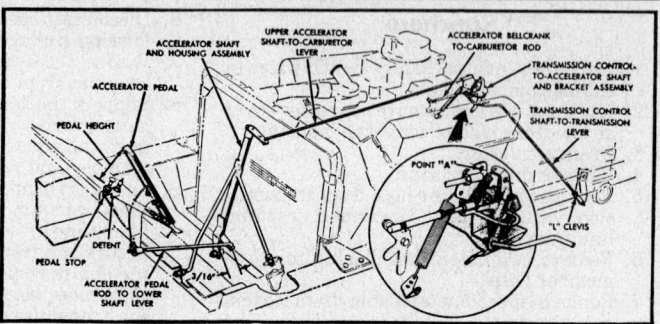

Fig. 18 Transmatic throttle linkage 1970–71 Tilt cab. Pedal height should be 4¼"

TRANSMATIC DRIVE
1970–71

For a detailed description on the operation and servicing of this transmission see the *Allison Chapter* elsewhere in this manual. The following material deals with linkage adjustments and removal of the unit from the truck.

Range Selector Linkage, Adjust

1. Place the selector lever at R.
2. Check the distance that the control cable adjusting threads extend above the sleeve assembled to the range selector arm, Figs. 15 and 16.
3. At the transmission, disconnect the range selector cable from the transmission control lever.
4. Shift the transmission control lever to R (all the way forward and upward).
5. Push the control cable up until the selector lever hits the R stop. Adjust the threaded sleeve so that the sleeve pin fits the hole in the control lever.
6. Assemble the sleeve to the lever.
7. From the driver's seat, feel for full engagement at each detent position before the lever hits its stop.

Throttle Linkage, Adjust

Conventional Cab, 1970–71

1. With transmission in Neutral and engine at normal operating temperature, check idle speed which should be 500–550 rpm.
2. Stop the engine and adjust the length of the accelerator bellcrank to carburetor rod until the carburetor lever at idle position enables a ¼" pin at Point A. Fig. 17.
3. With the pin in place, adjust the length of the accelerator shaft to transmission control shaft rod assembly to obtain a pedal height of 4 11/16".
4. Push the transmission control shaft to transmission rod assembly downward until the transmission lever is against its stop inside the transmission. Adjust the L clevis on the transmission control shaft to transmission rod assembly until the upper end of the rod enters freely into its mounting hole in the transmission control to accelerator shaft assembly.
5. Shorten the length of the rod by turning the L clevis clockwise three turns. Install the clevis and tighten the locknut. Remove the ¼" pin.
6. Adjust the accelerator pedal detent stop to just contact the underside of the pedal when the carburetor throttle lever contacts the full throttle stop on the carburetor. Depress accelerator pedal until all movement in the transmission control

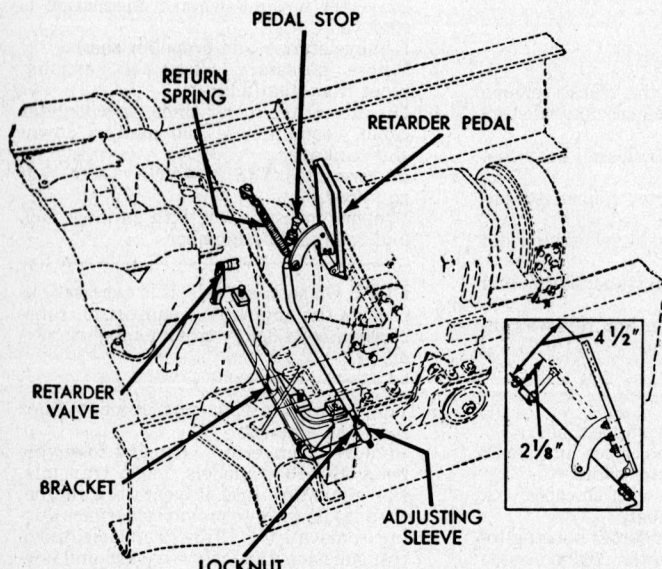

Fig. 19 Hydraulic retarder linkage. Conventional cab models (Typical)

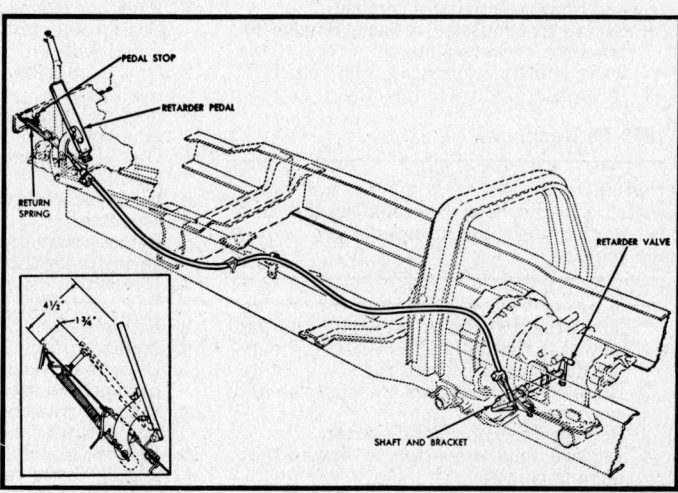

Fig. 20 Hydraulic retarder linkage. Tilt cab models

shaft to transmission rod assembly ceases. Adjust the pedal stop bolt to just contact the underside of the pedal.
7. Check linkage for free movement in all positions.

Tilt Cab, 1970–71

Adjustment procedures for these models are the same as those for conventional models except for pedal heights, Fig. 18.

Hydraulic Retarder Linkage, Adjust

Conventional Cab

1. Check hydraulic retarder pedal stop bolt height against dimension shown in Fig. 19. Adjust as required.
2. Disconnect hydraulic retarder control rod at transmission end. Pull retarder lever toward the rear of the transmission until retarder valve is heard and felt to bottom in the retarder casting.
3. Pull the control rod down until the pedal contacts its stop bolt.
4. Adjust control rod threaded sleeve until pin just fits in lever hole.
5. Lengthen control rod by rotating sleeve counterclockwise to provide 1/8" clearance between pedal and stop at full retarder application.
6. Assemble control rod to lever and tighten lock nut.
7. Check adjustment by depressing pedal against stop bolt. Just before pedal hits stop bolt, retarder valve should be felt to bottom in its body. Check for full release and readjust if necessary.

Tilt Cab

1. Adjust pedal retarder stop bolt height as shown in Fig. 20.
2. Disconnect retarder control cable at transmission.
3. Pull retarder lever toward rear of transmission until retarder valve is heard and felt to bottom in its body.
4. Pull retarder cable toward transmission until pedal is against its stop bolt.
5. With retarder valve bottomed (all the way to rear) and retarder pedal against its stop, adjust cable adjusting sleeve until sleeve pin just fits hole in lever.
6. Lengthen cable by turning sleeve counterclockwise to provide about 1/8" clearance between pedal and stop at full retarder application.
7. Assemble cable to lever.
8. Check adjustment by depressing pedal against its stop bolt. Retarder valve should be felt to bottom just before pedal hits the stop bolt.

Transmission, Replace

1. Loosen acorn nut on filter cover and drain transmission. When fluid stops flowing tighten filter cover nut.
2. On one-piece drive shaft models, disconnect shaft from pinion flange and from yoke at parking brake drum. *Do not remove the bolt that retains the flange on the transmission output flange.*
3. On two-piece drive shaft models, disconnect the coupling shaft from the yoke at the parking brake drum, then remove the center support bearing bracket. Move the forward end of the drive shaft out of the way.
4. Disconnect speedometer cable.
5. Remove fluid filler tube and breather hose.
6. Disconnect cable and TV rod from levers at transmission. Remove cable clamp bracket from housing.
7. Disconnect retarder linkage and remove cross shaft.
8. Disconnect parking brake linkage.
9. Remove fluid temperature warning light switch.
10. Disconnect oil cooler lines from fittings on retarder valve body, then remove forward fitting. Plug lines and valve body openings.
11. Remove flywheel housing dust shield.
12. Unfasten converter pump cover from flywheel (6 nuts).
13. Unfasten converter housing from frame cross member (2 bolts).
14. Remove nut from top of transmission rear support and cross member.
15. Raise rear of engine to take weight off cross member.
16. Support transmission with suitable jack.
17. Remove transmission rear support cross member.
18. Unfasten converter housing from flywheel housing.
19. Move converter and transmission away from engine until converter housing clears cross member, then lower the unit. If necessary, raise floor pan slightly to permit converter housing to clear cross member.
20. Reverse the foregoing procedure to install the transmission and check the adjustment of the linkage as outlined previously.

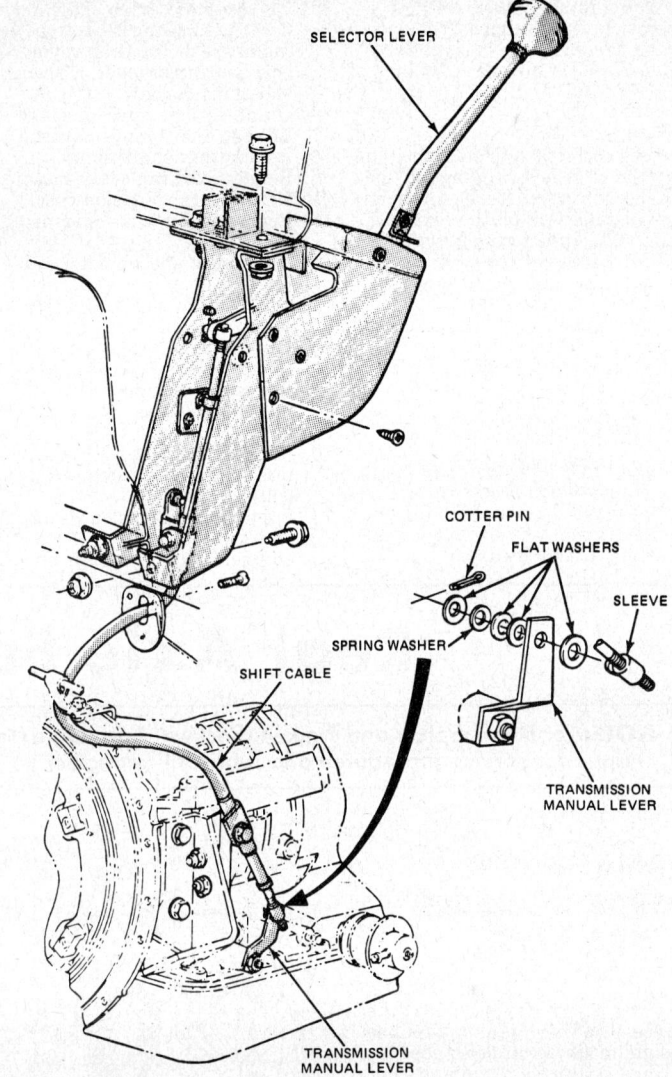

Fig. 21 AT-540, MT-640 & MT-650 range selector linkage (typical)

AT-540 & MT-640, 650

For a detailed description on the operation and servicing of this transmission see the *Allison AT-540 & MT-640, 650 Chapters* elsewhere in this manual. The following material deals with linkage adjustments and removal of the unit from the truck.

Range Selector Linkage, Adjust

AT-540

1. With engine stopped, position transmission selector lever in "R" position.
2. Disconnect shift cable sleeve at transmission manual lever, Fig. 21.
3. Shift transmission manual lever to "R" (all the way forward and upward).
4. With transmission manual lever in "R" position, adjust sleeve so that it freely enters into hole of manual lever.
5. Connect sleeve to manual lever with flat

Ford

washers, spring washer, and cotter pin.
6. Check operation in all ranges. It may be necessary to readjust sleeve slightly to obtain detent position in all drive ranges.

MT-640, 650

When linkage is correctly adjusted, the pin which engages the shift lever linkage at the transmission should move freely in each range. Proper installation of the external selector lever is imperative to the function of the transmission. Excessive torquing of the selector lever nut may damage the internal selector lever.

Refer to AT-540 procedure for selector linkage adjustment.

Transmission, Replace
1973–80

1. Remove right and left door sill scuff plates and transmission access cover.
2. On one piece drive shaft models, disconnect drive shaft from pinion flange and yoke at parking brake drum.
3. On two piece drive shaft models, disconnect the coupling shaft from yoke at parking brake drum, then remove center support bearing bracket. Place aside forward end of drive shaft.
4. On all models, disconnect parking brake linkage and remove parking brake drum from output shaft flange.
5. Remove parking brake handle and brackets from transmission case.
6. Remove filler tube and drain transmission.
7. Disconnect speedometer cable, oil cooler lines, shift cable, vacuum modulator line and remove modulator and shift cable clamp bracket from transmission.
8. Remove flywheel housing dust shield and converter to flywheel bolts.
9. Remove four upper and two lower converter housing to flywheel housing bolts.
10. Remove engine rear support lower insulators and loosen engine front support bolts.
11. Support transmission with a suitable jack and with a second jack, raise rear of engine, relieving weight from crossmember.
12. Remove engine rear support upper insulators and brackets from crossmember.
13. Remove the remaining converter housing to flywheel housing bolts and move transmission assembly rearward until converter housing contacts metal body. Then, tilt rear of transmission upward to clear crossmember and lower transmission from vehicle.
14. Reverse procedure to install.

1972

1. Remove right and left door scuff plates and place floor covering out of way.
2. Remove right and left front body bolt covers and front body bolts, then the two rear body bolt covers and body bolts.
3. Disconnect flex coupling from steering gear.
4. Raise body and place 4 × 4 inch wood blocks between frame and body, then lower body onto wooden blocks.
5. Follow steps 2 through 14 outlined under 1973–79 "Transmission, Replace" procedure.

Rear Axle Section

NOTE: For Eaton, Spicer and Timken (Rockwell) driving axles used on Ford Trucks, see the "name" chapter for service procedures and lubricant capacities

DANA/SPICER INTEGRAL HOUSING TYPE AXLE

This rear axle, Fig. 1, is a semi-floating type, while the axle shown in Fig. 1A is of the full-floating type. The drive pinion is of the over-hung design, mounted on pre-loaded taper roller bearings. Sealing of the pinion shaft is accomplished at the front end by a spring-loaded leather seal bearing on the companion flange, which is splined and secured to the pinion shaft by a nut.

Axle Shaft, Remove

Semi-Floating Axle
1. Raise vehicle and place stand jacks under rear axle housing.
2. Remove wheel and brake drum.
3. Remove four nuts from bearing retainer bolts on inside of axle flange.
4. Attach axle shaft puller, Fig. 2, and remove axle shaft and bearing assembly.
5. Install bolt and nut to hold brake backing plate on axle housing.

Full-Floating Axle
1. Raise vehicle and place stands under housing.
2. Remove axle shaft stud nuts and lockwashers.
3. Strike the center of the axle shaft flange with a hammer and drift to loosen the tapered dowels, remove the dowels.
4. Remove the axle shaft from the housing.

Bearing or Oil Seal, Replace

Semi-Floating Axle
1. With a chisel, nick soft ring next to bearing and remove ring. The ring need not be split, only nicked deep enough to allow removal.
2. Install a suitable press plate between axle flange and bearing and press bearing from shaft.
3. To replace oil seal, pry it out of housing with screwdriver.
4. Install new seal.
5. Install new bearing, pressing it on so it seats on the shaft against shoulder. Bearing retainer must be on axle shaft before bearing is installed.
6. Install new bearing retainer ring, being sure ring seats against bearing.

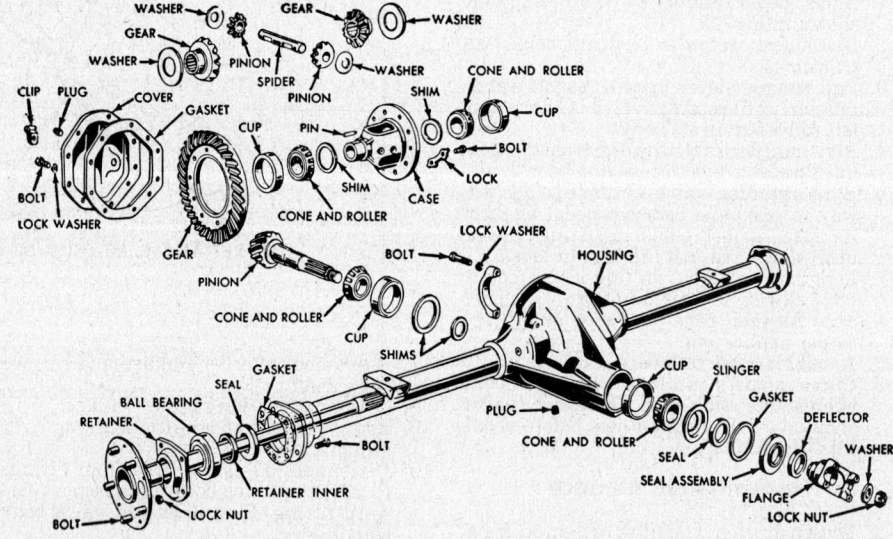

Fig. 1 Semi-floating integral housing hypoid rear axle

Full-Floating Axle
1. Remove the outer seal from the axle shaft flange studs.
2. Bend the lockwasher tab away from the locknut, and remove locknut, lockwasher and the adjusting nut.
3. With a wheel jack, raise the wheel to the point that all wheel weight is removed from the wheel bearings.
4. Remove the outer bearing cone and pull the wheel straight off the axle.
5. With a piece of hard wood which will just clear the outer bearing cup, drive the inner bearing cone and inner seal out of the wheel hub.

Ford

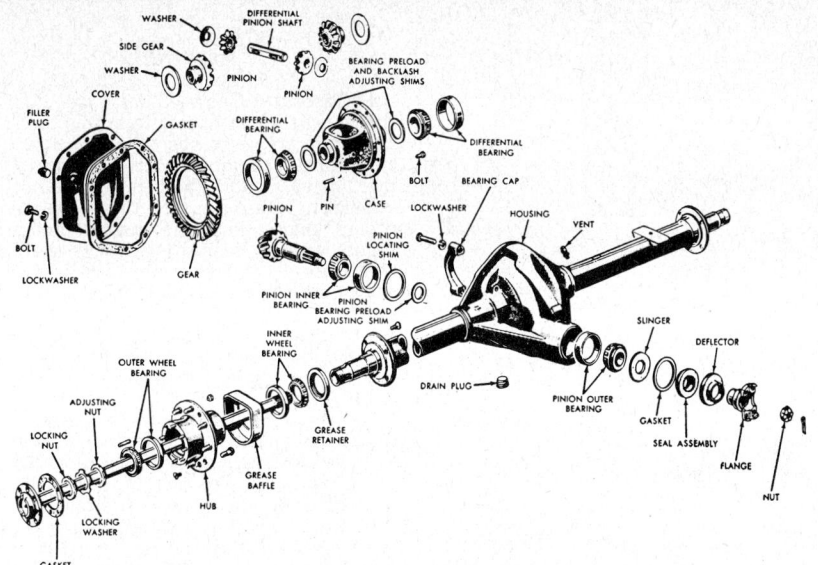

Fig. 1A Full-floating integral housing hypoid rear axle

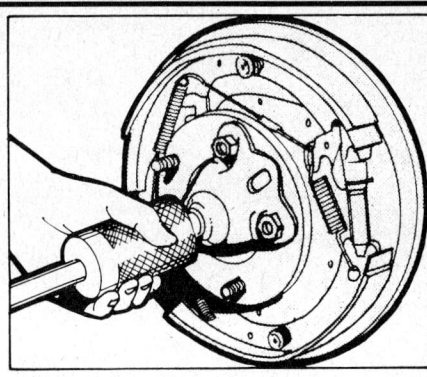

Fig. 2 Type of puller used to remove semi-floating axle shaft

6. Clean all the old grease or axle lubricant out of the wheel hub.

   NOTE: If axle lubricant is found in a wheel hub that has an outer seal, it means the seal or sealing surface has failed and should be replaced.

7. Inspect the bearing races and rollers for pitting, galling and erratic wear pattern. Inspect the rollers for end wear.
8. If bearing cups are to be replaced, drive them out with a drift.
9. Check for proper seating of new cups by trying to insert a .0015 inch feeler gauge between the cup and the hub.
10. A ring of wheel bearing grease as high as the cup should be placed in the hub on each side of both cups. These rings form a dam which prevents thinned grease from flowing out of the bearing.
11. Pack each bearing cone and roller assembly.
12. Place the inner bearing in the wheel hub and install a new hub inner seal.
13. Adjust the wheel jack so the wheel can be installed straight on the housing without damaging the inner seal.
14. Install the outer bearing and start the bearing adjuster nut.
15. On all models except 1975–80 E-250, 350 models:
    a. Torque adjuster nut to 50–80 ft. lbs., while rotating wheel.
    b. Back off adjuster nut to obtain a .001–.010 inch end play, the following number of turns: 1970–80, 3/8 turn. Install lockwasher.
    c. If adjusting nut is equipped with a locking dowel, make sure the lock washer hole aligns with the dowel.
    d. Torque lock nut to 110 ft. lbs. Recheck end play and correct if necessary.
    e. If lock washer has tabs, bend two tabs over adjusting nut and two tabs over lock nut.
16. On 1975–80 E-250, 350 models:
    a. Torque adjuster nut to 120–140 ft. lbs., while rotating wheel.
    b. Back off adjuster nut to obtain a .001–.010 inch end play, 1/8 to 1/4 of a turn.
    c. The locking wedge must cut a new groove in the nylon retainer within the 1/8 to 1/4 turn specified.

    NOTE: Replace the adjusting nut and locking wedge; if locking wedge cannot be installed into uncut nylon insert when adjusting nut is backed off.

Axle Shaft, Install

Semi-Floating Axle
1. Insert five new bolts and force heads down to flange on new axle.
2. Peen end of shoulder on bolts into countersink around bolt holes in flange.
3. Install new bearing as outlined above.
4. Remove temporary nut and bolt holding brake backing plate in place.
5. Install new retainer gasket.
6. Install axle shaft in housing. Outer race of bearing must seat against shoulder in axle housing.
7. Install nuts and washers on bearing retainer bolts and tighten securely.
8. Install brake drum and wheel.

Full-Floating Axle
1. Install the seal and gaskets on the axle shaft flange studs.
2. Install the axle shaft, tapered dowels, lockwashers and axle shaft flange nuts.
3. Adjust the brakes.

Rear Axle Assembly, Replace
1. Raise vehicle from floor and support with stand jacks under frame side rails.
2. Remove rear wheels.
3. Split rear universal joint.
4. Disconnect parking brake cable from equalizer rod and unfasten brake cable brackets from frame cross member.
5. Disconnect hydraulic brake line connection at rear axle housing.
6. Loosen and move shock absorbers out of the way.
7. While supporting axle housing with hydraulic jack, remove spring clips and lower axle assembly to the floor.
8. Reverse the foregoing procedure to install the rear axle assembly, being sure to bleed the brake system when the installation is completed.

FORD TYPE AXLE

Axle Shaft, Replace

Removal, Units with Ball Bearing
1. Remove wheel assembly.
2. Remove brake drum from flange.
3. Working through hole provided in axle shaft flange, remove nuts that secure wheel bearing retainer.
4. Pull axle shaft out of housing. If bearing is a tight fit in axle housing use a slide hammer-type puller. *Brake carrier plate must not be dislodged. Install one nut to hold the plate in place after axle shaft is removed.*

NOTE: On 1978–80 models, remove brake backing plate and secure to frame rail.

5. If the axle shaft bearing is to be replaced, loosen the inner retainer by nicking it deeply with a chisel in several places. The bearing will then slide off easily.
6. Press bearing from axle shaft.
7. Inspect machined surface of axle shaft and housing for rough spots that would affect sealing action of the oil seal. Carefully remove any burrs or rough spots.
8. Press new bearing on shaft until it seats firmly against shoulder on shaft.
9. Press inner bearing retainer on shaft until it seats firmly against bearing.
10. If oil seal is to be replaced, use a hook-type tool to pull it out of housing. Wipe a small amount of oil resistant sealer on outer edge of seal before it is installed.

Removal, Units with Roller Bearing
1. Remove wheel assembly.
2. Remove brake drum from flange.
3. Working through hole provided in axle flange, remove nuts securing wheel bearing retainer.
4. Pull axle shaft carefully from housing to prevent damage to outer seal rubber. Use a slide hammer type puller to remove tapered bearing cup from housing. Remove brake backing plate and secure to

1121

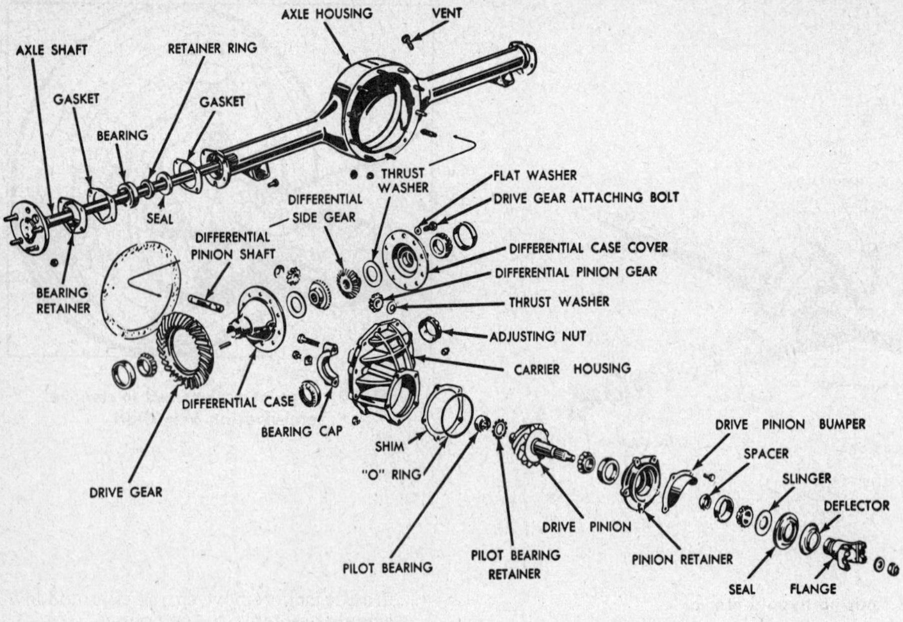

FORD

Fig. 3 Ford removable carrier rear axle

frame rail.
5. If the axle shaft bearing or seal is to be replaced, split the inner bearing retainer.
6. Press bearing from axle shaft.
7. Inspect machined surface of axle shaft and housing for rough spots that would affect sealing action of the oil seal. Carefully remove any burrs or rough spots.
8. Install outer retainer plate on axle shaft. Press lubricated seal and bearing onto shaft until firmly seated.

NOTE: Oil seal for rear drum brake equipped vehicles is different than that used on vehicles with rear disc brakes. Seals used with drum brakes have a gray metal colored outer rim, while seals used with disc brakes have a black or orange color.

9. Press new bearing retainer onto shaft until seated.

Installation
1. On 1978-80 models, place a new gasket on each side of brake carrier plate and slide axle shaft into housing. On models with roller bearing, ensure that outer seal is not fully mounted on the bearing.
2. Start the splines into the differential side gear and push the shaft in until bearing bottoms in housing.
3. Torque bearing retainer nuts 30-40 ft. lbs. on light duty axles, 50-75 ft. lbs. on heavy duty models.

FORD REMOVABLE CARRIER TYPE REAR AXLE

This rear axle, Fig. 3, is a banjo-housing hypoid in which the drive pinion is mounted $2\frac{1}{4}''$ below the centerline of the drive gear. The drive pinion is straddle-mounted in that two opposed tapered roller bearings support the pinion shaft at the front of the pinion gear and a straight roller bearing supports the pinion shaft at the rear of the pinion gear.

The pinion shaft and gear are assembled in the pinion retainer which is bolted to the carrier housing. Two carrier and differential cases are used to accommodate two bearing sizes. The right and left axle shafts are not interchangeable since the left shaft is shorter than the right.

Disassembly
1. Mark one differential bearing cap and bearing support to ensure proper assembly. Remove adjusting nut locks, bearing caps and adjusting nuts. Lift differential out of carrier.
2. Remove drive gear from differential case.
3. Drive out differential pinion shaft retainer and separate the differential pinion shaft and remove gears and thrust washers.
4. Remove drive pinion retainer from carrier. Remove O-ring from retainer.
5. Remove pinion locating shim. Measure shim thickness with micrometer.
6. If the drive pinion pilot bearing is to be replaced, drive the pilot end and bearing retainer out at the same time. When installing, drive the bearing in until it bottoms. Install a new retainer with the concave side up.
7. Mount the drive pinion retainer assembly in a holding fixture and remove pinion shaft nut and flat washer. Then remove universal joint flange, oil seal and slinger.
8. Remove pinion retainer from fixture and place a protective sleeve or hose on the pinion pilot bearing surface. Then press the pinion shaft out of front bearing cone and remove spacer.
9. Remove pinion rear bearing cone.
10. Do not remove pinion bearing cups from retainer unless they are worn or damaged. The flange and pilot are machined by locating on these cups after they are installed in the bores. If new cups are to be installed, make sure they are seated in the retainer by trying to insert a .0015" feeler gauge between cup and bottom of bore.

Assembly

Differential Case—Place a side gear and thrust washer in the differential case bore. *Lubricate all parts liberally with axle lubricant during assembly.* With a soft-faced hammer, drive pinion shaft into case only far enough to retain a pinion thrust washer and pinion gear. Place the second pinion and thrust washer in position. Drive the pinion shaft into place. Be careful to line up pinion shaft retainer holes. Place second side gear and thrust washer in position and install differential case cover. Install retainer. A pinion or axle shaft spline can be inserted in side gear spline to check for free rotation of differential gears.

Insert two $7/16'' \times 2''$ bolts through differential flange and thread them 3 or 4 turns into the drive gear as a guide in aligning the drive gear bolt holes. Press or tap the drive gear into position. Install and tighten the drive gear bolts evenly and alternately across the gear to 60-65 lb. ft. torque.

If the differential bearings have been removed, use a suitable press to install them.

Pinion and Retainer—Install the pinion rear bearing cone on the pinion shaft and install a new spacer on the shaft. Place the bearing retainer on the pinion shaft, then install the front bearing cone. *As the bearing is pressed into position, rock the pinion retainer. Do not press the bearing on the shaft, until all play is removed between retainer and bearings as the spacer may be compressed too much.*

Lubricate both bearings with axle lubricant. Place oil slinger in position. Coat the outside edge of a new oil seal with an oil-resistant sealer and press it into the bearing retainer. New seals need not be soaked before installation. Install the universal joint flange. Place the flat washer over the pinion shaft and start the pinion shaft nut.

Hold the flange and tighten the pinion shaft nut until a torque required to turn the pinion is 8-12 *inch* lbs. with used bearings or 17-27 *inch* lbs. with new bearings. As the pinion shaft nut is tightened, rotate the pinion shaft frequently to allow the bearing to seat.

Shim Selection—Manufacturing tolerances in the pinion bore dimensions are in the best operating position of the gears make an adjustment shim necessary. This shim is placed between the pinion retainer and the carrier, Fig. 3. An increase in the thickness of the shim moves the pinion *away* from the drive gear. Manufacturing objectives are to make axles requiring a .0015" shim and if a new assembly is being built, a .0015" shim should be used for a tentative buildup. Shims are available in .010" to .021" thicknesses in steps of .001".

Pinions and drive gears are marked, when matched, with the same number. Following the number on the pinion is a minus (−) or plus (+) followed by a number. If the pinion is marked "−1" it indicates that a shim .001" thinner than a standard shim for this carrier is required. A minus number means the pinion should be moved closer to the drive gear and a thinner shim is required. A plus number means the pinion should be moved farther from the drive gear and a thicker shim is required. A pinion marked zero (0) is a standard pinion.

To select a shim, measure the original shim with a micrometer. Note the dimensional mark on the original pinion. Compare the mark on the original pinion with the mark on the new pinion to determine how the original shim should be modified.

For example, if the original shim is .015"

Ford

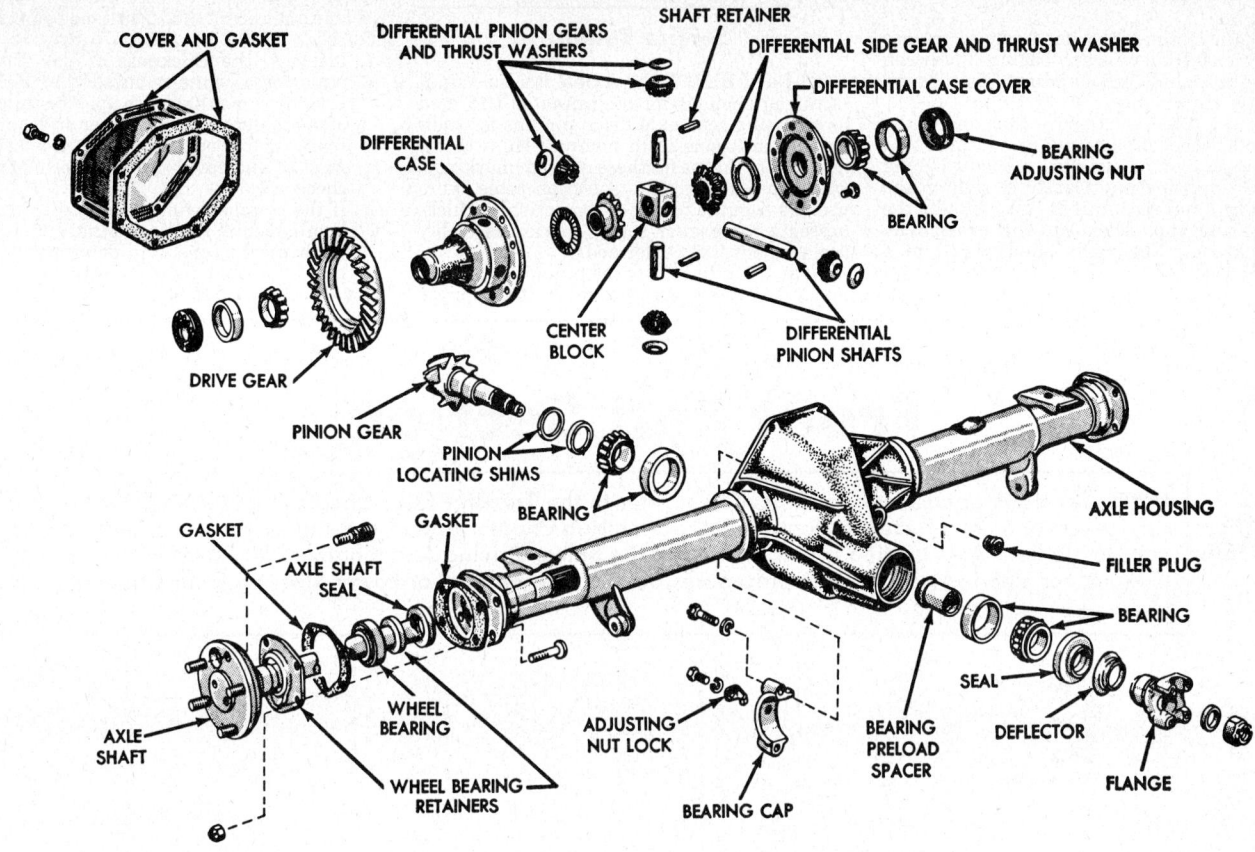

Fig. 4 Ford integral carrier rear axle disassembled

and the original pinion is marked "−1", the new pinion requires a +1 shim. Therefore, the new pinion requires a .002" thicker shim, and a .017" shim should be used. If the new pinion is marked the same as the old pinion, no shim change is required.

Backlash Adjustment—The threaded nut type of differential bearing adjustment is used.

FORD INTEGRAL CARRIER TYPE

All operations on the differential case assembly and drive pinion assembly may be performed with the axle housing in the truck, Fig. 4.

Differential & Pinion, Remove

1. Remove axle shafts as outlined for Spicer Integral Type.
2. Remove axle housing cover.
3. Remove drive shaft.
4. Mark one differential bearing cap and case so marks can be notched on reassembly.
5. Remove differential bearing adjusting lock nuts, cap bolts and bearing caps.
6. Lift out differential.
7. Remove drive pinion flange nut and flange. With soft faced hammer, drive pinion out of front bearing cone and remove it through rear of carrier casting.
8. Drive against front pinion bearing cone and drive flange seal and bearing cone out of front carrier casting.
9. If they are to be replaced, drive pinion bearing cups of casting with a drift. *When installed, make sure cups are properly seated in their bores. If a .0015" feeler gauge can be inserted between cup and bottom of its bore at any point around cup, cup is not properly seated.*
10. Remove pinion rear bearing cone. *Measure shim (under bearing cone) with a micrometer and record its thickness. If a new gear set is to be installed, a new shim will have to be selected. The original shim thickness is one of the factors involved in selecting the new shim thickness.*
11. Remove differential components from case.

Drive Pinion & Ring Gear Adjustment

Referring to Fig. 4, assemble drive pinion and related parts in housing. In replacing pinion, the original factory shim is used to select the proper replacement shim.

1. Measure thickness of original shim.
2. Note shim adjustment number on both the old pinion and the new one.
3. Refer to Fig. 5 to determine the correct amount of shim thickness change.
4. If the original shim pack was lost or a new carrier casting is being installed, substitute a nominal .018" shim for the original and follow the foregoing procedure for a trial build up. If further shim change is necessary it will be indicated in a tooth pattern check.

Pinion Bearing Preload

1. Insert flange into seal and hold it firmly against front bearing cone. Insert pinion shaft into flange.
2. Place flat washer on pinion shaft; start and tighten flange nut. While there is still end play in pinion shaft, flange and cone will be felt to bottom as nut is tightened.
3. From this point a much greater torque must be applied to turn the nut since the spacer must be collapsed. Also, from this point, the nut must be tightened very slowly and pinion shaft end play checked so preload does not exceed limits. *If preload exceeds limits, a new collapsible spacer must be installed.*
4. As soon as there is preload on the bearings, turn pinion shaft in both directions several times to seat bearing rollers.
5. Adjust preload on used bearings to 10–16 inch lbs. and new bearings to 17–27 inch lbs. Preload is measured with torque wrench on flange nut as nut is tightened.

Backlash and Differential Bearing Preload

1. Tighten differential bearing cap bolts to 40–50 ft. lbs. Then loosen cap bolts and retighten only to 5 ft. lbs.
2. Loosen right hand adjusting nut until it is away from cup. Tighten left hand nut until all ring gear backlash is eliminated.
3. Loosen left hand nut 1 to 1½ notches. Then tighten right hand nut 2 notches beyond the point where it contacts bearing cup. Rotate ring gear several revolutions in each direction while bearings are loaded to seat the bearings in their

1123

FORD

cups.
4. Again loosen right hand nut to release preload. If there is any backlash between gears, tighten left hand nut just enough to remove lash.
5. At this time, make sure that one of the slots in the left hand nut is so located that the lock can be installed without turning the adjusting nut. Carefully tighten the right hand nut until it just contacts the bearing cup. Then set the preload by tightening the right hand nut 2 to 3 notches.

Service Bulletin

All Ford Built Rear Axles: Recent manufacturing changes have eliminated the need for marking rear axle drive pinions for individual variations from nominal shim thicknesses. In the past, these pinion markings, with the aid of a shim selection table, were used as a guide to select correct shim thicknesses when a gear set or carrier assembly replacement was performed.

With the elimination of pinion markings, use of the shim selection table is no longer possible and the methods outlined below must be used.
1. Measure the thickness of the original pinion depth shim removed from the axle. Use the same thickness upon installation of the replacement carrier or drive pinion. If any further shim change is necessary, it will be indicated in the tooth pattern check.
2. If the original shim is lost, substitute a nominal shim for the original and use the tooth pattern check to determine if further shim changes are required.

Front End Section

NOTE: For transfer case service procedures, refer to the Transfer Case Chapter. For locking hub service procedures, refer to the Front Wheel Locking Hub Chapter. For differential assembly service, refer to the Rear Axle Section in this chapter or the Spicer Driving Axle Chapter elsewhere in this manual. For steering gear service procedures, refer to the Manual or Power Steering Gear Chapter.

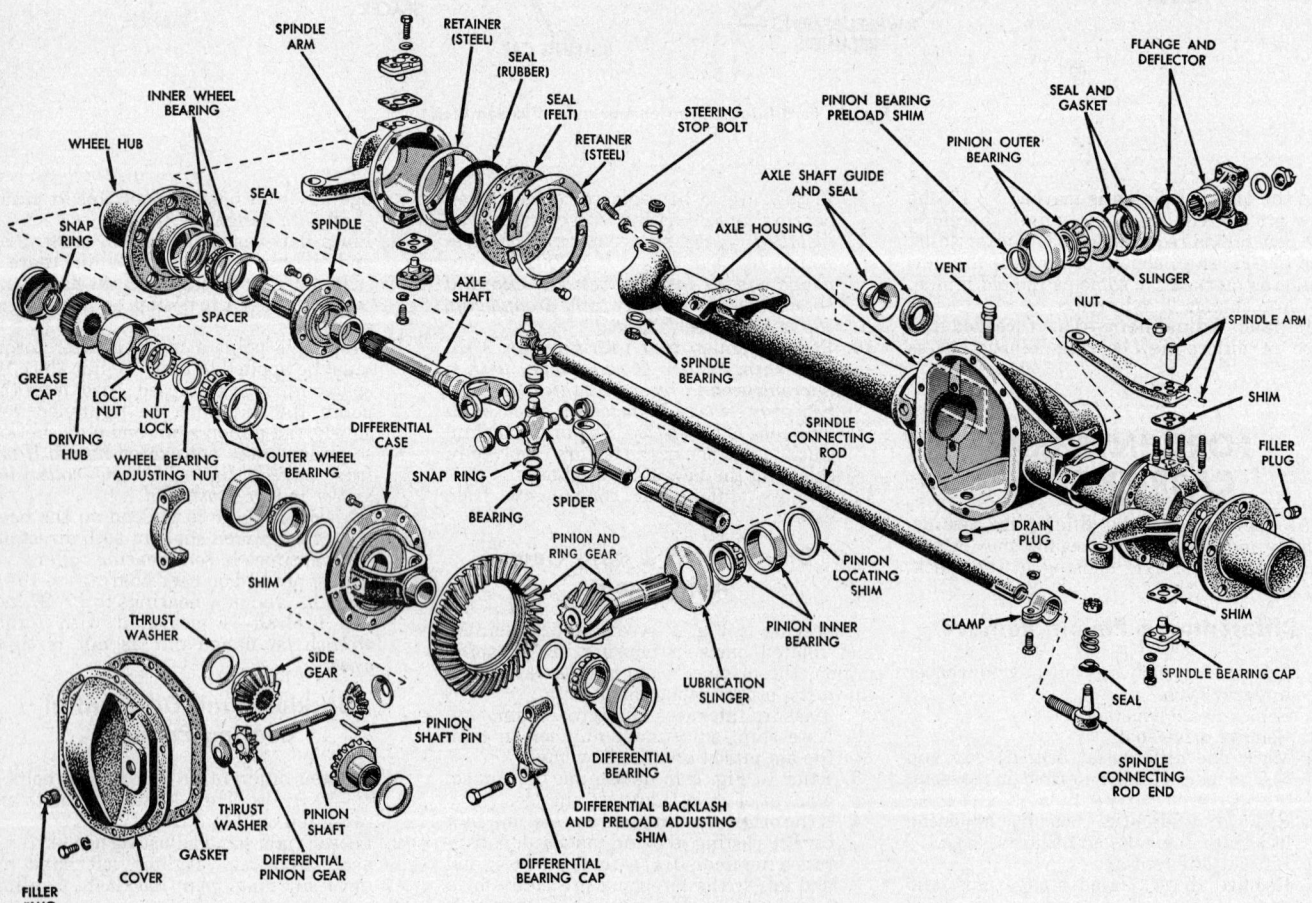

Fig. 1 Four wheel drive front axle assembly; closed spindle type (Typical)

Ford

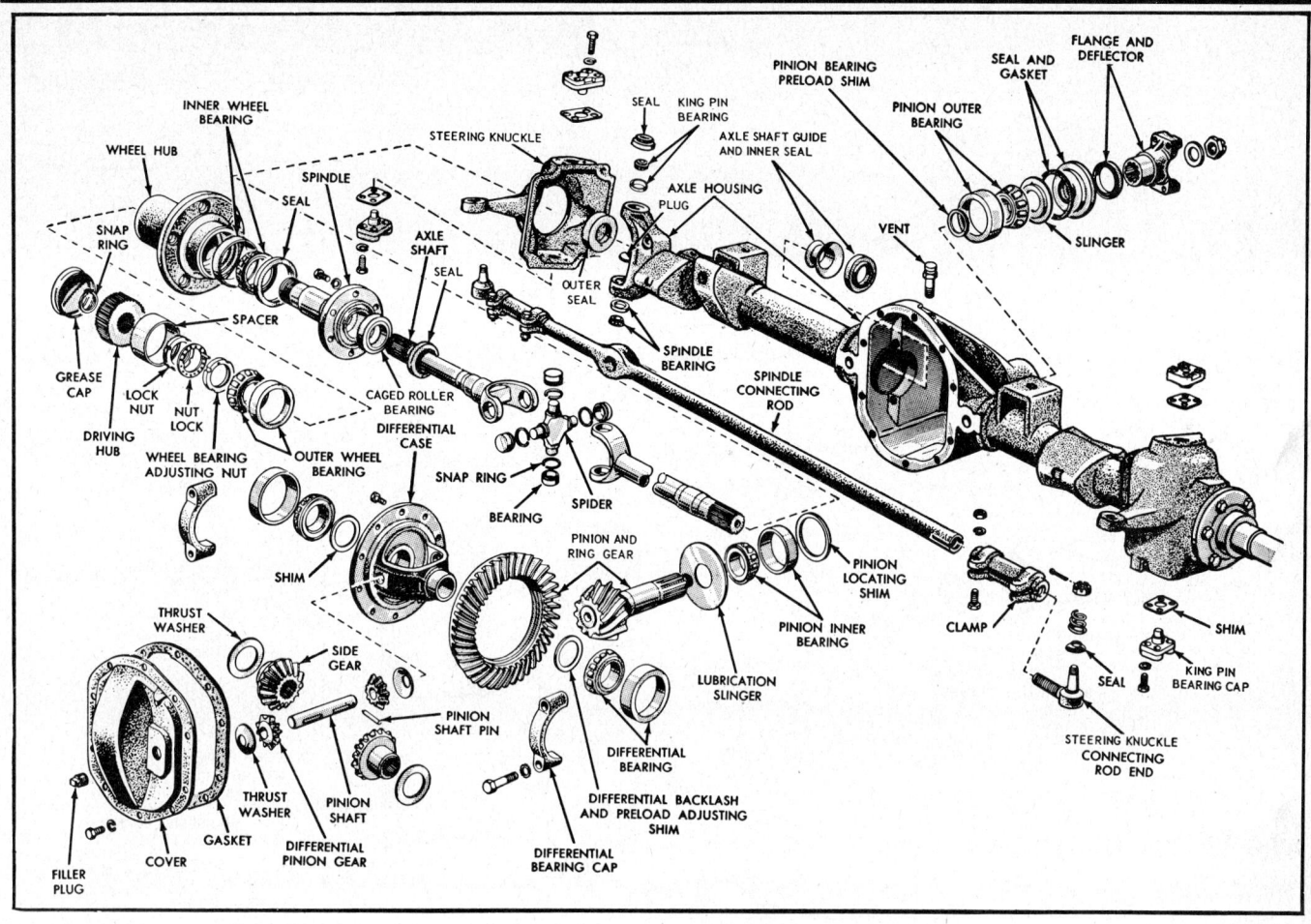

Fig. 2 Four wheel drive front axle assembly; open spindle type

1970-79 4 × 4 SERVICE

Front Axle Shaft

Closed Spindle Type
1. Raise truck on a hoist and then lower it so that the front axle is supported on a stand.
2. Referring to Fig. 1, remove hub dust cap and snap ring and slide splined driving hub from between outer axle shaft and wheel hub and drum.
3. After removing lock nut, washer and wheel bearing retainer nut from steering spindle, remove wheel, hub and drum as an assembly. The wheel outer bearing will be forced off the spindle at the same time.
4. Remove wheel inner bearing.
5. Place a drain pan under steering knuckle, and remove brake backing plate and spindle.
6. Pull outer axle shaft, universal joint and inner axle shaft from housing as an assembly.
7. Reverse procedure to install, then remove the steering knuckle plug and fill the knuckle with 1/2 pint of the proper lubricant.

Spindle Bearing

Removal
1. Referring to Fig. 1, remove the inner and outer axle shafts and U-joint from each end of the axle housing.
2. Disconnect upper spindle arm from steering drag link (left side only).
3. Disconnect spindle connecting rod (tie rod) from front spindle arm.
4. Remove oil seal retaining bolts from rear flange of steering knuckle and remove the two-piece retainer.
5. Remove upper spindle arm (left side) and integral bearing cap and shaft from steering knuckle. On the right side there is only a bearing cap and shaft assembly. Remove bearing preload shims.
6. Remove lower spindle bearing cap and shaft from steering knuckle.
7. Remove steering knuckle from axle housing yoke.
8. After removing upper and lower spindle bearings from the axle housing yoke, remove upper and lower bearing cups from yoke.
9. Remove felt, rubber and metal oil seal rings from axle housing.

Installation
Reverse the removal procedure to install the bearings. However, to mount the steering knuckle on the axle housing yoke, first fit the lower end of the knuckle over the bottom of the yoke so that the lower bearing will fit into the cup; then bring the entire knuckle into position on the yoke.

Place the bearing preload shims over the studs on the upper side of the knuckle and install the upper bearing cap and shaft. The shaft is inserted in the bearing and the cap is bolted to the upper side of the knuckle.

To check the bearing preload, place a torque wrench on one of the bearing cap nuts and pivot the knuckle on its bearings. As the knuckle is turned, a preload reading of 5 to 10 inch-pounds should register on the torque wrench. After removing or adding shims to establish correct preload, torque bearing cap nuts to 25-40 ft. lbs.

Front Axle, Open Spindle Type

Front Axle Shaft & Spindle
1. To remove, raise vehicle on a hoist.
2. Drain lubricant from axle. *This must be done to prevent lubricant flooding the outer axle housing when axle shaft is removed.*
3. Remove hub grease cap and driving hub retaining snap ring and slide splined hub from between axle shaft and wheel hub. Remove hub spacer.
4. Remove wheel bearing adjusting nut.
5. Remove wheel, hub and drum.
6. Remove inner bearing cone.
7. Remove brake carrier plate and secure it to one side to avoid damaging brake hose. Remove spindle.
8. Pull axle shaft from housing, working universal joint through bore of spindle arm. *At this point the following parts can be replaced without further disassembly of the axle: axle shaft, universal joint, axle housing outer seal, spindle bore seal, and*

1125

Ford

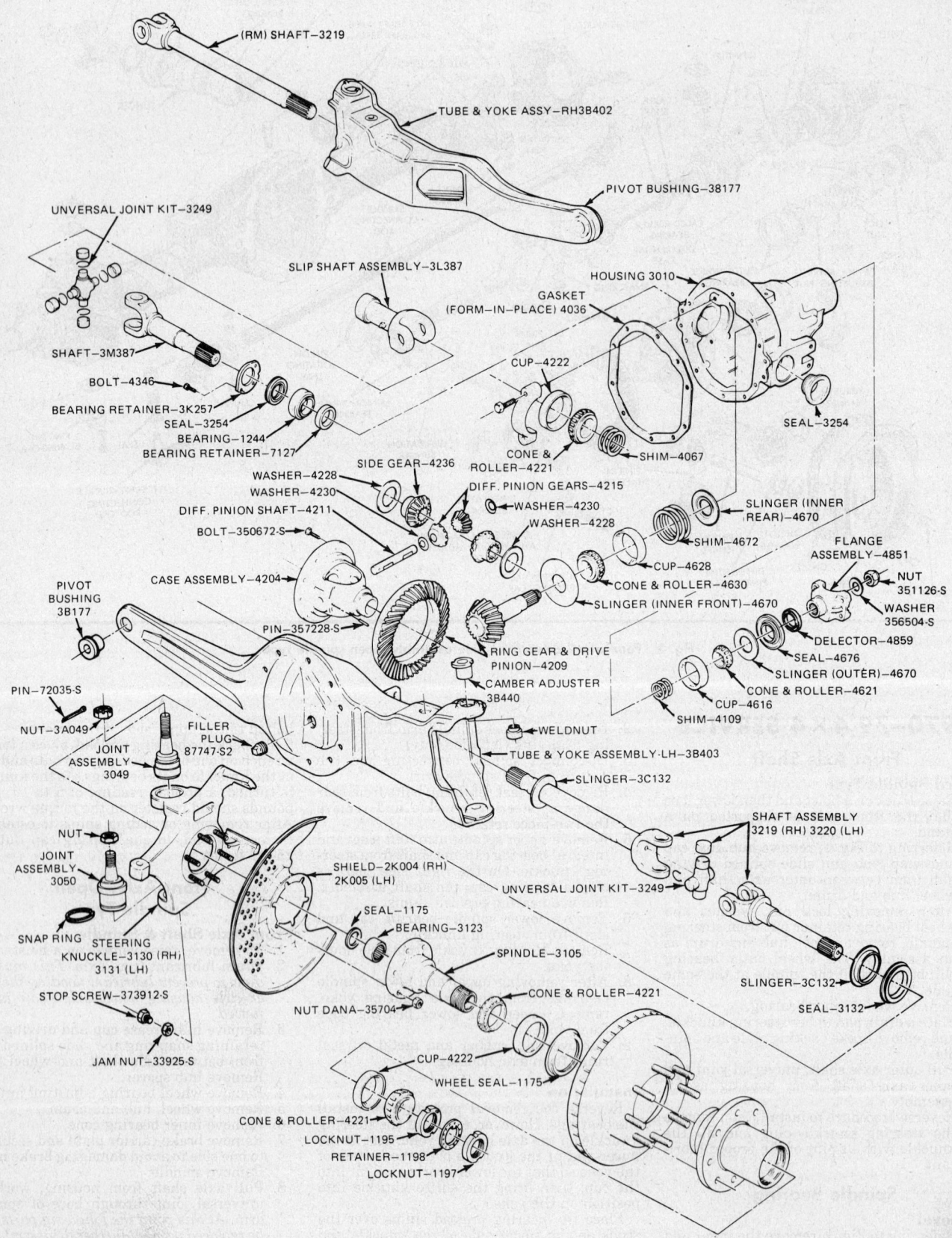

Fig. 3 Independent front driving axle. 1980 Bronco & F-150 4 Wheel Drive

Ford

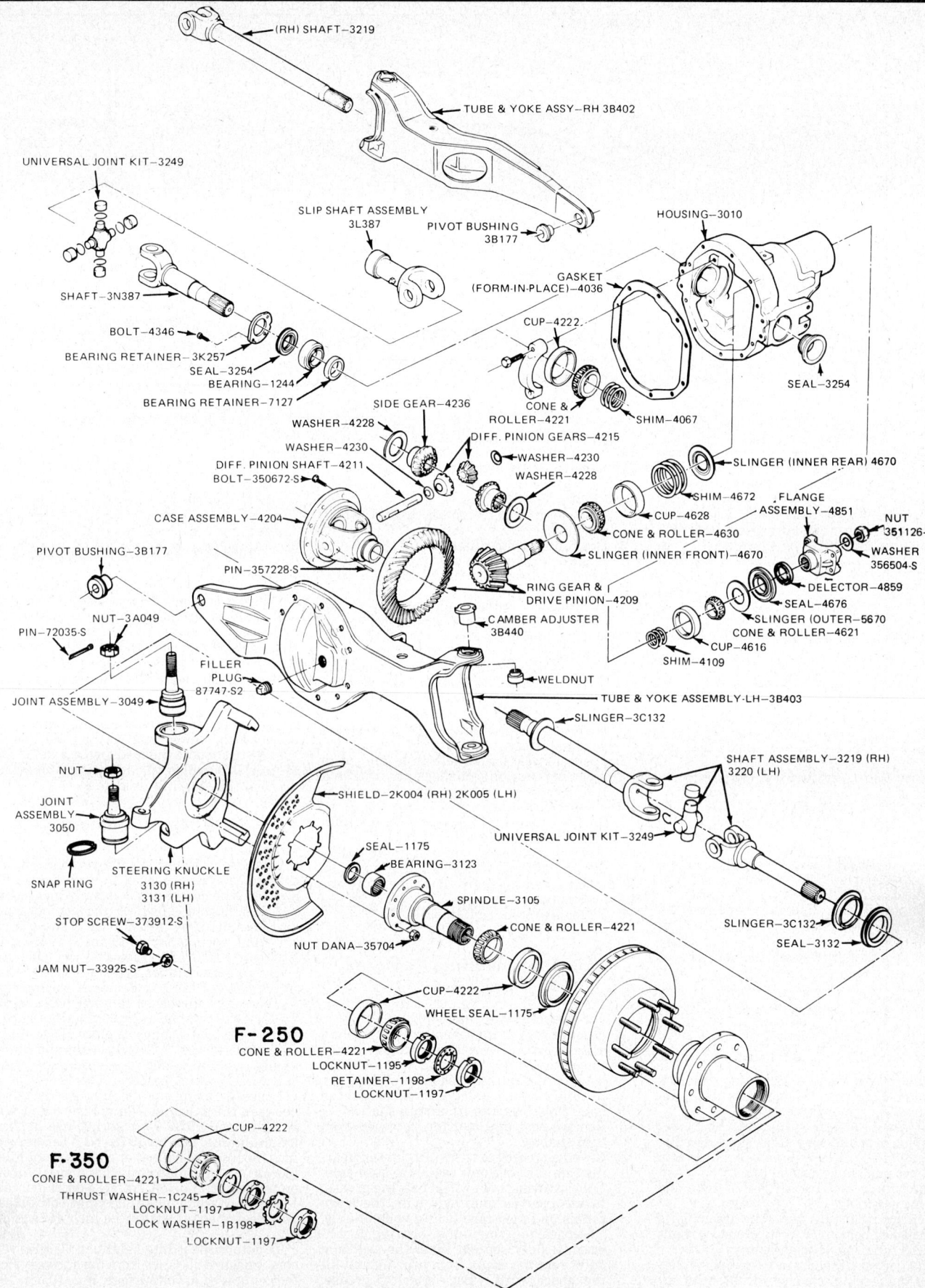

Fig. 4 Independent front driving axle. 1980 F-250, 350 4 Wheel Drive

Ford

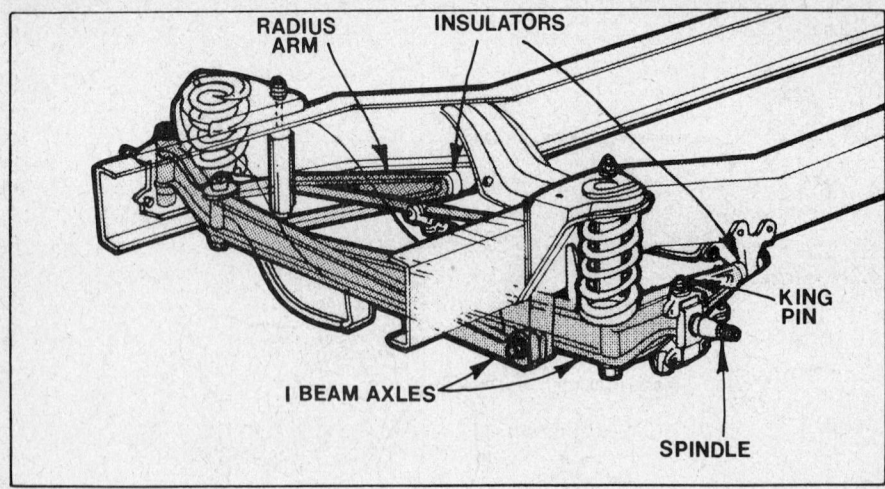

Fig. 6 Twin I-Beam front axle

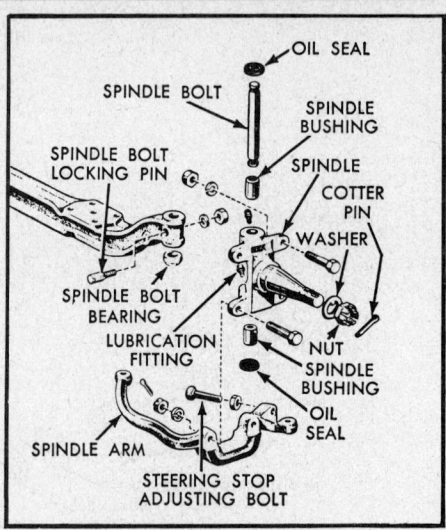

Fig. 7 Spindle used with twin I Beam front axle. Typical

spindle bore roller bearing.
9. To remove spindle arm (housing), disconnect steering connecting rod end from spindle arm and remove bearing caps and spindle arm on models without ball joints. On models with ball joints, loosen the nuts from upper and lower joints and separate the knuckle from the yoke.

NOTE: Discard the lower joint nut, replace with a new one.

10. Install knuckle into a vise and press out ball joints with suitable tool.
11. Reverse procedure to install.

1980 BRONCO F150, 250, 350 (4 × 4) SERVICE

Front Axle Assembly, Replace

1980 Bronco & F150, Fig. 3
1. Raise and support vehicle. Remove front wheels.
2. Drain fluid from differential.
3. Remove brake caliper, hub assembly, brake rotor, spindle, splash shield and axle shaft.
4. Position a jack under tube and yoke assembly and remove upper coil spring retainers.
5. Lower jack and remove coil spring, cushion and lower spring seat.

NOTE: Place caliper on frame or support caliper to prevent damage to brake hose.

6. Remove shock absorber, then steering knuckle. Refer to "Steering Knuckle, Replace" for removal procedure.
7. Remove stud and spring seat at upper radius arm and tube and yoke assembly. Remove bolt attaching lower radius arm to tube and yoke assembly.
8. Disconnect vent tube from left tube and yoke assembly.
9. Remove right tube and yoke assembly to crossmember pivot bolt. Remove right hand tube and yoke assembly.
10. Position jack and drain pan under differential housing. Remove differential attaching bolts from housing. Remove left tube and yoke assembly to crossmember pivot bolt. Remove left tube and yoke assembly.
11. Reverse procedure to install.

1980 F-250 & F-350, Fig. 4
1. Raise and support vehicle. Remove front wheels.
2. Drain fluid from differential.
3. Remove brake calipers, hubs, brake rotors, spindles, splash shields and axle shafts.
4. Position jack under right tube and yoke assembly. Disconnect shock absorber and leaf spring plate from tube and yoke assembly.
5. Remove steering knuckle from tube and yoke assembly. Refer to "Steering Knuckle, Replace" for removal procedure.
6. Disconnect vent tube from left tube and yoke assembly. Remove right tube and yoke assembly.
7. Position jack under left tube and yoke assembly. Disconnect shock absorber and leaf spring plate from tube and yoke assembly.
8. Remove steering knuckle assembly from left tube and yoke assembly.
9. Position jack and drain pan under differential housing. Remove differential attaching bolts. Remove left tube and yoke assembly.
10. Reverse procedure to install.

Axle Shaft Bearing, Replace, Figs. 3 & 4

1. Remove axle shaft assembly.
2. Remove axle shaft bearing retainer plate bolts, then pull stub shaft from housing.
3. Place stub shaft in vise and drill a 1/4 inch hole 3/4 through the bearing retainer.
4. Cut the retainer using a chisel across the hole. Press bearing from stub shaft.
5. Remove seal and bearing retainer from stub shaft.
6. Reverse procedure to install. Install bearing retainer and new seal onto stub axle. Lubricate seal with wheel bearing grease. Install bearing onto axle with the large radius on inner race facing yoke of axle. Press bearing, then install bearing retainer until fully seated. Push the seal and outer retainer away from bearing and fill the space with wheel bearing grease. Wrap a piece of tape around the space, then pull the retainer and seal against the bearing. This will force the grease into the bearing. Repeat until the grease is visible on the small end of rollers.

TWIN I-BEAM AXLE

As illustrated in Fig. 6 there are two I-beam axles, one for each front wheel. One end of each axle is attached to the spindle and a radius arm and the other end is attached to a frame bracket on the opposite side of the vehicle.

Each spindle is held in place on the axle by a spindle bolt which pivots in bushings pressed in the upper and lower ends of the spindle, Fig. 7. A thrust bearing is installed between the lower end of the axle and the spindle to support the load on the axle. A spindle arm is installed on each spindle for attachment to the steering linkage.

Wheel Alignment

1970-80
On these vehicles, the I-beams are not to be twisted or bent in order to correct caster or camber. The caster angle is built in, and cannot be adjusted, however the camber angle can be adjusted by the addition of shims under the front springs, or the substitution of the front springs. To increase camber, add shims (1/4 inch, part number 385795-S) with a maximum of two shims under each spring. Each 1/4 inch shim increases camber by 1/2 degree. To decrease camber, replace the front springs with lower load springs in place of the vehicle equipped springs. To check caster and camber angles, use the following procedure.

Before checking caster or camber, level the vehicle by placing equal height wooden blocks between the axle and frame, Figs. 8 and 9. On E series and 1970-77 F series, use 3 1/2 inch height blocks, and on 1978-80 F series, use 5 inch blocks. Use ballast or clamps to maintain blocks in place. Measure from a similar point on the right and left frame side rail to axle I-beam surface to make sure that both sides of vehicle are equal within 1/8 inch of each other.

To determine riding height on F series vehicles, measure distance from top surface of axle to spring seat lower surface, Fig. 10. On 1970 E series vehicles, measure distance from top surface of axle to bottom of crossmember

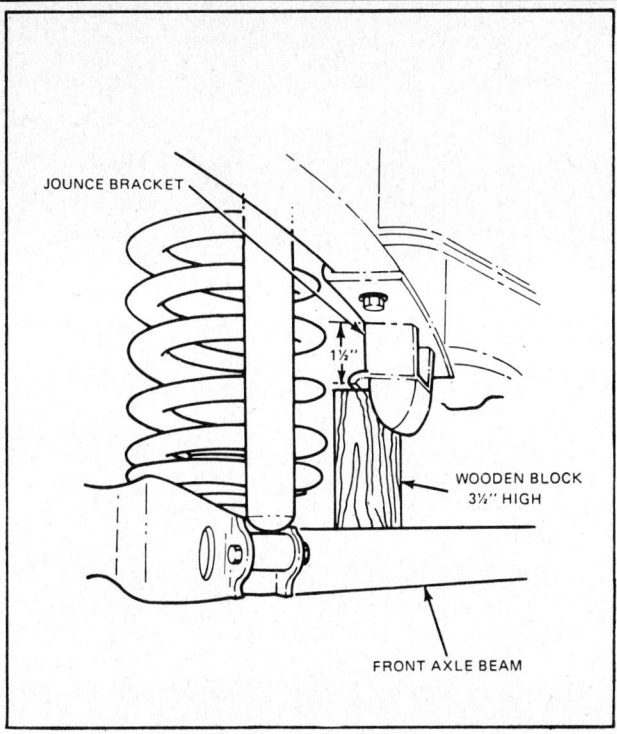

Fig. 8 Installation of wooden blocks to level vehicle. E series

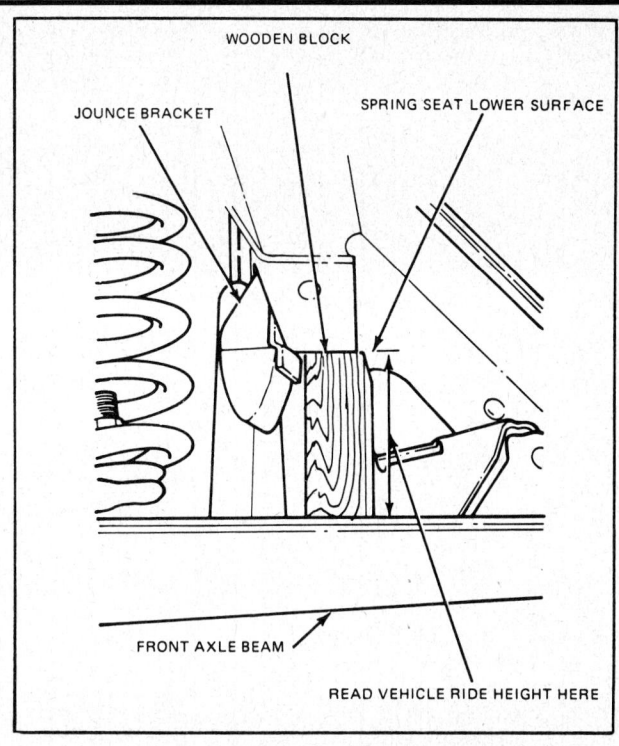

Fig. 9 Installation of wooden blocks to level vehicle. F series

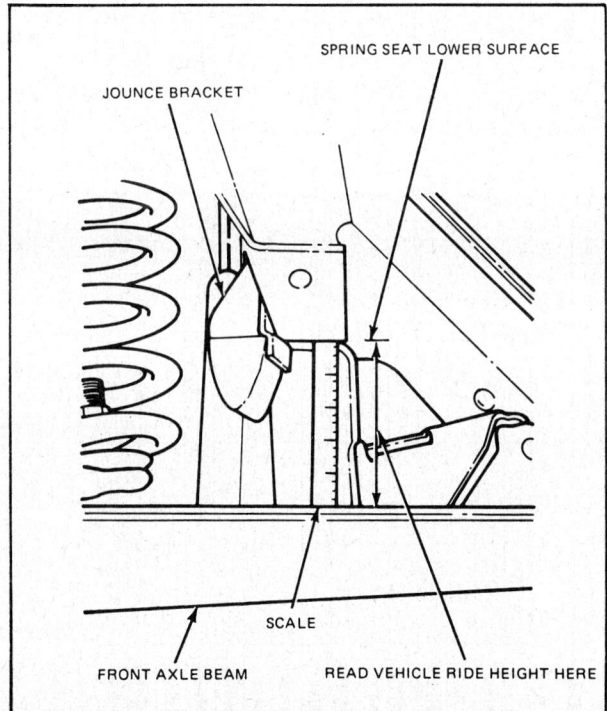

Fig. 10 Mesuring riding height. F series

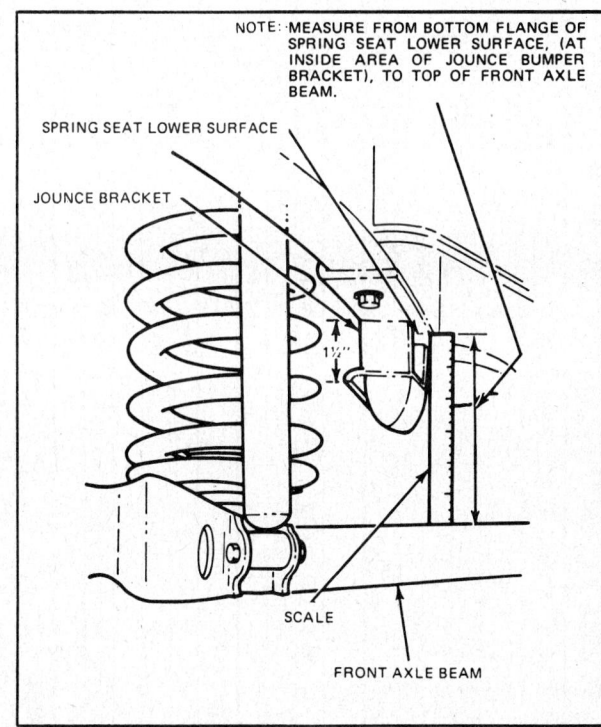

Fig. 12 Measuring riding height. 1977–79 E series

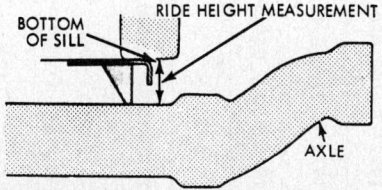

Fig. 11 Measuring riding height. 1971–76 E series

WHEEL ALIGNMENT SPECIFICATIONS CHART

1970

Riding Height, Inches		1 1/2	1 3/4	2	2 1/4	2 1/2	2 3/4	3	3 1/4	3 1/2	3 3/4	4	4 1/4	4 1/2	5	5 1/2	Toe In
E100, 200, 300	Caster	—	—	+5 1/8°	—	+4 1/2°	—	+3 1/4°	—	+1 7/8°	—	+°	—	—	—	—	1/8
	Camber	—	−1/16°	—	+1/2°	—	+1 1/2°	—	+2 1/4°	—	+3 1/4°	—	+4 3/8°	+2 1/4°	+3 1/4°	+4 3/8°	
F100, 250	Caster	—	—	—	—	—	—	+5 1/8°	—	+4 1/2°	—	+3 1/4°	—	+1 7/8°	+1°	—	1/8
	Camber	—	—	—	—	—	—	−1/16°	+2 1/4°	+1/2°	+3 1/4°	+1 1/2°	+4 3/8°	+2 1/4°	+3 1/4°	+4 3/8°	
F350	Caster	—	—	—	—	—	—	—	—	+5 1/8°	—	+4 1/2°	—	+3 1/4°	+1 7/8°	+1°	1/8
	Camber	—	—	—	—	—	+1 1/2°	−1/16°	+2 1/4°	+1/2°	+3 1/4°	+1 1/2°	+4 3/8°	+2 1/4°	+3 1/4°	+4 3/8°	

1971–73

Riding Height, Inches		3.87	4.12	4.37	4.62	4.87	5.12	5.37	5.62	5.87	6.12	6.37	6.62	Toe In
E300	Caster	—	—	+7 1/4°	—	+6 1/2°	—	+5 1/4°	—	+3 7/8°	—	+3°	—	3/32
	Camber	—	+7/8°	—	+5-8°	—	+1 1/2°	—	+2 3/8°	—	+3 1/8°	—	4°	

1971–74 F100, 250, 350

Riding Height, Inches		3	3.50	4	4.50	5	5.50	Toe In
F100, 250①	Caster	+5 1/4°	+4 1/2°	+3 1/4°	+1 7/8°	+1°	—	3/32
	Camber	+7/8°	+5/8°	+1 1/2°	+2 3/8°	+3 1/8°	+4 1/4°	
F35	Caster	—	+5 1/4°	+4 1/2°	+3 1/4°	+1 7/8°	+1°	3/32
	Camber	+7/8°	+5/8°	+1 1/2°	+2 3/8°	+3 1/8°	+4 1/4°	

1971–74 E100, 200 SERIES

Riding Height, Inches		3.69	3.99	4.19	4.44	4.69	4.94	5.19	5.44	5.69	5.94	Toe In
1971 E100, 200	Caster	—	+5 1/4°	—	+4 1/2°	—	+3 1/4°	—	+1 7/8°	—	+1°	33/32
	Camber	−7/8°	—	+5/8°	—	+1 1/2°	—	+2 3/8°	—	+3 1/8°	—	
1972–74 E100, 200	Caster	—	+8 1/4°	—	+7 1/2°	—	+6 1/4°	—	+4 3/4°	—	+4°	3/32
	Camber	−7/8°	—	+5/8°	—	+1 1/2°	—	+2 3/8°	—	+3 1/8°	—	

1971–76 F SERIES

Riding Height, Inches		2.25	2.75	3	3.25	3.50	3.75	4	4.25	4.50	4.75	5	5.25	5.50	Toe In
1971 F100, 250	Caster	—	—	+5 1/4°	—	+4 1/2°	—	+3 1/4°	—	+1 7/8°	—	+1°	—	—	3/32
	Camber	—	—	+7/8°	—	+5/8°	—	+1 1/2°	—	+2 3/8°	—	+3 1/8°	—	+4 1/4°	
1971 F350	Caster	—	—	—	—	+5 1/4°	—	+4 1/2°	—	+3 1/4°	—	+1 7/8°	—	+1°	3/32
	Camber	—	—	−7/8°	—	+5/8°	—	+1 1/2°	—	+2 3/8°	—	+3 1/8°	—	+4 1/4°	
1972–74 F100, 250①	Caster	—	—	+8 1/4°	—	+7 1/2°	—	+6 1/4°	—	+4 3/4°	—	+4°	—	—	3/32
	Camber	—	—	−3/4°	—	−1/2°	—	+1 1/22°	—	+2 3/8°	—	+3 1/4°	—	+4°	
1972–74 F250②, F350	Caster	—	+8 1/4°	—	+7 3/8°	—	+6 1/8°	—	+4 3/4°	—	+4°	—	—	—	3/32
	Camber	—	−3/4°	—	+1/2°	—	+1 1/2°	—	+2 1/2°	—	+3 1/4°	—	+4 1/4°	—	
1975 F100③, 250④	Caster	—	—	+8 5/8°	—	+7 3/8°	—	+6 1/4°	—	+4 7/8°	—	+3 7/8°	—	—	1/8
	Camber	—	—	−3/4°	—	+1/2°	—	+1 1/2°	—	+2 1/4°	—	+3 1/4°	—	+4 1/8°	
1975 F250⑤	Caster	—	+8 5/8°	—	+7 3/8°	—	+6 1/4°	—	+4 7/8°	—	+3 7/8°	—	—	—	1/8
	Camber	—	−3/4°	—	+1/2°	—	+1 1/2°	—	+2 1/4°	—	+3 1/4°	—	+4 1/8°	—	
1975 F100⑥, 150⑥, 250⑦	Caster	—	—	+8 5/8°	—	+7 3/8°	—	+6 1/4°	—	+4 7/8°	—	+3 7/8°	—	—	1/8
	Camber	−3/4°	—	+1/2°	—	+1 1/2°	—	+2 1/4°	—	+3 1/4°	—	+4 1/8°	—	—	
1975 F250⑧, 350	Caster	—	—	+8 5/8°	—	+7 3/8°	—	+6 1/4°	—	+4 7/8°	—	+3 7/8°	—	—	1/8
	Camber	—	—	−3/4°	—	+1/2°	—	+1 1/2°	—	+2 1/4°	—	+3 1/4°	—	+4 1/8°	

Continued

FORD

WHEEL ALIGNMENT SPECIFICATIONS CHART—Continued

1971–76 F SERIES—Continued

	Riding Height, Inches	2.25	2.75	3	3.25	3.50	3.75	4	4.25	4.50	4.75	5	5.25	5.50	Toe In
1976 F100③, 150③, 250③	Caster	—	—	—	—	+7⁷⁄₈°	—	+6³⁄₈°	—	+4⁷⁄₈°	—	+4¹⁄₄°	—	—	¹⁄₈
	Camber	—	−1¹⁄₂°	—	−⁵⁄₈°	—	+⁵⁄₈°	—	+1⁷⁄₈°	—	+3¹⁄₄°	—	+4¹⁄₄°	—	
1976 F250⑩, 350	Caster	—	—	—	—	—	—	+7⁷⁄₈°③⑩	—	+6³⁄₈°③⑩	—	+4⁷⁄₈°③⑩	—	+4¹⁄₄°③⑩	¹⁄₈
	Camber	−1¹⁄₂°	−⁵⁄₈°	—	−⁵⁄₈°	—	+1⁷⁄₈°	—	+3¹⁄₄°	—	—	—	—	—	
1976 F100⑥, 150⑥	Caster	—	—	—	—	+7⁷⁄₈°	—	+6³⁄₈°	—	+4⁷⁄₈°	—	+4¹⁄₄°	—	—	¹⁄₈
	Camber	—	−1¹⁄₂°	—	−⁵⁄₈°	—	+⁵⁄₈°	—	+1⁷⁄₈°	—	+3¹⁄₄°	—	—	—	

1975–76 E SERIES

	Riding Height, Inches	2.80	3	3.30	3.50	3.80	4	4.25	4.50	4.80	5	5.30	5.50	To In
E100, 150	Caster	—	—	—	+8⁵⁄₈°	—	+7³⁄₈°	—	+6¹⁄₄°	—	+4⁷⁄₈°	—	+3⁷⁄₈°	¹⁄₈
	Camber	—	−³⁄₄°	—	+¹⁄₂°	—	+1¹⁄₂°	—	+2¹⁄₄°	—	+3¹⁄₄°	—	+4¹⁄₈°	
E250	Caster	—	—	+8⁵⁄₈°	—	+7³⁄₈°	—	+6¹⁄₄°	—	+4⁷⁄₈°	—	+3⁷⁄₈°	—	¹⁄₈
	Camber	—	−³⁄₄°	—	+¹⁄₂°	—	+1¹⁄₂°	—	+2¹⁄₄°	—	+3¹⁄₄°	—	+4¹⁄₈°	
E350	Caster	—	—	+8⁵⁄₈°	—	+7³⁄₈°	—	+6¹⁄₄°	—	+4⁷⁄₈°	—	+4¹⁄₈°	—	¹⁄₈
	Camber	−³⁄₄°	—	+¹⁄₂°	—	+1¹⁄₂°	—	+2¹⁄₄°	—	+3¹⁄₄°	—	—	—	
1976 E100, 150	Caster	—	—	—	—	—	+7³⁄₄°	—	+6¹⁄₂°	—	+5³⁄₈°	—	+4¹⁄₄°	¹⁄₈
	Camber	—	—	—	—	—	+¹⁄₈°	—	+³⁄₄°	—	+1⁷⁄₈°	—	+2³⁄₄°	
1976 E250, 350	Caster	—	—	+6°	—	+4³⁄₄°	—	+3¹⁄₂°	—	+2³⁄₈°	—	+1¹⁄₄°	—	¹⁄₈
	Camber	—	−1¹⁄₄°	—	−1¹⁄₄°	—	−¹⁄₈°	—	+³⁄₄	—	+1⁷⁄₈°	—	+2³⁄₄°	

1977–79 E & F SERIES

	Riding Height, Inches	3.00–3.25	3.50–3.75	4.00–4.25	4.25–4.50	4.75–5.00	5.25–5.50	Toe In
1977 E100, 150	Caster	—	—	—	+3¹⁄₄° to +5³⁄₄°	+2° to +4¹⁄₂°	+³⁄₄° to +3¹⁄₄°	—
	Camber	—	—	—	−³⁄₄° to +³⁄₄°	−³⁄₄° to +3¹⁄₄°	+1¹⁄₂° to +3¹⁄₄°	¹⁄₃₂
1977–78 E250, 350	Caster	+7° to 9¹⁄₂°	+5³⁄₄° to +8¹⁄₄°	+6¹⁄₄° to +9°	+5³⁄₄° to +8¹⁄₄°	+4¹⁄₄° to +1¹⁄₄°	+3¹⁄₄° to +6°	¹⁄₃₂
	Camber	−¹⁄₂° to +1°	0 to +2¹⁄₄°	−1° to +³⁄₄°	−¹⁄₂° to +1¹⁄₄°	+¹⁄₂° to +2¹⁄₄°	+1¹⁄₂° to +3¹⁄₄°	
1977 F100, 150, 250⑪	Caster	+6¹⁄₂° to +8³⁄₈°	+5¹⁄₄° to +7³⁄₈°	+4¹⁄₂° to +7°	+4° to +6¹⁄₂°	+3¹⁄₈° to +5⁷⁄₈°	—	³⁄₃₂
	Camber	−¹⁄₂° to +1°	0 to +2¹⁄₄°	+³⁄₄° to +2¹⁄₂°	+1¹⁄₄° to +3°	+2° to +3³⁄₄°	—	
1977 F250⑫	Caster	+6¹⁄₂° to +9°	+5¹⁄₄° to +7³⁄₄°	+4° to +6¹⁄₂°	+3¹⁄₄° to +5¹⁄₂°	+2¹⁄₂° to +4°	—	³⁄₃₂
	Camber	−¹⁄₄° to +1¹⁄₂°	0 to +1³⁄₄°	+1¹⁄₄° to +3°	+1³⁄₄° to +3¹⁄₄°	+2³⁄₄° to +4¹⁄₈°	—	
1977 F250⑬⑭, 350	Caster	+7° to +9¹⁄₂°	+5³⁄₄° to +8¹⁄₂°	+5³⁄₄° to +8¹⁄₂°	+5¹⁄₄° to +7³⁄₄°	+4° to +6¹⁄₂°	—	¹⁄₈
	Camber	−¹⁄₄° to +1¹⁄₂°	−¹⁄₄° to +1¹⁄₄°	0 to +2¹⁄₄°	+³⁄₄° to +2¹⁄₂°	+1³⁄₄° to +3¹⁄₄°	—	
1978 E100, 150	Caster	—	—	+3³⁄₄° to +6¹⁄₂°	+3³⁄₄° to +5³⁄₄°	+2° to +4¹⁄₂°	+³⁄₄° to +3¹⁄₄°	³⁄₃₂
	Camber	—	—	−³⁄₄° to +¹⁄₂°	−¹⁄₂° to +³⁄₄°	+¹⁄₂° to +1³⁄₄°	+1³⁄₄° to +3¹⁄₄°	
1978 F100, 150, 250⑪	Caster	—	+6¹⁄₂° to +7³⁄₈°	+5° to +6¹⁄₂°	+4¹⁄₄° to +5⁷⁄₈°	+3¹⁄₈° to +4¹⁄₂°	—	³⁄₃₂
	Camber	—	0 to +1³⁄₄°	+³⁄₄° to +2¹⁄₂°	+1¹⁄₄° to +3°	+2° to +3³⁄₄°	—	
1978 F250⑫	Caster	+6⁷⁄₈° to +8³⁄₈°	+5³⁄₄° to +7°	+4¹⁄₈° to +5⁷⁄₈°	+3⁷⁄₈° to +5¹⁄₈°	+2¹⁄₂° to +4°	—	³⁄₃₂
	Camber	−¹⁄₄° to +1¹⁄₂°	+¹⁄₂° to +2¹⁄₄°	+1¹⁄₂° to +3°	+1³⁄₄° to +3¹⁄₄°	+2³⁄₈° to +4¹⁄₈°	—	
1978 F250⑬⑭, 350	Caster	+9° to +10¹⁄₄°	+7⁵⁄₈° to +8⁵⁄₈°	+6³⁄₈° to +7¹⁄₄°	+5³⁄₄° to +7°	+4¹⁄₈° to +5⁷⁄₈°	+1¹⁄₂° to +2³⁄₄°	³⁄₃₂
	Camber	−1° to +⁵⁄₈°	−¹⁄₄° to +1¹⁄₈°	+¹⁄₄° to +1¹⁄₂°	+³⁄₄° to +2¹⁄₂°	+1³⁄₄° to +3¹⁄₄°	+1¹⁄₂° to +2³⁄₄°	
1979 E100, 150	Caster	—	+5³⁄₄° to +7¹⁄₄°	+4¹⁄₂° to +5³⁄₄°	+4° to +5¹⁄₄°	+2¹⁄₂° to +4°	+2° to +3³⁄₄°	¹⁄₃₂
	Camber	—	−1¹⁄₂° to +¹⁄₄°	−¹⁄₂° to +1¹⁄₄°	0 to +1³⁄₄°	+1° to +2³⁄₄°		

Continued

1131

WHEEL ALIGNMENT SPECIFICATIONS CHART—Continued

1977–79 E & F SERIES—Continued

Riding Height, Inches		3.00–3.25	3.50–3.75	4.00–4.25	4.25–4.50	4.75–5.00	5.25–5.50	Toe In
1979 E250, 350	Caster	—	+8 1/2° to +9 3/4°	+7 1/8° to +8 1/2°	+6 1/2° to +7 3/4°	+5 1/4° to +6 1/2°	+4° to +5 1/2°	1/32
	Camber	—	−1 1/2° to +1/4°	−1/2° to +1 1/4°	0° to +1 3/4°	+1° to +2 3/4°	+2° to +3 3/4°	
1979 F100, 150, 250⑮	Caster	+7 3/4° to +9°	+6 1/4° to +7 5/8°	+5 1/8° to +6 1/2°	+4 1/2° to +5 7/8°	+3 1/4° to +4 5/8°	—	3/32
	Camber	−1 1/2° to +1/8°	−3/4° to +1°	0° to +1 5/8°	+3/8° to +2°	+1 1/4° to +2 3/4°	—	
1979 F250⑯	Caster	+8 3/8° to +7°	+5 7/8° to +7 1/8	+4 1/2° to +5 7/8°	+3 7/8° to +5 1/4°	+2 5/8° to +4°	—	3/32
	Camber	−1 1/2° to +1/8°	+7/8° to −3/4°	0° to +1 5/8°	+3/8° to +2°	+1 1/4° to +2 3/4°	—	
1979 F250⑬⑭, 350	Caster	+8 7/8° to +10 3/8°	+7 3/4° to +9°	+6 3/8° to 7 3/4°	+5 3/4° to +7 1/8°	4 1/2° to +5 7/8°	—	3/32
	Camber	−1 3/4° to −1/4°	−1 1/8° to +1/2°	−1/4° to +1 1/4°	0° to +1 5/8°	+3/4° to +2 3/8°	—	

1980 E SERIES

Riding Height, Inches		3.25–3.50	3.50–3.75	4.00–4.25	4.25–4.50	4.50–4.75	5.00–5.25	5.25–5.50	Toe In
E100, 150	Camber	−1 3/4° to −1/4°	−1 1/2° to +1/4°	−1/2° to +1 1/4°	0° to +1 3/4°	+1/2° to +2 1/4°	+1 1/2° to +3 1/4°	+2° to +3 3/4°	1/8°
	Caster	+6 1/4° to +8°	+5 3/4° to +7 1/4°	+4 1/2° to +5 3/4°	+4° to +5 1/4°	+3 1/4° to +4 1/2°	+2° to +3 1/4°	+1 1/2° to +2 3/4°	
E250, 350	Camber	−1 3/4° to −1/4°	−1 1/2° to +1/4°	−1/2° to +1 1/4°	0° to +1 3/4°	+1/2° to +2 1/4°	+1 1/2° to +3 1/4°	+2° to +3 3/4°	1/32°
	Caster	+9° to +10 1/2°	+8 1/2° to +9 3/4°	+7 1/8° to +8 1/2°	+6 1/2° to +7 3/4°	+5 3/4° to +7°	+4 5/8° to +6°	+4° to +5 1/2°	

1980 F SERIES

Riding Height, Inches		3.25–3.50	3.50–4.00	4.00–4.25	4.25–4.75	4.75–5.00	5.00–5.50	5.50–6.00	Toe In
F100, 150 (4×2)	Camber	−1 1/4° to +1 1/4°	−1/4° to +2 1/4°	+1/2° to +3°	+1 1/2° to +4°	—	—	—	3/32°
	Caster	+4° to +8°	+3° to +7°	+2° to +6°	+1° to +5°	—	—	—	
F250, 350 (4×2)	Camber	+1/4° to +2 3/4°	+1° to +3 1/2°	+2° to +4 1/2°	—	—	—	—	7/32°
	Caster	+2 3/4° to +6°	+1 3/4° to +5°	+3/4° to +4°	—	—	—	—	
F150, Bronco (4×4)	Camber	−1 3/4° to +1/2°	−3/4° to +1 1/2°	0° to +2 1/4°	+1° to +3 1/4°	+1 3/4° to +4°	—	—	1/16°
	Caster	+5° to +8°	+4° to +7°	+3° to +6°	+2° to +5°	+1° to +4°	—	—	
F250, 350 (4×4)	Camber	—	—	—	−4° to −1 1/4°	−2 3/4° to 0°	−1 1/2° to +1 1/4°	−1/4° to +2 1/2°	1/16°
	Caster	—	—	—	+3 1/2° to +5 3/4°	+3 1/4° to +5 1/2°	+3° to +5 1/4°	+2 3/4° to +5°	

①—Except 1972–73 heavy duty & 1974 7500-8050 GVW.
②—1972–73 heavy duty & 1974 7500-8050 GVW.
③—Except Super Cab.
④—Except 7500-8050 GVW & 6900 GVW with V8-460 engine.
⑤—6900 GVW with V8-460 engine.
⑥—Super Cab.
⑦—Super Cab 8100 GVW.
⑧—Super Cab except 8100 GVW.
⑨—Except 7800-8000 GVW.
⑩—F250 7800-8000 GVW.
⑪—Regular Cab 6200-6900 GVW.
⑫—Regular Cab 7800-8000 GVW & Super Cab 6350-7800 GVW.
⑬—Super Cab 8100 GVW.
⑭—Super Cab with standard suspension.
⑮—6200-6800 GVW.
⑯—Regular Cab 7700-7900 GVW & Super Cab 6300-7800 GVW.

Ford

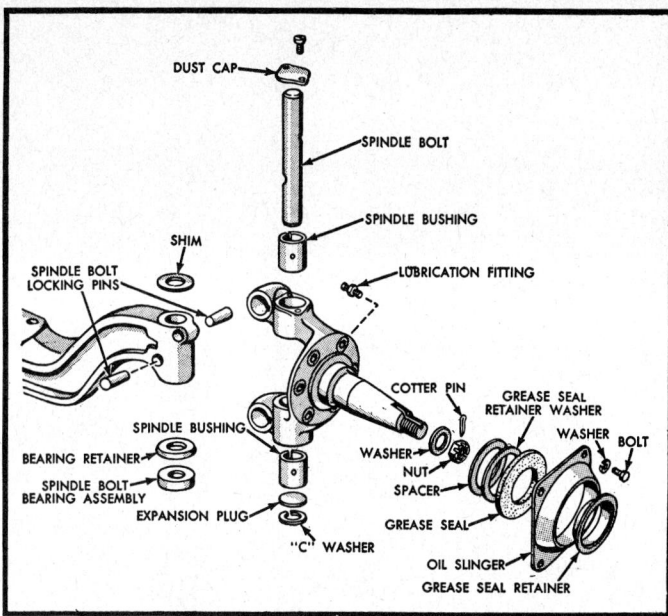

Fig. 13 Spindle used with 7000 thru 9000 lb. axles

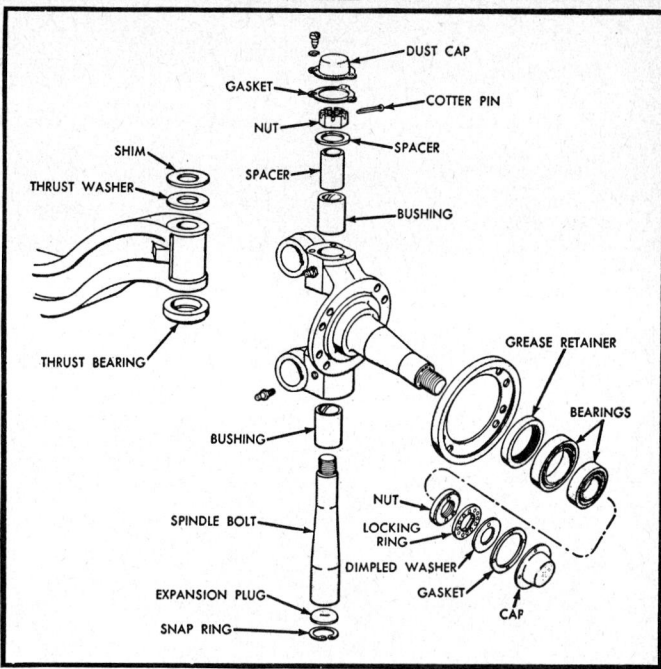

Fig. 14 Spindle used with 11,000 lb. axle

flange. On 1971–76 E series vehicles, measure from top surface of axle to bottom of sill, Fig. 11. On 1977–80 E series vehicles, measure from bottom of flange to spring seat lower surface at inside area of jounce bumper to top surface of axle, Fig. 12.

After determining the riding height, measure the caster and camber. Correlate the recorded actual vehicle ride height and recorded actual caster and camber angles with the "Wheel Alignment Specifications Chart" found in this section to determine which wheel is out of specifications if an excessive side to side variation exists. If caster and camber measurements exceed the maximum variance of 5/8 degree for camber and 1 1/2 degrees for caster, inspect for damage from suspension components and replace as necessary.

Alignment equipment indicates a true reading only when the vehicle's frame is horizontal. Therefore, if the frame is not level (due to tire, spring or load differences), the caster angle reading must be modified to compensate for the frame angles. If the front is higher than the rear, subtract the amount of angle from the reading. If the front is lower than the rear, add the angle. To check frame angle, use a spirit protractor, and take the frame angle measurement on the lower frame flange at the flat area immediately adjacent to the rear spring front hanger.

SINGLE I-BEAM AXLES

These axles are the I-beam type with the front wheel spindles attached to the ends of the axles, Figs. 13 and 14.

Each spindle is held in place on the axle by a spindle bolt. On 4000, 5000 and 5500 lb. axles, steel-backed, bronze bushings are pressed into the upper and lower ends of the spindle to provide bearing surfaces for the spindle bolt. Delrin bushings are used on 6000 through 11,000 lb-axles.

A thrust bearing is installed between the lower end of the axle and the spindle to support the load on the axle. A spindle arm, to which the steering linkage is attached, is installed on each spindle.

FRONT SUSPENSION

1980 Bronco & F-150 4 Wheel Drive

The independent front suspension on these vehicles is composed of a two piece front driving axle assembly, two coil springs and two radius arms, Fig. 15.

The front driving axle consists of two independent yoke and tube assemblies. One end of yoke and tube assembly is anchored to the frame. The other end of each yoke and tube assembly is supported by the coil spring and radius arm.

1980 F-250 & F-350 4 Wheel Drive

The independent front suspension on these vehicles has a two piece driving axle attached to the frame with two semi-elliptic leaf springs, Fig. 16. Each spring is clamped to the axle yoke with two U-bolts. The rear tube assembly of the spring rests in a rear hanger bracket. The front of the spring is attached to a shackle bracket.

1970–79 F-100, 150 4 Wheel Drive & Bronco

The front driving axle is attached to the frame with two coil springs, two radius arms and a track bar, Fig. 17.

The radius arms clamp around the axle tube and attach to frame brackets behind the front axle. A coil spring is attached to each radius arm directly above the axle and extends to the frame spring seat. The shock absorbers are attached to the frame and to brackets on the radius arm.

The track bar is mounted to a bracket on the left frame side member and extends to the right side of the axle housing.

Caster and camber angles are designed into the front axle and cannot be adjusted.

1970–79 F-250, 350 4 Wheel Drive

The front suspension on these vehicles consists of a driving axle attached to the frame with two semi-elliptic leaf type springs. Each spring is clamped to the axle with U-bolts. The front of the spring rests in a front hanger bracket, while the rear of the spring is attached to a shackle bracket. The shock absorbers are attached to a frame bracket at the top and to an axle bracket at the bottom.

Caster and camber are designed into the front axle. Camber is not adjustable, and caster is adjustable by using shims on 1970 vehicles only.

RANCHERO

1972–79

The front suspension, Fig. 18, has been redesigned with the coil spring mounted on the lower arm rather than the upper arm as in the past.

1970–71

Referring to Fig. 17, each front wheel rotates on a spindle. The upper and lower ends of the spindle are attached to ball joints that are mounted to an upper and lower control arm. The upper arm pivots on a bushing and shaft assembly that is bolted to the underbody. The lower arm pivots on a bolt that is located in an underbody bracket.

A coil spring seats between the upper arm and the top of the spring housing. A double-acting shock absorber is bolted to the arm and the top of the spring housing.

Struts, which are connected between the lower control arms and the underbody, prevent the arms from moving fore and aft.

Wheel Alignment

1972–80

Caster and camber can be adjusted by loosening the bolts that attach the upper suspen-

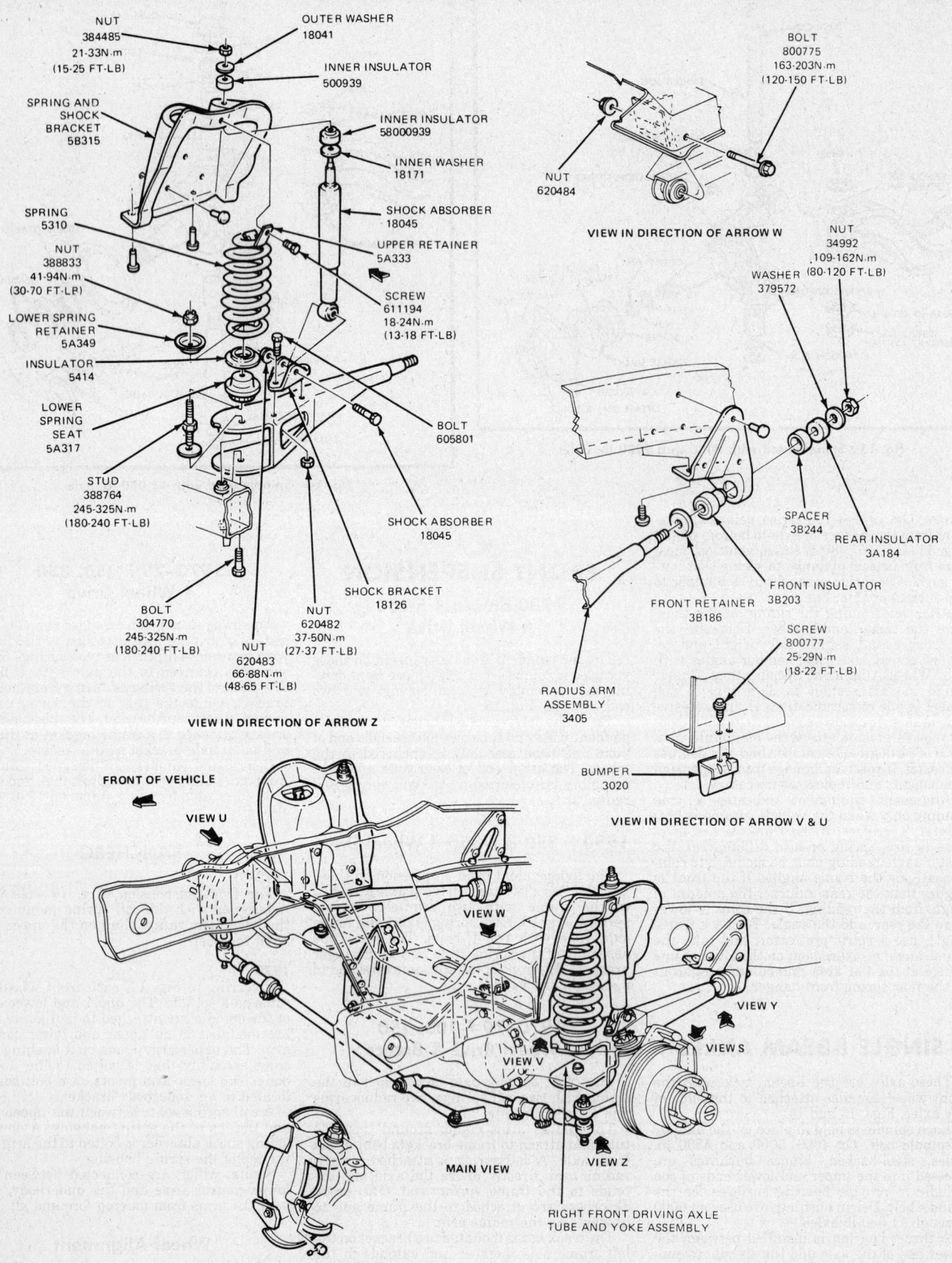

Fig. 15 Independent front suspension. 1980 Bronco & F-150 Four Wheel Drive

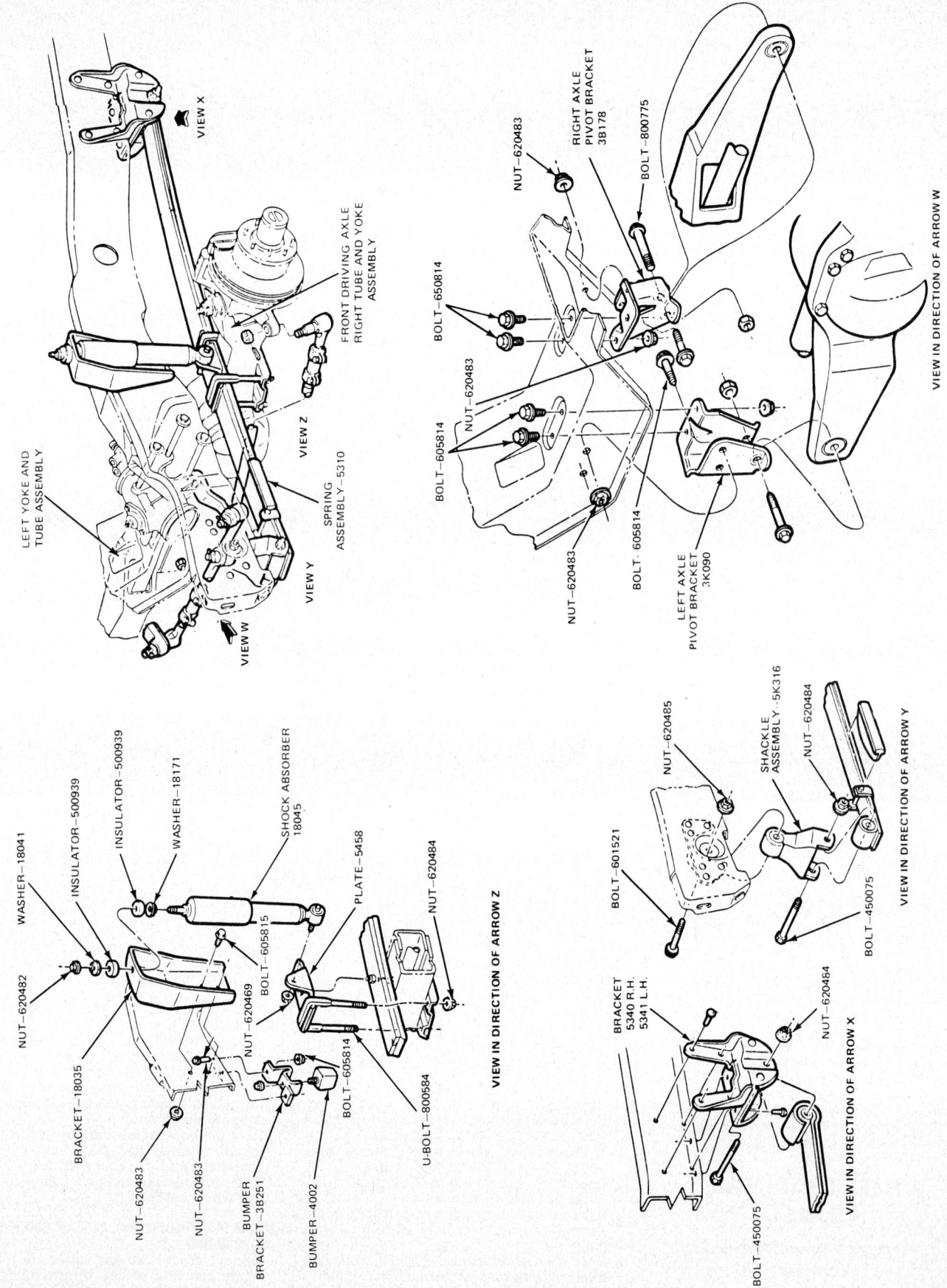

Fig. 16 Independent front suspension. 1980 F-250 & F-350 Four Wheel Drive

FORD

sion arm to the shaft at the frame side rail, and moving the arm assembly in or out in the elongated bolt holes, Fig. 18. Since any movement of the arm affects both caster and camber, both factors should be balanced against one another when making the adjustment.

Install the tool with the pins in the frame holes and the hooks over the upper arm inner shaft. Tighten the hook nuts snug before loosening the upper arm inner shaft attaching bolts, Fig. 20.

Caster Adjust
1. Tighten the tool front hook nut or loosen the rear hook nut as required to increase caster to the desired angle.
2. To decrease caster, tighten the rear hook nut or loosen the front hook nut as required.

NOTE: The caster angle can be checked without tightening the inner shaft retaining bolts.

3. Check the camber angle to be sure it did not change during the caster adjustment and adjust if necessary.
4. Tighten the upper arm inner shaft retaining bolts and remove tool.

Camber, Adjust
1. Install as previously outlined.
2. Loosen both inner shaft retaining bolts.
3. Tighten or loosen the hook nuts as necessary to increase or decrease camber.
4. Recheck caster angle.

1970-71
As shown in Fig. 21, caster is controlled by the front suspension strut. To obtain positive caster, loosen the strut rear nut and tighten the strut front nut against the bushing. To obtain negative caster, loosen the strut front nut and tighten the strut rear nut against the bushing.

Camber is controlled by the eccentric cam located at the lower arm attachment to the side rail. To adjust camber, loosen the camber adjustment bolt nut at the rear of the body bracket. Spread the body bracket at the camber adjustment bolt area just enough to permit lateral travel of the arm when the adjustment bolt is turned. Rotate the bolt and eccentric clockwise from the high position to increase camber or counterclockwise to decrease it.

Toe-In, Adjust

Check the steering wheel spoke position when the front wheels are in the straight-ahead position. If the spokes are not in the normal position, they can be adjusted while toe-in is being adjusted.
1. Loosen clamp bolts on each tie rod end sleeve.
2. Adjust toe-in. If steering wheel spokes are in their normal position, lengthen or shorten both rods equally to obtain correct toe-in. If spokes are not in normal position, make necessary rod adjustments to obtain correct toe-in and steering wheel spoke alignment.

WHEEL BEARINGS, ADJUST

Except 4 Wheel Drive Vehicles

Ranchero
1. With wheel rotating, torque adjusting nut to 17-25 ft. lbs.
2. Back off adjusting nut 1/2 turn and retorque nut to 10-15 inch lbs.
3. Place nut lock on nut so that castellations on lock are aligned with cotter pin hole in spindle and install cotter pin.
4. Check wheel rotation. If it rotates rough or noisily, clean or replace bearings.

1970-76 F-100 Thru F-350 & E-100 Thru E-350
1. Remove grease cap, cotter pin and nut lock.
2. While rotating wheel, torque adjusting nut to 17-25 ft. lbs. to seat bearings.
3. Install nut lock so a slot is aligned with cotter pin hole in spindle.
4. Back off adjusting nut and nut lock two slots of the nut lock and install cotter pin.
5. Check wheel rotation. If wheel rotates freely with no noticeable end play, adjustment is acceptable. If wheel is loose or if it rotates rough or noisily, the bearing cones, rollers and cups are dirty or worn and should be cleaned or replaced.
6. Install grease cap.

1977-80 F-100 Thru F-350 & E-100 Thru E-350, 1979-80 Bronco
1. Remove wheel and tire assembly, disc brake caliper and pads, dustcap, locknut, adjusting nut, washer and cotter pin.
2. Tighten wheel adjusting nut to 22-25 ft. lbs. while rotating disc brake caliper in opposite direction.
3. Back off wheel retention nut 1/8 turn and install retainer and cotter pin without any additional movement of nut.
4. Reinstall dustcap, caliper, pads and tire and wheel assembly.

1970-76 P-350 thru 500, 1977 P-500 & 1978-79 P-600
1. Remove grease cap and cotter pin.
2. While rotating wheel, torque adjusting nut to 40-55 ft. lbs. on 1970-76 models and 40-50 ft. lbs. on 1977-79 models to

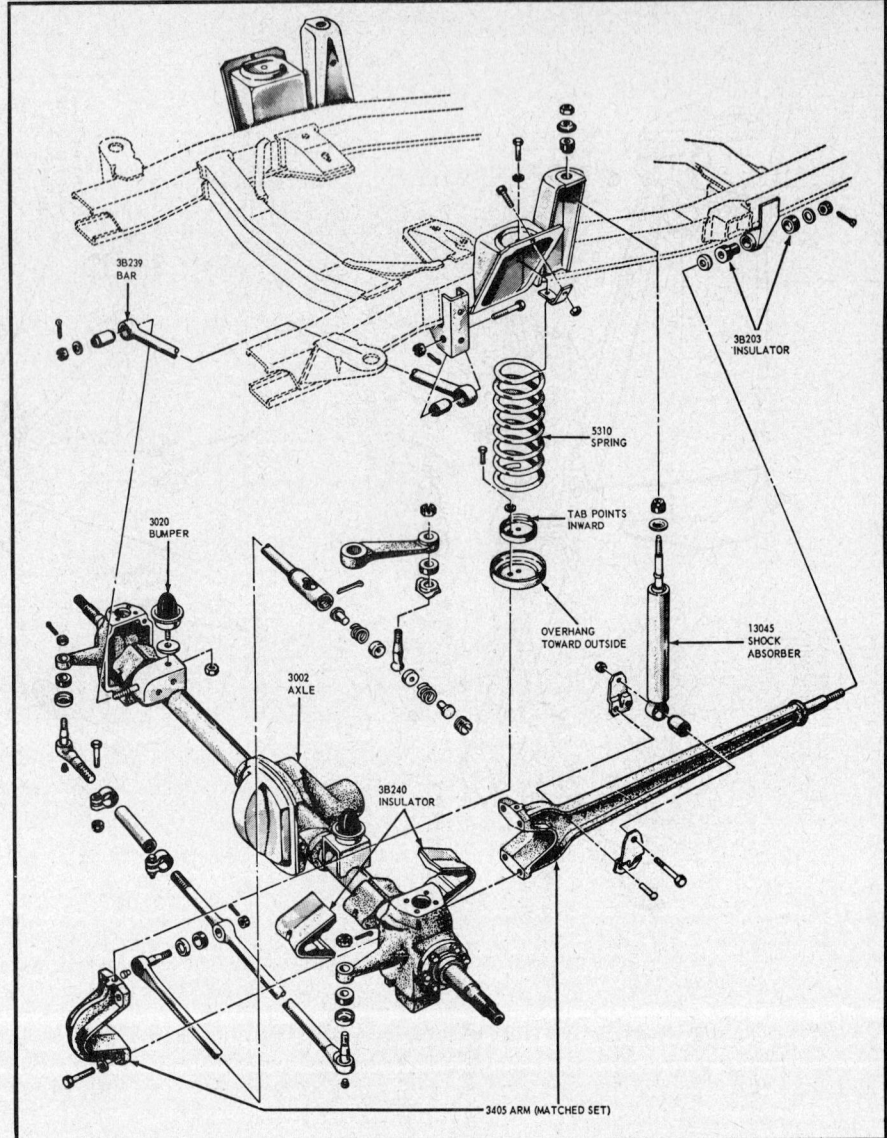

Fig. 17 Front suspension (Typical) F-100 & 150 4 wheel drive & Bronco. Less independent front suspension

Ford

1970–77 Vehicles With 12000 Pound Center Point Axle With Double Nut & Washer

1. Back off brake adjustment, then straighten lock washer and remove lock nut and washer.
2. While rotating wheel in both directions, torque adjusting nut to 100–125 ft. lbs. to seat bearings.
3. Back off adjusting nut one complete turn, then again, while rotating wheel in both directions, retorque adjusting nut to 40–55 ft. lbs.
4. Back off adjusting nut to obtain an initial .004–.010 inch end play between hub and spindle.
5. Install outer washer and lock nut and torque to 100–125 ft. lbs.
6. Final end play should be .001–.010 inch. Readjust if necessary.
7. Bend washer outward in two places on opposite sides of lock nut, to lock outer nut in position.
8. Install gasket and grease cap and readjust brakes.

NOTE: Final adjustment must not result in a preloaded bearing.

1970–77 Vehicles With 15000 Pound Axle With Double Nut & Lock Ring

1. Back off brake adjustment, then remove grease cap and gasket.
2. While rotating wheel in both directions, torque adjusting nut to 100–125 ft. lbs. to seat bearings.
3. Back off adjusting nut one complete turn, then while again rotating wheel in both directions, retorque nut to 40–55 ft. lbs.
4. Back off adjusting nut to obtain an initial .004–.010 inch end play between wheel hub and spindle.
5. Install lock ring making sure that adjacent dowel is inserted into a lock ring hole, then install washer with dimple indexed in one of the holes in lock ring.
6. Install lock nut and torque to 100–125 ft. lbs.
7. Recheck end play. Final bearing adjustment must allow .001–.010 inch end play. Readjust if necessary.
8. Bend lock washer in two places on opposite sides to lock nut in position.
9. Install gasket and grease cap, and readjust brakes.

NOTE: Final adjustment must not result in a preloaded bearing.

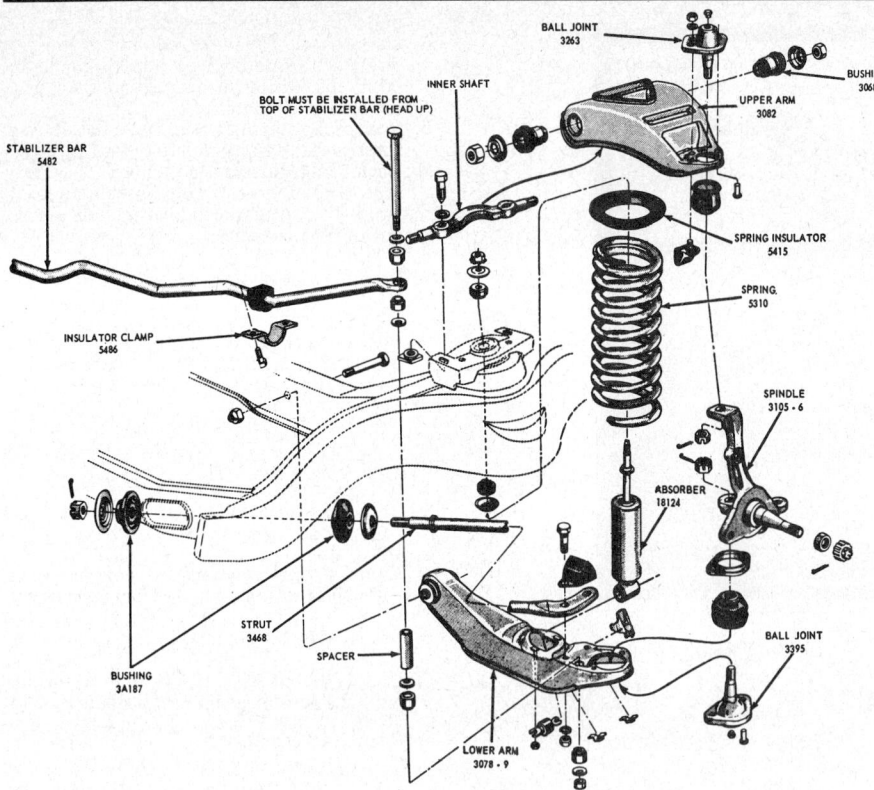

Fig. 18 Front suspension. 1972–79 Ranchero

seat bearings.

3. If necessary, back off adjusting nut to next slot so nut aligns with cotter pin hole, then back off nut two slots and install cotter pin.
4. Check wheel rotation. If wheel rotates freely with no noticeable end play, adjustment is acceptable. If wheel is loose, or if it rotates rough or noisily, the bearing cones, rollers and cups are dirty or worn and should be cleaned or replaced.
5. Install grease cap.

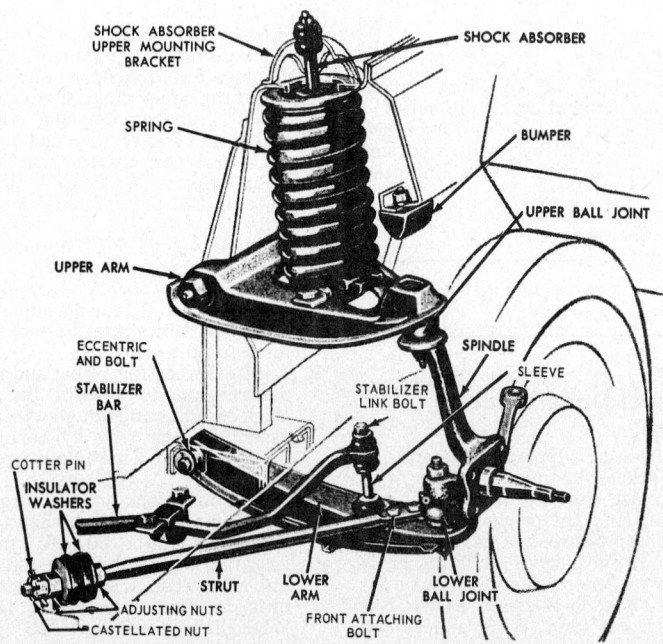

Fig. 19 Front suspension. 1970–71 Ranchero

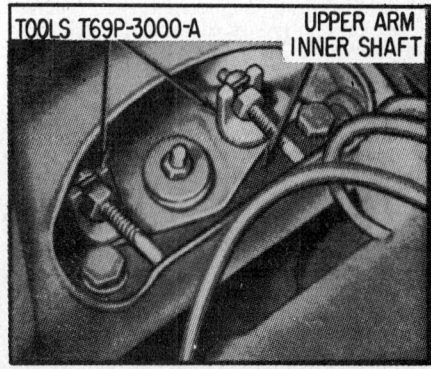

Fig. 20 Caster & camber adjustments. 1972–79 Ranchero

FORD

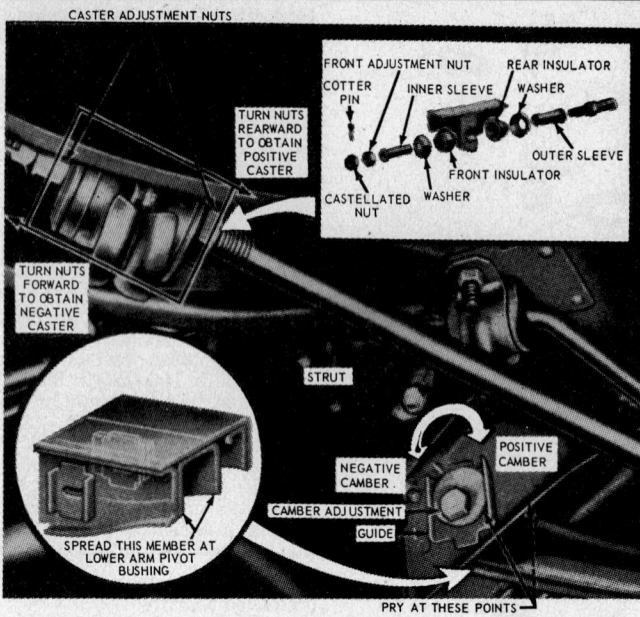

Fig. 21 Caster & camber adjustments. 1970-71 Ranchero

1970-80 Vehicles With 5000-7000 Pound Axles With Single Nut & Cotter Pin, 1980 Vehicles With 7000, 9000 & 12000 Pound Axles With Air Brakes

1. Back off brake adjustment, then remove grease cap and cotter pin.
2. While rotating wheel, torque adjusting nut to 70-100 ft. lbs. to seat bearings.
3. Back off adjusting nut one half turn, then hand tighten adjusting nut (13-17 inch lbs.) while moving top part of tire in and out.
4. If cotter pin hole lines up with slot in nut, insert a new cotter pin. If it does not, back off adjusting nut to align a slot with nearest cotter pin hole and install a new cotter pin. Adjustment should provide .001-.010 inch end play.
5. Install gasket and grease cap, then adjust brakes.

NOTE: Final adjustment must not result in a preloaded bearing.

1970-79 Vehicles With 9000 & 12000 Pound Axle With Double Nut & Lock Ring, 1980 9000 & 12000 Pound Axle With Double Nut, Lock Ring & Hydraulic Brakes

1. Back off brake adjustment, then remove gasket and grease cap and straight lock washer.
2. While rotating wheel in both directions, torque adjusting nut to 100-125 ft. lbs. to seat bearings.
3. Back off adjusting nut one complete turn, then while again rotating wheel in both directions, retorque adjusting nut to 50-70 ft. lbs.
4. Back off adjusting nut to obtain an initial end play of .004-.010 inch between hub and spindle.
5. Install lock ring making sure that adjusting nut dowel is inserted into lock ring, then install outer washer locating dimple in washer in one of the lock ring holes. Install lock nut and torque to 100-150 ft. lbs.
6. Recheck to make sure that final bearing adjustment is .001-.010 inch end play. Readjust if necessary.
7. Bend washer outward in two places to lock outer nut in position, then install gasket and grease cap and adjust brakes.

NOTE: Final adjustment must not result in a preloaded bearing.

1970-80 16000, 18000 & 20000 Pound Axle With Single Nut & Cotter Pin

1. Back off brake adjustment, then remove grease cap and gasket.
2. While rotating wheel in both directions, torque adjusting nut to 100-125 ft. lbs. to seat bearings.
3. Back off adjusting nut one complete turn, then while again rotating wheel in both directions, retorque adjusting nut to 50-70 ft. lbs.
4. If necessary, back off adjusting nut to align a slot with next cotter pin hole.
5. Using same cotter pin hole as a reference point, back off adjusting nut to next slot to allow wheel to rotate freely. End play should be .001-.010 inch.
6. Install cotter pin, gasket and grease cap and readjust brakes.

NOTE: Final adjustment must not result in a preloaded bearing.

4 Wheel Drive Vehicles

1970 All Models

1. Raise vehicle and support with stands.
2. Back off brake adjustment, if necessary.
3. Remove grease cap and driving hub retaining snap ring, then slide splined driving hub from between axle shaft and wheel hub. Remove driving hub spacer. If equipped with freerunning lock-out hub, refer to "FRONT WHEEL LOCKING HUBS" section and remove lock-out hub.
4. Using tool T59T-1197-B, remove lock nut and lock ring from spindle.
5. Using tool T59T-1197-B and a torque wrench, torque bearing adjusting nut to 50 ft. lbs. while rotating wheel back and forth to seat bearings.
6. Continue rotating wheel, then loosen and retorque adjusting nut to 30-40 ft. lbs.
7. Back off adjusting nut about 1/2 turn (135-150 degrees), then assemble lock ring by turning nut to nearest hole where dowel pin will enter.
8. Install outer lock nut and torque to 50 ft. lbs. Final end play of wheel when installed on spindle should be .001-.010 inch.
9. Install driving hub, spacer, snap ring and grease cap. If equipped with freerunning lock-out hub, install lock-out hub.
10. Install brake drum.

1971-72 Bronco & F-100

1. Raise vehicle and support with stands.
2. Back off brake adjustment, if necessary.
3. Remove hub grease cap and driving hub snap ring.
4. Remove splined driving hub and pressure spring. This may require prying slightly.
5. Remove wheel bearing lock nut and lock ring.
6. Using tool T59T-1197-B and a torque wrench, torque bearing adjusting nut to 50 ft. lbs. while rotating wheel back and forth to seat bearing.
7. Continue rotating wheel, then loosen adjusting nut and retorque to 30-40 ft. lbs.
8. Back off adjusting nut 1/4 turn, then assemble lock ring by turning nut to nearest notch where dowel pin will enter.
9. Install outer lock nut and torque to 50 ft. lbs. End play of wheel when installed on spindle should be .001-.010 inch.
10. Install pressure spring, driving hub and hub grease cap. If equipped with freerunning lock-out hubs, refer to "FRONT WHEEL LOCKING HUBS" section for installation of lock-out hub.
11. Adjust brakes.

1971-72 F-250

1. Raise vehicle and support with stands.
2. Back off brake adjustment, if necessary.
3. Remove hub grease cap and driving hub retaining snap ring, then slide splined driving hub from between axle shaft and wheel hub and remove driving hub spacer. If equipped with free running lock-out hubs, refer to "FRONT WHEEL LOCKING HUBS" section and remove lock-out hub.
4. Using tool T59T-1197-B, remove lock nut and lock ring from spindle.
5. Using tool T59-1197-B and a torque wrench, torque bearing adjusting nut to 50 ft. lbs. while rotating wheel back and forth to seat bearings.
6. Continue rotating wheel and then loosen and retorque to 30-40 ft. lbs.
7. Back off adjusting nut about 1/4 turn, then assemble lock ring by turning nut to nearest notch where dowel pin will enter.
8. Install outer lock nut and torque to 50 ft. lbs. End play of wheel when installed on spindle should be .001-.010 inch.
9. Install driving hub, spacer, snap ring and hub grease cap. If equipped with free running lock-out hubs, refer to "FRONT WHEEL LOCKING HUBS" section and install lock-out hub.
10. Adjust brakes, if necessary.

FORD

1971-78 F-600

1. Remove outer hub cap retaining screws and cap.
2. Remove retaining lock ring, screws and splined drive plate.
3. Straighten tab of lock washer and remove lock nut and washer. Discard lock washer.
4. While rotating wheel in both directions, torque adjusting nut to 50 ft. lbs., then back off adjusting nut 1/4 to 1/3 turn.
5. Place a new lock washer against adjusting nut and apply oil to outer surface of lock washer.
6. Turn lock nut up against lock washer and torque to 100-150 ft. lbs.
7. Bend one tab of lock washer over lock nut, and bend other tab of lockwasher over adjusting nut.

NOTE: Use a blunt tool when bending tabs to avoid making any chips which could cause damage to bearing.

8. Apply silastic sealer or equivalent to front and rear mounting surfaces of splined drive plate, then position drive plate and install retaining screws.
9. Install retaining lock ring, outer hub cap and retaining screws.

1973-77 F-250

NOTE: If vehicle is equipped with free running lock-out hubs, refer to "FRONT WHEEL LOCKING HUBS" section for removal and installation.

1. Raise vehicle and support with stands.
2. Remove free-running hubs, if equipped.
3. Remove grease cap, then using tool T59T-1197-B, remove lock nut and lock ring from spindle.
4. Using tool T59T-1197-B and a torque wrench, torque bearing adjusting nut to 50 ft. lbs. while rotating wheel in both directions to seat bearings.
5. Back off adjusting nut 1/4 turn, then assemble lock ring by turning nut to nearest notch for dowel pin installation.
6. Install outer lock nut and torque to 80-100 ft. lbs. on 1973-76 models, and 50-70 ft. lbs. on 1977 models.
7. Install grease cap. Install free-running hubs, if equipped.

1973-79 Bronco, 1973-76 F-100, 1977-79 F-150, 1978-79 F-250 & 1979 F-350

NOTE: If vehicle is equipped with free running lock-out hubs, refer to "FRONT WHEEL LOCKING HUBS" section for removal and installation

1. Raise vehicle and support with stands.
2. Back off brake adjustment, if necessary.
3. Remove grease cap and hub snap ring, then remove splined driving hub and pressure spring. This may require prying slightly.
4. Remove wheel bearing lock nut and lock ring.
5. Using tool T59T-1197-B and a torque wrench, torque bearing adjusting nut to 50 ft. lbs. while rotating wheel back and forth to seat bearings.
6. Back off adjusting nut 1/4 turn, then assemble lock ring by turning nut to nearest notch for dowel pin installation.

NOTE: The dowel pin must seat in a lock ring hole for proper bearing adjustment and wheel retention.

7. Install outer lock nut and torque to 80-100 ft. lbs. on 1973-76 models, 50-70 ft. lbs. on 1977 models and 50-80 ft. lbs. on 1978-79 models. Final end play of wheel when installed on spindle should be .001-.010 inch on all except 1979 F-250 with a Dana 44-9F axle, and .001-.006 inch on 1979 F-250 with a Dana 44-9F axle.
8. Install pressure spring, driving hub, snap ring and grease cap, then adjust brakes, if necessary.

1980 Bronco & F-150 Thru F-350

NOTE: If vehicle is equipped with free running lock-out hubs, refer to "FRONT WHEEL LOCKING HUBS" section for removal and installation.

1. Raise vehicle and support with stands.
2. Remove hub assembly, then using tool T59T-1197-B and a torque wrench, torque bearing inner adjusting nut to 50 ft. lbs. while rotating wheel back and forth to seat bearings.
3. Back off adjusting nut 1/4 turn, then assemble lock tab and outer locknut. Torque locknut to 50 ft. lbs. Bend at least one tab into a slot on both the inner adjusting nut and outer lock nut.
4. Final end play of wheel when installed on spindle should be .001-.006 inch.
5. Install hub assembly.

FRONT SPRING, REPLACE

1980 Bronco & F-150 4 Wheel Drive, Fig. 3

1. Raise and support vehicle.
2. Remove shock absorber to lower bracket attaching bolt.
3. Remove spring lower retainer attaching nuts from inside coil spring.
4. Remove spring upper retainer attaching screw and the upper retainer.
5. Place jack stands under frame side rails and lower axle to relieve spring tension.

NOTE: The axle must be supported when replacing spring and not be permitted to hang by the brake hose. If the length of the brake hose is not sufficient to permit spring replacement, it will be necessary to remove the disc brake caliper. Do not suspend caliper by brake hose, if removed.

6. Remove spring and lower retainer.
7. Reverse procedure to install.

1980 F-250 & 350 4 Wheel Drive, Fig. 4

1. Raise vehicle until weight is relieved from front spring with the front wheels still contacting floor. Support axle to prevent rotation.
2. Disconnect shock absorber lower end from U-bolt spacer, then remove U-bolts, cap and spacer.
3. Remove rear hanger bolt at rear of spring.
4. Remove front shackle bolt and remove spring.
5. Reverse procedure to install.

RADIUS ARM, REPLACE

1980 Bronco & F-150 4 Wheel Drive, Fig. 3

1. Raise and support vehicle under frame side rails.
2. Remove front spring as outlined under "Front Spring, Replace".
3. Remove nut attaching radius arm to frame bracket, then the radius arm rear insulator.
4. Remove bolt and stud attaching radius arm to axle.
5. Move axle forward and remove radius arm from axle, then pull radius arm from frame bracket.
6. Reverse procedure to install.

AXLE HOUSING PIVOT BUSHING, REPLACE

1980 Bronco, F-150 Thru F-350 4 Wheel Drive, Figs. 3 & 4

1. Raise and support vehicle, remove front wheels.
2. Remove front axle assembly from vehicle.
3. Remove pivot bushing from axle housing using suitable tool.
4. Reverse procedure to install.

STEERING KNUCKLE, REPLACE

1980 Bronco, F-150 Thru F-350 4 Wheel Drive, Figs. 3 & 4

1. Remove axle shaft and spindle from steering knuckle.
2. Disconnect tie rod from steering arm.
3. Remove upper ball joint nut and loosen lower ball joint nut. Strike upper ball joint stud to loosen ball joints.
4. Remove lower ball joint nut and remove knuckle from yoke tube.
5. Remove camber adjuster bushing from tube and yoke assembly.
6. Install knuckle into vise and press out ball joints using suitable tool.

NOTE: On some models, the lower ball joint is retained by a snap ring.

7. Reverse procedure to install. Install knuckle onto tube and yoke assembly, then install camber adjusting bushing with arrow pointing outward for "positive camber" or towards center of vehicle for "negative camber". Install new lower ball joint nut and torque both upper and lower ball joint nuts to 100 ft. lbs.

STEERING GEAR, REPLACE

1970-74 Econoline

1. Raise vehicle on hoist and remove attaching bolt from lower half of flex coupling.
2. Disconnect Pitman arm with suitable puller.
3. While supporting steering gear, remove three attaching bolts and lower steering gear.
4. Remove Pitman arm attaching nut. Remove Pitman arm.

Ford

5. Reverse procedure to install.

1975–80 Econoline

1. Raise and support front of vehicle, then disconnect flex coupling from steering shaft flange by removing two attaching nuts.
2. Disconnect drag link from pitman arm using tool No. 3290-C.
3. Remove pitman to sector shaft attaching nut and washer, then remove pitman arm from gear sector shaft using tool No. T64P-3590-F.
4. While supporting steering gear, remove bolts and washer attaching gear assembly to frame side rail and lower gear assembly from vehicle.

1970 F-100 2 Wheel Drive, 250 & 350

1. Remove the bolt that attaches the flex joint to the steering gear.
2. Raise front of vehicle and install stands.
3. Disconnect pitman arm from sector shaft.
4. If equipped with standard transmission, disconnect clutch return spring from the steering gear.
5. Remove the bolt that secures the parking brake cable clamp to the fender apron.
6. Unfasten and remove steering gear.
7. Reverse procedure to install.

1971–80 F-100-350 2 Wheel Drive

1. Remove bolt attaching flex coupling to steering gear. Remove brake line bracket.
2. Raise and support front of vehicle, then disconnect pitman arm from sector shaft using tool No. T64P-3590.
3. Remove steering gear to frame attaching bolts, then remove steering gear assembly.

1970–77 F-100 Thru 350 4 Wheel Drive & Bronco

1. Raise the vehicle on a hoist and remove the pitman arm from the sector shaft.
2. Unfasten the steering gear from the frame side rail and lower vehicle.
3. Remove the flex coupling bolt and nut from the coupling clamp.
4. Loosen the clamp on the steering shaft at end of steering column and separate the coupling from the gear input shaft by pushing the steering shaft toward the column.
5. Remove the flex coupling clamp from the steering gear input shaft and remove the gear from the frame side rail.
6. Reverse procedure to install.

1978–80 F-150 4 Wheel Drive & 1979–80 Bronco

Recirculating Ball Manual Steering Gear
1. Remove bolt attaching flex housing to coupling assembly shaft. Note alignment of bolt with groove in shaft.
2. Raise and support front of vehicle, then disconnect drag link from pitman arm using tool No. 3290-C.
3. Remove pitman arm nut and washer, then remove pitman arm from sector shaft using tool No. T64P-3590-F.
4. Support steering gear, then remove steering gear to frame attaching bolts and lower steering gear assembly from vehicle.

1978–80 F-150 4 Wheel Drive & Bronco

Worm & Roller Manual Steering Gear
1. Raise and support front of vehicle, then remove pitman arm attaching nut and washer.
2. Remove pitman arm from sector shaft using tool No. T64P-3590-F.
3. Remove bolts attaching steering gear to frame side rail, then lower front of vehicle.
4. Remove flex coupling clamp bolt and nut. Loosen clamp from coupling at end of steering column and separate coupling from steering gear input shaft by pushing steering shaft toward steering column.
5. Remove flex coupling clamp from steering gear input shaft, then remove steering gear assembly from vehicle.

1979–80 F-250 & 350 4 Wheel Drive

1. Remove two bolts attaching steering shaft to steering gear and column shaft.
2. Remove fan shroud attaching bolts and position shroud to right hand side of engine compartment.
3. Raise and support front of vehicle, then remove pitman arm nut and washer.
4. Disengage steering shaft coupling from steering gear shaft.
5. Remove steering gear to frame attaching bolts and lower steering gear assembly from vehicle.

F-B 500-800, 6000-7000

1. Loosen steering column lower clamp and slide clamp down.
2. Remove bolt and nut retaining pitman arm from sector shaft.
3. Remove retaining bolts and retaining strap if so equipped and remove steering gear from under vehicle.

L-N 500-900, 6000-9000, L-LT-LNT-W-WT 800-900, 8000-9000 & CL-9000

1. Remove Pitman arm.
2. Remove bolt and nut retaining U joint to steering gear shaft and slide joint off shaft.
3. Remove retaining bolts and straps if so equipped and remove steering gear.

P Series

1. Remove steering wheel.
2. Remove column bracket bolts from instrument panel.
3. Raise front of truck about 10 inches and install safety stands.
4. Remove pitman arm from sector shaft and remove steering gear retaining bolts.
5. Loosen steering column lower clamp.
6. Disconnect horn wire.
7. Move gear to left and remove it from beneath truck.
8. Reverse procedure to install.

C Series

1. Remove horn wire brush from steering column just below instrument panel bracket.
2. Remove U-joint upper nut and bolt.
3. Turn wheels to right and remove pitman arm from sector shaft.
4. Unfasten and remove steering gear with U-joint atttached.
5. Reverse procedure to install.

Ranchero with Integral Power Steering Gear

These models use an integral power steering gear which replaces the linkage power steering used previously. Remove the gear assembly as follows:
1. Disconnect pressure and return lines from gear and plug openings to prevent entry of dirt.
2. Remove two bolts that secure flex coupling to the gear and to the column.
3. Raise vehicle and remove pitman arm with suitable puller.
4. If vehicle is equipped with synchromesh transmission, remove clutch release lever retracting spring to provide clearance to remove gear.
5. Support gear and remove three gear attaching bolts.

Ranchero with Manual Steering Gear

1. Remove flex coupling bolts.
2. Remove pitman arm nut and remove pitman arm from sector shaft using a puller.
3. On vehicles with manual transmission it may be necessary to disconnect the clutch linkage and on V8 models it may be necessary to lower the exhaust system.
4. Unfasten and remove steering gear.

GMC

INDEX OF SERVICE OPERATIONS

> **NOTE:** This chapter contains service procedures on V6-305, 351, 379, 401, 432, 478 & V8-403, 455, 637 engines. Refer to Chevrolet Chapter for service procedures on 6-250, 292; V6-200, 229, 231; V8-267, 305, 307, 350, 366, 396, 400, 402, 427, 454 engines.

AXLES, DRIVING
	Page No.
Own Make Axle Service	1193
Eaton Axle Service	204
Spicer Axle Service	239
Timken Axle Service	241
Locking Differentials	192
Front Wheel Locking Hubs	505
Front Wheel Drive	1197

BRAKES
Adjustments	590
Air Brake Service	620
Anti-Skid Brakes	551
Bendix Twinplex Brake	608
Brake Booster Service	639
Disc Brakes	661
Hydraulic System Service	632
Parking Brake Service	612
Stopmaster Brake Service	599

CLUTCHES
Air-Hydraulic (Air-Pak)	468
Clutch Service	429
Hydraulic Clutch Controls	1181

COOLING SYSTEM
Cooling System Capacity	1142
Variable Speed Fans	10
Water Pump, Replace	1178

ELECTRICAL
Alternator Service	52
Dash Gauge Service	179
Distributors, Standard	141
Electronic Ignition	152
Generator Service	11
Ignition Coils and Resistors	7
Starting Motor Service	29
Starter Switch Service	21
Tune Up Service	2

ENGINE
	Page No.
Camshaft	1175
Crankshaft Rear Oil Seal	1175
Cylinder Head, Replace	1171
Piston and Rod, Assemble	1175
Rocker Arms	1172
Timing Case Cover	1174
Timing Gears	1175
Timing Chain	1175
Valves, Adjust	1172
Valve Guides	1174
Valve Lifters	1174
Valve Rotators	1172

ENGINE OILING
Crankcase Capacity	1142
Oil Pan, Replace	1176
Oil Pump Repairs	1176

FRONT SUSPENSION
Ball Joint Suspension	1201
Coil Spring Suspension	1200
Front Wheel Locking Hubs	505
Torsion Bar Suspension	1200

FUEL & EXHAUST
Blue Ox Compression Brake	677
Carburetor Adjustments	1178
Crankcase Ventilation	748
Emission Controls	750
Fuel Pump Service	183
Jacobs Engine Brake	678
L.P.G. Carburetion	190
Turbochargers	187

SPECIFICATIONS
Alternator and Regulator	1164
Carburetor Adjustment Specs.	1178
Crankshaft and Bearing	1167
Distributor	1157

	Page No.
Engine Tightening Torque	1168
General Engine Data	1145
Piston, Pin and Ring	1167
Starting Motor	1162
Tune Up	1148
Valve	1157
Wheel Alignment	1169

STEERING
Steering Gear, Replace	1204
Manual Steering Gear Service	680
Power Steering Gear Service	686

TRANSFER CASES | 469 |

TRANSMISSIONS, Manual
Own Make	1182
Clark	275
Fuller	289
New Process	329
Spicer	346
Warner	406, 1182

TRANSMISSIONS, Automatic
Allison AT-540, 543	510
Adjustments	1187
Allison MT-640, 643, 644, 650, 653 & 654CR	512
Adjustments	1187
Allison HT-740, 750	514
Pow-R-Flo	522
Adjustments	1192
Replace	1190
Turbo Hydra-Matic 200	541
Adjustments	1187
Turbo Hydra-Matic 250	544
Turbo Hydra-Matic 350	544
Adjustments	1188
Turbo Hydra-Matic 400, 475	538
Adjustments	1190

GMC

MODEL INDEX & ENGINE APPLICATION

ENGINE IDENTIFICATION—The GMC Service Parts Identification Plate is located inside the cab or on the truck firewall. Stamped on the plate is the model of the engine, transmission, auxiliary transmission, service brakes, front and rear axles. This information represents only the equipment on the vehicle when it was shipped from the factory.

Model	Year	Engine Make	Standard Engine Model	Crankcase Refill Capacity, Qts.	Cooling System Capacity, Qts.
SPRINT, 1971–77					
Sprint	1971–77	Chevrolet	6-250	4	12
Sprint	1971–73	Chevrolet	V8-307	4	15
Sprint	1974–75	Chevrolet	V8-350	4	15
Sprint	1976	Chevrolet	V8-305	4	17.2
CABALLERO					
Caballero	1978–79	Chevrolet	6-200	4	18.5
Caballero	1978–80	Buick	V6-231	4	15.5
Caballero	1980	Chevrolet	V6-229	4	18.7
2 AXLE CONVENTIONAL, 1970–80					
C-1500	1973–80	Chevrolet	6-250	4	15
C-1500	1979–80	Chevrolet	V8-305	4	17.6
C-1500	1973–80	Chevrolet	V8-307	4	16
C-1500	1974–80	Chevrolet	V8-350	4	18
CE-1500	1970–72	Chevrolet	V8-307	4	18
CM-1500	1970	Own	V6-305E	5	31 1/2
CS-1500	1970–71	Chevrolet	6-250	4	13
CS-1500	1972	Chevrolet	6-250	4	12
K-1500	1973–74	Chevrolet	6-250	4	13
K-1500	1975–80	Chevrolet	6-250	4	15
K-1500	1973	Chevrolet	V8-307	4	16
K-1500	1974–76	Chevrolet	V8-350	4	18
K-1500	1977–78	Chevrolet	V8-305	4	18
K-1500	1979	Chevrolet	V8-305	4	17.6
K-1500	1979–80	Chevrolet	V8-350	4	17.6
KE-1500	1970–71	Chevrolet	V8-307	4	18
KE-1500	1972	Chevrolet	8-307	4	16
KS-1500	1970–72	Chevrolet	6-250	4	13
CE-1550	1970–71	Chevrolet	V8-307	4	18
CE-1550	1972	Chevrolet	8-307	4	16
CS-1550	1970–71	Chevrolet	6-250	4	12
CS-1550	1972	Chevrolet	6-250	4	13
KE-1550	1970–71	Chevrolet	V8-307	4	18
KE-1550	1972	Chevrolet	8-307	4	16
KS-1550	1970–71	Chevrolet	6-250	4	12
KS-1550	1972	Chevrolet	6-250	4	13
C-2500	1979–80	Chevrolet	6-250	4	14.8
C-2500	1979–80	Chevrolet	V8-350	4	17.6
C-2500	1977–78	Chevrolet	V8-305	4	18
C-2500	1975–80	Chevrolet	6-292	5	15
C-2500	1973–76	Chevrolet	V8-350	4	18
C-2500	1974	Chevrolet	6-250	4	15
C-2500	1974	Chevrolet	V8-454	4	26
CE-2500	1970–72	Chevrolet	V8-307	4	18
CS-2500	1970–72	Chevrolet	6-250	4	12
K-2500	1974	Chevrolet	6-250	4	15
K-2500	1975–78	Chevrolet	6-292	5	15
K-2500	1973–76	Chevrolet	V8-350	4	18
K-2500	1977–78	Chevrolet	V8-305	4	18
K-2500	1979–80	Chevrolet	V8-350	4	18.0
KE-2500	1970–72	Chevrolet	V8-307	4	18
KS-2500	1970–72	Chevrolet	6-250	4	12
C-3500	1973–74	Chevrolet	6-250	4	15
C-3500	1975–80	Chevrolet	6-292	5	15
C-3500	1973	Chevrolet	V8-307	4	—
C-3500	1974–76	Chevrolet	V8-350	4	18
CE-3500	1970–72	Chevrolet	V8-307	4	18
CS-3500	1970–72	Chevrolet	6-250	4	12
K-3500	1977–80	Chevrolet	6-292	5	15
CE-4500	1970–72	Chevrolet	V8-350	4	21
CS-4500	1970	Chevrolet	6-250	4	12
CS-4500	1971–72	Chevrolet	6-250	4	16
PS-4500	1977–78	Chevrolet	6-292	5	17
C5D042	1979–80	Chevrolet	V8-350	5	21
CE-5000	1973–75	Chevrolet	V8-350	4	21
CS-5000	1973–74	Chevrolet	6-250	4	16
CS-5000	1975	Chevrolet	6-292	5	15
CS-5000	1976–78	Chevrolet	6-292	5	17
CE-5000	1975	Chevrolet	V8-350	5	18
CE-5000	1976–78	Chevrolet	V8-350	5	21
CM-5500	1970–72	Own	V6-305C	8	36
CE-5500	1970–72	Chevrolet	V8-350	4	20
CS-5500	1970–72	Chevrolet	6-292	5	17
CG-5500	1970	Own	V6-D478	8	29
CG-5500	1971–72	Own	V6-DH478	8	29
C6D042	1979–80	Chevrolet	V8-350	5	21
CM-6000	1973	Own	V6-305C	8	36
CM-6000	1974	Own	V6-379	8	36
CS-6000	1973–78	Chevrolet	6-292	5	17
CE-6000	1973–78	Chevrolet	V8-350	6	21
CD-6000	1977–78	Own	4-53N	14	23
CG-6000	1973–74	Own	V6-DH478	8	29
CD-6500	1978	Detroit	4-53T	14	23
CM-6500	1970	Own	V6-351	8	36
CM-6500	1971–72	Own	V6-351C	8	34
CM-6500	1973–74	Own	V6-379	8	34 1/2
CE-6500	1970	Chevrolet	V8-366	6	20 1/2
CE-6500	1971–78	Chevrolet	V8-366	6	33
CY-6500	1975	Caterpillar	V8-3708	—	44
C7D042	1979–80	Chevrolet	V8-366	6	33
HE-7500	1975–77	Chevrolet	V8-427	8	31.6
HE-7500	1978	Chevrolet	V8-427	8	36 1/2
HM-7500	1970	Own	V6-401	8	34 1/2
HM-7500	1971–72	Own	V6-401M	8	37
HM-7500	1973–74	Own	V6-432	8	37
HJ-7500A	1970	Own	V8-D637	12	39 1/2
HJ-7500	1971	Own	V8-DH637	12	47 1/2
HV-7500A	1970–71	Detroit	6V-53N	14	38
HV-7500	1972–78	Detroit	6V-53N	14	36 1/2
HY-7500	1975–77	Cat.	3208	10	50
HY-7500	1978	Cat.	320P	10	44
J8C042	1979–80	Chevrolet	V8-427	8	37
HC-9500	1971	Cummins	NHCT-270	36	61 1/2

Continued

GMC

MODEL INDEX & ENGINE APPLICATION—Continued

Model	Year	Engine Make	Standard Engine Model	Crankcase Refill Capacity, Qts.	Cooling System Capacity, Qts.
HC-9500	1972	Cummins	NTC-270	36	61½
HC-9500	1972–76	Cummins	NTC-290	28	61½
HC-9500	1977–78	Cummins	NTC-290	36	61½
HE-9500A	1970	Own	V8-637	12	42½
HE-9500	1971–72	Own	V8-637	12	51
J9C042	1979–80	Detroit	8V-71N	23	60
N9E042	1979–80	Detroit	8V-71N	23	92
N9F042	1979–80	Detroit	8V-71N	23	92

1970–80 3-AXLE CONVENTIONAL

Model	Year	Engine Make	Standard Engine Model	Crankcase Refill Capacity, Qts.	Cooling System Capacity, Qts.
C6D062	1979–80	Chevrolet	V8-366	6	33
C7D064	1979–80	Chevrolet	V8-366	6	33
HJ-9500	1977–78	Detroit	6V-92TT	18	57
HH-9500	1971	Detroit	8V-71NE	27	71
HH-9500	1972–78	Detroit	8V-71NE	27	80
HI-9500	1971–74	Detroit	6-71N	19	51.2
HI-9500	1975–78	Detroit	6-71N	22	51.2
HI-9500A	1970	Detroit	6-71NE	18	45
HN-9500	1970–74	Cummins	NHC-250	24	53
JE-7500	1975–77	Chevrolet	V8-427	8	31.6
JE-7500	1978	Chevrolet	V8-427	8	31½
JM-7500	1970	Own	V6-401	8	35½
JM-7500	1971–72	Own	V6-401M	11	37
JM-7500	1973–74	Own	V6-432	8	37
JJ-7500	1970	Own	V6-D637	12	39½
JJ-7500	1971	Own	V8-DH637	13½	47½
JV-7500A	1970	Detroit	6V-53N	19	38
JV-7500	1971–78	Detroit	6V-53N	14	36½
JY-7500	1975–78	Cat.	3208	10	7.5
J8C064	1979–80	Chevrolet	V8-427	8	37
JV-8500	1973	Detroit	6V-53N	—	36½
J9C064	1979–80	Detroit	8V-71N	23	60
JE-9500	1970	Own	V8-637	12	43
JE-9500	1971–72	Own	V8-637	12	51
JJ-9500	1977–78	Detroit	6V-92TT	18	57
JI-9500A	1970	Detroit	6-71NE	24	45
JH-9500	1971	Detroit	8V-71NE	27	71
JH-9500	1972–78	Detroit	8V-71NE	27	80
JI-9500	1971–74	Detroit	6-71N	19	51
JI-9500	1975–78	Detroit	6-71N	22	51
JN-9500	1970–74	Cummins	NHC-250	24	53
JC-9500	1971	Cummins	NHCT-270	36	61½
JC-9500	1972	Cummins	NTC-270	36	61½
JC-9500	1972–76	Cummins	NTC-290	28	61½
JC-9500	1977–78	Cummins	NTC-290	36	61½
JB-9500	1972–73	Cummins	V-903	18	61
ME-6500	1970	Chevrolet	V8-366	8	20½
ME-6500	1971–78	Chevrolet	V8-366	8	33.1
MM-6500	1974	Own	V6-432	8	36
MB-9500	1972–73	Cummins	V-903	18	61
MC-9500	1972–74	Cummins	NTC-350	28	63½
MC-9502	1978	Cummins	NTC-290	36	72
MI-9500A	1970	Detroit	6-71NE	24	45
MI-9500	1971–72	Detroit	6-71N	19	51
MH-9005	1977	Detroit	8V-71N	27	92
MH-9500A	1970–71	Detroit	8V-71NE	27	56
MH-9500	1972–76	Detroit	8V-71NE	27	73
MH-9502	1977–78	Detroit	8V-71N	27	92
MK-9005	1977	Detroit	8V-92	27	92
MK-9502	1977–78	Detroit	8V-92	27	92
N9E064	1977–80	Detroit	8V-71N	23	92
M9F064	1979–80	Detroit	8V-71N	23	92
MI-9501	1978	Detroit	6-71N	22	72
NI-9502	1977–78	Detroit	6-71N	22	72
NH-9502	1977–78	Detroit	8V-71N	27	92
NJ-9502	1977–78	Detroit	6V-92N	18	80
NC-9502	1977–78	Cummins	NTC-290	36	72

1970–80 2-AXLE TILT CAB

Model	Year	Engine Make	Standard Engine Model	Crankcase Refill Capacity, Qts.	Cooling System Capacity, Qts.
TM-5500	1970	Own	V6-305C	8	43½
TM-5500V	1971–72	Own	V6-305C	9	46.6
TE-5500	1970–72	Chevrolet	V8-350	4	28
TS-5500	1970–71	Chevrolet	6-292	5	23½
TG-5500	1970	Own	V6-DH478	13	35
TG-5500	1971–72	Own	V6-DH478	15	38
TE-6000	1973–75	Chevrolet	V8-350	6	29
TE-6000	1976–78	Chevrolet	V8-350	6	28.1
TE-6500	1977–78	Chevrolet	V8-366	6	35
TG-6000	1973–74	Own	V6-DH478	11	38½
TM-6000	1973–74	Own	V6-305C	8	46½
TM-6500	1970	Own	V6-351C	8	43½
TM-6500	1971–72	Own	V6-351C	9	45
TM-6500	1973–74	Own	V6-379	8	45
TE-6500	1970–78	Chevrolet	V8-366	6	35
W6N042	1979–80	Chevrolet	V8-350	5	28
W7N042	1979–80	Chevrolet	V8-366	6	35
TM-7500	1970	Own	V6-351C	8	42
TM-7500	1971–72	Own	V6-401M	11	47
TM-7500	1973–74	Own	V6-432	8	47
TV-7500A	1970	Detroit	6V-53N	19	33
TV-7500	1971–75	Detroit	6V-53N	16	31½
TE-9500A	1970	Own	V8-637	10	45½
TE-9500	1971–72	Own	V8-D637	12	54
TW-9500	1973	Detroit	6V-71N	—	54

1970–75 3-AXLE TILT CAB

Model	Year	Engine Make	Standard Engine Model	Crankcase Refill Capacity, Qts.	Cooling System Capacity, Qts.
WM-7500A	1970	Own	V6-401M	9	45½
WM-7500	1971–72	Own	V6-401M	11	47
WM-7500	1973–74	Own	V6-432	8	47
WV-7500	1972–75	Detroit	6V-53N	16	31½
WW-9500	1973	Detroit	6V-71N	—	54

1970–80 2-AXLE SET FORWARD TILT CAB

Model	Year	Engine Make	Standard Engine Model	Crankcase Refill Capacity, Qts.	Cooling System Capacity, Qts.
D9K042	1979–80	Detroit	8V-71N	23	72
D9L042	1979–80	Detroit	8V-71N	23	72
FI-9500A	1970	Detroit	6-71NE	18	48½
FH-9500A	1970	Detroit	8V-71NE	24	60½
FI-9502	1971–74	Detroit	6-71N	19	51
FI-9502	1975–78	Detroit	6-71N	22	51
FJ-9502	1975–76	Detroit	6V-92	18	73
FJ-9502	1977–78	Cummins	NTC-290	36	55
FH-9502	1971	Detroit	8V-71NE	27	56

Continued

GMC

MODEL INDEX & ENGINE APPLICATION—Continued

Model	Year	Engine Make	Standard Engine Model	Crankcase Refill Capacity, Qts.	Cooling System Capacity, Qts.
FH-9502	1972–78	Detroit	8V-71NE	27	73
FN-9502	1970–74	Cummins	NHC-250	24	53
FC-9502	1970–71	Cummins	NHCT-270	36	54½
FC-9502	1972	Cummins	NTC-270	36	55
FC-9502	1972–76	Cummins	NTC-290	28	55
FC-9502	1977–78	Cummins	NTC-290	36	55
FB-9502	1972–74	Cummins	V-903	18	61

1970–80 3-AXLE SET FORWARD TILT CAB

Model	Year	Engine Make	Standard Engine Model	Crankcase Refill Capacity, Qts.	Cooling System Capacity, Qts.
D9K064	1979–80	Detroit	8V-71N	23	72
D9L064	1979–80	Detroit	8V-71N	23	72
DI-9500A	1970	Detroit	6-71NE	18	48½
DH9500A	1970–72	Detroit	8V-71NE	24	60½
DI-9502	1971–74	Detroit	6-71N	19	51
DI-9502	1975–78	Detroit	6-71N	22	51
DH-9502	1971	Detroit	8V-71NE	27	56
DH-9502	1972–78	Detroit	8V-71NE	27	73
DN-9502	1970–74	Cummins	NHC-250	24	53
DC-9502	1970–71	Cummins	NHCT-270	36	54½
DC-9502	1972	Cummins	NTC-270	36	55
DC-9502	1972–76	Cummins	NTC-290	28	55
DC-9502	1977–78	Cummins	NTC-290	36	55
DB-9502	1972–78	Cummins	V-903	18	62
DJ-9502	1975–78	Detroit	6V-92	18	57
DK-9502	1975–76	Detroit	8V-92	27	74
DK-9502	1977–78	Detroit	8V-92	27	60
DP-9502	1972–78	Detroit	12V-71	34	98
DL-9502	1977–78	Cummins	KT450	40	21½
DR-9502	1977–78	Cat.	3406	32	69

1970–80 UNITIZED FORWARD CONTROL

Model	Year	Engine Make	Standard Engine Model	Crankcase Refill Capacity, Qts.	Cooling System Capacity, Qts.
G-1500	1979–80	Chevrolet	6-250	4	17
G-1500	1973–78	Chevrolet	6-250	4	15
G-1500	1973	Chevrolet	V8-307	4	16
G-1500	1974–75	Chevrolet	V8-350	4	16
G-1500	1976	Chevrolet	V8-350	4	18
GE-1500	1970–71	Chevrolet	V8-307	4	18
GE-1500	1972	Chevrolet	8-307	4	15.9
GS-1500	1970–71	Chevrolet	6-250	4	13
GS-1500	1972	Chevrolet	6-250	4	12.6
G-2500	1979–80	Chevrolet	6-250	4	17.2
G-2500	1979	Chevrolet	V8-350	4	20
G-2500	1973–78	Chevrolet	6-250	4	13
G-2500	1975–78	Chevrolet	6-292	5	15
G-2500	1973–75	Chevrolet	V8-350	4	16
G-2500	1976	Chevrolet	V8-350	4	18
GE-2500	1970	Chevrolet	V8-307	4	18
GE-2500	1971–72	Chevrolet	V8-350	4	18
GE-2500	1972	Chevrolet	8-350	4	16.1
GS-2500	1970–71	Chevrolet	6-250	4	13
GS-2500	1972	Chevrolet	6-250	4	12.6
G-3500	1979	Chevrolet	6-250	4	17.2
G-3500	1979–80	Chevrolet	V8-350	4	20
G-3500	1973–78	Chevrolet	6-250	4	13
G-3500	1975–78	Chevrolet	6-292	5	15
G-3500	1973–75	Chevrolet	V8-350	4	16
G-3500	1976	Chevrolet	V8-350	4	18
GE-3500	1971	Chevrolet	V8-350	4	18
GE-3500	1972	Chevrolet	8-350	4	16.1
GS-3500	1971–72	Chevrolet	6-250	4	13
TG-31303	1975–80	Chevrolet	V8-350	4	20
TG-31303	1976–78	Chevrolet	6-292	5	15
TG-31332	1979–80	Chevrolet	V8-350	4	20
TG-31603	1975–80	Chevrolet	V8-350	4	20
TG-31632	1979–80	Chevrolet	V8-350	4	20
TG-31603	1976–78	Chevrolet	6-292	5	15

1970–80 CHASSIS FORWARD CONTROL

Model	Year	Engine Make	Standard Engine Model	Crankcase Refill Capacity, Qts.	Cooling System Capacity, Qts.
P-1500	1973–74	Chevrolet	6-250	4	13
P-1500	1975–80	Chevrolet	6-292	5	14
PS-1500	1970–71	Chevrolet	6-250	4	21
PS-1500	1972	Chevrolet	6-250	4	13.5
P-2500	1973–74	Chevrolet	6-250	4	13
P-2500	1979	Chevrolet	V8-350	4	16.8
P-2500	1975–80	Chevrolet	6-292	5	14
P-2500	1973	Chevrolet	V8-307	4	14.9
P-2500	1974–76	Chevrolet	V8-350	4	17
PE-2500	1972	Chevrolet	V8-307	4	16.9
PE-2500	1970–71	Chevrolet	V8-307	4	18½
PS-2500	1970–72	Chevrolet	6-250	4	13½
P-3500	1973–74	Chevrolet	6-250	4	13
P-3500	1975–80	Chevrolet	6-292	5	14
P-3500	1973	Chevrolet	V8-307	4	14.9
P-3500	1979	Chevrolet	V8-350	4	16.8
P-3500	1974–76	Chevrolet	V8-350	4	17
P-3500	1974–75	Chevrolet	V8-454	4	27
PE-3500	1972	Chevrolet	V8-307	4	16.9
PE-3500	1970–72	Chevrolet	V8-307	4	18½
PE-3500	1971–72	Chevrolet	V8-350	4	16.9
PS-3500	1970–72	Chevrolet	6-250	4	13½
PS-4500	1970	Chevrolet	6-250	5	14
PS-4500	1977	Chevrolet	6-292	5	17
TP-30832	1979–80	Chevrolet	V8-350	4	19
TP-30832	1975–78	Chevrolet	V8-350	4	20
TP-31132	1979–80	Chevrolet	V8-350	4	19
TP-31132	1975–78	Chevrolet	V8-350	4	20
TP-31432	1975–80	Chevrolet	V8-350	4	20
TP-31832	1979–80	Chevrolet	V8-454	6	24.5
TP-31832	1975–78	Chevrolet	V8-454	4	25

1970–80 SCHOOL BUS CHASSIS

Model	Year	Engine Make	Standard Engine Model	Crankcase Refill Capacity, Qts.	Cooling System Capacity, Qts.
B6P042	1979–80	Chevrolet	V8-350	5	21
SM-5500M	1970–72	Own	V6-305C	8	36
SS-5500M	1970–72	Chevrolet	6-292	6	16
SG-5500	1970	Own	V6-D478	8	32½
SG-5500	1971–72	Own	V6-DH478	15	29
SE-5500	1970–72	Chevrolet	V8-350	4	20
SE-6000	1973–77	Chevrolet	V8-350	6	21
SE-6000	1978	Chevrolet	V8-350	5	25
SG-6000	1973–74	Own	V6-DH478	11	29
SM-6000	1973–74	Own	V6-305C	8	36
SS-6000	1973–74	Chevrolet	6-292	5	16½
RM-7500	1970–72	Own	V6-401M	9	41½
RM-7500	1973	Own	V6-432	—	40.7

GMC

GENERAL ENGINE SPECIFICATIONS

Year	Engine Model	Carb. Type	Bore & Stroke	Comp. Ratio	Horsepower @ R.P.M.	Torque Ft. Lbs. @ R.P.M.	Comp. Pressure Cranking Speed	Governed Speed R.P.M. Full Load	Normal Oil Pressure Lbs.
1970	6-250	1 Bore	3⁷/₈ × 3.53	8.5	155 @ 4200	235 @ 1600	130	②	40–60
	6-292	1 Bore	3⁷/₈ × 4.12	8.0	170 @ 4000	275 @ 1600	130	②	40–60
	V6-305C	2 Bore	4.25 × 3.58	7.75	170 @ 4000	277 @ 1600	⑦	3400	60
	V8-307①	2 Bore	3⁷/₈ × 3.25	9.0	200 @ 4600	300 @ 2400	150	②	30
	V8-350①	2 Bore	4.0 × 3.48	8.0	215 @ 4000	335 @ 2800	150	②	30
	V8-350①	4 Bore	4.0 × 3.48	9.0	255 @ 4600	355 @ 3000	150	②	30
	V6-351C	2 Bore	4.56 × 3.58	7.5	195 @ 3600	314 @ 1600	⑦	3600	60
	V8-366①	4 Bore	3.937 × 3.76	8.0	235 @ 4000	345 @ 2600	⑦	②	50–75
	V8-396①	4 Bore	4.094 × 3.76	9.0	310 @ 4800	400 @ 3200	150	②	50–75
	V6-401M	2 Bore	4.87 × 3.58	7.5	237 @ 4000	372 @ 1600	⑦	3400	60
	V8-427①	4 Bore	4.25 × 3.76	8.0	260 @ 4000	405 @ 2600	⑦	②	50–75
	V6-478M	2 Bore	5.125 × 3.86	7.5	254 @ 3700	442 @ 1400	⑦	3200	60
	V8-637	2 Bore	5.125 × 3.86	7.5	275 @ 2800	600 @ 1600	⑦	2800	60
1971	6-250	1 Bore	3.87 × 3.53	8.5	145 @ 4200	230 @ 1600	⑦	4000	40–60
	6-292	1 Bore	3.87 × 4.12	8.0	165 @ 4000⑧	270 @ 1600	⑦	3900	40–60
	V6-305C	2 Bore	4.25 × 3.58	7.75	170 @ 4000	277 @ 1600	⑦	3400	57
	V8-307①	2 Bore	3.87 × 3.25	8.5	200 @ 4600⑨	300 @ 2400⑩	⑦	—	30
	V8-350①	2 Bore	4.0 × 3.48	8.0	215 @ 4000	335 @ 2800	⑦	4000	30
	V8-350①	4 Bore	4.0 × 3.48	8.5	250 @ 4600	350 @ 3000	⑦	4000	30
	V6-351C	2 Bore	4.56 × 3.58	7.5	195 @ 3600	314 @ 1600	⑦	3600	57
	V8-366①	4 Bore	3.937 × 3.76	8.0	235 @ 4000	345 @ 2600	⑦	4000	40–55
	V8-402①	4 Bore	4.126 × 3.76	8.5	300 @ 4800	400 @ 3200	⑦	—	45–55
	V6-401M	2 Bore	4.87 × 3.58	7.5	237 @ 4000	372 @ 1600	⑦	3400	60
	V8-427①	4 Bore	4.251 × 3.76	8.0	260 @ 4000	405 @ 2600	⑦	4000	40–55
	V6-478M	2 Bore	5.125 × 3.86	7.5	254 @ 3700	442 @ 1400	⑦	3200	60
	V8-637	2 Bore	5.125 × 3.86	7.5	275 @ 2800	600 @ 1600	⑦	2800	60
1972	6-250	1 Bore	3.87 × 3.53	8.5	110 @ 3600	185 @ 1600	⑦	4000	40–60
	6-292	1 Bore	3.87 × 4.12	8.0	125 @ 3600	225 @ 2400	⑦	3900	40–60
	6-292	1 Bore	3.87 × 4.12	8.0	142 @ 3800	253 @ 2000	⑦	—	40–60
	V6-305C	2 Bore	4.25 × 3.58	7.75	—	—	⑦	3400	57
	V8-307①	2 Bore	3.87 × 3.25	8.5	135 @ 4000⑪	230 @ 2400⑪	⑦	—	30
	V8-350①	2 Bore	4.0 × 3.48	8.0	155 @ 4000⑪	280 @ 2400⑪	⑦	4000	30
	V8-350①	4 Bore	4.0 × 3.48	8.5	175 @ 4000⑪	290 @ 2400⑪	⑦	—	30
	V6-351C	2 Bore	4.56 × 3.58	7.0	154 @ 3600⑪	254 @ 1600⑪	⑦	3600	57
	V8-366①	4 Bore	3.937 × 3.76	8.0	200 @ 4000⑪	295 @ 2800⑪	⑦	4000	40–55
	V8-402①	4 Bore	4.126 × 3.76	8.5	210 @ 4000⑪	320 @ 2800⑪	⑦	—	45–55
	V6-401M	2 Bore	4.87 × 3.58	7.5	175 @ 3400⑪	298 @ 1600⑪	⑦	3400	60
	V8-427①	4 Bore	4.25 × 3.76	8.0	230 @ 4000⑪	360 @ 2400⑪	⑦	4000	40–55
	V8-454	4 Bore	4.251 × 4.00	8.5	270 @ 4000	390 @ 3200	⑦	—	40
	V6-478M	2 Bore	5.125 × 3.86	7.5	192 @ 3200⑪	371 @ 1400⑪	⑦	3200	60
	V8-637	2 Bore	5.125 × 3.86	7.0	219 @ 2800⑪	478 @ 1600⑪	⑦	2800	60
1973	6-250	1 Bore	3.87 × 3.53	8.25	100 @ 3600	175 @ 1600	⑦	3400	40–60
	6-292	1 Bore	3.87 × 4.12	8.0	120 @ 3600	215 @ 2000	⑦	3350	40–60
	6-292	1 Bore	3.87 × 4.12	8.0	130 @ 3600	225 @ 2000	⑦	3350	40–60
	V6-305C	2 Bore	4.25 × 3.58	7.75	148 @ 4000	238 @ 1600	⑦	3400	57
	V8-307①	2 Bore	3.875 × 3.25	8.5	115 @ 3600	205 @ 2000	⑦	—	30
	V8-307⑦	2 Bore	3.875 × 3.25	8.5	115 @ 3600	205 @ 2000	⑦	—	30
	V8-350①	2 Bore	4.00 × 3.48	8.5	145 @ 4000	255 @ 2400	⑦	4000	40
	V8-350①	4 Bore	4.00 × 3.48	8.5	155 @ 4000	255 @ 2400	⑦	4000	40
	V8-350①	2 Bore	4.00 × 3.48	8.0	160 @ 4000	265 @ 2400	⑦	4000	40
	V8-350①	4 Bore	4.00 × 3.48	8.5	175 @ 4000	260 @ 2800	⑦	4000	40
	V8-366①	4 Bore	3.937 × 3.76	8.0	200 @ 4000	310 @ 2800	⑦	4000	40–55
	V6-379	2 Bore	4.56 × 3.86	7.5	170 @ 3600	280 @ 1600	⑦	3400	57
	V8-427①	4 Bore	4.25 × 3.76	8.0	230 @ 4000	360 @ 2800	⑦	4000	40–55

Continued

GMC

GENERAL ENGINE SPECIFICATIONS—Continued

Year	Engine Model	Carb. Type	Bore & Stroke	Comp. Ratio	Horsepower @ R.P.M.	Torque Ft. Lbs. @ R.P.M.	Comp. Pressure Cranking Speed	Governed Speed R.P.M. Full Load	Normal Oil Pressure Lbs.
	V6-432	2 Bore	4.875 × 3.86	7.5	190 @ 3200	331 @ 1600	⑦	3200	60
	V8-350①	4 Bore	4.25 × 4.00	8.25	240 @ 4000	355 @ 2800	⑦	—	40
	V8-454	4 Bore	4.25 × 4.00	8.25	245 @ 4000	375 @ 2800	⑦	—	40
	V8-454①	4 Bore	4.25 × 4.00	8.25	250 @ 4000	365 @ 2800	⑦	—	40
	V8-455	4 Bore	4.125 × 4.250	8.5	—	—	⑦	—	—
	V6-478	2 Bore	5.125 × 3.86	7.0	192 @ 3200	371 @ 1400	⑦	3200	60
1974	6-250	1 Bore	3.875 × 3.53	8.5	100 @ 3600	175 @ 1600⑬	⑦	3600	40–60
	6-292	1 Bore	3.875 × 4.12	8.0	120 @ 3600	215 @ 2000	⑦	3600	40–60
	6-292	1 Bore	3.875 × 4.12	8.0	130 @ 3600	225 @ 2000	⑦	3600	40–60
	V6-305C	2 Bore	4.25 × 3.58	7.75	148 @ 4000	238 @ 1600	⑦	3400	57
	V8-350①	2 Bore	4.00 × 3.48	8.5	145 @ 3600	205 @ 2000	⑦	—	40
	V8-350①	4 Bore	4.00 × 3.48	8.5	155 @ 4000	255 @ 2400	⑦	—	40
	V8-350①	2 Bore	4.00 × 3.48	8.0	160 @ 4000	265 @ 2400	⑦	4000⑫	40
	V8-366①	4 Bore	3.937 × 3.76	8.0	200 @ 4000	310 @ 2800	⑦	4000⑫	40–55
	V6-379	2 Bore	4.56 × 3.86	7.5	170 @ 3600	280 @ 1600	⑦	3400	57
	V8-400①	2 Bore	4.125 × 3.75	8.5	150 @ 3200	295 @ 2000	⑦	—	40
	V8-400①	4 Bore	4.125 × 3.75	8.5	180 @ 3800	290 @ 2400	⑦	—	40
	V8-427①	4 Bore	4.25 × 3.76	8.0	230 @ 4000	360 @ 2800	⑦	4000	40–55
	V6-432	2 Bore	4.87 × 3.86	7.5	190 @ 3200	331 @ 1600	⑦	3200	60
	V8-454①	4 Bore	4.25 × 4.00	8.25	240 @ 4000	355 @ 2800	⑦	—	40
	V8-455	4 Bore	4.125 × 4.250	8.5	265 @ 4300	375 @ 2800	⑦	—	—
	V6-478	2 Bore	5.125 × 3.86	7.0	192 @ 3200	371 @ 1400	⑦	3200	60
1975	6-250	1 Bore	3.875 × 3.53	8.25	105 @ 3800	185 @ 1200	130	—	40–60
	6-292	1 Bore	3.87 × 4.12	8.0	120 @ 3600	215 @ 2000	130	—	40–60
	6-292	1 Bore	3.87 × 4.12	8.0	130 @ 3600	225 @ 2000	130	4000	40–60
	V8-350①	2 Bore	4.00 × 3.48	8.5	145 @ 3500	250 @ 2200	150	—	40
	V8-350①	2 Bore	4.00 × 3.48	8.0	160 @ 4000	265 @ 2400	150	4000	30
	V8-350①	4 Bore	4.00 × 3.48	8.5	155 @ 3800	250 @ 2800	150	—	40
	V8-350①	4 Bore	4.00 × 3.48	8.5	160 @ 3800	250 @ 2400	150	—	40
	V8-366①	4 Bore	3.937 × 3.76	8.0	200 @ 4000	305 @ 2800	—	4000	40–55
	V8-400①	4 Bore	4.126 × 3.76	8.5	175 @ 3600	305 @ 2000	150	—	40
	V8-427①	4 Bore	4.25 × 3.76	8.0	220 @ 4000	360 @ 2400	—	4000	40–55
	V8-454①	4 Bore	4.25 × 4.00	8.15	215 @ 4000	350 @ 2400	150	—	40
	V8-454①	4 Bore	4.25 × 4.00	8.15	245 @ 4000	355 @ 3000	150	—	40
	V8-454①	4 Bore	4.25 × 4.00	8.15	245 @ 4000	375 @ 2800	150	—	40
	V8-455	4 Bore	4.126 × 4.250	8.5	212 @ 3400	344 @ 2400	⑦	—	30–45
1976	6-250①⑭	1 Carb.	3.87 × 3.53	8.25	105 @ 3800	185 @ 1200	130	3800	40–60
	6-250①⑮	1 Bore	3.87 × 3.53	8.0	100 @ 3600	175 @ 1800	130	3600	40–60
	6-292①⑭	1 Bore	3.87 × 4.12	8.0	120 @ 3600	215 @ 2000	130	3600	40–60
	6-292①⑮	1 Bore	3.87 × 4.12	8.0	130 @ 3600	225 @ 2000	130	3600	40–60
	V8-305	2 Bore	3.736 × 3.48	8.5	140 @ 3800	245 @ 2000	155	—	32–40
	V8-350①⑭	2 Bore	4.00 × 3.48	8.5	145 @ 3800	250 @ 2200	150	—	40
	V8-350①⑮	2 Bore	4.00 × 3.48	8.0	160 @ 4000	265 @ 2400	150	—	30
	V8-350	4 Bore	4.00 × 3.48	8.5	165 @ 3800	260 @ 2200	150	—	32–40
	V8-350①⑭	4 Bore	4.00 × 3.48	8.5	165 @ 3800	260 @ 2400	160	—	40
	V8-350①⑮	4 Bore	4.00 × 3.48	8.5	165 @ 3800	255 @ 2800	160	—	40
	V8-366①⑯	4 Bore	3.937 × 3.76	8.0	195 @ 4000	290 @ 2800	150	4000	40–55
	V8-366①⑰	4 Bore	3.937 × 3.76	8.0	200 @ 4000	305 @ 2800	150	4000	40–55
	V8-400①	4 Bore	4.125 × 3.75	8.5	175 @ 3600	290 @ 2800	160	—	40
	V8-400①	4 Bore	4.125 × 3.75	8.5	175 @ 3600	305 @ 2000	160	—	40
	V8-427①	4 Bore	4.25 × 3.76	7.8	220 @ 4000	360 @ 2400	150	4000	40–55
	V8-454①⑭	4 Bore	4.25 × 4.00	8.25	245 @ 3800	365 @ 2800	160	—	40
	V8-454①⑱	4 Bore	4.25 × 4.00	8.15⑳	240 @ 3800	370 @ 2800	160	—	40
	V8-454①⑲	4 Bore	4.25 × 4.00	8.15⑳	250 @ 3800	385 @ 2800	160	—	40
	V8-455	4 Bore	4.126 × 4.250	8.5	212 @ 3400	344 @ 2400	⑦	—	30–45

Continued

GMC

GENERAL ENGINE SPECIFICATIONS—Continued

Year	Engine Model	Carb. Type	Bore & Stroke	Comp. Ratio	Horsepower @ R.P.M.	Torque Ft. Lbs. @ R.P.M.	Comp. Pressure Cranking Speed	Governed Speed R.P.M. Full Load	Normal Oil Pressure Lbs.
1977	6-250①③	1 Bore	3.87 × 3.53	8.25	110 @ 3800	195 @ 1600	—	—	40–60
	6-250①④	1 Bore	3.87 × 3.53	8.25	90 @ 3600	175 @ 1800	—	—	40–60
	6-292①⑭	1 Bore	3.87 × 4.12	8	120 @ 3600	215 @ 2000	130	—	40–60
	6-292①⑮	1 Bore	3.87 × 4.12	8	130 @ 3600	220 @ 2000	130	—	40–60
	V8-305①④	2 Bore	3.74 × 3.48	8.5	140 @ 3800	235 @ 2000	—	—	32–40
	V8-305①③	2 Bore	3.74 × 3.48	8.5	145 @ 3800	245 @ 2400	—	—	32–40
	V8-350①㉑㉒	4 Bore	4.00 × 3.48	8.5	170 @ 3800	270 @ 2400	160	—	40
	V8-350①㉑㉓	4 Bore	4.00 × 3.48	8.5	160 @ 3800	260 @ 2400	160	—	40
	V8-350①③	4 Bore	4.00 × 3.48	8.5	165 @ 3800	260 @ 2400	160	—	40
	V8-350①④	4 Bore	4.00 × 3.48	8.5	165 @ 3800	255 @ 2800	160	—	40
	V8-366①	4 Bore	3.937 × 3.76	8	200 @ 4000	305 @ 2800	150	—	40–55
	V8-400①	4 Bore	4.125 × 3.75	8.5	175 @ 3600	290 @ 2800	—	—	40
	V8-403	4 Bore	4.351 × 3.385	7.9	200 @ 3600	330 @ 2400	—	—	30–45
	V8-427①	4 Bore	4.25 × 3.76	—	220 @ 4000	360 @ 2400	150	—	40–55
	V8-454①③	4 Bore	4.25 × 4.00	8.5	245 @ 3800	365 @ 2800	—	—	40
	V8-454①④㉒	4 Bore	4.25 × 4.00	8.5	240 @ 3800	370 @ 2800	—	—	40
	V8-454①④㉓	4 Bore	4.25 × 4.00	8.5	250 @ 3800	385 @ 2800	—	—	40
	V8-455	4 Bore	4.126 × 4.250	8.5	212 @ 3400	344 @ 2400	⑦	—	—
1978	V6-200①㉔㉛	2 Bore	3.50 × 3.48	8.2	95 @ 3800	160 @ 2000	—	—	34–39
	V6-231①㉔㉛	2 Bore	3.80 × 3.40	8.0	105 @ 3800	180 @ 2000	—	—	37
	6-250①㉔	1 Bore	3.87 × 3.53	8.0	100 @ 3600	175 @ 1800	—	—	40–60
	6-292①㉔	1 Bore	3.87 × 4.12	8.0	130 @ 3600	220 @ 2000	—	—	40–60
	V8-305①㉔	2 Bore	3.74 × 3.48	8.5	140 @ 3800	245 @ 2400	—	—	—
	V8-350①㉔	4 Bore	4.00 × 3.48	8.5	165 @ 4000	270 @ 2400	—	—	—
	V8-366①㉔	4 Bore	3.937 × 3.76	8.0	200 @ 4000	305 @ 2800	—	—	—
	V8-400①㉔	4 Bore	4.125 × 3.75	8.5	170 @ 3600	290 @ 2800	—	—	—
	V8-403	4 Bore	4.35 × 3.38	7.9	200 @ 3600	330 @ 2400	⑦	—	30–45
	V8-427①㉔	4 Bore	4.25 × 3.76	8.1	220 @ 4000	360 @ 2400	—	4000	—
	V8-454①㉔	4 Bore	4.25 × 4.00	8.5	240 @ 3800	370 @ 2800	—	—	—
1979	V6-200①㉛	2 Bore	3.50 × 3.48	8.2	94 @ 4000	154 @ 2000	⑦	—	34–39
	V6-231①㉛	2 Bore	3.80 × 3.40	8.0	115 @ 3800	190 @ 2000	⑦	—	37
	6-250①㉕	2 Bore	3.87 × 3.53	8.3	130 @ 4000	210 @ 2000	—	—	40–60
	6-250①㉖	2 Bore	3.87 × 3.53	8.3	125 @ 4000	205 @ 2000	—	—	40–60
	6-250①㉗	2 Bore	3.87 × 3.53	8.3	130 @ 4000	205 @ 2000	—	—	40–60
	6-292①㉘㉙	1 Bore	3.87 × 4.12	7.8	115 @ 3400	215 @ 1600	—	—	40–60
	6-292①㉚	1 Bore	3.87 × 4.12	7.8	125 @ 3600	225 @ 2000	—	4000	40–60
	V8-267①	2 Bore	3.50 × 3.48	8.5	125 @ 3800	215 @ 2400	⑦	—	40
	V8-305①㉜	2 Bore	3.74 × 3.48	8.4	140 @ 4000	240 @ 2000	—	—	45
	V8-305①㉒㉛	4 Bore	3.74 × 3.48	8.4	160 @ 4000	235 @ 2400	⑦	—	45
	V8-305①㉓㉛	4 Bore	3.74 × 3.48	8.4	155 @ 4000	225 @ 2400	—	—	45
	V8-350①⑮	2 Bore	4.00 × 3.48	8.0	161 @ 3800	275 @ 2400	⑦	4000	30
	V8-350①⑭㉛	4 Bore	4.00 × 3.48	8.2	165 @ 3800	260 @ 2400	—	—	45
	V8-350①⑤⑭㉜	4 Bore	4.00 × 3.48	8.2	165 @ 3600	270 @ 2000	—	—	45
	V8-350①⑥⑭㉜	4 Bore	4.00 × 3.48	8.2	155 @ 3600	260 @ 2000	—	—	45
	V8-350①⑧⑭㉜	4 Bore	4.00 × 3.48	8.3	165 @ 3800	255 @ 2800	—	—	45
	V8-366①⑨⑯	4 Bore	3.937 × 3.76	7.6	180 @ 4000	290 @ 2400	—	4000	40–55
	V8-366①⑩⑰	4 Bore	3.937 × 3.76	7.6	190 @ 4000	305 @ 2400	—	4000	40–55
	V8-400①㉕	4 Bore	4.125 × 3.75	8.2	185 @ 3600	300 @ 2400	—	—	40
	V8-400①⑪	4 Bore	4.125 × 3.75	8.2	170 @ 3600	305 @ 1600	—	—	40
	V8-400①⑧	4 Bore	4.125 × 3.75	8.3	180 @ 3600	310 @ 2400	—	—	40
	V8-427①⑯	4 Bore	4.25 × 3.76	7.5	195 @ 3800	340 @ 2400	—	4000	40–55
	V8-427①⑰	4 Bore	4.25 × 3.76	7.5	210 @ 3800	350 @ 2400	—	4000	40–55
	V8-454①⑬	4 Bore	4.25 × 4.00	7.6	205 @ 3600	335 @ 2800	—	—	40
	V8-454①⑨	4 Bore	4.25 × 4.00	7.6	210 @ 3800	340 @ 2800	—	—	40
	V8-454①⑬⑰	4 Bore	4.25 × 4.00	7.6	225 @ 4000	365 @ 2400	—	4000	40–55

Continued

GMC

GENERAL ENGINE SPECIFICATIONS—Continued

Year	Engine Model	Carb. Type	Bore & Stroke	Comp. Ratio	Horsepower @ R.P.M.	Torque Ft. Lbs. @ R.P.M.	Comp. Pressure Cranking Speed	Governed Speed R.P.M. Full Load	Normal Oil Pressure Lbs.
1980	V6-229①	2 Bore	3.736 × 3.48	8.6	115 @ 4000	175 @ 2000	—	—	45
	V6-231①	2 Bore	3.80 × 3.4	8.0	110 @ 3800	190 @ 1600	—	—	45
	6-250①	2 Bore	3.876 × 3.53	8.25	—	—	—	—	—
	V8-267①	2 Bore	3.50 × 3.48	8.3	120 @ 3600	215 @ 2000	—	—	45
	6-292①㉙	1 Bore	3.876 × 4.12	7.8	115 @ 3400	215 @ 1600	—	—	50
	6-292①㉚	1 Bore	3.876 × 4.12	7.8	125 @ 3600	225 @ 1600	—	—	50
	V8-305①㉓	4 Bore	3.74 × 3.48	8.6	155 @ 4000	230 @ 2400	—	—	45
	V8-305①㉒	4 Bore	3.74 × 3.48	8.6	155 @ 4000	240 @ 1600	—	—	45
	V8-350①	2 Bore	4.0 × 3.48	8.0	161 @ 3800	275 @ 2400	—	4000	30
	V8-366①⑨	4 Bore	3.937 × 3.76	7.6	180 @ 4000	290 @ 2400	—	4000	40–55
	V8-366①⑩	4 Bore	3.937 × 3.76	7.6	190 @ 4000	305 @ 2400	—	4000	40–55
	V8-427①⑯	4 Bore	4.25 × 3.76	7.5	195 @ 3800	340 @ 2400	—	4000	40–55
	V8-427①⑰	4 Bore	4.25 × 3.76	7.5	210 @ 3800	350 @ 2400	—	4000	40–55
	V8-454①⑰	4 Bore	4.25 × 4.00	7.6	225 @ 4000	365 @ 2400	—	4000	40–55

①—See Chevrolet Chapter for service procedures on this engine.
②—Various speed stamped on governor.
③—Except heavy duty emissions.
④—Heavy duty emissions.
⑤—Light & medium duty emissions (G.V.W.R. 8500 lbs. or under) except Calif. & high altitude.
⑥—California light & medium duty emissions (G.V.W.R. 8500 lbs. or under) & high altitude emissions (G.V.W.R. 6000 lbs. or under).
⑦—Lowest reading must be within 80% of highest reading.
⑧—Heavy duty emissions (G.V.W.R. 8501 lbs. or above).
⑨—School bus chassis.
⑩—Except school bus chassis.
⑪—California light & medium duty emissions (G.V.W.R. 8500 lbs. or under).
⑫—4100 with AT 475 transmission.
⑬—Light & medium duty emissions (G.V.W.R. 8500 lbs. or under).
⑭—Light Duty.
⑮—Heavy Duty.
⑯—Single Exhaust.
⑰—Dual Exhaust.
⑱—Heavy Duty except California.
⑲—California Heavy Duty.
⑳—C1500/F44 and C1500-2500 models, 8.25:1.
㉑—Sprint.
㉒—Exc. Calif.
㉓—Calif.
㉔—Horsepower & torque ratings may vary slightly depending on application.
㉕—Light & medium duty emissions (G.V.W.R. 8500 lbs. or under) except Calif.
㉖—California Series 1500 Light duty emission (G.V.W.R. 6000 lbs. or under).
㉗—California Series 2500 & 3500 Light & medium duty emissions (G.V.W.R. 8500 lbs. or under).
㉘—P-1500-3500 & C & K-3500.
㉙—P4TO42.
㉚—C5D042 & CD6042.
㉛—Caballero.
㉜—Except Caballero.

TUNE UP SPECIFICATIONS

The following specifications are published from the latest information available. This data should be used only in the absence of a decal affixed in the engine compartment.

★ When using a timing light, disconnect vacuum hose or tube at distributor and plug opening in hose or tube so idle speed will not be affected.

● When checking compression, lowest cylinder must be within 80 percent of highest.

▲ Before removing wires from distributor cap, determine location of the No. 1 wire in cap, as distributor position may have been altered from that shown at the end of this chart.

Year & Engine	Spark Plug Type	Spark Plug Gap	Firing Orders Fig.▲	Ignition Timing BTDC①★ Man. Trans.	Ignition Timing BTDC①★ Auto. Trans.	Location	Curb Idle Speed② Man. Trans.	Curb Idle Speed② Auto. Trans.	Fuel Pump Pressure
1980									
V6-229	R45TS	.045	A	8°	12°	Damper	700/800	600/675D	4½–6
V6-231 Exc. Calif.	R45TSX	.060	B	—	15°	Damper	—	560/670D	3 Min.
V6-231 Calif.	R45TSX	.060	B	—	15°	Damper	—	600D	3 Min.
6-250 Exc. Calif.	R46TS	.035	C	10°	10°	Damper	450/750	450/650D	4½–6
6-250 C&G-1500 Calif.	R46TS	.035	C	10°	10°	Damper	425/750	425/600D	4½–6
6-250 C&G-2500 Calif.	R46TS	.035	C	10°	8°	Damper	425/750	425/600D	4½–6
6-292	R44T	.035	C	8°	8°	Damper	700	700N	4–5
V8-267	R45TS	.045	D	—	4°	Damper	—	500/600D	7½–9
V8-305 Caballero Exc. Calif.	R45TS	.045	D	4°	4°	Damper	700	500/600D	7½–9
V8-350 Caballero Calif.	R45TS	.045	D	—	4°	Damper	—	550/650D	7½–9
V8-305 Series 1500–3500	R45TS	.045	D	—	8°	Damper	600/700	500/600D	③
V8-350 2 Barrel Carb. B, C, P&W-4, 5, 6	R44T	.045	D	4°④	4°④	Damper	700	700N	7–9

Continued

GMC

TUNE UP SPECIFICATIONS—Continued

The following specifications are published from the latest information available. This data should be used only in the absence of a decal affixed in the engine compartment.

★ When using a timing light, disconnect vacuum hose or tube at distributor and plug opening in hose or tube so idle speed will not be affected.

● When checking compression, lowest cylinder must be within 80 percent of highest.

▲ Before removing wires from distributor cap, determine location of the No. 1 wire in cap, as distributor position may have been altered from that shown at the end of this chart.

Year & Engine	Spark Plug Type	Spark Plug Gap	Firing Orders Fig.▲	Ignition Timing BTDC①★ Man. Trans.	Ignition Timing BTDC①★ Auto. Trans.	Location	Curb Idle Speed② Man. Trans.	Curb Idle Speed② Auto. Trans.	Fuel Pump Pressure
1980—Continued									
V8-350 4 Barrel Carb.⑤	R45TS	.045	D	8°⑥	8°⑥	Damper	700	500/600D	③
V8-350 4 Barrel Carb. Exc. Calif.⑦	R44T	.045	D	4°	4°	Damper	700	700N	③
V8-350 4 Barrel Carb. Calif.⑦	R44T	.045	D	6°	6°	Damper	700	700N	③
V8-366	R43T	.045	D	8°	8°	Damper	700	700N	7–9
V8-400 G-2500	R45TS	.045	D	—	4°	Damper	—	500/600D	③
V8-400 K-2500 & G, K-3500 Exc. Calif.	R44T	.045	D	—	4°	Damper	—	700N	③
V8-400 K-2500 & G, K-3500 Calif.	R44T	.045	D	—	6°	Damper	—	700N	③
V8-427	R42T	.045	D	8°	8°	Damper	700	700N	7–9
V8-454 C-2500 & C, P-3500	R44T	.045	D	4°	4°	Damper	700	700N	7½–9
V8-454 C7D	R42T	.045	D	8°	8°	Damper	700	700N	7–9
1979									
V6-200	R45TS	.045	A	8°	12°	Damper	700/800	600/700D	4¼–5¾
V6-231 Exc. Calif. & High Alt.	R45TSX	.060	B	—	15°	Damper	—	⑧	3 Min.
V6-231 Calif. & High Alt.	R45TSX	.060	B	—	15°	Damper	—	600D	3 Min.
6-250 C, G & K-1500	R46TS	.035	C	10°	10°	Damper	425/750	425/600D	4½–6
6-250 C-2500, G-2500, 3500 Exc. Calif.	R46TS	.035	C	10°	10°	Damper	425/750	425/600D	4½–6
6-250 C-2500, G-2500, 3500 Calif.	R46TS	.035	C	6°	8°	Damper	425/750	425/600D	4½–6
6-292	R44T	.035	C	8°	8°	Damper	700	700N	4½–6
V8-267	R45TS	.045	D	4°	8°	Damper	600/700	500/600D	7½–9
V8-305 Caballero Exc. High Alt.	R45TS	.045	D	4°	4°	Damper	700	500/600D	7½–9
V8-305 Caballero High Alt.	R45TS	.045	D	—	8°	Damper	—	600/650D	7½–9
V8-305 C, G, K-1500 & C-2500	R45TS	.045	D	6°	6°	Damper	600/700	500/600D	③
V8-350 2 Barrel Carb. B, C, P&W-4, 5, 6	R44T	.045	D	4°	4°	Damper	700	700N	—
V8-350 4 Barrel Carb. Caballero	R45TS	.045	D		8°	Damper		600/650D	7½–9
V8-350 4 Barrel Carb.⑤	R45TS	.045	D	8°	8°	Damper	700	500/600D	③
V8-350 4 Barrel Carb.⑦	R44T	.045	D	4°	4°	Damper	700	700N	③
V8-366	R43T	.045	D	8°	8°	Damper	700	700N	6
V8-400 K-1500, 2500 & C-2500, 3500	R45TS	.045	D	—	4°	Damper	—	500/600D	③
V8-400 G, K-3500	R44T	.045	D	4°	4°	Damper	700	700N	③
V8-427	R42T	.045	D	8°	8°	Damper	700	700N	6
V8-454⑤	R45TS	.045	D	8°	8°	Damper	700	550/600D	7½–9
V8-454⑦	R44T	.045	D	4°	4°	Damper	700	700N	7½–9
V8-454 C-7D	R42T	.045	D	8°	8°	Damper	700	700N	6

Continued

GMC

TUNE UP SPECIFICATIONS—Continued

The following specifications are published from the latest information available. This data should be used only in the absence of a decal affixed in the engine compartment.

★ When using a timing light, disconnect vacuum hose or tube at distributor and plug opening in hose or tube so idle speed will not be affected.

● When checking compression, lowest cylinder must be within 80 percent of highest.

▲ Before removing wires from distributor cap, determine location of the No. 1 wire in cap, as distributor position may have been altered from that shown at the end of this chart.

Year & Engine	Spark Plug Type	Spark Plug Gap	Firing Orders Fig. ▲	Ignition Timing BTDC①★ Man. Trans.	Ignition Timing BTDC①★ Auto Trans.	Location	Curb Idle Speed② Man. Trans.	Curb Idle Speed② Auto Trans.	Fuel Pump Pressure
1978									
V6-200	R45TS	.045	A	8°	8°	Damper	700	600D	4¼–5¾
V6-231	R46TSX	.060	B	15°	15°	Damper	600/670D	600/670D	3 Min.
6-250 Exc. Calif. & High Alt.⑤	R46TS	.035	C	8°	8°	Damper	425/750	⑨	4–5
6-250 Calif.⑤	R46TS	.035	C	8°	10°	Damper	425/750	425/600D	4–5
6-250 High Alt.⑤	R46TS	.035	C	8°	12°	Damper	425/750	425/600D	4–5
6-250⑦	R46T	.035	C	6°	6°	Damper	450/600	450/600N	4–5
6-292 Series 1500–3500	R44T	.035	C	8°	8°	Damper	450/600	450/600N	4–5
6-292 Series 4500–6500	R44T	.035	C	8°	8°	Damper	600	600N	4–5
V8-305 Caballero Exc. Calif.	R45TS	.045	D	4°	4°	Damper	600	500D	7½–9
V8-305 Caballero Calif.	R45TS	.045	D	—	6°	Damper	—	600/700D	7½–9
V8-305⑤	R45TS	.045	D	4°	4°	Damper	600	500D	7½–9
V8-305⑦	R44T	.045	D	6°	6°	Damper	700	700N	7½–9
V8-350 2 Barrel Carb. Series 4500–6500	R44T	⑩	D	4°	4°	Damper	600	600N	7½–9
V8-350 4 Barrel Carb. Exc. Calif. & High Alt.⑪	R45TS	.045	D	6°	6°	Damper	700	500/600D	7½–9
V8-350 4 Barrel Carb. Calif.⑪	R45TS	.045	D	—	8°	Damper	—	500/600D	7½–9
V8-350 4 Barrel Carb. High Alt.⑪	R45TS	.045	D	—	8°	Damper	—	500/650D	7½–9
V8-350 4 Barrel Carb.⑤	R45TS	.045	D	8°	8°	Damper	700	500/600D	7½–9
V8-350 4 Barrel Carb. Exc. Calif.⑦	R44T	.045	D	8°	8°	Damper	700	700N	7½–9
V8-350 4 Barrel Carb. Calif.⑦	R44TX	.060	D	2°	2°	Damper	700	700N	7½–9
V8-366 Exc. Calif.	R44T	.045	D	8°	8°	Damper	700	700N	8¼
V8-366 Calif.	R44TX	.060	D	8°	8°	Damper	700	700N	8¼
V8-400⑤	R45TS	.045	D	—	4°	Damper	—	500/600D	7½–9
V8-400 Exc. Calif.⑦	R44T	.045	D	—	4°	Damper	—	700N	7½–9
V8-400 Calif.⑦	R44T	.045	D	—	2°	Damper	—	700N	7½–9
V8-403⑫	R46SZ	.060	E	—	—	Damper	—	—	5½–6½
V8-427 Exc. Calif.	R42T	.045	D	8°	8°	Damper	700	700N	8¼
V8-427 Calif.	R42TX	.060	D	8°	8°	Damper	700	700N	8¼
V8-454 Exc. Calif.⑤	R45TS	.045	D	—	8°	Damper	—	550/650D	7½–9
V8-454 Calif.⑤	R45TS	.045	D	—	8°	Damper	700	550/650D	7½–9
V8-454⑦	R44T	.045	D	8°	8°	Damper	700	700N	7½–9
1977									
6-250 Sprint Exc. Calif. & High Alt.	R46TS	.035	C	6°	8°	Damper	⑬	⑨	4–5
6-250 Sprint Calif.	R46TS	.035	C	—	6°	Damper	—	425/550D	4–5
6-250 Sprint High Alt.	R46TS	.035	C	—	10°	Damper	—	425/600D	4½–5½
6-250 Exc. Calif. & High Alt.⑤	R46TS	.035	C	8°	12°	Damper	425/750	⑨	4½–5½
6-250 Calif.⑤	R46TS	.035	C	6°	10°	Damper	425/850	425/600D	4½–5½
6-250 High Alt.⑤	R46TS	.035	C	—	12°	Damper	—	425/600D	4½–5½

Continued

GMC

TUNE UP SPECIFICATIONS—Continued

The following specifications are published from the latest information available. This data should be used only in the absence of a decal affixed in the engine compartment.

★ When using a timing light, disconnect vacuum hose or tube at distributor and plug opening in hose or tube so idle speed will not be affected.

● When checking compression, lowest cylinder must be within 80 percent of highest.

▲ Before removing wires from distributor cap, determine location of the No. 1 wire in cap, as distributor position may have been altered from that shown at the end of this chart.

Year & Engine	Spark Plug Type	Gap	Firing Orders Fig.▲	Ignition Timing BTDC①★ Man. Trans.	Auto Trans.	Location	Curb Idle Speed② Man. Trans.	Auto Trans.	Fuel Pump Pressure
1977—Continued									
6-250⑦	R46T	.035	C	6°	6°	Damper	450/600	450/600D	4½–5½
6-292 Series 1500–3500	R44T	.035	C	8°	8°	Damper	450/600	450/600N	4½–5½
6-292 Series 4500–6500	R44T	.035	C	8°	8°	Damper	600	600N	4½–5½
V8-305 Sprint	R45TS	.045	D	—	8°	Damper	—	500/650D	7½–9
V8-305⑤	R45TS	.045	D	8°	8°	Damper	600/700	500/650D	7½–9
V8-305⑦	R44T	.045	D	6°	6°	Damper	700	700N	7½–9
V8-350 2 Barrel Carb. Series 4500–6500	R44T	.035	D	4°	4°	Damper	600	600N	7½–9
V8-350 4 Barrel Carb. Exc. High Alt.⑭	R45TS	.045	D	—	8°	Damper	—	500/650D	7½–9
V8-350 4 Barrel Carb. High Alt.⑭	R45TS	.045	D	—	8°	Damper	—	600/650D	7½–9
V8-350 4 Barrel Carb. Calif. & High Alt.⑤	R45TS	.045	D	8°	8°	Damper	700	500/650D	7½–9
V8-350 4 Barrel Carb. Calif.⑤	R45TS	.045	D	6°	6°	Damper	700	500/650D	7½–9
V8-350 4 Barrel Carb. High Alt.⑤	R45TS	.045	D	—	6°	Damper	—	600/650D	7½–9
V8-350 4 Barrel Carb. Exc. Calif.	R44T	.045	D	8°	8°	Damper	700	700N	7½–9
V8-350 4 Barrel Carb. Calif.⑦	R44TX	.060	D	2°	2°	Damper	700	700N	7½–9
V8-366 Exc. Calif.	R43T	.045	D	8°	8°	Damper	700	700N	7½–9
V8-366 Calif.	R43TX	.060	D	8°	8°	Damper	700	700N	7½–9
V8-400 Exc. Calif.	R44T	.045	D	—	4°	Damper	—	700N	7½–9
V8-400 Calif.	R44T	.045	D	—	2°	Damper	—	700N	7½–9
V8-403 Exc. Calif.⑫	R46SZ	.060	E	—	12°⑮	Damper	—	600D	5½–6½
V8-403 Calif.⑫	R46SZ	.060	E	—	2°⑮	Damper	—	600D	5½–6½
V8-427 Exc. Calif.	R42T	.035	D	8°	8°	Damper	700	700N	7½–9
V8-427 Calif.	R42TX	.060	D	8°	8°	Damper	700	700N	7½–9
V8-454⑤	R45TS	.045	D	—	4°	Damper	—	600D	7½–9
V8-454⑦	R44T	.045	D	8°	8°	Damper	700	700N	7½–9
V8-455⑫	R46SX	.080	E	—	8°⑮	Damper	—	600D	5½–6½
1976									
6-250 Sprint	R46TS	.035	C	6°	6°	Damper	425/850	⑬	3½–4½
6-250 Exc. Calif.⑤	R46TS	.035	C	⑯	10°	Damper	425/900	425/550D	3½–4½
6-250 Calif.⑤	R46TS	.035	C	6°	10°	Damper	425/1000	425/600D	3½–4½
6-250⑦	R46T	.035	C	6°	6°	Damper	450/600	450/600N	3½–4½
6-292 Series 1500–3500	R44T	.035	C	8°	8°	Damper	450/600	450/600N	4–5
6-292 Series 4500–6500 Less H.E.I.⑰	R44T	.035	F	8°	8°	Damper	600	600N	4–5
6-292 Series 4500–6500 w/H.E.I.	R44T	.035	C	8°	8°	Damper	600	600N	4–5
V8-305 Sprint	R45TS	.045	D	6°	8°	Damper	800	600D	7–8½
V8-305 Series 1500 & 2500	R44T	.045	D	6°	6°	Damper	800	600D	7–8½
V8-350 2 Barrel Carb.⑤⑭	R45TS	.045	D	2°	6°	Damper	800	600D	7–8½

Continued

GMC

TUNE UP SPECIFICATIONS—Continued

The following specifications are published from the latest information available. This data should be used only in the absence of a decal affixed in the engine compartment.

★ When using a timing light, disconnect vacuum hose or tube at distributor and plug opening in hose or tube so idle speed will not be affected.

● When checking compression, lowest cylinder must be within 80 percent of highest.

▲ Before removing wires from distributor cap, determine location of the No. 1 wire in cap, as distributor position may have been altered from that shown at the end of this chart.

Year & Engine	Spark Plug Type	Gap	Firing Orders Fig.▲	Ignition Timing BTDC①★ Man. Trans.	Auto Trans.	Location	Curb Idle Speed② Man. Trans.	Auto. Trans.	Fuel Pump Pressure
1976—Continued									
V8-350 2 Barrel Carb. Less H.E.I.⑱⑲	R44T	.035	G	4°	4°	Damper	600	600N	7½–9
V8-350 2 Barrel Carb. w/H.E.I.⑱	R44T	.035	D	4°	4°	Damper	600	600N	7½–9
V8-350 4 Barrel Carb. Exc. Calif.⑤⑭	R45TS	.045	D	8°	8°	Damper	800	600D	7–8½
V8-350 4 Barrel Carb. Calif.⑤⑭	R45TS	.045	D	6°	6°	Damper	800	600D	7–8½
V8-350 4 Barrel Carb. Exc. Calif.⑦	R44TX	.060	D	8°	8°	Damper	600	600N	7–8½
V8-350 4 Barrel Carb. Calif.⑦	R44TX	.060	D	2°	2°	Damper	700	700N	7–8½
V8-366 Exc. Calif. Less H.E.I.⑲	R43T⑳	.035	G	8°	8°	Damper	700	700N	7½–9
V8-366 Exc. Calif. w/H.E.I.	R43T⑳	.035	D	8°	8°	Damper	700	700N	7½–9
V8-366 Calif.	R43TX㉑	.060	D	8°	8°	Damper	700	700N	7½–9
V8-400 Sprint	R45TS	.045	D	—	8°	Damper	—	600D	7–8½
V8-400 Series 1500–3500 Exc. Calif.	R44TX	.060	D	—	4°	Damper	—	700N	7–8½
V8-400 Series 1500–3500 Calif.	R44TX	.060	D	—	2°	Damper	—	700N	7–8½
V8-427 Exc. Calif. Less H.E.I.⑲	R42T㉒	.035	G	8°	8°	Damper	700	700N	7½–9
V8-427 Exc. Calif. w/H.E.I.	R42T㉒	.035	D	8°	8°	Damper	700	700N	7½–9
V8-427 Calif.	R42TX㉓	.060	D	8°	8°	Damper	700	700N	7½–9
V8-454⑤	R45TS	.045	D	—	㉔	Damper	—	600D	7–8½
V8-454⑦	R44T	.045	D	8°	8°	Damper	700	700N	7–8½
V8-455⑫	R46SX	.080	E	—	8°⑮	Damper	—	600D	5½–6½
1975									
6-250 Sprint Exc. Calif.	R46TX	.060	C	10°	10°	Damper	425/850	425/550D	3½–4½
6-250 Sprint Calif.	R46TX	.060	C	—	10°	Damper	—	425/600D	3½–4½
6-250 Series 1500–3500	R46TX	.060	C	10°	10°	Damper	425/900	425/550D	3½–4½
6-292 Series 1500–3500	R44TX	.060	C	8°	8°	Damper	450/600	450/600N	3½–4½
6-292 Series 4500–6500⑰	R44T	.035	F	8°	8°	Damper	600	600N	4–5
V8-350 2 Barrel Carb.⑤⑭	R44TX	.060	D	6°	6°	Damper	800	600D	7–8½
V8-350 2 Barrel Carb.⑱⑲	R44T	.035	G	4°	4°	Damper	㉕	550N	7½–9
V8-350 4 Barrel Carb.⑤⑭	R44TX	.060	D	6°	㉖	Damper	800	600D	7–8½
V8-350 4 Barrel Carb. Exc. Calif.⑦	R44TX	.060	D	8°	8°	Damper	600	600N	7–8½
V8-350 4 Barrel Carb. Calif.⑦	R44TX	.060	D	2°	2°	Damper	700	700N	7–8½
V8-366 Exc. Calif.⑲	R43T⑳	.035	G	8°	8°	Damper	700	700N	7½–9
V8-366 Calif.	R43TX	.060	D	8°	8°	Damper	700	700N	7½–9
V8-400 Sprint	R44TX	.060	D	—	8°	Damper	—	600D	7–8½
V8-400 Exc. Calif.⑦	R44TX	.060	D	4°	4°	Damper	700	700N	7–8½
V8-400 Calif.⑦	R44TX	.060	D	2°	2°	Damper	700	700N	7–8½
V8-427 Exc. Calif.⑲	R42T㉒	.035	G	8°	8°	Damper	700	700N	7½–9
V8-427 Calif.	R42TX	.060	D	8°	8°	Damper	700	700N	7½–9

Continued

GMC

TUNE UP SPECIFICATIONS—Continued

The following specifications are published from the latest information available. This data should be used only in the absence of a decal affixed in the engine compartment.

★ When using a timing light, disconnect vacuum hose or tube at distributor and plug opening in hose or tube so idle speed will not be affected.

● When checking compression, lowest cylinder must be within 80 percent of highest.

▲ Before removing wires from distributor cap, determine location of the No. 1 wire in cap, as distributor position may have been altered from that shown at the end of this chart.

Year & Engine	Spark Plug Type	Spark Plug Gap	Firing Orders Fig.▲	Ignition Timing BTDC①★ Man. Trans.	Ignition Timing BTDC①★ Auto Trans.	Location	Curb Idle Speed② Man. Trans.	Curb Idle Speed② Auto. Trans.	Fuel Pump Pressure
1975—Continued									
V8-454 Exc. Calif.⑤⑭	R44TX	.060	D	—	16°	Damper	—	㉗	7-8½
V8-454 Exc. Calif.⑦	R44TX	.060	D	8°	8°	Damper	500/700	500/700N	7-8½
V8-454 Calif.⑦	R44TX	.060	D	8°	8°	Damper	600	600N	7-8½
V8-455 Less H.E.I.⑫㉘	R45S	.040	H	—	8°⑮	Damper	—	600D	5½-6½
V8-455 w/H.E.I.⑫	R46SX	.080	E	—	8°⑮	Damper	—	600D	5½-6½
1974									
6-250㉙⑰	R46T	.035	F	8°	8°	Damper	850	600	3½-4½
6-250㉚⑰	R46T	.035	F	6°	6°	Damper	600N	600N	3½-4½
6-292⑰	R44T	.035	F	8°	8°	Damper	600N	600N	3½-4½
V6-305C⑰	CR44NS	.035	I	7½°	7½°	Damper	600N	600N	5-7
V6-379⑰	R43T	.035	I	5°	5°	Damper	575N	575N	5-7
V6-432⑰	R43T	.035	I	5°	5°	Damper	525N	525N	5-7
V6-478⑰	R43T	.035	I	7½°	7½°	Damper	525N	525N	5-7
V8-350⑲㉙㉛	R44T	.035	G	TDC	8°	Damper	900	600	7-8½
V8-350⑲㉙㉜	R44T	.035	G	8°㉝	8°㉞	Damper	900	600	7-8½
V8-350⑲㉚㉜	R44T	.035	G	4°	4°	Damper	600N	600N	7-8½
V8-350⑲㉟㉛	R44T	.035	G	4°	4°	Damper	600N	600N	7-8½
V8-366⑲	R43T	.035	G	8°	8°	Damper	700N	700N	7-8½
V8-400, Exc. Calif.⑭⑲㉛	R44T	.035	G	—	8°	Damper	—	600	7-8½
V8-400, Calif.⑭⑲㉜	R44T	.035	G	—	8°	Damper	—	600	7-8½
V8-427⑲	R42T	.035	G	8°	8°	Damper	700N	700N	7-8½
V8-454, 1500⑲	R44T	.035	G	10°	10°	Damper	800	600	7-8½
V8-454, 2500-3500⑲	R44T	.035	G	8°	8°	Damper	700N	700N	7-8½
V8-455⑫㉘	R45S	.040	H	—	8°	Damper	—	600	5½-6½
1973									
6-250 L.D.⑰	R46T	.035	F	6°	6°	Damper	700	600	3½-4½
6-250 H.D.⑰	R46T	.035	F	4°	4°	Damper	700	700N	3½-4½
6-292 Exc. Calif.⑰	R44T	.035	F	4°	4°	Damper	700	700N	3½-4½
6-292, Calif.⑰	R44T	.035	F	8°	8°	Damper	600	600N	3½-4½
V6-305C⑰	CR44NS	.040	I	7½°	7½°	Damper	525	525N	5½-7
V6-379⑰	R43T	.035	I	8°	8°	Damper	525	525N	5½-7
V6-432⑰	R43T	.035	I	8°	8°	Damper	525	525N	5½-7
V6-478M⑰	CR43N	.035	I	7½°	7½°	Damper	525	525N	5½-7
V6-478SN⑰	CR44NS	.040	I	5°	5°	Damper	500	500N	5½-7
V8-307 L.D.⑲	R44T	.035	G	4°	8°	Damper	600	900	5-6½
V8-307 H.D.⑲	R44T	.035	G	TDC	TDC	Damper	600	600	5-6½
V8-350 L.D. 1500-2500-3500⑲	R44T	.035	G	8°㊱	12°	Damper	900	600	7-8½
V8-350 H.D. 1500-2500-3500⑲	R44T	.035	G	4°	4°	Damper	600	600N	7-8½
V8-350 Exc. Calif. 5500-6500⑲	R44T	.035	G	4°	4°	Damper	600	600N	7½-9
V8-350 Calif. 5500-6500⑲	R44T	.035	G	6°	6°	Damper	700	700N	7½-9
V8-366 Exc. Calif.⑲	R43T	.035	G	8°	8°	Damper	550	550N	7½-9
V8-366 Calif.⑲	R43T	.035	G	8°	8°	Damper	750	750N	7½-9

Continued

1153

GMC

TUNE UP SPECIFICATIONS—Continued

The following specifications are published from the latest information available. This data should be used only in the absence of a decal affixed in the engine compartment.

★ When using a timing light, disconnect vacuum hose or tube at distributor and plug opening in hose or tube so idle speed will not be affected.

● When checking compression, lowest cylinder must be within 80 percent of highest.

▲ Before removing wires from distributor cap, determine location of the No. 1 wire in cap, as distributor position may have been altered from that shown at the end of this chart.

Year & Engine	Spark Plug		Ignition Timing BTDC①★				Curb Idle Speed②		Fuel Pump Pressure
	Type	Gap	Firing Orders Fig.▲	Man. Trans.	Auto Trans.	Location	Man. Trans.	Auto. Trans.	
1973—Continued									
V8-427 Exc. Calif.⑲	R42T	.035	G	8°	8°	Damper	550	550N	7½–9
V8-427 Calif.⑲	R42T	.035	G	8°	8°	Damper	750	750N	7½–9
V8-454 L.D.⑲	R44T	.035	G	10°	10°	Damper	900	600	7–8½
V8-454 H.D. Exc. Calif.⑲	R44T	.035	G	10°	10°	Damper	700	700N	7–8½
V8-454 H.D. Calif.⑲	R44T	.035	G	5°	8°	Damper	700	700N	7–8½
V8-455⑫㉘	R45S	.040	H	—	8°	Damper	—	600	5½–6½
1972									
6-250 Exc. Calif. K-2500 Suburban⑰	R46T	.035	F	4°	4°	Damper	700	600	3½–4½
6-250, Calif. K-2500 Suburban⑰	R46T	.035	F	TDC	TDC	Damper	700	600	3½–4½
6-292⑰	R44T	.035	F	4°	4°	Damper	700	700N	3½–4½
V6-351C⑰	CR43N	.035	I	7½°	7½°	Damper	600	600N	5–6½
V6-401⑰	CR43N	.035	I	7½°	7½°	Damper	525	525N	5–6½
V6-478M⑰	CR43N	.035	I	7½°	7½°	Damper	525	525N	5–6½
V6-478SN⑰	CR44NS	.040	I	7½°	7½°	Damper	500	500N	5–6½
V8-307, Exc. CK 20/30⑲	R44T	.035	G	4°	8°	Damper	900㊲	600	5–6½
V8-307, C, K-2500-3500⑲	R44T	.035	G	4°	4°	Damper	900㊲	600	7–8½
V8-350⑲	R44T	.035	G	4°	8°	Damper	800	600	7–8½
V8-350 Sprint 2 Barrel⑲	R44T	.035	G	6°	6°	Damper	900	600	7–8½
V8-350 4500–6500⑲	R44T	.035	G	4°	4°	Damper	600	600	7½–9
V8-366⑲	R43T	.035	G	8°	8°	Damper	550	550	7½–9
V8-402⑲	R44T	.035	G	8°	8°	Damper	750	600	7–8½
V8-427⑲	R43T	.035	G	8°	8°	Damper	550	550	7½–9
V8-454⑲	R44T	.035	G	8°	8°	Damper	750	600	7–8½
V8-637⑲	CR42N	.035	J	5°	5°	Damper	475	475	7½–9
1971									
6-250, G-1500⑰	R46T	.035	F	TDC	4°	Damper	750	600	3½–4½
6-250, G-2500-3500⑰	R46T	.035	F	TDC	4°	Damper	550	400/500	3½–4½
6-250, Exc. G Series⑰	R46TS	.035	F	4°	4°	Damper	550	500	3½–4½
6-292⑰	R44T	.035	F	4°	4°	Damper	550	500	3½–4½
V6-305C⑰	CR-44NS	.040	I	7½°	7½°	Damper	550	550	5½–7
V6-351C⑰	CR-43N	.035	I	5°	5°	Damper	550	550	5½–7
V6-401M⑰	CR-43N	.035	I	7½°	7½°	Damper	550	550	5½–7
V6-478M⑰	CR-43N	.035	I	5°	5°	Damper	750	750	5½–7
V8-307, G-Series⑲	R-45	.035	G	2°	2°	Damper	700	450/600	5–6½
V8-307, 200 H.P.⑲	R-45TS	.035	G	4°	8°	Damper	600	550	5–6½
V8-307, 215 H.P.⑲	R-45TS	.035	G	4°	4°	Damper	550	500	7–8½
V8-350, G-Series⑲	R-44	.035	G	TDC	4°	Damper	700	600	7–8½
V8-350, Exc. G-Series⑲	R-44TS	.035	G	4°	8°	Damper	600	550	7–8½
V8-350, 4500–6500⑲	R-44T	.035	G	4°	4°	Damper	500	500	7½–9
V8-366⑲	R-43T	.035	G	8°	8°	Damper	500	500	7½–9
V8-402⑲	R-44TS	.035	G	8°	8°	Damper	600	600	7–8½
V8-427⑲	R-44T	.035	G	8°	8°	Damper	500	500	7½–9
V8-637⑲	CR-42N	.035	J	5°	5°	Damper	400	400	5½–7

Continued

GMC

TUNE UP SPECIFICATIONS—Continued

The following specifications are published from the latest information available. This data should be used only in the absence of a decal affixed in the engine compartment.

★ When using a timing light, disconnect vacuum hose or tube at distributor and plug opening in hose or tube so idle speed will not be affected.

● When checking compression, lowest cylinder must be within 80 percent of highest.

▲ Before removing wires from distributor cap, determine location of the No. 1 wire in cap, as distributor position may have been altered from that shown at the end of this chart.

Year & Engine	Spark Plug Type	Gap	Firing Orders Fig.▲	Ignition Timing BTDC①★ Man. Trans.	Auto. Trans.	Location	Curb Idle Speed② Man. Trans.	Auto. Trans.	Fuel Pump Pressure
1970									
6-250, 292, 1500 Exc. G.⑰	R-46T㊳	.035	F	TDC	4°	Damper	750	400/500	3½-4½
6-250, 292, 2500-3500⑰	R-46T㊳	.035	F	TDC	4°	Damper	600	400/500	3½-4½
6-250, 292, G-Series⑰	R-46T㊳	.035	F	TDC	4°	Damper	700	400/500	3½-4½
6-250, 4500-6500⑰	R-46N㊳	.035	F	TDC	4°	Damper	550	500	4½-5
6-292, 4500-6500⑰	CR-44N	.035	F	TDC	4°	Damper	550	500	4½-5
V6-305C⑰	CR-44NS	.040	I	7½°	7½°	Damper	550	550	5-6½
V6-351C⑰	CR-43N	.035	I	10°	10°	Damper	550	550	5-6½
V6-401M⑰	CR-43N	.035	I	10°	10°	Damper	500-550	500-550	5-6½
V6-478M⑰	CR-43N	.035	I	10°	10°	Damper	500-550	500-550	5-6½
V8-307 1500 Exc. G.⑲	R-45	.035	G	2°	8°	Damper	700	450/600	5-6½
V8-307 2500-3500 Exc. G.⑲	R-45	.035	G	2°	8°	Damper	600	450/600	5-6½
V8-307 G-Series⑲	R-45	.035	G	2°	8°	Damper	700	400/600	5-6½
V8-350 Exc. P-Series⑲	R-44	.035	G	TDC	4°	Damper	700	600	7-8½
V8-350 P-Series⑲	R-44	.035	G	TDC	4°	Damper	600	500	7-8½
V8-350 4500-6500⑲	CR-43	.035	G	4°	4°	Damper	500	500	5-6½
V8-366⑲	CR-44N	.035	G	6°	6°	Damper	500	500	5-6½
V8-400⑲	R-44T	.035	G	4°	4°	Damper	700	600	7-8½
V8-427⑲	CR-44N	.035	G	6°	6°	Damper	500	500	5-6½
V8-637⑲	CR-42N	.035	J	10°	10°	Damper	400-425	400-425	5.5-7

①—B.T.D.C.—Before top dead center.
②—Idle speed on man. trans. vehicles is adjusted in Neutral & auto. trans. vehicles is adjusted in Drive (D) or Neutral (N) as specified. Where two idle speeds are listed, the higher speed is with the A/C or idle solenoid energized.
③—With vapor return line, 5½-7 psi.; less vapor return line, 7½-9 psi.
④—Non-governed California models, set at 2°BTDC.
⑤—Series 1500-3500 light duty emissions, GVWR 6000 lbs. & under.
⑥—C-1500 & 2500 series w/distributor model No. 1103339, set at 6° BTDC.
⑦—Series 1500-3500 heavy duty emissions, GVWR 6001 lbs. & above.
⑧—Less A/C, 550D RPM; with A/C, 560/670D RPM.
⑨—Less A/C, 425/550D RPM; with A/C, 425/600D RPM.
⑩—Exc. Calif. .035"; California, .045".
⑪—Caballero
⑫—Motor Home & Trans Mode.
⑬—Less A/C, 425/750 RPM; with A/C 425/800 RPM.
⑭—Sprint.
⑮—At 1100 RPM.
⑯—Exc. C-1500 w/ 4 spd. man. trans., 6° BTDC; C-1500 w/ 4 spd. man. trans., 10° BTDC.
⑰—Breaker point gap, new .019", used .016"; dwell angle, 31°-34°.
⑱—Series 4500-6500.
⑲—Breaker point gap, new .019", used .016"; dwell angle 28°-32°.
⑳—For predominately urban driving where spark plug fouling may occur, use R44T.
㉑—For predominately urban driving where spark plug fouling may occur, use R44TX.
㉒—For predominately urban driving where spark plug fouling may occur, use R43T or R44T.
㉓—For predominately urban driving where spark plug fouling may occur, use R43TX or R44TX.
㉔—Models less catalytic converter, 8° BTDC; models w/ catalytic converter, 12° BTDC.
㉕—Models less governor 450 RPM; models w/ governor, 550 RPM.
㉖—Sprint except Calif., 8° BTDC; Sprint California models and all series 1500-3500 models, 6° BTDC.
㉗—Sprint, 500/600D RPM; Series 1500-3500, 500/650D RPM.
㉘—Breaker point gap .016; dwell angle, 30°.
㉙—Series 1500
㉚—Series 2500-3500
㉛—With 2 barrel carb.
㉜—With 4 barrel carb.
㉝—Suburban exc. Calif., 6°; Calif., 4°.
㉞—Suburban and Rally Wagon exc. Calif., 12°; Calif. Suburban, 6°.
㉟—Series 5500-6500
㊱—C2500 Suburban, 2°.
㊲—Calif C-K, 950.
㊳—6-292 R44T.

Continued

GMC

TUNE UP NOTES—Continued

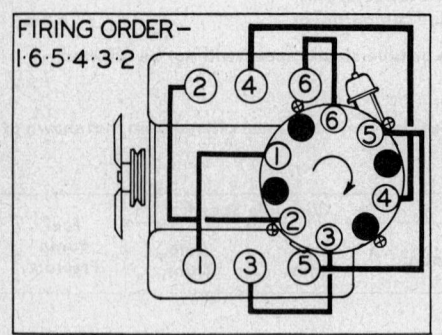

Fig. A

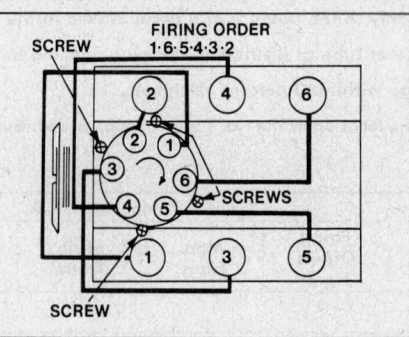

Fig. B

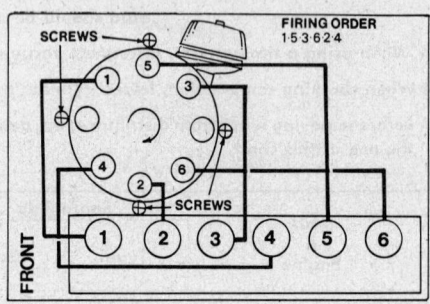

Fig. C

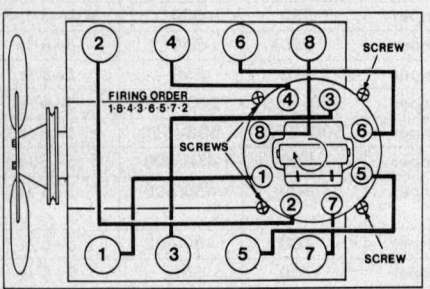

Fig. D

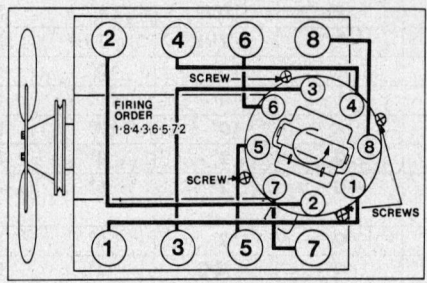

Fig. E

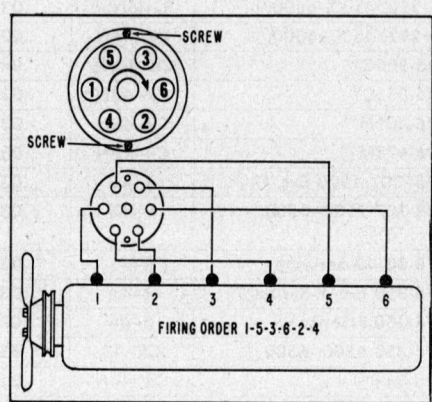

Fig. F

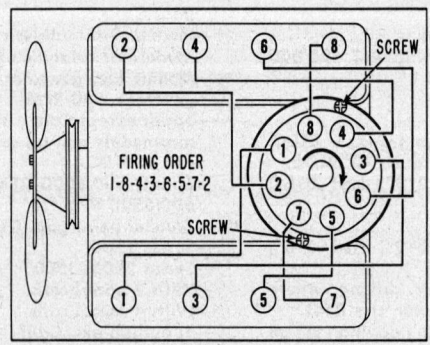

Fig. G

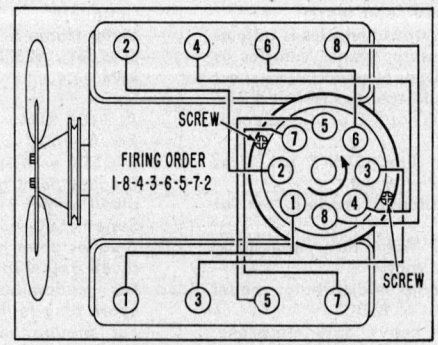

Fig. H

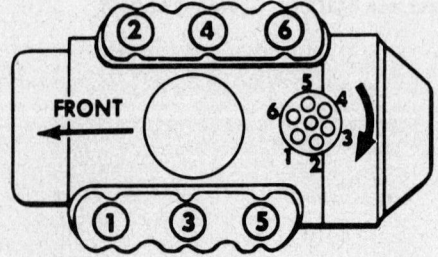

Fig. I

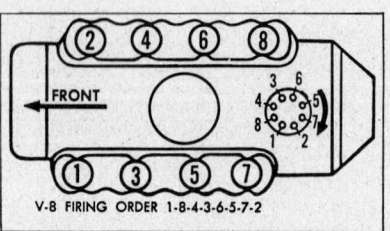

Fig. J

GMC

VALVE SPECIFICATIONS

Engine Model	Year	Valve Lash Int.	Valve Lash Exh.	Valve Angles Seat	Valve Angles Face	Valve Springs Installed Height	Valve Springs Pressure Lbs. @ In.	Valve Stem Clearance Intake	Valve Stem Clearance Exhaust	Stem Diameter, Std. Intake	Stem Diameter, Std. Exhaust
V6-200	1978–79	1 Turn③		46	45	1⁴⁵⁄₆₄	200 @ 1.25	.0010–.0027	.0010–.0027	.3410–.3417	.3410–.3417
V6-229	1980	1 Turn③		46	45	1⁴⁵⁄₆₄	①	.0010–.0027	.0010–.0027	.3410–.3417	.3410–.3417
V6-231	1978–79	—		45	45	1²³⁄₃₂	168 @ 1.327	.0015–.0032	.0015–.0032	.3402–.3412	.3405–.3412
V6-231	1980	—		45	45	1²³⁄₃₂	182 @ 1.34	.0015–.0035	.0015–.0035	.3402–.3412	.3405–.3412
6-250	1970–80	1 Turn③		46	45	1²¹⁄₃₂	186 @ 1.27	.0010–.0027	.0010–.0027	.3410–.3417	.3410–.3417
V8-267	1979–80	1 Turn③		46	45	1⁴⁵⁄₆₄	⑭	.0010–.0027	.0010–.0027	.3410–.3417	.3410–.3417
6-292	1970–80	1 Turn③		46	45	1⅝	179 @ 1.30	.0010–.0027	.0010–.0027	.3410–.3417	.3410–.3417
V6-305C	1970–74	.012H	.018H	②	②	—	200 @ 1.495	.0015–.0030	.0020–.0035	.3407–.3412	.3402–.3407
V8-305	1977	1 Turn③		46	45	⑩	⑪	.0010–.0027	.0010–.0027	—	—
V8-305	1978–79	1 Turn③		46	45	⑫	⑬	.0010–.0027	.0010–.0027	—	—
V8-305	1980	1 Turn③		46	45	1.7	④	.0010–.0027	.0010–.0027	.3410–.3417	.3410–.3417
V8-307	1970–73	1 Turn③		46	45	1²³⁄₃₂	200 @ 1.25	.0010–.0027	.0010–.0027	.3410–.3417	.3410–.3417
V8-350	1970–73	1 Turn③		46	45	1²³⁄₃₂	200 @ 1.25	.0010–.0027	.0010–.0027	.3410–.3417	.3410–.3417
V8-350	1974–76	1 Turn③		46	45	⑧	⑨	.0010–.0027	.0010–.0027	.3410–.3417	.3410–.3417
V8-350	1977	1 Turn③		46	45	⑩	⑪	.0010–.0027	.0010–.0027	—	—
V8-350	1978–80	1 Turn③		46	45	⑫	⑬	.0010–.0027	.0010–.0027	—	—
V6-351C	1970–72	.012H	.018H	②	②	1⁵⁹⁄₆₄	204 @ 1.92	.0020–.0030	.0025–.0040	.3725–.3730	.4340–.4345
V8-366	1970–79	1 Turn③		46	45	1¹³⁄₁₆	220 @ 1.40	.0010–.0027	.0012–.0029	.3715–.3722	.3713–.3720
V8-396	1970	1 Turn③		46	45	1⅞	240 @ 1.38	.0017–.0020	.0019–.0022	.3415–.3722	.3713–.3720
V8-400	1970–76	1 Turn③		46	45	1²³⁄₃₂	200 @ 1.25	.0010–.0027	.0012–.0027	.3410–.3417	.3410–.3417
V8-400	1977	1 Turn③		46	45	⑩	⑪	.0010–.0027	.0012–.0029	—	—
V8-400	1978–80	1 Turn③		46	45	⑫	⑬	.0010–.0027	.0012–.0029	—	—
V6-401	1970–72	.012H	.018H	②	②	1⁵⁹⁄₆₄	204 @ 1.92	.0015–.0030	.0025–.0040	.3725–.3730	.4340–.4345
V6-432	1973–74	.012H	.018H	②	②	1⁵⁹⁄₆₄	204 @ 1.92	.0015–.0030	.0019–.0036	.3725–.3730	.4344–.4351
V8-402	1971–72	1 Turn③		46	45	1⅞	240 @ 1.38	.0010–.0027	.0012–.0029	—	—
V8-427	1970–79	1 Turn③		46	45	1¹³⁄₁₆	220 @ 1.40	.0010–.0027	.0019–.0022	.3715–.3722	.3713–.3720
V8-454	1971–73	1 Turn③		46	45	1⅞	300 @ 1.38	.0010–.0027	.0012–.0027	—	—
V8-454	1974–77	1 Turn③		46	45	1⅞	300 @ 1.38	.0010–.0027	.0012–.0029	—	—
V8-454	1978–80	1 Turn③		46	45	1.80	220 @ 1.40	.0010–.0027	.0012–.0029	—	—
V6-478	1970–72	.012H	.018H	②	②	1⁵⁹⁄₆₄	204 @ 1.92	.0015–.0030	.0025–.0040	.3725–.3730	.4340–.4345
V8-637	1971–72	.010H	.018H	45	45	⑥	⑦	.0014–.0031	.0024–.0041	.3724–.3730	.4339–.4346

① —Intake, 175 @ 1.25; Exhaust, 190 @ 1.25.
② —Intake 30, exhaust 45.
③ —Tight from zero lash point.
④ —Intake, 175 @ 1.25; Exhaust, 184 @ 1.16.
⑤ —Intake, 180 @ 1.25; Exhaust, 190 @ 1⁵⁄₃₂.
⑥ —Inner spring 1⁵⁷⁄₆₄; outer spring 2³⁄₃₂.
⑦ —Inner spring—70 @ 1.397 inch; outer spring—154 @ 1.595.
⑧ —Intake 1²³⁄₃₂, exhaust 1⅝".
⑨ —Intake 200 @ 1.25"; exhaust 189 @ 1.20.
⑩ —Intake 1²³⁄₃₂, exhaust 1¹⁹⁄₃₂.
⑪ —Intake 194–206 @ 1.25; Exhaust 194–206 @ 1.16.
⑫ —Intake, 1.70; exhaust, 1.61.
⑬ —Intake, 180 & 1.25; exhaust, 190 @ 1.16.

DISTRIBUTOR SPECIFICATIONS

Year	Engine Model	Distributor Number	Rotation ①	Breaker Gap (New)	Dwell Angle Deg.	Breaker Arm Spring Tension	Centrifugal Advance Degrees @ R.P.M. of Distributor Advance Starts	Centrifugal Advance Degrees @ R.P.M. of Distributor Full Advance	Vacuum Advance Inches of Vacuum To Start Plunger	Vacuum Advance Max. Adv. Dist. Deg. @ Vacuum
1970–71	6-250	1110466	C	.019	31–34	19–23	1.5 @ 600	15 @ 2100	6 to 8	11.5 @ 17
	6-250	1110463	C	.019	31–34	19–23	1 @ 500	17 @ 2100	6 to 8	11.5 @ 17
	6-250	1110464	C	.019	31–34	19–23	1.5 @ 600	15 @ 2100	6 to 8	11.5 @ 17
	6-292	1110467	C	.019	31–34	19–23	1 @ 500	17 @ 2100	6 to 8	11.5 @ 17
	6-292	1110468	C	.019	31–34	19–23	1 @ 500	15 @ 2150	6 to 8	11.5 @ 17
	V6-305C	1110471	C	.019	31–34	19–23	1 @ 400	16 @ 1700	5 to 7	7.5 @ 12
	V6-351, 401, 478	1110478	C	.019	31–34	19–23	2 @ 510	12 @ 1750	3 to 5	7.5 @ 8.2
	V8-307	1110912	C	.019	28–32	19–23	2 @ 600	13 @ 2150	7 to 9	10.3 @ 17.8
	V8-307	1111481	C	.019	28–32	19–23	2.7 @ 600	15 @ 2250	5 to 7	8 @ 12.7
	V8-350	1111338	C	.019	28–32	19–32	2.9 @ 600	15 @ 2050	—	—
	V8-350	1111495	C	.019	28–32	19–23	2.9 @ 600	15 @ 2050	7 to 9	8 @ 15.75
	V8-350	1111955	C	.019	28–32	19–23	4.1 @ 700	15 @ 2250	6 to 8	13 @ 17.5

Continued

GMC

DISTRIBUTOR SPECIFICATIONS—Continued

Year	Engine Model	Distributor Number	Rotation ①	Breaker Gap (New)	Dwell Angle Deg.	Breaker Arm Spring Tension	Centrifugal Advance Degrees @ R.P.M. of Distributor		Vacuum Advance	
							Advance Starts	Full Advance	Inches of Vacuum To Start Plunger	Max. Adv. Dist. Deg. @ Vacuum
	V8-350, 400	1111500	C	.019	28–32	19–23	3.5 @ 600	15 @ 2100	7 to 9	8 @ 15.75
	V8-366, 427	1111337	C	.019	28–32	19–23	3.3 @ 600	18 @ 2200	—	—
	V8-637	1111944	C	.019	28–32	19–23	2 @ 550	14 @ 1800	3 to 5	9 @ 9.7
	V8-637	1111985	C	.019	28–32	19–23	3 @ 550	15 @ 1600	3 to 5	9 @ 9.7
1971	6-250	1110465	C	.019	31–34	19–23	4.5 @ 610	16 @ 2100	7 to 9	11.5 @ 16
	6-250	1110466	C	.019	31–34	19–23	4 @ 700	14 @ 2100	7 to 9	11.5 @ 16
	V8-307	1111481	C	.019	29–31	19–23	5 @ 800	14 @ 2150	6 to 8	7.5 @ 12
1972	6-250 20–30 Ser.	1110498	C	.019	31–34	19–23	.0 @ 465	12 @ 2050	8	11½ @ 16
	6-250 exc. "G" Ser.	1110489	C	.019	31–34	19–23	0 @ 465	12 @ 2050	8	11½ @ 16
	6-250 "G" Ser.	1110493	C	.019	31–34	19–23	0 @ 465	12 @ 2050	8	11½ @ 16
	6-292	1110486	C	.019	31–34	19–23	0 @ 430	10 @ 2000	8	9 @ 16
	V8-307 10 Ser.	1112040	C	.019	29–31	19–23	0 @ 340	10 @ 2100	8	10 @ 17
	V8-307 10 Ser.	1112041	C	.019	29–31	19–23	0 @ 400	12 @ 2150	8	10 @ 17
	V8-307 20–30 Ser.	1112043	C	.019	29–31	19–23	0 @ 400	10 @ 2100	8	7½ @ 15½
	V8-350	1112047	C	.019	29–31	19–23	0 @ 432	9 @ 2100	8	7½ @ 15½
	V8-350	1112046	C	.019	29–31	19–23	0 @ 400	12 @ 2150	8	7½ @ 15½
	V6-351C	1110478	C	.019	31–34	19–23	1 @ 510	12 @ 1750	3	7½ @ 8.2
	V8-366, 427	1111365	C	.016	28–32	19–23	1 @ 625	14 @ 2200	—	—
	V6-401, 478M	1110478	C	.016	31–34	—	0 @ 510	12 @ 1750	3–5	7½ @ 8¼
	V8-402	1112064	C	.019	29–31	19–23	0 @ 465	15 @ 2200	8	10 @ 17
	V8-454	1112052	C	.019	28–32	19–23	0 @ 428	11 @ 1950	8	10 @ 17
	V6-478SN	1110451	C	.016	31–34	—	0 @ 450	12 @ 1800	7–9	5 @ 14.9
	V8-637	1111985	C	—	28–32	—	1 @ 550	14 @ 1600	3–5	9 @ 9.7
1973	6-250	1110489	C	.019	31–34	19–23	1 @ 650	12 @ 2050	4	7½ @ 7
	6-250 exc. "G" Ser.	110499	C	.019	31–34	19–23	0 @ 465	12 @ 2050	7	6 @ 15
	6-250 10 Ser.	1110500	C	.019	31–34	19–23	0 @ 465	12 @ 2050	7	6 @ 15
	6-250 20–30 Ser.	1110493	C	.019	31–34	19–23	0 @ 465	12 @ 2050	8	11½ @ 16
	6-250 exc. "G" Ser.	1110489	C	.019	31–34	19–23	0 @ 465	12 @ 2050	8	11½ @ 16
	6-292 20–30 Ser.	1110486	C	.019	31–34	19–23	0 @ 430	10 @ 2000	9	9 @ 13
	6-292 exc. Calif.	1110486	C	.019	31–34	19–23	1½ @ 600	14 @ 2000	9	9 @ 16
	6-292 20–30 Ser.	1110518	C	.019	31–34	19–23	0 @ 465	7 @ 2050	10	5 @ 13
	6-292 Calif.	1110518	C	.019	31–34	19–23	1 @ 600	16 @ 2000	10	5 @ 13
	V6-305C, 379, 432	1110478	C	.019	31–34	19–23	1 @ 510	11 @ 1750	4	7½ @ 7
	V6-432 A.I.R.	1112674	C	.019	31–34	19–23	1 @ 510	11 @ 1750	—	—
	V8-307 10 Ser.	1112102	C	.019	29–31	19–23	0 @ 500	10 @ 2100	6	7½ @ 12
	V8-307 10 Ser.	1112227	C	.019	29–31	19–23	0 @ 500	12 @ 2150	6	7½ @ 12
	V8-307 20–30 Ser.	1112096	C	.019	29–31	19–23	0 @ 550	12 @ 2100	10	5 @ 15
	V8-350	1112094	C	.019	29–31	19–23	0 @ 550	7 @ 2100	6	7½ @ 14
	V8-350	1112093	C	.019	29–31	19–23	0 @ 550	9 @ 2100	6	7½ @ 14
	V8-350 20–30 Ser.	1112097	C	.019	29–31	19–23	0 @ 550	11 @ 2100	8	5 @ 13
	V8-350 exc. Calif.	1111364	C	—	28–32	—	1 @ 550	10 @ 1900	—	—
	V8-350 exc. Calif.	1112048	C	—	28–32	—	1 @ 600	10 @ 1900	8	8 @ 17
	V8-350 Calif.	1113171	C	—	29–31	—	1 @ 600	10 @ 2100	—	—
	V8-350 Calif.	1112092	C	—	29–31	—	1 @ 600	10 @ 2100	—	—
	V8-350 exc. Calif.	1111396	C	—	29–31	—	1 @ 550	10 @ 1900	—	—
	V8-350 Calif.	1111372	C	—	29–31	—	1 @ 600	10 @ 2100	—	—
	V8-366, 427	1111365	C	—	28–32	—	1 @ 625	13 @ 2200	—	—
	V8-366	1111370	C	—	28–32	—	1 @ 600	13 @ 2200	—	—
	V8-454 exc. 20–30 Sub.	1112113	C	.019	29–31	19–23	0 @ 550	7 @ 2100	6	10 @ 15
	V8-454 20 Ser. Sub.	1112504	C	.019	29–31	19–23	0 @ 550	7 @ 2100	8	7½ @ 15.5

Continued

GMC

DISTRIBUTOR SPECIFICATIONS—Continued

Year	Engine Model	Distributor Number	Rotation ①	Breaker Gap (New)	Dwell Angle Deg.	Breaker Arm Spring Tension	Centrifugal Advance Degrees @ R.P.M. of Distributor		Vacuum Advance	
							Advance Starts	Full Advance	Inches of Vacuum To Start Plunger	Max. Adv. Dist. Deg. @ Vacuum
1974	6-250 exc. "G" Ser.	1110499	C	—	31–34	—	0 @ 550	12 @ 2050	7	12 @ 15.5
	6-250 10 Ser.	1110500	C	—	31–34	—	0 @ 550	12 @ 2050	7	12 @ 15.5
	6-250 20–30 Ser.	1110520	C	—	31–34	—	0 @ 550	12 @ 2050	13	5 @ 13.5
	6-250 "G" Ser.	1110525	C	—	31–34	—	0 @ 550	12 @ 2050	13	5 @ 13.5
	6-292 20–30 Ser.	1110518	C	—	31–34	—	0 @ 550	12 @ 2050	10	5 @ 13.5
	V6-305, 379, 432	1112674	C	.019	31–34	—	2 @ 510	12 @ 1750	—	—
	V8-350 C,K, 10 Ser.	1112093	C	—	29–31	—	0 @ 550	9 @ 2100	6	7½ @ 14
	V8-350G, 10–30 Ser.	1112847	C	—	29–31	—	0 @ 550	9 @ 2100	3	7 @ 8.5
	V8-350 C,K,G	1112543	C	—	29–31	—	0 @ 500	11 @ 2100	6	7½ @ 14
	V8-350	1112848	C	—	29–31	—	0 @ 450	7 @ 2100	3	7 @ 8.5
	V8-350	1112844	C	—	29–31	—	0 @ 500	10 @ 2100	3	7 @ 8.5
	V8-350	1112849	C	—	29–31	—	0 @ 500	11 @ 2100	3	7 @ 8.5
	V8-350	1112097	C	—	29–31	—	0 @ 600	11 @ 2100	8	5 @ 13.5
	V8-350	1111364	C	—	28–32	—	1 @ 550	11 @ 1900	—	—
	V8-350	1111373	C	—	29–31	—	1 @ 550	11 @ 1900	—	—
	V8-350	1112149	C	—	28–32	—	1 @ 450	11 @ 1900	—	—
	V8-366	1111374	C	—	29–31	—	1 @ 625	14 @ 2200	—	—
	V8-366, 427	1111365	C	—	28–32	—	1 @ 625	14 @ 2200	—	—
	V8-454 C,K, 10 Ser.	1112113	C	—	29–31	—	0 @ 550	9 @ 2100	6	10 @ 15.7
	V8-454	1112504	C	—	29–31	—	0 @ 550	9 @ 2100	8	8 @ 16
	V8-454 C,K, 20–30	1112105	C	—	29–31	—	0 @ 550	10 @ 2100	6	12 @ 14.3
	V8-455	1112172	CC	.016	30	—	0–2 @ 575	9 @ 1700	4.5	12 @ 19
1975	6-250	1110650②	C	—	—	—	0 @ 550	8 @ 2100	4	7 @ 12
	6-250	1112863②	C	—	—	—	0 @ 550	8 @ 2100	4	9 @ 12
	6-292	1110518	C	.019	31–34	—	0 @ 650	13 @ 2050	9	5 @ 13
	6-292	1112887②	C	—	—	—	0 @ 550	12 @ 2100	10	5 @ 13
	V8-350	1112880②	C	—	—	—	0 @ 600	11 @ 2100	4	9 @ 12
	V8-350	1112888②	C	—	—	—	0 @ 550	8 @ 2100	4	9 @ 12
	V8-350	1112940②	C	—	—	—	0 @ 600	10 @ 2100	8	7½ @ 15½
	V8-350	1111364	C	—	28–32	—	0 @ 550	11 @ 1900	—	—
	V8-350	1111373	C	—	29–31	—	0 @ 550	11 @ 1900	—	—
	V8-350	1112149	C	—	28–32	—	0 @ 450	11 @ 1900	—	—
	V8-350, 400	1112884②	C	—	—	—	0 @ 575	11 @ 2100	8	5 @ 13
	V8-366	1111379	C	—	29–31	—	0 @ 625	14 @ 2200	—	—
	V8-366, 427	1111378	C	—	28–32	—	0 @ 625	14 @ 2200	—	—
	V8-366, 427	1112890②	C	—	—	—	0 @ 600	14 @ 2200	—	—
	V8-400	1112941②	C	—	—	—	0 @ 500	9½ @ 1725	8	5 @ 13
	V8-454	1112494②	C	—	—	—	0 @ 550	10 @ 2100	10	7 @ 17
	V8-454	1112869②	C	—	—	—	0 @ 550	10 @ 2100	6	10 @ 15
	V8-454	1112886②	C	—	—	—	0 @ 900	6 @ 2100	4	9 @ 7
	V8-454	1112943②	C	—	—	—	0 @ 550	9 @ 2100	6	10 @ 15
	V8-455	1112172	CC	.016	30	—	0–2 @ 575	9 @ 1700	4.5	12 @ 19
	V8-455	1112893②	C	—	—	—	0 @ 450	8 @ 1700	—	6 @ 20
	V8-455	1112945②	C	—	—	—	0 @ 450	8 @ 1700	—	2½ @ 19
1976	6-250	1110650②	C	—	—	—	0 @ 550	8 @ 2100	4	7½ @ 12
	6-250	1110666②	C	—	—	—	0 @ 500	10 @ 2100	4	12 @ 15
	6-250	1110667②	C	—	—	—	0 @ 500	10 @ 2100	4	7½ @ 12
	6-250	1112863②	C	—	—	—	0 @ 550	8 @ 2100	4	9 @ 12
	6-250	1112887②	C	—	—	—	0 @ 550	12 @ 2050	10	5 @ 13
	6-292	1110664②	C	—	—	—	0 @ 550	12 @ 2050	10	5 @ 13

Continued
1159

GMC

DISTRIBUTOR SPECIFICATIONS—Continued

Year	Engine Model	Distributor Number	Rotation ①	Breaker Gap (New)	Dwell Angle Deg.	Breaker Arm Spring Tension	Centrifugal Advance Degrees @ R.P.M. of Distributor		Vacuum Advance	
							Advance Starts	Full Advance	Inches of Vacuum To Start Plunger	Max. Adv. Dist. Deg. @ Vacuum
	6-292	1112887②	C	—	—	—	0–1 @ 600	13 @ 2050	9–11	8 @ 14
	V8-305	1112977②	C	—	—	—	0 @ 500	10 @ 1900	4	9 @ 12
	V8-305	1112999②	C	—	—	—	0 @ 500	10 @ 1900	4	5 @ 8
	V8-350	1112880②	C	—	—	—	0 @ 600	11 @ 2100	4	9 @ 12
	V8-350	1112885②	C	—	—	—	0–2 @ 550	11 @ 1900	—	—
	V8-350	1112888②	C	—	—	—	0 @ 550	8 @ 1200	4	9 @ 12
	V8-350	1112905②	C	—	—	—	0 @ 600	11 @ 2100	6	7½ @ 12
	V8-350	1112940②	C	—	—	—	0 @ 600	10 @ 2100	8	7½ @ 15½
	V8-350, 400	1112884④	C	—	—	—	0 @ 575	11 @ 2100	8	5 @ 13
	V8-366	1112890②	C	—	—	—	0–2 @ 600	14 @ 2200	—	—
	V8-400	1103203②	C	—	—	—	0 @ 500	7½ @ 1400	6	7½ @ 12
	V8-400	1102882②	C	—	—	—	0 @ 500	7½ @ 1400	8	7½ @ 15½
	V8-400	1112941②	C	—	—	—	0 @ 500	9½ @ 1725	8	5 @ 13
	V8-427	1112890②	C	—	—	—	0–2 @ 600	14 @ 2200	—	—
	V8-454	1112494②	C	—	—	—	0 @ 550	10 @ 2100	10	7½ @ 17
	V8-454	1112869②	C	—	—	—	0 @ 550	10 @ 2100	6	10 @ 15
	V8-454	1112886②	C	—	—	—	0 @ 650	6 @ 2100	4	9 @ 7
	V8-455	1112893③	CC	—	—	—	0 @ 450	8 @ 1700	8–10	6 @ 20
	V8-455	1112945③	CC	—	—	—	0 @ 450	8 @ 1700	14–15	2½ @ 19
1977	6-250	1110674②	C	—	—	—	0 @ 550	8 @ 2100	4	18 @ 12
	6-250	1110678②	C	—	—	—	0 @ 500	10 @ 2100	4	24 @ 15
	6-250	1110679②	C	—	—	—	0 @ 550	12 @ 2050	10	10 @ 13
	6-250	1110682②	C	—	—	—	0 @ 550	8 @ 2100	4	7½ @ 12
	6-250	1110692②	C	—	—	—	0 @ 550	10 @ 2100	4	9 @ 12
	6-292	1110679②	C	—	—	—	0 @ 550	12 @ 2050	10	10 @ 13
	6-292	1110680②	C	—	—	—	0 @ 550	12 @ 2050	10	10 @ 13
	V8-305	1103237②	C	—	—	—	0 @ 500	10 @ 1900	8	5 @ 13
	V8-305	1103239②	C	—	—	—	0 @ 600	10 @ 2100	4	7½ @ 10
	V8-305	1103252②	C	—	—	—	0 @ 500	10 @ 1900	4	9 @ 12
	V8-350	1103246②	C	—	—	—	0 @ 600	11 @ 2100	4	9 @ 12
	V8-350	1103248②	C	—	—	—	0 @ 600	11 @ 2100	4	5 @ 8
	V8-350	1103250②	C	—	—	—	0 @ 575	11 @ 2100	8	5 @ 13
	V8-350	1103251②	C	—	—	—	0 @ 500	13 @ 2200	—	—
	V8-350	1103253②	C	—	—	—	0 @ 550	11 @ 2300	4	9 @ 12
	V8-350	1103254②	C	—	—	—	0 @ 600	11 @ 2100	6	7½ @ 12
	V8-350	1103274②	C	—	—	—	0 @ 600	10 @ 2100	6	7½ @ 12
	V8-366, 427	1103241②	C	—	—	—	0 @ 550	13 @ 2200	—	—
	V8-400	1103249②	C	—	—	—	0 @ 500	9½ @ 1725	6	7½ @ 12
	V8-400	1103250②	C	—	—	—	0 @ 575	11 @ 2100	8	5 @ 13
	V8-454	1103238②	C	—	—	—	0 @ 550	10 @ 2100	10	7½ @ 17
	V8-454	1103240②	C	—	—	—	0 @ 550	10 @ 2100	6	10 @ 15
1978	V6-200	1110696②	C	—	—	—	0 @ 500	10 @ 1900	3	8 @ 6½
	V6-231	1110695②	C	—	—	—	0–3 @ 1000	9 @ 1800	7–9	12 @ 13
	V6-231	1110731②	C	—	—	—	0–2 @ 1000	9 @ 1800	4–6	8 @ 9
	6-250	1110715②	C	—	—	—	0 @ 500	10 @ 2100	4	9 @ 12
	6-250	1110717②	C	—	—	—	0 @ 550	12 @ 2050	4	9 @ 12
	6-250	1110719②	C	—	—	—	0 @ 550	8 @ 2100	4	9 @ 12
	6-250, 292	1110720②	C	—	—	—	0 @ 550	12 @ 2050	10	5 @ 13
	6-292	1110721②	C	—	—	—	0 @ 550	12 @ 2050	10	5 @ 13
	V8-305	1103237②	C	—	—	—	0 @ 500	10 @ 1900	8	5 @ 13
	V8-305	1103281②	C	—	—	—	0 @ 500	10 @ 1900	4	9 @ 12
	V8-305	1103282②	C	—	—	—	0 @ 500	10 @ 1900	4	10 @ 10
	V8-305	1103338②	C	—	—	—	0 @ 500	10 @ 1900	5	12 @ 12

Continued

GMC

DISTRIBUTOR SPECIFICATIONS—Continued

Year	Engine Model	Distributor Number	Rotation ①	Breaker Gap (New)	Dwell Angle Deg.	Breaker Arm Spring Tension	Centrifugal Advance Degrees @ R.P.M. of Distributor		Vacuum Advance	
							Advance Starts	Full Advance	Inches of Vacuum To Start Plunger	Max. Adv. Dist. Deg. @ Vacuum
	V8-350	1103250②	C	—	—	—	0 @ 575	11 @ 2100	8	5 @ 13
	V8-350	1103251②	C	—	—	—	0 @ 500	12 @ 2050	—	—
	V8-350	1103274②	C	—	—	—	0 @ 600	10 @ 2100	6	7½ @ 8
	V8-350	1103285②	C	—	—	—	0 @ 600	11 @ 2100	4	5 @ 8
	V8-350	1103286②	C	—	—	—	0 @ 550	11 @ 2300	4	9 @ 12
	V8-350	1103302②	C	—	—	—	0 @ 550	11 @ 2300	6	7½ @ 12
	V8-350	1103337②	C	—	—	—	0 @ 550	8 @ 1200	4	12 @ 10
	V8-350	1103339②	C	—	—	—	0 @ 550	11 @ 2300	4	5 @ 8
	V8-366, 427	1103241②	C	—	—	—	0 @ 550	13 @ 2200	—	—
	V8-400	1103249②	C	—	—	—	0 @ 500	9½ @ 1725	6	7½ @ 12
	V8-400	1103250②	C	—	—	—	0 @ 550	11 @ 2100	8	5 @ 13
	V8-400	1103301②	C	—	—	—	0 @ 500	9½ @ 1725	4	5 @ 8
	V8-454	1103238②	C	—	—	—	0 @ 550	10 @ 2100	8	5 @ 13
	V8-454	1103240②	C	—	—	—	0 @ 550	10 @ 2100	6	10 @ 15
	V8-454	1103358②	C	—	—	—	0 @ 550	10 @ 2100	4	7½ @ 10
1979	V6-200	1110696②	C	—	—	—	0 @ 500	10 @ 1900	2	8 @ 7½
	V6-200	1110756②	C	—	—	—	0 @ 700	7 @ 1900	2	12 @ 10
	V6-231	1110766②	C	—	—	—	0-2 @ 1000	8½ @ 1800	4	12 @ 12
	V6-231	1110767②	C	—	—	—	0-2 @ 1000	8½ @ 1800	3	10 @ 12
	6-250	1110717②	C	—	—	—	0 @ 550	12 @ 2050	4	9 @ 12
	6-250	1110749②	C	—	—	—	0 @ 550	8 @ 2100	4	5 @ 8
	6-292	1110753②	C	—	—	—	0 @ 550	12 @ 2050	4	5 @ 8
	V8-267	1103370②	C	—	—	—	0 @ 650	8 @ 2100	3	12 @ 10
	V8-267	1103371②	C	—	—	—	0 @ 500	11 @ 2200	3	12 @ 10
	V8-305	1103282②	C	—	—	—	0 @ 500	10 @ 1900	4	10 @ 11
	V8-305	1103368②	C	—	—	—	0 @ 500	10 @ 1900	4	5 @ 8
	V8-305	1103369②	C	—	—	—	0 @ 600	10 @ 2100	3	8 @ 6½
	V8-305	1103374②	C	—	—	—	0 @ 600	10 @ 2100	4	8 @ 7½
	V8-305	1103379②	C	—	—	—	0 @ 500	10 @ 1900	3	10 @ 8½
	V8-305	1103381②	C	—	—	—	0 @ 600	10 @ 2100	3	10 @ 7½
	V8-350	1103286②	C	—	—	—	0 @ 550	11 @ 2300	4	9 @ 12
	V8-350	1103302②	C	—	—	—	0 @ 550	11 @ 2300	6	7½ @ 12
	V8-350	1103339②	C	—	—	—	0 @ 550	11 @ 2300	4	5 @ 8
	V8-350	1103353②	C	—	—	—	0 @ 550	11 @ 2300	4	10 @ 11
	V8-350	1103372②	C	—	—	—	0 @ 550	11 @ 2300	4	7 @ 8
	V8-350	1103375②	C	—	—	—	0 @ 575	11 @ 2100	4	5 @ 8
	V8-400	1103301②	C	—	—	—	0 @ 500	9½ @ 1725	4	5 @ 8
	V8-400	1103375②	C	—	—	—	0 @ 575	11 @ 2100	4	5 @ 8
	V8-454	1103240②	C	—	—	—	—	—	—	—
	V8-454	1103358②	C	—	—	—	—	—	—	—
	V8-454	1103376②	C	—	—	—	0 @ 550	10 @ 2100	8	5 @ 13
1980	V6-229	1110696	C	—	—	—	0 @ 500	5 @ 1900	2	8 @ 7.5
	V6-229	1110756	C	—	—	—	0 @ 700	7 @ 1900	2	12 @ 10
	V6-231	1110766	C	—	—	—	0-2 @ 1000	6½-8½ @ 1800	4	12 @ 12
	V6-231	1110767	C	—	—	—	0-2 @ 1000	6½-8½ @ 1800	3	10 @ 12
	6-250	1110755	C	—	—	—	0 @ 550	12 @ 2050	5	8 @ 11.5
	6-250	1110747	C	—	—	—	0 @ 550	12 @ 2050	4	7.5 @ 12
	6-250	1110717	C	—	—	—	0 @ 550	12 @ 2050	5	8 @ 11.5
	6-250	1110749	C	—	—	—	0 @ 550	8 @ 2100	4	5 @ 8
	V8-267	1103371	C	—	—	—	0 @ 500	11 @ 2200	3	12 @ 10
	6-292	1110753	C	—	—	—	0 @ 550	12 @ 2050	4	5 @ 8
	V8-305	1103282	C	—	—	—	0 @ 500	10 @ 1900	4	10 @ 11

Continued

GMC

DISTRIBUTOR SPECIFICATIONS—Continued

Year	Engine Model	Distributor Number	Rotation ①	Breaker Gap (New)	Dwell Angle Deg.	Breaker Arm Spring Tension	Centrifugal Advance Degrees @ R.P.M. of Distributor		Vacuum Advance	
							Advance Starts	Full Advance	Inches of Vacuum To Start Plunger	Max. Adv. Dist. Deg. @ Vacuum
	V8-305	1103368	C	—	—	—	0 @ 500	10 @ 1900	4	5 @ 8
	V8-305	1103369	C	—	—	—	0 @ 600	10 @ 2100	3	8 @ 6.5
	V8-305	1103379	C	—	—	—	0 @ 500	10 @ 1900	3	10 @ 8.5
	V8-305	1103381	C	—	—	—	0 @ 600	10 @ 2100	3	10 @ 7.5
	V8-350	1103339	C	—	—	—	0 @ 550	11 @ 2300	4	5 @ 8
	V8-350	1103372	C	—	—	—	0 @ 550	11 @ 2300	4	7 @ 8
	V8-350	1103375	C	—	—	—	0 @ 575	11 @ 2100	4	5 @ 8
	V8-350	1103420	C	—	—	—	0 @ 900	12 @ 2000	10	5 @ 13
	V8-350	1103435	C	—	—	—	0 @ 550	11 @ 2300	3	8 @ 6.5
	V8-350	1103436	C	—	—	—	0 @ 550	11 @ 2300	3	10 @ 7.5
	V8-350	1103439	C	—	—	—	0 @ 500	9.5 @ 1725	4	7 @ 8
	V8-400	1103375	C	—	—	—	0 @ 575	11 @ 2100	4	5 @ 8
	V8-400	1103420	C	—	—	—	0 @ 900	12 @ 2000	10	5 @ 13
	V8-400	1103423	C	—	—	—	0 @ 500	9.5 @ 1725	4	7.5 @ 10
	V8-400	1103439	C	—	—	—	0 @ 500	9.5 @ 1725	4	7 @ 8
	V8-454	1103376	C	—	—	—	0 @ 550	10 @ 2100	8	5 @ 13

①—As viewed from top. C—Clockwise, CC—Counterclockwise.
②—High Energy Ignition System.

STARTING MOTOR SPECIFICATIONS

Starter Number	Brush Spring Tension Oz.①	Free Speed Test			Resistance Test ③		Lock Torque Test		
		Amps.	Volts	R.P.M.	Amps.	Volts	Amps.	Volts	Torque Ft. Lbs.
1107247	35	49–76②	10.6	6200–9400	270–310②	4.3	—	—	—
1107273	35	49–76②	10.6	6200–9400	270–310	4.3	—	—	—
1107274	35	65–100②	10.6	3600–5100	300–360	3.5	—	—	—
1107315	35	55–95②	10.6	3800–6000	300–360	3.5	—	—	—
1107320	35	65–100②	10.6	3600–5100	300–360	3.5	—	—	—
1107365	35	70–99②	10.6	7800–12000	410–480②	3.0	—	—	—
1107369	40	72②	11.8	6025	295–365	3.5	—	—	—
1107370	40	72②	11.8	6025	295–365	3.5	—	—	—
1107371	40	72②	11.8	6025	295–365②	3.5	—	—	—
1107372	35	55–95②	10.6	3800–6000	300–360	3.5	—	—	—
1107375	35	100②	10.6	3600	300–360②	3.5	—	—	—
1107376	35	95②	10.6	3800	300–360②	3.5	—	—	—
1107399	35	49–87②	10.6	6200–10700	290–425②	4.2	—	—	—
1107497	35	49–87②	10.6	6200–10700	290–425②	4.2	—	—	—
1107591	35	75–100②	10.6	6450–8750	720–870②	5.0	—	—	—
1107575	35	75–100②	10.6	6450–8750	720–870②	5.0	—	—	—
1107586	35	50–80②	9	5500–9000	—	—	—	—	—
1107681	35	65–100②	10.6	3600–5100	300–360	3.5	—	—	—
1107751	35	65–100②	10.6	3600–5100	300–360	3.5	—	—	—
1107752	35	55–95②	10.6	3800–6000	300–360	3.5	—	—	—
1108332	40	72②	11.8	6025	295–365	3.5	—	—	—
1108357	35	35–75②	9	6000–9000	—	—	—	—	—
1108338	35	55–80②	9	3500–6000	—	—	—	—	—
1108350	40	72	11.8	6025	295–365	3.5	—	—	—
1108360	35	55–80②	9	3500–6000	—	—	—	—	—
1108362	35	55–80②	9	3500–6000	—	—	—	—	—
1108363	40	72	11.8	6025	295–365	3.5	—	—	—

Continued

GMC

STARTING MOTOR SPECIFICATIONS—Continued

Starter Number	Brush Spring Tension Oz.①	Free Speed Test			Resistance Test③		Lock Torque Test		
		Amps.	Volts	R.P.M.	Amps.	Volts	Amps.	Volts	Torque Ft. Lbs.
1108364	40	35–75②	9	6000–9000	295–365	3.5	—	—	—
1108365	35	50–80②	9	5500–10500	—	—	—	—	—
1108367	35	50–80②	9	5500–10500	—	—	—	—	—
1108368	35	50–80②	9	5500–10500	—	—	—	—	—
1108369	—	35–75②	9	6000–9000	—	—	—	—	—
1108372	40	72	11.8	6025	295–365	3.5	—	—	—
1108385	—	65–95②	9	7500–10500	—	—	—	—	—
1108418	—	65–95②	9	7500–10500	—	—	—	—	—
1108425	35	40–105②	9	3500–6500	—	—	—	—	—
1108427	—	55–80②	9	3500–6000	—	—	—	—	—
1108430	—	65–95②	9	7500–10500	—	—	—	—	—
1108479	—	50–80②	9	5500–10500	—	—	—	—	—
1108480	—	50–80②	9	5500–10500	—	—	—	—	—
1108483	—	55–80②	9	3500–6000	—	—	—	—	—
1108484	—	35–75②	9	6000–9000	—	—	—	—	—
1108485	—	35–75②	9	6000–9000	—	—	—	—	—
1108486	—	35–75②	9	6000–9000	—	—	—	—	—
1108487	—	35–75②	9	6000–9000	—	—	—	—	—
1108488	—	35–75②	9	6000–9000	—	—	—	—	—
1108502	—	65–95②	9	7500–10500	—	—	—	—	—
1108522	—	65–95	9	7500–10500	—	—	—	—	—
1108550	—	50–80②	9	5500–9000	—	—	—	—	—
1108744	—	50–80②	9	5500–10500	—	—	—	—	—
1108746	—	50–80②	9	5500–10500	—	—	—	—	—
1108747	—	50–80②	9	3500–6000	—	—	—	—	—
1108748	—	65–90②	9	7500–10500	—	—	—	—	—
1108752	—	65–95②	9	7500–10500	—	—	—	—	—
1108753	—	65–95②	9	7500–10500	—	—	—	—	—
1108754	—	65–95②	9	7500–10500	—	—	—	—	—
1108761	—	65–95	9	7500–10500	—	—	—	—	—
1108774	—	50–80②	9	5500–10500	—	—	—	—	—
1108776	—	65–95②	9	7500–10500	—	—	—	—	—
1108778	—	50–80②	9	5500–10500	—	—	—	—	—
1108779	—	50–80②	9	5500–10500	—	—	—	—	—
1108780	—	50–80②	9	3500–6000	—	—	—	—	—
1108781	—	65–90②	9	7500–10500	—	—	—	—	—
1108782	—	65–90②	9	7500–10500	—	—	—	—	—
1108783	—	55–80②	9	3500–6000	—	—	—	—	—
1108774	—	55–80②	9	3500–6000	—	—	—	—	—
1108785	—	55–80②	9	3500–6000	—	—	—	—	—
1108787	—	35–75②	9	6000–9000	—	—	—	—	—
1108788	—	65–95②	9	7500–10500	—	—	—	—	—
1108792	—	35–75②	9	6000–9000	—	—	—	—	—
1108793	—	55–80②	9	3500–6000	—	—	—	—	—
1108799	—	50–80②	9	5500–10500	—	—	—	—	—
1109030	—	55–80②	9	3500–6000	—	—	—	—	—
1109032	—	35–75②	9	6000–9000	—	—	—	—	—
1109033	—	65–95②	9	7500–10500	—	—	—	—	—
1109034	—	65–95②	9	7500–10500	—	—	—	—	—
1109035	—	65–95②	9	7500–10500	—	—	—	—	—
1109052	—	65–95②	9	7500–10500	—	—	—	—	—
1109056	—	50–80②	9	5500–10500	—	—	—	—	—
1109059	—	65–95②	9	7500–10500	—	—	—	—	—
1109075④	—	35–75	9	6000–9000	—	—	—	—	—
1109075⑤	—	65–95	9	7500–10500	—	—	—	—	—

Continued

GMC

STARTING MOTOR SPECIFICATIONS—Continued

Starter Number	Brush Spring Tension Oz.①	Free Speed Test			Resistance Test③		Lock Torque Test		
		Amps.	Volts	R.P.M.	Amps.	Volts	Amps.	Volts	Torque Ft. Lbs.
1109076	—	65–95②	9	7500–10500	—	—	—	—	—
1109077	—	65–95②	9	7500–10500	—	—	—	—	—
1109078	—	55–80②	9	3500–6000	—	—	—	—	—
1109079	—	55–80②	9	3500–6000	—	—	—	—	—
1109086	—	95–120②	9	4000–7000	—	—	—	—	—
1109146	—	50–80②	9	5500–9000	—	—	—	—	—
1109631	—	95–120②	20	5500–7500	—	—	—	—	—
1109772	—	95–120②	20	5500–7500	—	—	—	—	—
1109798	—	50–80②	9	5500–10500	—	—	—	—	—
1113114	80	57–70②	11.5	5000–7400	—	—	500	3.3	22
1113169	80	57–70②	11.5	5000–7400	—	—	500	3.4	22
1113171	—	50–70②	9	3500–5500	—	—	—	—	—
1113183	80	70②	11.5	5000–7400	—	—	500	3.4	22
1113184	—	50–70②	9	3500–5500	—	—	—	—	—
1113202	—	57–70②	11.5	5000–7400	—	—	—	—	—
1113243	—	50–70②	9	3500–5500	—	—	—	—	—
1113379	80	65②	11.4	6000	—	—	500	3.2	28
1113659	80	125–165②	11.0	6300–8700	—	—	600	1.3	11
1113686	80	130–160②	11.0	5000–7000	—	—	—	—	—
1114068	80	100–155②	11.0	6300–9500	—	—	700	1.5	15
1114070	80	170②	11.0	6300	—	—	600	1.3	11
1114074	80	115–170②	11.0	6300–9500	—	—	700	1.5	15
1114086	—	140–190②	9	4000–7000	—	—	—	—	—
1114101	80	120–150	9	3000–4500	—	—	—	—	—
1114105	80	90–130②	11.5	5600–7600	—	—	600	2.5	16.5
1114121	80	90–130②	11.5	5600–7600	—	—	600	2.5	16.5
1114107	80	90–130②	11.5	5600–7600	—	—	600	2.5	16.5
1114135	—	90–130②	11.5	5600–7600	—	—	—	—	—
1114141	—	140–215②	9	4000–7000	—	—	—	—	—
1114143	—	140–190②	9	4000–7000	—	—	—	—	—
1114161	—	140–190②	9	4000–7000	—	—	—	—	—
1114163	—	120–150②	9	3000–4500	—	—	—	—	—
1114178	—	120–150②	9	3000–4500	—	—	—	—	—
1114733	—	140–190②	9	4000–7000	—	—	—	—	—

①—Minimum.
②—Includes solenoid.
③—Check capacity of motor by using a 500 ampere meter and a carbon pile rheostat to control voltage. Apply volts listed across motor with armature locked. Current should be as listed.
④—Exc. Heavy Duty.
⑤—Heavy Duty.

ALTERNATOR & REGULATOR SPECIFICATIONS

Year	Alternator					Regulator						
	Model	Field Current @ 80° F. 12 Volts	Cold Output @ 14 Volts		Rated Hot Output Amperes	Model	Field Relay			Voltage Regulator		
			Amperes @ 2000 R.P.M.	Amperes @ 5000 R.P.M.			Air Gap	Point Gap	Closing Voltage	Air Gap	Point Gap	Volts @ 125° F.
1970–72	1100825	4–4.5	—	58	61	Integral	—	—	—	—	—	—
	1100833	4–4.5	—	37	42	Integral	—	—	—	—	—	—
	1100834	2.2–2.6	25	35	37	1119515	.015	.030	1.5–2.7	—	.014	13.5–14.6
	1100838	2.2–2.6	25	35	37	1119515	.015	.030	1.5–2.7	—	.014	13.5–14.6
	1100839	2.2–2.6	28	40	42	1119515	.015	.030	1.5–2.7	—	.014	13.5–14.6
	1100842	2.2–2.6	28	40	42	1119515	.015	.030	1.5–2.7	.067	.014	13.5–14.6
	1100842	2.2–2.6	28	40	42	1119507	.015	.030	3.8–7.2	.067	.014	13.5–14.4
	1100849	2.2–2.6	33	58	61	1119507	.015	.030	3.8–.72	.067	.014	13.5–14.4
	1100849	2.2–2.6	33	58	61	1119515	.015	.030	1.5–2.7	.067	.014	13.5–14.6
	1100750	2.2–2.6	33	58	61	1119515	.015	.030	1.5–2.7	.067	.014	13.5–14.6
	1117128	2.22–2.4	40	126	130	1119507	.015	.030	3.8–7.2	.067	.014	13.5–14.4

Continued

GMC

ALTERNATOR & REGULATOR SPECIFICATIONS—Continued

| Year | Alternator | | | | | Regulator | | | | | | |
| | Model | Field Current @ 80° F. 12 Volts | Cold Output @ 14 Volts | | Rated Hot Output Amperes | Model | Field Relay | | | Voltage Regulator | | |
			Amperes @ 2000 R.P.M.	Amperes @ 5000 R.P.M.			Air Gap	Point Gap	Closing Voltage	Air Gap	Point Gap	Volts @ 125° F.
	1117128	2.22–2.4	40⑦	126⑧	130	1116374	—	—	—	—	—	—
	1117128	2.22–2.4	40⑦	126⑧	130	9000590	—	—	—	—	—	—
	1117141	4–4.5	—	—	—	Integral	—	—	—	—	—	—
	1117225	4.1–4.5	22⑦	65⑧	75	Integral	—	—	—	—	—	—
	1117231	4.1–4.5	22⑦	65⑧	75	Integral	—	—	—	—	—	—
	1117754	3.7–4.4	20⑦	55⑧	62	1116374	—	—	4.5–8	—	—	13.6–14.3
	1117754	3.7–4.4	20⑦	55⑧	62	1116378	—	—	2–4	—	—	13.6–14.3
	1117756	3.7–4.4	20⑦	55⑧	62	9000590	—	—	—	—	—	13.7–14.3
	1117765	4.1–4.6	20⑦	55⑧	62	1116374	—	—	4.5–8	—	—	13.6–14.3
	1117777	3.7–4.4	20⑦	55⑧	62	9000590	—	—	—	—	—	13.7–14.3
	1117782	4.14–4.62	20⑦	55⑧	62	1116378	—	—	—	—	—	13.6–14.3
1972	1102440	2.2–2.6	25	35	37	1119515	.015	.030	1.5–3.2	.067	.014	13.5–14.4
	1102452	2.2–2.6	25	35	37	1119515	.015	.030	1.5–3.2	.067	.014	13.5–14.4
	1102453	2.2–2.6	25	35	37	1119515	.015	.030	1.5–3.2	.067	.014	13.5–14.4
	1102455	2.2–2.6	33	58	61	1119515	.015	.030	1.5–3.2	.067	.014	13.5–14.4
	1102456	2.2–2.6	25	35	37	1119515	.015	.030	1.5–3.2	.067	.014	13.5–14.4
	1102458	2.2–2.6	28	40	42	1119515	.015	.030	1.5–3.2	.067	.014	13.5–14.4
	1102459	2.2–2.6	28	40	42	1119515	.015	.030	1.5–3.2	.067	.014	13.5–14.4
	1102463	2.2–2.6	33	58	61	1119515	.015	.030	1.5–3.2	.067	.014	13.5–14.4
	1100487	2.2–2.6	33	58	61	Integral	—	—	—	—	—	—
1973	1102349	4.0–4.5	—	37	42	Integral	—	—	—	—	—	—
	1102350	4.0–4.5	—	55	61	Integral	—	—	—	—	—	—
1973–74	1100497	4.4–4.9	—	36.6④	37	Integral	—	—	—	—	—	—
	1100573	4.0–4.5	—	37	42	Integral	—	—	—	—	—	—
	1100597	4.0–4.5	—	55	61	Integral	—	—	—	—	—	—
	1100934	4.4–4.5	—	36④	37	Integral	—	—	—	—	—	—
	1102346	4.0–4.5	—	37	42	Integral	—	—	—	—	—	—
	1102347	4.0–4.5	—	55	61	Integral	—	—	—	—	—	—
1974	1100080	—	54	73	80	Integral	—	—	—	—	—	—
	1100081	—	48	61	65	Integral	—	—	—	—	—	—
	1100547	4.0–4.5	—	37	42	Integral	—	—	—	—	—	—
	1100548	4.0–4.5	—	55	61	Integral	—	—	—	—	—	—
	1101022	4.0–4.5	—	74	80	Integral	—	—	—	—	—	—
	1102352	4.0–4.5	—	55	61	Integral	—	—	—	—	—	—
	1117141	4.0–4.5	—	110	105	Integral	—	—	—	—	—	—
	1100838	2.2–2.6	25	35	37	1119515	.015	.030	1.5–3.2	.067	.014	13.5–14.4
	1100842	2.2–2.6	28	40	42	1119515	.015	.030	1.5–3.2	.067	.014	13.5–14.4
	1100849	2.2–2.6	33	58	61	1119507	.015	.030	3.8–7.2	.067	.014	13.5–14.4
	1100849	2.2–2.6	33	58	61	1119515	.015	.030	1.5–3.2	.067	.014	13.5–14.4
	1117782	4.1–4.6	20①	55②	62	1116374	—	—	4.5–8	—	—	13.4–14.1
	1117782	4.1–4.6	20①	55②	62	1116378	—	—	2–4	—	—	13.4–14.1
	1102382	4.0–4.5	—	37	42	Integral	—	—	—	—	—	—
	1102383	4.0–4.5	—	55	61	Integral	—	—	—	—	—	—
	1100575	4.0–4.5	—	50	55	Integral	—	—	—	—	—	—
1975	655988	—	102	—	105	Integral	—	—	—	—	—	—
	1100080	4.4–4.9	52	72	80	Integral	—	—	—	—	—	—
	1100081	4.4–4.9	45	57	65	Integral	—	—	—	—	—	—
	1100497	4.4–4.9	—	33	37	Integral	—	—	—	—	—	—
	1100547	—	40	—	42	Integral	—	—	—	—	—	—
	1100548	—	57	—	61	Integral	—	—	—	—	—	—
	1100560	4.0–4.5	—	50	55	Integral	—	—	—	—	—	—
	1100575	4.0–4.5	—	50	55	Integral	—	—	—	—	—	—
	1100597	4.0–4.5	—	55	61	Integral	—	—	—	—	—	—

Continued

GMC

ALTERNATOR & REGULATOR SPECIFICATIONS—Continued

Year	Model	Alternator Field Current @ 80° F. 12 Volts	Cold Output @ 14 Volts Amperes @ 2000 R.P.M.	Cold Output @ 14 Volts Amperes @ 5000 R.P.M.	Rated Hot Output Amperes	Regulator Model	Field Relay Air Gap	Field Relay Point Gap	Field Relay Closing Voltage	Voltage Regulator Air Gap	Voltage Regulator Point Gap	Voltage Regulator Volts @ 125° F.
	1100838	3.0⑦	35	—	37	⑤	—	—	—	—	—	12.5–15.5
	1100842	3.0⑦	40	—	42	⑤	—	—	—	—	—	12.5–15.5
	1100849	3.0⑦	57	—	61	⑤	—	—	—	—	—	12.5–15.5
	1101022	—	—	—	80	Integral	—	—	—	—	—	—
	1102346	4.0–4.5	—	38	42	Integral	—	—	—	—	—	—
	1102347	4.0–4.5	—	55	61	Integral	—	—	—	—	—	—
	1102483	4.0–4.5	—	33	37	Integral	—	—	—	—	—	—
	1102493	4.0–4.5	—	38	42	Integral	—	—	—	—	—	—
	1117147	4.0–4.5	80	110	105	Integral	—	—	—	—	—	—
	1117225	4.1–4.5	—	77	75	Integral	—	—	—	—	—	—
	1117231	4.1–4.5	—	77	75	Integral	—	—	—	—	—	—
	1117782	4.1–4.6	20①	55②	62	⑥	—	—	—	—	—	12.5–15.5
	1117787	—	62⑧	—	65	—	—	—	—	—	—	12.5–15.5
1975–76	711925⑨	2.8	81	105④	105	Integral	—	—	—	—	—	—
	1101015	4.4–4.9	—	76	80	Integral	—	—	—	—	—	—
	1101016	4.4–4.9	—	76	80	Integral	—	—	—	—	—	—
	1101029	4.4–4.9	55	76	80	Integral	—	—	—	—	—	—
	1102497	4.0–4.5	30	57	61	Integral	—	—	—	—	—	—
	1102498	2.2–2.6	33	58	61	Integral	—	—	—	—	—	—
	1102499	4.0–4.5	25	38	42	Integral	—	—	—	—	—	—
	1102943	2.2–2.6	25	35	37	1119515	.015	.030	1.5–3.2	.067	.014	13.5–14.4
	1102944	2.2–2.6	28	40	42	1119515	.015	.030	1.5–3.2	.067	.014	13.5–14.4
	1102945	2.2–2.6	33	58	61	1119507	.015	.030	3.8–7.2	.067	.014	13.5–14.4
	1117481	3.6–4.3	68②	86③	90	Integral	—	—	—	—	—	—
1976	1100080	4.4–4.9	52	72	80	Integral	—	—	—	—	—	—
	1100081	4.4–4.9	45	57	65	Integral	—	—	—	—	—	—
	1117147	4.0–4.5	80	110	105	Integral	—	—	—	—	—	—
	1117225	4.1–4.5	—	77	75	Integral	—	—	—	—	—	—
	1117231	4.1–4.5	—	77	75	Integral	—	—	—	—	—	—
	1117782	4.1–4.6	20①	55②	62	1116378	—	—	2–4	—	—	13.4–14.1
1977–80	711925	2.8	81	105④	105	Integral	—	—	—	—	—	—
	1100080	4.4–4.9	52	72	80	Integral	—	—	—	—	—	—
	1100081	4.4–4.9	46	58	65	Integral	—	—	—	—	—	—
	1101016	4–4.5	—	76	80	Integral	—	—	—	—	—	—
	1101020	4.4–4.9	63	97	100	Integral	—	—	—	—	—	—
	1101028	4–4.5	—	76	80	Integral	—	—	—	—	—	—
	1101029	4.4–4.9	55	76	80	Integral	—	—	—	—	—	—
	1101030	4.4–4.9	55	76	80	Integral	—	—	—	—	—	—
	1101044	4–4.5	—	—	70	Integral	—	—	—	—	—	—
	1101071	4–4.5	—	—	70	Integral	—	—	—	—	—	—
	1102394	4–4.5	—	33	37	Integral	—	—	—	—	—	—
	1102474	4–4.5	—	57	61	Integral	—	—	—	—	—	—
	1102478	4–4.5	—	51	55	Integral	—	—	—	—	—	—
	1102479	4–4.5	—	51	55	Integral	—	—	—	—	—	—
	1102480	4–4.5	—	57	61	Integral	—	—	—	—	—	—
	1102484	4–4.5	—	38	42	Integral	—	—	—	—	—	—
	1102485	4–4.5	—	38	42	Integral	—	—	—	—	—	—
	1102486	4–4.5	—	57	61	Integral	—	—	—	—	—	—
	1102491	4–4.5	—	33	37	Integral	—	—	—	—	—	—
	1102497	4–4.5	30	57	61	Integral	—	—	—	—	—	—
	1102499	4–4.5	25	38	42	Integral	—	—	—	—	—	—
	1102841	4–4.5	—	38	42	Integral	—	—	—	—	—	—
	1102886	4–4.5	—	57	61	Integral	—	—	—	—	—	—

Continued

GMC

ALTERNATOR & REGULATOR SPECIFICATIONS—Continued

Year	Alternator					Regulator						
	Model	Field Current @ 80° F. 12 Volts	Cold Output @ 14 Volts		Rated Hot Output Amperes	Model	Field Relay			Voltage Regulator		
			Amperes @ 2000 R.P.M.	Amperes @ 5000 R.P.M.			Air Gap	Point Gap	Closing Voltage	Air Gap	Point Gap	Volts @ 125° F.
	1102887	4–4.5	—	38	42	Integral	—	—	—	—	—	—
	1102888	4–4.5	—	57	61	Integral	—	—	—	—	—	—
	1102889	4–4.5	—	33	37	Integral	—	—	—	—	—	—
	1103043	4–4.5	—	—	42	Integral	—	—	—	—	—	—
	1103044	4–4.5	—	—	63	Integral	—	—	—	—	—	—
	1103046	4–4.5	32	60	63	Integral	—	—	—	—	—	—
	1103088	4–4.5	—	—	55	Integral	—	—	—	—	—	—
	1103091	4–4.5	—	—	63	Integral	—	—	—	—	—	—
	1103092	4–4.5	—	—	55	Integral	—	—	—	—	—	—
	1103118	4–4.5	—	—	37	Integral	—	—	—	—	—	—
	1103161	4–4.5	—	—	37	Integral	—	—	—	—	—	—
	1103162	4–4.5	—	—	37	Integral	—	—	—	—	—	—
	1103169	4–4.5	—	—	63	Integral	—	—	—	—	—	—
	1117241	4.1–4.5	—	70	75	Integral	—	—	—	—	—	—
	1117244	4.1–4.5	—	70	75	Integral	—	—	—	—	—	—
	1117481	3.6–4.3	68②	86③	90	Integral	—	—	—	—	—	—
	1117732	3.6–4.3	72②	90③	90	Integral	—	—	—	—	—	—
	2009386	5–6	85	130⑩	130	Integral	—	—	—	—	—	—
	5104711	—	15⑩	75⑪	75	Integral	—	—	—	—	—	—
	5148785⑨	4	—	75⑪	75	Integral	—	—	—	—	—	—

①—At 1100 RPM.
②—At 2500 RPM.
③—At 6500 RPM.
④—At 7000 RPM.
⑤—Part number 1119507 or 1119515.
⑥—Part number 1116374 or 1116378.
⑦—Less than.
⑧—At 1800 RPM.
⑨—Leece-Neville Alternator.
⑩—At 600 RPM.
⑪—At 6000 RPM.

PISTON, PIN, RING, CRANKSHAFT & BEARING SPECIFICATIONS

Year	Engine Model	Piston Clearance	Ring End Gap		Wristpin Diameter	Rod Bearings		Main Bearings			Shaft End Play
			Comp.	Oil		Shaft Diameter	Bearing Clearance	Shaft Diameter	Bearing Clearance	Thrust on Bear. No.	
1970–80	6-250	⑬	.010	.015	.9271	1.999–2.000	㉓	㉒	㉔	5	.002–.006
1970–72	6-292	.0026–.0032	.010	.015	.9274	2.0990–2.1000	.0007–.0028	2.2983–2.2993	.0008–.0024	Rear	.002–.006
1973–80	6-292	.0026–.0036	.015	.015	.9271	2.099–2.100	㉓	㉒	㉕	Rear	.002–.006
1978–79	V6-200②	.0007–.0017	.010	.015	.9271	2.0986–2.0998	.0013–.0035	㉑	㉚	4	.002–.006
1980	V6-229	.0007–.0017	.010	.015	.9272	2.0986–2.0998	.0013–.0035	㉑	㉚	4	.002–.006
1978–80	V6-231②	.0008–.0020	.010	.015	.9392	2.2487–2.2495	.0005–.0026	2.4995	.0003–.0017	2	.004–.008
1970–71	V6-305	.0027–.0033	.017	.015	1.24	2.8107–2.8117	.0015–.004	③	④	3	.003–.008
1970–71	V6-351	.0027–.0033	.017	.015	1.24	2.8107–2.8117	.0015–.004	③	④	3	.003–.008
1970–71	V6-401	.0033–.0039	.017	.015	1.24	2.8107–2.8117	.0015–.004	③	④	3	.003–.008
1970–72	V6-478	.0039–.0045	.017	.015	1.24	2.8107–2.8117	.0015–.004	③	④	3	.003–.008
1970–72	V8-637	.0039–.0045	⑤	.017	1.24	2.8107–2.8117	.0015–.004	③	④	4	.003–.008
1979–80	V8-267	.0007–.0017	.010	.015	.9271	2.0986–2.0998	.0013–.0035	㉑	㉚	5	.002–.006
1977–80	V8-305②	.0007–.0017	.010	.015	.9272	㉘	.0013–.0035	㉑	⑭	5	.002–.006
1970–71	V8-307②	.0005–.0011	.015	.015	.9270	1.999–2.000	.004㉗	⑥	.004 Max.	5	.002–.006
1972–73	V8-307②	.0012–.0018	.015	.015	.9270	2.199–2.200	.0013–.0035	⑥	⑭	5	.002–.006
1970–71	V8-350②	.0010–.0016	.015	.015	.9272	2.099–2.100	.0007–.0028	⑦	⑧	5	.003–.011
1972–76	V8-350②	.0007–.0013	⑰	.015	.9272	2.199–2.200	.0013–.0035	⑥	⑭	5	.002–.006
1977–80	V8-350②	.0007–.0017	.010	.015	.9272	㉘	.0013–.0035	㉑	⑭	5	.002–.006
1970–79	V8-366②	.003–.004	.010	.010	.9896	2.199–2.200	.0014–.003	㉜	㉝	5	.006–.010
1970–79	V8-427②	.0034–.0044	.010	.010	.9896	2.199–2.200	.0014–.003	㉜	㉝	5	.006–.010
1970–71	V8-400②	.0018–.0028	.015	.015	.9895	2.1990–2.200	.0009–.0025	⑨	⑩	5	.006–.010
1975	V8-400②	.0014–.0020	.015	.015	.9272	2.099–2.100	.0013–.0035	⑱	⑭	5	.006–.010
1977–80	V8-400②	.0014–.0024	.010	.015	.9272	㉘	.0013–.0035	⑱	⑭	5	.002–.006

Continued

GMC

PISTON, PIN, RING, CRANKSHAFT & BEARING SPECIFICATIONS—Continued

Year	Engine Model	Piston Clearance	Ring End Gap		Wristpin Diameter	Rod Bearings		Main Bearings			Shaft End Play
			Comp.	Oil		Shaft Diameter	Bearing Clearance	Shaft Diameter	Bearing Clearance	Thrust on Bear. No.	
1972	V8-402②	.0018–.0026	.015	.015	.9827	2.1985–2.1995	.0009–.0025	⑮	⑯	5	.006–.010
1977–79	V8-403	.001–.002	.010	.015	.9805	2.1238–2.1248	.0004–.0033	㉛	㉖	3	.0035–.0135
1977–79	V8-454②	㉙	.010	.015	.9895–.9898	2.1985–2.1995	.0009–.0025	⑳	⑫	5	.006–.010
1980	V8-454	.003–.0040	.010	.015	.9896	2.2000–2.1990	.0009–.0025	①	㉗	5	.006–.010
1970–72	V8-454②	.0024–.0034	.015	.015	.9897	2.199–2.200	.0009–.0025	⑪	⑫	5	.006–.010
1973–76	V8-454②	.0018–.0028	.015	.010	.9896	2.1985–2.1995	.0009–.0025	⑪	⑫	5	.006–.010
1973–77	V8-455	.0010–.0020	.010	.015	.9805	2.4988–2.4998	.0004–.0033	2.9993–3.0003	⑲	3	.004–.008

①—Nos. 1, 2, 3, 4, 2.7481–2.7490"; No. 5, 2.7476–2.7486".
②—See Chevrolet Chapter for service procedures on this engine.
③—Rear bearing 3.1225–3.1235", others 3.123–3.124".
④—Rear bearing .0025–.0055", others .002–.005".
⑤—Top ring .026", 2nd ring .017".
⑥—Rear bearing 2.4479–2.4488. Others 2.4484–2.4493".
⑦—Rear 2.4479–2.4488", all others 2.4448–2.4493".
⑧—Rear .001–.006", all others .0008–.0024".
⑨—Nos. 1 and 2—2.7487–2.7496". Nos. 3 and 4—2.7481–2.7499". No. 5—2.7478–2.7488".
⑩—No. 1—.0007–.0019". Nos. 2, 3 and 4—.0013–.0025". No. 5—.0024–.0040".
⑪—No. 1, 2.7485–2.7494 inch; No. 2, 3, 4, 2.7481–2.7490; No. 5, 2.7478–2.7488".
⑫—No. 1, 2, 3, 4, .0013–.0025 inch; No. 5, .0024–.0040.
⑬—1970–77—.0005–.0015, 1978–80—.0010–.0020.
⑭—No. 1—.0008–.0020". Nos. 2, 3 and 4—.0011–.0023". No. 5—.0017–.0032".
⑮—No. 1, 2—2.7487–2.7496"; Nos. 3, 4, 2.7481–2.7490; No. 5, 2.7473–2.7483".
⑯—No. 1—.0007–.0019". Nos. 2, 3 and 4—.0013–.0025". No. 5—.0019–.0033".
⑰—Top ring .010", 2nd ring .013".
⑱—Nos. 1, 2, 3, 4 2.6484–2.6493; No. 5 2.6479–2.6488.
⑲—Nos. 1, 2, 3, 4, .0005"–.0021"; No. 5, .0020–.0034".
⑳—No. 1, 2.7485"–2.7494"; Nos. 2, 3, 4, 2.7481"–2.7490"; No. 5, 2.7478"–2.7488".
㉑—Front 2.4484"–2.4493"; Intermediate 2.4481"–2.4490"; Rear 2.4479"–2.4488".
㉒—Exc. 1978–80—2.2983–2.2993; 1978–80—2.2979–2.2994.
㉓—Exc. 1978–80—.0007–.0027; 1978–80—.0010–.0026.
㉔—Exc. 1978–80—.0003–.0029; 1978–80—Nos. 1 thru 6—.0010–.0024; No. 7—.0016–.0035.
㉕—Exc. 1978–80—.0008–.0034; 1978–80—Nos. 1 thru 6—.0010–.0024; No. 7—.0016–.0035.
㉖—No. 1, 2, 3, 4—.0005–.0021"; No. 5—.0015–.0031.
㉗—Nos. 1, 2, 3, 4, .0013–.0025"; No. 5, .0024–.0040".
㉘—1977—2.199–2.200"; 1978–80—2.0988–2.0998".
㉙—1977—.0024"; 1978–79—.0014–.0024".
㉚—Front .0008–.0020; Intermediate—.0011–.0023; Rear—.0017–.0032.
㉛—Nos. 2, 3, 4, 5—2.4995–2.4985"; No. 1—2.4998–2.4988".
㉜—Rear—2.7473–2.7483; All others—2.7481–2.7490.
㉝—Rear—.0029–.0045; All others—.0013–.0025.

ENGINE TIGHTENING SPECIFICATIONS★

★ Torque Specifications are for clean and lightly lubricated threads only. Dry or dirty threads produce increased friction which prevents accurate measurement of tightness.

Engine	Spark Plugs Ft. Lbs.	Cylinder Head Bolts Ft. Lbs.	Intake Manifold Ft. Lbs.	Exhaust Manifold Ft. Lbs.	Rocker Arm Shaft Bracket Ft. Lbs.	Rocker Arm Cover Ft. Lbs.	Connecting Rod Cap Bolts Ft. Lbs.	Main Bearing Cap Bolts Ft. Lbs.	Flywheel to Crankshaft Ft. Lbs.	Vibration Damper or Pulley Ft. Lbs.
6-250	⑦㉓	95㉕	20–25⑪	20–25⑫	None	㉖	35	65	60	③
6-292	⑦㉓	95㉕	㉗	㉗	None	㉖	40	65	110	60
V6-200④	20㉓	65	30	20	—	45⑭	45	70	60	60
V6-229④	22	65	30	20	—	45⑭	45	70	60	60
V6-231④	20	80	45	25	30	4	40	100	60	175
V6-305	22–27	65–72	20–25	15–20	20–25	—	55–65	130–140①	100–110	⑥
V6-305⑰	32	⑯	20–25	15–20	20–25	3–5	55–65	170–180⑤	100–110㉛	180–200
V6-351	22–27	65–72	20–25	15–20	20–25	—	55–65	130–140①	100–110	⑥
V6-379	15	⑯	20–25	15–20	20–25	3–5	55–65	170–180⑤	100–110㉛	240–260
V6-401	23–27	65–72	20–25	15–20	20–25	—	55–65	130–140①	100–110	⑥
V6-432	15	⑯	20–25	15–20	20–25	3–5	55–65	170–180⑤	100–110㉛	240–260
V6-478	23–27	65–72	20–25	15–20	20–25	—	55–65	130–140①	100–110㉛	⑥
V8-267④	22	65	30	20	—	45⑭	45	70	60	60
V8-283④	25	65	30	20	—	—	35	80	60	—
V8-305④②	15㉓	65	30	20	—	45⑭	45	70	60	60
V8-305④⑳	15㉓	65	30	20	—	45⑭	45	80㉔	60	60
V8-307④	25	65	30	20	—	—	35	80	60	—
V8-350④②	15㉓	65	30	20⑬	—	45⑭	45	70	60	60

Continued

GMC

ENGINE TIGHTENING SPECIFICATIONS★—Continued

★ Torque Specifications are for clean and lightly lubricated threads only. Dry or dirty threads produce increased friction which prevents accurate measurement of tightness.

Engine	Spark Plugs Ft. Lbs.	Cylinder Head Bolts Ft. Lbs.	Intake Manifold Ft. Lbs.	Exhaust Manifold Ft. Lbs.	Rocker Arm Shaft Bracket Ft. Lbs.	Rocker Arm Cover Ft. Lbs.	Connecting Rod Cap Bolts Ft. Lbs.	Main Bearing Cap Bolts Ft. Lbs.	Flywheel to Crankshaft Ft. Lbs.	Vibration Damper or Pulley Ft. Lbs.
V8-350④⑳	⑦㉓	65	30	20⑬	—	45⑭	35⑮	70㉘	60	—
V8-366④	⑦	80	30	25–30	50⑧	50⑭	㉚	⑨	65	85
V8-396④	25	80	30	20	—	—	30	110	65	85
V8-400④	15㉓	65	30	20	—	45⑭	45	80㉔	60	60
V8-402④	⑦	80	30	20	50⑧	4	55	100	60	85
V8-403	25	130	40	25	25⑲	7	42	80㉑	㉒	200–310
V8-427④	⑦	80	30	25–30	50⑧	50⑭	㉚	⑨	65	85
V8-454④	⑦㉓	80⑩	30	20	—	50⑭	50	110	65	85
V8-455	⑱	85	40	25	25⑲	7	42	120	60	160 min.
V8-637	23–27	130–135	20–25	15–20	20–25	—	55–65	170–180⑤	100–105	⑥

① —Rear (1/2″) 55–65.
② —Caballero
③ —Pressed on.
④ —See Chevrolet Chapter for service procedures.
⑤ —Rear and side (1/2″) 90–100 ft. lbs.
⑥ —With cone and washer: V6: 180–200. V8: 1½″ bolt. 190–210. V8: 2½″ bolt, 240–260. Without cone: 95–105 1970–478M, 637 engines; phosphate coated 180–200; cadium coated 240–260.
⑦ —5/8″ hex, tapered seat type 15 ft. lbs.; 13/16″ hex, gasket type 25 ft. lbs.
⑧ —Rocker arm stud.
⑨ —1970–72, inner bolts 100 ft. lbs., outer bolts 95 ft. lbs.; 1973–79, 105 ft. lbs.
⑩ —Aluminum head; short bolt, 65 ft. lbs.; long bolts, 75 ft. lbs.
⑪ —1973–74 engine 35 ft. lbs.
⑫ —1973–80 engine 30 ft. lbs.
⑬ —1973–80 engine inside bolts 30 ft. lbs.
⑭ —Inch pounds
⑮ —1973–80 engine 45 ft. lbs.
⑯ —7/16″ 60–65 ft. lbs.; 1/2″ 90–100 ft. lbs.
⑰ —1973–74.
⑱ —14 mm, 25 ft. lbs.; 18 mm, 35 ft. lbs.
⑲ —Rocker arm pivot bolt.
⑳ —Exc. Caballero.
㉑ —Rear 120 ft. lbs.
㉒ —Auto. trans., 60 ft. lbs.; manual trans., 90 ft. lbs.
㉓ —1979–80, 22 ft. lbs.
㉔ —Intermediate outer bolts, 70 ft. lbs.
㉕ —On 1976–80 engines; front left hand bolt 85 ft. lbs.
㉖ —1970, 55 inch lbs.; 1971–80, 45 inch lbs.
㉗ —1966–73, end clamps 20 ft. lbs., center bolts 30 ft. lbs.; 1974–76, 35 ft. lbs.; 1977–80 40 ft. lbs.
㉘ —1970–76, 70 ft. lbs., outer bolts on models w/4 bolt caps 65 ft. lbs.; 1977–79, 80 ft. lbs.; outer bolts on models w/4 bolt caps, 70 ft. lbs.
㉙ —1977–80, 80 ft. lbs.
㉚ —1970–72, 55 ft. lbs.; 1973–79, 7/16″ bolts 70 ft. lbs.; 3/8″ bolts 50 ft. lbs.
㉛ —1973–74 models w/MT 640 or MT 650 trans., 60–90 ft. lbs.

WHEEL ALIGNMENT SPECIFICATIONS

NOTE: For standard axle with vehicle level and weight on wheels.

Truck Model	Caster Deg.	Camber Deg.	Toe-In Inch	Kingpin Angle Deg.
1970 SERIES 1500 THRU 3500				
K1500	+4	+1–+3	1/8	—
CP1500, C1550	−1/4–+1/4	0–+1/2	1/8–1/4	—
G1500, 2500	+3/4	+1 1/4–+1 3/4	3/32–3/16	7 1/4
K1500, 2500	+3/4	+1/2–+1 1/2	3/32–3/16	—
P2500, 3500	−1/4–+1/4	0–+1/2	1/8–1/4	—
1971 SERIES 1500 THRU 3500				
C-P 1500	㉓	㉓	1/8–1/4	—
C-P 2500, 3500	㉓	㉓	1/8–1/4	—
G1500-3500	0°	+1/4	1/8–1/4	—
K1500, 2500	+4	+1 1/2	1/8–1/4	—
1972 SERIES 1500 THRU 3500				
C-P 1500	㉓	+1/4	3/16	—
C-O 2500, 3500	㉓	+1/4	3/16	—
G1500-3500	㉓	+1/4	3/16	—
K1500, 2500	+4	+1 1/2	3/16	—
Sprint	−1/2–+1 1/2	+1/4–+1 1/4	1/8–1/4	—
1973–74 SERIES 1500 THRU 3500				
CA, GA, PA 10-20-30	㉓	+1/4	3/16	—
KA 10-20	㉓	+1 1/2	3/16㉕	—
Sprint㉖	−1/2–+1 1/2	㉘	0–1/8	—
Sprint㉗	−1/2–+1/2	㉘	0–1/8	—
1975–78 SERIES 1500 THRU 3500				
C-1500, 2500, 3500	㉓	+1/4°	3/16	—
K-1500, 2500	+4①°	+1 1/2°②	0	—
G-1500, 2500, 3500	㉓	+1/4°	3/16	—
P-1500, 2500, 3500	㉓	㉓	3/16	—
P-30 Motor Home	㉓	㉓	5/16	—
Sprint㉖	+2 1/2–+1 1/2	㉘	0–1/8	—
Sprint㉗	⑦	㉘	0–1/8	—
Caballero㉖	+1/2–+1 1/2	0–+1	1/16–3/16	—
Caballero㉗	+2 1/2–+3 1/2	0–+1	1/16–3/16	—
1979–80 SERIES 1500 THRU 3500				
C-1500, 2500, 3500	㉓	+1/5	3/16	—
K-1500, 2500	8④	+1	0	—
K-3500	8④	+1	0	—
G-1500, 2500	㉓	+1/5	3/16	—
G-3500	㉓	+1/5	3/16	—
P-1500, 2500, 3500	㉓	㉓	3/16	—
P-30 Motor Home	㉓	㉓	5/16	—
Caballero㉖	+1	+1/2	1/8	—
Caballero㉗	+3	+1/2	1/8	—

Continued

GMC

WHEEL ALIGNMENT SPECIFICATIONS—Continued

NOTE: For standard axle with vehicle level and weight on wheels.

Truck Model	Caster Deg.	Camber Deg.	Toe-In Inch	Kingpin Angle Deg.
1970–72 SERIES 4000 THRU 6500				
CP4500	+2-+3	+1/2-+1 1/2	1/8-3/16	7 1/4
CS5500	+2-+3	+1/2-+1 1/2	3/32-3/16	7 1/4
CM6500⑩	+2-+3	+1/2-+1 1/2	3/16-3/16	7 1/4
M6500	+2-+3	⑫	1/8-7/32	⑤
CM6500⑪⑭	+2-+3	⑫	1/8-7/32	⑤
T5500-T6500⑩	+3/4-+1 3/4	+1-+2	1/8-1/4	7
T5500-T6500⑪	+3/4-+1 3/4	⑫	1/8-1/4	⑤
1973 SERIES 5000 THRU 6500				
C-50	+2-+3	+1/2-+1 1/2	1/8-3/16	7 1/4
S/C-60	+2-+3	+1/2-+1 1/2	3/32-3/16	7 1/4
C/M-65⑩	+2-+3	+1/2-+1 1/2	3/32-3/16	7 1/4
C/M-65⑪⑮	+2-+3	⑫	1/8-7/32	⑬
T-60⑩	+3/4-+1 3/4	+1-+2	1/8-1/4	7
T-60⑪	+3/4-+1 3/4	㉔	1/8-1/4	⑬
T-65⑩	+3/4-+1 3/4	+1-+2	1/8-1/4	7
T-65⑪	+3/4-+1 3/4	㉔	1/8-1/4	⑬
T-65⑮	+3/4-+1 3/4	㉔	1/8-1/4	⑬
1974 SERIES 4000 THRU 6500				
P-40-45	+2-+3	+1/2-+1 1/2	1/16-1/8	7 1/4
C-50	+2-+3	+1/2-+1 1/2	1/16-1/8	7 1/4
S/C-60	+2-+3	+1/2-+1 1/2	1/16-1/8	7 1/4
C/M-65	+2-+3	+1/2-+1 1/2	1/16-1/8	7 1/4
C/M-65⑪⑮	+2-+3	⑫	1/8-1/4	⑬
T-60⑩	+3/4-+1 1/4	+1-+2	1/16-1/8	7
T-60⑪	+3/4-+1 1/4	⑫	1/8-1/4	⑬
T-65⑩	+3/4-+1 1/4	+1-+2	1/16-1/8	7
T-65⑪	+3/4-+1 1/4	⑫	1/8-1/4	⑬
T-65⑮	+3/4-+1 1/4	⑫	1/8-1/4	⑬
1975–78 SERIES 4000 THRU 6500				
P-40-45	+2-+3	+1-+2	1/8-1/4	7 1/6
C-50	+2-+3	+1-+2	1/8-1/4㉞	7 1/6
S/C-60	+2-+3	+1-+2	1/8-1/4㉞	7 1/6
C/M-65⑩	+2-+3	+1-+2	1/8-1/4㉞	7 1/6
C/M-65⑪㊱	+2-+3	㉟	1/8-1/4㉞	⑬
C/M-65⑮	+2-+3	−1/4-+3/4	1/8-1/4㉞	⑬
T-60-65⑩	+3 1/2-+4 1/2	+1-+2	1/8-1/4㉞	7 1/6
T-60-65⑪㊱	+3 1/2-+4 1/2	㉟	1/8-1/4㉞	⑬
T-60-65⑮㉝	+3 1/2-+4 1/2	−1/4-+3/4	1/8-1/4㉞	⑬
1979–80 SERIES 4500–6500				
B6	+2	+1 1/2	1/8-1/4㉞	7 1/6
C5, 6	+2	+1 1/2	1/8-1/4㉞	7 1/6
P4	+2 1/2	+1 1/2	1/8-1/4㉞	7 1/6
W6	+4	+1 1/2	1/8-1/4㉞	7 1/6
1970 SERIES 7500				
HJ, HM, HV⑩	+2 1/8-+2 7/8	+1-+2	1/8-1/4	7
HJ, HM, HV	+1/2-+1 1/2	⑫	1/8-1/4	⑬
JJ, JM, JV⑪	+1/2-+1 1/2	−1/4-+3/4	1/8-1/4	7
JJ, JM, TV⑤	+1/2-+1 1/2	⑫	1/8-1/4	⑬
JM⑥	+1/2-+1 1/2	+1/2-+1 1/2	1/8-1/4	8
RM	+2 1/2-+3 1/2	⑫	1/8-1/4	⑬
TM7500A	+1/2	⑫	1/8-1/4	⑬
TM7500V	+3/4-+1 3/4	⑫	1/8-1/4	⑬
TV	+3/4-+1 3/4	+1/2-+2	1/8-1/4	7
WM⑪⑮	+1/2	⑫	1/8-1/4	⑬
WM⑯	+1/2	+1/2-+1 1/2	1/8-1/4	8
1971–72 SERIES 7500				
HJ, HM, HV⑩	+2-+3	+1-+2	1/16-1/8	7
HJ, HM, HV, JJ, JM⑮	+1/2-+1 1/2	⑫	1/16-1/8	⑬
JV, WV⑪⑮	+1/2-+1 1/2	⑫	1/16-1/8	⑬
JJ, JM, JV, WV㉙	+1/2-+1 1/2	+1/2-+1 1/2	1/16-1/8	5 1/2
RM⑪	+2 1/2-+3 1/2	⑫	1/16-1/8	⑬
TMA⑪⑮	+1/2	⑫	1/16-1/8	⑬
TMV, TV⑩	+3/4-+1 3/4	+1-+2	1/16-1/8	7
TMV, TV⑪⑮	+3/4-+1 3/4	⑫	1/16-1/8	⑬
WM⑪⑮	+1/2	⑫	1/16-1/8	⑬
1975–80 SERIES 7500				
C7	+2	+1 1/2	1/8-1/4㉞	7 1/6
HV⑩	+.9-+1.9	+1-+2	1/8-1/4㉞	7 1/6
HE, JE, JV, HV⑪	+1/2-+1 1/2	㉟	1/8-1/4㉞	⑬
HV, JV, JY⑮	+1/2-+1 1/2	−1/4-+3/4	1/8-1/4㉞	⑬
JV㉙	—	—	—	—
TV⑩	+3 1/2-+4 1/2	+1-+2	1/8-1/4㉞	7 1/6
TV⑪	+3 1/2-+4 1/2	㉟	1/8-1/4㉞	⑬
TV⑮	+3 1/2-+4 1/2	−1/4-+3/4	1/8-1/4㉞	⑬
W-7	+4	+1 1/2	1/8-1/4㉞	7 1/6
WV㉙	—	—	—	—
1979–80 SERIES 8500–9500				
D-9	0	+1/4	1/8-1/4㉞	5 3/4
J-8	+1 1/2	⑫	1/8-1/4㉞	⑬
J-9	+1 1/2	+1/4	1/8-1/4㉞	5 3/4
N-9	0	+1/4	1/8-1/4㉞	5 3/4
1972 SERIES 8700				
HM⑯㉜	+1/2-+1 1/2	+1/2-+1 1/2	1/16-1/8	8
1970 SERIES 9500				
HE, JE, MH⑪	+1/2-+1 1/2	⑫	1/8-1/4	⑬
HI, JI, MI, FN⑮	+1/2-+1 1/2	⑫	1/8-1/4	⑬
FC, FH, FI⑮	+1/2-+1 1/2	⑫	1/8-1/4	⑬
TE⑪	+1/2	⑫	1/8-1/4	⑬
TE⑮	+20	⑫	1/8-1/4	⑬
DC, DH, DI⑯	+1/2-+1 1/2	+1-+2	1/8-1/4	8
DC, DH, DI⑯	+1/2-+1 1/2	+1/2-+1 1/2	1/8-1/4	8
DN9502⑯	+1/2-+1 1/2	+1/2-+1 1/2	1/8-1/4	8
1971 SERIES 9500				
HE, HI, HN, J, MH, MI⑪⑮	+1/2-+1 1/2	⑫	1/16-1/8	⑬
TE⑪⑮	+1/2	⑫	1/16-1/8	⑬
J, MH, MI㉙	+1/2-+1 1/2	+1-+2	1/16-1/8	⑬
1972 SERIES 9500				
HC, HE, HI, HN, HM⑪⑮	+1/2-+1 1/2	⑫	1/16-1/8	⑬
HH, MB, MC, J, MH⑪⑮	+1/2-+1 1/2	⑫	1/16-1/8	⑬

Continued

GMC

WHEEL ALIGNMENT SPECIFICATIONS—Continued

NOTE: For standard axle with vehicle level and weight on wheels.

Truck Model	Caster Deg.	Camber Deg.	Toe-In Inch	Kingpin Angle Deg.
TE⑪⑮	+1/2	⑫	1/16-1/8	⑬
J, MH㉙	+1/2-+1 1/2	㉛	1/16-1/8	5 1/2
1975–78 SERIES 9500				
HC, HH, HI, JC, JH, JI⑪	+1/2-+1 1/2	㉟	1/8-1/4㉞	⑬
HC, HH, HI, JC, JH, JI, MH⑮	+1/2-+1 1/2	−1/4-+3/4	1/8-1/4㉞	⑬
JC, JH, JI, MH㉙	—			
1971–72 SERIES 9502				
FC, FH, FI, FN, DC, DH⑮	+1/2-+1 1/2	⑫	1/16-1/8	⑬
DI, DN, DP, DB, FB⑮	+1/2-+1 1/2	⑫	1/16-1/8	⑬
FC, FH, FI, FN, DC, DH㉙	+1/2-+1 1/2	+1/2-+1 1/2	1/16-1/8	5 1/2
DI, DN, DP, DB, FB⑨	+1/2-+1 1/2	+1/2-+1 1/2	1/16-1/8	5 1/2

Truck Model	Caster Deg.	Camber Deg.	Toe-In Inch	Kingpin Angle Deg.
1975–78 SERIES 9502				
D/F⑮	+1/2-+1 1/2	−1/4-+3/4	1/8-1/4㉞	5 3/4
D/F㉙	—			
D/F㉚	+1/2-+1 1/2	⑱	1/8-1/4㉞	—
1977⑮	−9/20-+11/20	−1/4-+3/4	1/8-1/4㉞	5 3/4
㉚	−7/15-+8/15	+2/5-+1 1/10	1/8-1/4㉞	5 1/2
⑲	−9/20-+11/20	+3/5-+1 1/4	1/8-1/4㉞	5 1/2
1978⑪⑮⑰	−11/20-+9/20	−1/4-+3/4	1/8-1/4㉞	—
⑲	−8/15-+7/15	⑧	1/8-1/4㉞	
㉚	−7/15-+8/15	⑧	1/8-1/4㉞	
1971–72 FE-900 & FE-970 AXLES				
FE-900	+1/2-+1 1/2	③	1/16-1/6	㉒
FE-970	−1-0	+1/2-+1 1/2	0	1
1975–78 MOTOR HOME				
1975–78	+1 1/2-+2 1/2	㉑	⑳	—

① —1977–78, 8°.
② —1977–78, no adjustment provision.
③ —Left side +1/2 to +1 1/2, right side +1 1/2 to +2 1/2.
④ —No adjustment provision.
⑤ —Left side 5 3/4°, right side 6 1/4°.
⑥ —Left side −1/4 to +3/4, right side −3/4 to +3/4.
⑦ —1977, belted tires, +1/2° to +1 1/2°; radial tires, +1 1/2° to +2 1/2°.
⑧ —Left −1/10 to +3/5, Right +2/5 to 1 1/10.
⑨ —Power steering +2 1/2 to +3 1/2.
⑩ —With front axle No. F070.
⑪ —With front axle No. F090.
⑫ —Right side −1/4, left side +1/4.
⑬ —Right side 6 1/4, left side 5 3/4.
⑭ —With front axle No. F110.
⑮ —With front axle No. F120.
⑯ —With front axle No. F160.
⑰ —With front axle No. F-120D.
⑱ —Left, 0° to 3/4°; Right 0 to 1/4°.
⑲ —With front axle No. FF-933.
⑳ —1975–76, 0 to 1/4" toe out; 1978, 1/16 to 3/16 toe-out.
㉑ —L.H., +1/2 to 1°; R.H., +1/4° to 3/4°.
㉒ —Left side 6, right side 7.
㉓ —For procedure and settings, see Wheel Alignment section of Chevrolet Truck Chapter. CMG C-P 1500 same as Chev. C, P-10. GMC C-P 2500–3500 same as Chev. C, P-20, 30. GMC G1500–3500 same as Chev. G 10–30.
㉔ —Left side −1/4 to +3/4, right side −3/4 to +1/4.
㉕ —1974, K-10 with full time four wheel drive toe-in 0".
㉖ —Manual steering.
㉗ —Power steering.
㉘ —Left +1/2 to +1 1/2°, right 0° to +1°.
㉙ —With front axle No. FL-901.
㉚ —With front axle No. FL-931.
㉛ —Left +1/2 to +1 1/2°, right +1° to +2°.
㉜ —With front axle No. FL-161.
㉝ —Air Brakes.
㉞ —For trucks using steel belted radial tires, zero toe-in.
㉟ —Left, −1/4° to +3/4°; Right, −3/4° to +1/4°.
㊱ —Hydraulic Brakes.

Engine Section

NOTE: Refer to Chevrolet Chapter for service procedures on 6-250, 292; V6-200, 229, 231; V8-267, 305, 307, 350, 366, 396, 400, 402, 427, 454 engines.

CYLINDER HEAD, REPLACE

V6 Engines

After installing cylinder head, run engine until normal operating temperature is reached. Then tighten cylinder head bolts in the sequence shown in Fig. 1 to the torque given in the *Engine Tightening* table. After head is properly tightened, adjust valve lash to the recommended clearance.

V8-403, 455 Motor Home

Some cylinder head gaskets are coated with a special lacquer to provide a good seal once the parts have warmed up. Do not use any additional sealer on such gaskets. If the gasket does not have this lacquer coating, apply suitable sealer to both sides.

Tighten cylinder head bolts a little at a time in three steps in the sequence shown in the illustrations. Final tightening should be to the torque specifications listed in the *Engine Tightening* table.

1. Drain radiator and cylinder block.
2. Disconnect spark plug wires and remove intake manifold.
3. Loosen exhaust pipe clamp at muffler then remove exhaust manifold bolts and position exhaust manifolds away from cylinder heads.
4. Remove valve cover (loosen or remove any accessory brackets that interfere).
5. Remove ground strap from right cylinder head.
6. Remove exhaust manifold, rocker arms and push rods from head to be removed.
7. Reverse removal procedure to install head, and tighten bolts in the sequence shown in Fig. 2.

V8-637

After installing cylinder head, run engine until normal operating temperature is reached. Then tighten cylinder head in the sequence shown in Fig. 3 to the torque given in the *Engine Tightening* table. After tightening head, adjust valve lash to the proper clearance.

1171

GMC

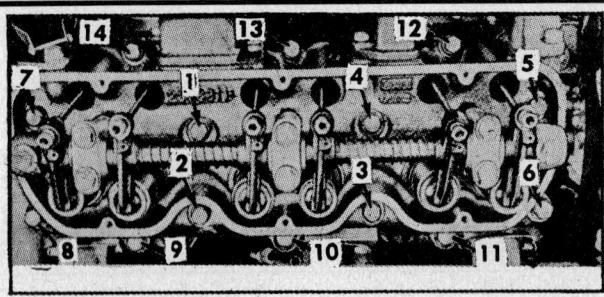

Fig. 1 Cylinder head tightening sequence. V6 engines

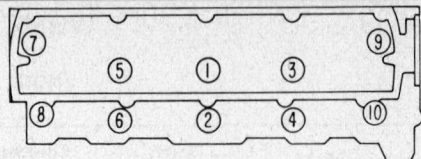

Fig. 2 Cylinder head tightening sequence. V8-403, 455

ROCKER ARM SERVICE

V6 Engines

Referring to Fig. 4, assemble rocker arms, springs and brackets on rocker arm shaft, then install end brackets. Lubricate all moving parts with engine oil.

Place steel washer on each bracket bolt, then locate rocker arm shaft and bracket assembly on cylinder head and start bracket bolts into tapped holes. Back off adjusting screws, then tighten bracket bolts evenly while holding adjusting screws in respective push rod sockets. *Use special bolt at position (1) (Fig. 4) to assure correct position of shaft (6).*

NOTE: Check length of special bolt, if 2 7/8 inch bolt is used install two flat washers under bolt. If 2 3/4 inch bolt is used install one flat washer under bolt.

Check clearance between shaft end brackets and rocker arms. Clearance should be approximately .030 inch. Adjust clearance by loosening end bracket bolts and relocate brackets as allowed by clearance in bracket bolt holes. Tighten shaft bracket bolts to specified torque as listed under "Engine Tightening Specifications".

Tighten cylinder head to specified torque and then adjust valve clearance.

V8-455 Motor Home

1. Remove valve cover.
2. Remove flanged bolts, rocker arm pivot and rocker arms, Fig. 5.
3. When installing rocker arm assemblies, lubricate wear surfaces with suitable lubricant. Torque flanged bolts to 25 ft. lbs.

V8-637

The rocker arms, shafts and brackets must be installed as shown in Fig. 6. Note that the thick spacer (8) Fig. 6 must be installed between rocker arm and bracket at end of the assembly where special bolt (9) is used.

Back out the adjusting screws sufficiently to prevent bending push rods or causing other damage when the assembly is installed. Tighten cylinder head to proper torque and then adjust valve lash.

VALVES, ADJUST

V6 & V8-637

With engine at operating temperature and rocker arm covers removed, turn adjusting

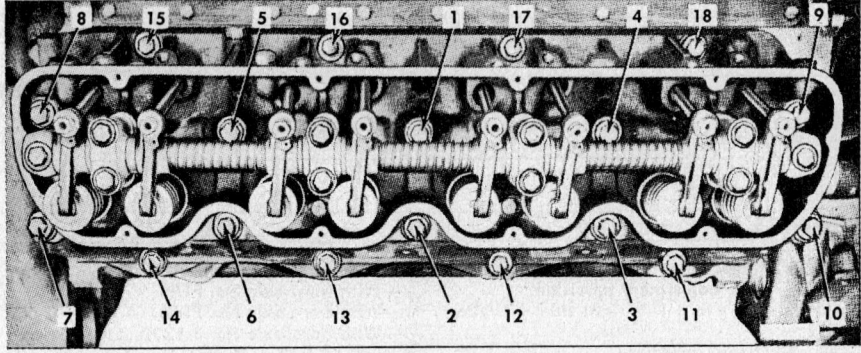

Fig. 3 Cylinder head tightening sequence. V8-637

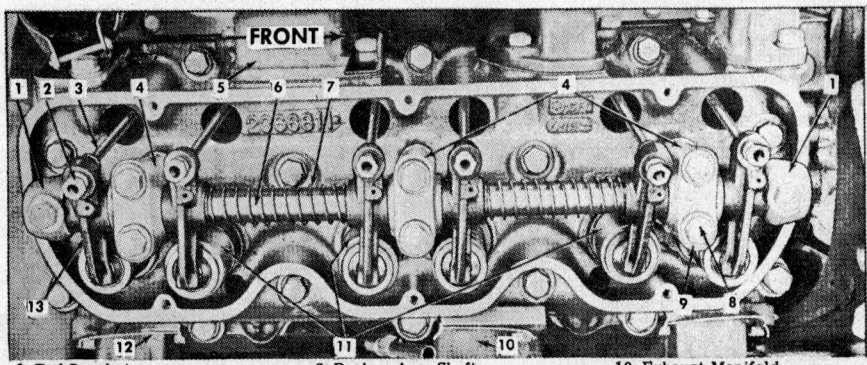

1 End Bracket
2 Adjusting Screw
3 Push Rod
4 Rocker Arm Shaft Bracket
5 Intake Manifold
6 Rocker Arm Shaft
7 Spring
8 Bracket Bolt
9 Flat Washer
10 Exhaust Manifold
11 Shields on Intake Valves
12 Exhaust Manifold Bolt Lock
13 Rocker Arm

Fig. 4 Rocker arms and shafts installed. V6 engines

nut on each rocker arm until proper clearance is obtained between valve stem and rocker arm. For proper clearance see *Tune-Up and Valve Specifications* table.

VALVE ROTATORS

All Engines Except V8-403, 455

The parts involved in the rotating mechanism, Fig. 7, are a special spring seat retainer, a pair of flat half-moon keys, a close fitting cap located on the valve stem and a specially constructed valve stem.

In order to accomodate valve expansion, the valve lash must be maintained. When camshaft rotation causes this lash or clearance to be taken up, the cap on the valve stem causes the valve keys to raise the spring retainer, removing the load on the valve springs from the valve *before* the valve is moved from its seat. A clearance of .002–.004" should be maintained between the end face of the valve stem and cap. This is the distance the spring retainer is moved *before* the valve is moved. The slow valve rotating motion is caused by the vibration of the valve, the flowing of exhaust gases around the valve head, and a slight rotating motion imparted to the valve

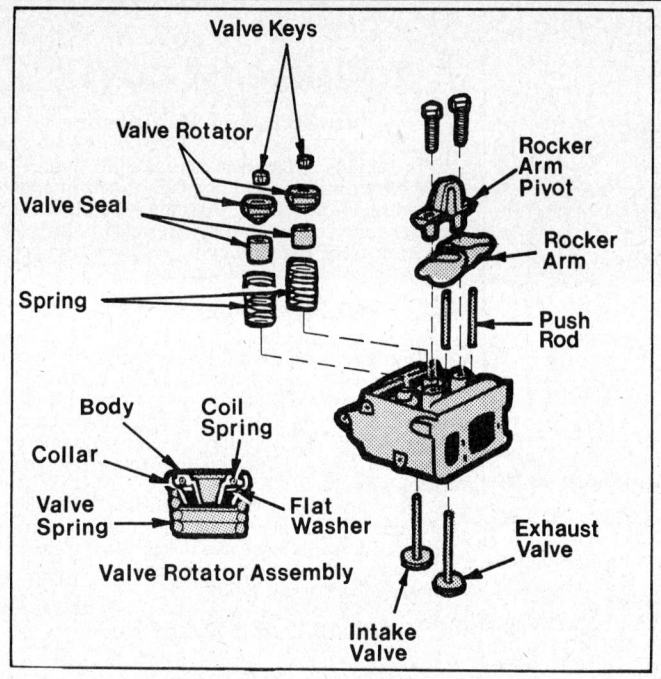

Fig. 5 Cylinder head exploded, V8-403, 455

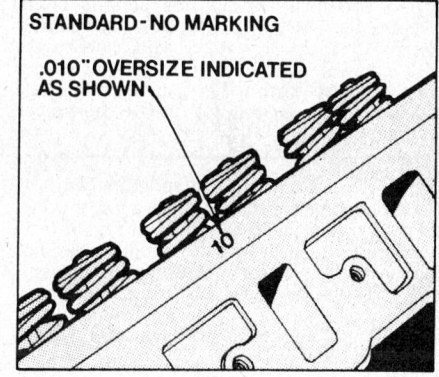

Fig. 8 Checking valve stem tips for rotator malfunction. V8-403, 455

by the valve spring.

Whenever valve work is being done, a check for clearance should be made by holding the assembled valve and rotating mechanism in the hands. With one hand, press down on the valve cap and turn the valve with the other hand. If the valve turns readily, it indicates that there is clearance present.

A special gauge is available to check this clearance. If the gauge indicates no clearance, grind off the end of the valve stem. If the clearance is too great, grind off the open end of the valve cap.

V8-403, 455 Motor Home

The rotator operates on a Sprag clutch principle utilizing the collapsing action of coil spring to give rotation to the rotor body which turns the valve, Fig. 5.

To check rotator action, draw a line across rotator body and down the collar. Operate engine at 1500 rpm, rotator body should move around collar. Rotator action can be in either direction. Replace rotator if no movement is noted.

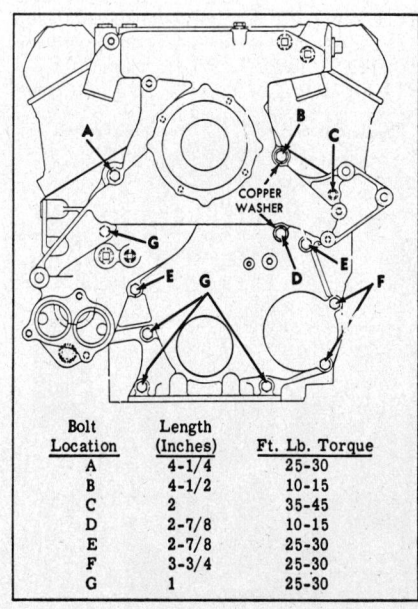

Fig. 9 Valve guide bore marking. V8-403, 455

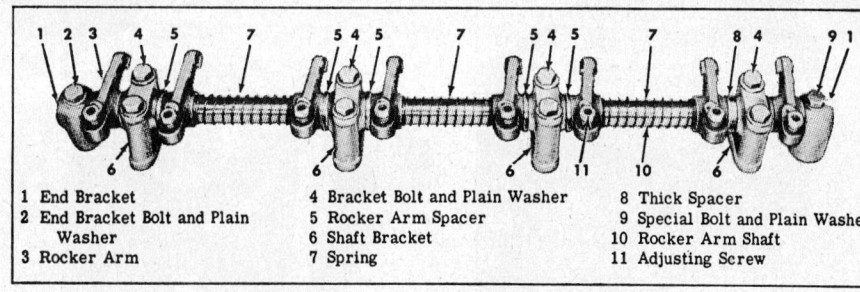

Fig. 6 Rocker arm assembly. V8-637

Fig. 7 Valve rotator and retaining parts, Six-cyl. engines. Typical of V8s

Bolt Location	Length (Inches)	Ft. Lb. Torque
A	4-1/4	25-30
B	4-1/2	10-15
C	2	35-45
D	2-7/8	10-15
E	2-7/8	25-30
F	3-3/4	25-30
G	1	25-30

Fig. 10 Front cover bolt arrangement and torque. V8-637

GMC

When servicing valves, valve stem tips should be checked for improper wear pattern which could indicate a defective valve rotator, Fig. 8.

VALVE GUIDES

Except V8-403, 455

Valve guides in these engines are an integral part of the head and, therefore, cannot be removed. For service, guide holes can be reamed oversize to accomodate one of several service valves with oversize stems.

Select the reamer for the smallest oversize which will provide a clean straight bore through the valve guide. After reaming, a new seat should be cut into the head to assure perfect seating of the new valve.

V8-403, 455 Motor Home

Valve stem guides are not replaceable, due to being cast in place. If valve guide bores are worn excessively, they can be reamed oversize.

If a standard valve guide bore is being reamed, use a .003″ or .005″ oversize reamer. For the .010″ oversize valve guide bore, use a .013″ oversize reamer. If too large a reamer is used and the spiraling is removed, it is possible that the valve will not receive the proper lubrication.

NOTE: Occasionally a valve guide will be oversize as manufactured. These are marked on the cylinder head as shown in Fig. 9. If no markings are present, the guide bores are standard. If oversize markings are present, any valve replacement will require an oversize valve. Service valves are available in standard diameters as well as .003″, .005″, .010″ and .013″ oversize.

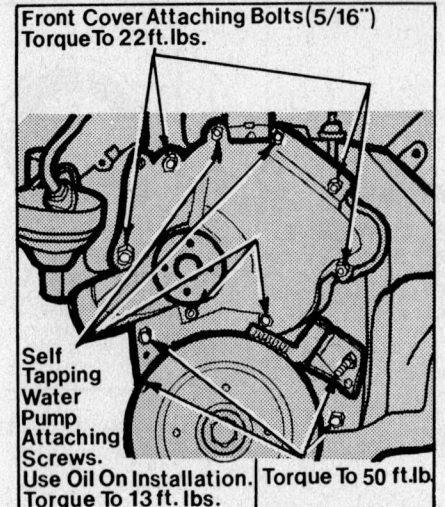

Fig. 11 Engine front cover bolts. V8-403, 455

2. Remove parts from lifter body.
3. Clean all parts and inspect for damage. If any parts are damaged, the entire lifter assembly should be replaced. The inertia valve in plunger for rocker arm lubrication should move when plunger is shaken.
4. To reassemble, invert plunger and set ball into hole in plunger. Place ball check valve retainer over ball and on plunger. Place check valve retainer spring over retainer. Assemble body over plunger assembly. Turn assembly over and install push rod seat. Compress plunger with push rod and install retainer.
5. Compress plunger to open oil holes and fill with SAE 10 oil. Work plunger up and down and refill.

TIMING CASE COVER

V6-305, 351 Engines

To remove cover, block crankshaft and remove retaining bolt and washer at front side of crankshaft pulley. Assemble a suitable puller and remove pulley. Remove bolts attaching front cover to cylinder block and jar cover loose with a lead hammer.

V6-401, 478, V8-637

To remove the cover, drain the cooling system and disconnect lower radiator hose. Disconnect external water by-pass at the intake manifold. Drop the oil pan. Take off radiator, shroud, fan blades, pulleys, vibration damper and fuel pump. Unfasten the cover from the block and lift it off.

When installing the front cover on V8-637 engines be sure to follow the bolt arrangement and torque as shown in Fig. 10. *Note that no lockwashers are used on any of the front cover bolts on the V8-637.*

V8-403, 455 Motor Home

NOTE: When it becomes necessary to replace the cover oil seal, the cover need not be removed.

1. Drain cooling system and disconnect heater hose, by-pass hose and both radiator hoses.
2. Remove all belts, fan and pulley, crankshaft pulley and pulley hub.
3. Remove oil pan.
4. Remove cover, timing, pointer and water pump assembly, Fig. 11.

HYDRAULIC VALVE LIFTERS

V8-403, 455

1. Hold plunger down with push rod. Using a small screw driver or awl, remove plunger retainer.

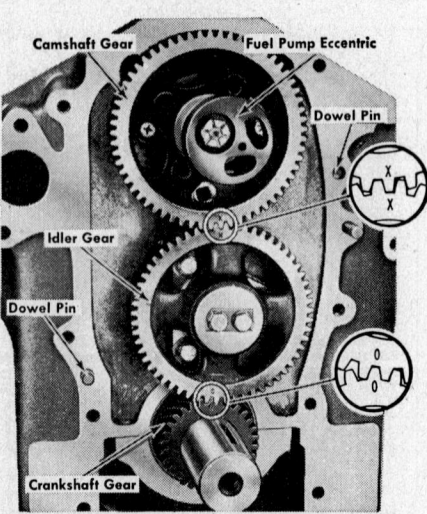

Fig. 12 Timing gear showing timing marks on V6-401, 432, 478 engines

1 Crankshaft	12 Camshaft Idler Gear
2 Oil Slinger	13 Balance Shaft Idler Gear
3 Crankshaft Gear	14 Thrust Plate
4 Lock Plates	15 Balance Shaft Front Weight
5 Plate Retaining Bolts	16 Hole Plug (Ball)
6 Gear Retaining Plate	17 Balance Shaft
7 Retaining Washer	18 Balance Shaft Gear
8 Self-Locking Bolt	19 Oil Seal O-Ring
9 Camshaft Thrust Plate Screw	20 Key
10 Fuel Pump Eccentric	
11 Camshaft Gear	

Fig. 13 Valve timing marks. V8-637

1 Bolt	8 Crankshaft
2 Cap	9 Crankshaft Sprocket
3 Thrust Plate Screw	10 Timing Marks
4 Dowel Hole	11 Camshaft Sprocket
5 Fuel Pump Eccentric	12 Eccentric Clamp Washer (Special)
6 Timing Chain	
7 Pulley Hub Key	

Fig. 14 Timing chain and sprocket details. V6-305, 351 and 379 engines

GMC

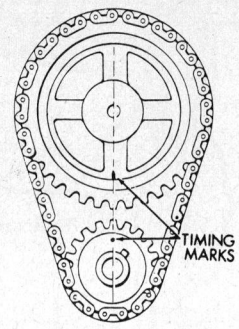

Fig. 15 Timing chain position. V8-403, 455

TIMING GEARS
V6-401, 432, 478

NOTE: When necessary to install a new camshaft gear, the camshaft will have to be removed as the gear is a pressed fit on the shaft.

For correct valve timing, the "X" marks on the camshaft and idler gears should be aligned, Fig. 12, and the "O" marks on the idler and crankshaft gears should be aligned.

V8-637

NOTE: When necessary to install a new camshaft gear, the camshaft will have to be removed as the gear is a pressed fit on the shaft.

For correct valve timing the marks should be aligned as shown in Fig. 13. When replacing front cover refer to Fig. 10 for bolt torque and arrangement.

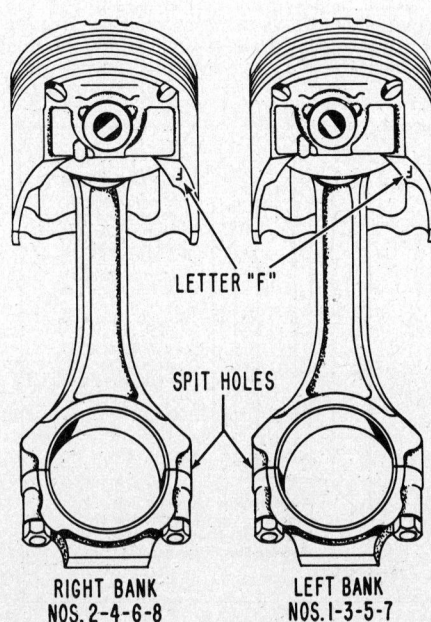

Fig. 17 Piston and rod assembly. V8-455

TIMING CHAIN
V6-305, 351, 379

When chain is properly installed, a straightedge aligned with the center of the crankshaft and camshaft will also be aligned with the timing marks as shown in Fig. 14. Install fuel pump eccentric at front side of camshaft sprocket. Special washer and bolt (1 and 12, Fig. 14 are used to retain eccentric and sprocket. Tighten bolt to a torque of 60–70 ft. lbs.

V8-403, 455 Motor Home

1. After removing front cover, remove fuel pump eccentric, oil slinger, crankshaft sprocket, chain and camshaft sprocket.
2. Install camshaft sprocket, crankshaft sprocket and timing chain together, aligning timing marks as shown in Fig. 15.
3. Install fuel pump eccentric with flat side rearward. Then install oil slinger and replace front cover, Fig. 11.

CAMSHAFT
V8-403, 455 Motor Home

1. Remove engine from vehicle.
2. Remove oil pan, crankshaft pulley and harmonic balancer and engine front cover.
3. Disconnect spark plug cables, then remove distributor cap and valve covers.
4. Remove intake manifold, rocker arms, push rods and valve lifters.

NOTE: Identify parts so they can be reinstalled in their original locations.

5. Remove fuel pump eccentric, camshaft gear, oil slinger and timing chain.
6. Remove camshaft by carefully sliding it out of engine.

CAUTION: Use care when removing camshaft to avoid damaging bearings.

7. Reverse procedure to install.

V6 & V8-637 Engines

Camshaft is supported on bushing type bearings and all journals are pressure lubricated. An oil trough just below camshaft holds oil into which the cam lobes dip as the camshaft rotates.

To remove the camshaft, remove thrust plate attaching bolts at front end of camshaft. Pull camshaft forward to remove from cylinder block. Remove key from keyway in camshaft, then remove thrust plate and gear spacer.

To install camshaft, apply engine oil to camshaft journals and cam lobes, then install camshaft in block. If spacer has been removed, install spacer with chamfer toward bearing journal and drive key into keyway. Install thrust plate. Sprocket is installed together with chain.

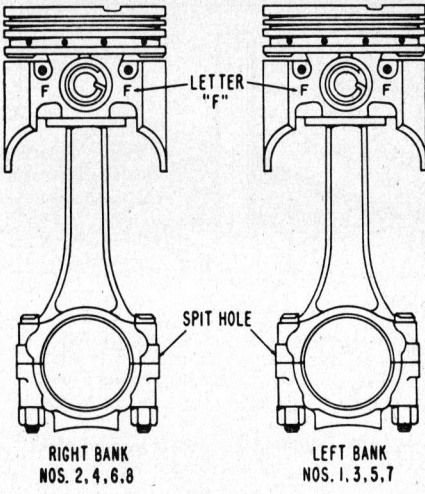

Fig. 16 Piston and rod assembly. V8-403

PISTONS & RODS, ASSEMBLE
V8-403, 455 Motor Home

Lubricate piston pin bore and piston pin to facilitate installation of pin, then position the connecting rod with its respective piston as shown in Figs. 16 and 17. Install piston and connecting rod assembly into engine with notches on top of piston towards front of engine. Position index tang on bearing cap on same side as index tang on connecting rod.

V6 & V8-637 Engines

Install piston and rod assembly using care to match the number on the rod and cap, Fig. 18. *Numbers for rods on right-cylinders must be toward right-hand side of crankcase, while numbers on rods for left-hand cylinders must be toward left-hand side of crankcase.*

CRANKSHAFT OIL SEAL, REPLACE
V8-403, 455 Motor Home

To replace upper rear main bearing seal, the crankshaft must be removed. After removing crankshaft use tool No. BT23-18 to install seal, Fig. 19.

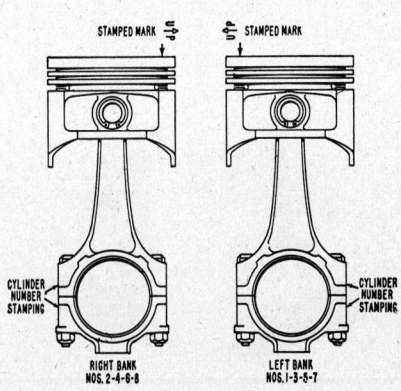

Fig. 18 Pistons assembled to rods. V8-637

GMC

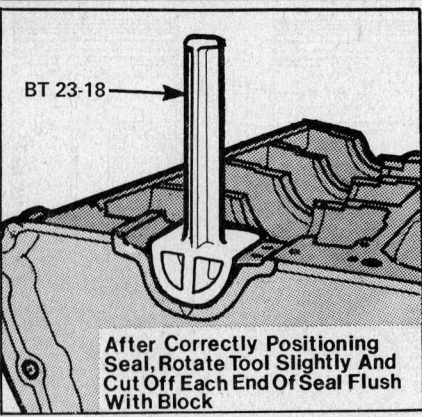

Fig. 19 Installing crankshaft rear oil seal. V8-403, 455

Lower rear main bearing seal can be installed with crankshaft in place and engine in vehicle. Remove oil pan, then the rear main bearing cap. Remove bearing and seal from cap. Position new seal in groove in bearing cap. Using tool BT23-18, hammer seal into groove. Rotate tool slightly, then cut seal ends flush with bearing cap surface. Pack seal end fibers away from edges, using a screw driver. Install bearing in cap, then install cap, lubricate bolt threads and torque to 120 ft. lbs. Install oil pan and lower flywheel cover.

V6 & V8-637 Engines

Crankshaft rear bearing oil seal consists of two pieces of special packing. One piece is installed in the groove in the rear bearing cap and the other piece is installed in a similar groove in the cylinder block, Fig. 20.

Position the rear bearing seal in the groove in the cylinder block. Lay an improvised mandrel, Fig. 21, in the bearing bore and strike the mandrel with a hammer to drive the seal into the groove. Install the seal in the bearing cap in a similar manner. Using a sharp knife, cut off both ends of each seal which project out of the grooves. When cutting off the ends of the seals, do not leave frayed ends which

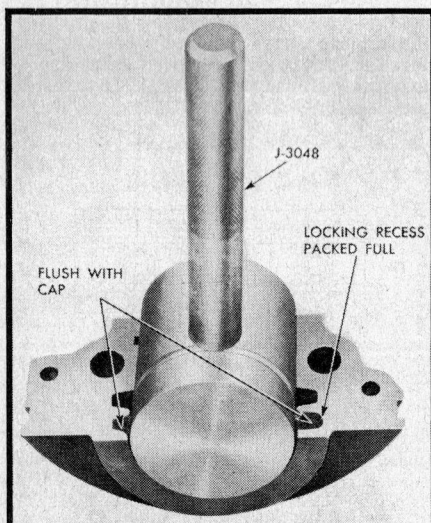

Fig. 21 Compressing oil seal in rear main bearing cap

would prevent proper seating of the bearing cap if the ends should extend between cap and cylinder block.

When installing rear bearing cap side seals, immerse the seals in diesel fuel oil prior to installation, and the exposed end of each side seal will protrude approximately .045", Fig. 22. *Do not cut off protruding ends of side seals.*

OIL, PAN, REPLACE

V6 & V8-637

Drain the oil, remove the oil pan attaching screws and lower the pan.

V8-403, 455 Motor Home

1. Remove transmission and final drive from vehicle.
2. Drain oil from engine, then disconnect relay tie rod from idler arm and relay lever and steering shock absorber from crossmember bracket.
3. Remove left hand lower venturi bracket and disconnect power steering pump.
4. Remove the four front support bolts and front motor mount bolts and position support aside.
5. Remove flywheel, then remove oil pan bolts.
6. Raise engine about 1 inch and remove oil pan.
7. Reverse procedure to install.

OIL PUMP REPAIRS

V6-305, 351 & 379

After removing the oil pan, remove oil inlet pipe and screen from pump. Remove two bolts attaching oil pump to cylinder block, then remove pump and drive shaft. Disassemble pump as suggested by Fig. 23, then inspect parts as follows:

1. Inspect ends of drive shaft which engage distributor and oil pump shafts. Replace shaft if excessively worn or damaged.
2. Check fit of inner rotor shaft in body. If excessive wear is indicated at either shaft or body, replace worn parts.
3. Place outer rotor in body and insert inner rotor and shaft in operating position. Check clearance between outer rotor and body and clearance between edge of inner rotor lobe and outer rotor with feeler gauge; if clearance exceeds .006", replace worn parts.
4. With rotors in pump body, place straightedge across rotors and body; then with feeler gauge measure clearance between rotors and straightedge, which should be .0011–.0034".
5. Use straightedge to check rotor side of pump cover for flatness. Also look for grooves and other evidence of wear on cover. Replace cover if not in good condition.
6. Relief valve spring should have 14.7 to 16.3 lbs. pressure when compressed to 1.69". Spring free length should be 2.72".

V6-401, 478, V8-637

After removing the oil pan and oil pump, disassemble the pump as follows, referring to Fig. 24.

Remove bolts that secure spinner valve cover, rotor cover and spinner housing to pump body and separate parts. Remove outer rotor and shaft and inner rotor from pump body.

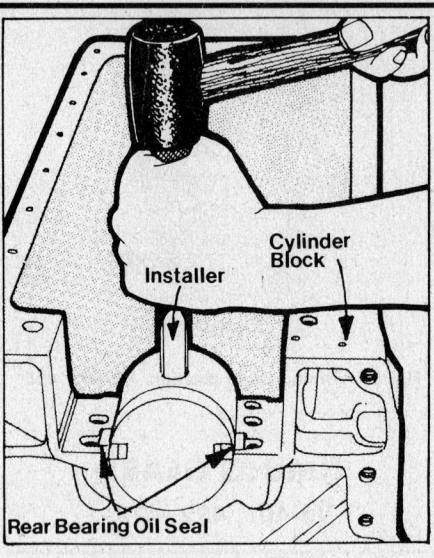

Fig. 20 Installing crankshaft rear oil seal. V6 and V8-637 engines

Remove relief valve spring cap, then remove spring and valve.

Inspection of Parts—Inner rotor and shaft assembly and outer rotor are furnished for service in matched sets. With rotors in pump body, place a straightedge across rotors and body and measure clearance with feeler gauge. Clearance should be .0011–.0064".

Use feeler gauge to check rotor side of rotor cover and spinner housing for flatness. Also look for grooves and other evidence of wear on pump cover.

Clean relief valve parts and check fit of valve in bore of pump. Valve must slide into bore smoothly.

Check fit of spinner valve shaft in cover and spinner valve housing in cover. If excessive clearance is evident, replace parts as necessary. Inspect thrust washer for wear. Clean passages through spinner shaft and passages including bleed hole in spinner cover.

Soak spinner valve and shaft in solvent, then note fit of valve in shaft. It should be possible to push valve endwise, and spring should move valve to closed position. If valve sticks or appears to be loose in shaft, obtain a new preadjusted valve assembly, for use when

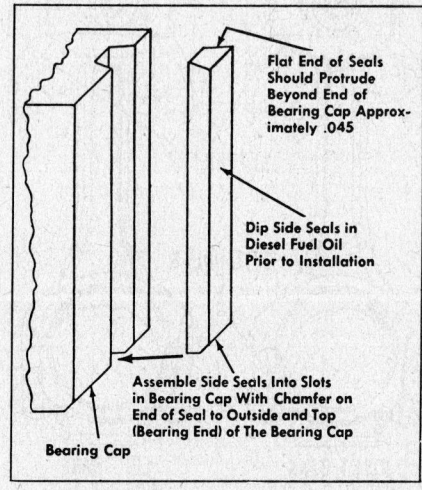

Fig. 22 Rear bearing cap side seal installation.

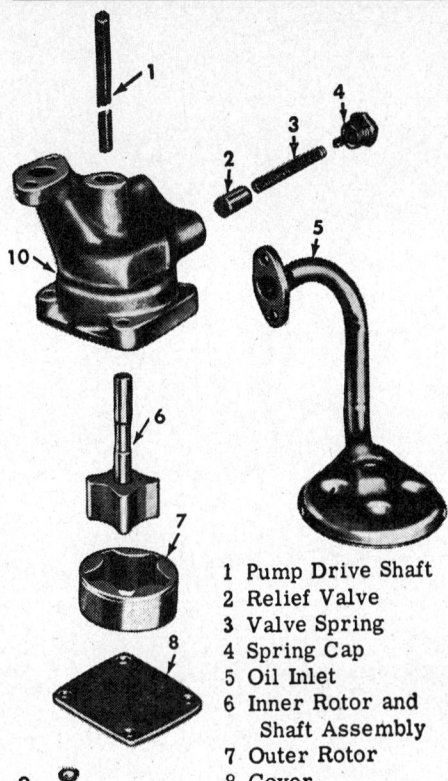

1. Pump Drive Shaft
2. Relief Valve
3. Valve Spring
4. Spring Cap
5. Oil Inlet
6. Inner Rotor and Shaft Assembly
7. Outer Rotor
8. Cover
9. Cover Bolt
10. Pump Body

Fig. 23 Oil pump on V6-305, 351 & 379 engines

reassembling pump unit. *Since special equipment is required for testing spinner valve operation, the valve adjustment should not be disturbed.*

Assembling Pump and Spinner Valve—
1. Install pressure relief valve parts in pump body in following order: valve, spring and spring cap. Tighten cap securely.
2. Lubricate shaft and inner rotor with engine oil and insert shaft into pump body.
3. Install outer rotor in body, then try turning inner rotor and shaft. Shaft must rotate without drag for six or more revolutions.
4. Install rotor cover and spinner housing and retain with two short self-locking bolts.
5. With oil pump inverted, drop coupling into slot in end of pump shaft. Set spinner valve and shaft in place at coupling, then place thrust washer on shaft and install governor spinner cover.

V8-403, 455 Motor Home
1. Remove oil pan and pump baffle. Remove attaching screws and remove pump and drive shaft extension.
2. To service the pump, refer to Fig. 25.
3. To install, insert the drive shaft extension through the opening in the block until the shaft mates into the distributor drive gear. Position pump onto rear main drive gear. Position pump onto rear main bearing cap and torque the attaching bolts to 35 ft-lbs.
4. Install oil pump baffle and pan.

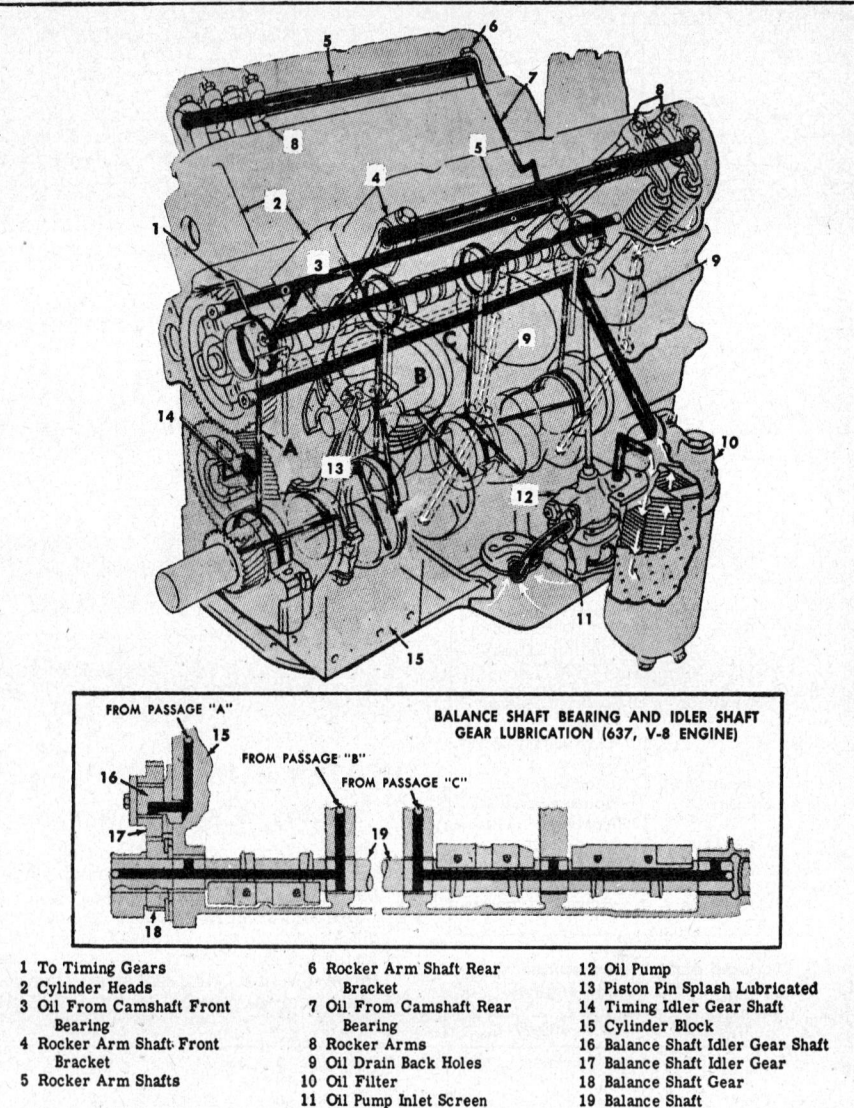

1. To Timing Gears
2. Cylinder Heads
3. Oil From Camshaft Front Bearing
4. Rocker Arm Shaft Front Bracket
5. Rocker Arm Shafts
6. Rocker Arm Shaft Rear Bracket
7. Oil From Camshaft Rear Bearing
8. Rocker Arms
9. Oil Drain Back Holes
10. Oil Filter
11. Oil Pump Inlet Screen
12. Oil Pump
13. Piston Pin Splash Lubricated
14. Timing Idler Gear Shaft
15. Cylinder Block
16. Balance Shaft Idler Gear Shaft
17. Balance Shaft Idler Gear
18. Balance Shaft Gear
19. Balance Shaft

Engine lubrication diagram. V6 engines and V8-637

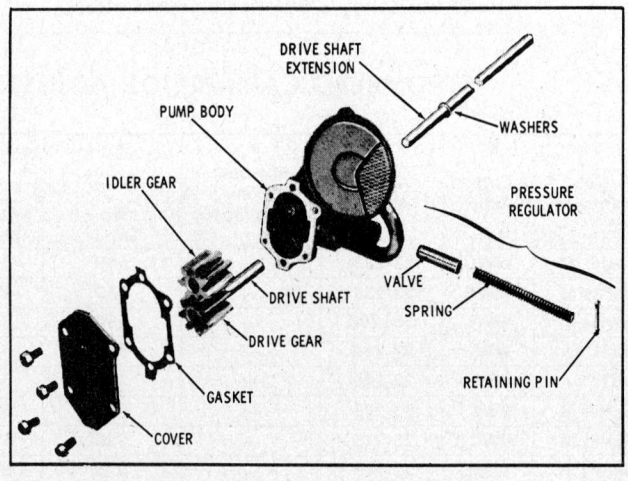

Fig. 25 Oil pump. V8-403, 455

GMC

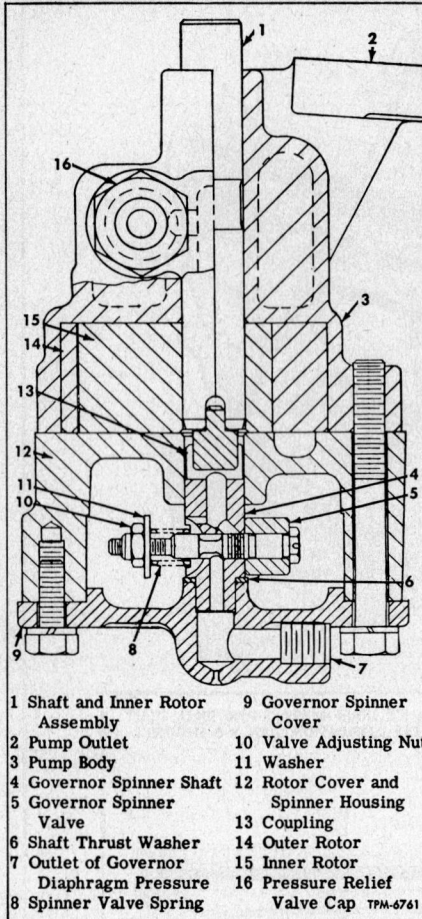

1 Shaft and Inner Rotor Assembly
2 Pump Outlet
3 Pump Body
4 Governor Spinner Shaft
5 Governor Spinner Valve
6 Shaft Thrust Washer
7 Outlet of Governor Diaphragm Pressure
8 Spinner Valve Spring
9 Governor Spinner Cover
10 Valve Adjusting Nut
11 Washer
12 Rotor Cover and Spinner Housing
13 Coupling
14 Outer Rotor
15 Inner Rotor
16 Pressure Relief Valve Cap   TPM-6761

Fig. 24 Oil pump and governor spinner valve. V6-401, 432, 478, V8-637 engines

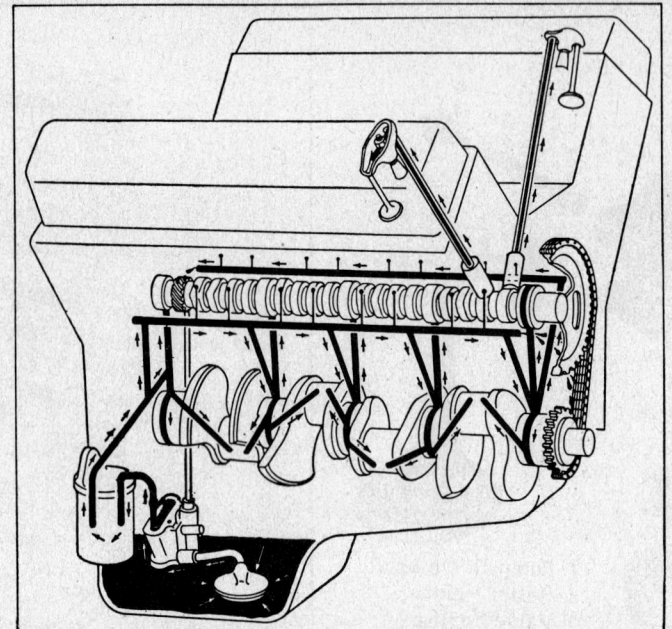

Engine lubrication diagram. V8-403, 455

WATER PUMP, REPLACE

V8-403, 455 Motor Home

1. Drain cooling system, then loosen all belts, disconnect bypass hose and remove heater hose from water pump.
2. Raise and properly support vehicle, then disconnect lower radiator hose from water pump.
3. Remove venturi ring seal strap, then fold venturi to shroud seal forward and over shroud.
4. Remove the four nuts retaining clutch assembly to water pump, then position fan and clutch assembly in the fan shroud, using care to avoid damaging the radiator.
5. Remove venturi ring and water pump pulley.
6. Disconnect power steering pump and left hand upper venturi ring bracket.
7. Remove water pump bolts and remove water pump.

Carburetor Section

NOTE: Refer to the Chevrolet Chapter for service procedures and specifications on Holley & Rochester carburetors.

STROMBERG CARBURETOR ADJUSTMENT SPECIFICATIONS

Year	Engine Application	Carb. Type	Carb. Model	Idle Mix. Screw Turns Open	Hot Idle Speed Eng. R.P.M. Std. Trans.	Hot Idle Speed Eng. R.P.M. Auto. Trans.	Float Level (Dry)	Float Coat	Pump Setting	Idle Vent Setting	Choke Setting
1970	V6-Series M	WWC	23-232	—	550	550	5/32	—	.190	—	—
	V6-Series M	WWC	23-233	—	550	550	5/32	—	.190	—	—
1971	V6-Series C	WWC	381296	—	550	550	.190	—	.420–.450		
1972	V6-351C	WW	23-244	—	550	—	.190	—	.420–.450		
	V6-351C	WW	23-248	—	550	—	.190	—	.420–.450		
	V6-Series M	WWC	23-243	—	525	525	7/32	—	3/16		
	V6-Series M	WWC	23-245	—	525	525	7/32	—	3/16		
	V6-Series M	WWC	23-246	—	525	525	7/32	—	3/16		

Continued

STROMBERG CARBURETOR ADJUSTMENT SPECIFICATIONS—Continued

Year	Engine Application	Carb. Type	Carb. Model	Idle Mix. Screw Turns Open	Hot Idle Speed Eng. R.P.M. Std. Trans.	Hot Idle Speed Eng. R.P.M. Auto. Trans.	Float Level (Dry)	Float Coat	Pump Setting	Idle Vent Setting	Choke Setting
	V6-Series M	WWC	23-247	—	525	525	7/32	—	3/16	—	—
	V6-Series M	WWC	23-249	—	525	525	7/32	—	3/16	—	—
	V6-Series M	WWC	23-250	—	525	525	7/32	—	3/16	—	—
	V6-478SN	WWC	23-243	—	500	500	7/32	—	3/16	—	—
	V8-637	WWC	23-251	—	475	475	7/32	—	3/16	—	—
1973	V6-305C, 379	WW	23-257	—	550	550	3/16	—	—	—	—
	V6-379	WW	23-258	—	550	550	3/16	—	—	—	—
	V6-432	WWC	23-259	—	550	550	7/32	—	—	—	—
	V6-432	WWC	23-260	—	550	550	7/32	—	—	—	—
1974	V6-305C, 379	WW	23-264	—	①	①	7/32	—	—	—	—
	V6-432, 478	WWC	23-265	—	525	525	7/32	—	—	—	—

①—V6-305C, 600 R.P.M.; V6-379, 575 R.P.M.

Stromberg WW-2 & WWC-3 Units, Figs. 1 & 2

Float Level

On 1970-72 models, hold tab on float firmly against needle valve and measure distance from top of fuel bowl to top of float, Fig. 3. On 1973-74 models, invert main body to allow float to rest on needle valve and measure distance between top rib of float and top of fuel bowl, Fig. 4.

Pump Adjustment, WW-2 models

On 1970-72 models, operate accelerator to properly seat check ball. Then with throttle valves fully closed, place a straight-edge across air horn and measure distance from straight-edge to top of pump piston rod. Open throttle valve and measure distance from straight-edge to top of piston rod. Subtract measurement taken with throttle valve fully closed from measurement taken with throttle valve fully open to determine pump rod travel. If the travel is not within .420 to .450", adjust by bending pump rod at point indicated. Minimum travel should be .160", Fig. 5.

On 1973-74 models, measure distance between top of pump link and air horn with throttle fully closed, Fig. 6. Distance should be .97 inch. Adjust by bending rod at point shown in Fig. 6.

Pump Adjustment, WWC-3 models

Measure total distance at point at top of pump lever travels when throttle lever is moved from closed to wide open position, Fig. 7. When necessary to adjust lever travel, bend pump rod at upper end.

Fast Idle Adjustment, Fig. 8

Check position of cam with choke valve fully open. Fast idle screw must clear cam when throttle is fully closed. If there is interference, bend link to allow fast idle cam to drop below fast idle screw with throttle plate closed and choke open. To adjust fast idle properly, locate end of fast idle screw flush with inner surface of lever, then turn screw IN 7½ turns as shown.

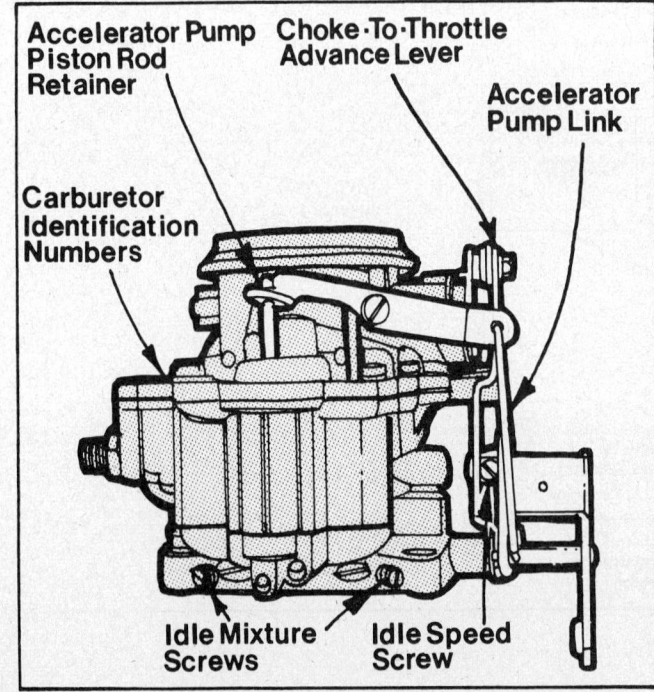

Fig. 1 Stromberg WW-2 Carburetor

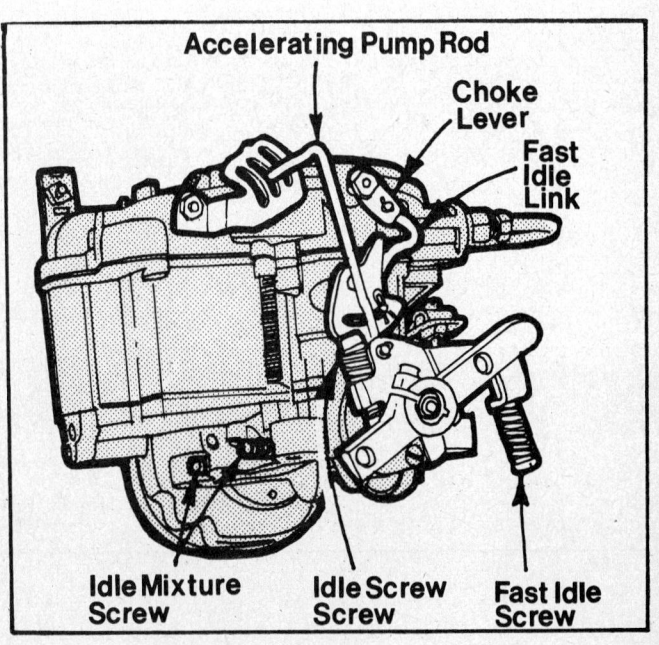

Fig. 2 Stromberg WWC-3 carburetor

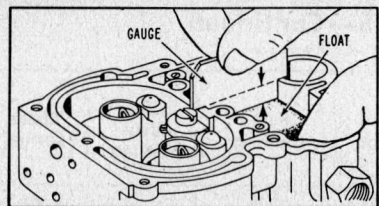

Fig. 3 Float level check. 1970-72 Stromberg

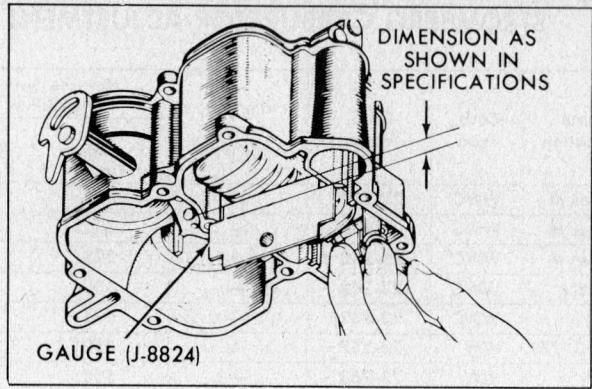

Fig. 4 Float level check. 1973-74 Stromberg

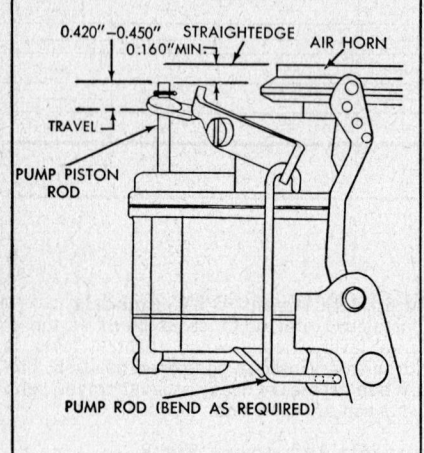

Fig. 5 Pump adjustment. 1970-72 WW-2 carburetor

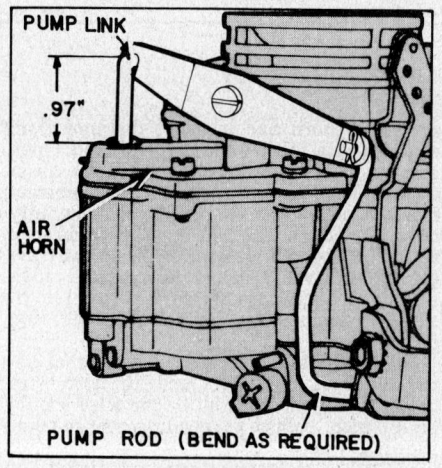

Fig. 6 Pump adjustment. 1973-74 WW-2 carburetor

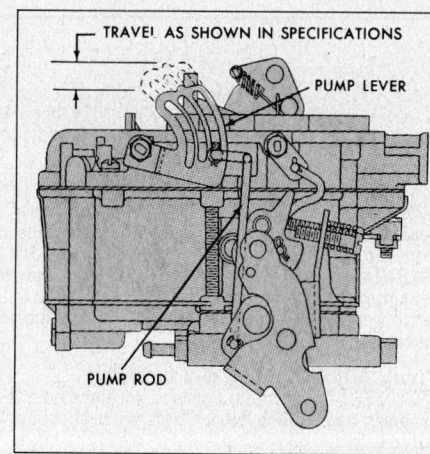

Fig. 7 Pump adjustment. WWC-3 carburetor

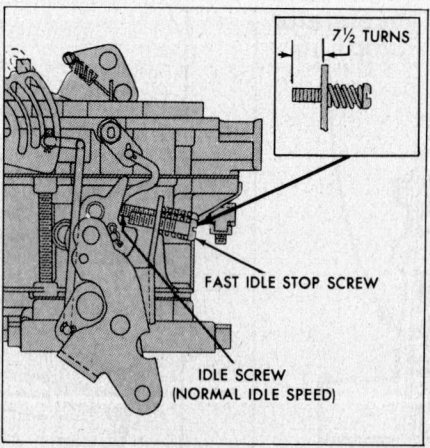

Fig. 8 Fast idle adjustment. WWC-3 carburetor

Clutch Section

NOTE: Refer to the Chevrolet Chapter for clutch adjustment procedure on models equipped with mechanical clutch controls.

HYDRAULIC CLUTCH CONTROLS

This system, Fig. 1, utilizes hydraulic pressure as a means of transmitting clutch pedal movement to the clutch release mechanism. The system consists of a pedal-operated master cylinder and a slave cylinder, interconnected with hydraulic lines. The clutch pedal is connected to the master cylinder push rod and the slave cylinder push rod is connected to the clutch throwout lever.

Maintenance

To maintain proper clutch operation, the system should be checked and serviced periodically as follows:
1. Maintain proper level of hydraulic fluid in master cylinder. At least once a year drain and flush entire clutch system and refill with new fluid.
2. Inspect entire clutch system regularly for fluid leakage. Leakage must be corrected immediately.
3. Make sure return spring at slave cylinder is not weak or broken.
4. Check and adjust if necessary the clutch pedal linkage as outlined below.

Clutch Control Linkage, Adjust

Two adjustments are required to obtain proper clutch control operation: Master cylinder push rod and slave cylinder push rod.

The purpose of the master cylinder push rod is to make sure the piston is resting all the way back against the piston stop with the end of the push rod barely contacting the piston. If the push rod is adjusted too long, the piston may never return far enough to clear the compensating port in the cylinder. This seals the line and the result is the same as riding the clutch all the time. If the push rod is too short, the pedal must be depressed too far before clutch disengages.

The slave cylinder push rod adjustment obtains the specified distance between wedge and adjusting nut when cylinder is not pressurized and release fork and bearing are held just in contact with clutch release levers, Fig. 2.

A slight reduction in pedal free travel at high engine rpm is normal; it is the result of centrifugal action on the clutch release lever weights. Do not change adjustment to obtain a definite free pedal travel dimension.

Before making adjustments, the hydraulic system must be free of air and the master cylinder must be filled to 1/2" below filler opening.

Master Cylinder Push Rod, Adjust

Before making adjustment, pull master cylinder boot back on push rod. Visually check to see that piston is firmly seated against piston stop. If it isn't, push rod is too long and should be shortened.

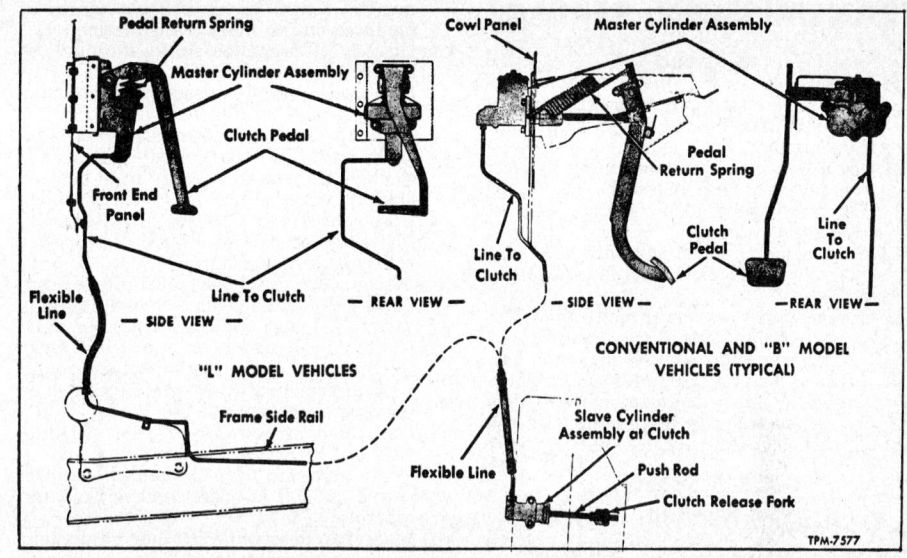

Fig. 1 Hydraulic clutch control system

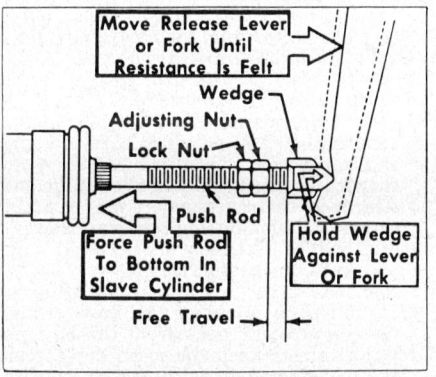

Fig. 2 Slave cylinder push rod adjustment

Conventional and "B" Models—Loosen lock nut on master cylinder push rod and turn hex portion of push rod as necessary to provide 1/16 inch free travel before push rod contacts master cylinder piston. Tighten lock nut on push rod.

Slave Cylinder Push Rod, Adjust

1. Disconnect clutch release fork retracting spring at side of clutch. *Do not apply pressure on clutch pedal while spring is disconnected.*
2. Bottom slave cylinder push rod and piston by pushing slave cylinder push rod toward front of engine as far as it will go.
3. Pull clutch release fork toward rear end of engine until clutch release bearing just contacts pressure plate release levers.
4. Referring to Fig. 2, measure clearance between wedge and adjusting nut, clearance should be as follows:

1970-72	Inline 6 & V8	3/16"
	V6	1/2"
	7500-9502 Series	1/4" to 1/2"
1973-74	Inline 6	23/64"
	V6	1/2"
	V8	13/32"
	7500-9502 Series	1/4" to 1/2"
1975-77	Inline 6	23/64"
	V8	13/32"

If necessary, adjust by turning adjusting nut at rear of wedge. Adjusting nut is the self-locking type. After making adjustment, connect clutch release fork return spring.

Bleeding System

The need for bleeding air from the system is generally indicated by a springy, spongy pedal action. The presence of air in the system is the result of low fluid level in the main cylinder, or if some part of the system has been opened. A bleeder valve is provided at the slave cylinder alongside of clutch.

The clutch master cylinder is accessible under the hood on conventional and "B" models, inside the cab and under dash on "L" models, and through the access door on "SP" models.

The plain end of bleeder hose can be slipped over end of bleeder valve. And the system can be bled by either the pressure or manual method in the same manner as when bleeding hydraulic brakes.

GMC

Manual Shift Transmission Section

NOTE: For Clark, New Process, Spicer and Warner transmissions used on GMC trucks, see the "name" chapter for service procedures and lubricant capacities

TRANSMISSION, REPLACE

3-Speed

1. Remove transmission rear support (if used) and disconnect propeller shaft from transmission.
2. Disconnect transmission control rods from levers at transmission.
3. Disconnect speedometer shaft at rear of transmission case.
4. Remove clutch housing underpan to gain access to the transmission lower mounting bolts.
5. Remove upper and lower mounting bolts, replacing guide pins in the upper holes.
6. Pull transmission straight back and out.
7. Install in the reverse order, using guide pins in the upper mounting holes to keep the transmission in alignment with the clutch housing during installation.

4 & 5 Speed
Light & Medium Duty

1. Remove access cover from cab floor.
2. On C.O.E. models, remove bellows and transmission control tower.
3. Disconnect speedometer shaft at rear of transmission case.
4. Disconnect transmission rear support (if used).
5. Disconnect propeller shaft.
6. On conventional models, remove hand brake lever and linkage at transmission.
7. Disconnect transmission strut rod (if used).
8. Remove clutch housing underpan.
9. Remove the two top transmission mounting bolts and replace with guide pins.
10. Remove lower mounting bolts.
11. With jack under transmission, move unit straight back and out.
12. Install in reverse order.

All Heavy Duty

The procedure to remove the transmission from the above model trucks is dependent generally upon the type of cab, type of body, and lifting equipment available in the shop. Operations other than those included in this procedure may be necessary if the vehicle has special equipment such as power take-off and controls.

The required operations will be obvious upon visual inspection of the vehicle. Therefore, the following instructions should be used as a guide in replacing a transmission.

1. Inside cab, remove seals and/or cover plates from floor above transmission.
2. If gearshift lever tower is removable, remove it. Some C.O.E. models have the gearshift lever clamped to a stub lever at the transmission cover. In such instances gearshift lever may be removed from stub lever instead of removing the complete tower assembly.
3. Remove hand brake lever and bracket when those items are mounted on the transmission cover. On some models it is necessary to detach the auxiliary transmission control lever bracket which is mounted on the main transmission.
4. Disconnect propeller shaft at flange at rear of transmission. If a separate auxiliary transmission is used, it may be necessary to remove the complete propeller shaft between the transmission and auxiliary unit to provide sufficient clearance to move transmission away from engine. On long wheelbase trucks with propeller shaft center bearing, remove center bearing bolts to allow movement of propeller shafts to provide clearance.
5. Disconnect clutch control linkage and, except when an auxiliary transmission is used, disconnect speedometer cable housing from connector on mainshaft rear bearing cap. Disconnect engine ground strap if attached to transmission case or clutch housing.
6. Disconnect strut rod from rear of transmission.
7. Drain lubricant from transmission and if power take-off is used, remove unit and controls.
8. Inspect to determine if other equipment or brackets must be removed to permit removal of transmission. On some trucks the exhaust pipe or support brackets must be removed.
9. *On trucks equipped with Fuller transmissions, the air pressure must be exhausted from the air system and the air line must be disconnected from the pressure regulator valve before transmission can be removed. Also the feed wire to the circuit switch must be disconnected.*
10. Place transmission dolly or jack under transmission and adjust to carry weight of transmission. Then remove the rear support (if used). If there is sufficient clearance, the rear support may remain on transmission during removal. However, it will be necessary to disconnect support from brackets at frame.
11. Remove bolts which attach clutch housing to flywheel housing and move transmission straight back from the engine, using care to keep the main drive gear shaft in alignment with the clutch disc hub.
12. If the transmission is to be disassembled, remove the clutch release mechanism and remove the hand brake mechanism and rear support members if these parts are installed at the rear of the transmission.

SAGINAW 3 SPEED

For service refer to "Chevrolet Truck Chapter, Manual Shift Transmission Section, 1970–80 Chevy Van Models & 1973–75 Vega 3 Speed."

SAGINAW 4 SPEED

For service refer to "Chevrolet Truck Chapter, Manual Transmission Section, 1973–75 Vega 4 Speed Transmission."

MUNCIE 3 SPEED, 1970–80

For service refer to "Chevrolet Truck Chapter, Manual Shift Transmission Section".

1976–80 TREMEC 3 SPEED

For service procedures, refer to the Ford Chapter, Transmission Section under "3 SPEED TRANS., 1970–80".

MUNCIE 4 SPEED, 1970–80

For service refer to "Chevrolet Truck Chapter, Manual Shift Transmission Section".

WARNER 4 SPEED, 1975–80 CABALLERO & SPRINT

Transmission Disassemble

1. Position transmission in 2nd gear, then remove side cover, gasket and both shift forks, Fig. 1.
2. Remove reverse shifter lock pin, Fig. 2, pull shifter shaft outward, disengaging lever from reverse gear.
3. Remove extension housing bolts and tap housing with a mallet to loosen, then pull extension housing rearward until idler shaft clears idler gear. Turn housing to left thereby freeing reverse shift fork from collar and remove housing.
4. Remove snap ring, then slide speedometer gear from mainshaft, remove second speedometer gear snap ring, Fig. 3.
5. Remove reverse gear from mainshaft, then slide rear reverse idler gear from rear bearing retainer.
6. Remove lock bolt from rear bearing retainer and drive locating pin from bearing retainer into case.
7. Rotate rear bearing retainer counterclockwise, providing access to rear of countershaft.
8. From front of case, using a dummy shaft, tap countershaft and key out the rear of case, Fig. 5.
9. Using a mallet, tap rear bearing retainer rearward, and remove mainshaft through rear of transmission.
10. Remove bearing rollers and washer from main drive gear bore.
11. Remove front reverse idler gear and thrust washer from case.
12. Remove fourth gear synchronizing ring from main drive gear.
13. Remove main drive gear bearing retainer from case, remove snap ring and washer from main drive gear, then press gear from bearing, Fig. 6.

GMC

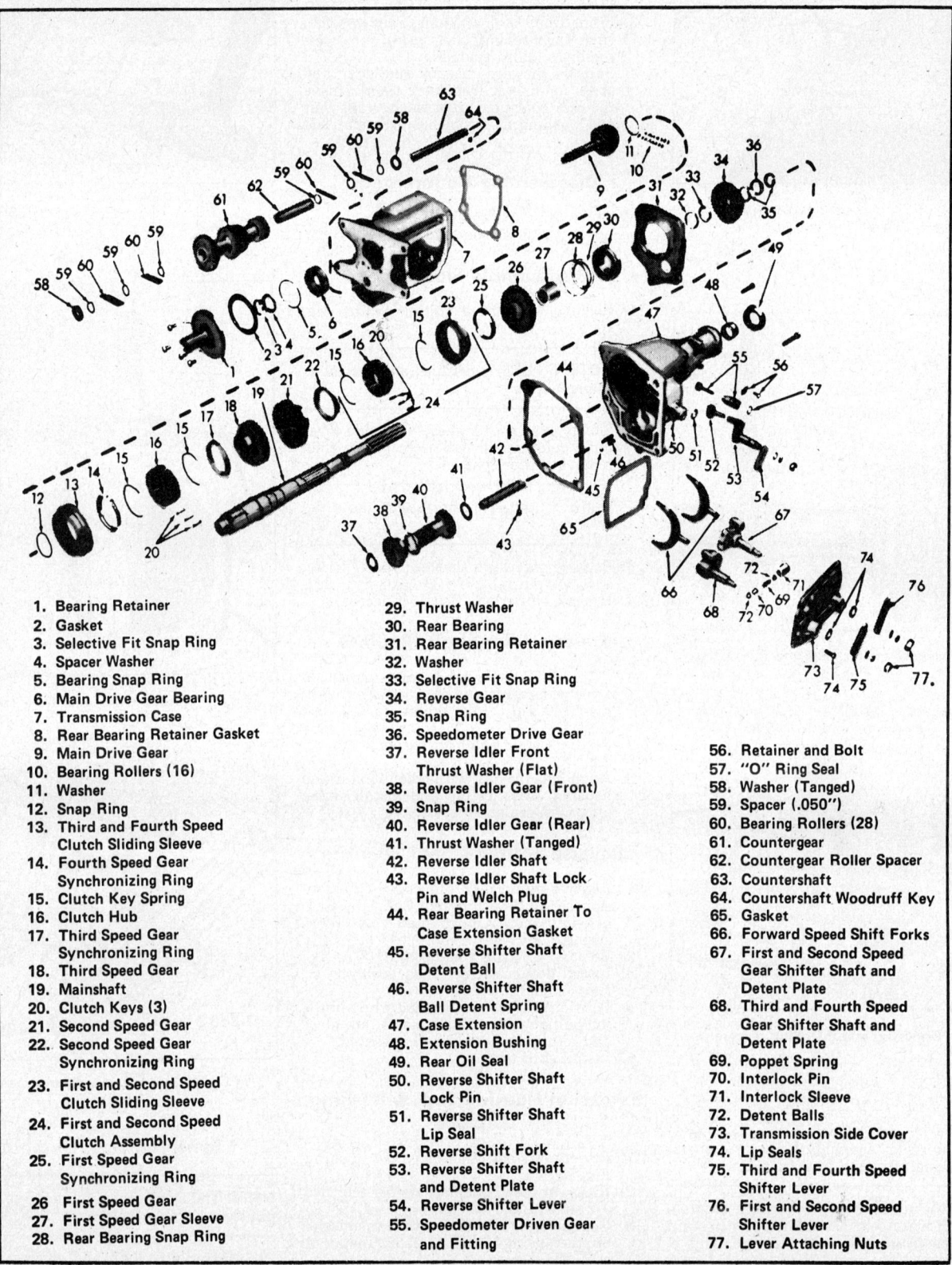

1. Bearing Retainer
2. Gasket
3. Selective Fit Snap Ring
4. Spacer Washer
5. Bearing Snap Ring
6. Main Drive Gear Bearing
7. Transmission Case
8. Rear Bearing Retainer Gasket
9. Main Drive Gear
10. Bearing Rollers (16)
11. Washer
12. Snap Ring
13. Third and Fourth Speed Clutch Sliding Sleeve
14. Fourth Speed Gear Synchronizing Ring
15. Clutch Key Spring
16. Clutch Hub
17. Third Speed Gear Synchronizing Ring
18. Third Speed Gear
19. Mainshaft
20. Clutch Keys (3)
21. Second Speed Gear
22. Second Speed Gear Synchronizing Ring
23. First and Second Speed Clutch Sliding Sleeve
24. First and Second Speed Clutch Assembly
25. First Speed Gear Synchronizing Ring
26. First Speed Gear
27. First Speed Gear Sleeve
28. Rear Bearing Snap Ring
29. Thrust Washer
30. Rear Bearing
31. Rear Bearing Retainer
32. Washer
33. Selective Fit Snap Ring
34. Reverse Gear
35. Snap Ring
36. Speedometer Drive Gear
37. Reverse Idler Front Thrust Washer (Flat)
38. Reverse Idler Gear (Front)
39. Snap Ring
40. Reverse Idler Gear (Rear)
41. Thrust Washer (Tanged)
42. Reverse Idler Shaft
43. Reverse Idler Shaft Lock Pin and Welch Plug
44. Rear Bearing Retainer To Case Extension Gasket
45. Reverse Shifter Shaft Detent Ball
46. Reverse Shifter Shaft Ball Detent Spring
47. Case Extension
48. Extension Bushing
49. Rear Oil Seal
50. Reverse Shifter Shaft Lock Pin
51. Reverse Shifter Shaft Lip Seal
52. Reverse Shift Fork
53. Reverse Shifter Shaft and Detent Plate
54. Reverse Shifter Lever
55. Speedometer Driven Gear and Fitting
56. Retainer and Bolt
57. "O" Ring Seal
58. Washer (Tanged)
59. Spacer (.050")
60. Bearing Rollers (28)
61. Countergear
62. Countergear Roller Spacer
63. Countershaft
64. Countershaft Woodruff Key
65. Gasket
66. Forward Speed Shift Forks
67. First and Second Speed Gear Shifter Shaft and Detent Plate
68. Third and Fourth Speed Gear Shifter Shaft and Detent Plate
69. Poppet Spring
70. Interlock Pin
71. Interlock Sleeve
72. Detent Balls
73. Transmission Side Cover
74. Lip Seals
75. Third and Fourth Speed Shifter Lever
76. First and Second Speed Shifter Lever
77. Lever Attaching Nuts

Fig. 1 Warner four speed transmission. 1975-80 Caballero & Sprint

GMC

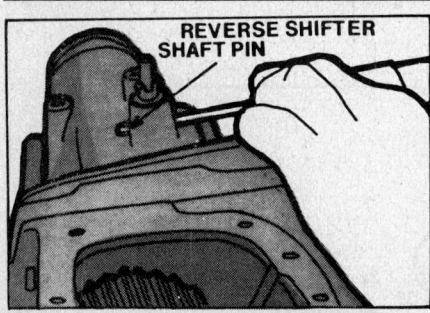

Fig. 2 Removing reverse shifter shaft lock pin

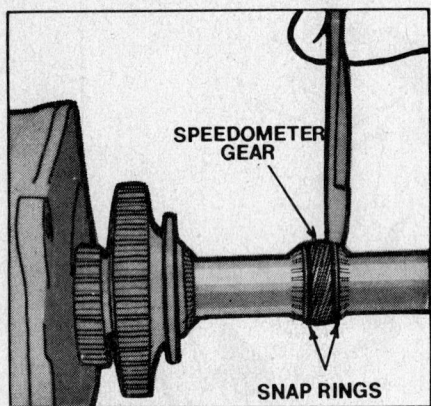

Fig. 3 Speedometer gear and snap rings

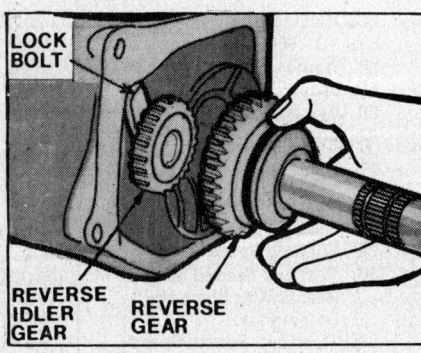

Fig. 4 Removing and installing reverse gear

14. Tap drive gear bearing from case, remove countergear assembly and 2 washers. Drive locating pin from case.

NOTE: It is not necessary to remove countershaft and main gear assemblies if only main drive gear bearing is to be replaced. This is accomplished by using tools J-22912 and J-8433-1, Fig. 7.

Disassemble Mainshaft

1. From rear of mainshaft, remove snap ring and slide rear bearing retainer from mainshaft, Fig. 8.
2. Remove rear bearing snap ring and washer.
3. From front of mainshaft, remove snap ring, then remove 3-4 synchronizer assembly and 3rd gear, Fig. 1.
4. Support forward face of 2nd gear and press mainshaft from rear then remove the rear bearing, thrust washer, 1st gear and bushing, 1-2 synchronizer and 2nd gear.

Disassemble Countergear

Remove dummy shaft, bearings rollers, spacers and tubular spacer, Fig. 9.

Disassemble Side Cover

1. Remove forks from shifter shafts, Fig. 10.

   NOTE: Forks are identical and are interchangeable.

2. Slowly push shifter shafts into side cover until detent balls fall from cover, then remove shifter shafts.

   NOTE: The 3-4 shifter shaft has a detent.

3. Remove interlock sleeve, poppet spring and lock pin.
4. Replace shifter shaft seals if necessary.

Reverse Idler Shaft, Replace

1. Remove thrust washer, use punch to drive welch plug and pin into idler shaft, Fig. 11, until idler shaft can be removed.
2. Position idler shaft in extension housing.
3. Align hole in shaft with hole in extension housing, drive in pin and install welch plug with sealer.

Reverse Shifter & Seal, Replace

1. Remove shifter fork, tap shaft into extension housing until detent ball falls from housing, then remove shaft and detent spring.
2. Remove "O" ring and discard.
3. Install detent spring, then position "O" ring on shaft.
4. Position ball on spring, then while pressing ball downward, slide shaft into place and rotate shaft until ball is seated.
5. Install shift fork.

Extension Housing Seal & Bushing, Replace

1. Pry out oil seal, then drive out bushing, Fig. 12.
2. Press in new bushing using tool No. J-21465-17 and J-8092.
3. Coat bushing and seal with transmission oil, then using tool No. J-21359 install oil seal, Fig. 13.

Drive Gear Bearing Oil Seal, Replace

Pry seal with screw driver. Position seal in bore and tap in with flat plate, Fig. 14.

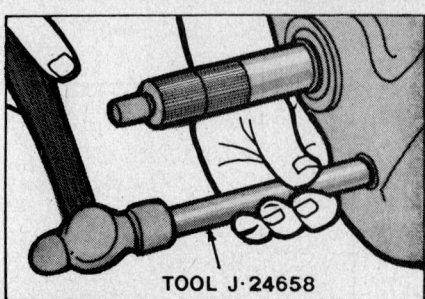

Fig. 5 Removing countershaft

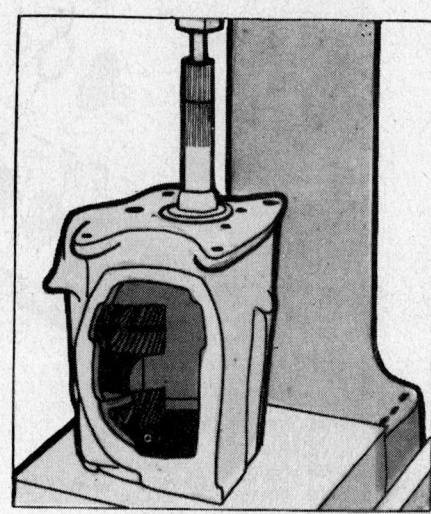

Fig. 6 Pressing drive gear from bearing

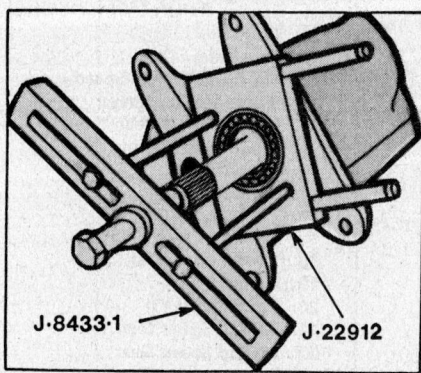

Fig. 7 Main drive gear bearing removal

Synchronizers, Overhaul

NOTE: The synchronizer clutch hub and sliding sleeve are replaced as an assembly.

1. Mark clutch hub and sliding sleeve so they can be installed in the same position, Fig. 15.
2. Press clutch hub from sliding sleeve, remove clutch keys and springs.
3. Install clutch keys and springs, align marks, install sliding sleeve on clutch hub.

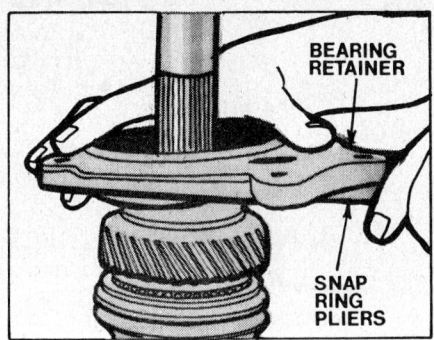

Fig. 8 Removing and installing rear bearing retainer

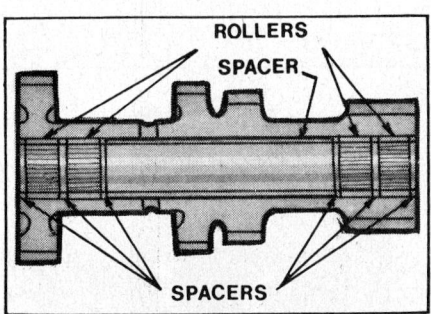

Fig. 9 Countergear assembly

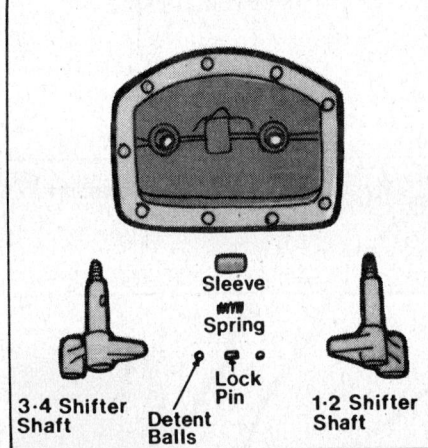

Fig. 10 Side cover assembly

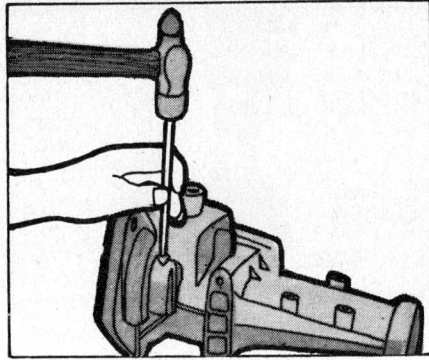

Fig. 11 Removing roll pin from reverse idler shaft

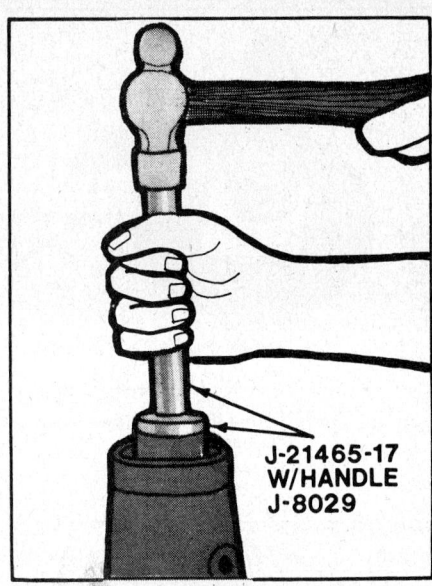

Fig. 12 Removing and installing extension housing bushing

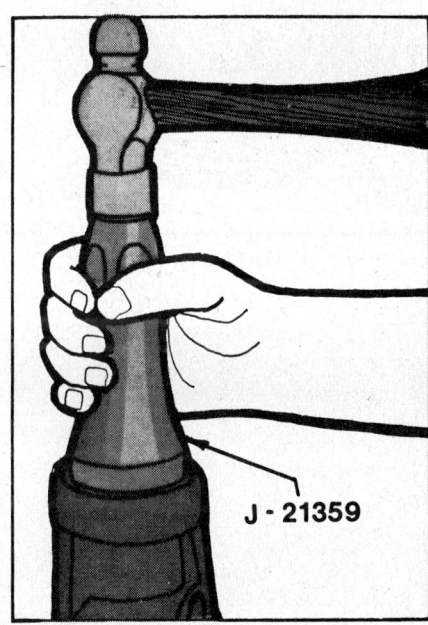

Fig. 13 Installing extension housing oil seal

Assemble Side Cover

NOTE: When assembling transmission always use new gaskets, oil seals and snap rings.

1. Install seals in shifter shaft bores, if removed.
2. Install 3-4 shifter shaft in bore, position in neutral, then install detent ball, interlock sleeve, poppet spring and lock pin, Fig. 10.
3. Position detent ball in other end of interlock sleeve, depress ball and install 1-2 shifter shaft.
4. Position 1-2 shifter shaft in 2nd gear and install shift forks.

Countergear Assemble & Install

1. Position dummy shaft in countergear bore and install tubular spacer.
2. Install spacer in bore. Using heavy grease to hold rollers in place, install 28 rollers, Fig. 9.
3. Install second spacer, 28 additional rollers and third spacer.
4. Install rollers and spacers in other end of countergear using above procedure.
5. Install thrust washers in each end of transmission case with tangs inserted in case recesses, using grease to hold washers in place.
6. Insert countershaft through rear of case, in turn forcing dummy shaft out through front of case. Install woodruff key on countershaft; tap countershaft until flush with rear of case.

Countergear End Play Check

Attach dial indicator, Fig. 16; check end play. If end play is greater than .025 in. new selective thrust washers must be installed.

Assemble Mainshaft

1. Front rear of mainshaft and install 2nd gear with hub facing rearward.
2. Position synchronizing rings on 1-2 synchronizer, then install synchronizer on mainshaft with hub facing forward.
3. Press 1st gear bushing on mainshaft until 2nd gear, 1-2 synchronizer and bushing are against mainshaft shoulder, Fig. 17.
4. Install 1st gear and inner race with gear hub facing front, then press rear bearing on mainshaft with snap ring groove facing front, Fig. 18.
5. Install spacer and selective thickness snap ring.

NOTE: Use the thickest snap ring that will fit in mainshaft groove.

6. Install 3rd gear with hub facing front and the 3rd gear synchronizing ring with notches facing front.
7. Install 3rd and 4th gear clutch assembly with the taper facing front.

NOTE: Ensure that keys in hub mate with notches in 3rd gear synchronizing ring.

8. Install selective thickness snap ring. Use thickness snap ring that will fit mainshaft groove.
9. Install locating pin in rear bearing retainer. Place bearing retainer over rear of mainshaft; spread retainer snap ring and align with groove in rear bearing, Fig. 18.
10. Using heavy grease, install 16 rollers and flat washer into main drive gear bore, Fig. 19.
11. Position 4th gear synchronizer ring on 3-4 synchronizer, aligning ring notches with hub keys.
12. Install front drive gear on main shaft.

GMC

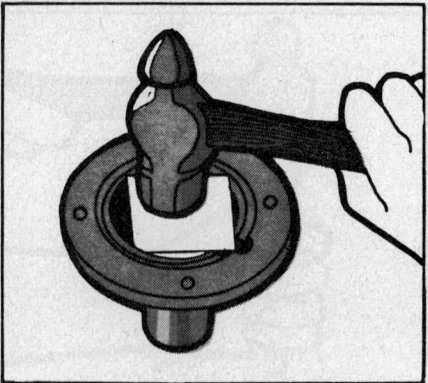

Fig. 14 Installing drive gear bearing retainer oil seal

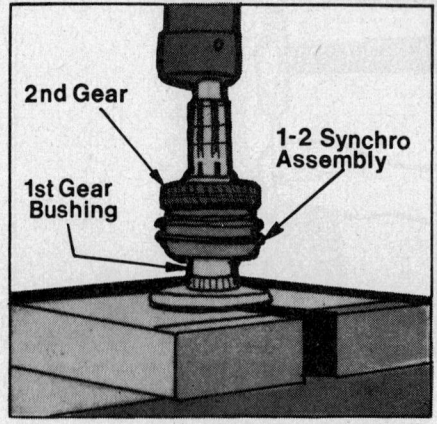

Fig. 17 Installing 2nd gear, 1–2 synchronizer assembly and 1st gear bushing

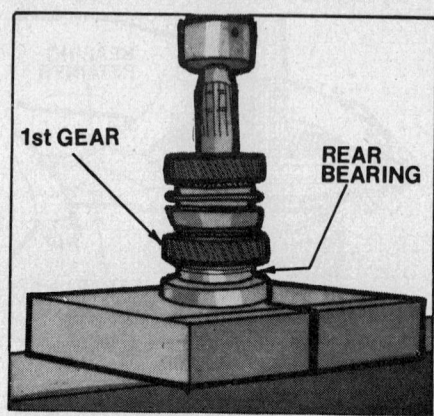

Fig. 18 Installing 1st gear and rear bearing

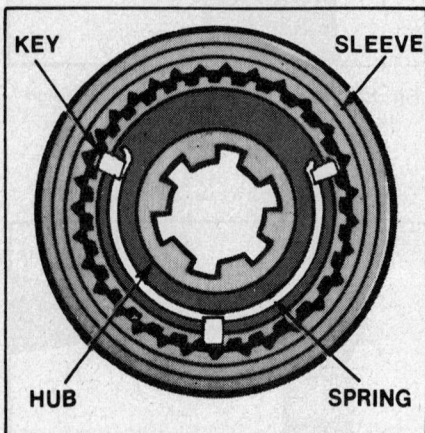

Fig. 15 Synchronizer assembly

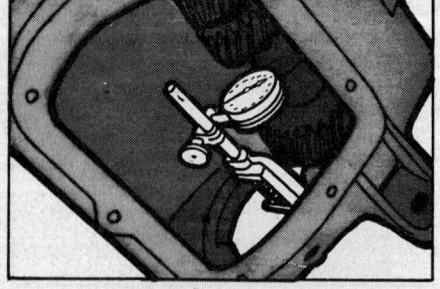

Fig. 16 Countergear end play check

Transmission Assemble

1. Install drain plug in transmission case.
2. Install thrust washer and front section of reverse idler gear with hub facing rear and position gasket on rear of transmission case.
3. Position synchronizers in neutral and install mainshaft in case. Install retainer locating pin and torque retainer lock bolt to 25 ft. lbs.
4. Tap main drive gear bearing into case. Using suitable tool, pull drive gear shaft forward, and tap bearing again until bearing bottoms on main drive gear and the washer and snap ring can be installed on main gear drive shaft, Fig. 20.
5. Install main drive gear bearing retainer and gasket, apply sealer to bolts and torque to 18 ft. lbs.
6. Install rear reverse idler gear, engaging splines with front section.
7. Install reverse sliding gear with hub facing rear, Fig. 4, then install the speedometer gear and two snap rings on mainshaft, Fig. 3.
8. Position gasket on rear bearing retainer and, install thrust washer on reverse idler shaft in extension housing.
9. Rotate reverse shifter shaft until fork is in full forward position. With synchronizer sleeves in neutral, slide extension housing over mainshaft. Guide reverse idler shaft into reverse idler gears, engaging fork on collar, then position shifter shaft in neutral.
10. Rotate reverse shifter shaft clockwise and push extension housing forward, aligning rear bearing retainer locating pin with extension housing. Apply sealer to bolts and torque long bolts to 40 ft. lbs., short bolts to 25 ft. lbs.
11. Install reverse shifter shaft lock pin.
12. Shift transmission into 2nd gear. The front synchronizer sleeve should be in neutral and the rear sleeve in forward position to engage 2nd gear synchronizer teeth.
13. Position slide cover and gasket to transmission case and index shift forks to shift collars, then install and torque side cover bolts to 18 ft. lbs.

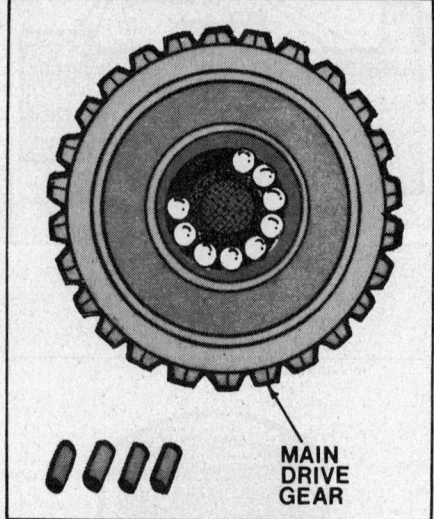

Fig. 19 Installing bearing rollers into main drive gear bore

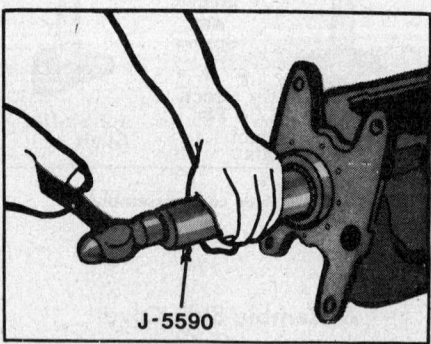

Fig. 20 Installing drive gear bearing

GMC

Automatic Transmission Section

ALLISON AT-540, MT-640, MT-650 & MT-654

Selector Linkage

1974–79 Models Exc. MT-654
1. Disconnect clevis from transmission shift lever and the control cable from transmission bracket. Also, remove cable retainer clips from underside of cab.
2. Remove range selector cover screws and lift range selector out to facilitate cable attachment inspection at selector lever and hanger.
3. Check cable at trunnion for dimension specified in View A-A, Figs. 1 and 2. This dimension is necessary to allow for proper cable length at clevis. If an adjustment is needed, remove cable from range selector lever and hanger assembly as follows:
    a. Remove trunnion locknut and disconnect cable from hanger anchor point.
    b. Mark location of trunnion, then remove trunnion with attached cable core from lever.

NOTE: Trunnion must be installed in original position hole since unsafe vehicle operation may result.

4. Loosen trunnion jam nut and rotate trunnion to obtain proper dimension, View A-A, Figs. 1 and 2. Install trunnion in original hole and tighten locknut.

NOTE: On 1977–79 models, the dimension in View A-A, Figs. 1 & 2 should be 1/2 inch.

5. Connect cable to hanger anchor point and torque nuts to 3–5 ft. lbs.
6. Install range selector cover and torque screws to 3–5 ft. lbs. and install the cable retainer clips to cab underside.
7. Connect cable to transmission bracket and tighten screws.
8. Place transmission shift lever in reverse position which is at the end of full counter-clockwise travel of lever and the range selector lever against stop in reverse position.
9. Loosen clevis jam nut and rotate clevis until clevis pin can be inserted through clevis and transmission shift lever holes. Then, rotate clevis one full turn clockwise to allow for cable backlash.
10. Connect clevis to lever with pin and a new cotter pin, however, do not spread cotter pin at this time.
11. Shift range selector lever through all ranges. The transmission detents should fully engage just before range selector lever contacts the stops incorporated in range selector cover.
12. Spread cotter pin and tighten jam nut against clevis.
13. Check adjustment for proper operation.

MT-654 Models

NOTE: Before making adjustment, ensure controls are not damaged and operate smoothly.

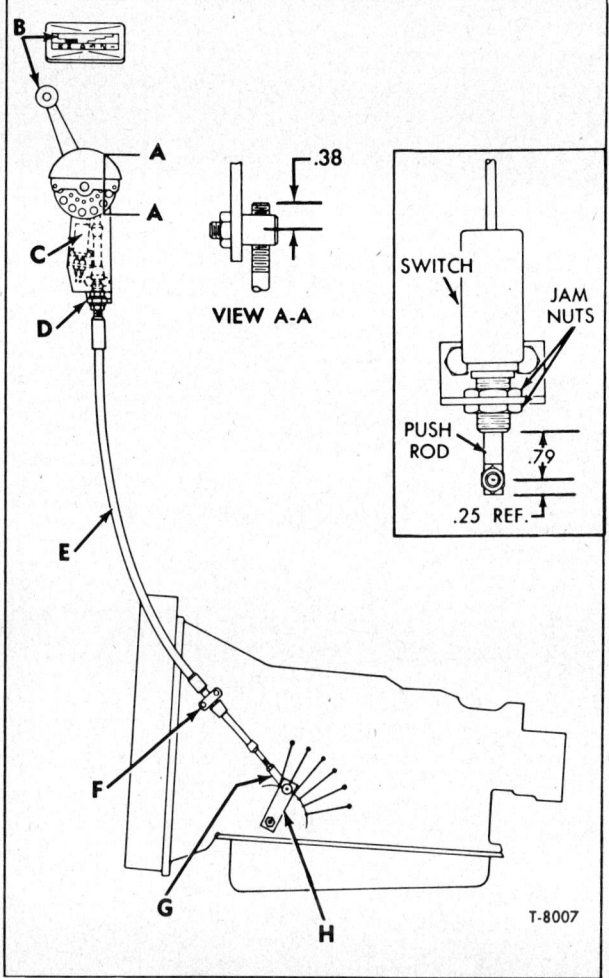

Fig. 1 Manual shift linkage. Allison AT-540

1. Place range selector lever against stop in "Reverse" position, Fig. 3.
2. Disconnect clevis from transmission lever.
3. Move transmission shift lever fully counterclockwise to "Reverse".
4. Loosen clevis jam nut and adjust clevis until holes on clevis and transmission lever are aligned, then install clevis pin. Adjust clevis 1/2 turn at a time until pin enters freely.
5. Turn clevis one full turn clockwise to allow for cable backlash.
6. Connect clevis to lever and secure with a new cotter pin.
7. Check for proper operation.

Exc. 1974–80 & MT-654 Models
1. Locate transmission selector lever (B), Fig. 1, against stop in "N" position.
2. Check cable for dimension shown in view A-A of Figs. 1 and 2 and adjust if necessary. Anchor cable to bracket at point (D).
3. Disconnect clevis (G) from manual shift lever (H). Anchor cable (E) securely to point (F).
4. Locate manual shift lever (H) in "N".

NOTE: Neutral position of manual shift lever is obtained by rotating lever completely forward, then back one notch.

5. Adjust clevis (G) for free entry of clevis pin through clevis and manual shift lever (H). Then shorten cable by rotating clevis 2 turns clockwise. Tighten jam nut against clevis; install clevis pin and secure with cotter pin.
6. Check operation in all ranges.

TURBO HYDRA-MATIC 200

Gearshift Linkage

1977 Sprint & 1978–80 Caballero Console Shift
1. Place shifter in "N" (NEUTRAL) position of the detent plate, Fig. 4.
2. Place transmission lever in "N" (NEUTRAL) position by moving lever clock-

1187

GMC

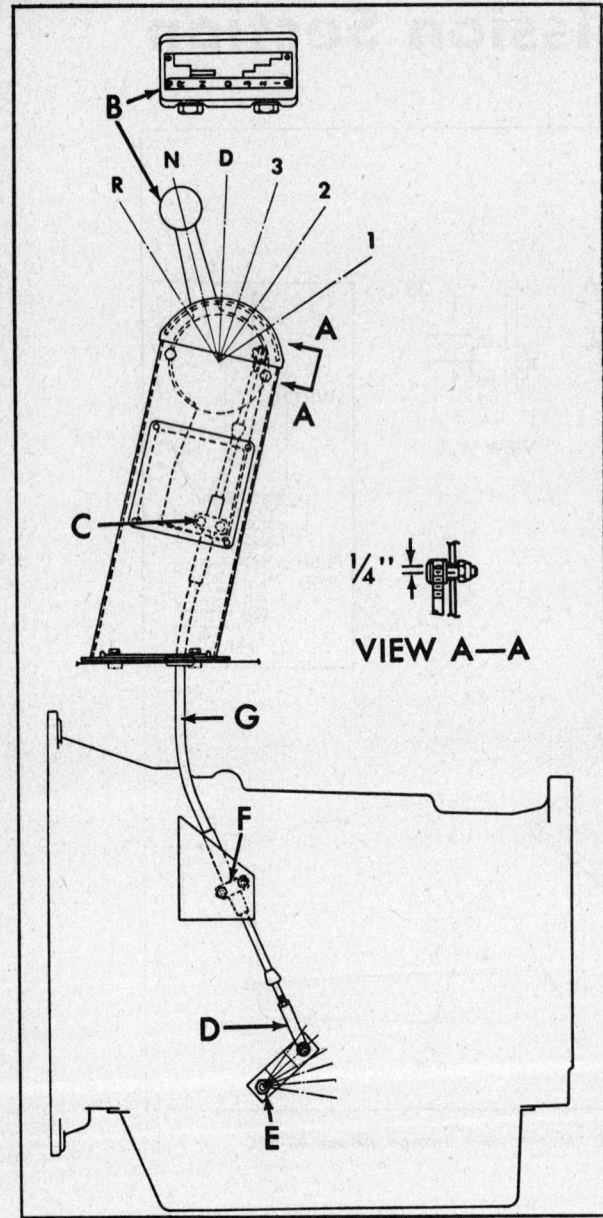

Fig. 2 Manual shift linkage. Allison MT-640, 650

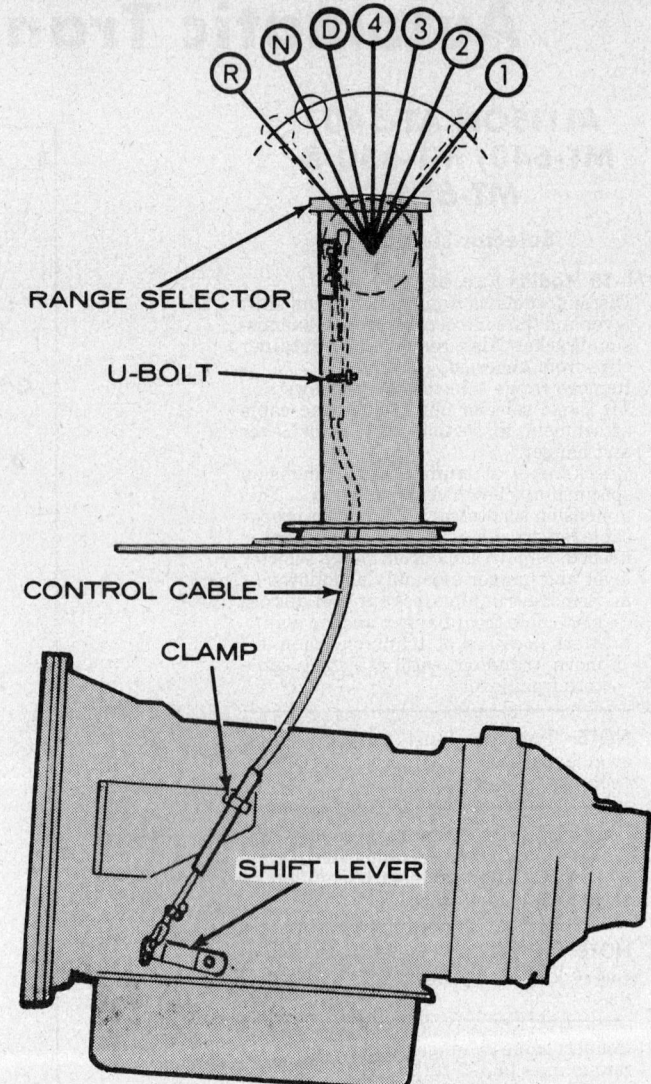

Fig. 3 Shift linkage adjustment. MT-654 models

wise to maximum detent "P" (PARK), then counterclockwise two (2) positions (NEUTRAL-N).
3. Install the pin and lock onto the fork with lever in "N". Adjust the rod length until hole in rod aligns with pin on shifter assembly, install rod onto pin.
4. Install washer and clip.

1977 Sprint & 1978-80 Caballero Column Shift
Refer to Fig. 5 for column shift adjustment.

TURBO HYDRA-MATIC 350

Gearshift Linkage

1973-80 Sprint & Caballero Console Shift
1. Loosen swivel screw so rod is free to move

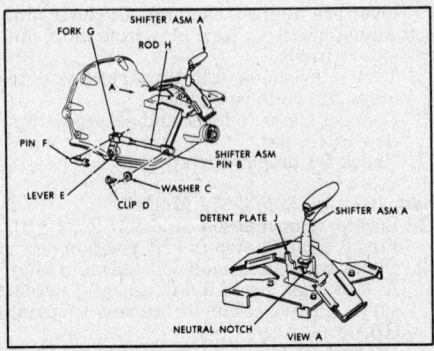

Fig. 4 Shift linkage adjustment. Turbo hydramatic 200 with console shift

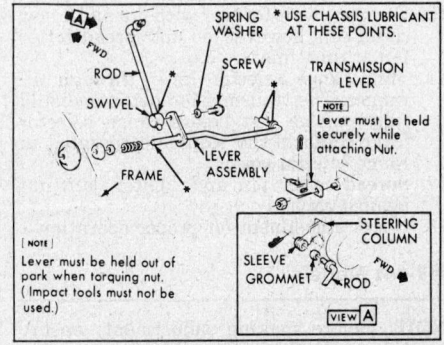

Fig. 5 Shift linkage adjustment. Turbo hydramatic 200 with column shift

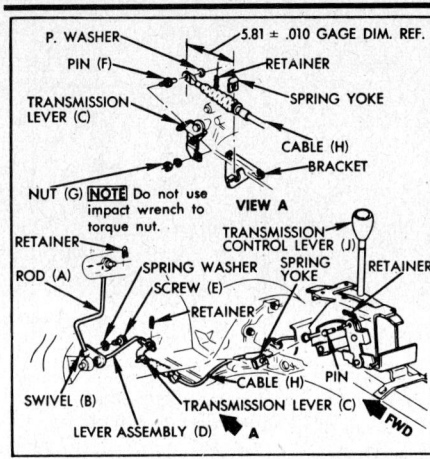

Fig. 6 Turbo hydra-matic 350 shift linkage. 1973-80 Sprint & Caballero console shift

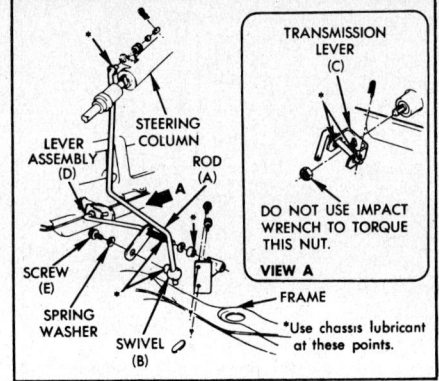

Fig. 7 Turbo hydra-matic 350 shift linkage. 1973-80 "CK" models Sprint & Caballero column shift, 1974-80 "P" models

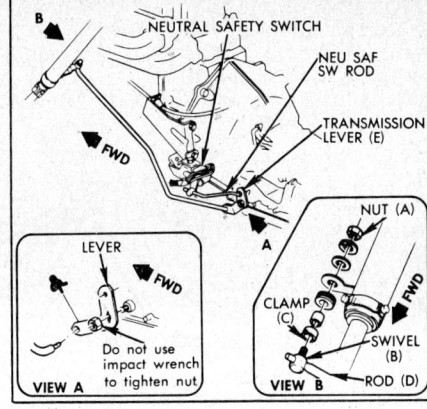

Fig. 8 Turbo hydra-matic 350 shift linkage. 1973 "P" models

in swivel, Fig. 6.
2. Place transmission control lever in Drive and loosen pin in transmission lever, so it moves in the slot.
3. Move transmission lever counterclockwise to L1 detent and then three detents clockwise to Drive position. Tighten nut on transmission lever to 20 ft. lbs.
4. Place transmission control lever in Park and ignition switch in the lock position and pull lightly against lock stop, then tighten swivel screw to 20 ft. lbs. Check for proper operation.

1973-80 "CK" Models, Sprint & Caballero Column Shift, 1974-80 "P" Models

1. Place transmission lever in Neutral by moving lever counter-clockwise to L1 detent then clockwise three detent positions to Neutral.
2. Place selector lever in Neutral as determined by mechanical stop on steering column. Do not use indicator as reference.
3. Assemble swivel, spring washer and screw to lever assembly then tighten screw to 20 ft. lbs., Fig. 7.

1973-80 "G" Models & 1973 "P" Models

1. Loosen swivel nut at steering column lever to allow free movement of swivel and clamp on rod.
2. Place transmission lever in Neutral position by moving lever counterclockwise to "L1" detent then clockwise three detent positions to Neutral.

3. Place selector lever in Neutral as determined by mechanical stop. Do not use indicator as reference.
4. On 1973 P models and 1973-74 G models, torque swivel nut to 18 ft. lbs., Figs. 8 & 9.
5. On 1975-80 G models, hold steering column lever against Neutral stop (Park position side) and torque swivel nut to 18 ft. lbs., Fig. 10.

1972 Sprint Console Shift
1. Place shift lever in Drive, Fig. 11.
2. Raise vehicle, disconnect cable from transmission lever and manually place transmission lever in Drive. Measure distance from rearward face of attachment bracket to center of cable attachment stud. This dimension should be 5.5". If not, loosen stud nut and move stud accordingly. Reinstall stud nut and adjust end of cable so that it fits freely on stud. Reinstall clip.

1972 Sprint Column Shift
1. Place selector lever in Drive as determined by the transmission detent.
2. Loosen adjustment swivel at cross shaft and rotate transmission lever so it contacts the Drive stop in the steering column.
3. Tighten swivel and recheck adjustment.
4. Readjust indicator needle if necessary to agree with the transmission detent positions.
5. Readjust neutral safety switch if necessary, Fig. 12.

1970-72 "G" Models
1. Refer to Fig. 13 and set transmission lever (E) in Drive position. Obtain Drive position by moving transmission lever counterclockwise as far as it will go to "L1" detent, then clockwise two detent positions to Drive position.
2. Attach control rod (D) to lever (E) and shaft assembly (B) if removed.
3. If necessary, assemble ring, washers, grommet, swivel, retainer, washer and nut loose on shaft assembly (B).
4. Insert control rod (C) in swivel and retainer and attach opposite end of control rod to shift lever on steering column.
5. Set shift lever in Drive position and tighten nut (F).

1970-72 "P" Models
1. Set selector lever at transmission in

Drive position. Obtain Drive position by moving transmission lever clockwise as far as it will go then counterclockwise two detent positions to Drive.
2. Raise shift lever and tube assembly to Reverse position. Assemble swivel and clamp over control shaft. Install lockwasher and nut on swivel, Fig. 14.
3. Move shift lever and tube assembly to Drive position and tighten clamp nut.

NOTE: When adjusted correctly, the following conditions must be met when moving steering column shift lever:

a. From Reverse to Drive travel, the transmission detent must be noted and related to indicated position on dial.
b. When Drive and Neutral position pull lever upward, then release. It must drop back into position with no restriction and have no other travel.

1970-72 "C" Models
Adjust as previously described for "P" models, Fig. 15.

Detent Cable Adjust

1970-71 Models
1. Refer to Fig. 16 and remove air cleaner and loosen detent cable screw at transmission.
2. With choke off and accelerator linkage properly adjusted, place carburetor throttle lever in wide open position.

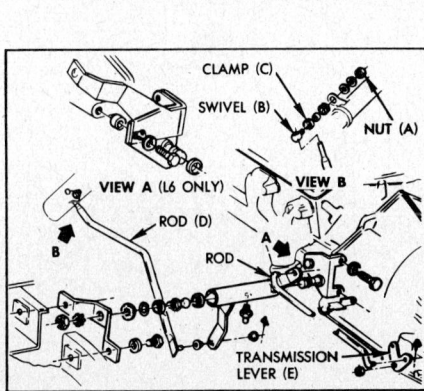

Fig. 9 Turbo hydra-matic 350 shift linkage. 1973-74 "G" models

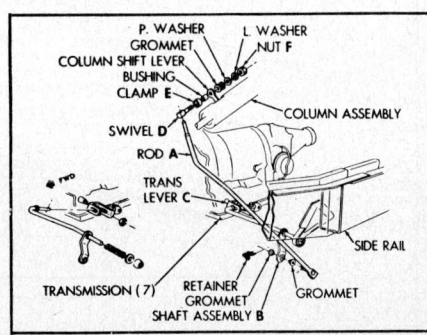

Fig. 10 Turbo hydra-matic 350 shift linkage. 1975-80 "G" models

GMC

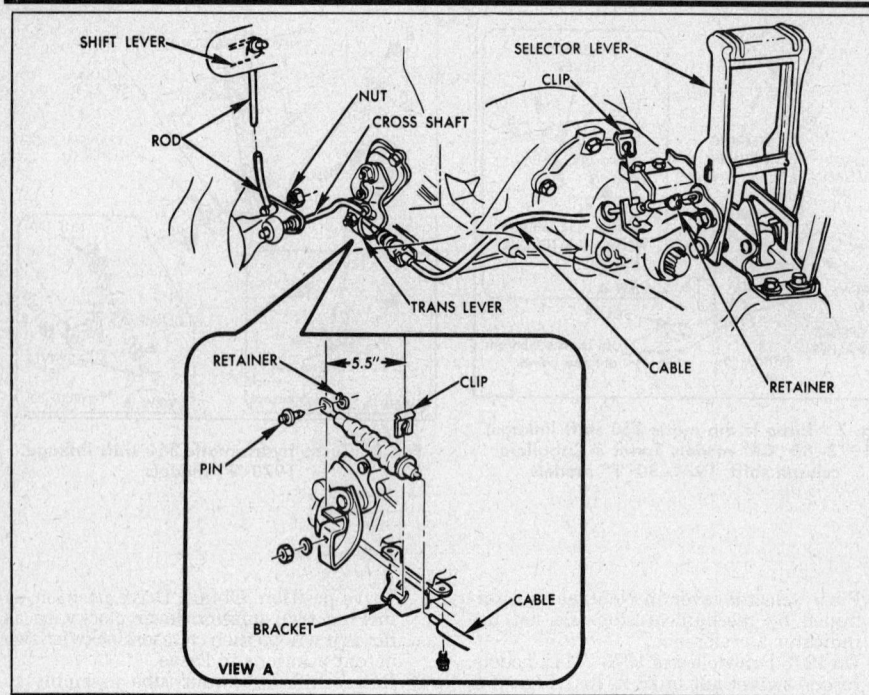

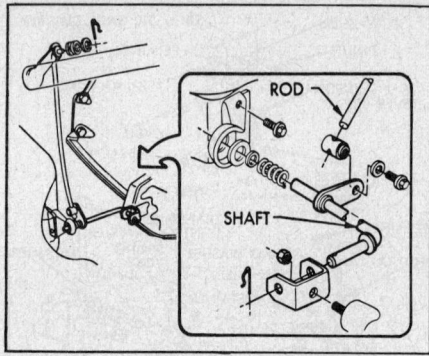

Fig. 12 Turbo hydra-matic 350 shift linkage. 1972 Sprint column shift

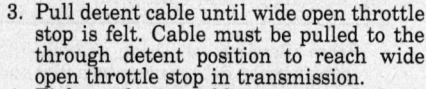

Fig. 11 Turbo hydra-matic 350 shift linkage. 1972 Sprint console shift

POW-R-FLO TRANS.

Transmission, Replace

Handi-Van

1. Support engine with jack and remove propeller shaft.
2. Disconnect control rods from transmission levers, and remove neutral safety switch wire harness.
3. Remove speedometer cable, vacuum line at modulator, and oil cooler lines at transmission.
4. Remove engine rear mount-to-bracket thru bolt.
5. Remove linkage cross shaft frame attaching bolts and accelerator linkage at bellcrank before lowering engine. Lower engine enough to allow rear engine mount housing to clear its support bracket.
6. Attach transmission jack on transmission.

3. Pull detent cable until wide open throttle stop is felt. Cable must be pulled to the through detent position to reach wide open throttle stop in transmission.
4. Tighten detent cable screws and check linkage for proper operation.

Disconnect downshift cable from snap-lock at cable mounting bracket, then position carburetor to wide open throttle and push snap-lock downward until top is flush with remainder of cable.

TURBO HYDRA-MATIC 400, 475

Adjustments are made as described previously by the TH-350.

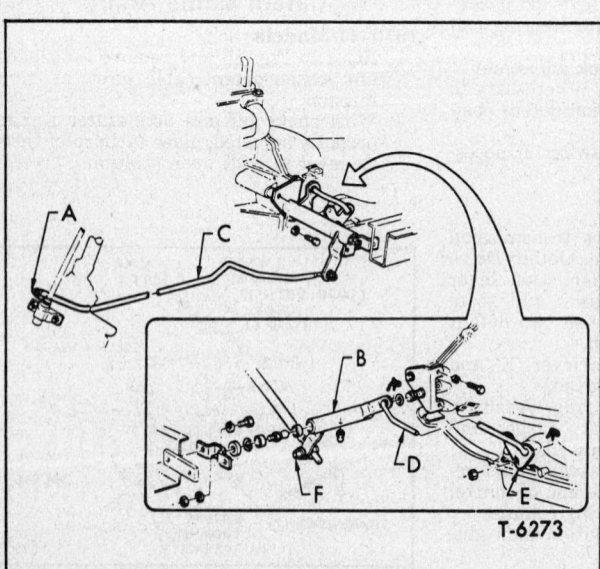

Fig. 13 Turbo hydra-matic 350 shift linkage. 1970–72 "G" models

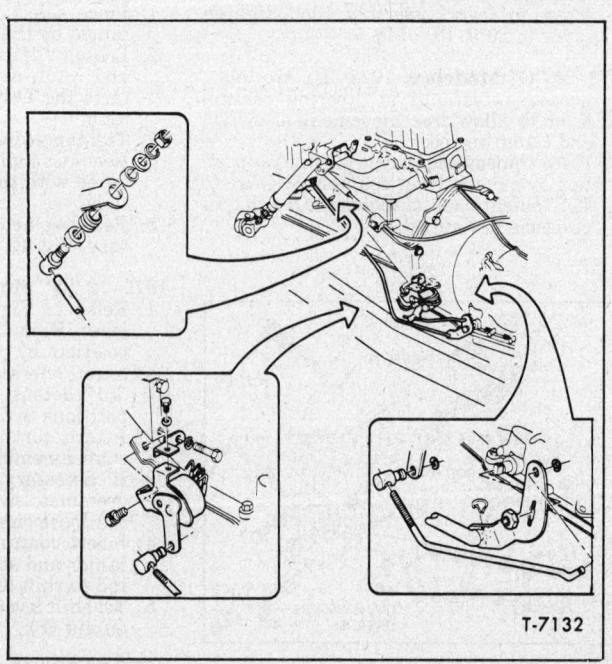

Fig. 14 Turbo-hydra-matic 350 shift linkage. 1970–72 "P" models

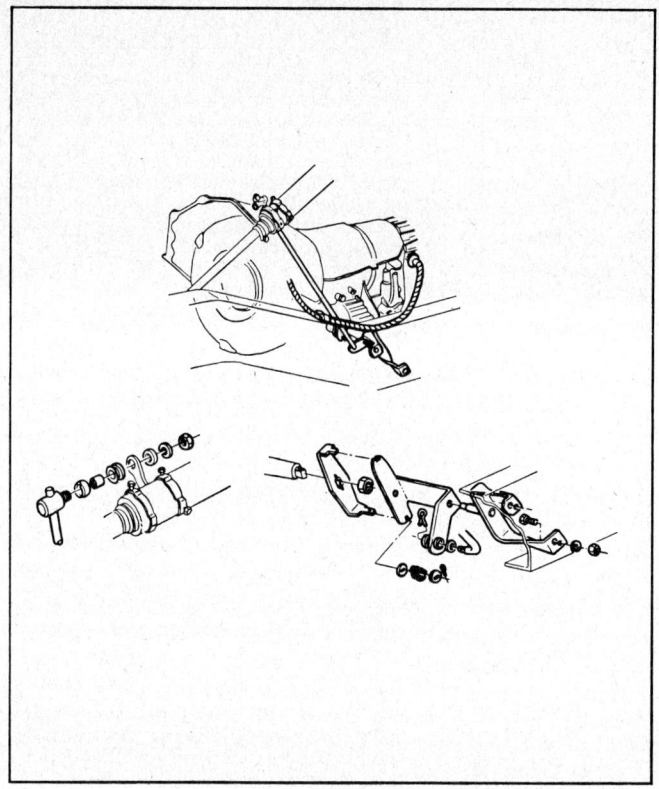

Fig. 15 Turbo hydra-matic shift linkage. 1970–72 "C" models

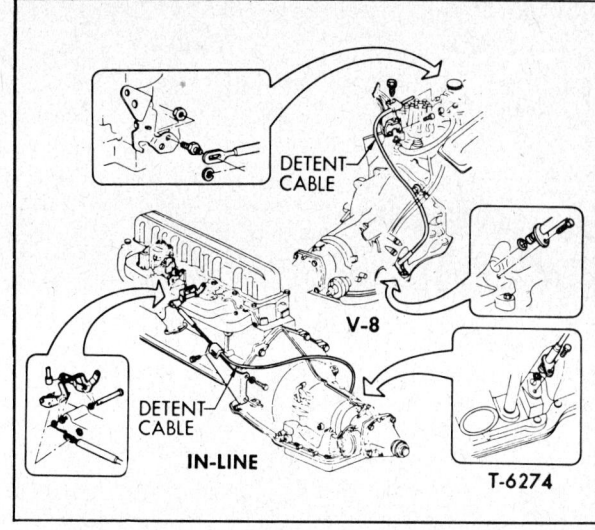

Fig. 16 Detent control cable. Turbo hydra-matic 350

7. Remove converter underpan. Scribe flywheel-converter relationship for reassembly, then remove flywheel-to-converter bolts.

NOTE: The "light" side of the converter is denoted by a blue stripe painted across the ends of the converter cover and housing. This marking should be aligned as closely as possible with the white stripe painted on the engine side of the flywheel outer rim (heavy side of engine) to maintain balance during reassembly.

8. Remove transmission housing-to-engine bolts.

NOTE: Observe converter when moving transmission rearward. If it does not move with transmission, pry it free of flywheel before proceeding. Keep front of transmission upward to prevent converter from falling out. Attach a length of strong wire to hold converter in position immediately after removal from engine.

9. Move transmission slightly to rear and downward and out of vehicle.
10. Reverse removal procedure to install transmission. Check for any oil leaks and adjust linkage as required.

Models Other Than Handi-Van
1. Disconnect vacuum modulator line and speedometer drive cable fitting at transmission. Tie lines out of the way.
2. Disconnect manual and TV control lever rods from transmission.
3. Disconnect propeller shaft from transmission.
4. Support transmission with jack or lift.
5. Disconnect engine rear mount on transmission extension, then remove transmission support crossmember.
6. Remove converter underpan, scribe flywheel-converter relationship, then remove flywheel-to-converter attaching bolts.

NOTE: The "light" side of the converter is noted by a "blue" stripe painted across the ends of the converter cover and housing. This marking should be aligned as closely as possible with the "white" stripe painted on the engine side of the flywheel outer rim (heavy side of engine) to maintain balance during assembly.

7. Support engine at oil pan rail with a jack or other suitable brace capable of supporting engine weight when transmission is removed.
8. Lower rear of transmission slightly so that upper transmission-to-engine bolts can be reached with a universal socket and long extension. Remove upper bolts.

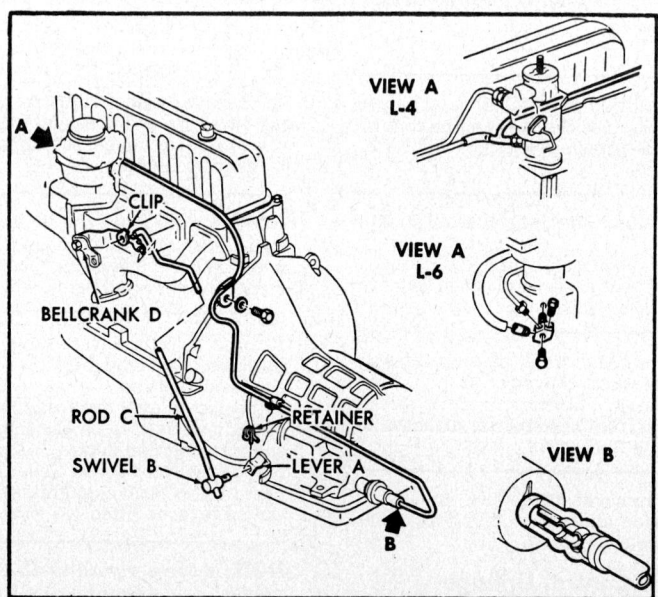

Fig. 18 Pow-R-Flo throttle valve linkage. Handi-Van

GMC

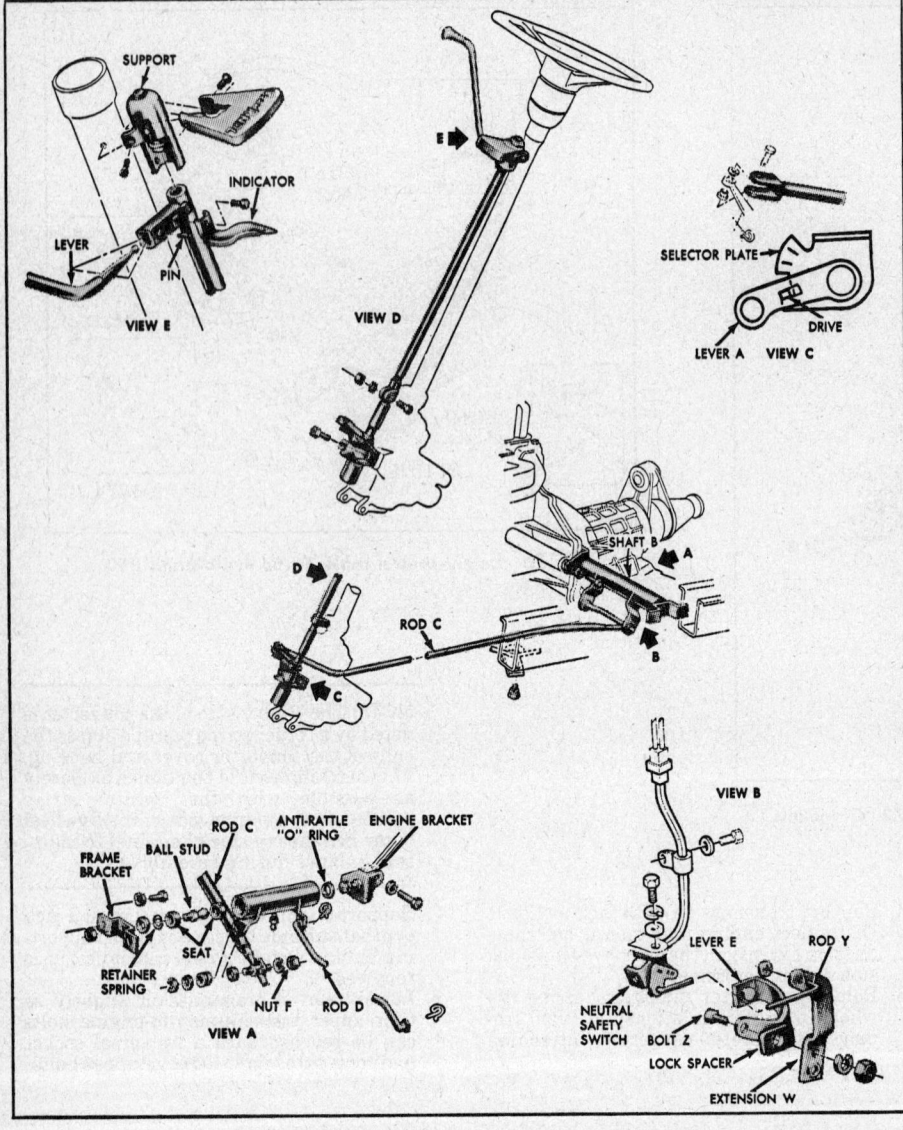

Fig. 17 Pow-R-Flo shift control linkage. Handi-Van

CAUTION: It is best to have a helper observe clearance of upper engine components while transmission rear end is being lowered.

9. Remove remaining transmission attaching bolts.
10. Remove transmission by moving it slightly to rear and downward, then remove from beneath vehicle.

CAUTION: Keep front of transmission upward to keep converter from falling out. Better still, attach a brace or strong wire across front of converter attached to housing.

11. Reverse removal procedure to install transmission and adjust shift linkage as outlined below.

Shift Control Linkage

1972 Sprint Column Shift
1. Shift tube and lever assembly must be free in mast jacket.
2. To check for proper adjustment, lift selector lever toward steering wheel. Allow selector lever to be positioned in D by transmission detent.

NOTE: Do NOT use the indicator pointer as a reference to position the selector lever. When performing linkage adjustment, pointer is adjusted last.

3. Release selector lever. Lever should be inhibited from engaging low range unless the lever is lifted.
4. Lift selector lever towards steering wheel and allow lever to be positioned in N by the transmission detent.
5. Release selector lever. Lever should now be inhibited from engaging reverse range unless lever is lifted.

NOTE: A properly adjusted linkage will prevent the selector lever from moving from beyond both the neutral detent and the drive detent unless the lever is lifted to pass over the mechanical stop in the steering column.

6. If an adjustment is required, place the selector lever in D as determined by the transmission detent (see Steps 2 and 3).
7. Loosen adjusting swivel at cross shaft and rotate the transmission lever so that it contacts the drive stop in the steering column, Fig. 12.
8. Tighten swivel and recheck adjustment.
9. Readjust indicator needle if required.

1972 Sprint Console Shift
Follow adjustment procedures under "Turbo Hydra-Matic 350" Gear Shift Linkage.

Handi-Van Models
Whenever linkage has been completely removed, as when replacing the transmission, the following procedure should be strictly adhered to.
1. Referring to Fig. 17, loosely assemble extension (W) to control lever (E), View B.
2. With both transmission and neutral safety switch (pinned) in neutral position, attach switch rod (Y) to neutral switch and lever extension (W). Tighten extension bolt (Z). Then remove pin from neutral switch.
3. Tube and lever (A) must be free in mast jacket. Be certain there is no bind.
4. Set lever (E) in "Drive" position. Obtain drive position by moving transmission lever counterclockwise to low detent, then clockwise one detent to drive.
5. Attach control rod (D) to extension lever (W) and shaft (B) with retainers (View A).
6. Assemble parts shown in View A loosely on shaft.
7. Insert control rod (C) in swivel and retainer and attach opposite end of tube and lever (View C).
8. Set tube lever in Drive position and tighten nut (F). Views A and C.

NOTE: When above procedure is adhered to, the following conditions must be met by manual operation of steering column shift lever: From reverse to drive position travel the transmission detent feel must be noted and related to indicated position on dial. When in "Drive" and "Reverse" position, pull lever upward (toward steering wheel) and then release. It must drop back into position with no restriction.

CAUTION: Any inaccuracies in the above adjustment may result in premature failure of the transmission due to operation without controls in full detent. Such operation results in reduced oil pressure and in turn partial engagement of the affected clutches. Partial engagement of the clutches with sufficient pressure to cause apparent normal operation of the vehicle will result in failure of clutches or other internal parts after only a few miles of operation.

Models Other Than Handi-Van & Sprint
1. With engine stopped, lift up on range selector lever and move lever to the position where transmission "Drive" detent is felt.
2. Slowly release lever to feel if shaft lever tang freely enters lock plate.
3. Check "Reverse" range in similar manner.
4. If tang does not freely enter tang in both drive and reverse ranges, adjust as fol-

GMC

lows.
5. Position range selector lever in driving compartment in "D". Disconnect shift control rod at its swivel attachment to shift control lever on lower end of mast jacket by loosening clamp nut.
6. Place transmission shift control outer lever in Drive position.

NOTE: Drive detent in transmission is the first clockwise detent position from fully counterclockwise detent or "L" position.

7. Hold shift control lever at lower end of mast jacket against Drive stop of range selector lock plate. With control rod through swivel, tighten clamp nut.
8. Test transmission shifts in all ranges.

Throttle Linkage, Adjust
Handi-Van
1. Referring to Fig. 18, transmission lever (A) must be rotated counterclockwise against internal transmission stop.
2. Assemble rod (C) to transmission lever.
3. Install swivel (B) on rod, and with accelerator lever in wide open position, adjust swivel on rod to freely enter hole in transmission lever.
4. Lengthen rod by rotating swivel three complete turns and install swivel in transmission lever.

Models Other Than Handi-Van
Throttle valve linkage must be adjusted so that when the carburetor throttle valve (or valves) is fully closed (hot idle) the transmission throttle valve lever must be all the way toward the rear of the transmission against its internal stop.

To make the adjustment, first disconnect the throttle linkage at the carburetor to relieve all tension from the rest of the linkage. Then disconnect the throttle rod from the throttle lever at the transmission. Hold the throttle lever back against its stop and adjust the throttle rod clevis, swivel or trunnion (whichever is used) so that the throttle rod can be attached to the throttle lever without moving the lever away from its stop. The throttle linkage at the carburetor can then be adjusted so that the carburetor throttle valve is fully closed (hot idle).

If a road test indicates that the shifts occur too early, shorten the rod a turn or two. If the shifts occur late, lengthen the rod a turn or two. Again road test and, if necessary, alter the adjustment as required to obtain the desired result.

Rear Axle Section

NOTE: For Chevrolet, Eaton, Spicer and Timken (Rockwell) driving axles used on GMC trucks, see the "name" chapters for service procedures and lubricant capacities

GMC SINGLE SPEED AXLE

Refer to Chevrolet Chapter for service procedures and specifications on Salisbury type axles.

These axles, being of the full floating type, enables removal of the axle shafts without removing the truck load or jacking up the rear axle. The drive pinion is stradle mounted, being supported at the rear end by a straight roller bearing and at the front end by a double row ball bearing, Fig. 1, or opposed tapered roller bearings, Fig. 1A.

Axle Shaft, Replace
Dowel Drive Type
1. Remove nuts attaching axle shaft flange to wheel hub.
2. Strike center of axle flange with a suitable hammer to loosen flange and split tapered dowels from hub studs. Remove split tapered dowels from studs.
3. Pull axle shaft from housing. Discard gasket.
4. Reverse procedure to install. Lubricate small end of axle shaft and install into housing using a new gasket. Torque 1/2 inch nuts to 50-60 ft. lbs. and 5/8 inch nuts to 90-110 ft. lbs.

NOTE: Ensure that clearance exists between nut and flange, Fig. 2. If no clearance is noted, replace worn parts as required.

Spline Drive Type
1. Remove hub cap retaining cap screws and hub cap.
2. Install a slide hammer adapter into tapped hole in axle flange.
3. Attach slide hammer onto adapter and remove axle shaft from housing, Fig. 3.
4. Reverse procedure to install. Lubricate small end of axle shaft and install into housing using a new gasket. Torque axle flange cap screws on 1974-76 models to 15-20 ft. lbs. 1977-79 models to 11-18 ft. lbs.

Wheel Bearings, Replace
1. Raise and support rear axle.

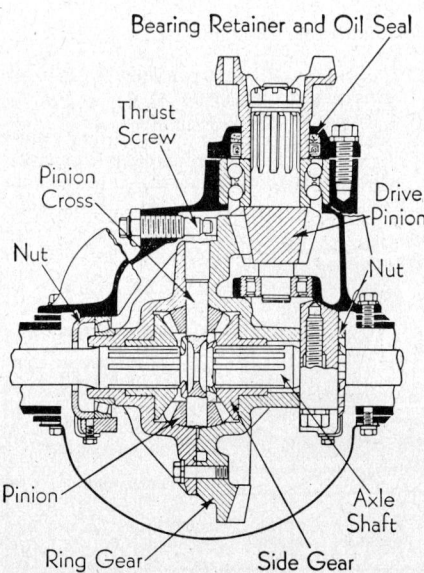

Fig. 1 Sectional view of differential carrier. GMC single speed with double row ball bearing

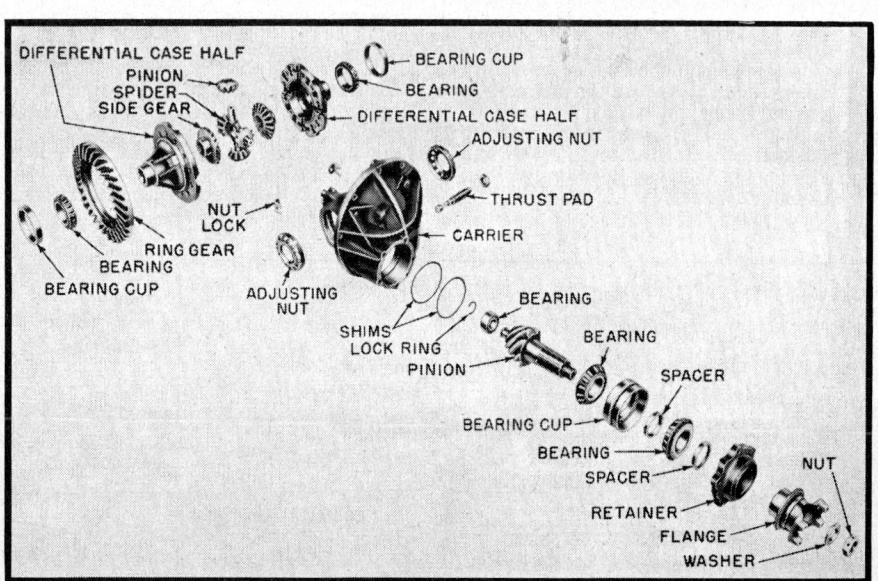

Fig. 1A Exploded view of differential carrier assembly. GMC single speed with tapered roller bearings

GMC

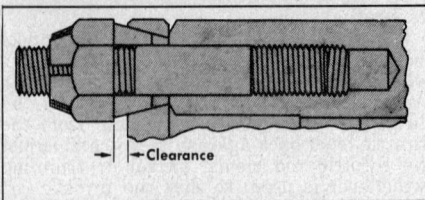

Fig. 2 Axle shaft flange to stud nut clearance. Dowel drive type axle shaft

2. Remove wheel and axle shaft.
3. Remove hub and drum, Figs. 4 & 5.

NOTE: On models equipped with spline drive type axle shafts, pull hub from axle housing using care not to drop outer wheel bearing.

4. Remove inner bearing and oil seal.
5. On models equipped with dowel type axle shafts, remove outer bearing race using suitable drift.
6. On models equipped with spline drive axle shafts, tap on outer race to relieve tension on bearing snap ring. Remove snap ring, then, using a suitable drift, drive on axle shaft spacer to remove outer bearing assembly from hub.
7. Reverse procedure to install. Refer to "Wheel Bearings, Adjust" for adjustment.

Wheel Bearings, Adjust

1. Raise and support rear axle.
2. Remove axle shaft as described in "Axle Shaft, Replace". Release brakes.
3. Remove bearing lock nut and nut lock or lock ring.
4. On models equipped with tapered bearing, torque adjusting nut to 50 ft. lbs. while rotating wheel, then back off 1/4 to 1/3 turn to obtain .001 to .007 inch end play. Then proceed as follows:
   a. On models equipped with type shown in section A of Fig. 6, align flat on adjusting nut with nearest lip of nut lock. Ensure that wheel spins freely, then install nut lock and lock nut. Torque lock nut to 135 ft. lbs. and bend one lip of nut lock over a flat of each nut.
   b. On models equipped with type shown in section B of Fig. 6, align nearest slot in adjusting nut with short tang on nut lock and bend tang into slot of nut. Install lock nut with slots outward and torque to 135 ft. lbs. Bend tangs of nut lock into slots of both nuts.
   c. On models equipped with type shown in section C of Fig. 6, align dowel pin of adjusting nut with nearest hole in lock ring. Install lock nut and torque to 250–300 ft. lbs.

   NOTE: Lock ring can be turned on either side to align hole with least movement of adjusting nut.

5. On models equipped with barrel bearing, torque adjusting nut to 75–100 ft. lbs. while rotating wheel back and forth to seat bearings. Back off adjusting nut a minimum amount to obtain as close to zero end play as possible. The wheel should rotate freely. Align the nearest slot in adjusting nut with short tang on nut lock and bend tang into slot of nut. Install lock nut with slots facing outward and torque to 250 ft. lbs. Bend tangs of nut lock into slots of both nuts.

Rear Axle, Replace

1. Raise vehicle from floor and support with stand jacks under frame side rails.
2. Remove rear wheels.
3. Disconnect propeller shaft from rear axle.
4. Swing propeller shaft to one side and tie to frame side rail.
5. Disconnect hydraulic or air brake line connection at rear axle housing.
6. Disconnect hand brake cables from cross shaft levers and remove cables from clamps on frame, if equipped.
7. Disconnect shock absorber links or eyes from anchor plates or anchor bracket, if equipped.
8. On all models, while supporting axle assembly with hydraulic jack, remove spring "U" bolts and lower axle assembly to floor.
9. Reverse procedure to install.

Service Note

The following operations may be performed without raising the truck or removing the axle assembly from the vehicle.

Differential Carrier, Replace

1. Drain lubricant, remove axle housing cover and axle shafts.
2. Disconnect propeller shaft from rear axle.
3. Swing propeller shaft to one side and tie to frame side rail.
4. Remove bolts or nuts which attach carrier to axle housing. Support carrier with floor jack and roll it from under truck.
5. Reverse procedure to install.

Differential Carrier, Disassemble

1. Loosen ring gear thrust pad adjusting screw and remove thrust pad.
2. Remove differential bearing adjuster locks, bearing cap screws and bearing caps.

NOTE: Mark bearing cap to carrier position to help reposition during assembly.

3. Remove differential and ring gear from carrier housing.
4. Remove pinion oil seal retainer, then the pinion and bearing assembly from carrier using suitable drift.

NOTE: Refer to Fig. 1, then remove pinion adjustment shims, making note of the number and total thickness of shims removed.

5. Remove pinion nut from shaft and press oil seal retainer and yoke from shaft.

Pinion Oil Seal, Replace

1. Remove old seal and packing from retainer.
2. Soak new seal and packing in light engine oil until saturated.
3. Clean seal bore of retainer.
4. Install felt packing into retainer, then lightly coat outer surface of oil seal with a suitable sealer and install into retainer

Fig. 3 Removing axle shaft. Spline drive type axle shaft

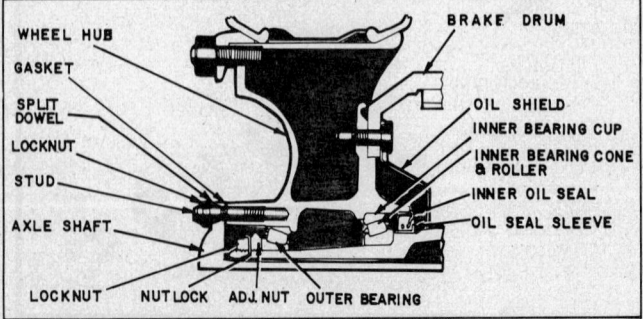

Fig. 4 Rear wheel hub and bearing sectional view. Dowel drive type axle shaft

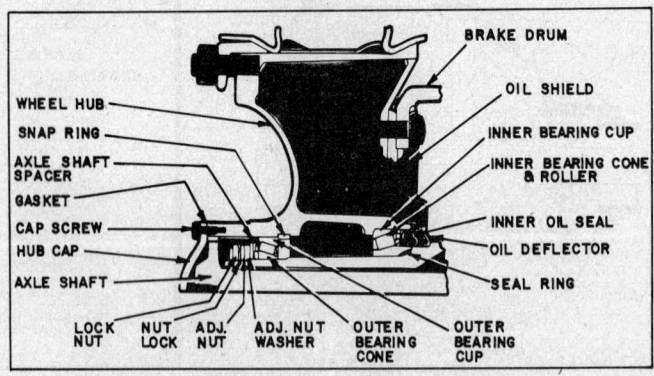

Fig. 5 Rear wheel hub and bearing sectional view. Spline drive type axle shaft

GMC

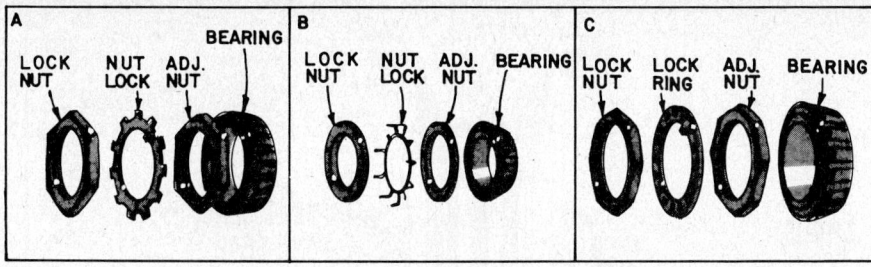

Fig. 6 Rear wheel bearing adjustment nuts. Full floating axle

with lip of seal facing towards inner side of retainer.

Pinion Bearing, Replace

1. Remove rear pinion bearing snap ring if equipped, and press bearing from shaft.
2. Press front pinion bearing from shaft. *On models with tapered roller bearings, the outer race, two inner race and roller assemblies and spacer should always be installed as a group as the spacer is preselected to give proper pinion bearing adjustment.*
3. On models with tapered roller bearings, press one new inner race and roller assembly on the pinion shaft, using a 2" pipe, applying pressure against the inner race. Large diameter of bearing race should be toward pinion. Place spacer and outer race on shaft and press on other inner roller. Small diameter of this race should be toward pinion.
4. On models with ball bearing, press new double row pinion bearing on shaft, using a piece of 2" pipe, applying pressure to inner race. Thus bearing must be installed so that extended portion of inner race is toward the back of pinion gear teeth.
5. On all models, press rear pinion bearing on shaft, using driver to apply pressure to inner race. Chamfered side of inner race should be toward pinion.
6. Install lock ring, if required.
7. Position pinion bearing oil seal retainer over hub of drive flange.
8. On all models, install drive flange and bearing retainer with washer and nut.
9. Tighten pinion shaft nut to a torque load of 220 ft. lbs. Lock nut with cotter pin.

Differential, Disassemble

1. Check differential case to make sure two halves are marked so they may be reassembled in the same position.
2. Remove attaching bolts and separate case from cover and remove pinion gears, spider and side gears.
3. Tap back of ring gear with soft hammer to remove gear from case.
4. Pull off differential bearings.

Differential, Assemble

1. Install differential bearings.
2. Install two guide pins to ring gear diametrically opposite each other. These pins can be made from 1/2"-20 × 2" capscrews with heads cut off and slotted for use of screwdriver.
3. Start guide pins through holes in case flange and tap ring gear on case.
4. Place differential pinions on spider. Then assemble side gears and pinions to left half or cover of differential.
5. Assemble ring half to left half, being sure to line up marks on both halves.
6. Install ring gear bolts and washers and tighten evenly until ring gear is flush with case flange.
7. Remove guide pins and install remaining bolts. Then torque all bolts to 150–160 ft. lbs. on 1970–78 models exc. H-110, 165 ft. lbs. on 1979 models exc. H-110, 100–110 ft. lbs. on 1970–78 model H-110, and 118 ft. lbs. on 1979 model H-110.

Differential Carrier, Assemble

1. Install differential bearings.
2. Install pinion assembly into carrier with new gasket. Torque pinion bearing retainer bolts to 160–170 ft.lbs. on 1970–78 H-110 thru H-150 model axles, 95 ft.lbs. on 1979 H-110 model, 98 ft.lbs. on 1979 H-135 model; 93 ft.lbs. on 1979 H-150 model, and 165 ft.lbs. on 1979 H-170 model.
3. Install differential assembly in carrier and install adjusting nuts.
4. Install differential bearing caps, making sure marks on caps line up with marks on carrier.
5. Install bearing cap bolts and tighten until lock washers just flatten out.
6. Adjust ring gear to pinion backlash and pinion depth as described in "Ring Gear and Pinion, Adjust" and "Pinion Depth, Adjust".
7. Torque differential bearing cap bolts to 205 ft.lbs. after final adjustments have been made.

Ring Gear & Pinion, Adjust

1. Loosen right hand adjusting nut and tighten left hand adjusting nut.
2. Continue tightening left adjusting nut until all backlash between ring gear and pinion is removed.
3. Back off left adjusting nut approximately two notches to a point where notch in nut is aligned with lock.
4. Tighten right adjusting nut firmly to force differential and planet assembly in solid contact with left adjusting nut. Loosen right adjusting nut until it is free of its bearing, then retighten snugly against bearing. Tighten right nut from one to two notches more to a locking position. This method provides for the proper pre-load on the bearings.
5. Mount a dial indicator on the housing and check the backlash between ring gear and pinion which should be .005" to .008". Whenever backlash is more than .008", loosen right adjusting nut one notch and tighten left nut one notch. If backlash is less than .005", loosen left nut one notch and tighten right nut one notch. When backlash has been adjusted, tighten bearing cap bolts securely. Again check backlash and then install adjuster locks.

Pinion Depth, Adjust

NOTE: On models equipped with ball bearings, pinion depth is not adjustable.

1. Paint ring gear teeth with a mixture of red lead and oil to produce a contact pattern.
2. Rotate pinion through several revolutions, applying pressure to the ring gear to develop a definite contact pattern.
3. Pinion depth is controlled by the shim pack between the pinion bearing seal retainer and the carrier.
4. Changing pinion depth will cause some change in ring gear backlash. After adjusting pinion depth, recheck backlash.

Ring Gear Thrust Pad, Adjust

Inspect the bronze tip of ring gear thrust pad and replace if worn. Install the thrust pad and tighten the screw until the bronze tip engages the back of the ring gear while rotating the gear. Back off the screw 1/12 of a turn and tighten lock nut. Make sure the screw does not turn during the locking process. This adjustment provides .005 to .007" clearance between ring gear and thrust pad.

GMC 2 SPEED AXLE

This axle, Fig. 7, is a planetary type which is shifted by the driver as operating conditions require. Movement of the control valve shift lever causes the shift chamber at the axle housing to select the desired speed range. The axle shafts and differential carrier can be removed for repair without removing the axle assembly from the vehicle.

Disassemble

1. Remove axle shafts.
2. Place jack under carrier and remove carrier-to-housing cap screws.
3. Break carrier loose with mallet and work it out of housing.
4. Place carrier in repair stand.
5. Remove anchor from carrier.
6. Remove shifter assembly.
7. Drive out shifter yoke shaft.
8. Slide shifter yoke and sleeve to the left, removing sleeve and yoke from end of sun gear.
9. Remove differential bearing adjusting lock from each side.
10. Remove oil trough.
11. Remove thrust screw and pad.
12. Remove differential bearing caps and adjusters.
13. Remove differential and planet assembly from housing.
14. Mark ring gear and both halves of planetary support case by marking lines on case and gear.
15. Remove drive gear from planetary support case and cover.
16. Lift off planet support case.
17. Remove thrust washer used between planet cover and differential.
18. Remove sun gear and four planet gears.
19. Mark or tag all gears so they can be reassembled exactly as removed.
20. Separate differential case halves. Case halves and spider are stamped on all four sides with matching numbers to assist in assembly.
21. Remove side gears and thrust washers

GMC

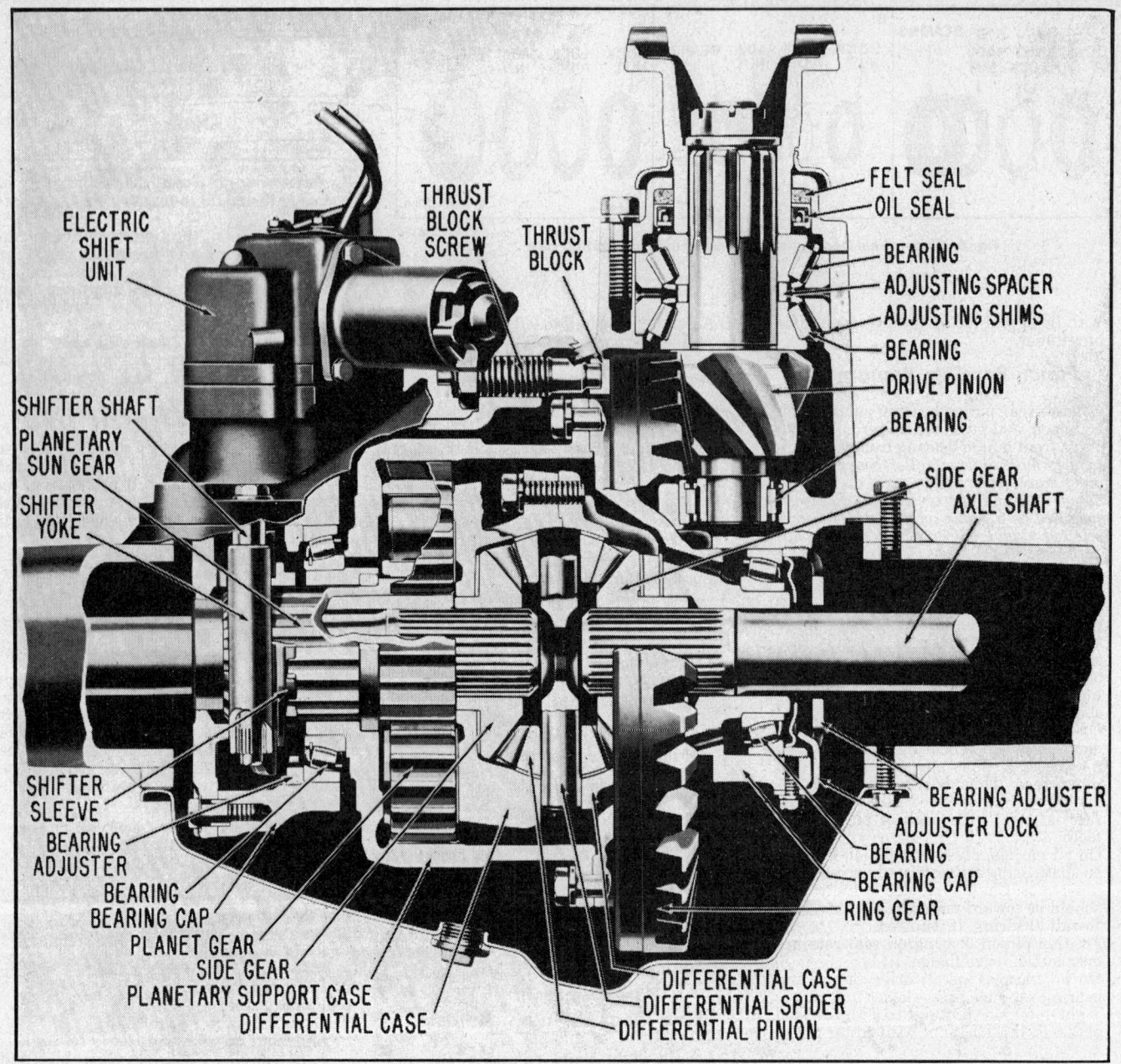

Fig. 7 GMC two-speed axle. Typical

from each case half.
22. Remove differential side bearings.
23. Loosen bolts attaching pinion bearing oil seal retainer to carrier. As bolts are loosened they will contact deflector flange on U-joint flange.
24. Tap universal joint yoke with mallet, driving pinion, bearings, and retainer assembly gradually from carrier housing while continuing to loosen attaching bolts.
25. Remove shims from carrier housing and note the amount required in back of the double thrust bearing.
26. Remove rear pinion bearing from carrier housing.
27. Separate U-joint yoke from pinion.
28. Remove pinion bearing oil seal retainer and seal from yoke.
29. Press off double thrust bearing.

Reassembly

Before axle is reassembled, make sure that all oil passages are thoroughly clean. Apply a thin coating of differential lubricant to all thrust and bearing surfaces to prevent scoring of parts when vehicle is first placed in service.

Pinion Assembly

1. Press bearing inner race on pinion.
2. Press double row thrust bearing on pinion.
3. Install pinion rear bearing in differential carrier.
4. Install original shim pack in carrier. Grease shims thoroughly. If original ring gear and pinion are reinstalled, use shims that were removed. If new gears are used, start with one .015" and .018" shim (total .022").
5. Position retaining cap screws and lock washers in oil seal retainer and install retainer on propeller shaft yoke.
6. Install new washer and nut and tighten securely.
7. Install pinion assembly into carrier and tap on yoke nut until cap screws can be started. Tighten cap screws alternately and evenly until pinion assembly is in place.

Differential and Planetary Assembly

1. Assemble differential parts into planetary half of case, then place plain half of

case over assembled parts. *Be sure that all parts are assembled as indicated by marks stamped or tagged at time of disassembly. Also see that side gear with longest hub is on bevel gear side.*
2. Fasten differential case halves and tighten securely.
3. Install bearing cones at planetary support case cover.
4. Place ring gear on wood blocks with gear teeth down and install several guide pins in ring gear bolt holes. Then position planetary case cover over guide pins with marks in alignment.
5. Place a thrust washer in planetary support case cover, then install the assembled differential in case cover.
6. Install the four planet gears on differential case with long hub of gears away from case.
7. Install large planetary support case over the assembled parts with marks in alignment.
8. Fasten two halves of planetary support case and bevel gear together.

Differential and Planetary Installation

1. Locate bearing races on each side, then install differential and planetary assembly in differential carrier.
2. Install differential bearing adjusting nuts on each side. See that oil baffle is in place in right adjusting nut.
3. Install differential bearing adjusting caps and dowels at each side.
4. Install cap bolts and lock washers and tighten snugly or until bearing adjusting nuts can just be turned.

Ring Gear and Pinion, Adjust

1. Loosen right hand adjusting nut and tighten left hand adjusting nut.
2. Continue tightening left adjusting nut until all backlash between ring gear and pinion is removed.
3. Back off left adjusting nut approximately two notches to a point where notch in nut is aligned with lock.
4. Tighten right adjusting nut firmly to force differential and planet assembly in solid contact with left adjusting nut. Loosen right adjusting nut until it is free of its bearing, then retighten snugly against bearing. Tighten right nut from one to two notches more to a locking position. This method provides for the proper pre-load on the bearings.
5. Mount a dial indicator on the housing and check the backlash between ring gear and pinion which should be .005" to .008". Whenever backlash is more than .008", loosen right adjusting nut one notch and tighten left nut one notch. If backlash is less than .005", loosen left nut one notch and tighten right nut one notch. When backlash has been adjusted, tighten bearing cap bolts securely. Again check backlash and then install adjuster locks.

Pinion Depth, Adjust

1. Coat ring gear teeth lightly with red lead or prussian blue. Then turn the pinion several revolutions in both directions while applying pressure to ring gear to create a load.
2. Examine the pattern on the ring gear. If the pinion depth is correct, the tooth pattern will be centered on the pitch line and toward the toe of the ring gear.
3. If the pattern is below the pitch line the pinion is too deep and it will be necessary to remove the pinion and increase the shim thickness between the pinion bearing retainer and differential carrier housing.
4. If the pattern is above the pitch line on the ring gear teeth, the pinion is too shallow and it will be necessary to decrease the shim thickness.
5. Checking the pinion depth will make some change in the backlash; therefore, it may be necessary to readjust the backlash.
6. Tighten the bearing cap screws, recheck backlash and install adjusting nut locks.
7. Install oil trough.

Ring Gear Thrust Pad Installation

1. Inspect the bronze tip on ring gear thrust pad and replace if worn.
2. Install thrust pad and tighten until pad contacts ring gear. Then back off 30° to obtain a clearance of .005" to .007". Tighten lock nut, making sure screw does not turn.

Shifter Assembly Installation

1. Install shifter yoke on sleeve and install assembled parts on sun gear.
2. Install shifter lever and shaft through adapter and housing, then into the shifter yoke, mating the two parts carefully to avoid damage to the splines. The shaft must be free to avoid binding when the shifter assembly is installed.
3. Position shift anchor at left of differential carrier with anchor knob in bushing and opposite end secured to bearing cap with cap screw and lock washer.

Differential Carrier Installation

1. With new gasket in place, place carrier on roller jack, using a suitable wood block as a support.
2. Use a long drift to align assembly and install it in axle housing.
3. Install and tighten cap screws securely.
4. Use new gasket and install electric shift units. (For service on the Electric shift unit, see the *Eaton Electric Shift section of the Rear Axles Chapter*.)

Front Wheel Drive

NOTE: For service procedure on transfer case used with four-wheel drive trucks, see Transfer Case Chapter

FRONT AXLE

The front axle is a Spicer unit equipped with steering knuckles, Figs. 1 and 2. To permit the turning and driving of the front wheels, the axle is equipped with steering knuckles and yoke and trunnion type universal joints. 1977–80 K3500 series incorporate king pins, while 1970–80 K1500 and 2500 series incorporate ball joints.

Ball Joint Adjustment

1970–80

Ball joint adjustment is generally necessary when there is excessive play in steering, irregular tire wear or persistent loosening of the tie rods.
1. Raise vehicle and support with jack stands placed just inside of front springs.
2. Disconnect drag link and tie rods to permit independent movement of each steering knuckle.
3. On 1970–76 models:
   a. Apply a torque wrench to one of the steering knuckles retaining stud nuts and check torque required to turn steering knuckle. Maximum torque required should be 15 ft. lbs. for 1970–71 or 20 ft. lbs. for 1972–76.

   NOTE: Steering knuckle should turn freely without vertical end play.

   b. If torque required is too low, remove upper ball joint cotter pin and locknut, then torque adjusting sleeve to 50 ft. lbs. and reinstall locknut and cotter pin.
   c. Recheck torque required to turn steering knuckle. If torque is still too low, retorque adjusting sleeve to 60 ft. lbs. as described previously.
   d. Recheck torque required to turn steering knuckle. If torque is still too low, replace parts as necessary to bring torque within specifications.
4. On 1977–80 models:
   a. Using a spring scale attached to tie rod mounting hole, determine amount of pull at right angles, required to keep knuckle assembly turning from a straight ahead position.
   b. If pull exceeds 25 lbs., remove upper ball stud nut, and loosen adjusting sleeve as required. Tighten ball stud nut and recheck turning effort.

Axle Assembly, Replace

1. Disconnect propeller shaft from front axle differential and raise front of vehicle until weight is removed from springs.
2. Disconnect connecting rod from steering arm, brake hoses from frame fittings and cap ends.
3. Disconnect the shock absorbers from axle brackets.
4. If equipped, disconnect axle vent tube from differential housing.

GMC

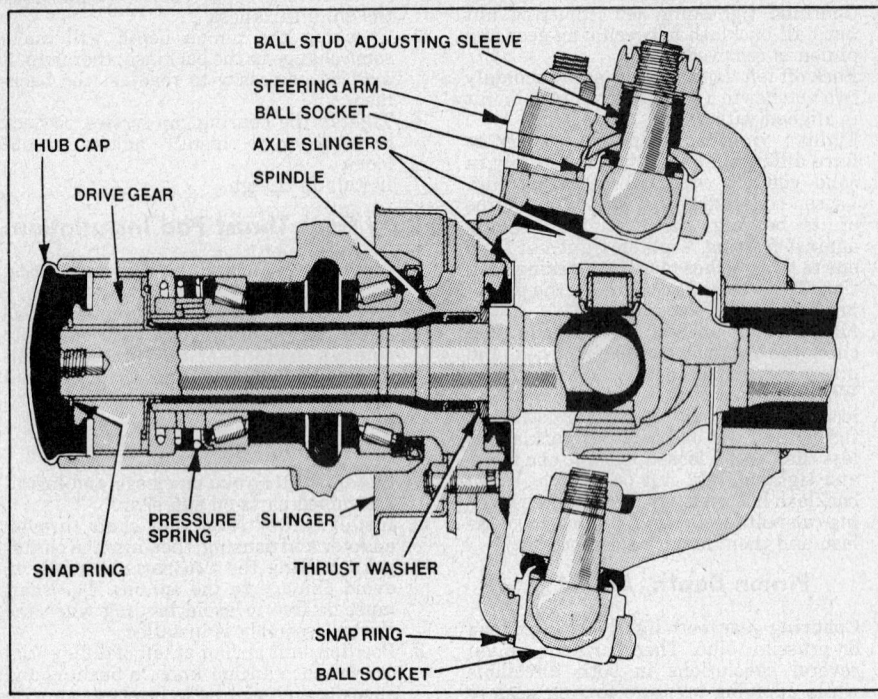

Fig. 1 Sectional view of front driving axle. 1970–80 Series K1500, K2500

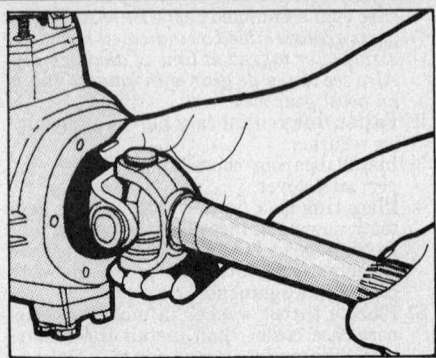

Fig. 3 Removing and installing axle shaft and U-joint

5. Remove "U" bolts from springs and axle assembly.
6. Raise vehicle to clear axle assembly and roll axle from front of vehicle.
7. Reverse procedure to install.

Axle Shaft, Replace

1. Remove hub and wheel bearings as described in "Hub and Wheel Bearing, Replace".
2. Remove spindle attaching nuts, then lightly tap spindle from steering knuckle.
3. Remove thrust washer and pull axle shaft assembly from axle housing, Fig. 3.
4. Reverse procedure to install. Torque spindle nuts to 45 ft.lbs. on 1970–76 K-1500 and 2500, 25 ft.lbs. on 1977–78 K-1500 and 2500, 60 ft.lbs. on 1977–80 K-3500, and 33 ft.lbs. on 1979–80 K-1500, 2500.

Axle Joint Repairs

1. Remove lock rings from trunnion bearings.
2. Support shaft yoke in a suitable vise.
3. With a brass drift and a hammer, tap on one end of trunnion bearing to drive the opposite bearing from yoke. Then, support other side of yoke and drive out remaining bearing.
4. Remove trunnion. Inspect and replace bearings if necessary, then lubricate with wheel bearing grease.
5. Replace trunnion and press bearings into yoke and over trunnion hubs far enough to install lock rings.
6. Gently tap yoke to seat bearings against lock rings.

Hub & Wheel Bearing, Replace

NOTE: On models with Free-Wheeling Hubs, refer to "Front Wheel Locking Hubs" chapter for locking hub removal.

1. Raise and support vehicle.
2. On models with locked hubs, Figs. 1 & 2:
   a. Remove hub cap and snap ring.
   b. Remove drive gear. On K-1500 and 2500 models, remove pressure spring. Place hand over drive gear and pry out using a screwdriver.
3. On all models, remove wheel bearing outer lock nut, lock ring and wheel bearing inner adjusting nut using suitable tool, Fig. 4.
4. Remove disc brake caliper and position out of the way.
5. Remove hub-and-disc assembly, outer wheel bearing and spring retainer plate:
   a. Remove inner wheel bearing and oil seal from hub using suitable drift.
   b. Remove inner and outer bearing cups from hub using suitable drift.
6. Reverse procedure to install. Refer to "Wheel Bearings, Adjust" for wheel bearing adjustment.

Wheel Bearings, Adjust

1. Remove dust cap or free wheeling hub, lockwasher and outer locknut.
2. Using suitable spanner wrench, torque inner adjusting nut to 50 ft.lbs. while rotating hub. Back off adjusting nut and retorque to 35 ft.lbs. while rotating hub, Fig. 4.
3. Back off adjusting nut 1/4 turn on 1970–72 models; or 3/8 turn on 1973–80 models.
4. On 1970–80 K-1500 and 2500 models, assemble lockwasher by turning nut to nearest hole in lockwasher, then install and torque locknut to 50 ft.lbs on 1970–78 models, and 80 ft. lbs. on 1979–80 models.
5. On 1977–80 K-3500 models, assemble lockwasher and locknut, then torque locknut to 65 ft.lbs. and bend one ear of lockwasher at least 30° over adjusting nut and another ear at least 60° over locknut.

NOTE: Hub assembly should have .001 to .010 inch end play.

6. Install dust cap or free wheeling hub.

Steering Knuckle, Replace

1970–80 K-1500, 2500 With Ball Joints

1. Remove axle shaft as described in "Axle Shaft, Replace".
2. Disconnect tie rod from steering arm.

CAUTION: If steering arm is removed from knuckle, discard the self-locking nuts and replace with new ones during installation. Torque nuts to 90 ft. lbs.

3. Remove cotter pin from upper ball joint stud nut, and remove retaining nuts from both ball joints.
4. Separate stud from yoke using suitable ball joint fork at lower joint and repeat at upper joint if required.

CAUTION: Do not remove upper ball joint adjusting sleeve from yoke unless ball joint is being replaced. If it is necessary to loosen the sleeve to remove the knuckle, only loosen the sleeve two threads. The non-hardened threads in the yoke can be easily damaged by the adjusting sleeve.

5. Reverse procedure to install.
6. Torque lower ball joint to 70 ft. lbs,

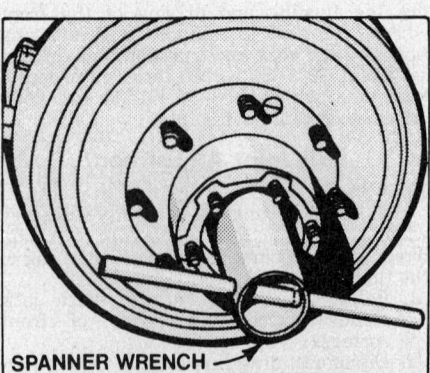

Fig. 4 Adjusting wheel bearing

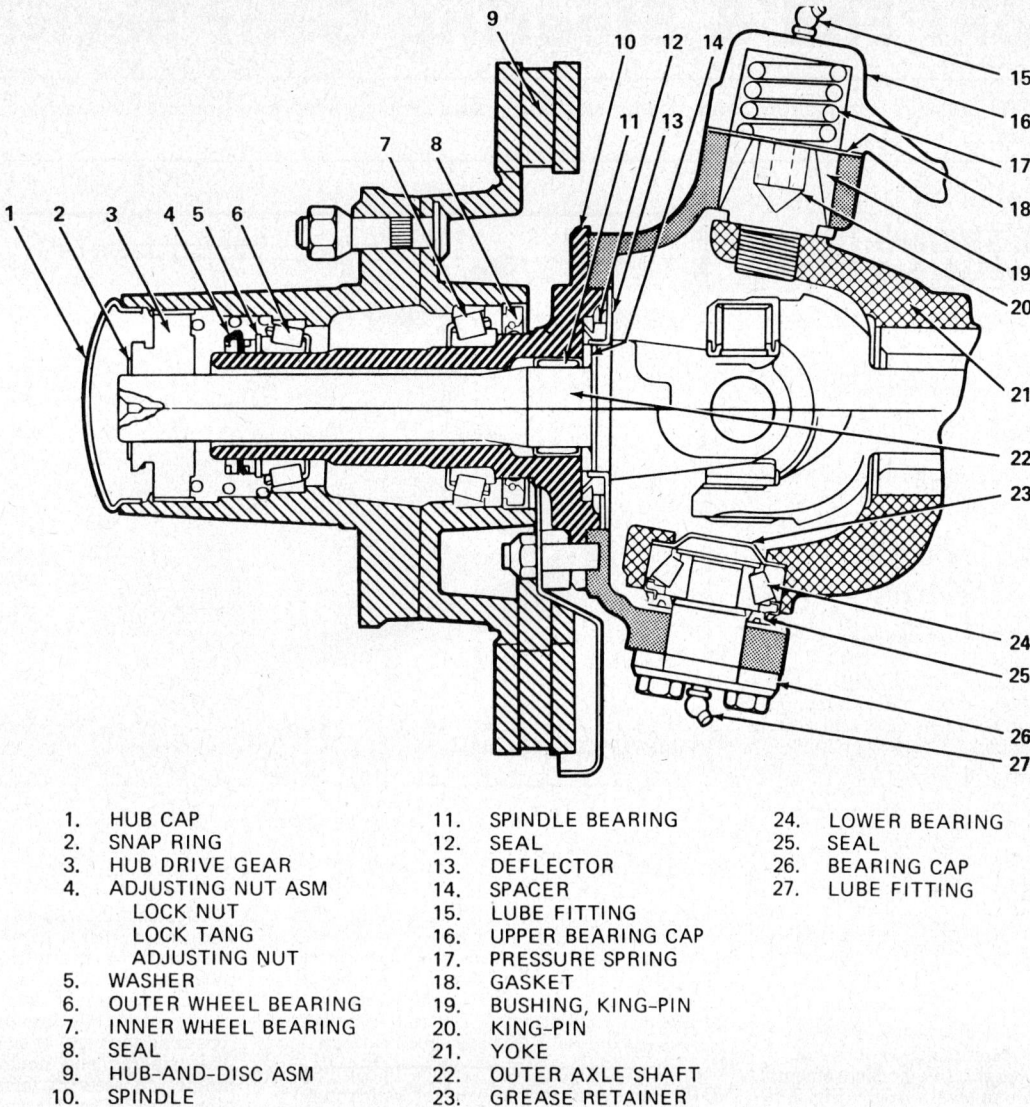

1. HUB CAP
2. SNAP RING
3. HUB DRIVE GEAR
4. ADJUSTING NUT ASM
   LOCK NUT
   LOCK TANG
   ADJUSTING NUT
5. WASHER
6. OUTER WHEEL BEARING
7. INNER WHEEL BEARING
8. SEAL
9. HUB-AND-DISC ASM
10. SPINDLE
11. SPINDLE BEARING
12. SEAL
13. DEFLECTOR
14. SPACER
15. LUBE FITTING
16. UPPER BEARING CAP
17. PRESSURE SPRING
18. GASKET
19. BUSHING, KING-PIN
20. KING-PIN
21. YOKE
22. OUTER AXLE SHAFT
23. GREASE RETAINER
24. LOWER BEARING
25. SEAL
26. BEARING CAP
27. LUBE FITTING

Fig. 2 Sectional view of front driving axle. 1975–80 K3500 series

adjusting sleeve to 50 ft. lbs, and upper ball joint to 100 ft. lbs. Torque tie-rod nut to 45 ft. lbs.

1977–80 K30 with King Pins

1. Remove axle shaft as described in "Axle Shaft, Replace".
2. Remove upper king pin cap by alternately loosening nuts to unload the compression spring. Withdraw the spring and gasket.
3. Remove the lower bearing cap and king pin.
4. Remove upper king pin tapered bushing and remove knuckle from yoke.
5. Remove upper king pin from yoke using a large breaker bar.
6. Reverse procedure to install.
7. Torque upper king pin to 500–600 ft. lbs, upper and lower bearing cap nuts to 70–90 ft. lbs, and spindle nuts to 60 ft. lbs.

Ball Joints, Service 1970–80 K10 & K20

1. Remove steering knuckle from axle assembly.
2. Remove lower ball joint snap ring.

NOTE: Lower ball joint must be removed before upper ball joint can be serviced.

3. Press lower ball joint from knuckle using suitable tool.
4. Press upper ball joint from knuckle using suitable tool.
5. Press new lower ball joint into knuckle until fully seated. Install snap ring.

NOTE: Lower ball joint does not have a cotter pin hole in stud end.

6. Press upper ball joint into knuckle until fully seated.

King Pins, Service 1977–80 K30

Refer to "Steering Knuckle, Replace" for king pin service.

Front End & Steering Gear Section

NOTE: Repairs on manual and power steering gears are covered in separate chapters. See Index.

COIL SPRING SUSPENSION

1970-80

This suspension, Fig. 1, consists of upper and lower control arms pivoting on steel threaded bushings on upper and lower arm shafts which are bolted to the front suspension crossmember.

For service procedures, see Chevrolet Truck chapter.

TORSION BAR SUSPENSION

1973-78 Motor Home

The front suspension consists of control arms, stabilizer bar, shock absorbers and right and left torsion bars. The front end of the torsion bar is attached to the lower control arm, and the rear of the torsion bar is mounted in an adjustable arm at the torsion bar crossmember. The riding height of the vehicle is controlled by this adjustment, Fig. 2.

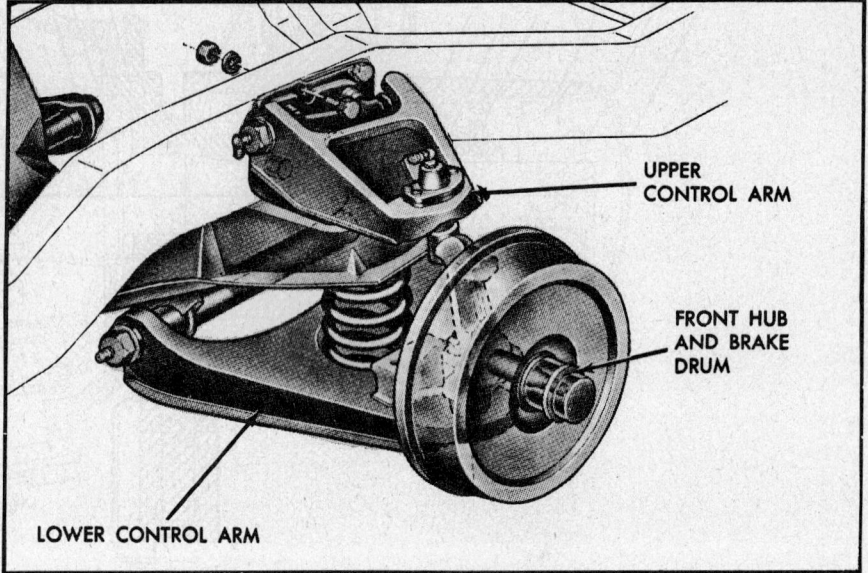

Fig. 1 Coil spring suspension. 1979-80 typical

Wheel Alignment, Adjust

Riding Height

The riding height must be checked and adjusted if necessary before checking and adjusting front wheel alignment. Before checking riding height, make sure that the vehicle is parked on a level surface and that tire pressure is to specification.

To check riding height, take measurements from top of oval hole to level surface, Fig. 3. If adjustments are required, proceed as follows:

CAUTION: Do not attempt to adjust riding height using the adjusting bolt only. The adjusting bolt will turn, but will strip the threads. Tool J-22517-02 must be used. This tool will adjust the riding height without loading the adjusting bolt.

1. Install tool J-22517-02 with pin of tool aligned in hole in crossmember, and seat center screw in dimple of torsion bar adjusting arm.
2. To raise vehicle, turn tool until proper height is obtained, then turn adjusting bolt until it contacts adjusting arm and remove tool.
3. To lower vehicle, raise adjusting arm from contact with adjusting bolt, then loosen adjusting bolt and lower adjusting arm with tool until proper riding height is obtained. Turn adjusting bolt until it contacts adjustment arm and remove tool.

Camber

1. Loosen nuts on upper control arm cam bolts.
2. Turn front cam bolt (inboard or outboard) to correct for 1/2 of incorrect setting.
3. Turn rear cam bolt (same way front bolt was turned) to correct for remaining 1/2 of incorrect setting.
4. Torque front and rear cam nuts to 80-95 ft. lbs. while holding bolts with another wrench so that camber is not changed.
5. Recheck adjustment. Do not readjust camber unless it exceeds specifications.

NOTE: Remove any weld splatter which may be on the cam adjustment surface. Weld splatter in this area will affect front end alignment.

Caster

1. Loosen front and rear cam nuts while holding bolts with another wrench to avoid changing camber.
2. Turn front cam bolt so that camber changes 1/4 of the desired amount of caster to be corrected.
3. Turn rear cam bolt so that camber now returns to corrected position.
4. Recheck caster setting.
5. Torque cam nuts to 90 ft. lbs., while holding bolt with another wrench so that final setting will not be changed.

Toe-In

1. Loosen tie rod adjusting sleeves clamp bolts.

NOTE: If the torque required to remove nut from bolt (from initial breakaway) exceeds 7 ft. lbs. discard the nuts and bolts. Apply penetrating oil between clamp and tube and rotate clamps until they rotate freely. Install new nuts and bolts to assure proper retention of parts at the specified torque.

2. With steering wheel set in straight ahead position, turn tie rod adjusting sleeves as necessary to obtain proper toe-in adjustment at curb load.
3. After adjustment has been completed, make sure that number of threads exposed at each end of sleeve are equal and that tie rod end housings are at right angles to steering arm. Position inner and outer tie rod clamps as shown in Fig. 4, and torque nuts to 20 ft. lbs.

Torsion Bars, Replace

Removal

1. Raise vehicle on a two post hoist.
2. Remove the nuts and center screw from tool J-22517-02, then position tool over crossmember with pin of tool in crossmember hole, Fig. 5. Install the nuts and counter screw on tool. Apply chassis grease to center screw threads and rounded end of screw.
3. Turn center screw until it seats in dimple of torsion bar adjusting arm, then remove torsion bar adjusting bolt and nut.

NOTE: Count and record number of turns required to remove adjusting bolt. The number of turns will be used upon installation to obtain original riding height.

4. Turn center screw of tool until tension on torsion bar is completely removed, then remove tool.
5. Repeat above procedure on opposite torsion bar.
6. Remove bolts and retainer from torsion bar crossmember at frame.
7. Disconnect exhaust pipe hanger from crossmember, then loosen pipe saddle U-

clamp and slide hanger rearward.
8. Move crossmember rearward until torsion bars are free and adjusting arms are removed.
9. Move torsion bar crossmember sideways to the extreme left, then move crossmembers upward and outward until opposite end clears exhaust pipe.
10. Remove torsion bars, and mark as to right or left to insure proper installation.

Installation

1. Install torsion bars in their proper locations.

   NOTE: New torsion bars are stamped on one end with an "L" for left side or an "R" for right side.

2. Install crossmember insulators, then install crossmember positioned about two inches rearward of its normal position.
3. Raise torsion bars to align with hole in crossmember, then move torsion bars forward so that torsion bars rest on edge of hole.
4. Insert torsion bar adjusting arm into crossmember and position it so that arm will engage torsion bar and the end of arm will be 1 3/4–2 inches below crossmember, then tap crossmember forward enough to engage bar into arm.
5. Repeat step 4 on opposite torsion bar.
6. Place crossmember in its normal position. Torsion bar should be through and flush with rear face of adjusting arm. If not, repeat steps 4 and 5, and pulling bar slightly out from lower control arm.
7. Install retainer over each insulator and torque nut to 10 ft. lbs.
8. Connect exhaust pipe hanger to crossmember and torque saddle and U-clamp nuts to 15 ft. lbs.
9. Place tool J-22517-02 over crossmember with pin of tool in hole in crossmember. Install the two nuts and center screw.
10. Turn center screw until adjusting arm is in position to allow installation of adjusting nut, then install adjusting nut and turn adjusting bolt the same number of turns as recorded in step 3 to obtain the original riding height.
11. Turn center screw until torsion bar tension is completely removed, then remove tool.
12. Repeat steps 9 thru 11 on opposite torsion bar.
13. Lower vehicle and check riding height. If necessary, readjust riding height as described previously.

Ball Joints, Check

1. Raise vehicle and place floor stands under left and right lower control arms as close as possible to each lower ball joint.

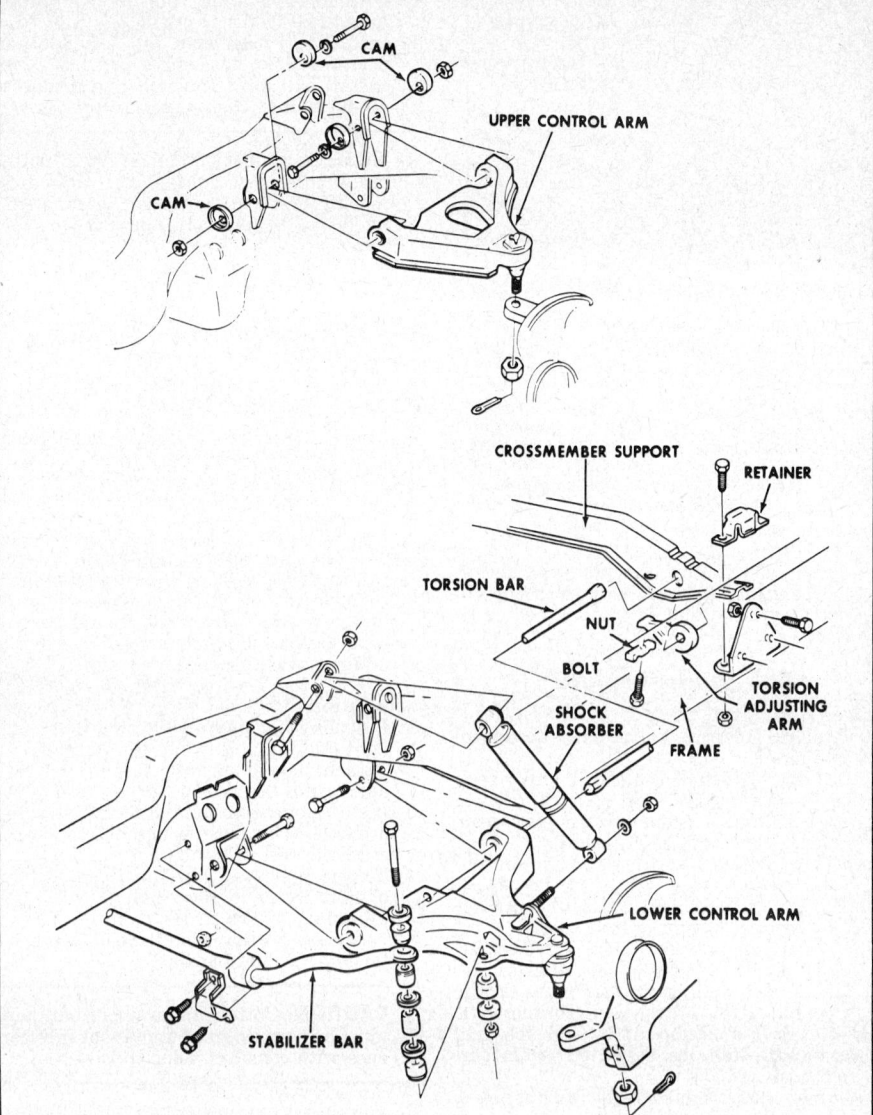

Fig. 2 Torsion bar front suspension. 1973–78 Motor Home

NOTE: Vehicle must be stable and not rock on floor stands.

2. Position a dial indicator on spindle nut to measure vertical travel, Fig. 6.
3. Use a pry bar between outer constant

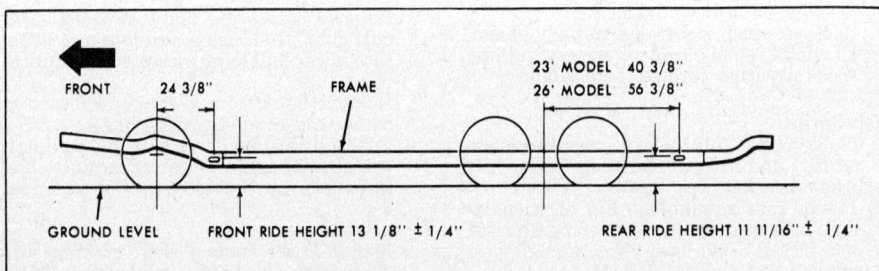

Fig. 3 Riding height dimensions. 1973–78 Motor Home

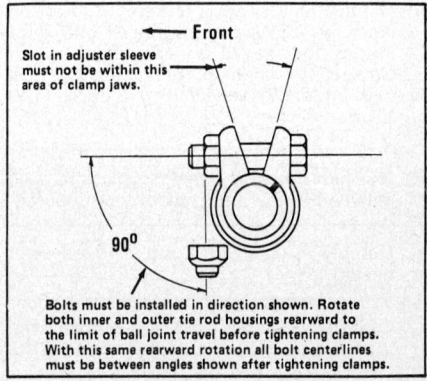

Fig. 4 Positioning tie rod clamp. 1973–78 Motor Home

GMC

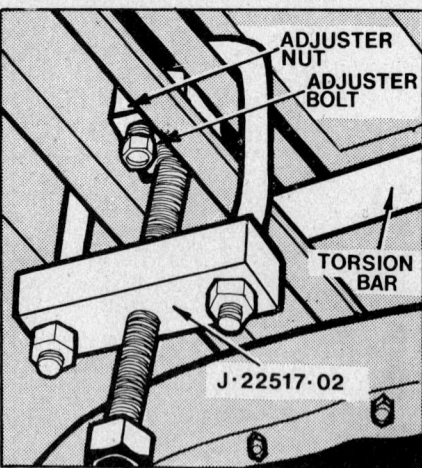

Fig. 5 Torsion bar removal tool installation. 1973-78 Motor Home

velocity joint outer race and lower control arm and pry up and down. Reading on dial indicator should not exceed .125 inch.

Ball Joints, Replace

Lower Ball Joint
1. Remove steering knuckle as described further on.
2. Using a 1/4 inch drill bit, drill side rivets to 1/2 inch depth. Then using a 1/2 inch drill bit, drill same rivets just deep enough to remove rivet heads.
3. Using a hammer and punch, drive out rivets.
4. Using a 5/8 inch drill bit, drill top rivet just enough to remove rivet head.
5. Using a hammer and punch, drive center rivet of ball joint out of control arm.
6. Install new ball joint with nuts facing toward side of control arm. Torque bolts to 25 ft. lbs. and top nut to 45 ft. lbs. and top nut to 45 ft. lbs. Stake top nut at four locations.
7. Install knuckle as described further on.
8. Check clearance from ball joint nut to drive axle outer joint. If there is no clearance, grind off nut, but not to exceed 1/16 inch.

Upper Ball Joint
1. Raise and support vehicle under lower control arms and remove wheel.
2. Remove upper ball joint stud cotter pin and nut, then disconnect brake hose clip from stud.
3. Using a hammer and brass drift, drive on steering knuckle until upper ball joint stud is disengaged from knuckle.
4. Raise control arm up, then using a 1/8 inch drill bit, drill rivet heads to a depth of 3/8 inch.

NOTE: If necessary, insert a block of wood between frame and control for support.

5. Using a 1/2 inch drill bit, drill off rivet heads.

CAUTION: Do not drill into control arm.

6. Using a hammer and punch, drive out rivets and remove ball joint.
7. Install new ball joint into control arm with bolts installed from the top. Torque nuts to 20 ft. lbs.
8. Install ball joint stud into knuckle and position brake hose clip over stud.
9. Install ball joint stud nut and torque to 40-60 ft. lbs., then install cotter pin.

NOTE: Do not back off nut to install cotter pin. If necessary, tighten nut to align hole in ball joint stud with slot in nut. Also make sure to bend cotter pin so as to avoid interference with constant velocity joint seal.

Steering Knuckle, Replace

Removal
1. Raise and properly support vehicle.
2. Remove wheel, hub and disc assembly.
3. Remove upper ball joint stud nut and disconnect brake line hose clip from stud.
4. Using a brass drift and hammer, strike steering knuckle to loosen upper ball joint stud.
5. Remove cotter pin and nut from tie rod end, then using a suitable puller, separate tie rod end from steering knuckle.
6. Remove cotter pin and nut from lower ball joint stud, then using a suitable tool, separate ball joint from steering knuckle and remove steering knuckle.

Installation
1. Position steering knuckle onto lower ball joint and install but not tighten nut.
2. Attach tie rod end to steering knuckle and install but do not tighten nut.
3. Install upper ball joint stud into steering knuckle, then place brake hose clip onto stud and install but do not tighten nut.
4. Torque upper ball joint nut to a minimum of 40 ft. lbs., and lower ball joint nut to a minimum of 100 ft. lbs. Tighten nuts as necessary to allow installation of new cotter pins. Do not back off nut.

CAUTION: Cotter pin on upper ball joint must be bent up so as to prevent interference with constant velocity joint seal.

5. Torque tie rod end nut to 40-50 ft. lbs., then install cotter pin. If necessary, tighten nut to allow installation of cotter pin. Do not back off nut.
6. Install hub and disc assembly and wheel.

Upper Control Arm, Replace

Removal
1. Raise vehicle and place floor stands under each lower control arm.
2. Remove shock absorber upper retaining bolt, then remove upper ball joint cotter pin and nut and disconnect brake hose clamp from ball joint stud.
3. Using a hammer and brass drift, drive on steering knuckle until upper ball joint is disengaged from knuckle.
4. Remove upper control arm cam assemblies, Fig. 2, and remove control arm by guiding shock absorber through access hole.

Installation
1. Guide upper control arm over shock absorber and install bushing ends into frame bracket.
2. Install cam assemblies, Fig. 2, then install ball joint stud into steering knuckle and install brake hose clip onto ball joint stud.
3. Install ball joint stud nut and torque to a minimum of 40 ft. lbs. Tighten nut as nec-

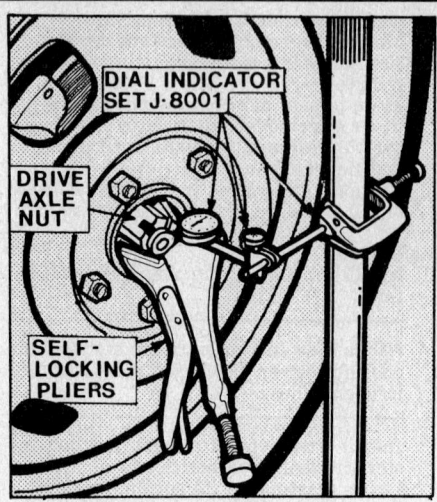

Fig. 6 Ball joint vertical check. 1973-78 Motor Home

essary to allow installation of new cotter pin. Do not loosen nut.

CAUTION: Cotter pin must be bent up so as not to interfere with constant velocity joint seal.

4. Install shock absorber upper retaining bolt.
5. Install wheel and lower vehicle.
6. Check front end alignment and adjust as necessary.

Lower Control Arm, Replace

Remove
1. Raise and support vehicle and remove wheel.
2. From tool J-22517-02, remove the two nuts and center screw, then place tool over crossmember support. Align pin of tool with hole in crossmember, then install the two nuts and screw on tool. Turn center screw until seated in dimple of torsion bar adjusting arm.
3. Remove torsion bar adjusting bolt and nut.

NOTE: Count and record number of turns required to remove adjusting bolt. The number of turns will be used upon installation to obtain original riding height.

4. Turn center screw of tool J-22517-02 until tension on torsion bar is completely removed then remove tool and torsion bar.
5. Disconnect shock absorber and stabilizer link from lower control arm and remove drive axle nut.
6. Remove cotter pin and nut from lower ball joint, then using suitable tool, separate lower ball joint from steering knuckle.
7. Remove bolts from lower control arm to frame and remove torsion bar.
8. Push inboard on drive axle and pull outward on knuckle to gain clearance, and remove lower control arm from knuckle.

Installation
1. Install lower control arm, making sure that shock absorber is guided onto lower control arm shock absorber, then guide ball joint stud into knuckle and install

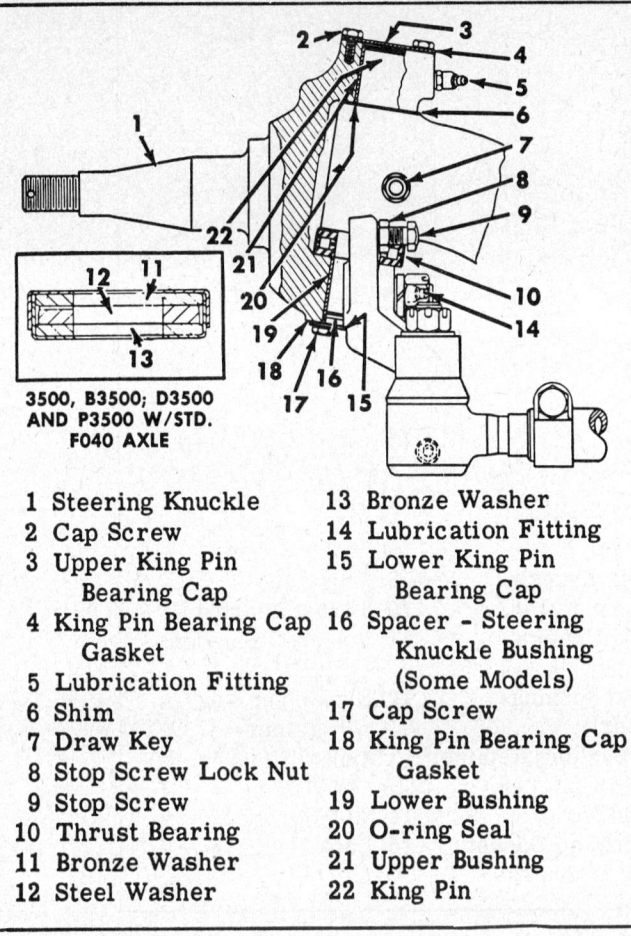

1 Steering Knuckle
2 Cap Screw
3 Upper King Pin Bearing Cap
4 King Pin Bearing Cap Gasket
5 Lubrication Fitting
6 Shim
7 Draw Key
8 Stop Screw Lock Nut
9 Stop Screw
10 Thrust Bearing
11 Bronze Washer
12 Steel Washer
13 Bronze Washer
14 Lubrication Fitting
15 Lower King Pin Bearing Cap
16 Spacer - Steering Knuckle Bushing (Some Models)
17 Cap Screw
18 King Pin Bearing Cap Gasket
19 Lower Bushing
20 O-ring Seal
21 Upper Bushing
22 King Pin

Fig. 7 Steering knuckle with single draw key. Typical F-050, 055, 070 model axles

1 Upper Draw Key (Short)
2 King Pin
3 Upper Bushing
4 Cap Gasket
5 King Pin Cap
6 Spacing Shim
7 Lower Draw Key
8 Thrust Bearing
9 Axle Center
10 Expansion Plug
11 Lock Ring
12 Lower Bushing
13 Steering Knuckle

Fig. 8 Steering knuckle with two draw keys. Typical 1970-79 F-161, 901, 921, 970; and 1975-79 F-120 model axles

but do not tighten stud nut.
2. Install lower control arm to frame bracket bolts. Install and torque nuts to 90 ft. lbs.
3. Torque ball joint stud nut to 100 ft. lbs., then install new cotter pin. Tighten nut as necessary to install cotter pin. Do not back off nut.
4. Install shock absorber nut and stabilizer link nut.
5. Coat both ends of torsion bar with chassis grease, then push front end of torsion all the way into control arm.
6. Insert adjusting arm into crossmember and position it 1 3/4–2 inches below centerline of crossmember. Slide torsion bar rearward until flush with rear face of adjusting arm.
7. Install tool J-22517-02 making sure that pin of tool is in hole in crossmember. Turn center screw of tool until adjusting arm is in position to permit installation of adjusting nut.
8. Apply chassis grease to adjusting bolt, then install and turn adjusting bolt the number of turns recorded in step 3 to obtain original riding height.
9. Loosen center screw of tool until tension is completely removed from tool and remove tool.
10. Install wheel and lower vehicle.
11. Check riding height and adjust if necessary as described previously.

I-BEAM FRONT AXLE

Front Axle, Replace

1. Raise and support vehicle at frame. Position floor jack under center of axle beam.
2. Remove wheels and hubs. Disconnect brake lines at axle, then the drag link from steering arm.
3. Remove U-bolt nuts and washer if equipped, and remove U-bolts.

NOTE: Note position of shims, spacer blocks, shock absorber brackets and dowel pins for proper reassembly.

4. Lower axle and remove from under vehicle.
5. Reverse procedure to install.

Steering Knuckle, Replace

1. Raise and support front axle.
2. Remove front wheels, hubs and bearings.
3. Remove brake components and disconnect tie rod from steering arm.
4. Remove steering arm from knuckle, if removable.
5. On models with single draw key, Fig. 7:
   a. Remove draw key nut and washer.

Thread nut onto draw key enough to protect key threads and drive on key to loosen. Remove key from knuckle using suitable drift.
   b. Remove upper and lower king pin caps and gaskets.
   c. Drive king pin out of knuckle using suitable brass drift. Remove knuckle, shims, thrust bearing and O-ring.
6. On models with two draw keys, Fig. 8:
   a. Remove upper king pin dust cap and on F-120, 921 axles, lower dust cap.
   b. On all except F-120, 921, remove lower expansion plug retainer and expansion plug.

NOTE: If plug will not come out, it will come out when king pin is removed.

   c. Remove both keys using suitable drift against small end of key.

NOTE: Keys were originally installed from opposite sides of center.

   d. Drive pin out of knuckle using suitable brass drift. Remove knuckle, shims and thrust bearing.
7. On models with tapered king pin, Fig. 9:
   a. Remove upper dust cap and gasket.
   b. On all except F-160 models, remove lower expansion plug retainer and plug.
   c. On F-160 models, remove lower king pin bushing retainer only if broken or damaged.
   d. On all models; remove cotter pin, king pin nut and steel spacer.

GMC

e. Drive pin out of knuckle using suitable brass drift. Remove knuckle, thrust washer and spacing washer from axle. Remove sleeve bushing.

8. Reverse procedure to install.

STEERING GEAR, REPLACE

1971-80 All Exc. 1971-72 G Models & Motor Home

1. Place front wheels in straight ahead driving position.
2. On C-K models, remove flexible coupling to steering shaft flange bolts. On P models, remove lower universal joint pinch bolt and mark position of universal joint to wormshaft.
3. On all models, mark position of pitman arm to pitman shaft, remove pitman shaft nut or pitman arm pinch bolt and, with a suitable puller, remove pitman arm from pitman shaft.
4. Remove steering gear to frame bolts and steering gear from vehicle.
5. On C-K models, remove flexible coupling pinch bolt and flexible coupling from steering gear wormshaft.
6. Reverse procedure to install.

1970 Exc. G Models

1. With wheels in straight ahead position, mark steering shaft and worm shaft relationship and loosen coupling-to-steering gear bolt.
2. Remove pitman arm retaining nut and, with suitable puller, remove pitman arm.
3. Remove steering gear-to-frame retaining bolts and remove steering gear.

1972 G Models

1. With the wheels in the straight ahead position (wormshaft flat at 12 o'clock), disconnect battery negative cable and remove the steering shaft flange to flexible coupling bolts.
2. Remove pitman arm retaining nut. Mark position of arm on shaft and with a suitable puller remove pitman arm.
3. Remove steering gear to frame retaining bolts and remove the steering gear and flexible coupling as an assembly.
4. Disconnect the flexible coupling from wormshaft.

1970-71 G Models

1. Remove steering wheel.

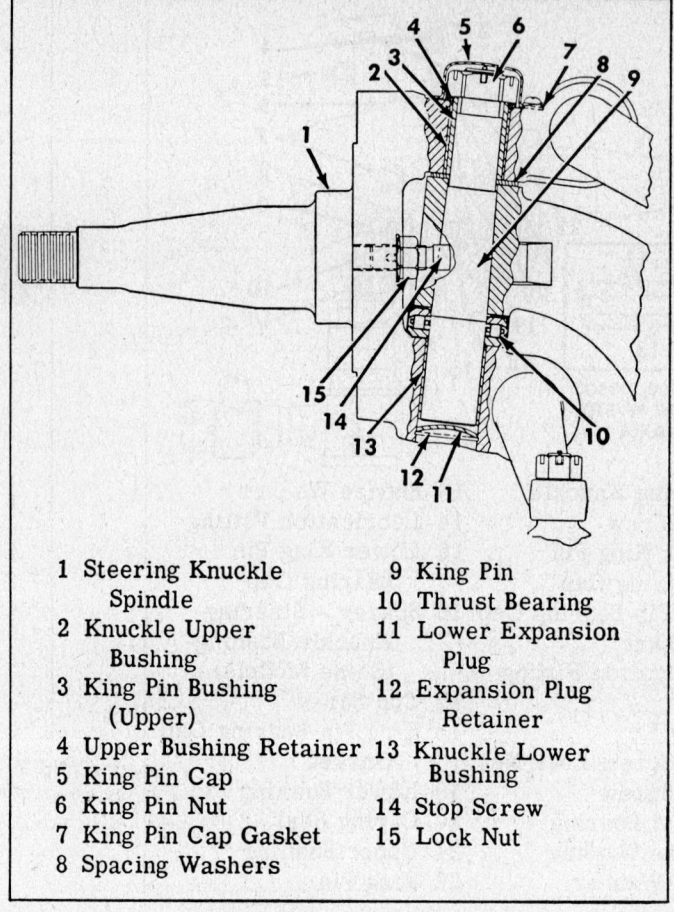

1. Steering Knuckle Spindle
2. Knuckle Upper Bushing
3. King Pin Bushing (Upper)
4. Upper Bushing Retainer
5. King Pin Cap
6. King Pin Nut
7. King Pin Cap Gasket
8. Spacing Washers
9. King Pin
10. Thrust Bearing
11. Lower Expansion Plug
12. Expansion Plug Retainer
13. Knuckle Lower Bushing
14. Stop Screw
15. Lock Nut

Fig. 9 Steering knuckle with tapered king pin. Typical 1970-74 F-120; and 1970-79 F-090, 160, 900 model axles

2. Raise vehicle and remove deflector and extension assembly, and disconnect pitman arm after marking relationship of pitman arm and sector shaft.
3. Disconnect brake pedal from lower pedal assembly.
4. Disconnect transmission shift linkage.
5. Remove steering gear mounting bolts.
6. From inside vehicle, remove brake pedal.
7. Pull back floor mat and disconnect toe pan seal and remove toe pan cover.
8. Remove mast jacket bracket from support and remove steering gear, and transmission controls as an assembly.
9. Disassemble mast jacket assembly as necessary.

1973-78 Motor Home

1. Disconnect power steering hoses from steering gear.
2. Remove pitman arm from pitman shaft using suitable puller.
3. Loosen steering shaft yoke cinch bolt.
4. Remove steering gear to frame rail attaching bolts, then the steering gear.
5. Reverse procedure to install. Torque steering gear mounting bolts to 70 ft. lbs. and pitman shaft nut to 160-210 ft. lbs.

INTERNATIONAL

INDEX OF SERVICE OPERATIONS

	Page No.
AXLES, DRIVING	
Eaton Axle Service	204
Spicer Axle Service	239
Timken Axle Service	241
Locking Differentials	192
Front Wheel Locking Hubs	505
Front Wheel Drive	1240
BRAKES	
Adjustments	590
Air Brake Service	620
Anti-Skid Brakes	551
Bendix Twinplex Brake	608
Brake Booster Service	639
Disc Brakes	661
Hydraulic System Service	632
Parking Brake Service	612
Stopmaster Brake Service	599
CLUTCHES	
Air-Hydraulic (Air-Pak)	468
Clutch Service	429
Hydraulic Clutch Controls	1238
COOLING SYSTEM	
Cooling System Capacity	1205
Variable Speed Fans	10
ELECTRICAL	
Alternator Service	52
Dash Gauge Service	179
Distributors, Standard	141
Electronic Ignition	152

	Page No.
Generator Service	11
Ignition Coils and Resistors	7
Ignition Timing	1226
Starting Motor Service	29
Starter Switch Service	21
Tune Up Service	2
ENGINE	
Camshaft and Bearings	1224
Crankshaft Rear Oil Seal	1225
Cylinder Head, Replace	1222
Engine, Replace	1221
Piston and Rod, Assemble	1224
Rocker Arms	1222
Timing Gears	1224
Timing Chain	1224
Valve Guides	1224
Valve Lifters	1224
Valve Rotators	1223
ENGINE OILING	
Crankcase Capacity	1205
Oil Pump Repairs	1205
FRONT SUSPENSION	
Ball Joint, Replace	1251
Coil Spring, Replace	1250
Front Wheel Locking Hubs	816
Torsion Bar Suspension	1249
Wheel Alignment, Adjust	1248
FUEL & EXHAUST	
Carburetor Adjustments	1227
Crankshaft Ventilation	748

	Page No.
Emission Controls	750
Fuel Pump Service	183
L.P.G. Carburetion	190
Turbochargers	187
SPECIFICATIONS	
Alternator and Regulator	1217
Carburetor Adjusting Specs.	1227
Crankshaft and Bearing	1219
Distributor	1213
Engine Tightening Torque	1220
General Engine Data	1208
Generator and Regulator	1218
Piston, Pin and Ring	1219
Rear Axle Capacities	1244
Starting Motor	1215
Transmission Capacities	1242
Tune Up	1210
Valve	1219
Wheel Alignment	1220
STEERING	
Manual Steering Gear Service	680
Power Steering Gear Service	686
TRANSFER CASES	469
TRANSMISSIONS, Manual	
Own Make	1240
Clark	275
Fuller	289
New Process	329
Spicer	346
Warner	406

MODEL INDEX & ENGINE APPLICATION

ENGINE IDENTIFICATION—Engine model takes the form of a prefix to the engine serial number. For example, a V-266 engine serial number would read V-266-000000. Engine numbers are located on machined boss on block.

Truck Model or Series	Year	Standard Engine Make	Standard Engine Model	Oil Pan Refill Capacity Qts.	Cooling System Capacity Qts.
SCOUT					
Scout	1970–71	Own	4-152, 196	4	11.6
Scout	1970–71	Own	V-304	6	18
Scout	1970–71	Jeep	PT-6-232	4	17
Scout II	1972–74	Own	4-196	4	11.6
Scout II	1973–74	Jeep	6-258	4	12
Scout II	1975–79	Own	4-196	4	14
LIGHT DUTY					
1000D	1970–71	Jeep	PT-6-232	4	12
1010	1972	Jeep	6-258	4	—
1100D	1970–71	Jeep	PT-6-232	4	12
1110	1972	Jeep	6-258	4	—
1200D	1970–71	Jeep	PT-6-232	4	17
1210	1972	Jeep	6-258	4	—

Truck Model or Series	Year	Standard Engine Make	Standard Engine Model	Oil Pan Refill Capacity Qts.	Cooling System Capacity Qts.
1300D	1970–71	Jeep	PT-6-232	4	17
1310	1972	Jeep	6-258	4	—
1500D	1970–71	Jeep	PT-6-232	4	17
1510	1972	Jeep	6-258	4	—
LOADSTAR					
1600	1970–71	Own	V-304	9	21
1600	1972–74	Own	V-345	10	22
1600	1975–78	Own	V-345	—	—
1600 4×4	1974	Own	V-304	—	—
1600 4×4	1975	Own	V-345	—	—
1610FC	1978	Own	V-345	—	—
1650	1978	Own	D-150	—	—
1700	1970–71	Own	V-304	9	21
1700	1972–74	Own	V-345	10	22
1700	1975–78	Own	MV-404	—	—

Continued

1205

INTERNATIONAL

MODEL INDEX & ENGINE APPLICATION—Continued

Truck Model or Series	Year	Standard Engine Make	Standard Engine Model	Oil Pan Refill Capacity Qts.	Cooling System Capacity Qts.
1700 4×4	1975–77	Own	V-345	—	—
1750	1970–72	Own	DV-462	10	42
1750	1973–74	Own	DV-550B	—	42
1750	1975–78	Own	D-150	12	—
1800	1970–74	Own	V-345	10	22
1800	1975–78	Own	MV-404	—	—
1850	1970–72	Own	DV-550	10	42
1850	1973–74	Own	DV-550B	—	42
1850	1975–78	Own	D-170	12	—
1890	1970–71	Own	V-345	10	22
1890-D	1970–71	Detroit	6V-53N	—	22
F-1800	1970–74	Own	V-345	10	22
F-1800	1975–78	Own	MV-404	—	—
F-1800-D	1970–71	Detroit	6V-53N	—	22
F-1850	1970–72	Own	DV-550	10	42
F-1850	1973–74	Own	DV-550B	—	42
F-1850	1975–78	Own	D-170	12	42
CO-1600	1970–71	Own	V-304	9	26
CO-1700	1970	Own	V-304	9	26
CO-1750	1970	Own	DV-462	10	42
CO-1800	1970	Own	V-345	10	27
CO-1850	1970	Own	DV-550	10	52.8

CARGOSTAR

Truck Model or Series	Year	Standard Engine Make	Standard Engine Model	Oil Pan Refill Capacity Qts.	Cooling System Capacity Qts.
CO-1610A	1970–71	Own	V-304	9	—
CO-1610A	1972–73	Own	V-345	10	22
CO-1610B	1974–79	Own	V-345	—	—
CO-1630A	1970–71	—	D-354	—	—
CO-1710A	1970–71	Own	V-304	9	—
CO-1710A	1972–73	Own	V-345	10	22
CO-1710B	1974	Own	V-345	—	—
CO-1710B	1975–79	Own	MV-404	—	—
CO-1730A	1970–71	Detroit	4-53N	14	—
CO-1750A	1970–71	Own	DV-452	10	—
CO-1810A	1972–73	Own	V-345	10	22
COF-1810A	1970–72	Own	V-345	10	—
COF-1810A	1973	Own	V-345	10	—
CO-1810B	1974	Own	V-345	—	—
CO-1810B	1975–79	Own	MV-404	—	—
CO-1830A	1970–71	Detroit	4-53N	14	—
CO-1850A	1970–72	Own	DV-550	10	—
CO-1850A	1973	Own	DV-550B	—	—
CO-1850B	1974	Own	DV-550B	10	—
CO-1850B	1975–79	Own	D-170	12	—
CO-1910A	1970–72	Own	VS-401	10	—
CO-1910B	1974	Own	VS-401	10	—
CO-1910B	1975–77	Own	VS-478	—	—
CO-1910B	1978	Own	V-537	—	—
CO-1950A	1970–71	Own	DV-550	10	—
CO-1950B	1974	Own	DV-550B	10	—
CO-1950B	1975–76	Own	D-170	12	—
CO-1950B	1977–79	Own	D-190	—	—
COF-1810B	1974	Own	V-345	—	—
COF-1810B	1975–79	Own	MV-404	—	—
COF-1910A	1970–73	Own	VS-401	10	—
COF-1910B	1974	Own	VS-401	10	—
COF-1910B	1975–76	Own	VS-478	—	—
COF-1910B	1977–79	Own	V-537	—	—
COF-1950A	1970–72	Own	DV-550	10	—
COF-1950A	1973	Own	DV-550B	—	—
COF-1950A	1974	Own	DV-550B	10	—
COF-1950B	1975–76	Own	D-170	12	—
COF-1950B	1977–79	Own	D-190	—	—

FLEETSTAR

Truck Model or Series	Year	Standard Engine Make	Standard Engine Model	Oil Pan Refill Capacity Qts.	Cooling System Capacity Qts.
F-1910A	1970–73	Own	RD-406	9	47.7
2000-D	1970–71	Cummins	NH-250	24	48
F-1910A	1973	Own	RD-406	9	47.7
F-2000-D	1970–71	Cummins	NH-230	24	48
F-2010A	1970–71	Own	RD-406	9	47.7
F-2010A	1972–74	Own	RD-450	9	47.7
F-2010A	1975–77	Own	VS-478	—	53
F-2010A	1978	Own	V-537	—	—
F-2050A	1970–72	Own	DV-550	10	57.3
F-2050A	1973–74	Own	DV-550B	—	57.3
F-2050A	1975–77	Own	D-170	—	—
F-2050A	1978	Own	D-190	—	—
F-2500A	1975	Own	D-170	12	57.3
F-2070A	1973–77	Detroit	6-71N	30	48
2010A	1970–74	Own	RD-450	9	47.7
2010A	1975–77	Own	VS-478	—	53
2010A	1978	Own	V-537	—	—
2050A	1970–72	Own	DV-550	10	57.3
2050A	1973–74	Own	DV-550B	—	57.3
2050A	1975–77	Own	D-170	12	57.3
2050A	1978	Own	D-190	—	—
2070A	1973–77	Detroit	6-71N	30	48
2110A	1970–73	Own	RD-450	9	47.7

TRANSTAR

Truck Model or Series	Year	Standard Engine Make	Standard Engine Model	Oil Pan Refill Capacity Qts.	Cooling System Capacity Qts.
4270	1973–75	Detroit	8V-71	27	67
4270	1973–77	Detroit	8V-71NE	27	67
4270	1978	Detroit	8V-71T	—	—
4270	1978–79	Detroit	6V-92TT	—	67
4370	1973–79	Cummins	NTC-290	34.5	54
4370	1973–77	Cummins	NH-230	32	54
F-4270	1973–75	Detroit	8V-71	27	67
F-4270	1973–77	Cummins	NTC-290	—	—
F-4270	1978	Detroit	8V-71T	—	—
F-4270	1978	Detroit	6V-92TT	—	67
F-4370	1973–79	Cummins	NTC-290	34.5	54
CO-4070A	1973	Cummins	NTC-290	34.5	55
CO-4070A	1973	Cummins	NH-230	32	55
CO-4070A	1973	Cummins	NH-250	32	55
CO-4070B	1974–79	Cummins	NTC-290	—	55
COF-4070A	1973	Cummins	NTC-290	34.5	55
COF-4070A	1973	Cummins	NH-230	32	55
COF-4070A	1973	Cummins	NH-250	32	55
COF-4070B	1974–79	Cummins	NTC-290	—	55
COF-5370	1978	Cummins	NTC-250	—	—

Continued

INTERNATIONAL

MODEL INDEX & ENGINE APPLICATION—Continued

Truck Model or Series	Year	Standard Engine Make	Standard Engine Model	Oil Pan Refill Capacity Qts.	Cooling System Capacity Qts.
TRAVELALL					
100 4×2	1974	Own	V-345	—	—
100 4×4	1974	Own	V-392	—	—
150 4×2	1975	Own	V-304	—	19
150 4×4	1975	Own	V-304	—	19
200 4×2	1974	Own	V-392	—	—
200 4×4	1974	Own	V-392	—	—
200 4×2	1975	Own	V-304	—	19
200 4×4	1975	Own	V-304	—	19
PAYSTAR					
5050 4×4	1973–74	Own	DV-550B	—	—
5050 4×4	1975–76	Own	D-190	12	—
5050 4×4	1977–79	Own	DT-466	—	—
5070 4×4	1973	Cummins	NH-230	32	—
5070 4×4	1974–79	Detroit	6-71N	—	—
5050 6×4	1973–74	Own	DV-550B	—	—
5050 6×6	1973–74	Own	DV-550B	—	—
COF-5370 6×4	1979	Cummins	NTC-250	—	—
F-5050 6×4	1975–76	Own	D-190	12	—
F-5050 6×4	1977–79	Own	DT-466	—	—
F-5050 6×4	1978	Cat	3208	—	—
F-5050 6×6	1975–76	Own	D-190	12	—
F-5050 6×6	1977–79	Own	DT-466	—	—
F-5070 6×4	1973–79	Detroit	6-71	30	—
F-5070 6×6	1974–79	Detroit	6-71	—	—
F-5050SF 6×4	1973–74	Own	DV-550B	—	—
F-5050SF 6×4	1975–76	Own	D-190	12	—
F-5050SF 6×4	1977	Detroit	6V-53	—	—
F-5050SF 6×4	1978–79	Own	DT-466	—	—
F-5050SF 6×4	1978	Cat	3208	—	—
F-5070SF 6×4	1973–79	Detroit	6-71N	30	—
S-SERIES					
1624	1979	Own	V-345	—	—
1724	1979	Own	V-345	—	26
1754	1979	Own	D-150	—	—
1824	1979	Own	MV-404	—	25
1824 4×4	1979	Own	V-345	—	—
1854	1979	Own	D-190	—	—
1854 4×4	1979	Own	D-170	—	—
1924	1979	Own	MV-404	—	26
F-1924	1979	Own	MV-404	—	26
F-1924 6×6	1979	Own	MV-404	—	26
F-1925	1979	Own	MV-404	—	26
1954	1979	Own	DT-466	—	37
F-1954	1979	Own	D-190	—	—
F-1954 6×6	1979	Own	D-190	—	—
1955	1979	Own	D-190	—	—
2125	1979	Own	V-537	—	—
F-2125 6×4	1979	Own	V-537	—	—
2155	1979	Own	DT-466	—	37
2275 4×2	1978–79	Detroit	6-71	—	—
F-2275 6×4	1978–79	Detroit	6-71	—	—
2524 4×2	1978–79	Own	V-537	—	—
F-2524 6×4	1978–79	Own	V-537	—	—
2554 4×2	1978–79	Own	DT-466	—	—
F-2554 6×4	1978–79	Own	DT-466	—	—
2574 4×2	1978–79	Detroit	6-71	—	—
F-2574 6×4	1978–79	Detroit	6-71	—	—
2575 4×2	1978–79	Detroit	6-71	—	—
F-2575 6×4	1978–79	Detroit	6-71	—	—
F-2624 6×4	1978–79	Own	V-537	—	—
F-2654 6×4	1978–79	Own	DT-466	—	—
F-2674 6×4	1978–79	Detroit	6-71	—	—
ACO, CO, VCO, DC, DCO SERIES					
CO-190	1970–72	Own	RD-406	9	27
COF-190	1970–72	Own	RD-406	9	27
CO-1950	1970–71	Own	DV-550	10	43
CO-200	1970–72	Own	RD-406	9	27
CO-220	1970–72	Own	RD-501	9	27
COF-1950	1970–71	Own	DV-550	10	43
VCO-190	1970–72	Own	V-401	10	46.5
VCOF-190	1970–72	Own	V-401	10	46.5
VCO-200	1970–72	Own	V-401	10	46.5
VCO-220	1970–72	Own	V-478	10	46.5
DCOF-195-H	1970–71	Cummins	NH-230	28	36
DCO-200	1971	Cummins	C-180	—	38.4
DCO-200	1970	Cummins	NH-180	28	38.4
DCO-205-H	1970–71	Cummins	NH-230	28	36
ALL WHEEL DRIVE MODELS					
1100D	1970–72	Own	PT-6-232	4	12
1200D	1970	Own	V-304	6	20
1200D	1971	Own	PT-6-232	4	17
1200D	1971	Own	V-266	—	17
1300D	1970	Own	V-304	6	20
1300D	1971	Own	PT-6-232	4	17
1300D	1971	Own	V-266	—	17
1600	1970–73	Own	V-304	9	21
1700	1970–72	Own	V-304	9	21
183-RE	1970–72	Own	V-345	10	41.5
193-RE	1970–72	Own	V-401	10	41.5
1603	1970–74	Own	V-304	9	21
1603	1975–78	Own	V-345A	—	—
1610-F.C.	1978	Own	V-345	—	—
1703	1970–74	Own	V-304	9	21
1703	1975–78	Own	V-345A	—	—
1723	1979	Own	V-345	—	—
1803	1970–78	Own	V-345	9	21.9
1823	1979	Own	MV-404	—	26
1853	1970–74	Own	RD-406	9	27
1853	1977–78	Own	D-170	—	—
1853-FC	1970–72	Own	RD-406	9	28

Continued

INTERNATIONAL

MODEL INDEX & ENGINE APPLICATION—Continued

Truck Model or Series	Year	Standard Engine Make	Standard Engine Model	Oil Pan Refill Capacity Qts.	Cooling System Capacity Qts.
METRO SERIES, MULTI-STOP & MOTOR HOME CHASSIS					
M-1100	1970–71	Own	4-196	4	15.6
M-1100	1972	Jeep	6-258	4	—
M-1200	1970	Own	4-196	4	—
M-1200	1971	Own	PT-6-232	4	15.6
M-1200	1972	Jeep	6-258	4	—
MA-1200	1970	Own	4-196	4	15.6
MA-1200	1971	Own	PT-6-232	4	12
MS-1210	1973–74	Jeep	6-258	4	15.6
MS-1210	1975	Own	V-345A	—	20
MHC-1310	1973–75	Own	V-392	—	24
M-1500	1970	Own	V-304	6	19.5
M-1500	1971	Own	PT-6-232	4	19.5
M-1500	1972	Jeep	6-258	4	—
MA-1500	1970	Own	V-304	6	—
MA-1500	1971	Own	PT-6-232	4	12
MS-1510	1973	Jeep	6-258	—	15.6
MS-1510	1974	Own	V-345	—	15.6
MS-1510	1975	Own	V-345A	—	20
MHC-1510	1973–75	Own	V-392	—	24
100, 110, 120, 130 SERIES					
100	1974	Jeep	6-258	4	12
100 4×4	1974	Own	V-304	—	17
140, 150, 160 SERIES					
150	1975	Own	V-304	—	19
150 4×4	1975	Own	V-304	—	19
200, 210, and 230 SERIES					
200	1974	Jeep	6-258	4	12
200 4×4	1974	Jeep	6-258	4	—
200	1975	Own	V-304	—	19
200 4×4	1975	Own	V-304	—	19
210	1970–72	Own	RD-450	9	28
210-D	1970	Cummins	NH-180	28	50
210-D	1971	Cummins	NH-200	—	50
F-210	1970–72	Own	RD-450	9	28
F-210-D	1970	Cummins	H-180	28	50
F-210-D	1971	Cummins	NH-200	—	50
F-230	1970–72	Own	RD-501	9	28
F-230-D	1970	Cummins	NH-180	28	50
F-230-D	1971	Cummins	NH-200	—	50
400 and 405 SERIES					
DC-400	1970–71	Own	DVT-573	21	54
DCF-400	1970–71	Own	DVT-573	21	54
D-400	1970–71	Cummins	NH-230	28	48
DF-400	1970–71	Cummins	NH-230	28	48
500 SERIES					
500	1974	Jeep	6-258	4	12
500	1975	Own	V-304	—	19
4000 CAB-OVER SERIES					
CO-4070-A	1970–71	Own	DVT-573	21	55
COF-4070-A	1970–71	Own	DVT-573	21	55
COF-4090-A	1970	Detroit	12V-71N	38	80
M SERIES					
M-412-CBE	1970	Own	RD-450	9	27.1
M-412-10	1971–72	Own	RD-450	9	—
M-412-50	1971	Own	DV-550	10	—
M-623-CBE	1970	Own	RD-450	9	27.1
M-623-10	1971–72	Own	RD-450	9	—
M-623-50	1971	Own	DV-550	10	—
M-6123-CBE	1970	Own	RD-450	9	27.1
M-6123-10	1971–72	Own	RD-450	9	—
M-6123-50	1971	Own	DV-550	10	—
M-8234-CBE	1970	Own	RD-450	9	27.1

GENERAL ENGINE SPECIFICATIONS

Year	Engine Model	Carb. Type	Bore & Stroke	Comp. Ratio	Horsepower @ R.P.M.	Torque Ft. Lbs. @ R.P.M.	Comp. Pressure Cranking Speed ①	Governed Speed R.P.M.	Normal Oil Pressure Lbs.
1970–71	OHV-4 4-196	1 Bore	4¹⁄₈ × 3²¹⁄₃₂	8.10	111 @ 4000	180 @ 2000	143	—	50
1972–74	OHV-4 4-196	1 Bore	4¹⁄₈ × 3²¹⁄₃₂	8.1	103 @ 4000	177 @ 2000	—	—	—
1975–79	OHV-4 ④ 4-196	1 Bore	4¹⁄₈ × 3²¹⁄₃₂	8.02	86 @ 3800	157 @ 2200	—	—	40–50
1979	OHV-4 ③ 4-196	1 Bore	4.125 × 3.656	8.02	79 @ 3600	155 @ 2000	—	—	40–50
1979	OHV-6 6-232	1 Bore	3.75 × 3.50	8.5	120 @ 4000	202 @ 1000	—	—	32
1972	OHV-6 6-258	1 Bore	3¾ × 3.895	8.0	140 @ 3800	235 @ 1200	—	—	13–37
1973–74	OHV-6 6-258	1 Bore	3¾ × 3.895	8.0	115 @ 3800	199 @ 2000	—	—	32
1970–72	OHV-6 .... PT-6-232	1 Bore	3¾ × 3½	8.5	145 @ 4300	215 @ 1600	145	—	32
1970–72	OHV-6 .... RD-406	2 Bore	4⅜ × 4½	7.13	193 @ 3200	373 @ 1600	125	2750	35–45
1973–74	OHV-6 .... RD-406	2 Bore	4⅜ × 4½	7.1	160 @ 2750	336 @ 1400	143	2750	35–45
1970–72	OHV-6 .... RD-450	2 Bore	4⅜ × 5	7.06	202 @ 3000	422 @ 1600	120	2600	35–45
1973–74	OHV-6 .... RD-450	2 Bore	4⅜ × 5	7.1	168 @ 2600	372 @ 1400	142	2600	35–45

Continued

INTERNATIONAL

GENERAL ENGINE SPECIFICATIONS—Continued

Year	Engine Model	Carb. Type	Bore & Stroke	Comp. Ratio	Horsepower @ R.P.M.	Torque Ft. Lbs. @ R.P.M.	Comp. Pressure Cranking Speed ①	Governed Speed R.P.M.	Normal Oil Pressure Lbs.
1970–72	OHV-6 .... RD-501	4 Bore	4½ × 5¼	6.78	215 @ 3000	451 @ 1600	120	2600	35–45
1973–74	OHV-6 .... RD-501	4 Bore	4½ × 5¼	6.8	181 @ 2600	406 @ 1400	145	2600	35–45
1970–71	OHV-V8 .... V-266	2 Bore	3⁵⁄₈ × 3⁷⁄₃₂	8.4	155 @ 4400	227 @ 2800	150	—	40–50
1970–72	OHV-V8 .... V-304	2 Bore	3⁷⁄₈ × 3⁷⁄₃₂	8.19	193 @ 4400	273 @ 2800	145	—	40–50
1973–74	OHV-V8 .... V-304	2 Bore	3⁷⁄₈ × 3⁷⁄₃₂	8.2	147 @ 3900	240 @ 2400	145	—	50
1973–74	OHV-V8 .... V-304	4 Bore	3⁷⁄₈ × 3⁷⁄₃₂	8.2	153 @ 3900	246 @ 2400	145	—	50
1975–77	OHV-V8 .... V-304	2 Bore	3⁷⁄₈ × 3⁷⁄₃₂	8.2	140 @ 3800	243 @ 2400	—	—	45
1978–79	OHV-V8 .... V-304A	2 Bore	3.875 × 3.219	8.19	144 @ 3600	247 @ 2400	—	—	40–50
1970–72	OHV-V8 .... V-345	2 Bore	3⁷⁄₈ × 3²¹⁄₃₂	8.05	197 @ 4000	309 @ 2200	140	3800	40–50
1973–74	OHV-V8 .... V-345	2 Bore	3⁷⁄₈ × 3²¹⁄₃₂	8.1	157 @ 3800	266 @ 2400	143	3800	50
1975–79	OHV-V8 .... V-345	2 Bore	3⁷⁄₈ × 3²¹⁄₃₂	8.05	158 @ 3600	288 @ 2000	—	—	45
1978–79	OHV-V8 .... V-345A	2 Bore	3.875 × 3.656	8.28	163 @ 3600	292 @ 2000	—	—	40–50
1973–74	OHV-V8 .... V-345	4 Bore	3⁷⁄₈ × 3²¹⁄₃₂	8.1	163 @ 3800	273 @ 2400	143	3800	50
1975–78	OHV-V8 .... V-345	4 Bore	3⁷⁄₈ × 3²¹⁄₃₂	8.05	168 @ 3800	288 @ 2000	—	3800	45
1970–72	OHV-V8 .... V-392	4 Bore	4⅛ × 3²¹⁄₃₂	8.02	236 @ 4000	357 @ 2800	143	3600	50
1973–74	OHV-V8 .... V-392	2 Bore	4⅛ × 3²¹⁄₃₂	8.0	191 @ 3600	299 @ 2800	143	3600	50
1973–74	OHV-V8 .... V-392	4 Bore	4⅛ × 3²¹⁄₃₂	8.0	194 @ 3600	308 @ 2800	143	3600	50
1975–77	OHV-V8 .... V-392	4 Bore	4⅛ × 3²¹⁄₃₂	8.02	187 @ 3600	307 @ 2400	—	—	45
1975–79	OHV-V8 .... V-392	4 Bore	4⅛ × 3²¹⁄₃₂	8.0	191 @ 3600	307 @ 2800	—	3600	45
1973–74	OHV-V8② V-400	2 Bore	4¹¹⁄₆₄ × 3¹¹⁄₁₆	8.25	211 @ 4000	326 @ 2800	—	—	37–75
1970–72	OHV-V8 .... V-401	2 Bore	4⅛ × 3¾	7.69	206 @ 3600	355 @ 1800	135	3400	50–60
1973–74	OHV-V8 .... V-401	2 Bore	4⅛ × 3¾	7.7	186 @ 3400	322 @ 2400	139	3400	40–55
1970–72	OHV-V8 Short VS-401	2 Bore	4⅛ × 3¾	7.69	206 @ 3600	355 @ 1800	135	3400	50–60
1973–76	OHV-V8 Short VS-401	2 Bore	4⅛ × 3¾	7.7	186 @ 3400	322 @ 2400	140	3400	40–55
1977	OHV-V8 Short VS-401	2 Bore	4⅛ × 3¾	7.69	180 @ 3400	339 @ 1700	—	3400	45–55
1975–79	OHV-V8 .... MV-404	2 Bore	4⅛ × 3¾	8.1	188 @ 3600	311 @ 2300	—	3600	44–50
1975–79	OHV-V8 .... MV-404	4 Bore	4⅛ × 3¾	8.1	210 @ 3600	336 @ 2800	—	3600	44–50
1975–79	OHV-V8 .... MV-446	4 Bore	4⅛ × 4³⁄₁₆	8.1	235 @ 3600	385 @ 2600	—	3600	44–50
1970–72	OHV-V8 .... V-478	2 Bore	4½ × 3¾	7.64	234 @ 3600	431 @ 1800	135	3400	50–60
1975–74	OHV-V8 .... V-478	2 Bore	4½ × 3¾	7.6	209 @ 3400	384 @ 2200	140	3400	40–55
1970–72	OHV-V8 Short VS-478	2 Bore	4½ × 3¾	7.64	234 @ 3600	431 @ 1800	135	3400	50–60
1973–75	OHV-V8 Short VS-478	2 Bore	4½ × 3¾	7.6	209 @ 3400	384 @ 2200	140	3400	40–55
1977	OHV-V8 Short VS-478	2 Bore	4½ × 3¾	7.64	234 @ 3600	409 @ 1800	—	3400	45–55
1975–79	OHV-V8 .... V-537	2 Bore	4.625 × 4.00	7.5	208 @ 3200	415 @ 2000	—	—	45–55
1975–79	OHV-V8 .... V-537	4 Bore	4.625 × 4.00	7.5	236 @ 3200	429 @ 2200	—	—	45–55
1970–72	OHV-V8 .... V-549	4 Bore	4½ × 4⁵⁄₁₆	7.57	257 @ 3400	505 @ 2000	135	3200	50–60
1973–76	OHV-V8 Short V-549	4 Bore	4½ × 4⁵⁄₁₆	7.6	227 @ 3200	446 @ 2000	140	3200	40–55
1970–72	OHV-V8 Short VS-549	4 Bore	4½ × 4⁵⁄₁₆	7.57	257 @ 3400	505 @ 2000	135	3200	50–60
1973–76	OHV-V8 Short VS-549	4 Bore	4½ × 4⁵⁄₁₆	7.6	227 @ 3200	446 @ 2000	140	3200	40–55
1977	OHV-V8 Short VS-549	4 Bore	4½ × 4⁵⁄₁₆	7.57	230 @ 3200	479 @ 1600	—	3200	45–55
1973–76	OHV-V8 Short FTVS-549	4 Bore	4½ × 4⁵⁄₁₆	7.6	232 @ 3200	446 @ 2000	140	3200	40–55
1977	OHV-V8 Short FTVS-549	4 Bore	4½ × 4⁵⁄₁₆	7.57	230 @ 3200	479 @ 1600	—	3200	45–55

①—Plus or minus 10 lbs.
②—See V8-401 in Jeep Chapter for service data.
③—Calif.
④—Exc. 1979 Calif.

INTERNATIONAL

TUNE UP SPECIFICATIONS

The following specifications are published from the latest information available. This data should be used only in the absence of a decal affixed in the engine compartment.

★ When using a timing light, disconnect vacuum hose or tube at distributor and plug opening in hose or tube so idle speed will not be affected.
● When checking compression, lowest cylinder must be within 80 percent of highest.
▲ Before removing wires from distributor cap, determine location of the No. 1 wire in cap.

Year & Engine	Spark Plug		Firing Order ▲	Ignition Timing BTDC①★		Mark Location	Curb Idle Speed		Fuel Pump Pressure
	Type	Gap		Man. Trans.	Auto. Trans.		Man. Trans.	Auto. Trans.②	
1980									
4-196	RJ-10Y	.035	③	TDC	TDC	Damper	700	700N	4–5½
V-304	RJ-10Y	.035	④	10°⑤	10°⑤	Damper	650	650N	4½–5¾
V-345 Scout	RJ-10Y	.035	④	7½°⑤	7½°⑤	Damper	700	700N	4½–5¾
V-345 Exc. Scout⑥	RJ-6	.030	④	5°⑤	5°⑤	Damper	625–675	625–675N	4½–5¾
V-345 Exc. Scout⑦	RJ-6	.030	④	TDC⑤	TDC⑤	Damper	625–675	625–675N	4½–5¾
V-392	RJ-6	.030	④	TDC⑤	TDC⑤	Damper	625–675	625–675N	4½–5¾
MV-404	RBN-13Y	.030	⑧	9°	9°	Damper	525–575	625–675N	4½–5¾
MV-446	RBN-13Y	.030	⑧	5°	5°	Damper	525–575	625–675N	4½–5¾
V-537	RN-11Y	.030	⑨	7°	7°	Damper	500–550	600–650N	4½–5¾
1979									
4-196	RJ-10Y	.035	③	TDC	TDC	Damper	700	700N	4–5½
V-304	RJ-10Y	.035	④	TDC⑤	TDC⑤	Damper	700	700N	4½–5¾
V-345 Scout	RJ-10Y	.035	④	TDC⑤	TDC⑤	Damper	700	700N	4½–5¾
V-345 Exc. Scout⑥	RJ-6	.030	④	5°⑤	5°⑤	Damper	625–675	625–675N	4½–5¾
V-345 Exc. Scout⑦	RJ-6	.030	④	TDC⑤	TDC⑤	Damper	625–675	625–675N	4½–5¾
V-392	RJ-6	.030	④	TDC⑤	TDC⑤	Damper	625–675	625–675N	4½–5¾
MV-404	RBN-13Y	.030	⑧	9°	9°	Damper	525–575	625–675N	4½–5¾
MV-446	RBN-13Y	.030	⑧	5°	5°	Damper	525–575	625–675N	4½–5¾
V-537	RN-11Y	.030	⑨	7°	7°	Damper	500–550	600–650N	4½–5¾
1978									
4-196	RJ-10Y	.035	③	TDC	TDC	Damper	525–575	525–575N	4–5½
V-304	RJ-10Y	.035	④	TDC⑤	TDC⑤	Damper	650–700	650–700N	4½–5¾
V-345 Exc. Calif.	RJ-6	.030	④	TDC⑤	TDC⑤	Damper	650–700	650–700N	4½–5¾
V-345 Calif.⑥	RJ-6	.030	④	5°⑤	5°⑤	Damper	625–675	625–675N	4½–5¾
V-345 Calif.⑦	RJ-6	.030	④	TDC⑤	TDC⑤	Damper	625–675	625–675N	4½–5¾
V-392 Exc. Calif.	RJ-6	.030	④	TDC⑤	TDC⑤	Damper	650–700	650–700N	4½–5¾
V-392 Calif.	RJ-6	.030	④	TDC⑤	TDC⑤	Damper	625–675	625–675N	4½–5¾
MV-404	RBN-13Y	.030	⑧	9°	9°	Damper	525–575	625–675N	4½–5¾
MV-446	RBN-13Y	.030	⑧	5°	5°	Damper	525–575	625–675N	4½–5¾
V-537	RN-11Y	.030	⑨	7°	7°	Damper	500–550	600–650N	4½–5¾
1977									
4-196	RJ-10Y	.035	③	TDC	TDC	Damper	525–575	525–575N	4–5½
V-304 Exc. Calif.⑩	RJ-10Y	.035	④	TDC⑤	TDC⑤	Damper	650–700	650–700N	4½–5¾
V-304 Calif.	RJ-10Y	.035	④	5°⑤	5°⑤	Damper	600–650	600–650N	4½–5¾
V-345 Exc. Calif.⑩	RJ-6	.030	④	TDC⑤	TDC⑤	Damper	650–700	650–700N	4½–5¾
V-345 Calif.⑥	RJ-6	.030	④	5°⑤	5°⑤	Damper	625–675	625–675N	4½–5¾
V-345 Calif.⑦	RJ-6	.030	④	TDC⑤	TDC⑤	Damper	625–675	625–675N	4½–5¾
V-392 Exc. Calif.⑩	RJ-6	.030	④	TDC⑤	TDC⑤	Damper	650–700	650–700N	4½–5¾
V-392 Calif.	RJ-6	.030	④	TDC⑤	TDC⑤	Damper	625–675	625–675N	4½–5¾
MV-404	RBN-13Y	.030	⑧	9°	9°	Damper	525–575	625–675N	4½–5¾
MV-446	RBN-13Y	.030	⑧	5°	5°	Damper	525–575	625–675N	4½–5¾
V-537	RN-11Y	.030	⑨	7°	7°	Damper	500–550	600–650N	4½–5¾
1976									
4-196	RJ-10Y	.035	③	TDC	TDC	Damper	525–575	525–575N	4–5½
V-304⑩	RJ-6	.030	④	TDC⑤	TDC⑤	Damper	650–700	650–700N	4½–5¾

Continued

INTERNATIONAL

TUNE UP SPECIFICATIONS—Continued

The following specifications are published from the latest information available. This data should be used only in the absence of a decal affixed in the engine compartment.

★ When using a timing light, disconnect vacuum hose or tube at distributor and plug opening in hose or tube so idle speed will not be affected.

● When checking compression, lowest cylinder must be within 80 percent of highest.

▲ Before removing wires from distributor cap, determine location of the No. 1 wire in cap.

Year & Engine	Spark Plug		Ignition Timing BTDC①★				Curb Idle Speed		Fuel Pump Pressure
	Type	Gap	Firing Order ▲	Man. Trans.	Auto Trans.	Mark Location	Man. Trans.	Auto. Trans.②	
1976—Continued									
V-345 Exc. Calif.⑩	RJ-6	.030	④	TDC⑤	TDC⑤	Damper	650–700	650–700N	4½–5¾
V-345 Calif.⑩	RJ-6	.030	④	5°⑤	5°⑤	Damper	625–675	625–675N	4½–5¾
V-392 Exc. Calif.⑩	RJ-6	.030	④	TDC⑤	TDC⑤	Damper	650–700	650–700N	4½–5¾
V-392 Calif.⑩	RJ-6	.030	④	TDC⑤	TDC⑤	Damper	625–675	625–675N	4½–5¾
MV-404	RBN-4	.030	⑧	9°	9°	Damper	525–575	525–575N	4½–5¾
MV-446	RBN-4	.030	⑧	5°	5°	Damper	525–575	525–575N	4½–5¾
V, VS-478⑪	RJ-6	.030	⑨	12°	12°	Damper	500–550	500–550N	4½–5¾
V-537	RN-11Y	.030	⑨	7°	7°	Damper	550–550	500–550N	4½–5¾
V, VS-549⑪	RJ-6	.030	⑨	7°	7°	Damper	550–550	500–550N	4½–5¾
1975									
4-196	RJ-10Y	.035	③	TDC	TDC	Damper	525–575	525–575N	4–5½
V-304⑫	RJ-6	.030	④	TDC⑤	TDC⑤	Damper	650–700	650–700N	4½–5¾
V-345 Exc. Calif.⑫	RJ-6	.030	④	TDC⑤	TDC⑤	Damper	650–700	650–700N	4½–5¾
V-345 Calif.⑫	RJ-6	.030	④	5°⑤	5°⑤	Damper	625–675	625–675N	4½–5¾
V-392 Exc. Calif.⑫	RJ-6	.030	④	TDC⑤	TDC⑤	Damper	650–700	650–700N	4½–5¾
V-392 Calif.⑫	RJ-6	.030	④	TDC⑤	TDC⑤	Damper	⑬	⑬	4½–5¾
MV-404	RBN-4	.030	⑧	9°	9°	Damper	525–575	525–575N	4½–5¾
MV-446	RBN-4	.030	⑧	5°	5°	Damper	525–575	525–575N	4½–5¾
V, VS-478	RJ-6	.030	⑨	12°	12°	Damper	500–550	500–550N	4½–5¾
V-537	RN-11Y	.030	⑨	7°	7°	Damper	500–550	500–550N	4½–5¾
V, VS-549	RJ-6	.030	⑨	7°	7°	Damper	500–550	500–550N	4½–5¾
1974									
4-196	UJ10Y	.030	③	4°	4°	Damper	575	575	4–5½
6-258	N12-Y	.035	⑭	3°	3°	Damper	700	700N	4–5½
V-304	J6	.030	④	TDC⑤	TDC⑤	Damper	675	675N	4½–5¾
V304A	J6	.030	④	TDC⑤	TDC⑤	Damper	675	675N	4½–5¾
V-345	⑬	.030⑯	④	TDC⑤⑰	TDC⑤⑰	Damper	675	675N	4½–5¾
V-392	⑬	.030	④	TDC⑤⑱	TDC⑤⑱	Damper	700	700N	4½–5¾
V-400	J6	.035	④	5°	5°	Damper	700	700N	—
V-401	J6	.027	⑨	7°	7°	Damper	600	600N	4½–5¾
RD-406	J6	.030	⑭	5°	5°	Damper	525	525N	3½–5½
RD-450	J6	.030	⑭	5°	5°	Damper	500㉒	500㉒	3½–5½
V8-478	J6	.027	⑨	10°	10°	Damper	500	500N	4½–5¾
RD-501	J6	.030	⑭	5°	5°	Damper	—	—	3½–5½
V-549	J6	.027	⑨	7°⑲	7°⑲	Damper	—	—	4½–5¾
1973									
4-196	UJ10Y	.030	③	4°	4	Damper	525	525N	4–5½
6-258	N12-Y	.035	⑭	3°	3°	Damper	700	700N	4–5½
V-304	J6	.030	④	TDC⑤	TDC⑤	Damper	700⑳㉓	700N⑳㉓	4½–5¾
V-304A	J6	.030	④	TDC⑤	TDC⑤	Damper	700⑳㉓	700N⑳㉓	4½–5¾
V-345	J6	.030	④	TDC⑤	TDC⑤	Damper	700⑳㉓	700N⑳㉓	4½–5¾
V-392	J6	.030	④	TDC⑤	TDC⑤	Damper	700	700N	4½–5¾
V-400	J6	.035	④	5°	5°	Damper	700	700N	—
V-401	J6	.027	⑨	7°	7°	Damper	600	600N	4½–5¾

Continued

INTERNATIONAL

TUNE UP SPECIFICATIONS—Continued

The following specifications are published from the latest information available. This data should be used only in the absence of a decal affixed in the engine compartment.

★ When using a timing light, disconnect vacuum hose or tube at distributor and plug opening in hose or tube so idle speed will not be affected.
● When checking compression, lowest cylinder must be within 80 percent of highest.
▲ Before removing wires from distributor cap, determine location of the No. 1 wire in cap.

Year & Engine	Spark Plug		Firing Order ▲	Ignition Timing BTDC ①★			Curb Idle Speed		Fuel Pump Pressure
	Type	Gap		Man. Trans.	Auto Trans.	Mark Location	Man. Trans.	Auto. Trans. ②	
1973—Continued									
RD-406	J6	.030	⑭	5°	5°	Damper	525	525N	3½–5½
RD-450	J6	.030	⑭	5°	5°	Damper	500㉒	500N㉒	3½–5½
V-478	J6	.027	⑨	10°	10°	Damper	500	500N	4½–5¾
RD-501	J6	.030	⑭	5°	5°	Damper	—	—	3½–5½
V-549	J6	.027	⑨	7°⑲	7°⑲	Damper	—	—	4½–5¾
1972									
4-196	UJ10Y	.030	③	4°	4°	Damper	700	550D	4–5½
PT-6-232	N14-Y	.035	⑭	TDC	TDC	Damper	—	—	4–5½
6-258	N12-Y	.035	⑭	TDC	TDC	Damper	700	550N	4–5½
V-304	J6	.030	④	TDC⑤	TDC⑤	Damper	475㉒㉓	475D㉒㉓	4½–5¾
V-304A	J6	.030	④	TDC⑤	TDC⑤	Damper	475㉒㉓	475D㉒㉓	4½–5¾
V-345	J6	.030	④	TDC⑤	TDC⑤	Damper	475㉒㉓	475D㉒㉓	4½–5¾
V-392	J6	.030	④	TDC⑤	TDC⑤	Damper	700	550D	4½–5¾
V-401	J6	.027	⑨	7°	7°	Damper	600	600N	4½–5¾
RD-406	J6	.030	⑭	5°	5°	Damper	525	525N	3½–5½
RD-450	J6	.030	⑭	5°	5°	Damper	500㉒	500N㉒	3½–5½
V-478	J6	.027	⑨	10°	10°	Damper	500	500N	4½–5¾
RD-501	J6	.030	⑭	5°	5°	Damper	—	—	3½–5½
V-549	J6	.027	⑨	7°⑲	7°⑲	Damper	—	—	4½–5¾
1971									
4-196	UJ10Y	.030	③	5°	5°	Damper	700	550D	4–5½
PT-6-232	N14Y	.035	⑭	TDC	TDC	Damper	700	550D	4–5½
6-258	N12Y	.035	⑭	TDC	TDC	Damper	—	—	4–5½
V-266	J8	.027	④	4°⑤	4°⑤	Damper			4½–5¾
V-304	J6	.027	④	TDC⑤	TDC⑤	Damper	475㉓㉒	475D㉓㉒	4½–5¾
V-345	J6	.027	④	TDC⑤	TDC⑤	Damper	475㉓㉒	475D㉓㉒	4½–5¾
V-392	J6	.027	④	TDC⑤	TDC⑤	Damper	700	550D	4½–5¾
V-401	J6	.027	⑨	7°	7°	Damper	600	600N	4½–5¾
RD-406	J6	.030	⑭	5°	5°	Damper	525	525N	3½–5½
RD-450	J6	.030	⑭	5°	5°	Damper	500㉒	500N㉒	3½–5½
V-478	J6	.027	⑨	10°	10°	Damper	500	500N	4½–5¾
RD-501	J6	.030	⑭	5°	5°	Damper	—	—	3½–5½
V-549	J6	.027	⑨	7°⑲	7°⑲	Damper	—	—	4½–5¾
1970									
4-196	UJ10Y	.030	③	5°	5°	Damper	700	700N	4–5½
PT-6-232	N14Y	.035	⑭	TDC	TDC	Damper	700	700N	4–5½
6-258	N12Y	.035	⑭	TDC	TDC	Damper	—	—	4–5½
V-266	J8	.027	④	4°⑤	4°⑤	Damper			4½–5¾
V-304	J6	.027	④	TDC⑤	TDC⑤	Damper	475㉓㉒	475D㉓㉒	4½–5¾
V-345	J6	.027	④	TDC⑤	TDC⑤	Damper	475㉒㉓	475D㉒㉓	4½–5¾
V-392	J6	.027	④	TDC⑤	TDC⑤	Damper	700	700N	4½–5¾
V-401	J6	.027	⑨	7°	7°	Damper	600	600N	4½–5¾
RD-406	J6	.030	⑭	5°	5°	Damper	525	525N	3½–5½
RD-450	J6	.030	⑭	5°	5°	Damper	500㉒	500N㉒	3½–5½
V-478	J6	.027	⑨	10°	10°	Damper	500	500N	4½–5¾
RD-501	J6	.030	⑭	5°	5°	Damper	—	—	3½–5½
V-549	J6	.027	⑨	7°⑲	7°⑲	Damper	—	—	4½–5¾

Continued

INTERNATIONAL

TUNE UP SPECIFICATIONS—Continued

①—B.T.D.C.—Before top dead center.
②—N: Neutral; D: Drive.
③—Cylinder numbering front to rear, firing order 1-3-4-2.
④—Cylinder numbering (front to rear), left bank, 1-3-5-7; right bank, 2-4-6-8. Firing order 1-8-4-3-6-5-7-2.
⑤—Timed at No. 8 cylinder, located on right bank, rear of engine.
⑥—Models equipped with Holley 2210C carburetor.
⑦—Models equipped with Holley 2300GLEG carburetor.
⑧—Cylinder numbering (front to rear), right bank, 1-3-5-7; left bank, 2-4-6-8. Firing order, 1-2-7-3-4-5-6-8.
⑨—Cylinder numbering (front to rear), left bank, 1-3-5-7; right bank, 2-4-6-8. Firing order, 1-8-7-3-6-5-4-2.
⑩—Breaker point gap, new .019", used .016"; dwell angle, 24°–34°.
⑪—Breaker point gap, new .017", used .014"; dwell angle, 28°–32°.
⑫—Breaker point gap, .015"; dwell angle, 28°–32°.
⑬—Models equipped with Holley 4150 G carburetor, 625–675N RPM; models equipped with Carter Thermo-Quad carburetor, 650–700N RPM.
⑭—Firing order 1-5-3-6-2-4.
⑮—Scout, 150–500, RJ10Y; 1600–1800, RJ6.
⑯—L.P.G. models .015 inch.
⑰—L.P.G. models 10°; Low compression engine 5°.
⑱—With Thermo Quad Carburetor or Low compression engine, 5°.
⑲—FTVS-549, 9°.
⑳—Carburetor list Nos. 4079-1, 4080-1, 4083-1, 4084-1, 6379, 6391, man. trans. 700 RPM, auto trans. 550 RPM in Drive; List Nos. 4594, 4595 550 RPM in Drive; List Nos. 4574, 4593, 600 RPM; List Nos. 6380, 6386, 6393, 6394, 700 RPM in Neutral with A/C on.
㉑—Calif. 675 RPM in Neutral.
㉒—Carburetor List Nos. 6398, 6398-1, 6438, 525 RPM.
㉓—Four barrel carb. 575 RPM.
㉔—Carburetor List Nos.

DISTRIBUTOR SPECIFICATIONS

Engine Application	Distributor Make	Distributor Model	Rotation Rotor End	Point Gap Inch	Dwell Angle Deg.	Breaker Arm Spring Tension Ounces	Centrifugal Advance Deg. @ Dist. R.P.M. Advance Starts	Centrifugal Advance Deg. @ Dist. R.P.M. Full Advance	Vacuum Advance Inches of Vacuum to Start Advance	Vacuum Advance Max. Adv. Dist. Deg. @ Vacuum
P.T., RD ENGINES										
	Delco-Remy	1110429	C	.019	28–35	17–21	5 @ 400	14 @ 1000	—	—
	Delco-Remy	1110479	CC	.019	31–34	17–21	1 @ 400	14 @ 2000	5 to 7	—
	Delco-Remy	1112276	C	.025	31–37	17–21	1 @ 300	14 @ 1350	—	—
	Delco-Remy	1112288	C	.025	31–37	17–21	1 @ 300	14 @ 1350	—	—
	Delco-Remy	1112293	C	.025	31–37	17–21	1 @ 300	14 @ 1350	—	—
	Delco-Remy	1112321	C	.025	31–37	17–21	1 @ 300	14 @ 1350	—	—
	Delco-Remy	1112324	C	.025	31–37	17–21	1 @ 250	10 @ 900	—	—
	Delco-Remy	1112341	C	.025	31–37	17–21	1 @ 300	14 @ 1350	—	—
	Delco-Remy	1112342	C	.025	31–37	17–21	1 @ 300	14 @ 1350	—	—
	Delco-Remy	1112355	CC	.025	31–37	17–21	1 @ 250	15 @ 1500	3 to 5	7½ @ 14
	Delco-Remy	1112359	C	.025	31–37	17–21	1 @ 300	14 @ 1350	—	—
	Delco-Remy	1112366	C	.025	31–37	17–21	1 @ 300	14 @ 1350	—	—
	Delco-Remy	1112370	C	.025	31–37	17–21	1 @ 300	11 @ 1600	—	—
	Delco-Remy	1112371	C	.025	31–37	17–21	1 @ 300	14 @ 1350	—	—
	Delco-Remy	1112397	C	.025	31–37	17–21	1 @ 225	14 @ 1050	3 to 5	7½ @ 14
	Delco-Remy	1112398	C	.025	31–37	17–21	1 @ 250	10 @ 900	—	—
	Delco-Remy	1112412	C	.025	31–37	17–21	1 @ 300	11 @ 1600	—	—
	Delco-Remy	1112416	CC	.019	28–35	17–21	2 @ 300	12 @ 1100	6 to 8	7½ @ 14
	Delco-Remy	1112417	C	.019	28–35	17–21	1 @ 350	14 @ 1350	—	—
	Delco-Remy	1112422	CC	.019	28–35	17–21	2 @ 300	12 @ 1100	6 to 8	7½ @ 14
	Delco-Remy	1112423	C	.019	28–35	17–21	1 @ 275	11 @ 1600	—	—
	Delco-Remy	1112424	CC	.019	28–35	17–21	1 @ 225	14 @ 1050	6 to 8	7½ @ 14
	Delco-Remy	1112429	C	.019	28–35	17–21	1 @ 300	11 @ 1600	—	—
	Delco-Remy	1112704	C	.019	28–35	17–21	1 @ 350	14 @ 1350	—	—
	Delco-Remy	1112705	C	.019	28–35	17–21	1 @ 300	11 @ 1600	—	—
	Delco-Remy	1112706	C	.019	28–35	17–21	1 @ 300	11 @ 1600	—	—
	Delco-Remy	1112714	C	.019	28–35	17–21	1 @ 350	14 @ 1350	—	—
	Delco-Remy	1112690	CC	.019	31–34	17–21	1 @ 375	15 @ 1350	—	—
	Delco-Remy	1112691	CC	.019	31–34	17–21	1 @ 300	12 @ 1750	—	—
	Delco-Remy	1112692	CC	.019	31–34	19–23	2 @ 350	12 @ 1750	—	—
V8 ENGINES										
V8-266, 304 & 345	Delco-Remy	1110953	C	.016	28–32	17–21	1 @ 350	16 @ 1800	3 to 5	7 @ 10
	Delco-Remy	1110954	C	.016	28–32	17–21	1 @ 350	14 @ 2100	3 to 5	7 @ 10

Continued

INTERNATIONAL

DISTRIBUTOR SPECIFICATIONS—Continued

Engine Application	Distributor Make	Distributor Model	Rotation Rotor End	Point Gap Inch	Dwell Angle Deg.	Breaker Arm Spring Tension Ounces	Centrifugal Advance Deg. @ Dist. R.P.M. Advance Starts	Centrifugal Advance Deg. @ Dist. R.P.M. Full Advance	Vacuum Advance Inches of Vacuum to Start Advance	Vacuum Advance Max. Adv. Dist. Deg. @ Vacuum
V8 ENGINES—Continued										
	Delco-Remy	1110966	C	.016	28–32	17–21	1 @ 350	14 @ 2100	3 to 5	7 @ 10
	Delco-Remy	1110967	C	.016	28–32	17–21	1 @ 350	18 @ 1900	3 to 5	7 @ 10
	Delco-Remy	1111002	C	.016	28–32	17–21	1 @ 350	16 @ 1800	3 to 5	7 @ 10
	Delco-Remy	1112740	C	.016	28–32	17–21	1 @ 350	16 @ 1800	3 to 5	7 @ 10
	Delco-Remy	1112743	C	.016	28–32	17–21	1 @ 350	14 @ 2100	3 to 5	7 @ 10
	Delco-Remy	1112744	C	.016	28–32	17–21	1 @ 350	14 @ 2100	3 to 5	7 @ 10
	Delco-Remy	1112745	C	.016	28–32	17–21	1 @ 350	16 @ 1800	3 to 5	7 @ 10
	Delco-Remy	1112752	C	.016	28–32	17–21	1 @ 350	14 @ 2100	3 to 5	7 @ 10
	Delco-Remy	1112753	C	.016	28–32	17–21	1 @ 350	14 @ 2100	3 to 5	7 @ 10
	Delco-Remy	1112771	C	.016	28–32	17–21	1 @ 375	12 @ 2100	3 to 5	7 @ 10
	Delco-Remy	1112772	C	.016	28–32	17–21	1 @ 375	12 @ 2100	3 to 5	7 @ 10
	Delco-Remy	1112775	C	.016	28–32	17–21	1 @ 375	12 @ 2100	3 to 5	7 @ 10
	Delco-Remy	1112776	C	.016	28–32	17–21	1 @ 350	14 @ 2100	3 to 5	7 @ 10
	Delco-Remy	1112777	C	.016	28–32	17–21	1 @ 350	16 @ 1800	3 to 5	7 @ 10
	Delco-Remy	1112778	C	.016	28–32	17–21	1 @ 350	16 @ 1800	3 to 5	7 @ 10
V-266, 304	Prestolite	285098-C91	—	.017	25–29	17–20	1 @ 350	14 @ 2000	5 to 7	14 @ 11
V-304, 345	Prestolite	285093-C91	—	.017	25–29	17–20	1 @ 350	14 @ 2000	5 to 7	14 @ 11
V-345	Prestolite	285096-C91	—	.017	25–29	17–20	1 @ 350	14 @ 2000	5 to 7	14 @ 11
①	Prestolite	291262-C92	—	②	25–29	17–21	1 @ 350	14½ @ 2000	5 to 7½	7 @ 11½
①	Prestolite	359206-C91	—	②	25–29	17–21	1 @ 350	14½ @ 2000	5 to 7½	7 @ 11½
V-304	Prestolite③	467073-C91③	C	.008④	26–32	—	2 @ 600	16.8 @ 2100	5 to 7	8 @ 15
V-304, 345	Prestolite	291260-C94	—	②	25–29	17–21	1 @ 350	14½ @ 2000	5 to 7½	7 @ 11½
V-304, 345	Prestolite	359217-C91	—	②	25–29	17–21	1 @ 350	14½ @ 2000	5 to 7½	7 @ 11½
V-304, 345	Prestolite	359220-C91	—	②	25–29	17–21	1 @ 350	14½ @ 2000	5 to 7½	7 @ 11½
V-304, 345	Prestolite③	461270-C91③	C	.008④	26–32	—	2 @ 550	16.7 @ 2200	5 to 7	6 @ 15
⑤	Prestolite③	463333-C91③	C	.008④	26–32	—	½ @ 300	14½ @ 2000	5 to 7½	8 @ 15
⑤	Prestolite③	463334-C91③	C	.008④	26–32	—	½ @ 300	17 @ 1800	4¾ to 6¼	8 @ 15
⑤	Prestolite③	463335-C91③	C	.008④	26–32	—	½ @ 300	14½ @ 2000	5 to 7½	8 @ 15
⑤	Prestolite③	463336-C91③	C	.008④	26–32	—	½ @ 300	17 @ 1800	4¾ to 6¼	8 @ 15
V-345	Prestolite③	448685-C91③	C	.014④	22–28	—	½ @ 400	17 @ 2000	5 to 7	4 @ 11
V-345	Prestolite③	461271-C91③	C	.008④	26–32	—	½ @ 400	12.4 @ 2000	5 to 7	6 @ 15
V-345	Prestolite③	461272-C91③	C	.008④	26–32	—	½ @ 400	12.4 @ 2000	5 to 7	6 @ 15
V-345 L.P.G.	Prestolite③	463330-C91③	C	.008④	26–32	—	1 @ 400	12½ @ 2000	5 to 7	8 @ 15
V-345 L.P.G.	Prestolite③	463331-C91③	C	.008④	26–32	—	1 @ 400	12½ @ 2000	5 to 7	8 @ 15
V-345 L.P.G.	Prestolite③	463332-C91③	C	.008④	26–32	—	1 @ 400	12½ @ 2000	5 to 7	8 @ 15
V-392	Prestolite	285092-C91	—	.017	25–29	17–20	1 @ 350	12 @ 2000	5 to 7	14 @ 11
V-392	Prestolite	285095-C91	—	.017	25–29	17–20	1 @ 350	12 @ 2000	5 to 7	14 @ 11
V-392	Prestolite	323418-C93	—	②	25–29	17–21	½ @ 350	12½ @ 2000	5 to 7	7 @ 11
V-392	Prestolite	359218-C91	—	②	25–29	17–21	½ @ 350	12½ @ 2000	5 to 7	7 @ 11
V-392	Prestolite	359221-C91	—	②	25–29	17–21	½ @ 350	12½ @ 2000	5 to 7	7 @ 11
V-392	Prestolite③	448686-C91③	C	.008④	26–32	—	2.7 @ 400	15 @ 2200	5 to 7	6 @ 15
V-392	Prestolite③	461273-C91③	C	.008④	26–32	—	½ @ 400	12.4 @ 2000	5 to 7	6 @ 15
V-392	Prestolite③	467034-C91③	C	.008④	26–32	—	3.6 @ 650	15½ @ 2000	5 to 7	8 @ 15
V-392	Prestolite③	467035-C91③	C	.008④	26–32	—	3.6 @ 650	15½ @ 2000	5 to 7	8 @ 15
V-392	Prestolite③	519861-C91③	C	.008④	26–32	—	½ @ 400	12.4 @ 2000	5 to 7	6 @ 15
V-400	Delco-Remy	1112215	—	.016	29–31	17–21	¾ @ 400	14¼ @ 2000	4 to 6	8¼ @ 13
V-400	Delco-Remy	1112904	—	.016	29–31	17–21	¾ @ 400	14¼ @ 2000	9 to 11	6 @ 15½
MV-404	Prestolite③	446916-C91③	CC	.008④	26–32	—	2 @ 600	12.4 @ 1900	5 to 7	4 @ 12
MV-404	Prestolite③	446920-C91③	CC	.008④	26–32	—	2 @ 600	12.4 @ 1900	5 to 7	4 @ 12
MV-404	Prestolite③	446921-C91③	CC	.008④	26–32	—	2 @ 600	12.4 @ 1900	5 to 7	4 @ 12
MV-446	Prestolite③	446917-C91③	CC	.008④	26–32	—	2 @ 600	12.4 @ 1900	10 to 12	4 @ 15
MV-446	Prestolite③	446918-C91③	CC	.008④	26–32	—	2 @ 600	12.4 @ 1900	10 to 12	4 @ 15

Continued

INTERNATIONAL

DISTRIBUTOR SPECIFICATIONS—Continued

Engine Application	Distributor Make	Distributor Model	Rotation Rotor End	Point Gap Inch	Dwell Angle Deg.	Breaker Arm Spring Tension Ounces	Centrifugal Advance Deg. @ Dist. R.P.M. Advance Starts	Centrifugal Advance Deg. @ Dist. R.P.M. Full Advance	Vacuum Advance Inches of Vacuum to Start Advance	Vacuum Advance Max. Adv. Dist. Deg. @ Vacuum
V8 ENGINES—Continued										
V-401, 549	Holley	1883-1	—	.016	28–32	17–20	1 @ 350	11 @ 1600	6 to 7	7 @ 11
L.P.G.	Holley	2293	—	.016	28–32	17–20	1 @ 350	7 @ 1600	5 to 6	5 @ 10
V-401, 549	Prestolite	286686-C93	—	②	25–29	17–21	½ @ 350	8 @ 1600	5½ to 7½	7 @ 11½
V-401, 549	Prestolite	359223-C91	—	②	25–29	17–21	½ @ 350	8 @ 1600	5½ to 7½	7 @ 11½
V-401, 549	Prestolite	359226-C91	—	②	25–29	17–21	½ @ 350	8 @ 1600	5½ to 7½	7 @ 11½
V-401, 549	Prestolite	359228-C91	—	②	25–29	17–21	½ @ 350	8 @ 1600	5½ to 7½	7 @ 11½
V-401, 549	Prestolite	359230-C91	—	②	25–29	17–21	½ @ 350	8 @ 1600	5½ to 7½	7 @ 11½
V-401, 549	Prestolite	359231-C91	—	②	25–29	17–21	½ @ 350	8 @ 1600	5½ to 7½	7 @ 11½
V-401, 549	Prestolite	359233-C91	—	②	25–29	17–21	½ @ 350	8 @ 1600	5½ to 7½	7 @ 11½
V-478	Prestolite	286684-C93	—	②	25–29	17–21	0 @ 350	12 @ 1600	5½ to 7½	7 @ 11¼
V-478	Prestolite	359227-C91	—	②	25–29	17–21	0 @ 350	12 @ 1600	5½ to 7½	7 @ 11¼
V-478	Prestolite	359229-C91	—	②	25–29	17–21	0 @ 350	12 @ 1600	5½ to 7½	7 @ 11¼
V-478	Prestolite	359232-C91	—	②	25–29	17–21	0 @ 350	12 @ 1600	5½ to 7½	7 @ 11¼
FOUR CYLINDER ENGINES										
4-196	Holley	3857-P	—	.017	42–48	17–20	1 @ 300	16 @ 1800	5 to 7	11 @ 14
4-196	Prestolite③	464359-C91③	C	.008④	26–32	—	5 @ 600	17.8 @ 2200	5 to 7	6 @ 15

①—V-266, 304, 345.
②—New .017", used .014".
③—Electronic breakerless ignition system.
④—Clearance between end of trigger wheel tooth and sensor.
⑤—V-304, 345 & 392 low compression engines.

STARTING MOTOR SPECIFICATIONS

Starter Part No.	Brush Spring Tension, Oz.	Free Speed Test Amperes	Free Speed Test Volts	Free Speed Test R.P.M.	Resistance Test④ Amperes	Resistance Test④ Volts	Lock Torque Test Amperes	Lock Torque Test Volts	Lock Torque Test Torque Ft.-Lbs.
BENDIX DRIVE TYPE									
1108009	24	70①	5.65	5500②	—	—	570	13.5	3.15
1108142	24	70①	11.3	6000②	—	—	530	16	6.7
1108221	24	70①	5.0	3500②	—	—	600	22	3.0
1108312	35	58–80	10.6	6750–10500	280–320	4.0	—	—	—
1108840	36–40	115①	11.6	7000②	—	—	570	20	2.3
1113336	48	30①	23.4	6000②	—	—	200	20	6.6
1113456	28–36	50①	11.5	3600②	—	—	500	34	3.25
1113458	28–36	50①	5.7	2300②	—	—	500	31	3.0
1113460	36	35①	23.5	3500②	—	—	200	28	6.6
1114000	80	75–115	11.5	5600–7600	—	—	600	16.5	2.5
1114089	80	75–115	11.5	5600–7600	—	—	600	16.5	2.5
DYER DRIVE TYPE									
1109715	36–40	100①	23	8000②	—	—	525	32	3.0
1113708	80	60–90	23	7000–10700	—	—	500	26	3.5
1113709	80	60–90	23	7000–10700	—	—	500	26	3.5
1113781	80	60–90	23	7000–10700	—	—	500	26	3.5
1113823	80	60–90	23	7000–10700	—	—	500	26	3.5
ENCLOSED SHIFT LEVER TYPE (Standard)									
1107220	35	55–80③	9	3500–6000	300–360	3.5	—	—	—
1107678	35	50–80③	9	5500–10500	270–310	4.3	—	—	—
1107679	35	55–80③	9	3500–6000	300–360	3.5	—	—	—
1107680	35	50–80③	9	3500–10500	300–360	3.5	—	—	—
1107709	35	50–80③	9	5500–10500	270–310	4.3	—	—	—
1107710	35	55–80③	9	3500–6000	300–360	3.5	—	—	—
1107742	35	40–105③	9	3500–6500	300–360	3.5	—	—	—

Continued

INTERNATIONAL

STARTING MOTOR SPECIFICATIONS—Continued

Starter Part No.	Brush Spring Tension, Oz.	Free Speed Test			Resistance Test ④		Lock Torque Test		
		Amperes	Volts	R.P.M.	Amperes	Volts	Amperes	Volts	Torque Ft.-Lbs.
EXPOSED SHIFT LEVER TYPE (Standard)—Continued									
1108233	—	20–30 ③	20	2250–2750	—	—	—	—	—
1108238	35	40–75 ③	20	3300–5600	385–435	15.0	—	—	—
1108278	—	50–80 ③	9	5500–10500	—	—	—	—	—
1108341	35	50–80 ③	9	5500–10500	300–360	3.5	—	—	—
1108384	35	50–80 ③	9	5500–10500	270–310	4.3	—	—	—
1108478	—	50–80 ③	9	5500–10500	—	—	—	—	—
1108515	—	50–80 ③	9	5500–10500	—	—	—	—	—
ENCLOSED SHIFT LEVER TYPE (Heavy Duty)									
1109630	—	95–120 ③	20	5500–7500	—	—	—	—	—
1109989	—	95–120 ③	20	5500–7500	—	—	—	—	—
1113167	80	57–70	9	3500–5500	—	—	500	22	3.4
1113172	80	57–70	9	3500–5500	—	—	500	22	3.4
1113217	—	50–70 ③	9	3500–5500	—	—	—	—	—
1113218	—	50–70 ③	9	3500–5500	—	—	—	—	—
1113626	80	75–105 ③	9	5000–7000	—	—	600	20	2.2
1113644	80	75–105 ③	9	5000–7000	—	—	600	20	2.2
1113655	80	75–105 ③	9	5000–7000	—	—	600	20	2.2
1113820	80	75–95 ③	20	5500–7500	—	—	500	26	3.5
1113914	80	75–95 ③	20	5500–7500	—	—	500	26	3.5
1113969	—	75–95 ③	20	5500–7500	—	—	—	—	—
1114052	80	120–150 ③	9	3000–4500	—	—	600	16.5	2.5
1114058	—	140–190 ③	9	4000–7000	—	—	—	—	—
114064	80	120–150 ③	9	3000–4500	—	—	600	19	2.5
1114066	80	120–150 ③	9	3000–4500	—	—	600	16.5	2.5
1114070	80	140–190 ③	9	4000–7000	—	—	700	15	1.5
1114071	80	120–150 ③	9	3000–4500	—	—	600	19	2.5
1114074	80	140–190 ③	9	4000–7000	—	—	700	15	1.5
1114076	80	140–190 ③	9	4000–7000	—	—	700	15	1.5
1114085	80	120–150 ③	9	3000–4500	—	—	600	16.5	2.5
1114088	80	140–190 ③	9	4000–7000	—	—	700	15	1.5
1114098	80	140–190 ③	9	4000–7000	—	—	700	15	1.5
1114102	80	140–190 ③	9	4000–7000	—	—	700	15	1.5
1114107	80	120–150 ③	9	3000–4500	—	—	600	16.5	2.5
1114112	—	120–150 ③	9	3000–4500	—	—	—	—	—
1114113	80	140–190 ③	9	4000–7000	—	—	700	15	1.5
1114116	80	120–150 ③	9	3000–4500	—	—	600	16.5	2.5
1114120	80	140–190 ③	9	4000–7000	—	—	700	15	1.5
1114122	80	120–150 ③	9	3000–4500	—	—	600	16.5	2.5
1114127	—	140–190 ③	9	4000–7000	—	—	—	—	—
1114128	—	140–190 ③	9	4000–7000	—	—	—	—	—
1114134	—	140–190 ③	9	4000–7000	—	—	—	—	—
1114145	—	140–190 ③	9	4000–7000	—	—	—	—	—
1114161	—	140–190 ③	9	4000–7000	—	—	—	—	—
1114165	—	140–190 ③	9	4000–7000	—	—	—	—	—
1114168	—	120–150 ③	9	3000–4500	—	—	—	—	—
1114171	—	140–190 ③	9	4000–7000	—	—	—	—	—
1114176	—	140–190 ③	9	4000–7000	—	—	—	—	—
1114180	—	120–150 ③	9	3000–4500	—	—	—	—	—
1114187	—	120–150 ③	9	3000–4500	—	—	—	—	—
1114189	—	120–150 ③	9	3000–4500	—	—	—	—	—
1114196	—	120–150 ③	9	3000–4500	—	—	—	—	—
1114197	—	140–190 ③	9	4000–7000	—	—	—	—	—

Continued

INTERNATIONAL

STARTING MOTOR SPECIFICATIONS—Continued

Starter Part No.	Brush Spring Tension, Oz.	Free Speed Test			Resistance Test④		Lock Torque Test		
		Amperes	Volts	R.P.M.	Amperes	Volts	Amperes	Volts	Torque Ft.-Lbs.
EXPOSED SHIFT LEVER TYPE									
1107156	24	70①	5.65	5500②	—	—	550	11	3.25
1107168	24	80①③	5.6	5500②	—	—	550	11	3.3
1107218	35	91①	10.6	3240②	330–395	3.5	—	—	—
1107689	35	112①	10.6	3240②	320–385	3.5	—	—	—
1108033	24	80①	5.67	5500②	—	—	600	14	3.0
1108042	24	80①	5.67	5500②	—	—	600	14	3.0
1108051	24	80①	5.67	5500②	—	—	600	14	3.0
1108153	24	70①	11.3	6000②	—	—	530	16	6.7
1108157	24	70①	11.3	6000②	—	—	530	16	6.7
1108161	24	70①	11.3	6000②	—	—	530	16	6.7
1108233	24	35①	23.5	2500②	—	—	265	19	19.1
1109930	24	35①	23.5	2500②	—	—	265	19	19.1
1109941	24	35①	23.5	2500②	—	—	265	19	19.1
1113001	28–36	50①	11.5	8000②	—	—	500	22	3.25
1113039	28–36	50①	5.7	5000②	—	—	500	21	3.0
1113040	28–36	50①	11.5	8000②	—	—	500	22	3.25
1113070	48	57–70③	11.5	5000–7400	—	—	500	22	3.4
1113081	48	57–70③	11.5	5000–7400	—	—	500	22	3.4
1113098	48	57–70③	11.5	5000–7400	—	—	500	22	3.4
1113108	28	32–40③	23.5	5800–6800	—	—	250	19.5	8.0
1113109	28	32–40③	23.5	5800–6800	—	—	250	19.5	8.0

①—Maximum.
②—Minimum.
③—Includes solenoid.
④—Check capacity of motor by using a 500 ampere meter and a carbon pile rheostat to control voltage. Apply volts listed across motor with armature locked. Amperage should be as listed.

ALTERNATOR & REGULATOR SPECIFICATIONS

Model	Alternator				Regulator						
	Field Current @ 80°F. 12 Volts	Cold Output @ 14 V		Rated Hot Output Amperes	Model	Field Relay			Voltage Regulator		
		Amperes @ 2000 R.P.M.	Amperes @ 5000 R.P.M.			Air Gap	Point Gap	Closing Voltage	Air Gap	Point Gap	Volts @ 125° F.
1100072⑥	4.4–4.9	45	57	65	Integral	—	—	—	—	—	13.2–14.4
1100073⑥	4.4–4.9	54	73	80	Integral	—	—	—	—	—	13.2–14.4
1100544⑥	—	—	—	37	Integral	—	—	—	—	—	13.3–15.6
1100588⑥	—	—	—	61	Integral	—	—	—	—	—	13.3–15.6
1100628⑥	1.90–2.30	25	35	37	1119507	.015	.030	3.8–7.2	.067	.014	13.5–14.4
1100629⑥	1.90–2.30	28	40	42	—	—	—	—	—	—	—
1100630⑥	1.90–2.30	21	30	32	—	—	—	—	—	—	—
1100633⑥	1.90–2.30	32	50	52	1119507	.015	.030	3.8–7.2	.067	.014	13.5–14.4
1100687⑥	2.2–2.6	21	30	32	—	—	—	—	—	—	—
1100688⑥	2.2–2.6	25	35	37	—	—	—	—	—	—	—
1100689⑥	2.2–2.6	28	40	42	—	—	—	—	—	—	—
1100690⑥	2.2–2.6	32	50	55	—	—	—	—	—	—	—
1100750⑥	2.2–2.6	33	58	61	—	—	—	—	—	—	—
1117070⑥	6.00–6.60	31①	58②	60	9000554	.014	.030	3.8–7.2	.075	—	13.2–14.2
1117078⑥	6.00–6.60	31①	58②	60	9000552	.014	.027	5.0–9.5	.075	—	13.2–14.2
1117089⑥	6.00–6.60	31①	58②	60	9000552	.014	.027	5.0–9.5	.075	—	13.2–14.2
1117090⑥	6.00–6.60	24③	80②	85	—	—	—	—	—	—	—
1117096⑥	3.60–4.00	23⑤	61②	60	—	—	—	—	—	—	—
1117115⑥	1.23–1.33	32③	98②	105	—	—	—	—	—	—	—
1117128⑥	2.22–2.40	40③	126②	130	—	—	—	—	—	—	—
1117143⑥	4.0–4.5	—	150	145	Integral	—	—	—	—	—	13.2–14.4
1117225⑥	4.1–4.5	—	77	75	—	—	—	—	—	—	—
1117753⑥	2.10–2.40	14③	55④	55	1119500	.015	.015	6.5–8.5	.067	.016	13.5–14.4

Continued

INTERNATIONAL

ALTERNATOR & REGULATOR SPECIFICATIONS—Continued

	Alternator				Regulator						
	Field Current @ 80°F. 12 Volts	Cold Output @ 14 V		Rated Hot Output Amperes		Field Relay			Voltage Regulator		
Model		Amperes @ 2000 R.P.M.	Amperes @ 5000 R.P.M.		Model	Air Gap	Point Gap	Closing Voltage	Air Gap	Point Gap	Volts @ 125° F.
1117754⑥	3.70–4.40	18③	62④	62	9000595	.015	.027	2.3–3.5	.075	—	13.2–14.2
1117756⑥	3.70–4.40	18③	62④	62	9000567	.014	.027	5.0–9.5	.075	—	13.2–14.2
8AL2026F⑦	1.8–2.5	—	—	37	8RD2001	—	—	—	—	—	13.3–13.95
8AL2033L⑦	1.8–2.5	—	—	42	8RD2001	—	—	—	—	—	13.3–13.95
513303-C91⑥	—	—	—	85	Integral	—	—	—	—	—	—
513542-C91⑧	2.9	—	—	105	Integral	—	—	—	—	—	—
514089-C91⑧	2.9	—	—	65	Integral	—	—	—	—	—	—
514251-C91⑧	—	—	—	130	Integral	—	—	—	—	—	—
517368-C91⑧	—	—	—	75	Integral	—	—	—	—	—	—
520443-C91⑧	2.9	—	—	105	Integral	—	—	—	—	—	—
521092-C91⑧	2.9	—	—	105	Integral	—	—	—	—	—	—

① —At 1000 R.P.M.
② —At 2500 R.P.M.
③ —At 1100 R.P.M.
④ —At 6500 R.P.M.
⑤ —At 5000 R.P.M.
⑥ —Delco-Remy.
⑦ —Motorola.
⑧ —Leece Neville.

GENERATOR & REGULATOR SPECIFICATIONS

★ To polarize generator, connect jumper wire from "hot" side of battery to armature terminal of generator.

	Generator					Regulator					
Gen. No. ①	Rotation and Ground Polarity ③	Brush Spring Tension, Oz.	Rated Cap. Amps.	Gen. Field Ground Location★	Field Current	Reg. No. ①	Cutout Relay		Voltage Setting	Current Setting	Current & Voltage Regulator Armature Air Gap, Inch
							Closing Voltage	Arm. Air Gap, In.			
1100337	C-N	28	25	External	1.50–1.62	1119000	12.2	.020	14.5	25	.075
1100374	C-N	28	25	External	1.50–1.62	1119000	12.6	.020	14.2	25	.075
1102005	C-P	28	30	External	1.48–1.62	1118839	12.2	.020	14.5	30	.075
1102034	C-N	28	30	External	1.48–1.62	1119001	12.6	.020	14.3	30	.075
11102044	C-N	28	30	External	1.48–1.62	1119003	12.2	.020	14.5	30	.075
1102169	C-N	28	20	External	1.62–1.82	1119245	12.6	.020	14.3	23	.075
1102182	C-N	28	20	External	1.62–1.82	1119245	12.6	.020	14.3	23	.075
1102191	C-N	28	30	External	1.69–1.79	1119001	12.6	.020	14.3	30	.075
1105008	C-P	28	50	External	1.77–1.93	1118838	12.2	.020	14.2	50	.075
1105876	C-N	28	25	External	1.62–1.82	1119000	12.2	.020	14.5	25	.075
1105941	C-N	28	20	External	1.54–1.67	1118902	12.2	.020	14.5	20	.075
1105946	C-N	28	25	External	1.54–1.67	1119000	12.2	.020	14.5	25	.075
1106805	CC-P	20	50	External	1.37–1.50	1118880	12.2	.020	14.2	50	.075
1106821	C-P	20	40	External	1.37–1.50	1118886	12.2	.020	14.5	40	.075
1106822	C-N	20	50	External	1.37–1.50	1119156	12.2	.020	14.2	50	.075
1106822	C-N	20	50	External	1.37–1.50	1118881	12.6	.020	14.2	50	.075
1106822	C-P	20	50	External	1.37–1.50	1118838	12.6	.020	14.2	50	.075
1106826	C-P	20	50	External	1.37–1.50	1118838	12.6	.020	14.2	50	.075
1106986	C-N	20	50	External	2.14–2.28	1119606	12.4	.020	14.2	50	②
1106987	C-N	28	35	External	2.14–2.28	1119611	12.2	.020	14.3	35	④

① —Stamped on plate riveted to housing or regulator base.
② —Current regulator air gap .075", voltage regulator gap .080".
③ —C—Clockwise. CC—Counterclockwise. N—Negative. P—Positive.
④ —Current regulator air gap .075", voltage regulator gap .067".

INTERNATIONAL

PISTON, PIN, RING, CRANKSHAFT & BEARING SPECIFICATIONS

Year	Engine Model	Wristpin Diameter	Piston Clearance, Inch	Ring End Gap, In. (Minimum) Comp.	Ring End Gap, In. (Minimum) Oil	Crank Pin Diameter, Inch	Rod Bearing Clearance, In.	Main Bearing Journal Diameter, In.	Main Bearing Clearance, Inch	Thrust On Bearing No.	Shaft End Play
1970	4-196	1.0624	.0035	.010	⑤	2.373–2.374	.0011–.0032	2.7484–2.7494	.001–.004	3	.001–.005
1971–77	4-196	1.0624	.0035	.013	.013	2.373–2.374	.0011–.0036	2.7484–2.7494	.001–.004	3	.003–.008
1970–74	6-258	.9306	.0009	.010	.015	2.0934–2.0955	.001–.002	2.4981–2.5001	.001–.002	3	.0015–.007
1970–74	RD-406	1.109	④	.025	.013	2.751–2.752	.0012–.0037	2.2495–2.2505	.0013–.0043	7	.006–.015
	RD-450	1.109	④	.025	.013	2.751–2.752	.0012–.0037	3.2495–3.2505	.0013–.0043	7	.006–.015
	RD-501	1.109	④	.025	.013	2.751–2.752	.0012–.0037	3.2495–3.2505	.0013–.0043	7	.006–.015
1970–71	V-266	1.0624	.0035	.010	⑤	2.373–2.374	.0011–.0033	2.7484–2.7494	.001–.004	3	.001–.005
	V-304	1.0624	.0035	.010	⑤	2.373–2.374	.0011–.0033	2.7484–2.7494	.001–.004	3	.001–.005
	V-345	1.0624	.0035	.010	⑤	2.373–2.374	.0011–.0033	2.7484–2.7494	.001–.004	3	.001–.005
1972–77	V-304	1.11248	.004	.010	⑤	2.373–2.374	.0009–.0034	2.7484–2.7494	.001–.004	3	.002–.010
1972–77	V-345	1.11248	.004	.010	⑤	2.373–2.374	.0009–.0034	2.7484–2.7494	.001–.004	3	.002–.010
1970–71	V-392	1.0624	.0035	.010	⑤	2.373–2.374	.0011–.0033	2.7484–2.7494	.001–.004	3	.001–.005
1972–77	V-392	1.11248	.004	.013	②	2.373–2.374	.0009–.0034	2.7484–2.7494	.001–.004	3	.002–.010
1973–74	V-400	1.006	.0010	.010	③	2.2485–2.2464	.001–.002	2.7474–2.7489	.001–.002	3	.003–.008
1970–71	V-401	1.312	.0035	.013	①	2.623–2.624	.0017–.0042	3.123–3.124	.0014–.0044	3	.004–.009
1972–74	VS-401	1.3118	.002	.013	.013	2.623–2.624	.0017–.0042	3.124–3.125	.0008–.0038	3	.006–.001
1975–77	MV-404	1.200	.0012	.013	.013	2.4980–2.4990	.0011–.0036	3.1228–3.1236	.0010–.0036		.0025–.0085
1975–77	MV-446	1.200	.0012	.013	.013	2.4980–2.4990	.0011–.0036	3.1228–3.1236	.0010–.0036		.0025–.0085
1970–71	V-478	1.312	.0035	.013	①	2.623–2.624	.0017–.0042	3.123–3.124	.0014–.0044	3	.004–.009
1972–75	VS-478	1.3118	.002	.013	.013	2.623–2.624	.0017–.0042	3.124–3.125	.0008–.0038	3	.006–.011
1970–71	V-549	1.312	.0035	.013	①	2.623–2.624	.0017–.0042	3.123–3.124	.0014–.0044	3	.004–.009
1972–77	VS-549	1.3118	.002	.013	.013	2.623–2.624	.0017–.0042	3.124–3.125	.0008–.0038	3	.006–.011
1970–71	PT-6-232	.9306	.0005	.010	⑤	2.0934–2.0955	.001–.002	2.4981–2.5001	.001–.002	3	.0015–.007

①—U-Flex ring-no clearance. Chrome face type .013".
②—No gap at ring joint. Steel rail gap .013 inch.
③—No gap at ring joint. Steel rail gap .0015 inch.
④—Top of skirt .0045 inch, bottom .002 inch.
⑤—No gap at ring joint. Steel rail gap .015".

VALVE SPECIFICATIONS

Engine Model	Valve Lash	Valve Angles Seat	Valve Angles Face	Valve Springs Installed Height	Valve Springs Pressure Lbs. @ In.	Valve Stem Clearance Intake	Valve Stem Clearance Exhaust	Stem Diameter, Std. Intake	Stem Diameter, Std. Exhaust
4-196	Zero①	②	②	③	188 @ 1.42	.001–.0035	.0015–.004	.372–.373	.414–.415
6-232	Zero①	④	④	—	195 @ 1⁷⁄₁₆	.001–.003	.001–.003	.3715–.3725	.3715–.3725
6-258	Zero①	④	④	—	195 @ 1⁷⁄₁₆	.001–.003	.001–.003	.3715–.3725	.3715–.3725
V-266	Zero①	45°	45°	—	195 @ 1¹³⁄₃₂	—	—	—	—
V-304	Zero①	45°	45°	³¹⁄₃₂	188 @ 1.429	.001–.0035	.0015–.004	.372–.373	.3715–.3725
V-304A	Zero①	45°	45°	⑤	188 @ 1.429	.001–.0035	.0015–.004	.372–.373	.3715–.3725
V-345	Zero①	45°	45°	⑤	188 @ 1.429	.001–.0035	.0015–.004	.372–.373	.3715–.3725
V-392	Zero①	45°	45°	③	188 @ 1.429	.001–.0035	.0015–.004	.372–.373	.3715–.3725
V-400	Zero①	⑥	⑥	—	⑦	.001–.003	.001–.003	.3715–.3725	.3715–.3725
V-401	Zero①	⑧	⑧	—	116 @ 1.663	.001–.0035	.0025–.0045	.434–.435	.433–.434
MV-404	Zero①	45°	45°	—	188 @ 1.429	.0011–.0028	.00165–.00235	.3721–.3728	.37165–.37235
RD-406	.024–.026H	⑧	⑧	—	137 @ 1⁴⁵⁄₆₄	.0015–.004	.002–.0045	.434–.435	.4335–.4345
MV-446	Zero①	45°	45°	—	188 @ 1.429	.0011–.00285	.00165–.00235	.3721–.3728	.37165–.37235
RD-450	.024–.026H	⑧	⑧	—	137 @ 1⁴⁵⁄₆₄	.0015–.004	.002–.0045	.434–.435	.4335–.4345
V-478	Zero①	⑧	⑧	—	116 @ 1.663	.001–.0035	.0025–.0045	.434–.435	.433–.434
RD-501	.024–.026H	⑧	⑧	—	137 @ 1⁴⁵⁄₆₄	.0015–.004	.002–.0045	.434–.435	.4335–.4345
V-537	Zero①	⑧	⑧	—	200 @ 1.39	.0016–.0034	.002–.0037	.4341–.4349	.4338–.4345
V-549	Zero①	⑧	⑧	—	116 @ 1.663	.001–.0035	.0025–.0045	.434–.435	.433–.434

①—Hydraulic lifters.
②—Intake, 30°; Exhaust 45°.
③—Intake, ³¹⁄₃₂; Exhaust 1¹¹⁄₆₄.
④—Intake, 30°; Exhaust 44°.
⑤—Intake, ³¹⁄₃₂; Exhaust 1³⁄₃₂.
⑥—Intake, 29°; Exhaust 44°.
⑦—Intake, 218 @ 1.365; Exhaust 218 @ 1.183.
⑧—Intake, 15°; Exhaust 45°.

INTERNATIONAL

ENGINE TIGHTENING SPECIFICATIONS★

★ Torque specifications are for clean and lightly lubricated threads only. Dry or dirty threads produce increased friction which prevents accurate measurement of tightness.

Engine	Spark Plugs Ft. Lbs.	Cylinder Head Bolts Ft. Lbs.	Intake Manifold Ft. Lbs.	Exhaust Manifold Ft. Lbs.	Rocker Arm Shaft Bracket Ft. Lbs.	Rocker Arm Cover Ft. Lbs.	Connecting Rod Cap Bolts Ft. Lbs.	Main Bearing Cap Bolts Ft. Lbs.	Flywheel to Crankshaft Ft. Lbs.	Vibration Damper or Pulley Ft. Lbs.
4-196 ⑤	28–30	90–100	40–45	40–45	14–16	—	45–55	75–80	45–55	100–110
4-196 ⑥	28–30	110	25–30	25–30	14–16	—	45–50	75–85	45–55	100–110
6-258	25–30	80–85	20–25	20–25	20–33	—	26–30	75–85	100–110	70–80
RD-372	28–30	100–110 ②	25–30	25–30	25–30	—	65–75	110–110	150–160	①
RD-406	28–30	100–110 ②	25–30	25–30	25–30	—	65–75	100–110	150–160	①
RD-450	28–30	100–110 ②	25–30	25–30	25–30	—	65–75	100–110	150–160	①
RD-501	28–30	100–110 ②	25–30	25–30	25–30	—	65–75	100–110	150–160	①
V-266	28–30	90–100	40–45	40–45	—	—	45–55	75–85	45–55	100–110 ③
V-304, 345	28–30	90–100	40–45	40–45	—	—	45–55	75–85	45–55	100–110 ③
V-392	28–30	90–100	40–45	40–45	—	—	40–45	75–85	45–55	100–110 ③
V-400	28	110	43	25	—	—	38	100	105	55
V-401	28–30	90–100	—	—	80–90 ⑦	—	60–70	100–110	90–100	①
MV-404	15	100–110	—	15–21	18–22 ⑦	4–7	42–46	70–90	—	80–100
MV-446	15	100–110	—	15–21	18–22 ⑦	4–7	42–46	70–90	—	80–100
V-478	28–30	90–100	—	—	80–90	—	60–70	100–110	90–100	①
V-549	28–30	90–100	—	—	80–90	—	60–70	100–110	90–100	①
PT-6-232	25–30	80–85	20–25	20–25	20–23	45–55 ④	26–30	75–85	100–110	70–80

① —Pressed on.
② —Oil supply bolt 75–85.
③ —Pulley hub bolt.
④ —Inch pounds.
⑤ —Prior to engine serial No. 37396.
⑥ —Engine serial No. 37396 & after.
⑦ —Rocker arm cap screw.

WHEEL ALIGNMENT SPECIFICATIONS

Front Axle Model ①	Caster, Degrees	Camber, Degrees	Toe-In, Inch	Kingpin Inclination, Degrees	Front Axle Model ①	Caster, Degrees	Camber, Degrees	Toe-In, Inch	Kingpin Inclination, Degrees
FA-1	1–3	1–2	0–1/8	4	FA-46	−1 to +1	1	0–1/8	8½
FA-3	0–1	1	0–1/8	8½	FA-48	⑨	½	0–1/8	4
FA-4	3	1½	0–3/16	7	FA-50	2–3	1	1/16–1/8	4
FA-5	⑤	⑤	⑤	—	FA-51	1–2	1½	1/32–3/32	8
FA-6	⑤	⑤	⑤	—	FA-52	1° 36′	1½	1/32–1/16	8
FA-7	⑤	⑤	⑤	—	FA-54	0	1½	1/32–1/16	8
FA-8	⑬	+½ to +1½	1/8–3/16	8	FA-57	2° 59′	Zero	1/16–1/8	—
FA-9	⑬	+½ to +1½	1/8–3/16	8	FA-58	2° 59′	1½	1/32–1/16	8
FA-10	2½–3½	1–2	0–1/8	4	FA-59	2° 59′	Zero	1/16–1/8	—
FA-11	0	1½	1/8	7½	FA-60	2–3	1	1/16–1/8	4
FA-12	⑨	½	0–1/8	4	FA-62	−1 to +1	1	0–1/8	8½
FA-13	0–1	1	0–1/8	8½	FA-63	−1 to +1	1	0–1/8	8½
FA-14	0	1½	1/8	7½	FA-65	2–3	1	1/16–1/8	4
FA-15	½	1½	1/8–3/16	7½	FA-68	1–3	½	0–1/8	4
FA-16	½	1½	1/2–3/16	7½	FA-69	⑦	½	1/16–3/16	4
FA-18	½	1½	1/8–3/16	8	FA-70	2–3	1	1/16–1/8	4
FA-19	½	1½	1/8–3/16		FA-71	2	½	0–1/8	⑥
FA-20	2–3	1	1/16–1/8	4	FA-72	2	½	1/16	4
FA-21	0	1½	1/8	7½	FA-73	2	½	0–1/8	⑥
FA-24	0	1½	1/8	7½	FA-74	⑦	½	1/16–3/16	⑥
FA-25	½	1½	1/8–3/16	8	FA-80	2–3	1	1/16–1/8	4
FA-28	⑩	½	0–1/8	4	FA-90	2–3	1	1/16–1/8	4
FA-30	2–3	1	1/16–1/8	4	FA-91	2	½	0–1/8	4
FA-40	2–3	1	1/16–1/8	4	FA-98	⑪	½	0–1/8	4
FA-41	2–3	1	1/16–1/8	4	FA-99	⑦	½	1/8–3/16	4
FA-43	−1 to +1	1	0–1/8	8½	FA-100	2–3	1	1/16–1/8	5½
FA-44	−1 to +1	1	0–1/8	8½	FA-101	⑫	½	0–1/8	⑥
FA-45	−1 to +1	1	0–1/8	8½					

Continued

INTERNATIONAL

WHEEL ALIGNMENT SPECIFICATIONS—Continued

Front Axle Model①	Caster, Degrees	Camber, Degrees	Toe-In, Inch	Kingpin Inclination, Degrees	Front Axle Model①	Caster, Degrees	Camber, Degrees	Toe-In, Inch	Kingpin Inclination, Degrees
FA-103	⑦	1/2	1/16–3/16	⑥	FA-228	2	1/2	0–1/8	5 1/2
FA-105	2–3	1	3/16–1/4	5 1/2	FA-229	2	1/2	0–1/8	5 1/2
FA-109	1	⑧	0–1/8	⑥	FA-230	—	—	—	—
FA-110	2–3	1	1/16–1/8	5 1/2	FA-231	—	—	—	—
FA-111	2–3②	1	3/16–1/4 ③	5 1/2	FA-232	—	—	—	—
FA-112	1/2–1 1/2④	1	1/16–1/8	1	FA-233	—	—	—	—
FA-113	1/2–1 1/2④	1	1/16–1/8	0	FA-239	—	—	—	—
FA-115	2–3②	1	3/16–1/4 ③	5 1/2	FA-309	1	⑧	0–1/8	⑥
FA-130	2–3	1	1/16–1/8	4	FA-329	1	⑧	0–1/8	⑥
FA-132	1/2–1 1/2	—	1/16–1/8	8	FA-339	1	⑧	0–1/8	⑥
FA-133	1/2–1 1/2	—	1/16–1/8	8	FA-340	1	⑧	0–1/8	⑥
FA-136	2	1/2	0–1/8	5 1/2					
FA-139	1	⑧	0–1/8	⑥					
FA-140	2–3	Zero	1/16–1/8	—					
FA-182	2–3	1	0–1/8	5 1/2					
FA-208	2–3	1	3/16–1/4	5 1/2					
FA-209	⑦	1/2	1/16–3/16	5 1/2					
FA-211	2–3	1	3/16–1/4	5 1/2					
FA-215	2–3	1	3/16–1/4	5 1/2					
FA-218	2–3	1	3/16–1/4	5 1/2					
FA-219	4 1/2	1/2	1/16–3/16	5 1/2					
FA-225	2	1/2	0–1/8	5 1/2					

①—Model is given on aluminized paper plate glued in truck cab.
②—Emeryville models 1/2–1 1/2 pos.
③—Emeryville models 1/16–1/8".
④—Center point steering 1/2–2° neg.
⑤—Refer to the wheel alignment procedure in the "Torsion Bar Suspension & Steering Gear" Section.
⑥—Left 4 1/4, right 4 1/2.
⑦—Manual Steering 3°, power steering 4 1/2°.
⑧—Left 1/4°, right 0°.
⑨—Except Motor Home +2°, Motor Home +4°.
⑩—Except Motor Home and Metro +1°, Motor Home +4°, Metro +3°.
⑪—Except Fleet Star 4 × 4 (+2°), Fleet Star 4 × 4 (+4°).
⑫—Except Fleet Star 6 × 4 (+2°), Fleet Star 6 × 4 (+4°).
⑬—Manual Steering −1°, Power Steering zero.

Engine Section

ENGINE, REPLACE

CAUTION: If the truck is equipped with LPG fuel system, be sure that the tank valves are tightly closed and all fuel is exhausted from the lines before starting any repair work on the fuel system.

Any trucks of this type which have been involved in an accident should not be brought into the shop for repair until the tanks and system is checked for possible leaks.

PT-6-232, 258

1. Drain cooling system and crankcase and disconnect battery ground cable.
2. Remove hood, radiator hoses and radiator.
3. Remove carburetor air cleaner and disconnect fuel line at fuel pump.
4. Disconnect exhaust pipe at manifold. Disconnect carburetor throttle and choke linkages.
5. Disconnect wiring harnesses from alternator, starter, temperature and oil pressure sending units and ignition coil.
6. Remove starter motor.
7. Disconnect power brake vacuum hose, power steering lines and freon compressor lines, if so equipped.
8. Disconnect vacuum line from rear of intake manifold.
9. Remove automatic transmission filler tube support if so equipped.
10. Attach lifting sling to engine and raise engine enough to remove load from engine mounts. Disconnect mounting brackets from crossmember.
11. Remove flywheel housing front cover. Remove five flywheel housing-to-crankcase bolts.
12. The engine must be pulled forward to clear the transmission main drive gear and clutch disc then raised and lifted out of the chassis.

NOTE: Use extreme care while removing engine to avoid damaging the clutch disc.

13. Reverse procedure to install.

V8 Engines

The engine is removed as an assembly complete with accessories, less the carburetor air cleaner. The transmission is separated from the engine at the flywheel housing. Drain the cooling system; drain points are located one on each side and toward the front of the cylinder block and the lower left of the radiator. Drain engine oil. Disconnect battery ground cable and tape the end of the terminal to avoid accidental grounding.

On V8-401, 461, 478, 549, tapped holes at the rear of the intake manifold and engine front cover are provided for lifting eye bolts.

On V8-266, 304, 345, 392, the engine lifting fixture can be attached to the intake manifold by utilizing the carburetor mounting capscrews with flat washers. *When installing the lifting fixture, the capscrews are to be installed finger tight; then tighten the capscrews one-half additional turn.*

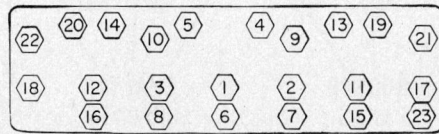

Fig. 1 Cylinder head tightening sequence. RD engines

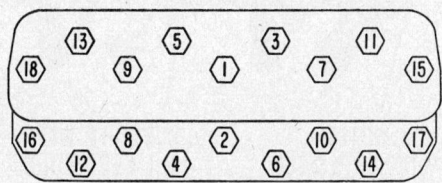

Fig. 2 Cylinder head tightening sequence. V-401, 478, 549

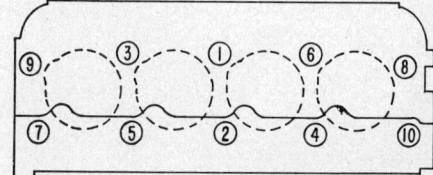

Fig. 3 Cylinder head tightening sequence. 4-196, V-266, 304, 345, 392 & MV 404, 446

INTERNATIONAL

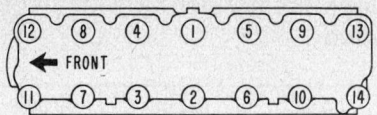

Fig. 4 Cylinder head tightening sequence. PT-6-232, 258

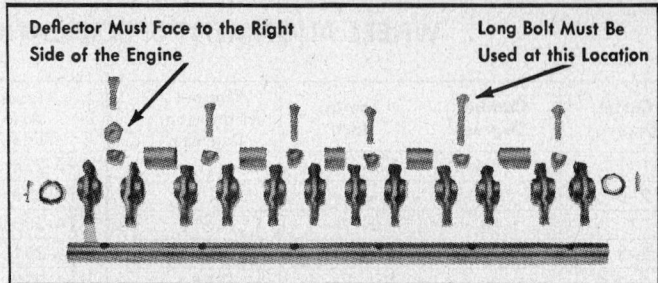

Fig. 5 Rocker arm assembly. Early PT-6-232, 258

4-196 Engines

1. Drain cooling system, crankcase and disconnect battery ground cable.
2. Remove fan blade, radiator, and other parts such as radiator cross braces, heater air ducts, etc., which may interfere with engine removal.
3. Remove carburetor linkage and engine wiring.
4. Remove fuel line from pump.
5. Disconnect exhaust pipe from manifold.
6. Install lifting fixture on engine.
7. Hoist engine enough to support it while disconnecting engine front mountings.
8. Separate engine from transmission by separating transmission from flywheel housing or flywheel housing from rear of engine.
9. Pull engine forward to clear clutch from transmission main drive gear shaft. Then tilt engine upward and remove from chassis.

RD Engines

1. Drain engine oil and cooling system.
2. Disconnect upper and lower hoses.
3. Remove air cleaner.
4. Disconnect vacuum line at manifold or air line at compressor when equipped with air brakes.
5. Disconnect coil wire, starter cable, engine ground strap and instrument sender unit wires.
6. Disconnect fuel line at fuel pump.
7. Disconnect throttle control linkage and remove choke wire at carburetor.
8. Remove hood and floor boards.
9. Remove fenders and grille as a unit.
10. Unfasten and remove radiator and its support.
11. Remove engine front mounting bolts from support bracket. These are the bolts at the front cross member.
12. Support transmission with floor jack or blocking. Then remove cap screws from around bell housing.
13. Disconnect exhaust pipe from manifold.
14. Attach engine sling to front and rear right side cylinder head bolts and remove engine from chassis.
15. Reverse procedure to install.

CYLINDER HEAD, REPLACE

All Engines

Cylinder heads should be tightened down by starting from the center, working outward from side to side and to the ends in the sequence shown in Figs. 1 to 4.

PT-6-232

CAUTION: The cylinder head bolt located at the left front corner of the head (No. 11, Fig. 4) must have the threads sealed to prevent cooling system leakage. Permatex No. 2 or equivalent is recommended.

ROCKER ARM SERVICE

Early PT-6-232, 258

The pressure supply for each rocker arm is obtained from No. 5 camshaft bearing located where the camshaft meters the flow of oil from the main lubrication gallery through a groove in the camshaft bearing surface to a gallery extending upwards to the cylinder head gasket surface. When installing the rocker arm shaft the oil holes must face down to the cylinder head, Fig. 5.

Late 6-232, 258

As shown in Fig. 6, the rocker arm assembly consists of a pair of rocker arms and one rocker arm bracket for each cylinder. When disassembling, keep parts in order to assure reassembly in their original position if in satisfactory condition.

4-196 Engines

As shown in Fig. 7, the rocker arm assembly consists of the shaft, shaft supports, rocker arms and spacers. The rocker arms are lubricated by oil supplied to the hollow shaft through an oil passage in one of the supports.

Formation of sludge in the oil passages of the rocker arms and shaft will restrict flow of oil to the rocker arm bushings and valves. Therefore, each time the assembly is removed, it should be disassembled and cleaned thoroughly.

When disassembling, keep parts in order to assure reassembly in their original position if in satisfactory condition.

If necessary to remove plugs from each end of shaft, drill or pierce one plug, then knock out the opposite plug with a steel rod. Working from the other end, knock out other plug.

When reassembling, lubricate rocker arm bushings with engine oil. Make sure the notches at ends of rocker arm shaft are up. Be sure to position the rocker arm support having the oil feed hole so that the oil hole will index with the oil feed hole in the cylinder head (third from rear, Fig. 7).

NOTE: Before installing push rods in 4-196

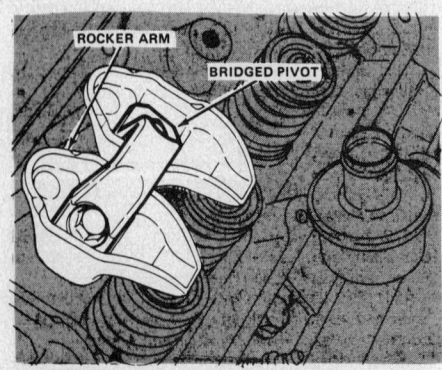

Fig. 6 Rocker arm removal. Late 6-232, 258

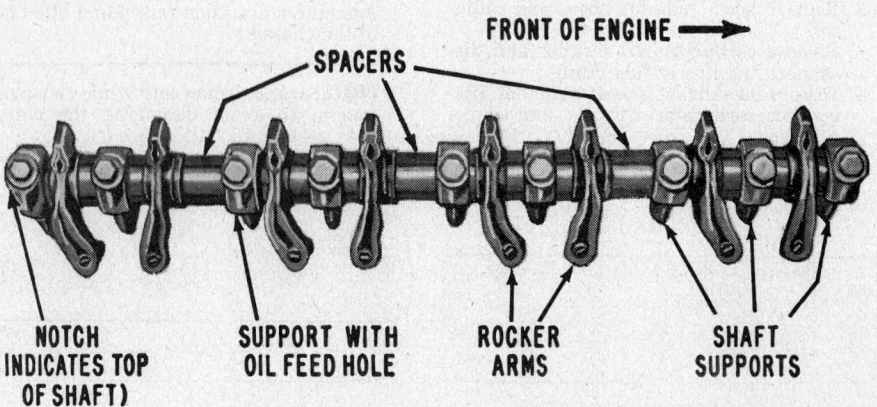

Fig. 7 Rocker arm assembly on 196 engines

INTERNATIONAL

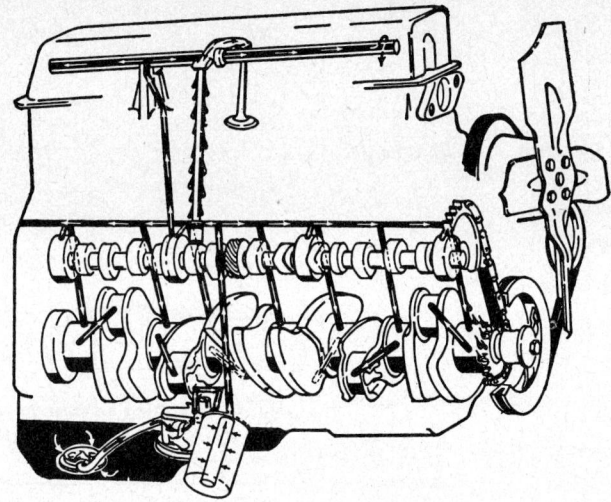

Engine lubrication. PT-6-232, 258

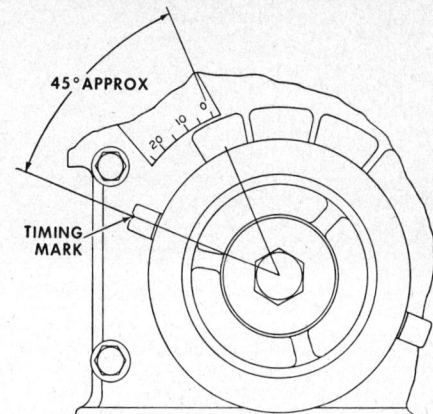

Fig. 8 Correct position of crankshaft pulley when installing push rod on 4-196.

engines, rotate the crankshaft to position the crankshaft pulley hub as shown in Fig. 8. This is to prevent possible damage to engine parts if the hydraulic lifters have not leaked down to operating position.

V-266, 304, 345, 392 Engines

When assembling the rocker arms, Fig. 9, make sure the notches at the end of the rocker arm shaft are facing upward. Also make sure the rocker arm shaft support incorporating the oil feed hole is located *third from rear on right bank and third from front on left bank*. Rocker arm shaft assemblies are interchangeable from one bank to another. Make sure rocker arms are correctly positioned to actuate the valves. Check all push rods for straightness by rolling on a flat surface. Replace any that are bent or have loose ends.

V-401, 478, 549 Engines

The rocker arm assemblies, Fig. 10, are removed from the engine as a unit. After removing the hair pin retaining rings and spring washers from the ends of the shaft, the shafts may be stripped of arms, springs and supports. Keep parts in order so they may be replaced in their original position if in satisfactory condition. Remove plugs from ends of shafts and clean all parts thoroughly, making sure all oil passages are open.

When assembling, make sure rocker arms are correctly positioned to actuate the valves. Be sure the rocker arm end supports incorporate the dowel sleeves for alignment to cylinder head.

MV-404, 446 Engines

The rocker arms on these engines are individually mounted and are retained by flange head bolts and pivot balls. Install the rocker arm components in original position.

Inspect the pivot surfaces of the rocker arms and pivot balls for signs of scuffing, pitting or excessive wear. Inspect the valve stem contact surface of the rocker arms for pitting. Replace any component found unsatisfactory.

RD Engines

The rocker arm assembly, Fig. 11, is composed of front and rear shafts joined at the center, on which are mounted the twelve rocker arms and four tension springs. The shafts are mounted on seven brackets, and are prevented from turning at the two center brackets which contain locking washers fitting into slots in the shaft. *Note that the third bolt from the rear on the left side of the cylinder head is drilled with an oil hole which supplies oil to the rocker arms.*

Inspect the component parts of the assembly as outlined for BD engines. And when new bushings are installed in the rocker arms they should be burnished and reamed to provide a clearance of .0015–.004″. Ream dimension is .8745–.8760″.

VALVE ROTATORS

RD Engines

The parts involved in the rotating mechanism are a special spring seat retainer, a pair of flat halfmoon keys, a close fitting cap located on the valve stem, and a specially constructed valve stem, Fig. 12.

In order to accomodate valve expansion, the valve lash must be maintained. When camshaft rotation causes this lash or clearance to be taken up, the cap on the valve stem causes the valve keys to lower the spring retainer, removing the load of the valve springs from the valve *before* the valve is raised from its seat. A clearance of .002–.006″ should be maintained between the end face of the valve stem and cap, Fig. 12. This is the distance the spring retainer is lowered *before* the valve is moved. The slow valve rotating motion is caused by vibration of the valve, the flowing of exhaust gases around the valve head, and a slight rotating motion imparted to the valve by the valve spring.

Whenever valve work is done, check the clearance, using the special gauge shown in Fig. 13. If there is no clearance, grind off the end of the valve stem. If the clearance is too great, grind off the open end of the valve cap.

4-196 & V8 Engines Exc. 400, 404, 446

The "Roto Cap" valve rotator may be used on the intake valve or both valves. 4-152, 196 and V8-304, 345 and 392 engines have the "Roto Cap" on the intake valve, Fig. 14. V8-401, 461, 478 and 549 engines, use the "Roto Cap" on both valves.

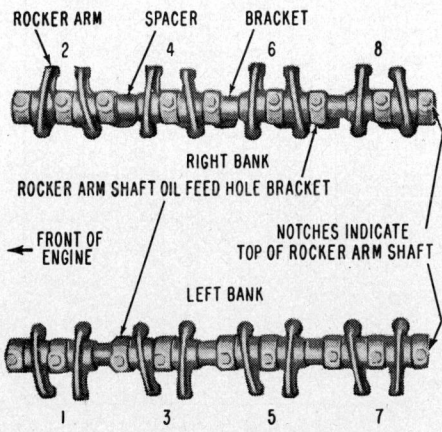

Fig. 9 Rocker arm assemblies. V-266, 304, 345, 392

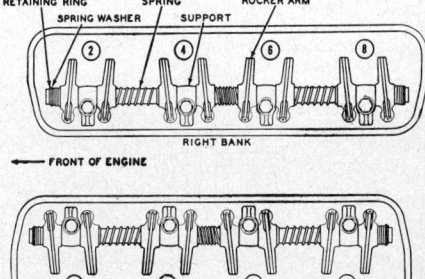

Fig. 10 Installation of rocker arms. V-401, 478, 549

INTERNATIONAL

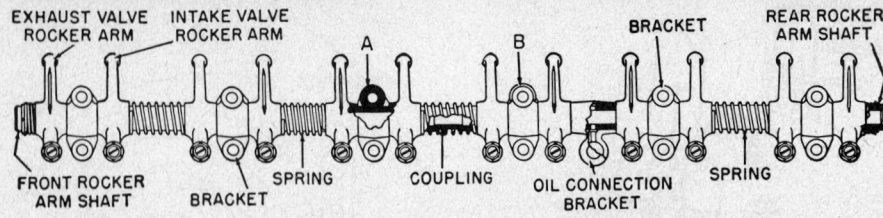

Fig. 11   Rocker arm assembly. RD engines

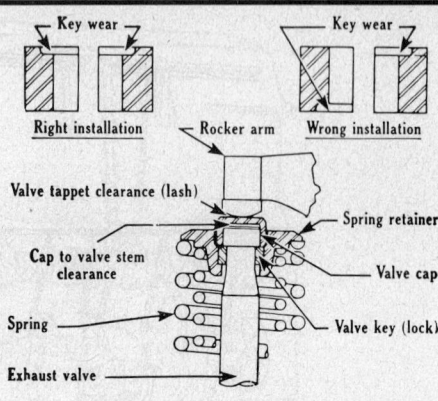

Fig. 12   Rotating exhaust valve mechanism. RD engines

VALVE GUIDES
PT-6-232, 258

Using a micrometer and a suitable telescope hole gauge, check the diameter of the valve stem in three places (top, center and bottom). Insert telescope hole gauge in valve guide bore, measuring at the center. Subtract the highest reading of valve stem diameter from valve guide bore center diameter to obtain valve-to-guide clearance. If clearance is not within specified limits, use the next oversize valve and ream bore to fit. Valves with oversize stems are available in .003", .015" and .030". Valve-to-guide clearance should be .001"–.003".

VALVE GUIDES, REPLACE

Clean valve guides with a suitable cleaning tool. Then check each valve guide with a "GO and NO-GO" gauge, if available; otherwise, use a new valve to check the fit. If the "NO-GO" portion of the gauge enters, the guide must be replaced.

Replacement is recommended for valve guides with diameters exceeding specifications, bell-mouthed more than .0005 inch or guides which are out-of round.

New guides should be installed so that the distance from the cylinder head to the top of the guide is as follows.

4-196 Intake	31/32"
4-196 Exhaust	1 11/64"
V-266	31/32"
V-304, V-345, V-392 Intake	31/32"
V-304, V-345 Exhaust	1 3/32"
V-392 Exhaust	1 11/64"
V-401, 461, 478, 549 Intake	1"
V-401, 461, 478, 549 Exhaust	1 1/16"
MV-404, 446 Intake	27/32"
MV-404, 446 Exhaust	1 1/8"
RD-406, 450, 501 Intake	1 1/16"
RD-406, 450, 501 Exhaust	1"

When guides are properly installed, they should be reamed to the following diameters:

4-196	.376–.377"
V-266, 304, 345	.374–.3755"
V-401, 461, 478, 549	.4365–.4380"
MV-404, 446	.374–.375"
RD	.4365–.4380"

VALVE LIFTERS
4-196, PT-6-232, 258 & V8 Engines

Hydraulic valve lifters, Figs. 15 and 16, are removed from the engine as an assembly. The lifters are removed by removing the valve cover, rocker arm and shaft assembly, then lifting out the push rods. If a lifter cannot be removed due to carbon build-up, use a carburetor solvent in the lifter bore. However, if an excessive amount of solvent is used, it will be necessary to change the engine oil. The lifters are also accessible by removal of the lifter covers.

As shown in Figs. 15 and 16, different designs of hydraulic lifters are used. When disassembling, do not mix the components of any lifter. Service kits of component parts are available for both types of lifters.

RD Engines

These lifters are of the mushroom type operating in guide holes bored in the cylinder block. To remove lifters, therefore, it is necessary to take out the camshaft and remove the lifters through the bottom of the engine.

The valve lifter bores have spring-loaded retainers in the block, Fig. 17, which are used to hold up the lifters when pulling out the camshaft. When the lifter is pushed up the retainer snaps into the groove at the top of the lifter. After the camshaft is installed, the lifters may be pushed down into position by the push rods.

TIMING GEARS OR CHAIN

When valves are correctly timed, the timing marks on the gears or sprockets should be adjacent to each other. Figs. 18 thru 21.

CAMSHAFT & BEARINGS
All Engines

Camshaft bearings should be installed in sets and care must be exercised to see that the oil holes in the bearings and the oil feed holes in the block are aligned to assure adequate lubrication.

Service Note

4-196 & V8-304, 345, 392

Camshaft bushings must be installed so as to provide running clearance between valve lifters and bushings as shown in Fig. 22.

PISTONS & RODS, ASSEMBLE
V-304, 345, 392

When assembling connecting rod to piston, the rod bearing tangs will be towards side of piston (marked "up"). It is important that piston and rod are assembled correctly so that when piston is installed in engine the chamfered side of each rod is located against the crankshaft face.

When installing piston in engine, position side of piston (marked "up") towards engine center line. Install bearing cap with corresponding number on same side as number on connecting rod. Torque connecting bolts to specifications as listed under "Engine Tightening Specifications."

CAUTION: If bolt is over tightened it must be replaced.

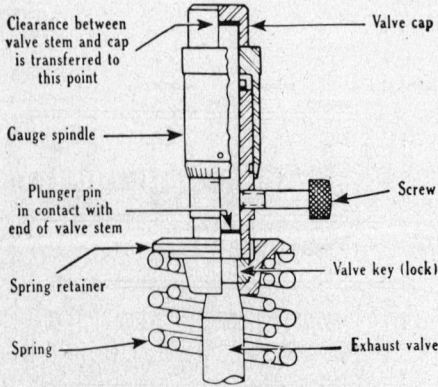

Fig. 13   Showing use of special gauge for checking clearance between valve stem and cap. RD engines

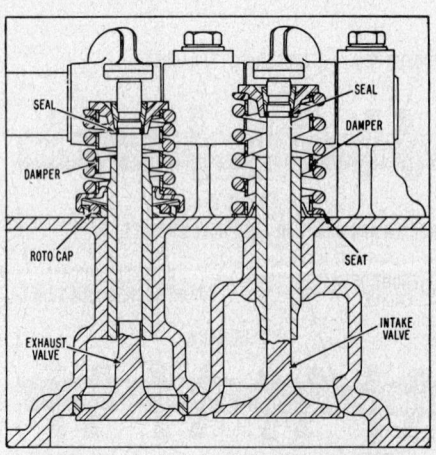

Fig. 14   Valves & related parts. 4-196 & V8-304, 345 & 392 (Typical of V8-401, 478 & 549)

INTERNATIONAL

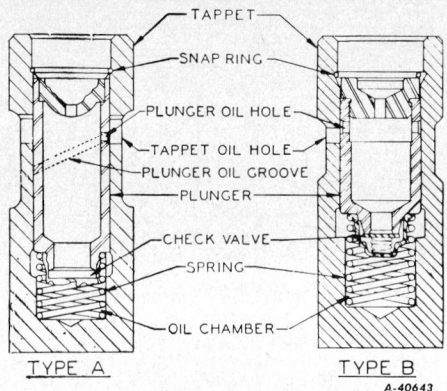

Fig. 15 Hydraulic valve lifters. V-401, 478, 549

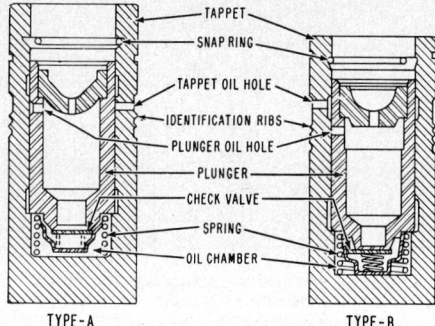

Fig. 16 Hydraulic valve lifters. V-266, 304, 345, 392

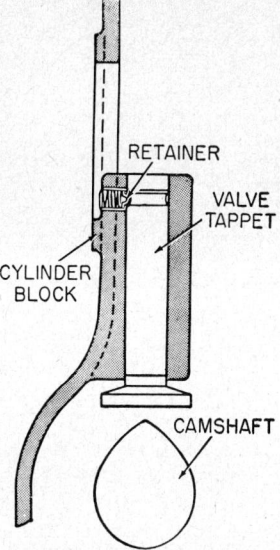

Fig. 17 Tappet and guide construction. RD engines

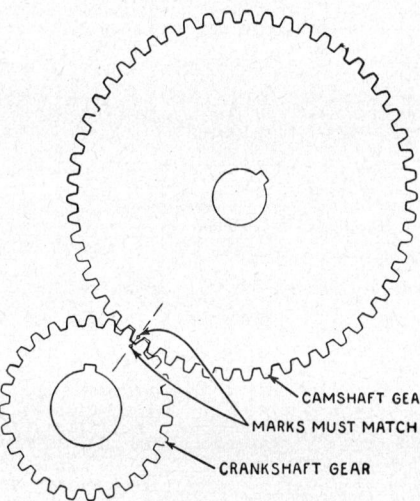

Fig. 18 Valve timing on 6 cylinder engines except PT-6-232

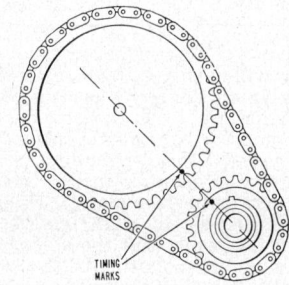

Fig. 19 Valve timing. PT-6-232, 258

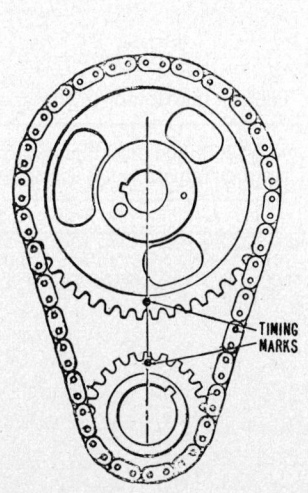

Fig. 20 Valve timing marks. V8-400

MV-404, 446

Before disassembling, mark piston on same side as large chamfer on connecting rod, so they can be assembled in the same position. New pistons may be installed either way on connecting rod.

When installing piston in engine the large chamfered side of each connecting rod must be located against the crankshaft face. The chamfer provides clearance at the crankshaft fillet.

V8-401, 478, 549 Engines

For correct assembly of the connecting rod to the piston, the rod bearing tangs will be toward the domed side of the piston (marked "up") for proper installation, Fig. 23. This is important in that the rod and piston must be assembled correctly so that when the piston is installed in the engine the chamfered side of each rod is located against the crankshaft face. The chamfer provides clearance at the crankshaft fillet.

Place the piston in a piston vise, and with the piston heated to approximately 200°, in a piston heater or boiling water, position the rod in the piston and install the piston pin.

6-Cyl. Engines

On RD engines, the step on the piston head must be installed in the cylinder on the side opposite to the camshaft, Fig. 24.

On PT-6-232, 232, 258 engines, assemble the piston and rod so that the notch in the piston head faces the front of the engine and the numbered side of the rod faces the camshaft side of the engine, Fig. 25.

4-196 Engines

For correct assembly of the connecting rod to the piston, the rod bearing locators (bearing tangs) must be toward the dome side (marked "up") of the piston. And when installed in the cylinder, the word "up" on the piston goes toward the top (camshaft) side of the engine.

CRANKSHAFT OIL SEAL, REPLACE

196 Engines

The rear main bearing oil seal can be replaced with the engine in the chassis by first removing the transmission, clutch and flywheel.

Position rear bearing oil seal on pilot No. SE-1942-2, then position pilot on installer No. SE-1942-1. Place installer and seal over crankshaft, drive seal into bore until flush with engine.

V8's and 6-Cyl.

Crankshaft rear bearing oil seal consists of two pieces of special packing. One piece is installed in the groove in the rear bearing cap and the other piece is installed in a similar groove in the cylinder block.

Position the rear bearing seal in the groove in the cylinder block. Lay an improvised mandrel in the bearing bore and strike the mandrel with a hammer to drive the seal into the groove. Install the seal in the bearing cap in a similar manner. Using a sharp knife, cut off both ends of each seal which project out of the grooves. When cutting off the ends of the seals, do not leave frayed ends which would prevent proper seating of the bearing cap if the ends should extend between cap and cylinder block.

OIL PUMP REPAIRS

196, V8's and 6-Cyl.

Conventional gear type oil pumps, located in the crankcase, are used on all engines.

1225

INTERNATIONAL

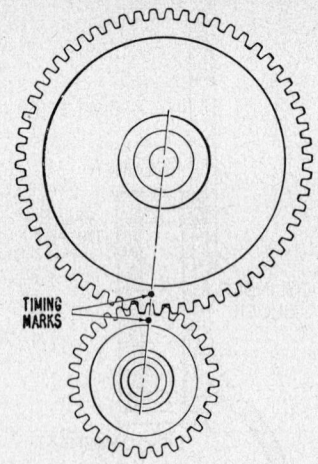

Fig. 21 Valve timing marks. V8 exc. 400

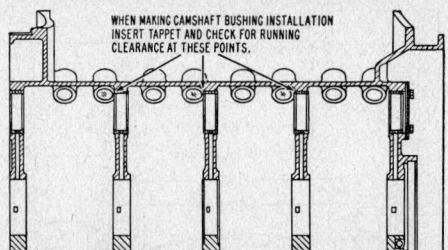

Fig. 22 Checking clearance between valve lifters and camshaft bearings. 4-196 & V8-304, 345, 392

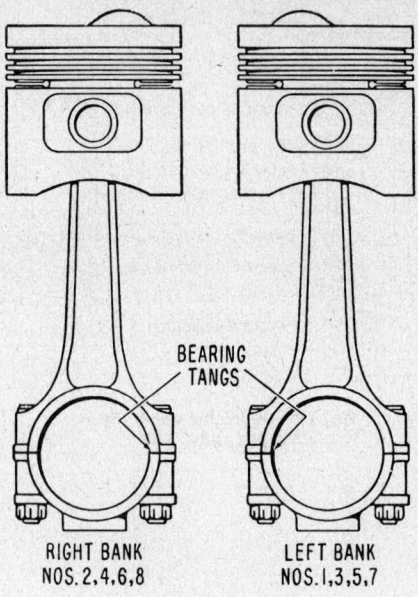

Fig. 23 Correct assembly of pistons and rods. V8-401, 478, 549 engines

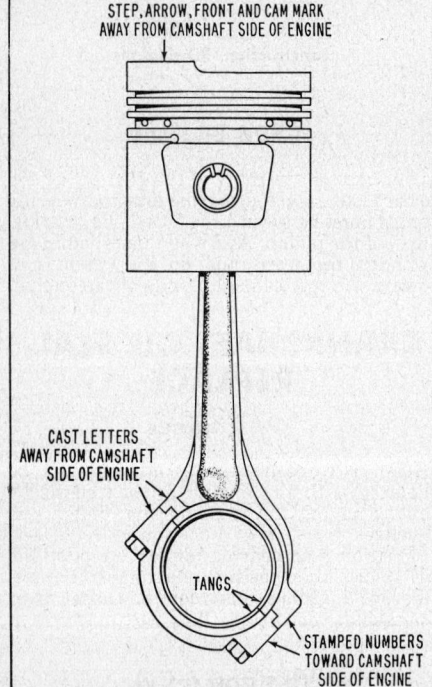

Fig. 25 Piston and rod assembly. PT-6-232, 258

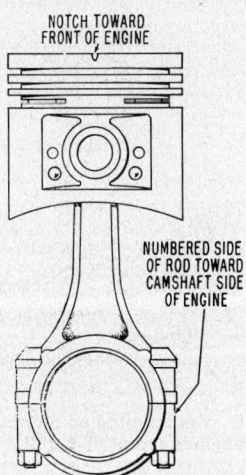

Fig. 24 Piston and rod assembly. RD engines

down on a surface plate with emery if necessary. Place the bottom cover on the pump and check the drive shaft end play. If end play is excessive (more than .006"), replace the drive and idler gears.

NOTE: Whenever the oil pump is removed, the distributor will have to be taken off as well in order to reinstall the pump without damage. The reason for this is that the slots in the end of the oil pump drive shafts must match the tangs on the end of the distributor drive shaft. If an attempt is made to install the pump while the distributor is in place, it will be difficult or impossible to align the slots and tangs with the result that the pump will be damaged when its mounting bolts are tightened. Be sure to retime the ignition when the oil pump and distributor are installed.

IGNITION TIMING

If a timing light is to be used to set ignition timing, disconnect the vacuum advance pipe to the carburetor and place a piece of tape over end of pipe. *This is important as carburetor trouble can affect timing adjustments.*

Lacking a power timing light, an accurate method of setting ignition timing with the engine stopped is with the aid of a jumper light. Be sure to use a light bulb that corresponds with the system voltage of the vehicle.

1. Remove distributor cap and rotor and see that the breaker gap is set according to specifications.
2. Rotate engine until No. 1 cylinder is at the ignition timing point as indicated by the timing pointer and timing mark being lined up with each other.
3. Connect the jumper light between distributor ignition terminal and ground.
4. Turn on ignition switch.
5. Loosen distributor and turn it in the direction of normal rotation until the points just close (light out). Then slowly turn distributor in the opposite direction just to the exact point that the light goes on. Tighten distributor in this position.

NOTE: On V-266, 304, 345 and 392 engines, connect timing light to No. 8 spark plug.

After removing the oil pan, the pump may be removed from its mounting and disassembled for repairs.

Inspect the pump gears for nicks or burrs. Inspect the bottom cover for wear and dress

INTERNATIONAL

Carburetor Section
CARBURETOR ADJUSTMENT SPECIFICATIONS

Carb. Make	Carb. Model	Carb. Part No.	Engine Application	Float Level (Dry)	Fuel Level (Wet)	Idle Mix. Screws Turns Open	Pump Link Position	Dashpot Clearance	Fast Idle Setting	Idle CO %
Carter	TQ	6550S, 6591S	V-345	1.06	—	—	Inner	⑨	.089–.109	1.5
		6551S	V-392	1.06	—	—	Inner	⑨	.089–.109	1.5
		6590S, 6592S	V-392	1.06	—	—	Inner	⑨	.089–.109	1.5
Holley	852-FFG	2691-A	RD-450	1¼	—	½	Center	—	—	—
		2410-1	V-461	1¼	—	½–¾	Center	—	—	—
		2409-2	V-401, VS-401	1¼	—	⅞–1⅛	Center	—	—	—
		3806	V-478, VS-478	1¼	—	½–¾	Center	—	—	—
		4329, 4330	RD-450	1¼	⅝	1½–2	#2 Hole	—	—	3
		4378, 4438	V-401, VS-401	1¼	⅝	1½–2	#2 Hole	—	—	3
		4679	V-401, VS-401	1¼	⅝	1½–2	—	—	—	3
		4331, 4332	V-478, VS-478	1¼	⅝	1½–2	#2 Hole	—	—	3
		4333, 4377	V-478, VS-478	1¼	⅝	1½–2	#2 Hole	—	—	3
Holley	2140-C	864-1	RD-501	¼	—	⅜–⅝	See Text	—	—	—
		977	RD-501	¼	—	⅜–⅝	See Text	—	—	—
		987-2	V-549	¼	—	1⅞–2⅛	See Text	—	—	—
		1348-1	V-549	¼	—	1⅞–2⅛	See Text	—	—	—
		2407	V-549	¼	—	1⅞–2⅛	See Text	—	—	—
		2408	V-549	¼	—	1⅞–2⅛	See Text	—	—	—
		2461	V-549	¼	—	1⅞–2⅛	See Text	—	—	—
		2486	V-549	¼	—	1⅞–2⅛	See Text	—	—	—
Holley	2140-G	4334, 4335	RD-501	¼	½	⅞	#2 Hole	—	—	3
		4334	RD-501	¼	½	⅞	#2 Hole	—	—	3
		864-1	RD-501	¼	½	⅞	#2 Hole	—	—	3
		977	RD-501	¼	½	⅞	#2 Hole	—	—	3
		4337, 4338	V-549, VS-549	¼	½	1½–2	#2 Hole	—	—	3
		4339, 4340	V-549, VS-549	¼	½	1½–2	#2 Hole	—	—	3
		4341	V-549, VS-549	¼	½	1½–2	#2 Hole	—	—	3
		4635	V-549, VS-549	¼	½	1½–2	#2 Hole	—	—	3
		4636	V-549, VS-549	¼	½	1½–2	#2 Hole	—	—	3
		4342, 4343	FTV, FTVS-549	¼	½	1½–2	#2 Hole	—	—	3
		4634, 4633	FTV-FTVS-549	¼	½	1½–2	#2 Hole	—	—	3
Holley	885-FFG	126582	RD-372	7/32	—	1¼–1¾	Center	—	—	—
		126583	RD-406	7/32	—	1–1½	Center	—	—	—
		260612	RD-406, 450	7/32	—	1–1½	Center	—	—	—
		4327	RD-406	7/32	½	1½–2	#2 Hole	—	—	3
		4328	RD-406	7/32	½	1½–2	#2 Hole	—	—	3
Holley	1904	3716	4-196	See Text	—	1	—	—	—	—
		3842	4-196E	See Text	—	1	—	—	—	—
Holley	1920	3993-1, 4487	4-196	—	27/32⑧	3	#2 Hole	.125–.155	—	—
		4591	4-196	—	27/32⑧	3	#2 Hole	.075–.125	—	—
		4405	6-232	—	27/32⑧	3	#2 Hole	.105–.135	—	—
		4542	6-232	—	27/32⑧	3	#2 Hole	—	—	—
Holley	1940C	6442	6-258	—	11/16	—	—	.070–.090	—	1.5
Holley	2210C	6443	V-304, 345	13/64①	½	—	—	.070–.090	—	1.5
		6443-1	V-304, 345	13/64①	½	—	—	.070–.090	—	1.5
		6776	V-304, 345	13/64①	½	—	—	.070–.090	—	1.5
		6620	V-345	13/64①	½	—	—	—	—	2
		6674-1	V-400	13/64①	½	—	—	.070–.090	—	1.5

Continued

INTERNATIONAL

CARBURETOR ADJUSTMENT SPECIFICATIONS—Continued

Carb. Make	Carb. Model	Carb. Part No.	Engine Application	Float Level (Dry)	Fuel Level (Wet)	Idle Mix. Screws Turns Open	Pump Link Position	Dashpot Clearance	Fast Idle Setting	Idle CO %
Holley	2300	1710	V-266, 304	—	3/8 ③	3/4	#1 Hole	1/16	—	⑥
		2977-2	V-304, 345	—	3/8 ③	3	—	.090–.120	⑤	⑥
		1710-4	V-304, 345	—	3/8 ③	3	—	.090–.120	⑤	⑥
		3991-1	V-304, 345	—	3/8 ③	3	—	.090–.120	⑤	3
		4079-1	V-304, 345	—	3/8 ③	3	—	.090–.120	⑤	3
		4308	V-304, 345	—	3/8 ③	3	—	.090–.120	⑤	3
		4306	V-304, 345	—	3/8 ③	3	—	.090–.120	⑤	3
Holley		4574	V-304, 345	—	3/8 ③	3	—	—	⑤	—
		4594	V-304, 345	—	3/8 ③	3	—	.090–.120	⑤	—
		4081-1	V-304, 345	—	3/8 ③	3	—	.090–.120	⑤	3
		4083-1	V-304, 345	—	3/8 ③	3	—	.090–.120	⑤	3
Holley	2300G	1706-2	V-304	—	3/8 ③	3	#2 Hole	—	.018–.020	—
		1707-2	V-345	—	3/8 ③	3	#2 Hole	—	.018–.020	—
		2979	V-304, 345	—	3/8 ③	3	—	—	.018–.020	⑥
		2980	V-304, 345	—	3/8 ③	3	—	—	.018–.020	⑥
		2975	V-304, 345	—	3/8 ③	3	—	—	.018–.020	⑥
		4310	V-304, 345	—	3/8 ③	3	—	—	.018–.020	3
		4311	V-304, 345	—	3/8 ③	3	—	—	.018–.020	3
Holley	2300C	3679-3	V-304, 345	—	3/8 ③	3	—	.090–.120	⑤	⑥
		2520-3	V-304, 345	—	3/8 ③	3	—	.090–.120	⑤	⑥
		3937-2	V-304, 345	—	3/8 ③	3	—	.090–.120	⑤	⑥
		3936-2	V-304, 345	—	3/8 ③	3	—	.090–.120	⑤	⑥
Holley	2300C	4078-1	V-304, 345	—	3/8 ③	3	—	.090–.120	⑤	3
		4080-1	V-304, 345	—	3/8 ③	3	—	.090–.120	⑤	3
		4082-1	V-304, 345	—	3/8 ③	3	—	.090–.120	⑤	3
		4084-1	V-304, 345	—	3/8 ③	3	—	.090–.120	⑤	3
		4307	V-304, 345	—	3/8 ③	3	—	.090–.120	⑤	3
		4309	V-304, 345	—	3/8 ③	3	—	.090–.120	⑤	3
		4593	V-304, 345	—	3/8 ③	3	—	—	⑤	—
		4595	V-304, 345	—	3/8 ③	3	—	.090–.120	⑤	—
Holley	4150	4237	V-392	—	⑦	⑩	—	—	.025	3
		4264	V-392	—	⑦	⑩	—	.060–.090	⑪	3
		4318	V-392	—	④	4	—	—	.025	—
		4320	V-392	—	④	4	—	.060–.090	.025	—
		4572	V-392	—	⑦	3	—	—	.025	—
		4601	V-392	—	⑦	3	—	.090–.120	—	—
		4601-1, 2	V-392	—	⑦	3	—	.090–.120	⑫	—
Holley	4150C	4312	V-392	—	⑦	⑩	—	—	—	⑬
		4313	V-392	—	⑦	⑩	—	.060–.090	—	⑬
		4319	V-392	—	④	4	—	—	.025	—
		4321	V-392	—	④	4	—	.060–.090	.025	—
		4599	V-392	—	⑦	3	—	—	—	—
		4602	V-392	—	⑦	3	—	.090–.120	—	—
		6390	V-392	—	⑦	3	—	.075–.105	—	1.0–1.5
Holley	4150G	1708	V-392	—	④	3/4	.015	—	.025	—
		4323	V-392	—	④	⑩	—	—	⑪	⑬
		4324	V-392	—	④	⑩	—	—	⑪	⑬
		6803	V-392	—	④	3	—	—	.010–.015	2
Holley	4160C	6444	V-392	—	⑦	—	—	.070–.090	—	1.5

①—Measure from flat on float to inner edge of bowl with carburetor held upside down.
②—Adjust to maximum vacuum, using a vacuum gauge.
③—At 5 1/2 psi fuel pump pressure.
④—Primary float 3/8", secondary float 5/8".
⑤—Zero clearance.
⑥—12–13 air fuel ratio.
⑦—Primary float 1/2", secondary float 5/8".
⑧—At 4 1/2 psi fuel pump pressure.
⑨—Manual Trans. .050"–.070"; Auto. Trans. .070"–.090".
⑩—1970–74 models, 3 turns.
⑪—1970–74 models, .010"–.015".
⑫—Man. trans., .025"; auto. trans. exc. Calif., .070"; auto. trans. Calif., .040".
⑬—1970–71 models, 3.0; 1972 models, 1.0–2.0; 1973–74 models, 2.0.

INTERNATIONAL

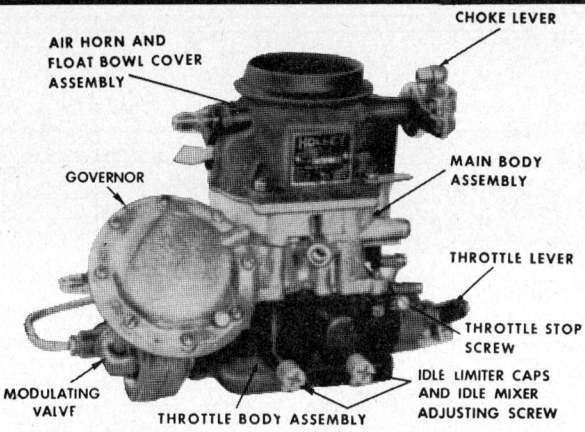

Holley Model 852-FFG carburetor

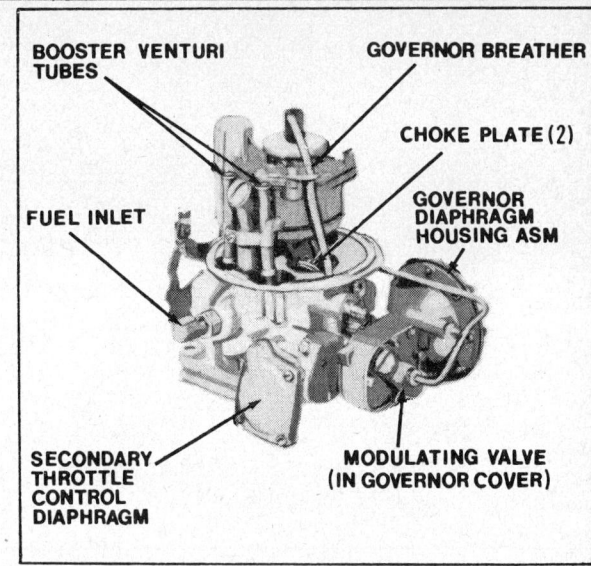

Holley Model 2140G carburetor

CARBURETOR ADJUSTMENTS

Holley 852-FFG

Float Level, Fig. 1

The float level can be set accurately when the air horn is off by gauging the distance between the bottom of the float and the flange surface of the air horn. Holding the air horn upside down (without gasket) and with the float in the closed position, measure the distance from the flange surface of the air horn to what would normally be the bottom side of the float, not the soldered seam. If the dimension is not as specified, bend the float arm up or down as required. Pushing the float toward the float chamber cover raises the level; pushing it away from the cover lowers the level.

Accelerating Pump Stroke, Fig. 2

When the engine does not accelerate properly, check the pump system for dirt. If the pump inlet check valve does not seat, fuel will return to the float bowl instead of discharging through the pump discharge passages. This can be checked by removing the main body cover and operating the pump with a small amount of fuel in the bowl. If the check ball is leaking, air or fuel will bubble back into the float bowl through the inlet hole. After cleaning this seat, extreme care should be taken when reinstalling the pump piston to be sure the piston is not damaged and that it contacts the cylinder wall. If the piston is not a snug fit against the cylinder wall, fuel will leak by the piston on acceleration, causing a weak discharge.

Holley 2140-G

Float Level, Fig. 3

To check the float level, lift the float to completely close the fuel inlet valve. Hold the float closed and place a straight edge across the float chamber so that one end of the straight edge rests on the rim of the float chamber and the other end rests on the center of the main body. Use a scale and measure the distance between the straight edge and the flat top surface of the float at a point farthest from the fuel inlet valve. Check both halves of float in this manner. If one side is lower than the other, bend that part of the float lever next to the float to correct the mis-alignment. The float level can be adjusted by bending the tab on the float lever that contacts the fuel inlet needle. Bend the tab up to lower or down to raise the float.

Accelerating Pump System

The pump system is provided with an adjustment for varying the quantity of pump discharge to meet seasonal requirements and climatic changes. The adjustment is made by changing the position of the pump link in the

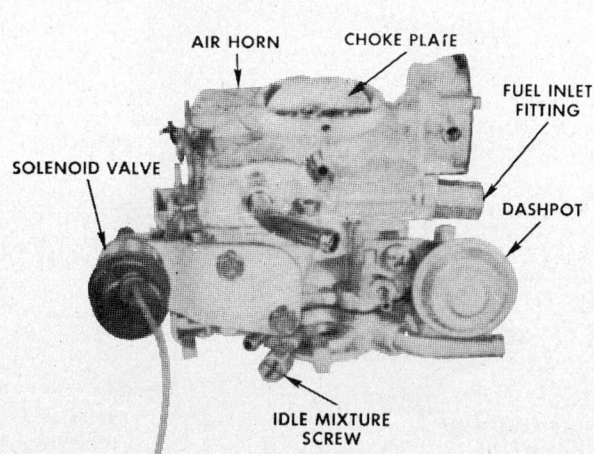

Holley Model 1940C carburetor

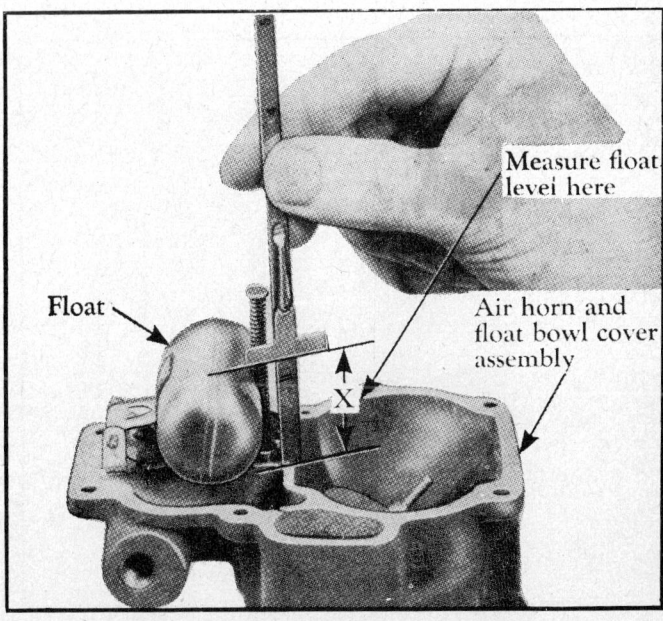

Fig. 1 Float level check. Holley 852-FFG

INTERNATIONAL

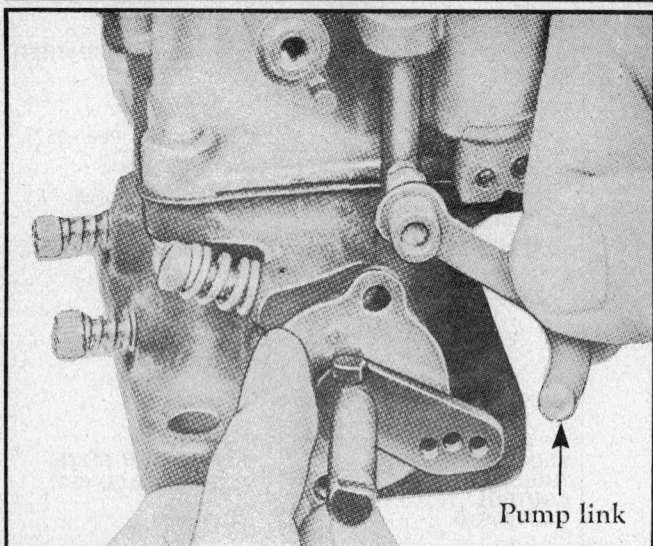

Fig. 2 Accelerating pump stroke. Holley 852-FFG

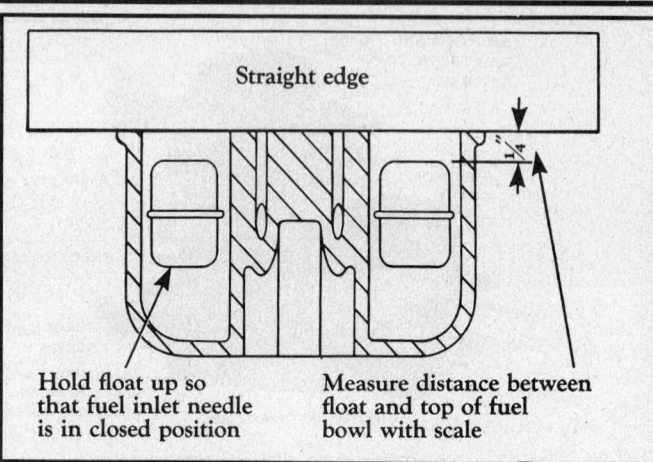

Fig. 2 Float level check. Holley 2140G and 885-FFG

holes located in the throttle lever. The hole most distant from the throttle shaft is the cold weather setting since it gives the longest stroke and greatest fuel discharge. The hole nearest the throttle shaft is used in hot weather.

Holley 885-FFG

Float Level

Check and adjust the float level as outlined for the 2140G carburetor and refer to Fig. 3.

Pump Setting, Fig. 4

The accelerating pump is provided with an adjustment for varying the quantity of the pump discharge to meet seasonal requirements and climatic changes. The adjustment is made by changing the position of the pump link in the holes provided in the throttle lever. The position farthest from the throttle shaft is the cold weather setting since it gives the longest stroke and the greatest discharge. The middle position gives the average setting, and the position nearest the throttle shaft is used in hot weather.

Holley 1904

Float Level, Fig. 5

Invert main body, allowing float to drop to closed position. Using the float gauge shown, check the setting on both the "touch," and "no touch" legs of gauge. The level of the float may be adjusted by bending the small tab in the float lever that contacts the head of the fuel inlet needle pin.

Dashpot Adjustment

The dashpot on carburetors for engines equipped with automatic transmission is to be adjusted after the idle speed and mixture settings have been completed. Close the throttle lever to the idle position. Set the dashpot adjusting screw to the clearance specified and with the dashpot diaphragm rod in fully compressed position. To assure an accurate adjustment, check the choke plate to be sure it remains fully open while setting the dashpot adjusting screw.

Holley 1940C

Float Level

With the Air Horn removed and carburetor body in an upright position, place a straight edge across the surface of the fuel bowl. The straight edge should just touch the toes of the float when the fuel inlet valve is held closed. Adjust by bending the float tang.

Fast Idle Cam Adjustment, Fig. 6

With throttle lever screw against second highest step, move choke plate toward closed position. Check clearance between choke plate and wall of air horn. Adjust by bending fast idle connector rod with a suitable tool.

Dashpot Adjustment

With engine at idle speed, depress dashpot plunger completely into dashpot. Measure clearance between plunger and throttle lever. Loosen jam nut and rotate dashpot to obtain specified clearance.

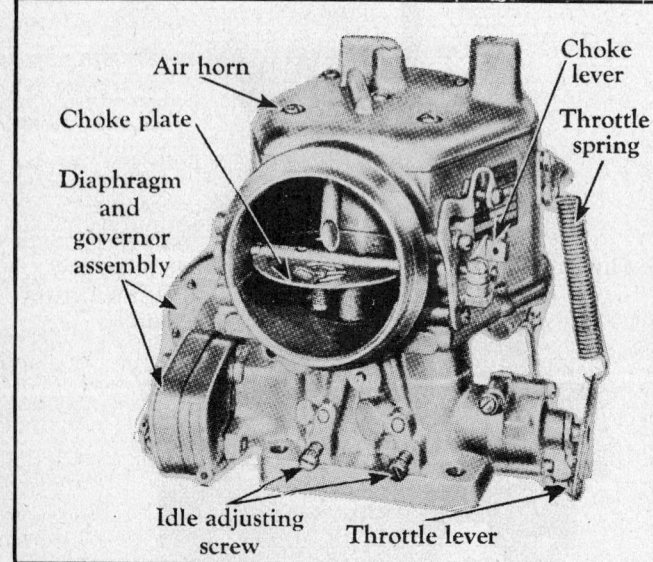

Holley Model 885-FFG carburetor

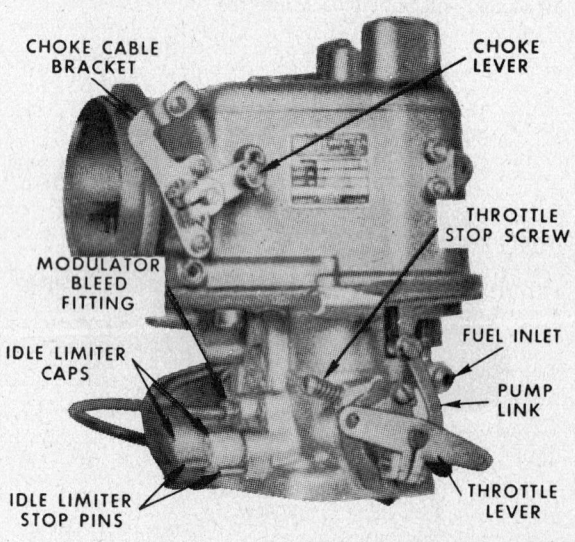

Accelerating pump stroke. Holley 885-FFG

INTERNATIONAL

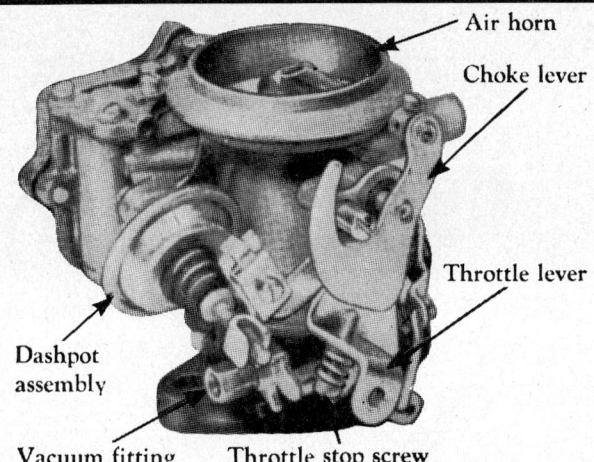

Holley 1904 carburetor used with automatic transmission

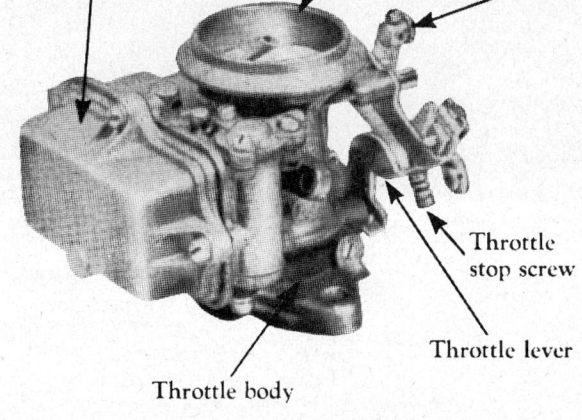

Holley Model 1904 carburetor used with standard transmission

Holley 2210C

Float Level, Fig. 7

Invert air horn so weight of float forces needle against seat. Measure clearance between top of float and float stop. Adjust by bending float lip toward or away from needle using a narrow blade screw driver.

Dashpot Adjustment

With engine at idle speed, depress dashpot plunger completely into dashpot. Measure clearance between plunger and throttle lever. Loosen jam nut and rotate dashpot to obtain specified clearance.

Holley 2300, 2300C, 2300G

Fast Idle, Model 2300G

Adjust fast idle stud so as to have the specified clearance between stud and fast idle cam when throttle plates are set for curb idle and choke plate is fully open.

Fast Idle, Model 2300, 2300C

Set throttle lever stop screw so that screw just touches fast idle cam at curb idle.

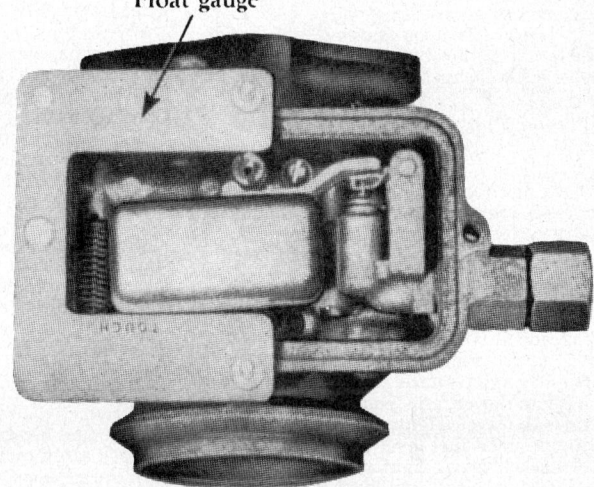

Fig. 5 Float level check. Holley 1904

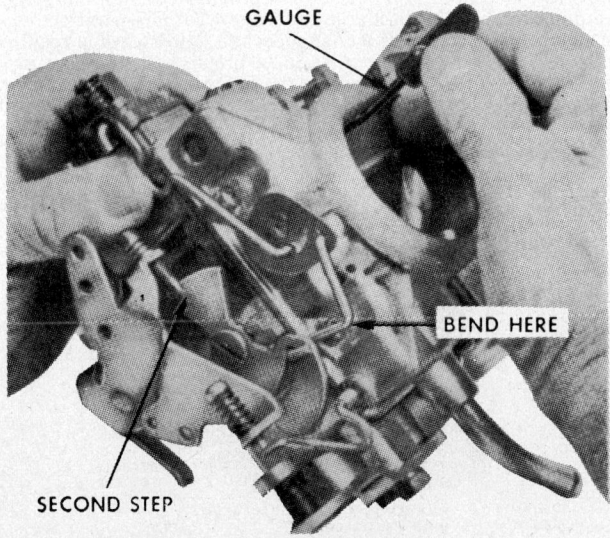

Fig. 6 Fast idle cam adjustment. Holley 1940C

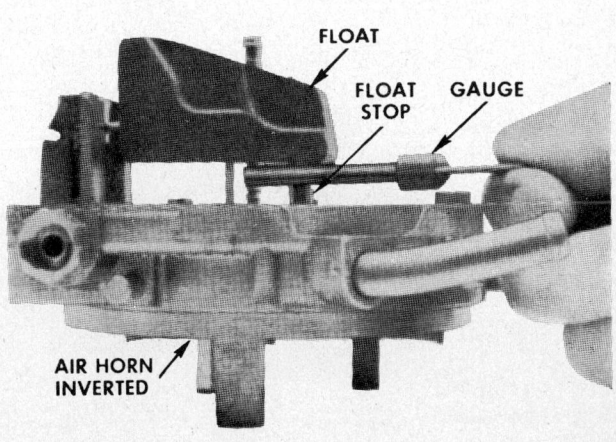

Fig. 7 Float level check. Holley 2210C

1231

INTERNATIONAL

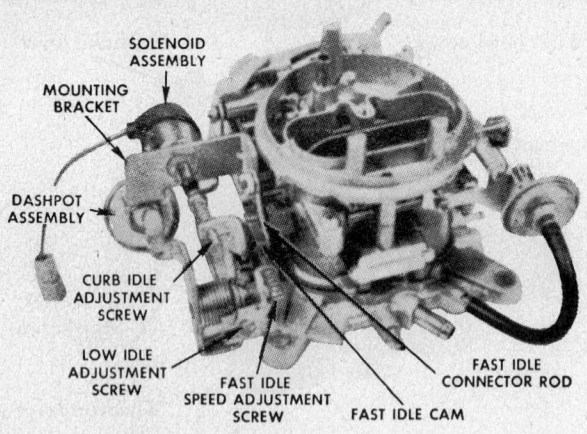

Holley Model 2210C—Early Production

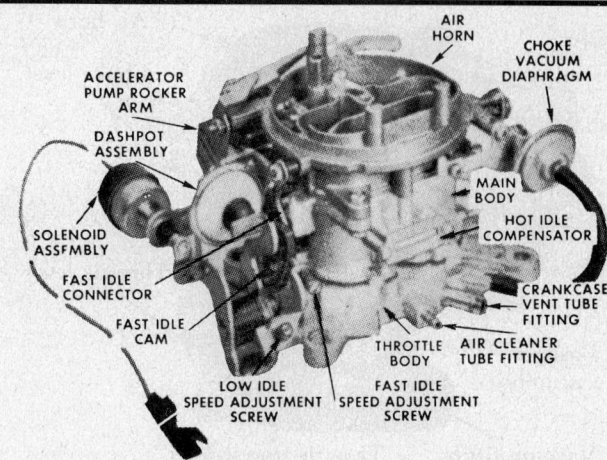

Holley Model 2210C—Late production

Dashpot Adjustment
Dashpot adjustment is made only after idle speed and mixture settings have been completed. Loosen dashpot jam nut and rotate complete dashpot to obtain the specified clearance between dashpot and throttle lever.

Fuel Level, Figs. 8 and 9
Check fuel pump pressure before changing fuel level. Pump pressure should be 5½ psi.
1. With ignition off and air cleaner removed, remove fuel bowl lower mounting screw (farthest from fuel inlet). Drain fuel into a shallow pan to purge bowl of possible dirt. Reinstall bowl screw.
2. Start engine and remove sight plug from bowl. The fuel level should be on line with threads at bottom of sight plug hole.
3. To adjust fuel level, loosen lock bolt slightly and turn the adjusting nut clockwise to lower and counterclockwise to raise the level. Tighten lock bolt. Operate engine until fuel level is stabilized, then recheck level at sight plug hole. Repeat adjustment until fuel level is correct.

Pump Discharge, Fig. 10
The adjustment that regulates the pump discharge is located at the override spring on the pump lever. With choke wide open and throttle set for curb idle, lengthen or shorten adjusting bolt until the bolt touches the diaphragm lever and takes up the slack in the linkage. Then lengthen the adjusting bolt ½ turn.

Holley 4150G

Fuel Level, Fig. 11
With vehicle on a level floor, operate engine until normal operating temperature has been reached. Place a suitable container below fuel level sight plug to collect any fuel spill over. Check each fuel bowl separately.

With engine stopped, remove air cleaner, fuel sight plug and gasket and check fuel level. The level within the bowl should be at the lower edge of the sight plug opening (plus or minus 1/16").

If the fuel level is too high or low, install sight plug, drain fuel bowl by loosening one lower retaining bolt from bowl and drain fuel into a suitable container. Install bolt and sight plug, and start engine to fill fuel bowl. Check level again before altering the float setting. This will eliminate the possibility of foreign material causing a temporary flooding condition.

If the fuel level requires adjustment, loosen the lock screw on top of the fuel inlet seat and turn the adjusting nut in or out as required to correct the fuel level. A 1/6 turn of the adjusting nut equals 3/64" in fuel level. Remove sight plug and recheck the level.

Fast Idle Adjustment, Fig. 12
The fast idle speed adjusting screw is located on the governor housing. Adjust the curb idle speed and mixture, then adjust the fast idle speed.

With choke plate wide open, adjust fast idle screw to provide the clearance specified between head of screw and fast idle cam. Check fast idle rpm, using a tachometer. If the fast idle is not within the limits of 900 to 1000 rpm, turn fast idle screw clockwise to decrease engine rpm or counter-clockwise to increase the rpm.

Accelerating Pump Lever, Fig. 13
1. Using a feeler gauge and with throttle plates wide open, there should be the specified clearance (minimum) between pump operating lever adjustment screw and pump arm when pump arm is depressed manually.
2. If adjustment is required, loosen lock nut and turn adjusting screw in to increase clearance and out to decrease clearance. One-half turn of screw is equal to approximately .015".
3. When proper adjustment has been made, hold screw in position with a wrench and tighten lock nut.

Accelerating Pump Stroke
To satisfy the requirements in various climates, the pump discharge can be adjusted. The bottom hole (No. 2) in the pump cam and throttle lever provides the maximum pump discharge for extreme cold weather, and the top hole (No. 1) provides the minimum pump discharge for warm weather operation.

If a change in the adjustment is required, make certain the proper hole in plastic pump cam, located behind throttle lever, is properly indexed with the numbered hole in the throt-

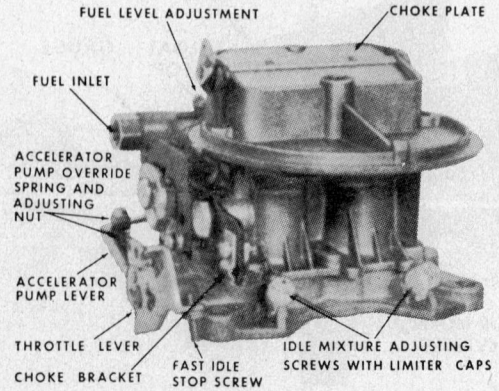

Holley Model 2300 carburetor

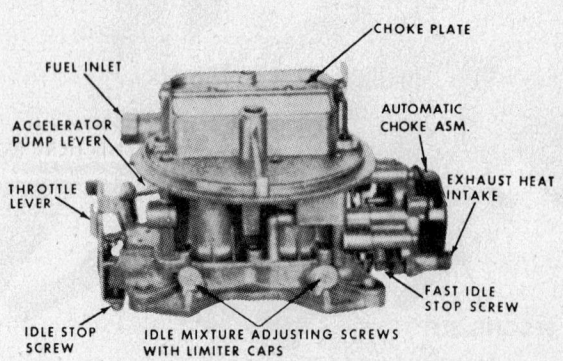

Holley Model 2300C carburetor

INTERNATIONAL

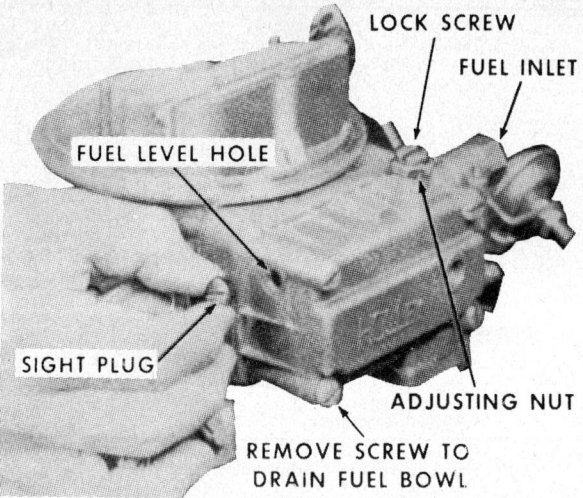

Fig. 8 Removing sight plug from fuel bowl. Holley 2300, 2300C, 2300G

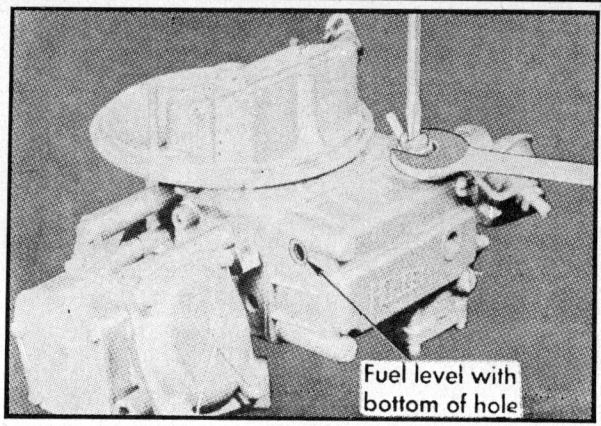

Fig. 9 Adjusting fuel level. Holley 2300, 2300C, 2300G

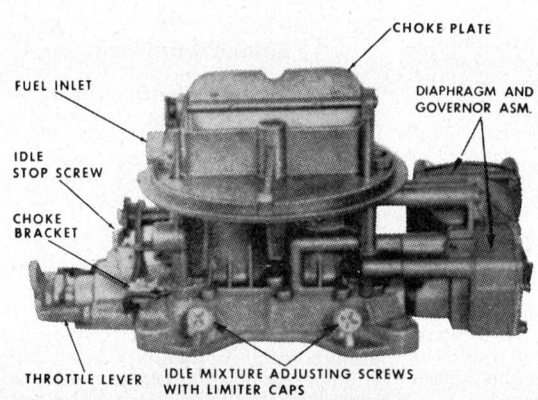

Holley Model 2300G carburetor

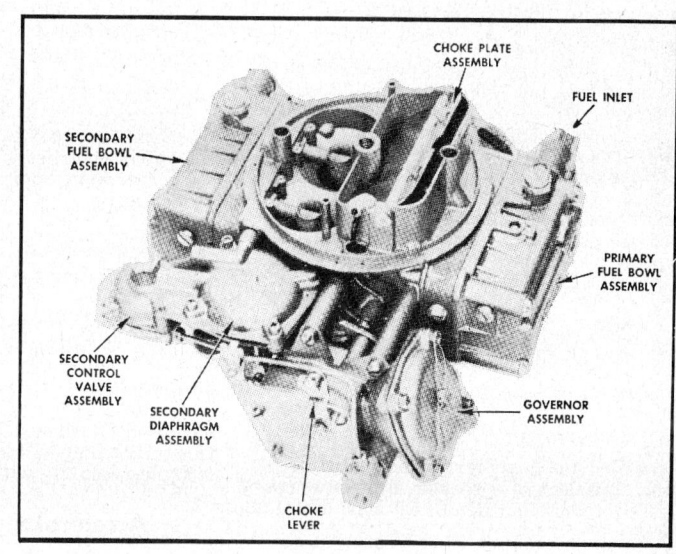

Holley Model 4150G

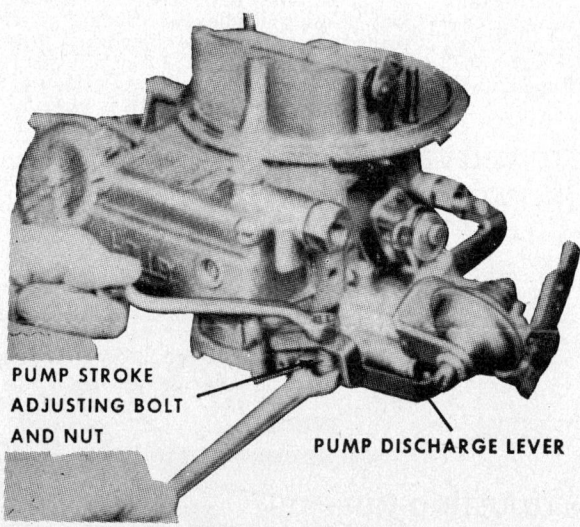

Fig. 10 Accelerating pump discharge adjustment. Holley 2300, 2300C, 2300G

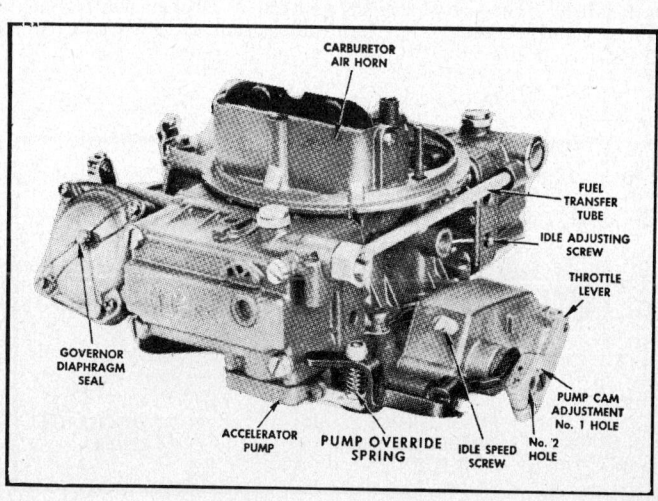

Holley Model 4150G

INTERNATIONAL

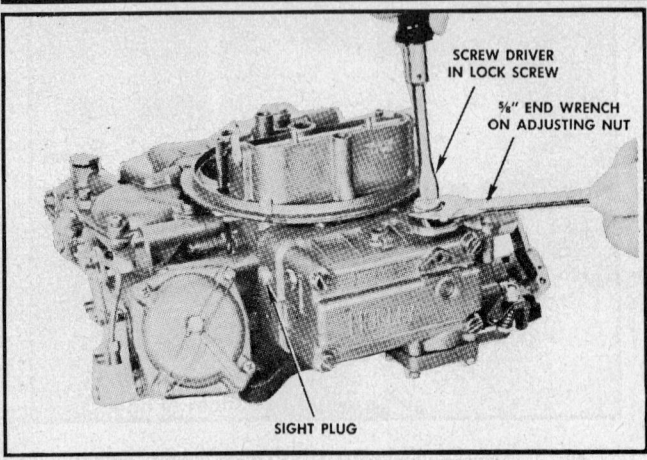

Fig. 11 Fuel level check. Holley 4150G

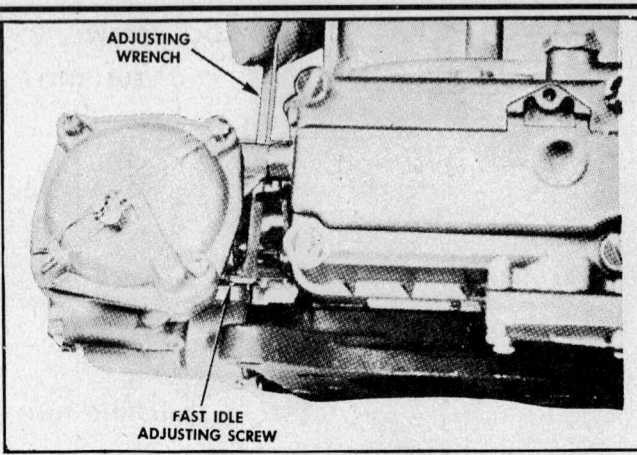

Fig. 12 Fast idle adjustment. Holley 4150G

tle lever before installing the retaining screw.

Holley 4160C

Float Level, Fig. 14

With bowl in an inverted position, adjust float so that top of float is parallel to bowl floor.

Dashpot Adjustment

With engine at idle speed, depress dashpot plunger completely into dashpot. Measure clearance between plunger and throttle lever. Loosen jam nut and rotate dashpot to obtain specified clearance.

CARTER TQ ADJUSTMENTS

Float Setting

Fig. 1—With bowl cover inverted, gasket installed and floats resting on seated needle, the dimension of each float from bowl cover gasket to bottom side of float should be 1.06 inch.

Secondary Throttle Linkage

Fig. 2—Block choke valve in wide open position and invert carburetor. Slowly open the primary throttle valves until it is possible to measure between lower edge of primary valve and its bore. If necessary to adjust, bend rod so primary and secondary stops both contact at same time.

Secondary Air Valve Opening

Fig. 3
1. With air valve in closed position, the opening along air valve at its long side must be at its maximum and parallel with air horn gasket surface.
2. With air valve wide open, the opening of the air valve at the short side and air horn must be 31/64 inch. The corner of air valve is notched for adjustment. Bend the corner with a pair of pliers to give proper opening.

Secondary Air Valve Spring Tension

Fig. 4—Loosen air valve lock plug and allow air valve to position itself wide open. With a long screwdriver that will enter center of tool positioned on air valve adjustment plug, turn plug counterclockwise until air valve contacts stop lightly, then turn an additional 1¼ turns. Hold plug with screwdriver and tighten lock plug securely with tool.

Accelerator pump stroke

Fig. 5—With engine at operating temperature, choke in wide open position, idle solenoid activated and engine idle speed adjusted to proper rpm, measure primary accelerator pump stroke. Measure distance between top of bowl cover to bottom of accelerator pump link. Dimension should be .328-.358 inch. Bend throttle connector rod at upper angle to adjust.

Position throttle lever just below secondary opening and measure secondary accelerator pump stroke. Measure distance between top of bowl cover and bottom of accelerator pump link. Dimension should be .120-.160 inch. Bend accelerator pump secondary pick-up tab to adjust.

Choke Control Lever

Fig. 6—Place carburetor on a flat surface. Close choke by pushing on choke lever with throttle partly open. Measure vertical distance between top of rod hole in control lever and base of carburetor (flat surface). Dimension should be 3.30 inch. Adjust by bending link connecting the two choke shafts.

Choke Diaphragm Connector Rod

Fig. 7—Apply a vacuum of 10 or more inches of Mercury to diaphragm to fully depress diaphragm stem. An auxiliary source like a distributor test machine can be used for this purpose. With air valve closed, adjust connector rod to give .020-.060 inch clearance between air valve and stop.

Vacuum Kick Adjustment

Fig. 8—With engine running, back off fast idle speed screw until choke can be closed to kick position at idle. Note number of screw turns so fast idle can be turned back to original adjustment. Insert a #35 drill between long side (lower edge) of choke valve and the air horn wall. Apply sufficient pressure on

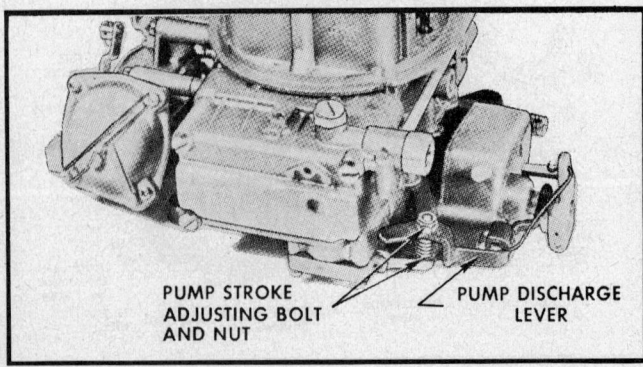

Fig. 13 Pump lever adjustment. Holley 4150G

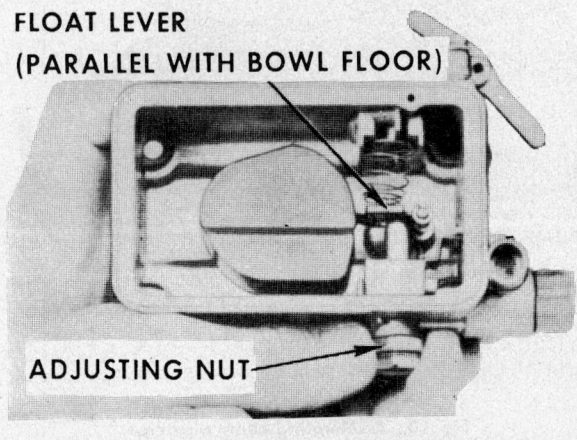

Fig. 14 Float level check. Holley 4160C

INTERNATIONAL

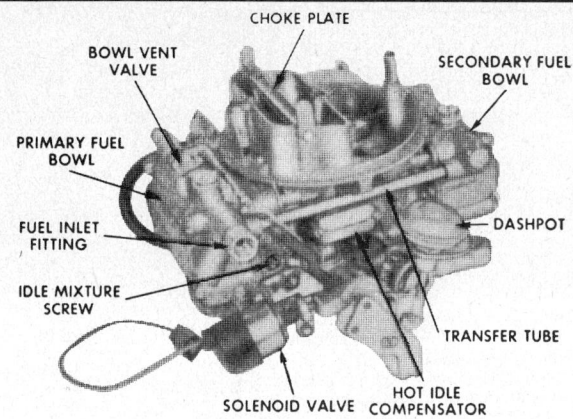

Holley Model 4160C carburetor

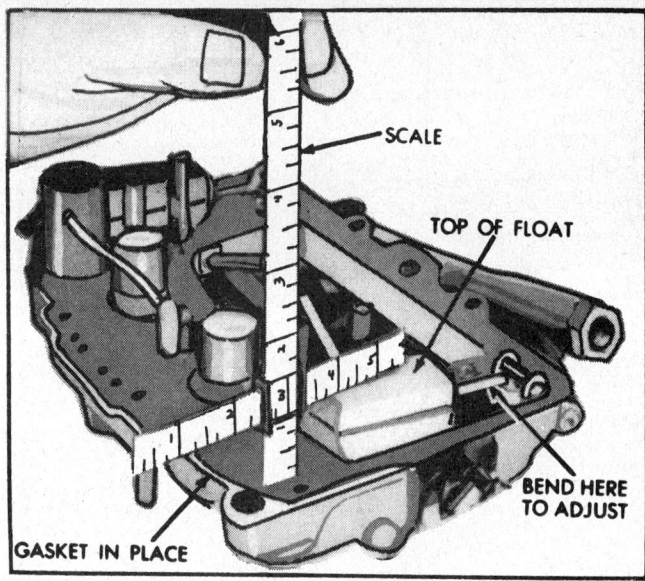

Fig. 1 TQ float setting

choke control lever to provide a minimum choke valve opening. The spring connecting the control lever to the adjustment lever must be fully extended for proper adjustment. Bend tang as shown to change contact with end of diaphragm rod. Do not adjust diaphragm rod. A slight drag should be felt as drill is being removed.

Fast Idle Cam & Linkage

Fig. 9—With fast idle adjusting screw on second step of fast idle cam, move choke valve toward closed position with light pressure on choke control lever. Clearance between choke valve lower edge and air horn wall should be .089–.109 inch. Adjust by bending fast idle connector rod at angle.

Choke Unloader Adjustment

Fig. 10—Hold throttle valves in wide open position and insert a .280–.320 inch gauge between long side (lower edge) of choke valve and inner wall of air horn. With finger lightly pressing against choke valve control lever, a slight drag should be felt as drill is withdrawn. Adjust by bending tang on fast idle control lever.

Secondary Throttle Lockout

Fig. 11—Move choke control lever to open choke position. Measure clearance between lockout lever and stop. Clearance should be .060–.090 inch. Adjust by bending tang on fast idle control lever.

Bowl Vent Valve Adjustment

Fig. 12—Remove bowl vent valve checking hole plug in bowl cover. With throttle valves at curb idle, insert a narrow ruler down through hole. Allow ruler to rest lightly on top of valve. Dimension should be .800–.830 inch. Adjust by bending bowl vent operating lever at notch. Install a new plug.

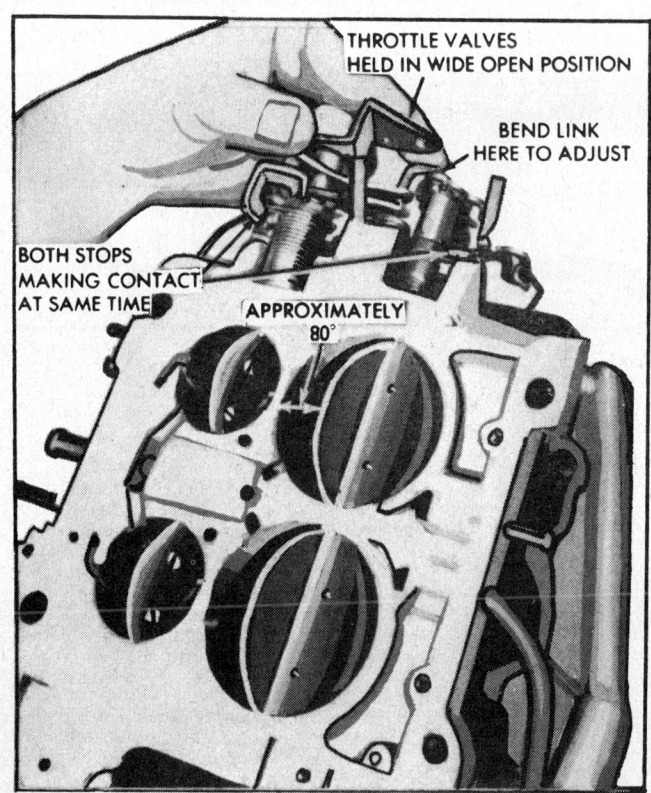

Fig. 2 TQ secondary throttle adjustment

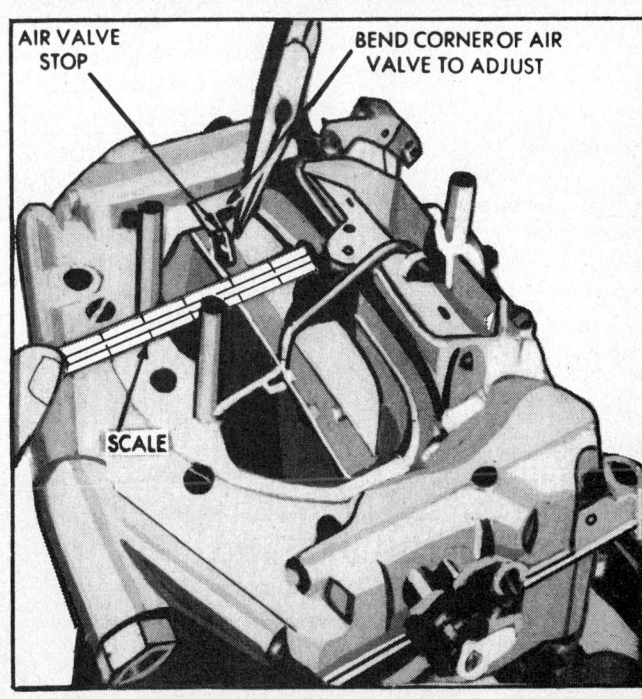

Fig. 3 TQ secondary air valve opening

INTERNATIONAL

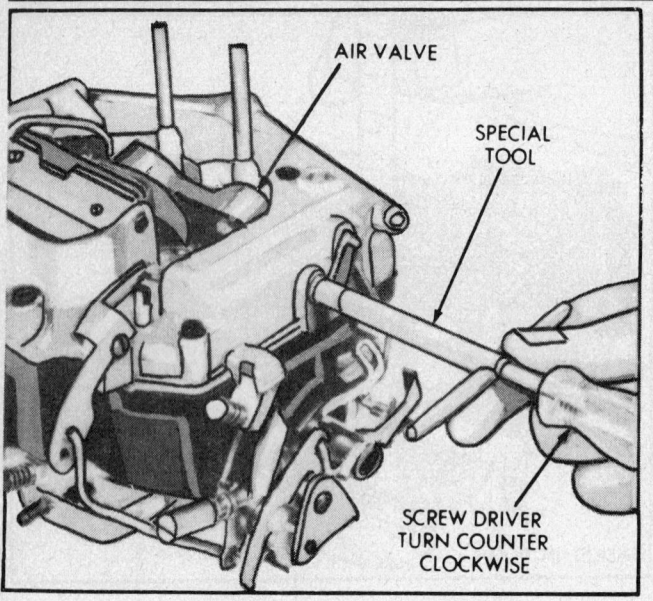

Fig. 4 TQ secondary air valve spring tension

Fig. 5 TQ accelerator pump stroke

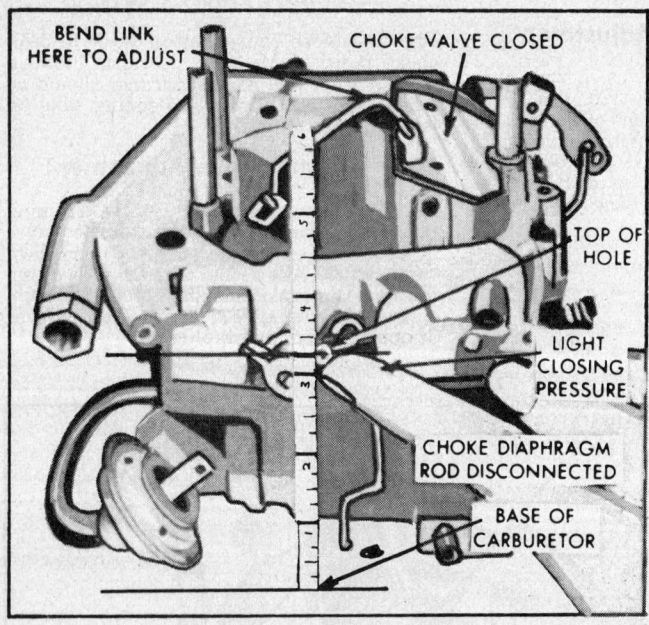

Fig. 6 TQ choke control lever adjustment

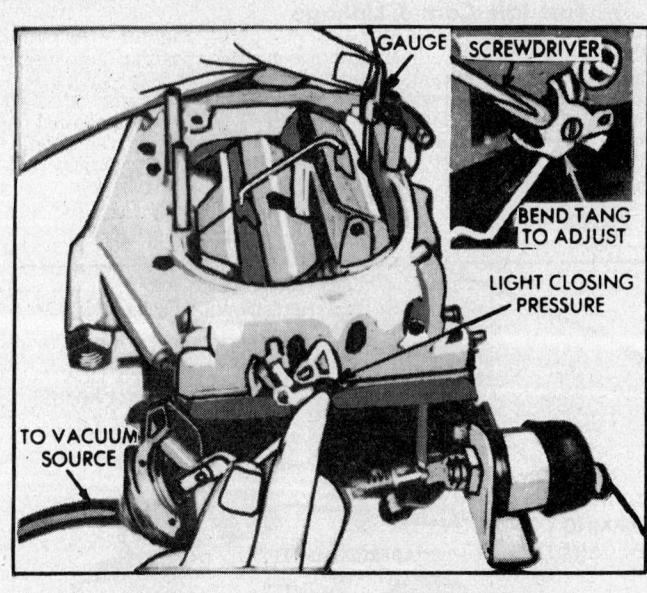

Fig. 7 TQ choke diaphragm connector rod

Fast Idle Speed Cam

NOTE: Disconnect and plug the EGR valve vacuum line.

Fig. 13—With engine off and transmission in Park or Neutral, open throttle slightly. Close choke valve until fast idle screw is positioned on second step of cam against shoulder of first step. Start engine and stabilize RPM, then adjust fast idle speed to 1550-1600 RPM.

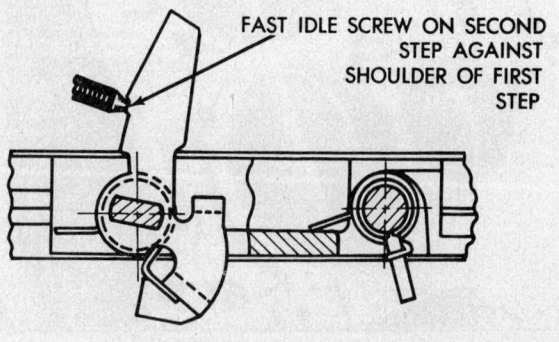

Fig. 13 TQ fast idle speed cam position

INTERNATIONAL

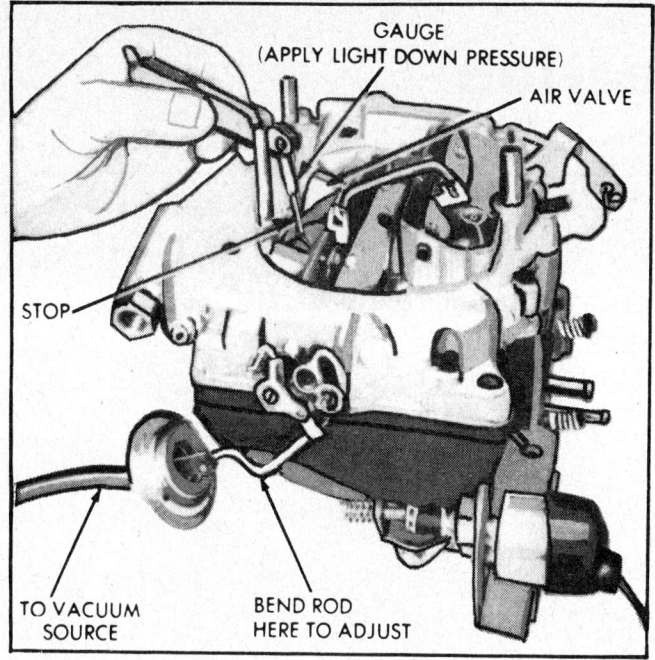

Fig. 8 TQ vacuum kick adjustment

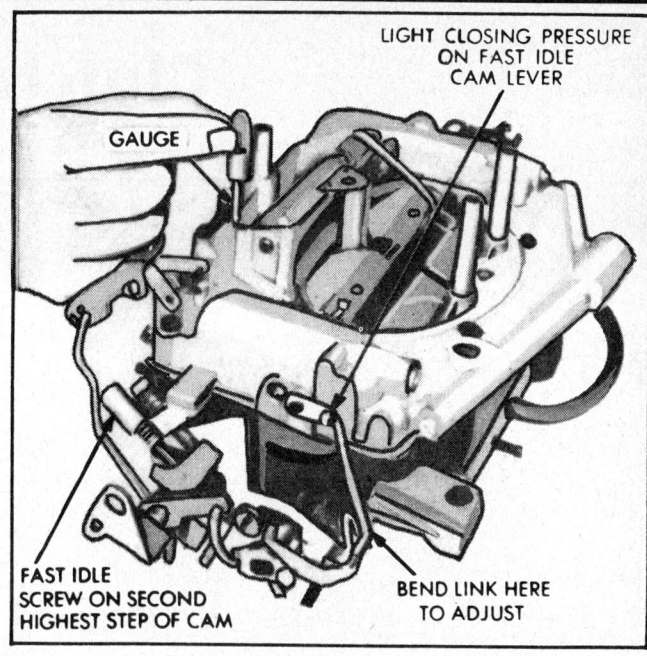

Fig. 9 TQ fast idle cam & linkage adjustment

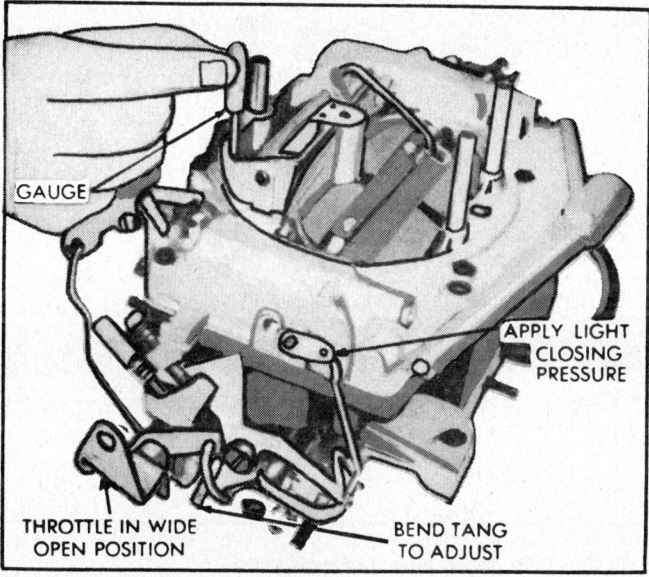

Fig. 10 TQ choke unloader adjustment

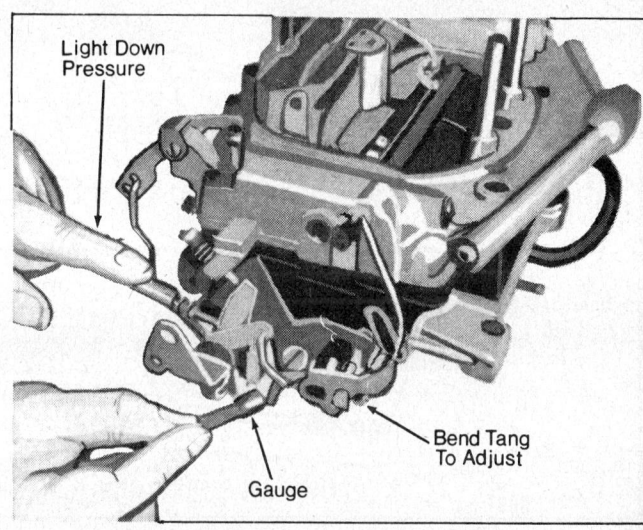

Fig. 11 TQ secondary throttle lockout

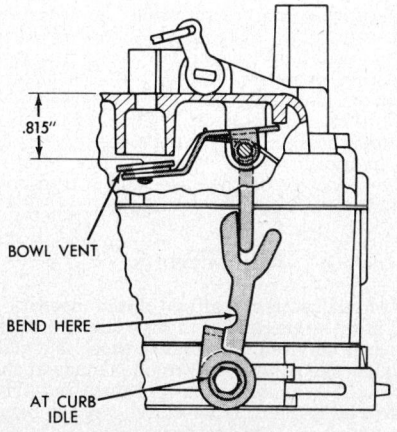

Fig. 12 TQ bowl vent valve adjustment

1237

INTERNATIONAL

Clutch Section

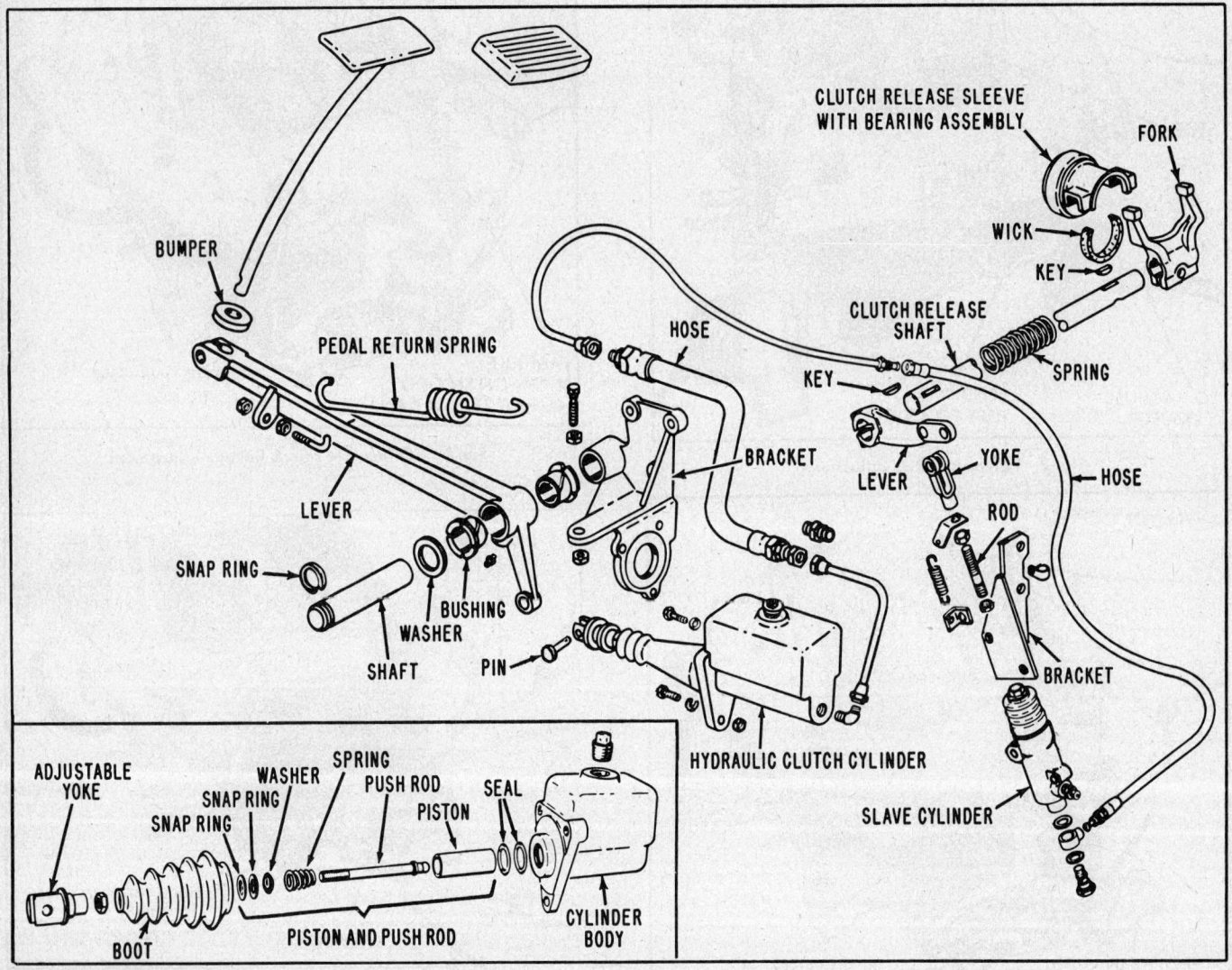

Fig. 1 Hydraulic clutch control. CM-75, 80, 110 and 1600 thru 1890 Models have suspended pedal

HYDRAULIC CLUTCH CONTROL

As shown in Figs. 1 and 2, the system consists of a pedal-operated cylinder, similar to a brake master cylinder, which transmits hydraulic fluid to the slave cylinder mounted on the transmission. The slave cylinder moves the clutch release bearing to engage and disengage the clutch. Tubing and flexible hose connect the two units.

The hydraulic cylinder is filled with high grade hydraulic brake fluid. To replenish fluid, fill the reservoir to within 3/4" from the top of the filler neck.

Bleeding System

Any air trapped inside the system will eventually bleed itself to the reservoir. However, this is not accomplished immediately and takes place over an extended period of clutch pedal operation. For this reason a bleeding operation should be performed whenever the units have been disassembled or fluid lines disconnected. The bleeding procedure is accomplished in the same manner as for hydraulic brake systems. The bleeder screw is located on the lower end of the slave cylinder.

Adjustments

Two adjustments affect clutch operation and must be checked each time the hydraulic clutch is serviced. The first of these is clutch pedal stroke adjustment which is made at the hydraulic cylinder piston and push rod. The second adjustment is for clutch release bearing clearance. This adjustment is made at the upper end of the slave cylinder.

Clutch Pedal, Adjust Except 1600-1890 & 80 Scout Models

1. With clutch pedal disconnected from hydraulic cylinder push rod, pull piston and push rod assembly its full length of stroke out of cylinder. *Be sure piston is held snugly against snap ring stop in end of cylinder.*
2. Hold clutch pedal up against pedal stop.
3. Adjust clevis yoke on end of piston push rod until yoke can be fastened to clutch pedal. Tighten jam nut on yoke. Install end pin and cotter pin.

1600 Thru 1890 & 80 Scout Models

1. Measure clutch pedal height from lower edge of clutch pedal lever to toe boards.

(Measurement should be made at 90° to toe boards).
2. If pedal height is not $5^{5/8}"$ for 1600 thru 1890 models or $6^{1/8}"$ for 80 Scout model. Loosen lock nut on master cylinder push rod and adjust push rod to obtain proper pedal height.

Clutch Release Bearing Clearance Except CM-75, 80, 110, 80 Scout and 1600 Thru 1890 Models

1. Remove slave cylinder push rod return spring, Fig. 3. Loosen clevis yoke lock nut on push rod. Remove cotter pin and clevis yoke end pin. Remove two hex head mounting bolts from slave cylinder body and move cylinder away from clutch release lever.
2. Move clutch release lever upward until release bearing contacts clutch release levers. With push rod in released position, turn clevis yoke until yoke hole indexes with clutch release lever hole when slave cylinder mounting holes are aligned with mounting bracket holes. *Be certain that clutch release bearing is held against release levers while completing this step.*
3. After completing Step 2, turn clevis yoke on to push rod $2^{1/2}$ turns which provides approximately $1/8"$ clutch release bearing-to-levers clearance. Tighten lock nut on push rod to keep clevis yoke from turning while reinstalling slave cylinder.
4. Reinstall slave cylinder. Connect clevis yoke and clutch release lever with end pin. Insert cotter pin. Recheck lock nut on push rod and install push rod return spring, keeping spring clips aligned.

CM-75, 80, 110

This adjustment should follow clutch pedal adjustment.
1. Depress clutch pedal until there is the feel of the release bearing contacting the clutch release levers.
2. Adjust the pedal free movement by loosening the lock nut on the slave cylinder and turning the push rod to obtain $1^{1/2}"$ pedal free movement.
3. Tighten lock nut and recheck pedal free movement.

1600 Thru 1890 Models

This adjustment should follow clutch pedal adjustment.
1. Loosen lock nut on clutch slave cylinder push rod. Remove cotter pin and yoke pin.
2. Move clutch release lever forward until release bearing contacts clutch release fingers. With slave cylinder push rod assembly retained in the released position (bottomed), turn yoke until yoke hole indexes with clutch release lever hole. Install yoke pin.
3. After completing step 2, remove yoke pin and shorten linkage by turning yoke 4 complete turns. Reassemble yoke pin and cotter pin and tighten lock nut on push rod assembly.

Scout 80

1. Loosen lock nuts on clutch release lever adjustment bolt located on slave cylinder mounting bracket.
2. Hold release lever so clutch release bearing contacts the clutch fingers. Move bolt until $1/16"$ clearance is obtained between

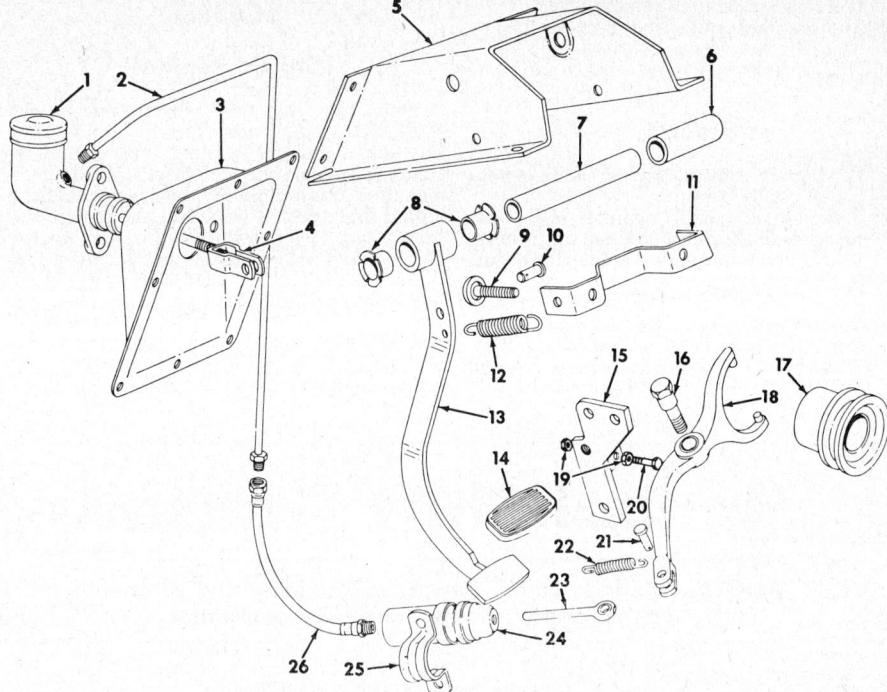

1. ASSEMBLY, master cylinder.
2. PIPE.
3. BRACKET, master cylinder.
4. CLEVIS and PUSH ROD.
5. BRACKET, pedal support.
6. SPACER, pedal shaft.
7. SHAFT, pedal.
8. BUSHING.
9. BUMPER, pedal stop.
10. PIN.
11. BRACKET, pedal stop.
12. SPRING, pedal return.
13. LEVER, clutch.
14. PAD PEDAL.
15. BRACKET, slave cylinder.
16. BOLT, clutch release fork.
17. BEARING, clutch release.
18. LEVER, clutch release.
19. NUT, lock.
20. BOLT, release lever adj.
21. PIN.
22. SPRING, release lever return.
23. PUSH ROD.
24. CYLINDER, slave.
25. CLIP.
26. HOSE.

Fig. 2 Hydraulic clutch control. 80 Scout

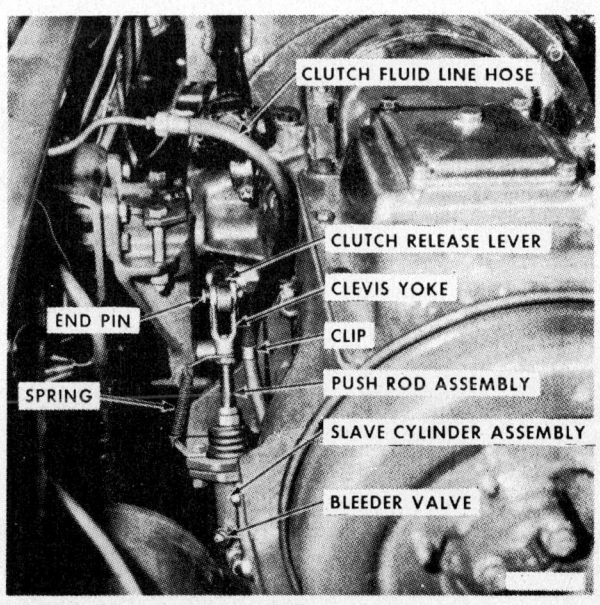

Fig. 3 Slave cylinder mounting details

INTERNATIONAL

bolt head and clutch release lever.
3. Tighten lock nuts and recheck clearance.

Scout II

1. Disconnect return spring and loosen clutch rod lock nut.
2. Hold clutch pedal against stop and lengthen or shorten clutch rod until there is zero clearance between the throw out bearing and clutch release fingers.
3. After obtaining zero clearance, rotate clutch two turns to obtain the desired 3/32 inch clearance between the throw out bearing and the clutch release fingers and tighten clutch rod lock nut.

SCOUT

Clutch, Replace

When removing the transmission for the purpose of gaining access to the clutch or for any other reason, extreme care should be taken to support the weight of the transmission until it is completely removed so that the clutch shaft splines will clear the clutch disc hub. There is a possibility of distorting the clutch disc which will then not permit a free release of the clutch.

When installing the clutch, position the disc and clutch assembly on the flywheel, using a stub shaft (or a spare clutch shaft) to align the clutch disc. Then tighten the cover-to-flywheel capscrews gradually and evenly.

Free Pedal Travel, Adjust

The clutch pedal should have a minimum of 1½" free movement before clutch pressure is felt. If pedal free movement is less than specified, an adjustment is necessary to provide adequate bearing-to-lever clearance.

On models with turnbuckle release rod, adjustment is made by loosening release rod lock nuts on each side of turnbuckle. Looking down on turnbuckle, turn it counter-clockwise to increase or clockwise to decrease free travel.

On models with adjustable end yokes, remove yoke pins and turn yokes up or down on release rod as required.

Manual Shift Transmission Section

NOTE: For Clark, Fuller, New Process, Spicer and Warner transmissions used in International trucks, see the "name" chapter for service procedures

MODELS T1, T2, T4

Disassemble, Figs. 1, 2

1. Take off control cover.
2. Remove universal flange nut and pull off flange.
3. Remove speedometer driven gear and front and rear bearing retainers.
4. Drive countershaft out rearward, allowing cluster gear to lie in case.
5. Pull main drive gear out through front.
6. Remove mainshaft front pilot bearing and push mainshaft far enough to rear to permit removal of speedometer drive gear and rear bearing.
7. Lift mainshaft and gears out through top.
8. Lift out cluster gear and washers.
9. Drive reverse idler shaft out through rear and lift out gear.
10. To disassemble mainshaft, slide the low and reverse sliding gear and synchronizer unit from the shaft. Release snap ring and take off the second speed gear, bushing and thrust washer.
11. Reverse the order of the above procedure to assemble the transmission.

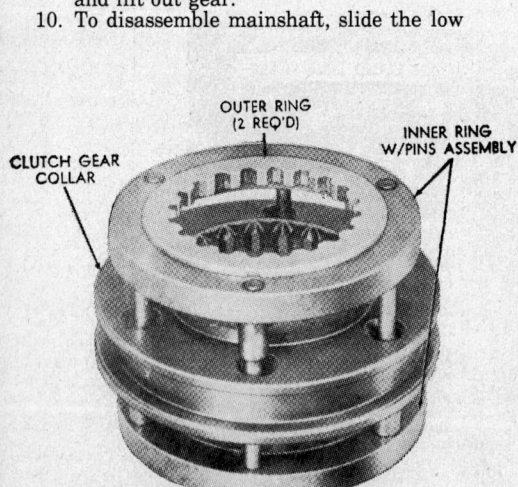

Fig. 2 On T1 and T2 transmissions the synchronizer consists of the parts shown plus the synchronizer clutch gear which is secured to the mainshaft with a snap ring

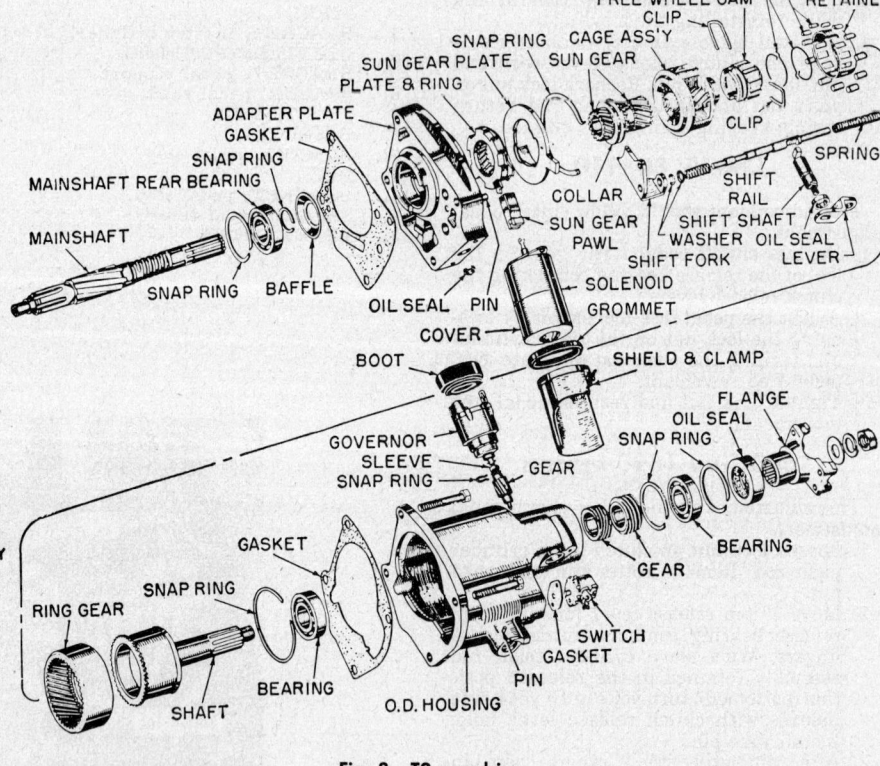

Fig. 3 T2 overdrive

T2, T8 O. D. TRANS.

Disassemble, Fig. 3

1. Drain lubricant.

INTERNATIONAL

2. Remove companion flange.
3. Remove lockout switch.
4. Remove governor.
5. Drive out tapered pin (from underside) which holds overdrive control shaft in case. Pull shaft with lever from case.
6. Remove screws which attach overdrive case and adapter to transmission. Tap end of output shaft lightly with a soft mallet and remove overdrive case. This prevents shaft and ring gear from being removed with case and spilling the 12 clutch rollers.
7. With case removed, slide governor and speedometer drive gear from shaft.
8. Reinstall one capscrew to hold adapter to transmission.
9. Remove shift rail adapter spring from inside of overdrive case. Pry out control shaft and output shaft oil seal from case. Discard seals and replace with new ones upon reassembly.
10. Remove outer snap ring, rear bearing and inner snap ring from shaft.
11. Remove output shaft and ring gear, catching 12 clutch rollers, Fig. 4.
12. Separate ring gear and output shaft by removing large snap ring.
13. Pry retaining clip that retains roller clutch assembly (free wheeling unit) to output shaft. Then remove free wheeling cam and pinion case assembly, Fig. 5. Remove retaining clip holding the two units together and separate.
14. Slide sun gear with shifting collar off end of transmission mainshaft and at the same time remove shift rail from case adapter.
15. Remove two snap rings which retain shifting collar to sun gear and separate collar and gear.
16. Remove "C" washer located on shift rail between shift fork and "C" washer cup. Then slide fork, "C" washer cup and reverse lock-up spring from shift rail.
17. Unfasten solenoid from case and turn clockwise 1/4 turn and remove from adapter.
18. Remove large snap ring located in adapter next to retainer plate with oil trough and remove parts.
19. Before further disassembly of the overdrive unit can be made, it will be necessary to partially disassemble the transmission as follows:
20. Remove transmission cover.
21. Remove main drive gear bearing retainer, noting that oil drain is located below.
22. Start main drive gear bearing out of case by tapping on outer race from inside of case. As soon as bearing is started, work it out of case by moving end of shaft from side to side.
23. Pull overdrive adapter and mainshaft toward rear of transmission case, lowering extended end of mainshaft to permit removal of synchronizer from inside of case. Remove snap ring and strip mainshaft.
24. Remove large snap ring holding bearing in adapter. Pull adapter off bearing and press bearing from mainshaft.
25. Turn transmission low and reverse shift lever shaft to its forward limits. This will provide clearance for removal of reverse lockout cam.

Assemble

1. Reverse the disassembly procedure to assemble the transmission and overdrive, observing the following:
2. Prior to assembling the overdrive unit, select correct thickness of snap ring that will secure (a) mainshaft rear bearing in overdrive case adapter (b) rear bearing to mainshaft, (c) retaining plate with oil trough in adapter, and (d) output shaft bearing in overdrive case with no perceptible end play.
3. Always install new gaskets and oil seals if unit has accumulated any extensive mileage or if damaged in removal.
4. When installing sun gear control plate and blocker ring assembly, *be sure* that the blocker ring and pawl are properly positioned. Position blocker ring so that pawl will be located between the two lugs of the blocker ring. The notched side of the pawl should be positioned so that the notch faces toward top of transmission.
5. The solenoid should be installed so that opening in end of solenoid is located to the bottom and that plunger is engaged and locked in pawl.
6. To facilitate installing output shaft and ring gear, apply heavy grease to roller clutch cage to hold the 12 rollers in position. Then, with low gear of transmission engaged, turn cage and rollers counterclockwise until the rollers are in their low positions on cam. Install output shaft and ring gear on pinion cage and roller clutch (free wheeling unit), turning the shaft to

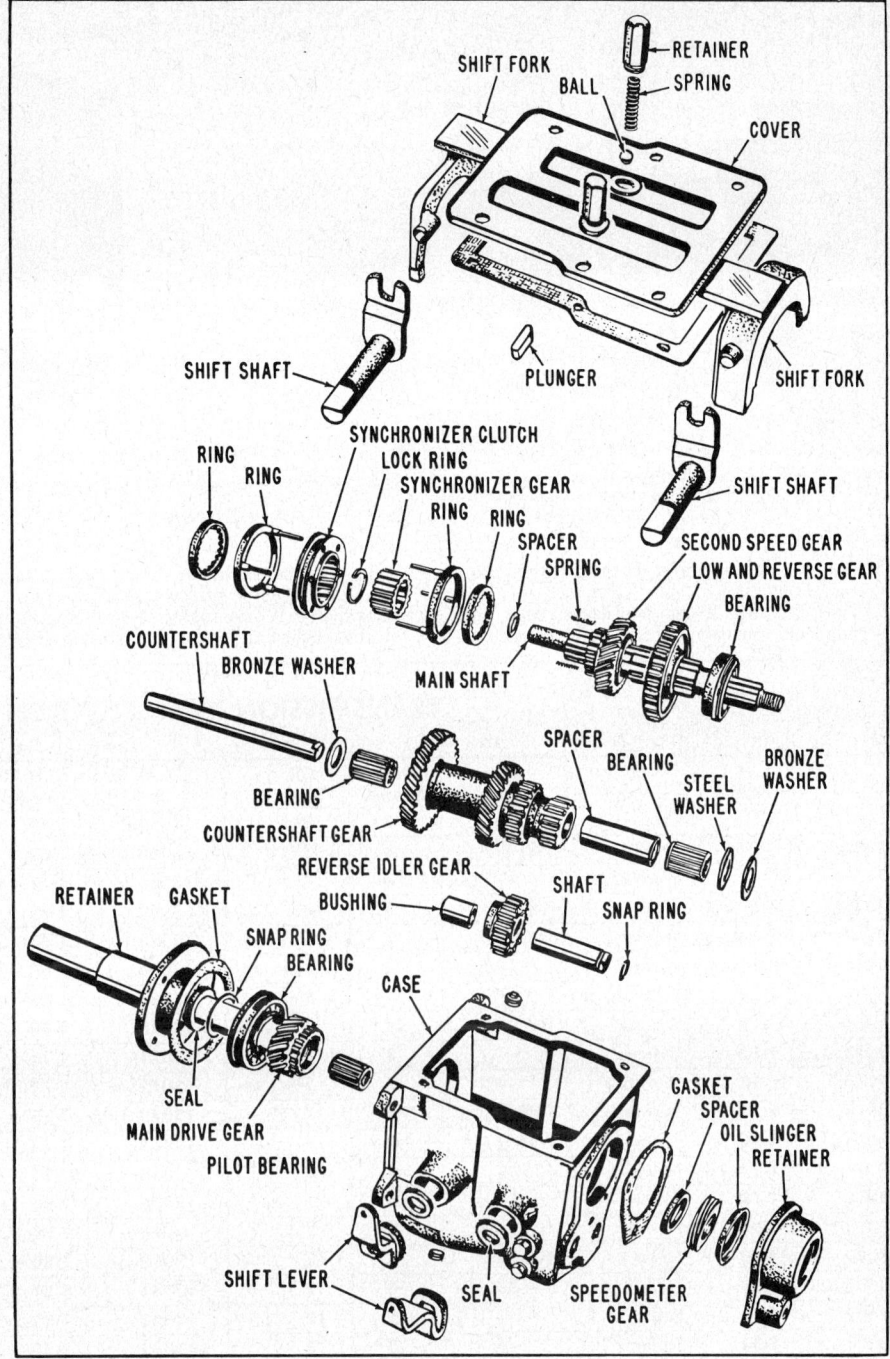

Fig. 1 Three speed transmission. Model T-1

1241

INTERNATIONAL

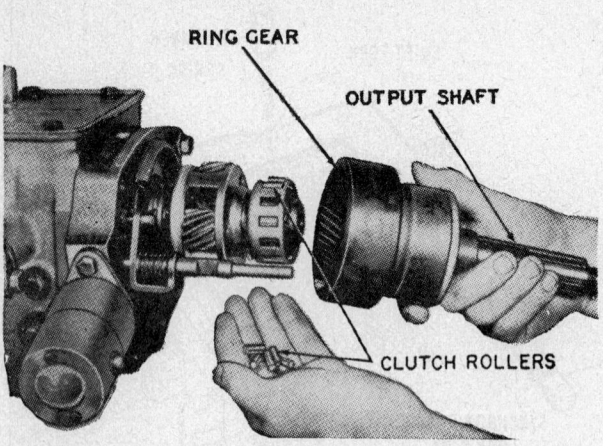

Fig. 4 Removing output shaft and ring gear

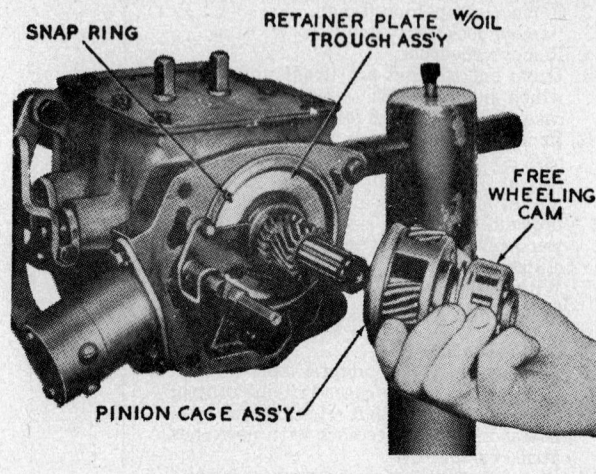

Fig. 5 Removing free wheeling shaft and pinion cage

the left as the outer race encloses the rollers.
7. Prior to installing overdrive case to adapter, position shift rail retractor spring in case. Insert a pilot in case through retractor spring to assure spring alignment. While installing case, guide shift rail through retracting spring. Pilot will be forced from case. *Be sure* slotted portion in shift rail is properly positioned to take overdrive control shaft before installing case.

TRANSMISSION IDENTIFICATION

I.H.C. Code[1]	I.H.C. Model	Mfr's Name	Mfr's Model	No. Speeds	Oil Pints	I.H.C. Code[1]	I.H.C. Model	Mfr's Name	Mfr's Model	No. Speeds	Oil Pints
13001	T-1	I.H.C	T-1	3	2½	13059	T-59	Fuller	5-A-620[2]	5	24
13002	T-2	I.H.C	T-2	3	3½	13060	T-60	Fuller	5-A-620[2]	5	24
13004	T-4	Warner	—	3	2½	13061	T-61	Fuller	5-A-62[2]	5	24
13005	T-5	Warner	T-87[2]	3	6	13062	T-62	Fuller	5-C-65[2]	5	24
13007	T-7	Warner	T-87[2]	3	6	13063	T-63	Fuller	5-C-650[2]	5	24
13008	T-8	Warner	—	3	3½	13064	T-64	Fuller	5-C-650[2]	5	24
13010	T-10	Warner	T-9[2]	4	5½	13068	T-68	Spicer	5652	—	—
13011	T-11	Warner	T-9[2]	4	5	13070	T-70	Fuller	5-C-65[2]	5	24
13013	T-13	Warner	—	3	2¾	13071	T-71	Fuller	5-C-65[2]	5	24
13014	T-14	Warner	—	3	2¾	13072	T-72	Fuller	5-C-65[2]	5	24
13015	T-15	Warner	T-98[2]	4	7	13073	T-73	Fuller	5-C-65[2]	5	26
13016	T-16	Warner	T-98[2]	4	7	13074	T-74	Fuller[3]	R-35[2]	7	16
13017	T-17, 18	New Process	435[2]	4	7	13075	T-75	Fuller[3]	R-46[2]	8	17
13018	T-18	Fuller	—	4	7	13076	T-76	Fuller[3]	R-46S[2]	8	17
13024	T-24	—	—	3	2½	13078	T-78	Fuller	5-C-65[2]	5	26
13030	T-30	Fuller	5-A-33[2]	5	12	13080	T-80	Fuller	10CB-650[2]	10	31
13031	T-31	Fuller	5-A-330[2]	5	12	13081	T-81	Fuller	10CB-65[2]	10	31
13032	T-32	Fuller	—	5	12	13082	T-82	Spicer	8125[2]	12	28
13033	T-33	Fuller	—	5	12	13083	T-83	Spicer	3152	5	28
13034	T-34	Fuller	—	5	12	13088	T-88	Spicer	5752C	—	—
13035	T-35	Fuller	—	5	12	13089	T-89	Spicer	8125[2]	12	28
13036	T-36	Fuller	—	5	12	13090	T-90	Fuller	10CB-650[2]	10	—
13039	T-39	Fuller	WG-11[2]	3	19	13091	T-91	Fuller	10CB-650[2]	10	—
13040	T-40	Spicer	4652[2]	5	13	13104	T-104	Fuller	5-H-74[2]	5	24
13041	T-41	Spicer	4753[2]	5	13	13105	T-105	Fuller	5-HA-74[2]	5	24
13044	T-44	Fuller	WG-11[2]	4	7	13106	T-106	Fuller	5-H-75[2]	5	24
13045	T-45	Fuller	—	4	7	13107	T-107	Fuller	5-HA-75[2]	5	24
13049	T-49	Fuller	WG-11[2]	3	19	13109	T-109	Allison	SA-1126J	6	—
13050	T-50	Fuller	5-A-430[2]	5	19	13110	T-110	Fuller	MT-41[2]	6	19
13051	T-51	Fuller	5-A-43[2]	5	19	13111	T-111	Fuller	MT-42[2]	6	19
13053	T-53	Fuller	—	5	19	13112	T-112	Fuller	MT-42[2]	6	19
13054	T-54	Fuller	—	5	19	13113	T-113	Allison	SA-1126J	6	—
13057	T-57	Fuller	5W-43[2]	5	19	13117	T-117	Allison	SA-1126J	6	—

Continued

INTERNATIONAL

TRANSMISSION IDENTIFICATION—Continued

I.H.C. Code①	I.H.C. Model	Mfr's Name	Mfr's Model	No. Speeds	Oil Pints	I.H.C. Code①	I.H.C. Model	Mfr's Name	Mfr's Model	No. Speeds	Oil Pints
13118	T-118	Allison	SA-1126J	6	—	13412	T-412	Fuller	5CW-65②	5	24
13119	T-119	Allison	SA-1126J	6	—	13413	T-413	Fuller	5CW-65②	5	26
13120	T-120	Allison	SA-1126J	6	—	13414	T-414	Fuller	5CW-650②	5	26
13121	T-121	Fuller	6352②	6	17	13418	T-418	—	—	4	7
13122	T-122	Fuller	MT-42	6	19	13419	T-419	—	—	4	7
13126	T-126	Fuller	5C-720	5	22	13422	T-422	Fuller	RT-613	—	—
13128	T-128	Fuller	RT-915②	15	28	13424	T-424	Fuller	RTO-613	—	—
13129	T-129	Fuller	RT-910②	10	25	13425	T-425	New Process	4590	4	8
13130	T-130	Fuller	—	10	39	13427	T-427	Warner	T-19	4	—
13132	T-132	Fuller	—	5	24	13428	T-428	Warner	T-19A	4	—
13135	T-135	Fuller	—	5	24	13429	T-429	IH	T-429	5	13½
13136	T-136	Fuller	—	5	24	13430	T-430	IH	T-430	5	13½
13137	T-137	Fuller	—	5	24	13431	T-431	IH	T-431	5	13½
13194	T-194	Fuller	RT-12509	—	—	13445	T-445	—	—	4	7
13197	T-197	Fuller	TO-955 All	—	—	13448	T-448	Fuller	RT-610	—	—
13204	T-204	Spicer	6352B	—	—	13451	AT-451	Allison	SA-1241-A	4	—
13208	T-208	Fuller	5C-720②	5	24	13454	AT-454	Allison	SA-1241-A	4	—
13209	T-209	Fuller	5C-720②	5	24	13456	T-456	Spicer	1007-3A	—	—
13210	T-210	Fuller	5C-720②	5	24	13457	T-457	Spicer	1211-3A	—	—
13211	T-211	Fuller	5C-72②	5	24	13459	T-459	Fuller	RTO-9513	—	—
13212	T-212	Fuller	5C-72②	5	24	13460	T-460	Fuller	RTOO-9513	—	—
13214	T-214	Fuller	5W-74②	5	24	13462	T-462	Fuller	RT-9513	—	—
13215	T-215	Fuller	5CA-720②	5	24	13463	T-463	Fuller	T-955 All	—	—
13216	T-216	Fuller	5CA-720②	5	24	13464	AT-464	Allison	SA-1317-A	4	—
13217	T-217	Fuller	5CA-720②	5	24	13465	AT-465	Allison	SA-1317-A	5	—
13218	T-218	Fuller	5CA-720②	5	24	13466	T-466	Fuller	TO-955 All	—	—
13219	T-219	Fuller	5WA-74②	5	24	13468	T-468	Fuller	RTO-12513	—	—
13220	T-220	Fuller	5A-1120②	5	29	13470	T-470	Fuller	RTO-958 LL	—	—
13223	T-223	Spicer	6352②	5	17	13471	T-471	Fuller	RT-9509A	—	—
13227	T-227	Fuller③	R-660②	10	—	13474	AT-474	Allison	SA-1270-B	4	—
13228	T-228	Fuller③	R-63②	10	30	13475	AT-475	Allison	SA-1270-B	5	—
13230	T-230	Fuller③	R-96C②	10	39	13478	T-478	Spicer	RP-8516-3A	—	—
13231	T-231	Fuller③	R-960C②	10	39	13480	T-480	Spicer	1010-2A	—	—
13233	T-233	Fuller	R-96A②	10	39	13482	T-482	Spicer	1252A	—	—
13234	T-234	Fuller	R-960A②	10	39	13486	AT-486	Allison	SA-1270-B	5	—
13252	T-252	Fuller	—	5	24	13487	T-487	Fuller	RT-12510	—	—
13298	T-298	Spicer	6352G	—	—	13488	AT-488	Allison	SA-1317-A	4	—
13316	T-316	Fuller	TO-955 All	—	—	13489	AT-489	Allison	SA-1317-A	4	—
13320	T-320	Spicer	6853C	—	—	13491	T-491	Spicer	1252A	—	—
13331	T-331	IH	T-331	3	3	13493	T-493	Fuller	12515	—	—
13331	T-331	Warner	T-15D	—	—	13494	T-494	IH	T-494	5	12
13332	T-332	IH	T-332	3	3	13495	T-495	IH	T-495	5	12
13332	T-332	Warner	T-15D	—	—	13496	T-496	IH	T-496	5	12
13345	T-345	Fuller	RTO-910②	10	25	13501	AT-501	Spicer	5831②	3 Aux.	10
13346	T-346	Fuller	RTO-915②	15	28	13510	AT-510	Fuller	2-A-45②	2 Aux.	10
13347	T-347	Fuller	T-905A	—	—	13522	AT-522	Spicer	7231②	3 Aux.	8
13348	T-348	Fuller	T-905B	—	—	13523	AT-523	Spicer	7231②	3 Aux.	8
13362	T-362	Fuller	TO-905C	—	—	13524	AT-524	Spicer	6041②	4 Aux.	8
13365	T-365	Fuller③	R-46②	8	—	13527	AT-527	Fuller	3-H-65②	3 Aux.	6½
13366	T-366	Fuller	—	10	39	13528	AT-528	Fuller	3-H-65②	3 Aux.	6½
13367	T-367	Fuller	—	10	39	13529	AT-529	Fuller	3-A-65②	3 Aux.	6½
13401	T-401	Fuller	5CW-62②	5	24	13530	AT-530	Fuller	3-A-65②	3 Aux.	6½
13402	T-402	Fuller	5CW-62②	5	24	13536	AT-536	Spicer	7041	—	—
13403	T-403	Fuller	5CW-62②	5	24	13539	AT-539	Spicer	8031②	3 Aux.	12
13404	T-404	Fuller	5CW-620②	5	24	13540	AT-540	Spicer	8031②	3 Aux.	12
13407	T-407	Chrysler	Loadflite	3	19	13546	AT-546	Spicer	8341②	4 Aux.	12
13411	T-411	Fuller	5CW-65②	5	26	13548	AT-548	IH	AT-548	4	12

Continued

INTERNATIONAL

TRANSMISSION IDENTIFICATION—Continued

I.H.C. Code①	I.H.C. Model	Mfr's Name	Mfr's Model	No. Speeds	Oil Pints
13551	AT-551	Spicer	8345②	5 Aux.	12
13552	AT-552	Spicer	R-8341	—	—
13601	AT-601	Fuller	2A-92	2 Aux.	12
13610	AT-610	—	3A-92	3 Aux.	12
13610	AT-610	—	3B-92	3 Aux.	12
13620	AT-620	Fuller	3T-92	3 Aux.	24

I.H.C. Code①	I.H.C. Model	Mfr's Name	Mfr's Model	No. Speeds	Oil Pints
13625	AT-625	Fuller	4M-112	4 Aux.	21
13630	AT-630	Spicer	8035②	3 Aux.	12

①—Code number is listed on Vehicle Inspection Card attached to left sun visor.
②—See the Stock Transmissions Chapter for repairs on this unit.
③—Roadranger transmission.

Rear Axle Section

NOTE: For Eaton and Timken (Rockwell) driving axles used on International trucks, see the "name" chapter for service procedures.

I.H.C. Code①	I.H.C. Model	Mfr's Name②	Axle Type③	Oil Pints
14001	RA-1	Spicer	S. R.	3
14002	RA-2	Spicer	S. R.	2
14003	RA-3	Spicer	S. R.	3
14004	RA-4	Spicer	S. R.	2.4
14005	RA-5	Timken	S. R.	6
14006	RA-6	Timken	S. R.	6
14009	RA-9	Spicer	S. R.	3
14010	RA-10	Timken	S. R.	6
14011	RA-11	Timken	S. R.	6
14012	RA-12	Spicer	S. R.	2.4
14013	RA-13	Spicer	S. R.	2.4
14014	RA-14	Spicer	S. R.	2.4
14015	RA-15	Timken	S. R.	6½
14016	RA-16	Spicer	S. R.	5½
14017	RA-17	Spicer	S. R.	5½
14018	RA-18	Spicer	S. R.	3
14019	RA-19	Spicer	S. R.	3
14020	RA-20	Timken	S. R.	6½
14021	RA-21	Spicer	S. R.	2
14023	RA-23	Spicer	S. R.	3
14024	RA-24	Spicer	S. R.	3
14025	RA-25	Timken	S. R.	9½
14026	RA-26	Timken	S. R.	8
14028	RA-28	Spicer	S. R.	3
14030	RA-30	Timken	S. R.	9½
14031	RA-31	Timken	S. R.	8
14032	RA-32	Timken	S. R.	8
14033	RA-33	Timken	S. R.	8
14035	RA-35	Timken	S. R.	12
14039	RA-39	Timken	S. R.	12
14043	RA-43	Timken	S. R.	24
14044	RA-44	Timken	S. R.	24
14045	RA-45	Timken	S. R.	22
14047	RA-47	Timken	S. R.	31½
14048	RA-48	Timken	S. R.	31½
14050	RA-50	Timken	S. R.	21
14051	RA-51	Spicer	S. R.	2½
14053	RA-53	Spicer	S. R.	6
14054	RA-54	Spicer	S. R.	6
14055	RA-55	Timken	S. R.	24

I.H.C. Code①	I.H.C. Model	Mfr's Name②	Axle Type③	Oil Pints
14057	RA-57	Timken	S. R.	31
14060	RA-60	Timken	S. R.	23
14063	RA-63	Spicer	S. R.	5¾
14065	RA-65	Timken	S. R.	31
14067	RA-67	Timken	S. R.	28
14070	RA-70	Timken	S. R.	30
14071	RA-71	Timken	S. R.	28
14072	RA-72	Timken	S. R.	—
14073	RA-73	Timken	S. R.	34
14074	RA-74	Timken	S. R.	—
14075	RA-75	Eaton	S. R.	34
14076	RA-76	Timken	S. R.	—
14078	RA-78	Timken	S. R.	34
14083	RA-83	Spicer	S. R.	6
14084	RA-84	Spicer	S. R.	6
14120	RA-120	Eaton	2 Sp.	13
14125	RA-125	Eaton	2 Sp.	11
14126	RA-126	Eaton	2 Sp.	13
14127	RA-127	Eaton	2 Sp.	13
14128	RA-128	Eaton	2 Sp.	13
14130	RA-130	Eaton	2 Sp.	11
14131	RA-131	Eaton	2 Sp.	11
14135	RA-135	Eaton	2 Sp.	16
14136	RA-136	Eaton	2 Sp.	20
14138	RA-138	Eaton	2 Sp.	20
14140	RA-140	Timken	2 Sp.	26④
14143	RA-143	Eaton	2 Sp.	16
14145	RA-145	Eaton	2 Sp.	18
14146	RA-146	Eaton	2 Sp.	22
14147	RA-147	Eaton	2 Sp.	22
14149	RA-149	Eaton	2 Sp.	20
14150	RA-150	Eaton	2 Sp.	22
14152	RA-152	Eaton	2 Sp.	28½
14155	RA-155	Eaton	2 Sp.	24
14157	RA-157	Eaton	2 Sp.	29½
14158	RA-158	Eaton	2 Sp.	34
14160	RA-160	Timken	2 Sp.	29
14162	RA-162	Timken	2 Sp.	28
14163	RA-163	Eaton	2 Sp.	22④
14165	RA-165	Timken	2 Sp.	29④

Continued

INTERNATIONAL

I.H.C. Code①	I.H.C. Model	Mfr's Name②	Axle Type③	Oil Pints	I.H.C. Code①	I.H.C. Model	Mfr's Name②	Axle Type③	Oil Pints
14167	RA-167	Timken	2 Sp.	32½	14346	RA-346	Timken	T.S.R.	⑪
14170	RA-170	Timken	2 Sp.	34④	14348	RA-348	Timken	T.D.	—
14172	RA-172	Timken	2 Sp.	31	14349	RA-349	Timken	T.D.	—
14175	RA-175	Timken	2 Sp.	37④	14351	RA-351	Timken	T.S.R.	⑰
14178	RA-178	Timken	2 Sp.	37④	14355	RA-355	Timken	T.S.R.	⑰
14180	RA-180	Eaton	2 Sp.	32	14356	RA-356	Eaton	T.D.R.	⑭
14181	RA-181	Eaton	2 Sp.	32	14360	RA-360	Eaton	T. 3 Sp.	⑭
14184	RA-184	Eaton	2 Sp.	13	14361	RA-361	Eaton	T. 3 Sp.	⑭
14186	RA-186	Eaton	2 Sp.	22	14364	RA-364	Rockwell	T.D.R.	⑲
14187	RA-187	Eaton	2 Sp.	13	14367	RA-367	Rockwell	T.D.R.	20
14189	RA-189	Eaton	2 Sp.	20	14368	RA-368	Rockwell	T.D.R.	⑳
14190	RA-190	Timken	2 Sp.	35	14370	RA-370	Timken	T.D.R.	28 Each
14191	RA-191	Timken	2 Sp.	60	14371	RA-371	Timken	T.D.R.	28 Each⑦
14192	RA-192	Eaton	2 Sp.	28	14372	RA-372	Timken	T.D.R.	28 Each
14196	RA-196	Eaton	2 Sp.	29½	14373	RA-373	Timken	T.D.R.	28 Each⑦
14197	RA-197	Eaton	2 Sp.	29½	14375	RA-375	Eaton	T.D.R.	22 Each⑱
14199	RA-199	Eaton	2 Sp.	29½	14383	RA-383	Timken	T.D.	—
14245	RA-245	Eaton	D.R.	22	14386	RA-386	Timken	T.S.R.	—
14246	RA-246	Eaton	D.R.	22	14387	RA-387	Timken	T.S.R.	—
14250	RA-250	Eaton	D.R.	22	14388	RA-388	Rockwell	T.S.R.	㉖
14252	RA-252	Eaton	D.R.	28.5	14390	RA-390	Eaton	T.S.R.	㉑
14255	RA-255	Eaton	D.R.	35	14391	RA-391	Eaton	2 Sp.	㉑
14270	RA-270	Timken	D.R.	36④	14392	RA-392	Eaton	D.R.	㉑
14272	RA-272	Timken	D.R.	31	14393	RA-393	Eaton	3 Sp.	㉑
14273	RA-273	Timken	D.R.	34	14395	RA-395	Eaton	D.R.	24
14275	RA-275	Timken	D.R.	38④	14399	RA-399	Eaton	T.D.	㉔
14276	RA-276	Timken	D.R.	38	14446	RA-446	Eaton	S.R.	㉓
14277	RA-277	Timken	D.R.	38	14448	RA-448	Eaton	2 Sp.	㉒
14286	RA-286	Eaton	D.R.	22	14449	RA-449	Eaton	D.R.	㉒
14290	RA-290	Timken	D.R.	34	14459	RA-459	Rockwell	T.S.R.	—
14292	RA-292	Eaton	D.R.	31	14460	RA-460	Rockwell	T.D.R.	⑳
14301	RA-301	Eaton	T.S.R.	11 Each⑤	14461	RA-461	Rockwell	T.S.R.	—
14302	RA-302	Eaton	S.R.	18	14462	RA-462	Rockwell	T.D.R.	⑲
14303	RA-303	Eaton	2 Sp.	18	14487	RA-487	Eaton	S.R.	㉓
14304	RA-304	Eaton	D.R.	㉓	14488	RA-488	Eaton	2 Sp.	㉓
14305	RA-305	Eaton	T.S.R.	14 Each⑤	14489	RA-489	Eaton	D.R.	㉓
14306	RA-306	Eaton	3 Sp.	24	14490	RA-490	Eaton	S.R.	㉑
14310	RA-310	Eaton	T.S.R.	⑥	14491	RA-491	Eaton	2 Sp.	㉑
14312	RA-312	Eaton	T.S.R.	⑭	14492	RA-492	Eaton	D.R.	㉑
14313	RA-313	Eaton	T. 2 Sp.	⑭	14495	RA-495	Eaton	T.D.R.	24 Each
14314	RA-314	Eaton	T.D.R.	⑭					
14315	RA-315	Timken	T.D.R.	⑮					
14316	RA-316	Timken	T.D.R.	⑮					
14317	RA-317	Timken	T.D.R.	28 Each					
14318	RA-318	Timken	T.S.R.	⑩					
14319	RA-319	Timken	T.S.R.	⑩					
14320	RA-320	Eaton	T.S.R.	⑨					
14323	RA-323	Eaton	T.S.R.	⑭					
14324	RA-324	Eaton	T. 2 Sp.	⑭					
14325	RA-325	Eaton	T.D.R.	⑭					
14328	RA-328	Timken	T.S.R.	⑪					
14329	RA-329	Timken	T.D.R.	—					
14330	RA-330	Timken	T.D.R.	22 Each⑦					
14331	RA-331	Timken	T.D.R.	22 Each					
14332	RA-332	Timken	T.S.R.	⑬					
14333	RA-333	Timken	T.S.R.	⑫					
14334	RA-334	Timken	T.S.R.	⑫					
14335	RA-335	Timken	T.D.R.	22 Each					
14336	RA-336	Timken	T.D.R.	22 Each⑦					
14341	RA-341	Timken	T.S.R.	⑯					

① — Code number is listed on Vehicle Specification Card attached to left sun visor.
② — See Rear Axles Chapter for repairs on Timken and Eaton Axles.
③ — S.R.: Single reduction. D.R.: Double reduction. 2 Sp.: Two speed. T.S.R.: Tandem drive single reduction. T.D.R.: Tandem drive double reduction. T. 2 Sp.: Tandem drive 2 speed. T. 3 Sp.: Tandem drive 3 speed.
④ — Add 1 pint to pinion cage when new or reconditioned drive unit is installed.
⑤ — Power divider 6½ pints.
⑥ — Forward axle 28, rearward axle 33, power divider 3.
⑦ — Interaxle differential 2 pints.
⑧ — Forward axle 27, rearward 24, interaxle differential 2.
⑨ — Forward axle 20, rearward 21, power divider 2.
⑩ — Forward axle 31, rearward 32, interaxle differential 2.
⑪ — Forward axle 31½, rearward 32, interaxle differential 2.
⑫ — Forward axle 34, rearward 31, interaxle differential 2.
⑬ — Forward axle 34, rearward 36, interaxle differential 2.

INTERNATIONAL

⑭—Forward axle 24, rearward 22.
⑮—Forward axle 26, rearward 28, interaxle differential 2.
⑯—Forward axle 25, rearward 26, interaxle differential 1.
⑰—Forward axle 23, rearward 24, interaxle differential 1.
⑱—Power divider 6 pints.
⑲—Forward axle 46, rearward 44; interaxle differential 2.
⑳—Forward axle 30, rearward 28, interaxle differential 2.
㉑—Forward axle 27, rearward 20.
㉒—Forward axle 43, rearward 34, interaxle differential 1.
㉓—Forward axle 24; rearward 18.
㉔—Forward axle 32, rearward 28, power drive 2.
㉕—Forward axle 33, rearward 32.

SPICER AXLE
Integral Housing Type

In as much as the axle tubes are pressed into the differential carrier to form a one-piece housing, the rear axle assembly must be removed from the chassis when it becomes necessary to overhaul the unit, Fig. 1.

AXLE SHAFT, REPLACE

1. Raise vehicle and support on jack stands. Remove wheels.
2. Remove brake drum with a suitable puller.
3. Disconnect brake lines at wheel cylinders.
4. Remove bolts securing seal retainer, bearing retainer, backing plate and shims. Retain shim for assembly.
5. Using a suitable puller, remove axle shaft from axle housing.

AXLE ASSEMBLY, REPLACE

1. Raise vehicle and support on jack stands. Remove wheels.
2. Disconnect brake lines and cables from housing and backing plate, then shock absorbers from lower mountings and propeller shaft from carrier.
3. Support axle with a suitable jack and remove leaf spring "U" bolts.
4. Lower axle assembly from vehicle.

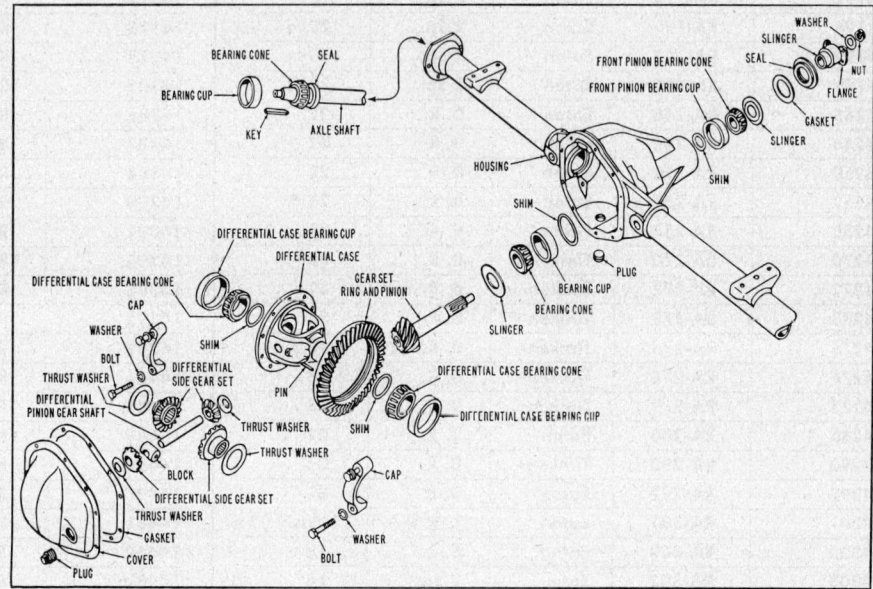

Fig. 1 Disassembled view of Spicer rear axle

Front Wheel Drive

SCOUT FRONT DRIVING AXLE

The differential carrier assembly is the same as the rear driving axle except that the front unit is full floating. The axle shafts can be removed without dismantling the steering knuckles.

Axle Shaft & Universal Joint

Removal
1. Referring to Figs. 1 and 2, remove hub cap and wheel.
2. Remove grease cap and snap ring.
3. Remove drive flange and gasket.
4. Remove brake drum.
5. Remove wheel bearing adjusting nut and washer.
6. Remove wheel hub with wheel bearing, taking care not to damage oil seal.
7. Disconnect brake hose at backing plate.
8. Remove six backing plate and wheel spindle bolts and washers.
9. Remove wheel bearing spindle with bushing.
10. Pull axle shaft and universal joint from axle housing.

Installation
1. Clean dirt from all parts.
2. Enter shaft and joint assembly into housing. Enter spline end of axle shaft into differential and push into place.
3. Install wheel bearing spindle with bushing.
4. Install backing plate and brake hose.
5. Pack wheel bearings with lubricant and install.
6. Assemble driving flange, wheel hub and drum.
7. Install wheel bearing lockwasher and adjusting nut. Tighten adjusting nut until there is a slight drag on bearings when hub is turned, then back off 1/6th of a turn.
8. Install lockwasher and lock nut; tighten nut and bend lip of lockwasher over lock nut.
9. Install snap ring, grease cap, wheel and hub cap.

Steering Knuckle Bearings

Replacement of steering knuckle bearings or bearing cups on the kingpin requires removal of the tie rod, brake drum, hub, wheel bearing, axle shaft, spindle and steering knuckle. The following procedure should be followed when removing the steering knuckle:

1. Referring to Figs. 1 and 2, remove studs and tapered capscrews holding kingpin bearing lower cap.
2. Remove studs and tapered capscrews holding kingpin bearing upper cap and shims.
3. Remove eight oil seal retaining capscrews.
4. Remove upper and lower steering knuckle bearing cone and cup.
5. Remove steering knuckle and seals.

Installation: When reinstalling the steering

knuckle, sufficient shims must be installed under the upper bearing cap so the proper tension may be maintained on the knuckle bearing. No shims are used on the lower bearing cap.

Shims are available in thicknesses of .005″, .010″, and .030″. Install one each of the three thicknesses over the studs on top of the knuckle. Then proceed as follows:
1. Install wheel bearing cups and cones, steering arm, bearing cap, bolts, lockwashers and nuts.
2. Check tension of bearings by hooking a spring scale around the steering arm ball.
3. Pull the scale at right angle to the steering arm. Take the reading when the arm is moving.
4. Remove or add shims until the load is approximately 25-35 pounds without the oil seal assembly in position.

Steering Knuckle Oil Seal

To remove the seal, remove the eight capscrews holding the steering knuckle oil seal in place and remove the seal.

Before installing the new seal, examine the spherical surface of the axle for scores or scratches that might damage the new seal. Roughness of any kind should be smoothed with fine emery cloth.

Lubrication

The front axle universal joints are lubricated by a constant supply of lubricant in the steering knuckle housings. A level plug for checking the lubricant level is located at the rear of each housing. Every 1,000 miles the level should be checked. The recommended capacity for each steering knuckle housing is 38 oz. Use viscous chassis lubricant.

MODELS FA-15, 16, 18, 19, 52

The axles covered in this section are front driving units of the Spicer, type incorporating hypoid gears and spherical steering knuckles. The axle shaft assemblies are full floating and may be removed without disassembling the steering knuckles.

Two different means of transmitting driving torque from the axle shaft to the wheel are employed in these axles. One type uses a drive flange having a splined ID to mate with the axle shaft splines. The flange is bolted to the wheel hub, thus transmitting driving torque from the axle shaft to the wheel hub, Fig. 2.

The second type has a drive gear splined both internally and externally, Fig. 3. The internal splines mate with the axle shaft splines and the external splines index with the splines on the inside of the wheel hub. Driving torque is carried from the axle shaft to the wheel hub through the splined drive gear.

NOTE: The different designs outlined above necessitate two different designs in front wheel locking hubs. For locking hub service, see the *Front Wheel Locking Hub Chapter*.

Axle Shaft & U-Joint

Axles Having Drive Flange, Fig. 2
1. Remove wheel and grease cap and snap ring from end of axle shaft.
2. Remove drive flange. If equipped with locking hubs, take out capscrews and remove clutch body. Lift off clutch body, holding it erect so as not to let drive pins fall out of body.
3. Remove hub body. Loosen setscrew and unscrew drag shoe from spindle.
4. Remove brake drum.
5. Remove wheel hub with wheel bearing.
6. Remove backing plate and wheel spindle bolts. Support backing plate to prevent damage to brake hose if hose is not disconnected.
7. Remove wheel spindle with bushing.
8. Pull out axle shaft and U-joint assembly.
9. Reverse procedure to install.

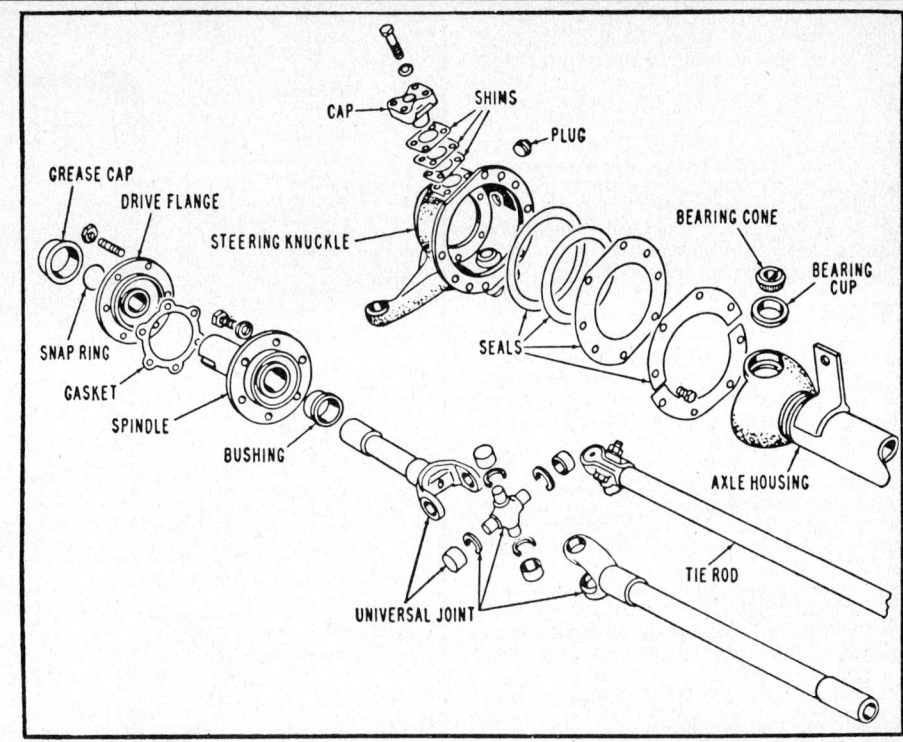

Fig. 1 Exploded view of 4 × 4 front axle shaft and universal joint

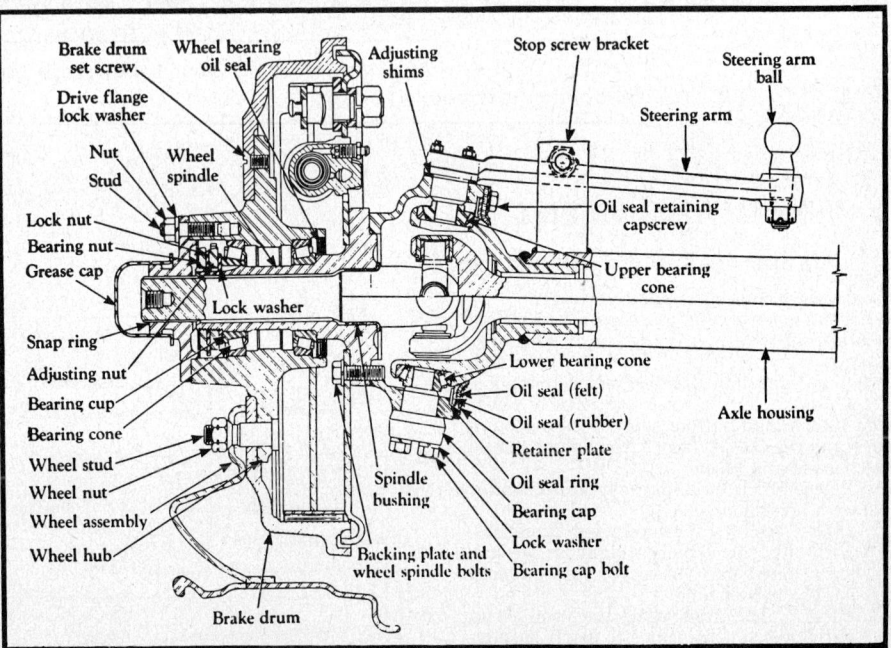

Fig. 2 Front wheel end assembly having drive flange

INTERNATIONAL

Axles Having Drive Gear, Fig. 3

1. Remove wheel. Lightly tap alternately around edge of hub cap until hub cap is removed.
2. If axle is equipped with locking hubs, remove setscrews securing hub clutch assembly to wheel hub. Drive pins may fall out of hub clutch when separated from wheel hub. Be certain to replace them upon reassembly.
3. Remove retaining ring from wheel hub if equipped with locking hubs.
4. Remove snap ring from axle shaft.
5. Pull drive gear out of wheel hub. If difficulty is encountered in removing drive gear, use an offset screwdriver and insert it into groove in drive gear and withdraw gear. If necessary, move wheel backward and forward to aid removal of gear.
6. Remove retaining ring and locking hub body (if equipped).
7. Remove wheel bearing outer nut and slide lock ring off axle shaft. Remove wheel bearing inner nut.
8. Pull drive gear spacer out of wheel hub.
9. Remove brake drum and slide wheel hub off spindle.
10. Remove grease guard and gasket from backing plate.
11. Unfasten spindle and backing plate from steering knuckle. Pull spindle with bushing off axle shaft.
12. Pull axle shaft and U-joint out of axle housing.
13. Reverse procedure to install.

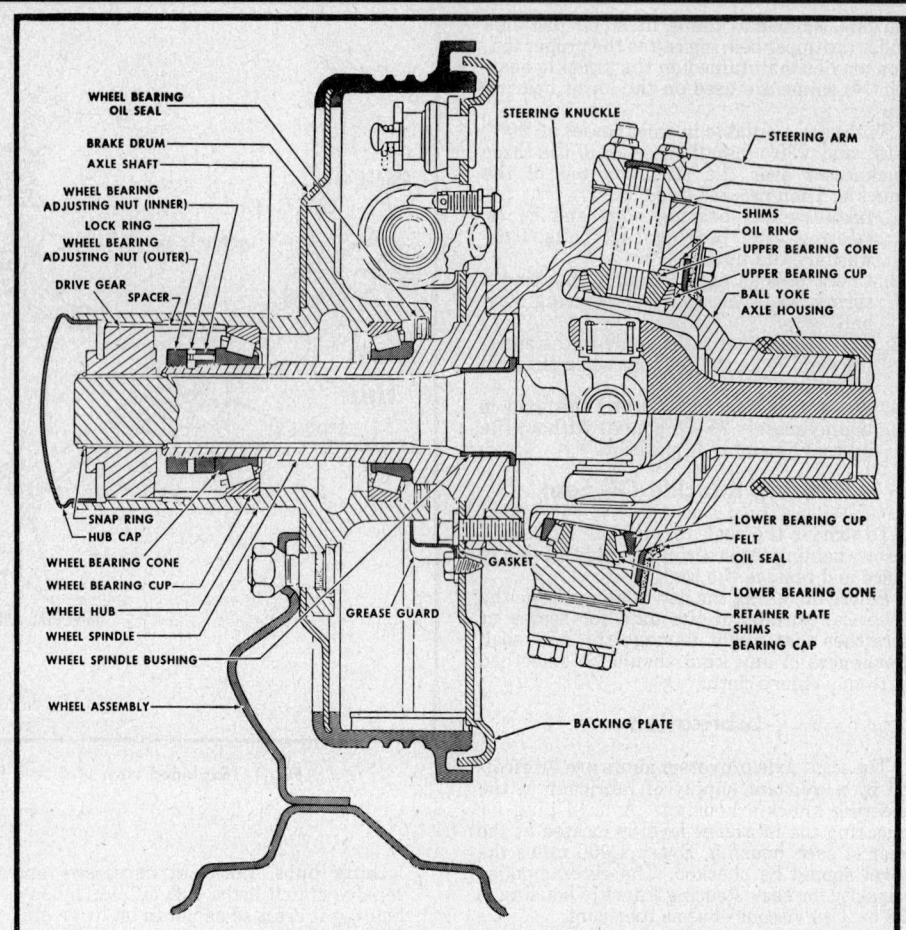

Fig. 3 Front wheel end assembly having drive gear

Front Suspension & Steering Gear

NOTE: Manual and power steering gear repairs are covered in separate chapters. See Index.

WHEEL ALIGNMENT

All Exc. FA-5, 6 & 7 Axles

Checking Front Suspension Height

Front suspension height should be checked before front wheels are aligned or whenever any service work is performed on the torsion bars. If suspension is not up to specifications, Fig. 1, measured between top edge of lower control arm and bottom edge of rubber bumper frame bracket as shown, the height should be checked and reset.

1. Place vehicle on alignment equipment or on a level floor.
2. Inflate tires to recommended pressures, with only the vehicle weight on the torsion bars (no passenger or unusual weight in vehicle).
3. Grasp front bumper and jounce vehicle up and down several times to settle suspension system.
4. Adjustment can be made by loosening or tightening the torsion bar retainer lever bolt, Fig. 2.

NOTE: If the difference between the two sides of the vehicle are within 1/8" of each other and are within the limits specified, they may be considered acceptable. If these values differ more than 1/8" or if one or both of them are outside the specified limits, the suspension height on both sides must be reset.

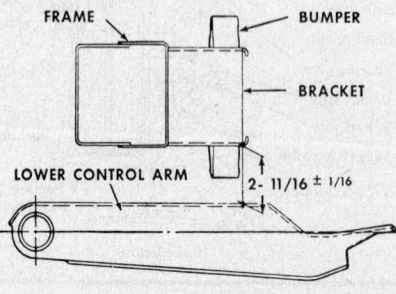

Fig. 1 Checking front suspension height

Camber, Adjust

1. Check front suspension height as described previously.
2. Referring to Fig. 2, loosen nut on camber adjusting bolt.
3. Turn camber bolt in the direction required to obtain a camber angle of one degree (plus or minus 1/2 degree).
4. Holding camber bolt, tighten nut to

INTERNATIONAL

81-135 ft. lbs. torque.

Caster, Adjust
1. Check front suspension height as described previously.
2. Loosen inner and outer nuts on threaded end of strut.
3. Adjust either the inner or outer nut to obtain a caster setting of two degrees *negative* (plus or minus 1/2 deg.).
4. After caster has been established, tighten nuts to 120-150 ft-lbs torque.

CAUTION: Make sure rubber insert washers are parallel with frame bracket when nuts are tightened.

5. Recheck caster after nuts are tightened.

Toe-In, Adjust
1. Check front suspension height as described previously.
2. Disconnect vertical link from left steering arm.
3. Position steering gear in mid-position.
4. Position left front wheel in straight ahead position.
5. Adjust vertical link so ball joint stud will enter hole in left steering arm with wheel in straight ahead position.
6. Insert ball stud in steering arm, install nut and tighten securely.
7. Recheck measurements. If toe-in is not within 1/8 to 3/16", it will be necessary to loosen clamp bolts on right vertical link sleeve and turn sleeve to obtain desired setting.

FA-5, 6 & 7 Axles

Checking Front Suspension Height
With aid of a pair of inside calipers, check the minimum gap from stop plate, welded on the underside of the suspension crossmember, to the ridge on the axle stop brackets located on the lower control arm, Fig. 3. Repeat axle gap measurement on both front wheels.

Camber, Adjust

NOTE: Always adjust camber first before adjusting caster.

1. Loosen nuts on front and rear cams of upper control arm inner pivot bolts, Fig. 4.
2. Adjust camber by simultaneously turning front and rear cam bolts clockwise to decrease positive camber and counter-clockwise to increase positive camber. Refer to "FA-5, 6 & 7 Wheel Alignment Specifications Chart."
3. Tighten nuts and check caster.

Caster, Adjust
1. Loosen nut on front cam of upper control arm pivot bolt, Fig. 4, and turn bolt counterclockwise to increase positive caster and clockwise to decrease positive caster. Refer to "FA-5, 6 & 7 Wheel Alignment Specifications Chart."
2. Tighten nut.
3. Loosen nut on rear cam of upper control arm pivot bolt and turn bolt clockwise to increase positive caster and counterclockwise to decrease positive caster. Refer to "FA-5, 6 & 7 Wheel Alignment Specifications Chart."
4. After camber and caster are adjusted to specifications, torque pivot bolt nuts to 65-75 ft. lbs.

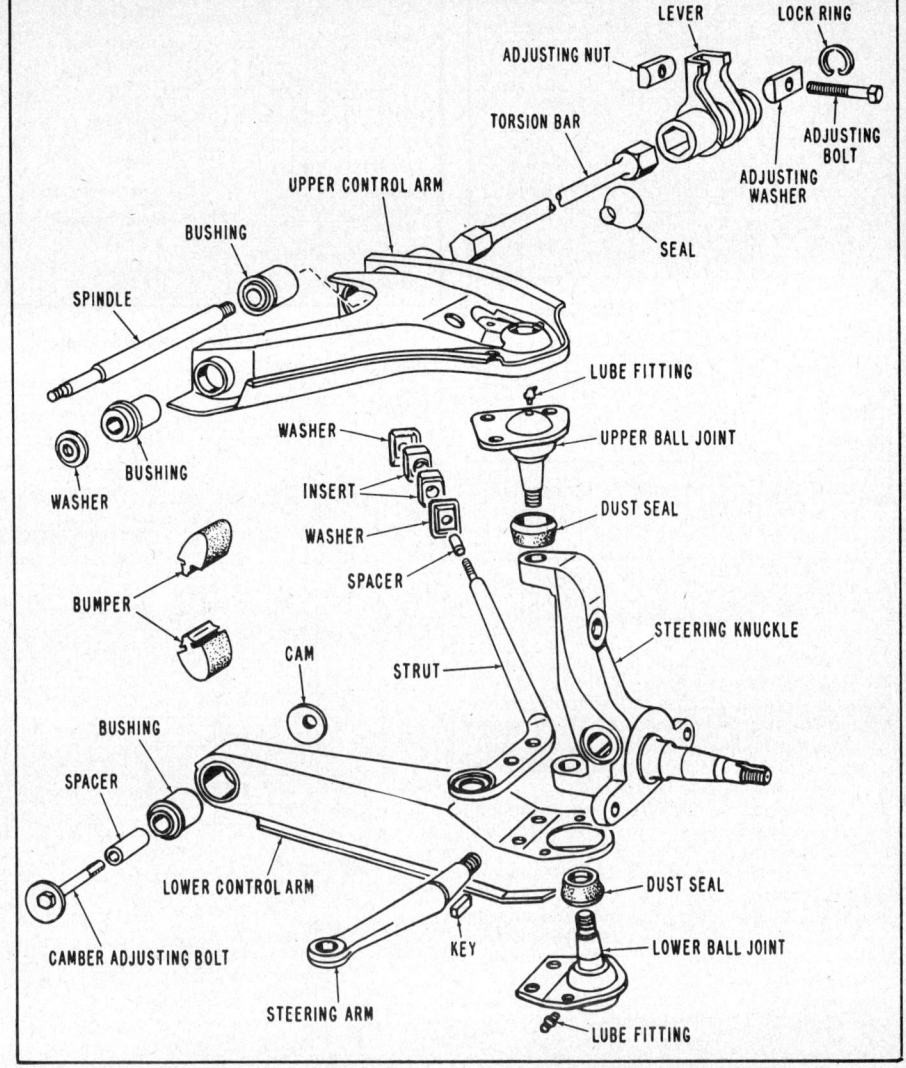

Fig. 2 Torsion bar suspension

Toe-In, Adjust

NOTE: Check all steering joints and make sure they are not binding or cocked to one side.

1. Check toe-in with pitman arm on center of travel of steering gear.
2. To adjust, loosen clamp bolt nuts and rotate turnbuckle as necessary. Refer to "FA-5, 6 & 7 Wheel Alignment Specifications Chart."
3. After correct alignment has been obtained, torque clamp bolt nuts to 25-35 ft. lbs.

TORSION BAR, REPLACE

The torsion bars are not interchangeable, side to side. The left-hand bar cannot be used on the right side and vice versa. The bars are marked "L" and "R" for left and right or stamped on the end of the rod. The bars should always be installed with these letters toward the rear of the vehicle. Also an arrow is stamped on the end of the bar to indicate the direction of wind-up for applying load application.

Removal

1. Referring to Fig. 2, raise vehicle with jack under frame crossmember.
2. Release load from torsion bar by loosening retaining lever adjusting bolt.
3. Remove retainer lever adjusting bolt, washer and nut and slide retainer lever from end of torsion bar.
4. Disengage torsion bar from upper control arm and slide bar to rear to remove from vehicle.

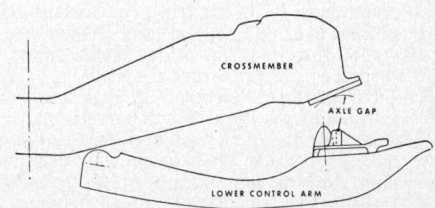

Fig. 3 Axle gap measurement

INTERNATIONAL

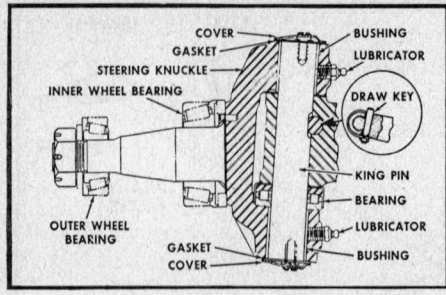

Steering knuckle using kingpin seal cap with hold-down screws

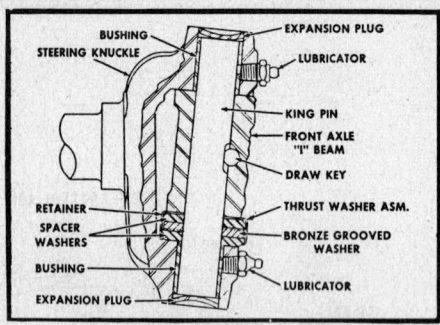

Steering knuckle using thrust bearing with bronze grooved washer

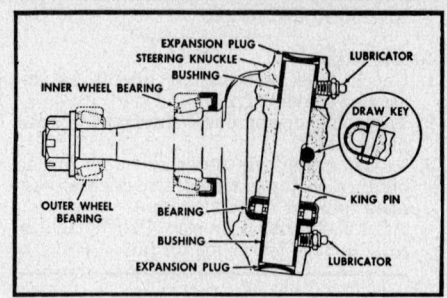

Steering knuckle with expansion type seal plugs

CAUTION: When removing torsion bars, be careful not to nick or scratch them as it may create a fracture.

Installation

1. With vehicle raised off floor, position torsion bar stamped with the letter "L" in upper control arm on left side of vehicle and bar stamped with letter "R" in upper control arm on right side of vehicle. Also make sure arrow stamped on end of bar is located toward rear of vehicle.
2. Position retainer lever on end of torsion bar so adjusting bolt can just be threaded into nut.
3. Install washer on adjusting bolt and insert bolt into retainer lever and bracket.
4. Install nut on adjusting bolt and adjust height of suspension as outlined below.
5. Always check caster and camber whenever torsion bars have been removed or replaced. Also check aiming of headlamps after setting front suspension height.

COIL SPRING, REPLACE

FA-5, 6 & 7 Axles

1. Raise vehicle and position two jack stands under frame.
2. Remove wheel and tire assembly.
3. Remove caliper, rotor, and brake shield from steering knuckle.

NOTE: Secure caliper to frame to prevent damage to brake hose.

4. Remove shock absorber.
5. Disconnect sway bar from axle bumper and wheel stop bracket, if equipped, then remove bumper and stop bracket from lower control arm.
6. Insert Compressor screw No. SE-2491-2 through shock absorber upper mounting hole in crossmember. Working through opening in lower control arm, assemble puller hook SE-2491-1 to compressor screw, then position puller hooks under second coil from bottom of spring.
7. Turn spring compressor until spring is unseated from lower control arm.
8. Remove cotter pins from upper and lower ball joint studs, then loosen lower ball joint stud nut approximately two turns.
9. Position tool No. SE-2493, Fig. 5, between upper and lower ball joint studs. Turn tool until a slight pressure is applied to lower

FA-5, 6 & 7 Axles Wheel Alignment Specifications Table

Axle Gap (Inch) Fig. 2	Caster, Degrees	Camber, Degrees		Toe-In, Inch
		Left	Right	
2.80	1½	⅛	−⅛	0–⅛
3.20	1	¼	0	0–⅛
3.60	½	¼	0	0–⅛
4.00	0	¼	0	0–⅛
4.40	−½	¼	0	0–⅛
4.80	−1	0	−¼	0–⅛
5.20	−1½	−¼	−½	0–⅛

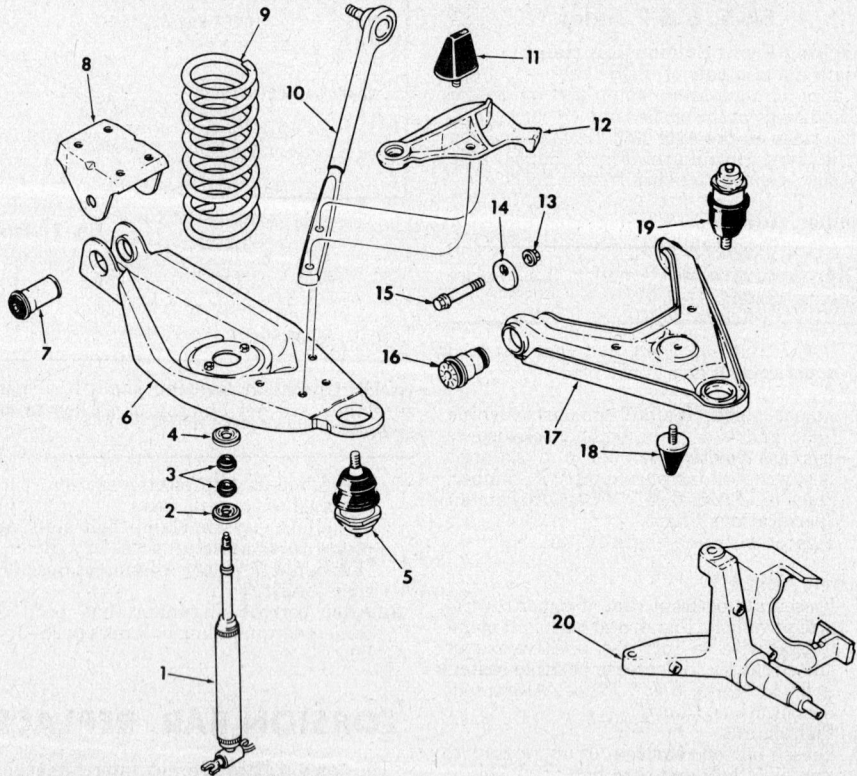

1. SHOCK ABSORBER
2. RETAINER
3. CUSHION
4. RETAINER
5. LOWER BALL JOINT
6. LOWER CONTROL ARM
7. BUSHING
8. BRACKET
9. COIL SPRING
10. CONTROL ARM ROD
11. BUMPER
12. WHEEL STOP BRKT.
13. NUT
14. CASTER ADJUST CAM
15. BOLT
16. BUSHING
17. UPPER CONTROL ARM
18. BUMPER
19. UPPER BALL JOINT
20. STEERING KNUCKLE

Fig. 4 Front suspension. FA-5, 6 and 7 models

ball joint stud, then tap steering knuckle to free stud.
10. Torque upper ball joint stud nut to 70–80 ft. lbs. on 100 models and 80–90 ft. lbs. on 200 models and install cotter pin.
11. Remove lower ball joint stud nut and lower control arm from steering knuckle.
12. Turn spring compressor until spring is unseated from crossmember, then remove compressor and spring.
13. Reverse procedure to install. Torque lower ball joint stud nut to 80–90 ft. lbs. on 100 models and 90–100 ft. lbs. on 200 models.

BALL JOINT, REPLACE

FA-5, 6 & 7 Axles

Upper Ball Joint
1. Raise vehicle and position two jack stands under frame.
2. Remove wheel and tire assembly and shock absorber.
3. Install spring compressor SE-2491 and puller hook SE-2491-1. Turn compressor screw until spring is unseated from lower control arm.
4. Using a suitable jack, support lower control arm at ball joint.
5. Remove cotter pins from upper and lower ball joint studs, then loosen upper ball joint stud nut approximately two turns.
6. Position tool No. SE-2493, Fig. 5, between upper and lower ball joint studs. Turn tool until a slight pressure is applied to the upper ball joint stud, then tap steering knuckle to free stud.
7. Torque lower ball joint stud nut to 80–90 ft. lbs. on 100 models and 90–100 ft. lbs. on 200 models and install cotter pin.
8. Remove upper ball joint stud nut and lift control arm from steering knuckle.

NOTE: Support upper control arm to prevent brake line from becoming damaged.

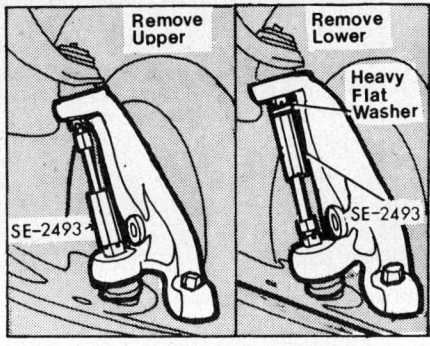

Fig. 5 Removing ball jont stud from steering knuckle

9. Using tool No. SE-2491-1, remove ball joint from control arm.
10. Install ball joint using tool No. 2491-1, thread ball joint into control arm until fully seated.
11. Pack dust cover 2/3 full with grease, then install dust cover on ball joint using tool No. SE-2495-2.
12. Place ball joint stud into steering knuckle, then install nut and cotter pin. Torque nut to 70–80 ft. lbs. on 100 models and 80–90 ft. lbs. on 200 models.
13. Using the jack, raise lower control arm until it contacts the spring.
14. Loosen spring compressor and lower jack.
15. Remove spring compressor.
16. Install shock absorber and wheel and tire assembly.

Lower Ball Joint
1. Remove spring as described under "Coil Spring Replace."
2. Remove lower control arm from frame bracket.
3. Position lower control arm in a vise.
4. Remove ball joint from control arm using tool No. 2494-2.
5. Install ball joint using tool No. 2494-2, thread ball joint into control arm until fully seated.
6. Pack dust cover 2/3 full with grease, then install dust cover on ball joint using tool No. 2495-1.
7. Remove control arm from vise and install on frame bracket.

JEEP

INDEX OF SERVICE OPERATIONS

AXLES, DRIVING
	Page No.
Service	1291
Eaton Axle Service	204
Spicer Axle Service	239
Timken Axle Service	241
Locking Differentials	192
Front Wheel Locking Hubs	505
Front Wheel Drive	1294

BRAKES
Adjustments	590
Air Brakes Service	620
Brake Booster Service	639
Disc Brakes	661
Hydraulic System Service	632
Parking Brake Service	612
Stopmaster Brake Service	599

CLUTCHES
Air-Hydraulic (Air-Pak)	468
Clutch Pedal, Adjust	1288
Clutch, Replace	1288
Clutch Service	429

COOLING SYSTEM
Cooling System Capacity	1252
Variable Speed Fans	10
Water Pumps	1270

ELECTRICAL
Alternator Service	52
Dash Gauge Service	179
Distributor, Replace	1270
Distributors, Standard	141
Electronic Ignition	152
Generator Service	11
Ignition Coils and Resistors	7
Starting Motor Service	29
Starter Switch Service	21
Tune Up Service	2

ENGINE
Camshaft	1268
Crankshaft Rear Oil Seal	1268
Cylinder Head, Replace	1261
Main & Rod Bearings	1268
Piston and Rod, Assemble	1268
Rocker Arms	1263
Timing Case Cover	1265
Timing Chain	1267
Timing Gears	1267
Valves, Adjust	1265
Valve Arrangement	1265
Valve Guides	1265
Valve Lifters	1265

ENGINE OILING
Crankcase Capacity	1252
Oil Pump, Repairs	1269

FRONT SUSPENSION
Front Wheel Locking Hubs	505
Wheel Alignment, Adjust	1297

FUEL & EXHAUST
Carburetor Adjustments	1271
Crankcase Ventilation	748
Emission Controls	750
Fuel Pump Service	183
L.P.G. Carburetion	190
Turbochargers	187

SPECIFICATIONS
Alternator and Regulator	1258
Carburetor Adjustments	1271
Crankshaft and Bearing	1258
Distributor	1256
Engine Tightening Torque	1259
General Engine Data	1252
Piston, Pin and Ring	1258
Starting Motor	1258
Tune Up	1254
Valve	1259
Wheel Alignment	1260

STEERING
Steering Gear, Replace	1297
Manual Steering Gear Service	680
Power Steering Gear Service	686

TRANSFER CASES
469, 1290

TRANSMISSIONS, Manual
Clark	275
Fuller	289
New Process	329
Spicer	346
Transmission, Replace	1289
Warner	406

GENERAL ENGINE SPECIFICATIONS

Year	Model or Series	Engine Make	Engine Model	Bore & Stroke	Piston Displ. Cu. In.	Comp. Ratio	Horsepower @ R.P.M.	Normal Oil Pressure P.S.I.	Oil Pan Refill Capacity Qts. ②	Cooling System Capacity Qts. ①
JEEP										
1970	CJ Series	Own	F4-134	3 1/8 × 4 3/8	134	6.7	75 @ 4000	35	4	12
1970-71	CJ Series	Buick	V6-225	3.750 × 3.400	225	9.0	160 @ 4200	33	4	10
1972-75	CJ Series	Amer. Mtrs.	6-232	3.750 × 3.500	232	8.0	100 @ 3600③	37-75	5	10 1/2
1977-78	CJ Series	Amer. Mtrs.	6-232	3.750 × 3.500	232	8.0	—	37-75	5	10 1/2
1972-75	Commando	Amer. Mtrs.	6-232	3.750 × 3.500	232	8.0	100 @ 3600③	37-75	5	10 1/2
1976	CJ, Chero., Wag.	Amer. Mtrs.	6-232	3.750 × 3.500	232	8.0	90 @ 3050	37-75	5	10 1/2
1970	DJ Dispatcher	Own	F4-134	3 1/8 × 4 3/8	134	6.7	75 @ 4000	35	4	12
1970-71	DJ Dispatcher	Buick	V6-225	3.750 × 3.400	225	9.0	160 @ 4200	33	4	10
1970-71	J-100 Series	Amer. Mtrs.	6-232	3.750 × 3.500	232	8.5	145 @ 4300	50	5	10 1/2
1970-71	J-100 Series	Buick	V8-350	3.800 × 3.850	350	9.0	230 @ 4400	37	4	15
1971	J-100 Series	Amer. Mtrs.	V8-360	4.08 × 3.44	360	8.5	245 @ 4400	37	4	13
1972-75	J-100 Series	Amer. Mtrs.	6-258	3.750 × 3.895	258	8.0	110 @ 3500③	37-75	5	10 1/2

Continued

JEEP

GENERAL ENGINE SPECIFICATIONS—Continued

Year	Model or Series	Engine Make	Engine Model	Bore & Stroke	Piston Displ. Cu. In.	Comp. Ratio	Horsepower @ R.P.M.	Normal Oil Pressure P.S.I.	Oil Pan Refill Capacity Qts. ②	Cooling System Capacity Qts. ①
JEEP—Continued										
1976	CJ, Chero., Wag.	Amer. Mtrs.	6-258	3.750 × 3.895	258	8.0	95 @ 3050	37–75	5	10½
1977–78	CJ Series	Amer. Mtrs.	6-258	3.750 × 3.895	258	8.0	—	37–75	5	10½
1977–78	Cherokee	Amer. Mtrs.	6-258	3.750 × 3.895	258	8.0	—	37–75	5	10½
1972–73	J-100 Series	Amer. Mtrs.	V8-360	4.08 × 3.44	360	8.5	175 @ 4000	37–75	4	13
1974–75	All	Amer. Mtrs.	V8-360④	4.08 × 3.44	360	8.25	175 @ 4000	37–75	4	—
1974–75	All	Amer. Mtrs.	V8-360⑤	4.08 × 3.44	360	8.25	195 @ 4400	37–75	4	—
1976	Chero., Wag.	Amer. Mtrs.	V8-360④	4.08 × 3.44	360	8.25	140 @ 3200	37–75	4	14
1976	Chero., Wag.	Amer. Mtrs.	V8-360⑤	4.08 × 3.44	360	8.25	165 @ 3500	37–75	4	14
1976	Chero., Wag.	Amer. Mtrs.	V8-401	4.16 × 3.68	401	8.25	205 @ 3500	37–75	4	14
1977–78	Chero., Wag.	Amer. Mtrs.	V8-360④	4.08 × 3.44	360	8.25	—	37–75	4	14
1977–78	Chero., Wag.	Amer. Mtrs.	V8-360⑤	4.08 × 3.44	360	8.25	—	37–75	4	14
1977	Chero., Wag.	Amer. Mtrs.	V8-401	4.16 × 3.68	401	8.25	—	37–75	4	14
1978	Chero., Wag.	Amer. Mtrs.	V8-401	4.16 × 3.68	401	8.30	—	37–75	4	14
1970	Jeepster	Own	F4-134	3⅛ × 4⅜	134	6.7	75 @ 4000	35	4	12
1970	Jeepster	Buick	V6-225	3.750 × 3.400	225	9.0	160 @ 4200	33	4	10
1971	Jeepster	Amer. Mtrs.	6-258	3.750 × 3.895	258	8.0	150 @ 3800	37	4	10½
1971	All	Amer. Mtrs.	V8-304	3.750 × 3.44	304	8.4	210 @ 4400	37	4	14
1972–75	CJ Series	Amer. Mtrs.	V8-304	3.75 × 3.440	304	8.4	150 @ 4200③	37–75	4	14
1976	CJ Series	Amer. Mtrs.	V8-304	3.750 × 3.44	304	8.4	120 @ 3200	37–75	4	14
1977–78	CJ Series	Amer. Mtrs.	V8-304	3.75 × 3.44	304	8.4	—	37–75	4	13
1979	All	Amer. Mtrs.	6-258	3.75 × 3.90	258	8.3	—	37–75	5	10.5
1979	All	Amer. Mtrs.	V8-304	3.75 × 3.44	304	8.4	—	37–75	4	13.0
1979	All	Amer. Mtrs.	V8-360	4.08 × 3.44	360	8.25	—	37–75	4	13.0
1980	CJ Series	Pontiac	4-151	4.00 × 3.00	151	8.2	—	37–75	3	7.8
1980	All	Amer. Mtrs.	6-258	3.75 × 3.90	258	8.0	—	37–75	5	10.5
1980	CJ Series	Amer. Mtrs.	V8-304	3.75 × 3.44	304	8.4	—	37–75	4	13
1980	All Exc. CJ	Amer. Mtrs.	V8-360	4.08 × 3.44	360	8.25	—	37–75	4	14
JEEP TRUCKS										
1970	J-2000, 3000	Amer. Mtrs.	6-232	3¾ × 3½	232	8.50	145 @ 4400	50	5	10½
	J-2000, 3000	Buick	V8-350	3.800 × 3.850	350	9.0	230 @ 4400	37	4	—
1971–75	J-2000	Amer. Mtrs.	6-258	3.750 × 3.895	258	8.0	110 @ 3500③	37–75	5	10½
1972–73	J-4000	Amer. Mtrs.	V8-360	4.08 × 3.44	360	8.5	175 @ 4000③	37–75	4	13
1974–75	All	Amer. Mtrs.	V8-360④	4.08 × 3.44	360	8.25	175 @ 4000	37–75	4	—
	All	Amer. Mtrs.	V8-360⑤	4.08 × 3.44	360	8.25	195 @ 4400	37–75	4	—
	All	Amer. Mtrs.	V8-401	4.16 × 3.68	401	8.25	215 @ 4200	37–75	4	—
1976	J-10, 20	Amer. Mtrs.	6-232	3.75 × 3.50	232	8.0	90 @ 3050	37–75	5	10½
	J-10, 20	Amer. Mtrs.	6-258	3.750 × 3.895	258	8.0	95 @ 3050	37–75	5	10½
	J-10, 20	Amer. Mtrs.	V8-360④	4.08 × 3.44	360	8.25	140 @ 3200	37–75	4	14
	J-10, 20	Amer. Mtrs.	V8-360⑤	4.08 × 3.44	360	8.25	165 @ 3500	37–75	4	14
	J-10, 20	Amer. Mtrs.	V8-401	4.16 × 3.68	401	8.25	205 @ 3500	37–75	4	14
1977–78	J-10	Amer. Mtrs.	6-258	3.750 × 3.895	258	8.0	—	37–75	5	10½
	J-10, 20	Amer. Mtrs.	V8-360④	4.08 × 3.44	360	8.25	—	37–75	4	14
	J-10, 20	Amer. Mtrs.	V8-360⑤	4.08 × 3.44	360	8.25	—	37–75	4	14
	J-10, 20	Amer. Mtrs.	V8-401	4.16 × 3.68	401	⑥	—	37–75	4	14
1979	All	Amer. Mtrs.	6-258	3.75 × 3.90	258	8.3	—	37–75	5	10.5
	All	Amer. Mtrs.	V8-304	3.75 × 3.44	304	8.4	—	37–75	4	13.0
	All	Amer. Mtrs.	V8-360	4.08 × 3.44	360	8.25	—	37–75	4	13.0
1980	All	Amer. Mtrs.	6-258	3.75 × 3.90	258	8.0	—	37–75	5	10.5
1980	All	Amer. Mtrs.	V8-360	4.08 × 3.44	360	8.25	—	37–75	4	14

① —With heater.
② —Add 1 qt. with filter change.
③ —Ratings are NET—as installed in vehicle.
④ —2 Bar. Carb.
⑤ —4 Bar. Carb.
⑥ —1977; 8.25, 1978; 8.30.

JEEP

TUNE UP SPECIFICATIONS

The following specifications are published from the latest information available. This data should be used only in the absence of a decal affixed in the engine compartment.

★ When using a timing light, disconnect vacuum hose or tube at distributor and plug opening in hose or tube so idle speed will not be affected.

⊙ When checking compression, lowest cylinder must be within 80 percent of highest.

▲ Before removing wires from distributor cap, determine location of the No. 1 wire in cap, as distributor position may have been altered from that shown at the end of this chart.

Year & Engine	Spark Plug		Ignition Timing BTDC①★				Curb Idle Speed②		Fuel Pump Pressure
	Type	Gap	Firing Order Fig. ▲	Man. Trans.	Auto. Trans.	Mark Fig.	Man. Trans.	Auto. Trans.	
1980									
4-151	R44TSX⑰	.060	E	12°	—	Damper	900	—	6½–8
6-258 CJ Models Exc. Calif.	③⑱	.035	A	8°	10°	Damper	700	500/600D	4–5
6-258 CJ Models Calif.	N13L⑱	.035	A	6°	8°	Damper	700	500/600D	4–5
6-258 Exc. CJ Models	④⑱	.035	A	8°	8°	Damper	700	700D	4–5
V8-304 Exc. Calif.	⑤⑱	.035	B	8°⑥	10°	Damper	700	500/600D	5–6½
V8-304 Calif.	⑤⑱	.035	B	5°	5°	Damper	700	500/600D	5–6½
V8-360	⑤⑱	.035	B	8°	8°	Damper	800	600D	5–6½
1979									
6-258 CJ Models	⑦	.035	A	6°	4°	Damper	700	600D	4–5
6-258 Exc. CJ Models	⑦	.035	A	8°	8°	Damper	600	600D	4–5
V8-304	⑤	.035	B	5°	8°	Damper	⑧	600D	5–6½
V8-360	⑤	.035	B	8°	8°	Damper	800	600D	5–6½
1978									
6-232 Exc. High Alt.	N13L	.035	A	5°	—	Damper	850	—	4–5
6-232 High Alt.	N13L	.035	A	10°⑨	—	Damper	600	—	4–5
6-258 1 Barrel Carb.⑩	N13L	.035	A	3°	8°	Damper	850	550D	4–5
6-258 1 Barrel Carb. Calif.	N13L	.035	A	8°	8°	Damper	850	550D	4–5
6-258 1 Barrel Carb. High Alt.	N13L	.035	A	10°⑨	10°⑨	Damper	600	550D	4–5
6-258 2 Barrel Carb.	N13L	.035	A	6°	6°	Damper	650	550D	4–5
V8-304	N12Y	.035	B	5°	⑪	Damper	750	700D	5–6½
V8-360 Exc. Calif.	N12Y	.035	B	5°	8°	Damper	750	700D	5–6½
V8-360 Calif.	N12Y	.035	B	—	10°	Damper	—	700D	5–6½
V8-401	N12Y	.035	B	5°	8°	Damper	750	700D	5–6½
1977									
6-232 Exc. High Alt.	N12Y	.035	C	5°	—	Damper	850	—	4–5
6-232 High Alt.	N12Y	.035	C	10°⑫	—	Damper	600	—	4–5
6-258 1 Barrel Carb.⑩	N12Y	.035	C	3°	8°	Damper	850	550D	4–5
6-258 1 Barrel Carb. Calif.	N12Y	.035	C	6°	8°	Damper	850	700D	4–5
6-258 1 Barrel Carb. High Alt.	N12Y	.035	C	10°⑬	10°⑫	Damper	600	550D	4–5
6-258 2 Barrel Carb.	N12Y	.035	C	6°	6°	Damper	650	550D	4–5
V8-304	RN12Y	.035	D	5°	⑩	Damper	700	700D	5–6½
V8-360, 401	RN12Y	.035	D	5°	8°	Damper	750	700D	5–6½
1976									
6-232	N12Y	.035	C	8°	—	Damper	600	—	4–5
6-258 Exc. Calif.	N12Y	.035	C	6°	8°	Damper	⑭	550D	4–5
6-258 Calif.	N12Y	.035	C	6°	8°	Damper	600	700D	4–5
V8-304 Exc. Calif.	N12Y	.035	D	5°	10°	Damper	750	700D	5–6½
V8-304 Calif.	N12Y	.035	D	5°	5°	Damper	750	700D	5–6½
V8-360, 401 Exc. Calif.	N12Y	.035	D	5°	8°	Damper	750	700D	5–6½
V8-360, 401 Calif.	N12Y	.035	D	5°	5°	Damper	750	700D	5–6½

Continued

JEEP

TUNE UP SPECIFICATIONS—Continued

The following specifications are published from the latest information available. This data should be used only in the absence of a decal affixed in the engine compartment.

★ When using a timing light, disconnect vacuum hose or tube at distributor and plug opening in hose or tube so idle speed will not be affected.

● When checking compression, lowest cylinder must be within 80 percent of highest.

▲ Before removing wires from distributor cap, determine location of the No. 1 wire in cap, as distributor position may have been altered from that shown at the end of this chart.

Year & Engine	Spark Plug Type	Spark Plug Gap	Firing Order Fig. ▲	Ignition Timing BTDC①★ Man. Trans.	Ignition Timing BTDC①★ Auto. Trans.	Mark Fig.	Curb Idle Speed② Man. Trans.	Curb Idle Speed② Auto. Trans.	Fuel Pump Pressure
1975									
6-232	N12Y	.035	C	5°	—	Damper	⑮	—	4–5
6-258	N12Y	.035	C	3°	3°	Damper	⑯	550D	4–5
V8-304	N12Y	.035	D	5°	—	Damper	750	—	5–6½
V8-360, 401	N12Y	.035	D	2½°	2½°	Damper	750	700D	5–6½
1974									
6-232⑲	N12Y	.035	C	5°	—	Damper	600	—	4–5½
6-258⑲	N12Y	.035	C	3°	3°	Damper	600	550D⑳	4–5½
V8-304㉑	N12Y	.035	D	5°	—	Damper	750	—	4–6½
V8-360㉑	N12Y	.035	D	5°	5°	Damper	750	700D⑳	4–6½
V8-401㉑	N12Y	.035	D	㉒	㉒	Damper	650	600D⑳	4–6½
1973									
6-232, CJ/DJ⑲	N12Y	.035	C	5°	—	Damper	700	—	4–5½
6-232, Commando⑲	N12Y	.035	C	5°	3°	Damper	600	550D	4–5½
6-258, CJ/DJ⑲	N12Y	.035	C	3°	—	Damper	700	—	4–5½
6-258, Exc. CJ/DJ⑲	N12Y	.035	C	3°	3°	Damper	600	550D	4–5½
V8-304㉑	N12Y	.035	D	5°	5°	Damper	750	700D	4–6½
V8-360㉑	N12Y	.035	D	5°	5°	Damper	750	700D	4–6½
1972									
6-232⑲	N12Y	.035	C	5°	5°	Damper	675	675D	4–5½
6-258⑲	N12Y	.035	C	3°	3°	Damper	675	600D	4–5½
V8-304㉑	N12Y	.035	D	5°	5°	Damper	725	650D	5–6½
V8-360㉑	N12Y	.035	D	5°	5°	Damper	725	650D	5–6½
1971									
6-232, Exc. Truck㉓	N14Y	.035	C	TDC	TDC	Damper	675	675	4–5½
6-232, Truck㉓	N14Y	.035	C	5°	—	Damper	550	—	4–5½
V6-225㉑	44S	.035	—	5°	5°	Damper	675	675	4½–5¾
V8-350㉑	45TS	.030	—	TDC	TDC	Damper	650	650N	4½–5¾
1970									
F4-134㉔	J8	.030	—	TDC	—	Pulley	675	—	2½–3¾
6-232, Exc. Truck㉓	N14Y	.035	C	TDC	TDC	Damper	675	675	4–5½
6-232, Truck㉓	N14Y	.035	C	5°	—	Damper	550	—	4–5½
V6-225㉑	44S	.035	—	5°	5°	Damper	675	675	4½–5¾
V8-350㉑	45TS	.030	—	TDC	TDC	Damper	650	650N	4½–5¾

① —B.T.D.C.-Before top dead center.
② —Idle speed on man. trans. vehicles is adjusted in Neutral & on auto. trans. equipped vehicles is adjusted in Drive unless otherwise specified. When two idle speeds are listed, the higher speed is with the A/C or idle solenoid energized.
③ —Except high altitude, man. trans. use N14LY, auto. trans. use N13L; high altitude, man. trans. use RN14LY, auto. trans. use RN13L.
④ —Except high altitude, use N14LY; high altitude, use RN14LY.
⑤ —Except high altitude, use N12Y; high altitude, use RN12Y.
⑥ —On hilly terrain, set at 12° BTDC.
⑦ —Except high altitude, use N13L; high altitude, use RN13L.
⑧ —Except Calif., 700 RPM; California, 750 RPM.
⑨ —At altitudes below 4000 ft., set at 5° BTDC.
⑩ —Except Calif. & high altitude.
⑪ —Except Calif., 10° BTDC; California, 5° BTDC.
⑫ —At altitudes below 4000 ft., set at 8° BTDC.
⑬ —At altitudes below 4000 ft., set at 6° BTDC.
⑭ —Except CJ models, 650 RPM; CJ models, 600 RPM.
⑮ —Except Calif., 700 RPM; California, 600 RPM.
⑯ —Except Calif., less EGR 700 RPM, with EGR 650 RPM; California, 600 RPM.
⑰ —AC.
⑱ —Champion.
⑲ —Breaker point gap, .016 inch; dwell angle, 31–34°.

Continued

JEEP

TUNE UP NOTES—Continued

⑳—Disconnect TCS wires at solenoid vacuum valve.
㉑—Breaker point gap, .016 inch; dwell angle, 29–31°.
㉒—Except heavy duty, 5° BTDC; heavy duty, 2½° BTDC.
㉓—Breaker point gap, .020 inch; dwell angle, 31–34°.
㉔—Breaker point gap, .020 inch; dwell angle, 37–43°.

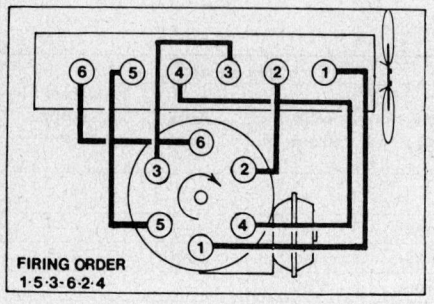

Fig. A

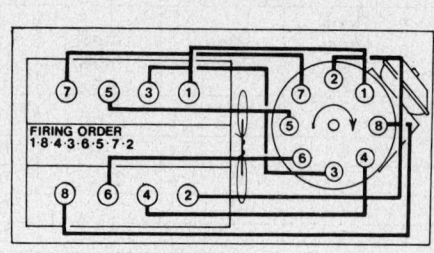

Fig. B

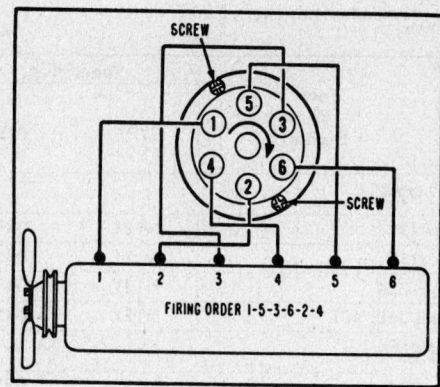

Fig. C

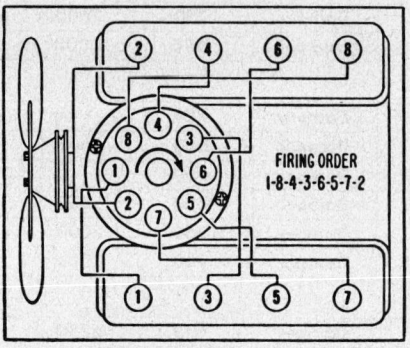

Fig. D

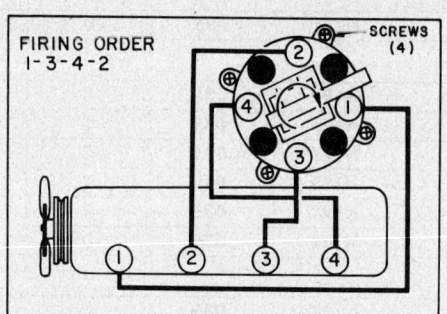

Fig. E

DISTRIBUTOR SPECIFICATIONS

★NOTE: If advance is checked on the vehicle, double the R.P.M. and degrees to get crankshaft figures.

Year	Engine	Distributor Part No.	Rotation	Breaker Gap	Dwell Angle	Breaker Arm Spring Tension	Centrifugal Advance Degrees @ R.P.M. of Distributor★		Vacuum Advance	
							Advance Starts	Full Advance	Inches of Vacuum To Start Plunger	Max. Adv. Dist. Deg. @ Vacuum
1970	F4-134	IAY-4401A	CC	.020	37–43	17–20	1 @ 425	13½ @ 1700	—	—
1970–71	6-232	1110320	C	.016	31–34	17–21	0 @ 400	7 @ 1100	—	6½ @ 11
	6-232	1110340	C	.016	31–34	17–21	0 @ 400	14 @ 2200	6	6½ @ 11
	6-232	1110366	C	.016–.021	31–34	17–21	1 @ 360	16 @ 2075	5–7	23 @ 16
	V8-327	1111025	CC	.016	28–32	17–21	0 @ 300	18 @ 1900	6	10 @ 15
	V8-327	1111130	CC	.016	28–32	17–21	1 @ 350	21 @ 1850	5–7	18 @ 15
	V6-225	1110342	C	.016	29–31	19–23	1 @ 500	14 @ 2100	6–8	19.5
	V6-225	1110376	C	.016	29–31	19–23	1 @ 500	14 @ 2100	6–8	19.5
	V8-350	1111330	C	.016	28–32	17–21	1 @ 500	15 @ 2300	6	18 @ 16
1972	Six	1110497	C	.016	31–34	17–21	½ @ 500	14 @ 2000	5	9 @ 11
	V8	1112111	C	.016	29–31	17–21	0–2 @ 550	15 @ 2000	5	9 @ 16

Continued

JEEP

DISTRIBUTOR SPECIFICATIONS—Continued

★NOTE: If advance is checked on the vehicle, double the R.P.M. and degrees to get crankshaft figures.

Year	Engine	Distributor Part No.	Rotation	Breaker Gap	Dwell Angle	Breaker Arm Spring Tension	Centrifugal Advance Degrees @ R.P.M. of Distributor★		Vacuum Advance	
							Advance Starts	Full Advance	Inches of Vacuum To Start Plunger	Max. Adv. Dist. Deg. @ Vacuum
1973	Six	1110522	C	.016	31–34	17–21	0–2½ @ 500	14 @ 2200	5	9 @ 13¼
	Six	1110523	C	.016	31–34	17–21	0–1 @ 550	15 @ 2200	5	9 @ 13¼
	V8	1112112	C	.016	29–31	17–21	0–1½ @ 500	14 @ 2000	5	8.25 @ 12½
	V8	1112179	C	.016	29–31	17–21	0–1 @ 400	17 @ 2200	5	8.25 @ 12½
	V8	1112214	C	.016	29–31	17–21	0–2¼ @ 450	17 @ 2200	4	8.25 @ 13
	V8	1112215	C	.016	29–31	17–21	0–3¼ @ 400	16 @ 2300	4	8.25 @ 13
1974	6-232, 258	1110529	C	.016	31–34	17–21	0–2 @ 500	14 @ 2300	5	9 @ 13
	V8-360①④	1112112	C	.016	29–31	17–21	0–1¾ @ 500	14 @ 2000	5	8.25 @ 12¾
	V8-304	1112179	C	.016	29–31	17–21	0–1 @ 400	17 @ 2200	5	8.25 @ 12¾
	V8-360②	1112215	C	.016	29–31	17–21	0–1½ @ 400	16 @ 2200	4	8.25 @ 13
	V8-360, 401⑤	1112215	C	.016	29–31	17–21	0–1½ @ 400	16 @ 2200	4	8.25 @ 13
1975	6-232, 258⑥	3224968	C	—	—	—	0–2 @ 600	15 @ 2250	5–7	9 @ 13
	6-232, 258⑧	3224969	C	—	—	—	0–2 @ 500	14 @ 2250	5–7	9 @ 13
	6-258⑦	3224969	C	—	—	—	0–2 @ 500	14 @ 2250	5–7	9 @ 13
	V8-304	3224965	C	—	—	—	0–2 @ 500	17 @ 2200	5–7	7½ @ 12½
	V8-360, 401②	3224746	C	—	—	—	0–4.5 @ 500	16 @ 2300	6	8½ @ 12.7
	V8-360, 401①	3225295	C	—	—	—	0–2 @ 500	14 @ 2000	5–7	17 @ 12½
1976	6-232, 258	3227331	C	—	—	—	0–.4 @ 500	6.25 @ 2200	5–7	8 @ 12.6
	V8-304②	3228263	C	—	—	—	0–2.8 @ 500	12 @ 2200	4–6	7.5 @ 12.7
	V8-304①	3228264	C	—	—	—	0–2.4 @ 500	14.5 @ 2200	5–7	7.5 @ 12.7
	V8-360, 401①	3228263	C	—	—	—	0–2.8 @ 500	12 @ 2200	4–6	7.5 @ 12.7
	V8-360, 401②③	3228265	C	—	—	—	0–2.7 @ 500	8.5 @ 2200	4–6	7.5 @ 12.7
1977	Six	3229719	C	—	—	—	0–1.8 @ 500	11 @ 2200	5–7	9 @ 12.7
	V8-304①③	3228264	C	—	—	—	0–2.4 @ 500	15½ @ 2200	5–7	8½ @ 11.4
	V8-304②	3228263	C	—	—	—	0–2.8 @ 500	13 @ 2200	4–6	8½ @ 11.7
	V8-360①	3228263	C	—	—	—	0–2.8 @ 500	13 @ 2200	4–6	8½ @ 11.7
	V8-360②	3228265	C	—	—	—	0–2.7 @ 500	9½ @ 2200	4–6	8½ @ 11.7
	V8-401	3228265	C	—	—	—	0–2.7 @ 500	9½ @ 2200	4–6	8½ @ 11.7
1978	Six	3232434	C	—	—	—	0 @ 400	9½ @ 2200	3–7	8 @ 13
	V8-304②⑨	3230443	C	—	—	—	0 @ 400	12 @ 2200	2–5	8 @ 12.7
	V8-304①③	3231340	C	—	—	—	0 @ 400	14½ @ 2200	2–7	8 @ 12.2
	V8-360①	3230443	C	—	—	—	0 @ 400	12 @ 2200	2–5	8 @ 12.7
	V8-360②	3231341	C	—	—	—	0 @ 300	8 @ 2200	2–5	8 @ 12.7
	V8-401	3231341	C	—	—	—	0 @ 300	8 @ 2200	2–5	8 @ 12.7
1979	6-258	3231915	C	—	—	—	0 @ 450	9½ @ 2200	2	12 @ 12
	6-258	3232434	C	—	—	—	9 @ 500	9 @ 2200	3	8 @ 13
	V8-304	3231340	C	—	—	—	0 @ 450	14½ @ 2200	3	8 @ 12
	V8-304	3233959	C	—	—	—	0 @ 600	13 @ 2200	3	16 @ 12
	V8-304	3234693	C	—	—	—	0 @ 500	13 @ 2200	2	12 @ 13
	V8-360	3233174	C	—	—	—	0 @ 450	8½ @ 2200	3	12 @ 13
	4-151	1110560	C	—	—	—	0 @ 475	8 @ 2100	3½–4½	11 @ 9½
1980	6-258	3235141	C	—	—	—	0 @ 450	7½ @ 2200	3	13½ @ 15¾
	V8-304	3231340	C	—	—	—	0 @ 425	16 @ 2200	2	9½ @ 12
	V8-304	3237198	C	—	—	—	0 @ 650	11 @ 2300	2½	12½ @ 12
	V8-304	3237199	C	—	—	—	0 @ 500	11½ @ 2200	2½	17½ @ 12
	V8-360	3233174	C	—	—	—	0 @ 400	9½ @ 2200	1¾	13 @ 11

①—Man. trans.
②—Auto. trans.
③—All Calif.
④—2 barrel carb.
⑤—4 barrel carb.
⑥—W/O EGR.
⑦—W/EGR.
⑧—California.
⑨—Exc. Calif.

JEEP

STARTING MOTOR SPECIFICATIONS

Year	Engine Model	Starter Number	Brush Spring Tension Oz.	Free Speed Test			Resistance Test		Lock Torque Test		
				Amps.	Volts	R.P.M.	Amps.	Volts	Amps.	Volts	Torque Ft. Lbs.
1970–71	F4-134	MCH-6203	42–53	65	5	4300	—	—	335	2.0	6.0
	F4-134	MCH-6215	42–53	65	5	4300	—	—	335	2.0	6.0
	F4-134	MDM-6005	31–47	50	10	5300	—	—	280	4.0	6.2
	F4-134	MDU-7004	32–40	50	10	5300	—	—	295	4.0	6.0
	F4-134	1108077	35	60	5	6000	—	—	600	3.0	15.0
	F4-134	1107746	24	75	10.3	6900	—	—	435	5.8	10.5
1970	6-232	MDY-8102A	32–40	60	10	4200	—	—	405	4.0	9.0
1970–71	V6-225	1107391	32–40	75	10.6	6200	—	—	—	—	—
1970	V8-350	1108380	35	65–100	10.6	3600–5100	—	—	300–360	3.5	—
1971	V-6	MHA-7008	32–40	43	10	9000	—	—	200	4	3.0
1972–77	All	—	40	65	12	9250	—	—	600	3.4	13.0
1978	6-232, 258 & V8-304	—	40	67	12	9356	—	—	—	—	—
	V8-360 & 401	—	40	77	12	9600	—	—	—	—	—
1979–80	Exc. 4-151	—	40	77	12	9600	—	—	—	—	—
1980	4-151	1109526	—	45–70	9	7000–11,900	—	—	—	—	—

ALTERNATOR SPECIFICATIONS

Year	Alternator			Rated Output		Field Current		Regulator			
	Make	Model	Ground Polarity	Amperes	Volts	Amperes ①	Volts	Model ②	Regulator Test @ 120°F.		
									Ampere Load	Altern. R.P.M.	Volts
1970	Motorola	A12NAM-451S	Negative	35	15	1.2–1.7	10	TVR-12-W14	10	1500	13.7–14.5
	Motorola	A-12NW-528	Negative	35	15	1.7–2.3	10	R-2-K-1	—	—	—
	Motorola	AP12NW-551③	Negative	40	15	1.2–1.7	12	TVR-12-W14	10	3500	13.65–14.65
	Motorola	A-12NW-552③	Negative	40	15	1.2–1.7	12	TVR-12-W14	10	3500	13.65–14.65
1970–71	Motorola	A-12NW-526	Negative	35	15	1.7–2.3	10	R-2-K-1	—	—	—
1972	Motorola	8AL2025F	Negative	37	15	1.8–2.5	12	8RB-2005	—	—	—
1973–74	Motorola	8AL2025F	Negative	37	15	1.8–2.5	12	8RD-2001	—	—	—
1975	Motorola	—	Negative	37		1.8–2.5	12	8RH-2003	—	—	—
	Motorola	—	Negative	51		1.8–2.5	12	8RH-2003	—	—	—
	Motorola	—	Negative	62		1.8–2.5	12	8RH-2003	—	—	—
	Delco-Remy	—	Negative	37	—	—	—	1116387	—	—	—
	Delco-Remy	—	Negative	55	—	—	—	1116387	—	—	—
	Delco-Remy	—	Negative	63	—	—	—	1116387	—	—	—
1976–77	Delco-Remy	—	Negative	37	—	④	12	1116387	—	—	—
	Delco-Remy	—	Negative	63	—	④	12	1116387	—	—	—
	Motorcraft	—	Negative	40	—	2.5–3	—	—	10		13.7–14.5
	Motorcraft	—	Negative	60	—	2.5–3	—	—	10		13.7–14.5
1978–80	Delco-Remy	—	Negative	37		4–5		1116387	—	—	—
	Delco-Remy	—	Negative	63		4–5		1116387	—	—	—

①—Excessive current draw indicates shorted field windings; no current draw indicates an open winding.
②—Regulator is a sealed assembly, requiring no adjustments.
③—Optional.
④—4–4.5 amps @ 80° F.

PISTONS, PINS, RINGS, CRANKSHAFT & BEARINGS

Year	Engine Model	Piston Clearance	Ring End Gap ①		Wristpin Diameter	Rod Bearings		Main Bearings			
			Comp.	Oil		Shaft Diameter	Bearing Clearance	Shaft Diameter	Bearing Clearance	Thrust on Bear. No.	Shaft End Play
1970	F4-134	.003	.008	.008	.812	1.9375–1.9385	.0005–.0025	2.3331–2.3341	.0014–.0029	1	.006 Max.

Continued

JEEP

PISTONS, PINS, RINGS, CRANKSHAFT & BEARINGS—Continued

Year	Engine Model	Piston Clearance	Ring End Gap ① Comp.	Ring End Gap ① Oil	Wristpin Diameter	Rod Bearings Shaft Diameter	Rod Bearings Bearing Clearance	Main Bearings Shaft Diameter	Main Bearings Bearing Clearance	Thrust on Bear. No.	Shaft End Play
1970	6-232	.001	.010	.015	.9306	2.0948–2.0955	.0010–.0020	2.4988–2.4995	.0010–.0020	3	.003–.007
1970	V6-225	.0002–.0023	.015	.015	.9394	2.000	.0002–.0023	2.2992	.0005–.0021	2	.004–.008
1970	V8-350	.0013–.0029	.010	.020	.9394	2.000	.0004–.0015	2.9995	.0004–.0015	3	.003–.009
1971–73	6-232	.0009–.0007	.010	.015	—	2.0934–2.0955	.001–.002	2.4986–2.5001	.001–.002	3	.0015–.007
1971–73	6-258	.0009–.0017	.010	.015	—	2.0934–2.0955	.001–.002	2.4986–2.5001	.001–.002	3	.0015–.007
1971–73	V8-304	.001–.0018	.010	.010	—	2.0934–2.0955	.001–.002	②	③	3	.003–.008
1973	V8-360	.0012–.002	.010	.015	—	2.0934–2.0955	.001–.002	②	③	3	.003–.008
1974–75	6-232	.0009–.0017	.010	.010	.9307	2.0934–2.0955	.001–.003	2.4986–2.5001	.001–.003	3	.0015–.0065
1974–75	6-258	.0009–.0017	.010	.010	.9307	2.0934–2.0955	.001–.003	2.4986–2.5001	.001–.003	3	.0015–.0065
1974–75	8-304	.0010–.0018	.010	.010	.9311	2.0934–2.0955	.001–.003	②	.001–.003	3	.003–.008
1974–75	V8-360	.0012–.0020	.010	.015	.9311	2.0934–2.0955	.001–.003	②	.001–.003	3	.003–.008
1974–75	V8-401	.0010–.0018	.010	.015	1.0011	2.2464–2.2485	.001–.003	②	.001–.003	3	.003–.008
1976–78	6-232	.0009–.0017	.010	.010	.9307	2.0934–2.0955	.0010–.0025	2.4986–2.5001	.001–.003	3	.0015–.0065
1976–80	6-258	.0009–.0017	.010	.010	.9307	2.0934–2.0955	.0010–.0025	2.4986–2.5001	.001–.003	3	.0015–.0065
1976–80	V8-304	.0010–.0018	.010	.010	.9311	2.0934–2.0955	.001–.003	②	④	3	.003–.008
1976–80	V8-360	.0012–.0020	.010	.015	.9311	2.0934–2.0955	.001–.003	②	④	3	.003–.008
1976–78	V8-401	.0010–.0018	.010	.015	1.0011	2.2464–2.2485	.001–.003	②	④	3	.003–.008

①—Fit rings in tapered bores for clearance listed in tightest portion of ring travel.
②—Rear, 2.7464–2.7479"; others 2.7474–2.7489".
③—Rear, .002–.003"; others .001–.002".
④—Rear, .002–.004"; others .001–.003".

VALVE SPECIFICATIONS

Year	Engine Model	Valve Lash Int.	Valve Lash Exh.	Valve Angles Seat	Valve Angles Face	Valve Spring Installed Height	Valve Spring Pressure Lbs. @ In.	Stem Clearance Intake	Stem Clearance Exhaust	Stem Diameter Intake	Stem Diameter Exhaust
1970	F4-134	.018C	③	45	45	④	73 @ 1.66	.0007–.0022	.0025–.0045	.3733–.3738	.3710–.3720
1970–71	6-232	Zero	Zero	①	②	1¹³⁄₁₆	88 @ 1¹³⁄₁₆	.0010–.0030	.0010–.0030	.3718–.3725	.3718–.3725
	V6-225	Zero	Zero	45	45	1⁴¹⁄₆₄	168 @ 1¼	.002–.0025	.0025–.003	.3407–.3412	.3402–.3407
	V8-350	Zero	Zero	45	45	1.727	180 @ 1.34	.0015–.0035	.0025–.0045	.3720–.3730	.3715–.3725
1971–78	6-232	Zero	Zero	⑤	②	1¹³⁄₁₆⑨	195 @ 1⁷⁄₁₆⑧	.001–.003	.001–.003	.3715–.3725	.3715–.3725
1971–78	6-258⑩	Zero	Zero	⑤	②	1¹³⁄₁₆⑨	195 @ 1⁷⁄₁₆⑧	.001–.003	.001–.003	.3715–.3725	.3715–.3725
1977–80	6-258⑪	Zero	Zero	⑤	②	1¹³⁄₁₆	⑫	.001–.003	.001–.003	.3715–.3725	.3715–.3725
1971–72	V8-304	Zero	Zero	①	⑥	1¹³⁄₁₆	218 @ 1²³⁄₆₄	.001–.003	.001–.003	.3715–.3725	.3715–.3725
1972	V8-360	Zero	Zero	①	⑥	1¹³⁄₁₆	218 @ 1²³⁄₆₄	.001–.003	.001–.003	.3715–.3725	.3715–.3725
1973–80	V8-304	Zero	Zero	⑤	②	1¹³⁄₁₆	⑦	.001–.003	.001–.003	.3715–.3725	.3715–.3725
1973–80	V8-360	Zero	Zero	⑤	②	1¹³⁄₁₆	⑦	.001–.003	.001–.003	.3715–.3725	.3715–.3725
1974–78	V8-401	Zero	Zero	⑤	②	1¹³⁄₁₆	213 @ 1²³⁄₆₄	.001–.003	.001–.003	.3715–.3725	.3715–.3725

①—Intake 30°, exhaust 45°.
②—Intake 29°, exhaust 44°.
③—Eaton face valve .012C, Thompson Roto Valve .016C.
④—Intake 140 @ 1¹³⁄₃₂", exhaust 110 @ 1¾".
⑤—Intake 30°, exhaust 44½.
⑥—Intake 29°, exhaust 44½.
⑦—1973, 218 lbs. @ 1²³⁄₆₄"; 1974–80, 213 lbs. @ 1²³⁄₆₄".
⑧—With valve rotators, 218 @ 1³⁄₁₆.
⑨—With valve rotators, 1⅝".
⑩—1 Barrel carb.
⑪—2 Barrel carb.
⑫—1977; 204 @ 1²³⁄₆₄, 1978–80; 195 @ 1¹³⁄₃₂.

ENGINE TIGHTENING SPECIFICATIONS★

★ Torque Specifications are for clean and lightly lubricated threads only. Dry or dirty threads produce increased friction which prevents accurate measurement of tightness.

Year	Engine	Spark Plugs Ft. Lbs.	Cylinder Head Bolts Ft. Lbs.	Intake Manifold Ft. Lbs.	Exhaust Manifold Ft. Lbs.	Rocker Arm Shaft Bracket Ft. Lbs.	Rocker Arm Cover Ft. Lbs.	Connecting Rod Cap Bolts Ft. Lbs.	Main Bearing Cap Bolts Ft. Lbs.	Flywheel to Crankshaft Ft. Lbs.	Vibration Damper or Pulley Ft. Lbs.
1970	F4-134	25–30	60–70	29–35	29–35	—	—	35–40	65–75	36–40	100–130

Continued

JEEP

ENGINE TIGHTENING SPECIFICATIONS★—Continued

★ Torque Specifications are for clean and lightly lubricated threads only. Dry or dirty threads produce increased friction which prevents accurate measurement of tightness.

Year	Engine	Spark Plugs Ft. Lbs.	Cylinder Head Bolts Ft. Lbs.	Intake Manifold Ft. Lbs.	Exhaust Manifold Ft. Lbs.	Rocker Arm Shaft Bracket Ft. Lbs.	Rocker Arm Cover Ft. Lbs.	Connecting Rod Cap Bolts Ft. Lbs.	Main Bearing Cap Bolts Ft. Lbs.	Flywheel to Crankshaft Ft. Lbs.	Vibration Damper or Pulley Ft. Lbs.
	6-232	25–30	80–85	20–25	20–25	—	45–55③	46–50	75–85	100–110	70–80
	V6-225	25–35	70–75	25–35	10–15	25–35	3–5	60–75	65–70	50–60	140–160
	V8-350	15	75	50	18	30	4	35	110	60	140–160
1971–72	6-232	25–30	80–85	20–25	20–25	19–22	45–55③	26–30	75–85	100–110	50–60
1971–72	6-258	25–30	80–85	20–25	20–25	19–22	45–55③	26–30	75–85	100–110	50–60
1971–72	V8-304	25–30	105–115	40–45	30–35	65–70④	45–55③	26–30	95–105	100–110	50–60
1972	V8-360	25–30	105–115	40–45	30–35	65–70④	45–55③	26–30	95–105	100–110	50–60
1973	6-232	22–33	95–115	37–47	20–30	—	48–58③	26–30	75–85	95–120	48–64
1973	6-258	22–33	95–115	37–47	20–30	—	48–58③	26–30	75–85	95–120	48–64
1974	6-232, 258	22–33	95–115	18–28	18–28	18–26	42–58③	26–30	75–85	95–120	48–64
1975–76	6-232, 258	22–33	95–115	18–28	18–28	16–26⑤	42–58③	30–35	75–85	95–120	48–64
1977–80	6-232, 258	22–33	95–115	18–28②	18–28②	16–26⑤	42–58③	30–35	75–85	95–120	70–90
1973	V8-304	22–33	95–120	37–47	20–30	65–70④	48–58③	26–30	90–105	95–120	48–64
1973	V8-360	22–33	95–120	37–47	20–30	65–70④	48–58③	26–30	90–105	95–120	48–64
1974	V8-304, 360	22–33	100–120	37–47	20–30	16–26⑤	42–58③	26–30	90–105	95–120	48–64
1974–76	V8-401	22–33	100–120	37–47	20–30	16–26⑤	48–58③	35–40	90–105	95–120	48–64
1975–76	V8-304, 360	22–33	100–120	37–47	20–30	16–26⑤	42–58③	30–35	90–105	95–120	48–64
1977–78	V8-401	22–33	100–120	37–47	20–30	16–26⑤	48–58③	35–40	90–105	95–120	80–100
1977–79	V8-304, 360	22–33	100–120	37–47	20–30	16–26⑤	42–58③	30–35	90–105	95–120	80–100
1980	4-157	7–15	81–103	34–40	34–40	17–23	77–83③	27–33	62–68	65–71	157–163
	V8-304, 360	22–33	100–120	37–47	②	16–26⑤	42–58③	30–35	90–105	95–115	80–100

①—Exhaust to intake manifold bolts & nuts, 45–55 ft. lbs.
②—Center two bolts, 20–30 ft. lbs.; outer four bolts, 12–18 ft. lbs.
③—Inch pounds.
④—Stud.
⑤—Rocker arm cap screw.

WHEEL ALIGNMENT SPECIFICATIONS

Model	Caster, Deg.	Camber, Deg.	Toe-In, Inch	Kingpin Inclination, Deg.
Utility Wagon	+3	+1	3/64–3/32	7 1/2
CJ & DJ Series	+3	+1 1/2	3/64–3/32	⑤
J-Series 2WD①	+3	+3/4 to +1	3/64–3/32	7 1/2
J-Series 2WD②③	+3	+1 1/2	3/64–3/32	7 1/2
J-Series②④	+4	+1 1/2	3/64–3/32	8 1/2
J-Series 4WD	+3	+1 1/2	3/64–3/32	7 1/2
Jeepster	+3	+1 1/2	3/64–3/32	7 1/2
Commando	+3	+1 1/2	3/64–3/32	7 1/2
Cherokee	+4	+1 1/2	3/64–3/32	8 1/2
Wagoneer	+4	+1 1/2	3/64–3/32	⑤
Series 13, 14	+3	+1 1/2	3/32–3/16	7 1/2
Series 23, 24	+3	+1 1/2	3/64–3/32	7 1/2
Series 33, 34	+3	+1 1/2	3/64–3/32	7 1/2
FJ-3	+3	+1 1/2	3/64–3/32	7 1/2
FJ-3A	+3	+1 1/2	3/64–3/32	7 1/2
F4-134	+3	+1 1/2	3/64–3/32	7 1/2
FC-150	+3	+1 1/2	3/64–3/32	7 1/2
FC-170	+3	+1 1/2	3/64–3/32	7 1/2

①—Independent front suspension.
②—Solid front axle.
③—Except 1974–80.
④—1974–80.
⑤—Except 1974–79, 7 1/2°; 1974–80, 8 1/2°.

Jeep

Engine Section

CYLINDER HEAD, REPLACE

4-134, Engines

Before the cylinder head is installed, make certain that all dirt and carbon is removed from both the head and block. File or hone all high spots.

Use a torque wrench when tightening down cylinder heads. Uneven or excessive tightening of nuts may distort cylinder bores, causing compression loss and excessive oil and consumption.

Tighten cylinder heads in the sequence shown in Fig. 1 tightening them a little at a time in the proper order a couple of times around before final tightening to the torque values given in the *Engine Tightening Chart*. After the engine has warmed up to operating temperature, recheck torque and tighten as required.

Be sure to check intake valve operating clearances after the final tightening.

Service Note

Tightening cylinder heads on F-head engines without removing rocker arms may be accomplished with a wrench having an 11/16″ box on one end and a 1/2″ square box on the other end. This, together with a torque wrench will do the job.

To gain access to No. 5 cylinder head bolt for head removal or for tightening head bolts, Fig. 1, the carburetor must be removed.

6-232, 258

1. Drain cooling system, then disconnect upper radiator hose and remove valve cover.
2. On 1970–72 and early 1974 engines, remove rocker arm and shaft assembly.
3. On 1973, late 1974 and 1975–80 engines, remove bridged pivot and rocker arm assemblies.

NOTE: Loosen each bridged pivot bolt one turn at a time to avoid breaking the bridge pivot. Also keep bridged pivots and rocker arms in same order as removed, so that they can be reinstalled in their original locations.

4. Remove push rods.

NOTE: Keep push rods in same order as removed, so that they can be installed in their original locations.

5. Remove intake and exhaust manifold bolts.
6. If equipped with air conditioning, remove idler bracket and loosen alternator belt, then remove compressor bracket bolts and set compressor aside.
7. Disconnect spark plug wires and temperature sending lead, then remove spark plugs and ignition coil and bracket assembly.
8. Remove cylinder head bolts and cylinder head.
9. Reverse removal procedure to install. Torque cylinder head bolts to the specification given in the Engine Tightening Chart and in the sequence shown in Fig. 2.

CAUTION: The cylinder head bolt located at the left front corner of the head (No. 11, Fig. 2) must have the threads sealed to prevent

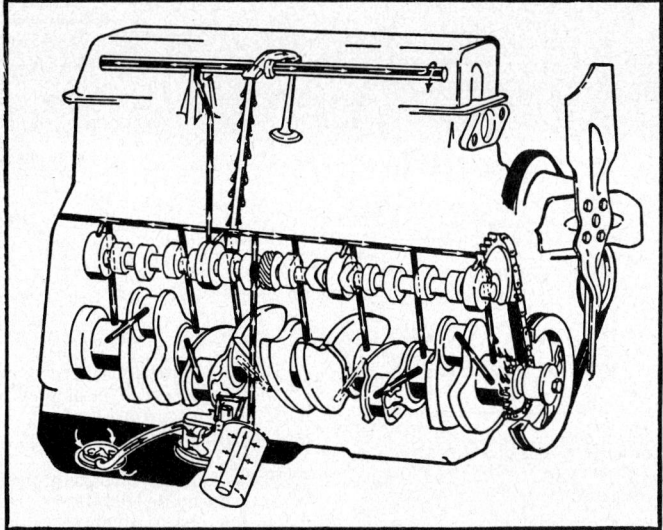

Engine oiling system. 1970–72 and early 1974 6-232, 258

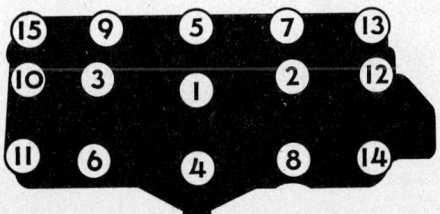

Fig. 1 Cylinder head tightening sequence. Four-cyl. F-head engines

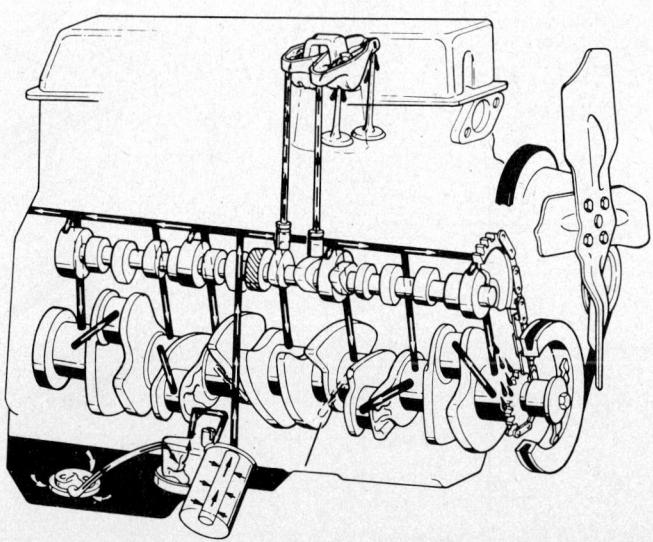

Engine oiling system. 1973, late 1974 & 1975–80 6-232, 258

JEEP

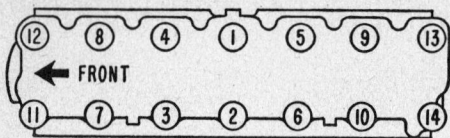

Fig. 2 Cylinder head bolt tightening sequence. 6-232, 258

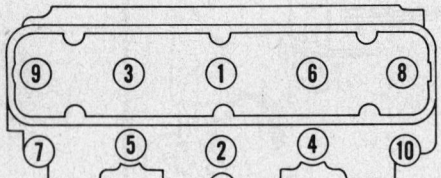

Fig. 3 Cylinder head tightening sequence. 1970–71 V8-350

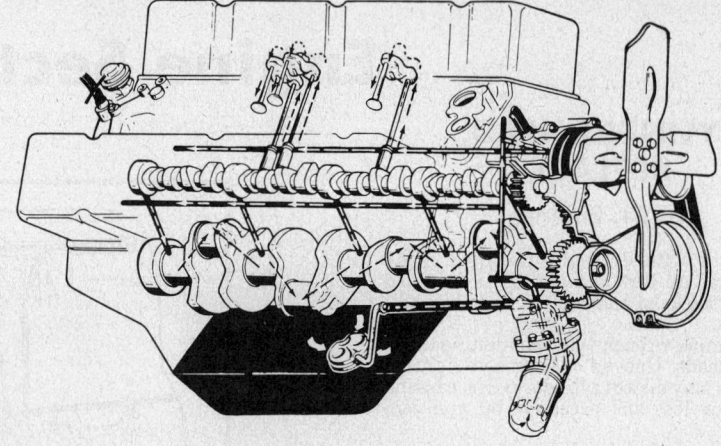

Engine oiling system. V8-304, 360, 401

coolant leakage. Permatex No. 2 or equivalent is recommended.

1970–71 V8-350

1. Drain coolant and disconnect battery.
2. Remove intake manifold.
3. When removing right cylinder head, remove Alternator and/or A/C compressor with mounting bracket and move out of the way. *Do not disconnect hoses from air compressor.* Disconnect A.I.R. pipe assembly if so equipped.
4. When removing left cylinder head, remove oil dipstick, power steering pump and/or A.I.R. pump with mounting bracket (if equipped) and move out of the way with hoses attached. Disconnect A.I.R. pipe if so equipped.
5. Disconnect exhaust manifold from head to be removed.
6. Remove rocker arm shaft and lift out push rods.
7. Remove cylinder head.
8. Reverse procedure to install and tighten bolts gradually and evenly in the sequence shown in Fig. 3.

V6-225

1. Drain cooling system.
2. Remove air cleaner. Disconnect all pipes and hoses from carburetor.
3. Remove ignition coil.
4. Disconnect temperature switch wire.
5. Disconnect accelerator and transmission linkage at carburetor.
6. Disconnect crankcase ventilator hose at valve.
7. Slide front thermostat by-pass hose clamp back on hose. Disconnect bypass hose at timing chain cover to allow coolant to drain from manifold. Disconnect upper radiator hose at outlet.
8. Disconnect heater hose at intake manifold.
9. Remove intake manifold and carburetor as a unit.
10. Disconnect spark plug wires at plugs and swing wires and retainer out of the way.
11. On right side, remove crankcase ventilator valve.
12. Remove rocker arm cover. Unfasten and remove rocker arm and shaft assembly. Oil baffle is mounted under rear bolts on right head assembly.
13. Remove push rods. If valve lifters are to be serviced, remove them at this time. If not, protect the lifters and camshaft from dirt by covering area with clean cloths.
14. Remove alternator and power steering pump bracket.
15. Unfasten and remove cylinder head with exhaust manifold attached.
16. Reverse removal procedure to install heads. Refer to the illustrations for correct location of bolts and tightening sequence, Fig. 4.

V8-304, 360, 401

1. Remove air cleaner and drain cooling system, then if equipped with Air Guard emission system, disconnect air hose from injection manifold.
2. Disconnect all hoses and electrical leads from intake manifold.
3. Remove valve covers, bridged pivot assemblies, rocker arms and push rods.

NOTE: Loosen each bridged pivot bolt one turn at a time to avoid breaking the bridged pivot. Also, keep rocker arms,

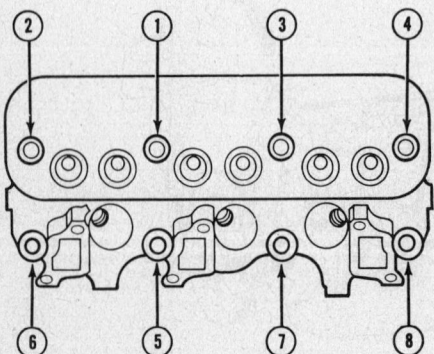

Fig. 4 Cylinder head tightening sequence. V6 engines

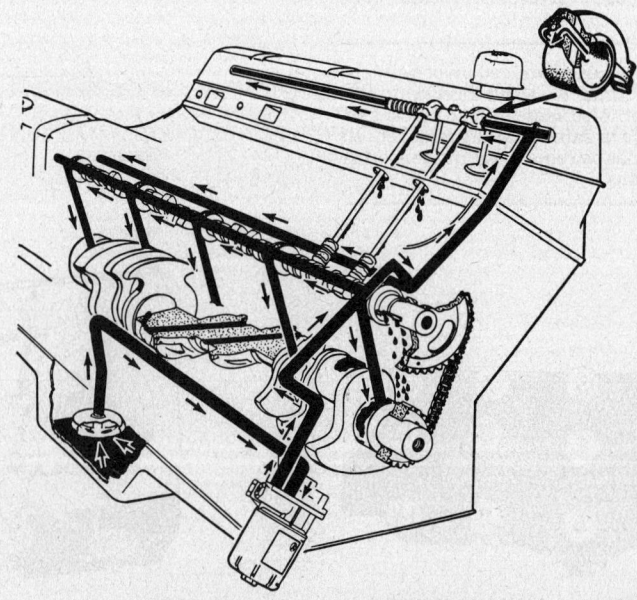

Lubrication diagram for V6-225 & V8-350

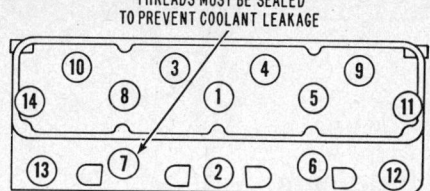

Fig. 5 Cylinder head tightening sequence. V8-304, 360, 401

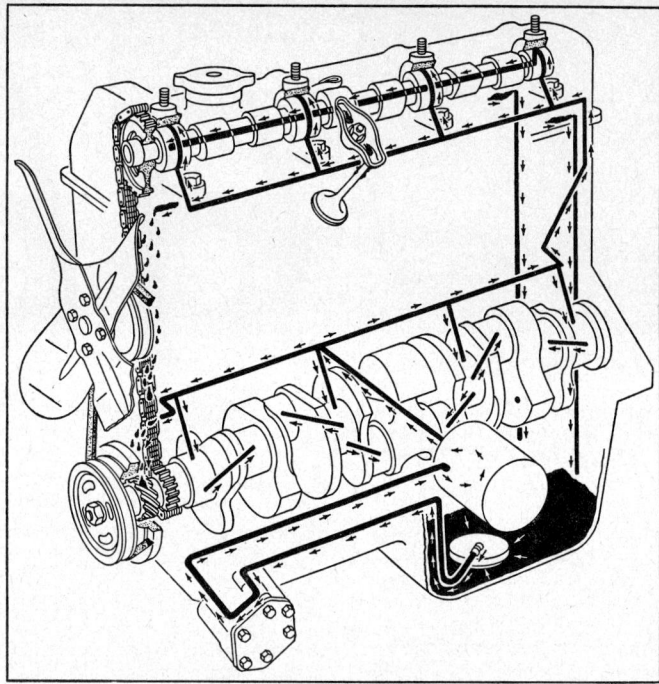

Lubrication diagram for Overhead Camshaft engine

bridged pivot and push rods in same order as removed so that they can be reinstalled in their original locations.

4. Disconnect spark plug wires and remove spark plugs.
5. Remove intake manifold and disconnect exhaust manifolds from cylinder head.
6. Loosen all drive belts, then if equipped with air conditioning, remove compressor bracket attaching bolts and set compressor aside.
7. Disconnect alternator support brace, power steering mounting bracket and Air Guard pump (if used) mounting bracket from cylinder head.
8. Remove cylinder head bolts and cylinder head.
9. Reverse removal procedure to install. First torque the cylinder head bolts to 80 ft. lbs. and in the sequence shown in Fig. 5, then finally torque the cylinder head bolts to the specifications given in the "Engine Tightening" chart.

NOTE: The cylinder block has two locating dowels on each bank to assist in lining up and holding the cylinder head and gasket in position during installation.

CAUTION: The No. 7 bolt shown in Fig. 5, second from front on the left bank, must have the threads sealed to prevent coolant leakage. Permatex No. 2 or equivalent is recommended.

ROCKER ARM SERVICE

F-Head Engines

To remove the rocker arm assembly, proceed as follows:
1. Remove carburetor air cleaner.
2. Disconnect spark plug wires.
3. Drain cooling system.
4. Remove rocker arm cover.
5. Remove rocker arm bracket screws and lift off rocker arm assembly.

Before disassembly, mark rocker arms, brackets and shaft so they can be reassembled in the original positions.

Sludge and gum formation in the rocker arms and shafts will restrict the normal flow of oil to the rocker arms and valves. Each time the rocker arm and shaft assemblies are removed they should be disassembled and thoroughly cleaned.

When disassembling rocker arms, place all parts on the work bench in their proper sequence to insure correct assembly.

Clean all sludge and gum formation from the inside and outside of the shaft. Clean oil holes and passages in the rocker arms and shafts. Clean the oil connector. Inspect the shafts for wear.

Check the ball ends of the rocker arms to be sure they are not pitted or rough. If used in this condition, it will be difficult to maintain valve clearances.

6-232, 258 Engines

On 1970-72 and early 1974 engines, the pressure supply for each rocker arm is obtained from No. 3 camshaft bearing location where the camshaft meters the flow of oil from the main lubricating gallery through a groove in the camshaft bearing surface to a gallery extending upwards to the cylinder head gasket surface, Fig. 6. On 1973, late 1974 and 1975-80 232, 258, oil is supplied through the valve lifters and hollow push rods. On 1970-72 and early 1974 232 and 258, install the rocker arm shaft with oil holes facing down toward the cylinder head, Fig. 7. The 1973, late 1974 and 1975-80 232, 258 engines have the intake and exhaust rocker arms pivoting on a bridged pivot assembly which is secured to the cylinder head by two cap screws, Fig. 8.

NOTE: The new rocker arms used on late 1974 engines (beginning with build date code 704 (A or E) 04, have been redesigned with the oil hole on the push rod end relocated, pointing away from the valve assemblies allowing for improved oil control, Fig. 9. Also, these rocker arms are not interchangeable with the 1973 type, since the camshaft and rocker arm ratio

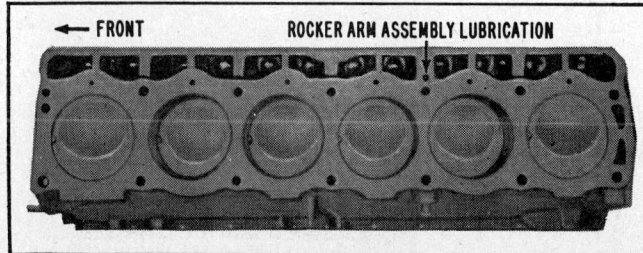

Fig. 6 Rocker arm lubrication gallery. 1970-72 & early 1974 6-232, 258

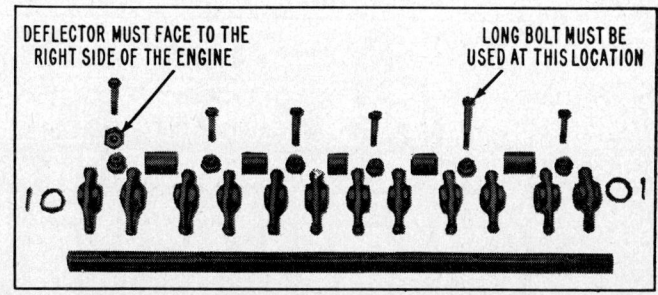

Fig. 7 Rocker arm assembly. 1970-72 and early 1974 6-232, 258

JEEP

Fig. 8 Rocker arms, push rod & pivot assembly. 1973, late 1974 & 1975–80 6-232, 258; 1973 V8-304 & all 1974–80 V8's.

Fig. 9 1973 (7300) & 1974 (7400) rocker arm identification.

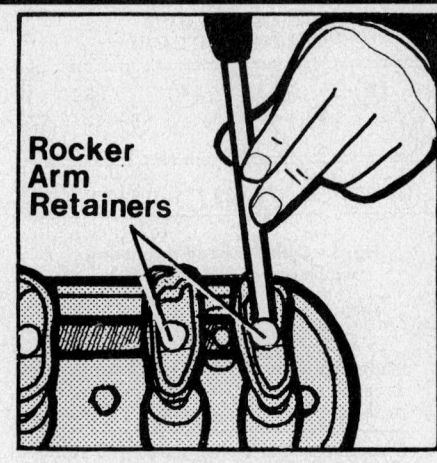

Fig. 10 Removing nylon retainer. 1970 V8-350

has been modified.

The exhaust valve train on certain engines, has been modified to incorporate valve rotators to improve valve durability.

NOTE: When replacing rocker arms on these engines, use only the cast type rocker arms, as they are designed to accommodate the valve rotators.

1970 V8-350

A nylon retainer is used to retain the rocker arm. Break them below their head with a chisel, Fig. 10. When replacing rocker assembly, position rocker arms so that external rib on each arm points away from rocker shaft bolt, Fig. 11.

V6-225

1. To disassemble, remove cotter pin, plain washer and spring washer from each end of rocker arm shaft.
2. Remove bracket bolts and slide rocker arms and brackets off shaft.
3. Clean and inspect all parts, taking care to clean out all oil holes. Replace parts that are excessively worn.
4. Assemble springs, rocker arms and brackets. *Note that two different rocker arms are used and that the valve ends of rocker arms slant away from the brackets.*
5. Install spring washer, flat washer and cotter pin on each end of shaft in the other shown in Fig. 12.

V8-304, 360, 401

These engines have individually mounted rocker arms consisting of a rocker arm retaining stud, rocker arm pivot ball, rocker arm and retaining nut to operate each valve, Fig. 13. The 1973 V8-304 and all 1974–80 V8 engines have the intake and exhaust rocker arms pivoting on a bridged pivot assembly which is secured to the cylinder head by two cap screws, Fig. 8.

On 1971–72 V8-304 & 1971–73 V8-360, 401 engines, the rocker arm studs are threaded into the cylinder head. The threads are of such design to cause an interference fit; therefore, care must be taken that replacement studs be installed until the hexagon head is flush with the cylinder head and torqued to 65–70 ft-lbs.

The push rods are hollow, serving as oil galleries for lubricating each individual rocker arm assembly. Prior to installing, the push rods should be cleaned thoroughly, inspected for wear and deposits which may restrict the flow of oil to the rocker arm assembly.

The push rods also serve as guides to maintain correct rocker arm to valve stem relationship; therefore, a contact pattern on the push rods where they contact the cylinder head is normal.

On 1971–72 V8-304 & 1971–73 V-360, 401 engines, when installing the rocker arm retaining nut, it is important that they be tightened until bottomed, using a torque of 20–25 ft-lbs.

Lubrication to each rocker arm is supplied by the corresponding hydraulic valve lifter. A metering system located in each valve lifter consists of a stepped lower surface on the push rod cap that contacts a flat plate, causing a restriction. The restriction meters the amount of oil flow through the push rod cap, hollow push rod, and upper valve train components. A loss of lubrication to the rocker arm could be caused by a restricted or plugged push rod or a defective hydraulic valve lifter.

CAUTION: Correct installation of push rods in these engines is critical and more than normal care must be taken upon installation. When placing the push rods through the guide hole in the cylinder head, it is important that the push rod end is inserted in the plunger cap socket. It is possible that the push rod may seat itself on the edge of the plunger cap which will restrict valve lifter rotation and lubrication to rocker arms.

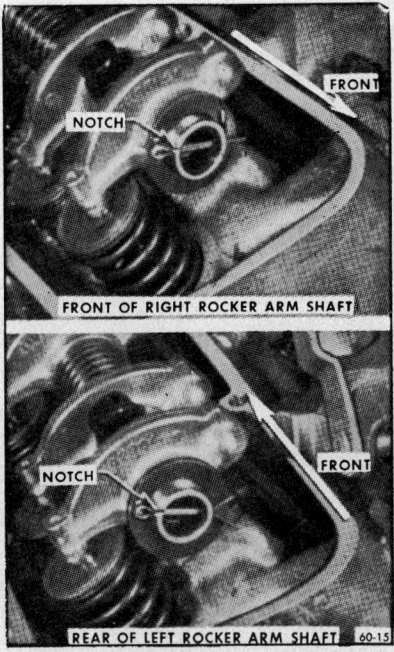

Fig. 12 Rocker arm shaft installation. V6-225

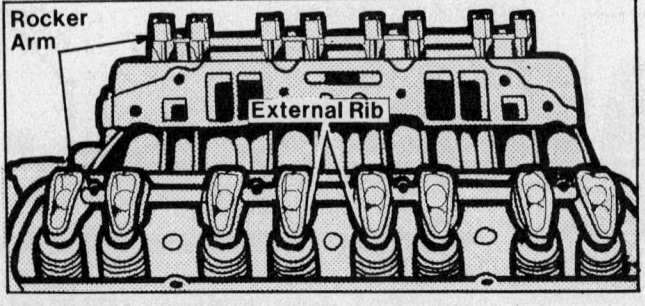

Fig. 11 Rocker arm positioned on shaft. 1970 V8-350

JEEP

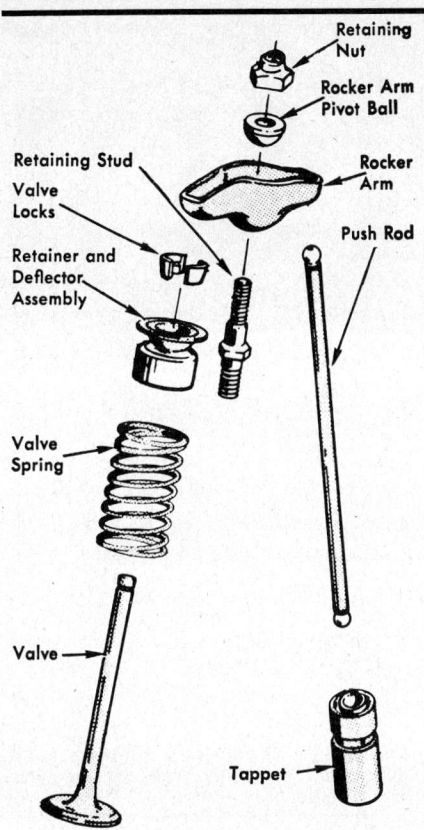

Fig. 13 Valve train assembly. 1972 V8-304 & 1972–73 V8-360

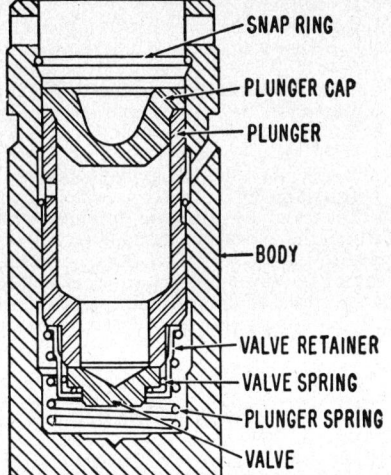

Fig. 14 Hydraulic valve lifter

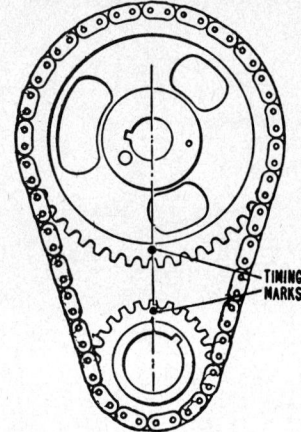

Fig. 16 Valve timing. V8 engine

It is recommended that, just prior to installation of the cylinder head covers, the engine be operated and the supply of lubrication to each rocker arm be visually inspected. If inspection reveals that an individual rocker arm is not being supplied with lubrication, the push rod and/or valve lifter must be inspected to determine the cause.

VALVE ARRANGEMENT

Front to Rear

V6 Left Head	E-I-E-I-I-E
V6 Right Head	E-I-I-E-I-E
All V8s	E-I-I-E-E-I-I-E
6-232, 258	E-I-I-E-I-E-E-I-E-I-I-E

VALVES, ADJUST

4-Cyl. F-Head Engines

The exhaust valves (in block) may be adjusted in the same manner as outlined for L-head engines. However, the intake valves may best be adjusted with the engine running after it has warmed up to operating temperature.

If the cylinder head has been tightened, be sure to recheck intake valve clearances and adjust as required.

VALVE GUIDES

6-232, 258, V8-304, 360, 401 Engines

Excessive valve stem-to-guide clearance will cause lack of power, rough idling and noisy valves, and may cause valve breakage. Insufficient clearance will result in noisy and sticky functioning of valves and disturb engine smoothness of operation.

Valve stem-to-guide clearances are listed in the *Engine Valve Specifications* table. By using a micrometer and a suitable telescope hole gauge, check the diameter of the valve stem in three places (top, center and bottom). Insert telescope hole gauge in valve guide bore, measuring at the center. Subtract the highest reading of valve stem diameter from valve guide bore center diameter to obtain valve-to-guide clearance. If clearance is not within specified limits, use the next oversize valve and ream bore to fit. Valves with oversize stems are available in .003", .015" and .030".

VALVE LIFTERS

6-232, 258, V8-304, 350, 360, 401

Valve lifters may be removed from their bores after removing the rocker arms and push rods. Adjustable pliers with taped jaws may be used to remove lifters that are stuck due to varnish, carbon, etc. Fig. 14 illustrates the type of lifter used.

TIMING CASE COVER

4 Cyl. Engines

1. Drain cooling system.
2. Remove radiator and grille or guard.
3. Remove cylinder head, valves and springs.
4. On L-head engines, remove manifolds.
5. Remove fuel and oil pumps.
6. Remove oil pan.
7. Remove crankshaft pulley.
8. Remove fan assembly.

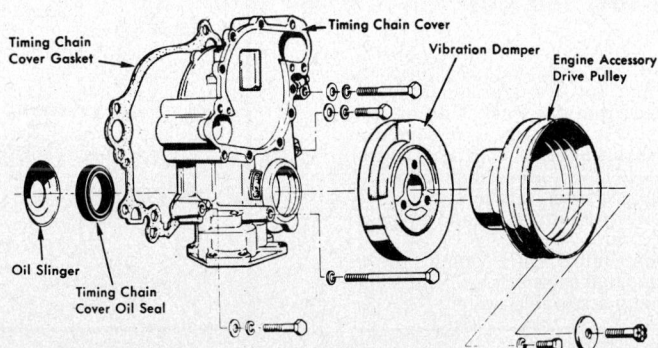

Fig. 15 Timing chain cover assembly V8-304, 360, 401

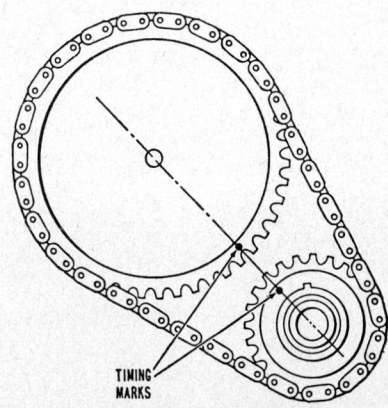

Fig. 17 Valve timing. 6-232, 258

JEEP

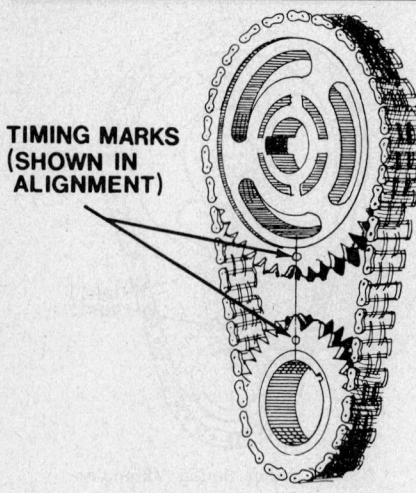

Fig. 18 Valve timing. V8-360, 401 with double row timing chain

seal on timing case cover.
8. Install timing case cover on engine, then the cover-to-block and oil pan-to-cover screws.
9. Torque the timing case cover-to-cylinder block screws to 5 ft. lbs. and the oil pan-to-timing case cover screws to 11 ft. lbs.
10. Install vibration damper, pulley, fan and hub assembly and the drive belts.

When installing the cover it is important that the cover be properly aligned when installing the vibration damper to prevent damage to the oil seal. This is accomplished by leaving the cover-to-block cap screws loose until the vibration damper has been partially installed. Then tighten the cover screws.

9. Remove engine front cover.

6-232, 258

1. Remove drive belts, fan and hub assembly, damper pulley and the vibration damper.
2. Remove oil pan-to-timing case cover screws and the cover-to-cylinder block screws.
3. Raise timing case cover enough to detach the retaining nibs of the oil seal from the bottom side of the cover. This prevents the seal end tabs pulling away from the tongues of the oil pan gasket which would cause an oil leak requiring oil pan removal to correct.
4. Remove timing case cover and gasket from engine.
5. Cut off oil pan seal end tabs flush with front face of cylinder block and remove seal.
6. Coat both sides of new timing case cover gasket with suitable sealer and position gasket on cylinder block.
7. Cut off tabs of a new pan seal. Coat seal end tabs with suitable sealer and position

V6-225 & V8-350

1. Drain cooling system and remove radiator.
2. Remove fan, pulleys and belts.
3. Remove crankshaft pulley and reinforcement.
4. If equipped with power steering, remove any pump bracket bolts attached to timing chain cover and loosen and remove any other bolts necessary that will allow pump and brackets to be moved out of the way.
5. Remove fuel pump.
6. Remove alternator and brackets.
7. Remove distributor cap and pull spark plug wire retainers off brackets on rocker arm cover. Swing distributor cap with wires attached out of the way. Disconnect distributor primary lead.
8. Remove distributor. *If chain and sprockets are not to be disturbed, note position of distributor rotor for installation in the same position.*
9. Loosen and slide clamp on thermostat by-pass hose rearward.
10. Remove bolts attaching chain cover to block.
11. Remove two oil pan-to-chain cover bolts and remove cover.
12. Reverse procedure to install.

CAUTION: Remove the oil pump cover and pack the space around the oil pump gears completely full of vaseline. There must be no air space left inside the pump. Reinstall the cover using a new gasket. This step is very important as the oil pump may lose its prime whenever the pump, pump cover or timing chain cover is disturbed. If the pump is not packed it may not begin to pump oil as soon as the engine is started.

V8-304, 360, 401

The timing chain cover is a die casting incorporating an oil seal at the vibration damper hub, Fig. 15. The crankshaft front seal is installed from the back side of the cover; therefore, it is necessary to remove the cover when replacement of the seal is required. To remove cover, proceed as follows:
1. Drain cooling system completely.
2. Remove lower radiator hose and by-pass hose from cover.
3. Remove distributor, fuel pump, drive belts, fan and hub assembly and vibration damper, using a suitable puller.

NOTE: It is not necessary to disconnect power steering or discharge air condition-

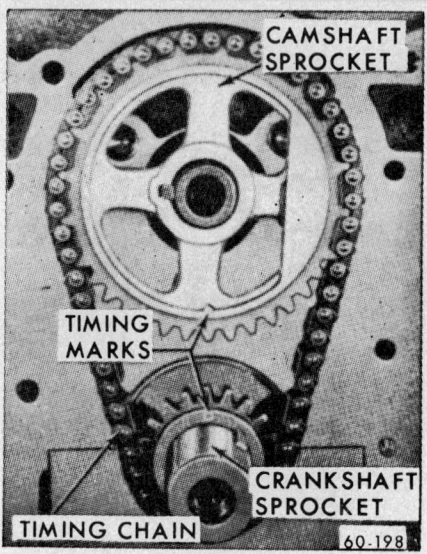

Fig. 19 Valve timing. V6-225

ing system (if equipped). Remove units from their mounting brackets and place them aside.

4. Remove two front oil pan bolts and the eight hex head bolts retaining the cover to the cylinder block.
5. Pull cover forward until free from locating dowel pins.
6. Remove used seal and clean seal bore and gasket surface of cover.
7. Apply sealing compound to outer surface of seal and a film of Lubriplate or equivalent to seal lips. Drive seal into cover bore until seal contacts outer flange of cover.

Installation of Cover

1. Prior to installation of cover, remove lower dowel pin from cylinder block.
2. Using a sharp knife or razor blade, cut oil pan gasket flush with cylinder block on both sides of oil pan.
3. Cut corresponding pieces of gasket from

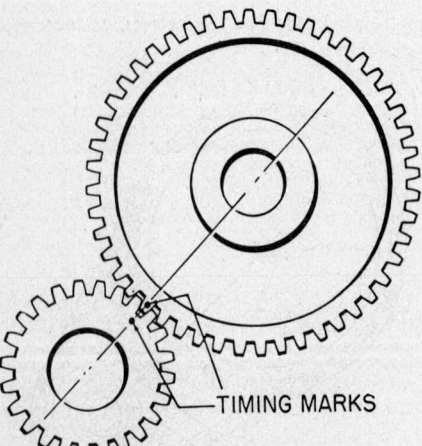

Fig. 20 Valve timing on four-cylinder engines

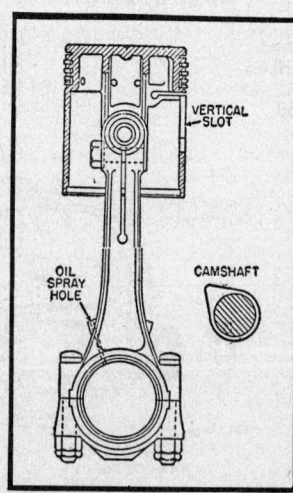

Fig. 21 Piston and rod assembly. 4 cyl. engines

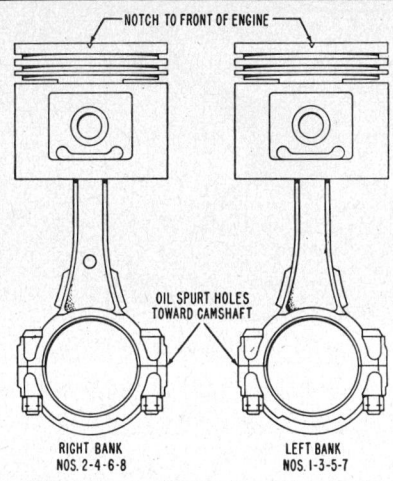

Fig. 22 Piston and rod assembly. V8-350

gines built after April 22, 1974 use a new double row roller type timing chain to improve timing chain durability, Fig. 18. This new timing chain is available as a service replacement item and should be installed when timing chain failures occur to eliminate recurrence of the problem. Installation of the new timing chain requires the use of a new heavy duty camshaft sprocket and crankshaft sprocket.

V6-225 & V8-350

1. With the timing case cover removed as outlined above, temporarily install the vibration damper bolt and washer in end of crankshaft.
2. Turn crankshaft so sprockets are positioned as shown in Figs. 16 and 19. Use a sharp rap on a wrench handle to start the vibration damper bolt out without disturbing the position of the sprockets.
3. Remove front oil slinger.
4. Remove camshaft distributor drive gear and fuel pump eccentric.
5. Use two large screwdrivers to alternately pry the camshaft sprocket then the crankshaft sprocket forward until the camshaft sprocket is free. Then remove camshaft sprocket and chain, and crankshaft sprocket off crankshaft.
6. To install, assemble chain on sprockets and slide sprockets on their respective shafts with the "0" marks on the sprockets lined up as shown.
7. Complete the installation in the reverse order of removal.

TIMING GEARS
4-Cyl. Engines

The camshaft is driven by a steel gear on the crankshaft and a fibre gear on the camshaft. Lubrication is positive through a jet pressed into the crankcase directly back of the contact point of the gears. When the gears are removed, check both the jet and oil passage to make sure they are clear.

When it becomes necessary to replace the timing gears, due attention must be given to the end play of both shafts and running clearance of the gears.

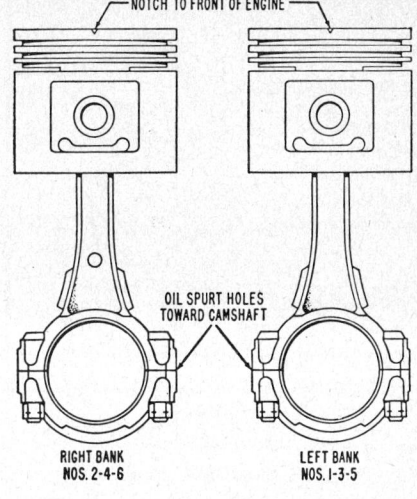

Fig. 23 Piston and rod assembly. V6-225

End play of the crankshaft is controlled by the running clearance between the crankshaft gear and gear thrust plate. The end play is adjusted by shims placed between the thrust plate and the end of the front main bearing. Shims .002 in. thick are available for this adjustment. When the thrust plate or washer is removed, be sure it is reinstalled with the beveled inner edge toward the crankcase.

End play of the camshaft is determined by the running clearance between the camshaft gear and thrust plate. The standard clearance is .003 to .0055 in. which is determined by the thickness of the camshaft gear thrust plate spacer. Should a check indicate not enough clearance, place a thin shim between the thrust plate spacer and the shoulder on the camshaft. Clearance may be reduced by dressing off the spacer slightly. Whenever the spacer is installed, make sure that the beveled inner edge is toward the rear.

End play of both the camshaft and crankshaft can best be measured with a dial indicator.

the replacement oil pan gasket set. Cement gasket to cover. Install replacement Neoprene oil pan seal into cover and align cork gasket tabs to the pan seal.

4. Apply a strip of sealing compound to both the cut-off oil pan gaskets at the oil pan to cylinder block location.
5. Replace cover in position, install oil pan bolts in cover, tighten evenly and slowly until cover aligns with upper dowel. Then install lower dowel through cover. Drive dowel in corresponding hole in cylinder block.
6. Install cover attaching bolts and torque to 20–30 ft-lbs.

TIMING CHAIN
6-232, 258, V8-304, 360, 401

When installing a timing chain, see that the timing marks on the sprockets are in line as shown in Figs. 16, 17 and 18.

NOTE: All V8-360 and 401 heavy duty en-

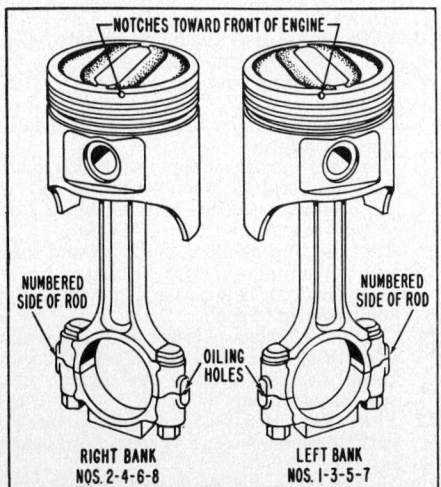

Fig. 24 Piston and rod assembly V8-401

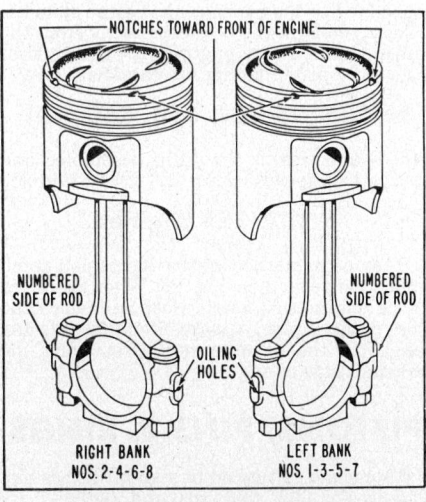

Fig. 25 Piston and rod assembly. V8-304 & V8-360 std.

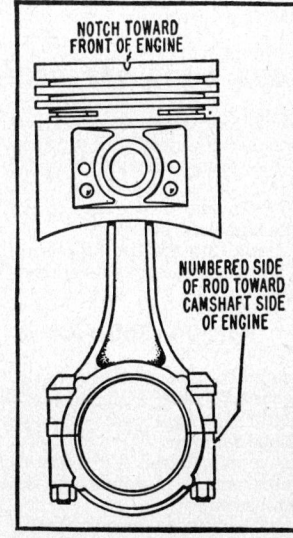

Fig. 26 Piston and rod assembly. 6-232, 258

JEEP

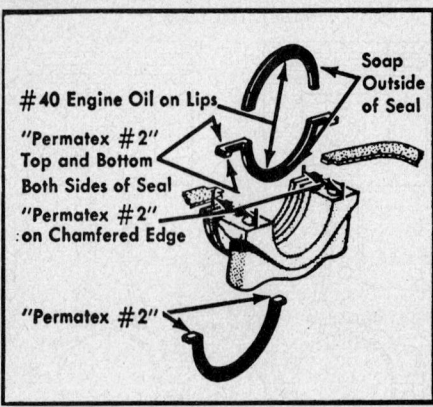

Fig. 27 Rear main bearing oil seal. 6-232, 258, V8-304, 360, 401

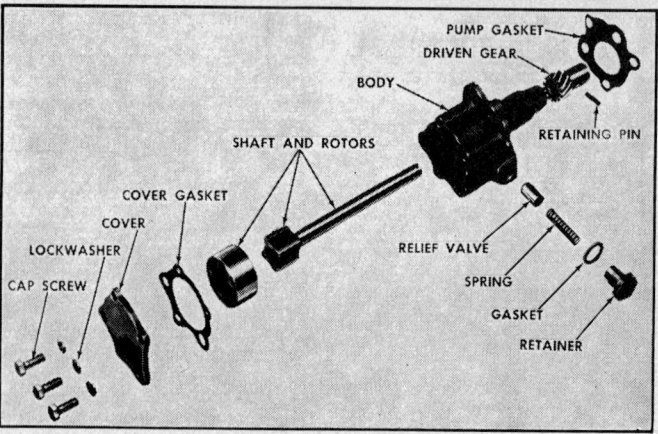

Fig. 28 Oil pump. 4-134

Standard running clearance between the gears is .000 to .002 in., which should be checked with a dial indicator.

To set the valve timing, install the crankshaft gear followed by the camshaft gear with the camshaft positioned to allow installation with the timing gear marks meshed, Fig. 20.

CAMSHAFT

4-134 Engines

To remove the camshaft, take off the gear cover as outlined previously and proceed as follows:

1. Remove fuel and oil pumps.
2. Remove camshaft gear and thrust plate.
3. Tie the valve lifters up at their highest point of travel with string wrapped around the adjusting screws and attach to manifold studs.
4. Withdraw camshaft from engine and, if necessary, take lifters out from below.
5. Replace the parts in reverse order of removal.
6. When installing the oil pump on 4-cyl. engines, refer to the section covering the oil pump because the pump gear must be properly meshed with the driving gear on the camshaft to correctly couple with the distributor shaft to maintain ignition timing.

V6-225, 6-232, 258, V8-350

To remove camshaft, remove all valve lifters. Take off timing chain and sprockets. Remove fuel pump, distributor and distributor oil pump drive gear. When withdrawing camshaft from engine, use care to avoid damage to the camshaft bearings.

When installing the timing chain, be sure to align the timing marks as shown in Figs. 16, 17 and 19.

V8-304, 360, 401

1. Disconnect battery ground cable.
2. Disconnect transmission cooler lines at radiator if so equipped.
3. Remove radiator.
4. Remove distributor, wires and coil.
5. Remove intake manifold and carburetor as an assembly.
6. Remove cylinder head covers, loosen rocker arms and remove push rods and lifters.
7. Dismount power steering pump.
8. Remove fan and hub, fuel pump and heater hose at water pump.
9. Remove alternator.
10. Remove vibration damper and pulley and lower radiator hose at water pump.
11. Remove timing chain cover, distributor-oil pump drive gear, fuel pump eccentric sprockets and chain.
12. Remove hood latch support bracket upper retaining screws and move bracket as required to allow removal of camshaft.

When installing the timing chain, be sure to align the timing marks as shown in Fig. 16.

PISTONS & RODS, ASSEMBLE

4-Cyl. Engines

Service Note

The oil spray hole in the rod must be on the side away from the camshaft (toward right side of vehicle). Because of the oil spray hole, No. 1 and 2 or No. 3 and 4 connecting rods cannot be interchanged for if they are reversed the spray hole will be on the wrong side. No. 1 and 3 or No. 2 and 4 can be interchanged.

As shown in Fig. 21, pistons should be assembled to the connecting rods so that the oil spray hole in the rod faces away from the camshaft side of the engine with the vertical slot in the piston facing the camshaft side.

V6-225, V8-304, 350, 360, 401

Rods and pistons should be assembled and installed as shown in Fig. 22, 23, 24 and 25.

6-232, 258 Engines

Pistons are marked with a depression notch on the top perimeter, Fig. 26. When installed in the engine this notch must be toward the front of the engine. Always assemble rods and caps with the cylinder numbers facing the camshaft side of engine.

PISTONS, PINS & RINGS

Pistons are furnished in standard sizes and oversizes of .002, .005, .010 and .020″.

Piston pins are furnished in oversizes of .003 and .005″.

Piston rings are available in .020″ oversizes.

MAIN & ROD BEARINGS

Both main and rod bearings are supplied in undersizes of .001, .002, .010 and .012″.

CRANKSHAFT OIL SEAL

4-Cyl. Engines

The rear main bearing is sealed against external leakage by a lip type neoprene seal with a metal core. The seal has the advantage of being able to be slipped into place without removing the crankshaft.

For easy installation, give the seal a coat of grease. Be careful not to coat the ends of the seal as they have sealing compound applied to them.

6-232, 258, V8-304, 360, 401 Engines

1. To replace the seal, Fig. 27, remove oil pan and scrape oil pan surfaces clean.
2. Remove rear main bearing cap.
3. Remove and discard oil seals.
4. Clean cap thoroughly.
5. Loosen all remaining main bearing cap screws.
6. With a brass drift and hammer, tap upper seal until sufficient seal is protruding to permit pulling seal out completely with pliers.
7. Wipe seal surface of crankshaft clean, then oil lightly.
8. Coat back surface of upper seal with soap, and lip of seal with No. 40 engine oil.
9. Install upper seal into cylinder block. *Lip of seal must face to front of engine.*
10. Coat cap and cylinder block mating surface portion of seal with Permatex No. 2 or equivalent, being careful not to apply sealer on lip of seal.
11. Coat back surface of lower seal with soap, and lip of seal with No. 40 engine oil. Place into cap, seating seal firmly into seal recess in cap.
12. Place Permatex No. 2 or equivalent on both chamfered edges of rear main bearing cap.
13. Install main bearings and install cap. Tighten all caps to 75–85 ft-lbs.
14. Cement oil pan gasket to cylinder block

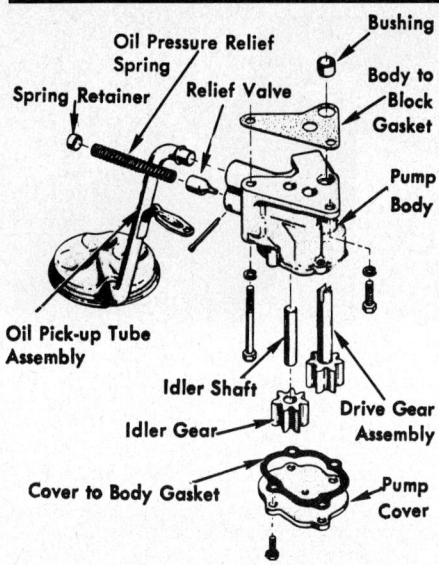

Fig. 29 Oil pump. 6-232, 258

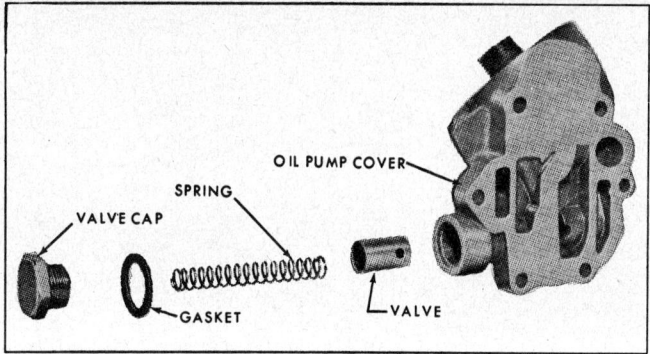

Fig. 30 Oil pump cover and by-pass valve. V6-225, V8-350

with tongue of gasket at each end coated with Permatex or equivalent before installing into rear main bearing cap at joint of tongue and oil pan front neoprene seal.
15. Coat oil pan rear seal with soap. Place into recess of rear main bearing cap, making certain seal is firmly and evenly seated.
16. Install oil pan and tighten drain plug securely.

V6-225, V8-350 Engines

A braided oil seal is pressed into the upper and lower grooves behind the rear main bearing. Directly in front of this seal is an oil slinger which deflects the oil back into the oil pan. Should the braided seal require replacement, the installation of the lower half is accomplished as follows:

With the bearing cap and lower bearing half removed, install a new seal so that both ends protrude above the cap. Tap the seal down into position or roll it snugly in its groove with a smooth rounded tool. Then cut off the protruding ends of the seal with a sharp knife or razor blade.

OIL PUMP

4-134

The oil pump is located externally on the left side of the engine. When necessary to remove the pump, first take off the distributor cap and note the position of the rotor so that the pump may be reinstalled without disturbing the ignition timing.

To install the pump without disturbing the timing, the pump gear must be correctly meshed with the camshaft driving gear to allow engagement of the driving key on the distributor shaft in the pump shaft driving slot without moving the distributor rotor. Assembly can be made only in one position because the slot and driving key are machined off center.

To disassemble the pump, Fig. 28, remove the cover and gasket. Hold a hand over the cover opening and, with the pump upside down, turn the shaft until the outer rotor slips out. Drive out the pin securing the drive gear to the shaft. Press the shaft out of the gear and slide the shaft and inner rotor out of the body.

Failure of the pump to operate at full efficiency may usually be traced to excessive end play in the rotor or excessive clearance between the rotors. The clearance between the outer rotor and pump body should also be checked.

End play of the rotors is controlled by the thickness of the cover gasket which is made of special material which can only be slightly compressed. Never use other than a standard factory gasket.

6-232, 258

Oil pump removal or replacement will not affect distributor timing as the distributor drive gear remains in mesh with the camshaft gear.

Upon disassembly of the oil pump, Fig. 29 locate a straight edge across the pump body and gears in the body and check the gear-to-cover clearance, which should not exceed .004″. A clearance of .008″ maximum should exist between gears and walls of pump body.

NOTE *The pump cover should be installed with the pump out of the engine and pump checked for freedom of operation before installation.*

The oil pressure relief valve, which is built into the pump, is not adjustable, the correct pressure being built into the relief valve spring.

V6-225, V8-350 Engine

1. To remove pump, take off oil filter.
2. Disconnect wire from oil pressure indicator switch in filter by-pass valve cap (if so equipped).
3. Remove screws attaching oil pump cover to timing chain cover. Remove cover and slide out pump gears. Replace any parts not serviceable.
4. Remove oil pressure relief valve cap, spring and valve, Fig. 30. Remove oil filter by-pass valve cap, spring and valve. Replace any parts of valve not serviceable.
5. Check relief valve in its bore in cover. Valve should have no more clearance than an easy slip fit. If any perceptible side shake can be felt, the valve and/or cover should be replaced.
6. The filter by-pass valve should be flat and free of nicks and scratches.

Assembly & Installation

1. Lubricate and install pressure relief valve and spring in bore of pump cover. Install cap and gasket. Torque cap to 30–35 ft-lbs.
2. Install filter by-pass valve flat in its seat in cover. Install spring, cap and gasket. Torque cap to 30–35 ft-lbs.
3. Install pump gears and shaft in pump body section of timing chain cover to check gear end clearance. If clearance is less than .0018″ check timing chain cover for evidence of wear.
4. If gear end clearance is satisfactory, remove gears and pack gear pocket *full* of vaseline, not chassis lube.
5. Reinstall gears so vaseline is forced into every cavity of gear pocket and between teeth of gears. *Unless pump is packed with vaseline, it may not prime itself when engine is started.*
6. Install cover and tighten screws alternately and evenly. Final tightening is 10–15 ft-lbs. torque. Install filter on nipple.

V8-304, 360, 401

The oil pump is driven by the distributor drive shaft, Fig. 31.

NOTE: Oil pump gear removal or replacement will not affect distributor timing as the distributor drive gear remains in mesh with the camshaft gear.

After removal of the oil pump cover and gasket, place a straight edge across the pump body and gears in their operational cavity and check the gear to end clearance with a feeler gauge, Fig. 32. The clearance should be .002–.006 in.

If the gear end clearance is less than specified, replace the timing chain cover and the gear and shaft assemblies.

Measure between the gear tooth and the pump body inner wall directly opposite the point of gear mesh, Fig. 33. Rotate the gears to check each tooth for .0005–.0025 in. clearance. If the gear to body clearance is more than specified, replace the idler gear, idler shaft and drive gear assembly.

NOTE: To ensure self-priming of the oil pump, the pump must be filled with oil prior to installation.

JEEP

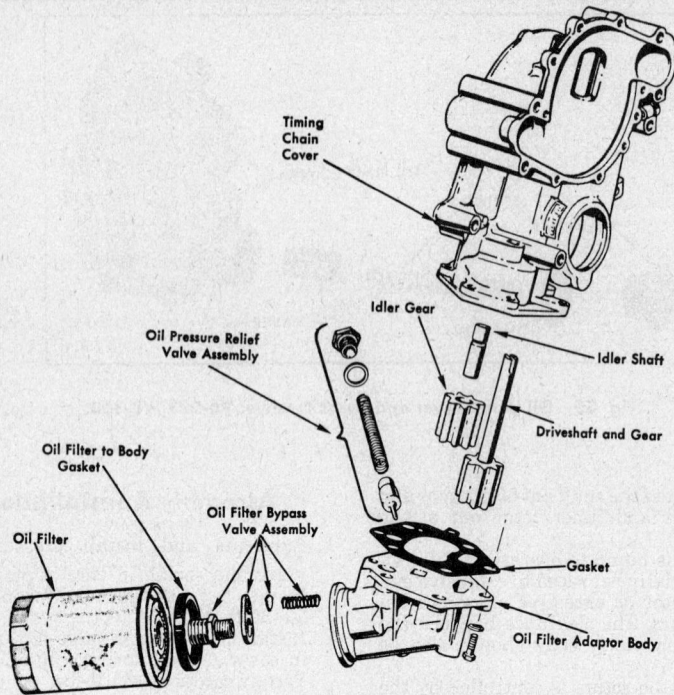

Fig. 31 Oil pump. V8-304, 360, 401

Fig. 32 Checking oil pump. Gear end clearance

coil terminal.
2. Remove distributor cap and rotor. *Mark position of rotor arm on distributor housing so distributor can be installed in same position.*
3. Remove vacuum line from distributor.
4. Remove distributor hold-down clamp.
5. Note relative position of distributor in block, then work it out of the engine.

Installation

1. Turn rotor about 1/8 of a turn counter-clockwise past the mark previously placed on the distributor housing.
2. Push the distributor down into the block with the housing in the normal "installed" position. *On gear-driven distributors, it may be necessary to move the rotor slightly to start gear into mesh with camshaft gear, but rotor should line up with mark when distributor is down in place.*
3. Tighten distributor clamp screw snugly and connect vacuum line, primary wire to coil, and install cap.

V8 Service Note

If the engine was disturbed while the distributor was removed from the engine, first crank the engine to bring No. 1 piston up on its compression stroke and continue cranking until the timing mark is adjacent to the timing indicator. Then rotate the distributor cam until the rotor is in position to fire No. 1 cylinder. Install the distributor as outlined above and set the ignition timing as directed below.

WATER PUMP, REPLACE

Remove the fan belt and blades, unfasten the pump from the cylinder block and lift it off. On some models, it may be necessary to loosen the radiator core and pull it forward in order to remove the water pump assembly.

NOTE: It will be necessary to remove some accessories and the mounting brackets and position aside to gain access to water pump.

DISTRIBUTOR, REPLACE

4-134

The distributor is mounted on the right side of the engine and is operated by a coupling on the oil pump shaft which is driven by a spiral gear on the camshaft.

1. Remove wires from the distributor cap, noting the order in which they are assembled to assure correct reassembly.
2. Remove primary lead from terminal post at side of distributor.
3. Disconnect vacuum tube.
4. Remove distributor cap.
5. Note position of rotor in relation to the distributor housing. Mark housing to facilitate installing and timing.
6. Remove screw holding distributor to crankcase and lift unit from engine.
7. Reinstall in the reverse order of removal and set the timing as outlined below.

6-232, 258, V8-304, 350, 360, 401

1. Disconnect distributor primary wire from

Carburetor Section

AUTOLITE/MOTORCRAFT 2100, 2150 CARBURETOR ADJUSTMENTS

Year	Carb. Part No.①	Float Level (Dry)	Float Level (Wet)	Choke Plate Pulldown Clearance	Pump Setting	Fast Idle Cam	Fast Idle Speed (on Car)	Choke Unloader Clearance	Dashpot	Choke Setting
1972	2DA2, 2RA2	3/8	3/4	.130	No. 3A②	.120	1600③	13/64	9/64	2 Rich
	2DM2	3/8	3/4	.140	No. 3A②	.130	1600③	13/64	7/64	1 Rich
1973	3DA2, 3RA2	3/8	3/4	.120	No. 3A②	.110	1600③	1/4	—	2 Rich
	3DM2	3/8	3/4	.130	No. 3A②	.130	1600③	1/4	9/64	1 Rich
1974	4DM2, 4DMJ2	23/32	25/32	.130	—	.130	1600④	1/4	9/64	2 Rich
	4RA2	23/32	25/32	.140	—	.130	1600④	1/4	—	2 Rich
	4RHD2	3/8	3/4	.140	—	.130	1600④	1/4	9/64	2 Rich
1975	5DM2, 5DM2J	.400	.78	.130	—	.130	1600④	1/4	.095	2 Rich
	5RHA2	.555	.93	.140	—	.130	1600④	1/4	—	2 Rich
	5RHM2	.555	.93	.140	—	.130	1600④	1/4	—	2 Rich
1976	6DA2J	.555	.930	⑤	—	⑥	1600⑦	.250	—	1 Rich
	6DM2	.555	.930	⑤	—	⑥	1600⑦	.250	.093	1 Rich
	6DM2J	.555	.930	⑤	—	⑥	1600⑦	.250	.093	2 Rich
	6RHA2, 6RHM2	.555	.930	⑤	—	⑥	1600⑦	.250	—	2 Rich
1977	6DA2J	.555	.930	.136	—	.126	1600⑦	.250	—	1 Rich
	6DM2	.555	.930	.132	—	.120	1600⑦	.250	.093	2 Rich
	6DM2J	.555	.930	.132	—	.120	1600⑦	.250	.093	1 Rich
	6RHA2, 6RHM2	.555	.930	.136	—	.115	1600⑦	.250	—	2 Rich
	7DA2A	.555	.930	.104	—	.089	1600⑦	.290	—	1 Rich
	7DM2A	.555	.930	.110	—	.089	1600⑦	.290	—	2 Rich
1978	8DM2A	.555	.930	.093	—	.078	1600⑦	.290	—	2 Rich
	8DM2	.555	.930	.132	—	.120	1500⑦	.250	—	2 Rich
	8DM2C	.555	.930	.132	—	.120	1500⑦	.250	—	1 Rich
	8DA2J	.555	.930	.136	—	.126	1600⑦	.250	—	1 Rich
	8DA2JC	.555	.930	.136	—	.126	1600⑦	.250	—	1 Rich
	6RHA2	.555	.930	.136	—	.115	1600⑦	.250	—	2 Rich
	6RHM2	.555	.930	.136	—	.115	1600⑦	.250	—	2 Rich
	8RHA2C	.555	.930	.136	—	.126	1600⑦	.250	—	2 Rich
1979	9DA2J	.555	.930	.128	—	.113	1600⑧	.300	—	1 Rich
	9DM2	.555	.930	.125	—	.120	1500⑧	.300	—	2 Rich
	9DM2C	.555	.930	.132	—	.120	1500⑧	.250	—	1 Rich
	9DM2H	.555	.930	.140	—	.125	1500⑧	.360	—	Index
	9RHA2	.555	.930	.113	—	.093	1600⑦	.350	—	2 Rich
	9RHM2	.555	.930	.104	—	.086	1500⑦	.348	—	2 Rich
1980	0DA2J	.375	.930	.128	—	.113	1600⑧	.300	—	1 Rich
	0DA2J2	.375	.930	.120	—	.106	1600⑧	.300	—	2 Rich
	0DM2A	.375	.930	.128	—	.113	1500⑧	.360	—	1 Rich
	0DMJ2	.375	.930	.113	—	.113	1500⑧	.300	—	2 Rich
	0DM2JC	.375	.930	.120	—	.106	1500⑧	.300	—	2 Rich
	0DHA2	.575	.930	.113	—	.086	1600⑧	.350	—	2 Rich
	0DHM2	.575	.930	.014	—	.081	1500⑧	.348	—	2 Rich

①—Located on tag attached to carburetor on casting.
②—With link in inboard hole in pump lever.
③—Engine hot and screw on highest step of cam.
④—Second step of cam.
⑤—V8-304 with manual trans.; .132". V8-304 with auto. trans.; .136". V8-360; .136".
⑥—V8-360; .115". V8-304 with manual trans.; .120". V8-304 with auto. trans.; .126".
⑦—On second step of fast idle cam with TCS and EGR disconnected.
⑧—Engine hot and EGR valve disconnected.

JEEP

Model 2100, 2150
Figs. 1 & 2

These carburetors have two main bodies—the air horn and throttle body. The air horn assembly, which serves as a cover for the throttle body, contains the choke plate and vents for the fuel bowl. The 1972-74 units use a fuel bowl vent valve.

A choke modulator assembly is incorporated in the 1972-80 2100 units, Fig. 3. The 1973-80 units have an additional port for the Exhaust Gas Recirculation (EGR) system.

The throttle plate, accelerating pump, power valve and fuel bowl are in the throttle body. The choke housing is attached to the throttle body.

The two bodies each contain a main and booster venturi, main fuel discharge, accelerating pump discharge, idle fuel discharge, and a throttle plate. An antistall dashpot is attached to the carburetor when the vehicle is equipped with an automatic transmission.

Float Level Adjustment

Fig. 4—This is a preliminary adjustment; the final adjustment must be made after the carburetor is mounted on the engine.

With air horn removed, float raised and fuel inlet needle seated, measure distance between top surface of throttle body and top surface of float.

Depress the float tab to seat the fuel inlet needle. The float height is measured from the gasket surface of the throttle body with gasket removed. If the float height is not as listed in the 2100 *Specifications Chart*, bend tab on float as required to achieve the desired setting.

Fuel Level Adjustment

Fig. 5—With vehicle on a level surface, operate engine until normal temperature is reached, then stop engine and check fuel level as follows:

1. Remove carburetor air cleaner.
2. Remove air horn retaining screws and carburetor identification tag.
3. Temporarily leave air horn and gasket in position on throttle body and start engine.
4. Allow engine to idle for several minutes, then rotate air horn and remove air horn gasket to gain access to float or floats.
5. While engine is idling, use a standard depth gauge to measure vertical distance from top machined surface of throttle body to level of fuel in bowl. The measurement must be made at least 1/4" away from any vertical surface to assure an accurate reading.
6. If the fuel level is not as listed in the 2100 *Specifications Chart*, stop the engine to avoid any fire hazard due to fuel spray when float setting is disturbed.
7. To adjust fuel level, bend float tab (contacting fuel inlet needle) upward in relation to original position to raise the fuel level, and downward to lower it.
8. Each time an adjustment is made to the float tab to alter the fuel level the engine must be started and permitted to idle for at least three minutes to stabilize the fuel level. Check fuel level after each adjustment until the specified level is achieved.
9. Assemble carburetor with a new air horn gasket. Then adjust idle speed and mixture, and anti-stall dashpot, if so equipped.

Accelerating Pump Adjustment

Fig. 6—The primary throttle shaft lever (overtravel lever) has 4 holes and the accelerating pump link has 2 holes to control the pump stroke for various atmospheric temperatures, operating conditions and specific engine applications.

NOTE: The stroke should not be changed from the specified setting.

1. To release rod from retainer clip, press tab end of clip toward rod. Then, at the same time, press rod away from clip until it is disengaged.
2. Position clip over specified hole in overtravel lever. Press ends of clip together and insert opening rod through clip and lever. Release clip to engage rod.

Choke Plate Clearance (Pulldown) Adjustment

1978-79 2100 Units

1. Loosen choke cover retaining screws and rotate cover 1/4 turn counterclockwise, then tighten one screw.
2. Disconnect choke heat inlet tube. Align fast idle speed adjusting screw with second step of fast idle cam.
3. Start engine without moving accelerator linkage. Turn fast idle cam lever adjusting screw counterclockwise three turns. Measure clearance between upper edge of choke valve and air horn wall, Fig. 7. Refer to 2100, 2150 Specification Chart.
4. Adjust by turning set screw on bottom of modulator.
5. Stop engine and connect choke heat tube. Adjust fast idle cam clearance.

Fig. 4 Float level adjustment 2100, 2150

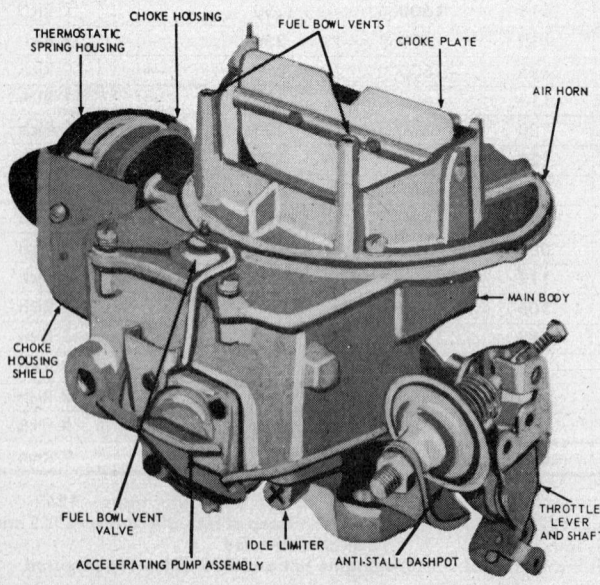

Fig. 1 Autolite/Motorcraft 2100 carburetor (Typical)

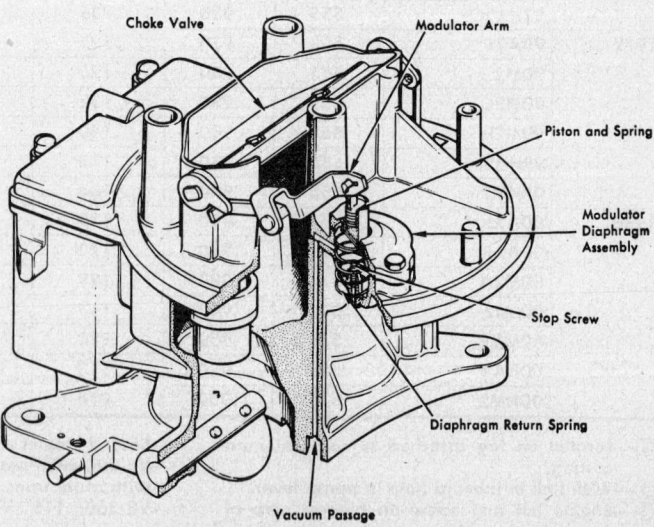

Fig. 3 Autolite/Motorcraft 2100 choke diaphragm assembly

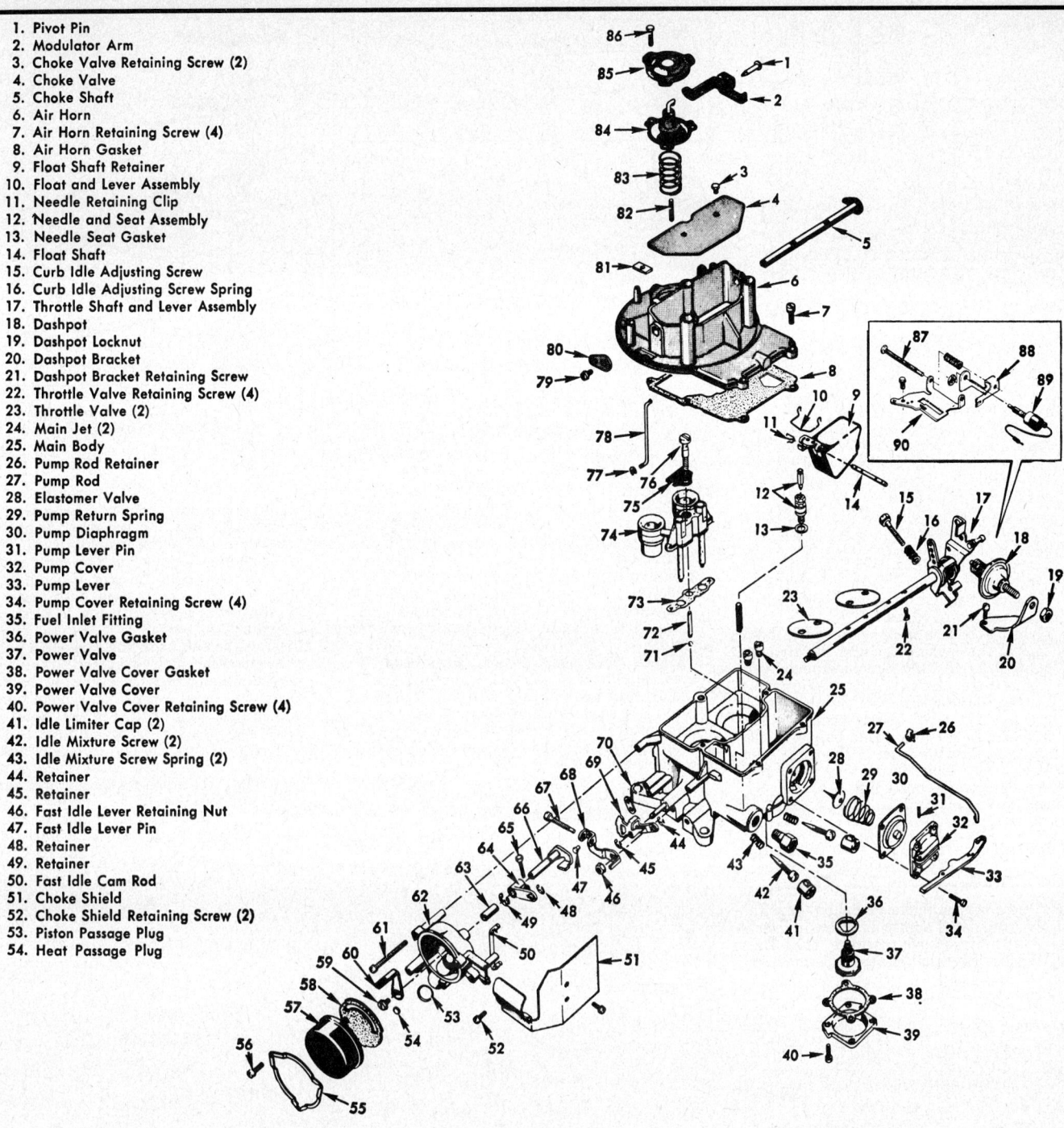

1. Pivot Pin
2. Modulator Arm
3. Choke Valve Retaining Screw (2)
4. Choke Valve
5. Choke Shaft
6. Air Horn
7. Air Horn Retaining Screw (4)
8. Air Horn Gasket
9. Float Shaft Retainer
10. Float and Lever Assembly
11. Needle Retaining Clip
12. Needle and Seat Assembly
13. Needle Seat Gasket
14. Float Shaft
15. Curb Idle Adjusting Screw
16. Curb Idle Adjusting Screw Spring
17. Throttle Shaft and Lever Assembly
18. Dashpot
19. Dashpot Locknut
20. Dashpot Bracket
21. Dashpot Bracket Retaining Screw
22. Throttle Valve Retaining Screw (4)
23. Throttle Valve (2)
24. Main Jet (2)
25. Main Body
26. Pump Rod Retainer
27. Pump Rod
28. Elastomer Valve
29. Pump Return Spring
30. Pump Diaphragm
31. Pump Lever Pin
32. Pump Cover
33. Pump Lever
34. Pump Cover Retaining Screw (4)
35. Fuel Inlet Fitting
36. Power Valve Gasket
37. Power Valve
38. Power Valve Cover Gasket
39. Power Valve Cover
40. Power Valve Cover Retaining Screw (4)
41. Idle Limiter Cap (2)
42. Idle Mixture Screw (2)
43. Idle Mixture Screw Spring (2)
44. Retainer
45. Retainer
46. Fast Idle Lever Retaining Nut
47. Fast Idle Lever Pin
48. Retainer
49. Retainer
50. Fast Idle Cam Rod
51. Choke Shield
52. Choke Shield Retaining Screw (2)
53. Piston Passage Plug
54. Heat Passage Plug
55. Choke Cover Retaining Clamp
56. Choke Cover Retaining Screw (3)
57. Choke Cover
58. Choke Cover Gasket
59. Thermostat Lever Retaining Screw
60. Thermostat Lever
61. Choke Housing Retaining Screw (3)
62. Choke Housing
63. Choke Shaft Bushing
64. Fast Idle Cam Lever
65. Fast Idle Cam Lever Adjusting Screw
66. Thermostatic Choke Shaft
67. Fast Idle Speed Adjusting Screw
68. Fast Idle Lever
69. Fast Idle Cam
70. Choke Housing Gasket
71. Pump Discharge Check Ball
72. Pump Discharge Weight
73. Booster Venturi Gasket
74. Booster Venturi Assembly
75. Air Distribution Plate
76. Pump Discharge Screw
77. Retainer
78. Choke Rod
79. Choke Lever Retaining Screw
80. Choke Lever
81. Choke Rod Seal
82. Stop Screw
83. Modulator Return Spring
84. Modulator Diaphragm Assembly
85. Modulator Cover
86. Modulator Retaining Screw (3)
87. Adjusting Screw
88. Carriage
89. Electric Solenoid
90. Mounting Bracket

Fig. 2 Exploded view of a typical 2100 two barrel carburetor

JEEP

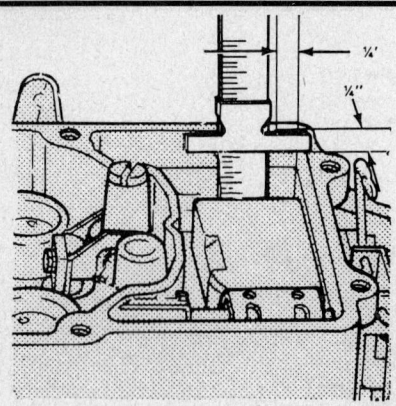

Fig. 5 Fuel level adjustment 2100, 2150

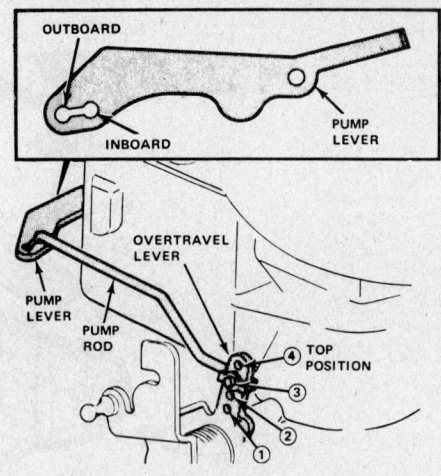

Fig. 6 Pump stroke adjusting points 2100, 2150

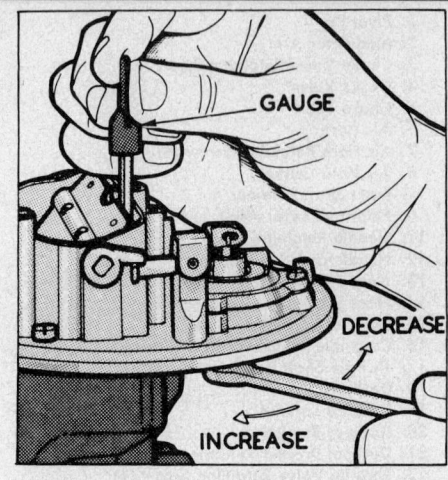

Fig. 7 Choke plate pulldown adjustment. 1978-80 2100 units

1972-77 2100 Units

1. Loosen the choke cover retaining screws. Rotate the choke cover 1/4 turn counter-clockwise (rich) from index and tighten the retaining screws. Disconnect the choke heat inlet tube.
2. Align the fast idle speed adjusting screw with the second step of the fast idle cam.
3. Start the engine without moving the accelerator linkage. Turn the fast idle cam lever adjusting screw out counter-clockwise 3 full turns.
4. Measure the clearance between the lower edge of the choke valve and the air horn wall. Refer to *2100 Specifications Chart* for the correct setting. Adjust by grasping the modulator arm securely with a pair of pliers at point "A" and twisting the arm at point "B" with a second pair of pliers. Twist toward the front of the carburetor to increase clearance and toward the rear to decrease clearance, Fig. 8.

CAUTION: Use extreme care while twisting the modulator arm to avoid damaging the nylon piston rod of the modulator assembly.

NOTE: Connect the choke heat tube. Turn the fast idle came lever adjusting screw in (clockwise) 3 full turns. Do not reset the choke cover until the fast idle cam linkage adjustment has been performed.

2150 Units

1. Set throttle on fast idle cam top step, then loosen choke thermostatic housing retaining screws and set housing 90° in rich direction.
2. Activate pulldown motor by manually forcing pulldown control diaphragm link in direction of applied vacuum or by applying vacuum to external vacuum tube.
3. Check clearance between lower edge of choke plate and center of carburetor air horn wall nearest fuel bowl Fig. 9. Refer to 2150 Specifications Chart. If clearance is not as specified, reset by adjusting diaphragm stop on end of choke pull-down diaphragm.

Fast Idle Cam Clearance

1. Loosen the choke thermostatic spring housing retainer screws and set the housing 90 degrees in the rich direction.
2. Position the fast idle speed screw at the kickdown step of the fast idle cam. The kickdown step is identified on most units by a V stamped on the cam. When a two-piece fast idle lever is used, a tang on the top lever will align with the V mark on the cam.
3. Be sure the cam is at the kickdown position while checking or adjusting the fast idle cam clearance. Check clearance between the lower edge of the choke plate and the air horn wall, Fig. 10. Refer to *2100 Specifications Chart*. Adjust clearance, by turning the fast idle cam clearance adjusting screw clockwise to increase and counterclockwise to decrease the clearance.
4. Set the choke thermostatic spring housing to specifications. Adjust the anti-stall dashpot, idle speed and fuel mixture.

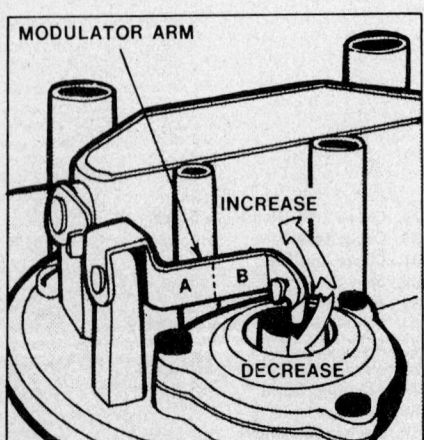

Fig. 8 Choke plate pulldown clearance 2100

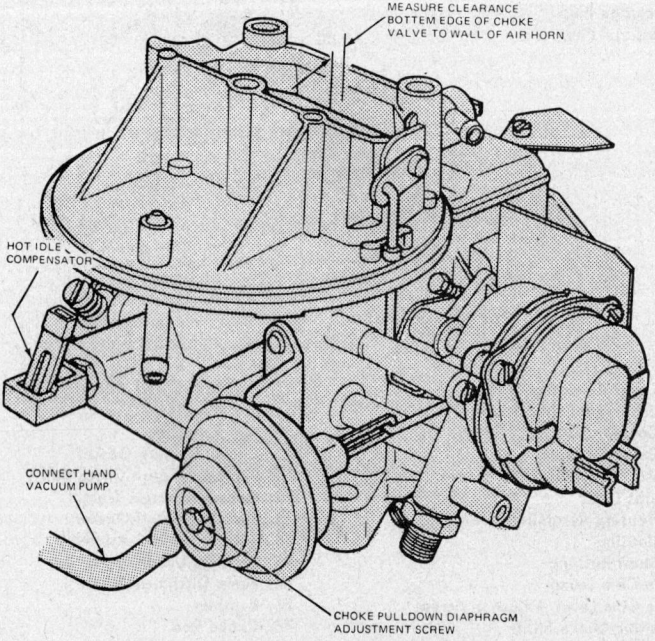

Fig. 9 Choke plate clearance adjustment. 2150

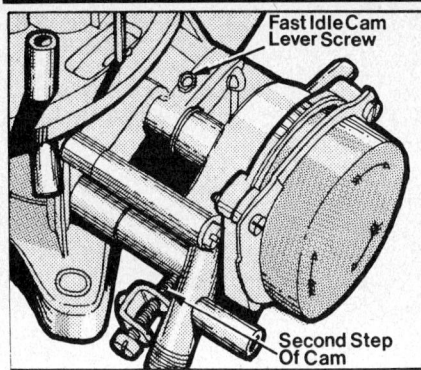

Fig. 10 Fast idle cam linkage adjustment 2100, 2150

Fig. 11 Choke unloader adjustment. 2100, 2150

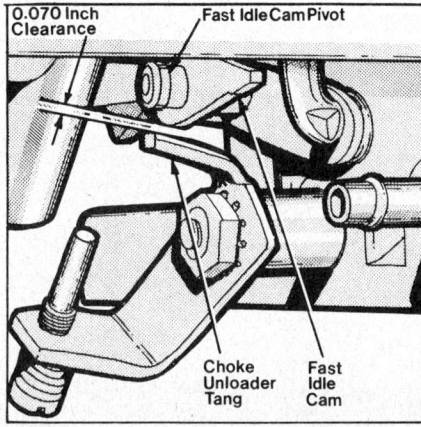

Fig. 12 Choke unloader to fast idle cam clearance. 2100, 2150

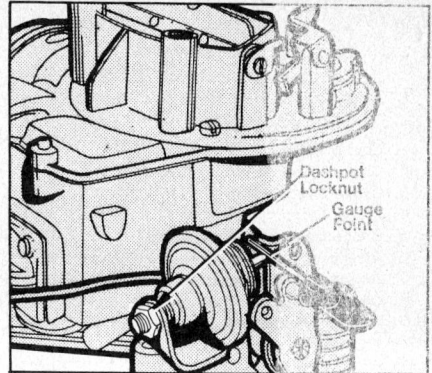

Fig. 13 Dashpot adjustment 2100, 2150

Unloader Adjustment

1. Hold throttle fully open and apply pressure on choke valve toward the closed position.
2. Measure clearance between lower edge of choke valve and air horn wall. Refer to the 2100 Specifications Chart.
3. Adjust by bending the unloader tang contracting fast idle cam, Fig. 11. Bending the tang toward the cam increases the clearance and bending the tang away from the cam decreases the clearance.

NOTE: Do not bend unloader tang downward from a horizontal plane.

4. On 1974-77 units, after making adjustment, open the throttle until the unloader tang is directly below the fast idle cam pivot. A clearance of .070 inch must be obtained between the unloader tang and the edge of the fast idle cam, Fig. 12.

Anti-Stall Dashpot Adjustment

Fig. 13—With engine idle speed and mixture properly adjusted and with engine at normal operating temperature, loosen dashpot lock nut. Hold throttle in closed position and depress plunger with screwdriver as shown. Check clearance between throttle lever and plunger tip. If clearance is not as listed in the 2100 Specifications Chart, turn dashpot in its bracket as required to obtain the desired clearance. Tighten lock nut.

AUTOLITE/MOTORCRAFT 4300 CARBURETOR ADJUSTMENTS

Year	Carb. Part No.①	Float Level	Choke Plate Pulldown Clearance	Pump Setting	Fast Idle Cam	Fast Idle Speed (Hot Engine)	Choke Unloader Clearance	Dashpot Setting	Choke Setting
1973	3TA4	13/16	3/16	Center	.160	1600②	.275	9/64	2 Rich
	3TM4	13/16	3/16	Center	.160	1600②	.275	9/64	2 Rich
1974	4TA4	13/16	11/64	—	.160	1600②	.325	—	2 Rich
	4THD4	13/16	11/64	—	.160	1600②	.325	9/64	2 Rich

①—Located on tag attached to carburetor on casting.   ②—Second step of cam.

MODEL 4300

The model 4300, Figs. 1 and 2, is a four barrel, three piece, separately cast design consisting of air horn, main body and mounting flange. A cast-in center fuel inlet has provision for a supplementary fuel inlet system. The fuel bowl is vented by an internal balance vent and a mechanical atmospheric vent operates during idle. An idle air by-pass system is designed to provide a consistent idle and a hot idle compensator is used to help stability.

The main (primary) fuel system has booster-type venturii cast integral with the air horn, and the main venturii are cast integral with the main body. The secondary throttle plates are mechanically operated from the primary linkage.

An integral hydraulic dashpot dampens sudden movement of the air valve plates to help prevent plate flutter and erratic engine operation.

The automatic choke system consists of a standard bimetal thermostat.

An electric assist choke is incorporated within the choke cover to speed up the opening of the choke valve when the underhood air temperature reaches approximately 95 degrees F.

A single fuel bowl supplies both the primary and secondary fuel systems. Pontoon-type floats are used to help stabilize fuel level during cornering and hill-climbing. The accelerator pump is of the piston type. It is located in the fuel bowl for more positive displacement and a safeguard against external leaks.

Float Setting

Fig. 3—Check clearance and alignment of float pontoons to gauge. Both pontoons should just touch gauge for proper setting. Align pontoons if necessary by slightly twisting pontoons.

Adjust the float level by bending the tab which contacts the fuel inlet needle.

JEEP

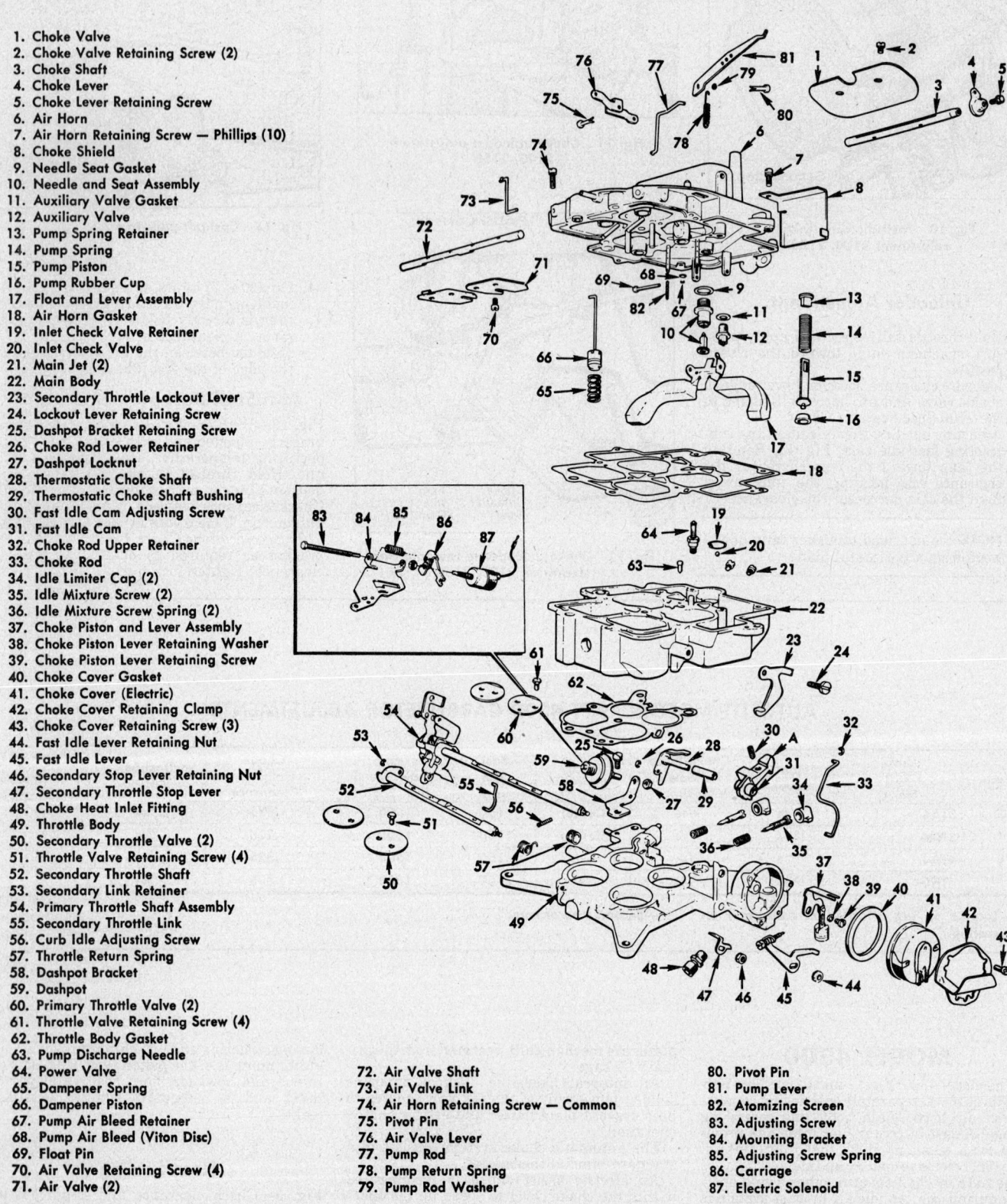

1. Choke Valve
2. Choke Valve Retaining Screw (2)
3. Choke Shaft
4. Choke Lever
5. Choke Lever Retaining Screw
6. Air Horn
7. Air Horn Retaining Screw — Phillips (10)
8. Choke Shield
9. Needle Seat Gasket
10. Needle and Seat Assembly
11. Auxiliary Valve Gasket
12. Auxiliary Valve
13. Pump Spring Retainer
14. Pump Spring
15. Pump Piston
16. Pump Rubber Cup
17. Float and Lever Assembly
18. Air Horn Gasket
19. Inlet Check Valve Retainer
20. Inlet Check Valve
21. Main Jet (2)
22. Main Body
23. Secondary Throttle Lockout Lever
24. Lockout Lever Retaining Screw
25. Dashpot Bracket Retaining Screw
26. Choke Rod Lower Retainer
27. Dashpot Locknut
28. Thermostatic Choke Shaft
29. Thermostatic Choke Shaft Bushing
30. Fast Idle Cam Adjusting Screw
31. Fast Idle Cam
32. Choke Rod Upper Retainer
33. Choke Rod
34. Idle Limiter Cap (2)
35. Idle Mixture Screw (2)
36. Idle Mixture Screw Spring (2)
37. Choke Piston and Lever Assembly
38. Choke Piston Lever Retaining Washer
39. Choke Piston Lever Retaining Screw
40. Choke Cover Gasket
41. Choke Cover (Electric)
42. Choke Cover Retaining Clamp
43. Choke Cover Retaining Screw (3)
44. Fast Idle Lever Retaining Nut
45. Fast Idle Lever
46. Secondary Stop Lever Retaining Nut
47. Secondary Throttle Stop Lever
48. Choke Heat Inlet Fitting
49. Throttle Body
50. Secondary Throttle Valve (2)
51. Throttle Valve Retaining Screw (4)
52. Secondary Throttle Shaft
53. Secondary Link Retainer
54. Primary Throttle Shaft Assembly
55. Secondary Throttle Link
56. Curb Idle Adjusting Screw
57. Throttle Return Spring
58. Dashpot Bracket
59. Dashpot
60. Primary Throttle Valve (2)
61. Throttle Valve Retaining Screw (4)
62. Throttle Body Gasket
63. Pump Discharge Needle
64. Power Valve
65. Dampener Spring
66. Dampener Piston
67. Pump Air Bleed Retainer
68. Pump Air Bleed (Viton Disc)
69. Float Pin
70. Air Valve Retaining Screw (4)
71. Air Valve (2)
72. Air Valve Shaft
73. Air Valve Link
74. Air Horn Retaining Screw — Common
75. Pivot Pin
76. Air Valve Lever
77. Pump Rod
78. Pump Return Spring
79. Pump Rod Washer
80. Pivot Pin
81. Pump Lever
82. Atomizing Screen
83. Adjusting Screw
84. Mounting Bracket
85. Adjusting Screw Spring
86. Carriage
87. Electric Solenoid

Fig. 2 Exploded view of a Autolite/Motorcraft 4300 4-barrel carburetor

JEEP

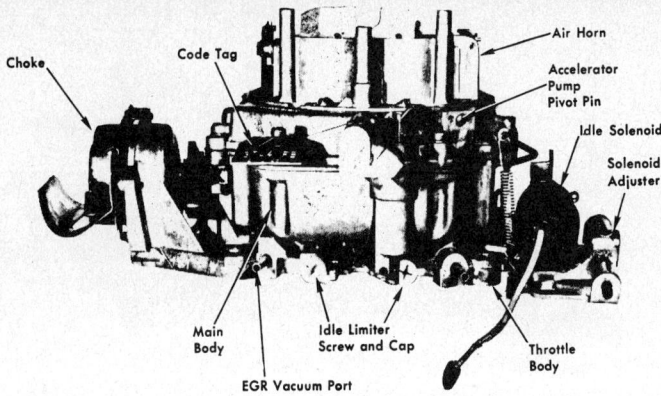

Fig. 1 Autolite/Motorcraft 4300 4-barrel carburetor

4. Pull the choke piston lever counterclockwise until the choke piston locks the wire gauge in place.
5. Hold the choke piston in this position and check the clearance between the lower edge of the choke valve and the air horn wall, Fig. 7. Refer to *4300 Carburetor Specifications Chart*.
6. Adjust by loosening the choke lever retaining screw and rotating the choke shaft.
7. Install choke cover and rotate it to specified setting, then tighten cover.

NOTE: The retaining screw has a left hand thread and must be turned clockwise to loosen.

Fast Idle Cam Linkage Adjustment

1. Rotate the choke cover 1/4 turn clockwise and tighten the retaining screws.
2. Operate the throttle to allow the choke valve to close completely.
3. Push down on the fast idle cam counterweight until the screw is in contact with the second step and against the shoulder of the high step.
4. Measure the clearance between the lower edge of the choke valve and the air horn wall, Fig. 8. Refer to *4300 Carburetor Specifications Chart*.
5. Adjust by turning the fast idle cam adjusting screw.
6. Loosen the choke cover retaining screw and adjust the choke. Refer to *4300 Carburetor Specifications Chart*.

Dashpot Adjustment

Set throttle to curb idle and fully depress the dashpot stem. Measure the clearance between the stem and the throttle lever Fig. 5. Refer to *4300 Specifications Chart*. Adjust by loosening the lock nut and turning the dashpot.

Fast Idle Speed Adjustment

NOTE: Make certain the curb idle speed and mixture are adjusted to specification before attempting to set the fast idle speed.

1. With the engine operating temperature normalized (hot), air cleaner removed and the tachometer attached, manually rotate the fast idle cam until the fast idle adjusting screw rests on the kickdown (middle) step of the cam.
2. Adjust by turning the fast idle adjusting screw inward or outward as required. Refer to *4300 Specifications Chart*.

Auxiliary Inlet Valve Adjustment

1. Turn the air horn assembly upright allowing the float to hang freely.
2. Push up on the float until the primary fuel inlet needle lightly contacts its seat.
3. While holding the float in this position, measure the clearance between the float level auxiliary tab and the auxiliary inlet valve plunger, Fig. 4.
4. Adjust by bending the tab. Refer to *4300 Specifications Chart*.

Accelerator Pump Stroke Adjustment

Fig. 5—The accelerator pump stroke has been calibrated to inject a pre-determined quantity of fuel into the air stream and help keep the exhaust emission level of the engine within the specified limits. The additional holes provided for pump stroke adjustment are for adjusting the stroke for specific engine applications.

NOTE: The stroke should not be changed from the specified setting.

If the pump stroke has been changed from the specified setting, refer to the following instructions to correct the stroke to specification. Before adjusting the accelerator pump stroke, measure the height of the pump piston. Adjust by bending the pump control rod to correct the piston stem height. Refer to *4300 Specifications Chart*.

Unloader Adjustment

With the throttle held fully open, apply pressure on the choke valve and measure the clearance between the lower edge of the choke valve and the air horn wall, Fig. 6. Refer to *4300 Specifications Chart*. Adjust by bending the tang on the fast idle lever which contacts the fast idle cam.

NOTE: For 1974, the unloader adjustment has been eliminated. It will be necessary to check for wide-open throttle to ensure proper unloading.

NOTE: Final unloader adjustment must be accomplished on vehicle. To make sure there is a full throttle opening, the throttle should be fully depressed with accelerator pedal to floor.

Choke Plate Pulldown Adjustment

1. Bend a .035 inch wire gauge at a 90 degree angle approximately 1/8 inch from the end.
2. Partially open the throttle and close the choke valve. This will move the fast idle cam and choke piston into the cold start position.
3. Hold the choke valve fully closed; release the throttle and the choke valve. Insert the wire gauge into the slot at the front of the choke piston passage, Fig. 7.

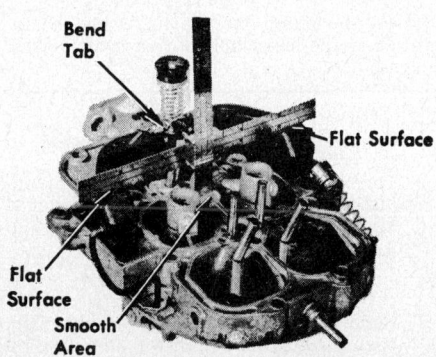

Fig. 3 Float adjustment 4300 4-barrel carburetor

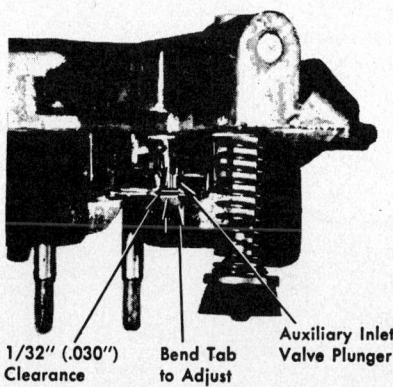

Fig. 4 Auxiliary inlet valve adjustment

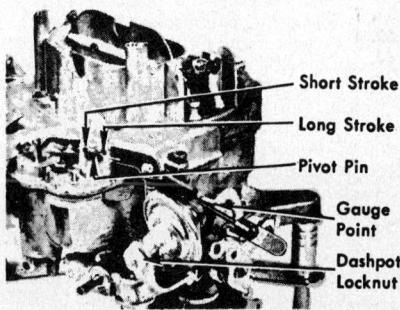

Fig. 5 Accelerator pump and dashpot adjustment

JEEP

Fig. 6 Unloader adjustment

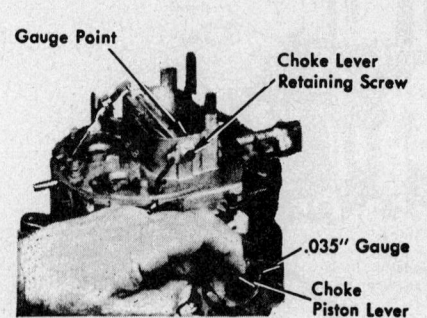

Fig. 7 Choke plate pulldown adjustment

Fig. 8 Fast idle cam linkage adjustment

MOTORCRAFT 4350 CARBURETOR ADJUSTMENTS

Year	Carb. Model (Code 9510)	Float Level (Dry)	Pump Setting (Hole No.)	Choke Plate Clearance (Pulldown)	Fast Idle Cam Linkage Setting	Fast Idle Speed (Hot Engine)	Auxiliary Inlet Valve Setting	Dechoke Clearance	Metering Rod Setting	Choke Setting
1975	5THA4	.90	Lower	.140	.160	1600①	.050	.325	.120	2 Rich
	5THA4D	29/32	Lower	.135	.135	1600①	.050	.325	.120	2 Rich
	5THM4	.90	Lower	.140	.160	1600①	.050	.325	.120	2 Rich
	5THM4D	29/32	Lower	.135	.135	1600①	.050	.325	.120	2 Rich
1976	6THA4	.90	—	.135	.135	1600①	.050	.325	—	2 Rich
	6THA4C	.90	—	.135	.135	1600①	.050	.325	—	2 Rich
	6THM4	.90	—	.135	.135	1600①	.050	.325	—	2 Rich
1977–78	6THA4	.90	Middle	.135	.135	1600①	.050	.325	.117	2 Rich
	6THA4C	.90	Middle	.135	.135	1600①	.050	.325	.112	2 Rich
	6THM4	.90	Middle	.135	.135	1600①	.050	.325	.108	2 Rich

①—On second step of cam with TCS solenoid and EGR disconnected.

MODEL 4350-4V ADJUSTMENTS

Accelerator Pump Stroke Adjustment

This piston-to-shaft pin position which is the only adjustment, is pre-set to deliver the correct amount of fuel for the engine on which it is installed and should not be changed from the specified setting. Do not attempt to adjust the accelerator pump stroke by turning the vacuum limiter level adjusting nut. This adjustment is pre-set and changing it could affect driveability.
1. Remove air horn assembly, then disconnect accelerator pump from operating lever by depressing spring and sliding arm out of pump shaft slot.
2. Disassemble spring and nylon keeper retaining adjustment pin. Refer to 4350 specifications chart. If pin is not in specified hole, remove it, reposition shaft in specified hole and reinstall pin, Fig. 1.

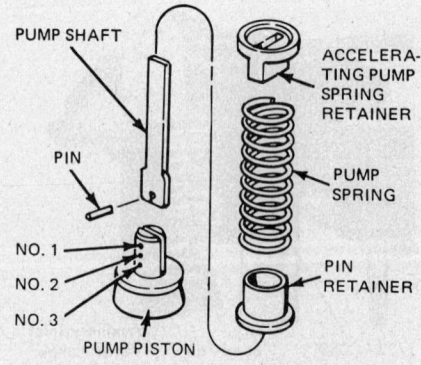

Fig. 1 Accelerating pump stroke adjustment

3. Slide nylon retainer over pin and position spring on shaft, then compress spring on shaft and install pump on arm.

Accelerating Pump Link Adjustment

NOTE: The pump throttle link must be installed in the lower hole of the throttle shaft lever, Fig. 2.

1. Turn out idle speed screw until primary throttle plates are completely seated in the bores.
2. Turn accelerating pump throttle link adjusting nut until notch in pump lever is aligned with index mark on air horn, Fig. 2.

Initial Choke Pulldown

1. Remove choke housing assembly, then open throttle about half-way and position fast idle adjusting screw on high step of fast idle cam.
2. Bend a .036" wire gauge at 90° angle,

Jeep

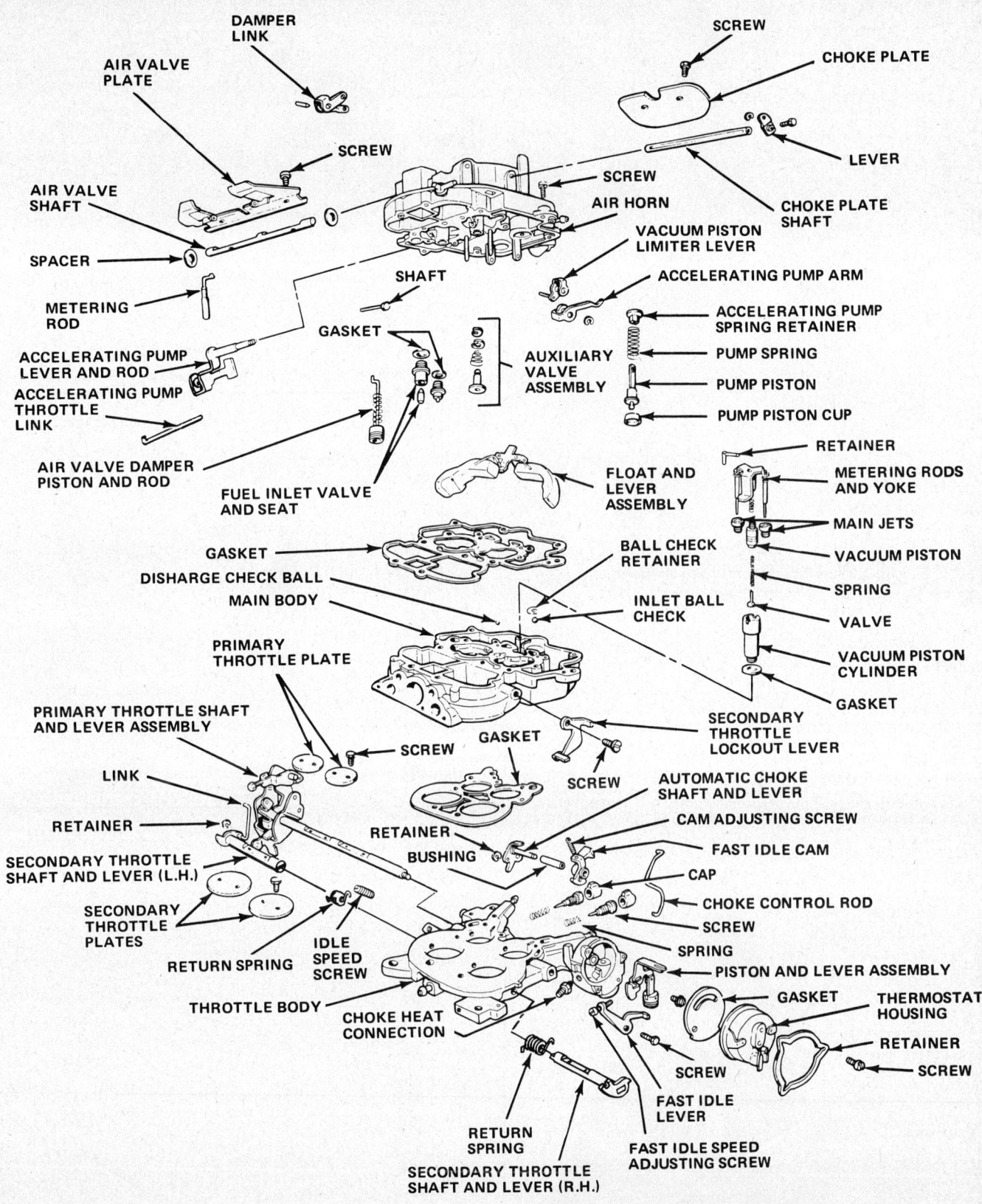

Exploded view of 4350 4V carburetor

JEEP

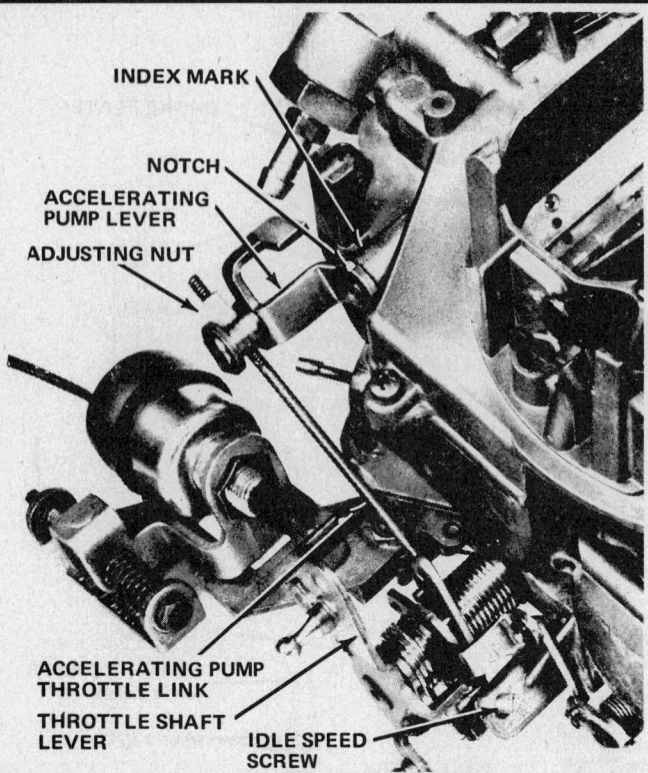

Fig. 2 Accelerating pump link adjustment

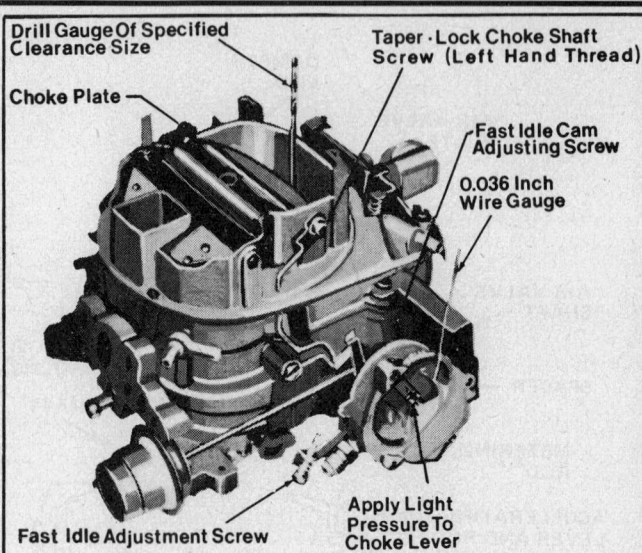

Fig. 3 Initial choke plate pulldown adjustment

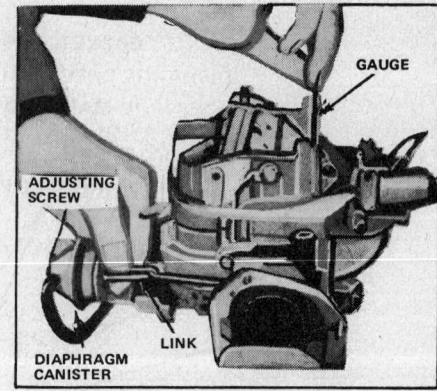

Fig. 4 Initial choke valve clearance

about 1/8" from end, then insert bent end of gauge between choke piston slot and upper edge of right hand slot in choke housing, Fig. 3.

3. Rotate choke lever counterclockwise until gauge is snug in piston slot, then apply light force to lever to hold gauge and move top of choke rod away from carburetor while moving bottom of rod toward carburetor to remove end play from linkage.

4. Using a drill gauge or pin of specified size, check clearance between lower edge of choke plate and wall, Fig. 3. Refer to 4350 specifications chart.

5. Adjust clearance to specifications, by turning lock screw on choke plate shaft 3 full turns in a clockwise direction. Pry choke lever from shaft to break taper lock. Choke lever should rotate freely on choke shaft.

6. With drill gauge and .036" wire gauge positioned as above, tighten, screw on choke shaft.

7. Install choke housing assembly.

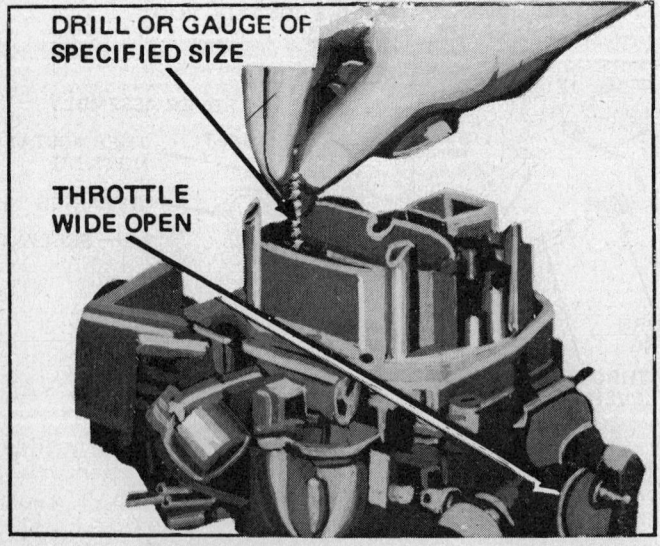

Fig. 5 Dechoke clearance adjustment

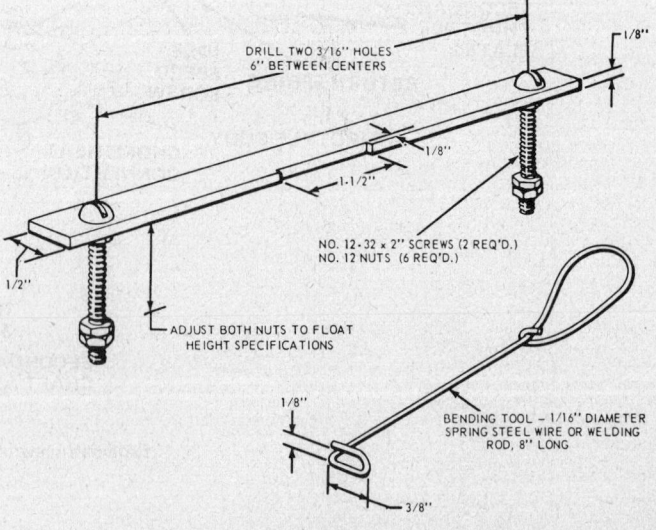

Fig. 6 Float setting gauge and bending tool

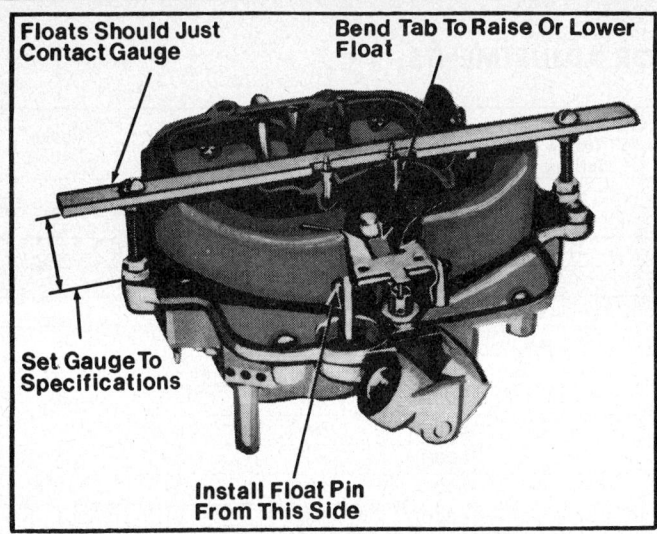

Fig. 7 Setting float level

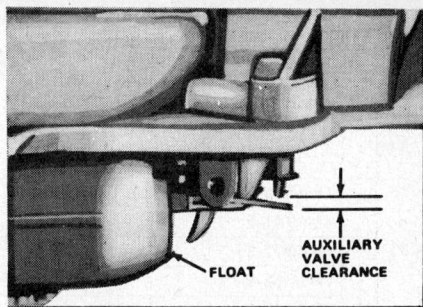

Fig. 8 Auxiliary inlet valve adjustment

Units With Vacuum Diaphragm

Initial Choke Valve Clearance
1. Loosen choke cover screws, open throttle and rotate choke cover until choke valve closes. Then, tighten one cover screw to hold cover in place.
2. Close throttle. The fast idle screw should be on top step of cam.
3. Bottom choke diaphragm on setscrew, however, do not press on links, Fig. 4.
4. Measure clearance between air horn and lower edge of choke valve, Fig. 4. Adjust by turning adjusting screw at rear of diaphragm housing.
5. Adjust fast idle cam linkage.
6. Loosen choke cover screw and set choke cover to specifications.

Choke Plate Indexing
1. Loosen choke lever attaching screw and pry lever from choke shaft to permit choke valve rotation.

NOTE: The choke lever attaching screw has a left hand thread.

2. Loosen choke cover screws and rotate cover 90° counterclockwise so the choke shaft lever contacts cam adjusting screw.
3. Position fast idle screw on top step of fast idle cam. Then, back off cam adjusting screw until clearance is obtained between screw and choke shaft lever.
4. Turn cam adjusting screw until it contacts choke shaft lever, then turn 6-7 additional turns.
5. Manually close choke plate and tighten choke shaft lever attaching screw.
6. Adjust initial choke valve clearance and fast idle cam linkage.
7. Set choke cover and tighten cover screws.

Dechoke (Unloader) Clearance
1. Hold throttle plate fully open and apply pressure on choke valve toward close position.
2. Measure clearance between lower edge of choke valve and air horn wall, Fig. 5. Refer to 4350 Specifications Chart.
3. Adjust clearance to specifications by bending unloader tang which contacts fast idle cam forward to increase or rearward to decrease clearance.

NOTE: Do not bend tang downward from a horizontal plane. After adjustment, make certain that there is at least .070 inch clearance between unloader tang and choke housing with throttle fully open.

Float Setting

To simplify float setting, refer to Fig. 6 for construction of an adjustable float gauge and float tab bending tool.
1. Adjust gauge to specified height and insert gauge into air horn, Fig. 7.
2. Check clearance and alignment of floats to gauge. Refer to 4350 Specifications Chart. Both floats should just touch gauge. If necessary, align floats by twisting floats slightly.
3. To raise float setting, insert open end of bending tool to right side of float lever tab between needle and float hinge. Raise float lever off needle and bend tab downward.
4. To lower float setting, insert open end of bending tool to left side of float lever tab between needle and float hinge. Support float lever and bend tab upward.
5. If above gauge is not available, invert upper body and measure distance from top of float to gasket surface of upper body. Adjust alignment and height of floats with bending tool as described previously.

Auxiliary Valve Setting

Check auxiliary valve clearance as shown in Fig. 8. If necessary to adjust clearance, use bending tool, Fig. 6. Refer to 4350 Specifications Chart.

Vacuum Piston & Metering Rods Adjustment

1. Remove air horn assembly. Depress metering rod hanger and turn vacuum piston adjusting screw and metering rod adjusting screws until metering rod hanger is fully sealed against vacuum cylinder topface, Fig. 8.
2. Hold metering rod hanger in full downward position and turn each metering rod adjusting screw clockwise until the metering rod hanger starts to rise. Metering rods are now properly positioned in relation to vacuum piston.
3. Turn vacuum piston adjusting screw clockwise until specified clearance between metering rod hanger and vacuum cylinder top face is obtained.

Fast Idle Cam

1. Loosen choke cover screws and rotate cover to align index marks on cover and housing. Then, rotate cover an additional 90° counterclockwise and tighten attaching screws.
2. Place fast idle speed adjusting screw on kickdown (center) step of fast idle cam. Fully close choke plate and check clearance between air horn and lower edge of choke plate. Adjust by turning fast idle cam adjusting screw, ensuring adjusting screw remains on kickdown step during adjustment.
3. Loosen choke cover screws and rotate cover to specified index mark and tighten cover screws.

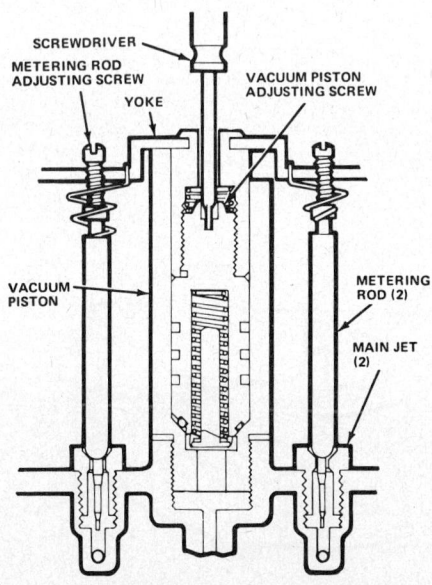

Fig. 9 Metering rod adjustment

JEEP

CARTER YF CARBURETOR ADJUSTMENTS

Year	Carburetor Model	Float Level	Float Drop	Idle Screw Turns Open	Pump Travel Setting	Fast Idle Setting	Choke Unloader Setting	Dashpot	Choke Setting
1970	YF-4366-S	17/64	—	1/2–2 1/2	—	—	—	1/8	—
	YF-4941-S	17/64	—	1/2–2 1/2	—	—	—	1/8	—
1971	YF-4002-S	17/64	—	—	—	—	—	—	—
	YF-4366-S	17/64	—	—	—	—	—	1/8	—
	YF-4941-S	17/64	—	—	—	—	—	1/8	—
	YF-6115-S	17/64	—	—	—	—	—	1/8	—
	YF-938SD	5/16	—	—	—	—	—	—	—
1972	YF-6287S	29/64	1 1/4	2	—	1600①	19/64	3/32	Index
	YF-6288S	29/64	1 1/4	2	—	1600①	19/64	3/32	Index
1973	YF-6299	29/64	1 1/4	—	—	1600①	9/32	3/32	1
	YF-6300	29/64	1 1/4	—	—	1600①	9/32	3/32	1
	YF-6401	29/64	1 1/4	—	—	1600①	9/32	3/32	1
1974	YF-6423	.476	1.38	—	—	1600①	.275	3/32	1
	YF-6431	.476	1.38	—	—	1600①	.275	3/32	1
	YF-6511	.476	1.38	—	—	1600①	.275	3/32	1
	YF-7001	.476	1.38	—	—	1600①	.275	—	1
	YF-7029⑭	.476	1.38	—	—	1600①	.275	.095	1 Rich
1975	YF-7040	.476	1.38	—	—	1600②	.275	.075	1 Rich
	YF-7041	.476	1.38	—	—	1600②	.275	.075	1 Rich
	YF-7043	.476	1.38	—	—	1600②	.275	—	1 Rich
1976	YF-7083	.476	1.38	—	—	1600②	.275	.075	1 Rich
	YF-7084	.476	1.38	—	—	1600②	.275	.075	2 Rich
	YF-7085	.476	1.38	—	—	1600②	.275	.075	1 Rich
	YF-7088	.476	1.38	—	—	1600②	.275	.075	1 Rich
	YF-7109	.476	1.38	—	—	1600②	.275	.075	2 Rich
1977	YF-7110	.476	1.375	—	—	1600①	.275	—	2 Rich
	YF-7111	.476	1.375	—	—	1800	.275	—	2 Rich
	YF-7151	.476	1.375	—	—	1600①	.275	—	1 Rich
	YF-7153	.476	1.375	—	—	1600①	.275	—	Index
	YF-7154	.476	1.375	—	—	1600①	.275	—	1 Rich
1978	YF-7201	.476	1.375	—	—	1600①	.275	—	Index
	YF-7228	.476	1.375	—	—	1600②	.275	—	1 Rich
	YF-7230	.476	1.375	—	—	1600②	.275	—	1 Rich

①—On second step of fast idle cam.
②—On second step of fast idle cam with TCS solenoid and EGR disconnected.

MODEL YF SERIES ADJUSTMENTS

Float Adjustment

Fig. 1—Invert the air horn assembly, and check the clearance from the top of the float to the bottom of the air horn with the float level gauge. Hold the air horn at eye level when gauging the float level. The float arm (lever) should be resting on the needle pin. Do not load the needle when adjusting the float. Bend the float arm as necessary to adjust the float level (clearance). Do not bend the tab at the end of the float arm. It prevents the float from striking the bottom of the fuel bowl when empty.

Float Drop Adjustment

Fig. 2—Hold air horn upright and measure maximum clearance from top of float to bottom of air horn with float drop gauge. Bend tab at end of float arm to obtain specified setting listed under YF Adjustment Specifications.

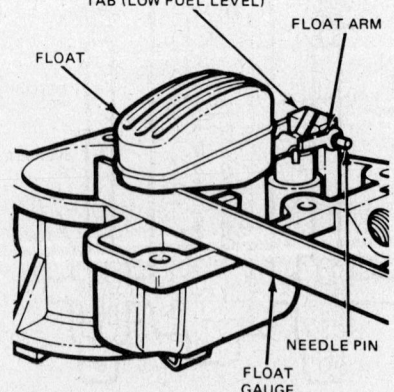

Fig. 1 YF float level adjustment

Metering Rod Adjustment

Figs. 3 & 4—Back out the idle speed adjusting screw until the throttle plate is closed tight in the throttle bore. Press down on upper end of diaphragm shaft until diaphragm bottoms in vacuum chamber. Metering rod should contact bottom of metering rod well, and metering rod should contact lifter link at the outer end nearest the springs and at supporting lug. For models not equipped with metering rod adjusting screw, adjust by bending lip of metering rod arm to which metering rod is attached, up or down as required. For models equipped with a metering rod adjusting screw, turn the adjusting screw until metering rod just bottoms in the body casting. For final adjustments turn metering rod ad-

JEEP

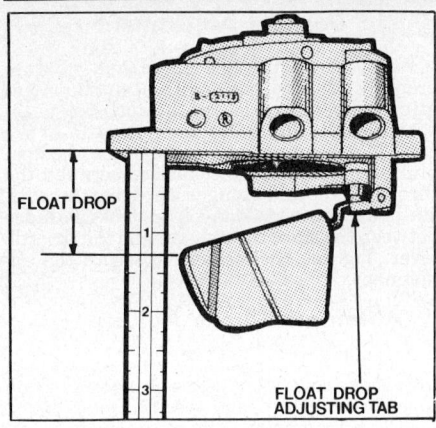

Fig. 2 YF float drop adjustment

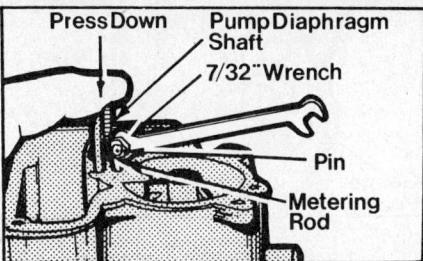

Fig. 3 YF metering rod adjustment. 1971-72

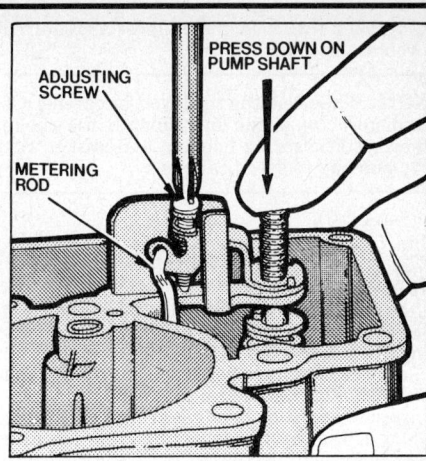

Fig. 4 YF metering rod adjustment. 1973-78

justing screw in (clockwise) one additional turn.

Fast Idle Cam Linkage Adjustment

1971

With engine off, open throttle slightly and close choke to position trip lever on highest step of fast idle cam. Start engine and check fast idle speed. Refer to YF Specifications Chart. To adjust, bend choke connector rod at lower angle. Repeat above procedure to check adjustment.

NOTE: The choke trip connector lever must not contact fast idle cam during adjustment.

1972-73

Partially open throttle and close choke to position fast idle cam into cold start position. Hold choke valve closed and release throttle. In this position, the fast idle adjusting screw must be aligned with index marks on back side of cam. To adjust, bend choke rod at its upper angle, Fig. 5.

1974-78

Position fast idle screw on second step of

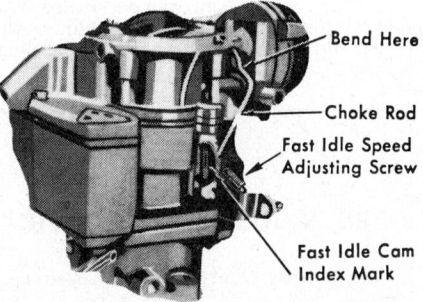

Fig. 5 YF fast idle cam linkage adjustment

fast idle cam and against shoulder of highest step, Fig. 5. Using a drill of specified size, check clearance between lower edge of choke plate and bore. Refer to YF Specifications Chart. To adjust, bend choke connector rod as required.

Fig. 7 YF choke plate pulldown adjustment 1972-78

Choke Unloader Adjustment

1971

With throttle valve held wide open and choke valve held toward closed position, there should be the clearance listed in the YF Specifications Chart between lower edge of choke valve and inner air horn wall, Fig. 6. Adjust by bending the unloader lug on choke trip lever. Bending the lug downward decreases clearance and bending lug upward increases clearance.

Choke Plate Pulldown Adjustment

1972-78

Bend a 0.025 in. diameter wire gauge at a 90 degree angle approximately 1/8-inch from one end. Insert the bent end of the gauge between the choke piston slot and the right hand slot in choke housing. Rotate the choke piston lever counterclockwise until gauge is snug in the piston slot. Exert a light pressure on choke piston lever to hold the gauge in place, then use a drill with a diameter equal to the specified pulldown clearance between the lower edge of choke plate and carburetor bore to check clearance, Fig. 7.

To adjust the choke plate pulldown clear-

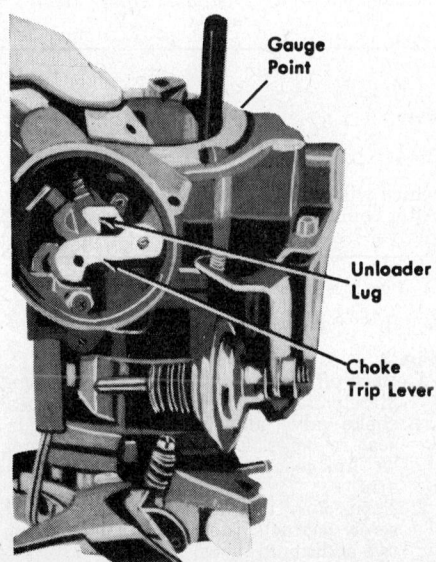

Fig. 6 YF unloader adjustment. 1971

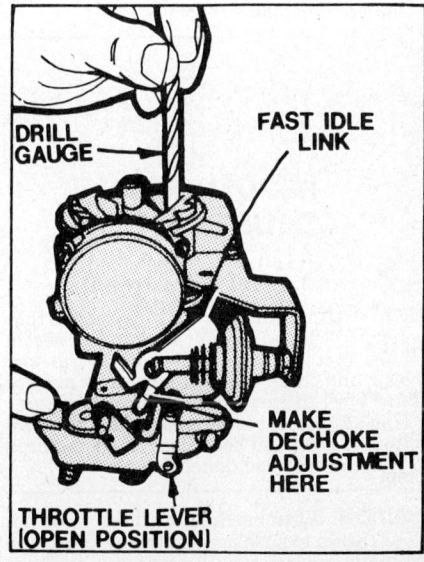

Fig. 8 YF dechoke adjustment. 1972-78

1283

JEEP

ance, bend the choke piston lever as required to obtain specified setting.

NOTE: When bending the lever, be careful not to distort the piston link. Install the choke thermostatic spring housing and gasket. Set the housing to specifications.

Dechoke Adjustment

1972-78

Hold the throttle plate fully open and close the choke plate as far as possible without forcing it. Use a drill of specified diameter to check the clearance between choke plate and air horn, Fig. 8. If clearance is not within specification, adjust by bending arm on choke trip lever of the throttle lever. Bending the arm downward will decrease the clearance, bend-

Fig. 9 YF dashpot adjustment

ing it upward will increase the clearance.

If the choke plate clearance and fast idle cam linkage adjustment was performed with the carburetor on the engine, adjust the engine idle speed and fuel mixture. Adjust dashpot (if so equipped).

Dashpot Adjustment

With the engine idle speed and mixture properly adjusted, the engine at normal operating temperature, loosen the anti-stall dashpot lock nut, Fig. 9. Hold the throttle in the curb idle position and depress the dashpot plunger. Measure the clearance between the throttle lever and plunger tip. Turn the anti-stall dashpot to provide $7/64'' \pm 1/64''$ clearance between the tip of the plunger and the throttle lever. Tighten the locknut to secure the adjustment.

Automatic Choke Adjustment

Loosen choke cover retaining screws and turn choke cover so that line or index mark on cover lines up with the specified mark listed in *YF Specifications Chart* on choke housing.

CARTER BBD ADJUSTMENT SPECIFICATIONS

See Tune Up Chart for hot idle speed.

Year	Carb. Model	Float Level	Vacuum Piston Gap	Initial Choke Valve Clearance	Choke Unloader	Fast Idle Cam	Automatic Choke Setting	Fast Idle Speed
1977-78	8107	.250	.040	.128	.280	.095	2 Rich	1700①
1979	8185	.250	.035	.140	.280	.110	1 Rich	1600③
	8186	.250	.035	.150	.280	.110	1 Rich	1500③
	8187	.250	.035	.140	.280	.110	1 Rich	1600③
	8188	.250	.035	.150	.280	.110	1 Rich	1500③
	8195	.250	.035	.140	.280	.110	1 Rich	②③
	8229	.250	.035	.128	.280	.095	1 Rich	1500③
1980	8253	.250	.035	.128	.280	.095	2 Rich	1850
	8254	.250	.035	.120	.280	.086	2 Rich	1700
	8255	.250	.035	.140	.280	.093	2 Rich	④
	8256	.250	.035	.128	.280	.093	2 Rich	1850
	8257	.250	.035	.128	.280	.095	2 Rich	1700
	8277	.250	.035	.116	.280	.081	1 Rich	1700

①—On second step of fast idle cam with TCS solenoid and EGR disconnected.
②—Manual trans.; 1500. Auto. trans.; 1600.
③—Engine hot with EGR valve disconnected.
④—Manual trans., 1700; auto. trans., 1850.

MODEL BBD ADJUSTMENTS

Float Level Adjustment

Fig. 1—With carburetor body inverted so that weight of floats ONLY is forcing needle against its seat, use a T-scale or the tool shown, and check the float level from surface of fuel bowl to crown of each float at center.

If an adjustment is necessary, hold floats on bottom of bowl and bend float lip as required to give the specified dimension.

CAUTION: When bending the float lip, do not allow the lip to push against the needle as the synthetic rubber tip (if used) can be compressed sufficiently to cause a false setting

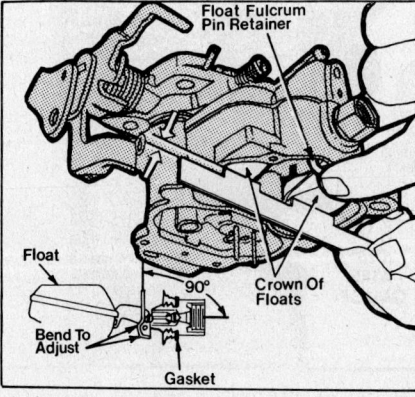

Fig. 1 BBD float level adjustment

which will affect correct level of fuel in bowl. After being compressed, the tip is very slow to recover its original shape.

Accelerator Pump

Fig. 2

1. Back off curb idle adjusting screw, completely closing throttle valve, then open choke valve, allowing throttle valves to seat in bores. Ensure accelerator pump "S" link is located in outer hole or pump arm.
2. Turn curb idle adjusting screw until screw contacts; stop, then rotate screw two additional turns.
3. Measure distance between air horn surface and top of accelerator pump shaft.

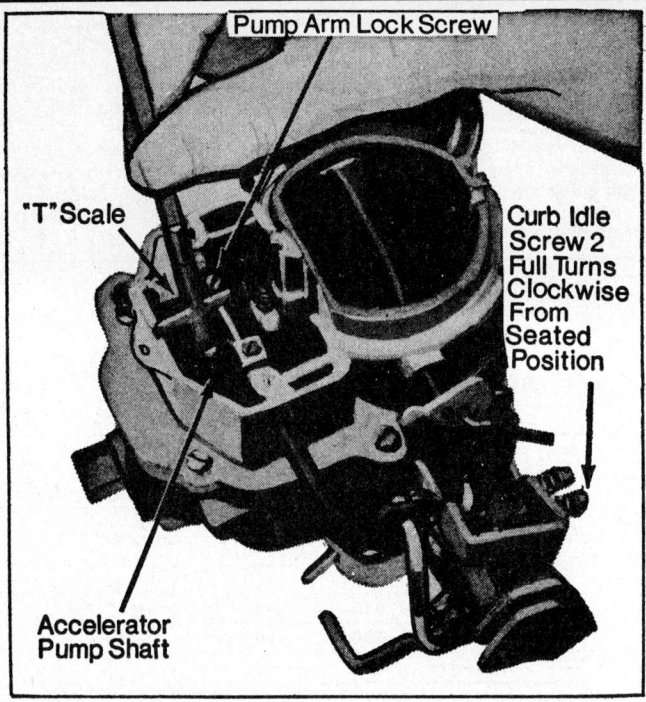

Fig. 2 BBD accelerating pump setting

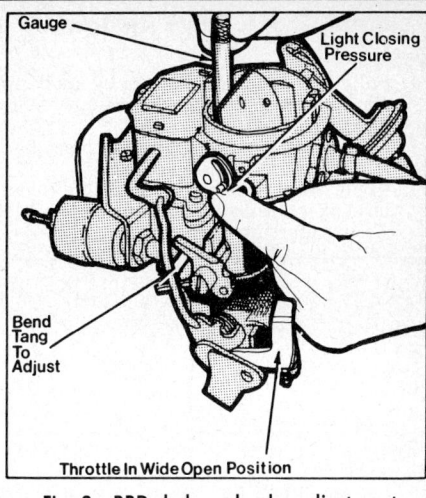

Fig. 3 BBD choke unloader adjustment

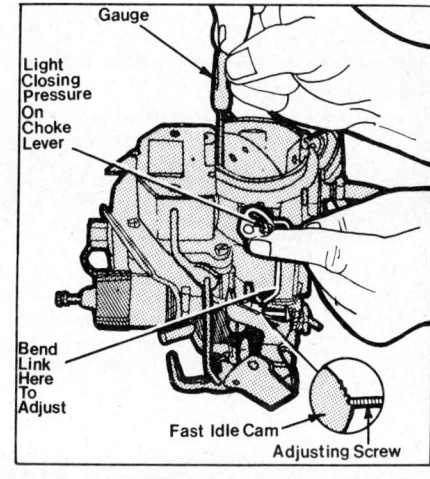

Fig. 4 BBD fast idle cam position adjustment

Refer to BBD Specifications Chart.
4. Adjust by loosening pump arm adjusting screw and rotating sleeve until proper dimension is obtained. Tighten adjusting screw.

Choke Unloader Adjustment

Fig. 3—The choke unloader is a mechanical device to partially open the choke valve at wide open throttle. It is used to eliminate choke enrichment during engine cranking. Engines that have been flooded or stalled by excessive choke enrichment can be cleared by the use of the unloader. Adjust as follows:
1. Hold throttle valve in wide open position. Insert the specified drill size between upper edge of choke valve and inner wall of air horn.
2. With a finger lightly pressing against choke valve, a slight drag should be felt as the drill is being withdrawn.
3. If an adjustment is necessary, bend unloader tang on throttle lever until specified opening has been obtained.

Fast Idle Cam Position

Fig. 4
1. With fast idle adjusting screw contacting second highest step on fast idle cam, move choke valve toward closed position with light pressure on choke shaft lever.
2. Insert the specified size drill between choke valve and air horn wall. An adjustment will be necessary if a slight drag is not obtained as drill is being removed.
3. Adjust by bending fast idle connector rod at lower angle.

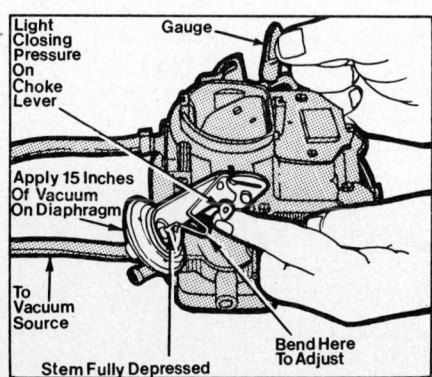

Fig. 5 BBD initial choke valve clearance adjustment

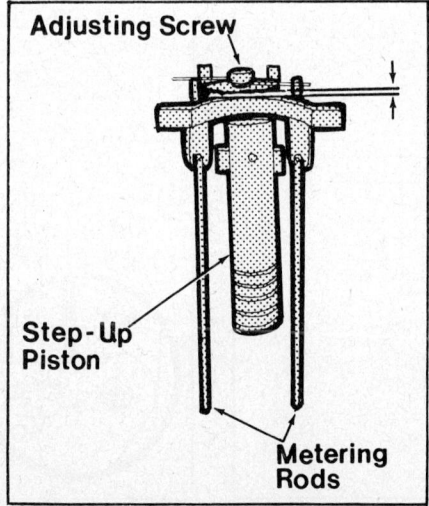

Fig. 6 BBD step-up piston adjustment

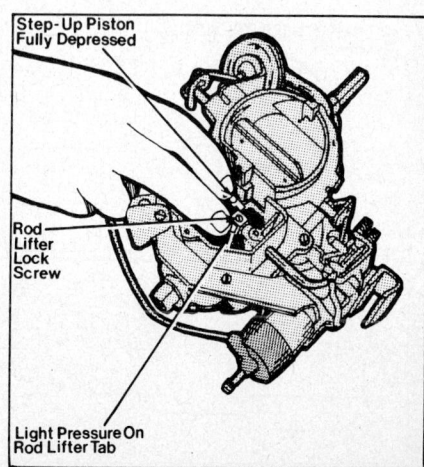

Fig. 7 BBD vacuum piston gap adjustment

JEEP

Initial Choke Valve Clearance
Fig. 5
1. Fully seat choke diaphragm by applying a minimum of 19 inches of mercury from an external vacuum source.
2. Open throttle valve slightly to place fast idle screw on high step of cam.
3. Apply light closing pressure to choke lever or rotate choke coil housing to apply closing pressure to choke.
4. Measure clearance between upper edge of choke plate and air horn wall. To adjust, bend diaphragm connector link.

Vacuum Piston Gap Adjustment
Figs. 6 & 7
1. Adjust vacuum piston gap to specifications. Rotate allen head screw on top of piston to adjust gap.
2. Install vacuum piston assembly into air horn bore, ensuring metering rods are positioned in the metering jets.
3. Back off curb idle screw until throttle valves are completely closed. Count number of turns so that screw can be returned to its original setting.
4. Fully depress piston and while applying moderate pressure on rod lifter, tighten rod lifter-screw.
5. Release piston and rod lifter and reset curb idle screw.

ROCHESTER TWO BARREL CARB. ADJUSTMENTS

Carb. Part No.①	Carb. Model	Year	Idle screw (Mixture) Turns Open	Float Level (Dry)	Float Drop	Pump Setting	Bowl Vent Clearance	Fast Idle Bench	Fast Idle On Car	Choke Unloader Clearance	Anti-Stall Dashpot Clearance	Choke Setting
7026082	2G	1971	2	1 3/32	1 7/8	1 5/32	—	3 Turns	675	.140	1/8	①
7026089	2G	1970	2	1 5/32	1 3/4	1 5/32	—	3 Turns	675	.140	1/8	①
7027082	2G	1971	2	1 5/32	1 7/8	1 5/32	—	3 Turns	675	.140	1/8	①
7027089	2G	1970	2	1 5/32	1 3/4	1 5/32	—	3 Turns	675	.140	1/8	①
7028088	2GV	1970	2	1 11/32	1 3/4	1 1/16	.025	3 Turns	650	.140	—	①
7041185	2G	1971	2	1 5/32	1 7/8	1 5/32	—	3 Turns	675	.140	1/8	①

①—Standard hole.

ROCHESTER 2G & GV

Float Level Setting
With air horn assembly inverted, measure distance from air horn gasket to toe of float. Bend float arm as required to obtain specified dimension, Fig. 1.

Float Drop
With air horn held right side up, measure dimension from gasket to notch at toe of float. Bend float tang as required to obtain the specified dimension, Fig. 2.

Pump Rod Adjustment
Back out idle stop screw to completely close throttle plates in bores. Measure from air cleaner flange to top of pump rod. Bend pump rod as required to obtain the specified setting, Fig. 3.

Choke Rod Adjustment
With idle stop screw in normal idle position, place idle stop screw on second step of fast idle cam and against shoulder of the high step. Bend tang on choke lever to obtain a .035" dimension between the upper edge of the choke valve and the wall of the air horn, Fig. 4.

Vacuum Break Adjustment
With vacuum break diaphragm plunger seated and choke valve closed so the vacuum break rod is at the end of the slot in the choke shaft lever, place a .065" gauge between the upper edge of the choke valve and the inside wall of the air horn. To adjust, bend vacuum break rod, Fig. 5.

Choke Unloader Adjuster
With throttle valves held wide open, dimension between upper edge of choke valve and inner wall of air horn should be .140". Bend unloader tang on throttle lever to adjust, Fig. 6.

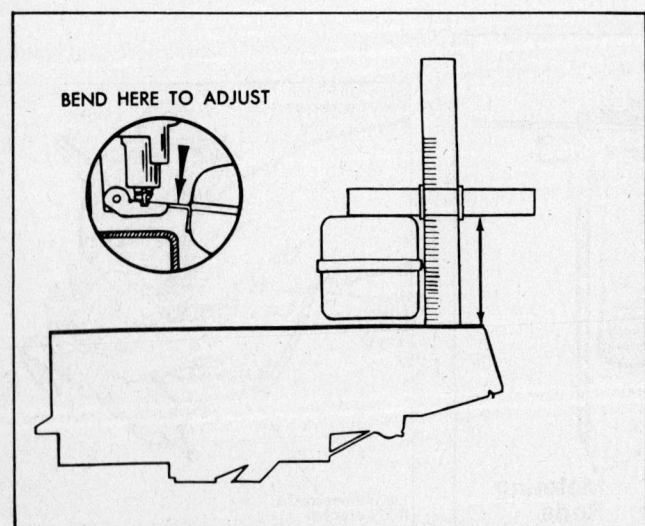

Fig. 1 Float level adjustment

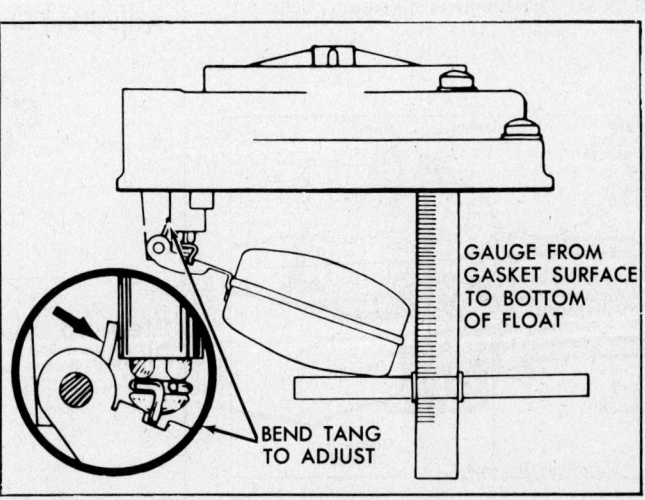

Fig. 2 Float drop adjustment

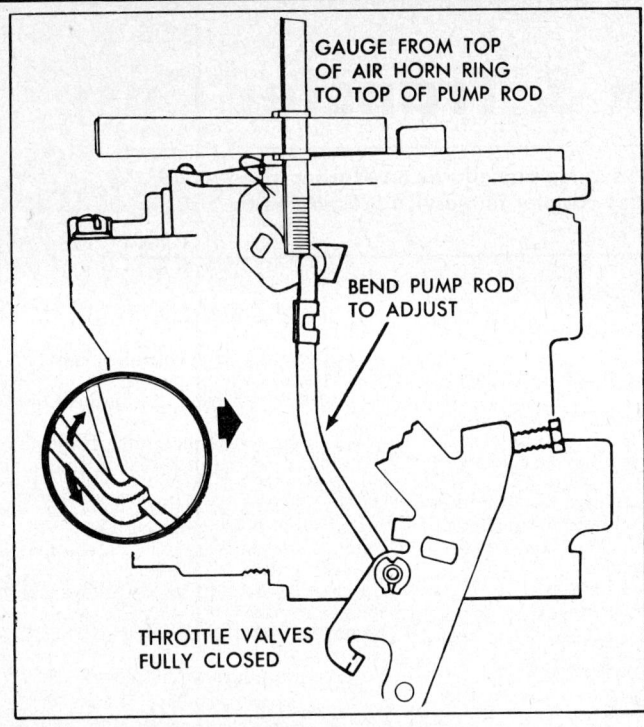

Fig. 3 Pump rod adjustment

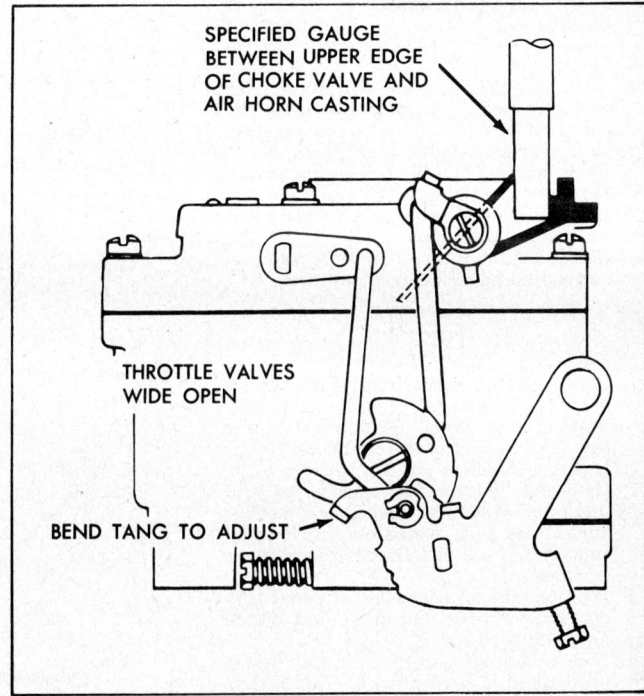

Fig. 4 Choke rod adjustment

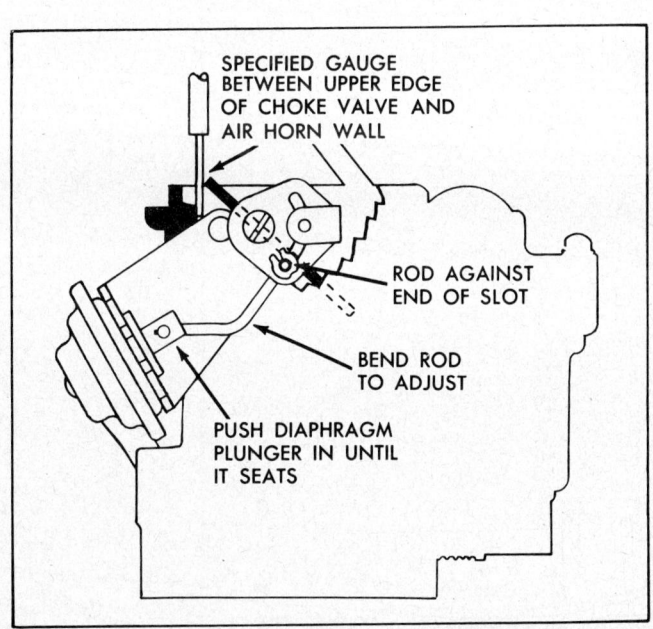

Fig. 5 Vacuum break adjustment

Fig. 6 Choke unloader adjustment

JEEP

Clutch, Transmission & Transfer Case

NOTE: Refer to the Warner Transmission chapter for service procedures on Warner transmissions used on these vehicles. Also refer to the Transfer Case chapter for service procedures on transfer cases used on these vehicles.

CLUTCH PEDAL, ADJUST

1970–71 All

Two types of clutch linkages are used on these vehicles. A clutch control cable type, Fig. 1, and a cross shaft tube and lever type, Fig. 2. The adjustment procedures for both types are as follows:

Cable Type, Fig. 1
1. Position clutch pedal against pedal support bracket stop.
2. Turn adjusting nut until slack is removed from cable and throw out bearing contacts pressure plate release levers or diaphragm.
3. Back off adjusting nut 2½ turns to obtain the desired ¾ inch free pedal travel.

Cross Shaft Tube & Lever Type, Fig. 2
1. With cross shaft positioned (V6 engines, 58°, and F4 engines, 52°) as shown in Fig. 2, and clutch pedal against pedal support bracket stop, turn cable adjusting nut until all slack is removed from the cable.
2. With cross shaft positioned in step 1, push clutch release lever rearward until the throwout bearing contacts the pressure plate release levers or diaphragm.
3. Remove clevis pin and turn cable adjusting clevis 2½ turns for V6 engines and 3 turns for F4 engines to obtain the desired ¾ inch pedal free play.
4. Release clutch lever, then reinstall cable clevis pin and lock clevis jam nut.

1972
1. Roll carpeting away from area directly behind clutch pedal, then measure distance at an angle of 90° from floor to the center of the face of the clutch pedal pad. If this distance is not 8 inches on CJ-5, CJ-6 and Commando models or 8⅜ inches on Wagoneer and Truck models, adjust stop bolt located on clutch pedal support bracket until the desired distance is obtained.
2. Position clutch pedal against pedal support bracket stop and disconnect clutch fork return spring.
3. Loosen ball adjusting nut at clutch fork until there is some slack in cable, then adjust ball adjusting nut until all slack is removed from cable and the throwout bearing contacts the pressure plate fingers.
4. Back off adjusting nut to provide the desired ¾ inch free pedal travel, then tighten jam nut and reconnect return spring.

1973–80
1. On 1973-75 models adjust bellcrank outer support bracket to obtain about ⅛ inch bellcrank end play.
2. Position clutch pedal against pedal support bracket stop.
3. Adjust the pedal to bellcrank push rod until bellcrank inner lever is parallel to front face of clutch housing and slightly forward from the vertical position.
4. Adjust clutch fork to bellcrank rod to obtain the following clutch pedal free travel: ⅜–⅝ inch on Cherokee, Commander, Truck and Wagoneer, ½–¾ inch on 1973-74 CJ/DJ, ⅞–1 inch on 1975-77 CJ and 1–1¼ inch on 1978-80 CJ.

CLUTCH ASSEMBLY, REPLACE

1970–71

J Series
1. Remove the transmission and transfer case, if so equipped, as outlined further on in this chapter.
2. Remove the pan from the flywheel housing.
3. Mark the pressure plate and flywheel so the clutch can be installed in the same position.
4. Remove clutch attaching bolts leaving two opposed to be removed last.
5. Remove the remaining bolts equally, a little at a time, to prevent distortion of clutch pressure plate and to relieve clutch springs evenly.
6. Remove clutch through flywheel housing pan opening.
7. Reverse procedure to install.

Except J Series
To remove the clutch, follow the procedure outlined in the transmission section for the

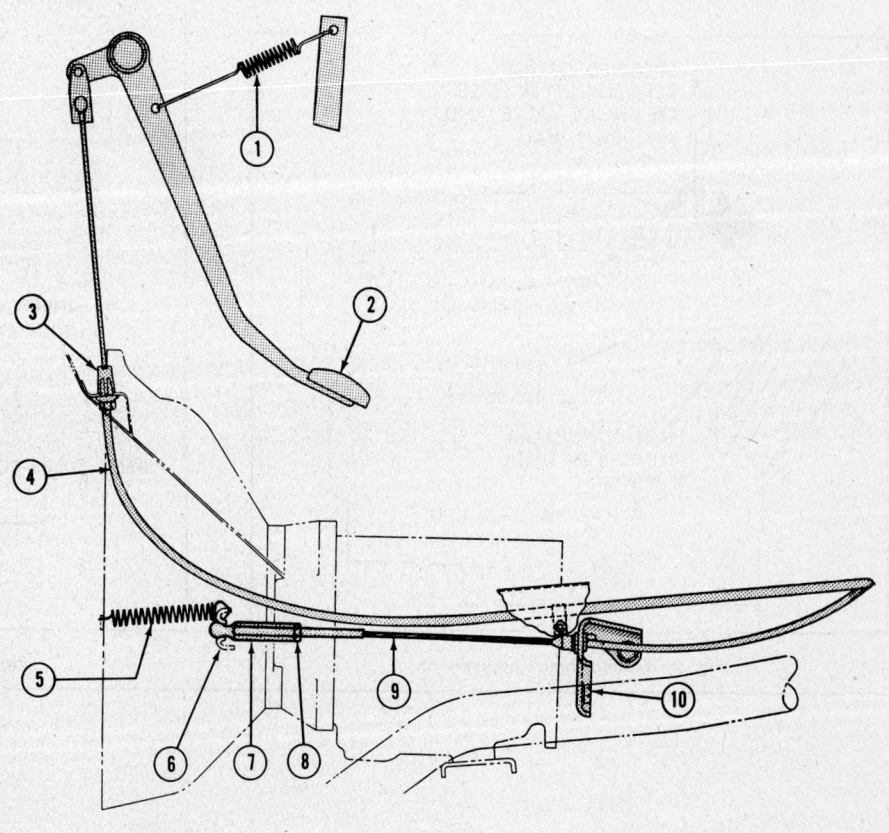

1—Retracting Spring (Clutch Pedal)
2—Clutch Pedal Assembly
3—Retainer
4—Clutch Cable Housing
5—Retracting Spring (Clutch Fork)
6—Clutch Fork
7—Ball Adjusting Nut
8—Lock Nut
9—Clutch Cable
10—Clutch Cable Support Bracket

Fig. 1 Cable type clutch control linkage

removal of the transmission or transmission and transfer case from the vehicle.

Remove the transmission and bell housing from vehicles not equipped with a transfer case. Then remove the clutch from the flywheel.

If the same clutch is to be reinstalled, mark both the pressure plate and flywheel so that the assembly may be installed in the same position.

Install the clutch in the reverse order of its removal and adjust the clutch control cable to establish the proper free pedal travel.

1972-80

Removal

1. Raise and support vehicle.
2. Remove transmission as outlined under "Transmission, Replace" procedure.
3. Remove starter motor.
4. Remove throwout bearing and clutch housing.
5. Mark position of pressure plate on flywheel for assembly reference.
6. Alternately loosen the pressure plate attaching bolts to relieve spring tension.

NOTE: The pressure plate bolts must be loosen evenly to prevent distortion of cover.

7. Remove pressure plate bolts, then the pressure plate and driven plate from flywheel.

NOTE: Place a mark on the side of the driven plate facing the flywheel for assembly reference.

8. Remove pilot bushing lubricating wick and soak wick in engine oil.

Installation

1. Lightly lubricate release lever pivots.
2. Install pilot bushing lubricating wick into crankshaft bore.
3. Install a suitable clutch alignment tool or a spare clutch shaft into driven plate hub.
4. Install assembled plate and tool on flywheel. Ensure that tool is seated fully in the pilot bushing.

NOTE: Ensure that the proper side of the driven plate faces the flywheel.

5. Place pressure plate on flywheel and over driven plate and alignment tool. Align pressure plate and flywheel using the marks made during removal. Install pressure plate attaching bolts finger tight.
6. Torque pressure plate evenly and alternately to 40 ft. lbs.
7. Install clutch housing and starter motor.
8. Install throwout bearing and waved washer, if used.
9. Install transmission.

TRANSMISSION, REPLACE

1972-80 All

1. Remove floor lever knob, trimming, boot, floor covering and pan.
2. On three-speed transmissions, remove shift control lever housing assembly and on four-speed transmissions, remove shift cap, spring retainer, spring, shift lever and pin.
3. Remove transfer case shift lever and bracket assembly.
4. Raise vehicle, remove front propeller shaft and disconnect rear propeller shaft from transfer case.
5. Disconnect speedometer cable, backup lamp switch and TCS switch wires, and brake cable.
6. On vehicles with V8 engines, disconnect exhaust pipes from manifolds.
7. Support transmission and engine with jacks and remove frame center crossmember.
8. Remove transmission to bell housing bolts and lower transmission slightly, then slide transmission and transfer case toward rear of vehicle until clutch shaft clears bell housing.

1970-71
Four Wheel Drive, Except J Series

1. Remove front and rear propeller shafts.
2. If vehicle is equipped with a power take-off, disconnect transfer case end of power take-off drive shaft.
3. Disconnect speedometer cable at transfer case.
4. Disconnect brake cable.
5. Support transmission and engine with jacks.
6. Remove nuts holding rear mounting to frame crossmember.
7. Remove transfer case snubbing rubber bolt nut at crossmember.
8. Remove shift lever or remote control rods.
9. Disconnect clutch release cable at bell crank at yoke end.

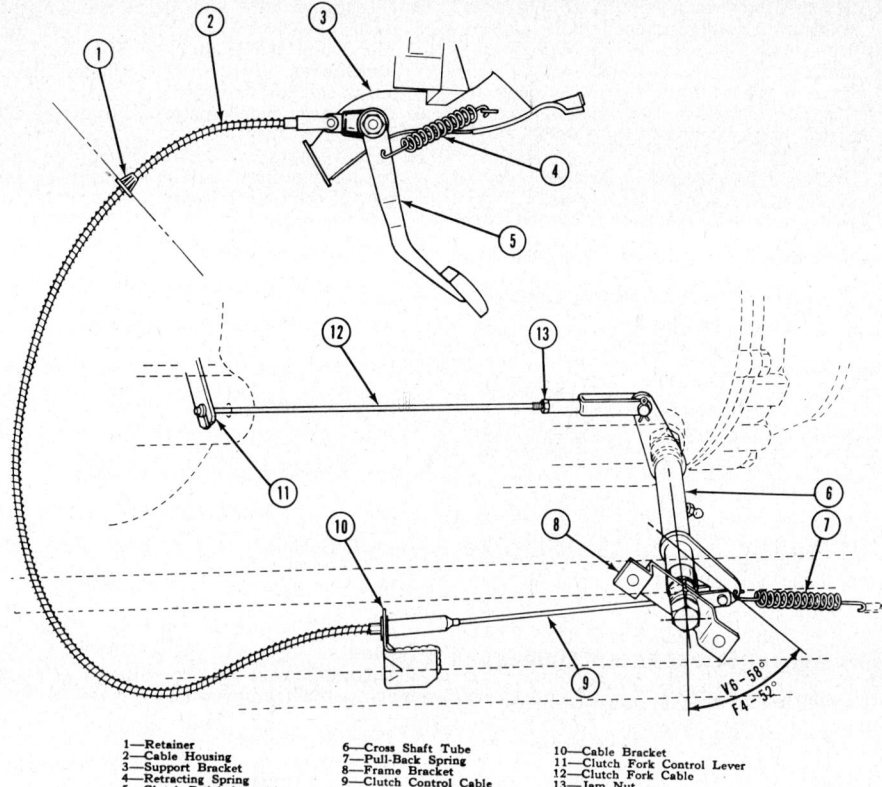

Fig. 2 Cross shaft and lever type clutch control linkage

1—Retainer
2—Cable Housing
3—Support Bracket
4—Retracting Spring
5—Clutch Pedal Assembly
6—Cross Shaft Tube
7—Pull-Back Spring
8—Frame Bracket
9—Clutch Control Cable
10—Cable Bracket
11—Clutch Fork Control Lever
12—Clutch Fork Cable
13—Jam Nut

10. Remove floor board inspection plate.
11. Remove transfer case shift lever pivot pin screw.
12. Remove transfer case shift lever pivot pin and remove levers. If vehicle is equipped with power take-off, remove shift lever plate screws and lift out lever.
13. Remove frame center crossmember.
14. Remove bolts holding transmission to bell housing.
15. Force transmission to right to disengage clutch control lever tube ball joint.
16. Lower jacks under engine and transmission and slide transmission and transfer case toward rear of vehicle until clutch shaft clears bell housing.

Separate Transmission From Transfer Case

1. Drain lubricant from both units.
2. Remove screws from cover on rear face of transfer case (if equipped with power take-off, remove power take-off shift housing).
3. Remove transfer case main drive gear from rear end of transmission mainshaft.
4. Remove shift tower from transmission.
5. In the absence of a transmission mainshaft retaining plate, loop a piece of wire around the mainshaft just back of the second speed gear. Twist the wire and attach one end to right hand front cover screw and the other end to left hand cover screw.
6. Draw wire tightly to prevent mainshaft from pulling out of transmission case when transfer case is removed.

JEEP

7. Separate the two housings, using care to see that the transmission mainshaft bearing, which bears in both housings, remains in the transmission case.
8. Reverse the removal procedure to attach the transmission to the transfer case and install the assembly in the vehicle.

4-Wheel Drive, J Series

1. Drain lubricant from transmission and transfer case.
2. Remove the transfer case as outlined further on in this chapter. The transfer case and the transmission can be removed as an assembly.
3. Remove the transmission access cover from the floor.
4. Disconnect shift rods from shift levers.
5. Disconnect speedometer cable.
6. Support engine with a jack and remove nuts holding rear mounting to crossmember.
7. Remove bolts holding transmission to flywheel housing.
8. Slide transmission assembly toward rear until main drive gear clears the flywheel housing and remove transmission from under vehicle.

Two-Wheel Drive, Except J Series

The following outline covers removal of transmission and overdrive. If not so equipped, disregard operations pertaining to overdrive.

1. Disconnect remote control rods at transmission.
2. Disconnect two wires from overdrive solenoid. *Tag wires and terminals to assure correct assembly.*
3. Disconnect two wires at overdrive rail switch. *Tag wires and terminals to assure correct assembly.*
4. Disconnect front universal joint, and speedometer cable at transmission. Have available an ordinary cork of correct size to close cable opening to prevent leakage of lubricant.
5. Disconnect overdrive control cable and conduit.
6. Remove rubber mounted saddle support at rear end of overdrive. Use care not to lose spacers. Remove overdrive.
7. Place jack under flywheel bell housing and raise it to support weight of housing.
8. Remove frame cross member with rubber insulators attached.
9. Place jack under engine to support engine when transmission is removed.
10. Thread out four screws attaching transmission to bell housing as far as possible and yet support weight of transmission. Pull transmission back to bolt heads which will provide approximately 3/4" opening between the two housings and at the same time relieve pressure on clutch release fork in bell housing.
11. Use a long screwdriver through opening in side of bell housing to pry clutch release fork from engagement with clutch release bearing carrier.
12. Complete removal of four transmission attaching screws and pull transmission back until clutch shaft clears bell housing and remove the assembly with release bearing carrier attached.

Two Wheel Drive, J Series

1. Drain the transmission.
2. Remove transmission access cover from the floor.
3. Disconnect shift rods from the control levers.
4. Remove propeller shaft by disconnecting it at the rear universal joint and pulling it out of the transmission.
5. Disconnect speedometer cable at transmission.
6. Remove nuts and lockwashers from the rubber mounted saddle support at the rear of the transmission. Use care not to lose the spacers.
7. Place a jack under the flywheel housing and raise the jack until the mounting bolts on the rubber insulator clear the crossmember.
8. Remove bolts attaching transmission to flywheel housing.
9. Pull transmission to the rear until it clears the crossmember and lower the transmission from the vehicle.

TRANSFER CASE

1970-71

Except J Series

In removing the transfer case, follow the procedure outlined under transmission removal.

J Series

The transfer case may be removed without removing the transmission. Proceed as follows:

1. Drain the transmission and transfer case oil. *It is not necessary to drain the automatic transmission.*
2. Disconnect parking brake spring from fuel tank flange and remove clevis pin from brake cable connecting bracket.
3. Remove the front propeller shaft.
4. Disconnect the rear propeller shaft at the transfer case. Slide the propeller shaft yoke back and move the shaft to one side.
5. Disconnect speedometer cable at transfer case.
6. Remove center cotter pin of shaft linkage at transfer case to disconnect shift linkage.
7. Remove wiring clips from light signal switches mounted on transfer case.
8. Remove exhaust pipe bracket bolts.
9. Remove bolts connecting transfer case to transmission and remove transfer case.

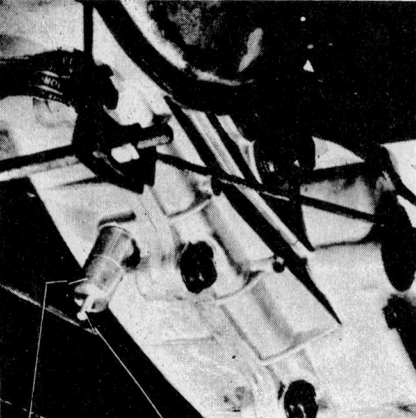

Chain Tension Gauge W-363   Protruding Plunger Indicates Good Chain

Fig. 3 Warner Quadra-Trac, drive chain tension check

1972-75

1. Remove shift lever knob, boot and shift lever.
2. Raise and support vehicle.
3. Drain transfer case lubricant.
4. Disconnect front and rear propeller shafts from output shaft yokes.
5. Disconnect parking brake cable from equalizer.
6. Disconnect speedometer cable from transfer case.
7. Remove transfer case to transmission attaching bolts. Install one 3/8 × 4 inch dowel pin on each side of case for use as guides during installation.
8. Remove transfer case from vehicle.
9. Remove transmission to transfer case gasket and discard.
10. Install a new transmission to transfer case gasket.
11. Reverse steps 1 through 8 to install.

1976-79

1. Remove shift lever knob, trim ring and boot from transmission.
2. Remove transfer case shift levers.
3. Remove floor covering, if equipped, then the transmission access cover from floorpan.
4. Raise and support vehicle.
5. Drain transfer case lubricant. On CJ models, drain transmission lubricant.
6. Disconnect torque reaction bracket from crossmember, if equipped.
7. On CJ models, place a jack stand under clutch housing to support engine and transmission, then remove rear crossmember.
8. On all models, disconnect front and rear propeller shafts from output shaft yokes.
9. Disconnect speedometer cable from transfer case.
10. On Cherokee and truck models, disconnect parking brake cable at equalizer and the exhaust pipe support bracket from transfer case.
11. On all models, remove transfer case to transmission attaching bolts.

NOTE: One attaching bolt is located at the front of the transfer case at the lower right corner of the transmission.

12. Remove transfer case from vehicle. Remove and discard transfer case to transmission gasket.
13. Install new transfer case to transmission gasket.
14. Reverse steps 1 through 12 to install.

1980

CJ Models

1. On models equipped with automatic transmission, remove shift lever knob, trim ring and boot from transfer case shift lever.
2. On models equipped with manual transmission, remove shift lever knob, trim ring and boot from transmission and transfer case shift levers.
3. On all models, remove floor covering, if equipped, then the transmission access cover from floorpan.
4. Raise and support vehicle. Drain lubricant from transfer case.
5. Place a jack stand under clutch housing to support engine and transmission, then remove rear crossmember.
6. Disconnect front and rear propeller shafts from output shaft yokes.

JEEP

7. Disconnect speedometer cable from transfer case.
8. Disconnect parking brake cable at equalizer, if necessary.
9. Disconnect exhaust pipe support bracket from transfer case, if equipped.
10. Remove transfer case to transmission attaching bolts.
11. Remove transfer case from vehicle.
12. Remove and discard transfer case to transmission gasket.
13. Install new transfer case to transmission gasket.
14. Reverse steps 1 through 11 to install.

Cherokee, Wagoneer & Truck Models
1. Raise and support vehicle.
2. Drain transfer case lubricant.
3. Disconnect front and rear propeller shafts from output shaft yokes.
4. Disconnect speedometer cable and indicator switch wires from transfer case.
5. Support transmission with a suitable jack and remove rear crossmember.
6. Disconnect parking brake cable guide from pivot, located at right frame rail, if necessary.
7. Remove bolts attaching exhaust pipe support bracket to transfer case, if necessary.
8. Remove transfer case to transmission attaching bolts.
9. Remove transfer case from vehicle.
10. Remove transfer case to transmission gasket and discard.
11. Install new transfer case to transmission gasket.
12. Reverse steps 1 through 9 to install.

WARNER QUADRA-TRAC
1973-78
Drive Chain Tension Check

Drain lubricant from transfer case and reinstall drain plug. Remove chain inspection plug and install chain tension gauge into hole. If chain tension is satisfactory, plunger will protrude past end of tool, Fig. 3. If plunger is flush or is recessed within tool, the drive chain has lost tension, requiring replacement.

Transfer Case, Removal
1. Disconnect front and rear propeller shafts from transfer case, mark universal joints for proper alignment during installation.
2. Remove exhaust system support bracket from transfer case.
3. Disconnect diaphragm control vacuum hoses, lock-out indicator switch wire and speedometer cable from transfer case.
4. Disconnect parking brake cable guide from frame right side pivot.
5. On CJ-7 models, place a support under clutch housing and remove rear crossmember.
6. Remove two transfer case to transmission bolts entering from front and the two bolts entering from rear and install guide pins in the upper holes.
7. Slide transfer case rearward until unit clears output shaft and guide pins, then remove assembly from vehicle.
8. Reverse procedure to install.

Reduction Unit, Removal
1. Raise vehicle on hoist.
2. Loosen bolts attaching reduction unit to transfer case and move unit rearward to drain oil from unit.
3. Loosen control lever cable retaining bolt and remove control cable from clamp bracket and control lever.
4. Remove reduction unit to transfer case bolts and move reduction unit rearward to clear transmission output shaft and remove unit from vehicle.
5. Reverse procedure to install.

TRANSFER CASE SHIFT LINKAGE, ADJUST

1. Disconnect adjustable link at transfer case.
2. On dual range transfer cases, move both transfer case shift rods out to the last detent position (maximum forward position). On single range cases, move the single shift rod to the first detent position (maximum rearward position). Make sure detents are fully seated.
3. Position transfer case shift lever knob in the forward position with 3/4" clearance between knob and floor pan.
4. With shift rods and lever knob positioned as above, adjust and install adjustable link.
5. Test operation in all positions. If necessary, readjust to eliminate any interference between shift lever knob and floor pan.

Rear Axle Section

NOTE: For unit overhaul procedure, refer to "Spicer Driving Axles" chapter.

AXLE SHAFT, REMOVE

1976-80 Semi-Floating-Tapered Shaft, Fig. 1

The hub and drum are separate units, and the hub and axle shaft are serrated to mate and fit together on the taper. Both are marked to insure correct assembly. The axle shaft and bearing assembly may be removed as follows:
1. Remove rear wheel, drum and hub, then disconnect parking brake cable at equalizer.

CAUTION: Do not use a slide hammer or knockout type puller to remove hub from axle shaft. Damage to the axle bearings or other components will result.

2. Disconnect brake tube from wheel cylinder and remove brake support plate assembly, oil seal and axle shims from axle shaft.

NOTE: Axle shaft end play shims are located on the left side only.

3. Using suitable puller, pull axle shaft and bearing from axle tube.

CAUTION: On models equipped with Twin Grip differential, do not rotate differential unless both axle shafts are in place.

1970-80 Semi-Floating - Flanged Shaft, Remove, Fig. 2

1. Raise and support vehicle and remove rear wheels.
2. Remove drum.
3. Remove axle retainer nuts using access hole in axle shaft flange.

NOTE: On 1970-77 models, remove access hole cup plug from flange to gain access to nuts.

4. Remove axle shaft from housing using suitable slide hammer. Remove bearing cup from housing.

1970-80 Full-Floating, Remove, Fig. 3

NOTE: It is not necessary to remove rear wheels to facilitate axle shaft replacement.

1. Remove axle flange nuts, lockwashers, and split washers retaining axle shaft flange.
2. Remove axle shaft from housing.

1970-71 Semi-Floating - Tapered Shaft, Remove, Fig. 4

1. Raise and support vehicle, remove hub cap and wheel.
2. Remove axle shaft cotter pin, nut and flat washer. Back off brake adjustment.
3. Remove wheel hub using suitable puller.

NOTE: Do not use a slide hammer or knockoff type puller. Damage to axle

JEEP

bearings or axle components will result.

4. Remove bearing retainer screws, brake dust protector, grease retainer, bearing retainer, brake assembly and shims from axle housing.
5. Disconnect brake line from brake assembly, then remove dust shield and bearing retainer.
6. Remove axle shaft and bearing assembly from housing using suitable slide hammer.

BEARING OR OIL SEAL, REPLACE

Semi-Floating - Tapered Shaft, Figs. 1 & 4

Remove and install axle shaft bearing using a suitable arbor press. Remove old oil seal from axle housing bore, clean bore and install new seal.

Semi-Floating - Flanged Shaft, Fig. 2

1. Remove oil seal from housing bore, clean bore and install new seal.
2. To remove bearing, drill 1/4 inch hole in retainer ring. Hole depth should be 3/4 of the ring thickness. Do not allow drill to contact axle shaft.
3. Use a large chisel to deeply nick the retaining ring. This will enlarge the ring, or split it, allowing it to be removed.

NOTE: Be certain not to damage axle shaft.

4. Cut through outer oil seal using a hacksaw, then remove seal from shaft.
5. Using suitable press, remove bearing from axle shaft. Remove retainer plate.
6. Reverse procedure to install. When installing new bearing, pack bearing with wheel bearing grease and install with cup rib ring facing axle flange.

Full-Floating Axle, Fig. 3

1. Remove axle shaft.
2. Bend lip of lockwasher and remove locknut and lockwasher.
3. Raise and support vehicle.
4. Remove adjusting nut, outer wheel bearing and pull the wheel straight off the axle.
5. Service wheel bearings as required.
6. Reverse procedure to install. Adjust wheel bearings as described in "Wheel Bearings, Adjust".

AXLE SHAFT, INSTALL

1976-80 Semi-Floating - Tapered Shaft, Fig. 1

Replace the parts in the reverse order of their removal. If the old parts are replaced and the shims have not been disturbed, the axle shaft end play should be correct when the parts are assembled. However, if a new shaft, bearing, differential carrier or housing has been installed, it will be necessary to check the end play.

The end play can be checked when all parts have been replaced except the wheel and hub.

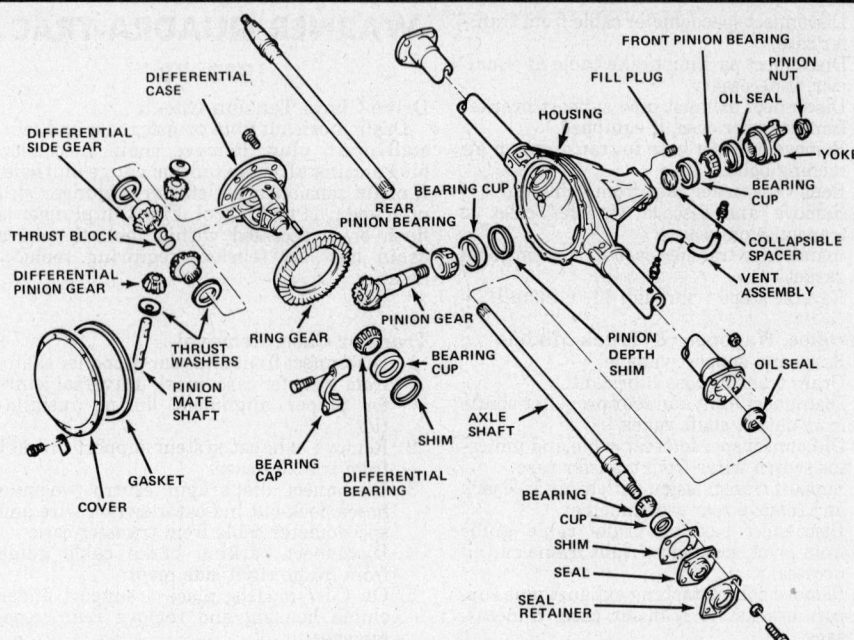

Fig. 1 Semi-Floating axle with tapered shaft. 1976-80

To make this check, rap each axle shaft after the nuts are tight to be sure the bearing cups are seated. Then place a dial indicator so that its stem contacts the end of the shaft and work the shaft in and out to determine the amount of existing end play. End play should be .004 to .008 inch. If an adjustment is necessary, remove the outer oil seal and brake support and add or remove shims as required. When making this adjustment, add or subtract shims on left side of axle only.

NOTE: *The application of a bead of sealing material such as "Pliobond" or "Permatex" to the outer diameter of axle tube flange and the brake support contact area is recommended. The sealing material will be used in addition to the gasket for improved sealing.*

When installing hub onto axle, install two well lubricated thrust washers and axle shaft nut. Tighten axle shaft nut until hub is installed to the dimensions shown in Fig. 5. Remove axle shaft nut and one thrust washer. Reinstall axle shaft nut and tighten to 250 ft. lbs. If cotter pin hole is not aligned, tighten the nut to the next castellation and install cotter pin.

NOTE: Do not use an original hub on a replacement axle shaft; use a new hub. A new hub may be installed on an original axle shaft providing the serrations on the shaft are not worn or damaged. Be certain that the hub and axle shaft are punch marked to insure proper alignment on installation. A replacement hub, which is not serrated, can be installed

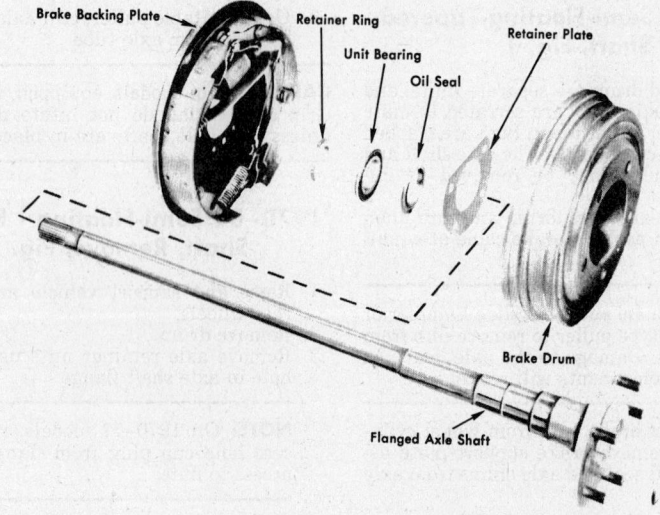

Fig. 2 Semi-Floating flanged axle shaft

JEEP

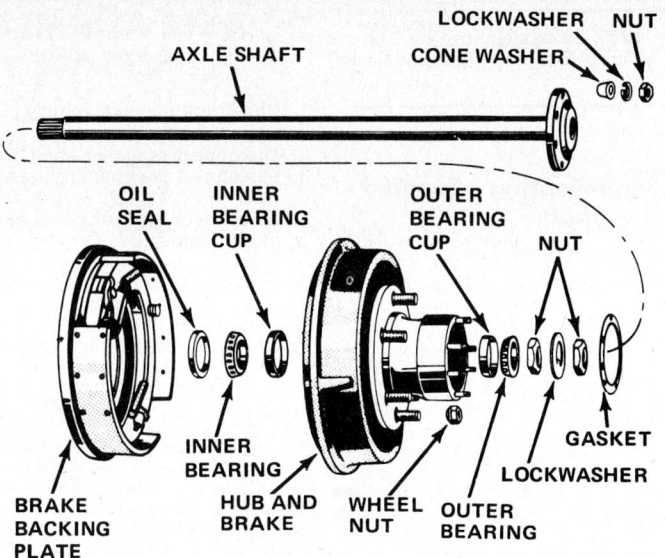

Fig. 3 Full-Floating axle with wheel bearing

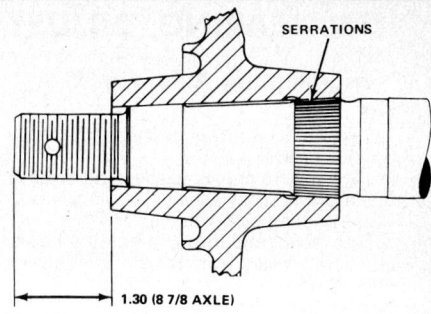

Fig. 5 Replacement hub installation measurement. 1976-80 with tapered shaft

1970-80 Full-Floating Axle Shaft, Fig. 3

1. Install new gasket on hub.
2. Install axle shaft and tighten nuts securely.

NOTE: It may be necessary to rotate wheel hub to align axle shaft splines with differential splines.

1970-71 Semi-Floating - Tapered Shaft, Fig. 4

Installation is the reverse of removal. Refer to "Wheel Bearing, Adjust" for wheel bearing adjustment procedure. Torque axle shaft nut to 150 ft. lbs.

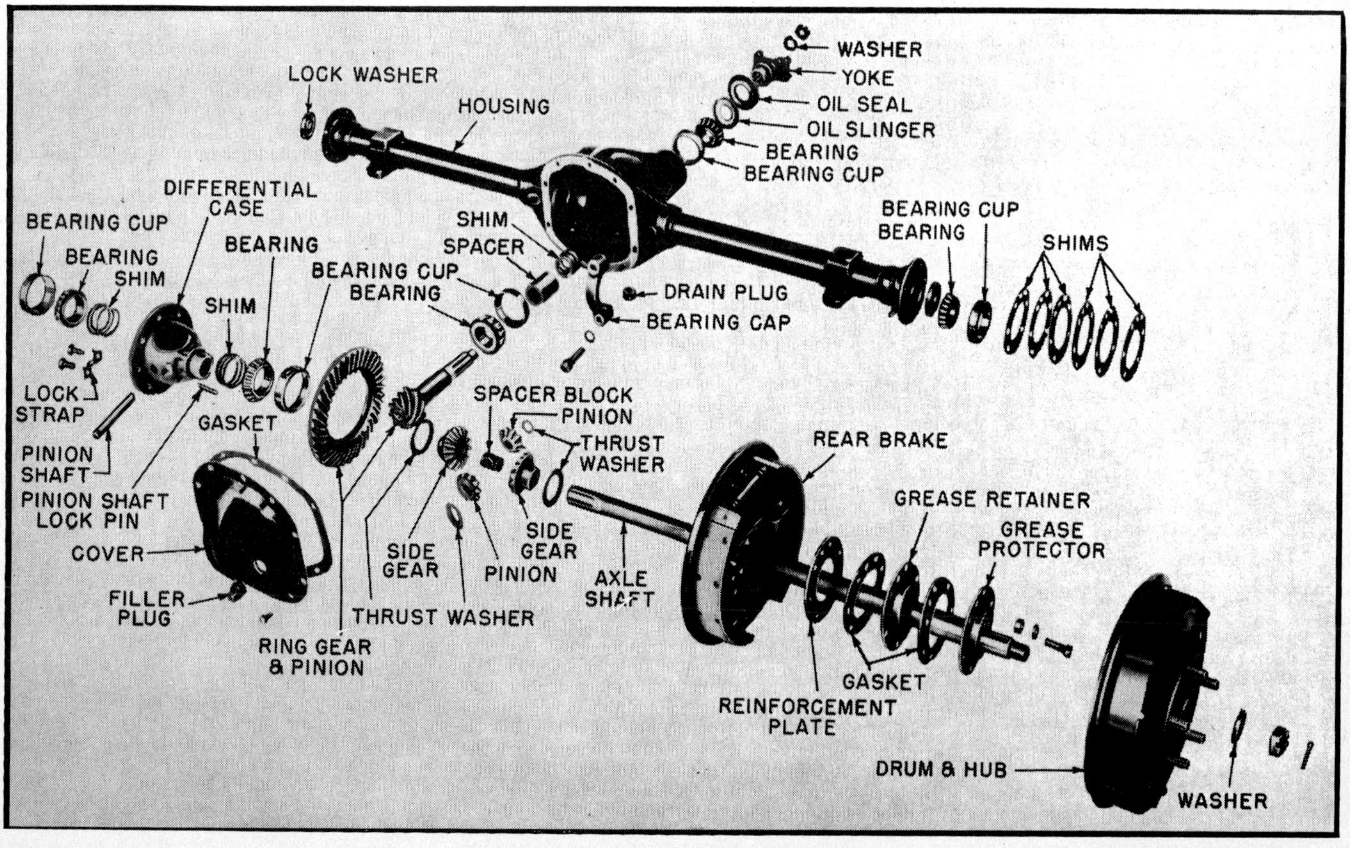

and serrations will be cut in the hub when installed on the shaft due to the difference in hardness of the shaft and the hub.

1970-80 Semi-Floating - Flanged Shaft, Fig. 2

1. Lubricate outer diameter of bearing cup and install axle shaft and bearing assembly into axle housing using care not to damage oil seal.
2. Install axle shaft retainer and backing plate to housing. Torque retainer nuts to 30 ft. lbs.
3. Install cup plug into axle flange hole if required.
4. Install brake drum and wheel. Lower vehicle.

Fig. 4 Semi-Floating axle with tapered shaft. 1970-71

JEEP

WHEEL BEARING, ADJUST

Full-Floating Axle, Fig. 3

1. Remove axle shaft as described in "Axle Shaft, Service".
2. Straighten lip of lockwasher and remove locknut and lockwasher.
3. Raise and support vehicle.
4. Rotate wheel and torque adjusting nut to 50 ft. lbs. to seat bearings. Back off nut 1/6 turn or until wheel rotates freely without lateral movement.
5. Install locknut and bend over lockwasher lip.

NOTE: On 1975–80 models, torque locknut to 50 ft. lbs. before bending lockwasher lip.

1970–71 Semi-Floating - Tapered Shaft

The bearing adjusting shims are located between the brake backing plate and axle flange, Fig. 4. Remove or install shims to provide an axle end play of .001 to .006 inch. Torque backing plate nuts to 30 ft. lbs.

AXLE ASSEMBLY, REPLACE

1. Raise and support vehicle. Remove rear wheels.
2. Disconnect propeller shaft from axle.
3. Disconnect parking brake cable to equalizer.
4. Disconnect hydraulic brake hose from tee at axle housing.
5. Disconnect shock absorbers from axle.
6. Support axle housing using a suitable jack, remove spring clips and lower axle to floor.
7. Reverse procedure to install.

Front Driving Axle Section

NOTE: For unit overhaul procedure, refer to "Spicer Driving Axles" chapter.

AXLE SHAFT, REPLACE

1977–80 CJ Models, Fig. 1

1. Raise and support vehicle, then remove wheel.
2. Remove brake caliper if equipped.
3. Remove hub cap and drive flange snap ring.
4. Remove rotor hub bolts, hub cover and gasket if equipped with disc brakes. On models with drum brakes, remove axle flange bolts.
5. Remove axle flange.
6. Straighten lip of lockwasher and remove outer nut, lockwasher, inner adjusting nut and bearing lockwasher.
7. Remove outer bearing and drum/rotor assembly.

NOTE: Do not damage oil seal.

8. Remove brake support plate or adapter and splash shield as equipped.
9. Remove spindle and spindle bearing, then slide out axle shaft assembly.
10. Reverse procedure to install. Torque inner adjusting nut to 50 ft. lbs. while rotating hub to seat bearings. Back off adjusting nut 1/3 turn on 1977–79 models and 1/6 turn on 1980 models. Install outer lockwasher and locknut. Torque locknut to 50 ft. lbs. and bend lip of washer over nut. On 1980 models, torque hub body bolts to 30 ft. lbs.

1974–80 Except CJ Models, Fig. 1

1. Raise and support vehicle.
2. Remove wheel and dust cover.
3. Remove axle shaft snap ring, drive gear and pressure spring. It may be necessary to pry drive gear from shaft with a suitable tool.
4. Remove wheel bearing locknut, lock ring, and wheel bearing adjusting nut.
5. Remove brake caliper and position aside if equipped.
6. Remove hub and drum or rotor assembly. Note that the spring retainer and outer bearing will slide out as the assembly is removed.
7. Remove nuts and bolt retaining spindle and disc brake shield, if equipped.
8. Remove spindle and disc brake shield, then slide axle shaft from housing.
9. Reverse procedure to install. Torque inner wheel bearing adjusting nut to 50 ft. lbs. while rotating wheel to seat bearings, then back nut off 1/4 turn on 1974–78 models, 1/3 turn on 1979 models and 1/6 turn on 1980 models. Install lockwasher with inner tab aligned with keyway in spindle. Turn inner adjusting locknut until the peg engages nearest hole in lockwasher. Install outer locknut and torque to 50 ft. lbs.

NOTE: Install spring retainer with cupped side facing toward center of vehicle.

1970–76 CJ & 1970–73 Except CJ Figs. 1 & 2

1. Remove drive flange hub cap and snap ring.
2. Remove axle flange bolts, lock washers and flat washers.
3. Have a helper apply the service brakes, then remove axle flange using suitable puller.
4. Release locking lip of lock washer and remove outer nut, lockwasher, adjusting nut and bearing lock washer.
5. Remove brake drum assembly with bearings. Use care not to damage oil seal.
6. Disconnect brake hose between front brake line and the flexible connection, then remove brake backing plate.
7. Remove spindle and spindle bushing.
8. Remove axle shaft and universal joint assembly.
9. Reverse procedure to install. Before installing drive flange, tighten bearing adjust-nut until a slight drag on the bearings is present as the hub is rotated. Then, back off nut approximately 1/6 turn and install lock washer and nut.

WHEEL BEARINGS, REPLACE & ADJUST

Refer to "Axle Shaft, Replace" for wheel bearing replacement and adjustment procedure.

STEERING KNUCKLE, REPLACE

Closed Knuckle Type, Fig. 2

1. Remove axle shaft as described in "Axle Shaft, Replace".
2. Remove oil seal retainer cap screws.
3. Remove the pivot pin cap screws, lock washers and pivot pins. Remove knuckle from yoke.
4. Reverse procedure to install. Check the pivot pin bearing preload as described in "Pivot Pin Bearing Preload, Adjust".

Open Knuckle Type, Removal, Fig. 1

1. Remove axle shaft as described in "Axle Shaft, Replace".
2. Disconnect tie rod from knuckle arm.
3. Remove lower ball stud jamnut and discard. Loosen upper ball stud nut until top of nut is flush with top of stud.
4. Unseat ball studs using suitable hammer. Remove upper ball stud nut and steering knuckle.
5. Remove upper ball stud split ring seat using suitable nut wrench.

Open Knuckle Type, Installation, Fig. 1

1. Install upper ball split ring seat until top of seat is flush with top of yoke.
2. Install steering knuckle on yoke then a new lower ball stud jamnut finger tight.
3. On 1972–74 models, position Nut Wrench W-355, Button SP-5583, Plate SP-5581 and Puller SP-5574, Fig. 3. On 1975–80

JEEP

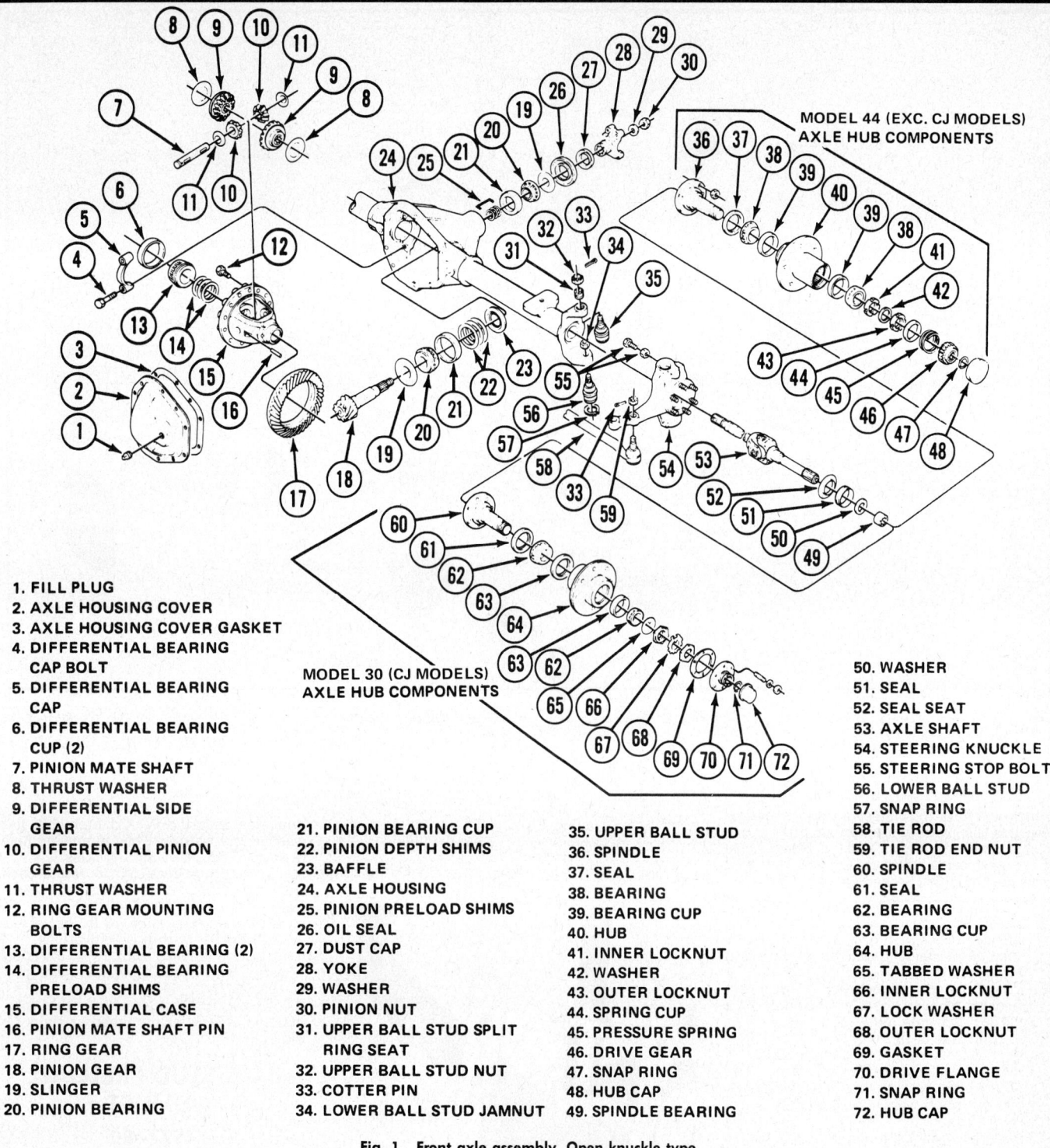

Fig. 1 Front axle assembly. Open knuckle type

1. FILL PLUG
2. AXLE HOUSING COVER
3. AXLE HOUSING COVER GASKET
4. DIFFERENTIAL BEARING CAP BOLT
5. DIFFERENTIAL BEARING CAP
6. DIFFERENTIAL BEARING CUP (2)
7. PINION MATE SHAFT
8. THRUST WASHER
9. DIFFERENTIAL SIDE GEAR
10. DIFFERENTIAL PINION GEAR
11. THRUST WASHER
12. RING GEAR MOUNTING BOLTS
13. DIFFERENTIAL BEARING (2)
14. DIFFERENTIAL BEARING PRELOAD SHIMS
15. DIFFERENTIAL CASE
16. PINION MATE SHAFT PIN
17. RING GEAR
18. PINION GEAR
19. SLINGER
20. PINION BEARING
21. PINION BEARING CUP
22. PINION DEPTH SHIMS
23. BAFFLE
24. AXLE HOUSING
25. PINION PRELOAD SHIMS
26. OIL SEAL
27. DUST CAP
28. YOKE
29. WASHER
30. PINION NUT
31. UPPER BALL STUD SPLIT RING SEAT
32. UPPER BALL STUD NUT
33. COTTER PIN
34. LOWER BALL STUD JAMNUT
35. UPPER BALL STUD
36. SPINDLE
37. SEAL
38. BEARING
39. BEARING CUP
40. HUB
41. INNER LOCKNUT
42. WASHER
43. OUTER LOCKNUT
44. SPRING CUP
45. PRESSURE SPRING
46. DRIVE GEAR
47. SNAP RING
48. HUB CAP
49. SPINDLE BEARING
50. WASHER
51. SEAL
52. SEAL SEAT
53. AXLE SHAFT
54. STEERING KNUCKLE
55. STEERING STOP BOLT
56. LOWER BALL STUD
57. SNAP RING
58. TIE ROD
59. TIE ROD END NUT
60. SPINDLE
61. SEAL
62. BEARING
63. BEARING CUP
64. HUB
65. TABBED WASHER
66. INNER LOCKNUT
67. LOCK WASHER
68. OUTER LOCKNUT
69. GASKET
70. DRIVE FLANGE
71. SNAP RING
72. HUB CAP

models, position Nut Wrench J-25158, Button J-25211-3, Plate J-25211-1 and Puller J-25215, Fig. 3.
4. Tighten puller screw until lower ball stud is held firmly seated. Torque jamnut to 85 ft. lbs. on CJ models, and 75 ft. lbs. on all other models. Remove puller and plate.
5. Torque upper ball stud split ring seat to 50 ft. lbs.
6. Install upper ball stud nut and torque to 100 ft. lbs. Install cotter pin.
7. Install tie rod to steering knuckle. Torque tie rod end nuts to 50 ft. lbs.
8. Install axle shaft as described in "Axle Shaft, Replace".

BALL STUDS, REPLACE

1. Remove steering knuckle as described in "Steering Knuckle, Replace".
2. Remove lower ball stud snap ring.
3. Using suitable tools, press lower and upper ball studs from steering knuckle.
4. Reverse procedure to install. Install a new replacement snap ring on the lower ball stud.

BALL STUD PRELOAD MEASUREMENT

1977–80

NOTE: Ball stud preload is measured when

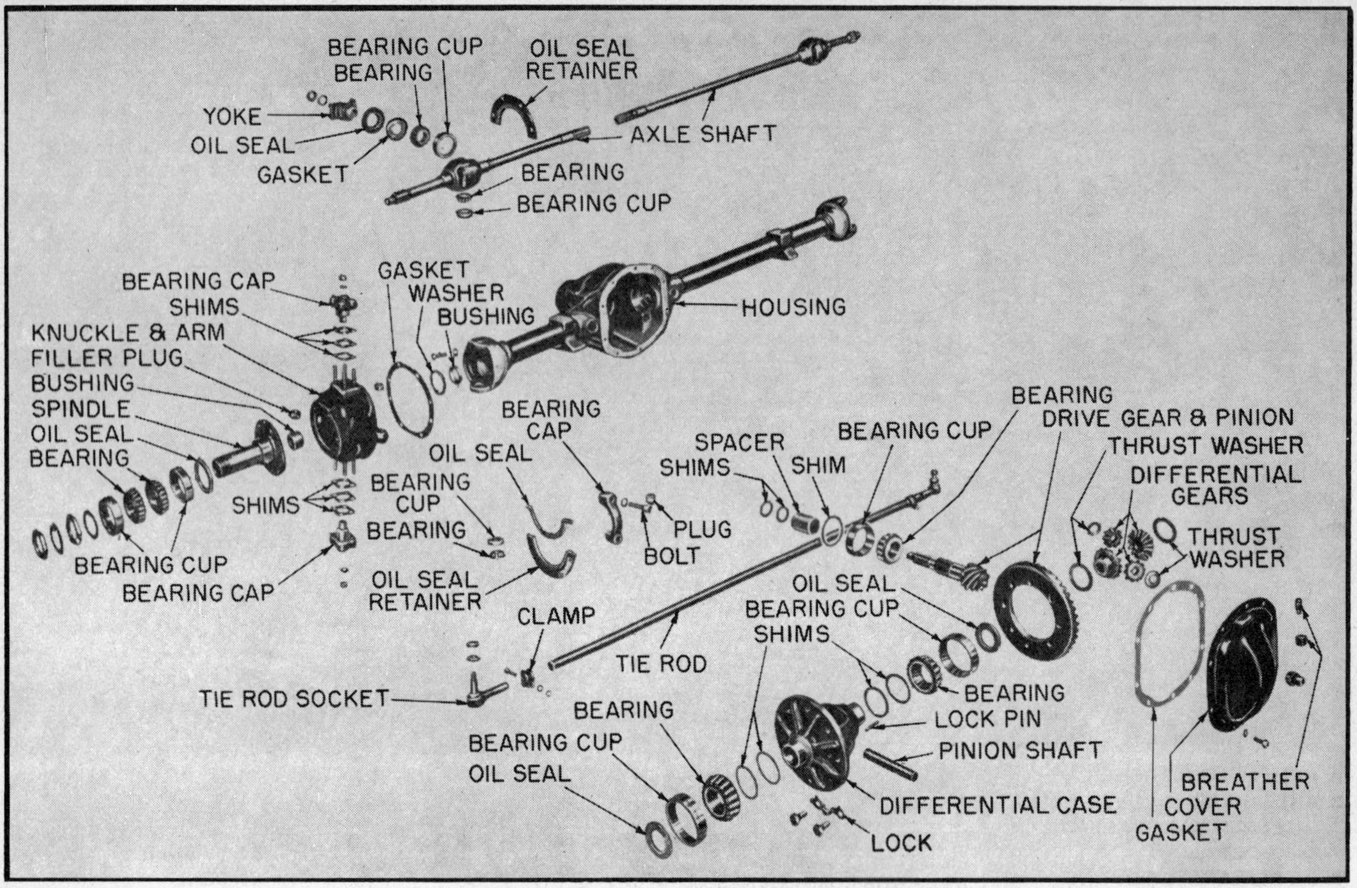

JEEP

Fig. 2 Front axle assembly. Closed knuckle type

vehicle exhibits high steering effort or slow return of the steering mechanism after turns. If this condition occurs and all other items affecting steering effort are normal, ball stud preload should be checked.

1. Raise and support vehicle. Remove front wheels.
2. Disconnect steering damper at tie rod if equipped.
3. Unlock steering column. Disconnect steering connecting rod at right-side of tie rod on CJ models; and on all other models, at right side of tie rod.
4. Remove cotter pin and nut attaching tie rod to right side steering knuckle.
5. Rotate both steering knuckles completely several times, working from right side of vehicle.
6. Assemble a socket and 0-50 ft. lb. torque wrench onto right tie rod attaching nut.

NOTE: Torque wrench must be positioned parallel with the steering knuckle arm.

7. Rotate steering knuckles slowly and steadily through a complete arc and measure torque required to rotate knuckles.
   a. If reading is less than 25 ft. lbs., turning effort at knuckles is normal. Check other steering components for defects or binding.
   b. If reading is greater than 25 ft. lbs., proceed to step 8.
8. Disconnect tie rod from both steering knuckles. Install a 1/2 × 1 inch bolt, flat washer and nut in tie rod mounting hole in each of the steering knuckles.
9. Measure torque required to rotate each steering knuckle as described previously.
   a. If torque is less than 10 ft. lbs., steering effort is within specifications.
   b. If torque is more than 10 ft. lbs., perform "Ball Stud Preload, Adjust" procedure.
10. If both steering knuckles are within specification, check for damaged or tight tie rod ends.

BALL STUD PRELOAD, ADJUST
1977-80

1. Remove front axle shafts as described in "Axle Shaft, Replace".
2. Loosen lower ball stud jamnut, then remove upper ball stud nut.
3. Unseat ball studs from yoke using suitable hammer.
4. Remove upper ball stud split ring seat and discard.
5. Remove lower ball stud jamnut and steering knuckle. Discard jamnut.
6. Clean upper ball stud split ring seat threads, lower ball stud taper in steering knuckle, threads and tapered surfaces of ball studs, and upper ball stud retaining nut threads.

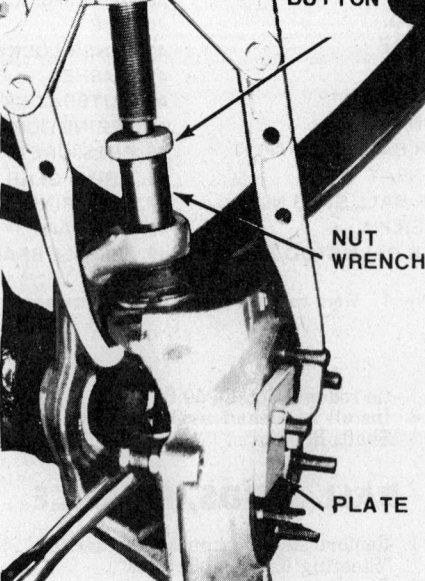

Fig. 3 Steering knuckle installation tools

7. Position steering knuckle on axle and install a new lower ball stud jamnut finger tight.
8. Install upper ball stud nut and torque 10-20 ft. lbs. to draw lower ball stud into yoke.

NOTE: Do not install upper ball stud split ring seat at this time.

9. Torque lower ball stud jamnut to 80 ft. lbs.
10. Remove upper ball stud nut and install a new split ring seat. Torque split ring seat to 50 ft. lbs. Install upper ball stud nut and torque to 100 ft. lbs. Align and install cotter pin.

NOTE: Do not loosen nut to align cotter pin holes. Tighten only enough to align the holes and install cotter pin.

11. Install front axle shafts and steering spindles loosely and measure turning effort of each steering knuckle as described in "Ball Stud Preload, Measurement".
    a. If turning effort is less than 10 ft. lbs., proceed to next step.
    b. If turning effort is more than 10 ft. lbs., replace upper and lower ball studs as described in "Ball Stuuds, Re-place".
12. Install front axle shafts and connect tie rod to steering knuckle arms. Torque tie rod end retaining nuts to 45 ft. lbs.
13. Attach connecting rod to tie rod. Torque connecting rod nut to 60 ft. lbs. on CJ models; and 75 ft. lbs. on all other models. Install steering damper if equipped.
14. Install front wheels and lower vehicle.

PIVOT PIN BEARING PRELOAD, ADJUST

NOTE: The pivot pin bearing preload is checked before installing the oil seal.

1. Check the preload in the bearing by hooking a spring scale in the tie rod socket hole in the steering arm with the steering knuckle in the straight ahead position.
2. Make note of the scale reading when the knuckle had just started its sweep. The reading should be 12-16 lb.
3. Shims are available in the following thicknesses: .003, .005, .010, and .030 inch. Add or remove shims from under top bearing cap to obtain this reading, Fig. 2.

JEEP

FRONT AXLE ASSEMBLY, REPLACE

1. Raise and support vehicle. Support at frame behind front springs.
2. Remove front wheels.
3. Disconnect front propeller shaft at axle.
4. Disconnect steering linkage from steering knuckles.
5. Disconnect shock absorbers from axle. Disconnect sway bar link bolts if equipped.
6. Disconnect brake hoses. Disconnect breather tube from axle if equipped.
7. Remove brake drums and support plates or brake calipers, hub, rotors and brake shields.
8. Support axle assembly with suitable jack.
9. On vehicles with springs mounted under the axle, remove nuts from spring clips. Remove spring clips, then disconnect springs from shackles by removing lower spring shackle bolts. Lower springs and slide axle assembly from under vehicle.
10. On vehicles with springs mounted on top of axle, remove nuts from spring to axle U-bolt clips. Remove spring clip plates and slide axle assembly from under vehicle.
11. Reverse procedure to install.

Front End and Steering Section

CAMBER & CASTER

Solid Axle Models

Camber is set into the axle assembly at time of manufacture and cannot be adjusted.

Caster may be adjusted by installing new front end components or caster shims between the axle pad and the springs.

Independent Suspension, J-Series

Camber is controlled by the attachment of the upper control arms to the ball joints through slotted holes in the control arms. To adjust camber, loosen the control arm to ball joint bolts and adjust to specification.

Caster is controlled by a strut bar which runs between the end of the axle and the frame side member. Adjustment is made by loosening the locknuts at each end of the strut tube, and rotating the tube until the specified setting is obtained.

TOE-IN, ADJUST

Position the wheels to a true straight ahead position with the steering gear also in a straight ahead driving position. Then turn both tie rod adjusting sleeves an equal amount until the desired toe-in setting is obtained.

MANUAL STEERING GEAR, REPLACE

J-Series, Cherokee, Commando, Truck & 1972-76 CJ, DJ

1. Disconnect steering gear from column by removing the flexible coupling nuts or flex coupling pinch bolt.
2. Disconnect the connecting rod from the steering arm.
3. Remove the bolts attaching the gear to the frame and remove the gear by sliding it slightly forward and to the right and lifting it out of the engine compartment.

1977-80 Models

1. Remove intermediate shaft to worm-shaft coupling clamp bolt and disconnect intermediate shaft.
2. Remove pitman arm nut and lockwasher, then separate pitman arm from steering gear shaft using a puller.
3. On all except CJ models, remove steering gear to frame bolts and remove steering gear.
4. On CJ models:
   a. Slightly raise left side of vehicle to relieve tension on left front spring, then place support stand under frame.
   b. Remove steering gear lower bracket to frame bolts.
   c. Remove steering gear upper bracket to crossmember bolts and remove gear.
   d. Remove bolts attaching upper bracket to tie plate and lower bracket to steering gear and remove brackets.
5. Reverse procedure to install. Apply Locktite 271 or equivalent to the steering gear to frame bolts, the bracket to gear bolts and the bracket to tie plate bolt. Torque steering gear to frame bolts and bracket to gear bolts to 70 ft. lbs., the bracket to tie plate bolt to 55 ft. lbs. and the coupling pinch bolt and nut to 45 ft. lbs.

NOTE: If there is a slightly rough feel after the steering gear is installed, turn the steering wheel completely to the left and then to the right for 10 to 15 complete cycles.

1970-71 CJ & DJ

4 Cylinder Engines

1. Remove turn signal unit from steering column, then remove steering column bracket to instrument panel retaining nuts.
2. Remove upper section of floor pan, then if used, disconnect shift rods from shift levers at lower end of steering column.
3. Disconnect horn wire at lower end of steering gear assembly.
4. Disconnect steering gear arm from steering gear, then remove the steering gear attaching bolts and remove the steering gear by lifting it up through the floor opening.

V6 Engines

1. Remove oil pan skid plate and disconnect the left exhaust pipe.
2. Disconnect drag link from steering gear and remove steering gear to frame attaching bolts.
3. Remove steering wheel and disconnect accelerator linkage, then remove upper floor pan assembly and disconnect turn signal switch.
4. Raise vehicle and remove steering gear and column assembly through the floor pan opening.

Forward Control Models

1. Remove steering wheel and turn signal unit from steering column.

JEEP

2. Remove floor panels at base of steering column and disconnect cable from clutch pedal.
3. Remove lower left panel from instrument panel and remove steering column clamp U-bolt.
4. Loosen radiator screen and swing it down for access to steering gear, and disconnect connecting rod from steering gear arm.
5. Remove steering gear retaining bolts and disconnect horn wire.
6. Remove steering gear arm from steering gear.
7. Remove steering gear by sliding gear housing shaft through frame opening and pulling assembly up and out of cab.

POWER STEERING GEAR, REPLACE
Exc. 1977-80

1. Disconnect pressure and return hoses from gear and plug hoses and gear ports to prevent contamination of system.
2. Disconnect steering gear from column by removing the flexible coupling nuts or flex coupling pinch bolt.
3. Remove pitman arm and the steering gear to frame bolts and remove gear from vehicle.
4. Reverse procedure to install.

1977-80 Models

1. Disconnect lines from gear. Plug lines to prevent entry of dirt and keep lines raised to avoid excessive fluid loss.
2. On all except CJ models, remove clamp bolt and nut attaching flex coupling to steering gear shaft and disconnect intermediate shaft.
3. On CJ models, remove clamp bolt and nut attaching intermediate shaft coupling to steering gear shaft and disconnect intermediate shaft.
4. Paint alignment marks on pitman shaft and pitman arm for assembly reference, then remove and discard the pitman arm nut and lockwasher. Use new nut and lockwasher.
5. Remove pitman using a puller.
6. On all except CJ models, remove steering gear to frame mounting bolts and remove steering gear.
7. On CJ models:
   a. Raise left side of vehicle to relieve tension on left front spring and place support stand under frame.
   b. Remove the three lower steering gear mounting brackets to frame bolts.
   c. Remove the two upper steering gear mounting brackets to crossmember bolts and remove steering gear and mounting brackets.
   d. Remove mounting bracket to gear attaching bolts and remove upper and lower mounting brackets from steering gear.
8. Reverse procedure to install. Apply Locktite 271 or equivalent to mounting bracket to steering gear bolts and to steering gear to frame bolts. Torque steering gear to frame bolts to 70 ft. lbs. on all except CJ models, and 55 ft. lbs. on CJ models, the mounting bracket to steering gear bolts to 70 ft. lbs., the flex coupling clamp bolt to 30 ft. lbs., the intermediate shaft coupling to steering gear bolt to 45 ft. lbs. and the pitman arm nut to 185 ft. lbs.

KENWORTH

INDEX OF SERVICE OPERATIONS

AXLES, DRIVING

	Page No.
Eaton Axle Service	204
Timken Axle Service	241
Locking Differentials	192
Front Wheel Locking Hubs	505

BRAKES

	Page No.
Adjustments	590
Air Brake Service	620
Brake Booster Service	639
Hydraulic System Service	632
Parking Brake Service	612
Stopmaster Brake Service	599

CLUTCHES

	Page No.
Air-Hydraulic Control	468
Clutch Linkage	...
Clutch Service	429

COOLING SYSTEM

	Page No.
Cooling System Capacity	1299
Variable Speed Fans	10

ELECTRICAL

	Page No.
Alternator Service	52
Dash Gauge Service	179
Distributor Service	141
Electronic Ignition	152
Generator Service	11
Ignition Coils and Resistors	7
Starting Motor Service	29
Starter Switch Service	21
Tune Up Service	2

FUEL & EXHAUST

	Page No.
Crankcase Ventilation	748
Emission Controls	750
Fuel Pump Service	183
L.P.G. Carburetion	190
Turbochargers	187

SPECIFICATIONS

	Page No.
Cooling System Capacity	1299
Crankcase Capacity	1299
Generator and Regulator	1299
Starting Motor	1299
Wheel Alignment	1300

STEERING GEARS

	Page No.
Manual Steering	680
Power Steering	686

TRANSFER CASES

	Page No.
	469

TRANSMISSIONS

	Page No.
Allison 6 Speed	518
Clark	275
Fuller	289
New Process	329
Spicer	346
Warner	406

KENWORTH

MODEL INDEX & ENGINE APPLICATION

ENGINE IDENTIFICATION—Kenworth identification nameplate can be found on the cab door. Stamped on the plate is the model of the engine, transmission, auxiliary transmission, rear axle and front axle. This data represents only the equipment on the vehicle when it was shipped from the factory.

Model	Engine Make	Basic Engine Model	Crankcase Refill Capacity, Qts.	Cooling System Capacity, Qts.	Model	Engine Make	Basic Engine Model	Crankcase Refill Capacity, Qts.	Cooling System Capacity, Qts.
C823S-2	①	①	②	③	W922S-12	①	①	②	③
C823S-12	①	①	②	③	W923	①	①	②	③
C824S-2	①	①	②	③	W923S-2	①	①	②	③
C824S-12	①	①	②	③	W923S-12	①	①	②	③
C825S-2	①	①	②	③	W924	①	①	②	③
C825S-12	①	①	②	③	W924S-2	①	①	②	③
K121	①	①	②	③	W924S-12	①	①	②	③
K122	①	①	②	③	W925	①	①	②	③
K123	①	①	②	③	W925S-2	①	①	②	③
K124	①	①	②	③	W925S-12	①	①	②	③
K125	①	①	②	③					
W921	①	①	②	③					
W921S-2	①	①	②	③					
W921S-12	①	①	②	③					
W922	①	①	②	③					
W922S-2	①	①	②	③					

①—Various Diesel engines are available. Consult nameplate to identify engine.
②—Capacity varies depending on engine installed.
③—Capacity varies depending on engine and radiator installed.

STARTING MOTOR SPECIFICATIONS

Unit Part No.	Rotation ①	Brush Spring Tension Oz.	No Load Test			Torque Test		
			Amperes	Volts	R.P.M.	Amperes	Volts	Torque Lb. Ft.
1113818	C	80	60–90	23	7000–10700	500	3.5	26
1113845	C	80	60–90	23	7000–10700	500	3.5	26
1113887	C	80	60–90	23	7000–10700	500	3.5	26

①—As viewed from drive end. C—Clockwise. CC—Counterclockwise.

GENERATOR & REGULATOR SPECIFICATIONS

★ To polarize generator, reconnect leads to regulator; then momentarily connect a jumper wire from the "Gen" to the "Bat" terminals of the regulator.

Generator						Regulator						
Gen. No.	Rotation	Brush Spring Tension, Oz.	Rated Cap. Amps.	Gen. Field Ground Location★	Field Current	Reg. No.	Cutout Relay		Voltage Setting	Current Setting	Current & Voltage Reg. Arm. Air Gap, In.
							Closing Voltage	Arm. Air Gap, In.			
1117090	①	10	85	Either	6.0–6.6	9000590	—	—	14	—	
1117094	①	10	85	Either	6.0–6.6	9000590	—	—	14	—	

①—Rotation may be in either direction.

KENWORTH

WHEEL ALIGNMENT SPECIFICATIONS

Front Axle Model	Caster, Deg.	Camber, Deg.	Toe-In, Inch	Kingpin Inclination, Deg.	Front Axle Model	Caster, Deg.	Camber, Deg.	Toe-In, Inch	Kingpin Inclination, Deg.
1-F-1①	0	1	1/4	0	F-7900④	1 1/2	1	1/8–1/4	8
2-F-1①	2–2 1/2	1	1/8	0	FE-900⑤	2–3	1	1/16	5 1/2
2-F-2①	1 1/2	0	1/16	0	FE-970⑤	1 1/2–1 3/4	1	1/16	0
3-F-1①	1 1/2	1	1/8–1/4	8	FF-901⑤	2–3	1	1/16	5 1/2
4-F-1①	1 1/2	1	1/8–1/4	8	FF-921⑤	2–3	1	1/16	5 1/2
DCA53-4③	2–2 1/2	1	1/8	0	FG-900⑤	1 1/2	1	1/16	8
DCA53-5③	2–2 1/2	1	1/8	0	FH-901⑤	3–4	1	1/16	5 1/2
FDS-20000②	0	3/4	1/16–1/8	0	FL-901⑤	3–4	1	1/16	5 1/2
FDS-22500②	1 1/2	3/4	1/16–1/8	8	FU-900⑤	1 1/2	0	1/16	0
FE-15③	2–2 1/2	1	1/8	0	27462⑤	1 1/2	1	1/16	8
FE-18③	2–2 1/2	1	1/8	0					
F-223④	5	0	1/8–1/4	0					
F-429④	3	0	1/8–1/4	0					
F-3200④	6 1/2	0	3/16–5/16	0					

①—Kenworth axle.
②—Clark axle.
③—Shuler axle.
④—Wisconsin (Rockwell) axle.
⑤—Timken (Rockwell) axle.

Clutch Linkage

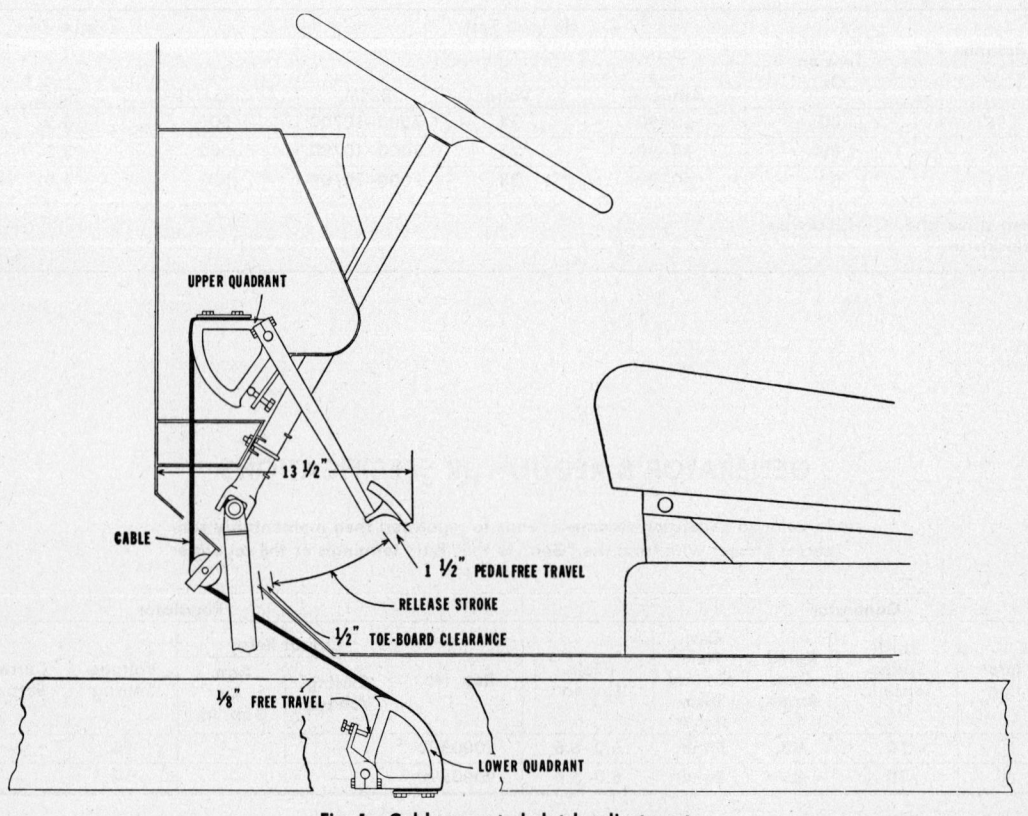

Fig. 1 Cable operated clutch adjustments

External Linkage Adjustment

1. Check the clutch pedal to be sure it is fully engaged (pedal up).
2. With the clutch in the engaged position, free travel clearance at the lever arm must not be more than 1/8" or less than 1/16".

NOTE: Use a 1/8" drill rod to establish proper clearance at adjusting setscrew, as the contact surface is not flat.

3. After setting the adjusting setscrew, check the clutch pedal to make sure there is sufficient free travel, Fig. 1.

Cable, Adjust

1. Loosen the locknut and turn adjusting setscrew so about 1/2" of setscrew protrudes on quadrant side.
2. Loosen two capscrews at either end of the cable.
3. Shorten or lengthen cable as necessary, being careful to lace cable in "figure eight" fasion, Fig. 2, at its connecting point on the quadrant.
4. Tighten capscrews.
5. Adjust setscrews so clearance is 1/8" as outlined in preceding External Linkage Adjustment.

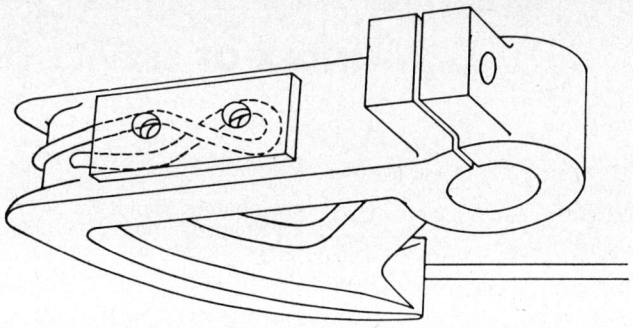

Fig. 2 Cable properly laced to quadrant

Cable, Replace

1. Remove old cable.

NOTE: When removing old cable from lower quadrant, note the number of turns that spring is wound on the quadrant (about 1½ turns).

2. Turn adjusting setscrew so about 1/2" of it is protruding on lower quadrant side.
3. Install cable on upper quadrant being sure to lace it properly as shown in Fig. 2 and tighten capscrews.
4. Thread cable past pulley and through guide.
5. Turn lower quadrant until it is in original position and fasten cable being sure to lace it properly.
6. Take up all slack in cable and tighten capscrews.
7. Adjust clutch as outlined previously.

MACK

INDEX OF SERVICE OPERATIONS

AXLES, DRIVING
	Page No.
Own Make Axle Service	1329
Eaton Axle Service	204
Timken Axle Service	241
Locking Differentials	192
Front Wheel Locking Hubs	505

BRAKES
Adjustments	590
Air Brake Service	620
Anti-Skid Brakes	551
Brake Booster Service	639
Hydraulic System Service	632
Parking Brake Service	612
Stopmaster Brake Service	599

CLUTCHES
Air-Hydraulic (Air-Pak)	468
Clutch Pedal, Adjust	1314
Clutch Service	429
Unishift Adjustment	1314

COOLING SYSTEM
Cooling System Capacity	1302
Variable Speed Fans	10
Water Pumps	1309

ELECTRICAL
Alternator Service	52
Dash Gauge Service	179
Distributors, Standard	141
Electronic Ignition	152
Generator Service	11
Ignition Coils and Resistors	7
Ignition Timing	1309
Starting Motor Service	29
Starter Switch Service	21
Tune Up Service	2

ENGINE
Camshaft and Bearings	1309
Crankshaft End Play, Adjust	1309
Crankshaft Rear Oil Seal	1309
Cylinder Head, Replace	1309
Piston Pins, Replace	1309
Piston and Rod, Assemble	1309
Timing Gears	1309
Valve Lifters	1309

ENGINE OILING
Crankcase Capacity	1302
Oil Pump Repairs	1309

FRONT SUSPENSION
Front Wheel Locking Hubs	505

FUEL & EXHAUST
Carburetor Adjustments	1310
Crankcase Ventilation	748
Emission Controls	750
Fuel Pump Service	183
L.P.G. Carburetion	190
Turbochargers	187

SPECIFICATIONS
Cooling System Capacity	1302
Crankcase Capacity	1302
Crankshaft and Bearings	1307
Distributor	1306
General Engine Data	1305
Generator and Regulator	1306
Piston, Pin and Ring	1307
Starting Motor	1307
Tune Up	1306
Valve	1306
Wheel Alignment	1308

STEERING
Manual Steering Gear Service	680
Power Steering Gear Service	686

TRANSFER CASES
	469

TRANSMISSIONS, Automatic
Allison AT-540, 543	510
Allison MT-640, 643, 644, 650, 653, 654 CR	512
Allison HT-740, 750	514
Allison 6 Speed	518

TRANSMISSIONS, Manual
Own Make	1316
Clark	275
Fuller	289
New Process	329
Spicer	346
Warner	406

MODEL INDEX & ENGINE APPLICATION

Truck Model	Engine Model ①	Crankcase Refill Capacity Qts.	Cooling System Capacity Qts.
DM & DMM MODELS			
DM401	END475	15	32
DM403	END465C	15	42
DM410	EN414A	8	32
DM487	ENDT475	16	37
DM487, S	ETZ477	—	—
DM492, S	3208 ⑫	—	—
DM606	ET673	—	—
DM606S	ETZ673E	—	—
DM607	END673	15	44
DM607	END673E	—	49
DM609	END707	19	49
DM611	ENDT673	15	52
DM611S, SX	ETZ673C	—	—
DM611S	ET673	—	—
DM612, S, SX	ETAZ673A	—	—
DM615	END684	⑧	56
DM640	END540A	13	58
DM685	ENDT675	19	57
DM685S, SX, S	ETZ675	—	—
DM686, S, X	ENDT676	—	58
DM807	END673	15	62
DM809	END707	19	62
DM811	ENDT673	—	62
DM811	ET673	—	—
DM811SX	ETZ673C	—	—
DM812, SX	ETAZ673A	—	—
DM815	END864	⑧	62
DM819	ENDT864	⑧	64
DM821ST, SX	ETAZ1000	—	—
DM831	NH220 ②	—	60
DM833	Super 250 ②	—	—
DM837	NHC250 ②	—	60
DM845	NTC335 ②	—	64
DM861	V903 ②	—	—
DM863	NTC335 ②	—	64
DM866ST	NTA400 ②	—	—
DM867, SX	NTC350 ②	—	—
DM885	ENDT675	19	64
DM885SX	ETZ676	—	—
DM886, SX	ENDT676	—	64
DM895	ENDT865	—	66
DM897	ENDT866	—	66
DM6076, S	END673	15	52
DML821SX	ETAZ1000	—	—
DML886SX	ENDT676	—	—
DMM612, S	ETAZ673A	—	—
DMM685	ENDT675	—	—

Continued

MACK

MODEL ENGINE & ENGINE APPLICATION—Continued

Truck Model	Engine Model ①	Crankcase Refill Capacity Qts.	Cooling System Capacity Qts.	Truck Model	Engine Model ①	Crankcase Refill Capacity Qts.	Cooling System Capacity Qts.	Truck Model	Engine Model ①	Crankcase Refill Capacity Qts.	Cooling System Capacity Qts.
DMM685S	ETZ675	—	—	F895	ENDT865	—	70	MB401	END475	15	38
DMM686, S	ENDT676	—	—	F985	ENDT675	—	62	MB402	EN402	8	36
DMM4876	ENDT475	—	37	F995	ENDT865	—	70	MB403	END465	15	42
DMM6076	END673E	—	44	**FL & FS MODELS**				MB410	EN414A	8	32
DMM6096	END707	—	—	FL707	END673	15	48	MB478	ENDT475	16	37
DMM6116	ENDT673	—	52	FL709	END707	19	53	MB483	6-53N③	—	—
DMM6856	ENDT675	—	58	FL711	ENDT673	15	55	MB487	ENDT475	15	42
MM6856S, SX	ETZ675	—	—	FL711L, LS	ENDLT673C	—	—	MB487P, S, T	ET477	—	—
DMM6866, SX	ENDT676	—	58	FL715	END864	⑧	59	MB47P, S	ETZ477	—	—
				FL719	ENDT864	⑧	59	MB491	V8-210②	—	—
F MODELS				FL731	NH220②	—	48	MB492	3208⑫	—	—
F607	END673	15	44	FL733	Super 250②	—	—	MB605	END673	15	44
F609	END707	19	⑦	FL737	NHC250②	—	48	MB606	ET673E	—	—
F609	END711	19	⑨	FL739	NHCT270②	—	48	MB607S	END673E	—	—
F611	ENDT673	15	④	FL747	NTC290L②	—	—	MB607	END673	15	49
F685	ENDT675	19	55	FL753	1674⑫	—	—	MB609	END707	—	49
F707	END673P	15	44	FL755	1693T⑫	—	—	MB611	ENDT673	—	52
F707	END673E	—	54	FL759	VT903L②	—	—	MB611S	ET673	—	—
F709	END711	19	⑦	FL759LS	ENDT865	—	—	MB685	ENDT675	—	56
F711	ENDT673	15	54	FL761	V903L②	—	—	MC487	ET477	—	—
F711T, ST	ETE673	—	—	FL763	NTC335②	—	54	MC487P, S	ETZ477B	—	—
F712T, ST	ETAZ673A	—	—	FL765	NTA370L②	—	—	MC492, S	3208⑫	—	—
F715	END864	⑧	55	FL767	NTC350L②	—	—	MC606	ET673	—	—
F719	ENDT864	⑧	60	FL769	8V71T③	—	—	MC606P, S	ETZ673E	—	—
F721ST, T	ETAZ1000	—	—	FL773	8V71③	—	66	MC685	ENDT675	—	—
F723	ENDT864A	⑧	60	FL781	6-71N③	—	—	MC685P, S	ETZ675	—	—
F726, ST	6V92TT③	—	—	FL785	ENDT675	19	55	MC686, S, P	ENDT676	—	—
F731	NH220②	—	—	FL786	ENDT676	—	55	MR487	ET477	—	—
F733	Super 250②	—	—	FL795	ENDT865	—	71	MR487P, S	ETZ477B	—	—
F737	NH250②	—	⑤	FL797	ENDT866	—	72	MR492, S	3208⑫	—	—
F741	NTO-6-B②	—	58	FL797LS	ENDT866	—	—	MR606	ET673	—	—
F743	V8-265②	—	48	FS711	ENDLT673C	—	55	MR606P, S	ETZ673E	—	—
F745	NT280②	—	52	FS733	Super 250②	—	—	MR685	ENDT675	—	—
F747	NTC290②	—	—	FS747	NTC290L②	—	—	MR685P, S	ETZ675	—	—
F747, ST	Formula 290②	—	—	FS753	1674⑫	—	—	MR686, S, P	ENDT676	—	—
F749	NHS②	—	52	FS755	1693T⑫	—	—	**R MODELS**			
F759	NHRS②	—	58	FS759	VT903L②	—	—	R401	END475	15	37
F759T, ST	VT903②	—	—	FS761	V903L②	—	—	R402	EN402	8	36
F761	V903②	—	—	FS673L, LS	NTC335	—	—	R403	END465C	15	42
F763	NTC335②	—	54	FS765	NTA370L②	—	—	R410	EN414A	8	32
F765	NT-380②	—	58	FS767	NTC350L②	—	—	R487	ENDT475	15	37
F765	NTA370②	—	—	FS769	8V71T③	—	—	R487P	ET477	—	—
F767	NTC350②	—	—	FS773	8V71N③	—	—	R487P	ETZ477	—	—
F767, ST	Formula 350②	—	—	FS781	6-71N③	—	—	R482	3208⑫	—	—
F769	8V71T③	—	—	FS785	ENDT675	—	55	R492P	3208⑫	—	—
F773	8V71N③	—	—	FS786	ENDT676	—	55	R567	END465D	15	40
F773	8V71NE③	—	—	FS795	ENDT865	—	71	R606	ET673E	—	—
F785	ENDT675	—	55	FS797	ENDT866	—	72	R606T	ETZ673E	—	—
F785ST, T	ETZ675	—	—	**H, HM, HMM, MB, MC & MR MODELS**				R607	END673P	15	⑥
F786, T	ENDT676	—	55	H693	ENDT673	15	52	R607	END673E	—	49
F795	ENDT865	—	70	HMM685	ENDT675	—	—	R609	END707	19	⑦
F797	ENDT866	—	70	HMM6856	ENDT675	—	58	R609	END711	19	⑨
F885	ENDT675	—	62	HMM6856S	ETZ675	—	—	R611	ENDT673	15	④

Continued

MACK

MODEL ENGINE & ENGINE APPLICATION—Continued

Truck Model	Engine Model ①	Crankcase Refill Capacity Qts.	Cooling System Capacity Qts.	Truck Model	Engine Model ①	Crankcase Refill Capacity Qts.	Cooling System Capacity Qts.	Truck Model	Engine Model ①	Crankcase Refill Capacity Qts.	Cooling System Capacity Qts.
R611	ENDT673C	—	57	RD686	ENDT676	—	57	RM686	ENDT676	—	—
R611T, ST	ETZ673	—	—	RD686S, SX	ENDT676	—	—	RM4874	END475	—	37
R612	ETAZ673	—	—	RD721SX	ETAZ1000	—	—	RM4874X	ET477	—	—
R612ST, T	ETAZ673A	—	—	RD731	NH230②	—	66	RM4874X, S	ETZ477	—	—
R615	END864	⑧	56	RD733	Super 250②	—	—	RM4876	ENDT475	—	37
R640	EN540A	13	58	RD747	NTC 290②	—	—	RM6004	ENDT475	—	—
R685	ENDT675	19	57	RD759	ENDT865	—	—	RM6074	END673E	—	44
R685ST, T	ETZ675	—	—	RD673	NTC335②	—	54	RM6076	END673E	—	44
R686	ENDT676	—	57	RD767SX	NTC350②	—	—	RM6114	ENDT673	—	52
R686ST, T	ENDT676	—	—	RD769SX	8V71T③	—	—	RM6114X	ETZ673	—	—
R707	END673	15	58	RD773	8V71N③	⑪	68	RM6116	ENDT673	—	52
R709	END707	19	60	RD785L	ENDT675	—	—	RM6854	ENDT675	—	58
R709	END711	19	60	RD795	ENDT865	—	68	RM6856, S	ENDT675	—	58
R711	ENDT673	15	60	RD797	ENDT866	—	68	RM6864, X	ENDT676	—	58
R711ST	Super 250②	—	—	RL456L, LS	1150⑫	—	—	RM6866, SX	ENDT676	—	58
R715	END864	⑧	62	RL457L, LS	1160⑫	—	—	RS456L	1150⑫	—	—
R719	ENDT864	⑧	64	RL483L, LS	6V-53N③	—	—	RS457L	1160⑫	—	—
R721S, ST	ETAZ1000	—	—	RL493L, LS	V555②	—	—	RS483L	6V-53N③	—	—
R731	NH220②	—	54	RL611	ET673	—	—	RS493L	V555②	—	—
R733	Super 250②	—	—	RL611L, LS	ENDLT673	—	—	RS611L, LS	ENDLT673	—	—
R737	NHC250②	—	54	RL611L, LS	ETZ673C	—	—	RS611L, LS	ETZ673C	—	—
R743	V8-265②	—	50	RL612L, LS	ETAZ673A	—	—	RS612L, LS	ETAZ673A	—	—
R747	NTC290②	—	—	RL626L, LS	6V92TA③	—	—	RS626L, LS	6V92TA③	—	—
R747ST	Formula 250②	—	—	RL673L, LS	RV-71N③	—	—	RS673L, LS	8V-71N③	—	—
R761	V903②	—	—	RL673L, LS	RV-71N③	—	—	RS673L	NTC335②	—	—
R763	NTC335②	—	66	RL673L	8V-71NE③	—	—	RS679LS	6V-71N③	—	—
R767	NTC350②	—	—	RL679L, LS	6V-71N③	—	—	RS685L, LS	ETZ675	—	—
R767ST	Formula 350②	—	—	RL685L, LS	ENDT675	—	—	RS686LS	ENDT676	—	—
R769	8V-71T③	—	—	RL685L, LS	ETZ675	—	—	RS711	ET673	—	—
R773	8V71C③	—	—	RL686L, LS	ENDT676	—	—	RS711	ENDLT673C	—	55
R773ST	8V-71N③	—	—	RL711	ET673	—	—	RS711L, LS	ETZ673C	—	—
R773ST	8V-71NE③	—	—	RL711	ENDLT673C	—	55	RS712L	ETAZ673E	—	—
R786	ENDT676	—	—	RL711L	ETZ673C	—	—	RS721L	ETAZ1000	—	—
R795	ENDT865	—	68	RL712L	ETAZ673E	—	—	RS733	Super 250②	—	—
R797	ENDT866	—	68	RL721L	ETAZ1000	—	—	RS747, L	NTC290L②	—	—
RD487	ENDT475	—	37	RL733	Super 250②	—	—	RS753	1674⑫	—	—
RD487P	ETZ477	—	—	RL747, L	NTC290L②	—	—	RS755	1693T⑫	—	—
RD487P, S	ET477	—	—	RL753	1674⑫	—	—	RS759	VT903L②	—	—
RD492, S	3208⑫	—	—	RL755	1693T⑫	—	—	RS761	V903L②	—	—
RD606	ET673E	—	—	RL759	VT903L②	—	—	RS765	NTA370L②	—	—
RD606S	ETZ673E	—	—	RL761	V903L②	—	—	RS767, L	NTC350L②	—	—
RD607	END673E	15	44	RL765	NTA370L②	—	—	RS769, L	8V71T③	—	—
RD611	ENDT673	15	52	RL767, L	NTC350L②	—	—	RS773	8V71N③	—	—
RD611	ENDT673C	15	57	RL769, L	8V71T③	—	—	RS781	6-71N③	—	—
RD611S, SX	ETZ673C	—	—	RL773	8V71N③	—	—	RS785	ENDT675	—	55
RD611P, S, SX	ET673	—	—	RL781	6-71N③	—	—	RS785L	ETZ675	—	—
RD612	ETAZ673	—	—	RL785	ENDT675	—	55	RS786, L	ENDT676	—	55
RD612S	ETAZ673A	—	—	RL785L	ETZ675	—	—	RS795	ENDT865	—	71
RD612SX	ETAZ673	—	—	RL786, L	ENDT786	—	55	RS797	ENDT866	—	72
RD615	END864	⑧	56	RL795	ENDT865	—	71	RWL711	ETZ673C	—	—
RD685	ENDT675	19	57	RL797	ENDT866	—	72	RWL712	ETAZ673A	—	—
RD685P, S, SX	ETZ675	—	—	RM685	ENDT675	—	—	RWL721	ETAZ1000	—	—
				RM685X	ETZ675	—	—	RWL747	Formula 290②	—	—

Continued

MACK

MODEL ENGINE & ENGINE APPLICATION—Continued

Truck Model	Engine Model ①	Crankcase Refill Capacity Qts.	Cooling System Capacity Qts.	Truck Model	Engine Model ①	Crankcase Refill Capacity Qts.	Cooling System Capacity Qts.	Truck Model	Engine Model ①	Crankcase Refill Capacity Qts.	Cooling System Capacity Qts.
RWL754	3406DIT⑫	—	—	U607	END673P	15	⑥	WL768L, LS	KT450②	—	—
RWL766	NTC400②	—	—	U609	END707	19	④	WL770L, LS	8V92TA③	—	—
RWL767	NTC350②	—	—	U609	END711	19	⑨	WL785	ENDT675	—	—
RWL768	KT450②	—	—	U611	ENDT673	15	④	WL785L, LS	ETZ675	—	—
RWL770	8V92TA③	—	—	U612	ETAZ673	—	—	WL786L, LS	ENDT676	—	—
RWL785	ETZ675	—	—	U612ST, T	ETAZ673A	—	—	WL795	ENDT865	—	—
RWL786	ENDT676	—	—	U615	END864	⑧	56	WL797	ENDT866	—	—
RWL711	ETZ673C	—	—	U626	6V92TT③	—	—	WS711	ENDT673C	—	—
RWL712	ETAZ673A	—	—	U626ST, TA	6V92TA③	—	—	WS711L, LS	ETZ673C	—	—
RWL721	ETAZ1000	—	—	U661	V903②	—	—	WS712L, LS	ETAZ673A	—	—
RWL747	Formula 290②	—	—	U685	ENDT675	19	57	WS721L, LS	ETAZ1000	—	—
RWL754	3406DIT⑫	—	—	U685ST, T	ETZ675	—	—	WS747L, LS	Formula 290②	—	—
RWL766	NTC400②	—	—	U686	ENDT676	—	57	WS754L, LS	3406 DIT⑫	—	—
RWS711	ETZ673C	—	—	U686ST, T	ENDT675	—	—	WS766L, LS	NTC400②	—	—
RWS712	ETAZ673A	—	—	U734ST	Formula 250②	—	—	WS767L, LS	Formula 350②	—	—
RWS721	ETAZ1000	—	—	U747ST	Formula 290②	—	—	WS768L, LS	KT450②	—	—
RWS747	Formula 290②	—	—	U767ST	Formula 350②	—	—	WS770L, LS	V92TA③	—	—
RWS754	3406DIT⑫	—	—	U769ST	8V71TA③	—	—	WS785	ENDT675	—	—
RWS766	NTC400②	—	—	U770ST	8V92TA③	—	—	WS785L, LS	ETZ675	—	—
RWS767	NTC350②	—	—	U795	ENDT865	—	—	WS786, L, LS	ENDT676	—	—
RWS768	KT450②	—	—	U797	ENDT866	—	—	WS795	ENDT865	—	—
RWS770	8V927A③	—	—	U795	ENDT865	—	74	WS797	ENDT866	—	—
RWS785	ETZ675	—	—	U797	ENDT866	—	74				
RWS786	ENDT676	—	—	**W MODELS**							
U MODELS				WL711	ENDT673C	—	—				
U92T	3208⑫	—	—	WL711L, LS	ETZ673C	—	—				
U401	END475	15	32	WL712L, LS	ETAZ673A	—	—				
U403	END465C	15	42	WL721L, LS	ETAZ1000	—	—				
U410	EN414A	8	32	WL747L, LS	Formula 290②	—	—				
U487	ENDT475	—	37	WL754L, LS	3406 DIT⑫	—	—				
U492T	3208⑫	—	—	WL766L, LS	NTC400②	—	—				
U567	END465D	15	40	WL767L, LS	Formula 350②	—	—				
U606	ET673	—	—								
U606T	ETZ673E	—	—								

①—Mack design unless otherwise noted.
②—Cummins engine.
③—Detroit diesel engine.
④—Radiator frontal area: 700 sq. in. 52 qts; 1000 sq. in. 60 qts.
⑤—Radiator frontal area: 700 sq. in. 42 qts.; 1000 sq. in. 52 qts.
⑥—Radiator frontal area: 560 sq. in. 44 qts.; 1000 sq. in. 60 qts.
⑦—Radiator frontal area: 700 sq. in. 49 qts.; 1000 sq. in. 60 qts.
⑧—High level 16 qts.; low level 12 qts.
⑨—Radiator frontal area; 700 sq. in. 50 qts., 1000 sq. in. 60 qts.
⑩—High level 20 qts.; low level 16 qts.
⑪—Caterpillar engine.

GENERAL ENGINE SPECIFICATIONS

ENGINE IDENTIFICATION—Engine model and serial number located on right front of cylinder block by timing case cover on Magnadyne engines; on Thermodyne engines on top of right front motor leg.

Engine Model	No. Cyls. & Valve Location	Bore & Stroke	Piston Disp. Cu. In.	Compression Ratio	Horsepower @ R.P.M.	Torque Ft. Lb. @ R.P.M.	Governor No-Load Setting R.P.M.	Governor Full-Load Setting R.P.M.	Normal Oil Pressure
707A	6 In Head	5 × 6	707	6.1	232 @ 2100	615 @ 1200	2150	2000	45–60
707B	6 In Head	5 × 6	707	6.4	232 @ 2100	615 @ 1200	2250	2100	45–60
707C	6 In Head	5 × 6	707	7.5	232 @ 2100	615 @ 1200	2250	2100	45–60
707C①	6 In Head	5 × 6	707	7.0	232 @ 2100	617 @ 1200	2250	2100	45–60

①—Latest production.

MACK

TUNE UP & VALVE SPECIFICATIONS

Engine Model	Firing Order	Spark Plugs Type⑮	Spark Plugs Gap	Ignition Timing Timing Mark	Ignition Timing Location	Cylinder Head Torque	Valve Face Angle	Valve Lash, Cold Intake	Valve Lash, Cold Exhaust	Valve Spring Pressure, Lb. @ In. Length
707A	153624	D14	.030	15BTC	③	150	②	.010	.025	110 @ 2⁵⁄₃₂④
707B	153624	D14	.030	13BTC	Flywheel	150	②	.010	.025	110 @ 2⁵⁄₃₂④
707B⑤	153624	D14	.030	16BTC	Flywheel	150	②	.018	.028	110 @ 2⁵⁄₃₂④
707C	153624	J6	.025	8BTC	Flywheel	150	②	.015	.025	110 @ 2⁵⁄₃₂④
707C①	153624	J6	.025	10BTC	Flywheel	150	②	.015	.025	110 @ 2⁵⁄₃₂④

①—Latest production.
②—Intake 30°, exhaust 45°.
③—Flywheel and vibration damper.
④—Outer spring.
⑤—Special service head, spark plugs on left side, washer necessary to locate exhaust valve rocker arm.

DISTRIBUTOR SPECIFICATIONS

Unit Part No. ①	Rotation ②	Cam Angle, Degrees	Breaker Gap, In.	Condenser Capacity, Mfds.	Breaker Arm Spring Tensions, Oz.	Centrifugal Advance Deg. @ R.P.M. of Dist. Advance Starts	Centrifugal Advance Deg. @ R.P.M. of Dist. Full Advance	Vacuum Advance Inches of Vacuum to Start Plunger Movement	Vacuum Advance Inches of Vacuum for Full Plunger Travel	Vacuum Advance Maximum Vacuum Advance, Dist. Degrees
1111541	CC	37	.018–.024	.20–.25	17–21	1 @ 350	8.5 @ 1100	4–6	9–11	15
1111780	CC	31–37	.022	.20–.25	17–21	1 @ 350	8.5 @ 1100	None	None	None
1111795	CC	31–37	.022	.20–.25	17–21	1 @ 275	10 @ 825	None	None	None
1111800	C	31–37	.022	.20–.25	17–21	1 @ 350	10 @ 1250	None	None	None
1111819	C	31–37	.022	.20–.25	17–21	1 @ 250	10 @ 1150	None	None	None
1111833	C	31–37	.022	.20–.25	17–21	1 @ 250	10 @ 1150	None	None	None
1111842	CC	31–37	.022	.20–.25	17–21	1 @ 275	12 @ 950	None	None	None
1111843	C	31–37	.022	.20–.25	17–21	1 @ 250	7 @ 825	None	None	None
1111844	C	31–37	.022	.20–.25	17–21	1 @ 250	7 @ 825	None	None	None
1111848	CC	31–37	.022	.20–.25	17–21	1 @ 300	9 @ 1100	None	None	None
1111849	C	31–37	.022	.20–.25	17–21	1 @ 250	8 @ 950	None	None	None
1111850	C	31–37	.022	.20–.25	17–21	1 @ 250	8 @ 950	None	None	None
1111878	C	31–37	.022	.20–.25	17–21	1 @ 250	8 @ 950	None	None	None

①—Stamped on plate riveted to housing.
②—As viewed from top; C—Clockwise.
　　CC—Counter-clockwise.

GENERATOR & REGULATOR SPECIFICATIONS

★ To Polarize Generator: For internally grounded systems, disconnect field lead from regulator and momentarily flash this wire to regulator battery terminal. For externally grounded systems, connect jumper wire from "hot" side of battery to armature terminal of generator.

Gen. No. ①	Rotation and Ground Polarity ③	Brush Spring Tension Oz.	Rated Cap. Amps.	Gen. Field Ground Location★	Field Current	Reg. No. ②	Cutout Relay Closing Voltage	Cutout Relay Arm. Air Gap, In.	Voltage Setting	Current Setting	Current & Voltage Regulator Arm. Air Gap, In.
1102120	C-P	28	30	External	1.69–1.79④	1118839	12.6	.020	14.3	30	.075
1102716	C-P	28	30	External	1.75–1.95⑤	1118302	6.4	.020	7.3	36	.075
1102746	C-P	28	40	External	1.87–2.0⑤	1118842	6.4	.020	7.3	42	.075
1106637	C-P	23	25	External	1.13–1.27④	1118214	12.8	.020	14.3	25	⑧
1106753	C-P	20	50	External	1.70–1.95⑤	1118335	6.4	.020	7.2	50	.075
1106757	C-P	20	50	External	1.70–1.95⑤	1118832	6.4	.020	7.3	55	.075
1106759	C-P	20	50	External	1.70–1.95⑤	1118333	6.4	.020	7.2	50	.075

Continued

MACK

GENERATOR & REGULATOR SPECIFICATIONS—Continued

★ To Polarize Generator: For internally grounded systems, disconnect field lead from regulator and momentarily flash this wire to regulator battery terminal. For externally grounded systems, connect jumper wire from "hot" side of battery to armature terminal of generator.

	Generator					Regulator					
Gen. No. ①	Rotation and Ground Polarity ③	Brush Spring Tension Oz.	Rated Cap. Amps.	Gen. Field Ground Location★	Field Current	Reg. No. ②	Cutout Relay		Voltage Setting	Current Setting	Current & Voltage Regulator Arm. Air Gap, In.
							Closing Voltage	Arm. Air Gap, In.			
1106805	CC-P	20	50	External	1.37–1.50 ④	1118838	12.8	.020	14.5	50	.075
1106810	C-P	20	50	External	1.37–1.50 ④	1118339	12.8	.020	14.3	50	.075
1106822	C-P	20	50	External	1.37–1.50 ④	1118838	12.8	.020	14.5	50	.075
1106822	C-P	20	50	External	1.37–1.50 ④	1118939	12.6	.020	14.3	55	.075
1106827	C-P	20	50	External	1.37–1.50 ④	1118368	12.8	.020	14.5	50	.075
1106916	C-P	20	40	External	1.37–1.50 ④	1118886	12.6	.020	14.3	40	.075
1106920	C-P	20	50	External	1.37–1.50 ④	1118838	12.8	.020	14.5	50	.075
1117567	C-P	25	120 ⑥	Internal	1.9–2.1 ⑦	1118544	12.8	⑨	14.1	120	⑩

①—Stamped on plate riveted to housing.
②—Stamped on regulator base.
③—P—Positive. C—Clockwise. CC—Counter-clockwise; as viewed from drive end.
④—At 12 volts.
⑤—At 6 volts.
⑥—Maximum output, both field circuits operating.
⑦—At 12 volts each set of fields.
⑧—Voltage regulator air gap, .070"; current regulator air gap, .080".
⑨—Actuating relay air gap, .035–.012"; point opening, .024–.031".
⑩—Voltage regulator air gap, .068–.082"; current regulator air gap, .088–.102".

PISTON, PIN, RING, CRANKSHAFT & BEARING SPECIFICATIONS

Engine Model	Wristpin Diameter	Piston Clearance Top of Skirt	Ring End Gap Minimum		Crankpin Diameter ①	Rod Bearing Clearance	Rod Bolt Torque	Main Bearing Journal Diameter ①	Main Bearing Clearance ③	Main Bolt Torque
			Comp.	Oil						
707A	1.43	.010	.017	.017	2.9975	.0015–.003	150	②	③	150
707B	1.43	.010	.017	.017	2.9975	.0015–.003	150	②	③	150
707C	1.43	.010	.017	.017	2.9975	.0015–.003	150	②	③	150

①—Crankshaft journal diameters are subject to a tolerance of plus or minus .0005".
②—Numbers 4 and 7, 3.4970"; all others, 3.4975".
③—Numbers 4 and 7, .002–.0045"; all others, .001–.0035".

STARTING MOTOR SPECIFICATIONS

Unit Part No. ①	Rotation ②	Brush Spring Tension, Ounces	No Load Test			Torque Test		
			Amperes	Volts	R.P.M.	Amperes	Volts	Torque Ft. Lb.
1107456	C	24–28	65	5.0	6000 ③	570	3.15	15
1107838	C	24–28	65	11.35	6000	450	7.5	15
1108863	C	36–40	100	23.0	8000	525	3.0	32
1108871	C	36–40	100	23.0	8000	525	3.0	32
1108874	C	36–40	100	23.0	8000	525	3.0	32
1108951	C	36–40	60	5.7	3300	675	3.15	30
1108956	C	36–40	65	11.3	5500	675	4.0	30
1109113	C	36–40	65	12.0	4500	725	4.8	44
1109151	C	36–40	65	11.4	6000	725	5.0	44
1109152	C	36–40	65	11.4	6000	725	5.0	44
1109441	C	36–40	70	11.3	4500	725	5.0	57
1109718	C	36–40	100	23.0	8000	525	3.0	32
1109729	C	36–40	100	23.0	8000	525	3.0	32
1113055	C	48 Min.	50	11.5	6000	500	3.3	22

Continued

MACK

STARTING MOTOR SPECIFICATIONS—Continued

Unit Part No. ①	Rotation ②	Brush Spring Tension, Ounces	No Load Test			Torque Test		
			Amperes	Volts	R.P.M.	Amperes	Volts	Torque Ft. Lb.
1113309	C	48 Min.	65	11.4	6000	500	3.2	28
1113330	C	48 Min.	65	11.4	6000	500	3.2	28
1113700	C	35 Min.	100	23.0	8000	500	3.0	28
1113708	C	35 Min.	100	23.0	8000	500	3.0	28
1113709	C	35 Min.	100	23.0	8000	500	3.0	28

①—Stamped on plate riveted to housing.
②—As viewed from drive end. C—Clockwise.
③—Free speed of 5000 R.P.M. for Bendix Type motors.

WHEEL ALIGNMENT SPECIFICATIONS

Toe-In on all axles except Rockwell 1/8" to 3/16".
Toe In on Rockwell axles 0 to 1/8".

Front Axle Model FA-	Caster, Degrees		Camber Degrees	Kingpin Angle Degrees
	Manual Steering	Power Steering		
1970–77 "DM" Models—6 Wheel Trucks & Dumpers				
532	1 to 3	4 to 6	1/2 to 1	7
W532	1 to 3	4 to 6	1/2 to 1	7
5321	1 to 3	4 to 6	1/2 to 1	7
534	1 to 3	4 to 6	1/2 to 1	8
5341	1 to 3	4 to 6	1/2 to 1	8
535	1 to 3	4 to 6	1/2 to 1	7
5351	1 to 3	4 to 6	1/2 to 1	7
W536	1 to 3	4 to 6	1/2 to 1	7
W537	1 to 3	4 to 6	1/2 to 1	7
600	1 to 3	4 to 6	1/2 to 1	3 1/2
601	1 to 3	4 to 6	1/2 to 1	3 1/2
6001	1 to 3	4 to 6	1/2 to 1	3 1/2
6011	1 to 3	4 to 6	1/2 to 1	3 1/2
604	1 to 3	4 to 6	1/2 to 1	5 1/2
6041	1 to 3	4 to 6	1/2 to 1	5 1/2
6042	1 to 3	4 to 6	1/2 to 1	5 1/2
6043	1 to 3	4 to 6	1/2 to 1	5 1/2
612	1 to 3	4 to 6	1/2 to 1	3 1/2
W612	1 to 3	4 to 6	1/2 to 1	3 1/2
701	1 to 3	4 to 6	1/2 to 1	3 1/2
702	1 to 3	4 to 6	1/2 to 1	3 1/2
703	1 to 3	4 to 6	1/2 to 1	3 1/2
1970–77 "DMM" Models				
6042	1 to 3	4 to 6	1/2 to 1	5 1/2
6044	1 to 3	4 1/2 to 6 1/2	1/2 to 1	5 1/2
1970–77 "F" Models—4 & 6 Wheel Trucks & Tractors				
532	1 to 3	4 to 6	1/2 to 1	7
L532	1 to 3	4 to 6	1/2 to 1	7
W532	1 to 3	4 to 6	1/2 to 1	7
5321	1 to 3	4 to 6	1/2 to 1	7
534	1 to 3	4 to 6	1/2 to 1	8
5341	1 to 3	4 to 6	1/2 to 1	8
535	1 to 3	4 to 6	1/2 to 1	7
L535	1 to 3	4 to 6	1/2 to 1	7
5351	1 to 3	4 to 6	1/2 to 1	7
W536	1 to 3	4 to 6	1/2 to 1	7
W537	1 to 3	4 to 6	1/2 to 1	7
604	1 to 3	4 to 6	1/2 to 1	5 1/2
6041	1 to 3	4 to 6	1/2 to 1	5 1/2
6042	1 to 3	4 to 6	1/2 to 1	5 1/2
6043	1 to 3	4 to 6	1/2 to 1	5 1/2
703	1 to 3	4 to 6	1/2 to 1	3 1/2
705	1 to 3	4 to 6	1/2 to 1	3 1/2
1970–77 "MB" Models—4 & 6 Wheel Trucks & Tractors				
532, W532	1 to 3	4 to 6	1/2 to 1	7
5321	1 to 3	4 to 6	1/2 to 1	7
534, 5341	1 to 3	4 to 6	1/2 to 1	8
L535	1 to 3	4 to 6	1/2 to 1	7
W536, W537	1 to 3	4 to 6	1/2 to 1	7
604, 6041	1 to 3	4 to 6	1/2 to 1	5 1/2
6042, 6043	1 to 3	4 to 6	1/2 to 1	5 1/2
W612	1 to 3	4 to 6	1/2 to 1	3 1/2
1970–77 "R", "RD", "RL", "RM" & "V" Models—4 & 6 Wheel Tractors, Trucks & Dumpers				
532, L532	1 to 3	4 to 6	1/2 to 1	7
W532	1 to 3	4 to 6	1/2 to 1	7
5321	1 to 3	4 to 6	1/2 to 1	7
534, 5341	1 to 3	4 to 6	1/2 to 1	8
535, L535	1 to 3	4 to 6	1/2 to 1	7
5351	1 to 3	4 to 6	1/2 to 1	7
535N	1 to 3	4 to 6	1/2 to 1	7
W536, W537	1 to 3	4 to 6	1/2 to 1	7
600, 601	1 to 3	4 to 6	1/2 to 1	3 1/2
6001, 6011	1 to 3	4 to 6	1/2 to 1	3 1/2
604, 6041	1 to 3	4 to 6	1/2 to 1	5 1/2
6042	1 to 3	4 to 6	1/2 to 1	5 1/2
6043	1 to 3	4 to 6	1/2 to 1	5 1/2
6044	1 to 3	4 1/2 to 6 1/2	1/2 to 1	5 1/2
612, W612	1 to 3	4 to 6	1/2 to 1	3 1/2

MACK

Engine Section

CYLINDER HEAD, REPLACE

All Engines

When removing a cylinder head a chisel or screw driver should never be used to pry it loose from the cylinder block. On L-head engines, use an eyebolt in the third or fourth spark plug hole, lifting up on the eyebolt while tapping lightly around the edges of the head with a lead or rawhide hammer or mallet. Be sure that all the head stud nuts or bolts have been removed before starting to remove the head.

In replacing the head, the stud nuts or bolts at the center of the head should be tightened first and then work outward from side to side and to the ends, Figs. 1 & 2.

Draw the nuts or bolts down evenly until all are normally tight. Then after the engine has run long enough to warm it up, make a final tightening with a torque wrench to the torque loads given in the *Tune Up & Valve Specifications* table.

On overhead valve engines, be sure to check the valve clearances after the final tightening.

VALVE LIFTERS

All Engines

On some engines, valve lifters are of the barrel type, operating in guide holes bored in the cylinder block. To remove lifters of this type, take off the engine side cover and take out the lifters.

Other engines have valve lifters which operate in removable guide clusters bolted to the cylinder block. To remove lifters of this type, merely unbolt the guide clusters from the block and take out the assembly.

Another design is where the lifters operate in bushings pressed in the block. These bushings may be pressed out after the lifters have been removed. After pressing in the new bushings, they should be reamed to provide the proper operating clearance and to eliminate any distortion which may have occurred during the replacement operation.

TIMING GEARS

All Engines

If the timing gears are removed for any reason, the camshaft must be timed when the gears are replaced. Before removing gears, make sure the timing marks are legible. And when replaced, valve timing will be correct if the marks on the camshaft and crankshaft gears are meshed.

CAMSHAFT & BEARINGS

All Engines

Camshaft bearings should be installed in sets and care must be exercised to see that the oil holes in the bearings are aligned with the oil feed holes in the block to assure adequate lubrication.

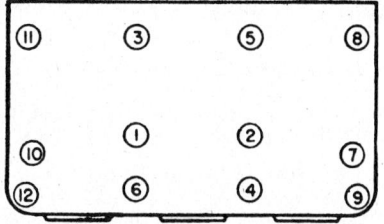

Fig. 1 Cylinder head tightening sequence. 431, 438, 464, 540 engines.

To assure proper camshaft fit on engines with crankcase separate from the cylinder block, line-ream camshaft bearings after the block is bolted in place.

PISTONS & RODS, ASSEMBLE

All Engines

If the pistons and rods have factory markings to indicate their position in the cylinders, assemble and install them according to these marks, or according to the marks made during removal if they were not otherwise marked, Fig. 4.

PISTON PINS, REPLACE

All Engines

In some engines, the pins are clamped in the rod, and when installing pins of this type, turn the notch in the pin to line up with the clamp screw hole in the rod to prevent damage to the clamp screw threads as it is being installed.

In other engines, the pins are of the floating type, being free to rotate in both the rod and piston bores. These pins are prevented from rubbing against the cylinder wall by either snap rings which fit in grooves in the piston bosses, or by aluminum plugs pressed in the ends of the pins.

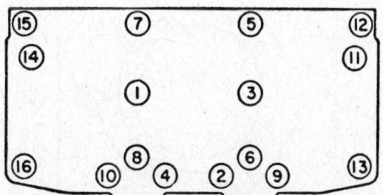

Fig. 2 Cylinder head tightening sequence. 707 engines

Pins should be selected that can be installed by pushing with the palm of the hand with piston at normal room temperature. To make assembly easier, however, heat the piston in boiling water for a few minutes to obtain maximum expansion of the metal and quickly insert the pin.

CRANKSHAFT END PLAY, ADJUST

All Engines

Through normal wear, crankshaft end play will seldom become excessive, but whenever new bearings are fitted, check the end play carefully and correct as required.

End thrust is controlled by thrust washers at the center main bearing. If end play is excessive, install new washers.

CRANKSHAFT OIL SEAL

All Engines

An oil slinger, integral with the crankshaft, behind the the rear main bearing, and a lead seal inserted in the flywheel housing at the rear of the slinger, Fig. 5, prevents oil leaking at this point.

OIL PUMP REPAIRS

All Engines

Conventional gear type oil pumps, located in the crankcase, are used on all engines. After removing the oil pan, the pump may be unfastened from its mounting and disassembled for repairs.

Inspect the pump gears for nicks or burrs. Inspect the bottom cover for wear and dress it down on a surface plate with emery if necessary. Place the cover on the pump and check the drive shaft end play. If end play is in excess of .006″, replace the drive and idler gears.

WATER PUMP REPAIRS

All Engines

The water pumps used on these engines are of the ball bearing type with sealing accomplished by a non-adjustable spring-loaded seal, Figs. 6 and 7. In servicing these pumps, note carefully the arrangement of the seal parts as they are removed so that the new seal may be assembled correctly.

IGNITION TIMING

All Engines

If a timing light is to be used to set ignition

MACK

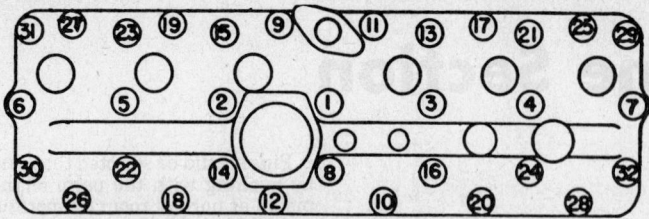

Fig. 3 Cylinder head tightening sequence. EN-291, 331 and 401 engines. The 402 engine has 34 studs

timing, disconnect the vacuum advance pipe to the carburetor and place a piece of tape over open end of pipe. *This is important as carburetor trouble can affect timing adjustments.*

Lacking a power timing light, an accurate method of setting ignition timing with the engine stopped is with the aid of a jumper light. Be sure to use a light bulb that corresponds with the system voltage of the vehicle.

1. Remove distributor cap and rotor and see that the breaker gap is set according to specifications.
2. Rotate engine until No. 1 cylinder is at the ignition timing point as indicated by the timing pointer and timing mark being lined up with each other.
3. Connect the jumper light between distributor ignition terminal and ground.
4. Turn on ignition switch.
5. Loosen distributor and turn it in the direction of normal rotation until the points just close (light out). Then slowly turn distributor in the opposite direction just to the exact point that the light goes on. Tighten distributor in this position.

HOLLEY CARBURETORS
AA-1G & 885-JJS

These carburetors, Figs. 8 and 9, are dual downdraft units incorporating an integral governor. The governor throttle mechanism is part of the carburetor and has been designed to provide the needed power required for moving the throttle to governing speeds as controlled by a separately driven governor rotor. The combination of these two units give instant response and accurate governing.

Fuel & Float Level

When checking the fuel level in an open vessel, under 3 lbs. pump pressure the level should measure $19/32''$ on AA-1G models and $5/8''$ on 885-JJS units. The measurement is taken below the surface of the float chamber cover (gasket in place) to the level of the fuel. The level may be corrected by bending the float arm.

The float level can be set when the air horn is off by gauging the distance between the bottom of the float and the flange surface of the air horn, Fig. 10. Holding the air horn upside down and the float in the closed position, measure the distance from the flange surface of the air horn to what would normally be the bottom side of the float (not the soldered seam). The correct distance should measure $1\,1/4''$ on AA-1G and $1\,3/8''$ on 885-JJS. Bend the float lever arm as required to correct the float level.

Idle Mixture

The idle mixture is controlled by the idle adjustment needles. Turning these needles in makes a leaner mixture and turning them out makes the mixture richer. Turn the needles in until they just touch the seats and back off one full turn.

When the engine has warmed up to operating temperature, alter the adjustment as required to obtain smooth performance. The range should be between 1 and $1\,1/2$ turns.

Accelerating Pump

The quantity of the fuel discharged by the accelerating pump can be controlled by changing the position of the pump link in the throttle lever. Of the three different positions (marked 1, 2 and 3) number 2 is the average setting, number 1 is for summer and 3 is for winter operation.

ZENITH CARBURETORS
28ADA10

This carburetor, Fig. 11, is a downdraft, single-barrel unit with a mechanically-operated accelerating pump and a manifold vacuum controlled power jet system.

Float Setting

Float height setting is measured from the gasket surface or parting line of the float chamber cover to the bottom of the float at the center, Fig. 12, with the fuel inlet valve seated (holding float chamber cover upside down). This distance should measure $1\,1/2''$.

Under three pounds fuel pump pressure the fuel level should measure $25/32''$.

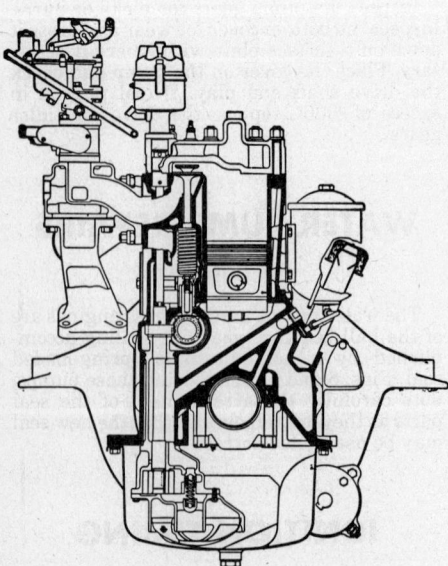

Section through EN-291, 331, 401 engines at intake valve

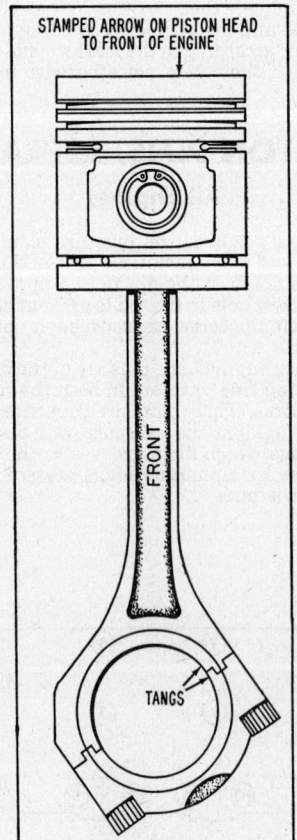

Fig. 4 Piston and rod assembly

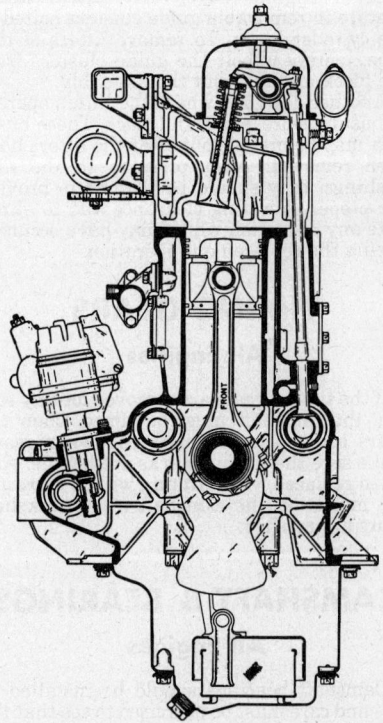

Section through EN-431A and 464 engines at piston and intake valve

MACK

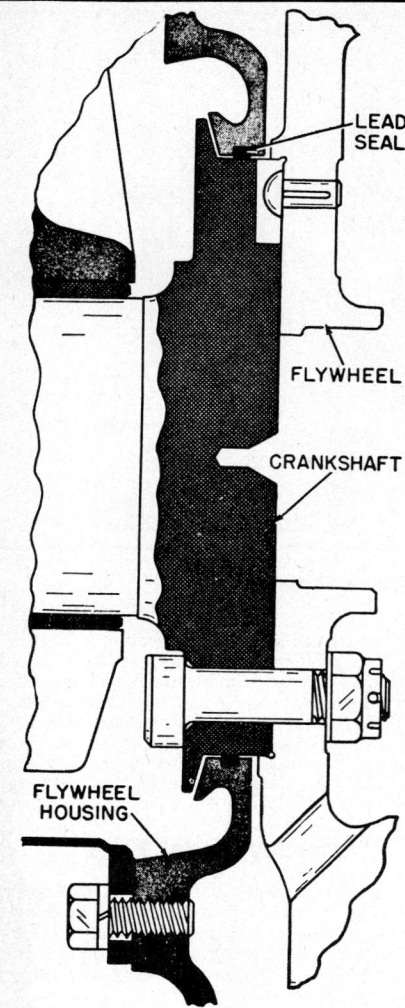

Fig. 5 Crankshaft rear oil seal. All engines

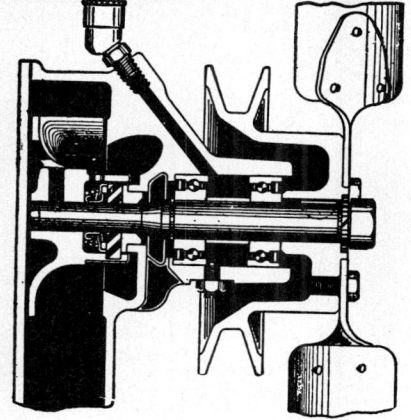

Fig. 6 Typical sealed type ball bearing water pump on engines using one fan belt

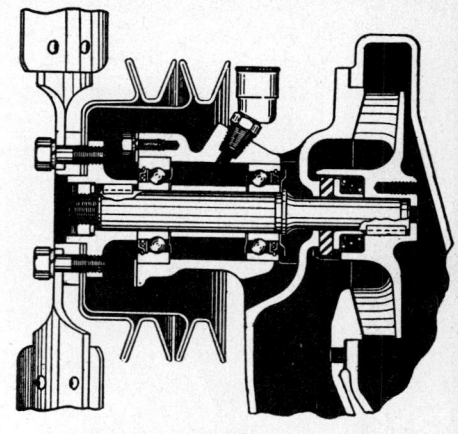

Fig. 7 Typical sealed type ball bearing pump on engines using dual fan belts

air and fuel to the engine without flooding when the vehicle is operated at extreme angles. The fuel chamber can be tipped at an angle to any position within a circle up to 45°. This feature is very helpful when the vehicle is operated in hilly country, in and out of excavations, on ramps, or when operated at side angles.

Float Setting

With the cover and float assembly held upside down and fuel inlet needle held closed, the distance indicated in Fig. 12 should be $1^{41}/_{64}"$.

Idle Mixture

For a preliminary adjustment, turn the needle into its seat and open one full turn. Run the engine until it reaches normal operating temperature and alter the adjustment as required to obtain smooth performance. The range should be 1 to 1½ turns open.

Zenith 63 Series

Zenith 63AW-12, 63AW-14 and 63AW-16 models are used on these engines, Fig. 14. They are single barrel, updraft carburetors with a manifold vacuum-controlled power and accelerating system. A removable venturi tube measures the volume of air which passes through the carburetor.

Float Setting

Float height setting is measured from the

Idle Mixture

For a preliminary adjustment, turn the idle adjusting needle into its seat and open one full turn. Run the engine until it reaches normal operating temperature and alter the adjustment as required to obtain smooth performance. The range should be between 1 and 1½ turns open.

Accelerator Pump

The accelerating jet and the pump spring control the rate of acceleration discharge. The stroke of the pump is controlled by the position of the rod in relation to the pump piston rod. The stroke can be varied by changing the position of the hairpin clip on the pump piston rod. The upper groove allows a half stroke. The center groove allows an intermediate or 3/4 stroke and the lower groove allows maximum or full stroke.

29D13 & 14

This carburetor, Fig. 13, is a downdraft carburetor with a concentric float bowl. This design assists in the proper metering of the

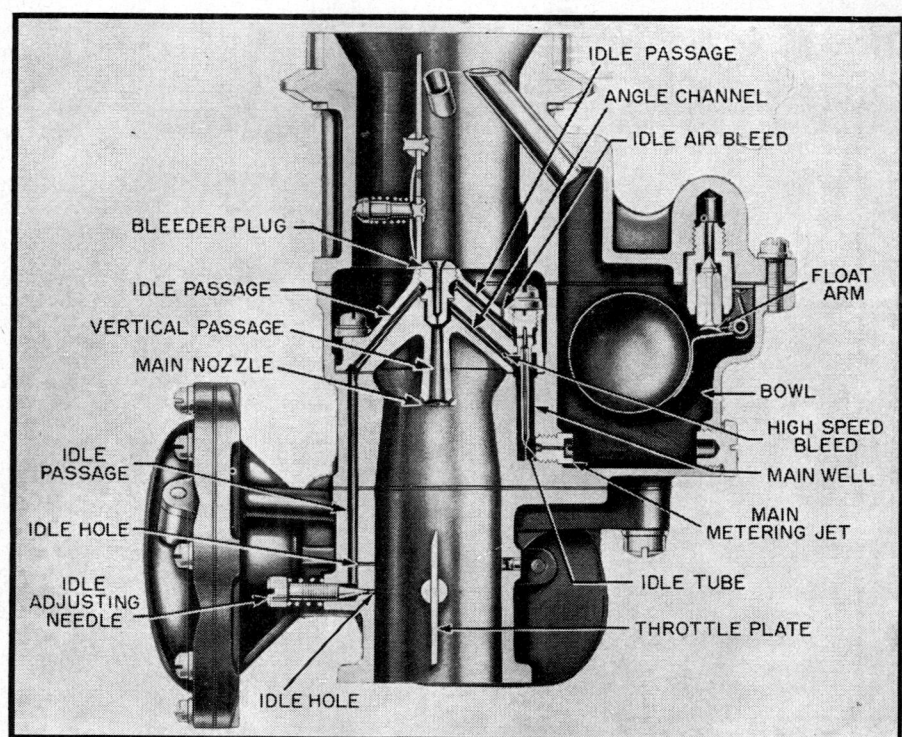

Fig. 8 Holley AA-1G carburetor

MACK

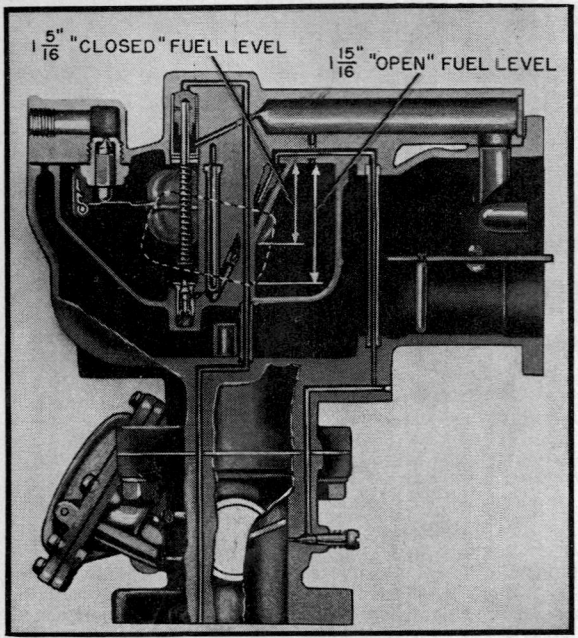

Fig. 9 Holley 885-JJS carburetor

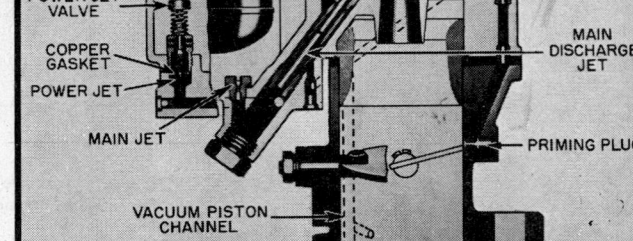

Fig. 11 Zenith 28 Series carburetor

gasket surface or parting line of the float chamber cover to the bottom of the float at the center, Fig. 12, with the fuel inlet valve seated (holding float chamber cover upside down). This distance should measure 1 19/32" on 63AW-12 carburetors and 2 1/64" for 63AW-14 and 63AW-16 units.

Under three pounds fuel pump pressure the fuel level should measure 55/64" on 63AW-12 units and 1 3/64" on 63AW-14 and 63AW-16 carburetors.

Idle Mixture

For a preliminary adjustment, turn the needle into its seat and open one full turn. Run the engine until it reaches normal operating temperature and alter the adjustment as required to obtain smooth performance. The range should be between 1 and 1 1/2" turns open.

Accelerator Pump

This adjustment is provided in the form of three grooves on the pump piston rod. The carburetor must be opened up and the vacuum pump piston assembly removed. Compress the spring toward the vacuum piston to permit moving the pump rod to the outer end of the slot in the pump piston base. At this point the slot is wide enough to permit removal of the rod.

There are three grooves near the end of the pump rod providing for three lengths of pump stroke. Install the pump piston in the groove nearest the end of the rod to obtain minimum or a half stroke; in the center groove for intermediate stroke, and in the third groove for maximum stroke. The spring holds the rod in the center of the pump piston base.

CARBURETOR GOVERNOR

Zenith

To change the governed speed, remove the seal wire and large seal plug, Fig. 15. Turn the main adjusting screw clockwise to increase or counter-clockwise to decrease governed speed. If the governor does not show definite response to changes of 1/4 to one full turn of the adjusting screw, it indicates a defective governor.

If the governor "surges" or "hunts" to a higher or lower engine speed, remove the small seal plug and turn the compensating spring adjusting screw 1/4 turn counter-clockwise until the surge is overcome.

If the governor does not respond quickly enough when governed speed is approached and the action "lags" or is "flat", turn the compensating adjusting screw clockwise until the symptom is overcome. Do not turn the adjustment more than 1/2 turn at a time without checking the performance of the vehicle on the road.

Holley Model 1174

Used with Holley carburetors, this governor, Fig. 16, is a vacuum controlled device featuring all the advantages of a mechanical governor without lengthy and complicated linkage. Should it become necessary to make any changes, proceed as follows:

To adjust the governor cut-off speed, remove the seal from the screw on the side of the governor housing and remove the screw. Rotate the engine until the end of the governor rotor, which carries the adjusting screw, is in line with the hole from which the screw was removed. Turn the adjusting screw clockwise to increase or counter-clockwise to decrease governed speed.

Whenever the governor has been disassembled and serviced, after reassembling turn the adjusting screw clockwise until it stops, then turn it counter-clockwise three full turns. Final adjustment is then made after the governor has been assembled to the engine.

The vacuum adjusting screw, Fig. 17, regulates the rpm spread between the governor full load cut-off speed and the no-load engine speed. Turning the screw clockwise will decrease the rpm spread. Turning it counter-clockwise will increase the spread. Changing the position of the screw will change the average governor speed and this should be corrected by the rotor adjusting screw.

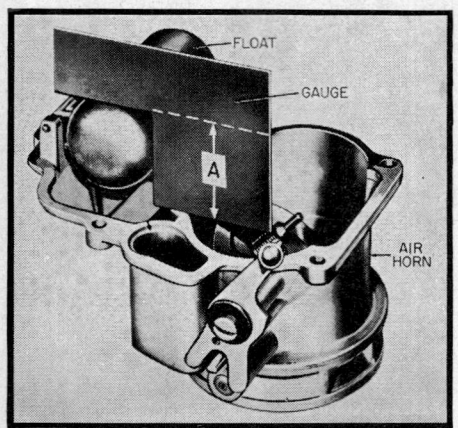

Fig. 10 Gauging float level. Holley carburetors

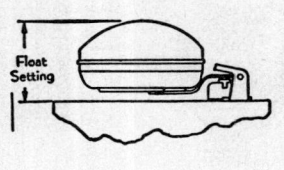 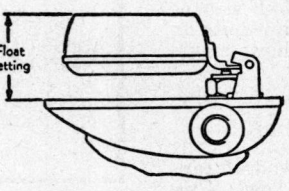 

Fig. 12 Zenith carburetor float settings

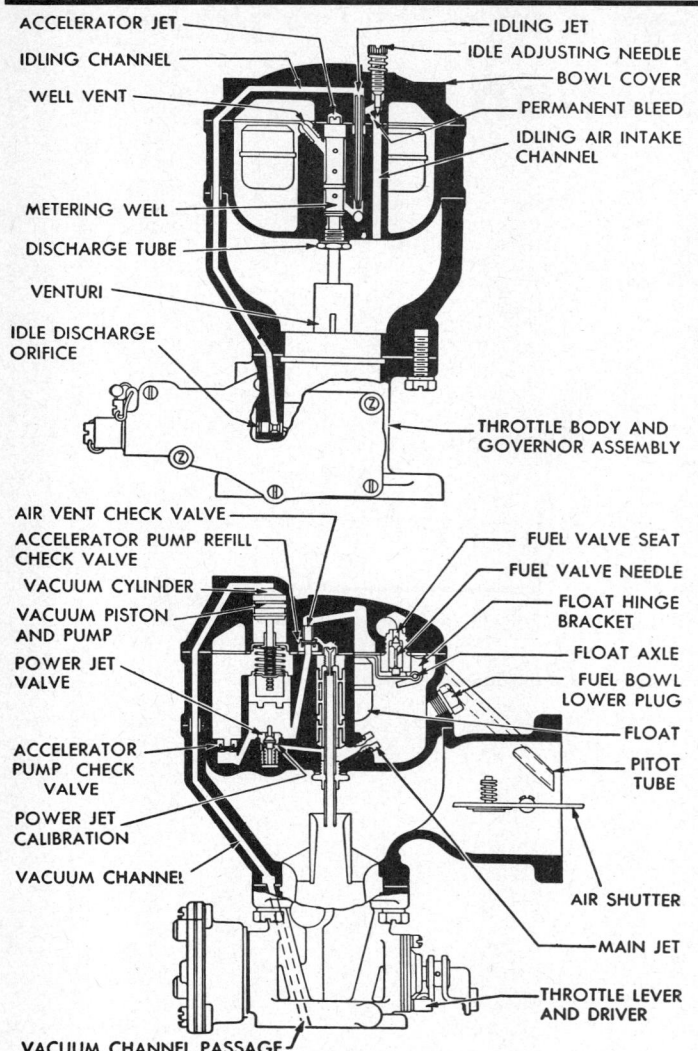

Fig. 13 Zenith 29 Series carburetor

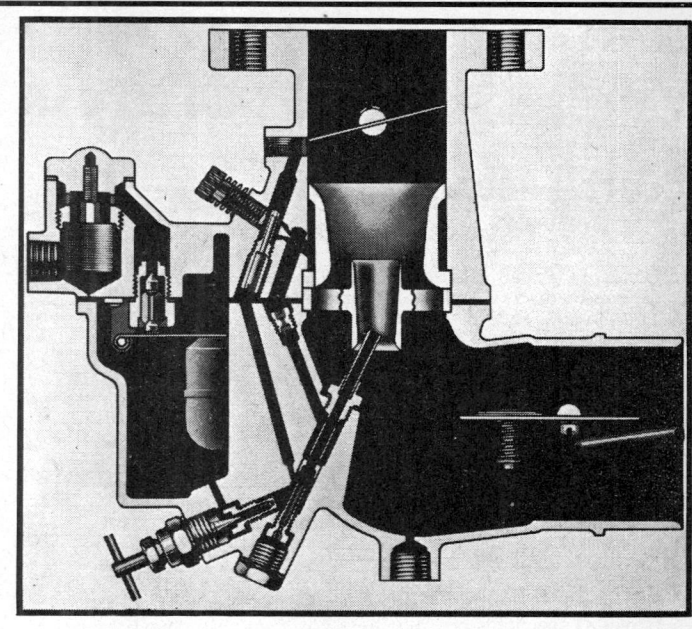

Fig. 14 Zenith 63 Series carburetor

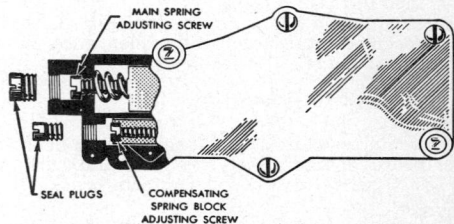

Fig. 15 Zenith carburetor governor adjustments

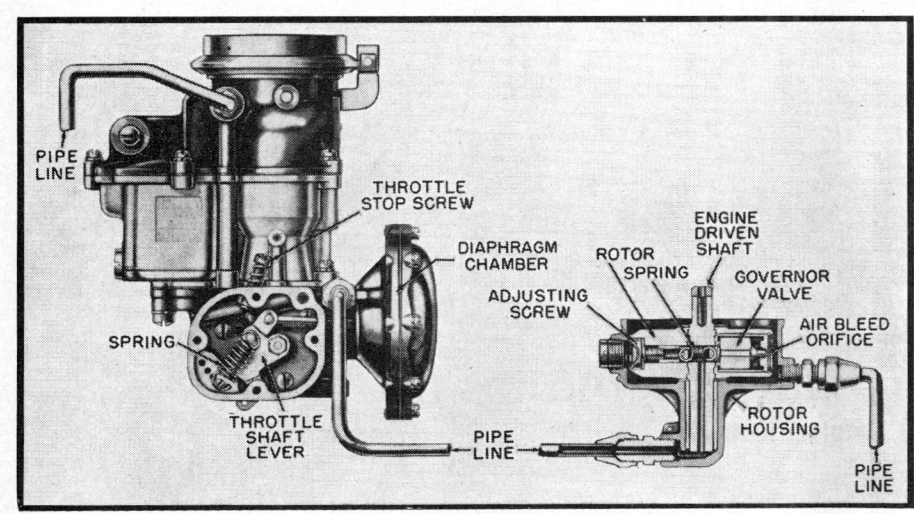

Fig. 16 Holley carburetor governor. Model 1174

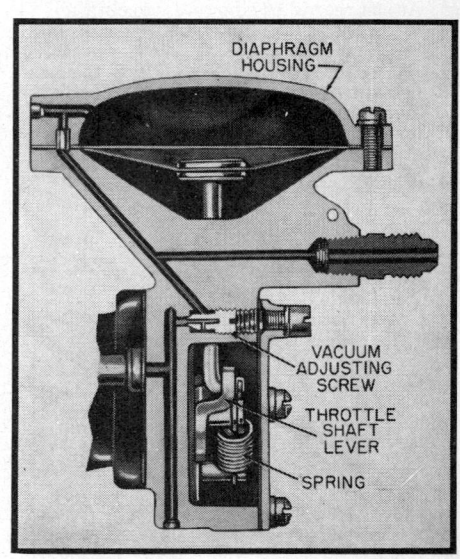

Fig. 17 Vacuum screw adjustment. Holley 1174 governor

MACK

Clutch Section

CLUTCH PEDAL, ADJUST

F Models

1. Connect and adjust rod (5), Fig. 1, to dimension (6) as specified in chart, Fig. 2. The setscrew should extend approximately 1 1/4 inch. Leave rod (3) disconnected.
2. Rotate setscrew (7) to obtain clutch bearing to collar clearance to specified dimension, Fig. 2.
3. Slide pedal located in lower arm, Fig. 6, to adjust clutch pedal to specified dimension (1), Fig. 2.
4. After cab is properly positioned, install and adjust rod (3) so lever (2) contacts roller with clutch pedal at full height.

MB Models

1. Rotate stop bolt (1) to obtain clutch pedal travel as specified, Fig. 3.
2. Adjust pull rod (2) to obtain dimension (3), Fig. 3, then adjust pull rod (4) to specified dimension in chart, Fig. 4.
3. With cab down and locked, adjust set screw (5), Figs. 3 & 5, to dimension specified in chart, Fig. 4.
4. If equipped adjust lever stop, Fig. 3, to specified total clutch collar clearance in chart, Fig. 4.

R Models

1. Compress clutch pedal seal against floor board approximately 1/8 inch and turn stop screw (4) until it contacts bracket, Fig. 6.
2. Loosen clamp bolt (1) and adjust pedal travel to 8 1/2 inches, then tighten clamp bolt and recheck pedal travel, Fig. 6.
3. Install pull rod (3), Fig. 6.
4. Adjust lower rod assembly (5), Figs. 7 & 8, to specified dimension (6) in chart, Figs. 9 & 10, then install the rod and retractor spring.
5. Adjust rear idler stop screw to obtain 13/16 vertical clearance to end of rod, Figs. 7 & 8.
6. Rotate set screw (7), Figs. 7 & 8, to specified dimension in chart, Fig. 11. If adjustment cannot be obtained, remove dog lever and move lever one spline in required direction.

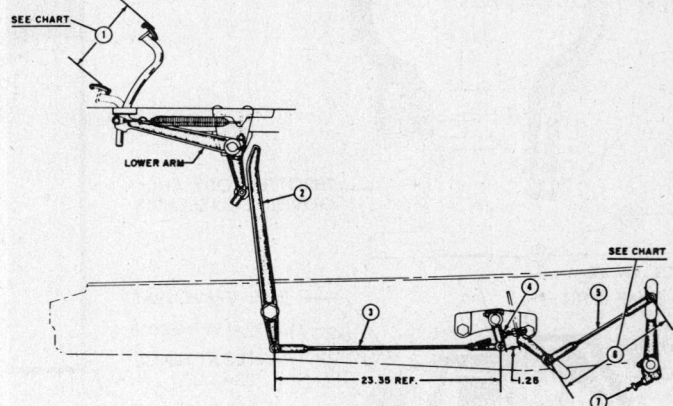

Fig. 1　Clutch linkage adjustment. F models

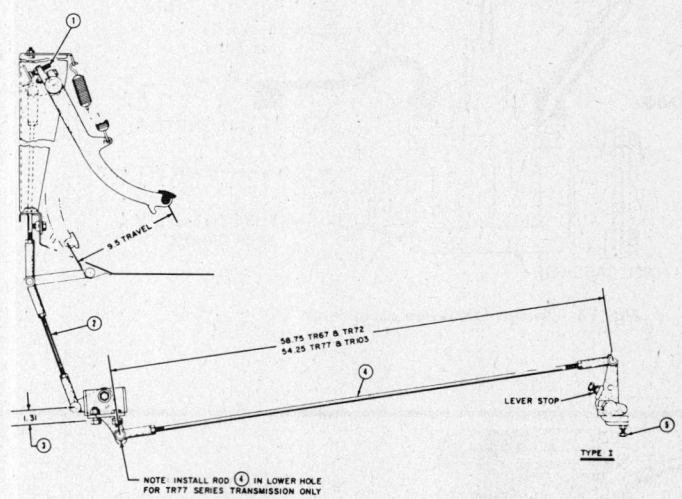

Fig. 3　Clutch linkage adjustment. MB models

ENGINE CLUTCH COMBINATION		DIM. ①	DIM. ⑥	
ENGINE	CLUTCH			
END-673 ENDT-673	CL-28	9.00	13.95	4-WHEEL
END-673 ENDT-673	CL-28	9.00	14.97	6-WHEEL
END-673 ENDT-673	CL-50	9.00	15.07	4-WHEEL
END-673 ENDT-673	CL-50	9.00	16.33	6-WHEEL
END-864	CL-50	8.50	12.58	4-WHEEL
END-864	CL-50	8.50	13.79	6-WHEEL
ENDT-864	CL-50	8.50	14.41	4-WHEEL
ENDT-864	CL-505	8.50	15.62	6-WHEEL

Fig. 2　Clutch pedal and rod adjustment chart. F models

NOTE: If clutch pedal pressure exceeds 65 lbs., recheck adjustment to ensure proper installation of components.

UNISHIFT ADJUSTMENT

Electrically Actuated

1. Adjust clutch linkages to specifications as described previously.
2. Determine clutch pedal position at which complete clutch disengagement occurs by gently attempting to shift transmission into 5th speed without depressing the clutch pedal, then depress clutch pedal. The point at which 5th speed engages is the point at which complete clutch disengagement occurs. At this point measure the distance from top of clutch pedal pad to floor.
3. Adjust position of collar in relation to clutch control trip switch occurs at point of complete clutch disengagement as determined previously.

Air Actuated

1. Determine clutch pedal position at which complete clutch disengagement occurs by gently attempting to shift transmission into 5th speed without depressing the

CLUTCH	RELEASE COLLAR TRAVEL		
	FREE	WORKING	TOTAL
CL-28 SERIES	.125	.375	.500
CL-47 SERIES	.062	.500	.562
CL-50 SERIES	.125	.500	.625
CL-40 SERIES EXCEPT CL-404	.125	.281	.406
CL-404	.125	.437	.562

Fig. 4 Clutch collar clearance chart. MB models

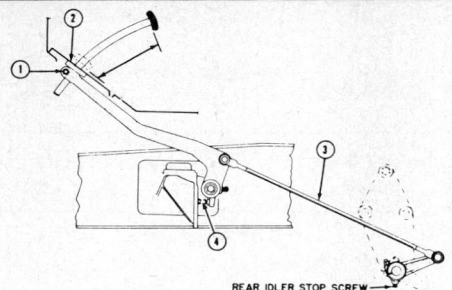

Fig. 6 Clutch linkage adjustment. R models

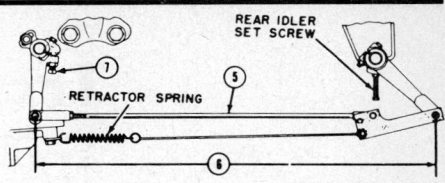

Fig. 8 Lower rod adjustment. R-400 series with or without unishift and R-500, 600 and 700 series without unishift

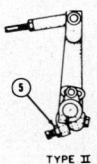

Fig. 5 Clutch release lever. Type II used on MB models

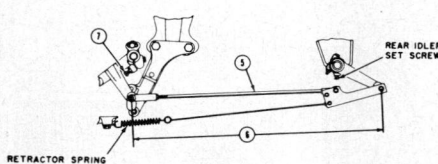

Fig. 7 Lower rod adjustment. R-500, 600 and 700 series with unishift

ENGINE, TRANS. AND CLUTCH COMBINATIONS			DIM 6
ENGINE	TRANS.	CLUTCH	
CUM-6	TR-72	CL-50	26.8
CUM-6	TR-72	CL-28	27.3
END(T) 673, 711 (R-600 ONLY)	TR-72	CL-28, 58	29.6
END-864 (R-615 ONLY)	TR-72	CL-50, 58	33.1
END-864 CUM. V-8-265 (R-700 ONLY)	TR-72	CL-28, 50, 58	36.4
END-673, 711 (R-700 ONLY)	TR-72	CL-28, 58	37.3

Fig. 9 Lower rod adjustment chart. R-500, 600 and 700 series with unishift

clutch pedal, then depress clutch pedal. The point at which 5th speed engages is the point at which complete clutch disengagement occurs. At this point measure the distance from top of clutch pedal pad to floor on all except MB models and from the top of clutch pedal pad to dash panel on MB models.

2. On F models, adjust length of rod (8), Fig. 12 to a point at which air valve starts to open and pedal position is 1/2 inch higher (further from floor) than that measured at complete clutch disengagement as determined in step 1.

3. On MB models, adjust length of rods (6 & 7), Fig. 13 to a point at which air valve starts to open and pedal position is 1/2 inch further from dash panel than that measured at complete clutch disengagement as determined in step 1.

4. On all models except F and MB, rotate unishift valve and bracket or valve and bracket to a point at which cam starts to open the unishift air valve 1/2 inch higher (further from floor) than that measured at complete clutch disengagement as determined in step 1.

ENGINE, TRANS. AND CLUTCH COMBINATIONS			DIM 6
ENGINE	TRANS. SERIES	CLUTCH	
CUM-6	TR-72	CL-50	26.8
CUM-6	TR-72	CL-28	27.3
END-465D	TR-67	CL-471, CL-405	29.6
END(T) 673, 711 (R-600 ONLY)	TR-72	CL-28, 58	29.6
END-475 END-465C	TR-103, 106 TR-77	CL-405, 471	31.3
END-864 (R-615 ONLY)	TR-72	CL-50, 58	33.1
END-864 CUM-V8-265 (R-700 ONLY)	TR-72	CL-28, 50, 58	36.4
END-673, 711 (R-700 ONLY)	TR-72	CL-28, 58	37.3

Fig. 10 Lower rod adjustment chart. R-400 series with or without unishift and R-500, 600 and 700 series without unishift

CLUTCH	RELEASE COLLAR TRAVEL		
	FREE	WORKING	TOTAL
CL-28 & 58 SERIES	.125	.375	.500
CL-40 SERIES EXCEPT CL-404	.125	.281	.406
CL-47 SERIES	.062	.500	.562
CL-50 SERIES	.125	.500	.625

Fig. 11 Clutch collar clearance chart. R models

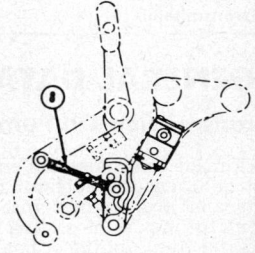

Fig. 12 Unishift adjustment. F models

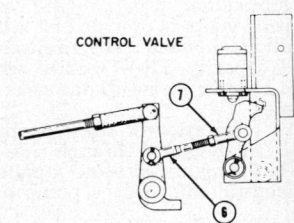

Fig. 13 Unishift adjustment. MB models

MACK

Transmission Section

For Clark, Fuller and Spicer transmissions used on Mack trucks, see the "name" transmission chapters for service procedures

Mack Unit No.①	Oil, Pints
TR-130	33
TR-671	15
TRD-67, 670	20
TRDX-670	19
TRD-675, 6750	24
TR-72, 720	22
TRD-72, 720	28
TRDX-720	28
TRD-725, 7250	30
TRT-72	30
TRQ-72, 720	36

Mack Unit No.①	Oil, Pints
TR-73②	12
TRL-107	
TR-771	11
TR-77	13
TRDX-770	14
TRD-775	15
TRQ-77	17

①—See name plate on transmission housing for model identification.
②—Fuller transmission.

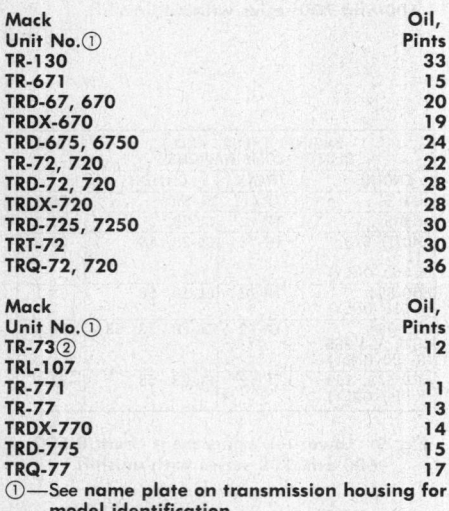

Fig. 1 Sectional view of typical Mack transmission oil pump and mainshaft drillings

GENERAL DATA

Transmission Oil Pump

All Mack-made transmissions employ constant mesh helical gears which run free on the mainshafts and are brought into selective engagement by means of sliding gear-type clutches. These free-running or floating gears run on thinshell bushings to maintain gear alignment with greater precision. However, because bushings require more positive provision for lubrication, pressure lubrication of these floating gears is provided by a built-in pump in all Mack-made transmissions except the small capacity TR-77 Series which is lubricated by gear throw-off and gear pumping action.

Pressure lubrication of these bushings is provided by oil delivered through rifle-drilled passages in the mainshafts and supplied by a simple eccentric shuttle-type pump built in the main drive pinion, Fig. 1. This pump has but one moving part—a double-ended reciprocating vane which dispenses with valves. Calculated leakage past the bronze nipple acting as a jumper tube, which conducts oil from the pump to the drilled mainshafts, supplies copious lubrication to the spigot bearings. Gravity feed oil reaches in the reverse cluster gear bearings through a rifle-drilled connecting hole in the supporting shaft.

All working and sliding parts of Mack-made transmissions are bathed in oil from gear throw-off when the engine is running; the countershaft being partially submerged in lubricant. To supply the pump, part of this gear throw-off is collected by a gutter high on the right-hand side of the case. Through a drilled connecting passage in the case, this oil is led to the eccentric space between the driving pinion shaft and its bearing cover. As the shaft turns, the pump vane reciprocates in its eccentric orbit and the vane ends pick up the oil and force it into the center passage through the bronze nipple to the mainshaft drillings.

Magnetic Cleaner Plug

Of course, clean oil in a transmission is essential to long life of gears and bearings. Minute particles of steel, dislodged as a result of wear, form an abrasive of great destructiveness and tend to circulate with the oil. This greatly increases the wear on gear teeth and bearings unless means are provided to separate them from the oil. To combat this, all Mack-made transmissions are provided with a magnetic oil cleaner plug. As viewed from the rear of the transmission, Fig. 2, the oil cleaner is located high inside the transmission case on the right-hand side above the level of the oil. It is so situated that it receives the throw-off from the upper gears. The cleaner consists of an integral open trough and

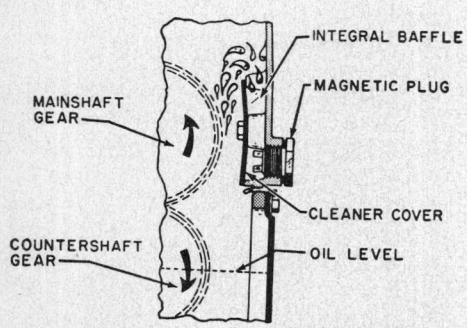

Fig. 2 Section through rear of transmission showing magnet cleaner plug

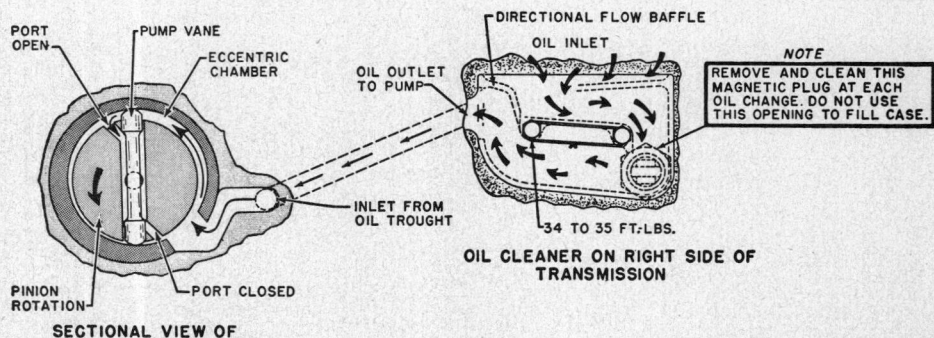

Fig. 3 Showing oil pump and oil cleaner

1316

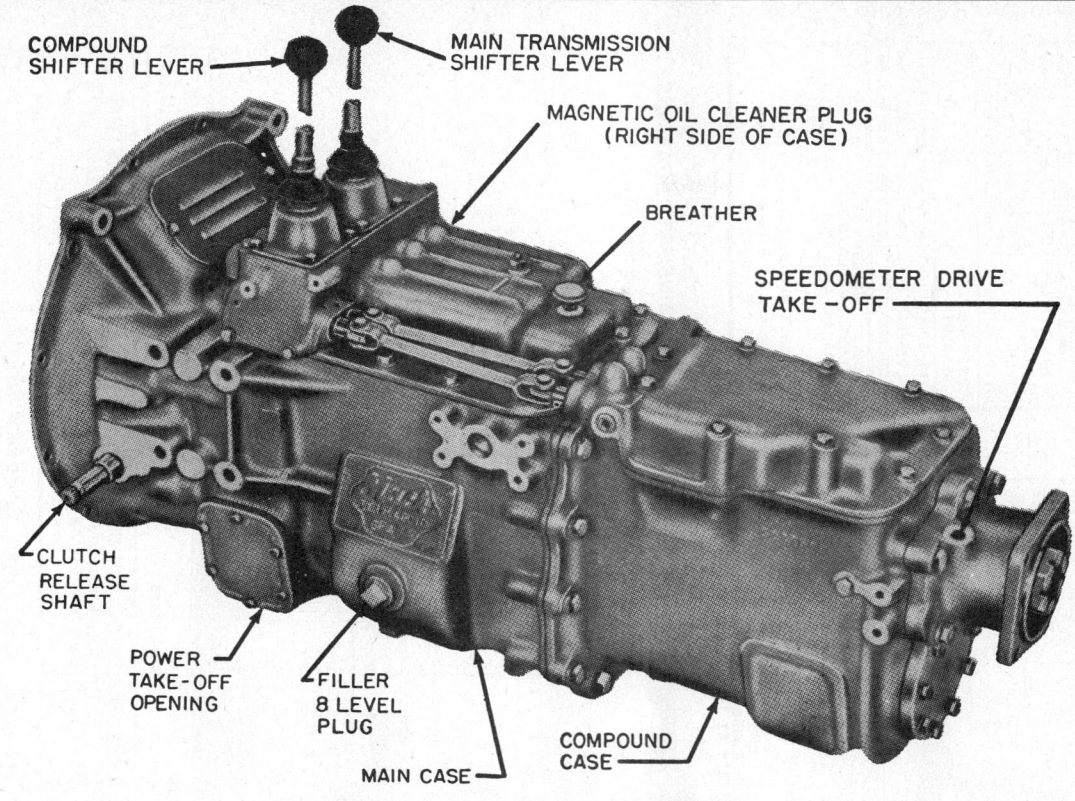

Fig. 4 Mack 20 speed TRQ-720 transmission

slanting baffle with a removable sheet metal cover, Fig. 3. At the bottom of the slanting baffle, a tapped hole in the case accomodates a large hex plug with a powerful built-in magnet installed from outside, Fig. 2.

It is not necessary to drain the case in order to remove the plug for cleaning or for removing sludge from the bottom of the trough. The oil cleaner plug may be removed at any time without losing any oil or disturbing other parts of the transmission. When removed, it carries all foreign matter with it which is easily removed from the magnet simply by wiping it clean. Remove sludge from the sump and then replace the plug in the case.

In the TR-51 and 13 Series of large Mack transmissions, magnetic drain plugs are also employed in addition to the magnetic cleaner plug to aid in extracting any magnetizeable particles from the lubricating oil.

MACK 20 SPEED TRQ-72, 720

Disassembly, Figs. 4 and 5

Unless a complete overhaul is necessary, remove only those parts required to gain access to the faulty parts. Do not disturb parts having press fits unless replacement is necessary. In that case, use proper press setups and pullers so that usable parts are not damaged. After cleaning all transmission parts with suitable solvent, inspect each part thoroughly. Replace worn or damaged parts, staked nuts, gaskets and cotter pins to avoid subsequent transmission failures.

1. After removing transmission from vehicle and cleaning externally, mount unit in a suitable overhaul stand. Remove hand brake parts, clutch release bearing assembly with return spring, clutch release shaft and yoke, P.T.O. covers and gear shifter hand control levers.
2. Remove both case covers and lay aside for bench disassembly. Engage sliding gear and ALL sliding clutches so that the entire gearset is locked up. Remove cotter pin from drive flange nut and then remove nut. Install standard puller and remove drive flange. Remove both rear bearing covers and save countershaft rear bearing shim pack intact. Slide speedometer gear off of mainshaft.
3. Remove all case-to-case dowel bolts and capscrews. With a large enough nylon headed mallet, tap compound case and separate it and the enclosed parts from the main case. Lay enclosed parts aside.
4. Remove mainshaft rear bearing retainer capscrews, oil tube, countershaft rear bearing cone clamp plate and capscrews. Remove countershaft front bearing cover capscrews and use jackscrews to remove the cover. Remove main driving pinion cover capscrews and cover. Carefully remove oil pump vane from pinion and save. To remove pinion, tap on gear end of pinion with a nylon mallet and work assembly out of case. Lay pinion aside.
5. Remove mainshaft spigot bearing inner race retaining snap ring. With 4th and 5th speed sliding clutch against bearing inner race, tap on clutch with nylon mallet and remove both parts from mainshaft. Pry key out of mainshaft spline. With a small tool, rotate 4th speed gear thrust washer one spline tooth and slide washer off of mainshaft.
6. Butt a soft drift forward end of mainshaft and with a hammer, drive mainshaft rearward to separate rear bearing from case.
7. Carefully slide gears, sleeve, thrust washer fixed and sliding clutches from mainshaft while withdrawing mainshaft from rear of main case. Remove sleeve Woodruff key from mainshaft. Place mainshaft in a vise with soft jaws and pry retaining ring off of mainshaft rear bearing 2-piece thrust washer. Pry 2-piece thrust washer out of groove in mainshaft. Turn mainshaft over and remove oil tube, retaining snap ring and compound mainshaft spigot bearing. Remove from vise and press mainshaft out of rear bearing retainer and front cone. Remove bearing cone spacer shims and save. Remove remaining bearing cone with a segmented-type puller.
8. Remove reverse gear shaft lock and with puller 17-T-1425, withdraw gear shaft from case. Remove cluster gear, bearings and bearing spacer from case.
9. Slide countershaft rearward and partially through rear bearing opening. Install segmented puller on rear bearing cones and remove. With a soft steel drift, remove rear bearing cup from main case. When using a drift, be very careful not to damage part or case and apply alternate equal blows to opposite sides to prevent cocking of part in the case.
10. Tilt forward end of countershaft upward and remove entire assembly from case. Remove countershaft front bearing inner race and gear snap ring. For shops having a small capacity hydraulic press, press off one countershaft gear at a time. For shops

MACK

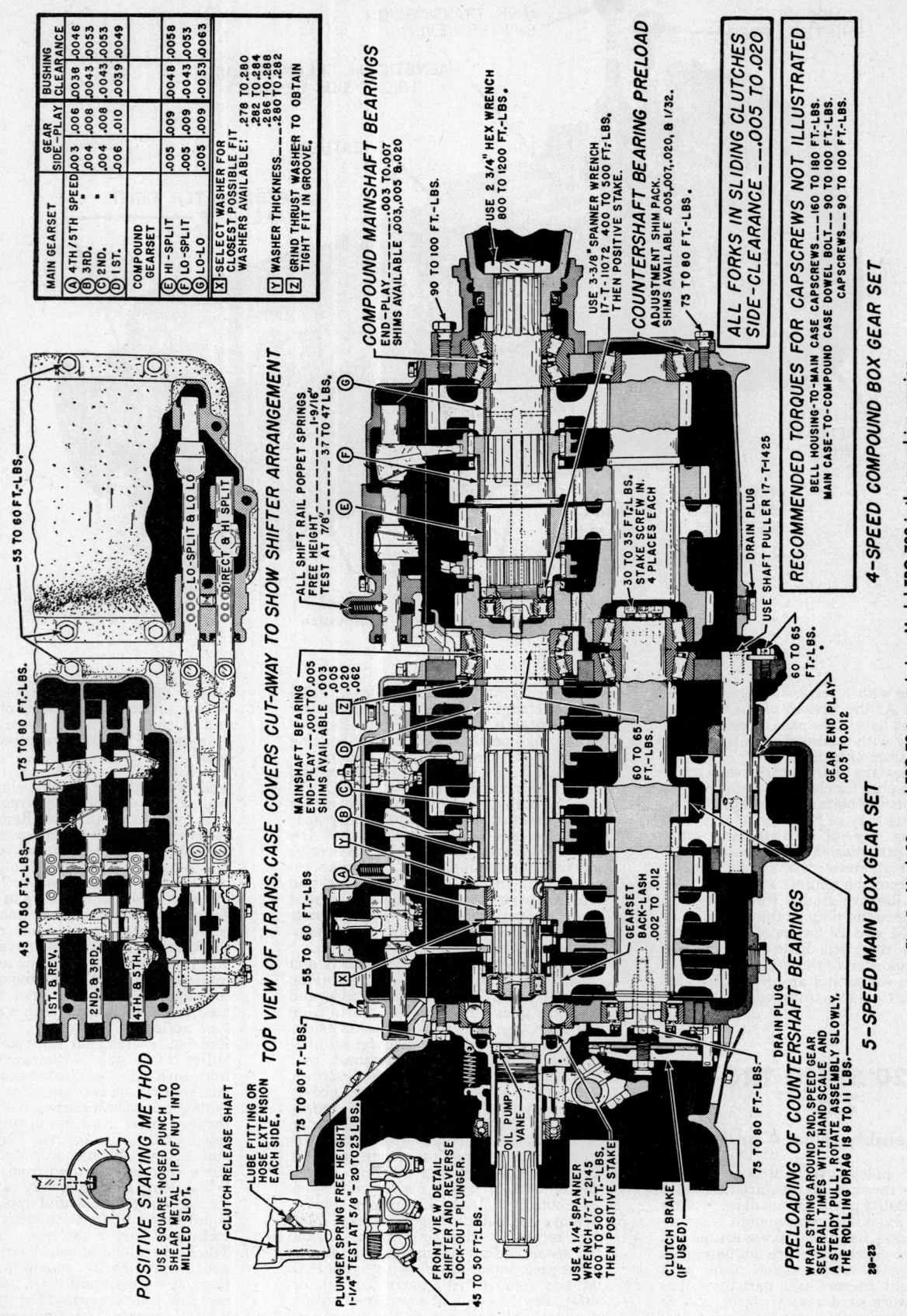

Fig. 5 Mack 20 speed TRQ-72 transmission. Model TRQ-720 is the overdrive version.

having a large capacity hydraulic press, place countershaft assembly in press, slide length of heavy tubing over countershaft integral gears to engage 3rd speed gear and remove all gears in one operation.
11. Clamp gear end of main driving pinion securely in large bench vise with soft jaws. Unstake pinion bearing nut and with a wrench, remove left-hand threaded nut. Remove ball bearing by pressing or tapping off. Turn pinion over and remove retaining snap ring and spigot bearing. Remove oil tube carefully and save.
12. Position compound case on arbor press table and press mainshaft out of case-mounted rear bearing retainer and cone. Carefully remove and save cone spacer and shims. Turn case over and remove compound mainshaft rear bearing retainer and compound countershaft rear bearing cup.
13. Press compound mainshaft out of LO-split gear, fixed clutch, LO-LO split gear, gear sleeve and rear bearing front cone. Turn shaft over and clamp in vise with soft jaws. Remove spigot bearing inner race from spigot, unstake nut and remove. Nut has left-hand threads. Slide fixed clutch, sliding clutch and HI-split gear off of shaft. Remove shaft from vise.
14. Remove bearing cup from compound countershaft constant-mesh gear. With segmented puller, remove rear bearing cone. Remove gears in hydraulic press one at a time or all in one operation, depending on capacity of press. Remove gear key from shaft.
15. Clamp flange of main case cover in bench vise and remove shifter and fork setscrews. Remove Welch plugs at shifter ends with shifter rails. Withdraw shifter rails from main case cover and at the same time remove shifters and shifter forks.

CAUTION: The spring-loaded balls over the shifter rails will fly out with CONSIDERABLE FORCE when released by withdrawing the rails. Therefore, it is advisable to hold a clean shop wiper over the holes while withdrawing the rails.

Be sure to save the balls, spring, and rail interlock pins for use at reassembly. Remove breather and toggle levers from top of cover.
16. Disassemble compound case cover in same manner. *Watch out for spring-loaded balls over rails when withdrawing rails from case.*

Inspection and Repair

1. Wash and clean all parts thoroughly in clean solvent and dry with moisture-free compressed air as damage to the bearing may result.
2. Replace bearings which are pitted and/or spalled. Replace lubricated bearings having excessive axial or radial clearances. Replace cases if outer races of bearings turn freely in case bores.
3. Replace gears having pitted or badly worn teeth. Replace gears with damaged internal or external teeth as a result of gear clashing. Floating gears having excessive radial clearance should be rebushed and bored to size.
4. Check all splines. If excessive wear is obvious, replace part or parts. Check thrust washers for scored surfaces or reduced thickness from excessive wear. Replace if either or both conditions prevail.
5. Check all gray iron parts for cracks and breaks. Case castings may be welded or brazed provided cracks do not extend into bearing bores or bolting surfaces. Replace or repair parts found to be damaged.
6. Check all other parts for wear and damage. Replace all parts that cannot be repaired or straightened. Replace all gaskets, damaged oil seals, O-rings, staked nuts and any part that shows mutilation. Replace poppet springs that have lost their tension. Clean up any threads that show mutilation.

Reassembly

NOTE: All working parts, especially the bearings, should be generously coated with SAE-30 oil while the transmission is being assembled. This will assure immediate lubrication when first starting and will prevent seizing of these parts. As moving parts are assembled, check frequently to see that they move freely.

1. Insert gear key in countershaft and press gears on one at a time. These gears have an interference fit and can be pressed on cold but for best results, the gears should be shrunk-fitted on shaft. With a heat lamp or hot oil, heat gears 270° to 300° F. for a period of not more than 1/2 hour. Oil shaft for each gear. Install gear snap ring, install front bearing inner race on spigot and retain with its snap ring.
2. Install countershaft front bearing in case. Install bearing cover and gasket. Place countershaft assembly in case with small end extending out of rear bearing opening. Install rear bearing cup in case. Install tapered roller bearing cones back-to-back on rear end of countershaft and secure with clamp plate. Position countershaft in front bearing.
3. Insert gear key in compound countershaft and press gears on one at a time. These gears have an interference fit and can be pressed on cold but for best results, the gears should be shrunk-fitted on shaft. With a heat lamp or hot oil, heat gears 270° to 300° F. for a period of not more than 1/2 hour. Oil shaft for each gear. Press bearing cup in front end of compound countershaft constant-mesh gear and bearing cone on rear end. Push countershaft rear bearing cup in compound case and install shim pack and bearing cover. Temporarily assemble compound countershaft, case-to-case gasket and compound case to the main case and countershaft.
4. Preload countershaft bearings as follows: Lubricate all bearings with SAE-30 oil. Wrap a string around countershaft 2nd-speed gear (largest integral gear) several times. Attach a spring scale to looped free end of string and with a steady pull, rotate the assembly SLOWLY. Repeat this operation and adjust thickness of rear bearing shim pack until the rolling-drag of 8 to 11 lbs.-pull is read on the scale. When correct shim pack thickness is established, remove compound case and compound countershaft from main case.
5. Position reverse cluster gear shaft so that slot in end of shaft will permit shaft lock to engage it. Start shaft into case. Assemble roller bearings and spacer in cluster gear. Position assembled gear in case and with a nylon hammer, tap shaft into case and gear. Install shaft lock and lock capscrew after tightening 60 to 65 ft.-lbs. with soft iron wire.
6. On bench, install compound mainshaft spigot roller bearing in end of mainshaft (compound driving pinion) and retain with snap ring. Place gear end of mainshaft in vise with soft metal jaws. Install rear bearing cone, bearing retainer with two cups, bearing retainer with two cups, bearing cone shims, front bearing cone and bearing split thrust washer. Adjust bearing shim pack thickness until end-play is .001 to .005" then press or drive positioning ring over split washer. Install 3rd-speed thrust washer Woodruff key in shaft.
7. Remove mainshaft from vise and start in main case through rear bearing hole. As mainshaft is advanced into working position, slide parts on mainshaft as follows: 1st-speed gear, reverse gear fixed clutch, reverse gear, 2nd-speed gear, 3rd-speed fixed and sliding clutches, 3rd speed gear, engage 3rd-speed gear through washer and 4th-speed gear sleeve with Woodruff key. Install 4th-speed gear on sleeve. Install 4th/5th-speed toothed thrust washer and with a small tool, move washer one tooth so that inner teeth align with mainshaft splines. Install washer key in deepened spline root and install 4th/5th-speed sliding clutch on splines and over inlaid key.
8. At this point the mainshaft rear bearing retainer should be seated in the main case. Install retainer capscrews and tighten 60 to 65 ft.-lbs., then lock heads together with soft iron wire. Install inner race of spigot bearing on front end of mainshaft and retain with snap ring.
9. Assemble mainshaft spigot bearing in gear end of main driving pinion and retain with snap ring. Turn pinion over and place in vise with soft metal jaws. Install pinion ball bearing and bearing nut. Tighten nut (left-hand thread) 400 to 500 ft.-lbs., the positive stake lip of nut to pinion in slot provided. Install oil tube in pinion gear end and install pinion assembly in transmission case. *Be very careful not to damage oil tube as it engages mainshaft.* Install oil pump vane in pinion and install bearing cover. Tighten cover capscrews 75 to 80 ft.-lbs.
10. At this point, the main case should be positioned in a vertical position with the pinion pointing downward. If overhaul stand is not used, block up bell housing so that end of pinion clears the floor.
11. Clamp compound mainshaft in vise with soft metal jaws or improvised holding device and assemble as follows: Slide HI-split floating gear and fixed clutch on front end of shaft, install clutch nut (left-hand threads) and tighten 400 to 500 ft.-lbs., then positive stake lip of nut to shaft in slot(s) provided. Install inner race of bearing on shaft spigot.
12. Slide LO-split floating gear on fixed clutch and install both parts on rear end of compound mainshaft. Install sliding clutch on fixed clutch. Install LO-LO-split gear sleeve on shaft then slide LO-LO floating gear on sleeve. Press bearing cone on shaft next to sleeve, install double-row cup, cone spacer and shims, then press rear cone on shaft. With a piece of tubing over flange splines, place assembly in a press and with a load on bearing cones, measure bearing end-play. Add or remove shims between cones until end-play is .003 to .007" as read on a dial gage,

MACK

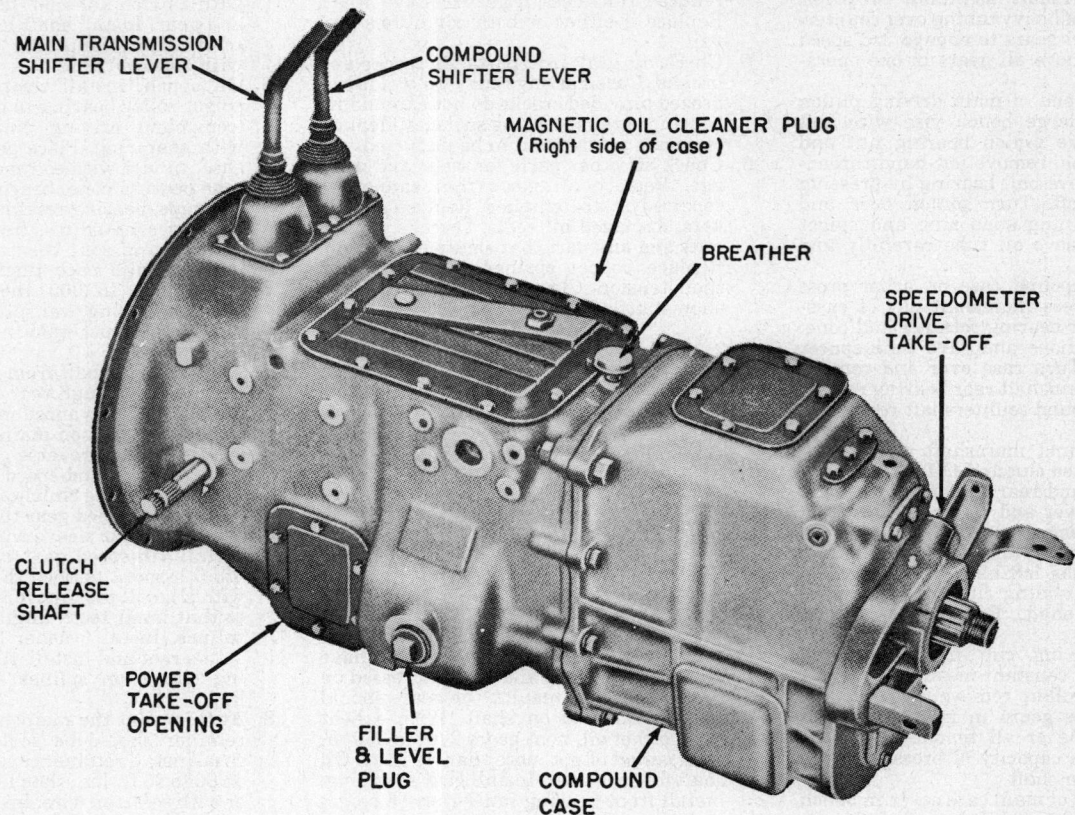

Fig. 6 Mack 20 speed TRQ-77 transmission

then remove double cup and rear bearing cone.

13. Slide HI-split clutch on its fixed clutch. Install interconnecting oil tube in end of mainshaft and carefully engage spigot of assembled compound mainshaft with oil tube and spigot bearing in end of mainshaft. *Be very careful not to damage oil tube as it engages compound mainshaft spigot.* Place compound countershaft (as-sembled earlier) on countershaft rear bearing cone and make sure all gears are properly meshed.

14. Paint end of main case with a good gasket sealer compound and install case-to-case gasket. Carefully lower compound case down over assembled parts and see that bearings are properly seated. Install case-to-case capscrews and dowel bolts. Tighten 90 to 100 ft.-lbs. Install double-row rear bearing cup in compound case. Install rear bearing cone and speedometer gear. Apply gasket sealer in case and gasket and install rear bearing retainer gasket. Install retainer and capscrews with lockwashers. Tighten capscrews 90 to 100 ft.-lbs. Dip drive flange oil seal in oil and install in rear bearing retainer. Install drive flange and nut. Return transmission to normal position.

15. Lock up gear train by engaging both sliding clutches of the compound gearset. Tighten drive flange nut 800 to 1200 ft.-lbs., then install nut cotter pin. Return all sliding clutches to their neutral positions.

16. Position main case cover in bench vise with soft metal jaws. Install transmission case breather and toggle shifter levers. Starting with 1st and reverse speed shifter rail, start rail in cover and shifter, with a small blunt tool compress detent ball and spring, push rail past compressed ball, through a shifter and into neutral position. Install large interlock pin next to rail just installed. Install 2nd and 3rd-speed rail in same manner. Install small interlock pin in 2nd and 3rd-speed rail then another large pin between. Install short 1st and reverse speed rail with fork then 4th and 5th-speed rail with fork and shifter. Install shifter and fork setscrews, tighten 45 to 50 ft.-lbs., then lock to shafts individually with soft iron wire. Install new Welch plugs in shifter rail openings. Remove from vise.

17. Place compound case cover in vise with soft metal jaws. Dip new rail oil seals in oil and install. Install LO-split rail in cover and fork. Install interlock pin between rails. Install HI-split rail in cover and fork. Install pipe plug in pin hole. Install fork setscrews and tighten 45 to 50 ft.-lbs. Remove cover from vise.

18. Apply gasket sealer compound to case openings and cover gaskets and install gaskets on cases. Position sliding gear and all sliding clutches in neutral position. Install both assembled covers and make sure the shifter forks engage the grooves in their mating parts. Install cover capscrews with lockwashers and tighten 55 to 60 ft.-lbs.

19. Apply sealer compound to all other cover gaskets and install covers and capscrews with lockwashers. Check for proper shifting and free rotation of gears. Install clutch release shaft, yoke bearing, return spring and any other external part that was removed for disassembly. Recheck all fasteners for correct torques and locking means. Install all plugs, then remove transmission from stand.

MACK 20 SPEED TRQ-77
Disassembly, Figs. 6 and 7

NOTE: Unless a complete overhaul is necessary, remove only those parts required to gain access to the faulty parts. Do not disturb parts having heavy press fits unless replacement is necessary. In that case, use proper press set-ups and pullers so that usable parts are not damaged. After cleaning all transmission parts with suitable solvent, inspect each part thoroughly. Replace worn or damaged parts, staked nuts, gaskets and cotter pins to avoid subsequent transmission failures.

1. After removing transmission from vehicle and cleaning externally, mount unit in a suitable overhaul stand. Remove hand brake parts, clutch release bearing assembly with return spring, clutch release shaft and yoke, P.T.O. covers and gear shifter hand control levers.

2. Remove ALL case covers and lay aside for bench disassembly. Engage sliding gear and ALL sliding clutches so that the entire gearset is locked up. Remove cotter pin from drive flange nut and then remove nut. Install standard puller and

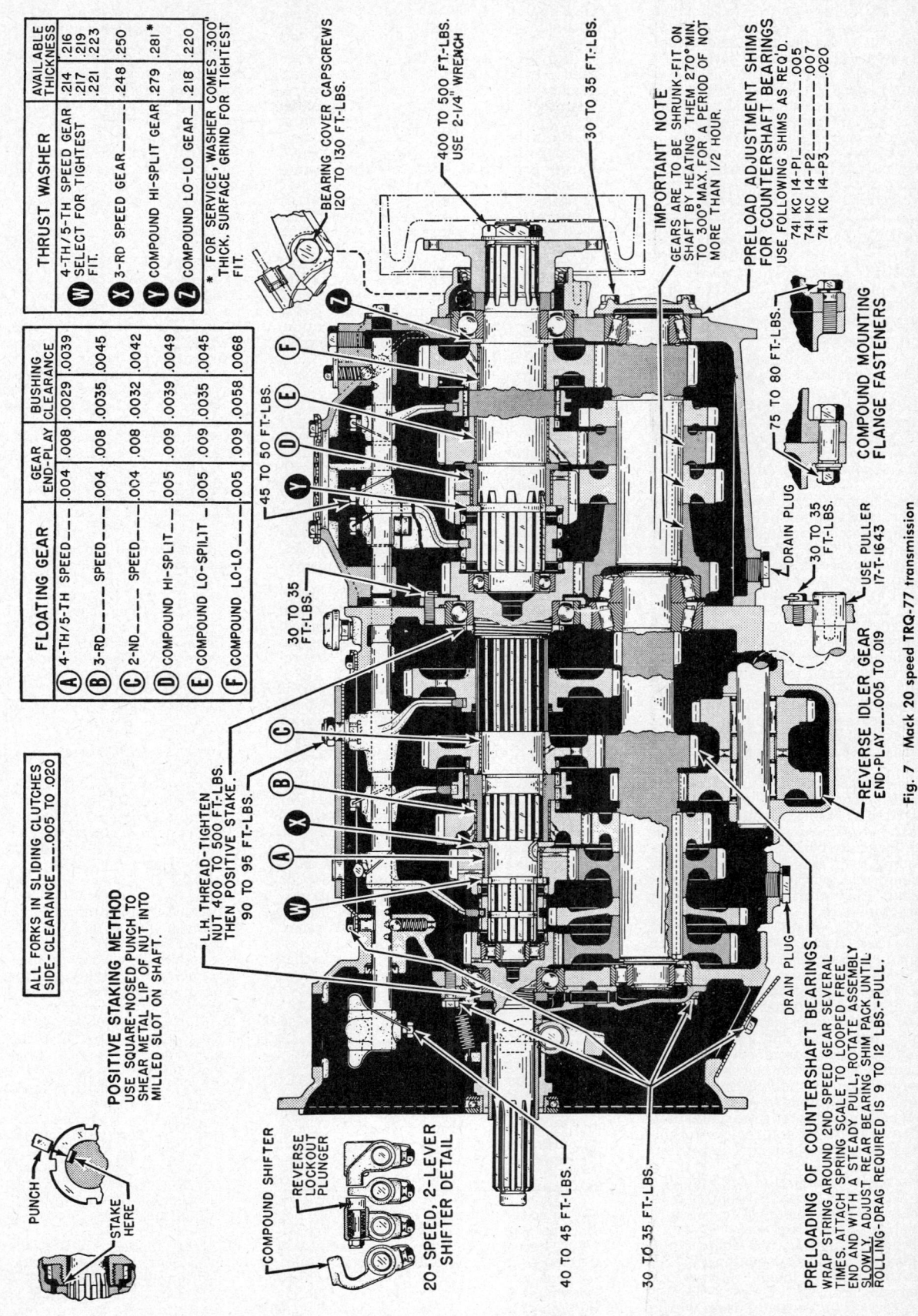

Fig. 7 Mack 20 speed TRQ-77 transmission

remove drive flange. Remove both rear bearing covers and save countershaft rear bearing shim pack intact. Slide speedometer gear off of mainshaft. Remove compound shifter rail ball poppet springs and balls. Through cover opening in top of compound case, remove setscrew from compound shifter control arm, withdraw long shifter rail from arm and both cases, then remove arm from compound case.

3. Remove setscrews from shifters and shifter forks in main case. Withdraw shifter rails from main case and at the same time remove shifters and shifter forks.

CAUTION: The spring-loaded balls under the shifter rails will fly out with CONSIDERABLE FORCE when released by withdrawing the rails. Therefore, it is advisable to hold a clean shop wiper over the holes while withdrawing the rails.

Be sure to save the balls, springs and rail interlock pin and balls for use at reassembly.

4. Remove all case-to-case dowels bolts and capscrews. With a large enough nylon headed mallet, tap compound case and separate it and the enclosed parts from the main case. Disassemble on clean bench.
5. Remove mainshaft rear bearing retainer capscrews and countershaft rear bearing snap ring. Remove main driving pinion bearing cover and countershaft front bearing cover capscrews. Remove bearing covers, connecting oil tube and tube seal as a unit and disassemble on bench.
6. Remove main driving pinion assembly from main case. Tap on gear end with nylon mallet if necessary to work it out of case. Clamp gear end securely in large bench vise with soft jaws. Unstake bearing nut and with wrench, remove nut. The threads are left-handed. Remove ball bearing by pressing or tapping off. Turn pinion over and remove retaining snap ring and spigot bearing from gear end of pinion.
7. Remove 4th/5th speed sliding clutch from mainshaft. Pry key out of mainshaft spline. With a small tool, rotate 4th speed gear thrust washer one spline and slide washer off of mainshaft.
8. Butt a soft drift against forward end of mainshaft and with a hammer, drive mainshaft rearward to separate rear bearing from case.
9. Carefully slide gears, sleeve, thrust washer, fixed clutch and sliding clutch from mainshaft while withdrawing mainshaft from rear of main case. Remove sleeve Woodruff key from mainshaft.
10. Clamp gear end of mainshaft securely in large bench vise with soft jaws. Remove retaining snap ring and pinion spigot bearing inner race from spigot end of mainshaft. Unstake rear bearing nut and with wrench, remove nut which also has a left-hand thread. Remove rear ball bearing and bearing retainer from mainshaft. Turn mainshaft over and remove retaining snap ring and compound mainshaft spigot bearing.
11. Remove reverse gear shaft lock and with puller 17-T-1643, withdraw gear shaft from case. Remove cluster gear, bearings and bearing spacer from case.
12. Slide countershaft rearward and partially through rear bearing opening. Install segmented puller on inside bearing cone and remove both cones. Remove countershaft case-mounted bearing parts with a soft steel drift. When using a drift, be very careful not to damage part of case and apply alternate equal blows to opposite sides to prevent cocking of part in the case.
13. Tilt forward end of countershaft upward and remove entire assembly from case. Remove countershaft front bearing retaining snap ring, bearing inner race and gear snap ring. For shops having a small hydraulic press, press off one countershaft gear at a time. For shops having a large capacity hydraulic press, place countershaft assembly in press, slide length of heavy tubing over countershaft integral gears to engage 3rd speed gear and remove all gears in one operation. Remove gear key.
14. Remove bearing cup from compound countershaft constant-mesh gear. With segmented puller, remove rear bearing cone. Remove gears in hydraulic press one at a time or all in one operation, depending on capacity of press. Remove gear key from shaft.

Inspection and Repair

1. Wash and clean all parts thoroughly in clean solvent and dry with moisture-free compressed air. Do not spin bearings with compressed air as damage to the bearing may result.
2. Replace bearings which are pitted and/or spalled. Replace lubricated bearings having excessive axial or radial clearances. Replace cases if outer races of bearings turn freely in case bores.
3. Replace gears having pitted or badly worn teeth. Replace gears with damaged internal or external teeth as a result of gear clashing. Floating gears having excessive radial clearance should be rebushed and bored to size.
4. Check all splines. If excessive wear is obvious, replace part or parts. Check thrust washers for scored surfaces or reduced thickness from excessive wear. Replace if either or both conditions prevail.
5. Check all gray iron parts for cracks and breaks. Case castings may be welded or brazed provided cracks do not extend into bearing bores or bolting surfaces. Replace or repair parts found to be damaged.
6. Check all other parts for wear and damage. Replace all parts that cannot be repaired or straightened. Replace all gaskets, damaged oil seals, O-rings, staked nuts and any part that shows mutilation. Replace poppet springs that have lost their tension. Clean up any threads that show mutilation.

Reassembly

NOTE: All working parts, especially the bearings, should be generously coated with SAE-30 oil while the transmission is being assembled. This will assure immediate lubrication when first starting and will prevent seizing of these parts. As moving parts are assembled, check frequently to see that they move freely.

Gaskets: So that the same instructions do not have to be repeated for every operation, we will state here that ALL new cover gaskets at final assembly are to be coated on BOTH sides with a good gasket sealer. When the attaching capscrews are tightened to their recommended torque values, the sealer will assure leakproof joints between the covers and the case. The metal shell of oil seals that contact whatever retains them, should also be coated lightly with a good gasket sealing compound before installation.

In most cases, it is easier to coat metal parts rather than the gasket. The dry gasket can be placed in position on the transmission case since the sealing compound is adhesive enough to hold the gasket until the cover is attached over it and fastened by capscrews.

As a further measure against oil leakage, additional sealing compound should be applied around the entire joint of each cover under which there is either a shim pack or a gasket.

1. Insert gear key in countershaft and press gears on one at a time. These gears have an interference fit and can be pressed on cold but for best results, the gears should be shrunk-fitted on shaft. With a heat lamp or hot oil, heat gears 270° to 300° F. for a period of not more than 1/2 hour. Oil shaft for each gear. Install gear snap ring, install front bearing inner race on spigot and retain with its snap ring.
2. Install countershaft front bearing in case. Place countershaft assembly in case with small end extending out of rear bearing opening. Install rear bearing cup in case. Install tapered roller bearings back-to-back on rear end of countershaft and retain with its snap ring. Position countershaft in front bearing.
3. Insert gear key in compound countershaft and press gears on one at a time. These gears have an interference fit and can be pressed on cold but for best results, the gears should be shrunk-fitted on shaft. With a heat lamp or hot oil, heat gears 270° to 300° F. for a period of not more than 1/2 hour. Oil shaft for each gear. Press bearing cup in front end of compound countershaft constant-mesh gear and bearing cone on rear end. Push countershaft rear bearing cup in compound case and install shim pack and bearing cover. Temporarily assemble compound countershaft, case-to-case gasket and compound case to the main case and countershaft.
4. Preload countershaft bearings as follows: Lubricate all bearings with SAE-30 oil. Wrap a string around countershaft 2nd-speed gear (largest integral gear) several times. Attach a spring scale to looped free end of string and with a steady pull, rotate the assembly SLOWLY. Repeat this operation and adjust thickness of rear bearing shim pack until the rolling-drag of 9 to 12 lbs.-pull is read on the scale. When correct shim pack thickness is established, remove compound case and compound cluster gear from main case. Then continue reassembly of main case.
5. Position reverse cluster gear shaft so that slot in end of shaft will permit shaft lock to engage it. Start shaft into case. Make sure that gear is not in reversed position. Assemble roller bearings and spacer in cluster gear. Position assembled gear in case and with a nylon hammer, tap shaft into case and gear. Install shaft lock and lock capscrew with soft iron wire after tightening 30 to 35 ft.-lbs.
6. On bench, install compound, mainshaft spigot ball bearing in end of mainshaft (compound driving pinion). Place gear end of mainshaft in vise with soft metal jaws. Place mainshaft rear bearing retainer on shaft, then install bearing. Install bearing nut (left-hand thread) and tighten 400 to 500 ft.-lbs. Positive stake lip of nut into slot or slots provided in the mainshaft for this purpose. Install bearing inner race on mainshaft spigot and

MACK

7. Remove mainshaft from vise and start in main case through rear bearing hole. As mainshaft is advanced into working position, slide parts on mainshaft as follows: 1st speed gear, 2nd speed gear, 3rd speed fixed and sliding clutches, 3rd speed gear, thrust washer Woodruff key, thrust washer, 4th/5th speed gear sleeve, gear and thrust washer. At this point, the mainshaft rear bearing should be seated in the main case. Install bearing retainer capscrews and tighten capscrews 30 to 35 ft.-lbs., then lock heads together with soft iron wire.

8. With a small tool, move 4th/5th speed gear thrust washer one tooth so that inner teeth align with mainshaft splines. Install washer key in deepened spline root and slide 4th/5th speed sliding clutch on splines and over inlaid key.

9. Assemble mainshaft spigot bearing in gear end of main driving pinion and retain with snap ring. Turn pinion over and place in vise with soft metal jaws. Install pinion ball bearing and bearing nut. Tighten nut (left-hand thread) 400 to 500 ft.-lbs. then positive stake lip of nut to pinion in slot provided. Install pinion assembly in transmission case. On bench, insert oil tube in main driving pinion bearing cover, slide rubber seal over tube and then assemble countershaft front bearing cover on free end of oil tube so that this assembly is ready to be installed on the main case as an assembly. Apply a good gasket sealer to the case and position bearing cover gaskets on case so that capscrew holes are aligned. (The sealer will hold the gaskets in place.) Apply gasket sealer to contacting surfaces of bearing covers and install covers over bearings. Install capscrews with lock-washers and tighten pinion cover and countershaft bearing cover capscrews 30 to 35 ft.-lbs.

10. At this point, the main case should be positioned in a vertical position with the pinion pointing downward. If overhaul stand is not used, block up bell housing so that end of pinion clears the floor.

11. Position compound mainshaft in arbor press with spigot end down. Slide LO-LO split floating gear and thrust washer on shaft. Remove snap ring from outer race of ball bearing and press bearing on shaft. Remove assembly from press and clamp in bench vise with soft metal jaws so that spigot end is up. Install LO/LO-LO split sliding clutch on splined shoulder of shaft. Slide LO-split floating gear and HI-split floating gear with sleeve on front end of compound mainshaft. Slide splined HI-split floating gear thrust washer on splines of compound mainshaft until it engages sleeve. With a small tool move thrust washer one tooth so that inner teeth align with mainshaft splines. Install washer key in deepened spline root so that it engages thrust washer and slot in HI-split floating gear sleeve. Slide DIRECT/HI-split sliding clutch on splined front end of compound mainshaft and over inlaid key, thus locking key in position. This sliding clutch is marked DIRECT on one end and it is *very important* that this end be assembled so that it will engage the driving pinion (mainshaft).

12. Loosen vise and hold assembled parts together while transferring assembled unit from bench to upright transmission. Install spigot end in ball bearing in gear end of driving pinion (mainshaft). Place previously assembled compound countershaft upright on rear bearing cone of main box countershaft and make sure all compound gears are properly meshed.

13. Paint end of main case with a good gasket sealer compound and install case-to-case gasket. Paint rim of gasket with sealer and lower compound case down over assembled shafts. Tap case into position so that bearings are seated properly, then install case-to-case capscrews and dowel bolts and tighten 75 to 80 ft.-lbs. Reinstall snap ring in outer race of compound mainshaft rear ball bearing. Install speedometer drive gear on shaft. Apply sealer compound and install rear bearing cover gasket and cover. Install cover capscrews with washers and tighten 120 to 130 ft.-lbs. Apply sealer compound to metal part of drive flange oil seal and install seal in rear bearing cover. Oil lip of seal, install drive flange and nut. Return transmission to normal position.

14. Lock up gear train by engaging sliding gear and all sliding clutches. Tighten flange nut 400 to 500 ft.-lbs. Install nut cotter pin.

15. Oil and install shifter oil seals in main case. On bench, install shifters on shaft ends. Starting with 1st and reverse speed shifter shaft, install spring and poppet ball in case, start shaft in case and with a blunt tool, compress spring-loaded detent ball and at the same time push shaft over ball. Engage 1st speed fork in sliding gear and push shifter shaft through fork hub and all the way into working position. Install fork setscrew, tighten and lock with soft iron wire. Install shifter shaft interlock ball next to shaft just installed, install poppet spring and ball in case for 2nd/3rd speed shaft, compress spring-loaded detent ball and pass 2nd/3rd speed shaft over it. Install interlock pin in shaft, engage 2nd/3rd speed fork with sliding clutch then push shaft on through and secure fork. Install interlock ball next to pin, start 4th/5th speed shifter shaft in case, compress detent spring-loaded ball and push shaft over it. Engage fork with 4th/5th speed sliding clutch and push shaft on through to working position. Secure fork to shaft. Tighten all shifter and fork set screws 45 to 50 ft.-lbs. Then lock with soft iron wire.

16. Through opening in top of compound case, install DIRECT/HI-split shifter fork in groove provided in sliding clutch. Also install LO/LO-LO split shifter fork in groove provided in its sliding clutch. Hold LO-LO split shifter fork in working position and insert its shift rail in compound case from the rear. Push rod in case and through hole in fork. Also hold rail shifter in working position and push rail through hole provided in shifter. Install setscrews in shifter and shifter fork. Make sure tapered end of setscrews enter locating detents in rail, then shift into neutral position. Install rail interlock ball in space provided between rails. While holding previously installed DIRECT/HI-split shifter fork in working position, insert its shift rail in compound case from the rear and push through hole provided in fork. Install fork setscrew and shift rail to neutral position.

17. Insert long compound control shift rail in hole provided in main case and push rearward until end appears at compound case. Engage compound control shifter arm in compound shifter slots and hold in working position. Continue pushing on long shift rail until it passes through control arm and into rear support hole. Install control arm setscrew. Tighten all four shifter and fork setscrews 40 to 50 ft.-lbs., then lock each setscrew to its rail with soft iron wire. Install compound shift detent balls and springs in holes provided at rear of case over the rails. Apply sealer to spring cover and rail end cover. Install gaskets, cover and capscrews with washers. Tighten capscrews 30 to 35 ft.-lbs.

18. Install travel-limiting pins for the shifter rails in holes provided. Check for free rotation of gears. Apply sealer compound to cover gasket and install on case. Assemble shifter toggle(s) to cover and install case cover. Install clutch release shaft, yoke, bearing return spring and any other external part that was removed for disassembly. Recheck all fasteners for correct torques. Install all plugs, then remove transmission from stand.

MACK 5 & 10 SPEED

In overhauling these transmissions, refer to Figs. 8, 9 and 10 and to the text which follows. Do not disturb sub-assemblies more than necessary to inspect parts and make repairs.

Disassembly

1. Remove case cover.
2. Lock gears by engaging two sliding clutches and remove drive flange.
3. On five speed units, remove mainshaft rear bearing cover.
4. Remove shifter rails and forks from main transmission.
5. Remove clutch collar, yoke and shaft.
6. On ten speed units, remove case-to-case capscrews and separate compound from main case.
7. On mono-shift units, remove shift cylinder and piston before separating cases. The internal parts of the monoshift compound cannot be removed with the case because the forward synchronizer is retained by the main transmission mainshaft. Tap shift rail and mainshaft as cases are separated. Then disassemble synchronizer as necessary to remove mainshaft and cluster gear.
8. Remove drive pinion bearing cover together with forward countershaft bearing cover.
9. On units with direct drive on fifth, pull drive pinion together with bearing forward from case.
10. Remove mainshaft rear bearing retainer and slide mainshaft rearward as far as possible. Slide 4th and 5th speed clutch from shaft. Pry key from mainshaft spline and remove star washer from floating gear. Slide remaining parts from mainshaft as shaft is withdrawn through rear bearing opening in case.
11. Remove reverse idler gear cluster.
12. Remove bearing covers and lower countershaft.
13. On units with direct drive on fourth, the main drive pinion may now be removed by detaching the bearing retainer ring and withdrawing the bearing and pinion assembly through inside of case.
14. On ten-speed units, to pull the bearing for countershaft removal, make split bearing cup and retainer ring to fit over forward bearing rollers.
15. Tilt forward end of countershaft upward and remove assembly from case.

Sub-Assemblies

Compound Mainshaft—On two-stick jobs,

1323

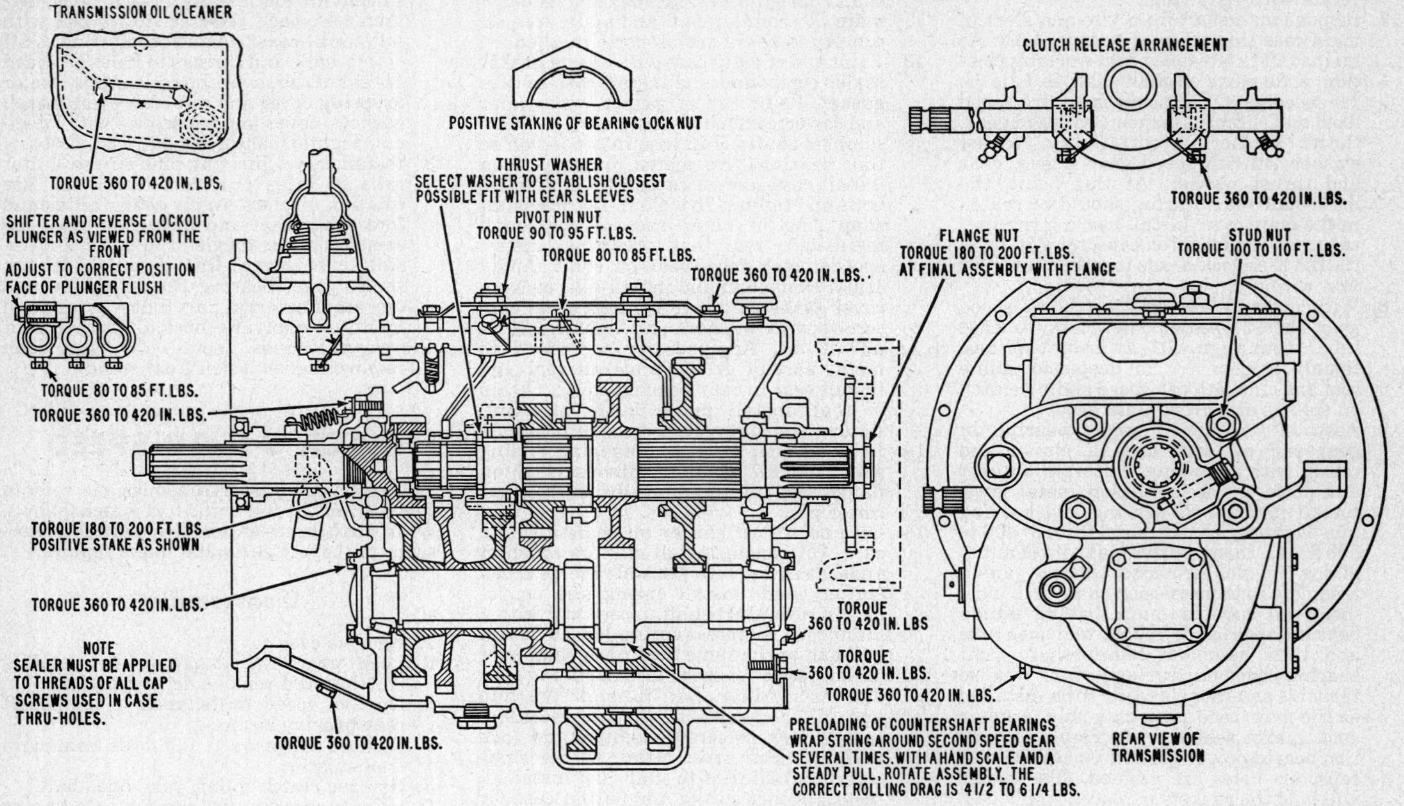

MACK

Fig. 8 Mack five speed transmission

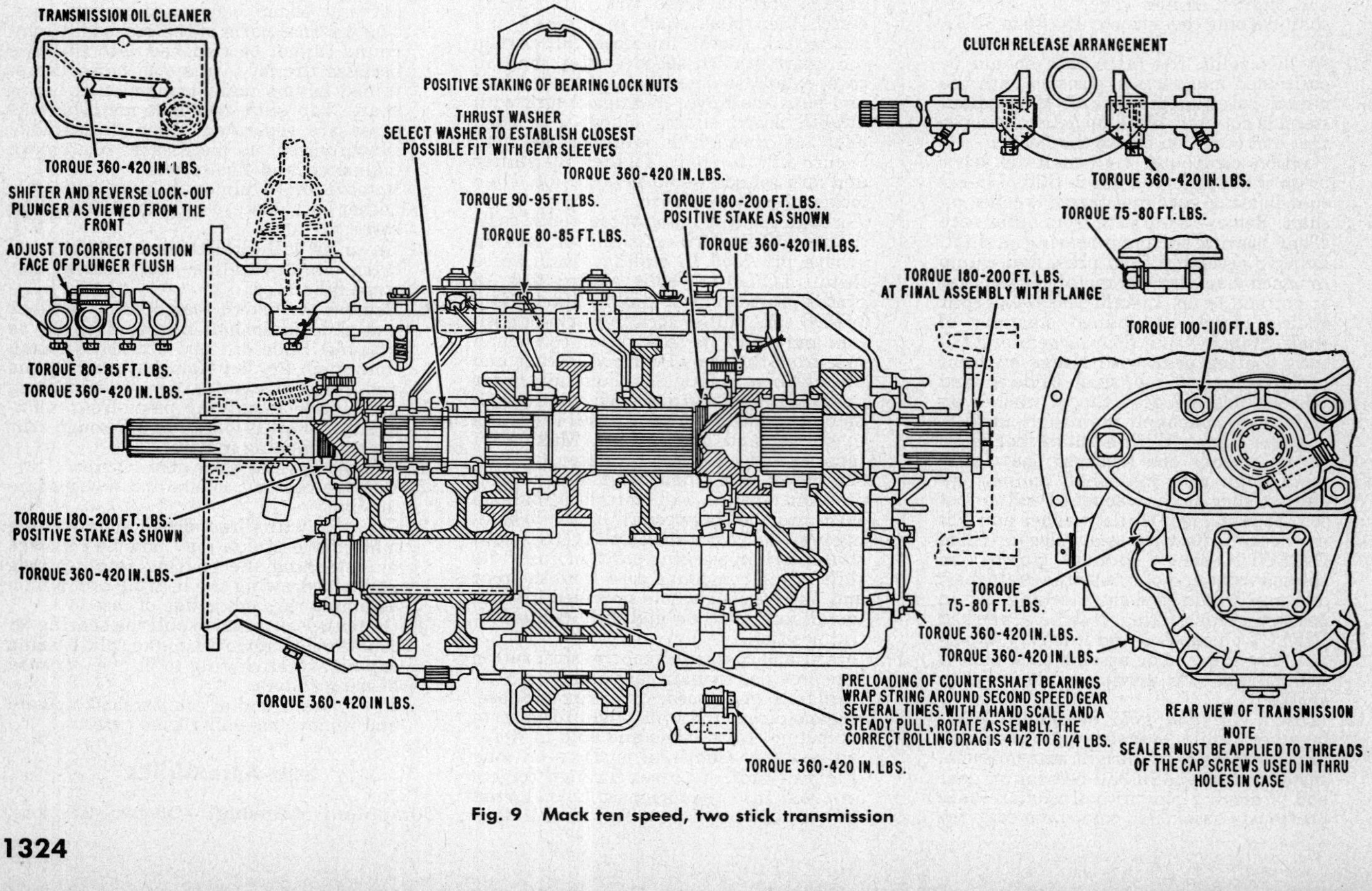

Fig. 9 Mack ten speed, two stick transmission

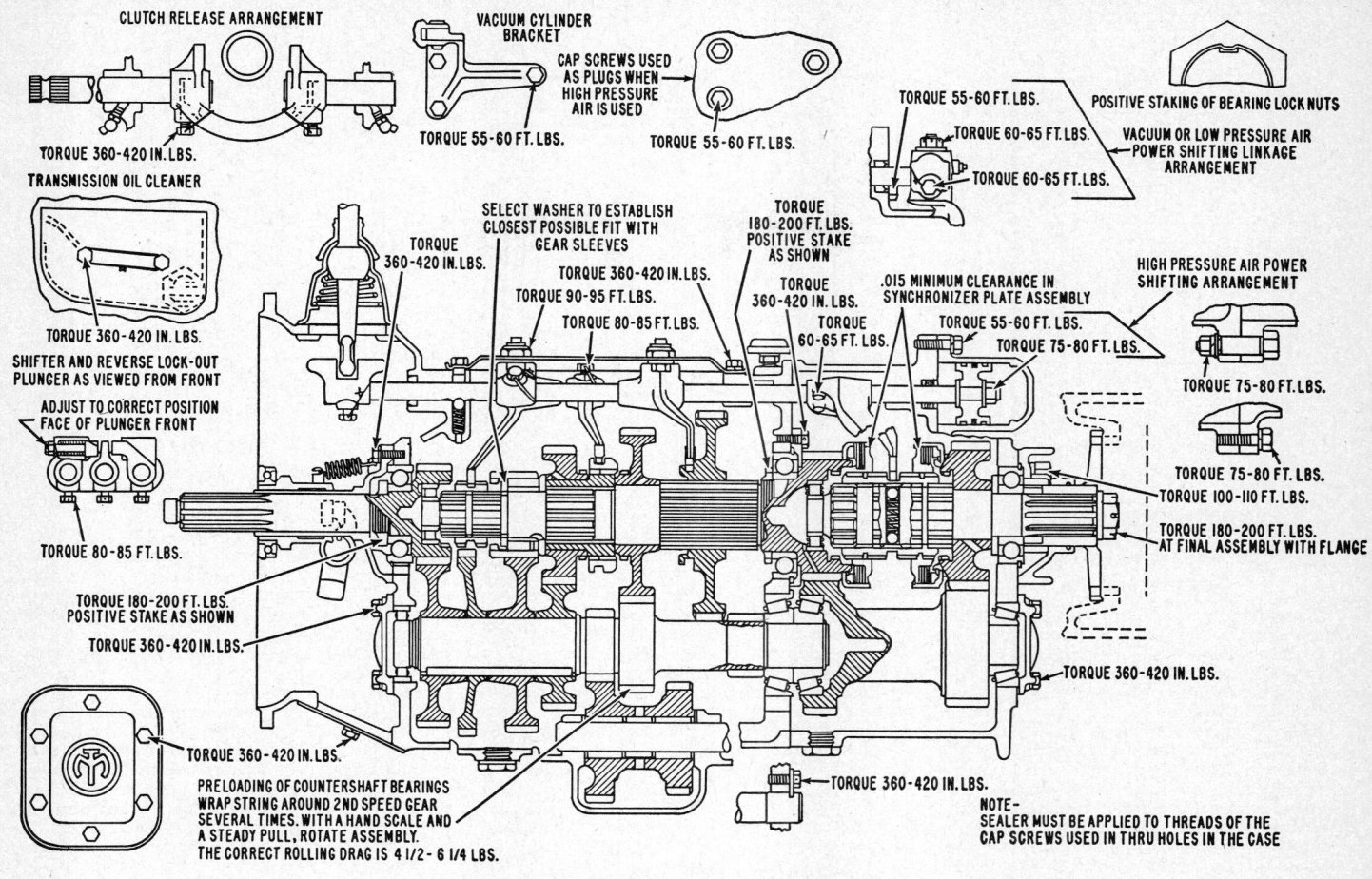

Fig. 10 Mack ten speed monoshift transmission

support floating gear on heavy tubing. Then press shaft through bearing and case.

Countershaft Gears—Remove countershaft front bearing inner race and gear snap ring from shaft. Slide length of heavy tubing over countershaft to engage 3rd speed gear. Place assembly in 75-ton press and remove all gears in one operation. Mated gears, if defective, must be replaced in matched sets.

Floating Gear Bushings—Be sure to align oil holes. Press bushings in .010" to .015" below face of bore and force bushing into four notches before burnishing. Lubricate broach with a water soluble oil mixture. Recess opposite end of bushing .035" to .040" after burnishing and then break sharp corner of bushing.

Reassembly

1. Lubricate all moving parts during assembly to insure initial lubrication when first run. As moving parts are assembled, check frequently to see that they are free.
2. Position countershaft and gear assembly in case.
3. Install countershaft bearing components (also compound case and countershaft when 10-speed) with trial shim pack under rear bearing cover. Wrap cord around 2nd speed gear and check for 9¼ to 12¼ lb. rolling drag. Make corrections by changing shim selection. Remove compound case and countershaft to allow installation of mainshaft.
4. Install main drive pinion.
5. Install reverse idler gear cluster.
6. Start mainshaft from rear of case and slide mainshaft components into place as shaft enters case, checking end play and clearance of components as assembly progresses.
7. On 10-speed units, assemble compound mainshaft and countershaft. When monoshift, be sure each synchronizer pack has .020" to .040" clearance.
8. Install shifter rails and forks, compound case (10-speed), case cover, bearing covers and drive flange.
9. Assemble clutch release collar on driving shaft pinion. Then install release shaft and yoke.

Shift Rail Rocker Pivot Pin, Adjust

The shifter mechanism includes a 1st and reverse shift rail rocker, carried by an adjustable eccentric pivot pin mounted in the transmission case cover. This arrangement not only shortens the shift into first speed and eliminates the awkward U-shift from 1st to 2nd speed as in some shift patterns, but at the same time, equalizes the travel length of each shift by bringing all forward shifts into orderly progression.

In overdrive transmissions, an additional rocker and pivot pin to operate the 4th and 5th speed sliding clutch, converts the shift pattern of these transmissions to that of the direct-drive units. Thus, either type of transmission has the same standard shift.

1. With engine running at idle speed and with hand shifter lever in neutral position, loosen the shift rail rocker pivot pin lock nut and adjust the pin as follows:
2. Left illustration, Fig. 11. Rotate pin to fore and aft position in one direction. If no gear clash is felt or heard, rotate pin to fore and aft position in the opposite direction. If no gear clash is felt or heard in either extreme eccentric position of the pin, reverse the rotation of the pin until flats are 90° to the transmission centerline and lock the pin in the halfway position.
3. Center illustration, Fig. 11. If gear clash is felt or heard in one direction and not in the fore and aft position in the opposite direction, move the pin back to the midpoint between point of gear clash and the fore and aft position. Lock pin at this midpoint.
4. Right illustration, Fig. 11. If gear clash is felt or heard in both directions, note position of flats, and position the pin midway between points of gear clash and lock in this position.

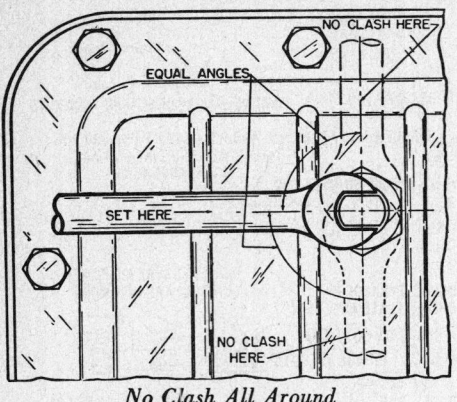 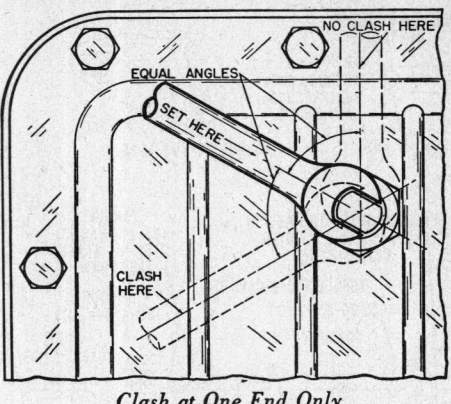 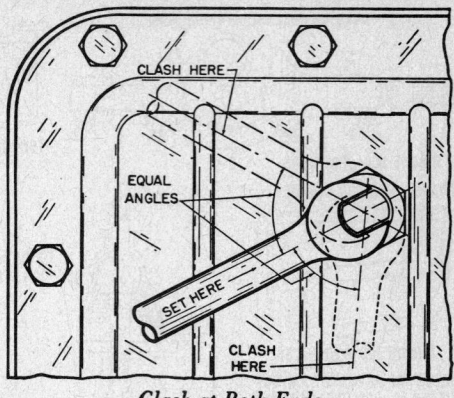

No Clash All Around — *Clash at One End Only* — *Clash at Both Ends*

Fig. 11 Adjustment of shift rail rocker eccentric pivot pin

MACK TRL-107
Five Speed with Three Countershafts

This transmission, Figs. 12 to 15, is a triple countershaft unit providing five speeds forward and one reverse. The five speed gearset is housed in an aluminum case that is constructed in two pieces for convenience of disassembly and reassembly.

Three countershafts are equally spaced around the input shaft. By distributing the load equally between three shafts, normal deflection is reduced to a minimum. The mainshaft gears are self-centered between the three countershafts, eliminating the need for gear bushings. The mainshaft gears are connected to the mainshaft only when engaged by a sliding clutch.

As shown in Fig. 15, all gears are of the spur type design and, with the exception of the reverse speed sliding gear, are in constant mesh with the countershaft gears. Other than reverse, driving engagement for the five forward speeds is effected by means of sliding clutches. Reverse is obtained by engaging reverse sliding spur gear with the three individually mounted idler gears. Conventional forks spanning the sliding clutches and reverse gear move these parts in response to the movement of the gear shifter and hand control lever.

A single row ball bearing supports the main driving pinion. The mainshaft is supported by a roller spigot bearing at the front end and a ball bearing at the rear. The countershafts are carried by a ball bearing and roller bearing combination. Ball bearings that are snap ring type provide shaft location, while the roller bearing is located adjacent to the more heavily loaded low range gears. In constant mesh with the countershafts, each of the three reverse idler gears revolves on a roller bearing mounted on a shaft.

Lubrication

All rotating and sliding parts of the transmission are bathed in oil from gear throw off when the engine is operating. However, the sliding clutches and mainshaft gears require more positive provision for lubrication, and for this reason, pressure lubrication of the clutches and gears is provided by a simple eccentric shuttle type pump built in the main driving pinion. As the pinion rotates the pump vane reciprocates in its eccentric housing, thus forcing lubricant under pressure through rifle drilled holes in the mainshaft to the sliding clutches and mainshaft gears. To supply the pump, oil from gear throw-off is collected by a trough located above the main driving pinion and is then gravity fed to the pump.

Removal of all foreign metallic particles within the transmission accomplished by two magnetic oil filters, one on each side of the case. The filter consists of an integral open trough and baffle arrangement with a removable sheet metal cover. At the bottom of the baffle, a tapped hole in the case accommodates a large hex plug with a built-in magnet installed from outside.

The oil from gear throw-off is collected by the filter and is made to pass the magnetic plugs that pull all ferrous metal particles out of the passing oil and holds them. After passing the magnet, clean and chip-free oil that rises to the outlet near the top of the filter and drops down into the transmission case. A magnetic drain plug is provided at the bottom of the case.

When the oil is hot, as when coming in from a run, the oil level of the transmission should be checked with the vehicle on level ground. To add oil, remove plug on right side of case and fill. The level should not be above the filler plug hole. At every check or change, always remove, clean and reinstall magnetic plugs on right and left side of case.

To change oil, remove magnetic drain plug and drain oil from case while hot. If necessary, also flush case with flushing oil and drain thoroughly. Clean and replace magnetic drain plug in case. Remove fill plug and fill with

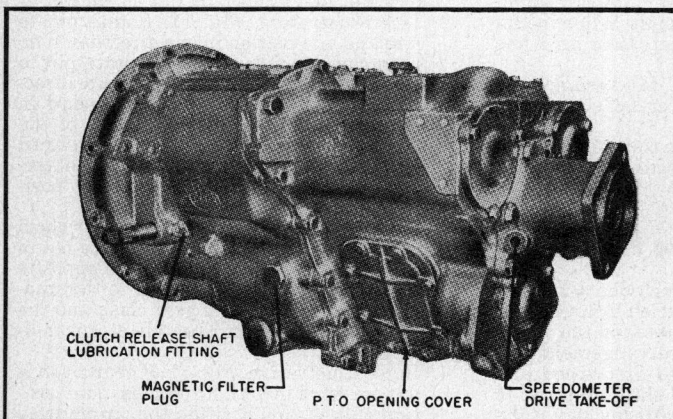

Fig. 13 Left rear view of Mack TRL-107 transmission

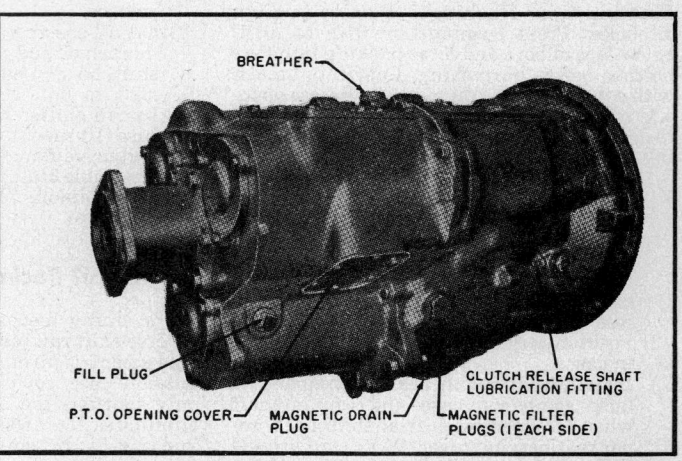

Fig. 14 Right rear view of Mack TRL-107 transmission

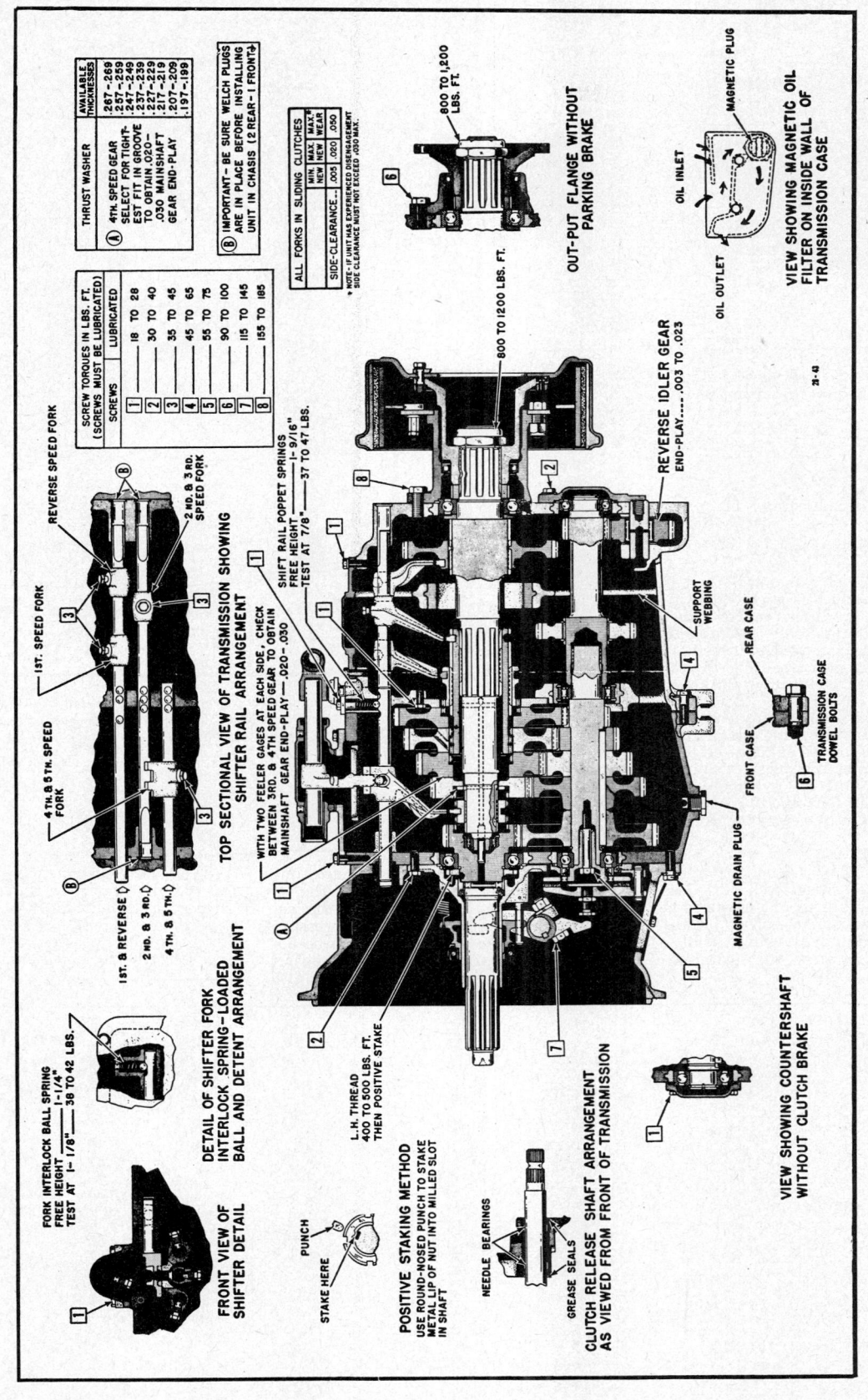

Fig. 12 Mack TRL-107 five speed triple countershaft transmission

MACK

Fig. 15 Skeletal view of Mack TRL-107 gearset (in support plates)

mild extreme pressure SAE-90 gear oil, year-round grade, to level of filler plug hole.

Clutch Brake, Fig. 16

In any unsynchronized transmission, the rapidity with which an upshift can be made is limited by the time it takes for the free-spinning clutch disc and countershaft assemblies to slow down to the slower rotating speed of the transmission mainshaft. In order to reduce this time element, Mack Clutch Brake is employed.

The clutch brake is assembled on the transmission lower countershaft, and since the countershaft is always connected to the clutch disc through the constant mesh driving pinion, action of the brake will overcome the tendency of the discs to continue to rotate at high speed when the clutch is disengaged.

Clutch Brake, Adjust

Remove inspection hole cover on bottom of bell housing. Loosen set screw lock nut. Depress clutch pedal to within 1/2" to 1" of the end of its travel. Adjust set screw so that brake pressure plate and lining assembly firmly contacts flange. Lock set screw with lock nut and install inspection hole cover.

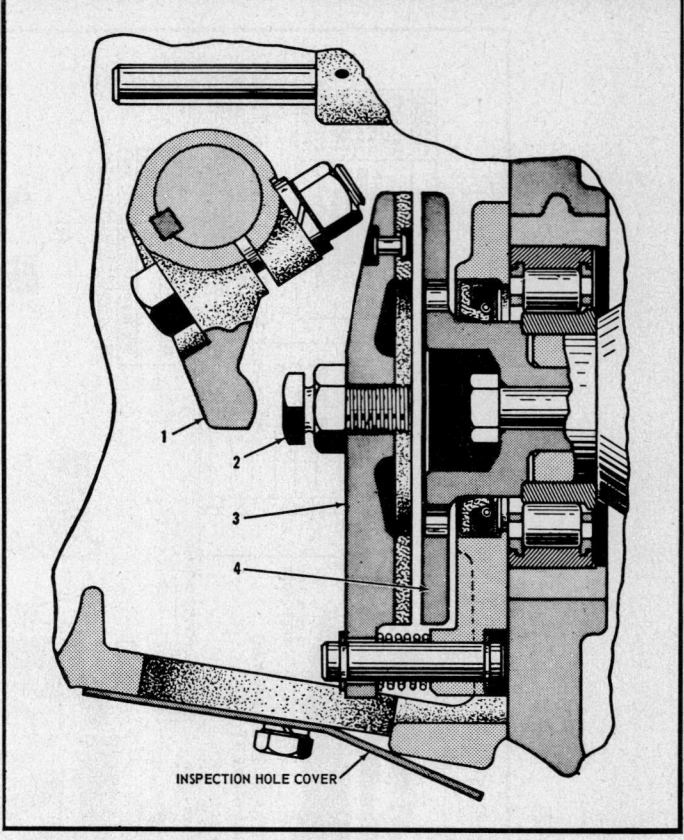

Fig. 16 Sectional view of Mack Clutch Brake. 1. Clutch throwout lever. 2. Adjusting screw. 3. Pressure plate and lining assembly. 4. Flange

NOTE: It must be remembered that each time a clutch adjustment is made to provide the 1/8" to 3/16" release bearing clearance, the set screw, which pushes the clutch brake pressure plate and lining assembly, must also be adjusted to suit location of clutch throwout lever. When initial wear on clutch driven disc has been used up and the spacers are to be removed, first move the set screw in to allow sufficient clearance with the throwout lever; then remove adjusting spacers. When the clutch cover is tightened down, readjust release bearing and clutch brake properly.

MACK

Rear Axle Section

NOTE: For Timken (Rockwell) driving axles, see the Timken chapter for service procedures

REAR AXLES

Mack Unit No.①	Type	Oil, Pts.
RAS-201	S.R.	8
RAS-202	S.R.	20
RAS-301	S.R.	26
RAS-507	S.R.	32
RAS-508	S.R.	32
RAS-509	S.R.	32
RAS-512	S.R.	32
RAD-111	D.R.	26
RAD-1141	D.R.	26
RAD-302	D.R.	31
RAD-303	D.R.	31
RAD-507	D.R.	31
RAD-508	D.R.	31
RAD-509	D.R.	31
RAD-512	D.R.	31
RAD-515	D.R.	31
RA2D-201②	2 Sp. D.R.	26
RA2D-301②	2 Sp. D.R.	29
RA2D-507②	2 Sp. D.R.	29
RA2D-508②	2 Sp. D.R.	29
RA2D-509②	2 Sp. D.R.	29
RA2D-510②	2 Sp. D.R.	34
RA2D-511②	2 Sp. D.R.	34
RA2D-512②	2 Sp. D.R.	29
RA2D-513②	2 Sp. D.R.	34
RA2D-514②	2 Sp. D.R.	34
SWS-50	Bogie	24③
SWD-32	Bogie	22½③
SWD-322	Bogie	22½③
SWDR-48	Bogie	31③
SWD-52-3-4	Bogie	8③
SWD-55-6-7-8	Bogie	8③
SWD-59	Bogie	22½③

①—Number located on axle housing.
②—This is a Timken axle.
③—Each axle.
S.R.—Single reduction. D.R.—Double reduction.
2-Sp. D.R.—Two-speed double reduction.

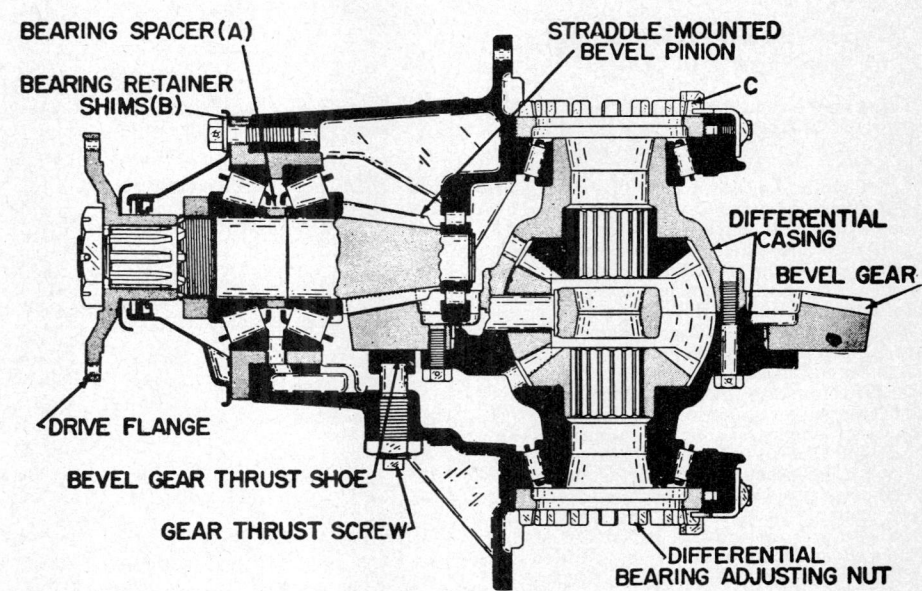

Fig. 1 Typical Mack single-reduction rear axle with straddle-mounted pinion

SINGLE REDUCTION AXLES

Type With Straddle-Mounted Pinion, Fig. 1

These single-reduction axle carriers have either a spiral bevel or hypoid gearset. Machined bosses on the differential bearing pedestal caps register against corresponding machined diameters in the axle housing to restrict pedestal deflection and thus insure proper meshing of the gearset under load.

The pinion and side gears of the four-pinion type differential are backed up by bronze washers to take the thrust, and the pinion gears are bronze bushed to the spider. These parts are enclosed in a differential case consisting of two mated halves bolted together, carried in a pair of tapered roller bearings. The bearings are mounted in the pedestals and can be adjusted by nuts at the outer cups. These nuts also permit positioning of the ring gear for proper tooth contact. Body-fitted capscrews secure the ring gear to the differential case.

The drive pinion is straddle-mounted, with

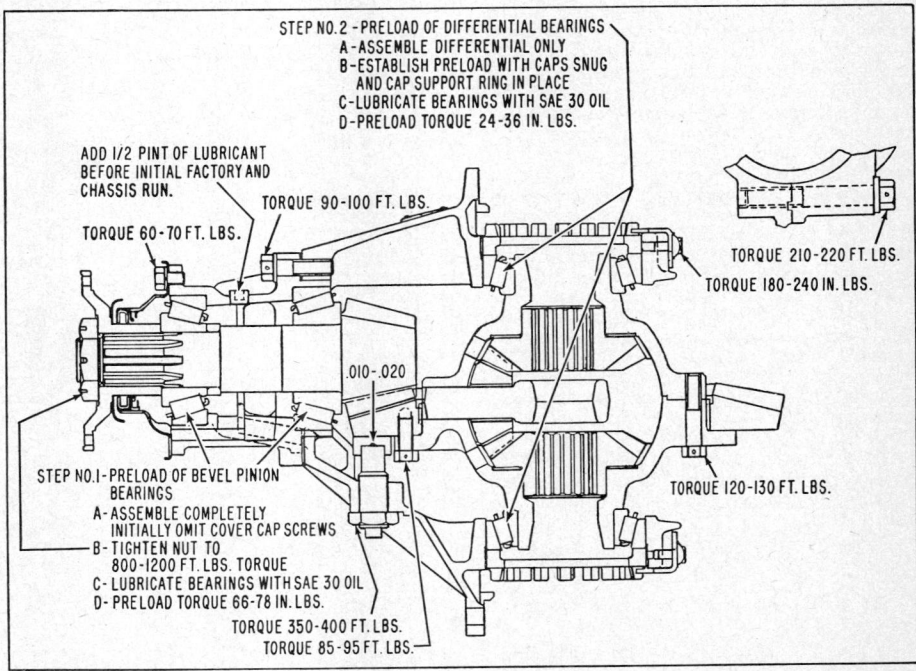

Fig. 2 Mack single-reduction carrier showing bearing preloads and screw torques

1329

MACK

a spigot bearing at the gear end. Two tapered roller bearings, back-to-back and carried in a separable housing, support the drive flange end and restrict end thrust. Bearing adjustment is obtained by varying the length of the spacer between the bearing cones, and tooth contact is adjusted by shims between the carrier and pinion bearings.

Deflection of the ring gear under load is restrained by an adjustable shoe, in back of the gear, opposite the point of contact with the drive pinion.

As a guide in servicing these axles, see the procedure outlined in the *Rear Axles* chapter for Timken Single-Reduction units.

Type Without Pinion Spigot Bearings, Figs. 2 & 3

These single-reduction axle carriers have a spiral bevel gearset. A separate housing, attached to the carrier housing by capscrews, is the mounting for the tapered roller bearings which carry the drive pinion. The ring gear and three-pinion differential are supported by another pair of tapered roller bearings mounted in the carrier housing differential bearing pedestals. Positively torqued capscrews are used in all bolting locations, thus eliminating the use of studs or bolts.

Machined bosses on the pedestal bearing caps register against corresponding machined diameters in the axle housing to restrict pedestal deflection and thus insure proper meshing of the gearset under load. Deflection of the ring gear under load is restrained by an adjustable shoe in back of the gear, opposite the point of contact with the drive pinion.

The drive pinion bearing arrangement has been designed so as to take the thrust load developed without endwise movement of the pinion. Bearing adjustment is obtained by varying the length of the spacer between the outer bearing cone and the shaft shoulder. Gear tooth contact is adjusted by varying the shim pack thickness between the carrier and drive pinion housings and adjusting the position of the ring gear.

The differential pinion and side gears are backed up by bronze washers to take the thrust, and the pinion gears are bronze bushed to the spider. The casing halves are machined with thick-walled steel forgings having wide, mated bolting flanges. A ring of capscrews clamp the casing halves together and thus form a rigid enclosure for the differential parts. This type of casing construction distributes driving torque and pressures equally. The left-hand differential casing has a splined pilot which engages internal splines of the ring gear. Another ring of capscrews attach the gear to the left-hand casing bolting flange. Driving torque is transmitted from the ring gear through the splines to the differential, thus relieving the gear capscrews of any shearing action. Slotted adjusting nuts, which bear against the differential bearing cups, are threaded to the pedestals to provide for the preloading of these bearings and also provide a means of positioning the ring gear for proper tooth contact.

One involute spline on the differential casing flanged half and the mating involute space on the ring gear are marked to facilitate aligning the ring gear bolt holes when assembling.

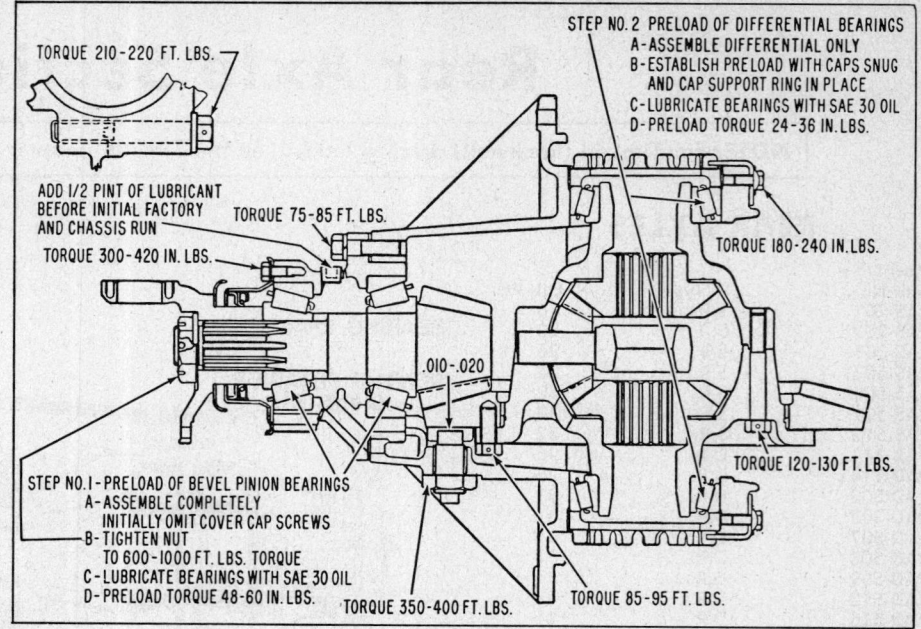

Fig. 3 Mack CRS-76 single-reduction carrier showing bearing preloads and screw torques

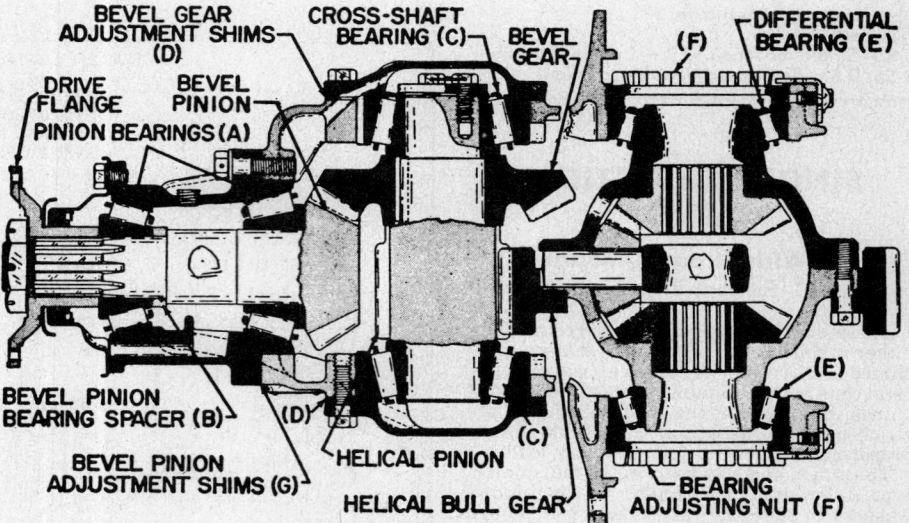

Fig. 4 Typical Mack double-reduction axle carrier

MACK

DOUBLE REDUCTION AXLES

A typical Mack double-reduction carrier is shown in Fig. 4. It has a spiral bevel gearset for the first reduction and helical gears for the second reduction.

Tapered roller bearings are provided throughout. And as is the case with the single-reduction carrier described above, the pinion bearings are preloaded by varying the length of the spacer between the bearings, and differential bearings are preloaded by adjusting nuts. The cross shaft bearings are preloaded by proper selection of shims. Proper pinion and ring gear tooth contact is obtained by varying shim packs "G" and "D", Fig. 4.

As a guide to servicing these carriers, see the *Rear Axle* chapter for double reduction repair procedures. Figs. 5 and 6 show the bearing preloads and screw torque requirements on two models of these carriers.

TANDEM AXLES

These tandem double-reduction axle carriers each have a spiral bevel gearset for the first reduction, spur gears for second reduction, and a three-pinion type differential. In addition, the forward carrier has an inter-axle power divider which consists of a driving cage, plungers, male and female cams. The driving cage carries two rows of stagger-indexed plungers which reciprocate between the male and female cam lobes when unequal resistance is offered by the cams and are stationary when equal resistance is offered. The female cam drives the forward carrier and the male cam, connected through the inter-axle propeller shaft, drives the rearward carrier.

A separable housing, fastened to the front of the forward carrier by capscrews, contains the inter-axle power divider with the drive pinion and through shaft in a quill arrangement. The pinion is carried in a pair of tapered roller bearings and has a spigotted roller bearing at the forward end to maintain power divider cage and outer cam alignment.

In the rearward carrier, the drive pinion shaft is carried by a pair of tapered roller bearings in a separable bearing housing which is fastened to the front of the carrier housing.

Beyond the differences stated above, both carriers are the same. The spur pinion shaft and spiral bevel gear mounted at right angles to the bevel pinion shaft, are carried by a pair of tapered roller bearings, one mounted in the carrier housing and the other in a separable bearing retainer. Proper bevel gear mesh is obtained by varying the thickness of the shim packs between the carrier housings and the pinion gear housings or retainers.

Body-fitted bolts clamp the bull gear to the differential casing which also carries the differential pinion gears. Long body-fitted through bolts clamp the casing between the casing covers, thus forming an enclosure for the differential side and pinion gears. This assembly turns in a pair of tapered roller bearings at the outer ends of the casing covers, the bearings being mounted in the carrier pedestals. Pre-loading of these bearings is provided for by a slotted adjusting nut threaded to the inboard side of the right-hand bearing cup.

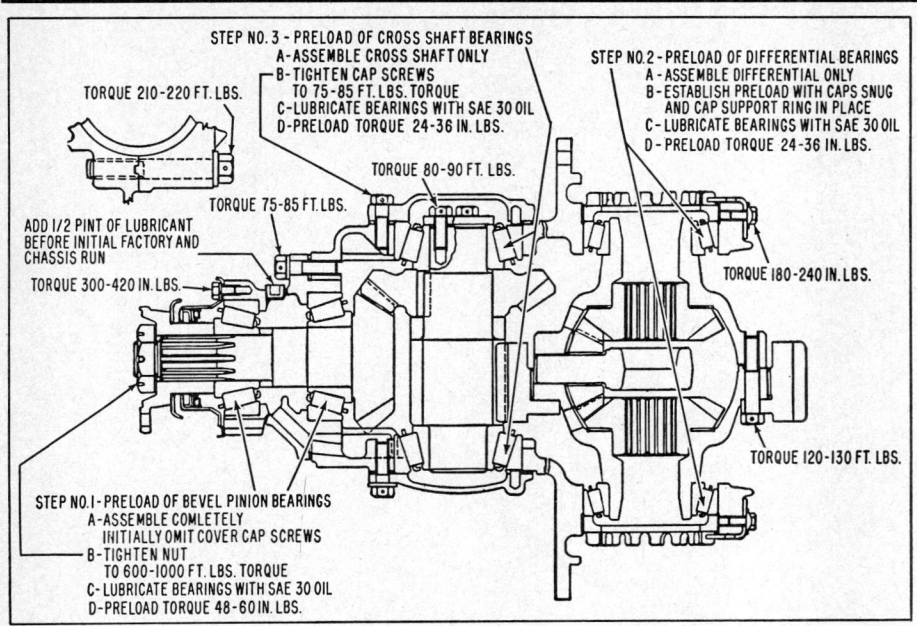

Fig. 5 Mack double-reduction carrier showing bearing preloads and screw torques

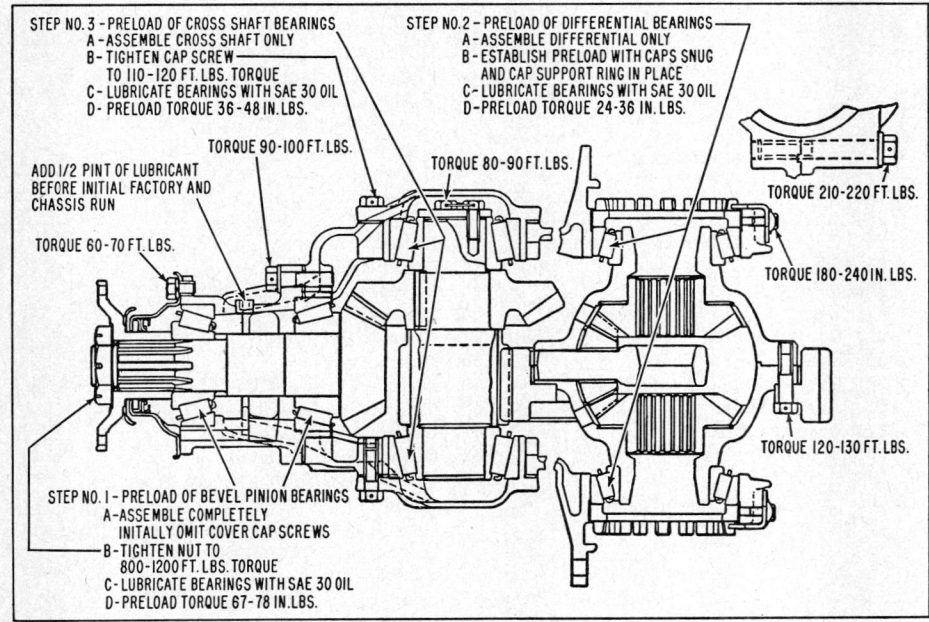

Fig. 6 Mack double-reduction axle carrier showing bearing preloads and screw torques

MACK

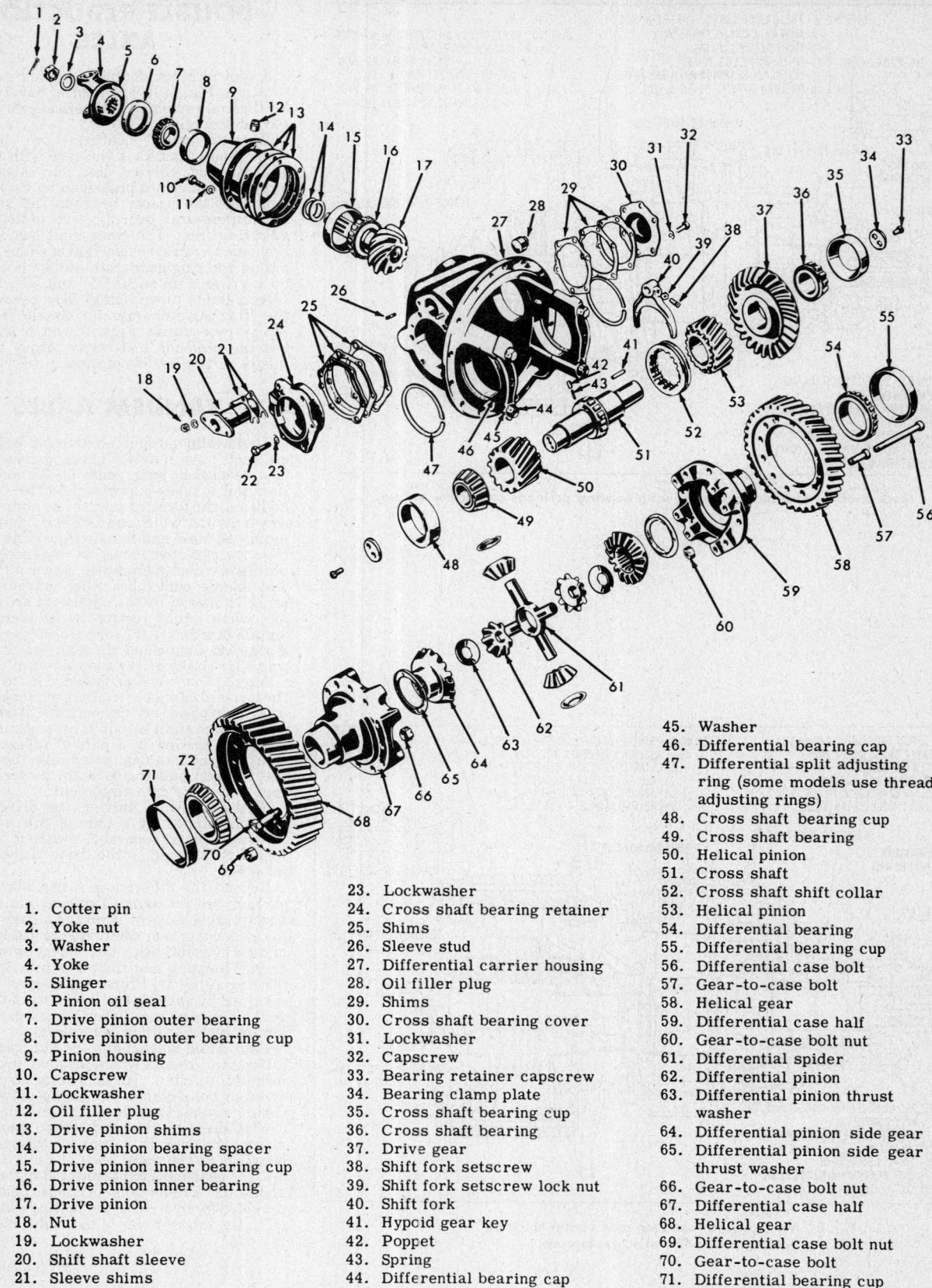

1. Cotter pin
2. Yoke nut
3. Washer
4. Yoke
5. Slinger
6. Pinion oil seal
7. Drive pinion outer bearing
8. Drive pinion outer bearing cup
9. Pinion housing
10. Capscrew
11. Lockwasher
12. Oil filler plug
13. Drive pinion shims
14. Drive pinion bearing spacer
15. Drive pinion inner bearing cup
16. Drive pinion inner bearing
17. Drive pinion
18. Nut
19. Lockwasher
20. Shift shaft sleeve
21. Sleeve shims
22. Capscrew
23. Lockwasher
24. Cross shaft bearing retainer
25. Shims
26. Sleeve stud
27. Differential carrier housing
28. Oil filler plug
29. Shims
30. Cross shaft bearing cover
31. Lockwasher
32. Capscrew
33. Bearing retainer capscrew
34. Bearing clamp plate
35. Cross shaft bearing cup
36. Cross shaft bearing
37. Drive gear
38. Shift fork setscrew
39. Shift fork setscrew lock nut
40. Shift fork
41. Hypoid gear key
42. Poppet
43. Spring
44. Differential bearing cap capscrew
45. Washer
46. Differential bearing cap
47. Differential split adjusting ring (some models use threaded adjusting rings)
48. Cross shaft bearing cup
49. Cross shaft bearing
50. Helical pinion
51. Cross shaft
52. Cross shaft shift collar
53. Helical pinion
54. Differential bearing
55. Differential bearing cup
56. Differential case bolt
57. Gear-to-case bolt
58. Helical gear
59. Differential case half
60. Gear-to-case bolt nut
61. Differential spider
62. Differential pinion
63. Differential pinion thrust washer
64. Differential pinion side gear
65. Differential pinion side gear thrust washer
66. Gear-to-case bolt nut
67. Differential case half
68. Helical gear
69. Differential case bolt nut
70. Gear-to-case bolt
71. Differential bearing cup
72. Differential bearing

Fig. 7 Two-speed, double reduction carrier assembly (Typical)

WHITE

INDEX OF SERVICE OPERATIONS

AXLES, DRIVING
	Page No.
Axle Identification	1350
Eaton Axle Service	204
Spicer Axle Service	239
Timken Axle Service	241
Locking Differentials	192
Front Wheel Locking Hubs	505

BRAKES
Adjustments	590
Air Brake Service	620
Brake Booster Service	639
Hydraulic System Service	632
Parking Brake Service	612
Stopmaster Brake Service	599

CLUTCHES
Air-Hydraulic (Air-Pak)	468
Clutch Service	429, 1351

COOLING SYSTEM
Cooling System Capacity	1333
Variable Speed Fans	10
Water Pumps	1347

ELECTRICAL
Alternator Service	52
Dash Gauge Service	179
Distributors, Standard	141
Electronic Ignition	152
Generator Service	11
Ignition Coils and Resistors	7
Ignition Timing	1348
Starting Motor Service	29
Starter Switch Service	21
Tune Up Service	2

ENGINE
Camshaft	1344
Crankshaft End Play, Adjust	1346
Cylinder Head, Replace	1341
Cylinder Liners	1345
Piston and Rod, Assemble	1345
Timing Gears	1344, 1345
Valves, Adjust	1342
Valve Lifters	1343
Valve Rotators	1342

ENGINE OILING
Crankcase Capacity	1333
Oil Pump Repairs	1346

FRONT SUSPENSION
Front Wheel Locking Hubs	505

FUEL & EXHAUST
Carburetor Adjustments	1348
Crankcase Ventilation	748
Emission Controls	750
Fuel Pump Service	183
L.P.G. Carburetion	190
Turbochargers	187

SPECIFICATIONS
Carburetor Adjustments	1348
Crankshaft and Bearing	1337
Distributor	1341
Engine Tightening Torque	1338
General Engine Data	1355
Generator and Regulator	1338
Piston, Pin and Ring	1337
Starting Motor	1339
Tune Up	1336
Valve	1336
Wheel Alignment	1337

STEERING
Manual Steering Gear Service	680
Power Steering Gear Service	686

TRANSFER CASES | 469 |

TRANSMISSIONS, Automatic
Allison AT-540, 543	510
Allison MT-640, 643, 644, 650, 653, 654 CR	512
Allison HT-740, 750	514
Allison 6 Speed	518

TRANSMISSIONS, Manual
Clark	275
Fuller	289
New Process	329
Spicer	346
Transmission Identification	1350
Warner	406

MODEL INDEX & ENGINE APPLICATION

ENGINE IDENTIFICATION—White service parts identification plate is attached to the left hand cab door. Stamped on the plate is the model of the engine, transmission, auxiliary transmission, rear axle and front axle. This represents only the equipment on the vehicle when it was shipped from the factory.

Truck Model	Year	Standard Engine Make	Standard Engine Model	Oil Pan Capacity Qts. Refill	Cooling System Capacity Qts.
1500 SERIES & COMPAC-VAN					
1500DP	1972	Perkins	6-354	14	23
1550	1970–72	White	6-170A	8	25
1550	1973–74	White	6-200A	8	—
1550D	1970–72	Cummins	C-180	—	—
1550D	1973	Detroit	6V-53N	—	—
1550J	1972	White	6-170A	—	—
1550PBT	1973–74	White	6-200A	8	—
1550PBTD	1972	Cummins	C-180	—	—
1550TD	1970	Cummins	C-180	—	—
1550TD	1973–74	Detroit	6V-53N	—	—
1550T	1970–72	White	6-170A	8	25
1550T	1973–74	White	6-200A	8	—
1564	1970–74	White	6-200A	8	—
1564T	1970–74	White	6-200A	8	25
1564D	1970	Cummins	C-180	—	—
1564TD	1970	Cummins	C-180	—	—
1564D	1973–74	Detroit	6V-53N	—	—
1564TD	1973–74	Cummins	V8-210	—	—
2000 SERIES					
2300	1970–71	White	6-130A	—	—
2300D	1970	Perkins	6-354	14	—
2300D	1971	Cummins	V8-185	—	—
2344	1970–71	White	6-170A	8	—

Continued

WHITE

MODEL INDEX & ENGINE APPLICATION—Continued

Truck Model	Year	Standard Engine Make	Standard Engine Model	Oil Pan Capacity Qts. Refill	Cooling System Capacity Qts.	Truck Model	Year	Standard Engine Make	Standard Engine Model	Oil Pan Capacity Qts. Refill	Cooling System Capacity Qts.
2344D	1970	Cummins	CF-160	16	—	7400TDB	1970	Cummins	NH-200	—	—
2344D	1971	Cummins	V8-185	—	—	74000TD-XRL	1970	Cummins	NHC-250	20	—
2364	1970–71	White	6-170A	—	—	7462T	1971–72	Cummins	NH-230	—	—
2364D	1970	Cummins	CF-160	—	—	7462TD	1970	Cummins	NH-230	—	—
2364D	1971	Cummins	V8-185	—	—	7462TDB	1970	Cummins	NH-230	—	—
2366	1970–71	White	6-170A	8	—	7464T	1971–72	Cummins	NH-230	—	—
2366D	1970	Cummins	CF-160	16	—	7464TD	1970	Cummins	NH-230	—	—
2366D	1971	Cummins	V8-185	—	—	7464TDB	1970	Cummins	NH-230	—	—
2386	1970–71	White	6-200A	—	—	7464TD-XRL	1970	Cummins	NHC-250	20	—
2386D	1970–71	Cummins	C-180	—	—	**9000 SERIES**					
4000 SERIES						9064DS	1970–75	Cummins	CF-160	16	20
4300	1970–73	White	6-200A	8	—	9064TD	1970	Cummins	NH-180	22	38
4300T	1970–73	White	6-200A	8	—	9300	1970–73	White	6-200A	8	—
4300D	1970	Cummins	CF-160	16	—	9300D	1970	Cummins	CF-160	16	—
4300D	1971	Cummins	V8-185	—	—	9300T	1970–73	White	6-200A	8	—
4300TD	1970	Cummins	CF-160	16	—	9300TD	1970	Cummins	CF-160	16	—
4300TD	1971	Cummins	V8-185	12	—	9300TD	1971	Cummins	V8-185	—	—
4300TD	1972	Cummins	C-180	—	—	9300TD	1972	Cummins	C-180	—	—
4364	1970–73	White	6-200A	8	—	9364	1970–79	White	6-186A	—	—
4364C	1973	Detroit	6V-53N	—	—	9364	1970–71	White	6-200A	—	—
4364D	1970	Cummins	CF-160	16	—	9364D	1970	Cummins	CF-160	16	—
4364D	1971	Cummins	V8-185	—	—	9364D	1971	Cummins	V8-185	—	—
C4364D	1970	Cummins	CF-160	16	—	9500TD	1970	Cummins	NHE-195	22	—
C4364	1971–72	GMC	6-478M	30	—	9500TD	1971–73	Cummins	NH-230	—	—
4500TD	1970	Cummins	NHE-195	22	—	9500TD-XRL	1970	Cummins	NHC-250	20	—
4500TD	1971–73	Cummins	NH-230	—	—	9562TD	1970	Cummins	NHE-195	22	—
4500TD-XRL	1970	Cummins	NHC-250	20	—	9562TD	1971–73	Cummins	NH-230	—	—
4564D	1970	Cummins	NHD-180	22	—	9564D	1970	Cummins	NHD-180	—	—
4564D	1971–73	Cummins	NH-230	—	—	9564D	1971–73	Cummins	NH-230	—	—
4564TD	1970	Cummins	NHE-195	22	—	9564TD	1970	Cummins	NHE-195	22	—
4564TD	1971–73	Cummins	NH-230	—	—	9564TD	1971–73	Cummins	NH-230	—	—
4564TD-XRL	1970	Cummins	NHC-250	20	—	9564TD-XRL	1970	Cummins	NHC-250	20	—
4600TD	1970	Cummins	NHE-195	22	—	**C SERIES**					
4600TD	1971–73	Cummins	NH-230	—	—	CM64	1974–76	Cummins	V-210	22	—
4664C	1973	Cummins	NH-230	—	—	CL64	1974–76	Cummins	NH-230	30	—
4664D	1970	Cummins	NHD-180	—	—	**R SERIES**					
4664TD	1970	Cummins	NHE-195	22	—	RB42	1973–75	Cummins	NTC-250	28	—
4664D	1971–73	Cummins	NH-230	—	—	RB42T	1973–75	Cummins	NTC-250	28	—
4664TD	1971–73	Cummins	NH-230	—	—	RB64	1973–75	Cummins	NTC-250	28	—
6000 SERIES						RB64T	1973–75	Cummins	NTC-250	28	—
6000D	1972–73	Cummins	NH-230	—	—	RBL42T	1973–74	Cummins	Super 250	—	—
6000T	1971	Cummins	NH-200	—	—	RBL42T	1975–76	Cummins	NTC-250	—	—
6000TD	1972–73	Cummins	NH-230	—	—	RB2L42T	1977	Cummins	Form. 290	—	—
6064D	1972–73	Cummins	NH-230	—	—	RB2L42T	1978	Cummins	Form. 290BC	—	—
6064T	1971–73	Cummins	NH-230	—	—	RB2L42TB	1978	Cummins	Form. 290BC	—	—
6064TD	1972–73	Cummins	NH-230	—	—	RBL64	1973–74	Cummins	Super 250	—	—
6000-06	1974	Cummins	NH-230	—	—	RBL64	1975–76	Cummins	NTC-250	—	—
6000T-06	1974	Cummins	NH-230	—	—	RBL64T	1973–74	Cummins	Super 250	—	—
6064-06	1974	Cummins	NH-230	—	—	RBL64T	1975–76	Cummins	NTC-250	—	—
6064T-06	1974	Cummins	NH-230	—	—	RB2L64T	1977	Cummins	Form. 290	—	—
7000 SERIES						RB2L64T	1978	Cummins	Form. 290BC	—	—
7400T	1971	Cummins	NH-200	—	—	RB2L64BT	1978	Cummins	Form. 290BC	—	—
7400T	1972	Cummins	NH-230	—	—	RBM42T	1973–74	Cummins	Super 250	—	—
7400TD	1970	Cummins	NH-200	—	—	RBM42T	1975–76	Cummins	NTC-250	—	—

Continued

WHITE

MODEL INDEX & ENGINE APPLICATION—Continued

Truck Model	Year	Standard Engine Make	Standard Engine Model	Oil Pan Capacity Qts. Refill	Cooling System Capacity Qts.	Truck Model	Year	Standard Engine Make	Standard Engine Model	Oil Pan Capacity Qts. Refill	Cooling System Capacity Qts.
RB2M42T	1977	Cummins	Form. 290	—	—	RC42TB	1975	Cummins	NTC-250	—	—
RB2M42T	1978	Cummins	Form. 290BC	—	—	RC64T	1973-74	Cummins	Super-250	—	—
RB2M42BT	1978	Cummins	Form. 290BC	—	—	RC64T	1975	Cummins	NTC-250	—	—
RBM64	1973-74	Cummins	Super 250	—	—	RC64TB	1974	Cummins	Super 250	—	—
RBM64	1975-76	Cummins	NTC-250	—	—	RC64TB	1975	Cummins	NTC-250	—	—
RB2M64	1977	Cummins	Form. 290	—	—	RC2L42T	1976-77	Cummins	Form. 290	—	—
RBM64T	1973-74	Cummins	Super 250	—	—	RC2L42T	1978-79	Cummins	Form. 290BC	—	—
RBM64T	1975-76	Cummins	NTC-250	—	—	RC2L64T	1976-77	Cummins	Form. 290	—	—
RB2M64T	1977	Cummins	Form. 290	—	—	RC2L64T	1978-79	Cummins	Form. 290BC	—	—
RB2M64T	1978	Cummins	Form. 290BC	—	—	RC2M42T	1978-79	Cummins	Form. 290BC	—	—
RB2M64BT	1978	Cummins	Form. 290BC	—	—	RC2M64T	1978-79	Cummins	Form. 290BC	—	—
RBS42	1975-76	Caterpillar	3208	12	25	RC2S42T	1976-77	Cummins	Form. 290	—	—
RB2S42	1977	Caterpillar	3208	—	—	RC2S42T	1978-79	Cummins	Form. 290BC	—	—
RBS42T	1973-74	Cummins	Super 250	—	—	RC2S64T	1976-77	Cummins	Form. 290	—	—
RBS42T	1975-76	Cummins	NTC-250	—	—	RC2S64T	1978-79	Cummins	Form. 290BC	—	—
RB2S42T	1977	Cummins	Form. 290	—	—	RCWL42T	1978-79	Cummins	Form. 290BC	—	—
RBS64	1973-74	Cummins	Super 250	—	—	RCWL64T	1978-79	Cummins	Form. 290BC	—	—
RBS64	1975-76	Cummins	NTC-250	—	—	RCWS42T	1978-79	Cummins	Form. 290BC	—	—
RB2S64	1977	Caterpillar	3208	—	—	RCWS64T	1978-79	Cummins	Form. 290BC	—	—
RBS64T	1973-74	Cummins	Super 250	—	—	RX42	1974	Caterpillar	1160	—	—
RBS64T	1975-76	Cummins	NTC-250	—	—	RX42	1975-76	Caterpillar	3208	—	—
RB2S64T	1977	Cummins	Form. 290	—	—	RX2-42	1977	Caterpillar	3208	—	—
RB2S64T	1978-79	Cummins	Form. 290BC	—	—	RX2-42	1978-79	Cummins	NTC-230	—	—
RBWL42T	1978-79	Cummins	Form. 290BC	—	—	RX42T	1974	Caterpillar	1160	—	—
RBWL42BT	1978-79	Cummins	Form. 290BC	—	—	RX42T	1975-76	Caterpillar	3208	—	—
RBWL64T	1978-79	Cummins	Form. 290BC	—	—	RX2-42T	1977	Caterpillar	3208	—	—
RBWL64BT	1978-79	Cummins	Form. 290BC	—	—	RX2-42T	1978-79	Cummins	Form. 290BC	—	—
RBWM42T	1978-79	Cummins	Form. 290BC	—	—	RX64	1974	Caterpillar	1160	—	—
RBWM42BT	1978-79	Cummins	Form. 290BC	—	—	RX64	1975-76	Caterpillar	3208	—	—
RBWM64T	1978-79	Cummins	Form. 290BC	—	—	RX2-64	1977	Caterpillar	3208	—	—
RBWM64BT	1978-79	Cummins	Form. 290BC	—	—	RX2-64	1978-79	Cummins	NH-230	—	—
RBWS42T	1978-79	Cummins	Form. 290BC	—	—	RX64T	1974-76	Cummins	NH-230	30	—
RBWS64T	1978-79	Cummins	Form. 290BC	—	—	RX2-64T	1977	Cummins	Form. 290	—	—
RC42T	1973-74	Cummins	Super-250	—	—	RX2-64T	1978-79	Cummins	Form. 290BC	—	—
RC42T	1975	Cummins	NTC-250	—	—						
RC42TB	1974	Cummins	Super 250	—	—						

①—See Chevrolet chapter for service on this engine.

GENERAL ENGINE SPECIFICATIONS

Engine Model	No. Cyls. & Valve Location	Bore & Stroke	Piston Displacement Cubic Inch	Compression Ratio	Horsepower @ R.P.M.	Torque Ft. Lb. @ R.P.M.	Engine Governed Speed	Normal Oil Pressure, Lbs.
6-110A	6 In Head	$3\frac{5}{8} \times 4\frac{1}{8}$	255	6.70	110 @ 3400	194 @ 1400	3400	40
120A	6 In Block	$3\frac{7}{8} \times 4\frac{1}{2}$	318	6.50	114 @ 2800	250 @ 1200	3000	30-35
130A	6 In Block	$4 \times 4\frac{1}{2}$	340	6.56	120 @ 3000	270 @ 1200	3000	30-35
6-130A	6 In Head	$3\frac{7}{8} \times 4\frac{1}{8}$	292	6.94	130 @ 3300	230 @ 1600	3300	40
140A	6 In Block	$3\frac{7}{8} \times 5\frac{1}{8}$	362	6.03	125 @ 3000	285 @ 1400	3000	30-35
6-145A	6 In Head	$4\frac{1}{8} \times 4\frac{1}{8}$	331	6.73	145 @ 3200	270 @ 1600	3200	40
150A	6 In Block	$4 \times 5\frac{1}{8}$	386	6.45	135 @ 3000	315 @ 1300	3000	30-35
6-170A	6 In Head	$4\frac{1}{8} \times 4\frac{1}{8}$	331	7.50	170 @ 3400	297 @ 1600	3400	40
6-185A	6 In Head	$4\frac{1}{4} \times 4\frac{1}{4}$	362	7.50	185 @ 3400	320 @ 1200	3400	40

Continued

WHITE

GENERAL ENGINE SPECIFICATIONS—Continued

Engine Model	No. Cyls. & Valve Location	Bore & Stroke	Piston Displacement Cubic Inch	Compression Ratio	Horsepower @ R.P.M.	Torque Ft. Lb. @ R.P.M.	Engine Governed Speed	Normal Oil Pressure, Lbs.
6-186A	6 In Head	4¼ × 4¼	362	7.50	186 @ 3400	320 @ 1200	3400	40
6-200A	6 In Head	4¼ × 4.7	400	①	200 @ 3400	365 @ 1600	3200	40
230A	6 In Block	4 × 4½	340	6.56	130 @ 3000	275 @ 1200	3000	50–55
250A	6 In Block	4 × 5⅛	386	6.45	145 @ 3000	328 @ 1250	3000	30–35
260A	6 In Block	4⅜ × 5	451	6.25	170 @ 3000	350 @ 1200	2800	40–45
280A	6 In Block	4⅝ × 5	504	6.00	184 @ 3000	405 @ 1200	2800	40–45
290A	6 In Block	4⅝ × 5	504	6.00	186 @ 3000	405 @ 1200	2800	40–45
380A	6 In Block	4⅝ × 5	504	6.00	185 @ 2900	405 @ 1400	2900	40–45
390A	6 In Block	4¾ × 5	531	6.40	200 @ 2900	440 @ 1400	2900	40–45
450A	6 In Block	4 × 5⅛	386	6.80	145 @ 3000	328 @ 1400	3000	50–55
460A	6 In Block	4 × 5⅛	386	6.80	159 @ 3000	336 @ 1400	3000	50–55
462A	6 In Block	4 × 5⅛	386	7.00	172 @ 3200	335 @ 1400	3200	50–55
470A	6 In Block	4½ × 5	477	6.60	200 @ 2900	395 @ 1400	2900	50–55
470G	8 In Head	4⅝ × 3½	470	8.10	250 @ 3400	312 @ 1800	3300	50–75
477A	6 In Block	4½ × 5	477	6.6	185 @ 2600	398 @ 1200	2600	50–55
490A	6 In Block	4¾ × 5	531	6.40	215 @ 2900	440 @ 1200	2900	50–55
531A	6 In Block	4¾ × 5	531	6.75	200 @ 2600	450 @ 1200	2600	50–55

①—Exc. 1972-73, 7.50; 1972-73, 8.0.

TUNE UP & VALVE SPECIFICATIONS

Engine Model	Firing Order	Spark Plugs Type⑥	Spark Plugs Gap	Ignition Timing Timing Mark	Ignition Timing Location	Valve Seat Angle, Degrees	Valve Clearance H-Hot C-Cold Intake	Valve Clearance H-Hot C-Cold Exhaust	Valve Spring Pressure, Lb. @ In. Length
6-110A	153624	⑦	.025	DC 1-10°	Damper	30	.015H	.015H	183 @ 1¹³⁄₃₂
120A	153624	⑦	.025	①	Flywheel	45	Zero	Zero	103 @ 2¹⁄₃₂
130A	153624	⑦	.025	①	Flywheel	45	Zero	Zero	103 @ 2¹⁄₃₂
6-130A	153624	⑦	.025	DC 1-10°	Damper	30	.015H	.015H	183 @ 1¹³⁄₃₂
140A	153624	⑦	.025	①	Flywheel	45	Zero	Zero	103 @ 2¹⁄₃₂
6-145A	153624	⑦	.025	DC 1-10°	Damper	30	.015H	.015H	183 @ 1¹³⁄₃₂
150A	153624	⑦	.025	①	Flywheel	45	Zero	Zero	145 @ 1.758
6-170A	153624	⑦	.025	DC 1-10°	Damper	30	.023C	.023C	183 @ 1¹³⁄₃₂
6-185A	153624	⑦	.025	DC 1-10°	Damper	30	.023C	.023C	183 @ 1¹³⁄₃₂
6-186A	153624	⑦	.025	DC 1-10°	Damper	30	.023C	.023C	183 @ 1¹³⁄₃₂
6-200A	153624	⑦	.025	DC 1-10°	Damper	30	.023C	.023C	183 @ 1¹³⁄₃₂
230A	153624	⑤	.025	Line	Flywheel	45	Zero	Zero	145 @ 1.758
250A	153624	⑤	.025	Line	Flywheel	45	Zero	Zero	145 @ 1.758
260A	153624	⑤	.025	Line	Flywheel	45	Zero	Zero	②
280A	153624	⑤	.025	Line	Flywheel	45	Zero	Zero	②
290A	153624	⑤	.025	Line	Flywheel	45	Zero	Zero	②
380A	153624	⑤	.025	Line	Flywheel	45	Zero	Zero	180 @ 1.827
390A	153624	⑤	.025	Line	Flywheel	45	Zero	Zero	180 @ 1.827
450A	153624	⑤	.025	Line	Flywheel	45	Zero	Zero	150 @ 1.758
460A	153624	⑤	.025	Line	Flywheel	45	Zero	Zero	150 @ 1.758
462A	153624	⑤	.025	Line	Flywheel	45	Zero	Zero	150 @ 1.758
470A	153624	⑤	.025	Line	Flywheel	45	Zero	Zero	182 @ 1.612
470G	15486372④	—	.025	6° BTC	Flywheel	30	.014H	.024H	213
477A	153624	⑤	.025	Line	Flywheel	45	Zero	Zero	182 @ 1.612
490A	153624	⑤	.025	Line	Flywheel	45	Zero	Zero	182 @ 1.612
531A	153624	⑤	.025	Line	Flywheel	45	Zero	Zero	182 @ 1.612

①—Line at bottom inspection hole or steel ball at side inspection hole.
②—Inner spring 95 @ 1.827", outer 104 @ 1.827".
③—Champion.
④—Cylinder numbering (front to rear): Right bank 1-2-3-4, left bank 5-6-7-8.
⑤—J6 for 14MM, D10 for 18MM.

WHITE

WHEEL ALIGNMENT SPECIFICATIONS

Model	Caster, Deg.	Camber, Deg.	Toe-In, Inch	Kingpin Inclination, Deg.	Model	Caster, Deg.	Camber, Deg.	Toe-In, Inch	Kingpin Inclination, Deg.
WC MODELS					**R SERIES**				
14, 16 Series	2⁵/₆	1	1/8	8	F3W-100 thru F6W-140②③	2⁵/₆	④	3/32	⑤
18 Series	2⁵/₆	1	1/8	8	F3W-100 thru F6W-140②⑥	5/6	④	3/32	⑤
20, PLT, 20B, 20T	2⁵/₆	1	1/8	8	FH, FL-901②	5/6	1	3/32	5 1/2
22 Series	2⁵/₆	1	1/8	8 1/2					
4000, 4200, 4400, & 9000 MODELS									
4000T, 9000	2 1/8	1	1/8	6					
4200T, 4400TD, 9000TD	2 1/8	1	1/8	6①					

①—FG-900 axle 8°, FE-990 and FD-900 5 1/2°.
②—Axle models.
③—Exc. tandem axle models.
④—Right, 1/3°; left, 1/2°.
⑤—Right, 6 2/3°; left, 6 1/2°.
⑥—Tandem axle models.

PISTON, PIN, RING, CRANKSHAFT & BEARING SPECIFICATIONS

Engine Model	Wristpin Diameter	Piston Clearance, Inch	Ring End Gap, In. (Minimum) Comp.	Ring End Gap, In. (Minimum) Oil	Crankpin Diameter, In.	Rod Bearing Clearance, In.	Main Bearing Journal Diameter, In.	Main Bearing Clearance, Inch	Thrust On Bearing No.	Shaft End Play
6-110A	1.125	.003④	.018③	.012	2.1705-2.1712	.001-.0032	2.4975-2.4982	.001-.0035	1	.004-.007
120A	1.000	.0030-.0035①	.010	.010	2.187-2.188	.002-.003	2.9995-3.0005	.003-.004	Center	.003-.007
130A	1.187	.0040-.0045①	.013	.013	2.187-2.188	.002-.003	2.9995-3.0005	.003-.004	Center	.003-.007
6-130A	1.125	.003④	.020③	.012	2.1805-2.1812	.001-.0032	2.5075-2.5082	.001-.0035	1	.004-.007
140A	1.000	.0030-.0035①	.010	.010	2.187-2.188	.002-.003	2.9905-3.0005	.003-.004	Center	.003-.007
6-145A	1.125	.004④	.020③	.012	2.1805-2.1812	.001-.0032	2.5075-2.5082	.001-.0035	1	.004-.007
150A	1.187	.005①	.010	.013	2.187-2.188	.002-.003	2.9995-3.0005	.003-.004	Center	.003-.007
6-170A	1.0625	.003④	.020③	.012	2.3093-2.3100	.001-.0032	2.7485-2.7492	.001-.0035	1	.004-.007
6-185A	1.0625	.003④	.020③	.017	2.3093-2.3100	.001-.0032	2.7485-2.7492	.001-.0035	1	.004-.007
6-186A	1.0624	.003④	.020③	.017	2.3093-2.3100	.001-.0032	2.7485-2.7492	.001-.0035	1	.004-.007
6-200A	1.0624	.003④	.020③	.017	2.3093-2.3100	.001-.0032	3.1235-3.1242⑥	.001-.0035⑤	1	.004-.007
230A	1.187	.005	.013	.013	2.187-2.188	.002-.003	2.9995-3.0005	.003-.004	Center	.003-.007
250A	1.187	.005	.010	.013	2.187-2.188	.002-.003	2.9995-3.0005	.003-.004	Center	.003-.007
260A	1.249	.005①	.013	.013	2.4995-2.5005	.003-.004	3.2495-3.2505	.0035-.0045	Center	.003-.007
280A	1.249	.005①	.013	.013	2.4995-2.5005	.003-.004	3.2495-3.2505	.0035-.0045	Center	.003-.007
290A	1.249	.005②	.013	.013	2.4995-2.5005	.003-.004	3.2495-3.2505	.0035-.0045	Center	.003-.007
380A	1.249	.005②	.013	.013	2.4995-2.5005	.003-.004	3.2495-3.2505	.0035-.0045	Center	.003-.007
390A	1.249	.005②	.013	.013	2.4995-2.5005	.003-.004	3.2495-3.2505	.0035-.0045	Center	.003-.007
450A	1.187	.005②	.013	.013	2.1868-2.1875	.002-.003	2.9995-3.0005	.003-.004	Center	.003-.007
460A	1.187	.005②	.013	.013	2.1868-2.1875	.002-.003	2.9995-3.0005	.003-.004	Center	.003-.007
462A	1.187	.005②	.013	.013	2.1868-2.1875	.002-.003	2.9995-3.0005	.003-.004	Center	.003-.007
470A	1.249	.005②	.013	.013	2.4995-2.5005	.003-.004	3.2495-3.2505	.0035-.0045	Center	.003-.007
470G⑦	1.3739	.0085-.0110	.013	.013	2.499-2.500	.0015-.0045	3.249-3.250	.0015-.0045	—	.004-.014
470G⑧	1.3739	.0085-.0110	.013	.013	2.499-2.500	.0015-.0045	3.499-3.500	.0015-.005	—	.004-.014
477A	1.249	.004	.013	.013	2.4995-2.5005	.002-.003	2.2495-2.2505	.0035-.0045	Center	.006-.013
490A	1.249	.005②	.013	.013	2.4995-2.5005	.003-.004	3.2495-3.2505	.0035-.0045	Center	.003-.007
531A	1.249	.004	.013	.013	2.4995-2.5005	.002-.003	2.2495-2.2505	.0035-.0045	Center	.006-.013

①—When checked with a 1" wide feeler it should require a 7 to 10 lb. pull on a spring scale to withdraw the feeler past the piston.
②—Piston is properly fitted when it can be moved by applying pressure with one or two fingers.
③—For top ring, 2nd ring .012".
④—When checked with 1/2" wide feeler gauge, a pull of 3 to 8 lbs. is required.
⑤—Front bearing .0014-.0039".
⑥—No. 1: 3.1231-3.1238.
⑦—Engine Se. No. Prefix "D".
⑧—Engine Se. No. Prefix "F".

WHITE

ENGINE TIGHTENING SPECIFICATIONS★

★ Torque Specifications are for clean and lightly lubricated threads only. Dry or dirty threads produce increased friction which prevents accurate measurement of tightness.

Engine	Spark Plugs Ft. Lbs.	Cylinder Head Bolts Ft. Lbs.	Intake Manifold Ft. Lbs.	Exhaust Manifold Ft. Lbs.	Rocker Arm Shaft Bracket Ft. Lbs.	Rocker Arm Cover Ft. Lbs.	Connecting Rod Cap Bolts Ft. Lbs.	Main Bearing Cap Bolts Ft. Lbs.	Flywheel to Crankshaft Ft. Lbs.	Vibration Damper or Pulley Ft. Lbs.
110A	①	100–105	—	—	—	—	65–70	85–90	—	—
120A	30	105–110	—	—	None	None	40–65	70–75	48–52	310–320
130A	30	105–110	—	—	None	None	40–65	70–75	48–52	310–320
6-130A	①	100–105	—	—	—	—	65–70	85–90	—	—
140A	30	105–110	—	—	None	None	40–65	70–75	48–52	310–320
6-145A	①	100–105	—	—	—	—	65–70	85–90	—	—
150A	30	105–110	—	—	None	None	50–65	80–90	48–52	200
6-170A	①	100–105	—	—	—	—	65–70	85–90	—	—
6-185A	①	100–105	—	—	—	—	65–70	85–90	—	—
6-186A	30	100–105	—	—	—	—	65–70	85–90	—	—
6-200A	30	100–105	—	—	—	—	65–70	85–90	—	—
230A	30	105–110	—	—	None	None	50–65	80–90	48–52	200
250A	30	105–110	—	—	None	None	50–65	70–75	48–52	200
260A	30	105–110	—	—	None	None	70–75	70–75	48–52	200
280A	30	105–110	—	—	None	None	70–75	70–75	48–52	200
290A	30	105–110	—	—	None	None	70–75	70–75	48–52	200
380A	28	105–110	—	—	None	None	80–120	80–90	48–52	200
390A	28	105–110	—	—	None	None	80–120	80–90	48–52	200
450A	28	105–110	—	—	None	None	50–65	80–90	40–44	200
460A	28	105–110	—	—	None	None	50–65	80–90	40–44	200
462A	28	105–110	—	—	None	None	50–65	80–90	40–44	200
470A, 477A	28	105–110	—	—	None	None	80–120	80–90	48–52	200
470G	25	100–105	25–30	30–32	100–105	—	②	175–185	115–120	95–105
490A, 531A	28	105–110	—	—	None	None	80–120	80–90	48–52	200

①—30 ft.-lbs. for 14MM, 34 ft.-lbs. for 18MM.
②—See text for template tightening method.

GENERATOR & REGULATOR SPECIFICATIONS

★ To Polarize Generator: For internally grounded systems, disconnect field lead from regulator and momentarily flash this wire to regulator battery terminal. For externally grounded systems, connect jumper wire from "hot" side of battery to armature terminal of generator.

	Generator					Regulator					
Gen. No. ①	Ground Polarity	Brush Spring Tension, Oz.	Rated Cap. Amps.	Gen. Field Ground Location★	Field Current	Reg. No. ②	Cutout Relay Closing Voltage	Cutout Relay Arm. Air Gap, In.	Voltage Setting	Current Setting	Current & Voltage Reg. Arm. Air Gap, In.
1102040	Neg.	28	30	External	1.48–1.62	1119001	12.6	.020	14.3	30	.075
1102040	Pos.	28	30	External	1.48–1.62	1118839	12.6	.020	14.3	30	.075
1102128	Pos.	28	30	External	1.69–1.79	1119673	12.4	.020	14.1	30	④
1102306	Pos.	28	35	External	1.69–1.79	1119673	12.4	.020	14.1	30	④
1102788	Pos.	28	45	External	1.87–2.0	1118828	6.4	.200	7.3	47	.075
1106751	Pos.	20	55	External	1.70–1.95	1118832	6.4	.020	7.3	55	.075
1106752	Pos.	20	45	External	⑤	1118834	6.4	.020	7.3	45	.075
1106757	Pos.	20	55	External	1.70–1.95	1118832	6.4	.020	7.3	55	.075
1106758	Pos.	20	45	External	⑤	1118834	6.4	.020	7.3	45	.075
1106801	Pos.	20	40	External	1.37–1.50	1118337	12.8	.020	14.3	40	.075
1106805	Pos.	20	50	External	1.37–1.50	1118838	12.8	.020	14.5	50	.075
1106808	Pos.	20	50	External	1.37–1.50	1118368	12.8	.020	14.3	50	.075
1106821	Pos.	20	40	External	1.37–1.50	1118886	12.8	.020	14.5	40	.075

Continued

WHITE

GENERATOR & REGULATOR SPECIFICATIONS—Continued

★ To Polarize Generator: For internally grounded systems, disconnect field lead from regulator and momentarily flash this wire to regulator battery terminal. For externally grounded systems, connect jumper wire from "hot" side of battery to armature terminal of generator.

Gen. No. ①	Ground Polarity	Brush Spring Tension, Oz.	Rated Cap. Amps.	Gen. Field Ground Location★	Field Current	Reg. No. ②	Cutout Relay Closing Voltage	Cutout Relay Arm. Air Gap, In.	Voltage Setting	Current Setting	Current & Voltage Reg. Arm. Air Gap, In.
1106821	Neg.	20	40	External	1.37–1.50	1118887	12.6	.020	14.3	40	.077
1106822	Neg.	20	50	External	1.37–1.50	1119156	12.6	.020	14.2	50	.075
1106822	Pos.	20	50	External	1.37–1.50	1118838	12.8	.020	14.5	50	.075
1106823	Neg.	20	50	External	1.37–1.50	1119156	12.6	.020	14.2	50	.075
1106909	Pos.	20	50	External	1.37–1.50	1118838	12.8	.020	14.5	50	.075
1106913	Pos.	20	50	External	1.37–1.50	1118838	12.8	.020	14.5	50	.075
1106932	Pos.	20	50	External	1.37–1.50	1118838	12.8	.020	14.5	50	.075
1106940	Pos.	20	50	External	1.45–1.60	1119672	12.4	.020	14.1	50	④
1106987	Pos.	20	35	External	2.14–2.28	1119158	12.2	.020	14.2	35	③
1117056	Pos.	10	60	—	6.0–6.7	—	—	—	—	—	—
1117057	Pos.	10	85	—	6.0–6.7	—	—	—	—	—	—
1117058	Neg.	10	85	—	6.0–6.6	—	—	—	—	—	—
1117070	Neg.	10	60	—	6.0–6.6	—	—	—	—	—	—
1117081	Pos.	10	60	—	6.0–6.6	—	—	—	—	—	—
1117090	Neg.	10	85	—	6.0–6.6	—	—	—	—	—	—
1117093	Pos.	10	60	—	6.0–6.6	—	—	—	—	—	—
1117094	Pos.	10	85	—	6.0–6.7	—	—	—	—	—	—
1117099	Neg.	10	85	—	6.0–6.6	—	—	—	—	—	—
1117116	Pos.	10	50	—	1.9–2.1	—	—	—	—	—	—
1117225	Neg.	—	75	—	4.1–4.5	—	—	—	—	—	—
1117232	Pos.	—	75	—	4.1–4.5	—	—	—	—	—	—
1117234	Pos.	—	75	—	4.1–4.5	—	—	—	—	—	—
1117235	Pos.	—	75	—	4.1–4.5	—	—	—	—	—	—
1117756	Neg.	—	62	—	4.14–4.62	—	—	—	—	—	—
1117763	Pos.	—	62	—	4.14–4.62	—	—	—	—	—	—
1117769	Pos.	—	62	—	4.14–4.62	—	—	—	—	—	—
1117778	Pos.	—	62	—	4.14–4.62	—	—	—	—	—	—
1117781	Neg.	—	62	—	4.14–4.62	—	—	—	—	—	—

① —Stamped on plate riveted to housing.
② —Stamped on regulator base.
③ —Voltage regulator air gap .080", current regulator air gap .075".
④ —Voltage regulator air gap, .067": current regulator air gap, .075".
⑤ —Main field 1.70–1.95 amps. Reverse field, .73–.83 amps.

STARTING MOTOR SPECIFICATIONS

Starter Number	Pinion Clearance	Brush Spring Tension Ounces	No Load Test Amperes	No Load Test Volts	No Load Test R.P.M.	Resistance Test② Amperes	Resistance Test② Volts	Lock Test Amperes	Lock Test Torque Ft-Lbs. Minimum	Lock Test Volts
1107037	—	24–28	75	5.7	5000	—	—	525	12	3.4
1107224	.010–.140	35	55–80①	9	3500–6000	300–360	3.5	—	—	—
1107506	.010–.140	35	50–80①	9	5500–9000	520–590①	3.5	—	—	—
1107541	—	35	75–95	10.6	6400–9500	545–600	3.5	—	—	—
1107542	.010–.140	35	50–80①	9	5500–9000	520–590①	3.5	—	—	—
1107578	.010–.140	35	50–80①	9	5500–9000	520–590①	3.5	—	—	—
1107671	—	35	112①	10.6	3240	—	—	320–385①	—	3.5
1107884	.010–.140	35	50–80①	9	5500–10500	270–310①	4.3	—	—	—
1107920	—	24–28	80	5.67	5500	—	—	600	14	3
1107972	—	24–28	80	5.67	5500	—	—	600	14	3

Continued

WHITE

STARTING MOTOR SPECIFICATIONS—Continued

Starter Number	Pinion Clearance	Brush Spring Tension Ounces	No Load Test			Resistance Test②		Lock Test		
			Amperes	Volts	R.P.M.	Amperes	Volts	Amperes	Torque Ft-Lbs. Minimum	Volts
1108111	—	24–28	70	10.0	7000	—	—	530	16	6.7
1108455	—	24–28	70	5	2500	—	—	600	28	6.7
1108533	—	24–28	70	10.0	2800	—	—	530	33	6.7
1108607	—	24–28	75	11.25	6000	—	—	615	29	5.85
1108621	1/64–9/64	24–28	75	11.25	6000	—	—	615	29	5.85
1108840	—	36–40	115	11.6	7000	—	—	570	20	2.3
1108863	3/16–1/4③	36–40	100	23	8000	—	—	525	32	3.0
1108872	3/16–1/4③	36–40	100	23.0	8000	—	—	525	32	3.0
1109173	—	36–40	65	11.4	6000	—	—	725	44	5
1109977	—	—	95–120①	20	5500–7500	—	—	—	—	—
1113328	—	48	65	11.4	6000	—	—	500	28	3.2
1113641	.010–.140	80	95	11.6	8000	—	—	600	20	2.2
1113658	—	—	130–160①	9	5000–7000	—	—	—	—	—
1113664	—	—	130–160①	9	5000–7000	—	—	—	—	—
1113670	—	—	130–160①	9	5000–7000	—	—	—	—	—
1113678	—	—	130–160①	9	5000–7000	—	—	—	—	—
1113708	3/16–1/4③	35–40	100	23.0	8000	—	—	500	28	3
1113800	3/16–1/4③	35–40	100	23.0	8000	—	—	500	28	3
1113842	23/64	80	60–90①	23	7000–10700	—	—	500	26	3.5
1113851	23/64	80	60–90①	23	7000–10700	—	—	500	26	3.5
1113855	23/64	80	60–90①	23	7000–10700	—	—	500	26	3.5
1113872	23/64	80	60–90①	23	7000–10700	—	—	500	26	3.5
1113887	—	—	75–95①	20	5500–7500	—	—	—	—	—
1113952	—	—	75–95①	20	5500–7500	—	—	—	—	—
1113968	—	—	75–95①	20	5500–7500	—	—	—	—	—
1114000	—	35	105	11.5	6000	—	—	600	19	2.3
1114052	—	—	120–150①	9	3000–4500	—	—	—	—	—
1114058	23/64	80	115–170①	11	6300–9500	—	—	700	15	1.5
1114070	—	—	140–190①	9	4000–7000	—	—	—	—	—
1114072	23/64	80	115–170①	11	6300–9500	—	—	700	15	1.5
1114077	—	—	120–150①	9	3000–4500	—	—	—	—	—
1114078	—	—	120–150①	9	3000–4500	—	—	—	—	—
1114086	23/64	80	115–170①	11	6300–9500	—	—	700	15	1.5
1114088	23/64	80	115–170①	11	6300–9500	—	—	700	15	1.5
1114096	—	—	120–150①	9	3000–4500	—	—	—	—	—
1114098	23/64	80	115–170①	11	6300–9500	—	—	700	15	1.5
1114110	—	—	140–190①	9	4000–7000	—	—	—	—	—
1114128	—	—	140–190①	9	4000–7000	—	—	—	—	—
1114135	—	—	120–150①	9	3000–4500	—	—	—	—	—
1114137	—	—	120–150①	9	3000–4500	—	—	—	—	—
1114143	—	—	140–190①	9	4000–7000	—	—	—	—	—
1114144	—	—	140–190①	9	4000–7000	—	—	—	—	—
1114145	—	—	140–190①	9	4000–7000	—	—	—	—	—
1114147	—	—	140–190①	9	4000–7000	—	—	—	—	—
1114154	—	—	140–190①	9	4000–7000	—	—	—	—	—
1114157	—	—	140–190①	9	4000–7000	—	—	—	—	—
1114158	—	—	140–190①	9	4000–7000	—	—	—	—	—
1114159	—	—	140–190①	9	4000–7000	—	—	—	—	—
1114161	—	—	140–190①	9	4000–7000	—	—	—	—	—
1114163	—	—	140–190①	9	4000–7000	—	—	—	—	—
1114164	—	—	140–190①	9	4000–7000	—	—	—	—	—
1114170	—	—	140–190①	9	4000–7000	—	—	—	—	—

①—Includes solenoid.
②—Check capacity of motor by using a 500 ampere meter and a carbon pile rheostat to control voltage. Apply volts listed across motor with armature locked. Current should be as listed.
③—Pinion travel.

WHITE

DISTRIBUTOR SPECIFICATIONS

Unit Part Number ①	Rotation ②	Cam Angle, Degrees	Breaker Gap, In.	Condenser Capacity, Mfds.	Breaker Arm Spring Tension, Oz. ③	Centrifugal Advance Deg. @ R.P.M. of Dist.		Vacuum Advance		
						Advance Starts	Full Advance	Inches of Vacuum to Start Plunger Movement	Inches of Vacuum for Full Plunger Travel	Maximum Vacuum Advance, Dist. Degrees
1110132	CC	31–37	.022	.20–.25	17–21	1 @ 425	9 @ 1600	5–7	16–18	7.5
1111790	C	31–37	.022	.20–.25	17–21	1 @ 375	9 @ 1300	4–6	13	7–8
1111866	C	38–45	.016	.20–.25	19–23	1 @ 275	15 @ 1150	None	None	None
1111905	C	38–45	.016	.20–.25	19–23	1 @ 450	15 @ 1700	None	None	None
1111922	C	38–45	.016	.18–.23	19–23	1 @ 450	13 @ 1875	None	None	None
1111923	C	28–35	.016	.18–.23	19–23	1 @ 425	12 @ 1700	None	None	None
1112254	C	35	.018–.024	.18–.23	19–23	1 @ 300	10 @ 1300	None	None	None
1112263	C	31–37	.022	.20–.25	17–21	1 @ 375	9 @ 1300	None	None	None
1112318	C	31–37	.022	.20–.25	17–21	1 @ 375	9 @ 1300	None	None	None
1112319	C	31–37	.022	.20–.25	17–21	1 @ 375	9 @ 1300	None	None	None
1112329	C	31–37	.022	.18–.23	19–23	2 @ 375	18 @ 1300	None	None	None
1112333	C	31–37	.022	.18–.23	19–23	2 @ 375	12 @ 1300	None	None	None

①—Stamped on plate riveted to housing.
②—As viewed from top; C—Clockwise. CC—Counter-clockwise.
③—Measurement taken from center of breaker point.

Engine Section

CYLINDER HEAD, REPLACE

Side Valve Engines

Cylinder heads should be tightened down by starting from the center and working outward from side to side and to the ends. Draw the nuts or bolts down evenly, repeating the operation until all are normally tight. After the engine has been run long enough to warm it up, a final tightening should be made in the sequence shown in Figs. 1 and 2 and to the torque given in the *Engine Tightening* chart.

Std. OHV Engines

When removing a cylinder head a chisel or screw driver should never be used to pry it loose from the cylinder block. Use an eyebolt in the third or fourth spark plug hole (6-cyl. engines), lifting up on the eyebolt while tapping lightly around the edges of the head with a lead or rawhide hammer or mallet. Be sure all the head stud nuts or bolts have been removed before starting to remove the head.

In replacing the head, the stud nuts or bolts at the center of the head should be tightened first and then work outward from side to side and to the ends. Draw the nuts or bolts down evenly until all are normally tight. After the engine has run long enough to warm it up, make a final tightening with a torque wrench to the torque loads given in the *Engine Tightening Chart* and in the sequence shown in Fig. 3.

470G Engine

Cylinder Head, Install
1. First make sure breather vent holes are plugged.
2. Place grommet retainers in water passages in block, small end up.
3. Lay head gasket on flat surface and place grommets in place by hand. Check grommet thickness; standard grommets are .065–.070" thick. *Resurfaced blocks require thicker head gaskets and grommets than new blocks.*
4. Install head gasket over ring dowels so that word TOP on gasket is visible. Be careful not to dislodge grommets as gasket is lowered over grommet retainers.
5. Install O-rings over dowels.
6. Install cylinder head over dowels.
7. Coat short capscrews with a suitable rust

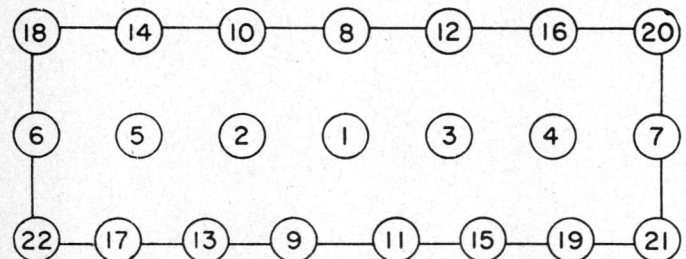

Fig. 1 Head tightening chart for side valve engine heads with 22 bolts

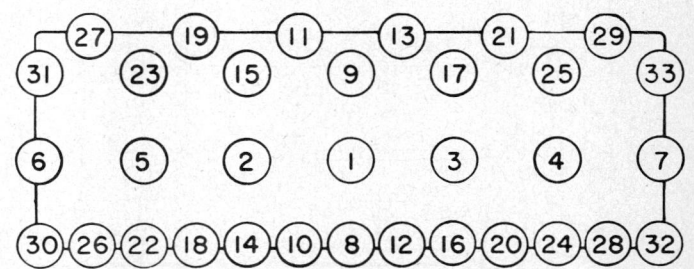

Fig. 2 Head tightening chart for side valve engine heads with 33 bolts

WHITE

Fig. 3 Cylinder head tightening sequence for overhead valve sixes

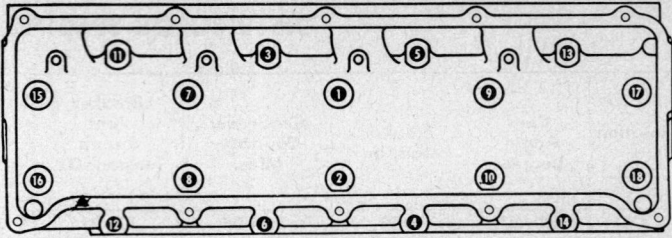

Fig. 4 Cylinder head tightening sequence. 470G engine

preventive and install. Snug tighten down in the sequence shown in Fig. 5. Final tightening is done later.

Valve Crossheads, Adjust
1. Insert crossheads over guides.
2. Hold crosshead firmly down on guide at stellite pad.
3. Run crosshead adjusting screw down until it just touches valve stem.
4. Torque adjusting screw lock nut to 20–30 ft-lbs.
5. Check clearance between crosshead and valve spring retainer with a wire feeler gauge; clearance should be .025".

Rocker Levers and Push Rods
1. Position rocker lever to cylinder head.
2. Coat rocker capscrews with a suitable rust preventive, and install in head.
3. Install push rods.
4. Check for a .010–.037" clearance between all rocker levers, spacers and lever brackets.

Tighten Cylinder Head Capscrews
1. Torque all capscrews to 100–105 ft-lbs in 25 ft-lb increments in the sequence shown in Fig. 4.

Push Rod Cavity Covers
1. Check for installation of pipe plugs in block.
2. Position cover with new gasket to block, and secure with flatwashers, lockwashers and capscrews.

Spark Plugs
1. Clean spark plug sleeve with a clean lint-free cloth.
2. Set spark plug gap at .025".
3. Install plugs and torque to 25 ft-lbs.

Spark Plug Adapter Tubes
1. Lubricate O-rings with engine oil.
2. Install O-rings in grooves of spark plug adapter tube.
3. Install adapter tube in cylinder head, secure with hold-down clamp and socket-head capscrew.

Cylinder Head Cover
1. After adjusting valves as outlined below, position new gasket to cylinder head cover.
2. Position cover on cylinder head.
3. Insert spark plug adapter tubes in bores, and secure cover to head with flatwashers, lockwashers and capscrews.

VALVES, ADJUST
470G Engine
1. Remove spark plug from No. 1 cylinder.
2. Turn engine over in direction of rotation.
3. As piston comes up to top of stroke, stick a small diameter rod into spark plughole and continue to turn engine over until it is at the top of its stroke and just before it starts to back down. This is top center.
4. Observe TC mark on flywheel through hole in bottom of flywheel housing. Also, see "VS" marks on vibration damper.
5. Shake both valve rocker levers, which should be free. If not free, a complete revolution is required before adjusting procedure should begin.
6. Loosen lock nut and back off adjusting screw. Insert feeler gauge between rocker lever and top of crosshead. Turn screw down until lever just touches gauge. Run adjusting screw nut down. Valve clearances are .014" for intake and .020" for exhaust valves.
7. Tighten adjusting screw nut to 70–80 ft-lbs.
8. After crossheads and valves are adjusted in this cylinder, rotate crankshaft 90-deg. in operating direction to the next cylinder corresponding to the firing order of the engine (1-5-4-8-6-3-7-2), Fig. 5, and repeat the above procedure.

NOTE: Two complete revolutions of the crankshaft are needed to set all crossheads and valves. Crossheads and valves can be adjusted for only one cylinder at any one crankshaft position.

Engines Other Than 470G

Adjust the valves to the clearances given in the *Tune Up & Valve Specifications* table. If the valves are to be adjusted warm, run the engine for about 30 minutes to normalize the expansion of all parts.

VALVE ROTATORS
Some Side Valve Engines

The parts involved in the rotating mecha-

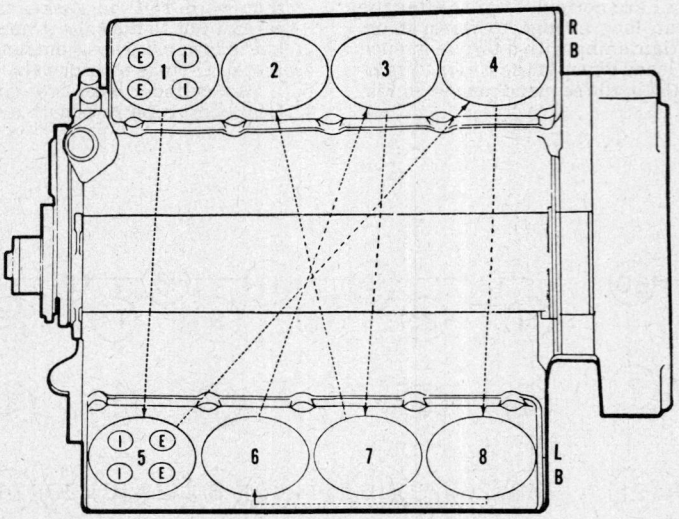

Fig. 5 Engine numbering and firing order diagram. 470G engine

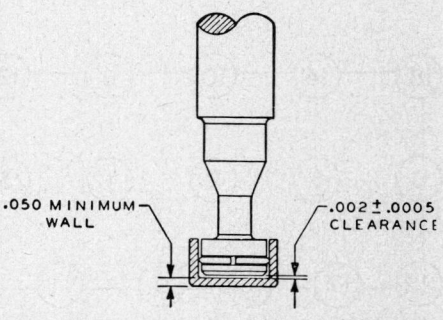

Fig. 6 Free valve stem-to-cap clearance. Side valve engines

WHITE

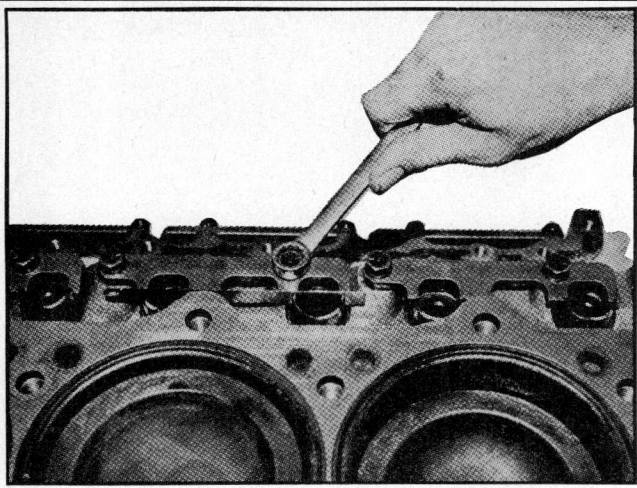

Fig. 7 Installing valve tapper plate. 470G engine

Fig. 9 Removing camshaft thrust plate capscrews. 470G engine

nism are special spring seat retainer, a pair of flat halfmoon keys, a close fitting cap located on the valve stem, and a specially constructed valve stem, Fig. 6

In order to accomodate valve expansion, the valve lash must be maintained. When camshaft rotation causes this lash or clearance to be taken up, the cap on the valve stem causes the valve keys to lower the spring retainer, removing the load of the valve springs from the valve *before* the valve is raised from its seat. The clearance shown in Fig. 6 should be maintained between the end face of the valve stem and cap. This is the distance the spring retainer is lowered *before* the valve is removed. The slow valve rotating motion is caused by vibration of the valve, the flowing of exhaust gases around the valve head, and a slight rotation motion imparted to the valve by the valve spring.

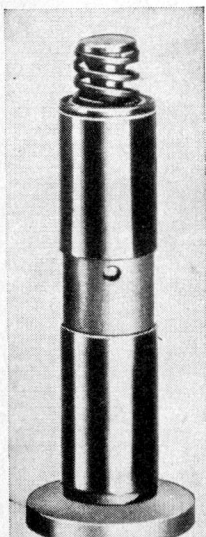 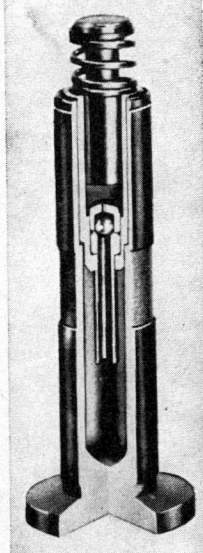

Fig. 8 Cutaway and exterior views of hydraulic valve lifter. Side valve engines

Whenever valve work is done, check the clearance, using a special gauge which is available for the purpose. If there is no clearance, grind off the end of the valve stem. If the clearance is too great, grind off the open end of the valve cap.

If the special gauge is not available, a check for clearance can be made by holding the assembled valve and rotating mechanism in the hands. With one hand press down on the valve cap and with the other hand turn the valve. If the valve turns readily at least it indicates that there is clearance present.

Std. OHV Engines

Increased exhaust valve lift is accomplished in these engines by the use of "Roto Valve" mechanism which is a special valve spring retainer and cap located on the end of the valve stem.

In operation, the rocker arm striking the cap lifts the retainer first, thus taking the spring load off the valve before lifting it from its seat. When the valve is in the raised position, it is free to rotate due to the vibration of the system.

When checking valve clearances, the feeler gauge is placed between the cap and socket as there is no other flat surface in the valve train.

VALVE LIFTERS

470G Engines

If the roller-type tappets (valve lifters) have been removed, install them as follows:
1. Install new spring clips on all tappets.
2. Install tappets in bores in block.
3. Hold tappet plate across tappet and tap lightly with a soft hammer to align tappets.
4. Place feeler gauge or shim between tappet plate and tappet, Fig. 7, to maintain .006–.014" clearance.
5. Secure tappet plate with lockwashers and capscrews, torquing capscrews to 18–20 ft-lbs.

Hydraulic Type

Fig. 8 illustrates the hydraulic lifter used in these engines. Because of the close fit between the cylinder and plunger, the plunger and cylinder should never be mismatched.

Failure of a hydraulic valve lifter is generally caused by an inadequate oil supply or dirt. An air leak at the intake side of the oil pump or too much oil in the engine will cause air bubbles in the oil supply to the lifters, causing them to collapse. This is a probable cause of trouble if several lifters fail to function, but air in the oil is an unlikely cause of failure of a single unit.

Remove the lock ring from the top of the lifter body and slide the complete unit out of the bottom of the lifter bracket. Take out the cylinder and plunger. Remove the plunger from the cylinder by twisting plunger counterclockwise to release the spring on the plunger.

Wash all parts in clean kerosene. *Never use gasoline or other fast drying agents.* Wash cylinder thoroughly until ball check rattles in cylinder.

To assemble, insert plunger in body. Plunger spring should be locked into cylinder body by turning clockwise with a twist of the plunger. Insert the lifter in the lifter bracket.

Before installing valve lifters in the engine, note the following items to make sure lifters are assembled properly. And be sure they are installed in the original position.
1. Ball check should rattle when cylinder unit is shaken.
2. Plunger should bounce back when pressed quickly into cylinder and released.
3. Plunger spring should be locked into cylinder body with a twist of the plunger.
4. Cylinder should slide smoothly into lifter body when free of oil.

Do not attempt to fill lifters with oil before assembly as this will be done automatically when the engine is running. After servicing and replacing the lifters, measure the clearance between the end of the plunger and valve stem. The valve must be fully seated. Use a feeler gauge to check the clearance, which should be from .040 to .080". If the clearance is more than .080", grind in the valve seat just enough to obtain the proper clearance. If the clearance is less than .040", carefully grind the end of the valve stem.

WHITE

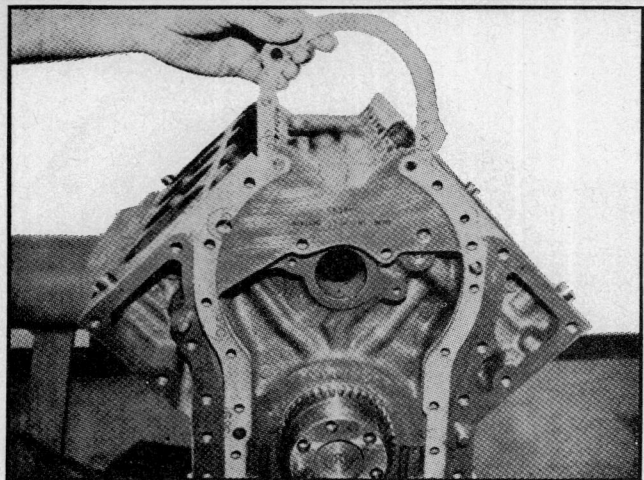

Fig. 10 Removing gear housing spacer plate. 470G engine

Fig. 11 Valve timing marks aligned. 470G engine

Std. OHV Engines

These engines are equipped with barrel type lifters which can be lifted out from above after taking out the push rods. With this construction the oil pan and camshaft need not be disturbed.

CAMSHAFT & TIMING GEARS

470G Engine

The gear housing, located at the rear of the engine, contains a set of three gears; camshaft gear, crankshaft gear and lubricating oil pump gear. The camshaft gear is a press fit on the camshaft which, of course, requires the removal of the camshaft. In order to do this, the following procedure must be followed:

Removal Procedure
1. Remove engine from vehicle.
2. Remove capscrews and washers securing oil pan to block, flywheel housing and front cover. Then lift off oil pan.
3. Remove two flywheel capscrews on opposite sides of flywheel. Insert two threaded studs, six inches long, to provide support for flywheel during removal. *Insert a wood block between crankshaft and cylinder block to prevent crankshaft from turning while removing capscrews.*
4. Remove remaining flywheel mounting capscrews.
5. In two holes provided, screw two flywheel mounting capscrews into flywheel. Turn in capscrews alternately to pull flywheel from crankshaft.
6. Remove capscrews and lift off flywheel, remove studs from crankshaft.
7. Remove pilot bearing from flywheel bore.
8. Unfasten flywheel housing from block and drive housing from dowels with block of wood or soft hammer.
9. Unfasten gear housing from block and, using a soft hammer, tap gear housing from dowels.
10. Remove lockplates and capscrews securing lubricating oil pump from block.
11. Remove capscrews and lockplates securing suction tube brackets and supports then lift off oil pump.
12. From behind camshaft gear, Fig. 9, unfasten camshaft thrust plate from spacer plate.
13. Rotate and lift camshaft slightly while pulling camshaft from block. *Do not remove gear from camshaft.*
14. Unfasten and lift off gear housing spacer plate, Fig. 10.

Installation Procedure
1. Position gear housing spacer plate with new gasket to rear of block. Gasket and plate must be flush with bottom of block.
2. Secure with lockplates and capscrews.
3. Install camshaft by lifting slightly and rotating it to assist in its installation.
4. Index "O" mark on camshaft gear with "O" mark on crankshaft gear to insure

Fig. 12 Checking camshaft end play 470G engine

Fig. 13 Checking camshaft gear backlash. 470G engine

WHITE

Fig. 14 Installing lubricating oil pump. 470G engine

Fig. 15 Checking oil pump drive gear backlash. 470G engine

correct timing, Fig. 11.
5. Secure camshaft thrust plate to block with new lockplates and capscrews.
6. With a dial indicator installed as shown, Fig. 12, check camshaft end play which must be .002–.005". If not within these limits, remove camshaft and change thrust washer.
7. Shift dial indicator to position shown in Fig. 13 and check gear train backlash which should be .003–.009". If backlash is not within limits, it is recommended that a complete new gear train be installed.

CAUTION: Insufficient gear lash or improperly mated gears will cause a noisy gear train and may cause gear failure.

8. Install lubricating oil pump, Fig. 14.
9. Attach dial indicator as shown in Fig. 15 and check oil pump drive gear backlash. Rotate gear by hand to advance position and "zero" the indicator. Back gear to retard position and note reading, which should be .002–.010". If not within limits, gear train must be replaced.
10. With new gasket in place, position gear housing to block over dowels and secure snugly with capscrews and washers.
11. Place dial indicator on end of crankshaft and check housing seal bore runout, which must not exceed .005". If run-out is excessive, remove housing and pull both dowels from block. Align housing to bore and ream for smallest permissible dowels. Install new pin dowels (use pin type only for replacement).
12. Remove gear housing and install new oil seal. Press seal into crankshaft bore from outside of housing until seal is flush with outer edge of bore.
13. Install flywheel housing and tighten capscrews in a criss-cross fashion gradually until all are tight; final tightening torque is 65–75 ft-lbs. Check housing face run-out with a dial indicator. Run-out should not exceed .008". If dowels were removed, ream dowel holes to the smallest permissible oversize and install new pin dowels.
14. Install two 1/2" × 6" long guide studs in crankshaft flange and install flywheel. Insert capscrews and tighten in a criss-cross fashion gradually; final torque

should be 100–105 lbs.
15. Install oil pan with new gasket. Tighten capscrews alternately and evenly. Torque 5/16" screws to 16–18 ft-lbs and 3/8" screws to 30–35 ft-lbs.

Overhead Valve Sixes

Before removing the timing gear cover it will be necessary to remove the oil pan and take out five fore-and-aft bolts between front oil pan arch and timing gear cover. Before removing cover bolts from front face, tap edge with soft hammer and lift off over two locating dowels.

TIMING GEARS

Side Valve Engines

Before removing timing gears be sure timing marks are legible. And when replaced valve timing will be correct if "X" marks on both gears are meshed as shown in Fig. 16.

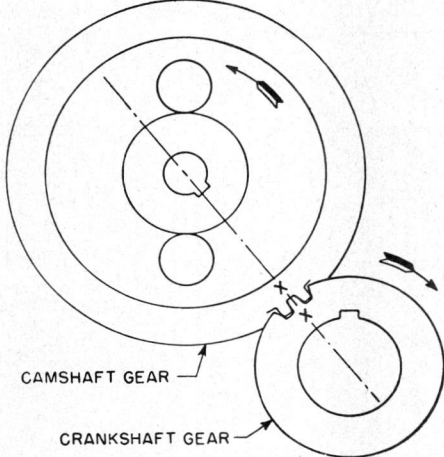

Fig. 16 Valve timing on all timing gear driven side valve engines

Std. OHV Engines

Both timing gears are punch-marked to automatically establish valve timing. On six-cylinder engines the punch-marks are aligned as shown in Fig. 17 with No. 6 piston on top of its firing stroke.

PISTONS & RODS, ASSEMBLE

470G Engine

Assemble pistons to rods so that when they are installed the numbered sides of rods will be toward outside of block.

NOTE: It is recommended that the connecting rod cap nuts be tightened as follows:

1. Tighten both nuts to 25–30 ft. lbs. Then tighten again to 50–55 ft-lbs.
2. Loosen both nuts completely to remove all tension. Then tighten them to 25 ft. lbs.
3. Advance nuts 60-deg. in 30-deg. increments.
4. When all assemblies are installed, push rods apart and check for .010–.018" clearance between rod on each crankpin, using feeler gauge at three locations around crankshaft.
5. Secure nuts by bending lockplate tangs against flat surface of nut.

All Except 470G

If the pistons and rods have factory markings to indicate their position in the cylinders, assemble and install them according to these marks, or according to the marks made during removal if they were not otherwise marked.

CYLINDER LINERS

470G Engine

Liners are the wet, replaceable sleeve type, precision machined to a uniform wall thick-

WHITE

ness to permit even expansion and contraction. The liners are a press fit in the top deck of the cylinder block and sealed at the lower bore with O-rings and crevice seals to prevent coolant leakage, Fig. 18.

All OHV Except 470G

Cylinder liners used in these engines are similar to those used in the Diesel engine but two O-ring seals are used at the lower bore to prevent coolant leakage.

When the liner is seated, check and make sure that top flange extends .002–.005″ above block. If flange is below planed surface of block it will not be sealed and held in place by the cylinder head and gasket which may then allow water leakage into the bore. Shims are available to correct sleeve protrusion.

CRANKSHAFT END PLAY, ADJUST

470G Engine

End thrust of the crankshaft is controlled by thrust rings behind the crank gear. To check the end play, proceed as follows:
1. Attach a dial gauge to block with contact point of gauge resting on crankshaft flange face.
2. Using a pry bar, pry crankshaft toward front of engine. Remove bar and set gauge at "0". Now pry crankshaft toward rear of engine and again remove pry bar.
3. Total gauge reading should be .004–.014″ with a new crankshaft and thrust rings.
4. Rotate crankshaft to see that it turns freely.
5. If end play is less than .004″, loosen capscrews slightly and shift crankshaft toward front of engine, then toward rear of engine. Retighten capscrews as outlined below, and recheck end play.

Tightening Procedure
1. Lubricate bolt threads and start main bearing cap side bolts (tightening these bolts will be done later).
2. Tighten both capscrews on each cap in 55–65 ft. lb. increments to a final torque of 175–185 ft. lbs.
3. Loosen all capscrews to remove all tension.

Fig. 17 Punch marks aligned for correct valve timing with No. 6 piston at top of its firing stroke. Overhead valve sixes

4. Repeat Step 2.
5. Tighten side bolts to 100–110 ft. lbs. in increments of 50–55 ft. lbs. using the sequence shown in Fig. 19.
6. Rotate crankshaft to see that it turns freely.

Side Valve Engines

Crankshaft end thrust is taken on the flanges of the center main bearing. Through normal wear end play will seldom become excessive but whenever new bearings are fitted, check the end play by forcing the crankshaft to the limit of its end play and check the clearance with a feeler gauge. If end play is greater than .007″, install new thrust bearing shells. If clearance is less than .003″, the bearing flanges may be dressed down to obtain the desired result.

Overhead Valve Engines

On six-cylinder engines crankshaft end thrust is taken up on the front main bearing. On early models it is controlled by flanges on the upper half only of this bearing. Later models have thrust flanges on upper and lower halves.

On V8 engines crankshaft end play is controlled by flanges on the rear main bearing.

A quick check of crankshaft end play can be made by anchoring a dial indicator to the chassis back of the radiator with the indicator on the front of the crankshaft pulley. Throwing the clutch in and out will cause a forward movement of the crankshaft to the extent of its end play. Using a piece of 2 × 4 wood ahead of the pulley, pry the crankshaft back (with foot off clutch pedal).

NOTE: *If check shows end play in excess of .012″, immediate correction of the condition is absolutely necessary because if the engine is allowed to run with excessive end play it will destroy the highly polished face of the crankshaft against which the bearing thrust flanges ride. Ultimately, this polished surface will be scored to the extent that a new thrust bearing will wear out in a very few miles. When this condition is reached the only correction is a new crankshaft.*

OIL PUMP REPAIRS

470G Engine

To remove the pump, follow the procedure given under *Camshaft and Timing Gears*. Disassembly of pump is an obvious operation. Clean and inspect all parts and replace those that are worn or damaged. Then assemble pump as follows:
1. Press idler shaft into pump body so that shaft protrudes 1.847″ above bottom surface of pocket.
2. Press driven gear on shaft flush to .035″ below surface of gear, Fig. 20.
3. Install driven gear and shaft into pump body; support drive shaft and press drive gear on shaft to the dimension shown in Fig. 20 (concave side toward gear body).
4. Slide idler gear over idler shaft.
5. Install cover to body, using new gasket. Torque capscrews to 180–205 inch lbs.
6. With dial indicator, check for

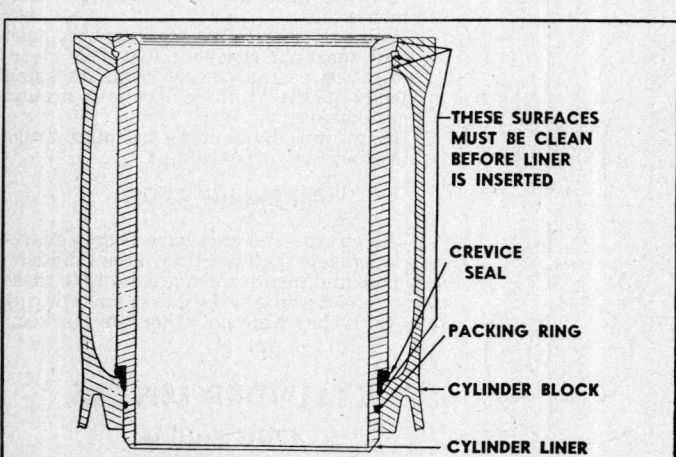

Fig. 18 Cylinder liner installed. 470G engine

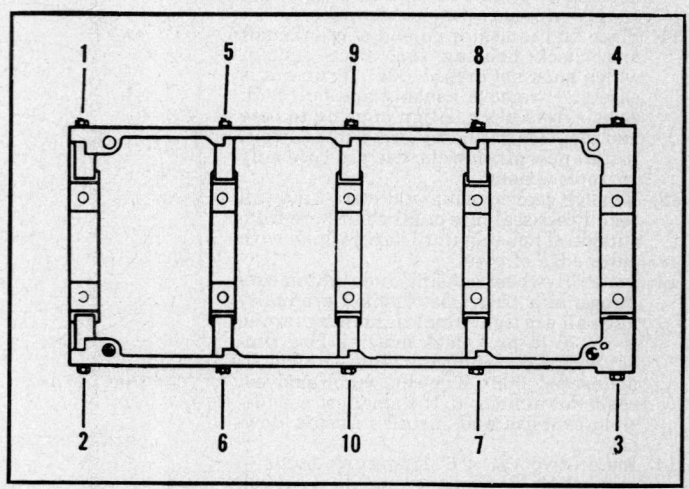

Fig. 19 Main bearing cap side bolt tightening sequence. 470G engine

WHITE

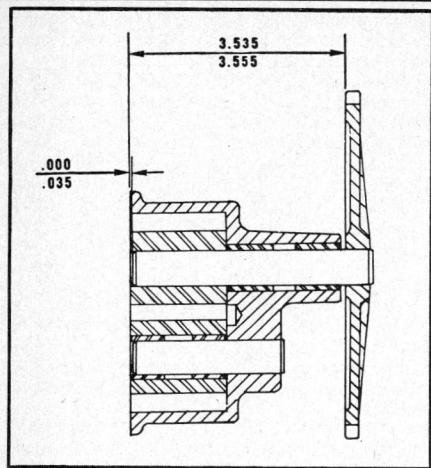

Fig. 20 Oil pump dimensions 470G engine

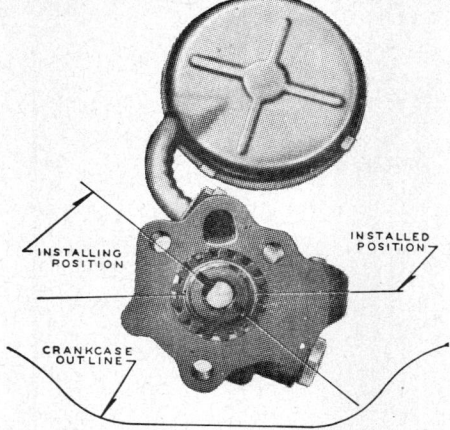

Fig. 21 Installing oil pump on overhead valve sixes

Fig. 22 Checking water pump impeller to body clearance. 470G engine

.0045–.0075″ end clearance on pump drive shaft.
7. Install regulator plunger and spring.

Side Valve Engines

These pumps can easily be disassembled by taking off the upper drive gear and bottom cover, after which the internal parts can readily be removed. Be sure to examine the pump pressure ball check, spring and seat, and if these parts show wear, new parts must be installed.

NOTE: On some engines, the oil pump is the rotor type. It is easily disassembled but the following are several points which should be noted when the pump is serviced.

1. The end clearance should be held to .0015 to .0045″ on the inner rotor and .001″ to .004″ on the outer rotor. These measurements are the difference between the depth of the counterbore in the body, including the gasket, and the length of the rotor. Always use a new gasket in assembling the pump.

2. The inner and outer rotor should have a tooth clearance of .002 to .010″.
3. The outer rotor outside diameter clearance should be from .003 to .010″. The clearance is measured between the outside diameter of the outer rotor and the inside diameter of the pump body.
4. Always install a new snap ring when the rotor has been removed from the shaft.
5. When assembled, the pump should turn finger free before installing on the engine.

NOTE: On 110A, 120A, 140A, 150A, 250A, whenever the oil pump is removed, it is advisable to remove the ignition distributor as well, since it is driven directly from an extension of the oil pump shaft.

To install the pump, crank the engine until No. 1 piston is on its compression stroke and stop when it is on top dead center, as indicated by the timing mark on the flywheel. With the engine in this position, install the oil pump. Replace the oil pump extension shaft. With the tongue on the lower end of the shaft in mesh with the oil pump shaft groove, check the position of the groove in distributor end of the extension shaft. Location of the oil pump drive gears may not permit exact positioning of the groove (45 degree angle from centerline of crankshaft); however, make sure the pump gear is not meshing one or more teeth off the prescribed position.

Installation, 6 Cyl. Engines

When installing oil pump, distributor should be removed to prevent interference by distributor shaft tongue.

If engine has been completely disassembled, oil pump should not be installed until crankshaft, camshaft and timing gears have been installed. Install oil pump as follows:

1. Turn engine over to No. 6 firing position. Be sure marks on timing gears are aligned as shown in Fig. 17.
2. Place oil pump distributor drive slot in position shown in Fig. 21. Note that slot is offset and that narrow segment of drive end is at top and rotated to the right.
3. Install long studs in two bolt holes in crankcase as pilots. Place gasket on pilot studs. Slide pump assembly into position in crankcase being careful not to turn gear before it meshes with drive gear on camshaft. As oil pump gear meshes with camshaft drive gear it rotates counter-clockwise approximately two teeth and slot then faces as shown in Fig. 21, installed position.
4. Mark No. 6 terminal position on distributor body and install distributor. Rotor should face No. 6 mark when distributor cap snap springs are in a line approximately parallel to cylinder block.

CAUTION: Do not tighten oil pump cap screws until distributor is installed. Check carefully to determine that distributor and oil pump assemblies rotate freely together after tightening pump fastenings.

WATER PUMP REPAIRS
470G Engine

Disassemble
1. Pull impeller from shaft.
2. Pull drive pulley from shaft.
3. Remove snap ring from groove in pump body.
4. Press on impeller end of shaft to remove shaft and bearing assembly. If small bearing remains in pump body, press it out.
5. Remove carbon face seal from body.
6. Remove slinger from shaft and press shaft from large bearing.
7. Clean and inspect all parts and replace those that show wear or damage.

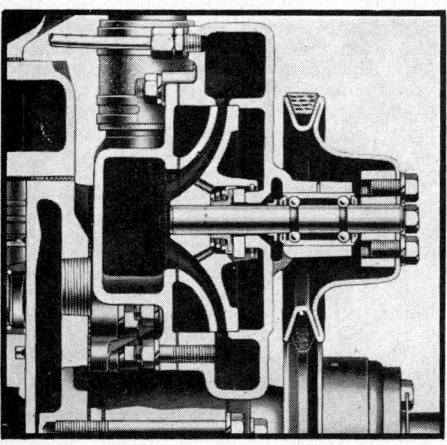

Fig. 23 Seated bearing type water pump

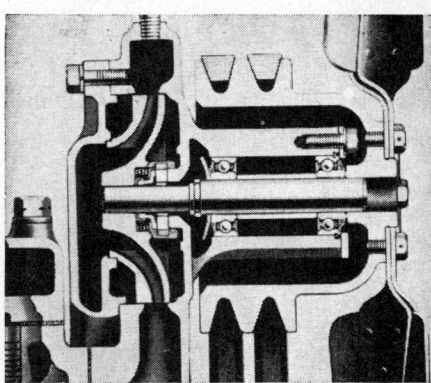

Fig. 24 Water pump with removable bearings

1347

WHITE

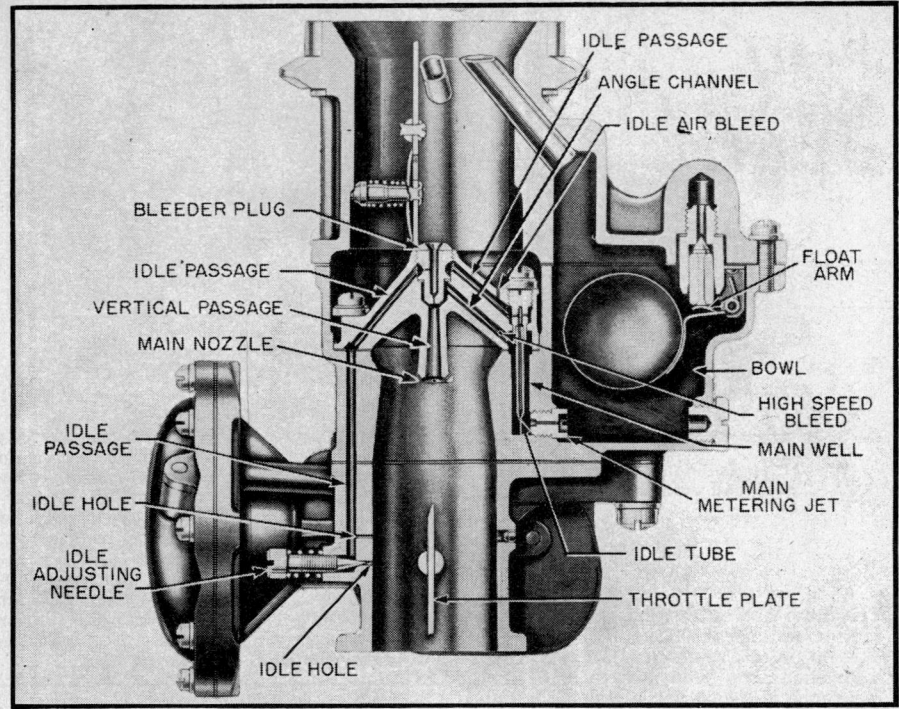

Fig. 25 Holley 847-FS carburetor. Typical of 852-FFC

Reassemble
1. Lubricate shaft and bearings with grease.
2. Pack bearings with grease.
3. Press small bearing on shaft with shielded side out toward impeller end of shaft until inner race seats against shoulder.
4. Press shaft into pump body bore.
5. Fill cavity of bore ½ to ⅔ full of grease.
6. Place large bearing over shaft and into bore of housing with shielded side out. Press bearing into its seat in housing bore.
7. Install large snap ring in pump body to secure bearings in place.
8. Support shaft on impeller end and press on drive pulley until pulley hub is tight against bearing inner race.
9. Apply suitable plastic lead sealer to bottom side or seat of carbon face seal driving flange.
10. Press in new carbon face seal. *Driving flange of seal case must seat on edge of bore in pump body.*
11. Support pump on pulley end of shaft; then press on impeller and maintain a .010–.020" clearance between impeller vanes and pump body, Fig. 22.

Sealed Bearing Type, Fig. 23

This type pump is packed with lubricant at the time of assembly and requires no further lubrication. When disassembling, carefully note the arrangement of the seal parts so that correct assembly may be assured.

Never soak the shaft and bearing assembly in cleaning solvent because it will dissolve the lubricant. To clean the shaft and bearing, merely moisten a cloth with cleaning fluid and wipe away any surplus lubricant or other foreign matter.

Be sure the face of the housing against which the thrust washer turns is smooth and true. If not, smooth it up with a special water pump facing cutter.

Removeable Bearing Type, Fig. 24

To service the pump, remove the fan pulley. Release the snap ring from the front bearing. Take off the rear cover plate. Press the shaft out of the impeller from the rear and remove the shaft and bearings as a unit. Press the shaft from the bearings, sleeve and slinger. Remove the seal from the impeller, noting the arrangement of the seal parts so that the new seal may be installed correctly.

Before assembling the pump, check the

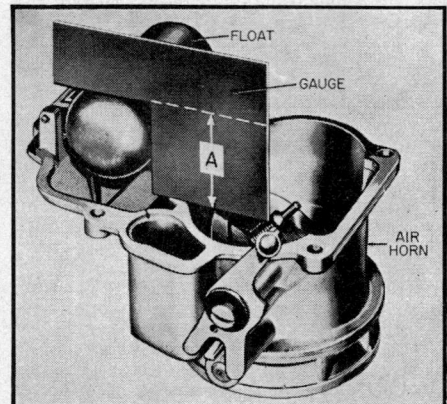

Fig. 26 Gauging float level. Holley carburetors

thrust face of the housing and if the surface is not smooth or true it should be smoothed up with a special water pump facing cutter.

To assemble the pump, apply a liberal quantity of grease to the bearings and to the shaft between the bearings. Then install the shaft and bearings in the housing as a unit. Press the impeller and seal assembly down onto the shaft, pressing it down just flush with the end of the shaft. Complete the assembly by installing the cover plate and fan pulley.

IGNITION TIMING

If a timing light is to be used to set ignition timing, disconnect the vacuum advance pipe to the carburetor and place a piece of tape over open end of pipe. *This is important as carburetor trouble can affect timing adjustments.*

Lacking a power timing light, an accurate method of setting ignition timing with the engine stopped is with the aid of a jumper light. Be sure to use a light bulb that corresponds with the system voltage of the vehicle.
1. Remove distributor cap and rotor and see that the breaker cap is set according to specifications.
2. Rotate engine until No. 1 cylinder is at the ignition timing point as indicated by the timing pointer and timing mark being lined up with each other.
3. Connect the jumper light between distributor ignition terminal and ground.
4. Turn on ignition switch.
5. Loosen distributor and turn it in the direction of normal rotation until the points just close (light out). Then slowly turn distributor in the opposite direction just to the exact point that the light goes on. Tighten distributor in this position.

HOLLEY CARBURETORS
Models 847-FS & 852-FFG

These carburetors are dual downdraft units incorporating an integral governor, Fig. 25. The governor throttle mechanism is part of the carburetor and has been designed to provide the needed power required for moving the throttle to governing speeds as controlled by a separately driven governor rotor. The combination of these two units gives instant response and accurate governing.

The carburetor and governor can be cleaned and serviced with ordinary tools and the governor rotor can be serviced independent of the carburetor. *Do not under any circumstances apply compressed air to an assembled carburetor as to do so may rupture the governor diaphragm.*

Fuel & Float Level

When checking the fuel level in an open vessel, under 4 lbs. (3 on 852) pump pressure the level should measure 11/16". The measurement is taken below the surface of the float chamber cover (gasket in place) to the level of the fuel. The level may be corrected by bending the float arm, Fig. 25.

The float level can be set when the air horn is off by gauging the distance between the bottom of the float and the flange surface of the air horn, Fig. 26. Holding the air horn upside down and the float in the closed position, measure the distance from the flange surface of the air horn to what would normally be the bottom side of the float (not the soldered seam). The correct distance should measure

$19/32''$ on 847 units and $1^{11}/_{32}''$ on 852 carburetors. Bend the float lever arm as required to correct the float level.

Idle Mixture

The idle mixture is controlled by the idle adjustment needles. Turning these needles in makes a leaner mixture and turning them out makes the mixture richer. Turn the needles in until they just touch the seats and back off one full turn.

When the engine has warmed up to operating temperature, alter the adjustment as required to obtain smooth performance. The range should be between 1 and $1\frac{1}{2}$ turns.

Accelerating Pump

The quantity of the fuel discharged by the accelerating pump can be controlled by changing the position of the pump link in the throttle lever. Of the three different positions (marked 1, 2 and 3) number 2 is the average setting, number 1 is for summer and 3 is for winter operation.

Models 885-JJG & 885-JJSG

These units are dual concentric carburetors with all metering jets and passages grouped together and located in the center of the float bowl. The float bowl is a separate unit, being suspended inside the main body from the main body cover. With this design the fuel is kept cool by circulation of the main air supply around and under the float bowl.

Fuel & Float Level

When checking the fuel level in an open vessel, under 5 lbs. pressure the fuel level should be $19/32''$ on 885-JJSG and $5/8''$ on 885-JJG. Measurement is taken from the float chamber cover with gasket in place to the level of the fuel in the bowl.

The float level can be set accurately by gauging the distance between the bottom of the floats and the chamber cover surface. When setting the float level, it is important that both the "Open" and "Closed" position of the floats be checked, Fig. 27.

To gauge the "Closed" position of the floats, hold the float chamber cover upside down. Then measure the distance from the float chamber gasket to what would normally be the bottom side of the free end of the floats.

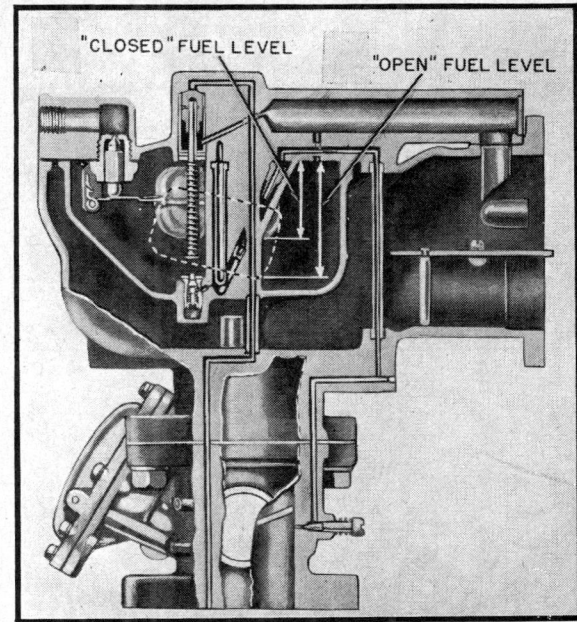

Fig. 27 Checking fuel level. Holley 885 carburetors

The distance should be $1^{5}/_{16}''$ on both models. Measurement is taken with fuel inlet valve in the closed position and the float chamber cover gasket in place. To correct the float setting for this position, the float lever arms should be bent up or down to bring the floats within the established limits and thus correct the fuel level for best operation. Pushing the floats up or toward the float cover, raises the fuel level, and down or away from the cover lowers the level.

The "Open" position is gauged by raising the floats up until the float stop arm comes to rest against the inlet needle housing. Then measure the float setting in the same manner as for the "Closed" position. The distance should measure $1^{15}/_{16}''$ on 885-JJSG ($1\frac{1}{4}''$ on 885-JJG) with the gasket in place and the float in the position illustrated in Fig. 27. Corrections for this setting can be made by bending the stop arm on the float lever.

Idle Mixture Setting

The idle needle valve setting from the closed position is from $3/4$ to $1\frac{1}{4}$ turns open. Care should be taken not to jam the needles against the seat tight enough to groove the points. If this occurs, the needles will have to be replaced before a satisfactory adjustment can be made.

When the engine has been warmed up, turn one idle needle in until the engine starts to slow down, then turn it out until it again slows down. A point midway between these two will be very close to the correct idle mixture. Repeat this procedure for the other needle. When this is done, cross check by repeating both of the above procedures. The idle speed should be reset, if necessary, between the above operations.

WHITE

Transmission & Rear Axles

TRANSMISSIONS
Transmission Identification

> **NOTE:** White model number stamped on plate attached to left-hand cab door. For service procedures and lubricant capacities on Clark, Fuller, New Process, Spicer and Warner transmissions, see the "name" chapters

White Model	Mfrs Model	Make	White Model	Mfrs Model	Make	White Model	Mfrs Model	Make
400B	T9A	Warner	524B	5A43	Fuller	574B	5A430	Fuller
418B	233F	Clark	525B	310V	Clark	581B	5AH650	Fuller
421B	5A650	Fuller	526B	318V	Clark	582B	305V	Clark
423B	8041	Spicer	527B	5AH65	Fuller	583B	315V	Clark
424B	185F	Clark	528B	308V	Clark	591B	5CW650	Fuller
426B	T98	Warner	529B	250V	Clark	800B	R45C	Fuller
427B	332F	Clark	530B	5CW65	Fuller	801B	R46	Fuller
501B	270V	Clark	531B	5AH65	Fuller	802B	R46S	Fuller
502B	205V	Clark	532B	5CW65	Fuller	1003B	303X	Clark
506B	5A65	Fuller	537B	5CW65	Fuller	1004B	403X	Clark
507B	290V	Clark	541B	5CW65	Fuller	1006B	10FB65	Fuller
509B	269V	Clark	551B	270 VO	Clark	1007B	R95C	Fuller
510B	5C72	Fuller	552B	205 VO	Clark	1026B	R63	Fuller
512B	4652	Spicer	556B	5A650	Fuller	1027B	R96	Fuller
513B	265V	Clark	557B	290 VO	Clark	1037B	R96S	Fuller
514B	300V	Clark	558B	8251	Spicer	1050B	10B1120	Fuller
515B	5A62	Fuller	559B	8051	Spicer	1056B	10FB650	Fuller
516B	5A65	Fuller	560B	5C720	Fuller	1057B	R950C	Fuller
517B	5A65	Fuller	561B	6453A	Spicer	1076B	R630D	Fuller
520B	295V	Clark	562B	4753	Spicer	1077B	R960	Fuller
521B	5A65	Fuller	565B	5A620	Fuller	1200B	8125	Spicer
522B	290V	Clark	566B	6455	Spicer			

REAR AXLES

> **NOTE:** See "name" chapters for service procedures and lubricant capacities on Eaton and Rockwell (Timken axles)

White Model	Mfrs Model	Make	White Model	Mfrs Model	Make	White Model	Mfrs Model	Make
90C	SD3010	Rockwell	322C	R301	Rockwell	407C	32M	Eaton
94C	SFD460	Rockwell	323C	17800	Eaton	408C	SW3020	Rockwell
106C	H100	Rockwell	324C	22501	Eaton	410C	SFD75H	Rockwell
108C	L100	Rockwell	325C	Q300	Timken	411C	SLDD	Rockwell
109C	F145	Rockwell	327C	QT300	Timken	412C	SQD	Rockwell
116C	E100	Rockwell	328C	19500	Eaton	413C	SQDD	Rockwell
132C	R101	Rockwell	329C	18800	Eaton	414C	SQW	Rockwell
135C	R101	Rockwell	333C	QT360	Rockwell	415C	SFDD4600	Rockwell
136C	H140	Rockwell	333TC	RT340	Rockwell	417C	SRDD	Rockwell
138C	L140	Rockwell	335C	R301	Rockwell	418C	SLHD	Rockwell
206C	H200	Rockwell	336C	H340	Rockwell	420C	SQDD	Rockwell
208C	L200	Rockwell	338C	L340	Rockwell	421C	SRDD	Rockwell
232C	R201	Rockwell	342C	16800	Eaton	422C	SLDD	Rockwell
235C	R201	Rockwell	389C	QT360	Rockwell	423C	SLD	Rockwell
306C	H300	Rockwell	389TC	RT340	Rockwell	424C	SQD	Rockwell
308C	L300	Rockwell	400C	36M	Eaton	425C	SQHD	Rockwell
315C	R301	Rockwell	401C	SFD4600	Rockwell	426C	38DS	Eaton
317C	13600	Eaton	402C	28M	Eaton	427C	34DS	Eaton
318C	16600	Eaton	403C	22M	Eaton	429C	SRHD	Rockwell
319C	17600	Eaton	404C	SW456	Rockwell	430C	SJHD	Rockwell
320C	18500	Eaton	405C	SW3456	Rockwell	433C	38DP	Eaton
321C	20500	Eaton	406C	SLD	Rockwell			

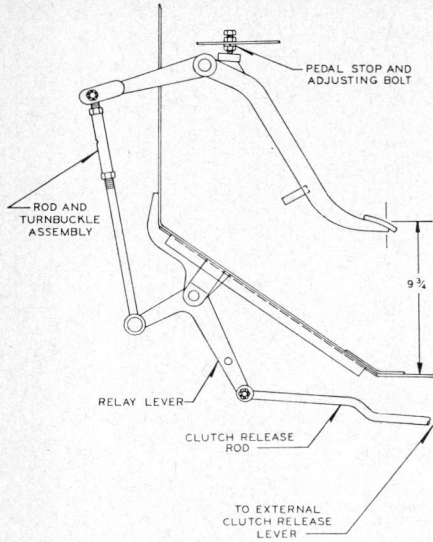

Fig. 1 Clutch linkage, 4000, 9000 and Road Boss series

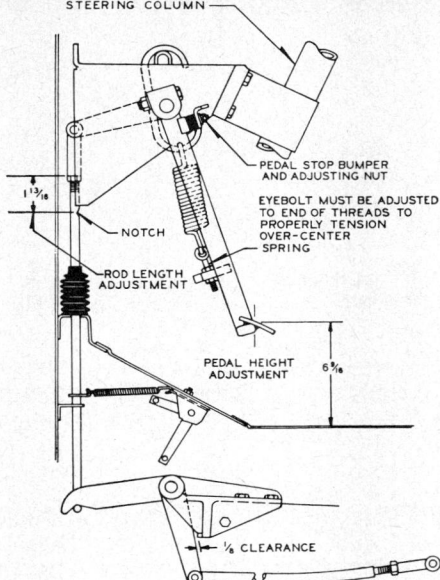

Fig. 2 Clutch linkage, 6000 series

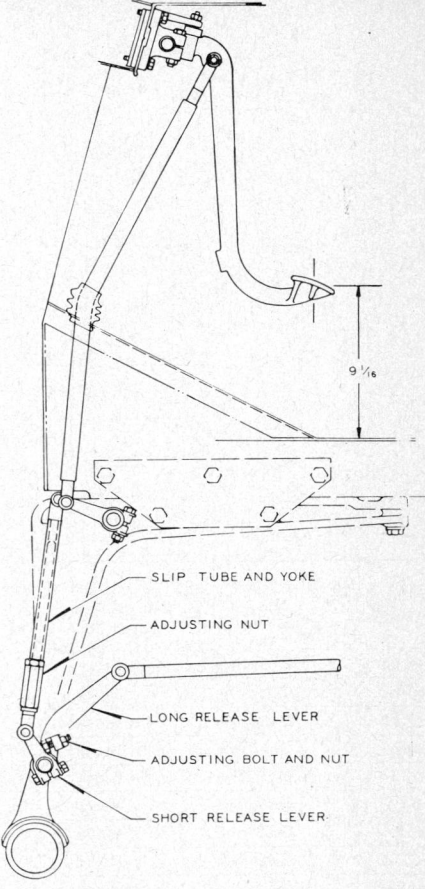

Fig. 3 Clutch linkage, 7400 and Road Commander series

CLUTCH LINKAGE ADJUSTMENT

4000, 9000 & Road Boss Series Fig. 1

1. Insert a 1/8 inch thick spacer between each yoke release lever finger and release bearing wear pad. Hold release yoke fingers firmly in contact with spacers by applying pressure to the external release lever while adjustments are being made.
2. Check clutch pedal height. If height is not 9 3/4 inches, turn pedal stop bolt as necessary to bring pedal height to specifications.
3. Loosen upper and lower jam nuts at turnbuckle in vertical linkage rod, then loosen turnbuckle until free play is obtained in linkage and retighten turnbuckle until all free play is just eliminated.

NOTE: Clutch pedal must be blocked in the "up" position or "clutch engaged" position while adjusting linkage.

4. Tighten jam nuts, remove spacers and check clutch pedal for free play.

6000 Series, Fig. 2

1. Insert a 1/8 inch thick spacer between each yoke release lever finger and release bearing wear pad. Hold release yoke fingers firmly in contact with spacers by applying pressure to the external release lever while adjustments are being made.
2. Check clutch pedal height. If height is not 6 9/16 inches, turn pedal stop adjusting nut as necessary to bring pedal height to specifications.
3. Loosen break-away clutch rod yoke jam nut.

NOTE: Jam nut is accessible from underneath instrument panel.

4. Tilt the cab and check clearance between relay lever and lever bracket. If clearance is not 1/8 inch, loosen jam nut, then disconnect clutch release rod and turn yoke as necessary to obtain desired clearance. After adjusting, reconnect release rod and tighten jam nut.
5. Rotate break-away clutch rod several turns to lengthen it, then return cab to driving position and check clearance between top of notch in relay rod and contact surface of break-away clutch rod.

NOTE: The 1 13/16 inch dimension shown in Fig. 2, is for assembly purposes only. Slight variations from this dimension are permissable when making final adjustments.

6. Tilt the cab and turn clutch rod as necessary until all clearance is just eliminated between the relay lever and clutch rod.
7. Return cab to driving position, then tighten clutch rod yoke jam nut, remove spacers from release bearing and check clutch pedal for free play.

7400 & Road Commander Series, Fig. 3

1. Insert a 1/8 inch thick spacer between each yoke release lever finger and release bearing wear pad. Hold release yoke fingers firmly in contact with spacers by applying pressure to the external release lever while adjustments are being made.
2. Check clutch pedal height. If height is not 9 1/16 inches, turn pedal stop adjusting bolt as necessary to bring pedal height to specifications.
3. Tilt the cab, then back off clutch rod jam nut to end of threads and turn adjusting nut to shorten slip tube end of adjustable clutch rod.
4. Loosen lock nut and turn adjusting bolt inward until there is clearance between bolt head and short release lever, then turn adjusting bolt outward until bolt head just contacts short release lever and tighten lock nut.

NOTE: Clutch pedal must be blocked in "up" position or "clutch engaged" position while adjustments are being made.

5. Return cab to driving position, then turn adjustable clutch rod adjusting nut until all clearance is just eliminated between the adjusting nut and slip yoke flange and tighten jam nut.
6. Remove spacers from release bearing and check clutch pedal for free play.

STOCK ENGINE SPECIFICATIONS

AUTOMOTIVE TYPE

Continental

ENGINE IDENTIFICATION—Model stamped on plate attached to engine.

GENERAL ENGINE SPECIFICATIONS

Engine Model	Type	No. Cyls. & Valve Location	Bore and Stroke	Piston Displacement Cu. In.	Compression Ratio	Horsepower @ R.P.M.	Torque Lb. Ft. @ R.P.M.	Normal Oil Pressure, Lbs.	Engine Oil Capacity Qts.①
F-4140	Gasoline	4 In Block	3 3/16 × 4 3/8	140	6.99	52 @ 3200	108 @ 1600	35–40	4
F-4162	Gasoline	4 In Block	3 7/16 × 4 3/8	162	7.02	58 @ 3200	122 @ 1600	35–40	4
F-6186	Gasoline	6 In Block	3 × 4 3/8	186	6.70	77 @ 3500	142 @ 1600	35–40	5
F-6209	Gasoline	6 In Block	3 3/16 × 4 3/8	209	6.70	90 @ 3500	160 @ 1600	35–40	5
F-6226	Gasoline	6 In Block	3 5/16 × 4 3/8	226	6.70	99 @ 3500	180 @ 1600	35–40	5
K-6271	Gasoline	6 In Head	3 5/8 × 4 3/8	271	6.40	115 @ 3200	216 @ 1400	40–50	7
M-6271	Gasoline	6 In Block	3 5/8 × 4 3/8	271	7.70	97 @ 3000	209 @ 1400	40–50	7
K-6290	Gasoline	6 In Head	3 3/4 × 4 3/8	290	6.40	123 @ 3200	232 @ 1400	40–50	7
M-6290	Gasoline	6 In Block	8 3/4 × 4 3/8	290	6.70	108 @ 3000	226 @ 1400	40–50	7
K-6330	Gasoline	6 In Head	4 × 4 3/8	330	6.40	147 @ 3200	266 @ 1800	40–50	7
M-6330	Gasoline	6 In Block	4 × 4 3/8	330	6.70	125 @ 3000	258 @ 1400	40–50	7
M-6363	Gasoline	6 In Block	4 × 4 13/16	363	6.70	146 @ 3000	304 @ 1600	40–50	7
K-6363	Gasoline	6 In Head	4 × 4 13/16	363	6.50	162 @ 3200	300 @ 1800	40–50	7
B-6371	Gasoline	6 In Block	4 1/8 × 4 5/8	371	6.50	124 @ 3000	284 @ 1400	40–50	7
T-6371	Gasoline	6 In Head	4 1/8 × 4 5/8	371	6.40	144 @ 3000	297 @ 1400	40–60	7
B-6427	Gasoline	6 In Block	4 5/16 × 4 7/8	427	6.50	142 @ 3000	328 @ 1200	40–50	8
T-6427	Gasoline	6 In Head	4 5/16 × 4 7/8	427	6.40	170 @ 3000	350 @ 1400	40–60	8
U-6501	Gasoline	6 In Head	4 1/2 × 5 1/4	501	6.20	178 @ 2600	414 @ 1200	55–65	14
R-6513	Gasoline	6 In Head	4 1/2 × 5 3/8	513	6.00	192 @ 2800	422 @ 1400	55–65	14
R-6572	Gasoline	6 In Head	4 3/4 × 5 3/8	572	6.00	220 @ 2800	464 @ 1200	55–65	14
R-6602	Gasoline	6 In Head	4 7/8 × 5 3/8	602	6.00	232 @ 2800	484 @ 1200	55–65	14
S-6749	Gasoline	6 In Head	5 3/8 × 5 1/2	749	6.00	250 @ 2800	574 @ 1400	55–65	18
S-6820	Gasoline	6 In Head	5 5/8 × 5 1/2	820	6.83	275 @ 2800	628 @ 1400	55–65	12
V-8603	Gasoline	8 In Head	4 3/4 × 4 1/4	603	7.00	240 @ 3200	500 @ 1400	50	18
TD-6427	Diesel	6 In Head	4 5/16 × 4 7/8	427	14.50	116 @ 2400	307 @ 1300	40–50	18
RD-6572	Diesel	6 In Head	4 3/4 × 5 3/8	572	14.50	172 @ 2400	423 @ 1300	40–60	18
SD-6802	Diesel	6 In Head	5 9/16 × 5 1/2	802	14.70	225 @ 2200	620 @ 1300	55–65	20
VD-8603	Diesel	8 In Head	4 3/4 × 4 1/4	603	15.80	182 @ 2800	470 @ 1300	50	12

①—Capacity of crankcase only, less filters.

STOCK ENGINES

TUNE UP & VALVE SPECIFICATIONS

Engine Model	Firing Order	Spark Plug Gap	Breaker Gap	Ignition or Injection Timing		Cylinder Head Torque Ft. Lb.	Valve Seat Angle Degrees	Valve Clearance H-Hot C-Cold		Valve Spring Pressure (Minimum) Lbs. @ Inch Length	
				Mark	Location			Intake	Exhaust	Outer	Inner
F-4140	1342	.025	.022	9°BTDC	Flywheel	②	③	.014H	.014H	96 @ 1²⁷⁄₆₄	⑤
F-4162	1342	.025	.022	9°BTDC	Flywheel	②	③	.014H	.014H	96 @ 1²⁷⁄₆₄	⑤
F-6186	153624	.025	.020	①	Flywheel	②	③	.014H	.014H	103 @ 1⅜	⑤
F-6209	153624	.025	.020	①	Flywheel	②	③	.014H	.014H	96 @ 1²⁷⁄₆₄	⑤
F-6226	153624	.025	.020	①	Flywheel	②	③	.014H	.014H	96 @ 1²⁷⁄₆₄	⑤
K-6271	153624	.025	.020	½°BTDC	Flywheel	②	③	.018H	.022H	77 @ 1.01	⑤
M-6271	153624	.025	.020	¼°BTDC	Flywheel	②	③	.017H	.020H	115 @ 1.52	⑤
K-6290	153624	.025	.020	8°BTDC	Flywheel	②	③	.018H	.022H	77 @ 1.01	⑤
M-6290	153624	.025	.020	½°BTDC	Flywheel	②	③	.017H	.020H	115 @ 1.52	⑤
K-6330	153624	.027	.020	8°BTDC	Pulley	②	③	.018H	.022H	77 @ 1.01	⑤
M-6330	153624	.025	.020	½°BTDC	Flywheel	②	③	.017H	.020H	115 @ 1.52	⑤
M-6363	153624	.025	.020	½°BTDC	Flywheel	②	③	.017H	.020H	115 @ 1.52	⑤
K-6363	153624	.027	.020	5°BTDC	Pulley	②	③	.017H	.022H	77 @ 1.01	⑤
B-6371	153624	.025	.020	IGN	Flywheel	②	③	.017H	.022H	137 @ 1.31	⑤
T-6371	153624	.025	.020	①	①	②	③	.018H	.022H	125 @ 1.11	57 @ 1.01
B-6427	153624	.025	.020	³⁄₁₆"BTDC	Flywheel	②	③	.017H	.022H	137 @ 1.31	⑤
T-6427	153624	.025	.020	³⁄₁₆"BTDC	Flywheel	②	④	.018H	.022H	125 @ 1.11	57 @ 1.01
U-6501	153624	.025	.020	①	①	②	③	.017H	.022H	47 @ 1²⁵⁄₃₂	⑤
R-6513	153624	.025	.020	⅝"BTDC	Flywheel	2	③	.018H	.024H	153 @ 1.61	86 @ 1.36
R-6572	153624	.025	.020	⅝"BTDC	Flywheel	②	③	.018H	.024H	153 @ 1.61	86 @ 1.36
R-6602	153624	.025	.020	IGN	Flywheel	②	③	.018H	.024H	153 @ 1.61	86 @ 1.36
S-6749	153624	.025	.020	8°BTDC	Flywheel	②	③	.020H	.024H	200 @ 2³⁄₁₆	100 @ 2¹⁄₃₂
S-6820	153624	.025	.020	8°BTDC	Flywheel	②	③	.020H	.024H	200 @ 2³⁄₁₆	100 @ 2¹⁄₃₂
V-8603	—	.025	.020	3°BTDC	Pulley	105	③	.020H	.028H	81 @ 2⅛	48 @ 1⅞
TD-6427	153624	None	None	32°BTDC	Flywheel	②	④	.018H	.022H	69 @ 1.54	29 @ 1.45
RD-6572	153624	None	None	30°BTDC	Flywheel	105	③	.020H	.024H	78 @ 2¼	⑤
SD-6802	153624	None	None	38°BTDC	Flywheel	②	③	.020H	.024H	93 @ 2¾	—
VD-8603	—	None	None	—	Pulley	105	45	.022H	.024H	78 @ 2¼	—

①—Timing varies with type of vehicle operation.
②—For ⅜" 35–40, ⁷⁄₁₆" 70–75, ½" 95, ⁹⁄₁₆" 135, ⅝" 150.
③—Intake 30, exhaust 45.
④—Intake 15, exhaust 45.
⑤—Single spring used.

PISTONS, PINS, RINGS, CRANKSHAFT & BEARINGS

Engine Model	Piston Clearance	Wrist Pin Diameter	Ring End Gap (Minimum)		Rod Bearings			Main Bearings		
			Comp.	Oil	Shaft Diameter	Bearing Clearance	Rod Bolt Torque Ft. Lb.	Shaft Diameter	Bearing Clearance	Main Bolt Torque Ft. Lb.
F-4140	.002	.859	.008	.007	1.9365–1.9375	.0002–.0022	①	2.249–2.250	.0002–.0024	①
F-4162	.002	.859	.007	.007	1.9365–1.9375	.0002–.0022	①	2.249–2.250	.0002–.0024	①
F-6186	.003	.859	.007	.007	1.9365–1.9375	.0002–.0022	①	2.249–2.250	.0002–.0024	①
F-6209	.002	.859	.007	.008	1.9365–1.9375	.0002–.0022	①	2.249–2.250	.0002–.0024	①
F-6226	.002	.859	.010	.008	2.0619–2.0627	.0000–.0018	①	2.3744–2.3752	.0000–.002	①
K-6271	.004	1.109	.013	.013	2.248–2.249	.0009–.0029	①	2.623–2.624	.0015–.0037	①
M-6271	.004	1.109	.008	.008	2.248–2.249	.0009–.0029	①	2.623–2.624	.0015–.0037	①
K-6290	.005	1.109	.013	.013	2.248–2.249	.0009–.0029	①	2.623–2.624	.0015–.0037	①
M-6290	.005	1.109	.008	.008	2.248–2.249	.0009–.0029	①	2.623–2.624	.0015–.0037	①
K-6330	.005	1.109	.013	.013	2.248–2.249	.0009–.0029	①	2.623–2.624	.0015–.0037	①

Continued

STOCK ENGINES

PISTONS, PINS, RINGS, CRANKSHAFT & BEARINGS—Continued

Engine Model	Piston Clearance	Wrist Pin Diameter	Ring End Gap (Minimum)		Rod Bearings			Main Bearings		
			Comp.	Oil	Shaft Diameter	Bearing Clearance	Rod Bolt Torque Ft. Lb.	Shaft Diameter	Bearing Clearance	Main Bolt Torque Ft. Lb.
M-6330	.005	1.109	.011	.010	2.248–2.249	.0009–.0029	①	2.623–2.624	.0015–.0037	①
M-6363	.005	1.109	.011	.010	2.248–2.249	.0009–.0029	①	2.623–2.624	.0015–.0037	①
K-6363	.005	1.109	.013	.013	2.248–2.249	.0009–.0029	①	2.623–2.624	.0015–.0037	①
B-6371	.005	1.250	.011	.007	2.498–2.499	.001–.003	①	2.873–2.874	.0015–.0037	①
T-6371	.005	1.250	.013	.013	2.498–2.499	.001–.003	①	2.873–2.874	.0015–.0037	①
B-6427	.005	1.250	.013	.013	2.498–2.499	.001–.003	①	2.873–2.874	.0015–.0037	①
T-6427	.005	1.250	.013	.013	2.498–2.499	.001–.003	①	2.873–2.874	.0015–.0037	①
U-6501	.005	1.500	.010	.010	2.7475–2.7485	.0011–.0036	①	2.7475–2.7485	.0011–.0041	①
R-6513	.005	1.500	.010	.010	2.999–3.000	.0012–.0028	①	3.249–3.250	.0022–.0046	①
R-6572	.005	1.500	.010	.010	2.999–3.000	.0012–.0028	①	3.249–3.250	.0022–.0046	①
R-6602	.006	1.500	.010	.010	2.999–3.000	.0012–.0028	①	3.249–3.250	.0022–.0046	①
S-6749	.008	1.750	.017	.022	3.499–3.500	.0015–.0045	①	3.749–3.750	.0016–.0046	①
S-6820	.008	1.750	.022	.022	3.499–3.500	.0015–.0045	①	3.749–3.750	.0016–.0046	①
V-8603	.002	1.500	.013	.015	3.124–3.125	.0016–.0042	①	3.499–3.500	.0018–.0044	①
TD-6427	.006	1.250	.013	.013	2.498–2.499	.001–.003	①	2.873–2.874	.0015–.0037	①
RD-6572	.006	1.500	.010	.010	2.999–3.000	.0012–.0028	①	3.249–3.250	.0022–.0046	①
SD-6802	.007	1.750	.013	.013	3.499–3.500	.0015–.0045	①	3.749–3.750	.0016–.0046	①
VD-8603	.005	1.500	.013	.013	3.124–3.125	.0016–.0042	①	3.499–3.500	.0018–.0044	①

①—5/16" 20–25, 3/8" 35–40, 7/16" 70–75, 1/2" 85–95, 9/16" 100–110.

Hall-Scott-Hercules

ENGINE IDENTIFICATION—Model stamped on plate attached to engine.

GENERAL ENGINE SPECIFICATIONS

Engine Model	Type	No. Cyls. & Valve Location	Bore and Stroke	Piston Displacement Cu. In.	Compression Ratio	Horsepower @ R.P.M.	Torque Ft. Lb. @ R.P.M.	Normal Oil Pressure, Lbs.	Engine Oil Capacity Qts.
190-2	Gasoline	6 In Head	5¼ × 6	779	6.00	240 @ 2200	625 @ 1300	80	20
190-5	Gasoline	6 In Head	5¼ × 6	779	6.00	240 @ 2200	625 @ 1300	80	20
590-GV-3	Gasoline	6 In Head	5 × 5	590	6.60	239 @ 2800	490 @ 1600	60	12
590-GV-4	Gasoline	6 In Head	5 × 5	590	6.60	239 @ 2800	490 @ 1600	60	12
590-BV-1	L.P.G.	6 In Head	5 × 5	590	8.70	256 @ 2800	530 @ 1600	60	12
590-GH-1	Gasoline	6 In Head	5 × 5	590	6.60	239 @ 2800	490 @ 1600	60	18
590-BH-1	L.P.G.	6 In Head	5 × 5	590	8.70	256 @ 2800	530 @ 1600	60	18
779	Gasoline	6 In Head	5¼ × 6	779	6.00	240 @ 2200	625 @ 1300	80	20
935-B-1	L.P.G.	6 In Head	5¾ × 6	935	8.10	330 @ 2400	880 @ 1400	60	22
935-G-1	Gasoline	6 In Head	5¾ × 6	935	6.40	294 @ 2400	820 @ 1400	60	22
1091-B-1	L.P.G.	6 In Head	5¾ × 7	1090	8.10	357 @ 2200	1070 @ 1200	60	22
1091-G-1	Gasoline	6 In Head	5¾ × 7	1090	6.40	318 @ 2200	945 @ 1400	60	22
6156-B-1	L.P.G.	6 In Head	5¾ × 6	935	8.10	342 @ 2400	890 @ 1400	60	22
6156-G-1	Gasoline	6 In Head	5¾ × 6	935	6.40	310 @ 2400	812 @ 1300	60	22
6182-B-1	L.P.G.	6 In Head	5¾ × 7	1091	8.10	368 @ 2200	1091 @ 1100	60	22
6182-G-1	Gasoline	6 In Head	5¾ × 7	1091	6.50	332 @ 2200	960 @ 1200	60	22

STOCK ENGINES

TUNE UP & VALVE SPECIFICATIONS

Engine Model	Firing Order	Spark Plug Gap	Breaker Gap	Ignition Timing Mark	Ignition Timing Location	Cylinder Head Torque Ft. Lb.	Valve Seat Angle Degrees	Valve Clearance Intake H-Hot C-Cold	Valve Clearance Exhaust H-Hot C-Cold	Valve Spring Pressure (Minimum) Lbs. @ Inch Length Inner	Valve Spring Pressure (Minimum) Lbs. @ Inch Length Outer
190-2	153624	.025	.018	①	Flywheel	④	②	.022C	.022C	110 @ 1¹⁵⁄₁₆	143 @ 2
190-5	153624	.025	.018	①	③	④	②	.022C	.022C	110 @ 1¹⁵⁄₁₆	143 @ 2
590-GV-3	153624	.025	.020	"5"	③	⑤	45	.021C	.021C	80 @ 1¾	144 @ 1³⁄₁₆
590-GV-4	153624	.025	.020	"5"	③	⑤	45	.021C	.021C	80 @ 1¾	144 @ 1³⁄₁₆
590-BV-1	153624	.015	.020	"10"	③	⑤	45	.021C	.021C	80 @ 1¾	144 @ 1³⁄₁₆
590-GH-1	153624	.025	.020	"5"	③	⑤	45	.021C	.021C	80 @ 1¾	144 @ 1³⁄₁₆
590-BH-1	153624	.015	.020	"10"	③	⑤	45	.021C	.021C	80 @ 1¾	144 @ 1³⁄₁₆
779	153624	.025	.018	①	Flywheel	④	②	.022C	.022C	110 @ 1¹⁵⁄₁₆	143 @ 2
935-B-1	142635	.016	.021	¾"BTDC	Flywheel	⑥	②	.021C	.031C	105 @ 1¹⁵⁄₁₆	138 @ 2
935-G-1	142635	.016	.021	¾"BTDC	Flywheel	⑥	②	.021C	.031C	105 @ 1¹⁵⁄₁₆	138 @ 2
1091-B-1	142635	.016	.021	¾"BTDC	Flywheel	⑥	②	.021C	.031C	105 @ 1¹⁵⁄₁₆	138 @ 2
1091-G-1	142635	.016	.021	¾"BTDC	Flywheel	⑥	②	.021C	.031C	105 @ 1¹⁵⁄₁₆	138 @ 2
6156-B-1	142635	.016	.021	1½"BTDC	Flywheel	⑥	②	.021C	.031C	110 @ 1¹⁵⁄₁₆	143 @ 2
6156-G-1	142635	.016	.021	1½"BTDC	Flywheel	⑥	②	.021C	.031C	110 @ 1¹⁵⁄₁₆	143 @ 2
6182-B-1	142635	.016	.021	⅝"BTDC	Flywheel	⑥	②	.021C	.031C	110 @ 1¹⁵⁄₁₆	143 @ 2
6182-G-1	142635	.016	.021	⁵⁄₁₆"BTDC	Flywheel	⑥	②	.021C	.031C	110 @ 1¹⁵⁄₁₆	143 @ 2

①—Three flywheel teeth before TDC mark on flywheel.
②—Intake 30°, exhaust 45°.
③—Flywheel and crankshaft pulley.
④—½" 35, ¾" 215.
⑤—Small 35, large 185.
⑥—Large 240, small nuts 40.

PISTONS, PINS, RINGS, CRANKSHAFT & BEARINGS

Engine Model	Piston Clearance	Wrist Pin Diameter	Ring End Gap (Minimum) Comp.	Ring End Gap (Minimum) Oil	Rod Bearings Shaft Diameter	Rod Bearings Bearing Clearance	Rod Bolt Torque Ft. Lb.	Main Bearings Shaft Diameter	Main Bearings Bearing Clearance	Main Bolt Torque Ft. Lb.
190-2	.0105	1.400	.013	.025	2.7475–2.7480	.004	130–140	3.247–3.2475	.004	180–200
190-5	.0105	1.400	.013	.025	2.7475–2.7480	.004	130–140	3.247–3.2475	.004	180–200
590-GV-3	.003	1.500	.017	.013	2.9970–2.9975	.003	100–120	3.248–3.2485	.004	130–140
590-GV-4	.003	1.500	.017	.013	2.9970–2.9975	.003	100–120	3.248–3.2485	.004	130–140
590-BV-1	.003	1.500	.017	.013	2.9970–2.9975	.003	100–120	3.248–3.2485	.004	130–140
590-GH-1	.003	1.500	.017	.013	2.9970–2.9975	.003	100–120	3.248–3.2485	.004	130–140
590-BH-1	.003	1.500	.017	.013	2.9970–2.9975	.003	100–120	3.248–3.2485	.004	130–140
779	.0105	1.400	.013	.025	2.7475–2.7480	.004	130–140	3.274–3.2475	.004	180–200
935-B-1	.006	1.6247	.020	.013	3.2468–3.2473	.0035	130–140	3.4968–3.4973	.004	180–200
935-G-1	.006	1.6247	.020	.013	3.2468–3.2473	.0035	130–140	3.4968–3.4973	.004	180–200
1091-B-1	.006	1.6247	.020	.013	3.2468–3.2473	.0035	130–140	3.4968–3.4973	.004	180–200
1091-G-1	.006	1.6247	.020	.013	3.2468–3.2473	.0035	130–140	3.4968–3.4973	.004	180–200
6156-B-1	.006	1.6247	.020	.013	3.2468–3.2473	.0035	130–140	3.4968–3.4973	.004	180–200
6156-G-1	.006	1.6247	.020	.013	3.2468–3.2473	.0035	130–140	3.4968–3.4973	.004	180–200
6182-B-1	.006	1.6247	.020	.013	3.2468–3.2473	.0035	130–140	3.4968–3.4973	.004	180–200
6182-G-1	.006	1.6247	.020	.013	3.2468–3.2473	.0035	130–140	3.4968–3.4973	.004	180–200

STOCK ENGINES

Hercules

ENGINE IDENTIFICATION—Model stamped on plate attached to engine.

TUNE UP & VALVE SPECIFICATIONS

Engine Model	Firing Order	Spark Plug Gap	Breaker Gap	Ignition or Injection Timing Mark	Ignition or Injection Timing Location	Cylinder Head Torque Ft. Lb.	Valve Seat Angle Degrees	Valve Clearance H-Hot Intake	Valve Clearance C-Cold Exhaust	Valve Spring Pressure (Minimum) Lbs. @ Inch Length Outer	Valve Spring Pressure (Minimum) Lbs. @ Inch Length Inner
DFXE	153624	None	None	27° BTDC	Flywheel	350	45	.010H	.016H	94 @ 3	57 @ $2^{21}/_{32}$
DFXH	153624	None	None	27° BTDC	Flywheel	350	45	.010H	.016H	124 @ $1^{25}/_{32}$	96 @ $1^{21}/_{32}$
DIX-4-D	153624	None	None	30° BTDC	Flywheel	158	45	①	①	49 @ 1.21	34 @ 1.09
DIX-6-272	153624	None	None	30° BTDC	Flywheel	158	45	①	①	49 @ 1.21	34 @ 1.09
DJXC	153624	None	None	26° BTDC	Flywheel	157	45	①	①	55 @ 1.40	37 @ 1.28
DJXH	153624	None	None	29° BTDC	Flywheel	157	45	①	①	55 @ 1.40	37 @ 1.28
DOOD	1243	None	None	25° BTDC	Flywheel	157	45	①	①	55 @ 1.40	37 @ 1.28
DRXC	153224	None	None	30° BTDC	Flywheel	②	45	①	①	48 @ 1.45	30 @ 1.33
DWXLD	153624	None	None	24° BTDC	Flywheel	158	45	①	①	84 @ $1^{37}/_{64}$	74 @ $1^{31}/_{64}$
HXE	153624	.025	.020	DC 1–6	Flywheel	105	30	.010H	.016H	84 @ $3^{5}/_{32}$	50 @ $2^{13}/_{16}$
IXB	1243	.025	.020	DC 1–4	Flywheel	40	30	.006H	.008H	42 @ $1^{3}/_{16}$	③
JXC, JXD	153624	.025	.020	DC 1–6	Flywheel	④	45	①	①	58 @ 1.60	③
JXLD	153624	.025	.020	DC 1–6	Flywheel	④	⑤	①	①	58 @ 1.60	③
QXD, QXLD	153624	.025	.020	DC 1–6	Flywheel	⑦	30	①	①	40 @ $1^{9}/_{32}$	③
RXC	153624	.025	.020	DC 1–6	Flywheel	⑧	45	①	①	102 @ $2^{5}/_{32}$	③
RXLDH	153624	.025	.020	DC 1–6	Flywheel	80	⑩	①	①	102 @ $2^{5}/_{32}$	③
TDC-895	153624	None	None	—	—	350	45	.010H	.016H	57 @ $2^{21}/_{32}$	94 @ $2^{31}/_{32}$
WXLC-3	153624	.025	.020	DC 1–6	Flywheel	⑨	30	.012H	.016H	102 @ $2^{5}/_{32}$	③
G-14, 1600	1342	.018	31–34	6° BTDC	Flywheel	60–85	—	.015	.015	—	—
G-20, 2300	1243	.031	.022	TDC	Flywheel	—	—	.016H	.016H	72 @ 1.292	—
G-3000	153624	.031	.022	6° BTDC	Flywheel	—	—	.016H	.016H	72 @ 1.292	—
G-3400	153624	.031	.022	TDC	Flywheel	—	—	.016H	.016H	72 @ 1.292	—
D-4800	153624	None	None	20° BTDC	Flywheel	140	—	.010C	.010C	—	—

① —See Instruction Plate on engine.
② —For ⅝" nuts 175, for 1" nuts 280.
③ —Single spring used.
④ —Nuts 65, screws on manifold side 75, screws marked "1041" 100, other screws 85.
⑥ —Exhaust 45°, intake 30° or 45°.
⑦ —Nuts 60, screws with washers 100.
⑧ —Cap screws 75, nuts 85.
⑨ —Cap screws 75, nuts 100.
⑩ —Intake 30°, exhaust 45°.

PISTONS, PINS, RINGS, CRANKSHAFT & BEARINGS

Engine Model	Piston Clearance	Wrist Pin Diameter	Ring End Gap (Minimum) Comp.	Ring End Gap (Minimum) Oil	Rod Bearings Shaft Diameter	Rod Bearings Bearing Clearance	Rod Bolt Torque Ft. Lb.	Main Bearings Shaft Diameter	Main Bearings Bearing Clearance	Main Bolt Torque Ft. Lb.
DFXE	.009	2.00	.018	.022	3.309–3.310	.003–.0055	263	4.499–4.500	.005–.006	260
DFXH	.0145	2.00	.018	.022	3.309–3.310	.003–.0055	263	4.499–4.500	.005–.006	260
DIX-4-D	.006	1.125	.012	.012	2.372–2.373	.003–.004	150	2.747–2.748	.003–.0045	①
DIX-6-272	.006	1.125	.012	.012	2.372–2.373	.003–.004	150	2.747–2.748	.003–.0045	①
DJXC, H	.0055	1.187	.018	.018	2.497–2.498	.003–.004	175	2.997–2.998	.003–.0045	②
DOOD	.0055	1.187	.018	.018	2.497–2.498	.003–.004	175	2.997–2.998	.003–.0045	②
DRXC	.0075	1.625	.018	.018	2.997–2.998	.003–.004	175	3.497–3.498	.003–.004	175
DWXLD	.0125	1.50	.015	.015	2.747–2.748	.0045–.0055	③	3.497–3.498	.0045–.0055	175
HXE	.006	1.50	.020	.020	2.997–2.998	.003–.004	263	3.497–3.498	.003–.004	④
IXB	.0035	.75	.015	.015	1.747–1.748	.001–.0015	42	1.987–1.988	.002–.0025	77
JXC, JXD	⑫	1.00	.015	.015	1.987–1.988	.0025–.003	56	2.497–2.498	.0035–.004	⑤
JXLD	.005	1.125	.015	.015	1.987–1.988	.0025–.003	56	2.497–2.498	.0035–.004	⑤
QXD, QXLD	⑬	.875	.015	.015	1.987–1.988	.001–.0015	39	2.497–2.498	.002–.003	⑤
RXC	.0045	1.25	.015	.015	2.622–2.623	.002–.003	⑦	2.997–2.998	.003–.004	⑧

Continued

STOCK ENGINES

PISTONS, PINS, RINGS, CRANKSHAFT & BEARINGS—Continued

Engine Model	Piston Clearance	Wrist Pin Diameter	Ring End Gap (Minimum)		Rod Bearings			Main Bearings		
			Comp.	Oil	Shaft Diameter	Bearing Clearance	Rod Bolt Torque Ft. Lb.	Shaft Diameter	Bearing Clearance	Main Bolt Torque Ft. Lb.
RXLDH	.0065	1.50	.015	.015	2.997–2.998	.004–.0045	158	3.497–3.498	.0045–.005	175
TCD-895	.008	2.00	.018	.018	3.309–3.310	.0035–.0045	263	4.449–4.500	.005–.006	260
WXLC-3	.0045	1.31	.015	.015	2.247–2.248	.0015–.0025	⑨	2.622–2.623	.0025–.0035	⑩
D-15, 17, 2000	.005	1.2498	.010	.010	2.373–2.374	.001–.003	—	2.8734–2.8744	.0009–.0034	—
D-21, 2300	.005	1.2498	.010	.010	2.373–2.374	.001–.003	—	2.8734–2.8744	.0009–.0034	—
D-30, 3400	.005	1.2498	.010	.010	2.373–2.374	.001–.003	—	2.8734–2.8744	.0009–.0034	—
G-1400	.002	—	.012⑪	.015	1.9979–1.9987	.001–.0028	30–35	2.2477–2.2485	.0004–.002	55–60
G-1600	.002	—	.010	.015	1.9979–1.9987	.0013–.0031	30–35	2.2477–2.2485	.0009–.0035	55–60
G-20, 2300	.003	1.2498	.010	.010	2.373–2.374	.001–.003	—	2.8734–2.8744	.0009–.0034	—
G-30, 3400	.003	1.2498	.010	.010	2.373–2.374	.001–.003	—	2.8734–2.8744	.0009–.0034	—

①—Front, center and rear 105, intermediate 85.
②—For ⅝" nuts 95, for ½" nuts 78.
③—For ½" nuts 158, for 9/16" nuts 225.
④—Front & inter. 210, center and rear 192.
⑤—Front and inter. 70, center and rear 60.
⑦—For ½" 105, for 9/16" 115.
⑧—Front and center 123, center and rear 105.
⑨—For ½" 105, for 7/16" 53.
⑩—Front & inter. 70, center and rear 75.
⑪—Top compression ring .013.
⑫—Model JXC, .0035; Models JXD, .0045.
⑬—Model QXD, .003; Models QXLD, .0035.

GENERAL ENGINE SPECIFICATIONS

Engine Model	Type	No. Cyls. & Valve Location	Bore and Stroke	Piston Displacement Cu. In.	Compression Ratio	Horsepower & R.P.M.	Torque Ft. Lb. & R.P.M.	Normal Oil Pressure, Lbs.	Engine Oil Capacity Qts.
DFXE	Diesel	6 In Head	5⅝ × 6	895	14.80	227 @ 2100	685 @ 2100	50	24
DFXH	Diesel	6 In Head	5¾ × 6	935	14.80	260 @ 2100	750 @ 1200	50	24
DIX4D	Diesel	4 In Head	3⅝ × 4	166	15.50	57 @ 3000	120 @ 1500	30	①
DIX6-272	Diesel	6 In Head	3 11/16 × 4¼	272	15.50	103 @ 3000	202 @ 1800	30	①
DJXB	Diesel	6 In Head	3½ × 4½	260	15.50	77 @ 2600	178 @ 1300	45	①
DJXC	Diesel	6 In Head	3¾ × 4½	298	15.50	83 @ 2600	208 @ 1300	45	①
DJXH	Diesel	6 In Head	3¾ × 4½	298	15.50	99 @ 2600	234 @ 1400	45	①
DOOD	Diesel	4 In Head	4¼ × 4½	255	15.50	79 @ 2600	183 @ 1400	30	①
DRXC	Diesel	6 In Head	4⅝ × 5¼	529	15.00	147 @ 2200	400 @ 1100	30	①
DWXLD	Diesel	6 In Head	4¼ × 5	426	15.50	142 @ 2600	328 @ 1600	40	①
D-1500	Diesel	3 In Head	3¾ × 4½	149	17.50	46 @ 2600	113 @ 1500	40	①
D-1700	Diesel	3 In Head	4 × 4½	169	17.50	50 @ 2600	128 @ 1500	40	①
D-2000	Diesel	4 In Head	3¾ × 4½	198	17.50	70 @ 2600	156 @ 1500	40	①
D-2120	Diesel	4 In Head	3⅞ × 4½	—	—	—	—	40	①
D-2300	Diesel	4 In Head	4 × 4½	226	17.50	73 @ 2600	182 @ 1400	40	①
D-3000	Diesel	6 In Head	3¾ × 4½	298	17.50	114 @ 3000	244 @ 1400	40	①
D-3000T	Diesel	6 In Head	3¾ × 4½	298	17	117 @ 2000	308 @ 2000	—	①
DH-3000	Diesel	6 In Head	3¾ × 4½	298	17.50	101 @ 2400	229 @ 1800	—	①
D-3400	Diesel	6 In Head	4 × 4½	339	17.50	115 @ 2600	276 @ 1400	40	①
D-4800	Diesel	6 In Head	4 9/16 × 4⅞	478	18	143 @ 2400	350 @ 1800	45	①
G-1400	Gasoline	4 In Head	3⅞ × 3	141	8.0	58 @ 2800	115 @ 2000	40	①
G-1600	Gasoline	4 In Head	4 × 3¼	163	8.0	60 @ 2400	140 @ 1400	40	①
G-2000	Gasoline	4 In Head	3¾ × 4½	198	7.50	78 @ 2400	185 @ 1400	35	①
G-2300	Gasoline	4 In Head	4 × 4¼	226	7.50	81 @ 2200	207 @ 1400	35	①
G-3000	Gasoline	6 In Head	3¾ × 4½	298	7.50	117 @ 2400	270 @ 1300	35	①
G-3400	Gasoline	6 In Head	4 × 4½	339	7.50	132 @ 2400	310 @ 1300	35	①
HXE	Gasoline	6 In Block	5¾ × 6	935	6.20	227 @ 2000	750 @ 900	35	①
IXB	Gasoline	4 In Block	3¼ × 4	133	6.50	46 @ 3200	92 @ 1800	20	①

Continued

STOCK ENGINES

GENERAL ENGINE SPECIFICATIONS—Continued

Engine Model	Type	No. Cyls. & Valve Location	Bore and Stroke	Piston Displacement Cu. In.	Compression Ratio	Horsepower & R.P.M.	Torque Ft. Lb. & R.P.M.	Normal Oil Pressure, Lbs.	Engine Oil Capacity Qts.
JXC	Gasoline	6 In Block	3¾ × 4¼	282	6.50	103 @ 3200	207 @ 1400	26	①
JXD	Gasoline	6 In Block	4 × 4¼	320	6.50	112 @ 3200	240 @ 1400	26	①
JXLD	Gasoline	6 In Block	4 × 4½	339	6.50	131 @ 3200	272 @ 1400	26	①
L-237	Gasoline	6 In Block	3 7/16 × 4¼	236.7	—	79 @ 2400	185 @ 1400	—	—
QXD	Gasoline	6 In Block	3 7/16 × 4⅛	230	6.50	78 @ 3200	167 @ 1500	26	①
QXLD	Gasoline	6 In Block	3 7/16 × 4¼	237	6.50	92 @ 3200	190 @ 1400	26	①
RXC	Gasoline	6 In Block	4⅝ × 5¼	529	6.30	143 @ 2400	372 @ 1100	26	①
RXLDH	Gasoline	6 In Block	4¾ × 5¼	558	6.50	181 @ 2600	443 @ 1400	36	①
TCD-895	Diesel	6 In Head	5⅝ × 6	895	14.80	318 @ 2000	846 @ 1800	50	①
WXLC-3	Gasoline	6 In Block	4¼ × 4¾	404	6.50	139 @ 2600	312 @ 1300	26	①

①—Depends upon type of oil pan used.

Waukesha

ENGINE IDENTIFICATION—Model stamped on plate attached to engine.

GENERAL ENGINE SPECIFICATIONS

Engine Model	Type	No. Cyls. & Valve Location	Bore and Stroke	Piston Displacement Cu. In.	Compression Ratio	Horsepower @ R.P.M.	Torque Ft. Lb. @ R.P.M.	Normal Oil Pressure, Lbs.	Engine Oil Capacity, Qts.①
135-DK	Diesel	6 In Head	4¼ × 5	426	16.80	140 @ 2400	326 @ 1600	40	12
135-DKB	Diesel	6 In Head	4¼ × 5	426	16.8	147 @ 2800	328 @ 1600	40	12
135-DKBS	Diesel	6 In Head	4¼ × 5	426	16.8	185 @ 2800	400 @ 1800	40	12
135-GKB	Gasoline	6 In Head	4¼ × 5	426	6.25	148 @ 3000	337 @ 1200	40	12
135-GZ	Gasoline	6 In Head	4⅜ × 5	451	6.30	153 @ 2800	351 @ 1300	40	12
135-GZB	Gasoline	6 In Head	4⅜ × 5	451	6.30	153 @ 2800	354 @ 1200	40	12
140-GK	Gasoline	6 In Head	4½ × 5½	525	6.40	155 @ 2250	420 @ 1000	40	10
140-GKB	Gasoline	6 In Head	4½ × 5½	525	6.40	220 @ 3200	466 @ 1800	40	10
140-GZ	Gasoline	6 In Head	4⅝ × 5½	554	6.40	170 @ 2250	468 @ 1000	40	10
140-GZB	Gasoline	6 In Head	4⅝ × 5½	554	6.40	226 @ 3200	490 @ 1800	40	10
145-GK	Gasoline	6 In Head	5¼ × 6	779	6.20	240 @ 2400	594 @ 1000	40	18
145-GKB	Gasoline	6 In Head	5¼ × 6	779	6.20	260 @ 2400	640 @ 1000	40	18
145-GZ	Gasoline	6 In Head	5⅜ × 6	817	6.30	250 @ 2400	630 @ 1200	40	18
145-GZB	Gasoline	6 In Head	5⅜ × 6	817	6.30	268 @ 2400	652 @ 1200	40	18
148-DK	Diesel	6 In Head	5¼ × 6	779	16.50	197 @ 2000	584 @ 1000	40	18
148-DKB	Diesel	6 In Head	5¼ × 6	779	16.50	200 @ 2100	584 @ 1000	40	18
148-DKBS	Diesel	6 In Head	5¼ × 6	779	16.50	280 @ 2100	706 @ 1800	40	18
180-DLC	Diesel	4 In Head	3½ × 3¾	144	17.10	45 @ 2400	102 @ 1800	25-30	5
180-GLB	Gasoline	4 In Head	3½ × 3¾	144	7.00	45 @ 2400	118 @ 1600	25-30	5
185-DLC	Diesel	6 In Head	3½ × 3¾	216	17.10	60 @ 2400	152 @ 1000	25-30	8
185-GLB	Gasoline	6 In Head	3½ × 3¾	216	7.00	67 @ 2400	176 @ 1400	25-30	8
190-DLCA	Diesel	6 In Head	3¾ × 4	265	17.00	85 @ 2600	191 @ 1400	25-30	7
190-GLB	Gasoline	6 In Head	3¾ × 4	265	7.00	77 @ 2200	223 @ 1200	25-30	7
195-DLCA	Diesel	6 In Head	4 × 4	302	17.00	98 @ 2800	221 @ 1800	25-30	7
195-GKA	Gasoline	6 In Head	4⅛ × 4	320	6.20	125 @ 3200	263 @ 1600	25-30	7
195-GL	Gasoline	6 In Head	4 × 4	302	6.20	85 @ 2400	240 @ 1200	25-30	7
197-DLC	Diesel	6 In Head	4 × 4	302	18.50	91 @ 2800	216 @ 1600	40	7
197-DLCS	Diesel	6 In Head	4 × 4	302	18.50	131 @ 2800	275 @ 1800	40	7
MZA	Gasoline	6 In Block	4¼ × 4¾	404	5.60	130 @ 3000	289 @ 1000	40	8
WAKB	Gasoline	6 In Head	6¼ × 6½	1197	7.00	280 @ 1800	997 @ 1000	40	32

Continued

STOCK ENGINES

GENERAL ENGINE SPECIFICATIONS—Continued

Engine Model	Type	No. Cyls. & Valve Location	Bore and Stroke	Piston Displacement Cu. In.	Compression Ratio	Horsepower @ R.P.M.	Torque Ft. Lb. @ R.P.M.	Normal Oil Pressure, Lbs.	Engine Oil Capacity, Qts. ①
WAKC	Gasoline	6 In Head	6¼ × 6½	1197	7.00	290 @ 1800	1020 @ 1000	40	32
WAKD	Diesel	6 In Head	6¼ × 6½	1197	16.50	224 @ 1600	840 @ 1000	40	32
WAKDB	Diesel	6 In Head	6¼ × 6½	1197	16.50	258 @ 1800	845 @ 1000	40	32
WAKDBS	Diesel	6 In Head	6¼ × 6½	1197	16.50	400 @ 1800	1400 @ 1200	40	32
ROILINE									
H540	Gasoline	V8 In Head	4½ × 4¼	540	6.70	170 @ 2400	430 @ 900	40	②
H570	Gasoline	V8 In Head	4⅝ × 4¼	570	7.45	218 @ 2400	509 @ 1600	50	②
H844	Gasoline	V8 In Head	5¼ × 4⅞	844	6.70	300 @ 2400	637 @ 1500	30-40	②
H884	Gasoline	V8 In Head	5⅜ × 4⅞	884	7.62	320 @ 2400	770 @ 1500	50	②

①—Sump capacity only. Add for filters, etc. ③—H844 and H884 20 qts., T-H844 and T-H884 front sump 16 qts., center sump 20 qts.
②—H540 16 qts., T-H540 9 qts.

TUNE UP & VALVE SPECIFICATIONS

Engine Model	Firing Order	Spark Plug Gap	Breaker Gap	Ignition or Injection Timing Mark	Ignition or Injection Timing Location	Cylinder Head Torque (Oiled) Inch Lbs.	Valve Seat Angle Degrees	Valve Clearance ⑨ C-Cold Intake	Valve Clearance ⑨ C-Cold Exhaust	Valve Spring Pressure (Minimum) Lbs. @ Inch Length Outer	Valve Spring Pressure (Minimum) Lbs. @ Inch Length Inner
135-DK	153624	None	None	⑧	Flywheel	2000–2100	45	.011C	.023C	82 @ 2⁵⁄₁₆	①
135-DKB	153624	None	None	FP⑧	Flywheel	2000–2100	45	.011C	.023C	82 @ 2⁵⁄₁₆	①
135-DKBS	153624	None	None	FP⑧	Flywheel	2000–2100	45	.011C	.023C	82 @ 2⁵⁄₁₆	①
135-GKB	153624	.025	.018	Dist.⑧	Flywheel	2000–2100	45	.011C	.023C	82 @ 2⁵⁄₃₂	①
135-GZ	153624	.025	.018	⑧	Flywheel	2000–2100	45	.011C	.023C	82 @ 2⁵⁄₃₂	①
135-GZB	153624	.025	.018	Dist.⑧	Flywheel	2000–2100	45	.011C	.023C	82 @ 2⁵⁄₃₂	①
140-GK	153624	.025	.018	Dist.⑧	Flywheel	2400–2500	②	.013C	.019C	86 @ 1²¹⁄₃₂	55 @ 1⁷⁄₁₆
140-GKB	153624	.025	.018	Dist.⑧	Flywheel	2400–2500	②	.013C	.025C	177 @ 1⁴¹⁄₆₄	①
140-GZ	153624	.025	.018	Dist.⑧	Flywheel	2400–2500	②	.013C	.019C	177 @ 1⁴¹⁄₆₄	①
140-GZB	153624	.025	.018	Dist.⑧	Flywheel	2400–2500	②	.013C	.025C	177 @ 1⁴¹⁄₆₄	①
145-GK	153624	.025	.018	Dist.⑧	Flywheel	③	②	.013C	.024C	118 @ 2³⁄₈	81 @ 2¹⁄₁₆
145-GKB	153624	.025	.018	Dist.⑧	Flywheel	③	②	.013C④	.030C④	265 @ 1⁶³⁄₆₄	①
145-GZ	153624	.025	.018	Dist.⑧	Flywheel	③	②	.013C	.024C	265 @ 1⁶³⁄₆₄	①
145-GZB	153624	.025	.018	Dist.⑧	Flywheel	③	②	.013C④	.030C④	265 @ 1⁶³⁄₆₄	①
148-DK	153624	None	None	⑧	Flywheel	3500–3600	45	.015C	.028C	158 @ 2³⁄₈	100 @ 2¹⁄₁₆
148-DKB	153624	None	None	FP⑧	Flywheel	3500–3600	45	.015C	.028C	158 @ 2³⁄₈	100 @ 2¹⁄₁₆
148-DKBS	153624	None	None	FP⑧	Flywheel	3500–3600	45	.015C	.028C	158 @ 2³⁄₈	100 @ 2¹⁄₁₆
180-DLC	1243	None	None	FP⑧	Flywheel	1350–1400⑦	45	o010C	.020C	48 @ 1⁵⁄₁₆	①
180-GLB	1243	.025	.018	Dist.⑧	Flywheel	1100–1200	45	.010C	.020C	48 @ 1¹⁵⁄₁₆⑤	45 @ 1⁴⁷⁄₆₄⑥
185-DLC	153624	None	None	FP⑧	Flywheel	1350–1400⑦	45	.010C	.020C	48 @ 1¹⁵⁄₁₆	①
185-GLB	153624	.025	.018	Dist.⑧	Flywheel	1100–1200	45	.010C	.020C	48 @ 1¹⁵⁄₁₆⑤	45 @ 1⁴⁷⁄₆₄⑥
190-DLCA	153624	None	None	FP⑧	Flywheel	1350–1400⑦	45	.010C	.020C	71 @ 1¹⁹⁄₃₂	①
190-GLB	153624	.025	.018	Dist.⑧	Flywheel	1100–1200	45	.008C	.022C	48 @ 1¹⁵⁄₁₆⑤	45 @ 1⁴⁷⁄₆₄⑥
195-DLCA	153624	None	None	FP⑧	Flywheel	1350–1400⑦	45	.010C	.020C	124 @ 1¹⁵⁄₁₆	①
195-GKA	153624	.025	.018	Dist.⑧	Flywheel	1100–1200	45	.015C	.023C	124 @ 1¹⁵⁄₁₆	①
195-GL	153624	.025	.018	Dist.⑧	Flywheel	1100–1200	45	.008C	.022C	124 @ 1¹⁵⁄₁₆	①
197-DLC	153624	None	None	FP⑧	Flywheel	1350–1400	45	.010C	.020C	124 @ 1¹⁵⁄₁₆	①
197-DLCS	153624	None	None	FP⑧	Flywheel	1350–1400	45	.008C	.020C	124 @ 1¹⁵⁄₁₆	①
MZA	153624	.025	.018	Dist.⑧	Flywheel	875–900	45	.099C	.020C	101 @ 1²¹⁄₃₂	①
WAKB	153624	.025	.018	Dist.⑧	Flywheel	2400–2500	②	.018C	.038C	50 @ 3¹⁵⁄₃₂	56 @ 3⁵⁄₃₂
WAKC	153624	None	None	FP⑧	Flywheel	3500–3600	②	.018C	.038C	50 @ 3¹⁵⁄₃₂	56 @ 3⁵⁄₃₂
WAKD	153624	None	None	FP⑧	Flywheel	3500–3600	②	.018C	.038C	50 @ 3¹⁵⁄₃₂	56 @ 3⁵⁄₃₂
WAKDB	153624	None	None	FP⑧	Flywheel	3500–3600	②	.014C	.024C	50 @ 3¹⁵⁄₃₂	56 @ 3⁵⁄₃₂
WAKDBS	153624	None	None	FP⑧	Flywheel	3500–3600	②	.014C	.024C	50 @ 3¹⁵⁄₃₂	56 @ 3⁵⁄₃₂
ROILINE											
H540	⑩	.023–.028	.018	TDC	Flywheel	1075–1100	45	.015C	.020C	106 @ 1.6	①
H570	⑩	.023–.028	.018	TDC	Flywheel	1075–1100	45	.015C	.020C	100 @ 1.8	①

Continued

STOCK ENGINES

TUNE UP & VALVE SPECIFICATIONS—Continued

Engine Model	Firing Order	Spark Plug Gap	Breaker Gap	Ignition or Injection Timing		Cylinder Head Torque (Oiled) Inch Lbs.	Valve Seat Angle Degrees	Valve Clearance⑨ C-Cold		Valve Spring Pressure (Minimum) Lbs. @ Inch Length	
				Mark	Location			Intake	Exhaust	Outer	Inner
H844	⑩	.023–.028	.018	TDC	Pulley	1075–1100	45	.015C	.020C	132 @ 1.8	①
H884	⑩	.023–.028	.018	TDC	Pulley	1075–1100	45	.015C	.020C	150 @ 1.9	①

①—Single spring used.
②—Intake 30°, exhaust 45°.
③—Long 2400–2500, short 1800–1850.
④—With sodium-cooled exhaust valves intake .011C, exhaust .020C.
⑤—Intake valve spring.
⑥—Exhaust valve spring.
⑦—Cap screws with former 3/16" hole drilled through to be torqued 950–100. Present hole (3/16 top—1/8 bottom) torque to 1150–1200.
⑧—Engines with degree marks instead of stamped marks on flywheel have timing data noted on engine.
⑨—Valve clearances stamped on WAUKESHA engine name plate for cold settings only.
⑩—1L-4R-4L-2L-3R-3L-2R-1R.

PISTONS, PINS, RINGS, CRANKSHAFT & BEARINGS

Engine Model	Piston Clearance	Wrist Pin Diameter	Ring End Gap (Minimum)		Rod Bearings			Main Bearings		
			Comp.	Oil	Shaft Diameter	Bearing Clearance	Rod Bolt Torque (Oiled) Inch Lbs.	Shaft Diameter	Bearing Clearance	Main Bolt Torque Inch Lbs.
135-DK	.0065	1.50	.015	③	2.999–3.000	.001–.0035	1300–1350	3.249–3.250	.0015–.0045	1500–1600
135-DKB	.0065	1.50	.015	③	2.999–3.000	.001–.0035	1300–1350	3.249–3.250	.0015–.0045	1500–1600
135-DKBS	.0065	1.50	.015	③	2.999–3.000	.001–.0035	1300–1350	3.249–3.250	.0015–.0045	1500–1600
135-GKB	.003	1.50	.015	③	2.999–3.000	.001–.0035	1300–1350	3.249–3.250	.0015–.0045	1500–1600
135-GZ	.003	1.50	.015	③	2.999–3.000	.001–.0035	1300–1350	3.249–3.250	.0015–.0045	1500–1600
135-GZB	.003	1.50	.015	③	2.999–3.000	.001–.0035	1300–1350	3.249–3.250	.0015–.0045	1500–1600
140-GK	.006①	1.375	.030	.015	2.624–2.625	.001–.003	1150–1200	3.249–3.250	.002–.004	1550–1600
140-GKB	.006	1.375	.030	.015	2.624–2.625	.001–.003	1150–1200	3.249–3.250	.002–.004	1550–1600
140-GZ	.006	1.375	.030	.015	2.624–2.625	.001–.003	1150–1200	3.249–3.250	.002–.004	1550–1600
140-GZB	.006	1.375	.030	.015	2.624–2.625	.001–.003	1150–1200	3.249–3.250	.002–.004	1550–1600
145-GK	.007②	1.625	.030	.020	2.999–3.000	.001–.003	800–825	3.499–3.500	.002–.004	3200–3300
145-GKB	.0075	1.625	.030	.020	2.999–3.000	.001–.003	800–825	3.499–3.500	.002–.005	3200–3300
145-GZ	.007	1.625	.030	.020	2.999–3.000	.001–.003	800–825	3.499–3.500	.002–.004	3200–3300
145-GZB	.007	1.625	.030	.020	2.999–3.000	.001–.003	800–825	3.499–3.500	.002–.005	3200–3300
148-DK	.007	1.875	.035	.015	3.374–3.375	.0015–.004	800–825	4.249–4.250	.002–.0047	3500–3600
148-DKB	.007	1.875	.035	.015	3.374–3.375	.0015–.004	800–825	4.249–4.250	.002–.0047	3500–3600
148-DKBS	.007	1.875	.035	.015	3.374–3.375	.0015–.004	800–825	4.249–4.250	.002–.0047	3500–3600
180-DLC	.0045	1.25	.014	.007③	2.249–2.250	.001–.0015	550–600	2.249–2.250	.002–.003	1050–1100
180-GLB	.002	1.25	.010	.007	2.249–2.250	.0005–.0015	525–550	2.249–2.250	.0002–.0032	1050–1100
185-DLC	.0045	1.25	.014	.007③	2.249–2.250	.0005–.0015	550–600	2.249–2.250	.0002–.0032	1050–1100
185-GLB	.002	1.25	.010	.007	2.249–2.250	.0005–.0015	525–550	2.249–2.250	.0002–.0032	1050–1100
190-DLCA	.0045	1.25	.015	.010③	2.624–2.625	.0005–.003	1050–1100	2.624–2.625	.0015–.0045	1300–1350
190-GLB	.0035	1.25	.015	.010	2.4365–2.4375	.0005–.0015	675–700	2.624–2.625	.0005–.0035	1300–1350
195-DLCA	.005	1.25	.015	.010③	2.624–2.625	.0005–.0015	1050–1100	2.624–2.625	.0015–.0045	1300–1350
195-GKA	.0035	1.25	.013	③	2.624–2.625	.0005–.003	675–700	2.624–2.625	.0015–.0045	1300–1350
195-GL	.0045	1.25	.013	③	2.249–2.250	.0005–.0015	1050–1100	2.624–2.625	.0005–.003	1300–1350
197-DLC	.006	1.250	.015	.010③	2.624–2.625	.0005–.003	1050–1100	2.624–2.625	.0015–.0045	1500–1600
197-DLCS	.006	1.250	.015	.010③	2.624–2.625	.0005–.003	1050–1100	2.624–2.625	.0015–.0045	1500–1600
MZA	.004	1.00	.013	.015	2.249–2.250	.001–.003	800–825	2.624–2.625	.0015–.0035	1150–1200
WAKB	.009	1.875	.045	.020	3.374–3.375	.0015–.004	1025–1050	3.999–4.000	.0025–.005	3500–3600
WAKC	.009	1.875	.045	.020	3.374–3.375	.0015–.004	1025–1050	3.999–4.000	.0025–.005	3500–3600
WAKD	.009	2.187	.035	.020	3.749–3.750	.002–.0045	1300–1350	4.749–4.750	.0024–.0058	3500–3600
WAKDB	.009	2.187	.035	.020	3.749–3.750	.002–.0045	1300–1350	4.749–4.750	.0024–.0058	3500–3600
WAKDBS	.009	2.187	.035	.020	3.749–3.750	.002–.0045	1300–1350	4.749–4.750	.0024–.0058	3500–3600
ROILINE										
H540	.002–.0035	1.2499	.012 Min.	.012 Min.	2.748–2.749	.0011–.0036	800–825	3.2481–3.2490	.0014–.0044	1300–1350
H570	.002–.0035	1.2499	.012 Min.	.012 Min.	2.748–2.749	.0011–.0036	800–825	3.2481–3.2490	.0014–.0044	1300–1350
H844	.003–.005	1.4999	.015 Min.	.015 Min.	3.248–3.249	.0013–.0043	1075–1100	3.7480–3.7490	.002–.005	1775–1825
H884	.003–.005	1.4999	.015 Min.	.015 Min.	3.248–3.249	.0013–.0043	1075–1100	3.7480–3.7490	.002–.005	1775–1825

①—For aluminum; cast iron .0045".
②—For aluminum; cast iron .0055".
③—U-Flex ring—no gap.

Farm Tractor Specifications

ALLIS-CHALMERS WHEEL TYPE
TUNE UP SPECIFICATIONS

Tractor Model	Firing Order	Spark Plug Gap	Breaker Gap Distributor	Breaker Gap Magneto	Ignition Mark Location	Ignition Mark Retarded Timing BTC	Ignition Mark Full Advance Timing BTC	Valve Lash Intake	Valve Lash Exhaust	Cylinder Head Torque
D-10, D-12 ③	1243	.025	.022⑪	—	Flywheel	"DC"	"F"	.013H	.013H	80–85
D-10, D-12 ④	1243	.025	.022⑪	—	Flywheel	"Center"	"F"	.009H	.015H	80–85
D-14	1243	.030	.020⑪	—	Flywheel	"DC"	"F"	.013H	.013H	80–85
D-15 Gasoline	1243	.025	.022⑪	—	Flywheel	"Center"	"F-25"	.009H	.015H	80–85
D-15 LPG	1243	.020	.022⑪	—	Flywheel	"Center"	"F-25"	.009H	.015H	80–85
D-15 Diesel	1342	—	—	—	①	①	①	.010H	.019H	95–100
D-17 Gasoline	1243	.025	.022⑪	—	Flywheel	TDC	"F"	.013H	.013H	②
D-17 LPG	1243	.020	.022⑪	—	Flywheel	TDC	"F"	.013H	.013H	②
D-17 Diesel	153624	—	—	—	⑤	①	①	.010H	.019H	100
D-19 Gasoline	153624	.025	.022	—	Pulley	TDC	25°	.015H	.020H	110–120
D-19 LPG	153624	.025	.022	—	Pulley	TDC	25°	.015H	.020H	110–120
D-19 Diesel	153624	—	—	—	Pulley	⑤⑩	⑤⑩	.015H⑥	.015H⑥	110–120
D-21, D-21 Series II Diesel	153624	—	—	—	Pulley	34°⑤	⑤	.015H	.015H	130–140
160 Diesel	123	—	—	—	Pulley	24°	—	⑨	⑨	55–60
170, 175 Gasoline	1243	.025	.022⑫	—	Flywheel	TDC	"F-25"	.011H	.015H	②
170, 175 Diesel	1342	—	—	—	⑦	⑦	⑦	.010H	.010H	80–85
180, 185, 190 Gasoline	153624	.025	.016	—	Pulley	—	26°	.020H	.025H	150
180, 185, 190 Diesel	153624	—	—	—	Pulley	⑧		.015H	.015H	150
190 XT Gasoline	153624	.025	.016	—	Pulley	⑧	26°	.020H	.025H	150
190 XT LPG	153624	.020	.016	—	Pulley	—	27°	.020H	.025H	150
190 XT Diesel	153624	—	—	—	Pulley	26°⑤	⑤	.015H	.015H	130
200 Diesel	153624	—	—	—	Pulley	24°⑤	⑤	.015H	.015H	150
210, 220 Diesel	153624	—	—	—	Pulley	24°⑤	⑤	.015H	.015H	130–140
7000 Diesel	153624	—	—	—	Pulley	18°⑤	⑤	.015H	.015H	150
7030 Diesel	153624	—	—	—	Pulley	24°⑤	⑤	.015H	.015H	150
7040 Diesel	153624	—	—	—	Pulley	16°⑤	⑤	.015H	.015H	150
7050 Diesel	153624	—	—	—	Pulley	26°⑤	⑤	.015H	.015H	150
7060 Diesel	153624	—	—	—	Pulley	18°⑤	⑤	.015H	.015H	150
7080 Diesel	153624	—	—	—	Pulley	22°⑤	⑤	.015H	.015H	150

①—For injection timing on early production models, timing lines on cam, governor drive plate and injection pump housing should be aligned. On late production models, pointer on timing gear cover should be aligned with correct timing mark on crankshaft pulley, timing lines on governor plate and cam should then be aligned.
Timing for late production models are as follows;
Injection pump part number.

A.C.	Roosa Master	BTDC
4512325	DBGFC429-1AF	22°
4513634	DBGFC429-5AF	22°
4508945	DGFCL629-12A	23°
4513839	DBGFC637-12AJ	16°
4513839	DBGFC637-14AJ	16°
4514022	DBGFC637-17AJ	16°
4514812	DBGFC637-32AJ	16°

②—1/2" capscrews 90–95 ft. lbs.; 7/16" capscrews 70–75 ft. lbs.
③—Before Serial No. D-10-3501 and D-12-3001.
④—Serial No. D-10-3501 and up, D-12-3001 and up.
⑤—For injection timing, pointer on timing gear cover should be aligned with correct timing mark on pulley. Timing lines on governor plate and cam should then be aligned.
⑥—Late camshaft (4513204) was used after Serial No. D-01498. Set lash .010H for intake and .019H for exhaust.
⑦—The "c" timing mark should align with straight edge of snap ring with No. 1 piston at 22° BTDC.
⑧—180, 185; 26°; 190; 28°.
⑨—.010 Hot; .012 Cold.
⑩—

Pump No.	Engine No.	BTDC
4513709	Before 121791	16°
4514017	121791 to D-01498	16°
4514557	D-01499 to D-03150	20°
4514756	After D-03150	20°

⑪—Dwell angle 25°–34°.
⑫—Dwell angle 31°–34°.

FARM TRACTORS

PISTONS, PINS, RINGS, BEARINGS & CRANKSHAFT

Tractor Model	Cyl. Bore Size In.	Piston Clearance	Pin Diam.	Ring End Gap Minimum		Rod Bearings		Rod Bolt Torque	Main Bearings		Cap Bolt Torque
				Comp.	Oil	Crankpin Diameter	Bearing Clearance		Journal Diameter	Bearing Clearance	
D-10, D-12	④	.0015–.003	.8134	.009	.007	1.936–1.937	.001–.003	35–40	2.749–2.750	.002–.004	90–95
D-14	3 1/2	.002–.004	.8134	.007	.007	1.9365–1.9375	.0006–.0027	35–40	2.748–2.749	.002–.004	90–95
D-15	3 1/2 ⑤	.002–.004	.8134	.009	.007	1.9365–1.9375	.0006–.0027	35–40	2.748–2.749	.002–.004	90–95
D-15 Diesel	3 9/16	.004–.0065	.9996	⑪	⑪	1.9975–1.9985	.0015–.0035	30–40	2.497–2.498	.0023–.0045	130
D-17	4	.0025–.0045	.9894	.009	.015	2.374–2.375	.001–.003	45	2.9995–3.000	.0014–.0035	85
D-17 Diesel	3 9/16	.004–.0065	.9996	⑫	.008	1.9975–1.9985	.0015–.0035	35–40	2.497–2.498	.0023–.0045	130
D-19	3 9/16	.0023–.0048	.9996	①	.014	1.9975–1.9985	.0011–.0036	40–50	2.4970–2.4980	.0013–.004	120–130
D-19 Diesel	3 9/16	.004–.0065	.9996	②	.007	1.9975–1.9985	.0011–.0036	40–50	2.4970–2.4980	.0013–.004	120–130
D-21 Diesel	4 1/4	.0065–.009	1.5016	③	.013	2.7470–2.7485	.001–.004	⑥	3.247–3.248	.0019–.0051	170–190
D-21 Series II Diesel	4 1/4	.0025–.005	—	.013	.008	2.7470–2.7485	.001–.004	⑥	3.247–3.248	.0019–.0051	170–190
160 Diesel	3.6	.006–.008	1.2499	.009	.009	2.2485–2.2490	.0025–.004	45–50	2.7485–2.7490	.0025–.004	110–115
170, 175 Gasoline	4	.0025–.004	.9894	.009	.015	2.3745–2.375	.001–.003	45–55	2.9995–3.000	.001–.004	130–140
170, 175 Diesel	3 7/8	.007	1.375	.015	.011	2.499–2.4995	.0015–.003	65–70	2.9985–2.999	.0025–.0045	145–150
180, 185 Gas	3 3/4	.0015–.004	1.2516	.008	.013	2.373	.0009–.0034	40–45	2.7475	.0016–.0043	130–140
180, 185 Diesel	3 7/8	.0035–.006	1.2516	⑨	⑩	2.373	.0009–.0034	40–45	2.7475	.0016–.0043	130–140
190 Gasoline	3 3/4	.0015–.004	1.2516	.008	.013	2.373	.0009–.0034	40–45	2.7475	.0016–.0043	130–140
190 Diesel	3 7/8	.0035–.006	1.2516	⑨	⑩	2.373	.0009–.0034	40–45	2.7475	.0016–.0043	130–140
190XT Gasoline	3 7/8	.0015–.004	1.2516	⑦	.013	2.373	.0009–.0034	40–45	2.7475	.0016–.0043	130–140
190XT LPG	3 7/8	.0015–.004	1.2516	⑦	.013	2.373	.0009–.0034	40–45	2.7475	.0016–.0043	130–140
190XT Diesel	3 7/8	.0035–.006	1.2516	⑨	⑩	2.373	.0009–.0034	40–45	2.7475	.0016–.0043	130–140
200 Diesel	3 7/8	.0045–.007	1.2516	⑧	.010	2.373	.0009–.0034	40–45	2.7475	.0016–.0043	130–140
210, 220 Diesel	4 1/4	.0025–.005	—	.013	.008	2.7470–2.7485	.001–.004	⑥	3.247–3.248	.0019–.0051	170–190
7000 Diesel	3 7/8	.0045–.007	1.2516	⑧	.010	2.3720–2.3735	.0009–.0034	40–45	2.7465–2.7480	.0016–.0043	130–140
7030 Diesel	4 1/4	.0025–.005	1.5012	⑬	.009	2.7470–2.7485	.001–.004	⑭	3.2470–3.2480	.0019–.0051	170–190
7040 Diesel	4 1/4	.0025–.005	1.5012	⑬	.009	2.7470–2.7485	.001–.004	⑭	3.2470–3.2480	.0019–.0051	170–190
7050 Diesel	4 1/4	.0025–.005	1.5012	⑬	.009	2.7470–2.7485	.001–.004	⑭	3.2470–3.2480	.0019–.0051	170–190
7060 Diesel	4 1/4	.0025–.005	1.5012	⑬	.009	2.7470–2.7485	.001–.004	⑭	3.2470–3.2480	.0019–.0051	170–190
7080 Diesel	4 1/4	.0025–.005	1.5012	⑬	.009	2.7470–2.7485	.001–.004	⑭	3.2470–3.2480	.0019–.0051	170–190

①—Top ring .007", others .014".
②—Top ring .022", others .014".
③—Top ring .030"; others .015".
④—Serial No. D-10-3501, D-12-3001 and up 3 1/2"; prior to these models 3 3/8".
⑤—Series II, 3 5/8".
⑥—Prior to engine serial #3D-09649, 65–70 ft. lbs.; later models, 80–85 ft. lbs.
⑦—Top ring .014", others .017".
⑧—Top ring, .019"; 2nd ring, .015"; 3rd ring, .015".
⑨—Top ring, .017"; 2nd ring—early 190 .017"; others, .013". 3rd ring—early 190 .017"; others, .012".
⑩—3 piece ring, .013"; others, .015".
⑪—Top, 4th & 5th .007"; others .014".
⑫—Top, .008"; 2nd & 3rd, .015"; 4th .014".
⑬—Top ring, .013"; 2nd & 3rd rings, .009".
⑭—Early models with six point cap screws, 60–70 ft. lbs.; late models with socket head screws, 80–85 ft. lbs.

J. I. CASE

TUNE UP SPECIFICATIONS

Tractor Model	Firing Order	Spark Plug Gap	Breaker Gap		Ignition Mark			Valve Lash		Cylinder Head Torque
			Distributor	Magneto	Location	Retarded Timing BTC	Full Advance Timing BTC	Intake	Exhaust	
200B	1342	.025	.020	.010	Flywheel	DC	—	.014C	.014C	60–65
300 Gasoline	1342	.025	.020	.010	Flywheel	7/32 ②	—	.014C	.014C	60–65
300 LP-Gas	1342	.025	.020	.010	Flywheel	3/32 ①	—	.014C	.014C	60–65
300 Diesel	1342	—	—	—	Flywheel ⑪	26° BTC ⑫	—	.014C	.014C	60–65
300B Gasoline	1342	.025	.020	.010	Flywheel	③	—	.014C	.014C	70–75
300B LP-Gas	1342	.025	.020	.010	Flywheel	3/32 ①	—	.014C	.014C	60–65
300B Diesel	1342	—	—	—	Flywheel ⑪	26° BTC ⑫	—	.014C	.014C	70–75
350	1342	.025	.020	.010	Flywheel	IGN	—	.014C	.014C	95–100
400 Gasoline	1342	.025	.020	.010	Pulley	TDC	26° BTC	.012C	.020C	100
400 Diesel	1342	—	—	—	Flywheel ⑪	⑫ ⑭	27° BTC	.012C	.012C	100
400B Gasoline	1342	.025	.020	.010	Flywheel	③	—	.014C	.014C	60–65

Continued

FARM TRACTORS

TUNE UP SPECIFICATIONS—Continued

Tractor Model	Firing Order	Spark Plug Gap	Breaker Gap Distributor	Breaker Gap Magneto	Ignition Mark Location	Retarded Timing BTC	Full Advance Timing BTC	Valve Lash Intake	Valve Lash Exhaust	Cylinder Head Torque
400B LP-Gas	1342	.025	.020	.010	Flywheel	3/32"①	—	.014C	.014C	60–65
430 Gasoline	1342	.025	.020	—	Flywheel	4° BTC	—	.014C	.014C	95–100
430 Diesel	1342	—	—	—	Flywheel⑪	8° BTC⑫	—	.014C	.014C	⑨
440 Gasoline	1342	.025	.020	—	Flywheel	4° BTC	—	.014C	.014C	60–65
470 Gasoline	1342	.025	.020	—	Flywheel	4° BTC	—	.014C	.014C	95–100
470 Diesel	1342	—	—	—	Flywheel⑪	8° BTC⑫	—	.014C	.014C	⑨
500 Diesel	153624	—	—	—	Pulley⑩	26° BTC⑫	—	.012C	.012C	98–102
500B Gasoline	1342	.025	.020	—	Flywheel	③	—	.014C	.014C	95–100
500B LP-Gas	1342	.025	.020	.010	Flywheel	3/32"①	—	.014C	.014C	95–100
530 Gasoline	1342	.025	.020	—	Flywheel	4° BTC	—	.014C	.014C	95–100
530 Diesel	1342	—	—	—	Flywheel⑪	8° BTC⑫	—	.014C	.014C	⑨
540 Gasoline	1342	.025	.020	—	Flywheel	4° BTC	—	.014C	.014C	95–100
570 Gasoline	1342	.025	.020	—	Flywheel	4° BTC	—	.014C	.014C	95–100
570 Diesel	1342	—	—	—	Flywheel⑪	8° BTC⑫	—	.014C	.014C	⑨
600 LP-Gas	153624	.025	—	.010	Pulley	3° BTC	23° BTC	.012C	.020C	98–102
600 Diesel	153624	—	—	—	Pulley⑩	28° BTC⑫	—	.012C	.012C	98–102
600B Gasoline	1342	.025	.020	.010	Flywheel	③	—	.014C	.014C	95–100
600B LP-Gas	1342	.025	.020	.010	Flywheel	3/32"①	—	.014C	.014C	95–100
630 Gasoline	1342	.025	.020	—	Flywheel	4° BTC	—	.014C	.014C	95–100
630 Diesel	1342	—	—	—	Flywheel⑪	8° BTC⑫	—	.014C	.014C	⑨
640 Gasoline	1342	.025	.020	—	Flywheel	4° BTC	—	.014C	.014C	95–100
700B Gasoline	1342	.025	.020	.010	Pulley	TDC	26° BTC	.012C	.020C	100
700B Diesel	1342	—	—	—	Pulley⑩	27° BTC⑫	—	.012C	.012C	100
730 Gasoline	1342	.025	.020	—	Pulley	2° ATC	—	.015C	.025C	⑧
730 LPG	1342	.020	.020	—	Pulley	5° ATC	—	.015C	.025C	⑧
730(C) Diesel	1342	—	—	—	Pulley⑩	33° BTC⑫	—	.025C	.025C	⑧
740(C) Gasoline	1342	.025	.020	—	Pulley	5° BTC	27° BTC	.015C	.025C	—
740(C) LP-Gas	1342	.020	.020	—	Pulley	5° BTC	27° BTC	.015C	.025C	—
770 Gasoline	1342	.025	.020	—	Flywheel	5° ATC	28° BTC	.015C	.025C	210
770 Diesel	1342	—	—	—	Pulley⑩	29° BTC⑫	—	.015C	.025C	210
800B Gasoline	1342	.025	.020	.010	Pulley	TDC	④	.012C	.020C	100
800B Diesel	1342	—	—	—	Pulley⑩	31° BTC⑫	—	.012C	.012C	100
830 Gasoline	1342	.025	.020	—	Pulley	2° ATC	—	.015C	.025C	⑧
830 LPG	1342	.020	.020	—	Pulley	TDC	—	.015C	.025C	⑧
830(C) Diesel	1342	—	—	—	Pulley⑩	29° BTC⑫	—	.025C	.025C	⑧
840(C) Gasoline	1342	.025	.020	—	Pulley	2° ATC	30° BTC	.015C	.025C	—
840(C) LP-Gas	1342	.020	.020	—	Pulley	2° BTC	34° BTC	.015C	.025C	—
870 Gasoline	1342	.025	.020	—	Flywheel	5° ATC	28° BTC	.015C	.025C	210
870 Diesel	1342	—	—	—	Pulley⑩	29° BTC⑫	—	.015C	.025C	210
900B LP-Gas	153624	.025	.020	.010	Pulley	⑤	⑥	.012C	.020C	98–102
900B Diesel	153624	—	—	—	Pulley⑩	⑦	—	.012C	.012C	98–102
930 Gasoline	153624	.025	.020	—	Pulley	4° BTC	—	.015C	.025C	⑧
930 LPG	153624	.020	.020	—	Pulley	2° ATC	—	.015C	.025C	⑧
930 Diesel	153624	—	—	—	Pulley	29° BTC	—	.012C	.012C	⑧
970 Gasoline	153624	.025	.020	—	Flywheel	5° ATC	28° BTC	.015C	.025C	210
970 Diesel	153624	—	—	—	Flywheel⑪	29° BTC⑫	—	.015C	.025C	210
1030 Diesel	153624	—	—	—	Pulley⑩	32° BTC⑫	—	.025C	.025C	—
1070 & 1090 Diesel	153624	—	—	—	Pulley⑩	30° BTC⑫	—	.015C	.025C	210
1170 Diesel	153624	—	—	—	Pulley⑩	30° BTC⑫	—	.015C	.025C	210
1175 Diesel	153624	—	—	—	Pulley⑩	30° BTC⑫	—	.015C	.025C	210
1200	153624	—	—	—	Pulley⑩	31° BTC⑫	—	.025C	.025C	145–150
1270	153624	—	—	—	Pulley⑩	30° BTC⑫	—	.015C	⑬	210

Continued

FARM TRACTORS

TUNE UP SPECIFICATIONS—Continued

Tractor Model	Firing Order	Spark Plug Gap	Breaker Gap		Ignition Mark			Valve Lash		Cylinder Head Torque
			Distributor	Magneto	Location	Retarded Timing BTC	Full Advance Timing BTC	Intake	Exhaust	
1370	153624	—	—	—	Pulley⑩	30° BTC⑫	—	.015C	⑬	210
1570	153624	—	—	—	Pulley⑩	25° BTC⑫	—	.015C	⑬	210

①—Before IGN mark.
②—Before DC mark.
③—With distributor IGN, with magneto DC.
④—Auto-Lite 26° BTC, Wico 28° BTC.
⑤—With distributor 2° BTC, with magneto 3° BTC.
⑥—With distributor 26° BTC, with magneto 23°.
⑦—PES pump 31° BTC, PSB pump 28° BTC.
⑧—Head stud nuts. 100 ft. lbs.; head cap screws 145–150 ft.-lbs.
⑨—Head stud nut 95–100 ft. lbs., head cap screws 110–115 ft. lbs.
⑩—With timing correct mark on pulley & pointer on front cover aligned, align timing mark on injection pump housing with timing mark on drive gear hub.
⑪—With timing marks on flywheel & flywheel housing aligned, align timing mark on governor cage with timing mark on cam ring.
⑫—Injection timing.
⑬—Cold .025"; hot .020".
⑭—Before pump serial No. 8104711, 26° BTDC; after pump serial No. 8104711, 27° BTDC.

PISTONS, PINS, RINGS, BEARINGS & CRANKSHAFT

Tractor Model	Cyl. Bore Size In.	Piston Clearance	Pin Diam.	Ring End Gap Minimum		Rod Bearings		Rod Bolt Torque	Main Bearings		Cap Bolt Torque
				Comp.	Oil	Crankpin Diameter	Bearing Clearance		Journal Diameter	Bearing Clearance	
200B	3 1/8	.003	.8592	.010	.010	1.9365–1.9375	.0015–.002	45–50	2.249–2.250	.0015–.002	95
300 Diesel	3 3/8	.004	1.1251	.010	.010	2.0615–2.0625	.0006–.0031	45–50	2.374–2.375	.0009–.0036	90
300 Gas	3 3/8	.003	.8592	.010	.010	1.9365–1.9375	.0015–.002	35–40	2.249–2.250	.0015–.002	95
300B Diesel	3 3/8	.004	1.1251	.010	.010	2.0615–2.0625	.0006–.0031	45–50	2.374–2.375	.0009–.0036	90
300B Gas	3 3/8	.003	.8592	.010	.010	1.9365–1.9375	.0015–.002	35–40	2.249–2.250	.0015–.002	95
350	3 9/16	.003	.9990	.010	.010	2.0605–2.0615	.0015–.002	45–50	2.623–2.624	.0015–.002	95
400 Gas	4	.004	1.3584	.013	.013	2.748–2.749	.0015–.0036	100	2.249–2.250	.002–.0046	150
400 Diesel	4	.0045	1.3584	.013	.013	2.748–2.749	.0013–.0038	100	2.998–2.999	.0016–.0046	150
400B	3 3/8	.003	.8592	.010	.010	2.0605–2.0615	.0015–.002	45–50	2.623–2.624	.0015–.002	95
430 Gasoline	3 3/8	.003	.8592	.010	.010	2.0605–2.0615	.0015–.002	45–50	2.623–2.624	.0015–.002	95
430 Diesel	3 13/16	.005	1.2498	.010	.010	2.0605–2.0615	.001–.0035	45–50	2.873–2.874	.0008–.0038	95
440	3 3/8	.003	.8592	.010	.010	2.0605–2.0615	.0015–.002	45–50	2.623–2.624	.0015–.002	95
470 Gasoline	3 3/8	—	.8592	.010	.010	2.0605–2.0615	.0015–.002	45–50	2.623–2.624	.0015–.002	95
470 Diesel	3 13/16	.005	1.2498	.010	.010	2.0605–2.0615	.001–.0035	45–50	2.873–2874	.0008–.0038	95
500	4	.004	1.3584	.013	.013	2.748–2.749	.0013–.0038	100	2.998–2.999	.0016–.0046	150
500B	3 9/16	.003	.9990	.010	.010	2.0605–2.0615	.0015–.002	45–50	2.623–2.624	.0015–.002	95
530 Gasoline	3 1/2	.003	.9994	.010	.010	2.0605–2.0615	.0005–.0025	45–50	2.623–2.624	.0015–.002	95
530 Diesel	3 13/16	.005	1.2498	.010	.010	2.0605–2.0615	.001–.0035	45–50	2.873–2.874	.0008–.0038	95
540	3 1/2	.003	.9994	.010	.010	2.0605–2.0615	.0005–.0025	45–50	2.623–2.624	.0015–.002	95
570 Gasoline	3 1/2	—	.9994	.010	.010	2.0605–2.0615	.0005–.0025	45–50	2.623–2.624	.0015–.002	95
570 Diesel	3 13/16	.005	1.2498	.010	.010	2.0605–2.0615	.001–.0035	45–50	2.873–2.874	.0008–.0038	95
600 Diesel	4	.005	1.3584	.013	.010	2.748–2.749	.0013–.0038	100	2.998–2.999	.0016–.0046	150
600 Gas	4	.004	1.3584	.013	.010	2.748–2.749	.0015–.0036	100	2.998–2.999	.0016–.0046	150
600B	3 9/16	.003	.9990	.010	.010	2.0605–2.0615	.0015–.002	45–50	2.623–2.624	.0015–.002	95
630	3 13/16	.005	1.2498	.010	.010	2.0605–2.0615	②	45–50	2.873–2.874	.0008–.0038	95
640	3 13/16	.004	.9994	.018	.010	2.0605–2.0615	.001–.002	45–50	2.873–2.874	.0008–.0038	95
700B Gas	4	.004	1.3584	.013	.010	2.748–2.749	.0013–.0038	100	2.998–2.999	.0016–.0046	150
700B Diesel	4 1/8	.0045	1.3584	.013	.010	2.748–2.749	.0013–.0038	100	2.998–2.999	.0016–.0046	150
730, 730C Diesel	4 1/8	.005	1.3584	.013	.010	2.748–2.749	.0013–.0038	100	2.998–2.999	.0016–.0046	150
730 Non-Diesel	4	.004	1.3585	.013	.010	2.748–2.749	.0015–.0036	100	2.998–2.999	.0016–.0046	150
740, 740C	—	.004	1.3584	.013	.010	2.748–2.749	.0015–.0036	100	2.998–2.999	.002–.0046	150
770 Gasoline	4	.0035	1.3584	.013	.015	2.748–2.749	.0013–.0038	95–105	2.998–2.999	.0016–.0046	145–155
770 Diesel	4 1/8	.005	1.4994	.013	.015	2.748–2.749	.0013–.0038	95–105	2.998–2.999	.0016–.0046	145–155
800B Diesel	4 1/8	.0045	1.3584	.013	.010	2.748–2.749	.0013–.0038	100	2.998–2.999	.0016–.0046	150

Continued

FARM TRACTORS

PISTONS, PINS, RINGS, BEARINGS & CRANKSHAFT—Continued

Tractor Model	Cyl. Bore Size In.	Piston Clearance	Pin Diam.	Ring End Gap Minimum Comp.	Ring End Gap Minimum Oil	Rod Bearings Crankpin Diameter	Rod Bearings Bearing Clearance	Rod Bolt Torque	Main Bearings Journal Diameter	Main Bearings Bearing Clearance	Cap Bolt Torque
800B Gas	4	.004	1.3584	.013	.010	2.748–2.749	.0015–.0036	100	2.998–2.999	.0016–.0046	150
830, 830C Diesel	4 3/8	.005	1.4994	.013	.015	2.748–2.749	.0013–.0038	100	2.998–2.999	.0016–.0046	150
830 Non-Diesel	4 1/4	.004	1.3585	.013	.010	2.748–2.749	.0015–.0036	100	2.998–2.999	.0016–.0046	150
840, 840C	—	.004	1.3584	.013	.015	2.748–2.749	.0015–.0036	100	2.998–2.999	.002–.0046	150
870 Gasoline	4 3/8	.004	1.3584	.013	.169	2.748–2.749	.0013–.0038	95–105	2.998–2.999	.0016–.0046	145–155
870 Diesel	4 5/8	.005	1.7994	①	.013	2.998–2.999	.0013–.0038	95–105	3.488–3.489	.0016–.0046	145–155
900B Diesel	4	.005	1.3584	.014	.010	2.748–2.749	.0013–.0038	100	2.998–2.999	.0016–.0046	150
900B Gas	4	.004	1.3584	.014	.010	2.748–2.749	.0015–.0036	100	2.998–2.999	.0016–.0046	150
930 Diesel	4 1/8	.005	1.3584	.013	.010	2.748–2.749	.0013–.0038	100	2.998–2.999	.0016–.0046	150
930 Non-Diesel	4	.004	1.3585	.013	.010	2.748–2.749	.0015–.0036	100	2.998–2.999	.0016–.0046	150
940	—	.005	1.3584	.013	.010	2.748–2.749	.0015–.0036	100	2.998–2.999	.002–.0046	150
970 Gasoline	4	.0035	1.3584	.013	.015	2.748–2.749	.0013–.0038	95–105	2.998–2.999	.0016–.0046	145–155
970 Diesel	4 1/8	.005	1.4994	.013	.015	2.748–2.749	.0013–.0038	95–105	2.998–2.999	.0016–.0046	145–155
1030	4 3/8	.0045	1.4995	.013	.015	2.748–2.749	.0013–.0038	100	2.998–2.999	.0016–.0046	150
1070 & 1090 Diesel	4 3/8	.005	1.4993	①	.010	2.748–2.749	.0013–.0038	95–105	2.998–2.999	.0016–.0046	145–155
1170 Diesel	4 3/8	.005	1.6244	.013	.010	2.748–2.749	.0013–.0038	95–105	2.998–2.999	.0016–.0046	145–155
1175 Diesel	4 3/8	.004–.006	1.6244–1.6246	.013	.010	2.748–2.749	.0013–.0038	95–105	2.998–2.999	.0016–.0046	145–155
1200	4 3/8	.0045	1.4995	.013	—	2.748–2.749	.0013–.0038	100	2.998–2.999	.0016–.0046	150
1270	4 3/8	.004–.006	1.6244–1.6246	①	.010	2.748–2.749	.0013–.0038	95–105	2.998–2.999	.0016–.0046	145–155
1370	4 5/8	.0045–.0055	1.7994–1.7996	.015	.010	2.998–2.999	.0013–.0038	95–105	3.498–3.499	.0016–.0046	145–155
1570	4 5/8	.005	1.7795	.015	.016	2.998	.0013–.0038	100	3.498–3.499	.0016–.0046	145–155

①—Top compression .015, all others .013.
②—Diesel .001–.0035; non-Diesel .001–.002.

JOHN DEERE

TUNE UP SPECIFICATIONS

Tractor Model	Firing Order	Spark Plug Gap	Breaker Gap Distributor	Breaker Gap Magneto	Ignition Mark Location	Ignition Mark Retarded Timing BTC	Ignition Mark Full Advance Timing BTC	Valve Lash Intake	Valve Lash Exhaust	Cylinder Head Torque
40	1–2	.025	.022	—	Flywheel	3° BTC	25° BTC	.012C	.012C	105
50 Gasoline	1–2	.030	.022	—	Flywheel	5°	20°	.020H	.020H	104
50 All Fuel	1–2	.030	.022	—	Flywheel	TDC	25°	.020H	.020H	104
50 LP-Gas	1–2	.030	.022	—	Flywheel	5°	10°	.020H	.020H	104
60 Gasoline	1–2	.030	.022	—	Flywheel	5°	20°	.020H	.020H	150
60 All Fuel	1–2	.030	.022	—	Flywheel	TDC	25°	.020H	.020H	150
60 LP-Gas	1–2	.030	.022	—	Flywheel	10°	5°	.020H	.020H	150
70 Gasoline	1–2	.030	.022	—	Flywheel	10°	15°	.020H	.020H	208
70 All Fuel	1–2	.030	.022	—	Flywheel	TDC	25°	.020H	.020H	208
70 LP-Gas	1–2	.030	.022	—	Flywheel	10°	5°	.020H	.020H	208
80 Diesel	1–2	—	—	—	Flywheel④	No. 1 Inj.③	—	.015H	.020H	275
320, 330	1–2	.025	.022	—	Flywheel	3°	31°	.012C	.012C	105
420, 430	1–2	.025	.022	—	Flywheel	2°	28°	.015C	.015C	90
435 Diesel	1–2	—	—	—	①	①③	①	—	.009H	175
440 Gasoline	1–2	.025	.022	—	Flywheel	2°	28°	.015C	.015C	90

Continued

FARM TRACTORS

TUNE UP SPECIFICATIONS—Continued

Tractor Model	Firing Order	Spark Plug Gap	Breaker Gap Distributor	Breaker Gap Magneto	Ignition Mark Location	Ignition Mark Retarded Timing BTC	Ignition Mark Full Advance Timing BTC	Valve Lash Intake	Valve Lash Exhaust	Cylinder Head Torque
440 Diesel	1-2	—	—	—	①	①③	①	—	.012C	85-95
520, 530	1-2	.030	.022	—	Flywheel	TDC	20°	.020H	.020H	104
620, 630	1-2	.030	.022	—	Flywheel	TDC	20°	.020H	.020H	150
720, 730 Gasoline	1-2	.030	.022	—	Flywheel	TDC	20°	.020H	.020H	275
720, 730 Diesel	1-2	—	—	—	Flywheel	No. 1 Inj.③	—	.020H	.020H	275
820, 830 Diesel	1-2	—	—	—	Flywheel④	No. 1 Inj.③	—	.015H	.020H	275
820, 830 Diesel	123	—	—	—	Pulley⑤	12°③	—	.014H	.018H	110
1010 Gasoline	1342	.025	.025	—	Flywheel	2°	28°	.012C	.018C	125
1010 Diesel	1342	—	—	—	Flywheel⑥	TDC③	—	.012C	.018C	125
1020 Gasoline	123	.025	.020	—	Pulley	—	30°	.014C	.022C	110
1020 Diesel	123	—	—	—	Flywheel⑦	12°③	30°	.014C	.018C	110
1520 Gasoline	123	.025	.020	—	Pulley	TDC	28°	.014C	.022C	110
1520 Diesel	123	—	—	—	Flywheel⑧	12°③	—	.014H	.018H	110
1530 Diesel	123	—	—	—	Flywheel⑨	—	—	.014C	.018C	110
2010 Gasoline	1342	.025	.022	—	Flywheel	2°	28°	.012C	.018C	125
2010 Diesel	1342	—	—	—	Flywheel⑥	TDC③	—	.012C	.018C	125
2020 Gasoline	1342	.025	.020	—	Pulley	—	30°	.014C	.022C	110
2020 Diesel	1342	—	—	—	Flywheel⑩	12°③	30°	.014C	.018C	110
2030 Gasoline	1342	.025	.020	—	Pulley	—	30°	.014C	.022C	110
2030 Diesel	1342	—	—	—	Flywheel⑨	12°③	—	.014C	.018C	110
2040 Diesel	123	—	—	—	⑯	③⑯	—	.014	.018	110
2440 Diesel	1342	—	—	—	Pulley⑪	TDC	7°	.014	.018	95
2510 Gasoline	1342	.025	.020	—	Pulley	TDC	30°	.014C	.022C	110
2510 Diesel	1342	—	—	—	Flywheel⑪	TDC③	—	.014C	.018C	110
2520 Gasoline	1342	.025	.020	—	Pulley	TDC	30°	.014C	.022C	110
2520 Diesel	1342	—	—	—	Flywheel⑪	TDC③	—	.014C	.018C	110
2630 Diesel	1342	—	—	—	Pulley⑪	TDC	7.5°	.014	.018	110
2640 Diesel	1342	—	—	—	Pulley⑪	TDC	6°	.014	.018	95
2840 Diesel	153624	—	—	—	⑯	③⑯	—	.014	.018	110
3010 Gasoline	1342	.025	.022	—	Flywheel	TDC	20°	.015C	.028C	115
3010 Diesel	1342	—	—	—	Flywheel⑫	10°③	10°	.018C	.018C	115
3020 Gasoline	1342	.025	.022	—	Flywheel	5° ATC	20°	.015H	.028H	115
3020 LP-Gas	1342	.025	.022	—	Flywheel	TDC	25°	.015H	.028H	115
3020 Diesel	1342	—	—	—	Flywheel⑫	TDC③	—	.018H	.018H	115
4010 Gasoline	153624	.025	.022	—	Flywheel	TDC	20°	.015C	.028C	115
4010 LP-Gas	153624	.015	.022	—	Flywheel	TDC	25°	.015C	.028C	115
4010 Diesel	153624	—	—	—	Flywheel⑫	14°③	14°	.018C	.018C	115
4020 Gasoline	153624	.025	.022	—	Flywheel	5°ATC	20°	.015H	.028H	115
4020 LP-Gas	153624	.025	.022	—	Flywheel	TDC	25°	.015H	.028H	115
4020 Diesel	153624	—	—	—	Flywheel⑫	TDC③	—	.018H	.018H	115
4030 Diesel	153624	—	—	—	②	TDC③	—	.014C	.018C	110
4230 Diesel	153624	—	—	—	②	TDC③	—	.018C	.028C	130
4320 Diesel	153624	—	—	—	Flywheel⑫	TDC③	—	.018C	.022C	130
4401 Diesel	1-2	—	—	—	①	①③	①	.009H	.009H	175
4430 Diesel	153624	—	—	—	②	TDC③	—	.018C	.028C	130
4520 Diesel	153624	—	—	—	Flywheel	TDC③	—	.018	.022	130
4620 Diesel	153624	—	—	—	Flywheel	TDC③	—	.018C	.022C	130
4630 Diesel	153624	—	—	—	②	TDC③	—	.018C	.028C	130
5010 Diesel	153624	—	—	—	Flywheel⑬	TDC③	—	.015H	.022H	170
5020 Diesel	153624	—	—	—	Flywheel⑬	—	—	.018H	.028H	170
6030 Diesel	153624	—	—	—	②⑬	TDC③	—	.018	.028	175

Continued

FARM TRACTORS

TUNE UP NOTES—Continued

① —Timed at fuel injector using gauge provided by General Motors.
② —Pump window.
③ —Injection pump timing.
④ —With timing marks on flywheel and timing gear housing aligned, align scribe mark on No. 1 injection pump plunger follower with index mark on window of the pump body.
⑤ —Timing on 830 tractor models cannot be checked. On 820 models prior to pump serial #047753 and after #082143, after timing pin is set with flywheel, timing marks on governor cage and pump cam should align. On 820 models between pump serial #047753 and #082142 use of flywheel and pump timing pins are necessary. If both pins index at same time, timing is correct.
⑥ —Align "DC" timing mark on flywheel with timing mark on clutch housing, timing marks on governor cage and cam ring should now align.
⑦ —On pump models before serial #60326 and after #117500, after flywheel pin is inserted, governor weight retainer and pump cam timing lines should align. On pump models between serial #60327 and #117499, use of flywheel and pump timing pins are necessary. If both pins index at same time, timing is correct.
⑧ —On pump models between serial #83759 and #117499, use of flywheel and pump timing pins are necessary, if both index at same time, timing is correct. On pump models after serial #117500, after flywheel pin is inserted, governor weight retainer and pump cam timing lines should align.
⑨ —On some models the CAV rotor pump was installed, in this case timing cannot be checked. In all other cases after flywheel pin has been inserted, governor weight retainer and pump cam timing lines should align.
⑩ —On pump models before #50303 and after #117500, after flywheel pin has been installed, governor weight retainer and pump cam timing lines should align. On pump models between serial #50304 and #117499, use of flywheel and pump timing pins are necessary, if both pins index at same time, timing is correct.
⑪ —On pump model DBG and JDB after flywheel pin has been inserted, governor weight retainer and pump cam timing lines should align. On pump model CDC and CBC use of flywheel and pump timing pins are necessary. If both pins index at same time, timing is correct.
⑫ —With marks on flywheel and flywheel timing window aligned, align scribe lines on governor cage and cam ring.
⑬ —With timing marks on flywheel and timing pointer aligned, align scribe marks on the cam and governor cage.
⑭ —With timing pin inserted into threaded hole on flywheel housing and hole on flywheel, align timing line on pump drive hub with pointer mark.
⑮ —Naturally aspirated—with timing mark on flywheel and mark on rear of timing window aligned, align timing lines on governor weight retainer and cam. Turbocharged—with timing mark on pulley aligned with notch on timing cover, align timing mark on pump drive hub with pointer mark.
⑯ —Injection pump timing gears are stamped with two timing marks, "3" or "4". Use timing mark "3" when timing a three or six cylinder engine. The injection pump is properly timed when timing mark "3" on pump timing gear is directly below timing tool, when tool is placed between center lines of crankshaft & injection pump shafts.

PISTONS, PINS, RINGS, BEARINGS & CRANKSHAFT

Tractor Model	Cyl. Bore Size In.	Piston Clearance	Pin Diam.	Ring End Gap Minimum		Rod Bearings			Main Bearings		
				Comp.	Oil	Crankpin Diameter	Bearing Clearance	Rod Bolt Torque	Journal Diameter	Bearing Clearance	Cap Bolt Torque
40	4	.005	1.1878	.013	.013	2.498–2.499	.001–.0035	55–60	2.397–2.398	.001–.0035	140
50	4¹¹⁄₁₆	.0075	1.4167	①	①	2.7492	.001–.004	85	⑧	.004–.006	100
60	5½	.007	1.7497	①	①	2.99925	.001–.004	105	⑨	.004–.006	150
70	⑩	.008	1.7498	①	①	3.3743	.001–.004	85	3.2495	.0045–.0065	150
80 Diesel	6⅛	.010	2.3547	①	①	3.9991–4.0005	.0015–.0049	210	4.4975–4.4985	④	150
320, 330	4	.004	1.1878	.013	.010	2.498–2.499	.001–.0035	55–60	2.397–2.398	.001–.0035	140
420, 430	4¼	.004	1.1878	.013	.103	2.498–2.499	.001–.0035	55–60	2.397–2.398	.001–.0035	140
435	3⅞	.0057	1.3748	.020	.010	2.499–2.500	.0044–.0084	40–45	2.999–3.000	.002–.004	125
440 Gas	4¼	.004	1.1878	.013	.013	2.498–2.499	.001–.0035	55–60	2.397–2.398	.001–.0035	140
440 Diesel	3⅞	.0037	—	.020	.010	2.499–2.500	.0044–.0084	40–45	2.999–3.000	.002–.004	125
520, 530	4¹¹⁄₁₆	.0057	1.4168	①	①	2.874–2.875	.001–.004	85	2.8735–2.8745	.004–.006	100
620, 630	5½	.006	1.7497	①	①	3.3736–3.375	.0011–.0041	105	②	②	150
720, 730 Gas	6	.008	2.3547	①	①	3.748–3.749	.002–.005	85	4.4975–4.4985	④	⑪
720, 730 Diesel	6⅛	.010	2.3547	①	①	3.748–3.749	.002–.005	208	4.4975–4.4985	④	⑪
820, 830	6⅛	.010	2.3547	①	①	3.9991–4.0005	.0015–.0049	210	4.4975–4.4985	④	150
820, 830 Diesel	3.86	.0028–.0052	1.1877	①	①	2.748–2.749	.0012–.0042	60–70	3.1235–3.1245	.0011–.0041	⑫
1010 Gas	3½	.003	1.1877	.010	.010	2.3085–2.3095	.0014–.004	40–45	2.9974–2.9984	.0016–.0046	145
1010 Diesel	3⅝	.0055	1.1877	.010	.010	2.3085–2.3095	.0014–.004	40–45	2.9974–2.9984	.0016–.0028	145
1020 Gasoline	3.86	.0034	1.1877	①	①	2.3085–2.3095	.0014–.0044	40–45	3.1235–3.1245	.0011–.0041	85
1020 Diesel	3.86	.0030–.0054	1.1877	①	①	2.7480–2.7490	.0012–.0042	60–70	3.1235–3.1245	.0011–.0041	85
1520 Gasoline	4.02	.0024	1.1877	①	①	2.748–2.749	.0012–.0042	60–70	3.1235–3.1245	.0011–.0041	85
1520 Diesel	4.02	.0015–.0039	1.1877	①	①	2.748–2.749	.0012–.0042	60–70	3.1235–3.1245	.0011–.0041	85
1530 Diesel	4.02	.0015–.0039	⑬	①	①	2.748–2.749	.0012–.0044	60–70	3.1235–3.1245	.001–.0041	110
2010 Gas	3⅝	.003	1.1877	.010	.010	2.3085–2.3095	.0014–.004	40–45	2.9974–2.9984	.0016–.0046	145
2010 Diesel	3⅞	.0055	1.1877	.010	.010	2.3085–2.3095	.0014–.004	40–45	2.9974–2.9984	.0016–.0046	145
2020 Gasoline	3.86	.0034	1.1891	①	①	2.3085–2.3100	.0014–.0044	40–45	3.1235–3.1245	.001–.0041	85
2020 Diesel	3.86	.0030–.0054	1.1891	①	①	2.7480–2.7490	.0012–.0042	60–70	3.1235–3.1245	.001–.0041	85
2030 Gasoline	4.02	.0024	⑬	①	①	2.3085–2.3100	.0014–.0044	40–45	3.1230–3.1240	.0016–.0046	85

Continued

FARM TRACTORS

PISTONS, PINS, RINGS, BEARINGS & CRANKSHAFT—Continued

Tractor Model	Cyl. Bore Size In.	Piston Clearance	Pin Diam.	Ring End Gap Minimum Comp.	Ring End Gap Minimum Oil	Rod Bearings Crankpin Diameter	Rod Bearings Bearing Clearance	Rod Bolt Torque	Main Bearings Journal Diameter	Main Bearings Bearing Clearance	Cap Bolt Torque
2030 Diesel	4.02	.0015–.0039	⑬	①	①	2.7480–2.7490	.0012–.0042	60–70	3.1230–3.1240	.0016–.0046	85
2040 Diesel	4.02	.005	1.3750	①	①	2.748–2.749	.0012–.0040	60–70	3.1230–3.1240	.0012–.004	85
2510 Gasoline	3.86	.0023–.0047	1.1877	①	①	2.3085–2.3095	.0014–.0044	40–45	3.1235–3.1245	.001–.004	85
2510 Diesel	3.86	.0018–.0042	1.1877	①	①	2.7480–2.7490	.0012–.0042	60–70	3.1235–3.1245	.001–.004	85
2840 Diesel	4.02	.005	1.3750	①	①	2.748–2.749	.0012–.0040	60–70	3.1230–3.1240	.0012–.004	85
3010 Gas	4	.006⑤	1.2497	.013	.013	2.9985–2.9995	.0015–.0045	105	3.3720–3.3730	.0031–.0061	150
3010 Diesel	4 1/8	⑥	1.4997	.013	.013	2.9985–2.9995	.0015–.0045	125	3.3720–3.3730	.0031–.0061	150
3020 Gasoline	4 1/4	.0055	1.250	.013	.013	2.998–2.999	.0015–.0045	90	3.3715–3.3725	.0031–.0061	150
3020 Diesel	4 1/4	.0035	1.500	.013	.013	2.998–2.999	.0015–.0045	125	3.3715–3.3725	.0031–.0061	150
4010 Gas	4	.007⑤	1.2497	.015	.015	2.9980–2.9990	.0015–.0045	105	3.3730–3.3740	.0031–.0061	150
4010 Diesel	4 1/8	⑦	1.4997	.015	.015	2.9980–2.9990	.0015–.0045	125	3.3730–3.3740	.0031–.0061	150
4020 Gasoline	4 1/4	.0055	1.250	.013	.013	2.998–2.999	.0015–.0045	90	3.3715–3.3725	.0031–.0061	150
4020 Diesel	4 1/4	.0035	1.500	.013	.013	2.998–2.999	.0015–.0045	125	3.3715–3.3725	.0031–.0061	150
4030 Diesel	4 1/4	.0015–.0039	1.1877	①	①	2.7480–2.7490	.0012–.0042	65	3.1230–3.1240	.0017–.0047	85
4230 Diesel	4 1/4	.0027–.0053	1.5000	①	①	2.9980–2.9990	.0015–.0045	100–110	3.3715–3.3725	.0017–.0047	150
4401 Diesel	3 7/8	.0057	1.3748	.020	.010	2.499–2.500	.0044–.0084	45–50	2.999–3.000	.002–.004	125
4430 Diesel	4 1/4	.0027–.0041	1.6250	①	①	2.7480–2.7490	.0015–.0045	100–110	3.3715–3.3725	.0017–.0047	150
4520 Diesel	4 1/4	.0023–.0047	1.625	①	①	2.9985	.0015–.0045	110	3.372	.0017–.0047	150
4630 Diesel	4 1/4	.0027–.0041	1.6250	①	①	2.7480–2.7490	.0015–.0045	100–110	3.3715–3.3725	.0017–.0047	150
5010 Diesel	4 3/4	.0065	1.750	.013	.013	3.498–3.499	.0015–.0045	160	3.748–3.749	.0031–.0061	170
5020 Diesel	4 3/4	.0028–.0052	1.750	.013	.013	3.498–3.499	.0015–.0045	160	3.748–3.749	.0031–.0061	175
6030 Diesel	4 3/4	.0058–.0082	1.8742	—	—	3.498–3.499	.0024–.0054	160	3.748–3.749	.0019–.0049	180

①—Rings are provided with proper gap by supplier.
②—Right 3.399–3.400, left 2.749–2.750.
③—Right .005–.007, left .004–.006.
④—Right and left .006–.008, center .0021–.0055.
⑤—Thrust side.
⑥—Thrust side .006, anti-thrust side .020.
⑦—Thrust side .0065, anti-thrust side .017.
⑧—Right 2.624, left 2.249.
⑨—Right 2.9995, left 2.7495.
⑩—Diesel 6 1/8″, non-Diesel 5 7/8″.
⑪—Center 50, right and left 75.
⑫—820: 85 ft. lbs.; 830: 110 ft. lbs.
⑬—Early models: 1.1886–1.1896; Late models: 1.376–1.377.

FORD

TUNE UP SPECIFICATIONS

Tractor Model	Firing Order	Spark Plug Gap	Breaker Gap Distributor	Breaker Gap Magneto	Ignition Mark Location	Ignition Mark Retarded Timing BTC	Ignition Mark Full Advance Timing BTC	Valve Lash Intake	Valve Lash Exhaust	Cylinder Head Torque
501, 601, 701 Gas	1243	.027	.025	—	Flywheel	4°	24°	.015H	.015H	65–70
501, 601, 701 LPG	1243	.027	.025	—	Flywheel	7°	27°	.015H	.015H	65–70
501, 601, 701 Diesel	1243	—	—	—	Flywheel⑥	26°⑤	—	.015H	.015H	100–105
600, 700 Gas	1243	.027	.025	—	Flywheel	8°	30°	.015H	.015H	65–70
600, 700 LPG	1243	.030	.025	—	Flywheel	11°	33°	.015H	.015H	65–70
800, 900 Gas	1243	.027	.025	—	Flywheel	5°	27°	.015H	.015H	65–70
800, 900 LPG	1243	.030	.025	—	Flywheel	8°	30°	.015H	.015H	65–70
801, 901 Gas	1243	.027	.025	—	Flywheel	4°	24°	.015H	.015H	65–70
801, 901 LPG	1243	.030	.025	—	Flywheel	7°	27°	.015H	.015H	65–70
801, 901 Diesel	1243	—	—	—	Flywheel⑥	18°⑤	—	.015H	.015H	100–105
100, 1600 Diesel	12	—	—	—	⑪	⑤⑪	—	.016H	.016H	108–111
1801 Gas	1243	.027	.025	—	Flywheel	4°	20°	.015H	.015H	65–70
1801 Diesel	1243	—	—	—	Flywheel⑥	18°⑤	—	.015H	.015H	100–105
2000 Gas	123	.025	.025	—	Flywheel	3°②	—	.015H	.018H	105–115

Continued

FARM TRACTORS

TUNE UP SPECIFICATIONS—Continued

Tractor Model	Firing Order	Spark Plug Gap	Breaker Gap Distributor	Breaker Gap Magneto	Ignition Mark Location	Ignition Mark Retarded Timing BTC	Ignition Mark Full Advance Timing BTC	Valve Lash Intake	Valve Lash Exhaust	Cylinder Head Torque
2000 Diesel	123	—	—	—	Flywheel⑨	19°⑤	—	.015H	.018H	105–115
2030 Gas	1243	.027	.025	—	Flywheel	4°	24°	.015H	.015H	65–70
2030 Diesel	1243	—	—	—	Flywheel⑥	26°⑤	—	.015H	.015H	100–105
2600 Gas	123	.025	.025	—	Flywheel	2°	—	.016H	.019H	110
2600	123	—	—	—	Flywheel⑫	23°⑤	—	.016H	.019H	110
3000 Gas	123	.025	.025	—	Flywheel	3°②	—	.015H	.018H	105–115
3000 Diesel	123	—	—	—	Flywheel⑨	19°⑤	—	.015H	.018H	105–115
3600, 4100, 4600, 4600 SU Gas	123	.025	.025	—	Flywheel	4°	—	.016H	.019H	110
3600, 4100, 4600, 4600 SU Diesel	123	—	—	—	Flywheel⑫	23°⑤	—	.016H	.019H	110
4000 Gas	123	.025	.025	—	Flywheel	3°②	—	.015H	.018H	105–115
4000 Diesel	123	—	—	—	Flywheel⑨	4°	24°	.015H	.015H	65–70
4030, 4040 Gas	1243	.027	.025	—	Flywheel	4°	24°	.015H	.015H	65–70
4030, 4040 Diesel	1243	—	—	—	Flywheel⑥	18°⑤	—	.015H	.015H	100–105
5000, 7000 Gas	1342	.025	.025	—	Flywheel	2°②	—	.015H	.018H	105–115
5000, 7000 Diesel	1342	—	—	—	Flywheel⑦	19°⑤	—	.015H	.018H	105–115
5600 Diesel	1342	—	—	—	Flywheel⑦	19°⑤	—	.016H	.0194	105–115
6000 Gas	153624	.030	.025	—	Damper	4°	24°	.015H	.015H	95–105
6000 Diesel	153624	—	—	—	Damper⑧	26°⑤	—	.015H	.015H	95–105
6600, 6700 Gas	1342	.025	.025	—	Flywheel	2°	—	.015H	.018H	105–115
6600, 6700 Diesel	1342	—	—	—	Flywheel⑦	19°⑤	—	.015H	.018H	105–115
7600, 7700 Diesel	1342	—	—	—	Flywheel⑦	23°⑤	—	.015H	.018H	105–115
8000, 8600, 8700 Diesel	153624	—	—	—	Flywheel⑦	23°⑤	—	.015H	.018H	④
9000, 9600, 9700 Diesel	153624	—	—	—	Flywheel⑦	23°⑤	—	.015H	.018H	④
Major Diesel	1243	—	—	—	Flywheel⑩	26°⑤	—	.015H	.012H	85–90
Power	1243	—	—	—	Flywheel⑩	26°⑤	—	.015H	.012H	85–90
Super Major	1243	—	—	—	Flywheel⑩	③⑤	—	.015H	.012H	85–90
NAA	1243	.027	.025	—	F;ywheel	8°	31°	.015H	.015H	65–70
Dextra Models	1243	—	—	—	Flywheel	①	—	.010H	.010H	55–60

①—With vacuum governor injection pump, 26° "spill" mark. With "Minimec" mechanical governor injection pump, 20° "spill" mark.
②—With vacuum advance line disconnected.
③—With vacuum governor injection pump, 23°. With "Minimec" mechanical governor injection pump 21°.
④—8000, 8600, 9000 & 9600 (1/2" bolts), 110 ft. lbs.; 8700 & 9700 (9/16" bolts), 160 ft. lbs.
⑤—Injection pump timing.
⑥—Align flywheel timing mark with index mark on timing port, then check to ensure scribe lines on governor cage and cam are aligned.
⑦—With timing mark on flywheel and arrow on timing hole aligned, align timing mark on the drive gear adapter hub with timing mark on pump housing.
⑧—With timing mark on vibration damper on timing gear cover aligned, align timing mark on injection pump drive flange with pointer on injection pump front cover.
⑨—C.A.V. pump—align scribe line on pump with "O" mark on engine front plate. Simms pump—with timing mark on flywheel and arrow on timing hole aligned, align timing mark on pump flange with scribe line.
⑩—Align crankshaft pulley with pointer at front of engine, timing mark drive coupling should then be aligned with mark on timing plate attached to pump.
⑪—Injection pump is properly timed when timing marks on pump drive gear & idler gear are aligned & marks on pump coupling & pump drive gear are aligned.
⑫—Injection pump is properly timed when scribed line on pump body is aligned with "O" mark on engine front plate.

PISTONS, PINS, RINGS, BEARINGS & CRANKSHAFT

Tractor Model	Cyl. Bore Size In.	Piston Clearance	Pin Diam.	Ring End Gap Minimum Comp.	Ring End Gap Minimum Oil	Rod Bearings Crankpin Diameter	Rod Bearings Bearing Clearance	Rod Bolt Torque	Main Bearings Journal Diameter	Main Bearings Bearing Clearance	Cap Bolt Torque
501, 601, 701 Gas	3.44	.003	.9122	.010	.010	2.2978–2.2988	.0004–.002	45–50	2.4974–2.4988	.0007–.0023	100–105
501, 601, 701 Diesel	3.56	.007	1.1242	.010	.010	2.2978–2.2988	.0004–.002	45–50	2.4974–2.4988	.0007–.0023	100–105
600, 700 Gas	3.44	.003	.9122	.010	.010	2.2978–2.2988	.0004–.002	45–50	2.4974–2.4988	.0007–.0023	100–105
800, 900 Gas	3.90	.003	.9122	.010	.010	2.2978–2.2988	.0004–.002	45–50	2.4974–2.4988	.0007–.0023	100–105

Continued

FARM TRACTORS

PISTONS, PINS, RINGS, BEARINGS & CRANKSHAFT—Continued

Tractor Model	Cyl. Bore Size In.	Piston Clearance	Pin Diam.	Ring End Gap Minimum		Rod Bearings		Rod Bolt Torque	Main Bearings		Cap Bolt Torque
				Comp.	Oil	Crankpin Diameter	Bearing Clearance		Journal Diameter	Bearing Clearance	
801, 901, 1801 Gas	3.90	.003	.9122	.010	.010	2.2978–2.2988	.0004–.002	45–50	2.4974–2.4988	.0007–.0023	100–105
801, 901, 1801 Diesel	3.90	.007	1.2492	.010	.010	2.2978–2.2988	.0004–.002	45–50	2.4974–2.4988	.0007–.0023	100–105
1000	3.54	.006	1.26	.012	.012	2.3602–2.3610	.0023–.0510	51–54	2.6752–2.6760	.0016–.0004	—
1600	3.54	.006	1.26	.012	.012	2.3602–2.3610	.0023–.0510	51–54	2.6752–2.6760	.0016–.0004	—
2000 Gas	4.2	.0027	1.4998	.012	.013	2.749–2.750	③	60–65	3.3714–3.3722	.0022–.0045	115–125
2000 Diesel	4.2	.0075	1.4998	.012	.013	2.749–2.750	③	60–65	3.3714–3.3722	.0022–.0045	115–125
2030 Gas	3.44	.003	.9122	.010	.010	2.2978–2.2988	.0004–.002	45–50	2.4974–2.4988	.0007–.0023	100–105
2030 Diesel	3.56	.007	1.1242	.010	.010	2.2978–2.2988	.0004–.002	45–50	2.4974–2.4988	.0007–.0023	100–105
2600 Gas	4.2	.0032	1.4998	.015	.015	2.749–2.750	.0021–.0042	60–65	3.3714–3.3722	.0022–.0045	115–125
2600 Diesel	4.2	.0080	1.4998	.015	.015	2.749–2.750	.0021–.0042	60–65	3.3714–3.3722	.0022–.0045	115–125
3000 Gas	4.2	.0027	1.4998	.012	.013	2.749–2.750	③	60–65	3.3714–3.3722	.0022–.0045	115–125
3000 Diesel	4.2	.0075	1.4998	.012	.013	2.749–2.750	③	60–65	3.3714–3.3722	.0022–.0045	115–125
3600 Gas	4.2	.0032	1.4998	.015	.015	2.749–2.750	⑪	60–65	3.3714–3.3722	.0022–.0045	115–125
3600 Diesel	4.2	.0080	1.4998	.015	.015	2.749–2.750	⑪	60–65	3.3714–3.3722	.0022–.0045	115–125
4000 Gas	4.4	.0032	1.4998	.012	.013	2.749–2.750	③	60–65	3.3714–3.3722	.0022–.0045	115–125
4000 Diesel	4.4	.008	1.4998	.012	.013	2.749–2.750	③	60–65	3.3714–3.3722	.0022–.0045	115–125
4100 Diesel	4.4	.0075	1.4998	.015	.015	2.749–2.750	⑪	60–65	3.3714–3.3722	.0022–.0045	115–125
4030, 4040 Gas	3.90	.003	.9122	.010	.010	2.2978–2.2988	.0004–.002	45–50	2.4974–2.4988	.0007–.0023	100–105
4030, 4040 Diesel	3.90	.007	1.2492	.010	.010	2.2978–2.2988	.0004–.002	45–50	2.4974–2.4988	.0007–.0023	100–105
4600	4.4	.0034	1.4998	.015	.015	2.749–2.750	⑪	60–65	3.3714–3.3722	.0022–.0045	100–105
4600 Diesel	4.4	.0080	1.4998	.015	.015	2.749–2.750	⑪	60–65	3.3714–3.3722	.0022–.0045	115–125
4600 SU	4.4	.0034	1.4998	.015	.015	2.749–2.750	⑪	60–65	3.3714–3.3722	.0022–.0045	115–125
4600 SU, Diesel	4.4	.0080	1.4998	.015	.015	2.749–2.750	⑪	60–65	3.3714–3.3722	.0022–.0045	115–125
5000, 7000 Gas	⑤	⑤	1.6248	.012	.013	⑧	③	60–65	⑨	.0022–.0045	115–125
5000, 7000 Diesel	⑤	⑤	1.6248	.012	.013	⑧	③	60–65	⑨	.0022–.0045	115–125
5600 Diesel	4.2	.0080	1.4999	.015	.015	2.7496–2.7504	③	60–65	3.3713–3.3723	.0022–.0045	115–125
6000 Gas	3.62	.0015	.9122	.010	.010	2.2980–2.2988	.0024–.006	45–50	2.4963–2.4971	.0021–.0039	100–105
6000 Diesel	3.62	.005	1.1242	.010	.010	2.2980–2.2988	.0024–.006	45–50	2.4963–2.4971	.0021–.0039	100–105
6600	4.4	.0037	1.4999	.015	.015	2.7496–2.7504	③	60–65	3.3713–3.3723	.0022–.0045	115–125
6600 Diesel	4.4	.0085	1.4999	.015	.015	2.7496–2.7504	③	60–65	3.3713–3.3723	.0022–.0045	115–125
6700 Diesel	4.4	.0085	1.4999	.015	.015	2.7496–2.7504	③	60–65	3.3713–3.3723	.0022–.0045	115–125
6700	4.4	.0037	1.4999	.015	.015	2.7496–2.7504	③	60–65	3.3713–3.3723	.0022–.0045	115–125
7600 Diesel	4.4	.0085	1.6248	.015	.015	2.7496–2.7504	③	60–65	3.3713–3.3723	.0022–.0045	115–125
7700 Diesel	4.4	.0085	1.4999	.015	.015	2.7496–2.7504	③	60–65	3.3714–3.3723	.0022–.0045	115–125
8000, 9000 Diesel	4.4	.008	1.4998⑦	⑥	.013	2.749–2.750	③	60–65	3.3713–3.3718	.0022–.0045	115–125
8600 Diesel	4.4	⑩	1.4998	.012	.013	⑧	③	60–65	⑨	.0020–.0045	115–125
8700 Diesel	4.4	⑩	1.4998	.012	.013	⑧	③	60–65	⑨	.0020–.0045	115–125
9600	4.4	⑩	1.6248	.012	.013	⑧	③	60–65	⑨	.0020–.0045	115–125
9700	4.4	⑩	1.6248	.012	.013	⑧	③	60–65	⑨	.0020–.0045	115–125
"Major Diesels"	3 15/16	.004	①	.011	.011	2.4997–2.5005	.002–.0035	55–60	3.0002–3.0010	.0025–.004	④
NAA	3.44	.002	.9122	.010	.010	2.2978–2.2986	.0004–.002	45–50	2.4974–2.4982	.0007–.0023	95–105
Dexta	3 1/2	.0045	1.250	.010	.009	2.2485–2.2490	.002–.0035	②	2.7485–2.7490	.0025–.0045	90–95
Super Dexta	3.6	.0055	1.250	.010	.009	2.2485–2.2490	.002–.0035	②	2.7485–2.7490	.0025–.0045	90–95

①—Before Eng. No. 1425097, 1.250 inch. After Eng. No. 1425096, 1.375".
②—With cadmium plated nuts 50–55 ft-lbs. Unplated nuts 65–70 ft-lbs.
③—Aluminum bearings .0025–.0046 inch, copper lead bearings .0017–.0038 inch.
④—With 1/2" capscrews, 70–75 ft. lbs. with 9/16 inch capscrews, 95–100 ft. lbs. with 5/8 inch capscrews, 115–120 ft. lbs.
⑤—Prior to July 20, 1968, 4.2 inch; after, 4.4 bore. 4.2 bore, gas, .0027 inch 4.2 bore, diesel, .0075; 4.4 bore, gas, .0032 inch; 4.4 bore, diesel, .008 inches.
⑥—Top ring .012; all others .010.
⑦—9000 Series, 1.6248.
⑧—Blue 2.7496–2.750; Red 2.750–2.7504.
⑨—Blue 3.3713–3.718; Red 3.3718–3.3723.
⑩—Cyl. # 1–5, .008–.009 inch; cyl # 6, .010–.011 inch.
⑪—Aluminum bearing .0021–.0042 inch; copper lead bearing .0017–.0038 inch.

FARM TRACTORS

INTERNATIONAL HARVESTER
TUNE UP SPECIFICATIONS

Tractor Model	Firing Order	Spark Plug Gap	Breaker Gap		Ignition Mark			Valve Lash		Cylinder Head Torque
			Distributor	Magneto	Location	Retarded Timing BTC	Full Advance Timing BTC	Intake	Exhaust	
100	1342	.023	.020	.013	Pulley	3rd Notch	30°①	.014H	.014H	65
Hydro 100	153624	—	—	—	Flywheel⑳	18°⑰	—	.020H	.025H	165
130	1342	.023	.020	.013	Pulley	4th Notch	26°①	.014H	.014H	65
140	1342	.023	.020	.013	Pulley	DC	22°①	.014H	.014H	65
154 Lo-Boy	1342	.023	.020	—	Pulley	TDC	16°	.015C	.015C	45
Farmall Cub	1342	.023	.020	.013	Pulley	TDC	16°	.013C	.013C	45
IH Cub, Cub Lo-Boy	1342	.023	.020	.013	Pulley	TDC	16°	.013C	.013C	45
200	1342	.023	.020	.013	Pulley	3rd Notch	30°①	.014H	.014H	65
230	1342	.023	.020	.013	Pulley	4th Notch	30°①	.014H	.014H	65
240	1342	.023	.020	.013	Pulley	DC	30°①	.014H	.014H	65
B275 Diesel	1342	—	—	—	Pulley㉕	20°⑰	—	.020H	.020H	70–75
300	1342	.023	.020	—	Pulley	Last Notch	④	.017H	.017H	70
300 HC	1342	.023	.020	—	Pulley	Last Notch	④	.017H	.017H	70
300 Utility	1342	.023	.020	.013	Pulley	Last Notch	④	.017H	.017H	70
330	1342	.023	.020	—	Pulley	TDC	30°	⑥	⑥	65
340 Gas	1342	.023	.020	—	Pulley	TDC	30°	⑥	⑥	65
340 Diesel	1342	—	—	—	Pulley㉖	3° ATC⑰	1°	.027H	.027H	115
350	1342	.023	.020	—	Pulley	Last Notch	④	.017H	.017H	70
350 HC	1342	.023	.020	—	Pulley	Last Notch	④	.017H	.017H	70
350 Diesel	1342	—	—	—	Pulley㉓	1st Notch⑰	—	.014H	.014H	70
350 Utility	1342	.023	.020	.013	Pulley㉓	Last Notch⑰	④	.017H	.017H	70
354 Gas	1342	.024	.014	—	Pulley	5°	39°	.020H	.020H	75–80
354 Diesel	1342	—	—	—	Pulley㉕	TDC⑰	—	.020H	.020H	75–80
364 Diesel	1342	—	—	—	Flywheel㉕	16°⑰㉕	—	.020H	.020H	75–80
400 Gas	1342	.023	.020	—	Pulley	Last Notch	⑤	.017H	.017H	110
400 Diesel	1342	—	—	—	Pulley㉔	Last Notch⑰	—	.017H	.017H	120
404	1342	.023	.020	—	Pulley	DC	20°	.014H	.020H	80–90
W400 Gas	1342	.023	.020	—	Pulley	Last Notch	⑤	.017H	.017H	110
W400 Diesel	1342	—	—	—	Pulley㉔	Last Notch⑰	—	.017H	.017H	120
B414 Diesel	1342	—	—	—	Flywheel㉕	TDC⑰	—	.020H	.020H	75–80
B414 Gas	1342	.024	.014	—	Pulley	5°	39°	.020H	.020H	75–80
424, 444 Diesel	1342	—	—	—	Flywheel㉚	16°⑰	—	.020H	.020H	75–80
424, 444 Gas	1342	.023	.020	—	Pulley	TDC	17°	.014H	.020H	80–90
450 Gas	1342	.023	.020	—	Pulley	Last Notch	⑤	.017H	.017H	110
450 Diesel	1342	—	—	—	Pulley㉔	Last Notch⑰	—	.017H	.017H	120
W450 Gas	1342	.023	.020	—	Pulley	Last Notch	⑤	.017H	.017H	110
W450 Diesel	1342	—	—	—	Pulley㉔	Last Notch⑰	—	.017H	.017H	120
454 Gas	1342	.023	.020	—	Pulley	TDC	17°	.027H	.027H	90
454 Diesel	132	—	—	—	Pulley㉑	14°⑰	—	.010H	.012H	90
460, 560 Gas	153624	②	.021	—	Pulley	2°	③	.027H	.027H	90
460, 560 Diesel	153624	—	—	—	Pulley㉖	3°⑰	25°	.027H	.027H	115
464 Gas	1342	.023	.020	—	Pulley	TDC	20°	.027H	.027H	90
464 Diesel	132	—	—	—	Pulley㉑	14°⑰	—	.010H	.012H	90
504 LPG	1342	.015	.020	—	Pulley	TDC	25°	.016H	.020H	70–75
504 Gas	1342	.023	.020	—	Pulley	TDC	20°	.016H	.020H	70–75
504 Diesel	1342	—	—	—	Pulley㉖	2° ATC⑰	—	.027H	.027H	110–120
544 Gas	1342	.023	.020	—	Pulley	TDC	20°	.027H	.027H	90
544 Diesel	1342	—	—	—	Pulley㉑	14°⑰	—	.010H	.012H	90
574, 674 Gas	1342	.023	.020	—	Pulley	TDC	20°	.027H	.027H	90

Continued

FARM TRACTORS

TUNE UP SPECIFICATIONS—Continued

Tractor Model	Firing Order	Spark Plug Gap	Breaker Gap Dis-tributor	Breaker Gap Magneto	Ignition Mark Location	Ignition Mark Retarded Timing BTC	Ignition Mark Full Advance Timing BTC	Valve Lash Intake	Valve Lash Exhaust	Cylinder Head Torque
574, 674 Diesel	1342	—	—	—	Pulley(21)	14°(17)		.010H	.012H	90
600, 650 Gas	1342	.023	.020	.013	Pulley	TDC	40°	.017H	.017H	160
600, 650 Diesel	1342	—	—	—	Pulley(27)	TDC(17)	8°	.017H	.017H	150
606 Gas	153624	.023	.020	—	Pulley	2°	—	.027H	.027H	90
606 LPG	153624	.015	.020	—	Pulley	3°	—	.027H	.027H	90
606 Diesel	153624	—	—	—	Pulley(26)	3°(17)	—	.027H	.027H	115
656 Diesel	153624	—	—	—	Pulley(28)	TDC(17)	—	.027H	.027H	85–95
656 LPG	153624	.015	.020	—	Pulley	2°	24°	.027H	.027H	85–95
656 Gasoline	153624	.023	.020	—	Pulley	2°	19°(31)	.027H	.027H	85–95
660 Gas	153624	(2)	.021	—	Pulley	2°	(3)	.027H	.027H	90
660 Diesel	153624	—	—	—	Pulley(26)	TDC(17)	8°	.027H	.027H	115
666 Hydro 70 Gas	153624	.023	.020	—	Pulley(20)	TDC	18°	.027H	.027H	90
666, Hydro 70 Diesel	153624	—	—	—	Pulley(20)	18°(17)	—	(32)	.021H	165
686, Hydro 86 Gas	153624	.023	.020	—	Pulley	TDC	—	.027H	.027H	90
686, Hydro 86	153624	—	—	—	Pulley(20)	18°(17)	—	(32)	.021H	165
686, Hydro 86	153624	—	—	—	Pulley(21)	8°(17)	—	.010H	.012H	90
706 Gasoline	153624	.023	.020	—	Pulley	(11)	(12)	.027H	.027H	90
706 LP-Gas	153624	.015	.020	—	Pulley	2° BTC	24°	.027H	.027H	90
706 Diesel	153624	—	—	—	Pulley(18)(22)(29)	(7)(17)	—	(13)	(13)	(14)
756 Gas	153624	.023	.020	—	Flywheel	1°	18°	.027H	.027H	90
756 LPG	153624	.015	.020	—	Flywheel	2°	24°	.027H	.027H	90
756 Diesel	153624	—	—	—	Flywheel(18)	14°(17)	—	.010H	.012H	90
766 Gas	153624	.023	.020	—	(15)	1°	18°	.027H	.027H	90
766 Diesel	153624	—	—	—	Flywheel(20)	18°(17)	—	.012H	.021H	165
806 Gasoline	153624	.023	.020	—	Flywheel	TDC	22°	.027H	.027H	90
806 LP-Gas	153624	.015	.020	—	Flywheel	2°BTC	24°	.027H	.027H	90
806 Diesel	153624	—	—	—	Flywheel(22)(29)	(8)(17)	—	.013H	.025H	135
826 Gas	153624	.023	.020	—	Pulley	TDC	22	.027H	.027H	135
826 LP-Gas	153624	.015	.020	—	Pulley	2°	24	.027H	.027H	135
826 Diesel	153624	—	—	—	(15)(18)	16°(17)	—	.010H	.012H	135
856 Gas	153624	.023	.020	—	Flywheel	TDC	22°	.027H	.027H	90
856 LPG	153624	.015	.020	—	Flywheel	2°	24°	.027H	.027H	90
856 Diesel	153624	—	—	—	Flywheel(22)	6°(17)	—	.013H	.025H	135
966 Diesel	153624	—	—	—	Flywheel(20)	18°(17)	—	.020H	.025H	165
1026 Diesel	153624	—	—	—	Flywheel(19)	6°(17)	—	.013H	.025H	135
1066 Diesel	153624	—	—	—	Flywheel(20)	18°(17)	—	.020H	.025H	165
1206 Diesel	153624	—	—	—	Flywheel(22)	8°(17)	—	.013H	.025H	135
1256 Diesel	153624	—	—	—	Flywheel(22)	6°(17)	—	.013H	.025H	135
1456 Diesel	153624	—	—	—	Flywheel(22)	2° ATC(17)	—	.013H	.025H	135
1466 Diesel	153624	—	—	—	Flywheel(20)	18°(17)	—	.020H	.025H	165
1468 Diesel	18736542	—	—	—	Pulley(16)	30°(17)	—	.014H	.016H	110
1566 Diesel	153624	—	—	—	Flywheel(20)	15°(17)	—	.020H	.025H	165
1568 Diesel	18736542	—	—	—	Pulley(16)	30°(17)	—	.014H	.014H	110
2404	1342	.023	.020	—	Pulley	DC	20°	.014H	.020H	80–90
2424, 2444 Diesel	1342	—	—	—	Flywheel(30)	16°(17)	—	.020H	.020H	75–80
2424, 2444 Gasoline	1342	.023	.020	—	Pulley	TDC	17°	.014H	.020H	80–90
2504 Gas	1342	.023	.020	—	Pulley	TDC	20°	.016H	.020H	70–75
2504 LPG	1342	.015	.020	—	Pulley	TDC	25°	.016H	.020H	70–75
2504 Diesel	1342	—	—	—	Pulley(26)	2° ATC(17)	—	.027H	.027H	110–120
2544 Gas	1342	.023	.020	—	Pulley	TDC	20°	.027H	.027H	90
2544 Diesel	1342	—	—	—	Pulley(21)	14°(17)	—	.010H	.012H	90
2606 Gas	153624	.023	.020	—	Pulley	2°	—	.027H	.027H	90
2606 LPG	153624	.015	.020	—	Pulley	3°	—	.027H	.027H	90

Continued

FARM TRACTORS

TUNE UP SPECIFICATIONS—Continued

Tractor Model	Firing Order	Spark Plug Gap	Breaker Gap Distributor	Breaker Gap Magneto	Ignition Mark Location	Ignition Mark Retarded Timing BTC	Ignition Mark Full Advance Timing BTC	Valve Lash Intake	Valve Lash Exhaust	Cylinder Head Torque
2606 Diesel	153624	—	—	—	Pulley㉖	3°⑰	—	.027H	.027H	115
2656 Gas	153624	.023	.020	—	Pulley	2°	⑩	.027H	.027H	85–95
2656 Diesel	153624	—	—	—	Pulley㉘	⑨⑰	—	.027H	.027H	110–120
2706 Gasoline	153624	.023	.020	—	Pulley	⑪	⑫	.027H	.027H	90
2706 LP-Gas	153624	.015	.020	—	Pulley	2° BTC	24°	.027H	.027H	90
2706 Diesel	153624	—	—	—	Pulley⑱㉒㉙	⑦⑰	—	⑬	⑬	⑭
2756 Gas	153624	.023	.020	—	Flywheel	1°	18°	.027H	.027H	90
2756 LPG	153624	.015	.020	—	Flywheel	2°	24°	.027H	.027H	90
2756 Diesel	153624	—	—	—	Flywheel⑱	14°⑰	—	.010H	.012H	90
2806 Gasoline	153624	.023	.020	—	Flywheel	TDC	22°	.027H	.027H	90
2806 LP-Gas	153624	.015	.020	—	Flywheel	2° BTC	24°	.027H	.027H	90
2806 Diesel	153624	—	—	—	Flywheel㉒㉙	⑧⑰	—	.013H	.025H	135
2856 Gas	153624	.023	.020	—	Flywheel	TDC	22°	.027H	.027H	90
2856 LPG	153624	.015	.020	—	Flywheel	2°	24°	.027H	.027H	90
2856 Diesel	153624	—	—	—	Flywheel㉒	6°⑰	—	.013H	.025H	135
21206 Diesel	153624	—	—	—	Flywheel㉒	8°⑰	—	.013H	.025H	135
21256	153624	—	—	—	Flywheel㉒	6°⑰	—	.013H	.025H	135
21456	153624	—	—	—	Flywheel㉒	2° ATC⑰	—	.013H	.025H	135

①—Magneto running time 35°.
②—Gasoline .025", LP-Gas .016".
③—Gasoline 30°, LP-Gas 25°.
④—Kerosene 30°, gasoline 22°, LP-Gas 16°.
⑤—Kerosene 30°, gasoline 25°, LP-Gas 16°.
⑥—Before Eng. No. 100501, .014H. After Eng. No. 100501, intake .016H, exhaust .020".
⑦—TDS, with Roosa-Master injection pump; 40° mark with 1H pump; 14° with Bosch pump.
⑧—8° BTDC with Roosa-Master injection pump; 50° mark with 1H pump.
⑨—TDC up to #67874, after #67874 w/std. trans. 3° BTDC, or 1° BTDC w/auto. trans.
⑩—W/std. trans. 19° BTDC, w/auto. trans. 22° BTDC.
⑪—Early TDC; late 1° BTDC.
⑫—Early, 22°; late, 18°.
⑬—Early, intake and exhaust .027H. Late, intake .010H, exhaust .012H.
⑭—115 ft. lbs.; late 90 ft. lbs.
⑮—Pulley or flywheel.
⑯—With timing marks on crankshaft pulley & pointer aligned, insert 1/4" diameter rod in front cover engaging hole in pump drive hub.
⑰—Injection timing.
⑱—Robert Bosch pump; with timing marks on flywheel & clutch housing aligned, align timing points on roller retainer ring.
⑲—With timing marks on flywheel & clutch housing or hydrostatic drive housing aligned, align timing mark on injection pump cam ring with timing mark on pointer.
⑳—With timing marks on flywheel & clutch housing or hydrostatic housing aligned, align timing mark on injection pump hub with timing pointer.
㉑—With timing marks on pulley & timing gear cover aligned, align timing line on pump face cam with timing pointer on roller retaining ring.
㉒—Roosa-Master pump; with timing marks on flywheel & clutch housing aligned, align injection pump cam ring with timing mark on pump mounting flange.
㉓—With timing marks on pulley & timing gear cover aligned, align timing marks on drive plate, cam & pump housing.
㉔—With timing marks on pulley & crankcase front cover aligned, align timing marks on drive plate, cam & pump housing.
㉔—With timing marks on pulley & crankcase front cover aligned, align mark on pump drive gear with mark on gear hub groove.
㉕—With mechanical governor; align timing marks on flywheel & left front flange of clutch housing, then align timing mark on front end plate with timing mark on pump mounting flange. With pneumatic governor; measure the distance from marker on pulley to timing pointer which should be 1 1/8" or 20° BTDC.
㉖—With timing marks on pulley & timing gear cover aligned, align timing mark on pump cam with timing mark on governor weight retainer.
㉗—With the timing marks on front flange of pulley & crankcase front cover aligned, align timing mark on gear hub with timing mark on injection pump drive gear.
㉘—With timing marks on pulley & timing pointer aligned, align timing marks on governor drive plate & cam ring.
㉙—I H Model RD; with timing mark on flywheel aligned with timing pointer, align timing mark on governor weight shaft with scribe line on front side of pump timing hole opening.
㉚—With timing marks on flywheel & left front flange of the clutch housing aligned, align timing mark on front end plate with timing mark on pump mounting flange.
㉛—With Hyd. drive, 22° BTDC.
㉜—Prior to serial No. 2505, .012H; Serial No. 2505 & later, .016H.

PISTONS, PINS, RINGS, BEARINGS & CRANKSHAFT

Tractor Model	Cyl. Bore Size In.	Piston Clearance	Pin Diam.	Ring End Gap Minimum Comp.	Ring End Gap Minimum Oil	Rod Bearings Crankpin Diameter	Rod Bearings Bearing Clearance	Rod Bolt Torque	Main Bearings Journal Diameter	Main Bearings Bearing Clearance	Cap Bolt Torque
Hydro 70, 86 Non Diesel	3 3/4	.0027	.8748	.010	.010	2.373–2.374	.0009–.0034	50	2.748–2.749	.0012–.0042	80
Hydro 70, 86 Diesel	3.875	.0055	1.6249	.014	.010	2.5185–2.5193	.0029–.0055	63	3.1484–3.1492	.0029–.0055	⑰

Continued

FARM TRACTORS

PISTONS, PINS, RINGS, BEARINGS & CRANKSHAFT—Continued

Tractor Model	Cyl. Bore Size In.	Piston Clearance	Pin Diam.	Ring End Gap Minimum		Rod Bearings			Main Bearings		
				Comp.	Oil	Crankpin Diameter	Bearing Clearance	Rod Bolt Torque	Journal Diameter	Bearing Clearance	Cap Bolt Torque
Hydro 100	4.300	.045–.0065	1.6248–1.6250	⑱	.010–.020	2.9977–2.9990	.0018–.0051	130	3.3742–3.3755	.0018–.0051	115
100, 130, 140	3 1/8	.0015	.9193	.010	.010	1.749–1.750	.001–.0035	45	2.124–2.125	.001–.0035	75
154	2 5/8	.002	.6875	.007	.007	1.498–1.499	.002–.003	—	1.623–1.624	.002–.003	55
200, 230, 240	3 1/8	.0015	.9193	.010	.010	1.749–1.750	.001–.0035	45	2.124–2.125	.001–.0035	75
B275 Diesel	3 3/8	.0031	1.1022	.012	.015	1.749–1.750	.001–.0029	30–35	2.124–2.125	.002–.004	⑯
300, 300U ①	3 9/16	.0035	1.1090	.010	.010	2.2975–2.2985	.0011–.0037	40	2.5575–2.5585	.0011–.0037	75
300, 300U ②	3 9/16	.0025	.8748	.010	.010	2.2975–2.2985	.0011–.0037	40	2.5575–2.5585	.0011–.0037	75
330, 340	3 1/4	.0015	.9193	.010	.010	1.749–1.750	.001–.0035	45	2.124–2.125	.001–.0035	75
340 Diesel	3 11/16	.0045	1.1248	.015	.010	2.373–2.374	.0007–.0015	50	2.748–2.749	.0012–.0042	80
350, 350U	3 5/8	.0025	.8748	.010	.010	2.2975–2.2985	.0011–.0037	40	2.5575–2.5585	.0011–.0037	75
350 Diesel	3 3/4	.005	1.1092	.015	.010	2.2475–2.2485	.0006–.0031	40	2.374–2.375	.0009–.0036	105
354 Diesel	3 3/8	.0031	1.1022	.012	.010	1.7495–1.75	.001–.0029	30–35	2.124–2.125	.002–.004	⑯
354 Gas	3 3/8	.0031	1.1022	.012	.012	1.7495–1.75	.001–.0029	30–35	2.124–2.125	.002–.004	⑯
364	3.500	.0031–.0039	1.1021–1.1024	.010–.015	.010–.015	1.7495–1.750	.001–.0029	40–45	2.124–2.125	.002–.004	⑲
400, W400 ①	4	.0035	1.3126	.013	.013	2.5475–2.5485	.0011–.0037	55–60	2.8075–2.8085	.002–.003	100
400, W400 ②	4	.003	.9998	.013	.013	2.5475–2.5485	.0011–.0037	55–60	2.8075–2.8085	.002–.003	100
400D, W400D	4	.005	1.3126	.015	.010	3.2485–3.2495	.002–.003	115	3.7475–3.7485	.0018–.0048	③
404	3 1/4	.0015	.8592	.010	.010	1.7495	.0009–.0039	45	2.1245	.0009–.0039	75–80
B414 Diesel	3 1/2	.0031	1.1022	.010	.010	1.7495–1.750	.0010–.0035	40–45	2.124–2.125	.0020–.0041	⑯
B414 Gas	3 3/8	.0031	1.1022	.012	.012	1.7495–1.750	.0010–.0035	40–45	2.124–2.125	.0020–.0041	⑯
424, 444 Diesel	3 1/2	.0031	1.1022	.010	.010	1.7495–1.750	.001–.0029	40–45	2.124–2.125	.002–.004	⑯
424, 444 Gas	3 3/8	.001	.8592	.010	.018	2.059–2.060	.0009–.0039	43–49	2.6235–2.6245	.0009–.0039	⑯
450, W450	4 1/8	.003	.9998	.013	.013	2.5475–2.5485	.0011–.0037	55–60	2.8075–2.8085	.002–.003	100
450D, W450D	4 1/8	.005	1.3126	.015	.010	3.2475–3.2485	.002–.003	115	3.7475–3.7485	.0018–.0048	③
454 Non-Diesel	3 3/8	.005	.8592	.010	.010	2.059–2.060	.0009–.0039	43–49	2.748–2.749	.0012–.0042	75–85
454, 464 Diesel	3 7/8	.0047	1.4172	.014	.010	2.5185–2.5193	.0023–.0048	45	3.1484–3.1492	.0029–.0055	⑤
460, 560	3 9/16	.0025	.8748	.010	.010	2.373–2.374	.0009–.0034	50	2.748–2.749	.0012–.0042	80
460D, 560D	3 11/16	.005	1.1248	.015	.010	2.373–2.374	.0009–.0034	50	2.748–2.749	.0012–.0042	80
464 Non-Diesel	3 9/16	.005	.8748	.010	.010	2.373–2.374	.0009–.0034	④	2.748–2.749	.0012–.0042	75–85
504 Gas	3 3/8	.0015	.859	.015	.010	2.059–2.060	.0009–.0039	40–45	2.625–2.6245	.0009–.0039	75–80
504 Diesel	3 11/16	.005	1.1248	.015	.010	2.373–2.374	.0009–.0034	40–50	2.748–2.749	.0012–.0042	75–85
544 Gas	3 13/16	.0025	.87485	.010	.018	2.3735	.0009–.0034	④	2.7485	.0012–.0042	75–80
544 Diesel	3 7/8	.0042	1.41725	.014	.010	2.5185–2.5193	.0023–.0048	63	3.1484–3.1492	.0029–.0055	⑤
574 Non-Diesel	3 13/16	.005	.8748	.010	.010	2.373–2.374	.0009–.0034	④	2.748–2.749	.0012–.0042	75–85
574 Diesel	3 7/8	.0047	1.4172	.014	.010	2.5185–2.5193	.0023–.0048	45	3.1484–3.1492	.0029–.0055	⑤
600, 650	4 1/2	.004	1.5001	.012	.012	2.9965–2.9975	.002–.005	85–90	3.2475–3.2485	.0019–.0049	125
600D, 650D	4 1/2	.008	1.5001	.013	.013	2.7475–2.7485	.0019–.0049	55–60	4.1225–4.1235	.002–.005	③
606 Non-Diesel	3 9/16	.0025	.8748	.010	.010	2.3735	.0009–.0034	50	2.7485	.0012–.0042	80
606 Diesel	3 11/16	.005	1.1248	.015	.010	2.3735	.0009–.0034	50	2.7485	.0012–.0042	80
656 Non-Diesel	3 9/16	.0025	.87485	.010	.010	2.3735	.0009–.0034	45–55	2.7485	.0012–.0042	75–85
656 Diesel	3 11/16	.0025	1.1248	.015	.010	2.3735	.0009–.0034	45–55	2.7485	.0012–.0042	75–85
660	3 9/16	.0025	.8748	.010	.010	3.373–2.374	.0009–.0034	50	2.748–2.749	.0012–.0042	80
660D	3 11/16	.005	1.1248	.015	.010	2.373–2.374	.0009–.0034	50	2.748–2.749	.0012–.0042	80
666 Non-Diesel	3 3/4	.0025	.8748	.010	.010	2.3730–2.3740	.0009–.0034	45–50	2.748–2.749	.0012–.0042	80
666 Diesel	3.875	.0055	1.6249	.010	.010	2.9977–2.9990	.0018–.0051	130	3.3742–3.3755	.0018–.0051	115
674 Non-Diesel	3 13/16	.005	.8748	.010	.010	2.373–2.374	.0009–.0034	④	2.748–2.749	.0012–.0042	75–85
674 Diesel	3 7/8	.0047	1.4172	.014	.010	2.5185–2.5193	.0023–.0048	45	3.1484–3.1492	.0029–.0055	⑤
686 Non-Diesel	3 3/4	.0025	.8748	.010	.010	2.373–2.374	.0009–.0034	50	2.748–2.749	.0012–.0042	80
686 Early Diesel	3.875	.0055	1.6249	.014	.010	2.5185–2.5193	.0018–.0051	⑰	3.3742–3.3755	.0018–.0051	115
686 Late Diesel	3.875	.0039–.0047	1.4172	.014	.010	2.5185–2.5193	.0023–.0048	63	3.1484–3.1492	.0029–.0055	115
706 Non-Diesel	⑥	.0025	.87485	.010	.010	2.373–2.374	.0009–.0034	④	2.748–2.749	.0012–.0042	80
706 Diesel	⑦	⑧	⑨	.015	.010	⑩	⑪	④	⑬	⑭	⑮
756 Non-Diesel	3 3/4	.0010	.87485	.010	.010	2.373–2.374	.0009–.0034	④	2.748–2.749	.0012–.0042	80
756 Diesel	3 7/8	.0039	1.4172	.014	.010	2.5185–2.5193	.0023–.0048	63	3.1484–3.1492	.0029–.0055	⑤

Continued

FARM TRACTORS

PISTONS, PINS, RINGS, BEARINGS & CRANKSHAFT—Continued

Tractor Model	Cyl. Bore Size In.	Piston Clearance	Pin Diam.	Ring End Gap Minimum		Rod Bearings			Main Bearings		
				Comp.	Oil	Crankpin Diameter	Bearing Clearance	Rod Bolt Torque	Journal Diameter	Bearing Clearance	Cap Bolt Torque
766 Non-Diesel	3 3/4	.0045	.8748	.010	.010	2.373–2.374	.0009–.0034	④	2.748–2.749	.0012–.0042	80
766 Diesel	3 7/8	.0065	1.6249	.010	.010	2.9977–2.9990	.0018–.0051	130	3.3742–3.3755	.0018–.0051	115
806 Non-Diesel	3 13/16	.0015	.87485	.010	.010	2.373–2.374	.0009–.0034	④	2.748–2.749	.0012–.0042	80
806 Diesel	4 1/8	.004	1.4999	.017	.014	2.998–2.999	.0018–.0051	105	3.3742–3.3755	.0018–.0051	115
826 Non-Diesel	3 13/16	.0045	.8748	.010	.010	2.373–2.374	.0009–.0034	④	2.748–2.749	.0012–.0042	80
826 Diesel	3 7/8	.0047	1.4172	.014	.010	2.5185–2.5193	.0023–.0048	45	3.1484–3.1492	.0029–.0055	⑰
856 Non-Diesel	3 3/16	.0010	.87485	.010	.010	2.373–2.374	.0009–.0034	④	2.748–2.749	.0012–.0042	80
856 Diesel	4 5/16	.0049	1.4999	.017	.014	2.998–2.999	.0018–.0051	105	3.3742–3.3755	.0018–.0051	115
966 Diesel	4.3	.0065	1.6249	.016	.010	2.9977–2.9990	.0018–.0051	130	3.3742–3.3755	.0018–.0051	115
1026 Diesel	4.321	.0069	1.6249	.013	.013	2.998–2.999	.0018–.0051	105	3.3742–3.3755	.0018–.0051	115
1066 Diesel	4.3	.0065	1.6249	.016	.010	2.9977–2.9990	.0018–.0051	130	3.3742–3.3755	.0018–.0051	115
1206 Diesel	4 1/8	.0043	1.4999	.017	.014	2.9983	.0018–.0051	105	3.3745	.0018–.0051	115
1256 Diesel	4 5/16	.0049	1.4999	.017	.014	2.998–2.999	.0018–.0051	105	3.3742–3.3755	.0018–.0051	115
1456 Diesel	4 5/16	.0049	1.6249	.017	.014	2.998–2.999	.0018–.0051	105	3.3742–3.3755	.0018–.0051	115
1466, 1566	4.300	.0045–.0065	1.6248–1.6250	⑱	.010–.020	2.9977–2.9990	.0018–.0051	130	3.3742–3.3755	.0018–.0051	115
1468, 1568	4.500	.006–.007	1.4998–1.5000	.013–.023	.013–.028	2.753–2.754	.0019–.0044	55⑳	3.123–3.124	.0018–.0048	130
2404	3 1/4	.0015	.8592	.010	.010	1.7495	.009–.0039	45	2.1245	.0009–.0039	75–80
2424, 2444 Diesel	3 1/2	.0031	1.1022	.010	.010	1.7495–1.750	.001–.0029	40–45	2.124–2.125	.002–.004	⑯
2424, 2444 Gas	3 3/8	.0015	.8592	.010	.018	2.059–2.060	.0009–.0039	43–49	2.6235–2.6245	.0009–.0039	⑯
2504 Gas	3 3/8	.0015	.859	.015	.010	2.059–2.060	.0009–.0039	40–45	2.6235–2.6245	.0009–.0039	75–80
2504 Diesel	3 11/16	.005	1.1248	.015	.010	2.373–2.374	.0009–.0034	40–50	2.748–2.749	.0012–.0042	75–85
2544 Gas	3 13/16	.0025	.87485	.010	.018	2.3735	.0009–.0034	④	2.7485	.0012–.0042	75–80
2544 Diesel	3 7/8	.0042	1.41725	.014	.010	2.5185–2.5193	.0023–.0048	63	3.1484–3.1492	.0029–.0055	⑤
2606 Non-Diesel	3 9/16	.0025	.8748	.010	.010	2.3735	.0009–.0034	50	2.7485	.0012–.0042	80
2606 Diesel	3 11/16	.305	1.1248	.015	.010	2.3735	.0009–.0034	50	2.7485	.0012–.0042	80
2656 Gas	3 9/16	.0025	.87485	.010	.010	2.3735	.0009–.0034	45–55	2.7485	.0012–.0042	80
2656 Diesel	3 11/16	.0035	1.1248	.015	.010	2.3735	.0009–.0034	45–55	2.7485	.0012–.0042	80
2706 Non-Diesel	⑥	.0025	.87485	.010	.015	2.373–2.374	.0009–.0034	④	2.748–2.749	.0012–.0042	80
2706 Diesel	⑦	⑧	⑨	.015	.010	⑩	⑪	⑫	⑬	⑭	⑮
2756 Non-Diesel	3 3/4	.0010	.87485	.010	.010	2.373–2.374	.0009–.0034	④	2.748–2.749	.0012–.0042	80
2756 Diesel	3 7/8	.0039	1.4172	.014	.010	2.5185–2.5193	.0023–.0048	63	3.1484–3.1492	.0029–.0055	⑤
2806 Non-Diesel	3 13/16	.0015	.87485	.010	.010	2.373–2.374	.0009–.0034	④	2.748–2.749	.0012–.0042	80
2806 Diesel	4 1/8	.004	1.4999	.017	.014	2.998–2.999	.0018–.0051	105	3.3742–3.3755	.0018–.0051	115
2856 Non-Diesel	3 13/16	.0010	.87485	.010	.010	2.373–2.374	.0009–.0034	④	2.748–2.749	.0012–.0042	80
2856 Diesel	4 5/16	.0049	1.4999	.017	.014	2.998.2.999	.0018–.0051	105	3.3742–3.3755	.0018–.0051	115
21206 Diesel	4 1/8	.0043	1.4999	.017	.014	2.9983	.0018–.0051	105	3.3745	.0018–.0051	115
21256 Diesel	4 5/16	.0049	1.4999	.017	.014	2.998–2.999	.0018–.0051	105	3.3742–3.3755	.0018–.0051	115
21456 Diesel	4 5/16	.0049	1.6249	.017	.014	2.998–2.999	.0018–.0051	105	3.3742–3.3755	.0018–.0051	115

① — Heavyweight.
② — Lightweight.
③ — Center 260 ft. lbs., others 160 ft. lbs.
④ — Place Bolt—50 ft. lbs. Pitch Bolt 45 ft. lbs.
⑤ — Bolt Marked 10K—80 ft. lbs. Marked 12K—97 ft. lbs. with lubricated threads.
⑥ — Early series 3 9/16; late, 3 3/4.
⑦ — Early series 3 11/16; late, 3 7/8.
⑧ — Early series, .005; late, .0039.
⑨ — Early series, 1.1247; late, 1.4172.
⑩ — Early series 2.373–2.374; late, 2.5185–2.5193.
⑪ — Early series, .0009–.0034; late, .0023–.0048.
⑫ — Early series, 45–50 ft. lbs.; late, 63 ft. lbs.
⑬ — Early series, 2.748–2.749; late, 3.1484–3.1492.
⑭ — Early series, .0012–.0042; late, .0029–.0055.
⑮ — Early series, 80; late, see note ⑤.
⑯ — Pitch bolt 70–75 ft. lbs.; Place bolt 80–85 ft. lbs.
⑰ — Bolt marked 10K or 10-9: 80 ft. lbs.; marked 12K or 12-9: 97 ft. lbs.; marked 10.9: 115 ft. lbs.; marked 12.9: 140 ft. lbs.
⑱ — Top ring, .016"–.126"; Second ring, .020"–.030".
⑲ — Pitch bolts, 70–75 ft. lbs.; place bolts, 80–85 ft. lbs.
⑳ — Tighten nut 1/6 turn after 55 ft. lbs. torque is reached.

FARM TRACTORS

MASSEY-FERGUSON
TUNE UP SPECIFICATIONS

Tractor Model	Firing Order	Spark Plug Gap	Breaker Gap		Ignition Mark			Valve Lash		Cylinder Head Torque
			Distributor	Magneto	Location	Retarded Timing BTC	Full Advance Timing BTC	Intake	Exhaust	
MF-25 Diesel	1342	—	—	—	Pulley⑤	18°②	—	.012C	.012C	40–42
MF-35 Gas	1342	.025	.022	—	Flywheel	5°	—	.013H	.013H	70–75
MF-35 Diesel	123	—	—	—	Flywheel⑩	18°②	—	.010H	.010H	55–60
TO-35 Gas	1342	.025	.022	—	Flywheel	5°	—	.013H	.013H	70–75
TO-35 Diesel	1342	—	—	—	Flywheel⑪	①	—	.012C	.008C	50–60
F-40	1342	.025	.022	—	Flywheel	5°	—	.013H	.013H	70–75
MF-50, MH-50	1342	.025	.022	—	Flywheel	5°	—	.013H	.013H	70–75
MF-65 Gas	1342	.026	.022	—	Flywheel	6°	26–30°	.016H	.018H	70–75
MF-65 LP-Gas	1342	.026	.022	—	Flywheel	4°	24–28°	.016H	.018H	70–75
MF-65, Diesel	1342	—	—	—	Flywheel⑫	④②	—	.010H	.010H	55–60
MF-85, 88 Gas	1342	.026	.022	—	Flywheel	5°	—	.016H	.018H	100–110
MF-85, 88 LPG	1342	.026	.022	—	Flywheel	4°	—	.016H	.018H	100–110
MF-85, 88 Diesel	1342	—	—	—	Flywheel⑬	20°②	—	.014H	.014H	130–140
MF-90, 90 WR Gas	1342	.026	.022	—	Flywheel	5°	—	.016H	.018H	100–110
MF-90, 90 WR LPG	1342	.026	.022	—	Flywheel	4°	—	.016H	.018H	100–110
MF-90, 90 WR Diesel	1342	—	—	—	Flywheel⑭	16°②	—	.010H	.010H	105–110
MF-130 Diesel	1342	—	—	—	Pulley⑨	18°②	—	.012C	.012C	40–42
MF-135 Special Gas	1342	.025	.022	—	Flywheel	6°	26°	.013	.013	70–75
MF-135 Non Diesel	1342	.025	.022	—	Flywheel	6°	30°	.013H	.013H	70–75
MF-135 Diesel	123	—	—	—	Flywheel⑭	20°②	—	.010H	.010H	55–60
MF-150 Non-Diesel	1342	.025	.022	—	Flywheel	6°	26°	.013H	.013H	70–75
MF-150 Perkins Gas	123	.025	.021	—	Flywheel	12°	26°	.012	.015	55–60
MF-150 Diesel	123	—	—	—	Flywheel⑭	20°②	—	.010H	.010H	55–60
MF-165 Non-Diesel	1342	.025	.022	—	Flywheel	6°	26°	.016H	.018H	70–75
MF-165 Perkins Gas	1342	.025	.022	—	Pulley	12°	36°	.012	.015	85–90
MF-165 Diesel	1342	—	—	—	Flywheel⑭	24°②	—	.010H	.010H	55–60
MF-175 Diesel	1342	—	—	—	Flywheel⑫	23°②	—	.010H	.010H	70–75
MF-175 Gas	1342	.025	.022	—	Pulley	6°	26°	.016	.018	70–75
MF-180 Perkins Gas	1342	.025	.022	—	Pulley	10°	32°	.012	.012	85–90
MF-180	1342	.025	.022	—	Pulley	6°	26°	.016H	.018H	85
MF-202	1342	.025	.022	—	Flywheel	5°	—	.013H	.013H	70–75
MHF-202	1342	.025	.022	—	Flywheel	5°	—	.013H	.013H	70–75
MF-204	1342	.025	.022	—	Flywheel	5°	—	.013H	.013H	70–75
MV-230 Gas	1342	.025	.020	—	Flywheel	8°	27°	.011H	.013H	70–75
MF-230 Diesel	123	—	—	—	Flywheel⑯	16°②	—	.010H	.010H	70–75
MF-235 Gas	1342	.025	.020	—	Flywheel	8°	28°	.011H	.013H	70–75
MF-235 Diesel	123	—	—	—	Flywheel⑯	24°②	—	.010H	.010H	70–75
MF-245 Gas	1342	.025	.020	—	Flywheel	8°	28°	.011H	.013H	70–75
MF-245 Diesel	123	—	—	—	Flywheel⑯	24°②	—	.010H	.010H	70–75
MF-255 Gas	1342	—	.022	—	Flywheel	12°	—	.012H	.015H	90–95
MF-255 Diesel	1342	—	—	—	Flywheel⑱	26°②	—	.010H	.010H	70–75
MF-265 Gas	1342	—	.022	—	Flywheel	11°	—	.012H	.015H	95–100
MF-265 Diesel	1342	—	—	—	Flywheel⑲	23°②	—	.010H	.010H	95–100
MF-275 Diesel	1342	—	—	—	Flywheel⑳	24°②	—	.010H	.010H	95–100
MF-285 Diesel	1342	—	—	—	Pulley⑤	20°②	—	.010H	.010H	85–90
MF-303 Gas	1342	.025	.020	—	Flywheel	DC	18°	.014H	.014H	105
MF-303 Diesel	1342	—	—	—	Flywheel⑨	22°②	—	.014H	.014H	105
MH-333 Gas	1342	.025	.020	—	Flywheel	DC	18°	.014H	.014H	105
MH-333 LP-Gas	1342	.025	.020	—	Flywheel	DC	18°	.016H	.016H	105

Continued

FARM TRACTORS

TUNE UP SPECIFICATIONS—Continued

Tractor Model	Firing Order	Spark Plug Gap	Breaker Gap		Ignition Mark			Valve Lash		Cylinder Head Torque
			Distributor	Magneto	Location	Retarded Timing BTC	Full Advance Timing BTC	Intake	Exhaust	
MH-333 Diesel	1342	—	—	—	Flywheel⑨	22°②	—	.014H	.014H	105
MF-404 Gas	1342	.025	.020	—	Flywheel	DC	18°	.014H	.014H	135
MF-404 Diesel	1342	—	—	—	Flywheel⑨	③	—	.014H	.014H	135
MF-406 Gas	1342	.025	.020	—	Flywheel	DC	18°	.014H	.014H	105
MF-406 Diesel	1342	—	—	—	Flywheel⑨	22°②	—	.014H	.014H	105
MH-444 Gas	1342	.025	.020	—	Flywheel	DC	18°	.014H	.014H	135
MH-444 LP-Gas	1342	.025	.020	—	Flywheel	DC	16°	.016H	.016H	135
MH-444 Diesel	1342	—	—	—	Flywheel⑨	③	—	.014H	.014H	135
MF-1001 Gas	1342	.025	.020	—	Flywheel	DC	18°	.014H	.014H	105
MF-1001 Diesel	1342	—	—	—	Flywheel⑨	22°②	—	.014H	.014H	105
MF-1080	1342	—	—	—	Pulley⑤⑧	28°②	—	.012C	.012C	⑮
MF-1085	1342	—	—	—	Pulley⑤⑧	20°②	—	.012C	.012C	⑮
MF-1100 Gas	153624	.025	.016	—	Flywheel	2°	—	.012C	.022C	95
MF-1100 LP Gas	153624	.025	.016	—	Flywheel	DC	—	.012C	.022C	95
MF-1100 Diesel	153624	—	—	—	Flywheel⑯	22°②	—	.012C	.012C	85
MF-1105 Diesel	153624	—	—	—	Flywheel⑰	26°②	—	.010H	.010H	85
MF-1130 Diesel	153624	—	—	—	Flywheel⑯	28°②	—	.012C	.012C	85
MF-1135 Diesel	153624	—	—	—	Flywheel⑰	30°②	—	.010H	.010H	85
MF-1150 Diesel	18754362	—	—	—	Flywheel⑦	30°②	—	.012C	.012C	120–125
MF-1155	18754362	—	—	—	Pulley	28°	—	.012C	.012C	120–125

①—Injection pump without automatic advance 17° BTC, with automatic advance 13° BTC.
②—Injection pump timing.
③—APE injection pump 32½° BTC, PSB pump 25° BTC.
④—With Perkins engine 4A-203 timing is 18°, with Perkins engine AD4-203, 24°.
⑤—With timing mark on crankshaft pulley and timing pointer aligned, align scribe mark on injection pump rotor with square end of snap ring.
⑥—When flywheel timing mark "STAT" is centered with pointer, "E" mark scribed on pump rotor should be aligned with square end of the snap ring.
⑦—With timing mark on flywheel and notch on inspection hole aligned, align slot in tab on injection pump camshaft with center of sight hole.
⑧—Early models use flywheel.
⑨—APE pump—with timing mark on flywheel and pointer on inspection port aligned, align timing line on pump drive gear hub with timing line on front flange of pump housing. PSB pump—with timing mark on flywheel and pointer on inspection port aligned, align line mark on apex of pump plunger drive gear teeth with mark on housing.
⑩—When flywheel timing mark "Spill 18" is aligned with the center of the timing window, "E" mark scribed on pump rotor should be aligned with scribed line at lower hole of pump snap ring.
⑪—With ¼" rod inserted into timing hole on flywheel housing and corresponding hole on flywheel, align scribe line on pump flange with scribe line on adapter housing.
⑫—When flywheel timing mark "SPILL" is aligned with center of timing window, on regular diesel letter "C" on injection pump rotor should be aligned with lower hole of snap ring, on Direct injection diesel, letter "B" on injection pump rotor should be aligned with lower end of snap ring.
⑬—With timing mark on flywheel and timing pointer aligned, align scribe line on governor cage with scribe line on cam ring.
⑭—When flywheel timing mark "STAT" is centered with pointer, "E" mark scribed on pump rotor should be aligned with line scribed on snap ring.
⑮—Engines before serial #312VA1148, 105-110; Engines serial #318VA1148 and after, 85–90.
⑯—With no. 1 piston on compression, align the correct degree mark on flywheel with timing in housing, then align "E" mark on injection rotor with square end of snap ring.
⑰—With no. 1 piston on compression and "Static Timing" mark is aligned in timing window, align "F" mark on injection rotor with square end of snap ring.
⑱—With 26° mark on flywheel centered in timing hole, align "B" mark on injection rotor with square edge of snap ring.
⑲—With 23° mark on flywheel aligned with pointer, align "C" mark on injection rotor with square edge of snap ring.
⑳—With pointer halfway between 23° & 25° mark on flywheel, align "C" mark on injection rotor with square edge of snap ring.

PISTONS, PINS, RINGS, BEARINGS & CRANKSHAFT

Tractor Model	Cyl. Bore Size In.	Piston Clearance	Pin Diam.	Ring End Gap Minimum		Rod Bearings		Rod Bolt Torque	Main Bearings		Cap Bolt Torque
				Comp.	Oil	Crankpin Diameter	Bearing Clearance		Journal Diameter	Bearing Clearance	
MF-25	3⅛	.005	.9376	.012	.009	1.9995–2.000	.0015–.003	30–35	2.248–2.2485	002–.0035	80–85
MF-35 Gas.	3 5/16	.0012	.8592	.010	.010	1.9365–1.9375	.0015–.0025	35–40	2.249–2.250	.0015–.0025	90
MF-35 Diesel	3.6	—	1.250	.009	.013	2.2485–2.2490	.002–.0035	70–80	2.7485–2.7490	.0025–.0045	115
TO-35 Gas	3 5/16	.0012	.8592	.010	.010	1.9365–1.9375	.0015–.0025	35–40	2.249–2.250	.0015–.0025	90
TO-35 Diesel	3 5/16	.004	1.1249	.009	.018	2.3110–2.3115	.002–.0035	65–70	2.7515–2.7520	.002–.0035	①
F-40	3 5/16	.0012	.8592	.010	.010	1.9365–1.9375	.0015–.0025	35–40	2.249–2.250	.0015–.0025	90
MF-50	3 5/16	.0012	.8592	.010	.010	1.9365–1.9375	.0015–.0025	35–40	2.249–2.250	.0015–.0025	90

Continued

FARM TRACTORS

PISTONS, PINS, RINGS, BEARINGS & CRANKSHAFT—Continued

Tractor Model	Cyl. Bore Size In.	Piston Clearance	Pin Diam.	Ring End Gap Minimum		Rod Bearings			Main Bearings		
				Comp.	Oil	Crankpin Diameter	Bearing Clearance	Rod Bolt Torque	Journal Diameter	Bearing Clearance	Cap Bolt Torque
MH-50	3 5/16	.0012	.8592	.010	.010	1.9365–1.9375	.0015–.0025	35–40	2.249–2.250	.0015–.0025	90
MF-65 Gas	3.58	.002	1.1251	.010	.010	2.0615–2.0625	.007–.0027	35–40	2.374–2.375	.0005–.0027	90
MF-65 Diesel	3.6	—	1.2498	.009	.009	2.2485–2.2490	.002–.0035	70–80	2.7485–2.7490	.0025–.0045	115
M-85, 88	3 7/8	.003	1.109	.013	.013	2.248–2.249	.0014–.0024	70–75	2.264–2.625	.0005–.0027	85–95
M-85, 88 Diesel	4	.0035	1.250	.013	.013	2.7475–2.7485	.0013–.0038	85–95	2.873–2.874	.0015–.0035	130–140
M-90, 90 WR Gas	3 7/8	.003	1.109	.013	.013	2.248–2.249	.014–.024	70–75	2.624–2.625	.0005–.0027	85–95
M-90, 90 WR Die.	4 1/2	.0035	1.4375	.011	.014	2.7483–2.749	.0028–.0045	100–105	2.9985–2.999	.003–.0055	140–150
MF-85 Gas	3 7/8	.003	1.1092	—	—	2.248–2.249	.0014–.0024	70–75	2.624–2.625	.0005–.0027	90
MF-85 Diesel	4	.004	1.2498	—	—	2.7475–2.7485	.0013–.0038	85–95	2.873–2.874	.0015–.0035	135
MF-88 Gas	3 7/8	.003	1.1092	—	—	2.248–2.249	.0014–.0024	70–75	2.624–2.625	.0005–.0027	90
MF-88 Diesel	4	.004	1.2498	—	—	2.7475–2.7485	.0013–.0038	85–95	2.873–2.874	.0015–.0035	135
MF-130	3 1/8	.005	.9376	.012	.009	1.9995–2.000	.0015–.003	30–35	2.248–2.2485	.002–.0035	80–85
MF-135 Diesel	3.6	.006	1.250	.009	.009	2.2485–2.2490	.0025–.004	45–50	2.7485–2.749	.003–.005	④
MF-135 Gas	3.6	.003	.8592	.010	.010	1.9365–2.9375	.0003–.0023	40–45	2.249–2.250	.0005–.0027	85–95
MF-135 Spec. Gas	3.312	.0025	.8591	.010	.010	1.9365–1.0375	.0003–.0023	40–45	2.249–2.250	.0005–.0027	85–95
MF-150 Diesel	3.6	.006	1.250	.009	.009	2.2485–2.2490	.0025–.004	45–50	2.7485–2.7490	.003–.005	④
MF-150 Gas	3.6	.003	.8592	.010	.010	1.9365–1.9375	.0003–.0023	40–45	2.249–2.250	.0005–.0027	85–95
MF-165 Diesel	3 3/8	.006	1.250	.009	.009	2.2485–2.2490	.0025–.004	45–50	2.7485–2.7490	.004–.005	④
MF-165 Gas	3.6	.003	1.1251	.010	.010	2.0615–2.0625	.0007–.0027	40–45	2.374–2.375	.000–.0027	85–95
MF-165 Diesel	3.6	.005–.007	1.24975	.009	—	2.2485–2.249	.0025–.004	45–50	2.7485–2.749	.003–.005	④
MF-165 Gas	3 7/8	.007	1.3749	.018	.014	2.499–2.4995	.0015–.003	65–70	2.9985–2.999	.0025–.0045	145–150
MF-165 Gas	3.58	.0012	.8592	.10	.10	1.9365–1.9375	.0015–.0025	35–40	2.249–2.250	.0015–.0025	90
MF-175 Diesel	3 7/8	.007	1.3749	.018	.014	2.499–2.4995	.0015–.003	65–70	2.9985–2.999	.0025–.0045	145–150
MF-175 Gas	3 13/16	—	1.250	.010	.010	2.0615–2.0625	.0007–.0027	40–45	2.374–2.375	.0005–.0028	85–95
MF-175 Gas	3 7/8	—	.9998	.016	.012	2.499–2.4995	.0015–.003	65–70	2.9985–2.999	.0025–.0045	145–150
MF-180 Gas	3 13/16	.007	1.3749	.018	.014	2.499–2.4995	.0015–.003	65–70	2.9985–2.999	.0025–.0045	145–150
MF-180 Diesel	3 7/8	.007	1.3749	.018	.014	2.499–2.4995	.0015–.003	65–70	2.9985–2.999	.0025–.0045	145–150
MF-180 Gas	3 7/8	—	.9998	.016	.012	2.499–2.4995	.0015–.003	65–70	2.9985–2.999	.0025–.0045	145–150
MF-202	3.58	.0012	.8592	.010	.010	1.9365–2.9375	.0015–.0025	35–40	2.249–2.250	.0015–.0025	90
MHF-202	3 5/16	.0012	.8592	.010	.010	1.9365–1.9375	.0015–.0025	35–40	2.249–2.250	.0015–.0025	90
MF-204	3 5/16	.0012	.8592	.010	.010	1.9365–1.9375	.0015–.0025	35–40	2.249–2.250	.0015–.0025	90
MF-303 Gas	3 5/16	.003	1.1092	.013	.013	2.248–2.249	.0008–.0029	75–85	2.624–2.625	.0005–.0032	90
MF-303 Diesel	3 11/16	.004	1.1092	.013	.010	2.248–2.249	.0008–.0029	75–85	2.264–2.625	.0005–.0032	90
MH-333 Gas	3 11/16	.003	1.1092	.013	.013	2.248–2.249	.0008–.0029	75–85	2.624–2.625	.0005–.0032	90
MH-333 Diesel	3 11/16	.004	1.1092	.013	.010	2.248–2.249	.0008–.0029	75–85	2.624–2.625	.0005–.0032	90
MF-404 Gas	3 11/16	.003	1.2499	.013	.013	2.498–2.500	.0005–.0025	85–95	2.873–2.874	.0015–.0035	105
MF-404 Diesel	4	.004	1.2499	.007	.007	2.498–2.500	.0005–.0025	85–95	2.873–2.874	.0015–.0035	135
MF-406 Gas	4	.003	1.1092	.013	.013	2.248–2.249	.0008–.0029	75–85	2.624–2.625	.0005–.0032	90
MF-406 Diesel	3 11/16	.004	1.1092	.013	.010	2.248–2.249	.0008–.0029	75–85	2.624–2.625	.0005–.0032	90
MH-444 Gas	4	.003	1.2499	.013	.013	2.498–2.500	.0005–.0025	85–95	2.873–2.874	.0015–.0035	105
MH-444 Diesel	4	.004	1.2499	.007	.007	2.498–2.500	.0005–.0025	85–95	2.873–2.874	.0015–.0035	135
MF-1001 Gas	3 11/16	.003	1.1092	.013	.013	2.248–2.249	.0008–.0029	75–85	2.624–2.625	.0005–.0032	90
MF-1001 Diesel	3 11/16	.004	1.1092	.013	.010	2.248–2.249	.0008–.0029	75–85	2.624–2.625	.0005–.0032	90
MF-1100 Gas	4 1/8	.003	1.3748	.013	—	2.624–2.625	.0005–.0030	85–90	2.624–2.625	.0015–.0045	110
MF-1100 Diesel	3 7/8	.007	⑤	.018	.014	2.499–2.4995	.0015–.0030	65–70	2.9985–2.999	.0025–.0045	145–150
MF-1130 Diesel	3 7/8	.007	⑤	.021	.015	2.499–2.4995	.0015–.0030	65–70	2.9985–2.999	.0025–.0045	145–150
MF-1080, 1085 Diesel	4.5	.006–.008	1.4375	⑥	.018	2.7483–2.749	.002–.0042	100–105	2.9985–2.999	.0025–.0045	140–150
MF-1150	4 1/4	.005–.007	1.6249	.017	.017	3.248–3.2485	.0023–.0042	90–95	3.9967–3.9972	.004–.0063	190–200

① —Front and rear bearing housing to block 18–20 ft. lbs., center bearing housing to block 39–42 ft. lbs., upper to lower bearing housing 25–30 ft. lbs.
② —Front bearing, non-diesel 135–145 ft.-lbs., diesels 195–205.
③ —After Serial No. 17300000.
④ —Bearings with shim washers and lock tabs 90–95; without washers and locks 110–115.
⑤ —1.3748 on models without turbocharger and 1.4998 on models with turbocharger.
⑥ —Top Comp. .018.—2nd & 3rd .014.

FARM TRACTORS

MINNEAPOLIS-MOLINE
TUNE UP SPECIFICATIONS

Tractor Model	Firing Order	Spark Plug Gap	Breaker Gap Distributor	Breaker Gap Magneto	Ignition Mark Location	Ignition Mark Retarded Timing BTC	Ignition Mark Full Advance Timing BTC	Valve Lash Intake	Valve Lash Exhaust	Cylinder Head Torque
UB Gasoline	1342	.024	.022	—	Flywheel	—	3⁷⁄₈"④	.008H	.010H	⑦
UB Distillate	1342	.028	.022	—	Flywheel	—	4¹⁄₈"④	.008H	.010H	⑦
UB LP-Gas	1342	.024	.022	—	Flywheel	—	4¹⁄₈"④	.008H	.010H	⑦
UB Diesel	1342	—	—	—	Flywheel②	27°⑪	—	.008H	.010H	⑨
UTS Gasoline	1342	.024	.022	—	Flywheel	—	3⁷⁄₈"④	.008H	.010H	⑦
UTS Distillate	1342	.028	.022	—	Flywheel	—	4¹⁄₈"④	.008H	.010H	⑦
UTS LP-Gas	1342	.024	.022	—	Flywheel	—	4¹⁄₈"④	.008H	.010H	⑦
UTS Diesel	1342	—	—	—	Flywheel②	27°⑪	—	.008H	.010H	⑨
U-302 Gasoline	1342	.024	.022	—	Flywheel	DC-1	15°	.010H	.018H	95–100
U-302 LP-Gas	1342	.021	.022	—	Flywheel	DC-1	16°	.010H	.018H	95–100
Jet Star Gasoline	1342	.024	.022	—	Flywheel	3°	28°	.008H	.010H	75–80③
Jet Star LP-Gas	1342	.015	.022	—	Flywheel	3°	28°	.008H	.010H	75–80③
Jet Star Diesel	1342	—	—	—	Flywheel②	27°⑪	—	.008H	.010H	75–80③
4 Star Gasoline	1342	.024	.022	—	Flywheel	3°	28°	.008H	.010H	75–80③
4 Star LP-Gas	1342	.015	.022	—	Flywheel	3°	28°	.008H	.010H	75–80③
4 Star Diesel	1342	—	—	—	Flywheel②	27°⑪	—	.008H	.010H	75–80③
4 Star Super Gaso.	1342	.024	.022	—	Flywheel	3°	28°	.008H	.010H	75–80③
4 Star Super LP-Gas	1342	.015	.022	—	Flywheel	3°	28°	.008H	.010H	75–80③
4 Star Super Diesel	1342	—	—	—	Flywheel②	27°⑪	—	.008H	.010H	75–80③
5 Star Gasoline	1342	.024	.022	—	Flywheel	—	3¹⁄₈"④	.008H	.010H	⑧
5 Star LP-Gas	1342	.024	.022	—	Flywheel	—	2⁷⁄₈"④	.008H	.010H	⑧
5 Star Diesel	1342	—	—	—	Flywheel②	29°⑪	—	.008H	.010H	⑩
M5 Gasoline	1342	.024	.020	—	Flywheel	—	3¹⁄₈"④	.008H	.010H	⑧
M5-LP-Gas	1342	.015	.020	—	Flywheel	—	2⁷⁄₈"④	.008H	.010H	⑧
M5 Diesel	1342	—	—	—	Flywheel②	⑤⑪	—	.008H	.010H	⑩
G-VI LP-Gas	153624	.015	.022	—	Flywheel	—	24°	.008H	.010H	⑧
G-VI Diesel	153624	—	—	—	Flywheel②	⑥⑪	—	.008H	.010H	⑩
335 Gasoline	1342	.024	.021	—	Flywheel	—	24°	.008H	.010H	75③
335 LP-Gas	1342	.021	.021	—	Flywheel	—	25°	.008H	.010H	75③
445 Gasoline	1342	.024	.021	—	Flywheel	DC-1	25°	.008H	.010H	75③
445 Distillate	1342	.026	.021	—	Flywheel	—	28°	.008H	.010H	75③
445 LP-Gas	1342	.021	.021	—	Flywheel	—	28°	.008H	.010H	75③
M-504 Gasoline	1342	.023	.022	—	Flywheel	DC1-4	3¹⁄₈"	.010H	.020H	⑧
M-504 LP-Gas	1342	.015	.022	—	Flywheel	DC1-4	2⁷⁄₈"	.010H	.020H	⑧
M-504 Diesel	1342	—	—	—	Flywheel②	⑤⑪	—	.010H	.018H	⑩
M-602 Gasoline	1342	.023	.022	—	Flywheel	DC1-4	25°	.010H	.020H	170–175
M-602 LP-Gas	1342	.015	.022	—	Flywheel	DC1-4	25°	.010H	.020H	170–175
M-602 Diesel	1342	—	—	—	Flywheel②	⑤⑪	—	.010H	.018H	⑫
M-604 Gasoline	1342	.023	.022	—	Flywheel	DC1-4	25°	.010H	.020H	170–175
M-604 LP-Gas	1342	.015	.022	—	Flywheel	DC1-4	25°	.010H	.020H	170–175
M-604 Diesel	1342	—	—	—	Flywheel②	⑤⑪	—	.010H	.018H	⑫
M-670 Gasoline	1342	.025	.022	—	Flywheel	—	11°	.010H	.022H	170–175
M-670 LP-Gas	1342	.015	.022	—	Flywheel	—	10°	.010H	.022H	170–175
M-670 Diesel	1342	—	—	—	Flywheel②	9°⑪	—	.010H	①	⑫
G-705 LP-Gas	153624	.015	.022	—	Flywheel	DC1-4	25°	.010H	.020H	170–175
G-705 Diesel	153624	—	—	—	Flywheel②	⑤⑪	—	.010H	.018H	⑫
G-706 LP-Gas	153624	.015	.022	—	Flywheel	DC1-4	25°	.010H	.020H	170–175

Continued

FARM TRACTORS

TUNE UP SPECIFICATIONS—Continued

Tractor Model	Firing Order	Spark Plug Gap	Breaker Gap Distributor	Breaker Gap Magneto	Ignition Mark Location	Ignition Mark Retarded Timing BTC	Ignition Mark Full Advance Timing BTC	Valve Lash Intake	Valve Lash Exhaust	Cylinder Head Torque
G-706 Diesel	153624	—	—	—	Flywheel②	⑤⑪	—	.010H	.018H	⑫
G-707 LP-Gas	153624	.015	.022	—	Flywheel	—	25°	.012C	.022C	170–175
G-707 Diesel	153624	—	.022	—	Flywheel②	11°⑪	—	.012C	.020C	⑫
G-708 LP-Gas	153624	.015	.022	—	Flywheel	—	25°	.012C	.022C	170–175
G-708 Diesel	153624	—	.022	—	Flywheel②	11°⑪	—	.012C	.020C	⑫
G-900 Gasoline	153624	.025	.021	—	Flywheel	—	13°	.012C	.028C	170–175
G-900 LP-Gas	153624	.015	.021	—	Flywheel	—	16°	.012C	.028C	170–175
G-900 Diesel	153624	—	.021	—	Flywheel②	2°⑪	—	.015C	.022C	⑫
G-950 Gasoline	153624	.025	.021	—	Flywheel	—	13°	.012C	.028C	170–175
G-950 LP-Gas	153624	.015	.021	—	Flywheel	—	16°	.012C	.028C	170–175
G-950 Diesel	153624	—	.021	—	Flywheel②	2°⑪	—	.015C	.022C	⑫
G-955 LP-Gas	153624	.015	.021	—	Flywheel	—	16°	.012C	.028C	170–175
G-955 Diesel	153624	—	—	—	Flywheel②	2°⑪	—	.015C	.022C	⑫
G-1000 Gasoline	153624	.025	.021	—	Flywheel	—	12°	.012C	.028C	170–175
G-1000 LP-Gas	153624	.015	.021	—	Flywheel	—	15°	.012C	.028C	170–175
G-1000 Diesel	153624	—	.021	—	Flywheel②	6°⑪	—	.015C	.022C	⑫
G-1000 Vista LP-Gas	153624	.015	.021	—	Flywheel	—	15°	.012C	.028C	170–175
G-1000 Vista Diesel	153624	—	.021	—	Flywheel②	6°⑪	—	.015C	.022C	⑫
G-1050 Gasoline	153624	.025	.021	—	Flywheel	—	12°	.012C	.028C	170–175
G-1050 LP-Gas	153624	.015	.021	—	Flywheel	—	15°	.012C	.028C	170–175
G-1050 Diesel	153624	—	.021	—	Flywheel②	2°⑪	—	.015C	.022C	⑫
G-1350 LP-Gas	153624	.015	.021	—	Flywheel	—	17°	.010C	.028C	170–175
G-1350 Diesel	153624	—	.021	—	Flywheel②	4°⑪	—	.010C	.020C	⑫
G-1355 LP-Gas	153624	.015	.021	—	Flywheel	—	17°	.010C	.028C	170–175
G-1355 Diesel	153624	—	—	—	Flywheel②	4°⑪	—	.010C	.020C	⑫

①—M-670 Super Diesel .015H; all others .018H.
②—All models, align flywheel with correct timing mark. With APE pump, timing mark on gear flange should align with mark on pump body. With PSB pump, timing mark on pump coupling flange should align with timing pointer. With Roosa-Master pump, timing lines on governor cage and pump cam should align.
③—With cold engine.
④—Before DC-1 or DC-1-4 mark.
⑤—APE pump 40° BTC, PSB pump 30° BTC, Roosa pump 10° BTC.
⑥—APE pump 42° BTC, PSB pump 30° BTC, Roosa pump 11° BTC.
⑦—Camshaft side 100–105, exhaust manifold side 85–90.
⑧—Camshaft side 125–130, exhaust manifold side 105–110.
⑨—5/8″ studs on camshaft side 100–105, 85–90 on exhaust manifold side, 9/16″ studs 70.
⑩—5/8″ studs on camshaft side 125–130, 105–110 on exhaust manifold side. 9/16″ studs 85–90.
⑪—Injection timing.
⑫—Torque 9/16″ nut to 130–135 ft. lbs. and 5/8″ nuts to 170–175 ft. lbs.

PISTONS, PINS, RINGS, BEARINGS & CRANKSHAFT

Tractor Model	Cyl. Bore Size In.	Piston Clearance	Pin Diam.	Ring End Gap Minimum Comp.	Ring End Gap Minimum Oil	Rod Bearings Crankpin Diameter	Rod Bearings Bearing Clearance	Rod Bolt Torque	Main Bearings Journal Diameter	Main Bearings Bearing Clearance	Cap Bolt Torque
UB, UTS Gas	4 1/4	.0045	1.2499	.020	.020	2.5770–2.5775	.0015–.0024	80–85	2.9110–2.9120	.0014–.0044	①
UB, UTS Diesel	4 1/4	.007	1.4999	.015	.015	2.9115–2.9120	.0024–.0039	80–85	2.9110–2.9120	.0014–.0044	②
U-302	3 3/4	.004	.9995	.010	.010	2.625	.0015–.003	70–75	④	⑤	60–65
Jet Star Gas	3 5/8	.003	.9995	.010	.010	2.625	.0015–.003	70–75	④	⑤	60–65
Jet Star Diesel	3 5/8	.005	1.2500	.010	.010	2.625	.0015–.003	70–75	④	⑤	⑥
4 Star Gas	3 5/8	.003	.9995	.010	.010	2.625	.0015–.003	70–75	④	⑤	60–65
4 Star Diesel	3 5/8	.005	1.2500	.010	.010	2.625	.0015–.003	70–75	④	⑤	⑥
5 Star Gas	4 1/4	.005	1.2499	.020	.020	2.5770–2.5775	.0009–.003	80–85	2.9110–2.9120	.0014–.0044	①
5 Star Diesel	4 5/8	.008	1.4999	.013	.013	2.9115–2.9120	.0009–.003	80–85	2.9110–2.9120	.0014–.0044	②
M5 Gas	4 5/8	.005	1.2499	.013	.013	2.9110–2.9120	.0009–.003	80–85	2.9110–2.9120	.0014–.0044	①
M5 Diesel	4 5/8	.008	1.4999	.013	.013	2.9115–2.9120	.0009–.003	80–85	2.9110–2.9120	.0014–.0044	②

Continued

FARM TRACTORS

PISTONS, PINS, RINGS, BEARINGS & CRANKSHAFT—Continued

Tractor Model	Cyl. Bore Size In.	Piston Clearance	Pin Diam.	Ring End Gap Minimum		Rod Bearings			Main Bearings		
				Comp.	Oil	Crankpin Diameter	Bearing Clearance	Rod Bolt Torque	Journal Diameter	Bearing Clearance	Cap Bolt Torque
G-VI Gas	4¼	.0045	1.2499	.020	.020	2.5770–2.5775	.0009–.003	80–85	2.9110–2.9120	.0014–.0044	①
G-VI Diesel	4¼	.007	1.4999	.015	.015	2.9115–2.9120	.0009–.003	80–85	2.9110–2.9120	.0014–.0044	②
335 Gas	3⅝	③	.9994	.010	.010	2.6245–2.6250	.0011–.0027	70–75	④	.0015–.0036	60–65
335 Diesel	3⅝	③	.9994	.010	.010	2.6245–2.6250	.0011–.0027	70–75	④	.0015–.0036	60–65
445 Gas	3⅝	.0035	.9994	.010	.010	2.6245–2.6250	.0011–.0031	70–75	④	⑤	60–65
445 Diesel	3⅝	.0035	.9994	.010	.010	2.6245–2.6250	.0011–.0031	70–75	④	⑤	60–65
M-504 Gas	4⅝	.005	1.250	.013	.013	2.9110–2.9120	.0009–.003	80–85	2.9110–2.9120	.0014–.0044	①
M-504 Diesel	4⅝	.008	1.500	.013	.013	2.9115–2.9120	.0009–.003	80–85	2.9110–2.9120	.0014–.0044	③
M-602 Gas	4⅝	.005	1.250	.013	.013	2.9100–2.9120	.0009–.003	80–85	2.9110–2.9120	.0014–.0044	①
M-602 Diesel	4⅝	.008	1.500	.013	.013	2.9115–2.9120	.0009–.003	80–85	2.9110–2.9120	.0014–.0044	②
M-604 Gas	4⅝	.005	1.250	.013	.013	2.9110–2.9120	.0009–.003	80–85	2.9110–2.9120	.0014–.0044	①
M-604 Diesel	4⅝	.008	1.500	.013	.013	2.9115–2.9120	.0009–.003	80–85	2.9110–2.9120	.0014–.0044	②
M-670 Gasoline	4⅝	.0007–.0009	1.2497–1.2500	.020–.030	.020–.030	2.9110–2.9120	.0009–.0030	⑩	2.9110–2.9120	.0014–.0044	①
M-670 LP Gas	4⅝	.0007–.0009	1.2497–1.2500	.020–.030	.020–.030	2.9110–2.9120	.0009–.0030	⑩	2.9110–2.9120	.0014–.0044	①
M-670 Diesel	4⅝	.0007–.0009	1.4997–1.5000	.015–.020	.015–.020	2.9115–2.9120	.0009–.0030	⑩	2.9110–2.9120	.0044–.0044	⑨
G-705 Gas	4⅝	.005	1.250	.013	.013	2.9110–2.9120	.0009–.003	80–85	2.9110–2.9120	.0014–.0044	①
G-705 Diesel	4⅝	.008	1.500	.013	.013	2.9115–2.9120	.0009–.003	80–85	2.9110–2.9120	.0014–.0044	②
G-706 Gas	4⅝	.005	1.250	.013	.013	2.9110–2.9120	.0009–.003	80–85	2.9110–2.9120	.0014–.0044	①
G-706 Diesel	4⅝	.008	1.500	.013	.013	2.9115–2.9120	.0009–.003	80–85	2.9110–2.9120	.0014–.0044	②
G-707 Gas	4⅝	.0045	1.2495	.013	.013	2.9115–2.9120	.0009–.003	80–85	2.911–2.912	.0014–.0044	①
G-707 Diesel	4⅝	.007	1.4995	.013	.013	2.9115–2.9120	.0009–.003	80–85	2.911–2.912	.0014–.0044	②
G-708 Gas	4⅝	.0045	1.2495	.013	.013	2.9115–2.9120	.0009–.003	80–85	2.911–2.912	.0014–.0044	①
G-708 Diesel	4⅝	.007	1.4995	.013	.013	2.9115–2.9120	.0009–.003	80–85	2.911–2.912	.0014–.0044	②
G-900 Gas	4¼	.0045	1.2495	.020	.015	2.9115–2.9120	.0014–.0039	70–75	2.911–2.912	.0014–.0044	⑦
G-900 Diesel	4⅜	.005	1.4995	.015	.010	2.9115–2.9120	.0014–.0039	70–75	2.911–2.912	.0014–.0044	⑦
G-950 Gas	4¼	.0045	1.2495	.020	.015	2.9115–2.9120	.0014–.0039	70–75	2.911–2.912	.0014–.0044	⑦
G-950 Diesel	4⅜	.005	1.4995	.015	.010	2.9115–2.9120	.0014–.0039	70–75	2.911–2.912	.0014–.0044	⑦
G-955 Gas	4¼	.0055	1.2495	.020	.015	2.9115–2.9120	.0014–.0039	70–75	2.911–2.912	.0014–.0044	⑦
G-955 Diesel	4⅜	.006	1.8745	.015	.010	2.9115–2.9120	.0014–.0039	70–75	2.911–2.912	.0014–.0044	⑦
G-1000 Gas	4⅝	.006	1.2495	.016	.013	2.9115–2.9120	.0014–.0039	70–75	2.911–2.912	.0014–.0044	⑦
G-1000 Diesel	4⅝	.007	1.4995	.016	.013	2.9115–2.9120	.0014–.0039	55–60	2.911–2.912	.0014–.0044	⑦
G-1000 Vista Gas	4⅝	.006	1.2495	.016	.013	2.9115–2.9120	.0014–.0039	70–75	2.911–2.912	.0014–.0044	⑦
G-1000 Vista Diesel	4⅝	.007	1.4995	.016	.013	2.9115–2.9120	.0014–.0039	55–60	2.911–2.912	.0014–.0044	⑦
G-1050 Gas	4⅝	.006	1.2495	.016	.013	2.9115–2.9120	.0014–.0039	70–75	2.911–2.912	.0014–.0044	⑦
G-1050 Diesel	4⅝	.007	1.4995	.016	.013	2.9115–2.9120	.0014–.0039	55–60	2.911–2.912	.0014–.0044	⑦
G-1350 Gas	4⅝	.006	1.2495	.016	.013	2.9115–2.9120	.0014–.0039	70–75	2.911–2.912	.0014–.0044	⑦
G-1350 Diesel	4¾	.007	1.8745	.017	.015	3.498–3.499	.0023–.0053	80	3.498–3.499	.0033–.0053	⑧
G-1355 Gas	4⅝	.007	1.2495	.016	.013	2.9115–2.9120	.0014–.0039	70–75	2.911–2.912	.0014–.0044	⑦
G-1355 Diesel	4¾	.008	1.8745	.017	.015	3.498–3.499	.0023–.0053	80	3.498–3.499	.0033–.0053	⑧

① — Front 140, others 100–105.
② — Front 200, others 100–105.
③ — Iron pistons .0035", aluminum, .004.
④ — Rear 2.9995–3.000, others 2.7495–2.7500.
⑤ — Rear .0015–.0035, others .0015–.004.
⑥ — Rear bearing 60–65 ft.-lbs., others 90–100.
⑦ — Front 240, others 140.
⑧ — Front 200, others 108–112.
⑨ — Front, 195–205 ft. lbs.; others, 170–175 ft. lbs.
⑩ — M670 & M670 Super, 70–75 ft. lbs.; all others 80–85 ft. lbs.

FARM TRACTORS

OLIVER
TUNE UP SPECIFICATIONS

Tractor Model	Firing Order	Spark Plug Gap	Breaker Gap Distributor	Breaker Gap Magneto	Ignition Mark Location	Ignition Mark Retarded Timing BTC	Ignition Mark Full Advance Timing BTC	Valve Lash Intake	Valve Lash Exhaust	Cylinder Head Torque
Super 44	1342	.025	.020	—	Flywheel	TDC	IGN	.014H	.014H	70-75
Super 55 HC	1243	.025	.022	—	Flywheel	TDC	IGN-HC	.009C	.015C	96
Super 55 D	1243	—	—	—	Flywheel⑩	FP	—	.009C	.019C	115
66 HC	1243	.025	.022	.015	Flywheel	TDC	IGN-HC	.009C	.016C	96
66 KD	1243	.025	.022	.015	Flywheel	5°	IGN-KD	.009C	.016C	96
66 D	1243	—	—	—	Flywheel⑩	FP	—	.009C	.016C	115①
Super 66 HC	1243	.025	.022	—	Flywheel	TDC	IGN-HC	.010C	.016C	96
Super 66 D	1243	—	—	—	Flywheel⑩	FP	—	.010C	.020C	115①
77 LPG, 77HC	153624	.025	.022	.015	Flywheel	TDC	IGN-KD	.009C	.016C	96
77 KD	153624	.025	.022	.015	Flywheel	5°	IGN-HC	.009C	.016C	96
77D	153624	—	—	—	Flywheel⑩	FP	—	.009C	.016C	115①
Super 77 HC	153624	.025	.022	—	Flywheel	TDC	IGN-HC	.010C	.016C	96
Super 77 D	153624	—	—	—	Flywheel⑩	FP⑭	—	.010C	.020C	115①
88 HC	153624	.025	.022	.015	Flywheel	TDC	IGN-HC	.009C	.016C	96
88 LPG	153624	.025	.022	.015	Flywheel	TDC	IGN-HC	.009C	.016C	96
88 KD	153624	.025	.022	.015	Flywheel	5°	IGN-KD	.009C	.016C	96
88 D	153624	—	—	—	Flywheel⑩	FP⑭	—	.009C	.016C	115①
Super 88 HC	153624	.025	.022	—	Flywheel	TDC	IGN-HC	.010C	.016C	96
Super 88 D	153624	—	—	—	Flywheel⑩	FP⑭	—	.010C	.020C	115①
Super 99	132	—	—	—	Flywheel	—	—	—	.009H	170
440	1342	.025	.020	—	Flywheel	TDC	4 IGN	.014H	.014H	70-75
550 HC	1243	.025	.022	—	Flywheel	TDC	IGN-HC	.009C	.015C	96
550 D	1243	—	—	—	Flywheel⑩	FP⑭	—	.009C	.019C	115①
660 HC	1243	.025	.022	—	Flywheel	TDC	IGN-HC	.010C	.016C	96
660 D	1243	—	—	—	Flywheel	FP	—	.010C	.020C	115①
770 HC	153624	.025	—	—	Flywheel	TDC	IGN-HC	.010C	.016C	96
770 D	153624	—	—	—	Flywheel	FP⑭	—	.010C	.020C	115①
880 HC	153624	.025	.022	—	Flywheel	TDC	IGN-HC	.010C	.016C	96
880 D	153624	—	—	—	Flywheel⑩	FP⑭	—	.010C	.020C	115①
950 HC	153624	.025	.022	—	Flywheel	4½°	IGN	.009C	.016C	100
950 D	153624	—	—	—	Flywheel	—	—	.009C	.016C	115
990	132	—	—	—	Flywheel	—	—	—	.009H	170
995	132	—	—	—	Flywheel	—	—	—	.009H	170
1550, 1555 Gasoline	153624	.025	④	—	Flywheel	TDC	—	.010C	.016C	115①
1550, 1555 Diesel	153624	—	—	—	Flywheel⑪	2° ATC⑭	—	.010C	.020C	115①
1558, 1555 LPG	153624	.025	④	—	Flywheel	TDC	—	.010C	.016C	115①
1600 Gasoline	153624	.025	.016	—	Flywheel	⑤	—	.014C	.023C	115
1600 LPG	153624	.025	.016	—	Flywheel	5° BTC	—	.014C	.023C	115
1600 Diesel	153624	—	—	—	Flywheel⑪	7° BTC⑭	—	.010C	.020C	115
1650, 1655 Gasoline	153624	.025	.025	—	Flywheel	TDC	—	.020C	.030C	115
1650, 1655 LPG	153624	.025	.025	—	Flywheel	TDC	—	.020C	.030C	115
1650, 1655 Diesel	153624	—	—	—	Flywheel⑪	⑥⑭	—	⑦	.030C	⑧
1750 Gasoline	153624	.025	.025	—	Flywheel	2° BTDC	—	.020C	.030C	130
1750 Diesel	153624	—	—	—	Flywheel⑪	4° BTC⑭	—	.030C	.030C	③
1755 Gasoline	153624	.025	.025	—	Flywheel	2°	26°	.019C	.029C	129
1755 Diesel	153624	.025	—	—	Flywheel⑪	2°⑭	26°	.029C	.029C	⑨
1880A Gasoline	153624	.025	.022	—	Flywheel	"O"	—	.014C	.023C	130
1880A LPG	153624	.022	.022	—	Flywheel	4° BTC	—	.014C	.023C	130
1800A Diesel	153624	—	—	—	Flywheel⑪	8° BTC⑭	—	②	②	130
1800B-C Gasoline	153624	.025	.016	—	Flywheel	2° BTC	—	.014C	.023C	130
1800B-C LPG	153624	.022	.016	—	Flywheel	7° BTC	—	.014C	.023C	130

Continued

FARM TRACTORS

TUNE UP SPECIFICATIONS—Continued

Tractor Model	Firing Order	Spark Plug Gap	Breaker Gap Distributor	Breaker Gap Magneto	Ignition Mark Location	Ignition Mark Retarded Timing BTC	Ignition Mark Full Advance Timing BTC	Valve Lash Intake	Valve Lash Exhaust	Cylinder Head Torque
1800B-C Diesel	153624	—	—	—	Flywheel⑪	2° BTC⑭	—	②	②	130
1850 Gasoline	153624	.025	.025	—	Flywheel	"O"	—	.014C	.023C	130
1850 LPG	153624	.025	.025	—	Flywheel	2° BTC	—	.014C	.023C	130
1850 Diesel	153624	—	—	—	Flywheel⑯	28° BTC⑭	—	.012C	.012C	85
1855 Gasoline	153624	.025	.025	—	Flywheel	TDC	24°	.019C	.029C	129–133
1855 Diesel	153624	.025	—	—	Flywheel⑪	TDC	24°	.029C	.029C	⑨
1900, 1950 Diesel	1342	—	—	—	Flywheel	—	—	—	.009H	—
1950T Gasoline	153624	.025	.025	—	Flywheel	2°	—	.020C	.030C	129–133
1950T Diesel	153624	—	—	—	Flywheel⑪	4°⑭	—	.030C	.030C	⑮
2050–2150	153624	—	—	—	Pulley⑫	20°⑭	—	.010C	.017C	130
1955 Diesel	153624	.025	—	—	Flywheel⑪	2°⑭	—	.029C	.029C	⑨
2255 Diesel	12734568	—	—	—	⑬	16°	—	.015C	.025C	

① —Drilled screw 96–100.
② —Intake (A, b) .010C, exhaust .016C. Intake (C) .017C, exhaust .027C.
③ —Tighten six center capscrews to 150 ft. lbs.; all others to 133 ft. lbs.
④ —1550, .016; 1555, .025.
⑤ —231 cu. in., TDC; 248 cu. in., 2°.
⑥ —2° BTC; On series 1650 after tractor serial number 187 586-000 and all series 1655, 4° BTC.
⑦ —Indirect injection .020C; direct injection .050C.
⑧ —Indirect injection, 131 ft. lbs.; direct injection, tighten six center capscrews from 147–150 ft. lbs., all others to 131 ft. lbs.
⑨ —Tighten 1 through 8, 11 & 12, 180 ft. lbs.; tighten 9, 10, 13 & 14, 133 ft. lbs.
⑩ —With timing mark "FP" aligned with flywheel timing port notch, align line mark on injection pump coupling hub with timing pointer on front face of pump.
⑪ —With correct timing mark on flywheel aligned with pointer, timing lines in injection pump window should be exactly aligned.
⑫ —With timing mark on crankshaft damper and pointer on timing gear cover aligned, align pump timing pointer with mark on pump drive hub.
⑬ —With timing pin inserted into slot on injection pump camshaft, thread a timing gear cover cap screw into tapped hole on camshaft gear. If capscrew is centered in timing hole, pump is correctly timed.
⑭ —Injection pump timing.
⑮ —Capscrews 1–8, 11 and 12, 180 ft. lbs.; capscrews 9, 10, 13 and 14, 133 ft. lbs.
⑯ —With timing mark on flywheel and pointer on timing hole aligned, align "F" mark on injection pump rotor with scribe line on snap ring.

PISTONS, PINS, RINGS, BEARINGS & CRANKSHAFT

Tractor Model	Cyl. Bore Size In.	Piston Clearance	Pin Diam.	Ring End Gap Minimum Comp.	Ring End Gap Minimum Oil	Rod Bearings Crankpin Diameter	Rod Bearings Bearing Clearance	Rod Bolt Torque	Main Bearings Journal Diameter	Main Bearings Bearing Clearance	Cap Bolt Torque
Super 44	3 3/16	.003	.8592	.007	.008	1.9365–1.9375	.0002–.0022	45–50	2.249–2.250	.0002–.0024	105
Super 55 HC	①	.002	1.2495	.010	.010	2.249–2.250	.0005–.0015	46–50	2.249–2.250	.0005–.0035	90
Super 55 D	①	.002	1.2495	.010	.010	2.249–2.250	.0005–.0015	46–50	2.249–2.250	.0005–.0035	90
66 HC, 66 KD	3 1/2	.002	1.2495	.012	.010	1.999–2.000	.0005–.0015	46–50	2.249–2.250	.0005–.0035	90
66 D	3 1/2	.002	1.2495	.012	.010	1.999–2.000	.0005–.0015	46–50	2.249–2.250	.0005–.0035	90
Super 66 HC	3 1/2	.002	1.2495	.012	.010	2.249–2.250	.0005–.0015	46–50	2.249–2.250	.0005–.0035	90
Super 66 D	3 1/2	.002	1.2495	.012	.010	2.249–2.250	.0005–.0015	46–50	2.249–2.250	.0005–.0035	90
77 Gas	3 1/2	.002	1.2495	.012	.010	1.999–2.000	.0005–.0015	46–50	2.249–2.250	.0005–.0035	90
77 Diesel	3 1/2	.002	1.2495	.012	.010	1.999–2.000	.0005–.0015	46–50	2.249–2.250	.0005–.0035	90
Super 77 HC	3 1/2	.002	1.2495	.012	.010	2.249–2.250	.0005–.0015	46–50	2.249–2.250	.0005–.0035	90
Super 77 D	2 1/2	.002	1.2495	.012	.010	2.249–2.250	.0005–.0015	46–50	2.249–2.250	.0005–.0035	90
88 Gas	4	.002	1.2495	.012	.010	2.249–2.250	.0005–.0015	46–50	2.624–2.625	.0005–.0035	90
88 Diesel	4	.002	1.2495	.012	.010	2.249–2.250	.0005–.0015	46–50	2.624–2.625	.0005–.0035	90
Super 88 HC	4	.002	1.2495	.012	.010	2.437–2.438	.0005–.0015	56–58	2.624–2.625	.0005–.0035	110
Super 88 D	4	.002	1.2495	.012	.010	2.437–2.438	.0005–.0015	56–58	2.624–2.625	.0005–.0035	110
Super 99	4 1/4	.006	1.500	.015	.013	2.749–2.750	.0015–.003	70	3.499–3.500	.0015–.003	185
440	3 3/16	.003	.8592	.007	.008	1.9365–1.9375	.0002–.0022	45–50	2.249–2.250	.0002–.0024	105
550 HC	①	.002	1.2495	.010	.010	2.249–2.250	.0005–.0015	46–50	2.249–2.250	.0005–.0035	90
550 D	①	.002	1.2495	.010	.010	2.249–2.250	.0005–.0015	46–50	2.249–2.250	.0005–.0035	90
660 HC	3 1/2	.002	1.2495	.012	.010	2.249–2.250	.0005–.0015	46–50	2.249–2.250	.0005–.0035	90

Continued

FARM TRACTORS

PISTONS, PINS, RINGS, BEARINGS & CRANKSHAFT—Continued

Tractor Model	Cyl. Bore Size In.	Piston Clearance	Pin Diam.	Ring End Gap Minimum		Rod Bearings			Main Bearings		
				Comp.	Oil	Crankpin Diameter	Bearing Clearance	Rod Bolt Torque	Journal Diameter	Bearing Clearance	Cap Bolt Torque
660 D	3 1/2	.002	1.2495	.012	.010	2.249–2.250	.0005–.0015	46–50	2.249–2.250	.0005–.0035	90
770 HC	3 1/2	.002	1.2495	.012	.010	2.249–2.250	.0005–.0015	46–50	2.249–2.250	.0005–.0035	90
770 D	3 1/2	.002	1.2495	.012	.010	2.249–2.250	.0005–.0015	46–50	2.249–2.250	.0005–.0035	90
880 HC	3 3/4	.002	1.2495	.012	.010	2.437–2.438	.0005–.0015	56–58	2.624–2.625	.0005–.0035	110
880 D	3 3/4	.002	1.2495	.012	.010	2.437–2.438	.0005–.0015	56–58	2.624–2.625	.0005–.0035	110
950 HC	4	.003	1.250	.015	.013	2.249–2.250	.0005–.0015	90	2.624–2.625	.0005–.003	110
950 D	4	.003	1.250	.015	.013	2.249–2.250	.0005–.0015	90	2.624–2.625	.0005–.003	110
990	4 1/4	.006	1.500	.015	.013	2.749–2.750	.0015–.003	70	3.499–3.500	.0015–.003	185
995	②	.006	1.500	.015	.013	2.749–2.750	.0015–.003	70	3.499–3.500	.0015–.003	185
1550, 1555 Gas	3 5/8	.002	1.2495	.010	.010	2.249–2.250	.0005–.0015	46–50	2.249–2.250	.0002–.0032	90
1550, 1555 Diesel	3 5/8	.002	1.2495	.010	.010	2.249–2.250	.0005–.0015	46–50	2.249–2.250	.0002–.0032	90
1600 Non-Diesel	②	.0025	1.2495	.010	.010	2.249–2.250	.0005–.0015	46–50	2.624–2.625	.0005–.0035	110
1600 Diesel	3 3/4	.003	1.2495	.010	.010	2.436–2.437	.0005–.0015	56–60	2.624–2.625	.0005–.0035	110
1650, 1655 Non-Diesel	3 3/4	.003	1.2495	.010	.010	2.249–2.250	.0005–.0015	46–50	2.624–2.625	.0005–.0035	110
1650, 1655 Diesel	3 7/8	③	1.2495	.010	.010	2.436–2.437	.0005–.0015	④	2.624–2.625	.0015–.0045	131
1750 Gasoline	3 7/8	.0035	1.2495	.010	.010	2.4365–2.4375	.0005–.0015	46–50	2.624–2.625	.0015–.0045	131
1750 Diesel	3 7/8	.002	1.2495	.010	.010	2.4365–2.4375	.0005–.0015	46–50	2.624–2.625	.0015–.0045	131
1755 Gasoline	3 7/8	.003	1.2495	.010	.015	2.4365–2.4375	.0005–.0015	44–46	2.624–2.625	.0015–.0045	127–133
1755 Diesel	3 7/8	.003	1.2495	—	.010	2.4365–2.4375	.0005–.0015	44–46	2.624–2.625	.0015–.0045	129–133
1800 Non-Diesel	3 7/8	.0025	1.2495	.010	.010	2.436–2.437	.0025 Max.	56–58	2.624–2.625	.0015–.0045	130
1800 Diesel	3 7/8	.004	1.2495	.010	.010	2.436–2.437	.0025 Max.	56–58	2.624–2.625	.0015–.0045	130
1850 Non-Diesel	3 7/8	.0025	1.2495	.010	.010	2.436–2.437	.0025 Max.	56–58	2.624–2.625	.0015–.0045	130
1850 Diesel	3 7/8	.004	1.3749	.010	.010	2.499–2.500	.0025 Max.	65–70	2.998–2.999	.0025–.0045	145
1855 Gasoline	3 7/8	.003	1.2495	.010	.015	2.4365–2.4375	.0005–.0015	44–46	2.624–2.625	.0015–.0045	129–133
1855 Diesel	3 7/8	.003	1.2495	.014	.010	2.4365–2.4375	.0005–.0015	44–46	2.624–2.625	.0015–.0045	129–133
1900, 1950 Diesel	3 7/8	.007	1.3748	.020	.010	2.499–2.500	.0025 Max.	40–45	2.999–3.000	.0013–.0042	125
1950T Gasoline	3 7/8	—	1.2495	.010	.015	2.4365–2.4375	.0005–.0015	46–50	2.624–2.625	.0015–.0045	129–133
1950T Diesel	3 7/8	.002	1.2495	.014	.010	2.4365–2.4375	.0005–.0015	46–50	2.624–2.625	.0015–.0045	129–133
1955 Diesel	3 7/8	.003	1.2495	.014	.010	2.4365–2.4375	.0005–.0015	44–46	2.624–2.625	.0015–.0045	129–133
2050–2150	4.56	.005–.0075	1.6248	.021	.021	2.996–2.997	.002–.0055	100	3.620–3.621	.002–.0055	100
2255 Diesel	4 1/2	—	1.4999	.015	.010	2.7496–2.7504	.0015–.0045	27–33	3.4995–3.500	.0015–.0045	165–185

①—Prior to Ser. No. 72832, 3 1/2"; after Ser. No. 72831, 3 5/8".
②—Prior to Ser. No. 137613, 3 1/2"; after Ser. No. 137612, 3 5/8".
③—Direct injection (1650–1655), .002; indirect injection (1650), .004.
④—Direct injection (1650–1655), 46–50; indirect injection (1650), 56–58.

WHITE

TUNE UP SPECIFICATIONS

Tractor Model	Firing Order	Spark Plug Gap	Breaker Gap		Ignition Mark			Valve Lash		Cylinder Head Torque
			Distributor	Magneto	Location	Retarded Timing BTC	Full Advance Timing BTC	Intake	Exhaust	
2-70 Gasoline	153624	.025	.025	—	Flywheel	21° BTC	—	.020C	.030C	112–117 ③
2-70 Diesel	153624	—	—	—	Flywheel	4° BTC ①	—	.030C	.030C	④
2-85, 2-105 Diesel	153624	—	—	—	—	30° BTC	—	.010H	.010H	100
2-135, 2-155 Diesel	153624	—	—	—	Pulley	20° BTC ②	—	.010C	.025C	160
2-150	153624	—	—	—	Flywheel	4° ATC ①	—	.010C	.020C	170–175

①—With correct timing mark on flywheel aligned with pointer, timing lines in injection pump window should be exactly aligned.
②—With correct timing mark on crankshaft damper aligned with pointer, timing lines in injection pump window should be exactly aligned.
③—Torque oil screw to 96–100 ft. lbs.
④—Inner six bolts, 147–150 ft. lbs.; outer eight bolts, 129–133 ft. lbs.
⑤—Torque front nut securing water manifold flange to 100–105 ft. lbs.